Who's Who in the South and Southwest

**Biographical Reference Works
Published by Marquis Who's Who**

Who's Who in America

Who Was Who in America

    Historical Volume (1607-1896)

    Volume I (1897-1942)

    Volume II (1943-1950)

    Volume III (1951-1960)

    Volume IV (1961-1968)

    Volume V (1969-1973)

    Volume VI (1974-1976)

Who Was Who in American History—Arts and Letters

Who Was Who in American History—The Military

Who Was Who in American History—Science and Technology

Who's Who in the Midwest

Who's Who in the East

Who's Who in the South and Southwest

Who's Who in the West

Who's Who of American Women

Who's Who in Government

Who's Who in Finance and Industry

Who's Who in Religion

Who's Who in American Law

Who's Who in the World

Who's Who Biographical Record—Child Development Professionals

Who's Who Biographical Record—School District Officials

World Who's Who in Science

Directory of Medical Specialists

Marquis Who's Who Publications/Index to All Books

Travelers' Guide to U.S. Certified Doctors Abroad

Who's Who in the South and Southwest®

Including Alabama, Arkansas, Florida, Georgia, Kentucky, Louisiana, Mississippi, North Carolina, Oklahoma, South Carolina, Tennessee, Texas, Virginia, West Virginia, Puerto Rico, the Virgin Islands, and Mexico

17th edition
1980-1981

Marquis Who's Who, Inc.
200 East Ohio Street
Chicago, Illinois 60611 U.S.A.

Copyright © 1975, 1976, 1978, 1980 by Marquis Who's Who Incorporated. All rights reserved. No part of this publication may be reproduced, stored in a retrieval system, or transmitted in any form or by any means, electronic, mechanical, photocopying, recording or otherwise, without the prior written permission of the publisher, except in a magazine or newspaper article referring to a specific listee.

Library of Congress Catalog Card Number 50-58231
International Standard Book Number 0-8379-0817-5
Product Code Number 030242

Manufactured in the United States of America
1 2 3 4 5 6 7 8 9 10

Table of Contents

Preface.. vi

Standards of Admission... vii

Key to Information in this Directory.............................. viii

Table of Abbreviations.. ix

Alphabetical Practices... xiv

Biographies... 1

Southern and Southwestern Biographees in
Who's Who in America.. 837

Preface

The mid 1900s saw a dramatic increase both in population and in commercial and industrial activity in the Southern and Southwestern areas of the United States. Attracted by the climate, the wealth of raw materials, the large labor force and numerous markets, manufacturing industries built thousands of factories. Mass production of the automobile and the expansion of paved highways also contributed to the growth of the region's economy, particularly in the Southwest.

Today, mining is one of the biggest industries in the Southwest. Texas supplies almost 6% of the world's petroleum, two-fifths of the nation's natural gas, and about one-half of the country's sulfur. The Southern region derives most of its income from the manufacture of chemicals, textiles, furniture and food.

This growth could not have been achieved without the efforts of educated, experienced, responsible individuals. Because these individuals are of decided reference interest, both locally and nationally, it is appropriate to record their achievements in this new edition of *Who's Who in the South and Southwest.*

This 17th Edition represents our editors' attempts to recognize particular merit and to satisfy reference interest — to record the latest and the continuing accomplishments of individuals involved in all significant fields of endeavor in the South and Southwest.

Assiduously reviewed, revised and amended, this 17th Edition offers up-to-the-minute coverage of a broad range of key individuals based on position or individual achievement. Our editors have made every effort to present a balanced picture of achievement in the South and Southwest. To assure such balance in compilation of the volume, a list of essential names is made up of those men and women who are so eminent that their omission would fault the usefulness of the book. In the great majority of cases, these individuals have furnished their own data, thus assuring a high degree of accuracy. In some cases where individuals have failed to supply information, Marquis staff members compile the data through careful and independent research. Sketches compiled in this manner are denoted by an asterisk. As in previous editions, biographees are given the opportunity to review prepublication proofs of their sketches to make sure they are correct.

Marquis Who's Who editors exercise the utmost care in preparing each biographical sketch for publication. Occasionally, however, errors do occur despite all precautions taken to minimize such occurrences. All users of this directory are requested to draw the attention of the publisher to any errors found, so that corrections can be made in a later edition.

The 17th Edition contains more than 19,000 names from the region embracing Alabama, Arkansas, Florida, Georgia, Kentucky, Louisiana, Mississippi, North Carolina, Oklahoma, South Carolina, Tennessee, Texas, Virginia, West Virginia, Puerto Rico, and the Virgin Islands. Because of its own importance and its contiguity to the Southwestern United States, Mexico is also covered in this volume.

The persons sketched in this volume represent a broad spectrum of achievement in virtually every significant field of endeavor. Included are executives and officials in government, business, education, religion, the press, civic affairs, the arts, cultural affairs, law and other fields. This edition also includes significant contributors in such fields as contemporary art, music and science.

The question is often asked, "How do people get into a Who's Who volume?" Name selection is based on one fundamental principle: reference value.

Biographees of *Who's Who in the South and Southwest* can be classified into two basic categories: (1) Persons who are of regional reference importance to colleagues, librarians, researchers, scholars, the press, historians, biographers, participants in business and civic affairs, and others with specific or general inquiry needs. (2) Individuals of national reference interest who are also of such regional or local importance that their inclusion in the book is essential to its serviceability; there is a minimum of duplication with these names between this volume and *Who's Who in America.* In recognition of the complementary relationship between these two Marquis publications, this 17th Edition of *Who's Who in the South and Southwest* contains a listing of all those biographees of the South and Southwestern regions whose sketches appear in the 41st Edition of *Who's Who in America.*

In the editorial evaluation that resulted in the ultimate selection of names in this directory, an individual's desire to be listed was not sufficient reason for inclusion; rather it was the individual's demonstrated merit that ruled. Similarly, wealth or social position was not a criterion; only occupational stature or achievement in some field affecting the development of the Southern and Southwestern region of North America influenced selection. Indeed, many of the biographees are engaged in fields marked far more by service than by monetary reward. And, of course, this volume lists worthy individuals regardless of their race or ethnic origin.

Thus, on every level, this 17th Edition of *Who's Who in the South and Southwest* carries on the tradition of excellence established in 1899 with the publication of the first edition of *Who's Who in America.* The essence of that tradition is reflected in our unceasing effort to produce reference works that are responsive to the needs of their users throughout the world.

Standards of Admission

The foremost consideration in determining possible biographees of *Who's Who in the South and Southwest* is the extent of an individual's reference interest. Such reference interest is judged on either of two factors: (1) the position of responsibility held, or (2) the level of significant achievement attained.

Admissions based on the factor of position include:

Members of the U.S. Congress

Federal judges

Governors of states covered by this volume

State attorneys general

Judges of state and territorial courts of highest appellate jurisdiction

Mayors of major cities

Heads of the major universities and colleges

Heads of leading philanthropic, educational, cultural, and scientific institutions and associations

Chief ecclesiastics of the principal religious denominations

Principal officers of national and international businesses

Others chosen because of incumbency, authorship, or membership

Admission based on individual achievement, on the other hand, must be decided by a judicious process of evaluating qualitative factors. To be selected on this basis, a person must have accomplished some conspicuous achievement—something that distinguishes him from the vast majority of his contemporaries. He or she may scarcely be known in the local community, but may be widely recognized in some special field of endeavor. Such a person often is one whose work is better known than his/her name.

Key to Information in this Directory

❶ FULTON, SAMUEL GARDNER ❷ banker; **❸** b. Roanoke, Va., May 9, 1923; **❹** s. Oliver and Lorraine (Gardner) F.; **❺** B.A., Furman U., 1944; **❻** m. Rachel Harrison, Dec. 24, 1946; **❼** children—Sallie Jo Fulton Potter, Walter James, Frances Ruth Fulton Palmer, Cecily Louise Fulton McBride. **❽** Teller, Union Nat. Bank, Decatur, Ga., 1947-50, trust officer, 1950-57, v.p. trusts, 1957-65, pres., 1965-75, pres., chmn. bd., 1975—, also dir.; lectr. banking Decatur Jr. Coll., 1968—. **❾** Chmn. Decatur United Fund, 1969; active Decatur chpt. ARC; mem. Decatur City Council, 1965-68, 71-74; bd. dirs. Salvation Army Home. **❿** Served with USNR, 1944-46; PTO. **⓫** Decorated Bronze Star; named Man of Yr., Decatur Jaycees, 1969; recipient Outstanding Alumnus award Furman U., 1976. **⓬** Mem. Am. Banker's Assn., AIM, Decatur Banker's League (pres. 1967-68, dir. 1970—), Phi Delta Theta. **⓭** Democrat. **⓮** Baptist. **⓯** Clubs: Decatur Country, Decatur Athletic, Masons (Shriner). **⓰** Contbr. articles to profl jours **⓱** Home: 28 Hidden Hollow Rd. Decatur GA 30032 **⓲** Office: 350 Peachtree St. Decatur GA 30034

Key

❶ Name
❷ Occupation
❸ Vital Statistics
❹ Parents
❺ Education
❻ Marriage
❼ Children
❽ Career
❾ Civic and political activities
❿ Military record
⓫ Awards and certifications
⓬ Professional and association memberships
⓭ Political affiliation
⓮ Religion
⓯ Clubs (including lodges)
⓰ Writings and special achievements
⓱ Home address
⓲ Office address

The biographical listings in *Who's Who in the South and Southwest* are arranged in alphabetical order according to the first letter of the last name of the biographee. Each sketch is presented in a uniform order as in the sample sketch above. The many abbreviations used in the sketches are explained in the Table of Abbreviations.

Table of Abbreviations

The following abbreviations and symbols are frequently used in this Directory

∗ (An asterisk) following a sketch indicates that it was researched by the Marquis Who's Who editorial staff and has not been verified by the biographee.

A.A. Associate in Arts
AAAL American Academy of Arts and Letters
AAAS American Association for the Advancement of Science
AAHPER Alliance for Health, Physical Education and Recreation
A. and M. Agricultural and Mechanical
AAU Amateur Athletic Union
AAUP American Association of University Professors
AAUW American Association of University Women
A.B. Arts, Bachelor of
AB Alberta
ABC American Broadcasting Company
AC Air Corps
acad. academy, academic
acct. accountant
acctg. accounting
ACDA Arms Control and Disarmament Agency
ACLU American Civil Liberties Union
A.C.P. American College of Physicians
A.C.S. American College of Surgeons
ADA American Dental Association
a.d.c. aide-de-camp
adj. adjunct, adjutant
adj. gen. adjutant general
adm. admiral
adminstr. administrator
adminstrn. administration
adminstrv. administrative
adv. advocate, advisory, adviser
advt. advertising
A.E. Agricultural Engineeer
A.E. and P., AEP Ambassador Extraordinary and Plenipotentiary
AEC Atomic Energy Commission
aero. aeronautical, aeronautic
aerodyn. aerodynamic
AFB Air Force Base
AFL-CIO American Federation of Labor and Congress of Industrial Organizations
AFTRA American Federation TV and Radio Artists
agr. agriculture
agrl. agricultural
agt. agent
AGVA American Guild of Variety Artists
agy. agency
A&I Agricultural and Industrial
AIA American Institute of Architects
AIAA American Institute of Aeronautics Astronautics
AID Agency for International Development
AIEE American Institute of Electrical Engineers
AIM American Institute of Management
AIME American Institute of Mining, Metallurgy, and Petroleum Engineers
AK Alaska
AL Alabama
ALA American Library Association
Ala. Alabama
alt. alternate
Alta. Alberta
A&M Agricultural and Mechanical
A.M. Arts, Master of
Am. American, America
AMA American Medical Association

A.M.E. African Methodist Episcopal
Amtrak National Railroad Passenger Corporation
AMVETS American Veterans of World War II, Korea, Vietnam
anat. anatomical
ann. annual
ANTA American National Theatre and Academy
anthrop. anthropological
AP Associated Press
APO Army Post Office
apptd. appointed
apt. apartment
AR Arkansas
ARC American Red Cross
archeol. archeological
archtl. architectural
Ariz. Arizona
Ark. Arkansas
Arts D. Arts, Doctor of
arty. artillery
ASCAP American Society of Composers, Authors and Publishers
ASCE American Society of Civil Engineers
ASHRAE American Society of Heating, Refrigeration, and Air Conditioning Engineers
ASME American Society of Mechanical Engineers
assn. association
asso. associate
asst. assistant
ASTM American Society for Testing and Materials
astron. astronomical
astrophys. astrophysical
ATSC Air Technical Service Command
AT&T American Telephone & Telegraph Company
atty. attorney
AUS Army of the United States
aux. auxiliary
Ave. Avenue
AVMA American Veterinary Medical Association
AZ Arizona

B. Bachelor
b. born
B.A. Bachelor of Arts
B. Agr. Bachelor of Agriculture
Balt. Baltimore
Bapt. Baptist
B.Arch. Bachelor of Architecture
B.A.S. Bachelor of Agricultural Science
B.B.A. Bachelor of Business Administration
BBC British Broadcasting Corporation
B.C.,BC British Columbia
B.C.E. Bachelor of Civil Engineering
B.Chir. Bachelor of Surgery
B.C.L. Bachelor of Civil Law
B.C.S. Bachelor of Commerical Science
B.D. Bachelor of Divinity
bd. board
B.E. Bachelor of Education
B.E.E. Bachelor of Electrical Engineering
B.F.A. Bachelor of Fine Arts
bibl. biblical
bibliog. bibliographical
biog. biographical
biol. biological
B.J. Bachelor of Journalism
Bklyn. Brooklyn
B.L. Bachelor of Letters
bldg. building
B.L.S. Bachelor of Library Science

Blvd. Boulevard
bn. battalion
B.&O.R.R. Baltimore & Ohio Railroad
bot. botanical
B.P.E. Bachelor of Physical Education
br. branch
B.R.E. Bachelor of Religious Education
brig. gen. brigadier general
Brit. British, Britannica
Bros. Brothers
B.S. Bachelor of Science
B.S.A. Bachelor of Agricultural Science
B.S.D. Bachelor of Didactic Science
B.S.T. Bachelor of Sacred Theology
B.Th. Bachelor of Theology
bull. bulletin
bur. bureau
bus. business
B.W.I. British West Indies

CA California
CAA Civil Aeronautics Administration
CAB Civil Aeronautics Board
Calif. California
C.Am. Central America
Can. Canada, Canadian
CAP Civil Air Patrol
capt. captain
CARE Cooperative American Relief Everywhere
Cath. Catholic
cav. cavalry
CBC Canadian Broadcasting Company
CBI China, Burma, India Theatre of Operations
CBS Columbia Broadcasting System
CCC Commodity Credit Corporation
CCNY City College of New York
CCU Cardiac Care Unit
CD Civil Defense
C.E. Corps of Engineers, Civil Engineer
CENTO Central Treaty Organization
CERN European Organization of Nuclear Research
cert. certificate, certification, certified
CETA Comprehensive Employment Training Act
CFL Canadian Football League
ch. church
Ch.D. Doctor of Chemistry
chem. chemical
Chem. E. Chemical Engineer
Chgo. Chicago
chirurg. chirurgical
chmn. chairman
chpt. chapter
CIA Central Intelligence Agency
CIC Counter Intelligence Corps
Cin. Cincinnati
Cleve. Cleveland
climatol. climatological
clin. clinical
clk. clerk
C.L.U. Chartered Life Underwriter
C.M. Master in Surgery
C.& N.W.Ry. Chicago & Northwestern Railway
CO Colorado
Co. Company
COF Catholic Order of Foresters
C. of C. Chamber of Commerce
col. colonel
coll. college
Colo. Colorado
com. committee
comd. commanded
comdg. commanding

comdr. commander
comdt. commandant
commd. commissioned
comml. commercial
commn. commission
commr. commissioner
condr. conductor
Conf. Conference
Congl. Congregational
Conglist. Congregationalist
Conn. Connecticut
cons. consultant, consulting
consol. consolidated
constl. constitutional
constn. constitution
constrn. construction
contbd. contributed
contbg. contributing
contbn. contribution
contbr. contributor
Conv. Convention
coop., co-op. cooperative
CORDS Civil Operations and Revolutionary Development Support
CORE Congress of Racial Equality
corp. corporation, corporate
corr. correspondent, corresponding, correspondence
C.&O.Ry. Chesapeake & Ohio Railway
C.P.A. Certified Public Accountant
C.P.C.U. Chartered property and casualty underwriter
C.P.H. Certificate of Public Health
cpl. corporal
CPR Cardiac Pulmonary Resuscitation
C.P.Ry. Canadian Pacific Railway
C.S. Christian Science
C.S.B. Bachelor of Christian Science
CSC Civil Service Commission
C.S.D. Doctor of Christian Science
CT Connecticut
ct. Court
CWS Chemical Warfare Service
C.Z. Canal Zone

d. daughter
D. Doctor
D.Agr. Doctor of Agriculture
DAR Daughters of the American Revolution
dau. daughter
DAV Disabled American Veterans
D.C., DC District of Columbia
D.C.L. Doctor of Civil Law
D.C.S. Doctor of Commercial Science
D.D. Doctor of Divinity
D.D.S. Doctor of Dental Surgery
DE Delaware
dec. deceased
def. defense
Del. Delaware
del. delegate, delegation
Dem. Democrat, Democratic
D.Eng. Doctor of Engineering
denom. denomination, denominational
dep. deputy
dept. department
dermatol. dermatological
desc. descendant
devel. development, developmental
D.F.A. Doctor of Fine Arts
D.F.C. Distinguished Flying Cross
D.H.L. Doctor of Hebrew Literature
dir. director
dist. district
distbg. distributing
distbn. distribution

distbr. distributor
disting. distinguished
div. division, divinity, divorce
D.Litt. Doctor of Literature
D.M.D. Doctor of Medical Dentistry
D.M.S. Doctor of Medical Science
D.O. Doctor of Osteopathy
D.P.H. Diploma in Public Health
D.R. Daughters of the Revolution
Dr. Drive
D.R.E. Doctor of Religious Education
Dr.P.H. Doctor of Public Health, Doctor of Public Hygiene
D.S.C. Distinguished Service Cross
D.Sc. Doctor of Science
D.S.M. Distinguished Service Medal
D.S.T. Doctor of Sacred Theology
D.T.M. Doctor of Tropical Medicine
D.V.M. Doctor of Veterinary Medicine
D.V.S. Doctor of Veterinary Surgery

E. East
E. and P. Extraordinary and Plenipotentiary
Eccles. Ecclesiastical
ecol. ecology, ecological
econ. economic
ECOSOC Economic and Social Council (of the UN)
E.D. Doctor of Engineering
ed. educated
Ed.B. Bachelor of Education
Ed.D. Doctor of Education
edit. edition
Ed.M. Master of Education
edn. education
ednl. educational
EDP electronic data processing
Ed.S. Specialist in Education
E.E. Electrical Engineer
E.E. and M.P. Envoy Extraordinary and Minister Plenipotentiary
EEC European Economic Community
EEG electroencephalogram
EEO Equal Employment Opportunity
EKG electrocardiogram
E.Ger. German Democratic Republic
elec. electrical
electrochem. electrochemical
electrophys. electrophysical
elem. elementary
E.M. Engineer of Mines
ency. encyclopedia
Eng. England
engr. engineer
engring. engineering
entomol. entomological
environ. environmental, environment
EPA Environmental Protection Agency
epidemiol. epidemiological
Episc. Episcopalian
ERA Equal Rights Amendment
ERDA Energy Research and Development Administration
ESEA Elementary and Secondary Education Act
ESSA Environmental Science Services Administration
ethnol. ethnological
ETO European Theatre of Operations
Evang. Evangelical
exam. examination, examining
exec. executive
exhbn. exhibition
expdn. expedition
expn. exposition
expt. experiment
exptl. experimental

F.A. Field Artillery
FAA Federal Aviation Administration
FAO Food and Agriculture Organization (of the UN)
FBI Federal Bureau of Investigation
FCA Farm Credit Administration
FCC Federal Communication Commission
FCDA Federal Civil Defense Administration
FDA Food and Drug Administration
FDIA Federal Deposit Insurance Administration
FDIC Federal Deposit Insurance Corporation
F.E. Forest Engineer
FEA Federal Energy Administration
fed. federal
fedn. federation
fgn. foreign
FHA Federal Housing Administration
fin. financial, finance
FL Florida
Fla. Florida
FMC Federal Maritime Commission
FOA Foreign Operations Administration
found. foundation
FPC Federal Power Commission
FPO Fleet Post Office
frat. fraternity
FRS Federal Reserve System
FSA Federal Security Agency
Ft. Fort
FTC Federal Trade Commission

G-1 (or other number) Division of General Staff
Ga., GA Georgia
GAO General Accounting Office
gastroent. gastroenterological
GATT General Agreement of Tariff and Trades
gen. general
geneal. genealogical
geod. geodetic
geog. geographic, geographical
geol. geological
geophys. geophysical
gerontol. gerontological
G.H.Q. General Headquarters
G.N.Ry. Great Northern Railway
gov. governor
govt. government
govtl. governmental
GPO Government Printing Office
grad. graduate, graduated
GSA General Services Administration
Gt. Great
GU Guam
gynecol. gynecological

hdqrs. headquarters
HEW Department of Health, Education and Welfare
H.H.D. Doctor of Humanities
HHFA Housing and Home Finance Agency
HI Hawaii
hist. historical, historic
H.M. Master of Humanics
homeo. homeopathic
hon. honorary, honorable
Ho. of Dels. House of Delegates
Ho. of Reps. House of Representatives
hort. horticultural
hosp. hospital
HUD Department of Housing and Urban Development
Hwy. Highway
hydrog. hydrographic

x

IA Iowa
IAEA International Atomic Energy Agency
IBM International Business Machines Corporation
IBRD International Bank for Reconstruction and Development
ICA International Cooperation Administration
ICC Interstate Commerce Commission
ICU Intensive Care Unit
ID Idaho
IEEE Institute of Electrical and Electronics Engineers
IFC International Finance Corporation
IGY International Geophysical Year
IL Illinois
Ill. Illinois
illus. illustrated
ILO International Labor Organization
IMF International Monetary Fund
IN Indiana
Inc. Incorporated
ind. independent
Ind. Indiana
Indpls. Indianapolis
indsl. industrial
inf. infantry
info. information
ins. insurance
insp. inspector
insp. gen. inspector general
inst. institute
instl. institutional
instn. institution
instr. instructor
instrn. instruction
internat. international
intro. introduction
IRE Institute of Radio Engineers
IRS Internal Revenue Service
ITT International Telephone & Telegraph Corporation

J.B. Jurum Baccalaureus
J.C.B. Juris Canonici Bachelor
J.C.L. Juris Canonici Lector
J.D. Juris Doctor
j.g. junior grade
jour. journal
jr. junior
J.S.D. Jurum Scientiae Doctor
J.U.D. Juris Utriusque Doctor
Judge Adv. Gen. Judge Advocate General

Kans. Kansas
K.C. Knights of Columbus
K.P. Knights of Pythias
KS Kansas
K.T. Knight Templar
Ky., KY Kentucky

La., LA Louisiana
lab. laboratory
lang. language
laryngol. laryngological
LB Labrador
lectr. lecturer
legis. legislation, legislative
L.H.D. Doctor of Humane Letters
L.I. Long Island
lic. licensed, license
L.I.R.R. Long Island Railroad
lit. literary, literature
Litt. B. Bachelor of Letters

Litt. D. Doctor of Letters
LL.B. Bachelor of Laws
LL.D. Doctor of Laws
LL.M. Master of Laws
Ln. Lane
L.&N.R.R. Louisville & Nashville Railroad
L.S. Library Science (in degree)
lt. lieutenant
Ltd. Limited
Luth. Lutheran
LWV League of Women Voters

m. married
M. Master
M.A. Master of Arts
MA Massachusetts
mag. magazine
M.Agr. Master of Agriculture
maj major
Man. Manitoba
M.Arch. Master in Architecture
Mass. Massachusetts
math. mathematics, mathematical
MATS Military Air Transport Service
M.B. Bachelor of Medicine
MB Manitoba
M.B.A. Master of Business Administration
MBS Mutual Broadcasting System
M.C. Medical Corps
M.C.E. Master of Civil Engineering
mcht. merchant
mcpl. municipal
M.C.S. Master of Commercial Science
M.D. Doctor of Medicine
Md., MD Maryland
M.Dip. Master in Diplomacy
mdse. merchandise
M.D.V. Doctor of Veterinary Medicine
M.E. Mechanical Engineer
ME Maine
M.E. Ch. Methodist Episcopal Church
mech. mechanical
M.Ed. Master of Education
med. medical
M.E.E. Master of Electrical Engineering
mem. member
meml. memorial
merc. mercantile
met. metropolitan
metall. metallurgical
Met. E. Metallurgical Engineer
meteorol. meteorological
Meth. Methodist
Mex. Mexico
M.F. Master of Forestry
M.F.A. Master of Fine Arts
mfg. manufacturing
mfr. manufacturer
mgmt. management
mgr. manager
M.H.A. Master of Hospital Administration
M.I. Military Intelligence
MI Michigan
Mich. Michigan
micros. microscopic, microscopical
mil. military
Milw. Milwaukee
mineral. mineralogical
Minn. Minnesota
Miss. Mississippi
M.I.T. Massachusetts Institute of Technology
mktg. marketing
M.L. Master of Laws
MLA Modern Language Association
M.L.D. Magister Legnum Diplomatic

M.Litt. Master of Literature
M.L.S. Master of Library Science
M.M.E. Master of Mechanical Engineering
MN Minnesota
mng. managing
Mo., MO Missouri
mobLzn. mobilization
Mont. Montana
M.P. Member of Parliament
M.P.E. Master of Physical Education
M.P.H. Master of Public Health
M.P.L. Master of Patent Law
Mpls. Minneapolis
M.R.E. Master of Religious Education
M.S. Master of Science
MS Mississippi
M.Sc. Master of Science
M.S.F. Master of Science of Forestry
M.S.T. Master of Sacred Theology
M.S.W. Master of Social Work
MT Montana
Mt. Mount
MTO Mediterranean Theatre of Operations
mus. museum, musical
Mus.B. Bachelor of Music
Mus.D. Doctor of Music
Mus.M. Master of Music
mut. mutual
mycol. mycological

N. North
NAACP National Association for the Advancement of Colored People
NACA National Advisory Committee for Aeronautics
NAD National Academy of Design
N.Am. North America
NAM National Association of Manufacturers
NAPA National Association of Performing Artists
NAREB National Association of Real Estate Boards
NARS National Archives and Record Service
NASA National Aeronautics and Space Administration
nat. national
NATO North Atlantic Treaty Organization
NATOUSA North African Theatre of Operations
nav. navigation
N.B., NB New Brunswick
NBC National Broadcasting Company
N.C., NC North Carolina
NCCJ National Conference of Christians and Jews
N.D., ND North Dakota
NDEA National Defense Education Act
NE Nebraska
N.E. Northeast
NEA National Education Association
Nebr. Nebraska
neurol. neurological
Nev. Nevada
NF Newfoundland
NFL National Football League
Nfld. Newfoundland
N.G. National Guard
N.H., NH New Hampshire
NHL National Hockey League
NIH National Institutes of Health
NIMH National Institute of Mental Health
N.J., NJ New Jersey
NLRB National Labor Relations Board
NM New Mexico
N.Mex. New Mexico
No. Northern

NOAA National Oceanographic and Atmospheric Administration
NORAD North American Air Defense
NOW National Organization for Women
N.P. Ry. Northern Pacific Railway
nr. near
NRC National Research Council
N.S., NS Nova Scotia
NSC National Security Council
NSF National Science Foundation
N.T. New Testament
NT Northwest Territories
numis. numismatic
NV Nevada
NW Northwest
N.W.T. Northwest Territories
N.Y., NY New York
N.Y.C. New York City
N.Z. New Zealand

OAS Organization of American States
Ob-Gyn obstetrics-gynecology
obs. observatory
O.D. Doctor of Optometry
OECD Organization of European Cooperation and Development
OEEC Organization of European Economic Cooperation
OEO Office of Economic Opportunity
ofcl. official
OH Ohio
OK Oklahoma
Okla. Oklahoma
ON Ontario
Ont. Ontario
ophthal. ophthalmological
ops. operations
OR Oregon
orch. orchestra
Oreg. Oregon
orgn. organization
ornithol. ornithological
OSRD Office of Scientific Research and Development
OSS Office of Strategic Services
osteo. osteopathic
otol. otological
otolaryn. otolaryngological

Pa., PA Pennsylvania
P.A. Professional Association
paleontol. paleontological
path. pathological
P.C. Professional Corporation
PE Prince Edward Island
P.E. Professional Engineer
P.E.I. Prince Edward Island
PEN Poets, Playwrights, Editors, Essayists and Novelists (international association)
penol. penological
P.E.O. women's organization (full name not disclosed)
pfc. private first class
PHA Public Housing Administration
pharm. Pharmaceutical
Pharm.D. Doctor of Pharmacy
Pharm.M. Master of Pharmacy
Ph.B. Bachelor of Philosophy
Ph.D. Doctor of Philosophy
Phila. Philadelphia
philharm. philharmonic
philol. philological
philos. philosophical
photog. photographic

phys. physical
physiol. physiological
Pitts. Pittsburgh
Pkwy. Parkway
Pl. Place
P.&L.E.R.R. Pittsburgh & Lake Erie Railroad
P.O. Post Office
PO Box Post Office Box
polit. political
poly. polytechnic, polytechnical
P.Q. Province of Quebec
P.R., PR Puerto Rico
prep. preparatory
pres. president
Presbyn. Presbyterian
presdl. presidential
prin. principal
proc. proceedings
prod. produced (play production)
prof. professor
profl. professional
prog. progressive
propr. proprietor
pros. atty. prosecuting attorney
pro tem pro tempore
PSRO Professional Services Review Organization
psychiat. psychiatric
psychol. psychological
PTA Parent-Teachers Association
PTO Pacific Theatre of Operations
pub. publisher, publishing, published
publ. publication
pvt. private

quar. quarterly
q.m. quartermaster
Q.M.C. Quartermaster Corps
Que. Quebec

radiol. radiological
RAF Royal Air Force
RCA Radio Corporation of America
RCAF Royal Canadian Air Force
R.D. Rural Delivery
Rd. Road
REA Rural Electrification Administration
rec. recording
ref. reformed
regt. regiment
regtl. regimental
rehab. rehabilitation
rep. representative
Rep. Republican
Res. Reserve
ret. retired
rev. review, revised
RFC Reconstruction Finance Corporation
R.F.D. Rural Free Delivery
rhinol. rhinological
R.I., RI Rhode Island
R.N. Registered Nurse
roentgenol. roentgenological
ROTC Reserve Officers Training Corps
R.R. Railroad
Ry. Railway

s. son
S. South
SAC Strategic Air Command
SALT Strategic Arms Limitation Talks
S.Am. South America
san sanitary
SAR Sons of the American Revolution

Sask. Saskatchewan
savs. savings
S.B. Bachelor of Science
SBA Small Business Administration
S.C., SC South Carolina
SCAP Supreme Command Allies Pacific
Sc.B. Bachelor of Science
S.C.D. Doctor of Commercial Science
Sc.D. Doctor of Science
sch. school
sci. science, scientific
SCLC Southern Christian Leadership Conference
SCV Sons of Confederate Veterans
S.D., SD South Dakota
SE Southeast
SEATO Southeast Asia Treaty Organization
sec. secretary
SEC Securities and Exchange Commission
sect. section
seismol. seismological
sem. seminary
sgt. sergeant
SHAEF Supreme Headquarters Allied Expeditionary Forces
SHAPE Supreme Headquarters Allied Powers in Europe
S.I. Staten Island
S.J. Society of Jesus (Jesuit)
S.J.D. Scientiae Juridicae Doctor
SK Saskatchewan
S.M. Master of Science
So. Southern
soc. society
sociol. sociological
S.P. Co. Southern Pacific Company
spl. special
splty. specialty
Sq. Square
sr. senior
S.R. Sons of the Revolution
S.S. Steamship
SSS Selective Service System
St. Saint
St. Street
sta. station
statis. statistical
stats. statistics
S.T.B. Bachelor of Sacred Theology
stblzn. stabilization
S.T.D. Doctor of Sacred Theology
subs. subsidiary
SUNY State University of New York
supr. supervisor
supt. superintendent
surg. surgical
SW Southwest

TAPPI Technical Association of Pulp and Paper Industry
Tb Tuberculosis
tchr. teacher
tech. technical, technology
technol. technological
Tel.&Tel. Telephone & Telegraph
temp. temporary
Tenn. Tennessee
Ter. Territory
Terr. Terrace
TESL Teaching English as a Second Language
Tex. Texas
Th.D. Doctor of Theology
theol. theological
Th.M. Master of Theology
TN Tennessee
tng. training

topog. topographical
trans. transaction, transferred
transl. translation, translated
transp. transportation
treas. treasurer
TV television
TVA Tennessee Valley Authority
twp. township
TX Texas
typog. typographical

U. University
UAW United Auto Workers
UCLA University of California at Los Angeles
UDC United Daughters of the Confederacy
U.K. United Kingdom
UN United Nations
UNESCO United Nations Educational, Scientific and Cultural Organization
UNICEF United Nations International Children's Emergency Fund
univ. university
UNRRA United Nations Relief and Rehabilitation Administration
UPI United Press International
U.P.R.R. Union Pacific Railroad
urol. urological
U.S. United States
U.S.A. United States of America
USAAF United States Army Air Force
USAF United States Air Force

USAFR United States Air Force Reserve
USAR United States Army Reserve
USCG United States Coast Guard
USCGR United States Coast Guard Reserve
USES United States Employment Service
USIA United States Information Agency
USIS United States Information Service
USMC United States Marine Corps
USMCR United States Marine Corps Reserve
USN United States Navy
USNG United States National Guard
USNR United States Naval Reserve
USO United Service Organizations
USPHS United States Public Health Service
U.S.S. United States Ship
USSR Union of the Soviet Socialist Republics
USV United States Volunteers
UT Utah

VA Veterans' Administration
Va., VA Virginia
vet. veteran, veterinary
VFW Veterans of Foreign Wars
V.I., VI Virgin Islands
vice pres. vice president
vis. visiting
VISTA Volunteers in Service to America
VITA Volunteers in Technical Service
vocat. vocational
vol. volunteer, volume

v.p. vice president
vs. versus
VT., VT Vermont

W. West
WA Washington
WAC Women's Army Corps
Wash. Washington
WAVES Women's Reserve, U.S. Naval Reserve
WCTU Women's Christian Temperance Union
W. Ger. Germany, Federal Republic of
WHO World Health Organization
WI Wisconsin
Wis. Wisconsin
WSB Wage Stabilization Board
WV West Virginia
W. VA. West Virginia
WY Wyoming
Wyo. Wyoming

YK Yukon
YMCA Young Men's Christian Association
YMHA Young Men's Hebrew Association
YM & YWHA Young Men's and Young Women's Hebrew Association
YWCA Young Women's Christian Association
yr. year

zool. zoological

Alphabetical Practices

Names are arranged alphabetically according to the surnames, and under identical surnames according to the first given name. If both surname and first given name are identical, names are arranged alphabetically according to the second given name. Where full names are identical, they are arranged in order of age—those of the elder being put first.

Surnames beginning with De, Des, Du, etc., however capitalized or spaced, are recorded with the prefix preceding the surname and arranged alphabetically, under the letter D.

Surnames beginning with Mac are arranged alphabetically under M. This likewise holds for names beginning with Mc; that is, all names beginning Mc will be found in alphabetical order after those beginning Mac.

Surnames beginning with Saint or St. all appear after names that would begin Sains, and such surnames are arranged according to the second part of the name, e.g., St. Clair would come before Saint Dennis.

Surnames beginning with prefix Van are arranged alphabetically under letter V.

Surnames containing the prefix Von or von are usually arranged alphabetically under letter V; any exceptions are noted by cross references (Von Kleinsmid, Rufus Bernhard; see Kleinsmid, Rufus Bernhard von).

Compound hyphenated surnames are arranged according to the first member of the compound.

Compound unhyphenated surnames common in Spanish are not rearranged but are treated as hyphenated names.

Since Chinese names have the family name first, they are so arranged, but without comma between family name and given name (as Lin Yutang).

Parentheses used in connection with a name indicate which part of the full name is usually deleted in common usage. Hence Abbott, W(illiam) Lewis indicates that the usual form of the given name is W. Lewis. In alphabetizing this type name, the parentheses are not considered. However if the name is recorded Abbott, (William) Lewis, signifying that the entire name William is not commonly used, the alphabetizing would be arranged as though the name were Abbott, Lewis.

Who'sWho in the South and Southwest

AARONSON, ALFRED ENOCH, real estate exec.; b. N.Y.C., Oct. 31, 1893; s. Lionel E. Z. and Cynthia Thelma (Robins) A.; student Columbia U., 1911-12; m. Millicent Lubetkin, Oct. 5, 1915; children—Grace (Mrs. Judah Goldin), Alice (Mrs. Dov Zlotnick). Pres., Tuloma Oil Co., Tulsa, 1915-26; v.p. Leavell Coal Co., Tulsa, 1920-45; v.p. Commonwealth Co., Tulsa, 1925-35; organizer, v.p. Looboyle, Inc., 1930-57, Consumers Oil Stas. Inc., 1930-57; pres. Court Arcade Bldg. Co., Tulsa, 1936—; dir. 4th Nat. Bank Tulsa. Chmn. Keep Gilcrease Mus. for Tulsa, 1954-55; chmn. Downtown Bus. Com., Tulsa Met. Area Bus. Com., 1959; chmn. Tulsa City and County Library Com., 1960-66; chmn. bldg. com. Tulsa Psychiat. Found., 1962; organizer Tulsa County Hist. Soc., 1962; mem. Tulsa Community Relations Com., 1962-66; mem. Okla. Human Rights Commn., 1963-66, hon. mem., 1967—; hon. mem. S.W. Center Human Relations, U. Okla., 1962; hon. mem. Urban League, 1963, NCCJ, 1964; pres. Tulsa Jewish Community Council, 1944, Gilcrease Inst. Am. History and Art, 1956-58. Recipient Distinguished Service award U. Okla., 1966, Sertoma award, 1969, Okla. Library Assn. award, 1966, awards City of Tulsa, 1967, 69; Civitan Leadership award, Tulsa, 1973, Am. State Bank award, 1975; named Distinguished Hon. Alumnus, Langston U., 1966; to Okla. Hall of Fame, 1975. Fellow U. Okla., 1970—. Mem. Tulsa Bldg. Owners and Mgrs. Assn. (past pres.). Mason (Shriner), Lion (hon.), Rotarian (hon.); mem. B'nai B'rith. Club: Summit (Tulsa). Home: 1782 E 30th St Tulsa OK 74114 Office: Court Arcade Bldg 6th and Boulder Av Tulsa OK 74103

ABBOTT, BENJAMIN EDWARD, JR., corp. exec.; b. Washington, Dec. 7, 1928; s. Benjamin Edward and Agnes (Campbell) A.; B. Indsl. Engring., U. Fla., 1953; m. Ellianna Gray, May 22, 1955; children—Celeni, Dawn, Mark, Scott. Indsl. engr. E.I. DuPont de Nemours & Co., Martinsville, Va., 1951, Allis Chalmers, Milw., 1953, Pensacola (Fla.) Naval Air Sta., 1955-61; mem. exec. staff Dr. Wernher von Braun, Marshall Space Flight Center, NASA, Huntsville, Ala., 1961-68; v.p., dir. Investors Corp. of Am., Birmingham, 1968-75, Internat. Resorts, Inc., 1970-75; pres. Resort Properties Realty Co., 1975, Profl. Realty Services, Inc., 1976-77, Energy Systems Engrs., Inc., Birmingham, 1978—. Served to lt. (j.g.) USNR, 1953-55. Registered profl. engr., Ala., Fla. Mem. Am. Inst. Indsl. Engrs. (sr.), Nat. Soc. Profl. Engrs., Assn. Energy Engrs., ASHRAE, Pi Kappa Phi. Home: Route 2 Box 116-B Alpine AL 35014 Office: Energy Systems Engrs 1055 24th St S Birmingham AL 35202

ABBOTT, EDITHGENE BECRAFT, educator; b. Rushville, Ind., June 3, 1916; d. Frank William and Pearle (Casey) Becraft; R.N., U. Cin., 1940; B.S. in Edn., Oglethorpe U., Atlanta, 1958; M.Ed., Emory U., 1959; Ed.D. (Regents scholar 1967-68), U. Ga., 1973; m. Frank Sparks, Mar. 21, 1941; children—J. Michael, Patricia Abbott Friend, James M.; m. 2d. Martin L. Abbott, Jan. 16, 1972. Kindergarten tchr., then public sch. tchr., 1953-59; vis. prof. Emory U., 1960-63; asst. prof. edn. Oglethorpe U., 1964-67; asst. prof. U. S.Fla., Tampa, 1968-70; mem. faculty Ga. Coll., Milledgeville, 1970—, prof. edn., 1979—, chmn. dept. childhood edn., 1979—. Mem. Nat. Council Tchrs. English, Ga. Assn. Tchrs. English, Nat. Middle Sch. Assn., Nat. Assn. Edn. Young Children, Ga. Assn. Young Children. Republican. Home: 1679 Pine Valley Rd Milledgeville GA 31061 Office: Georgia Coll Milledgeville GA 31061

ABBOTT, HERSCHEL LEE, JR., lawyer; b. Little Rock, Sept. 4, 1941; s. Herschel Lee and Wanda Cathryn (Jones) A.; certificate U. Birmingham (Eng.), 1962; B.A., Tulane U., New Orleans, 1963, LL.B., 1966; m. Anne Elizabeth Hamilton, Dec. 21, 1963; children—Cathryn Boyd, Herschel Lee III. Asst. dean students Tulane U., 1965-66; asso. prof. lit. Altus (Okla.) Jr. Coll., 1966-70; admitted to La. bar, 1966; lectr. bus. law Far East div. U. Md., Bien Hoa, Republic Vietnam, 1969-70; asso. lawyer firm Jones, Walker, Waechter, Poitevent, Carrere & Denegre, New Orleans, 1970-73, partner, 1973—. Mem. subcom. to revise La. Partnership Laws La. State Law Inst., 1975—. Mem. bishop and council Episcopal Diocese La.; bd. dirs. New Orleans Area Health Planning Council, 1974—, 1st v.p., 1975, pres., 1976-77. Served to capt., USAF, 1966-70; Vietnam. Decorated Bronze Star medal, Cross of Galantry with Palm (Vietnam). Mem. New Orleans, La., Am. bar assns., Omicron Delta Kappa, Kappa Delta Phi, Phi Sigma Alpha, Phi Delta Phi. Democrat. Episcopalian. Clubs: Bienville, Stratford, Pickwick, New Orleans Country, Pendennis, Plimsoll. Home: 4201 Cleveland Pl Metairie LA 70003 Office: 225 Baronne St New Orleans LA 70112

ABBOTT, ROBERT EARL, JR., city ofcl.; b. Dallas, Aug. 17, 1935; s. Robert Earl and Jane Ann (Hines) A.; B.S., Hardin Simmons U., 1960; M.Urban and Regional Planning, Va. Poly. Inst. and State U., 1970; D.P.A., N.Y. U., 1979; m. Betty Jeanette Deaver, July 24, 1965; 1 son, Mark Arthur. Sr. city planner City of Richmond (Va.), 1969-71; dir. mayors' council N. Hudson Council Mayors, Hudson County, N.J., 1971-73; exec. dir. Regional Planning Commn., Thomas Jefferson Planning Dist. Commn., Charlottesville, Va., 1973-78; cons. City of Newport News (Va.), 1978—; lectr. U. Va., Va. Commonwealth U., Va. Poly. Inst. and State U. Served with AUS, 1960-62, 63-67. Mem. Am. Inst. Cert. Planners, Am. Planning Assn., Soc. for Advancement Mgmt. Baptist. Home: 316 Camellia Dr Charlottesville VA 22903 Office: PO Box 1533 Newport News VA 23601

ABBOTT, THOMAS BENJAMIN, educator; b. Atlasburg, Pa., June 27; s. Thomas Rankin and Emma Elizabeth (Behling) A.; B.A., Muskingum Coll., 1943; M.A., Case Western Res. U., 1948; Ph.D., U. Fla., 1957; m. Lee Margaret Parsons, Dec. 29, 1945; children—John P., Amy P. Dir. speech therapy programs RoseMary Home for Crippled Children, Cleve., 1948-49; asst. prof. speech Minn. Stat. Coll. at St. Cloud, 1949-53; instr. U. Fla. at Gainesville, 1955-57; lectr. U. So. Calif., Los Angeles, 1957-58; prof. Baylor U., Waco, Tex., 1958-63; prof. speech U. Fla. at Gainesville, 1963—, chmn. dept., 1978—; cons. Office Edn., 1966—; mem. adv. council Commr. Edn. Fla., 1969—. Bd. dirs. Fla. Easter Seal Soc., 1966—, pres., 1968-70; bd. dirs. Nat. Easter Seal Soc., 1979—. Served with AUS, 1943-45. Fellow Am. Speech and Hearing Assn.; mem. Fla. Speech and Hearing Assn. (pres. 1968-69), Speech Communication Assn., Nat. Council for Exceptional Children. Edit. cons. Jour. Speech and Hearing Disorders, 1966-69. Home: 1502 NW 31st St Gainesville FL 32605 Office: Dept Speech Univ Florida Gainesville FL 32611

ABBOTT, WILLIAM ORVEL, mfg. co. exec.; b. Houston, May 30, 1938; s. Orvel Cullen and Eunice (Cline) A.; student San Jacinto Jr. Coll., 1964-66; m. Barbara Mae Elizabeth Koenig, Aug. 2, 1957; children—Steven Cullen, Derek Lane. Sheet metal mechanic Tex. Instruments, 1967-69; with Sheet Metal Products, Inc., Houston, 1969—, gen. mgr., 1971-76, pres., owner, 1976—; founder, pres. AKS, Houston, 1978—; co-founder, sec. Pasco, 1978-79. Served with USNR, 1957-58. Mem. Nat. Tool and Die Assn., Am. Mgmt. Assn. Republican. Methodist. Club: Pineforest Country. Office: 1751 Stebbins Dr Houston TX 77043

ABCHAL, GEORGE LEE, decorating co. exec.; b. St. Louis, Aug. 13, 1938; s. George Francis and Helen Lenore (Marsh) A.; student Kans. U., 1958; B.A. in Bus., Pratt Inst., 1961; m. Victoria Ann Anderson, Dec. 10, 1973; children—Mia, Joseph, Alexandra. Pres., Images, Inc., Pompano Beach, Fla., 1973—; v.p. Vec Trak Research & Devel., Inc., N.Y.C., 1970-72, Carbo-Jet Inc., Ft. Lauderdale, Fla., 1967-70; pres. Spooner Motors, Inc., St. Louis, 1958-60. Bd. govs. Boys' Club Broward County, 1973—. Served with U.S. Army, 1961-67. Mem. Am. Soc. Interior Decorators, Am. Inst. Design. Democrat. Roman Catholic. Club: Civitan. Office: 1543 N Dixie Hwy Pompano Beach FL 33060

ABDO, PETER FREDERICK, office machines co. exec.; b. Methuen, Mass., Jan. 31, 1921; s. Nackley and Teresa (Kalil) A.; student parochial schs.; m. Charlena Fayed, Jan. 10, 1954; children—Charles, Peter. Br. mgr. Dictapone Corp., 1953-63; founder South Fla. Office Machines, West Palm Beach, 1963; pres. Advanced Bus. Products, West Palm Beach, 1973-78; owner, operator South Fla. Leasing Co.; pres. Abson Corp., D.B.A. Advanced Bus. Products of Miami; dir., sec. Bus. Machines, Inc. Served with AUS, 1940-43, USAAF, 1943-45. Recipient award Fla. Med. Records Assn., 1979. Mem. Nat. Office Machine Dealers Assn. Clubs: West Palm Beach Country, Wellington Country, Mayacoo Country, West Palm Beach Rotary (dir. 1972, 75, 79, 80). Home: 236 Old Country Rd West Palm Beach FL 33411 Office: PO Box 1507 West Palm Beach FL 33402

ABDULRAHMAN, MUSTAFA SALIH, educator; b. Sulaimaniah, Iraq, June 15, 1930; s. Salih and Ammina Al-Haj (Mohammad) A.; came to U.S., 1956; B.S., Baghdad (Iraq) U., 1952; M.S., Rutgers U., 1958; Ph.D., Ia. State U., 1964. Chief engr. Baghdad U., 1964-65; asso. prof. civil engring. U. Miss., University, 1965—. Cons. engr., land developer, Oxford, Miss., 1968—. Named Outstanding Tchr., Sch. Engring., U. Miss., 1968. Mem. ASCE, Am. Soc. Engring. Edn., Am. Concrete Inst., Miss. Engring. Soc., Chi Epsilon. Home: 2204 Church St Oxford MS 38655 Office: PO Box 1251 University MS 38677

ABEL, PAUL LOUIS, educator; b. Clarksdale, Miss., Nov. 23, 1926; s. Paul Louis and Elizabeth (Campbell) A.; B.Mus., Eastman Sch. Mus., 1948; M.Mus., U. Rochester, 1950; m. Adeline Marie Tifft, Aug. 27, 1952; children—Paul, Mark, Charles, Andrew; m. 2d, Genevieve Robinson, Jan. 30, 1968; 1 son, Leo. Instr., U. Mont., Missoula, 1950-54; prof. La. State U., Baton Rouge, 1954—. Choir dir. Broadmoor Presbyn. Ch., Baton Rouge, La., 1971—. Recipient Benjamin award for mus. composition, 1962; H.M. (Hubb) Cotton award for outstanding teaching La. State U. Found., 1978; named Outstanding Educator, 1975. Mem. Am. Fedn. Musicians, Mus. Educator's Nat. Conf., Am. Guild Organist, Phi Mu Alpha Sinfonia, Phi Kappa Lambda, Omicron Delta Kappa. Office: Sch Music La State U Baton Rouge LA 70803

ABEL, THOMAS CRAWFORD, hosp. edn. adminstr.; b. New Orleans, Sept. 13, 1929; s. John Vaughan and Myrle Louise (Satterlee) A.; B.Div., New Melleray Abbey, 1967; M.S. in Social Studies, Miss. State U., 1971; m. Mary Ann Dziak, Aug. 14, 1971; children—Carrie Ann, Christopher Vaughan, Jonathan Dziak, David Thomas. Ordained priest, 1963; founder, coordinator New Monastery, Brooksville, Miss., 1968-71; resource cons. Head Start, Prairie Opportunity Program, Macon, Miss., 1969; reading instr. Chambliss Children's Home, Tuskegee (Ala.) Inst., 1971-72; tchr. learning disabilities, Central Ala. Youth Service, Tremont Sch., Selma, Ala., 1972-73; dir. group homes, Selma, 1973-75; exec. dir. Brantwood Ch. Home, Montgomery, Ala., 1975-77; formed Ten Agency Child Care Consortium, Montgomery, 1976; dir. edn. St. Margaret's Hosp., Montgomery, 1977-79; founder, coordinator New South Lifestyles, Intentional Community, Wetumpka, Ala., 1977; active in local and state health edn. confs.; chmn. Health Educators Tri County Consortium, Montgomery, 1978-80. Exec. sec. pastoral council Roman Catholic Diocese of Mobile. Mem. Ala. Soc. Adlerian Psychology (pres.), Nat. League Nursing. Democrat. Home: Route 1 Box 75 Wetumpka AL 36092 Office: PO Drawer 311 834 Adams St Montgomery AL 36101

ABELLA, ROSA MARGARITA, librarian; b. Havana, Cuba, Feb. 13, 1920; d. Faustino and Rosa (Schmidt) Abella; Tecnica Bibliotecarria, U. Habana, 1956, Dr. Filosofia y Letras, 1958. Came to U.S., 1961, naturalized, 1969. Librarian, Biblioteca Instituto de la Habana, 1952-59; head librarian circulation dept. Biblioteca Nacional Jose Marti, Havana, 1959-61; prof., librarian Otto G. Richter Library, U. Miami, Coral Gables, Fla., 1961—. Past pres. Seminar on Acquisitions of Library Materials. Mem. Inst. Internat. Edn. Club: Cuban Women's. Contbr. articles to profl. jours. Home: 7541 SW 62 St Miami FL 33155 Office: University of Miami Library Coral Gables FL 33124

ABELS, MAC JON, florist; b. Peaster, Tex., Mar. 17, 1930; s. Benjamin Joseph and Ida Laney (Allison) A.; grad. Weatherford Jr. Coll., 1949; B.S., Tex. Christian U., 1953; m. Patricia Anita Black, Apr. 19, 1964; children—Lallene Jeanine Rector, Melody Anita Rector. Asst. personnel mgr. Continental Oil Co., Ft. Worth, 1953-54, mktg. sr. price clk., 1954-64; propr., mgr. Lillian Simons Flowers, Inc., Ft. Worth, 1965—; floral designer, 1950—; lectr. floral design various schs. and clubs, 1973—; designer Gard All White Show, Chgo., 1970. Adviser Jr. Achievement, Ft. Worth, 1960—. Bd. dirs. Tex. Girls Choir, 1973—; mem. adv. bd. Tarrant County Jr. Coll., Ft. Worth, 1974—. Mem. Am. Inst. Floral Designers (guest speaker 1973—, designer nat. symposium 1973), Tex. State (v.p. 1968—), Ft. Worth (pres. 1974—) florist assns., Soc. Am. Florists, Profl. Floral Commentators Internat., Ft. Worth C. of C. Democrat. Methodist (bd. chmn. 1970-71, trustee 1971-72, bd. dirs. Met. Bd. missions 1972-73). Mason, Elk, Kiwanian (pres. 1973). Contbr. articles on floral design to various profl. mags. Home: 1732 Sheffield Pl Fort Worth TX 76112 Office: 3621 W 7th St Fort Worth TX 76107

ABERCROMBIE, MARY LOUISE, plastic packaging co. exec.; b. Woodruff, S.C., Dec. 11, 1937; d. Paul Henry and Valma Mary (Perry) Fincher; student bus. Young Harris Jr. Coll., 1954-55; children—Kathryn Darlene, Robert Perry, Laura Lynn. Sec. patent dept. Cryovac div. W.R. Grace & Co., Duncan, S.C., 1962-65, sec. purchasing dept., 1968-73, purchasing asst., 1973-76, buyer, 1976—; sec. purchasing and physics dept. U. N.C., Chapel Hill, 1965-66. Mem. Purchasing Mgmt. Assn. Carolinas-Va. (2d vice chmn. Upper S.C. chpt. 1979-80). Home: 620 Edwards St Woodruff SC 29388 Office: Cryovac div WR Grace & Co PO Box 464 Duncan SC 29334

ABERCROMBIE, RALPH MCCALL, JR., hosp. adminstr.; b. Charlotte, N.C., Sept. 26, 1928; s. Ralph McCall and Mamie Lucille (Schenck) A.; B.A. in Polit. Sci., U. N.C., 1958; cert. hosp. adminstrn. Charlotte Meml. Hosp., 1960; m. Elizabeth Joanne Hovis, Feb. 7, 1953; children—Ralph McCall III, Jeffry Hunter, James Malcomb, Anne Elizabeth. Asst. adminstr. Spartanburg (S.C.) Hosp., 1960-63; adminstr. Tuomey Hosp., Sumter, S.C., 1963—; dir. Blue Cross S.C. Served with U.S. Army, 1950-53. Paul Harris fellow, 1976. Fellow Am. Coll. Hosp. Adminstrs.; mem. S.C. Hosp. Assn. (dir.), Am. Hosp. Assn. Methodist. Clubs: Sunset Country (pres. 1974), Rotary (club pres. 1971-72, dist gov. 1975-76). Office: 16 W Calhoun St Sumter SC 29150

ABERNATHY, BOBBY FRANKLIN, petroleum co. exec.; b. Athens, Tex., June 25, 1933; s. George R. and Mary Lou (Jernigan) A.; B.S. in Petroleum Engring., U. Tex., Austin, 1955; postgrad. U. Western Ont.; m. Donna Childers, Feb. 28, 1963; children—Julie Ann, Scott Franklin. Various engring. positions Amoco Prodn. Co., U.S. and Can., 1955; exec. v.p., dir. Quasar Petroleum Ltd., Calgary, Alta., 1972-73; v.p. Am. Quasar Petroleum Co., Ft. Worth, 1973-76; sr. v.p. exploration and prodn., dir. Champlin Petroleum Co., Ft. Worth, 1976—; dir Calnev Pipe Line Co. Former Republican precinct chmn. Tarrant County; mem. Tarrant County Rep. Com.; founder, 1st chmn. Fort Worth Polit. Action Com. Recipient Cedrick K. Ferguson medal Soc. Petroleum Engrs., 1965. Mem. Am Petroleum Inst., Ind. Petroleum Assn. Am. (v.p. Tex.-Central area), N.Mex. Oil and Gas Assn., Internat. Oil Scouts Assn., Tex. Mid-Continent Oil and Gas Assn., Tex. Ind. Producers and Royalty Owners Assn., West Central Tex. Oil and Gas Assn., Natural Gas Soc. N. Tex., Internat. Assn. Drilling Contractors, W. Tex. C. of C. (dir.). Methodist. Clubs: Ft. Worth, Shady Oaks Country, Ft. Worth Petroleum. Office: Champlin Petroleum Co PO Box 9365 Fort Worth TX 76107

ABERNATHY, HARRY HOYLE, JR., lawyer; b. Statesville, N.C., Mar. 28, 1925; s. Harry Hoyle and Pearl (Frazier) A.; B.S., Appalachian State U., 1950; LL.B., U. S.C., 1958, J.D., 1970; m. Elizabeth Ball, Aug. 31, 1948; children—Harry H., Donna Cooper. Tchr. public schs., Iredell County, N.C., 1953-54; salesman Bratgen & Kluge, 1954-55; adjuster Harleysville Mutual Ins. Co., Fayetteville, N.C., 1958-59; admitted to S.C. bar, 1958; individual practice law, Great Falls, S.C., 1958—; city atty., Great Falls, 1968—; bd. dirs. Lancaster-Chester County Public Defender's Corp. Pres., Great Falls United Fund, 1973-74. Served with USAAF, 1943-46, USAF, 1950-51. Mem. S.C. Bar Assn., Chester County Bar Assn. (v.p.), S.C. City Atty.'s Assn., S.C. Librarians Assn., Phi Alpha Delta. Democrat. Methodist. Clubs: Masons, Scottish Rite. Home: 20 Argonne St Great Falls SC 29055 Office: PO Box 488 Great Falls SC 29055

ABERNETHY, BYRON ROBERT, arbitrator; b. Beach, N.D., Feb. 18, 1909; s. William Marlborough and May (Stockwell) A.; B.A., N.D. State Coll., Dickinson, 1933; M.A., U. N.D., 1938; Ph.D., U. Iowa, 1941; m. Helen Bessie Prchal, Oct. 8, 1938; children—Byron Robert, William Albert, Janet Mae Abernethy Simmons. Regional wage stblzn. dir. Nat. Wage Stblzn. Bd., Dallas, 1942-45; vice-chmn. Nat. War Labor Bd., Dallas 1945-46, regional dir., chmn. regional bd., 1951-53; prof. gov. Tex. Tech. Coll., 1947-57; asso. prof. econs. Western Res. U., 1946-47; profl. arbitrator labor-mgmt. relations, Lubbock, Tex., 1957—; mem. presdl. emergency bds., 1961, 63, 68; mem. atomic energy labor mgmt. relations panel, 1968; mem. Nat. Def. Exec. Res.; participant 198th Wilton Park Internat. Conf., Eng., 1978; instr. social sci. Jr. Coll. Albert Lea (Minn.), 1938-40; asst. prof. polit. sci. U. N.D., 1937-38; registrar State Tchrs. Coll., Dickinson, N.D., 1934-36. Del. Nat. Conv. Democratic party, 1956. Mem. Nat. Acad. Arbitrators (v.p. 1976-78, bd. govs. 1961-63), Am. Arbitration Assn., Indsl. Relations Research Assn. Unitarian. Author: Liberty Concepts in Labor Relations, 1943; Constitutional Limitations on the Legislature, 1959; Some Persisting Questions Concerning the Constitutional State Executive (selected for Permanent White House Library), 1960; editor: Private Elisha Stockwell, Jr. Sees the Civil War (E. Stockwell, Jr.) (Civil War Book of Month Club selection), 1958. Home: 3306 37th St Lubbock TX 79413 Office: 3102 50th St Lubbock TX 79413

ABLARD, RUSSELL ALLYN, mgmt. specialist; b. Williamsburg, Iowa, Mar. 14, 1933; s. Glenn Lortz and Alice Rebecca (Jones) A.; B.S. in Commerce, U. Iowa, 1959; m. Marsha Ann Coats, June 22, 1957; children—Susan Jeanette, Jeffrey Allyn. Mem. mktg. services staff Collins Radio, Cedar Rapids, Iowa, 1956-58; staff mem. program mgmt., engring. adminstrn., Dallas, 1959-68, mgr. corporate mktg. adminstrn., 1968-71 mgr. sales analysis, corporate fin., 1971-73; mgr. program planning, control Collin/Rockwell Internat., Dallas, Newport Beach, Calif., 1973-76, controller comml. satellite communications Rockwell Internat., Dallas, 1976-78, mgr. advanced devel., 1979—; seminar instr. program mgmt. Indian Guide dir. YMCA, Garland, Tex., 1966-69; committeeman Boy Scouts Am., 1971-75; sec., treas. Garland High Sch. Booster Club, 1975—. Mem. Nat. Mgmt. Assn. (certified mgr.). Republican. Methodist. Home: 2418 Newcastle Dr Garland TX 75041 Office 1200 N Alma Rd Richardson TX 75080

ABLE, VIRGINIA NEIL, counselor; b. Albany, Ga., Nov. 27, 1946; d. Eugene Walter and Mary Louise (Chadwick) Able; A.A., N. Greenvile Jr. Coll., 1965; B.A., Furman U., 1967; student Southwestern Bapt. Theol. Sem., 1967-68; M.Ed., U. S.C., 1975; div.; 1 son, Roy Douglas White. Tchr., John De la Howe Sch., McCormick, S.C., 1966-67; visitor Poly. Bapt. Ch., Ft. Worth, Tex., 1968-70; counselor Alice Birney Middle Sch., Charleston Heights, S.C., 1975-78; interim prof. Citadel Mil. Coll., Charleston, S.C., 1978;

counselor Batesburg-Leesville Middle Sch., Leesville, S.C., 1978—. Mem. S.C. Legis. Com. Elem. Counselors, 1978—. Named Counselor of Year, S.C. Middle Sch., 1980. Mem. Charleston County Middle Sch. Counselors Assn. (chmn. 1976-77), S.C. Sch. Counselors Assn. (v.p. 1977-78, exec. bd. 1977—), S.C. (treas. 1978-79, mem. exec. bd. 1977—, licensure com. 1978—, chmn. membership com. 1979—), Am. personnel and guidance assns., S.C., Am. assns. non-white concerns, S.C. Assn. Sch. Counselors. Baptist.

ABLES, RICHARD FRANK, chem. engr.; b. Coffeyville, Kans., Nov. 16, 1935; s. Frank Clifford and Lillian Elizabeth (Gerdes) A.; B.S. in Chem. Engring., U. Tex. at Austin, 1964; m. Frances Ligi, Aug. 18, 1956; children—Alicia, Brian, Mark. Engr. DuPont Co., New Johnsonville, Tenn., 1964-67, research engr., 1967-70, sr. research engr., Starke, Fla., 1970-71, tech. supr., 1971-79, engring. asso., 1979—. Scoutmaster Boy Scouts Am., 1964-77. Served with AUS, 1954-56, 61-62. Mem. Am. Inst. Chem. Engrs. (chmn. sect. 1972-73), Soc. Mining Engrs. Club: Lions. Home: PO Box 881 Keystone Heights FL 32656 Office: PO Box 753 Starke FL 32091

ABLON, ARNOLD NORMAN, accountant; b. Ft. Worth, July 12, 1921; s. Esir R. and Hazel (Dreeben) A.; B.S., La. State U., 1941; M.B.A., Northwestern, 1942; m. Carol Sarbin, July 25, 1962; children—Jan Ellen, Elizabeth Jane, William Neal, Robert Jack. Lectr. accounting So. Methodist U., 1946-47; auditor Levine's Dept. Stores, 1947-49; accountant Peat, Marwick, Mitchell & Co., 1946-47; sr. partner Arnold N. Ablon and Co., C.P.A.'s, Dallas, 1949—; partner Troth & Ablon, investments; dir. Ablon Enterprises, Inc., 1st Continental Enterprises, Inc. Bd. dirs. The Greenhill Sch., Spl. Care Sch., June Shelton Sch., Temple Emanu-El. Served as capt. F.A., AUS, World War II. Mem. Am. Inst. C.P.A.'s, Tex. Soc. C.P.A.'s, Nat. Assn. Accountants. Mason (Shriner). Clubs: Variety Internat., Dallas, Dallas Athletic, Columbian, City, Engineers. Office: 1620 Republic Nat Bank Bldg Dallas TX 75201

ABLON, BENJAMIN MANUEL, accountant; b. Dallas, Feb. 12, 1929; s. Esir R. and Hazel (Dreeben) A.; B.B.A., So. Meth. U., 1948; M.B.A., Northwestern, 1949; LL.B., Harvard, 1956; m. Renee Angrist, Jan. 6, 1962 (div. Oct. 1969); 1 son, Edward Lawrence. Admitted to Tex. bar, 1956, D.C. bar, 1957; with tax rulings div. IRS, Washington, 1956-60; asso. law firm, N.Y.C., 1960-62; accountant, tax mgr. Price Waterhouse & Co., N.Y.C., 1963-68; accountant, partner Arnold N. Ablon & Co., C.P.A.'s, Dallas, 1968—. Served to lt. USAF, 1951-53. Mem. Am. Inst. C.P.A.'s, Tex. Soc. C.P.A.'s, State Bar Tex., Am. Assn. Attys.-C.P.A.'s, Dallas Estate Planning Council, Beta Gamma Sigma. Contbr. articles to profl. jours. Home: 5917 Sandhurst St Dallas TX 75206 Office: Republic National Bank Bldg Dallas TX 75201

ABNEY, JAMES MARION, JR., dentist; b. Macon, Ga., Oct. 14, 1939; s. James Marion and Mae (Lockeby) A.; A.B., Emory U., 1961, D.D.S., 1966; m. Sandra Stewman, June 22, 1963; children—Marian Lynn, Mary Kate. Individual practice dentistry, Smyrna, Ga., 1968—; asso. prof. Emory U. Sch. Dentistry, 1968-79; asst. chief dental service Cobb Gen. Hosp., 1971—, cons. gen. dentistry cleft palate team. Bd. dirs. Cobb County Youth Mus., Southeastern region UNICEF; chmn. Kennasaw Mountain Chpt. March of Dimes. Mem. Cobb County C. of C., Am., Ga. dental assns., Northwestern Dist., Cobb County dental socs., Atlanta Gnathological Soc., Terminus Dental Study Club (pres.), Psi Omega, Sigma Alpha Epsilon. Republican. Episcopalian. Clubs: Hampton Farms Tennis and Swim, Horseshoe Bend Country; Smyrna Rotary (pres.). Home: 333 Hunters Ridge Marietta GA 30060 Office: 1900 The Exchange Suite 200 Atlanta GA 30339

ABOU-DONIA, MOHAMED BAHIE, toxicologist, pharmacologist, educator; b. Domiat, Egypt, Nov. 3, 1939; came to U.S., 1961, naturalized, 1977; s. Ahmad Awad and Fathia Abdo (Abou-Hindia) A.D.; B.S., Alexandria U., 1960; Ph.D., U. Calif., Berkeley, 1967; m. Martha May Davis, Feb. 1, 1968; children—Tarek, Sheref, Suzanne. Research asso. biochemistry and biophysics Tex. A&M U., College Station, 1967-70; asst. prof. pesticide chemistry Alexandria U., 1971-73; research asso. physiology and pharmacology, Med. Center, Duke U., Durham, N.C., 1973-74, asst. prof. pharmacology, 1975-79, asso. prof., 1979—. United Arab Republic scholar, 1962-67, NIH postdoctoral fellow, 1974-76. Mem. AAAS, Am. Assn. Pathology, Am. Chem. Soc., Am. Coll. Toxicology, Am. Inst. Chemistry, Am. Soc. Neurochemistry, Am. Soc. Pharmacology and Exptl. Therapeutics, Entomol. Soc. Am., N.Y. Acad. Scis., N.C. Acad. Scis., Soc. Neurosci., Soc. Toxicology, Soc. Environ. Toxicology and Chemistry. Contbg. author, contbr. articles to profl. publs. Home: 106 Catawba Ct Chapel Hill NC 27514

ABRAHAM, GEORGE G., stockyards and meat packing exec.; b. Scranton, Pa., June 15, 1906; s. Samuel H. and Ann (Arnof) A.; student U. Chgo., 1924-25, Law Sch. U. Memphis, 1925-28; m. Celia Gold, Dec. 1, 1928; children—Hubert, LeRoy. Sales mgr., sec., pres. Abraham Bros. Packing Co., Memphis, 1925-50; plant mgr. Wison and Co., Memphis, 1950-55; pres. Ill. Packing Co., Chgo., 1955-61; asst. to chmn. bd., Hygrade Packing Co., Detroit, 1961-66; chmn. bd. Dixie Nat. Stockyards, Abraham Cattle Co., Memphis, 1966—; mem. Nat. War Meat Bd., Washington, 1942-46. Recipient service recognition 4-H Clubs of Am., 1966, Dist. Grand Lodge B'Nai B'Rith, 1976. Mem. Memphis Agr. Club, Am. Meat Inst., Livestock Mktg. Assn. Republican. Jewish. Clubs: Ridgeway Country, B'nai B'rith, Masons, Scottish Rite, Shrine. Home: 505 S Perkins Rd Memphis TN 38117 Office: 1460 Warford St Memphis TN 38108

ABRAHAM, GEORGE LESTER, research economist; b. Andover, S.D., Sept. 12, 1925; s. Paul Leo and Mary Cecila (Langhammer) A.; B.S., U. Mo., 1950; m. Virginia Mae Walz, May 24, 1952; children—Mary, Kathleen, Donna, Joseph, David, Susan, Edward. Economist, provisions asst. Cudahy Foods, Omaha, 1950-54; research asso., asso. John J. Madigan Assos., Omaha, 1954-61; dir. market and econ. research, v.p., dir. Cudahy Foods, 1961-63; v.p., dir. Madigan-Abraham Assos., Inc., Sarasota, Fla., 1963-69; pres., dir., owner Abraham & Assos., Inc., Sarasota, 1969—. Commr. Whitfield Zoning Dist., Sarasota, 1974-75; fin. officer, bd. dirs., treas. Cardinal Mooney Sch., Sarasota, 1969-79. Served with U.S. Army, 1945-46. Mem. Am. Agrl. Econs. Assn., Phi Eta Sigma, Delta Gamma Sigma. Democrat. Roman Catholic. Home: 1125 Chevy Chase Dr Sarasota FL 33580 Office: 1627 Whitfield Ave Sarasota FL 33580

ABRAHAM, JOHN ROBERT, JR., mfg. co. exec.; b. Wallins, Ky., Jan. 8, 1934; s. John Robert and Lillie Wilma (Howard) A.; B.S., U. Tenn., Chattanooga, 1959; A.S. in Plastics Technology, N.Y. U., 1974; m. Sherry Louise Sidener, May 24, 1974; children—John Robert III, Michael Paul, Jason Robert. Prodn. mgr. Plastics div. Am. Can Co., Washington, N.J., 1962-71; prodn. mgr. Am. Standard Co., Paintsville, Ky., 1972, Ball Plastics Co., Evansville, Ind., 1972-73; mgr. plastics Amana Refrigeration Inc., Fayetteville, Tenn., 1974—. Served with USAF, 1953-56. Mem. Soc. Plastics Engrs., Soc. Plastics Industry, NRA. Pres. Young Republicans Club, 1969-71. Home: Route 6 Box 37 Orchard Hill Rd Fayetteville TN 37334 Office: Wilson Pkwy Fayetteville TN 37334

ABRAMSON, LOUIS, JR., ret. oil co. exec., cons. petroleum industry; b. Shreveport, La., Oct. 24, 1903; s. Louis and Bella Gladys (Loewenstein) A.; B.A., La. State U., 1924; postgrad. Tulane U. Med. Sch., 1924-25; m. Marion Pfeifer, June 6, 1925 (dec. 1965); 1 dau., Lucie Lee Abramson Wing; m. 2d, Ruth Herron, 1965. Mktg. exec. W.E. Winship Fuel Oil Co., New Orleans, 1925-28; asst. traffic mgr. Chalmette Petroleum Corp., New Orleans, 1928-29, asst. sales mgr., 1929-30, sales mgr., 1930-32, asst. to pres., 1930-32; owner, pres. Intercoastal Oil Corp., New Orleans, 1932-36; pres., dir. Pinnacle Oil Co., New Orleans, 1936-53, Petrolane Gas Co., New Orleans, 1936-72, So. Solvents & Chems. Corp., 1945-72; cons. petroleum products and industry, 1932—; chmn. liquified petroleum gas subcom. Petroleum Adminstrn. for War, 1942. Founder, pres. Citizens Action League, New Orleans, 1940-45; mem. Statewide Planning for Vocat. Rehab., La., 1967. Named hon. state senator La. Mem. Nat. Liquified Petroleum Gas Assn. (pres. 1941-43, Saley award 1958), La. State Alumni Assn., Petroleum Club. Democrat. Jewish. Clubs: Lamplighter, Audubon Golf; So. Yacht. Author: Inside the Petroleum Industry, 1977. Address: 4512 James Dr Metairie LA 70003

ABSE, DAVID WILFRED, physician, educator; b. Cardiff, Wales, Mar. 15, 1915; came to U.S., 1951, naturalized, 1956; B. Surgery, Welsh Nat. Sch. Medicine, 1938; diploma in Psychol. Medicine, U. London, 1940; M.D., U. Wales, 1948; m. Elizabeth Smith. Intern, Cardiff Royal Infirmary, 1937-38; resident Monmouthshire Mental Hosp., Wales, 1939-42; prof. psychiatry U. N.C., Chapel Hill, 1952-60, dir. postgrad. edn. in psychiatry, 1954-58; mem. faculty Washington Sch. Psychiatry, 1970-75; prof. psychiatry dept. behavioral medicine and psychiatry U. Va., Charlottesville, 1962—; dir. psychiat. edn. St. Alban's Pvt. Psychiat. Hosp., Radford, Va., 1980—. Fellow Am. Psychiat. Assn., Royal Coll. Psychiatrists, Brit. Psychol. Soc.; mem. Am Psychoanalytic Assn., Va. Neuropsychiat. Soc., Va. Psychoanalytic Soc. (pres. 1978-80), AMA, Brit. Med. Assn. Author: Hysteria and Related Mental Disorders, 1966. Home: 1852 Winston Rd Charlottesville VA 22903 Office: Box 190 U Va Med Center Charlottesville VA 22903

ABT, FRED WILLIAM, pub. accountant, ins. agent; b. Cullman, Ala., Jan. 25, 1926; s. Willy E. and Julia (Hasenbein) A.; B.S., U. Ala., 1949; m. Irene Hughes, Aug. 10, 1948; children—Jeanne (Mrs. Richard M. Bunis), William C., James F. Pub. accountant specializing in income tax Fred W. Abt, Cullman, 1950—, owner, 1965; ins. agt. Abt Ins. Agy., Cullman, 1950—, owner, 1965—. Pres. Ala. Assn. Retarded Children, 1965-68. Bd. dirs. Cullman County (Ala.) Assn. Retarded Children, 1960-75, pres., 1960-62; bd. dirs. Cullman County United Fund, 1960-73, pres., 1969-70. Served with AUS, 1944-46. Decorated Bronze Star; recipient William Crawford Gorgas award Ala. Med. Assn., 1970. Mem. Am. Legion (post comdr. 1966-67), Cullman Civitan Club (pres. 1970-71), VFW, Ala. Assn. Pub. Accountants, Nat. Soc. Pub. Accountants, Ret. Officers' Assn., Ala. Assn. Ins. Agts. Lutheran (fin. sec. 1955-56). Elk. Home: 502 8th St SE Cullman AL 35055 Office: 322 1/2 1st Ave SE Cullman AL 35055

ACERS, MAURICE WILSON, lawyer; b. Dallas, Aug. 27, 1907; s. Austin Edward and Effie Elizabeth (Holsomback) A.; B.A., So. Meth. U., 1929; postgrad. Harvard U., 1929-30, 61, 76; J.D., U. Tex., Austin, 1934; certificate of attainment Met. Police Coll., London, 1938; m. Ebby Halliday, Apr. 18, 1965. Admitted to Tex. bar, 1934, U.S. Supreme Ct. bar, 1937; atty. RFC, Dallas, 1932; individual practice law, Dallas, 1934; spl. agt., spl. agt.-in-charge, insp. and dir. personnel FBI, 1934-47; v.p., gen. mgr. Shary Products Co., Mission, Tex., 1947-49; pres. Tex. Citrus Fruit Growers Exchange, Inc., Mission, 1949-51; exec. sec. to Gov. Allan Shivers of Tex., 1951-55; commr. Tex. Employment Commn., Austin, 1955-61; pres. Acers Investment Co., Austin; chmn. bd., gen. counsel Ebby Halliday Realtors, 1961—. Pres., Tex. United Fund 1959-61, chmn. bd., 1962; pres. United Way/Capital Area, 1961, chmn. bd., 1962; pres. Tex. United Community Services, 1969-70, chmn. bd., 1971—; nat. rep., mem. adv. council USO; pres. Austin High Sch. PTA, 1960-61; dist. chmn. U.S. savs. bonds program Dept. Treasury, 1963-73, recipient Liberty Bell award, 1968, Twin Seal award, 1973; pres. Beautify Tex. Council, 1972-75, recipient Bluebonnet award; bd. dirs. United Way Am., Inc., YMCA. Mem. Am., Jefferson County, Travis County, Dallas bar assns., State Bar Tex., Nat. Assn. Realtors, Internat. Real Estate Fedn. (world pres. profl. and ednl. exchange sec. 1977—, dir. 1980—), Am. Automobile Assn., Mid-Continent Oil and Gas Assn. Mem. Christian Ch. (elder, vice chmn. bd. 1978-80, chmn. bd. 80—). Clubs: Rotary (dist. gov. 1965-66), Masons, Shriners, Yachting of Am. Home: 8515 Preston Rd Dallas TX 75225 Office: Westgate Suite 1509 1122 Colorado St Austin TX 78701 also 5920 Sherry Ln Dallas TX 75225

ACKEL, FRED JOHN, dentist; b. Gloversville, N.Y., Mar. 28, 1927; s. Fred and Anna Azar (Ackel) A.; student Clarkson Coll. Tech., 1944-45, U.S. Merchant Marine Acad., 1945-46; B.S., Hartwick Coll., 1950; D.D.S., Georgetown U., 1954; m. Mildred Krause, July 15, 1950 (div. Oct. 1969); children—Debra Ann, Gary Fredric, Kimberly Jean. Individual practice dentistry, Ft. Lauderdale, Fla., 1957—. Mem. Fla. State Bd. Health, 1967-68; mem. Broward County Health Planning and Developmental Council, 1973—; mem. Fla. State Racing Commn., 1968-71. Pres. Broward County Young Republicans, 1961-63; chmn. Young Ams. for Freedom, 1962-65; del. Rep. Nat. Conv., 1964; chmn. Citizens for Goldwater-Miller, Nat. Draft Goldwater Com., Broward County, 1964; chmn. Rep. Citizens Com., Broward County, 1965-71. Trustee Coral Oaks Med. Dental Bldg. Enterprises. Served from 1st lt. to capt. USAF, 1954-56. Fellow Acad. Gen. Dentistry; mem. ADA (chmn. dels. ann. meeting 1969), Internat. Coll. Dentists, Pierre Fauchard Acad., Broward County (pres. 1965-66), Fla. (trustee 1972—, pres. 1979-80) dental assns., Am. Prosthodontic Soc., Am. Acad. Periodontology, Am. Equilibration Soc., Am. Assn. Dental Editors. Roman Catholic. Club: Player's. Editor Broward County Dental Review, 1968—, Atlantic Coast Dental Explorer, 1973—. Home: 4821 NE 26th Ave Fort Lauderdale FL 33308 Office: 2655 E Oakland Park Blvd Fort Lauderdale FL 33306

ACKER, DAVID DE PEYSTER, engr., educator; b. Newark, Oct. 12, 1921; s. David De Peyster and Lillian Mulford (Gillmor) A.; B.S. in Mech. Engring., Rutgers U., 1948, M.S., 1950; m. Lillian Radcliff Work, Apr. 9, 1949; children—Suzanne Clark, Maritta Fairchild. Tool designer Wright Aero. Corp., Paterson, N.J., 1940-42; design engr. Am. Tool Engring. Co., N.Y.C., 1942; asst. to chief engr. Bright Star Battery Co., Clifton, N.J., 1945-46; instr. mech. engring. Rutgers U., 1948-51, Va. Polytech. Inst., summer 1950; with N.Am. Rockwell Corp., El Segundo, Calif., 1951-70, mem. sr. tech. staff, sr. v.p. research and engring., 1966-70; staff engr., dir. def. research and engring. Office Sec. Def., Washington, 1970-73; asso. dean adminstrn., prof. mgmt. Def. Systems Mgmt. Coll., Ft. Belvoir, Va., 1973—; instr., vis. lectr. UCLA, 1957-68; lectr. various univs. Served with AUS, 1942-45. Decorated Bronze Star medal. Recipient certificate of Merit Electronic Industries Assn., 1974, Outstanding Performance award Def. Systems Mgmt. Coll., 1975, 77, 78, 79. Mem. ASME (chmn. exec. com. mgmt. div., 1973-74; mem. gen. engring. dept. policy bd. 1975, 76, 78, 79, 80; recipient awards), Am. Soc. Engring. Edn., Nat. Soc. Profl. Engrs. (affiliate), Sigma Xi. Presbyterian. Contbr. engring. articles to profl. lit. Home: 7723 Timon Dr McLean VA 22102 Office: Def Systems Mgmt Coll Fort Belvior VA 22060

ACKER, PAUL EDWIN, electronics co. exec.; b. Dallas, Feb. 6, 1954; s. Noble Acker; B.B.A., U. Tex., Arlington, 1976; postgrad U. N. Fla. Driver, then salesman Pete Jones Furniture Co., Arlington, 1969-76; sales rep. Morse Chain div. Borg-Warner Corp., Ithaca, N.Y., 1976-77; personnel communications rep. Motorola Communications & Electronics Co., Jacksonville, Fla., 1977—. Men. N. Fla. Home Builders Assn., Jacksonville Exec. Businessmen's Assn. Democrat. Roman Catholic. Home: 4158 Dalry Dr Jacksonville FL 32216 Office: 7820 Arlington Express Suite 640 Jacksonville FL 32211

ACKER, W. L. (LOU), univ. ofcl.; b. Amarillo, Tex., Mar. 24, 1937; s. Doyle and Jewel (Talley) A.; B.S., Sam Houston State U., 1974; m. Peggy Ann Thompson, Jan. 1, 1959; 1 son, Kelly Michael Kennedy. Dir. adminstrv. services bur. Dallas County Sheriffs Dept., 1965-76; chief campus police dept. North Lake Coll., Irving, Tex., 1977—; dir. Omega Team, Inc. (Dallas). Served with AUS, 1955-57; capt. Tex. State Guard. Certified Tex. peace officer; certified instr. Tex. Commn. Law Enforcement Standards and Edn. Mem. Internat., Tex. police assns., Assn. U.S. Army, Am. Def. Preparedness Assn., Tex. State Guard Assn., Nat. Mil. Intelligence Assn., U.s. Armor Assn., Res. Officers Confederate Alliance, Confederate State Militia, Am. Soc. Indsl. Security, Nat. Rifle Assn., Internat. Assn. Chiefs Police, S.C.V., Ft. Chickamauga Nat. Hist Soc. Democrat. Lutheran. Clubs: Masons, Shriners. Author: The Office of Sheriff in Texas, 1975. Home: 3502 Palm Dr Mesquite TX 75150 Office: North Lake College Irving TX 75062

ACKERMAN, LOIS VOLK, retail exec.; b. Sharon, Pa., Aug. 17, 1934; d. Louis and Sara Greenberger; B.B.A. magna cum laude, U. Pitts., 1955; m. Lawrence Volk, Dec. 25, 1955 (dec.); children—Valerie, David, Pamela; m. 2d, Sidney Ackerman, Sept. 3, 1978. Instr., demonstrator Burroughs Corp., Pitts., 1956; owner, mgr., pres. Star Pharmacy, Inc., North Fort Myers, Fla., 1971—; pres. Star Gifts Inc., Fort Myers. Mem. Gift and Decorative Accessories Assn., Jewelers Council, Nat. Assn. Retail Druggists (asso.), Beta Gamma Sigma. Democrat. Jewish. Club: Rotary Ann's. Home: 1715 Marina Terr North Fort Myers FL 33903 Office: 1240 N Tamiami Trail North Fort Myers FL 33903

ACKERMAN, ROBERT FEATHERSTON, physician; b. Memphis, Apr. 21, 1919; s. Robert William and Marie Keith (Featherston) A.; B.S., Southwestern Coll. Memphis, 1942; M.S. in Physiology, U. Tenn., 1943, M.D., 1943; M.S. in Medicine, U. Minn., 1949; m. Patricia Clare Robeson, Feb. 16, 1965; children—Ruth, David, Robert Featherston, Todd. Intern, Presbyn. Hosp. Chgo., 1943-44, asst. resident in medicine, 1944; fellow in medicine Mayo Found., Rochester, Minn., 1945, 47-49; practice medicine specializing in internal medicine, Memphis, 1950—; asst. prof. div. medicine and preventive medicine U. Tenn. Coll. Medicine, Memphis, 1950-65, clin. asso. prof. medicine, 1950—; mem. staff Bapt. Meml., City of Memphis, St. Joseph, Meth. hosps. Served to capt., M.C., U.S. Army, 1945-47. Tenn. Heart Assn. grantee, 1950-54, Memphis Heart Assn. grantee, 1950-54, USPHS grantee, 1960-65. Diplomate Am. Bd. Internal Medicine. Fellow A.C.P., Am. Coll. Cardiology; mem. Am. Soc. Internal Medicine, Am., Tenn. diabetes assns., Memphis-Shelby County Med. Soc., Am., Memphis heart assns., AMA, Sigma Xi, Chi Beta Phi. Republican. Episcopalian. Club: Raquet of Memphis. Contbr. articles on clin. investigations and cardiovascular pathology to sci. jours. Home: 112 S Yates Rd Memphis TN 38117 Office: 910 Madison Ave Memphis TN 38103

ACKERMAN, ROY ALAN, research co. exec.; b. Bklyn., Sept. 9, 1951; s. Jack and Estelle (Kuchlik) A.; B.S in Chem. Engring., Poly. Inst. Bklyn., 1972; M.S., M.I.T., 1974; Ph.D., U. Va., 1980; m. Janet Sharon Ostrow, July 4, 1974. Chem. engr. Tri-Flo Research Labs., Bellmore, N.Y., 1972-74; sr. project engr. Thetford Corp., Ann Arbor, Mich., 1975; dir. research and devel. ASTRE, Charlottesville Va., 1976—, gen. mgr., 1977—. Samuel Ruben scholar, 1968-72. Accredited profl. chem. engr. Mem. ACLU, Am. Soc. Artificial Internal Organs, Am. Inst. Chem. Engrs., Water Pollution Control Fedn., Soc. Indsl. Microbiology, N.Y. Acad. Scis., Assn. Advancement Med. Instrumentation, Tau Beta Pi, Sigma Xi. Contbr. articles to profl. jours. Patentee artificial kidney, dialysate supply systems, mutant bacteria which degrade ammonia. Home: 3135 Shore Rd Bellmore Harbor NY 11710 Office: PO Box 5072 Charlottesville VA 22905

ACKERS, LARRY DALE, radio sta. exec.; b. Lubbock, Tex., Aug. 21, 1938; s. Dale and Johnnie (Robert) A.; B.A. in Bus. Adminstrn., Tex. Christian U., 1961; m. Leona Bailey, Nov. 26, 1969; 1 child, Pepper D. With Sta. KFDA-TV, Amarillo, Tex., 1963-72; salesman Sta. KRRV, Sherman, Tex., 1972; salesman, sta. mgr. Sta. KENM, Portales, N.Mex., 1972-75; owner, mgr. Sta. KEND, Lubbock, 1975—. Bd. dirs. W. Tex. Children's Found., 1977-78, pres., 1979—. Mem. Lubbock Advt. Club (dir.). Mem. Diciples of Christ. Office: 2112 Broadway St Lubbock TX 79401

ACOR, JOHN ALBERT, animal hosp. adminstr.; b. Waterloo, N.Y., July 24, 1944; s. Harold Lahr and Letha L. (Allen) A.; A.A., Orlando Jr. Coll., 1969; B.S.B.A., Fla. Technol. U., 1971; m. Geneva Charlotte Keene, Nov. 18, 1966; children—John Brannen, Erick Ryan. Electromech. designer Saturn V and F-111 fed. govt. projects, Daytona Beach, Fla. and Rochester, N.Y., 1965-72; mfrs.' rep. Supro Corp., Orlando, Fla., 1972-73; owner, operator Acor Industries, Inc., drywall products mfg., Vero Beach, Fla., 1973-74; adminstr. Westside Animal Hosp., Vero Beach, 1975—; salesman Sun Realty of Fort Pierce, Inc., Vero Beach. 1979—. Chmn. City of Vero Beach Parks, Planning and Zoning Commn., 1975—; bd. dirs. Taxpayers Assn. Indian River County (Fla.), 1976—, sec., 1979, pres., 1980; v.p. Republican Club of Indian River County, 1978; chmn. Beach Erosion Control Com., 1977—. Served with USN, 1963-65. Mem. Am. Entrepreneurs Assn., Internat. Wealth and Success, Delta Sigma Pi (life). Republican. Methodist. Office: Westside Animal Hosp 1795 10th Ave Vero Beach FL 32960

ACRES, NORMAN CLIFTON, mfg. co. exec.; b. Scott County, Oneida, Tenn., June 4, 1926; s. Audney and Thelma Delna A.; student Draughons Bus. Coll., 1947-49, La. State U. Sch. Banking, 1967-69, U. Tenn. Mgmt. Sch., 1976; m. Pauline Sexton, Jan. 13, 1951; children—Auther, Paula Linda, Tammie. Vets. service officer, Scott County, Tenn., 1949-51; dir. Plateau Electric Coop., Oneida, Tenn., 1951-53; bookkeeper Swain Lumber Mills, Helenwood, Tenn., 1952-60; mill supt. Elgin Wood Products (Tenn.), 1960-61; mgr. First Nat. Bank, Oneida, 1961-67; v.p. personnel Hughett Industries, Inc., Helenwood, Tenn., 1967—. Dir., Indsl. Devel. Bd. Scott County; capt. Scott County Rescue Squads; mem. Scott County Election Commn.; dir. Tenn. Assn. Rescue Squads; bd. dirs. Easter Seals, Tenn. Emergency Med. Technicians Assn. Served with U.S. Army, 1944-47. Decorated Bronze Star, Purple Heart. Mem. Am. Mgmt. Assn., Tenn. Emergency Med. Technicians Assn. (dir.), Tenn. Law Enforcement Assn., Tenn. Oil and Gas Assn. (dir.), Am. Legion, VFW. Republican. Baptist. Clubs: 40 and 8, Masons. Home: PO Box 114 Helenwood TN 37755 Office: PO Box 38 Helenwood TN 37755

ACZEL, THOMAS, research chemist; b. Nagykanizsa, Hungary, Dec. 18, 1930; came to U.S., 1959, naturalized, 1964; s. Joseph and Elisabeth (Fischer) Z.; Sc.D., U. Trieste (Italy), 1954; m. Mollie D. Goodman, July 15, 1962; children—Joseph Israel, Stephen Max, Elisabeth Anne, Bettina Vera. Research scientist Exxon Research and Engring. Co., Baytown, Tex., 1959—, sr. research asso., 1976—; cons. Oak Ridge Nat. Labs., 1975-77. Vice pres. Friends of Sterling Mcpl. Library, Baytown, 1977-79; bd. dirs. Baytown Symphony Orch., 1976-78. Recipient profl. award Baytown Soc. Profl. Chemists, 1967. Mem. ASTM (vice chmn. E-14, chmn. sect. M, research and devel. div. IV), Am. Chem. Soc. (research award 1969, dir. S.E. Tex. sect., chmn. continuing edn. com., profl. award 1978), Am. Soc. Mass Spectrometry (chmn. nominating com.). Jewish. Club: B'nai B'rith. Contbr. chpts. to books, numerous sci. articles to profl. publs. Office: PO Box 4255 Baytown TX 77520

ADAIR, JOE RONALD, tile mfg. co. exec.; b. San Angelo, Tex., Feb. 25, 1940; s. Pat and Beth (Hicks) A.; B.B.A., Angelo State U., 1969; m. Elaine Couch, Jan. 11, 1960; 1 dau., Christy Lynn. With Monarch Tile Mfg. Co., Florence, Ala., 1965—, Eastern regional sales mgr., 1978—. Mem. Republican Nat. Com., 1971—; dir. Am. Security Council, 1974, mem. nat. adv. bd., 1975; mem. adv. com. Connally for Pres., 1979-80. Served with AUS, 1959-60. Mem. Am. Mgmt. Assn., Research Inst. Am., Producers Council, Tile Council Am., Am. Security Found. Republican. Baptist. Clubs: Admirals, Ambassadors, Gas Light, Turtle Point Yacht and Country. Home: 309 Knights Bridge Rd Florence AL 35630 Office: Box 999 Rickwood Rd Florence AL 35630

ADAIR, WILLIAM MICHAEL advt. co. exec.; b. Winfield, Ala., May 10, 1933; s. James Carl And Clara (Mason) A.; B.A.A., Auburn U., 1955; m. Jacqueline Waller, Nov. 19, 1955; children—Jennifer Ann, Lauri Lu. Asst. advt. mgr. Ampex Magnetic Tape Inc., Opelika, Ala., 1960-61; asso. creative dir., advt. services mgr., nat. sales promotion mgr. Coca-Cola USA, Atlanta, 1962-71; pres. Kesler/Klaxon, Inc., Atlanta, 1971-74; chief exec. officer, chmn. bd. Adair Advt., Inc., Atlanta, 1974—; lectr. in field. Regional public relations dir. Polaris council Boy Scouts Am., Atlanta, 1971-77; mem. exec. com. Atlanta Cancer Soc., 1977. Served with S.C., U.S. Army, 1957-60. Named Atlanta Good Guy Sta. WSB, 1975. Mem. Atlanta Advt. Club, Atlanta C. of C., Atlanta Better Bus. Bur., Auburn Alumni Assn. Republican. Baptist. Office: 2 Northside 75 Suite 333 Atlanta GA 30318

ADAM, GERARD RENE, II, accountant; b. New Orleans, July 14, 1953; s. Gerard R. and June Violet (Burke) A.; B.S. with honors in Acctg., U. New Orleans, 1975; m. Linda Maisicot, Mar. 19, 1976; 1 son, Gerard Rene III. In-charge acct. Ernst & Ernst, New Orleans, 1975-76; chief acct. East Jefferson Gen. Hosp., Metairie, La., 1976-78; sr. acct. corporate auditing HAI, Inc., Nashville, 1978-79, INA, Inc., Nashville, 1979—. C.P.A., La. Active Big Brothers La., Special Olympics. Mem. Am. Inst. C.P.A.'s, Hosp. Financial Mgmt. Assn., La. State Soc. C.P.A.'s, Tenn. Hosp. Assn., Beta Gamma Sigma, Phi Kappa Beta. Democrat. Roman Catholic. Home: 810 Bellevue Rd A-228 Nashville TN 37221 Office: 4525 Harding Rd Nashville TN 37205

ADAMS, ALFRED BERNARD, JR., chem. engr.; b. Asbury Park, N.J., Oct. 15, 1920; s. Alfred Bishop and Julia Ruth (Wiseman) A.; B.S., Ga. Inst. Tech., 1943; postgrad. Wayne U., 1946-47; m. Claudia Neff, Dec. 28, 1942; children—Alfred B. III, Tamara (Mrs. Carl Edward Dohn, Jr.), Carla (Mrs. William H. York, Jr.). Sr. project engr. Pennwalt Corp., Wyandotte, Mich., 1946-50; sales mgr. Goslin-Birmingham Mfg. Co. (Ala.), 1950-61; field chem. engr. Eimco Corp., Birmingham, 1961-62; prin. engr. Thiokol Chem. Co., Brunswick, Ga., 1962-64; sr. staff air pollution engr. Rust Engring. Co., Birmingham, 1964—. Tchr. air pollution course Auburn U. Extension Sch., also U. Wis. Extension Sch.; guest lectr. tech. soc. meetings. Mem. Pub. and Environmental Health Adv. Com. for 5 counties in Ala., 1973-76; mem. environ. adv. com. FEA, 1975. Served with AUS, World War II; ETO. Decorated Purple Heart. Registered profl. engr., Ala., Fla., Mich., Ga. Mem. TAPPI, Air Pollution Control Assn. (past chmn. So. sect.). Contbr. articles to profl. jours. Home: 4063 Woodland Ave Pinson AL 35126 Office: Rust Engring Co PO Box 101 Birmingham AL 35201

ADAMS, ALLEN, state legislator N.C., lawyer; b. Greensboro, N.C., Jan. 15, 1932; s. Joseph Allen and Marion (Crawford) A.; A.B., U. N.C., Chapel Hill, 1952, J.D., 1954; m. LeNeve Foster Hodges, June 1953; children—Ann Caroline, Jefferson Hodges, Spencer Allen; m. 2d, Betty Eichenberger, June 1977. Admitted to N.C. bar, 1954; practice in Raleigh, 1958—, partner firm Sanford, Adams, McCullough & Beard, and predecessor firm, 1967—; mem. N.C. Ho. of Reps. from 15th Dist., 1974—. Chmn., Wake County Pub. Library Bd., 1970-75; pres. Wake County Young Democrats, 1964; chmn. Wake County Dem. Party, 1968-72. Served as comdr. Judge Adv. Gen's Corps, USNR, 1955-58. Mem. Am. Bar Assn., N.C. Acad. Trial Lawyers. Home: 224 Woodburn Rd Raleigh NC 27605 Office: PO Box 389 Raleigh NC 27602

ADAMS, ANDREW STANFORD, govt. ofcl.; b. San Francisco, July 8, 1922; s. Edward Lewis and Eva Jane (Kurowsky) A.; A.A., San Francisco City Coll., 1942; B.S., U. Calif. at Berkeley, 1949, Ph.D., 1954; m. Anke Peters, Oct. 2, 1967; 1 dau., Arva Petra. Profl. baseball player, 1946-50; tchr., adminstr. Contra Costa (Calif.) Pub. Schs., 1951-55; civilian edn. and tng. officer Naval Ordnance Test Sta., China Lake, Calif., 1955-56; supr., prin. San Luis Obispo County (Calif.) Pub. Schs., 1956-60; supr. Freedom (Calif.) Pub. Schs., 1960-62; asst. to supr., dir. instructional services Clark County (Nev.) Pub. Schs., Las Vegas, 1962-64; dir. ednl. affairs and selections VISTA, OEO, also chief ednl. programs br. OSA, Washington, 1964-70; supt. schs. Kansas City (Mo.) Pub. Schs., 1970-73; dep. dir. edn. and rehab. services VA, Washington, 1973-74; U.S. commr. Rehab. Services, HEW, 1974-77; staff asst. policy, budget and adminstrn. Office of Sec., Dept. Interior, 1977—; prof. mgmt. sci. and edn. various univs. Served with USAAF, 1942-45. Contbr. articles to profl. jours. Address: River House Apt B-409 1600 S Joyce St Arlington VA 22202

ADAMS, BARBARA COLE, counselor; b. Atlanta, Feb. 17, 1941; d. Herschel Eugene and Rose Belle (Dumas) Cole; B.A., Emory U., 1963; M.A., U. Ala., 1972; postgrad. U. Ala.; m. John Bradley Adams, July 6, 1963. Tchr. elementary sch. Tuscaloosa Pub. Schs., 1963-73, elementary guidance counselor, 1973—, coordinator elementary guidance services, 1976—. Chmn. Tuscaloosa Juvenile Agy. Council, 1976-77; bd. dirs. Parents Anonymous Mem. Ala. (dir. 1976-78), Am. sch. counselors assns., Am., Ala. personnel and guidance assns., NEA, Ala. Edn. Assn., Profl. Educators Tuscaloosa, Kappa Delta Epsilon, Kappa Delta Pi, Alpha Delta Kappa, Kappa Kappa Gamma. Home: 5007 10th Ave E Tuscaloosa AL 35405 Office: 1100 21st St E Tuscaloosa AL 35405

ADAMS, BEULAH GRACE JENKINS (MRS. ADDISON FRANK ADAMS), abstract co. exec.; b. Bastrop, Tex., Nov. 29, 1909; d. Hartford and Beulah Alice (Hemphill) Jenkins; B.A., Baylor U., 1930; postgrad. U. Tex., 1933, 39, U. Colo., 1934; m. Addison Frank Adams, Dec. 26, 1938; children—Forrest Jenkins, Alice Ann (Mrs. Charles Woodrow Miller). Tchr., Bastrop Pub. Schs., 1930-41; v.p., mgr. Bastrop County Abstract Co., Inc., 1942—. Mem. AAUW, Tex. State Geneal. Soc., Am., Tex. land title assns., Am. Assn. Petroleum Landmen, Delta Kappa Gamma. Baptist. Home: 1707 Pecan St Bastrop TX 78602 Office: 901 Main St PO Box 550 Bastrop TX 78602

ADAMS, BILLY JOE, bus. coll. dean.; b. Forney, Tex., June 2, 1919; s. Garland John William and Bula Mae (Willmon) A.; B.S., Tex. A. and M. U., 1941, Ph.D., 1977; M.B.A., Tulane U., 1960; m. Martha Irelene Albright, July 19, 1942; children—Jack Lynn, Patricia Adams Manny. Chief accountant. asst. treas. Goldrus Drilling Co., Houston, 1946-47; chief accountant, office mgr. Gallery & Hurt, Houston, 1947-48; commd. 2d lt. U.S. Army, advanced through grades to col., 1963; bn. comdr., Korea, 1953-54; staff officer Pentagon, 1955-58; dir. computer simulation div. Army Logistics Mgmt. Center, Ft. Lee, Va., 1960-64, chief evaluation div., combat service support group, 1964-65; ret., 1965; asst. prof. Tex. Christian U., Fort Worth, 1965-66; asst. dir. exec. devel. programs Tex. A. and M. U., College Station, 1966-70, asst. dean Coll. Bus. Adminstrn., 1970—, dir. exec. devel. programs, 1970—, asst. prof. mgmt., 1967—, dir. office continuing edn., 1978—; dir. Orna Metals Casting Co., Bryan, Tex. Served with AUS, 1941-46. Decorated Legion of Merit, Bronze Star with oak leaf. Mem. Data Processing Mgmt. Assn., Am. Soc. Tng. and Devel., Tex. Assn. Community Service and Continuing Edn., Beta Gamma Sigma, Sigma Iota Epsilon. Mem. Christian Ch. (Disciples of Christ). Editor Tex. Bus. Exec., 1975—. Home: 1207 Neal Pickett St College Station TX 77840 Office: Office on Continuing Edn Tex A and M U College Station TX 77843

ADAMS, CRAWFORD WILLIAM, cardiologist; b. Springfield, Mass., Sept. 15, 1915; s. E. Crawford and Doris (Roane) A.; B.S., U. Mass., 1938; M.D., Boston U., 1942; m. Barbara Ann Simpkins, Nov. 27, 1943; children—Jeffrey Paul, Patricia Ann, Cynthia Louise Adams Sumerville, Stephen Roane, Barbara Jean Adams Langston, Crawford William, Doris Elizabeth, Diane Elaine Adams Allison, Nancy Marie Adams Gregg, John Thomas, Joan Theresa, Anne Melissa. Intern Boston City Hosp., 1942-43, resident, 1942-43, 46-47; practice medicine specializing in cardiology, Nashville, 1945—; mem. staff St. Thomas Hosp., Vanderbilt U., Bapt., Nashville Met., Nashville Meml. hosps.; asso. clin. prof. medicine Vanderbilt U. Med. Sch., Nashville, 1966—, Meharry Med. Sch., Nashville, 1950—. Chmn. Brentwood Acad. Fund Drive, 1971-72; pres. Middle Tenn. council Boy Scouts Am., 1967-69, bd. dirs., 1963—; mem.-at-large Nat. council, 1965—; bd. dirs. Jr. Achievement, 1968-69, YMCA, 1974-75. Served to maj. USAAF, 1943-46. Recipient Beaver award Boy Scouts Am., 1963, Eagle Scout Recognition dinner, 1972; named hon. citizen Tenn., 1967. Fellow Am. Coll. Chest Physicians (exec. council 1966—, pres.-elect 1974-75, pres. 1975-76), Am. Coll. Angiology, Am. Coll. Cardiology (bd. govs. 1973-76), Internat. Cardiovascular Soc., Am. Geriatrics Soc., Sci. Council and Internat. Coll. Angiology, Council on Clin. Cardiology Am. Heart Assn., A.C.P., Royal Soc. Health Gt. Britian; mem. Tenn. (dir. 1967—), Middle Tenn. (dir. 1959—, chmn. bd. dirs. 1968-69) heart assns., Nashville Acad. Medicine and Davidson County Med. Soc. (chmn. program com. 1964-65), Nashville Soc. Internal Medicine (chmn. program com. 1962-64), Upper Cumberland Med. Soc. (pres. 1963-64), Clin. Cardiac Research Found. (chmn. bd. dirs. 1968—), AMA (chmn. sect. chest diseases 1966-67), Nashville Cardiovascular Soc. (pres. 1974-75). Author: Clinical Electrocardiography, 1964. Asso. editor Diseases of the Chest, 1965-67, sr. editor, 1967-72; editorial cons. Am. Jour. Cardiology, 1968—, Heart and Lung, 1975-78, Hosp. Media, 1976-77. Contbr. numerous articles to profl. jours. Home: 4115 Legend Hall Nashville TN 37215 Office: 402 21st and Hayes Med Bldg Nashville TN 37203

ADAMS, DAVID HOLMES, lawyer, constrn. co. exec.; b. Paintsville, Ky., Oct. 6, 1948; s. Stuart Holmes and Geneva L. (Honeycutt) A.; B.S., Pikeville Coll., 1970; J.D., U. Louisville, 1972; married; 1 son, David Holmes. Vice pres. Adams Constrn. Corp., Pikeville, Ky., 1970—; admitted to Ky. bar, 1972; asso. Hinton, Hall & Todd, 1972—; v.p. Adams Corps., WLSI Radio Sta. Mem. Ky. Bar Assn., Pike County Bar Assn., Phi Delta Tau, Delta Theta Phi. Clubs: Kiwanis, Shriners. Home and Office: PO Box 2853 Pikeville KY 41501

ADAMS, EDWARD QUINCY, broadcasting co. exec.; b. Chgo., Oct. 3, 1926; s. Edward Richmond and Frances Ruth (Cummings) A.; B.S., Northwestern U., 1950; m. Nancy Lane Thomas, Jan. 10, 1959; children—Marion Frances, Abigail Quincy. Salesman TV Advt. Reps., 1959-65; gen. sales mgr. sta. KDKA-TV, Pitts., 1965-68; sr. v.p., gen. mgr. sta. WCIX-TV Coral TV Corp., Miami, Fla., 1969—. Served with USNR, 1944-46, 50-52. Home: 12855 Old Cutler Rd Miami FL 33156 Office: 1111 Brickell Ave Miami FL 33131

ADAMS, ERNESTINE, editor; b. Hartville, Mo., Apr. 14, 1905; d. Ernest James and Betty (Cottengim) Adams; B.J., U. Mo., 1926; postgrad. New Sch. Social Research, Columbia, 1929, N.Y. U., 1938, So. Meth. U., 1943-45. Pub., Owner Logan County News, Crescent, Okla., 1930-37; advt. dept. Neiman Marcus, Dallas, 1943; editor Petroleum Engr. Pub. Co., Dallas, 1943-77, dir. Search Enterprises subs., 1969-77; editor Energy Publs. div. Harcourt, Brace, Jovanovich, Dallas, 1977—. Named 1st Oil Woman of Yr., Internat. Petroleum Expn., 1953; recipient Editorial Achievement award, Am. Bus. Press, 1963, Matrix award, Theta Sigma Phi, 1964. Mem. Women in Communication, Chi Omega, Pi Epsilon Tau. Presbyn. Clubs: Press (charter) (Dallas); Desk and Derrick (charter) (Dallas). Home: 2818 Fondren Dallas TX 75205 Office: 800 Davis Bldg Dallas TX 75202 also 6611 Snider Plaza Dallas TX 75205

ADAMS, EZRA JOHN, educator; b. Darnell, La., Aug. 30, 1923; s. John Washington and Corinne (Hargrove) A.; B.A. in Journalism, N.E. La. State Coll., 1956; M.A., La. State U., 1964; m. Catherine Geraldine Ward, Nov. 2, 1956; 1 adopted dau., Janet Shadowens; 1 dau., Gayla Dawn Miller. Reporter, state editor Morning World, Monroe, La., 1954-56; pub. relations dir. Parish Recreation and Parks Commn., Baton Rouge, 1956-57; salesman, newsman radio sta. WJBO, Baton Rouge, 1957-58; reporter Morning Adv., Baton Rouge, 1958; mng. editor Rural La., Assn. La. Elec. Coops., Opelousas, 1959-63; pub. information rep. La. Dept. Agr., Baton Rouge, 1963-64; dir. publs. Southeastern La. Coll., Hammond, 1964-66, asst. prof. journalism, 1964-66; pub. relations rep. Internat. Paper Co., Bastrop, La., 1966-68; student Am. history doctoral program Northwestern State U. La., Natchitoches, 1968-69, prof. journalism, 1969—. Served with USAAF, 1942-46, USAF, 1951-53. Mem. Assn. Edn. in Journalism (charter mem. newspaper div.), Sigma Delta Chi, Tau Kappa Epsilon. Democrat. Baptist. Clubs: Lions, Masons.

ADAMS, FRANCES GRANT, office procedures cons.; b. Springfield, Ill.; d. Daniel Harmon and Adah (Morris) Grant; A.B., U. Ill., 1960; student Ill. Wesleyan U., 1938-39, U. Miami, (Fla.), 1945, Am. Inst. Banking, 1959-60; m. Jack R. Adams, Oct. 24, 1945 (dec. 1975); children—Jack Richard, Jr., Alexander Beall, Frances Grant II. Sec., Ill. Senate, 1936; sec., bus. mgr. Wesleyan U. Ill., 1938-39; sec. to chief staff Flying Tng. Command, USAAF, 1951, personnel supr. U.S. Army Air Base, Ephrata and Moses Lake, Wash., 1941-42; job classification and adminstrv. survey analyst Canal Zone, 1942-44; sec. to comdr. USAF Res. Wing, Pitts., 1951-55; sec. to mayor City of Wheeling (W.Va.), 1955-59; sec. W.Va. Ho. of Dels., 1965-66, 77-78, 79-80; mem. D.A.R., 1947—, nat. vice chmn. Service for vet. patients, 1968-71, editor W.Va. news, 1965-71, W.Va. state parliamentarian, 1979-80, dir. No. dist. 1980—; nat. chmn. pub. relations Nat. Soc. Women Descs. Ancient and Honorable Arty. Co., 1974-77; mem. Nat. League Am. Pen Women, 1949—, nat. 3d v.p., 1971-72, nat. rec. sec., 1966-68, nat. chmn. orgn., 1972-74, nat. chmn. commemorative endowment fund, 1976-80, W.Va. pres. 1980—. Mem. AAUW, Magna Charta Dames, Colonial Order of the Crown, Order of Washington, Phi Beta Kappa. Democrat. Presbyterian. Home: Route 1 Box 63 Elkins WV 26241

ADAMS, GEORGE EMERY, educator; b. Gary, Ind., Mar. 9, 1942; s. John Emery and Katherine Ellen (Cassiday) A.; B.A. in Math., Manchester Coll., 1963; M.A. (NSF fellow) U. Ill., 1967; postgrad. (univ. fellow) Fla. State U., 1969-71; m. Elvira Elizabeth Bene, June 24, 1967; children—Robert Edward Lee, Kelly Elizabeth. Math. tchr. public schs., Cleve., 1963-66; asst. prof. math. Manchester Coll., N. Manchester, Inc., 1967-69, 71-72; prof. math. Montreat-Anderson Coll., Montreat, N.C., 1972—, chmn. dept. math.; teaching asst. Fla. State U., 1970-71. Deacon, Montreat Presbyn. Ch., 1976—. Recipient Tchr. of Year award. 1976, 78. Mem. Math. Assn. Am. Republican. Home: 211 Chapel Rd Black Mountain NC 28711 Office: PO Box 846 Montreat NC 28757

ADAMS, HARRY CASPER, educator; b. McIntire, Iowa, Mar. 23, 1932; s. Edward and Pauline (Hemann) A.; B.S., U. Pitts., 1964; M.Ed., U. West Fla., 1978; m. Roberta L. Allen, Aug. 8, 1953; children—Steven Russell, Janet Lynn, Kathryn Ann, Carol Diane. Enlisted in USAF, 1951, advanced through grades to lt. col., 1969; command pilot, 1971; chief safety Norton AFB, San Bernardino, Calif., 1972; dep. dir. safety Patrick AFB, Fla., 1974; ret., 1974; mgr. engring. tech. program Gulf Coast Community Coll., Panama City, Fla., 1975—, asst. prof., 1979—. Decorated Air medal, Bronze Star. Mem. Fla. Assn. Community Colls., Fla. Vocat. Assn. Democrat. Roman Catholic. Home: 931 E Pierson Dr Lynn Haven FL 32444 Office: 5130 W Hwy 98 Panama City FL 32401

ADAMS, HAZEL GREENLEE REDFEARN (MRS. PAYTON F. ADAMS II), educator; b. Monroe, N.C., Nov. 12, 1905; d. Ephraim Eugene and Rebecca (Laney) Redfearn; student Radford Coll., 1924; A.B., U. Ky., 1940, M.A., 1953; postgrad. U. Nebr., 1955; m. Payton F. Adams II, July 11, 1928; children—Payton F. III, Juliette Greenlee Adams Hawk. Elementary tchr. Larchmont Sch., Norfolk, Va., 1924-28, Winchester (Ky.) City Schs., 1943-53; supr. Clark County (Ky.) Schs., 1953-61; supr. student tchrs. Ky. Wesleyan Coll., 1945-48; instr. Wesleyan Coll., Macon, Ga., 1960; named asst. prof. edn. Dakota Wesleyan U., Mitchell, S.D., 1961, asso. prof. edn. and psychology, 1961-70; asso. prof. early childhood edn. Pfeiffer Coll., Misenheimer, N.C., 1970-77, adviser Student Edn. Assn., 1972-73. Chmn., Clark County Community Council, 1950-52, Clark County Recreation Bd., 1955-60; supr. Teen-Town, Winchester, 1954-60. Recipient Honor award State of Ky., 1960; mem. advisory council Southeastern Christian Coll. Mem. AAUP, AAUW, NEA, S.D. Edn. Assn., DAR (treas. chpt. 1974-80), Assn. Supervision Curriculum Devel., Assn. for Childhood Edn., Mitchell Bus. and Profl. Women, Nat. Trust Hist. Preservation, Ky. Hist. Soc., First Settlers Homemakers Club (family life chmn.), Albemarle Bus. and Profl. Women (pres. 1972-73), Assn. United Meth. Women, Phi Kappa Phi (pres. 1964-66), Delta Kappa Gamma (pres. 1964-66), Pi Gamma Mu. Methodist. Mem. Order Eastern Star. Clubs: Winchester Music, Daniel Boone Music; Winchester Hist., Nat. Hist., Ky. Hist., Christian Women's, Clark County Hosp. Aux.; Author: The Inimitable Educator: Robert E. Lee. Home: 136 College St Winchester KY 40391 Office: Pfeiffer Coll Misenheimer NC 28109

ADAMS, HERBERT FLEET, JR., dentist; b. Montross, Va., Dec. 26, 1933; s. Herbert Fleet and Virginia Carlton (Baker) A.; B.S., Va. Poly. Inst. and State U., 1951-55; D.D.S., Med. Coll. Va., 1959; m. Mary Elizabeth Diracour, Aug. 5, 1962; 1 dau., Elizabeth Carlton. Pvt. practice orthodontics, Petersburg, Va., 1967—. Served with U.S. Army, 1959-62. Licensed dentist, Va., 1959. Mem. Am. Assn. Orthodontists, So. Soc. Orthodontists, Va. Orthodontic Soc., Am. Dental Assn., Va. Dental Assn., Southside Va. Dental Soc., Sons of Confederate Vets. Home: Rt 2 #6 Wedgewood Farms Petersburg VA 23803 Office: 15 Goodrich Ave Petersburg VA 23803

ADAMS, JACQUELINE, artist; b. Ennis, Tex., Sept. 24, 1935; d. Woodson Bryan and Sarah Elizabeth (Hickox) Adams; B.A., Tex. State Coll. Women, 1956; postgrad. Tex. Women's U., 1956-58. Dir. occupational therapy Children's Service, Nebr. Psychiat. Inst., Omaha, 1958-60; occupational therapist St. Joseph's Hosp., Omaha, 1960-62; tchr. art Bryant, Ark., 1962—; designer, dir. Jacqueline's Originals, Bryant, 1971—; founder Jonah Co., 1978; one-man shows Ark. State Capitol 1970, El Dorado (Ark.) Fine Arts Center, 1970, Seabrooks Gallery Memphis, 1971, A & B Originals Gallery, Dallas, 1971; exhibited in group shows Bryant Art Galleries, Harrison, Ark., 1970-74, Art Fair Art Gallery, Little Rock, 1970-74, Sketch Box Art Gallery, Little Rock, 1969, S.E. Ark. Art Gallery, Pine Bluff, 1972, Internat. Galleries, Houston, 1973, others; exhibited in 14 states, 1975, 12 states and Can., 1976; represented in permanent collections various cities. Mem. Ark. Art Center, Am. Therapy Assn. Clubs: Arkansas Kennel (Little Rock); Southeast Arkansas Kennel (Pine Bluff). Home: Box 86 Bryant AR 72022

ADAMS, JAMES CARLIE, II, engring. co. exec.; b. Raleigh, N.C., Aug. 25, 1941; s. James Carlie and Julia Brown (Hobbs) A.; B.S., N.C. State U., 1963; m. Harriet Dana Heard, Aug. 17, 1968; children—James Carlie, Shannon Dana. Vice pres. Hobbs-Adams Engring. Co., Suffolk, Va., 1968—; pres. Pioneer processers, Suffolk, 1971—, Two Adams Co., Willow Springs, N.C., 1976—; v.p. J.C. Adams, Inc., Willow Springs, 1973—, So. Processors Corp., Cullman, Ala., 1975—; partner Rainbow Barley Tobacco Warehouse, Mountain City, Tenn., Planters Tobacco Whse., Fuquay Springs, N.C.; dir. United Va. Bank, Norfolk. Served with U.S. Army, 1964. Mem. Am. Peanut Research and Edn. Assn., Forest Products Research Soc., Nat. Peanut Council, Nat. Bark Producers Assn. (v.p. 1976—, dir. 1976—), Jr. C. of C., Kappa Alpha. Club: Elks Home: 825 Craig Dr Suffolk VA 23434 Office: 1100 Holland Rd Suffolk VA 23434

ADAMS, JAMES IRWIN, r.r. exec.; b. Ackerman, Miss., Apr. 1, 1926; s. Irwin Asa and Josie (Morehead) A.; B.S., U. Tenn., 1948; m. Barbara Joyce Sullivan, Dec. 20, 1946; children—James R., David A., Elizabeth A., Robert A. Supr., Pa. R.R., Phila., Chgo., Johnstown and Harrisburg, Pa., Harrington, Del., Williamsport, Pa., Pitts., 1949-63; gen. supt. communications and signals L. & N. R.R., Louisville, 1963-69, chief engr., 1969-73, asst. v.p. engring., 1973-77, asst. v.p. transp., 1977-79, asst. v.p. ops., 1979—. Scoutmaster, mem. council Boy Scouts Am. Served with USAAF, 1944-45. Named Ky. col. Registered profl. engr., Pa., Tenn., Ky. Mem. Ky. Soc. Profl. Engrs., Am. Radio Relay League, Nat. Rifle Assn. (life), Roadmasters and M.W. Assn., Am. Assn. Railroads, Am. Ry. Engring. Assn., Eta Kappa Nu, Kappa Alpha. Republican. Baptist. Club: L & N Golf (pres. 1975-76, dir.). Home: 5416 Old Heady Rd Jeffersontown KY 40299 Office: 908 W Broadway Louisville KY 40201

ADAMS, JAMES NORMAN, microbiologist; b. Bklyn., Nov. 4, 1932; s. James Thomas and Anna Gertrude (Feldzaman) A.; B.S., U. Ky., 1954; Ph.D., U. Ga., 1961; m. Margie Beatrice McDaniel, Sept. 6, 1955; children—Bruce E., Leah E., Connie J., Thomas M. Research asst. Okla. State U., Stillwater, 1955-56; research fellow U. Ga., Athens, 1959-62, asst. prof., 1962-63; mem. faculty U. S.D., Vermillion, 1963-75, asst. prof., 1963-67, asso. prof., 1967-71, prof. microbiology, 1971-75, acting chmn., 1970-71; prof., coordinator med. microbiology Sch. Medicine, U.S.C., Columbia, 1975—; vis. lectr. U. Minn., 1964, Loyola U. Stritch Sch. Medicine, Chgo., 1971, Med. Coll. Ga., 1972, Universidad de los Andes, Merida, Venezuela, 1974, Universidad Nacional Autonoma de Mexico, 1975; cons. on research Polish Acad. Sci., Wroclaw, Poland, 1976. Served with U.S. Army, 1957-61. USPHS career devel. awardee, 1966-75. Fellow Am. Acad. Microbiology; mem. AAAS, Am. Soc. Microbiology, Soc. for Gen. Microbiology, Soc. for Indsl. Microbiology, Genetics Soc. Am., Sigma Xi, Phi Kappa Phi, Tau Kappa Epsilon (U.S.D. chpt. advisor 1967-70), Clubs: Am. Radio Relay League. Developer conjugation system in bacterial genus Nocardia; cons. editor The Aquarium Jour., 1961-66; asso. editor Biology of Actinomycetes and Related Organisms, 1975—; advisory com. Bergey's Manual of Determinative Bacteriology, 1966-70; review Indsl. Microbial Genetics; mem. editorial bd. Jour. Bacteriology, 1973—; invited reviewer Internat. Jour. Systematic Bacteriology, 1969, Canadian Jour. Microbiology, 1972—; contbr. articles to profl. jours. Home: 730 Shadow Brook Dr Columbia SC 29210 Office: U S C Columbia SC 29208

ADAMS, JESSE EARL, physician, surgeon; b. Lexington, Ky., Dec. 5, 1925; s. Jesse E. and Esther Francis (Nicholson) A.; B.S., U. Ky., 1945; M.D., Harvard, 1948; m. Hattie Boeswetter, Feb. 21, 1959; 1 son, Jesse Earl III. Rotating intern Harper Hosp., Detroit, 1948-49; intern in surgery Vanderbilt Hosp., 1949-50, resident, 53-55; resident Med. Coll. Va. Hosp., 1950-51, U. Va. Hosp., 1955-56; vis. surgeon Rigshospitolet, Copenhagen, Denmark, 1956; asst. prof. surgery Vanderbilt U. Sch. Medicine, Nashville, 1956-60, dir. S.R. Light Lab. for Surg. Research, 1958-60; mem. Assn. Thoracic and Cardiovascular Surgery, Chattanooga, 1961—. Past pres. bd. dirs., mem. exec. com. Chattanooga Area Heart Assn.; past chmn. Chattanooga-Hamilton County Air Pollution Control Bd.; bd. dirs. Tenn. Regional Health Program; v.p. State Vol. Mut. Ins. Co. Served with USAF, 1951-52. Diplomate Am. Bd. Surgery, Am. Bd. Thoracic Surgery. Fellow A.C.S.; mem. Am. (past rep. councilor), So. thoracic socs., Am. Coll. Chest Physicians, A.M.A., Tenn. Med. Assn. (ho. of dels.), Chattanooga-Hamilton County Med. Soc. (past pres.), Am. Assn. Thoracic Surgery, Southeastern Surg. Congress, Soc. Thoracic Surgeons, Tenn thoracic Soc. (past pres., mem. exec. com.), Tenn. Tb and Respiratory Disease Assn. (mem. exec. com.), Tenn. Heart Assn. (past pres., dir., past chmn. program com., research com.). Contbr. articles on cardiac, thoracic and vascular surgery to med. jours. Home: 224 N Crest Rd Chattanooga TN 37404 Office: 1000 E 3d St Chattanooga TN 37403

ADAMS, JEWEL HAMILTON, realtor; b. Bryant, Ark., May 15, 1924; d. Andrew Wilson and Bessie Jane (Hughes) Hamilton; student realty U. So. Ala., 1971; m. Sherley Bain Adams, June 1, 1941; children—Sherley Lewis II, Andrew W. Hamilton, Carol Lynn Hall. Editor soc. newspapers Morehouse Enterprise, Bastrop, La., 1950-52; salesman mut. funds Investors Diversified Services, Mobile, Ala., 1958; sales exec. real estate Robert Bros., Inc., Mobile, 1960-72; v.p. Adams Real Estate, Inc., Mobile, 1972—. Residential chmn. ARC, 1949-50, Cancer Soc., 1951-52; mem. Mobile Beautification Bd. Mem. Ala. Assn. Realtors (dir. 1973-75), Mobile County Bd. Realtors (dir. 1969-70), Million Dollar Sales Club, Nat. Assn. Realtors (women's council), Realtors Nat. Mktg. Inst. Republican. Methodist. Clubs: Skyline Country. Home: 3808 N Llewelyn Dr Mobile AL 36608 Office: 272 S Mc Gregor at Airport Mobile AL 36608

ADAMS, JIM MILLS, chem. co. exec.; b. Sioux Falls, S.D., Aug. 4, 1936; s. Paul Avery and Ferne (Mills) A.; B.S. in Chem. Engring., S.C. Sch. Mines and Tech., 1958; M.S. in Nuclear Engring., U. Wash., Seattle, 1960, Ph.D., 1962; m. Sherrell D. Shurtz, Oct. 11, 1958; children—Cynthia Ann, Christopher Charles. Engring. specialist, prin. investigator Aerojet Gen. Co., Sacramento, 1962-68; sr. scientist, mgr. engring. Hoffmann LaRoche, Inc., Nutley, N.J., 1968-75; mgr. Bushy Park (S.C.) plant Haarmann & Reimer Corp., Charleston, S.C., 1975-78; pres. Haarmann & Reiner Corp., Springfield, N.J., 1980—; cons. med. instrumentation devel. Served with AUS, 1959. H.L. Dougherty Ednl. Found. grantee, 1954-58; W. Alton Jones fellow, 1959-61. Mem. Am. Mgmt. Assn., Am. Phys. Soc., AAAS, Sigma Xi (past chpt. pres.). Author, patentee optics, spectroscopy, thermodynamics. Address: 211 Hobcaw Dr Mount Pleasant SC 29464

ADAMS, JOHN AMOS, III, restaurant chain exec.; b. Washington, May 20, 1945; s. John A. and Lucille (Simmons) A.; B.S., Mont. State U., 1967; M.B.A., Bellarmine Coll., 1977; D.B.A., Calif. Western U., 1980; m. Maria E. Rolling, Mar. 22, 1971. Field sales mgr. Ford Motor Co., Dearborn, Mich., 1971; regional credit mgr. Brandeis Machinery & Supply Corp., Louisville, 1975-78; dir. budget and planning Burger Queen Enterprises, Inc., Louisville, 1978—. Mem. Republican Nat. Com., 1967—. Served with inf. AUS, 1968-71; Vietnam. Decorated Air medal, Bronze Star with oak leaf cluster, Purple Heart, Vietnamese Cross of Gallantry with star. Mem. Nat. Assn. Accts., Am. Mgmt. Assn., Inst. Mgmt. Acctg., Assn. M.B.A. Execs., Planning Execs. Inst., Res. Officers Assn. U.S.A. Republican. Methodist. Home: 12401 Croswinds Dr Middletown KY 40243 Office: 4010 DuPont Sq PO Box 6014 Louisville KY 40206

ADAMS, JOHN BRADLEY, psychologist; b. Sarasota, Fla., Jan. 28, 1938; s. J. Bradley and Dorothy May (Price) A.; B.S., U. Fla., 1960; Ph.D., U. Ala., 1974; m. Barbara Ann Cole, July 6, 1963. Chief programmer bd. dirs. Human Devel. Inst., Atlanta, 1961-63; clin. psychologist Ala. State Hosp., Bryce Hosp., Tuscaloosa, 1963-78, pvt. practice, Tuscaloosa, 1978—. Mem. Am. Psychol. Assn., Am. Personnel and Guidance Assn., Soc. Police and Criminal Psychology, Am. Assn. Correctional Psychologists. Ala. Psychol. Assn. Republican. Episcopalian. Club: Kiwanis. Home: 5007 10th Ave E Tuscaloosa AL 35405 Office: First Federal Bldg Tuscaloosa AL 35401

ADAMS, JOHN J., constrn. engr.; b. N.Y.C., Mar. 19, 1933; s. John V. and Domenica (DeMarco) A.; Asso. Applied Sci., SUNY, 1952; student Cooper Union, 1962-63, Adelphi U., 1978; m. Diane L. Benton, Nov. 16, 1952; children—John, Keith, Scott, Brian. Structural steel detailer Bethlehem Steel Co., 1952-54; from draftsman to designer checker N.Y.C. Transit Authority, 1954-62, specification writer, 1962-70, supervising specification writer, 1970-73, program control mgr., 1973-77; owner cons. John J. Adams Constrn. and Archtl. Specification, Commack, N.Y., 1965-77; chief specification engr. Kaiser Transit Group, Post, Buckley, Schuh & Jernigan, Inc., Miami, 1977-79, constrn. mgr. Kaiser Transit Group, 1979—. Mem. Nat. Soc. Profl. Engrs., Constrn. Specifications Inst., Fla. Engring. Soc. Office: 46 SW 1st St Miami FL 33130

ADAMS, K.S., JR., bus. exec.; b. Bartlesville, Okla., 1923; ed. U. Kans., 1943. Chmn., Adams Resources & Energy, Inc., Houston, KSA Industries, Inc., Adams Petroleum Center, Inc., Bud Adams Ranches, Houston Oilers Profl. Football Team, Inc., River Garden Farms, S.W. Lincoln-Mercury, Inc., S.W. Motor Leasing; adv. dir. First City Nat. Bank of Houston, Allied Am. Bank, Houston; v.p. Travel House of Houston. Trustee Profl. Football Hall of Fame; mem. exec. bd. Sam Houston Area council Boy Scouts Am.; mem. adv. bd. dirs. Children's Oncology Services Tex. Served with USNR, 1943-46. Named Houston Salesman of Yr., 1960, Mr. Sportsman of 1961, Westerner of Yr., 1969. Mem. Tex. Ind. Producers and Royalty Owners Assn., Ind. Petroleum Assn. Am., Houston Assn. Petroleum Landmen, Houston Geol. Soc., Sigma Chi. Clubs: River Oaks Country, Petroleum (Houston). Office: PO Box 844 Houston TX 77001

ADAMS, LAMAR TAFT, physician; b. Hiawassee, Ga., Apr. 9, 1938; s. Cecil Taft and Julia Nadine (Wilson) A.; B.S., Wake Forest U., 1959; M.D., Bowman Gray Sch. Medicine, 1965. Intern, N.C. Bapt. Hosp., 1965-66, resident in internal medicine, 1966-69; staff physician VA Hosp., Mountain Home, Tenn., 1971-72; chief med.-surg. services Ga. Regional Hosp., Augusta, 1973-74; asst. prof., med. dir. physician's asst. tng. program Med. Coll. Ga., Augusta, 1974-75; practice medicine specializing in internal medicine, Monroe, Ga., 1975—. Served with USAF, 1969-71. Mem. Phi Rho Sigma. Baptist. Contbr. articles to med. jours. Home: Box 669 Monroe GA 30655 Office: Alcova St Monroe GA 30655

ADAMS, LARRY JOE, welding supply co. exec.; b. Evansville, Ind., Mar. 30, 1945; s. Oscar Winfield and Clara Helen (Carpenter) A.; B.B.A., U. Houston; m. Beverly Ann Land, July 29, 1966. Sales engr. Am. Cryogenics, Houston, 1966-70, Acme Oxygen, Houston, 1969-70, Tex. Oxygen Co., Houston, 1970-71; pres. Welding Products of Tex., Houston, 1971—. Mem. Nat. Welding Supply Assn., Am. Welding Soc., Tex. Concrete Pipe Assn. Methodist. Office: 8443 Airline St Houston TX 77037

ADAMS, LAWRENCE H., pub. utility exec.; b. W. Palm Beach, Fla., Feb. 11, 1927; s. Harry L. and Pauline (Kraynick) A.; student Purdue U., 1944, U. Miami, 1951, Harvard Advanced Mgmt. Program, 1974; m. Arminta Gregg, Oct. 27, 1951; children—Larry, Ron, Thad. Ops. mgr. Fla. Power & Light Co., Miami, 1949-57, mgr. consumer services, 1957-67, comml. mgr., 1967-73, gen. S.E. div., 1973-76, So. div., 1976—. Trustee, U. Miami, 1974-77, chmn. student affairs com., 1976-78; bd. dirs. Greater Miami YMCA, 1967-73; exec. bd. dirs. Jr. Achievement of Broward County (Fla.), 1973-76; campaign chmn., pres. elect United Way Broward County, 1975-76; chmn. Broward County chpt. ARC, 1975-76; founding dir. Fellowship of Christian Athletes, Ft. Lauderdale and Miami, 1964—; coordinator activities Broward Minutemen Bicentennial Commn., 1975-76; exec. bd. Boy Scouts Am., Ft. Lauderdale and Miami, 1973—; co-chmn. Unit D, United Way Dade County (Fla.), 1976-80; v.p. Ft. Lauderdale C. of C., 1975; bd. dirs. Ft. Lauderdale Downtown Devel. Authority, 1975-76; chmn. subcom. for econ. devel. Greater Miami C. of C., 1976-77; vice chmn. Met. Dade County Indsl. Devel. Authority, 1977—; mem. Com. of 100, Broward Indsl. Bd., 1973-76. Served with USAF, 1944-46. Named Outstanding Businessman of Broward County, Broward Sales and Mktg. Assn., 1975. Mem. Ft. Lauderdale Exec. Assn., U. Miami Alumni Assn. (pres. 1973). Democrat. Baptist. Clubs: Riviera Country, Rod and Reel Club Miami, Am. in Miami, Miami, 200 of Greater Miami, Tiger Bay. Home: 730 Saldano Ave Coral Gables FL 33143 Office: PO Box 529311 Miami FL 33152

ADAMS, LEON ASHBY, otolaryngologist; b. Four Oaks, N.C., Feb. 23, 1923; s. L.A. and Alice Thorne (Patterson) A.; B.S., U. N.C., 1944; M.D., U. Va., 1946; postgrad. U. Pa. Grad. Sch., 1951; m. Jean Crichton Davis, Dec. 22, 1947; children—Leon Ashby III, Crichton Alston Thorne, Joseph Mayo Atkinson. Intern, Phila. Gen. Hosp., 1946-47; resident in otolaryngology U.S. Naval Hosp., Phila. and U. Pa. Hosp., 1948-49, 51-52; practice medicine specializing in otolaryngology, Princeton, N.J., 1951-73, Wilson, N.C., 1973—; mem. staff Wilson Meml. Hosp., Carolina Clinic; mem. teaching staff U. Pa. Hosp., 1951-56, Rutgers U. Sch. Medicine, 1971-73. Served with USN, 1946-50. Diplomate Am. Bd. Otolaryngology. Mem. AMA, Pan Am. Med. Assn., Am. Acad. Ophthalmology and Otolaryngology, Royal Soc. Health (Eng.), Med. Soc. N.C., Magna Carta Barons. Republican. Clubs: St. Anthony (N.Y.C.).

ADAMS, LORAN LEON, JR., med. technologist; b. New Braunfels, Tex., Aug. 15, 1947; s. Loran Leon and Martha Elizabeth (Mosley) A.; B.S. in Med. Tech., Southwestern Union Coll., 1970; children—Stacie Christeen, Jeffrey Scott. Staff technologist Harris Hosp., Ft. Worth, 1970, supr. serology dept., 1971-75, instr. Sch. Med. Tech., 1971-75, microbiology sect. chief, 1976-77; asst. chief technologist, microbiology sect. chief Huguley Meml. Hosp., Ft. Worth, 1977-78, chief technologist, 1978—. Mem. Am. Soc. Med. Technologists, Am. Soc. Microbiologists, Tex. Soc. Microbiologists, North Tex. Soc. Microbiologists, Am. Soc. Clin. Pathologists (affiliate). Seventh-Day Adventist. Home: 6818 S Hulen Apt 243 Fort Worth TX 76133 Office: 11801 S Freeway Fort Worth TX 76115

ADAMS, LOUIS WILLIAM, clergyman; b. Fort Worth, Dec. 29, 1929; s. James Oran and Marguerite Elizabeth (Horony) A.; B.A., Tex. Christian U., 1954, Th.M., 1973, D.Ministry, 1975; M.Div., Austin Presbyterian Theol. Sem., 1966, postgrad., 1967-68; m. Dolores Ann Reid, July 19, 1967; 1 dau., Wendy Kaye. Commd. 2d lt. USAF, 1954, advanced through grades to capt., 1960; ret., 1963; ordained to ministry Presbyterian Ch., 1966; asso. exec. sec. Presbyn. Synod Tex., also chaplain Ramsey unit Tex. Dept. Corrections, Rosharon, Tex., 1966-73; dir. Azle (Tex.) Pastoral Counseling Center, 1976-79; interim dir. Pastoral Care and Tng. Center Tex. Christian U., Fort Worth, 1979—; supply pastor First Presbyn. Ch., Cumby, Tex., 1974-75, Union Hill Presbyn. Ch., Joshua, Tex., 1976—. Chaplain, CAP, 1973-74, 77—. Bd. dirs. Tex. Corrections Assn. Fellow Am. Protestant Correctional Chaplains Assn. (regional v.p. 1969-72), Am. Assn. Pastoral Counselors (diplomate); mem. Am. Assn. Marriage and Family Therapists (clin. mem.), Alpha Chi, Pi Sigma Alpha, Theta Phi. Home: 2913 Carson St Fort Worth TX 76117

ADAMS, MARGRETT LINDLEY, educator; b. Booneville, Miss., Nov. 19, 1914; d. Charles Edward and Bessie Aldridge L.; B.A., Blue Mountain Coll., 1937; M.B.E., Ga. State U., 1964; Ed.D., U. Ga., 1974; m. Emmett Womack Adams, Jr., July 18, 1937 (div.); children—Emmett Lindley, Margaret Carol. Tchr., DeKalb County (Ga.) Sch. System, 1949-62; prof. Young Harris Coll., 1962-68; teaching asst. U. Ga., 1968-70, 73-74; vocat. office tng. coordinator Elbert County (Ga.) Sch. System, 1970-73; asso. prof., dir. grad. bus. edn. program Valdosta (Ga.) State Coll., 1974—. Nat. Tchr. Edn. scholar, 1961. Mem. Nat. Bus. Edn. Assn., Am. Bus. Communications Assn., Am. Vocat. Assn., Nat. Assn. Tchr. Educators for Bus. and Office Edn., So. Bus. Edn. Assn., Ga. Bus. Edn. Assn., Ga. Council Bus. Tchr. Educators, AAUP, AAUW, Delta Pi Epsilon, Phi Delta Kappa, Bus. and Profl. Women's Club (past pres.). Democrat. Methodist. Asso. editor Ga. Bus. Edn. Armchair Bull., 1977-78; sect. editor Nat. Assn. Bus. Tchr. Edn. Rev., 1979-80. Office: Dept Secretarial Adminstrn and Bus Edn Box 189 Valdosta State Coll Valdosta GA 31601

ADAMS, PATRICIA SWISHER, audiologist; b. Yokohoma, Japan, Apr. 21, 1955; d. George Ronald and Kinuko Swisher; B.S. in Speech Pathology-Audiology, W.Va. U., 1976, M.S., 1978; m. Paul Edward Adams, Jr., May 14, 1977. Audiologist C.E. Haislip, M.D., Inc., Fairmont, W.Va., 1978—. Mem. Am. Speech Language Hearing Assn., W.Va. Speech and Hearing Assn., Phi Kappa Phi. Democrat. Methodist. Home: 1111 Valley View Ave Morgantown WV 26505 Office: 1836 Locust Ave Fairmont WV 26554

ADAMS, PERRY RONALD, coll. adminstr.; b. Parkersburg, W.Va., Sept. 16, 1921; s. Russell Douglas and Beulah Grace (Cunningham) A.; A.B., U. Ky., 1943, M.A., 1948; Ed.D. (Kellogg fellow), U. Fla., 1965; m. Ann Mallory Gillespie, Dec. 25, 1943; children—Suzanne (Mrs. Frank Markwell), Sally (Mrs. Robert Barrios). Instr., U. Ky., 1948-53; dir. music U. Fla., 1953-63; dean instrn. Polk Jr. Coll., Winter Haven, Fla., 1965-69; provost No. Va. Community Coll., Annandale, 1969-70; pres. Paul D. Camp Community Coll., Franklin, Va., 1970-79; vice-chancellor Va. Community Coll. System, Richmond, 1979—; adjudicator various high sch. music contests, 1953—; mem. fin. adv. com. Va. Council Higher Edn., 1970—, also mem. adv. com. on instructional progress; mem. adv. council of pres. Va. Community Coll. System; dir. United Va. Bank Va. Trustee, Southampton Hosp. Served with USNR, 1942-47; MTO, ETO, PTO. Mem. Am. Assn. Higher Edn., Am. Assn. Jr. Colls., So. Assn. Colls. and Schs. (accreditation com.), Phi Mu Alpha (nat. councilman), Ruritan Club (dir.), Va., Franklin-Southampton, Suffolk (dir.) chambers commerce, Phi Delta Kappa, Kappa Delta Pi. Baptist (bd. deacons). Clubs: Rotary, Cypress Cove Country. Home: 10811 Whitaker Wood Rd Richmond VA 23229 Office: PO Box 1558 Richmond VA 23212

ADAMS, RICHARD LEON, banker; b. Scottsbluff, Nebr., July 19, 1921; s. Clyde Charles and Elizabeth (Sullivan) A.; student Okla. A. and M. Coll., 1940; diploma La. State U. Sch. Banking, 1963; m. Mildred Catherine Moody, Oct. 29, 1945; children—Janine Elaine, Richard Leon, Nancy Sue Adams Yawn, Charles C., Donna Jo. Clk., Scottsbluff Nat. Bank, 1937-41, teller, loan clk., 1945-47; with First Nat. Bank in Palm Beach (Fla.), 1947—, auditor, 1947-51, asst. cashier, 1953-57, asst. v.p., 1957-61, v.p., 1961-68, exec. v.p., 1968—; pres., vice chmn. bd. Palm Beach Mall Bank, West Palm Beach, Fla., 1970—. Pres. Palm Beach County Heart Assn., 1974-75; adv. bd. Salvation Army, 1970—; bd. dirs. Palm Beach County Comprehensive Community Mental Health Center, Palm Beach Symphonette, Fla. Heart Assn.; bd. dirs. Fla. Bankers Assn. Ednl. Found., chmn., 1971-72, pres., 1979-80. Served to maj. USAAF, 1941-46, USAF, 1951-53. Decorated D.F.C., Air medal with cluster. Mem. Am. (exec. com. real estate and housing, governing council 1979-80), Fla. (chmn. credit div. 1972-73, v.p. 1977—) bankers assns., Soc. Real Estate Appraisers, Palm Beach Sales and Mktg. Assn., Palm Beach Islanders (treas., bd. dirs.), Air Force Assn., Navy League. Palm Beach (dir., v.p. 1979-80), West Palm Beach (dir.) chambers commerce, Quiet Birdmen, Flying Alligators. Methodist (mem. ch. bd., trustee 1960—). Kiwanian (dir.). Club: Sailfish (bd. govs. 1970—). Home: 3101 Embassy Dr West Palm Beach FL 33401 Office: 255 S County Rd Palm Beach FL 33480

ADAMS, RICHARD STEVEN, textile co. exec.; b. Macon, Ga., Oct. 17, 1944; s. James Clarence and Nellie Ernestine (Ellerbee) A.; A.E., So. Tech. Inst., Marietta, Ga., 1965; m. Brenda Jones Adams, Mar. 5, 1965; children—Richard S., Katherine Ashley. Dept. mgr. Thomaston Mills (Ga.), 1965-73; sales and tech. service rep. Barber Colman Co., Gastonia, N.C., 1973-76; sales mgr. textiles North Chem. Co., Marietta, Ga., 1976—. MMem. Am. Mgmt. Assn., So. Textile Assn., Am. Assn. Textile Tech., Ala. Textile Operating Execs. Democrat. Baptist. Clubs: Kiwanis, Jaycees. Home: Rt 1 Cobb's Way Anderson SC 29621 Office: PO Box 769 Marietta GA 30061

ADAMS, RUSSELL LEE, clin. psychologist; b. Jefferson, Tex., Mar. 2, 1941; s. Irby Ray and Verda Mae (Griffen) A.; B.B.A., Tex. A. and M. U., 1962; M.A., S.W. Tex. State U., 1964; Ph.D., U. Tex., 1967; m. Carolyn Sue Pulley, Aug. 8, 1964; children—Scott, David. Mem. faculty U. Tex. Med. Sch., San Antonio, 1969-78, chief psychology consultation service Audie L. Murphy VA Hosp., San Antonio, 1973-78; dir. clin. psychology internship program U. Okla. Health Scis. Center, Oklahoma City, 1978—. Bd. dirs. Touch Narcotic Rehab. Inc. Served to capt. AUS, 1967-69. Diplomate Am. Bd. Profl. Psychology. Mem. Am., Tex., Southwestern, Bexar County (pres. 1972) psychol. assns. Democrat. Baptist (bd. deacons 1969—). Contbr. articles to profl. jours. Home: 1600 Thunderbird Edmond OK 73034 Office: PO Box 26901 Oklahoma City OK 73190

ADAMS, SALVATORE CHARLES, lawyer; b. N.Y.C., July 10, 1934; s. Charles Joseph and Rose (Scala) A.; B.C.E., Rensselaer Poly. Inst., Troy, N.Y., 1955; M.S., U. Conn., 1961; J.D., U. Miami (Fla.), 1968; m. Linda Lewis Pollock, Mar. 31, 1973; children by previous marriage—Mark Charles, Scott Shepherd, David James, Christopher Amos. Constrn. estimator Bechtel Corp., San Francisco, 1957-58; planning and econ. feasibility cons., Hartford, Conn., 1958-63; mem. faculty U. Conn., Storrs, 1958-63; project mgr. Rader & Assos., cons. engrs., Miami, 1963-65; pres. Motivation Cons., Miami, 1965-68; admitted to Fla. bar, 1968; practiced in Miami, 1968-70; propr. S. Charles Adams & Assos., Ft. Lauderdale, 1971—; counsel City of Pompano Beach (Fla.), 1972-76; chief municipal judge City of North Lauderdale, 1974-77; asso. municipal judge City of Coconut Creek (Fla.), 1974-77; pres., dir. Atlantic Concession Assos., Inc., 1977—; dir. Biltmore Mgmt. Corp.; prof. Nova U., Coral Springs, Fla. Served with USNR, 1955-57. Recipient Pres.'s award Broward County Bar Assn., Alumni Key award Rensselaer Poly. Inst. Mem. Am. Trial Lawyers Assn., Am., Fla., North Broward (treas.) bar assns., Nat. Inst. Municipal Law Officers, Fla., Broward County (dir.) municipal judge's assns., Lambda Chi Alpha, Delta Theta Phi. Author: Land Use and Municipal Finance, 1961. Office: 1300 Stirling Rd Suite 9B Dania FL 33004

ADAMS, TED ANTHONY, accountant; b. Raceland, La., Oct. 24, 1953; s. Edwey Joseph and Alice Mary (Federine) A.; B.S., Nicholls State U., 1976. Computer programmer trainee Lafource Telephone Co., Larose, La., 1973-74; payroll accountant Tidewater Marine Service Co., Morgan City, La., 1977, chief accountant, 1978—. Democrat. Roman Catholic. Office: PO Box 2407 Morgan City LA 70380

ADAMS, TIM, pub. relations exec.; b. Nov. 23, 1943; s. Leroy and Ruby (Lucas) A.; student Bethune Cookman Coll., 1961-64, Stetson U., 1964-65; B.S., Universal Sci. Acad.; student So. Coll., Fla., 1973-75. Property accountant W. Tex. Utilities Co., Abilene, 1967-68; dir. Jobmobile, T.M. Services Inc., Orlando, Fla., 1968-70, pres., 1969-71, chief exec. officer, 1968-70; adminstrv. asst. Orange County (Fla.) Econ. Opportunity Inc., Orlando, 1969-70; counselor Bethune Cookman Coll., Daytona Beach, Fla., 1973-74; counselor Orlando Tng. Center, 1974-75; public relations cons., 1975—; census bur. supr., 1969-70. Exec. v.p. Tex. Community Action Agy., Abilene, 1967-68. Served with USAF, 1965-67. Mem. West Central Orlando C. of C., Am. Bus. League, Alpha Phi Omega. Home: PO Box 1172 2404 Monte Carlo Trail Orlando FL 32802

ADAMS, WILLIAM ROGER, historian; b. Mpls., Nov. 4, 1935; s. Jacob and Clara (Jordan) A.; B.A., U. Minn., 1961, M.A., 1967; Ph.D., Fla. State U., 1974; m. LaVonne May Turgeon, June 24, 1961; children—James, April. Officer, USIS, 1963-69; asst. prof. history Fla. State U., 1972-75; exec. dir. Fla. Bicentennial Commn., 1975-77; dir.

Hist. St. Augustine (Fla.) Preservation Bd., 1977—; bd. dirs. Fla. Trust Hist. Preservation. Served with AUS, 1955-57. Author articles in field. Home: 2002 Versailles Ct Tallahassee FL 32308 Office: PO Box 1987 St Augustine FL 32084

ADAMSON, JAMES ROBERT, real estate co. exec.; b. Birmingham, Ala., Nov. 12, 1925; s. John Lamar and Nora (Williams) A.; student Auburn U., 1945-47; m. Eugenia Douthitt Martin, June 29, 1951; 1 son, John Martin. Realtor-appraiser, Laurel, Miss., 1952-79; owner James R. Adamson Real Estate, Laurel, 1952—. Served with C.E., U.S. Army, World War II; ETO. Mem. Nat. Assn. Realtors, Am. Right of Way Assn., Nat. Assn. Real Estate Appraisers, Nat. Assn. Review Appraisers, Miss. Assn. Realtors, Miss. Bd. Realtors (dir.), Laurel Bd. Realtors (pres., Realtor of Year 1968), Sigma Phi Epsilon. Episcopalian. Club: Laurel Country. Home: 1433 Amy Rd Laurel MS 39440 Office: 1134 Hwy 15 N Laurel MS 39440

ADCOCK, EVA JACQUELINE, musician, educator; b. San Pedro, Calif., Mar. 8, 1925; d. Joseph and Irene (Titus) Blumberg; A.A., Chaffey Coll., 1944; B.A., U. Calif., Berkeley, 1946; M. Mus. Edn., Fla. State U., 1968, Ph.D., 1970; m. Howard L. Adcock, Jr., Feb. 1, 1947; children—Mary Jane, Joel F., Christy Beth. Tchr. choral and gen. music pub. schs., Fla., Ohio, Tenn.; prof. music edn. Western Carolina U., Cullowhee, N.C., 1970—; changing voice clinician and researcher; clogging and dulcimer clinician; mem. Council for Preservation Mountain Dance and Music. Mem. Music Educators Nat. Conf., Internat. Soc. Music Edn., Am. Choral Dirs. Assn., Coll. Music Soc. (life), U. Calif. (life), Fla. State U. (life) alumni assns., N.C. State Employees Assn. Methodist. Home: PO Box 982 Cullowhee NC 28732 Office: Dept Music Western Carolina U Cullowhee NC 28723

ADCOCK, KEN RAYBURN, data processing profl.; b. Smithville, Tenn., Apr. 20, 1941; s. Sherman Clifford and Mary Frances (Ferrell) A.; B.S. in Math., Tenn. Technol. U., 1964; M.B.A., U. Tenn., 1976; m. Charlotte Robinson, June 13, 1964; children—Ray, Jonathan. Sci. programmer Arnold Engring. Devel. Center, Arnold Air Force Sta., Tenn., 1965-70; project programmer Bowater Inc., Calhoun, Tenn., 1970-73, mgmt. sci. specialist, 1973-76, mgmt. sci. analyst, 1976—. Certified data processor. Mem. Assn. Computing Machinery, Inst. Mgmt. Sci. Home: Route 2 Westbrook Circle Cleveland TN 37311 Office: Bowater Inc MIS Calhoun TN 37309

ADCOCK, SANDRA WILLIAMS, nurse; b. Albemarle, N.C., June 4, 1938; d. Hugh Irvin and Christine Louise (Swann) Williams; student E. Carolina U., 1957-58; diploma Rex Hosp. Sch. Nursing, Raleigh, N.C., 1962; m. Frederick Dale Adcock, June 12, 1959; children—Frederick Dale, Dana Michelle. Staff nurse medicine-surgery Rex Hosp., 1962-65, 68-70, staff nurse dept. emergency, 1970-74, head nurse, 1974—; instr. emergency clinician program E. Carolina U.; instr. Wake County (N.C.) Emergency Med. Services; cert. CPR instr., Am. Heart Assn. Nursing coordinator N.C. State Fair; mem. nursing service com., 1st aid com. ARC. Mem. Nat. Emergency Dept. Nurses Assn., Greater Carolina Chpt. N.C. Emergency Dept. Nurses Assn., N.C. Emergency Med. Services Council (adv. 1974—). Democrat. Methodist. Home: 6808 Buckhead Dr Raleigh NC 27609 Office: 1311 Saint Mary's St Raleigh NC 27603

ADCOCK, WILLIS ALFRED, electronics co. exec.; b. St. Johns, Que., Can., Nov. 25, 1922; s. William Arthur and Luella (White) A.; came to U.S., 1936, naturalized, 1944; B.S. cum laude, Hobart Coll., 1943; Ph.D., Brown U., 1948; M.L.A., So. Meth. U., 1975; m. Sara McCoy Whiddon, Dec. 28, 1970; children from previous marriage—William John, Robert Charles, Edward James, Margaret Eleanor Adcock Boshart. Mem. staff Woods Hole (Mass.) Oceanographic Inst., 1943-44; mem. tech. staff Clinton Labs., Oak Ridge, 1944-46; mem. tech. staff Stanolind Oil & Gas Co., Tulsa, 1948-53; mgr. devel. dept., mgr. integrated circuits dept. Tex. Instruments, Inc., Dallas, 1953-64; tech. dir. Sperry Semicondr., Norwalk, Conn., 1964-65; mgr. advanced planning, tech. devel. areas Tex. Instruments Inc., Dallas, 1965-75, asst. v.p. consumer products activity, 1975-78, prin. fellow asst. v.p. corporate research devel. and engring., 1978—. Fellow IEEE; mem. Nat. Acad. Engring., Am. Chem. Soc., Phi Beta Kappa, Sigma Xi. Episcopalian. Patentee in field. Contbr. articles to profl. jours. Home: 5409 Castlewood Rd Dallas TX 75229 Office: MS132 PO Box 225936 Dallas TX 75265

ADDISCOTT, DEREK HERBERT, publisher; b. Plymouth, Eng., Apr. 14, 1910; s. Herbert C. and Claire (Roberts) A.; student Oundle Coll., Eng., 1924-28, Stevens Inst. Tech. 1928-29; m. Katharine W. Bray, Nov. 23, 1944: children—Gayle K., Lynn C. Office mgr. Hamilton Watch Co., Lancaster, Pa., 1939-41; mgr. orgn. planning and procedures div. RCA, Camden, N.J., 1941-50; mgr. indsl. engring. PanAm. Airways, Cape Kennedy, Fla., 1954-58, mgr. data processing, 1958-67; pub. Eau Gallie, Fla., 1967—. Councilman, Town of Palm Shores, Fla., 1960-61, vice mayor, 1961-63, mayor, 1963-74. Mem. Planning Zoning Commn., Palm Shores, Brevard County Civilian-Mil. Relations Council. Bd. dirs. Brevard Symphony Orch. Mem. Am. Mgmt. Assn., Moonwalk Commemorative Assn. (pres. 1972), Sigma Nu. Democrat. Episcopalian. Home: 4895 N Harbor City Blvd Palm Shores Melbourne FL 32935 Office: PO Box 399 Eau Gallie FL 32935

ADDISON, HAROLD VICTOR, petroleum co. exec.; b. Shongaloo, La., Oct. 12, 1922; s. I.T. and Gladys Alline (Lee) A.; student La. Tech. U., 1940-43, 46-48, U. Denver, 1950-51, Centenary Coll., 1953. With Marathon Oil Co., Shreveport, La., 1953-58; gen. mgr. Anabaco, Oklahoma City, 1958-65; asst. land mgr. Eason Oil Co., Oklahoma City, 1965—. Served with USAF, 1949-51. Decorated Purple Heart, Bronze Star. Mem. Nat. Assn. Div. Order Analysts (chmn.), Am., Oklahoma City assns. petroleum landmen, Okla. Mus. Art (patron), Arklatex Landsman Assn., Geneal. Research Soc., N.Y. Philharmonic Soc. (hon.), Sigma Alpha Iota, Tau Kappa Epsilon (past pres.), Alpha Lambda Tau (corr. sec.). Republican. Episcopalian. Home: 4949 Skillman #152 Dallas TX 75206 Office: PO Box 2880 Dallas TX 75221

ADDISON, MARY JANE, clubwoman; b. Beaumont, Tex.; d. Henry Davis and Corinne (Carter) Pond; R.N., Jefferson Davis Sch. Nursing, 1945; m. Eugene Morse Addison, Mar. 10, 1946; children—Eugene Morse, Paul Davis. Mem. choir First Baptist Ch.; den mother Cub Scouts, 6 years, recipient Den Mothers award, 1961; pres. Huntsville (Tex.) PTA, 1955-56, v.p. dist. bd., 1956-57, state life mem. PTA, 1967; pres. Women's Missionary Union, First Bapt. Ch., 1965-68; chmn. heritage com. Mayor's Bicentennial Com., 1974-76; pres. Woman's Forum, Tex. Fedn. Womens Clubs, 1972-74, 80—; named Woman of Year, 1974; life mem. Hosp. Aux., pres., 1971-72; active Sam Houston Meml. Mus., Walker County Hist. Survey Commn., Tex. Hist. Found.; bd. dirs. Community Choir; chmn. Huntsville Beautification, 1979—. Decorated Grand Peiory of Am. Order St. John of Jerusalem, dame Knights Hospitaller. Mem. African Violet Soc. Am., Daus. Republic of Tex. (pres. Houston chpt. 1970-75, 79—, registrar 1975-77, state rec. sec. gen. 1973-75, state 1st v.p. gen. 1975-77, pres. gen. 1977-79, dir. 1979—), DAR (regent Mary Martin Elmore Scott chpt. 1972-74), Daughters Am. Colonists (regent Capt. John Utie chpt., state corr. sec. 1977-79), UDC (dist. rec. sec. 1974-76), Colonial Dames Am., Walker County Geneal. Soc., San Jacinto Mus. History Assn., Victorian Soc. (charter mem. Tex. chpt.), Tex. Hist. Assn., Lone Star Hist. Assn. (state adv. com.), Am., Tex. (pres. 38th Dist. 1977—) nurses assns., AMA, Tex., Tri-County (past pres.) med. auxs. Clubs: Garden (past pres.); Univ. Women. Address: Huntsville TX 77340

ADDLEMAN, DORIS JOAN HURST, med. center exec.; b. Fort Worth, Nov. 20, 1937; d. Walter Eugene and Helen Lorraine (Hornsby) Hurst; student Tex. Christian U., 1955-58; m. LeRoy Andrew Addleman, Aug. 30, 1969; children—Kendra Allison, Tracy Diane, LeAnna Lynn. Chief med. technologist Arlington (Tex.) Meml. Hosp., 1959-62, Diagnostic Lab., Arlington, 1963-64, NASA Manned Spacecraft Center, Houston, 1965-67; med. technologist Southeast Clin. Labs., Houston, 1967-68, NASA Manned Spacecraft Center, Brown-Root-Northrup, Houston, 1968-69; adminstr. coordinator research lab., biol. lab. research technologist VA Med. Center, Temple, Tex., 1969-70; co-owner Mouse House, Killeen, Tex., 1970-71; med. technologist House Med. Clinic, Killeen, Tex., 1971-72; chief med. technologist Hillandale Meml. Hosp., Killeen, 1972-73, Anatomic and Clin. Pathology Labs., Garland, Tex., 1973-74; sales asst. lab. dir., tech. rep. client services, Southwest Med. Labs., Dallas, 1974-75; med. technologist VA Med. Center, Blood Bank, Dallas, 1975-78, adminstrv. officer Radiology Service, 1978—. Mem. Am. Soc. Clin. Pathologists, Am. Hosp. Radiology Adminstrs. Republican. Lutheran. Home: 925 Young Blvd DeSoto TX 75115 Office: Veterans Administration Med Center Radiology Service 4500 S Lancaster Rd Dallas TX 75216

ADEM, JULIAN, research meteorologist; b. Tuxpan, Veracruz, Mex., Jan. 8, 1924; s. Jorge and Almas (Chahin) A.; Civil Engr., Nat. U. Mex., 1948; Ph.D., Brown U., 1953; postgrad. in meteorology Internat. Meteorol. Inst., Stockholm, Sweden, 1955-56; m. Martha Diaz de Leon, Sept. 8, 1958; children—Julian, Alejandro. Research asst. U. Mex., Mexico City, 1948-50, prof., 1954, 57-65, 71—; research asst. Brown U., Providence, 1952-53; research asso. Internat. Meteorol. Inst., Stockholm, 1955-56; asst. dir. Inst. Geophysics, Mexico City, 1957-59, dir., 1959-62, 71-77; dir. Centro de Ciencias de la Atmosfera, 1977; vis. prof. U. Hamburg (Germany) 1961-62, Max Planck Institut für Meteorologie, W. Ger., 1978; research meteorologist Nat. Weather Service, Washington, 1965-71; vis. sr. research asso. Lamont Geol. Obs. Columbia U., 1979—. Mem. Am. Geophys. Union, Am. Meteorol. Soc., El Colegio Nacional, Union Geofisica Mexicana (pres. 1960—), Sociedad Mexicana de Fisica, Sociedad Matematica Mexicana, Academia de la Investigacion Cientifica, N.Y. Acad. Scis, Geofisica Internacional (dir. jour. 1960-77). Contbr. articles to profl. jours. Home: 14 Nabor Carrillo Mexico City 20 DF Mexico Office: Centro de Ciencias de la Atmósfera Ciudad Universitaria Mexico City 20 DF Mexico

ADEN, ARTHUR LAVERNE, engr.; b. Ford County, Ill., Feb. 1, 1924; s. Johann Franzen and Ida Magda (Hafermann) A.; student (scholar) N. Ill. State Coll., 1941-43, U. Mich., 1943-44; postgrad. Harvard U., 1944-45, M.A. (Gordon McKay scholar), 1948, M.E.S. (NRC predoctoral fellow), 1949, Ph.D., 1950; m. Leona A. Hoff, June 21, 1944; children—Donald A., Charles R., Sherry L., Gary D. With Thunderstorm Research Project, Orlando, Fla. and Clarksville, Ohio, 1946-47; sect. head Cambridge (Mass.) Research Center, 1950-53; asst. lab mgr., engring. mgr. Sylvania Electric Products, Mountain View, Calif., 1953-58; with Motorola, Inc., v.p. Motorola Instrumentation and Control, Inc., mgr. ops. solid state div., asso. dir. research and devel. mil. electronics div., Phoenix, 1958-63; with Xerox Corp., 1963—, v.p. electro optical systems, Pasadena, Calif., 1963-72, tech. dir. Xerox Edn. Group, 1972, sr. planning specialist office systems and office products divs., Dallas, 1973-79, prin. engr. office products div., 1979—; cons. Dept. Def. book on electronic countermeasures U. Mich., 1958-59. Served with USAAF, 1943-46. Fellow IEEE (Phoenix sect. award 1963); mem. Am. Phys. Soc., Am. Mgmt. Assn., Sigma Xi, Sigma Zeta. Lutheran. Contbr. sect. to book, articles to jours.; patentee in field. Office: 1341 W Mockingbird Ln Dallas TX 75247

ADER, PAUL FASSETT, author; b. Asheville, N.C., Oct. 20, 1919; s. Olin Peter and Alice Estella (Fassett) A.; B.A., Duke U., 1940; M.A., U. N.C., 1949; m. Cicely Frances Peeples, June 7, 1949; children—Donald Andrew, Rosalind Frances, Alison Estelle. Commd. capt. U.S. Air Force, 1951, advanced through grades to lt. col., 1969; ret., 1969; mgr. Asbury Nutrition Center for Sr. Citizens, San Antonio, 1974—. Served with USAAC, 1941-45. Decorated Air Force Commendation medal. Mem. Phi Beta Kappa. Methodist. Author: We Always Come Back, 1945; The Leaf Against the Sky, 1947; How To Make A Million at the Track, 1977. Home: 519 Serenade Dr San Antonio TX 78216

ADKINS, BARBARA L., accountant; b. Sugarland, Tex., Oct. 26, 1946; d. Thomas H. and Patricia A. Adkins; student Tex. Christian U., 1972, in Bus. Adminstrn., U. Dallas, 1978—. With Pier 1 Imports, 1973—, dir. European acctg., 1973-76, mgr. mdse. stats., 1977, asst. to exec. v.p., 1977-78, merchandising systems analyst, Ft. Worth, 1978—. Active Young Republicans, 1972. Mem. Ft. Worth Profl. Women's Assn. Methodist.

ADKINS, DAVID CRISP, athletic dir.; b. Greenville, N.C., June 9, 1939; s. William David and Vera Belle (Baker) D.; B.S., Atlantic Christian Coll., Wilson, N.C., 1964; M.Ed., U. N.C., Chapel Hill, 1965; m. Susan Rush, Mar. 31, 1962; children—Kimberly Susan, David Gregory, Amanda Heitman, Callie Baker. Instr. phys. edn. Atlantic Christian Coll., spring 1964, dir. athletics, soccer coach, asst. prof. phys. edn., 1972—; asst. prof., dir. intramural athletics N.C. State U., Raleigh, 1965-72. Mem. Nat. Intramural Sports Council (rep. 1971), Nat. Assn. Intercollegiate Dirs. Athletics (dist. chmn. 1973, exec. com. 1979-80; named Dist. Soccer Coach of Year 1976, 78, 79), N.C. Assn. Health, Phys. Edn. and Recreation (v.p. recreation 1969, exec. com. recreation div. So. dist. 1970), Nat. Intercollegiate Soccer Ofcls. Assn., Nat. Soccer Assn. Am., Phi Epsilon Kappa. Club: Rotary. Home: 1008 Rollingwood Dr Wilson NC 27893 Office: Box 5328 Atlantic Christian Coll Wilson NC 27893

ADKINS, EDWARD CLELAND, lawyer; b. Villisca, Iowa, Aug. 11, 1926; s. Esse Clarence and Elsie Mae (Cline) A.; B.S., U.S. Naval Acad., 1949; J.D., U. Mich., 1957; m. Claudia Rae Kangas, Sept. 17, 1955; children—Pamela, Philip, Paul. Admitted to Ohio bar, 1957, Fla. bar, 1963, Mich. bar, 1965; engr., supr. Ford Motor Co., Wayne, Mich., 1954-57; asso. firm Arter & Hadden, Cleve., 1957-64; trial counsel Gen. Motors Corp., Detroit, 1964-70; partner firm Carlton, Fields, Ward, Emmanuel, Smith & Cutler, Tampa, Fla., 1970—; pres. Flobar, Inc., Tampa, 1975-78; lectr. in field. Served with USN, 1949-54, capt. USNR. Mem. Am., Fla., Hillsborough bar assns., Am. Judicature Soc., Tampa C. of C. Republican. Lutheran. Clubs: Tower, Palma Ceia Golf, Shriners, Masons, Order Eastern Star. Contbr. articles in field to legal jours. Home: 3938 Venetian Dr Tampa FL 33614 Office: 1900 Exchange Nat Bank Bldg Tampa FL 33602

ADKINS, JOSEPH VINCENT, publisher, editor; b. Chgo., Apr. 19, 1935; s. Joseph Vincent and Anita A.; ed. high sch.; m. Mary Joyce Buyck, Sept. 2, 1959; children—Joseph Vincent III, Corey, Marcia, Gary Jamilla. Owner, operator Right Angle Spltys., Chgo., 1962-63, Integral Spltys., 1963-70; editor and pub. Direction in Atlanta, 1971—. Served with U.S. Army, 1957-59. Pub. Ashanti Coloring Book, 1973. Office: 3020 Forrest Park Rd SE Hapeville GA 30354

ADKINS, RICHARD EUGENE, petroleum co. exec.; b. Bakersfield, Calif., Feb. 4, 1922; s. Walter Edwin and Addie (Woodward) A.; A.A., Bakersfield Coll., 1941; B.S., U. So. Calif., 1948; m. Mimi Thornton, Feb. 15, 1946 (dec. Dec. 1967); children—Corey (Mrs. Chester Robinson), Anthony, Scott, Lorraine; m. 2d, Jo Ann Yeager, Apr. 3, 1969. With Petrolane, Inc., Atlanta, 1951—, v.p., 1967—. Served with USAAF, 1942-45. Decorated D.F.C. Mem. Wash., Mont., Ga. Liquid Petroleum gas assns. Clubs: Rotary, Lions. Home: 2826 Evans Dale Circle Atlanta GA 30340 Office: 2965 Flowers Rd S 109 Atlanta GA 30341

ADKINS, WILLIAM WITTY, SR., city utility adminstr.; b. Rockingham County, N.C., July 28, 1917; s. John Everette and Linnie Byron (Witty) A.; B.S. in Chem. Engring., N.C. State U., 1939; m. Doris Geraldine Bailey, Jan. 16, 1942; children—Lynn (Mrs. Gordon Logan), William Witty. Supt. Water and Sewer Dept., Asheboro, N.C., 1939-51; dir. Dept. Utilities, Burlington, N.C., 1951-56; asst. gen. mgr., chief engr. Commn. Pub. Works, Greenville, S.C., 1956-67, gen. mgr., 1967—. Recipient George C. Franklin award N.C. League Municipalities, 1956. Mem. Am. Water Works Assn. (chmn. sects. 1951, 1969, Warren Fuller Man of Year award 1957, Wiedman award 1972), Am. Pub. Works Assn., Water Pollution Control Fedn. (chmn. chpt. 1951, sect. 1963), Greenville C. of C. Methodist (adminstrv. bd.). Club: Kiwanis (pres. 1951). Home: 15 Burgundy Dr Greenville SC 29615 Office: 206 S Main St Greenville SC 29602

ADKISON, DUANE TURNER, mortgage bank exec.; b. Jacksonville, Fla., Nov. 19, 1937; s. Joe Turner and Louise (Fenner) A.; B.A., U. Fla., 1959, postgrad., 1963-64; m. Carol Dee Boykin, Aug. 12, 1962; children—Paul McEwen, Mark Carter. Vice pres., Wachovia Mortgage Co., Winston-Salem, N.C., 1965-74; pres., chief exec. officer So. Nat. Mortgage Co., Charlotte, N.C., 1974—, also dir. Served with USN, 1959-63. Mem. Am., Carolinas mortgage bankers assns. Club: Kiwanis. Republican. Episcopalian. Home: 4617 Mullens Ford Rd Charlotte NC 28211 Office: PO Box 32246 Charlotte NC 28232

ADKISSON, DAVID FLINTOFF, coll. pres.; b. Ashland City, Tenn., Aug. 21, 1912; s. Samuel Henry and Ruth (Flintoff) A.; B.S., Middle Tenn. State Coll., 1935; M.A., George Peabody Coll., 1946; Ed.D., U. Tenn. 1960; m. Odessa Duncan, Feb. 2, 1940; 1 dau., Barbara Ann. Tchr. pub. schs., Cheatham County, Tenn., 1935-42, prin., South Fulton, Tenn., 1942-44, Bristol, Tenn., 1946-50; supt. schs., Watertown, Tenn., 1944-46, Bristol, Tenn., 1956-67; regional supr. Tenn. Dept. Edn., 1950-53; county dir. instrn. Knox County, Tenn., 1953-55; instr. U. Tenn., 1955-56; pres. Cleveland (Tenn.) State Community Coll., 1967—. Mem. Nat. (life), Tenn. (life) congresses parents and tchrs., Nat., Tenn. edn. assns., Phi Kappa Phi, Phi Delta Kappa. Methodist. Clubs: Masons, Rotary. Home: 1211 Greenwood Trail Cleveland TN 37311

ADLER, ROBERT, photog. co. exec.; b. N.Y.C., Dec. 25, 1906; s. Hyman and Freida (Byers) A.; student Ohio State U., 1925-27; m. Rosa Schuman, Aug. 5, 1933; 1 son, Michael Frederic. With advt., editorial depts. Cleve. Plain Dealer, 1927-32; advt. mgr. Lorain (Ohio) Times Herald, 1933-34; pub. Lorain Shopper, 1935-37; pub. Springfield (Ohio) Shopper, 1935-41; pub. Springfield Tabloid Times, Springfield Jour., 1939; owner Robert Adler Advt. Agy., Springfield, 1941-45; pres. Click Camera Shops, Inc., Springfield, 1945-63, Rapid Photo, Inc., Springfield, 1953-62, A & H Realty Co., Springfield; pres. Tru-Foto, Inc., Springfield 1953-64, now chmn. bd.; chmn. bd. Foto-Color Co., Dayton, Ohio, 1960—, Rapid Mail Co., Dayton, Tru-Foto, Inc. N.J., Tru-Foto, Inc., Atlanta, Photo Enterprises, Indpls., Progressive Industries Corp., Dayton; mem. adv. bd. Summit Bank, Tamarac, Fla. Mem. 4th Study Mission to Israel, 1957, Springfield Commn. Downtown Improvement Com., 1962. Pres. Retail Mchts. Council Springfield, United Jewish Appeal, Bonds for Israel; chmn. bd. So. Ohio Coll., 1967-74; bd. dirs. Springfield Devel. Council, Boy Scouts Am., Jr. Achievement, North Broward County Jewish Fedn.; vice chmn. Nat. Anti-Defamation League, also mem. Soc. Fellows. Recipient David Ben Gurion award State of Israel Bonds, Leadership award Ft. Lauderdale Jewish Fedn. Mem. Springfield C. of C. (dir.), Wisdom Soc. Jewish religion (v.p. dir. temple). Clubs: Masons, Rotary, B'nai B'rith, Woodlands Country (bd. govs., award 1978) (Ft. Lauderdale). Author, producer, photographer (films), Hong Kong Clicking, 1960, Israel, 1961. Home: 5719 Coco Palm Dr Fort Lauderdale FL 33319 Office: 2030 Kuntz Rd Dayton OH 45404

ADOMIAN, GEORGE, mathematician, educator; B.S., M.S. in Elec. Engring., U. Mich.; Ph.D. in Theoretical Physics, U. Calif., 1963. Research asso. U. Mich. Electronics Def. Group, 1951-53; head theoretical studies group, sr. scientist, project head Hughes Aircraft Co., 1953-64; prof. math. and engring. Pa. State U., 1964-66; prof. math. U. Ga., Athens, 1966—, now David Crenshaw Barrow prof. math., dir. Center for Applied Math.; sr. scientist, cons. Hughes Aircraft, 1978; cons. Nat. Acad. Scis.; mem. Nat. Def. Panel on Undersea Warfare, 1973. Fellow AAAS; mem. Sigma Xi. Asso. editor Jour. Nonlinear Analysis and Applications, 1977-80, Jour. Math. Analysis and Applications, 1979—; cons. editor Jour. Math. Armenian Acad. Scis.-USSR, 1980—; reviewer for numerous jours. Address: Center for Applied Math Tucker Hall U Ga Athens GA 30602

ADRION, WILLIAM RICHARDS, computer scientist; b. Alexandria, La., Nov. 2, 1943; s. Vernon Richards and Mary Leone (Carlock) A.; B.S., Cornell U., 1966, M.Engring., 1967; Ph.D., U. Tex., Austin, 1971; m. Jacqueline M. Cotner, July 3, 1971; 1 dau., Carrie Buchanan. Computer engr. Honeywell Co., Boston, 1969-70; asst. prof. U. Tex. Austin, 1971-72; asst. prof. Oreg. State U., Corvallis, 1972-76; program dir. theoretical computer sci. NSF, 1976-78, program dir. computer sci. spl. projects, 1980—; computer scientist Nat. Bur. Standards, Washington, 1978-80, mgr. software engring. group Inst. Compter Sci. and Tech., 1979-80; cons. Honeywell Tektronix. Inc., Applied Theory Assos.; professorial lectr. Am. U., Washington. Recipient NSF Sustained Superior Performance award, 1977; Dow Am. Soc. Engring. Edn. Outstanding Young Faculty award, 1975. Mem. N.Y. Acad. Scis., Assn. Computing Machinery, IEEE, Soc. Indsl. and Applied Math, Cornell Soc. Engrs., Sigma Xi, Phi Kappa Phi. Contbr. articles to profl. jours. Home: 5007 N 34th Rd Arlington VA 22207 Office: NSF Washington DC 20550

AFFELDT, HARLEY PAUL, coll. adminstr.; b. Cleve., Mar. 31, 1926; s. Harley August and Lydia F. (Schmidt) A.; B.S., Va. Poly. Inst. and State U., 1950, M.Ed., 1958; m. Virginia Fanning, June 14, 1952; 1 son, James Kent. Tchr. indsl. arts, Portsmouth, Va., 1950-52; sales rep. IBM, Norfolk, Va., 1955-57; tchr. public schs., Portsmouth, 1958-60; asso. dir. Indsl. Edn. Center, Winston-Salem, N.C., 1960-63; dir. student services Forsyth Tech. Inst., Winston-Salem, 1963-66; dir. Richmond Tech. Center, dir. vocat. adult edn., Richmond, 1966-71; pres. Forsyth Tech. Inst., Winston-Salem, 1971—. Bd. dirs. Winston-Salem Goodwill Industries, Industries for Blind; bd. dirs. Wesley Found., 1974-77, Experiment in Self Reliance, 1974—. Served with USAF, 1944-46. Mem. Am. Vocat. Assn. (life), N.C.

Vocat. Assn., Am. Tech. Edn. Assn., N.C. Assn. Community Edn., N.C. Adult Edn. Assn., N.C. Community Coll. Adult Edn. Assn., N.C. Community Coll. Pres.'s Assn. Democrat. Methodist. Clubs: Stratford Rotary, Ardmore Community, Masons. Home: 301 Pineridge Dr Winston-Salem NC 27104 Office: 2100 Silas Creek Pkwy Winston Salem NC 27103

AFIELD, WALTER EDWARD, psychiatrist, health care adminstr., educator; b. N.Y.C., Dec. 28, 1939; s. Walter Edward and Mollie Evelyn (McGovern) A.; A.B., U. Pa., 1956; M.D., Johns Hopkins, 1960; m. Nancy Browning, Dec. 27, 1973. Intern, Grady Meml. Hosp. and Emory U. Med. Sch., 1960-61; resident in psychiatry Mass. Mental Health Center, Boston, 1961-64; resident in child psychiatry Judge Baker Guidance Center, Boston, 1963-64, Mass. Gen. Hosp., 1966-67; teaching fellow in psychiatry Harvard Med. Sch., 1961-64, teaching fellow in child psychiatry, 1966-67; asst. prof. psychiatry Johns Hopkins Sch. Medicine, 1967-70, dir. child psychiatry Johns Hopkins Hosp., 1967-70; med. dir. Tampa Bay Neuropsychiat. Inst., Tampa, Clearwater, St. Petersburg, Sarasota, 1970—; prof., chmn. dept. psychiatry U. S.Fla. Coll. Medicine, 1970-74, clin. prof., 1974—. Cons. VA, 1970—, Mayor of Tampa, 1970—, Tampa Area Mental Health Bd., 1970—; examiner adult, child and adminstrv. bds. Am. Bd. Psychiatry and Neurology, 1970—. Trustee McDonald Tng. Center, Hillsborough County Mental Health Assn.; pres. Fla. Lyric Opera, Tampa. Served with USAF, 1964-66. Recipient Mayor's award for outstanding contributions to the cultural and profl. life of Fla. Tampa C. of C., 1974. Mem. AMA, Am. Psychiat. Assn., Am. Coll. Psychiatrists. Republican. Roman Catholic. Clubs: University, Tower, Tampa Yacht. Contbr. articles to profl. jours. Home: 4619 Bay to Bay Blvd Tampa FL 33609 Office: 4700 N Habana Ave Tampa FL 33615

AGATHER, VICTOR NEILS, investment banker; b. Kalispell, Mont., Aug. 21, 1912; s. Alfons A. and Martha Bertha (Neils) A.; B.S., Georgetown U., 1934; M.B.A., Harvard U., 1936; m. Fifi O'Connor, Aug. 31, 1940; children—Merrilee, Anne, Neils, John. With Shields & Co., 1936-40; exec. v.p. La Consolidada, S.A., Mexico City, 1946-59; pres. Intercon, S.A., Mexico City, 1959—. Served to col. USAAF, 1940-45. Office: Intercon SA CV Monte Caucaso 915 4 Mexico 10 Mexico

AGEE, THOMAS ANDERSON, gas co. exec.; b. Little Rock, Feb. 20, 1943; s. Frank Lawrence and Margaret Catherine (Oliphant) A.; B.B.A., Little Rock U., 1968; m. Martha Cornelia Daughenbaugh, June 9, 1963; children—Thomas Anderson II, Kenneth Lawrence (Larry). Asst. to gen. sales mgr. Ark. La. Gas Co., Shreveport, La., 1966-73, internal auditor, 1973-74, sr. internal auditor, 1974-75, asst. mgr. internal auditing, 1975-77, chief auditor, 1977—. lectr. in field. Bd. dirs. Pulaski County (Ark.) Spl. Sch. Dist., 1969-73; founder Oak Grove Athletic Assn., 1972-73; bd. dirs. Econ. Opportunity Agy. Area 6-B, Pulaski County, 1972-73. C.P.A., La. Mem. Am. Inst. C.P.A.'s, La. Soc. C.P.A.'s, Inst. Internal Auditors. Democrat. Methodist. Home: 445 Mohican St Shreveport LA 71106 Office: Ark La Gas Co 525 Milam St Shreveport LA 71151

AGEE, WILLIAM CAMERON, art mus. adminstr.; b. N.Y.C., Sept. 26, 1936; s. William Herman and Elsie (Burgess) A.; B.A., Princeton U., 1960; M.A., Yale U., 1963; m. Elita Vesta Taylor, Sept. 10, 1966; children—Cintra Cady, Matthew Titus. Dir. research project on New Deal and arts Archives Am. Art, Detroit, 1964-65; asso. curator Whitney Mus. Am. Art, N.Y.C., 1966-70, Mus. Modern Art, N.Y.C., 1968-70; dir. exhbns. and collections Pasadena (Calif.) Art Mus., 1970-71, dir., 1971-74; dir. Mus. Fine Arts, Houston, 1974—. Instr. art Yale, 1962-63, U. Mich., Ann Arbor, 1965, Sch. Visual Arts, N.Y.C., 1969-70; mem. rev. panels Nat. Endowment for Arts, from 1974, nat. adv. com., 1975—. Mem. Assn. Art Mus. Dirs. Office: Mus Fine Arts PO Box 6826 Houston TX 77005*

AGERTON, WILLIAM REID, editor; b. Dale County, Ala., Aug. 6, 1939; s. Roscoe and Lizzie (Hughes) A.; B.S., Auburn U., 1964, M.Ed., 1965; m. Anne Weed, Dec. 3, 1960; children—Lori Anne, Vicki Lynn, Jill Michele. Extension farm agt., photo journalism agt., Mobile, Ala., 1965-70; area field rep. Ala. Farm Bur. Fedn. S.W., 1970-71; asso. editor to editor Ala. Farm Bur. News, Montgomery, 1971-75; extension editor publs. Ga. Coop. Extension, Athens, 1975-79; editor Potash and Phosphate Inst., Atlanta, 1979—. Former pres. Gaines Sch. P.T.A. Served with AUS, 1957-60, 62. Recipient Gold medal Farm Bur. News, 1974. Mem. Agrl. Communicators in Edn., Montgomery Assn. Bus. Communicators (past pres.), Nat. Agrl. Mktg. Assn., Kappa Delta Pi. Methodist. Club: Civitan (pres.). Home: 5282 Enchanted Cove Lilburn GA 30247 Office: 2801 Buford Hwy NE Atlanta GA 30329

AGNEW, MARY KATHRYN, univ. adminstr.; b. Birmingham, Ala., Apr. 8, 1923; d. James Richard and Ida Clementine (Wilson) Finley; B.S., Howard Coll., 1943; diploma U.S. Savs. and Loan Inst., 1961; M.A., U. Ala., 1973, Ed.D., 1979; m. Norman McKee Agnew, Apr. 12, 1957; 1 son by previous marriage, William Jackson Ray. Tchr. chemistry and social studies Jefferson County (Ala.) Bd. Edn., 1943-45; with mortgage loan dept. Duckworth-Morris Real Estate, Inc., Tuscaloosa, Ala., 1950-52; with First Fed. Savs. & Loan Assn. Tuscaloosa, 1952-65, loan officer, asst. sec., 1957-65; with Coll. Edn., U. Ala., University, 1965—, exec. asst., fin. mgr. Gen. Assistance Center, 1975-77, asst. dean Coll. Mgmt. and Fin., 1977—, asst. prof., 1979—. Bd. dirs. Ala Credit Union, 1976—, sec.-treas., 1977, pres., 1978. Mem. Pi Tau Chi, Kappa Delta Pi, Phi Delta Kappa, Alpha Phi. Presbyterian. Clubs: Univ. Women's, Univ., Indian Hills Country, Masquer's. Home: 147 Fox Run Tuscaloosa AL 35406 Office: PO Box Q Coll Edn University AL 35486

AGREDA, VICTOR HUGO, chem. engr.; b. Bolivia, Oct. 16, 1953; s. Jose Hugo and Maria Basilia (Zurita) A.; came to U.S., 1971, naturalized, 1977; B.S. in Chemistry, B.S. in Chem. Engring., N.C. State U., 1975, M.S. in Chem. Engring., 1977, Ph.D., 1979; m. Carla Hyatt Leonard, Mar. 10, 1973; 1 son, Victor Hugo. Process engr. Perry Electronics, Raleigh, N.C., 1973-74; teaching asst. chem. engring. N.C. State U., Raleigh, 1975-77, lab. mgr. coal gasification lab. chem. engring. dept., 1977-79; chem. engr., process systems Tenn. Eastman Co., Kingsport, 1979—. Mem. Am. Inst. Chem. Engrs., Am. Chem. Soc., Nat. Soc. Profl. Engrs., Phi Eta Sigma, Phi Kappa Phi, Pi Kappa Phi, Tau Beta Pi. Home: 1000 University Blvd F-56 Kingsport TN 37660 Office: B-150B Tenn Eastman Co Kingsport TN 37662

AGUAM, ABUL SENON, surgeon; b. Ganassi, Lanao, Philippines, Apr. 13, 1937; s. Sultan Aguam and Bai Senon (Malaco) Dipatuan; A.A., Far Eastern U., Manila, 1956, M.D., 1962; m. Zenaida Canilao; 1 son, Denton; children by previous marriage—Angela, Andrea, Robert. Intern, St. Michael's Hosp., Milw., 1963-64; resident in gen. surgery Columbus Hosp., N.Y.C., 1965-69; chief resident in cardiovascular and thoracic surgery N.Y. Med. Coll., N.Y.C., 1970-71; asso. dir. dept. surgery Hosp. for Joint Diseases and Med. Center, N.Y.C., 1973-77, attending surgeon, 1977-78; clin. asso., dept. surgery Mt. Sinai Sch. Medicine, N.Y.C., 1975, asst. prof. surgery, 1977-78; practice medicine specializing in surgery, Mt. Pleasant, Tex., 1978—; mem. staff Titus County Meml. Hosp. Diplomate Am. Bd. Surgery. Fellow A.C.S., Am. Coll. Angiology, N.Y. Acad. Scis., N.Y. Acad. Medicine; mem. AMA, N.Y. State, N.Y. County med. socs., N.Y. State Soc. Surgeons, Am. Profl. Practice Assn., Smithsonian Inst. (nat. asso.), Soc. Philippine Surgeons in Am. (bd. govs.). Democrat. Moslem. Contbr. articles to med. jours. Home: 415 Brookwood St Mount Pleasant TX 75455 Office: 1114 N Jefferson St Mount Pleasant TX 75455

AGUILA, DANIEL DUMUK, graphic arts exec.; b. Manila, Philippines, Sept. 24, 1928; s. Doroteo A. and Donata B. (Dumuk) A.; B.F.A., U. Philippines, 1952; grad. student mass communications, ednl. TV, Syracuse (N.Y.) U.; m. Norma Alampay, Sept. 24, 1960; children—Normalinda, Dina Belle, Daniel Bliss. Came to U.S., 1956. Co. artist Philippines Am. Life Ins. Co., Manila, 1952-56; tech. expert mass communication Philippine Rural Reconstn. Movement, Manila, 1960-62; art dir., v.p. Asian Newsweekly Examiner, Philippines, 1965-67; art cons. The Upper Room, Nashville, 1967-68; art dir. Robert G. Fields Advt., Nashville, 1967-72, channel 8, WDCN-TV, Nashville, 1972-75, Fin. Instn. Services, Inc., 1976—; editorial cartoonist Filipino Reporter, N.Y. and Calif., 1975—; lectr. mass. communications U. Philippines, 1963-64; free-lance writer, 1956—. Vice pres. Art Assn. Philippines, 1965-67; Philippines dir. Nat. Press Club Philippines, 1965-66; pres. Soc. Philippine Illustrators and Cartoonists, 1965-66; mem. Citizens Council for Mass Media, Manila, 1963-67. Pub. relations dir. Friends of Marcos, presdl. campaign, 1965. Recipient Outstanding Sillimanian award in communication arts, 1976, other awards in art, journalism and broadcasting. Ramon Roces art scholar, 1948-49; Harold Stassen grantee, 1956-58. Mem. Art Dirs. Club Nashville (pres. 1975), Internat. Assn. Bus. Communicators (v.p. chpt. 1979), United Meth. Communications (mgr.-at-large 1977-80). Editor: The First Couple of the Philippines, 1965. Home: 3906 Wallace Ln Nashville TN 37215 Office: PO Box 40726 Nashville TN 37204

AHEARN, GEORGE PATRICK, chem. co. exec.; b. Bklyn., Oct. 14, 1935; s. Maurice Joseph and Antoinette (Mantone) A.; B.A., City U. N.Y., 1957; M.S., Rutgers U., 1959, Ph.D., 1960; m. Mary Grace Avena, July 4, 1960; children—John Patrick, Allison Clare. Research chemist Exxon Research and Engring. Co., 1960-63; research supr., head dept. Exxon Prodn. Research Co., 1963-71; product exec. Exxon Chem. Co., N.Y.C., 1971-74, div. mgr. Exxon Chem. Co. U.S.A., Houston, 1974—; research fellow Rutgers U., 1959-60, teaching fellow, 1958-59. Mem. Am. Chem. Soc., Am. Mgmt. Assn., Am. Inst. Metall. and Mining Engrs. Roman Catholic, Phi Lambda Upsilon. Patentee in field. Office: 1333 W Loop S Houston TX 77024

AHEARN, JOHN FRANCIS, JR., natural resource co. exec.; b. Waterbury, Conn., May 19, 1921; s. John Francis and Anna E. (Kane) A.; A.B., Brown U., 1944; M.B.A., Stanford U., 1955; m. Mary Louise Gardner, Jan. 7, 1956. Mgr. agrl. mktg. Kern County Land Co., Bakersfield, Calif., 1955-61, mgr. corp. planning, San Francisco, 1962-65; dir. corp. planning J. I. Case Co., Racine, Wis., 1965-67; v.p. corp. planning and devel. So. Natural Resources, Inc., Birmingham, Ala., 1968—. Served with USN, 1944-46, 50-53. Republican. Roman Catholic. Clubs: Shoal Creek, Mountain Brook, Relay House. Home: 207 Eagle View Shoal Creek AL 35094 Office: PO Box 2563 Birmingham AL 35202

AHEARN, MICHAEL JOHN, hematologist; b. Jacksonville, Tex., June 6, 1936; s. John Tom and Reba (Raye) A.; B.A., U. Tex., 1958, M.A., 1961, Ph.D., 1965; m. Joyce Donaho Ramey, June 6, 1964. Asso. prof. lab. medicine U. Tex. System Cancer Center M.D. Anderson Hosp., Houston, 1965—; mem. faculty U. Tex. Sch. Allied Health Scis., U. Tex. Grad. Sch. Biomed. Scis. Mem. Am. Assn. Cancer Research, Electron Microscope Soc. Am., Tex. Soc. Electron Microscopy, Sigma Xi. Baptist. Contbr. numerous articles on oncological hematology to profl. jours. Home: 2200 Willowick St Houston TX 77027 Office: Dept Lab Medicine MD Anderson Hosp Med Center Houston TX 77030

AHEARNE, DANIEL PAUL, physicist; b. New Britain, Conn., Apr. 23, 1931; s. Daniel Paul and Balbena (Balowski) A.; B.S., Calif. State U., 1962; postgrad. U. N.Mex., 1967-70, N.Mex. Inst. Tech., 1968-69, U. Calif. at Los Angeles, 1963-65; m. Germaine Marie, Feb. 7, 1954; children—Michael, Douglas. Served with U.S. Army, 1948-57; research engr. N.Am. Aviation, Inc., Anaheim, Calif., 1963-65; physicist, analyst TRW Systems, Redondo Beach, Calif., 1965-66; systems analyst USAF Weapons Lab., Kirtland AFB, N.Mex., 1966-69; chief scientist U.S. Army Safeguard Communications Agy., Ft. Huachuca, Ariz., 1969-70; pres. Mesa Cons. Corp., Albuquerque, 1970-73; asso. adminstr. FEA, Washington, 1974; pres. Total Energy Applications & Mgmt., Inc., Springfield, Va., Albuquerque, 1975—; cons. ERDA, Office Tech. Assessment, U.S. Congress, Ark. Electric Coop. Corp., Western Minn. Municipal Power Agency, Commonwealth P.R. Exec. dir. N.Mex. Democratic Party, 1970-73, S.W. organizer for v.p. campaign, 1972, tech. adviser to N.M. gov., 1971-72; active Nat. Dem. Club. Decorated D.S.C., Silver Star medal, Bronze Star medal, Purple Heart with clusters. AEC nuclear sci. fellow, 1962, N.Am. Aviation work-study fellow, 1964. Mem. Am. Phys. Soc., Fedn. Am. Scientists, N.Y. Acad. Sci., Ala. Acad. Sci., Am. Acad. Polit. and Social Sci., Am. Physicists Assn., AAAS, Sigma Pi Sigma. Roman Catholic. Patentee in field. Home: 7221 Briarcliffe Dr Springfield VA 22153

AHLBURN, BYRON TROTTER, physicist; b. Cin., Feb. 1, 1939; s. Byron Edward and Veta Mae (Trotter) A.; B.S., Yale U., 1961; M.S. (E.J. Noble Found. grantee), Purdue U., 1963, Ph.D. (E.J. Noble Found. grantee), 1969; m. Carol Louise Vilter, June 15, 1963; 1 son, Andrew Robert. Research asso. Coordinated Sci. Lab., U. Ill., Urbana, 1969-70; head engring. sect. Tex. Instruments Inc., Dallas, 1970—. Mem. Friends of Dallas Public Library. Mem. Am. Phys. Soc., Texins Assn., Yale Sci. and Engring. Assn., Sigma Xi. Presbyterian (ruling elder). Club: Dallas Yale. Contbr. articles to profl. jours. Patentee in field. Home: 11340 Quail Run Dallas TX 75238 Office: MS 35-Tex Instruments Inc 13500 N Central Expressway Dallas TX 75222

AHLM, ANNETTE MARIE, speech pathologist, hosp. supr.; b. Herrin, Ill., Aug. 4, 1943; d. Johnnie and Eda Josephine (De Zutti) Cavalli; student So. Ill. U., 1961-63, Panama C.Z. Coll., 1969; B.A., Our Lady of the Lake U., 1974, M.A., 1976; children—Lisa, Charles, Michele. Speech-lang. pathologist Villa Rosa Annex, Santa Rosa Med. Center, San Antonio, 1976-77; dir. speech pathology St. Benedict's Hosp., San Antonio, 1977—; practicum supr. students Our Lady of Lake U., SW Tex. U. and St. Mary's U.; family counseling for rehab. patients St. Benedict's Hospice team, 1978—. Our Lady of Lake U. grad. fellow, 1976-77. Mem. Am. Speech and Hearing Assn. (cert. clin. competence), Tex. Speech and Hearing Assn., San Antonio Speech, Lang. and Hearing Assn. Home: 3502 5100 NW Loop 410 San Antonio TX 78229 Office: St Benedict's Hosp 323 E Johnson St San Antonio TX 78204

AHLSTROM, RICHARD MATHER, chem. co. exec.; b. Painesville, Ohio, Nov. 25, 1934; s. William McKinley and Janice (Mather) A.; A.B., Harvard U., 1956; exec. program Amos Tuck Sch. Bus. Adminstrn., 1974; m. Beverly Sowle, Apr. 6, 1957; children—Thomas Richard, Michael Christopher. With Diamond Shamrock Corp., Cleve., 1960—, treas. fgn. subs., 1964-65, mgr. adminstrn. chem. div., 1966-67, asst. treas. corp., 1968-71, treas. corp., 1971-76, v.p. fin. 1976; dir. Tex. Commerce Bank, Dallas, Stouffer's Inn on the Square. Bd. dirs. Tex. Taxpayers Assn.; trustee Fine Arts Assn. Mem. Nat. Acctg. Assn., Fin. Execs. Inst., Ohio Archaeol. Soc. (chpt. dir.). Clubs: Treas.'s of Cleve. (dir.), Cleve. Athletic, Bent Tree Country. Named Boss of Year, Am. Businesswomens Assn., 1971. Office: Diamond Shamrock Corp 2300 Southland Center Dallas TX 75201

AHLSTROM, ROBERT GEORGE, travel agy. exec.; b. Mpls., June 14, 1931; s. Rueben Guthart and Anna Charlotte (Lindquist) A.; student U. Minn., 1955-59. Travel agt. Travel Center, Anchorage, 1959-66; mgr. group tour and conv. div. Trade Wind Tours of Hawaii, Honolulu, 1966-73, 75-76; v.p. Consites Internat., Ltd., Honolulu, 1973-75, Travel Planners, Inc., San Antonio, 1976—; pres. TPI-Hawaii, 1978. Vice chmn. conv. com. Hawaii Visitors Bur., 1973-75. Served with USAF, 1951-55. Recipient Recognition awards Lions, Western Airlines, Sheraton Hotels Hawaii. Mem. Am. Soc. Assn. Execs. (asso.), Am. Soc. Travel Agts., Fgn. Travel Club, Phi Mu Alpha. Home: 126 Teakwood San Antonio TX 78216 Office: 350 GPM Bldg San Antonio TX 78216

AHMAD, FARRUKH IFTIKHAR, geophysicist; b. Aligarh, India, June 15, 1945; came to U.S., 1967; s. Iftikhar and Firdos Sualeha (Alam) A.; B.Sc. (unv. merit scholar, AEC scholar), Aligarh U., 1964, M.Sc. (Gold medal), 1966; M.S., U. Mass., Amherst, 1971, Ph.D., 1975. Asst. prof. Aligarh U. 1966-67; teaching asst., then teaching asso. U. Mass., 1968-73; with Seiscom Delta, Inc., Houston, 1974-77, supr. marine seismic processing, 1975-77; project geophysicist Gulf Sci/Tech. Co., Houston, 1977—. Bd. dirs. India Culture Center Greater Houston, 1976—; vcl. lang. and arts com. Houston Ind. Sch. Dist. Mem. Soc. Exploration Geophysicists, Am. Geophys. Union, AAAS, Geophys. Soc. Houston (editor 1979--), Geol. Soc. Houston, Sigma Xi. Club: Toastmasters Internat. Author papers in field. Home: 10110 Forum Park Dr Apt 208 Houston TX 77036 Office: Gulf Sci and Tech Co PO Box 36506 Houston TX 77036

AHMANN, DONALD HENRY, mfg. co. exec.; b. Struble, Iowa, Jan. 9, 1920; s. Henry F. and Philomena (Wictor) A.; student Trinity Coll., 1937-39; B.S. in Chemistry, Iowa State U., Ames, 1941, Ph.D., 1948; m. H. Anne Harvey, Sept. 24, 1945; children—Richard S., Carol (Mrs. Thomas P. Beresford), Rebecca (Mrs. Patrick Mahoney), Sarah, Kathryn, Elizabeth. Jr. chemist AEC Ames Lab. Iowa State U., Ames, 1942-48; research asso. Knolls Atomic Power Lab., Gen. Electric Co., Schenectady, 1948-50, mgr. phys. chemistry, 1950-55, mgr. chemistry and chem. engring., 1955-57, mgr. chemistry and chem. engring. Vallecitos Atomic Lab., Pleasanton, Calif., 1957-67, mgr. chemistry and metallurgy Vallecitos Atomic Lab., Pleasanton, 1967, mgr. materials sci. and tech. Nuclear Systems Programs, Cin., 1967-69, mgr. engring. Neutron Devices Dept., St. Petersburg, Fla., 1969—. Mem. Am. Chem. Soc., Am. Soc. for Metals, Am. Nuclear Soc., Am. Vacuum Soc., AAAS, Phi Kappa Phi, Phi Lambda Upsilon. Home: 660 Bluff View Dr Belleair Bluffs FL 33540 Office: PO Box 11508 St Petersburg FL 33733

AHMED, AHMED ELSAYED, educator; b. Cairo, Egypt, Aug. 21, 1942; s. Ahmed Aly and Sna Yousf (Elshorbagy) A.; came to U.S., 1969, naturalized, 1975; B.S., Cairo (Egypt) U., 1966; Ph.D., U. Minn., 1975; m. Dalal Fouad, June 24, 1969; children—Tamer, Hazem. Research specialist Niles Co. for Pharms., Cairo, Egypt, 1966-69; jr. scientist U. Minn., Mpls., 1969-70, teaching asst., 1970-74, postdoctoral research fellow, NIH fellow dept. pharmacology, 1975-77, mem. grad. sch. biomed. scis., 1977—; asst. prof. pathology, pharmacology and toxicology U. Tex. Med. Br., Galveston, 1977—, lectr. courses, seminars in fields. Recipient NIH Nat. Individual Research Service award, 1975-77, achievement award pharm. scis. Alexandria (Egypt) U., 1963, Melondy fellowship award, U. Minn., 1973; prin. investigator, co-investigator grants. Mem. Am. Chem. Soc., AAAS, Sigma Xi, Rho Chi. Contbr. articles, abstracts in field to profl. publs. Home: 314 Tuna Ave Galveston TX 77550 Office: Dept Pathology University Texas Medical Branch Galveston TX 77550

AHMED, SHEIK BASHEER, educator; b. Kurnool, India, Jan. 1, 1934; s. S. Mohammad Hussain and K. Aminabi; came to U.S., 1961, naturalized, 1972; B.A., Madras U., 1955; M.A., Osmania U., 1957; M.S., Tex. A. and M. U., 1963, Ph.D., 1966; m. Alice Pearce, Sept. 21, 1968; 1 dau., Ivy Amina. Asst. prof. econs. Tenn. Tech. U., 1966-68; asst. prof. quantitative methods Ohio U., 1968-70; asso. prof. bus. adminstrn. Western Ky. U., Bowling Green, 1970-73, prof., 1973—; vis. fellow Center Internat. Studies, Princeton U., 1977-78; cons. Oak Ridge Nat. Lab., Econ, Inc., Regional Sci. Research Center, MTI. Mem. IEEE (pres. Systems, Man, and Cybernetics Soc. 1980-81), Ops. Research Soc., World Future Soc., Am. Inst. Decision Scis., Fedn. Am. Scientists, AAAS. Club: Rotary. Author: Quantitative Methods for Business, 1974; Nuclear Fuel and Energy Policy, 1979; also articles. Address: 912 Highland Dr Bowling Green KY 42101

AHN, YOUNG WHAN, physician, educator; b. South Korea, May 16, 1940; s. Kyu S. and Boon (Nam) A.; came to U.S., 1967, naturalized, 1977; M.D., Kyung Pook U. Sch. Medicine, 1964; m. Kyung J. Lee, Mar. 20, 1966; children—Kelly J., Steven Ahn. Intern, Bronx Lebanon Hosp., Bronx, N.Y., 1967; resident Highland Park (Mich.) Park Gen. Hosp., 1968-72; mem. faculty Emory U. Sch. Medicine, Atlanta, 1973—, asso. prof. obs.-gyn. 1979—; cons. Emory U. Hosp., Crawford W. Long Meml. Hosp. Served with Korean Army, 1964-67. Recipient Physicians Recognition awards in Continuing Med. Edn., AMA, 1978. Fellow Am. Coll. Obstetrics and Gynecology; mem. State Bd. Med. Examiners, AMA, Am. Coll. Obstetrics and Gynecologists, Am. Gynecol. Laparoscopists Assn., Assn. Profs. Obstetrics and Gynecologists. Home: 436 Rue Andeleys St Stone Mountain GA 30309 Office: 80 Butler St Atlanta GA 30303

AHRENS, FREDERICK PHILLIP, JR., lawyer, diversified mfg. co. exec.; b. Kansas City, Mo., Oct. 6, 1937; s. Fred Phillip and Adeline Artilda (Cutsforth) A.; B.S. in Economics, Xavier U., 1959, M.B.A., 1962; J.D., Marquette U., 1962; m. Carolyn Joan Thomas, Jan. 17, 1962 (div.); children—Tracey Elizabeth, Sean Frederick. Admitted to Wis. bar, 1962, Mich. bar, 1963; indsl. relations positions Ford Motor Co., Dearborn, Mich., 1962-65; indsl. relations mgr. Internat. Harvester, various locations, 1965-70; div. dir. indsl. relations Paper Mate div. Gillette Co., Chgo., 1970-73; group indsl. relations dir. Gen. Instrument Co., Hicksville, N.Y., 1973-74; v.p. corporate indsl. relations Wylain, Inc., Dallas, 1974—; tchr. labor law and economics Ohio U., Belmont, 1968-70. Served in USAFR, 1962. Mem. Am., Mich., Wis., Tex. bar assns., Am. Mgmt. Assn., Am. Soc. Personnel Adminstrs. Roman Catholic. Clubs: Prestonwood Country, Willow Bend Polo and Hunt. Office: Wylain Inc 17250 Dallas Pkwy Dallas TX 75248

AHUJA, VIJAY, computer scientist; b. India, Nov. 21, 1942; came to U.S., 1967; s. Yog Dhyan and Shakuntla (Grover) A.; M.S. in Computer Sci., U. N.C., 1970, Ph.D. in Computer Sci., 1976; m. Neeta Seth, Aug. 29, 1969; children—Vinita, Anant. Adv. scientist IBM, Research Triangle Park, N.C., 1970—; program/session chmn. confs. on computers and networks. Mem. Assn. Computing Machinery, Sigma Xi. Hindu. Contbr. papers in field to publs. Home: 6216

Lakerun Ct Raleigh NC 27612 Office: IBM Research Triangle Park NC 27709

AICHBHAUMIK, DIBYAJYOTI, research scientist; b. Netrokona, Bangladesh, Jan. 5, 1944; came to U.S., 1971, naturalized, 1977; s. Dibyendu and Jyotsna (Goon) A.; B.S. (Merit scholar), U. Calcutta, 1965; M.S. (Univ. fellow), Wayne State U., Detroit, 1972, Ph.D., 1976; m. Nilu Datta, Feb. 4, 1971; 1 son, Niladri. Foundry trainee Howrah Iron & Steel Corp., Calcutta, summers 1963-65; jr. engr., sr. engr., project engr. Kuljian Corp., Calcutta, 1965-71; fellow, research asst., part-time mem. faculty Wayne State U., 1971-76; sr. research metallurgist Nat. Steel Corp., Weirton, W.Va., 1976—; cons. Named Best Student of Year, ASTM, 1972-73. Mem. Am. Soc. Metals, Metall. Soc., AIME, Nat. Soc. Profl. Engrs., ASME, Indian Inst. Metals, Sigma Xi. Hindu. Contbr. articles to profl. jours. Home: 3336 Pennsylvania Ave Weirton WV 26062 Office: R and D Center National Steel Corp Weirton WV 26062

AIDMAN, CAROLYN BETH, counselor, planner; b. Akron, Ohio, Mar. 27, 1948; d. Sol and Jeanne (Whitehouse) A.; B.A., B.S.W., Fla. State U., 1969, M.S., 1971, Ph.D., 1980. Pvt. practice counseling, tng. cons., tchr. tng., Tallahassee, 1966—; clin. social worker Fla. State Hosp., Chattahoochee, 1971-72; elem. sch. counselor Leon County Public Schs., Tallahassee, 1972-76; planner, evaluator, dir. tng. project Fla. Dept. Health and Rehab. Services, Tallahassee, 1976-77; rep. Tchr. Edn. Center, Fla. State U., Fla. A&M U. 1974-77. Mem. exec. com. Democratic Party, Leon County, 1975-79; chmn. sch. meal and nutrition subcom. Leon County Sch. Dist. Adv. Com., 1976-79; action auction team leader Sta. WFSU-TV, 1977; chmn. bd. dirs. Leon County Public Library, 1979. Law Enforcement Assistance Adminstrn. grantee, 1976—. Mem. Am. Personnel and Guidance Assn., Fla. Personnel and Guidance Assn., Phi Delta Kappa. Democrat. Contbr. articles in field to profl. jours. Home: 240 Perkins St Tallahassee FL 32301

AIKEN, ELIZABETH BOONE, journalist; b. Chattanooga, Tenn.; d. Benjamin Arthur and Janey Pickel Boone; student McKenzie Bus. Coll., 1932-34, Bob Jones Coll., 1936-37, Auburn U.; m. William Craig Aiken, Apr. 16, 1938; children—William Craig, Elizabeth Boone. Clk.-receptionist Dixie Foundry Co., Cleveland, Tenn., 1934-48; news editor Central Ala. Electric Coop., 1956-59; news corr., photographer Montgomery Advertiser, 1951-59, Ala. Jour., 1952-54, UPI, 1952-59, Prattville Progress, 1952-59, Birmingham (Ala.) News, 1953—, WSFA-TV, Montgomery, Ala., 1954—. Charter chmn. Prattville com. Girl Scouts U.S.A.; charter chmn. Prattville Cub Scouts Com.; chmn. Autauga County Vol. Spl. Ser. ARC; Autauga County chmn. Christmas Seal campaign, Easter Seal campaign; mem. Prattville Planning Commn.; charter mem. Service League, Prattville; adult adviser to young people, dir. union vacation Bible sch., supt. jr. dept. Prattville Presbyterian Ch.; pres. Women of Ch.; chmn. religious edn. E. Ala. Presbytery; bd. dirs. Lee County chpt. Ala. Soc. Crippled Children and Adults. Recipient award of merit Ala. Hist. Commn., 1976; Big N award Birmingham News, 1972; certificate of appreciation Prattville chpt. Future Farmers Am., 1956, Salvation Army, 1961, Selma YMCA, 1963, Barbour County Ret. Sr. Vols. Program, 1977; dist. service award Boy Scouts Am., 1960; Communication award Ala. Easter Seal Soc., 1975; named hon. mem. State Future Farmers Am., 1957. Mem. Nat. Press Photographers Assn., Ala. Women's Press Assn., Ala. Hist. Assn., Autauga County Heritage Assn., Auburn Heritage Assn., Lee County Hist. Soc. (charter), DAR. Club: Pilot (Service award 1979, named Auburn Pilot of Yr. 1969). Author: Will Howard Smith and McQueen Smith Farms, 1971. Home: 410 Cary Dr Auburn AL 36830

AIKENS, LUCILE BALLOON, educator; b. Madison County, Fla., Aug. 1, 1924; married, 5 children. Diploma elementary edn. Edward Waters Coll., 1946; B.S. in Elementary Edn., Fla. A. and M. U., 1954, M. in Elementary Edn., 1959. Prin. elementary sch., Canton and Pine Hill Sch., Lovett, Fla., 1947-52; tchr., Madison County (Fla.) Tng. Sch., 1952-66; reading tchr. Madison High Sch., 1967-71; reading diagnostician, Madison County Middle Schs., 1971—. Named Tchr. of Year, Madison Sch., 1978-79. Mem. Fla. Tchrs. Assn., Fla. Edn. Assn., Internat. Reading Assn., Madison Edn. Assn. Home: PO Box 465 Madison FL 32340 Office: Madison Middle School Madison FL 32340

AILOR, JAMES RICHARD, EPD cons.; b. Raleigh, N.C., June 27, 1947; s. William Henry and Clara Louise (Horne) A.; B.S. in Biology, Randolph Macon Coll., 1969. Programmer, Reynolds Metals Co., Richmond, Va., 1966-69; student asst., EDP, Randolph Macon Coll., Ashland, Va., 1966-69; systems programmer Philip Morris, Inc., Richmond, Va., 1969-72; dir. dept. info. systems Med. Coll. Va., Richmond, 1972-77; med. EDP cons. Compucare Inc., McLean, Va., 1977—; cons. health care; participant hosp. EDP seminars. Pres. Evergreen Sq. Homeowners Assn., 1977—. Mem. Assn. Computing Machinery (chpt. v.p. 1968-69), Electronic Computing Health Oriented, AAAS. Author publs. in field. Home: 10327 Bushman Dr Oakton VA 22124 Office: Compucare Inc Suite 602 1970 Chain Bridge Rd McLean VA 22104

AILOR, WILLIAM HENRY, JR., research engr.; b. Knoxville, Tenn., July 15, 1917; s. William Henry and Eda Mae (Hacker) A.; B.S. cum laude, U. Tampa, 1939; B. Chem. Engring., N.C. State U., 1948; m. Clara Louise Horne, May 1, 1942; children—William H., James Richard, David Callahan. Research chemist A.C.L. R.R., Jacksonville, Fla., 1948-53; spl. lectr., research engr. N.C. State U., Raleigh, 1953-54; research engr. Reynolds Metals Co., Richmond, Va., 1954—; adj. prof. math. Va. Commonwealth U., Richmond, 1959-79. Pres. Westwood Civic Assn., 1966—. Bd. dirs. Richmond council Boy Scouts Am., chmn. Capitol Dist. council. Served with USNR, 1942-46, 52-53. Recipient Silver Beaver award Boy Scouts Am. Fellow ASTM (award of merit 1970), AAAS; mem. Nat. Assn. Corrosion Engrs., U.S. Naval Inst. Democrat. Methodist. Mason. Editor: Metal Corrosion in the Atmosphere, 1966; Handbook on Corrosion Testing and Evaluation, 1971; Engine Coolant Testing, 1980. Home: 6009 S Crestwood Ave Richmond VA 23226 Office: Metallurgical Research Div Reynolds Metals Co Richmond VA 23261

AINSWORTH, CHARLES LEN, univ. adminstr., educator; b. San Angelo, Tex., Apr. 29, 1933; s. Nina H. (Morton) A.; B.A., Tex. Tech U., 1953, M. Ed., 1958, Ed.D., 1963; m. Peggy Louise Price, July 31, 1953; children—Price Len, Charles Lewis. Tchr., El Paso (Tex.) Public Schs., 1955-56; tchr., prin. Lubbock (Tex.) Ind. Sch. Dist., 1956-63; adminstr. Big Spring (Tex.) Ind. Sch. Dist., 1963-66; area dir. Southwestern Coop. Ednl. Lab., Albuquerque, 1966-68; asso. prof. edn. Tex. Tech U., Lubbock, 1967-72, prof., 1972—, asst. dean grad. sch., 1970-73, asso. v.p. acad. affairs, 1973—; cons. ednl. agys. Served with U.S. Army, 1953-55. Am. Council on Edn. adminstrv. internship, fellow, 1972-73. Mem. Am. Assn. Colls. Tchr. Edn., NEA, Tex. State Tchrs. Assn., Am. Assn. State Colls. and Univs. Author: The Turtle and the Rabbit Run a Race, bilingual children's book, 1971; editor: Teachers and Counselors for Mexican American Children, 1969; contbr. articles to profl. publs. Home: 3002 69th St Lubbock TX 79413 Office: Dept Edn Tex Tech U W Broadway Lubbock TX 79409

AINSWORTH, JOHN MICHAEL, health system exec.; b. Jackson, Miss., Nov. 15, 1951; s. Wilburn Eugene and Johnnie Elizabeth (Barlow) A.; B.A., Millsaps Coll., 1973; M.B.A., Harvard U., 1976. Mktg. mgr. S.Central Bell Telephone Co., Jackson, 1973-74; dir. fin. and mktg. Miss. Meth. Rehab. Center, Jackson, 1976-78, v.p., 1978—; instr. fin. Millsaps Coll., 1978-79; pres. Video Univ., Inc., Ainsworth Cons. Corp. Co-chmn., Handicapped Housing Project; del. Leadership Miss. Conclave, White House Conf. on Handicapped. Mem. Am. Assn. Hosp. Planners, Internat. Union Health Edn., Am. Mgmt. Assn., Am. Coll. Hosp. Adminstrs., Miss. Hosp. Assn., Miss. Econ. Council. Methodist. Clubs: Exchange, Harvard Miss. (dir.). Author workbook: Debt Management for Small Business; multi-media materials: Spinal Injury Learning Series (Brit. Med. Assn. award, Chgo. Film Festival), Diabetes Learning Program, Bottom Line. Home: 904B Glastonbury Circle Jackson MS 39221 Office: PO Box 4878 Jackson MS 39216

AIRTH, ALFRED THOMAS, lawyer; b. Live Oak, Fla., Feb. 2, 1906; s. Henry Franklin and Elizabeth Putnam (Porter) A.; student U. of the South, 1924-25; LL.B., U. Fla. at Gainesville, 1930, J.D., 1967; m. Elizabeth Rogers, Aug. 19, 1931. Admitted to Fla. bar, 1930; gen. practice law, Live Oak, 1931-42; gen. mgr. Radford Constrn. Co., 1945-48; gen. practice law, Live Oak, 1949-66; sr. partner law firm Airth, Sellers & Lewis and predecessor firms, Live Oak, 1966—; dir., counsel First Comml. Bank of Live Oak, 1931-42, First Nat. Bank of Live Oak, 1951-80; dir., counsel North Fla. Telephone Co., 1953—, also sec., 1953-59, treas., 1967—; dir., counsel First Fed. Savings & Loan Assn. of Live Oak, 1962-80, also sec., 1962-80. Mem. Fla. House Reps., 1928-30; pros. atty. Suwannee County (Fla.), 1933-41, 58-72; atty. Bd. County Commrs., Suwannee County, 1933-41, 63-75; state atty. Third Jud. Dist., State of Fla., 1942; atty. City of Live Oak, 1953-75; atty. Suwannee County Sch. Bd., 1957-69. Bd. dirs. Children's Home Soc. Fla., 1960—; trustee U. of the South, Sewanee, Tenn., 1948-63. Served from lt. to comdr. USNR, 1942-45. Decorated Commendation medal with star; named Man of the Year, Suwannee County, 1956. Fellow Am. Coll. Probate Council; mem. Am., Third Circuit bar assns., Fla. Bar (gov. 1951-55), Lawyers' Title Guaranty Fund (trustee 1969-74), Suwannee County C. of C. (pres. 1953), Suwannee County Jr. C. of C. (pres. 1939), Phi Gamma Delta. Democrat. Episcopalian (vestryman 1932-52, treas. 1932-42, sr. warden 1948-50; del. diocesan, gen. convs.; chancellor Diocese Fla., 1956-60; Distinguished service award 1976). Rotarian (dir. 1938-42, pres. 1939). Home: 114 Westmoreland St Live Oak FL 32060 Office: 105 N Ohio Ave Live Oak FL 32060

AJALAT, DICK SABA, dentist; b. Bklyn., Sept. 25, 1927; s. Saba D. and Mary B. (Curry) A.; B.S., Columbia, 1951; D.D.S., Med. Coll. Va., 1957; m. Sybil Dawahare, Feb. 24, 1957; children—Stephen Joseph, Mary Nell. Pharmacist, Schleigers & Peoples Drug, Newport News, Va., 1951-53, Standard Drugs, Richmond, Va., 1953-56, Mc Guire Pharmacy, Richmond, 1957; pvt. practice dentistry, Springfield, Va., 1957—. Pres., Civitan Club, Springfield, 1961-62; sec. Amara Civic Club, 1962-63; pres. Springfield YMCA, 1966-67, Coop Sch. Handicapped Children, 1965-68; bd. dirs. St. George Orthodox Ch., Washington, 1966, 79, St. Peter and Paul Orthodox Antiochian Christian Ch., Bethesda, Md.; mem. Friendship Vets. Fire Engine Co., Alexandria, Va., 1970—. Served with USCG, 1946-48. Lic. dentist, Va., 1957. Mem. ADA, Vt. (del. 1979), No. Va. dental assns., Fairfax Dental Soc., Med. Coll. Va. Alumni Assn., VFW (post surgeon 1969-77), Delta Sigma Theta, Xi Psi Phi. Address: 6115 Blacklick Rd Springfield VA 22150

AJAX, MICHAEL FLEMING, physicist; b. Salt Lake City, May 8, 1936; s. William Theodore and Kathryn Ridley (Fleming) A.; B.S. in Physics and Math., U. Tex., El Paso, 1964, M.S. in Physics and Math., 1967; m. Shirley Ann Michels, Apr. 21, 1962; 1 dau., Deianira Ann. Instr. math. Edn. Center, Ft. Bliss, Tex., 1960-63, dir. evening program, 1963-67; asst. to dir. Kidd Meml. Seismic Obs. and Research Lab., U. Tex., El Paso, 1964-67; sr. research scientist applied physics div. S.W. Research Inst., San Antonio, 1967—; cons. in acoustics, noise prediction and control. Served in U.S. Army, 1955-59. Mem. Acoustical Soc. Am., ASME, Sigma Pi Sigma. Presbyterian. Author: Handbook for Noise Control at Gas Pipeline Facilities, 1977. Home: 6309 War Hawk Dr San Antonio TX 78238 Office: 6220 Culebra Rd San Antonio TX 78284

AKEJU, RUFUS OLORUNTOYIN, polit. scientist, educator; b. Lagos, Nigeria, May 25, 1947; came to U.S., 1970, naturalized, 1971; s. Dauda and Bada A.; B.A. in Polit. Sci., U. Calif., Berkeley, 1973; M.A. in Internat. Affairs, Ohio U., 1974; Ph.D. (fellow), Howard U., 1977. Tchr. English lit., geography and history Fed. Ministry of Edn., Lagos, Nigeria, 1968-70; ethnic studies asst. (part-time) U. Calif., Berkeley, 1971-72; sales agt. Hearthstone Ins. Co. of Mass., San Francisco office, 1973; research asst. Sch. of Law, Howard U., Washington, 1974-76, spl. asst. to dean Grad. Sch., 1974-76; asst. prof. govt. and public affairs Tenn. State U., Nashville, 1977—, faculty rep., 1977—, urban affairs coordinator, 1980—; panelist 4th Ann. Third World Workshop, Govs. State U., Park Forest South, Ill., 1978; cons. to Population Studies Group, Tempo Center for Advanced Studies, Washington, 1975, Trevecca Nazarene Coll., Nashville, 1979-79; area rep. operation crossroads Africa Inc., Nashville, 1977—. Recipient Cert. of Laud and Honor, Tenn. State U. Sch. Arts and Scis., 1979. Mem. Am. Polit. Sci. Assn., Am. Acad. Polit. and Social Sci., Am. Soc. Internat. Law, Internat. Studies Assn., Nat. Hist. Soc., African Studies Assn., Internat. Humanist and Ethical Union Assn., Alpha Phi Alpha, Gamma Beta Phi (hon.), Gamma Kappa chpt. of Pi Sigma Alpha. Contbr. articles on polit. economy and internat. relations to scholarly publs. Office: Tenn State Univ Nashville TN 37203

AKERMAN, JOSEPH LAX, physician; b. Savannah, Ga., June 24, 1921; s. Walter E. and Marian (Lax) A.; student Vanderbilt U., 1940-42; M.D., Tulane U. Sch. Medicine, 1951; m. Orfa Mae Palko, Jan. 2, 1950; children—Joseph Lax, Marian Beth, Amos Tappan, John Michaels, Mary Louise. Intern USPHS, Galveston, Tex., 1951-52; resident USPHS Hosp., Memphis, 1952, med. staff, 1952; individual practice medicine, Apopka, Fla., 1953—; physician Plymouth Citrus Products Coop. plant, 1958—, Plymouth Citrus Growers Assn. (Fla.), 1958—, Gen. Electric Lamp Plant, Plymouth, 1969—; cons. physician for numerous owners in foliage plant industry. Pres. Central Fla. council Boy Scouts Am., 1968, 69, 70, v.p. council, 1973-76, council, 1973-76, council commr., 1966, 67, 71-73, mem. nat. council, 1965—, program chmn. Area VI, 1972-74, area cub scout chmn., 1972-78; mem. nat. council Cub Scout Com., 1968—. Served with U.S. Army, 1943-46, USAF, 1946-51; ATO, ETO. Recipient Silver Beaver award Fla. council Boy Scouts Am., Silver Antelope award, 1977; Vigil Honor, Order of Arrow, 1968, named Man of Yr. Orange County YMCA, 1969, 1 of Top 10 Citizens Apopka, 1968, 69, 70. Mem. various med. socs., Kappa Alpha. Presbyn. (ruling elder). Club: Apopka Sertoma (charter pres.; chmn. bd. 1969-70, 70-71; gov. N.E. Fla. dist. 1972-73, Heart of Fla. dist. 1973-74, state dir. 1974-76; internat. dir. 1976-78; named Distinguished Club pres., dist. gov.). Home: 220 N Washington St Apopka FL 32703 Office: 125 S Park PO Box 1107 Apopka FL 32703

AKERS, CHARLES DAVID, lawyer; b. Atlanta, Jan. 6, 1948; s. James Ires and Lillian M. A.; B.A., Vanderbilt U., 1970, J.D., 1973. Admitted to Tenn. bar, 1973; legis. atty. Tenn. Legis. Council Com., Nashville, 1974-75; staff atty. Tenn. Dept. Public Health, Div. Water Quality Control, Nashville, 1976-78, staff atty. Office of Gen. Counsel, Tenn. Dept. Public Health, 1979, legis. coordinator, 1979—. Mem. Tenn. Bar Assn., Am. Bar Assn., Mensa, Nashville Area Jr. C. of C. Republican. Unitarian. Office: Tenn Dept Public Health Cordell Hull Bldg Nashville TN 37219

AKERS, MICHAEL JAMES, pharm. scientist; b. Beech Grove, Ind., Aug. 24, 1946; s. James Linwood and Helen Garmon (Thompson) A.; B.A., Wabash Coll., 1968; Ph.D., U. Iowa, 1972; m. Mary Margaret Wilder, June 8, 1968; children—Scott Michael, Ryan Matthew, Allison Michelle. Research investigator Searle Labs., Skokie, Ill., 1972-74; sr. scientist Alcon Labs., Ft. Worth, 1974-77; asst. prof. pharmacy U. Tenn., Memphis, 1977—; cons. to pharm. industry on parenteral medications. Fellow Am. Found. Pharm. Edn.; mem. Am. Pharm. Assn., Parenteral Drug Assn., Am. Assn. Colls. Pharmacy, Rho Chi, Phi Lambda Upsilon. Presbyterian. Contbr. articles to profl. jours. Home: 2181 Woodcreek St Germantown TN 38138 Office: College of Pharmacy U Tenn Center Health Sciences Memphis TN 38163

AKERS, WILBURN HOLT, paleontologist; b. Lawton, Okla., Oct. 18, 1918; s. Dennis Randolph and Veannous Ann (Holt) A.; B.S. in Geology, U. Okla., 1941, M.S. in Geology, 1947; Ph.D., Tulane U., 1971; m. Beverly J. Pecunia; children—Glenn Alan, Denise Aline, Robert Dell. Sr. staff paleontologist Chevron Oil Co., New Orleans, 1948—. Cons. dept. earth scis. Tulane U., New Orleans, 1974—. Commr. New Orleans area Council Boy Scouts Am., 1966-69, Silver Beaver, 1965. Served with AUS, 1941-45; NATOUSA, Italy. Fellow Geol. Soc. Am.; mem. Sigma Xi (research award 1971). Democrat. Unitarian (bd. dirs. 1975, pres. 1977—). Research, publs. on foraminifera, calcareous nannofossils. Home: 3920 Lolan Ct Marrero LA 70072 Office: 1111 Tulane Ave New Orleans LA 70112

AKERS, WILLIAM WALTER, univ. adminstr.; b. Panola County, Tex., Dec. 31, 1922; s. Oscar Walter and Lela (Malone) A.; B.S., Tex. Tech U., 1943; M.S., U. Tex., 1944; Ph.D., U. Mich., 1951; m. Nancy Tressel, Mar. 1, 1947; children—Susan Elaine, Carol Lorraine. Engr., Atlantic Refining Corp., Dallas, 1947; cons. to various chem. industries, 1947-65; mem. faculty Rice U., Houston, Tex., 1947—, prof. chem. engring., 1956—, chmn. dept. chem. engring., 1955-66, dir. Bio-Med. Engring. Lab., 1963-69, asst. to pres., 1973-74, dir. of univ. relations, 1974, v.p. external affairs, 1975—; mem. council Oak Ridge Inst. Nuclear Studies, 1958-63; tech. adviser to Yugoslavia, 1962; mem. U.S.-Afghanistan Ednl. Consortium, 1963-70; research project dir. Baylor Coll. of Medicine, 1965-70; mem. bio-med. engring. fellowship com. NIH, 1967-70. Trustee, St. Luke's Hosp., Houston, 1975-79; bd. dirs. S. Main Center Assn., 1976—. Served with C.E., U.S. Army, 1942-43; ETO. Recipient Distinguished Engring. Alumnus award Tex. Tech. U., 1967. Mem. Am. Chem. Soc., Am. Inst. Chem. Engrs. (award 1967), Houston Philos. Soc., Am. Soc. Artificial Organs, Council on Fgn. Relations, Sigma Xi, Tau Beta Pi. Episcopalian. Contbr. numerous articles on chem. engring. and bio-med. engring. to profl. jours. Home: 5214 Green Tree Rd Houston TX 77027 Office: Rice Univ PO Box 1892 Houston TX 77001

AKIN, RALPH HARDIE, JR., geologist, oil co. exec.; b. Decatur, Ill., Oct. 18, 1938; s. Ralph Hardie and Darla Iris (Sutterfield) A.; B.S. in Geology, Centenary Coll., 1960; M.S. in Geology, U. Tulsa, 1966; m. Anna Elaine Fleming, June 28, 1974; 1 dau., Jennifer Aimee; children by previous marriage—Laura Elizabeth, Michael Hardie. Geologist petroleum exploration Apache Corp., Tulsa, Houston, 1961-67; geologist Ada Oil Co., Houston, 1967-59, exploration mgr., 1969-70; sr. v.p. T. C. Bartling & Assos., Houston, 1971-76; pres. Akin Energy Corp., Houston, 1976—. Served with AUS, 1960-61. Mem. Am. Assn. Petroleum Geologists, Soc. Exploration Geophysicists, Houston Geol. Soc., Geophys. Soc. Houston, Am. Assn. Petroleum Landmen, Kappa Alpha Order. Home: 823 Daria Houston TX 77079 Office: Akin Energy Corp 920 Americana Bldg Houston TX 77002

AKINS, DOROTHY LOUISE, cons.; b. Lake Charles, La., Sept. 7, 1931; d. Joseph B. and Elouieese C. (Barousse) A.; B.A., McNeese State U., Lake Charles, 1952, Ed.D. (Delta Kappa Gamma scholar 1976), 1978; M.Ed. St. Louis U., 1956. Tchr., counselor Calcasleu Parish (La.) schs., Lake Charles, 1952-78, spl. services cons. to coordinate testing, 1978—. Mem. Am. Personnel and Guidance Assn., La. Personnel and Guidance Assn., La. Assn. Measurement and Evaluation (pres.), Calcasieu Counselors Assn., Delta Kappa Gamma. Democrat. Roman Catholic. Home: 2601 Elms St Lake Charles LA 70601 Office: 1120 W 18th St Lake Charles LA 70601

AKMAL, RUTH, Realtor; b. Norman, Okla., Feb. 8, 1930; d. Ollie M. and Alcidene Smith Grimwood; m. Mohamed Gawid Akmal, Apr. 22, 1948; children—Mohamoud Gawid, Kenneth Paul, Barbara Diana, Omar Gawid, Deenar Gawid. Owner, mgr. Akmal Realty, Houston, 1967-80. Mem. Houston Livestock Show and Rodeo Assn. Democrat. Methodist. Home: 5005 Georgi Ln Apt 17 Houston TX 77092

AL-ABDULLA, HAMID MOHAMMED, physician; b. Diwaniya, Iraq, Apr. 29, 1935; s. Haj Mohammed and Fatima Mahmud (Tiwaij) Al-A.; M.D., U. Baghdad Coll. Medicine, 1958; m. Linda Lee Ruttig, June 27, 1964; children—Safaa Hamid, Susan-Lee Hamid. Intern, Christ Hosp., Jersey City, 1961-62; resident internal medicine Franklin Sq. Hosp., Balt., 1963-64, Cook County Hosp., Chgo., 1964-66; fellow cardiology Univ. Hosps., Cleve., 1966-67, St. Vincent Charity Hosp., Cleve., 1967-68; asst. cardiologist Highland View Hosp., Cleve., 1968-70; dir. cardiovascular lab. VA Hosp., Des Moines, 1970-73; pvt. practice cardiology and internal medicine, Richmond, Va., 1973—; mem. staff Richmond Meml. Hosp., St. Mary's Hosp., Retreat Hosp., Drs. Hosp. Mem. Sleepy Hollow Civic Assn., Richmond, 1973—; v.p. Iraqi Grads. Assn., Fairfax, Va. Served with Iraqi Army, 1958-59. Diplomate Am. Bd. Internal Medicine, Am. Bd. Cardiovascular Disease. Fellow A.C.P., Am. Coll. Cardiology, Am. Coll. Angiology, Am. Coll. Chest Physicians; mem. Am. Heart Assn. Moslem. Contbr. articles to med. jours. Office: 3604 Monument Ave Richmond VA 23230

ALALA, JOSEPH BASIL, JR., lawyer, accountant; b. Aleppo, Syria, Apr. 29, 1933; s. Joseph Basil and Waheda (Tall) A.; B.S. in Bus. Adminstrn., U. N.C., 1957, J.D. cum laude, 1959; m. Nell Powers, Dec. 19, 1954; children—Sharon J., Tracy M., Joseph B. III. Accountant, Arthur Anderson & Co., Charlotte, N.C., 1959-62; admitted to N.C. bar, 1959; partner firm Garland & Alala, Gastonia, N.C., 1963—; lectr. on taxes various C.P.A. and bar seminars; profl. devel. lectr. various profl. assns. Bd. dirs. Garrison Community Found., Belmont Abbey Coll.; past mem. bd. trustees, comm. finance com. St. Michael's Cath. Ch.; pres. Jr. C. of C., 1964. Served with M.P., U.S. Army, Korean War. Mem. Am. Judicature Soc., Am. Bar Assn., Am. Assn. Atty.-C.P.A.'s, N.C., Gaston County bar assns., Am. Inst. C.P.A.'s, N.C. Assn. C.P.A.'s, Nat. Assn. Accts. Clubs: Grand Knights of Malta, Rotary Internat. (dir. Gastonia chpt.), Gaston Country. Home: 1216 South St Gastonia NC 28052 Office: 192 South St Gastonia NC 28052

ALAVI, SEYED MOHAMMAD, surgeon; b. Rafsanjan, Iran, Mar. 21, 1936; came to U.S., 1969, naturalized, 1979; m. Karim and Farkhondeh (Saberi) A.; M.D., Tehran Med. Sch. (Iran), 1961; m. Mansoureh Sabouhi Moghadam, Feb. 6, 1961; children—Dineh, Dorsay, Amir H. Rotating intern Sina U. Hosp., Tehran, 1960-61, surg. resident, 1961-65; asst. prof. surgery Tehran Med. Sch., 1966-69; surg. intern SUNY, Syracuse, 1969-70, resident in surgery, 1970-71; resident in surgery St. Francis Hosp., U. Ill., Peoria, 1971-74; practice medicine specialzing in gen. surgery, El Paso, Tex., 1974—; clin. prof. Med. Sch., Juarez, Mexico, 1975—; mem. staff Eastwood Hosp., Providence Hosp., Hotel Dieu Hosp. Diplomate Am. Bd. Surgery. Fellow ACS; mem. AMA, Tex. Med. Assn., El Paso County Med. Soc., Southwestern Surg. Congress, Ednl. Council Fgn. Med. Grads. Moslem. Contbr. articles in field to Jour. Surg. Research, Iranian jours. Home: 10629 Vista Alegre St El Paso TX 79935 Office: 10301 Gateway W El Paso TX 79925

ALBA, ENRIQUE, business exec.; b. Havana, Cuba, July 15, 1946; s. Ramon and Josefina (Lamelas) A.; came to U.S., 1962, naturalized, 1973; B.A. in Psychology with honors, U. Fla., 1970, Ed.M., 1971, Ph.D. in Ednl. Psychology, 1972; m. Carmen Regueira, Dec. 20, 1969; children—Anna Christina, Brenda Lisa. Staff psychologist Searcy Hosp., Mount Vernon, Ala., 1972, unit dir., 1972-74; cons. in edn., Miami, Fla., 1974-75; chmn., chief exec. officer Ednl. Systems Engring. Corp., Miami, 1976—; exec. v.p. Alba Indsl. Corp., 1979—; instr. Mercy Coll., Miami, 1977—; cons. in ednl. psychology Miami-Dade Community Coll., 1976—. Bd. dirs. Substance Abuse Task Force, 1975. Mem. Am. Psychol. Assn., Assn. for Advancement of Behavior Therapy, Am. Ednl. Research Assn., Latin C. of C. U.S. Democrat. Office: 940 W 22d St Hialeah FL 33010

ALBACH, HENRY JOHN, IV, lawyer; b. Dallas, Mar. 26, 1949; s. Henry John and Greta Nobel (Edgren) A.; B.A. magna cum laude, Tufts U., 1971; postgrad. (Ziegler Ednl. Fund fellow), U. Tex. Law Sch., 1976; m. Susan Albaugh, Oct. 2, 1971. Staff asst., chief investigator Dallas Civil Liberties Union, summers 1969, 70, 71; mem. research staff Center for Advancement of Criminal Justice, Harvard, 1971-72; staff dir. joint com. on prison reform, Tex. Legislature, Austin, 1973-75; regional dir. Nat. Council on Crime and Delinquency, Central Mountain Service Center, Austin, 1975-77; exec. dir. Tex. Council Crime and Delinquency, 1977-78; partner firm Albach Gutow Rosenberg & Blume, Dallas, 1978—; cons. criminal justice. Coordinator, Dallas Students for McCarthy, 1968; state coordinator Students for Humphrey-Muskie, Mass., 1968; mem. steering com. Students for McGovern, Boston, 1972; pres. Tex. Coalition for Juvenile Justice. Mem. Am. Bar Assn., Tex. Bar Assn., Dallas Bar Assn., ACLU, Tex. Corrections Assn. Democrat. Editor: The Criminal Justice System in Texas, 1975. Home: 4723 Swiss Ave Dallas TX 75204 Office: One Lemmon Park E 3627 Howell Suite 217 Dallas TX 75204

ALBERGA, ALTA W., artist; b. Tuscaloosa, Ala.; d. James Richard and Leila Savannah (Sullivan) Wheat; m. Alvyn Clyde Alberga, Dec. 3, 1930. Instr. art Wichita State U., 1954-55, Webster Coll., St. Louis, 1961, Presbyn. Coll., Clinton, S.C., 1969-74; tchr. Tempo Gallery, Greenville, S.C., 1978—, Greenville County Mus. Art Sch., 1977—; one woman shows include Wichita State U., 1955, St. Louis Artists Guild, 1961, N.C. State U., 1966, Presbyn. Coll., 1972, U. S.C. at Lancaster, 1974, Pickens County Mus., 1979, Greenvill Artists Guild, 1979; group exhbns. include City Art Mus., St. Louis, S.W. Am. Artists, Tulsa, Gibbs Gallery, Charleston, S.C., S.E. Center Contemporary Art, Winston-Salem, N.C., Greenville County Mus. Art, 1979; represented in permanent and pvt. collections. Mem. Artists Equity N.Y., Art Students League N.Y., S.C. Artists Guild, Greenville Artists Guild (bd. dirs.), Southeastern Graphics Council, Internat. Platform Assn. Home: 11 Overton Dr Greenville SC 29609

ALBERGOTTI, LILA FRETWELL, musician; b. Anderson, S.C., July 31, 1929; d. Raymond and Lila (Brownlee) F.; B.Mus., Salem Coll., 1950; m. William Greer Albergotti, Mar. 31, 1951; children—Samuel Fretwell, Raymond Mackay, Mary Argoe, Paul McAlpin. Choir dir. Good Hope Presbyn. Ch., Iva, S.C. Bd. dirs. Children's Bur. S.C., 1968—, chmn., 1976-77; chmn. bd. dirs. Anderson County Meals on Wheels, 1976—; bd. dirs. People Attempting to Help, Inc., 1976—, Anderson-Oconee Council on Aging, 1973—; mem. Mayor's Com. on Hiring the Handicapped, 1978. Recipient Sertoma Service to Mankind award (local, district & regional), 1977. Mem. Presbyn. Music Assn. Democrat. Episcopalian. Clubs: Anderson Women's, Anderson Garden, Anderson County. Home: 406 Shannon Way Anderson SC 29621

ALBERS, DONALD DEEN, mfg. co. exec.; b. Corley, Iowa, Jan. 3, 1927; s. Rudolph Claus and Lauena (Trimble) A.; B.S., U. Iowa, 1948; postgrad. U. Mich., 1950; m. Sandra Jean Anfin, Feb. 12, 1955; children—William, Susan, Robert, Kathryn. With Ford Motor Co., Detroit, 1948-55, Chrysler Corp., Detroit, 1955-62; cons. Arthur Young & Co., 1962-64; exec. v.p. Tex. Refinery Corp., Ft. Worth, 1964-68; pres. Am. Excelsior Co., Arlington, Tex., 1968-77, vice chmn. bd., 1977-79; partner Vantage Co., Dallas, 1980—; dir. Tex. Refinery Corp., Columbia Investment Corp. Chmn. bd. trustees Ft. Worth Country Day Sch., 1978—; bd. trustees United Fund, 1965-68. Served with U.S. Army, 1944-46. Mem. C. of C., Am. Mgmt. Assn. Republican. Clubs: Colonial Country, 2001, Export-Import, Fin., Salesmanship, Mktg. Home: 3412 Overton Park W Fort Worth TX 76109 Office: 2525 Stemmons Freeway Dallas TX 75207

ALBERS, MORRIS EDWARD, govt. ofcl.; b. nr. LaGrange, Tex., Jan. 9, 1924; s. Odell Walter and Irene Catherine (Wessels) A.; B.S., Tex. A&M U., 1947; m. Vivian H. von Minden, Dec. 19, 1946; children—Morris Edward II, Moira K., Mary M., Margaret E., James H. Vocat. agr. tchr., 1947-48; work unit conservationist Soil Conservation Service, 1949-54; county supr. Farmers Home Adminstrn., 1955-59; mgmt. analyst U.S. Air Force, 1959-64, supervisory procurement analyst, 1965-69, supervisory contract negotiator, 1970-75, procurement specialist, 1976-77, supervisory contract adminstrn., 1978-79, dep. chief mfg. and contract adminstrn. div., directorate of contracting and mfg. San Antonio Air Logistics Center, 1979—. Chmn. credit com. St. Gregory's Fed. Credit Com., 1965-75. Served with U.S. Army, 1943-46. Decorated Purple Heart. Mem. Nat. Contract Mgmt. Assn. (cert. profl. contracts mgr.), Soc. Logistics Engrs., Res. Officers Assn., Kelly Mgmt. Club. Roman Catholic. Home: 3023 Gainesborough Dr San Antonio TX 78230 Office: San Antonio Air Logistics Center SA-ALC/PMD Kelly Air Force Base TX 78241

ALBERS, RICHARD LEE, lawyer, bank exec.; b. Omaha, June 27, 1942; s. Richard Henry and Rose Cecelia (Foley) A.; B.S. in Bus. Mgmt. cum laude, Western Ky. State U., 1964; J.D., Nashville YMCA Night Law Sch., 1972; m. Patricia May Fussell, July 17, 1971. Asst. nat. bank examiner U.S. Treasury Dept., Nashville, 1965-68; auditor Nashville City Bank & Trust Co., 1968-70, asst. v.p., auditor, 1970-72, v.p., auditor, comptroller, 1972-75; admitted to Tenn. bar, 1973, U.S. Tax Ct., 1975; partner firm Morrow & Albers, Nashville, 1975—. Mem. Am., Tenn., Nashville bar assns., Internat. Platform Assn., Am. Judicature Soc., Am. Trial Lawyers Assn., Tenn. Trial Lawyers Assn., Dickson County (Tenn.) Farm Bur. Club: Kiwanis (pres. 1979-80). Home: 5131 Brucewood Dr Nashville TN 37211 Office: 3221 Nolensville Rd Nashville TN 37211

ALBERT, EMIL RICHARD, III, businessman; b. Tulsa, Oct. 9, 1941; s. Emil Richard and Mary Kathryn (McCarthy) A.; B.A., Washington and Lee U., 1963; m. Margaret Huffman, Aug. 31, 1974; children—Pelham, Emil Richard, Paige, Brooke. Salesman, Alexander & Alexander, Inc., N.Y.C., 1964-66; pres. E.R. Albert Ins. Agy., Inc., 1966-68; pres. Albert & Tate, Inc., Tulsa, 1968-73; v.p. Albert Equipment Co., Inc., Tulsa, 1973-76, pres., chief operating officer, 1976—; dir. Bank of Tulsa, Fo-Mac, Inc., S.C.S., Inc., S.E. Leasing, Inc. Dir. Philbrook Mus. Served with U.S. Army, 1966-68. Mem. Young Pres. Orgn. Episcopalian. Home: 1505 E 29th St Tulsa OK 74136 Office: 7794 E 42d Tulsa OK 74145

ALBERT, LOIS ELDORA, archaeologist; b. Alva, Okla., June 2, 1938; d. Clinton Lawrence and Daisy Madeleine (Thau) Wilson; B.S., Northwestern State Coll., 1960; M.S., Okla. State U., 1963; postgrad. Okla. City U., summers 1967, 68; postgrad. Central State Coll., 1967-68; M.A., U. Okla., 1974; m. Abbott H. Albert. Chemistry lab. teaching asst. Northwestern State Coll., Alva, Okla., 1957-60; grad. research asst. Dept. Biochemistry, Okla. State U., Stillwater, 1960-62; research asst. div. gastroenterology U. Colo. Med. Center, Denver, 1962-64, Okla. Med. Research Found., Oklahoma City, 1964-66, dept. microbiology U. Okla. Health Sci. Center, Oklahoma City, 1966-70, summer 1974, part-time, 1970-72; archaeol. asst. dept. anthropology, U. Okla., Norman, summer 1971, grad. asst., 1972-73, sec. I, 1975-76, research asst. I, 1976-78, acting dir. Okla. Archaeol. Survey, 1978-79, research asst., 1979—; with Okla. Hwy. Dept., Oklahoma City, summer 1975; project dir. Prehistoric People of Okla. film series planning project, 1979; Okla. Humanities Com. grantee, 1979. Mem. Am. Chem. Soc., Am. Assn. Stratigraphic Palynologists, Soc. for Am. Archaeology, Soil Sci. Soc. Am., Soc. for Archaeol. Sci., AAAS, Sigma Xi, D.A.R., Okla. Soc. Mayflower Descs. Series editor Studies in Okla.'s Past, Okla. Archaeol. Survey, 1978-79, Prehistoric People of Okla., 1979—; contbr. articles in field to profl. jours. Office: 1335 S Asp St Norman OK 73019

ALBERT, RUDOLPH MILTON, JR., chemist; b. Pulaski, Va., Sept. 20, 1938; s. Rudolph Milton and Shirley Mae (Gleason) A.; B.A., King Coll., 1960; M.S., Va. Poly. Inst. and State U., 1962; Ph.D., U. Fla., 1973; m. Carol Elaine Goedert, Sept. 6, 1960; children—Mary Elizabeth, Laura Elaine, Robert Milton, Rebecca Lynn, Daniel Lawrence. Chemist, Glidden Co., Jacksonville, Fla., 1962-68 (merged with SCM Corp., 1966), chemist organic chemistry div. SCM Corp., 1973-78, mgr. devel., 1978—. Mem. Am. Chem. Soc. Democrat. Presbyterian. Patentee in field. Home: 3520 NW 26th Terr Gainesville FL 32605 Office: PO Box 389 Jacksonville FL 32601

ALBERTS, BRUCE ERWIN, mktg. and sales exec.; b. Chgo., Jan. 10, 1937; s. Erwin Olaf and Ann Marie (Winsler) A.; B.S., U. Wis., 1960; postgrad. Roosevelt U., 1975-76; m. Joan Marese Doll, Aug. 8, 1958; children—Lisa Renee, David Michael, Karin Marese. Comml. rep. Gen. Telephone Co. of Wis., Plymouth, 1960-62, local comml. mgr., 1962-63; asst. mgr. Kroger Co., Fond Du Lac, Wis., 1963-65; salesman Oscar Mayer & Co., Milw., 1965-66; dist. sales mgr. Oscar Mayer & Co., Chgo., 1966-68, asst. plant sales mgr., 1968-71; regional sales engr. Omeco, St. John & Co., Omaha, 1971-72; nat. sales mgr. Foodservice div. La Choy Food Products, Archbold, Ohio, 1972-75; nat. mktg. mgr. Beatrice Foods, Chgo., 1975-76; nat. sales and mktg. mgr. Gebhardt Mexican Foods, San Antonio, 1976—. Pres., Elk Grove Village (Ill.) Homeowners Assn., 1971; dir. Hidden Forest Homeowners Assn., 1978; bd. dirs. Elk Grove Little League, 1976. Served with USMC, 1954-55. Recipient Certificate of Merit, Foodservice Mktg., Beatrice Foods, 1977. Mem. Instl. Food Mfrs. Assn. (asst. chmn. mktg. com. 1976-78), Internat. Foodservice Mfrs. Assn., Nat. Automatic Merchandisers Assn., Tex. Restaurant Assn. Roman Catholic. Club: Woodlake Country. Home: 1232 Weeping Willow Dr San Antonio TX 78232 Office: PO Box 7130 Station A San Antonio TX 78285

ALBERTS, HAROLD, lawyer; b. San Antonio, Apr. 3, 1920; s. Bernard H. and Rose (Cassel) A.; LL.B., U. Tex., 1942; m. Rose M. Gaskin, Mar. 25, 1945; children—Linda Rae, Barry Lawrence. Tchr., U. Tex., 1942; admitted to Tex. bar, 1943; gen. practice law, Corpus Christi, Tex., 1946—. Pres., Jewish Welfare Fund Corpus Christi, 1948; charter vice chmn. of the Southwest Regional Anti-Defamation League, 1953, chmn., 1969-72; also chmn. Brotherhood Week, 1957; chmn Nueces County chpt. ARC, 1959-61; mem. campaign exec. com., chmn. meetings United Community Services, 1961; chmn. Coastal Bend Council on Alcoholism, 1974-76; pres. Combined Jewish Appeal, 1974-76; v.p. Little Theatre Corpus Christi, 1964—; moderator Friday Morning Group, 1970, weekly TV pub. service program, 1975-76; chmn. Corpus Christi NCCJ, 1967-69, mem. nat. bd. dirs., 1974-77; bd. dirs. Tex. State Assn. for Mental Health. Served to lt. USNR, 1942-46. Mem. Am., Tex., Nueces County bar assns. Clubs: Masons (32 deg.), Kiwanis (pres. 1962), B'nai B'rith (pres. 1955, past v.p. Tex.). Home: 618 Dolphin Pl Corpus Christi TX 78411 Office: Wilson Tower Corpus Christi TX 78401

ALBERTSON, DAVID ALLEN, surgeon; b. Roanoke, Va., Oct. 27, 1947; s. Horace Allen Albertson and Marie (Patterson) Albertson Lawson; B.S., Hampden-Sydney Coll., 1969; M.D., U. Va., 1972; m. Martha Kennedy, Dec. 27, 1969. Intern, N.C. Baptist Hosp., Winston-Salem, 1972-73, resident in gen. surgery, 1973-77; fellow in surg. endocrinology Boston U. Med. Center, 1977-78; instr. surgery Bowman Gray Sch. Medicine, Winston-Salem, 1978-79, ass. prof., 1979—; mem. staffs N.C. Bapt. Hosp., Forsyth Meml. Hosp.; physician adviser Piedmont Med. Found. Diplomate Am. Bd. Surgery. Fellow Royal Coll. Surgeons (Can.); mem. AMA, A.C.S., Southeastern Surg. Congress, Assn. for Acad. Surgery, N.C. Med. Soc., N.C. Thoracic Soc., Forsyth County Med. Soc. Presbyterian. Office: Dept Surgery Bowman Gray Sch Medicine Winston-Salem NC 27103

ALBERTSON, GARY ROGER, physician; b. Watonga, Okla., Nov. 1, 1945; s. Lloyd Roger and Joyce Marie (Pekrul) A.; B.S., Southwestern State U., 1966; D.O., Kirksville (Mo.) Coll. Osteopathy and Surgery, 1970; m. Twila Zalynn Gallman, Aug. 16, 1944; children—Darron, Kristyl. Intern, Carson City (Mich.) Osteo. Hosp., 1970-71; gen. practice osteo. medicine, Ashley, Mich., 1973-74, Muleshoe, Tex., 1974—; mem. staff W. PLains Med. Center, Muleshoe, 1974—, dir., 1975—, chief staff, 1977—; health officer Bailey County, Tex., 1975—. Bd. dirs. Heart Assn., Muleshoe, 1975-77. Served to capt. U.S. Army, 1971-73. Diplomate Am. Bd. Family Practice. Fellow Am. Acad. Family Physicians; mem. South Plains Chpt. Family Practice (dir., v.p. 1978—), Tex. Acad. Family Practice, Sigma Sigma Phi, Psi Sigma Alpha. Mem. Assemblies of God Ch. Home: 1904 W Ave H Muleshoe TX 79347 Office: 708 S 1st St Muleshoe TX 79347

ALBERTSON, HAROLD D., elec. engr., educator; b. Parsons, Kans., Dec. 28, 1931; s. George Dewey and Mamie Irene (Harrell) A.; B.S. in Math. and Elec. Engring., U. Houston, 1953; M.S. in Elec. Engring., So. Methodist U., 1960; Ph.D. (Tex. Instruments fellow), U. Tex., 1968; m. Margaret Elna Bodden, Aug. 8, 1953; 1 dau., Anne. Systems engr. Chance Vought Aircraft, Dallas, 1953-58; design engr. Tex. Instruments, Inc., Dallas, 1958-61, program mgr., 1961-65, mem. tech. staff, 1968-73; instr. physics Eastfield Coll., Dallas, 1972-73; instr. electro-mech. and fluid power tech. Richland Coll., Dallas, 1973-77, chmn. math. and tech. div., 1977-78, dean instructional sers., 1978—. Mem. steering com. Southwest Simulation Council, 1971-72. Mem. IEEE (chmn. Dallas chpt. 1971-72), Sigma Xi, Tau Beta Pi. Home: 7660 Chalkstone St Dallas TX 75240 Office: 12800 Abrams Rd Dallas TX 75231

ALBRIGHT, BOYCE SINGLETON, supt. schs.; b. Haleyville Ala., Apr. 27, 1924; s. Virgie Hugh and Tiney (Posey) A.; student U. Ala., 1943, Ed.D., 1976; B.A., Howard Coll., 1948; M.A., George Peabody Coll., 1952. Head coordinator Vets. Tng. Program, Haleyville, 1948-61; tchr. Haleyville Schs., 1952-61, supt. schs., 1971—; coordinator trade and indsl. edn. Haleyville High Sch., 1960-61; supt. schs. Winston County (Ala.), 1961-71; state chmn. Profl. Relations and Tchr. Welfare Com. Mem. Ala. Com. for Better Schs., 1961—. Trustee N.W. Ala. State Jr. Coll., Samford U., 1977—; bd. dirs. N. Ala. Rehab. Center, Birmingham. Served with AUS, World War II. Named Alumni of Year Haleyville Schs., 1973. Mem. Ala. Edn. Assn. (mem. state legislative com., dist. pres. elect, state chmn. joint com.), Ala. Assn. Sch. Adminstrs. (state exec. com.), NEA, A., Distributive Edn. Clubs Am. (hon. life), Ala. Congress Parents and Tchrs. (hon. life), Internat. Platform Assn., Am. Legion, VFW, C. of C., Kappa Phi Kappa. Alpha Phi Omega, Omicron Delta Kappa, Pi Kappa Alpha. Mason., Lion (pres., dep. dist. gov., zone chmn.). Home: PO Box 149 Haleyville AL 35565 Office: 1800 E 20th St Haleyville AL 35565

ALBRIGHT, COOPER EUGENE, engring. co. exec.; b. West Monroe, La., Aug. 27, 1927; s. George Cooper and Verlie Lurline (Williams) A.; M.E., Internat. Corr. Schs., 1960; m. Gracie Pearl Bradley, Dec. 29, 1968; children—George Allen, Paul Randall, Carole Jean; stepchildren—Tanya Lane Bodo, Gary Lang Koger, Patricia Ann Sveda. With Internat. Paper Co., 1948-69, project engr., Pine Bluff, Ark., 1958-65, sr. project engr., Bastrop, La., 1965-67, Mobile, Ala., 1967-69; sr. project engr. Southland Paper Mills, Houston, 1969-74; mgr. process services Brown & Root, Inc., Houston, 1974—. Mem. adv. council DeMolay, Pine Bluff, 1964; mem. airport adv. com. Bastrop City Countil, 1966. Served with USNR, 1945-46, 50-51. Registered profl. engr., Ala., La., Miss., Okla., S.C., Tex., Wis. Mem. Nat., Tex. socs. profl. engrs., ASME, Houston Engring. and Sci. Soc. Republican. Baptist. Clubs: Lake Forest Country (Mobile); Masons (32 deg.). Patentee device for pulp fiber removal. Home: 5723 Claridge Dr Houston TX 77096 Office: Brown & Root Inc PO Box 3 Houston TX 77001

ALBRIGHT, JOHN GROVER, chemist, educator; b. Winfield, Kans., June 29, 1934; s. Penrose Strong and Mary (Lucas) A.; B.A., Wichita U., 1956; Ph.D., U. Wis., 1962; m. Sharon Rae Rudd, June 11, 1960; children—Mary Kathrine, David Louis. Postdoctoral fellow Australian Nat. U., Canberra, 1963-65; research fellow Inst. Enzyme Research, Madison, Wis., 1965-66; asst. prof. chemistry Tex. Christian U., 1966-72, asso. prof., 1972—; vis. prof. chemistry Lawrence Livermore Lab. summers 1969, 72, 77, 78, 79. Mem. sci. adv. com. Southwestern Coll., Winfield, 1976—. Mem. Am. Chem. Soc. Congregationalist. Club: Lions. Contbr. articles to profl. publs. on liquid diffusion. Home: 4332 Lanark St Fort Worth TX 76109

ALBRITTON, ROBERT BYNUM, lawyer; b. Andalusia, Ala., Feb. 1, 1905; s. William Harold and Anne (Mashburn) A.; LL.B., U. Ala., 1930; m. Carrie Veal, Aug. 16, 1928; 1 son, William Harold III. Admitted to Ala. bar, 1930, since practiced in Andalusia; mem. firm Powell, Albritton & Albritton, 1930-48, Albrittons & Rankin, 1948-76, Albrittons & Givhan, 1976—; dir., gen. counsel, Ala. Textile Products Corp., Troy Textiles, Enterprise Mfg. Co., Evergreen Textiles, Inc., Elba Apparels, Andala Co., to 1968; gen. counsel, sec., dir. Plumbing Supply Co. Mem. Ala. Law Inst. Adv. Com. for Revision of Probate Code; mem. U. Ala. Pres.'s Cabinet; pres. Lurleen B. Wallace Jr. Coll. Found.; mem. task force on evaluation Ala. State Bar, task force liaison with com. state bar presidents. Bd. dirs. U. Ala. Law Sch. Found. Fellow Am. Coll. Probate Counsel, Am. Inst. Mgmt.; mem. Ala. (pres. 1971-72, mem. permanent com. on Ala. Constn.), Am. (past chmn. real estate, probate and trust sect.), Covington County (pres. 1955) bar assns., Fedn. Ins. Counsel, Ala. Law Inst. (council), Am. Judicature Soc., Ala. Def. Lawyers Assn., World Assn. Lawyers (a founder), Farrah Law Soc., Am. Acad. Polit. and Social Sci., Internat. Platform Assn., Kappa Sigma, Phi Delta Phi. Presbyn. (deacon). Rotarian. Clubs: Andalusia Country (past pres.); Fort Walton (Fla.) Yacht. Editorial adv. bd. Ala. Lawyer. Home: 723 Albritton Rd Andalusia AL 36420 Office: 109 Opp Ave Andalusia AL 34620

ALBRITTON, WILLIAM HAROLD, III, lawyer; b. Andalusia, Ala., Dec. 19, 1936; s. Robert Bynum and Carrie (Veal) A.; diploma Marion Inst. (Ala.), 1955; A.B., U. Ala., 1959, LL.B., 1960; m. Jane Rollins Howard, June 2, 1958; children—William Harold IV, Benjamin Howard, Thomas Bynum. Admitted to Ala. bar, 1960; mem. firm Albrittons & Rankin, Andalusia, 1962-76, firm Albrittons & Givhan, 1976—; dir. TV Cable Co., Andalusia. Chmn., Andalusia Bd. Zoning Adjustment, 1963-64. Mem. Ala. Republican Exec. Com., 1967—; mem. Covington County Rep. Exec. Com., 1967—, chmn., 1970—. Bd. dirs. Covington County chpt. Ala. Soc. Crippled Children and Adults, 1970—. Served to capt. AUS, 1960-62. Mem. Am., Ala. (chmn. ins. programs com. 1978—), Covington County (pres. 1973) bar assns., Andalusia C. of C. (pres. 1967-68), Nat. Assn. R.R. Trial Counsel, Am. Judicature Soc., Ala. Def. Lawyers Assn. (dir. 1970-72, pres. 1976-77), Internat. Assn. Ins. Counsel, Assn. Ins. Attys., U. Ala. Farrah Law Soc., Trial Lawyers Am., Phi Beta Kappa, Phi Delta Phi, Omicron Delta Kappa, Alpha Tau Omega. Presbyterian (elder). Clubs: Andalusia Country (pres. 1977), Rotary (pres. 1979). Home: 730 Albritton Rd Andalusia AL 36420 Office: 109 Opp Ave Andalusia AL 36420

ALCORN, ROBERT STANLEY, ins. agy. exec.; b. San Antonio, Nov. 23, 1949; s. Lloyd Donald and Alberta Marie A.; B.S.B.A., U. Ark., 1972; m. Patricia Elaine Partney, Oct. 5, 1979. Computer, teller, bookkeeper First Nat. Bank, Newport, Ark., 1972-74; ins. office mgr. McCartney, Manning, McDonald & Guinn, Inc., Newport, 1974-76; office mgr., agt. Armstrong Ins. Agy., Tuckerman, Ark., 1976—; owner, real estate broker Jackson County Realty, Tuckerman, 1977—. Mem. Ind. Ins. Agts. Ark. Democrat. Roman Catholic. Club: Service (Tuckerman). Home: PO Box 1050 Tuckerman AR 72473 Office: PO Box 882 Tuckerman AR 72473

ALDER, DIANE LINDSAY, market researcher; b. Chgo., May 26, 1952; d. James Lewis and Gloria June A.; B.A. with high honors, So. Meth. U., 1973; M.B.A., U. Tex., Austin, 1975. Analyst market research, corp. planning Mercantile Nat. Bank, Dallas, 1975-77; mgr. market research Shakey's Inc., Dallas, 1977-78; mgr. research project Bloom Agy., Dallas, 1978—; cons. market research. Mem. Am. Mktg. Assn., Dallas Ad League II, Phi Beta Kappa, Kappa Mu Epsilon, Alpha Lambda Delta, Chi Omega. Home: 9255 Locarno Dallas TX 75243 Office: Bloom Agy PO Box 225975 3000 Diamond Park Dr Dallas TX 75265

ALDERETE, JOSEPH FRANK, med. service adminstr., psychiatrist; b. Las Vegas, N.Mex., Sept. 10, 1920; s. Jose P. and Adela R. (Armijo) A.; B.S. in Chemistry and Biology, Tex. Western Coll., 1950; M.D., Nat. U. Mex., 1959; m. Christine Krajewski, June 24, 1964; children—Joseph Frank, Sarah A. Intern USPHS Hosp., Balt., 1959-60; resident in psychiatry USPHS Hosp., Lexington, Ky., 1960-62; sr. resident in psychiatry U. Hosp., U. Okla. Sch. of Medicine, Oklahoma City, 1962-63; practice medicine specializing in psychiatry, Balt., 1963-65, Springfield, Mo., 1965-67, Atlanta, 1968—; staff psychiatrist USPHS Hosp., Balt., 1963-65; chief of psychiat. service U.S. Med. Center for Fed. Prisoners, Springfield, Mo., 1965-67; clin. and research fellow in electroencephalography Mass. Gen. Hosp.-Harvard, Boston, 1967-68; clin. instr. psychiatry Emory U. Sch. of Medicine, Atlanta, 1968—; chief med. officer, hosp. dir. U.S. Penitentiary Hosp., Atlanta, 1968-78; asst. regional flight surgeon So. Dist., ARTCC, Atlanta, 1978—; psychiat. cons. to Student Health Office, Okla. State U., Stillwater, 1962-63, U.S. Fed. Reformatory, El Reno, Okla., 1962-63. Served with USAF, 1944-48, to capt. AUS, 1948-50. Mem. AMA, Am. Psychiat. Assn., Am. Soc. Clin. Hypnosis, So. EEG Soc., Am., Internat. acads. of law and psychiatry, Acad. of Psychosomatic Medicine, Atlanta Med. Soc., Clin. Soc. of USPHS, Phi Rho Sigma. Contbr. articles to profl. jours. Home: 4130 E Brockett Creek Ct Tucker GA 30084 Office: 299 Woolsey Rd Hampton GA 30228

ALDERMAN, JAMES E., justice Fla. Supreme Ct.; b. Fort Pierce, Fla., Nov. 1, 1936; s. B. E. and Frances (Allen) A.; B.A., U. Fla., 1958, LL.B., 1961; m. Jennie T. Thompson, Mar. 3, 1961; 1 son, James Allen. County judge St. Lucie County (Fla.), 1971-72; circuit judge 19th Jud. Circuit Fla., 1973-76; appellate judge 4th Dist. Ct. Appeals Fla., 1976-78; justice Supreme Ct. Fla., 1978—. Episcopalian. Office: Supreme Ct Bldg Tallahassee FL 32304

ALDERMAN, LOUIS CLEVELAND, JR., coll. pres.; b. Douglas, Ga., Aug. 12, 1924; s. Louis Cleveland and Minnis Amelia (Wooten) A.; A.A., S.Ga. Coll., 1942; A.B., Emory U., 1946; M.S., U. Ga., 1949; postgrad. Columbia, summers 1951-54; Ed.D. (Ford found. fellow), Auburn U., 1959; m. Anne Augusta Whipple, Dec. 31, 1952; children—Amelia Anne, Louis Cleveland III, Fielding Dillard, Jonathan Augustus. USPHS grad. research asst. U. Ga., 1948-49, instr. biology, Rome Center, 1949-50, dir., asst. prof. biology, Savannah Center, 1950-51, Rome Center, 1951-56, Columbus Center, 1956-59; dir. U. Ky., Henderson Coll., 1959-64; pres. Middle Ga. Coll., Cochran, 1964—. Trustee Middle Ga. Coll. Found.; mem. advisory council U. System of Ga.; bd. dirs. Bleckley County Hosp. Authority, Cochran Community House; trustee Ga. Rotary Student Fund; chmn. Cochran-Bleckley Bicentennial Com.; pres. Cochran-Bleckley-Bicentennial Celebration, Inc.; chmn. 8th dist. Ga. State C. of C. Travel Council. Served to sgt. U.S. Army, 1942-46; PTO. Recipient Good Citizenship award Civitan Club, 1955; Club Service award Rotary Internat., 1968-69, Outstanding Rotarian award, 1976; Chmn. of Year award Ga. State C. of C., 1979. Mem. Assn. Higher Edn., Ga. Hist. Soc., SAR, NEA, Ga. Assn. Colls., Ga. Assn. Educators, Ga. Assn. Jr. Colls. (exec. com. 1967-70, pres. 1968-69), Pulaski Hist. Commn. (v.p., bd. dirs.), Ga. Heart Assn. (12th dist. chmn. and cabinet mem.), Cochran-Bleckley C. of C. (1st v.p., dir., v.p.), Phi Delta Kappa, Phi Theta Kappa, Sigma Nu, Phi Beta Lambda, Gamma Beta Phi. Democrat. Baptist (deacon, former chmn. bd. deacons). Rotarian (bd. dirs. 1965-69, 76-79, pres. 1967-68, gov. dist. 692 1976-77), Order Ky. Cols., Magna Charta Barons, Descs. Knight of the Garter, S.A.R. (organizing pres. chpt. 1979). Clubs: Uchee Trail Country, Stateman. Author: Focus on Change, 1964; Fifty Years as Middle Georgia College, 1967; Education in the American Colonies, 1971; History of Old Richland Church, 1972; Signers of The Declaration of Independence, 1974. Contbr. articles to profl. jours. Home: Old Chester Rd Cochran GA 31014 Office: 101 Sanford Hall Middle Ga Coll Cochran GA 31014

ALDOUS, DUANE LEO, educator; b. Albuquerque, Nov. 2, 1930; s. Clarence Moroni and Sarah Eunice (Robinson) A.; B.S., U. N.Mex., 1953, Ph.D., 1961; m. Barbara Kekauoha, July 21, 1955; children—Keith K., Valerie K., Jeffrey N., Melanie K., Wade K. Teaching asst. U. N.Mex., 1956-58; research chemist E.I. duPont, Kinston, N.C., 1962-68; asst. prof. pharm. chemistry Xavier U. La., New Orleans, 1968-71, asso. prof., 1971—, acting dean, 1973, dean Coll. Pharmacy, 1974—. Bishop, Metairie ward Ch. of Jesus Christ of Latter Day Saints, 1978—. Served with U.S. Army, 1953-56. Mem. Am. Chem. Soc., Am. Assn. Colls. Pharmacy, AAUP, Internat. Soc. Heterocyclic Chemists, La. Pharmacists Assn., Sigma Xi, Kappa Psi. Home: 5917 Marcie St Metairie LA 70003 Office: 7325 Palmetto St New Orleans LA 70125

ALDREDGE, JAMES HENRY, JR., counselor; b. Danville, Va., May 8, 1917; s. James Henry and Bessie (Wagner) A.; B.S. in Bus. Adminstrn., Va. Poly. Inst. and State U., 1941, M.Ed. in Vocat. Edn., 1971. With Danville Industries, Inc. (Va.), 1947-65, asst. sec.-treas., 1953-58, sec.-treas., 1958-65; indsl. coop. tng. coordinator Petersburg (Va.) Public Schs., 1965-67, vocat. guidance counselor, 1967—; vocat. edn. cons. Served to maj. Insp. Gen.'s Dept. and Coast Arty. Corps, U.S. Army, 1941-46. Cert. guidance counselor Va. Bd. Edn.; lic. profl. counselor, Va. Mem. NEA, Am. Vocat. Assn., Am. Personnel and Guidance Assn., Nat. Vocat. Guidance Assn., Am. Sch. Counselor Assn., Nat. Assn. Trade and Indsl. Educators, Va. Edn. Assn., Va. Vocat. Assn., Va. Personnel and Guidance Assn., Va. Vocat. Guidance Assn., Va. Sch. Counselor Assn., Va. Trade and Indsl. Educators, Petersburg Edn. Assn., Va. Poly. Inst. Alumni Assn. (past pres. Danville area). Methodist. Clubs: Golf (Danville); Lions (Petersburg); Masons (past master), K.T., Shriners. Home: 1551 Berkeley Ave Petersburg VA 23803 Office: Petersburg Pub Schs 3101 Johnson Rd Petersburg VA 23803

ALDRICH, DOUGLAS FORD, info. systems cons.; b. Troy, N.Y., July 18, 1951; s. Theodore Henry and Zelma Edith (Blackman) A.; A.A.S., Purdue U., 1971, B.S., 1974; M.B.A., Ind. U., 1978; m. Debra Ann Shipman, Feb. 6, 1971; children—Dara Jeanette, Amanda Lee. With GTE Data Services, Ft. Wayne, Ind., 1970-72; programmer Lincoln Nat. Corp., Ft. Wayne, 1972-74; systems project leader Cummins Engine Co., Columbus, Ind., 1974-78; mgr. info. systems cons. Arthur Young Co., Dallas, 1978—; instr. Ind. U.-Purdue U., Indpls., 1975-78; speaker nat. seminar Computer Security Inst. Cert. data processor, data processing auditor. Mem. Assn. EDP Auditors, Assn. of MBA Execs. Home: 1700 Windsong Trail Richardson TX 75081 Office: 2900 Republic Bank Bldg Dallas TX 75201

ALDRICH, LYMAN DAVENPORT, real estate investment co. exec.; b. N.Y.C., Aug. 14, 1943; s. Lyman D. and Elizabeth (Franklin) A.; B.B.A., U. Miss., 1966; grad. Stonier Grad. Sch. Banking, Rutgers U., 1973. Vice-pres. First Nat. Bank of Memphis, 1967-76; pres. Aldrich & Assos., Memphis, 1976—, also dir.; co-founder, past chmn. bd. regents Memphis Sch. Banking. Fund raising chmn. St. Jude Hosp., 1972; co-chmn. fund raising Memphis Arts Council, 1972; vice-chmn. Mayor's Youth Guidance Commn., 1975; Memphis div. treas. Am. Cancer Soc., 1972; mem. exec. com. Forum for a Better Memphis, 1976-77; v.p. Beale St. Devel. Corp., 1971-75; founder, pres. Memphis In May Internat. Festival Soc., 1976, chmn., 1977; co-founder pres. Memphis Music, Inc., 1973-74; mem. exec. com. Memphis Cotton Carnival Assn., 1972-76. Recipient Pioneer award for downtown devel., 1979. Mem. Memphis Area C. of C. (dir. 1976-78). Republican. Episcopalian. Clubs: University of Memphis, Petroleum, Delta, Phoenix of Memphis. Home: 107 S Front St Memphis TN 38103 Office: 66 S Front St Memphis TN 38103

ALDRIDGE, CLAUDIA KAY, counselor; b. Houston, Oct. 14, 1942; d. Claude Bryant and Florence Estelle (Ritz) Aldridge; B.A., Tex. Christian U., 1964; M.A., U. Houston, 1974. Tchr. minimal brain injured Houston Ind. Sch. Dist., 1966-69, speech pathologist, 1969-73, diagnostic tchr., 1973-74, elementary sch. counselor, 1974—; trainee in speech pathology Houston VA Hosp., 1966, U. Houston Drug Abuse Counselors' Program, 1975, Summer Inst. Social Service Workers, 1976—. Mem. Houston Symphony Chorale, 1967-72, Houston Gilbert and Sullivan Soc., 1965-68. Certified secondary sch. tchr., speech pathologist, sch. counselor. Mem. Am. Personnel and Guidance Assn., Houston Tchrs. Assn., NEA, Mortar Board, Delta Gamma, Phi Beta. Mem. Christian Ch. Home: 800 S Post Oak Apt 99 Houston TX 77056 Office: 3830 Richmond Houston TX 77027

ALDRIDGE, IRIS RUTH SMITH, ednl. adminstr.; b. Kinston, N.C., Dec. 25, 1926; d. Heber and Lena Melissa (Spain) Smith; B.S., E. Carolina U., 1952, M.A., 1962, Ed.S., 1976; postgrad. U. N.C., Greensboro, 1957, 63; m. Carl Francis Aldridge, Aug. 14, 1945; children—Linda Jeanne, Heber Carl, Lorelei. High sch. home econs. tchr., Deep Run, N.C., 1954-60; vocat. rehab. home econs. tchr., supr. mentally retarded, Kinston, N.C., 1960-65; high sch. guidance counselor, South Lenoir, 1965-72; acad. dir. Lenoir County Sch., Kinston, 1972—. Pres. County 4-H Leaders Orgn., 1975-76, adult leader, 1970-80, named outstanding Adult 4-H Leader, 1977. Recipient Tchr. of Yr. award S. Lenoir High Sch. PTA, 1969. Mem. Nat. Assn. Educators, Assn. Supervision and Curriculum Devel., N.C. Assn. Educators (past pres. local unit), Dist. Home Econs. Assn. (past pres.). Democrat. Baptist. Club: Order Eastern Star. Home: Route 5 Box 318 Kinston NC 28501 Office: 201 E King St Kinston NC 28501

ALDRIDGE, RICHARD CAMPBELL, JR., nurseryman; b. Center Point, Tex., Mar. 9, 1925; s. Richard Campbell (Sr.) and Tweena (Lange) A.; grad. high sch.; m. Meredith Emily Bailey, May 7, 1941; children—Donald Wayne, Mark Vinton, Connie Lynn Aldridge Brannan, Gwenda Aldridge Neel, David Richard. With Aldridge Nursery, Inc., Von Ormy, Tex., 1940—, gen. mgr., 1960-74, pres., 1974—. Bd. trustees S.W. Ind. Sch. Dist., 1957, v.p., 1960-62, pres., 1963-78. Mem. exec. com. Bexar County Fedn. Sch. Bds., 1970-78, Bexar County Mental Health and Mental Retardation Assn., 1971-73; life mem. Tex. PTA, Nat. PTA. Served with USCG, 1943-46; PTO. Mem. Am. (lt. gov. 1973-75, gov. 1975—), San Antonio (hon. life), Tex. (regional dir. 1973-77, v.p. 1976-77, pres. 1978-79) assns. nurserymen, Internat. Platform Assn., Tex. Hort. Soc. (dir. 1979), Youth for Christ Assn. Democrat. Baptist. Address: Route 1 Box 8 Von Ormy TX 78073

ALEWINE, JAMES WILLIAM, financial exec.; b. Williamston, S.C., Apr. 26, 1930; s. David Andrew and Ruby Mae (Moore) A.; B.A., Carolina Sch. Commerce, 1961; m. Bobbie Sue Crawford, June 18, 1949; children—David, Susan. With Daniel Internat. Corp., 1947—, mgr. internal audit, Greenville, S.C., 1970-72, adminstrv. mgr. M & M div., 1972-73, fin. adminstr., Jenkinsville, S.C., 1973-77, mgr. accounting M-E-T Group, Greenville, 1977-78, asst. treas., 1978—. Served with USN, 1952-55. Cert. internal auditor, S.C. Mem. Inst. Internal Auditors (pres. Palmetto chpt. 1975-76). Baptist. Clubs: Masons (past grand high priest, knight York grand cross of honour), Elks. Home: 2 Broad St Williamston SC 29697 Office: Daniel Bldg Greenville SC 29602

ALEXANDER, ANDREW BUCHANAN, computer programmer; b. Harrodsburg, Ky., Mar. 9, 1942; s. James Menifee and Gladys (Davenport) A.; student U. Ky., 1960-66; m. Patricia Gale Sutton, Mar. 22, 1968; children—Gladys Lee, Ann Frances. Clk., Hoover Food Store, Harrodsburg, 1958; cashier, clk. Kroger Co., Harrodsburg, 1958-65; systems programmer U. Ky. Computing Center, Lexington, 1966-67, lead analyst/programmer, 1971—, instr., 1974. Served with U.S. Army, 1964. Mem. Data Processing Mgmt. Assn., Systems Mgmt. Assn. Democrat. Presbyterian. Club: Ky. Cols. Musical compositions include: A Christmas Fantasia, 1975; An Improvisation on Greensleeves, 1976; Petite Noel, 1976; Kyrie Eleison, 1976; contbr. articles to profl. jours. Office: Computing Center McVey Hall U Ky Lexington KY 40506

ALEXANDER, AUBREY MURRAY, JR., radiologist; b. New Orleans, Feb. 19, 1924; s. Aubrey Murray and Mary Theresa (James) A.; B.S., La. State U., 1943, M.D., 1946; m. Shirley Mary Simeon, Sept. 29, 1946; children—Rebecca, Aubrey III, Susan, Barbara. Intern, New Orleans Charity Hosp., 1946-47, resident, 1948-49, 51-54; practice medicine specializing in radiology, Alexandria, La., 1954—; radiologist, cons. St. Francis Cabrini Hosp., Huey P. Long Charity Hosp., Pineville, La., VA Hosp., Pineville; clin. instr. dept. medicine Med. Sch., Tulane U., New Orleans; pres. La. State Health Coordinating Council. Pres. Caula Community Theatre, 1965-67. Served in USAF, 1949-51. Mem. Am. Coll. Radiology, Am. Coll. Nuclear Medicine Am. Soc. Nuclear Medicine, AMA, La., Rapides Parish (pres.) med. socs., La. Radiol. Soc. (past pres.). Democrat. Roman Catholic. Home: 3409 Parkway Dr Alexandria LA 71301 Office: 3330 Masonic Dr Alexandria LA 71301

ALEXANDER, BEATRICE WITTE, educator; b. Fredericksburg, Tex., Jan. 1, 1922; d. Oliver Bernard and Will Mignon (Whiting) Witte; B.A., Tex. Woman's U., 1942; M.A., U. Tex., Austin, 1946; m. Theodor Walter Alexander, Sept. 6, 1947; children—Richard Witte, Ronald Walter. Instr. fgn. langs. Tex. Tech. U., Lubbock, 1945-61, asst. prof. French, 1961-71, asso. prof., 1971—. Recipient first Pi Delta Phi Nat. award for chpt. moderators, 1969. Mem. Modern Lang. Assn. Am., Am. Assn. Tchrs. French, South Central Modern Lang. Assn., AAUW. Methodist. Contbr. articles to profl. jours. Home: 3405 25th St Lubbock TX 79410 Office: Box 4649 Dept Classical and Romance Langs Tex Tech U Lubbock TX 79409

ALEXANDER, DANNY LEVERT, educator; b. Dumas, Tex., Sept. 12, 1950; s. Aubrey Levert and Effie Estle (Johnson) A.; B.S., U. Ala., 1972, M.A., 1973, Ed.S., 1974. Tchr. social studies Eleanor McMain Magnet Secondary Sch., New Orleans, 1975—. Mem. Am. Personnel and Guidance Assn., Am. Sch. Counselor Assn., U. Ala. Alumni Assn., U. Ala. Capstone Found. Assn., Phi Delta Kappa. Democrat. Baptist. Home: 1020 Esplanade St Apt 203 New Orleans LA 70116 Office: 5712 S Claiborne Ave New Orleans LA 70125

ALEXANDER, DIETRICH BIEMANN, JR., bldg. components mfg. and constrn. co. exec.; b. Greenwood, S.C., Aug. 28, 1902; s. Dietrich Biemann and Lillian (Malone) A.; B.C.E., The Citadel, 1922; LL.B., Woodrow Wilson Coll. Law, 1938; postgrad. Babson Inst., summers 1940-41; m. Merridy Wefing, Mar. 3, 1930; children—Dietrich Biemann III, Merridy Wefing (Mrs. Alexander Lloyd), Stanton Malone. Tchr., coach Thomas Indsl. Inst., De Funiak Springs, Fla., 1922-23; with Atlantic Steel Co., Atlanta, 1923-45, asst. sec.-treas. 1925-45; admitted to Ga. State bar, 1938; partner Mitchell & Alexander Lumber Co., Daytona Beach, Fla., 1945-49; chmn. bd., chief exec. officer Prefab Bldg. Components, Holly Hill, Fla., 1969—; pres. Alexander Constrn. Co., Holly Hill, 1969—; pres. Daytona Beach Builders Exchange, 1962. Mem. Daytona Beach Zoning Bd., 1947-50; mem. Recreation and Parks Adv. Council, Region IV, State of Fla., 1972—; pres. Daytona Community Chest, 1948; chmn. camping com. Central Fla. council Boy Scouts Am., 1956-62; bd. visitors Embry-Riddle U., 1971—. Mem. Fla. Bldg. Material Dealers Assn. (pres. 1958-59), Daytona Beach C. of C. (v.p. 1953, dir. 1952-55), Daytona Beach Mchts. Assn. (dir. 1947-51), U.S. Navy League. Episcopalian (sr. warden 1962, vestryman 1954-62). Clubs: Kiwanis (pres. Daytona Beach, 1949), Piedmont Driving (hon. life mem.) (Atlanta); University of Volusia County (dir. 1963-68, pres. 1966), Halifax River Yacht, Daytona Beach Quarterback. Home: The Pendleton Club 1224 S Peninsula Dr Daytona Beach FL 32018 Office: 336 11th St Holly Hill FL 32017

ALEXANDER, E. CURTIS, ednl. cons.; b. Norfolk, Va., Sept. 24, 1941; s. Albert Tilton and Fidelia (Holley) A.; A.B. in Sociology, Norfolk State Coll., 1967; M.S. in Edn., Bank St. Coll. of Edn., N.Y.C., 1970; certificate Inst. African Studies U. Ghana, 1970; Ed.M., Tchrs. Coll., Columbia U., 1972, Ed.D., 1977; D.D., Universal Bible Inst., 1974; postgrad. Makerere U., Uganda, 1976, U. of Dar Es Salaam, Tanzania, 1976; m. Barbara Johnson, July 2, 1966; children—Kwame, Sia, Nataki. Ordained to ministry Baptist Ch., 1972; community organizer Morningside Heights Inc., N.Y.C., 1967-68; social caseworker for div. of day care Dept. of Social Services, N.Y.C., 1967-69; nat. talent pool cons. Leadership Tng. Inst. for Career Opportunities Program, U.S. Office of Edn., Washington, 1972-74; instr. of early childhood Barber-Scotia Coll., Concord, N.C., 1970-71; adminstrv. dir. Logan Homes Day Care Center, Concord, N.C., 1971; asst. prof. of urban edn. Antioch Grad. Sch. of Edn., N.Y.C., 1971-72; asst. prof. of early childhood edn. William Paterson Coll. of N.J., 1972-74, adj. prof. edn. Tombrock Coll., N.J., 1973-74; adminstrv. dir. Unity and Work Sch., Paterson, N.J., 1973-74, founder child-centered pre-sch. program, 1973; asst. prof. early childhood edn. A. and T. State U., Greensboro, N.C., 1975; ednl. cons. to Johnston County (N.C.) Community Action Program, 1972—, Council of Ind. Instns., N.Y.C., 1973—, Bd. of Global Missions, United Meth. Ch., 1974—, William M. Young & Associates, Oak Park, Ill., 1975—; human and race relations cons. Med. Center Hospitals Complex, Norfolk, Va., 1975—; mem. adj. faculty dept. sociology Norfolk (Va.) State Coll., 1975-76; adj. lectr. on African-Am. history Tidewater Community Coll., Chesapeake, Va., 1976-77, also counselor, 1974-75; regional coordinator for kindergarten-early childhood Ednl. Dist. IV, State Dept. Pub. Instruction, Fayetteville, N.C., 1974-75; pres. E. Curtis Alexander Associates, Chesapeake, 1977—; examiner team staff of Cosmetology Accrediting Commn., Washington, 1977—. Recipient Meritorious Service award Community Day Nursery Assn., 1971, Outstanding Community Service award Philemon Pre-Sch. Nursery, 1973; certified tchr., N.Y., Va. Fellow Internat. Inst. of Community Services; mem. Internat. Adult Edn. Assn., Nat. Assn. of Black Social Workers, Nat. Assn. for Edn. of Young Children, Am. Assn. of Sex Educators, Counselors and Therapists, Assn. of Evang. Institutional Chaplains, AAUP, Fayetteville Child Devel. Council (adviser 1974-77), Phi Delta Kappa, Kappa Delta Pi. Contbr. articles on teaching and childhood edn. to profl. jours. Home: 925 Main Creek Rd Chesapeake VA 23320 Office: 1045 Bells Mill Rd Chesapeake VA 23320

ALEXANDER, EUGENE DENNY, athletic dir.; b. Detroit, Oct. 5, 1945; s. Frank and Viva Elaine A.; B.S., Aquinas Coll., 1967; M.A., Central Mich. U., 1974; m. Linda Lee Jones, Dec. 2, 1967; children—Darwyn, Brandi. Tchr. bus., basketball coach Detroit East Catholic High Sch., 1967-72; instr., asst. basketball coach Central Mich. U., 1972-78; dir. athletes, head basketball coach Xavier U., New Orleans, 1978—. Mem. AAHPER. Baptist. Home: 5014 Howard Ave New Orleans LA 70125 Office: 7325 Palmetto St New Orleans LA 70125

ALEXANDER, EWELL FREDERICK, fund-raising cons.; b. Independence, Mo., June 27, 1923; s. Alvin Paul and Mary Angeline (Ross) A.; student Graceland Coll., 1941-42, U. Mo., 1944-45; m. Audentha Rogers, Nov. 24, 1943; children—Linda Gail Alexander Dickens, Michael Grant, Dana Alexander Taylor. Announcer, Midland Broadcasting Co., Kansas City, Mo., 1945-54; fund-raising cons. and not-for-profit corp. mgmt. cons. for various groups including: Reformed Ch. of Am., N. Ark. Conf. of United Meth. Ch., Inst. of Ch. Renewal, Atlanta, Kidney Found. of Tenn., Methodist Hosp., Memphis, Wheaton (Ill.) Acad., Research Hosp., Kansas City, Mo., Le Bonheur Childrens Hosp., Memphis; participant in seminars and confs. throughout U.S.; founder Philadelphia Ch., 1978. Served with USAF, 1942-44. Contbr. articles in field to profl. jours. Home and Office: 6978 Neshoba St Germantown TN 38138

ALEXANDER, GEORGE MOYER, bishop; b. Jacksonville, Fla., May 15, 1914; s. George and Monimia (Starratt) A.; student U. Fla., 1935; B.A., U. of South, 1938, B.D., 1939, S.T.M., Grad. Sch. Theology, 1957, D.C.L., 1973; D.D., Va. Theol. Sem., 1957; S.T.D., Seabury-Western Theol. Sem., 1957; m. Mary Danto Bedell, May 25, 1935; children—Stephen Gray, John Rowell. Ordained priest Episcopal Ch., 1940; priest-in-charge St. Mary's, Green Cove Springs, Fla., 1939-42; rector St. Mark's, Palatka, Fla., 1942-44, Holy Trinity Ch., Gainesville, Fla., 1945-48, Trinity Ch., Columbia, S.C., 1949-55; fellow Gen. Theol. Sem., 1955-56; dean Sch. Theology, U. of South, 1956-73; consecrated bishop Diocese of Upper S.C., 1973; lectr. St. Augustine's Coll., Canterbury, 1960. Mem. Diocese of Fla. (sec. 1941-48), Diocese of Upper S.C. (sec. 1953-54), Nat. Council Episcopal Ch.; dep to Gen. Conv. P.E. Ch. Chmn. County Welfare Bd., Alachua County, Fla. Bd. dirs. Community Chest, United Fund; bd. regents U. of South, 1950-55. Author: The Handbook of Biblical Personalities, 1962; Henry Disbrow Phillips, 1968. Contbr. articles to church publs. Office: PO Box 1789 Columbia SC 29202

ALEXANDER, JAMES ATWELL, poultryman; b. Stony Point, N.C. July 23, 1911; s. J. Will and Mary Emma (Alexander) A.; A.B. Davidson Coll., 1929, M.A., 1931; student Colo. Sch. Mines, 1930, postgrad. U. N.C., 1932-34 ; m. Anna Pauline Hill, Dec. 23, 1938; children—Mary Anna, Eva Pauline. Seismologist Shell Oil Co., Houston, 1937-40; owner, mgr. Alexander Poultry Farm, Stony Point, 1940— bd. of dirs. Alexander County Water Corp. Chmn. Alexander County Poultry Council, 1953-55, Catawaba Soil Conservation Dist. Conservation Dist. Suprs., 1949-51; mem. adv. com. poultry test, 1958—; mem. gen. bd. Northwestern Bank, 1971—. Mem. Bd. Commrs., Alexander County, 1950-54, Welfare Bd., 1952-54, Alexander County Planning Bd., 1969—; mem. N.C. State Bd. Agr., 1955—; mem. Gov.'s Adv. Com. Nuclear Energy, N.C., 1957—; mem. N.C. Gov.'s Council on Occupational Health, N.C. Gov.'s Council on Rehab.; chmn. N.C. Gov.'s Adv. Com. Agr., 1965—; mem. exec. com. Gov's Council for Econ. Devel. Mem. Fair Commn., Dixie Classic Fair, Winston-Salem, N.C. Bd. dirs. Alexander County Hosp.; exec. com. N.C. Agrl. Found., 1965—, v.p., 1967; adv. com. Sch. Agr. N.C. State U. Named Man of the year, Grange of Alexander County, N.C., 1957, Alexander County C. of C., 1967; N.C. Outstanding Farm Mgr., 1965, N.C. County Agrl. Agts. award, 1971; named to N.C. Poultry Hall Fame, 1976. Mem. N.C. Acad. Sci., N.W. N.C. Devel. Assn. (pres., chmn agrl div. award 1969), C. of C. (dir.), N.C. Egg Mktg. Assn. (pres. 1961-62), N.C. Poultry Council (pres. 1963), N.C. Vocat. Agrl. Tchrs. Assn. (hon.), N.C. Agribusiness Council (exec.

com.), Sigma Xi, Gamma Sigma Epsilon, Gamma Sigma Delta, Sigma Gamma Epsilon. Democrat. Lion (charter mem., zone chmn.). Home: Stony Point NC 28678

ALEXANDER, JAMES EDWIN, bus. exec.; b. Indianola, Iowa, Feb. 16, 1930; s. James Eugene and Lillian Esther (Gamble) A.; B.A., U. Pacific, 1959; S.T.B., Boston U., 1962; M.A., Claremont Grad. Sch., 1965; Ph.D., Vanderbilt U., 1972, postgrad. in Law, 1976; m. Joan Frances Harris, June 28, 1952; children—James Michael, Michele Alene, Marsha Ann. Chief engr. Radio Sta. KJOY, Stockton, Calif., 1955-59; instr. broadcasting U. Pacific, 1956-59, lectr. Bible, 1963-65; owner, operator Stockton Teletronics, 1956-59; studio engr. Radio Sta. WHDH, Boston, 1960; teaching fellow Boston U., Coll. Bus. Adminstrn., 1960-62; ordained to ministry Methodist Ch., 1960; pastor Gleasondale (Mass.) Meth. Ch., 1960-62; asso. pastor Central Meth. Ch., Stockton, 1962-65, Claremont (Calif.) Meth. Ch., 1966-67; dir. printed resources Meth. Bd. Edn., United Meth. Ch., Nashville, 1967-70, asst. gen. sec., 1970-75, exec. dir. communications, 1976-78; exec. dir. The Other Sch. System, Inc., 1978—; pres. Music City Thirty, Inc., 1979—; dir. Public Service Satellite Corp. Mem. Calif. Gov.'s Council on Aging, 1964-65, panel distinguished scholars New Media Bible, 1975—; mem. exec. bd. Christian Youth Publs., 1967-75; mem. adv. com. Nat. Orgns. Corp. for Public Broadcasting, 1974—; mem. Lake Placid Winter Olympics Com., 1977-80. Served with USN, 1947-55. Decorated Letter of Commendation; recipient Walker awards for excellence in classical studies U. Pacific, 1956, 57, 58, citation Senate and Assembly State of Calif. for TV series, 1965; Jacob Sleeper fellow Boston U., 1965. Mem. Am. Acad. Religion, Am. Mgmt. Assn., Nat. Assn. Ednl. Broadcasters, Soc. Bibl. Lit., Religious Pub. Relations Council, Soc. for Antiquity and Christianity. Author: Abstracts from Federal Communications Law, 1958; Audiovisual Facilities for Churchmen, 1970; Ethical Factors in Management Decision, 1972; Mass Media Models of Education, 1975; Emerging Developments in Educational Television, 1976; Footprints in Space: Religious Applications of Communications Satellites, 1977; contbr. articles to religious publs. Exec. producer The Other School System, 1978. Home: 712 Adkisson Ln Nashville TN 37205 Office: PO Box 840 Nashville TN 37202

ALEXANDER, JANIE OLIVIA SMALLS, counselor; b. Savannah, Ga., Aug. 22, 1923; d. Frank James and Georgia Ann Smalls; B.S., Savannah State Coll., 1942; M.A., N.Y. U., 1964; m. Jonathan C. Alexander, July 24, 1944; children—Jonathan C., Sharon Ann. Elementary tchr. George W. Carver Sch., Bryan County, Ga., 1942-43; music tchr. Tompkins High Sch., Savannah, 1944-65, Cuyler Jr. High Sch., Savannah, 1965-73; sch. counselor Sprague Elem. Sch., Jackson and Florance St. Elem. Schs., Barnard Sch., Savannah, 1973-79, ret., 1979; cons. in field, Savannah, 1979—. Active YMCA, NAACP. Recipient Nat. Alumni Assn. Savannah State Coll. award, 1968; service awards Bd. Public Edn. City of Savannah, 1979, Ga. Assn. Educators, 1979; Tchr. of Yr. awards Tompkins High Sch., 1963-64, music trophy, 1962, plaque, 1971, service award 1976; Tchr. of Yr. awards Cuyler Jr. High Sch., 1967-68, PTA service awards, 1966, 67, 70; outstanding service plaque Jackson Elem. Sch. and community, 1979. Mem. NEA, Chatham County Edn. Assn., Am. Personnel and Guidance Assn., Nat. Piano Guild. Presbyterian. Home: 1110 W 42nd St Savannah GA 31401

ALEXANDER, LAMAR, gov. Tenn.; b. Blount County, Tenn., July 3, 1940; B.A., Vanderbilt U.; J.D., N.Y. U., 1965; m. Leslee Kathryn Buhler, Jan. 4, 1969; children—Drew, Leslee, Kathryn, Will. Admitted to Tenn. bar, 1965; asso. firm Fowler, Rountree, Fowler and Robertson, Knoxville, Tenn., 1965; former law clk. U.S. Ct. Appeals for 5th Circuit, New Orleans; campaign coordinator for Howard Baker's U.S. Senate race, 1966; legis. asst. to U.S. Senator Howard Baker, Washington, 1967-69; exec. asst. to counselor in charge congressional relations White House, Washington, 1969-70; mgr. gubernatorial campaign of Winfield Dunn, Tenn., 1970; partner firm Dearborn & Ewing, Nashville, 1971; founder, co-chmn. Tenn. Citizens for Revenue Sharing, 1971; founder, 1st chmn. Tenn. Council on Crime and Delinquency, 1973; polit. commentator TV sta., Nashville, 1975-77; spl. counsel to Senate minority leader Howard Baker, 1977; gov. State of Tenn., Nashville, 1979—. Mem. Am. Bar Assn., Phi Beta Kappa. Republican. Presbyterian. Office: Office of Gov State Capitol Bldg Nashville TN 37219

ALEXANDER, LOUIS, writer, educator; b. N.Y.C., Mar. 15, 1917; s. Louis I. and Gertrude (Seydel) A.; B.S. in Mktg., U. Newark, 1941; M. Letters in Journalism, U. Houston, 1961 m. Paulette Marlowe, Dec. 23, 1948 (div. Dec. 20, 1968); children—Kathryn, Marjory Lynn; m. 2d, Mildred Nootsie Crowe, Aug. 8, 1976. Reporter, county editor Houston Chronicle, 1947-57; free-lance writer for mags. and newspapers, 1957—; instr., then asst. prof. journalism U. Houston, 1954—; corr. Wall Street Jour., 1959-75, Newsweek, 1964—, Nat. Pub. Radio, 1972—; dir. All-Media Properties, Inc., Houston, Radio Sta. KEYH. Mem. Bellaire Parks and Recreation Commn., 1957-60; mem. fin. subcom. Sch. Adv. Com., Bellaire, 1976-77; mem. citizens adv. bd. Met. Transit Authority, 1978—. Served with USAAF, 1942-45; to capt. USAF, 1951-52; lt. col. Res. Decorated D.F.C., Air medal with three oak leaf clusters. Mem. Aviation/Space Writers Assn., Assn. Petroleum Writers, Assn. Edn. in Journalism, Nat. Conf. Editorial Writers. Club: Press (Houston). Author: Beyond the Facts, 1975. Home: 704 Mulberry Ln Bellaire TX 77401 Office: Sch Communication U Houston TX 77004

ALEXANDER, MARY LOUISE, educator; b. Ennis, Tex., Jan. 15, 1926; d. Emmett F. and Florence (Hill) Alexander; B.A., U. Tex., 1947, M.A., 1949, Ph.D., 1951. Instr., research asst. Genetics Found., U. Tex., Austin, 1944-51, postdoctoral research fellow, 1952-55, research scientist Genetics Found., 1962-68; postdoctoral fellow biology div. AEC, Oak Ridge, 1951-52; research asso. U. Tex.-M.D. Anderson Hosp. and Tumor Inst., Houston, 1956-58, asst. biologist, 1959-62; asso. prof. biology S.W. Tex. State U., San Marcos, 1967-69, prof., 1969—. Research cons. Brookhaven Nat. Lab., Upton, N.Y., 1955; research participant Oak Ridge Inst. Nuclear Studies, Tenn., 1951-77. Nat. Cancer Inst. fellow Inst. Animal Genetics, Edinburgh, Scotland, 1960-61. Mem. Genetics Soc. Am., Radiation Research Soc., Am. Soc. Human Genetics, Sigma Xi, Gamma Phi Beta, Phi Sigma, Alpha Epsilon Delta. Home: Hunter's Glen Route 2 Box 119 San Marcos TX 78666

ALEXANDER, ROBERT HAROLD, psychologist; b. Alton, Ill., Sept. 18, 1918; s. Harold C. and Florence M. (Steiner) A.; B.A., Washington U., St. Louis, 1940, M.A., 1948, Ph.D., 1953; 1 son, Richard Robert. Psychometrist, VA 1946-47; instr. Washington U., 1947-48; chief area psychologist Ill. Dept. Pub. Instrn., 1949-55; chmn. dept. psychology Mac Murray Coll., Jacksonville, Ill., 1955-57; research dir. Springfield (Ill.) Mental Health Clinic, 1956-57; clin. psychologist in pvt. practice, Springfield, 1957-68, Jacksonville, Fla., 1968—. Served from 2d lt. to capt. AUS, 1941-45; ETO. Recipient Gold medal Fla. Mental Health Assn., 1976; licensed psychologist, Ill., Fla. Mem. Am., Fla., psychol. assns., Am. Soc. Clin. Hypnosis, Am. Assn. Marriage, Family Counselors, Internat. Soc. Hypnosis, U.S. Power Squadron. Clubs: Masons, Shriners. Editor socially and emotionally maladjusted sect. Dictionary of Edn., 1958. Home: 7901 Bay Meadows Circle E #358 Jacksonville FL 32216 Office: 2137 Park St Jacksonville FL 32217

ALEXANDER, RON DURWOOD, elec. equipment mfg. co. exec.; b. Phoenix, Sept. 2, 1942; s. George Clude and Clotell (Poore) A.; B.A., So. Meth. U., 1963; m. Celia Cadaval, Jan. 9, 1975; children—Andres, Anthony. With Lake Catherine Footwear, Inc., Hot Springs, Ark., 1963-70, personnel dir., 1965-70; dir. mfg. Montego Bay Treading Co., Buenos Aires, Argentina, 1970-75, Neco de Mex. div. Sunbeam Corp., Matamoros, Mex., 1975—. Chmn. bd. Garland County Mental Health Soc., Hot Springs, 1972; bd. dirs. Garland United Fund, 1965-68, mem. budget com., 1964-67; bd. dirs. YMCA, 1965-68. Republican. Methodist. Clubs: Rotary, Lions. Office: PO Box 4519 Brownsville TX 78520

ALEXANDER, THEODOR WALTER, educator; b. Vienna, Austria, Aug. 1, 1919; s. Gustav and Gisela (Rubel) A.; B.S., Tex. Tech. U., 1946, M.S., 1947; m. Beatrice Witte, Sept. 6, 1947; children—Richard Witte, Ronald Walter. Instr., Tex. Tech. U., Lubbock, 1947-53, asst. prof., 1954-58, asso. prof., 1959-67, prof. German, 1968—; vis. asso. prof. U. Tex., Austin, summer 1960. Served with AUS, 1941. Recipient Distinguished Teaching award Standard Oil (Ind.) Found., Inc., 1969. Mem. Modern Lang. Assn. Am., Am. Assn. Tchrs. German, South Central Modern Lang. Assn., Internat. Arthur Schnitzler Research Assn. Contbr. articles to profl. jours. Home: 3405 25th St Lubbock TX 79410 Office: Box 4579 Tex Tech U Lubbock TX 79409

ALEXANDER, THOMAS EATON, JR., mfg. co. exec.; b. New Orleans, July 28, 1912; s. Thomas Eaton and Dora A. (Hingle) A.; B.S., Tulane U., 1935; m. Jeanne Perrodin, July 28, 1951; children—Thomas Eaton III, Sidney D., James H. Mech. engr. Equitable Equipment Co., New Orleans, 1936-39, sales engr. 1939-44; sales and service engr. Crane Packing Co., Baton Rouge and New Orleans, 1944-58; pres. KP Industries, mfr. check valves, Baton Rouge, 1967—; pres. Power Packing Co., Inc., mfr. mech. seals and packings, Baton Rouge, 1958—. Registered profl. engr., La. Mem. Am. ASME (dir. Baton Rouge chpt. 1966-70), Baton Rouge Council Engrs. and Sci. Soc. (pres. 1961), La.ngrs. Soc. (pres. Baton Rouge 1960), Nat. Soc. Profl. Engrs. Methodist (dir. 1969—). Clubs: Sherwood Forest Country, City. Home: 11308 Goodwood Blvd Baton Rouge LA 70815 Office: 2769 Mission St Baton Rouge LA 70805

ALEXANDER, THOMAS WILLIS, ins. exec.; b. Charlotte, N.C., Jan. 11, 1910; s. Thomas W. and Alice (Spruill) A.; B.S., U. N.C., 1932, postgrad. exec. program, 1956-57; m. Shirley Haywood, Feb. 18, 1939; 1 son, Thomas W.H. With S.H. Kress Co., Roanoke, Va., 1932-33; dep. commr. N.C. Revenue Dept., Raleigh, 1933-40; with State Capital Life Ins. Co., Raleigh, 1945-69, exec. v.p., 1967-69, treas., 1947-69, dir., 1955-69, exec. v.p. (through merger Durham Life Ins. Co.), 1970-75, pres., 1973-75; pres. treas., Haywood Real Estate Co., Raleigh, 1947—; dir. N.C. Nat. Bank, Raleigh, Durham Life Broadcasting Service, Raleigh, 1970—; chmn. N.C. Bus. Devel. Corp., 1973—. Chmn., N.C. Bd. Assessment, 1967-71; chmn. N.C. Tax Study Commn., 1965-66. Treas., Research Triangle, 1959—, dir., 1970—; pres. United Fund, 1964; chmn. bd. trustees St. Mary's Coll., 1975-80. Served to lt. comdr. USNR, 1940-45; PTO. Mem. U. N.C. Alumni Assn. (pres. 1958-59), Delta Kappa Epsilon. Rotarian (pres. 1955-56). Clubs: Carolina Country, Circle (Raleigh); Coral Bay (Atlantic Beach, N.C.). Home and Office: 2831 Exeter Circle Raleigh NC 27608

ALEXANDER, WILLIAM ALANSON, III, architect; b. Plainfield, N.J., Apr. 19, 1942; s. William A. and Ida Belle Durham (Davis) A.; B.Arch., Ga. Inst. Tech., 1965; m. Jo Ann Charter, July 8, 1978; 1 dau., Lisa L. Project mgr. Harland Bartholomew, Atlanta, 1965-67; asso. Mudano Assos., Clearwater, Fla., 1972-76; pres. Alexander & Assos., Chartered Architects/Planners, Clearwater, 1976—. Served with USAF, 1967-72. Decorated D.F.C. Mem. AIA, Greater Clearwater C. of C. (bd. govs. 1979—, chmn. beautification council 1978-79). Republican. Presbyterian. Home: 1916 Granada Ct Clearwater FL 33516 Office: 1437 S Belcher Rd Suite 120 Clearwater FL 33516

ALEXANDER, WILLIAM TASSE, III, oil storage tanks mfg. co. exec.; b. Mecklenburg County, N.C., Feb. 1, 1904; s. William Tasse and Mary Charlotte (Watkins) A.; A.B., U. N.C., Chapel Hill, 1927; m. Sarah Margaret Land, July 10, 1943; children—Sarah Land, Margaret Stafford, Mary Neal (dec.). Insp., Retail Credit Co., Atlanta, 1928-37; pres., treas. William T. Alexander & Co., Charlotte, N.C., 1947—. Served with U.S. Army, 1942-43. Mem. Am. Welding Soc. (chmn. Charlotte sect. 1973-74), NAM, Southeastern Steel Tank Fabricators Assn. (pres.), Charlotte Engrs. Club. Republican. Presbyterian. Club: Univ. City Civitan. Home: Route 10 Box 362 Charlotte NC 28213 Office: PO Box 9022 Charlotte NC 28299

ALEXANDER, WILLIAM VOLLIE, JR., congressman; b. Memphis, Jan. 16, 1934; s. William V. and Eulalia (Spencer) A.; student U. Ark., 1951-53; B.A., Southwestern at Memphis, 1957; LL.B. Vanderbilt U., 1960; 1 dau., Alyse Haven. Admitted to Tenn. bar, 1960, Ark. bar, 1963; law clk. to chief judge U.S. Dist. Ct., Memphis, 1960-61; asso. Montedonico, Bonne, Gilliland, Heiskell & Loch, Memphis, 1961-63; partner Swift & Alexander, Osceola, Ark., 1963-69; former dir. Osceola Riverport Authority; former commr. Arkansas Waterways Commn.; mem. 91st-96th Congresses from 1st Dist. Ark., asst. Democratic whip. Former bd. dirs. Osceola YMCA; East Ark. council Boy Scouts Am.; bd. dirs. Mississippi County YMCA, Southwestern at Memphis. Mem. Am. Acad. Polit. and Social Sci., Nat. Assn. Underwater Diving Instrs., Kappa Sigma, Phi Delta Phi. Episcopalian. Clubs: Masons, Rotary (pres., dir.). Office: Cannon House Office Bldg Washington DC 20515

ALEXEFF, IGOR, educator; b. Pitts., Jan. 5, 1931; s. Alexander and Tamara (Tchirkow) A.; B.A., Harvard U., 1952; M.S., U. Wis., 1955, Ph.D., 1959; m. Anne I. Fabina, Feb. 4, 1954; children—Alexander, Helen. Research engr. Westinghouse Corp., Pitts., 1952-53; NSF postdoctoral fellow U. Zurich, Switzerland, 1959-60; group leader controlled thermonuclear fusion Oak Ridge Nat. Lab., 1960-71; prof. elec. engring. U. Tenn., 1971—; vis. prof. Inst. Plasma Physics, Nagoya, Japan, 1973, Phys. Research Lab., Ahmedabad, India, 1975, physics dept. U. Natal, Durban, S.Africa, 1976, Universidade Federal Fluminense Niteroi, Rio de Janeiro, 1978; organizer Plasma Physics Workshop, U.S. and India, 1976; chmn. Gordon Research Conf. on Plasma Physics, 1974. Registered profl. engr., Tenn. Fellow Am. Phys. Soc.; mem. IEEE (asso. editor Transactions on Plasma Sci.; organizer 1st Internat. Conf. on Plasma Sci. 1974, pres. Oak Ridge chpt.), Nuclear and Plasma Sci. Soc. of IEEE (sec.). Contbr. articles to profl. jours. Home: 2790 Turnpike Oak Ridge TN 37830 Office: Ferris Hall U Tenn Knoxville TN 37916

ALFORD, CHARLES AARON, JR., physician, educator; b. Birmingham, Ala., Dec. 8, 1928; s. Charles Aaron and Lorine Hortense (Cummings) A.; B.S., U. Ala., 1951, M.D., 1955; postgrad. in virology Harvard U., 1962-65; m. Mary Elizabeth Akeroyd, Aug. 25, 1962; children—Caroline Cummings, Susan Elizabeth. Intern, U. Ala. Hosp., Birmingham, 1955-56, resident, 1956-58; instr. pediatrics U. Ala., 1960-62, asst. prof., 1965-66, asso. prof., 1966-67, Meyer prof. pediatric research, 1967—, prof. microbiology, 1972—, sr. scientist cancer research tng. program, 1973—. Cons. Center for Disease Control; Ralph Platou vis. prof. pediatrics Tulane U., New Orleans, 1972; mem. nat. com. Joint Pediatric Council, 1973-74, Combined Acad. Council, 1973-74; mem. panel control viral infections, virology task force Nat. Inst. Allergy and Infectious Diseases; mem. Nat. Adv. Child Health and Human Devel. Council, 1979—. Served to lt. M.C., USNR, 1958-60. Mem. Soc. Pediatric Research (pres. 1973-74), Am. Assn. Immunologists, Nat. Insts. Child Health and Human Devel. (chmn. maternal and child health research com. 1974-75), Am. Pediatric Soc., So. Soc. Pediatric Research, Am. Acad. Pediatrics, Am. Fedn. Clin. Research, Am. Soc. Microbiology, Am. Pub. Health Assn., Par Am. Med. Assn., Fedn. Am. Scientists, Infectious Disease Soc. Am., Sigma Xi. Editor: Pediatric Research, 1976—. Home: 3000 Southwood Rd Birmingham AL 35223

ALFORD, FARRA MCRAE, real estate exec.; b. Lexington, Ky., Dec. 22, 1949; s. William Van Meter and Daisy Ruth (Woltz) A.; B.S. in Mktg. (athletic scholar), U. Ala., 1973; m. Katherine Park Samford, Nov. 22, 1975; 1 dau., Katherine McRae. Shopping center mgr. Consol. Devels., Inc., Lexington, 1973-74; mktg. mgr. Miracon, Inc., Lexington, 1974—; pres. Real Estate Mktg., Inc.; owner, operator First Lexington Co., 1977—. Rep. for C.D.I. to Internat. Council Shopping Centers. Mem. Delta Kappa Epsilon. Republican. Presbyterian. Clubs: Rotary, Varsity Lettermans U. Ala., Idle Hour Country. Home: 418 Queensway Dr Lexington KY 40502 Office: 2216 Young Dr Suite 2 Lexington KY 40505

ALFORD, FREDERICK FERGUS, JR., warehousing co. exec.; b. Dallas, Mar. 17, 1931; s. Frederick Fergus and Olita (McCoy) A.; B.B.A., So. Methodist U., 1952; m. Bertha Olmsted Worthington, Dec. 18, 1954; 1 dau., Bertha Worthington. Asst. to pres. Alford Refrigerated Warehouses Inc., Dallas, 1953-56, v.p., 1956-58, pres. Gulf Coast div., Corpus Christi, Tex., 1964—, pres., chief exec. officer, Dallas, 1964—; owner Flying A Ranch, Rosser, Tex., 1972—. Treas., bd. dirs. Tejas council Girl Scouts U.S.A., 1972—. Served as 2d lt. USAF, 1952-53. Mem. Am. Warehousemen's Assn., Nat. Assn. Refrigerated Warehouses, Nat. Assn. Practical Refrigeration Engrs., AIM, So. Inst. Mgmt., Am. Mgmt. Assn. (pres.'s council), Council Phys. Distbn. Mgmt., Soc. Advancement Mgmt., Nat. Rifle Assn., Navy League U.S., Nat. Frozen Food Distbrs. Assn., Tex. Shrimp Assn., Sheriff's Assn. Tex., Am. Prodn. and Inventory Control Soc., Total Distbn. Plan For Am. (pres. 1972-73, 76-77), Metroplex Polled Hereford Assn. (pres. 1973—), Propeller Club of U.S., Sigma Iota Epsilon, Kappa Sigma. Presbyterian. Clubs: Dallas Press, Dallas Country, Dervish, Brookhollow Golf, City. Home: 3819 McFarlin Blvd Dallas TX 75205 Office: PO Box 5088 Dallas TX 75222

ALFORD, GEARY SIMMONS, psychologist; b. McComb, Miss., Apr. 11, 1945; s. Percy Knapp and Murrell Ellen (Dodds) A.; diploma Goethe Inst., Germany, 1965-66; B.A., Millsaps Coll., 1968; Ph.D., U. Ariz., 1972; m. Catherine Elizabeth Alford, Oct. 16, 1976. NIMH trainee U. Ariz., 1969-70; NIDA-NIAAA postdoctoral fellow Baylor Coll. Medicine, Tex. Research Inst. Mental Scis., Houston and U. Miss. Med. Center, 1975-77; asst. prof. psychiatry-psychology, clin. asst. prof. family medicine U. Miss., Jackson, 1972—; dir. Protective Service Life Ins. Co., 1976—. Diplomate Am. Bd. Profl. Psychology. Sigma Xi scholar, 1971; Fellow Behavior Therapy and Research Soc. (clin.); mem. Am. Psychol. Assn., Miss. Psychol. Assn. (pres. 1977-78), Assn. Advancement Behavior Therapy, Undersea Med. Soc., Sigma Xi. Episcopalian. Contbr. articles to profl. jours., chpts. to books. Office: Dept Psychiatry and Human Behavior U Miss Medical Center 2500 N State St Jackson MS 39216

ALFORD, JAMES DURHAM, educator; b. Danville, Ky., July 15, 1928; s. Otis Durham and Viola Mae (Raynes) A.; student Freed Hardeman Jr. Coll., 1948; B.S., U. Ky., 1957; M.B.A., 1959; m. Rose Raines, Jan. 24, 1949; children—James Harold, Linda (Mrs. Roger Paher), David Alan, Barbara Gail. Supr. accounts Ky. Dept. Revenue, Frankfort, 1961-65; exec officer Ky. Dept. Finance, Frankfort, 1965-68; asso. prof. bus. adminstrn. Eastern Ky. U., Richmond, 1969—. Pres., Band Parents Assn., 1967-68; asst. scoutmaster Blue Grass council Boy Scouts Am., 1962-63, scoutmaster, 1963-67. Mem. Am. Finance Assn., Financial Mgmt. Assn., Financial Analysts Assn. Mem. Ch. of Christ (elder 1972-74). Home: Pleasant Ridge Dr Route 10 Richmond KY 40475 Office: Eastern Ky U Richmond KY 40475

ALFORD, MARY DONNELLY, bookkeeping service exec.; b. New Orleans, June 19, 1931; d. James Philip and Amelia Gertrude (Lafranz) Donnelly; student Loyola U., New Orleans, 1950, La. State U., 1952, New Orleans Bapt. Theol. Sem., 1963, Acad. Computer Tech., 1973; m. William Seaborn Alford, Apr. 15, 1950; children—Patricia, Amelia, JoAnn, Frances Marie, William Nicholas, John, James. Owner, mgr. Alford Bookkeeping & Acctg. Service, Gretna, La., 1949—; dir. Danny's Fried Chicken, A & B Real Estate Co., Pyramid Services, Tastee Donuts #32; cons. Recipient cert. Kiwanis Club, 1970. Mem. Nat. Small Bus. Assn., Am. Mgmt. Assn., Nat. Assn. Women Bus. Owners, Terrytown Civic Assn. Democrat. Roman Catholic. Club: Eastern Star. Contbr. articles newspapers. Home and Office: 509 Farmington Pl Gretna LA 70053

ALFORD, (VIRGINIA) SUE BOWEN, ednl. adminstr.; b. Mpls., Nov. 4, 1928; d. Joel Charles and Frances Virginia (Hannah) Bowen; student U. Tex., Austin, 1945, Lamar U., 1946-47; B.S. in Edn. and Psychology, N. Tex. State U., 1950; M.A. in Speech Pathology, N.Mex. State U., 1967; postgrad. in ednl. adminstrn. U. Tex., El Paso, 1976-79; m. Hoy Ernest Alford, Aug. 6, 1947 (div.); children—Shirley Jane, Annette Jo, Carla Lynn. Tchr., Chaves County (N.Mex.) schs., 1950-51, St. Clement's Epis. Sch., 1964-65; speech pathologist Las Cruces (N.Mex.) schs., 1967-70, N.Mex. State U., Las Cruces, 1968; spl. edn. appraisal cons. Region XIX Edn. Service Center, El Paso, Tex., 1970-73, coordinator regional deaf-blind program, 1975-77, coordinator regional Child Find/Child Serve Program, 1977—. Mem. Am. Speech and Hearing Assn. (cert. of clin. competency in speech pathology), Assn. for Children with Learning Disabilities, Tex. State Tchrs. Assn., AAUW, El Paso Mental Health Assn. (profl. bd. dirs. 1977—), El Paso Speech and Hearing Assn., N.Mex. State U. Alumni Assn. (dir.), Alpha Delta Kappa. Republican. Methodist. Home: 3329 Shedfield Pl El Paso TX 79925 Office: 6611 Boeing St PO Box 10716 El Paso TX 79997

ALFORD, WALLACE WAYNE, educator; b. Brownsville, Miss., Apr. 19, 1931; s. Howard Luther and Willia Catherine (Carsley) A.; B.A., Miss. Coll., Clinton, 1956, M.A., 1960; Ph.D., George Peabody Coll. Tchrs., 1965; postgrad. La. State U., 1956-57, U. Miss., 1960; m. Catherine LaNelle Miller, July 25, 1953; children—Deborah Lynn, Robert Wayne, Rogena Leigh. Tchr., adminstr. Jackson (Miss.) Public Schs., 1959-62; head English dept. Lander Coll., Greenwood, S.C., 1965-66; acad. dean William Carey Coll., Hattiesburg, Miss., 1966-67, Wayland Bapt. Coll., Plainview, Tex., 1967-73; head edn. dept. Union U., Jackson, Tenn., 1973—. Minister music North Jackson (Tenn.) Bapt. Ch., 1975-79, Emmanuel Bapt. Ch., Humboldt, Tenn., 1979—. Served with USN, 1949-53. Recipient Outstanding Service award Tenn. Assn. Retarded Citizens, 1978. Mem. Tenn. Assn. Tchr. Educators, Sigma Tau Delta, Alpha Phi Omega. Contbr. articles to profl. jours. Home: 102 Tuckahoe Rd Jackson TN 38301 Office: Dept Edn Union U Jackson TN 38301

ALFORD, XELPERT GURNEY, ret. florist; b. Cedar Rapids, Nebr., Sept. 10, 1904; s. Will and Agnes Emma A.; grad. U. Rochester, 1924, Ohio State U., 1928; m. Elizabeth Argus, June 27, 1927; children—Jane, Gwen; m. 2d, Elcy L. Miller, June 28, 1969. Storeman, Du Bois Press, Rochester, N.Y., 1926-35; owner Alford Printing Service, 1928-29; expeditor Eastman Kodak Co., Rochester, 1940-53; ad man, proofreader Times-World Corp., Roanoke, Va., 1938-69; supt. Miller Printing Co., Asheville, N.C., 1953-54; owner Gurney Gardens, Salem, Va., 1969-78; cons., writer, speaker local garden clubs, local TV. Democratic committeeman, Rochester, N.Y., 1946-54; mem. screening com. United Fund Application Amounts, 1946-50. Mem. Va., Roanoke Valley florists assns., Am. Gloxinia & Gesneriad Soc. Presbyterian (elder). Club: Masons. Home: 4435 Wyndale Ave SW Roanoke VA 24018

ALGEO, MARK ANTHONY, speech pathologist; b. Springfield, Ohio, Mar. 26, 1951; s. C. Dean and Nellie E. (O'Neal) A.; M.S., U. S.Fla., Tampa, 1974; m. M. Christine Ryan, July 12, 1975; children—Katherine Ellen, Maura Elizabeth. Head counsellor Good Counsel Camp, Floral City, Fla., 1968-74; chmn. speech and lang. dept. Citrus County schs., Inverness, Fla., 1974—; pvt. practice speech pathology, 1975—; pres. Fla. Council Stutterers, 1973. Cert. tchr., Fla. Mem. Am. Speech, Lang. and Hearing Assn., Council Exceptional Students, Coordinators Speech and Lang. in Schs., Fla. Speech, Lang. and Hearing Assn., Greater Citrus County Jaycees (v.p. 1976; Jaycee of Quarter award 1976). Roman Catholic. Home: 1506 Eden Dr Inverness FL 32650 Office: 1507 W Main St Inverness FL 32650

ALIAS, FRED VINCENT, hotel and motel exec.; b. Clarksdale, Miss., Sept. 12, 1946; s. William Anthony and Aline (Faccini) A.; B.B.A. in Mktg. and Sales, U. Miss., Oxford, 1968; m. Rebecca Susan Hendee, Apr. 23, 1977. Public relations attache to gov. Miss., 1968-69; from sales rep., Los Angeles to sr. v.p. mktg. and advt. Holiday Inns, Inc., Memphis, 1969-73; v.p. mktg., then v.p. devel. W.B. Johnson Properties, owner, operator 11 Holiday inns and 6 Marriott hotels, Atlanta, 1973-78, exec. v.p., 1979—; mem. nat. adv. com., advt. and mktg. com. Internat. Assn. Holiday Inns; speaker, cons. in field. Active local United Way, Campus Crusade for Christ. Served with Air N.G., 1969-75. Recipient numerous salesmanship awards. Mem. Hotel Sales Mgmt. Assn., Discover Am. Tour Orgn., Nat. Tour Brokers Assn., U. Miss. Alumni Assn. Roman Catholic. Clubs: Cherokee Town and Country, Commerce (Atlanta). Home: 3355 Chatham Dr Atlanta GA 30305 Office: 2175 Parklake Dr NE Suite 103 Atlanta GA 30345

ALINDOGAN, JESULIN BARANDA, surgeon; b. Juban, Sorsogon, Philippines, June 2, 1936; s. Cecilio Orteza and Canuta (Baranda) A.; came to U.S., 1964; A.A., Letran Coll., Philippines, 1957; M.D., Sansto Thomas U., Philippines, 1962; m. Darlene Ann Weinlein, Aug. 19, 1977; 3 children. Intern, Mercy Hosp., Hamilton, Ohio, 1964-65, resident, 1965-66; resident Trumbull Meml. Hosp., Warren, Ohio, 1966-69; preceptorship in gen. surgery Samaritan Hosp., Troy, N.Y., 1969-71; emergency room physician St. Clare's Hosp., Schenectady, 1974-77; pvt. practice medicine, surgeon, Estelline, S.C., 1977-78, Gainsville, Va., 1978-79, Supply, N.C., 1979—; mem. staffs Brunswick County Hosp., Supply. Diplomate Am. Bd. Surgery. Mem. S.D. State Med. Assn. Roman Catholic. Home: 140 Greensboro St Holden Beach NC 28462 Office: Brunswick County Med Center Supply NC 28462

ALLAIN, WILLIAM A., state ofcl.; b. 1928; grad. U. Notre Dame; LL.B., U. Miss. Admitted to bar, 1950; formerly asst. atty. gen. State of Miss., atty. gen., 1980—. Office: Office Atty Gen 450 High St PO Box 220 Jackson MS 39205*

ALLAIRE, PAUL EUGENE, mech. engr.; b. Bristol, Conn., Sept. 23, 1941; s. Orien J. and Josephine M. A.; B.E., Yale U., 1963, M.E., 1964; Ph.D., Northwestern U., 1972; m. Janet Anne Hoglund, July 4, 1971; 1 son, Timothy Joseph. Lectr., Ethiopian Telecommunications Inst., Peace Corps, 1964-66; asst. prof. mech. engring. Meml. U. Nfld., St. John's, 1971-72; asso. prof. mech. engring. U. Va., Charlottesville, 1972—. Mem. ASME, Am. Soc. Lubrication Engrs. Editor: (with S.M. Rohde and C.J. Maday) Topics in Fluid Film Bearing and Rotor Bearing System Design and Optimization, 1979, Fundamentals of the Design of Fluid Film Bearings, 1980. Home: 112 Hilton Dr Charlottesville VA 22901 Office: Mechanical and Aerospace Engineering Dept U Va Charlottesville VA 22903

ALLAUN, SAMUEL PLUMMER, diversified co. exec.; b. Newport News, Va., Jan. 6, 1947; s. William Edwin and Madeliene Elliott (Huffman) A.; student N.C. Weslyan U., 1965, Old Dominion U., 1965, 69-70, Tyler (Tex.) Coll., 1966, Christopher Newport Coll., 1967, U. Va., 1971; m. Marilynne Moore Freeman, June 15, 1979; children by previous marriage—Augusta Christian, Adam Finch. Mktg. mgr. Great Atlantic Agy., Newport News, 1970-71; v.p., treas. Bulkeley Corp, Newport News, 1971—, Allaun Corp., Newport News, 1971—, Va. Distbrs. Supply, Inc.; asst. sec. Bright Blue Prodns., Inc.; sec. Energy Economy, Inc. Trustee, Gloucester County (Va.) Day Sch., 1976-78; mem. exec. com. No. Star dist. Boy Scouts Am. Served with USNR, 1967-68. Mem. Hampton Rds. Acad. Alumni Assn. (pres. 1975). Episcopalian. Clubs: James River Country, Ware River Yacht, Abingdon Men's (past pres.). Home: Route # 629 Indian Point Gloucester VA 23061 Office: 123 30th St Newport News VA 23607

ALLBRITTON, JOE LEWIS, publisher; b. D'Lo, Miss., Dec. 29, 1924; s. Lewis A. and Ada (Carpenter) A.; LL.B., Baylor U., 1949, LL.D. (hon.), 1964, J.D., 1969; L.H.D., Calif. Bapt. Coll., 1973; m. Barbara Jean Balfanz, Feb. 23, 1967; 1 son, Robert Lewis. Admitted to Tex. bar. 1949; since practiced in Houston; mem. firm Clawson, Allbritton & Clawson, 1950-53, Allbritton, McGee & Hand, 1961-64; dir. Perpetual Corp., Los Angeles, 1958—, pres., 1965-76, 78—, chmn. bd., 1973—; chmn. bd. Pierce Nat. Life Ins. Co., Los Angeles, 1958-72, 75—, dir., 1958—; chmn. bd. Pierce Bros., Los Angeles, 1958-66, 68-72, dir. 1958—; chmn. bd. Mineral Oil Refining Co., Dickinson, Tex., 1963-68; pres., dir. San Jacinto Savings Assn., Houston, 1956-68; dir. Bank of the Southwest Nat. Assn., Houston, 1964-69, mem. exec. com., 1965-69; chmn. exec. com., dir. Houston Citizens Bank & Trust Co., 1969-75, pres., 1970-73, chmn. bd., chief exec. officer, 1970-75; chmn. exec. com. First Internat. Bancshares, Inc., Dallas, 1972-74, dir. 1972-75; chmn. bd., pres. First Allef (Tex.) Bank, 1972-73; pub. The Washington Star, 1974-77; chmn. bd. The Evening Star Newspaper Co., 1974-78, Allbritton Communications Co., 1976—, WJLA, Inc., 1976—, Washington Star Syndicate, 1976-78; chmn. bd. First Nat. Bank Tomball (Tex.), 1970-75, Houston Internat. Bank Luxembourg, S.A., Grand Duchy of Luxembourg, 1972-79, Exchange Bank, Houston, 1974, University Bancshares, Inc., Houston, 1975—; dir. Southwestern Pub. Service Co., Amarillo, Tex., 1965-74, Gene Murphee Corp., Houston, 1970-77, Astrodomain Corp., Houston, 1970-72, H.F. Ahmanson & Co., Los Angeles, 1972-77, First Internat. Bancshares Ltd., London, 1973-74; dir. First Fed. Savings & Loan Assn., Dallas, 1971-72, adv. dir. 1972-74. Mem. Hosp. Adv. Council, Tex. Dept. Health, Austin, 1965-66, Fgn. Mission Bd., So. Bapt. Conv., Richmond Va., 1966-73, Tulane Bus. Sch. Council, Tulane U., New Orleans, 1972-74, Energy Crisis Council, State of Tex., Austin, 1973-75; chmn. Tex. Offshore Terminal Commn., Austin, 1973-75; bd. dirs. Houston Symphony Soc., 1960-77, mem. exec. com., 1972-77, v.p., treas., 1972-75; bd. dirs. Inst. Internat. Edn., N.Y.C., mem. So. Regional Adv. Bd., Houston, 1972-74; bd. dirs. Meridian House Internat., Washington, 1974-77, Internat. Sch. Law, Washington, 1975-78, Newspaper Advt. Bur., N.Y., 1976-78, Met. Bd. Trade, Washington, 1975-79; trustee Baylor U. Coll. Medicine, Houston, 1959-68, chmn. bd. trustees, 1965-68; trustee Baylor U., Waco, Tex., 1959-68, mem. exec. com., 1960-68; trustee Mus. Fine Arts, Houston, 1971-75, v.p., 1972-75, mem. adv. bd., 1975—; trustee Fed. City Council, Washington, 1975—. Served with USN, 1943-46. Recipient Distinguished Alumni award Pi Kappa Delta, 1963. Mem. Am. Bar Assn., State Bar Tex., Houston C. of C. (dir. 1973-74). Baptist (chmn. bd. trustees 1953-71). Office: 2777 Allen Pkwy Suite 829 Houston TX 77019 also Washington DC

ALLDERDICE, THOMAS GILMORE, mech. engr.; b. Hagerstown, Md., Aug. 13, 1916; s. Fitzhugh Berry and Lillian Fletcher (Martin) A.; student St. Petersburg Jr. Coll., 1934-35; B.C.E., U. Fla., 1948; m. Ada Frances Runyon, Mar. 11, 1950; 1 dau., Mary Frances. With Russell & Axon, cons. engrs., Daytona Beach, Fla., 1948-49; with Reynolds, Smith & Hills, architects, engrs. and planners, Jacksonville, Fla., 1949—, now supervisory mech. engr. Served with AUS, 1935-41, 42-46. Decorated Purple Heart, Combat Infantryman's Badge; recipient citation War Dept., 1946. Registered profl. engr., Fla., W.Va. Mem. Nat. Soc. Profl. Engrs., ASME, Fla. Engring. Soc., Tau Beta Pi, Sigma Tau. Presbyterian (elder). Patentee water system freeze protection valve. Home: 12816 Aladdin Rd Jacksonville FL 32223 Office: PO Box 4850 Jacksonville FL 32201

ALLEE, W. ARTHUR, educator; b. Lynnville, Iowa, Oct. 30, 1914; s. William and Finis (White) A.; B.S. in Commerce, State U. Iowa, 1945, M.A., 1948, Ph.D., 1955. Cashier 1st State Bank, Lynnville, 1935-42; asst. prof. U. Ill., 1953-56; prof. U. Houston, 1956-78, prof. emeritus, 1978—. Named Tex. Bus. Edn. Tchr. of Year, Tex. Bus. Edn. Assn., 1974; recipient Mountain-Plains Leadership award, Mountain-Plains Bus. Edn. Assn., 1978. Fellow Huguenot Soc. London; mem. Internat. Soc. Bus. Edn. (Pres.'s award 1975), Am. Records Mgmt. Assn. (pres. Houston chpt. 1971-72), Tex., Nat. bus. edn. assns., London Soc. Genealogists, Houston Genealogical Form, Pi Omega Pi (nat. pres. 1977, 78), Delta Pi Epsilon, Delta Sigma Pi, Phi Kappa Phi, Phi Delta Kappa. Mem. Soc. of Friends. Contbg. author: Secretarial Handbook, 1977.

ALLEN, BENJAMIN HARRISON, psychologist; b. Goldsboro, N.C., Apr. 7, 1931; s. Benjamin Harrison and Nancy J. (Hagy) A.; B.A., Wofford Coll., 1956; M.A., Peabody Coll., 1957, Ph.D., 1962; m. Martha Payne, July 10, 1952; children—Martha Jean, and Mary Joan (twins), John Charles. Sch. psychologist City Public Schs., Nashville, 1958-61; psychol. cons. Bd. Health, Wilmington, N.C., 1961-63; asso. prof. psychology E. Carolina Coll., Greenville, N.C., 1963-65; asst. prof. dept. spl. edn. Fla. State U., Tallahassee, 1965-68; asso. prof. dept. spl. edn. U. Ga., Athens, 1968-69; dir. div. mental retardation Dept. Mental Health, Montgomery, Ala., 1969-70; program cons., project dir., manpower utilization project Fla. Dept. Rehab., Tallahassee, 1969-70; dir. programs and services Sunland Regional Center, Ft. Myers, Fla., 1970-74; dir. Southwestern Va. Tng. Center for Mentally Retarded, Hillsville, 1974—. Served with Submarine Service, USN, 1949-53. NIMH grantee, 1956-58. Mem. Am. Psychol. Assn., Am. Assn. Mental Deficiency (pres. Fla. chpt. 1973-74, pres. Va. chpt. 1978, 1st v.p. region IX, 1979-80), Council for Exceptional Children, Nat. Assn. Retarded Children. Presbyterian. Club: Lions (pres. 1980). Home: Route 3 Box 20B Hillsville VA 24343 Office: Southwestern Va Tng Center Route 1 Box 196 Hillsville VA 24343

ALLEN, CHARLES MICHAEL, computer engr., educator; b. New Castle, Pa., Sept. 1, 1942; s. Charles Moore and Betty Jane (Wise) A.; B.S. in E.E., Carnegie Inst. Tech., 1964, M.S., 1965; Ph.D., SUNY, Buffalo, 1968; m. Kathleen Rita Riemer, Sept. 4, 1965; children—Charles Reed, James Michael. Engring. asst. CIA, summers 1963, 64; engring. asso. Bell Telephone of Pa., summer 1965; engr. Sylvania Electric Co., Buffalo, 1966-67; research asst./instr. SUNY, Buffalo, 1965-68, asst. prof., 1968-74; engr. Lenlab Inc., Lockport, N.Y., 1967-74; asso. prof. computer engring. U. N.C., Charlotte, 1974—; linear/digital electronics cons. Sec.-treas., chmn. bd. edn. Assumption Sch., 1975—. Mem. IEEE (chpt. sec.-treas. 1978-80, vice chmn. 1979-80), Internat. Soc. for Multiple Valued Logic, Assn. for Computing Machinery. Roman Catholic. Club: Queen City Optimists (dir. 1975-76, treas. 1976-77, v.p. 1977-78). Home: 6541 Grove Park Blvd Charlotte NC 28215 Office: EAD Dept Univ of NC Charlotte NC 28223

ALLEN, CHERYL JONES, educator; b. Beaumont, Tex., Mar. 21, 1942; d. Charles Henry and Olga Mabel (Taylor) Jones; B.S., Lamar U., 1964, counseling certification, 1975; M.Ed., U. Houston, 1970; m. Bob Glenn Allen, June 1, 1963; 1 dau., Angela Kay. Profl. model, 1950; ballet instr., 1956, 57; tchr. speech, drama and English, East Chambers Ind. Sch. Dist., Winnie, Tex., 1964-76; instr. dept. communication Lamar U., 1976-77; counselor East Chambers Sch. Dist., Winnie, 1976—. Mem. worship com. First United Methodist Ch. Mem. AAUW, NEA, Tex. Speech Communication Assn. (dist. chmn.), Tex. Secondary Theatre Conf., Tex. Personnel and Guidance Assn., S.E. Tex. Speech and Drama Assn. (past pres.), Sabine-Neches Guidance Assn., Beta Sigma Phi, Alpha Chi Omega Alumnae Assn., Phi Kappa Phi, Pi Kappa Delta, Nat. Forensic Assn., Tex. Tchrs. Assn. Democrat. Home: PO Box 150 Winnie TX 77665 Office: PO Box 417 Winnie TX 77665

ALLEN, CLARENCE BOYCE, writer, civic leader; b. Latta, S.C., Mar. 17, 1899; s. William Benjamin and Theodosia (Cox) A.; B.A., Furman U., 1921; postgrad. Yale U., 1925-27; LL.B., U. S.C., 1932, M.A., 1938, J.D., 1970; m. Eupha Lee McComas, Nov. 11, 1936; 1 dau., Martha Lee (Mrs. James Andrew Elkins, Jr.). Admitted to S.C. bar, 1932; mem. firm Dargan & Paulling, Darlington, S.C., 1933-34; farmer nr. Latta, 1935-71; tchr. pub. schs., Georgetown County, S.C., 1947-53, Lee County, S.C., 1953-56, Dillon County, S.C., 1956-71. Mem. Pee Dee Regional Devel. and Planning Council Task Force, 1972—; vice chmn. Dillon County Hist. Preservation Commn., 1972—; mem. Dillon County Bicentennial Com., 1974—. Chmn. bd. trustees Dillon County Library, 1973-77. Mem. Dillon County Hist. Soc. (pres. 1971-72), Phi Beta Kappa. Baptist (deacon 1938—). Clubs: Masons, Lions, Civitan. Author: Edwin Arlington Robinson: A Critical Analysis of His Poetic Contributions, 1938; English for Everyday Use, 1967; History of Dalcho Lodge, 1970; History of Catfish Creek Baptist Church, 1971; History of Antioch Baptist Church, 1973; William Benjamin and Theodosia Allen Family, 1973; History of Latta Library, 1974; Joel Allen House and Related Personalities, 1977; entry Dillon County sites Nat. Register Historic Places: Early Cotton Press, 1972, Joel Allen House, 1974, Catfish Creek Bapt. Ch., 1975. Address: 311 Richardson St Latta SC 29565

ALLEN, CLIFTON JUDSON, clergyman, editor; b. Latta, S.C., Nov. 7, 1901; s. William Benjamin and Theodosia (Cox) A.; B.A., Furman U., 1923, D.D., 1960; Th.M., So. Baptist Theol. Sem., 1928, Ph.D., 1932; m. Hattie Bell McCracken, Aug. 22, 1930; children—Judson Boyce, Rosalind (Mrs. John C. Barker), Robert Moore. Prin., Minturn (S.C.) High Sch., 1923-25; tutor Greek N.T., So. Bapt. Theol. Sem., 1928-31; ordained to ministry So. Bapt. Ch., 1926; pastor in McHenry, Ky., 1926-29, Utica, Ky., 1929-32, Fairmont, N.C., 1932-36, Statesville, N.C., 1936-37; asso. editorial sec. Sunday sch. bd. So. Bapt. Conv., 1937-44, editorial sec., 1945-68; rec. sec. So. Bapt. Conv., 1966-77; vis. prof. Southeastern Bapt. Theol. Sem., 1972-76, Carson-Newman Coll., 1977; Sec. commn. Christian teaching and tng. Bapt. World Alliance, 1957-65, chmn., 1965-70; mem. exec. com. Bapt. Conv. N.C., 1935-37; mem. internat. Sunday sch. lesson com. div. Christian edn. Nat. Council Chs., 1942-68, chmn., 1960-67, mem. div. assembly, 1957-63; radio broadcaster, 1945-72. Recipient E.Y. Mullins Denominational Service award So. Baptist Theol. Sem., 1970. Democrat. Rotarian. Quarternion. Author: The Gospel According to Paul, 1956; Points for Emphasis (ann.), 1953-74; Affirmations of Our Faith, 1972; Life Is Worth Your Best, 1980; also curricular materials. Chmn. editorial com. Ency. of Southern Baptists 1958; gen. editor Broadman Bible Commentary, 12 vols., 1969-72. Home: 1019 Kearns Ave Winston-Salem NC 27106

ALLEN, CONSTANCE OLLEEN, artist, designer; b. Camphill, Ala., June 10, 1923; d. Alonza Evans and Sara Alvesta (Jones) Adcock; student George Washington U., 1942-44; m. Byron B. Webb, Oct. 12, 1947; children—Martha Ellen, Alan James, Deana Olleen; m. 2d. Walt Allen, Mar. 11, 1976. Painter, 20 Indian Chiefs in Indian Hall of Fame, Duncan, Okla., 1972-73; commd. to paint hist. paintings of South Central Okla., 1978; instr. U. Sci. and Arts of Okla., 1974-75; owner, dir. The Studio Gallery, Chickasha, Okla., 1979—. Winner over 50 awards in competitions, 1967-78. Mem. Internat. Soc. Artists, Okla. Art Guild, Artists Equity, Okla. Watercolor Assn., Lawton-Ft. Sill Art Guild. Home: 2009 Carolina Ave Chickasha OK 73018

ALLEN, DIANA UPTAIN, nursing home adminstr.; b. Guntersville, Ala., Mar. 3, 1948; s. Mann and Ruth (Bearden) Uptain; B.S. in Human Services, U. Tenn., Chattanooga, 1975; m. Charles Clay Allen, June 10, 1978. Med. sec. Team Evaluation Center, Chattanooga, 1967-72; dir. social service Hamilton County (Tenn.) Nursing Home, Chattanooga, 1975-80 Meml. Hosp., Chattanooga, 1980—. Expt. in Internat. Living Study Abroad Program scholar, 1974; Sarah Key Patten scholar, 1974. Mem. Soc. Hosp. Social Work Dirs., Am. Hosp. Assn., Tenn. Soc. Health Care Social Workers, Pi Gamma Mu. Home: 1764 Pine Needles Trail Chattanooga TN 37421 Office: 2500 Citico Ave Chattanooga TN 37404

ALLEN, DONALD COLE, mfg. exec.; b. Dallas, Sept. 9, 1922; s. Raymond Daniel and Anne Elizabeth (Cole) A.; student Murray State Tchrs. Coll., 1943, U. Ga., 1945, So. Meth. U., 1948; J.D., LaSalle U., 1968; A.B., B.L.S., Syracuse U., 1972; Ph.D., Walden U., 1975; m. Mary Jane Dunn, July 11, 1942; children—Dianne (Mrs. Glen Fry), Cynthia (Mrs. Tom Jennings). Sales rep. Rice Stix Co., St. Louis. 1950-55; terr. mgr. Ely & Walker Co., Memphis, 1955-62, regional sales mgr., 1962-65, 1st v.p., gen. sales mgr., 1965-69, pres., 1969—. Asso. mem. Field Sales Mgmt. Inst., Syracuse U., 1962-63; research asso. So. Meth. U., 1950-65. Served with USNR, 1942-45. Mem. Sales Exec. Club, Sales and Mktg. Execs. Internat. Methodist. Contbr. articles in field to profl. jours. Home: 754 Shady Grove Memphis TN 38138 Office: 823 E Holmes Rd Memphis TN 38116

ALLEN, DOROTHY NIXON, county agy. adminstr.; b. Cleve., June 7, 1927; d. Samuel and Pearl (Johnson) A.; student public schs., Cleve.; m. Robert Lee Allen, June 12, 1944 (dec. 1962); children—Robert Lee, Barbara Allen Simons, Harold N. Various home nursing positions, Raleigh, N.C., 1946-75; librarian (part-time) Richardson B. Harrison Library, Raleigh, 1964; head dept. J.C. Penney & Co., Raleigh, 1965; community worker Wake County Opportunities, Inc., Raleigh, 1966-67, dep. dir., 1968, exec. dir., 1969—. Mem. Mayor's Community Relations Com., Raleigh, 1975-77; mem. adv. bd. Central Youth Offenders Community Vol. Program, 1976-78; mem. State Health Coordinating Council, State of N.C., 1979—; bd. dirs. Youth Action Group, 1972-74, Raleigh Youth Council, 1973-75, Wake Advancement Center, 1974-77, N.C. Consumer Council, 1977-79. Named Parent of Yr., J.W. Ligon High Sch. PTA, 1963, Citizen of Yr., Omega Psi Phi; recipient Outstanding Community Service award St. Augustine Coll. Social Club, 1970, St. Augustine Coll., 1972. Mem. N.C. Community Action Assn. (pres. 1972-74, dir. 1976—), Nat. Assn. Community Devel., LWV, NAACP, Raleigh Citizens Assn. Democrat. Club: Junior Women's. Home: PO Box 25321 Raleigh NC 27611 Office: 567 E Hargett St Raleigh NC 27610

ALLEN, EDGAR JENNESS, broadcasting co. ofcl.; b. West Palm Beach, Fla., Feb. 5, 1947; s. Edgar Jenness and Violet M. Allen; B.S., Youngstown (Ohio) State U., 1970; m. Jacklyn Dale Gillam, Aug. 10, 1968; children—Mindy Joy, Lindsay Noelle. Sales rep. Susquehanna Broadcasting Co., Toledo, 1973-74, regional sales mgr., 1974, sta. mgr. Sta. WHLQ, Canton, Ohio, 1974-76; local and regional sales rep. Sta. WNCI, Nationwide Communications, Inc., Columbus, Ohio, 1976; regional mgr. Radio Advt. Bur., Roswell, Ga., 1977—. Republican. Lutheran. Address: 9640 N Pond Roswell GA 30076

ALLEN, EDWARD DUDLEY, clin. psychologist; b. Spartanburg, S.C., Mar. 19, 1936; s. Robert Benjamin Dudley and Edna Mae (Moore) A.; B.A., Wofford Coll., 1968; M.A., Furman U., 1970; Ph.D., Mt. Yunah Coll., 1975; m. Georgia A. Kalangis, Mar. 4, 1956; children—Edward Dudley, Michael Andrew. Juvenile counselor Spartanburg County (S.C.) Family Ct., 1966-69; psychologist Whitten Village, S.C. Dept. Mental Retardation, Clinton, 1969-70; psychologist Spartanburg Mental Health Center, S.C. Dept. Mental Health, 1970—. Cons. Spartanburg County Sch. Systems. Mem. adv. bd. SPARTA, Project for Autistic Children, Spartanburg, 1973-75. Bd. dirs. Spartanburg Girls' Home; bd. dirs. Charles Lea Center, 1969-70, vice-chmn., 1970-71, chmn., 1970-71. Mem. Spartanburg Jaycees (S.C. Recognition of Merit 1959, Nat. Recognition of Merit 1959, Internat. Recognition of Merit 1960), Am., Southeastern psychol. assns., Am. Acad. Polit. and Social Sci., Pi Kappa Alpha. Baptist. Contbr. articles to profl. jours. Home: Route 3 Spartanburg SC 29301 Office: 149 E Wood St Spartanburg SC 29303

ALLEN, ELIZABETH ANN, ednl. adminstr.; b. Cullman, Ala., Oct. 20, 1939; d. John W. and Ann E. Rowe; Asso. in Applied Sci., Calhoun Community Coll., 1974; B.S., Athens Coll., 1976; m. Walter L. Allen III, Feb. 15, 1977; children by previous marriage—Charles J. Gorman Jr., William Barry Gorman, Mitchell Dale Gorman. Dental asst., Cullman, Ala., 1956-59, Birmingham, Ala., 1960-61; dental asst. supr. U. Ala. Sch. Dentistry, Birmingham, 1962-71, dental aux. coordinator, 1971-73; dir. dental assisting program John C. Calhoun Community Coll., Decatur, Ala., 1973-77, seminar dir. continuing edn., 1973-77; dir., chief instr. dental assisting program Trenholm State Tech. Coll., Montgomery, Ala., 1978—. Mem. Ala. Dental Assts. Assn. (pres. elect. 1979, Browning Trophy award 1975, 76), Birmingham Dental Assts. Soc. (pres. 1973, Onzalee Blatzer award 1972), Council Dental Edn. (rev. com. for dental aux. edn. 1976-79), Ala. Vocat. Ednl. Assn., Decatur-Athens Dental Assts. Soc. (pres. 1976), 2d Dist. Dental Assts. Soc. (pres. 1979—), Am. Dental Assts. Assn. Methodist. Club: Arrowhead Country. Contbr. revs. to profl. jours. Home: 310 Arrowhead Dr Montgomery AL 36106 Office: 1225 Air Base Blvd Montgomery AL 36108

ALLEN, EMORY RAWORTH, educator; b. Augusta, Ga., Jan. 21, 1935; s. Ernest Mason and Virginia (Williamson) A.; B.S. in Biol. Scis., U. Md., 1959; postgrad. Brown U., 1959; Ph.D. in Anatomy, U. Pa., 1964; m. Rae Heine, Dec. 19, 1957; children—Ronald Joseph, Dennis Raymond, Raworth Douglas, Robert Francis. Asst. instr. dept. anatomy U. Pa., Phila., 1964-65; instr. U. Pitts., 1965-66, asst. prof., 1966-71; asso. prof. dept. anatomy Med. Center, La. State U., New Orleans, 1971—. Mem. Bayou Liberty Civic Assn., 1971—. Served with USNR, 1954-56. USPHS predoctoral fellow, 1960-64, postdoctoral fellow, 1964-65; Muscular Dystrophy Assn. grantee, 1968-72. Mem. Internat. Acad. Pathology (lectr. 1970), La. Soc. Electron Microscopy (pres. 1980—), Sigma Xi. Contbr. to profl. jours. Home: Dubisson Rd Slidell LA 70458 Office: 1100 Florida Ave New Orleans LA 70119

ALLEN, ENSIL ROSS, reptile show exec.; b. Pitts., Jan. 2, 1908; s. Charles Leslie and Florence May (Martin) A.; student Stetson U., 1928; children—Betty Allen Landers, Robert Ross, John William, Thomas Carl, Kenneth Martin, Craig Lawrence, Sidney Janes. Founder Ross Allen's Reptile Inst., Silver Springs, Fla., 1929—; owner Indian Prairie Farm, 1970—, Ross Allen Reptile World, Sarasota, Fla., 1976—; stockholder Ross Allen Wildlife Park, N. Ft. Meyers, Fla.; animal handler and stunt man numerous films; TV and radio appearances. Mem. Fla. Commn. on Indian Affairs, 1969-71. Recipient Conservation award Fla. Dept. Agr., 1965; certificate of merit Fla. Bd. Conservation, 1965; Fla. Govs.'s Conservation award, 1970; award for contbn. to Fla. exhibit World's Fair, 1964; Silver Beaver award Boy Scouts Am., 1963, Distinguished Eagle Scout award, 1972; awards Tex. Med. Assn., Pa. Athletic Club. Mem. Internat. Crocodilian Soc. (founder, pres.), Nat. Audubon Soc. (pres. Ft. King chpt. 1968-70), Phila. Zool. Soc. (life). Contbr. numerous publs. in field to profl. jours. Discoverer several reptile species. Address: 13 Marilyn Ave St Augustine FL 32084

ALLEN, FLOYD LEE, chem. co. exec.; b. Houston, Feb. 21, 1943; s. Arthur and Lurlene (Moseley) A.; student North Tex. State U., 1960-63; B.A., Houston Bapt. Coll., 1969; m. Geraldine Lee Tiffany, Dec. 28, 1963; children—Darin Arthur, Melissa Lee. Instr., Houston Bapt. Coll., 1969-70; research chemist Milchem Inc., Houston, 1970-73, offshore cons., 1973-74, supr. specialty products div., 1974-78, product advisor, 1978—. Cons. Ecology Control Inc.; v.p., dir. Kemah Marina Inc., Nassau Bay, Tex., 1973—. Mem. Soc. Petroleum Engrs., Am. Chem. Soc. Patentee in field. Home: 9611 Galston St Spring TX 77379 Office: PO Box 22111 Houston TX 77027

ALLEN, FRANCES BARNES, nurse; b. Cotton Valley, La., Dec. 7, 1918; d. John Sidney and Bettie Clara (Merritt) Barnes; R.N., Vicksburg (Miss.) Hosp., 1946; m. Edward H. Allen, Mar. 23, 1945; children—Edward H., Betty Marie, Barbara Melissa. Staff nurse Vicksburg Hosp., 1946; operating room supr. Humpheries County Hosp., Belzonia, Miss., 1950-51; staff nurse St. Francis Hosp., Monroe, La., 1960-61; head nurse Glenwood Hosp., West Monroe, La., 1964-71, emergency dept. supr., 1971—. Served with Cadet Nurses Corps, 1944-46. Recipient Balfour medal, Vicksburg Hosp., 1946. Mem. La. Nurses Assn., Monroe Dist. Nurses Assn. (bd. dirs.), Glenwood Head Nurses and Suprs. (sec.), Am. Nurses Assn., Emergency Dept. Nurses Assn., Am. Cancer Soc., Am. Heart Assn. Baptist. Clubs: N.E. Univ. Women's, Univ. Women's Book, Ouachita Cowbells, La. Cow Bells. Home: 4100 Blanks St Monroe LA 71203 Office: Glenwood Hospital McMillan and Thomas Rd West Monroe LA 71291

ALLEN, FRANK CARROLL, banker; b. Hazlehurst, Miss., Nov. 10, 1913; s. Walter Scott and May (Ellis) A.; A.A. with high honors, Copiah-Lincoln Jr. Coll., Wesson, Miss., 1933; student Am. Inst. Banking, 1935, 36, 37, 47, 49; m. Clara Marnee Alford, June 23, 1937; children—Marnee Louise, Susan Carroll, Elizabeth Jane. Bookkeeper, teller Georgetown Bank (Miss.), 1933-34, cashier, dir., 1937-41; bookkeeper Deposit Guaranty Bank & Trust Co., Jackson, Miss., 1934-37; bank examiner, Miss., 1942-46; cashier, dir. Brookhaven Bank & Trust Co. (Miss.), 1947-49; pres., dir. Lawrence County Bank, Monticello, Miss., 1949-65; pres. Monticello Bank (now br. Deposit Guaranty Nat. Bank), 1966-78; chmn. adv. bd. Monticello/Newhebron Bank brs., 1966—; adv. bd. Deposit Guaranty Nat. Bank, Jackson, 1966—; chmn. bd. Ins. & Realty Underwriters, 1970-75, dir., 1959-76. Bd. dirs. Miss. Econ. Council, 1950-53; commr. Monticello Planning Bd., 1964-74; bd. dirs. S.W. Miss. Devel. Assn., 1960-75. Chmn. scholarship bd. Monticello Mfg. Co., 1960-72; exec. bd. Andrew Jackson council Boy Scouts Am., 1975—. Served to 1st lt. AUS, 1942-46. Mem. Am. (chmn. Miss. dist. 7 on U.S. Savs. Bonds 1952—), Miss. (chmn. bank mgmt. com. 1948-49, group v.p. 1948-49) bankers assns., Monticello C. of C. (pres. 1951-53, 60-61, dir. 1951—), Newcomen Soc. N. Am. Democrat. Baptist (deacon 1953—, Sunday sch. supt. 1958-60). Club: Lion (pres. Monticello 1954-55). Home: PO Box 297 Monticello MS 39654 Office: PO Box 458 Monticello MS 39654

ALLEN, FRED EDWIN, mailing list cons.; b. Mt. Pleasant, Tex., May 12, 1928; s. Claud E. and Lillie (Brownlee) A.; B.S., East Tex. U., 1949; m. Mildred Craghead, Mar. 19, 1955; 1 dau., Linda. Nat. sales mgr. Royal Typewriter Co., N.Y.C., 1954-62; sales mgr. Bus. Equipment group Litton Industries, N.Y.C., 1962-66; founder, pres. List Mgmt., Inc. (div. Fairfield Communities Land Co. 1971). Rye, N.Y., 1966-73; founder, pres. Fred E. Allen, Inc., Mt. Pleasant, 1973—, now chmn. bd.; chmn. bd. Superior Graphics & Stationery Corp., Listfinder Corp.; dir. Am. Nat. Bank (all Mt. Pleasant). Vice chmn. bd. Titus County Meml. Hosp. Served with U.S. Army, 1952-54. Mem. Mailing List Industry Assn. (charter pres. 1970-72), Mailing List Mgrs. and Compilers Assn., Direct Mail Mktg. Assn., Tex. (dir.), East Tex. (pres.) Angus assns. Republican. Methodist. Home: Route 7 PO Box 133AA Mount Pleasant TX 75455 Office: PO Box 470 Mount Pleasant TX 75455

ALLEN, FREDERICK ROGER, civil engr., trade assn. exec.; b. Boston, Aug. 10, 1939; s. Roger Aylmer and Marguerite Elizabeth (Augustine) A.; B.S. in Civil Engring., Va. Poly. Inst., 1967, M.S., 1968; m. Carolyn Vivian Lobban, June 20, 1964; children—Lynn, Larry. Staff engr. Byrd, Tallamy, Mac Donald & Lewis, Cons. Engrs., Falls Church, Va., 1968-71; product devel. engr. Nat. Crushed Stone Assn., Washington, 1971-73, dir. tech. services, 1973-77; exec. dir. N.C. Aggregates Assn., Raleigh, 1977—; participant Insts. Orgn. Mgmt., 1974-77. Served with U.S. Army, 1963-66. Decorated Vietnam Service medal. Recipient Engr.-in-Tng. of Year award No. Va. chpt. Va. Soc. Profl. Engrs., 1974; registered profl. engr., N.C., Va. Mem. Am., Carolina socs. assn. execs., ASTM, Am. Pub. Works Assn., AIME, ASCE, Nat., N.C., socs. profl. engrs. Presbyterian. Clubs: Raleigh Engrs., Raleigh Racquet. Contbr. articles on concrete and aggregates to profl. jours. Home: 7508 Harps Mill Rd Raleigh NC 27609 Office: N C Aggregates Assn PO Box 30603 Raleigh NC 27612

ALLEN, GARY CURTISS, educator; b. Stockton, Calif., July 18, 1939; s. Curtiss Wright and Helen Lucille (McElroy) A.; B.S. in Chemistry (Owens-Ill. Co. scholar), Stanford U., 1961; M.A. in Geology, Rice U., 1963; Ph.D. in Geochemistry, U. N.C., Chapel Hill, 1968; m. Ruth Lee Mayeux, June 5, 1965; children—Adrienne Lucille, Christopher Gary. Sect. head geochemistry-petrology Va. Div. Mineral Resources, 1966-68; asst. prof. La. State U., New Orleans, 1968-72; asso. prof. U. New Orleans, 1972-78, prof. earth scis., 1978—; pres. Sunbelt Assos., Inc., New Orleans, 1978—. Novice League baseball coach New Orleans Recreation Dept., 1976, 78. NASA fellow, 1963-66. Mem. Geol. Soc. Am., Am. Chem. Soc., Mineral. Soc., Geochem. Soc., Carolina Geol. Soc., Sigma Xi (pres. U. New Orleans, 1977-78), Sigma Gamma Epsilon. Researcher metamorphic petrology, archaeol. geochemistry, mineralogy, environ. affairs; contbr. articles to sci. jours. Home: 6961 Mayo Blvd New Orleans LA 70126 Office: Dept Earth Sciences Univ New Orleans New Orleans LA 70122

ALLEN, HERBERT, steel works exec.; b. Ratcliff, Tex., May 2, 1907; s. Jasper and Leona (Matthews) A.; B.S. in Mech. Engring., Rice Inst., 1929; m. Helen Daniels, Aug. 28, 1937; children—David Daniels, Anne (Mrs. Jonathan Taft Symonds), Michael Herbert. Engaged in miscellaneous research, 1929-31; chief engr. Abercrombie Pump Co., Houston, 1931-35; chief engr. Cameron Iron Works, Inc., 1935-41, v.p. engring. and mfg., 1942-50, v.p., gen. mgr., 1950-66, pres., 1966-73, chmn. bd., 1973-77, also dir.; dir. Tenneco Inc., Tex. Commerce Bank, Big Three Industries, Inc. Bd. dirs. Tex. Tech. U., 1963-69, Houston Symphony Soc., 1971—; trustee emeritus William Marsh Rice U. Named Engr. of Year, San Jacinto chpt. Tex. Soc. Profl. Engrs., Inventor of Year, Houston Patent Attys. Assn., 1977. Registered profl. engr., Tex. Fellow ASME (hon. mem.); mem. C. of C. (bd. dirs. 1952-54, 62, v.p. 1954-55), Am. Inst. Mining, Metall. and Petroleum Engrs., Am. Petroleum Inst., Nat. Acad. Engring., Newcomen Soc. N. Am., Tex. Soc. Profl. Engrs., Houston Engring. and Sci. Soc., Houston Philos. Soc., Tau Beta Pi, Episcopalian. Clubs: Ramada, River Oaks Country, Petroleum, Houston, Bayou; Metropolitan (N.Y.). Patentee in field. Home: 3207 Groveland Ln Houston TX 77019 Office: PO Box 1212 Houston TX 77001

ALLEN, JANIE ARNOLD, educator; b. Jackson, Miss., Sept. 21, 1938; d. Frank Steele and Virgillee (Holloway) Arnold; B.S., Miss. U. for Women, 1959; M.S., U. So. Miss., 1970, Ph.D., 1973; m. Edgar Allen III, Jan. 31, 1959; 1 dau., Kellie Autumn. Tchr., Natchez, Miss., 1959-60, Meridian, Miss., 1961-62, Jackson, Miss., 1963-64; tchr., primary coordinator Jackson (Miss.) Acad., 1964-68; asso. prof. dept. curriculum and instrn. U. So. Miss., Hattiesburg, 1973—; dir. Literacy Program, First Bapt. Ch., 1970-77; chmn. Project Hope, 1976; elementary edn. cons. Forrest Gen. Hosp., 1977-78; reading/lang. arts cons. Holmes County Sch. System, 1970, Lumberton Sch. System, 1973, Perry County Sch. System, 1974, Columbia Sch. System, 1976, Heidelberg Sch. System, 1977. Active Hattiesburg Civic Arts Council, Hattiesburg Cancer Crusade. U. So. Miss. grad. fellow, 1968-70. Mem. Internat. Reading Assn. (pres. S. Miss. council 1974-75), Assn. Miss. Tchr. Educators, Nat. Assn. Jr. Auxiliaries (chmn. scholarship project Hattiesburg chpt. 1978-79), Forrest County Miss. U. for Women Alumnae (pres. 1974-75), Phi Delta Kappa (chpt. sec. 1977-78), Delta Kappa Gamma (chpt. rec. sec. 1976-78). Kappa Delta Pi, Pi Tau Chi. Baptist. Club: Nat. Assn. Miniature Enthusiasts (sec. S. Miss. chpt. 1978-79). Home: 203 Wildwood Trace Hattiesburg MS 39401 Office: So Sta Box 8296 Hattiesburg MS 39401

ALLEN, JOHN DAVID, lawyer, cons.; b. Rochester, N.Y., Aug. 20, 1944; s. Woodrow Wilson and Ann Veronica (Nugent) A.; B.A., U. Rochester, 1965, M.B.A., 1966; J.D., Cath. U. Am., 1978; postgrad. Sch. Exec. Devel. U. Ga., Athens, 1975; m. Mary Mullins, July 11, 1970. Branch mgr. Arlington (Va.) Fairfax Savs. and Loan Assn., 1970-73; v.p. 1st Fed. Savs. and Loan Assn., Alexandria, Va., 1973-78; v.p., dir. Washington ops. Instl. Pension Cons.'s Data Corp., N.Y.C., 1978—; instr. Inst. Fin. Edn., 1974—. Served to capt. inf. U.S. Army, 1966-70. Decorated D.S.C., Silver Star, Bronze Star, Purple Heart. Mem. Alexandria C. of C., Assn. M.B.A. Execs., Inst. Fin. Edn. Democrat. Roman Catholic. Clubs: Optimists, Masons. Home: 8412 Huerta Ct Alexandria VA 22309 Office: PO Box 15093 Alexandria VA 22314

ALLEN, JOHN ELDRIDGE, historian, former govt. ofcl.; b. Morehead City, N.C., Sept. 11, 1911; s. Arthur Vincent and Annie (Willis) A.; B.B.A., U. Miami (Fla.), 1934; M.A., George Washington U., 1937; postgrad. Am. U., 1937; m. Mary Josephine Edwards, June 11, 1949, 1 son, Mark Edwards. Info. aid NRA, Washington, 1935; tech. aid Dept. Treasury, 1935-39; records asst. Dept. Agr., 1940-41; social research supr. Works Progress Adminstrn., Fed. Works Agy., 1941-42; tech. analyst, writer depts. Army and Defense, 1948-57; asst. exec. dir. Lincoln Sesquicentennial Commn., Nat. Archives, 1958-59; research, writer Abraham Lincoln Sesquicentennial Tributes, 1959-61; instr. social sciences U. Miami, 1961-62, housing asst. Dept. Residence Halls, 1963-74; evening instr. social sci. Miami-Dade Community Coll., 1966; research and writing, 1962—; adv. reorgn. Congress, U.S. Senate Rules and Procedures Rules and Adminstrn. Com., 1963-64; mem. adv. panel govtl. transition planning Carter Adminstrn., 1976-77. Mem. dedication group Statue of Nathan Hale, Dept. Justice Bldg., 1948; mem. Joint Com. Honor Plaques Washington homes nine former Chief Justices U.S., 1948-49; mem. advisory panel Gt. Lawgivers sculptored portraits House Chamber U.S. Capitol, 1949-50; vice chmn. joint birthday celebration honoring George Washington, 1952, also program dir. pub. celebration honoring Thomas Jefferson, Washington, 1952; chmn. Abraham Lincoln's 150th birthday anniversary program Lincoln Mus., Washington, also mem. com. Nat. Lincoln Sesquicentennial Dinner, 1959; speaker program honoring U.S. Grant, Washington, 1959; mem. div. historic sites and bldgs. Nat. Capital Sesquicentennial Commn., Washington, 1950. Served from ensign to lt. comdr., USNR, 1942-46; PTO; Res., 1946-55. Recipient Abraham Lincoln medallion Lincoln Sesquicentennial Commn., 1960; Service plaque Hialeah Boy Scouts Am. Cub Pack, 1961; Service plaque Beta Sigma Rho Fraternity, 1962. Mem. Columbia Hist. Soc. (rec. sec. 1949-52, v.p. 1953-54), Lincoln Group D.C. (past pres., charter), S.A.R. (past pres. D.C., Presidential Insignia medal 1957, service certificate 1968; nat. trustee 1953-54), U.S. Capitol Hist. Soc. (founding mem.), U.S. Supreme Ct. Hist. Soc. (founder), George Washington Law Assn., Renaissance Soc. Am. (founding mem.), U. Miami Gen. Alumni Assn. (dir. 1961-64, chmn. Spring reunion 1962; chmn. devel. council 1962-63), U. Miami Alumni Fund Century Club (charter, organizer chmn. 1963), U.S. Olympic Soc. (charter), Nat. Archives U.S. (asso.), Cousteau Soc., Nat. Trust Hist. Preservation, World-Wide Acad. Scholars (asso.). Democrat. Methodist. Club: University (sec. 50th Anniversary Celebration com. 1954) (Washington). Editor and historian: Allen Personal Papers and Historical Journals, 1973—. Contbr. articles to profl. jours. Home: 7339 SW 82nd St South Miami FL 33143

ALLEN, KAREN SUE, clin. psychologist; b. Columbus, Ga., Mar. 12, 1943; d. William Arthur and Elizabeth Marie (Juengling) Drowns; B.S., U. Idaho, 1965, M.S., 1967; Ph.D., U. Md., 1973; m. Dr. Reuben Michael Allen, Apr. 24, 1974; 1 dau., Brandwyd Michele. Research psychologist Friends Psychiat. Research, Catonsville, Md., 1968-70; psychologist Great Oaks Center, Silver Spring, Md., 1971-73; intern Walter Reed Army Hosp., 1973-74; chief psychology service, Ft. Hood, Tex., 1974-76; asst. prof. psychiatry Thomason Hosp., Tex. Tech. Med. Sch., El Paso, 1977-78; asst. prof. family medicine La. State U. Med. Sch., Shreveport, 1979—; adj. coll. lectr. Howard Community Coll., Columbia, Md., 1971-72; cons. Coppers Cove Sch. System, Tex. and Sabine Valley Mental Health/Mental Retardation Bd., Marshall and Longview, Tex., 1975-76, Killeen (Tex.) Child Abuse Bd., 1975-76. Served to capt. M.S.C., AUS, 1973-76. Licensed, certified psychologist, Tex., Va.; lic. clin. psychologist, Va. Mem. Am., Tex. psychol. assns. Script writer, editor Step Behind Series, 3 films, 1972; also articles, self-instructional monographs, tapes for med. sch. teaching; composer: Flowers Bloom Forever, 1972; Time Has Gone to Sleep, 1972; Tomorrow's Children, 1972. Home: 3 Wood Fern Ln Haughton LA 71037

ALLEN, KERMIT, cons. engring. co. exec.; b. Denison, Tex., July 26, 1933; s. Kermit and Pauline (McGill) A.; student Arlington (Tex.) State Coll., 1951-54; B.S., Tex. A. and I. U., 1957; m. Terry Emery, Aug. 4, 1978; children—Michael Blair, Sally Ann, Susan Ann. Engr., Phillips Petroleum Co., Odessa, Tex., 1957-60; mgr. Mesquite Gas Products Inc., Odessa, 1960-62; chief engr. Permian Brine Sales & Service Co., Odessa, 1962-66; sr. v.p. solution mining Fenix & Scisson Inc., Tulsa, 1966—. Cons. underground storage. Registered profl. engr., Tex. Mem. Nat. Soc. Profl. Engrs., Am. Inst. Mining, Metall. and Petroleum Engrs., So. Gas Assn., Engring. Soc. Tulsa. Club: Tulsa Country. Contbg. author: Society of Mining Engineers Mining Engring. Handbook, 1973. Contbr. articles on underground storage of hydrocarbons in salt caverns to profl. jours. Home: 4912 S Darlington Tulsa OK 74135 Office: 1401 S Boulder Tulsa OK 74119

ALLEN, LEE NORCROSS, historian, univ. dean; b. Shawmut, Ala., Apr. 16, 1926; s. Leland Norcross and Dorothy Herbert (Whitaker) A.; B.S., Auburn U., 1948, M.S., 1949; Ph.D., U. Pa., 1955; m. Catherine Ann Bryant, Aug. 24, 1963; children—Leland, Leslie Catherine. Instr., Eastern Baptist Coll., St. David's, Pa., 1952-53, asst. prof., 1953-55, asso. prof., 1955-57, prof., 1957-61; prof. history Samford U., Birmingham, Ala., 1961—, dean Sch. Grad. Studies, 1965—, dean Coll. Arts and Scis., 1975—. Served with AUS, 1944-46. Paul Harris fellow, 1977. Mem. Am. Hist. Assn., So. Hist. Assn., Ala. Hist. Assn., So. Bapt. Hist. Soc., Ala. Bapt. Hist. Soc. Baptist. Club: Shades Valley Rotary (pres. 1969-70). Author: History of Ruhama Baptist Church 1819-1969, 1969; The First 150 Years: First Baptist Church, Montgomery, Alabama, 1829-1979, 1979; contbr. articles to profl. jours. Home: 24 Pine Crest Rd Birmingham AL 35223 Office: Samford U Birmingham AL 35229

ALLEN, LEWIS, JR., oil and gas operator, rancher; b. Hallettsville, Tex., Oct. 16, 1925; s. Lewis and Elma (Appelt) A.; B.A., U. Tex., 1949. Landman Deep Rock Oil Co., Tex. and La., 1950-54; ind. trader oil and gas properties, 1954—; rancher, South Central Tex., 1954—. Mem. Am. Assn. Petroleum Landmen, Tex. Ind. Producers and Royalty Owners Assn. (past dir., mem. state petroleum issues com.), Tex. SW cattle raisers assns., Ind. Cattlemen's Assn., Chi Phi. Methodist. Club: Petroleum (Houston). Home: 904 E 3d Hallettsville TX 77964 Office: PO Box 124 Hallettsville TX 77964

ALLEN, LORETTA BELLE BROOME (MRS. CLARENCE CANNING ALLEN), artist, journalist; b. Caney, Kans., June 22, 1916; d. Floyd Leroy and Lillie Elizabeth (Trumbly) Broome; student Anatomy Studios, 1933-34, Fed. Art Schs., 1934-36, Famous Writers Sch., 1959-61; m. Marcellus Davis Douglass, Dec. 20, 1934; 1 son, Jesse Davis; m. 2d, Clarence Canning Allen, Feb. 4, 1957. Costume designer Pat Rooney Studios, Oklahoma City, 1934-35; illustrator Dona Dress & Robe Co., Oklahoma City, 1933-36; designer Dona Dress & Robe Mfg. Co., Oklahoma City, 1968-71; columnist Southside Times, Tulsa, 1971—, Bixby (Okla.) shows 1973—; exhibited art in one woman at Tulsa Studio Club Gallery, Fourth Nat. Gallery, Tulsa Little Theatre Gallery; exhibited art in group shows at Oklahoma City Art Center, Allen Art Group, Fourth Nat. Gallery, Tulsa, Tulsa Garden Center, 1978, 79, Tulsa Psychiat. Found. Center, 1980; represented art in permanent collections at Osage County Mus., Pawhuska, Okla. Tchr. drawing adult class Allen Art Studio, Tulsa, 1959-61. Mem. Tulsa Press Club (v.p. 1960-62), Assn. Am. Editorial Cartoonists (v.p. aux. 1967-68), Am. Artist Profl. League, Philbrook Art Mus. and Aux., Tulsa Opera Guild, Tulsa Geneal. Soc., Tulsa Civic Ballet Guild. (illustrator booklet-program 1975, 76). Democrat. Address: 1645 E 17th Pl Tulsa OK 74120

ALLEN, LULLAVEE ROGERS, educator; b. Shuqualak, Miss., Sept. 23, 1919; d. Will and Zeacie Earnestine (Perry) Rogers; B.S., Tenn. State U., Nashville, 1939, M.S., 1977; postgrad. Fisk U., Nashville, 1951-54; m. Howard Verdell Allen, Aug. 16, 1960; 1 son, Howard Verdell. Tchr. home econs. Decatur High Sch., Decaturville, Tenn., 1939-44, supr., 1939-44; supr. Children's Detention Home, Nashville, 1945-47; tchr. public schs., Nashville, 1947-73, Stokes Sch., 1972—. Hostess, USO, 1942-44; leader Girl Scouts Am., Nashville, 1952-62; sponsor Jr. Red Cross, Nashville, 1963-68. Meharry Med. Coll. grantee, 1973, Vanderbilt U. grantee, 1974. Mem. Nat. Council Negro Women (chmn. social services 1973), LaComrade Bridge Club (pres. 1969-73), Couples Club (treas. 1973), Nashville Sigma Shadows (v.p. 1972), Basileus, Zeta Phi Beta. Home: 4004 Drakes Branch Rd Nashville TN 37218 Office: Stokes Sch 3701 Belmont Blvd Nashville TN 37215

ALLEN, MARYON PITTMAN, U.S. senator; b. Meridian, Miss. Nov. 30, 1925; d. John D. and Tellie (Chism) Pittman; student U. Ala., 1944-47, Internat. Inst. Interior Design, 1970; m. Joshua Sanford Mullins, Jr., Oct. 17, 1946 (div. Jan. 1959); children—Joshua Sanford III, John Pittman, Maryon Foster; m. 2d, Senator James Browning Allen, Aug. 7, 1964 (dec. 1978); 1 stepson, James Browning Allen. Office mgr. Dr. Alston Callahan, Birmingham, Ala., 1959-60; bus. mgr. psychiat. clinic U. Ala. Med. Center, Birmingham, 1960-61; agt. Protective Life Ins. Co., Birmingham, 1961-62; women's editor Sun Newpapers, Birmingham, 1962-64; columnist The Birmingham News, 1964—; writer syndicated weekly column Reflections of a News Hen; v.p. Emerald Valley Corp.; partner J.D. Pittman Partnership Co.; U.S. senator from Ala., 1978—. Mem. com. to choose artist of yr. Birmingham Festival Arts, 1967—; v.p. Ladies Senate Red Cross, Ala. Arts Commn.; mem. Blair House Fine Arts Commn., 1974—; Democratic presdl. elector, 1968; trustee Children's Fresh Air Farm, Birmingham, 1947—. Recipient Ala. Press. Assn. 1st place award, 1962, 63, also various state and nat. press awards for typography, fashion writing, food pages. Mem. Birmingham Com. 100 Women (charter), Arlington Hist. Assn. (dir. 1968—), Ala. Hist. Commn. (mem. at large), Antiquarian Soc. Gadsden, Gadsden Art Assn, U.S. Capitol Hist. Soc., Nat. Trust Historic Preservation. Presbyterian. Clubs: Music Study, Gadsden Country, Music (Gadsden); Mountain Laurel Garden; Am. Newspaper Women's (membership com.), 91st Congress, Congressional, 1925 F Street (Washington). Office: 6205 Dirksen Senate Office Bldg Washington DC 20510

ALLEN, OTIS WILMUTH, ednl. adminstr.; b. Vine Grove, Ky., Feb. 13, 1912; s. Fred P. and Alice Mell (Peterson) A.; B.S., Western Ky. U., 1937; M.S., Ohio State U., 1940; postgrad. Miss. State U., 1954-59, U. Miss., 1960-61, Columbia U., 1960, U. So. Miss., 1962, Delta State U., 1963-65; m. Helen Tucker Farris, Sept. 6, 1941; children—Alice, Rebecca, Otis Wilmuth, Helen Gay, James Fredrick. Dir., Greenwood-Leflore County (Miss.) Civil Def., 1957-69; instr. Greenwood-Leflore Hosp. Sch. Nursing, 1945-56; instr. for meter and instrument constrn. Supreme Electronics, Greenwood, 1942-44; tchr. and head dept. sci. Greenwood High Sch., 1941-56; prin. Hynes Elem. Sch., Meade County, Ky., 1933-36; tchr. Bowling Green (Ky.) Jr. High and Sr. High Sch., 1937-41; supt. edn. Leflore County Schs.,

Greenwood, 1956—. Organizer, Outdoor Conservation Edn. Lab., 1968—; trustee Miss. Delta Jr. Coll., 1956—; mem. adv. com. Gov.'s Conf. on Edn., 1972, Gov.'s Conf. on Sch. Fin. Study, 1973-74; mem. Gov.'s Conf. on Early Childhood Edn., 1975, Gov.'s Conf. on World of Work, 1975, Gov.'s Quality Edn. Com., 1974-76; mem. Miss. Stering Com. for Sch. Fin. Study, 1976-78, Miss. State Com. on Certification, 1976-78, Miss. State Com. on Grad. Requirements, 1976-78; bd. dirs. Miss. Alliance for Arts Edn., 1976—; mem. Criminal Justice Planning Commn., 1976-77; bd. dirs. Cottonlandia Ednl. and Recreational Found., 1968—, 1st pres., 1973-75; leadership tng. chmn. Delta council Boy Scouts Am., 1942-55; adv. bd. Salvation Army, 1945—; bd. dirs. Golden Age Nursing, 1955—; charter mem. Greenwood Leflore County Kidney Assn. Recipient Most Outstanding Young Man in Greenwood award Jr. C. of C., 1946; Most Outstanding Citizen of Leflore County award Lions, 1962; Outstanding Civilian award U.S. Dept. Def., 1966; Conservation Educator of the Year, Miss. Wildlife Fedn., 1971; Outstanding Community Leadership award Miss. Valley State U., 1975; Golden Deeds award Exchange club, 1973; Outstanding Service award Miss. Indsl. Arts Edn., 1970; Cert. of Achievement, Nat. Acad. for Sch. Execs., 1958, 60; Ford Found. fellow, 1952-53; Disting. award Miss. Acad. Scis., 1980. Mem. Am. Assn. Sch. Adminstrs., Miss. Edn. Assn. (legis. com. 1958-60), Miss. Assn. Sch. Adminstrs. (pres. 1960-61, bd. dirs. 1960-62), Miss. Assn. Sch. Supts. (pres. 1977-78), Miss. Assn. County Supts. (pres. 1957-58), NEA, Nat. Sci. Tchrs. Assn., So. Assn. Colls. and Schs., Miss. Conservation Edn., Miss. Classroom Tchrs. Assn., Miss. Congress of Parents and Tchrs., Greenwood Edn. Assn. (1st pres. 1948-49, bd. dirs. 1950-56), Leflore County Edn. Assn., Outdoor Conservation Edn. Lab., Miss. Friends of the Arts, Smithsonian Asso., Nat. Audubon Soc., Leflore County Hunting and Fishing Assn., Ducks Unltd. Baptist. Clubs: Rotary, Gold Patro Greater Greenwood Found. of Arts, Leflore County Country. Contbr. articles in field to profl. jours. Patentee in field. Home: 1200 S Boulevard Greenwood MS 38930 Office: PO Box 544 Greenwood MS 38930

ALLEN, REUBEN PHILLIP, JR., lawyer; b. Arkadelphia, Ark., Nov. 26, 1917; s. Reuben P. and Georgia (Rutledge) A.; B.A., Henderson State U., 1939; M.A., U. Ark., 1941; J.D., U. Tex., 1952; m. Bernadette McLean, June 24, 1948; children—Reuben Philip, Bruce Edward. Tchr. public schs., Ark., 1939-41; admitted to Tex. bar, 1952; practice law, Yorktown, Tex., 1952-59; atty. real estate div. U.S. Army C.E., Ft. Worth dist., 1959—; partner firm Allen & John, Attys., Ft. Worth, 19—; lectr. Tarrant County Jr. Coll., 1975-79. Chmn. ARC, DeWitt County, 1954; chmn. Longhorn council Dewitt County Boy Scouts Am., 1957; pres. Heart of Tex. Council, Cerebral Palsy Assn., 1960-61, 61-62; pres. Tarrant County Services for Hearing Impaired, 1977-78, 78-79. Served with USAF, 1941-50, ret. lt. col. Res. Mem. Tex. Bar Assn., Fed. Bar Assn., Am. Legion, VFW, Sons of Hermann, Fed. Bus. Assn., U. Ark. Alumni Assn., U. Tex. Alumni Assn., Henderson State U. Alumni Assn., Ret. Officers Assn., Res. Officers Assn. Baptist. Clubs: Masons, Shriners, Order Eastern Star, Nat. Sojourners, Gideons Internat., Lions, Carswell AFB Officers. Home: 5013 Saint Lawrence Rd Fort Worth TX 76103 Office: 1101 WT Waggoner Bldg Fort Worth TX 76102

ALLEN, RICHARD WILLIAM, fin. exec.; b. Monson, Mass., Dec. 7, 1929; s. Leonard Delvil and Kathrine Cecila (Repasky) A.; B.A./B.S., Am. Internat. Coll., 1957; postgrad. Tampa Coll., 1973; m. Lorraine M. Swiderski, June 19, 1954; children—Lorraine Mary, Richard William, Carla Jean, Gary John. Chief acct. Ludlow Papers Corp., Ware, Mass., 1958-61; controller Jarvis & Jarvis Co., Palmer, Mass., 1961-65, Zero Mfg. Co., Monson, 1965-71; treas. Trak Microwave Corp., Tampa, Fla., 1971—. Served with CIC, U.S. Army, 1947-53; ETO. Mem. Nat. Assn. Accts., AMVETS (fin. officer 1960-66). Democrat. Roman Catholic. Home: 6416 Olympia Ave Tampa FL 33614 Office: 4726 Eisenhower Blvd Tampa FL 33614

ALLEN, ROBERT CHARLES, physician, biochemist; b. Pueblo, Colo., Aug. 12, 1945; s. Noel Charles and Gladys Louise (Puig) A.; B.S., Southeastern La. U., 1967; Ph.D., Tulane U., 1973, M.D., 1977; m. Joan Marie Lindsay, June 26, 1976; 1 son, Robert Lindsay. Asso. in biochemistry Tulane U., New Orleans, 1973-76; intern Brooke Army Med. Center, Ft. Sam Houston, Tex., 1977-78, infectious disease officer, Inst. Surg. Research and Clin. Investigation Service, 1978—. Served with U.S. Army, 1968-70. Recipient award La. Pathology Soc., 1977; Leah Seidman Shaffer award, Tulane U., 1977; cert. physician, surgeon La. Mem. Am. Soc. Microbiology, Am. Chem. Soc., Am. Soc. Photobiology, Biophys. Soc., Reticuloendothelial Soc., Am. Fedn. Clin. Research, AMA, Sigma Xi. Med. research in field of biochemistry and immunology. Home: 3215 Woodcrest Dr San Antonio TX 78209 Office: Box 455 Brooke Army Med Center US Army Fort Sam Houston TX 78234

ALLEN, ROBERT LOUIS, univ. ofcl.; b. Stockton, Ala., Sept. 12, 1935; s. Dan and Susie (Thomas) A.; B.S., Ala. A&M U., 1961; M.A., U. Iowa, 1968; m. Clara Juliette Blackshear, Dec. 21, 1964; 1 son, Quentin B. Instr. printing Fla. A&M U., Tallahassee, 1961-66, dir. publs., 1970-71, dir. univ. relations, 1971—; copy editor and columnist Decatur (Ill.) Herald newspapers, 1968-70. Mem. citizens adv. com. Leon County Democratic Exec. Com., 1979—. Served with U.S. Army, 1954-57. Recipient Outstanding Service award Student Govt. Assn., Fla. A&M U. Mem. Fla. Public Relations Assn. (dir. 1978-79), So. Public Relations Fedn., Public Affairs Council of State of Fla. Univ. System (mem. legis. coordinators team 1978—), Nat. Assn. of State Univs. and Land Grant Colls. (chmn. 1978-79), Leon County Parents Assn. for Gifted Children (pres. 1980-81), Tallahassee Urban League, Tallahassee C. of C., NAACP, Kappa Alpha Psi. Baptist. Contbr. news and feature stories to state and local newspapers; producer, host weekly TV and radio programs. Home: 251 Little John Trail Tallahassee FL 32312 Office: Fla A&M U PO Box 368 Tallahassee FL 32307

ALLEN, ROLAND HAROLD, lawyer, businessman; b. Waco, Tex., Apr. 16, 1921; s. Albert Sidney and Ida (Neel) A.; J.D., Baylor U., Waco, 1951; m. Elnora Lee Daniel, July 18, 1953; children—Donna Carol, James Edwin, William Harold. Admitted to Tex. bar, 1951; law clk., liaison with mil. and vets. reps. Office U.S. Congressman, Washington, 1951-52; asso. firm Eugene E. Piper, Borger, Tex., 1953; partner Gassaway & Allen and predecessor firms, Borger, 1954-68; asst. atty. gen. of Tex., Austin, 1969-79. Engaged in oil gas bus., Borger, 1955—, real estate investments, 1958—; sec., dir. Indsl. Dynamics, Inc., Borger, 1961-69; atty. Panhandle Bank & Trust Co., Borger, 1954-68, 1st Savs. & Loan Assn., Borger, 1955-68. Dist. chmn. Nat. Fedn. Ind. Bus., 1963-68; mem. Tax Equalization Bd., Borger, 1965-67, chmn., 1967. Precinct chmn. Democratic party, 1960-62. Bd. dirs. Hutchinson County Child Welfare, 1967-69; trustee land trust, Amarillo, Tex., 1965-69; trustee, sec. N.W. Tex. Masonic Home and Sch. Ednl. Found., 1963—. Served with USMC, 1942-46; PTO. Decorated Purple Heart. Mem. Am., Borger (pres. 1957), Travis County bar assns., State Bar Tex., Am. Judicature Soc., Am. Legion, Delta Theta Phi. Baptist. Mason (Shriner, 32 deg., editor Tex. Freemason 1980—). Clubs: Exchange (pres. 1957), Country (Borger). Home: 2903 Clarice Ct Austin TX 78731

ALLEN, THOMAS JEFFERSON, educator, range scientist; b. Wortham, Tex., Aug. 4, 1925; s. Frank and Rubye Margaret (Holmes) A.; A.S., John Tarleton Jr. Coll., 1948; B.S., Tex. A & M U., 1949, Ph.D., 1969; M.A., Sul Ross State U., 1960; m. Billye Scarbrough, Dec. 15, 1946; children—Desiee (Mrs. Patrick Marek), Thomas Jefferson, Forrest Frank. Tchr. vocat. agr. Marathon (Tex.) Ind. Sch. Dist., 1955-57, Alpine (Tex.) Ind. Sch. Dist., 1957-59; asst. range specialist Tex. Agrl. Expt. Sta., Marfa, 1957-59; range scientist Tex. A & M U., Marfa, 1960-63, Tex. Agr. Expt. Sta., Pecos, Tex., 1963-67; asst. prof. Tex. A & M U., 1969-74, Tex. Agr. Expt. Sta., Vernon, Tex., 1974-79; adminstr. tech. programs SDHPT, 1979—. Vice pres. College Station (Tex.) Little League, 1970-74. Served with USNR, 1942-45. Mem. Soc. Range Mgmt., Am. Soc. Plant Physiologists, Weed Sci. Am., Sigma Xi. Baptist. Contbr. articles to profl. jours. Home: 502 Sara St Round Rock TX 78664 Office: 11th & Brazos Austin TX 78701

ALLEN, WALTER GREGORY, JR., coll. adminstr.; b. LaFayette, Ala., Aug. 8, 1924; s. Walter G. and Ruth W. (Wooddy) A.; B.S., Auburn U., 1947; M.B.A., U. Fla., 1966, Ed.D., 1974; m. Jo Ann Long, Oct. 12, 1952; ; 1 dau., Vivian Jo Ann. Asst. prodn. dir., cost engr. John H. Swisher & Sons, Inc., Jacksonville, Fla., 1947-52; dir. Colonial Properties, Inc., Jacksonville, 1952—; chmn. dept. mgmt. Jones Bus. Coll., Jacksonville, 1967-71; instr. econs., mgmt. and accounting Fla. Jr. Coll., Jacksonville, 1967-73, coordinator bus. adminstrn. dept., 1973—. Mem. YMCA, Jacksonville, 1950—; mem. Manpower Advisory Council, 1977—, Jacksonville Community Relations Commn., 1976—; trustee Edward Waters Coll., 1976—. Served to 1st lt. USAAF, 1942-46. Recipient Manuscript award Nat. Assn. Accountants, 1975 76, Most Valuable Mem. award, 1976, Community Service award City of Jacksonville, 1975; Community Service and Humanitarian award NAACP, 1974; named Tchr. of the Year, Jones Bus. Coll., 1971. Registered profl engr., Ga.; licensed gen. contractor, Fla.; licensed real estate broker. Mem. Nat. Accounting Assn. (v.p. edn. 1976—, dir. 1975), Sales and Mktg. Execs. Internat., Jacksonville Bd. Realtors, Am. Mgmt. Assn., Am. Soc. Mil. Engrs., Nat. Soc. Profl. Engrs., Soc. Advancement Mgmt., AAUP, Fla. Assn. Community Colls., Am. Assn. Community and Jr. Colls., Am., Fla., Duval County vocational edn. assns., Nat. Assn. Bus. Educators, Jacksonville Area C. of C., U. Fla. Alumni Assn. (pres.'s council 1974—), Auburn U. Alumni Assn., Phi Theta Pi, Phi Delta Kappa. Episcopalian. Contbr. articles to profl. jours. Clubs: Univ., Ponte Vedra, Sawgrass, Ye Mystic Revellers. Home: 1508 Campbell Ave Jacksonville FL 32207 Office: 3116 Atlantic Blvd Jacksonville FL 32207

ALLEY, BARRETT LEQUATTE, publisher; b. N.Y.C., Oct. 29, 1934; s. Paul Richter and Maxine (McKinney) A.; B.S., Mich. State U., 1958; m. Karen Adair, Jan. 19, 1979; 1 son, Paul Edward. Media buyer Benton & Bowles, N.Y.C., 1958-61; media supr. Kenyon and Eckhardt Advt., Inc., N.Y.C., 1961, asst. media dir., Detroit, 1961-63, v.p., media dir., Chgo., 1963-66, v.p., dir. programs and TV, N.Y.C., 1966-69; sr. v.p. mktg. Burton Sohigian Advt., Detroit, 1969-72; pub., founder Indian River Life Mag., Vero Beach, Fla., 1972—; chmn., chief exec. officer Tampa Bay Life Mag., 1980—. Pres., Indian River County United Way. Mem. Fla. Mag. Assn. (treas.). Republican. Episcopalian. Club: Rotary (Ft. Lauderdale). Address: Box 1118 Vero Beach FL 32960

ALLEY, CARL QUILLIN, fence co. exec.; b. Gate City, Va., Aug. 29, 1918; s. Lloyd and Callie (Quillin) A.; m. Irene; children—James, Susan, Robert. With Sears, Roebuck & Co., Roanoke, Va. and Miami, Fla., 1937-76; exec. v.p. Pan Nat. Fence Mfg. Co., Bay Harbour, Fla., 1976—, also dir.; sec.-treas. Chain Link Mfg. Inst. Served in USAF, 1945-48. Republican. Home: 150 NW 100 Ter Miami Shores FL 33150 Office: 1135 Kane Concourse Bay Harbour FL 33154

ALLEY, CLYDE DUNN, chemist, mfg. co. exec.; b. Nashville, Aug. 27, 1931; s. Clyde Dunn and Corinne (Lee) A.; B.S., U. Tenn., 1954, Ph.D., 1959; m. Peggy Anne White, Aug. 18, 1956; children—Michael Paul, Jeffrey Scott, Pamela Lee. Chief thermodynamics group Thiokol Chem. Corp., Huntsville, Ala., 1959-61; dir. preliminary design and analysis, Northrop Carolina Inc. (now Chemtronics Inc.), Asheville, N.C., 1961-64, tech. dir. 1965-70, mgr. chem. research, 1970-73; mgr. devel. Mason & Hanger, Silas Mason Co. Inc., Pantex Plant, Amarillo, Tex., 1973—; Recipient U.S. Air Force Systems Command award, 1964; Petroleum Research Fund grantee, 1959—. Mem. Am. Chem. Soc., AIAA, Am. Def. Preparedness Assn., Sigma Xi. Baptist.

ALLEY, ERNEST ROBERTS, cons. engr.; b. Greenville, Miss., Sept. 17, 1938; s. Ernest Hayes and Thelma Minon (Roberts) A.; B.E. in Civil Engring., Vanderbilt U., 1960, M.S., 1972; m. Marion Catherine Spelta; children—E. Roberts, Laura Elizabeth, Aime Catherine, Emma Lynne. Project engr. Oman Constrn. Co., Inc., Memphis, 1960-61; sr. engr. J.R. Wauford & Co., Donelson, Tenn., 1961-68; pres. Alley & Brown, Inc., Nashville, 1968-71; v.p. Hart-Freeland-Roberts, Inc., Nashville, 1971-74; pres. E. Roberts Alley & Assos., Inc., Brentwood, Tenn., 1974-80, Alley, Young & Baumgartner, Inc., Brentwood, 1980—. Active Boy Scouts Am. Served with U.S. Army, 1960-61. Mem. Am. Water Works Assn., Water Pollution Control Fedn., ASCE, Nat. Soc. Profl. Engrs., Am. Cons. Engrs. Council, Nashville C. of C. Presbyterian. Club: Rotary. Home: 6030 Sherwood Ct Nashville TN 37215 Office: PO Box 496 Brentwood TN 37027

ALLEY, J. T., JR., city ofcl.; b. Lubbock, Tex., June 26, 1923; s. J.T. and Edna Ann (Mullins) A.; student FBI Nat. Acad., 1952, Tex. Technol. U., 1955-56, U. Okla., 1962, U. Louisville, 1963, U. Tex., 1967; m. Wanda Qwenelle Lewis, Oct. 6, 1976; children—Mary Ann (Mrs. David Andy Wilkinson), Patricia K. (Mrs. Vasa Spurling), Billie D'Arlene (Mrs. Robert Jay Schwinkendorf), Jaye Tori (Mrs. Brian Harrison). Patrolman, Lubbock Police Dept., 1946-47, sgt., 1947-51, capt., 1951-57, chief of police, 1957—; mem. criminal justice adv. com. South Plains Assn. Govts., 1979-80. Bd. dirs. Lubbock State Sch., 1979-80. Served with USMC, 1942-46. Mem. Am. Fedn. Police, Internat. Assn. Chiefs of Police (chmn. emergency planning com. 1972—). Methodist. Rotarian (dir. 1968-70). Home: 3608 Knoxville Dr Lubbock TX 79423 Office: Box 2000 Lubbock TX 79457

ALLGOOD, MYRALYN FRIZZELLE, educator; b. Atlanta, Mar. 2, 1939; d. Murray and Sybil (Cowart) Frizzelle; B.A. magna cum laude, Samford U., 1961; postgrad. Instituto Tecnologico y de Estudios Superiores de Monterrey (Mex.), 1961, U. Nacional Autonomo de Mex., 1963; M.A., U. Ala., 1963; m. Stephen Craig Allgood, Apr. 11, 1964; 1 dau., Allison Lucienne. Prof. Spanish, Samford U., Birmingham, Ala., 1963—. Student summer missions coordinator Rio Grande River Ministry, Baptist Gen. Conv., Tex., 1975-80. Recipient Macon award for excellence in teaching Samford U., 1978. Mem. Ala. Assn. Fgn. Lang. Tchrs. (hostess and local arrangements coordinator ann. meeting 1977-80), MLA, So. Conf. Lang. Teaching, Am. Assn. Tchrs. Spanish and Portuguese (state sec.-treas. 1974-75, state v.p. 1975-76, state pres. 1976-77), Southeastern Conf. Latin Am. Studies, Am. Council on Teaching Fgn. Langs., Birmingham Fgn. Lang. Council, Birmingham Spanish Club, Phi Kappa Phi, Sigma Delta Pi, Pi Kappa Phi, Kappa Delta Epsilon, Kappa Delta Pi, Zeta Tau Alpha (acad. adv.). Baptist. Office: Dept Fgn Langs Samford U Birmingham AL 35209

ALLGOOD, THOMAS FORREST, state senator; b. Augusta, Ga., Sept. 10, 1928; s. Forest Verdell and Lovie (Young) A.; grad. Augusta Coll., 1949; LL.B., Emory U., Atlanta, 1952, LL.D., 1970; m. Thelma Ray, Apr. 1, 1956. Pres. Ins. Adjusting Service, Inc., Augusta, 1953-58; admitted to Ga. bar, 1952; sr. partner firm Allgood and Child, Augusta, 1954—; mem. Ga. Senate from 22d Dist., 1976—. Served with AUS, 1946-47. Mem. VFW. Democrat. Methodist. Club: Augusta Golf. Address: PO Box 1523 Augusta GA 30903

ALLISON, CLAUDE FERRELL, assn. exec., lawyer; b. Pensacola, Fla., Apr. 7, 1921; s. Claude Alexander and Leona Eloise (Edgar) A.; B.A., Rollins Coll., 1948; J.D., Jones U., 1976; m. Dorothy Winifred Devis, Feb. 25, 1945; children—Sally Anne Allison Behel, Claude Ferrell, Arvie MacKinnon. Advt. copywriter Young & Rubicam, N.Y.C., 1948; pub. accountant Raymond Holdsworth & Co., Boston, 1948-50; asst. office mgr. Amoskeag Co., Boston, 1950-51; pres., gen. mgr. Charlie Wilkerson Gas Co., Pensacola, Fla., 1951-72; exec. dir. Ala. LP-Gas Assn., Montgomery, 1972—; admitted to Ala. bar, 1977; dir. Fla. LP-Gas Assn., 1968-71, sec.-treas., 1971-72; pres., dir. Greater Pensacola Gas Inst., 1968—, Gas Inst. W. Fla., 1961-62. Chmn. bd. dirs. Escambia Christian Sch., Pensacola, 1970-72. Served with USN, 1941-45. Recipient Algernon Sydney Sullivan award Rollins Coll., 1948. Mem. Am. Soc. Assn. Execs., Ala. Council Assn. Execs., Hwy. Users Conf., Ala. Trial Lawyers Assn., Am., Ala. bar assns., Pi Gamma Mu, Phi Kappa Psi. Democrat. Mem. Chs. of Christ. Club: Capital City Kiwanis (Montgomery, Ala.). Home: Route 1 Box 237 Shorter AL 36075 Office: 660 Adams Ave Suite 394 Montgomery AL 36104

ALLISON, FRANK EDWARD, SR., architect; b. San Saba, Tex., Nov. 7, 1929; s. Benjamin Rush and Gladys Mae (Karnes) A.; B.Arch., Tex. A. and M. U., 1951; m. Maxine G. Nickles, Nov. 26, 1952; children—Tina Denise, Brenda Day, Frank Edward, Melissa Dawn. Engring. draftsman H. E. Bovay Engrs., Houston, 1953-54; project architect/prodn. capt. Pitts, Mebane & Phelps, Beaumont, Tex., 1954-59; prin. Frank E. Allison Assos., Beaumont, 1959-61; dir. planning/project dir. Welton Becket Assos., Houston, 1961-63, project architect, N.Y.C., 1963-66; prin. Allison Assos., Houston, 1966—; pres. AIA Corp. and Allison/Walker Interests, Houston, 1973—; gen. partner Atrium Greenbriar Partnership, 6776 Regency Partnership, 2323 Voss Partnership, West Forest Ltd., Atrium 525 Venture, Atrium 6420 Partnership, Atrium 2600 Partnership, Atrium 523 Venture, Atrium Westwood Ltd., Atrium 210; pres. High Sign, Inc., Stratasource, Inc. Recipient Disting. Student award Tex. A. and M. U., 1950, 51, Design awards Houston Light & Power, 1972; registered architect, Tex., La., N.Y., Fla., Okla., Ga. Mem. AIA, Nat. Council Archtl. Registration Bds., Tex. Soc. Architects, Am. Soc. Planning Ofcls., Urban Land Inst. Author: Comparative Wall Analysis, 1957; Matrix of CBD, 1959; Land-Use Tract Analysis, 1962; Theory and Planning of Satellite Shopping Centers, 1962; Land Use Study, 1962; High Rise Apartment Feasibility Study, 1963; Marina Resort Development, 1963; Design and Development of the Atrium Office Building, 1975. Home: 6200 Claridge St Houston TX 77096 Office: 9898 Bissonnet-One Houston TX 77036

ALLISON, IRL, pianist, music educator; b. Warren, Tex., Apr. 8, 1896; s. John Van and Mary Cleona (Richardson) A.; A.B., Baylor U., 1915, A.M., 1922; D.Mus. (hon.), Southwestern Conservatory, Dallas, 1947; LL.D., Hardin-Simmons U., 1954; attended Chgo. Mus. Coll., summer 1915, Columbia U., 1920-21, summers 1942, U. Tex., 1943; Dr. Music (hon.), Houston Conservatory, 1954; piano study Ezra Rachlin, Rudolph Hoffman, Josef Evans, Percy Grainger, Ernest Hutcheson, Harold von Mickwitz, Walter Gilewicz; m. Jessie Johnson, July 3, 1918 children—Mary J. (dec.), John (dec.), Irl, Lucille (Mrs. Therl Ockey). Dean music Rusk Coll., 1918-19; instr. piano Baylor Coll. Women, 1921-23; dean fine arts Montezuma Coll., 1923-27; dean music Hardin-Simmons Univ., 1927-34. Founder, pres. Nat. Guild Piano Tchrs.; pres. Am. Coll. Musicians, 1934-60; founder Golden Rule Peace Movement and originator World Peace Programs (radio), 1948; mgr. Nat. Piano-Playing Auditions (founder), 1929-60; editor Piano Guild Notes, 1951-60. Mem. Music Tchrs. Nat. Assn., Music Educators Nat. Conf., Nat. Music Council, Author: Through the Years; Our George. Compiler editor Irl Allison Piano Library, 33 vols. Contbr. to newspapers, music publications. Co-founder, donor $10,000 grand prize Van Cliburn Internat. Quadrennial Piano Competition. Home: 1500 Murray Ln Austin TX 78703

ALLISON, JAMES CLAYBROOKE, II, broadcasting co. exec.; b. Mason County, Ky., May 26, 1942; s. James Claybrooke, and Frances Orme A.; B.A. in Radio-TV, U. Ky., 1964; m. Rosa Lee Parr, Aug. 29, 1965; children—Frances Michelle, James Claybrooke, III. Announcer, Sta. WVLK, 1964-65; news dir., Sta. WCMI, 1965; news reporter Sta. WLAP, Lexington, Ky., 1965-68, announcer, copywriter, 1968-69, asst. gen. mgr., ops. dir., 1969-70, gen. mgr., 1970—. Vice-pres., Ky. chpt. Leukemia Soc. Am., 1977—; bd. dirs. Big Bros./Big Sisters, Lexington, 1979—. Mem. Sales and Mktg. Execs. Lexington (dir. 1978—), Ky. Assn. Broadcasters. Democrat. Club: Lions. Office: 3549 Russell Cave Rd PO Box 11670 Lexington KY 40577

ALLISON, JIMMY EARL, elec. utility engr.; b. Palo Pinto County, Tex., Nov. 8, 1941; s. Joseph Earl and Desla Frances (Camp) A.; A.A., Weatherford (Tex.) Jr. Coll., 1962; B.S. in Elec. Engring., Arlington State Coll. (now U. Tex., Arlington), 1965. Jr. engr. Tex. Elec. Service Co., Big Spring, 1970, asso. engr., Fort Worth, 1970-76; elec. engr. Tex. Utilities Generating Co., 1976-77, Tex. Electric Service Co., Fort Worth, 1977—. Served with USNR, 1966-70. Registered profl. engr., Tex. Mem. IEEE. Mem. Ch. of Christ. Home: 2801 Wildplum St Arlington TX 76015 Office: PO Box 970 Fort Worth TX 76101

ALLISON, JOHN WALLACE, JR., power cons.; b. Middlesboro, Ky., Dec. 16, 1920; s. John Wallace and Rosa Belle (Phillips) A.; B.M.E., U. Tenn., 1950; m. Margaret Taylor, Jan. 27, 1943; children—John Wallace, April Allison Behringer, Amy. Comml. service adviser Tex. Power & Light Co., Waco, 1951-52, power cons., Dallas, 1952, So. div., Waco, 1953-74, sr. power cons., 1974—. Chief judge, mem. adv. bd. Central Tex. Regional Sci. Fair, 1963-78; pres. Waco chpt. USO, 1968—; Waco com. chmn. Tex. Tech. Edn. Adv. Found. Served to lt. col. USAAF, 1942-46. Decorated Air medal. Mem. Air Force Assn. (Tex. State pres. 1970, dir. 1968—), Tex. Mfrs. Assn. (dir. 1974-75), Tex. Assn. Bus. Democrat. Baptist. Clubs: Kiwanis of Waco, Waco City. Home: 3113 Alexander St Waco TX 76708 Office: 3600 Franklin Ave Waco TX 76703

ALLISON, MARSHALL LORETZ, lawyer; b. Lavonia, Ga., Mar. 3, 1897; s. Thomas F. and Gertrude (Bost) A.; B.S., Young Harris Coll., 1915; m. Marion W. Wilbanks, Aug. 27, 1919; 1 dau., Julia Carolyn (Mrs. Robert J. Urick). Admitted to Ga. bar, 1926, U.S. Supreme Ct., 1936; practiced in Lavonia, 1926-36, city atty., 1926-36; asst. atty. gen. Ga., Atlanta, 1937-38, 38-41, 43-45; judge No. Jud. Circuit Ga., Lavonia, 1938; law asst. to chief justice Ga. Supreme Ct., 1941-42; pvt. practice law, Atlanta, 1945-53, Lavonia, 1953—; apptd. mem. Jud. Council Ga., 1962-64. Trustee, Young Harris Coll., 1942—. Served with F.A., U.S. Army, World War I. Mem. Am., Ga. bar assns.,

Bar Assn. No. Jud. Circuit Ga., Am. Legion (1st comdr.). Methodist (steward). Lion (1st pres.). Author: Compiled Opinions of Attorney General of Georgia, 1939-41, 1941-43. Address: 55 Bowman St Lavonia GA 30553

ALLISON, MELODY POTTS, nurse; b. Jefferson County, Tenn.; R.N., E. Tenn. Bapt. Hosp. Sch. of Nursing, Knoxville, 1955; B.S., St. Mary-of-the Woods Coll., St. Mary-of-the-Woods, Ind., 1976; M.Ed. summa cum laude, U. Louisville, 1977; m. Lawrence Allison; children—Deborah Lea, Jennifer Faye, Stuart James, Patricia Ann. With Blount Meml. Hosp., Maryville, Tenn., 1955-66, U. Tenn., Knoxville, 1966-69, 71-74, Alcoa (Tenn.), 1969-71, Suburban Hosp., Louisville, 1974-78; with Morton F. Plant Hosp., Clearwater, Fla., 1978—, asst. dir. nursing, 1978—. Mem. Nat. League for Nursing, Am. Soc. Nursing Adminstrs., Iota Lambda Sigma. Home: 1105 Melba Ct Largo FL 33540 Office: Morton F Plant Hosp 323 Jeffords St Clearwater FL 33517

ALLISON, PATRICIA HELBING, assn. exec.; b. Tulsa, June 22, 1935; d. Carl John and Lucile Clarice (McElwee) Helbing; student Bishop Toolen Jr. Coll. for Women, 1949, Fla. State U., Tallahassee, 1952-53; m. John McLean Allison, Jr., June 16, 1962; children—John McLean III, Carl John. Inventory clk. Jackson Grain Co., Tampa, Fla., 1952-54; customer service Tampa Electric Co., 1954-62; freelance market researcher, Tampa, 1963-68; exec. dir. Suncoast council Girl Scouts U.S.A., Tampa, 1978—. Mem. Citizens Adv. Bd. Sta. WEDU-TV, Public Broadcasting Service, Tampa, 1979—; pres. Tampa Jr. Mus., 1973-74; mem. budget adv. com. Tampa City Council, 1975-77; pres. Hillsborough Assn. Vol. Coordination, 1976-77; mem. council of execs. Tampa and Pinellas United Way, 1978—; active Hillsborough County Youth Collaboration; treas. Jr. League of Tampa, Inc., 1971-72; pres. parents club Christ the King Roman Cath. Ch., 1976-77, chmn. sch. bd., 1977-78, pres. parish council, 1979-80. Mem. Tampa C. of C., Tampa Fedn. Garden Clubs (fin. chmn. 1968), Delta Delta Delta. Democrat. Home: 3224 Fountain Blvd Tampa FL 33609 Office: Suncoast Council Girl Scouts USA 3711 Watrous Ave Tampa FL 33609

ALLMAN, MARIAN ISABEL, ophthalmologist; b. Birmingham, Ala., Feb. 18, 1946; d. William Claxton and Reva Elizabeth (White) A.; B.A., Fisk U., 1966; M.D., Meharry Med. Coll., 1970. Intern, George W. Hubbard Hosp., Nashville, 1970-71; resident in ophthalmology H.G. Phillips Hosp., St. Louis, 1971-74; fellow in ophthalmology Washington U., St. Louis, 1971-72; fellow in ophthalmic pathology U. Pa., 1974-76; staff ophthalmologist VA Hosp., Tuskegee, Ala., 1976-77; chief ophthalmology sect. VA Med. Center, Tuskegee, 1977—, dir. residency program, 1977—. Joseph Goldberger fellow, 1969; NIH trainee, 1974-76. Diplomate Am. Bd. Ophthalmology. Mem. Am. Acad. Ophthalmology, Ala. Acad. Ophthalmology, Am. Assn. Ophthalmology, Assn. Research and Vision Ophthalmology, AMA, Nat. Med. Assn., Med. Assn. Ala. Baptist. Contbr. articles to profl. jours. Home: 166 Pinetree Dr Montgomery AL 36117 Office: VA Medical Center Tuskegee AL 36083

ALLMAN, MARTHA KINZER, nurse; b. Pulaski, Va., May 24, 1938; s. Henry Brinson and Louise Ratcliffe K.; L.P.N., Haywood County Hosp., Waynesville, N.C., 1965; A.S.D., E. Tenn. State U., 1972; m. Boyce Allman, Nov. 3, 1952; children—Nancy, Bane, Laura, Gray. Sec., N.Y. Life Ins. Co., Christinsburg, Va., 1962, County Agent Office, Christinsburg, 1963; coordinating nurse surgery Holston Valley Hosp., Kingsport, Tenn., 1965-73; operating room supr. Indian Path Hosp., Kingsport, 1973—. Mem. Tenn. Nurses Assn., Tenn. Soc. Nursing Service Dirs., Assn. Operating Room Nurses (dir. chpt. 5, 1978—), Operating Room Research Inst. Home: Route 1 Box 2A Gate City VA 24251 Office: Indian Path Hospital Kingsport TN 37660

ALLMON, JOSEPH THURMAN, textile co. exec.; b. Mize, Miss., Mar. 20, 1921; s. William Richard and Susan Elizabeth (Huff) A.; student East Central Jr. Coll., 1938-40; B.A., Miss. Coll., 1942; Th.M., So. Bapt. Sem., 1945; postgrad. N.Y. U., 1948; m. Vauda Carolyn Burson, Sept. 25, 1945; 1 son, Warren Douglas. Personnel dir. Riegel Textile Corp., Conover, N.C., 1957-59, supr. mgmt. devel., N.Y.C., 1959-63, dir. indsl. relations, Ware Shoals, S.C., 1963-69, v.p. indsl. relations, 1969-73, v.p., Greenville, S.C., 1973—; adj. prof. mgmt. U. S.C., Columbia, 1974-75. Pres. Greenville Urban League, 1974-76; vice chmn. council affiliate press. Nat. Urban League, 1975-76; chmn., bd. trustees Ednl. Resources Found.; civil service commr., Greenville; chmn. Goodwill Industries Upper S.C. Served with USNR, 1945-46. Mem. Silver Bay Indsl. Mgmt. Conf. (past chmn.). Republican. Unitarian. Editor: How to Organize and Conduct a Management Development Group, 1950. Home: 101 E Lanneau Dr Greenville SC 29605 Office: Green Gate Park Greenville SC 29606

ALLPHIN, NYLEN LEE, JR., chemist; b. Laramie, Wyo., Feb. 25, 1937; s. Nylen Lee and Grace Phyllis (Hassell) A.; B.S., Brigham Young U., 1959; postgrad. U. Denver, 1960-61; Ph.D., U. Colo., 1964; m. Patricia Gail Adolf, Dec. 21, 1956; children—Nyla, Allan Lee, Eric Bruce, Kevin Dee, James Wayne, Owen Louis, Loreen, Darren, Susan, Andrew Nylen. Chemist, Marathon Oil Research Center, Denver, 1959-61; research chemist Chevron Research Co., Richmond, Calif., 1964-76; exec. v.p. Pearsall Chem. Corp., Houston, 1976-79; gen. mgr. Johann Haltermann, Ltd., Houston, 1979—; instr. chemistry U. Colo., 1961-64. Mem. Am. Chem. Soc., Am. Soc. Lubrication Engrs., Sigma Xi, Alpha Chi Sigma. Mormon (stake pres.). Contbr. articles to profl. publs. Patentee in field. Home: 12211 Coachman's Ln Pinehurst TX 77362 Office: 5050 Westheimer Houston TX 77056

ALLRED, GARY ERMON, baking co. exec.; b. Detroit, Nov. 18, 1951; s. E. Roy and Wilma F. (White) A.; B.S. in Bus. Adminstrn., U. Tenn., 1976; children—W. Courtney, Lauren O., Hannah R. Warehouse mgr. Red Kap Industries, Nashville, 1971-73; dock foreman Smith's Transfer Corp., Nashville, 1973-76; dir. acctg. and fin. Tenn. Doughnut Corp., Nashville, 1976—, also corp. sec. Recipient Citizenship award Rotary Club. Democrat. Club: Civitan (pres. 1968-69). Home: PO Box 53 Lakewood Rd Fairview TN 37062 Office: 2975 Armory Dr Nashville TN 37204

ALLRED, PHILLIP LANCE, audiologist; b. Provo, Utah, Dec. 25, 1937; s. Everett Lance and Helen Almira (Duke) A.; B.S. in Bus., Brigham Young U., 1969, M.S. in Audiology, 1974; Ph.D. in Audiology, U. Utah, 1980; m. Lenna Hodnett, June 24, 1967; children—Eric Joseph, Mark Edward, Alysia, Shannon, Christie Lyn, Gary Thomas, Sherry LaRae. Audiological research asst. U. Utah, 1974-76, clin. audiologist Geriatric Clinic, 1974-76; specialist in hearing aids and electronystagmography U. Utah Hosp., 1974-76; asst. prof. audiology Sam Houston State U., Huntsville, Tex., 1976—; pvt. practice audiology, Huntsville, Tex., 1979—; cons. to schs., industry, and physicians. Com. mem. Cub Scouts, Huntsville, 1978—. Served with USN, 1956-60. Mem. Am. Speech and Hearing Assn., Utah Audiology Soc., Tex. Speech and Hearing Assn., Acad. Dispensing Audiologists. Republican. Mormon. Office: Dept Clin Edn Sam Houston State U Huntsville TX 77341

ALLRED, WILLIAM DAVID, state legislator Tex.; b. Austin, Nov. 27, 1933; s. James V. and Joe Betsy (Miller) A.; B.A., Tex. Christian U., 1955; M. Journalism, Columbia, 1961; m. Patricia Lee Moyer, June 18, 1960; children—Rebecca Lee, Stephen David, James Moyer. Various positions Washington bur. Houston Post, 1961-63; mem. staff U.S. Senator Ralph Yarborough of Tex., 1958-59, U.S. Rep. Ray Roberts of Tex., 1963; investigator Govt. Activities Subcom. Ho. of Reps., Washington, 1964-65; mem. Tex. Ho. of Reps., 1967—; lectr. in field. Served with U.S. Army, 1955-57. Licensed minister Disciples of Christ, 1970—. Home: 1567 Mesquite St Wichita Falls TX 76302 Office: PO Box 5066 Wichita Falls TX 76307

ALLS, WILLARD JESS, JR., pharmacologist; b. Paducah, Ky., July 6, 1938; s. Willard Jess and Catherine Mae (Fields) A.; B.S. in Pharmacy, U. Ky., 1962; m. Martha Jean Harding, Aug. 7, 1960; 1 son, Joe Mark. Chief pharmacist Hopkins County Hosp., Madisonville, Ky., 1962-64; dir. pharmacy services Murray (Ky.)-Calloway County Hosp., 1975—; mem. faculty Freed Hardeman Coll., Henderson, Tenn., summers 1972-77; lectr. Murray State U.; pres. Calloway County Council Drug Edn., 1968-73; bd. dirs. Jackson Area Council Health Edn. Services, 1976—. Pres. Murray Middle Sch. PTA, 1973-75; bd. dirs. Mid-South Youth Camp, 1977—, Internat. Bible Coll., 1977—; lay preacher Ch. of Christ, 1962—; deacon Univ. Ch. of Christ, Murray. Recipient Mc Kesson and Robbins Service award, 1967; named Ky. Pharmacist of Year, Ky. Pharm. Assn., 1971; Ky. col., 1970; Duke of Paducah, 1976; Outstanding Young Man of Murray, Murray Jaycees, 1972; recipient Distinguished Service award Calloway County Council Drug Edn., 1972, 73, 74; Recognition award W. Ky. Vocat.-Tech. Sch., Paducah, 1976. Mem. Am., Ky. (past pres.; E.R. Squibb award 1967) socs. hosp. pharmacists, Am., Ky. (President's award 1971), 1st Dist. pharm. assns., Phi Delta Chi. Club: Murray Kiwanis (Distinguished Service award 1971). Author: What The Christian Should Know About Drug Use and Abuse, 1972; What The Christian Should Know About Alcoholism, 1974; Christianity and Tobacco, 1978; also articles. Home: 1610 Keenland St Murray KY 42071 Office: 803 Poplar St Murray KY 42071

ALLSBROOK, OGDEN OLMSTEAD, JR., educator; b. Wilmington, N.C., July 1, 1940; s. Ogden Olmstead and Elizabeth Barringer (Warren) A.; A.B., Wake Forest U., 1962; Ph.D., U. Va., 1966. Asst. prof. econs. U. Miami, Coral Gables, Fla., 1965-66; operations research analyst U.S. Dept. Def., Washington, 1966-68; asst. prof. econs. U. Ga., Athens, 1968-73, asso. prof. econs., 1973—, dir. grad. programs in econs., 1974—. Lectr. U. Md., College Park, 1967-68. Served to capt. AUS, 1966-68. Decorated Army Commendation medal. Mem. Am., So., Western econs. assns., Pub. Choice Soc., Atlanta Econs. Club, Omicron Delta Epsilon, Lambda Chi Alpha. Lutheran. Author: The Utilization of Military Resources, 1968; A Survey of Army Automated Cost Models, 1968. Home: 315 S Pope St Athens GA 30605

ALMANZA, HELEN KATHERINE PLUMMER, educator; b. Stonewall, Okla., Aug. 4, 1939; d. Frank Slater and Jo Ethel (Black) Plummer; B.A., U. Tex., Austin, 1960, M.A., 1970, Ph.D., 1980; m. Albert Almanza, Apr. 1, 1961; children—Albert Boone, Katherine Elizabeth. Speech pathologist Austin (Tex.) Ind. Sch. Dist., 1960-62; tchr. El Paso (Tex.) Presch. for Deaf and Hard of Hearing, 1963-65; speech pathologist Jourdanton Ind. Sch. Dist., 1966-68; teaching asst. dept. speech U. Tex., Austin, 1968-69; speech pathologist Brown Schs., 1970; cons. spl. edn. Edn. Service Center, Region XIII, Austin, 1971—; adv. State Edn. Agy., Bur. Edn. for Handicapped, U.S. Office Edn., Tex. Assn. Children with Learning Disabilities. Den mother Boy Scouts Am., 1970-72; jr. high youth dir. United Meth. Ch., 1968-70; pres. Dill Elementary PTA, 1973-74, O'Henry Jr. High, 1979-80; chmn. security for fiesta Laguna Gloria Art Guild, 1973-76; bd. mem. Capital Area Rehab. Center, 1978—; bd. dirs. Evaluation tng. Consortium, Western Mich. U., 1979—. Recipient Tchr. Edn. div. Service award Internat. Council Exceptional Children, 1978; Calcasieu scholar, 1956; Rehab. Services Adminstrn. fellow, 1969; EPDA fellow, 1970. Mem. Am. Speech and Hearing Assn., NEA, Am. Assn. Edn. Severely/Profoundly Handicapped, Am. Assn. Mental Deficiency, Tex. State Tchrs. Assn., Tex. Assn. Suprs. and Curriculum Dirs., Phi Delta Kappa, Phi Kappa Phi. Contbr. articles in field to profl. jours. Home: 2206 Meadowbrook St Austin TX 78703 Office: 7703 N Lamar Blvd Austin TX 78752

ALMEIDA, JOSÉ AGUSTÍN, educator; b. Waco, Tex., Aug. 28, 1933; s. Jesse M. and Teodora (Mancillas) A.; B.A., Baylor U., 1961; M.A., U. Mo., 1964, Ph.D., 1967; m. Maritza Barros, Sept. 5, 1964; 1 son, José Rodolfo. Teaching asst. U. Mo., Columbia, 1961-66; instr. Baylor U., Waco, 1962-63; asst. prof. dept. Romance langs. U. N.C., Greensboro, 1966-77, asso. prof., 1977—, chmn. Latin Am. studies; vis. prof. Elmira (N.Y.) Coll., summer 1967; asst. prof. Inst. in Middle Am., summer 1968-69; cons. verbal-active teaching method Hampton Inst., 1976, 77; lectr. First Internat. Congress of Picaresque Lit., Madrid, Spain, 1976. Active Common Cause, ACLU. Served with USAF, 1953-57. Nat. Endowment for Humanities fellow, 1970. Mem. Modern Lang. Assn. Am., S.Atlantic Modern Lang. Assn., Am. Assn. Tchrs. Spanish and Portuguese, Internat. Assn. Hispanists, Sigma Delta Pi, Democrat. Roman Catholic. Author: (with Stephen C. Mohler and Robert R. Stinson) Descubrir y crear, 1976; La crítica literaria de Fernando de Herrera, 1976. Home: 1410 Valleymede Rd Greensboro NC 27410

ALMEIDA Y MERINO, ADALBERTO, archbishop; b. Bachiniva, Chihuahua, Mexico, June 5, 1916; s. Luis Almeida Alderete and Maria Merino Saenz; grad. in Philosophy, Theology and Canon Law, Gregorian U., Rome, 1945. Ordained priest Episcopal Ch.; archbishop of Chihuahua; prof. theology, 1946-56; founder, pres. Comision Episcopal de Pastoral Social; pres. Commn. Sacred Music and Arts; mem. Comision de Medios de Comuncacion Social. Mem. Episc. Conf. Mexico. Author: Cartas Pastorales. Office: Av Cuauhtemoc N deg 1828 Chihuahua Chihuahua Mexico

ALMON, JANET NEWTON, advt.-pub. relations exec.; b. Chgo., Oct. 29, 1945; d. William Edward Newton and Mildred Faye (Sorensen) Betten; B.A. in Journalism, U. Ariz., 1967. Dir. info. Wytheville Community Coll., 1967-70; dir. pub. relations, advt. Orsborn Agy., Tucson, 1970-72, 73-74; women's reporter Ariz. Daily Star, Tucson, 1972-73; dir. pub. relations and advt. Nathan Co., Dallas, 1973-76; dir. communications Haldane Assos., Houston, and cons. to nat. orgn., 1976-79; dir. account services Bentley Group, San Antonio and Houston, 1976-79; pres. Almon Assos., Advt./Public Relations, San Antonio, 1979—. Bd. dirs. Big Bros. and Sisters, Alamo Area. Named 1 of Top 10 Presswomen, Nat. Assn. Press Women, 1972; recipient 1st, 2d and 3d Pl. awards Ariz. Presswomen-Nat. Assn. Press Women, 1971, 72, 73, Pub. Service award Pima County (Ariz.) Mental Health Assn., 1970, 71, 72, 73, S.W. Advt. Fedn. award, 1972. Mem. Public Relations Soc. Am., San Antonio Advt. Fedn., Women in Communications. Clubs: Death Valley Yacht and Racquet (founder, commodore), Royal and Ancient Ethical Marching Guard Duck Band. Author: Newspaper Editing Handbook, 1968. Home and Office: 8800 Starcrest 211 San Antonio TX 78217

ALONSO, ANTONIO ENRIQUE, lawyer, editor; b. Havana, Cuba, Aug. 31, 1924; J.D., U. Havana, 1946, Ph.D. in Humanities, 1952; postgrad. Fairleigh Dickinson U., 1968, Coll. St. Teresa, 1971, Iowa State U., 1973, Washington U., St. Louis, 1973; came to U.S., 1959; m. Daisy Ojeda, 1950; children—Margarita, Antonio, Henry, Jorge. Public defendant High Ct. of Las Villas Province (Cuba), 1946-49; tchr. Spanish lit. Valladares Acad., Cienfuegos, Cuba, 1948-52; ofcl. atty. Provincial Govt. Cuba, 1950-52; 1st undersec. of Treasury, Republic of Cuba, 1952-54; prof. tax law U. Jose Marti, Cuba, 1953-58; mem. Ho. of Reps., Congress Republic of Cuba, 1954-58; prof. criminal law U. Cienfuegos, 1958-60; editor stats. dept. Informes sobre Cuba, Miami, Fla., 1959-61; fin. columnist Agencia de Informaciones Periodisticas, Miami, 1963-69; dir. and lectr. Christian orientation 3d Summer Camp, YMCA, Miami, 1963-67; prof. public speech (Spanish), Inst. de Accion Social, Miami, 1964-65; prof. modern langs. dept. Coll. Saint Teresa, Winona, Minn., 1968-74, freshman adv., 1971-74, fgn. student adv., 1970-74, dir. Latin Am. area studies program, 1971-74; prof. grad. summer program Saint Mary's Coll., Minn., 1968-73; editor La Hacienda mag., Miami, 1974—; admitted to Fla. bar, 1976. Recipient Nat. Order of Merit, Republic of Cuba, 1957; named Outstanding Citizen of Cienfuegos (Cuba), 1957; Ricardo Dolz award, 1947. Mem. MLA, Am. Assn. Tchrs. Spanish and Portuguese, Midwest Assn. Latin Am. Studies, Cath. U. Assn., Nat. Assn. Fgn. Student Affairs (grantee 1973), Fedn. Cuban Educators in Exile, Cuban Tchrs. in Exile, Cuban Soc. Internat. Law (nat. award 1946), AAUP, N.W. Assn. Latin Am., Wis. Council Latin Americanists, Cuban Soc. Criminal Law, Sigma Delta Pi. Clubs: Kiwanis, Rotary, K.C. Author: Antonio Maceo. The Commandments of the Fatherland, 1954; Dynamic Budgets, 1956; Violation of Human Rights by the Government of Cuba, 1962; History of the Communist Party of Cuba, 1970; contbr. articles to publs. in Latin Am. and U.S. Home: 11125 SW 128 Ct Miami FL 33186 Office: 1699 Coral Way Suite 315 Miami FL 33145

ALONSO, CARLOS VICTOR, hydraulic engr.; b. Buenos Aires, Argentina, Jan. 18, 1934, came to U.S., 1964, naturalized, 1973; s. José and Natalia (Brossa) A.; Mech.Eng., U. Buenos Aires, 1963; M.Sc., U. Iowa, 1967, Ph.D., 1970; m. Beatriz Luisa Palatini, June 14, 1965; 1 dau., Diane. Research engr. Iowa Inst. Hydraulics Research, Iowa City, 1970-71; asst. prof. civil engring. U. Miss., 1971-74; research hydraulic engr. U.S. Dept. Agr. Sedimentation Lab., Oxford, Miss., 1974—; adj. asso. prof. civil engring. U. Miss., 1974—. Mem. ASCE (chmn. sedimentation task com. 1979-81), Internat. Assn. Hydraulic Research, Am. Geophys. Union. Contbr. articles to profl. jours. Office: PO Box 1157 Oxford MS 38655

AL-SHAIEB, ZUHAIR FOUAD, geologist, educator; b. Damascus, Syria, Sept. 28, 1940; came to U.S., 1967, naturalized, 1977; s. Fouad and Rosette (Sabbagh) Al-S.; B.S., U. Damascus, 1963, diploma edn., 1964; M.S., U. Mo., Rolla, 1969, Ph.D., 1972; m. Rebekah Peterson, Aug. 22, 1970; 1 son, Johnny. Tchr. earth sci. Shaiwk Coll., Kuwait, 1965-66; research and teaching asst. U. Mo., Rolla, 1967-72; asst. prof. geology Okla. State U., Stillwater, 1972-76, asso. prof., 1976—; cons., lectr. in field. NSF, U.S. Dept. Energy grantee. Mem. Geol. Soc. Am., AIME, Nat. Geog. Soc., Sigma Xi, Sigma Gamma Epsilon, Phi Kappa Phi. Contbr. articles to sci. publs., pioneering researcher uranium geochemistry in peralkaline rocks, also investigator clay minerals' diagenesis and effect on sandstone reservoir properties. Home: 721 W Lakeshore Dr Stillwater OK 74074

ALTCHULER, STEVEN IRA, research physiologist; b. N.Y.C., Aug. 1, 1951; s. Murray and Lyn (Atkins) A.; B.S., M.I.T., 1973, Ph.D., 1978. Teaching asst. M.I.T., Cambridge, 1975-77, research asst., 1977-78; research physiologist NASA, Johnson Space Center, Houston, 1978—; nutrition cons.; lectr. in field. Asst. capt. emergency aid stas. ARC, 1975-77, capt., 1977-78, disaster services caseworker, 1977-78, action team vol., 1977—; merit badge counselor Nassau County and Cambridge councils Boy Scouts Am., 1969-74; medic Clear Lake Emergency Med. Corps, 1978—, bd. dirs., 1979—; instr. Am. Heart Assn., 1974-79, instr.-trainer, 1979—. Recipient award Rensselaer Poly. Inst., 1969; Frederick Gardner Fassett, Jr. award, 1973; numerous awards ARC, 1969-79; Vicks fellow, 1976-77; Grumman Aerospace Corp. scholar, 1969-73. Mem. AAAS, Am. Statis. Assn., Houston Calcium Research Group, N.Y. Acad. Sci., Nutrition Today Soc, Sigma Xi. Contbr. articles to sci. jours. Office: NASA/Johnson Space Center Biomed Labs Houston TX 77058

ALTER, RONALD, educator; b. N.Y.C., Mar. 27, 1939; s. Manny and Charlotte (Harris) A.; B.S., City Coll. N.Y., 1960; M.A. (Teaching fellow 1960-62; NSF Summer fellow 1962), U. Pa., 1962, Ph.D. (Research fellow 1962-64), 1965; m. Arlene Barbara London, Nov. 16, 1963; children—Roy Samuel, Robin Damian, Tao Daniel. Asst. prof. math. U. Calif., Los Angeles, 1964-67; math. analyst Litton Systems, Inc., Beverly Hills, Cali., 1966; asso. research scientist System Devel. Corp., Santa Monica, Calif., 1968-69; asst. prof. math. and computer sci. U. Ky., Lexington, 1970-71, asso. prof. computer sci., 1971—, dir. grad. studies dept. computer sci., 1973-74; faculty research participant Oak Ridge Nat. Lab., summer 1975. Postdoctoral research fellow System Devel. Corp., 1967-68. Mem. Am. Math. Soc., Math. Assn. Am. (Ky. rep. 1976—), Assn. for Computing Machinery. Contbr. articles to profl. jours. Home: 521 N Broadway Lexington KY 40508

ALTIERI, PABLO IVAN, physician; b. P.R., May 16, 1943; s. Pablo Altieri and Monsita Nieto; M.D., U. P.R., 1967; m. Emma, June 2, 1967; children—Pablo Ivan, II, Mariemma. Intern, Univ. Hosp.-U. P.R. Med. Sch., 1967-68, resident, 1968-71; research fellow, clin. instr. Ohio State U., 1972-73; dir. cardiovascular lab. U. P.R. Med. Sch., 1975—, asso. prof. medicine, 1975—, also faculty pres. Served with M.C., USAF, 1973-75. Mem. Am. Fedn. Clin. Research, Am. Heart Assn. (dir. P.R. chpt. 1975, Distinguished Mem. 1975), AMA. Roman Catholic. Club: Rotary (Humacao, P.R.). Office: PO Box 23134 U PR Sta Rio Piedras PR 00931

ALTMAN, STEVEN, univ. adminstr.; b. Jacksonville, Fla., Oct. 24, 1945; s. I. Harold and Estelle A.; B.A., UCLA, 1967; M.B.A., U. So. Calif., 1969, D.B.A., 1975; m. Judy Ovadenko, Feb. 8, 1969. Asst. dean Sch. of Bus., U. So. Calif., Los Angeles, 1969-72; asst. prof. Sch. of Bus., Fla. Internat. U., Miami, 1972-75, asso. prof. mgmt., 1975—, chmn. div. mgmt., 1972-77, asst. v.p. acad. affairs, 1977-78, asso. v.p. acad. affairs, 1978—; 1975—; labor arbitrator; cons. Mem. grad. council Embry Riddle Aero. U., 1974-76. Recipient gold medal Freedoms Found., 1971. named Outstanding Faculty mem. Fla. Internat. U., 1975; named Spl. Master Fla. Public Employees Relations Commn., 1976—. Mem. Am. Arbitration Assn., Indsl. Relations Research Assn., Acad. of Mgmt., Am. Soc. for Pub. Adminstrn., Internat. Personnel Mgmt. Assn., Soc. Profls. in Dispute Resolution, Beta Gamma Sigma. Author numerous books; contbr. articles to profl. jours Office: Fla Internat U Tamiami Trail Miami FL 33199

ALTOM, WILLIAM HARVEY, constrn. co. exec.; b. Knoxville, Tenn., Dec. 22, 1925; s. W. Luther and L. Kate (Hicks) A.; B.S.E.E., U. Tenn., 1949; m. E. Jane Brett, June 7, 1947; children—Mark W., Kathleen S., Teresa A. Elec. distbn. engr. Pub. Service Co. of Colo., Denver, 1949-50; elec. engr. Howard P. Foley Co., Denver, 1950-51, Phila., 1952-53; mech. supt. Turner Constrn. Co., Chattanooga, Cin.,

N.Y.C., 1953-62, contract mgr., N.Y.C., Cin., 1962-70, project mgr., Houston, 1970-73, v.p., mgr. Houston terr., 1974—. Served with U.S. Army, 1943-46. Club: Petroleum of Houston. Home: 1306 Chardonnay Rd Houston TX 77077 Office: 3336 Richmond Ave Houston TX 77046

ALTSHULER, HAROLD LEON, pharmacologist; b. N.Y.C., June 8, 1941; s. Jack and Sophie (Goldberg) A.; B.S., Cornell U., 1964; Ph.D., U. Calif., Davis, 1972; m. Marilyn Bornstein, Jan. 25, 1964; children—Jason, Dana. Research asst. Sandoz Pharms. Co., Hanover, N.J., 1963-64, Parke-Davis and Co., Ann Arbor, Mich., 1964-65, Oklahoma City U., 1966; lab. supr. Nat. Center Primate Biology, Davis, Calif., 1967-71; research asso. U. Calif. Med. Sch., Davis, 1971-72; sect. head Tex. Research Inst. Mental Scis., Houston, 1972—; asst. prof. pharmacology Baylor Coll. Medicine, Houston, 1972—; clin. asso. prof. psychology U. Houston, 1974—. Grantee Pharm. Mfrs. Assn., 1974-75. Fellow Am. Coll. Clin. Pharmacology; mem. Soc. Neuroscis., AAAS, ASPET, Western Pharmocology Soc., Am. Assn. Lab. Animal Sci., Phi Kappa Phi. Editor: Behavior and Brain Electrical Activity, 1975. Home: 2043 Masters Ln Missouri City TX 77459 Office: 1300 Moursuund Ave Houston TX 77025

ALTSHULER, KENNETH Z., psychiatrist; b. Paterson, N.J., 1929; B.A., Cornell U., 1948; M.D., U. Buffalo, 1952; D.Sc. (hon.), Gallaudet Coll., Washington, 1972. Rotating intern Kings County Hosp., 1952-53; resident in psychiatry Bronx VA Hosp., 1955-56, N.Y. Psychiat. Inst., 1956-58; practice medicine specializing in psychiatry, N.Y.C., 1958-77; prof. psychiatry, chmn. dept. U. Tex. Southwestern Med. Sch., Dallas, 1977—; attending psychiatrist Home for Aged and Infirmed Hebrews, N.Y.C., 1957-58, Presbyn. Hosp., 1958-77; sr. research scientist N.Y. State Psychiat. Inst., 1958-60, asso. research scientist, 1960; guest lectr. N.Y. Sch. Psychiatry, 1960-62; cons. neuropsychiatry U.S. Naval Hosp., St. Albans, 1962-65; mem. sensoring study sect., div. grants HEW, Vocational Rehab. Adminstrn., 1966-71; tng. analyst Columbia U. Psychoanalytic Clinic for Tng. and Research, 1969-77; unit chief deafness unit Rockland Psychiat. Center and N.Y. State Psychiat. Inst., 1966-77; chief psychiatrist Isabella Geriatric Center, 1958-77; project dir. Trauma and Sleep Physiology, 1976; asst. in psychiatry Columbia U. Sch. Medicine, 1958-59, instr., 1959-63, research asso. psychiatry, 1963-67, asst. clin. prof., 1967-71, asso. clin. prof., 1971-75, prof. clin. psychiatry, 1975-77, dir. undergrad. med. edn. in psychiatry Coll. Physicians and Surgeons, 1974-77. Recipient Wilson award in genetics and preventive psychiatry, 1961; diplomate Am. Bd. Psychiatry. Fellow Am. Coll. Psychiatrists; mem. AAAS, AMA, Am. Psychiat. Assn. (certificate of significant achievement 1976), Am. Psychoanalytic Assn., Assn. Psychoanalytic Medicine (Merit award 1965), N.Y. Acad. Scis., N.Y. State, New York County med. socs., Am. Psychopath. Assn., Assn. Dirs. Med. Sch. Edn. in Psychiatry, Inc. (v.p. 1976-77). Author 5 books and numerous articles in fields of genetics, early total deafness, psychoanalysis, and sleep and dreams as they relate to psychiatry. Address: Southwestern Med Sch U Tex Health Sci Center 5323 Harry Hines Blvd Dallas TX 75235

ALVAREZ, JESSICA HELEN (SCANLAN), speech pathologist; b. El Paso, Tex., June 20, 1953; d. Norbert John and Helen Evelyn (Dyer) S.; B.S., Coll. of Charleston (S.C.), 1976; M.S., Tex. Tech. U., 1978; m. Edward Alvarez, Jr., July 14, 1979. Grad. asst., bilingual speech pathologist/diagnostician St. Mary's of Plains Hosp. and Rehab. Center, Lubbock, Tex., 1978-79, cons., ancillary staff, 1979—; grad. asst., speech pathologist/diagnostician, asso. and asst. dir. Speech and Hearing Center Inc., Lubbock, 1978-79, asst. dir., 1979; early childhood/speech lang. specialist Northside Sch. Dist., San Antonio, 1979—. bilingual speech/lang. pathologist Bexar County. Mem. S. Plains Speech and Hearing Assn., Nat. Student Speech and Hearing Assn., Am. Speech and Hearing Assn. Roman Catholic. Researcher Myasthenia Gravis, cleft palate, early childhood nutrition. Home: 9202 Woodheather San Antonio TX 78250

ALVAREZ, SALVADOR, educator; b. San Isidro, Tex., Apr. 6, 1924; s. Octaviano and Eduviges (Lopez) A.; B.A., Tex. A&I U., Kingsville, 1950, M.A., 1952; Ph.D., U. Tex., 1973; m. Irma Diva Ramos, Aug. 13, 1950; children—Carmen, Irma Lamar, Sandy, Norma Linda, Marco Antonio. Elem. sch. tchr., Premont, Tex., 1949-53; automobile salesman, 1953-59; high sch. tchr., Corpus Christi, Tex., 1959-65; supr. fgn. lang., div. instrn. Corpus Christi Public Schs., 1965-71; prin. Carroll Lane Elem. Sch., Corpus Christi, 1972; asso. prof. edn. Tex. A&I U., 1972—, dir. bilingual specialization masters degree program, 1974-79; mem. regional interviewing com. Tchr. Exchange Program, HEW, 1969-79. Served with AUS, 1943-45. Recipient cert. merit HEW, 1972, City of Kingsville, 1959; fellow U. Ariz., 1954, Central Wash. State U., 1967, U. Tex., 1969-70. Mem. Nat. Assn. Bilingual Edn., Am. Assn. Tchrs. Spanish and Portuguese (chpt. pres. 1970), Teaching English to Speakers Other Langs. Assn., Tex. Assn. Coll. Tchrs., Phi Delta Kappa, Sigma Delta Pi. Democrat. Roman Catholic. Home: 4629 Stonegate Way Corpus Christi TX 78411 Office: Edn Dept Box 196 Tex A&I Univ Kingville TX 78363

ALVAREZ-BEJAR, ROMAN, educator; b. Colima, Colima, Mex., May 4, 1940; s. Jose Roman and Ana (Bejar-Ortiz) A.; B.A., Nat. U. Mex., 1965; M.S. (Nat. Inst. Sci. Research grantee), U. Calif. at Berkeley, 1969, Ph.D. (Nat. Inst. Sci. Research grantee 1970-71, Nat. Council Sci. and Tech. 1972), 1972; m. Carmen Varea Gilabert, May 7, 1965; children—Francisco Roman, Maria Jose. Prof. physics U. Sonora (Mex.), 1965-67; asst. research geophysicist U. Calif. at Berkeley, 1972-73; prof. geophysics nat. U. Mex., Mexico City, 1973—. Prin. investigator lunar sample program NASA, 1974-78; mem. com. for charter of Latin-Am. Union of Geophysics, Rio De Janeiro, Brazil, 1975. Mem. Nat. Council Sci. and Tech., AAAS, Meteoritical Soc., Soc. Exploration Geophysicists, European Assn. Exploration Geophysicists, Am. Geophys. Union, Union Geofisica Mexicana, Union Iberoamericana de Geofisica. Clubs: Mundet, Casablanca. Home: 57 Rinconada Atlamaya Mexico 20 D F Mexico Office: Instituto de Geofisica UNAM Mexico 20 D F Mexico

ALVES, REX DOUGLAS, accountant, educator; b. Tampa, Fla., Aug. 7, 1935; s. Clifford and Alma Lucile (Peters) A.; B.S., Fla. So. Coll., 1958; M.C.S., Rollins Coll., 1970; m. Joan Costen Edwards, June 29, 1961 (div. Mar. 1971); m. 2d, Carol Ann Howard, Feb. 14, 1976. Internal revenue agt. IRS, Orlando, Fla., 1960-71; partner Stanaland & Alves, C.P.A.'s, Orlando, 1971-72; practice accounting, Orlando, 1972—. Adj. instr. Rollins Coll., Winter Park, Fla., 1970-79; ofcl. staff grader for cert. internal auditor exam. Inst. Internal Auditors, 1975—. C.P.A., Fla. Mem. Am. Inst. C.P.A.'s, Fla. Inst. C.P.A.'s, Pi Kappa Phi, Delta Sigma Pi. Home: 2649 Cayman Way Winter Park FL 32792 Office: 222 Comstock West PO Box 1545 Winter Park FL 32790

ALVIS, RICHARD DARWIN, indsl. engr.; b. Birmingham, Ala., May 7, 1949; s. Richard Emanuel and Katie Davis (Cobb) A.; B.S. in Indsl. Engring., Auburn U., 1973. Project engr. Deering Millikan Inc., LaGrange, Ga., 1972, Diversified Industries Opelika, Ala., 1972; indsl. engr. Am. Cast Iron Pipe Co., Birmingham, 1973—. Sponsor Jefferson County Jr. Achievement Group, 1976, 77; head community service project Brimingham Police Dept., 1975. Served with Ala. Air Nat. Guard, 1970-76. Recipient award Nat. Center for Productivity and Quality of Working Life, 1975. Mem. Am. Inst. Indsl. Engrs. (chmn. region VII 1976-77, chmn. community affairs Birmingham chpt. 1974—), Jaycees, Nat. Profl. Engrs., Am. Mgmt. Assn., Am. Foundrymen's Soc., Nat. Mgmt. Assn., Soc. Mfg. Engrs. Democrat. Baptist. Home: 4941 43d Way N Birmingham AL 35217 Office: PO Box 2727 Birmingham AL 35202

ALY, ADEL AHMED, educator; b. Fayoum, Egypt, Oct. 30, 1944; came to U.S., 1969, naturalized, 1976; s. Ahmed Mohamed and Naeema (El-Ghatit) A.; B.Sc., U. Cairo, 1966; M.S., N.C. State U., 1972; Ph.D., Va. Poly. Inst. and State U., 1974. Teaching asst. N.C. State U., Raleigh, 1969-72; teaching asst. Va. Poly. Inst. and State U., Blacksburg, 1972-74; asst. prof. indsl. engring. U. Okla., Norman, 1975-78, asso. prof., 1978—. Registered profl. engr., Okla. Mem. Nat. Soc. Profl. Engrs., Am. Inst. Indsl. Engrs. (sr.), Am. Soc. Engring. Edn., Ops. Research Soc. Am., Soc. Mfg. Engrs., Inst. Mgmt. Sci., Sigma Xi, Tau Beta Pi, Alpha Pi Mu, Pi Mu Epsilon. Republican. Moslem. Home: PO Box 2295 Norman OK 73070 Office: U Okla Sch Industrial Engineering Norman OK 73019

AMADEO, JOSE H., physician, educator; b. N.Y.C., July 16, 1928; s. H. R. and Carmen (Nigaglioni) A.; B.Sc., Ursinus Coll., 1948; M.D., Jefferson Med. Coll., 1952; m. Patricia Carron; children—Jose F. Javier, Luis Robert, Carmen Patricia; children (by previous marriage)—Mary Martha, Jose H., John Michael, Jennifer. Intern Jefferson Med. Coll. Hosp., Phila., 1952-53, resident surgery, 1953-57, Am. Cancer Soc. fellow, 1956-57; instr. surgery Jefferson Med. Coll., 1959-61; chief surg. service San Juan (P.R.) VA Hosp., 1961—, prof. surgery U. P.R. Sch. Medicine, San Juan, 1961—. Mem. Phila. Dist. Health and Welfare Council, 1960-61. Served to capt. M.C., USAF, 1957-59; now col. P.R. Army N.G. Diplomate Am. Bd. Surgery, Am. Bd. Thoracic Surgery, Nat. Bd. Med. Examiners. Fellow A.C.S., Internat. Soc. Surgery; mem. AMA, Pan Am. Med. Assn., Soc. Thoracic Surgery, Assn. Mil. Surgeons U.S., Am. Fedn. Clin. Research, Soc. for Surgery of Alimentary Tract, Southeastern Surg. Congress, Res. Officers Assn., Alpha Omega Alpha, Alpha Kappa Kappa. Republican. Roman Catholic. Contbr. articles to med. and surg. publs. Home: PO Box 10837 Caparra Heights PR 00922 Office: VA Hospital San Juan PR 00936

AMATO, ALBERT LOUIS, dentist; b. Atlanta, Ga., Sept. 10, 1947; s. Jack and Emily B. (Benbenisty) A.; D.D.S., Emory U., 1972; certificate in endodontics U. Wash., 1976; m. Faye Shain, June 6, 1971; children—Erica Leigh, David Ian. Clin. instr. U. Wash., Seattle, 1975-76; pvt. practice endodontics, Marietta, Ga., 1976—; clin. instr. endodontics Emory U., Altanta, 1976—. Served with USAF, 1972-74. Licensed dentist, Ga., 1972. Mem. Am., Ga., N.W. Dist. dental assns., Cobb County Dental Soc., Am., Ga. assns. endodontists, Alpha Omega, Omicron Kappa Upsilon. Home: 3360 Indian Hills Dr NE Marietta GA 30067 Office: 848 Church St Ext NW Marietta GA 30060

AMBROGGIO, LUIS ALBERTO, mktg. co. exec.; b. Cordoba, Argentina, Nov. 11, 1945; s. Ernesto Pedro and Perla (Lutereau) A.; M.B.A., Va. Poly. Inst., 1977; Ph.D., Cath. U., Argentina, 1967; postgrad Cath. U. Am., 1973; m. Lillian A. Abohasen, Aug. 26, 1972; children—Luis Alberto II, Xavier Ignacio. Guest cons. Pan Am. Devel. Found., 1968, White House Com. on Spanish Speaking People Opportunities, UN, 1969; dep. div. chief Argentinian embassy, Washington, 1970-75; pres. AIM Enterprises, aerospace mktg., Washington, 1976—; bus. mgr. Made in Latin Am. mag., 1976-78; rep. aircraft mfg. cos., Washington. Mem. Ibero Am. C. of C. Washington (dir.), No. Va. Export Import Assn., Am. Mktg. Assn., Nat. Assn. Fgn Student Affairs, Nat. Aviation Club, Pi Gamma Mu. Roman Catholic. Home: 2413 Sweetbay Ln Reston VA 22091 Office: 11250 Roger Bacon Dr Unit 12 Reston VA 22090

AMBROSE, JAMES PAUL, fin. planner; b. Ft. Lauderdale, Fla., Jan. 23, 1938; s. Paul Crumbly and Effie Valerie (Cheek) A.; B.S., Fla. So. Coll., 1960; m. Judith Ann Shannon, Apr. 17, 1965; children—Sheryl Ann, James Paul. Account exec. Reynolds Securities, Inc., Ft. Lauderdale, 1965-75, mgr. investment planning, 1975-76, v.p. sales, 1976-77; v.p. investment Dean Witter Reynolds, Ft. Lauderdale, 1978—; fin. columnist. Served with U.S. Army, 1961-63. Cert. tchr., Fla.; registered mgr., N.Y. Stock Exchange; cert. fin. planner, Coll. Fin. Planning. Mem. Assn. Investment Brokers, Internat. Assn. Fin. Planners, Delta Sigma Pi. Republican. Methodist. Clubs: Masons, Shriners. Home: 5241 NE 17th Ave Fort Lauderdale FL 33334 Office: Dean Witter Reynolds 3535 Galt Ocean Dr Fort Lauderdale FL 33308

AMBROSE, PAUL CARLSEN, mag. publishing co., advt. exec.; b. Newport, R.I., Jan. 22, 1952; s. Russell Louis and Daphne (Abraham) A.; B.S. in Bus. Adminstrn., Old Dominion U., Norfolk, Va., 1977. Surveyor, Tidewater Constrn. Corp., Norfolk, 1972-76; advt. salesman, then advt. mgr. Mace & Crown, Old Dominion U., 1975-77; v.p. Fortnight Mag. Co., Inc., Norfolk, 1977; owner Advantage Advt., 1979—. Mem. CAP, 1976—; dist. chmn. Va. Young Democrats, 1977-79. Mem. Downtown Norfolk Assn., Norfolk Jaycees, Order Sons Italy, Alpha Kappa Psi. Roman Catholic. Clubs: 21st St. Ski, Tidewater Advt. Home: 812 Round Bay Rd Norfolk VA 23502 Office: 602 E Liberty St Chesapeake VA 23324

AMBUHL, JANE DUTTON HALL, musician; b. Frankfort, Ky., Dec. 31, 1925; d. Martin Luther and Mary Elizabeth (Dutton) Hall; B.A., John B. Stetson U., 1945; M.Ed., U. Houston, 1970; m. John Clifton Ambuhl, Feb. 16, 1946; children—John Frederick, Martin Hall, Janette Marie Ambuhl McNaspy, Allen Christian. Organist, First Bapt. Ch., Fort Myers, Fla., 1943, DeLand, Fla., 1944-45, Presbyn. Chs. in Tenn., 1954-56; also chs. in Tex.; substitute organist various chs., 1966—; pvt. practice teaching music. Lake Jackson, Tex., 1958—; founder, dir. Youth Chamber Ensemble; mem. Brazosport (Tex.) Fine Arts Council; musical accompanist Brazosport Music Theatre, 1977—. Mem. Brazoria County chpt. Tex. Fedn. Democratic Women. Mem. Nat. Assn. Organ Tchrs. (adjudicator), Nat Guild Piano Tchrs. (adjudicator, Hall of Fame), Brazosport Music Tchrs. Assn. (past pres., treas. 1979-80), Tex. Music Tchrs. Assn., Music Tchrs. Nat. Assn., AAUW, Inter-Am. Soc., UN Assn. U.S.A., Acad. Polit. Sci., Center for Study Dem. Instns., Nat. Hist. Soc. Baptist. Home and Office: 506 Sycamore Lake Jackson TX 77566

AMERMAN, ALMERON EARL, JR., lawyer; b. Houston, Oct. 16, 1911; s. Almeron Earl and Cordelia (Bostick) A.; B.A., Rice U., 1932; LL.B., Tex. U., 1935; m. Dorothy Blackburn Kenyon, May 27, 1936; children—Cora (Mrs. Robert Blackbird), Mary (Mrs. George Walteon Weir), June (Mrs. Frank Jeff Dyke Jr.), Dorothy (Mrs. Milton Allen). Admitted to Tex. bar, 1935, since practiced in Houston; mem. firm Fouts, Amerman and Moore, 1935-51. Served with USNR, 1943-45. Mem. Am., Houston, Tex. bar assns., Delta Kappa Epsilon. Democrat. Mem. Christian Ch. Home: 407 Pinehaven St Houston TX 77024 Office: 1001 Bankers Mortgage Bldg Houston TX 77002

AMES, HAROLD STANCEY, automotive corp. adminstr.; b. Sturgis, Ky., Dec. 29, 1939; s. Rosser Louis and Virginia Frances (Liles) A.; student Carver State Jr. Coll., Mgmt. Sch., 1976; m. Bernice Wells, Feb. 21, 1960; children—Rebecca Gay, Regina Kay, Rita Marlene. Carpenter Alloway Lumber Co., Sturgis, Ky., 1957, then Berg & Diehl Home Bldrs., Mobile, Ala.; foreman Allen Construction Co., Mobile, then carpenter foremen, 1970-73; assembler Continental Motors Corp., Mobile, 1967-70, 1973-74, supervisor, 1974—. Advisor Jr. Achievement. Recipient certificate of appreciation, Nat. Mgmt. Assn., Mem. Nat. Mgmt. Assn. (booster 1975-76, 1976-77), Baptist. Club: Mason. Home: 144 Alton St Mobile AL 36609 Office: Teledyne Continental Motors Brookley Complex Mobile AL 36609

AMICK, JIM PHILLIP, mktg. exec.; b. Groom, Tex., Oct. 5, 1949; s. Howard West and Edith Vivian (Gibson) A.; student Amarillo Jr. Coll., 1968; B.J. with honors, U. Tex., 1972. Dir. mktg. Barry Gilling Water Co., Austin, Tex., 1969-73; owner Amick & Browder Advt., Austin, 1974; property mgr./mktg. dir. First Mortgage Co., Houston, 1975-77; dir. advt. Sturm Interests, Houston, 1977-78; dir. advt. and mktg. Nash Phillips/Copus, Austin, 1978—. Mem. Am. Mktg. Assn., Austin Assn. Builders, Austin Assn. Builders Sales and Marketing Council. Republican. Club: Austin Ad. Home: 8117 Ceberry St Austin TX 78759 Office: 6010 Brooks St Austin TX 78752

AMIDON, ROGER LYMAN, educator; b. Burlington, Vt., Apr. 8, 1938; s. Ellsworth L. and Mae L. Amidon; B.A., U. Vt., 1960; M.A., U. Iowa, 1965, Ph.D. (USPHS trainee 1965-66), 1968; m. Jo Ann Reiland, Aug. 1, 1968. Mem. faculty U. Iowa, 1966-77, asso. prof. hosp. and health adminstrn., 1973-77; exec. sec., researcher Nat. Center Health Services Research, HEW, 1975-76; prof., chmn. dept. health adminstr. U. Okla. Sch. Public Health, 1977—, also dir. Am. Indian Grad. Program in Health Adminstrn.; cons. in field. Served with USAR, 196 -62 Mem. AAAS, AAUP, Am. Hosp. Assn., Am. Public Health Assn., Internat. Hosp. Fedn., Atlantic Salmon Assn., Grenfell Assn. Am., Miramichi Salmon Assn. Author papers in field; editorial adv. bd. Am. Coll. Nursing Home Adminstrs. Home: 728 NE 21st St Oklahoma City OK 73105 Office: Box 26901 Oklahoma City OK 73190

AMIN, MUHAMMAD, surgeon; b. Pakistan, May 7, 1945; came to U.S., 1968; s. Feroze and Rehmat (Begum) Khan; F.Sc., Govt. Coll., Sahiwal, Pakistan, 1962; M.B., B.S., Nishtar Med. Coll., Multan, Pakistan, 1967; m. Nighat Jabin Ara, June 20, 1968; children—Tabassum, Asna. Rotating intern St. Mary's Hosp., Bklyn., 1968-69; resident in surgery St. Michael Hosp., Newark, 1969-70, Bronx-Lebanon Hosp., 1970-74; attending surgeon Morrisania-North Central Bronx Hosp., 1974-77; commd. maj. M.C., U.S. Air Force, 1977; gen. surgeon USAF Hosp., Tyndall AFB, Fla., 1977—. Fellow Internat. Coll. Surgeons; mem. AMA, Assn. Mil. Surgeons. Home: 2701 Delta St Tyndall Air Force Base FL 32403 Office: US Air Force Hospital Tyndall Air Force Base FL 32403

AMIR-MOEZ, ALI REZA, mathematician, educator; b. Teheran, Iran, Apr. 7, 1919; s. Mohammad and Fatema (Gorgestani) A.-M.; B.A., U. Teheran, 1942; M.A., U. Calif. at Los Angeles, 1951, Ph.D., 1955. Came to U.S., 1947, naturalized, 1961. Instr. math. Teheran Tech. Coll., 1942-46; asst. prof. math. U. Idaho, 1955-56, Queens Coll., N.Y.C., 1956-60, Purdue U., 1960-61; asso. prof. U. Fla., Gainesville, 1961-63; prof. math. Clarkson Coll., Potsdam, N.Y., 1963-65; prof. math. Tex. Tech. U., Lubbock, 1965—. Served to 2d lt. Persian Army, 1936-38. Decorated Honor emblem Persian Royal Ct., medal Pro Mundi Beneficio Academia Brasileira de Ciencias Humanas. Mem. Am. Math. Soc., Math. Assn. Am., Sigma Xi, Pi Mu Epsilon. Author: Elements of Linear Space, 1961; (play) Kaleeheh & Demneh, 1962; Three Persian Tales, 1961, Matrix Techniques Trigonometry and Analytic Geometry, 1964; Mathematics and String Figures, 1966; Classes Residues et Figures ovec Ficelle, 1968; Extreme Properties of Linear Transformations and Geometry in Unitary Spaces, 1971; Elements of Multilinear Algebra, 1971; Linear Algebra of the Plane, 1973. Contbr. articles to math. jours. on proper and singular values of linear operators and matrices. Office: Dept Math Texas Tech U Lubbock TX 79409 Dept Math Texas Tech U Lubbock TX 79409

AMJAD, HASSAN, hematologist, oncologist; b. Jhang, Pakistan, Nov. 27, 1947; came to U.S., 1971; s. Jaffar Hussain and Anwer Fatima Jaffary; M.D., Punjab U., King Edward Med. Coll., Pakistan, 1970; m. Lolita Paragas Quezon, Oct. 27, 1973; children—Urooj, Quartel-Ayne, Shabnaum. Asst. clin. instr. medicine SUNY, Buffalo, 1972-73; instr. medicine Wayne State U., Detroit, 1976-77; asst. clin. prof. medicine Marshall U., W.Va., 1977—; physician VA Hosp., Beckley, W.Va.; cons. hematologist Beckley Appalachian Regional Hosp. Recipient Burton Brown medal in medicine, 1970; diplomate Am. Bd. Internal Medicine. Fellow A.C.P.; mem. Am. Fedn. Clin. Research, AAAS, Am. Soc. Hematology. Contbr. articles on blood and cancer-related disorders, sickle cell disease to profl. jours. Home: 200 Veterans Ave Beckley WV 25801 Office: Veterans Administration Hospital Beckley WV 25801

AMMONS, WILLIAM HENRY, II, ednl. adminstr.; b. Ballinger, Tex., Oct. 28, 1919; s. Oscar and Adel (Bean) A.; B.S., Tex. Coll., 1947; cert. in Adminstrn. and Supervision, Prairie View (Tex.) A&M U., 1953; postgrad. (NSF grantee), Tex. So. U., Houston, 1963, A.B.D., 1974-77; M.Ed., W.Tex. State U., 1969; postgrad. Tex. A&M, Coll. Sta., 1970-71; m. Ann Juanita Glover, Apr. 11, 1947; children—William Howard, Adele Valcine, Deborah Ann, Marsha. Prin., coach Booker T. Washington High Sch., Sweetwater (Tex.) Ind. Sch. Dist., 1947-50 Bridie Stephenson Elementary-High Sch., Rotan (Tex.) Ind. Sch. Dist., 1951-52, Booker T. Washington High Sch., Breckenridge (Tex.), Ind. Sch. Dist., 1952-53; counselor, math. instr. Amarillo AFB, Tex., 1955-58; head sci. dept., tchr. Carver High Sch., Amarillo Ind. Sch. Dist. 1958-65; counselor USDA Job Corps, Heber, Ariz., 1966-68; dean of men Tex. Coll., Tyler, 1968-71, dir. Upward Bound project, 1971-76, asst. to pres. for advanced instl. devel. program coordinator, 1977—, cons. residence hall clinic, counseling guidance seminar, reality therapy, acad. advisement. Auditor Tyler Orgn. of Men, 1973; mem. com. Explorers, Boy Scouts Am., 1979. Served with USAF 1944-76. NSF fellow, 1959, 60, 63. Mem. Nat. Assn. Student Personnel Adminstrs., Am. Personnel and Guidance Assn., Tex. Assn. Student Personnel Adminstrs., Tex. Vocat. Guidance Assn., Assn. for Supervision and Curriculum Devel., Phi Delta Kappa, Phi Delta Psi, Alpha Kappa Mu, Kappa Alpha Psi, Mu Chi Sigma (v.p., 1942-43). Democrat. Baptist. Clubs: Masons, Shriners. Condr. research coll. govt.; author handbook of Upward Bound, 1973, Tutor's Acad. Handbook, 1978. Home: Route 16 Box 754 Tyler TX 75701 Office: 2404 N Grande Ave Tyler TX 75702

AMOROSO, EUGENE VINCENT, foods co. exec.; b. Chgo., Feb. 18, 1935; s. Cuono and Vincenzia (Nastasia) A.; B.S., Loyola U., 1957, M.S., 1960; postgrad. U. Mich.; m. Joan Marie Pucci, May 10, 1958; children—Debbie, Lisa. Asst. to dir. psychol. research Buchen Advt. Co., Chgo., 1959-60; mktg. research analyst, mktg. research mgr. Elgin Watch Co. (Ill.), 1960-63; mktg. mgr. Anchor Hocking Glass, Lancaster, Ohio, 1963-66; mktg. research coordinator, mgr. new products research Ford Motor Co., Dearborn, Mich., 1966-68; with Am. Motors Corp., Detroit, 1968-77, v.p. mktg. group, to 1977; v.p., dir. mktg. foods div. Coca-Cola Co., Houston, 1977—. Bd. dirs. Cystic Fibrosis Found., Houston, 1979. Served with U.S. Army, 1957-59. Mem. Am. Mgmt. Assn., Am. Mktg. Assn. Republican. Roman Catholic. Clubs: Houston, Houstonian. Home: 11 Stonegate Houston TX 77024 Office: 7 04 Old Katy Houston TX 77024

AMORUSO, ANTHONY VINCENT, JR., dermatologist; b. Englewood, N.J., Dec. 5, 1947; s. Anthony Vincent and Mildred June (Berardi) A.; B.S., Manhattan Coll., 1969; M.D., Creighton U., 1973. Intern, Creighton U. Affiliated Hosp., Omaha, 1973-74; resident in dermtology SUNY, Buffalo, 1974-77; physician, dermatologist MacGregor Med. Clinic Assos., Houston, 1977-78; cons. dermatologist Tex. Dept. Corrections, Huntsville, 1978-79; practice medicine specializing in dermatology, Stafford, Tex., 1978—; mem. staff Hermann Hosp., S.W. Meml. Hosp., Alief Gen. Hosp., Westbury Hosp., Med. Center Del Oro; instr. Baylor U., Houston, 1978—, U. Tex. Med. Sch., Houston, 1979—. Recipient Physicians Recognition award Am. Acad. Dermatology, 1977, AMA, 1980; diplomate Am. Bd. Dermatology. Mem. Am. Acad. Dermatology, Dermatology Found., Houston Dermatol. Assn., Tex. Med. Assn., Southewestern Dermtatology Assn., Tex. Dermatol. Assn. Roman Catholic. Home: 12218 Brookvalley Dr Houston TX 77071 Office: 12110 Murphy Rd Stafford TX 77477

AMORY, OTIS TAYLOR, JR., Realtor, mortgage banker; b. Newport News, Va., Feb. 7, 1922; s. Otis Taylor and Marcie (Tuck) A.; B.A. in Econs., U. Va., 1947, M.B.A., 1949, postgrad. Law Sch., 1950; m. Deborah A. Bayne, Nov. 18, 1977; children by previous marriage—Elise A. Amory Crosswy, Marcie T., O. Taylor, III, Thomas Nelson, Jane Page. Pres., co-owner Commwealth Realty and Mortgage Corp., 1976—; pres. McLean (Va.) Mortgage Co., 1977; owner Otis T. Amory, Realtor; chmn. adv. com. No. Va. Community Coll.; coordinator real estate U. Va.; lectr. in real estate fin., planning, sales and brokerage; cons. U.S. Savs. and Loan League; profl. witness U.S. Superior Ct., Washington. Mem. state and county coms. Republican Party. Served with USN, 1941-45. Decorated Navy Cross, D.F.C. Mem. Nat. Assn. Realtors, Va. Assn. Realtors, No. Va. Bd. Realtors, Nat. Assn. Home Builders, Va. Assn. Home Builders, No. Va. Builders Assn., Mortgage Bankers of Am., No. Va. Mortgage Bankers Assn., U. Va. Alumni Assn. (life), U.S. Lawn Tennis Assn., Middleburg (Va.) Tennis Assn. Author: The Real Estate Practitioner, 1977. Home: 600 Stonewall Ave Middleburg VA 22117 Office: 1301 Beverly Rd McLean VA 22101

AMOS, MARVIN CYRIL, airline exec.; b. Seymour, Ind., July 29, 1924; s. David Lawrence and Mary Eva (Hill) A.; B.A., Hanover (Ind.) Coll., 1949; m. Anne Addison, June 11, 1949; children—Patrick Marvin, Joanne Lee, Mark Alan, Judy Mitchell, Steven Lawrence. Edn. specialist RCA, Indpls., 1956-57; mgr. edn. and profl. placement, mgr. profl. placement and devel. Hotpoint div. Gen. Electric Co., Chgo., 1957-62; asst. to pres., dir. indsl. relations Wright Aero. div. Curtiss-Wright Corp., Woodbridge, N.J., 1962-64; dir. planning and research, dir. personnel, v.p. personnel Eastern Air Lines Inc., Miami, 1965-76, v.p. personnel and corporate adminstrn., 1976-78, sr. v.p. personnel and corporate adminstrn., 1978—. Trustee Hanover (Ind.) Coll., 1971—, chmn. bldgs. and grounds com., 1973—; bd. dirs. Sanibel Moorings Assn., 1975—. Served with U.S. Army, 1943-46, 51-53. Named alumnus of year Hanover Coll., 1976. Mem. Greater Miami C. of C. Republican. Roman Catholic. Club: Riviera Country. Home: 7745 SW 138th Terr Miami FL 33158 Office: Eastern Air Lines Inc Miami Internat Airport Miami FL 33148

AMOS, WILLIAM G., constrn. co. exec.; b. Columbus, Ga., Feb. 5, 1935; s. William G. and Isabel (Floyd) A.; B.S., Auburn U., 1957; m. Patricia Gunn, June 8, 1957; children—Leigh, Lynn. Project mgr. The Jordan Co., Columbus, Ga., 1959-64; adminstrv. asst. Rep. Howard H. Callaway, Washington, 1965-66; innkeeper Callaway Gardens, Pine Mountain, Ga., 1967-69; pres. Amos Constrn. Co., Valdosta, Ga., 1969—. Pres. United Way, 1978-79; commr. Valdosta-Lowndes Planning Commn., 1971—. Served to 1st lt. USMC, 1957-59. Mem. Assn. Gen. Contractors (dir. Ga. br.). Republican. Presbyterian. Clubs: Valdosta Country (past pres.), Rotary (past pres.), Elks. Home: 1205 Hickory Dr Valdosta GA 31601 Office: PO Box 1184 Valdosta GA 31601

AMOS, WILLIAM LAFAYETTE, JR., obstetrician, gynecologist, ins. co. exec.; b. Miami, Fla., June 29, 1944; s. William LaFayette and Olivia Diamond A.; B.S. in Applied Biology, Ga. Inst. Tech., 1966; M.D., Med. Coll. Ga., 1970; m. Janet Ann Eastburn, Dec. 18, 1965; children—Ashley Paige, William LaFayette III. Intern, Baylor U. Med. Center, Dallas, 1970-71, resident in ob-gyn, 1971-74; practice medicine specializing in ob-gyn, Columbus, Ga., 1975—; asst. med. dir. Am. Family Life Assurance Co., Columbus, 1975-76, v.p., med. dir., 1976—; mem. staffs Med. Center, Drs. Hosp., St. Francis Hosp., Columbus; dir. Am. Family Corp. Bd. dirs. Columbus chpt. Am. Cancer Soc., 1976—, chmn. profl. edn. com., 1977, med. v.p., 1979—state adviser Ga. Soc. Med. Assts., 1976—; mem. Mayor's Com. to Study Feasibility of New Hosp., 1978-79. Served to lt. comdr. USNR, 1974-75. Diplomate Am. Bd. Obstetrics and Gynecology. Fellow Am. Coll. Obstetricians and Gynecologists; Mem. AMA (Physicians Recognition award 1978), Am. Assn. Gynecologic Laparoscopists, Am. Assn. Life Ins. MMed. Dirs., So. Med. Assn., Am. Fertility Soc., Med. Assn. Ga., Muscogee County Med. Soc. Methodist. Clubs: Columbus Ski (treas. 1978-79), Ga. Tech (pres 1979-80)(Columbus). Home: 2700 Lynda Ln Columbus GA 31904 Office: 2021 Warm Springs Rd Columbus GA 31904

AMRAM, VICTOR JUAN, export co. exec.; b. Santiago de Cuba, Cuba, Nov. 24, 1926; came to U.S., 1961, naturalized, 1970; s. Jose Victor and Estrella Maria (Ortiz) A.; B.S., Colegio Baldor, Havana, Cuba, 1946; Exec. Accountant, Peirce Sch. Bus. Adminstrn., Phila., 1948; m. Consuelo Odriozola Baizan, Dec. 17, 1950; children—Maria Carolina, Maria Teresita, Jose Carlos, Consuelo Maria, Victor Juan, Francisco Jose. Mfrs. rep. and commn. agt. Jose V. Amram & Son, Havana, 1948-53; gen. mgr. Especialidades Veterinarias, S.A., Havana, 1953-61; sales rep. F.A. Galbraith of West Palm Beach (Fla.), in P.R., 1961-63; v.p., gen. mgr. Galbram Inc., San Juan, P.R., 1962-69; dir. sales and mktg. for Latin Am., Babson Bros., 1969—; instr. Dale Carnegie Inst., 1967-69. Mem. Am. Mgmt. Assn. Republican. Roman Catholic. Home: 901 SW 101st Ave Miami FL 33174 Office: 2100 S York Rd Oak Brook IL 60521

ANAND, HARISH C., neonatologist; b. New Delhi, India, July 5, 1948; came to U.S., 1973, naturalized, 1976; s. Ram M. and Vidya W. (Soni) A.; student Delhi U., 1964-65; M.D., Christian Med. Coll., Punjab U., 1970; m. Parveen Gujral, Nov. 10, 1973; children—Rishi G., Akash G. Clin. instr. Charity Hosp., New Orleans, 1975-77; asst. prof. pediatrics Tulane U., New Orleans, 1977—. Mem. AMA, So. Perinatal Assn., Orleans Parish Med. Soc. Home: 2109 Colombo Dr Harvey LA 70058 Office: 1415 Tulane Ave New Orleans LA 70112

ANANTHAKRISHNAN, CHITTUR VISWANATHAN, physician; b. Calicut, Kerala, India, May 17, 1945; came to U.S., 1975; s. Chittur S. and Rajam Viswanathan; M.B., B.S., Christian Med. Coll., India, 1967; m. Santosh Kumari Dass, June 28, 1969; children—Aiyer Viswanathan, Aiyer Sapna, Aiyer Sheetal. Rotating intern Christian Med. Coll. Hosp., Punjab, India, 1967, house surgeon, 1968, registrar in orthopaedics, 1969; teaching fellow in anatomy Queens U., Kingston, Ont., Can., 1969-70; resident in surgery Jewish Hosp., Cin., 1970; resident in phys. medicine and rehab. Kingston Gen. Hosp., 1970-71; resident in orthopaedics U. Alta. Hosps., Edmonton, Alta., Can., 1971-72; resident in surgery Bronx (N.Y.) Lebanon Hosp. Center, 1972-73; resident orthopaedics Meml. U. of Nfld., St. Johns, 1973-74; resident in phys. medicine McMaster U., Hamilton, Ont., Can., 1974-75; orthopaedic arthritis fellow U. Colo. Med. Center, Denver, 1975-76; practice medicine specializing in orthopaedic surgery, Lubbock, Tex., 1976—; asst. prof. dept. orthopaedic surgery, phys. medicine and rehab. Tex. Tech. U. Sch. Medicine, 1976-78, asst. clin. prof., 1978—; med. dir. dept. phys. medicine and rehab. St. Mary of the Plains Hosp., Lubbock, 1978—; vis. prof. Christian Med. Coll., Ludhiana, India, 1978. Diplomate Am. Bd. Orthopaedic Surgery. Mem. Tex. Med. Assn., AMA, Lubbock Garza Crosby County Med. Soc., Lubbock Soccer Assn. (coach 1977—). Club: Lions. Home: 1802 Atlanta St Lubbock TX 79416 Office: 3716 21st St Lubbock TX 79410

ANCHOR, KENNETH NORMAN, clin. psychologist; b. Detroit, July 19, 1945; s. Bernard and Pearl (Dashkin) A.; B.S. with honors, U. Mich., 1967; M.A., U. Conn., 1970, Ph.D., 1972; m. Felicia Nancy Figlarz, June 15, 1969; children—Jessica Michelle, Stephanie Nicole. Asst. prof. psychology George Peabody Coll., Nashville, 1972; asso. dir. Vanderbilt U. Interuniv. Psychol. and Counseling Center, Nashville, 1974—, asso. prof. psychology, 1975—; co-founder Behavior Mgmt. Cons., Nashville, 1974—; vocat. expert Social Security Adminstrn.; cons. in field. John F. Kennedy Center for Human Devel. grantee, 1974-75; recipient Dr. Barbara Brown award, 1979. Diplomate Am. Bd. Profl. Psychology. Mem. Am. Psychol. Assn., Am. Assn. Biofeedback Clinicians, Assn. Advancement of Behavior Therapy, Biofeedback Soc. Am., Midwestern Psychol. Assn., Tenn. Psychol. Assn. Co-author numerous articles on self disclosure, behavior therapy, maladaptive aggression and stress mgmt.; founding editor Am. Jour. Clin. Biofeedback; editorial bd. mem. Clin. Neuropsychology; editorial reviewer Jour. Personality, Jour. Counseling Psychology, Jour. Community Psychology. Office: Peabody Coll of Vanderbilt U Nashville TN 37203

ANDERS, HOWELL KENDRICK, JR., hosp. food service adminstr.; b. Shreveport, La., Jan. 4, 1950; s. Howell Kendrick and Myrtis (Boodie) A.; student in indsl. mgmt. La. Tech. U., 1972, in food service mgmt. Auburn U., 1979; m. Judy Jan Womack, Feb. 25, 1977. Asst. dir. dietary services Sara Mayo Hosp., New Orleans, 1973-74, Physicians and Surgeons Hosp., Shreveport, 1974; dir. dietary services Panola Gen. Hosp., Carthage, Tex., 1974-78, Baptist Med. Center, Montgomery, Ala., 1978—. Project chmn. U.S. Jaycees, 1973-74. Named an Outstanding Young Man Am., 1975. Mem. East Tex. Hosp. Food Service Dirs. (v.p. 1978). Home: 2233 Semmes Dr Montgomery AL 36106 Office: 2105 E South Blvd Montgomery AL 36111

ANDERS, LOUISE THOMPSON, ednl. adminstr.; b. Greenville, S.C., Sept. 30, 1919; d. Haskey B. and Eliza Campbell (Floyd) Thompson; B.S. in Elementary Edn., Furman U., Greenville, 1956, M.A. in Guidance and Psychology, 1958; Ed.S., U. S.C., Columbia, 1973, Ph.D. in Edn., 1976; m. John W. Anders; 1 dau., Patricia Anders Dulaney. Tchr. Beaufort (S.C.) Schs., 1956-58, prin. elementary sch., 1958-65, title I dir., 1965-68, dir. adult edn., 1970-75, prin. U.S. Govt., Laurel Bay, 1968-70; nat. cons. migrant edn. Mem. S.C. State Task Force Juvenile Discipline; bd. dirs. Speech and Hearing Clinic; chmn. bd. dirs. Day Care and Kindergarten Beaufort Baptist Ch., also tchr. adult class; supr. establishment Alternative High Sch. and Sch. for Exceptional Children, Beaufort County; mem. S.C. Dept. Edn. task force on Public Sch. Fin. Act, Crusade for Better Edn. task force; mem. Gov.'s Council Citizen Participation in Edn. Active state adv. council drug and substance abuse. Mem. AAUW (pres. 1958), S.C. Elementary Prins. Assn. (pres. 1969-70), Internat. Reading Assn., Wil Lou Gray Reading Council (pres.) United Profl. Adult Continuing Edn. Assn., S.C. Supervision Curriculum Assn., S.C. Adult Edn. Dirs. Assn. (pres. 1974-75), S.C. Assn. Sch. Adminstrs. (past pres.). Named Career Woman of Year, S.C., 1969, Outstanding Adult Educator, 1973. Baptist. Home: 906 Forest Ln Beaufort SC 29902 Office: Drawer 309 Beaufort SC 29902

ANDERSON, AARON STEPHEN, retail store exec.; b. Louisville, Miss., May 11, 1947; s. Aaron Quitman and Winnie Ruth (Reynolds) A.; B.S., Miss. State U., 1969; M.B.A., U. So. Miss., 1972; grad. Gemological Inst. Am.; m. Sherry LaBarreare, Nov. 1, 1975. Mgr. jewelry dept. Medco Jewelry Corp., Pascagoula, Miss., 1975-77; mgr. Zales Jewelers, Natchez, Miss., 1977—. Mem. Alpha Tau Omega, Delta Sigma Pi. Baptist. Clubs: Jaycees, Masons, Shriners, Lions (dir.). Home: 106 Espero Ave Natchez MS 39120 Office: 350 John Junkin Dr Natchez MS 39120

ANDERSON, ANITA JONES, audiologist; b. Phila., Mar. 21, 1945; d. Howard Z. and Ethel M. Fretz; M.A. in Audiology, So. Meth. U., 1968, M.A. in Speech Pathology, 1968; m. L. W. Anderson, Jr.; 1 son, Eric R. Jones. Clin. audiologist Callier Center Communication Disorders, Dallas, 1968-74; dir. audiology Garland Meml. Hosp., Garland, Tex., 1974-75; with Tex. Dept. Human Resources, 1976—, dir. Tex. Medicaid Hearing Aid Program, 1977—. Mem. Am. Speech and Hearing Assn., Tex. Speech and Hearing Assn., Tex. Public Employees Assn. Episcopalian. Office: Tex Dept Human Resources Hearing Aid Program John H Reagan Bldg Austin TX 78701

ANDERSON, B(ILLY) LYNN, systems exec.; b. Electra, Tex., Aug. 10, 1940; s. Sherman Lyman and Billie Irene (Bourland) A.; B.B.A., E. Tex. State U., 1972; m. Sidney Inez Kirkpatrick, Sept. 2, 1960; children—Sherman Lynn, Brian Keith, William Gregory, Michael Gary. With E-Systems, Greenville, Tex., 1959—, sr. data processing planning analyst, 1966-69, supr. planning services, 1970-72, gen. supr. inventory control, 1973, mgr. logistics support Presdnl. aircraft, 1974—. Mem. Nat. Property Mgmt. Assn. (cert. property mgr.), Am. Mgmt. Assn. (asso.). Democrat. Baptist. Home: Route 2 Box 66B Greenville TX 75401 Office: E-Systems Box 1056 Greenville TX 75401

ANDERSON, BRUCE MORGAN, computer scientist; b. Battle Creek, Mich., Oct. 8, 1941; s. James Albert and Beverly Jane (Morgan) A.; B.S. in Elec. Engring., Northwestern U., 1964; M.S. in Elec. Engring., Purdue U., 1966; Ph.D. in Elec. Engring. (NASA fellow), Northwestern U., 1973; m. Jeannie Marie Hignight, May 24, 1975; children—Ronald, Michael, Valerie, John, Carolyn. Research engr. Zenith Radio Corp., Chgo., 1965-66; asso. engr. Ill. Inst. Tech. Research Inst., Chgo., 1966-68; sr. electronics engr. Rockwell Internat., Downers Grove, Ill., 1973-75; computer scientist Argonne (Ill.) Nat. Lab., 1975-77; software systems engr. Tex. Instruments, Dallas, 1977—; computer cons. depts. geography, transp., econs., sociology and computer sci. of Northwestern U., instr. computer sci. Mem. IEEE, Assn. Computing Machinery, Sigma Xi, Eta Kappa Nu, Theta Delta Chi. Contbr. articles to tech. jours. Home: 2716 Teakwood Ln Plano TX 75075 Office: Texas Instruments MS 269 PO Box 226015 Dallas TX 75266

ANDERSON, CARL EMIL, tng. and documentation specialist; b. North Easton, Mass., May 3, 1930; s. John Andrew and Eva Matilda A.; m. Nelda Mae, Mar. 20, 1953; children—David Bruce, Brenda Gayle. Tng. and documentation specialist RCA Internat. Corp., Patrick AFB, Fla., 1958—. Bd. dirs. ARC, Brevard County, Fla., 1973; treas. Cocoa (Fla.) Presbyn. Ch., 1979, 80. Served with USAF, 1951-55; Korea. Home: 1507 Emory Ln Cocoa FL 32922 Office: RCA International Corp PO Box 4308 Patrick AFB FL 32925

ANDERSON, CHARLES HILL, lawyer, state ofcl.; b. Chattanooga, June 16, 1930; s. Ray and Lois (Entrekin) A.; J.D., U. Tenn., 1953; m. Virginia R. Baker, May 5 1956; children—Eric Scott, Alicia Lea, Burton Hill. Admitted to Tenn. bar, 1953; practice law, Chattanooga, 1953-60; asso. gen. counsel Life & Casualty Ins. Co. Tenn., Nashville, 1960-69; U.S. atty. Middle Dist. of Tenn., Nashville, 1969-77; practice law, Nashville, 1977-79; asst. adj. gen. Tenn. Army N.G., Nashville, 1979—. Mem. Atty. Gen.'s Adv. Com. of U.S. Attys., 1973-77; del. Tenn. Constl. Conv., 1965. Served to brig. gen. Army N.G., 1979—. Mem. Am. Bar Assn., Tenn. Bar Assn., Nashville Bar Assn., Assn. Life Ins. Counsel, Phi Delta Phi, Phi Kappa Phi. Presbyterian. Editor Tenn. Law Rev., 1951-53. Office: Nat Guard Hdqrs 3041 Sidco Dr Nashville TN 37204

ANDERSON, CLARENCE LEE, oil co. exec.; b. Kermit, Tex., Oct. 11, 1943; s. ClarkMarion and Golden Elizabeth (Roach) A.; B.B.A., S.W. Tex. U., 1966; m. Nina Proctor, Jan. 22, 1966; children—Blake, Kelli. Ter. salesman Shell Oil Co., Houston, 1967-71, retail tng. instr., St. Louis, 1971-73, area mgr., Indpls., 1973-77; pres. Benton Service Oil Co. (Ky.), 1977—, exec. dir. Pres., Gilbertsville PTO, 1978, Indian Guides YMCA, 1976. Mem. Shell Oil Co. Laurel Soc. (awardee 1975), Key Oilman Com. Ind., U.S. Jaycees, Petroleum Marketers Assn. Ky. (dir. 1979—), Ind. Petroleum Speakers Bur., Ky. Shell Gobbers Assn. (brand chmn. 1979—), Marshall County C. of C., Ky. Western Waterland Assn., Nat. Fedn. Independent Businessmen, Pi Kappa Alpha. Methodist. Club: Masons. Home: Rt 7 Box 239E Hwy 1422 Benton KY 42025 Office: PO Box 96 92 N Main St Benton KY 42025

ANDERSON, CLAUDE TAYLOR, physician; b. Chapin, Ill., Aug. 12, 1921; s. William and Daisy Irene (Taylor) A.; B.A., Knox Coll., 1947; B.A. (Rhodes scholar), Oxford (Eng.) U., 1951, B.Sc., 1951, M.A., 1956; M.D., Yale U., 1953; M.Sc., U. Rochester, 1963; m. Evelyn R. Hamburger, June 3, 1950, (div. Nov., 1978); children—Marshall W., Scni Jo, Rebecca L., Ross M., Laurie J. Intern, Cleve. City Hosp., 1953-54, resident, 1954-57; commd. 1st lt. M.C., U.S. Air Force, 1953, advanced through grades to col., 1972; internist Scott AFB Hosp., 1957-60; chief internal medicine U.S. Air Force Acad. Hosp., 1960-62; staff officer Transp. Commn. Surg. Office, Scott AFB, Ill., 1963-65; staff officer, Randolph AFB, Tex., 1965-69; comdr. U.S. Air Force Hosp., South Ruislip, Eng., 1969-72; ret., 1972; immunology fellowship U. Tex., 1973-76, instr. Health Sci. Center, 1976-78; dir. South Tex. Immunology Lab., Inc., San Antonio, 1979—; asst. clin. prof. U. Tex. Health Sci. Center, 1978—. Decorated Air medal with five oak leaf clusters, D.F.C., Meritorious Service medal, Legion of Merit; recipient Ferris prize in anatomy, 1948; diplomate Am. Bd. Internal Medicine, Am. Bd. Allergy and Immunology. Fellow A.C.P.; mem. Phi Beta Kappa, Sigma Xi, Alpha Omega Alpha. Democrat. Home: 1012 Ivy Ln San Antonio TX 78209 Office: 7342 Oak Manor Dr San Antonio TX 78229

ANDERSON, CLAYTON EARLE, constrn. exec.; b. Leavenworth, Kans., Feb. 16, 1932; s. Herbert Thomas and Kathryn Francis (Walter) A.; B.S., U. Kans., 1954; m. Carolyn Jan Bryant, Feb. 3, 1961; children—Jan Cecile, Michael William, John Clayton, Eric Lee. Resident engr. Cities Service Oil Co., Bartlesville, Okla., 1954-61; constrn. engr., supt. R.L. Frailey, Inc., Perry, Okla., 1961-65; sr. resident engr. Gen. Electric Co., RECO, Schenectady, 1965-69; dir. constrn. Walt Disney World, Buena Vista Land Co., Orlando, Fla., 1969-73; dir. engring. and constrn. Ringling Brothers Barnum & Bailey Circus World, Orlando, 1973-74; project mgr. Leisure Properties Ltd., Tallahassee, 1974—; mgr. St. George Island Utilities. Tribal chief YMCA Indian Guides, 1971; umpire Rolling Hills Little League, 1972-73; pres. St. George Island (Fla.) Homeowners Assn. Served to 1st lt. USAF, 1954-56. Named Ky. Col. Registered profl. engr., Okla., Fla.; cert. water treatment and wastewater treatment plant operator. Home: 3601 Westmoreland Tallahassee FL 32303 Office: 1 Ocean West St George Island FL 32328

ANDERSON, CURTIS ANDREW, oil co. exec.; b. Victoria, Ill., Sept. 17, 1913; s. August S. and Emma Carolyn (Palm) A.; student Tex. A. and M. U., 1940; grad. Command and Gen. Staff Sch., 1946; m. Rowena Meyer, Nov. 23, 1941; children—Mary (Mrs. Carl B. Bertrand), Karen (Mrs. Ward Roberson), Curtis Andrew. Petroleum engr. Sun Oil Co., Beaumont, Tex., 1946-70, Houston, 1970-72; v.p., mgr. Ada Belle Oil Co., Beaumont, 1957-75. Fuel cons. Varibus Corp., Beaumont, 1973—; pres. Hardin County Salt Water Co., 1968-77. Served to maj. USAAF, 1940-46. Home: 1755 Karen Ln Beaumont TX 77706 Office: Lock Drawer 2237 Beaumont TX 77704

ANDERSON, DARLENE WEEKS, counselor; b. Ft. Polk, La., Oct. 27, 1953; d. Franklin Eugene and Cleo Gelena W.; student Northwestern State U. La., 1971-73; B.A., Winthrop Coll., 1974; M.Ed., U. S.C., 1976; counselor cert. The Citadel, 1977; m. L. McTier Anderson, Aug. 4, 1979. Tchr., Ashwood Central Sch., Bishopville, S.C., 1974-75; nat. colonizer Sigma Sigma Sigma Nat. Sorority, Woodstock, Va., 1975; admissions counselor U. S.C., Spartanburg, 1976; residence counselor Coll. of Charleston (S.C.), 1976-77; dir. student services Columbia (S.C.) Coll., 1977-79; guidance counselor Clarke Central High Sch., Athens, Ga., 1979—. Recipient Outstanding Service award Columbia Coll., 1979; profl. tchr. certs., S.C. Mem. Am. Personnel and Guidance Assn., Am. Coll. Personnel Assn., Nat. Assn. Student Personnel Adminstrs., Southeastern Coll. Personnel Assn., S.C. Coll. Personnel Assn., Winthrop Coll. Alumnae Assn. Columbia, Sigma Sigma Sigma (v.p. Columbia alumnae chpt.), Panhellenic. Methodist. Home: 815 S Milledge Ave Apt 6 Athens GA 30605 Office: 350 S Milledge Ave Athens GA 30606

ANDERSON, DEWAYNE HENRY, planning cons.; b. Chgo., Jan. 26, 1937; s. Henry Monrad and Florence (Alleman) A.; B.Arch., Miami U., Oxford, Ohio, 1959; M. Urban Planning, U. Ill., 1966; m. Suzanne Marille Kinney, May 4, 1963; children—Lisa Aileen, DeWayne Henry. Architect, Perkins & Will, Chgo., 1962-64; asso. Milo Smith & Assos., Tampa, Fla., 1966-68; mgr. Atlanta office Candeub, Fleissig & Assos. Planning Cons., Newark, 1968-70; pres., dir. Eric Hill Assos., Inc., Atlanta, also Winston-Salem, N.C., 1970-77; chmn. Anderson, Benton Holmes, Inc., Winston Salem, 1977—. Bd. dirs. Winston-Salem Downtown Ch. Center, 1973-74, Winston-Salem/Forsyth County Voluntary Action Center, 1974-79; mem. Winston-Salem Adv. Budget Commn., 1979—. Served to capt. USMCR, 1959-61. Mem. Am. Inst. Cert. Planners (pres. N.C. chpt. 1975-77). Episcopalian. Democrat. Rotarian. Home: 801 Oaklawn Ave Winston Salem NC 27104 Office: PO Box 21 Winston Salem NC 27102

ANDERSON, DONALD LEE, clergyman; b. Litchfield, Ill., May 31, 1929; s. Robert James and Nita Mae (McDonald) A.; B.A., William Jennings Bryan Coll., 1951; Ph.D., U. Tex. at Austin, 1971; m. Jeanne Rodgers, Nov. 2, 1950; children—Cheryl Anderson Dugger, Kathy Anderson Markham, Merri Lee. Ordained minister Baptist Ch., 1949; pastor First Bapt. Ch., Agua Dulce, Tex., 1951-53, Mathis, Tex., 1953-56, Kerrville, Tex., 1956-60, Kingsville, Tex., 1960-63, Manor Bapt. Ch., San Antonio, 1963-72; exec. dir. Ecumenical Center for Religion and Health, San Antonio, 1972—; clin. asso. prof. psychiatry U. Tex. Health Sci. Center, San Antonio, also clin. asso. prof. family practice, adj. asso. prof. obstetrics and gynecology; mem. adv. council on human life values Santa Rosa Med. Center. Bd. dirs. San Antonio

Children's Center. Licensed psychologist, Tex. Mem. Am., Tex., Southwestern psychol. assns., Am. Assn. Marriage and Family Counselors. Clubs: Rotary, Torch. Contbr. articles profl. jours. Home: 16410 Ledge Way San Antonio TX 78232 Office: 4507 Medical Dr San Antonio TX 78229

ANDERSON, DONALD ROGER, physician; b. Mpls., June 27, 1946; s. Bennie L. and Dorothy C. (Golden) A.; B.S., Creighton U., 1968; M.D., 1972; m. Marie Jeanne Seaman, June 1, 1968; children—David John, Karin Jo. Intern, Creighton U. Affiliated Hosps., Omaha, 1972, resident internal medicine, 1972-75; staff physician Clark (S.D.) Clinic, 1975-79; staff physician, partner Bartron Clinic, Watertown, S.D., 1975—; asst. clin. prof. dept. medicine U. S.D. Med. Sch., 1976-79; chmn. Watertown Ambulance Com., 1976—; chief staff St. Ann's Hosp., 1979; dir. spl. care unit Meml. Med. Center, Watertown, 1978-79; chmn. coronary care com., mem. exec. com. Combined Med. Staff, St. Ann's and Meml. Med. Center, Watertown, 1978-79; chief Internal Medicine Clinic, Brooke Army Med. Center, Ft. Sam Houston; mem. profl. ednl. com. Am. Cancer Soc., S.D. chpt., 1978-79; mem. Tb Control Center for N.E. S.D., 1977-79; mem. tumor bd. Meml. Med. Center, 1975-79. Diplomate Am. Bd. Internal Medicine. Mem. AMA, Am. Heart Assn., Kidney Found., A.C.P., Am. Soc. Internal Medicine, S.D. State Med. Assn. Clubs: Optomist, Elks. Home: Beach Pavilion Box 548 Fort Sam Houston San Antonio TX 78234

ANDERSON, EDMUND THEODORE, III, petroleum engr., oil, gas and geothermal exploration co. exec.; b. Shreveport, La., Nov. 27, 1912; s. Harry Edmond and Grace Sophia (Showalter) A.; B.S. in Petroleum Engring., Okla. U., Norman, 1940; m. Lillian Gartin, Dec. 27, 1941; children—Mary Lavelle (Mrs. Raymond Boll), Edmund Theodore IV. Timekeeper, Pipeline Constrn. Co., Miss. and W. Tex., 1930-31; roustabout Sims Oil Co. and Gypsy Oil Co., 1931-35; petroleum engr. Dowell Inc., Midland, Tex., Seagraves, Tex., Levelland, Tex., 1940-41, Midland, 1944-49; petroleum engr. Dow Chem. Co., Freeport, Tex., 1941-44; petroleum engr. C. T. McLaughlin Co., Snyder, Tex., 1949-50; exec. in charge of exploration, devel. oil, gas firm Joseph I. O'Neill, Midland, 1950—, exec. in charge exploration, devel. for oil, gas and geothermal energy, 1960—. Registered profl. engr., Tex. Mem. Ind. Petroleum Assn. Am. (dir. 1973-74), Midland Petroleum Club. Republican. Roman Catholic. Elk, K.C. Club: Midland Country (pres. 1962). Home: 2521 Humble St Midland TX 79701 Office: 410 W Ohio St PO Box 2840 Midland TX 79702

ANDERSON, ERIC CHARLES, computer specialist; b. Barberton, Ohio, July 5, 1946; s. Harold Roy and Ethel May (Coolman) A.; B.Sc., U. Akron, 1968; m. Ruta Ariihohoa, July 7, 1976; 1 son, Charles. Physicist equipment devel. lab. U.S. Nat. Weather Service, Silver Spring, Md., 1970; mathematician Naval Command Systems Support Activity, Washington, 1971-73; computer specialist Navy Regional Data Automation Center, Norfolk, Va., 1973—. Served with USNR, 1968-75. Mem. Am. Def. Preparedness Assn. Home: 11 Bristol Circle Chesapeake VA 23320 Office: FTSD NARDAC Norfolk VA 23511

ANDERSON, FLETCHER CLARK, educator; b. Birmingham, Ala., Dec. 7, 1939; s. Fletcher Campbell and Alla Glass (Southall) A.; A.B., Birmingham-So. Coll., 1962, B.Music Edn., 1962; postgrad. U. Ill., 1962-63, M.S. in Music Edn., 1967; Ed.D. in Music Edn., U. Ga., 1978; m. Virginia Fullerton, Aug. 17, 1963; children—Charles, Joseph, Patrick. Gen. music tchr. Area III elem. schs., Atlanta, 1963-65; choral and gen. music tchr. Elizabethtown (Ky.) High Sch., 1965-66; asst. prof. music Edinboro (Pa.) State Coll., 1967-70; asso. prof. music Wesleyan Coll., Macon, Ga., 1970—, acting chmn. dept., 1979-80; dir. music Centenary United Meth. Ch. Chmn. troop 80 com. Piedmont Dist. council Boy Scouts Am. Mem. Music Educators Nat. Conf., Ga. Music Educators Assn. (chmn. elect coll. div., state student adv. 1979-80, research chmn. 1977-79), Am. Guild Organists, Coll. Music Soc. Home: 367 Wesleyan Dr Macon GA 31210 Office: Music Dept Wesleyan Coll Macon GA 31201

ANDERSON, GARY STEPHEN, real estate developer; b. Greensboro, N.C., Mar. 12, 1946; s. Rex Monty and Dorothy (Means) A.; B.S., M.I.T., 1968; M.S. (N.Am. Rockwell fellow), U. So. Calif., 1970; M.B.A., Harvard U., 1972; m. Linda Augusta McNealey, Aug. 23, 1969; children—Kathryn, Christopher. Asso. devel. mgr. Sea Pines Co., Hilton Head Island, S.C., 1972-73; v.p. finance Moss Creek Devel. Corp., Hilton Head Island, 1973-79; pres. Anderson Devel. Corp., Hilton Head Island, 1979—; dir. Mayrand, Inc. Trustee Sea Pines Montessori Sch. Home: 25 Victoria Dr Hilton Head Island SC 29928 Office: 5 Office Park Rd Hilton Head Island SC 29928

ANDERSON, GARY SWEN, hydrologist; b. Sioux City, Iowa, July 18, 1939; s. Swen Lars and Ruth Eleanor (Johnson) A.; student U. Colo., 1957-58; B.A., Augustana Coll. (Ill.), 1961; M.S., Iowa State U., 1963; postgrad. U. Alaska, 1963-65; m. Judith Ann Thompson, Dec. 18, 1965; 1 son, Gregory Swen. Asso. investigator Iowa State U., 1961-63; geologist Alaskan Geology br. U.S. Geol. Survey, summers 1963-64, geologist engring. geology Alaskan Terrain and Permafrost sect., Fairbanks, 1963-64, hydrologist Water Resources Div., Anchorage, 1965-77, asst. dist. chief, Richmond, Va., 1978—; Eagle scout Boy Scouts Am., 1957. Iowa State U. research grantee, 1961. Mem. Geol. Soc. Am., Arctic Inst. N.Am., Am. Geophys. Union, Soc. Engring. Geologists, Assn. Profl. Geol. Scientists, Am. Water Resources Assn., Am. Water Well Assn., Alaskan Geology Soc., Alaska Ground-Water Assn. (pres. 1976), Sigma Gamma Epsilon. Contbr. articles to profl. jours. Home: Route 2 Box 31 Hanover VA 23069 Office: 200 W Grace St Richmond VA 23220

ANDERSON, HAYWARD SULLIVAN, educator; b. Thomasville, Ga., Nov. 30, 1920; s. Walter and Leroy (McCloud) A.; B.S., Savannah (Ga.) State Coll., 1946; B.S., Northwestern U., 1949; M.B.A., N.Y. U., 1952; D.B.A. (Univ. doctoral research fellow 1957-58), Harvard U., 1961; m. Althea Mayme Williams, Mar. 19, 1966. Asst. prof. bus. W.Va. State Coll., Institute, 1953-56; prof. bus. adminstrn. Savannah State Coll., 1959-69, 73—, chmn. div., 1959-69; prof. bus. Jackson (Miss.) State Coll., 1969-72, chmn. div., 1969-72, dean Sch. Bus. and Econs., 1972. Mem. Ga. adv. council SBA, 1969; bd. dirs. Jackson Nat. Bus. League, 1970-72; bd. dirs. Jackson Urban League, 1972; bd. dirs. Savannah Area Minority Contractor Assn., 1976—, chmn. bd., 1978—; mem. adv. bd. dirs. YWCA, 1976—; mem. Chatham County-Savannah Met. Planning Commn., 1977—. Served to 1st lt. AUS, 1943-46, 50. Mem. Am. Accounting Assn., Am. Mktg. Assn., AAUP (pres. local chpt. 1967-69, mem. exec. com. Ga. conf. 1968-69), Harvard Bus. Club of Atlanta, So. Bus. Adminstrn. Assn. (mem. exec. com. 1972-73), Savannah Area C. of C. (mem. bus. task force 1977—), Phi Delta Kappa. Home: PO Box 3655 4301 Whatley Ave Savannah GA 31404

ANDERSON, HERBERT EUGENE, JR., water treatment equipment mfg. co. exec.; b. Muskogee, Okla., Aug. 19, 1944; s. Herbert Eugene and Anna Margaret (Gotwals) A.; student Oklahoma City U., 1962-64; B.S.E.E., Washington U., St. Louis, 1967; m. Martha Beth Hazlewood, Sept. 14, 1974. Jr. engr., Monsanto Co., St. Louis, 1967-71, sr. engr., 1971; v.p. H.E. Anderson Co., Muskogee, Okla., 1971-76, pres., 1976—; dir. 1st Nat. Bank & Trust Co. of Muskogee. Bd. dirs. Kelly B. Todd Cerebral Palsy and Neuromuscular Found., Baptist. Clubs: Rotary (pres. Muskogee 1978-79), Wauhillau Outing, Masons, Elks. Office: HE Anderson Co 2100 Anderson Dr Muskogee OK 74401

ANDERSON, HOWARD PALMER, state senator; b. Crystall Hill, Va., May 25, 1915; B.A., Coll. William and Mary, 1940; LL.B., U. Richmond, 1948; m. Mildred Graham Webb. Admitted to Va. bar, 1948; practice law, Halifax, Va., 1950—; mem. Va. Ho. of Dels., 1958-71, Va. State Senate, 1972—. Trustee, Patrick Henry Meml. Found.; mem. Halifax County Sch. Bd., 1952-57. Served with USNR, World War II. Mem. Va. Bar Assn., Halifax County Bar Assn., U. Richmond Law Sch. Assn., Halifax County C. of C., Am. Legion, VFW. Baptist. Clubs: Lions, Masons, Sportsman (Halifax). Office: PO Box 847 Halifax VA 24558

ANDERSON, HUBERT MAXWELL, JR., mfrs. rep.; b. Brewster, Fla., Mar. 12, 1939; s. Hubert Maxwell and Louise (Whidden) A.; B.E.E., U. Fla., 1963; postgrad. Alexander Hamilton Inst. Bus., 1969-70; m. Marie Lou Franceschini, Feb. 18, 1966; children—Allan Max, Maurice Enrique, Max Robert. Design engr. IT&T Research and Devel. Lab., San Juan, P.R., 1964-66; engr. RCA Info. System div., West Palm Beach, Fla., 1967-68; v.p. E. Franceschini Assos., Santurce, P.R., 1968-78; pres. M. Anderson Co. Inc., 1978—. Served with AUS, 1959. Mem. IEEE, Mfrs. Agts. Nat. Assn., Armed Forces Communications Assn., Am. Mgmt. Assn. Clubs: Caparra (P.R.) Country, Caribe Hilton Swimming and Tennis (San Juan, P.R.). Home: Calle Cerezo #5 Urb San Patricio Guaynabo PR 00657 Office: Edificio El Monte Mall Hato Rey PR 00918

ANDERSON, JACK OLAND, coll. pres.; b. Mich., Aug. 5, 1921; s. Seymour and Laura (Fox) A.; student Ferris State Coll.; B.S., Central Mich. U., 1948; M.A., U. Mich., 1950; Ed.D., Mich. State U., 1962. Tchr. public schs., Mich., 1949-59; asst. instr. Mich. State U., 1959-62; dir. edn. Lansing (Mich.) Bus. Inst., 1963-65; exec. dir. Lockyear Bus. Coll., 1965-66; acad. dean Detroit Coll., 1966-69; pres. Bristol (Tenn.) Coll., 1969—; past chmn., mem. Sullivan County Vocat. Adv. Com. Served to capt. U.S. Army, 1942-46. Mem. Tenn. Bus. Coll. Assn. (past pres. and dir.), Southeastern Bus. Coll. Assn. (past pres. and dir.), Bristol C. of C. (dir. 1978—, chmn. congressional action 1979). Baptist. Club: Bristol Rotary. Address: PO Box 763 Bristol TN 37620

ANDERSON, JAMES WILLIAM, TV exec., writer, publisher; b. Webster Groves, Mo., July 29, 1926; s. James W. and Cecelia (Bertels) A.; B.S. in Mktg., St. Louis U., 1949. Mem. mktg. dept. Philip Morris Co., 1949-51, Westinghouse Co., 1951-54; troubleshooter, then sales promotion mgr. Midwest Dist. ABC TV Network, 1960-64; books include: The UHF Explosion, 1967, The New York Indie Phenomenon, 1968, A $250,000,000 Salesman Tells How to Sell Condominiums, 1973, How To Live Rent Free, 1978. Curator, Lemon City, Fla., 1978. Served with USN, 1944-46. Republican. Home and office: 701 NE 67th St Miami FL 33138

ANDERSON, JAY MORGAN, mortgage co. exec.; b. South Boston, Va., Apr. 29, 1936; s. Florence Lee Whitt; B.S., Va. Poly. Inst. and State U., 1975; M.S., Radford Coll., 1976; J.D., Blackstone Sch. Law, 1976; m. Helen H. Booth, 1963; 1 son, Jay Morgan. Vice pres. Pyrmaid Publ. Co., Greensboro, N.C., 1959-62; pres. Va. Carolina Mortgage Co., Roanoke, Va., 1962-68; chmn. bd. Mortgage Co. Am., Roanoke, 1969—. Served with AUS, 1954-56. Republican. Office: Box 1191 Roanoke VA 24006

ANDERSON, JOHN CARLIN, JR., bus. exec.; b. Washington, Aug. 7, 1944; s. John Carlin and Bonnie Blanche (Nichols) A.; B.S., George Mason U., 1973, postgrad., 1973-74; m. Carol Lee Gilbert, Oct. 8, 1978. Asst. gen. mgr., v.p. The Van House Inc., Alexandria, Va., 1974-76; gen. mgr., pres., chmn. bd. The Van House of Richmond, 1976—; chmn. bd. John C. Anderson, Inc., Richmond, 1976—. Served with Air N.G., 1966-76, USAF, 1968-69. Mem. Kappa Sigma, Beta Epsilon Phi, Omicron Delta Epsilon. Presbyterian. Office: 1319 W Broad St Richmond VA 23220

ANDERSON, JOHN CARSON, JR., electric utility exec.; b. Whiteville, N.C., May 27, 1937; s. John Carson and Mary Elneda (Long) A.; student Presbyterian Jr. Coll., 1956; m. Anna Pearl Mercer, July 26, 1959; children—Anna Gaye, Wynna Renea, Emily Marijon. Resident engr. So. Engring. Co., Atlanta, 1956-61; ops. engr. Little River Electric Coop., Inc., Abbeville, S.C., 1961-67; asst. gen. mgr. Berkeley Electric Coop., Inc., Moncks Corner, S.C., 1967-71; v.p. Black River Electric Coop., Inc., Sumter, S.C., 1971—; trustee Central Electric Power Coop., Inc., v.p., 1975—; mem. Wateree Community Action Com. of Weatherization, 1976—; pres. S.C. Electric Coops. Employees Credit Union, 1974—, S.C. Farmer Coop. Council, 1976—. Mem. Nat. Rural Electric Coop. Assn., S.C. Assn. Electric Coops. (dir.). Democrat. Methodist. Clubs: Masons, Elks (chpt. officer), Exchange (dist. pres. 1976-77), Optimists. Home: 5 Foxfire Ln Wedgefield SC 29160 Office: PO Box 130 Sumter SC 29150

ANDERSON, JOHN HENDERSON, educator, ret. army officer; b. Bklyn., Oct. 3, 1929; s. Alexander Paul and Elizabeth May (Henderson) A.; B. Gen. Edn., U. Omaha, 1965; grad. U.S. Army Command and Gen. Staff Coll., 1966; M.S., Troy State U., 1973; m. Mary Eleanor Kraus, Sept. 12, 1952; children—Virginia, John, Scott. Commd. 2d lt. U.S. Army, 1952, advanced through grades to lt. col., 1968; various command and staff positions in arty. and aviation units, U.S., Korea, Vietnam, W. Ger., 1951-68; chief evaluation div. Office of Dir. Instruction, U.S. Army Aviation Sch., Ft. Rucker, Ala., 1968-71, ret., 1971; sr. instr. Army Jr. ROTC program Daleville (Ala.) High Sch., 1971—; coach Ala. State High Sch. championship rifle team, 1977, 78, 79, 80, Trindoc Nat. Interscholastic championship rifle team, 1979. Decorated Legion of Merit, Bronze Star with three oak leaf clusters, Purple Heart, Air medals (10). Mem. Am. Personnel and Guidance Assn., Am. Coll. Personnel Assn., Assn. U.S. Army, Army Aviation Assn. Am. (charter, life mem.), VFW, Ret. Officers Assn. (dir. Ft. Rucker chpt.). Home: 1102 Holiday Ln Ozark AL 36360 Office: USAIG JROTC Daleville High Sch Daleville AL 36322

ANDERSON, JOHN JOSEPH BAXTER, nutritionist; b. Cleve., June 12, 1934; s. Francis M. and Phyllis Suzette (Wallbridge) A.; B.A., Williams Coll., 1956; M.A.T., Harvard U., 1958; M.A., Boston U., 1962; Ph.D., Cornell U., 1966; m. Elizabeth Elsemore, Aug. 17, 1957; children—Edward E., John P., Timothy W. Instr., Bradford (Mass.) Jr. Coll., 1959-62; trainee Cornell U., Ithaca, N.Y., 1962-66; asst. prof. physiology U. Ill., Urbana, 1966-72; asso. prof. Sch. Public Health, U. N.C., Chapel Hill, 1972-77, prof., 1977—. Mem. AAAS, Am. Public Health Assn., Nutrition Today Soc., Am. Inst. Nutrition, Fedn. Am. Socs. for Exptl. Biology, Am. Physiol. Soc. Author: (with others) Human Ecology, 1975; Editor: Applied Nutrition for Health Professions, 1977; Parturient Hypocalcemia, 1971; contbr. articles to profl. jours. Home: 15 Rogerson Dr Chapel Hill NC 27514 Office: Dept Nutrition Sch Public Health U NC Chapel Hill NC 27514

ANDERSON, JUSTICE CONRAD, educator, missionary; b. Bay City, Tex., Feb. 13, 1929; s. Conrad Roy and Eunice May (Justice) A.; B.A., Baylor U., 1950, M.A., 1951; M.Div., Southwestern Bapt. Theol. Sem., 1955, Th.D., 1965; m. Mary Ann Elmore, June 1, 1949; children—Sandra Jean, Timothy Justice, Bradley Pryse, Suzanne Renee. Ordained to ministry So. Bapt. Conv.; pastor Tex., 1949-57; missionary, prof. ch. history and homi letics Internat. Bapt. Theol. Sem., Buenos Aires, 1957-74; prof. missions Southwestern Bapt. Theol. Sem., Fort Worth, 1974—. Named Man of Merit, Baylor U., 1979. Mem. Bapt. Hist. Soc., Internat. Assn. Missions, Am. Soc. Missiology. Clubs: Ridglea Country. Author: The Manual of Ecclesiology, 1974; The Manual of Homiletics for Laymen, 1963; A History of the Baptists, Vol. I, 1978. Contbr. articles to profl. jours. Home: 4628 Brandingshire Pl Fort Worth TX 76133 Office: Box 22206 Fort Worth TX 76122

ANDERSON, LAVERE FRANCIS SHOENFELT (MRS. FRENCH ANDERSON), author, editor; b. Muskogee, Okla., Apr. 15, 1907; d. George Burket and Jessie Jonesia (Jordan) Shoenfelt; B.A., U. Tulsa, 1928; postgrad. Columbia U., 1928, U. Okla., 1951; m. French Anderson, June 16, 1928; children—Jessica (Mrs. L.G. Nidiffer), Audrey (Mrs. Thomas C. Thixton), W. French. Reporter, Tulsa Daily World, 1930-42, book editor, 1942-50, 52-76; also free-lance writer. Instr. creative writing U. Tulsa, 1942-50, 52-68, Philbrook Art Center, 1953-61; lectr., panel mem. Regional Writers' Conf., Drury Coll., Springfield, Mo. Active Girl Scouts U.S., YWCA. Mem. Nat. League Am. Pen Women, Am. Assn. U. Women, D.A.R., Theta Sigma Phi, Delta Delta Delta. Presbyn. Clubs: Tulsa Press, University. Author children's books: A Story a Day to Read Aloud, 1962; Stories About America, 1963; Animal Stories, 1964; Abraham Lincoln, 1965; Robert Todd Lincoln, 1967; Sitting Bull, 1970; Quanah Parker, 1970; Abe and the River Robbers, 1971; Frederic Remington, 1971; Tad Lincoln, 1971; Allan Pinkerton, 1972; Black Hawk, 1972; Martha Washington, 1973; Johnny Appleseed, 1974; Saddles and Sabers, 1975; Mary Todd Lincoln, 1975; Mary McLeod Bethune, 1976; Balto, 1976; Svea, 1977. Contbr. fiction and non-fiction to mags., book chpts. to anthologies, paperback reprints, syndication, fgn. edits., broadcasting, Braille, audiovisual edn. Home: 232 E 27th Pl Tulsa OK 74114

ANDERSON, LEWIS DANIEL, surgeon; b. Greensboro, Ala., Oct. 13, 1930; s. Thomas Jefferson and Frances (Daniel) A.; student Emory U., 1947-49; M.D., U. Pa., 1953; M.S. in Orthopedic Surgery, U. Tenn., 1960; m. Stella Stickney Cobbs, July 7, 1951; children—Evelyn C., Lewis Daniel, Tunstall C., Lida T. Intern, U. Pa. Hosp., 1953-54, resident in gen. surgery, 1954, 56-57; resident orthopedic surgery Campbell Clinic, Memphis, 1957-60; practice medicine specializing in orthopedic surgery, Memphis, 1960-77, Mobile, Ala., 1977—; asso. prof. orthopedic surgery U. Tenn. Center for the Health Scis., Memphis, 1965-71, prof., 1971-77, asst. to chancellor for clin. ops., 1975-77; mem. active staff City of Memphis Hosp., 1960-77, med. dir., 1972-75; mem. attending staff Bapt. Meml. Hosp., 1960-77, U. Tenn. Hosp., 1975-77, U.S. Ala. Med. Center Hosp., 1977—, Providence Hosp., 1977—; mem. cons. staff St. Joseph Hosp., 1960-77, Le Bonheur Children's Hosp., 1960-77, St. Jude's Children's Hosp., 1964-77, Tenn. Psychiat. Inst., 1965-77, Mobile Infirmary, 1977—, Med. Center Hosp., Selma, Ala., 1978—; prof., chmn. dept. of orthopaedic surgery U. of South Ala. Coll. of Medicine, Mobile, 1977—. Mem. edn. com. U. Tenn. Campbell Found. Residency Program, 1962-77. Served with M.C., USN, 1954-56. Am.-Brit.-Can. Orthopedic Assn. Exchange fellow, 1967; diplomate Am. Bd. Orthopedic Surgery. Fellow A.C.S.; mem. Am. Acad. of Orthopedic Surgeons (sec. com. on continuing edn. 1969-73, mem. adv. com. on edn. 1974-75), Am. Orthopedic Assn., Tenn. Orthopedic Assn., Va. Orthopedic Soc. (hon. mem.). Ala. Orthopedic Soc., Clin. Orthopedic Soc., Orthopedic Research Soc., Med. Soc. of Mobile County, Med. Soc. State of Ala., Assn. for Acad. Surgery, Am. Assn. of Orthopedic Chairmen (mem. com. undergrad. edn. 1977—), Willis C. Campbell Orthopaedic Club (sec. 1970-73), AMA, So. Med. Assn., Société Internat. de Chirurgie Orthopédique et de Traumatologie, Sigma Xi, Alpha Omega Alpha. Episcopalian. Contbr. numerous articles on orthopedic surgery to med. jours.; contbr. book revs. in field to profl. jours.; editorial bd. Contemporary Orthopedics, 1979—. Home: 1907 Old Shell Rd Mobile AL 36607 Office: 2451 Fillingim St Mobile AL 36617

ANDERSON, LINDA LOUISE, telephone co. exec.; b. Farmington, Ky., Mar. 20, 1926; d. Romuald and Ruby Ophelia (Cook) Spalding; grad. Mayfield Bus. Coll., 1946; m. Jack Anderson, Nov. 25, 1949; 1 son, Jack Stevens. Sec., Production and Mktg. Adminstrn., Mayfield, Ky., 1943-50; sec., bookkeeper Sheriff's Office, Mayfield, 1950-51; with W. Ky. Rural Telephone Coop., Mayfield, 1951—, office mgr., 1979—. Recipient award U.S. Dept. Agr. Grad. Sch. Acctg., 1955. Mem. Nat. Telephone Coop. Assn., U.S. Ind. Telephone Assn., Ind. Telephone Pioneer Assn., Ky. Telephone Assn., Tenn. Telephone Assn., Mayfield Emblem Bus. and Profl. Woman's Club (sec.-treas.). Democrat. Roman Catholic. Home: 616 Central Ave Mayfield KY 42066 Office: 237 N 8th St Mayfield KY 42066

ANDERSON, LYN D., food co. exec.; b. Louisville, Aug. 11, 1944; s. Vernon D. and Eleanor D. (Thuftedal) A.; B.A. in Acctg., St. Cloud State U., 1966, M.B.A., 1969; m. Janice Marie Burski, Mar. 22, 1969; children—Kimberly Lynn, Jennifer Marie, Brian Lyn. Staff acct. Gen. Mills Inc., 1969-70; acct., Gen. Mills Chems., Inc., Mpls., 1971-72, fin. analyst, 1972-73, sr. fin. analyst, 1973-74; mgr. budgeting Tom's Foods subs. Gen. Mills, Inc., Columbus, Ga., 1975-77, asst. dir. acctg., 1977-78, dir. acctg., 1978—. Adviser Jr. Achievement; treas., head trustee Lutheran Ch. of the Redeemer. Served with U.S. Army, 1967-69; Vietnam. Decorated Army Commendation medal. Mem. Nat. Assn. Accts. (dir. Columbus chpt.), Inst. Mgmt. Acctg. (cert. mgmt. acct.). Home: 6121 Seaton Dr Columbus GA 31904 Office: Tom's Foods Subs Gen Mills Inc PO Box 60 Columbus GA 31902

ANDERSON, MABLE BELL, educator; b. Birmingham, Ala., Sept. 7, 1930; d. I.C. and Beatrice (Craddock) Bell; B.S. (inst. scholar), Tuskegee Inst., 1950; M.A. (univ. scholar), Mich. State U., 1952; Ed.D., Pa. State U., 1965; postgrad. Grambling Coll., summer 1960, Bank St. Coll. Edn., summer 1967, Yeshiva U., summer 1967; postdoctoral Western Ky. U., 1968, U. Ga., 1974; m. Furman C. Anderson, June 9, 1958 (div. May 1965). Instr. home econs. and health Fayette County Tng. Sch., Fayette, Ala., 1950-51; tchr.-trainer in home econs. edn. and child devel. Grambling Coll. 1952-54; mem. faculty child devel. and family relationships Miles Coll., Birmingham, 1954-60; presch. asst. tchr. Pa. State U., 1961-62; dir. Migrant Day Care Center, Dept. Child and Family Welfare, Harrisburg, Pa., summer 1961, social caseworker, summer 1962; prof. child devel., chmn. grad. studies in home econs. Tenn. A. and I. State U., 1963-66; prof. elementary edn. Western Ky. U., Bowling Green, 1966-69, supr. student tchrs. in elementary edn., 1966; prof. Center for Early Childhood Personnel Devel., State Coll. Ark., Conway, 1969-70; prof. edn., coordinator early childhood edn., 1970-77, asso. dir. tchr. corps. Albany (Ga.) State Coll., 1970-72; adminstr. Birmingham Bd. Edn., 1977-79; dir. acad. devel. Miles Coll., Birmingham, 1979—; guest lectr. Head Start Tchr. Tng. programs George Peabody Coll., Pa. State U., 1965; workshop leader, 1966—; rep. Ky. Com. on Early Childhood Edn., 1966-70; adviser, cons. kindergartens, day care centers, 1967—; chmn. Dougherty County Task Force in comprehensive Early Childhood Devel. programs cons. Warren County-Bowling Green Assn. Mental Retardation, 1966-70, Coll. of Ozarks, Clarksville, 1969-70; lectr., cons. P.R. Dept. Edn., San Juan, 1971; mem. Citizen's Advisory Com., Albany, 1972—; bd. dirs., tech. advisor So. Ky. Econ.

Opportunity Council, 1967-70, Child Devel. Asso. Consortium, 1972—, Ga. Accreditation Commn., 1972-77; participant conf. on changing sex roles, Dubrovnik, Yugoslavia, 1975; lectr. in field; research in Child Devel.; mem. Assn. Childhood Edn. Internat. (dir. 1970-73), Nat. Council Family Relations (dir. 1969-73), Ky. Edn. Assn., Nursery-Kindergarten NEA, Am. Assn. Sch. Adminstrs., Am. Home Econs. Assn., AAUW, AAUP, Groves Conf. Family Life, Alpha Kappa Mu, Omicron Nu, Kappa Delta Phi, Phi Delta Kappa. Asso. editor Family Coordinator, 1973—. Home: PO Box 8331 Birmingham AL 35218

ANDERSON, MALCOLM WYLIE, JR., mfg. co. exec.; b. Tampa, Fla., May 3, 1944; s. Malcolm Wylie and Bertilla (Garcia) A.; grad. Bus. U. Tampa, 1964; B.A., U. South Fla., 1969, M.A., 1972, postgrad., 1974-76; m. Joanne Wilson, July 16, 1977; 1 son, Trevor Scott. Tchr., Hillsborough County Sch. Bd., Tampa, Fla., 1969-70, resource tchr., 1970-72, program coordinator, 1972-74; cons. U. South Fla., Tampa, 1973-74; supr. exceptional student edn. Pasco County Sch. Bd., Land O'Lakes, Fla., 1974-77; regional sales mgr. west coast Lykes-Pasco Packing Co., Dade City, Fla., 1977-78, Worldwide mil. mktg. mgr., 1979—. Mem. Am. Logistics Assn., Am. Mgmt. Assn., U. South Fla. Alumni Assn. Democrat. Baptist. Home: 100 Elm St San Antonio FL 33576 Office: Lykes Pasco Packing Co PO Box 97 Hwy 301 Dade City FL 33525

ANDERSON, MARIAN MCCUTCHEN (MRS. WILLIAM WHITE ANDERSON), hosp. adminstr.; b. Bishopville, S.C., June 2, 1913; d. Robert Othello and Florence (Jenkins) McCutchen; student U. S.C., 1930-32, 36; grad. Draughan's Bus. Coll. 1936; m. William White Anderson, May 30, 1941 (dec. May 1949);children—Susan Anderson (Mrs. Donald Eugene Mathis), McCutchen Brooks. Chief clk. Selective Service Bd., 1941-42; sec.-bookkeeper Ashwood Area Vocational Sch., Bishopville, 1949-50; bookkeeper Lee County Meml. Hosp., Bishopville, 1950-58, adminstr., 1958-75. Mem. Santee-Wateree Health Planning Council. Bd. dirs. Lee County Mental Health Assn., Lee County chpt. ARC, Mem. Am., S.C. hosp. assns., Hosp. Fin. Mgmt. Assn. (life mem.; Follmer and founders award for outstanding service S.C. chpt. 1966, sec. 1966-75), Internat. Platform Assn., French Huguenot Soc., Soc. Magna Charta Dames. Presbyn. Home: 211 S Heyward St Bishopville SC 29010 Office: Church St Extension Bishopville SC 29010

ANDERSON, MARINO RAUL, pool products co. exec.; b. Quito, Ecuador, Apr. 18, 1925 (father Am. citizen); s. Louis Henry and Matilde (Rivadeneira) A.; B.A. in Govt. and Econs., So. Meth. U., 1948; M.A. in Internat. Law, Universidad Central, Quito, 1951; children—Paul Louis, Eva Marie, Charles Marino. With Shell Oil Co., Ecuador, 1944-46, Jack Danciger Investments, Ft. Worth, 1951-55, Murray Cotton Gin, Dallas, 1955-58, Lone Star Steel Co., Dallas, 1958-60, Intercontinental Enterprises, Duesseldorf, W. Ger., 1960-63, Continental Cotton Gin, Prattville, Ala., 1963-66, Wayne Mfr., Mexico City, 1966-68, Merc. Nat. Bank, Dallas, 1968-70, Dresser Industries, Dallas, 1970-73; with Seablue Internat. div. Meridian Enterprises Inc., 1973—, mgr. internat. ops., 1979—. Served with U.S. Army, 1949-51. Mem. Am. Soc. Internat. Execs., Internat. Trade Assn. Dallas. Republican. Roman Catholic. Home: 8403 Oak Stream St Dallas TX 75243 Office: Seablue Internat IMG Div Meridan Enterprises Inc 5355 McConnel Ave Los Angeles CA 90066

ANDERSON, MARY BAKER, guidance counselor; b. Monroe County, Miss., Dec. 6, 1931; d. Hamilton William and Ellie Elkin (Wood) Baker; B.S. in Elem. Edn., Miss. State Coll. Women, 1953; M.A. in Guidance Counseling, Columbia U., 1960; m. John Crowell Anderson, Dec. 27, 1959; children—Charles William, Mary Caroline, John Andrew. Tchr. public schs., Miss., Fla., Ala. and Ga., 1953-78; guidance counselor Rocky Mountain Sch., Cobb County Sch. System, Marietta, Ga., 1978-79, adminstrv. asst. sch. system, 1979—; chmn. Cobb County Polit. Action Com. Edn., 1975-79; vol. tutor for children with learning disabilities. Mem. steering com. Mountain View Presbyn. Ch., Cobb County, 1974-77. Mem. NEA (chmn. dist. polit. action com. 1976-79), Am. Personnel and Guidance Assn., Ga. Assn. Educators, Cobb County Assn. Educators, LWV, Alpha Delta Kappa. Democrat. Home: 3390 Vandiver Dr Marietta GA 30066 Office: 2400 Rocky Mountain Rd Marietta GA 30066

ANDERSON, PATRICIA ETTA, advt. exec.; b. Filbert, W.Va., Jan. 18, 1942; d. Thomas Allen and Martha Louise (Crigger) A.; A.A., Brevard Community Coll., 1975; B.S., U. Central Fla., 1979. Mng. editor Dope Sheet, Norfolk Va., 1961-64, Beachcomber Newspaper, Ship Bottom, N.J., 1964-70; compositor Brevard Printing Co., Cocoa, Fla., 1971-75; free lance composition, Orlando, Fla., 1975-76; advt. dir. Cody Publs., Inc., Kissimmee, Fla., 1976-79; asst. exec. dir. FLBMDA, Inc., Orlando, Fla., 1980—. Served with U.S. Navy, 1961-64. Mem. Internat. Assn. Printing House Craftsmen, Nat. Assn. Female Execs. Democrat. Methodist. Address: 905 Lee Rd Orlando FL 32810

ANDERSON, PATRICIA HOUSLEY, ednl. adminstr.; b. Sumrall, Miss., Nov. 11, 1937; married, 1 child. B.S. with honors in Elem. Edn., U. So. Miss., Hattiesburg, 1962, M.S. Ednl. Adminstrn., 1966. Tchr. Columbia (Miss.) City Schs., 1962-68, librarian, 1968-69, tchr. reading, 1969-71; supr. Title I Marion County schs., Columbia, Miss., 1971—. Mem. Internat. Reading Assn., NEA, Miss. Ednl. Assn. Certified in counseling, psychology, ednl. adminstrn. Recipient Outstanding Young Educators award Marion County, Miss., 1966. Home: Route 6 Box 286A Columbia MS 39429 Office: 211 Newsom Bldg Columbia MS 39429

ANDERSON, R. BRUCE W., educator; b. Evanston, Ill., Oct. 10, 1938; s. Edward Ralph and Ruth E. (Wilmot) A.; A.B., Stanford U., 1961; M.A., Northwestern U., 1965; Ph.D. (NIMH fellow), Duke U., 1970; m. Birgit Vendelbo, June 21, 1963; children—Britt V., Belinda E., Bodil J. Instr. sociology Northwestern U., 1963-65; asst. prof. sociology Carroll Coll., Waukesha, Wis., 1965-67, U. Man. (Can.) Winnipeg, 1971-73; asso. prof. U. Tex. at Arlington, 1973—, also instr. Danish lang., 1979; cons. in field. Bd. dirs. Winnipeg Pollution Probe, 1971-72; pres. bd. dirs. Cowtown Co-op., 1978-79; bd. dirs. SOS Ambulance Dist. Postdoctoral fellow Center Study Aging and Human Devel., Duke, 1969-71. Mem. Am., Internat. sociol. assns., So. Sociol. Soc., Am. Statis. Assn., Soc. Intercultural Edn., Tng. and Research, Alpha Kappa Delta, Alpha Delta Sigma. Contbr. articles to profl. jours., also chpts. in books. Corr. editor Sociolinguistics Newsletter, 1974—. Office: Dept Sociology U Texas Arlington TX 76019

ANDERSON, RAE ROY, art gallery exec.; b. Danielson, Conn., Apr. 29, 1927; d. Onesime and Delina (Morin) Roy; B.A., Wayne U., Detroit, 1948; postgrad. N.Y. Sch. Interior Design, 1956; m. William R. Anderson, Nov. 20, 1973. Adminstrv. asst. Douglas Furniture Corp., El Segundo, Calif., 1948-58; mfrs. rep. various firms, 1958-69; founder, dir. Quadrangle Galleries, Dallas, 1968—. Coordinator, Retrospective Exhbn., Norton Mus., Shreveport, La., 1974. Mem. Nat. Home Fashions League (charter). Republican. Presbyterian. Club: Las Colinas. Address: PO Box 656 McAllen TX 78501

ANDERSON, RANDALL HAROLD, coll. exec.; b. Ft. Worth, Mar. 28, 1952; s. Edwin Harold and Virginia Katherine (de Bruyn) A.; student Tex. Tech. U., 1972-73; B.B.A. cum laude, Midwestern State U., 1975; M.B.A., Tarleton State U., 1980; m. Jean Elizabeth Foster, Aug. 25, 1972; 1 son, Randall Clayton. Staff acct. Arthur Anderson & Co., Ft. Worth, 1975-76; sr. acct. Lockhart & Co., C.P.A.'s, Ft. Worth, 1976-78; bus. mgr. Weatherford (Tex.) Coll., 1978—. Bd. dirs., treas. Parker County (Tex.) United Way, 1978—. Served with USMC, 1970-72. C.P.A., Tex. Mem. Am. Inst. C.P.A.'s, Tex. Soc. C.P.A.'s, Tex. Assn. Public Jr. Coll. Bus. Officers, Tex. Jr. Coll. Tchrs. Assn., Phi Theta Kappa. Republican. Mem. Ch. of Christ. Club: Optimist (dir. 1977-80). Home: 1212 Vivienne St Weatherford TX 76086 Office: 308 E Park Ave Weatherford TX 76086

ANDERSON, RICHARD JOHN, social worker, educator; b. Kewanee, Ill., Mar. 25, 1929; s. Carl H. and Dorothea F. A.; B.A., U. Denver, 1950; M.S.W., U. Ill., 1955; Ed.D., Ill. State U., 1968; m. Martha Bishop, June 23, 1951; children—Kimball, Julene. Asso. prof. social work U. Ill., 1969-74; prof. social work and edn. U. Ga., Athens, 1974—. Served with USAF, 1951-53. Grad. fellow, 1964-65; cert. Acad. Cert. Social Workers; cert. social worker, cert. sch. adminstr., Ill. Mem. Nat. Assn. Social Workers, Council Social Work Edn., Mental Health Assn., Phi Delta Kappa. Author: Georgia Law Relating to Minors, 1979; editor-in-chief Jour. Social Work in Edn., 1978; contbr. articles to profl. jours. Office: School of Social Work University of Georgia Athens GA 30602

ANDERSON, RICHARD LOUIS, phys. chemist; b. Hale Center, Tex., Nov. 27, 1935; s. John Louis and Daisy Belle (Caudle) A.; B.S. in Chemistry, M.I.T., 1958; Ph.D. in Phys. Chemistry, Rice U., 1965; m. Barbara Ellen Follmer, Oct. 10, 1976; children—Lisa Helene, Teresa Louise; 1 stepdau., Vanessa Ellen Hedges. Research physicist Nat. Bur. Standards, Washington, 1963-71; scientist Physikalisch-Technische Bundesanstalt, Braunschweig, W. Ger., 1971-74; head metrology lab. Oak Ridge Nat. Lab., 1974-79, group leader, measurements research group, instrumentation and controls div. Oak Ridge Nat. Lab., 1979—. Treas. Oak Ridge Civic Music Assn., 1976-79, Oak Ridge Symphony, 1978-79, Oak Ridge Community Band, 1979—. Recipient Disting. Authorship award Nat. Bur. Standards, 1971; 1st place award, jour. articles E. Tenn. Soc. for Tech. Communications, 1978. Mem. Am. Vacuum Soc., IEEE, Am. Soc. Metals, Sigma Xi. Unitarian. Home: 112 Garnet Ln Oak Ridge TN 37830 Office: Oak Ridge Nat Lab PO Box X Bldg 3500 Oak Ridge TN 37830

ANDERSON, RICHARD MCLEMORE, physician; b. Gainesville, Fla., Mar. 3, 1930; s. Montgomery Drummond and Myrtle (McLemore) A.; B.S., U. Fla., 1951; M.D., Emory U., 1958; m. Leewood Shaw, Mar. 21, 1959; children—Richard M., Bruce D. Intern, Grady Meml. Hosp., Altanta, 1958-59; resident in internal medicine U. Fla. Teaching Hosp., 1959-61, research fellow, 1961-62; practice medicine specializing in internal medicine, Gainesville, 1962—; attending physician Alachua Gen., N. Fla. Regional hosps.; clin. instr. medicine U. Fla., 1965—; chief of staff Alachua Gen. Hosp., 1973-75, dir., 1978—. Served with USAF, 1951-54. Diplomate Am. Bd. Internal Medicine. Mem. AMA, Fla. Med. Assn., Alachua County Med. Soc. (past v.p.), Am. Soc. Internal Medicine, Alpha Omega Alpha. Presbyterian (elder). Club: Rotary (pres. 1980) (Gainesville). Home: 631 N W 28th St Gainesville FL 32607 Office: 106 S W 10th St Gainesville FL 32601

ANDERSON, RICHMOND KARL, physician, educator; b. Bangalore, India, Dec. 6, 1907 (parents Am. citizens); s. Karl Edwin and Emma Jennie (Wardle) A.; B.A., Cornell Coll., Mt. Vernon, Iowa, 1929, D.Sc., 1958; M.S. in Biochemistry, Northwestern U., 1931, Ph.D. in Biochemistry, 1934, M.D., 1937; M.P.H., Johns Hopkins, 1948; m. Cleo Hildayne Holland, July 14, 1935; children—Karl Elmo, Dale Kristin (Mrs. Niall Finlayson), Karen Cleo (Mrs. James Holden), Royce Richmond. Asst. physiol. chemistry Med. Sch. Northwestern U., Chgo., 1929-34, research fellow, 1934-35; instr. biochemistry Tulane U., New Orleans, 1935-38; intern Alameda County (Calif.) Hosp., Oakland, 1938-39; asso. dir. labs., resident in medicine Buffalo City Hosp., E.J. Meyer Meml. Hosp., 1939-42; Rockefeller Found., N.Y.C., 1942-64, spl. fellow N.C., 1942-43, mem. field staff, Mexico, 1943-45, India, 1948-55, asst. dir. biol., med. research, N.Y.C., 1956-57, asso. dir. med., natural scis., 1958-64; dir. tech. assistance div. Population Council, N.Y.C., 1964-70; program dir. Josiah Macy, Jr., Found., N.Y.C., 1970-71; dir. internat. programs office Carolina Population Center U. N.C. at Chapel Hill, 1971-74, dir. African health tng. instn. project, 1973-75, sr. cons. internat. programs office, 1974-75, prof. dept. nutrition Sch. Pub. Health, 1973—; head field study div. Internat. Fertility Research Program, Chapel Hill, 1975-77. Instr. medicine U. Buffalo, 1939-42; adj. prof. Inst. Nutrition Scis. Columbia, 1962-64; mem. internat. tech. cooperation, assistance panel Pres.'s Sci. Adv. Com., 1966-67; mem. missions on population, nutrition World Bank, India, 1971, 72, Indonesia, 1973. Served with USPHS, 1945-47; Diplomate Am. Bd. Preventive Medicine, Am. Bd. Nutrition. Fellow Am. Pub. Health Assn., AAAS; mem. Am. Inst. Nutrition, Am. Coll. Preventive Medicine, Soc. Tropical Medicine, Hygiene, Population Assn. Am., Phi Beta Kappa, Sigma Xi, Alpha Omega Alpha. Editor: (with others) Family Planning and Population Programs — A Review of World Developments, 1965. Contbr. articles to profl. publs. Home: Carol Woods Apt 190 Chapel Hill NC 27514

ANDERSON, ROBERT CLETUS, univ. adminstr.; b. Birmingham, Ala., July 18, 1921; s. Allie Cletus and Dana Beatrice (Hilliard) A.; B.S., Auburn U., 1942; M.A., U. N.C., 1948; Ph.D., N.Y. U., 1950; m. Margaret Campbell Spidle (div.); children—Margaret Campbell, William Robert; m. 2d, Evalce R. Pilgrim. Research asst. U. N.C., 1946-47; asst. to dean N.Y. U., 1948-50; dir. Grad. Sch., Memphis State U., 1950-53; exec. asso. So. Regional Edn. Bd., Atlanta, 1953-55, asso. dir., 1955-57, dir., 1957-61; exec. v.p. Auburn U., 1961-65; v.p. research, prof. sociology U. Ga., Athens, 1965—, pres. U. Ga. Research Found., 1978—. Mem. Surgeon Gen.'s Cons. Group on Med. Edn., 1958-59; mem. edn. adv. com. W.K. Kellogg Found., 1960-64; mem. Joint Council on Ednl. Communications, 1961-70, v.p., 1965-67. Served with U.S. Army, 1942-46. Decorated Purple Heart. Mem. Am. Council Edn., Am. Assn. Higher Edn., Nat. Council Univ. Research Adminstrs., Phi Kappa Phi, Alpha Tau Omega, Alpha Kappa Delta, Kappa Delta Pi, Omicron Delta Kappa, Phi Delta Kappa. Home: 110 Holmes Ct Athens GA 30606 Office: Grad Studies Research Center U Ga Athens Ga 30602

ANDERSON, ROBERT GORDON, JR., educator; b. Greensboro, N.C., Nov. 7, 1945; s. Robert Gordon and Mary Elizabeth (LaRogue) A.; B.A., St. Andrews Presbyn. Coll., 1967; M.A., Am. U., 1972, postgrad., 1972—; m. Margaret Virginia Gamble, June 21, 1968; 1 dau., Mary Margaret. Vis. prof. African Studies S.C. Assn. Ind. Colls., 1968-70; grad. asst. Am. U., Washington, 1970-72; dir. polit. studies Presbyn. Coll., Clinton, S.C., 1972-79; asso. acad. dean for curriculum devel., dir. internat. studies, asso. prof. polit. sci. St. Andrews Presbyn. Coll., Laurinburg, N.C., 1979—, dir. and dean summer and winter sessions, dir. continuing edn. program; Am. Coll. and Univ. for Internat. and Intercultural Studies and U.S. Dept. State rep. to African Univs., 1976, 77. Alderman, Clinton City Council, 1976—, mayor pro tem, 1976—; S.C. exec. com. Democrat Party, 1976-78; del. Dem. Nat. Conv., 1976; exec. com. Laurens County Dem. Party, 1976—; asst. dir. Carter Presdl. campaign, 5th Congressional Dist. S.C., 1976—; bd. dirs. Gleams Community Action, 1975-77. Served with USAFR, 1964-70. Mem. Alumni Assn. St. Andrews Presbyn Coll. (pres. 1976), Am., So., S.C. polit. sci. assns., Assn. So. Africanists, Municipal Assn. S.C., AAUP, African Studies Assn., Assn. for Sharing in Internat. Studies (exec. dir.), Pi Sigma Alpha, Pi Gamma Mu. Democrat. Presbyterian. Club: Rotary. Home: Route 6 Windmere Dr Laurinburg NC 28352 Office: St Andrews Presbyn Coll Laurinburg NC 28352

ANDERSON, ROBERT GRAHAM, architect; b. Vienna, Austria, Sept. 2, 1927; s. Donald B. and Marian A.; student Miami U., Oxford, Ohio, 1946-48; B.Arch., N.C. State U., Raleigh, 1952; M.Arch., Harvard U., 1957; m. Cleo Lucas, Nov. 24, 1954; children—Linda K., Donald G., Kim S. With Pace Assos. & Mies Van Der Rohe, Chgo., 1952-53, Colbert & Assos., New Orleans, 1953-56, Smith/Selew Assos., Boston, 1956-57; asst. prof. Tex. A&M Coll., 1957-58, C.R.S. Architects, Bryan, Tex., 1957-58; asso. prof. Auburn (Ala.) U., 1958-62, U. So. Calif., 1962-68; chmn. architecture and engring. U. Miami (Fla.), 1968-70; dean Coll. Architecture, U. N.C., Charlotte, 1970-75, prof., 1975—; mem. Fla. Bd. Arch., 1968-70. Chmn. Charlotte Housing Authority; cons. Redevelopment Commn. Served with USNR, 1944-46. Lic. architect, La., N.C. Mem. AIA, Assn. Collegiate Schs. Architecture. Home: 1431 Runnymede Ln Charlotte NC 28211 Office: Coll Architecture U NC Charlotte NC 28223

ANDERSON, RONNIE JOE, physician, educator; b. Chickasha, Okla., Sept. 6, 1946; s. Ted J. and Ruby Alice (Harston) Anderson Benjamin; B.S., Southwestern U. Okla., 1969; M.D., U. Okla., 1973; m. Sue Ann Anderson, Apr. 12, 1975; children—Sarah Elizabeth, Daniel Jerrod. Intern, U. Tex. Affiliated Hosps., Dallas, 1973-74, resident in internal medicine, 1973-76, chief resident in medicine, 1975-76; asst. prof. medicine Health Sci. Center, U. Tex., Dallas, 1976—, chmn. ambulatory care - emergency medicine, 1976—, asst. dean clin. affairs, 1979; med. dir. ambulatory care Parkland Meml. Hosp., 1979; adv., cons. in field. Bd. dirs. Addison, Carrollton, Coppell and Farmer's br. chpt. Am. Heart Assn., 1979. Diplomate Am. Bd. Internal Medicine, Am. Bd. Med. Examiners. Mem. Dallas County Med. Soc., Tex. Med. Assn., AMA, A.C.P., Nat. Assn. Residents and Interns, Soc. for Research and Edn. in Primary Care Internal Medicine. Home: 3511 Whitehall St Dallas TX 75229 Office: Dept Internal Medicine Health Sci Center U Tex 5323 Harry Hines Blvd Dallas TX 75235

ANDERSON, ROY LEONARD, JR., mfg. co. exec.; b. Vincennes, Ind., Mar. 3, 1948; s. Roy Leonard and Georgia Rose (Patheal) A.; B.S., U. Tex., 1971; m. Catherine Elaine Springfield, Dec. 9, 1977; 1 son, Jeff Springfield. Buyer toys, sporting goods Titches Dept. Stores, Dallas, 1971-74; purchasing agt. Alcon Labs., Ft. Worth, Tex., 1974-77, mgr. purchasing operations, 1977-79, corporate purchasing mgr., 1979—. Active Boy Scouts Am., Arlington, Tex., 1969-75; coach Little League Baseball, 1978—; chpt. advisor Phi Delta Theta, U. Tex., Arlington, 1976—. Mem. Phi Delta Theta (pres. alumni assn. 1974). Presbyterian. Club: Optimist. Office: 6201 S Freeway Fort Worth TX 76101

ANDERSON, SAMUEL EDWARD, ins. agt.; b. Pine Flats, Pa., Aug. 12, 1946; s. James Wesley and Anna (Gibbons) A.; B.S. in Acctg., Wheeling (W.Va.) Coll., 1975; A.B. in Acctg., Cambria Rowe Bus. Coll., 1970; m. Rosemary Beatrice Coyle, July 25, 1971; 1 son, Mihcael Thomas. Staff acct. S.R. Snodgrass & Co., Wheeling, 1970-76; gen. agt. Anderson & Assos., Wheeling, 1976—, also sales rep. real estate Pilot Realty, Michael D. Donahis, and Davis Real Estate, Wheeling, 1976—. Bus. drive chmn. Ohio County chpt. Am. Cancer Soc.; co-chmn. public relations com. United Way, 1979—. Recipient Cert. of Appreciation, Am. Cancer Soc. Served with USAF, 1965. Mem. Nat. Assn. Realtors, Nat. Assn. Accts. (past dir.), Wheeling Jaycees (dir. 1979—), W.Va. Jaycees (mgr. govtl. affairs 1979-80). Republican. Presbyterian. Club: Rotary. Office: PO Box 227 Wheeling WV 26003

ANDERSON, THOMAS NOLAN, ret. editor; b. Chgo., Feb. 14, 1918; s. Louis Sidney and Vera Estella (Nolan) A.; A.B., Lake Forest (Ill.) Coll., 1942; m. Barbara Blanchard, Nov. 8, 1954; children—David, Ray. Self employed radio commentator until 1964; editor Fla. Dept. Natural Resources, Tallahassee, 1964-75, editor Fla. Conservation News to 1977. Chmn. Fla. Conservation Council. Served with AUS, 1942-43. Mem. Fla. Outdoor Writers' Assn. (life), Fla. Nature Conservancy, Fla. Wildlife Fedn. Author: Complete Guide to Florida Fishing, 1974. Home: 1112 S Magnolia Dr Apt M101 Tallahassee FL 32301

ANDERSON, THOMAS PEDEN, JR., environ. engr.; b. Westminster, S.C., Feb. 20, 1908; s. Thomas Peden and Pearl (Hutchinson) A.; B.S. in Civil Engring., Clemson U., 1931; M.S. in San. Engring., U. N.C., 1958; m. Helen Sewell Anderson, Jan. 2, 1937; children—Ann Anderson Williams, Helen Anderson Richardson. Bridge draftsman, designer Dept. Hwy State of S.C., 1931, 34-35; asst. engr. County of Pinellas, Clearwater, Fla., 1932-33; with S.C. State Bd. Health, Columbia, 1936-74, dir. water supply div., 1961-72, chief Bur. Water Hygiene and Spl. Services, 1973-74; sec., treas. S.C. State Bd. Cert. Environ. Systems Operators, Columbia, 1974—. Served with U.S. Army, 1941-46. Mem. Am. Water Works Assn. (past sec. treas., chmn. S.E. sect., recipient George Warren Fuller award 1971), Water and Pollution Control Assn. of S.C., S.C. Public Health Assn., S.C. State Employees Assn., Am. Assn. Ret. Persons, Tau Beta Pi. Presbyterian (elder). Clubs: Kiwanis, Am. Legion. Home: 1218 Sherwood Rd Columbia SC 29204

ANDERSON, THOMAS WAYNE, mgmt. engr.; b. Montgomery, Ala., Dec. 10, 1946; s. Orville Lynn and Ann Leona (Kennedy) A.; B.Indsl. Engring., U. Fla., 1970; m. Catherine Lee Sullivan, Mar. 15, 1969; children—Melissa Joy, Heather Lee. Systems rep. computer div. RCA, Tallahassee, 1970-71: dir. mgmt. systems engring. U. Fla., Gainesville, 1971-75; dir. mgmt. engring. Sarasota (Fla.) Meml. Hosp., 1975-77; dir. mgmt. systems engring. Bapt. Med. Centers, Birmingham, Ala., 1977-78; dir. systems devel. U. Ala. Hosps., Birmingham, 1978—. Served with USN, 1966. Recipient Coll. of Engring. Service Key, 1970. Mem. Am. Inst. Indsl. Engrs. (L.J. Turaville achievement award 1970, speaker confs. 1975, 79), Hosp. Mgmt. Systems Soc. (speaker conf. 1977), Am. Hosp. Assn. Democrat. Baptist. Collaborator: Changing Patterns of Psychiatric Inpatient Care in a University General Hospital, 1975; co-author: A Study of Components of Nursing Job Satisfaction, 1977. Home: 637 Wilderness Rd Pelham AL 35124 Office: 619 S 19th St Birmingham AL 35233

ANDERSON, URSULA MARY, physician; b. Cheshire, Eng., 1929; d. Francis David and Beatrice Mary Anderson; came to U.S., 1958; ed. Loreto Coll., Llandudno, North Wales, U. Liverpool (Eng.), U. London (Eng.), Yale; m. Lino H. Dominguez, May 10, 1969. Formerly sr. asst. med. officer of health, Reading, Eng.; pediatric cons. N.C. State Bd. Health, 1960-62; dir. maternal and child health Erie County (N.Y.) Health Dept., 1962-69; now med. cons. maternal and child health Region IV, HEW; asso. clin. prof. pediatrics N.Y. State U. at Buffalo, 1962-69; asso. attending pediatrician Buffalo Childrens

Hosp., 1962-69; chief div. community health Hosp. for Sick Children, Toronto, Ont., Can., 1969-72; asso. prof. pediatrics U. Toronto, 1969-73; now asso. clin. prof. Emory U., Atlanta. Cons., Head Start, 1965-69, WHO, 1970-71; chmn. N.Y. State Task Force on Health Manpower, 1968-69. Fellow Am. Acad. Pediatrics, Am. Pub. Health Assn.; mem. World, Brit., Canadian med. assns., Pan Am. Med. Fedn. Author articles in field. Home: 503 Old Canton Rd Marietta GA 30067 Office: 50 7th St NE Altanta GA 30323

ANDERSON, VIRGINIA SWITZER, audiologist; b. New Orleans, June 9, 1949; d. James C. and Jeanne M. (Maddox) Switzer; B.A., La. State U., 1971; M.S., Vanderbilt U., 1972; postgrad. U. No. Colo., 1973, Colo. State U., 1979. Speech therapist Baton Rouge (La.) State Mental Health Center, summer 1970; tchr. hearing impaired Biloxi (Miss.) Mun. Sch. Dist., 1973; med. diagnostic audiologist Coastal Med. Center, Biloxi, 1973-74, Dr. Donald Todd and Dr. Don Bryan, Otolaryngologists, Pensacola, Fla., 1974-75; clin. audiologist Bapt. Hosp., Speech and Hearing Clinic, Pensacola, 1975; clin. and rehab. audiologist Communication Disorder Center, St. Vincent Infirmary, Markham and Univ., Little Rock, 1975-77, Jenkins Meml. Children's Center, Pine Bluff, Ark., 1977—; audiology cons. to Com. on Early Intervention, Pascagoula, Miss., 1974. Mem. Am. Speech and Hearing Assn., Ark. Speech and Hearing Assn. (pres. elect. 1979), Am. Audiology Soc., Gulf Coast Speech and Hearing Soc., Ark. Assn. for Hearing Impaired Children (bd. dirs. 1977), So. Audiol. Soc., Soc. Med. Audiology, Ark. Council of Audiology (chmn. 1975-76), Am. Acad. of Mental Deficiency, Council Exceptional Children, Sigma Alpha Eta, Alpha Delta Pi. Club: Centurion. Contbr. articles in field to profl. jours. Home: 1105 Kings Mountain Dr Little Rock AR 72211 Office: 2410 Rike Dr Pine Bluff AR 71603

ANDERSON, W. E. (ANDY), writer, film producer; b. Carlinville, Ill., Dec. 2, 1903; s. Crittenden Henry Crawford and Nellie (Patchen) A.; ed. Tex. A. and M. Coll.; m. Mabel Mae Rooks, Nov. 15, 1930. With Nat. Life & Accident Ins. Co., Dallas, 1933-54; gen. partner Adventurers Assos., producer hunting films; producer, narrator, participant Hollywood prodn. Big Game Hunting in North America; dir., producer, narrator Wildlife and mem. hunting film Big Game Trails, 1973. Leader's Round Table of Tex., 8 yrs. Past bd. dirs. YMCA, West Dallas Social Center. Mem. S.A.R., Tex. A. and M. U. Lettermen's Assn. (founder). Methodist (mem. adminstrv. bd., fin. com., chmn. new pledge com.). Clubs: Lions (past chmn. membership com. Oak Cliff club, health and welfare com., civic com., interstate and internat. pub. relations com., Achievement award 1962, Monarch award 1964); Oak Cliff Country (charter), Dallas Woods and Water (charter; 1st chmn. big game hunting com.); Century (Tex. A. and M. U.). Author poem: The Hunter's Dream; stories: Bushytails of the Llano; Duke, the Story of a Bird Dog; with Deep in the Heart of Texas; Johnnie's Lucky Day, with illustrations; Skyline Meadows, 1954; King Caribou, 1954; Sleek and Glossy, 1954; A Texan Meets a Silvertip, 1957; Five from Which to Choose, 1957. Contbr. articles to Am. Hunter Mag., Sports Afield, Sports Afield Hunting Ann., Am. Hunter, Tex. Game & Fish, Guns mag., Alaskan Sportsman, Am. Rifleman, Field and Stream, Outdoor Life mag. Home: 955 Sam Dealey Dr Dallas TX 75208

ANDERSON, WALTER ALWIN, county govt. ofcl.; b. Homerville, Ga., Nov. 26, 1942; s. Thomas Alwin and Jean A.; B.B.A., Armstrong State Coll., 1976; m. Signe Michelle Kuhn, July 9, 1976; children—William A., John R., Amber, Wendy, Hollis. Technician, Miss. Air N.G., 1968-70; clk. Bd. Commrs., Liberty County, Ga., 1970-72, chief appraiser, mem. Bd. Tax Assessors, 1972—, chmn., sec., 1973-76. Served with USAF, 1960-68. Cert. appraiser, Ga. Mem. Internat. Assn. Assessing Ofcls., Assn. Fed. Appraisers, Ga. Assn. Assessing Ofcls., Liberty County Bd. Tax Assessors, Ft. Stewart Impact Coordination Com. Baptist. Home: PO Box 143 US Hwy 82 Hinesville GA 31313 Office: PO Box 81 Courthouse Sq Hinesville GA 31313

ANDERSON, WILLIAM, air force officer; b. Somerville, Mass., Feb. 27, 1939; s. William Alexander and Ellen Louise (Shea) A.; B.Gen. Studies, U. Nebr., Omaha, 1973; M.S. in Systems Mgmt., U. So. Calif., 1978; m. Rose Angela Bracciante, Jan. 5, 1968. Served as enlisted man U.S. Air Force, 1956-73; communications equipment installer, 1957-67, computer maintenance technician, 1973; commd. 2d. lt., 1973, advanced through grades to capt., 1977; chief organizational maintenance br. 340 CAMS, Altus AFB, Okla., 1978-79, Barksdale AFB, La., 1979—. Office: 8 AF/LGM Barksdale AFB LA 71110

ANDERSON, WILLIAM EVAN, internist, educator; b. Mankato, Minn., Sept. 7, 1927; s. Evan Ernest and Naomi (Ahlskog) A.; A.B., Gustavus Adolphus Coll., 1950; M.D., U. Minn., 1954; m. Ramona Marie Baker, Mar. 26, 1951; 1 son, Evan William. Intern, St. Luke's Hosp., Duluth, Minn., 1954-55; resident in internal medicine VA Hosp., Mpls., 1955-58; instr. medicine U. Minn., 1958-60; asst. prof. medicine W.Va. U., Morgantown, 1960-67, asso. prof., 1967-74, prof., 1974—, chmn. div. gastroenterology, 1967—; cons. gastroenterologist VA Hosp., Clarksburg, W.Va. Served with USNR, 1945-46. Diplomate Am. Bd. Internal Medicine, subsplty. Bd. Gastroenterology. Mem. W.Va., Monongalia County med. assns., Alpha Omega Alpha. Lutheran. Home: 625 Sylvan Pl Morgantown WV 26505 Office: West Virginia University Medical Center Morgantown WV 26506

ANDES, JOAN KEENEN, EDP service co. exec.; b. Clarksburg, W.Va., Apr. 23, 1930; d. Ree Marvin and Mary Ruth (Pyle) Groghan; m. Ralph Paul Andes, Sept. 29, 1976; children—Paula Annette Keenen Skelton, William Ree Keenen, Donald Monroe Dreyer. Statis. typist State of W.Va., 1948-49, Frederick Koshkin C.P.A., Beaumont, Tex., 1950-56, Arthur Greenspan, C.P.A., 1956-60; founder Machine Accounting and Computing Services, Beaumont, 1960-68; founder Joan Keenen Automated Ent Keypunch Sch., Beaumont, 1965-71; founder pres. Joan Keenen Automated Employment, 1965-71; founder, pres. Applied Data Processing Techniques, Inc., Beaumont, 1968—. Mem. Data Processing Mgmt. Assn. (numerous offices, coms.). Democrat. Mem. Ch. of Christ. Club: Soroptomist. Home: 1410 Marshal Place Dr Beaumont TX 77706 Office: 2635 McFaddin Beaumont TX 77702

ANDES, WILLARD ABE, physician; b. Miami, Fla., Feb. 19, 1942; s. Willard F. and Jewell E. (Whiddon) A.; B.A., U.N.C., 1964; M.D., Tulane U., 1968; m. Glenda M. Gilmore, Oct. 2, 1972; children—Cecily Elizabeth, Melanie Ann. Intern, Barnes Hosp., St. Louis, 1968-69; resident in medicine Tulane U., 1969-71, fellow in hematology, 1971-72, 75-76; practice medicine specializing in hematology Tulane Med. Center, New Orleans; asst. prof. medicine Tulane U., New Orleans, 1976—; vis. scientist Oxford U. Haemophilia Centre, 1976-77. Served as maj. U.S. Army, 1972-75. Mem. AMA, Am. Burn Assn., Alpha Kappa Kappa. Republican. Presbyterian. Contbr. articles to profl. jours. Home: 74 Versailles Blvd New Orleans LA 70125 Office: 1430 Tulane Ave Tulane University Medical School New Orleans LA 70112

ANDRE, CARL FERDINAND, lawyer; b. Terry, Miss., Apr. 16, 1929; s. Andreas Ferdinand and Mittie Theresa (Slyhart) A.; B.A., U. Miss., 1950; M.A., La. State U., 1952; LL.B., Jackson Sch. Law, 1966; m. Martha Yerger, Aug. 4, 1951; children—Sigrid Elizabeth, Carl Ferdinand Yerger, Sarah Hester. Account exec. Godwin Advt. Agy., Jackson, Miss., 1956-66; admitted to Miss. bar, 1966; dir. govtl. services Miss. Research & Devel. Center, Jackson, 1966-68; asst. atty. gen. State of Miss., Jackson, 1968-72; individual practice law, Jackson, 1972—. Served as officer USAF, 1953-55. Mem. Am. Bar Assn., Miss. State Bar, Hinds County Bar Assn., Miss. Def. Lawyers Assn., Am. Soc. Hosp. Attys., Nat. Assn. Coll. and Univ. Attys., Sigma Alpha Epsilon. Episcopalian. Home: 4445 Audubon Park Dr Jackson MS 39211 Office: Unifirst Bldg Jackson MS 39205

ANDREASEN, SAMUEL GENE, clergyman, counselor; b. Kearney, Nebr., May 7, 1927; s. Fred and Ester E. (Gotobed) A.; B.A., Sterling Coll., 1951; M.Div., Columbia Theol. Sem., 1954; Th.M., Winona Lake Sch. Theology, 1968; M.A., Central Mich. U., 1973; Ed.S., Ariz. State U., 1974, Ed.D., 1976; m. Rachel M. Poe, May 29, 1959; children—Paul S., Cathye E. Farmer, Iowa, 1944-48; ordained to ministry Presbyterian Ch. in U.S., 1954; pastor chs., Diagonial and Clearfield, Iowa, 1954-56, Grace Presbyn. Ch., Aikin, S.C., 1957-60; counselor Clinic of Physicians and Surgeons, Mesa, Ariz., 1973-76; coordinator religious services and religious edn. Partlow State Sch., Tuscaloosa, Ala., 1976—; cons. counselor USAF Bases; guest speaker Meth. Confs. on Mental Retardation. Pres. Ida Redbird Elementary Sch. PTA, Mesa, 1975-76; coach Pop Warner Football, Mesa, 1975-76, Little League Baseball, Mesa, 1973-76; chaplain CAP. Served to maj. USAF, 1962-71, lt. col. Res. Mem. Am. Psychol. Assn., Am. Assn. Pastoral Counselors, Am. Assn. Marriage and Family Counselors, Am. Personnel and Guidance Assn., Ariz. Adult Edn. Assn., DAV. Republican. Contbr. articles to The Chaplain. Office: Partlow State Sch PO Box 1730 Tuscaloosa AL 35401

ANDREASON, GEORGE EDWARD, univ. adminstr.; b. Seattle, July 4, 1932; s. Alfred M. Andreason and Alberta (Brewer) Andreason Thompson; B.S. in Bus. Adminstrn., Tex. Wesleyan U., Ft. Worth, 1960; M.P.A. (Ford. Found. scholar), Ind. U., 1966; Ph.D., Clayton U., St. Louis, 1979; m. Carolyn A. McKown, June 30, 1973; 1 son, Paul Edward. Program analyst U.S. Army, Washington, 1963-64; asst. chief mgmt. analysis div. FAA, Ft. Worth, 1964-67, chief mgmt. analysis div., Oklahoma City, 1968-70, exec. officer, 1970-71; mgmt. cons. Dept. Transpo., 1966-67; asst. dir. IRS, Denver, 1971-72, asst. regional commr. adminstrn., Dallas, 1972-74, dist. dir., Denver, 1974, asst. dir. dir., St. Louis, 1974-76; dir. adminstrv. services McLennan Community Coll., Waco, Tex., 1976-77; v.p. bus. and adminstrn. U. Mary Hardin-Baylor, Belton, Tex., 1977—; partner McGregory Assos., bus. and mgmt. cons., McGregor, Tex. Served with USN, 1951-55. Recipient Career Edn. award FAA and Nat. Inst. Public Affairs, 1965. Fellow Nat. Inst. Public Affairs; mem. Am. Soc. Public Adminstrn., Personnel and Mgmt. Assn., Nat. Coll. and Univ. Bus. Officers, So. Assn. Coll. and Univ. Bus. Officers, Belton C. of C. Baptist. Clubs: Rotary (Belton); Masons (master McGregor 1977, Tex. dist. dep. grand master 1980) (McGregor and Ft. Worth). Home: PO Box 181 McGregor TX 76657 Office: U Mary Hardin-Baylor MHB Station Belton TX 76513

ANDREW, CLARK ELLIOTT, JR., oil co. exec.; b. Highland Park, Mich., July 18, 1935; s. Clark Elliott and Texie Keller A.; student U. Mich., 1953-55; B.S. in Bus. Adminstrn., Wayne State U., 1960; P.M.D., Harvard U., 1976; m. Marcia Joan Ericson, Aug. 14, 1957; children—Vicki Lynn, Clark Elliott III, Amy. With Acme Steel Co., Detroit, 1958-60; sales rep. Sun Oil Co., Detroit, 1960-67, product mgr., Phila., 1967-69, dist. mgr. Marcus Hook, Pa., 1969-74, div. mgr., Tulsa, 1975-80; v.p. Arkansas Valley Petroleum Co., Tulsa, 1980—. Mem. Am. Chem. Soc., Mid-Continent Harvard Bus. Sch. Club. Republican. Presbyterian. Clubs: Petroleum (Tulsa); Cedar Ridge Country. Home: 7715 S Quebec St Tulsa OK 74136 Office: 8014 S Memorial St Tulsa OK 74133

ANDREW, KENNETH RAY, recreational mgmt. co. exec.; b. Stillwater, Okla., Feb. 18, 1938; s. Carl S. and Arta Fay A.; student Okla. State U., 1955-60; m. Roberta Rae McConnell, Jan. 14, 1945; children—Carl S. II, Kenneth Ray, Megan Rae. Real estate investor, Stillwater, 1959—; pres., chmn. bd. Racquet Times, Inc., Stillwater, Okla. Served with USAF, 1960-62. Republican. Home: 5105 Woodland Dr Stillwater OK 74074 Office: 1225 N Perkins Rd Stillwater OK 74074

ANDREWS, BETHLEHEM KOTTES, chemist; b. New Orleans, Sept. 18, 1936; d. George Leonidas and Anna Mercedes (Russell) Kottes; B.A. with honors in Chemistry, Newcomb Coll., Tulane U., 1957; m. William Edward Andrews, May 9, 1959; children—Sharon Leslie, Keith Edward. Chemist wash wear investigation, So. Regional Research Center, Sci. and Edn. Adminstrn., Dept. Agr., New Orleans, 1958-63, research chemist wash wear investigation, cotton textile chemistry lab., 1968-70, research chemist spl. products research, cotton textile chemistry lab., 1976—; scientist-supr. Grace King High Sch. Lab. Tech. Tng. Program. Recipient outstanding professionalism citation New Orleans Fedn. Businessman's Assn., 1977, Women of Yr. award in profl. category, 1978; La. Heart Assn. grantee, 1957. Mem. Am. Chem. Soc., Am. Assn. Textile Chemists and Colorists, Fiber Soc., Phi Beta Kappa, Sigma Xi, Phi Mu. Democrat. Roman Catholic. Clubs: P.E.O., Southern Yacht. Contbr. chpts. to books, articles to sci. jours; patentee. Office: So Regional Research Center Sci and Edn Adminstrn Dept Agr 1100 Robert E Lee Blvd New Orleans LA 70124

ANDREWS, CHARLES HAYNES, economist, univ. adminstr.; b. Waycross, Ga., Nov. 30, 1937; s. Charles Haynes and Louise Rebecca (McQuaig) A.; A.B. magna cum laude, Mercer U., 1960; Ph.D., Vanderbilt U., 1967; m. Lorraine Lynn, Aug. 24, 1974; children—Charles Haynes, William Edward. Asst. prof. econs. Stetson U., 1964-67, asst. prof., chmn. dept. econs., 1967-70, asso. prof., chmn. dept., 1970-73; asso. prof., chmn. econs. dept. Mercer U., Macon, Ga., 1973-74, James D. Stetson asso. prof. econs., 1974-76, James D. Stetson prof., 1976—, dean Sch. Bus. and Econs., 1978—; dir. Ga. Bank & Trust Co.; econ. cons. civil litigation. Ambassador Greater Macon C. of C., 1979. Woodrow Wilson nat. fellow, 1960-61; Earhart fellow, 1961-62; Fgn. Area fellow Ford Found., 1963. Mem. Am. Econ. Assn., So. Bus. Adminstrn. Assn., So. Econ. Assn. Methodist. Author: The Economic Performance of the Comparria de Acero del Pacifico S.A., 1970; editor, contbr. Mercer Bus. Bull., 1976—. Home: 1610 Adams St Macon GA 31201 Office: School of Business and Economics Mercer University Macon GA 31207

ANDREWS, CLAUDE LEONARD, psychologist; b. Scotland Neck, N.C., Jan. 13, 1943; s. Leland Waverly and Annie Grey (Hyde) A.; B.A., St. Andrews Presbyn. Coll., 1965; M.Div., Princeton Theol. Sem., 1969; M.Ed., U. Ga., 1972, Ed.D., 1978; m. Carol Gladys Cooper, June 10, 1967. Ordained to ministry Presbyterian Ch., 1969; chaplain intern U. N.C., Chapel Hill, 1967-68; clin. chaplain intern Central State Hosp., Milledgeville, Ga., 1969-70; marriage counselor, psychologist, family housing U. Ga., Athens, 1972-74; psychologist Edgecombe Nash Mental Health Center, Tarboro, N.C., 1974-77; psychologist, psychol. examiner Creative Living Assos., Tarboro, 1975—; mem. faculty U. Ga., Edgecombe Tech. Inst.; cons. psychol. services. Mem. policy council Nash-Edgecombe Econ. Devel., Inc., 1974-76. Recipient Leslie Rucker award Rucker Found; 1961; Lucy Steele Scholar, 1961-63. Mem. Am. Personnel and Guidance Assn., Am. Coll. Personnel Assn., Am. Assn. Sex Edn. Counselors and Therapists, Nat. Council Family Relations, Assn. Clin. Pastoral Edn., Am. (asso.), N.C. psychol. assns., Am. Assn. Mental Health Counselors, Edgecombe County Hist. Soc., Friends of Library, Phi Kappa Phi, Kappa Delta Pi. Democrat. Club: Hilma Country (Tarboro). Home: 309 St John St Tarboro NC 27886 Office: Creative Living Assos 309 St John St Tarboro NC 27886

ANDREWS, DUANNE WARREN, banker, former army officer; b. Kingfisher, Okla., Jan. 22, 1931; s. Thomas M. and Freda M. (Jones) A.; student U. Calif., Tokyo, 1953, Mary Hardin Baylor Coll., 1956, San Antonio Coll., 1962-65, U. Md., 1968-70; B.A., Our Lady of the Lake U., 1974; student U.S. Armed Forces Inst., Heidelberg (Germany) Press Sch. m. Darle Eloise Sullivan, Oct. 14, 1952; children—Danny Wayne, Delisa Ann, Diana Lynn, Susan Margaret. Enlisted in U.S. Army, 1949, advanced through grades to lt. col., 1966; rifle platton leader, N.Korea, 1952-53; personnel officer, Ft. Hood, Tex., 1956-58; hdqrs. staff officer, Ft. Sam Houston, Tex., 1971-72; ret., 1972; personnel officer The Main Bank, San Antonio, 1972-73, personnel dir., 1973-78, v.p., 1978—; guest lectr. various univs. and colls. in Tex., 1974-76. Neighborhood commr. Transatlantic council Boy Scouts Am., 1969-70; Little League baseball mgr., 1963-64; mem. vocat. edn. adv. bd. San Antonio Ind. Sch. Dist., 1973-76; participant Tex. Gov.'s Conf. on Aging for Pre-Retirement Planning, 1978; mem. San Antonio Area Vocat. Office Edn. Adv. Com., 1977-80, chmn., 1979-80; dir. U.S. Sr. Olympic Gymnastic Championships, 1976; mem. Bexar County Sr. Citizens Council, 1972—; mem. Nat. USO Council, 1964-65; mem. staff Tex. Folklife Festival, Inst. Tex. Cultures, San Antonio, 1973, 74; mem. bd. mgrs. S. Tex. AAU, 1975-76. Decorated Air medal, Purple Heart, Bronze Star; named Hon. Spl. Dep. Sheriff, Kingfisher, Okla., 1949; recipient Spl. Merit award Nat. Recreation Soc., 1967. Mem. Am. Inst. Banking, Bank Adminstrn. Inst., San Antonio Personnel and Mgmt. Assn., Am Soc. Tng. and Devel., Internat. Mil. Sports Council Acad., San Antonio C. of C. (life). Baptist. Home: 7768 Woodridge San Antonio TX 78209 Office: 911 N Main Ave San Antonio TX 78296

ANDREWS, EDWIN EVERTS, prosthodontist, forensic odontologist; b. Syracuse, N.Y., July 30, 1934; s. George Bouton and Marie (Buggeln) A.; B.S., Syracuse U., 1956; D.M.D., Fairleigh Dickinson U., 1963; M.Ed., Central State U., 1976 m. Patricia Ann McCarthy, Nov. 27, 1963; 1 son, Mark Robert. Intern Upstate Med. Center, Syracuse, 1963-64; resident in prosthetics N.Y. U., 1964-66; practice prosthetics, Syracuse, 1966-72; chief maxillofacial prosthetics State Univ. Hosp. Upstate Med. Center, Syracuse, 1967-72; asst. prof. maxillofacial prosthodontist U. Mo. Sch. Dentistry, Kansas City, 1972-73; asso. prof., chmn. maxillofacial prosthetics U. Okla. Coll. Dentistry, Oklahoma City, 1973-77; pvt. practice prosthodontics and maxillofacial prosthetics, Oklahoma City, 1977—; attending maxillofacial prosthetics U. Hosp, Children's Meml. Hosp, 1973, Presbyn. Hosp., 1976—. Health Scis. Center, Oklahoma City. Cons. VA Hosp, Oklahoma City, Muskogee, Okla., 1973—, Okla. Office of Chief Med. Examiner, 1974—, FAA, 1974—. Served USAF, 1956-58 maj. Res. Diplomate Am. Bd. Prosthodontics, Am. Bd. Forensic Odontology. Fellow Am. Coll. Prosthodontists, Am. Acad. Forensic Scis., Am. Acad. Maxillofacial Prosthetics; mem. Dental Assn., Am. Prosthodontic Soc., Am. Soc. Forensic Odontology, Fedn. Prosthodontic Orgns., Internat. Reference Orgn. in Forensic Medicine and Scis., Okla. State Dental Assn., Oklahoma County (Okla.) Dist. Dental Soc. Home: 16 Oakwood Dr Oklahoma City OK 73121 Office: 1117 N Shartel Ave Oklahoma City OK 73103

ANDREWS, HARVEY WELLINGTON, med. lab. exec.; b. Stowe Twp., Pa., Sept. 9, 1928 s. Robert W. and Theresa R. (Reis) A.; B.B.A. cum laude, U. Pitts., 1952; M.B.A., Harvard U., 1957; m. Jane Garland, Aug. 9, 1969; children—Marcia Lynne Glynis Susann, Elizabeth Jane. With Gen Electric Co., Syracuse, N.Y., 1952-55, Scovill Mfg. Co., Waterbury, Conn., 1957; comptroller Alcon Labs., Inc., Ft. Worth, 1958-61, comptroller, treas., 1961-65, v.p. finance, 1964-68; founder, pres. Medimation, Inc., Ft. Worth, 1968—, also dir.; dir. Med. Scis. Computer Corp., First's Clin. Labs., Hereford Med. Labs., Dalworth Med. Labs.; founder, dir. Tarrant Health Maintenance Orgn., Inc.; founder, dir., pres. Tarrant Health Protection Plan, Inc., 1978—. Bd. dirs., mem. exec. com. Fort Worth Opera Assn. Served with AUS, 1946-48. Mem. AAAS, Am. Acad. Polit. and Social Scis., Ft. Worth C. of C., Soc. Advancement Mgmt., TCU Pres.'s Roundtable Assn., Order Artus, Scabbard and Blade, Sigma Alpha Epsilon. Lutheran. Clubs: Rotary, Masons (32 deg.), Golden Eagle Assn., Fort Worth Boat, Colonial Country, Century II, Met. Knife and Fork. Home: PO Box 1786 3124 Chaparral Ln Fort Worth TX 76101 Office: 1300 Summit Ave Suite 314 Fort Worth TX 76102

ANDREWS, IKE FRANKLIN, congressman; b. Bonlee, N.C., Sept. 2, 1925; s. Archie F. and Ina (Dunlap) A.; student Mars Hill Coll.; B.S., U. N.C., 1950, LL.B., 1952; m. Pat Goodwin, 1977; children by previous marriage—Alice, Nina Patricia. Admitted to N.C. bar, 1952; partner Andrews & Stone, Siler City, 1966-72; mem. 93d-96th Congresses from N.C. Mem. N.C. Senate, 1959-61; mem. N.C. Ho. of Reps., 1961-67, 69, 71, majority leader, speaker pro-tem, 1971. Bd. govs. U. N.C., 1959-71 chancellor selection com., 1971. Served with F.A., AUS, 1943-45. Decorated Bronze Star medal, Purple Heart. Mem. Siler City C. of C., Am. Legion. Democrat. Baptist. Club: Rotary. Office: 2446 Rayburn House Office Bldg Washington DC 20515

ANDREWS, JAMES RHEUBEN, surgeon; b. New Orleans, May 2, 1942; M.D., La. State U., 1967; m. Joanie Andrews; children—Andy, Amy, Archi. Fellow in hand surgery and athletic medicine U. Va., Charlottesville, 1962; intern USPHS Hosp., San Francisco, 1967-68, resident, 1968, Indian Hosp., Anchorage, 1969; resident Tulane Orthopaedics, 1969-70, Med. Center, Columbus, Ga., 1970-71, VA Hosp., Pineville, La., 1971; fellow in knee surgery and athletic injuries U. DeLyon, 1972; practice medicine specializing in orthopaedic surgery, Columbus, 1973—; mem. staff Med. Center, St. Francis Hosp., Doctors Hosp. (all Columbus); instr. sports medicine Tulane U., 1974-77, asso. clin. prof., 1977—; cons. athletic teams. Mem. Muscogie County Med Soc., Ga. Med. Assn., So. Med. Assn., AMA, Herodicus Soc. (sec. 1976-77, v.p. 1977-78, pres. 1978-79), Ga. Orthopaedic Soc., Am. Acad. Orthopaedic Surgeons, Am. Orthopaedic Soc. Sports Medicine, Internat. Knee Soc., Nat. Athletic Trainers Assn., Ala. Orthopaedic Soc., Arthritis Found. (dir. Ga. chpt. 1974-77). Appeared on numerous TV shows. Contbr. articles to profl. jours. Office: Hughston Orthopaedic Clinic Columbus GA 31902

ANDREWS, JAY DONALD, marine biologist; b. Bloom, Kans., Sept. 9, 1916; s. Jay Straney and Eva Mildred (Dilley) A.; B.S. in Agr., Kans. State Agrl. Coll., 1938; Ph.D. in Biology, U. Wis., 1947; m. Mary Stuart Hornsby, Mar. 23, 1948; children—Donna Gay, Jay Stuart. With Va. Inst. Marine Sci., Gloucester Point, 1946—, sr. marine scientist, 1957—; prof. marine sci. Coll. William and Mary, Williamsburg, Va., 1957—. Served with inf. U.S. Army, 1941-45. Mem. Nat. Shellfisheries Assn. (hon. mem., editor Proc. 1960-62), Ecol. Soc. N.Am., Am. Inst. Biol. Scis., Va. Acad. Sci., Atlantic Estuarine Research Soc., Phi Kappa Phi, Alpha Zeta. Methodist. Author articles on ecology of shellfish, especially oysters, epizootiology of shellfish diseases. Home: 11 Cornwallis Rd Yorktown VA 23690 Office: Va Inst Marine Scis Gloucester Point VA 23062

ANDREWS, JOSEPH PATRICK, state ofcl.; b. Washington, Jan. 11, 1939; B.S. in Social Sci., Va. Commonwealth U., 1963, M.S. in Applied Psychology 1968; M.P.A., George Washington U., 1977. Caseworker, Richmond (Va.) Social Service Bur., 1963-65; rehab. counselor Va. Dept. Rehabilitative Services, 1966-68; tchr. Chesterfield County (Va.) Public Schs., 1968-69; adminstrv. intern Va. Dept. Corrections, 1969-70; human research developer Va. Dept. Housing and Community Devel., 1973-79; asst. dir. staff devel. Va. Dept. Welfare, Richmond, 1979—. Served with U.S. Army, 1957-58. Mem. Va. Council for Social Welfare, Am. Soc. Public Adminstrn., Nat. Ry. Hist. Soc. Roman Catholic. Club: K.C., Cath. Single Adults. Home: 2246 Concord Ave Richmond VA 23234 Office: Va Dept Welfare 8007 Discovery Dr Richmond VA 23288

ANDREWS, MARTIN FITZGERALD, educator; b. Danville, Va., July 12, 1924; s. William Oscar and Ela Allen (Rainey) A.; B.S., Randolph Macon Coll., 1952, postgrad., 1961; M.Ed., U. Va., 1963; student Duke U., 1949-50, Union Coll. (N.Y.), 1953; m. Marian June Shuff, July 8, 1950; children—William Earle, Ela Virginia, Douglas Martin, Marian June. Tchr., head sci. dept. Petersburg (Va.) High Sch., 1953-57; ednl. specialist, writer U.S. Army, Quartermaster Sch., Fort Lee, Va., 1957-59; head sci. dept. Thomas Dale High Sch., Chester, Va., 1959-61; head sci. dept., tchr. Miller Sch. of Albemarle, Miller School, Va., 1962—. Scoutmaster Boy Scouts Am., 1953-55; capt. CAP, 1976—. Served with USN, 1943-46, 50-51; Korea; ret. Res. Gen. Electric fellow, 1953. Mem. Am. Soc. Aerospace Edn., Va. Acad. Sci., Va. Herpetological Soc., Va. Ornithol. Soc., Nat. Wildlife Fedn., Va. Wildlife Soc., Cousteau Soc., Am. Numismatic Assn., Kappa Sigma, Beta Beta Beta. Methodist. Home: PO Box 146 Miller School VA 22901 Office: Miller School VA 22901

ANDREWS, MARY SUE, oil co. rep.; b. Chattanooga, Sept. 26, 1940; d. Olen and Aileen (Cooper) Vardaman; student So. Methodist U., 1979; m. James Wortham Andrews, Nov. 29, 1961; children—Haydon Willson, Jeffery Sterling, Daniel Walter. Various secretarial positions, 1958, 60-69; public relations asst. Atlantic Richfield Co., Dallas, 1969—. Mem. exec. com. Sch. Vol. Program, Dallas, 1973—; mem. Women's Center Dallas, 1975—; adv. com. Arts Magnet High Sch., Dallas, 1979—; sec. Employer's Affirmative Action Com., Dallas, 1974-79. Recipient various certs. appreciation. Mem. Public Relations Soc. Am., Dallas Advt. League (dir. 1978-79). Republican. Home: 2311 Spring Hill Dr Dallas TX 75228 Office: 411 N Akard St Dallas TX 75221

ANDREWS, MITCHELL DEWAYNE, physician; b. Enid, Okla., May 24, 1944; s. Mitchell S. and Truel Eva (Melton) A.; B.S., Baylor U., 1966; M.D., U. Okla., 1970. Intern in medicine Johns Hopkins Hosp., Balt., 1970-71; resident in medicine U. Okla. Health Scis. Center, Oklahoma City, 1971-72, chief resident in medicine, 1974-75, fellow in nephrology, 1975-76, dir. housestaff program dept. medicine, 1978—; asst. prof. medicine U. Okla. Coll. Medicine, 1976—; asst. chief of medicine Univ. Hosp. and Clinics, Oklahoma City, 1978—. Served with USPHS, 1972-74. Diplomate Am. Bd. Internal Medicine. Mem. A.C.P. (teaching and research scholar, 1976-79), Am. Soc. Internal Medicine, Assn. of Program Dirs. in Internal Medicine, Alpha Omega Alpha. Office: PO Box 26901 University of Oklahoma Health Sciences Center Oklahoma City OK 73190

ANDREWS, RICHARD FRANCIS, ins. agy. exec., kennel exec.; b. N.Y.C., Sept. 19, 1936; s. William R. and Mary J. (O'Neil) A.; B.S., Fordham U., 1958; m. Barbara Fripp, Nov. 9, 1969; 1 son, Gordon. Vice pres. James A. Kennedy Co., Inc., Miami, Fla., 1961-67; pres. Andrews & Co., Inc., Miami, 1967—; pres. Dick Andrews, Inc., greyhound racing kennel, Miami, 1971—; guest lectr. and instr. for Dade County Public Safety Dept. Served to capt. U.S. Army, 1958-60. Finished 1st and 2d Irish-Am. Classic greyhound race, 1979, finished 1st, 1970. Mem. Best Recommended Ins. Adjusters, Nat. Assn. Ind. Adjusters, South Fla. Claimsmen Assn., Nat. Greyhound Assn. Roman Catholic. Jewelry recoveries include Brasher Doubloon for Yale U. Sterling Mus., 1968 and Katherine the Gt. silver collection, 1972. Office: 1901 Brickell Ave Miami FL 33129

ANDREWS, SYDNEY DIAMOND, state ofcl.; b. Tallahassee, July 23, 1915; s. Thomas Edwin and Annie (Vause) A.; student Fla. State U., 1935; diploma in analytical chemistry Internat. Corr. Schs., 1937; student Biarritz U., France, 1945; m. Winifred Jackson, Nov. 10, 1938; 1 dau., Carol Sue Andrews Liedy. With Fla. Dept. Agr. and Consumer Services, Tallahassee, 1933—, chief analyst, 1947-61, chief petroleum inspection bur., 1961-63, asst. dir. div. standards, 1963-68, dir. div. standards, 1968—; mem. U.S. Metric Bd. Pres., Suwannee River Area council Boy Scouts Am., 1969-71. Served with C.E., U.S. Army, 1944-46; ETO. Recipient Silver Beaver award Boy Scouts Am., 1965; Tallahassee Rotary Club Paul Harris fellow, 1975. Mem. ASTM (v.p.), Nat. Conf. Weights and Measures (chmn. 1974-75), So. Conf. Weights and Measures, Nat. Scalemen's Assn., U.S. Metric Assn., Am. Nat. Metric Council. Clubs: Capital City Country, Rotary (pres. Tallahassee Chpt. 1960-61, dist. govt. 1965-66). Home: 1133 Myers Park Dr Tallahassee FL 32301 Office: Fla Dept Agr and Consumer Services Mayo Bldg-Lab Complex Tallahassee FL 32301

ANDREWS, VERA JEAN, apparel mfg. co. exec.; b. Chester County, S.C., Jan. 1, 1941; d. Burt M. Andrews and Ersie S. Andrews Stewart; student Clemson U., 1962, Fashion Inst. Tech., 1964, U. S.C., 1967-69. With Skyline Mfg. Co., Camden, S.C., 1959—, dir. mfg., 1974—. Mem. adv. bd. Kershaw County Vocat. Sch., 1979-81, co-author tng. manual. Recipient Disting. Service award City of Camden, 1963; Disting. Service cert. Kershaw County Vocat. Sch., 1978. Mem. Am. Mgmt. Assn., Am. Apparel Mfg. Assn. (edn. com.), Bus. and Profl. Women's Club (pres. local club 1969, chmn. state standing com. 1968), S.C. Needle Trade Assn. Home: 100 Chesnut St Camden SC 29020 Office: Dicey Creek Rd Camden SC 29020

ANDREWS, WILLIAM COOKE, physician; b. Norfolk, Va., June 7, 1924; s. Charles James and Jean Curry (Cooke) A.; A.A., Princeton U., 1946; M.D., Johns Hopkins U., 1947; m. Elizabeth Wight Kyle, Nov. 10, 1951; children—Elizabeth Randolph, William Cooke, Susan Carrington. Intern, N.Y. Hosp., 1947, resident in obstetrics and gynecology, 1948-50, 52-53; practice medicine specializing in obstetrics and gynecology, Norfolk, Va., 1953—; asst. in obstetrics and gynecology Cornell U. Med. Sch., 1948-50, 52-53; mem. attending staff Med. Center Hosp.; mem. vis. staff DePaul Hosp.; prof. obstetrics and gynecology Eastern Va. Med. Sch., Norfolk, 1975—, pres. faculty senate, 1976-77. Chmn. Bicentennial Commn., City of Norfolk, 1969-71; commr. Community Promotion Commn., 1971-73, chmn., 1973—; bd. dirs. Va. League for Planned Parenthood, 1966-68; pres. Norfolk chpt. Planned Parenthood, 1966-68. Served with M.C., USN, 1950-52. Named Hon. Officer of the Most Excellent Order of the Brit. Empire, Queen Elizabeth II, 1967. Diplomate Am. Bd. Obstetrics and Gynecology. Fellow Am. Coll. Obstetricians and Gynecologists, Am. Assn. Obstetricians and Gynecologists; mem. Am. Fertility Soc. (dir. 1970-73, pres. 1977), Med. Soc. of Va., Norfolk Acad. Medicine, Va., Tidewater obstet. and gynecol. socs., Continental Gynecol. Soc., So. Med. Assn., AMA, South Atlantic Assn. Obstetricians and Gynecologists, Norfolk C. of C. (chmn. armed forces com. 1966-68, v.p. 1968-69, pres. 1970), Internat. Fedn. Fertility Socs. (asst. treas. 1974—), Navy League U.S. (pres. Hampton Roads council 1968-70, nat. dir. 1970-74), English Speaking Union U.S. (pres. Norfolk-Portsmouth br. 1964-66), Planned Parenthood Fedn. Am. (cons. nat. med. com. 1975—). Presbyterian. Club: Norfolk Yacht and Country (commodore 1966). Contbr. articles in field to profl. jours. Home: 929 Graydon Ave Norfolk VA 23507 Office: 903 Medical Tower Norfolk VA 23507

ANDREWS, WILLIAM EUGENE, metal bldg. mfg. co. exec.; b. Augusta, Ga., May 9, 1943; s. William David and Mildred Opal (Aldridge) A.; B.S., Miss. State U., 1964, M.B.A., 1980; m. Marilynn Dana Knox, Mar. 21, 1975; children—Wendy Paige, William Christopher, Scott Eugene. Auditor, tax cons. Coopers & Lybrand, Birmingham, Ala., 1964-69; div. controller Mitchell Engring. Co. div. Ceco Corp., Columbus, Miss., 1969—. Mem. Miss. Econ. Council, 1972-79. Served with USAR, 1965-71. C.P.A., Miss. Mem. Columbus-Lowndes C. of C., Miss. Soc. C.P.A.'s, Am. Inst. C.P.A.'s. Republican. Presbyterian. Club: Rotary. Home: Route 7 Box 113A Columbus MS 39701 Office: PO Box 911 Columbus MS 39701

ANDREWS, WILLIAM FREDERICK, interior designer; b. Allentown, Pa., Jan. 29, 1946; s. Herbert Eugene and Alma (Kleinbach) A.; A.A., Palm Beach Jr. Coll. 1966; B.A. in Design, U. Fla. 1970. Owner, designer William F. Andrews-Cons., Delray Beach, Fla., 1970—; instr. Palm Beach (Fla.) Jr. Coll. 1977. Recipient Design award, Bronze medal U. Fla. 1970; Merit award AIA, 1977. Profl. mem. Am. Soc. Interior Designers, nat. bd. dirs. 1980—. Republican. Lutheran. Interior designer Temple Beth El, Boca Raton, Fla., STP Corp., Boca Raton; project designer Sea Ridge Condominium, Gulfstream, Fla., 1976, Bull-Nose table series, Office Suites Inc., Chgo., 1975; project designer, developer Palm Trail Pl. Condominium, Delray Beach, Fla., 1978. Home: 4300 N Ocean Blvd Delray Beach FL 33444 Office: 100 NE 5th Ave Delray Beach FL 33444

ANDRIN, GEORGE EDMUND, state agy. ofcl.; b. Los Angeles, Apr. 11, 1927; s. George and Katherine W. (Kubisiak) A.; B.B.A., U. Ga., 1952; postgrad. U. Wis., 1964-69; m. Peggy Braswell, June 7, 1952; children—George, Katherine, Susan, Rebecca. Personnel asso. Gen. Motors Corp., 1953-58; sales account exec. Prudential Ins. Co., 1959-64; tng. dir. Ga. Dept. Revenue, 1964-69; tng. specialist Ga. Dept. Human Resources, Atlanta, 1969—; pres. Andrin & Assos., Atlanta, 1972—. Active Boy Scouts Am. Served with USNR, 1946. Recipient Service award Atlanta council Camp Fire Girls, 1979. Mem. Am. Assn. Mental Deficiency (Ga. state membership chmn.), Am. Soc. Tng. and Devel., Trout Unltd., Alpha Kappa Psi. Roman Catholic. Home: 4092 Navajo Trail NE Atlanta GA 30319

ANDRIOT, JEANNE KURZ, counseling center exec.; b. Cin., May 30, 1924; d. John Gaylord and Ellen Elsie (Wardwell) Huber; A.A. with highest distinction, No. Va. Community Coll., 1972; B.A. with high distinction, George Mason U., 1974, M.A. in Psychology, 1976; m. John Leo Andriot, June 30, 1944; children—Mary Ellen, Judith Lynn, Donna, Wendy, John Wayne, Laurie. Cost accounting clk. King Machine Tool Co., Cin., 1943-44; asso. dir. Documents Index, Arlington and McLean, Va., 1953-70, v.p. bd., 1974—; dir. Center for Counseling Families, Fairfax, Va., 1976—, pres. bd., 1976—; founding pres., chmn. bd. Juvenile Assistance, McLean, 1967-70. Bd. deacons Lewinsville Presbyterian Ch., McLean, 1961-64, mem. of session, 1967-70. Certified asso. profl. counselor, Va. Mem. Am. Personnel and Guidance Assn., Am. Assn. Marriage and Family Counselors (asso.), Phi Theta Kappa, Alpha Chi, Psi Chi (founding pres. George Mason chpt. 1973-74). Democrat. Home: 6451 Madison Ct McLean VA 22101 Office: 3541 Chain Bridge Rd Suite 6 Fairfax VA 22030

ANDUJAR, JOHN J., physician; b. Chgo., Jan. 26, 1912; s. M.A. and Lily (Kurzenknabe) A.; B.S., Pa. State U., 1930; M.D., Temple U., 1934; postgrad. Union U., 1935-36, Cornell U., 1942; m. Elizabeth Richards, Aug. 16, 1935; children—Betty Jo, Linda Lee. Intern Harrisburg Gen. Hosp., 1934-35, Meml. Hosp., N.Y.C., 1942-43, Bender Hygienic Lab., Albany, N.Y., 1935-36; asso. prof. U. Ark., 1937-38; practice of medicine, Ft. Worth, 1938—; prof. med. technology Tex. Christian U., 1938-50; dir. Ft. Worth Med. Labs., Doctors Hosp. Labs., Ft. Worth Dept. Health Labs., Texas Dept. Health Regional Labs.; cons. pathologist USPHS, John Peter Smith hosps., Carswell AFB Sta. Hosp. Past pres. Tarrant County Crime Commn., Am Pathology Found., World Pathology Found. Diplomate Nat. Bd. Med. Examiners, Am. Bd. Pathology (past pres.). Fellow Am. Soc. Clin. Pathologists (past. pres.), A.C.P., Coll. Am. Pathologists (founder); mem. AAAS, AMA, Am. Assn. Blood Banks (founder), Am. Assn. Phys. and Surg., Am. Cancer Soc., Soc. Am. Bacteriologists, Pan-Am. Med. Assn., Tex. Acad. Internal Medicine, Assn. Mil. Surgeons U.S., Internat. Acad. Pathology, Am. Public Health Assn., Tex. Acad. Sci., Tex. Hosp. Assn., Tex. Pub Health Assn., Tex. Soc. Pathologists (past pres.), Tarrant County Med. Soc. (past pres.), Internat. Council Soc. Pathology, Royal Soc. Health, World Assn. Soc. Pathology (pres. 1969-72), Tarrant County Mental Health Soc., Phi Beta Pi. Presbyterian. Clubs: Fort Worth Boat, Torch. Address: PO Box 1118 Fort Worth TX 76101

ANEJA, ARUN PAL, chem. engr.; b. Jullunder, India, Nov. 21, 1948; s. Gopal Singh and Raj Rani (Sapra) A.; B.Tech., Indian Inst. Tech., 1970; M.S., N.C. State U., Raleigh, 1972, Ph.D., 1974; Sr. research engr. polyesters Monsanto Co., Research Triangle Park, N.C., 1974-78, engring. specialist, research and devel., 1978—. Instr. water safety ARC. Mem. Am. Inst. Chem. Engrs. (chmn. N.C. sect. 1978-79), Indian Inst. Chem. Engrs., AAAS, N.C. Acad. Sci., Analog Hybrid Computer Edn. Soc., Sigma Xi. Sikh. Home: 2328 Airline Dr Raleigh NC 27607 Office: PO Box 12274 Monsanto Co Research Triangle Park NC 27709

ANEJA, VINEY PAL, chem. engr.; b. Jullender, India, Nov. 21, 1948; s. Gopal Singh and Raj Rani (Aneja) A.; came to U.S., 1971; B.Tech., Indian Inst. Tech., Kanpur, India, 1971; Ph.D., N.C. State U., 1977. Mem. sci. staff dept. applied sic. Brookhaven Nat. Lab., Upton, N.Y., 1973-75; sr. scientist Northrop Services, Inc., Research Triangle Park, N.C., 1976—. Mem. Am. Inst. Chem. Engrs., AAAS, Sigma Xi. Home: 2711 Everett Ave Raleigh NC 27607 Office: PO Box 12313 Research Triangle Park NC 27709

ANGEL, JOSE FERNANDO, physician; b. Colombia, S. Am., Dec. 30, 1942; s. Jose and Cecilia de Gomez A.; M.D., Javeriana U. (Colombia), 1968; m. Sylvia Jimenez, Dec. 14, 1968; children—Andres, Carolina. Intern, The Meml. Hosp., Pawtucket, R.I., 1972-73; resident in anesthesiology Baylor Coll. Medicine, Houston, 1973-74, Med. Coll. Wis., Milw., 1974-76; practice medicine specializing in anesthesiology, Cedars of Lebanon Med. Center, Miami, Fla., 1979—; anesthesiologist Meml. Med. Center, Savannah, Ga., 1976-79. Diplomate Am. Bd. Anesthesiology. Fellow Am. Coll. Anesthesiologists; mem. Am. Soc. Anesthesiologists, Dade County Med. Assn., AMA. Roman Catholic. Address: 5741 SW 132d Terr Miami FL 33156

ANGEL, VERA FAY, real estate co. exec.; b. Covington, Ky., Oct. 7, 1928; d. Loren Jerome and Clara Blaine (McNay) Rusk; grad. high sch.; m. James Bird Angel, June 20, 1947; children—Terry Lee, Daryl Jay, Paula Kya Angel Wing. Owner, Vera Angel Realty, Covington, 1957—; dir. Kenton-Boone Bd. Realtors, 1976—, pres., 1979. Mem. Covington City Commn., 1968-71; vice chmn. No. Ky. chpt. Am. Cancer Soc., 1976-77, chmn., 1977-78, local chmn. and state dir., 1974; chmn. Kenton County Heart Fund, 1977. Mem. No. Ky. C. of C. (dir. 1975-77, 1st v.p. 1980), Kenton-Boone Bd. Realtors, Nat., Ky. (sec. 1978) assns. realtors, No. Ky. Homebuilders Assn., Latonia Bus. Assn. Democrat. Baptist. Home: 47 Madonna Ln Cold Spring KY 41076 Office: 3631 Decoursey Ave Covington KY 41015

ANGLIN, RAYMOND HARVEY, convenience stores co. exec.; b. Mexia, Tex., June 9, 1946; s. Ulyses Harvey and Alice Thelma (Jones) A.; student architecture Hampton Inst., 1964-69; cert. in effective constrn. mgmt. U. New Orleans, 1979; cert. in energy mgmt. in bldgs. N.Y. U., 1976; cert. in constrn. planning and estimating Tex. Christian U., 1973; cert. in basic mgmt. devel. Nat. Convenience Stores, 1975, cert. in advanced mgmt. devel., 1979. With Nat. Convenience Stores Inc., Houston, 1971—, constrn. coordinator, 1974-76, mgr. constrn./equipment, 1977-78, mgr. store planning, 1979—; design and planning cons. for light comml. bldg. Mem. indsl. adv. com. Houston Community Coll. Mem. Black Coalition for Econ. Devel., Am. Inst. Design and Drafting, Nat. Car Wash Council. Baptist. Home: 2806 Ashmont St Missouri City TX 77459 Office: 3200 Travis Houston TX 77003

ANGLIN, W(ILLIAM) E(NGLISH), judge; b. Burnsville, N.C., Oct. 24, 1907; s. Geo. W. and Carrie (English) A.; B.S., U. N.C., 1934, LL.B., 1934, replaced by J.D., 1969. Admitted to N.C. bar, 1934, U.S. Dist. Ct. bar Western Dist., N.C., 1934; practiced under own name in Burnsville, N.C., 1934-42, 46-65; resident superior ct. judge, 1965-75, emergency superior ct. judge, 1975-77, ret. Served to comdr. USNR, 1942-46; PTO. Mem. N.C. Bar Assn., Theta Chi, Phi Delta Phi. Office: PO Box 217 Burnsville NC 28714

ANGUIZOLA, GUSTAVE A., educator, author; b. Panama City, Panama, Feb. 28, 1927; B.A., U. Evansville, 1948; M.A. (fellow), Ind. U., 1950, Ph.D., 1953; M.S., Mich. State U., 1953; postgrad. Am. Sch. Classics and Archaeology, Athens, Greece, 1964, Stanford U., 1975. With U.S. Dist. Engrs. Corps, C.Z., 1941-44; prof. econs. and govt., chmn. dept. Morris (S.C.) Coll., 1960-61; prof. Latin Am. history and govt. N.C. State U., Elizabeth City, 1961-62, chmn. dept., 1962-63; vis. prof. Latin Am. instns. N.Y. State U., 1962, 63; asst. prof. history polit. sci. Purdue U., 1963-66; asso. prof. history polit. sci. Chgo. State U., 1967-68; asst. prof. history polit. sci. U. Tex., Arlington, 1966—. Spl. asst. to mayor Chgo. for Pan Am. Games, 1959; cons. in field; mem. adv. bd. Am. Security Council. Recipient grand prize, gold medal Sesquicentennial Commn. for Panama Canal, 1953; Hays-Mundt award, 1953, Fulbright-Hays award, 1964-65; NSF grantee, 1975. Mem. Am., So., European, Nat. hist. assns., AAUP, Conf. Latin Am., Renaissance Soc. Am., Western Social Sci. Assn., Am. Ednl. League, Council Inter-Am. Security, Instituto Panamericano de Geografia e Historia, Interam. Soc., Classical Soc., Am. Security Council. Club: Westerners (Ft. Worth). Author: Violation of Human Rights and Civil Liberties in Panama, 1977, 78; Isthmian Political Instability: 1821-1975, 1976, 77; The Power of Persistence: Bunau-Varilla and Panama, 1979. Home: 920 Appleton St Arlington TX 76010 also 2909 W Logan Blvd Chicago IL 60647 Office: Box 19488 University of Texas Station Arlington TX 76019 also PO Box 2138 Panama City Panama

ANLYAN, WILLIAM GEORGE, surgeon, univ. ofcl.; b. Alexandria, Egypt, Oct. 14, 1925; s. Armand and Emmeraude (Nazar) A.; B.S. magna cum laude, Yale U., 1945, M.D., 1949; D.Sc. (hon.), Rush Med. Coll., 1973; m. Barbara Ellen Echols, July 5, 1973; children by previous marriage—William George, John Peter, Louise, Barbra, Laura. Intern, resident, instr., asso. in surgery Duke Hosp., Durham, N.C., 1949-53, asst. prof. surgery, 1958-61, prof. surgery, 1961—; asso. dean Sch. Medicine, Duke U., 1963, dean, 1964-69, v.p. health affairs, 1969—. Chmn. vice pres.'s com. Durham VA; surg. cons. Durham VA Hosp. Chmn. regents Nat. Library Medicine, 1971-72. Recipient award for disting. achievement Modern Medicine, 1974; Gov's award for disting. meritorious service, 1978; Markle scholar med. sci., 1953-58; diplomate Am. Bd. Surgery, Am. Bd. Thoracic Surgery. Fellow A.C.S.; mem. AMA (adv. com. med. sci. 1972—), Soc. Univ. Surgeons, Soc. Vascular Surgery, Internat. Cardiovascular Soc., Soc. Clin. Surgery, Am. Heart Assn., Soc. Med. Adminstrs., Inst. Medicine of Nat. Acad. Sci., Council Deans (chmn. 1968-69), Coordinating Council Med. Edn. (chmn. 1973-74), So. Med. Assn., Surg. Biology Club II, Am. Surg. Assn., So. Surg. Assn., Halsted Soc., Allen O. Whipple Surg. Soc., Assn. Am. Med. Colls. (chmn. 1970-71), Assn. Acad. Health Centers (pres. 1975), Sigma Xi, Alpha Omega Alpha. Club: Rotary. Mem. Editorial bd. Pharos, 1968—. Home: 1516 Pinecrest Rd Durham NC 27705

ANOATUBBY, BILL J., Chickasaw Nation ofcl.; b. Denison, Tex., Nov. 8, 1945; s. Joseph Morris and Opal Fay (Mitchell) A.; A.A. in Bus., Murray State Coll., 1970; B.S. in Acctg., East Central State U., 1972; m. Janice Marie Loman, Dec. 23, 1967; children—Chris, Brian. Acct., office mgr. Am. Plating Co., Duncan, Okla., 1972-74; acct. Little Giant Corp., Oklahoma City, 1974-75; health dir., controller Chickasaw Nation, Ada, Okla., 1975-78, spl. asst. to gov., 1978—, lt. gov., 1979—; pres. Chickasaw Credit Assn., 1975—; cons. Indian Youth Leadership Conf., East Central U., 1979. Bd. dirs. So. Okla. Devel. Assn. Served with Army N.G., 1963-69. Mem. Intertribal Council of the Five Civilized Tribes. Democrat. Baptist. Home: Route 3 Box 169-D Ada OK 74820 Office: Arlington and Miss Box 1548 Ada OK 74820

ANSARI, AFTAB ALAM, immunologist, immunogeneticist; b. Allahabad, India, July 1, 1950; came to U.S., 1973; s. Abdul Azis and Amina (Khatoon) A.; B.S., Gorakhpur U. (India), 1966; M.S., Aligarh Muslim U. (India), 1968, M.Phil., 1970, Ph.D., 1971. Asso. lectr. Aligarh Muslim U., 1970-73; vis. fellow NIH, Bethesda, Md., 1974-76; vis. asso. Nat. Inst. Environ. Health Scis., Research Triangle Park, N.C., 1977-78, vis. scientist, 1978—; clin. asst. prof. dept. medicine U. N.C., Chapel Hill, 1979—. Council Sci. and Indsl. Research fellow, 1968-70; NIH fellow, 1974-76. Mem. Genetics Soc. Am., Indian Soc. Biol. Chemists, Environ. Mutagen Soc., Am. Assn. Immunologists, AAAS, Sigma Xi. Islamic. Contbr. articles to profl. jours. Research on mutagenesis in mammals with respect to early detection of carcinoma in humans. Home: 109 Seasons Dr Raleigh NC 27614 Office: PO Box 12233 Research Traingle Park NC 27709

ANSEL, HOWARD CARL, educator, univ. adminstr.; b. Cleve., Oct. 18, 1933; s. Alex Sandor and Celia Ansel; B.S., U. Toledo, 1955; M.S. in Pharmacy, U. Fla., 1957, Ph.D. in Pharmaceutics, 1959; m. Suzanne Marie Klein, Aug. 14, 1960; children—Lori Sue, Michael Louis, Jeffrey Stephen. Asst. prof. pharmacy U. Toledo, 1959-62; asst. prof. U. Ga., Athens, 1962-65, asso. prof., 1965-69, head dept. pharmacy Sch. Pharmacy, 1968-77, prof. pharmacy, 1969—, dean Sch. Pharmacy, 1977—; mem. adv. panel FDA, 1972-73. Fellow Am. Found. Pharm. Edn.; mem. Am. Pharm. Assn., Ga. Pharm. Assn., Acad. Pharm. Scis., Am. Assn. Colls. Pharmacy, Sigma Xi, Rho Chi, Phi Kappa Phi. Club: Rotary. Author books in field. Home: 598 Forest Rd Athens GA 30605 Office: Sch Pharmacy Univ of Ga Athens GA 30602

ANTHONY, BERYL FRANKLIN, JR., congressman; b. El Dorado, Ark., Feb. 21, 1938; s. Beryl Franklin and Oma Lee (Roark) A.; B.S., U. Ark., 1961, J.D., 1963; m. Sheila Foster, Aug. 4, 1962; children—Alison, Lauren. Admitted to Ark. bar; asst. atty. gen. Ark., 1964-65; dep. pros. atty. Union County, 1966-70; pros. atty. 13th Jud. Dist. Ark., 1971-76; legal counsel Anthony Forest Products Co., El Dorado, 1977; pvt. practice, El Dorado, 1977—; mem. 96th Congress from 4th Dist. Ark.; pres. Ark. Pros. Attys. Assn., 1975; dir. Union Fidelity Savs. and Loan Assn., El Dorado. Recipient Outstanding Young Man award El Dorado Jaycees, 1973. Mem. Ark. Bar Assn., Ark. Forestry Assn. (sec., dir. 1977). Democrat. Episcopalian. Office: 506 Cannon House Bldg Washington DC 20515

ANTHONY, JON ANDRÉ, restaurant and food catering co. exec.; b. Ft. Worth, July 26, 1937; s. Wallace M. and Ruby J. (Fuller) Farrar; student Tex. Christian U., 1955-57, Armstrong Coll., 1962, Westchester Coll., 1963-66, U. Tex., Arlington, 1967; B.A., So. Meth. U., 1974; m. Brandy Kay Herbert, July 9, 1977; children—Tijuana René, Christian Shea (by previous marriage). With Garber & Katz, C.P.A.'s, White Plains, N.Y., 1960-66; comptroller Matlock Land Co., Ft. Worth, 1967; with Omnus Corp., Dallas, 1968, Transam. Corp., Dallas, 1969-71, Trinity Valley Foods, Dallas, 1971-72; comptroller, gen. mgr. 7-J Corp., Dallas and Houston, 1972-79; owner County Fair Foods, Houston, 1979—. Mem. Mobile Indsl. Catering Assn. (dir. 1978-79), Nat., Tex. restaurant assns., Am. Contract Bridge League (nat. master), Mensa. Address: PO Box 1465 Pearland TX 77581

ANTHONY, PAMELA K., advt. exec.; b. Athens, Ohio, Apr. 19, 1946; d. Gaylord Charles and Wanda Maye (Jaynes) Ray; B.S. in Edn., Ohio U., 1968; children—Kim, Jill. Tchr., U.S. Govt., Tokyo, 1972-73; advt. dir. Neighbor Newspapers, Tampa, Fla., 1974-77; pres. Fla. Newspaper Reps., St. Petersburg, Fla., 1978—; pub. Community Consumer News & TV Facts, St. Petersburg, 1980—; mgmt. and sales cons. Mem. Am. Advt. Fedn., St. Petersburg Advt. Fedn., St. Petersburg C. of C., Audit Bur. Circulation (asso.). Republican. Office: 538 Central Ave Saint Petersburg FL 33701

ANTHONY, ROGER PARSONS, elec. co. exec.; b. Bryn Mawr, Pa., July 11, 1944; s. Frederick and Marjorie A.; A.B. in Econs., Syracuse U., 1966. Controller power cooling systems div. Westinghouse Electric Corp., 1974-75, fin. mgr. combustion turbine div., Phila., 1975-76, fin. mgr. medium power transformer div., Sharon, Pa., 1976-77, controller Charlotte (N.C.) turbine plant, 1978—. Mem. Am. Mgmt. Assn., Jr. C. of C. (v.p. 1973-74, sec. 1972-73). Republican. Presbyterian. Home: 222 Providence Square Dr Charlotte NC 28211 Office: PO Box 7002 Charlotte NC 28217

ANTHONY, WILLIAM WALLACE, polit. scientist; b. Marblehead, Mass., Sept. 9, 1920; s. Luther and Lillian A.; B.A., Tarleton State U.; M.A., Tex. A&M U.; M. Urban Planning, U. Houston, then Ph.D. Commd. officer U.S. Army, 1943, advanced through grades to maj.; ret., 1965; mem. faculty Tex. A&M U., College Station, 1970—. NASA fellow, 1972. Mem. Am. Acad. Polit. and Social Scis., Acad. Polit. Sci., Am. Acad. Arts and Scis., Am. Polit. Sci. Assn., Assn. Asian Studies. Democrat. Home: Box 3146 College Station TX 77840 Office: Dept Polit Sci Tex A&M U College Station TX 77843

ANTOINE, JANET ANNE ABRATH, rehab. counselor; b. Chgo., Nov. 1, 1945; d. Karl Frederick and Aniele Domitilda (Chappas) Abrath; student Loyola U., Chgo., 1963-66, B.A., 1969; postgrad. U. S.C., 1974, Mich. State U., 1975; M.Pub.Service, Western Ky. U., 1977; m. Lawrence Verne Antoine, Sept. 4, 1964; children—Lawrence Verne, Dennis Patrick. With directorate personnel and community activities Ft. Gordon (Ga.), 1972-75; tchr. Catholic edn. br., directorate personnel and community activities Fort Knox (Ky.), 1976-77, counselor Army community service, 1976-77, counselor human resource center, 1977-78; now staff Ky. Dept. Human Resources Bur. Social Services, 1977—. Area chmn. Muscular Dystrophy Campaign, Augusta, Ga., 1974; active in scouting and PTA. Mem. Am., Ky. personnel and guidance assns., AAUW, Mil. Police Wives (treas. 1972-74). Roman Catholic. Home: 1334 S 2d St Louisville KY 40208 Office: 200 S 7th St Louisville KY 40202

ANYIWO, JOSHUA CHUKWUKA, found. exec.; b. Oguta, Nigeria, Jan. 13, 1946; s. Jonathan A. and Harriet (Eziofu) A.; B.A., M.A., Cambridge U., 1969; Ph.D., Colo. State U., 1971; 1 son, Michael Ifeanyi Obinna. Sr. engr. Boston Edison Co., 1973-74; sr. cons. systems engr. Fed. Govt. Nigeria, Lagos, 1975-76; asso. prof. math and engring. Hampton (Va.) Inst., 1977-79; chief exec. officer Kcamies Found., Ark, Va., 1978—. Mem. Sigma Xi. Club: Kameez.

APELT, WALTER EDWARD, real estate co. exec.; b. San Antonio, Tex., Dec. 10, 1942; s. Armin Otto and Ella Anna (Joraschy) A.; B.E.E., U. Va., 1965; m. Patricia Ann Smith, July 10, 1965; children—Kathleen Elizabeth, Wendy Christine, Laura Ann. Project engr. Teledyne Avionics, Charlottesville, Va., 1969-71; co-owner Lant Realty Assos., Inc., Charlottesville, 1971-74, Mgmt. Services Corp., Charlottesville, 1971-74, Omega Constrn. Corp., Charlottesville, 1971-74; dist. dir. Century 21 Real Estate, Norfolk, Va., 1974; exec. v.p. Realty World Corp., Washington, 1974-77; regional dir., owner Realty World Mid-Atlantic region, Norfolk, Va., 1977—; pres., dir. Realty Specialists, Inc. Served to capt. USAF, 1965-69. Mem. Nat., Va. assns. realtors, Newport News-Hampton Beach Bd. Realtors, Realtors Nat. Mktg. Inst., Sales and Mktg. Inst. Lutheran. Home: 154 Pasture Rd Poquoson VA 23662 Office: 6330 Newtown Rd Norfolk VA 23502

APINIS, JOHN, chemist; b. Katvari, Latvia, Mar. 20, 1933; s. Augusts and Marta (Gravelsins) A.; B.S., Clemson U., 1960; m. Johnnie Verena Burden, Feb. 6, 1960. Came to U.S., 1949, naturalized, 1954. Apprentice, Am. Thread Co., Willimantic, Conn., 1951-52, Leiss Velvet Mfg. Co., Willimantic, 1952-53; asst. plant chemist Burlington Industries, Wake Finishing Co., Raleigh, N.C., 1960-65, plant chemist, 1965-75, mgr. dept. dyeing, 1975-76, tech. coordinator, 1976—. Served with AUS, 1953-55. Mem. Am. Assn. Textile Chemists and Colorists. Clubs: Elks, Rotary (v.p. 1963-64, pres. 1964-65, dir. 1963-66), Raleigh Music, Questers (v.p. 1977-78, pres. 1978-79), Raleigh Clemson Alumni (pres. 1976-77). Research in textile color computer and chromosorter. Home: 2205 Millbrook Rd Raleigh NC 27604 Office: Box 2748 Raleigh NC 27602

APPEL, WILLIAM GEORGE, assn. exec.; b. Pitts., Dec. 13, 1925; s. Ellwood and Charlotte (Wiertheimer) A.; student Inst. Orgn. Mgmt., Mich. State U., 1968-70, U. Del., 1976-77; grad. Inst. Orgnl. Mgmt., U. Del., 1978; div.; 1 son, Robert William; m. 2d, Nancy; 1 dau., Kandy Lynn. Shipping clk. Paramount Pictures, Pitts., 1948-50, booker, Atlanta, 1950-51; booker Universal Pictures, Atlanta, 1951-54, salesman, Cin., 1954-57; sales engr. Shower Door Co. Am., Atlanta, 1958-61; v.p. sales A-B Real Estate & Constrn. Co., Smyrna, Ga., 1961-63; gen. sales mgr. King-Williams Land Co., Smyrna, 1963-64; asst. v.p. Potter & Co., Smyrna, 1964-66; pres. Ga. Automotive Wholesalers Assn., Atlanta, 1966—; sec. GAWA Services, Inc., 1972—, sec.-treas. credit union, 1974-77. Mem. Heart Assn. Fund, 1965, 76. Served with AUS, 1944-46; ETO. Recipient Distinguished Service award So. Automotive Show, 1969, 74, 77. Mem. Automotive Wholesalers Assn. Execs. (chmn. liaison com. 1971-74, chmn. edn. com. 1970-75, sec. 1969-70, v.p. 1970-71, pres. 1971-72), Ga. Soc. Assn. Execs. (sec. treas. 1968-71, sec. 1973-74, v.p. 1974-75, dir. 1967-68, 76-78, pres.-elect 1979-80, pres. 1980—), Automotive Booster Club, Am. Soc. Assn. Execs. (cert. assn. exec.), Internat. Platform Assn., Airline Passengers Assn. Contbg. columist Automotive Aftermarket News, 1971-72, Cotton Pickers jour. Atlanta Automotive Boosters, 1970—. Home: 1741 Oak Ridge Circle Stone Mountain GA 30087 Office: 2193 Northlake Pkwy Suite 35 Tucker GA 30084

APPLE, MELVIN J., optometrist; b. Charleston, W.Va., Oct. 9, 1940; s. Gerald and Dora (Cohen) A.; student W.Va. U., 1955-58; D.Optometry, Ill. Coll. Optometry, 1961; m. Ursula Frances Hand, June 3, 1963; children—Marc, Michele. Individual practice optometry, Boca Raton, Fla., 1968—. Cons. visually related learning disabilities to various schs. Div. Children's Med. Services; mem. institutional health services com. Health Planning Council. Mem. adv. bd. Gables Acad. and Learning Success Center, 1970—. Served to capt. USAF, 1961-68. Fellow Am. Acad. Optometry, Coll. Optometrists in Vision Devel.; mem. Am., Fla., Palm Beach County (pres. 1974-75) optometric assns. Kiwanian. Home: 719 Elm Tree Ln Boca Raton FL 33432 Office: 900 NW 13th St Boca Raton FL 33432 also 3434 Lake Ida Rd Delray Beach FL 33445

APPLEGATE, WALTER THOMAS, clergyman; b. Lewis County, Ky., May 17, 1931; s. Benjamin Lewis and Mildred Ellen (Cooper) A.; B.A., Asbury Coll., 1954; B.D., Asbury Theol. Sem., 1957; M.Div., Asbury Theol. Sem., 1964, postgrad., 1978—; D.D., Mo. Bible Inst., 1978; m. Bonnie Jo Crawley, Apr. 1, 1956; 1 dau., Angela Susan. Ordained deacon United Meth. Ch., 1962, elder, 1964; pastor United Meth. Ch., Maysville (Ky.) Dist., 1959-64, Ashland (Ky.) Dist., 1965-71, Lexington (Ky.) Dist., 1972-75; pastor First United Meth. Ch., Prestonsburg, Ky., 1975—; chaplain Ky. Village Reform Sch., Lexington, 1956-58, Floyd County (Ky.) High Sch., 1978—, Highlands Mt. Manor Nursing Home, Prestonburg, 1977—; sec. Dist. Bd. Evangelism, United Meth. Ch., 1975; mem. conf. bd. discipleship United Meth. Ch., 1975. Sec.-treas. Prestonsburg Sr. Citizens Housing, 1976, Highlands Ch. Housing, 1978; sec. Prestonsburg Ministerial Bd., 1977-79. Mem. Highlands United Meth. Ministerial Assn. (pres. 1978), Floyd County Ministerial Assn. (pres. 1977-79). Democrat. Contbr. articles to profl. jours. Home: 54 S Arnold Ave Prestonsburg KY 41653 Office: 60 S Arnold Ave Prestonsburg KY 41653

APPLEMAN, BUFORD MARION, mgmt. cons. co. exec.; b. Fullerton, Calif., May 20, 1925; s. Milford Harold and Bessie Amelia (Olson) A.; A.A., Fullerton Jr. Coll., 1948; B.B.A., U. Tex., 1950; m. Virginia H. Maufrais, Apr. 28, 1946; children—Vicki, Susan. Indsl. engr., service mgr., dist. sales mgr. Tex. Foundries, Lufkin, 1950-62; mgr. asphalt sales Douglas Oil Co., Los Angeles, mgr. corp. planning, 1962-66; asst. to pres. Challenge-Cook Bros., Los Angeles, 1966-67; mgr. nat. account sales Taylor Machine Co., Louisville, Miss., 1967-68; v.p. leasing and maintenance contracts Crane Carrier Corp., Tulsa, 1968-74; prin. Appleman & Assos., Tulsa, 1974—; pres. Appleman Profit Systems, Inc., also Century Leasing, Inc., Tulsa, 1978—. cons. ready-mix concrete industry. Served with USAAF, 1943-46; ETO. Mem. Nat. Ready Mixed Concrete Assn. Republican. Presbyterian. Home: 7051 E 53d St Tulsa OK 74145

APPLETON, WAYNE CRAIG, chemist; b. Kearny, N.J., Jan. 24, 1947; s. Raymond Minor and Alice Patricia (Gage) A.; B.A., Rutgers State U., 1969; M.S, Utah State U., 1972; Ph.D., So. Ill. U., 1975; m. Leota Marie Hoard, Mar. 18, 1979; stepchildren—John R., Julienne E. Robert A. Welch postdoctoral fellow Tex. A&M U., 1975-76; sr. research chemist Velsicol Chem. Corp., Ann Arbor, 1976-78; area chemist EI duPont de Nemours & Co., Inc., Belle, W.Va., 1978, area supr. analytical methods group, 1978—. Mem. Am. Chem. Soc., AAAS, Sigma Xi, Phi Lambda Upsilon. Republican. Episcopalian. Home: 1418 Virginia St E Charleston WV 25301 Office: EI duPont de Nemours & Co Inc Belle WV 25015

APPLEY, LAWRENCE A., assn. exec.; b. Nyack, N.Y., Apr. 22, 1904; s. Joseph Earl and Jessie (Moore) A.; A.B., Ohio Wesleyan U., 1927, LL.D. (hon.), 1946; LL.D. (hon.), Bethany Coll., 1951, St. Lawrence U., 1951, Colgate U., 1955; Litt.D. (hon.), Bryant Coll., 1970; m. Ruth G. Wilson, Sept. 1, 1927 (dec. 1977); children—Ruth Ann (Mrs. Albert Gleaves Cohen), Judith (Mrs. William K. Schatz). Served as instr. Colgate U., 1927-30; personnel mgr. Buffalo div. Socony Mobil Oil Co., Inc., 1930-34, ednl. dir., N.Y.C., 1934-41; v.p. Vick Chem. Co., N.Y.C., 1941-46, dir., 1945-47; v.p., dir. Montgomery Ward & Co., Chgo., 1946-48; pres. Am. Mgmt. Assn., 1948-68, chmn., 1968-74, chmn. emeritus, 1974—; dir. emeritus Brunswick Corp.; dir. Nat. Can Corp., Oneida, Ltd., Kuhlman Corp., Kohler Co., Devonshire Street Fund, Investment Trust of Boston. Adviser on adminstrv. orgn. CSC, 1938-41; expert cons. to sec. of war on civilian personnel, 1941-42; exec. dir., later dep. chmn. War Manpower Commn., Washington, 1943-44; mem. personnel policy com. Hoover Commn., 1948, personnel adv. com. AEC, 1948-52; pres. Truman's Adv. Com. on Mgmt. 1949-52, U.S. Commn. on Intergovtl. Relations, 1953-54; mem. U.S. Bus. Ethics Adv. Council, 1961-63. Pres. Glen Ridge (N.J.) Bn. Forum, 1945-46, Bd. of Edn., 1940-46. Trustee emeritus Colgate U. Recipient War Dept. citation for meritorious civilian service, 1944; Presdl. citation Medal for Merit, 1946: Skipper Allen award Nat. Assn. Train Dirs., 1958; Human Relations award, 1952, Taylor Key Soc. Advancement Mgmt., 1961; Henry Laurence Gantt medal, 1963; Horatio Alger award, 1971. Fellow Internat. Acad. Mgmt.; mem. Am. Mgmt. Assn. (v.p. charge personnel div. 1942-44, dir., mem. exec. com. 1944-47), ASME (chmn. exec. com. mgmt. 1945), Soc. Advancement Mgmt., Am. Morgan Horse Assn. (pres. 1970-73, chmn. 1973-74), Phi Beta Kappa Assos., Phi Beta Kappa, Omicron Delta Kappa, Chi Phi, Delta Sigma Rho, Sigma Iota Epsilon. Author: Management in Action; Management Evolution; Values in Management; A Manager's Heritage; Formula for Success. Home: 1536 SE 15th Ct Deerfield Beach FL 33441

APT, NORMA ABRAMSON, speech pathologist; b. Greenville, Tex., Jan. 31, 1929; s. Meyer and Ida Rae (Beleck) Abramson; B.A., Tex. Christian U., 1951; M.A., Emerson Coll., 1953; m. Donald G. Apt, Aug. 15, 1953 (div. 1957); 1 son, William Burt. Speech pathologist lang. clinic Mass. Gen. Hosp., Boston, 1952-56, Baylor U. Med. Center, 1959-67, Parkland Hosp., Dallas, 1959-63; pvt. practice speech pathology, Dallas, 1959-67, 72—; supr. speech and hearing Methodist Hosp., Bklyn., 1968-72; cons. Richardson Med. Center, Dallas; vis. lectr. dept. orthodontics Baylor Coll. Dentistry, Dallas, 1976; U.S. Govt. trainee U. Miami Sch. Medicine, summer 1959. Mem. Am. Speech and Hearing Assn., Tex. Speech and Hearing Assn., Dallas Assn. Speech Pathologists and Audiologists, MENSA. Jewish. Author, pub.; What's In A Number?, 1978.

APTON, RALPH JULIUS, investment adviser, business and fin. cons.; b. Cologne, Germany, Oct. 16, 1930; s. Adolph A. and Erna (Neu) A.; brought to U.S., 1935, naturalized, 1940; B.A., U. Chgo., 1950, M.B.A., 1954; m. Renate Sickinger, Dec. 30, 1959; children—Kory Kim, Keith Jerrard. Fgn. trade and investment asst. AID, Washington, 1954; asst. indsl. analyst, New Delhi, India, 1955-57; dep. regional tech. aids coordinator for Latin Am., Mexico City, 1957-59; dep. exec. sec. Pres. Task Force for Fgn. Economic Assistance, Washington, 1960-61; chief mgmt. analysis br. Bur. for Latin Am. Affairs, Washington, 1962; devel. loan officer, Quito, Ecuador, 1963-65, AID del. to Ecuadorian Hwy. Transp. Com., 1963-65; chief preinvestment loans Inter-Am. Bank, Washington, 1966-76; real estate operator; pres. Apton Investment Adviser, Inc.; chmn., treas. Tack N' Teake, Ltd.; cons. Dominion Sash & Door Corp., Leaf Co.; instr. U.S. Dept. Agr. Grad. Sch. Trustee, Stonewall Dairy Farm. Mem. Am. Fin. Assn., Am. Mktg. Assn., Psi Upsilon. Clubs: U. Chgo. (dir.), Internat. (Washington); River Bend Country (Va.); Quito Golf and Tennis. Home: 9610 Beach Mill Rd Great Falls VA 22066 Office: 6736 Old McLean Village Dr McLean VA 22101

ARANA, ORLANDO ANTONIO, surgeon; b. Matanzas, Cuba, May 20, 1925; s. Francisco Manuel and Rita Maria A.; B.S., Matanzas Inst., 1942; M.D., Havana U., 1951; m. Suelena Maria Sires, July 14, 1958; children—Orlando, Silvia, Cynthia Lynn, Anthony Kerwin. Intern, Marymount Hosp., Cleve., 1963-64; resident in surgery St. Francis Hosp., Miami Beach, Fla., 1964-65; resident in surgery Mt. Sinai Hosp., Miami Beach, 1965-68, chief surg. resident, 1967-68; practice medicine specializing in surgery, Miami, 1968—; staff Coral Gables Hosp., Miami, 1972—, chief of surgery, 1977-78. Diplomate Am. Bd. Surgery. Fellow A.C.S. mem. AMA, Fla. Med. Assn., Dade County Med. Assn., Fla. Assn. Gen. Surgeons. Republican. Roman Catholic. Clubs: Ocean Reef, Racquet. Office: Suite 402 1850 S W 8th St Miami FL 33135

ARANDA, MIGUEL ANGEL, surgeon; b. Chihuahua, Chih, Mexico, Nov. 25, 1939; s. Miguel and Rebeca (Gomez) A.; student English Lang. Inst., Ann Arbor Mich., 1957; M.D., U. Chihuahua, 1964; m. Bertha Lucia Vargas, Oct. 31, 1964; children—Berta Miriam Irais, Rebeca Cristina Isabel, Miguel Angel, Jorge Xavier, Alejandro Manuel. Trained in legal medicine, Mexico City, 1971, aerospace medicine, 1972; prof. legal medicine Sch. Law, U. Chihuahua, 1965—, prof. legal medicine Med. Sch., 1972—, asso. prof. surgery, 1968—; head teaching dept. Univ. Hosp.; vis. prof. U. Ill. Med. Center, Chgo., 1975. Dean (dir.) Clinic Sanatorio Mederno, Chihuahua City. Served with Instituto Regional, 1957. Mem. Asociacion de Medicos Egresados de la Universidad Autonoma de Chihuahua, Asociacion Mexicana de Cirugia General, Colego Nacional de Medicina Psicosomati, Civil Aviation Med. Assn., Aerospace Med. Assn., Asociacion Latino Americana de Medicina de Aviacion y del Espacio, Sociedad de Cirugia del Hosp. Juarez. Roman Catholic. Club: Country of Chihuahua. Contbr. articles to profl. jours. Home: 1400 26th St Chihuahua Chih Mexico Office: 510 Bolivar St Chihuahua Chih Mexico

ARANGO, ABELARDO DE JESUS, surgeon; b. Medellin, Colombia, July 6, 1944; s. Abelardo and Julia (Restrepo) A.; B.S. cum laude, U. Antioquia (Colombia), 1960, M.D. summa cum laude, 1967; m. Janet Lynn Rossi, May 14, 1971; children—Julia Cristin, Jeanette Lynn, Abelardo. Intern, U. Antioquia Sch. Medicine, Medellin, 1966-67; NIH research fellow U. Miami Sch. Medicine, 1968; surg. intern Jackson Meml. Hosp., 1968, resident in surgery, 1969-72, NIH fellow in trauma, 1973-75, instr. surgery, 1973-74, asst. prof., 1975, clin. asst. prof., 1975—; practice medicine specializing in surgery, Miami; fellow in surgery U. Tex. Southwestern Med. Sch., Dallas, vis. asst. prof., 1973-74. Diplomate Am. Bd. Surgery. Fellow A.C.S.; mem. Am. Trauma Soc., Assn Acad. Surgery, Fla. Assn. Gen. Surgery, Fla. Med. Assn., So. Med. Assn., Dade County Med. Assn. Roman Catholic. Home: 17203 SW 79th Pl Miami FL Office: 3661 S Miami Ave Suite 910 Miami FL 33131

ARAU, ANTHONY JOHN, advt. exec.; b. Quincy, Mass., Nov. 25, 1926; s. Anthony and Helen (Boyle) A.; B.A., U. Chgo., 1951, postgrad., 1952-54; m. Eleanor Kittredge White, Aug. 27, 1949 (div. 1968); children—Eleanor Kittredge, Anthony James; m. 2d, Barbara Pearson Pettingell, 1971. Research asst., staff editor Indsl. Relations Center, U. Chgo., 1952-54; advt. mgr. U. Chgo. Press, 1954-56; advt. copywriter, N.Y.C., 1956-57; copy and creative chief Reader's Digest Books & Records, 1957-62; pres. Arau Assos., Inc., direct mail advt., N.Y.C. and Paris, 1962-71; creative cons., Miami, Fla., 1971-79; pres., creative dir. Arau & Co. Direct Mktg., Inc., Coral Gables, Fla., 1979—; lectr. to profl. mktg. and pub. groups, nat. and regional direct mktg. assns. Writer Ill. Young Democrats, 1952-56; cons. Fla. State Democratic Com., 1972; cons. Jack Orr Mayoral Campaign, Miami, 1972; bd. dirs. Mental Health Assn. Westchester County (N.Y.), 1966-70. Served with U.S. Army, 1944-46; PTO. Recipient Nat. Direct Mail Leader award Direct Mail Mktg. Assn., 1965, 66, 67, 68, 69; Gov.'s award, Fla. State Addy award Am. Advt. Fedn., 1978, Nat. and Miami Regional Addy awards, 1978. Mem. ACLU. Democrat. Contbr. articles to newspapers and profl. jours. Office: Arau & Co Direct Mktg Inc 4601 Ponce De Leon Blvd Coral Gables FL 33146

ARAUZ, CARLOS GASPAR, city ofcl.; b. Havana, Cuba, Jan. 6, 1949; came to U.S., 1960, naturalized, 1974; s. Agnelio Alejandro and Mariana (Rodriguez) A; B.S., Loyola U., Los Angeles, 1970; M.S., Ga. Inst. Tech., 1975, postgrad., 1975—. Bacteriologist, Emory U. Hosp., Atlanta, 1970-72; research psychologist Atlanta Regional Commn., 1973-74; dir. personnel City of College Park (Ga.); indsl. psychology cons. Lockheed Ga. Co., Marietta, 1976; asst. dir. human resources City of Miami, 1976—; cons. govt. and industry. Bd. dirs. New World Bicultural Generation, Inc. Mem. Internat. Personnel Mgmt. Assn. (young personnel profl. award N. Ga. 1975; pres. N. Ga. chpt. 1976, S. Fla. chpt. 1978, v.p. So. region 1979-80), Am. Soc. Personnel Adminstrn., Fla. Public Personnel Assn., Internat. City Mgmt. Assn., S.E. Psychol. Assn., Sigma Xi. Roman Catholic. Club: Lake Arrowhead Yacht and Country. Office: PO Box 330708 Miami FL 33133

ARBIB, JOHN A., constrn. co. exec.; b. Lawrence, N.Y., Sept. 18, 1924; s. Robert Simeon and Edna (Henry) A.; student Pa. State Coll., 1942-43, Ala. Polytech. Inst., 1943, Columbia U., 1946-47; m. Leonore Grandlinger, June 5, 1949; children—John Paul, Peter Laurence, Diane Lynn. Partner, Robert S. Arbib & Co., N.Y.C., 1946-57; pres. Arbib Building Corp., Margate, Fla., 1958-62; pres. Custom Craft Homes of So. Fla., Inc., Boca Raton, 1962-65; v.p. VR Corp., Hallandale, Fla., 1965-68; v.p. Royal Palm Beach Colony Inc., Hallandale, 1968-72, St. Petersburg, Fla., 1971-72; v.p., gen. mgr. Pinebrook Bldg. Corp., Pembroke Pines, Fla., 1972-76; v.p. Pasadena Homes, Inc., gen. mgr. Pinebrook div., 1976—; pres. Home Owners Warranty Corp. of South Fla., 1974-76, v.p., 1977—; dir. Home Owners Warranty Corp., Washington, 1974—, mem. exec. com., 1979-80. Pres., Lakeville Estates, N.Y. Civic Assn., 1953-54; mem. Fla. Condominium Commn., 1972—; mem. Gov.'s Econ. Adv. Com., 1980—. Bd. dirs. Progress for Dade County, Fla., 1973—, Broward County Urban League, 1980—. Mem. Broward County Bd. Rules and Appeals, 1975—, mem. exec. com., 1979-80. Served with AUS, 1943-46; ETO. Named Builder of Month, Gen. Electric Corp., Oct. 1971. Mem. Builders Assn. S. Fla. (dir. 1966—, pres. 1973; Pres.'s award 1975, Builder of Year 1976), Fla. Home Builders Assn. (dir. 1969—, area v.p. 1973, sec. 1977, treas. 1978, pres. 1980), Nat. Assn. Home Builders (dir. 1970—, chmn. bus. mgmt. com. 1975-76, vice chmn. consumer affairs com. 1977, resolutions com. 1979), Constrn. Council Fla. (pres. 1975, cir. 1974—). Democrat. Unitarian (dir. 1965-70), pres. Ft. Lauderdale ch. 1969). Home: 5561 SW 8th St Plantation FL 33317 Office: PO Box 8360 Pembroke Pines FL 33024

ARBUCKLE, VANCE JOSEPH, advt. agy. exec.; b. Hobart, Okla., Aug. 4, 1936; s. Jesse William and Mary Etta (Gibson) A.; student U. Ark., 1955-57; B.A., Wichita State U., 1959. Copywriter, Rumrill-Hoyt Advt., N.Y.C., 1960-66, Grey Advt., N.Y.C., 1967-72; v.p., asso. creative dir. Noble-Dury Advt., Nashville, 1972-76; asso. creative dir. D'Arcy-MacManus, Masius, St. Louis, 1976-77; v.p., creative dir. Abbott Advt. Agy., Lexington, Ky., 1977—; guest lectr. U. Ky; chmn. Lexington Ad Awards. Recipient CLIO award 1976; One Show award N.Y. Art Dirs. Club, 1975, ANDY award, 1975; ADDY award Am. Advt. Fedn., 1974. Mem. Lexington Advt. Club (1st v.p. 1979-80), Mensa. Club: Lexington Tennis. Home: 3320 Montavesta Lexington KY 40502 Office: 101 Jerrico Dr Lexington KY 40579

ARBURN, ROBERT WILLIAM, architect; b. Pueblo, Colo., June 10, 1933; s. Darwin William and Ethel Marie (Lamb) A.; student (scholar) Denver U., 1951-52; B.Arch. (Univ. scholar), U. Tex., 1956; m. Lavonne Leatrice Kennedy, Sept. 14, 1955; children—Donald Joseph, Ginger Ann. Designer, Dean Eichelberger, Houston, 1956; designer Monroe Licht & Higgins, El Paso, Tex., 1957; architect Davis-Foster & Thorpe, El Paso, 1958, Carroll & Daueble, El Paso, 1959-61, Bartlett Cocke & Assos., El Paso, also San Antonio, 1961-71; pvt. practice architecture, 1971-73; architect Robert Arburn & Assos., San Antonio, Arburn-Reitzer & Assos., Inc., San Antonio, 1973-75, Robert Arburn & Assos., 1975—; architect Randolph-Brooks Fed. Credit Union, Randolph AFB, 1973; chmn. bd. So. Manor Nursing Homes, Inc. Recipient Malon D. and Luna M. Thatcher Found. award, 1956; Outstanding Design award U.S. Air Force, 1976; Excellence in Architecture award Dept. of Def., 1976. Mem. Tex. Soc. Architects (mem. criminal justice com.), AIA, Constrn. Specifications Inst. Clubs: Masons, Shriners, Rotary, Toastmasters (pres. 1971-72) (San Antonio). Home: 122 Dogwood St San Antonio TX 78213 Office: 774 Isom Rd San Antonio TX 78216

ARCAMONTE, HUMBERT VINCENT, clin. social worker; b. Westchester County, N.Y., Feb. 11, 1930; s. Humbert and Lucia (Gentile) A.; B.A., U. Miami, Coral Gables, Fla., 1955, postgrad. in psychology, 1956; M.S.W., Fla. State U., Tallahassee, 1960; m. Ana Maria Roque, Aug. 17, 1956; children—Ana Maria, Edward, Steven. Clin. social worker alcoholic rehab. program State of Fla., 1960-63; pvt. practice individual, group and family psychotherapy, Dania, Fla., 1963—; group therapist Meml. Hosp., Hollywood, Fla., Sec., Escombia County Mental Health Assn., 1961. Served with U.S. Army, 1952-54. Cert., Acad. Cert. Social Workers. Fellow Fla. Soc. Clin. Social Workers (pres.); mem. Nat. Assn. Social Workers. Home: 4216 Arthur St Hollywood FL 33021 Office: 158 N Federal Hwy Dania FL 33004

ARCEMENT, BILLY PAUL, chemist; b. Labadieville, La., June 3, 1939; s. Herman Joseph and Isabelle Ann (St. Germain) A.; B.S., Nicholls State U., 1961, postgrad. 1971-73; M.Ed., La. State U., 1965; m. Ernestine Marie Veron, Feb. 17, 1962; children—Stacie Marie, Corey Paul, Patrick Veron, Mary Katherine. Coach, tchr. sci. Assumption High Sch., Napoleonville, La., 1962-64, Donaldsonville (La.) High Sch., 1965-69; chemist Triad Chems., Donaldsonville, 1969-73; chief chemist Melamine Chems., Donaldsonville, 1973—. Coach, Recreation League Donaldsonville, 1972—. Served with Army N.G., 1961-62. Mem. TAPPI, Greater Baton Rouge Indsl. Mgmt. Council (v.p. 1978-80, pres. 1980—). Democrat. Roman Catholic. Club: Ascension Cath. Men's (pres. 1978-79). Home: 108 Magnolia Dr Donaldsonville LA 70546 Office: PO Box 748 Donaldsonville LA 70346

ARCENEAUX, GEORGE, JR., judge; b. New Orleans, May 17, 1928; s. George and Louise (Austin) A.; B.A., La. State U., 1949; LL.B., Am. U., 1957; m. Mary Elizabeth Martin, Aug. 17, 1954; children—Mary Elizabeth, George III, Robert Martin. Program dir. Radio Sta. KCIL, Houma, La., 1949; state editor Daily Advertiser, Lafayette, 1949-50; legis. asst. Senator Allen J. Ellender, Washington, 1952-56, adminstrv. asst., 1957-60; admitted to La. bar, 1959; practiced in Houma, 1960-79; mem. firm Duval, Arceneaux, Lewis & Funderburk, 1960-79; U.S. dist. judge Eastern Dist. La., New Orleans, 1979—. Chmn., Houma-Terrebonne Regional Planning Commn., 1963-69. Served with AUS, 1950-51. Mem. Am., La., Terrebonne Parish (pres. 1964-65) bar assns., C. of C. (dir. 1963, pres. 1966-67). Methodist. Clubs: Plimsoil, Internat. House (New Orleans); Univ. (Washington); Rotary (dir. 1963, pres. 1966, dist. gov. 1971-72). Home: 2 El Paso Dr Houma LA 70360 also 3201 Saint Charles Ave New Orleans LA 70115 Office: 500 Camp St New Orleans LA 70130

ARCENEAUX, JULES MENOU, oil field service co. exec.; b. Bay St. Louis, Miss., July 7, 1925; s. Eddie Joseph and Marie Violette (Menou) A.; student Millsaps Coll., 1943-44, U. Ala., 1946; B.S., U. Southwestern La., 1949; m. Patricia J. Miller, Sept. 8, 1951; children—Mary Patrice, Jules M., Mary Katherine, Mary Alice, Mary Margaret. Asst. store mgr., city salesman Nat. Supply Co., 1949-51; sales rep. Mutual of N.Y. Life Ins. Co., 1951; with Eastman Oil Well Surveying Co., Houma, La., 1952-56, dist. mgr., 1954-56; mgr. Gammaloy Ltd., Lafayette, La., 1956—; bd. chmn. Vacco Wireline Service, Inc., 1969—; dir. Petroleum Machinery and Tool Co., D. H. Castille, Inc. Pres., Lafayette Public Library Bd., 1953-68, Our Lady of Fatima Parish Council, 1979, Lafayette Juvenile and Young Adult Rehab. Program. Served with USN, 1943-46. Mem. Am. Petroleum Inst., Nat. Assn. Drilling Contractors, AIME. Democrat. Clubs: Civitan, K.C. Home: 110 Oak View Blvd Lafayette LA 70503 Office: PO Box 51602 Lafayette LA 70505

ARCENEAUX, WILLIAM, ednl. adminstr.; b. Lafayette, La., Aug. 19, 1941; B.A., U. Southwestern La., 1962; M.A., La. State U., 1965; Ph.D., 1969. Instr. history La. State U., 1966-67; asst. prof. Northwestern State U., Natchitoches, La., 1967-69; asso. prof., chmn. dept. history So. U., New Orleans, 1969-72; exec. dir. La. Coordinating Council for Hihger Edn., Baton Rouge, La., 1972-75; commr. higher edn. State of La., Baton Rouge, 1975—. Mem. State Higher Edn. Execs. Officers Assn., Am., La. hist. assns., Fgn. Relations Assn. New Orleans. Democrat. Roman Catholic. Club: Rotary. Home: 8956 Norfolk Dr Baton Rouge LA 70809 Office: Suite 1530 1 American Pl Baton Rouge LA 70825

ARCHER, ALICE DURHAM, sociologist; b. Greenville, S.C., Jan. 29, 1915; d. James Willis and Bertha Lee (Walker) Durham; B.A., Clark Coll., 1936; M.A., Atlanta U., 1940; postgrad. Ohio State U., 1961-67; vis. prof. scholar Harvard U., 1971; m. Leonard Courtney Archer, Aug. 31, 1940; 1 dau., Alice Lenore. Womens editor Atlanta Daily World, 1936-39; dir. news service Central State Coll., Wilberforce, Ohio, 1951-57; dir. Fellowship House, Cin., 1957-58; exec. sec. Mus. Modern Art, Cin., 1958; mem. faculty Tenn. State U., Nashville, 1958—, asst. prof. sociology, 1958—. Bd. dirs. YWCA, 1959-60; pres. Nashville Links, Inc., 1962-64, Nashville Girl Friends, Inc., 1976-78. Mem. So. Sociol. Assn., AAUP. Democrat. Baptist. Clubs: Ardent Gardeners, X-3, Finesse, Entre Nous Bridge. Author articles in field. Home: 2214 Murphy Ave Nashville TN 37203 Office: 3500 Centennial Blvd Nashville TN 37203

ARCHER, CARL MARION, oil and gas co. exec.; b. Spearman, Tex., Dec. 16, 1920; s. Robert Barton and Gertrude Lucille (Steeds) A.; student Tex. U., Austin, 1937-39; m. Peggy Garrett, Aug. 22, 1939; children—Mary Frances, Carla Lee. Pres., Anchor Oil Co., Spearman, Tex., 1959—, Carl M. Archer Farms, Spearman, 1960—; gen. mgr. Speartex Grain Co., Spearman, 1967—, Speartex Oil & Gas Co., 1974—; dir. Panhandle Bank & Trust Co., Borger, Tex. Chmn. County Democratic Com., 1969—. Mem. Tex. Grain Dealers Assn., Ind. Royalty Owners and Producers Assn., Nat. Grain Dealers Assn., Am. Petroleum Landmen Assn., Nat., Tex. bankers assns. Mem. Ch. of Christ. Clubs: Perryton, Borger Country, Amarillo. Home: 304 S Endicott Spearman TX 79081 Office: 514 Collard St Spearman TX 79081

ARCHER, WILLIAM REYNOLDS, JR., congressman; b. Houston, Mar. 22, 1928; s. William Reynolds and Eleanor (Miller) A.; student Rice U., 1945-46; B.B.A., U. Tex., 1949, LL.B., 1951; m. Patricia Moore, Nov. 21, 1953; children—William Reynolds III, Richard Moore, Sharon Leigh, Elizabeth Ann, Barbara Elise. Admitted to Tex. bar; pres. Uncle Johnny Mill, Inc., Houston, 1953-61, W.R. Archer, Inc., 1961—; partner firm Harris, Archer Parks & Graul, 1967-72; dir. Heights State Bank, 1967-71; mem. 92d-96th congresses from 7th Tex. Dist., mem. ways and means com. Councilman, mayor pro-tem City of Hunters Creek Village, Tex., 1955-62. Bd. dirs. Houston Soc. for Prevention of Cruelty to Animals. Served from pvt. to 1st lt., USAF, 1951-53; capt. Res. Recipient Man of Yr. award Sigma Alpha Epsilon, 1968, Outstanding Alumnus award St. Thomas High Sch., 1971; Man of Year award Dist. 7 B'nai B'rith, 1973, NAB Watchdog of Treasury award, 1974; NFIB Guardian of Small Bus. award, 1973; Brotherhood award NCCJ, 1980. Mem. Houston Bar Assn., State Bar Tex., Phi Delta Phi. Republican. Roman Catholic. Office: 1024 Longworth House Office Bldg Washington DC 20515

ARCHIBALD, GEORGE JOLLEY, coll. adminstr.; b. Atlanta, Feb. 10, 1946; s. George Osborne and Elma Jolley A.; A.B., W. Ga. Coll., 1968, M.Ed., 1973, Bd.S., 1979; m. Sylvia Sue Carter, June 5, 1976. Asst. to dean Sch. Edn., W. Ga. Coll., Carrollton, 1974—. Served with USCG, 1968-71. Mem. Am. Personnel and Guidance Assn., Phi Delta Kappa. Club: Sportsman's (pres. 1975-76) (Carrollton, Ga.). Home: 223 Carroll St Carrollton GA 30117 Office: Sch Edn W Ga Coll Carrollton GA 30118

ARCHIBALD, JOHN DUNCAN, library adminstr., geographer; b. Winnipeg, Man., Can., Nov. 9, 1942; s. Ralph George and Norma Gwendolyn (Jones) A.; came to U.S., 1943, naturalized, 1966; B.A. in Geography and Econs., Ohio Wesleyan U., 1964; M.A. in Geography, San Diego State Coll., 1968; M.S. in Library Sci., U. Tenn., 1972; postgrad. So. Ill. U., 1969, N.C. State U., 1973-74, N.C.A. and T. State U., 1977, U. Idaho, 1979; M.A. in Mgmt. and Supervision, Central Mich. U., 1978; m. Brigitte Edith Zapp, Aug. 29, 1970; children—David Andrew, Elizabeth Anna. Planning aid San Diego County Planning Dept., 1966-67; instr. geography Eastern N.Mex. U., Portales, 1968-69; asst. prof. geography Mansfield (Pa.) State Coll., 1969-70; grad. teaching asst. in geography U. Tenn., Knoxville, 1970-71; instr. geography James Sprunt Tech. Inst., Kenansville, N.C., 1972-73; dir. Duplin County (N.C.) Dorothy Wightman Library, Kenansville, 1972-79; dir. Mishawaka (Ind.)-Penn Public Library, 1979—; tchr. Duplin County Schs. Extended Day Program, 1976-78. Participant ann. auditions Nat. Guild of Piano Tchrs., Dallas, 1953-60. Sec., publicity mgr. Duplin County Bi-centennial Commn., 1974-76; mem. Kenansville Bi-centennial Commn. 1974-76, Kenansville Fire Dept. and Rescue Squad, 1975-76, Kenansville Gov.'s Award Com., 1975-76; mem. exec. com. Duplin County Task Force Improvement of Reading, 1975-76; mem. Duplin County Helpline, 1975-76. U.S. Office Edn. grantee, 1969, 78. Mem. ALA (pub. library assn. starter list new br. collections com., pub. relations services to libraries com.), Ind. Library assn., Am. Natural Hygiene Assn., Kappa Kappa Psi. Baptist. Contbr. articles to newspaper columns. Home: 1 Bayberry Ct Greensboro NC 27405 Office: 209 E Lincoln Way E Mishawaka IN 46544

ARD, HOWARD ANTHONY, computer systems engr.; b. Pensacola, Fla., July 13, 1943; s. Anthony Ard and Lois (Anger) Fink; B.S.Ch.E., U. South Ala., 1972; m. Glenda Jean Sessions, July 20, 1968; children—John Wesley, Marcus Kevin. Quality control engr. Monsanto Co., Pensacola, 1972-74, systems engr., 1974-78, sr. systems engr., 1978-79, supr. process systems applications, 1979—. Past adv. Jr. Achievement of Pensacola; Sunday sch. tchr. Ensley Beams of Life Mission, Pensacola. Served with arty. U.S. Army, 1966-69. Recipient Achievement awards Monsanto Co., 1977, 78. Democrat. Home: 13 E Duke St Pensacola FL 32504 Office: PO Box 12830 Pensacola FL 32575

ARDAIOLO, FRANK PALMA, univ. dean; b. Bklyn., Oct. 21, 1948: s. Salvatore P. and Helen C. Ardaiolo; B.A. (coll. acad. scholar 1966-70), Assumption Coll., 1970; M.S. (NDEA fellow 1970), Ind. U., 1974, Ed.D., 1978; m. Joleen Phifer, Mar. 18, 1978. Asst. coordinator residence life Ind. U., 1971-74; dir. residence life, asso. dean students Belmont (N.C.) Abbey Coll., 1974-76; research asso. Ind. U., 1977-78; asso. dean student affairs U. S.C., Columbia, 1978—. Mem. Am. Coll. Personnel Assn., Am. Personnel and Guidance Assn., Nat. Assn. Student Personnel Adminstrs. Roman Catholic. Author papers in field. Home: 7648 Sumter Hwy Apt 189 Columbia SC 29209 Office: West Wing Russell House Univ SC Columbia SC 29208

ARDEN, DENIS EDMUND, architect; b. Cleve., Sept. 8, 1946; s. Jon Edmund and Marie Eva (Stelma) A.; B.Arch., U. Fla., 1969, M.A. in F.A., 1976; m. Marjorie Miller, Oct. 3, 1970. Draftsman, Ferendino, Grafton, Spillis, Candela, Miami, Fla., 1966, 67, 70; architect-designer Watson, Deutschman & Lyon, Miami, 1969-70; pres. Arden-Green-Architects, Inc., Miami, 1972—; lectr. in field; guest appearances on tv for Architecture-The Future of Miami, 1975. Recipient AIA Design award for Apogee Townhouse Project, Miami, 1976; Archtl. Record Mag. Nat. Design award, 1976; Design award, Biscayne West-Design the Year 2000, Nat. Urban Design competition, Miami, 1976. Office: 3298 Mary St Suite 4 Miami FL 33133

ARDITTI, FRED DAVID, economist, educator; b. N.Y.C., Jan. 30, 1939; s. David Aaron and Marie Arditti; B.S. in Elec. Engring., M.I.T., 1960, M.S. (fellow) in Indsl. Mgmt., 1962, Ph.D. in Econs. (Ford Found. fellow), 1966; 1 dau., Elizabeth Marie. Economist, Rand Corp., Santa Monica, Calif., 1965-67; asst. prof. U. Calif., Berkeley, 1968-71; asso. prof. dept. econs. U. Fla., Gainesville, 1971-73, prof., 1973-74, Walter J. Matherly prof. of fin. and econs., 1974—, chmn. dept. econs., 1977—; cons. to Dept. of Energy, 1976-79. Mem. Chgo. Bd. Trade's Ednl. Adv. Com., 1977-79. Mem. Am. Econ. Assn., Am. Fin. Assn. Contbr. numerous articles on fin. and econs. to profl. jours. Office: Dept of Economics 100 Mathelry Hall Univ of Florida Gainesville FL 32611

ARDOIN, KENNETH ALLEN, pharm. co. exec.; b. Alexandria, La., Dec. 15, 1942; s. Francis Allen and Mary Elizabeth (Edwards) A.; B.S. in Econs., U. Southwestern La., 1964; cert. Baylor U., 1974; m. Mary Annette Butler, July 22, 1967; children—Brett Allen, Scott David, Michelle Annette. Med. service rep. Roerig div. Pfizer Inc., Little Rock, 1969, hosp. mgr., New Orleans, 1969-71, dist. mgr., Chgo., 1971-77, Dallas, 1977—. Coach, Little League, Little Rock and Chgo., 1966-76; coach baseball YMCA, Dallas, 1977—; coach soccer, Dallas, 1977—. Named Dist. mgr. of Yr., 1972. Roman Catholic (parish adv. council 1979, mem. choir). Clubs: Dallas N. Soccer Assn., St. Theresa's Mens (pres. 1968-69), All Saints Mens (pres. 1979—). Home: 16306 Fallkirk St Dallas TX 75248

ARDOIN, RAY BURKE, acct.; b. Evangeline Parish, La., May 25, 1938; s. Ray John and Tessie (Guillory) A.; B.S., U. Mo., 1959; M.B.A., Stanford U., 1963; Ph.D., Ben Franklin U., Phila., 1976; m. Denise Rand, Dec. 23, 1974; children—James Ray, Angelique. Prin., owner Ray B. Ardoin & Assos., Denham Springs, La., 1966—. Continental Oil Co. fellow, 1966. Mem. Accts. Assn. La. (ednl. chmn.), Am. Acctg. Assn., Nat. Soc. Public Accts., Baton Rouge Assn. Accts. (pres.). Democrat. Roman Catholic. Club: Kiwanis (treas.). Home: Rt 4 Box 812 Denham Springs LA 70726 Office: 205 Florida Blvd Denham Springs LA 70726

ARECHAVALETA, CARMEN LATOUR, real estate co. exec.; b. Havana, Cuba, July 8, 1940; d. Eduardo and Carmen E. (Soto Padrera) Latour; B.A., Villanova U., Havana, Cuba, 1960; m. Ramon Arechavaleta, July 6, 1963; children—Ramon E., Cristina, Lilian, Victor. Realtor asso., sales mgr. Latin Am. div. Rose Grodon Realty, Miami, Fla., 1964-73; v.p., treas. Realty Center Miami, Inc., 1973—. Mem. Nat. Assn. Realtors, Miami, Coral Gables bds. realtors. Roman Catholic. Club: Big Five. Home: 2900 DeSoto Blvd Coral Gables FL 33134 Office: 5523 SW 8th St Miami FL 33134

ARESU, BERNARD CAMILLE, educator; b. Constantine, Algeria, June 15, 1944; came to U.S., 1967; Licence es Lettres, U. Montpellier, 1967; Ph.D., U. Wash., 1975; m. Carolyn Shore, Aug. 7, 1976. Instr., French, U. Va., 1967-68; lectr. comparative lit., continuing edn. U. Wash., 1968-76; asst. prof. dept. French Rice U., Houston, 1977—, asso. Baker Coll., 1978—. Fulbright-Hays grantee, 1967. Mem. MLA, Internat. Comparative Lit. Assn., Philol. Assn. Pacific Coast, South-Central MLA. Contbr. articles in field to profl. jours. Office: Dept French Rice U Houston TX 77001

ARGO, JAMES ROLAND, pharmacist; b. Gadsden, Ala., June 7, 1921; s. George Franklin and Mattie Elizabeth (Erwin) A.; B.S. in Pharmacy, Samford U., 1948; m. Mary Lee Rushing, Sept. 8, 1946; children—James Roland, Mary Carol, Lee Ann. Pharmacist, Lane Drug Co., Montgomery, Ala., 1948-50, Montgomery Apothecary, 1950-51; owner, mgr. Argo Drug Co., Millbrook, Ala., 1954-57; chief pharmacist VA Med. Center, Montgomery, 1951—; lect. hosp. pharmacy Sch. of Pharmacy, Auburn U. Chmn. bd. Methodist Ch. Served with USNR, 1942-45; ETO. Mfem. Am. Soc. Hosp. Pharmacists, Am. Pharm. Assn., Ala. Soc. Hosp. Pharmacists (charter), Ala. Pharm. Assn. Club: Masons (past master). Home: 2311 Edgewood Rd Millbrook AL 36054 Office: 215 Perry Hill Rd Montgomery AL 36109

ARMAND, RUTH HALL, ret. counselor; b. Mansfield, La., Dec. 8, 1915; d. Guy Bridges and Mary (Christian) Hall; A.A., Dodd Coll., 1935; B.S., La. Poly. Inst., 1937; M.Ed., Northwestern State U. La., 1958, postgrad., 1969-75; m. Lawrence B. Armand June 1948; children—Lawrence B., James Hall. Home mgmt. supt. FHA, Avoyelles, La., 1938-46; home demonstration agt. La. Extension Service, Avoyelles, 1946-48; tchr. home econs. Avoyelles Parish Sch. System, 1948-71, reading specialist, 1971-76, guidance counselor, 1976-79, Marksville Sr. High Sch., 1959-79. Chief RADEF decontamination Avoyelles Parish CDA, 1966—; tng. officer, 1975—. Mem. Am., La. personnel and guidance assns., Am., La. (La. Sr. High Counselor of Year 1978-79) assns. sch. counselors, Am., La. vocat. counselors assns., Avoyelles Guidance Assn. (pres. 1977-79), Alpha Delta Kappa (pres. chpt. 1963-65). Democrat. Baptist. Club: Ladies Golf Assn., Avoyelles Golf and Country. (v.p. golf 1977—). Home: 721 Washington St S Marksville LA 71351

ARMBRISTER, DOUGLAS KENLEY, surgeon; b. Emory, Va., Feb. 20, 1934; s. Victor Stradley and Naomi Lucile (Byrd) A.; B.A., B.S., Emory and Henry Coll., 1955; M.D., U. Va., 1959, M.S. in Surgery, 1962; m. Nancy Sherri Douglas, Apr. 30, 1960; children—Valerie Lynne, Victor Kenley, Christopher Douglas, Karen Leigh. Intern, U. Va. Med. Center, Charlottesville, 1959-60, resident in surgery, 1960-62, 64-66, chief resident, asst. attending surgeon, 1966-67; practice medicine specializing in gen. surgery, Marion, Va., 1967—; mem. staff Smyth County Community Hosp., 1967—, pres. staff, 1973, chmn. surg. service, 1976—; surg. cons. Southwestern VA State Mental Hosp.; mem. S.W. Va. Comprehensive Health Planning Council, 1974-77, v.p., 1976-77; mem. Va. Regional Med. Program Cancer Com., 1968-70; mem. state advisory group Va. Regional Med. Program, 1971-75; pres. S.W. Va. Health Systems Agency Sub-Area Council, 1977; bd. dirs. S.W. Va. PSRO, 1978—; mem. Medico-Legal Malpractice Rev. Panels (2). Served with M.C., USAF, 1962-64. Diplomate Am. Bd. Surgery. Fellow A.C.S. (state trauma com. 1977), mem. Va., Muller surg. socs., Va., S.W. Va., Smyth County (pres. 1971) med. socs. Republican. Methodist. Home: Keller Ln Marion VA 24354 Office: Med Arts Bldg Radio Hill Dr Marion VA 24354

ARMEL, DANIEL EUGENE, mfg. co. exec.; b. Columbus, Ohio, Apr. 16, 1917; s. Charles Daniel and Octa Eugene (McCann) A.; student Ohio State U., 1935-39, Ariz. State U., 1945-46; m. Cledith Ellen Smith, Feb. 25, 1967; children—Daniel Edward, Julie Sallyann. Mgr. cost control Goodyear Aircraft Corp., Akron, Ohio and Phoenix, 1940-48; mgr. Ariz. Pacific Fin. Corp., Phoenix, 1945-48; chief acct. Miller Foundry div. Lennox Furnace Co., Columbus, 1948-50; exec. v.p. Cert. Credit Corp., Cert. Life Assurance Co. and affiliated cos., Columbus and Houston, 1950-54, pres., 1954-58, chmn. bd., 1958-63; pres. Orleans Mgmt. Corp., New Orleans, 1964-68; fin. cons., 1968-76; pres., dir. Telcom Data Corp., Huntsville, Ala., 1976—; gen. partner Computer Equipment Ltd., Huntsville, 1976—; v.p., dir. Commerce Centers Corp., New Orleans, 1976—; chmn. bd., chief exec. officer, dir. Metlduct Corp., Morgan City, La., 1976—; corporate cons. in mergers and acquisitions, 1968—. Active Camp Fire Girls, Inc., greater New Orleans area, 1968—. Recipient William H. Pohlman award, 1973. Mem. Am. Soc. Metals, Ohio State U. Alumni Assn., Am. Acctg. Soc., Am. Fin. Soc., Internat. Council of Shopping Centers. Home: 579 Deerfield Rd Gretna LA 70053 Office: Care Metlduct Corp Hwy 90 W Patterson LA 70309

ARMITAGE, SHELLEY SUE, educator; b. Fort Worth, June 17, 1947; d. Robert Allen and Dorothy (Dunn) A.; B.A., Tex. Tech U., 1969, M.A., 1971; Ph.D., U. N.Mex., 1981. Reporter, columnist Vega (Tex.) Enterprise, 1961-65; teaching asst. Tex. Tech U., Lubbock, 1969-71; asst. prof. English, Tarrant County Jr. Coll., Hurst, Tex., 1971—; grad. asst. U. N.Mex., Albuquerque, 1979-80; freelance writer and photographer; tech. writing cons.; lectr. U. Asmara (Ethiopia), 1974; alt. U.S. Olympic Women's Basketball Team, 1976. Recipient various awards and grants. Mem. AAUW, MLA, Western Lit. Assn., Am. Studies Assn. Contbr. poetry to mags., articles to profl. jours. Home: PO Box 239 Vega TX 79092 Office: Am Studies Dept U NMex Albuquerque NM 87131

ARMS, THOMAS OLEN, chem. engr.; b. Greenville, S.C., Aug. 23, 1930; s. James Tolley and Nora Lee (Pittman) A.; B.S. in Chem. Engring., Clemson U., 1957; m. Ella Carolyn Stokes, Oct. 13, 1950; children—Larry Thomas, Kenneth Olen, Alvin Dale, Randall Scott. Engr. in charge pilot plant Deering-Milliken Research Corp.,

Pendleton, S.C., 1957; dir. mfg. Milliken Chem., Inman, S.C., 1958-67; asst. mgr. chem. div. J.P. Stevens & Co., Inc., Piedmont, S.C., 1967—. Served with USAF, 1947-48, U.S. Army, 1950-52; Korea. Mem. Am. Inst. Chem. Engrs. Republican. Baptist. Home: 624 Stafford Ave Spartanburg SC 29302 Office: PO Box 428 Piedmont SC 29673

ARMSTRONG, ALICE KATHRYN, civic worker; b. Stevenson, Ala., July 14, 1925; d. Percy Dixon and Alice(Mann) A.; student Gulfpark Coll., 1942; A.B., U. Ky., 1947. Sec., Chickamauga Cedar Co., Inc., Stevenson, Ala., 1950-59, pres., 1959-63, cons., 1963-65. Chmn. devel. bd. City of Stevenson Hist. Assn., 1976—; bd. dirs. Jackson County Hist. Assn., Scottsboro, Ala., 1977—. Recipient Hist. award merit, 1976; named Col., State of Ala., 1977. Mem. Stevenson Downtown Merchants Assn. Episcopalian. Home: Armstrong Rd Stevenson AL 35772

ARMSTRONG, DONALD LEIGH, assn. exec.; b. Evanston, Ill., Mar. 14, 1931; s. James William and Francele (Harris) A.; A.B., U. Ky., 1953; M.A., Western Ky. U., 1972; m. Anne Barnett, June 10, 1957; children—Bryan Leigh, Catherine Anne. Public info. officer Commonwealth of Ky., Frankfort, 1962-67; dir. mem. relations Am. Public Welfare Assn., Chgo., 1967-68; dir. public relations Western Ky. U., Bowling Green, 1969-79; exec. dir. Ky. Press Assn., 1979—. Served to lt. col. USAF, 1953-55, 68-69. Decorated Air Force Commendation medal. Mem. Air Force Assn., N.G. Assn., Ky. Press Assn., Council for Advancement and Support of Edn., Soc. Profl. Journalists-Sigma Delta Chi. Democrat. Presbyterian (elder). Club: Frankfort Rotary. Author: 1947-1977: Mustangs to Phantoms, 1977; editor: (cartoon book) File-13 by Coyle, 1978; editor Western Alumnus, 1970-79, Ky. Press., 1979—. Home: 202 Paul Sawyier Dr Frankfort KY 40601 Office: 63 Fountain Pl Frankfort KY 40601

ARMSTRONG, ELIZABETH LOUISE (MRS. BOB JUNIUS ARMSTRONG), lawyer; b. Houston; d. Bruno Julius and Margaret Louise (Kehr) Reich; B.A., U. Houston, 1952; m. Bob Junius Armstrong, June 28, 1952; children—Pamela Beth, Robert Paul and Cynthia Ann (twins). Admitted to Tex. bar, 1956, U.S. Dist. Court, U.S. Court of Appeals, U.S. Supreme Ct.; practice law, Lake Jackson, Tex. Mem. City of Lake Jackson Tax Equalization Bd., 1970, chmn. 1971; mem. budget and admissions com. Brazoria County United Fund, 1970; trustee Brazoria County Sch. Bd., 1972—, chmn., 1975-77; mem. Tex. State Bd. Edn., 1977—. Mem. State Bar Tex. (mem. pub. affairs com. 1971—), Brazoria County Bar Assn. (dir. 1966-68, sec., treas. 1971-72), Delta Kappa Gamma, Home: 90 Van Winkle Dr Lake Jackson TX 77566 Office: 628 Dixie Dr PO Box 124 Lake Jackson TX 77566

ARMSTRONG, ELMER E., accountant; b. Monmouth, Ill., Dec. 20, 1904; s. Elmer Ellsworth and Alice (Logan) A.; A.A., Kansas City Jr. Coll., 1921; postgrad. Centenary Coll., 1942-43; m. Ruth Marie Dale, July 25, 1925; children—Dale E., Lenora Ann (Mrs. Steve Cowel). Mem. editorial staff Kansas City Jour., 1920-22, Kansas City Kansan, 1922-25; editor Alva Record, Okla., 1922; account specialist Burroughs Adding Machine Co., 1925-45; with Smith, Cole, Armstrong & Filipowski, and predecessor, C.P.A.'s, Shreveport, La., 1945—, sr. partner, 1952—; treas. Honor Oil Co., Inc., Shreveport, 1951—. Lectr. advanced accounting Centenary Coll. of La., 1950-52, So. States Accounting Conf., Savannah, Ga., Conf. Lawyers and C.P.A.'s, U. Miss. at Hattiesburg, 1951; dean Shreveport Sch. Theology, 1968—. Mem. NCCJ, Shreveport, 1968—, dir. Speakers Bur., 1969—, chmn. Brotherhood Week, 1972; chmn. Shreveport Housing Authority, 1967-79; mem. lay adv. council Perkins Sch. Theology, So. Meth. U., Dallas. Bd. dirs. Mental Health Assn. N.W. La., 1975-76. C.P.A., La., Okla., Tex. Mem. Soc. La. C.P.A.'s (pres. Shreveport 1967-68), Am. Inst. C.P.A.'s, Shreveport C. of C., Internat. Platform Assn., Am. (dist. treas.), Shreveport (v.p. 1970-71) rose socs., Nat. Writers Club. Methodist (steward; dir. adult tchrs. 1963-66; dist. dir. adult ministries Shreveport dist. 1968—, lay del. La. Annual Conf. 1975, 77). Kiwanian (treas. 1952-56, bd. dirs. 1969-71, Shreveport), Toastmaster (dist. gov. 1952). Clubs: Shreveport Petroleum, Univ. Home: 1402 Audubon Pl Shreveport LA 71105 Office: Smith Cole Armstrong & Filipowski 800 Lane Bldg Shreveport LA 71101

ARMSTRONG, GEORGE BERT, govt. ofcl.; b. Atlanta, Aug. 21, 1939; s. Lionel and Josephine (Bell) A.; M.S.W., Fla. State U., 1967; B.A., Ga. State U., 1964; m. Mary Christine Harmon, Dec. 30, 1971; children—Travis A., Robin Christina. Supr. child welfare programs Fulton County Dept. Family and Children Services, Atlanta, 1967, vol. services dir. all programs, 1970, staff devel. supr., 1972-75; field rep. II, tng. coordinator Ga. Dept. Human Resources, Atlanta, 1975—. Mem. adv. bd. Vol. Atlanta, 1970-72, Sr. Citizens of Atlanta, 1970-72. Recipient Faithful Service award State of Ga., 1977, 79. Mem. Nat. Assn. Social Workers, Ga. Conf. Social Work, Am. Public Welfare Assn., Child Welfare League Am. Methodist. Clubs: S.E. Antique Bottle (past pres.), Nat. Button, Beer Can Collectors Am. Office: 618 Ponce de Leon Ave Atlanta GA 30308

ARMSTRONG, JERRY LOY, real estate investment counselor; b. Kannapolis, N.C., Oct. 23, 1933; s. James L. and Marie T. (Thorneburg) A.; student N.C. State U., 1952-54, U. N.C., 1954, U. Ga., 1956; m. Nancy Barger, June 3, 1952; 1 son, Kevin. Sports editor Kannapolis Daily Ind., 1955-56; state editor, sports editor Columbus (Ga.) Ledger-Enquirer Newspapers, 1958-60; editor Playground Daily News, Ft. Walton Beach, Fla., 1961-62; real estate broker, investment counselor, pres. Armstrong & Assos., Inc., Ft. Walton Beach, 1962—; v.p. Garden Properties Realty, Inc., Elgin Realty, Inc.; gen. mgr. Ft. Walton Sq. Shopping Center; owner Bayou Gazette. Served with AUS, 1956-58. Mem. Ft. Walton Beach Bd. Realtors, Pensacola Bd. Realtors, Fla. Assn. Realtors, Nat. Assn. Real Estate Bds., Nat. Real Estate Inst., Nat. Farms and Land Brokers, Am. Mgmt. Assn., Inst. Bus. Mgmt. Democrat. Lutheran. Clubs: Rotary, YMCA, Boys. Home: 218 Sotir St NW Fort Walton Beach FL 32548 Office: Suite 12 Fort Walton Sq 99 Eglin Pkwy Fort Walton Beach FL 32548

ARMSTRONG, NEWTON EELLS, indsl. mgr., systems engr.; b. E. Cleve., Jan. 6, 1919; s. Newton George and Ellen (Griswold) A.; B.A., Ohio State U., 1940; M.S., S.E. Inst. Tech., 1977; m. Carolyn Williams Little, Nov. 5, 1975; children—Newton E., Andrew M., John M. Tech. engr. in electronics IBM Corp., Endicott, N.Y., 1954-56; mgr. control div. Dresser Industries, SIE Div., Houston, research mgr. automation div.; program mgr. Gen. Dynamics, San Diego and Ft. Worth, design specialist, engring. mgmt. systems specialist, product mgr., to 1964; gen. mgr. Hunt Electronics Co., Dallas, 1965-67; mktg. mgr. Automation Tech., Dallas, 1967; salesman Carey & Asso., Houston, 1970-72; sales engr. Daniel Industries, Houston, 1972-74; program mgr. Sci Systems Inc., Houston and Huntsville, Ala., 1974, now applications engr.; instr. pipeline automation U. Tex. Extension Coll. Treas., Afton Village Civic Club, Houston, 1956-58. Served to maj. USAR, 1940-46, 1948-50, 51-53; Korea. Mem. Instrument Soc. Am. Author: Control, The Answer to Increased Pipeline Profits, 1958; contbr. articles in field to profl. jours. Home: 2021 Highridge Ave #11F Huntsville AL 35802 Office: 8600 S Memorial Pkwy Huntsville AL 35802

ARMSTRONG, PAMELA ANN, data processing exec.; b. Opelousas, La., Dec. 21, 1948; d. David Albert and Margaret Ouida (Culley) A.; B.A., U. Iowa, 1970; postgrad. DeCordova Mus. Sch., 1978-79. Promotion mgr. Witt-Armstrong Equipment Co., Hopkinton, Mass., 1970-78; store mgr. Denim Den, Bradenton, Fla., 1978-79; dept. head data processing interphase dept. Tropicana Products, Inc., Bradenton, 1979—. Mem. Am. Mgmt. Assn., U. Iowa Alumni Assn., Ringling Mus. Assn., DeCordova Mus. Assn., Jr. League Boston. Home: 706 Pearl Ave Sarasota FL 33580 Office: Tropicana Products Bradenton FL

ARMSTRONG, WALTER PRESTON, JR., lawyer; b. Memphis, Oct. 4, 1916; s. Walter Preston and Irma Lewis (Waddell) A.; A.B., Harvard U., 1938, J.D., 1941; D.C.L. (hon.), Southwestern at Memphis, 1961; m. Alice Kavanaugh McKee, Nov. 3, 1949; children—Alice Kavanaugh, Walter Preston. Admitted to Tenn. bar, 1940, practiced in Memphis, 1941—; asso. firm Armstrong, Allen, Braden, Goodman, McBride & Prewitt, and predecessors, Memphis, 1941—, partner, 1948—; commr. for Promotion Uniformity of Legis. in U.S. for Tenn., 1947-67. Mem. Tenn. Hist. Commn., 1969—; pres. bd. edn. Memphis City Schs., 1956-61; mem. Tenn. Higher Edn. Commn., 1967—, chmn., 1974-75. Served from pvt. to maj. AUS, 1941-46. Hon. French consul, 1978—. Fellow Am. Bar Found. (sec. 1960-62), Am. Coll. Trial Lawyers; mem. Am. (ho. of dels. 1952-75), Tenn. (pres. 1972-73), Memphis and Shelby County, Inter-Am., Internat. bar assns., Assn. Bar City N.Y., Am. Law Inst., Am. Judicature Soc., Nat. Conf. Commns. on Uniform State Laws (pres. 1961-63), Harvard Law Sch. Assn. (sec. 1957-58), Order of Coif, Phi Delta Phi, Scribes (pres. 1960-61), Omicron Delta Kappa. Author articles in field. Home: 1530 Carr Ave Memphis TN 38104 Office: One Commerce Sq Memphis TN 38103

ARNETT, EUGENE BRITTON, JR., dentist; b. Lexington, Ky., Nov. 1, 1929; s. Eugene and Frances (Kirk) A.; B.S., Georgetown Coll., 1951; D.M.D., U. Louisville, 1956; m. Sharkey Utley, Oct. 31, 1953; children—Eugene Britton III, Allison Sharkey, Claire Elisabeth. Pvt. practice dentistry, Louisville, 1956-60, Owens Med. Center, 1960—. Mem. Ky. Bd. Dental Examiners; v.p. Ky. State Bd. Dentistry, 1971, pres., 1972. Bd. govs. U. Louisville, 1974-78; mem. Ky. Derby Festival Com., 1977-79. Served from A/b to A/2c, USAF, 1951-52. Mem. Louisville Dist., Ky. (ho. of dels. 1976—), Am. dental assns., Am. Assn. Dental Examiners, Order Ky. Colonels, Pierre Fauchard Acad., Kappa Alpha (life), Delta Sigma Delta (life), Phi Delta. Democrat. Baptist (deacon). Clubs: Hurstbourne Country; Lions. Charter mem. Ky. Athletic Hall of Fame. Home: 2802 Lime Kiln Ln Louisville KY 40222 Office: 4122 Shelbyville Rd Louisville KY 40207

ARNETT, PENELOPE SUSAN, nurse; b. Cleve., Mar. 4, 1948; d. Raymond Harry and Nancy Margaret (Moore) Pratt; diploma Fairview Gen. Hosp. Sch. Nursing, Cleve., 1969; B.S. Nursing, Med. Coll. Ga., 1974, M.S. Nursing, 1975; m. Jerry Lorris Arnett, June 6, 1970; children—Andrea Felicia, Jay Bryan. Staff nurse Lakewood Hosp. (Ohio), 1969, St. Joseph Hosp., Augusta, Ga., 1971-74, Med. Coll. Ga., Augusta, 1975; instr. Clemson (S.C.) U., 1975-76; asst. prof. U. S.C., Aiken, 1976—. Served with Army Nurse Corps, 1968-71. Mem. Am. Nurses Assn., Ga. Nurses Assn., Sigma Theta Tau. Democrat. Roman Catholic. Home: 106 Oakhurst Dr North Augusta SC 29841 Office: 171 University Pkwy Aiken SC 29801

ARNETT, ROBERT KENNETH, urologist; b. Huntington, Tex., May 21, 1919; s. Ralph Clint and Minnie Day (Welch) A.; student Stephen F. Austin State Coll., 1937-39; student U. Tex., 1939-40, M.D., 1943; m. Alice June Holton, July 27, 1946; children—Lizabeth Len Arnett Medford, Robert Kenneth, Darwin Philip. Intern, Hermann Hosp., Houston, 1943-44, resident in surgery and urology, 1944-45, 48, 49; practice medicine specializing in urology, Lufkin, Tex., 1950—; dir. Home Savs. and Loan Assn. of Lufkin, 1959—, Lufkin Nat. Bank, 1968—. Mem. Angelina County Planning Bd., 1951; mem. Lufkin Ind. Sch. Dist. Bd. Edn., 1957-75, pres., 1960-61. Served to capt. M.C., U.S. Army, 1946-47. Diplomate Am. Bd. Urology. Mem. Angelina County Med. Soc., Am. Bd. of Med. Specialties (voting rep. 1974-77), AMA, Tex., So. med. assns., Am. Urol. Assn., S. Central sect. Am. Urol. Assn., Tex. Assn. Genito-Urinary Surgeons. Baptist. Home: 714 Pine Tree Ln Lufkin TX 75901 Office: 1113 Ellis Ave Lufkin TX 75901

ARNETTE, CHARLES BYRON, antique dealer; b. Murfreesboro, Tenn., Mar. 16, 1918; s. Charles B. and Sara Catherine (Hall) A.; student Middle Tenn. State U., 1935-36, U. Tenn., 1936-37, Watkins Inst., 1939, U. Tenn. Ext., 1947-48; m. Sara Louise Kimery, Sept. 16, 1948; children—Dana Lyne, Cheryl Lou, Patrick Ken, Lorrie Jane. Owner, Angus Packing Co., Murfreesboro, 1948-56; owner Arnette Auction Galleries, Murfreesboro, 1956—. Rutherford County rep. Mid-Cumberland Tourism Com., 1974-75; bd. dirs. Middle Tenn. Christian Sch., 1964—, chmn. bd., 1968-73. Served with AUS, 1943-46. Mem. Tenn. Auctioneers Assn. (pres. 1965-66), Murfreesboro Antique Dealers Assn. (pres. 1976-77). Home: Route 4 Murfreesboro TN 37130 Office: 300 W Castle St Murfreesboro TN 37130

ARNOLD, CLARENCE EDWARD, JR., coll. adminstr.; b. Eastville, Va., May 18, 1944; s. Clarence Edward and Nicey Edith (Press) A.; B.S., Va. State Coll., 1970, M.Ed., 1974; postgrad. Howard U., 1979—; m. Linda Eileen Arnette, June 19, 1971; 1 dau., Sherri Mignon. Home-sch. coordinator Petersburg (Va.) High Sch., 1970-71; tchr. McGuffy Edn. Center, Charlottesville, Va., 1971-72; juvenile and comestic relations counselor 16th Dist. Ct. Service Unit, Charlottesville, 1973-74; instr./coordinator audio visual services dept. J. Sargeant Reynolds Community Coll., Richmond, Va., 1974—; tchr. ednl. TV prodn. and photography Va. State U., 1977-78. Mem. Central Va. Child Devel. Bd., 1974; mem. citizens adv. council WWBT-TV, 1977; mem. adv. council WTVR-TV AM and FM, 1979—. Served with U.S. Army, 1968-70. Decorated Bronze Star; NDEA Ednl. Media Inst. for Trainers Tchrs. grantee, 1972-73. Mem. Assn. Ednl. Communications and Tech., Community Coll. Assn. Instrn. and Tech., Va. Ednl. Media Assn., Va. Television Reps. in Higher Edn., NAACP (v.p. Richmond br. 1976—, bd. mem. Va. state conf. 1978—). Roman Catholic. Club: Masons. Home: 2222 Maplewood Ave Richmond VA 23220 Office: PO Box 12084 108 E Grace St Richmond VA 23241

ARNOLD, EDNA EARLE SMITH, author; b. Cullman, Ala., Aug. 28, 1911; d. Jesse Harden and Lula Florence (Winn) Smith; A.B., Huntingdon Coll., Montgomery, 1932; m. Henry Frank Arnold, Aug. 27, 1934; children—Henry Frank, Ann Arnold. Tchr. English, Hanceville (Ala.) High Sch., 1932-34; co-editor, co-owner Cullman Tribune, 1937-68; freelance writer, Cullman, 1968—; novel: Beyond Tomorrow, 1978; editor: (with others) If Walls Could Talk, 1977. Sec. Cullman Bi-Centennial Com.; vol. ARC, Cullman; mem. Cullman County Mus. Bd., 1974—. Episcopalian. Clubs: Ala. Fedn. Women's (v.p. 1948-50), Book (past pres.), Music (past pres.), Federated (past pres.). Home: 500 5th Ave NE Cullman AL 35055

ARNOLD, FRANCES ANDERSON (ANDY), nurse; b. Donna, Tex., Aug. 8, 1918; d. Thomas Edgar and Kate Una (Beard) Anderson; R.N., McAllen Sch. Nursing, 1941; m. Ray E. Arnold, Nov. 7, 1943 (div.). Night supr. McAllen (Tex.) Hosp., 1941; office nurse, Harlingen, Tex., 1943; dir. central service Valley Bapt. Med. Center, Harlingen, 1969—. Bd. dirs. Am. Cancer Soc.; chmn. bd. dirs. RSVP (Ret. Sr. Vol. Program). Mem. Am. Nurses Assn. Tex. Nurses Assn., Dist. 14 Tex. Nurses Assn. (pres.), Tex. Soc. Central Service (bd. dirs., pres.). Republican. Mem. Christian Ch. (Disciples of Christ). Clubs: Toastmistresses (council pres., 1978), Confederate Air Force Cullpepper Angel. Home: Dixieland Manor #64 Harlingen TX 78550 Office: Valley Baptist Medical Center Box 2588 Harlingen TX 78550

ARNOLD, G(EORGE) ROBERT, title ins. exec., lawyer; b. Gary, Ind., Mar. 12, 1940; s. Floyd E. and Ruby (Roberts) A.; A.A., Orlando (Fla.) Jr. Coll., 1960 J.D., Stetson U., 1964; M.C.S., Rollins Coll., 1970; m. Flora Ann Way, July 9, 1964; children—G. Robert, G. Richard. Admitted to Fla. bar, 1964; atty. Lawyers' Title Guaranty Fund, 1964-70, v.p. legal, 1971-72, v.p. ops., 1972-74, sr. v.p., 1974—; exec. v.p. Lawyers' Title Services, Inc., 1974-78; adv. land title recordation project HUD, 1978-79. Bd. dirs. Tom Skinner Clubs, 1971—, sec., 1972—; bd. dirs. Sevilla Homeowners Assn., 1979—. Served with USAR, 1965-71. Recipient Faith in God award Orlando Jaycees, 1972. Mem. Am. Bar Assn. (exec. council real property, probate and trust law sect.), Orange County Bar Assn., Nat. Assn. Bar-Related Title Insurers (past pres.), Fla. Bar (past chmn. real property, probate and trust law sect., exec. council econs. of law sect.), Orlando C. of C. (sports com.). Republican. Clubs: North Orlando Kiwanis, Orlando Optimist (past dir., sec.). Editor The Fund Concept, 1973—. Home: 1663 Barcelona Way Winter Park FL 32789 Office: 32 W Gore St PO Box 2671 Orlando FL 32802

ARNOLD, GLEN ELDRED, mgmt. cons.; b. Shreveport, La., Nov. 4, 1931; s. Eulice Eldred and Myrtle Elizabeth (Comalander) A.; student La. Tech. U., 1949-52; B.S. in Acctg., Centenary Coll., La., 1960; postgrad. So. Meth. U., 1970; m. Delores Nickels, Aug. 15, 1952; children—David Bruce, James Rendall. Plant accountant Ark. La. Gas Co., Shreveport, La., 1955-56, jr. engr. trainee, 1956-57, asst. supr. gen. accounting dept. 1957-59; traveling auditor So. Union Gas Co., Dallas, 1960-62, methods engr., 1962-63, data systems analyst, 1963-65, compensation mgr., 1965-69; corp. dir. personnel Great Southwest Corp. and subs.'s Six Flags, Inc. and GSC Devel. Corp., Arlington, Tex., 1969-72; sr. prin. with Hay Assos., mgmt. cons.'s, Dallas, 1972—; instr. Eastfield Jr. Coll., Dallas, 1973-76. Served to sgt. U.S. Army, 1953-54. Mem. Am. Soc. Personnel Adminstrn., Dallas Personnel Assn., Am. Mgmt. Assn. (guest lectr. 1966—), Kappa Alpha, Omicron Delta Kappa, Pi Kappa Delta. Democrat. Baptist. Office: 12700 Park Central Dallas TX 75251

ARNOLD, JAMES LYNN, broadcasting co. exec. b. Marion, Ind., Sept. 20, 1946; s. Clifford Ward and Sabrah Maxyne A.; grad. U. Ariz., 1969; m. Ruth Marie Becher, July 29, 1967; children—Kristin Dyann, Jeffrey Lawton. Studio technician Sta. WTAF-TV, Marion, 1962-64; asst. news dir. Sta. WBAT, Marion, 1965; disc-jockey Sta. KTKT, Tucson, 1965-67; program dir. Sta. KHYT, Tucson, 1967-69; prodn. mgr. Sta. KHOS, Tucson, 1969-70; program dir. Stas. WGOM/WMRI, Marion, 1970-72; ops. mgr. Sta. KCUB, Tucson, 1972-78; gen. mgr. Stas. KROD/KLAQ, El Paso, Tex., 1978—. Served with N.G. USAF. Mem. El Paso Assn. Radio Stas. (dir.), Nat. Assn. Broadcasters, Jaycees, El Paso C. of C. Club: Rotary. Office: 4141 Pinnacle St #120 El Paso TX 79902

ARNOLD, LOUIS WALKER, clergyman; b. Garrard County, Ky., Jan. 17, 1914; s. Edward Lawrence and Texie Bell (Agee) A.; student So. Baptist Sem., Louisville, 1942; D.D., Pioneer Theol. Sem., 1953; student U. Ky., 1955; D.Litt., Colonial Acad., 1956. Ordained to ministry Baptist Ch., 1933; pastor Fellowship Bapt. Ch., Lexington, Ky., 1950-57, Central Bapt. Ch., Cin., 1945-47; flying pastor, preaching from airplane over powerful PA system; fgn. missionary; radio preacher on network stas.; evangelist; owner Arnold Publs., Nicholasville, Ky., 1965—; past pres. Blue Grass Bible Inst., Internat. Fellowship Fundamentalists. Ky. Col., Hon. Commr. Agr., Ky., Hon. Dep. Sheriff, Jessamine County, Adm., Cherry River Navy (W.Va.). Author: Way of Revival, 1947; God's Message for This Hour, 1944; Miracle of Israel, 1978. Composer numerous gospel songs. Contbr. articles to religious pubs. Home and Office: Route 3 Box 148-D Bethel Rd Nicholasville KY 40356

ARNOLD, LUCILLE EDNA COCKRIEL, med. group adminstr.; b. Indpls., Oct. 14, 1926; s. George W. and Cleo A. (DuChemin) C.; student Purdue U., 1944-46, Ind. U., 1946-48; m. William Arnold, June 22, 1947; 1 son, Tab. With Foster Bros., Weber, Toledo, 1957-59; gen. bookkeeper, fin. bookkeeper Ind. Bank, Ft. Wayne, Ind., 1965-68; tchr. Payne (Ohio) Elem. Sch., 1966-68; bus. mgr. Pediatrics Assos., Hollywood, Fla., 1970-77; adminstr. Internal Medicine Assos. of Hollywood (Fla.), 1977—; dir. Prudential Bank Fla.; med./bus. cons. Mem. Am. Coll. Med. Group Adminstrs., Med. Group Mgmt. Assn., Fla. Med. Group Mgmt. Assn. (past treas.). Club: Order Eastern Star. Home: 732 48th Ave Plantation FL 33317 Office: Internal Medicine Assos of Hollywood 750 S Federal Hwy Hollywood FL 33020

ARNOLD, LUTHER BISHOP, JR., research chemist; b. Duluth, Minn., Aug. 9, 1907; s. Luther Bishop and Maude (McVeety) A.; A.B., Carleton Coll., 1929; student U. Paris (France), 1926; A.M., Harvard U., 1930, Ph.D., 1933; m. Erna Andersen, Oct. 10, 1947; 1 son, Luther Kristian. Research asst. Harvard U., 1933; research chemist to group leader organic chemistry E.I. duPont de Nemours & Co., Inc., 1933-41, research supr. rayon dept., 1941-43; asst. dir. chemistry div. metall. lab. Manhattan Project, U. Chgo., 1943-45; asst. to pres. Arthur D. Little, Inc., 1945-47; pres., treas. Vikon Chem Co., Inc., Burlington, N.C., 1947—; cons. pesticide registrations, 1979—; chmn. So. Textile Research Conf., 1961, treas., 1962—, chmn. adv. bd., 1976—. Chmn. bd. dirs. Burlington Boys' Choir, 1974-77; pres. Alamance County chpt. N.C. Symphony, 1977-78. Fellow AAAS; mem. Am. Assn. Textile Chemists and Colorists (permanent mem. tech. com. research, chmn. com. antimicrobial activity), Am. Chem. Soc., ASTM. Episcopalian. Clubs: Rotary, Alamance Country. Contbr. articles to chem. jours. Patentee in field. Home: 1614 Woodland Ave Burlington NC 27215 Office: PO Box 1520 Burlington NC 27215

ARNOLD, PHILIP MILLS, chem. engr.; b. Springfield, Mo., Feb. 9, 1911; s. Anthony L. and Mary Genevieve (Hodnett) A.; B.S., Washington U., 1932, Chem. E., 1941. Chem. engr. research div. Phillips Petroleum Co., 1937-48, asst. mgr. chem. dept., 1948-50, mgr. research and devel. dept., 1950-64, v.p. research and devel., 1964-76. Mem. Nat. Acad. Engring., Indsl. Research Inst. (pres. 1964-65), AAAS, Coordinating Research Council (dir. 1964-75, pres. 1969-71), Internat. Union Pure and Applied Chemistry (mem. bur. 1969-75, exec. com. 1971-75), World Petroleum Congress (mem. permanent council 1965-71, com. on scholarly communication with Peoples Republic of China 1976-79). Address: Box 1457 Bartlesville OK 74003

ARNOLD, PHILLIP HAYES, sound engr., producer; b. Knoxville, Tenn., July 13, 1942; s. Harold H. and Icesy (Hayes) A.; music student U. Tenn., 1960-62; student U.S. Army Signal Sch., 1964; m. Mary Ellen Davis, June 19, 1971; 1 son, Jason Phillip. Musician and leader The Deltas, rock group, 1960-63; asst. in charge of stacks Tenn. State Library, 1963-64; specialist E-5 U.S. Army Dept. Def. Info. Sch.,

Indpls., 1964-67; sound engr. TV Radio and Film Commn. of Methodist Ch. (name later changed to United Meth. Communications), Nashville, 1967-77; free lance sound engr., 1977—; co-producer film Minnie Remembers; producer country music, including: You Don't Have to Be a Baby to Cry; Poor Wilted Rose; tchr. rec. Nashville State Tech. Inst. Served with U.S. Army, 1964-67. Mem. Nashville Assn. Musicians, Am. Fedn. Musicians, Nat. Acad. Rec. Arts and Scis., Country Music Assn., Soc. Motion Picture and TV Engrs., Audio Engring. Soc. Episcopalian. Home: 206 Acklen Park Dr Nashville TN 37203

ARNOW, HERBERT IRVING, aerospace engr.; b. Lithuania, Oct. 12, 1912; s. Samuel and Sarah (Sharenson) A.; came to U.S., 1919; B.S. in Engring., Northeastern U., 1935; m. Ruth Dorothy Davidoff, July 4, 1944; - children—Lenore Phillipa, Robert Lewis. Design engr. Gen. Elec. Co., Lynn, Mass., 1937-41; naval architect U.S. Navy Dept. Subship, Quincy, Mass., 1941-46; aero. engr. U.S. Naval Air Systems Command, Bethpapge, N.Y., 1953-62, Norfolk, Va., 1962-79; instr. engring. Hofstra Coll., 1958. Certified fallout shelter analyst Dept. Def. Mem. Am. Def. Preparedness Assn. Address: 2611 NW 56th Ave Lauderhill FL

ARNOW, WINSTON EUGENE, fed. judge; b. Micanopy, Fla., Mar. 13, 1911; s. Joseph Leslie and Mabel (Thrasher) A.; B.S. in Bus. Adminstrn., U. Fla., 1932, J.D., 1933; m. Frances Day Cease, Jan. 11, 1941; 1 dau., Ann. Admitted to Fla. bar, 1933; research clk. Supreme Ct. Fla., 1934; gen. practice, Gainesville, Fla., 1935-42; mem. firm Clayton, Arnow, Duncan, Johnston, Clayton & Quincey, Gainesville, 1946-67; judge U.S. Dist. Ct., No. Dist. Fla., Pensacola, 1968—, chief judge, 1969—; chmn. steering com. Fla. Civil Practice Before Trial. Served to maj. AUS, 1942-46. Recipient Distinguished Alumni award U. Fla., 1972. Fellow Am. Coll. Probate Counsel; mem. Am. Bar Assn., Fla. Bar, Am. Law Inst., Soc. Bar 1st Jud. Circuit, Am. Judicature Soc., Order of Coif (hon.), Scabbard and Blade, Fla. Blue Key, Sigma Phi Epsilon, Phi Delta Phi, Tau Kappa Alpha, Phi Delta Epsilon. Clubs: Pensacola Country, Pensacola Rotary. Contbr. articles to profl. jours. Office: US Dist Ct PO Box 12347 Pensacola FL 32581

ARNWINE, DON LEE, hosp. adminstr.; b. Ponca City, Okla., Oct. 2, 1932; B.Sc., Central State U., Okla., 1957; M.S. in Hosp. Adminstrn., Northwestern U., 1959; hon. doctorate Morris Harvey Coll., 1974; m. Norma Arnwine; children—Devon, Andrea. Resident U. Colo. Med. Center, 1958-59, adminstrv. asst., 1959-60, asst. dir. hosps., 1960-61, dir. hosps., 1961-72; pres. Charleston (W.Va.) Area Med. Center, 1972—. Served with M.C., U.S. Army, 1953-55. Fellow Am. Coll. Hosp. Adminstrs.; mem. Am. (del.-at-large 1971-74, 75-77, Council on Legis. 1977—), W.Va., Colo. (pres. 1969) hosp. assns. Office: Charleston Area Med Center 1210 Elmwood Ave Box 1547 Charleston WV 25326

ARONOV, OWEN WILLIAM, real estate exec.; b. Montgomery, Ala., Oct. 23, 1951; s. Aaron Morris and Marjorie (Schoenbaum) A.; B.S. in Bus. Adminstrn., U. Ala., 1974; M.B.A., Cert. real estate, So. Methodist U., 1975. Propr. Aronov Realty Co., shopping center devel. and mgmt., Montgomery, 1975—; also dir. numerous affiliated cos.; chmn. real estate com. U. Ala. Bd. dirs. Ala. Kidney Found., Montgomery Kidney Found., 1978—, Montgomery Family Guidance Center, 1977—; v.p. Jewish Fedn. Montgomery. Mem. Montgomery Bd. Realtors (dir.), Ala. Realtors Assn. (chmn. polit. action com.), U. Ala. Commerce and Exec. Soc., Beta Gamma Sigma, Omicron Delta Kappa. Jewish. Home: 630 Plymouth St Montgomery AL 36103 Office: Aronov Realty Co PO Box 1951 Montgomery AL 36106

ARRINGTON, EDWARD LEE, JR., banker; b. Bassett, Va., Aug. 18, 1946; s. Edward Lee and Mollie Elizabeth (Frye) A.; certificate in accounting Denville Community Coll., 1967; certificate Am. Inst. Banking, 1974; B.A. in Sociology, Asbury Coll., Wilmore, Ky., 1973; preliminary tchrs. cert. Evang. Tchrs. Tng. Assn., 1977; grad. Sch. for Bank Adminstrn., U. Wis., 1980; m. Brenda Faye Eanes, June 25, 1966; children—Angela Kay, Eric Lee. Ins. agt. Interstate Life & Accident Ins. Co., 1967-68; with Valley Veneer Co., Inc., Bassett, Va., 1968; with Frye Oil Corp., Bassett, 1968-69, dir., 1970—, v.p., 1970—; computer programmer Bassett Furniture Industries, Inc., 1969, Mid-State Financial Corp., Lexington, Ky., 1970-73; asst. ops. officer Piedmont Trust Bank, Martinsville, Va., 1973—. Div. co-chmn. Martinsville United Fund, 1975; Christian edn. dir., 1973-79, Sunday sch. tchr., mem. bd. Clearview Wesleyan Ch., Martinsville, ch. sec., 1978—; active Va. dist. Wesleyan Ch. Am.; treas. Clearview Sch. PTA, 1979-80. Home: 801 Ainsley St Martinsville VA 24112 Office: PO Box 4751 Martinsville VA 24112

ARRINGTON, LANCE HARDY, quality mgmt. cons.; b. Columbus, Ga., Oct. 16, 1938; s. Clarence Hardy and Virginia Madge (Tucker) A.; B.E.E., Ga. Tech. U., 1961; postgrad. managerial economics N.C. State U., 1968-70; m. Geraldine Carol Burks, Sept. 11, 1960; children—Elaine Camille, Tracy Lynn. Sr. engr. ITT Telecommunications, Raleigh, N.C., 1964-65, mgr. engring. adminstrn., 1965-66, mgr. product engring., 1966-68, quality dir., 1968-70, mgr. quality engring. ITT European Hdqrs., Brussels, 1972-77, dir. quality ITT Fed. Electric Corp., Paramus, N.J., 1977-78, dir. quality ITT Telecommunications Tech. Center, Shelton, Conn., 1978-79; dir. quality Gen. Datacom Industries, Westport, Conn., 1970-72; pres. Philip Crosby Assos., Winter Park, Fla., 1979—; internat. lectr. quality mgmt. Recipient Ring of Quality award ITT, 1976. Mem. Am. Soc. Quality Control, Eta Kappa Nu. Home: 1208 Alexa Dr Winter Park FL 32789 Office: 201 W Canton Ave Winter Park FL 32789

ARRINGTON, ZARA PITTMAN, food service adminstr.; b. Coffeeville, Miss., Jan. 8, 1917; d. James Richard and Dora Ann (Bobbitt) Pittman; student Water Valley Nursing Sch.; cert. food service supr. U. N.D., 1976; children—Bobby Gene, Margaret Ann, Larry Dean, Martha Fay, Ralph Pittman. Dir. food service Calhoun County Hosp., Bruce, Miss., 1951-65; owner, mgr. Bruce Motel Restaurant, 1965-67; dir. food service Yalobusha Gen. Hosp., Water Valley, Miss., 1968—, Yalobusha County Nursing Home, 1973—. Pres., PTA, 1950, Bruce Fine Arts Club, 1957. Mem. Bruce C. of C., Bruce Mchts. Assn. Baptist. Club: Eastern Star (worthy matron 1955-56). Author: Zara's Cookbook. Home: PO Box 334 Bruce MS 38915 Office: PO Box 728 Water Valley MS 38965

ARSENAULT, ALBERT JOSEPH, JR., educator; b. Berlin, N.H., July 20, 1927; s. Albert Peter and Mathylda (Lemieux) Arseneau; B.S. in Bus. Adminstrn., Boston Coll., 1952, M.A., 1958, M.B.A., 1970; m. Beatrice Juliette Labonte, Aug. 14, 1954; children—Richard, Denis. Tchr. French and Latin, Randolph (Mass.) Public Schs., 1957-70; instr. econs. N.H. Coll., Manchester, 1970-71; prof. acctg. Hillsborough Community Coll., Tampa, Fla., 1971—, chmn., 1972-78; tax cons. Moteland Hotel and small businesses. Treas. Maritime Found.; bd. dirs. Consumer Inc. Served with USMC, 1952-55. Mem. Am. Accounting Assn. (tax div., jr. coll. div., chmn. Fla. mems., coordinator jr. coll. div.), Am. Mgmt. Assn., Am. Fedn. Teachers-NEA (treas. coll. chpt., active collective bargaining, 1976-78), Phi Beta Kappa (hon., chpt. sponsor). Democrat. Roman Catholic. Club: K.C. Speaker public hearings against Fla. Power Co., radio and TV against fuel shortage. Home: 1556 Belleair Rd Clearwater FL 33516 Office: Hillsborough Community College PO Box 22127 Tampa FL 33622

ARSUAGA, ANIBAL L., mcht.; b. Old San Juan, P.R., Sept. 25, 1918; s. Luis and Carmen (Casellas) A.; B.A., U. P.R., 1949; m. Zayda Llenza, May 26, 1967; children—Anibal, Maria de Lourdes, Angel R., Zayda Sanchez. Office mgr. Armco Internat. Corp., San Juan, 1941-43; mgr. advt. dept. P.R. World Jour., San Juan, 1943-44, staff writer, 1944-45; legal translator Translation Bur., P.R. Legislature, 1945-47; indsl. salesman Ulpiano Casal, Inc., San Juan, 1947-50, treas., gen. mgr., 1950-56; pres. Annibal L. Arsuaga, Inc., Hato Rey, P.R., 1956—, Arsuaga & Santana, Inc., Hato Rey, 1957—, Arblas Indsl. Supplies, Hato Rey, 1959—, Polychems., Inc., Trujillo Alto, P.R., 1962-71; mem. advisory council SBA, 1969. Founder, pres. Asociacion Puertorriquena de Empresarios Cristianos, 1962; v.p. Aspira de P.R., 1976-77; bd. dirs. United Fund P.R., 1973—, Am. Cancer Soc., 1976—; steering com. U. Cayey, 1977—. Named Small Bus. Person of Year, SBA, 1976. Mem. Asociacion de Comerciantes en Materiales de Construccion (pres. 1965), C. of C. P.R. (sec., dir. 1974-75, 1st v.p. 1975-76, pres. 1976-77), Mech. Contractors Assn. P.R., Water Pollution Control Assn. (affiliate), Home Builders Assn. P.R. (affiliate), Gen. Contractors Assn. P.R. (affiliate), Mrs. Assn. P.R. (affiliate), Sales and Mktg. Assn. San Juan (hon.), Ateneo de P.R., Art Student League San Juan, Phi Sigma Alpha. Roman Catholic. Home: 93 Romerillo St Santa Maria Rio Piedras PR 00927 Office: GPO Box 71326 San Juan PR 00936

ARTHUR, BRADLEY DOUGLAS, sculptor; b. Tampa, Fla., July 20, 1953; s. Donald Morton and Sandra Carrol (Esrick) A.; apprentice with Hugh Dumont, Coconut Grove Sch. Art, 1970; student U. South Fla., 1971-75, Sarah Lankiance Coll., France, 1977; apprentice Yasuo Mizui, France, studio of Silverio Palio, Italy, 1979. Sculpture exhibited Hollywood (Fla.) Mus., 1971, Avery Fisher Hall, Lincoln Center, N.Y.C., 1978, 79, Lynnkottler Galleries, N.Y.C., 1978, 79, N.Y. U., 1979, N.Am. Sculpture Exhbn., Golden, Colo., 1979, Pietrasanta, Italy, 1979; founder metal sculpture program Miami Beach (Fla.) High Sch., 1971, Be-Art, art co., 1976; innovator Found-Objects Assemblege in sculpture; copyrighted sculpture was design logo for ABC and Olympics, 1976, stone carving King and Queen, 1977; creative cons. firms N.Y.C., Fla., and abroad; condr. seminars in field. Recipient award Lincoln Center, 1978, Spontaneous Patience award Tampa Bay Art Center, 1977. Office: 207 E Davis Blvd Tampa FL 33606

ARTHUR, SUSAN, librarian; b. nr. Pineville, Ky.; d. John M. and Lettie (McKeehan) Arthur; student Cumberland Coll., 1932-34; A.B., Berea Coll., 1936; B.S. in L.S., U. Ky., 1948. High sch. tchr. English and social studies, Pineville, 1937-41; high sch. librarian, 1941-48; asst. librarian Henderson State Tchrs. Coll., Arkadelphia, Ark., 1951-52; asst. librarian Union Coll., Barbourville, Ky., 1952-54; tchr. English, Barbourville High Sch., 1954-56; serials librarian, instr. library sci. Berea Coll., 1956-60; classified librarian in tech. manuals Transp. Research Center, U.S. Army, Ft. Eustis, Va., 1960-61; librarian, Barbourville City Schools, 1969—. Mem. pub. library bd. for Knox County, 1953-55. Mem. AAUW (local br. pres. 1965-67), AAUP, Garden Club of Ky. (Mt. Laurel dist. dir. 1975-77). Mem. Disciples of Christ Ch. Clubs: Barbourville, Garden (pres. 1969-74, dist. dir. 1975—). Home: 601 N Main St Barbourville KY 40906

ARTHUR, WILLIAM JAMES, coll. dean; b. Lynchburg, Va., Aug. 12, 1930; s. Leonard C. and Mary B. Arthur; student Lynchburg Coll., 1951-53; B.S.B.A., U. Va., 1955, M.B.A., 1957, D.B.A., 1969; m. Barbara Ann Bailey, Aug. 18, 1952; children—Stephen M., Susan C., David S. Pres., Dornin-Adams Co., Lynchburg, 1963-65; v.p. Lynchburg Coll., 1965-71; chmn. dept. acctg. U. No. Fla., 1971-75; dean Coll. Bus. Adminstrn., Tenn. Tech. U., 1975—; dir. bank; cons. in field. Served with USN, 1949-51. Mem. Am. Acctg. Assn., So. Bus. Adminstrn. Assn. (dir., sec.-treas.), Phi Kappa Phi, Beta Gamma Sigma, Omicron Delta Kappa. Methodist. Author: A Financial Planning Model for Private Colleges, 1972; contbr. articles to profl. jours.

ASCHERL, JOHN LAWRENCE, elec. engr.; b. N.Y.C., May 19, 1931; s. Anthony Peter and Rose Ellen (Gabrini) A.; B.S., U.S. Mcht. Marine Acad., 1955; m. Margaret Barone, Sept. 15, 1956; children—Nancy Ann, Michael John, Laura, Steven Eric. Engr., United Fruit Co., 1955-56; div. engr. Tex. Bd. State Hosps. and State Schs., 1956-60; design engr. B. Segal Jr. Cons., Austin, Tex., 1960-61; chief engr. Powell Elec. Mfg. Co., Houston, 1961-63; v.p. Engineered Elec. Equipment Co., Houston, 1964-70; mgr. mktg., elec. div. Hutchinson Hayes Internat. Co., Houston, 1970-73; pres. Elec. Power Systems Internat., Houston, 1973-79, H S Power Systems Inc., Houston, 1979—; sr. exec. Hawker Siddeley Power Engring., U.K., 1979—. Pres. PTA, 1969-71. Served to comdr. USNR, 1951-79. Lic. marine engr. Mem. IEEE. Republican. Roman Catholic. Home: 5316 Valerie St Bellaire TX 77401 Office: 8850 Katy Freeway Suite 118 Houston TX 77024

ASH, MARY KAY WAGNER (MRS. MELVILLE JEROME ASH), cosmetic co. exec.; b. Hot Wells, Tex.; d. Edward Alexander and Lula Vember (Hastings) Wagner; student U. Houston, 1942-43; m. Melville Jerome Ash, Jan. 6, 1966; children—Marylyn (Mrs. Robert Cates), Ben Rogers, Richard Rogers. Mgr., Stanley Home Products, Houston, 1939-52; nat. tng. dir. World Gift Co., Dallas, 1952-63; founder, chmn. Mary Kay Cosmetics, Inc., Dallas, 1963—. Mem. chancellor's council U. Tex. Recipient Bus. Woman of Yr. award Assn. for Corp. Growth, 1977, Cosmetic Career Woman of Yr. award, 1978, Dale Carnegie Leadership award, 1978, Ky. Gov.'s Ambassador of Good Will award, 1978; named Hon. Citizen, Bardstown, Louisville. Mem. Bus. and Profl. Women's Club. Office: 8787 Stemmons Freeway Dallas TX 75247

ASH, MICHAEL LEE, coll. adminstr.; b. Bradford, Pa., Sept. 29, 1952; s. Paul M. and Ann M. (Hayes) A.; B.A. in Edn., Oral Roberts U., 1974; M.Guidance and Counseling, Tulsa U., 1980; m. Beth Carol Gilliland, May 9, 1974. Instr. phys. edn. Oral Roberts U., 1974-76, dir. intramural sports, 1974-79, dean men, dir. housing, 1976—. Bd. dirs. Tulsa Youth for Christ; Tchr. Sunday sch. Central Assembly, Tulsa. Recipient Outstanding Service award Oral Roberts U., 1974, Youth for Christ Service award 1976. Mem. Am. Personnel and Guidance Assn., Okla. Personnel and Guidance Assn., Okla. Ofcls. Assn., U.S. Jaycees, Phi Beta Delta. Republican. Home and Office: 7777 S Lewis St Tulsa OK 74171

ASH, THOMAS GRAY, bank exec.; b. Casper, Wyo., July 6, 1939; s. Kenneth John and Marion Gertrude (Gray) A.; B.A., Stanford U., 1962; M.B.A., U.S.C., 1975; m. Arlayne Marie Plutte, May 1, 1965; children—Christopher Joseph, Timothy Kenneth. Sr. systems analyst System Devel. Corp., Santa Monica, Calif., 1965-67; asst. div. mgr., market planning div. Wilbur Smith & Assos., Cola, S.C., 1967-70; v.p., data processing dir. First Nat. Bank of S.C., Columbia, 1970—; adj. prof. U. S.C., 1977-78. Served with USAF, 1962-65. Decorated Air Force Commendation medal. Mem. adv. bd. Cardinal Newman High Sch., 1979—; v.p. East Columbia Dixie Youth Baseball Commn., 1978—. Mem. Am. Bankers Assn. (edn. com.), S.C. Bankers Assn. (chmn. ops. com.), Data Processing Mgmt. Assn., Assn. Systems Mgrs. Republican. Roman Catholic. Clubs: Wildewood Country, Hunting Creek Swim and Racquet (pres. 1976-77). Home: 108 Steeplechase N Columbia SC 29209 Office: First National Bank of South Carolina 1628 Browning Rd Columbia SC 29210

ASHBAUGH, LAWRENCE LLOYD, educator; b. Warren, Pa., Dec. 20, 1941; s. Frank Harold and Bertha (Johnson) A.; B.S. Ed., Clarion State Coll., 1964; M.Ed., Pa. State U., 1966, Ed.D., 1969. Spl. edn. tchr. Bellwood (Pa.) Antis High Sch., 1964-65; work study tchr. Loysville (Pa.) Youth Devel. Center, 1966-67; asso. prof. spl. edn. Western Mich. U., Kalamazoo, 1969-75; asso. prof. U. Tulsa, 1975—; due process hearing officer State of Okla., 1978—. Bd dirs. Respite Care Program for Handicapped, 1975—. U.S. Dept. Edn. fellow, 1965-66, 67-69. Mem. Okla. Assn. Children with Learning Disabilities (child protection and advocacy team 1978—), Am. Assn. Mental Deficiency, Council Exceptional Children, Am. Ednl. Research Assn., Assn. Children with Learning Disabilities, Am. Assn. Edn. Severely/Profoundly Handicapped, Phi Delta Kappa. Office: Sch Edn U Tulsa Tulsa OK 74104

ASHBY, EUGENE CHRISTOPHER, chemist, educator; b. New Orleans, Oct. 25, 1930; s. Anthony and Ida A.; B.S., Loyola of the South, 1951; M.S., Auburn U., 1953; Ph.D., U. Notre Dame, 1956; m. Carolyn Turner; children—Chris, Steve, Terry, Marie, Julie, Angie, Rachael. Research chemist Ethyl Corp., Baton Rouge, 1956-63; asst. prof. chemistry, now Regents prof. Ga. Tech. U., Atlanta, 1963—. Recipient Lavoisier medal French Chem. Soc., 1971; Sloan fellow, 1965-67; Guggenheim fellow, 1978-79. Mem. Am. Chem. Soc., Sigma Xi. Roman Catholic. Contbr. articles to sci. jours. Office: Sch Chemistry Ga Tech Atlanta GA 30332

ASHBY, JOHN EDMUND, JR., mktg. exec.; b. Dallas, Mar. 5, 1936; s. John Edmund and Lillian Eloise (Cox) A.; B.B.A., U. Tex., 1957; m. Martha Caroline Isabel de Larios, June 25, 1975; children—Nancy Suzanne, Shelley Bickham, Elizabeth Ann, Vicki Suzanne Anderson, Dana Elizabeth Strickland. Salesman, IBM, Corpus Christi, 1959-63, San Antonio, 1963-64; mktg. mgr. St. Louis Recognition Equipment Inc., Dallas, 1964-67, v.p. mktg. N.Am., Japan, 1967—. Served with USMCR, 1957-59. Recipient Sales award IBM, 1964. Mem. Sales and Mktg. Execs. Inc. (award 1961), Beta Theta Pi. Republican. Presbyn. Club: Royal Oaks Country. Home: 3429 Cornell Ave Dallas TX 75205 Office: PO Box 22307 Dallas TX 75222

ASHBY, RANDOLPH WILLIAM, air force officer, meteorologist; b. Sebring, Fla., May 18, 1943; s. William Kenneth and Betty Anne (Lane) A.; B.S. in Chemistry (Honors at Entrance), U. Calif. at Davis, 1965; Meteorologist Certification, U. Okla., Norman, 1967; M.S. in Meteorology, U. Wis., Madison, 1972, Ph.D. in Meteorology; distinguished grad. Air Force Inst. Tech. Program, 1976; children—Karen E., Kevin M. Commd. 2d. lt. U.S. Air Force, 1966, advanced through grades to maj., 1977, served wing weather officer, K.I. Sawyer AFB, Mich., 1967-70, staff meteorologist to Air Force Flight Test Center, Edwards AFB, Calif., 1972-74, staff weather officer Dept. Defense, Los Angeles AFS, 1976-79, Air Command and Staff Coll., Maxwell AFB, Ala., 1979—. Pres. bd. dirs. Edwards Preschool, Inc., 1973-74, Eagle Scout, Boy Scouts Am. Named Outstanding Jr. Officer of Yr., 3d. Weather Wing, 1969; NSF research gratnee, 1972-75. Mem. Am. Meteorol. Soc., Air Force Assn., U. Calif. Alumni Assn. (life), U. Wis. Alumni Assn. (life), Sigma Xi. Home: 3836 Governors Dr A-203 Montgomery AL 36111 Office: ACSC/EDO-1 Maxwell AFB AL 36112

ASHCRAFT, RONALD EUGENE, jewelry co. exec.; b. Hertha, Kans., Oct. 1, 1936; s. Willis Vaughn and Fannie Mae (Archer) A.; A.A., Pueblo Coll., 1956; B.Mus.Ed., U. Colo., 1958; certificate in diamonds Gemological Inst. Am., 1970; m. Joy Hill, Dec. 29, 1974; 1 son, Brian Eugene; 1 dau. (by previous marriage), Julie. Tchr. pub. schs., Monte Vista, Colo., 1958-59, Denver-Adams County, 1960-63, Denver-Ashcraft Piano Studios, 1960-69; engaged in piano sales and service, Denver, 1963-69, Dallas, 1969-72; owner, pres. Ronald Ashcraft Assos., Inc., Dallas, 1973—. Served with U.S. Army, 1959. Mem. Diamond Dealers Club N.Y., Jewelers Bd. Trade (asso.). Clubs: Park Cities Rotary, Brookhaven Country, Lancers. Office: 334-3 World Trade Center PO Box 58157 Dallas TX 75258

ASHCRAFT-GINGRICH, CAROLYN WOLFE, psychologist; b. Waxhaw, N.C.; d. John Carl and Carolyn Leola (Ray) Wolfe; B.S., U. N.C.; M.A., then Ph.D., George Peabody Coll., Nashville, 1963; m. Tom Ashcraft; children—Anne Carolyn, Thomas Wolfe; m.2d, Gerald Gingrich. Mem. faculty Tenn. State U., 1966-67, U. Tenn., 1967-69, LaSalle Coll., Phila., 1969-72, U. Pa., 1970-75; psychologist Thomas Jefferson U., Phila., 1974, Overbrook Sch. Blind, Phila., 1975, Fla. Sch. Deaf and Blind, 1976-78, Human Devel. Center, Newport Richey, Fla., 1978-79; pvt. practice psychology, Tampa; faculty U. Tampa, 1979—, leader workshops in edn. psychology. Bd. dirs. St. Augustine (Fla.) Assn. Mental Retardation, 1976-77. Lic. psychologist, Tenn., Pa., cert., Fla.; mem. Nat. Register Health Providers in Psychology. Fellow Pa. Psychol. Assn.; mem. Am. Psychol. Assn., Southeastern Psychol. Assn., Fla. Psychol. Assn. Author papers in field, manual in gen. psychology. Home: 8808 Bay Point Dr 107B Tampa FL 33615 Office: U Tampa FL also 718 Buffalo Ave Tampa FL

ASHCROFT, WENDY JANE, educator; b. Urbana, Ill., Mar. 5, 1953; d. Samuel Clemens and Ethel English (Thompson) A.; B.A., Southwestern at Memphis, 1975; postgrad. Memphis State U., 1976—. Tchr. mentally retarded Shelby County Schs., Memphis, 1975—, asst. dir. Camp Shenandoah, Winchester, Va., 1976-79. Certified water safety instr., first aid instr., CPR instr. ARC. Mem. Council for Exceptional Children, Found. for Exceptional Children, Am. Assn. Mental Deficiency, Nat. Assn. for Retarded Citizens, Tenn. Assn. for Retarded Citizens, Memphis-Shelby County Assn. for Retarded Citizens (pres. 1979—), NEA, Tenn. Edn. Assn., Shelby County Edn. Assn., Mortar Bd., Alpha Omicron Pi. Home: 5654 Los Gatos Dr Apt 2 Memphis TN 38118 Office: 2085 Cordes Rd Germantown TN 38138

ASHE, VICTOR HENDERSON, lawyer, state senator; b. Knoxville, Tenn., Jan. 1, 1945; s. Robert Lawrence and Martha (Henderson) A.; B.A. in History, Yale U., 1967; J.D., U. Tenn., 1974. Admitted to Tenn. bar, 1977; partner firm Morton, Lewis & Krieg, Knoxville, 1977—; mem. Tenn. Ho. of Reps., 1968-74; mem. Tenn. Senate, 1975—; mem. East Tenn. Devel. Dist. Bd., 1975—. Named Outstanding Young Man of Yr., Tenn. Jaycees, 1976. Mem. Knoxville Urban League, E. Tenn. Heart Assn. Republican. Baptist. Club: Civitan. Office: PO Box 1382 Knoxville TN 37901

ASHER, FRED M., counseling psychologist; b. Ranger, Tex., July 12, 1948; s. J.B. and Maxine (Jacoby) A.; B.S., U. Tex.; M.S., East Tex. State U., Ph.D., 1977; m. Deborah Lynne Collins, Aug. 31, 1975. Asst. instr. U. Tex., 1972-73; resident counselor East Tex. State U., Commerce, 1973-74; univ. counselor Tex. A. and I. U., Kingsville, 1974-75; dir. counseling and student devel. U. Dallas Grad. Sch., 1977—; pvt. practice counseling psychology, psychol. and psychometric cons.; clin. dir. PsyCore Inst. for Human Relations. Mem. Am. Psychol. Assn., Tex. Psychol. Assn., Am. Personnel and Guidance Assn., Psi Chi, Sigma Delta Pi (pres.), Phi Delta Kappa.

Democrat. Research and publs. in field. Home: 6817 John Dr Fort Worth TX 76118 Office: Univ of Dallas-Braniff Dallas TX 75061

ASHER, VERNON, justice of peace; b. Rio Vista, Tex., Feb. 10, 1915; s. James Washington and Pattie Eva (Stratton) S.; student public schs., Joshua, Tex.; m. Dovie King, Aug. 1, 1978. Justice of peace, Cleburne, Tex., 1964—. Served with inf. U.S. Army, 1942-46; ETO. Decorated Purple Heart, Bronze Star. Democrat. Baptist. Clubs: Elks, Odd Fellows, 40 and 8. Home: PO Box 1532 Cleburne TX 76031

ASHINGTON-PICKETT, MICHAEL DEREK, constrn. co. exec.; b. London, Oct. 11, 1931; s. Edward Robert and Mary Dorothy (Trewhella) Ashington-Pickett; came to U.S., 1965, naturalized, 1971; Civil and Structural Engring. degrees London U., 1956; m. Sandra Helen Smart, Nov. 20, 1976; children—Mary Hillary, Michael Derek II. Constrn. mgr. various firms in Eng., 1956-63; pres. So. Precast Holdings, London, Eng., 1963-65, Ashington-Pickett Constrn. Corp., Inc., Orlando, Fla., 1965—, Country Side Properties, Inc., Orlando, 1972—; chmn. Orlando Constrn. and Licensing Bd., 1974; lectr. for Brit. Council, 1963-65. Served as officer Brit. Army, 1950-52; Korea. Recipient Distinguished Service award Orange County Bicentennial Commn., 1976. Mem. home builders assns. Am. (past dir.), Mid-Fla. (pres., dir.; Disting. Service award 1973), Fla. (past dir.), Orlando Jaycees, Sommeller Guild. Mem. Ch. of Eng. Clubs: Kiwanis, Citrus. Home: 1307 Malcolm St Orlando FL 32806 Office: PO Box 20252 Orlando FL 32814

ASHKAR, FUAD SALAMAH, physician, educator; b. Broumana, Lebanon, June 13, 1935; s. Salameh A. and Helen (Mufarij) A.; came to U.S., 1962, naturalized, 1972; B.S., Am. U. of Beirut (Lebanon), 1958, M.D., 1962; m. Theresa Nelson, May 31, 1968; children—Anda Theresa, Alexander Fuad. Intern Am. U. Hosp., Beirut, Lebanon, 1961-62; resident Jackson Meml. Hosp., Miami, and NIH, 1962-68; instr. medicine U. Miami (Fla.), 1968-69, instr. radiology, medicine, 1969-71, asst. prof., 1971-74, asso. prof., 1974—; staff physician Jackson Meml. Hosp., Miami, 1968—, dir. nuclear metabolic sect. and radio assay lab., 1968—; staff physician Mt. Sinai Hosp., Miami, 1968—. Decorated Medal of the National Order of the Cedars Chevalier Rank (Lebanon). Mem. A.A.A.S., AMA, Am. Diabetes Assn., Soc. Nuclear Medicine, Am. Thyroid Assn., Endocrine Soc., Fla. Assn. Nuclear Physicians (pres.), Am. Coll. Nuclear Medicine, Alpha Omega Alpha. Author: Practical Nuclear Medicine, 1974; A Study Guide in Nuclear Medicine, 1975; Thyroid and Endocrine System Investigation with Radionuclides and Radioassays, 1979; contbr. articles to profl. jours. Patentee in field. Home: 6500 SW 79 Ct Miami FL 33143 Office: 1700 NW 10th Av Miami FL 33136

ASHLER, PHILIP FREDERIC, cons.; b. N.Y.C., Oct. 15, 1914; s. Philip and Charlotte (Barth) A.; B.B.A. cum laude, St. John's Coll., 1935; M.B.A., Harvard, 1937; postgrad. Indsl. Coll. Armed Forces, 1956; Sc.D., Fla. Inst. Tech., 1969; LL.D., U. West Fla., 1969; m. Jane Porter, Mar. 4, 1942 (dec. 1968); children—Philip Frederic, Robert Porter, Richard Harrison; m. 2d, Elise Barrett Duvall, June 21, 1969; stepchildren—Richard Edward Duvall, Jeffries Harding Duvall. Enlisted USMCR, 1932; commd. ensign U.S. Navy, 1938, advanced through grades to rear adm., 1959; dir. Office of Small Bus., Dept. Def., Washington, 1948-51; mem. joint staff Joint Chiefs of Staff, Washington, 1957-59; ret., 1959; dir. devel. Pensacola Jr. Coll., 1960-68; vice chancellor adminstrn. State U. System Fla., Tallahassee, 1968-70, exec. vice chancellor, 1970-75; treas. State of Fla., 1975-76, also ins. commr., state fire marshal; advisor for econ. devel. Gov. of Fla., 1977; sec. of commerce, 1977-79; pres. Philip F. Ashler & Assos., Tallahassee, internat. trade and devel., 1979—; rep. NATO Sci. Session, W.Ger., 1973; mem. Inter-Am. Congress on Psychology, Bogota, Colombia, 1974; guest lectr. U. Belgrade (Yugoslavia), 1973; mem. Dist. Export Council, U.S. Dept. Commerce, 1978—. Mem. Fla. Edn. Council, 1967-68, Fla. Council of 100, 1976—; commr. from Fla., Edn. Commn. of States, 1967-68; mem. legis. advisory council So. Regional Edn. Bd., 1966-68; chmn. Fla. Civil Def. Advisory Council, 1966-69; mem. State Bd. Ind. Colls. and Univs. Fla.; mem. Select Council on Post-High Sch. Edn., 1967-68; chmn. bd. Fla. Council Internat. Devel. Mem. Fla. Ho. of Reps., 1963-68. Treas. Internat. Cardiology Found., 1973-78; bd. dirs. Fla. Heart Assn., 1963—, chmn., 1969-71; chmn. Fla. Med. Liability Ins. Commn., 1975-76; bd. dirs. Am. Heart Assn., 1971-76, LeMoyne Art Found., Tallahassee, Tallahassee Meml. Hosp., Internat. Cardiology Fedn., Geneva, 1974-78; dir. U.S. Fidelity and Guaranty Co., Balt., Fidelity & Guaranty Life Ins. Co., Balt., Lewis State Bank, Tallahassee. Decorated Bronze Star with Combat V; recipient Kiwanis Internat. Disting. Service award, 1965; Am. Heart Assn. Disting. Service award, 1965, 71, Disting. Achievement medal, 1975; St. Petersburg Times Legislative award, 1967. Mem. Nat. Assn. Ins. Commrs. (vice chmn. exec. com. 1976, chmn. com. valuation bonds and other securities 1975-76), Fla. C. of C. (chmn. internat. bus. com.), Internat. C. of C. (U.S. council 1979—), S.E. U.S.-Japan Assn. (vice chmn.), Kappa Delta Pi. Democrat. Episcopalian (lay reader). Mason (32 deg., Shriner), Rotarian. Clubs: Capital City Country (dir.), Fla. Econs. (Tallahassee), Capital City Tiger Bay (bd. chmn.) (Tallahassee); Curzon House (London). Home: 2115 E Randolph Circle Tallahassee FL 32312 also 11 Riad Sultan Kasbah Tangier Morocco

ASHLEY, BILLY HILTON, chemist; b. Shreveport, La., Sept. 24, 1930; s. Joe and Thedis Beatrice (Leone) A.; B.A., Baylor U., 1951; M.L.A., Southern Methodist U., 1972; m. Patriica Anne Petty, Sept. 30, 1970; children—Daniel Hilton, Billy Hilton, Douglas Marlon, Brian K., Brenda K. Chief engr. Gulf Coast Mud Co., 1956-58; founder, pres. President Labs., Inc., Shreveport, La., 1958-62; drilling engr. Analytical Logging Co., Tyler, Tex., 1962-67; plant chemist LaGloria Oil & Gas Co., Tyler, 1967—; cons. chemist East Tex. Testing Labs. and Gas Services, Inc., Tyler, 1973—. Mem. chemistry text book com. Tyler Ind. Sch. Dist., 1968; election judge, Republican, Presdl. election, 1976; head swim coach, 8 and under, AAU, Shreveport, 1960-62. Hon. lt. col. Ala. Militia. Mem. Am. Ordnance Assn., Am. Chem. Soc., Smith County Hist. Soc., Am. Petroleum Inst., Am. Inst. Mech. Engrs. Episcopalian. Clubs: Tyler Swim. Home: Route 6 Box 329-D Tyler TX 75704 Office: Box 840 Commerce and McMurry Sts Tyler TX 75710

ASHLEY, CARL THOMAS, chemist; b. Lexington, Ky., Apr. 13, 1941; s. Carl Thomas and Thelma Elizabeth (Bowles) A.; A.B., Transylvania Coll., 1963; M.S., Marshall U., 1967; m. Linda Marie Ramsey, June 30, 1963; children—Lara Claire, David Porter. Chemist, Ashland Oil & Refining Co. (Ky.), 1964-66; dir. math. Math. and Sci. Center, Richmond, Va., 1968-69; devel. chemist IBM, Lexington, Ky., 1969; speaker Internat. Conf. Organic Coatings Sci. and Tech., Athens, Greece, 1978. Recipient Public Service award, 1974, Disaster Service award ARC, 1977. NSF fellow, 1963; Ashland Oil fellow, 1967. Mem. Am. Chem. Soc., Am. Radio Relay League, Blue Grass Amateur Radio Club (pres. 1974-75), Holleian Soc. Mensa. Mem. Christian Ch. (Disciples of Christ). Home: 591 Cricklewood Dr Lexington KY 40505 Office: 740 New Circle Rd Lexington KY 40511

ASHLOCK, JAMES ROBERT, airline exec.; b. Baird, Tex., Dec. 3, 1932; s. Ralph and Frances Elizabeth (Cochran) A.; B.A. in Journalism, Tex. A & M U., 1954; M.A., Columbia U., 1957; m. Elizabeth Louise Scott, Aug. 8, 1959; children—Mary Frances, William Ralph, Jennifer Scott. News editor Pecos (Tex.) Enterprise, 1954-55; state editor San Angelo (Tex.) Standard, 1955-56; reporter Kansas City (Mo.) Star, 1957-60; pub. relations specialist TWA, N.Y.C., 1960-62; transport editor Aviation Week and Space Tech., N.Y.C., Washington, 1962-66; pub. relations specialist Eastern Airlines, Washington, Miami, 1966—. Asst. All-Americans council Democratic Nat. Com., 1968; pres. Colonial Dr. Citizens Assn., 1978-79. Mem. Fla. Engring. Soc. (mem. pub. relations adv. com. 1972—), Aviation Space Writers Assn. (dir. 1973-74), Greater Miami Aviation Assn. (pres. 1976-77), Greater Miami C. of C. (exec. bd. 1976—). Home: 15600 Palmetto Club Dr Miami FL 33157 Office: Eastern Airlines Miami Internat Airport Miami FL 33148

ASHMAN, LEE EARLE, computer co. exec.; b. Norwalk, Conn., Sept. 27, 1929; s. William Earle and Lucy Smith (Hall) A.; B.S., U.S. Naval Acad., 1952, postgrad., 1958-59; m. Rita Marie Todd, July 4, 1958; children—Therese, Rita, William, Michael, Mary, Christina. Commd. ensign USN, 1952, advanced through grades to lt. comdr., 1962; served in USS Remey, 1952-56, USS Pursuit, 1956-57; with Office Chief Naval Ops., 1959-60; served in USS Dealey, 1961-62, USS Dash, 1962-63; with Naval Command Systems Support Activity, 1963-67; engring. mgr. Logicon, Inc., Falls Church, Va., 1968-71; dist. marketing mgr. System Devel. Corp., Falls Church, 1972-73; dir. corporate devel. Techplan Corp., Falls Church, 1973-76; pres. Sci. Analysis and Research Corp., Vienna, Va., 1975—; mktg. mgr. Semcor, Inc., Arlington, Va., 1976—. Mem. IEEE, Assn. Computing Machinery, Clark's Crossing Homes Assn. (pres., dir. 1976—), Assn. Old Crows, Mensa, S.A.R. Contbr. articles profl. jours. Home: 9807 Peppermill Pl Vienna VA 22180 Office: 2341 Jefferson Davis Hwy Arlington VA 22202

ASHTON, GUY THEODORE, sociologist-anthropologist, educator; b. Gainesville, Fla., Feb. 25, 1941; s. Jonathan R. and Myra M. (Knettle) A.; A.B., Grinnell Coll., 1963; M.A., U. Ill., 1968, Ph.D., 1972; m. Ruth Urrego de Ashton, Sept. 12, 1967; children—Juan Enrique, Mayra Alicia. Fulbright lectr. (asst. prof.) dept. anthropology U. Los Andes, Bogota, Colombia, 1969-71; asst. prof. dept. sociology and anthropology InterAm. U., Hato Rey, P.R., 1972-75, asso. prof., 1977—; asst. prof. dept. anthropology Northeastern Ill. U., Chgo., 1975-77. NSF grantee, 1968-70. Fellow Am. Anthropology Assn., Soc. for Applied Anthropology; mem. Soc. Colombiana de Antropologia, Current Anthropology, Caribbean Studies Assn. Editorial bd. Revista/Review Interamericana, 1978—. Home: 1001 Fordham St Univ Gardens Rio Piedras PR 00927 Office: PO Box 1293 Hato Rey PR 00919

ASHTON, SAMUEL COLLIER, research exec.; b. Hohenwald, Tenn., Sept. 26, 1922; s. Arch Will and Lula Earle (Collier) A.; student Tenn. Poly. Inst., 1938-40; B.S. in Elec. Engring., U.S. Naval Acad., 1945; m. Rita Jane Anderson, Oct. 18, 1947; 1 son, Craig Collier. Head cryogenic lab. Texaco Co., Long Beach, Calif., 1947-48; asst. dir. fin., bus. and facilities, phys. sci. div. Stanford Research Inst., Menlo Park, Calif., 1948-59; corp. v.p. fin., procurement and facilities Research Triangle Inst., Research Triangle Park, N.C., 1959—. Served to ensign, USN, 1945-47. Mem. Am. Defense Preparedness Assn. (chmn. Carolinas chpt., 1955). Republican. Episcopalian. Club: Hope Valley Country (Durham, N.C.). Participant in orgn. and devel. of Research Triangle Inst., campus and bldgs. Home: 3104 Buckingham Rd Durham NC 27707 Office: Research Triangle Park NC 27709

ASHWORTH, CHARLES CLAYTON, broadcasting co. exec.; b. Mt. Vernon, Ind., Nov. 12, 1927; s. Charles Fredrick and Faye Henrietta (McCarty) A.; grad. in bus. mgmt., LaSalle Extension U., Chgo., 1958; m. Maria Luisa Bono, Apr. 21, 1978; children by previous marriage—Denise Jean, Clayton Charles. Acct. exec. Sta. WABB, Mobile, Ala., 1962-64; sr. acct. exec. Sta. WSGN, Birmingham, Ala., 1964-71; sales mgr. Sta. WRBC, Jackson, Miss., 1971-72; gen. sales mgr. Sta. WVOL, Nashville, 1972-73; broadcast sales cons. Educasting Systems Inc., N.Y.C., 1973, Sta. WMCV-TV, Nashville, 1973-79; exec. v.p. Taber Broadcasting Co., El Paso, 1974—, also asst. sec. Bd. dirs. Am. Heart Assn., El Paso, 1974—. Served with U.S. Maritime Service, 1944-46. Mem. Tex. Assn. Broadcasters, El Paso C. of C., Nat. Fedn. Independent Bus. Clubs: Downtown Lions (named Lion of Month (3) 1974, Outstanding Lion 1976-77). Office: 5710 Trowbridge St El Paso TX 79925

ASHWORTH, KENNETH HAYDEN, ednl. adminstr.; b. Abilene, Tex., Feb. 24, 1932; s. Harold Laverne and Mae Beatrice (Grote) A.; B.A., U. Tex., 1958, Ph.D., 1969; M. Pub. Adminstrn., Syracuse U., 1959; children—Rodney Brian, Karen Grace. Asst. commr. coordinating bd. Tex. Coll. and Univ. System, Austin, 1965-69, commr. higher edn., 1976—; vice-chancellor for academic affairs U. Tex. System, Austin, 1969-73; exec. v.p. U. Tex. at San Antonio, 1973-76; mem. commn. on colls. So. Assn. Colls. and Schs. Served with USN, 1951-55. Mem. Philos. Soc. of Tex., Sembradores de Amistad, Phi Beta Kappa, Phi Delta Kappa, Phi Kappa Phi, Pi Sigma Alpha. Democrat. Unitarian. Clubs: Rotary, Town and Gown. Author: Scholars and Statesmen, 1972; American Higher Education in Decline, 1979. Home: 6631 Valleyside Rd Austin TX 78731 Office: PO Box 12788 Austin TX 78711

ASKEW, REUBIN O'DONOVAN, govt. ofcl., former gov. Fla.; b. Muskogee, Okla., Sept. 11, 1928; s. Leo and Alberta (O'Donovan) A.; B.S. in Public Adminstrn., Fla. State U., 1951; LL.B., U. Fla., 1956; postgrad. Denver U.; LL.D. (hon.), Fla. So. Coll., Lakeland, 1972, U. Notre Dame, 1973, U. Miami, 1975, U. West Fla., 1978, Barry Coll., Miami, 1979; D.P.A. (hon.), Rollins Coll., Winter Park, Fla., 1972; L.H.D., Eckerd Coll., St. Petersburg, Fla., 1973, Stetson U., Deland, Fla., 1973, Bethune-Cookman Coll., 1975, St. Leo (Fla.) Coll., 1975; m. Donna Lou Harper, Aug. 11, 1956; children—Angela Adair, Kevin O'Donovan. Admitted to Fla. bar, 1956; practice law, Pensacola, Fla., 1956-70, partner firm Levin, Askew, Warfield, Graff and Mabie, 1958-70; asst. county solicitor Escambia County (Fla.), 1956-58; mem. Fla. Ho. of Reps., 1958-62; mem. Fla. Senate, 1962-70, pres. pro tem, 1969, 70; gov. Fla., 1971-79; partner firm Greenberg, Traurig, Askew, Hoffman, Lipoff, Quentel & Wolff, P.A., Miami, 1979; apptd. Pres.'s U.S. trade rep., Washington, 1979—; chmn. Edn. Commn. of States, 1973, Select Commn. Immigration and Refugee Policy, 1979; vice chmn. So. Govs. Conf., 1973-74, chmn., 1974-75; chmn. Nat. Democratic Govs. Conf., 1976-77, Nat. Govs. Conf., 1977, 78; chmn. So. Growth Policies Bd., 1977—; chmn. Presdl. Adv. Bd. Ambassadorial Appointments, 1977-79. Past pres. Western div. Children's Home Soc. Fla., Pensacola Oratorio Soc.; bd. dirs. City of Hope; past mem. state exec. com. Fla. Tb and Health Assn.; keynote speaker Democratic Nat. Conv., 1972. Past pres. bd. dirs., past mem. state exec. com. Fla. Assn. for Retarded Children; past bd. dirs. Pensacola YMCA, United Fund, Heart Assn. Served with AUS, 1946-48, to capt. USAF, 1951-53. Recipient John F. Kennedy Profiles in Courage award B'nai B'rith, 1971; Nat. Wildlife Fedn. award, 1972; Outstanding Conservationist of Yr. award Fla. Audubon Soc., 1972; Herbert H. Lehman Ethics award, 1973; Gen. William Booth award Salvation Army, 1973; John F. Kennedy award Nat. Council Jewish Women, 1973, Herbert Harley award Am. Judicature Soc., 1975; Theodore Roosevelt award, 1975; vis. Chubb fellow Yale U., 1976; vis. fellow Harvard U., 1979; Leadership Honor award Am. Inst. Planners, 1978; medal of honor Fla. Bar Found., 1979; Disting. Community Service award Brandeis U., 1979. Mem. Am. Bar Assn., Dade County Bar Assn., Fla. Bar, Am. Judicature Soc. (dir. 1979—), Am. Legion, Phi Alpha Delta, Delta Tau Delta, Alpha Phi Omega. Democrat. Presbyn. (elder). Mason (Shriner), Rotarian. Home: 9855 SW 89 Ct Miami FL 33176 Office: US Trade Rep 1800 G St NW Suite 712 Washington DC 20506

ASKINS, PANSY MCCAULEY, telephone co. exec.; b. Greenville, S.C., Jan. 2, 1905; d. William Henry and Anna Robert (Fowler) McCauley; B.S., Limestone Coll., 1929; m. Harold William Askins, Dec. 5, 1931; children—Hannah Cauley Askins Lancaster, Harold William. Tchr., Blue Ridge Mission Sch., nr. Stuart, Va., 1929-30, Pleasant Retreat Sch., Greenville County, S.C., 1930-31; v.p., sec. Chesnee Telephone Co. (S.C.), 1932-65, pres., chmn. bd., 1965—. Treas., 1st Baptist Ch. of Chesnee, 1932-36, pres. woman's missionary union, 1936-37. Limestone Coll. scholar, 1925-26. Mem. S.C. Ind. Telephone Assn., Nat. Telephone Co-op. Assn., Palmetto Ind. Telephone Pioneer Club, Alumni Assn. Limestone Coll., Sr. Citizens of Greenville and Spartanburg County, N. Greenville Jr. Coll. Alumni Assn. Clubs: Rose Garden (pres. 1969-70, v.p. 1978-79), Chesnee Women's. Home: 205 N Alabama Ave Chesnee SC 29323 Office: 208 S Alabama Ave Chesnee SC 29323

ASTIN, WILLIAM LINDEN, JR., mfg. co. exec.; b. Danville, Va., Apr. 15, 1936; s. William Linden and Myrtle Irene (Brown) A.; B.A. in Chemistry, Lenoir Rhyne Coll., N.C., 1956; M.S. in Bus. Edn., U. Richmond, 1964; m. Norma Anne Ellis, May 28, 1956; children—LeAnne Ellis, Wade Linden. Chemist, Allied Chem. Corp., Hopewell, Va., 1956-62, market research analyst, N.Y.C., 1962, product devel. mgr., 1962-64; mgr. market research Mobil Chem. Co., Richmond, Va., 1964-65, mgr. planning and budgets, 1965-69, mgr. mktg. services, 1969-70; corp. devel. and planning asso. Reynolds Internat., Richmond, 1970-72; v.p. corp. div. Copolymer Rubber and Chem. Corp., Baton Rouge, 1972-75; mgr. planning and analysis Freeport Minerals Corp., Uncle Sam, La., 1975-79, mgr. adminstrn., New Orleans, 1979—. Mem. Chem. Mktg. Research Assn. Republican. Unitarian. Club: Southwood Racquet. Home: 1346 Havenwood Dr Baton Rouge LA 70815 Office: Freeport Queensland Nickel Co New Orleans LA 70161

ASTLER, VERNON BENSON, physician; b. Wyoming, Ohio, Sept. 5, 1925; s. Vernon Wolfert and Blanche (Benson) A.; student Miami U., 1943-45; M.D., Temple U., 1949; M.S., U. Mich., 1953; m. Louise Menge, Aug. 9, 1949 (div.); children—Kim Louise, Kristy Lee, Douglas Vernon; m. 2d, Diane Rosacker, Dec. 31, 1969. Intern Univ. Hosp., Ann Arbor, Mich., 1949-50, resident, 1950-57; practice medicine, specializing in surgery, Boynton Beach, Fla., 1958—; mem. staff Bethesda Hosp., Boca Raton Hosp., Doctors Hosp., Lake Worth, Fla.; chmn. bd. Pinco Ins. Co., Fla. Physicians Ins. Reciprocal. Mem. Fla. State Bd. Med. Examiners (pres. 1971-73). Mem. Fla. Council of 100. Served with M.C. AUS, 1953-55. Diplomate Am. Bd. Surgery. Fellow A.C.S., Southeastern Surg. Congress; mem. Am. Hosp. Assn. (com. on physicians 1974-76), Fla. Med. Assn. (gov. 1971—, pres. 1975-76), Frederick A. Coller Surg. Soc., A.M.A., Delray Beach C. of C., Sigma Nu, Phi Chi. Mason (Shriner), Kiwanian. Clubs: Little (Gulfstream, Fla.); Sapphire Valley Country (N.C.); Quail Ridge Tennis (Boynton Beach, Fla.); Hunter's Run Golf and Tennis. Home: 3268 N Ocean Blvd Gulfstream FL 33444 Office: Med Arts Center 2800 S Seacrest Blvd Boynton Beach FL 33435

ATCHLEY, BOBBIE JOYCE, nurse; b. Bradley County, Tenn., June 20, 1935; d. Johnnie Bob and Mazie Annas (Whaley) Woody; licensed practical nurse, 1960; A.Nursing cum laude, Cleveland (Tenn.) State Community Coll., 1976; m. William L. Atchley, Aug. 24, 1957; children—Richard Stephen, William Leon. Staff nurse Bradley Meml. Hosp., Cleveland, Tenn., 1961-64, charge nurse, 1974—; office nurse Ivan C. Humphries, Jr. M.D., Cleveland, 1964-74; past mem. Tenn. Mid-South Regional Med. Program, Tenn. Med. Malpractice Rev. Bd. Mem. Am., Tenn. (sec. Dist. 14) nurses assns. Democrat. Baptist. Home: 1104 Key St NW Cleveland TN 37311

ATHERTON, JAMES CHRISTIAN, educator; b. Bolivar, La., Aug. 4, 1915; s. James G. and Mary (Matthews) A.; B.S., La. State U., 1935, M.S., 1947; Ed.M., U. Ill., 1949, Ed.D., 1950; m. Ruth Victoria Cash, Nov. 26, 1937; children—James Christian, George A., Ruth V. Tchr., Loranger (La.) High Sch., 1935-42, 45-46, prin., 1946-48; prof. agrl. edn. U. Ark., Fayetteville, 1950-65, La. State U., Baton Rouge, 1965—. Pres. tchr. tng. sect. So. Regional Conf. Agrl. Edn., 1957-58; v.p. So. Agrl. Edn. Conf., 1971-72. Served to lt. col. U.S. Army, 1942-45. Recipient Distinguished Service award in agrl. edn. So. Regional Conf. Agrl. Edn., 1962; outstanding service citation, Nat. Vocat. Agrl. Tchrs. Assn., 1968; hon. state farmer degree, Ark., La. Future Farmers Am., 1955, 67. Mem. Am. Vocat. Assn., Nat. Vocat. Agr. Tchrs. Assn., Am. Assn. Tchr. Educators in Agr. (editor Jour. 1966-70), Alpha Tau Alpha (nat. 1st v.p. 1965-69), Phi Kappa Phi, Alpha Zeta, Gamma Sigma Delta, Phi Delta Kappa. Democrat. So. Baptist. Co-author Essential Aspects of Career Planning and Development, 2d edit., 1977; editor Ark. Service Bull., 1955-65; regional editor Agr. Edn. mag., 1955-62, 64-80; contbr. articles to profl. jours. Home: 5099 S Pollard Pkwy Baton Rouge LA 70808

ATHERTON, JAMES EARL, paper co. exec.; b. Leesburg, Fla., Aug. 31, 1939; s. Louis James and Minnie Frances (Watson) A.; m. Wanda Gladys Dahl, Nov. 1, 1975; 1 dau., Wendy Ann. Sales engr. Lummus Cotton Gin Co., Columbus, Ga., 1959-61; sales service mgr. Internat. Paper Co., Houston, 1961-64; salesman Eccor Corp., Houston, 1964-66; salesman Moore Paper Co., Houston, 1966-69, sales mgr., 1969-71, gen. sales mgr., 1971-75, exec. v.p. sales and mktg., 1975—. Mem. Nat. Paper Trades Assn., Internat. Bus. Forms Industries, Assn. Ind. Corrugated Convertors. Home: 15811 Fleetwood Oaks Houston TX 77079 Office: Moore Paper Co 100 Hogan St PO Box 805 Houston TX 77001

ATKINS, CARL CLYDE, fed. judge; b. Washington, Nov. 23, 1914; s. Carl Clyde and Marguerite Agnes (Criste) A.; student U. Miami, 1931-32; J.D., U. Fla., 1936; m. Esther M. Castillo, Jan. 18, 1937; children—Julie Atkins Landrigan, Carla Atkins Schulte (dec.), Carl Clyde. Admitted to Fla. bar; practice law, Stuart, Fla., 1936-41, Miami, Fla., 1941-66; judge U.S. Dist. Ct. So Dist. Fla., Miami, 1966—. Pres., Archdiocesan Council Catholic Men, 1958-69. Trustee Biscayne Coll., Miami, Mercy Hosp., Miami; adminstrv. bd. Barry Coll., Miami. Recipient Outstanding Catholic award NCCJ, Fla. region, 1959. Mem. Fla. Bar (pres. 1960-61), Am. (ho. of dels. 1961-66), Dade County (pres. 1954-55) bar assns., Phi Alpha Delta, Phi Kappa Tau. Clubs: Miami; Coral Gables Country. Contbr. articles to legal jours. Home: 2040 Country Club Prado Coral Gables FL 33134 Office: US Dist Ct US Courthouse 300 NE 1st Ave Miami FL 33101

ATKINS, HANNAH DIGGS, state legislator Okla.; b. Winston-Salem, N.C., Nov. 1, 1923; d. James T. and Mabel (Kennedy) Diggs; B.S., St. Augustine's Coll., 1943; B.L.S., U. Chgo., 1949; postgrad. Oklahoma City U., 1963-64, U. Okla., 1968; m. Charles N. Atkins, May 24, 1943; children—Edmund Earl, Charles N., Valerie Ann. Reporter Winston-Salem Jour. and Sentinel, also tchr. French, Atkins (N.C.) High Sch., 1945-48; research asst. biochemistry MeHarry Med. Sch., 1948-49; reference librarian Fisk

U., 1949; sch. librarian Kimberley Park Elementary Sch., Winston-Salem, 1950-51; br. librarian Oklahoma City Pub. Libraries, 1953-56; reference librarian Okla. State Library, 1962-63, chief gen. reference div., acting law librarian, 1963-68; mem. Okla. Ho. of Reps., 1968—, mem. from 97th Dist., 1973—, chairperson mental health and retardation com. Instr. law Oklahoma City U.; instr. library sci. U. Okla.; reference librarian Library USA, N.Y. World's Fair, 1964. Mem. task force early childhood edn. Edn. Commn. States; past pres. Vis. Nurse Assn., Oklahoma City; mem. exec. bd. Community Action Program, Oklahoma City. Del. nat. assembly Nat. Black Polit. Conv., 1972, 74; mem. Okla. Women's Caucus, 1972; chairperson Okla. Black Polit. Caucus, 1972—; mem. exec. com. Nat. Conf. State Legislatures, 1976; chmn. Nat. Assn. Black Women Legislators, 1976—; mem. Dem. Nat. Com., 1976—. Mem. nat. and regional exec. bd. Family Ser. Assn. Am. Named Outstanding Soror, Midwest region Alpha Kappa Alpha, 1965; Woman of Year, Theta Sigma Phi, 1968; Southwestern Regional Citation award Phi Delta Kappa, 1976; named Nat. Pub. Citizen of Yr., Nat. Assn. Social Workers, 1975; Woman of Yr., Shawnee chpt. NOW, 1976. Mem. ALA, Am. Assn. Law Librarians (past pres. Southwestern chpt.), N.A.A.C.P., Urban League (Community Service award Oklahoma City 1977), Jack and Jill Am. (past regional dir.), Links, Phi Beta Kappa, Alpha Kappa Alpha. Democrat. Home: Route 4 Box 799 Oklahoma City OK 73111 Office: Room 334 State Capitol Oklahoma City OK 73105

ATKINS, ORIN ELLSWORTH, oil co. exec.; b. Pitts., June 6, 1924; s. Orin E. and Dorothy (Whittaker) A.; student Marshall U., Huntington, W.Va., 1942-43, 46-47, LL.D., 1970; student U. Pa., 1943-44; LL.B., U. Va., 1950; m. Kathryn Agee, Nov. 25, 1950; children—Randall, Charles. Admitted to W. Va. bar, 1950, Ky. bar, 1952; with Ashland Oil & Refining Co. (Ky.), 1950—, exec. asst., 1956-59, adminstrv. v.p., 1959-65, pres., chief exec. officer, 1965-72, chmn. bd., chief exec. officer, 1972—, dir.; dir. Cin. br. Fed. Res. Bank Cleve., 1968-71. Served with AUS, 1942-46. Mem. Am., W.Va., Ky. bar assns., Conf. Bd. Presbyn. Office: 1409 Winchester Ave Ashland KY 41101

ATKINSON, BRUCE ERROL, physician; b. Greenwood, Miss., Dec. 21, 1946; s. Errol Ward and Mabel (Blackwell) A.; B.S., U. Miss., 1968, M.D. magna cum laude, 1971; m. Sandra Faye Parkinson, Dec. 27, 1969; 1 son, George Michael. Intern, Parkland Meml. Hosp., Dallas, 1971-72; resident in internal medicine Univ. Hosp., Jackson, Miss., 1972-75, chief resident, 1974-75; practice medicine specializing in internal medicine, Amory, Miss., 1975—, Tupelo, Miss., 1979—. Diplomate Am. Bd. Internal Medicine. Chmn. deacons 1st Baptist Ch., Amory, 1977-78. Mem. Miss. Med. Assn. (jud. council 1977—), Miss. Soc. Internal Medicine (pres. 1979—), A.C.P. Club: Rotary. Home: Route 2 Box 343-A Amory MS 38821 Office: PO Box 119 Amory MS 38821

ATKINSON, EVELYN ROREX, architect; b. Panhandle, Tex., Dec. 29, 1931; d. Joe and Lydia (Lill) Rorex; student West Tex. State Coll., 1949-50; B.Arch., Tex. Technol. Coll., 1955; married; 2 stepchildren. Draftsman, designer to campus landscape architect Tex. Technol. Coll., 1953-55; draftsman, designer Parks and Recreation Dept., Lubbock, Tex., 1953-55, Atcheson, Atkinson and Cartwright, architects and engrs., Lubbock, 1955-71; partner Atcheson, Atkinson, Cartwright and Rorex, architects and engrs., Lubbock, 1971-74, Atkinson, Atkinson & Assos., architects, 1975—. Bd. dirs. Lubbock Cultural Affairs Council, 1971-76. Registered architect, Tex. Mem. A.I.A. (corporate; Outstanding Grad. Student award Panhandle chpt. 1955, treas. 1970), Alpha Chi. Democrat. Methodist. Home: 3201 29th St Lubbock TX 79410 Office: 1214 14th St Lubbock TX 79401

ATKINSON, JUNE MARGARET, physician; b. Coventry, Eng., Oct. 20, 1932; d. Sydney and Margaret Ina Birch; came to U.S., 1968, naturalized, 1973; M.D., Welsh Nat. Sch. Medicine, Cardiff, Wales, 1956; children—Rachel Sian Henllan-Jones, Rhiannon Mari Henllan-Jones; m. John W. Atkinson, Dec. 1978. Intern in gen. medicine, gen. surgery, and psychiatry, Wales and Eng., 1956-59; gen. practice medicine, Cardiff, Wales, 1959-63, Jamaica, B.W.I., 1963-68; resident in obstetrics and gynecology Beth Israel Hosp., Boston, 1968-72; physician for ambulatory obstet. and gynecol. services Volusia County (Fla.) Health Dept., 1972-75; dir. Lake County Pub. Health Dept., Tavares, Fla., 1975—. Bd. dirs. Lake County chpt. Am. Cancer Soc. Diplomate Am. Bd. Obstetrics and Gynecology. Fellow Am. Coll. Obstetricians and Gynecologists; mem. Brit., Fla. med. assns., Lake County Med. Soc., Am., Fla. (pres. 1979-80) pub. health assns., Fla. Assn. County Health Officers, Audubon Soc., Am. Forestry Assn. Club: Hillhouse Bath and Tennis. Home: 3B Bunker Hill St Mount Dora FL 32757 Office: 421 W Main St Tavares FL 32778

ATKINSON, JUNE ST. CLAIR, educator; b. Bedford, Va., Aug. 19, 1948; d. Clarence William and Emily Catherine St. Clair; B.S., Radford (Va.) Coll., 1969; M.S. in Edn., Va. Poly. Inst. and State U., Blacksburg, 1974. Bus. edn. tchr., Roanoke County (Va.), 1969-72; coop. office occupations coordinator Mecklenburg County, Charlotte, N.C., 1972-76; chief cons. bus. edn. N.C. Dept. Public Instnr., Raleigh, 1976—; part-time instr. Internat. Mgmt. Council, Charlotte, 1973-76; cons. in field. Mem. Adminstrv. Mgmt. Soc. (internat. chmn. edn./bus. interaction com. 1979-80), Nat. Bus. Edn. Assn., Am. Vocat. Assn., N.C. Bus. Edn. Assn., N.C. Vocat. Assn., So. Bus. Edn. Assn., N.C. Employees Assn. Republican. Baptist. Editor curriculum materials. Home: 1134 Collington Dr Cary NC 27511 Office: 100 W Edenton St Raleigh NC 27611

ATKINSON, MARJORIE FAGEN, librarian; b. Ormond Beach, Fla., June 3, 1917; d. William H. and Ruth Marie (Seabloom) Fagen; B.A., La. State U., 1940; M.A., Fla. State U., 1956; children—Judith R., T. Prescott, John L., William R. Asst. librarian Montgomery County (Ala.) Library, 1956-57; librarian Huntingdon Coll., Montgomery, 1957-58, Air University Library, Maxwell AFB, Ala., 1959—, library historian, 1967—. Mem. Spl. Libraries Assn., Ala., Southeastern library assns., Beta Phi Mu, Phi Kappa Phi, Phi Alpha Theta, Phi Sigma Iota, Sigma Delta Pi. Episcopalian. Home: 636 Ponce De Leon Ave Montgomery AL 36106 Office: Air U Library Maxwell AFB AL 36112

ATKINSON, WILLIAM JAMES, JR., internist; b. Mobile, Ala., July 4, 1917; s. William J. and Gertrude C. (Smith) A.; B.A., Amherst Coll., 1939; M.D., U. Pa., 1943; M.S. in Internal Medicine, St. Louis U., 1949; m. Glenda E. Street, Oct. 29, 1949; children—Glenda Street, Regina Creswell, William James III. Intern, Phila. Gen. Hosp., 1943-44; resident in medicine St. Louis City Hosp., 1946-48; resident in cardiology St. Louis U., 1948-49; practice medicine specializing in internal medicine and cardiology, Mobile, Ala., 1949—; mem. staff Mobile Gen. Hosp., 1949—, chmn. dept. medicine, 1958-69; mem. staff Mobile Infirmary, Providence Hosp.; chmn. bd. Diagnostic and Med. Clinic, P.A., 1973—; clin. asso. prof. medicine U. Ala., 1964—; asso. prof. medicine U. So. Ala., 1973—. Served as capt. M.C., U.S. Army, 1944-46. Decorated Bronze Star medal. Diplomate Am. Bd. Internal Medicine, Am. Bd. Cardiovascular Disease. Fellow A.C.P., Am. Coll. Cardiology, Am. Coll. Chest Physicians; mem. Am., Ala. (chmn. bd. 1956) heart assns., AMA, Am. Soc. for Clin. Pharmacology and Therapeutics, Mobile C. of C. Republican. Episcopalian. Clubs: Rotary, Mobile County, Mobile Yacht (Mobile). Home: 3965 Byronell Ct Mobile AL 36609 Office: 1217 Government St Mobile AL 36604

ATNIP, MICHAEL GRANT, ins. co. exec.; b. Ft. Worth, July 8, 1948; s. Reuben Roy and Elsie Jean A.; B.A. in Math., U. Tex., Austin, 1971; postgrad. U. Tex., Arlington, 1973-74; M.B.A., Baylor U., 1977; m. Betty Ann Ebarb, Feb. 17, 1973; children—Michael Grant, Melanie Dawn. Mgmt. trainee Southland Life Ins. Co., Dallas, 1971-73, systems analyst, 1973-75; adminstrv. asst. to v.p. adminstrn. Am.-Amicable Life Ins. Co., Waco, Tex., 1975-76, mgr. policy issue, 1976, mgr. adminstrv. systems, 1976-78, asst. v.p. adminstrv. systems and planning, 1978-80, v.p. adminstrv. systems and planning, 1980—. Campaign worker Downtown Dallas YMCA, 1973-74, United Way, Waco, 1976. Served with USAFR, 1970-76. Fellow Life Mgmt. Inst.; mem. Life Office Mgmt. Assn., S.W. Systems Devel. Com., Beta Gamma Sigma, Sigma Iota Epsilon. Baptist. Club: Lake Oaks Country (Waco). Office: Am-Amicable Life Ins Co 425 Austin Ave Waco TX 76701

ATON, JAMES KEYES, JR., physician; b. St. Petersburg, Fla., Feb. 13, 1933; s. James Keyes and May (Griffith) A.; student U. Fla., 1950-52; B.A., Emory U., 1954; M.D., U. Md., 1958; m. Margaret Joan Hall, Nov. 21, 1956; children—Keyes, Herbert, Randy, Tracy. Intern, Med. Coll. Hosp., Charleston, S.C., 1958-59; resident, U. Md., Balt., 1959-62; practice medicine specializing in dermatology, Salisbury, Md., 1963-65; with VA, Balt., 1965-67; commd. capt. U.S. Army, 1968, advanced through grades to col., 1974; chief dermatology Eisenhower Army Med. Center, Augusta, Ga., 1974—; asst. prof. dermatology Med. Coll. Ga., Augusta, 1974—. Recipient "A" Profl. Designator award (certificate of achievement), Dept. Army, 1978. Mem. AMA, Am. Acad. Dermatology, Balt. City and Md. med. socs. Episcopalian. Home: 3615 Bermuda Circle W Augusta GA 30909 Office: Dermatology Clinic DDEAMC Ft Gordon GA 30905

ATWILL, JOSEPH HARVEY, JR., radiologist; b. Florence, S.C., Nov. 10, 1923; s. Joseph Harvey and Blanche Susan (Taylor) A.; B.S., U. S.C., 1944; M.D., Med. U. S.C., 1947; m. Pauline Garr Fillingim, Sept. 5, 1945; children—Beth Lee, Joseph Harvey, James Steven, Pauline Bailey. Intern, Med. Center, Jersey City, 1947-48; resident Roper Hosp., Charleston, S.C., 1951-54; gen. practice medicine, Columbia, S.C., 1948-49; radiologist Orangeburg (S.C.) Regional Hosp., 1954—; pres. Radiology Assos., Orangeburg, 1969—; dir. adv. bd. Standard Savs. & Loan, Orangeburg, 1970—. Trustee, Orangeburg Dist. 5 pub. schs., 1956-74, chmn., 1971-74; dir. S.C. Sch. Bd. Assn., 1962-70. Served with to capt., M.C., U.S. Army, 1949-51. Fellow Am. Coll. Radiology; mem. AMA, S.C. Med. Assn., S.C. Radiol. Soc., Radiol. Soc. N.Am., So. Med. Assn., C. of C. (v.p. 1965-66). Methodist. Club: Rotary (pres. 1960). Home: 339 Club Acres Orangeburg SC 29115 Office: 550 Carolina Ave Orangeburg SC 29115

ATWOOD, SAUNDRA LEE, hosp. ofcl.; b. Miami, Fla., Apr. 5, 1946; d. Norman R. and Helen S. A.; B.S. in Advt., U. Fla., 1968. Editor, Western Temporary Services, San Francisco, 1968-70; advt. copywriter Jordan Marsh Stores, Miami, 1972-74; advt. copy chief Gold Triangle Stores, Miami, 1974; asst. dir. public relations Miami Heart Inst., 1975-77; dir. public relations Parkway Gen. Hosp., Miami, 1977—. Recipient MacEachern award Nat. Coll. Hosp. Pub. Relations, 1976; award for community service Fla. Hosp. Assn. Public Relations Council, 1978, awards for vol. effort communications, community service, internal program, 1979. Mem. Fla. Hosp. Assn. (chmn. health edn. com.), Am. Soc. Hosp. Public Relations, Internat. Assn. Bus. Communicators, S. Fla. Hosp. Public Relations Assn. (pres.), Fla. Hosp. Public Relations Council (dir.), N. Dade C. of C. (dir.), N. Miami Beach C. of C., N. Miami C. of C., Greater Miami C. of C. Home: 9100 S W 137th Terr Miami FL 33176 Office: Parkway Gen Hosp 160 NW 170th St North Miami Beach FL 33169

AUDA, STEPHEN PETER, surgeon; b. N.Y.C., Oct. 1, 1943; s. Mario L. and Flora M. (Ollearis) A.; M.D., U. Torino, Italy, 1970; m. Pierangela Gannio, July 29, 1967; children—Sonia, Mario, Michael. Intern in gen. Surgery SUNY, Bklyn. and Kings County Hosp. Center, 1971-72, resident in gen. surgery, 1972-77; fellow in surg. oncology Nat. Cancer Inst., Bethesda, Md., 1977-79; practice medicine specializing in gen. and vascular surgery and surg. oncology, Riverdale, Ga.; mem. staffs South Fulton Hosp., Clayton Gen. Hosp., Henry Gen. Hosp.; clin. asso. in radiation therapy Emory U., Atlanta, 1979—; sr. research scientist Ga. Inst. Tech., Atlanta, 1979. Served with USPHS, 1977-79. Diplomate Am. Bd. Surgery. Mem. AMA, Assn. Mil. Surgeons of U.S., N.Y. Acad. Scis., Assn. Clin. Oncologists of Ga., Sigma Xi. Office: 181 Upper Riverdale Rd Riverdale GA 30274

AUERBACH, ANITA L., clin. psychologist; b. Flushing, N.Y., Dec. 23, 1946; d. Ben and Gussie (Zuckerman) Weiss; B.A. cum laude (N.Y. state regents scholar), SUNY, Buffalo, 1968, M.A. (regents fellow), 1970; Ph.D., George Washington U., 1977; m. Steven Miles Auerbach, May 25, 1969. Chief of research, youth crime control project D.C. Dept. Correction, 1970-74; clin. intern pschology No. Va. Tng. Center, Fairfax, 1974-75, staff psychologist, 1975-76, chief psychol. services, 1976—; pvt. practice clin. psychology, McLean, Va., 1979—; cons. Arlington Mental Health Clinic, Sheltered Occupational Center, Inc., Arlington and Fairfax Mental Health Services Bd. lectr. psychology Washington Tech. Inst., 1972-73, George Mason U., 1978—. Mem. family adv. edn. bd. Joseph P. Kennedy Jr. Found., 1977-79; mem. regional appeals bd. No. Va. Pub. Schs., 1977-79. Mem. Va. Acad. Clin. Psychologists, No. Va. Soc. Clin. Psychologists, Am. Psychol. Assn., Va. Psychol. Assn., Psi Chi, Alpha Lambda Delta. Home: 7116 Matthew Mills Rd McLean VA 22101 Office: 1449 Dolley Madison Blvd McLean VA 22101

AUGSBURGER, MYRON (SHENK), coll. pres., clergyman; b. Elida, Ohio, Aug. 20, 1929; s. Clarence A. and Estella (Shenk) A.; B.A., Eastern Mennonite Coll., 1955, Th.B., 1958; B.D., Goshen Coll., 1959; Th.M., Union Theol. Sem., Richmond, Va., 1961, Th.D., 1964; LL.D., Houghton Coll., 1966, Alderson-Broaddus Coll., 1972; m. Esther L. Kniss, Nov. 28, 1950; children—John, Michael, Marcia. Ordained to ministry Mennonite Ch., 1951; pastor of students Eastern Mennonite Coll., 1953-54, asst. prof., theology Eastern Mennonite Coll. and Eastern Mennonite Sem., 1962-65, prof., pres., 1965—; chmn. Council Mennonite Colls., Council Mennonite Sems.; bd. dirs. Presbyn. Ministers Fund; mem. Adv. Council for Pvt. Colls. in Va. Mem. Council for Advancement Small Colls. Club: Rotary. Author books, the most recent being: The Broken Chalice, 1971; The Expanded Life, 1972; Walking In The Resurrection, 1976; Faithful Unto Death, 1978; contbr. articles to profl. jours. Office: Eastern Mennonite Coll Harrisonburg VA 22801

AUGUSTINE, NORMAN RALPH, aerospace co. exec.; b. Denver, July 27, 1935; s. Ralph Harvey and Freda Irene (Immenga) A.; B.S., Princeton U., 1957, M.S., 1959; postgrad. Columbia U., 1958, U. Calif. at Los Angeles, 1959-60, U. So. Calif., 1960; m. Margareta Engman, Jan. 20, 1962; children—Gregory Eugen, René Irene. Research asst. Princeton U., 1957-58; chief engr. Douglas Aircraft Co., Inc., Santa Monica, Calif., 1958-65; asst. dir. research and engring. Office Sec. Def., Washington, 1965-70, cons., 1971-73; v.p. advanced systems, missiles and space div. LTV Aerospace Corp., Dallas, 1970-73; asst. sec. Army, Washington, 1973-75, under sec., 1975-77; cons. Dept. of Army, 1970-73, Exec. Office of Pres., 1971-73, and Office Sec. Def., 1971-73, 78—; v.p. tech. ops. Martin Marietta Aerospace Co., Bethesda, Md., 1977—; dir. Internat. Laser Systems, Inc.; mem. policy council Def. Systems Mgmt. Coll., 1973-76; mem. research and tech. advisory com. NASA, 1973-76. Fund raiser YMCA, Arlington, Tex., 1971-72; chmn. nat. program evaluation com. Boy Scouts Am., 1975—; pres. bd. visitors Am. U. Undergrad. Program in Procurement, Acquisitions and Grants Mgmt.; mem. advisory bd., dept. aero. and mech. engring. Princeton U. Recipient Meritorious Service medal Sec. Def., 1970, Distinguished Civilian Service medal U.S. Army, 1975, Distinguished Service medal Dept. Def., 1973, 77. Asso. fellow Inst. Aeros. and Astronautics (v.p. pub. policy, dir.); mem. Am. Def. Preparedness Assn. (chpt. dir.), Am. Helicopter Soc. (dir. 1974-75), Aerospace Industries Assn. (exec. com. Tech. Council), Soc. Logistics Engrs. (bd. advisers), Nat. Security Indsl. Assn. (vice chmn. exec. com. on command and control), Phi Beta Kappa, Sigma Xi, Tau Beta Pi. Presbyterian. Asso. editor: Def. Systems Mgmt. Rev., 1977—; mem. advisory bd. Jour. of Def. Research, 1971—. Home: 1329 Merrie Ridge Rd McLean VA 22101 Office: Martin Marietta Aerospace Corp 6801 Rockledge Dr Bethesda MD 20034

AUKLAND, ELVA DAYTON, educator; b. Arlington, Va., Apr. 25, 1922; d. William A. and Helen Gertrude (Rollins) Dayton; A.B. cum laude, Wheaton Coll., 1943; M.S., U. Minn., 1946; m. Merrill Forrest Aukland, June 18, 1949; children—Bruce Michael, Duncan Dayton, Rebecca Elizabeth. Teaching asst. U. Minn., 1943-46; instr. botany Ohio Wesleyan U., Delaware, 1946-49; instr. zoology and microbiology Ohio U., Athens, 1949-50; bacteriologist E.R. Squibb & Sons, New Brunswick, N.J., 1951-53; tchr., chmn. sci. dept. Washington-Lee High Sch., Arlington, 1962-78; tchr. T. C. Williams High Sch., Alexandria, Va., 1978—; dir. Insect Zoo, Smithsonian Instn., 1972. Commr., Arlington Parks and Recreation Commn., 1971-77; mem. Environ. Improvement Commn., Arlington County, 1977—; bd. dirs. No. Va. Conservation Council. Named Outstanding Tchr. Sci. and Math., Washington Acad. Sci., 1966. Mem. Am. Inst. Biol. Scis., Va. (Outstanding Tchr. 1975), Va. Jr. (dir.) acads. sci., Nat. Sci. Tchrs. Assn., Nat., So., Va. edn. assns., Am. Chem. Soc., Wilderness Soc., Audubon Soc., Delta Kappa Gamma, Phi Theta Kappa. Editor sci. tchrs. sect. Va. Jour. Sci., 1971-76. Home: 2412 N Columbus St Arlington VA 22207

AURIOLES, GABRIEL, educator, mgmt. cons.; b. Havana, Cuba, Mar. 9, 1917; s. Diego and Otilia A.; B.Ch.E., Tulane U., 1938; M.Ed., Fla. Atlantic U., 1975, Ed.D., 1977; m. Beatriz Navarrete, Apr. 11, 1948; children—Maria Beatriz, Gabriel, Vivian. With Procter & Gamble Co., Havana, 1938-48, 50-57, Mex., 1948-50; prof. Villanova U., Havana, 1952-60; v.p., gen. mgr. Extractora Cubana Aceites Vegetales, S. A., Havana, 1957-60; mgmt. cons., Mexico, El Salvador, Honduras, Nicaragua, Costa Rica, Brazil, 1960-73; prof., indsl. engring. dir. Anahuac U., Mexico City, 1971-73; asso. prof. indsl. tech., dept. chairperson Fla. Internat. U., Miami, 1978—; Office Minority Bus. Enterprise grantee, 1977. Mem. Interam. Businessmen's Assn. (dir. 1978—), Am. Inst. Indsl. Engrs., Inst. Food Technologists, Am. Soc. Safety Engring., Am. Indsl. Hygiene Assn., Am. Soc. Engring. Edn., Am. Inst. Chem. Engrs., Internat. Assn. Arson Investigators. Roman Catholic. Home: 1731 SW 103d Ave Miami FL 33165 Office: Fla Internat U Indsl Systems Tamiami Trail Miami FL 33199

AUSTELL, JOSEPH ROBERTS, community coll. adminstr.; b. Greenville, S.C., Mar. 5, 1920; s. Joseph Hopson and Edna (Roberts) A.; B.S.I.E., Clemson A&M U., 1941, M.S.I.E., 1955; postgrad. Va. Poly. Inst., 1975; m. Frances Jones, May 30, 1946; children—Susan Lee, Cynthia Ann. High sch. tchr., Kannapolis, N.C., 1941; tchr. music and indsl. arts, Elkin, N.C., 1949-51; enlisted U.S. Army Air Corps, 1941, advanced through grades to lt. col. USAF, 1965; ret., 1967; dir. Wilkes Community Coll., Wilkesboro, N.C., 1968—; mem. faculty U. Md., 1955-58, Trenton State U., 1965-66, McKendree Coll., 1961, Clemson U., 1951-55; edn. cons.; profl. musician; symphony dir. 1968-70; dir. Wilkes Community, Coll. Jazz Ensemble, 1975—. Bd. dirs. Foothill Arts Council, 1968-70; mem. exec. bd. Arts Council; N.C. vis. artist coordinator, 1978-80. Mem. N.C. Educators Assn., Mu Beta Psi. Baptist. Author: A Study of Industrial Arts Programs in South Carolina, 1958. Home 357 South St Elkin NC 28621 Office: Drawer 120 Wilkesboro NC 28697

AUSTIN, JACK, constrn. co. exec.; b. Waco, Tex., Jan. 6, 1917; s. Howard Walter and Rena Margret (Culverhouse) A.; ed. high sch.; m. Edith Threlkeld, Aug. 11, 1942; children—Bobby Jack, Larry Douglas. Various constrn. jobs, 1933-42; supt. Inge-Hayman Constrn. Co., Dallas, 1944-47, Nathan Wohlfeild Gen. Constrn. Co., Dallas, 1948, Leslie Crockett, Austin, Tex., 1949-54; with Austin-Wright Constrn. Co., Inc., Oklahoma City, 1954—, gen. mgr., 1956—, exec. v.p., 1963—; pres. A&W Lumber Co., Oklahoma City, 1968—; owner Jack Austin & Assos., La Feria, Tex., 1970—. Served with USAAF, 1942-43. Mem. Asso. Gen. Contractors, Nat. Rifle Assn. Clubs: Masons (32 deg.), Shriners. Home: 600 S Canal St Box 968 La Feria TX 78559 Office: Jack Austin & Assos PO Box 968 La Feria TX 78559

AUSTIN, JOHN PAUL, beverage co. exec.; b. La Grange, Ga., Feb. 14, 1915; s. Samuel Yates and Maude (Jernigan) A.; A.B., Harvard, 1937, LL.B., 1940; m. Jeane Weed, July 14, 1950; children—John Paul, Samuel Weed. Admitted to N.Y. bar, 1940; practiced in N.Y.C., 1940-41, 45-49; mem. legal dept. Coca-Cola Co., 1949-50, exec. v.p., 1961-62, pres., dir., 1962—, chief exec. officer, 1966—, chmn. bd., 1970—; exec. v.p. Coca-Cola Export Corp., 1958-59, pres., dir., 1959—; dir. Federated Dept. Stores, Inc., Morgan Guaranty Trust Co., N.Y.C., Gen. Electric Co., Trust Co. Ga., Atlanta, Dow Jones & Co., Inc. Served as lt. comdr. USNR, 1942-45. Clubs: Racquet and Tennis, Links (N.Y.C.); Blind Brook Golf (Purchase, N.Y.); Capitol City, Peachtree Golf (Atlanta). Office: 310 North Ave NW Atlanta GA 30313

AUSTIN, LARRY D., composer, educator; b. Duncan, Okla., Sept. 12, 1930; s. Jess Clemens and Thais Sylva (Newburn) A.; B.M., N. Tex. State U., 1951, M.M., 1952; postgrad. U. Calif., Berkeley, 1955-58; m. Edna Navarro, Oct. 31, 1953; children—Don, Elizabeth, David, Thais, Aurora. Asso. in music U. Calif., Berkeley, 1955-58; asst. prof. music U. Calif., Davis 1958-64, asso. prof., 1964-70, prof., 1970-72; prof. music, dir. Systems Complex for Studio and Performing Arts, U. South Fla., Tampa, 1972-78; prof. music N. Tex. State U., Denton, 1978—. Served with U.S. Army, 1952-55. Recipient Distinguished Composer award Music Tchrs. Nat. Assn., 1974. Mem. Am. Soc. Univ. Composers, Broadcast Music Inc., Am. Composers Alliance. Democrat. Roman Catholic. Compositions include: Accidents, 1967, Improvisations for Orchestra with Jazz Soloist, 1961, Phantasmagoria: Fantasies on Ives' Universe Symphony, 1974-77. Home: 2109 Woodbrook Dr Denton TX 76201 Office: North Tex State U Denton TX 76203

AUSTIN, LELA FRENCHA MONTGOMERY, guidance counselor; b. Lake City, S.C., Nov. 1, 1932; d. James Lee and Mable (Peterson) Montgomery; B.S., Claflin Coll., 1954; M.Ed., S.C. State

Coll., 1967; m. Harry James Austin, June 5, 1953; children—Debra Irene, James P. Tchr. sci. and biology Camerontown Elem. and Carver High Sch., Lake City, 1954-59; guidance counselor Carver High Sch., 1959-70, Lake City High Sch., 1970—. Active NAACP, Council Negro Women; mem. adv. council Florence County Alcohol and Drug Abuse. Mem. S.C. Sch. Counselor Assn., United Teaching Profession, Am. Personnel and Guidance Assn., Am. Sch. Counselor Assn., S.C. Personnel and Guidance Assn., S.C. Assn. Non-white Concerns, United Meth. Women (v.p. Florence dist., Mother of Yr. 1976), Zeta Phi Beta. Club: Order Eastern Star. Home: Route 1 Box 7 Cades SC 29518 Office: PO Box 1157 Lake City SC 29560

AUSTIN, STEPHEN GREGG, accountant; b. Brevard, N.C., May 17, 1952; s. Wendell Gregg and Gloria M. (Foster) A.; B.S. in Acctg., Bob Jones U., 1974; M.B.A., U. Ga., 1976; m. Gail R. Huff, June 26, 1976; 1 dau., Krista G. Bus., math. tchr. Athens (Ga.) Christian Sch., 1975-76; intern Price Waterhouse & Co., Chgo., 1974, auditor, Atlanta, 1976—; public acct., fin. cons. Faith Christian Schs., Ellenwood, Ga. Loaned exec. Met. Atlanta United Way, 1976; treas. Fellowship Baptist Ch., 1977; chmn. Bob Jones U. Ga. Banquet, 1978. C.P.A., Ga. Mem. Ga. Soc. C.P.A.s, Beta Alpha Psi. Republican. Home: 3681 N Decatur Rd M1 Decatur GA 30033 Office: Price Waterhouse & Co 3700 1st Nat Bank Tower Atlanta GA 30303

AUTEN, MELVIN RAY, psychol. cons.; b. Merced, Calif., Sept. 5, 1944; s. Ray L. and Mary Luciel (Fox) A.; B.S., E. Central Okla. State U., 1967, M.Ed., 1970; Ed.D., East Tex. State U., 1980; m. Carol Elaine Owen, June 28, 1968; 1 child—Krista Renae. Tchr., Konawa (Okla.) Schs., 1968, Chickasha (Okla.) Schs., 1969, Watonga (Okla.) Schs., 1970; counselor Shawnee (Okla.) Schs., 1971, Altus AFB, Okla., 1972, VA, Dallas, 1976, E. Tex. State U., Commerce, 1977; dir. counseling Barksdale AFB, Bossier City, La., 1973; adjunct prof. Okla. State U., Stillwater, 1972-73; psychol. cons., clin. dir. Okla. Children's Center, Muskogee, 1978—. Served with U.S. Army, 1964. Mem. Am., Tex. personnel and guidance assns., Am. Coll. Personnel Assn., Psi Chi, Phi Delta Kappa. Democrat. Baptist. Club: Kiwanis. Contbr. article in field. Home: 315 S 30 St Muskogee OK 74401

AVANT, DAVID ALONZO, JR., realty co. exec., photographer; b. Tallahassee, Fla., Apr. 11, 1919; s. David Alonzo and Fenton Garnett (Davis) A.; B.A., U. Fla., 1940; M.A., Cornell U., 1941; postgrad. Sch. Modern Photography, N.Y.C., 1946, Winona (Ind.) Sch. Photography, 1951; B.A., Fla. State U., 1958; m. Anne Leigh Wilder, Nov. 22, 1961 (div. Mar. 4, 1976); children—David Alonzo III, Eugenia Tatum Davis. Instr. art Fla. State U., Tallahassee, 1946-47; partner, owner, color portrait photographer L'Avant Studios, Tallahassee, 1947—; partner firm Avant Offices & Apts., Tallahassee, 1953—; partner Avant Tree Farms, Tallahassee, 1964—; dir. Indian Hills Estates, Tallahassee Br. Fla. Fed. Savs. & Loan. Pres. Old St. Augustine (Fla.) Estates, 1968. Chmn. Armed Forces Day Tallahassee, 1958. Bd. dirs. Salvation Army. Served to lt. col., USAAF, 1941-68. Named Territorial Krewe Chief Springtime Tallahassee Festival, Tallahassee Sesquicentennial Com., 1974. Mem. U.S. Navy League (v.p. 1975-76), Tallahassee Jaycees (dir.), Profl. Photographers' Assn. Am. (Master of Photography certificate 1964), Am. Soc. Photographers, Fla. Photographers' Assn., Fla. Pub. Relations Assn. (dir., Gold award 1966), Tallahassee Art League (pres. 1954-54), Tallahassee Camellia Club (pres. 1953-54 68-69), Soc. Cincinnati of Md., Tallahassee Sons Am. Revolution (pres. 1957-58, 76-77, 77-78), Order of First Families Va., Order Founders and Patriots Am., Soc. Colonial Wars, Order Loyalists and Patriots, Soc. Descendants Colonial Clergy, Jamestowne Soc., Soc. War of 1812, S.R., Flagon and Trencher, Mil. Order World Wars, Mil. Order Fgn. Wars, Order Stars and Bars, Sons Confederate Vets., Huguenot Soc. S.C., St. Andrew's Soc. Tallahassee. Democrat. Methodist (steward). Rotarian. Author: (with others) More Money Selling Portraits, 1956; Tallahassee Sesquicentennial Pageant, 1974; Florida Pioneers and Their Alabama, Georgia, Carolina, Maryland and Virginia Ancestors, 1974. Contbr. articles to profl. photog. jours. Pub. Like a Straight Pine Tree, 1971; Professional Raccoon Trapping, 1979; The Davis-Wood Family of Gadsden County, Florida, 1979. Home: 2312 Don Patricio Dr Tallahassee FL 32304 Office: Box 1711 207 W Park Ave Tallahassee FL 32302

AVARY, BOB C., mgmt. cons.; b. Pecos, Tex., Nov. 26, 1933; s. J. C. and Helen E. (Elrod) A.; student Tex. A&M U., 1950-53; children—Bobby, Johnny, Sammy, Billy. Pres., Bob Avary and Assos., Odessa, Tex. Mem. Monahans C. of C. (dir.), Am. Soc. Tng. and Devel., Internat. Transactional Analysis Assn. Democrat. Clubs: Jaycees (pres.), Kiwanis (pres.). Home: 3128 Magill Odessa TX 79763 Office: 3211 Kermit Hwy Odessa TX 79762

AVEDIKIAN, SOUREN ZACHARIA, chem. exec., cons.; b. Sivas, Armenia in Turkey, July 3, 1911; came to U.S., 1921, naturalized, 1927; s. Zacharia H. and Veron Z. (Ghazarian) A.; B.A., Columbia U., 1932, M.A., 1933, Ph.D., 1934; m. Araxia Baliozian, Jan. 16, 1943. With Avedikian & Co., Pompano Beach, Fla., 1932—, mng. dir., 1969—; with Chicopee Mfg. Corp., Milltown, N.J., 1957-58; dir. engring. devel. center Lummus Co., Newark, 1960-61; dir. research and devel. Rai Research Corp., Long Island City, N.Y., 1964-65; tech. coordinator chem. prodn. dept. Hoffman-LaRoche, Inc., Nutley, N.J., 1967-68; dir. summer conf. Fairleigh Dickinson U., 1966. Served with Chem. Corps, U.S. War Dept., 1936-47. N.Y. State scholar, 1928-32; recipient Am. Chem. Soc. prize, 1928; U.S. Army Dept. Commendation for Meritorious Civilian Service for outstanding performance of duty, 1940-47. Fellow AAAS, Am. Inst. Chemists; mem. Armenian Gen. Benevolent Union, Am. Chem. Soc. (emeritus), Am. Inst. Chem. Engrs., Electrochem. Soc., Air Pollution Control Assn., Am. Water Works Assn., Water Pollution Control Fedn., Fla. Pollution Control Assn., Inst. Food Technologists, TAPPI, Columbia Coll. Alumni Assn., Engring. Sch. Alumni Assn., N.Y. Acad. Sci., Sigma Xi, Phi Beta Kappa, Phi Lambda Upsilon. Republican. Armenian Ch. Clubs: Chemists, Masons. Patentee in field. Address: 1012 N Ocean Blvd Apt 909 Pompano Beach FL 33062

AVEN, ALEXANDER PHIPPS, mgmt. cons. exec.; b. San Antonio, Aug. 23, 1929; s. William Ralph and Rhoma (Phipps) A.; B.S., U. Okla., 1951; M.B.A., Harvard, 1955; m. Camilla Lytle, Dec. 26, 1951; children—William Cobb, Margaret Farrar. Geologist, Brit. Am. Oil Producing Co., Denver, Casper, Wyo., 1951-55, Continental Oil Co., 1955-57; v.p., dir. Eason Oil Co., Oklahoma City, 1957-64; petroleum cons., 1964-69; sr. partner Resource Analysis & Mgmt. Group, Oklahoma City, 1969—; pres. Ellex Transp., Inc., 1974-77, dir., 1974-79; pres., dir. Fain-Porter Prodn. Co., Oklahoma City, 1977—; v.p. Kerr Consol. and predecessors, 1977—. Asso. bus. Oklahoma City U., 1964-71; cons. to adminstr. NASA, 1966-70; vice chmn. Okla. Energy Adv. Council, 1973-74. Mem. alumni adv. council Sch. Geology and Geophysics, U. Okla. Served with USAF, 1955-57. Mem. Am. Assn. Petroleum Geologists, Am. Assn. Petroleum Landmen, Assn. Profl. Geol. Scientists. Episcopalian. Clubs: Economic of Okla. (pres. 1973-74), Men's Dinner, Harvard Business School Okla. (pres. 1965; dir. 1964-67), Beacon, Petroleum (Oklahoma City); University (Washington). Home: 1213 Larchmont Ln Oklahoma City OK 73116 Office: First Nat Center Oklahoma City OK 73102

AVERBUCH, PHILIP FRED, orthopedic surgeon; b. Bklyn., Nov. 28, 1941; s. Maurice and Dorothy (Bindelglass) A.; A.B., Columbia U., 1963; M.D., Tufts U., 1967; m. Judith Hope Rosenberg, June 18, 1964; children—Amy Lynn, Robert Neil. Intern, Hosp. for Joint Disease, N.Y.C., 1967-68; resident in orthopedic surgery Hosp. for Joint Diseases, N.Y.C., 1968-72; practice medicine specializing in orthopedic surgery, Tamarac, Fla., 1974—; staff Univ. Community Hosp., 1974—, chief of staff, 1979—, chief of surgery, 1975-77, asst. chief of staff, 1977-79, dir. phys. medicine, 1974—; staff Margate Gen. Hosp., 1974—, chief of surgery, 1976-78, dir. phys. medicine, 1974-78. Served to maj. M.C., U.S. Army, 1972-74. Diplomate Am. Bd. Orthopedic Surgery. Fellow Am. Acad. Orthopedic Surgeons, A.C.S., Internat. Coll. Surgerons; mem. AMA, Fla., Broward County med. assns. Jewish. Developer new type short arm cast. Home: 3180 NW 114th Terr Coral Springs FL 33065 Office: 7301 N University Dr Tamarac FL 33321

AVERY, EDWINA AUSTIN, lawyer; b. Silver Creek, N.Y., Oct. 11, 1896; d. Llewellyn Philip and Harriet (Robinson) Austin; J.D., M.P.L., Nat. U. Law, 1927; student George Washington U., 1928-30, Dept. Agr. Grad. Sch., 1928-31, 41-42; m. Hastings Palmer Avery, June 11, 1924 (dec. June 13, 1973); children—Cecilia Ann (dec.), Barbara Ann (Mrs. Homer Dean Huffman). Admitted to D.C. bar, 1926, U.S. Supreme Ct. bar, 1938; with U.S. Govt., 1918-58, clk. with Office Adj. Gen., 1918-22, Dept. Interior, 1922-24, successively clk., asst. editor, asso. editor Bur. Plant Industry, Dept. Agr., 1924-43, editor, later naturalization examiner Immigration and Naturalization Service, Dept. Justice, 1943-58; practice law, 1958—; also cons. in immigration and nationality law. Chmn. Govt. Workers Council, 1929-37; only woman mem. Blue Ribbon Zoning Com.; only woman pres. Diston Heights Civic Assn., 1966-67. Trustee O. E. Howe Home for Unfortunate Girls, 1954—. Recipient citation D.C. State Fedn. Bus. and Profl. Women's Clubs. Mem. Am., D.C., Fed., Women's (pres. 1933-35) bar assns., Nat. Assn. Women Lawyers, League Women Voters, D.A.R., Bus. and Profl. Women's Club, West Coast (Fla.) George Washington U. Alumni Assn. (pres. 1973-74), Kappa Beta Pi (grand dean 1943-47). Christian Scientist. Author: A Welcome to U.S.A. Citizenship (Freedoms Found. award), 1951; (motion picture script) Twentieth Century Pilgrim (Freedom Found. award); It Did Happen Here; also TV scripts, articles. Editor and compiler: Laws and Regulations, Immigration and Naturalization Service, 1944; Laws Applicable to Immigration and Nationality, 1952. Address: 1991 42d St N Saint Petersburg FL 33713

AVIGAEL, JACK RONALD, banker; b. Laredo, Tex., Oct. 21, 1949; s. Lester W. and Selma F. (Franklin) A.; B.S. cum laude, U. Pa., 1968; M.B.A., U. Tex., 1975; m. Cindy West, May 20, 1973; children—Joshua Joseph, Stacy Michaela. With Permanent Univ. Fund, U. Tex., Austin, 1972-75; sr. v.p., investment officer Laredo (Tex.) Nat. Bank, 1975—. Bd. dirs. Hillel Found., Austin, 1975, Agudas Achim Synagogue, Laredo, 1977—. Recipient Houston Soc. Fin. Analysts award, 1974. Mem. Fin. Analysts Fedn., San Antonio Soc. Fin. Analysts. Jewish. Clubs: B'nai B'rith, Austin Investment, Lions. Home: 102 McPherson St Laredo TX 78041 Office: PO Box 59 Laredo Nat Bank Laredo TX 78040

AVINGER, JUNITA HUNT, educator; b. Brownwood, Tex., Jan. 4, 1920; d. Benjamin Franklin and Laura Peachie (Chrane) Hunt; B.S. in Edn., Tex. Technol. U., 1955, M.S. in Edn., 1960; postgrad. U. Tex., Austin, 1970-71; Ed.D., Baylor U., 1974; m. William Herschel Avinger, Aug. 26, 1939; children—James Herschel, John Ross. Elem. tchr. Lubbock (Tex.) Ind. Sch. Dist., 1955-66; asst. prof. Abilene (Tex.) Christian U., 1966-73, asso. prof., 1973-78, prof. edn., 1978—, prof. reading, dir. reading clinic; cons. Right to Read, Tex. Ind. Sch. Dists. of Anson, Stamford, Abilene, Edn. Service Center Region XIV, Ginn and Co. Named Tchr. of Year, Abilene Christian U., 1971. Mem. Tex. Tchrs. Assn., Tex. Assn. Profs. of Reading, Tex. Assn. Improvement of Reading, Internat. Reading Assn. (cons. nat., state, regional, local workshops, mem. Big Country Council, Tex. Council), Phi Kappa Phi, Delta Kappa Gamma, Kappa Delta Pi, Delta Kappa Gamma (scholar, 1969-74). Democrat. Mem. Chs. of Christ. Club: Faculty Wives of Abilene Christian U. Researcher in field; editor DISTAR III, Sci. Research Assos. Home: 910 Harwell Abilene TX 79601 Office: Abilene Christian U 1600 Campus Cts Abilene TX 79601

AVRIGIAN, HARRY CASPER, indsl. mgmt. exec.; b. Phila., Nov. 23, 1921; s. Harry Toros and Nevart A.; diploma city and county planning and plan implementation U. Mo., 1976; m. Bernice Bess, May 15, 1943; children—Barry, Brian, Diane. Machinist Nat. Def. Tng. Inst., Phila., 1938-40; Baldwin Locomotive Works, Eddystone, Pa., 1940-41; armament machinist Empire Ordnance Co., Phila., 1941-42; indsl. mgmt. cons., 1948-69; with Western States Exploration, Inc., Salt Lake City, 1972—, chief exec. officer, chmn. bd., 1975—; cons. UN Habitat and Human Settlement Found., Nairobi, Kenya. Active SCORE program SBA, 1970-72. Served with U.S. Army, 1942-45; ETO. Mem. U.S. Indsl. Council, Am. Concrete Inst., Nat. Precast Concrete Assn., Forest Products Research Assn., Internat. Assn. for Housing Sci. Episcopalian.

AXELRAD, SYLVIA ROSEN, real estate broker; b. Phila., June 15, 1912; d. Samuel Daniel and Dora (Friedman) R.; student pub. schs., Miami, Fla.; m. Jack Harry Axelrad, Feb. 14, 1932; children—Moise, Samuel, David, Sandra. Real estate broker Sylvia Axelrad, Houston, 1937—. Licensed real estate broker, Tex., 1978. Home and office: 5500 N Braeswood St Apt 181 Houston TX 77096

AXTELL, KENNETH HAROLD, hosp. adminstr.; b. Medina, N.Y., May 1, 1932; s. Harold Ralph and Elizabeth Frances (Cole) A.; B.A., Kalamazoo Coll., 1959; M.H.A., Med. Coll. Va., 1961; m. Margaret Beth Youngs, Aug. 16, 1958; children—Deborah Lynn, Martha Beth, Philip Kenneth. Adminstrv. resident Jefferson Hosp., Roanoke, Va., 1960-61, asst. adminstr., 1961-64; adminstr. Bedford (Va.) County Meml. Hosp., 1964-68; asso. adminstr. Meml. Hosp., Danville, Va., 1968-76; pres., chief exec. officer Williamsburg (Va.) Community Hosp., 1976—; mem. adv. bd. Va. Fed. Savs. and Loan Assn.; mem. Eastern Va. Health Systems Agy. Bd.; mem. Peninsulas Emergency Services Council. Fellow Am. Coll. Hosp. Adminstrs.; mem. Va. Hosp. Assn., Tidewater Hosp. Council. Republican. Methodist. Club: Rotary. Home: 43 Mile Course Kingsmill Williamsburg VA 23185 Office: 1238 Mt Vernon Ave Williamsburg VA 23185

AXTELL, OLIVER, chem. co. exec.; b. York, Nebr., Sept. 5, 1926; s. Oliver and Myrtle (Bonner) A.; B.S. in Chem. Engring., Rice U., 1944; S.M. in Chem. Engring., Mass. Inst. Tech., 1947; m. Patricia Ann Dill, Apr. 9, 1955; children—Bonnie Jean, Steven Brian. With Celanese Chem. Co., N.Y.C., 1951—, econ. evaluation engr., 1955-63, mgr. comml. information, 1963—. Mem. Bd. Adjustment, Fanwood, N.J., 1970-76; mem. Union County Republican Com., 1963-69. Fellow Am. Inst. Chem. Engrs.; mem. Am. Chem. Soc., Sigma Xi, Phi Lambda Upsilon. Republican. Methodist. Patentee in field. Home: 7722 Chattington St Dallas TX 75248 Office: 1250 Mockingbird Ln Dallas TX 75247

AXTMAN, WILLIAM HENRY, assn. exec.; b. Medford, Mass., Mar. 2, 1924; s. Albert John and Marian Agusta (Hatch) A.; student Northeastern U., Boston, 1942-43, Tufts U., 1943-44, Western New Eng. Coll., 1959-65; m. Gwendolyn Ruth Austin, Aug. 10, 1946; children—Marian Axtman Thompson, Wendell Albert, Kathleen Axtman Fisher, Virginia Elaine Axtman Adams. Madelyn Ruth. Service supr. Met. Petroleum Co., Boston, 1950-57; chmn. dept. heating, power tech. Springfield (Mass.) Tech. Inst., 1957-67; asst. tech. dir. Nat. Oil Fuel Inst., N.Y.C., 1967-68; asst. exec. dir. Am. Boiler Mfrs. Assn., Arlington, Va., 1968-79, exec. dir., 1979—. Coordinator Evening Trade Sch., Springfield, 1966-67; Disaster chmn. Springfield Red Cross, 1963-65. Served with USNR, 1942-67. Mem. Am. Soc. Heating and Refrigeration Engrs., ASME, Beta Gamma Epsilon. Methodist. Tech. editor Fuel Oil, Oil Heat Mag., 1965—; Contbr. numerous articles to profl. jours. Home: 10712 Montgomery Dr Manassas VA 22110 Office: 1500 Wilson Blvd Arlington VA 22209

AYAD, JOSEPH MAGDY, psychologist; b. Cairo, Egypt, May 21, 1926; s. Fahim Sayed and Victoria Gabour (El-Masri) A.; came to U.S., 1949, naturalized, 1961; B.A. in Social Scis., Am. U., Cairo, 1946; M.A. in Clin. Psychology (Univ. scholar), Stanford U., 1952; Ph.D. in Clin. Psychology (Univ. scholar), U. Denver, 1956; m. Widad Fareed Bishai, May 29, 1954; children—Fareed Merritt, Victor Maher, Michael Joseph, Mona Elaine. Lectr., Fitzsimmons Army Hosp., Denver, 1953-54; staff psychologist Cons. Psychol. Services, Denver, 1954-55; psychologist, Denver, 1956-57, High Plains Neurol. Center, Amarillo, Tex., 1957—. Pres. JMA Cattle Co., Amarillo, 1973—; v.p., treas. Filigon Inc., Amarillo, 1962-75, pres., 1976—; cons. psychologist Tex. Dept. Pub. Welfare. Mem. profl. adv. bd. Amarillo Mental Health Assn., 1968-69. Mem. Amarillo Child Welfare Bd., 1961-63; area chmn. U. Denver Fund Raising Campaign, 1963; mem. profl. adv. bd. St. Paul's Meth. Ch. Sch. for Children with Learning Disabilities, Amarillo, 1969-70. Recipient Grad. Sr. award in Philosophy Am. U. at Cairo, 1946. Mem. Am. Psychol. Assn., Am. Assn. Marriage and Family Counselors, Am. Nat. Cattlemen's Assn., Potter-Randall County (Tex.) Psychol. Soc. (pres. 1974). Presbyn. Club: Amarillo Country. Contbr. articles to profl. jours. Home: 4239 Erik St Amarillo TX 79106 Office: 2301 W 7th St Amarillo TX 79106

AYARS, ALBERT LEE, ednl. adminstr.; b. Kettle Falls, Wash., Sept. 17, 1917; s. Glen Garrison and Ama Belle (Jennings) A.; B.A., Wash. State U., 1939, B.Ed., 1940, M.A., 1942, D.Ed., 1956; m. Frances Louise Schaaf, June 21, 1941; children—Cheron Marie Ayars Holman, Judith Louise, Albert Lee, Danielle Jo Ayars Alexander, Garrison Hubert, Debora Ann Ayars Dillon, Theodora Ama, Virginia Darlene. Tchr., Davenport (Wash.) High Sch., 1940-42; prin. Colville (Wash.) High Sch., 1942-45; supt. public schs., Omak, Wash., 1945-49, Sunnyside, Wash., 1949-52; asso. dir. Joint Council on Econ. Edn., N.Y.C., 1952-53; dir. edn. dept. Hill and Knowlton, Inc., N.Y.C., 1953-65; v.p. John W. Hill Found., 1956-65; supt. Spokane Public Schs., 1965-72, Norfolk (Va.) Public schs., 1972—; vis. prof., lectr. numerous univs. Mem. United Communities Fund Bd., 1972-78; mem. Norfolk Symphony Bd., 1978; mem. 4-H Adv. Council, 1976—; adv. bd. Tidewater (Va.) Assn. for Mental Health, 1976—; bd. dirs. Urban League of Tidewater, 1978—. Mem. Am. Assn. Sch. Adminstrs., Va. Assn. Sch. Adminstrs., Edn. Assn. Norfolk, Joint Council Econ. Edn. (dir.), Va. Council Econ. Edn. (trustee), Phi Kappa Phi, Phi Delta Kappa, Kappa Delta Pi. Baptist. Clubs: Rotary, Masons, Shriners. Author: Administering the People's Schools, 1957; How to Plan a Community Resources Workshop, 1975; co-author: The Teenager and Alcohol, 1970; The Teenager and the Law, 1978. Contbr. articles to profl jours. Office: PO Box 1357 Norfolk VA 23501

AYERS, ANNE LOUISE, edn. specialist; b. Albuquerque, Oct. 22, 1948; d. F. Ernest and Gladys (Miles) Ayers; B.A. (scholar), U. Kans., 1970; M.Ed., Seattle Pacific U., 1971; postgrad. Coll. William and Mary, 1978-79. Staff cons. student devel. Central Wash. State Coll., Ellensburg, 1971-72; dir. residence edn. centers Aerospace Def. Command for Mont. and N.D., Chapman Coll., Orange, Calif., 1972-74, also instr. psychology; instr. psychology Hampton (Va.) Inst., 1975-77; edn. service specialist Fort Monroe, Va., 1975-77; edn. specialist Fort Eustis, Va., 1977-79, Nat. Mine Safety and Health Adminstrn., Beckley, W.Va., 1979—. Humble Oil Leadership scholar, 1971. Mem. Am. Personnel and Guidance Assn., Federally Employed Women, Nat. Assn. Women Deans, Adminstrs. and Counselors, Nat. Assn. Student Personnel Adminstrs., Nat. Def. Transp. Assn., Internat. Platform Assn., Va. Sheriffs Assn. (hon.). Methodist. Club: Toastmasters.

AYERS, JAMES GILBERT, elec. mfg. co. exec.; b. Concord, N.C., Aug. 22, 1949; s. Karie Lee and Ethel Marjorie (Royston) A.; B.S. in Accounting, Auburn U., 1972; m. Margaret Carol Knox, Aug. 29, 1970; 1 son, Jonathan Karie. Staff accountant Swift Textiles Co., Columbus, Ga., 1972-73; mgr. cost accounting Kendall, Inc., Athens, Ga., 1973-74; asst. ops. controller Reliance Elec. Co., Flowery Branch, Ga., 1974-75, materials control supr., 1975-76, controller, 1976—. Mem. Nat. Assn. Accountants, Am. Mgmt. Assn., Am. Production and Inventory Control Soc. Home: Route 1 Box 70 A Flowery Branch GA 30542 Office: PO Box 250 Flowery Branch GA 30542

AYERS, JAMES LEE, naval officer, health care adminstr.; b. Seneca, S.C., Feb. 1, 1945; s. James Samuel and Ethel (Ivester) A.; A.S. in Sci. magna cum laude, Tidewater Community Coll., 1973; B.S. in Health Care Adminstrn., George Washington U., 1975; m. Mary Jeanette Davis, Mar. 18, 1968; children—Aaron Keith, Wendy Renee. Enlisted in U.S. Navy, 1963, advanced through grades to lt.; with 2d bn. 3d Marines, Vietnam; command duty officer USS Beacon; ensign Med. Service Corps; now chief of fiscal and supply service, comptroller Naval Hosp., Roosevelt Rds., P.R. Decorated Purple Heart. Mem. Assn. Mil. Surgeons U.S., Am. Hosp. Assn., Am. Soc. Mil. Comptrollers, Phi Theta Kappa. Republican. Mem. Christian and Missionary Alliance. Address: US Naval Hospital Miami FL 34051

AYERS, NICKY ALEXANDRIDES, pub. sch. counselor; b. Athens, Greece, Oct. 5, 1924; d. George Alexander and Martha Maria (Papadopoulos) Alexandrides; came to U.S., 1952, naturalized, 1953; B.A., Cameron U., 1972; M.Ed. in Guidance and Counseling, Okla. U., 1974; m. Conrad L. Ayers, Jr., July 29, 1950; children—Conrad Alekos, Martha Nicky. Sec., Am. embassy, Athens, Greece, 1947-50; counselor Lawton (Okla.) Public Sch., 1973—. Cert. psychometrist and sch. psychologist, Okla., cert. reading specialist. Recipient Distinguished Alumna award Cameron U., 1977. Mem. Am., Okla. personnel and guidance assns., NEA, Okla. Edn. Assn., Profl. Educators Assn. Lawton, Okla. Psychol. Assn., Okla. Sch. Psychol. Assn., Council for Exceptional Children (treas. chpt. 1977-78), Lawton Reading Council, Assn. Childhood Edn. Lawton, Phi Kappa Phi. Democrat. Greek Orthodox. Clubs: Knife and Fork, Lawton Woman's Forum. Home: 24 NW 56th St Lawton OK 73505 Office: 4912 Avalon St Lawton OK 73501

AYERS, STEPHEN CURTIS, communications co. exec.; b. Radford, Va., Aug. 28, 1954; s. Herbert Curtis and Nancy Jean (Kanode) A.; Asso. Applied Sci., Va. Western Coll., 1972-74; student New River Coll., 1974-76; asso. Inst. for Cert. of Engring. Technicians, 1976; m. Karen Ann Van Krey, July 4, 1975. Freelance electronics sales, photography, Va., 1968-72; photographer, sports editor, circulation mgr. Blacksburg (Va.) Sun, 1969-71; communications dispatcher Town of Blacksburg, 1972-76; co-owner

Profl. Communications Inc. (formerly HiLo Electronics Co.), Blacksburg, 1975-77; regional sales mgr. Universal Communication Systems Inc., telephone systems, Roanoke, Va., 1977—; pres. Blacksburg Answering Service Enterprises, 1978—. Vice pres. Blacksburg Vol. Fire Dept. and First Aid Crew, 1977—; bd. dirs. Western Va. Emergency Med. Services Council, Mem. Asso. Public Safety Communications Officers, Asso. Telephone Answering Exchanges. Mem. Ch. of God. Home: 806 Airport Rd Blacksburg VA 24060 Office: Universal Communication Systems Inc 1401 Municipal Rd Roanoke VA 24012

AYERS, WALTER CARY, trade assn. exec.; b. Stuart, Va., Jan. 9, 1942; s. Cary Goode and Nellie Irene (Hazelwood) A.; student Ferrum Jr. Coll., 1960-62; B.A. in Govt., Coll. William and Mary, 1964; m. Evelyn Lynn Parker, May 3, 1969; 1 son, Walter Cary. Field rep. Va. Farm Bur., 1965-68, dir. pub. affairs, 1968-72; dir. pub. affairs and research Va. C. of C., 1972-74; exec. v.p. Va. Agribus. Council, 1974-76; exec. dir. Va. Petroleum Industries, Richmond, 1976—; sec.-treas. Va. Motor Vehicle Conf. Pres. Friends of the Industry of Agr., Va., 1975-76. Served with AUS, 1964-65. Mem. Va. Soc. Assn. Execs., Va. Travel Council, Va. C. of C., Va. Farm Bur. Fedn. Baptist. Home: 9018 Michaux Ln Richmond VA 23229 Office: 1809 Staples Mill Rd Richmond VA 23220

AYERS, WILLIAM MITCHELL, hosp. emergency services mgr.; b. Guntersville, Ala., Dec. 4, 1949; s. Robert Jay and Hellon (Chambers) A.; A.S. in Nursing, Polk Community Coll., 1970; m. Betty Waggoner, Jan. 8, 1972; children—Mary Michelle, Courtney Danielle. Orderly/grad. nurse Heart of Fla. Hosp., Haines City, 1966-70, staff, charge, med., surg. cardiac nurse, 1974; staff nurse med. and surg. intensive care Landstuhl (Germany) Army Hosp., 1973-74; mgr. emergency services Winter Haven (Fla.) Hosp;., 1974—; CPR instr., trainer Am. Heart Assn., ARC; emergency med. technician instr. Polk Community Coll. Vol. advisor child and spouse abuse; provider advanced cardiac life support, 1978; mem. Gov.'s Task Force on Emergency Med. Services. Served with USAF, 1970-74. Decorated D.S.M. Mem. Fla. Nurses Assn., Emergency Dept. Nurses Assn. (pres. Fla. coordinating council), ARC (Outstanding Service award 1978), Am. Heart Assn. (v.p. Polk County chpt. 1977-78, Award of Distinction 1978), Polk County Emergency Med. Services Council (sec. 1978-79). Methodist. Clubs: Foresters, Kiwanis. Contbr. articles to profl. publs. in field. Home: PO Box 1101 Dundee FL 33838 Office: 200 Ave F NE Winter Haven FL 33880

AYLSWORTH, CLARK, mut. fund exec.; b. St. Joseph, Mo., Apr. 4, 1920; s. George Allyn and Josephine Esterly (Clark) A.; student Yale U., 1938-41; B.S., U. Calif., 1956; M.S., Tex. A&M U., 1962; m. Fern Ann MacManus, June 17, 1976; children—DeAnn Ellisor, Clark Allyn, James F. Drake III. Commd. 2d lt. U.S. Army Air Force, 1942, advanced through grades to capt., 1944, separated, 1945, recalled to duty, 1951, advanced through grades to lt. col., 1965; ops. and flying assignments in U.S. and Orient, 1951-54; chief analysis and programming U.S. Air Force Command Post, Pentagon, Arlington, Va., 1964-68, ret., 1968; pres. Growth Research & Mgmt. Inc., United Services Fund, Inc., Universal City, Tex., 1968—, also dir.; dir. Auric United Corp. Decorated D.F.C., Air Medal with 9 oak leaf clusters; Croix de Guerre with Palm (France); Silliman scholar, 1938. Republican. Episcopalian. Clubs: Woodlake Country, Fair Oaks Country. Office: Growth Research & Mgmt Inc 110 E Byrd Blvd Universal City TX 78148

AYTES, GENE THERON, coal co. exec., florist; b. Morgan County, Tenn., Sept. 11, 1935; s. Clayton M. and Flossie (Mathews) A.; ed. high sch.; m. Betty Collins, Mar. 24, 1953; children—Sheila, Loretta, Phillip, Angela, Timothy. Staff, Morgan County (Tenn.) Hwy. Dept., 1954-59; operator heavy equipment A.B. Long Constrn. Co., Tenn., 1959-67; operator, foreman, owner, operator Aytes Coal Co., Wartburg, Tenn., 1967—; owner, pres. Morgan County Florist, 1972—, Aytes Inc., 1973—, Wage Coal Inc., 1975—, Four Seasons Inc., 1975—, A&G Enterprises, 1975—, A&H Coal Co., 1975—, Holco Inc., 1975—, Aytes Coal Sales, 1979— (all Wartburg). Served with USCGR, 1953-54. Mem. Facts About Coal in Tenn., Nat. Fedn. Ind. Bus. Baptist. Home and Office: Box 351 Wartburg TN 37887

AYUS, JUAN CARLOS, physician; b. Buenos Aires, Argentina, Feb. 25, 1941; came to U.S., 1973, naturalized, 1976; s. Jose and Matilde A.; B.S. with honors, Coll. 17, Buenos Aires, 1960; M.D., U. Buenos Aires, 1967; m. Maria Giudici, June 27, 1971; children—Sebastian, Mariana. Intern, Meml. Hosp., U. Mass., 1973-74; resident U. Buenos Aires, 1968-71, U. Minn., 1974-75; teaching fellow U. Buenos Aires, 1971-72, instr. dept. medicine, 1971-72; fellow dept. medicine U. Calif., San Francisco, 1975-77; chief renal service Ben Taub Gen. Hosp., Houston, 1977—; asst. prof. medicine Baylor Coll. Medicine, Houston, 1977—. Vice pres. Argentinian House of Houston, 1979—. Served with Army of Argentina, 1961-62. Nat. Kidney Found. research fellow, 1976-77. Diplomate Am. Bd. Internal Medicine. Fellow A.C.P.; mem. Am. Soc. Nephrology, Am. Soc. Clin. Research, Internat. Soc. Nephrology, Latin Am. Soc. Nephrology. Roman Catholic. Home: 10306 Balmforth St Houston TX 77096 Office: Baylor Coll Medicine 1200 Moursund Ave Houston TX 77030

AZAD, HARDAM SINGH, environ. engr.; b. Punjab, India, Aug. 10, 1938; s. Jaswant Singh and Mohinder Kaur (Grewal) Vaid; came to U.S., 1963, naturalized, 1973; B.A. in Econs. and Polit. Sci., Punjab U., Chandigarh, India, 1961; B.S. in Civil Engring., Kans. State U., Manhattan, 1964; M.S. in San. Engring., U. Mo., Columbia, 1965; Ph.D. in Environ. Engring., U. Mich., Ann Arbor, 1968; m. Jagdesh Kaur Dhaliwal, Aug. 22, 1965; children—Ishnella Mohinder, Jaspaul Singh. Supr. environ. lab., wastewater treatment plant ops. mgr. Abbott Labs., N. Chgo., 1968-70; mgr. indsl. wastewater research and devel. Monsanto Enrvio-Chem. Systems Co., Dayton, Ohio and Chgo., 1970-72; mgr. environ. control, project mgr. Davy McKee Internat., Chgo. and San Mateo, Calif., 1972-75; dir. projects and engring. NUS Corp., Rockville, Md. and Houston, 1975—. Named Exemplary Am. Citizen Council Met. Chgo., 1974. Mem. Am. Inst. Chem. Engrs., Water Pollution Control Fedn. Republican. Sikh. Editor: Industrial Wastewater Management Handbook, 1976. Home: 310 Big Hollow Ln Houston TX 77042 Office: NUS Corp 11511 Katy Freeway Suite 500 Houston TX 77079

BAALKE, JOSEPH HOWARD, III, meteorologist, counselor; b. Oak Park, Ill., Nov. 28, 1949; s. Joseph Howard and Marie Helen (Bruno) B.; B.S., U. North Ala., 1977, M.A., 1979; m. Judith B. Marciniak, Mar. 1, 1969; 1 son, Kevin Brian. Meteorologist, TVA, Muscle Shoals, Ala., 1975—; pvt. practice counseling, Muscle Shoals, 1979—. Served with USAF, 1968-75. Mem. Nat. Weather Assn., Am. Mental Health Counselors Assn., Phi Kappa Phi.

BAAMONDE, JOSEPH, JR., pharm. co. exec.; b. Tampa, Fla., Aug. 31, 1944; s. Joseph and Lupe (Randon) B.; B.A., Parsons Coll., 1972; m. Judith Frisk, June 9, 1973; 1 dau., Jennifer Judith. With Mallinckrodt, Inc., Brandon, Fla., 1973—, regional sales mgr. S.E. region, 1978—. Pres., Luth. Churchmen of Salem Luth. Ch., Peoria, Ill., 1977. Named Mgr. of Yr., Mallinckrodt, Inc., 1978. Mem. Am. Mgmt. Assn., Profl. Pharm. Mfrs. Reps. Assn. (v.p. Peoria 1976-77), Theta Chi. Republican. Address: 1306 Brandonwood Dr Brandon FL 33611

BABB, DONALD QUENTIN, entomologist, exterminator; b. Dalton, Ga., Oct. 11, 1950; s. Quentin Marion and Dot (Ford) B.; A.S., Dalton Jr. Coll., 1970; B.S. in Entomology, U. Ga., 1972; m. Judy Ann Kinnett, Aug. 17, 1971; 1 dau., Fawn Yonah. Research staff U.S. Dept. Agr., summer 1972; Fla. mgr. Stephenson Chemicals Co., Orlando, 1972-73; agent U. Ga. Extension Dept., Rome, 1973; inspector Ga. Dept. Agr., Atlanta, 1973-74; tng. and tech. dir. Met. Exterminating Co., College Park, Ga., 1974-75; pres. Babb Exterminating Co., Douglasville, Ga., 1975—. Democrat. Baptist. Clubs: Jaycess, Kiwanis. Home and Office: 6259 Shallowford Way Douglasville GA 30135

BABB, (JOSEPH) GLENN, newspaper editor; b. Columbia, Mo., June 30, 1894; s. Jeremiah Glenn and Clara Louise (Beauchamp) B.; A.B., U. Mo., 1914, B.J., 1915; m. Katharine Cecelia Elder, June 10, 1931; children—Jeremy Glenn (dec.), Sara Leighton. Reporter, news editor, editor Japan Advertiser, Tokyo, 1915-23; AP corr., editor, Tokyo, Peking, Mukden, Shanghai, N.Y.C., San Francisco, Washington, 1924-48, fgn. news editor, 1942-48; editor, pub. Bedford (Va.) Democrat, 1949-61; editor Bedford Bull.-Democrat, 1961—. Served as 1st lt. U.S. Army, 1917-19. Home: 1512 Woodland Rd Bedford VA 24523 Office: Bedford Bull-Democrat E Main St Bedford VA 24523

BABB, ROBERT MARION, univ. computer adminstr.; b. Henderson, Ky., May 19, 1943; s. F. M. and Bobbie Lois (Overby) B.; B.S.B., Murray State U., 1970, M.A.Ed., 1971, S.C.T., 1973; Ed.D. (U. Ky. Research Found. fellow), U. Ky., 1976; m. Sherion Dian Hurst, June 14, 1965; children—Susan Renee, Dora Lee, Kara Marion. Salesman, L.S. DuBois Wholesale Drug, Paducah, Ky., 1965-68; coordinator data processing Paducah Community Coll., 1971-73; asst. prof. data processing Ark. State U., 1974-77, dir. computer services, 1977—. Deacon, Walnut St. Bapt. Ch., Jonesboro, Ark., 1978—, vice chmn. fin. com., 1978-80, ch. tng. dir., 1977-78. Served with USAR, 1966—. Decorated Army Commendation medal. Mem. Data Processing Mgmt. Assn., Phi Delta Kappa. Baptist. Office: PO Drawer AAA State University AR 72467

BABER, WILBUR H., JR., lawyer; b. Shelby, N.C., Dec. 18, 1926; s. Wilbur H. and Martha Corinne (Allen) B.; B.A., Emory U., 1949; postgrad. U. N.C., 1949-50, U. Houston, 1951-52; J.D., Loyola U., New Orleans, 1965. Admitted to La. bar, 1965, Tex. bar, 1966; practice law, Hallettsville, Tex. Served with U.S. Army. Mem. Am., La., Tex. bar assns., La. Engring. Soc., Tex. Surveyors Assn. Methodist. Club: Rotary. Office: PO Box 294 Hallettsville TX 77964

BABETTE, ANITA, photographer; b. Detroit, Aug. 27, 1939; d. Alfred and Mae (Klein) Greenstein; student in photography and silversmithing Centro Superior de Artes Aplicadas, Mexico City, 1960-61; B.A., Wayne State U., 1962, postgrad. in Spanish, 1965; postgrad. Cuban culture program U. Miami (Fla.), 1967-68. Asst. photographer audio-visual prodn. dept. Wayne State U., 1958-59; owner, operator Fotografia A.B.G., San Juan, P.R., 1963-65; aerial and archtl. photographer Photog. Services, Miami, 1967-69; photographer for postcards, guide books Dukane Press, Hollywood, Fla., 1969-70; pres., comml. photographer Ad/Photographics, Inc., Miami, 1971—; participant radio interviews Photography as a Career, Sta. WKYN, San Juan and Sta. WIOD, Miami, 1964-69; ofcl. photographer Fla. Furniture Mart, 1974-75; speaker in field; lectr. comml. photography Miami Photography Coll., 1971. Recipient 1st Pl. prize Club Fotografico de Mexico Nat. Photog. Competition, 1960, 2d Pl. prize, 1960; winner competition Indsl. Photography mag., 1979. Mem. Nat. Home Fashions League, Fla. Profl. Photographers (Salon of Photography cert. of Merit 1967, 69), Southeastern Profl. Photographers Assn., Profl. Photographers Am., Am. Soc. Mag. Photographers, Wayne State U. Alumni Assn., Internat. Center Photography, Young Profls., Nat. Assn. Women Bus. Owners. Democrat. Contbr. photographs to mags. for covers, feature articles, to guide books, articles to profl. jours.; research and devel. of method of photographing gems, metallic objects, reflective surfaces. Office: 3614 SW 3d Ave Miami FL 33145

BACH, BERT COATES, univ. ofcl.; b. Jenkins, Ky., Dec. 14, 1936; s. Bert C. and Rowena W. (Coates) B.; A.B. in English, Eastern Ky. U., 1958; M.A., George Peabody Coll., 1959; Ph.D. in English, N.Y. U., 1966; m. Diana Miller, Aug. 25, 1957; children—Bert Coates, Nancy Elizabeth. Asst. prof. English, W.Ga. Coll., Carrollton, 1959-61; instr. dept. English, Manhattan Coll., N.Y.C., 1961-64, asst. prof., 1964-66; asso. prof. English, Eastern Ky. U., Richmond, 1966-67, prof. English, 1967-70, chmn. English composition program, 1967-70; prof. English, Millikin U., Decatur, Ill., 1970-75, asst. to v.p. acad. affairs, 1974-75, chmn. dept. English, 1970-73; dean Coll. Arts and Scis., U. Tenn., Chattanooga, 1975-78, exec. dean of faculty, 1978—; manuscript cons. to Harper & Row, pubs., 1969—. Del. to Democratic Conv., Ky., 1964; bd. dirs. Chattanooga Symphony Assn., 1978—; trustee Richland Community Coll., Decatur, 1971-75. Am. Council on Edn. fellow, 1973-74. Mem. MLA, Nat. Council Tchrs. English, Am. Assn. Higher Edn., Phi Kappa Phi. Presbyterian. Author: Dickens' Great Expectations: A Guide, 1967; (with Gordon Browning) Fiction for Composition, 1968, Drama for Composition, 1973; (with William A. Sessions and William Walling) The Liberating Form: A Handbook-Anthology of English and American Poetry, 1972; contbr. essays on lit. criticism to scholarly jours. Home: 2883 Old Britain Circle Chattanooga TN 37421 Office: U Tenn Chattanooga TN 37402

BACHI, MICHAEL MARIO, artist, educator; b. Genoa, Italy, Mar. 1, 1920 (parents Am. citizens); s. Angelo Luigi and Alcisa (Cardinale) B.; B.A., Oklahoma City U., 1951; M.F.A., U. Okla., 1953, postgrad., 1953; postgrad. Southeastern State Coll., Durant, Okla., 1954, Instituto de Allende, San Miguel De Allende, Gt., Mexico, 1964; m. Mable Naomi Baker, Apr. 5, 1947. Tchr. art McAlester (Okla.) Jr. and Sr. High Schs., 1953-56; prof., head dept. art Rio Grande (Ohio) Coll., 1956-57; asst. prof. art Wis. State Coll., Superior, 1957-60; asst. prof. art Chadron (Nebr.) State Coll., 1960-62; prof. art Central State U., Edmond, Okla., 1962—, mem. faculty governance com., 1968-69, mem. faculty senate, 1969-70, 76-77, 79-80; exhibited in one man shows: Henson Gallery, Yukon, Okla., 1966, Ballet Theatre Sch., Oklahoma City, St. Paul's Cathedral, Oklahoma City, 1968; exhibited in group shows Philbrook Mus., Tulsa, 1953, Okla. U. Show at Forum Gallery, N.Y.C., 1954, Tweed Gallery, Duluth, Minn., 1959, galleries Superior, Wis., 1958, Norman, Okla., 1963, Yukon, 1966, Oklahoma City, 1967. Faculty Show, Okla. Sci. and Arts Found., 1965, Okla. Painting and Sculpture Biennial, 1971, Balcony Art Gallery, Oklahoma City, 1971; executed mural Midland Coop. Supermarket, Superior, 1959; tchr. water color Okla. Sci. and Art Found. Faculty, 1965-66. Mem. Gov.'s Council on Arts and Humanities, 1966. Served with USAAF, 1941-45. Decorated Bronze Star medal with five clusters. Mem. Contemporary Art Found. Oklahoma City, AAUP (exec. com. local chpt.), Kappa Pi, Delta Phi Delta. Democrat. Home: 3700 Mason Hills Dr Edmond OK 73034

BACHI, NAOMI MABEL, guidance counselor; b. Weatherford, Okla., Mar. 26, 1916; d. Albert James and Maybell Rebecca (Patton) Baker; student Oklahoma City U., 1947-49, Rio Grande Coll., 1956-57; Chadron (Nebr.) State Tchrs. Coll., 1961-62, Central State U., 1965; m. Michael Mario Bachi, Apr. 5, 1947. Admissions and records clk. Central State U., Edmonds, Okla., 1963-64, records asst., 1964-71, admissions and records counselor, 1971-72, admissions counselor for fgn. students, 1972-74, asso. internat. student advisor, 1974—. Mem. Edmond Democratic Women's Club, Nat. Assn. Fgn. Student Affairs, Central State U. Dames. Home: 3700 Mason Hills Dr Edmond OK 73034 Office: Internat Office Central State U Edmond OK 73034

BACHMAN, JOHN ANDREW, JR., engr.; b. Washington, Apr. 26, 1926; s. John Andrew and Margaret Eleanor (Hauf) B.; B.Aero. Engring., Ga. Inst. Tech., 1951; m. Mary Irene Dougherty, Dec. 27, 1952; children—Barbara Lee (dec.), Robert J., John D., Thomas A., Lisa Marie. Jr. engr. Boeing Co., Seattle, 1951-52; aerodynamist Chase Aircraft Co., Trenton, N.J., also Fairchild Aircraft Co., Hagerstown, Md., 1953-54; engring. cons. Washington area, 1955-57; staff engr. Honeywell Inc., Mpls. and Washington, 1957-68; regional mgr. Ground Transp. div. LTV Corp., Washington, 1968-73; with Mitre Corp., McLean, Va., 1973-77; passenger rail systems program mgr. Unified Industries Inc., Alexandria, Va., 1977—. Active Boy Scouts Am., 1938-72. Served with USNR, 1944-46. Asso. fellow Am. Inst. Aeros. and Astronautics (sect. council 1976-78); mem. Am. Def. Preparedness Assn. Presbyterian. Author publs. in field. Home: 205 Yoakum Pkwy Apt 626 Alexandria VA 22304 Office: 5400 Cherokee Ave Alexandria VA 22312

BACHMAN, ROBERT JOHN, respiratory therapist, hosp. adminstr.; b. Syracuse, N.Y., June 21, 1951; s. James Edward and Mary Jane (Burke) B.; A.A.S., SUNY Upstate Med. Center, Syracuse, 1971; student Ga. State U., Atlanta. Staff technician Meml. Hosp., Syracuse, 1970-71; staff therapist Duke U. Med. Center, Durham, N.C., 1971-72; staff Grady Meml. Hosp., Atlanta, 1972-75, asst. chief respiratory therapy, 1973-75, acting chief, 1975; dir. respiratory care services Crawford W. Long Meml. Hosp., Emory U., Atlanta, 1975—; clin. faculty Ga. State U., 1977—, Emory U., 1977—; asso. examiner Nat. Bd. Respiratory Therapy. Named among outstanding young men Am., U.S. Jaycees, 1978; registered respiratory therapist. Mem. Ga. Soc. Respiratory Therapy (pres.-elect 1979, Pres.'s cert. 1978), Ga. Thoracic Soc., Am. Assn. Respiratory Therapy (chmn. membership sers. com. 1979—), Alpha Eta. Office: Respiratory Care Sers Dept Crawford W Long Meml Hosp of Emory U 35 Linden Ave Atlanta GA 30308

BACHMANN, KATHRYN HODGES, artist, illustrator; b. Henry County, Ala., Nov. 29, 1924; d. Chester Lee and Lottie Lee (Brackin) Hodges; student Troy State U., 1944-45, U. Ala., 1958-59; grad. Famous Artist Sch., 1959; m. Norman Edgar Bachmann, Dec. 24, 1945. Free-lance comml. artist, Dothan, Ala., 1959-61; civil service tng. aids illustrator U.S. Army, Ft. Rucker, Ala., 1961-77; now art tchr. in pvt. practice; one-woman shows: Municipal Civic Center Gallery, Panama City, Fla., 1969, Houston Meml. Library, 1969, 73; exhibited various local group shows; represented in permanent collections: Houston Meml. Library, Dothan, pvt. collections. Mem. Ala., Wiregrass art leagues, Mobile (Ala.) Art Assn., Nat. Hist. Soc., Henry County Hist. Soc., Am. Orchid Soc., United Daus. of the Confederacy. Home: Route 1 Box 336 Dothan AL 36301

BACHNER, JOHN PHILIP, pub. relations and mgmt. cos. exec.; b. Boston, Nov. 8, 1944; s. Barnard and Bertha (Bellar) B.; A.B., Harvard, 1966; m. Marcia L. Davis, Aug. 7, 1966; children—Bernard David, Lissa Suzanne. Screenplay writer Screen Presentations, Inc., film prodn. co. Washington, 1967-68; account exec. Hoffman Assos., Inc., Silver Spring, Md., 1968-71; pres. Bachner Communications, Inc., communications-mktg. co., Silver Spring, 1971—; pres. Bachner Mgmt. Systems, multiple assn. mgmt. co. Silver Spring, 1973—; v.p. Gt. Equitations, Inc., Gt. Falls, Va., 1977—; exec. dir. Cons. Engrs. Council of Met. Washington, Silver Spring, 1971—, Property Mgmt. Assn. Met. Washington, Silver Spring, 1973—, Washington Area Council Engring. Labs., Silver Spring, 1975—, Property Mgmt. Assn. Am., Silver Spring, 1979—, Chem. Specialties Assos., Ltd., Silver Spring, 1979—; exec. sec. Assn. Soil, Found. Engrs., Silver Spring, 1973—; chmn. bd. Constrn. Industry Tech., Inc., Silver Spring, 1973—. Exec. dir. Spruce Knob Assn., Silver Spring, 1975—. Author: Marketing and Promotion for Design Professionals, 1977; writer 25 motion pictures; contbr. numerous articles to profl. publs., popluar mags. Home: 9206 Sterling Montaque Dr Great Falls VA 22066 Office: 8811 Colesville Rd Silver Spring MD 20910

BACKER, WARREN HOWARD ALONZO, food co. exec.; b. New Orleans, Jan. 22, 1930; s. Albert Fredrick and Leota Emily (Alonzo) B.; student Soule Coll., 1946-47; B.A., Tulane U., 1951; m. Jean C. Smith, Sept. 18, 1954; children—Karen E., Cheryl E., Warren Howard Alonzo. Pres., Backer-LeJeune, Inc., New Orleans, 1972—, also dir.; partner B-L Realty Co.; dir. Nat. Bank Commn. in Jefferson, Backer Realty Co., Lafayette Savs. & Loan Assn. Mem. grad. sch. adv. bd. Tulane U., 1972—; mem. pres.'s adv. council Jesuit High Sch., New Orleans; mem. bd. City Park, New Orleans, 1965—. Served with USAF, 1950-52. Mem. Nat. (nat. dir. 1964-67), New Orleans (pres. 1968) food brokers assns. Club: Rotary. Home: 7441 Canal Blvd New Orleans LA 70124 Office: PO Box 9279 Metairie LA 70055

BACKUS, NANCY AHRBECKER, real estate co. exec.; b. Indpls., July 22, 1932; d. Frederick Walter and Frances Irene (Peters) Ahrbecker; B.S., Purdue U., 1954; A.M.T., Ind. U., 1958; postgrad. Columbia U., 1970; children—John Carlton, Frederick William. Tchr. speech pathology various schs., 1958-70; real estate broker Re/Max Properties, Houston, 1977—. Mem. Am. Speech and Hearing Assn., Houston Bd. Realtors, Tex. Bd. Realtors, Acad. Real Estate, Houston Property Exchange. Republican. Presbyterian. Home: 12514 Pine Rock Houston TX 77024 Office: Re/Max Properties 14760 Memorial Dr Suite 303 Houston TX 77079

BACKUS, RICHARD PAUL, banker; b. Cleve., Mar. 9, 1936; s. William F. and Helen C. Backus; B.S.F.S. with honors, Georgetown U., 1956; M.B.A. with honors, U. of Americas, Mexico City, 1966; grad. Advanced Mgmt. Program, U. Hawaii, 1976; postgrad. U. Tex., Dallas, 1973-79; m. Feb. 23, 1957; children—Rebecca Lynn, Richelle Louise, David Paul. With First Nat. City Bank of N.Y., 1960-72, resident v.p., Hong Kong, 1970-72, various Latin Am. positions, 1960-72; v.p. Republic Nat. Bank, Dallas, 1972-73, sr. v.p., 1973—; lectr., chmn. various seminars Am. Mgmt. Assn.; lectr. U. Tex., Dallas, Southwestern Grad. Sch. Banking at So. Meth. U. Treas., bd. dirs. Dallas chpt. Amigos de las Americas, 1977-78, 78-79; mem. Pan Am. com. Tex. State Fair, 1977-79. Served with USMC, 1956-60. Mem. Dallas C. of C., Bankers Assn. Fgn. Trade, Am. Inst. Banking, North Tex. Commn. Clubs: 2001, Brookhaven Country, Rush Creek Yacht. Office: PO Box 225961 Dallas TX 75265

BACON, CHARLES EDWARD, newspaper publisher; b. Oklahoma City, Apr. 16, 1951; s. William J. and Una Opal (Keeter) B.; B.J., U. Okla., 1973; m. Susan L. Marshall, June 9, 1978. Pub., Sayre (Okla.) Jour., 1973—; advisor, prodn. supt. Sayre Jr. Coll. newspaper, 1975-78, Sayre High Sch. newspaper, 1976—. Sec., Beckham County Election Bd., 1979—; bd. dirs. Sayre Meml. Hosp., 1974-77, vice chmn., 1976-77; chmn. United Fund drive, Sayre, 1975-76; bd. dirs. Okla. Symphony; bd. visitors U. Okla., 1974-77; mem. corrections sub-com. Criminal Justice Standards and Goals Project, Okla., 1976-77; chmn. bd. United Meth. Ch., Sayre, 1978-79. Mem. Women in Communications, Okla. Press Assn., Nat. Newspaper Assn., Sayre C. of C. (dir. 1973-77), Western Okla. Hist. Soc. (bd. dirs. 1976-78), Okla. Heritage Assn., Sayre Jaycees, Kappa Alpha, Kappa Tau Alpha, Sigma Delta Chi. Democrat. Club: Sayre Rotary (pres. 1978-79). Home: 705 N Broadway Sayre OK 73662 Office: 110 N 4th St Sayre OK 73662

BACON, H(ENRY) STUART, psychologist; b. Boston, Sept. 23, 1925; s. Henry Stuart and Teresa Regina (Gammons) B.; B.A., U. Mass., 1949; M.S., U. Tenn., 1951, Ph.D., 1953; children—Stuart, Christopher, Geoffrey, Susan, Carolyn, Paul, Laura. Chief clin. psychologist Western State Hosp., Bolivar, Tenn., 1953-55; psychologist Psychiat. Services, Knoxville, 1955-62; pvt. practice clin. psychology, Knoxville, 1962—; pres. Vol. State Rehab. Assn., 1971-72, East Tenn. Substance Abuse Council, 1974-76. Served with U.S. Army, 1943-46; ETO. Mem. Am. Bd. Examiners in Profl. Psychology (diplomate), Am. Psychol. Assn., Tenn. Psychol. Assn. (pres. 1974-75), Internat. Transactional Analysis, Nat. Rehab. Assn., Am. Group Psychotherapy Assn., Southwestern Group Psychotherapy Soc. (pres. 1967-68). Roman Catholic. Office: 4803 Lyons View Pike Knoxville TN 37919

BACON, PHILLIP, geographer, educator, author; b. Cleve., July 10, 1922; s. Hollis Phillip and Emma (Schneider) B.; student The Citadel, 1940-41; A.B., U. Miami, 1946; M.A., George Peabody Coll. for Tchrs. (now Vanderbilt U.), 1951, Ed.D., 1955; m. Dorothy Willey; children—Laura Jane (Mrs. Robert C. Fraser), Phillip Everett. Tchr. social studies Castle Heights Mil. Acad., Lebanon, Tenn., 1946-47, Army and Navy Acad., Carlsbad, Calif., 1948-53; grad. asst. geography George Peabody Coll. for Tchrs., 1953-55, dean Grad. Sch., 1963-64, acting dir. Library Sch., 1964; asst. prof. geography U. Pitts., 1955-57; vis. asst. prof. geography Columbia Tchrs. Coll., 1956-57, asso. prof., 1957-60, prof., 1960-63, 64-66; prof. geography and social studies edn. U. Wash., Seattle, 1966-71, co-dir. tri-univ. project in elementary edn., 1967-71; prof. geography U. Houston, 1971—, chmn. dept. geography, 1973-77, chmn. dept. anthropology, 1973-75. Vis. prof. geography U. Colo., summer 1961, N.C. Central U., spring 1966, U. Tex., summer 1966, Seattle Pacific U., summers 1977-80, U. Wash., 1965, 79; NSF vis. scientist, 1969-71. Mem. editorial adv. bd. World Book Ency., 1965—; bd. cons. World Book Atlas, 1965-70, chmn. area studies com., 1969—; cons. editor Golden Press, 1958-61; cons. book div. Time, Inc., 1960-69; cons. social sci. project Ednl. Research Council Am., 1962-70; mem. steering com. High Sch. Geography Project, 1965-70; cons. U.S. Office Edn., 1964-76; mem. Wash. Social Studies Adv. Commn., 1968-71; curriculum cons. Served with USNR, 1942-45. Recipient award for distinguished undergrad. teaching U. Wash., 1971; Teaching Excellence award U. Houston, 1975, 79. Fellow Royal Geog. Soc., Am. Geog. Soc. N.Y., Nat. Council for Geog. Edn. (pres. 1966, Distinguished Service award 1974); mem. Assn. Am. Geographers (councillor 1976-79, chmn. publs. com. 1977-79), NEA, Am. Assn. Higher Edn., Nat. (sec. Geography Spl. Interest Group 1977-78), Tex. councils social studies, Geographic Educators Tex. (founder, co-dir. S.E. Tex. region), S.W. Social Sci. Assn., Vanderbilt Alumni Assn. (dir. 1979—), Sigma Xi, Sigma Alpha Epsilon, Phi Delta Kappa, Omicron Delta Pi, Phi Kappa Phi, Kappa Delta Pi, Gamma Theta Upsilon, Pi Gamma Mu. Presbyterian. Club: Explorers. Author: Australia, Oceania, and the Polar Lands, 1961; North America, 1961; Golden Book Picture Atlas of the World, 6 vols., 1961; Children's Picture Atlas of the World, 1966; Children's Picture Atlas in Colour, 1966; (with Norman Carls and Frank E. Sorenson) Knowing Our Neighbors in the United States, 1966; Knowing Our Neighbors in the United States and Canada, 1966; Regions Around The World, 1976; (with R.R. Boyce) Towns and Cities, 1976; (with others) The United States and Canada, 1970; (with P.V. Greco) The Story of Latin America, 1970; Field Media Kit series, 1973; (with Byron Strong and W.B. Conroy) America In Space and Time, 1976. Editor: Focus on Geography, Key Concepts and Teaching Strategies, 1970; co-editor: Foundations of World Regional Geography Series, 1970-73. Cons. editor Life Pictorial Atlas of the World, 1961, Jour. of Geography, 1967-70, Where and Why?, 1972, 80; co-dir. Addison-Wesley Elementary Social Studies Series, 1975; mem. editorial adv. bd. Social Edn., 1976—. Contbr. chpts. to books and yearbooks, articles and revs. to profl. jours. Home: 2627 Amherst St West University Pl Houston TX 77005 Office: 527 Philip Guthrie Hoffman Hall U Houston Houston TX 77004

BACON, PHYRNE YOUENS, mathematician; b. Holbrook, Ariz., Jan. 2, 1936; d. Willis George and Cynthia (Tanner) Youens; B.A., Rice Inst., Houston, 1959; M.S., U. Tenn., 1963; M.A., U. Fla., 1971, Ph.D., 1974; m. Philip Bacon, Mar. 12, 1966; children—Jennie Webb Marquess, Cynthia Marquess. Engr. lab. Sperry Rand Corp., 1959-61; self-employed research mathematician, 1974—. NASA trainee, 1963-66. Address: 3101 NW 2d Ave Gainesville FL 32607

BACON, WILLIAM ARTHUR, lawyer; b. Durant, Miss., Feb. 8, 1912; s. James Webster and Zouella (Guess) B.; LL.B., U. Miss., 1935; m. Carolee Meyer Pratt, Mar. 15, 1941; 1 son, William A. Admitted to Miss. bar, 1935; city atty. (Durant), Miss., 1935-40; asst. U.S. dist. atty. So. Dist. Miss., 1942, 46; state bond atty. Miss., 1951—; city atty. Pearl (Miss.), 1973—. Mem. Miss. Ho. of Reps., 1936-40. Pres. Crestview Home, 1957-64, Miss. Children's Home Soc, 1964-76, Jackson YMCA, 1963-64. Served as lt. USNR, 1942-46. Mem. Am., Miss., Hinds County (pres. 1959-60) bar assns., Jackson Photog. Soc. (pres 1957), Miss. State Bar (pres. 1970-71), Fed. Bar Assn., Miss. Mcpl. Attys. Assn. (pres. 1978-79), Am. Judicature Soc. Democrat. Episcopalian (vestryman). Clubs: Gulf States Camera (pres. council), Men's Y (pres. 1947); Kiwanis (pres. 1956), Jackson Country, River Hills (dir.). Home: 3909 Pinewood Dr Jackson MS 39211 Office: Plaza Bldg PO Box 15 Jackson MS 39205

BACOT, HENRY PARROTT, JR., art historian, mus. curator; b. Shreveport, La., Dec. 13, 1941; s. Henry Parrott and Martha Jane (Van Loan) B.; B.A., Baylor U., 1963; M.A., State U. N.Y., 1972; m. Barbara Evlyn SoRolle, Aug. 1, 1970. Curator, Anglo-Am. Art Mus., La. State U., Baton Rouge, 1967—, asst. prof. fine arts, 1967—. Mem. bd. Found. for Hist. La., 1972-74; sponsor Am. Friends of Attingham Summer Sch., Inc., 1977—; mem. Citizens Com. for Preservation of Old State Capitol, 1977—. Mem. Soc. Archtl. Historians, Victorian Soc. Am., Friends of Cast Iron Architecture, Decorative Arts Soc. Republican. Episcopalian. Home: 2800 July St #19 Baton Rouge LA 70808 Office: PO Box 20249 La State U Baton Rouge LA 70893

BADDERS, HURLEY EDMUND, hist. agy. dir.; b. Cedartown, Ga., June 21, 1931; s. Herald Edmund and Parilee (Parker) B.; grad. pub. high sch.; m. Barbara Ann Storey, Nov. 12, 1955; children—Barbara April, Parker Lanier. Asst. state news editor Anderson (S.C.) Ind., 1957-61, news dir., 1961-68; exec. dir. Pendleton Dist. Hist. and Recreational Commn., 1968—. Cons. several comml. firms. Mem. So. Travel Dirs. Council, 1970-76; exec. bd. S.C. Fedn. Museums, 1971-75, pres., 1976-78; chmn. leisure resources com. Appalachian Council Govts., 1972-75; mem. exec. council Confedn. S.C. Hist. Socs., 1974-76, vice chmn., 1976-78, chmn., 1978-80; S.C. regional coordinator Am. Revolution Bicentennial, 1974—; bd. dirs. S.C. Travel Council; permanent v.p. S.C. Hall of Fame, Inc.; treas. Discover Upcountry Carolina Assn., 1979—; bd. mem. Appalachian Hist. Preservation Adv. Com., 1978—; exec. bd. Anderson YMCA, 1980—; trustee Anderson Heritage, Inc. Served with USNR, 1951-53. Recipient award for news reporting S.C. Press Assn., 1960, award for in-depth reporting, 1963; named Leisure Resources Man of Year, Appalachian Council Govts., 1976. Mem. Anderson Area C. of C. (tourism chmn. 1970), Am. Assn. Museums, Nat. Trust Hist. Preservation, Anderson County Hist. Soc. (exec. council 1977—, v.p. 1978—), Assn. State and Local History, Am. Booksellers Assn. Baptist. Author: Pendleton Historic District, 1973; Broken Path: The Cherokee Campaign of 1776, 1976. Editor: Old Stone Church, 1973. Home: 2517 Lindale Rd Anderson SC 29621 Office: 125 E Queen St Pendleton SC 29670

BADDLEY, JAMES RICHARD, assn. exec.; b. Water Valley, Miss., June 15, 1938; s. Richard Henry and Virginia (Lee) B.; B.A., U. Miss., 1960, M.S., 1963; postgrad. Creighton U., 1965, Auburn U., 1967; m. Melvanna Lee Handley, Mar. 13, 1963; children—Melanie Ann, Scot Lee, Virginia Marie. Instr., Hinds Jr. Coll., 1965-71, dir. allied health programs, 1971-74; asst. dean Sch. Health Related Professions, U. Miss. Med. Center, Jackson, 1974-75; v.p. edn. Miss. Hosp. Assn., Jackson, 1975—; exec. dir. Miss. Hosp. Assn. Ednl. Found. Mem. Am. Soc. Health Manpower, Edn. and Tng., Am. Hosp. Assn. Baptist. Office: PO Box 16444 Jackson MS 39206

BADGETT, JIMMIE LEON, fire sci. educator; b. Winters, Tex., Feb. 24, 1937; s. Howard Lloyd and Veda Rae (McDonald) B.; B.A., Hardin Simmons U., 1960; M.P.A., S.W. Tex. State U., 1978; m. Charlotte Ann Lynch, Feb. 18, 1961; children—Christi Kalyn, Regina Gaye. Ins. agt. Farmers Ins. Group, Abilene, Tex., 1966-72; realtor, owner operator Big Country Real Estate Co., Abilene, 1964-72; lt. Abilene Fire Dept., 1960-72; tng. cons. Commn. on Fire Protection Personnel Standards and Edn., Austin, Tex., 1972—; fire sci. instr. Austin Community Coll.; asst. chief CE-Bar Vol. Fire Dept.; chief Lake Ridge Vol. Fire Dept.; cons. Community Coll. of Air Force. Mem. Abilene Housing Authority, 1970-71; chmn. Centex chpt. ARC, 1974. Certified master fire service instr. Mem. Internat. Soc. Fire Service Instrs. (organizer Tex. chpt.), Nat. Fire Protection Assn., Nat. Assn. Fire Sci. and Adminstrn., Austin Soc. Pub. Adminstrs., Am. Inst. Planners, Am. Soc. Planning Ofcls., Tex. State Assn. Fire Fighters, Austin Fire Safety Bd., Internat. Fire Service Training Assn., Pi Gamma Mu, Delta Tau Kappa. Democrat. Baptist. Clubs: Classic Am. LaFrance Coterie, Masons, Shriners. Home: 9704 Lake Ridge Dr Austin TX 78746 Office: 510 S Congress Suite 406 Austin TX 78704

BADILLO, JORGE, surgeon; b. Mexico City, Mex., Oct. 24, 1928; s. Ricardo J. and Carmen L. (Gonzalez) B.; came to U.S., 1957, naturalized, 1971; B.S. in Biology, Mex. U., 1944; M.D., Escuela Medico Militar, 1950; children—Kenneth, Erick. Intern Central Army Hosp., Mexico City, 1951-53; resident in cancer surgery Roswell Park Med. Inst., Buffalo, 1957-59, surgeon in head and neck cancer research, 1959-61; resident in surgery Alexandria (Va.) Hosp., 1964-65, Scott & White Hosp., Temple, Tex., 1965-67; attending surgeon St. Joseph Hosp., Houston, 1967—, instr. surgery, 1967—. Diplomate Am. Bd. Surgery. Fellow ACS; mem. Soc. Head and Neck Surgeons, Tex. Med. Assn., Harris County Med. Soc., Roswell Park Surg. Soc. Republican. Roman Catholic. Club: Braircliff in Lake Travis (Austin). Contbr. numerous articles in cancer research to profl. jours. Office: 2101 Crawford St Houston TX 77002

BADOUH, EDWARD, JR., lawyer; b. Houston, Feb. 7, 1945; s. Edward and Rubylien B.; B.B.A., Tex. U., 1967; J.D., St. Mary's U., 1970. Admitted to Tex. bar, 1971; mem. staff. Congressman George Bush, 1970; partner ifrm firm Badouh and Badouh, Houston, 1971—; judge, municipal ct., City of New Braunfels, Tex., 1971-73; chmn. Aquasonic Lures, Inc., Cibolo, Tex., 1977—; dir. New Braunfels Abstract. Dir. Community Chest, New Braunfels, 1974-75; dir. San Antonio Livestock Show and Rodeo, 1975—; dir. Gonzales (Tex.) Warm Springs Hosp., 1972-77, pres., 1978-80. Served to lt. U.S. Army, 1970-71. Mem. Am., S. Central Tex., Comal County (v.p.), San Antonio Jr. bar assns., S. Tex., New Braunfels C. of C., New Braunfels Indsl. Found., State Bar Tex. Episcopalian. Home: 245 S Seguin St New Braunfels TX 78130 Office: PO Box 1010 New Braunfels TX 78130

BAER, CHARLES MICHAEL, exec. elec. engr.; b. Balt., Oct. 20, 1909; s. Charles Edward and Dorothy (Fuchs) B.; B.S. in Mil. Engring., U.S. Mil. Acad., 1932; grad. Nat. War Coll., 1950; m. Esther Debelius, Nov. 1, 1932; children—Charles Michael, Alan LeRoy, Esther Sandra (Mrs. Thomas R. Savoie). Commd. 2d lt. Signal Corps, U.S. Army, 1932, advanced through grades to brig. gen., 1957; comdr. joint communications activities Okinawa Invasion, 1945; mem. staff Joint Chiefs Staff, 1950-53; signal officer 2d Army, Ft. Meade, Md., 1953-56; chmn. European mil. communications coordinating com., chmn. civil emergency communications planning com. NATO, Paris, 1956-59; comdt. U.S. Army Signal Sch. and comdg. gen. Ft. Monmouth, N.J., 1959-62; ret., 1962; European rep. G.T. & E. Co., 1962-64; with State Dept., 1965; asst. chief scientist Communications Satellite Corp., Washington, 1966-74. Bd. dirs. Am. Club, Paris, 1963-64. Decorated Legion of Merit with oak leaf cluster. Sr. mem. I.E.E.E.; charter mem. Armed Forces Communications Electronics Assn. Mason (Shriner). Club: Army-Navy (Washington). Home: 3864 N Chesterbrook Rd Arlington VA 22207

BAER, DAVID CLYDE, architect-engr.; b. Maitland, Mo., Feb. 28, 1904; s. Hiram Cyrus and Charlotta Eleanor (Meeker) B.; student U. Colo., 1923-24, U. Minn., 1925-27, U. Tex., 1931-34; m. Gyneth Stugard, 1930 (div. 1931); m. 2d, Mayne Mary Collins, 1933 (div. 1966); children—Robert Goldwin, David Collins, Carolyn Marie; m. 3rd. Gladys Evelyn Johnson, 1966 (dec. 1973); m. 4th Vinnie Dee Coffman, 1979. Archtl. draftsman, Edinburg, Tex., 1928-31, Austin, Tex., 1928-33; prin. David C. Baer, architect, Austin, 1934-42, Houston, 1949—; hosp. archtl. designer Faulkner & Kingsbury, architects, Washington, 1944-45, Rather Moore & Assos., Houston, 1946-49, office mgr., 1947-49; cons. to Calhoun Tungate Jackson & Dill, architects, Houston, 1973-76; lectr. dept. architecture U. Houston, 1965-68. Bd. dirs. Family Service Center, Houston, 1960-68, pres., 1965-68. Served with C.E., U.S. Army, 1942-44. Fellow AIA (Kemper award 1957); mem. Constrn. Specifications Inst., Tex. Soc. Architects (dir. 1942-44, chmn. public relations com. 1951-54). Methodist. Clubs: Masons (32 deg.), Shriners, Sierra, Exchange. Maj. works include: Jones Youth Bldg., St. Paul's United Meth. Ch., Houston, 1959, Tazewell (Va.) Community Hosp., 1973, Wythe County (Va.) Health Center, 1977. Address: 1200 Bissonnett Houston TX 77005

BAERWOLF, CECILIA BEALDA CLAUSSEN, owner gift shop; b. Ironwood, Mich., May 6, 1923; d. John Frank and Mabel (Schroeder) Claussen; cert. Rice Bus. Coll., 1968; A.S., Trident Tech. Coll., 1979; m. Louis August Baerwolf, July 28, 1969; children by previous marriage—Linda M. Thomas, Michael Paul, Robert Frederick Thomas, Patrick Alan Thomas, Theresa Christine Thomas. Govt. food insp. Charleston County Sch. Dept., Charleston, S.C., 1967-68; credit mgr. Diana Dress Shop, Charleston, 1968-69; 2d shift supr. Manhattan Shirt Co., Charleston Heights, S.C., 1971; owner, operator Home Gift Shoppe, Lineville, N.C., 1979—; cons. and instr. in arts and crafts. Vol. worker Democratic Party, Davenport, Iowa, 1948-51; v.p. P.T.A., San Francisco, 1958-59.

BAETZMAN, FRED ERNEST, JR., diversified co. exec.; b. Leesburg, Fla., June 10, 1934; s. Fred E. and Alice (Lowrey) B.; B.S., The Citadel, Charleston, S.C., 1956; postgrad. U. Ga., 1956-57; m. Sandra Kay, Aug. 18, 1958; children—Kerry Ann, Kristi Kay. Contracts, mktg. Dynatronics Inc., Orlando, Fla., office in Washington, 1960-65; mktg. Vector Aydin Co., Orlando, 1965-67; mktg. United Aircraft Co., Orlando, 1967-69; v.p. Telemetry Sale Co., Orlando, 1969-71; v.p. Pricon Inc., Haiti, 1969-73, pres., 1973-75, also dir.; pres. UniRep Inc., Orlando, 1973—, Haitan Electronics Mfg. Co.; dir. Aerosci Corp.; real estate broker, 1970—. Served as pilot USAF, 1957-60. Mem. Armed Forces Communication and Electronics Assn., U.S. Air Force Assn., Electronic Warfare Assn., Central Fla. Real Estate Assn., Haitian Mfg. Assn. Presbyterian. Club: Lake Beresford Yacht. Home: 6419 Wynglow Ln Orlando FL 32808 Office: Pricon Inc Box 17713 Orlando FL 32810

BAFALIS, LOUIS ARTHUR, congressman; b. Boston, Sept. 28, 1929; s. Louis J. and Vesta (Reenstierna) B.; A.B., St. Anselm's Coll., 1952; m. Mary Elizabeth Lund, Feb. 18, 1956; children—Renee Louise, Gregory Louis. Investment banker, Palm Beach, Fla., 1970—; mem. Fla. Ho. Reps., 1964-66, Senate, 1966-70; mem. 93d-96th Congresses, 10th Dist. Fla. Vice chmn. Palm Beach County ARC, 1963-67; hon. dir. South Fla. Fair and Expn., 1965-70; county chmn. Muscular Dystrophy Assn., 1970. Candidate for Gov. Fla., 1970; chmn. Republican Nat. Govts. Conf., 1968. Served to capt. AUS; Korea. Mem. North Palm Beach C. of C., Palm Beach Gardens Jaycees. Mason. Home: Cresciente 401 S 7150 Estero Blvd Fort Myers Beach FL 33931 Office: 2433 Rayburn House Office Bldg Washington DC 20515

BAFFES, CHRIS GUS, surgeon; b. New Orleans, May 23, 1931; s. Gus and Tina (Bores) B.; B.S., Tulane U., 1953, M.D., 1955; m. Kathy Reitenbach, Apr. 7, 1967; children—Cyndie, Laura, Karen, Greg, Glen, Sharon, Tina. Intern, Charity Hosp., New Orleans, 1955-56, resident gen. and thoracic surgery, 1956-61; practice medicine specializing in surgery, Chgo., 1953—; mem. staff Swedish Covenant Hosp., Chgo.; asst. prof. surgery Rush Med. Coll., Chgo., 1974—. Served to capt. AUS, 1961-63. Fellow A.C.S., Am. Coll. Chest Physicians, Am. Coll. Angiology; mem. N.Y. Acad. Sci. Contbr. articles to profl. jours. Home: 6319 Louisville St New Orleans LA 70124

BAGBY, WILLIAM RARDIN, lawyer; b. Grayson, Ky., Feb. 19, 1910; s. John Albert and Nano (Rardin) B.; A.B., Cornell U., 1933; LL.B., U. Mich., 1936; postgrad. Northwestern U., 1946-47; m. Elizabeth Hinkel, Nov. 22, 1975; 1 son from previous marriage, John Robert. Admitted to Ky. bar, 1937, Ohio bar, 1952; practiced in Grayson, 1937-43; city atty., Grayson, 1939-41, judge, 1941-43; counsel U.S. Treasury, 1946-54; practiced law, Lexington, Ky., 1954—. Prof. law U. Ky., 1956-57; pub. Enquirer, Grayson, 1937-43. Mem. Lexington-Fayette County Bd. Adjustment, 1965—. Trustee, Bagby Music Lovers' Found., N.Y.C.; v.p., gen. counsel Headley-Whitney Mus., 1979—. Served as lt. USNR, 1944-46. Mem. Am., Ky., Ohio bar assns., Kappa Sigma, Democrat. Episcopalian. Clubs: Rotary, Iroquois Hunt, Keeneland, Spindletop; Wichita Country. Home: 228 Market St Lexington KY 40508 Office: First Nat Bldg Lexington KY 40507

BAGGETT, DURWARD AUGUSTUS, physician; b. Smackover, Ark., Dec. 30, 1924; s. David A. and Thelma (Collins) B.; B.S., U. Tex.-Austin, 1949, M.D., U. Tex.-Galveston, 1959; m. Vadis Dale Park, Apr. 7, 1946; children—Mary Ann Baggett McGuffin, David D. Chemist, Cities Service Refining Corp., Lake Charles, La., 1949-51; research chemist Dow Chem. Co., Freeport, Tex., 1951-55; intern Brackenridge Hosp., Austin, 1959-60; family practice as physician and surgeon, Austin, 1960—; chief of staff Brackenridge Hosp., 1976. Served with USNR, USMCR, 1942-46. Diplomate Am. Bd. Family Practice. Fellow Am. Acad. Family Physicians; mem. AMA, Tex. (council ann. sessions), Travis County med. assns., Tex. (chmn. sci. program com.), Travis County (pres. 1966) acads. family physicians, Sigma Xi, Phi Theta Kappa. Baptist. Clubs: Masons (32 deg.), Shriners. Patentee in chem. field. Home: Austin TX Office: 3006 Red River Austin TX 78705

BAGGETT, JIMMY DEAN, hydrologic engr., govt. ofcl.; b. Vernon, Tex., Jan. 11, 1935; s. Frank Bunos and Martha Lois (Lemon) B.; B.Arch., Tex. Tech U., 1956; m. Glenda Faye Johnson, Jan. 24, 1958; children—Carolyn, Cathy. Supervisory hydrologic engr. Corps Engrs., Ft. Worth, 1967-71, chief hydraulics br., 1972—. Mem. U.S. com. Internat. Commn. on Large Dams, 1971—. Served with C.E., AUS, 1956-57. Recipient Community Service award Tarrant County United Fund, 1974, certificate of achievement Corps Engrs., 1958. Registered profl. engr., Tex. Mem. Nat., Tex. socs. profl. engrs., Soc. Am. Mil. Engrs., Ft. Worth Fed. Bus. Assn. (pres., certificate of appreciation 1974), Res. Officers Assn. (sec.-treas. Ft. Worth chpt.), Nat. Congress Parents and Tchrs., Tex. Tech U. Ex-Students Assn., Dallas-Ft. Worth Metroplex Recreation Council. Democrat. Baptist. Designer, operator flood control structures in 9 river basins of Tex. Home: 1114 Sproles St Fort Worth TX 76126 Office: 819 Taylor St Fort Worth TX 76102

BAGGETT, WILLIAM ROBERT, metal products mfg. exec.; b. Atlanta, Jan. 12, 1936; s. Eruee and Annie Mildred (Millirons) B.; student Ga. State U., Atlanta, 1956; m. Patricia Irene Towns, Oct. 15, 1955; 1 dau., Patricia Carlene. Spl. agt. Vulcan Life Ins. Co. 1956-58; gen. agt. Peach State Ins. Co., 1958-61; v.p. Nat. Factors Corp., also pres. Nat. Factors Investment Corp., 1969-71; v.p. Ga. Factors Corp., also pres. Monitor Mfg. Co., 1971—; pres. Monitor Distbg. Co., Atlanta, 1972—; dir. Ga. Factors, Nat. Wholesalers, Monitor Mfg. Co., Monitor Distbg. Co. Bd. dirs. Arlington Schs., 1974-77, vice chmn., 1975-78; indsl. chmn. United Way, 1975. Recipient award Vulcan Life Ins. Co., 1957, St. Regis Paper Co., 1974. Mem. Ga. Bus. and Industry Assn., South Fulton C. of C., Metal Mfg. Assn. Republican. Baptist. Clubs: Lakeside Country, Horseshoe Bend Country, Landings Country. Home: 2525 Spalding Dr Dunwoody GA 30338 Office: 4736 Frederick Dr SW Atlanta GA 30336

BAGGS, LEAH L. BATES (MRS. LINTON DANIEL BAGGS, JR.), civic worker; b. Franklinville, N.Y.; d. William Henry and Arlie Mae (Bozworth) Bates; A.B., Barnard Coll., 1922; student spl. courses various univs.; m. Linton Daniel Baggs, Jr., Oct. 1, 1926; children—Joan Bates (Mrs. Herbert A. McKenzie, Jr.), Linton Daniel III. Hon. bd. dirs. Macon Community Concert Assn., 1968—, pres., 1959-64; bd. dirs. Middle Ga. Camellia Soc., v.p. Macon Grand Opera Assn., 1954—; vice regent Ga. div. Magna Charta Dames, 1968-70, regent, 1970-72; hon. state regent Daus. Am. Colonists, 1962, nat. chmn. colonial heritage com., 1962-64; com. chmn. Ga. br. Sons and Daus. of Pilgrims Soc., 1954-55. Mem. AAUW, Ga. Soc. Mayflower Descs. (corr. sec. 1960-62), Pilgrim John Howland Soc., D.A.R., Middle Ga. Hist. Soc. (charter mem.). Am., Ga., Middle Ga. (dir. 1974—), S.C. camellia socs., Nat. Trust for Historic Preservation, Sigma Alpha Iota. Presbyterian. Clubs: Barnard Coll. (v.p. 1967-72), Morning Music (pres. 1951-53), Atlanta Music, Capitol City Atlanta (Atlanta); Idle Hour Country (Macon, Ga.). Home: 1137 N Jackson Springs Rd Macon GA 31211

BAGGS, LINTON DANIEL, JR., corp. exec.; b. Bainbridge, Ga., Dec. 27, 1902; s. Dr. Linton Daniel and Madge Ione (Morgan) B.; student Mercer U., 1920-21, Pace Inst., 1921-22; m. Leah Bates, Oct. 1, 1926; children—Linton Daniel III, Joan Bates (Mrs. Herbert Alonzo McKenzie, Jr.). Accountant, L. D. Baggs & Co., Macon, Ga., 1923-46; v.p. Jacksonville Broadcasting Co. (Fla.), 1942-52; pres. Community Broadcasting Co., Asheville, N.C., 1946-49, Bibb Transit Co., Macon, 1949-67, Coca Cola Bottling Co., Hannibal, Mo., Coca Cola Bottling Co., Kankakee, Ill., Coca Cola Bottling Co., Dubuque, Iowa, all until 1967; sec.-treas. Brower-Baggs Press, Inc., North Miami, Fla., 1967—; dir. Ga. Bank & Trust Co., Macon, Peeler Hardware Co. Mem. Ga. Bd. Accountants, 1953-58. Bd. regents Univ. System of Ga. C.P.A., Ga. Mem. Ga. Soc. C.P.A.'s, Am. Inst. C.P.A.'s, Am., Middle Ga. (pres. 1961-62, dir. 1968—) camellia socs., Sigma Nu. Presbyterian. Mason, Rotarian (pres. 1957-58), Elk. Clubs: Idle Hour (Macon); Capitol City (Atlanta). Home: 1137 N Jackson Springs Rd Macon GA 31211 Office: 12365 W Dixie Hwy North Miami FL 33161

BAGGS, WILBUR JAMES, JR., gynecologist; b. Balt., Nov. 10, 1919; s. Wilbur James and Evelyn Thistle (McCoy) B.; B.A., U. Richmond, 1940; M.D., Med. Coll. Va., 1943; m. Virginia Cockes, Oct. 2, 1947; children—Beverly Lynn, Barbara Denise. Intern, Charity Hosp. La., New Orleans, 1944; resident Norfolk (Va.) Gen. Hosp., 1946-47, Charity Hosp. La., 1947-50; practice medicine specializing in gynecology, New Orleans, 1950, Newport News, Va., 1951—. Served with USN, 1944-46. Diplomate Am. Bd. Ob-Gyn. Fellow A.C.S.; mem. Am. Thermographic Soc., Soc. Study Breast Disease, Med. Soc. Va. Episcopalian. Club: James River Country (Newport News). Office: 328 Main St Newport News VA 23601

BAGLEY, RONALD EVERETT, fin. analyst; b. Niagara Falls, N.Y.; s. Augustus and Eula (Lee) B.; A.A.S., Orange County Community Coll., 1967; B.S., U. Buffalo, 1972; M.B.A., Syracuse U., 1976; m. Alleen Todd; children—Daria Patrice, Ronald Demetric. Liaison engr. Bell Aerosystems Co., Niagara Falls, 1967-69; engr. Gen. Electric Co., Roanoke, Va., 1972-75; buyer IBM, Lexington, Ky., 1976-77, sr. staff asst., 1977-78, mgr. purchasing plans and controls, 1978-79, fin. analyst lab. ops., 1979—; mktg. instr. Ky. Bus. Coll., 1976—; pres. Tech. Mktg. Program Orgn. Gen. Electric Co., 1974-75. Mem. council Program to Increase Minority Engring. Grads., 1973-75. Recipient Profl. Excellence award Gen. Electric Co., 1974, 75. Mem. NAACP (chpt. v.p. 1966-67), Am. Mgmt. Assn., Assn. MBA Execs. Home: 3205 Carriage Lane Circle Lexington KY 40502 Office: 740 New Circle Rd Lexington KY 40511

BAGWELL, CHARLES MALCOLM, civil engr.; b. Lawrenceville, Ga., May 25, 1934; s. John Daniel and Julia Ellen (Morcock) B.; B.C.E., Ga. Inst. Tech., 1959; m. Susan Grovia Brender, Nov. 8, 1964; children—Jennifer Ann, Tyler Ernst. Civil engr. Ga. Hwy. Dept., Atlanta, 1959-63, Dept. Housing and Urban Devel., Atlanta, 1963-65; civil engr. Urban Renewal, Atlanta, 1965-67; civil engr., planner HEW, Constrn. Services, Office of Edn., Atlanta, 1967-71; civil engr. Fac. Engring. Constrn. Agy., HEW, Atlanta, 1971—. Registered profl. engr., Ga. Served with AUS, 1954-56. Home: 137 Lancelot Way Lawrenceville GA 30245

BAGWELL, GINGER GAYE CAPPS, counselor; b. Mangum, Okla., Nov. 26, 1946; d. Travis Bowles and Virginia Myrie (Dorrill) Capps; B.S. in Edn., U. Okla., 1969; M.Ed. in Counseling, W. Tex. State U., 1978; m. Paul Wesley Bagwell, June 26, 1965; 1 son, Paul Wesley. Tchr. English, Austin Jr. High Sch., Amarillo, 1969-72; placement specialist, women's programs Amarillo (Tex.) Coll., 1978—; vol. instr. English to fgn.-speaking adults, 1972-73. Mem. Am. Personnel and Guidance Assn., AAUW, High Plains Personnel and Guidance Assn., Pharm. Aux. Republican. Baptist. Club: Amarillo Town. Home: 1010 Crockett St Amarillo TX 79102 Office: PO Box 447 Amarillo TX 79178

BAGWELL, LEWIS HOBSON, JR., broadcasting co. exec.; b. Clinton, S.C., June 15, 1926; s. Lewis Hobson and Eunice Elizabeth (Painter) B.; student Clemson U., 1943-44, Presbyn. Coll., Clinton, S.C., 1946-48; m. Rudy Elizabeth Craine, Dec. 15, 1945; children—Zane, Cathy, Susan. Mgr. Cherokee Theatre, Gaffney, S.C., 1948-50; salesman Maxwell Bros. & Wilkes Furniture Co., Clinton, 1950-57; salesman Suburban Radio Group, Clinton, 1957-60, mgr., 1960-67, v.p., gen. mgr. stas. WJJJ/WVVV radio, Christiansburg, Va., 1967—, also dir. radio stas. WJJJ, WVVV, WHHV, WSVM, WZKY, WEGO, WPEG. Served with USNR, 1944-46. Mem. Christiansburg C. of C. (dir. 1970). Baptist (deacon). Clubs: Rotary (dir. 1976), Masons (32 deg.), Shriners. Contbr. articles on western films for film collectors' mags. Home: 370 Summit Ridge Rd Christiansburg VA 24073 Office: PO Box 30 1780 N Franklin St Christiansburg VA 24073

BAHAKEL, CY N., broadcasting exec.; b. Birmingham, Ala., Apr. 12, 1921; B.A., U. Ala., 1943, J.D., 1945; m. Beverly B. Boyd, 1951; children—Vevann, Suzanne, Cy, Marybeth, Amy, Steve. Practice law, Tuscaloosa, Ala., 1945-47; pres. Bahakel Stas., also Sta. WCCB-TV, Charlotte, N.C. Trustee, United Community Service, Charlotte, Wingate Coll.; bd. dirs. Charlotte Jr. Achievement; mem. exec. bd. Mecklenburg council Boy Scouts Am.; bd. dirs. Billy Graham Charlotte Crusade, 1972, Law Enforcement Assistance Found., Charlotte, Charlotte Symphony Assn.; mem. N.C. State Senate, 1972-76. Recipient Pres.'s award Gardner-Webb Coll., 1976; Abe Lincoln award, 1977; Founder's award N.C. Heart Assn. Served with U.S. Army, 1944-45. Mem. Charlotte C. of C. Baptist. Office: WCCB 1 TV Pl Charlotte NC 28205

BAHAR, DAVID, physician, educator; b. Balikesir, Turkey, Mar. 1, 1915; s. Bohor Salamon and Miriam (Bonfil) B.; came to U.S., 1956, naturalized, 1967; B.A., Kabatas Coll. for Boys, Istanbul, Turkey, 1934; M.D., U. Istanbul, 1940; m. Natica May Cooze, Apr. 15, 1962; children—Barbara Lynne (Mrs. Gerald Hartenberger), Donna Jean, David Winchester. Intern Army Hosp., Konya, Turkey, 1941-42; resident 3d Med. Service U. Hosp., Istanbul, Turkey, 1943-46; chief Tb Dispensary, Eyub, Istanbul, 1946-56; research fellow Baylor Coll. Medicine, Houston, 1956-59, instr. medicine, 1959-61, asst. prof., 1963-66; clin. dir. Tb div. Jefferson Davis Hosp., Houston, 1960-62, med. dir., 1963-66; med. dir., supt. Hale Meml. Hosp., Tuscaloosa, Ala., 1967-77; staff physician VA Hosp., Tuscaloosa, Druid City Hosp., Tuscaloosa; mem. adj. faculty Coll. Community Health Scis., U. Ala., Tuscaloosa, 1974-77, asso. prof. medicine, 1977—; cons. in chest Bryce Hosp., Partlow State Sch. and Hosp. Mem. Ala. Tb Hosp. Assn. (pres. 1968-71), Ala. (pres. 1971-72), Am. thoracic socs., Tuscaloosa County Med. Soc., Med. Soc. State Ala., Am. Coll. Chest Physicians. Democrat. Clubs: Indian Hills Country, University (Tuscaloosa). Author: Psychopathia Sexualis-Krafft-Ebbing, 1950; Les Jours De L'Homme-Besençon, 1948. Research, publs. in Tb. Home: 2566 14th St E Tuscaloosa AL 35401 Office: 809 University Blvd E Tuscaloosa AL 35401

BAHN, GILBERT SCHUYLER, mech. engr.; b. Syracuse, N.Y., Apr. 25, 1922; s. Chester Bert and Irene Eliza (Schuyler) B.; B.S., Columbia U., 1943; M.S. in Mech. Engring., Rensselaer Poly. Inst., 1965; Ph.D. in Engring., Columbia Pacific U., 1979; m. Iris Cummings Birch, Sept. 14, 1957 (dec.); 1 son, Gilbert Kennedy. Chem. engr. Gen. Electric Co., Pittsfield, Mass., 1946-48, devel. engr., Schenectady, 1948-53; sr. thermodynamics engr. Marquardt Co., Van Nuys, Calif., 1953-54, research scientist, 1954-64, research cons., 1964-70; engring. specialist LTV Corp., Hampton, Va., 1970—. Mem. JANNAF Performance Standardization Working Group, 1966—, thermochemistry working group, 1967-72; propr. Schuyler Tech. Library, 1952—. Active Boy Scouts Am., 1958-78. Served to capt. USAAF, 1943-46. Recipient Silver Beaver award Boy Scouts Am., 1970. Registered profl. engr., N.Y., Calif. Mem. ASME, Am. Chem. Soc., Spl. Libraries Assn., Combustion Inst. (sec. western states sect. 1957-71), Soc. for Preservation Book of Common Prayer. Episcopalian (vestryman 1968-70). Author: Reaction Rate Compilation for the H-O-N System, 1968. Founding editor Pyrodynamics, 1963-69; proceedings editor Kinetics, Equilibria and Performance of High Temperature Systems, 1960, 63, 67. Contbr. articles to profl. jours. Home: 615 Brandywine Dr Newport News VA 23602 Office: 3221 N Armistead Ave Hampton VA 23666

BAHNER, THOMAS MAXFIELD, lawyer; b. Little Rock, Nov. 26, 1933; s. Carl Tabb and Catharine (Garrott) B.; B.S., Carson Newman Coll., 1954; B.D., So. Bapt. Theol. Sem., 1957; LL.B., U. Va., 1960; m. Sara Minta McIntyre, Sept. 28, 1957; children—Maxfield Tabb, Minta Susan, Margaret Catharine. Admitted to Va., Tenn. bars, 1960, asso. firm Kefauver, Duggan and McDonald, Chattanooga, 1960-62; partner firm Duggan, McDonald and Bahner, Chattanooga, 1962-64, firm Chambliss, Bahner Crutchfield Gaston & Irvine, Chattanooga, 1964—. Pres. United Cerebral Palsy Greater Chattanooga, 1966-67; mem. allocations steering com. United Fund Greater Chattanooga, 1970—, vice chmn. com., 1972-73. Bd. dirs. Chattanooga Council Alcoholism, 1964-65, Team Evaluation Center Inc., Chattanooga, 1965-70, Chattanooga Symphony, 1978—; bd. dirs. Orange Grove Sch. and Center for Retarded, Chattanooga, 1962—, pres., 1973-75, chmn., 1975—; mem. Hamilton County Sch. Bd., 1969-74; mem. adv. bd. Carson-Newman Coll., Jefferson City, Tenn., 1969—, trustee, sec., 1975—; mem. Tenn. and Am. Sch. Bds. Assn. Mem. Chattanooga (pres. 1969-70), Tenn. (lectr. 1965, bd. govs. local bar conf. 1969-71, bd. govs. 1975—, pres. elect 1979—), Am. bar assns., Va. State Bar, Tenn. Def. Lawyers Assn., Assn. Past Presidents Chattanooga Bar Assn., Am. Judicature Soc., Estate Planning Council (bd. dirs. 1971-72), Baptist (deacon). Club: Mountain City (Chattanooga). Office: 1111 Maclellan Bldg 721 Broad St Chattanooga TN 37402

BAIER, ALAN LEIGH, bus. exec.; b. White Plains, N.Y., July 1, 1941; grad. Taft Sch., Watertown, Conn., 1959; B.A. in Polit. Economy, Williams Coll., 1963; LL.B., Duke, 1966; m. Alyse Gautier Lucas Corcoran. Admitted to Ga. bar; with firm Hansell, Post, Brandon &Dorsey, Atlanta, 1966-69; now pres., chmn. bd. Baier Corp., Atlanta; chmn. bd. First Atlanta Equity Corp., Restoration Atlanta, Inc.; adv. bd. Citizens Trust Bank. Hon. French consul for State Ga.; mem. Atlanta Community Relations Commn. Bd. dirs. Atlanta Council Internat. Visitors; bd. sponsors Atlanta Symphony Orch. Mem. Atlanta Arts Alliance, Atlanta, Ga. bar assns., Atlanta Music Club (mem. men's adv. com.), Central Atlanta Progress. Kiwanian. Clubs: Atlanta Polo, Commerce, Capital City, Lawyers (Atlanta); Carolina Yacht (Charleston, S.C.). Home: Glenwoods 1632 Ponce de Leon Ave NE Atlanta GA 30307 Office: Baier Corp Equitable Bldg PO Box 1827 Decatur GA 30031

BAIER, RONALD ANTON, structural engr.; b. Flushing, N.Y., Sept. 7, 1943; s. Anton and Margaret (von der Heydt) B.; B.E. in Civil Engring., City Coll. N.Y., 1967; M.E., U. Fla., 1970. Assembly and test engr. Boeing Co., Cocoa Beach, Fla., 1967-69; field engr. Pitts. Testing Lab., Miami, Fla., 1970-71; design engr. Alpine Engineered Products Inc., Pompano Beach, Fla., 1971-72, Arthur L. Bromley, cons. engr., Ft. Lauderdale, Fla., 1972-74, Jenkins & Charland, cons. engrs., Ft. Lauderdale, 1974; pvt. practice cons. structural engring., Ft. Lauderdale, 1974—; v.p. Southeastern Engring. Testing Lab., 1973—; constrn. mgr. Roof Structures, Inc., Ft. Lauderdale, 1976-77; dir. structural engring. Craven, Thompson & Assos., Ft. Lauderdale, 1977; prin. Herbert M. Schwartz & Assos., Cons. Engrs., Miami, 1978—. Registered profl. engr., Fla., N.Y. Mem. ASCE (asso.), Fla. Engring. Soc., Am. Concrete Inst., Nat. Soc. Profl. Engrs., Mensa. Republican. Roman Catholic. Home: 67 NE 20th St Wilton Manors FL 33305

BAILEY, ALFRED WILLIAM, veterinarian, state ofcl.; b. Lamont, Wash., Sept. 1, 1935; s. Fred and Ila (Schuster) B.; D.V.M., Wash. State U., 1960; m. Patricia Catherine Seals, Dec. 27, 1960; children—Barbara Ellen, Bryan David. Individual practice vet. medicine, Victoria, B.C., Can., 1960, Seattle, 1963-64; vet. med. officer Dept. Agr., Ellensburg, Wash., 1964-70; supervisory vet. med. officer Consumer and Mktg. Service Consumer Protection programs Dept. Agr., Phoenix, 1970-72; circuit supr. Animal and Plant Health Inspection Service, Corvallis, Oreg., 1972-75; dir. meat and poultry inspection program Okla. Dept. Agr., Oklahoma City, 1975—. Served to capt., Vet. Corps, AUS, 1961-63. Recipient Dept. Agr. merit award superior performance, 1968. Mem. Nat. Assn. Fed. Veterinarians, Wash., Am., B.C., Intermountain, Canadian vet. med. assns., U.S. Animal Health Assn. (com. public health and environ. quality), Am. Assn. Food Hygiene Veterinarians. Clubs: Masons, Elks. Home: 10200 Ski Dr Oklahoma City OK 73132 Office: 312 NE 28th St Oklahoma City OK 73105

BAILEY, AMOS PURNELL, clergyman; b. Grotons, Va., May 2, 1918; s. Louis William and Evelyn (Charnock) B.; B.A., Randolph-Macon Coll., 1942, D.D., 1956; B.D., Duke, 1948; Th.M., Union Theol. Sem., 1957; postgrad. Columbia U., 1948, Ecumenical Inst., Jerusalem, 1979-80; m. Ruth Martin Hill, Aug. 22, 1942; children—Eleanor Carol (Mrs. Thomas T. Harriman), Anne Ruth (Mrs. Peter S. Page), Joyce Elizabeth (Mrs. David L. Richardson II), Jeanne Purnell (Mrs. Paul H. Dodge). Ordained to ministry United Methodist Ch., 1942; student pastor, Emporia, Va., 1938; pastor Richmond (Va.), 1938-43, New Kent (Va.) Circuit, 1943-44, Oak Grove Ch., Norfolk, Va., 1948-50, Grace Ch., Newport News, Va., 1950-54, Centenary Ch., Richmond, 1954-61; dist. supt. Richmond dist. Meth. Ch., 1961-67; sr. minister Reveille Ch., Richmond, 1967-70; asso. gen. sec. Div. Chaplains, United Meth. Ch., Arlington, Va., 1970-79; v.p. Nat. Meth. Found., 1979—. Mem. Meth. Commn. Higher Edn. 1960-70, v.p. 1961; mem. Meth. Interbd. Council, 1960-70, Meth. Chaplains Commn., 1964-70; mem. World Meth. Council; del. S.E. Jurisdictional Confs. United Meth. Ch., 1964, 68; mem. Gen. Conf., 1964, 66, 68, 70, World Meth. Conf., London, Eng., 1966, Denver, 1971, Dublin, Ireland, 1976; mem. com. pastoral care, v.p. com. on ministry to servicemen Nat. Council Chs.; pres. joint radio com. S.E. Jurisdiction and S.C. Jurisdiction, 1968-76, S.E. Jurisdiction Communications Commn., 1968-76; mem. program and coordinating councils United Meth. Ch.; mem. family life com. Meth. Hist. Soc., mem. Council of secs., 1970-72; dir. Interpretation, Interagy. Staff Com. on Research. Chmn. adv. bd. VA Chaplaincy; mem. Armed Forces chaplains Bd.; trustee, mem. exec. com. trustees Randolph-Macon Coll., 1960-74; trustee, mem. exec. com. So. Sem., 1966-76; bd. dirs. Va. Meth. Advocate, 1952-66; bd. visitors Duke Div. Sch., 1962-68; bd. mgrs. Richmond YMCA, 1960-68. Served with Chaplain Corps, AUS, 1945-47. Mem. Duke Div. Alumni Assn. (past pres.), Coll. Chaplains, Assn. Mental Health Chaplains. Kiwanian. Author: syndicated column Daily Bread, 1945—; syndicated radio devotional Daily Bread, 1945-69; The Night Pastor, religious counseling radio stas., 1955-69, Sunshine and Shadows, 1967-70. Meth. speaker on The Protestant Hour, 1962, 71. Contbr. articles to publs. in U.S., Can., Eng., Australia, Japan; contbr. to Ency. of World Methodism. Home: 7815 Falstaff Rd McLean VA 22101 Office: PO Box 9344 Arlington VA 22109

BAILEY, CHARLES WILLIAMS, III, realtor, elec. engr.; b. Spartanburg, S.C., July 26, 1925; s. Charles W. and Katherine F. (Ford) B.; B.E.E., Clemson U., 1947; M.E.E., N.C. State U., 1949; m. Dorothea Theresa Lamb, Feb. 5, 1960; children—Elizabeth Mary, Susan Margaret, Charles Williams IV. Asst. prof. elec. engring. The Citadel, S.C., 1949-51; design engr. Westinghouse Electric Corp., Balt., 1951-54; sales engr. Mpls. Honeywell, Charlotte, N.C., 1954-55; v.p. M.N. Weir & Sons, Inc., Pompano Beach, Fla., 1955-58; asst. to gen. mgr. Arvida Corp., Miami, 1958-61, asst. to pres., 1961-63; v.p. Arvida Realty Sales, Inc., Miami, 1963-71; pres. Bailey & Casey, Inc., Miami, 1971—; developer apt. units, Pompano Beach, 1969-76. Served with U.S. Army, 1944-46. Mem. Am. Soc. Appraisers (pres. S. Fla. chpt. 1966-67), Nat. Assn. Rev. Appraisers, Fla. Assn. Mortgage Brokers, Real Estate Securities and Syndication Inst., Bldg. Owners and Mgrs. Inst. Internat., Inst. Real Estate Mgmt., Nat. Inst. Farm and Land Brokers, Miami Bd. Realtors, Fla. Assn. Realtors, Internat. Real Estate Fedn. Republican. Presbyterian. Clubs: Key Biscayne Yacht, Key Biscayne Beach; Univ. (Miami), Miami, 200 Club, Bankers. Inventor underwater breathing electronic device. Contbr. articles to profl. jours. Home: 701 S Mashta Dr Key Biscayne FL 33149 Office: 1220 AmeriFirst Bldg Miami FL 33131

BAILEY, DAN LEE, univ. adminstr.; b. Mullens, W.Va., Feb. 28, 1945; s. James Robert and Rosa Belle (Farmer) B.; B.S., Concord Coll., Athens, W.Va., 1967; M.S., U. Tenn., Knoxville, 1971; m. Linda G. Campbell, Aug. 20, 1977; 1 dau., Alecia Kaye. Agt., Prudential Ins. Co., Bluefield, W.Va., 1968-69; div. bus. mgr. Oak Ridge (Tenn.) Asso. Univs., 1969—, treas. employees fed. credit union, 1973-76, pres. bd., 1977. Mem. Tennessee Valley Personnel Assn. Club: Broadacres Recreation (pres. bd. 1975). Home: 1020 Parrish Rd Knoxville TN 37919 Office: PO Box 117 Oak Ridge TN 37830

BAILEY, GARRICK ALAN, anthropologist; b. Hartshorne, Okla., Aug. 13, 1940; s. Linus Eugene and Alma Kathleen (Townsend) B.; B.A., U. Okla., 1963; M.A., U. Oreg., 1968, Ph.D., 1970; m. Roberta Joan Glenn, Sept. 10, 1965. Instr. anthropology U. Tulsa, 1968-70. Asst. prof., 1970-76, asso. prof., 1976—, chmn. dept. anthropology, 1976-79. Mem. Indian health adv. com. Indian Health Service, Health Services Adminstrn., HEW, 1975-78; mem. Indian com. Philbrook Art Center, 1978—; bd. dirs. Tulsa Indian Emphasis Program, 1975-78. Fellow Am. Anthrop. Assn.; mem. Soc. for Applied Anthropology, Soc. for Med. Anthropology, Am. Soc. Ethnohistory, Am. Ethnological Soc. Congregationalist. Author: Changes in Osage Social Organization: 1673-1906, 1973. Home: 2623 E 21st St Tulsa OK 74114 Office: 600 S College Tulsa OK 74104

BAILEY, GEORGE PHILIP, life ins. co. exec.; b. Oklahoma City, Oct. 28, 1948; s. George W. and Ela Beth B.; B.A., Abilene Christian Coll., 1970; m. Gaye Waters, June 6, 1975; children—Kimberly Jill. Bible salesman Southwestern Pub. Co., Nashville, 1967-68; dept. mgr., salesman Sears Roebuck & Co., Abilene, Tex., 1968-71; asst. store mgr. Star Furniture Co., Harlingen, Tex., 1971-73, store mgr., Edinburg, Tex., 1973-75; sr. asso. Pilot Life Ins. Co., McAllen, Tex., 1975—. Recipient Nat. Quality award Nat. Assn. Life Underwriters, 1979; Eagle Scout. Mem. Nat. Assn. Life Underwriters, Tex. Assn. Life Underwriters, Upper Valley Assn. Life Underwriters (dir. McAllen, Tex. 1979-80), Edinburg C. of C. (retail chmn. 1974-75), Nat. Forensic League, Tex. Leaders Round Table. Mem. Ch. of Christ. Club: Rotary (pres. 1978-79) (Edinburg, Tex.). Home: 206 Montevideo St Edinburg TX 78539 Office: 1006 McAllen State Bank Tower McAllen TX 78501

BAILEY, GRACIE MASSENBERG, coll. ofcl.; b. Sussex County, Va., Feb. 25, 1936; d. Ernest Royal and Maxine (Stith) Massenberg; B.S., Va. State Coll., 1958, M.Ed., 1970; postgrad. Va. Poly. Inst. and State U., 1977—; m. Erling Bailey, Dec. 24, 1958; children—LaVetta Faye, Erling. Tchr. bus. edn. Public Schs. Amelia County (Va.), 1958-60; Sussex County Public Schs., 1961-63, Dinwiddie County (Va.) Public Schs., 1963-74; asso. prof. bus. edn., computer mgmt. Richard Bland Coll., Petersburg, Va., 1974—, dir. personnel affirmative action EEO, 1976—, adminstrv. asst. to pres., 1978—; salesman Hartford Variable Annuity Life Ins. Co., 1960-79. Mem. Am. Bus. Women's Assn. (sec. 1973), AAUP, Am. Assn. Adminstrv. Women in Higher Edn., Adv. Council Ednl. Computing State of Va. Baptist. Home: Rt 1 Box 204B5 Petersburg VA 23803 Office: Rt 1 Box 77A Petersburg VA 23803

BAILEY, HELEN MCSHANE, historian; b. Gardner, Kans., Oct. 17, 1916; d. Harry Cramer and Maude (Kramer) McShane; B.A., Bethany Nazarene Coll., 1938; m. James Edwin Bailey, Feb. 23, 1946; children—James Edwin, Barbara Ann (Mrs. William Lance Crawford). Adminstrv. asst. Office of Chief of Staff, U.S. Army, Washington, 1941-48, historian ofcl. history WWII; 1948-58; research asst. George C. Marshall Research Found., Washington, 1958-59; historian Orgn. Joint Chiefs of Staff, Dept. Def., Washington, 1968—. Mem. Am. Hist. Assn., Am. Com. on History of Second World War, Soc. Historians Am. Fgn. Relations. Republican. Lutheran. Home: 9451 Lee Hwy Apt 815 Fairfax VA 22031 Office: Room 1B-717 The Pentagon Washington DC 20301

BAILEY, HENRIETTA, ednl. counselor; b. Malvern, Ark., July 4, 1921; d. Henry and Alberta (Barker) Fanning; B.S., Philander Smith Coll., Little Rock, 1949; M.A., Columbia U., 1956; m. Edward Ernest Bailey, June 29, 1949; children—Edward Ernest, Julia Alberta, Laura Roegenia. Social studies instr. Malvern Colored High Sch., 1941-51, Wilson High Sch., Malvern, 1952-64, counselor, 1965-70, counselor Malvern High Sch., 1971—; mem. Ark. Adv. Council on Secondary Edn., Ark. Textbooks Selection Com. Mem. Hot Spring County Drug Abuse Bd., 1965; bd. dirs. Upward Bound Project, Ouachita U., Arkadelphia, Ark., 1955—, Ouachita Regional Counseling and Mental Health Center, Hot Springs, Ark., 1973-74, Hot Spring-County Center for Exceptional Children and Adults, 1974—. Mem. Am. Personnel and Guidance Assn., Nat., Ark. edn. assns., AAUW, Bus. and Profl. Womens Clubs. Mem. African Methodist Episcopal Ch. Home: 313 S Walnut St Malvern AR 72104 Office: 525 E Highland St Malvern AR 72104

BAILEY, JACK BENNETT, hosp. mgmt. co. exec.; b. Clay County, Tenn., Aug. 29, 1940; s. Jack Marcom and Lockie Marie (Reed) B.; B.S. in Bus. Adminstrn., Tenn. Tech. U., 1969; m. Lyla Evelyn French, Oct. 19, 1968; children—Mark Bennett, Caroline Jennings. Mem. audit staff Ernst & Ernst, C.P.A.'s, Nashville, 1969-72; controller Coliseum Park Hosp., Macon, Ga., 1972-73; asst. controller, audit mgr. Hosp. Corp. Am., 1973-74; regional coordinator Humana, Inc., Mobile, 1974-75, asst. regional mgr., 1975—. Served with USAR, 1958-61. Named Ky. col., 1978; C.P.A., Tenn. Mem. Am. Inst. C.P.A.'s, Hosp. Fin. Mgmt. Assn., Am. Coll. Hosp. Adminstrs., Tenn. Soc. Cert. Accountants, Mobile C. of C. Democrat. Episcopalian. Club: Skyline Country. Home: 5505 Oak Park Ct Mobile AL 36609 Office: 4 Winthrop Sq 800 Hillcrest Rd Mobile AL 36609

BAILEY, JAMES LOVELL, ret. state ofcl.; b. Portland, Tenn., Dec. 18, 1907; s. James Johnson and Annie May (Lovell) B.; student Bowling Green U., 1925, Middle Tenn. State Tchrs. Coll., 1926-29, Western Ky. State Coll., 1929-30, George Washington U., 1931-33, U. Tenn., 1938-41; m. Fairrelle Brown, June 1, 1940 (dec. Dec. 1976); 1 dau., Annie Elizabeth (Mrs. Richard Genung); m. Hester W. Brown, Apr. 29, 1979. With U.S. Bur. of Census, 1930-32, U.S. Dept. of Agr., 1933-37; with Tenn. Dept. Conservation, Nashville 1937-76, dir. ednl. service, 1957-76; organized 1st soil conservation dist. in Tenn., 1940; mem. Tenn. Conservation Commn., 1978—, sec., 1980—. Pres. Davidson County (Tenn.) chpt. Muscular Dystrophy Assn., 1957; mem. garden com. Tenn. Bot. Gardens and Fine Arts Center, Nashville, 1969—; mem. Vol. State Coll. Adv. and Devel. Council, 1976—; charter mem., bd. dirs. Tenn. Environ. Council, 1970-77, life mem., 1977—; bd. dirs. Tenn. Beautiful, 1972; trustee West Coast Christian Corp. Served with USNR, 1942-45. Recipient awards including Cartter Patten award Tenn. Conservation League, 1963, Key Man award Conservation Edn. Assn., 1967, Gov.'s Conservationist of Year award, 1971, silver seal Nat. Council State Garden Clubs, 1973, Forestry Recognition award Soc. Am. Foresters, 1976. Fellow Soil Conservation Soc. Am. (pres. Tenn. council chpts. 1961, regional rep., conservation history com.); mem. Middle Tenn. Conservancy Council, E. Tenn. Edn. Assn., Nat. Assn. Conservation Edn. and Publicity (pres. 1949), Conservation Edn. Assn., Highland Rim (dir.) Hist. Soc., Dickson County Hist. Soc.; Nat. Wildlife Fedn., Tenn. Assn. Preservation Antiquities, Nat. Trust for Historic Preservation, Bowen Campbell House Assn. (v.p.), Common Cause, Tenn. Fedn. Garden Clubs Inc. (life). Mem. Ch. of Christ. Club: Nashville Torch (pres. 1963-64). Author: Our Land and Our Living, 1940. Asso. editor Tenn. Conservationist, 1959-72, editor-in-chief, 1972-76, editor emeritus, 1976—. Home: Route 2 Box 102 White Bluff TN 37187

BAILEY, JOHN ALAN, computer systems adminstr.; b. Arkansas City, Kans., Nov. 10, 1934; s. Coral Marion and Hattie Vista (Baehler) B.; B.S., U. Tex., 1957; M.S., U. Tulsa, 1958. Petroleum engr. Shell Oil Co., 1958-62; petroleum engr. Sinclair Oil and Gas Co., 1962-64, sr. engr., systems analyst, 1964-69; systems mgr. info. services div. U. Tulsa, 1969-75, dir. info. services div., 1975—, adj. asst. prof. computer sci., 1970—. Active Boy Scouts Am. Registered profl. engr., Tex. Mem. Soc. Petroleum Engrs., IEEE, Assn. Computing Machinery, Brit. Computer Soc. Home: 7705 S Gary Pl Tulsa OK 74136 Office: 1133 N Lewis Ave Tulsa OK 74110

BAILEY, JOHN ALBERT, educator; b. Liverpool, Eng., June 8, 1937; s. John Albert and Phylis Caterine (Monk) B.; B.Sc., Birmingham (Eng.) Coll. Advanced Technology, 1957; B.Sc. in Metallurgy, Univ. Coll. Swansea (Eng.), 1960, Ph.D., 1963; m. Anne Thomas, May 7, 1963. Came to U.S., 1963, naturalized, 1973. Asso. prof. Ga. Inst. Tech., Atlanta, 1963-67; mem. faculty N.C. State U., Raleigh, 1967—, prof. 1970—. Cons. Celanese Fibers Co., Charlotte. Recipient research grants NSF, 1964, 66, 72, 74, NASA, 1964, 72, 75. Chartered engr. Fellow Instn. Metallurgists; mem. ASME, Inst. Metals, Soc. Mfg. Engrs., Sigma Xi, Phi Kappa Phi. Contbr. profl. jours. Home: 1214 Gray Owl Garth Cary NC 27511 Office: Dept Mechanical and Aerospace Engring NC State Univ Raleigh NC 27650

BAILEY, JOHN JAMES, JR., ins. agy. exec.; b. Athens, Ohio, Aug. 30, 1931; s. John James and Dorothy Mae B.; B.S., Coll. William and Mary, 1957; m. Phyllis Lane, Apr. 11, 1951; children—Debra K. Crimmins, Denyse R. Megginson, Dena Ann. Pres., Asso. Cons., Newport News, Va., 1959—; pres., dir. Asso. Ins. Marketing, Inc., Virginia Beach, Va., 1974—, Ins. Cons., Inc., Virginia Beach, 1977—; v.p., chmn. bd. Union Plan Adminstrs., Norfolk, Va., 1965—; partner, chmn. Employee Benefits Computer Co., Norfolk, 1976—; partner Asso. Claims Services; gen. agt. Guardian Life Ins. Co., Virginia Beach, 1977—. Bd. dirs. Oceans Condominium Owners' Council, Virginia Beach, Virginia Beach United Meth. Ch.; mem. parents council Va. Wesleyan Coll., Norfolk. Served with USAF, 1950-54. Registered health underwriter. Mem. Nat. Life Underwriters Assn., Nat. Health Underwriters Assn., Norfolk Life Underwriters Assn. Methodist. Clubs: Cavalier Golf and Yacht (past dir.), Sertoma (past dir.). Home: 4004 Oceanfront 901 Virginia Beach VA 23451 Office: 900 Commonwealth Pl Suite 6 Virginia Beach VA 23462

BAILEY, KENNETH DUANE, cons., educator; b. Valentine, Nebr., Oct. 14, 1938; s. Dale Cooke and Maude Ellen (Garner) B.; student Calif. State Poly., Pomona, 1959-61; B.A., Midwestern U., Wichita Falls, Tex., 1965, M.A., 1967; Ph.D. (univ. fellow), U. Md., College Park, 1975; children—Kevin Duane, Brian David, Scott Wayne, Karen Denise. Lectr. govt., politics U. Md., 1967-69; asst. prof. polit. sci. U. Ark., Fayetteville, 1969—; research cons. to Gov. Ark., 1975-76. Pres. Opinion Survey, Research Corp. Polit. cons., research asso. Cranford/Johnson/Hunt & Assos., Little Rock, 1973-76; election analyst sta. KFSM-TV, Fort Smith, Ark., 1974—. Tech. advisor Fayetteville Citizens' Participation Com., 1973-75; del. Ark. State Democratic Conv., 1974; co-chmn. com. on spl. edn. Springdale Citizen's Edn. Evaluation Com. Served with USAF, 1961-65. Recipient Ark. Certificate of Merit Gov. David Pryor, 1975. Mem. Am., Midwest, So., Southwestern, Western polit. sci. assns., Center for Study of Presidency, Roper Pub. Opinion Research Center, Am. Assn. for Pub. Opinion Research, Alpha Chi, Pi Sigma Alpha. Contbr. articles in field to profl. jours. Home: PO Box 1865 Fayetteville AR 72701

BAILEY, KINCHEON HUBERT, JR., educator; b. Zebulon, N.C., Dec. 21, 1921; s. Kincheon Hubert and Ellen Florence (Williams) B.; student Lake Forest Coll., 1941; B.S., U.S. Mil. Acad., 1945; M.Ed. (NSF fellow), Pa. State U., 1967; D.Ed., N.C. State U., 1975; m. Tommye Lou Williams, Dec. 18, 1948; children—Kincheon Hubert III, Linda Lou (Mrs. William Hux), Beth Ellen, Laura Jane, Nancy Margaret. Commd. 2d lt. U.S. Army, 1945, advanced through grades to lt. col., 1963, ret., 1966; dir. tech. edn. Holding Tech. Inst., Raleigh, N.C., 1967-72, instr. electronics, 1972—, head electronics dept., 1976—; adviser John Wiley & Sons, N.Y.C., 1972—. Emergency coordinator Am. Radio Relay League, Wake County, Raleigh, 1971-79, Army MARS, N.C., 1977—. Decorated Silver Star. Mem. Raleigh Amateur Radio Soc., IEEE (chmn. membership and transfers com. eastern N.C. 1970-79, counsellor Wake Tech. Inst. student br. 1973—), Wake Tech. Inst. Amateur Radio Soc. (trustee 1970—), Pa. State U. Alumni Assn., Am. Security Council, Citizens for Decent Lit., Friends of Library N.C. State U., Mil. Order World Wars, Assn. Grads. U.S. Mil. Acad., SCV (comdr. Raleigh 1976—, N.C. 1978—), Kappa Sigma. Club: Northbrook Country (Raleigh). Home: 701 Currituck Dr Raleigh NC 27609

BAILEY, LLOYD WHITFIELD, physician; b. Phila., Mar. 24, 1928; s. Clarence Whitfield and Olive (Magnusson) B.; B.S., Wake Forest Coll., 1949; M.D., Jefferson Med. Coll. Phila., 1953; postgrad. U. Pa. Grad. Sch. Medicine, 1957-58; m. Ann Witherspoon Lewis, July 29, 1955 (div. 1977); children—Lloyd Whitfield, Linda Lee, Joan Lewis, Intern, Jefferson Med. Coll. Hosp., Phila., 1953-54; resident Wills Eye Hosp., Phila., 1958-60; practice medicine, specializing in ophthalmology, Rocky Mount, N.C., 1960—; mem. staff Nash Gen. Hosp., Rocky Mount Sanatorium. Chmn. disaster com. ARC, Rocky Mount, 1963-69; chmn. Rocky Mount-Nash-Edgecombe Support Your Local Police Com., 1974—. Mem. Nash County Republican Exec. Com., 1966-68; Presdl. elector for 2d Congl. Dist. N.C., 1968; mem. exec. com. Am. party of N.C., 1970-71, 74-76. Served with USAF, 1955-57. Recipient Liberty award Congress of Freedom, 1969. Mem. So. Med. Assn. (life), Med. Soc. State N.C., N.C. (com. on eye care and eye banks 1963-79, ho. of dels. 1969-73, 74-78, 80, pres.-elect 1980), Nash County med. socs., Am. Assn. Ophthalmology, Wills Eye Hosp. Soc., N.C. Soc. Ophthalmology, Assn. Am. Physicians and Surgeons (del. 1974-80, N.C. membership chmn. 1974-75), Am. Assn. Councils of Med. Staffs Pvt. Hosps. (area dir. 1975-76), U.S. Power Squadron, Ducks Unltd., John Birch Soc. (chpt. leader 1967-68; life), Nat. Rifle Assn., Kappa Alpha, Phi Chi. Baptist. Club: Gun, Benvenue Country (bd. govs. 1975-78). Home: 3813 Hawthorne Rd Rocky Mount NC 27801 Office: 109 Foy Dr Rocky Mount NC 27801

BAILEY, ROBERT CLIFTON, biometrician; b. Richmond, Va., Mar. 29, 1941; s. James Edward and Florence (Miles) B.; B.S., Randolph Macon Coll., 1962; M.S., Iowa State U., 1964; Ph.D. (NIH spl. fellow 1970-71) Emory U., 1972; m. Susan C. Goodman, Mar. 20, 1965; children—Linda Carol, Alice Kerry. Fellow and asso. in stats. and biometrics Emory U., Atlanta, 1964-72; asso. prof. stats. Morris Brown Coll., Atlanta, 1967-73; math. statistician FDA, Washington, 1973-75; command statistician Naval Med. Research Inst., Bethesda, Md., 1975—. Mem. Am. Statis. Assn., Biometric Soc., AAAS, Inst. Math. Stats., Phi Beta Kappa, Sigma Xi, Chi Beta Phi. Home: 6507 Divine St McLean VA 22101 Office: Naval Med Research Inst Bethesda MD 20014

BAILEY, ROBERT PENDLETON, plastics co. exec.; b. Lynchburg, Va., Aug. 21, 1932; s. John Pendleton and Pearl Lee (Burnette) B.; B.B.A., Tulane U., 1957, B.S. in Chemistry, 1960; S.A.I., U. Chgo., 1961; student Columbia U., 1964; m. Carole Kay Eaton, Aug. 27, 1961; children—Gregory Pendleton, Beth Allison. Mktg. asst. Exxon, New Orleans, 1956-59, product mgr. trainee, 1959-60, tech. chem. sales, 1960-64; div. mgr. U.S.I., Div. Nat. Distillers, Chgo. and Memphis, 1964-69; s. dist. mgr. No. Petrochems. Co., Atlanta, 1969-72; spl. products mgr. nat. div. PMS Corp., Atlanta, 1972-77, nat. accounts coordinator, 1977—, mktg. mgr., 1977—. Advisor Jr. Achievement, Evanston, Ill., 1963. Served with USN, 1951-53. Decorated Am. Spirit Honor medal by combined armed forces; named outstanding div. mgr., U.S.I. Div. Nat. Distillers, 1968; licensed nat. starter, Sports Car Club Am. Mem. Midwest Chem. Mktg. Assn. (charter mem., sec. 1962, treas. and social chmn. 1963), Chem. Mfgs. Assn. (nat. entertainment chmn. 1963, nat. com. Aerosol Div. 1963-64), Chgo. Soap, Perfume and Extract Assn., Soc. Plastics Engrs., Soc. Cosmetic Chemists, Cin. Drug and Chem. Assn., Soc. Paint Tech., Chgo. Drug and Chem. Assn., Louisville, Cin., Chgo. paint and lacquer assns. Republican. Episcopalian. Clubs: W.C.T., Peachtree World of Tennis, Kingsley Racquet and Swim, Flying Col., ALTA (Atlanta). Home: 2366 N Peachtree Way Dunwoody GA 30338 Office: 6685 Marbut Rd Lithonia GA 30058

BAILEY, ROLAND DEAN, nuclear fuel service co. exec.; b. Erwin, Tenn., Nov. 20, 1938; s. Harley L. and Mable (Tipton) B.; B.S. in Bus. Mgmt., East Tenn. State U., 1968, postgrad., 1968-70; m. Linda Ann Waldrop, June 1, 1963. File clk. FBI, Washington, 1959-60; prodn. operator Nuclear Fuel Services, Inc., Erwin, 1960-68, adminstrv. asst., 1968-71, mgr. indsl. relations, 1971—. Mem. blood com. ARC, 1971-80; mem. Erwin Planning Commn., 1979—, sec., 1979—; bd. dirs. YMCA, Erwin; mem. Unicoi County Vocat. Edn. Adv. Com.; mem. bus. adminstrn. adv. council E. Tenn. State U. Served with U.S. Army, 1961-63. Mem. Am. Soc. Personnel Adminstrs., Johnson City Personnel Assn., Tri-Cities Adminstrv. Mgmt. Soc. (dir. 1980). Republican. Presbyterian. Clubs: Erwin Kiwanis (dir. 1978-79), Erwin Elks. Home: 605 Mohawk St Erwin TN 37650 Office: Nuclear Fuel Services Inc Carolina St Erwin TN 37650

BAILEY, RONALD BERESFORD, educator; b. Fort Pierce, Fla., Feb. 5, 1936; s. Harry Augustus and Ruth Geneva (Finlayson) B.; B.S. in Polit. Sci. magna cum laude, Fla. A. and M. U., 1958; M.A. in Polit. Sci. (Woodrow Wilson fellow), U. Ill., 1959, Ph.D. in Polit. Sci. (John Hay Whitney fellow 1959, YMCA-Univ. Bailey scholar 1960), 1965. Teaching fellow U. Ill., Urbana, 1960-64; lectr. history U. Md., Heidelberg, Germany, 1965-66; asso. prof., chmn. dept. polit. sci. Atlanta U., 1966-68; asst. prof. St. Louis U., 1968-70; asso. prof. polit. sci., black studies Washington U., St. Louis, 1970-71; asso. prof. social scis., polit. sci., asst. dean Univ. Coll. U. Fla., Gainesville, 1971-73, asso. prof. social scis., polit. sci., 1974-76; prof., chmn. dept. polit. sci. Fla. A. and M. U., Tallahassee, 1976—; cons. HUD, 1972, N.Y. Dept. Civil Service, Albany, 1974. Served to capt., AUS, 1965-66; Germany. Am. Council on Edn. fellow, 1973-74. Mem. Am. Polit. Sci. Assn., Nat. Conf. Black Polit. Scientists, So. Polit. Sci. Assn., Alpha Kappa Mu, Kappa Delta Pi, Pi Sigma Alpha, Omega Psi Phi. Democrat. Episcopalian. Contbr. articles to profl. jours. Home: 1112 S Magnolia Dr Apt I-103 Tallahassee FL 32307 Office: Dept Polit Sci and Pub Mgmt Fla A and M U Tallahassee FL 32307

BAILEY, ROY JACKSON, educator; b. Baker, La., July 16, 1933; s. James Holloway and Dorothy (Jackson) B.; B.A., La. State U., 1960; M.B.Ed., U. Miss., 1978; m. Glenda Deason, Nov. 4, 1962; 1 son, Michael. With Baton Rouge Police Dept., 1954-60, Vicksburg (Miss.) Evening Post, 1960-63, 67-69, Assn. La. Elec. Coops., 1964-67, Miss. Restaurant Assn., Jackson, 1969-72; instr. hotel motel restaurant mgmt. N.E. Miss. Jr. Coll., Booneville, 1972—; cons. hospitality industry. Served with Army NG, 1954—. Mem. Miss. Restaurant Assn. (hon. dir.), Distbv. Edn. Clubs Am., Miss. Assn. Distbv. Edn. Tchrs., Am. Vocat. Assn., Miss. Bus. Edn. Assn., Nat. Restaurant Assn., Miss. Non Commd. Officers Assn., Delta Phi Epsilon. Democrat. Episcopalian. Home: Parkwood Gardens Booneville MS 38829 Office: Waller Center NE Miss Jr Coll Booneville MS 38829

BAILEY, SAMUEL HERBERT, shipbldg. co. exec.; b. Phila., July 21, 1943; s. Herbert Otis and Mary Bailey; B.S., Pa. State U., 1967; m. Mary Susan Bruno, Feb. 24, 1973; 1 dau., Jessica Sarah. Mgr. dept. computer applications Avondale Shipyards, Inc., New Orleans, 1975-76, mgr. dept. engring. standards, 1976—. Served to lt. USN, 1967-75; Vietnam, Korea. Mem. ASTM (chmn. shipbldg. standard sub-com.), Soc. Naval Architects and Marine Engrs., Am. Def. Preparedness Assn., Engring. Reprographics Soc., Am. Inst. Design and Drafting. Republican. Episcopalian. Club: Colonial Golf and Country. Developed many cost saving standards. Home: 9616 Marsha Dr River Ridge LA 70123 Office: PO Box 50280 New Orleans LA 70150

BAILEY, WILLIAM CHARLES, physician; b. Jacksonville, Fla., Aug. 4, 1939; s. Cecil C. and Augusta D. (Mann) B.; B.A., Washington and Lee U., 1961; M.D., Tulane U., 1965; m. Bonnie Shaw, June 8, 1963; children—William Charles, John Faison-Oates, Evans Cecil. Rotating intern Charity Hosp., New Orleans, 1965-66, resident in internal medicine, 1968-70; NIH fellow in pulmonary disease Tulane U. Sch. Medicine, New Orleans, 1970-72; dir. Bur. Tb Control, City of New Orleans Health Dept., 1970-73; Tb control officer, dir. inhalation therapy and respiratory ICU, Charity Hosp. of La., New Orleans, 1971-73; asst. prof. medicine Tulane U. Sch. Medicine, New Orleans, 1972-73; practice medicine specializing in pulmonary medicine, Birmingham, Ala., 1973—; med. dir. Bur. Communicable Diseases, Jefferson County Health Dept., Birmingham, 1973-78, cons., 1978—; Tb. coordinator Ala. Dept. Public Health, 1973—; asso. chief staff edn. VA Med. Center, Birmingham, 1976—, chief pulmonary disease sect., 1973—; asst. prof. medicine U. Ala. Sch. Medicine, Birmingham, 1973-75, asso. prof., 1975-79, prof., 1979—, asst. dean edn., 1976—. Deacon, Briarwood Presbyn. Ch., Birmingham, 1974-75, elder, 1975—; bd. dirs. Briarwood Christian Sch., 1978—. Served with USPHS, 1966-68. Diplomate Am. Bd. Internal Medicine and Pulmonary Disease. Fellow A.C.P., Am. Coll. Chest Physicians; mem. Am. Thoracic Soc. (mem. council 1976—, exec. com. 1977—, chmn. Tb Sci. Assembly 1976-77), Ala. Thoracic Soc. (pres. 1975-76), Am. Public Health Assn., Internat. Union Against Tb (mem. com. epidemiology and stats. 1979—), AMA, Med. Assn. Ala., Jefferson County Med. Soc., Ala. Public Health Assn. (chmn. Tb. sect. 1976-77), Christian Med. Soc. (Ho. of Dels. 1977—, trustee 1980—). Contbr. numerous articles on pulmonary disease to med. jours. Home: 4212 Caldwell Mill Rd Birmingham AL 35243 Office: 700 S 19th St Birmingham AL 35233

BAIN, EMILY JOHNSTON, artist, educator; b. Forest Hill, La., July 28, 1911; d. Daniel Roger and Necy Ann (Hicks) Johnston; B.A., Northwestern State U., La., 1932; M.A. in Edn. and Art (Univ. fellow), La. State U., 1940; M.A. in English, Tulane U., 1961; m. Robert Edward Zeigler, July 1, 1940 (dec. May 1945); 1 dau., Nora Ann Zeigler; m. 2d, Alonzo Wesley Bain, June 1, 1949 (dec. Jan. 1976); 1 dau., Emily Carolyn. Tchr. public schs., La., 1932-39, East Baton Rouge Parish, 1968-70, Tex. Pub. Schs., 1970-77; art tchr. pub. schs., Kilgore, Tex., 1940-43, Dallas, 1945, 47-48, New Orleans, 1953-65, Grand Prairie, 1965-68; supr. art pub. schs. La. Dept. Edn., 1948-49; one-woman shows: Kilgore High Sch., 1943; group shows: Kottler Galleries, N.Y.C., 1977, Ligoa Duncan Gallery, N.Y.C., Raymond Duncan Gallery, Paris, 1979. Mem. Nat. Soc. Lit. and Arts, Internat. Soc. Artists, Am. Security Council, Tex. State Tchrs. Assn. (life), La. Ret. Tchrs. Assn., Nat. Writers Club, Delta Kappa Gamma. Democrat. Baptist. Club: Woman's of Grand Prairie (Tex.). Paintings included in: Artists U.S.A., 1976, 77, 78, 80. Home and Office: 834 Valley View Dr Grand Prairie TX 75050

BAIN, WILLIAM DONALD, JR., chem. co. exec., lawyer; b. Rochelle, Ill., July 1, 1925; s. William Donald and Gretchen Ann (Kittler) B.; B.S., U. Pa., 1947; LL.B., Washington and Lee U., 1949; m. Pauline Alexander Thomas, Jan. 14, 1950; children—Elizabeth Kittler, Anne Alexander, Nancy Hemenway. Admitted to S.C. bar, 1951; field rep. mortgage loan dept. Travelers Ins. Co., Hartford, Conn., 1949, Cleve., 1949-50, Orlando, Fla., 1950-51; field rep. Moreland McKesson Chem. Co., Spartanburg, S.C., 1951-60, exec. v.p., 1960-65, pres., 1965—; regional v.p. McKesson Chem. Co., 1978—, chmn. bd. Spartanburg Bank & Trust Co.; dir. Spartan Radiocasting Co., Chemtech Industries, St. Louis. Mem. Spartanburg City Sch. Bd., 1956-72, chmn., 1963-72. Exec. committeeman Republican Party, 1972—; trustee Mary Black Meml. Hosp., Converse Coll.; mem. Washington and Lee U. Alumni Bd., 1978—. Served with USAAF, 1943-45. Mem. S.C. Bar Assn., Spectator Club (pres. 1973-74), Sigma Alpha Epsilon, Phi Alpha Delta. Episcopalian. Clubs: Rotary (pres. 1975-76, now dir.), Country of Spartanburg, Piedmont (pres. 1973, 74). Home: 194 Westminster Dr Spartanburg SC 29302 Office: PO Box 2169 Spartanburg SC 29304

BAINE, JAMES EVERITT, lawyer, oil co. exec.; b. Boston, Oct. 20 1941; s. Rodney Montgomery and Aline Asha (Everitt) B.; B.B.A., U. Ga., 1964, M.A. in Econs., 1970; J.D., U. Miss., 1968; m. Edith Turley, Aug. 27, 1967; 1 son, John Anderson. Asst. prof. fin. U. So. Miss., Hattiesburg, 1968-69; admitted to Miss. bar, 1968, Ark. bar, 1972; atty. Gillespie & Gillespie, Raymond, Miss., 1969-70; atty., asst. sec. Murphy Oil Corp., El Dorado, Ark., 1970—; sec. Deltic Farm & Timber Co., Inc., El Dorado, 1972—; dir. REDI, Inc., Conway, Ark. State campaign chmn. Ark. chpt. Nat. Multiple Sclerosis Soc., 1977; chmn. bd. dirs. El Dorado YWCA, 1978—. Served with U.S. Army, 1964-65. Recipient Hope Chest award Nat. Multiple Sclerosis Soc., 1977, M. Keith Upson Meml. award U.S. Jr. C. of C., 1975. Mem. Am. Bar Assn., Arbitration Assn., Delta Theta Phi (nat. vice-chancellor 1979-81). Republican. Presbyterian. Home: 807 Brookwood St El Dorado AR 71730 Office: Murphy Bldg 200 Jefferson St El Dorado AR 71730

BAINE, JOHN RAYMOND, found. exec.; b. Paragould, Ark., Nov. 20, 1909; s. Albert and Willie T. (Hay) B.; B.A., Ouachita Coll., 1930; m. Alice May Brennan, Oct. 24, 1936; 1 son, William Brennan. Pub. sch. prin., Columbus, Ark., 1931-32; employee U.S. Ho. of Reps., Washington, 1932-38; singer, N.Y.C., 1938-42; polit. officer U.S. Dept. State, Washington, Milan and Rome, Italy, and Lisbon, Portugal, 1945-69; treas. Waterford (Va.) Found., 1970-71, 74—, pres., 1972-73. Pres., Va. Mus. Fine Arts, Loudoun County, 1972-74, Loudoun County Restoration and Preservation Soc., 1976—. Served to capt. AUS, 1942-45. Clubs: Waterford Players (dir.); Leesburg (Va.) Bridge (pres.); Army and Navy. Home: Meeting House Waterford VA 22190 Office: Waterford Found Waterford VA 22190

BAINE, WILLIAM BRENNAN, med. epidemiologist; b. Washington, Aug. 10, 1945; s. John Raymond and Alice (Brennan) B.; A.B., Princeton U., 1966; M.D., Vanderbilt U., 1970; m. Martha Scott, Aug. 30, 1969; 1 son, Britton Alexander. Intern dept. medicine Cleve. Met. Gen. Hosp., 1970-71, asst. resident, 1971-72; epidemic intelligence service officer Center for Disease Control, Atlanta, 1972-74; resident dept. internal medicine Parkland Meml. Hosp., Dallas, 1974-75; fellow in infectious diseases, dept. internal medicine U. Tex. Southwestern Med. Sch., Dallas, 1975-77; med. epidemiologist Center for Disease Control, Atlanta, 1977-79, assigned to Istituto Superiore di Sanità, Rome, Italy, 1979—. Fellow Am. Coll. Physicians; mem. Am. Fedn. Clin. Research, AAAS, Am. Soc. Microbiology, Soc. Epidemiologic Research. Episcopalian. Club: Colonial. Author articles on enteric bacterial infections, Legionnaires' disease. Home: 1433 Council Bluff Dr NE Atlanta GA 30345 Office: Center for Disease Control Atlanta GA 30333 also c/o Science Attache Am Embassy Rome APO New York NY 09794

BAINES, DONALD DEAN, air force officer; b. Boise, Idaho, May 28, 1938; s. Kenneth Rodney and Eula Louise (Matlock) B.; B.S., Colo. State U., 1960; M.S., Troy State U., 1974; Ph.D., Columbia Pacific U., 1980; m. Jacque Lee Snyder, Feb. 17, 1962; children—Trevor Dean, Troy Douglas, Trent Darrin, Ty Dustin, Torrey Dana. Commd. 2d lt. USAF, 1960, advanced through grades to lt. col.; dir. profl. personnel mgmt. course Air Univ., Maxwell AFB, Ala., 1977—; mgmt. cons., lectr., behavioral scientist. Decorated DFC, Air Medal. Mem. Okaloosa County Council on Aging, Montgomery Mental Health Agy., Air Force Assn., Am. Mgmt. Assn., Troy State U. Alumni Assn. Home: 202 Poplar St Prattville AL 36067 Office: LMDC/DPM Maxwell AFB AL 36112

BAINES, ROBERT EMMETT, ins. co. exec.; b. Poughkeepsie, N.Y., Dec. 29, 1922; s. Robert and Laura Anna (Briggs) B.; B.A., So. Methodist U., 1949; m. Kathryn Rose Feagin, Sept. 4, 1949; children—Robert Ellis, Jack Clifford, Lawrence Arthur. Asst. actuary Republic Nat. Life Ins. Co., Dallas, 1950-61, v.p. data processing, 1961-73; sr. v.p. adminstrn. Consol. Am. Life Co., Jackson, Miss., 1973—; also dir. Served with USN, 1943-46. Mem. Actuaries Club Southwest, Life Ins. Assn. Miss. (sec. treas.), Life Office Mgmt. Assn.

(fellow Life Mgmt. Inst.), Ins. Acctg. and Statis. Assn. Methodist. Club: Lions. Home: 4605 Nordell St Jackson MS 39206 Office: 308 N West St Jackson MS 39205

BAINES, TYRONE RANDOLPH, polit. scientist, univ. adminstr.; b. Exmore, Va., Feb. 22, 1943; s. Hilton and Clarease (Dillard) B.; A.B., Morgan State U., 1965; M.S.W., U. Pa., 1967; M.A. (Woodrow Wilson fellow), U. Md., 1971, Ph.D., 1972; m. Shereatha Bethel, June 3, 1967; children—Tyrone Randolph II, Tonita. Dir. adolescent day care program Community Service Inc., Phila., 1965; dir. summer youth program OEO, Washington, 1969-71; dir. public adminstrn. program N.C. Central U., 1972—, Durham, N.C., asst. prof. polit. sci., 1972-74, asso. prof., 1975—; mem. faculty CSC Fed. Exec. Inst., 1974; fellow Harvard U. Inst. for Ednl. Mgmt., 1977. Pres. Durham (N.C.) Acad. Parents Council; candidate for Durham County Bd. Commrs.; mem. Durham Com. on Black Affairs; mem. Durham City Council Adv. Bd. Served to capt. U.S. Army, 1965-67. Rockefeller fellow, 1978-79. Mem. Am. Soc. Public Adminstrn., Nat. Assn. Schs. Public Adminstrn. and Affairs, Nat. Inst. Public Mgmt., Conf. Minority Public Adminstrs. (award 1975), Omega Psi Phi. Home: 5314 Shady Bluff Rd Durham NC 27704 Office: NC Central U Durham NC 27707

BAIR, ANNA WITHERS, educator, musician; b. Mayodan, N.C., Aug. 12, 1916; d. Percy Lawson and Lydia Lucile (Williamson) W.; A.B. cum laude, Salem (N.C.) Coll., 1936, Mus.B. cum laude, 1937; postgrad. Royal Sch. Ch. Music, Eng., summer 1962; M.A., DePaul U., Chgo., 1969; postgrad. Duke U., 1967, Coll. William and Mary, 1969-72; m. Clifford Edwin Bair, June 16, 1938; children—Anna Elizabeth, Mary Ellen, Lucile Withers. Mem. music faculty Salem Coll., 1937-39; organist Home Moravian Ch., Winston-Salem, N.C., 1937-38, 40; organist, choir dir. Christ Moravian Ch., Winston-Salem, N.C., 1943-48, Calvary Moravian Ch., Winston-Salem, 1948-53; choir master-organist St. Mary's Epis. Ch., High Point, N.C., 1955-64, St. Paul's Epis. Ch., Edenton, N.C., 1965-68; mem. fine arts faculty Coll. of Albemarle, Elizabeth City, N.C., 1965—, chmn. dept. fine arts, 1972—; pvt. tchr. piano and organ, 1943—. Mem. Edenton Hist. Commn. Named Outstanding Tchr., Coll. of Albemarle, 1973, 75; Elizabeth City Musician of Yr., 1975; Nat. Endowment Humanities grantee, 1974. Mem. Am. Guild Organists (asso.), Nat. Soc. Colonial Dames Am., Nat. Trust for Historic Preservation, N.C. Lit. and Hist. Soc., Wachovia Hist. Assn., Pasquotank Hist. Assn., Delta Kappa Gamma. Elizabeth City Music Club. Democrat. Moravian. Home: 2108 Rivershore Rd Elizabeth City NC 27909 Office: Dept Fine Arts Coll of Albemarle Elizabeth City NC 27909

BAIR, CLIFFORD EDWIN, educator, musician; b. Goldsboro, Pa., Apr. 14, 1907; s. Daniel B. and Mina Rheinhardt (Shelley) B.; student Coll. City N.Y., 1924-25; Mus.B., Chgo. Musical Coll., 1928, Mus.D., 1948; m. Anna Elizabeth Withers, June 16, 1938; children—Anna (Mrs. Ellis Lewis Aycock), Ellen (Mrs. William Dale Stancil), Lucile (Mrs. C.B. Jackson). Acting head music dept. Battle Creek (Mich.) Coll., 1928-29; head voice and opera dramatics dept. Wayne (Neb.) State Coll., 1934-36, Salem Coll., Winston-Salem, N.C., 1936-45; vis. prof. voice and opera workshop, Wake Forest (N.C.) Coll., 1948-63; prof. music Coll. of Albemarle, Elizabeth City, N.C., 1964-72, dir. fine arts dept., 1968-72, prof. emeritus, 1972—. Buffo tenor Breslau (Germany) Stadt Theater, 1930, Salzburg (Austria) Festival Prodns., 1932, Am. and Civic Opera Co., Chgo., Detroit Civic Opera Co., 1932-34; opera producer Asheville (N.C.) Mozart Festival, 1938-41, Piedmont (N.C.) Arts Festival, 1942-50, Fla. Lyric Theater, Miami Beach, 1961, Columbia (S.C.) Fine Arts Festival, 1962, DePaul U. Opera Festivals, Chgo., 1965-67; founder, dir. Bel Canto Boys Choir, Winston-Salem, 1940-46, Civic Opera Assns. in Mt. Airy, N.C., 1944-50, Greensboro, N.C., 1945-49, Raleigh, N.C., 1946-49, Charlotte, N.C., 1948-54; co-dir. N.C. Festival Opera Schs., Salem Coll., 1941, 43, U. N.C. at Greensboro, 1942, 44, Western Carolina Coll., N.C., 1945-50; opera dir. Inspiration Point Fine Arts Colony, Eureka Springs, Ark. Bd. dirs. Winston-Salem Civic Music Assn., 1938-64, Winston Salem Little Theater, 1941-45; trustee Winston Salem Arts Council, 1951-60, Albemarle Area Arts Council, 1965-72. Mozarteum Found. grantee, 1932. Recipient Musician of Year award Elizabeth City, 1969, Distinguished Achievement award Albemarle Area Devel. Assn., 1972, Distinguished Service award Charlotte (N.C.), 1968, Nat. Honor award D.A.R., 1975. Mem. Music Tchrs. Nat. Assn., Fedn. Music Clubs (nat. opera chmn. 1943-47), Nat. Assn. for Opera (founder, pres. 1944-47), Nat. Assn. Tchrs. Singing (dir. 1944-48), Nat. Opera Assn. (dir. 1955-59), AAUP, Nat. Music Council (dir. 1944-47), Am. Acad. Tchrs. Singing, Elizabeth City Music Club, Charlotte (N.C.) Musicians Union. Mem. Moravian Ch. (dir. choirs 1954-64). Kiwanian. Editor: Vocal Score Stage Guide, Mozart's Bastien and Bastienne, 1940. Contbr. articles on opera to various mags. and book chpts. Home: 2108 Rivershore Rd Elizabeth City NC 27909 Office: Fine Arts Dept College of the Albemarle Elizabeth City NC 27909

BAIR, RONALD LEHMAN, psychotherapist; b. Williamsport, Pa., Jan. 1, 1937; s. Clyde Donald and Marjorie Lenore (Bendle) B.; student Temple U., 1954-55, Ursinus Coll., 1955-56; B.D., Christian Congl. Div. Sch., 1964; Th.D., Zion Theol. Sem., 1969; m. Sandra Ann Adams, Apr. 6, 1974; children—Ronald Lehman, Kevin J., Guy D., Jimmy, Janell. Exec. dir. Consulting Center, Williamsport, Pa., 1965-72; exec. dir. Christian Counseling Center, West Palm Beach, Fla., 1972—; staff psychologist Palm Beach County, Fla., 1977—; pvt. practice psychotherapist, West Palm Beach, 1969—. Bd. dirs. Project Rescue, Inc., 1979—, Tamarac Symphonic Pops Orch., Nova U., 1979—. Diplomate Am. Bd. Med. Examiners. Mem. Am. Psychotherapy Assn., Am. Counseling Assn., Nat. Psychol. Assn., Assn. Christian Counselors, Assn. Christian Marriage Counselors. Republican. Mem. Christian Ch. Club: Elks. Author: (with H.E. Lindsay) Clinical Hypnosis, 1969. Editor, Observer, 1974—, Graymatter, 1978—. Home: 1401 20th Ave N Lake Worth FL 33460 Office: PO Box 2436 Brass Bldg West Palm Beach FL 33402

BAIRD, BRUCE DOUGLAS, surgeon; b. Butler, Pa., Dec. 24, 1943; s. William Kenneth and Virginia Belle (Rumbaugh) B.; student Case Western Res. U., 1961-62; B.S. cum laude, U. N.H., 1965; M.D., U. Vt., 1969; m. Heidi Anne Grethe, May 24, 1969; children—Chardie Lynn, Spencer Kenneth. Intern Albany (N.Y.) Med. Center, 1969-70; resident Med. U. S.C., Charleston, 1970-72, 73-74, chief resident surgery, teaching fellow, 1974-75; research fellow VA Hosp., Charleston, 1972-73; asso. dir. surg. edn. Roanoke (Va.) Meml. Hosps., 1978—; asst. prof. surgery U. Va. Served with USNR, 1975—. Recipient Carl A. Moyer award Am. Burn Assn., 1973; diplomate Am. Bd. Surgery. Republican. Presbyterian. Contbr. articles to profl. jours. Home: 6120 Flamingo Dr SW Roanoke VA 24018 Office: Roanoke Meml Hosps PO Box 13367 Roanoke VA 24033

BAIRD, HARRY HAYNES, surgeon; b. Mars Hill, N.C., Oct. 11, 1918; s. Thomas and Nan (Wallin) B.; A.B., U. N.C., 1938; M.D., Washington U., St. Louis, 1942; m. Cornelia Wallace, Aug. 13, 1940; children—Wallace, Harry, Alice. Intern, Barnes Hosp., St. Louis, 1942-43, resident, 1943-47; practice medicine, specializing in urol. surgery, Charlotte, N.C., 1947—; mem. staff Presbyn. Hosp.; chmn. dept. urology Charlotte Meml. Hosp., 1967-70; dir. So. Nat. Bank; lectr. urology seminary U. Louisville, 1950. Mem. Morehead Scholarship Selection Com. U. N.C., 1967—; trustee Mars Hill Coll., 1952-75. Diplomate Am. Bd. Urology. Fellow Internat. Coll. Surgeons, A.C.S., Southeastern Surg. Congress; mem. Am. Urol. Assn. Baptist. Clubs: Rotary, Charlotte Country. Contbr. articles to profl. publs. Home: 4112 Robinwood Dr Charlotte NC 28212 Office: 1012 Kings Dr Charlotte NC 28207

BAIRD, HAYNES WALLACE, pathologist; b. St. Louis, Jan. 28, 1943; s. Harry Haynes and Mary Cornelia (Wallace) B.; B.A., U. N.C., 1965, M.D., 1969; m. Phyllis Jean Tipton, June 26, 1965; children—Teresa Lee, Christopher Wallace, Kelly Wallace. Intern, N.C. Meml. Hosp., Chapel Hill, 1969-70, resident in pathology, 1970-72, chief resident in pathology, 1972-73; asso. pathologist Moses H. Cone Meml. Hosp., Greensboro, N.C., 1973—; individual practice medicine, specializing in pathology Greensboro, 1973—; clin. asst. prof. U. N.C., Chapel Hill, 1978—; clin. lectr. chemistry U. N.C., Greensboro, 1973—. Bd. dirs. Greensboro unit Am. Cancer Soc. Diplomate Am. Bd. Pathology. Fellow Coll. Am. Pathologists; mem. Am., So. med. assns., Am. Soc. Cytology, Am. Soc. Clin. Pathologists, Internat. Acad. Pathology, N.C., Guilford County med. socs., N.C. Soc. Pathologists (sec.-treas. 1977-79), Greensboro Acad. Medicine. Methodist. Home: 2805 New Hanover Dr Greensboro NC 27408 Office: 1200 N Elm St Greensboro NC 27420

BAIRD, HOWARD D., food co. exec.; b. Chgo., Apr. 21, 1926; s. Harold D. and Gertrude (Raymond) B.; B.A., St. Cloud State U., 1950; postgrad. Northwestern U., 1960; children—Bruce Edward, Steven Frederick, Douglas Harold, Grant Howard. Mgr. personnel and labor relations Armour & Co., Chgo., 1952-67; v.p. indsl. relations Tyson Foods Co., Springdale, Ark., 1967—. Served with USN, 1944-46: PTO. Mem. NAM, Nat. Right to Work Com., Northwest Ark. Personnel Mgrs. Assn. Conservative Republican. Episcopalian. Office: PO Drawer E Springdale AR 72764

BAIRD, HOWARD MELVILLE, JR., pub. sch. adminstr.; b. Oakland, Calif., Sept. 30, 1918; s. Howard M. and Ruthedra B. (Eichner) B.; A.B., U. Pitts., 1948; M.A.E., U. Fla., 1961, postgrad. in Guidance (NDEA grantee), 1962; certificate in Advanced Grad. Studies in Guidance and Counseling (NDEA grantee) Boston U., 1966; m. Martha Carr Mills, Aug. 9, 1958; children—William Ludwig, Cynthia Merla Baird Hobson. Laborer Carr Coal Co., Wilkinsburg, Pa., 1936-37; clk. Joseph Horn & Co. Dept. Store, Pitts., 1937-39; salesman ins. Sun Life Assurance, Wilkinsburg, 1950-51; salesman paints Sherwin-Williams Paint Co., Wilkinsburg, 1952-53; law messenger firm Reed, Smith, Shaw & McClay, Pitts., 1939-41; auto painter Bauman Chevrolet Co., Wilkinsburg, 1941-43; clk. purchasing dept. clk. U.S.S. H.C. Frick Coke, Pitts., 1943-50; tchr. Monroeville (Pa.) Jr. High, 1954-55, Jefferson Jr. High, Jacksonville, Fla., 1955-62; counseling psychologist Jos. Stilwell Jr. High Sch., 1962-64, Wolpson Sr. High Sch., 1965-66 (both Jacksonville); dir. secondary curriculum devel. Duval County (Fla.) Pub. Schs., Jacksonville, 1971—. Chmn. Monroeville (Pa.) Civi Orgn., 1953-54; mem. Duval County Sch. Bd. Legis. Com., 1975. Mem. Am., N.E. Fla. psychol. assns., Assn. Supervision and Curriculum Devel., Duval County, Fla. assns. supervision and curriculum devel., Am. Contract Bridge League, Phi Delta Kappa. Unitarian (dir. religious edn. 1965-68). Mason (32 deg.), Kiwanian. Author: Rationale-Design-Tools for a P.P.S. Team Approach, 1970; Touch-Tell Teaching, 1970; Pupil Personnel Services in Duval County, 1971. Home: 1339 Hollywood Ave Jacksonville FL 32205 Office: 1741 Francis St Jacksonville FL 32209

BAIRD, JOHN DAVID, ins. exec.; b. Evanston, Ill., Sept. 22, 1937; s. Guy C. and Mary L. (Ellerbush) B.; B.B.A., U. Tex., 1959, postgrad. in law, 1959-60; m. JoAn R. Novotny, June 10, 1960; children—Colleen, Karin, Brian. From sr. ins. clk. to ins. supr. Tenneco Inc., Houston, 1961-65; asst. corporate risk mgr. Anderson, Clayton & Co., Houston, 1965-68; mgr. corporate ins. G.W. Murphy Industries, Houston, 1968; corporate ins. mgr. Tracor, Inc., Austin, Tex., 1968-73, corporate mgr. financial services, 1973—; sec.-treas., dir. Baird's Village Hobby Shop Inc., 1977—. Guest speaker U. Tex. Grad. Sch. Bus.; corporate ins. cons. Bd. dirs. N.W. Austin Little League, 1973-76; pres., 1974-75; bd. dirs. N.W. Vikings Jr. Football, 1973-77, pres., 1975; bd. dirs. Brackenridge Hosp., 1976-78, N.W. Austin Pony-Colt League, 1977-79; mem. budget com. United Way, 1975—. Served to lt. AUS, 1960-61. Mem. Nat. Assn. Accountants (dir. Austin area chpt. 1972-76, v.p. 1975), Soc. Chartered Property and Casualty Underwriters (pres. Central Tex. chpt. 1973-74, treas. 1980—), Risk and Ins. Mgmt. Soc., Austin C. of C., Austin Heritage Soc., Austin Citizens League, NW Austin Civic Assn., Delta Sigma Phi. Roman Catholic. Club: Austin Runners. Home: 4004 Greystone Dr Austin TX 78731 Office: 6500 Tracor Ln Austin TX 78721

BAIRD, LARRY DON, clergyman; b. Abilene, Tex., Sept. 23, 1949; s. Delmar Lee and Frances Elizabeth (Robertson) B.; student Cisco Jr. Coll., 1977—; student Hendrick Meml. Hosp. Sch. Vocational Nursing, 1972-73; m. Mary Margaret Ledbetter, Dec. 22, 1970; 1 son, Shannon Kirk. Nurse, Hendrick Meml. Hosp., Abilene, 1973-75, Abilene Area Dialysis Center, 1975-76; ordained minister United Pentecostal Ch. Internat., 1973; evangelist, 1976-77; instr. for deaf San Diego Pub. Schs., 1971-72, United Pentecostal Ch., 1973-77. Served with USN, 1970-72. Republican. Home and office: 1336 Grape St Abilene TX 79601

BAIRD, RICHARD BALFE, systems planner; b. Toledo, June 18, 1924; s. Walter Balfe and Alma (Braunschweiger) B.; B.S. in Aero. Engring., Purdue U., 1949; M.S. in Internat. Affairs, George Washington U., 1966; certificate mil. sci. Air War Coll., 1966; m. Barbara Ann Wumer, Dec. 27, 1946; children—Carol Anne, Catherine Louis. Aircraft test engr. Air Force Dept., 1949-57, task scientist, 1957-60, supervisory aerospace engr., 1960-63, gen. engr., 1963-67, aerospace engr., propulsion and aeronautics, Washington, 1967-79; ret., 1979; with System Planning Corp., Arlington, Va., 1979—; tech. cons. Served with USAAF, 1943-46. Registered profl. engr., Ohio, Ind., Va. Mem. Am. Legion, Farm Bur., Delta Chi. Methodist. Clubs: Ruritan; George Washington U. Contbr. articles profl. jours. Home: Route 1 Box 145 Aldie VA 22001 Office: 1500 Wilson Blvd Arlington VA 22209

BAIRD, WILLIAM BRUCE, lawyer; b. Louisville, Feb. 11, 1933; s. David Wallace and Mary Eleanor (Newman) B.; B.A. summa cum laude, U. Louisville, 1957; J.D., U. Va., 1960; m. Dixie M. Baird; children by previous marriage—William Bruce, Douglas C., Alexander T. Admitted to Ohio bar, 1960, Ky. bar, 1962; asso. atty. firm Taft, Stettinius & Hollister, Cin., 1960-62; asso. firm Middleton, Reutlinger & Baird, Louisville, 1962-65, partner, 1965-72, sr. partner, 1972—. Bd. dirs. Arthritis Found., Louisville chpt., 1969-72, Salvation Army Boys' Club, Louisville, 1974-76. Served with AUS, 1953-55. Mem. Ohio State, Louisville, Ky. bar assns. Republican. Roman Catholic. Clubs: Harmony Landing Country, Pendennis (Louisville). Home: 447 University Ave Louisville KY 40206 Office: 501 S 2d St Louisville KY 40202

BAKER, BAXTER LEE, sch. psychologist; b. Brewton, Ala., Feb. 6, 1951; s. Ollie Baxter and Mary Ann (Strawbridge) B.; A.S., Jefferson Davis State Jr. Coll., 1971; B.S., Auburn U., 1974; M.S., Jacksonville State U., 1975; m. Ivey Liles. Secondary sch. sci. tchr. Greenville (Ala.) Acad., 1974; patient affairs officer U.S. Army-MEDDAC, Ft. McClellan, Ala., 1974; counselor Escambia County Schs., Brewton, Ala., 1975-77, sch. psychologist, 1978—; grad. asst. U. Ala., 1977-78, counselor for new student orientation and Capstone Honors Program, summers 1976—; instr. Patrick Henry Jr. Coll., Monroeville, Ala., 1978—. Recipient cert. of achievement for outstanding service Ft. McClellan, 1974. Mem. Am. Personnel and Guidance Assn., Nat. Assn. Sch. Psychologists, Am. Sch. Counselors Assn., Assn. Measurement and Evaluation in Guidance, Council for Exceptional Children, Council for Ednl. Diagnostic Services, NEA, Ala. Assn. Sch. Psychologists, Ala. Council for Indian Edn., Ala. Edn. Assn., Ala. Personnel and Guidance Assn., Kappa Delta Pi (v.p.), Psi Chi. Methodist. Office: PO Box 307 Brewton AL 36426

BAKER, BRUCE A., psychologist, educator; b. Rochester, N.Y., Feb. 21, 1927; s. Frances A. and Dorothy M. (Geisinger) B.; B.A., Am. U., 1955, M.A., 1963; postgrad. in Edn. Va. Poly. Inst. and State U., 1970—; m. Dolores J. Martin, Apr. 6, 1953; children—Paul Manuel, Philip Bruce, Patricia Maria Dolores. Instr. Fairfax County (Va.) Sch. System, 1955-67; sr. psychologist No. Va. Community Coll., Annandale, 1967-71; dean student services Paul D. Camp Community Coll., Franklin, Va., 1971-73, coordinator spl. programs, 1973-74, asst. prof. psychology, 1974—; pvt. practice marriage and family counseling, Franklin, 1975—; clin. psychologist, therapist Western Tidewater Mental Health Clinic, Suffolk and Franklin, 1972-75. Cons. to pres. Compromatics div. Industrionics Inc., Arlington, Va., 1970-71, Disability Determination Dept. Vocat. Rehab., Richmond, Va., 1962-65. Mem. Franklin-Southampton (Va.) Drug com. City Council, Franklin, 1972-74. Bd. dirs. Idlewood Sch. for Retarded Children, Suffolk, 1972-73. Served with AUS, 1944-45. Recipient Outstanding Sci. Teaching award for No. Va. NSF, 1956. Mem. Am. Psychol. Assn. (asso.), Franklin C. of C. Episcopalian (vestryman 1968-71). Rotarian. Home: 121 Oakwood Dr Franklin VA 23851

BAKER, BRUCE ROBERT, elec. engr.; b. Passaic, N.J., Oct. 31, 1946; s. Byard Leonard and Florence Johanne (Hoegel) B.; B.S., U. Wash., 1968; postgrad. U. Fla., 1969-71; m. Becky Cartee, Aug. 9, 1975. Elec. engr., NASA, Kennedy Space Center, Fla., 1968—, mem. launch team Apollo 8, 10, 12-17, Skylab 1-3, Apollo-Soyuz test project, Space Shuttle. Mem. IEEE, Titusville (sec. 1970-71), Mims-Scottsmoor (treas. 1971-72, state dir. 1972-73) jr. chambers commerce. Home: 5400 Kathy Dr Titusville FL 32780 Office: VE ETD 21 Kennedy Space Center FL 32899

BAKER, CATHY M., lawyer; b. Baxley, Ga., Jan. 12, 1947; d. Thomas Peyton Jr. and Mary Jacqueline (Fennell) Miles; B.A., Mercer U., J.D., W.F. George Sch. of Law, 1971; m. James E. McCoy, Jr., June 11, 1971; 1 dau., Jacqueline Amelia; m. 2d, James M. Baker, Nov. 17, 1979. Admitted to Ga. bar, 1972; partner firm Miles & Baker, Baxley, 1971—; city atty. Surrency, Ga., 1973—. Treas. Appling County Assn. for Retarded Citizens, Baxley, 1973, 74. Mem. Am., Ga. bar assns., Phi Alpha Delta, Alpha Gamma Delta (treas. 1967). Baptist. Home: PO Box 484 Baxley GA 31513 Office: PO Box 412 Baxley GA 31513

BAKER, CLIFFORD HOWARD, mktg. research co. exec.; b. Paoli, Ind., Oct. 14, 1932; s. James A. and Alice (Limeberry) B.; B.S., U.S. Mil. Acad., 1956; M.S., Purdue U., 1965; Ph.D. in Econs., Statistics and Indsl. Psychology, N.C. State U., 1972; m. Joan B. Meyer, Feb. 4, 1958; children—Steven Conrad, Bradford Nelson, Paul Milton, Jeffrey Todd, Douglas Ross. Indsl. mktg. exec. Tex. Instruments, Dallas, 1959-61; market research exec. Gen. Motors Corp., Kokomo, Ind., 1961-65; supr. market analysis Corning Glass Works, Raleigh, N.C., 1965-70; pres. Indsl. Edn. Inst., Raleigh, 1970—. Served with AUS, 1956-59. Recipient Nat. Def. Service medal West Point, 1956. Mem. I.E.E.E., Assn. Grads. West Point, Adminstrv. Mgmt. Soc. Mem. Ch. of Christ. Home: 4816 Deerwood Dr Raleigh NC 27612 Office: 4509 Creedmoor St Raleigh NC 27612

BAKER, ERIC WHITE, social worker; b. Louisville, July 27, 1947; s. Dallard G. and Dora Etta (White) B.; A.B., Bellarmine Coll., 1970; M.S. in Social Work, U. Louisville, 1974. With Ky. Dept. for Human Resources, Shelbyville, 1970—, now supr. social services; pvt. practice family, marital and individual counseling, Louisville, 1977—. Bd. dirs. So. Regional Inst.; incorp. bd. dirs. Reproductive Health Center, Louisville, 1973; communication cons. Tri-County Com. on Aging; active Ky. chpt. for Prevention of Child Abuse. Cert. social worker, Ky.; hon. Ky. Col. Mem. Am. Coll. Social Workers, Acad. Cert. Social Workers, Nat. Assn. Social Workers, Am. Public Welfare Assn., Internat. Transactional Analysis Assn., Ky. Council on Crime and Delinquency, Child Welfare League Am., Audubon Soc. Democrat. Roman Catholic. Home: 8126 Lake Terr Apt 11 Louisville KY 40222 Office: PO Box 206 Shelbyville KY 40065 also 1313 Lyndon Ln Suite 215 Louisville KY 40222

BAKER, FRANK HAMON, univ. dean, animal scientist; b. Stroud, Okla., May 2, 1923; s. DeWitt and Maude Emma (Hamon) B.; B.S., Okla. State U., 1947, M.S., 1951, Ph.D., 1954; m. Meloncee Gaynelle Gray, May 25, 1946; children—Rilda, Necia, Twila, Dayna. County agt. Delaware County (Okla.), 1947-48; agrl. instr. VA, Ramona, Okla., 1948-50; grad. asst. Okla. State U., 1951-53, extension livestock specialist, 1958-62, dean agr., prof., 1974—; asst. prof. animal sci. Kans. State U., 1953-55; asso. prof. animal nutrition U. Ky., 1955-58; nat. coordinator extension animal sci. Dept. Agr., Washington, 1962-66; chmn. dept. animal sci. U. Nebr., 1966-74. Served with U.S. Army, 1943-45: ETO. Decorated Purple Heart; recipient Outstanding Service award Dept. Agr., 1965, Spl. Merit award, 1966, Continuing Service Beef Improvement, 1974; Agrl. Achievement award AKSRABEN Found., 1974. Fellow Am. Soc. Animal Sci. (pres. 1974), AAAS; mem. Council Agrl. Sci. and Tech. (pres. 1979), Am. Meat Sci. Assn., Am. Inst. Biol. Sci., Blue Key, Sigma Xi, Gamma Sigma Delta, Epsilon Sigma Phi, Alpha Zeta. Democrat. Methodist. Clubs: Kiwanis, Block and Bridle. Research, numerous publs. in field. Office: Coll Agr Okla State U Stillwater OK 74074

BAKER, GEORGE DORSET, data processing forms corp. exec.; b. London, Eng., Feb. 8, 1926; s. William Alfred and Aileen (Dorset) B.; student London Poly. Inst., 1948-50; came to U.S., 1958, naturalized, 1969. Mgmt. trainee John Dickinson & Co., London, 1948-52, v.p. prodn., Hamilton, Ont., Can., 1952-58; gen. mgr. Data Forms, Inc., Rochester, N.Y., 1958-64; pres. Datagraphic, Inc., Rochester, N.Y., Atlanta, 1964—, Datacheck, Inc., Dallas; lectr. Distributive Edn. Clubs Am., 1971-74. Mem. nat. advisory council Nat. Fedn. Independent Bus., 1972—, N.Y. state chmn., 1972—. Served to capt. Brit. Army, 1942-48. Mem. Nat. Fedn. Ind. Business (state chmn. 1972—), Forms Mfrs. Credit Assn. (chmn. 1969-70). Contbr. articles to various publs. Home: 98 Goldrush Circle Atlanta GA 30328 Office: 875 Johnson Ferry Rd NE Suite 550 Atlanta GA 30342

BAKER, GERRY SAYLORS, civic worker; b. Ennis, Tex., May 17, 1925; d. Joseph Benjamin and Myrtle Lorene (Long) Saylors; student Tex. State Coll. for Women, 1943; B.A., Tex. U., 1956; postgrad. Princeton Sem., 1946-47, Houston U., 1972; m. Daniel Arthur Baker, Aug. 31, 1946; children—Rebecca Ann Baker, Daniel Arthur Baker. Tchr., Sunday sch., Wynnewood Presbyterian Ch., Dallas, 1947-57, Grace Presbyn. Ch., Houston, 1957—; asst. to dir. Presbyn. Devel. Fund., Houston, 1962-63; diamond appraiser, 1979—. Mem. Woman's Club Houston (chmn. fine arts com. 1972), Tex. Fine Arts

Assn. (regional dir. 1972) Art League Houston, Houston Civic Arts Assn., Nat. League Am. Pen Women, Houston Gem and Mineral Soc. Republican.

BAKER, GLENN EARL, educator; b. Goosecreek, Tex., Oct. 4, 1933; s. Robert Easley and Jessie Katherine (Groesbeeck) B.; student U. Tex. at El Paso, 1951-52; B.S., Tex. A. and M. U., 1956, M.Ed., 1961, Ed.D., 1966; postgrad. U. No. Colo., 1964, U. Md., 1965; m. Judy Kay Hunzeker, Dec. 22, 1967; children—John Konrad, Robert Arthur. Tchr. pub. schs., Tex., 1958-64; asso. prof. Wayne (Nebr.) State Coll., 1966-71, chmn. dept. indsl. edn., 1971; asso. prof. U. Mo., Columbia, 1971-74; asso. prof., coordinator grad. studies in indsl. arts N.C. State U., Raleigh, 1974-77; asso. prof. indsl. edn. dept. Tex. A. and M. U., College Station, 1977—; cons. K. & E. Co., Hoboken, N.J., 1968, Mo. Dept. Edn., 1971-74; mem. adv. bd. Indsl. Edn. Mag., 1977—. Served to staff sgt., AUS, 1956-58; Korea. Recipient Faculty Research award Wayne State Found., 1968; Mo. Dept. Edn. grantee, 1973-74; N.C. State U. grantee, 1975-76; Tex. Edn. Agy. grantee, 1979-80. Mem. Nebr. Edn. Assn. (sec. 1969-70), Nebr. Indsl. Tchr. Educators (pres. 1968-69), Am. Indsl. Arts Assn., Am. Council on Indsl. Arts Tchr. Edn., Am. Vocat. Assn., Tex. Coll. Indsl. Arts Assn. (state advisor), Nat. Assn. Indsl. Tchr. Edn., Am. Indsl. Arts Student Assn. (dir. 1979), Am. Soc. Engring. Edn., Magna Carta Barons, Epsilon Pi Tau (laureate trustee), Iota Lambda Sigma, Phi Delta Kappa, Phi Kappa Tau, DeMolay. Club: Lions. Author: (with Leonard Crow) Electricity Fundamentals, 1972; (with L. Dayle Yeager) Wood Technology, 1974; Construction Techniques, 1976; (with others) The Meaning and Value of Work, 1973. Contbr. articles to profl. jours. Home: 2804 Normand Dr College Station TX 77840 Office: Indsl Edn Dept Tex A and M U College Station TX 77843

BAKER, HELEN VAUGHAN BURDIN, educator; b. New Orleans, May 20, 1937; d. John Joseph and Helen Rose (Broussard) Burdin; B.A., H. Sophie Newcomb, 1959; M.A., U. Southwestern La., 1970, Ph.D., 1975; m. Larry Eugene Baker, Aug. 22, 1959; children—Larry Eugene, Elizabeth, David. Teaching asst. U. Southwestern La., 1969-73, asst. prof. history, 1975-77, dir. Women in La. Collection, Center for La. Studies, 1977—; cons. Lafayette Natural History Mus. and Planetarium. Recipient John Snell Meml. prize, 1971; La. Com. for the Humanities grantee, 1978-79; Nat. Endowment for Humanities grantee, 1980-81. Mem. Am. Hist. Assn., So. Hist. Assn. (editor European History newsletter 1979—), La. Hist. Assn., Southwestern Social Sci. Assn., Attakapas Hist. Assn. (pres. 1972-74), So. Assn. Women Historians, Coordinating Council for Women in the Hist. Profession, Western Assn. German Studies. Democrat. Roman Catholic. Author: (with Amos E. Simpson) Death of an Old World, 1914-1945, 1972, Genesis of a New World, 1945-Present, 1978. Contbr. articles to profl. jours. Home: 1104 Marilyn Dr Lafayette LA 70503 Office: Women in Louisiana Collection University of Southwestern Louisiana Lafayette LA 70504

BAKER, HORACE ANSON, JR. (PAT), advt. agy. exec.; b. Wills Point, Tex., Dec. 30, 1933; s. Horace Anson and Janet Williams (Lybrand) B.; B.S. in Journalism, So. Meth. U., Dallas, 1955; M.A. in Radio-TV Advtg., U. Houston, 1956. Pub. relations editor U.S. Plywood Corp., N.Y.C., 1959-63; partner Lamb-Baker & Assos. Advt. Co., Dallas, 1963-65; dir. advt., sales promotion Employers Ins. of Tex., Dallas, 1965-70; mgr. advtg., Sales promotion Redman Industries Inc., Dallas, 1970-72; account exec. McCrary-Powell Advt. Co., Dallas, 1972-74; pres. Baker and Burnett Advt., Inc., Dallas, 1974—. Pres. Dallas Met. Ballet, 1975-77; adv. dir. Dallas Shakespeare Festival, 1975-76. Precinct chmn. Republican Party, 1967. Served with AUS, 1956-58. Ky. col. Fellow Northwood Inst.; mem. Dallas C. of C., Dallas Advt. League, Soc. Profl. Journalists, 500 Inc. of Dallas, Assemblage of Dallas, Sigma Delta Chi, Lambda Chi Alpha. Methodist. Author of After the Attack, TV film for Tex. Heart Assn. Home: 3883 Turtle Creek Blvd Dallas TX 75219 Office: 3707 Rawlins Suite 216 Dallas TX 75219

BAKER, HOWARD HENRY, JR., U.S. senator, lawyer; b. Huntsville, Tenn., Nov. 15, 1925; s. Howard Henry and Dora (Ladd) B.; student U. of South, Tulane U.; J.D., U. Tenn., 1949; LL.D., Tusculum Coll.; D.C.L., Southwestern U., Memphis; m. Joy Dirksen, Dec. 22, 1951; children—Darek, Cynthia. Former partner law firm Baker, Worthington, Barnett & Crossley; former chmn. bd. First Nat. Bank, Oneida, Tenn.; U.S. senator from Tenn., 1966—, minority leader, 1977—; chmn. Tenn. del. Republican Nat. Conv., 1968. Served to lt. (j.g.) USNR, 1943-46. Mem. Am., Knoxville, Scott County bar assns., Bar Assn. Tenn., Scarabbean Soc., Pi Kappa Phi. Presbyn. Office: 4123 Dirksen NSOB Washington DC 20510

BAKER, IRA LEE, journalist; b. Fairwood, Va., Sept. 5, 1915; s. Joseph Franklin and Celia (Blackburn) B.; B.A., Wake Forest Coll., 1936; M.A., Columbia U., 1952; postgrad. U. Ill., U. Wis., U. Tenn., Syracuse U.; M.Sc. in Journalism, U. Ill., 1963. Instr. English, N.C. State Coll., Raleigh, 1946-50, asst. extension editor State Coll. Extension Service and mng. editor Extension Farm-News, 1950-51; head journalism dept. Furman U., Greenville, S.C., 1951-65; asso. prof. journalism and English, High Point (N.C.) Coll., 1965-68; prof. journalism East Carolina U., Greenville, 1968—, columnist, mem. editorial staff Communication: Journalism Education Today, 1977—; corr. Religion News Service, 1953—; permanent advisor S.C. Collegiate Press Assn. Publicity chmn. Wake County council N.C. Symphony Orch., 1947-51; active Raleigh Music Club, Raleigh Little Theatre, 1946-51, Greenville Little Theater, 1951—; mem. alumni council Wake Forest Coll., 1964; relationships chmn. Pitt County council Boy Scouts Am., 1975; del. S.C. Republican Conv., 1958. Served with USAAF, 1942-44. Recipient Scholastic Pioneer award Nat. Scholastic Press Assn., 1970; named Distinguished Newspaper Adviser, Nat. Council Coll. Publs. Advisers, 1973. Mem. Am. Assn. Coll. and Univ. Profs. (v.p. Furman U. chpt.), Am. Assn. Tchrs. Religious Journalism, Assn. Ednl. Journalism (state dir.), S.C. Press Assn., Nat. Council Coll. Publs. Advisers (membership chmn. dist. III 1967-68), Pub. Relations Soc. Am. (asso.), S.C. Assn. Coll. Publs. Advisers (pres. 1957—), South Atlantic Modern Lang. Assn., Pitt County (N.C.) Hist. Soc., (publicity chmn.) SAR, Sigma Delta Chi, Tau Kappa Epsilon, Alpha Phi Gamma (nat. pres. 1968-70). Baptist. Co-author: Modern Journalism, 1961; mem. adv. bd. Student Writer; chmn. adv. bd. Cerebral Palsy News of S.C.; mem. bd. editors Scholastic Mag.; mem. book reviewing staff Greensboro News, 1960, Richmond News Leader, 1975; editor The Collegiate Journalist; contbr. book revs. to Raleigh News and Observer, 1968—, Richmond (Va.) News Leader, 1974—, also articles to Ency. So. Bapts., 1958. Address: Box 2707 East Carolina U Greenville NC 27834

BAKER, JAMES LINTON, JR., plastic and reconstructive surgeon; b. Somerville, N.J., May 4, 1936; s. James Linton and Dorothy Ann (Murray) B.; B.S., Fla. So. Coll., 1958; student U. Miami Sch. Medicine, 1958-59; M.D., U. Amsterdam, 1964; m. Wiesje Knap, May 3, 1963; children—Cynthia Louise, Dana Arlette. Intern Monmouth Med. Center, Long Branch, N.J., 1964-65, resident gen. surgery, 1965-69; resident plastic surgery Orange Meml. Hosp., Orlando, Fla., 1969-71; practice medicine specializing in plastic and reconstructive surgery, Orlando, Fla., 1971—; chief plastic surgery Holiday Hosp., Orlando, Lucerne Gen. Hosp., Orlando; attending plastic surgeon Orange Meml. Hosp. Bd. dirs. Central Fla. Devel. Com., 1975—. Recipient Outstanding Intern and Resident awards, Monmouth Med. Center, 1964, 69. Mem. A.C.S., Am. Soc. Plastic and Reconstructive Surgeons, Am., Fla. cleft palate assns., Internat. Acad. Cosmetic Surgery, Am. Soc. Aesthetic Plastic Surgeons, Internat. Clin. Soc. Plastic Surgeons, Plastic and Maxillofacial Soc. N.E. Fla. Clubs: University, Citrus, Country (Orlando, Fla.). Contbr. articles to med. jours.; producer 5 med. movies. Home: 1216 Buckwood Dr Orlando FL 32806 Office: 400 W Morse Blvd Winter Park FL 32789

BAKER, JOHN DAVID, real estate developer; b. Columbia, S.C., July 5, 1955; s. David and JoAnn (Schreiber) B.; student U. South Fla., 1973-76; B.S., U. S.C., 1977. Acct., property mgr., salesman Keenan Co. Realtors, Columbia, 1976-79; broker-in-charge, property mgr. Baker & Baker, Columbia, 1979—. Mem. exec. com. Midlands chpt. March of Dimes, 1978—; state treas. Ann. Good Health Appeals Campaign, 1980; membership chmn. Downtown Action Council, Downtown Action Club; mem., past treas. Carolina Carillon Christmas Parade, Columbia. Mem. Inst. Real Estate Mgmt., Columbia Jaycees (state dir. 1978). Democrat. Judaism. Home: 1520 Senate St Apt 2-G Columbia SC 29201 Office: PO Box 11700 Columbia SC 29211

BAKER, JOHN JAY, oncologist; b. Charles Town, W.Va., June 1, 1941; s. Jonathan Jefferson and Dorothy Elizabeth B.; B.A., U. Mich., 1963; M.D., Wayne State U., 1968; m. Judith May Reinhardt, July 5, 1969; 1 son, Jonathan Jordan. Intern, Butterworth Hosp., Grand Rapids, Mich., 1968-69; resident in internal medicine, 1971-73, fellow in med. oncology, 1973-75; practice medicine Ga. Oncology Hematology Clinic, Marietta, 1975—; mem. staff Kennestone Hosp., Marietta, Northside and Crawford hosps., Atlanta. Served with M.C., USN, 1969-71; Vietnam. Decorated Bronze Star. Diplomate Am. Bd. Internal Medicine. Mem. So. Med. Assn., Med. Assn. Ga., Med. Assn. Atlanta, Cobb County Med. Soc., Am. Soc. Clin. Oncology, Clin. Oncology Assn. of Ga. Office: 737 Church St Marietta GA 30060

BAKER, JOHN LANGSTON, air-conditioning equipment co. exec.; b. Oklahoma City, Oct. 10, 1930; s. John Wesley and Bessie Lou (Crouch) B.; B.S.M.E., U. Okla., 1953; m. Beverly Jean Goudelock, May 31, 1953; children—Marsha Lynn Baker Roberts, John Scott. Field application engr. Carrier Air Conditioning Co., Dallas, 1953-58, sales engr., Oklahoma City, 1958-64, br. mgr., Oklahoma City, 1964-71, dist. mgr., Dallas, 1971—. Group chmn. United Way of Dallas, 1973, firm chmn., 1974—; patron Richardson Symphony Orch. Served with USNR, 1954-55; ETO. Recipient Expert Rifle medal. Mem. Am. Soc. Heating, Refrigerating and Air Conditioning Engrs., Nat. Soc. Profl. Engrs., Nat. Rifle Assn. (life), Dallas Mus. Fine Arts, Res. Officers Assn., Shakespeare Guild, U. Okla. Alumni Assn. (life), Pi Kappa Alpha. Republican. Mem. Disciples of Christ. Ch. (elder, chmn. gen. bd.). Clubs: Brookhaven Country, Rotary. Home: 5 Pebblebrook Circle Richardson TX 75080 Office: 10838 N Central Expressway POB 30642 Dallas TX 75230

BAKER, KATHRYN TAYLOR, social worker; b. Trenton, Tenn., Jan. 5, 1925; d. John Andrew and Alma Lou (Wharey) Taylor; B.S., U. Tenn., 1945, M.S., 1954; postgrad. U. Chgo., 1950, Vanderbilt U., 1951; m. John Baker, Sept. 30, 1972. Home demonstration agt. U. Tenn. Agrl. Extension Service, Hardeman County, 1946-49, Dyer County, 1949-50; child welfare worker Tenn. Dept. Public Welfare, Dyer County, 1951-53; med. social worker LeBonheur Children's Hosp., Memphis, 1954-57; med. social cons. Child Devel. Center, U. Tenn. Coll. Medicine, Knoxville, 1957-59; social worker Children's Med. Center, Tulsa, 1959-60; asst. prof. social work, dir. med. social work dept. U. Tenn. Coll. Medicine, Memphis, 1960-68, asso. prof. social work, 1972—; dir. community services Memphis Regional Med. Program, 1968-76; dir. regional clinic program U. Tenn. Child Devel. Center, Memphis, 1976—. Mem. admissions bd. Arlington Devel. Center, 1974—; hon. bd. dirs. Am. Cancer Soc., 1974—; bd. dirs. Goodwill Industries, 1975—, W. Tenn. AGAPE, 1975—; mem. human rights com. Happy Acres Home Life Center, 1976—. Fellow Am. Assn. on Mental Deficiency; mem. Acad. Cert. Social Workers, Nat. Registry of Clin. Social Workers, AAUP (chpt. sec.-treas. 1976), Nat. Assn. Social Workers, Nat. Conf. on Social Welfare, Tenn. Conf. on Social Welfare, Tenn. Hosp. Assn., Tenn. Soc. Health Care Social Workers, Sigma Kappa (life). Democrat. Mem. Chs. of Christ. Club: U. Tenn. Faculty, Memphis Social Workers. Contbr. articles in field to profl. jours.; editor 14 reference books on health and health related resources in mid-South area, 1961-76. Home: 1818 Mignon Ave Memphis TN 38107 Office: 711 Jefferson Ave Memphis TN 38105

BAKER, KERRY ALLEN, food processing exec.; b. Selmer, Tenn., Sept. 21, 1949; s. Austin Clark and Betty Ann (Brooks) B.; B.I.E., Ga. Inst. Tech., 1971; M.B.A., Ga. State U., 1973. With dept. law State of Ga., 1971-73; commd. 2d lt. U.S. Army, 1973, advanced through grades to capt., 1977; assembly and transport platoon leader 1st 12th Lance F.A., Ft. Sill, Okla., 1973-74; adminstrv. officer weapons dept. F.A. Sch., Ft. Sill, 1974-77; instr. logistics br. weapons dept., Ft. Sill, 1977; div. engr. N.W. Ga. div. Gold Kist Poultry, Ellijay, 1977—. Mem. Am. Inst. Indsl. Engrs., Am. Mgmt. Assn., Soc. Advancement Mgmt., Soc. Am. Mil. Engrs., Scabbard and Blade, Sigma Phi Epsilon, Pi Delta Epsilon, Alpha Phi Omega. Baptist. Club: Masons, Order St. Barbara. Home: 824 Larry Ln Decatur GA 30033 Office: PO Box 467 Ellijay GA 30540

BAKER, L. ALLEN, JR., data processing adminstr.; b. El Paso, Tex., Mar. 7, 1950; s. Leo A. and Betty B.; B.S., W. Tex. State U., 1972; m. Debra Lynn Wheeler, Jan. 5, 1973; 1 son, Matthew Allen. Programmer, analyst Textar Corp., Arlington, Tex., 1972-74, systems and programming mgr., 1974-76; project mgr. Tex. Instruments, Dallas, 1976; mgr. data processing Core Labs., Inc., Dallas, 1976—. Mem. Data Processing Mgmt. Assn. Baptist. Office: 7501 Stemmons Freeway Dallas TX 75247

BAKER, LORAN FRANCIS, hosp. food adminstr.; b. Gastonia, N.C., Jan. 6, 1925; s. John Curtis and Dessie (Phillips) B.; student Backester Sch. Lie Detection, 1960, Treasury Sch. Intelligence, 1960; m. Ruth T. Trueblood, Mar. 29, 1965; children—Brenda, Michael, Kimberly, Karen. Enlisted U.S. Coast Guard, 1942, advanced through grades to chief petty officer, 1964, ret., 1965; with U.S. Post Office, 1965; dietary mgr., food adminstr. Albemarle Hosp., Elizabeth City, N.C., 1966—. Club: Elks. Office: Albemarle Hospital Elizabeth City NC 27909

BAKER, MARTHA ANN, nurse; b. Lee's Summit, Mo., Mar. 24, 1934; d. Chris Arthur and Lillie May (Harris) Ohmsieder; B.S., U. Kans., 1956; M.Ed., U. Nev., 1970; postgrad. N. Tex. State U., 1975—; postgrad. Tex. Women's U., 1974-77; m. Russell G. Baker, Apr. 5, 1958; 1 dau., Martha Lynn. Instr. nursing U. Kans., 1956-58; sch. nurse Neosho (Mo.) Pub. Schs., 1958-60; staff nurse Washoe Med. Center, 1963-64; asst. prof. instr. nursing Orvis Sch. Nursing, U. Nev., Reno, 1964-65, 70-71; asst. prof. nursing Baylor U., Dallas, 1971—. HEW fellow, 1968-69. Mem. AAUW, Am. Nurses Assn., Assn. for Care Children in Hosps. Presbyterian. Club: Brookhaven Country. Home: 1408 Northridge Ct Carrollton TX 75006 Office: 3616 Worth St Dallas TX 75204

BAKER, MARY JANE, ednl. counselor; b. Cherokee County, Ala., Oct. 6, 1944; d. King S. and Allie (Rinehart) Baker; B.S., Jacksonville State U., 1966; M.A., U. Ala., 1968, postgrad., 1979—; postgrad. Troy State U., 1977. Counselor student affairs West Ga. Coll., 1967-71; counselor, fgn. student adviser Troy State U., 1971-79; staff reference library U. Ala., University, 1979—. Mem. Pike County (Ala.) Mental Health Bd. Mem. AAUW (corp. rep. Troy State U., 1977-78), Troy Bus. and Profl. Women (internat. affairs rep. 1977-78), Ala. Library Assn., Nat. Assn. Women Deans, Counselors, Am., Ala. personnel, guidance assns., So. Coll. Personnel Assn., Internat. Students Cultural Orgn. Legion Aux. Home: Route 3 Centre AL 35960

BAKER, MICHAEL ALAN, lawyer; b. Shreveport, La., Sept. 27, 1945; s. Troy L. and Ethel M. (Harmon) B.; B.B.A., U. Houston, 1968, J.D. cum laude, 1971; children—Emily Jo, Dwight Alan. Accountant, J.K. Lasser & Co., Houston, 1968-71; admitted to Tex. bar, 1971; mem. firm Fulbright & Jaworski, Houston, 1971-72; atty. Browning-Ferris Industries, Inc., Houston, 1972—. Adj. prof. law Bates Coll. Law U. Houston, 1971—. Vol. for Vols. in Tech. Assistance. Served to capt. Finance Corps, AUS, 1971. Houston Inst. for Urban Studies fellow, 1970-71; Bates Coll. Law Teaching fellow, 1970. Mem. Tex. Soc. C.P.A.'s, Tex. State Bar, Houston, Am. (regional chmn. pub. contract law sect.) bar assns., Phi Sigma Kappa, Alpha Phi Omega, Phi Delta Phi. Editor: Houston Law Rev., 1970-71. Office Fannin Bank Bldg Houston TX 77025

BAKER, MICHAEL GEORGE MYRON, coll. ofcl.; b. Fremont, Ohio, Nov. 15, 1946; s. William E. and Elizabeth Baker; student U. Del., 1977; m. Sue Ann Lambright, Sept. 26, 1964; children—Phillip B., Amy Lyne, Wynn M. Ins. agt., Sandusky, Ohio, 1969-70, Findlay, Ohio, 1971-72; asst. sales mgr. C.H. Gundlach & Sons, Sandusky, 1970; mgr. Clancy's Inc., Orrville, Ohio, 1975-77; automobile salesman, Orrville, 1977-78; public relations coordinator Winston-Salem (N.C.) Bible Coll., 1978—. Deacon, Orrville Ch. of Christ, 1978, chmn. evangelism com., 1978, v.p. Growing Christian Sunday sch. class, 1977-78. Recipient various salesmanship awards. Mem. Assn. Instl. Devel. Officers, Devel. Assn. Christian Instns., Christian Amateur Radio Fellowship. Home: 309 Mountainbrook Dr King NC 27021 Office: 4117 Northampton Dr Winston-Salem NC 27105

BAKER, RALEIGH OTTO, JR., clergyman; b. Charlotte, N.C., Sept. 1, 1922; s. Raleigh Otto and Ruth Lillian (Bickett) B.; B.A. cum laude, Wake Forest Coll., 1950; B.D., Southwestern Bapt. Theol. Sem., Ft. Worth, 1953; D.Min., Luther Rice Sem., Jacksonville, Fla., 1974; m. Phyllis Ann McKinnon, Dec. 19, 1948; children—Jeannie Lynn, William Raleigh. Ordained to ministry So. Bapt. Conv., 1950; pastor chs. in Tex., N.C. and Va., 1951-73; dir. devel. Va. Bapt. Homes, Culpeper 1973-77, adminstr. Va. Bapt. Home, Culpeper, 1977—; adv. Sch. Long-Term Care, Va. Commonwealth U., 1978-80. Served with USAAF, 1943-46. Recipient M.E. Dodd Meml. award So. Bapt. Radio and TV Commn., 1977. Mem. Am. Assn. Homes Aging (ho. of dels. 1978-79), Va. Assn. Non-Profit Homes Aging (pres. 1977-79, dir. 1979-80; Adminstr. of Year award 1979), So. Bapt. Assn. Ministries with Aging (1st v.p. 1980-81), Bapt. Public Relations Assn. Author articles, book revs. in field. Address: PO Box 191 Culpeper VA 22701

BAKER, ROBERT FLOWERS, lawyer; b. Durham, N.C., Dec. 15, 1935; s. Lenox Dial and Rosa Virginia (Flowers) B.; B.A., Davidson (N.C.) Coll., 1958; J.D., Duke U., 1961; m. Billie Faye Edwards, June 12, 1958; children—William Lenox, Debra Dial, Robert Flowers. Admitted to N.C. bar, 1961; asso. firm Spears, Barnes & Baker, Durham, 1963-67, partner, 1967—; dir. Guaranty State Bank (Durham). Chmn. div. United Fund of Durham, 1965; trustee Episcopal High Sch., Alexandria, Va., 1978—. Served with Intelligence Corps, AUS, 1961-63. Mem. Am., N.C. (bd. govs. 1973-77, chmn. com. practical tng. 1972-77, chmn. membership com. 1978, chmn. advanced trial techniques com. 1979-80), Durham County (N.C.) (exec. com. 1972—, treas. 1977, v.p. 1978-79 pres. 1979-80) bar assns. Clubs: Kiwanis (pres. 1975-76), Hope Valley Country (bd. govs., v.p. 1975). Home: 3112 Cornwall Rd Durham NC 27707 Office: 433 W Main St Durham NC 27702

BAKER, ROY VERBLE, JR., agrl. engr.; b. Littlefield, Tex., Oct. 9, 1938; s. Roy Verble and Brena (Cook) B.; B.S. in Agrl. Engring., Tex. A and M U., 1951; M.S. in Agrl. Engring. (Nat. Cotton Council fellow), Clemson (S.C.) U., 1962; m. Pamela Sue Roden, May 9, 1970; 1 dau., Jennifer Michelle. Research engr. Southwestern Cotton Ginning Research Lab., U.S. Dept. Agr.-Agrl. Research Service, Mesilla Park, N.Mex., 1962-68, dir. lab. South Plains Cotton Ginning Research Lab., Lubbock, Tex., 1968—. Cons. IBRD, Washington, 1973. Mem. Am. Soc. Agrl. Engrs., Sigma Xi, Tau Beta Pi, Phi Kappa Phi, Alpha Zeta. Democrat. Baptist. Contbr. articles to profl. jours. Home: 5411 76th St Lubbock TX 79424 Office: Route 3 Box 213 AAA Lubbock TX 79401

BAKER, RUSSELL MONTEZ, lawyer; b. Celeste, Tex., Mar. 11, 1906; s. William Perry and Kathleen (Bolte) B.; grad. So. Meth. U., 1928; m. Ollie Marie Dedman, Aug. 26, 1927; children—Harriet Kay, Russell Montez. Admitted to Tex. bar, 1929, asso. Caldwell, Gillen, Francis & Gallagher, Dallas, 1929-32; jr. partner Caldwell, Gillen, Francis & Gallagher, 1932-38; mem. firm Caldwell, Baker & Jordan, Dallas, 1938-59; now sr. mem. firm Baker & Foreman; founding mem. Roscoe Pound Am. Trial Lawyers Research Center; research fellow Southwestern Legal Found. Fellow Am. Coll. Trial Lawyers, Tex. Bar Found.; mem. Assn. Trial Lawyers Am., Am. Judicature Soc., Law Sci. Acad., Law Sci. Found. Am., Internat. Acad. Trial Lawyers (bd. govs. 1975, dean of Acad. 1978-79), Tex. Assn. Plaintiff Attys. (pres.), Internat. (patron), Am. (nuclear energy com. 1971-73), Tex., Dallas bar assns., Am. Bd. Trial Advs., Internat. Soc. Barristers, Delta Chi. Clubs: Dallas Athletic, Dallas Athletic Country, Cosmopolitan (internat. pres. 1950-51). Editor Am. Trial Lawyers Assn. Law Jour. Home: 6256 Lupton Dr Dallas TX 75225 Office: Suite M-110 North Mall Campbell Centre 1 8350 N Central Expressway Dallas TX 75206

BAKER, SHERRY LYNN, art critic; b. Atlanta, Sept. 21, 1949; s. Marvin Napolean and Flora Florence (Ensley) B.; B.A., Am. U., 1972, grad. fellow, 1973. Public relations writer Joe Sports Assos., Atlanta, 1974-76; art critic, contbg. editor Atlanta Gazette, 1975-78; public info. officer Atlanta Dept. Parks, Libraries and Cultural Affairs, 1977-78; public relations dir. DeKalb County Recreation, Parks and Cultural Affairs, 1980—; freelance art critic, 1978—; bd. dirs. City Center Dance Theatre, Atlanta, 1977—; asso. editor Contemporary Art/Southeast, 1977; author hist. catalogue on quilts. Art criticism fellow Nat. Endowment Arts, 1978. Mem. Women in Film, Atlanta Prodn. Alliance. Address: 1823 Indiana Ave Atlanta GA 30307

BAKER, THOMAS LINDSAY, historian, mus. curator; b. Cleburne, Tex., Apr. 22, 1947; s. Garnell A. and Mary Lois (Miller) B.; B.A., Tex. Tech. U., 1969, M.A., 1972, Ph.D., 1977. Research asso., lectr., program mgr. History of Engring. Program Tex. Tech. U., 1970-75, 77-79; Fulbright lectr. Tech. U. Wroclaw (Poland), 1975-77; asso. curator history Panhandle-Plains Hist. Mus., Canyon, Tex., 1978—. Mem. Am. Hist. Assn., Western Hist. Assn., Tex. State Hist. Assn., Internat. Molinological Soc., Polish Am. Hist. Assn. (adv. council),

Nat. Trust Hist. Preservation, Am. Assn. State and Local History, Tex. Folklore Soc., Gamma Theta Upsilon. Author: Water for the Southwest, 1973; Early History of Panna Maria, 1975; First Polish Americans, 1978. Contbr. articles to profl. jours. Home: PO Box 7 WT Station Canyon TX 79016 Office: Panhandle Plains Hist Mus PO Box 967 WT Station Canyon TX 79016

BAKER, WILLIAM ANDERSON, JR., ins. agt.; b. Laurel, Miss., Feb. 14, 1929; s. William Anderson and Myrtis (Alford) B.; B.S., Tulane U., 1955; m. Gary Taylor Gillis, June 8, 1956; children—Carlotta Kraft, Lindsey Alford, William Anderson. Trainee, Kaiser Aluminum Co., Balt., 1955-56; mech. engr. Waldemar S. Nelson Inc., New Orleans, 1956-58; exec. v.p. Gillis, Ellis & Baker, Inc., ind. ins. agts., New Orleans, 1958—; dir. Bell Tire, Inc., Jacksonville, Fla. Treas., Orleans Neighborhood Centers, 1968; bd. dirs. Family Service Soc. New Orleans, 1966-70; bd. dirs. Kingsley House, New Orleans, 1963—, pres., 1970-72. Served with USNR, 1948-52. Decorated Air medal. Mem. Ind. Ins. Agts. Am., Ind. Ins. Agts. La. (pres. 1971-72), Ind. Ins. Agts. Greater New Orleans (sec. 1978—), Soc. C.P.C.U. (pres. Deep South chpt. 1966), Nat. Assn. Casualty and Surety Agts. Republican. Episcopalian. Clubs: Pickwick, New Orleans Lawn Tennis, New Orleans Country, Essex. Home: 1123 Octavia St New Orleans LA 70115 Office: 135 St Charles Ave Suite 700 New Orleans LA 70130

BAKER, WILLIAM DUNCAN, aero. engr.; b. Macon, Ga., Sept. 27, 1950; s. Alfred Stanley and Koma Jo (Johnson) B.; B.S. in Aero. Engring., Tex. A. and M. U., 1971; m. Martha Kathryn Sackett, Apr. 11, 1971 (div. 1979); children—Gray Duncan, Ryan Patrick; m. 2d, Katherine Ann Doster, Nov. 10, 1979 (div. 1980). System safety engr. Boeing Co., Houston, 1971-72, 74-75, logistics engr., Seattle, 1972-74; liaison engr. Bell Helicopter Co., Amarillo, Tex., 1975-76; safety engr. Occupational Safety and Health Adminstrn., U.S. Dept. Labor, Austin, Tex., 1976-77; liaison engr. Bell Helicopter Textron, Amarillo, 1977—; pres. Baker Enterprises, Amarillo. Registered profl. engr., Tex. Mem. Nat., Tex. socs. profl. engrs., Alpha Phi Omega, Tau Beta Pi, Sigma Gamma Tau. Home: PO Box 30711 Amarillo TX 79120 Office: PO Box 31100 Amarillo TX 79120

BAKER, WILLIAM HOWARD, univ. dean; b. Speedwell, Tenn., June 17, 1931; s. William and Alma (LeMarr) B.; B.A., Lincoln Meml. U., 1949-53; M.A., Tenn. Technol. U., 1968; Ed.D., U. Tenn., 1972; m. Barbara Ann Brittain, June 8, 1958; children—Kevin, Ann. Program and news dir. Sta. WMIK, Middlesboro, Ky., 1955-62; gen. mgr. Sta. WJAX, Jacksonville, Fla., 1962-66; adminstrv. asst. student services Tenn. Technol. U., Cookeville, 1966-68, asst. to pres., 1968-72, dean univ. services, 1972-75, dean univ. devel., 1975—, asso. prof. ednl. adminstrn., 1972—; cons. in pub. relations and advt., 1970—. Mem. Ky. Gov.'s Adv. Com. on Tourism, 1961, Ky. Com. on Traffic Safety, 1959; pres. Putnam Co. chpt. Am. Cancer Soc., 1977—. Served with U.S. Army, 1953-55. Mem. NEA, Tenn. Edn. Assn., Am. Edn. Fin. Conf., Council for Advancement and Support Edn., Lincoln Meml. U. Alumni Assn. (pres. 1959-60), Kappa Delta Pi, Phi Delta Kappa, Omicron Delta Kappa, Phi Delta Theta, Phi Kappa Phi. Democrat. Methodist. Club: Lions (local, zone, dist. officer 1957-62). Co-author: Workbook in School-Community Relations, 1976; author: A Christmas Notebook, 1977. Home: 1139 Mount Vernon Rd Cookeville TN 38501 Office: Box 5047 Tenn Technol U Cookeville TN 38501

BAKKER, HARRY (JOHN), lawn mower and adult tricycle mfg. co. exec.; b. Groningen, Netherlands, May 5, 1944; s. William John and Anne B.; student Calvin Coll., Grand Rapids, Mich., 1965-67; m. Betty Iosinga, Dec. 9, 1967; children—Mark, Conrad, Ben. Farmer, Londesboro, Ont., Can., 1967-72; pres. Tested Steel Products Ltd., Calgary, Alta., Can., 1972-77; pres. Trail Mate Inc., Bradenton and Sarasota, Fla., 1977—. Pres. Harbor Woods Homeowners Assn., 1978—; chmn. bd. Christian Reformed Ch., Bradenton, 1978—. Home: 5203 5th Ave Dr NW Bradenton FL 33505 Office: Trail Mate Inc 6050 Palmer Blvd Sarasota FL 33582

BALABANIS, THEOFILOS GEORGE, food service co. exec.; b. Mytilene, Greece, Nov. 19, 1933; s. George Theofilos and Elizabeth Michael (Paleologos) B.; came to U.S., 1935; B.S. in Hotel Adminstrn., Pa. State U., 1955; children—Joseph, Chad, Elizabeth Ann, Georgeanna Lee. Mgr., The Hut Restaurant, Martinsville, Va., 1963—; pres. Henry County Restaurants, Inc., Martinsville, 1965—, So. Host Inn, Inc., Martinsville, 1974. Bd. dirs. Martinsville and Henry County chpt. Am. Cancer Soc.; com. chmn. United Fund; adv. bd. Salvation Army; Served to 1st lt., inf., USAR, 1955-57. Mem. Va. Restaurant Assn. (chmn., dir.), C. of C., Pa. State Hotel and Restaurant Soc., Pa. State Alumni Assn., Am. Philatelic Soc., Phi Kappa Psi. Republican. Greek Orthodox. Clubs: Rotary, Masons, Shriners, Elks. Home: PO Box 3565 Martinsville VA 24112 Office: Virginia Ave Collinsville VA 24078

BALASSO, ANTHONY ANDREW, lawyer; b. Newark, Jan. 26, 1938; s. Marshall Joseph and Madeline Bertha (Fiori) B.; student St. Peters' Coll., 1956-58; B.A., U. Fla., 1960; J.D., Stetson U., 1966. Admitted to Fla. bar, 1966; asso. firm Wolfe, Bonner & Hogan, Clearwater, Fla., 1966-69; asso. firm Miller, Tucker, Roth & Prominski, Pompano Beach, Fla., 1969; asso. firm William G. Miller, Jr., Pompano Beach, 1971-73; partner firm, Miller, Zachman & Balasso, Profl. Assn., Pompano Beach, 1974—. Asst. county atty. Pinellas County, Fla., 1970; asst. city atty., Wilton Manors, Fla., 1971—. Co-chmn. Miss Clearwater Pageant Clearwater Jaycees, 1969; judge Miss St. Petersburg (Fla.) Pageant, 1970. Served with AUS, 1960-62. Mem. Fla. Bar, Am., Broward County, North Broward bar assns., Lawyers' Title Guaranty Fund, Am. Judicature Soc., Phi Delta Phi. Republican. Roman Catholic. K.C. (3 deg.). Home: Shore Club 1905 N Atlantic Blvd Apt E-5A Fort Lauderdale FL 33305 Office: PO Box 1239 Pompano Beach FL 33061

BALD, MARGARET, librarian; b. Pitts., Sept. 3, 1913; d. Edmond James and Margaret (Siemon) Bald; A.B., Asbury Coll., 1934; B.S., Carnegie Inst. Tech., 1935. Asst. Carnegie Library, Pitts,, 1935-37; asst. librarian Carnegie Steel Corp., 1937-40; asst. Pasadena Pub. Library, 1940-44; various positions U.S. Navy Dept., 1944-48; librarian Bob Jones U., Greenville, 1948—. Mem, Am., S.C. library assns. Home: Bob Jones Univ Greenville SC 29614

BALDINGER, CHARLENE LOIS, guidance counselor; b. Cin., Sept. 24, 1948; d. Bruce Charles and Shirley Lois (Grosardt) Baldinger; A.B. in Sociology, Eastern Ky. U., 1970, M.A., 1971. Tchr., Campbell County schs., Alexandria, Ky., 1971-73, counselor, 1973—. Youth dir. St. Paul's United Ch. Christ, Alexandria, 1971-77, mem. ch. and minsitry com., 1972-77, mem. bd. Christian edn., 1977—. NSF grantee, 1972. Mem. Am., Ky., Campbell County (chmn. polit. action com. 1976) edn. assns., Am., Ky., No. Ky. (pres. elect 1977-78) personnel and guidance assns. Club: Job's Daus. Home: 830 Alexandria Pike Fort Thomas KY 41075 Office: 8004 Alexandria Pike Alexandria KY 41001

BALDWIN, ALBERT LESLIE, govt. ofcl.; b. Lumberton, N.C., Aug. 4, 1938; s. Leslie Evans and Pauline (Register) B.; B.S. in Sci. Edn., U. N.C., 1960, M.P.H. in Health Adminstrn., 1971; m. Betty Thompson, Mar. 25, 1961; children—Albert Leslie, Sarah Beth. Health rep., public health advisor venereal disease br. Communicable Disease Center, HEW, Fayetteville, N.C., 1961-63, supervisory public health advisor, Fresno and San Francisco, Calif., 1963-65, public health analyst TB br. National Communicable Disease Center, Atlanta, 1965-66, public health advisor, Richmond, Va., 1966-68, statistics and program analysis unit, Atlanta, 1968-72, chief program analysis sub-unit, Atlanta, 1972-73, mgmt. analyst Region IV Mgmt. Analysis and Data Br. Office of Mgmt. Support, 1973-74, Office of Regional Dir. Adminstrn. and Mgmt., 1974-77, exec. dir. Southeastern Fed. Regional Council, 1978—; dir. student intern program Region IV, Sec. of HEW; mem. HEW staffing task forces, Washington, 1976, 77. Ruling elder, chmn. Christian edn. Clairmont Presbyn. Ch. Served with U.S. Army, 1960-61. Mem. Am. Soc. Public Adminstrn., U. N.C. Alumni Assn. Contbr. articles in field to publs. Home: 3163 Boxwood Dr Atlanta GA 30345 Office: Suite 2121 101 Marietta Tower Atlanta GA 30323

BALDWIN, CAROL WILLARD, govt. ofcl.; b. Frederick, Md., Aug. 20, 1948; d. Daniel Sylvester and Ethel (Bussard) Willard; student Bridgewater Coll., 1966-67, Frederick Community Coll., 1967-70; mgmt. cert. U. Md., European Div., 1977; B.A., Methodist Coll., 1980; m. Robert Earl Baldwin, Aug. 24, 1968. With Govt. Employees Ins. Co., Washington, 1968-70, Towson, Md. br., 1970-73, sales and service specialist, 1970-72, sr. sales and service specialist, 1972-73; acctg. technician, then budget analyst U.S. Army, Heidelberg, W. Ger., 1976-77; ednl. counselor Ft. Bragg campus Meth. Coll., Fayetteville, N.C., 1978-79; contract specialist U.S. Air Force, Pope AFB, N.C., 1979—. Mem. Porsche Club Am., Mensa. Republican. Lutheran. Home: 204 Summerhill Ct Fayetteville NC 28303 Office: Contracting Office Pope AFB NC 28308

BALDWIN, CLYDE PARRIS, environ. engr.; b. Frankfort, Ky., Mar. 30, 1941; s. Clyde M. and Marjorie Clellen (Parris) B.; B.S. in Civil Engring., U. Ky., 1965, M.S. in Civil Engring., 1968, Profl. Engr., 1969; m. Jo Anne Booth, July 10, 1961; children—Clyde Ray, Allen Douglas. Student and research technician Ky. Dept. Hwys., 1959-65; civil engr. for maintenance Ky. Dept. Transp., 1965-66; san. engr. for municipalities Ky. Water Pollution Control Commn., Frankfort, 1966-68, prin. environ. engr. indsl. waste, 1968-73, prin. environ. engr. permits program, 1973-75, chief environ. engr. permits and enforcement program, 1975—; lectr. continuing edn. Coll. Engring. U. Ky.; chmn. Ohio River Water Sanitation Commn., Nat. Pollutant Discharge Elimination System Com. Served with AF ROTC, 1959-62. Recipient Merkel award Arnold Air Soc., 1961; Ky. Col.; Ky. Adm. Mem. Ky. Soc. Profl. Engrs. (pres. 1976, state dir.), Am. Pub. Works Assn. (bd. dirs. Ky. chpt. 1977), Frankfort Jaycees, Delta Tau Delta, U. Ky. Alumni Assn. Democrat. Mem. Disciples of Christ. Home: 303 Ute Trail Frankfort KY 40601 Office: U S 127 S Century Plaza Frankfort KY 40601

BALDWIN, ESTHER LILLIAN, pianist, composer; b. Chgo.; d. George and Minnie (Neidigh) Baldwin; pvt. study Dr. Francis Hemington, Chgo.; Mus. B., Columbia Sch. Music and Art, in 1946; Mus. D.; widow. Tchr., dir. Baldwin Music Studios, Columbia, S.C., 1927—; concert pianist, 1946—; composer Sonata in C Major; Sonata in D Major. Mem. faculty, adjudicator Nat. Guild Piano Tchrs. Bd. govs. Exec. and Profl. Hall of Fame. Named to Hall of Fame Piano Guild U.S.A. Fellow Internat. Inst. Arts and Letters; mem. Internat. Pianist's Guild, Nat. Guild Piano Tchrs. (chmn. Columbia chpt.), Am. Coll. Musicians, Internat. Platform Assn., Musicians Club Am. Home: Apt 118 Davis Hotel 1712 Sumter St Columbia SC 29201 Studio: 1712 Sumter St Columbia SC 29201

BALDWIN, JACK LYELL, entomologist; b. Haskell, Tex., Feb. 14, 1949; s. Frank Lyell and Hilda Margaret (Kretschmer) B.; B.S., Tex. A & M U., 1971, M.S., 1972; m. Anne Frierson, Aug. 7, 1971; children—Belinda Marie, Priscilla Michelle, Kimberly Leigh. Field devel. biologist Agrl. Chem. div. ICI U.S., Inc., Goldsboro, N.C., 1974-77; research asst. Okla. State U., Stillwater, 1977—. Served with U.S. Army, 1972-74. Mem. Entomol. Soc. Am., Southwestern Entomol. Soc., Am. Registry Profl. Entomologists. Contbr. articles to profl. jours. Home: 1417 N Arrington St Stillwater OK 74074 Office: Dept Entomology Oklahoma State U Stillwater OK 74074

BALDWIN, PHILLIP LESLIE, banker; b. Rome, Ga., Apr. 6, 1953; s. Walter Lewis and Martha Jo (Carver) B.; B.S., W. Ga. Coll., 1971-73; m. Brenda Turner Thrasher, Oct. 18, 1975. With Trust Co. Bank, Atlanta, 1973-75; asst. v.p., ops. mgr., asst. br. mgr. First Ga. Bank, Atlanta, 1976—. Recipient Easter Seals award, 1979; United Way award, 1979; Ga. Youth Leadership Council award, 1978. Mem. Am. Inst. Bankers, Atlanta Jr. C. of C. (dir. 1976—, v.p. 1978—, named Jaycee of Month, Dir. of Yr. 1977-78). Methodist. Clubs: Horse Shoe Bend Civic, Horse Shoe Bend Athletic. Home: 2765 Cold Spring Trail Marietta GA 30064 Office: PO Box 1700 Atlanta GA 30301

BALENTINE, JOHN LEROY, III, govt. ofcl.; b. Hollywood, Calif., Apr. 14, 1948; s. John L. and Roberta E. (Wyatt) B., Jr.; B.A., San Fernando Valley State Coll., 1969; M.A., U. So. Calif., 1972; Ph.D., Jackson State U., 1976; m. Eva April Grimm, Sept. 20, 1975. Community services specialist Los Angeles Bd. Edn., 1967-69; spl. asst. community relations program Office of Mayor, City of Los Angeles, 1969-75; safety coordinator Los Angeles Dept. Recreation and Parks, 1975-76; pres. Total Travel Internat., Inc., Nashville, 1976-78; program evaluator Office of Comptroller of Treasury, State of Tenn., Nashville, 1978—. Bd. dirs. Recreation and Youth Services Planning Council, Los Angeles, 1970-76. Exec. bd. Greater Los Angeles Youth Adv. Council, 1968-73; bd. dirs. Calif. Council on Children and Youth, 1969-73. Jehovah's Witness. Clubs: Aircraft Owners and Pilots Assn., U.S. Ski Assn., Young Nashvillians, Nat. Travel. Recipient certificate of apprecation for community service, Mayor Sam Yorty, 1972, Human Relations Commn., Los Angeles, 1971, Youth Advisory Council, Los Angeles, 1975. Office: Andrew Jackson State Office Bldg Suite 1530 Nashville TN 37219

BALENTINE, ROBERT CHAPMAN, mathematician; b. Poteau, Okla., Dec. 29, 1934; s. Fred Roosevelt and Eula Ruth (Chapman) B.; B.S., Baylor U., 1957; postgrad. Tex. A. and M. U., 1957-58, 60; Patsy Lee Byrum, June 30, 1962 (div. Aug. 1971); children—David Michael, Timothy Charles. Mathematician, Army Ballistic Missile Agy., Redstone Arsenal, 1958-61, NASA Johnson Space Center, Hampton, Va., 1961-62, NASA, Huntsville, Ala., 1962—, space telescope software mgr., 1979—. Baptist. Home: 336 Jack Coleman Dr NW Huntsville AL 35805 Office: EE61 Marshall Space Flight Center Huntsville AL 35812

BALES, MARY AVARY, nurse; b. Atlanta, July 22, 1940; d. Eugene Carlston, Sr., and Florence Elizabeth (Cox) Bales; R.N., Ga. Bapt. Hosp., 1961. Staff nurse to asst. dept. mgr. emergency room Ga. Bapt. Hosp., Atlanta, 1961-66, 67-71; office and scrub nurse Dr. Warren F. Brown, Atlanta, 1967; house supr. 7-3 shift Clayton Gen. Hosp., Riverdale, Ga., 1971-76; house supr. West Paces Ferry Hosp., Atlanta, 1976, clinician emergency room and med. floor, 1978—; capt., tng. officer emergency med. services div. Clayton County Fire Dept., Jonesboro, Ga., 1976-78; CPR affiliate faculty Ga. Heart Assn. Cert. emergency med. technician instr., Ga. Co-founder 2d state approved basic emergency med. technician tng. course Clayton County, Ga., 1973. Home: 2577 Stratford Ln Morrow GA 30260 Office: 3200 Howell Mill Rd NW Atlanta GA 30327

BALESTRERO, GREGORY, indsl. tng. cons. co. exec.; b. N.Y.C., July 16, 1947; s. Christopher Emmanuel and Rose (Giolito) B.; B.S.I.E., Ga. Inst. Tech., 1970; m. Frances Marie Higgins, Feb. 25, 1978. Asst. gen. mgr. Nat. Tng. Aids, Atlanta, 1974-76; dir. tng. Nat. Tng. Services, Atlanta, 1976-79; v.p., dir. tng. and devel. Nat. Tng. Aids and Services, Atlanta, 1979—, bd. dirs., 1976—; cons. in field. Served with Missiles, F.A., U.S. Army, 1971-74. Mem. Nat. LP-Gas Assn., Am. Gas Assn., Nat. Fire Protection Assn. Democrat. Roman Catholic. Home: 865 Old Tucker Rd Stone Mountain GA 30087 Office: Nat Tng Aids & Services 1756 Wilwat Dr Suite A Norcross GA 30093

BALINT, DENNIS ANDREW, mktg. exec.; b. Bayonne, N.J., Oct. 17, 1945; s. Andrew Joseph and Martha (Babey) B.; B.S. in Indsl. Mgmt., St. Peters Coll., 1970; m. Oct. 7, 1978. With Am. Home Products Corp., Boyle-Midway Div., N.Y.C., 1966-74; sr. brand mgr., asst. to v.p. sales William Underwood Co., Westwood, Mass., 1974-77; v.p. mktg. Mauna Loa Macadamia Nut Corp., Atlanta, 1977—. Mem. C. of C., Ga. Bus. and Industry Assn., Made in Hawaii Assn. Home: 6937D Roswell Rd Atlanta GA 30328 Office: 875 Johnson Ferry Rd Atlanta GA 30342

BALL, ALLEN, health care exec.; b. Tuscaloosa, Ala., June 28, 1941; s. Ed and Lucinda (Scott) B.; B.A., Calif. State U., Dominquez Hills, 1971, M.A., 1974; A.A., E. Los Angeles Jr. Coll., 1961; m. Jacqueline Foster, Oct. 17, 1961; children—Malaika, Mboya, Zoleka, Chen Hraumah. Cons. Charles R. Drew Postgrad. Med. Sch., Los Angeles, 1970-75, editor, public relations, 1971-73; laison, tchr. Compton Unified Sch. Dist. and Tchr. Corps, Compton, Calif., 1973-75; resource devel. specialist TVA, Chattanooga, 1975-76; project dir. Red Bay (Ala.) Hosp., 1976-77; exec. dir. So. Rural Health Care Consortium, Red Bay, 1977—. Served with U.S. Army, 1958-61. Mem. Am. Rural Health Assn. (mem. corporate bd.), Internat. Human Health Found., Am. Public Health Assn., Nat. Assn. Community Health Centers, Nat. Rural Primary Care Assn. (corporate bd.), Am. Mgmt. Assn. Editor, founder Black Guard, 1969-70; editor Community Health News, 1971-73. Home and Office: PO Drawer N Red Bay AL 35582

BALL, BERNARD CAUDILL, art instr.; b. Upland, W.Va., Oct. 25, 1908; s. Calvin Casby and Mattie Minerva (Beard) B.; A.B., Marshall U., 1938; M.A., Ohio State U., 1941; m. Alverta Ellen McCoy, Aug. 22, 1936; children—Barbara Ann, David Michael. Teacher art, head dept. Parkersburg (W.Va.) High Sch., 1938-43; supr. indsl. design dept. Curtiss Wright and N.Am. Aircraft corps., Columbus, Ohio, 1943-53; advt. mgr. Champion Co., Springfield, Ohio, 1953-59; advt. mgr. White Superior div. White Motor Corp., Springfield, 1959-69; art instr. Port Charlotte (Fla.) Cultural Center, 1972—. Pres., Charlotte County Art Guild, Inc., 1976-78. Mem. Nat. Soc. Lit. and the Arts, Internat. Soc. Artists, Art Council S.W. Fla., Friends of the Arts, Sun Coast Watercolor Soc. Author, photographer articles on diesel engine installations. Home: 152 Salem Ave Port Charlotte FL 33952

BALL, HALLIE SUTTLE, nurse, hosp. ofcl.; b. Williamsburg, W.Va., July 14, 1923; d. Tyler Finley and Ethel B. (Judy) Suttle; R.N., St. Francis Sch. Nursing, Charleston, W.Va., 1943; B.A., W.Va. State Coll., Institute, 1978; m. Dale Edward Ball, Sept. 4, 1947. Staff nurse St. Francis Hosp., Charleston, 1944-45; relief nurse A., Viscose Co., Nitro, W.Va., 1947-48; pvt. duty nurse Charleston Hosp., 1949-54; supr. Kanawha Valley Meml. Hosp., Charleston, 1954-71, dir. nursing, 1972—. Adv. com. nursing program U. Charleston. Mem. Nat. Soc. Hosp. Nursing Service Adminstrs., W.Va. Soc. Hosp. Nursing Service Adminstrs., Phi Alpha Theta (pres. chpt. 1975—), Alpha Kappa Mu. Democrat. Mem. Ch. of God. Clubs: Order of Eastern Star, Quota (charter, pres. chpt. 1955, gov. 1st Dist. 1961). Home: 303 Highland Ave South Charleston WV 25303 Office: Kanawha Valley Meml Hosp 1014 Virginia St E Charleston WV 25301

BALL, IVAN ESTUS, utility co. exec.; b. Ages, Ky., July 5, 1923; s. Alex and Maude (Crider) B.; student Eastern Ky. State Tchrs. Coll., 1939-41; B.S. in Accounting, Bowling Green Coll. Commerce, 1948; m. Madaline Cornett, Oct. 18, 1946 (div. 1952); 1 dau., Lynn Estes (Mrs. George John Hume); m. 2d, Mona Elizabeth Gilbert, Sept. 25, 1954; 1 stepdau., Penelope Elizabeth (Mrs. Burton G. Goldstein). With Peoples Water & Gas Co., Miami Beach, Fla., 1948-58, financial v.p., 1957-58; with Tampa Gas Co. (Fla.), 1955-57, fin. v.p., 1957; controller So. Gulf Utilities, 1959-60; controller City Gas Co. Fla., Hialeah, 1961, fin. v.p., asst. sec., asst. treas., 1966—, also dir.; v.p. finance, asst. sec., asst. treas., dir. Essel Corp., 1973—; mgmt. cons. Stone & Webster Service Corp., 1962-65. Served with USAAF, 1941-45. Decorated Bronze Star medal. Mem. Gas Inst. Greater Miami, Am. Gas Assn., C. of C., 14th Air Force Assn., Flying Tigers, Miami Shores Men's Golf Assn., Beta Pi. Democrat. Clubs: Miami Shores Country, Basset Hound (Am.), South Fla. Basset Hound, Greater Miami Dog. Home: 800 NE 97th St Miami Shores FL 33138 Office: 955 E 25th St Hialeah FL 33013

BALL, JAMES ANDREW, pediatrician; b. Dallas, June 10, 1925; s. Clifford Crozier and Eunice (Fraley) B.; B.S., So. Methodist U., 1948; M.D., U. Tex., Galveston, 1948; m. Judith Lee Nave, Oct. 18, 1973; children—Suzanne, James A., Patrice Ball Jackson. Intern, Santa Rosa Hosp., San Antonio, 1948-49; resident in pediatrics Children's Med. Center, Dallas, 1953-54; practice medicine specializing in pediatrics, Dallas, 1955—; mem. staff Convulsive Clinic, Southwestern Med. Sch., 1955-74, also clin. asst. prof. pediatrics; medico, Honduras, 1967. Served with M.C., U.S. Army, 1948-51. Decorated Combat Med. badge, Legion of Merit, Bronze Star medal. Mem. AMA, Am. Acad. Pediatrics, Tex. Pediatric Soc., Tex. Med. Assn., Dallas Clin. Assn., Dallas County Med. Soc. Republican. Presbyterian. Office: 202 C Lake Highlands Village Dallas TX 75218

BALL, LEWIS EDWIN, II, diesel and turbine generator sets co. exec.; b. Huntsville, Tex., July 1, 1931; s. William Perry and Mary Ethel (Osborne) B.; B.B.A., U. Tex., Austin, 1952; m. Marion Buchanan, June 5, 1954. Mgr., Ernst & Whinney, C.P.A.'s, Houston, 1952-71; v.p., treas. Stewart & Stevenson Services, Inc., Houston, 1971—, also dir.; v.p., treas. C. Jim Stewart & Stevenson, Inc., Houston, 1971—, Machinery Acceptance Corp., Houston, 1971—. Bd. dirs. Soc. for Performing Arts, Houston; treas., trustee Houston Mus. Natural Sci.; mem. allocation com. Cultural Arts Council of Houston; bd. dirs. Retina Research Found.; mem. trustees com. Am. Assn. Museums. C.P.A., Tex. Mem. Am. Inst. C.P.A.'s, Tex. Soc. C.P.A.'s (dir.), Nat. Assn. Accountants, Fin. Execs. Inst., Houston C. of C. Methodist (vice chmn. adminstrn. bd.). Clubs: Houston Country, Ramada, Garden of the Gods, Riverhill. Home: 6122 Valley Forge Houston TX 77057 Office: Box 1637 Houston TX 77001

BALL, SUZIE MORRIS, communications sales exec.; b. Memphis, Dec. 3, 1946; d. William Benjamin and Loretta Mae (Duncan) Morris; student U. Tenn., 1965-66; m. Timothy Allen Ball, Jan. 29, 1966; children—Helen Loretta, Timothy Allen. With Motorola Communications & Electronics, Inc., Decatur, Ga., 1975—, zone sales mgr., 1977—. Del., Ga. Rep. Conv., 1972; exec. sec. Floyd

County Rep. Party, 1972. Mem. Soc. Broadcast Engrs. Republican. Episcopalian. Home: 1082 Village Rd Stone Mountain GA 30088 Office: PO Box 1920 Decatur GA 30031

BALL, THOMAS PRIOLEAU, JR., physician; b. Charleston, S.C., Jan. 30, 1932; s. Thomas Prioleau and Teresa (Daniel) B.; B.S., The Citadel, 1954; M.D., Emory U., 1958; m. Patricia Mengedoht, Feb. 13, 1954; children—Teresa V., Patricia M., Elizabeth E., Thomas Prioleau III. Intern, Grady Meml. Hosp., Atlanta, 1960-61, resident in urology, 1962-66; commd. 2d lt. USAF, 1957, advanced through grades to col., 1973; chief aerospace medicine Dover AFB, Del., 1959-62; chief urology David Grant USAF Hosp., 1966-68, Wiebaden (Germany) USAF Hosp., 1968-73; chief urology, dir. urol. tng. Wilford Hall USAF Med. Center, Lackland AFB, Tex., 1973-79, dir. Air Force med. manpower, 1979—; asso. prof. U. Tex., San Antonio, 1973—. Diplomate Am. Bd. Urology, Nat. Bd. Med. Examiners. Fellow A.C.S.; mem. AMA, Internat. Soc. Urology, Am. Urol. Assn., Soc. Air Force Clin. Surgeons, Soc. Govt. Service Urologists (pres.). Republican. Episcopalian. Editor Weekly Urology Update. Home: 3103 Knight Robin St San Antonio TX 78209 Office: Wilford Hall USAF Med Center Lackland AFB TX 78236

BALL, WILBERT R., educator; b. Va., Oct. 5, 1934; s. George H. and Lily Mae B.; A.B., Fairmont State Coll., 1958; M.Ed., Miami U., Oxford, Ohio, 1962; Ed.D. (fellow), Ind. U., 1971; m. Doris M. Wilson, May 25, 1954; children—Micah D., Susan L., Donna R. Chmn., tchr. indsl. arts Public Schs., Carlisle, Ohio; tchr., Public Schs., Phoenix; asst. prof. indsl. arts edn. E. Carolina U., Greenville, N.C., now prof. counseling and guidance; human relations cons. Served with AUS, 1953-55. Mem. White House Conf. on Children and Youth, 1970. Mem. Am. Personnel and Guidance Assn., Assn. Counselor Educators and Suprs., N.C. Personnel and Guidance Assn. Democrat. Home: 1615 Longwood Dr Greenville NC 27834 Office: Counseling Center East Carolina U Greenville NC 27834

BALLANTINE, THOMAS AUSTIN, JR., fed. judge; b. Louisville, Sept. 22, 1926; s. Thomas Austin and Anna Marie (Pfeiffer) B.; student Northwestern U., 1944-46; B.A., U. Ky., 1948; LL.B., U. Louisville, 1954; m. Nancy A. Armstrong, June 10, 1953; children—Thomas Austin, III, Nancy Adair, Brigid A., Joseph A. Admitted to Ky. bar, 1954; asso. firm McElwain, Dinning, Clarke & Winstead, Louisville, 1954-64; dep. commr. Jefferson County (Ky.) Circuit Ct., 1958-62, circuit judge, 1964-77; commr. Jefferson County Fiscal Ct., 1962-64; judge U.S. Dist. Ct., Western Dist. Ky., 1977—; instr. U. Louisville Law Sch., 1969-75. Bd. dirs. Louisville Urban League, 1958-64, chmn., 1963-64; bd. dirs. NCCJ, Louisville, 1960-65, Health and Welfare Council, Louisville, 1969, Louisville Thetrical Assn., 1970. Mem. Louisville Bar Assn., Ky. State Bar. Democrat. Roman Catholic. Club: Pendennis. Office: 247 US PO and Courthouse Louisville KY 40202

BALLANTINE, WILLIAM THOMAS, JR., offshore oil co. exec.; b. Balt., Mar. 4, 1945; s. William Thomas and Margaret A. (Hancock) B.; B.S., U.S. Naval Acad., 1967; M.S., Ga. Inst. Tech., 1968; m. Carol Ann Roberts, June 15, 1968; 1 dau., Tara Susan. Commd. ensign U.S. Navy, 1967, advanced through grades to lt., 1973; chief engr. USS Bigelow, 1970-72; material officer Desron 8 staff, 1972-73; ret., 1973; project engr. Exxon Co., Houston, 1973-74; mgr. marine constrn. Zapata Tech. Services Corp., Houston, 1974-75; mgr. maintenance and repair Zapata Marine Service, Inc., 1975-76, v.p. engring. and maintenance, 1976-79, sr. v.p. engring. and maintenance, 1979, sr. v.p. ops., engring. and maintenance, 1979—. Active Dads Club, 1974-78, Athletic Club, 1976-78. Mem. ASME, Am. Mgmt. Assn., Houston Engring. and Sci. Soc., Soc. Naval Architects and Marine Engrs. Republican. Methodist. Home: 4223 Little Berry St Houston TX 77088 Office: PO Box 4240 Houston TX 77001

BALLARD, GEORGE SPEIGHTS, JR., fin. exec.; b. Monticello, Ga., July 27, 1919; s. George Speights and Willie Maude (Benton) B.; grad. McCallie Sch., Chattanooga, 1936; A.B., Emory U., Atlanta, 1940; M.B.A., Harvard, 1942; m. Marguerite Louisa Candler, Feb. 3, 1973. With Coca-Cola Co., Atlanta, 1947-52; mgr. corporate fin. Underwood, Neuhaus & Co., Houston, 1953-64; spl. asst. SBA, Washington, 1965-66; asso. dir. devel. Emory U., Atlanta, 1966-68; v.p. fin. West Lumber Co. and subsidiary Asso. Distbrs., Inc., also treas. West Leasing Corp. and West Fin. Corp., Atlanta, 1968-75; self-employed as pvt. investor, 1975—. Served with USN, 1942-46, capt. Res. ret. Mem. Phi Beta Kappa, Omicron Delta Kappa. Episcopalian. Author: Long-Term Financing for Retailers, 1962. Home: 3092 Argonne Dr NW Atlanta GA 30305

BALLARD, GLENN ARLEN, ednl. adminstr.; b. Pitts., Dec. 28, 1931; s. Jack S. and Florence Irene (Dunn) B.; B.S., U. Pitts., 1955; M.A. (NSF grantee), U. Denver, 1965; m. Ann Claire Henry, Feb. 11, 1955; children—Glenn Arlen, Carol Tracey, Paula Jane, Catherine Alane. Tchr. math. Kiski Sch., Saltsburg, Pa., 1955-65; head Upper Sch., Graland Country Day Sch., Denver, 1965-67; headmaster Brownell-Talbot Sch., Omaha, 1967-71, Hockaday Sch., Dallas, 1971-79, Kinkaid Sch., Houston, 1979—. Trustee Winston Sch., Dallas, 1974—, Dallas Arts Found., 1972-75; mem. adv. bd. Dallas Women for Change Fedn., 1975-78. Mem. Ind. Schs. Assn. (pres. S.W. 1978-80), Country Day Sch. Headmasters Assn., Delta Tau Delta. Clubs: University, Houston. Home: 202 Kinkaid School Dr Houston TX 77024 Office: 201 Kinkaid School Dr Houston TX 77024

BALLARD, HARRY HAROLD, security co. exec.; b. Madison, W.Va., May 9, 1944; s. Harry Carter and Florence Effie (Walker) B.; m. Joyce Lynn Watson, Apr. 20, 1974; children—Bethany Lynne, Shannon Leigh. Mgr., Lums, Inc., Woodbridge, Va., 1970-72; area mgr. The Wackenhut Corp., South Charleston, W.Va., 1973-78; owner, partner, v.p. sales Asterisk Security, Inc., 1978—. Served with U.S. Army, 1962-70. Mem. Am. Soc. Indsl. Security (v.p., programs chmn., chmn.), VFW. Club: Lion (mem. internat. police congress). Office: 88 Kanawka Terr Saint Albans WV 25177

BALLARD, JAMES ALAN, geophysicist; b. Rockingham, N.C., Aug. 13, 1929; s. William Douglas and Deborah Anne (Jones) B.; B.S., U. N.C., 1953, M.S., 1959, Ph.D., 1979; m. Betsy Lee Bowie, Dec. 27, 1953; children—William Mark, Robert Clay, Joel Bowie, Mary Eleanor. Geophysicist, Ind. Exploration Co., Houston, 1953-54; oceanographer U.S.N. Hydrographic Office, Suitland, Md., 1959-62, supervisory oceanographer, Oceanographic Office, Washington, 1962-75; research oceanographer, Naval Ocean Research and Devel. Activity, Nat. Space Tech. Labs., Miss., 1976-78, geophysics programs mgr., 1978—; tech. adv. Md. Geol. Survey, 1974-75. Trustee, Prince Georges County (Md.) Public Schs., 1965-69. Served with AUS, 1954-56. Mem. Soc. Exploration Geophysicists, Southeastern Geophys. Soc., Am. Geophys. Union, Potomac Geophys. Union, Sigma Xi. Presbyterian. Clubs: Toastmasters, Picayune Band Boosters. Contbr. articles to profl. jours. Home: 1520 4th Ave Picayune MS 39466 Office: Naval Ocean Research and Devel Activity Nat Space Tech Labs Station MS 39529

BALLARD, JOHN WAYNE, gas co. exec.; b. Hosston, La., Aug. 26, 1914; s. John William and Nora (Wynn) B.; student Centenary Coll., Shreveport, La., 1941-45; m. Annie Lee Bickham, July 3, 1937; children—John R., Milton R. Admitted to La. bar, 1952, Lab. technician, Shoreline Oil Co. (La.), 1934-37, Talco Asphalt & Refinery, 1937-41, Stanolind Oil & Gas Co., Vivian, La., 1941-42; chief chemist Princeton Refining Co., Shreveport, La., 1942-45; asst. chief engr., asst. chief chemist Bayou State Oil Co., 1946-55, asst. supt., 1948-55; v.p., plant supr. Caddo Pine Island Corp., Shreveport, 1955-68, pres., gen. mgr., 1968—; dir. Caddo Trust & Savs. Bank, Belcher, La. pvt. practice law, Oil City, La., 1952—. Democrat. Baptist. Clubs: Rotary, Masons. Office: Rt 1 Box 60 Oil City LA 71061

BALLEISEN, CAROLYN KIMMELFIELD, lawyer; b. Bklyn., June 12, 1930; d. Isadore M. and Belle (Stern) Kimmelfield; A.B. cum laude, Barnard Coll., 1950; J.D. (Harlan Fiske Stone scholar), Columbia U., 1952; m. Donald H. Balleisen, Apr. 8, 1960; children—Ellen Margaret, Wendy Sue, Edward James. Admitted to N.Y. State bar, 1953, Ky. bar, 1971; research asst. income tax project Am. Law Inst., 1952-53; asso. mem. firm Lord Day & Lord, N.Y.C., 1953-59; revision editor Rabkin & Johnson Fed. Income Gift & Estate Taxation Reporter, N.Y.C., 1959-60, 67-68; vis. asso. prof. law U. Louisville, 1969-70; tax cons., Louisville, 1970—; dir. Ky. Housing Corp., 1973-78. Vice pres. Ky. Dance Council, 1972-79; v.p. Nat. Council Jewish Women, Louisville, 1973-77, chmn. state pub. affairs, 1977—; mem. citizens adv. group Jefferson County Office Housing and Community Devel., 1973—, vice chmn., 1979—; chmn. adv. com. Community for Ednl. Excellence, 1976-77; chmn. steering com. Louisville Area Coalition for Human Needs and Budget Priorities, 1977-78; pres. Louisville Ballet Co., 1978-79; bd. dirs. Metro United Way, 1977—; mem. community adv. bd. Kentuckiana Public TV Corp.; mem. task force on legislation and funding Jefferson County Bd. Edn., 1978—. Recipient Hannah Solomon award Louisville sect. Nat. Council Jewish Women, 1980. Mem. Am., Ky., Louisville bar assns. Democrat. Jewish. Club: Women's City. Editor Columbia Law Rev., 1951-52; author: West's Federal Practice Manual, 1980. Home: 3102 Runnymede Rd Louisville KY 40222

BALLEW, ALVIN ONESIMUS, food mgmt. co. exec.; b. Greenville, S.C., May 11, 1926; s. Issac A. and Cora P. (Brookshire) B.; m. Betty Cooke, Sept. 25, 1946; children—Charlene, Nancy, Janet, Alan O. With Walgreen Drug Co., 1942-44; served as enlisted man U.S. Navy, 1944-46; with So. Ry., 1946; served as enlisted man U.S. Air Force, 1946-66; self-employed, 1966-67; with Handy Andy Inc., San Antonio, 1967-77; with Greyhound Food Mgmt. Co./Prophet Foods Co., San Antonio, 1977—, dist. mgr., 1977—, dir. sales, 1968—, regional ops. dir., 1972—. Sec. PTA, 1957-59; bd. dirs. Rainbow Girls, 1963-66. Decorated Air Force Commendation medal with 2 oak leaf clusters. Mem. Nat. Restaurant Assn., Am. Mgmt. Assn., Ret. Enlisted Ret. Assn. Republican. Lutheran. Clubs: Masons, Shriners. Home: 3818 Starhill St San Antonio TX 78218

BALLEW, HAROLD CARL, lab. technologist; b. Seneca, S.C., Dec. 7, 1935; s. James Irvin and Emma (Timms) B.; B.S. in Biology, Furman U., 1957; M.S. in Zoology, Bacteriology, Clemson (S.C.) U., 1958; m. Jean Hedgepath, Dec. 8, 1962; children—Harold Carl, Kimberly Jean. Lab. technologist, tchr. diagnostic virology Center for Disease Control, Atlanta, 1963—; real estate agt. Barrett Realty Co., Decatur, Ga., 1971-75. Served with AUS, 1960-62. Mem. Am. Soc. Microbiology, Am. Chem. Soc., Alpha Epsilon Delta. Baptist. Author: The Zooplankton Population of Controlled Aquaria, 1958. Home: 2281 Deer Ridge Dr Stone Mountain GA 30083 Office: 1600 Clifton Rd NE Atlanta GA 30333

BALLIETT, JOHN WILLIAM, business cons.; b. Rochester, N.Y., Sept. 10, 1947; s. Charles G. and Burnetta E. Balliett; B.S. in Physics, Grove City (Pa.) Coll., 1969; postgrad. U. Rochester; m. Betsy Jane VanPatten, Jan. 25, 1969. Engr., Eastman Kodak Co., Rochester, 1969-70; with Tropel Inc., 1970-74, mktg. mgr., 1973-74; co-founder, exec. v.p., dir. Quality Measurement Systems Inc., Penfield, N.Y., 1974-77; pres. QMS Internat. Inc., Penfield, 1976-77; v.p. parent co. EG&G, 1977-78; pres. Balliett Assos., Inc., Sarasota, Fla., 1978—; bus. cons., Sarasota, 1978—. Patentee optical and measurement systems. Home: Shore Lane Boca Grande FL 33921 Office: Sarasota Bank Bldg Suite 703 Sarasota FL 33577

BALLINGER, JOHN KENNETH, lawyer; b. Muncie, Ind., Sept. 8, 1900; s. Lane L. and Viola (Stoner) B.; B.A., Ohio Wesleyan U., 1923; postgrad. U. Miami (Fla.), 1936; m. Lucille Carroll, Sept. 8, 1926; children—Carol Jo (Mrs. Robert S. Gregg), Margaret Ann (Mrs. Michael McCain). Reporter, Miami (Fla.) Herald, 1924, city editor, 1925, polit. editor, 1926-36; admitted to Fla. bar, 1937; pvt. practice law, Miami, 1937-40; asst. atty. gen. Fla., Tallahassee, 1940-41, 1965-70; pvt. practice law, Tallahassee, 1946-62; pres. Tallahassee Cablevision Corp., 1962-64, also owner WBGM-FM radio sta., Tallahassee; counsel Fla. Assn. Realtors, Tallahassee, 1970-77. Instr. law of press Fla. State U., Tallahassee, 1951. Mem. Fla. Ednl. TV Commn., 1957-61. Pres., Leon County (Fla.) Community Council, 1951; state rep. Leon County, 1952-56. Served to col. with 21st Field Arty., U.S. Army, 1918-19, USAAF, 1942-46. Mem. Am., Fla., Tallahassee bar assns., Tallahassee C. of C. (pres. 1949), Phi Delta Theta. Democrat. Methodist. Kiwanian. Club: Capital City Country (Tallahassee). Author: Miami Millions, 1932; Florida Real Estate Handbook, 1979; asst. editor Fla. Statutes, 1941. Home: 819 E Park Ave Tallahassee FL 32302 Office: 222 S Monroe St Tallahassee FL 32302

BALLOU, LEONARD ROSS, musician, historian; b. Staten Island, N.Y., May 19, 1926; s. John Jackson and Edna Nelson (De Hart) B.; B.A., Fisk U., Nashville, 1949; M.A., Va. State U., 1964; divorced; children—Joyce Lerita, Leonard Ross, Howard Nelson De Hart, Vicki Janice. Instr. music Fla. A&M U., 1947-49; chmn. music dept. St. Augustine's Coll., Raleigh, N.C., 1949-51; tchr. music Ala. State U., 1952-60; asst. prof. Va. State U., 1960-61; tchr. Overbrook High Sch., Phila., 1961-62; mem. faculty Elizabeth City (N.C.) State U., 1962—, asst. prof. music, 1963—, dir. instl. research, archivist. Mem. Pasquotank County (N.C.) Tricentennial Commn., 1963. Mem. N.C. Assn. Instl. Research (charter, past com. chmn.), Am. Guild Organists, Soc. Ethnomusicology, Am. Musicol. Soc., Soc. Coll. and Univ. Planning, Soc. Am. Archivists, Albemarle Pan-Hellenic Council (chpt. pres. 1968-70), Assn. Instl. Research, Alpha Phi Alpha (past chpt. pres., N.C. state dir., regional exec. sec., com. chmn.; various awards and citations). Democrat. Episcopalian. Address: Box 19 Elizabeth City State Univ Elizabeth City NC 27909

BALNICKY, ROBERT GABRIEL, clergyman; b. Elizabeth, N.J., Apr. 18, 1922; s. Harry and Irene (Sawicky) B.; student Pensacola Jr. Coll., 1949, Emory U., 1950, Columbia Theol. Sem., Decatur, Ga., 1952; B.Min., M.Min., Internat. Bible Inst. and Sem., Orlando, Fla., 1979; m. Annette Virginia Hawkins, Dec. 24, 1977; children by previous marriage—Richard Ozzie, Barbara Gail. With Merck & Co., Rahway, N.J., 1939-42; pastor Troy (N.C.) Presbyn. Ch., 1952-55, 1st Presbyn. Ch., Ocean Drive Beach, S.C., 1955-56, McCutchen Meml. Ch., Union, S.C., 1956-60, Fairfield Presbyn. Ch., Pensacola, Fla., 1960-64; founder, pastor Trinity Bible Ch., Pensacola, 1964-70; pastor Inskip Presbyn. Ch., Knoxville, Tenn., 1970-72; founding pastor Grace Presbyn. Ch., Knoxville, 1973-74; pastor Handsboro Presbyn. Ch., Gulfport, Miss., 1979—; chaplain Pay Cash Wholesale Grocery, 1972-74; counseling center dir. Christian Broadcasting Network, Inc., Knoxville, 1975-76; pres. Robert G. Balnicky Evang. Assn., Inc.; pres. Union County (S.C.) Ministers Assn., 1957; chmn. Enoree Presbytery Com. Evangelism, 1956-60; mem. com. evangelism S.C. Synod, 1956-60; chmn. bd. dirs. Pensacola Youth for Christ; bd. dirs. Fla. Alcohol-Narcotics, Inc., Fla. United Christian Action, Inc.; mem. adv. bd. Community Action Program, Am. Security Council. Lt. col., chaplain Fla. CAP, 1965-70; dep. wing chaplain Tenn. CAP, 1970-74, dep. chaplain S.E. Region CAP, 1974—. Served as aviation machinist's mate, flight engr. 1st class USN, 1942-49. Recipient Four Chaplains citation Chapel Four Chaplains, Phila., 1960; Meritorious Service award, 1973, Grover Loening Aerospace award, 1974 (both CAP). Mem. Am. Legion (state chaplain S.C. 1956-58, post comdr. 1953-54; grad. Am. Legion Coll., Indpls. 1954; mem. nat. press assn.; chmn. S.C. religious emphasis com. 1956-58, mem. nat. comdr.'s flying squadron; mem. Century Club 1954-55), 40 and 8 (grand aumonier S.C.; state chaplain 1957-59, aumonier nat., nat. chaplain 1959-60; local chaplain 1961-70), Navy League, World Ministry Fellowship (pres. 1966-68), Nat. Assn. Evangs., Internat. Order St. Luke the Physician. Club: Masons (32 deg.). Office: PO Box 6652 Gulfport MS 39501

BALOGA, JUDY MARIE, real estate exec.; b. Cleve.; d. Jack and Mary A. (Nigro) Oldenburg; student Richland Coll., 1971—; children—Jeff, Annette. Exec. sec. Erie Lackawanna R.R., Cleve., 1956-68; realtor asso. Sam Fullilove Realtors, Shreveport, La., 1969-71, Regal Realtors, Dallas, 1971-74; v.p., office mgr., relocation coordinator McKee, Inc., Realtors, Richardson, Tex., 1974—. Mem. Nat. Assn. Realtors, Real Estate Nat. Mktg. Inst., Greater Dallas Bd. Realtors, League Women Voters, Richardson C. of C., Realtors Richardson (chmn. 1977, mem. state edn./profl. standards com. 1979), Promenade Merchants Assn. Democrat. Roman Catholic. Home: 1902 Caprock St Richardson TX 75080 Office: 1705 Promenade St Richardson TX 75080

BALSLEY, HOWARD LLOYD, educator; b. Chgo., Dec. 3, 1913; s. Elmer Lloyd and Katherine (McGlashing) B.; A.B., Ind. U., 1946, M.A., 1947, Ph.D., 1950; postgrad. John Hopkins, 1947-48, U. Chgo., summer 1948; m. Irol Verneth Whitmore, Aug. 24, 1947. Asst. prof. econs. U. Utah, Salt Lake City, 1949-50; asso. prof. econs., dir. Sch. Bus., Russell Sage Coll., Troy, N.Y., 1950-52; asso. prof. econs. Washington and Lee U., Lexington, Va., 1952-54; prof. bus. statistics, head dept. bus. and econ. research La. Tech. U., Ruston, 1954-65; prof. bus. adminstrn. and statistics Tex. Tech. U., Lubbock, 1965-75; head dept. econs. and finance, prof. econs. and statistics U. Ark. at Little Rock, 1975—. Served with USAAF, 1943-46. Mem. Am. Econ. Assn., Am. Statis. Assn., Southwestern Social Sci. Assn., Am. Inst. Decision Scis. Author: (with James Gemmell) Principles of Economics, 1953; Readings in Economic Doctrines, vols. 1 and 2, 1961; Introduction to Statistical Method, 1964; Quantitative Research Methods for Business & Economics, 1970; (with Vernon Clover) Business Research, 1974; Basic Statistics for Business and Economics, 1978. Home: 11408 E Stoney Point Little Rock AR 72211

BALSLEY, IROL WHITMORE (MRS. HOWARD L. BALSLEY), educator; b. Venus, Nebr., Aug. 22, 1912; d. Sylvanus Bertrand and Nanna (Carson) Whitmore; B.A., Nebr. State Coll., Wayne, 1933; M.S., U. Tenn., 1940; Ed.D., Ind. U., 1952; m. Howard Lloyd Balsley, Aug. 24, 1947. Tchr. high schs., Osmond and Walthill, Nebr., 1934-37; asst. prof. Ind. U., 1942-49; lectr. U. Utah, 1949-50, Russell Sage Coll., 1953-54; prof. office adminstrn. La. Tech. U., 1954-65, also head dept. office adminstrn., 1963-65; prof. bus. edn. Tex. Tech. U., 1965-72, prof. edn., 1972-75; prof. adminstrv. services U. Ark. at Little Rock, 1975-80; adj. prof. Hardin-Simmons U., Abilene, Tex., 1980—; coordinator of USAF clk.-typist tng. program Pa. State U., 1951, inst., head office tng. sect. TVA, 1941-42; editorial asst. South-Western Pub. Co., 1940-41. Mem. Nat. Bus. Edn. Assn. (past pres. research found.). Nat. Assn. for Bus. Tchr. Edn., Adminstrv. Mgmt. Soc., Tex. Bus. Edn. Assn., Nat. Collegiate Assn. Secs. (co-founder, past pres., nat. exec. sec. 1976—), Am. Bus. Communication Assn., Pi Lambda Theta, Delta Pi Epsilon (past nat. sec.), Beta Gamma Sigma, Phi Delta Kappa, Pi Omega Pi, Sigma Tau Delta, Alpha Psi Omega, Delta Kappa Gamma. Author: (with Wanous) Shorthand Transcription Studies, 1968; (with Robinson) Integrated Secretarial Studies, 1963; (with Wood and Whitmore) Homestyle Baking, 1973; Century 21 Shorthand, Vol. I, 1974, (with Robert Hoskinson) Vol. II, 1974; Self-Paced Learning Activities for Century 21 Shorthand, Vol. I, 1977. Address: Box 1127 H-SU Station Abilene TX 79698

BALZER, LARRY DALE, physician; b. Liberal, Kans., Apr. 3, 1945; s. Lawrence John and Martha A. (Wiens) B.; B.S. in Biology, Panhandle A&M Coll., Goodwell, Okla., 1967; M.D., U. Okla., 1971; m. Diana Susan Kiser, Nov. 29, 1975; 1 dau., Keli Dawn. Resident in family practice Scott AFB, Ill., 1975-77, chief resident, 1977; practice medicine specializing in family medicine, Sherman, Tex., 1978—; med. examiner FAA, 1979—; med. cons. Tex. Mental Health and Retardation Center, 1978—. Served to maj. M.C., USAF, 1972-78. Diplomate Am. Bd. Family Practice. Mem. Sherman C. of C., Tex. Med. Assn., Grayson County Med. Soc., Am. Acad. Family Practice, Am. Soc. Clin. Hypnosis, Internat. Soc. Hypnosis. Republican. Baptist. Office: 207 W Mulberry St Sherman TX 75090

BANAS, NORMA ELISCU, ednl. guidance service co. exec.; b. N.Y.C., July 28, 1933; d. Frank and Mildred (Norman) Eliscu; B.Ed., U. Miami, 1957, M.Ed., 1965; children—Suzanne, Joanne. Tchr. pub. schs., Miami, Fla., 1951-52; instr. reading clinic U. Miami, 1960-62; dir. curriculum McGlannan Clin. Sch., Miami, 1963-67; pres., dir. curriculum Ednl. Guidance Services, Inc., Miami, 1967—; cons. pub. and pvt. sch. systems. Bd. dirs. Dade County Youth Fair Assn. Mem. Assn. Children with Learning Disabilities. Author: (with I.H. Wills) Success Begins With Understanding, 1972; Identifying Early Learning Gaps, 1975; Prescriptive Teaching: Theory Into Practice, 1976; New Approaches to Success in the Classroom, 1975; Help for the Adolescent, 1978; WISC-R Prescriptions, 1978; Prescriptions from the DTLA. Home: 9360 SW 66th St Miami FL 33173 Office: 7200 SW 39th Terr PO Box 557251 Miami FL 33155

BANDER, NORMAN ROBERT, communications and info. mgmt. cons.; A.B., Dartmouth, 1954; postgrad. Harvard, Columbia, U. Pa., N.Y. U. Former sales research dir. Benton & Bowles, Inc., N.Y.C.; media program research dir. Lennen & Newell, Inc., N.Y.C.; dir. mktg., test analysis Gillette Co., Boston; dir. creative communication evaluation and advt. research J. Walter Thompson Co., N.Y.C.; pres. Bander & Assos., Sarasota, Fla., 1968—. Served as clin. psychologist M.C., AUS, 1954-56. Mem. Am. Mktg. Assn. Clubs: Dartmouth, Yale (N.Y.C.). Author studies on mktg. and advt. effectiveness, consumer behavior and pub. opinion. Office: PO Box 190 Sarasota FL 33578

BANDY, ANNETTE BINGHAM, govt. ofcl.; b. Alva, Okla., May 19, 1946; d. Irwin Drake and Louise (Parker) Bingham; student Stephen F. Austin State U., 1964-65, E. Tex. State U., 1965-67; B.A., U. Tex., 1968, postgrad., 1968-69, 75. Editor, The Lone Star, Tex. Sch. for the Deaf, Austin, 1968-69; public info. officer Tex. Office Econ. Opportunity, Austin, 1969; reporter Selma (Ala.) Times Jour., 1970; mgmt. analyst U.S. Army Med. Materiel Agy., Pacific, Okinawa, Japan, 1971-73; public info. officer U.S. Dept. Labor, Dallas, 1973—. Pub. chmn. Benefit Air Show, Exptl. Aircraft Assn.

and Aerobatic Club of Am., Dallas, 1976. Recipient Labor Dept. Spl. Achievement award, 1979; named Most Valuable Mem., Dallas Women in Communications, 1977. Mem. Women in Communications (chpt. pres. 1977-78), Public Info. Officers Assn. Office: 555 Griffin Sq Bldg Room 220 Dallas TX 75202

BANE, GILBERT WINFIELD, JR., marine scientist, environmentalist; b. San Diego, Dec. 11, 1931; s. Gilbert Winfield and Eva (Chaffin) B.; B.S., San Jose State Coll., 1954; M.S., Cornell U., 1961, Ph.D., 1963; m. Anneka Wright, Nov. 5, 1971; children—Victoria, Cynthia, Robert. Scientist, Inter-Am. Tropical Tuna Commn., San Diego also Mancora, Peru, 1954-58; biol. oceanographer Star-Kist Foods, Inc./Ghana Fisheries Dept., West Africa, 1959-60; dir. fisheries U. P.R., 1963-65; asst. prof. marine scis. U. Calif., Irvine, 1955-59; asso. prof. L.I. U., 1959-73; dir. marine scis., environ. studies U. N.C., Wilmington, 1973—. Mem. N.C. Marine Resources Center Advisory Bd., 1974—; mem. monitor commn. Comml. & Sports Fisheries Advisory Council, 1979—; dir. Southeast Consortium for Underwater Research, 1978—, Southeastern Consortium for Undersea Research, 1979—. Fellow Explorers Club; mem. Am. Fisheries Soc., Am. Soc. Icthyologists and Herpetologists, Am. Soc. Limnologists and Oceanographers, Am. Inst. Fisheries Research Biologists. Author: Bay Fishes of Northern California, 1970; Fishes of Southern California, 1965; Ecology of Tunas and Tuna Bait in Gulf of Guinea, 1961; Biology of the Atlantic Yellowfin Tuna, 1963. Office: PO Box 3725 Wilmington NC 28406

BANE, JERRY WILLIAM, surgeon; b. Frost, Tex., Apr. 15, 1940; s. Wilford Virles and Ruby (Mitchell) B.; B.A., So. Meth. U., 1962; M.D., U. Tex. SW Med. Sch., 1968; m. Marsha Ann Sutherland, Aug. 1, 1961; children—Marc William, Margaret Ann. Intern, VA Hosp., Dallas, 1968-69; surg. resident U. Miss., Jackson, 1969-73; practice medicine specializing in surgery, Arlington, Tex., 1975—. Served with M.C., U.S. Army, 1973-75. Diplomate Am. Bd. Surgery. Mem. A.C.S., AMA, Tex. Med. Assn., Tarrant County Med. Assn., Ft. Worth Surg. Soc. (Arlington br.). Methodist. Home: 4101 Shady Valley Dr Arlington TX 76013 Office: 801 W Randol Mill Rd Arlington TX 76012

BANICK, OLIVIA ANN MARIE, ins. underwriter; b. Pomona, Calif., Feb. 13, 1945; d. Vincent William and Maryann (Munchak) B.; B.S., Syracuse U., 1966; M.S., Tex. Women's U., 1977. Home economist, nutritionist N.Y. State Electric & Gas Co., N.Y.C., also Cornell U., Ithaca, N.Y., 1966-68; adminstrv. supr. Vis. Nurse Assn. Dallas, 1972-76; nutritionist Parkland and Med. City hosps., Dallas, 1976-78; underwriter Travelers Ins. Co., Dallas, 1978—. Served to capt. USAF, 1968-72. Mem. Res. Officers Assn., Air Force Assn. Republican. Roman Catholic. Club: Syracuse U. Alumni. Address: 7978 Cliffbrook St Apt 2016 Dallas TX 75240

BANKIT, PAUL, educator; b. Milw., June 16, 1929; s. Joseph and Sally Josephine B.; student engring., U. Wis., 1946-50; B.G.E., U. Nebr., 1960; M.B.A., Mich. State U., 1966, Ph.D., 1972; m. Esther Lilly Halvorsen, July 8, 1950; children—Eric J., Paula A. Commd. 2d lt., U.S.Army, 1952, advanced through grades to col., 1978; armor unit comdr., Ft. Hood, Tex., 1954-57; aviation officer, Germany, 1957-59; instr. Ft. Rucker, Ala., 1959-60, test pilot, 1961-64; combat pilot, Vietnam, 1966-67; div. chief Combat Devels. Command, Ft. Eustis, Va., 1967-70; comdr. Transp. Engring. Agy., Washington, 1973-76; ret., 1978; prof. mgmt. sci. Christopher Newport Coll., Newport News, Va., 1978—; cons. Ketron Corp., Washington. Decorated Legion of Merit, Bronze Star, Air Medals; named lectr. of year Army Logistics Mgmt. Center, 1974; recipient achievement award Boy Scouts Am., 1968. Mem. Ops. Research Soc. Am., Am. Mktg. Assn., Acad. Mgmt., Am. Mgmt. Assn. Republican. Lutheran. Club: Masons. Author: Logistics Systems Design, 1972; Logistics Systems Analysis, 1975. Home: 174 D'Lane Dr Newport News VA 23602 Office: Christopher Newport College Box 6070 Newport News VA 23606

BANKS, ANDREI THEOFANO, architect; b. Newport News, Va., Sept. 28, 1947; s. Lee Riley and Cleopatra Maxine (White) B.; B.Arch., Howard U., 1970; m. Carolyn Iredell Conyers, Dec. 29, 1967; children—Andrei Theofano, Dyon Anthony, Tavares Annette. Draftsman, Dudley, Morrisette & Cederquist, Architects, Norfolk, Va., 1970-72; project mgr., architect Livas & Assos., Norfolk, 1972-74; project architect Williams & Tazewell & Assos., Norfolk, 1974-78; prin. Andrei T. Banks, AIA, Norfolk, 1978—. Mem. AIA, Young Profls. Tidewater, Mut. Investment Club Va. Democrat. Pentecostal. Club: Barraud Park Racket. Home: 1062 Rainey Dr Norfolk VA 23504 Office: 201 Granby Mall Suite 301 Norfolk VA 23510

BANKS, HARVEY DAVID, counselor; b. Birmingham, Ala., Nov. 21, 1945; s. Allen Banks and Mary Alice (Bennett) Banks Jones; B.A., Paine Coll., 1968; M.S., Troy State U., 1973; m. Ruth Roberts, Aug. 23, 1970; children—Melanee Rochelle, Pamela Michelle. Tchr., Sylauga High Sch. (Ala.), 1968-69; instr. Daniel Payne Coll., Birmingham, 1969-70; tchr. Kinston (Ala.) High Sch., 1974; social worker Dale County Dept. Pensions and Security, Ozark, Ala., 1974-75; guidance counselor Fort Jackson (S.C.) Army Edn., 1975—; mem. part time faculty U.S.C., Columbia. Served with AUS, 1970-74; Vietnam. Paine Coll. scholar, 1964. Mem. Am. Personnel and Guidance Assn., S.C. Personnel and Guidance Assn., S.C. Assn. Higher Continuing Edn., Assn. Counselor Edn. and Supervision, Phi Delta Kappa. Democrat. Baptist. Home: 1924 Quaker Rd Columbia SC 29206 Office: Army Edn Center Fort Jackson SC 29207

BANKS, PAUL EDWARD, data processing co. exec.; b. Bingham Canyon, Utah, Dec. 20, 1938; s. Merlin Dean and Lillie Eliza (Hodges) Christensen; Asso. B.A., Kennesaw Jr. Coll., 1978; student Ga. State U., 1979—; m. Shirley Ann Sypriano, Feb. 8, 1959; children—Terri, Vicki, Paul, Joseph. Served as enlisted man U.S. Air Force, 1955-76; commd. 2d lt. U.S. Air Force, advanced through grades to sr. master sgt., 1976; programmer/analyst U.S. Air Force, 1963-73; computer systems supt. U.S. Air Force, Montgomery, Ala., 1973-76, ret., 1976; programmer/analyst L'eggs Products, Inc., Atlanta, 1976, systems analyst, 1976-77, mgr. ops., 1977-79, data center mgr., 1979—; cons. data entry incentive systems. Mem. Community Welfare Services Com., 1967—. Decorated Air Force Meritorious Service medal with oak leaf cluster; named Mil. Citizen of Yr., Montgomery, Ala., 1974. Mem. Data Entry Mgrs. Assn. (v.p.), Honeywell Users N. Ga. Republican. Mormon. Home: 3581 Paul Samuel Rd Kennesaw GA 30144 Office: L'eggs Products Inc 500 Interstate N Atlanta GA 30339

BANKS, REBECCA BETH, ins. broker; b. Bellaire, Ohio, Jan. 22, 1951; d. John A. and Mary L. (Troyanovich) Balek; cert. of completion Offshore Oil Sch., U. Tex., 1977; m. David W. Banks, Oct. 15, 1976. With Associated Gen. Contractors, Washington, 1970-71, Am. Internat. Underwriters, Tulsa, 1971-73, Marsh & McLennan, Inc., Tulsa, 1973-75; mktg. ofcl. So. Marine and Aviation Underwriters, 1975-76; asst. v.p., br. mgr. J.H. Blades, Inc., Tulsa, 1976—. Mem. Okla. Surplus Lines Assn., Internat. Assn. Drilling Contractors (hon.), Met. C. of C. Republican. Presbyterian. Home: 2233 E 22d Pl Tulsa OK 74114 Office: 5800 E Skelly Dr Tulsa OK 74135

BANKS, ROBERT THOMAS, JR., religious assn. exec.; b. Griffin, Ga., Apr. 13, 1931; s. Robert Thomas and Estelle (Clark) B.; B.A., Baylor U., 1953; M.R.E., Southwestern Bapt. Theol. Sem., 1956; m. Martha Jane Sibley, Aug. 27, 1952; children—Sibyl Ann, Brenda Lee, Brian Nelson. Sec. Royal Ambassadors Bapt. Gen. Conv. Okla., Oklahoma City, 1954-68, dir. dept. brotherhood, 1968-73; exec. asst. brotherhood commn. So. Bapt. Conv., Memphis, 1974-76, program dir., 1976—. Cons. camps; dir. Camp Hudgens for Royal Ambassadors, McAlester, Okla., 1960-74. Mem. camp bd. YMCA, Oklahoma City, 1969-74. Bd. dirs. Sooner Alcohol-Narcotics Edn. Mem. Am. Camping Assn. (pres. chpt. 1960-63, regional Honor award 1963). Democrat. Baptist. Contbr. articles to profl. jours. Home: 1825 Malabar St Germantown TN 38138 Office: 1548 Poplar Ave Memphis TN 38104

BANKS, SARA LYNN, educator, counselor; b. Elizabeth, N.J., Apr. 19, 1939; d. Irving Romeon and Coralie Russell (Rayne) Groves; B.A. magna cum laude, U. Md., 1971; M.A., Ball State U., 1973; m. Douglas Trent Banks, Jan. 11, 1962; children—Elizabeth Lynn, Douglas Trent, Kimberly Erin. Tchr. English, Iran-Am. Soc., Tehran, 1960-62; counselor psychiat., drug detoxification ward, U.S. Army Hosp., Heidelberg, Ger., 1972-73; adjustment counselor for physically and emotionally and mentally handicapped, Brevard Achievement Center, Rockledge, Fla., 1974-76; tchr., counselor for socially maladjusted Juvenile Supervision Center, Titusville, Fla., 1976—. Vol. social worker ARC, 1971-72; vol. dir. Friends For Youth, 1973-74. Mem. Am. Personnel and Guidance Assn., Internat. Transactional Analysis Assn., Inst. Rational Emotive Therapy. Republican. Home: 325 Miami St Indialantic FL 32903 Office: 1800 S DeLeon St Titusville FL 32780

BANKS, VIRGINIA ANNE, assn. exec.; b. Dallas, Mar. 19, 1949; d. James Houston and Mary Virginia (Bussey) Banks; B.J., U. Tex., 1971. Reporter, Austin (Tex.) Am.-Statesman, 1969; pub. relations asst. to lt. gov. State of Tex., Austin, 1970; traveling cons. Alpha Omicron Pi sorority, Indpls., 1971-73, adminstrv. asst., 1973-74, traveling cons. program coordinator, 1974-77, internat. rush chmn., 1976-77, internat. v.p. for ops., 1977—; pub. info. officer Tex. Dept. Community Affairs, Austin, 1974-76; asst. dir. communications State Bar Tex., Austin, 1976-78, asso. editor Tex. Bar Jour., 1978-79, mng. editor, 1979—. Bd. dirs. Lone Star council Girl Scouts U.S.A., 1970-71, 73-75, troop leader, 1970-71, mem. troop camp com., 1968-70, chmn. pub. relations com., 1973-75; mem. steering com. Gov.'s statewide immunization campaign. Mem. Women in Communications, Am. Judicature Soc., Humane Soc. Austin and Travis County, Nat. Assn. Bar Execs., Alpha Omicron Pi. Methodist. Contbr. articles to various mags. Home: 3108 W Terrace Dr Austin TX 78731 Office: PO Box 12487 Capitol Station Austin TX 78711

BANKS, WARREN EUGENE, lawyer, educator; b. Hot Springs, Ark., Feb. 1, 1929; s. Warren Eugene and Helen Frances (Shaw) B.; B.S. in Bus. Adminstrn., U. Ark., Fayetteville, 1950, J.D., 1953, M.B.A., 1960, Ph.D., 1968; postgrad. Georgetown U. Law Center, 1957, U. Colo., 1962-63; m. Carolyn Beth Duty, Dec. 27, 1952; children—Karen Marie, Keith Randolph. Admitted to Ark. bar, 1953; asso. firm C. T. Cotham, Atty., Hot Springs, 1953; investigator GAO, Washington, 1955-57; instr. fin. U. Ark., 1957-59, asst. prof., 1959-64, asso. prof., 1964-70, prof., 1970—, head dept. fin., 1978—, part time faculty Sch. Law, 1957—; research asst. in securities analysis to prof. Harold Dulan, Participating Annuity Life Ins. Co., Fayetteville, 1960-63; lectr. sems., speaker to profl., acad. groups. Served to 1st lt. USAF, 1953-55. Recipient Faculty Achievement award Ark. Alumni Assn., 1973. Mem. Southwestern Fin. Assn., Fin. Mgmt. Assn., Ark. Bar Assn., Am., So. Regional bus. law assns., Am. Trial Lawyers Assn., Omicron Delta Kappa, Beta Gamma Sigma, Beta Alpha Psi, Alpha Kappa Psi, Sigma Pi, Phi Alpha Delta. Episcopalian. Contbr. articles to profl. jours. Home: 1109 Sunset Dr Fayetteville AR 72701

BANKS, WILSON HARPER, airport mgr.; b. Munday, Tex., June 11, 1916; s. Wesley Fannin and Jessie Kezar (Wilson) B.; B.A., U. Philippines, 1954; grad. Air Command and Staff Coll., 1947-48, Air War Coll., 1951-52; m. Marcia Jacqueline Smith, 1943; children—Sue Ann, Wilson Harper, Ronald D., Jacquie Banks Becker. Commd. flying cadet, USAAF, 1938, advanced through grades to col., USAF, 1951; comdr. 90th Bomb Group, S.W. Pacific, 1944; vice comdr. 13th Air Force, Clark Field, Philippines, 1953-55; comdr. Lackland AFB, 1958-60, 3560th Pilot Tng. Wing, Webb AFB, Tex., 1961-63; chief of staff Air U., Maxwell AFB, Ala., 1966-69; ret., 1969; dir. aviation City of Midland (Tex.), 1969—. Decorated Legion of Merit with oak leaf cluster, D.F.C., Air medal with 2 oak leaf clusters, Commendation medal (3); named Boss of Year in Midland, Secs. Assn., 1970. Mem. Am., Tex. (pres. 1974-76) assns. airport execs., Air Force Assn., Ret. Officers Assn., Order Daedalians. Club: Kiwanis. Home: 3600 Jordan St Midland TX 79703 Office: PO Box 6305 ATS Midland TX 79701

BANKSTON, WILLIAM CALVIT, govt. ofcl.; b. Darlington, La., Jan. 29, 1937; s. William Cyrus and Jonnie Irene (Calvit) B.; B.A., U. Southwestern La., 1963; M.S.W., La. State U., 1965; m. Eleanor Grace Lefegure, Aug. 2, 1958; children—William Calvit, Katherine, Susan, Elizabeth. Clin. social worker E. La. State Hosp., Jackson, La., 1965-66; adminstr. Crowley Mental Health Center, Crowley, La., 1966-70; dep. asst. sec. Office of Hospitals La. Dept. Health and Human Resources, Baton Rouge, 1972-78, Office of Mental Health, Bur. Substance Abuse, 1978—. Cert. social worker. Mem. Nat. Assn. Social Workers, Acad. Cert. Social Workers, Delta Sigma Phi, Psi Chi, Pi Gamma Mu. Methodist. Home: 1779 Pollard St Baton Rouge LA 70808 Office: Office of Mental Health Bureau of Substance Abuse 200 Lafayette St Baton Rouge LA 70801

BANNOURA, NASSER YACUB, county ofcl.; b. Jerusalem, Jan. 23, 1940; came to U.S., 1962, naturalized, 1969; s. Yacub Nasser and Nazha (Garfeh) B.; student Jerusalem Inst., 1958-62; m. Norma Zaloudek, Oct. 30, 1962; children—Michelle, James. Tour conductor, Jerusalem, 1960-62; tour promoter Downers Grove Travel Co. (Ill.), 1962-64; owner, mgr. Accent House, gift shop, Downers Grove, 1963-65; data processing trainee Bell Tel. Lab., Naperville, Ill., 1965-69; opns. mgr. info. systems Brownard County, Fort Lauderdale, Fla., 1970—; cons. Sunair Electronics Co., Fort Lauderdale. Chmn. photographic restoration com. Broward County Hist. Commn., 1977-78. Mem. Govt. Mgmt. Info. Scis. Assn., Syrian Lebanese Club Fort Lauderdale (pres.), Syrian Lebanese Club Fla (v.p.). Club: Masons. Roman Catholic. Home: 908 NW 30th Ct Wilton Manors FL 33311 Office: 201 SE 6th St Fort Lauderdale FL 33301

BAÑOS, JOSE LUIS, bank exec.; b. New Orleans, Aug. 25, 1918; s. Jose Rodrigo and Julia (Sussman Del Olmo) B.; B.B.A., Tulane U., 1939, LL.B., 1946; m. Catherine Dunbar Bensabat, June 20, 1947; children—Catherine Banos Eustis, Julia Banos Poitevent, Margot Banos Jones, Jose Luis, George. Mem. staff dept. fgn. banking Whitney Nat. Bank of New Orleans, 1946-49, asst. mgr., 1949-53, mgr., 1953-59, v.p., 1959—; co-owner, mgr. White Plantation, Thibodaux, La. Past chmn. pres. council, trustee St. Mary's Dominican Coll.; bd. dirs. City of New Orleans Delgado Albania Plantation Commn., Internat. Trade Mart; mem. exec. com., past pres. Internat. House; vice chmn. planned gifts com. Tulane U.; past pres. bd. Sociedad Española. Served to lt. comdr. U.S. Navy, 1941-46. Decorated Knight comdr. Order Isabel la Catolica (Spain); knight Mil. and Hospitaller Order St. Lazarus of Jerusalem; knight Equestrian Order of Holy Sepulchre of Jerusalem. Mem. Am., La. bar assns., Am. Inst. Banking, Phi Delta Theta. Clubs: Boston, Pickwick, Plimsoll, New Orleans Country, Wyvern. Home: 9 Richmond Pl New Orleans LA 70115 Office: 228 Saint Charles Ave New Orleans LA 70130

BANTLE, WILLIAM CHARLES, consumer goods mfg. co. exec.; b. Two Rivers, Wis., Aug. 25, 1940; s. Clarence G. and Germain I. (Goetz) B.; B.S. in Mech. Engring., U. Wis., 1963; M.S. in Mech. Engring., Wayne State U., 1965, M.B.A., 1968; m. Mary E. Durkee, June 22, 1963; children—Kristin Marie, Kelly Elain. With Chrysler Corp., 1963-69; plant mgr. Proto Tool div. Ingersoll Rand Co., Los Angeles, 1969-76; v.p. mfg. Ajax Forging & Casting div. Allegheny Ludlum Industries, Detroit, 1976-78, Disston div. Sandvik Co., Danville, Va., 1978—; instr. Colo. Springs (Colo.) Community Coll., 1971-73. Bd. dirs. Goodwill Industries. Mem. Va. Mfrs. Assn. Clubs: Danville Golf, Rotary. Home: 553 Downing Dr Danville VA 24541 Office: Disston Div Sandvik Co Route 29 N Danville VA 24541

BAPTIE, CHARLES, photographer, printer, publisher; b. Munhall, Pa., Mar. 13, 1914; s. Charles and Constance B.; m. Joan Pratt, Jan. 1, 1970; 1 son by previous marriage, Ronald. Photographer, Trans World Airways, Pitts., 1933-34, Capital Airlines, Washington, 1935-45; freelance photographer Annandale, Va., 1945—; illustrator numerous books; owner, operator Charles Baptie Studios, Annandale, 1945—; cons. graphic arts. Mem. Photog. Soc. Am. (asso.), Nat. Press Club, Nat. Photographers Assn. Author: (with Ollie Atkins) Camera on Assignment, 1958; (with Hope Ridings Miller) Great Houses of Washington, D.C., 1970; (with Jack Lloyd) How to Play Baseball; (with Margaret MacBeth Seiler) Mid the Hills of Pennsylvania, 1980; picture editor 16-vol. United States History, 1963—; photo illustrator Guest House of the Presidents (Eleanor Lee Templeman), 1980. Office: 4124 Village Ct Annandale VA 22003

BARAB, ANNE ELLIOTT, life ins. co. exec.; b. Ft. Worth, Oct. 2, 1947; d. Edmonds LeCato and Virginia Terry (Tutt) Guerrant; B.A., Tex. Christian U., 1969; m. Stuart Barab, Mar. 20, 1971. Various managerial positions Southwestern Bell Telephone Co., Dallas, 1969-72; methods analyst The Trinity Cos., 1973-75; methods analyst Planned Mktg. Associates, subs. K Mart, Dallas, 1975-76, fin. analyst, 1976-77, mktg. ops. coordinator, 1977-78, mgr. market planning, 1978, dir. market adminstrn., 1978-79, asst. v.p. mktg. 1979—. Vol. United Way of Met. Dallas. Fellow Life Office Mgmt. Inst.; mem. Assn. for Systems Mgmt., Women For Change, Delta Gamma. Home: 653 Goodwin Dr Richardson TX 75081 Office: 200 Treadway Plaza Dallas TX 75235

BARANSY, MARVIN LEE, JR., oil co. exec.; b. Trenton, N.J., Jan. 12, 1938; s. Marvin Lee and Violet (Larson) B.; A.A., Palm Beach Coll., 1965; B.A., Fla. Atlantic U., 1966; m. Julia Ann Moore, Feb. 21, 1963; children—Matthew, Steven. Sales rep. Union Oil Co., Atlanta, 1966-67, mgr. car care center, Norfolk, Va., 1967-70, mem. spl. outlets devel. staff, Chgo., 1971-72, tng. mgr., Memphis, 1972-74, Birmingham, Ala., 1974-78, merchandiser, advt. and sales promotion, 1978-80, mgr. interstate truck stops, 1980—. Served with USAF, 1959-62. Recipient R.C. Mendel award, 1965. Mem. Am. Soc. Testing and Devel., Soc. Automotive Engrs. Presbyterian. Clubs: Masons (Sherman, Tex.); Rotary, Toastmasters. Home: 2112 Granada Ln Charlotte NC 28211 Office: 4801 Independence Blvd Charlotte NC 28212

BARANYAI, PAUL DONALD, pipeline co. exec.; b. Detroit, Dec. 1, 1938; s. Paul and Mildred B.; B.S., Mich. State U., 1961, M.S., 1963; m. Janet Marilyn Roebke, June 16, 1962; children—Deborah Rowe, Bonnie Beth. Dist. devel. geologist Chevron, U.S.A., New Orleans, 1977; supr. regional exploration Kerr McGee Corp., Houston, 1978; mgr. offshore exploration Natural Gas Pipeline Co., Houston, 1979—. Mem. New Orleans Geol. Soc., Houston Geol. Soc., Am. Assn. Petroleum Geologists, Houston Assn. Chief Geologists, Sigma Xi. Republican. Presbyterian. Home: Rt 14 Box 1096D Conroe TX 77302 Office: PO Box 283 Houston TX 77001

BARBAKOW, DENNIS, psychologist; b. Princeton, W.Va., Sept. 16, 1949; s. Yankee and Libby B.; B.A. cum laude, Concord Coll., 1971; M.S.W., U. Ala., 1974, Ph.D. in Psychology, 1976; m. Penny Lane, Jan. 30, 1972. Instr. behavioral studies U. Ala., Tuscaloosa, 1974-76; cons. Birmingham (Ala.) City Sch. System, 1976; dir. treatment services Central Ala. Youth Service, Selma, 1976-77; regional dir. community services Ala. Dept. Mental Health, Tuscaloosa, 1977—; mem. adj. faculty U. Ala. Sch. Social Work, 1976—; mem. profl. adv. bd. Tuscaloosa County Mental Health Assn. Vice pres. Temple Emanuel, Tuscaloosa, 1978-79, pres. elect. Mem. Am. Ednl. Research Assn., Assn. Cert. Social Workers, Am. Assn. Correctional Psychologists, Ala. Juvenile Justice Assn., Am. Assn. Mental Deficiency. Author: A Study of Violence in A Southern Metropolitan School System, 1976. Home: 119 Vestavia Hills Northport AL 35476 Office: PO Box 864 Tuscaloosa AL 35402

BARBANEL, SIDNEY MANUEL (SID), med. instruments mfg. co. exec.; b. Savannah, Ga., Mar. 5, 1936; s. Leon and Ann M. (Kramer) B.; student U.S. Naval Acad., 1956, Coll. Charleston, 1957-58; B.A., Oglethorpe U., 1960; m. Anne Matthias, Mar. 16, 1961; children—Amy Laura, Bonnie Lynne. Salesman, Dun & Bradstreet, Inc., 1960-64; Purdue Frederick Co., Atlanta, 1964-68, Medtronic, Inc., Atlanta, 1968-69; So. div. mgr. sales and mktg. Cordis Corp., Atlanta, 1969-74; mgr. ARCO Med. Products Co. subs. Atlantic Richfield Corp., Pitts., 1974-76; exec. v.p. sales Intermedics Inc., Freeport, Tex., 1976—; v.p. Intermedics Intraocular, Inc., 1976-78; lectr. in field. Bd. visitors Oglethorpe U., 1979. Served with USN, 1954-56. Named to Pres.'s Club, Medtronic, Inc., 1969, Loyalty Club, Oglethorpe U., 1978; recipient cert. Ga. Heart Assn., 1972. Mem. Assn. Advancement Med. Instrumentation, Am. Mgmt. Assn., N.Am. Soc. Pacing and Electrophysiology. Sales and Mktg. Execs., Citadel Devel. Found., James Edward Oglethorpe Soc. Club: Masons. Office: 240 Tarpon Inn Village Freeport TX 77541

BARBEAU, DENNIS WILLIAM, marital and family therapist; b. Red Bud, Ill., Oct. 10, 1947; s. William Joseph and Bertha Elizabeth (Mueller) B.; B.A., Lewis U., 1969; M.Div., St. Meinrad Sch. Theology, 1973; M.A., U. South Fla., 1977; m. Sandra A. Wuebbels, Dec. 28, 1974. Instr., St. Petersburg Cath. High Sch., 1973-74; tchr., music dir., counselor Corpus Christi Parish and Sch., Tampa, Fla., 1974-76; asso. diocesan dir. religious edn. Diocese of St. Petersburg, 1976-77; diocesan dir., adminstr., therapist Cath. Marriage Counseling Center, Diocese of St. Petersburg, 1977—; cons. in field. Mem. Am. Assn. Marriage and Family Therapy, Am. Personnel and Guidance Assn., Am. Mental Health Counselors Assn., Assn. Religious and Value Issues In Counseling. Roman Catholic. Office: 12945 Seminole Blvd Largo FL 33540

BARBER, BYRON EDWARD, real estate devel. exec.; b. Chico, Calif., Oct. 31, 1946; s. Ernest E. and Janice Y. B.; B.B.A., S.W. Tex. State U., 1970; M.A. in Bus., Webster Coll., 1978; m. Kay M. Tinsley, June 14, 1975. Pres., Byron Enterprises and Bybar Music Pub. Co., 1967-70; mktg. rep. Ellison Industries, San Antonio, 1977-79; gen. partner, chief exec. officer BBS Devel. Group, San Antonio, 1977—; pres. Byron Barber, Inc., San Antonio, 1978—; pilot Tejas Airlines,

San Antonio, 1979, comml. real estate broker Henry S. Miller Co., San Antonio, 1979—; mng. mem. Pat Booker Rd. and Coronado-Booker Joint Ventures. Served with USAF, 1970-77. Mem. Nat. Assn. Home Builders (Million Dollar Circle 1977, 78), Lambda Chi Alpha. Home: 1906 Deer Mountain St San Antonio TX 78232

BARBER, CHARLES EDWARD, journalist; b. Miami, Fla., Oct. 30, 1939; s. James Plemon and Margaret Katherine (Grimes) B.; A.A., Santa Fe Community Coll., 1971; m. Judith Margaret Tuck, May 28, 1960; children—Janet Lynn, Christopher Edward. Prodn. mgr. dept. student publs. U. Fla., Gainesville, 1966-68, ops. mgr., 1968-70, asst. dir., 1970-72, dir., 1972-73, dir. div. publs., 1974; prodn. mgr. State Univ. System Press, Gainesville, 1975-76; pres., gen. mgr. Campus Communications, Inc., Gainesville, 1976—; cons. in field. Mem. citizens adv. council Stephen Foster Elem. Sch., Gainesville, 1973-77; mem. Friends of Five, 1975-77, Friends of the Library, 1975-77; chmn. book com. Fla. State Prison, 1973—; bd. dirs. Gainesville High Sch. Band Boosters, 1978-79; mem. pres.'s council U. Fla., 1978—; mem. Leadership Gainesville, 1979; pack com. chmn. Cub Scouts Am., 1977-78. Served with USCGR, 1957-65. Recipient Nat. 1st Place for Editorial Writing, Hearst Found., 1965; named nation's most disting. bus. adv. to coll. press, 1978. Mem. Am. Advt. Fedn., Am. Newspaper Pubs. Assn., Coll. Newspaper Bus. and Advt. Mgrs., Fla. Scholastic Press Assn., Fla. Newspaper Advt. Execs., Alligator Press Council (moderator 1979), Gainesville Advt. Fedn., (dir. 1979—), Inst. Newspaper Controllers and Fin. Officers, Internat. Newspaper Promotion Assn., Nat. Council Coll. Publs. Advisers, Printing Industries Fla., So. Coll. Advt. in Newspapers, Gainesville Area C. of C. (com. of 100), Soc. Profl. Journalists, Alligator Alumni Assn. (dir.), Sigma Delta Chi (treas. No. Fla. chpt. 1972-75), Alpha Phi Gamma. Democrat. Baptist (chmn. bd. deacons). Club: Kiwanis. Adv. editor Fla. Quar., 1973-74; contbr. articles in field to profl. jours. Home: 4205 NW 21st St Gainesville FL 32605 Office: PO Box 14257 Gainesville FL 32604

BARBER, FRANKLIN WESTON, food cons.; b. N.Y.C., July 3, 1912; s. Frank Weston and Vernie Dell (Clement) B.; B.S., Aurora Coll., 1934; M.S., U. Wis.-Madison, 1942, Ph.D. in Microbiology, 1944; m. Natalie Eaton, Feb. 25, 1937; 1 dau., Susan Vernie (Mrs. Burton Broman). Lab. technician H.P. Hood & Sons, dairy, Boston, 1937-40; instr. bacteriology U. Wis.-Madison, 1940-44; research asst. Golden State Co. Ltd., dairy, San Francisco, 1944-45; head dept. bacteriology Kraftco Inc., Glenview, Ill., 1945-53, chief fundamental research, 1953-57, asso. mgr., 1957-60, div. research dir., 1960-64, dir. regulatory compliance, 1964-75; food cons., Ft. Myers, Fla., 1975—. Chmn. joint expert com. milk hygiene FAO/WHO, 1959; mem. expert adv. panel environ. health WHO, 1959-75. Mem. Am. Soc. Microbiology, Am. Dairy Sci. Assn., Assn. Food and Drug Ofcls., Internat. Assn. Milk, Food and Environ. Sanitarians (pres. 1958-59; citation 1962), Chemists Soc. S.W. Fla., Inst. Food Technologists, Sigma Xi. Author papers in field. Address: 1584 Cumberland Ct Fort Myers FL 33907

BARBER, JEFFREY BRUCE, hosp. adminstr.; b. Houston, June 19, 1944; s. Wilbur S. and Mary E. (Zischang) B.; B.A. in Psychology, U. Houston, 1970; postgrad. Va. Poly. Inst., 1974-75; M.B.A., U. Houston, 1979. Vol., program coordinator U.S. Peace Corps, Dominican Republic, 1966-69, dir., Venezuela, Chile, 1970-73; asso. dir. U.S. Sister City Program, Washington, 1974-76; dir. tng. and devel. Foodmaker, Inc., Houston, 1977-78; dir. personnel adminstrn. and devel. St. Joseph Hosp., Houston, 1978—; bus. cons., Houston and Washington, 1976-79. Mem. internat. activities com. Capital Area council Boy Scouts Am., Washington, 1975-76; bd. dirs. Springfield Village Homeowners Assn., 1975-76; v.p. Hemisports Internat. Cons. Service, 1974-79; mem. student adv. council U. Houston, 1970. Recipient Certificates of Appreciation, U.S., 1970, Am. Revolution Bicentennial Adminstrn., 1976, U.S. Sister City Program, 1976, Dominican Republic, 1969. Mem. Am. Soc. Tng. and Devel., Am. Mgmt. Assn., Tex. Hosp. Assn., Tex. Soc. Hosp. Educators, Adminstrv. Mgrs. Soc. Methodist. Home: 5212 Humble Camp Rd Dickinson TX 77539 Office: 1919 La Branch St Houston TX 77002

BARBER, RICHARD MARTIN, religious denomination exec.; b. Gainesville, Fla., May 10, 1926; s. George Allen and Emma Lucile (Martin) B.; B.A., U. Fla., 1950, M.Ed., 1962; M.Div., New Orleans Bapt. Sem., 1955; D.Ministry, Southeastern Baptist Sem., 1980; m. Dorothy Jean Matthews, Aug. 3, 1952; children—Christopher, Richard, Bruce, Chester, Sherri. Ordained to ministry, Southern Baptist Convention, 1948; pastor Pine Mount Bapt. Ch., Live Oak, Fla., 1948, Providence Village Bapt. Ch., Providence, Fla., 1948-55, Spring Park Bapt. Ch., Jacksonville, Fla., 1955-59; McIntosh (Fla.) Bapt. Ch., 1963-64; Southside Bapt. Ch., Lake City, Fla., 1964-67; Oak Griner Bapt. Ch., Ocala, Fla., 1967-71; dir. missions Santa Fe River Assn., Gainesville, Fla., 1971-76; dir. annuity dept. Fla. Bapt. Conv., Jacksonville, Fla., 1976—. Served with USMCR, 1944-46, 50-51. Mem. Lake City (Fla.) Ministerial Alliance (pres. 1966-67), Fellowship of Dirs. Missions of So. Bapt. Conv. Democrat. Home: 4033 St Isabel Dr E Jacksonville FL 32211 Office: 1230 Hendricks Ave Jacksonville FL 32207

BARBER, RICHARD PAUL, textile chemist; b. New Bedford, Mass., Apr. 12, 1928; s. Charles Joseph and Margaret (George) B.; B.S., Bradford-Durfee Tech. Inst., 1951; M.S., Inst. Textile Tech., 1953; M.S., SUNY Coll. Forestry, 1956; m. Martha Borden May, Apr. 2, 1955; 1 son, Richard Paul. Research chemist Inst. Textile Tech., Charlottesville, Va., 1953-55; research chemist, engr. Syracuse (N.Y.) U. Research Inst., 1957-59; dir. research Mooresville Mills (N.C.) div. Burlington Industries, 1960-74, dir. research and devel. Sportswear div., 1974-78. Nat. Starch fellow, 1955; grantee Am. Cyanamide Co., Allied Chem. Co. Fellow AAAS; mem. Am. Assn. Textile Chemists and Colorists (chmn. Piedmont sect. 1972, nat. council 1973-75), Am. Chem. Soc., N.C. Acad. Sci., Sigma Xi, Phi Lambda Upsilon, Alpha Chi Sigma, Epsilon Phi Phi. Roman Catholic. Clubs: Toastmasters (pres. Mooresville 1962), Elks. Researcher, patentee in field. Home: 805 Fieldstone Rd Mooresville NC 28115

BARBER, WILLIAM JOSEPH, SR., clergyman; b. Free Union Community, Jamesville, N.C., Mar. 21, 1927; s. Benjamin Luther and Lettice Ann (Keyes) B.; B.S., St. Augustine's Coll., 1949; M.S., Butler U., 1959; B.D., Christian Theol. Sem., 1959; certificate in adult edn. Ind. U., 1965; postgrad. Lexington Theol. Sem., 1977; certificate in clin. pastoral edn. John Umstead Mental Hosp., N.C., 1977; m. Eleanor Lucille Patterson, Nov. 25, 1961; children—William Joseph II, Charles Edger. Tchr. Warrenton (Ga.) High Sch., 1949-52; counselor Eastside Christian Center, Indpls., 1952-53; staff asst., cannery and gardens Flanner House, Indpls., 1954-59, work camp dir., 1954-59; field worker Washington (N.C.) 2nd Norfolk (Va.) dist. Disciples of Christ, 1958-59; social case worker Marion County Dept. Pub. Welfare, Indpls., 1955-57; ordained to ministry Christian Ch., 1956; student pastor Market St. Christian Ch., Carthage, Ind., 1954-57, High St. Christian Ch., Carlisle, Ky., also 2d Christian Ch., North Middletown, Ky., 1959-60; pastor, dir. Hillside Christian Center, Indpls., 1962-65; tchr. sci. and math. Booker T. Washington Jr. High Sch., Indpls., 1960-63; instr. adult evening sch. Crispus Atticus High Sch., Indpls., 1961-63; asso. campus minister, instr. dept. humanities Jarvis Christian Coll., Hawkins, Tex., 1965-66; field worker Tex. Christian Missionary Fellowship, Hawkins, 1965-66; interim pastor 2d Christian Ch., Farmville, N.C., 1968-70; tchr. math. and sci. Washington County (N.C.) schs., 1966-70; coordinator agrl. coops. Martin County Community Action, Inc., Williamston, N.C., 1970, econ. developer, 1971-73; asso. econ. devel. coordinator, 1973-77; energy coordinator Martin County Community Action, 1976-77. Historian, Eastern Seaboard, Gen. Assembly, Chs. of Christ, Disciples of Christ, 1952—, cons. minister, ednl., polit. and socio-econ. affairs Washington and Norfolk dist. assembly Disciples of Christ, 1968—, sec., trustee dist. assembly, 1977-78, chmn. bd. trustees dist. assembly, 1978—, gen. evangelist, chmn. com. on evangelism Gen. Assembly, 1973—. Chaplain Indpls. C.A.P., 1960-65. Founding mem. bd. dirs. Washington County Civic and Charitable Assn.; bd. dirs. Martin County Coop. Assn., Inc., Rodgers Community Produce and Products Coop., Inc., Martin Indsl. Devel. Assn., Inc., N.C. Fedn. Chil Devel. Centers, Inc., N.C. Community Action; adv. bd. N.C. Sr. Citizens Fedn., 1975—. Served with USNR, 1945-46. Mem. N.C. Folklore Soc., Disciples Christ Hist. Soc., Alpha Phi Alpha. Author: Disciple Assemblies of North Carolina. Home: PO Box 253 Free Union Community Jamesville NC 27846 Office: Washington (NC) and Norfolk (Va) Dist Assembly Disciples of Christ Inc PO Box 28 Roper NC 27970

BARBOUR, LAWRENCE CHARLES, textile co. exec.; b. Salem, Ill., Nov. 3, 1948; s. Richard Edelen and Marjorie Lee (Lange) B.; B.A. in History, The Citadel, 1975; m. Nancy Lynn Gamble, May 18, 1974. Shipping clk. United Parcel Service, Charleston, S.C., 1973-75; mgmt. trainee Milliken & Co., Saluda, S.C., 1975-76, shift mgr., 1976-77, mgr. texturing dept., 1977-80, quality control mgr., 1980—. Served with USN, 1967-71; Viet Nam. Republican. Roman Catholic. Clubs: Sertoma, U.S. Senatorial. Office: Route 4 Hwy 378 Saluda SC 29138

BARBOUR, ROBERT FRANKLIN, C.P.A., fin. exec.; b. Wirt, Okla., June 29, 1930; s. Frank Burney and Bonnie Caroline (Barton) B.; B.S., Okla. A. and M. Coll., 1955; m. Dolores Dawson, Nov. 23, 1950. Internal auditor Halliburton Oil Well Cementing Co., Duncan, Okla., 1955-58; comptroller Compania Halliburton de Cementacion Y Fomento, Maracaibo, Venezuela, S.Am., 1958-62; C.P.A., Harrison, Ark., 1962-73; fin. analyst Jobbers' Motor Supply Inc., Harrison, 1973-77, v.p., 1977—; with Guaranty Savs. and Loan Assn., Harrison, 1977—. Treas. John Paul Hammerschmidt re-election Com. to U.S. Ho. Reps., 1970-77. Served with U.S. Army, 1948-50. Mem. Am. Inst. C.P.A.'s, Ark. State Soc. C.P.A.'s, Am. Mgmt. Assn., Beta Alpha Psi. Democrat. Baptist. Lion. Home: Cottonwood Rd PO Box 35 Harrison AR 72601

BARBOUR, THOMAS D., oil refining and mfg. co. exec.; b. Tulsa, Aug. 19, 1928; s. Clifford Wayne and Ireane (Deane) B.; B.S.Ch.E., U. Okla., 1951; m. Charlene Gay Elliott, Aug. 4, 1950; children—Nancy Lamm, Thomas Deans. With Allied Materials Corp. (div. Entex Inc. 1979), 1950—, pres., Oklahoma City, 1969-79, pres., chmn. bd., 1979—; dir. Entex, Inc., Houston, Union Bank & Trust Co., Oklahoma City. Vice pres. Greater Oklahoma City YMCA. Served to 1st lt. USAF, 1951-53. Mem. Am. Petroleum Refiners Assn. (dir.), Ind. Petroleum Refiners Am. (dir.), Nat. Petroleum Refiners Assn. (dir.), Asphalt Roofing Mfrs. Assn. (dir.). Republican. Methodist. Clubs: Oklahoma City Golf and Country, Men's Dinner of Oklahoma City. Office: PO Box 12340 Oklahoma City OK 73157

BARCELLONA, WAYNE JOSEPH, biologist, educator; b. Chgo., Sept. 22, 1940; s. Anthony and Mamie (Griffin) B.; A.B., U. So. Calif., 1962, M.S., 1965, Ph.D., 1970; m. Joan Marie Gabriele, June 20, 1970; children—Margo Elaine, Mario David. Postdoctoral fellow U. Tex. M.D. Anderson Hosp., Houston, 1970-72; research asso. Med. Br., U. Tex., Galveston, 1972-73; asso. prof. biology Tex. Christian U., Ft. Worth, 1973—. Asso. dir. Ft. Worth Regional Sci. Fair, 1979—. NIH postdoctoral trainee, 1970-72. Mem. AAAS, Am. Inst. Biol. Scis., Am. Soc. Andrology, N.Y. Acad. Sci., Soc. Devel. Biology, Soc. for Study of Reprodn., Tex. Acad. Sci., Tex. Soc. Electron Microscopy. Office: Dept Biology Tex Christian U Fort Worth TX 76129

BARCELO, BRUCE EARL, info. systems cons.; b. Jacksonville, Fla., June 21, 1952; s. Mike Ramon and Gladyse W. (Passmore) B.; A.B. in Govt. and Urban Planning (Rufus Choate Scholar, Braitmeyer fellow), Dartmouth Coll., 1974; m. Mary Ann Magers, Apr. 8, 1978. Fin. mgr. Strickland's Restaurant, Jacksonville, 1974-76; cabinet aide, exec. asst. to sec. of state of Fla., Tallahassee, 1976-78; dir. mgmt. systems and planning Fla. Dept. State, 1978-79; sr. cons., prin. Documanagement Corp., Tallahassee, 1979—; asso. Thomas E. Norman and Assos., Tallahassee, 1979—. Mem. Assn. Records Mgrs. and Adminstrs. (dir. Tallahassee chpt.). Roman Catholic. Club: F.A.D.C. Home: 850 E College Ave Tallahassee FL 32301

BARCENAS, CAMILO GUSTAVO, physician; b. Managua, Nicaragua, Sept. 18, 1944; came to U.S., 1969; s. Camilo and Margarita (Levy) B.; M.D., U. Nicaragua, 1968; m. Aurora Cardenas, Dec. 22, 1969; children—Margarita, Marcela, Camilo. Intern, Managua (Nicaragua) Gen. Hosp., 1967-68, Mt. Sinai Hosp., U. Conn., 1969; resident internal medicine Baylor Coll. Medicine, Houston, 1970-72; chief resident St. Luke's Episcopal Hosp., Houston, 1971; chief resident VA Hosp., Houston, 1972; fellow nephrology U. Tex. Health Sci. Center, Dallas, 1972-74; practice medicine specializing in internal medicine, Dallas, 1974-76, Houston, 1976—; chief home dialysis unit VA Hosp., Dallas, 1974-75, chief hemodialysis unit, 1975; chief nephrology sect. St. Luke's Episcopal Hosp., Houston, 1976—; asst. prof. medicine U. Tex. Health Sci. Center, Dallas, 1974-75; clin. asst. prof. medicine Baylor Coll. Medicine, Houston, 1976-79, clin. asso. prof., 1979—. Gen. sec. Juventud Social Christiana, 1968. Diplomate Am. Bd. Internal Medicine. Fellow A.C.P.; mem. Internat. Soc. Nephrology, Houston Soc. Internal Medicine, Am. Soc. Nephrology, Harris County Med. Soc., Tex. Med. Assn., Colegio Medico Nicaraguense. Roman Catholic. Contbr. articles on nephrology to med. jours. Office: 6720 Bertner St Houston TX 77030

BARCINAS, GASPAR ZAMORAS, physician; b. Tagbilaran, Bohol, Philippines, Jan. 6, 1937; came to U.S., 1964, naturalized, 1980; M.D., Univ. of the East (Philippines), 1963; m. Maxima, 1964; children—Gaspar Zamoras, Gary, Grace, Gina. Intern, U. of East Hosp., Quezon City, Philippines, 1962-63; instr. biochemistry Univ. of the East Coll. Medicine, 1963-64; resident in gen. practice Robinson Meml. Hosp., Ravenna, Ohio, 1964-66; resident in gen. surgery St. Elizabeth Hosp., Youngstown, Ohio, 1966-70, chief resident, 1970; practice medicine specializing in gen. surgery, Bridgeport, W.Va., 1970—; chief of surgery United Hosp. Center, Clarksburg, W.Va., 1978-79; Diplomate Am. Bd. Family Practice. Mem. AMA, W.Va. Med. Assn., Am. Acad. Family Practice, Harrison County Med. Soc. (dir.). Republican. Roman Catholic. Contbr. article to med. jour. Home: PO Box 160 Bridgeport WV 26330 Office: 103 Doctors Dr Bridgeport WV 26330

BARCLAY, JAMES RALPH, psychologist, educator; b. Grand Rapids, Mich., May 6, 1926; s. Gordon William and Ruth Margaret (Christensen) B.; A.B., Sacred Heart Sem., Detroit, 1947; M.A., U. Mich., 1956, Ph.D., 1959; m. Lisa Kurez, Dec. 29, 1954; children—Anne, Robert, Gregory, Christopher. Tchr., Boy's Republic, Detroit, 1952-53; child welfare worker State of Minn., 1953-54; instr. dept. edn. U. Detroit, 1955-58; sch. psychologist Redford Univ. Schs., Detroit, 1956-59; vis. lectr. U. Mich., 1959; asst. prof., asso. prof., prof., dir. U. Counseling Center, Idaho State U., 1959-64; prof., coordinator Sch. Psychology Program, Calif. State Coll., Hayward, 1964-69; prof., chmn. dept. ednl. psychology and counseling U. Ky., Lexington, 1969—; cons. Idaho Dept. Edn., Oakland Schs., Louisville, U.S. Office Edn. Proposal Rev. Mem. Bd. Psychol. Examiners Idaho., 1962-64; pres. Ednl. Skills Devel., Inc., Lexington. Diplomate Am. Bd. Profl. Examiners in Psychology. Fellow Am. Psychol. Assn. (exec. com.); mem. Am. Ednl. Research Assn., Am. Personnel and Guidance Assn., Phi Delta Kappa. Author: Counseling Psychology and Philosophy, 1968; Controversial Issues in Testing, 1968; Foundations of Counseling Strategies, 1971; editorial cons. Measurement and Evaluation in Guidance, 1969-73, Personnel and Guidance Jour., 1972-75, Sch. Psychology Digest, Jour. Sch. Psychology; editor Personnel and Guidance Jour., 1978—; contbr. articles to profl. jours. Home: 1672 Linstead Dr Lexington KY 40504

BARCUS, SAMUEL WRIGHT, III, mgmt. cons. co. exec.; b. Temple, Tex., July 24, 1946; s. Samuel Wright and Frances B.; B.B.A., U. Tex., 1971; M.B.A., U. Houston, 1974. Bus. systems analyst Tex. Instruments, Dallas, 1971-74; dir. planning and systems Symbiotics Internat., Houston, 1974-76; Sr. mgr. Price Waterhouse & Co., Nashville, 1976—. Chmn. fin. com. Versailles Townhome Owners Assn., Nashville, 1979—. Mem. Planning Execs. Inst. (pres. Nashville chpt. 1979-80), Assn. Systems Mgmt. (dir. Nashville chpt. 1979-80). Clubs: Md. Farms Racquet, Cumberland. Home: 3000 Hillsboro Rd #77 Nashville TN 37215 Office: First American Center Nashville TN 37238

BARCZAK, VIRGIL JOSEPH, mineralogist; b. Toledo, Ohio, Nov. 29, 1931; s. Joseph Anthony and Rosalie (Obarski) B.; B.S., U. Mich., 1958, M.S., 1959; M.E.A. in Indsl. Mgmt., Oklahoma City U., 1966; m. Patricia Kathleen Sullivan, June 6, 1959; children—Kathleen, Steven, David, Thomas. Research petrographer ceramic div. Champion Spark Plug Co., Detroit, 1959-64; research mineralogist Kerr-McGee Corp., Oklahoma City, 1964—. Served with USMC, 1952-55. Fellow Geol. Soc. Am.; mem. Mineral. Soc. Am., Mineral. Assn. Can., Am. Ceramic Soc. (co-recipient Ross Coffin Purdy award 1966), Am. Inst. Ceramic Engrs. Contbr. articles to profl. jours. Home: 2500 NW 109th St Oklahoma City OK 73120 Office: Kerr-McGee Corp Tech Center Oklahoma City OK 73102

BARDILL, DONALD RAY, army officer; b. Lancing, Tenn., Nov. 4, 1934; s. Martin C. and Vema E. (Wells) B.; student Centre Coll., 1953-55; B.A., U. Tenn., 1956, M.S. in Social Work, 1958; D. Social Work, Smith Coll., 1967; m. Norma J. Garrett, Sept. 15, 1956; children—Amy Jean, Amanda Jane. Commd. 2d lt. Med. Service Corps, U.S. Army, 1958, advanced through grades to lt. col., 1973; chief social work service Walter Reed Gen. Hosp., Washington, 1968-70, researcher Walter Reed Army Inst. Research, 1970-71, asst. chief psychiatry dept., 1971-73, acting chief dept., 1973-75, dir. edn. and tng. Social Work Service, 1975-78; prof. Fla. State U., Tallahassee, 1978—, also dean; cons. health sers. sect. Gen. Motors Corp., 1976—, prof., Nat. Cath. Sch. Social Service, Washington, 1968-78; mem. faculty Smith Coll., Northampton, Mass., 1974-75; cons. family therapy D.C. Family and Child Services, 1967-71. Fellow Nat. Assn. Social Workers; mem. Am. Assn. Marriage and Family Therapists, Acad. Certified Social Workers, Am. Group Psychotherapy Assn., Am. Family Therapy Assn., Council Social Work Edn. Author: Family Group Casework, 1964; Thank God I'm a Teenager, 1976. Home: 3022 Fermanagh Dr Tallahassee FL Office: Sch Social Work Fla State U Tallahassee FL 32308

BARDT, NATHAN NORMAN, pub. accountant; b. Bklyn., Nov. 29, 1922; s. Andrew S. and Fannie (Tolkan) B.; B.B.A., Pace Coll., 1950; Ph.D. (hon.), Colo State Christian Coll.; m. Patricia Faber, June 19, 1949; children—David R., Allison Sue, Leslie Ellen. Individual practice accounting, Rockville Centre, N.Y. Cons. on estate planning. Served with Signal Corps, AUS, 1941-44. Mem. Am. Inst. C.P.A.'s, N.Y. State Soc. C.P.A.'s, Fla. Inst. C.P.A.'s. Nat. Soc. Pub. Accountants, Accountants Assn. N.Y. (trustee 1957), Empire State Assn. Pub. Accountants, Tax Inst. Lion (treas. 1961-62); mem. B'nai B'rith. Home: 3310 S Ocean Blvd Highland Beach FL 33431 Office: 119 N Park Ave Rockville Centre NY 11570

BARDWELL, ANN SKINNER, family and child devel. specialist; b. Lexington, Ky., Jan. 2, 1930; d. Richard Norton and Ethel Margaret (Barnes) Skinner; B.S., U. Ky., 1953; M.S., Ohio State U., 1965, Ph.D., 1968; div.; children—Robert E., Carolyn Ann. Family devel. specialist Ohio State U., 1967-69, chief of home econs., asso. prof. Nisonger Center and Sch. Home Econs., 1969-74; program dir. Nelsonville Children's Center, Nelsonville, Ohio, 1974-75; chairperson Dept. Home Econs., Eastern Ky. State U., 1975-77; pres. AB Assos., Human Services Cons.'s, Lexington, Ky., 1977—. Treas., Democrats for Fayette County, 1979-80; bd. dirs. Columbus (Ohio) Planned Parenthood, Mountain Maternal Health, Berea, Ky. Mem. Am. Assn. Mental Deficiency (chairperson gen. sect. 1978-79), Am. Home Econs. Assn. (chmn. rehab. com. 1970-73), Ohio Council Family Relations, So. Assn. Children Under Six, Am. Home Econs. Assn., Ky. Home Econs. Assn., Southeastern Assn. Mental Deficiency, Nat. Assn. Edn. Young Children. Democrat. Presbyterian. Club: Quota. Address: 3163 Richmond Rd RFD #5 Lexington KY 40511

BAREFIELD, PAUL ACTON, educator; b. Mobile, Ala., Sept. 3, 1938; s. Collis W. and Eula Mae (Acton) B.; B.A., Samford U., Birmingham, Ala., 1960; M.A., L. State U., Baton Rouge, 1962, Ph.D., 1966; m. Catherine Elaine Saladin, Dec. 20, 1963; children—Kirsten Wells, Quinn Acton, Eric Kelly. Asst. prof., dir. forensics Moorhead (Minn.) State Coll., 1964-66; asst. prof. communication, dir. forensics, dir. forum U. Okla., Norman, 1966-70, asso. prof., 1970-77; prof. head dept. speech U. Southwestern La., Lafayette, 1977—; sr. asso. Situation Dynamics, Inc., Crofton, Md., and Balt., 1971-72; lectr., condr. workshops. Postdoctoral research grantee U. Okla. Found., 1969. Mem. Speech Communication Assn., So. Speech Communication Assn., Central States Speech Communication Assn., La. Speech Communication Assn., Am. Studies Assn., Am. Soc. Tng. and Devel., Omicron Delta Kappa, Phi Kappa Phi, Delta Sigma Rho, Tau Kappa Alpha. Contbr. articles profl. jours; cons. editor So. Speech Jour. Home: 220 Woodvale St Lafayette LA 70503 Office: PO Box 43650 U Southwestern La Lafayette LA 70504

BAREFOOT, SHERWOOD WASHINGTON, physician; b. Benson, N.C., July 24, 1913; s. Allen Leon and Emma Kitsey (Tart) B.; B.S., U. N.C., 1936; M.D., Duke U., 1938; m. Christine Long, Mar. 20, 1937; children—Sherwood Washington, Susan Waters. Intern, resident in medicine/dermatology Duke U. Med. Center, Durham, N.C., 1938-40, fellow in dermatology, 1945-47; research fellow in chemotherapy Bellevue Hosp., N.Y.C., 1940-41; practice medicine specializing in dermatology, Greensboro, N.C., 1947—; clin. asso. in dermatology Duke U. Med. Sch., 1947—; asso. clin. prof. dermatology U. N.C. Med. Sch., 1970—; mem. staff Wesley Long Hosp.; cons. Greensboro Hosp.; mem. staff, pres. med. bd. Moses H. Cone Hosp. Bd. dirs. Fellowship Hall, 1969—. Served from 1st lt. to maj., M.C., AUS, 1941-46: ETO. Mem. AMA, Am. Acad. Dermatology, N. Am. Clin. Dermatol. Soc., N.C. Med. Soc., Guilford County Med. Soc. (pres. 1969). Contbr. articles to profl. jours. Home: 3107 Madison Ave Greensboro NC 27403 Office: 1030 Professional Village Greensboro NC 27401

BARFIELD, ARNOLD BARTO, JR., oil co. exec.; b. Texarkana, Tex., Apr. 27, 1931; s. Arnold Barto and Mildred Ione (Elliott) B.; B.S. in Agrl. Econs., Tex. A. & M. Coll., 1958; m. Ruby Rose Britzman, Dec. 30, 1959; children—Brenda Renee, Arnold Barto III. Pres., Barfield's Furniture and Butane Co., New Boston, Maud, Tex., 1958—; distbr. Gulf Oil Co., New Boston, Tex., 1970—, Clarksville, Tex., 1973—, mem. govt. advt. council, 1976—. Mem. sch. bd., New Boston, Tex., 1962—. Served with M.C., U.S. Army, 1952-56. Mem. Tex. Farm Bur., Tex. LP Gas Assn., Tex. Oil Marketers Assn., Tex. Retail Furniture Assn., Tex. Brahman Assn., Pan Am. Zebu Assn., New Boston C. of C. Clubs: Lions, Masons, Shriners. Home: 309 Runnels St New Boston TX 75570 Office: Hwy 8 N New Boston TX 75570

BARFIELD, BOURDON REA, banker; b. Amarillo, Tex., Oct. 28, 1926; s. Bourdon Ivy and Oliver Rea (Eakle) B.; B.B.A., U. Tex., 1951; m. Carolyn Grissom, Jan. 4, 1951; children—Deyanne, Amanda, Bourdon Ivy, John Callaway. Vice pres. Barfield Corp., Amarillo, 1951-57, pres., 1957—; dir. Mr. Burger Inc.; pres. Pembrooke Corp., Amarillo, 1969—, Guaranty Mortgage Corp., Amarillo. Mem. Durett Scholarship Com. Amarillo Pub. Schs., 1951—; area chmn. Crusade for Freedom, 1957; pres. Amarillo Symphony Orch., 1959-61; chmn. Citizens' Action Program, Amarillo, 1961-63; mem. exec. com. U. Tex. Dads' Assn., 1975—; mem. dist. Democratic Congressional Campaign Com., 1962-65, chmn., 1969; bd. dirs. Dallas Civic Opera, 1962, St. Andrew's Day Sch., Amarillo, 1962, Family Service Inc., Amarillo, 1969, Amarillo Art Center, 1972—; chmn. bd. dirs. Amarillo Pub. Library, 1963. Recipient Young Man of Year award Jr. C. of C., 1960, award of Honor Downtown Amarillo Unltd. for Redevel. Work., 1966. Mem. Amarillo (pres. 1961), U.S. (dir. civic devel. com. 1960) chambers commerce, Jovian, 49ers, Beta Theta Pi. Episcopalian (lay reader, vestryman 1958-61). Clubs: Masons (32 deg.), Rotary, Amarillo Country, Palo Duro. Home: 3201 Ong St Amarillo TX 79109 Office: 1620 Tyler St Amarillo TX 79105

BARFIELD, LOUISE LOGAN, educator, concert pianist; b. Macon, Ga., Feb. 17, 1944; d. Ernest Michael and Helen Logan (Clisby) B.; student Wesleyan Conservatory Sch. Fine Arts, Macon; 1950-62; A.A., Stephens Coll., 1964, B.F.A., 1965; dip. Juilliard Sch. Music, 1967, M.S., 1968; student Aspen Sch. Music, summer 1966, Conservatorio di Santa Cecilia (Rome), 1968-69, Academia di Chigiana (Siena, Italy), summer 1969, Temple U., summer 1971, Tanglewood Inst. Music, summer 1972. Faculty piano Marymount Internat. Sch., Rome, 1969-70, Wesleyan Coll., Macon, Ga., 1974-77; faculty of piano Mercer U., Macon, 1978—; pvt. teaching piano, Macon, 1970—; lectr. in field; adjudicator for piano competitions, 19——; classical record critic The Audio Jour., 1978—; concert tour, Brazil, summer 1980. Recipient Joseph Maerz award, Macon, 1962; Emetaz scholar, Stephens Coll., 1963-65; Sigma Gamma Gamma scholar, Stephens Coll., 1964-65; William G. Helis Found. scholar, The Juilliard Sch., 1965-68, Edward Bromberg scholar, 1967-68; Fulbright-Hays grantee, Rome, 1968-70; Michael Vinciguerra grantee, 1969-70 (Rome); Boston U. scholar, 1972; Internat. Acad. Nice (France) scholar, 1979. Mem. Macon Piano Tchrs. Guild, Ga. Music Tchrs. Assn., Macon Concert Assn. (dir. 1978-81), Macon Music Tchrs. Assn., Soc. of Colonial Dames of Am. (mem. Macon town com.), Jr. League of Macon. Christian Scientist. Clubs: Macon Morning Music (pres. 1980-81), Macon, Federated Music. Home: 711 Forest Hill Rd Macon GA 31210 Office: 1400 Coleman Ave Macon GA 31201

BARGEON, HERBERT ALEXANDER, JR., lawyer; b. Fayetteville, N.C., May 23, 1934; s. Herbert Alexander and Violet (Geilfuss) B.; B.S. in Bus. Adminstrn., U. Va., 1956; LL.B., U. Fla., 1968; m. Gail Freer, Mar. 14, 1963; children—Brett Elizabeth (by previous marriage), Herbert Alexander III, Violet Gail. Admitted to Fla. bar. Pres., chmn. bd. Royal Poinciana Playhouse, Palm Beach, Fla. Served to 2d lt. AUS, 1957. Mem. Am. Bar Assn. Republican. Presbyterian. Club: Poinciana (Palm Beach). Home: 256 Palmo Way Palm Beach FL 33480 also Barker's Creek Whittier NC 28789 Office 70 Royal Poinciana Plaza Palm Beach FL 33480

BARGER, WILLIAM JOSEPH, advt. exec.; b. Rahway, N.J., Apr. 28, 1944; s. William Early and Eve F. Barger; A.B., Hope Coll., Holland, Mich., 1966; M.B.A., Western Mich. U., 1968; 1 son, William Charles. With advt. and sales dept. Gen. Foods Corp., 1968-71, Ralston-Purina Co., 1971-75; pres. Nashville Sound Studios Inc., 1975—. Mem. Country Music Assn., Nat. Assn. Broadcasters. Presbyterian. Composer numerous mus. pieces. Office: 1719 West End St Nashville TN 37203

BARGINEAR, JO GRACE, counselor; b. Pearsall, Tex., June 26, 1941; d. Edward Frederick and Helen Mildred (Young) Earnest; A.A., Victoria Jr. Coll., 1961; B.S., U. Houston, 1964, M.Ed., 1967. Tchr. spl. edn. Lampkin Elem. Sch., Cypress-Fairbanks (Tex.) Ind. Sch. Dist., 1964-68, M.R. Wood Sch., Ft. Bend Ind. Sch. Dist., 1968-75; counselor Blue Ridge Elem. Sch., Ft. Bend Dist., 1975—. Named Outstanding Tchr., 1976-77. Mem. NEA, Tex. Tchrs. Assn., Tex. Classroom Tchrs. Assn., Am. Personnel and Guidance Assn. Methodist. Home: 5203 Heatherbook St Houston TX 77045 Office: 500 Dulles Ave Stafford TX 77477

BARHAM, CHARLES CLEM, lawyer, state senator; b. Ruston, La., Apr. 20, 1934; s. Charles Emmett and Carice (Hilburn) B.; B.A., La. Tech. U., 1956; LL.B., La. State U., 1958, J.D., 1968; m. Jo Ann Frasier, Aug. 10, 1954; children—Karla Ann, Charles Emmett, Lori. Mem. firm Barham, Wright & Barham, Ruston, 1958-73; partner firm Barham, Campbell and Adkins, Ruston, 1973-75, firm Barham, Adkins & Coleman, Ruston, 1975—; dir. 1st Nat. Bank of Ruston; mem. La. State Senate, 1964-72, 76—. Mem. Lincoln Parish Bar Assn., Am. Bar Assn., La. Bar Assn., La. Trial Lawyers Assn., Am. Trial Lawyers Assn. Democrat. Methodist. Office: 101 S Trenton St Ruston LA 71270

BARHAM, JAMES WESLEY, educator; b. Shidler, Okla., Nov. 29, 1947; s. Claybern Oscar and Ruth Lee (Longley) B.; B.S. in Edn., Kans. State Coll., 1969; M.S. in Edn., Northeastern State U., Tahlequah, Okla., 1977; m. Marcia Marie Snow, June 21, 1969; children—James Wesley II, Claybern Douglas. Tchr., Vera (Okla.) Public Schs., 1969-70; tchr. Justus Public Sch., Claremore, Okla., 1970—, asst. prin., 1979—. Deacon, lay minister Meml. Heights Baptist Ch., Claremore. Mem. NEA, Okla. Edn. Assn., Kappa Delta Pi, Pi Alpha Theta. Democrat. Home: 304 Falletti St Claremore OK 74017 Office: PO Box 864 Claremore OK 74017

BARHAM, ROBERT LEE, utility co. exec.; b. Haw River, N.C., June 20, 1938; s. Athel Birch and Sudie Mae (Rorer) B.; A.B., Elon Coll., 1963; M.S., N.C. State U., 1969, postgrad., 1969, 70, 71; m. Betsy Anne Carden, Sept. 1, 1963; 1 dau., Robin Anne. Tchr., N.C. schs., 1963-70; asso. dean for continuing edn. Durham Tech. Inst., 1970-73; mem. recruiting, mgmt. devel. and benefits adminstrn. staff Carolina Power & Light Co., Asheville, N.C., 1973-78, div. personnel rep., 1979—; cons. tech. sch. curriculum design N.C., S.C., 1973-77. Mem. adv. bd., community vol. Durham County (N.C.) Dept. Corrections, 1971; mem. Asheville Mayor's Com. on Employment of the Handicapped. Mem. Asheville Area C. of C. (mem. legis. affairs com.), Am. Soc. Personnel Adminstrn., Western N.C. Personnel Assn., N.C. Cooperative Edn. Assn. (past pres.), Phi Kappa Phi. Republican. Mem. United Ch. of Christ. Clubs: Valley Springs Lions; Burlington Toastmasters (pres. 1962), Burlington Sertoma (chmn. bd. dirs. 1963); West Raleigh Exchange. Home: 20 Tuckaway Dr Asheville NC 28803 Office: PO Box 15240 Asheville NC 28803

BARINKA, LAWRENCE LOUIS, mathematician; b. Oak Park, Ill., Nov. 21, 1939; s. Ludvik R. and Marie R. Barinka; B.S.E., U. Mich., 1962, M.S.E., 1963; Ph.D., U. Va., 1972; m. Sandra Rae Deitrich, June 11, 1960; 1 dau., Karen Diane. Research engr. Beloit (Wis.) Corp., 1963-66; sr. engr. Babcock & Wilcox, Lynchburg, Va., 1966-70, sr. mathematician, 1970-73, mgr. applied math., 1973—; session chmn. Internat. Conf. Structural Mechanics, Berlin, 1971; mem. standards com. Am. Nat. Standards Inst., 1979—. NSF fellow, 1968-69; registered profl. engr., Va. Mem. ASME, Assn. Computing Machinery, Am. Nuclear Soc. (Cert. of Appreciation 1979, standards com. 1977—, gen. chmn. biennial topical meeting, Williamsburg, Va. 1979), Soc. Indsl. and Applied Math., Sigma Xi. Club: Fripp Island Beach. Author tech. papers in applied math. and mechanics. Home: 3301 Sky View Pl Lynchburg VA 24503 Office: PO Box 1260 Lynchburg VA 24505

BARKER, A. CLIFFORD, electronics co. exec.; b. Phoenix, June 7, 1933; s. Alva Clifford and Gertrude Theresa (Gertzen) B.; B.S. with highest honors in Engring. (W. Coast Electronics Mfrs. Assn. scholar), U. Calif., Los Angeles, 1959, M.S., 1962; m. Shirley Ray Mueller, May 30, 1975; children—Alexandra Caton, Adrienne Caren. Tech. staff Litton Industries, Beverly Hills, Calif., 1959-63; dir. advanced navigation systems Teledyne Systems Co., Hawthorne, Calif., 1963-67; exec. v.p. Internat. Engring. Co., Arlington, Va., 1967-70; v.p. Teledyne Hastings-Raydist, Hampton, Va., 1970-73; pres., chmn. bd. Navidyne Corp., Hampton, 1973—. Mem. nat. council John Birch Soc., 1968—; first violinist with Peninsula Symphony Orch., 1970—. Served with USMC, 1953-56. Recipient Tau Beta Pi Most Outstanding Student award, U. Calif., Los Angeles, 1959. Mem. Inst. Navigation, IEEE, Internat. Omega Assn. (treas., bd. dirs. 1975), Tau Beta Pi. Contbr. articles on marine and airborne navigation systems to publs.; patentee in field of electronic navigation systems. Home: 46 James River Ln Newport News VA 23606 Office: 11824 Fishing Point Dr Newport News VA 23606

BARKER, CHARLES LAWRENCE, physician; b. Murfreesboro, Tenn., Sept. 27, 1946; s. Joe Don and Dorothy Mae (McBroom) B.; B.S., Middle Tenn. State U., 1968, M.S., 1970; Ph.D., Baylor U., 1973; M.D., U. Tenn., 1978; m. JoAnn Dolezal, July 13, 1974; children—Joseph Lawrence, Michael Glen. Instr. chemistry McLennan Community Coll., Waco, Tex., 1970-72; instr. chemistry Mary Hardin-Baylor Coll., Belton, Tex., 1972, asst. prof., 1973-74, chmn. dept., 1974-75; intern in medicine City of Memphis Hosp., 1978-79, resident in obstetrics-gynecology, 1979—. Robert A. Welch fellow, 1970-73. Mem. AMA, Am. Chem. Soc., Sigma Xi, Sigma Nu. Republican. Baptist. Home: 21 Neely St Apt 101 Memphis TN 38105 Office: City of Memphis Hospital 860 Madison Ave Memphis TN 38104

BARKER, JOHANNA MCGRAW, sch. counselor; b. Shreveport, La., Mar. 13, 1947; d. John Boyd and Anna Holmes (Hinckley) McGraw; B.S., Centenary Coll. of La., 1968; M.Ed., Northwestern State U., 1972, postgrad. 1974; m. James Arthur Barker, Aug. 10, 1968; 1 son, John Thurston. Tchr. lang. arts, social studies Lakeshore Jr. High Sch., Shreveport, 1968-71; tchr. lang. arts J.S. Clark Jr. High Sch., Shreveport, 1971-73; elem. career counselor Caddo Parish Schs., Shreveport, 1973-74; Title I elem. counselor 32 schs., 1974-78, sec. counselor, 1978-79; counselor Broadmoor Jr. High Sch., Shreveport, 1979—; conductor various summer workshops; cons. in field; presentor program Am. Personnel and Guidance conv., 1979. Area chmn. ticket sales Shreveport Symphony, 1979-80. Mem. La. Vocat. Guidance Assn., Caddo Sch. Counselors Assn., Caddo Assn. Educators, Am. Personnel and Guidance Assn., Chi Omega, Alpha Delta Kappa. Democrat. Presbyterian. Club: Caddo Parish Adminstrs. Contbr. articles in field to profl. jours. Home: 613 Jonathan Clay Dr Shreveport LA 71106 Office: 441 Atlantic St Shreveport LA 71105

BARKER, KENNETH RAY, educator; b. Memphis, Oct. 30, 1939; s. Ray Whitman and Etta Mae (Sexton) B.; B.S. Southwestern U., Memphis, 1961; M.S., U. Miss., 1963; Ph.D., U. Tex., 1966; m. Marilyn Ann Koteras, May 22, 1971; children—Ray Clinton, Dara Lorraine. Instr. cell biology U. Tex., Austin, 1966, NIH fellow, 1967; research fellow U. Witwatersrand, Johannesburg, S. Africa, 1968; asso. prof. biology Canisius Coll. Buffalo, 1969-80; vis. prof. U. Tex. at Austin, 1976-77. Served with M.C., U.S. Army, 1958. Sigma Xi grantee, 1963-64; Am. Philos. Soc. grantee, 1967-68; Am. Heart Assn. grantee, 1967-68. Mem. AAAS, Am. Cell Biology, Can. Soc. Genetics. Author: A Lab Manual of Comparative Anatomy; contbr. articles to profl. jours. Home: 209 W Barton Ave Greenwood MS 38930

BARKER, PAUL LAWRENCE, counseling specialist; b. Oakland, Calif., June 15, 1947; s. L.V. and Dorothy Evelyn (Worden) B.; B.A., Miss. Coll., 1969; M.Ed., Miss. State U., 1974; m. Teresa Mynelle Terry, July 8, 1967; children—Micheal, Jeffery, Sharon. Employment counselor III, Miss. Employment Security Commn., Meridian, 1969-77, state counseling specialist, Jackson, 1977—. Mem. Am. Personnel and Guidance Assn., Nat. Employment Counselors Assn., Internat. Assn. Personnel Employment Security, Miss. Employment Counselors Assn. (pres. 1978), Miss. Personnel and Guidance Assn. (dir. 1978), Clinton Jaycees (dir. 1979; citation 1978). Baptist. Home: 101 Trailwood Dr Clinton MS 39056 Office: 1520 W Capital St Jackson MS 39205

BARKER, STEPHEN LEE, mfg. co. exec.; b. New Kensington, Pa., May 30, 1941; s. Erwin H. and Mildred F. Barker; B.Engring. Sci., Fenn Coll., 1964; m. Patricia S. Sullivan, Apr. 9, 1977; children—Raymond, Michael, Bridget. Coop. student, application engr. Johnson Controls, Inc., Cleve., 1960-64, sales engr., Louisville, 1964-70, sales engr., Pitts., 1970-76, br. mgr., Charleston, W.Va., 1976—; dir. Energy Holdings, Inc. Mem. ASHRAE. Republican. Jewish. Club: Rotary (sec., v.p., pres.). Home: 1506 Rockford Ct Charleston WV 25314 Office: Box 8543 South Charleston WV 25303

BARKER, THOMAS LEE, city ofcl.; b. WestPoint, Ga., July 29, 1912; s. Novatus Lee and Lillian (Croft) B.; student Ala. Poly. Inst., 1942, U. Ga., 1965; m. Martha Elizabeth Hooten, June 29, 1933; children—Carolyn Croft Barker Scott, Diane Woodfin, Martha Ann Barker Rogers. Insp., West Point Mfg. Co., Fairfax, Ga., 1934-35; supt. Nat. Life and Accident Co., 1935-45; safety dir. Kilby Steel, 1941-47, ins. bus., 1947-54; salesman Anniston Hardware Co., 1954-62; mgr. Anniston Housing Authority, 1962-74, exec. dir., 1974—. Instr., ARC, 1952, chmn. bd. Faith Sch., Anniston; ruling elder Presbyterian Ch., 1962—. Served with Army NG, 1929-31. Mem. Nat. Assn. Housing and Redevel. Ofcls. (chmn. public relations com. Southeastern Regional Council), Public Housing Authorities/Dirs. Assn., Anniston C. of C., Ala. Assn. Housing and Redevelopment Authorities. Clubs: Masons, Civitan (sec. treas.). Patentee stencil attachment for tire setter, automatic stop for textile inspection machine. Home: 2 Alice Ridge Rd Anniston AL 36201 Office: 500 Glen Addie Ave Anniston AL 36202

BARKER, WILLIAM DANIEL, hosp. adminstr.; b. New Orleans, July 21, 1926; s. William Daniel and Ada (Will) B.; B.B.A., Emory U., 1949; M.H.A., Ga. State U., 1966; m. Nancy Pool, Sept. 23, 1949; children—Nancy Louise, Julia Ann, William Daniel, III, Marion DeVilbus. Asst. adminstr. Griffin (Ga.) Spalding County Hosp., 1950-51; adminstr. Winder (Ga.) Barrow Hosp., 1951-52; cons. Ga. Dept. Public Health, Atlanta, 1952-55; bus. mgr. John L. Hutcheson Meml. Hosp., Ft. Oglethorpe, Ga., 1955-56, asst. adminstr., 1956-60; asst. dir. Crawford W. Long Meml. Hosp. of Emory U., 1960-72, adminstr., 1972—; dir. Ga. Savs. & Loan Assn., Blue Cross Blue Shield of Atlanta; trustee Woodruff Med. Center of Emory U.; asso. prof. preventive medicine and community health Emory U. Sch. Medicine, 1978—. Deacon, Second Ponce de Leon Baptist Ch., Atlanta. Served with U.S. Army, 1944-46. Decorated Bronze Star; recipient R. C. Williams award Ga. State U., 1966, Disting. Alumni award Ga. State U. Alumni Assn., 1979. Fellow Am. Coll. Hosp. Adminstrs. (Ga. regent 1972-75); mem. Am. Hosp. Assn. (chmn. bd. trustees 1979), Ga. Hosp. Assn. (pres. 1966-67), Hosp. Fin. Mgmt. Assn. (pres. Ga. chpt. 1957). Clubs: Kiwanis, Ansley Golf (Atlanta). Home: 50 South Prado Atlanta GA 30309 Office: 35 Linden Ave Atlanta GA 30308

BARKER, WILLIAM MCKINLEY, textile co. exec.; b. Alva, Okla., May 25, 1931; s. Elisha McKinley and Ruby Louisa (Branch) B.; student accounting Palmer Bus. Coll., 1956-59; m. Ann Gloria Usry, Sept. 3, 1949; children—William Wayne, John McKinley, David Branch. Cost accountant John P. King Mfg. Co., Augusta, Ga., 1955-57; div. controller Riegel Textile Corp., Johnston, S.C., 1957-67, Ware Shoals, S.C., 1967-70, Trion, Ga., 1970-76, adminstrv. mgr., Fries, Va., 1977—. Sec. treas. Trion (Ga.) Community Found., 1970-76; state exec. committeeman Edgefield County (S.C.) Republican Party, 1963-64; treas. Chattooga County (Ga.) Presbyn. Ministries, 1974-76. Mem. Data Processing Mgmt. Assn. (local pres. 1967), Galax-Carroll-Grayson C. of C. (pres. 1979). Home: 502 W Stuart Dr Galax VA 24333 Office: Fries Textile Co Fries VA 24330

BARKIN, JAMIE STEVEN, physician; b. N.Y.C., June 1, 1943; s. Arthur and Mazie G. (Tannenbaum) B.; M.D., U. Miami (Fla.), 1970. Intern, U. Miami Affiliated Hosps., 1970-71, med. resident, 1971-73, fellow in gastroenterology, 1973-75, asst. prof. medicine, div. gastroenterology, 1975—, asst. prof. dept. oncology, 1978—; mem. attending active staff Jackson Meml. Hosp., VA Hosp., U. Miami Hosps. and Clinics. Served as maj., M.C., U.S. Army, 1971—. Diplomate Am. Bd. Internal Medicine, Am. Bd. Gastroenterology. Recipient award VA, 1977. Fellow Am. Coll. Gastroenterology, A.C.P.; mem. Am. Soc. Internal Medicine, Am. Soc. Gastrointestinal Endoscopy, Fla. Soc. Gastrointestinal Endoscopy (v.p. 1978), Am. Pancreatic Soc., AMA, So. Med. Assn., Am. Gastroenterol. Assn., Alpha Omega Alpha. Contbr. articles on gastroenterology to profl. jours. and books. Office: U Miami Sch Medicine Div Gastroenterology PO Box 520875 Miami FL 33152

BARKLEY, CAROLYN ESTHER, broadcasting exec.; b. Austin, Tex., Nov. 21, 1944; d. Edward M. and Hermine Winifred (Pearce) Barkley; B.J., U. Tex. at Austin, 1967. Pub. information specialist City Austin (Tex.) Parks and Recreation Dept., 1967-69; community info. coordinator City Austin City Mgr.'s Office, 1969-70, City Austin Pub. Info. Dept., 1970; dedication office staff mem. L.B. Johnson Library Dedication Office, U. Tex. at Austin, 1971; spl. asst. to campaign dirs. Dolph Briscoe for Gov. State Hdqrs., Austin, 1972; dir. pub. relations United Way Capital Area, Austin, 1973-76; sales account exec. Sta. KTVV-TV, Austin, 1976—. Del. Travis County Dem. Conv., 1968, 72; alt. del. Tex. Dem. Conv., 1974; bd. dirs. Austin YWCA, 1979—. Named Miss Austin Aqua Beauty, Austin Aqua Festival, 1970, Top Salesman in Austin, 1978. Mem. Austin Advt. Club (sec.-treas. 1979-80). Democrat. Home: 2501 E St Elmo Rd Austin TX 78744 also 1200 Kenwood Ave Austin TX 78704 Office: 908 W Martin Luther King Blvd PO Box 490 Austin TX 78767

BARKLEY, G. RICHARD, elec. engr.; b. Lucerne, Mo., July 15, 1934; s. George Austin and Velma Geneveve (Lowry) B.; B.E.E., Okla. State U., 1960; children—Yvonne, Travis, Robin. With Gen. Dynamics Co., San Diego, Calif., 1960-70, field engr., 1960-62, sci. computer programmer, 1963, electromagnetic compatability engr., 1964-70; motel owner, mgr., Sedalia, Mo., 1970-75; research engr. underwater acoustics devel. program Applied Research Lab., Austin, Tex., 1976—. Served with Signal Corps, U.S. Army, 1954-57. Registered profl. engr., Tex. Mem. IEEE. Home: 1406 Massengale Round Rock TX 78664 Office: PO Box 8029 Austin TX 78712

BARKLEY, PAUL HALEY, JR., architect; b. Washington, Sept. 24, 1937; s. Paul Haley and Mary Barrett (Brewer) B.; B.Arch., U. Va., 1960; student Ecoles d'Art Americaines, Fontainebleau, France, 1959; m. Jeanette Frances Nickerson, Dec. 20, 1975. Archtl. designer Strang & Childers, Architects, Annandale, Va., 1960-61; project designer Alan J. Lockman, Architect, Washington, 1962-63; design asso. D.G. Chase & Assos., Architects, Alexandria, Va., 1964; partner Barkley Pierce Assos., Architects & Planners, Falls Church, Va., 1965-79, Barkley Pierce O'Malley, Falls Church, 1980—; lectr. architecture U. Va. Div. Continuing Edn., 1966—. Mem. bd. archtl. rev. Town of Vienna (Va.), 1971-74; mem. policy guidance com. City of Falls Church, 1973-74, mem. bus. and profl. devel. commn., 1975—, chmn., 1978-80; mem. exec. com. Fairfax-Falls Church United Way, 1978-79; bd. mgmr. Fairfax County YMCA, 1976—, treas., 1979. Served with USAF, 1961-62. Margaret Thompson Biddle fellow, 1959; registered architect, Va., Md., D.C. Mem. AIA (nat. conv. steering com. 1974, dir. Va. Soc. 1978-79, treas. Va. 1980), Nat. Trust Hist. Preservation (asso.), Bldg. Ofcls. and Code Adminstrs. Internat. (profl. mem.), Greater Falls Church C. of C. (pres. 1976, dir. 1975-79). Methodist. Archtl. works include Falls Church Community Center, 1967, 301 Office Bldg., Falls Church, 1969, Vega Precision Labs., Inc., 1972, Tollgate of Falls Church, 1978, First Va. Bank, Arlington, 1979. Home: 311 Chestnut St Falls Church VA 22046 Office: 111 Park Pl Falls Church VA 22046

BARKSDALE, ARLEN O'NEIL, investment and devel. co. exec.; b. San Diego, Apr. 8, 1945; s. Earlie Nathaniel and Carmen Pauline (Wilson) B.; A.A., Weatherford Coll., 1967; B.S., U. Tex., Arlington, 1969; M.A., Rice U., 1971, Ph.D., 1972; m. Ruby Diane Haynes, June 3, 1966; children—Julie Elisabeth, Shane Arlen. Prodn. planner Aerospace div. LTV, Grand Prairie, Tex., 1967; lab. technician, materials research Bell Helicopter, Ft. Worth, 1968; ops. mgr. silicon mfg. Tex. Instruments, Sherman, 1973-77; chmn. bd., chief exec. officer Cory Enterprises, Inc., Weatherford, Tex., 1977—; chmn. bd. Tex. & So. Quarter Horse Jour., 1979—; owner Sealcrest Homes, 1977—, Barksdale Orchards, 1975—, Hytec Engring. Consultants, 1974—. Served with USAF, 1963-65. AEC spl. fellow, 1969-72; NDEA fellow, 1972-73; U. Tex. grantee, 1967-69. Mem. Am. Phys. Soc., C. of C., Tex. Quarter Horse Assn., Am. Forestry Assn., Smithsonian Instn., AAAS, Phi Beta Kappa, Sigma Xi. Clubs: Lions,

DeMolay. Contbr. articles to profl. jours. Home: 906 Scarlet Rd Weatherford TX 76086 Office: Willow Park Shopping Center Weatherford TX 76086

BARKSDALE, ELOISE EVANS, poet; b. Dardanelle, Ark., Aug. 1, 1906; d. Lewis Allen and Nelle (Goodman) Evans; student Central Bapt. Coll., 1924-25, U. Ark., 1925-26, Ark. Poly. Coll., 1929; m. William Donoho Barksdale, June 1, 1930; children—William Evans, Lewis Donoho. Tchr. music Dardanelle Pub. Schs., 1926-28; feature writer, reporter Ark. Democrat, Little Rock, 1929-30; organist chs. and temples, Ark., 1930-60; tchr. Fort Smith (Ark.) Pub. Schs., 1958-66; book reviewer S.W. Times Record, Fort Smith, 1965-68; author: (poetry) Remembering is Music, 1968 (Poets Roundtable award); poems in mags., newspapers and anthologies. Named Poet of the Present in Ark., 1968. Mem. Ark. State Pioneers Assn., (pres. chpt. 1972-77), Poets Roundtable Ark., Nat. League Am. Pen Women (pres. Fort Smith br. 1974), Roundtable Poets Fort Smith (pres. 1962-78), Haiku Soc. Am., D.A.R., P.E.O. (composer state song), Chi Omega Alumni Assn. Methodist. Home: 2515 S N St Fort Smith AR 72901

BARKSDALE, ETHELBERT COURTLAND, educator; b. Arlington, Tex., Apr. 9, 1944; s. E.C. and Marjorie M. Barksdale; B.A., U. Tex., Arlington, 1965; M.A., Ohio State U., 1968, Ph.D., 1971. Lectr., U. Calif., Irvine, 1971-72; asso. prof. German and Slavic langs. and lits. U. Fla., Gainesville, 1972—. NDEA fellow, 1965-68. Mem. Am. Assn. Advancement Slavic Studies, Modern Lang. Assn. Mem. Christian Ch. Author: The Dacha and the Duchess, 1974; Cosmologies of Consciousness, 1980; Daggers of the Mind, 1979. also articles. Home: 1333 S Pecan St Arlington TX 76010 Office: 261 ASB Univ Fla Gainesville FL 32611

BARKSDALE, HUDSON LEE, SR., state senator, ins. agt.; b. Barksdale, S.C., Jan. 28, 1907; s. John Wesley and Mary Caroline B.; A.B., S.C. State Coll., 1936; M.A., Columbia U. Tchrs. Coll.; postgrad. Glass Boro Tchrs. Coll.; m. Katie Marcelle Knuckles, July, 1943; children—Nealy Jeanne Barksdale Keith, Hudson Lee. Pres., B & B Ins. Agy., Inc., Spartanburg, S.C.; mem. S.C. State Senate; 2d vice chmn. edn. com. S.C. Ho. of Reps. Recipient various awards, including cert. recognition City of Spartanburg, 1977, Service to Mankind award Sertoma, 1977; Barksdale Blvd. named after him. Mem. NEA (life; Human Rights award 1967), NAACP, Alpha Phi Alpha. Democrat. Methodist. Contbr. articles to profl. publs. Office: 157 1/2 N Church St Spartanburg SC 29301

BARKSDALE, RICHARD DILLON, civil engr.; b. Orlando, Fla., May 2, 1938; s. William Spruil and Lucile (Dillon) B.; A.S., So. Tech. Inst., 1958; B.C.E., Ga. Inst. Tech., 1962, M.S., 1963; Ph.D. (Univ. scholar), Purdue U., 1966; m. Bonnie Alice McClung, Nov. 16, 1962; children—Cheryl Lynn, Richelle Denise. Successively asst. prof. civil engring., asso. prof., prof. Ga. Inst. Tech., Atlanta, 1965—; v.p. Soil Systems, Inc., Marietta, Ga., 1972—, Soil Systems of the Carolinas, 1976—; spl. lectr. So. Tech. Inst., Marietta, 1958-60; dir. Soil Systems, Inc., Geotech. Research, Inc., Marietta; cons. and speaker in field. Recipient Ga. Engring. Soc. award, 1962; Am. City Aid-to-Edn. award, 1962; NSF grantee, 1966-67. Mem. ASCE (past pres. Ga. sect., chmn. nat. com. on structural design of roadways, recipient Norman medal 1978), Transp. Research Bd. (chmn. com. on strength and deformation characteristics of pavement sects.), Phi Kappa Phi (pres. Ga. Inst. Tech. chpt. 1979, recipient Scholarship award 1962). Republican. Baptist. Club: Apalachee Sportsman (pres.). Contbr. numerous articles in field to tech. jours. Home: 1306 Christmas Ln NE Atlanta GA 30329 Office: Sch Civil Engring Ga Inst Tech Atlanta GA 30332

BARLEY, STEVEN LEE, tobacco co. exec.; b. South Boston, Va., Dec. 10, 1949; s. Abner and Mae (Boelte) B.; B.S., Va. Poly. Inst. and State U., 1973; M.S., Va. Commonwealth U., 1978; m. Deborah J. Jenkins, May 24, 1975. Audit sr., Touche Ross & Co., Washington and Richmond, 1973-76; mgr. internal auditing Best Products Co., Inc., Richmond, 1976-78; audit mgr. Philip Morris Inc., Richmond, Va., 1978—; adj. instr. J. Sargeant Reynolds Community Coll., Richmond, 1978—. C.P.A., Va.; cert. data processing. Mem. Inst. Internal Auditors (seminar leader), Va. Soc. C.P.A.'s, Am. Inst. C.P.A.'s, Electronic Data Processing Auditors Assn. Republican. Home: 7841 Provincetown Dr Richmond VA 23235 Office: PO Box 26603 Richmond VA 23261

BARLOW, CHARLIE (CHUCK), duplicating equipment mfg. co. exec.; b. Jackson, Ga., Nov. 7, 1949; s. Eulus Paul and Helen Louise (Carr) B.; B.S., Morris Brown Coll., 1971; m. Shirley Ann McCou, Apr. 29, 1973; children—Algernon Nicole, Charlie F., Shayla C. Retail mgmt. trainee Abraham & Straus, N.Y.C., 1970; mgmt. trainee MONY Ins. Co., N.Y.C., 1971; sales rep. Xerox Corp., Atlanta, 1973-75, sales specialist, St. Petersburg, Fla., 1975-79, sales mgr. community involvement/public relations, 1979-80, br. mktg. mgr., Atlanta, 1980—. Mem. policy bd. Pinellas Headstart; bd. dirs. Urban League, Big Brothers, OIC, Bethel Baptist Ch. Served with AUS, 1971-73. Mem. Alpha Phi Alpha. Clubs: Rotary (dir.), Toastmasters (area gov., pres.). Home: 11454 132d Ave N Largo FL 33540 Office: 1801 Peachtree Rd NE Atlanta GA 30309

BARLOW, DONAL EDWARD, physician; b. Dermott, Ark., Dec. 23, 1921; s. Edward Ethelbert and Nina Perry (Brian) B.; student Hendrix Coll., 1939-42; M.D., U. Ark., 1946; m. Mary Jane Stormont, Oct. 22, 1949. Intern, Crawford W. Long Meml. Hosp., Atlanta, 1946-47; resident in obstetrics and gynecology U. Ark. Med. Center, Little Rock, 1949-50, 52-55; individual practice obstetrics and gynecology, Joplin, Mo., 1955-60; group practice obstetrics and gynecology F. Hood Craddock Meml. Clinic, Sylacauga, Ala., 1960—; mem. staff Sylacauga Hosp. dir. City Nat. Bank, Sylacauga. Served with AUS, 1947-49, 50-52. Diplomate Am. Bd. Obstetrics and Gynecology. Mem. AMA, Ala. Med. Assn., Talladega County Med. Soc., Am. Coll. Obstetrics and Gynecology, Ala. Assn. Obstetrics and Gynecology. Presbyn. Club: Rotary. Home: 19 Huntington Dr Sylacauga AL 35150 Office: 308-14 Hickory St W Sylacauga AL 35150

BARLOW, HERMAN ZULCH, JR., univ. adminstr.; b. Houston, Oct. 8, 1949; s. Herman Zulch and Billie (Hunter) B.; B.A., Houston Bapt. U., 1972; M.Ed., U. Houston, 1974; D.Phil., Cambridge U., 1977; 1 dau., Meredith Arden. Admissions counselor Houston Bapt. U., 1972, dir. admissions, 1973-78, v.p. for devel., 1978—. Dir. music Westbury United Meth. Ch., 1972—; music dir. Symphony N. of Houston, 1976—. Recipient Disting. Alumnus award Houston Bapt. U., 1974. Mem. Council for Advancement and Support of Edn., S.W. Soc. Fund Raisers, Am. Acad. Polit. and Social Sci., Am. Acad. Arts and Scis., Am. Assn. for Higher Edn., Nat. Assn. Coll. Admissions Counslors, Am. Assn. Collegiate Registrars and Admissions Officers, Tex. Personnel and Guidance Assn., Houston Personnel and Guidance Assn., Internat. Platform Assn., Am. Symphony Orch. League, Tex. Orch. Dirs. Assn., Am. Choral Dirs. Assn., Tex. Choral Dirs. Assn., Fellowship of United Meth. Musicians, Music Educators Nat. Conf., Tex. Music Educators Assn., Houston Choral Soc., Phi Mu Alpha, Kappa Alpha Order, Omicron Delta Kappa. Office: 7502 Fondren St Houston TX 77074

BARLOW, LARRY STEPHEN, air force officer; b. San Diego, Oct. 2, 1948; s. James Rudolph and Eunice (Cox) B.; B.A. in Bus., U. Puget Sound, 1970; M.S. in Mgmt., Troy State U., 1975; m. Sally Ann Llewellyn, July 21, 1973; children—Debra Erin, Patrick Kevin. Commd. 2d lt. USAF, 1970, advanced through grades to capt., 1974; chief adminstrn. communications div. Hdqrs. Mil. Airlift Command, 1970-72; adminstrv. officer Tan Son Nhut Air Base, Saigon, Vietnam, 1972-73, RAF Woodbridge, U.K., 1973-76; student Edn. with Industry, Xerox Corp., Rochester, N.Y., 1976-77; chief adminstrv. systems Air U., Maxwell AFB, Ala., 1977—. Decorated Air Force Commendation medal. Mem. Internat. Word Processing Assn., Nat. Micrographics Assn. Lutheran. Office: 3800/DAY Maxwell AFB AL 36112

BARLOW, MARJORIE RUTH, ednl. cons., family therapist; b. Ralls, Tex., Jan. 23, 1929; d. Odie B. and Ola Victoria (Kiker) McNeely; student W. Tex. State U., 1944; B.B.A., Tex. A & I U., 1947, M.S., 1966; Ph.D., U. Nebr., 1978; m. James M. Robinson, 1947 (dec. 1962); children—Anna Kathleen Robinson Brown, James Michael, Victoria Kaye, Edward McNeely; m. Marlyn Paul Barlow, June 8, 1964; 1 dau., Cynthia Christine. Tchr. elemen. schs., Mercedes and Kingsville, Tex., 1948-55; counselor high sch. Kingsville (Tex.) Ind. Sch. Dist., 1966-68; exec. dir. Family Guidance Services, Kingsville, Tex., 1973-79; marriage and family therapist Psychol. Service Center, Corpus Christi, Tex., 1979—; adj. prof. Tex. A & I U., Kingsville; ednl. cons., bus. and schs., 1973—. Mem. Am. Assn. Marriage and Family Therapists, Am. Personnel and Guidance Assn., Internat. Transactional Analysis Assn. Methodist. Home: 1726 W Santa Gertrudis St Kingsville TX 78363 Office: 1202 3d St Corpus Christi TX 78404

BARNACK, ROBERT FRANCIS, communications equipment engr., mfg. co. exec.; b. Scranton, Pa., Apr. 4, 1929; s. Jacob and Veronica Francis (Yuhar) B.; student in elec. engring. Gettysburg Coll. and George Washington U., 1955-57; m. Elizabeth Ann Waggoner, July 30, 1966; children—Veronica Dale, Randi, Michael. Communications specialist, chief signal office Dept. Army, 1950-62; sr. communications systems engr. Tele-Signal Corp., Hicksville, N.Y., 1962-65; mktg. mgr. No. Radio Co., N.Y.C., 1965-70; pres., chief exec. officer Potomac Marine & Aviation, Inc., Arlington, Va., 1970—. Served with U.S. Army, 1951-53. Mem. Washington Telecommunications Soc., Aircraft Owners and Pilots Assn., Armed Forces Communications Equipment Assn., Ind. Telephone Pioneers Assn. (past pres. Washington chpt.). Clubs: Old Dominion Boat (past commodore); Toastmasters Internat. (past v.p. Arlington chpt.). Home: 4607 N 38th St Arlington VA 22207 Office: 1400 N Uhle St Arlington VA 22201

BARNARD, BENNIE GARY, asso. architect, mktg. cons.; b. Waxahachie, Tex., Mar. 25, 1949; s. Bennie Rollen and Gracy Catherine (Ellis) B.; student Central Tex. Coll., 1969-71; m. Gaila Fae Edwards, Mar. 29, 1969; children—John Rollen, Andrea Faye, Robert Vernon. Draftsman, Walter Carrington Co., Austin, Tex., 1970-71; job capt. Dorr E. Hampton, AIA, Austin, 1971, John D. Byrum, Austin, 1971-72, Lundgren & Maurer, AIA, Austin, 1972-74, Eugene Wukasch Arch./Engr., Austin, 1974-75; asso. Jan Grierson, Inc., AIA, Austin, 1975—; pres. Barnard & Assos., mktg. cons., Austin, 1979—. Minister youth, Shenandoah Bapt. Ch., Leander, Tex. Home: 16106 Awalt Dr Austin TX 78734 Office: 5840 Balcones Dr Austin TX 78731

BARNARD, D. DOUGLAS, JR., Congressman; b. Augusta, Ga., Mar. 20, 1922; s. D. Douglas and Lucy (Burns) B.; B.A., Mercer U., 1943, postgrad. Walter F. George Sch. Law, 1948; m. Naomi Elizabeth Holt, Dec. 15, 1946; children—Pamela, Lucy, D.Douglas, III. Bookkeeper, teller, cashier, v.p., exec. v.p. Ga. R.R. Bank, 1948-63, 68-76; exec. sec. Gov. Carl E. Sanders, 1963-67; mem. Ga. Bd. Transp., 1966-76; mem. 95th-96th Congresses from 10th Ga. Dist. Deacon, First Bapt. Ch., Augusta; chmn. Richmond County (Ga.) Democratic Exec. Com., 1955-60; mem. State Dem. Exec. Com., 1963-66; bd. dirs. Augusta Boys Club; trustee Mercer U. Served with Fin. Corps, U.S. Army, 1943-45. Named Outstanding Man of Year, Augusta, 1957. Mem. Augusta C. of C., Phi Delta Theta, Phi Alpha Delta. Office: 418 Cannon House Office Bldg Washington DC 20515

BARNARD, WILLIAM DEAN, historian; b. Birmingham, Ala., Sept. 18, 1942; s. Cecil Dean and Dorothy (Bates) B.; A.B., Birmingham So. Coll., 1964; Ph.D. (Woodrow Wilson fellow, Va. Wilson fellow, Edward R. Stettinius, Jr. fellow), U. Va., 1971; m. Hollinger Farmer, Dec. 22, 1964; children—William Harrison II, Margaret Pace, Joshua Bates. Mem. faculty U. South Ala., 1968-72; asso. dir. acad. affairs Ala. Commn. Higher Edn., 1973-77; asst. to chancellor acad. program devel. U. Ala., 1977-79, asso. prof. history, 1979—, chmn. dept., 1979—. Chmn. Ala. Com. Humanities and Public Policy, 1978-79; v.p. Tuscaloosa (Ala.) chpt. ARC, 1979-80; pres. Verner Sch. PTA, Tuscaloosa, 1979-80. Mem. Am. Hist. Assn., Orgn. Am. Historians, So. Hist. Assn., Ala. Hist. Assn., Ala. Assn. Historians, Newcomen Soc. N.Am. Author: Dixiecrats and Democrats: Alabama Politics 1942-50, 1974. Home: 17 Pinemont Dr Tuscaloosa AL 35406 Office: PO Box 1936 University AL 35486

BARNARD, WILLIAM KENNETH, oil co. exec.; b. Rugby, Tex., Feb. 1, 1933; s. William Harold and Lucy Pearl (Moore) B.; A.A., Paris (Tex.) Jr. Coll., 1952; B.A., U. Tex. at Austin, 1954; M.S., N. Tex. State U., Denton, 1964, Ph.D., 1978; m. Ruth Castillo Flores; children—Stephen Harold, Patricia Sue. Store mgr., Sears, Roebuck & Co., Jacksonville, Tex., 1960-61, Montgomery Ward's, Grand Prairie, Tex., 1964; personnel mgr. Northpark store J.C. Penney, Dallas, 1966-68; adminstr. wage and salary Tex. Pacific Oil Co. Inc., Dallas, 1968-69, supr. office services, 1969-70, mgr. tng. and devel., 1970-76, mgr. employee relations, 1976—. Pres., chmn. bd. Forbes Highland Dancers, Inc. Served as spl. agt. CIC, U.S. Army, 1955-58. Accredited exec. in personnel Am. Soc. Personnel Adminstrs. Mem. Am. Soc. Tng. and Devel., Am. Psychol. Assn., Tex. Psychol. Assn., Am. Soc. Personnel Adminstrs., Dallas Personnel Assn., Acad. Mgmt., Southwestern Acad. Mgmt., Mensa. Office: 1700 One Main Pl Dallas TX 75250

BARNES, BEN F., constrn. co. exec., former state ofcl.; b. Gorman, Tex., Apr. 17, 1938; s. B.F. Barnes; student Tarleton State Coll., Tex. Christian U., U. Tex. at Austin; LL.D., McMurry Coll., Tex. Tech U., St. Edwards U.; m. Nancy Sayers; children—Greg, Amy, Scott, Brian. Lt. gov. State of Tex., 1969-73; owner, pres. Herman Bennett Co., Brownwood, Tex., 1973—. Mem. Tex. Ho. of Reps., 1960-68, chmn. rules com., 1963, speaker, 1965-68. Chmn. Tex. legislative council and legis. budget bd., 1969-73; chmn. So. conf. Council State Govts., 1967-68, mem. exec. com., 1968-70; pres. Nat. Legis. Conf., 1968-69. Named one of 10 outstanding young men in U.S., U.S. Jr. C. of C., 1970. Mem. Tex. Jr. C. of C. (one of 5 outstanding young Texans 1965), S.W. Cattle Growers Assn. Methodist. Elk. Home: Brownwood TX 76801 Office: Herman Bennett Co Brownwood TX 76801

BARNES, CARL COLUMBUS, credit union exec.; b. Corinth, Miss., Nov. 2, 1923; s. Columbus Franklin and Mary Loubettie B.; student LaSalle U., 1952-61; grad. cert. courses Credit Union Nat. Assn., 1978; m. Bettye Sue Williams, Sept. 4, 1950; 1 dau., Conchita Carlene Barnes Hansford. Agt., supt. Nat. Life & Accident Ins. Co., Nashville, 1948-49; quality control technician Naval Ammunition Depot, Hawthorne, Nev., 1950-51, gen. mgr. Employees Fed. Credit Union, 1951-61; pres., chief exec. officer Knoxville TVA Employees Credit Union, 1951—; chmn. State Credit Union Share Ins. Corp. Gov. apptd. mem. Nev. Econ. Devel. Bd., 1950-51. Mem. Credit Union Execs. Soc. (chmn.; cert.), Tenn. Credit Union League (past dir.). Democrat. Clubs: LeConte, Masons. Office: 507 Market St Knoxville TN 37901

BARNES, CARNELL MARTIN, counselor, marriage and family therapist; b. Odell, Okla., May 12, 1933; d. Carval Anderson and Roberta (Hamil) Martin; B.S., Southeastern Okla. State U., 1963, M.S., 1966; postgrad. doctoral program Tex. Woman's U., 1977—; children—James Wayne, Joe Bill, Jerry Bob Barnes. Tchr. vocat. home econs., Maud, Okla., 1963-64, Bokchito, Okla., 1964-67, Spurger, Tex., 1967-68, Winnie, Tex., 1968-72; tchr. learning disabilities, Wise County, Tex., 1972-73; counselor spl. edn., Mesquite, Tex., 1973-76, asso. sch. psychologist, 1976-77, coordinator appraisals, 1977-78, coordinator spl. edn. counseling, 1978-79; counselor marriage and family Creative Counseling Center, Dallas, 1978—, also bd. dirs. Cert. tchr., Okla., Tex.; cert. counselor, Tex. Mem. Am. Assn. Marriage and Family Therapy (asso.), Am. Personnel and Guidance Assn., Tex. Council on Family Relations, Delta Kappa Gamma. Home: 1625 South Pkwy Mesquite TX 75149 Office: Creative Counseling Center 6060 N Central Expressway Dallas TX 75206

BARNES, CHAPLIN BRADFORD, assn. exec.; b. New Haven, Apr. 7, 1941; s. Irston Roberts and Lidorra (Putney) B.; B.A., Yale Coll., 1962, LL.B., 1965; postgrad. Univ. Coll., Oxford U., 1965-67; m. Lila Cummings, May 13, 1972; children—Sarah Chaplin, Diana Brewster. Asso. firm Breed, Abbott & Morgan, N.Y.C., 1968-69; asst. to pres. Nat. Audubon Soc., N.Y.C., 1969-73, dir. internat. activities, 1973-78; pres. Piedmont Environ. Council, Warrenton, Va., 1979—. Dir. Rachel Carson Council, Inc. Mem. Watch Hill (R.I.) Chapel Soc. (trustee). Episcopalian. Clubs: Union (N.Y.C.); Misquamicut (Watch Hill, R.I.). Office: 28-C Main St Warrenton VA 22186

BARNES, CHARLES HERBERT, JR., engring. cons. co. exec.; b. Appomattox, Va., June 7, 1938; s. Charles Herbert and Ruby (Harris) B.; B.S C.E., Va. Poly. Inst., 1964; M.S.C.E. (Univ. fellow), W.Va. U., 1966; m. Barbara Anne Dunn, Dec. 14, 1963; children—Kevin, David. Transp. planning engr. Va. Dept. Hwys. and Transp., Richmond, 1964-68; dir. traffic and planning City of Petersburg (Va.), 1968-71; asso. Wiley & Wilson, Inc., Lynchburg, Va., 1971-73, project mgr., 1973—. Mem. Lynchburg Bd. Zoning Appeals, 1977—. Fellow Inst. Transp. Engrs.; mem. Nat. Soc. Profl. Engrs., Va. Soc. Profl. Engrs., Am. Inst. Cert. Planners, Transp. Research Bd. Methodist. Club: Kiwanis (dir. Lynchburg 1978-80). Home: 2212 Longwood Rd Lynchburg VA 24503 Office: Wiley & Wilson Inc 2310 Langhorne Rd Lynchburg VA 24501

BARNES, HENSON PERRYMOORE, lawyer, state senator; b. Bladen County, N.C., Nov. 18, 1934; s. Lalon Lem and Mabel (Cumbee) B.; A.A., Wilmington Coll., 1958; A.B., U. N.C., 1959, LL.B., D.H.L., William Carter Coll., 1979; m. Kitty Allen, Aug. 24, 1961; children—Rebecca, Amy. Admitted to N.C. bar; individual practice law, Goldsboro, N.C.; partner firm Barnes, Braswell & Haithcock, Goldsboro; mem. N.C. Ho. of Reps., 1975-76, N.C. Senate, 1976—. Served with U.S. Army, 1953-56. Mem. N.C. Bar Assn., Am. Bar Assn., N.C. Acad. Trial Lawyers. Democrat. Baptist. Clubs: Masons, Shriners, Civitan. Office: 231 E Walnut St Goldsboro NC 27530

BARNES, HERSCHIEL SEVIER, lawyer; b. Cookeville, Tenn., Dec. 19, 1919; s. Herschiel Sevier and Susan Gertrude (Tinnon) B.; B.S., George Peabody Coll., 1940; J.D., Vanderbilt U., 1948; m. Vivian Jean Hicks, Dec. 22, 1950; children—Amy, Joel, Thomas. Tchr. pub. schs., St. Petersburg, Fla., 1939-40; admitted to Tenn. bar, 1947; practiced in Cookeville, Tenn., 1948—; mem. firm Crawford & Barnes, 1949-71, Crawford, Barnes & Acuff, 1971—. Dir. Crest Lawn Meml. Cemetery, Citizens Bank of Cookeville. City atty., Cookeville, 1948-52; referee in bankruptcy Northeastern div. Middle Dist. Tenn., 1954-58. Chmn. bd. Cookeville Gen. Hosp., 1968-72, trustee, 1964-72. Served with AUS, 1941-45; ETO. Decorated Purple Heart. Mem. Tenn. Bar Assn. (chmn. uniform laws com. 1976-77), Putnam County Veterans' Orgn. (trustee 1973—), Phi Delta Phi, Order of Coif. Democrat. Methodist (chmn. adminstrv. bd. 1971; lay leader 1972). Home: 957 Sunset Dr Cookeville TN 38501 Office: 101 S Jefferson Ave Cookeville TN 38501

BARNES, HUGH WILLIAM, state dept. adminstr.; b. North Wilkesboro, N.C., Apr. 24, 1948; s. T. Glenn and Selma E. (Oxford) B.; B.S., Appalachian State U., 1970; m. Sally Agatha Myers, May 3, 1975; 1 dau., Autumn L. Spl. asst. to gov. State of N.C., 1973, dir. field services Dept. Transp., 1973-75, tech. writer Dept. Human Resources, 1975, head forms mgmt. unit, Raleigh, 1975-79, mgr. methods and procedures br., 1979—. Mem. Am. Inst. Indsl. Engrs., Bus. Forms Mgmt. Assn., Am. Maltese Assn., Victorian Soc. Am., Samoyed Club of Am. Club: Rotary. Home: 316 E Jones St Raleigh NC 27601 Office: 325 N Salisbury St Raleigh NC 27611

BARNES, JIMMIE FRANKLIN, JR., sociologist; b. Charleston, Miss., July 17, 1944; s. Jimmie Franklin and Alcola B.; B.S., Miss. Valley State U., 1965; M.A., Miss. State U., 1969, Ph.D., 1979; m. Janice Wilder, Apr. 30, 1966; children—Kyra, Joi. Social worker Coahoma Opportunities Inc., Clarksdale, Miss., 1965-66; instr. Mary Holmes Coll., West Point, Miss., 1969-70; instr. Miss. State U., Starkville, 1972-73; asso. prof. dept. social sci. Miss. Valley State U., Itta Bena, Miss., 1973—; cons. N. Miss. Rural Legal Services. Sec. Miss. Adv. Council on Drug Abuse; mem. Leflore County health adv. bd. Miss. Action for Progress. NDEA fellow, 1968-71. Mem. Mid-South Sociol. Assn., Acad. Criminal Justice Scis., Soc. Miss. Archivists, Nat. Assn. Blacks in Criminal Justice. Baptist. Home: Box 303 Itta Bena MS 38941 Office: Dept Social Sci Miss Valley State U Itta Bena MS 38941

BARNES, JOHN EVAN, JR., clergyman; b. Pratt City, Ala., July 9, 1911; s. John Evan and Hattie (Pollard) B.; A.B., Samford U., 1934; Th.M., So. Bapt. Theol. Sem., 1937; D.D., Miss. Coll., 1948; m. Marion Stallworth, Aug. 25, 1936; children—Frances Marilyn, John Evan III, Elizabeth Carson. Ordained to ministry Bapt. Ch., 1932; pastor 1st Bapt. Ch., Atmore, Ala., 1937-42, West Point, Miss., 1942-44, Main St. Bapt. Ch., Hattiesburg, Miss., 1944—. Pres. Miss. Bapt. Conv., 1953-54, chmn. edn. commn., 1965—, chmn. commn. on bds., 1956—; pres. So. Bapt. Sunday Sch. Bd., 1964—; pres. bd. dirs. So. Bapt. Hosp. Commn., 1957—; chmn. bd. trustees Wm Carey Coll., Hattiesburg, 1979—. Co-chmn. United Gives Fund, Hattiesburg, 1955—. Kiwanian (dir. 1946). Writer tract, Is It Right, 1951; also articles. Home: 1001 Estelle St Hattiesburg MS 39401 Office: 1101 Main St Hattiesburg MS 39401

BARNES, KENNETH O'NEAL, SR., utilities co. ofcl.; b. Durham, N.C., Mar. 13, 1942; s. Wyatte Wasdon and Margaret Helen (O'Neal) B.; A.A., Wingate Jr. Coll., 1963; B.A. in Bus. Adminstrn., E. Carolina U., 1965; m. Betty Lou Dowdy, Dec. 17, 1967; children—Elizabeth

Lee, Kenneth O'Neal. With right of way sect., div. hwys. N.C. Dept. Transp., 1965-67; with Carolina Power & Light Co., Wilmington, N.C., 1967—, right of way agt. Wilmington dist., 1970—. Deacon, receiving treas. Winter Park Presbyn. Ch. Served with Army N.G., 1967. Mem. Am. Right of Way Assn. Democrat. Clubs: Masons (master Orient Lodge #345, 1977), Scottish Rite, Shrine (drum and bugle corps 1969-74). Home: 104 Mary Ave Castle Hayne NC 28429 Office: PO Box 1110 Wilmington NC 28402

BARNES, LATHA MIMBS, chemist, educator; b. Adrian, Ga., Dec. 13, 1935; d. Lester Lee and Edna Truman (Stone) Mimbs; A.B., Berry Coll., 1957; M.S., U. Miss., 1959; Ph.D., Ga. State U., 1978; m. David Barnes, June 4, 1962; children—Sharon Louise, Susan Elizabeth. Teaching asst. U. Miss., Oxford, 1957-59; asst. prof. chemistry West Ga. Coll., Carrollton, 1959—. Mem. Am. Chem. Soc., Ga. Acad. Sci., Nat. Sci. Tchrs. Assn., AAUP, Phi Delta Kappa. Democrat. Methodist. Clubs: Katie Downs Service Guild, Bus. and Profl. Women's. Author: Workbook for Theoretical Chemistry, 1977; contbr. articles to profl. jours. Home: Route 2 Box 417D Carrollton GA 30117 Office: West Ga Coll Carrollton GA 30118

BARNES, LOUI JOSEPH, JR., writer, curator; b. Gadsden, Ala., Apr. 17, 1920; s. Loui Joseph and Myrtle Grace (Woodson) B.; student Auburn U., 1946; B.S., Jacksonville State U., 1949; M.S., U. Ala., 1978; m. Mabel Kathryn Thornton, July 20, 1947; children—Robert Samuel, Pamela Irene. Coach, Walnut Grove (Ala.) High Sch., 1949-52; with civil service U.S. Air Force, Gadsden and Mobile, Ala., 1952-58, U.S. Army, 1958-72, Huntsville, Ala., 1966-72; owner curator Indian Mus. Gadsden, Noccalula Falls, Ala., 1979—; lectr. in field. Chmn. heritage com. Bicentennial, Gadsden, 1975-76; chmn. Patriots Days, Gadsden, 1974-79. Served with U.S. Army, 1939-45; MTO, NATDUSA; served with USAR, 1956—. Decorated Army Commendation medal; named Soldier of Yr., Ala. U.S. Army Res., 1974. Mem. N.E. Ala. Geneal. Soc. (pres. 1966), Etowah County Hist. Soc., Ala. Hist. Soc. (exec. bd.), Ala. High Sch. Football Ofcls. Assn. Baptist. Clubs: Odd Fellow, Lions, Jacksonville State U. Alumni Assn. (bd. govs. 1975-80). Author: Man on a Mountain, 1966; John Wisdom - Citizen Soldier, 1979; Fighting Game Cocks, 1980. Home: Route 11 Box 109 Gadsden AL 35903 Office: Noccalula Falls Mus Gadsden AL 35901

BARNES, MAGGIE LUE SHIFFLETT (MRS. LAWRENCE BARNES), nurse; b. nr. Spur, Tex., Mar. 29, 1931; d. Howard Eldridge and Sadie Adilene (Dunlap) Shifflett; student Cogdell Sch. Nursing, 1959-60; Western Tex. Coll., 1972-76, grad. Meth. Hosp. Sch. Nursing, Lubbock, Tex., 1975; B.S. in Nursing, W. Tex. State U., 1977; m. T.C. Fagan, Jan. 1950 (dec. Feb. 1952); 1 son, Lawayne L.; m. 2d, Lawrence Barnes, Sept. 2, 1960. Floor nurse D.M. Cogdell Meml. Hosp., Snyder, Tex., 1960-64, medication nurse, 1964-76, asst. evening supr., 1976-78, charge nurse, after 1973, now evening nursing supr. Den mother Cub Scouts Am., Holliday, Tex., 1960-61; mem. PTA, Snyder, Tex., 1960-69; adviser Sr. Citizens Assn.; mem. Tri-Region Health Systems Agency. Mem. Vocational Nurses Assn. Tex. (mem. bd. 1963-65, div. pres. 1967-69), Emergency Dept. Nursing Assn. Apostolic Faith Ch. (sec., treas. 1956-58). Home: Route 1 Box 9B Hermleigh TX 79526 Office: Med Arts Center DM Cogdell Meml Hosp Snyder TX 79549

BARNES, MELVER RAYMOND, chemist; b. nr. Salisbury, N.C., Nov. 15, 1917; s. Oscar Lester and Sarah Albertine (Rowe) B.; A.B. in Chemistry, U. N.C. at Chapel Hill, 1947. Chemist Pitts. Testing Labs., Greensboro, N.C., 1949; chemist N.C. State Hwy. & Pub. Works Commn., Raleigh, 1949-50; chemist Edgewood (Md.) Arsenal, 1951-61; chemist Dugway (Utah) Proving Ground, 1961-70; pvt. sci. research, Linwood, N.C., 1971—. Served with AUS, 1942-45. Fellow Intercontinental Biog. Assn., Internat. Inst. Community Service, Harry S. Truman Library Inst.; mem. Am. Chem. Soc., Am. Phys. Soc., AAAS, Am. Soc. Distinguished Citizens, Soc. Am. Mil. Engrs., Internat. Platform Assn., UN Assn. U.S.A., Gen. Alumni Assn. U. N.C., U. Calif. at Los Angeles Alumni Assn., Smithsonian Assos. Author classified reports. Home: Rt 1 Box 424 Linwood NC 27299

BARNES, (WILMER) RAY, janitorial service co. exec.; b. Bomerton, Tex., Feb. 18, 1935; s. William Elmo and Edith Mae B.; student Midwestern State U., 1960-63; m. Jean Ann Rutledge, Oct. 11, 1952; children—Donna, Cindy, Julie. Route supr. Times Pub. Co., 1952-54; founder, pres. Barnes Maintenance Co., Inc., Wichita Falls, Tex., 1954—; founder WRB Properties, 1964. Bd. dirs. YMCA, Campfire Girls, Sr. Citizens, Boys Club; deacon 1st Baptist Ch. of Wichita Falls. Mem. Nat. Fedn. Ind. Businessmen, Action Council, S.W. Assn. Bldg. Service Contractors (pres. 1977-78), Internat. San. Suppliers Assn., Carpet Cleaners Assn., Wichita Falls Bd. Commerce and Industry (ambassador), U.S. C. of C., Gideons Internat. (past pres. Wichita Falls chpt.). Republican. Club: Miwestern State U. M, Rotary, Sertoma (chpt. pres. 1966-67), Masons. Home: 2422 Brentwood St Wichita Falls TX 76308 Office: 603 Burnett St Wichita Falls TX 76301

BARNES, RICHARD CHARLES, realtor; b. Woodstock, Ill., May 14, 1923; s. C. Percy and Ruth A. (Clements) B.; B.S. in Marketing and Mgmt., U. Ill., 1947; m. June Hood, May 18, 1974; children by previous marriage—Linda Sue (Mrs. R. Reinholtz), Ronda A., Barbara R. Asst. to v.p. Mitchell Furniture Co., Mt. Vernon, Ill., 1947-51; mgr. radio sta. WMIX, Mt. Vernon, 1949-51; real estate salesman, broker Anaconda Properties Corp., Ft. Lauderdale, Fla., 1951-55, v.p., 1953-55; partner Allstate Realty, Plantation, Fla., 1955-60; owner, mgr. R.C. Barnes, Inc., 1960—; propr. West Broward Financial Center, Plantation, 1961—. Pres., propr. Continental Finance Corp., Plantation, 1962—; founder Eastern Ins. Agy., Plantation, 1959, sec., treas., 1959-70. Mem. Ft. Lauderdale Bd. Realtors and Multiple Listing Services, Inc., 1964—. Pres. Parkway Middle Sch. P.T.A., 1962-63. Mem. Broward County (Fla.) Indsl. Bd., 1964-65; vice chmn. City of Plantation Bd. of Adjustment, 1963-64; chmn. City of Plantation Planning and Zoning Bd. Served to 1st lt. AUS, 1943-46; ETO. Decorated Purple Heart, Bronze Star medal. Mem. Greater Plantation C. of C. (pres. 1965-66, dir. 1966—), Nat. Assn. Real Estate Bds., Nat. Inst. Real Estate Brokers, Fla. Assn. of Realtors, Ft. Lauderdale Bd. of Realtors, Alpha Sigma Phi. Kiwanian (dir. 1973-75). Home: 709 SW 44th Av Plantation FL 33317 Office: 4310 W Broward Blvd Plantation FL 33317

BARNES, ROY EUGENE, lawyer; b. Atlanta, Mar. 11, 1948; s. William Columbus and Agnes Louise (Bradford) B.; A.B., U. Ga., 1969; J.D. cum laude, 1972; m. Edna Marie Dobbs, Aug. 16, 1970; children—Albert Harlan, Martha Allison, Mary Alyssa. Admitted to Ga. bar, 1972, U.S. Circuit Ct. bar, 1973, U.S. Supreme Ct. bar, 1978; asst. dist. atty. Cobb Jud. Circuit, Marietta, Ga., 1972-73; individual practice law, Marietta, 1973-75; Sr. partner firm Barnes and Browning, Marietta, 1975—; mem. Ga. Senate, 1974-76, 76-78, 78—; bd. dirs. 1st Nat. Bank Cobb County, 1978—. Served to capt. USAR, 1972-79. Named 1 of 5 Outstanding Young Men of Ga., Ga. Jaycees, 1975. Mem. Am. Bar Assn., Am. Trial Lawyers Assn., Am. Judicature Soc. Democrat. Methodist. Clubs: Kiwanis, Jaycees, Masons. Home: 639 Maran Ln Mableton GA 30059 Office: 191 Lawrence St Marietta GA 30060

BARNES, RUDOLPH COUNTS, JR., lawyer; b. Columbia, S.C., Sept. 16, 1942; s. Rudolph C. and Ella Caroline (Carson) B.; A.B. with honors in Polit. Sci., The Citadel, 1964; J.D., U. S.C., 1967; m. Jeanette Neville Wall, Aug. 29, 1964; children—Tracie Neville, Rudolph Counts, Ashley Carson. Admitted to S.C. bar, 1967; asst. atty. gen. S.C. Tax Commn., Columbia, 1967; partner firm Barnes, Austin & Ellison, Columbia, 1971—; dir. So. Bank & Trust Co.; instr. bus. law U. Md., Far East Div., 1969-70; mem. S.C. adv. com. U.S. Civil Rights Commn., 1977. Chmn., Emphasis on Edn., Columbia, 1977; pres., dir. Richland-Lexington Council on Aging, 1973-75; v.p., dir. Jr. Achievement Greater Columbia, 1972—; dir., chmn. Devel. Council Columbia Urban Service Center, 1973-76; chmn. law enforcement subcom. Greater Columbia Community Relations Council, 1971-77; bd. dirs. Opportunities Industrialization Center S.C.; trustee Oliver Mission; mem. Columbia City Council, 1978—, Central Midlands Regional Planning Council, 1978—. Served with JAGC, AUS, 1967-71. Mem. Am., S.C. (chmn. banking subcom.), Richland County, Okinawa bar assns., S.C. Income Property Assn., Am. Judicature Soc., World Peace Thru Law Soc., Greater Columbia C. of C. (chmn. com. to assist relocation Ugandan refugees 1973—, Outstanding Achievement award 1975). Methodist (lay mem. urban work com. S.C. Conf. 1971—). Clubs: Summit, Columbia Luncheon. Home: 2400 Wheat St Columbia SC 29205 Office: Bankers Trust Tower PO Box 11921 Columbia SC 29211

BARNES, RUSSELL MILLER, air line exec.; b. Columbia, Ky., Apr. 30, 1927; s. George O. and Effie M. (Miller) B.; B.S. in Elec. Engring., U. Ky., 1950; M.S. in Indsl. Mgmt. (Sloan fellow), Mass. Inst. Tech., 1964; m. Margaret L. Harding, July 8, 1952; children—Randall, Lisa. Field engr. Philco Corp., Phila., 1950-54; sr. field engr. Nat. Scientific Labs., Washington, 1954-55; planning engr. Pan Am. World Airways, Inc., Patrick AFB, Fla., 1955-57, mgr. program mgmt., 1957-60, mgr. range devel., 1960-63, operations mgr., 1965-70, v.p. aerospace service div., 1970-76, v.p. contract services, 1976—; pres. Pan Am. Tech. Services, Inc., Patrick AFB, 1974—. Bd. dirs. United Way of Brevard County (Fla.), 1970-72, Brevard County YMCA, 1960-63. Served with USNR, 1945-46. Asso. fellow Am. Inst. Aeros. and Astronautics; mem. Nat. Contract Mgmt. Assn. Mem. Christian Ch. Home: 685 Kenwood Ct Satellite Beach FL 32937 Office: 1325 N Atlantic Ave Cocoa Beach FL 32931

BARNES, VIRGIL EVERETT, geologist; b. Chehalis, Wash., June 11, 1903; s. Charles N. and Della (Matheny) B.; B.S., Wash. State Coll., M.S., 1927; Ph.D., U. Wis., 1930; m. Mildred Louise Adlof, Sept. 28, 1932; children—Virgil Everett II, Mildred Louise, Elizabeth Ann. Teaching fellow geology Wash. State Coll., Pullman, 1925-27; curator Geology Mus., U. Wis., Madison, 1927-29; geologist Mineral Lands Survey, Wis. Geol. Survey, Madison, summer, 1928; prospector Dominion Explorers, Ltd., Toronto, Ont., Can., summer, 1929; research fellow Am. Petroleum Inst., Austin, Tex., 1930-31; jr. topographic engr. Amarillo, Tex., 1933-35; geologist, research scientist Bur. Econ. Geology and dept. geol. scis. U. Tex., Austin 1935-77, prof. emeritus, 1977—, cons., 1977-78; cons. to various mining cos., 1973—. NSF grantee, 1960-72. Mem. Am. Geophys. Union, Am. Assn. Petroleum Geologists, Geol. Soc. Am., Austin Geol. Soc., Geochem. Soc., Mineral. Soc. Am., Soc. Econ. Paleontologists and Mineralogists, Internat. Assn. Paleontology, Am. Quaternary Assn., Meteoritical Soc., AAAS, Sigma Xi, Sigma Gamma Epsilon, Gamma Alpha. Club: Faculty. Author: (with Mildred A. Barnes) Tektites, 1973; contbr. articles to sci. jours. Home: 207 E 33rd St Austin TX 78705 Office: PO Box X University Station Austin TX 78712

BARNES, WILLIAM ARMSTEAD, JR., counselor; b. Richmond, Va., May 2, 1946; s. William Armstead and Virginia Belle (Twisdale) B.; B.A., Coll. of William and Mary, 1968, M.Ed., 1974. Tchr., Tidewater Acad., Wakefield, Va., 1970-72; tchr., coach, asst. prin. Claremont Manor Acad., Claremont, Va., 1970-74; tchr., coach Prince George Jr. High Sch., Disputanta, Va., 1974-77; counselor N.B. Clements Jr. High Sch., Prince George, Va., 1977—. Served with U.S. Army N.G., 1968-76. Mem. Prince George Edn. Assn., Va. Edn. Assn., NEA, Richmond Personnel and Guidance Assn., Va. Personnel and Guidance Assn., Am. Personnel and Guidance Assn., Am. Sch. Counselors Assn. Methodist. Club: Prince George Athletic Booster (dir. 1978-79). Home: Route 1 Box 132G Disputanta VA 23842 Office: Route 3 Box 25 Prince George VA 23875

BARNESS, LEWIS ABRAHAM, physician; b. Atlantic City, N.J., July 31, 1921; s. Joseph and Mary (Silverstein) B.; A.B., Harvard U., 1941, M.D., 1944; M.A. (hon.), U. Pa., 1971; m. Elaine Berger, June 14, 1953; children—Carol, Laura, Joseph. Intern, Phila. Gen. Hosp., 1944-45; resident Children's Med. Center, Boston, 1947-50; asst. chief, then chief dept. pediatrics Phila. Gen. Hosp., 1951-72; vis. physician U. Pa. Hosp., 1952-57, acting chief, then chief, 1957-72; mem. faculty U. Pa. Sch. Medicine, 1951-72, prof. pediatrics, 1964-72; prof. pediatrics, chmn. dept. U. So. Fla. Med. Sch., Tampa, 1972—. Served to capt. AUS, 1945-46. Recipient Lindback Teaching award U. Pa., 1963; Borden award nutrition, 1972. Mem. Am. Pediatric Soc. (recorder-editor 1964-75), Soc. Pediatric Research, Am. Acad. Pediatrics (chmn. com. on nutrition 1975—), Am. Inst. Nutrition, AAAS, Sigma Xi, Alpha Omega Alpha. Author: Pediatric Physical Diagnosis Yearbook, edits. 1-4, 1957—. Editor: Advances in Pediatrics, 1976—. Home: 548 W Davis Blvd Tampa FL 33606

BARNETT, BENJAMIN LEWIS, JR., physician, educator; b. Woodruff, S.C., July 22, 1926; s. Benjamin Lewis and Mattie Bernice (Skinner) B.; B.S., Furman U., 1946, LL.D., 1978; M.D., Med. U. S.C., 1949; m. Annalyne Louise Hall, Oct. 25, 1958; children—Benjamin Lewis III, Jane Kristen. Intern, Protestant Episcopal Hosp., Phila., 1949-50; pvt. practice gen. medicine, Woodruff, 1950-70; asso. prof. family practice Med. U. S.C., Charleston, 1970-74, prof. family practice, 1974-77, asst. dir. family practice residency program, 1970-75, chief undergrad. curriculum, 1970-77, vice chmn. dept. family practice, 1973-77, asst. dean for student affairs, 1975-77; mem. clin. staff Med. U. Hosp., Charleston County Hosp., 1970-77; Walter M. Seward prof., chmn. dept. family practice U. Va. Sch. Medicine, 1977—; family practice physician-in-chief U. Va. Med. Center Hosp., 1977—; chief of staff Woodruff Hosp., 1966-69; vis. lectr. numerous med. schs.; Stoneburner lectr. Med. Coll. Va., 1975; Daniel Drake lectr. U. Cin., 1976; Robert P. Walton lectr. Med. U. S.C., 1978; Goodlark prof. U. Tenn. Med. Sch., 1979; health officer Town of Woodruff, 1950-54. Mem. Spartanburg County Bd. Edn., 1968-70, sec., 1969-70; mem. drug adv. council S.C. Dept. Social Services, 1973-75. Trustee, Bethea Bapt. Home for Aged, Darlington, S.C., 1972-73. Served with USNR, 1954-56. Named Citizen of Year, Woodmen of World, 1968; recipient Golden Apple award for clin. teaching Student AMA, 1973; Thomas W. Johnson award Am. Acad. Family Physicians, 1976. Diplomate Am. Bd. Family Practice (mem. exam. bd. 1975—, dir. 1976—, pres. 1980—). Mem. AMA (mem. residency rev. com. for family practice 1974-79), Va., Albemarle County med. socs., Soc. Tchrs. Family Medicine (v.p. 1974, sec.-treas. 1975—), Am., S.C. (v.p. 1973, pres. 1975-76) acads. family practice, Spartanburg County Med. Soc. (v.p. 1968), Am. Philatelic Soc., Am. Manuscript Soc., Furman U. Alumni Assn. (dir. 1972-77), Alpha Omega Alpha (faculty councilor), Alpha Kappa Kappa (pres. 1948) Kappa Alpha. Baptist (deacon, chmn. bd.). Mason (32 degree). Editor S.C. Family Physician, 1973-74. Contbr. articles to med. jours. and textbooks. Home: 2406 Northfields Rd Charlottesville VA 22901

BARNETT, BERNARD HARRY, lawyer; b. Helena, Ark., July 13, 1916; s. Harry and Rebecca (Grossman) B.; student U. Mich., 1934-36; J.D., Vanderbilt U., 1940 ; m. Marian Spiesberger, Apr. 9, 1949; 1 son, Charles Dawson. Admitted to Ky. bar, 1940; pvt. practice, Louisville, 1940-42; asso. firm Woodward, Dawson, Hobson & Fulton, 1946-48; partner firms Bulitt, Dawson & Tarrant, 1948-52, Greenebaum, Barnett, Wood & Doll, 1952-70, Barnett & McConnell, 1972, Barnett, Greenebaum, Martin & McConnell, 1972-74, Barnett, Alagia, Greenebaum, Miller & Senn, 1974-75, Barnett & Alagia, 1975—; dir. Bank of Louisville, Cook United, Inc., Fuqua Industries, Inc. Mem. adv. group Joint Com. on Internal Revenue Taxation, U.S. Congress, 1953-55, Com. on Ways and Means, U.S. Ho. of Reps., 1956-58. Chmn., Louisville Fund, 1952-53; mem. nat. exec. com., nat. campaign cabinet United Jewish Appeal, 1959—, nat. chmn., 1967-71; chmn. Louisville United Jewish Appeal, 1968-69. Mem. Louisville and Jefferson County Republican Exec. Com., 1954-60; chmn. Ky. Rep. Finance Com., 1955-60. Trustee Spalding Coll., Louisville, 1975—, Norton Gallery and Sch. Art, 1980—, Benjamin N. Cardozo Sch. Law, 1979—. Served as lt. USNR, 1942-45. Mem. Am., Ky., Louisville bar assns. Home: Apt 1024 The Glenview 5100 Brownsboro Rd Louisville KY 40222 Office: 17th Floor Kentucky Home Life Bldg Louisville KY 40202

BARNETT, BETTY MARTIN, nurse; b. Mira, La., Dec. 4, 1929; d. Joe and Carrie Belle (Bundy) Martin; diploma Shreveport Charity Hosp. Sch. Nursing, 1950; B.S.N., Northwestern State U., 1957; children—Mary K., Janet M., Rebecca A., Cynthia D. Staff nurse operating rm. Shreveport (La.) Charity Hosp., 1950, staff nurse orthopedics, 1951, head nurse dept. medicine, 1952-54, asst. supr. orthopedics, 1954-73, asst. dir. nursing, 1973-76, asso. dir. nursing, 1976—. Mem. Shreveport Dist. Nurses Assn., La. Nurses Assn., Am. Nursing Assn., Gen. Fedn. Women's Clubs, Sigma Theta Tau, Beta Chi, Lambda Alpha. Democrat. Mem. Ch. of Christ. Address: 1541 Kings Hwy Shreveport LA 71130

BARNETT, CRAWFORD FANNIN, JR., physician; b. Atlanta, May 11, 1938; s. Crawford Fannin and Penelope Hollinshead (Brown) B.; student Taft Sch., 1953-56, U. Minn., 1957; A.B. magna cum laude, Yale, 1960; postgrad. (Davison scholar) Oxford (Eng.) U., 1963; M.D. (Trent scholar), Duke, 1964; m. Elizabeth McCarthy Hale, June 6, 1964; children—Crawford Fannin III, Robert Hale. Intern internal medicine Duke U. Med. Center, Durham, N.C., 1964-65, resident, 1965; resident internal medicine Wilmington (Del.) Med. Center, 1965-66; dir. Tenn. Heart Disease Control Program, Nashville, 1966-68; practice medicine, specializing in internal medicine, Atlanta, 1968—; mem. staff Crawford Long, Northside, Ga. Bapt., Grady Meml., Jessie Parker Williams, Doctors Meml., West Paces Ferry, Piedmont, hosps. (all Atlanta); mem. teaching staff Vanderbilt Med. Center, Nashville, 1966-68, Crawford Long Meml. Hosp., 1969—; clin. instr. internal medicine, dept. medicine Emory U. Med. Sch., Atlanta, 1969—. Vice pres., dir. Preferred Equities Corp., 1970—. Bd. govs. Doctors Meml. Hosp., 1971—; bd. dirs. Atlanta Speech Sch., 1976—, Historic Oakland Cemetery, 1976—, So. Turf Nurseries, 1977—, Tech Industries, 1978—. Served as surgeon USPHS, 1966-68. Fellow Am. Geog. Soc.; mem. Am. Fedn. Clin. Research, Council Clin. Cardiology, Am., Ga., Atlanta med. assns., Am., Ga. heart assns., Am., Ga. socs. internal medicine, Am. Assn. History Medicine, Ga., Atlanta (dir. 1976—) hist. socs., Ga., Nat. Trust for Historic Preservation, Internat. Hippocratic Found. Soc. (Greece), Faculty of History of Medicine and Pharmacy Worshipful Soc. Apothecaries of London (Eng.), Atlanta Com. on Fgn. Relations (chmn. exec. com.), So. Council on Internat. and Pub. Affairs, Newcomen Soc., Atlanta Clin. Soc., Victorian Soc. Am. (bd. advisers Atlanta chpt. 1971—), Mensa, Gridiron, Phi Beta Kappa. Episcopalian. Clubs: Piedmont Driving, Yale (dir. 1970-74), Nine O'Clocks (Atlanta); Pan Am. Doctors (Hidalgo, Mexico). Contbr. articles to profl. publs. Home: 2739 Ramsgate Ct NW Atlanta GA 30305 Office: 3250 Howell Mill Rd NW Atlanta GA 30327

BARNETT, DONALD OWEN, mech. engr.; b. Cleve., Sept. 9, 1936; s. Harold Earl and Anna (Bran) B.; B.S. in Mech. Engring. (Foundry Ednl. Found. grantee 1956-58), U. Ky., 1958; M.S. in Engring., U. Ala., 1966, Ph.D. (NASA trainee, NSF trainee), Auburn U., 1970; m. Connie Lynn Baldwin, Nov. 18, 1972; children—Michael, Stephen, Kathleen, Sandra, Christopher, JoAnna. Research engr. NASA, Cleve., 1958-60, aerospace technologist Huntsville, Ala., 1963-65; mech. engr. U.S. Air Force, Dayton, Ohio, 1960-63; mgr. aerothermodynamics br. Northrop Co., Huntsville, 1966-73; sr. research engr., head laser velocimetry and electro optics ARO, Inc., Tullahoma, Tenn., 1973-78; asso. prof. mech. engring. U. Ala., Birmingham, 1978—. Mem. ASME, Am. Soc. Engring. Edn., Sigma Xi. Methodist. Contbr. articles to profl. jours.; developer single beam transit time laser velocimeter. Home: 1524 Melrose Pl Homewood AL 35209 Office: Dept Mech Engring U Ala Birmingham AL 35294

BARNETT, FRANKLIN DEWEES, physician; b. Ft. Thomas, Ky., Aug. 1, 1935; s. Harry T. and Elizabeth (McKeny) B.; A.B., Asbury Coll., Wilmore, Ky., 1957; student Bowman Gray Sch. Medicine, 1957-58; M.D., U. Kans., 1961; m. Louise Baillod, Oct. 23, 1976; children—Julie, Brian, Kelly, Colin. Intern, Wesley Hosp., Wichita, Kans., 1962; resident obstetrics and gynecology U. Okla. Health Scis. Center, 1964-67; practice medicine specializing in obstetrics and gynecology, Midwest City, Okla., 1967—; chief obstetrics-gynecology Midwest City Meml. Hosp.; asso. clin. prof. Okla. Health Scis. Center. Diplomate Am. Bd. Obstetrics and Gynecology. Mem. Am. Coll. Obstetrics and Gynecology, Am. Assn. Gynecol. Laparoscopists, Am. Fertility Soc. Rotarian. Served with USAF, 1962-64. Office: 2801 Parklawn Dr Midwest City OK 73110

BARNETT, HARVEY LESTER, JR., communications co. exec.; b. Mobile, Ala., Mar. 3, 1952; s. Harvey Lester and Marie (Hodge) B.; B.A., U. South Ala., 1974; m. Flora Alleen Woodruff, June 15, 1974; 1 dau., Abigail Billings. With A.B. Dick Products Co. of Mobile, 1974—, gen. mgr., 1976-78, pres., 1978—, named to Co. Hall of Fame, 1977. Mem. Mobile Jaycees (Outstanding Service citation 1975), Theta Xi Alumni (advisor 1977-78). Republican. Episcopalian. Clubs: Rotary (asst. editor Newsletter 1977), U. South Ala. Alumni Century. Office: AB Dick Products Co of Mobile 201 Virginia St Mobile AL 36603

BARNETT, JOSEPH TOWNSEND, architect; b. Norton, Va., Aug. 10, 1927; s. John Edward and Margaret (Stryker) B.; B.S. in Architecture cum laude, Clemson (S.C.) U., 1951; m. Elizabeth Haaga, June 25, 1955; children—Elizabeth Claire, Margaret Anne, Caroline Marie. With archtl. firms in Memphis, 1953-76; propr. Joseph T. Barnett, architect, Memphis, 1976-77; chief architect Allen & Hoshall, Inc., 1978—; asso. prof. Memphis State U., 1974-77. Bd. dirs. Ave Maria Home Aged, Birthright Memphis. Served with AUS, 1945-46, to 1st lt. C.E., AUS, 1951-53; Korea. Decorated Commendation medal. Mem. AIA (pres. Memphis chpt. 1979), Serra Club. Roman Catholic. Home: 1593 Dearing Rd Memphis TN 38117 Office: 2430 Poplar Ave Memphis TN 38112

BARNETT, JUANITA MCMILLAN, librarian; b. Hope, Ark., May 3, 1915; d. David Williams and Leila Belle (Allen) McMillan; B.A., Ouachita Bapt. U., 1936; B.L.S., George Peabody Coll. Tchrs., 1937; m. James Russell Barnett, Aug. 14, 1938 (dec. July 1954); children—Judy Barnett Jennings, Barbara Barnett Galbraith. Librarian, Ouachita Bapt. U., Arkadelphia, Ark., 1936-40, 56—. Mem. Am. (state membership com. 1964), Southwestern, Ark. (2d v.p. 1964, chmn. coll. sect. 1959-60) library assns., Ark. Found. Asso. Colls. (sec. com. librarians 1966-67, pres. com. librarians 1970, 77), Clark County Hist. Assn. (charter, asst. exec. sec. 1972—). Presbyn. (sec. 1954-56, deacon 1971-76, elder 1977—). Editor 2d edit. Periodical Holdings in the Ark. Found. Asso. Colls., 1963. Home: 610 Pine St Arkadelphia AR 71923 Office: Riley Library Ouachita Bapt U Arkadelphia AR 71923

BARNETT, LEROY ELLIOT, airport exec.; b. New Smyrna Beach, Fla., Aug. 13, 1936; s. Leroy Elliot and Ruth Viola (Waters) Barnett; A.S. in Elec. Engring., Daytona Beach Jr. Coll., 1961; B.S. in Aviation Mgmt., Embry-Riddle U., 1971; grad. USAF Air U., Air Command and Staff Coll., Indsl. Coll. Armed Services; m. Patricia Achue, Jan. 1, 1962; children—Ian Lee, Rian Kel. Meteorol. technician Pan Am. Airways, USAF Eastern Test Range, 1961-64, recovery engr., 1964-66, chief recovery engr., 1966-68, staff engr., 1968-70; mgr. New Smyrna Beach Municipal Airport, 1972—; v.p. Impco, Fla., Ltd., Miami, 1975—; dir. ops. Southeast region CAP. Served with USAF, 1953-58. Recipient Service award CAP, 1968; licensed comml. pilot. Mem. Am. Assn. Airport Execs., Fla. Airport Mgrs. Assn., Fla. Civil Def. Assn., Nat. Aerospace Edn. Assn., Air Force Assn. Home: 804 E 11th Ave New Smyrna Beach FL 32069 Office: PO Box 890 New Smyrna Beach FL 32069

BARNETT, LOUIS, JR., apparel mfg. co. exec.; b. Mobile, Ala., Oct. 25, 1943; s. Louis and Wilhelmenia (Wilson) B.; A.B., Ala. State U., 1969; m. Shirley Jackson, Apr. 27, 1974; 1 dau., Nicole Renee. Staff worker Selma Project, Tuscaloosa, Ala., 1970-72; dir. Greene County Devel. Center, Eutaw, Ala., 1972-74; pres. Eutaw Apparel Corp., (Ala.), 1975—. Mem. Presidents' Club, Democratic party. Served with U.S. Army, 1962-65. Recipient Leadership award Extension Service, 1975, Econ. Devel. award Greene County Commn., 1975. Mem. Nat. Small Bus. Assn., Nat. Assn. Black Mfrs., Inc., Alpha Phi Alpha. Methodist. Home: 413 Roebuck Ave Eutaw AL 35462 Office: PO Box 531 Eutaw AL 35462

BARNETT, RONALD DAVID, agronomist; b. Texarkana, Ark., Nov. 20, 1943; s. Herman Clark and Agnes Margret (Nolte) B.; B.S.A., U. Ark., 1965, M.S., 1968; Ph.D., Purdue U., 1970; m. Pamela P. Barnett, Nov. 4, 1961; children—Penny, Brad, Amy. Agronomist, U. Fla., Quincy, 1970—, asso. prof., 1975—, asso. agronomist, 1975—. Mem. Am. Soc. Agronomy, Crop Sci. Soc. Am., Am. Genetics Assn., AAAS, Council of Agrl. Sci. and Tech., Soil and Crop Sci. Soc. Fla. Baptist. Club: Rotary (past pres.). Contbr. articles to profl. jours. Home: Route 2 Box 186 Quincy FL 32351 Office: Rt 3 Box 638 Quincy FL 32351

BARNETT, WILLIAM WOODSON, JR., ednl. adminstr.; b. Lexington, Mo., Oct. 23, 1920; s. William Woodson and Elizabeth (Slusher) B.; A.A., Wentworth Mil. Acad., 1939; B.S., U. Mo., 1941, M.A., 1949; m. Ann Mahler, Oct. 29, 1946; 1 son, Theodore Mahler. Accounting clk. Gen. Electric Co., Bridgeport, Conn., 1941-42; commd. 2d lt. U.S. Army, 1942, advanced through grades to lt. col., 1954, ret., 1965; instr. Wentworth Mil. Acad., Lexington, 1965-67; prof. journalism Schreiner Coll., Kerrville, Tex., 1967—, dir. publicity and student publs., 1967-75, dir. admissions, 1975-76, dir. student fin. aid, 1975—. Chmn. service unit Salvation Army, 1970-72; mem. Bd. Conv. Activities, City of Kerrville, 1976-78; sec. bd. dirs. Hill Country Arts Found., 1977—; exec. com. TASFAA, 1978—. Decorated Bronze Star medal with oak leaf cluster; recipient George C. Marshall medal Command and Gen. Staff Coll., 1961. Presbyterian (elder). Kiwanian (pres. 1976-77). Home: Schreiner Campus Kerrville TX 78028 Office: Schreiner Coll Kerrville TX 78028

BARNETTE, VOLNEY THEODORE, JR., water treatment products co. exec.; b. Tryon, N.C., Jan. 13, 1934; s. Volney Theodore and Mattie Mae (Ashmore) B.; B.S., Furman U., 1955; m. Roxie Ann Ford, Jan. 5, 1958; children—William Theodore, Melissa Anne, Amy Caroline. Asst. to plant chemist, food product div. Union Carbide Corp., Loudon, Tenn., 1958-62, plant chemist, 1962-66; devel. engr. Fiber Ind., Inc., Salisbury, N.C., 1966-73; prodn. engr. Texfi Industries, New Bern, N.C., 1973-77; quality control engr. Hoechst Fibers, Spartanburg, S.C., 1977-79; sales chemist Guardian Ipco, Birmingham, Ala., 1979—. Served with U.S. Army, 1957. Mem. Am. Soc. Quality Control (cert. quality control engr.). Baptist. Home: 228 Heather Dr Spartanburg SC 29301 Office: PO Box 43067 Route 13 Box 409 Birmingham AL 35243

BARNEY, CHARLES LESTER, petroleum co. exec.; b. Shreveport, La., Nov. 4, 1925; s. Lester K. and Ruby Lee (Meeks) B.; B.S., Petroleum Engr., La. State U., 1949; m. Frances Jenkins, Oct. 13, 1944; children—Jerry, Charles, Merilyn. Ops. mgr. Mobil Can., 1964-66; gen. mgr., exploration and producing Mobil Germany, 1966-70; producing mgr. Mobil Internat., 1970-71, planning mgr., 1971-72, mgr., acquisitions and concessions, 1972-74; corp. producing mgr. Mobil, 1974-75; v.p. drilling and prodn. Superior Oil Co., Houston, 1975-78, sr. v.p., prodn., sales, mfg. and planning, 1978—, also dir.; chmn. bd., chief exec. officer McIntyre Mines Ltd., Can., 1979; chmn. bd., dir. Can. Superior Oil Ltd. Served with USN, 1945-46. Mem. Soc. Petroleum Engrs., Mid-Continent Oil and Gas Assn. Episcopalian. Office: PO Box 1521 Houston TX 77001

BARNHART, BOBBY JAMES, thermal insulation contracting and distbn. co. exec., air conditioning co. exec.; b. Hondo, Tex., Sept. 5, 1927; s. George Bob and Sadie Gwendolyn (Earnest) B.; B.S. in Mech. Engring., U. Tex., 1949; postgrad. Central Mo. State Coll., 1945, Brown U., 1945-46; m. Alice Lorene Fritts, July 4, 1947; children—Bobby James, Marie Adele, Thomas Roy. Sales engr. Fulcher Air Conditioning Co., Austin, Tex., 1949-50; estimator, engr. Barnhart Plumbing & Heating Co., Austin, 1953; founder, pres. Cinbar Corp., Austin, 1953—, Barnhart Mfg. & Supply Co. Inc., Austin, 1959—. Served with USNR, 1945-46, 51-53; China, Korea. Registered profl. engr., Tex. Mem. Tex., Southwestern Cattle Raisers Assn., Am. Soc. Heating and Air Conditioning Engrs. (pres. chpt. 1961-62), ASME, Nat., Tex. socs. profl. engrs., V.F.W., Confederate Air Force. Baptist. Clubs: Headliners (Austin); Masons, Shriners, Elks. Home: 12612 N Lamar Blvd Austin TX 78753 Office: 12800 N Lamar Blvd Austin TX 78753

BARNHART, JOE EDWARD, educator; b. Knoxville, Tenn., Nov. 1, 1931; s. Clifford Edward and Irene Marie (Snyder) B.; B.A., Carson-Newman Coll., 1953; M.A. in Div., So. Bapt. Theol. Sem., 1956; Ph.D., Boston U., 1964; postgrad. Harvard U., summer 1959; m. Mary Ann Shropshire, Dec. 27, 1953; children—Ritschl Edward, Linda Jane. Asst. prof. philosophy Carson-Newman Coll., Jefferson City, Tenn., 1957-58; instr. philosophy Western Carolina U., 1961-64; asst. prof. philosophy U. Redlands (Calif.), 1964-66, dept. coordinator, 1964-66; lectr. philosophy and religion U. Calif., Riverside, 1965-66; asso. prof. Parsons Coll., Fairfield, Iowa, 1966-67; prof. philosophy N. Tex. State U., Denton, 1967—. Mem. Southwestern Philos. Soc., Am., N. Tex. (pres. 1973-74) philos. assns., Soc. for Sci. Study of Religion, Am. Acad. Religion, AAUP (pres. 1963-64), So. Soc. for Philosophy and Psychology. Author: The Billy Graham Religion, 1972; Religion and the Challenge of Philosophy, 1975; The Study of Religion and Its Meaning: New Explorations in Light of Karl Popper and Emile Durkheim, 1977; contbr. articles to scholarly jours.; asso. editor Southwestern Jour. Social Edn., 1970. Home: 606 Headlee Ln Denton TX 76201 Office: N Tex State U Denton TX 76203

BARNHILL, JOHN WILLIAMSON, JR., ice cream co. exec.; b. Brenham, Tex., Nov. 18, 1936; s. John Williamson and Cecilia Low (Morriss) B.; B.J., U. Tex., Austin, 1959; m. Katherine Jane Cook, Aug. 22, 1959; children—Jane Elizabeth, John Williamson III, Ted Cook. Asst. pres. sec. to Gov. Tex., 1958-59; editorial staff writer Houston Press, 1959-60; dir. sales promotion Blue Bell Creameries, 1961-64; gen. mgr. Houston br., 1964-72, gen. sales mgr., Brenham, Tex., 1972—, v.p. sales, 1977—, also dir. Trustee, Brenham Ind. Sch. Dist., 1974-75; bd. dirs. Vol. Services Council Brenham State Sch., 1976—, Bohne Meml. Hosp., Brenham, 1979—; ruling elder Brenham Presbyterian Ch., 1974—; chmn. Brenham Parks and Recreation Bd., 1979—; pres. Washington County chpt. Am. Heart Assn., 1979-80, Brenham Maifest Assn., 1979—. Served to 1st lt. U.S. Army, 1961-62. Mem. U. Tex. Ex-Students Assn. (life, pres. Washington County 1976-77), Washington County C. of C. (dir. 1974-76), Mktg. Communications Execs. Internat. (pres. Houston chpt. 1969-70), Dairy Products Inst. Tex. (dir. 1974-76), Tex., Houston retail grocers assns., Houston Livestock Show and Rodeo (life), Heritage Soc. Washington County (life), Kappa Alpha (pres. Houston chpt. alumni orgn. 1969-70). Clubs: Brenham Gun and Rod, Brenham Rotary (pres. 1975-76, gov.'s rep. dist. 589 1978-79). Home: Old Chappell Hill Rd Route 1 Brenham TX 77833 Office: PO Box 1807 Loop 577 Brenham TX 77833

BARNHILL, WILLIAM EDWARD, elevator mfg. co. exec.; b. Cairo, Ill., Jan. 30, 1933; s. George William and Mabel Audry (Peck) B.; A.A., Paducah Jr. Coll., 1959; student Memphis State U., 1960-61; m. Barbara Jean Dykes, Feb. 20, 1954; children—Marcelyn, Robert, Traci, Ronald. Inventory control mgr. Metal Goods Co., Memphis, 1964-67; material analyst, elevator div. Dover Corp., Horn Lake, Miss., 1967-74, sr. buyer, 1974-76, purchasing mgr., 1976—. Served with U.S. Army, 1953-55. Mem. Am. Mgmt. Assn., Nat. Assn. Purchasing Mgmt., Memphis Assn. Purchasing Mgmt. Home: 1806 St John's Pl Memphis TN 38116 Office: PO Box 468 Horn Lake MS 38637

BARNS, WILLIAM DERRICK, educator; b. Fayette County, Pa., Apr. 3, 1917; s. William Post and Lida (Williams) B.; A.B., Pa. State U., 1939, M.A., 1940; Ph.D., W.Va. U., 1947; m. Doretha Mae Clayton, Sept. 3, 1947. Instr. history Pa. State U., University Park, 1939-40; instr. history W.Va. U., Morgantown, 1940-47, asst. prof., 1947-54, asso. prof., 1954-77, prof., 1977—. Field agt. Am. Friends Service Com., 1944-46. Mem. AAUP (co-founder W.Va. conf. 1961, dir. 1961-71), Agrl. History Soc., Am. Hist. Assn., Orgn. Am. Historians, W.Va. Hist. Assn. of Coll. and Univ. Tchrs. (co-founder 1959, pres. 1962-63), English-Speaking Union, W.Va. Civil Liberties Union (co-founder, dir. 1970-79, v.p. 1979—), Phi Kappa Phi, Phi Alpha Theta, Pi Gamma Mu, Alpha Tau Omega. Mem. Soc. of Friends. Author: The Granger and Populist Movements in West Virginia, 1873-1914, 1947; Highlights in West Virginia's Agricultural History, 1863-1963, 1963; The West Virginia State Grange: The First Century, 1873-1973, 1973; contbr. articles in field to profl. jours. Home: 512 Beverly Ave Morgantown WV 26505 Office: Dept History WVa U Morgantown WV 26506

BARNWELL, THOMAS OSBORN, JR., civil engr.; b. Charleston, S.C., Mar. 12, 1947; s. Thomas Osborn and Joyce (Towles) B.; B.S., Clemson U., 1969, M.S., 1971; m. Gilda Jean Turner, Feb. 26, 1972; 1 son, Courtney Carter. Sanitary engr. U.S. EPA, Region IV, Athens, Ga., 1971-77, civil engr. ORD, 1977—. Served with USAR, 1972. Mem. ASCE, Water Pollution Control Fedn., Am. Water Resources Assn., Tau Beta Pi, Phi Kappa Pi, Chi Epsilon. Episcopalian. Home: 145 Arthur Circle Athens GA 30605 Office: EPA College Station Rd Athens GA 30613

BARON, FREDERICK MARTIN, lawyer; b. Cedar Rapids, Iowa, June 20, 1947; s. Abraham and Rose (Levin) B.; B.A., U. Tex. at Austin, 1968, J.D., 1971; m. Wendy Flatow, June 9, 1968; children—Andrew Michael, Courtney Melaine. Law clk. U.S. Commn. on Civil Rights, Washington, 1970; admitted to Tex. bar, 1971, U.S. Supreme Ct. bar, 1977; mem. firm Baron & Cowley, Dallas. Mem. Am., Dallas bar assns., Am., Tex., Dallas trial lawyers assns., Lawyers Involved for Tex., Tex. Law Rev. Ex-editors Assn. Democrat. Home: 7015 Lakewood Blvd Dallas TX 75214 Office: 1400 Dallas Fed Savs Tower Dallas TX 75225

BARON, IRA SAUL, mgmt. and tax consulting co. exec.; b. Bklyn., Nov. 8, 1948; s. Morris and Janet B.; B.A., U. Fla., 1971. Corporate controller Community Newspapers Corp., Miami, 1971-72; v.p. Nat. Funding Corp. Am., Miami, 1972; pres. Baron & Assos., Gainesville, Fla., 1973—; dir. Old Fla. Co., Newsstand Services, Inc., Adams-Johnson, Inc., Cosgrave Properties, Inc., Gainesville Personnel Services, Inc. Mem. Gainesville Bd. Realtors, Fla. Assn. Realtors, Alachua County Humane Soc., Gainesville C. of C. Republican. Club: Turkey Creek Country. Home: 5813 NW 26th St Gainesville FL 32601 Office: PO Box 14036 Gainesville FL 32604

BARONA, NARSES MONTES DE OCÁ, chem. engr.; b. Cali, Colombia, Feb. 14, 1932; s. Victor Manuel and Sara (Montes de Oca) B.; came to U.S., 1962, naturalized, 1976; Chem.E., U. Valle, Cali, 1953; M.Sc. in Chem. Engring., Carnegie-Mellon U., 1956; postgrad. in Chem. Engring. Poly. Inst. Bklyn., 1957; Ph.D. in Chem. Engring., U. Houston, 1964; m. Luz Marina Munoz Rengifo, Dec. 25, 1958; children—Narses, Luz Elisa. Asst. prof. chem. engring. U. Valle, 1953-54, prof., 1954-62, sec. Sch. Chem. Engring., 1954-58, head dept. chem. engring., 1957-58, dean engring., 1958-62; research engr. in process design, evaluation and devel. Ethyl Corp., Baton Rouge, 1964-76, sr. engr., cons., 1976—, cons. research group, 1972—; lectr. on reactor design, U.S., South America; Hon. prof. U. Central Quito (Equador), 1959. Mem. Am. Inst. Chem. Engrs., Am. Chem. Soc., Colombian Inst. Chem. Engr. (pres. 1957), Nat. Soc. Engring. Colombia, Peruvian Inst. Chem. Engrs. (miembro correspondiente 1977), Internat. Neighbors, Sigma Xi. Republican. Roman Catholic. Club: Toastmasters. Contbr. articles on chem. engring. to profl. jours.; specialty reactor designer. Home: 2947 Myrtle Ave Baton Rouge LA 70806 Office: Ethyl Corp Baton Rouge LA 70821

BARONDESS, STUART HENRY, radio sta. exec.; b. N.Y.C., Apr. 1, 1927; s. William H. and Belle (Toplitz) B.; B.A. cum laude, Norwich U., 1949; m. Shirley Spiegel, Apr. 1, 1955; children—David Paul, Mark Adam. Publicity, sales promotion, TV prodn. WTVJ, Miami, Fla., 1950-57; script writer for Gabriel Heatter, Mut. Network, 1951; sta. mgr. KCUL Radio, Ft. Worth, 1957-58; account exec. WNJR Radio, gen. sales mgr. WRAP Radio, Rollins, Inc., Norfolk, Va., 1959-77; gen. sales mgr. WOWI-FM/WPCE-AM Radio, Norfolk, 1977—. Served with inf., AUS, 1945-46; ETO. Honored by Womens Aux. Norfolk Community Hosp. for efforts in promoting broadcast campaign for heart machine, 1973. Home: 100 Conference Ct Virginia Beach VA 23462 Office: WOWI-FM/WPCE-AM Norfolk VA 23501

BARONE, ANTHONY JOSEPH, sales exec.; b. Leroy, N.Y., July 25, 1917; s. Joseph Anthony and Jovana (Maloni) B.; student Ithaca Coll., 1936-40; m. Betty Lou Poe, May 20, 1966; children—John Barone, Marietta, Toni-Ann. Mgr. Western Auto Stores, Newark, also Passaic, Paterson, N.J., 1941-49; gen. agt. Gen. Am. Life Ins. Co., Miami, Fla., 1960-64; salesman franchises, Birmingham, Ala., 1965-70; pres. Organ Center, Inc., Sound Advt. Media, Inc., Huntsville, 1970—. Mem. Sales and Mktg. Execs. Assn., Internat. Platform Assn., C. of C., Phi Mu Alpha. Democrat. Roman Catholic. Clubs: Elks, Lions. Home: 404 Weatherly Rd Huntsville AL 35803 Office: 2007 N Memorial Pkwy Huntsville AL 35810

BARONE, BARTOLO MARIANO, neurosurgeon; b. Poughkeepsie, N.Y., May 15, 1934; s. Bartolo and Gertrude (Granata) B.; B.S., Georgetown U., 1955; M.D. (Nat. Polio Found. fellow summers, 1956, 58), 1959; M.S., McGill U., 1962; m. Mary Pringle Herrin, Sept. 21, 1974; children by previous marriage—Florence, Caroline, Elizabeth; stepchildren—Dolph Rustin, Raiford Rustin. Rotating intern U. Chgo., 1959-60; resident neurosurg. surgery, McGill U., 1960-65; practice medicine specializing in neurosurgery Washington, 1965-66, Charleston, S.C., 1968—; mem. staff Roper hosp. (pres. 1975-76), St. Francis Xavier Hosp., S.C., Charleston County Hosp.; cons. neurosurgeon Med. U.S.C. Hosp.; lectr. neurosurgery McGill U., 1964-65; asst. prof. neurosurgery Georgetown U., 1965-66; asst. clin. prof. neurosurgery Med. U. S.C., 1968-74, asso. clin. prof., 1974—. Adv. Council Pollution Control Bd. Charleston County, 1970-72; pres. PTA Cathedral Sch. Charleston, 1971-72; bd. dirs. Roper Hosp., Charleston, 1977—. Served as chief neurosurgery, U.S. Naval Hosp., Charleston, 1966-68. NIH postdoctoral fellow, 1960, 64. Named Boss of Year, Charleston Chap. Am. Bus. Women's Assn., 1972. Diplomate Am. Bd. Neurol. Surgery. Fellow Am. Coll. Surgeons; mem. Med. Soc. S.C., Charleston County Med. Soc., AMA, S.C. Med. Assn. (council 1979—), So. Med. Assn., So. Neurosurg. Soc., Am. Assn. Neurol. Surgeons, Congress Neurol. Surgeons, Trident C. of C. Roman Catholic. Honorable Order of Ky. Cols. Clubs: Carolina Yacht, Sertoma. Contbr. articles in field to profl. jours. Home: TH-17 Dockside 330 Concord St Charleston SC 29401 Office: 315 Calhoun St Charleston SC 29401

BARONE, BETTY LOU, advt. exec., music co. exec.; b. Miami, Fla., Nov. 26, 1925; d. John Hal and Julia Elizabeth (White) Poe; student pub. schs., Miami; m. Anthony J. Barrone, May 20, 1966; children—Robert E. Rainey Jr., Terry L. Rainey, Dorothea M. Lowe, Sunny Ann Clowdus. Constrn. exec. Rainey Land Co., Inc., Miami, 1954-57; pvt. practice interior decoration, Miami, 1964-66, Huntsville, Ala., 1968-71; exec. Organ Center, Inc., Huntsville, 1969—; sec.-treas. Soound Advt. Media, Inc., Huntsville, 1975—. Mem. Huntsville C. of C., Huntsville Better Bus. Bur., Huntsville Advt. Club. Democrat. Home: 404 Weatherly Rd SE Huntsville AL 35803 Office: 2007 N Memorial Pkwy Huntsville AL 35810

BARR, CAMERON BOYD, hosp. adminstr.; b. New Orleans, Oct, 4, 1947; s. Thomas and Virginia Adelaide (Boyd) B.; B.A., So. La. U., 1969, M.Ed., 1971; M.P.H., Tulane U., 1975; m. Marcia Katherine Comeaux, Jan. 13, 1973; children—Virginia Lee, Thomas Boyd. Tchr., Tangipahoa Parish Sch. System, Amite, La., 1970-73; personnel asst. So. Bapt. Hosp., New Orleans, 1973-74, adminstrv. resident, 1974-75, adminstrv. asst. to exec. dir., 1975-78, adminstr. extended care unit, 1976-78 data processing liaison officer, 1977-78 adminstr. for planning and agy. relations, 1980—; acting exec. dir. Children's Hosp., New Orleans, 1978-80. Chmn. fin. com. Ch. of the Covenant, Presbyn., 1975-78. Named Outstanding First Year Tchr., Phi Delta Kappa. Mem. Am. Hosp. Assn., Am. Coll. Hosp. Adminstrs., La. Hosp. Assn., New Health Care Mgrs. Assn., Sigma Tau Gamma. Democrat. Home: 2225 Chestnut St New Orleans LA 70130 Office: 200 Henry Clay Ave New Orleans LA 70118

BARR, CAROL GELO, ednl. counselor; b. Searsmont, Maine, July 11, 1942; d. Clarence Edwin and Alice Nina (White) Gelo; B.A. with distinction, U. Maine, 1964; M.Ed., Coll. William and Mary, 1971, postgrad., 1975—; m. Herman Ernest Barr, June 15, 1963; children—Jonathan Roland, Thomas Herman, Jennifer Lee. Tchr. French pub. and pvt. schs., Newport News, Va., 1965-66, 73-74; guidance counselor Newport News Pub. Sch. System, 1974-77, dir. guidance, 1977-80, supr. guidance, 1980—. Mem. Am., Peninsula, Va. Personnel and Guidance Assns., Am. Sch. Counselor Assn., Assn. Specialists in Group Work. Episcopalian. Office: 51 Copeland Ln Newport News VA 23601

BARR, JAMES BRUCE, interior design co. exec., fin. cons.; b. Buffalo, Mar. 23, 1945; s. Bertram and Bertha (Marcus) B.; B.S. in Mgmt., Fairleigh Dickinson U., 1968; M.B.A. in Fin. and Investments, Bernard Baruch Grad. Sch., 1971; m. Gayle Hoffman, Mar. 19, 1966; children—Ronald, Rachael. Acct., Rayette Faberge Co., Jersey City, 1968-69; div. acct. Sun Chem. Co., Kearny, N.J., 1969; fin. analyst CIT Fin. Corp., N.Y.C., 1969-71; budget mgr. BVD Corp., N.Y.C., 1971, Gen. Devel. Corp., Miami, Fla., 1974-76; mgr. profit planning and analysis Aristar, Inc., Miami, 1972-74; mgr. corp. planning Modular Computer Systems, Inc., Ft. Lauderdale, Fla., 1976-79; v.p. Designs of Times, Inc., Coral Springs, Fla., 1979—; fin. cons., 1973—; adj. prof. Broward Community Coll., 1978—. Tchr.'s lic.; ins. lic.; real estate lic.; mut. fund lic. Mem. Planning Execs. Inst. (founder, dir., treas. Miami and Ft. Lauderdale chpts.), Nat. Assn. Securities Dealers, Ft. Lauderdale Area Bd. Realtors. Democrat. Jewish. Author: Credit Procedure Manual for Banks, 1976. Home: 8521 NW 19th Dr Coral Springs FL 33065 Office: 11471 W Sample Rd Coral Springs FL 33065

BARR, NONA LEE, speech pathologist; b. Florence, Ala., July 11, 1934; d. Joseph Allen and Beulah Mae (Futrell) Behel; student David Lipscomb Coll., Nashville, 1952-54; B.S., U. Houston, 1965, M.A. (grad. fellow 1966-68), 1968; Ph.D., Pacific Western U., Encino, Calif., 1978; m. Luther L. Barr, July 3, 1954: 1 dau., Lori Lee. Elementary sch. tchr. Cheasapeake Public Schs., Norfolk, Va., 1959-61; tchr. Children's Acad., Houston, 1965-67; speech pathologist La Porte (Tex.) Ind. Sch. Dist., 1967-68, Home Health Services La., Inc., 1968-79, St. Charles Gen. Hosp., New Orleans, 1974-78, Jefferson Parish Public Schs., Gretna, La., 1979—; dir. Grad. Speech Clinic, U. Houston, summer 1979—; bd. dirs. Southeastern Health System; cons. in field. Cert. tchr., Tex., La.; lic. speech pathologist, La. Mem. Am. Speech and Hearing Assn., Am. Acad. Pvt. Practice in Speech Pathology and Audiology (dir.), La. Speech and Hearing Assn (pres. 1975-76), Willowdale Civic Assn., Rolling Stones Gem and Mineral Club. Republican. Mem. Ch. of Christ. Author papers in field. Home: 2509 Ingrid Ln Metairie LA 70003 Office: 1450 Jefferson St Gretna LA 70053

BARR, RAY LAMAR, retail bus. machine co. exec.; b. West Monroe, La., Sept. 4, 1932; s. Roy Levi and Mattie Ruth (Griggs) B.; grad. public schs., Monroe, La.; m. Bette Jo Bamburg, Sept. 12, 1952; children—Roger Lewis, Mark Stuart. Salesman, Barr Typewriter Co., Monroe, 1952-55 sales coordinator Olin Mathieson Corp., West Monroe, 1955-58 sales rep. Home Office Supply, West Monroe, 1958-61, Bell & Howell Co., New Orleans, 1961-62; sales trainee

Victor Comptometer Corp., Nashville, 1962, sales mgr., 1963-69, br. mgr., Baton Rouge, 1969-75; owner, mgr. All-American Business Machine Co., Chattanooga, 1975—; cons. bus. edn. dept. La. State U., 1970-75. Mem. Twin City Symphony Orch., Monroe, 1960-62; Little Theatre, Monroe, 1960-62, Nashville, 1962-69. Mem. Ind. Cash Register Dealers Assn., Nat. Office Machine Dealers Assn. Baptist. Clubs: Masons, Shriners, Optimists, Sertoma (inter-club activities dir. 1978, v.p. 1979). Office: All American Bus Machine Co 739 McCallie Ave Chattanooga TN 37403

BARR, SIGVARD CHARLES, registered nurse; b. Ft. Collins, Colo., Aug. 27, 1953; d. Charley Lewis and Ruthmae (Helvick) B.; student Southwestern Union Coll., 1973; B.S. in Nursing, Union Coll., 1975; postgrad. Tex. Women's U., 1975—. Staff nurse med-surg. floors St. Paul's Hosp., Dallas, 1975; public health nurse Dallas County, 1975-76; charge nurse Mesquite (Tex.) Meml. Hosp., 1976; instr. Sch. Nursing, Southwestern Adventist Coll., 1976-77, relief instr., 1978; morning clin. coordinator nursing service Huguley Meml. Hosp., Ft. Worth, 1977-79, cardiac rehab. nurse, 1979—; CPR tchr.-trainer Am. Heart Assn., mem. CPR task force, Tarrant County, Tex., 1979-80. Mem. SW Basketball Ofcls. Assn. Adventist. Home: PO Box 552 Keene TX 76059 Office: PO Box 6337 Fort Worth TX 76115

BARR, WALLACE WESLEY, III, shipbuilding exec.; b. Bogalusa, La., Mar. 24, 1944; s. Wallace Wesley and Theone Patricia (Switzer) B.; B.S. in Psychology, Loyola U., New Orleans, 1977; m. Sharon Ann DiFatta, Apr. 13, 1973; children—Wallace Wesley IV, Sean Santo. Employment rep. space div. Chrysler Corp., New Orleans, 1965-68; mgr. sales, officer Commuter Airline-Jet Air Leasing and Central Tex. Airlines, New Orleans, 1969-70; asst. gen. mgr. Marine Splty. and Mill Supply, New Orleans, 1971-72; dir. emergency med. sers. State of La., New Orleans, 1972-73; gen. mgr. Blvd. Motors, 1973-74; personnel mgr. Avondale Shipyards, Inc., New Orleans, 1975-79; corporate dir. adminstrn. Equitable Shipyards, Inc., New Orleans, 1979—. Mem. bus. and distributive edn. adv. council Jefferson Parish Public Schs., 1978—; mem. vocat.-tech. task force La. Dept. Edn., 1979—. Served with USNG, 1965-71; served with U.S. Army, 1967. Recipient Key to City, New Orleans, 1972. Licensed instrument and ground instr. FAA; licensed 3d class radiotelephone operator with broadcast endorsement FCC; comml. pilot; licensed real estate agt. La. Mem. Internat. Assn. Personnel in Employment Security, Am. Soc. Personnel Adminstrn., Personnel Mgmt. Assn. New Orleans, New Orleans Jr. C. of C., New Orleans and River Region C. of C. (vocat.-tech. edn. com.). Republican. Roman Catholic. Home: 4805 Perry Dr Metairie LA 70002 Office: PO Box 8001 New Orleans LA 70182

BARRAR, ANNETTE KNIGHT, nurse, educator; b. Darlove, Miss., Feb. 25, 1939; d. Charlie Matthew and Wilda Helen (Bagley) K.; B.S., U. Ala., 1961; M.N., U. Fla., 1965; m. Harold Hayes Barrar, Aug. 2, 1975. Staff nurse, supr. and instr. Children's Hosp., Birmingham, Ala., 1961-64; instr. nursing Jones Jr. Coll., Ellisville, Miss., 1964-65; instr. nursing Rockingham Community Coll., Reidsville, N.C., 1966-69; clin. specialist pediatric nursing Guilford County Health Dept., Greensboro, N.C., 1969-72; asst. prof. Sch. Nursing Miss. U. for Women, Columbus, 1972—, dir. asso. degree program, 1973—, acting dean, 1980. Mem. Nat. League for Nursing, Am. Nurses Assn., Miss. Nurses Assn., Dist. 17 Nurses Assn., Miss. Council of Deans and Dirs. Methodist. Home: 207 Curtis Rd Columbus MS 39701

BARRERA, GLORIA ALICIA ESQUIVEL, sch. counselor; b. San Antonio, Oct. 5, 1942; d. Jesús Esquivel and Esperanza Badillo Esquivel Méndez; B.S., Our Lady of Lake Coll., San Antonio, 1965, M.Ed., 1969, cert. in counseling, 1972; M.A., cert. in mgmt., U. Tex., San Antonio, 1975; m. Fred Barrera, Dec. 26, 1965; 1 son, Fred. Tchr., San Antonio Sch. Dist., 1965-71, 72-75, dep. dir. Headstart, 1971, counselor, 1975—. Chmn. publicity PTA, St. Martin Hall Sch., San Antonio, 1976-78. Mem. NEA, Am. Personnel and Guidance Assn., Tex. Tchrs. Assn., Tex. Classroom Tchrs. Assn., Tex. Personnel and Guidance Assn., San Antonio Tchrs. Council (1st v.p. 1978-79), San Antonio Dist. Counselors Assn. (treas.; rights and responsibilities chmn.), S. Tex. Personnel and Guidance Assn., LWV, Mexican-Am. Bus. and Profl. Women's Club (social chmn.). Address: 11207 Whisper Sound San Antonio TX 78230

BARRETT, ANTHONY WILLIAM, city adminstr.; b. Chickasha, Okla., July 31, 1943; s. William Henry and Eda Lane (Chappel) B.; B.S. in History and Polit. Sci., Va. Wesleyan Coll., 1971; postgrad. Wake Forest U., 1970-71, in mcpl. adminstrn. U. N.C., 1976-77; m. Margaet Kathryn Johnson, Sept. 11, 1966; children—Amy Marlane, Christi Ann, Creighton Russell. Asst. county adminstr. Isle of Wight County (Va.), 1971-72, county adminstr., 1972-74; county adminstr. Pittsylvania County (Va.), 1974-76; city mgr. City of Nags Head (N.C.), 1976—. Active Boy Scouts Am., 1958-75; trustee Va. Wesleyan Coll., 1977—, chmn. student activities welfare com., 1978—, chmn. retention, enrollment, recruitment com., 1979. Served with USAF, 1965-68. Recipient Citizen Leadership award Northside Rotary Club, 1969; Walter Cecil Rawls Leadership award, 1961; named an Outstanding Young Man Am., U.S. Jaycees, 1978. Mem. Am. Soc. Public Adminstrs., Internat. City Mgrs. Assn., N.C. Assn. City and County Mgrs. Assn., Am. Legion (vice comdr. club 1971-72). Club: Va. Ruritan. Democrat. Office: Town of Nags Head PO Box 99 Nags Head NC 27959

BARRETT, BERNARD MORRIS, JR., plastic and reconstructive surgeon; b. Pensacola, Fla., May 3, 1944; s. Bernard Morris and Blanche (Lischkoff) B.; B.S., Tulane U., 1965; M.D., U. Miami, 1969; m. Julia Mae Prokop, Nov. 26, 1972; children—Beverly Frances, Julie Blaine. Surg. intern Meth. Hosp. and Ben Taub Hosp., Houston, 1969-70; resident in gen. surgery Baylor Coll. Medicine, Houston, 1970-71, UCLA, 1971-73; resident in plastic surgery U. Miami (Fla.) Affiliated Hosps., 1973-75, chief resident in plastic surgery, 1975; fellow in plastic surgery Clinica Ivo Pitanguy, Rio de Janeiro, Brazil, 1973; instr. in surgery Baylor Coll. Medicine, 1970-71, clin. instr. plastic surgery, 1977—; instr. surg. emergencies Los Angeles County Paramedics, 1972-73; plastic surgery coordinator for jr. med. students Sch. Medicine U. Miami, 1975; practice medicine specializing in plastic and reconstructive surgery, Houston, 1976—; pres., chmn. bd. dirs. Plastic and Reconstructive Surgeons, P.A., Houston, 1978—; attending physician Jr. League Clinic, Tex. Children's Hosp., Houston, 1977—; clin. asso. in plastic surgery U. Tex. Med. Sch., Houston, 1976—; instr. surg. emergencies Harris County Community Hosp.; dir. Am. Physicians Ins. Exchange, Dallas, Doctor's Center Hosp., Houston, Southwestern Bank, Stafford, Tex.; cons. physician Houston Oilers, 1978—; attending physician Ontario (Calif.) Motor Speedway, 1972-73. Served to lt. comdr. M.C., USNR, 1969-74. Surg. exchange scholar to Royal Coll. Surgeons, London, 1968. Diplomate Am. Bd. Plastic Surgery. Fellow A.C.S.; mem. Am. Soc. Plastic and Reconstructive Surgeons, Royal Soc. Medicine, Michael E. DeBakey Internat. Cardiovascular Surg. Soc., Denton A. Cooley Cardiovascular Surg. Soc., Tex. Med. Assn., Tex. Soc. Plastic Surgery, Harris County Med. Assn., Houston Soc. Plastic Surgery, D. Ralph Millard Plastic Surg. Soc. (v.p., 1977-79, sec., treas., 1975-77), U. Miami Sch. Medicine Nat. Alumni Assn. (bd. dirs., 1975-77), Alpha Kappa Kappa (pres., 1968-69). Clubs: University, Houstonian; Royal Biscayne Racquet; Commodore (Key Biscayne, Fla.). Inventor Barrett Sterling Surgigrip; author: Patient Care in Plastic Surgery, 1979; contbr. articles to med. publs., presentations to profl. confs.; hon. dep. sheriff Harris County, Tex. (Houston). Office: 7000 Fannin St Suite 2150 Houston TX 77030

BARRETT, JACQUELYN HARRISON, state law enforcement tng. council ofcl.; b. Charlotte, N.C., Nov. 4, 1950; d. Cornelius Edwin and Ocie (Perry) Harrison; B.A., Beaver Coll., 1972; M.A., Atlanta U., 1973; m. Edwin Morris Barrett, Jr., July 10, 1971; children—Kimberly Christine, Alan Harrison. Adult edn. instr. Atlanta Bd. Edn., 1972-75; criminal justice planner City of East Point, Ga., 1975-76; tng. specialist Ga. Peace Officers Standards and Tng. Council, Decatur, 1976—, curriculum coordinator, 1977-79, supr. law enforcement studies, 1979—. Law Enforcement Tng. Inst. grantee Boston U., 1979. Mem. Am. Soc. for Tng. and Devel. Office: Ga Peace Officer Standards and Tng Council Suite 1 4301 Memorial Dr Decatur GA 30032

BARRETT, MICHAEL BAKER, historian, educator; b. Honolulu, Oct. 12, 1946; s. John P. and Bernice (Baker) B.; A.B., The Citadel, 1968; M.A., U. Mass., 1969, Ph.D. (NDEA fellow), 1977; m. Sara Harriet McKerley, Sept. 20, 1969; 1 son, Michael M. Lectr. history U. Mass., Amherst, 1973-74, 75-76; instr. history The Citadel, Charleston, S.C., 1976-78, asst. prof., 1978—; reviewer European mil. history Library Jour., 1977—. Served with U.S. Army, 1969-71. Germanistic Soc. Am. fellow, 1974-75; Fulbright fellow, 1974-75; Citadel Devel. Found. fellow, 1977. Mem. Am. Hist. Assn., Am. Mil. Inst., Conf. Group Central European History, U.S. Army Armor Assn., Res. Officers Assn., Phi Alpha Theta, Phi Kappa Phi. Roman Catholic. Club: K.C. Contbr. articles to hist. jours. Address: Dept History The Citadel Charleston SC 29409

BARRETT, ROBERT ELLINGTON, ins. co. exec.; b. Jacksonville, Fla., Aug. 24, 1934; s. Clarence Gray and Marie (Ellington) B.; B.S., U. Fla., 1956; m. Elizabeth Allene Teagle, July 19, 1957; children—Robert Ellington, Shari Lynn. Vice-pres. Peninsular Glass Co., Jacksonville, Fla., 1959-61; controller Duval County Sch. Bd., Jacksonville, 1961-63; from salesman to sales mgr. Employers Ins. Wausau, Miami, 1963—. Mem. Fla. Gov.'s Com. Total Employment, 1967—. Served to 1st lt. U.S. Army, 1957-59, col. Res. Mem. Sales and Mktg. Execs. Miami (pres. 1970-72), Res. Officers Assn., Fla. Sheriffs Assn., U. Fla. Alumni Assn. Chmn. deacons Baptist Ch., Miami, 1971-74, ch. treas., 1977-79. Home: 10950 SW 59th Terr Miami FL 33173 Office: 7600 Red Rd Suite 205 South Miami FL 33143

BARRETT, ROLIN FARRAR, cons. engr.; b. White Sulphur Springs, W.Va., Aug. 25, 1937; s. Leonard Ward and Edna Coble (Farrar) B.; B.M.E., N.C. State U., 1959, M.M.E., 1962, Ph.D. (Shell Oil Co. fellow) in Mech. Engring., 1965; m. Dixie Linda Hobbs, Sept. 10, 1960; children—Rolin Farrar, Claire Hobbs. Instr. mech. and aerospace engring. dept. N.C. State U., Raleigh, 1962-65, asst. prof., 1965-68, asso. prof., 1968-73, prof., 1973-77, adj. prof., 1977—, asst. adminstrv. dean for research, 1973-76; dir. research and devel. Harrington Mfg. Co., Raleigh, 1976-77; pvt. cons., 1977—; cons. to legal and ins. professions, pvt. industry, govt. agys.; lectr. in indsl. safety, product liability, biomech. interests, auto safety. Recipient numerous grants for research, 1965—. Mem. Am. Inst. Aeros. and Astronautics (chmn. Carolina sect. 1969-70), ASME (chmn. Eastern N.C. sect. 1975-76, sec. region IV, 1976—), Soc. Automotive Engrs., ASTM, Am. Soc. for Metals, Sigma Xi, Phi Kappa Tau. Home: 705 Vick Ave Raleigh NC 27612 Office: Suite 116 Alleghany Bldg 3701 National Dr also PO Box 30188 Raleigh NC 27622

BARRETT, ROSS STANTON, speech pathologist, educator; b. Cin., Jan. 24, 1944; s. Herbert Ross and Joyce Stanton B.; B.S., U. Cin., 1970, M.S., 1976; postgrad. N.Y. Inst. Fin., 1972; m. Karen Hawver, Aug. 12, 1978. Adminstrv. asst. dept. trust Central Trust Bank, Cin., 1970-71; account exec., investment advisor Bartlett & Co., Cin., 1971-72; instr. psychology Hollins Coll., Roanoke, Va., 1976—, staff speech pathologist Hollins Communications Research Inst., 1976—; cons. Communication Devel. Corp. Recipient Eastman Kodak cert. of Merit, 1959. Mem. Am. Speech and Hearing Assn. (cert. clin. competence), AAUP. Republican. Episcopalian. Home: 5755 Oakland Blvd Roanoke VA 24019 Office: Dept Psychology Hollins College Hollins VA 24020

BARRETT, RUSSELL WAYNE, computer systems specialist; b. Parkersburg, W.Va., Aug. 6, 1939; s. Delbert Hall and Bess Mae (Hiley) B.; B.A., Marietta Coll., 1964; postgrad. Wittenberg U., 1973, U. Wis., 1974, W.Va. U., 1977-80; m. Linda Lee Law, Oct. 30, 1960; children—Michael Wayne, Joyce Ann, Susan Lynn. With E.I. DuPont de Nemours & Co., Inc., Parkersburg, 1959-80, supr. cost acctg., 1964-69, bus. specialist, 1969-73, mgr. EDP, 1973-75, specialist computer systems, 1975-80; instr. computer sci. Parkersburg Community Coll., 1976-79. Mem. City of Parkersburg Charter Bd., 1969-70; mem. City of Parkersburg City Council, 1970-73, pres., 1974-78. Named Outstanding Young Man, W.Va. Jaycees, 1972, Outstanding Local Pres., 1972. Mem. Data Processing Mgmt. Assn. Republican. Methodist. Clubs: Elks, Moose. Research on revenue sharing, community devel. block grants. Home: 829 S Arundel Dr Florence SC 29501 Office: PO Box 3000 Florence SC 29501

BARRETT, WILLIAM ARVEL, hosp. exec.,; b. Bluefield, W.Va., Aug. 16, 1919; s. Lawrence Witten and Beatrice (Massey) B.; B.B.A., Ga. State Coll., 1957; m. Dorothy Clements, Sept. 21, 1947 (div); children—William Arvel III (dec.), Johnny, Perry, Joy; m. 2d, Frances S. Whitley, Oct. 24, 1970. Asst. adminstr. Ga. Bapt. Hosp., Atlanta, 1955-58; adminstr. Athens (Ga.) Gen. Hosp., 1958-72; pres. Heritage Nursing & Convalescent Center, Inc., 1965—, Barrett Convalescent Center, Inc., 1966, Spring Valley Convalescent Center, Elberton, Ga.; cons. Elberton-Elbert County Hosp.; owner B-G Farm. Past trustee Ga. Hosp. Assn. Served with Med. Service Corps, AUS, 1943-46, 51-54. Fellow Am. Coll. Nursing Home Adminstrs., mem. Am. Coll. Hosp. Adminstrs., Ga. Hosp. Service Assn. (past (trustee Columbus), Ga. Nursing Home Adminstrs. (past dir.). Baptist. Home: 315 Ashton Dr Athens GA 30606 Office: 960 Hawthorne Ave Athens GA 30601

BARRINGER, JOHN WILLIAM, farmer, cotton merchant; b. Memphis, Apr. 5, 1940; s. Lewis T. and Josephine David (Davenport) B.; B.S., Memphis State U., 1964, J.D., 1964; m. Elizabeth Jane Guffee, June 5, 1964; children—Josephine Davenport, John W. With L.T. Barringer Co., Cotton mchts., Memphis, 1964—, asst. to pres., 1965—; farmer, rancher, Collierville, Tenn. Mem. Pres.' Export Council, 1979—; bd. dirs. Memphis Acad. Art. Mem. Tenn. Bar Assn., Memphis and Shelby County Bar Assn., Nat. Cotton Council, Agr. Council Am. (dir.), Am. Cotton Shippers Assn., Nat. Cattlemens Assn., Am. Soybean Assn. Democrat. Presbyterian. Club: Memphis Country. Home: 54 East Parkway N Memphis TN 38104 Office: PO Box 87 Memphis TN 38101

BARRINGER, THAD JONES, psychiatrist; b. Florence, S.C., Mar. 13, 1927; s. John Laurence and Belva Haynesworth (Jones) B.; B.S. in Chemistry, Davidson Coll., 1949; M.D., Vanderbilt U., 1953; m. Audrey Anne Adams, June 26, 1948; children—Ann Laurence, Thad Jones, William Kennon, Elizabeth Adams. Rotating intern St. Thomas Hosp., Nashville, 1953-54; asst. resident psychiatry Vanderbilt U. Hosp., Nashville, 1954-55; asst. resident psychiatry U. Cin., Cin. Gen. Hosp., 1955-57, also chief alcoholism clinic, 1956-57; practice medicine specializing in psychiatry Raleigh, N.C., 1960—; mem. staff Wake Meml. Hosp., Raleigh, N.C., 1960—, chief psychiat. service, 1966-67, 70-71, chief med. staff, 1973; mem. staff Rex Hosp., Raleigh, 1959—, Holly Hill Hosp., Raleigh, 1978—; cons. staff Raleigh Community Hosp., 1978—. instr. dept. psychiatry Med. Sch. Duke U., 1957-62; cons. VA Hosp., Durham, 1959-62; sr. attending staff and cons. Dorothea Dix Hosp., Raleigh, 1966-73; dir. Mental Health Center Raleigh and Wake County, N.C., 1959-62. Pres. PTA Martin Jr. High Sch., Raleigh, 1962-63; pres. bd. dirs. Holly Hill Hosp., Raleigh, 1977—. Served with USN, 1945-46. Diplomate Am. Bd. Neurology and Psychiatry. Fellow Am., So. psychiat. assns.; mem. Am. Coll. Psychiatry, AMA, Med. Soc. N.C., Wake County Med. Soc., Am. Soc. Clin. Hypnosis, N.C. Neuropsychiat. Assn. (pres. 1975-77), Southeastern Psychiat. Assn. (pres. 1967-68), Acad. Psychosomatic Medicine, Raleigh Acad. Medicine, Raleigh Acad. Psychiatry (pres. 1967), N.C. Mental Health Clinic Assos. (pres. 1959). Contbr. articles in field to profl. jours. Home: 5615 Lambshire Dr Raleigh NC 27612 Office: 3900 Browning Pl Suite 201 Raleigh NC 27609

BARRINGTON, BRUCE DAVID, data processing exec.; b. Chgo., Apr. 9, 1942; s. Arthur Richard and Lorene Cora (Powell) B.; B.S. in Math., Bradley U., 1964; m. Gayle Ann Wilcoxen, June, 1970; children—Arthur Richard, II, Kenneth Alan. Systems analyst Caterpillar Tractor Co., Peoria, Ill., 1965-67; mgr. hosp. systems devel. McDonnell Douglas Automation Co., Peoria, 1961-73; founder, dir. HBO & Co., Atlanta, 1973—. Mem. Peoria Assn. System Mgmt. (pres. 1971-72). Clubs: Country of Peoria; Lighthouse Point (Fla.) Yacht and Country, Country of Coral Springs. Developer computer software. Office: 4450 NE 31st Ave Lighthouse Point FL 33064

BARRON, BOBBY CURTIS, educator; b. Cobb County, Ga., Jan. 19, 1932; s. Thomas Terry and Evelyn (Morris) B.; A.S., Kennesaw Coll., 1970; B.S., U. Ga., 1970, M.Ed., 1972, Ed.S., 1976; m. Yvonne Irene Salladay, Aug. 1, 1954; children—Katherine Yvonne, Debra Anne, Linda Elaine, Bobbie Jean. Enlisted U.S. Air Force, 1953, served to 1961; head dept. electronics Dekalb Community Coll., Clarkston, Ga., 1961-66; head dept. electronics Iowa Central Community Coll., Ankeny, 1966-68; nat. dir. Edn. Inc., Balt., 1968; evening dir. Pickens Area Tech. Sch., Jasper, Ga., 1969-76; dir. vocat. edn. Etowah High Sch., Woodstock, Ga., 1976—; cons. vocat. edn. expansion and bldg. programs. Mem. adminstrv. bd. Hickory Flat Methodist Ch. NSF grantee, 1965. Named Sr. Engring. Technician. Mem. Am. Vocat. Assn. (life), Ga. Vocat. Assn., NEA, Ga. Edn. Assn., Navy Res. Assn. Home: Route 5 Box 141 Canton GA 30114 Office: Etowah High Sch Route 3 Puntam Mill Pd Woodstock GA 30188

BARRON, BRYANT MOORE, retail home and auto products store exec.; b. Amite County, Miss., Mar. 21, 1938; s. Wiley C. and Frankie (Moore) B.; A.A., S.W. Miss. Jr. Coll., 1961; B.S. in Personnel Mgmt., Miss. State U., 1966; m. Carol Lindsey, Dec. 29, 1963; 1 dau., Melissa Carole. Dairy farmer, Amite County, 1956-59; mgr. trainee J.C. Penney Co., Gulfport, Miss., 1962-64; hourly personnel rep. Ford Motor Co., Louisville, 1966; job analyst and labor relations specialist RCA, Bloomington, Ind., 1966-71; div. personnel mgr. Kellwood Co., Monticello, lMiss., 1971-77; owner, operator Western Auto Asso. Store, Liberty, Miss., 1978—. Bd. dirs. Miss. Regional Blood Center, Amite County of S.W. Miss. Jr. Coll. Mem. Am. Soc. Personnel Adminstrn. (accredited personnel mgr.), Miss. Econ. Council, Liberty C. of C. (v.p. 1979), S.W. Miss. Jr. Coll. Alumni Assn., Miss. State U. Alumni Assn. (pres. Lawrence County chpt. 1977). Baptist. Club: Masons. Home and Office: PO Drawer H Liberty MS 39645

BARRON, MARCELLINE ANTOINETTE, educator; b. Detroit, Jan. 27, 1941; d. Joseph A. and Irene L. (Turman) B.; B.S., U. Detroit, 1962, M.A., 1967; Ph.D., U. Mich., 1974. Tchr. mathematics Columbus Jr. High Sch., Detroit, 1962-65; tchr. chemistry, physics and mathematics Edwin Denby High Sch., Detroit, 1965-75; asst. prof. sci. edn. Manhattanville Coll., Purchase, N.Y., 1975-77, prof., acting dir. dept. teacher edn., 1977-78; dir. music and liturgy St. John's U. Parish, Stillwater, Okla., 1978—. Awarded silver medal of distinction and merit by Bishop of Sora, Italy, 1977. Mem. AAUP, Nat. Sci. Tchrs. Assn., AAAS, Assn. Educators of Tchrs. of Sci., Smithsonian Assos., Sch. Sci. and Mathematics Assn. Roman Catholic. Church organist, 1954-58; first chair violinist local community orchestra, 1955-58; contralto soloist, San Moritz Chamber Orchestra and Chorale, Stamford, Conn., concert tours with choirs, Poland, 1976, Italy, 1977, soloist with Phila. Orchestra, 1971, Detroit Symphony, 1970; pvt. voice tchr.; author: Coping with Chemistry Creatively, 1974. Home: PO Box 190 Stillwater OK 74074 Office: St Johns Univ Parish Stillwater OK 74074

BARRON, ORAN JAMES, JR., rancher; b. Athens, Tex., May 29, 1916; s. Oran James and Mavit (Hardin) B.; student U. Ariz., 1933, Tex. Western U,, 1934-35; m. Eleonora Prudence Swenson, Feb. 20, 1942; children—Oran James III, Helen Mavit (Mrs. Ronald Day), Amanda Hope (Mrs. Kevin Coyle). Owner Spur Hdqrs. Ranch, Spur Tex., 1946—; pres. Caprock Telephone Co. Inc., Spur 1955—, Tongue River Ranch Corp., 1978—; dir. Swenson Land & Cattle Co., N.Y.C., 1959-78. Mem. Tex. Water Resources Research Adv. Com., 1968-71; mem. Tex. Brush and Range Improvement Com., 1969—; mem. Tex. Agrl. Water Com., 1972—, pres., 1973—; chmn. Beef Devel. Task Force, 1974-77. Chmn. Dickens County (Tex.) Bd. Edn., 1956-78; pres. Dickens County Water Control and Improvement Dist. 1, 1962-70. Dir. Tex. Exptl. Ranch Com., 1958—. Served to maj. AUS, 1941-45. Decorated Bronze Star with oak leaf cluster. Mem. Am. Soc. Animal Sci., Am. Soc. Range Mgmt., Tex. Cattle Feeders Assn. (dir. 1967—, treas. 1972-73, 1st v.p. 1974-75, pres. 1976-77), Am. Nat. Cattlemen's Assn. (dir. 1974—), Nat. Livestock and Meat Bd. (dir. 1975—). Address: Route 1 Spur TX 79370

BARRON, OSCAR NOEL, oil prodn. research co. advisor; b. Burleson County, Tex., Feb. 4, 1929; s. Tom Joe and Lillian (Robinson) B.; B.S. in Chem. Engring., Rice U., 1948, postgrad., 1948-49; postgrad. U. Houston, 1957-59; m. Billie Lewis, Aug. 24, 1951; children—Noelie, William Lewis, Kaydell. With Exxon Co., 1949—, roustabout, Danciger, Tex., 1949-50, engr., Houston, 1950-60, supervising engr., Kingsville, Tex., 1960-63, sr. supervising engr., Corpus Christi, 1963-66, div. prodn. engr., Midland, Tex., 1967-69, sr. tech. advisor, New Orleans, 1969-71, div. gas engr., Houston, 1971-79; advisor Exxon Prodn. Research Co., Houston, 1980—; adv. com. Sch. Gas Tech. Kilgore, Tex., 1971. Registered profl. engr. Tex., La. Mem. Soc. Petroleum Engrs., Gas Processors Assn. (program chmn. 1965-66), Am. Petroleum Inst. (publ. rev. com. 1967-70), Tau Beta Pi. Presbyn. (ruling elder). Home: 133 Jeb Stuart Lane Conroe TX 77302 Office: 3120 Buffalo Speedway Houston TX 77039

BARRON, ROGER L., research co. exec.; b. Washington, Nov. 22, 1934; s. Bryton and Ella Rosalie (Lillibridge) B.; B.S., Princeton U., 1955; postgrad. (NSF fellow) Cambridge (Eng.) U., 1955-56; M.S. (Sperry Gyroscope fellow), Mass. Inst. Tech., 1957; m. Virginia Gayle Young, Sept. 11, 1956; children—Rowena L. Barron Crittenden, Andrew Roger, Jenifer Gayle, David William. Engr., Nat. Bur.

Standards, Washington, 1954-57; v.p. Dodco, Inc., Princeton, N.J., 1957-60, mem. tech. staff Melpar, Inc., Falls Church, Va., 1960-61; pres. Adaptronics, Inc., McLean, Va., 1961—, chmn., 1972—. Treas., Turnpike Baseball League, 1973; pres. Wakefield Forest Elementary Sch. PTA, 1976-77. Holder 4 nat. records, also numerous maj. awards in model aviation competition. Mem. Am. Inst. Aeros. and Astronautics, IEEE (nat. vice chmn. Systems, Man and Cybernetics Soc. div. 1970), Instrument Soc. Am. (sr.), Acad. Model Aeros. (leader), Am. Soc. Nondestructive Testing, Am. Radio Relay League. Presbyterian. Contbr. to numerous tech. publs., articles on adaptive control, signal processing advanced computation techniques, aerospace trajectory mechanics to profl. jours. Patentee in field. Home: 8605 Ardfour Ln Annandale VA 22003 Office: Adaptronics Inc 1750 Old Meadow Rd McLean VA 22102

BARRON, THOMAS WILLIS, lawyer, Realtor; b. Newnan, Ga., Apr. 9, 1949; s. Lindsey Hand and Genet Louise (Heery) B.; B.A., Emory U., 1971; J.D., Mercer U., 1974; m. Margaret Rose Maclennan, Aug. 17, 1973; children—Catharine Lindsey, Thomas Willis. Salesman Lindsey's, Inc., Newnan, 1968—; admitted to Ga. bar, 1974, Ga. Supreme Ct. bar, 1974, U.S. Ct. Appeals, 5th Circuit, 1974; asso. firm Sanders, Mottola, Haugen, Wood & Goodson, Newnan, 1974-77; individual practice law, 1977—; co-owner, broker, house counsel Lindsey's Inc.; dir. Coweta Devel., Inc., Consol. Devel. and Investment Corp. Bd. dirs. Coweta County United Way, 1974—, Coweta County Central Health Council, 1974—, Newnan-Coweta chpt. ARC, 1977—; deacon 1st Bapt. Ch. Newnan, 1975—. Mem. Newnan-Coweta Bd. Realtors, Am., Newnan-Coweta, Coweta Circuit bar assns., State Bar Ga., Am. Trial Lawyers Assn., Newnan-Coweta Assn. for Retarded Citizens, Coweta Circuit Bar Assn., Ducks Unltd. Baptist. Club: Newnan Country (dir.). Home: 63 Lundy St Newnan GA 30263 Office: 12 Jackson St Newnan GA 30263

BARROSO, FERNANDO JOSE MANUEL LUIS, educator; b. Havana, Cuba, June 6, 1933; s. Carlos Fabian and Dulce Maria Maxima (Garcia-Lavin) B.; student Nat. Bus. Coll., Roanoke, Va., 1950-52; LL.B., U. Havana, 1952-56, 59-60; M.Ed., Ph.D., U. Va., 1966-70. Came to U.S., 1961, naturalized, 1970. Jr. partner firm Zaldivar-Barroso, Havana, 1960-61; office clk. Wayne Mfg. Corp., Waynesboro, Va., 1962-63; instr. Spanish, Staunton (Va.) Mil. Acad., 1963-65, Shenandoah Coll., Winchester, Va., 1966-67; jr. instr. Spanish, U. Va., Charlottesville, 1967-69; asst. prof. Spanish, Madison Coll. (now James Madison U.), Harrisonburg, Va., 1969-70, asso. prof., 1970-76. Mem. Modern Lang. Assn., Am. Assn. Tchrs. Spanish and Portuguese. Roman Catholic. Author: El Naturalismo en La Pardo Bazán, 1973; Introducción al estudio de la civilización española, 1976. Home: 135 Campbell St Harrisonburg VA 22801

BARROW, ALLEN EDWARD, U.S. judge; b. Okemah, Okla., Jan. 22, 1914; s. Alfred E. and Minnie Lee (Coffelt) B.; student Okla. A. and M. Coll., 1935-36; B.A., U. Okla., 1936; postgrad. U. Tulsa; LL.B., Southeastern State Coll., 1942; m. Dorothy Elaine Dalton, Oct. 2, 1942; children—Allen Edward, Karla Elaine, Mary Celeste. With FBI, 1940-42; admitted to Okla. bar, 1942, also Supreme Ct. U.S.; pvt. practice, Tulsa, 1946-50, 54-62; counsel Southwestern Power Adminstrn., Dept. Interior, Tulsa, 1950-54; chief judge U.S. Dist. Ct. No. Dist. Okla., 1962—. Adv. bd. Tulsa Salvation Army, from 1956. Mem. bd. A.R.C. Served to maj. AUS, 1942-46. Recipient Alumni award Tulsa U. Sch. Law, 1975. Mem. Am., Okla. (Outstanding Service award 1959) bar assns., S.A.R. (pres. Okla. 1954), Delta Theta Phi, Phi Eta Sigma, Sigma Chi (pres. alumni assn. 1950; Significant Sig. award 1975). Democrat. Mem. Christian Ch. Office: Room 472 US Courthouse Tulsa OK 74103*

BARRY, JOHN TIMOTHY, fin. analyst; b. New Haven, Aug. 26, 1920; s. John Peter and Mary Ann (Moynihan) B.; B.A. in Econs., Yale U., 1941; postgrad. New Haven Coll., 1949-51, U. Ark. Law Sch., 1967-68; m. Evelyn Flather, Jan. 18, 1945; children—John Peter, Patricia Barry Fisk, Eugene Flather. Sr. cost clk. Gen. Motors Corp., Trenton, N.J., 1941-42, 46; cost accountant New Haven Clock & Watch Co., 1946-47, chief cost, gen. accountant, 1949-51; cost accountant, paymaster Voos Cutlery Co., New Haven, 1947-49; plant controller Timex Corp., Little Rock, 1951-74, sr. fin. analyst, 1974—; dir., sec., treas., co-owner The Knit Shop, Inc., Sherwood, Ark., 1972—. Alderman, Sherwood, 1957-62, budget dir., 1962-66. Served with USAAF, 1942-46. C.P.A., Ark. Mem. Ark. Soc. C.P.A.'s, Am. Inst. C.P.A.'s, Nat. Assn. Accountants. Democrat. Roman Catholic. K.C. Club: North Hills Country. Home: 507 Country Club Rd Sherwood AR 72116 Office: Box 1676 Little Rock AR 72203

BARRY, THOMAS MARTIN, JR., civil engr.; b. Chgo., Oct. 8, 1926; s. Thomas Martin and Alice Margaret (Laux) B.; B.S., U.S. Mil. Acad., 1950; M.S. in Civil Engring., U. Ill., 1956; m. Shirley Anne Ackerman, June 17, 1950; children—Thomas Howard, Patricia Anne (Mrs. Larry G. Barnes). Commd. 2d lt., C.E., U.S. Army, 1950, advanced through grades to lt. col., 1967; assigned to Hdqrs. 8th Army, Korea, 1965-66, Hdqrs. Army Materiel Command, Washington, 1966-68; engr. Safeguard Ballistic Missile Def. System, Huntsville, Ala., 1968-71; ret., 1971; sr. engr. Mid-South Distbrs., Jacksonville, Ala., 1971-72; project mgr. Jacksonville (Fla.) Dept. Pub. Works, 1972-73, engring. mgr. downtown devel., 1973—. Served with USAAF, 1944-45. Decorated Meritorious Service medal, Army Commendation medal, Bronze Star medal. Registered profl. engr., Ala., Fla., Ga., Miss., Tenn., Va. Mem. Soc. Am. Mil. Engrs. (pres. post 1978-79), Am. Pub. Works Assn., Inst. Mcpl. Engrs. Club: Exchange. Home: 4455 Confederate Point Rd Apt 15A Jacksonville FL 32210 Office: 1207 City Hall 220 E Bay St Jacksonville FL 32202

BARTEAU, JOHN FRANK, steel bldg. co. exec.; b. Springfield, Mass., Jan. 20, 1928; s. John Frank and Mary Elizabeth (Hunt) B.; student Norwich U., 1945-46; B.A., Lehigh U., 1952, B.S. in Mech. Engring., 1953; m. Frances Melba Crouch, July 15, 1954; children—John Frank III, Gilbert James, Suzanne Carlson, Peter Hunt. Dir. engring. AMF, York, Pa., 1953-70; mgr. spl. projects York Industries (Pa.), 1970-71; group v.p. Church's Fried Chicken, San Antonio, 1972-79; pres. Far West Products Co. subs. Church's Fried Chicken, San Antonio, 1979—. Served with U.S. Army, 1946-47. Mem. Phi Beta Kappa, Tau Beta Pi, Pi Tau Sigma, Pi Mu Epsilon, Phi Eta Sigma. Home: Route 2 Box 2382 Boerne TX 78006 Office: PO Box 5369 San Antonio TX 78284

BARTEL, LARRY DAN, ophthalmologist; b. Kokomo, Ind., Nov. 1, 1942; s. Walter Daniel and Bernice Fern (Stover) B.; B.S., Ind. U., 1964, M.D., 1967; m. Betsy Ann Toppe, June 1, 1963; children—Kyle Damon, Deirdre Lynne. Intern, U.S. Naval Hosp., San Diego, 1967-68; resident ophthalmology U. N.C. Meml. Hosp., Chapel Hill, 1972-75, McPherson Hosp., Durham, N.C., 1972-75; practice medicine specializing in ophthalmology, Rock Hill, S.C.; mem. staffs York Gen. Hosp.; adj. prof. Human Devel. Center, Winthrop Coll. Bd. dirs. York County Council on Alcohol and Drug Abuse, 1978—; chmn. Grace Lutheran Ch., 1979—. Served with USN, 1966-72. Diplomate Am. Bd. Ophthalmology. Mem. Am. Acad. Ophthalmology, Am. Assn. Ophthalmology, S.C. Soc. Ophthalmology (exec. com.), Physicians Edn. Network, So. Med. Assn., York County Med. Soc. Clubs: Rotary, Elk. Office: 1565 Ebenezer Rd PO Box 2874 CRS Rock Hill SC 29730

BARTH, ALF OTTO, architect; b. Risor, Norway, Aug. 5, 1921; s. Haakon Hjalmar and Emilie (Evensen) B.; came to U.S., 1929, naturalized, 1943; B.Arch. with honors, U. Fla., 1953; m. Mary Jayne Ingram, Apr. 28, 1951; children—Kathleen Elizabeth, Paul Haakon. Architect, dir. sch. planning Polk County, Fla., 1956-60; asso. dir. sch. planning Dade County, Fla., 1960-64; coordinating architect Orange County (Fla.) Schs., 1964-65; architect in charge Charles W. Cole & Son, South Bend, Ind., 1966; chief architect Dade County, 1968-79; cons. architect, 1956—; prin. works include Oakland Elementary Sch., Haines City, Fla., 1960; Sanctuary for Grace Luth. Ch., Winter Haven, Fla., 1960, ednl. bldg., 1967; addition Redeemer Luth. Ch., Miami Shores, Fla., 1961; Immanuel Luth. Ch., Tavernier, Fla., 1967; ednl. bldg. Concordia Luth. Ch., Miami, 1966. Chmn. Dade County Archtl. Selection Com., 1968-74, Dade County Archtl. Certification Com., 1974-79. Bd. dirs. Eastridge Retirement Village, Miami, 1963-64; mem. Dade County Transit Advisory Com., 1974—. Served with USNR, 1943-46; U.S. Army, 1947-50. Mem. AIA (dir. local chpt. 1964), Nat. Council Archtl. Registration Bds., Am. Arbitration Assn., Am. Pub. Works Assn., Gargoyle (historian), Phi Kappa Phi. Lutheran (chmn. trustees 1961-65). Mason, Odd Fellow. Home: 7581 SW 58th St Miami FL 33143 Office: 44 W Flagler St Miami FL 33130

BARTHA, LOUIS ALEXANDER, accountant; b. Toledo, June 18, 1917; s. Stephen Joseph and Susan (Piszkaly) B.; student Berea Coll., 1935-36, Ohio State U., 1936, U. Ill., 1936-39, 40; m. Ruth Kathryn Woodson, May 18, 1942; 1 son, Gregory Woodson. Accountant, Louis A. Bartha C.P.A., Midland, Tex., 1945—; sec.-treas., dir. Palafox Exploration Co., Midland, 1957—; v.p., dir. Scharbauer Cattle Co., Midland, 1958—; sec.-treas., dir. Scharbauer Bros. & Co., 1958—, Alamositas Cattle Co., 1958—; sec., dir. Ranching Enterprises, Inc., 1966-70. Mem. Tex. State Bd. Pub. Accountancy, 1958-67. Chmn. Midland County Democratic Exec. Com., 1948-52. Sec., dir. Midland Fair, Inc., 1950-65; treas., dir. Midland Indsl. Plan, Inc., 1954-65; sec., dir. Prairie Found., Midland, 1957—; chmn. Midland County Draft Bd., 1966—. C.P.A., Tex. Trustee Midland Ind. Sch. Dist., 1957-63, sec., 1959-63. Served to capt. USAAF, 1941-45. C.P.A., Tex. Mem. Am. Inst. C.P.A.'s, Tex. Soc. C.P.A.'s, Accounting Research Assn., Financial Mgmt. Assn., Am. Accounting Assn. Rotarian. Home: 905 Bedford Dr Midland TX 79701 Office: 1st Nat Bank Bldg Midland TX 79701

BARTHOLOMEW, SAMUEL WILSON, JR., lawyer; b. Columbus, Ga., July 6, 1944; s. Samuel Wilson and Charlene Anne (Oakes) B.; B.S., U.S. Mil. Acad., 1966; J.D., Vanderbilt U., 1973; m. Vicki Lynn Hurd, Sept. 13, 1967; children—Samuel Wilson, Anne St. Clair, William Hurd. Admitted to Tenn. bar, 1973; legislative asst. U.S. Senator Howard H. Baker, 1971-72, campaign dir. Re-Election Campaign, U.S. Sen. Baker, 1972; dir. corporate devel. First Amtenn Corp., Nashville, Tenn., 1973-75; exec. v.p., chief operating officer Guaranty Mortgage Co., Nashville, 1975-76; sr. v.p. mktg. First Am. Nat. Bank, Nashville, 1976-77; sr. partner law firm Bartholomew, Cleary & Mudter, Nashville, Tenn., 1977—; adj. prof. Vanderbilt Law Sch., 1974—. Sec.-treas. Met. Nashville Health & Ednl. Facilities Bd., 1975—; adv. bd. U.S. Senate Veterans Affairs Com., 1974-77. Trustee, Watkins Inst.; bd. dirs. Salvation Army; bd. dirs. Cumberland Mus. & Sci. Center. Served to capt. AUS, 1962-70. Decorated Bronze Star medals (3). Mem. Nashville, Am., Tenn. bar assns. Presbyterian (elder). Clubs: Army Navy Country, Belle Meade Country, Cumberland, Am. Legion, Mason, Scottish Rite. Home: 317 Walnut Dr Nashville TN 37205 Office: Bartholomew Cleary & Mudter First Am Center Nashville TN 37238

BARTLETT, CHARLES SAMUEL, JR., cons. geologist; b. Asheville, N.C., Oct. 20, 1929; s. Charles Samuel and Frances Coit (Weaver) B.; B.S. in Geology, U. N.C., 1951, M.S., 1967; Ph.D., U. Tenn. at Knoxville, 1974; m. Sarah Jean Schaefer, June 16, 1951; children—Katherine Ann, Linda Carol. Seismograph crew computer Superior Oil Co., Ardmore, Okla., 1955; field geologist, Gulf Oil Corp., Fort Smith, Ark., 1955-61; area geologist J.M. Huber Corp., Oklahoma City, 1961-65; instr. geology Pembroke (N.C.) State U., 1966-67; asso. prof. geology Emory and Henry Coll., Emory, Va., 1967—; NSF teaching fellow, 1970-71, researcher, Egypt, 1976; cons. geologist, Abingdon, Va., 1972—. Bd. dirs. Mt. Rodgers Citizens Devel. Corp., 1971—, v.p., 1975-79; bd. dirs. Washington County Bicentennial Commn.; People-to-People ambassador, Russia, Egypt, Italy, 1979. Served with USN, 1951-55. Faculty research fellow NASA, Johnson Space Center, 1977-78. Mem. Am. Assn. Petroleum Geologists, Am. Inst. Profl. Geologists, Geol. Soc. Am., Nat. Assn. Geology Teachers, Va. Acad. Sci. (sec. 1979—), Archeol. Soc. Va., Ark. Archeol. Soc., Bristol Gem and Mineral Soc. Contbr. articles in field to profl. jours. Home: Route 6 Box 447 Abingdon VA 24210 Office: 102 S Court St Abingdon VA 24210

BARTLETT, JACK ARNOLD, acct.; b. Dallas, May 23, 1947; s. Roger Frost and Dorothy Louise (Loop) B., Jr.; B.B.A., North Tex. State U., 1969, M.B.A., 1971; postgrad (teaching fellow) Mich. State U., 1971-72; m. Barbara Faye Niemeier, Aug. 29, 1971. Teaching fellow N. Tex. State U., Denton, 1969-71; auditor Arthur Andersen & Co., Dallas, 1969, 72-73; v.p., controller Cambridge Cos., Dallas, 1973-79; mgr. tax dept. Murski, Hicks & Co., C.P.A.s, 1979—. C.P.A., Tex. Mem. Tex. Soc. C.P.A.'s, Am. Accounting Assn., Tex. Hist. Soc., Common Cause, Blue Key, Beta Gamma Sigma, Beta Alpha Psi, Alpha Chi. Home: 3830 Farmbrook Ct Apt 452 Dallas TX 75234 Office: 701 First Internat Bldg Dallas TX 75270

BARTLETT, JOE HAROLD, ednl. adminstr.; b. Evergreen, Ala., Apr. 9, 1921; s. Joe Mack and Mamie Evelyn (Davis) B.; A.A., Lamar Jr. Coll., 1941; student So. Meth. U., 1945-46; B.S., N. Tex. State U., 1948, M.S., 1950; m. Glenna Joyce Graham, June 11, 1948; children—Glynese, Hal Bryan. Tchr., coach Sonora (Tex.) High Sch., 1948, Union Grove High Sch., Gladewater, Tex., 1949-51; athletic dir., coach Raymondville (Tex.) High 1952-56; tchr., coach Thomas Jefferson High Sch., Dallas, 1956-63; asst. adminstr. service centers Dallas Ind. Sch. Dist., 1964-66, adminstr. service center, 1966-78, mgr. bus. services, 1978—. Served with USAAF, 1942-45; PTO. Decorated D.F.C., Air medal with 6 oak leaf clusters. Mem. Assn. Sch. and Bus. Ofcls. of U.S. and Can., Tex. Assn. Sch. Bus. Ofcls., Dallas High Sch. Coaches Assn., Tex. Coaches Assn., Dallas County Adminstrs. Assn., Dallas Sch. Adminstrs. Assn. Republican. Baptist. Office: Dallas Ind Sch Dist 2517 S Ervay St Dallas TX 75215

BARTLETT, ROBERT CHARLES, phys. therapist; b. Syracuse, N.Y., Aug. 29, 1931; s. Charles Henry and Gertrude M. (Willis) B.; B.S. in Edn., Springfield (Mass.) Coll., 1954; cert. in phys. therapy, N.Y. U., 1957, M.A. in Phys. Therapy, 1959; m. Judy Wagnon, Sept. 14, 1964; children—Charles Henry III, Jessica Lynn. Staff phys. therapist N.Y. U. Med. Center, 1957-58, sr. phys. therapist, 1958-62, instr. Grad. Sch. Medicine, 1959-63; dir. program services United Cerebral Palsy Assn. N.Y. State, Inc., 1962-71; acting chmn. program in occupational therapy SUNY Downstate Med. Center, Bklyn., 1973-75, prof., chmn. program in phys. therapy, 1971-76; prof., chmn. dept. phys. therapy Duke U. Med. Center, Durham, N.C., 1976—; mem. task force study of United Health Founds., United Cerebral Palsy Assn., Inc., 1969-72; mem. residential living rev. com. Accreditation Council Facilities for Mentally Retarded, Joint Commn. Accreditation of Hosps., 1970; participant conf. on cert. in allied health professions Assn. Schs. of Allied Health Professions, 1971; mem. steering com. Study of Cert. of Selected Health Professions, 1972-73. Served with USN, 1954-56. Mem. Am. Phys. Therapy Assn. (past pres. N.Y. chpt., Past Pres. award 1970, Disting. Service award Greater N.Y. dist. 1970, commendation 1979, past nat. pres., dir.), World Confedn. Phys. Therapy, Nat. Health Council (dir.). Office: Box 3965 Duke University Medical Center Durham NC 27710

BARTOLO, ADOLPH MARION, food co. exec.; b. Cairo, Egypt, Apr. 12, 1929; s. Edgar Charles and Emma C. (Borrelli) B.; came to U.S., 1947, naturalized, 1953; B.S. in Chem. Engring., La. State U., 1950; m. Joycelyn Mary Bergeron, June 7, 1950; children—Pamela Bridget, Edgar Charles II, Janice Ann, Mary Elizabeth. From chem. engr. to asst. supt. Southdown Sugar, Inc., Houma, La., 1951-58; with Imperial Sugar Co., Sugarland, Tex., 1958—, v.p. refinery ops., 1968—, also dir.; dir. Cane Sugar Refiners Research Project, 1965—; dir. Sugar Industry Technologists, Inc., pres., 1976-77. Mem. La. State U. Found., 1966-68. Mem. Am. Inst. Chem. Engrs., U.S. Nat. Com. Sugar Anaylsis. Roman Catholic. Lion (pres. Sugarland 1960-61). Clubs: Exchange (Fort Bend); Sugar Creek Country (Sugarland). Home: 303 S Belknap St Sugarland TX 77478 Office: PO Box 9 Sugarland TX 77478

BARTON, ALEXANDER JAMES, ecologist, educator; b. Mt. Pleasant, Pa., May 9, 1924; s. Paul Carnahan and Barbara (Eggers) B.; B.S., Franklin and Marshall Coll., 1946; M.S., U. Pitts., 1957; m. Arlene Florence Arment, Oct. 6, 1945; children—Sandra, Lynne, Alexander James III. Herpetologist, Highland Park Zool. Gardens, Pitts., 1946-52; instr. biology Stony Brook (N.Y.) Sch., 1952-63, dir. admissions and fin. aid, 1957-63; profl. asst. NSF, Washington, 1963-65, profl. asso., 1965-70, program dir. sci. instructional materials devel., 1970—; adj. asst. prof. biology C.W. Post Coll., Brookville, N.Y., 1961-63; dir. Savannah (Ga.) Natural History Mus., 1957; chmn. Fed. Interagency subcom. Internat. Environ. Edn., 1976-78; mem. U.S. delegation UN Conf. on Environ. Edn., Tbilisi, USSR, 1977; cons. sci. books Doubleday & Co., 1962-64. Scoutmaster Allegheny County council Boy Scouts Am., Pitts., 1947-52, mem. nat. adv. com., 1950-54, mem. exec. council Suffolk County council, 1957-63; mem. Internat. Com. on Endangered Reptiles and Amphibians, 1967-74. Pres., Arlington Rose Found., 1970-71. Served to capt. USNR, 1943-45. Mem. Acad. Ind. Scholars (charter mem.), Potomac Rose Soc. (1st v.p. 1972-73, pres. 1974-75, dir. 1976—), Am. Rose Soc. (vice chmn. Colonial dist. 1971-72, cons. rosarian 1970—, chmn. nat. long-range planning com. 1973-75; accredited rose show judge 1970-77, life judge 1978—, gen. chmn. nat. conv. 1981), Assn. Admissions Officer Inc. Secondary Schs. (pres. 1959-62), AAAS, Am. Inst. Biol. Sci., Ecol. Soc. Am., others. Presbyn. (deacon 1946—, lay preacher 1954-65, tchr. adult bible class 1964-68). Contbr. numerous articles, papers to profl publs. Home: 3818 N Vernon St Arlington VA 22207

BARTON, CARL BART, cons.; b. Mansfield, Ohio, June 9, 1935; s. John J. and Sophia A. B.; B.E.E., U. Detroit, 1958; M.B.A., Lamar U., 1977, D.Engring., 1980; m. Marianne Patrick, Nov. 26, 1959; children—Amy, John J. II, C. Bart II, Jennifer. Systems engr. process control IBM, 1962-69; chmn., pres. Systems Cons. Corp., Beaumont, Tex., 1969-70; v.p., dir. Asso. Computer Services, Inc., Houston, 1970-71; cons. Sybron/Taylor, Beaumont, 1971—; dir. Internat. Tech. Inst., Pitts., 1976-69, Mgmt. Insts. Unlimited, Beaumont, 1978-80, Congress Internat. Tech., Pitts., 1976-80. Served with Signal Corps, U.S. Army, 1958-59. Recipient Literary Gold medal Freedom Found., 1955. Mem. Tex. Council Econ. Edn., C. of C. (mem. world trade com.), Leadership Beaumont, Eta Kappa Nu. Roman Catholic. Office: PO Box 5572 Beaumont TX 77702

BARTON, GEORGE EDWIN, community assn. exec.; b. Troy, Ohio, May 20, 1922; s. Harold Mitchell and Edna Helene (Douglass) B.; student Baldwin-Wallace Coll., 1940-43; B.A., U. Md., 1969; m. Gladys Louise Scheck, Dec. 6, 1944; 1 dau., Karen Helen. Commd. ensign, U.S. Navy, 1944, advanced through grades to capt., 1968; staff implementer for nat. mil. conmand center Def. Communications Agy., Arlington, Va., 1965-69; chief communications plans officer Hdqrs. U.S. European Command, Stuttgart, W.Ger., 1969-71; dep. dir. ops. and mgmt. Joint Tactical Communications Office, New Shrewsbury, N.J., 1971-74; chief of staff U.S. Naval Base, Guantanamo Bay, Cuba, 1975-76, ret., 1976; mgr. Assn. of Poinciana Villages, Inc., Kissimmee, Fla., 1976—. Decorated Bronze Star, Joint Service Commendation medal, Legion of merit with gold star. Mem. Naval Inst., Armed Forces Communications-Electronics Assn., Fla. City and County Mgmt. Assn., Community Assn. Inst. Republican. Home: 716 E Brassie Ln Kissimmee FL 32741 Office: 1 S Doverplum Ave Kissimmee FL 32741

BARTON, HUGH MITCHELL, JR., physicist; b. Kilgore, Tex., Jan. 27, 1918; s. Hugh Mitchell and Lila Ann (Goodman) B.; B.A. in Physics with honors, U. Tex., 1938; M.S., Poly. Inst. Bklyn., 1950; m. Margaret Louise Nance, June 6, 1942; 1 son, Hugh Mitchell III. Research physicist Phillips Petroleum Co., Bartlesville, Okla., 1938-42, 43-48, 49—. Bklyn., 1948-49; physicist U. Chgo. Metall. Lab., 1943-44; lectr. advanced electronics Okla. U., 1944-45. Active Boy Scouts Am., 1965-70; mem. ch. St. Luke's Episcopal Ch., Bartlesville, Okla., 1968-69, 71-74, sr. warden, 1970-71, diocesan del., 1969-71. Recipient citation Office Sci. Research and Devel., 1946; medal Am. Nuclear Soc./Atomic Indsl. Forum, 1962. Fellow AAAS; mem. Am. Phys. Soc., IEEE Nuclear and Plasma Sci. Soc., Sigma Xi. Clubs: Elks, Masons (32 deg.). Contbr. articles to profl. jours; patentee petroleum tech. Home: 2006 S Dewey Ave Bartlesville OK 74003 Office: Phillips Petroleum Co 370A Petroleum Lab 1 Bartlesville OK 74004

BARTON, JACK QUINN, lawyer, instr., police chief; b. Denison, Tex., Nov. 27, 1932; s. Joseph R.T. and Marion (Quinn) B.; B.A., U. Tex., 1960, J.D., 1962; m. Vena Barton; children—Robert Barry, Catherine Eileen, Joseph Lawrence, Raymond Edward, Jerry Quinn. With Corpus Christi (Tex.) Police Force, 1956-57; admitted to Tex. bar, 1962; practiced in San Francisco, 1962-63; law book editor Matthew Bender Co.; city atty. Denton, Tex., 1963-72; instr., dir. police N. Tex. State U., Denton, 1972—, legal adviser, 1973-77. Cons. municipal law to various cities. Mem. Decisions for Denton Com., 1969—; chmn. Denton March of Dimes, 1969; bd. dirs. Denton Area Tchrs. Credit Union, 1977—; trustee Optimist Meml. Found., Fairhaven Home for Aged, Denton; bd. dirs., chmn. finance com. Cross Timbers council Girl Scouts Am. Served with AC, USNR, 1951-55. Mem. Am., Tex., Denton County bar assns., Tex. Trial Lawyers Assn. K.C. Club: Breakfast Optimist (pres. 1972-73). Author: How to Pick a Lawyer, 1977; Beyond the Third Step, 1978. Home: 1207 Ridgecrest Circle Denton TX 76201

BARTON, JAMES HOWARD, physician; b. Murphy, N.C., Apr. 14, 1931; s. Guy Arvil and Esta (Swaim) B.; B.A., U. N.C., 1953, M.S. in Pub. Health, 1958; M.D., Med. Coll. Ga., 1962; m. Barbara Nell Brown, June 18, 1957; children—Gregory Jay, Steven Lyle, Leslie Kay. Intern, Spartanburg Gen. Hosp., 1962-63; gen. practice medicine, Social Circle, Ga., 1963—. Mem. Walton County Bd. Health, Served with AUS, 1954-56. Mem. Am., Ga. med. assns. Methodist (trustee). Lion (pres. Social Circle 1975). Home: 356 N

Cherokee St Social Circle GA 30279 Office: PO Box 468 Social Circle GA 30279

BARTON, MURRAY GEORGE, educator; b. Bronx, Sept. 13, 1925; s. Joseph and Fannie (Brill) B.; B.S., City Coll. N.Y., 1948; M.S.S.W., Boston U., 1950; postgrad. U. Chgo., 1951-54, U. Minn., 1956-60; m. Elaine Carr, Dec. 25, 1948; children—Francine Claire, Douglas Kenneth, Gary Mark. Program dir. Community Center, Chgo., 1950-51; psychiat. social worker VA Hosp., Hines, Ill., 1951-54; clin. instr. grad. schs. social work U. Ill. and Loyola U., Chgo., 1951-56; program supr. VA Hosp., Mpls. and clin. instr. Grad. Sch. Social Work, U. Minn., Mpls., 1956-60; chief social work service VA Hosp., Madison and asst. prof. Med. Sch., U. Wis. and Grad. Sch. Social Work, Madison, 1960-64; chief Social Work Service, VA Hosp., Albany, N.Y. and asst. prof. Med. Sch., Union Coll., Albany, and Grad. Sch. Social Work, State U. N.Y. and Syracuse (N.Y.) U., 1964-70; asst. chief social work service VA Med. Center, Little Rock and asst. prof. Grad. Sch. Social Work, U. Ark., Little Rock, 1970—; cons. Family Service Assn., Albany, 1964-70, Cerebral Palsy Center, Albany, 1964-70; social work instr. Skidmore Coll., Saratoga Springs, N.Y., 1965-70, Sienna Coll., Loudonville, N.Y., 1965-70, Carondolet Coll., 1965-70. Served with U.S. Army, 1943-45; ETO. Decorated Bronze Star medal, Croix de Guerre. Mem. Nat. Assn. Social Workers, Acad. Cert. Social Workers, Am. Hosp. Assn., Assn. Hosp. Educators. Unitarian. Contbr. articles in field to profl. jours. Home: 24 Laffite Circle North Little Rock AR 72116 Office: VA Med Center North Little Rock AR 72114

BARTON, ROBERT KENNETH, obstetrician, gynecologist, former naval officer, educator; b. Fountain City, Ind., Feb. 23, 1922; s. Kenneth Merle and Ethel Alta (Alexander) B.; B.S., Ball State U., 1943; postgrad. Cornell U., 1943-44; M.D., U. Cin., 1948; m. Mary Catherine Core, June 14, 1954; children—Mary Catherine, Molly Caroline. Commd. lt. j.g. U.S. Navy, 1948, advanced through grades to capt., 1974; intern Bethesda (Md.) Naval Hosp., 1948-49, resident in obstetrics gynecology, 1949-50; resident in obstetrics gynecology Chelsea (Mass.) Naval Hosp., 1952-53, San Diego Naval Hosp., 1953-57; staff Naval Hosp. Camp Lejeune, N.C., 1957-59; sr. med. officer Naval Support Activities, London, 1959-62; chief obstetrics gynecology, Quantico, Va., 1962-64, Naval Hosp., Bsoton, 1964-68; dep. comdg. surgeon, Vietnam, 1968-69; dir. profl. div. Bur. Medicine, Washington, 1969-73; spl. asst. comdg. officer Nat. Naval Med. Center, Bethesda, Md., 1973-74; ret., 1974; asso. clin. prof. Boston U. Med. Sch., 1964-68; clin. instr. Tufts U. Sch. Medicine, 1964-68; asso. prof. Ob-Gyn Mich. State U., East Lansing, 1974-78; dir. Ob-Gyn Saginaw (Mich.) Coop. Hosps., 1974-78; chief staff, pvt. practice Ob-Gyn, Emerald Hodgson Hosp., U. of South, Sewanee, Tenn., 1978—. Diplomate Am. Bd. Obstetrics Gynecology. Fellow Am. Coll. Obstetricians Gynecologists, A.C.S., Royal Soc. Medicine, Am. Fertility Soc., Assn. Mil. Surgeons, AMA. Republican. Episcopalian. Home: PO Box 130 Sewanee TN 37375

BARTOO, EUGENE CHESTER, educator; b. Wellsboro, Pa., Jan. 31, 1940; s. Eldred Lewellyn and Viola May (Mudge) B.; B.S., Pa. State U., 1961; M.Ed., SUNY, Buffalo, 1966, Ed.D., 1972; m. Ruth G. Walker, June 27, 1961; children—Steven, James, Thomas, Jennifer. Tchr. math., public schs., N.Y., 1961-69; adminstrv. dir. curriculum and instrn. Griffith Inst., N.Y., 1970-71; asst. prof. edn. Case Western Res. U., Cleve., 1971-78; asso. prof., head dept. curriculum and instrn. U. Tenn., Chattanooga, 1978—. Elder, Presbyn. Ch. NDEA fellow, 1963-66. Mem. Am. Ednl. Research Assn., Assn. Supervision and Curriculum Devel., Nat. Soc. Study of Edn., Phi Delta Kappa. Democrat. Contbr. chpts. to books, articles to profl. jours. Home: 8115 Angie Dr Chattanooga TN 37421 Office: 313 Hunter Hall McCallie Ave Chattanooga TN 37402

BARTOW, GENE, athletic dir.; b. Browning, Mo., Aug. 18, 1930; s. T. I. and Almeda (Gooch) B.; B.S. in Edn., N.E. Mo. State U., 1952; M.A., Washington U., St. Louis, 1957; m. Ruth Huffine, Dec. 24, 1952; children—Mark, Murry, Beth. Head basketball coach Central Mo. State U., 1961-64, Valparaiso (Ind.) U., 1964-70, Memphis State U., 1970-74, U. Ill., 1974-75, UCLA, 1975-77; dir. athletics U. Ala., Birmingham, 1977—. Served with AUS, 1952-54. Democrat. Methodist. Club: Rotary. Author: Winning Basketball, 1978. Home: 2636 Creekview Birmingham AL 35226 Office: University Sta Birmingham AL 35294

BARTSCHT, WALTRAUD ERIKA, educator, costume designer; b. Munich, Germany, Oct. 16, 1924; d. Bruno and Edith Frida (Snell) Gutensohn; came to U.S., 1952, naturalized, 1959; diploma Deutsche Meisterschule Füer Mode, Munich, 1949; M.A., So. Meth. U., Dallas, 1966; m. Heri Bert Barscht, Mar. 31, 1950; 1 son, Martin Donald. Fashion designer, 1949-65, Dallas, 1954-65; instr. German, U. Dallas, Irving, Tex., 1966-69, asst. prof., 1969—; designer theatrical costumes Knox Street Theater, Dallas, U. Dallas Drama Dept.; textile compositions exhibited Dallas galleries, Purdue U., and elsewhere, 1961—; textile chancel appts. Perkins Chapel So. Meth. U., St. Paul's Luth. Ch., Brenham, Tex. Mem. Tex. Fgn. Lang. Assn., South Central Modern Lang. Assn., Am. Assn. German Tchrs. (regional chmn. N. Central Tex. 1972-75), Dallas Goethe Center (founding mem.). Lutheran. Translator: Goethe's Das Maerchen, 1972. Translator poems in Kerygma, 1961, Constantin Review, 1974; contbr. articles to Schatzkammer, Rice Univ. Studies. Home: 1125 Canterbury Ct Dallas TX 75208 Office: University of Dallas Irving TX 75061

BASH, RON, athletic dir.; b. Trenton, N.J., Feb. 20, 1940; s. Joseph and Theresa Bash; B.S., Temple U., Phila., 1966; Ed.M., Boston U., 1967, Ed.D. (teaching fellow 1969-71), 1972; m. Barbara Lynn Gross, Oct. 14, 1978. Asst. Basketball coach, dir. intramurals U. Alaska, 1968-69; head basketball coach, asst. prof. phys. edn. York (N.Y.) Coll., 1973-74, SUNY, Stony Brook, 1974-78; dir. athletics, head basketball coach, asso. prof. phys. edn. Longwood Coll., Farmville, Va., 1978—. Named News Media Coach of Year, 1977; Man of Year, L.I. Assn., 1978; Coll. Coach of Yr., 1978-79, 79-80. Mem. Nat. Assn. Basketball Coaches, AAHPER, AAUP. Home: Rt 3 Box 73 Farmville VA 23901 Office: Longwood Coll Farmville VA 23901

BASINGER, ANDREW MARSHALL, II, lawyer; b. Greensboro, N.C., Aug. 10, 1939; s. Pryde William and Irene McRae (Matheson) B.; B.A. in Polit. Sci., U. N.C., Chapel Hill, 1962, LL.B., 1965; m. Virginia Dowdell Anderson, Aug. 19, 1966; children—Virginia Holt, Andrew Marshall III. Admitted to N.C. bar, 1965; agt. Lawyers Title Ins. Co. of N.C., Charlotte, 1965; asso. firm Bradley, Gebhardt, DeLaney & Millette, Charlotte, 1966-67; asso. firm Grier, Parker, Poe, Thompson, Bernstein, Gage & Preston, Charlotte, 1967-71, partner, 1971—. Chmn. crusade Am. Cancer Soc., Charlotte, 1969, pres., 1970, bd. dirs., exec. com., 1967—; mem. Salvation Army Boys' Club Council, Charlotte, 1971—, sec., 1973, 74, 75. Named one of top ten Outstanding Young Men of Mecklenburg County (N.C.) Charlotte Jr. C. of C., 1968. Mem. 26th Jud. Dist., N.C. bar assns., Sigma Chi, Phi Delta Phi. Presbyterian (deacon, counselor vocat. guidance program). Clubs: Charlotte Country, Charlotte Cotillion, Carrousel. Home: 855 Museum Dr Charlotte NC 28207 Office: 1100 Cameron-Brown Bldg Charlotte NC 28204

BASKIN, ROY HOWARD, JR., surgeon; b. Cameron, Tex., Oct. 10, 1916; s. Roy Howard and Toressa (Denson) B.; B.A., U. Tex., Austin, 1939; M.D., U. Tex., Galveston, 1942; m. Lowrey Waldene Burleson, Oct. 14, 1943; children—Roy Howard, III, Leland Burleson, John Spencer, Intern, U.S. Naval Hosp., Corpus Christi, 1942-43; resident Mayo Clinic, Rochester, Minn., 1947-52; pvt. practice surgery, Waco, Tex., 1952—; pres. staff Hillcrest Hosp., 1968, Providence Hosp., 1964— mem. McLennan County (Tex.) Bd. Health, 1972-75. Pres. Waco Symphony Assn., 1977-78, Waco Soc. for Hist. Preservation, 1966-67; trustee ofcl. bd. Austin Ave. United Methodist Ch., Waco, chmn., 1965-67, lay leader, 1959-61. Served as lt. M.C., USN, 1942-47. Fellow A.C.S. (pres. No. Tex. chpt. 1972); mem. McLennan County Med. Soc. (pres. 1972), Tex. Surg. Soc. (1st v.p. 1975-76, counselor 1980—), Tex. Med. Assn. (chmn. surg. sect. 1964) AMA, Tex. Mayo Alumni Assn. (pres. 1980), Phi Eta Sigma, Phi Beta Kappa, Alpha Omega Alpha. Clubs: N.W. Waco Rotary, Ridgewood Country. Co-author sect. on colon polyps in med. tex. Home: 2832 Braemar St Waco TX 76710 Office: 2115 N 34 St Waco TX 76708

BASLER, LOREN STANLEY, oil co. supr.; b. Wilson County, Kans., June 21, 1925; s. Aleck M. and Annie (Badger) B.; m. Dorothea L. Shaw, June 23, 1946; children—Stanley L., Kathleen. Asst. engr. Beatrice Foods Co., Parsons, Kans., 1946-47; with Phillipes Petroleum Co., Bartlesville, Okla., 1947—, bldg. engr., 1951-53, ops. supr., 1953—. Active various civic orgns. Served with USN, 1943-46; PTO. Mem. VFW (life). Republican. Methodist. Clubs: Bartlesville Sportsman, Masons. Office: Phillips Petroleum Co Town Power Plant Bartlesville OK 74004

BASS, CORNELIUS GRAHAM, oil jobber exec.; b. Latta, S.C., May 28, 1918; s. Howard H. and Sarah (Carmichael) B.; B.S. in Bus. Adminstrn., U. S.C., 1940; m. Ann Blair, May 23, 1942 (div. Jan. 1976); children—Ann Blair (Mrs. James E. Crowder, III), Cornelius Graham. With The Latta Cotton Co., 1940-41; asst. mgr. Dilmar Oil Co., Latta, 1941-42; mgr. Santee Oil Co., 1945-47, sec.-treas., 1947-71, v.p., 1971—, gen. mgr., 1947—; partner, gen. mgr. S & P Tire Co., Kingstree, S.C., 1949—; sec.-treas., gen. mgr. Services, Inc., Kingstree, 1950-71; pres. Warsaw Mfg. Co., Kingstree, 1958-63; pres. Bass Farms, Inc., Latta, 1963—; pres. Santee Broadcasting Co., Inc. (radio sta. WDKD), 1965-69, treas., 1970-75; pres. Kingstree Indsl. Devel. Corp., 1958—, Sunrise, Inc., 1976—, SUNUP, Inc., 1976—, Airport Beverage Corp., 1976—, TAB Enterprises, Inc., 1973—; sec.-treas. King's Tree Inn, Inc., 1967-70. Mem. Williamsburg Planning Commn., 1967—; chmn. Williamsburg County Bd. Edn., 1957-62. Served with AUS, World War II. Decorated Bronze Star. Mem. Kingstree C. of C. (v.p. 1956-58), S.C. Oil Jobbers Assn. (pres. 1954-55). Moose (past gov. Kingstree). Clubs: Kingstree Country (pres.), Optimist (past pres.), Lions (past pres.). Home: 1601 Fulton Ave Kingstree SC 29556 Office: Santee Oil Co Inc Hwy 52 N Kingstree SC 29556

BASS, JACK SOLOMON, author, journalist; b. Columbia, S.C., June 24, 1934; s. Nathan and Esther (Cohen) B.; A.B., U. S.C., 1956, M.A., 1976; m. Carolyn E. McClung, Mar. 3, 1957; children—Kenneth Nathan, David Louis, Elizabeth Rose. Copy editor News and Courier, Charleston, S.C., 1960-61; editor, pub. West Ashley Jour., Charleston, 1961-63; reporter Columbia (S.C.) Record, 1963-65; govtl. affairs editor The State, Columbia, 1966; bur. chief Charlotte Observer, Columbia, 1966-73; research fellow Duke U., Durham, N.C., 1973-75; writer-in-residence S.C. State Coll., Orangeburg, 1975-78; research fellow U. S.C. Law Sch., Columbia, 1978—. Served with USNR, 1956-60. Nieman fellow Harvard U., 1965-66. Mem. Soc. Nieman Fellows, Sigma Delta Chi. Jewish. Author: (with J. Nelson) The Orangeburg Massacre, 1970; Porgy Comes Home: South Carolina After 300 Years, 1972; (with W. DeVries) The Transformation of Southern Politics, 1976; The Four, 1980. Home: 3508 Fox Hall Rd Columbia SC 29204

BASS, JAMES ROGER, lawyer; b. San Antonio, Oct. 28, 1940; s. James Ozie and Mae (Kenedy) B.; B.B.A., Tex. A & M U., 1963; J.D., St. Mary's U., 1966; m. Darlene Hunter, Aug. 25, 1962; children—Wendy Ann, James Hunter. Admitted to Tex. bar, 1966; asso. firm. Waitz, Bretz & Collins, San Antonio, 1970-73; pres. firm James R. Bass, Inc., San Antonio, 1973—. Mem. San Antonio Bar Assn., State Bar Tex. Home: 3614 Hunter's Point San Antonio TX 78230 Office: 9002 Wurzbach Rd San Antonio TX 78240

BASS, LUTHER DEWITTE, scientist, mathematician, educator; b. Telfair County, Ga., Feb. 28, 1919; s. Croma and Evie (Williams) B.; A.B., Mercer U., 1949, M.Ed., 1954; postgrad. Fla. State U., 1957, Auburn U., 1961, 62, 65; m. Lillian Larkey (dec.), Mar. 27, 1948; 1 son, James L. Tchr., Coffee County (Ga.) Sch., 1946-63; prof. sci. and math. S. Ga. Coll., Douglas, 1963—, chmn. div. natural sci. and math., 1977—. Mem. City of Douglas Beautification Com., 1976—. Served with U.S. Army 1941-46. Mem. Ga. Assn. Edn., NEA. Presbyterian. Home: 321 W Cherry St Douglas GA 31533

BASS, WILLIAM KEAYS, SR., beverage co. exec.; b. Norfolk, Va., July 9, 1929; s. Louis Tulane and Muriel DeRinze (Carpenter) B.; B.S., Fla. State U., 1952; m. June Marie Cason, Dec. 28, 1952; children—William Keays, Patti Jo. With The Coca-Cola Co., Atlanta, 1952-79, Fla., 1979—, salesman fountain sales dept., 1952-59, spl. rep. fountain sales, 1959-61, supr. Navy sales fountain sales, 1961-66; asst. mgr. pub. relations, 1966-71, mgr. pub. relations services, 1971—, corp. affairs mgr. So. area, 1979—. Mem. Pub. Relations Soc. Am., Ga. Hospitality and Travel Assn. (dir.), Atlanta C. of C. (sports com.), Ga. Press Assn., Fla. Public Relations Assn., Greater Orlando C. of C. Republican. Episcopalian. Clubs: Atlanta Stadium, Atlanta Press, Braves 400 (pres. 1969), Atlanta Flames Booster (v.p.), Atlanta Press (dir. 1975), Henderson High Sch. Booster (pres. 1972) (Atlanta). Office: Coca-Cola Co Suite 525 Sun Bank Bldg Lake Buena Vista FL 32830

BASS, WILLIAM MICHAEL, roof truss co. exec.; b. Tyler, Tex., May 25, 1949; s. William Woodrow and Wilda Atrell (Thompson) B.; B.A. in Math., U. Tex., Arlington, 1973; m. Susan Elaine Nicholls, Aug. 7, 1970; 1 dau., Lindsay Nicole. With Timber Tech., Inc., Arlington, Tex., 1974—, plant mgr., 1977-79, v.p., gen. mgr., 1979—. Bd. dirs. Arlington Girls Club, 1978. Mem. Nat. Assn. Home Builders, Component Mfrs. Council. Republican. Baptist. Home: 2912 Glasgow Dr Arlington TX 76015 Office: 1707 S Peyco St Arlington TX 76017

BASSETT, CONSTANCE COLT, investment co. exec.; b. Buffalo, Feb. 1, 1915; d. Henry Van Schaick and Julia Kennett (Whitaker) Colt; student Chateau Brillamont, Lausanne, Switzerland, 1928-30, Ecole Vinet, Lausanne, 1930-32; m. William B.K. Bassett, Sept. 15, 1943; children—Carroll C., Nancy L., Constance K., Julia Bassett Aronson. Sec. Free French, Radio City, N.Y.C., 1941-42; coordinator info. and Office Strategic Services, 1942-45; treas. Sterling Security Corp., Bernardsville, N.J., from 1954, pres., 1975—; vice chmn. Bassett Found., Inc., 1973—; pres. Moorland Farms of S.C., 1978—. Club: Springdale Hall (Camden, S.C.). Home: Box 43 Route 3 Camden SC 29020 Office: PO Box 302 Pottersville NJ 07979

BASSETT, HARRY HOOD, banker; b. Flint, Mich., May 6, 1917; s. Harry Hoxie and Jessie Marie (Hood) B.; B.S., Yale U., 1940; children—Harry Hood, George Rodney, Patrick Glenn; m. 2d, Florence Schust Knoll, June 22, 1958. Asst. trust officer First Nat. Bank, Palm Beach, Fla., 1940-42, chmn. bd., 1965-71, also dir.; asst. v.p. First Nat. Bank, Miami, 1947-48, dir., 1947-48, v.p., 1948-56, asst. to pres., 1951—, chmn. exec. com., 1959—, pres., 1962-66, chmn. bd., 1966-76; dir. Wometco Enterprises, Eastern Airlines, Inc.; chmn. bd. S.E. Banking Corp., Inc. Mem. Orange Bowl Com.; chmn. emeritus U. Miami. Served as pilot Civil Coastal Patrol (anti-submarine), 1941-42; 1st lt. USAAF, 1944-46. Decorated Air medal. Mem. Fla. Bankers Assn., Assn. Res. City Bankers (dir.), Assn. Bank Holding Co. Episcopalian. Clubs: Bath, Miami; River (N.Y.C.); Lyford Cay (Nassau, Bahamas); Everglades (Palm Beach, Fla.); Biscayne Bay (Fla.) Yacht; Bohemian (San Francisco); Met. (Washington). Home: Coconut Grove FL 33133 Office: 100 S Biscayne Blvd Miami FL 33131

BASSETT, HENRIETTA ELIZABETH (BETH BASSETT), musician, composer, educator; b. Dallas, Mar. 25, 1932; d. Sidney Carl and Edna May (Shands) B.; B.A., Baylor U., 1952. Organist, pianist Baptist chs., Mesquite, Tex., 1945—; dir. plays and musicals in elem. schs. and Bapt. chs., Mesquite, 1950—; pvt. tchr. piano, Waco and Mesquite, 1948—; pvt. instr. organ, theory and composition, Mesquite, 1952—; tchr. music elem. Mesquite Ind. Sch., 1952-53; dir., adminstr. Music Camp Acad., Mesquite, 1949—; chmn. Mesquite Center, Nat. Piano-Playing Auditions, 1972-78, Nat. Organ-Playing Auditions, 1972-78; composer the First Christmas (cantata) (1st place award Am. Coll. Musicians), 1965, Fireworks (solo piano), 1972, Sleepy (solo piano), 1972, Stepping High (solo piano), 1972, Name That Tune (3 pianos, 12 performers) (1st place award Am. Coll. Musicians), 1975, Ten Little Indians (emsemble, 2 pianos, 10 performers), 1975, The Water Wheel, 1977. Named to Piano Guild Hall of Fame, 1972. Mem. Nat., Tex. music tchrs. assns., Am. Coll. Musicians, Nat. Assn. Organ Tchrs., Nat. Guild Piano Tchrs., Mesquite Area Music Tchrs. Assn., Baylor Alumni Assn. (life). Author: Requirements for Elementary Harmony Certificate, 1955; Intermediate Harmony Certificate, 1960; Intermediate Review, 1957; Listen, Then Do, I, 1975; Music Rudiments, 1973; Basic Fundamentals, 1977. Address: Route 2 Box 180 Mesquite TX 75182

BASSETT, JOHN EDWARD, psychologist; b. Saranac Lake, N.Y., July 6, 1941; s. Merritt and Doris (Parrott) B.; B.A. in Psychology, U. of Maine, in Portland, 1968; M.A. in Clin. Psychology, Memphis State U., 1971, Ed.D., 1973; m. Joanne Lee Howard, May 15, 1971; children—Johneen Marie, Stephanie Howard. Staff psychologist Pineland Hosp. and Tng. Center, Pownal, Maine, 1967-68, S. Portland (Maine) Sch. System, 1968-69, Arlington (Tenn.) Hosp., 1970-71, Tenn. Psychiatric Hosp., Memphis, 1971-72; dir. self mgmt. program Shelby County Penal Farm, Memphis, 1972—. Served with U.S. Coast Guard, 1959-63. Licensed psychologist, Tenn. Mem. Am., Southeastern, Maine, Memphis psychological assns., Assn. Advancement of Behavior Therapy, Am. Assn. Correctional Psychologists. Mem. editorial review bds. Jour. of Applied Behavior Analysis, Jour. Community Psychology, Quarterly Jour. Corrections; contbr. research and 41 articles in field. Home: 2073 Cranberry Dr Memphis TN 38134 Office: Shelby County Penal Farm Memphis TN 38134

BASTIAN, ROYAL RICHARD, III, bank exec.; b. New Orleans, July 5, 1946; s. Royal R. and Elizabeth M. B.; B.A. in History, U. Pa., 1969; postgrad. Stonier Grad. Sch. Banking, Rutgers U., 1972-75; m. Georgeanne Call, 1966; children—Jonathan, Matthew. Vice pres. Provident Nat. Bank, Phila., to 1975; v.p. Bank Okla., Tulsa, 1975-77; exec. v.p. Republic Bank & Trust Co., Tulsa, 1977, pres., chief exec. officer, 1978—. Vice chmn., trustee Tulsa Indsl. Authority; bd. dirs. Arts and Humanities Council Tulsa. Republican. Club: So. Hills Country. Office: PO Box 1656 Tulsa OK 74101

BASTO, JOHN DAVID, aluminum co. exec.; b. Harrisonburg, Va., Mar. 7, 1944; s. John William and Helen Shipp (Bowers) B.; B.S., The Citadel, 1966; M.Commerce, U. Richmond, 1973; m. Marion Graham Culler, Dec. 29, 1967; children—John David, Jr., Marion Graham. Structural engr. sect. dir. Lockwood-Green Engrs., Spartanburg, S.C., 1966-67; structural dept. head Piedmont Engrs. & Architects, Charleston, S.C., 1967-68; with Reynolds Metal Co., Richmond, Va., 1968—, staff asst. monumental div., 1968-70, structural engr. mill products div., 1970-72, market mgr. archtl. and bldg. products div., 1972-73, market dir. Reynolds Aluminum Supply, 1973—. Episcopalian. Club: Westwood Racquet. Contbr. articles to profl. jours. Home: 12 Hampton Hills Ln Richmond VA 23226

BATCHELLER, JOE ANN DEMING (MRS. DAVID SPRINGSTEEN BATCHELLER), business exec.; b. Jacksonville, Fla., Dec. 11, 1932; d. Osmer St. Clair and Lorena (Jones) Deming; A.A., Stephens Coll., 1952; B.A., U.N.C., 1955; m. David Springsteen Batcheller, Aug. 8, 1957; children—Elizabeth St. Clair, Osmer Deming, John Alden. Sec., Seminole Oil Co., Miami, 1957, pres., dir., 1961—; sec., dir. Blue Grass Plant Foods, Inc., Cynthiana, Ky., 1958; chmn. bd. dirs. Superior Plant Foods, Inc., Lakeland, Fla., 1958; v.p., dir. Pensacola Petroleum Co., Inc. (Fla.), 1961—, Top Power Stations, Inc., Miami, 1961—; chmn. bd. Blue Water Mobile Home Subdiv., Inc. Travernier, Fla., 1967—; pres. Blue Waters Mobile Home Sales, Inc. Bd. dirs. Miami Heart Inst., 1970—, v.p. aux., 1970—; trustee Miami Heart Inst., 1973—, v.p., 1975—; adv. bd. Convent of Sacred Heart, 1973—; co-chmn. Debutant Com. Miami, 1977. Mem. Young Patronesses of Opera, Symphony Club, Beaux Arts, Opera Guild, Vizcayans, D.A.R., English Speaking Union (v.p. Miami br. 1975—), Pi Beta Phi. Republican. Episcopalian. Home: 4595 Sabal Palm Rd Bay Point Miami FL 33137

BATCHELOR, PATRICK CASEY, lawyer; b. El Dorado, Ark., Sept. 15, 1946; s. George Wallin and Margaret Francis (Casey) B.; B.S., Baylor U., Waco, Tex., 1969, J.D., 1973; m. Carolyn Reynolds, June 30, 1974; children—Kelly Anne, J. Casey. Admitted to Tex. bar, 1973; 1st asst. criminal dist. atty. Navarro County, Corsicana, Tex., 1973-74, criminal dist. atty., 1975—; instr. Navarro Coll. Police Acad., 1974. Bd. dirs. Navarro County United Fund, 1976; deacon Westminster Presbyterian Ch., 1980. Mem. Am., Navarro County (pres. 1975) bar assns., State Bar Tex., Nat. Dist. Attys. Assn., Tex. Dist. and County Attys. Assn., Corsicana C. of C., Phi Alpha Delta. Democrat. Club: Corsicana Rotary (dir.). Home: 1824 Dartmouth Ln Corsicana TX 75110 Office: Navarro County Courthouse Corsicana TX 75110

BATCHO, PATRICIA JOAN, banker; b. Balt., Dec. 19, 1941; d. David B. and Gurtice A. (Chester) Cash; student Fla. State U., 1958-60, Coll. San Mateo, 1963-65, Fla. Sch. Banking, U. Fla., 1977; m. Joseph Batcho; 4 children. With 1st Nat. Bank of San Jose (Calif.), 1964-69, operations officer Saratoga-Quito br., 1965-69; v.p. revolving credit depts. Exchange Nat. Bank of Tampa (Fla.), 1970—. Mem. Fla. Bankers Assn. (bd. dirs.), Nat. Assn. Bank Women, Am. Inst. Banking, Tampa, Temple Terr. chambers commerce. Democrat. Roman Catholic. Clubs: Temple Terrace Golf and Country, Tampa Arts. Office: PO Box 1809 Tampa FL 33601

BATEMAN, CLINTON FRANK, accounting firm exec.; b. Fort Worth, May 2, 1940; s. Leonard Clinton and Frances (Ramsey) B.; B.B.A., Baylor U., 1962; m. Susan Smith, June 16, 1962; children—Stacie, Robyn, Kara. Supr. audit staff firm Coopers &

Lybrand, Dallas, 1961-66; partner firm Myron Anderson & Co., Midland, Tex., 1966-67; pres. firm Bateman & Co., Inc., Houston, 1967—, also chmn. bd.; mng. partner Wellington Group, real estate developers, Houston; partner, dir. Ancient Mariner, Inc., restaurant chain; instr. dept. acctg. So. Methodist U., 1966. Treas., mem. bd. dirs. Widowed, Inc., Houston, 1971—. Recipient Spl. Service award Vols. in Tech. Assistance, 1973. C.P.A., Tex. Mem. Am. Inst. C.P.A.'s, Tex. Soc. C.P.A.'s (dir.), Baylor U. Ex-students Assn. (dir.). Baptist. Gospel singer. Home: 12319 Queensbury Houston TX 77024 Office: 4041 Richmond Ave Houston TX 77027

BATEMAN, JOHN ROGER, investment holding co. exec.; b. Medford, Oreg., Sept. 21, 1927; s. Joseph Nielson and Bessie Mabel (Jackson) B.; student U. Redlands, 1944-45, Mont. Sch. Mines, 1945, Colo. Coll., 1945-46, San Diego State Coll., 1948; B.S. with honors, U. Calif., Berkeley, 1951, M.B.A., 1952; m. Dorothy Jane Blasingame, Mar. 23, 1949; children—David, Sally, Susan. Accounting trainee Standard Oil Co. Calif., San Francisco, 1952; sr. accountant Slavik & Ponder, C.P.A.'s, Corpus Christi, Tex., 1953-57; chief accountant Coastal States Gas Corp., Corpus Christi, 1957-59, treas., 1959-66, v.p. fin., 1963-66; mng. partner Bateman Investments, Corpus Christi, 1967—, Bateman Luxor Group Ltd., 1969-76, Bateman Alamo Group Ltd., 1971-74, Bateman Meridian Group Ltd., 1972-75; pres., chmn. bd. Bay Fabricators, Inc., 1973—, dir., 1972—; pres., chmn. bd. Bay Industries, Inc., 1975—, Bateman Industries, Inc., 1976—, Bay Heat Transfer Corp., 1977—; v.p., treas., dir. Integral Petroleum Corp., 1973-75, Integral Energy Corp., 1975—, Camden Drilling Co., 1974—, Integral Drilling Co., 1974—; dir. Guaranty Nat. Bank, 1972-75, chmn. exec. com., 1973-74. Bd. dirs., pres., treas. Little Theatre Corpus Christi, 1964-68; ofcl. bd. 1st United Methodist Ch., 1964-67, 70-73, 78—; bd. govs. United Way Coastal Bend, 1964-67, 73—, campaign chmn., 1977; exec. council USO, 1971-73; bd. dirs. Camp Fire Girls, 1967-69; state del. Republican Party Tex., 1972, 76, Nat. Rep. Senatorial Com., 1978—. Served to lt. (j.g.) USNR, 1945-50. C.P.A., Calif., Tex. Mem. Tex. Soc. C.P.A.'s, Navy League U.S., Phi Beta Kappa, Beta Alpha Psi, Beta Gamma Sigma, Alpha Lambda Nu. Clubs: Corpus Christi Country, Pharoah's Country (dir., treas. 1972-75), Town, Nueces, Rotary (dir. 1976-77, 78—). Home: 1015 Luxor St Corpus Christi TX 78412 Office: PO Box 2267 Corpus Christi TX 78403

BATES, EDWARD ELLETT, JR., lawyer; b. Wilmington, N.C., May 6, 1945; s. Edward Ellett and Sarah Cleveland (Beard) B.; B.A. in English, Washington and Lee U., 1967; J.D., U. Ga., 1972; m. Laura Helen Rassman, Aug. 28, 1969; 1 dau., Elizabeth Tyler. Admitted to Ga. bar, 1972; partner firm Hurt, Richardson, Garner, Todd & Cadenhead, Atlanta. Mem. High Mus. Art, Atlanta, 1974—. Mem. Am., Atlanta bar assns., State Bar of Ga., Atlanta Council Younger Lawyers. Clubs: Ansley Golf, German of Atlanta (pres. 1979), Lawyers of Atlanta. Home: 2541 Dellwood Dr NW Atlanta GA 30305 Office: 1100 Peachtree Center Harris Tower 233 Peachtree St Atlanta GA 30303

BATES, HAMPTON ROBERT, JR., pathologist; b. Roanoke, Va., Feb. 1, 1933; s. Hampton Robert and Mary Mildred (Crowder) B.; B.S., Roanoke Coll., 1953; M.D., Med. Coll. Va., 1957; m. Carole Harrison Young, Apr. 12, 1958; children—Hampton Robert III, Catherine Louise. Intern, Med. Coll. Va. Hosp., Richmond, 1957-58, resident in pathology, 1958-63; practice medicine specializing in pathology and nuclear medicine, Richmond, 1963—; pathologist Johnston-Willis Hosp., Chippenham Hosp.; v.p. Clin. Lab. Consultants, Inc., Richmond, 1976—; forensic pathologist Richmond Met. Area, 1959—. Diplomate Am. Bd. Pathology, Am. Bd. Nuclear Medicine. Fellow Coll. Am. Pathologists (life), Am. Soc. Clin. Pathologists; mem. Am. Coll. Nuclear Physicians (charter), AMA, Med. Soc. Va., Richmond Acad. Medicine. Episcopalian. Contbr. articles on descriptive, exptl. and forensic pathology to med. jours. Home: 641 Mobrey Dr Richmond VA 23235 Office: 7101 Jahnke Rd Richmond VA 23225

BATES, JOHN WILLIAM, cons. engr.; b. Mobile, Ala., Nov. 11, 1903; s. Alfred Absalom and Margaret Ellen (Green) B.; B.S., Auburn U., 1924; m. Ruth Ann Sawders, Apr. 15, 1940. Efficiency engr. Duquesne Light Co., Pitts., 1925-27; with U.S. Steel Corp., Youngstown, Ohio, 1927-44, dist. chief engr., 1940-44; gen. mgr. Acero del Pacifico, N.Y.C. and Concepcion, Chile, 1944-50; pres. La Hacienda Corp., Fisherman's Wharf Inc. (Fla.), 1960; pres., chmn. bd. Brobolan Corp., Clearwater, Fla., 1950—. City commr. Clearwater, 1953-54, Indian Rocks, Fla., 1956-60, 58-60; pres. Clearwater Civic Assn., 1952. Registered profl. engr., Ohio, Fla. Mem. Assn. Iron and Steel Engrs. (pres. 1929, 31), Am. Inst. Electric Engrs. (dir. 1930-31), Engrs. Soc. Western Pa. (dir. 1932-33), Clearwater C. of C. (pres. 1952-53), Gulf Breeze C. of C. (pres. 1955-57). Republican. Episcopalian. Home: 11920 Gulf Blvd Treasure Island FL 33706 Office: 377 La Hacienda Indian Rocks Beach FL 33703

BATES-NISBET, (CLARA) ELISABETH, lawyer, sch. adminstr., piano tchr., poet, songwriter; b. Houston, Dec. 4, 1902; d. William David and Kate Broocks (Arnall) Bates; B.A., U. Tex., 1938; M.A., U. Houston, 1941; LL.B., South Tex. Sch. Law, 1937. Tchr. pub. schs., Houston, 1923-49, prin., 1950-73, ret. prin. James Arlie Montgomery Elementary Sch.; admitted to Tex. bar, 1937; tchr. piano. Houston, 1928—. Life mem. chancellor's council U. Tex., Austin, Tex. Congress Parents and Tchrs. Mem. State Bar Tex., Houston Bar Assn., Tex. Tchrs. Assn. (life), Ex-Students Assn. U. Tex. at Austin (life), Tex. Geneal. Soc., Magna Charta Dames (organizing charter mem. East Tex. Colony 3d vice regent courier Round Table Tex. div. 1962-66), Tex. Hist. Assn. (patron, life), Colonial Dames XVII Century (registrar Col. John Alston chpt., mem. nat. com. on Am. history), Alston-Williams-Boddie-Hillard Soc. N.C., Colonial Order Crown, San Augustine County Hist. Soc. (charter), San Jacinto Descs., Inc., Daus. Republic Tex. (organizing charter mem. Ezekial Cullen chpt., rec. sec. gen., compiler and editor annuals 1963-65, state 2d v.p. gen., chmn. orgn. 1965-67), Officers Gen. Club, Soc. Descs. Charlemagne, D.A.R. (Tejas chpt. regent 1966-68, mem. nat. coms.), Soc. Descs. Knights of Order of Garter, Plantagenet Soc., Daus. Am. Colonists (organizer charter mem. LaSalle chpt.), U.D.C., Sovereign Colonial Soc. Ams. Royal Descent, Dames of Ct. of Honor, Daus. of Founders and Patriots of Am., Freedoms Found. Valley Forge (Houston women's chpt.), Internat. Platform Assn., Smithsonian Instn., Bates Family of Old Va. Assn., Jamestowne Soc., Delta Kappa Gamma (Eta Delta chpt. 1st v.p. 1966-68, life mem.), Nat. Soc. Poets. Co-founder Perpetual Endowment Fund Daus. Republic Tex., also perpetually endowed Presdl. scholarship in law, history, govt. or music U. Tex. at Austin, and Kate Broocks Bates award for research in Tex. history Daus. Republic Tex.; founder Kate Harding Bates Parker Award Fund for Jr. Historians orgn. of Tex. Hist. Assn., Emma Broocks Arnal perpetual endowment Okla. U., Norman. Address: 2305 Woodhead St Houston TX 77019

BATIE, BOBBY (BOB) NEAL, health care adminstr.; b. Guntersville, Ala., Sept. 16, 1938; s. Robert Wilford and Thelma Lou (Powers) B.; B.S., Berea Coll., 1960; M.A., Pepperdine U., 1975; m. Kay Kirby, Nov. 2, 1968; children—Debra Lynn, Robert Neal; 1 stepdau., Katherine. Staff, Kemper Ins. Cos., Chgo., summer 1959, Fed. Mut. Ins. Co., Decatur, Ill., 1960-63; underwriter Gulf Life Ins. Co., Jacksonville, Fla., 1963-67; with Blue Cross and Blue Shield of Fla., Jacksonville, 1967—, also dir.; adj. prof. Fla. State U., 1976—, Pepperdine U., 1976—. Recipient Fla. Coop. Edn. Clubs award, 1971; Kemper Ins. Found. grantee, 1957—. Mem. Adminstrv. Mgmt. Soc. (pres. 1973-74, diamond merit award 1977), Life Office Mgmt. Assn., Nat. Productivity Work Mgmt. Group, Berea Coll. Alumni Assn. (pres. 1978—). Democrat. Contbr. articles to profl. publs. Home: 4178 Churchwell Rd Jacksonville FL 32210 Office: Blue Cross and Blue Shield of Fla 532 Riverside Ave Jacksonville FL 32231

BATISTE, DONALDO RICARDO, speech pathologist; b. New Orleans, Jan. 20, 1953; s. Ernest and May del (Head) B.; B.A. magna cum laude (La. Bd. Edn. scholar 1974-75), Nicholls State U., 1975; postgrad. La. State U., 1975-76; M.Ed. summa cum laude, Southeastern La. U., 1979. Speech pathologist Terrebonne Parish Sch. Bd., Houma, La., 1976-77; speech and lang. specialist, cons. dept. corrective speech and lang. New Orleans Pub. Schs., 1977—; instr. dept. continuing edn. So. U., New Orleans, 1978—. Organist, St. Bridget Catholic Ch., 1966-75; cons. Terrebonne Voters League, 1972-75, mem., 1972—. Named Educator of Yr., New Orleans public schs., 1979. Mem. Am. Speech, Lang. and Hearing Assn., La. Speech and Hearing Assn., La. Assn. Educators, Thibodaux Aid to Hearing Assn., Greater New Orleans Communication Disorders Forum, Council for Exceptional Children, Assn. for Supervision and Curriculum Devel., Phi Kappa Phi, Phi Eta Sigma (v.p.), Kappa Delta Pi. Office: 1651 N Tonti St New Orleans LA 70119

BATTAGLIA, MARGARET ELIZABETH, restaurant owner; b. Elizabeth, N.J., Oct. 10; d. Rocco Marion and Elizabeth Anne (Nugent) Nittoli; R.N., Elizabeth Gen. Hosp.; m. Richard Battaglia, Oct. 31, 1948 (dec. 1972); children—Margaret Battaglia McAndrew, Richard, Robert. Co-owner, operator Jake's, Inc., Stuart, Fla., 1974—. Office: 423 S Federal Hwy Stuart FL 33494

BATTELL, WILLIAM PUTNAM, ret. marine corps officer, bank exec.; b. Mediapolis, Iowa, Dec. 26, 1906; s. Frederick Louis and Harriet Elizabeth (Chapman) B.; student Iowa State Coll., 1924-27, also marine corps, army and navy profl. schs.; m. Jean Finklea Bateman, Feb. 7, 1979. Enlisted in USMC, 1927, commd. 2d lt., 1930, advanced through grades to maj. gen.; assigned communications and electronics, 1927-48, supply, 1948-65; Q.M. Gen. Marine Corps, 1963-65; ret., 1965; pres., dir. Sun City Center Bank (Fla.), 1971-72, chmn. bd., 1972—. Mem. corp. Nat. Capitol USO Club; organizer, pres. S.W. Ga. Cerebral Palsy Assn.; mem. adv. com. Hillsborough County Charter Commn., v.p. Sun City Center Civic Assn., 1969-70, pres., 1971. Mem. Nat. Def. Transp. Assn. (v.p.), Def. Supply Assn. (hon. pres.), Armed Forces Mgmt. Assns. (bd. govs.), Am. Legion, Ret. Officers Assn., Nat. Assn. Uniformed Services, Old Timer Communicators So. Calif., Am. Inst. Banking, Vet. Wireless Operators Assn., Soc. Wireless Pioneers, S.W. Fla. Srs. Golf Assn., Marine Corps Combat Corrs. Assn., Internat. Platform Assn. Clubs: Rotary (pres. Ruskin-Sun City 1975-76), Sun City Center Men's (pres.); Valdosta (Ga.) Country. Home: 401 Blackhawk Circle Sun City Center FL 33570

BATTEN, JAMES WILLIAM, educator; b. Goldsboro, N.C., Aug. 5, 1919; s. Albert LeMay and Lydia Annie (Davis) B.; A.B., U. N.C., 1940, M.A., 1947, Ed.D., 1960: postgrad. Columbia U., 1942; m. Sara Magdalene Storey, June 1, 1945. Tchr., Glendale High Sch., Kenly, N.C., 1940-41, Wilmington Jr. Coll., 1946-47; tchr., coach Princeton (N.C.) High Sch., 1947-50; prin. Micro (N.C.) High Sch., 1950-58; teaching fellow, narrator Morehead Planetarium, Chapel Hill, N.C., 1958-60; asso. prof. E. Carolina U., Greenville, N.C., 1960-62, prof. edn., 1962—, chmn. dept. secondary edn., 1967—, also asst. dean Sch. Edn. Active in civic affairs. Served to lt. comdr. USNR, 1941-46. Mem. NEA, N.C. Assn. Educators (chpt. pres. 1961-62), Nat. Sci. Tchrs. Assn., Assn. for Supervision and Curriculum Devel., Phi Delta Kappa (pres. 1961-62), Horace Mann League, Nat. Soc. Study of Edn., Am. Ednl. Research Assn., N.C. Lit. and History Assn., Kappa Delta Pi (counselor 1967-74). Democrat. Baptist (deacon). Lion (pres. 1949-51). Author: Our Neighbors in Space, 1962, rev. edit., 1969; Research as a Tool for Understanding, 1965; Stars, Atoms, and God, 1968; (with J. Sullivan Gibson) Soils, 1970, rev. edit., 1977; Understanding Research, 1970, rev. edit., 1972; Human Perspectives in Educational Research, 1973; Rumblings of a Rolling Stone, 1974; Procedures in Educational Research, 1975, rev. edit., 1978; contbr. numerous articles profl. jours. Home: 1014 E Wright Rd Greenville NC 27834

BATTEN, RICHARD KENNETH, foundry exec.; b. Adel, Iowa, Aug. 17, 1918; s. Paul LaVerne and Ida Belle (Gray) B.; A.A., Chaffey Coll., 1939; student Santa Monica Tech. Coll., 1940; m. Betty Green, Jan. 4, 1942; children—Barbara Ellen, Richard Kenneth, Nancy Julia. Vice pres. All Am. Aircraft Co., Long Beach, Calif., 1946-47; dist. mgr. S.W. U.S., Piper Aircraft Co., Lockhaven, Pa., 1948-52; owner, pres. Okla. Aircraft Sales, distbr. for Okla. of Piper Planes, 1952-58; v.p., dir. Acme Foundry & Machine Co., Blackwell, Okla., 1979—. Served with AC, USN, 1940-46. Decorated Silver Cross, Air medal with 2 oak leaf clusters. Mem. Am. Soc. Metals, Am. Foundry Soc. (chmn. Plains States chpt.). Republican. Methodist. Office: PO Box 520 Blackwell OK 74631

BATTIN, BARBARA ELLEN, found. dir.; b. N.Y.C., Mar. 5, 1949; d. Milton A. and Katherine A. (Banks) Lessler; B.S. cum laude, Ohio U., Athens, 1972. Traffic dir., exec. sec., talent duties Sta. WRFD, Columbus, Ohio, 1972-73; dir. public relations Central Ohio Lung Assn., Columbus, 1973-74; dir. bldg. fun raising, asst. mgr. chpt. Tri-State Blood Center and Huntington-Cakell County chpt., ARC, Huntington, 1974-77; exec. dir. Huntsville (Ala.) Hosp. Found. Inc., also dir. devel. Huntsville Hosp., 1977—; cons. in field. Bd. dirs. Madison County ARC. Recipient Creative Achievement award Ad Club of Huntington (W.Va.), 1975. Mem. Nat. Assn. Hosp. Devel., Nat. Edn. Com., Nat. Soc. Fund Raising Execs. (sr.), Indsl. Devel. Assn., AAUW (at large), Public Relations Council Ala. (dir. N. Ala. chpt. 1978—), Huntsville Women's Center (pres. 1978—), Huntsville Interfaith Transp. Service (dir. 1978—). Democrat. Jewish. Club: Toastmaster (sec., v.p. Huntington Centennial 1975-77). Home: 2616 Pansy St Huntsville AL 35801 Office: Huntsville Hosp 101 Sivley Rd Huntsville AL 35801

BATTIN, (ROSABELL HARRIET) RAY, psychologist, audiologist; b. Rock Creek, Ohio; d. Harry Walter and Sophia (Boldt) Ray; A.B., U. Denver, 1948; M.S., U. Mich., 1950; Ph.D., U. Fla., 1959; postgrad. U. Miami (Fla.) Sch. of Medicine, 1957, U. Iowa, 1958; m. Tom C. Battin, Aug. 24, 1949. Instr. in speech pathology U. Denver, 1949-50; audiologist Ann Arbor (Mich.) Sch., 1950-51; audiologist Houston (Tex.) Speech and Hearing Center, 1954-56; dir. speech pathology-psychology Hedgecroft Hosp. and Rehab. Center, Houston, 1956-59; audiologist with Drs. Guilford, Wright and Draper, Houston, 1959-63; pvt. practice in psychology, audiology and psycholinguistics, Houston, 1959—; clin. instr. dept. otolaryngology U. Tex. Sch. Medicine, Galveston, from 1964; dir. of audiology vestibulography and speech pathology lab. Houston Ear Nose and Throat Hosp. Clinic, 1963-73; lectr. The First Word program Sta. KUHT-TV, 1959; guest lectr. to various workshops and schs., 1959—. Licensed psychologist, Tex. Recipient Gold award for Ednl. Exhibit, Am. Acad. Pediatrics, 1969. Fellow Am. Speech and Hearing Assn. (profl. services bd. 1967-70, com. on pvt. practice 1971-74), World Acad. Inc.; mem. Acad. Pvt. Practice in Speech Pathology and Audiology (pres. 1968-70), Am. Psychol. Assn., Tex. Speech and Hearing Assn. (v.p. 1968), Cleft Palate Assn., Tex., Houston psychol. assns., Acad. of Aphasia, Internat. Assn. of Logopedics and Phoniatrics, Am. Auditory Soc., Orthopsychiat. Assn., Am. Biofeedback Soc., Tex. Biofeedback Soc., Sigma Alpha Eta. Author: (with C. Olaf Haug) Speech and Language Delay, 1964; Vestibulography, 1974; Private Practice: Guidelines for Speech Pathology and Audiology, 1971; editor (with Donna R. Fox) Private Practice in Audiology and Speech and Language Pathology, 1978; contbr. articles in field to profl. jours.; author (with Irvin A. Kraft) The Dysynchronous Child (film), 1971. Home: 3337 Meadow Lake Ln Houston TX 77027 Office: Battin Clinic 3931 Essex Ln Houston TX 77027

BATTIN, ROBT. DAVIS, JR., clergyman; b. Mpls., Oct. 8, 1929; s. Robert Davis and Harriot Ada (MacMurray) B.; B.S., U. Ala., 1953; M.Div., Episcopal Sem. S.W., 1956; M.Ed., Miss. Coll., 1973; m. Charlotte Alice Wilson, Feb. 7, 1953; children—Barbara, Deborah, Brenda, Leslie, Nancy. Ordained to ministry Episcopal Ch., 1956; rector, Calvary Ch., Americus, Ga., 1958-62, St. Agustine Ch., Augusta, Ga., 1962-66; asso. rector, headmaster Ch. of Advent, Birmingham, Ala., 1956-70; headmaster St. Andrew's Sch., Jackson, Miss., 1970-73; rector, headmaster Holy Nativity Ch. and Sch., Panama City, Fla., 1973—. Served with AUS, 1956-58. Fellow in Celtic ch. history, 1961. Mem. Nat. Assn. Episcopal Schs. (elementary bd. 1973—), Kappa Delta Pi. Home: 125 N Lakewood St Panama City FL 32401 Office: 1005 Second Plaza Panama City FL 32401

BATTLE, ALLEN OVERTON, JR., educator, psychologist; b. Memphis, Nov. 19, 1927; s. Allen Overton and Florence Louise (Castelvecchi) B.; B.S., Siena Coll., 1949; M.A., Cath. U. Am., 1953, Ph.D., 1961; certificate in clin. psychology U. Tenn. Coll. Medicine, 1953; m. Mary Madeline Vroman, June 14, 1952; 1 son, Allen Overton. Instr. dept. psychiatry U. Tenn. Coll. Medicine, 1956-61, asst. prof., 1961-67, asso. prof., 1966-72, prof., 1972—, chief div. clin. psychology, 1974—; chief clin. psychologist U. Tenn. Mental Health Center, 1971-78; vis. lectr. Southwestern U. at Memphis, 1962—; cons. USPHS, Suicide and Crisis Intervention Service; mem. Mayor's Commn. on Alcohol and Drug Abuse, 1974-77. Bd. dirs. Runaway House, St. Peter's Home for Children. Recipient Disting. Service award Tenn. Dept. Mental Health, 1971. Diplomate Am. Bd. Profl. Psychology. Mem. Am., Tenn. psychol. assns , Am. Anthrop. Assn., N.Y. Acad. Sci., AAAS, Brit. Soc. Projective Techniques, Sigma Xi. Contbr. articles to profl. jours. Author: Clinical Psychology for Physical Therapists, 1975. Home: 2220 Washington Ave Memphis TN 38104 Office: 66 N Pauline St Memphis TN 38105

BATTLE, FRANK, mgmt. specialist, former army officer; b. Indianola, Miss., July 15, 1929; s. Frank and Hattie M. (Taylor) B.; Sr.; B.S., So. U., 1958; diploma N.W. Inst. Med. Tech., 1958; M.B.A., Fairleigh Dickinson U., 1976, M.P.A., 1977. postgrad. U.S. Army Command and Gen. Staff Coll., 1969, Air War Coll., 1973; m. Ethel Beatrice Hines, Dec. 28, 1955. Research asst. Sch. of Medicine, Vanderbilt U., Nashville, 1958-62; commd. 1st lt. U.S. Army, 1952, advanced through ranks to lt. col., 1968; served as transp. corps officer, Ft. Eustis, Va., Ft. Benning, Ga., McGuire AFB, N.J., 1952-57; served to inspector gen.-comdr. transp. corps, Ft. Meade, Md., Ft. Monmouth, N.J., Korea, Vietnam, Germany, 1962-77; tech. buyer purchasing dept. Tenn. State U., Nashville, 1978—; M.P.A. intern City of Long Branch, N.J., 1976. Mem. Civilian Review Action Com., Korea, 1970-71; mem. fin. com. Gordon Meml. United Meth. Ch., Nashville. Recipient meritorious certificate Methodist Bishop of Korea, 1953. Mem. Am. Soc. for Pub. Adminstrn., Assn. M.B.A. Execs., Soc. Logistics Engrs., Am. Acad. Polit. and Social Sci., Assn. U.S. Army, Nat. Def. Transp. Assn., Fairleigh Dickinson U. Century Club, Fairleigh Dickinson U. Alumni Assn., Transp. Corps Museum Found., VFW, Ret. Officers Assn., Alpha Phi Alpha, Zeta Epsilon Lambda (chmn. budget com. 1975-77). Methodist. Club: Methodist Men's. Contbr. article to profl. jour. Home 8132 Cloverland Dr Nashville TN 37211 Office: Tennessee State U 3500 Blvd Nashville TN 37203

BATTLE, LUCY TROXELL (MRS. J.A. BATTLE), educator; b. Bridgeport, Ala., June 28, 1916; d. John Price and Emily Florence (Williams) Troxell; student Ala. Coll., 1934-35; B.S., Fla. So. Coll., 1949; postgrad. U. Fla., 1950, 52, Fla. State U., 1963; M.A., U. South Fla., 1968; m. Jean Allen Battle, Aug. 25, 1940; 1 dau., Helen Carol (Mrs. George Clipper Salmon, Jr.). Asst. postmaster, Bridgeport, Ala., 1936-40; asst. dir. personnel office Sebring (Fla.) AFB, 1942-44; tchr. Cleveland Ct. Sch., Lakeland, Fla., also Forest Hill Sch., Carrollwood Sch., Tampa, Fla., 1949-64; dean of girls Greco Jr. High Sch., Tampa, 1964-67; counselor Plant High Sch., Tampa. Bd. dirs. Tampa Oral Sch. for Deaf, Internat. Cultural and Econ. Center, Tampa. Recipient Outstanding Service award Fla. So. Coll. Woman's Club, 1942. Mem. NEA, Am. Childhood Edn. Internat., Fla., Hillsborough County personnel and guidance assns., AAUW, Delta Kappa Gamma, Kappa Delta Pi, Phi Mu. Methodist. Club: Carrollwood Golf and Tennis. Author: (with J.A. Battle) New Idea in Education. Contbr. articles to profl. jours. Home: 11011 Carrollwood Dr Tampa FL 33618 Office: 2415 S Himes Ave Tampa FL 33609

BATTLE, MARY VROMAN, educator; b. Marshall, Minn., Sept. 8, 1926; d. Alois and Idalie (Vercoutere) Vroman; B.A. in English and French, Coll. St. Teresa, 1948; M.A. in Speech and Drama, Cath. U., 1954; m. Allen Overton Battle, June 14, 1952; 1 son, Allen Overton III. Tchr. English, Albany (Minn.) Sr. High Sch., 1948-49; librarian, Landon, Md., 1951-52; tchr. speech Lennox Sch. Retarded, Memphis, 1952-53; jr. high sch. tchr. English, Latin and sci., Washington, 1952-56; dean of studies Southwestern High Sch. Scholars Program, Memphis, 1967-71; instr. English, Memphis State U., 1956—. Founder, participant tutoring project. Mem. NEA, Tenn. Edn. Assn., Tenn. Philological Assn., Renaissance Soc., AAUW, MLA, Shelby-Memphis Council Tchrs. of English. Roman Catholic. Brown belt in karate. Home: 2220 Washington Ave Memphis TN 38104 Office: Dept English Memphis State U Memphis TN 38152

BATTLE, MINNIE, educator; b. Mar. 4, 1943; d. Glover and Harriett (Bobo) B.; A.S., Coahoma Jr. Coll., 1965; B.S., Alcorn State U., 1967; student Miss. State U., 1972-73; M.Ed., Delta State U., 1974; Ednl. Specialist, Jackson State U., 1979. Sec., Patton Lane High Sch., Batesville, Miss., 1962-63; sec. Utica Jr. Coll., 1967-73, secretarial tng. tchr., 1973—, continuing edn. tchr., 1974—, sec. to student activity com., 1977—. Pianist, Mt. Olive M.B. Ch., Pine Grove M.B. Ch., Mt. Zion M.B. Ch., Utica, Miss. Mem. Am. Vocat. Assn., Miss. Vocat. Assn. for Educators, Nat. Bus. Edn. Assn., Miss. Bus. and Office Assn., Miss. Bus. Edn. Assn., Alpha Kappa Alpha, Phi Beta Lambda. Home: Route 2 Box 296 Batesville MS 38606 Office: PO Box 51 Utica Jr Coll Utica MS 39175

BATTLE, MORRIS FONTAINE, aerospace co. exec.; b. Texarkana, Ark., July 23, 1927; s. Morris Sheppard and Margaret Josephine (Fontaine) B.; B.S.E.E., Tex. A. & M. U., 1944; M.S., U. N.Mex., 1957; M.B.A., U. So. Calif., 1966; m. Gloria Faye Horst, June 9, 1964; children—Terry Lynn, Morris Edward. Tech. dir. Air Force Missile Devel. Center, 1954-60; v.p. Aerolab Devel. Co., Pasadena, Calif.,

1960-63; dir. advanced missiles LTV Inc., Dallas, 1963-66; regional mgr. defense div. Brunswick Corp., Fort Walton Beach, Fla., 1966—; guest prof. Texarkana Engring. Coll., 1955-57. Dist. commr. Boy Scouts Am., 1955-59. Served to maj. U.S. Army, 1947-54. Decorated Purple Heart with four clusters, D.F.C., D.S.C. Registered profl. engr., Tex., N.Mex. Mem. Am. Def. Preparedness Assn., Air Force Assn., AIAA, AIEE, Naval Inst., DAV, Field Artillery Assn., Soc. Naval Architects and Marine Engrs., Fort Walton Beach C. of C. (dir. 1972-79), Old Crows. Republican. Episcopalian. Clubs: Soc. Crew Bowlegs, Ret. Officers (bd. mem.). Author: Basic Analogue Computers, 1956. Home: 386 Gardner Dr Fort Walton Beach FL 32548 Office: Suite 105/106 98 Miracle Strip Pkwy Fort Walton Beach FL 32548

BATTON, KENNETH DUFF, EDP adminstr.; b. Greenwood, S.C., May 30, 1942; s. Roy L. and Heppie Duff (Mayson) B.; B.S., Mankato State U., 1970; m. Deborah Dean Solsaa, Feb. 14, 1965; children—James Stanislaus, Michele Dean. EDP programmer operator Josten's, Inc., Owatonna, Minn., 1964-65; programmer, analyst, sr. analyst Mankato (Minn.) State U., 1965-70; EDP mgr. Associated Coll. Central Kans., 1971-72; EDP mgr. U. Va., Charlottesville, 1973-74; sr. mgr. U. Va. Med. Center, 1975-77; systems cons. Glen Raven Mills (N.C.), 1977; sr. asso. PRC Data Services Co., McLean, Va., 1977-78; dep. project mgr. Computer Center, Exec. Office of Pres., Washington, 1978; project mgr. Alaska Fed. Data Processing Center, Anchorage, for PRC Computer Center, Inc., McLean, Va., 1978—; instr. computer sci. colls. Mem. Data Processing Mgmt. Assn. (chpt. pres. 1977—). Republican. Home: Route 4 Greenwood SC Office: PRC Computer Center Inc 7670 Old Springhouse Rd McLean VA 22101

BATTS, LEMIA CLARENCE, JR., chem. engr.; b. Rose Hill, N.C., Mar. 11, 1945; s. Lemia Clarence and Annie (Smith) B.; B.S. in Chem. Engring., N.C. State U., 1970; m. Scarlet Elaine Fowler, Feb. 19, 1972. Engring. technician Starch div. Standard Brands Co., Clinton, Iowa, 1967-69; design engr. Am. Enka Co. (N.C.), 1970-72, sr. design engr., 1972-74, project engr., 1974-77, cost engr., 1977—, process engr., 1978—. Dir. sr. high div. 1st Baptist Ch., Asheville, N.C., 1975, Sunday sch. supt., 1979—; chmn. Jaycees Elderly Assistance Program, Asheville, 1976; bd. dirs. Caring for Children, Asheville, 1976—. Named Jan. Jaycee of Month, 1977. Mem. Am. Inst. Chem. Engrs. Home: 1 Melbourne Pl Asheville NC 28801 Office: Enka NC 28728

BAUCH, JOY COULTER, ret. sch. counselor, musician; b. Knoxville, Tenn., Jan. 15, 1923; s. Roy Elton and Della Mae (Coulter) B.; B.A., U. Tenn., 1948, M.S., 1952; postgrad. InterAm. U., Mex., 1968; m. Mary Regina Householder, June 10, 1949; 1 son, Henry Coulter. Tchr., counselor for Knoxville City Schs., 1949-76; office methods tng. officer TVA, summers 1967-76, clk. in word processing unit, 1976—; organist and choir dir. four chs. in Knoxville, 1947-79; organist Powell United Meth. Ch., 1979—. Served with C.E., U.S. Army, 1943-46. Recipient Service award City Schs. of Knoxville, 1976. Mem. NEA, Tenn., East Tenn. edn. assns., Knoxville Tchrs. League, Tenn., East Tenn. personnel and guidance assns., Pan-Am. League of Knoxville (pres. 1971-73, 75-77, adviser 1977—), Profl. Employees Internat. Union, Phi Delta Kappa. Methodist. Home: Route 1 Box 275 Powell TN 37849 Office: TVA 400 Commerce St SL63 Knoxville TN 37902

BAUCUM, INEZ ONO, social worker; b. Sulphur, Okla., Aug. 21, 1915; d. David Robert and Mary Hattie (Conyers) B.; student E. Central U., Ada, Okla., 1933-36; A.B., U. Okla., 1939; postgrad. Tulane U., New Orleans, 1944-45; M.S.W., U. Chgo., 1948; postgrad. Pepperdine U., 1975. Checker, Okla. Tax Commn., State Capitol, 1938-39; social worker Okla. Dept. Public Welfare, Old Age and Aid to Families with Dependent Children, 1939-44; social worker Okla. Child Welfare, Oklahoma City, 1944-55; social worker Children's Home, Lubbock, Tex., 1955—; instr. social work Lubbock Christian Coll., 1971—. Mem. exec. com. South Plains Health Systems Bd., 1975—; del. White House Conf. Children and Youth, 1960. Recipient 20th Century Christian Publ.'s Woman award; Family Ser. Assn. Am. Recognition award, 1979, Social Worker of Year award Nat. Assn. Social Workers. Mem. Nat. Assn. Social Workers (pres.), Acad. Cert Social Workers, Tex. United Community Services, Lubbock Christian Coll. Faculty. Mem. Ch. of Christ. Contbr. articles and poetry to profl. jours. Home: 2705 23d St Lubbock TX 79410 Office: PO Box 2824 Lubbock TX 79408

BAUER, JOHN HENRY, accountant; b. Evansville, Ind., Dec. 23, 1940; s. Joseph S. and Estelle J. (Corressell) B.; B.S., St. Edward's U., 1962; postgrad. South Tex. Coll. Law, 1966; m. Junia Lee Oakleaf, Sept. 24, 1966; children—Julie Ann, Jill Jaye, John Joseph. Staff accountant Coopers & Lybrand, C.P.A.'s, Houston, 1962-73, partner, 1973—. Instr. accounting St. Thomas U., 1969. Chmn. bd. trustees St. Edwards U., Austin, Tex. Served with AUS, 1962. Recipient Coronat award St. Edward's U., 1972. C.P.A., Tex. Mem. Am. Inst. C.P.A.'s, Tex. Soc. C.P.A.'s, Houston Jr. C. of C. (dir. 1968-69). Republican. Roman Catholic. Home: 21 Hickory Ridge Houston TX 77024 Office: 1010 Jefferson St Houston TX 77001

BAUGH, MARY ROSE, educator; b. Twin City, Ga., Aug. 24, 1935; d. Eustice Brinson and Sallie Mae (Canady) Turner; B.S. in Home Econs., U. Ga., 1957, Ph.D., 1978; M.Ed. in Counseling, U. Md., 1966; m. Marvin Hamilton Baugh, June 28, 1959; children—Frank, Rosemary, Jamie, Marty. Tchr. English Newton County High Sch., Covington, Ga., 1957; Manpower and Devel. Tng. Act counselor Prince George's Sch. Nursing, Washington, 1966-67; prof. dept. edn. Ga. Coll., Milledgeville, 1969—. Mem. Baldwin County (Ga.) Democratic Exec. Com., 1970-76; sec. treas. Baldwin County Recreation Commn., 1960—. Served with USAF, 1957-60. Recipient Res. Officers Assn. Minuteman award, 1960; Mod Mothers March Chm. award, 1972. Mem. Assn. Supervision and Curriculum Devel., Am., Ga. personnel and guidance assns., Am. Coll. Personnel Assn., Assn. Humanistic Edn. and Devel., Assn. for Specialists in Group Work, Ga. Coll. Personnel Assn. Methodist. Clubs: Milledgeville Music, Old Capitol Hist. Soc., Ga. Coll. Women's Ga. Coll. Drummers. Home: Rt 1 Box 222 Milledgeville GA 31061 Office: Kilpatrick Edn Center Ga Coll Milledgeville GA 31061

BAUGHN, ROBERT ELROY, microbiologist; b. Chanute, Kans., Jan. 31, 1940; s. Berryman Thomas and Oella Louise (Smith) B.; B.S., The Citadel, 1963; M.S. (USPHS fellow), U. Tenn., 1966; Ph.D. (NIH fellow), U. Cin., 1975; m. Myra Donell Phillips, Dec. 12, 1965; children—Heather Lynne, Brenna Gayle. Microbiologist, Hutcheson Meml. Tri-County Hosp., Ft. Oglethorpe, Ga., 1969-71, Parkridge Hosp., Chattanooga, 1971; instr. dept. dermatology and dept. microbiology and immunology Baylor Coll. Medicine, 1975-77, asst. prof., 1977—. Served as capt. AUS, 1967-69. Mem. Am. Soc. Microbiology, Am. Soc. Clin. Pathology, Reticuloendothelial Soc., Sigma Xi. Contbr. articles to profl. jours. Home: 11003 Atwell Dr Houston TX 77096 Office: Dept Infectious Diseases VA Hosp Bldg 211 2002 Holcombe Houston TX 77211

BAUKNIGHT, CLARENCE BROCK, wholesale, retail co. exec.; b. Anderson, S.C., May 14, 1936; B.S., Ga. Inst. Tech., 1958; s. John Edward and Theodosia (Brock) B.; m. Harriet League, June 29, 1959; children—Harriet League, Clarence Brock. Dist. mgr. Wickes Corp. (and predecessor), Atlanta, 1960-65; exec. v.p. Builder Marts of Am., Inc., Greenville, S.C., 1965-70, pres., 1970—, also dir.; dir. Citizens Builder Marts, Frank Ulmer Lumber Co. (both Greenville), Parks Lumber Co. (Gainesville, Ga.), Westwood Lumber Co. (Rocky Mount, N.C.). Mem. Indsl. Mgmt. Soc., Young Presidents Orgn., Phi Delta Theta. Methodist (adminstrv. bd.). Mason (Shriner). Clubs: Greenville Country, Poinsett (Greenville); Wildcat Cliffs, Highlands Country (Highlands, N.C.). Home: 111 Rockingham Dr Greenville SC 29607 Office: Builder Marts of Am PO Box 47 Greenville SC 29602

BAUM, GEORGE FREDERICK, JR., banker; b. Corsicana, Tex., Dec. 17, 1932; s. George Frederick and Priscilla Camille (Hartzell) B.; student Oxford U., Eng., 1953; A.B., Harvard U., 1955; LL.B., So. Meth. U., 1963; m. Catherine Margaret McLemore, May 1, 1965; children—George Frederick, Mary Katherine, Edward McLemore, Elizabeth Hartzell. Partner, Baum Properties, 1957—; admitted to Tex. bar, 1963; enforcement atty. SEC, Fort Worth, 1963-64; estate tax atty. U.S. Treasury Dept., Dallas, 1964-66; practiced law, Dallas, 1966-69; sec., gen. counsel Capital S.W. Corp., Dallas, 1969-76, MESBIC Fin. Corp., 1977-78; asst. gen. counsel Mich. Gen. Corp., 1976-79; pres. First Bancorp Capital Inc., 1979—. Served with USAF, 1955-57. Mem. Am., Tex. (sec.-treas. corporate counsel sect. 1976-77, chmn.-elect 1977-78, chmn. 1978-79), Dallas (sec.-treas. corporate council sect. 1975-76, vice chmn. 1976-77, chmn. 1977-78), bar assns., S.W. Legal Found., U.S. (nat. dir. 1963), Tex. (v.p. 1963) jr. chambers commerce, Assn. For Corporate Growth, Inc. (dir. Dallas-Ft. Worth chpt. 1978-79), Sons Republic Tex. (1st v.p. Dallas chpt. 1973, pres. 1974-75), Am. Soc. Corporate Secs., Inc., Mil. Order World Wars. Mem. Christian Ch. Club: Harvard (co-chmn. schs. com. 1966-68) (Dallas). Home: 4331 Lorraine Ave Dallas TX 75205 Office: 100 N Main St Corsicana TX 75110

BAUMAN, SANDRA RENEE SPIEGEL, nurse; b. N.Y.C., June 30, 1949; d. Siegmund and Ruth (Josias) Spiegel; student Boston U., 1967-70; B.S. in Nursing, Adelphi U., 1971, postgrad., 1973-74; postgrad. Barry Coll., 1978; m. H. Lee Bauman, Nov. 3, 1978. Staff nurse educator, obstetrics Albert Einstein Hosp., N.Y.C., 1971-72, head nurse newborn nurseries, 1973-74; asst. instr. maternity nursing St. Johns Riverside Hosp., 1972-73; head nurse obstetrics, nurseries, high risk nursery Mt. Sinai Hosp., Miami Beach, Fla., 1974-78; clin. nursing supr., div. pediatrics Jackson Meml. Hosp., Miami, 1978, coordinator div. clin. edn., 1978-79, quality assurance coordinator Maternal/Child Hosp. Center, 1979—; mem. Fla. State Bd. Nursing, 1979—; CPR instr., 1978. Mem. Am. Nurses Assn., Fla. Nurses Assn., Sigma Theta Tau. Contbr. articles to RN mag. Office: Jackson Meml Hosp 1611 NW 12th Ave Miami FL 33136

BAUMANN, ALAN FREDERIC, actuary; b. Boston, June 11, 1947; s. Frederic Francis and Phyllis B.; student U.S. Naval Acad., 1965-69: B.A. in Math., SUNY, Geneseo, 1976; postgrad. N. Tex. State U., 1977, U. Tex., Dallas, 1977—; m. Carol Curataio, Dec. 29, 1973. Actuary, Republic Nat. Life Ins. Co., Dallas, 1976-79, Blue Cross and Blue Shield, Dallas, 1979—. Served with USN, 1965-71. Cert. secondary math. tchr., N.Y. Home: 821 Via Altos Mesquite TX 75150 Office: Main at N Central Expy Dallas TX 75201

BAUMANN, DANIEL BRUCE, civil engr.; b. Perryton, Tex., Mar. 30, 1952; s. Bruce Endres and Clara Nell (Lathem) B.; B.S., Tex. Tech. U., 1974; m. Delania Wynn Allen, July 27, 1974. Civil engr. U.S. Army C.E., Durant, Okla., 1974—. Mem. Nat., Tex. socs. profl. engrs., Nat. Rifle Assn., Phi Kappa Phi. Methodist. Club: Lions. Home: 1713 Cedar Ridge Circle Durant OK 74701 Office: 1515 Main St Durant OK 74701

BAUMBACH, DONALD OTTO, educator; b. Oil City, Pa., June 25, 1926; s. Otto Ernest and Erna Eva (Zielke) B.; B.S., Syracuse U., 1954; M.S., Pa. State U., 1959, Ph.D., 1962; postgrad. Clarkson Coll. Tech., Potsdam, N.Y., 1979—; m. Leona May Anderson, Oct. 26, 1962; 1 son, Timothy Donald. Chemist, Solvay Process div., Allied Chem. Corp., Moundsville, W.Va., 1954-56; research chemist Lord Mfg. Corp., Erie, Pa., 1962-65; sr. research chemist Tex. U.S. Chem. Co., Parsippany, N.J., 1965-68; asst. prof. chemistry St. Paul's Coll., Lawrenceville, Va., 1970-77; vis. instr. Eastern Ill. U., 1978-79. Served with Signal Corps, AUS, 1944-46, 47-50; ETO. Allied Chem. Corp. fellow, Pa. State U., 1959; Nat. Urban League summer research fellow, 1974-76; Hampton Inst. summer research fellow, 1977. Mem. N.Y. Acad. Scis., Am. Chem. Soc., Sigma Xi, Phi Lambda Upsilon, Sigma Gamma Epsilon. Presbyterian (deacon 1966). Address: PO Box 897 Prescott AZ 86302

BAUMBERGER, THEODORE SHRIVER, state agy. exec.; b. Glasgow, Ky., Aug. 28, 1925; s. Perry Alvin and Helen (Shriver) B.; B.A., U. Louisville, 1949, M.A., 1950; Ph.D., U. Okla., 1961; m. JoAnn Dodson, Apr. 12, 1948; children—Erick Theodore, Andrea Leigh, Brent Lane; m. 2d, Susan Kay Kirk, June 29, 1975. Exec. sec. Ky. Com. for Children and Youth, Mid-Century White House Conf., Louisville 1950-51; adminstrv. asst. acting dir. div. sch. health Ky. Dept. Health, Louisville, 1951-52; supr. psychol. unit Okla. Dept. Instns., Social and Rehab. Services, 1954-59, supr. div. state homes and schs., 1960-68, acting supr. psychol. unit, 1960-68, adminstrv. asst., 1968-69, project dir. Juvenile Delinquency Planning Unit, Council Juvenile Delinquency, 1969-77; adminstrv. asst., supr. Okla. Div. Ct. Related and Community Services, 1977—; practicum supr. Psychol. Clinic, U. Okla., 1953-54, 58-68, staff psychologist Guidance Service, 1959-60, cons. Psychol. Clinic, 1961-68, adj. asst. prof., 1963-68; individual practice psychotherapy, Norman, Okla., 1963-70; cons. psychologist Okla. Bd. Pub. Affairs, 1956-59, Peace Corps Tng. Program, U. Okla., 1965-67, Oklahoma City Bd. Edn., 1966-69, Griffin Meml. Central State Hosp., 1968—, Fed. Bur. Prisons, El Reno Reformatory, 1969—, DePt. Health, Edn. and Welfare, 1971—, others; mem. profl. adv. bd. North Oklahoma City Mental Health Center. Sec. Okla. Bd. Examiners Psychologists, 1965-67, chmn., 1967-68. Mem. Okla. Gov.'s Com. on Vocat. Rehab., 1966-67, Correctional Task Force, 1973—; vice-chmn. therapeutic adv. council drug abuse and alcoholism Okla. Dept. Mental Health, 1972—; mem. adv. com. Okla. Commr. Narcotics and Dangerous Drugs Control, adv. task force criminal process edn. Okla. State Regents Higher Edn., 1973, numerous others. Served with USAAF, 1943-45. Mem. Am., Southwestern, Okla. (past pres.) psychol. assns., Am. Acad. Psychotherapists, Am. Group Psychotherapy Assn., Southwestern Group Psychotherapy Soc., Am. Pub. Welfare Assn., Nat. Assn. Tng. Schs. and Juvenile Agys., Nat., Okla. (mem. adv. com.) councils on crime and delinquency), Nat. Coll. Juvenile Ct. Judges (awards com.), Okla. Psychiat. Soc., Okla. Group Process Soc., Okla. Health and Welfare Assn., Sigma Chi Sigma, Delta Upsilon, Psi Chi, Delta Phi Alpha. Democrat. Methodist. Home: 616 NW 41st St Oklahoma City OK 73118 Office: PO Box 25352 Oklahoma City OK 73125

BAUMGARDNER, HAYNES MADDEN, realtor, air force officer; b. Wellington, Tex., July 27, 1920; s. Joseph Bailey and Eva Lyle (Godfrey) B.; B.S. in Animal Husbandry, Tex. Tech. U., 1942; postgrad. U. Ala., 1948; M.A. in Personnel Mgmt., George Washington U., 1956; postgrad. U. Md., 1961-62; m. Myrnavae Aileen Barkley, Dec. 6, 1943; children—Haynes Madden, Jan Barkley. Commd. aviation cadet USAF, 1942, advanced through grades to col., 1965; command pilot, navigator, ret., 1972; realtor Baumgardner's Matador Realtors Inc., Lubbock, Tex., 1973—; chmn. bd. Matador Realtors Inc., Lubbock, 1973—. Active Boy Scouts Am., Silver Beaver, 1971. Decorated D.F.C., Air medal with four bronze oak leaf clusters, Legion of Merit. Named Outstanding Angel Flight Advisor in Nation AFROTC, 1970; recipient Outstanding Unit award USAF, 1971. Mem. Air Force Assn. (life, charter), Lubbock C. of C., State Assn. Tex. Pioneers, Air Force Aid Soc. (life), USAF Hist. Found. (life), Order of Daedalians (life), West Tex. Museum Assn., Century Club Tex. Tech. U., Nat., Tex. assns. realtors, Farm, Land Inst., Tex. Soc. Farm, Land Brokers. Methodist. Clubs: Masons, Shriners. Home: 3706 68th St Lubbock TX 79413 Office: 5602 Slide Rd Lubbock TX 79414

BAUMGARDNER, JAMES LEWIS, educator; b. Bristol, Va., Jan. 26, 1938; s. John Richard and Roxie Katherine (Lewis) B.; A.A., Bluefield Jr. Coll., 1957; B.A., Carson-Newman Coll., 1959; M.A., U. Tenn., Knoxville, 1964, Ph.D., 1968; children—Ellen Lorena, James Michael. Asst. prof. history Carson-Newman Coll., Jefferson City, Tenn., 1964-67, asso. prof., 1967-73, prof., 1973—, chmn. history-polit. sci. dept., 1974—; ordained to ministry Baptist Ch., 1955. Interim mem. Jefferson County (Tenn.) Bd. Sch. Commrs., 1978. Served with U.S. Army, 1959-62. Mem. Am. Hist. Assn., Acad. Polit. Sci., Orgn. Am. Historians, So. Hist. Assn., So. Bapt. Hist. Soc., Phi Alpha Theta. Republican. Contbr. articles to learned jours. Office: Box 1929 Carson-Newman Coll Jefferson City TN 37760

BAUMLI, GEORGE RAYMOND, civil engr.; b. Marble, Colo., Apr. 9, 1929; s. Jacob and Marie (Bosshart) B.; B.C.E., U. Colo., 1957; m. Mary Jo Ryden, Dec. 26, 1954; children—Gregory, Mark, Christopher. Chief of planning Calif. Dept. Water Resources, Sacramento, Red Bluff and Los Angeles, 1957-78; div. engr. Internat. Boundary and Water Commn., El Paso, Tex., 1978—. Chmn., Red Bluff (Calif.) City Planning Commn., 1972-73. Served with AUS, 1950-52. Mem. ASCE (chmn. project formulation commn. irrigation and drainage div. 1978-79), U.S. Commn. Internat. Commn. on Large Dams. Democart. Episcopalian. Contbr. articles to tech. jours. Home: 6216 Pino Real El Paso TX 79912 Office: 4110 Rio Bravo El Paso TX 79902

BAUR, CATHERINE TORNILLO, nurse, hosp. adminstr.; b. Boston, Aug. 6, 1941; d. Mario Anthony and Helen Elizabeth (Platt) Tornillo. B.S., U. Conn., 1964; M.P.H., Yale U., 1976; postgrad. U. Pa., 1976; m. Edward G. Baur, Apr. 17, 1976; children—Grayson E., David A. Balla, Drew A., Julia W. Balla. Psychiat. staff nurse VA Hosp., West Haven, Conn., 1964; public health nurse Guilford (Conn.) Vis. Nurse Assn., 1965; head nurse birth defects U. Kans. Med. Center, Kansas City, 1966-68; intern Conn. Mental Health Center, New Haven, 1974; coordinator emergency med. service State of Conn., Hew Haven, 1974-77; asst. dir. nursing service Univ. Hosp. of Jacksonville (Fla.), 1977, asst. exec. dir. nursing, also dir. nursing, 1977—. Mem. Democratic Town Com., Roxbury, Conn., 1974-76; mem. New Haven CD adv. bd., 1975-76; adv. bd. Fla. Jr. Coll. Mem. NE Fla. Soc. Nursing Ser. Adminstrs. (sec. 1977—), Am. Soc. Nursing Ser. Adminstrs., Fla. Soc. Nursing Ser. Adminstrs. Home: 526 Lora St Neptune Beach FL 32233 Office: Univ Hosp of Jacksonville 655 W 8th St Jacksonville FL 32209

BAUR, MARIAN KROGMAN, educator; b. Cleve., Feb. 15, 1935; d. Wilton Marion and Virginia Madge (Lane) Krogman; B.S.N., Emory U., 1958; M.S.N., U. Ala., 1972; m. Gerd Robert Baur, May 6, 1958; children—Arthur William, Kathleen Elizabeth. Staff nurse various hosps., Fla., Ala., 1958-60; instr. Tenn. Valley State Tech. Vocat. Sch., Decatur, Ala., 1960-65; dir. nursing Decatur Gen. Hosp., 1965-66, adminstrv. dir., 1968-72; faculty U. Ala., Huntsville, 1972—, now asso. prof. nursing, chmn. Upper Div., Sch. of Nursing and acting chmn. Grad. Program. Active PTA, ARC, others; active Morgan County Republican Party. Served with Nurses Corps, U.S. Army, 1956-59. Mem. AAUW, Am. Nurses Assn., Nat. League for Nursing, Dau. of Am. Revolution, Sigma Theta Tau, Kappa Delta Pi. Episcopalian. Office: PO Box 1247 Huntsville AL 35807

BAUTCH, R. THOMAS, guidance counselor; b. Racine, Wis., Mar. 1, 1949; s. Roman Thomas and Rita Marie (Cullen) B.; B.S., U. Wis.-Whitewater, 1971, M.S., 1973; postgrad. Nova U., 1977—. Tchr., coach Eustis (Fla.) High Sch., 1973-74; guidance counselor Lake County Area Vo-Tech. Center, Eustis, 1974—, chmn. student services dept., 1975—; v.p. Xanthus Corp., Tavares, Fla., 1978—. Vol. counselor Youth Programs Inc., Tavares, 1973, recipient certificate of appreciation, 1974, 76; chmn. bd. dirs. Epilepsy Assn. Central Fla. Inc., Orlando, 1979—; bd. dirs. Helpline Inc., Umatilla, Fla., 1977—, recipient cert. of appreciation, 1977. Mem. Am., Fla., Central Fla. (pres.) personnel and guidance assns., Nat. Vocat. Guidance Assn., Am., Fla. vocat. assns., Fla. Career Devel. Assn., Lake-Sumter Employment Resources Council. Roman Catholic. Home: Rt 3 Box 256 Tavares FL 32778 Office: 2001 Kurt St Eustis FL 32726

BAUTSCH, VIRGINIA BELLE, city ofcl.; b. Dallas, Dec. 9, 1923; d. Harry Clay and Sarah Adelle (Slaughter) Coleman; student Dallas Art Museum, summers 1940, 41, Dallas Evening Sch., 1942-43, Met. Bus. Sch., 1945; m. Hilton Basil Bautsch, Dec. 21, 1947 (div. 1961); 1 son, Robert Hilton. Various clerical and stenography positions for bus. firms and schs. in Dallas, 1938-41; black and white etch and color copyist Manzer Studios, Dallas, 1941-42, sec., 1943-44; stenographer dept. water works City of Dallas, 1942-43, City Mgr.'s Office, 1945, sec. water works dept., 1946-52, sec. to city property mgr. pub. works dept., 1972, sec. dept. revenue and taxation, 1972-77, sec. psychol. services unit police dept., 1977—; exec. sec. A. Harris & Co., Dallas, 1954-55, Tex. Power & Light Co., Dallas, 1955-58, Republic Nat. Bank of Dallas, 1961-66, 67-68; notary pub., 1978—. Mem. Am. Bus. Women's Assn. (mem.-at-large), Tex. Notary Pub. Assn., Am. Philatelic Soc., Nat. Trust Historic Preservation. Baptist. Home: 5829 1/2 Prospect Ave Dallas TX 75206

BAXTER, GENE KENNETH, engring. mgmt. exec.; b. Emmett, Idaho, Sept. 4, 1939; s. Glen Wilton and Mable Velhelmina (Casper) B.; A.A., Boise Jr. Coll., 1959; B.S. in Mech. Engring., U. Idaho, 1961; M.S. in Aero. Engring. (NDEA fellow 1961-64), Syracuse (N.Y.) U., 1966, Ph.D. in Mech. Engring., 1971; m. Laraine Marie Mitchell, Jan. 20, 1968; children—Gretchen Lynn, Aaron Gregory. Engr. gas dynamics Pratt and Whitney Aircraft Co., East Hartford, Conn., 1961; teaching and research asst. Syracuse U., 1962-67; engr. heating, ventilation and air conditioning Galson and Galson Cons. Engrs., Syracuse, 1968; sr. mech. engr., staff engr. Electronic Systems div. Gen. Electric Co., Syracuse, 1968-77, advanced project mgr. mech. systems Space div., Daytona Beach, Fla., 1977, mgr. mech. design engring., 1977—; tchr. N.Y. State profl. engrs. refresher course, Syracuse, 1975-76. Chmn. fin. com. United Ch. of Christ, Liverpool, N.Y., 1974-77, chmn. bd. trustees, 1977; ruling elder Ormond Beach (Fla.) Presbyn. Ch., 1979—, chmn. stewardship com., 1979—. Recipient Achievement award for excellence in machine design Machinery Mag., 1961; Raymond J. Briggs award Idaho State Bd. Engring. Examiners, 1961; licensed profl. engr., N.Y. State. Mem. IEEE (sr. mem.; chmn. Daytona sect. 1979—), ASME, Nat. Soc. Profl. Engrs., Gen. Electric Speakers Bur., Sigma Xi, Phi Kappa Phi, Tau Beta Pi, Phi Theta Kappa. Club: Tomoka Oaks Country (Ormond Beach). Author numerous papers on gas dynamics, mech. structures, vibrations and thermal design; dir. projects creating state-of-the-art visual simulation and tng. systems, data processing and automated digital controls for electronic systems. Home: 10 Pebble Beach Dr Ormond Beach FL 32074 Office: Gen Electric Co PO Box 2500 Daytona Beach FL 32015

BAXTER, GEORGE WILLIAM, JR., educator; b. Moresville, Tenn., Oct. 8, 1925; s. George William and Lenora (Long) B.; A.B., Emory U., 1946; M. Div. cum laude, Yale, 1951; M.A., George Peabody Coll., 1968, Ph.D., 1969; m. Jane Elizabeth Farrar, Aug. 28, 1959; children—George William III, Elizabeth Lynne. Instr. religion Fla. So. Coll., Lakeland, 1959-60, asst. acad. dean, registrar, 1960-66; prof., chmn. dept. psychology King Coll., Bristol, Tenn., 1969—, Mary Reynolds Babcock prof. pscyhology, 1970-79, chmn. div. social scis., 1970-80. Chmn. bd. Offender Aid and Restoration of Bristol. Served with USNR, 1943-45. Mem. Am. Assn. Higher Edn., Am., Southeast psychol. assns., Soc. Psychol. Study Social Issues, Soc. Scientific Study Religion, Phi Beta Kappa. Methodist (adminstrv. bd. 1970—, chmn. social concerns commn. 1975-79). Contbr. articles to profl. publs. Home: 928 Florida Ave Bristol TN 37620

BAXTER, HARRY STEVENS, lawyer; b. Ashburn, Ga., Aug. 25, 1915; s. James Hubert and Anna (Stevens) B.; A.B. summa cum laude, U. Ga., 1936, LL.B. summa cum laude, 1939; postgrad. Yale U., 1939-40; m. Edith Ann Teasley, Apr. 4, 1943; children—Anna Katherine (Mrs. Paul Worley) (dec.), Nancy Julia (Mrs. John Adams Sibley III). Admitted to Ga. bar, 1941; instr. U. Ga. Law Sch., Athens, 1941; asso. Smith Kilpatrick Cody Rogers & McClatchey, Atlanta, 1942-51; partner Kilpatrick & Cody, Atlanta, 1951—; mem. State Bd. Bar Examiners Ga., 1960-66, chmn., 1961-66; mem. Ga. Jud. Qualifications Commn., 1979—; dir. Latex Contrns. Co., Atlanta. Pres., Atlanta Community Chest, 1963; mem. bd. visitors U. Ga. Law Sch., 1965-68, chmn., 1965-66, chmn. alumni adv. com. on reorgn., 1962-64; chmn. chancellor's alumni adv. com. on selection of pres. U. Ga., 1966-67; gen. co-chmn. Joint Ga. Tech.-Ga. Devel. Fund, 1967; trustee U. Ga. Found., chmn., 1973-76; trustee William E. Honey Found., St. Joseph's Infirmary, Atlanta. Served with AUS, 1942-45. Recipient Distinguished Alumnus award U. Ga. Law Sch., 1967. Fellow Am. Bar Found.; mem. Am. Law Inst., Am., Ga., Atlanta bar assns., Atlanta C. of C. (dir. 1959-62), Atlanta Legal Aid Soc. (pres. 1956-57), Phi Beta Kappa, Phi Beta Kappa Assos., Phi Kappa Phi, Omicron Delta Kappa, Phi Delta Phi, Clubs: Capital City (pres. 1965-67), Lawyers (pres. 1958-59), Piedmont Driving, Commerce, University Yacht. Home: 3197 Chatham Rd NW Atlanta GA 30305 Office: Equitable Bldg 100 Peachtree St NW Atlanta GA 30303

BAXTER, IDA MAE ALLEN (MRS. WALTER LAWRENCE BAXTER), educator; b. Morgan, Tex., Dec. 19, 1930; d. Joseph Flanary and Saphronia Anne (Womack) Allen; certificate Tarleton State Coll., 1950; B.B.A., Southwest Tex. State U., 1952; M.Ed., Colo. State U., 1967; m. Walter Lawrence Baxter, Apr. 21, 1951; children—Jessica Ann (Mrs. Douglas B. Hart), Dana Mae, Allen Lawrence. Stenographer Tex. Dept. Welfare, Glen Rose, 1949; typist Houston Power and Light Co., 1950; tchr. Mathis (Tex.) Ind. Sch. Dist., 2953-58, East Central Ind. Sch. Dist., San Antonio, 1958-59, New Caney (Tex.) Ind. Sch. Dist., 1959-60, Uvalde (Tex.) Ind. Sch. Dist., 1960-64; instr. data processing programming Southwest Tex. Jr. Coll., Uvalde, 1965—. Faculty adviser Bapt. Student Union, S.W. Tex. Jr. Coll., 1971-75. Recipient Outstanding Faculty Mem. award Southwest Tex. Jr. Coll., 1972-73. Mem. Tex. State Tchrs. Assn., Tex. Jr. Coll. Tchrs. Assn., Soc. Data Educators, Tex. Assn. Ednl. Data Systems, AAUW (rec. sec. 1972-74, corr. sec. 1968-70, pres. 1978—). Baptist (tchr. coll. and career dept. 1970-77). Club: Music (Uvalde, Tex.). Home: 705 Skylane Dr South Uvalde TX 78801

BAXTER, OSCAR FITZ-ALAN, V, real estate broker; b. Norfolk, Va., Apr. 6, 1945; s. Oscar Fitz-Alan IV and Lucy Gordon (Bailey) B.; B.B.A., Campbell Coll., 1972; m. Kathryn Matilda Barnhill, Aug. 26, 1972. Salesman, Sam Miriello & Assos., Inc., Dunn, N.C., 1972; sales mgr. Baxter Realty Corp., Norfolk, Va., 1973, v.p., 1975—; bd. dirs. Multiple Listing Service of Tidewater, Inc., Virginia Beach, 1975-76, 77—, sec.-treas., 1976, v.p., 1977—; pres. Shorehaven Group, Inc., Norfolk, 1975, dir., 1975—; pres., chmn. bd., dir. Heritage Corp. of Va., 1976—. Served with USN, 1965-69; Vietnam. Lic. real estate broker, Va., 1975; cert. property mgr. Mem. Norfolk/Chesapeake Bd. Realtors (dir. 1975—), Va. (dir. 1976-77), Nat. assns. realotrs, Inst. Real Estate Mgmt., Norfolk C. of C. Clubs: Million Dollar Sales, Kiwanis. Home: 3004 Milford Ln Virginia Beach VA 23452 Office: 6040 Virginia Beach Blvd Norfolk VA 23502

BAXTER, ROBERT FRANCIS, physician; b. N.Y.C., Nov. 14, 1926; s. Frank Henry and Frances Anna (Felton) B.; B.S., Roanoke Coll., 1951; postgrad. Va. Poly. Inst., 1952-53; M.D., U. Va., 1957; m. Nancy Carolyn McFall, Aug. 19, 1950; children—Frances Lee, Robert Francis (dec.), Mary Pat, Beth Ann, Nancy Jo. Ordained minister, Ch. of God; intern U. Va. Hosp., 1957-58; staff physician Grundy (Va.) Hosp., 1958-62, chmn. family practice and med. dept., 1969—; practice medicine specializing in family practice, Grundy, Va.; dir. Standard Savs. & Loan Assn. Pres. Buchanan County Assn. Mentally Retarded, 1965-70; mem. health advisory com. S.W. Va. Community Coll., 1969—; bd. dirs. YMCA Buchanan County, Nat. Assn. Med. Examiners, Ford Philpott Evangelistic Assn. bd. visitors King Coll., Bristol, Va. 1975—; co-chmn. Buchanan County Fuel-A-Thon, 1975-76; chmn. Christian Crusade, Buchanan County, 1975-76, 77. Served in USNR, 1943-46. Diplomate Am. Bd. Family Practice. Fellow Am. Acad. Family Practice (charter mem.); mem. AMA, Va. Acad. Family Practice (bd. dirs.), Va. Med. Soc., Am. Soc. Contemporary Medicine and Surgery, So. Med. Assn., Buchanan Dickinson Med. Soc. (pres.) Buchanan County Ministerial Assn. (hon.). Liberal Democrat. Club: Moose. Home: Box 66 Vansant VA 24656 Office: Grundy Hosp Inc Grundy VA 24614

BAXTER, TURNER BUTLER, office products co. exec.; b. Dermott, Ark., Mar. 13, 1922; s. Robert Wiley and Sallie Hollis (Murphy) B.; B.B.A., U. Tex., 1947; M.B.A., Pepperdine U., Los Angeles, 1976; m. Pauline Taylor Bond, June 7, 1947; children—David Bond, Paula Taylor. With Rio Grande Nat. Life Ins. Co., Dallas, 1947-67, sr. v.p., 1963-67; engaged in investments, 1967-75, 79—; pres. Shelby Office Supply Inc., Dallas, 1975-79. Pres. Dallas Health and Sci. Museum, 1953-56; adv. bd. Dallas Community Chest Trust Fund, 1976—; v.p. Circle Ten council Boy Scouts Am., 1970-74. Served with USAAF, 1943-46. Recipient Silver Beaver award Boy Scouts Am., 1968. Mem. Salesmanship Club Dallas. Methodist. Clubs: Kiwanis (pres. 1966), Dallas Country, Petroleum (Dallas). Home: 5815 B E University Dallas TX 75206 Office: PO Box 297 Dallas TX 75221

BAYAZEED, ABDO FARES, petroleum engr.; b. Damascus, Syria, Aug. 20, 1924; s. Fares Abdo and Waheebeh (Azizeyah) B.; came to U.S., 1947, naturalized, 1959; student Jr. Coll. Wentworth Mil. Acad., 1947-51; B.S. in Petroleum Engring., U. Okla., 1955; m. Dorothy Fay Gant, Oct. 11, 1957; children—Fares, David, Raina, Jason (dec.), Nadia. Petroleum engr. Sinclair Oil & Gas Co., Tulsa, 1957-60; petroleum engr. Layton Oil Co., Independence, Kans., 1960-62; petroleum engr. petroleum prodn. research Energy Research, Devel. Adminstrn. U.S. Bur. Mines, Bartlesville, Okla., after 1962, now with Bartlesville Energy Tech. Center Dept. Energy. Chmn. arrangement com. Sci. Fair, Bartlesville, 1967, judge, 1968; mem. Tech. Career Adv. Com., 1967—, bd. dirs., 1968-71, chmn. edn. com., 1970, Bartlesville; mem. youth com. YMCA, Bartlesville, 1969-70, advisor Jr. Hi-Y Club, 1969-70. Recipient award of Honor Wentworth Mil. Acad., 1950. Mem. Soc. Petroleum Engrs. (chmn. career adv. com. 1968-71), Bartlesville Gem, Mineral Soc. Contbr. articles to profl. jours. Home: 432 SE Queenstown Bartlesville OK 74003 Office: PO Box 1398 Bartlesville OK 74003

BAYNE, JAMES LARRY, materials engr.; b. Spartanburg, S.C., Jan. 9, 1952; s. James Leroy and Delia Hester (Edwards) B.; B.S., U. S.C., 1973; m. Elizabeth Andrews, Sept. 3, 1977. Technician, Deering-Milliken Research Co., Spartanburg, S.C., 1969-72; mech. technician Michelin Tire Corp., Greenville, S.C., 1974-77, materials handling engr., 1977—. Mem. ASME. Baptist. Office: Michelin Tire Corp Antioch Church Rd Greenville SC 29602

BAYS, KIRK VAN, ins. co. exec.; b. Springfield, Mo., June 22, 1951; s. Robert Newell and Gertha Bernice (Huddleston) B.; B.S. in Bus. Adminstrn. (scholar), Nicholls State U., 1973; postgrad. U. Tex., 1978-79; m. Cindy Fondren, June 9, 1973. Credit mgr. Terrebonne Bank & Trust Co., Houma, La., 1973-74; agt. Aetna Life & Casualty Co., New Orleans, 1974-75, agt., asst. supr., Tampa, Fla., 1975-76, estate and bus. analysis mgr., Dallas, 1976—; cons. Pres. Young Republicans, Thibodaux, La., 1972-73; mem. Nat. Rep. Com., 1976—. Recipient Nat. Sales Achievement award, 1974-77; Nat. Quality award, 1975-77; Man of Yr. award Aetna Life & Casualty, New Orleans, 1974, Tampa, 1975; named to Million Dollar Roundtable, 1975-76; recipient Sales Mgmt. award, 1976, 77, 78. Mem. Nat. Assn. Life Underwriters, Dallas Assn. Life Underwriters, Fellowship of Christian Athletes. Baptist. Home: 1704 Tulane Dr Richardson TX 75081 Office: 8350 N Central Expressway Suite M-2100 Dallas TX 75206

BAYS, ROBERT PAYNE, internist; b. Woodland, Miss., Mar. 19, 1921; s. Fred Barry and Sara Louise (Payne) B.; B.S., Miss. State Coll., 1942; M.D., Vanderbilt U., 1945; m. Lilburn Catherine Sandoz, Dec. 13, 1946; children—Robert Payne, Bonnie Lee, Katherine Elizabeth. Intern, Gorgas Meml. Hosp., Ancon, C.Z., 1946-47, resident, 1946-47; asst. resident Strong Meml. Hosp., Rochester, N.Y., 1949-50; resident in internal medicine Scott and White Clinic, Temple, Tex., 1950; fellow pathology Strong Meml. Hosp., Rochester, 1948, fellow hematology, 1948-49; chief med. services U.S. Med. Center, Springfield, Mo., 1951-53; pvt. practice internal medicine, Shreveport, La., 1953—; pres., Bays and Herold Med. Corp., Shreveport, 1970—; clin. asso. prof. La. State U. Med. Sch., Shreveport, 1967—; bd. dirs. Doctors Hosp., Inc., Shreveport, 1963-67, vice chmn., 1967, exec. com., 1967-71; dir. Savs. Life Ins. Co., 1974—, med. dir., 1975—. Served with U.S. Army, 1942-45, 46-48; USPHS, 1950-53. Diplomate Am. Bd. Internal Medicine, Bd. Life Ins. Medicine. Fellow ACP; mem. Am. Soc. Internal Medicine, Am. Fedn. Clin. Research, Am. Heart Assn., AAAS, Am. Assn. Life Ins. Med. Dirs., La Soc. Internal Medicine (pres. 1958-61). Contbr. articles to profl. jours. Home: 5513 Flagstone Dr Shreveport LA 71119 Office: 1121 Louisiana Ave Shreveport LA 71101

BAYSHORE, CHARLES ALEXANDER, optometrist; b. Hagerstown, Md., Aug. 30, 1919; s. Lloyd Mehring and Helen Lucetta (Purdy) Basehoar; O.D., Pa. State Coll., 1940; m. Bradylee Blackwell, Feb. 23, 1975; children—Donald, Beverly, Margo. Pvt. practice optometry, Orlando, Fla., 1945—; adj. prof. Coll. Optometry, U. Houston, 1980; cons. in field. Served with USAF, 1950-54. Decorated Bronze Star. Mem. Am., Fla. optometric assns., Am. Acad. Optometry, Internat. Soc. Contact Lens Specialists (recipient Sir Frederik Herschel Gold medal 1976). Contbr. articles in field to profl. jours. Home: 2013 Countryside Circle S Orlando FL 32804 Office: 214 E Marks St Orlando FL 32803

BEACH, DOROTHY RIGDON (DORE), counseling psychologist; b. Bklyn., Sept. 24, 1933; d. Lynn S. and Mary E. (Marine) Rigdon; M.A. in Counseling, U. South Fla., 1972; Ed.D., Nova U., 1975; m. Eugene Hamilton Beach, Oct. 9, 1967; children by previous marriage, Daryl S. Mattson, Dana L. Mattson. Acad. adviser U. South Fla., Tampa, 1972-74, univ. counseling psychologist, 1974—, asst. prof. guidance Coll. Edn. Pres. bd. dirs. Women's Survival Center, Tampa, 1978; bd. dirs. Children's Home, Inc., Tampa, 1979—. Mem. Am. Assn. Higher Edn., Am. Personnel and Guidance Assn., Am. Coll. Personnel Assn., Am. Sch. Counselor Assn., League Women Voters, Athena Soc. (pres. 1978-79), NOW, Phi Kappa Phi, Psi Chi, Phi Theta Kappa. Cert. sch. psychologist, Fla. Home: 19102 Lutz Lake Fern Rd Lutz FL 33549 Office: U South Fla Fowler Ave Tampa FL 33620

BEACH, ELIZABETH CAROLINE, psychiatrist; b. Spartanburg, S.C., Dec. 3, 1910; d. Henry and Ella Martha (Zaloudek) Kreisinger; A.B., Cornell U., 1931; M.D., Albany Med. Coll., 1943; certified in psychoanalysis New Orleans Psychoanalytic Inst., 1956; m. Kenneth Harold Beach, Sept. 17, 1948; children—Pamla Laura, Jennifer Lynn. Intern, L.I. Coll. Hosp., Bklyn., 1944; resident in psychiatry Psychiat. Inst. Presbyn. Hosp., 1945, Bellevue Hosp., N.Y.C., 1946; practice medicine specializing in psychiatry and psychoanalysis, Houston, 1960—; instr. New Orleans Psychoanalytic Inst., 1958-59; asst. clin. prof. psychiatry Baylor U. Mem. Am. Med. Women's Assn., Tex. Med. Assn., Am. Psychiat. Assn., AMA, Harris County Med. Soc., Houston Soc. Psychiatry and Neurology. Episcopalian. Home: 10 S Briar Hollow Ln Houston TX 77027 Office: 2121 Sage Rd Suite 320 Houston TX 77056

BEACH, ROBERT OLIVER, computer exec.; b. Washington, June 25, 1932; s. Oliver Fairmont and Aldora (Stone) B.; student George Washington U., 1950-51, 57-62; m. Allie A. Lamb, Aug. 14, 1976; children by previous marriage—Patricia Ann, Robert Edward, Michael Oliver, John Roger. With Engring. Research Corp., 1951-52; design engr. Nems-Clarke, 1952-55; project engr. Frederick Research Corp., 1955-59; project mgr. Am. Machine & Foundry Co., 1959-62; pres., founder SAID, Inc., Falls Church, Va., 1962—, Systems, Analyses, Instrumentation & Devel., 1977—; pres. Quick Copy, Inc., 1972—, Air Parcel Delivery, Inc., 1974—; real estate broker; comml. airplane pilot; cons. mktg. and finance; v.p. Interstate Service Corp.; high sch. faculty adviser devel. data processing curriculum, 1971. Mem. Falls Church Bicentennial Commn., 1975—. Mem. Data Processing Mgmt. Assn., UNIVAC Users Assn., Aircraft Owners and Pilots Assn., Falls Church C. of C. Club: Optimist (charter). Home: 500 N Roosevelt Blvd Falls Church VA 22044 Office: 417 W Broad St Falls Church VA 22046

BEACHAM, WOODARD DAVIS, physician; b. McComb, Miss., Apr. 10, 1911; s. Woodard D. and Ida (Felder) B.; B.A., U. Miss., 1932; B.S., 1933; M.D., Tulane U., 1935. Intern, Charity Hosp. of La., New Orleans, resident obstetrics and gynecology, sr. vis. surgeon, 1948-74, cons., 1975—; prof. clin. gynecology and obstetrics Tulane U. Sch. Medicine, 1949—; obstetrician and gynecologist So. Bapt. Hosp., pres. staff, 1961; past pres. surg. staff Charity Hosp., New Orleans; cons. Beacham Meml. Hosp. Magnolia, Miss., Hotel Dieu Sisters Hosp., New Orleans, Methodist Hosp., New Orleans; practice medicine specializing in obstetrics and gynecology, 1940-74, in gynecology, 1975—. Pres. Beacham Corp., 1964-79. Recipient A.C.S. med. records prize, 1943; Spl. award So. Bapt. Hosp., 1979. Diplomate Am. Bd. Obstetrics and Gynecology. Fellow A.C.S. (gov. as rep. obstet., gynecol. sect. AMA 1955-60, gov. as rep. Am. Gynecol. Soc. 1961-63; adv. council gynecology and obstetrics 1963-67, chmn. council 1967, past pres. La. chpt.), Am. Gynecol. Soc. (council 1959, 60), Am. Assn. Obstetricians and Gynecologists (com. on maternal welfare 1960, v.p. 1970-71), Am. Coll. Obstetricians and Gynecologists (first pres., nominating com. 1972, liaison com. with Internat. Fedn. Gynecology and Obstetrics 1973—, chmn. president's group, Distinguished Service award 1976); mem. So. Gynecol. and Obstet. Soc. (pres. 1967), Am. (chmn. sect. obstetrics and gynecology 1957-58), So. (chmn. sect. on obstetrics 1949, mem. council 1961-63, gen. chmn. arrangements ann. meeting 1972, 2d v.p. 1972, 1st v.p. 1973, Distinguished Service award 1975) med. assns., Internat. House New Orleans (founder; dir. 1974—, exec. com. 1977—), Internat. Trade Mart, C. of C., La., Orleans Parish med. socs., New Orleans Grad. Med. Assembly (past pres.), New Orleans Gynecol. and Obstet. Soc. (past pres.), Conrad G. Collins Obstetric and Gynecologic Soc. Tulane U. (1st pres.), Central Assn. Obstetricians and Gynecologists (asst. sec. 1950-52), Am. Assn. Med. Colls., U. Miss. Alumni Assn. (dir. 1962-65, past pres. New Orleans; named to Hall of Fame 1976), Philippine Obstet and Gynecol. Soc. (hon.), AAAS, Assn. Profs. Gynecology and Obstetrics, Peruvian (hon.), Paraguayan (hon.) obstet. and gynecol. socs., Royal Soc. Medicine, Tulane Med. Alumni Assn. (sec. 1971-73, v.p. 1974-75, pres. 1976-77), Sigma Xi, Alpha Omega Alpha, Phi Chi (grand presiding sr., nat. pres. 1970-73, trustee 1973—), Beta Theta Pi. Methodist (chmn. pastor-parish relations com., chmn. trustees, mem. adminstrv. bd.). Clubs: Plimsoll, New Orleans Country, Circumnavigators, Tulane Green Wave. Author: (with Robert J. Crossen and Dan W. Beacham) Synopsis of Gynecology (5th edit.), (with Dan W. Beacham) 6th edit., 1963, 7th edit., 1967, 8th ed., 1972, 9th edit., 1977. Editor for gynecology and obstetrics Stedman's Med. Dictionary, 23d edit. Contbr. to publs. in field. Home: 1527 S Carrollton Ave New Orleans LA 70118 Office: 4240 Magnolia at General Pershing St New Orleans LA 70115

BEACHLEY, CHARLES EDWARD, JR., surgeon; b. Nutley, N.J., Feb. 25, 1924; s. Charles Edward and Ruth Edna (Baitzell) B.; A.B., Johns Hopkins, 1945; M.D., Harvard, 1947; m. Joan Elizabeth Nichols, Apr. 3, 1948; children—Charles Edward III, Ann (Mrs. Lynn Patrick Martin), Holly Gail (Mrs. Russell Brear), Pamela Ruth. Intern U. Pitts. Med. Center, 1947-48; resident in surgery N.Y. U. Bellevue Med. Center, 1943-53; pvt. practice gen. surgery, Mt. Lebanon, Pa., 1955-57, Paris, Tex., 1957—. Served with USAF, 1953-55. Diplomate Am. Bd. Surgery. Fellow A.C.S.; mem. Community Concert Assn. Paris, Phi Beta Kappa, Omicron Delta Kappa, Phi Delta Epsilon, Alpha Tau Omega. Episcopalian. Club: Masons. Home: 2980 Hubbard St Paris TX 75460 Office: 2850 Lewis Ln Paris TX 75460

BEACHLEY, MICHAEL CHARLES, radiologist; b. Harrisburg, Pa., Nov. 14, 1940; s. Kenneth Gumbert and Carolyn Elizabeth (Jones) B.; A.B., Dartmouth U., 1962, B.M.S., 1963; M.D., Harvard U., 1965; m. Deborah Rowe Samson, July 27, 1963; children—Kenneth, Barbara, William. Intern in surgery Med. Coll. Va., Richmond, 1965-66, resident in radiology, 1966-69, instr. radiology, 1970, faculty, 1972—, acting chmn. dept. radiology, 1976, prof., chmn. dept. radiology, 1977—; cons. McGuire VA Hosp., 1977—; fellow in radiol. pathology Armed Forces Inst. Pathology, Washington, 1969. Vice. pres. College Hills Civic Assn., 1975—. Served to maj. M.C., U.S. Army, 1970-72. Diplomate Am. Bd. Radiology. Fellow Am. Coll. Radiology; mem. AMA, Am. Heart Assn., Med. Soc. Va., Richmond Acad. Medicine, Radiol. Soc. N.Am., Ridgetop Recreation Assn. (dir. 1979), Assn. Univ. Radiologists, Am. Roengten Ray Soc., Richmond Radiol. Soc. (sec.-treas. 1978-79), Soc. Chmn. Acad. Radiology Depts. Contbr. chpt. to book, revs. and med. articles to profl. jours. Home: 500 Gardiner Rd Richmond VA 23229 Office: Box 2 VCU/Med Coll Va Richmond VA 23298

BEACHUM, GRAHAM CARSON, city ofcl.; b. Marshville, N.C., Mar. 24, 1921; s. Clyce William and Sarah Ruth (Stigall) B.; student Va. Poly. Inst., 1938-40; B.A., George Washington U., 1960, M.A., 1960; m. Claudette Anne Hampton, Feb. 26, 1946; children—Glenda Anne, Graham Carson, Gary Hampton, Elizabeth Jane. Commd. pilot USAF, 1941, advanced through grades to col., asst. air attache Am. embassy, Turkey, 1952-53; civil engr. charge rebuilding air bases Germany, 1953-55, Templehof, Berlin, 1964-68; assigned Pentagon, 1960-64; command civil engr., Vietnam, 1968-69; ret., 1971; asst. dir. public works City of Raleigh (N.C.), 1971—. Decorated Legion of Merit, Bronze Star, Purple Heart, D.F.C., Air medal (4). Mem. Internat. City Mgrs. Assn., Am. Public Works Assn. Democrat. Episcopalian. Clubs: Lions, Masons. Home: 7609 Harps Mill Rd Raleigh NC 27609 Office: PO Box 590 Raleigh NC 27602

BEADLES, CLENN HARRIS, ins. co. exec., agrl. investment analyst; b. Vicksburg, Miss., June 6, 1922; s. Charles C. and Carrie Elizabeth (Browder) B.; B.S. in Agrl. Econs., La. State U., 1951; m. Mary Elizabeth Mottley, Aug. 21, 1942; children—Glenn Harris, Mary Catherine, Jessaca Ann. With Conn. Gen. Life Ins. Co., Hartford, 1951—, Dallas, 1968—, 2d v.p.-agrl. investment div., 1966—; dir. Congen Properties, Inc. Served with U.S. Army, 1942-45. Mem. Nat. Assn. Rev. Appraisers (certified), Am. Soc. Farm Mgrs. and Rural Appraisers, Alpha Zeta. Methodist. Club: Masons. Home: 4037 Northview Ln Dallas TX 75229 Office: 910 Stemmons Tower North Dallas TX 75207

BEADLES, MICHAEL WAYNE, social worker; b. Richmond, Va., Oct. 26, 1944; s. James Lawrence and Corrine (Lane) B.; B.S., Va. Commonwealth U., 1967, M.S.W., 1972; m. Beverly Gail Knowles, Aug. 5, 1967; 1 son, Barry Wayne. Casework supr. BonAir Learning Center (Va.), 1972-74; mgr. program and planning youth region Va. Dept. Corrections, Richmond, 1974—. Mem. Eastern Henrico FISH, 1974—. Served in U.S. Army, 1968-71. Mem. Nat. Assn. Social Workers, Acad. Cert. Social Workers, Am. Corrections Assn., Va. Corrections Assn., Va. Council on Social Welfare (state bd. dirs.), Va. Assn. Vols. in Criminal Justice. Methodist. Club: Fairfield Civitan (sec. 1979-80). Home 209 Stuttaford Dr Sandston VA 23150 Office: 302 Turner Rd Richmond VA 23225

BEAHN, RAYMOND ANGLUM, II, leasing co. exec.; b. Worcester, Mass., Oct. 18, 1932; s. Raymond Anglum and Ann Elizabeth (O'Toole) B.; B.S., Boston Coll., 1958; children from previous marriage—Raymond Anglum, Jennifer Ann, Meghan Elizabeth. Sales rep. Gen. Electric Credit Corp., N.Y.C., 1960-61, br. mgr., Mpls., 1961-63, mgr., 1963; gen. mgr., founder Minnesco Corp. subs. 3M Co., 1963-66; asst. treas. Boeing Co., Seattle, 1966-67; v.p., asst. gen. mgr. Airlift Internat., Miami, Fla., 1967-68; pres., owner Med. Mktg. Inc., Miami, Fla., 1969-73; pres. S.E. 1st Leasing, Inc. subs. S.E. Banking Corp., Miami, 1974—; mng. dir. S.E. Corp. Fin. Advisors Service of S.E. First Nat. Bank Miami, 1979—. Served with AUS, 1952-54. Mem. Assn. Registered Bank Holding Cos., Assn. Equipment Lessors, Bankers Club Miami. Clubs: Riviera Country, Innisbrook; Tarpon Springs (Fla.) Country. Home: 2201 Brickell Ave Miami FL 33131 Office: 100 Biscayne Blvd S Miami FL 33131

BEAIRD, CHARLES T., publisher; b. Shreveport, La., July 17, 1922; s. James Benjamin and Mattie Connell (Fort) B.; B.A., Centenary Coll., 1966; Ph.D. in Philosophy, Columbia, 1972; m. Carolyn Williams, Feb. 6, 1945; children—Susan Beaird McCormick, Marjorie (Mrs. M. Buie Seawell, Jr.), John B. Vice pres., asst. gen. mgr. J.B.

Beaird Corp., Shreveport, 1946-57; cons. oil and investments, Shreveport, 1957-59; pres. Beaird-Poulan Inc., Shreveport, 1959-73; chmn. bd. Beaird-Poulan div. Emerson Electric Co., 1973-76; pres., pub. Shreveport Jour., 1976—; dir. Fed. Res. Bd. Dallas, 1972-78, dep. chmn., 1973-78; adj. prof. Centenary Coll., Shreveport, 1969—. Mem. Caddo Parish Police Jury, 1956-60. Chmn. Caddo Parish Republican Exec. Com., 1952-56. Bd. suprs. So. U. La., 1975-76; bd. dirs. Woodrow Wilson Nat. Fellowship Found., Princeton, N.J., 1975-78. Served to capt. USMCR, 1943-46. Clubs: Shreveport, Shreveport Country, Univ. (Shreveport). Home: 7030 E Ridge Dr Shreveport LA 71106 Office: PO Box 31110 Shreveport LA 71130

BEALL, BARBARA JEANNE (MRS. E. D. BEALL), auto supply co. exec.; b. El Paso, Tex., July 25, 1931; d. Edward Charles Martin, Sr., and Martha Julia (Yager) Steiner; ed. Tex. Women's U.; m. Ellis DeBerry Beall, Mar. 2, 1952 (dec. July 1978); children—Roger Ellis, Linda Gail. Mathematician, Butler Bros.; mathematician, courier Dallas Fed. Res. Bank; tech. illustrator to dept. head Chance Vought; owner (under name Jeanne DeBerry) DeBerry Art Studio; owner, operator E.D. Beall's Auto Supply, Metro Alternator & Starter Service, Red Bird Car Wash and Mobil Sta., and Ed Beall's Service Center, Dallas. Mem. Automotive Wholesalers of Tex., Ind. Garageman's Assn., Internat. Car Wash Assn., Service Sta. Assn., Better Bus. Bur., Oak Cliff C. of C. Office: 2817 S Westmoreland St Dallas TX 75233

BEALL, GARY WAYNE, phys. and inorganic chemist; b. Granbury, Tex., Aug. 15, 1950; s. Wayman Worth and Wanda Faye (Keith) B.; B.S., Tarleton State U., 1972; M.S., Baylor U., 1974, Ph.D., 1975; m. Joy Lynne Ferris, Apr. 14, 1976; 1 dau., Cherish Ann. Robert A. Welch research fellow Baylor U., Waco, Tex., 1975-77; research chemist Oak Ridge (Tenn.) Nat. Lab., 1977-79; research chemist, group leader Radian Corp., Austin, Tex., 1980—; cons. minerals and precious metals, energy dispersive X-Ray diffraction, radiochemistry. NSF research grantee, 1975-76; Oak Ridge Nat. Lab. seed research grantee, 1979. Mem. Am. Chem. Soc., N.Y. Acad. Sci., Sigma Xi. Baptist. Contbr. research papers in field to profl. publs. Home: 11814 Rustle Ln Austin TX 78750 Office: 8500 Shoal Creek Blvd Austin TX 78766

BEALL, KENNETH SUTTER, JR., lawyer; b. Evanston, Ill., Aug. 9, 1938; s. Kenneth Sutter and Helen Canton (Koenig) B.; B.A., Washington and Lee U., 1961, LL.B., 1963; m. Blair Hamilton Bissett, May 23, 1975; children—Kevina Anne, Hunter Bissett, Baret Bissett. Admitted to Fla. bar, 1964; mem. firm, dir. Gunster, Yoakley, Criser, Stewart & Hersey, P.A., Palm Beach, Fla., 1964—. Chmn. Palm Beach County (Fla.) Environ. Control Hearing Bd., 1970—; bd. dirs. Palm Beach Habilitation Center, Whitehall Found., Inc. Served with USMCR, 1963-69. Mem. Am., Palm Beach County bar assns., Fla. Bar, Fed. Bar Assn. (pres. chpt. 1979-80). Democrat. Roman Catholic. Clubs: Everglades, Bath and Tennis (Palm Beach). Home: 130 Algoma Rd Palm Beach FL 33480 Office: 251 S County Rd Palm Beach FL 33480

BEALL, ROSS HORACE, librarian; b. Jamestown, N.D., July 9, 1889; s. Nesbit Ross and Emma (Bowdoin) B.; B.S., Coe Coll., 1921; M.A., U. Iowa, 1924, Ph.D., 1932; m. Pauline Begley, June 1, 1938; 1 son, Ross B. Supt. pub. schs., Andrew, Iowa, 1910-12, Keystone, Iowa, 1915-16, Miles (Iowa) Consol. Sch., 1916-27, Bellevue, Iowa, 1932-38; elementary sch. prin., Tulsa, 1932-38; asso. prof. edn. U. Tulsa, 1938-44, head dept. edn., 1944-58, prof. emeritus; dir. Tulsa Edn. Found. Sch. for Children with Learning Disabilities, 1958-61; founder, librarian University Village Retirement Home, Tulsa, 1971—. Mem. NEA (life), Am. Psychol. Assn. Republican. Unitarian. Address: 8555 S Lewis St Tulsa OK 74136

BEAMISH, PATRICIA MARY, psychologist; b. Nashville, Feb. 19, 1952; d. Richard Joseph and Josephine (Phelps) Beamish; B.A., U. Fla., 1973, M.Ed., Specialist in Edn., 1975; Ed.D. W.Va. U., 1979. Lab. supr. Precision Teaching of Fla., Gainesville, 1973-74; resident dir. Gainesville Open House, 1974-75; drug abuse counselor Fla., Correctional Instn., Lowell, 1975-76; counselor West Liberty (W.Va.) State Coll., 1976—; counselor W.Va. U. Counseling Center, Morgantown, 1977—; trainer vols. for Crisis Hotline, Wheeling, W.Va., Corner Drug Store, Gainesville; counseling psychologist U. Tex., El Paso, 1979-80. Mem. Am. Personnel and Guidance assn., Coll. Student Personnel Assn., Am. Mental Health Counselors Assn., Assn. Counselor Edn. and Supervision, Nat. Vocat. Guidance Assn., Assn. Specialists in Group Work. Democrat. Home: 1219 N Oregon El Paso TX 79902 Office: UTEP Counseling Service El Paso TX 79968

BEAMON, LAFAYETTE RUEBEN, JR., architect; b. Greenwood, S.C., Oct. 14, 1931; s. Lafayette Rueben and Verdell (Jones) B.; B.Arch., U. So. Calif., 1959; m. Juliet Dobbs Blackburn, Apr. 28, 1979; children by previous marriage—Darryl L., LaVette D., Reginald J. Pres. Archos Internat. Inc., archtl. planning and engring., Atlanta, 1979—; pres. Uni-Venture, 1977—, Structural Concepts, Inc.; mem. Atlanta Bldg. Code Adv. Bd., 1975—. Served with USAF, 1950-53. Mem. AIA, NAACP, Audubon Soc., Nat. Urban League, Ga. Conservancy, Sierra Club. Democrat. Club: Mercury Track (organizer). Home: 2700 The Fontainebleau SW Atlanta GA 30331 Office: 1231 W Peachtree St NW Atlanta GA 30308

BEAN, FRANK WILSON, food co. exec.; b. Bloomington, Ill., Jan. 14, 1940; s. Wilson R. and Beatrice (Mill) B.; B.S. in Advt., U. Fla., 1962, M.A. in Journalism, 1963; m. Joyce Travis Whitsel, June 11, 1960; children—Brenton Sewell, Kimberly Whitsel. Staff rep. in pub. relations Coca-Cola Co., Atlanta, 1968-74, mgr. corp. news services group, 1974-76; project mgr. Internat. Sports for U.S. and Can., 1976—; adj. prof./instr. advt./salesmanship DeKalb Community Coll., Atlanta, 1972—. Served to capt., 25th Air Div., USAF, 1963-67. Mem. Atlanta Jaycees (v.p. 1972-74), Pub. Relations Soc. Am. (accredited), Pi Kappa Alpha. Episcopalian. Club: Capital City (Atlanta). Editor: McChord AFB Guide, Newspaper (weekly), 1963-67. Home: 275 Forrest Lake Dr NW Atlanta GA 30327 Office: 310 N Ave Atlanta GA 30313

BEAN, LARRY, lawyer; b. Salina, Kans., Nov. 19, 1935; s. Lawrence Lee and Stella Vivian (Sias) B.; student U. Colo., 1953-55; B.S., Kans. State U., 1957; LL.B., So. Meth. U., 1960; children by previous marriage—Scott, Marla. Admitted to Tex. bar, 1960; asso. firm Jackson, Walker, Winstead, Cantwell & Miller, Dallas, 1960-66, partner, 1966—. Lectr. law So. Meth. U., Dallas, 1963-66; chmn. Oil, Gas Tax Inst. Southwestern Legal Found., Dallas, 1968-71, chmn. div. taxation, 1971-73. Bd. dirs. Larry and Jane Harlan Found., Hillvale Ednl. Assn. Served to 1st lt., AUS, 1960-66. Mem. Am. (vice-chmn. natural resources com. tax sect. 1972-74, chmn. 1975-77), Tex., Dallas bar assns., Phi Gamma Delta. Home: 7928D Royal Ln Dallas TX 75230 Office: 4300 First Nat Bank Bldg Dallas TX 75202

BEAN, MARVIN LEVON, mfg. co. exec.; b. Clarksville, Ark., Mar. 27, 1938; s. Marvin Luther and Realon (Houston) B.; student Coll. Ozarks, 1955-56, 78-79; m. Anna Estelle Smith, Sept. 6, 1956; 1 dau., Cynthia Diane. Machinist, Majestic Tool & Engring. Co., Rockford, Ill., 1959-64; tool and die maker Walker Die Tool & Engring. Co., Atlanta, 1966-71; tool and die supr. Singer Co., Clarksville, Ark., prodn. engr. 1972-74, sr. mfg. engr., supr., 1977—; mem. adv. com. tool and die program Petit Vocat. Tech. Sch., Morrillton, Ark., 1972-73. Mem. Am. Mgmt. Assn. Democrat. Baptist. Singer, composer gospel songs. Home: Rt 3 Box 56A Clarksville AR 72830 Office: Singer Co Clark and Cline Rd Clarksville AR 72830

BEAN, RICHARD ANDREW, chem. co. exec.; b. Atlanta, Jan. 29, 1947; s. James Lewis and Mildred Belle (Witherington) B.; B.A., Incarnate Word Coll., 1975; student Ga. Inst. Tech., 1965-69; m. Sharon Elaine Wilkie, Dec. 15, 1969; 1 dau., Teresa Karen. Area supr. sales Drew Chem. Corp., Cin., 1977—. asso. instr. Baylor U., 1974-77. Active Big Brothers, San Antonio, 1972-75; youth adv. North East Christian Ch., San Antonio, 1974-76, Crestwood Christian Ch. (Ky.), 1979. Served with AUS, 1969-77. Registered med. technologist. Mem. Am. Soc. Clin. Pathologists. Clubs: Porsche of Am., Ky. Cols. Home: 11313 Corston Ct Louisville KY 40222 Office: 4000 Executive Park Dr Cincinnati OH 45241

BEANE, DOROTHY GENE MOORE, med. editor; b. Ft. Worth, May 8, 1927; d. Elmer Harrison and Rossye Leila (Cornelius) Moore; A.B., N.Mex. Highlands U., 1950; postgrad. Chgo. Tchrs. Coll., 1958, Art Inst. Chgo., 1959; m. Ralph Clements Beane, May 22, 1964; 1 dau., Linda Alison Aldridge. Tchr. English and psychology, also librarian pub. sch. system, Newark and Hardy, Ark., 1949-51; practice accounting, Batesville, Ark., 1951-55; editor World Book Ency., Chgo., 1958-59; asst. editor U. Tex. System Cancer Center, M.D. Anderson Hosp. and Tumor Inst., Houston, 1959-65, asso. editor, 1965-67, 70-76, coordinator editorial services, 1976-79, head dept. sci. publs., 1979—; asst. instr., editor radiology and neurophysiology Baylor Coll. Medicine, Houston, 1967-69; asst. prof. med. and tech. writing U. Tex. Health Scis. Center, Houston, 1971-76, lectr. dental and tech. writing Dental Br., 1973; instr. piano, 1947-49, drawing and painting, 1951-55; editorial cons. Beane Photography and Advt., Houston, 1970—. Invited press relations officer ann. meetings Am. Assn. Cancer Research, 1963, 64; asst. investigator oncological word bank Nat. Cancer Inst. grant, 1967. Mem. Pi Beta Phi. Episcopalian. Home: 3902 Coleridge St Houston TX 77005

BEARD, BOB J., energy co. exec.; b. El Paso, Feb. 8, 1932; s. Raymond and Thera (Hughes) B.; B.S. (Franklin Found. scholar), U. Houston, 1956; m. Emmajean Ewald, Nov. 2, 1951; children—Bradley Kent, Donald Ray, Lana Jean, Robert J. Mgr. natural gas dept. Delhi-Taylor Oil Corp., Dallas, also v.p. subsidiaries Delhi Pipeline Corp., Natural Gas Gathering Corp., 1956-60; exec. v.p. Gulf Energy & Devel. Corp., San Antonio, 1960-63, pres., chief exec. officer, dir., 1963—; organizer, dir. First Nat. Bank of Zapata (Tex.), 1962-64; dir. Central Park Bank. Former mem. adv. council Coll. Bus. Adminstrn., Trinity U.; trustee Northside Ind. Sch. Dist., San Antonio, 1967-74, pres., 1971-73. Mem. Tex. Ind. Producers and Royalty Owners Assn. (exec. com. 1975-77, v.p.), Ind. Producers Assn. Am., Soc. Petroleum Engrs. Home: 21120 Babcock Rd Route 15 Box 237D San Antonio TX 78228 Office: PO Box 17349 San Antonio TX 78217

BEARD, CHARLES HAYDEN, communications co. exec.; b. Springtown, Tex., Mar. 8, 1937; s. W.P. and Helen W. Beard; student Westherford Jr. Coll., 1954-55, N. Tex. State U., 1956-57; m. Sally Ann Colgin, Nov. 25, 1960; children—Laurie E., Charles Andrew. Mgr., N.Y. Life Ins. Co., 1961-62; chief sta. property So. Airways, 1963-64; facility engr. Dept. Def., 1965-69; SW regional v.p. mktg. Aerotron, Inc., 1970-71; Gulf Coast regional v.p. mktg. Harris R. F. Communication, Inc., 1972-74; pres. CSSI, Inc., Weatherford, Tex., 1975—. Mem. IEEE, Radio Club Am., Assn. Police Communication Officers, Armed Forces Communication and Electronic Assn., Petroleum Electronic Suppliers Assn. Republican. Mem. Christian Ch. (Disciples of Christ). Club: Lions. Office: CSSI Inc 206 Wiggs St Suite 1 Weatherford TX 76081

BEARD, ELIZABETH LETITIA, physiologist; b. New Orleans, Apr. 2, 1932; d. Howard Horace and Irene (Handley) B.; B.A. in Biology cum laude, Tgx. Christian U., 1952, B.S. in Med. Tech. cum laude, 1953, M.S. in Med. Tech., 1955; postgrad. Smith Coll., 1953-54, Vanderbilt U., 1954-55; Ph.D. in Animal Physiology, Tulane U. Sch. Medicine, 1961. Instr. dept. biol. scis. Loyola U., New Orleans, 1955-58, asst. prof., 1958-62, 62-68, prof., 1968—; research asso. dept. physiology Tulane U., 1960-63, prof. biology med. reinforcement and enrichment program Sch. Medicine, 1968—; grantee reviewer NIH, 1975, 76; mem. project rev. com. New Orleans Area Health Planning Council, 1974-77, mem. bd. dirs., 1975-77. Pres. sch. bd. Holy Name Elem. Sch., New Orleans, 1976-79; mem. New Orleans Mus. Art, N.Y. Met. Mus. Art; soprano soloist, mem. choir Christ Ch. Episcopal Cathedral, 1967—; soprano soloist Holy Name of Jesus Choir, 1976—; chmn. coll. div. La. Heart Assn., 1975—; chmn. judges for zoology, sr. div. Greater New Orleans Sci. Fair, 1974-76; Loyola rep. La. Commn. on Aging, 1958; mem. grad. research com. La. chpt. Am. Heart Assn., 1970-72, undergrad. research com., 1977—, edn. com., 1980—. Libby research fellow La. Heart Assn., 1958-61; NIH grantee, 1962-64, 67-69; La. Heart Assn. grantee, 1966-67; Edward Schleider Found. grantee, 1974-77. Mem. Am. Physiol. Soc., Soc. Exptl. Biology and Medicine, N.Y., New Orleans (sec. 1957-60) acads. scis., AAUP, AAAS, Sigma Xi. Contbr. articles to sci. jours. Home: 6127 Garfield St New Orleans LA 70118 Office: 6363 Saint Charles Ave New Orleans LA 70118

BEARD, KENNETH EUGENE, dentist; b. Flint, Mich., Nov. 30, 1946; s. Herbert Hoover and Dorothy Faye (Cox) B.; student Lee Coll., 1964-67, Flint Jr. Coll., 1965; D.D.S., U. Mich., 1971; m. Judy Faye Owens, Dec. 15, 1966; children—Brian Kendall, Darleah, Sharee, Blake Adam. Gen. practice dentistry, Chattanooga, Tenn., 1971-72, Cleveland, Tenn., 1973—. Bd. dirs. Boy's Club, 1973—, YMCA, 1979—. Mem. ADA, Tenn. Dental Assn., Cleveland Dental Soc. (pres. 1977—), 3rd Dist. Dental Soc. Club: Optimist. Home: 1450 Everhart Dr Cleveland TN 37311 Office: 590 Church St NE Cleveland TN 37311

BEARD, ROBERT GRUBER, newspaper advt. dir.; b. Plainfield, N.J., Jan. 1, 1927; s. William Martin and Jessie Louisa (Gruber) B.; B.A., Princeton U., 1950; m. Betty Jane Huntley, Nov. 27, 1954; children—Barbara Ann, William Huntley. Sales corr., expense analyst, public relations Prentice-Hall Pub. Co., N.Y.C., 1950-52; editor-advt. mgr. Farmers Fedn. News, Asheville, N.C., 1952-58; advt. salesman, retail advt. mgr., asst. advt. dir., advt. dir. Asheville Citizen-Times, 1958—. Bd. trustees Meml. Mission Hosp.; chmn. public relations com. ARC, 1976-77; active United Way Asheville and Buncombe County, chmn. public relations com., 1976-78; bd. dirs. Asheville Art Mus., 1976-78; asst. scoutmaster Daniel Boone Council Boy Scouts Am., 1969-78, com. mem. Troop 8; mem. usher's guild, Sunday Sch. tchr. First Presbyn. Ch. Served with USAAF, 1945-46. Recipient honors from history dept., Princeton U., 1950. Mem. Midtlantic Newspaper Advt. Execs. Assn., Newspaper Advt. Bur., Asheville Merchants Assn. (dir.), Mid-City Merchants Council (dir., 1st. v.p.), Western N.C. Advt. Fedn. (dir., 1st. v.p.), Central Asheville Assn. (dir.), Western N.C. Heritage Center (dir.), Asheville Sales and Mktg. Execs. Club (dir., 1978, Sales Exec. of Year, 1979), U.S. C. of C. (One of 20 Top Salespersons in U.S. 1979), Asheville Area C. of C. (life). Republican. Clubs: Asheville Civitan (dir., pres., 1958-59, sec. 1963-68, 73—), Princeton Club of Western N.C., Carolina Mountain Hiking, SCV, Land of Sky Antique Car.

BEARD, ROBIN, congressman; b. Knoxville, Tenn., Aug. 21, 1939; grad. Montgomery Bell Acad., Nashville, 1957; B.A., Vanderbilt U., 1961; m. Catherine Rieniets, 1963; children—Robin John, Lisa Paige. State commr. personnel, 1970-72; mem. 93d-96th Congresses from Tenn., mem. armed services com., select com. on narcotics abuse and control. Served to capt. USMC, 1962-65; lt. col. Res. Office: 229 Cannon Office Bldg Washington DC 20515

BEARD, W(ILLIAM) ROBINSON COOK, lawyer; b. White Plains, N.Y., Oct. 29, 1940; s. David Fleming and Margaret Letcher (Cook) B.; B.A., Williams Coll., 1962; J.D., U. Va., 1965; m. Barbara Lynn Waterfill, June 14, 1969; children—Sarah Kelly and Barbara Breckinridge (twins). Admitted to Va. bar, 1965, Ky. bar, 1967; law clk. Ky. U.S. Dist. Ct. Eastern Dist., Lexington, 1965-66; partner firm Stites, McElwain & Fowler, Louisville, 1966—. Bd. dirs. Ky. Country Day Sch., Louisville, 1971-74, 75-80, sec., 1975-80; bd. dirs. Better Bus. Bur. of Greater Louisville, 1974—. Mem. Louisville, Ky., Am. bar assns., Va. State Bar, Soc. Colonial Wars, S.R., Jamestown Soc. Democrat. Episcopalian. Clubs: Harmony Landing Country, Pendennis. Home: 541 Barberry Ln Louisville KY 40206 Office: 3400 First Nat Tower Louisville KY 40202

BEARDEN, HAROLD IRWIN, bishop; b. Atlanta, Mar. 8, 1910; s. Lloyd and Mary (DaCosta) B.; A.B., Morris Brown Coll., 1933, D.D., 1962; B.D., Turner Theol. Sem., 1951; D.D., Campbell Coll., 1949, Kittrell Coll., 1963; LL.D. (hon.), Daniel Payne Coll., 1949, Monrovia Coll., Africa, 1955, Wilberforce U., 1964; m. Lois Minerva Mathis, June 12, 1931; children—JoAnn, Harold Irwin, Gloria, Lloyd, Sharon, Richard. Ordained deacon African Methodist Episcopal Ch., 1930, ordained elder, 1931, consecrated bishop, 1964; pres. Bishop's Council, Wilberforce, Ohio, 1973-74; presiding bishop Sixth Episc. Dist. of African Meth. Episc. Ch., State of Ga., Atlanta, 1976—; Episc. rep. A.M.E. Ch. to Inauguration of Pres. Carter, 1977; acting presiding elder, 1960-62. Pres., Atlanta br. NAACP, 1958-59; chmn. bd. trustees Morris Brown Coll., 1976—, Turner Theol. Sem., 1976—; bd. dirs. Atlanta U. Center, 1976—; trustee Southview Cemetary, Atlanta; cons. Democratic Primary Mcpl. Div., 1979-80. Recipient Religious Achievement award Morris Brown Coll., 1964; honored by Bd. Commrs. Fulton County (Ga.), 1978; named Outstanding Citizen, Ga. Senate, 1978. Mem. Phi Beta Sigma. Club: Masons. Chmn. compilation com. Book of Discipline, A.M.E. Ch., 1976-80. Office: 208 Auburn Ave Atlanta GA 30303

BEARDSLEE, FREDERICK PARDEE, ret. mgmt. cons.; b. Chgo., Aug. 6, 1910; s. James B. and Ethel (Pardee) B.; A.B., Carleton Coll., Northfield, Minn., 1932; M.B.A., Harvard U., 1934; m. Elma Peggs Drake, Dec. 2, 1950. Sr. cons. Turton Assos., Cleve., 1955-66; v.p. mktg. Serex, Inc., Twinsburg, Ohio, 1966-71; sr. cons. Career Mgmt., Inc., Cleve., Atlanta and Asheville, N.C., 1971-79. Mem. Service Corps Ret. Execs. Served to lt. comdr. USNR, 1942-46. Decorated Navy Commendation ribbon. Mem. Am. Soc. Naval Engrs. Republican. Presbyterian. Clubs: Etowah Golf, Buckhead Civitan, Shriners. Home: PO Box 916 Etowah NC 28729

BEARDSWORTH, DONALD EUGENE, ednl. adminstr.; b. Clinton, Iowa, Jan. 2, 1921; s. Arthur E. and Hazel M. (Higgins) B.; student Northeastern State Coll., Tahlequah, Okla., 1939-41; m. Janyce Estelle McDorman, Feb. 3, 1968; children—Donald Eugene, Jerry Lee, Mary Carol Beardsworth Anderson. Vice pres., cashier Comml. Bank, Muskogee, Okla., 1946-52; v.p. Bank of N.Mex., Albuquerque, 1952-54; pres. Citizens Bank, Albuquerque, 1962-66, LSI/Draughon Sch. Bus., Oklahoma City, 1967-72, Nettleton Bus. Coll., Omaha, 1972-73, Internat. Bus. Coll., El Paso, Tex., 1973—; pres. Fin. Aid, Inc., 1976—; real estate and ins. agt., Albuquerque, 1955-62. Mem. City Council Muskogee, 1950-52. Served with AUS, 1943-46. Mem. Southwestern Comml. Schs. Assn. (pres. 1977—), Tex. Assn. Pvt. Schs. (dir., pres. 1980-81), Nat. Assn. Ind. Colls. and Schs., Tex. Tchrs. Assn., Nat. Rehab. Assn., Okla. Writers Guild. Democrat. Methodist. Clubs: El Paso, El Paso Internat., Kiwanis (pres. Highland-Albuquerque 1960, v.p. El Paso). Editor N.Mex. Realtor, 1962-63. Home: 9001 McFall St El Paso TX 79925 Office: 4121 Montana St El Paso TX 79903

BEARSKIN, ALVIN WESLEY, ret. archtl. engr.; b. Wyandotte, Okla., Jan. 6, 1919; s. John and Myrtle (Shaw) B.; B.S. in Archtl. Engring., Okla. State U., 1955; postgrad. Tulsa U., 1955-56, Okla. U., 1965-66, U. Ala. at Huntsville, 1970; m. Mae Evelyn Wilson, Aug. 18, 1946; 1 dau., Mary Kay (dec.). Liaison engr. Douglas Aircraft, Tulsa, 1955-58; aerospace engr. USAF civil service Tinker AFB, Okla., 1958-66, Marshall Space Flight Center-NASA, Huntsville, Ala., 1966-77. Served with AUS, 1942-46, 50-52. Registered profl. engr., Okla., Ala. Mem. Nat., Ala., N.E. Ala. socs. profl. engrs. Club: Masons. Home: 3345 Robin Rd Paris TX 75460

BEASLEY, DAVID MULDROW, state legislator; b. Lamar, S.C., Feb. 26, 1957; s. Richard Lee and Jacqueline Adele (Blackwell) B.; student Clemson U., 1975-78, U. S.C., 1978-79. Aide to Sen. Strom Thurmond, 1975; mem. S.C. Ho. of Reps., 1978—. Democrat. Methodist. Club: Lions. Office: State Capitol Columbia SC

BEASLEY, ERNEST WILLIAM, JR., endocrinologist; b. Atlanta, May 7, 1924; s. Ernest William and Arrinda Elizabeth (Eidson) B.; M.D., Georgetown U., 1949; m. Ann Lee Jeffreys, July 1, 1950; children—Janet Ann, Ernest William III, Mary Elizabeth, Barbara Elaine. Intern, Walter Reed Hosp., Washington, 1949-50; resident in internal medicine VA Hosp.-Grady Meml. Hosp.-Emory U. Hosp., Atlanta; practice medicine specializing in family practice, Atlanta, 1955-65, in internal medicine, Atlanta, 1966-75, in endocrinology, Atlanta, 1975—; chief endocrinology and metabolism Ga. Bapt. Med. Center; asso. dept. internal medicine Emory U.; cons. endocrinology Crawford Long Hosp. of Emory U.; cons. Ga. Assn. Retarded Children, 1955-65; dir. Diabetes Assn. Atlanta, 1976. Served with AUS, 1943-45, M.C., U.S. Army, 50-52. Diplomate Am. Bd. Internal Medicine, Am. Bd. Family Practice. Mem. A.C.P. Med. Assn. Atlanta, Med. Assn. Ga., AMA, Am. Soc. Internal Medicine, Am. Diabetes Assn. Methodist. Club: Cherokee Country. Address: 478 Peachtree St NE Atlanta GA 30308

BEASLEY, FREDERICK ALEXANDER, lawyer; b. Salley, S.C., July 23, 1943; s. Percy Eugene and Amelia (Schroder) B.; A.B., Duke U., 1965; J.D., U. S.C., 1970; m. Susan Mobley McGarity, Aug. 10, 1974; children—Sarah Elizabeth, Amelia Schroder. Admitted to S.C. bar, 1970, Ga. bar, 1971; atty., trust examiner Fed. Res. Bank Atlanta, 1970-72; asso. firm Jones & Somers, Atlanta, 1972-74; partner firm Somers & Altenbach, Atlanta, 1974-75; trust officer So. Bank & Trust Co., Columbia and Orangeburg, S.C., 1975—. Bd. dirs. Children's Bur. S.C., 1977—, vice-chmn., 1979. Served as officer USN, 1965-67. Mem. Am., Ga., S.C. (chmn. fiduciary law com.), Richland County bar assns., Am. Bankers Assn., Columbia Estate Planning Council, Sigma Chi, Phi Delta Phi. Episcopalian. Clubs: Summit, Iron Dukes; Houndslake Country (Aiken, S.C.). Home: 5 Dinwood Circle Columbia SC 29204 Office: Box 728 Southern Bank & Trust Co Columbia SC 29202

BEASLEY, GEORGE REED, govt. ofcl.; b. Old Hickory, Tenn., Aug. 1, 1930; s. Leo and Georgia Ray (Reed) B.; grad. Gupton Coll. Mortuary Sci., 1952; m. Katherine Gray Tomlinson, Aug. 16, 1966; children—Reita Faye, George Reed. Operating engr. Union Carbide Corp., Oak Ridge, Tenn., 1953-77; dir. apprenticeship and tng. U.S. Dept. Labor, West Tenn. Area, Memphis, 1977—. Dep. commnr. labor State of Tenn., 1973-75; v.p. Tenn. State Labor Council, 1969-73; bd. dirs. City of Hope Found., 1973-75. Served with AUS, 1947-51. Mem. Internat. Union Operating Engrs., DAV. Club: Stonebridge Country. Mason. Home: 9390 Barley Mills Rd Memphis TN 38134 Office: 167 N Main St Room 209 Memphis TN 38103

BEASLEY, JERE LOCKE, former lt. gov. Ala., lawyer; b. Tyler, Tex., Dec. 12, 1935; s. Browder L. and Florence (Camp) B.; B.S., Auburn U., 1959; LL.B., U. Ala., 1962; m. Sara Baker, Mar. 15, 1958; children—Jere Locke, Julia Anne, Linda Lee. Admitted to Ala. bar, 1962; practice law in Tuscaloosa, 1962-64, Clayton, 1964-71, Montgomery, 1979—; mem. firm Beasley, Williams & Robertson, 1969-71; lt. gov., Ala., 1971-78, acting gov., 1972; chmn. Gov.'s Fiscal Com., 1975-78; vice chmn. State Reorgn. Commn., 1975-78; chmn. Ala. Govtl. Relations Commn., 1971-78. Home: 2208 Rosemont Dr Montgomery AL 36111 Office: 300 S Hull St Montgomery AL 36104

BEASLEY, JOHN CORNELL, cosmetic co. exec.; b. Hinds County, Miss., Feb. 19, 1942; s. Johnie C. and Helen (Coleman) B.; B.S. in I.E., Ga. Inst. Tech., 1960-65, postgrad. (NDEA fellow), 1966-68; m. Rebecca R. Brown, Sept. 15, 1964; children—John Cornell, Beau, Shannon. Project engr. U.S. Army Missile Command, Huntsville, Ala., 1960-64; internal cons. and line mgr. Ethyl Corp., Baton Rouge, Newnan, Ga., 1965-69; pvt. real estate sales and devel., Atlanta, 1969-74; sr. cons. Arthur Young & Co., Dallas, 1974-75; v.p. mfg. group Mary Kay Cosmetics, Dallas, 1975—, dir., 1979—; faculty U. Tex., Dallas, 1977—; cons. in field. Mem. Am. Inst. Indsl. Engrs. Club: Bent Tree Country. Home: 7210 Arbor Oaks Dallas TX 75248 Office: 1330 Regal Row Dallas TX 75247

BEASLEY, KATHERINE TOMLINSON, nurse, hosp. ofcl.; b. Tazewell County, Va., Dec. 19, 1938; d. Henry Grant and Lillian Gray (Beavers) Tomlinson; R.N., Johnston Meml. Hosp. Sch. Nursing, 1961; m. George Reed Beasley, Aug. 11, 1966; 1 son, George Reed II. Asst. supr. operating room Smyth County Community Hosp., Marion, Va., 1962-65; supr. nursing service Johnston Meml. Hosp., Abingdon, Va., 1966; head nurse St. Mary's Med. Center, Knoxville, 1967-71; coordinator quality assurance Oak Ridge Hosp., 1972-78; dir. quality assurance Meth. Hosps. Memphis, 1978—. Bd. dirs. Anderson County (Tenn.) Health Council, 1972-76; home health care adv. bd. Oak Ridge Dept. Public Health, 1972-76; home health care adv. bd. Upjohn Health Care Services, Knoxville, Tenn., 1974-78; task force for Oak Ridge chpt. Assn. for Children with Learning Disabilities, 1976—. Mem. Nat. League for Nursing, Nat. Assn. for Practitioners in Infection Control (charter), Nat. Assn. for Quality Assurance Practitioners (charter), Am. Soc. for Nursing Service Adminstrs., Am. Hosp. Assn., Tenn. Assn. Quality Assurance Practitioners, Tenn. Hosp. Assn. Democrat. Home: 9390 Barley Mills Rd Memphis TN 38134 Office: Nursing Service Office Meth Hosp Central Unit 1265 Union Ave Memphis TN 38104

BEASLEY, MARCIA LOU TURPIN, army officer, dietitian; b. Indpls., Feb. 27, 1938; d. D. John and Mona Belle (Albright) Turpin; B.S., Purdue U., 1960; M.H.A., Baylor U., 1969; m. Allen Oswald Beasley, Sept. 6, 1975; stepchildren—Gwendolyn Beasley McCall, Ossie Allen Beasley, Michelle Lynn Beasley. Commd. 2d lt. U.S. Army, 1960, advanced through grades to lt. col., 1979—; dietetic intern Walter Reed Army Med. Center, Washington, 1960-61; chief prodn. and service br. Food Service Div., Irwin Army Hosp., Ft. Riley, Kans., 1961-63; asst. instr. Kans. State U., Manhattan, 1963-64; asst. chief Clin. Dietetics Br., Food Service Div., Walter Reed Army Med. Center, Washington, 1964-67; dietetic cons. 43d Med. Group, Rep. of Vietnam, 1969-70; dir. Food Service Div., 2d Gen. Hosp., Landstuhl, Germany, 1970-72; chief clin. dietetics br. Food Service Div., Walter Reed Army Med. Center, Washington, 1972-75, chief prodn. and service br., 1973-75; dir. Food Service Div., Martin Army Hosp., Ft. Benning, Ga., 1975-80; ret., 1980; adj. instr. Coordinated Undergrad. Program in Dietetics Auburn (Ala.) U., 1977—. Decorated Army Commendation medals with 2 oak leaf clusters, Bronze Star medal. Mem. Columbus Dist. Dietetic Assn. (pres. 1979—), Am. Hosp. Assn., Ga. Dietetic Assn., Soc. for Nutrition Edn., Am. Dietetic Assn., Ga. Soc. for Allied Health Profls., Women in Communication, Phi Mu. Episcopalian. Clubs: Order Eastern Star D.A.R. Home: Route 2 Box 400 B Floral City FL 32636 Office: Martin Army Hosp Fort Benning GA 31905

BEASLEY, RONALD DOUGLAS, mfg. co. exec.; b. Columbus, Ga., Apr. 8, 1948; s. S. Douglas and Margaret O. B.; B.S. in Bus. Adminstrn., The Citadel, Charleston, 1970; M.B.A., Golden Gate U., 1973; 1 dau. Sales rep. Riegel Textile Corp., various locations, 1972-74; agent Equitable Life Assurance Soc. U.S., Charleston, 1974-75; mgmt. trainee Cooper River Fed. Savings & Loan, Charleston, 1976-79; employment supr. for personnel Control-o-fax Corp., Stone Mountain, Ga., 1980—. safety and tng. officer County of Charleston, S.C., 1976—; lectr. Coll. Charleston, Med. U. S.C., Trident Tech. Coll., Rice Coll.; cons. in field. Vol. Trident United Way, Charleston, 1976-78. Served with USAF, 1970-72. Recipient Disting. Service award Nat. Mgmt. Assn., 1979. Mem. Nat. Life Underwriters Assn., S.C. Life Underwriters Assn. Mem. Fellowship of Christian Athletes. Club: Exchange. Home: 215 Clubroad Circle Apt 17 Stone Mountain GA 30083 Office: 1510 Stone Ridge Rd Stone Mountain GA 30083

BEASON, DONALD RAY, educator; b. Heflin, Ala., May 27, 1935; m. Sylvan Calvin and Jennie Alma (Vise) B.; B.S., U. Ala., 1957, M.B.A., 1960, postgrad. 1961-63, 64-65. Instr. econs. Auburn U., 1960-61; instr. accounting Northeastern U., 1963-64; asst. prof. acctg. Jacksonville State U., 1965-67; asso. prof. acctg. Xavier U., 1967—, chmn. dept. bus. adminstrn. and econs., 1970—. IBM Summer Faculty fellow., 1969. Mem. Am. Acctg. Assn., So. Bus. Adminstrn. Assn., Southwestern Bus. Adminstrn. Assn., Am. Inst. Decision Scis., Nat. Assn. Mgmt. Edn., Chi Alpha Phi, Beta Alpha Psi, Omicron Delta Gamma. So. Baptist. Home: 2855 St Charles Ave New Orleans LA 70115 Office: Xavier U New Orleans LA 70125

BEASON, EDWARD STEWART, surgeon; b. Birmingham, Ala., June 13, 1937; B.A., Vanderbilt U., 1959; M.D., Med. Coll. Ala.; m. Barbara T., June 3, 1959; children—Stewart, Allison, Ted, David. Rotating intern Carraway Meth. Hosp., Birmingham, 1963-64; resident in surgery N.C. Bapt. Hosp., 1968-70; resident plastic surgery Baroness Erlanger Hosp., Chattanooga, 1971-72; mem. faculty Bowman Gray Sch. Medicine, Winston-Salem, N.C., 1972—, asst. prof., 1974—; mem. staff N.C. Bapt. Hosp. of Bowman Gray Sch. Medicine; mem. courtesy staff Forsyth Meml. Hosp., also mem. med. adv. bd. Mem. troop com. local council Boy Scouts Am.; basketball coach Central YMCA Youth League, 1975-78; mem. adv. bd. Salvation Army, Winston-Salem, N.C.; mem. father's com. Forsyth Country Day Sch., 1977-79, chmn., 1978-79. Served to capt. USAF, 1966-68. Diplomate Am. Bd. Surgery. Mem. Am. Soc. Plastic and Reconstructive Surgery, Southeastern Soc. Plastic and Reconstructive Surgery, Am. Burn Assn., N.C. Soc. Plastic, Maxillofacial and Reconstructive Surgery, Am. Cleft Palate Assn., N.C. Med. Soc., Forsyth County Med. Soc., AMA. Methodist. Contbr. articles to med. jours. Home: 710 Quarterstaff Rd Winston-Salem NC 27104 Office: Dept Clinics Bowman Gray Sch Medicine Winston-Salem NC 27103

BEATON, JOHN MCCALL, educator; b. Huntly, Scotland, June 21, 1944; s. Walter William and Elizabeth Helen (McCall) B.; came to U.S., 1971; B.Sc. with honors, U. Aberdeen (Scotland), 1966, M.Sc., 1969; Ph.D., U. Ala., 1973; m. Eleanor Rose, Apr. 20, 1968; 1 dau., Katie Leigh. Fellow, Med. Research Council, Aberdeen, 1966-69; sr. research asst. Addiction Research Found., Toronto, Ont., Can., 1969-71; research asso. in psychiatry U. Ala., Birmingham, 1971-73, instr., 1973-74, asst. prof. psychiatry and pharmacology, 1974-76, asso. prof., 1976—. Pres. Vestavia Knolls Townhouse Assn. Inc., Birmingham, 1975-76. Mem. Brit. Psychol. Soc., Soc. Neuroscis., Am. Psychophysiol. Soc. for Study Sleep, Collegium Internat. Neuropsychopharmicum, Am. Soc. Pharmacology and Exptl. Therapeutics. Contbr. articles to profl. jours. Home: 3764 White Ln Birmingham AL 35216

BEATTIE, JACK ROBERT, dentist; b. Bay City, Mich., Oct. 2, 1934; s. Aaron Joseph and Sadie Evelyn (Young) B.; B.A., Mich. State U., 1956; D.D.S., U. Mich., 1960; M.S., Western Reserve U., 1963; m. Ernestine Linda Johnson, June 27, 1959; children—John Robert, Jeffrey Lind, Kimberly Young, Beattie. Orthodontist, Orlando, Fla., 1963—. Guest lectr. Internat. Acad. Stomatology, Lima, Peru, 1965. Chmn. Orange County (Fla.) Republican Exec. Com., 1968-75; mem. Fla. delegation Rep. Nat. Conv., 1968, 72. Recipient Milo Hellman Research award Am. Assn. Orthodontists, 1964. Mem. Am. (state del.), Fla., Central Dist., Orange County dental assns., Fla. Orthodontic Soc., Am. Assn. Orthodontists (state del., chmn. So. del. 1971-77), So. Soc. Orthodontists. Mem. All-Am. Collegiate Swimming Team, 1955. Home: 561 Via Lugano Winter Park FL 32789 Office: 341 N Mills Orlando FL 32803

BEATTY, SAMUEL ALSTON, justice Ala. Supreme Ct.; b. Tuscaloosa, Ala., Apr. 23, 1923; s. Eugene C. and Rosabelle (Horton) B.; B.S. in Commerce and Bus. Adminstrn., U. Ala., 1948, J.D., 1953; LL.M., Columbia U., 1959, J.S.D., 1964; m. Maude Applegate, Jan. 19, 1949; children—Rosa Beatty Lord, Eugene A. Admitted to Ala. bar, 1953; pvt. practice, Tuscaloosa, 1953-56; mem. faculty U. Ala. Law Sch., 1955-70, prof. law, 1963-70, asst. dean, 1969-73; vis. prof. law U. Cin. Law Sch., 1966-67; asso. dir. Ala. Defender Project, 1967-70; dean, prof. law Mercer U. Law Sch., 1970-72, adj. prof., 1972-74; v.p., trust officer First Nat. Bank & Trust Co., Macon, Ga., 1972-74; asst. atty. gen., chief civil div. State of Ala., 1974; partner firm Henley & Beatty, Tuscaloosa and Northport, Ala., 1975-76; asso. justice Ala. Supreme Ct., 1976—; adj. prof. U. Ala. Grad. Sch., 1975—; speaker, lectr. in field. Served to maj. USAAF, 1942-45; PTO. Decorated Air medal with 9 oak leaf clusters. Mem. Am. Bar Assn., Ala. Bar Assn., Tuscaloosa County Bar Assn., Nat. Orgn. Legal Problems Edn., Farrah Order Jurisprudence, Order Coif, Phi Alpha Delta. Democrat. Methodist. Contbr. articles to legal jours.

BEAUCHAMP, JEFFERY OLIVER, engr.; b. Alice, Tex., Jan. 19, 1943; s. Charles Kirkland and Lila Arminda (Calk) B.; B.S. in Mech. Engring., U. Houston, 1968, M.S. in Mech. Engring., 1973; m. Toni Ramona Nobler, Sept. 7, 1963. Mech. designer Great Lakes Petroleum Service, Houston, 1963-64; mech. engr. Elliott Co. div. Carrier Corp., Houston, 1964-68; research asst. U. Houston, 1968-70; mech. design chief engr. Mallay Corp., Houston, 1970-74; project mgr. Fluor Engrs. & Constructors, Houston, 1974-79; pres. INTERMAT Materials Mgmt. Engrs., Houston, 1979—; cons. in field; speaker, lectr. Registered profl. engr., Tex. Mem. Nat., Tex. (Outstanding Young Engr. 1974) socs. profl. engrs., Engrs. Council Houston (treas.), ASME, Profl. Engrs. in Industry, Inst. Internat. Edn., Common Cause, Amnesty Internat., Sierra Club, Houston Mus. Fine Arts, Los Angeles County Mus., Smithsonian Assos., Sigma Xi, Phi Kappa Phi, Pi Tau Sigma. Contbr. articles to profl. jours. Home: 2636 Albans Rd Houston TX 77005 Office: 3333 Eastside Suite 200 Houston TX 77098

BEAUCHAMP PEREZ-GUERRA, ANGEL DEXTER, audiologist; b. Bayamon, P.R., Apr. 4, 1928; s. Angel and Consuelo (Perez-Guerra) B.; B.A., U. P.R., 1965; M.A., N.Y. U., 1971, M.S., 1973; m. Clarisa Lopez, June 3, 1950; children—Angel Dezter, Maritza, Enida, Daniel Baxter. Tchr. indsl. arts, P.R., 1946-76; prin. Sierra Bayman Sr. High Sch., 1976-77, Rexville Sr. High Sch., 1977-78; gen. supr. P.R. Dept. Edn., Hato Rey, 1978-79; instr. audiology Med. Sci. Sch. U. P.R., Rio Piedras, 1973-76; part-time instr., 1976— pvt. practice audiology, owner Villa Nevarez Speech and Hearing Center, Rio Piedras, 1976—. Mem. Am. Speech and Hearing Assn. (dir. hearing conservation program), P.R. Tchrs. Assn. Mem. Ch. of Christ. Home: Calle Rio Corozal A-11 Estancias de Riohondo Bayamon PR 00619 Office: Villa Nevarez Speech and Hearing Center 403 Villa Nevarez Profl Center Rio Piedras PR 00927

BEAURLINE, LOYD ARTHUR, realtor; b. St. Paul, Aug. 26, 1921; s. Arthur Willard and Mathilda Bertha (Waller) B.; B.A., Carleton Coll., 1943; m. Mary Jane Busch, Apr. 15, 1944; children—Edward A., Alan L., Sally A. Beaurline Kelly, Andrew G. Pres., Bluebird Coach Lines, Lyons, Ill., 1950-57, Beaurline Investment Corp., Edinburg, Tex., 1957—, A. W. Beaurline Corp., Edinburg, 1965—, B. I. C. Realty, Cook, Minn., also Edinburg, 1965—. Served with USNR, 1943-46. Clubs: Masons, Shriners. Home: 812 Volz Ln Mission TX 78572 Office: 106 S 12th Ave Edinburg TX 78539

BEAVEN, WILLIAM FREDRICK, social worker; b. Uniontown, Ky., July 31, 1947; s. Charles Donald and Delores June (Ashby) B.; B.S., Murray State U., 1972; M.S.W., U. Ky., 1975; children—Wendy Carol, Ronnie LeAnn, Brea Ashby. Counselor, Breckinridge Job Corps Center, Morganfield, Ky., 1968-72; social worker Western State Hosp., Hopkinsville, Ky., 1972-73, U. Ky., Lexington, 1973-75; dir. Higgins Learning Center, Morganfield, 1977—. Served with U.S. Army, 1966-68. Decorated Army Commendation medal. Mem. Nat. Assn. of Pvt. Residential Facilities (dir. 1978-81), Nat. Assn. Social Workers, Acad. Cert. Social Workers, Nat. Assn. Retarded Citizens. Democrat. Roman Catholic. Home: Box 606 Uniontown KY 42461 Office: Route 4 Morganfield KY 42437

BEAVER, BRIDGET SMITH, educator; b. Okmulgee, Okla., Sept. 13, 1947; d. Roy William and Una Angeline (Acord) Smith; B.S. in English Edn., Northeastern Okla. State U., 1968; M.A., U. Tulsa, 1974; m. Mose Arty Beaver, June 1, 1968; children—John Matthew, Angela Brooke. Tchr. English, Bixby (Okla.) High Sch., 1968-73, Okmulgee (Okla.) High Sch., 1973-74; instr. English, speech, humanities Connors State Coll., Warner, Okla., 1974—. Mem. Nat. Council Tchrs. English, Higher Edn. Alumni Council, Okla. Edn. Assn., Okla. Council Tchrs. English, Connors State Coll. Instrs. Assn. Home and Office: Connors State Coll Warner OK 74469

BEAVERS, RICHARD ALLEN, dentist; b. Durham, N.C., Oct. 3, 1944; s. William Olive and Eunice Margaret (Brass) B.; B.S. in Biology, Wake Forest U., 1967; M.A. in Biology (Greensboro Wildlife Club scholar), U. N.C., Greensboro, 1975; D.D.S., U. N.C., Chapel Hill, 1979; 1 dau., Debran Margaret. Grad. teaching asst. U. N.C., Greensboro, 1972-74, instr. in microbiology, 1974; instr. in math. and sci. Guilford Tech. Inst., 1974-75; resident in gen. practice of dentistry Univ. Hosp., Seattle, 1979-80; mem. profl. edn. com. Orange County unit, N.C. div. Am. Cancer Soc., 1978-79. Bd. dirs. Univ. Baptist Ch. Kindergarten-Day Care Center, 1975-79. Served with USNR, 1968-72. Recipient Am. Acad. Oral Pathology award, 1979, Pierre Fauchard Acad. award, 1979; Pfeiffer research fellow, 1978. Mem. ADA, Internat. Lymnology Soc., N.C. Dental Soc., Am. Assn. Dental Schs., Am. Soc. Dentistry for Children, Bapt. Med. Dental Fellowship, Sigma Xi, Omicron Kappa Upsilon, Delta Sigma Delta. Home: 1104 Hobbs Rd Greensboro NC 27410 Office: Univ Hosp Dental Service SC-62 Seattle WA 98195

BEAVERS, THOMAS CLAUDE, paper distbn. co. exec.; b. Hillsboro, Tex., Feb. 22, 1922; s. Thomas Claude and Luella (Dickson) B.; student James Milliken U., 1944; m. Theresa G. McSherry, Dec. 12, 1950; children—Danny, Darlene, Denise, David, Donald. Salesman, Carpenter Paper Co., Dallas, 1944-50, El Paso, Tex., 1950-59; co-owner, operator Bryan Office Supply Co., Artesia, N.Mex., 1960-61; sales mgr. Blake, Mollit & Towne, Los Angeles, 1962-69, mgr. printing papers, 1969-71; gen. mgr. Am. Papers Co., Denver, 1971-73 pres., co-owner Bosworth Papers Inc., Houston, 1973—. Served with U.S. Army, 1941-44. Mem. Gulf Coast Printing Industries. Clubs: Plaza, Sugar Creek Country, Craftsman, Houston City. Home: 2318 Country Club Dr Sugarland TX 77478 Office: PO Box 2528 1512 Center St Houston TX 77001

BEAZLEY, CURTIS EDWARD, air force officer; b. Scooba, Miss., Sept. 13, 1928; s. Curtis Atwood and Louise (Stribling (McWilliams) B.; A.A., E. Miss. Jr. Coll., 1946; B.S., Miss. State Coll., 1951, postgrad. in petroleum geology, 1950-51; B.S. in Meteorology, Fla. State U., 1952; grad. Armed Forces Staff Coll., 1966; M.P.A., Auburn U., 1980; m. Sara Patricia Richardson, Jan. 26, 1958; children—Rebecca, Sara Alison. Commd. 2d lt. USAF, 1951, advanced through grades to lt. col., 1968; served as weather officer, pilot, meteorologist, Brookley AFB, Ala., 1952, Seoul, Korea, 1953-54, Bolling AFB, Nat. Weather Analysis Center, Washington, 1954; student pilot, Kinston, N.C. and Vance AFB, Okla., 1954-55; comdr. Base HQ. Squadron, Ardmore AFB, Okla., 1955-56; pilot C-124 aircraft Larson AFB, Washington, 1956-58; aerial weather reconnaissance officer Shaw AFB, S.C., 1958-61; weather officer, Hanau, Germany, 1961-64; comdr. weather sta. Godman Army Airfield, Ft. Knox, 1964-65; aircraft comdr. C-141 aircraft flight comdr., aircrew mgmt. officer Robins AFB, Ga., 1966-71; weather comdr., staff weather officer OSAN AFB, Korea, 1971-72, Maxwell AFB, Ala., 1972-75. Active supporter numerous civic functions overseas as well as in U.S. Served with U.S. Army, 1946-48. Decorated Meritorious Service medal with 2 oak leaf clusters, Air medal with cluster, AF outstanding unit award with 4 clusters, combat readiness medal with cluster, WWII victory medal, Army of Occupation medal (Italy), Nat. Def. Service medal with bronze service star, Korean service medal with 2 bronze service stars, Armed Forces expeditionary medal, Vietnam service medal with 1 silver and 1 bronze service star, 2 Republic of Korea Presl. unit citations, UN service medal and Republic of Vietnam campaign medal. Mem. AF Assn., Sigma Gamma Epsilon, Sigma Pi, Pi Sigma Alpha. Baptist (deacon, Sunday sch. tchr.). Clubs: Coll. Band, Dip and Strike Geology Club, Masons. Address: 3832 Rouse Ridge Rd Montgomery AL 36111

BECK, CHARLES VERNON, broadcasting exec.; b. Bernice, La., Nov. 2, 1931; s. Leo and Etta Lucile (Davidson) B.; diploma Tyler (Tex.) Comml. Coll., 1951; m. Bobbie Jean Lunceford, Oct. 16, 1951; children—Charles Glenn, Ted Newton. Radio engr. Texoma Broadcasting Co. 1951-60; chief engr. Broadcasting Assos., 1960-75; pres. Mustang Broadcasting Co., Wichita Falls, Tex., 1975—; cons. engr. Vernon Beck Eclectonics, 1965—; mem. CATV com. City of Wichita Falls. Recipient various public service awards. Mem. Soc. Broadcast Engrs., Nat. Assn. Broadcasters, Radio Advt. Bur. Democrat. Baptist. Home: 6716 Gen Custer St Wichita Falls TX 76310 Office: PO Box 1794 Wichita Falls TX 76307

BECK, DORRIS DILLS, librarian, media specialist; b. Cullowhee, N.C., Jan. 18, 1933; d. Jesse Grady and Gracie Ellen (Green) Dills; B.S. in Edn., Western Carolina U., 1955, M.S. in Edn. in Audiovisual, 1972; m. Samuel F. Beck, Dec. 19, 1953; children—Teresa Kay, Susan Lynn. Circulation librarian, asst. librarian Western Carolina U., 1955-65; counselor, dep. dir. Neighborhood Youth Corps, Sylva, N.C., 1966-68; librarian Southwestern Tech. Inst., Sylva, 1968-71, dir. Learning Resource Center, 1971-73; media coordinator Fairview Elementary Sch., Sylva, 1973—. Pres. Sylva Elementary Sch. PTA, 1970-72. Mem. Southeastern, N.C. library assns., Ednl. Media Assn., NEA, N.C. Edn. Assn., Classroom Tchrs. Assn., Phi Kappa Phi. Baptist. Compiler manuals. Home: 126 Old Dillsboro Rd Sylva NC 28779 Office: Fairview Elementary Sch Sylva NC 28779

BECK, EARL RAY, educator; b. Junction City, Ohio, Sept. 8, 1916; s. Ernest Ray and Mary Francis (Helser) B.; A.B., Capital U., 1937; M.A., Ohio State U., 1939, Ph.D., 1942; m. Marjorie Lois Culbertson, Nov. 7, 1944; children—Ann, Mary Sue. Instr., Capital U., Columbus, Ohio, 1942-43, Ohio State U., Columbus, 1946-49; asst. prof. Fla. State U., Tallahassee, 1949-52, asso. prof., 1952-60, prof. history, 1960—, chmn. dept. history, 1967-72; vis. faculty U. Ky., Lexington, 1948, La. State U., 1955, Tulane U., 1959, Duke U., Durham, N.C., 1968. Served with U.S. Army, 1943-46. Mem. Am. Hist. Assn., So. Hist. Assn., Soc. Spanish and Portuguese History, Conf. Group Central European History, Com. for Study of History of Second World War. Democrat. Presbyterian. Author: Verdict on Schacht, 1955; Death of the Prussian Republic, 1959; Contemporary Civilization, 1959; On Teaching History in Colleges and Universities, 1966; Germany Rediscovers America, 1968; A Time of Triumph and of Sorrow - Spanish Politics during the Reign of Alfonso XII, 1874-1885, 1979. Home: 2514 Killarney Way Tallahassee FL 32308 Office: Dept of History Fla State Univ Tallahassee FL 32306

BECK, ESTHER ANN, psychologist; b. Providence, May 23, 1940; d. William Tillinghast and Esther Ann (DeWitt) Broomhead; A.A., Enterprise State Jr. Coll., 1968; B.S. magna cum laude, Troy State U., 1970; M.S., Auburn U., 1971, Ph.D., 1973; m. Edward Rubin Beck, Aug. 14, 1958. Asso. prof. psychology Auburn U., Montgomery, coordinator mental health center, 1974-75, clin. psychologist Psychol. Service Center, 1974—; pvt. practice psychology, Montgomery, 1974—; cons. in field. NDEA fellow, 1970-73; name Outstanding Profl. in Human Services, Am. Acad. Human Services, 1974-75. Mem. Am. Psychol. Assn. (legis. liasion for Ala., 1977-79), Ala. Psychol. Assn. (legis. chmn. 1976-78), AAUW (chmn. fellowships and ednl. founds., 1976-77), Assn. Licensed Psychologists in Ala. (sec.treas. 1976-78), Southeastern Psychol. Assn., Biofeedback Soc. Contbr. articles to profl. jours. Home: 350 N Anton Dr Montgomery AL 36105 Office: Auburn Univ Psychol Dept I-85 Campus Montgomery AL 36109

BECK, GEORGE PRESTON, physician; b. Wichita Falls, Tex., Oct. 21, 1930; s. George P. and Amanda (Wilbanks) B.; B.S., Midwestern U., 1951; M.D., U. Tex., 1955; m. Constance Carolyn Krog, Dec. 22, 1953; children—Cara Elizabeth, George P., Howard W. Intern, John Sealy Hosp., 1955-56; resident anesthesiology Parkland Meml. Hosp., Dallas, 1959-62, vis. staff, 1964—; practice medicine, specializing in anesthesiology, Lubbock, Tex., 1964—; chief staff Meth. Hosp., Lubbock, 1967-68; asst. prof. anesthesiology Southwestern Med. Sch., Dallas, 1962-64, asst. clin. prof., 1964-71, asso. clin. prof. anesthesiology U. Tex. Med. Br. at Galveston, 1971—; owner Gt. Plain Ballistics Corp., 1967—. Pres. found. bd. Tex. Tech U., 1972—. Served with USAF, 1956-59. Diplomate Am. Bd. Anesthesiology. Fellow Am. Coll. Anesthesiologists; mem. Am., Tex. (pres. 1974) socs. anesthesiologists, Tex., Lubbock County med. socs., Lubbock Surg. Soc. (pres. 1969). Lutheran (pres. ch. council 1965-66, pres. congregation 1965-66). Author: The Ideal Anesthesiologist, 1960; Mnemonics as an Aid to the Anesthesiologist, 1961; Anterior Approach to Sciatic Nerve Block, 1962. Home: 4601 W 18th St Lubbock TX 79416 Office: PO Box 16385 Lubbock TX 79490

BECK, LEE RANDOLPH, scientist, educator; b. Chgo., Mar. 7, 1942; s. John Joseph and Beverly (Deitz) B.; B.A., U. Dubuque, 1965; M.S., N.Mex. Highland U., 1966; Ph.D. (USPHS predoctoral fellow), Wash. State U., 1970; m. Marjorie Collisson, Aug. 13, 1966; children—John Christopher, Jessica Leigh. Postdoctoral fellow Ohio State U., 1970-72; asst. prof. U. Ala., Birmingham, 1972-73, asso. prof., dir. Human Reprodn. Biol. Lab., 1978—; cons. Stolle Research and Devel. Corp. Mem. Soc. Study of Reprodn., N.Mex. Highlands Honor Soc., Am. Fertility Soc., Sigma Xi, Phi Kappa Phi. Contbr. numerous articles profl. jours.; patentee in field. Home: 2550 Dunmore Pl Birmingham AL 35226 Office: University Sta Birmingham AL 35294

BECK, NANCY MANN MCCONNICO (MRS. EARL CRAFTON BECK, JR.), civic leader; b. Memphis, Aug. 31, 1931; d. John Davis and Pauline (Hilton) McConnico; grad. So. Sem. and Jr. Coll., 1949; m. Dean Carlton DuBois, Aug. 19, 1951 (div. Nov. 1963); children—Denise Hilton, Dean Carlton; m. 2d, Earl C. Beck, Jr., Jan. 31, 1971; 1 son, John Harrington. Asst. buyer, sportswear John Gerber Co., Memphis, 1950-51; fashion coordinator J. Hilton McConnico, Designer, Memphis, 1963-65; buyer, mgr. Bridal Salon, Goldsmiths, Memphis, 1965-70, French Room, 1970-71; v.p. Beck Distbg. Co., 1970-73; v.p. Crittenden Fine Arts Patron's League, 1977-78; chmn. Children's Art Day, Memphis, 1976-78; chmn. Women's coordination Billy Graham Crusade, Crittenden County, 1978; sec.-treas. Rivertown Devels., Inc. Press relations Hunter Lane for mayor, 1967; bd. dirs., v.p. Memphis Symphony League, pres., 1980—. Mem. Memphis Arts Council, Memphis Symphony League. Episcopalian. Clubs: Town and Country Garden (pres.) (Hughes, Ark.), Josephine Circle (past pres.) (Memphis). Home: Casa Lorraine Plantation Hughes AR 72348

BECKELHEIMER, CHRISTINE ELIZABETH CAMPBELL, nurse; b. Oak Hill, W.Va., Sept. 6, 1916; d. Charles Earl and Macie Avis (Boothe) Campbell; diploma in nursing Somerset Hosp., Somerville, N.J., 1938; B.S. in Nursing Edn., Hunter Coll., 1954; M.A. in Nursing Service Adminstrn., Tchrs. Coll. Columbia U., 1959, profl. diploma, 1961, postgrad, 1961-65; m. Joseph Howard, June 6, 1941 (dec.); 1 dau., Mary Elizabeth; m. 2d, Harry Abrahamsen, Oct. 10, 1943; 1 dau., Cherri Georgette; md. 3d, Robert Ernest Beckelheimer, Jan. 18, 1980. Staff nurse obstetrics Somerset Hosp., 1939; staff nurse Goldwater Meml. Hosp., Welfare Island, N.Y.C., 1939-40, research nurse, 1940-41; staff nurse St. Vincent's Hosp., N.Y.C., 1941-43; lab. asst. Am. Cyanamid Co., Bound Brook, N.J., 1943; charge nurse Paul Kimball Hosp., Lakewood, N.J., 1943-44; staff nurse to head nurse Pinewald Hosp., Bayville, N.J., 1944-46; staff nurse Morrisania City Hosp., Bronx, N.Y., 1946-49, head nurse, 1949-50, clin. instr., 1950-54; instl. insp. Dept. Hosps. City of N.Y., 1954-58; supr. edn. City Hosp., Elmhurst, N.Y., 1958-60, research asst. Fedn. of the Handicapped, 1962-63; research asso. Yeshiva U. Lincoln Hosp., N.Y.C., 1963-64; asst. coordinator exchange grad. nurse program St. Luke's Hosp., N.Y.C., 1964-65, asst. dir. nursing service inservice edn., 1966-67; cons. research and hosp. nursing service Nat. League Nursing, N.Y.C., 1968-70, acting dir. research (cons.), 1970-71; asso. prof. nursing W.Va. Inst. Tech., 1971-73, chmn. dept. nursing, 1973-75; coordinator patient care Raleigh Gen. Hosp., Beckley, W.Va., 1975-78, dir. hosp. inservice, 1978-79. USPHS Nurse Research fellow, 1961-63; USPHS grantee, 1965-66. Mem. Am., W.Va. nurses assns., Am., N.Y.C. pub. health assns., N.Y. Acad. Scis., Aerospace Med. Assn., Tchrs. Coll. Nurses Alumni Assn., Hunter Coll. Alumni Assn., Pi Lambda Theta, Kappa Delta Pi, Am. Legion Aux., DAR, United Daus. of Confederacy, Wittenfort Long Rifles, Mountaineer Flintlock Rifles, Rosicrucian Order. Author: Cristabel Manalacor of Veltakin, 1970; The Cruachan and the Killane, 1970; The Mortal Immortals, 1971; The Golden Olive, 1972; The Bride of Kilkerran, 1972. Home: 213 Washington Ave Oak Hill WV 25901

BECKELHYMER, PAUL HUNTER, clergyman, educator; b. Trenton, Mo., Nov. 23, 1919; s. Earl Errett and Corinne (Caffrey) B.; A.B., Park Coll., 1941; B.D., U. Chgo., 1944; D.D., Christian Theol. Sem., 1959; m. Betty Jane Courtney, Aug. 19, 1951; children—Helen Corinne, Anna Christine, Carolyn Jean. Ordained to ministry Christian Ch., 1942; minister North Shore Christian Ch., Chgo., 1944-46; minister Kenton (O.) Christian Ch., 1946-53; minister Hiram (Ohio) Christian Ch., 1953-66; asso. prof. homiletics Brite Div. Sch. Tex. Christian U., Fort Worth, 1966—; tutor Rosemont Community Sch., Fort Worth, 1974—; vis. fellow Princeton Theol. Sem., 1978; Wells preacher Tex. Christian U. Ministers' Week, 1979. Mem. Panel of Scholars Christian Ch., 1956-63, v.p. Bd. Higher Edn., 1961, bd. dirs. Council on Christian Unity, 1963-66. Named Alumnus of Year Div. Sch. U. Chgo., 1974. Mem. Acad. Homiletics (exec. com. 1976-78), Assn. Profl. Edn. Minstry, Pi Kappa Delta, Theta Phi. Democrat. Author: Meeting Life on Higher Levels, 1956; Questions God Asks, 1961; Hocking Valley Iron Man, 1962; Dear Connie, 1967. Editor: The Vital Pulpit of the Christian Church, 1969; The Word We Preach, 1970. Contbr. numerous articles to religious and profl. jours. Home: 5725 Whitman Ave Fort Worth TX 76133

BECKER, CAROLINE, epidemiologist; b. Williamsville, Mo., Nov. 20, 1924; d. Coulton Meldrom and Grace (Dulaney) Becker; student U. Mo., 1942-45; A.B. in Chemistry, Vanderbilt U., 1946; M.D., Johns Hopkins U., 1950; m. Ernest Croft Long, Feb. 6, 1954; 1 son, Croft Coulton. Intern, Duke U. Med. Center, Durham, N.C., 1950-51, resident in internal medicine, 1951-54, USPHS fellow, 1953, research asso. in exptl. surgery and virology, 1956-63; Boots fellow Wright Fleming Inst., London, 1954-56; Pan-Am. Health Orgn./WHO cons. in virology, Costa Rica, 1964; asst. prof. epidemiology Sch. Public Health, U. N.C., Chapel Hill, 1965-79, asso. prof., 1979—; cons. N.C. Heart Assn., Evans County (Ga.) cardiovascular studies. Pres., Home Health Agy. of Chapel Hill, 1976—. Recipient Founder's award N.C. Heart Assn., 1979. Mem. Soc. Epidemiol. Research, Am. Public Health Assn., N.C. Public Health Assn., Am. Med. Women's Assn., Johns Hopkins Med. and Surg. Assn., Am. Coll. Preventive Medicine, Elisha Mitchell Sci. Soc. (sec.-treas. 1979—), Johns Hopkins U. Alumni Assn. (schs. com. 1979—), Sigma Xi. Methodist. Contbr. articles on hypertension to med. jours. Home: Route 7 Box 218 Durham NC 27707 Office: Dept Epidemiology U NC Sch Public Health Rosenau Hall #201 H Chapel Hill NC 27514

BECKER, CHARLES HERBERT, structural engr.; b. York, Pa., July 4, 1904; s. Bernard Calvin and Anna Irene (Heckert) B.; grad. Wilson Engring. Sch., Cambridge, Mass., 1934; m. Thelma J. Karcher, Dec. 27, 1924; children—Nedra Karcher Escobedo, Donna Karcher Cashatt. Structural engr. bridge div. Tex. Hwy. Dept., Austin, 1944-48; sr. engr. Monsanto Chem. Co., Texas City, 1940-44; pvt. practice as structural cons., Austin, 1948—. Deacon, First Baptist Ch., Austin. Registered profl. engr., Tex., Ala. Mem. Tex. Soc. Profl. Engrs. Republican. Home: 7497 Chevy Chase St Apt 103 Austin TX 78752 Office: Suite 20 12703A Research Blvd Austin TX 78759

BECKER, MAYER GIL, data systems corp. exec.; b. Bklyn., July 2, 1951; s. Jack Jacob and Susan Faye (Balter) B.; B.Sc., Jacksonville U., 1974; M.B.A., Memphis State U., 1977; m. Joyce Reiter, Dec. 16, 1978. Sales rep. Eastern Airlines, Inc., 1971-74; dir. ops. Beth Sholom Synagogue, Memphis, 1975-76; partner Becker & Myers, Mgmt. Cons., Memphis, 1976-77; sales, exec. v.p. Minimax Data Systems, Inc., Memphis, 1977—. Mem. budget sub-com. United Way of Greater Memphis, 1975—; mem. investigation commn. ct. system City of Memphis, 1977; mem. City/County Alcohol and Drug Abuse Commn., 1979. Mem. Data Processing Mgmt. Assn., Assn. M.B.A. Execs., Zionist Orgn. Am. (life), Beta Gamma Sigma. Jewish. Club: B'nai B'rith. Home: 2195 Ealing Circle #2 Germantown TN 38138 Office: Minimax Data Systems Inc Suite 240 4646 Poplar Ave Memphis TN 38117

BECKMAN, GAIL MCKNIGHT, lawyer, educator; b. N.Y.C., Apr. 8, 1938; d. Irland McKnight and Elizabeth (Hurlock) Beckman; grad. Baldwin Sch., 1955; B.A., Bryn Mawr Coll., 1959; J.D., Yale, 1963; diploma (Fulbright scholar), U. Tubingen (Germany), 1960; M.A., U. Pa., 1966. Admitted to Pa. bar, 1964, Ga. bar, 1972, D.C. bar, 1964, U.S. Supreme Ct. bar, 1968; counsel Legal Aid Soc. Phila., 1961; asso. firm Morgan, Lewis, Bockius, Phila., 1963-66; lectr. law U. Glasgow (Scotland), 1967-71; asso. prof. law Ga. State U., Atlanta, 1971-76, prof., 1976—; vis. scholar Harvard Law Sch., 1980; research asso. Am. Philos. Soc., 1966-69. Mem. Phila., Atlanta, Ga., Am. (chmn. com. Internat. Ct. of Justice 1968-75, internat. estate problems 1974-79, vice chmn. legal problems aged 1979—) bar assns., Internat. Acad. Probate Trust Law, Yale Law Assn. Ga. (vice chmn. 1975-77), AAUW, Jr. League Atlanta, Nat. Soc. Colonial Dames Am., Yale Club Ga., Bryn Mawr Club Atlanta (founder, pres. 1976), St. Andrew's Soc. Atlanta (founder, sec., 1971). Presbyterian. Club: Commerce. Contbr. articles to books and profl. jours. Home: 3200 Lenox Rd C-400 Atlanta GA 30324 Office: Ga State U Atlanta GA 30303

BECKNER, LEE ALLEN, sales tng. mgr.; b. Chester, W.Va., Feb. 10, 1930; s. John Alman and Grace Lorraine (Morgan) B.; B.S., Weber State Coll., 1972; postgrad. U. Utah, 1972-73. Enlisted in U.S. Air Force, 1948, advanced through grades to master sgt., 1959, ret., 1968; staff tng. officer Thiokol Chem. Corp., Clearfield, Utah, 1968-70; dir. confs. and insts. Webert State Coll., Ogden, Utah, 1971-72; dir. continuing edn., asst. to pres. Westminster Coll., Salt Lake City, 1973; mgr. tng. and devel. br. IRS, Ogden, 1974-79; mgr. sales tng. foods div. Coca Cola Co., Houston, 1979—; tchr. and cons. in field of career devel. Established 1st drug abuse center, Ogden, 1q72. Decorated Air Force Commendation medal with oak leaf cluster. Mem. Am. Soc. for Tng. and Devel. (nat. v.p. 1979, nat. dir. 1977-78), Utah Adult Edn. Assn. (dir. 1971-72), Utah Fed. Trainers Assn. (pres. 1978). Home: 8402 Raylin Dr Houston TX 77055

BECKWITH, EDSON EMERSON, airline exec.; b. Frankfort, N.Y., Oct. 28, 1930; s. H. Elting and Laura May (Speece) B.; B.A., Hamilton Coll., 1953; m. Beatrice Jane Houseman, Aug. 12, 1961; children—John E., Amy S., Andrew McL. Banker, Chase Manhattan Bank, N.Y.C., 1957-66; asst. treas. Pepsico Inc., N.Y.C., 1966-70; v.p. fin. King Resources, Denver, 1971; v.p. Braniff Internat. Corp., Dallas, 1972-80, sr. v.p., 1980—. Trustee, Hamilton Coll., 1979—. Served with Fin. Corps, U.S. Army, 1953-56. Mem. Fin. Exec. Inst. (chpt. dir. 1974—, v.p. 1978-79, pres. 1979-80), Treas. Group N.Y.C. Club: Union League (N.Y.C.). Home: 4729 Melissa Ln Dallas TX 75229 Office: PO Box 61747 Dallas-Ft Worth Airport Dallas TX 75261

BECNEL, ALBERT THOMAS, ednl. adminstr.; b. Taft, La., June 24, 1916; married, 2 children. B.S. in Vocat. Edn., La. State U., Baton Rouge, 1939; M.Ed. in Guidance, Adminstrn. and Supervision, Nicholls State U., Thibodaux, La., 1968. Tchr., supr. St. John Parish Schs., Reserve, La., 1939-64, supt. schs., 1964—. Chmn. Reserve Charity to Birth Defects March Dimes Fund, 1964—. Mem. La. Assn. Sch. Supts., La. Assn. Sch. Execs., La. Tchr. Assn., NEA, La. Edn. Assn., Phi Delta Kappa. Home: PO Box 191 134 W 1st St Reserve LA 70084 Office: PO Box AL W 10th St Reserve LA 70084

BEDA, MICHAEL FRANCIS, machinery co. exec.; b. Omaha, Nov. 6, 1945; s. Frank Stanley and Veronica Ann (Rojewski) B.; B.S., Iowa State U., 1969; m. Wanda Jane Gillispie, May 25, 1974. Application and sales engr. Layne-Western Co., Kansas City, Mo., 1969; application engr. Marley Co., Kansas City, 1970-72; br. mgr. Process Equipment Co., Oklahoma City, 1972—. Adviser, Jr. Achievement, 1970-72. Registered profl. engr., Okla. Mem. Nat., Okla. socs. profl. engrs., Am. Soc. Heating, Refrigeration and Air Conditioning Engrs., Beta Theta Pi. Democrat. Roman Catholic. Club: Oklahoma City Ski. Home: 2141 NW 113th St Oklahoma City OK 73120 Office: 4500 N Sewell St Oklahoma City OK 73118

BEDDIE, GEORGE JAMES, JR., life ins. sales and service co. exec.; b. Barre, Vt., Dec. 22, 1941; s. George James and Mae JoAnna (Houghton) B.; student Whittier Coll., 1959-61; m. Carol Jeanne Pike, Aug. 27, 1961; 1 son, J. Paul. With Mut. Benefit Life Ins. Co., Sacramento, N.Y., N.J., 1963-71, gen agt., New Orleans, 1971—; owner, operator Ins. Planning Assos., New Orleans, 1971—. Active Boy's Club Am. Mem. Nat. Assn. Life Underwriters, Gen. Agts. and Mgrs. Conf. Republican. Methodist. Club: Krewe of Bacchus. Office: 135 St Charles Ave Suite 500 New Orleans LA 70130

BEDELL, CONALY WILLIAM, advt. exec.; b. Harrison, Ark., June 7, 1936; s. Calvin Wallis and Nell Drue (McAllister) B.; B.A., U. Tulsa, 1958; postgrad. U. Tulsa, U. Ark.; m. Frances Fletcher Smith, May 22, 1970; children—Daniel, Catherine, Virginia. Edn. editor Tulsa Tribune, 1959-60; staff reporter Life mag., 1961-62; freelance writer mags. including Life, Sat. Eve. Post, Ladies Home Jour., 1963-68; pres. Bedell Inc., Fort Smith, Ark., 1968—. Vice pres. advt. United Fund, 1975; bd. dirs. Fort Smith Heritage Found., 1975-78, Westark Community Coll., 1976—. Mem. Southwestern Assn. Advt. Agencies, Am. Mktg. Assn., Fort Smith-Van Buren Advt. Fedn. (dir. 1976-78), Tulsa Press Club, U. Tulsa Alumni Assn., Sebastian County Hist. Soc. Clubs: Hardscrabble Country, Town of Fort Smith. Home: 4103 S 35th St Fort Smith AR 72903 Office: 515 N 6th St Fort Smith AR 72901

BEDENBAUGH, ANGELA LEA OWEN (MRS. JOHN HOLCOMBE BEDENBAUGH), chemist; b. Seguin, Tex., Oct. 6, 1939; d. Wintford Henry and Nelia Melanie (Fischer) Owen; B.S. cum laude, U. Tex., 1961; Ph.D., U. S.C., 1967; m. John Holcombe Bedenbaugh, Dec. 27, 1961; 1 dau., Melanie Celeste. Lab. instr. U. Tex. at Austin, 1960-61; research asso. in chemistry U. So. Miss., Hattiesburg, 1967—. Bd. dirs. Forrest-Stone Area Opportunity, Inc., 1970-72, mem. exec. com. bd., 1972. Mem. Am. Chem. Soc., Sci. Research Soc. N. Am. (sec.-treas. U. So. Miss. br. 1967-69, pres. 1973-74), N.Y. Acad. Scis., Bus. and Profl. Women's Club, League Women Voters, Delta Kappa Gamma (1st v.p. Alpha Beta chpt. 1972-74, pres. 1974-76; chmn. Zeta state research com. 1973-77, chmn. state world fellowship com. 1979-81, internat. research com. 1976-78), Nat. Women's Polit. Caucus. Methodist (adminstrv. bd. 1974-75). Club: U. So. Miss. Faculty Wives (2d v.p. 1971-72). Contbr. articles to profl. jours. Patentee in field. Office: Box 8466 Southern Station Hattiesburg MS 39401

BEDENBAUGH, GEORGE ROSCOE, broadcasting exec.; b. Newberry County, S.C., Jan. 17, 1944; s. William Woodrow, Sr. and Martha Elise (Hawkins) B.; student U. S.C., 1962-63, Newberry Coll., 1965-66; m. Peggy Ann Chapman, Oct. 17, 1965; children—Karman Jay, Bradley Dee, Aaron Clark. Technician, Wicker's Radio & TV, Prosperity, S.C., 1959-62; announcer Sta. WKDK, Newberry, 1963-66; announcer, salesman Sta. WPCC, Clinton, S.C., 1966-67; indsl. salesman Dixie Radio Supply Co., Columbia, S.C., 1967-68; program dir. Sta. WKMG, Newberry, 1968-71, dir., gen. mgr., 1971-77, exec. v.p., gen. mgr., 1977—, also chief engr.; exec. v.p. Service Radio Co. Inc. Bd. dirs. Newberry County Devel. Bd., 1975—, Newberry County dist. Boy Scouts Am., 1977-78, planning div. United Way of the Midlands, 1977-78; mem. Prosperity Town Planning Commn., 1975-77; mem. Prosperity Am. Bicentennial Com., 1975-76; pres. Newberry County unit Am. Cancer Soc., 1974-75, chmn. bd., 1975-76; bd. dirs., treas. Assn. Greater Newberry, 1978—. Mem. S.C. Broadcasters Assn., C. of C. (dir.). Lutheran (mem. ch. council 1974-76, asst. sch. supt. 1976-78). Club: Newberry Sertoma (pres. 1972-73, chmn. bd. 1973-74, pres. honor club 1973). Home: Route 2 Box 16 Glenn St Ext Newberry SC 29108

BEDFORD, JOHN JOSEPH, aerospace engr.; b. Galveston, Tex., Sept. 23, 1950; s. Wendell J. and Mildred Alice (Brown) B.; B.S., Tex. A. and M. U., 1973, M.Engring., 1975; m. Carlotta Ann Malone, Aug. 19, 1972; 1 son, Sean Jeffrey. Aerospace engr., space shuttle guidance and control mechanics McDonnell Douglas Tech. Service Co., Houston, 1975-79; project engr. extra-vehicular activity space shuttle hardware Internat. Latex Corp., Houston, 1979—. Registered profl. engr., Tex. Mem. Tex. A. and M. Former Students Assn., Sigma Gamma Tau. Democrat. Home: 1314 N Noble Rd Texas City TX 77590 Office: 16903 Buccaneer St Houston TX 77058

BEDFORD, MADELEINE ALANN PECKHAM (MRS. CHARLES FRANCIS BEDFORD), civic worker; b. Ontario, Calif., Jan. 25, 1910; d. Allen Lewis and Madeleine (Elliott) Peckham; A.B., U. Calif. at Berkeley, 1930, M.A., 1937; LL.D. (hon.), Tex. Christian U., 1973; m. Charles Francis Bedford, Dec. 30, 1930; children—Madeleine Alann, Frances Ellen, Charlotte Jean. Supr. tchr. tng. and counseling, in charge testing Univ. High Sch., U. Calif. at Berkeley, 1931-38; tchr. English to fgn. born San Leandro (Calif.) Evening Schs., 1931-38. Treas., Tarrant County Day Care Assn., 1953-54; pres. Ft. Worth and Tarrant County council Camp Fire Girls, 1961-63, pres. nat. council, 1965-68; pres. Ft. Worth Lit. Council, 1963-65; v.p. Tarrant County United Fund and Community Council, 1963-66, mem. exec. com. bd. dirs., 1963—, chmn. speakers tours film div. United Way Met. Tarrant County, 1973, chmn. planning and research div., 1973-75, v.p., 1973-75; pres. Ft. Worth chpt. Am. Field Service, 1964-66; chmn. budget sub-com. United Fund, 1959-68; sec. Tex. United Community Services, 1968-70, v.p., 1970-73, pres., 1973-75, hon. chmn. bd., 1975—; mem. Mid-Am. Regional Vol. Task Force United Way Am., 1973-75, Tex. rep. for UNICEF, 1969—; mem. gov.'s steering com. White House Conf. on Children and Youth, 1970, chmn. task force com. for Tex. on internat. relations, 1970; chmn. Met. div. Crusade of Hope campaign, 1970; chmn. Mayor's Council on Youth Opportunity, Fort Worth, 1971-72; chmn. Tarrant County Task Force Aging, 1972-74; fin. and sec. social services adv. com. Tex. Dept. Pub. Welfare, 1974-75, chmn. com., 1975-76; bd. dirs., mem. advisory council adult basic edn. Tarrant County chpt. ARC, 1966-69; bd. dirs. United Cerebral Palsy, pres., 1976-77, chmn. bd., 1977—; v.p. United Cerebral Palsy of Tex., 1978; bd. dirs. Tarrant County Community Action Agy., Tarrant County Community Council, Tex. Social Welfare Assn.; mem. com. on nat. agy. support United Way Am., 1975—; mem. Child Care '76, Tarrant County; trustee Assn. for Grad. Edn. and Research North Tex., 1971-74, 78—, Tex. Christian U., 1975—; bd. dirs. Nat. Conf. Social Welfare, 1976—; bd. visitors Add-Ran Coll., Tex. Christian U., 1971—; mem. Housing Rehab. Project for Ft. Worth, 1975—. Recipient Gulick award Camp Fire Girls, 1961, Wo-He-Lo award, 1968; award of Excellence for Outstanding Leadership and Service Tarrant Co. Community Council, 1964, Civic award First Lady Ft. Worth Altrusa, 1966; Hercules award, planning and research div. United Way Met. Tarrant County, 1977. Mem. Ft. Worth Lecture Found., Mortar Board, Phi Beta Kappa (pres. Ft. Worth 1958-59), Alpha Chi Omega, Pi Sigma Alpha. Episcopalian. Club: Ft. Worth Woman's (past pres. history sect.). Home: 7 Westover Rd Fort Worth TX 76107

BEDIER, ROGER HENRY, energy prodn. and sers. exec.; b. Rochester, N.Y., Nov. 21, 1933; s. Henry Peter and Ida (Seitz) B.; B.Ch.E., U. Detroit, 1958; M.B.A., U. Chgo., 1964; m. Susan K. Stephens, June 6, 1970; children—John, Lynne, Amy, Jennifer. Dir. group planning Dresser Industries Tool Group, Chgo., 1973-78; dir. corp. planning Gen. Portland, Inc., Dallas, 1967-73; v.p. corp. planning Reading & Bates Corp., Tulsa, 1978—. Mem. Lincolnshire Planning Commn., 1976-77. Mem. Am. Mgmt. Assn. (Disting. Service award 1968), Assn. Corp. Growth, Planning Execs. Inst. Republican. Methodist. Clubs: Tulsa, Cedar Ridge Country. Home: 10320 S 67th E Ave Tulsa OK 74133 Office: 3800 1st National Tower Tulsa OK 74103

BEDOYA, RICARDO, radiologist; b. Cali, Colombia, Feb. 7, 1940; s. Ricardo and Lina (Garcia) B.; M.D., Javeriana U., 1964; m. Patricia Guzman, Apr. 7, 1968; children—Lina Maria, Ricardo A., Patricia Michelle. Intern, Mt. Sinai Hosp., Miami Beach, Fla., 1970-71; chief resident in radiology U. Hosp. of Jacksonville (Fla.), 1971-74; staff radiologist Lake Shore Hosp.-Lake City (Fla.) Med. Center, 1974—. Diplomate Am. Bd. Radiology. Mem. AMA, Am. Coll. Radiologists, Columbia County Med. Soc. (v.p.), Fla. Med. Assn., Radiol. Soc. N. Am., Am. Coll. Nuclear Physicians. Roman Catholic. Home and Office: 600 N Church St Lake City FL 32055

BEEBE, WILLIAM THOMAS, airline exec.; b. Los Angeles, Jan. 26, 1915; s. Dewey Sheldon and Elsie (Thomas) B.; B.B.A., U. Minn., 1937; m. Nancy Lee Gragg, Feb. 3, 1951; children—Marshall J., Linda Lee, Deborah Susan. Coll. trainee Gen. Electric Co., 1938-40; personnel mgr. United Aircraft Corp., Hartford, Conn., 1940-46; v.p. Delta Air Lines, Inc., Atlanta, 1947-67, sr. v.p. adminstrn., 1967-70, pres., 1970-71, chmn. bd., 1971—, also dir.; dir. Citizens & So. Nat. Bank, Provident Life & Accident Ins. Co., Am. Bus. Products, Inc. Former mem. Atlanta Bd. Edn.; mem. nat. adv. council Nat. Multiple Sclerosis Soc.; chmn. Ga. Soc. Prevention Blindness; trustee U. Minn. Found. Episcopalian. Office: Hartsfield Atlanta Internat Airport Atlanta GA 30320

BEELENDORF, RICHARD EDWARD, bus. exec.; b. Manchester, Conn., Aug. 26, 1936; s. Eugene Frank and Bernice T. (Rubacha) B.; student Coll. Advanced Traffic, 1969-70; B.A., Chapman Coll., 1978; m. Connie Jo Hale, Dec. 22, 1957; children—Lisa Ann, Douglas Brian, Scott Andrew. Chief cashier K & R Delivery, Des Plaines, Ill.,

1962-66; asst. gen. mgr. Larsen Trucking, Bensonville, Ill., 1966-69; ops. supr. Airborne Freight Corp., Chgo., 1969-70; traffic and warehouse mgr. McGraw Edison Co., Algonquin, Ill., 1970-73; distbn. mgr. M & M/Mars Inc., Albany, Ga., 1973—; vice chmn. freight task force C. of C., 1975. Sgt. at arms Jaycees, 1960, sec., 1961, 2d v.p., 1962, 1st v.p., 1963, pres., 1964. Served with USAF, 1955-59. Named Man of Yr., Des Plaines C. of C., 1962, Spoke award, 1960. Mem. S.W. Ga. Transp. Club (dir. 1974, v.p. 1975-76), McHenry County Transp. Club (v.p. 1972-73), Fox Valley Transp. Club (dir. 1971-72, v.p. 1973), U.S. P.O. Council (dir. 1976—). Clubs: Radium Country, Elks. Office: PO Box 3289 Albany GA 31706

BEEMAN, ROBERT LAWRENCE, steel co. exec.; b. Dallas, Dec. 25, 1937; s. Robert Herrin and Frances Fay (Jones) B.; B.S. in Mech. Engring., So. Meth. U., 1961; m. Suzanne Stemmons, Feb. 3, 1961; children—Robert Lawrence, Michael Leslie, Michelle Robin. Engr. Aeros. div. Ling Temco Vought, Dallas, 1961-63; pres. Merco Mfg., Inc., Dallas, 1964—. Past pres. Children Inc.; pres. June Shelton Sch. and Evalvation Center, 1975—; bd. dirs. Metro YMCA, 1975—, Harding Coll., Searcy, Ark., 1969—, Quorum 50, 1964—; past chmn. Christian Acad. Oak Cliff. Mem. Steel Deck Inst. (pres. 1976-77), ASME. Office: 2075 W Commerce St Dallas TX 75208

BEENHAKKER, ARIE, economist; b. Haarlem, The Netherlands, June 29, 1934; s. Peke and Adriana Cornelia (Lams) B.; certificate comml. corr. in Dutch, English, French, German, Bus. Coll., Alkmaar, Holland, 1954; Doctorandus in Devel. Econs. and Bus. Adminstrn., (Dutch Govt. fellow 1958-61), U. Netherlands, Rotterdam, 1961; Ph.D. (Inst. World Affairs fellow 1961, Fulbright fellow 1961, Ford Found. fellow, 1962-64), Purdue U., 1964; m. Ann Daugherty, June 18, 1965. Asst. to pres. Wyomissing Corp., Reading, Pa., 1964-65; asst. prof. Grad. Sch. Bus. McGill U., Montreal, Que., Can., 1965-67; econ. devel. adviser Ford Found., N.Y.C., to Govt. Nepal, 1967-71, Nigeria, 1971-73; prof. finance and mgmt. Coll. Bus. Adminstrn., U. South Fla., Tampa, 1973—; cons. pvt. indsl. firms Can.; cons., Surinam, 1978. Chmn. finance com. Protestant Congregation, Nepal, 1968-70. Served to 1st lt. Royal Dutch Arty., 1955-58. Recipient govt. research grants, 1976-79. Mem. Inst. World Affairs, Am. Econs. Assn., Financial Mgmt. Assn., Am. Soc. Pub. Adminstrn. Author: A Kaleidoscopic Circumspection of Development Planning, 1973; Nepal's Fourth Plan, 1970-75; contbg. author: The Physical Development of Kathmandu Valley, 1970; contbr. articles to profl. jours. Address: 16408 Shagbark Pl Route 1 Tampa FL 33618

BEERS, WILLIAM TOWNSEND, elec. engr.; b. Halifax, Nova Scotia, Can., May 13, 1919; s. George Henry and Gladys Florence (Townsend) B.; m. Katherine Ann Harmon, Jan. 1, 1948. Project engr. Raytheon Co., Waltham, Mass., 1941-43, 1945-57; group engr. Martin-Marietta Co., Orlando, Fla., 1957-60; pres. Peninsular Electronics Corp., Orlando, 1961-71, dir., 1961-71; sr. mem. tech. staff Wood-Ivey Systems Corp., Orlando, 1973—; cons. electronic research. Served with USAAF, 1943-45. Decorated Air medal with oak leaf cluster. Mem. Nat. Hist. Soc., Nat. Geog. Soc. Patentee in sensing device for abnormal tire conditions. Home: 7139 Conway Circle Orlando FL 32809 Office: 3535 Forsyth Rd Orlando FL 32807

BEESLEY, CRAIG CARROLL, psychiatrist, educator; b. Cin., Nov. 17, 1943; B.S. with honors (NSF grantee), Purdue U., 1965; M.D., U. Cin., 1969. Intern, Jackson Meml. Hosp., Miami, Fla., 1969-70, resident, 1970-71, 74-75, fellow in psychiatry, 1975; faculty dept. psychiatry Walter Reed Army Med. Center, Washington, 1976-78; clin. instr. dept. psychiatry Georgetown U., Washington, 1977-78; asst. prof. dept. psychiatry U. Miami Sch. Medicine, 1978—, asst. dir. consultation-liaison service, 1978—. Served with M.C., U.S. Army, 1972-73, 76-78. Mem. AAAS, AMA, Dade County Med. Assn., Am. Psychiat. Assn., S. Fla. Psychiat. Soc., N.Y. Acad. Scis., Alpha Epsilon Delta. Office: Dept Psychiatry (D29) U Miami Sch Medicine PO Box 016960 Miami FL 33101

BEESLEY, JESSE C., sculptor; b. Murfreesboro, Tenn., Oct. 1, 1901; student U. Va., 1920-21, Princeton U., 1921-24. Editor, This Week Mag., N.Y.C.; public relations exec. Gen. Motors Corp.; pub. Daily News Jour., Murfreesboro; editor seven publs. Prentice Hall, N.Y.C.; sculptor; works represented in permanent collections. Recipient numerous art awards. Author: Bachelor's Cookbook; contbr. feature articles to popular mags. including Vogue and American Mercury. Address: 512 E College St Murfreesboro TN 37130

BEESON, MARY RUTH (PETE), mgmt. cons.; b. Glen Rose, Tex., Nov. 15, 1913; d. Quentin Orestes and Maude Elma (Embree) Gaither; student Wright's Law Sch., 1931, U. Tex., 1934, San Antonio Coll., 1937; student St. Mary's U., 1937-39, Am. U., 1952-53; m. Charles Edward Beeson, Nov. 15, 1940; children—Peter Gaither Embree, Caroline Jane. Exec. asst. to state dir. of ops., Works Progress Adminstrn., San Antonio, 1935-40; certifying officer, adminstrv. asst. Civilian Personnel Office, Army Air Force, San Antonio Aviation Cadet Center, 1941-46; personnel officer IRS, Washington, 1957-63, employment officer, Austin Service Center, 1963-74, chmn. Fed. Women's Program Planning Com., 1963-68, chmn. Equal Employment Opportunity Planning Com., Austin Service Center, 1963-73, mem. regional commr.'s adv. com. on Fed. Women's Program, IRS, Dallas, 1972-74; cons. in personnel mgmt., Austin, 1976—; cons. on curriculum, Camp Gary Job Corps, 1965. Chmn. Parent Edn. Com., Falls Church Sch., 1952-54; mem. exec. com. Community Coordinated Child Care Com., Austin, 1968-72; mem. adv. commn. to Tex. Legis. Council's study on the handicapped, Austin, 1970-73; mem. adv. com. on vocat. office edn. to Austin Ind. Sch. Dist., 1965-69, also adv. com.; chmn. mayor's Com. on Developmental Child Care, Austin, 1970-75; chmn. Mayor's Commn. on Status of Women, Austin, 1970-75; mem. Austin Commn. on Status of Women, 1975—. Recipient Outstanding Service to the Deaf award Tex. Edn. Agy., 1967, Distinguished IRS Worker for the Handicapped award IRS Commr., 1972, commendation Pres.'s Com. on Employment of Handicapped, 1974. Mem. Internat. Personnel Mgmt. Assn., Am. Mgmt. Assn., Austin Personnel Assn. Unitarian. Clubs: Austin Country, Altrusa. Inventor: insulated coaster, Hycab, car wastebasket. Home: 2700 Valley Springs Rd Austin TX 78746 Office: 2700 Valley Springs Rd Austin TX 78746

BEEUWKES, LAMBERT BAER, broadcast sta. mgmt. cons.; b. Balt., May 6, 1907; s. John Christian and Elizabeth (Baer) B.; grad. Balt. Poly. Inst., 1926; student Johns Hopkins, 1926-28; m. M. Eleanor Byerly, Oct. 14, 1936; 1 son, Foster L. Aero. constrn. and exptl. design aircraft Ford-Stout, Fokker, Glenn L. Martin, 1928-35; radio sta. mgmt. and constrn. stas. KYW, WXYZ, WROV, WDAS, WLAW, Mich. Radio Network MBS, NBC, 1936-70; sales dir. NBC Radio Network, 1970-72; personal mgr. The Lone Ranger, 1942-45. Inventor retractable wing, boundary layer laminar flow control; pioneer broadcast techniques such as telephone giveaway, continuous news program, guarantee sales compensation. Address: 4596 Mountain Creek Dr Roswell GA 30075

BEGGS, JAMES RANDY, systems analyst; b. Greenwood, S.C., Dec. 14, 1949; s. James Grady and Lucy (Hill) B.; B.S., Ga. Tech. Inst., 1972; postgrad bus. adminstrn. Ga. State U., 1977—; m. Marilyn S. Woods, Sept. 24, 1977. Med. technologist Crawford W. Long Hosp., Atlanta, 1972-73; intelligence analyst Naval Ocean Surveillance Info. Center, Washington, 1973-76, instr., 1973-76; systems analyst Grady Meml. Hosp., Atlanta, 1976-78; sr. systems analyst Ga. Power Co., Atlanta, 1978—. Mem. Greater Washington Ga. Tech. Alumni Club (pres. 1973-75, sec. treas. 1975-76), Am. Mgmt. Assn., Am. Assn. Indsl. Engrs., Hosp. Mgmt. Systems Soc., Am. Hosp. Assn., Ga. Hosp. Assn., Chi Phi. Office: 270 Peachtree St NE Atlanta GA 30303

BEHAR, RAYMOND JACK, urologist; b. Orange, N.J., Nov. 1, 1938; s. Jack Victor and Mary (Mushabac) B.; B.A. cum laude, Washington and Jefferson Coll., 1960; M.D., N.Y. U., 1964; m. Susan Zeisler, May 31, 1965; children—Jessica, Jordan, Ryan, Jennifer. Intern, Albert Einstein Coll. Medicine-Bronx Municipal Hosp. Center, 1964-65, resident in surgery, 1965-66, resident in urology, 1969-72; pvt. practice urology, New Port Richey, Fla., 1972—; asst. instr. surgery (urology) Albert Einstein Coll. Medicine, 1971-72; chief of surgery Community Hosp. of New Port Richey, 1975-77, asst. chief staff, 1976-79, chief of staff, 1979—. Served with M.C., U.S. Army, 1966-69. Diplomate Am. Bd. Urology. Fellow A.C.S., Am. Urol. Assn.; mem. Am. Assn. Clin. Urologists, Fla. Urol. Assn., AMA, Fla., Pasco County med. assns. Republican. Jewish. Contbr. articles to med. jours. Home: 1732 Hickory Gate Dr N Dunedin FL 33528 Office: 310 High St New Port Richey FL 33552

BEIGHLEY, SIDNEY LAMBERT, III, television sta. exec.; b. Jacksonville, Fla., Feb. 3, 1951; s. Sidney Lambert, Jr. and Ila B.; A.A., Fla. Jr. Coll., 1971; B.S. in Advt., U. Fla., 1973. Advt. mgr. Fla. Alligator, Gainesville, 1973; account exec. Sta. WCJB-TV, Gainesville, 1973-74; account exec. Sta. KPOL, Los Angeles, 1974-76; regional account exec. Sta. WTVT, Tampa, Fla., 1976-78, nat. sales mgr., 1978—; mem. Advt. Adv. Council to U. Fla. Recipient Bay Area Addy award for prodn. Bay Area Crime Prevention campaign, 1978; Branny award for best actor for performance in Butterflies Are Free, Village Players, Brandon, Fla., 1977. Mem. Am. Advt. Fedn. (founder, past pres. Bay Area Ad Club II div., Eastern regional chmn. Ad Club II div.). Club: St. Augustine Young Life (co-founder 1970-71). Home: 4141 Bayshore Blvd #702 Tampa FL 33611 Office: PO Box 22013 Tampa FL 33622

BEITZEL, BARBARA ANN, ret. army officer, occupational therapist; b. Chico, Calif., July 25, 1930; d. Richard Sherburn and Violet Marguerite (Yuhnke) B.; B.A. in Occupational Therapy, San Jose State Coll., 1953. Lt. col. U.S. Army, 1969; occupational therapist, Washington, 1954, Honolulu, 1956-58, Denver, 1958-60, Ft. Riley, Kans., 1960-62, San Francisco, 1962-64, San Antonio, 1964, Phoenixville, Pa., 1965-67, Tokyo, 1967-69, chief occupational therapy, El Paso, 1969-71, 73-75, Frankfurt/Main, Germany, 1971-73, ret., 1975. Home: 5344 Cornell El Paso TX 79924

BEKKEDAHL, NORMAN, chemist; b. Shelly, Minn., Mar. 16, 1903; s. Ole and Martha (Ueland) B.; B.S., U. Minn., 1925; M.S., George Washington U., 1929; Ph.D., Am. U., 1931; m. Katherine Audrick, Sept. 2, 1943; 1 dau., Bonnie. With Nat. Bur. Standards, 1928-68, dep. chief polymers div., 1964-68, cons., 1968—. Recipient Meritorious Service award Dept. Commerce, 1954. Fellow Washington Acad. Scis.; mem. Am. Chem. Soc. (councillor 1945-49, chmn. membership com. 1953, dir. div. rubber chemistry 1951, chmn. editorial bd. Rubber Revs. 1957-59, Charles Goodyear medal rubber div. 1967), Chem. Soc. Washington (pres. 1942), Sigma Xi. Club: Cosmos (Washington).

BELANGER, JOSEPH WARREN, mfg. co. exec.; b. Boston, Mar. 18, 1930; s. Joseph and Mary (Silva) B.; B.S. in Bus. Adminstrn., Boston U., 1955; m. Helen Marie Coyne, Oct. 11, 1952; children—Joseph Michael, Mary Kelley, Shana Leigh. With A.W. Chesterton Co., Stoneham, Mass., So. area sales mgr., Mobile, Ala., 1955—; pres. Mech. Seals & Packing Co., Shreveport, La., 1973-78. Served with USMC; Korea. Mem. TAPPI, Paper Industry Mgmt. Assn. Roman Catholic. Address: 4601 Bit and Spur Rd Mobile AL 36608

BELAY, LEUL, educator; b. Gondar, Ethiopia, Mar. 20, 1942; s. Haile and Yetemegne Mersha; Ph.D., U. Mo., 1972; m. Marie Burnett, Aug. 28, 1973. Instr. lang. UCLA, summer 1964, U. Utah, Salt Lake City, summer 1967; instr. bus. Alcorn A&M U., Lorman, Miss., 1967-69; asst. prof. mgmt. Jackson (Miss.) State U., 1973—. Mem. Soc. for Advancement of Mgmt., So. Mgmt. Assn., Case Study Assn. Coptic Orthodox. Contbr. articles, cases to profl. publs. Office: Dept Business Jackson State University Jackson MS 39217

BELCHER, DANNY CHESTER, educator; b. Pikeville, Ky., Jan. 1, 1945; s. Claude and Georgia B.; m. Lois Reynolds; 1 son, Johnny. B.S. in Bus., Psychology and Economics, Morehead (Ky.) State U., 1967, M.A. in Guidance and Counseling, 1970. Guidance counselor Jenkins (Ky.) Ind. Sch. Dist., 1971-73, 74—; dean admissions Alice Lloyd Coll., Pippa Passes, Ky., 1973-74; instr. mgmt. and human relations skills Beth Elkhorn Corp. Mem. NEA, Ky., Jenkins ed. assns., Ky. Personnel and Guidance Assn. Author: (with David Banks and Danny C. Belcher) Individual or Group Assestment and Profile. Baptist. Home: Box 38 Dorton KY 41520 Office: Jenkins High Sch Jenkins KY 41537

BELCHER, DON, educator; b. Chambers County, Ala., Jan. 25, 1941; s. John Buren and Mildrgd Claudine (Turnham) B.; B.S., Samford U., 1964; M.A., U. Ala., 1966; Ed.D., Auburn U., 1973; m. Georgia Marie Sentell, May 29, 1965; children—Kimberly, Karen. Tchr., Minor Elementary Sch., Birmingham, Ala., 1964-66; counselor Birmingham Bd. Edn., 1966-67; counselor U. Ala., Birmingham, 1967-69, dir. admissions, asst. prof. edn., 1971-76, 77—; teaching asst. dept. counselor edn. Auburn U., 1969-71; asst. prof. edn. Troy State U.-Europe, 1976-77; cons. office of admissions Daniel Payne Coll. Recipient Outstanding Alumni award Sigma Chi Zeta of Lambda Chi Alpha, 1975. Mem. Am., Ala. personnel and guidance assns., Am., So. coll. personnel assns., Am. Assn. Collegiate Registrars and Admissions Officers, Nat. Assn. Fgn. Student Affairs, Nat. Assn. Student Personnel Adminstrs., Nat. Assn. Coll. Admissions Counselors, So. Assn. Collegiate Registrars and Admissions Officers, Ala. Assn. Collegiate Registrars and Admissions Officers, Ala. Council Student Personnel Educators, Phi Delta Kappa, Omicron Delta Kappa. Home: 3488 Sheila Dr Birmingham AL 35216 Office: 1101 10th Ave S Birmingham AL 35294

BELCHER, DON WESLEY, assn. exec.; b. Old Hickory, Tenn., Aug. 23, 1938; s. W.C. and Nell (Wesley) B.; B.S. in Journalism, U. Tenn., 1960; m. Judith Hoeltje Johnston, Aug. 17, 1968; children—C. Allyn, Beverly Ellen. Dir. research Middle Tenn. Indsl. Devel. Assn. Inc., Nashville, 1964-68, Nashville Area C. of C., 1968—; mem. adv. bd. Sta. WDCN-TV, 1972-79. Mem. facilities planning com. YWCA Nashville, 1975; mem. Mayor's Council on Youth Opportunity, Nashville, 1969-73, chmn., 1972-73; mem. U. Sch. of Nashville, pub. relations com., 1975-76; pres. Mid Cumberland Council on Alcohol and Drug Abuse, 1976—; bd. dirs. Council of Community Services, 1977—, Nashville Panel; adv. bd. Tenn. State Abuse Counselor Cert. Com.; bd. dirs. Nashville Pro Musica, mem. chamber choir, 1972-73; bd. dirs. Nashville chpt. Amigos de las Americas; active community theatre, Nashville. Served with U.S. Army, 1961-64. Mem. Am. Mktg. Assn., Am. C. of C. Execs. (research council), Am. C. of C. Researchers Assn. (pres. 1973-74), Am. Statis. Assn., Middle Tenn. Health Careers Council. Home: Rt 1 Box 62 Pegram TN 37143 Office: 161 4th Ave North Nashville TN 37219

BELCHER, RODNEY LYNN, surgeon; b. Roanoke, Va., Nov. 2, 1931; s. Albert Lynn and Marguerite Gaynell (Tanner) B.; pre-med. student U. Notre Dame (Ind.), 1952; M.D., U. Miami (Fla.), 1956; M.S. in Orthopaedic Surgery, Mayo Clinic and Found., Rochester, Minn., 1963; m. Dawn Amelia Dayton, Jan. 2, 1953; children—Christopher Lynn, Mark Dayton. Intern Georgetown U. Service, D.C. Gen. Hosp., Washington, 1956-57; resident, orthopaedic surg. fellow Mayo Clinic, 1960-63, asst. to staff dept. orthopaedic surgery, 1963; practice medicine specializing in orthopaedic surgery, Arlington, Va., 1963—; mem. staffs Arlington, VA, Dr.'s, Georgetown U. hosps.; chmn. emergency room com. Arlington Community Hosp., 1965-70, 72-75, chief dept. orthopaedic surgery, 1975; aviation med. examiner FAA, 1972-80; hon. cons. surgery, orthopaedics, sr. lectr. surgery, orthopaedics U. Dar Es Salaam (Tanzania, East Africa), 1970-72; asst. clin. prof. orthopaedics, surgery Georgetown U., 1969-78. Served to lt., M.C., USNR, 1957-60. Diplomate Nat. Bd. Med. Examiners, Am. Bd. Orthopaedic Surgery. Fellow A.C.S., Am. Acad. Orthopaedic Surgeons; mem. Arlington Country (Va.) Med. Soc. (sec. 1975), Va. Orthopaedic Soc., Washington Orthopaedic Club, Am. Trauma Soc. (founding), Eastern Orthopaedic Assn. (charter), Am., Va. med. socs., Nat. Pilots Assn. (Safe Pilot award 1973), Exptl. Aircraft Assn., Sigma Xi. Bahai religion. Home: 2807 N Quebec St Arlington VA 22207 Office: 1029 N Stuart St Arlington VA 22201

BELCHER, WILLIAM ALVIS, rancher, veterinarian; b. Del Rio, Tex., Aug. 25, 1918; s. Clifton C. and Willie (Cochran) B.; D.V.M., Tex. A. and M. U., 1943; postgrad. Mich. State U., Colo. State U.; m. Hazel Arledge, Sept. 8, 1937; children—Willie Ellen Langham, Madge Elizabeth (Mrs. Jim Keys). Gen. practice vet. medicine, Crystal City, Tex., 1943-46; rancher, Brackettsville, Tex., 1946—; owner, operator Shirley Commn. Co.-Ft. Worth Stockyard 1956-59; area veterinarian Tex. Animal Health Commn., 1965—; 1st v.p. Del Rio Wool and Mohair Co., 1950—; chmn. bd. dirs. San Antonio br. Dallas Fed. Res. Bank. County chmn. Screw Worm Eradication Program, 1961—; veterinarian in charge Tex. Screw Worm Program; Mem. Am. Vet. Med. Assn., Tex. S.W. cattle raiser's assn., Tex. Sheep and Goat Raiser's Assn. (dir.), Tex. Angus Assn. (dir.). Address: PO Box 588 Bracketville TX 78832

BELEN, INES MILAGROS, psychologist, educator; b. Santurce, P.R., Aug. 27, 1945; 1 dau., Enrique Ludovico Belen Trujillo and Rosa Maria Espinosa; B.A. magna cum laude, U. P.R., 1967; M.A. with honors, Caribbean Center for Advanced Studies, 1975, Ph.D. with honors, 1977; postgrad. law sch. U. P.R., 1967-68; m. Miguel Angel Rivera Reta; children—Negroni, Mirca Joan, Alvarez Elizabeth Eunice. Clin. psychologist P.R. Dept. Social Service, San Juan, 1970-75, sch. psychologist, 1971-75; prof. psychology Interam. U., Hato Rey, P.R., 1975—; supr. grad. program Caribbean Center for Advanced Studies, Santurce, 1977-78; pvt. practice as clin. psychologist Hato Rey, 1970—; cons. in field. Mem. Am. Psychol. Assn., Am. Assn on Mental Deficiency, Asociacion pro Ciudadonos Retardadas.

BELFIGLIO, VALENTINE JOHN, educator; b. Troy, N.Y., May 28, 1934; s. Edmond Liberato and Mildred Elizabeth (Sherwood) B.; B.S., Union U., 1956; M.A., U. Okla., Norman, 1967, Ph.D., 1970; 1 son by previous marriage, Valentine Edmond. Grad. asst., instr. U. Okla., 1967-70; asso. prof. polit. sci. Tex. Woman's U., Denton, 1970—. Reviewer textbooks in internat. politics Holbrook Press, Boston, 1973-75. Served with USAF, 1959-67. Tex. Woman's U. Instl. Research grantee, 1973-74, 76-77; postdoctoral fellow Republic of South Africa, 1976; Nat. Endowment for Humanities grantee, 1978. Mem. Internat. Studies Assn. (sec.-treas. region 1974-76), Am. Polit. Sci. Assn., AAUP, MENSA, Kappa Psi. Democrat. Roman Catholic. Author: The United States and World Peace, 1971; American Foreign Policy, 1979. Contbr. numerous articles on internat. relations, Asian politics to profl. jours. Home: 2707 Douglas St Apt 107 Dallas TX 75219 Office: Box 23974 Tex Woman's U Denton TX 76204

BELGER, JOSEPH HUGH, ceramic engr.; b. Hemingway, S.C., Nov. 17, 1931; s. William Jake and Wista Willis (Haselden) B.; B.S., Clemson U., 1965; m. Dorothy Mc Millan, June 26, 1955; children—Joseph Hugh, Gregory Mc Millan, Stacey Elizabeth. Cartographer, machine design draftsman E. I. DuPont, Aiken, S.C., 1952-63; asst. plant mgr. Richtex Corp., Columbia, S.C., 1965-66, plant mgr., 1966-69, prodn. mgr., 1969-70; ceramic engr. Lingl Corp., Paris, Tenn., 1970—, v.p., 1971—; dir. Comml. Brick Corp., Wewoka, Okla. Mgr. Babe Ruth League Baseball, 1972, pres., 1973. Mem. Am. Ceramic Soc. (sec. 1970-71, vice-chmn. 1971-72, chmn. elect. 1972-73, chmn. structural clay products div. 1973-74, mem. com. nomenclature 1977—), Canadian Ceramic Soc. Baptist. Elk. Home: Anderson Dr Paris TN 38242 Office: PO Box 1059 Paris TN 38242

BELK, IRWIN, mcht., former state senator; b. Charlotte, N.C., April 4, 1922; s. William Henry and Mary Leonora (Irwin) B.; student Davidson Coll., U. N.C., 1946; m. Carol Grotnes, Sept. 11, 1948; children—William, Irene Belk Miltimore, Marilyn Bryan, Carl. Trained in mdse. field since childhood; chmn. bd. Monroe Hardware Co., Belk Enterprises, Inc.; v.p., dir. Belk Group of Stores, Charlotte; chmn. bd. P.M.C., Inc., Raleigh, N.C.; exec. v.p. finance Belk Stores Services, Inc., Charlotte; dir. First Union Nat. Bank, Stonecutter Mills, Spindale, N.C. Fidelity Bankers Life Ins. Co., Richmond, Va., Adams-Millis Corp., Lumbermen's Mut. Casualty Co. Chmn. bd. Belk Found. Mem. N.C. Ho. of Reps., 1959-60, 61-62; N.C. state senator, 1960-61, 63-66; mem. N.C. Legislative Council, 1963-64, Legislative Research Commn., 1965-66; del. Nat. Democratic Conv., 1956, 60, 64, 68, 72; Democratic nat. committeeman, 1969-72. Mem. finance com., trustee U. N.C., Charlotte; trustee, mem. finance com. Queens Coll.; dir. Bus. Found. N.C.; mem. ho. of dels., local dir. Am. Cancer Soc.; bd. dirs. N.C. Med. Adv. Council U. N.C.; past pres. Carolinas Carrousel; bd. dirs. Charlotte Opera Assn. (mem. finance bd.), Hist. Found. Presbyn. and Reformed Chs.; bd. assos. Mars Hill Coll., Campbell Coll.; bd. advisers Chowan Coll.; mem. adv. council Wingate Coll.; bd. govs. U. N.C., Chapel Hill; bd. assos. Meredith Coll.; bd. counselors Erskine Coll.; bd. dirs., past pres. N.C. Soc. Prevention Blindness; bd. dirs. Bus. Found. N.C., Ednl. Found., Inc. (both Chapel Hill); mem. bd. Wake Forest U. Sch. Bus. Served as sgt., 8th Air Force, World War II. Named One of 10 Outstanding Young Men in Charlotte, 1954, 55, 56, 57. Mem. N.C. Mchts. Assn. (past pres., state dir.), Charlotte C. of C. (dir.), Charlotte Mchts. Assn., Kappa Alpha, Delta Sigma Pi. Presbyn. (past deacon, elder; past pres. men's council Synod of N.C.). Mason (shriner), Lion (past dist. gov.). Clubs: Executives (dir., past pres.), Charlotte Country, Myers Park Country, Charlotte City (Charlotte); Raleigh City; Sky (N.Y.C.). Home: 2519 Richardson Dr Charlotte NC 28211 Office: 308 E 5th St Charlotte NC 28201

BELK, JOHN MONTGOMERY, dept. store exec.; b. Charlotte, N.C., Mar. 29, 1920; s. William Henry and Mary (Irwin) B.; B.S. in Econs., Davidson Coll., 1941; m. Claudia Watkins, Feb. 20, 1971. With Belk Stores Services, Inc., Charlotte, 1941—, pres., 1955—, also dir; dir. Wachovia Bank & Trust Co., Charlotte, Wachovia Corp., Winston-Salem, N.C., Integon Inc., Winston-Salem, So. Radio Corp., Charlotte, Coca-Cola Bottling Co. Consol., Charlotte, Assos. Corp. N.A. Mem. exec. bd. Southeast region Boy Scouts Am., 1958—, mem. nat. exec. bd.; mayor of Charlotte, 1969-77; chmn. bd. visitors Davidson Coll.; bd. dirs. Athletic Found. U. N.C., Charlotte, Research Triangle Found., Tom Haggai & Assos. Found., N.C. Sports Hall Fame, Mint Mus. Served to capt. AUS, 1943-45. Recipient Silver Beaver award Boy Scouts Am., 1955, Silver Antelope award, 1962, Distinguished Eagle Scout award, 1974. Mem. Charlotte C. of C. (pres. 1964, sr. bd. 1975—), Am. Mgmt. Assn. (past dir.), Nat. Retail Mchts. Assn. (chmn. 1974), World Bus. Council, Omicron Delta Kappa, Mason (Shriner). Home: 435 Hempstead Pl Charlotte NC 28207 Office: 308 E 5th St Charlotte NC 28234

BELKEN, DONALD CLYDE, ins. exec.; b. Aransas Pass, Tex., Aug. 11, 1932; s. Frank William and Doris Elizabeth (Vaughan) B.; student U. Corpus Christi, 1955-57; m. Susan Cullwell, Oct. 6, 1978; children—Donald F., Brian D., Randall L., Stephen A. Partner, mgr. Belken Ins. Agy., Aransas Pass, 1954-60; spl. agt. Traders and Gen. Ins. Co., San Antonio, 1960; br. mgr. Floyd West & Co., Crum & Forster Group, San Antonio, 1960-73; risk and ins. mgr. USAF Non-appropriated Funds, Randolph AFB, Tex., 1973-74; risk and ins. mgr. Farm & Home Savs. Assn., San Antonio, also exec. v.p. Consol. Agys. Tex., Inc., 1974—, also dir. Served to col. U.S. Army. Mem. Risk and Ins. Mgmt. Soc., Tex. Savs. and Loan League (co-chmn. ins. com.), Nat. Savs. and Loan League (ins. com.). Episcopalian. Home: 3501 Wellsprings Dr San Antonio TX 78230 Office: Farm Home Savs Assn 615 NW Loop 410 San Antonio TX 78216

BELL, BETTIE MARTIN, accountant; b. Atlanta, Nov. 20, 1930; d. Roy Lee and Etta Lee (Stell) Martin; student public schs., Fulton County, Ga.; m. Eddie Richard Bell, July 2, 1949 (dec.); children—Donna Victoria, Darrell Michael, Dale Marie. With 1st Nat. Bank Atlanta, 1947-51, Bank of Ga., 1953-55; mem. staff credit dept. Sears Roebuck & Co., Atlanta, 1952-53, Brown Mfg. Co., Atlanta, 1955-63; acctg. staff Atlanta Housing Authority and Urban Renewal, 1963-65, IRS, Chamblee, Ga., 1966-67; with Noble Inns Corp., Atlanta, 1965—, controller, 1976—. Mem. Ga. Assn. Hospitality Accts. (v.p., pres., chmn. bd.), Atlanta Tax Club, Am. Mgmt. Assn., Internat. Assn. Hospitality Accts.

BELL, BRYAN, real estate, oil investment exec., educator; b. New Orleans, Dec. 15, 1918; s. Bryan and Sarah (Perry) B.; B.A., Woodrow Wilson Sch. Pub. and Internat. Affairs, Princeton, 1941; M.A., Tulane U., 1962; m. Rubie S. Crosby, July 15, 1950; children—Rubie Perry, Helen Elizabeth, Bryan, Beverly Saunders, Barbara Crosby. Pres., Tasso Plantation Foods, Inc., New Orleans, 1945-66; partner 5 Bell Oil Cos., New Orleans, 1962—, also 12 apt. complexes, The Bell-Drumm Co., New Orleans, 1970—; pres. Bell & Assos., Inc., New Orleans, 1970—; dir. Royal St. Louis, Inc., Prentiss Creosote and Forest Products Inc., Sandy Hook Industries Inc., Creative Prodns. and Displays, Inc., Marine Concrete Structures, Inc. Instr. econs. of real estate devel. Sch. Architecture, Tulane U., New Orleans, 1967—. Mem. Garden Dist. Assn., 1964—; bd. dirs. United Fund for Greater New Orleans Area, 1964-71, pres., 1968-69; chmn. Human Talent Bank Com., New Orleans, 1969—. Mem. City Planning Commn., New Orleans, 1956-58; bd. dirs. Met. Area Com., 1968—, pres., 1975—; bd. dirs. Bur. Govtl. Research, 1966—, pres., 1971—; chmn. com. Met. Leadership Forum, 1969—; mem. bd. New Orleans Area Health Council, 1966-70. Bd. dirs. Tulane-Lyceum, 1947-51, Family Service Soc., 1951-58, pres., 1956-58; bd. dirs. St. Martin's Protestant Episcopal Sch., 1964-68, Metairie Park Country Day Sch., 1967-71; bd. dirs. Trinity Episcopal Sch., chmn., 1958-68; chmn. Trinity Christian Community, 1975—; bd. dirs. Christian Spirit of '76 Com., Fedn. Chs., 1975—, named Layman of Year, 1977. Served to 1st lt. AUS, World War II. Mem. New Orleans C. of C., Princeton Alumni Assn. La. (pres. 1962-63), Fgn. Relations Assn. Democrat. Episcopalian (vestry 1960—, jr. warden 1968-70, sr. warden 1970-72, sr. counsellor 1975—). Clubs: Internat. House, Boston, New Orleans Lawn Tennis, Wyvern, Lakeshore, Pickwick, Pendennis. Address: 1331 3d St New Orleans LA 70130

BELL, CAROLINE LEE SPEARS, ednl. counselor; b. Ft. Worth, Apr. 18, 1932; d. Wilbur R. and Elizabeth C. (Lewis) Spears; B.S., So. Meth. U., 1952, M.L.A., 1971; Ed.M., N. Tex. State U., 1972, postgrad. 1976—; children—Pamela Bell Morris, James Forrest Bell, Jack Leslie Bell, Patricia Lee Bell. Dental asst., bookkeeper to dentist, Dallas, 1955-69; tchr. Richardson Ind. Sch. Dist., Dallas, 1969-75, coordinating counselor, 1975-78, spl. services counselor, 1978—; admissions officer N. Tex. State U., 1972; intern Counseling Center, Eastfield Community Coll., summer, 1978. Girl scout leader Tejas council Girl Scouts U.S., 1960-80; instr. first aid ARC, 1964-80; Cub Scout den mother cons., 1962-67; music librarian for Ch. choir St. John's Episcopal Ch., 1966-69. Cert. tchr., Tex.; cert. counselor, Tex. Mem. Am. Personnel and Guidance Assn., Tex. Personnel and Guidance Assn., Tex. State Tchrs. Assn., Richardson Educators Assn., AAUW, Altrusa. Episcopalian. Clubs: Pearl Richie Art (social chmn. 1958-64, art award 1957, 67, 76, 78), Lake Highlands Band. Author: Curriculum Guide for Life Science. Home: 9715 Wisterwood Dr Dallas TX 75238 Office: 10301 Kingsley Rd Dallas TX 75238

BELL, CLARENCE ELMO, state senator Ark.; b. Camden, Ark., Feb. 1, 1912; s. Joseph Dudley and Dona (Massengale) B.; A.B., Ouachita Bapt. U., 1934; M.A., U. Ark., 1940; m. Hope Raney, Aug. 16, 1936; children—Joseph Dudley, Beverly (Mrs. William Kinneman), Barbara (Mrs. Richard Blaine). High sch. prin., coach, Parkin, Ark., 1935-39; coach, Marked Tree, Ark., 1939-40; supt. schs., Parkin, 1941-63; with Ark. La. Gas Co., Little Rock, 1963—, dir., 1972—. Named Layman of Yr. in Edn., Ark., 1972; Conservationist of Yr., Ark., 1966. Rotarian. Home: 26 Church St Parkin AR 72373

BELL, DAVID PAIGE, hosp. adminstr.; b. Gallipolis, Ohio, June 7, 1944; s. Hollie Paige and Hortense Pearl (Hogue) B.; B.S., W. Va., U., 1968; M.B.A., W. Va. Coll. Grad. Studies, 1973; Ph.D., Ohio U., 1979; m. Roberta Ann Steel, June 10, 1967; 1 dau., Robin Ann. Pharmacist, Rogers Pharmacy, Morgantown, W. Va., 1965-69; mgr. Cohen Drug Stores, Charlestown, W. Va., 1969-72; dir. pharmacy service, Camden Clark Hosp., Parkersburg, W. Va., 1972-78, dir. human resources, 1978—; faculty Parkersburg Community Coll.; cons. in field. Mem. W. Va. Adv. Com. Pharmacy Consultants. Named W.Va. Hosp. Pharmacist of Year, 1977. Mem. W. Va. Soc. Hosp. Pharmacists (pres. 1977—), Am. Pharmacists Assn., Am. Soc. Hosp. Pharmacists, Am. Soc. Personnel Adminstrs., Am. Soc. Hosp. Personnel Adminstrs., Am. Coll. Hosp. Adminstrs., Res. Officers Assn., Am. Mgmt. Assn., Phi Delta Kappa, Phi Kappa Phi, Delta Sigma Rho, Phi Kappa Sigma. Club: Elks. Home: 4500 10th Ave Vienna WV 26105 Office: Camden Clark Hosp 800 Garfield Ave Parkersburg WV 26101

BELL, DOROTHY LOVETT, mental health adminstr.; b. Selma, Ala., Nov. 24, 1935; d. George H. and Susena V. Lovett; B.S., Ala. State Coll., 1957; M.A., U. Ala., 1973; postgrad. U. Ala., 1979—; m. Curtis Leon Bell, Sept. 5, 1960; 1 dau., Stephanie Jeaneane. Clk., U.S. Air Force, Brookley AFB, Ala., 1959-62; tchr. Mobile County (Ala.) Sch. System, 1962-72; tng. coordinator children's services Mobile Mental Health Center (Ala.), 1972-75, supr./coordinator transitional services, 1976-79; counselor pvt. practice, sch. cons. mental health, 1973-76. Sec. exec. bd. dirs. Opportunities Industrialization Center, Mobile, 1976—. Cert. tchr., Ala. Mem. Am. Personnel and Guidance Assn., Ala. Personnel and Guidance Assn., Mobile County Personnel and Guidance Assn., Am. Rehab. Counseling Assn., Assn. for Non-White Concerns in Personnel and Guidance. Democrat. Baptist. Office: Mobile Mental Health Center 1004 S Ann St Mobile AL 36605

BELL, EDWARD THOMAS, mfg. co. exec.; b. Metropolis, Ill., Mar. 1, 1942; s. Leonard Thomas and Violet A. (Robinson) B.; grad. Louisville Tab and Computer Coll., 1968; m. Sandra Kay Weaks, Dec. 11, 1965; 1 son, Edward Thomas. Marketing rep. Honeywell, Nashville, 1972-75, sr. marketing rep., 1975-76, br. sales mgr., 1977, br. marketing mgr., 1977—; instr. data processing Shawnee Coll. (Karnak, Ill.). Active Big Bros. Am. Served with AUS, 1960-68. Named salesman of year Honeywell So. Region, 1976. Mem. Data Processing Mgmt. Assn. Methodist. Clubs: Maumell Golf and Country, Masons, Elks. Home: 1414 Stonehenge Pl Little Rock AR 72204 Office: 6701 W 12th St Little Rock AR 72204

BELL, ESTHER BERNICE, occupational therapist; b. Los Angeles, June 1, 1930; d. Clifford and Esther Midlred (Haug) Bell; B.S., U. Calif. at Los Angeles, 1951; certificate occupational therapy U. So. Calif., 1954; M.A., Tex. Woman's U., 1971. Staff therapist Tex. Rehab. Hosp., Gonzales, 1954-62, dir. occupational therapy, 1962—. Chmn. clin. council Tex. Woman's U., 1964-78; mem. adv. com., occupational therapy asst. program St. Phillips Coll., San Antonio, 1973-77. Fellow Am. Occupational Therapy Assn. (sec. 1978—); mem. Tex. Occupational Therapy Assn. (del. 1971-77, v.p. 1977-79), Tex. Occupational Therapist of Year 1971), Tex. Rehab. Assn., Beta Sigma Phi. Home: 203 McClure St Gonzales TX 78629 Office: Box 58 Gonzales TX 78629

BELL, FRANCIS LANEY, textile exec.; b. Lancaster, S.C., May 20, 1917; s. John Ulysse and Mayme (Gregory) B.; B.S., Clemson U., 1938; student exec. program U. N.C., 1961-62; m. Mary Alice Jones, Jan. 12, 1942; children—Francis Laney, Ira Jones. Instr. chemistry Clemson U., 1938-39; with Springs Mills, Inc., Ft. Mill, S.C., 1939—, now v.p. personnel adminstrn.; dir. Leroy Springs & Co., Inc. Chmn. S.C. Bd. Tech. and Comprehensive Edn. Served to capt. USAAF, 1941-46. Mem. S.C. C. of C. (dir.), Am. Legion, Scabbard and Blade, 40 and 8, Blue Key, Sigma Tau Epsilon. Mem. Asso. Ref. Presbyterian Ch. Moose. Home: 614 W Barr St Lancaster SC 29720 Office: Springs Mills Inc White St Fort Mill SC 29715

BELL, HATTIE MAE, educator; b. Guadalupe County, Tex.; d. Julius and Hedwig (Stolte) Stahl; B.S. in Elementary Edn., S.W. Tex. State U., San Marcos, 1938, M.A. in Spl. Edn., 1950; m. Thomas E. Bell, 1977. Tchr. phys. edn., volleyball coach Harlandale Ind. Sch. Dist., San Antonio, 1943-70, dir. spl. edn., 1970—. Mem. community advisers council Trinity U., 1974—; mem. adv. council, region XX, Ednl. Service Center, 1974—. Mem. NEA, Tex. State Tchrs. Assn., Council for Exceptional Children, Assn. for Retarded Citizens. Pi Gamma Mu, Delta Psi Kappa. Named one of Ten Outstanding Women, San Antonio Express and New Pub. Co., 1972. Certified prin., supt., Tex. Home: Route 4 Box 132 Sequin TX 78155 Office: 902 March Ave San Antonio TX 78214

BELL, HENRY M., JR., banker; b. Jan. 23, 1928; s. Henry B.; student The Citadel, 1944-46; B.S., Yale U., 1948; m. Nell Allen; children—Henry M., John Allen. Pres., chmn. bd. Citizens First Nat. Bank of Tyler (Tex.). Mem. adv. bd. Mother Frances Hosp.; vestryman Christ Episcopal Ch., Tyler, also sr. warden; bd. dirs. United Way Greater Tyler, Tyler Indsl. Found.; bd. dirs., mem. exec. com. Tex. Eastern U. Ednl. Found.; bd. dirs. Tyler YMCA, Tyler United Fund, East Tex. Symphony Assn., Tex. Rose Festival Assn.; chmn. bd. Smith County ARC; trustee Tex. Chest Found.; trustee, chmn. Tchr. Retirement System Tex. Served with U.S. Army. Named Tyler's Outstanding Citizen; recipient T.B. Butler award, 1971. Mem. Tyler C. of C. (dir.), Robert Morris Associates, Tyler Petroleum Club (dir.). Clubs: Rotary (pres.), Masons. Office: PO Box 2020 100 E Ferguson St Tyler TX 75701

BELL, J. THOMAS, JR., anatomist, educator; b. Columbus, Ga., Aug. 30, 1926; s. J. Thomas and Mary Nell (Neal) B.; D.V.M., U. Ga., 1952; Ph.D., U. Minn., 1956; children—Tom, Elizabeth, Ansley. Asst. prof. anatomy Iowa State U., 1956-59; asso. prof. Mich. State U., 1959-62; prof., head dept. anatomy U. Ga., 1962-74; dean Sch. Vet. Medicine Ahmadu Bello U., Nigeria, 1974-77; prof. anatomy, dir. scis. basic to medicine Miss. State U., 1977—. Served with USNR, 1943-46. Mem. Am. Assn. Vet. Anatomists, AVMA, Internat. Assn. Aquatic Animal Medicine, Conf. Research Workers in Animal Diseases in N.Am., Miss. Vet. Med. Assn. Republican. Episcopalian. Club: Kiwanis. Contbr. articles to profl. jours. Home: 515 Spruce Ln Starkville MS 39759 Office: Drawer V Miss State U Mississippi State MS 39762

BELL, JAMES BRUCE, profl. photographer; b. Pelzer, S.C., Sept. 8, 1909; s. James Bert and Ellie Dee (Bruce) B.; student Am. Sch. Photography, 1936, Windna Sch. Photography, 1959; m. Eva Louise Matheson, Oct. 8, 1933; children—Harold Bruce, James Milton. Reporter, photographer Greenville (S.C.) News, 1951; owner, pres., photographer Bell Studio, Seneca, S.C., 1940;. Charter mem. Oconee County (S.C.) Planning Commn., 1954. Mem. Profl. Photographers Am., S.C., Southeastern profl. photographers assns., Oconee County Hist. and Recreational Soc., Oconee County (S.C.) Apple Festival Assn., Nat. Assn. Watch and Clock Collectors, Foothills Antique Club. Oconee Community Theatre. Baptist. Contbr. photographic works to books, newspapers, mags. Home: 110 S 2d St Seneca SC 29678 Office: 105 N Fairplay St Seneca SC 29678

BELL, JAMES CARLTON, aero-mech. engr., aerospace mfg. co. exec.; b. Jefferson, Pa., Sept. 12, 1933; s. James Carlton and Geraldine Lora (Pryor) B.; B.S. in Engring. Sci., Cleve. State U., 1957; m. Roberta K. Keller, Sept. 10, 1955; children—Robert J., Gary L., Ronald K., Lora J. Research and devel. engr. in aero-mech. programs Goodyear Aerospace Corp., Akron, Ohio, 1957-60, project engr., 1960-68, engring. group leader of electromech. antenna systems, 1964-70, program mgr. electromagnetic pulse simulator systems, 1968-72, engring. rep., 1971-72; asst. chief engr. seal systems devel. Bell Aerospace Co., New Orleans, 1972-73, chief engr., 1973—. Mgr. div. United Fund Campaign, 1969-70. Recipient Top Producer Campaign award YMCA, 1971, 72. Mem. AIAA (nat. tech. com.), Soc. Naval Architects and Marine Engrs., Lighter Than Air Soc. Methodist. Contbr. articles on various structural design systems to tech. jours. Patentee in field. Home: 3710 Rue Michelle New Orleans LA 70114 Office: 13800 Gentilly Rd New Orleans LA 70189

BELL, JOANNE IRENE, educator; b. Huntington, Pa., Aug. 1, 1928; d. George C. and Alma (Love) Bell; B.A., Juanita Coll., Huntington, 1949; M.S.W., U. Pa., 1954; postgrad. U. Md., 1967-70. Social worker, acting dir. Child Welfare Service, Lewistown, Md., 1949-52; supr. Balt. Dept. Social Services, 1954-61; div. dupr. San Francisco Dept. Social Services, 1961-66; instr. social welfare extension U. Calif., Berkeley, 1961-66; specialist HEW, Washington, 1966-67; asso. prof. social work U. Ky., Lexington, 1970-77, asso. prof., 1977—; cons. in field; chmn. Exceptional Children Adv. Com., 1972-75; adv. bd. Bluegrass Employment and Tng. Program, 1976; adv. bd. GROW, mem. Children's Services Com., 1960, Regional Crime Commn. Juvenile Delinquency, 1975-76. Fellow Pa. Dept. Social Welfare, 1952-53, U.S. Children's Bur., 1967-69; grantee Ky. Research Found., 1976. Mem. Council Social Work Edn., Nat. Assn. Social Work, AAUP. Roman Cath. Author in field. Home: Shalcey Farm Route 1 Box 94 Wilmore KY 40390 Office: 629 Patterson Office Tower U Ky Lexington KY 40506

BELL, LINDA CLEGHORN, nurse; b. LaFayette, Ga., July 17, 1942; d. James Roy and Katie Louise (Atkins) Cleghorn; R.N., Ga. Bapt. Hosp., Atlanta, 1963; student Cadek Conservatory Music, Chattanooga, 1964-65; m. Fred A. Bell, Jan. 2, 1976; children—John David, William Zachary; 1 stepdau., Angela Renee. Dir. nursing Kitchen Hosp., LaFayette, Ga., 1963-67; staff nurse operating rm. Hutcheson Meml. Hosp., Ft. Oglethorpe, Ga., 1967-71, pediatric unit supr., 1972-74, operating rm. supr., 1974-78, dir. dept. operating rm. nursing, 1978—. Tchr., cons. Girl Scouts U.S.A.; mem. Chattanooga Opera, 1964-67; mem. allocations com. Chattanooga Area United Fund, 1979-80. Mem. Assn. Operating Rm. Nurses, Southeastern Surg. Nurses Assn. Democrat. Baptist. Home: Rt 1 Box 254 Rockspring GA 30739 Office: 100 Gross Crescent Fort Oglethorpe GA 30742

BELL, LUCILLE LOWERY, nurse-anesthetist; b. Jacksonville, Fla., Apr. 6, 1924; d. Benjamin and Mary Lowery; student Edward Waters Coll., 1939-41; diploma Brewster Hosp. Sch. Nursing, 1942; grad. anesthesia Cook County Hosp., 1947. Sec., treas. Fed. Duval Enterprises, Inc., Jacksonville, 1957; founder Nightengale Home Nursing Care Class, Inc., Jacksonville, 1975; nurse, counselor Greater Jacksonville Econ. Opportunity Program. Bd. dirs., trustee Mt. Ararat Convalescent Home; bd. dirs. YWCA, Jacksonville. Certified in psychiat. nursing Fla. Bd. Health; recipient Distinguished Service citation Fla. div. Am. Cancer Soc., 1966. Mem. Am. Nurses Assn., LWV, Chi Eta Phi (charter). Baptist.

BELL, LUCY BUTLER, psychologist, educator; b. Rutherford County, Tenn., Sept. 23, 1947; d. William Harden and Mattie Raybon Butler; B.A., Fisk U., 1969; M.A., George Peabody Tchrs. Coll., 1972; m. Donald T. Bell, June 10, 1978. Instr. dept. psychology and edn. Daytona Beach (Fla.) Community Coll., 1972—, chmn. dept. behavioral scis., 1977—. Mem. Fla. Assn. Jr. and Community Colls., Assn. Human Potential Seminar Trainers and Leaders, AAUP, Am. Assn. Women in Jr. and Community Colls., Assn. Chmn. of Heads of Psychology Depts. Democrat. Methodist. Office: PO Box 1111 Daytona Beach FL 32015

BELL, MERTYS WARD (MRS. THOMAS EDWARD BELL), coll. dean; b. Arlington, Ga., July 13, 1917; d. Richard Christopher and Carol Odessa (Clements) Ward; A.B., Ga. Coll., 1937; B.L.S., U. N.C., 1942, postgrad., 1966; m. Thomas Edward Bell, Dec. 12, 1942; children—John Bruce, Lisa Ann. Librarian, Douglas (Ga.) Public Schs., 1937-40; dist. library supr. WPA Ga., Savannah, 1940-42; dir. Athens (Ga.) Regional Library, Athens, 1942-43; br. library supr. King County Public Library, Seattle, 1943-46; cataloger Greensboro (N.C.) Public Schs., 1955-60; librarian Guilford Tech. Inst., Jamestown, N.C., 1963-66, dir. learning resources, 1969-72, dean learning resources, 1972—; librarian Rockingham Community Coll., Wentworth, 1966-68; acquisitions librarian U. N.C., Greensboro, 1968-69; sec.-treas. T.E. Bell Constrn. Co., Inc., 1972—; mem. vis. teams So. Assn. Colls. and Schs., 1968—. Mem. adv. council Guilford County Bicentennial Commn., 1975—; chmn. GTI Bicentennial Com., 1975—; pres. Learning Resources Assn., N.C. Community Coll., 1967-68. Mem. NEA, N.C. Assn. Educators, Community Coll. Assn. Instruction and Tech., ALA, N.C. (sec.-treas. jr. coll. sect. 1973-75, v.p., pres. elect 1979—), Southeastern library assns., Guilford County Geneal. Soc. (rec. sec. 1975-76), Delta Kappa Gamma, Historic Jamestown Soc.; Phi Rho Pi, Pi Gamma Mu, Delta Kappa Gamma. Presbyterian (ruling elder). Club: Guilford Library (pres. 1973-74 Greensboro). Home: 5608 Scotland Rd Greensboro NC 27407 Office: PO Box 309 Jamestown NC 27282

BELL, PAUL BUCKNER, lawyer; b. Charlotte, N.C., July 29, 1922; s. George Fisher and Carrie (Savage) B.; B.S., Wake Forest U., 1947, J.D. cum laude, 1948; m. Betty Sue Trulock, May 3, 1952; children—Paul B., Morris Trulock, Betty Fisher, Douglas Savage. Admitted to N.C. bar, 1948; patent atty.; pres. firm Bell, Seltzer, Park & Gibson, Charlotte, 1948—. Dir. Pilot Research Corp., Southland Investors, Inc., Idlewild Farms, Inc., Charpat Investment Corp.; lectr. Practising Law Inst., 1974; guest lectr. patent law Wake Forest U. Sch. Law, 1974-80. Trustee, Mecklenburg Presbytery, Alexander Children's Center, Presbyn. Home of Charlotte, Mountain Retreat Assn.; v.p. The Presbyn. Found. Served as 1st lt. USAAF, 1943-46. Mem. Am., N.C., Mecklenburg bar assns., Am. Patent Law Assn., Licensing Execs. Soc., Sigma Phi Epsilon, Phi Alpha Delta. Presbyterian (elder). Clubs: Charlotte City, Charlotte Country, Charlotte Textile (past pres.), Grandfather Golf and Country; Union League (N.Y.C.). Home: 4001 Foxcroft Rd Charlotte NC 28211 Office: 1211 E Morehead St PO Box 10337 Charlotte NC 28237

BELL, ROBERTA JOYCE, credit union exec.; b. San Antonio, Tex., Dec. 8, 1939; d. Robert A. and Margaret J. (Collins) Smith; student Del Mar Coll., 1956-57, U. Houston, 1977-79; m. Richard D. Bell, Mar. 9, 1957; children—Richard D., Margaret A., Patrick S. Owner, operator Bell's Telephone Ser., Falfurrias, Tex., 1961-66; with Fluor Credit Union, Houston, 1969—, treas., mgr., 1977—, also dir. Mem. Credit Union Women Mgrs. Assn. Democrat. Roman Catholic. Club: Fluor Public Affairs (sec. 1978-79). Home: 6235 Lymbar St Houston TX 77096 Office: 4620 N Braeswood St Houston TX 77096

BELL, STEPHEN SCOTT, elec. engr., meter co. exec.; b. Oshkosh, Wis., Feb. 22, 1938; s. Edwin Paul and Dorothy Comfort (Partridge) B.; B.S. in Elec. Engring., U. Wis., Madison, 1964, M.S. in Elec. Engring., 1965, Ph.D., 1969; m. Carolyn Upham Sawyer, Sept. 11, 1959; children—Catherine Lee, Jeffrey Arthur. Instr. elec. engring. U. Wis., Madison, 1965-69; asst. prof. Coll. Applied Sci. and Engring., U. Wis., Milw., 1969-71; research engr. Badger Meter Inc., Milw., 1971-73, prin. engr. Precision Products div., Tulsa, 1973-75, supr. research engring., 1975-79, mgr. engring., 1979—. Served with USMC, 1957-60. Recipient Disting. Instr. awards U. Wis. chpt. Eta Kappa Nu and Polygon Bd., 1969; registered profl. engr., Wis. Mem. IEEE, AAAS, Sigma Xi, Eta Kappa Nu. Republican. Home: 3648 S Florence Pl Tulsa OK 74105 Office: Precision Products div Badger Meter Inc 6116 E 15th St Tulsa OK 74112

BELL, WAYNE HARVEY, sem. adminstr.; b. Dayton, Wash., June 9, 1919; s. Harry Leach and Inez Fay (Fortune) B.; A.B., Transylvania U., 1940, D.D. (hon.), 1957; B.D., Lexington Theol. Sem., 1943; m. Virginia Marsh, June 10, 1944; children—Brenda, Marsha, David, Laura, Kendall. Ordained to ministry Disciples of Christ Ch., 1940; minister 1st Christian Ch., Shelbyville, Ky., 1942-51, 7th St. Christian Ch., Richmond, Va., 1951-60, Vine St. Christian Ch., Nashville, 1960-74; pres. Lexington Theol. Sem., 1974—; bd. dirs. div. higher edn. Christian Ch., Disciples of Christ; mem. gen. bd. Christian Ch., bd. dirs. ch. fin. council. Mem. Council on Christian Unity (bd. dirs.).

Club: Rotary. Home: 220 Clinton Rd Lexington KY 40502 Office: 631 S Limestone Lexington KY 40508

BELL, WILLIAM ARTHUR, JR., chem. technologist; b. Knox County, Tenn., Nov. 24, 1916; s. William Arthur and Nola Mildred (Hibbs) B.; B.A., Maryville Coll., 1940; postgrad. U. Tenn., 1941-42; USN electronics officer trainee Princeton U., 1944, M.I.T., 1945; m. Anna Leece Williams, July 14, 1942; children—William Kenneth, Karen Kay. Teaching fellow U. Tenn., 1940-41; insp. FDA, Biloxi, Miss., 1941-42; insp., analyst Fed. Security Agy., New Orleans and St. Louis, 1946-47; with Union Carbide Corp. at Oak Ridge Nat. Lab., 1947—, ops. engr., 1947-75, devel. group leader isotopes sect., chem. tech. div., 1975—; U.S. participant Atomic Energy Research Establishment, Harwell, Eng., 1961. Served with USNR, 1942-46. Mem. Sigma Xi. Contbr. articles to profl. jours.; patentee isotope separation by electromagnetic process. Home: 112 Fulton Ln Oak Ridge TN 37830 Office: PO Box X 9204-3 Oak Ridge Nat Lab Oak Ridge TN 37830

BELL, WILLIAM JACK, educator; b. nr. Norcatur, Kans., Nov. 1, 1915; s. James S. and Ruth (Diefendorf) B.; B.A., B.S., Emporia Kans. State Tchrs. Coll., 1937, M.S, 1940; Ph. D., U. Mo., 1949; m. Marjorie May Andrews, May 9, 1942. Tchr. high sch., Colby, Kan., 1937-42; reporter-editor Colby Free Press-Tribune, 1937-42; grad. asst., instr. U. Mo. Sch. Journalism, 1946-49; asst. prof. U. Okla. Sch. Journalism, 1949-51; photographer Daily Oklahoman, Oklahoma City, summer 1951; prof. journalism, head journalism and graphic arts dept. East Tex. State U., Commerce, 1951—. City commr., Commerce, 1960-64, mayor pro-tem, 1964-66, 74—, mayor, 1967-70; chmn. Airport Adv. Bd., 1971-74. Bd. dirs. Sulphur River Municipal Water Dist., 1971-72. Mem. exec. com. NetSeO Trails council Boy Scouts Am., 1953-57. Served with USNR, 1942-45. Mem. Am. Soc. Journalism Sch. Adminstrs., Sports Information Dirs. (coordinator 68—; nat. pres. 1965-67) Nat. Assn. Intercollegiate Athletics (Hall of Fame 1970), C. of C. (dir. 1955-57, 59-62; 69-72), Tex. Journalism Edn. Council (exec. com. 1972-73), Phi Delta Kappa (historian 1957-69), Sigma Delta Chi. Lion (pres. 1959-60, dep. dist. gov. 1962-64). Home: 2500 Washington St Commerce TX 75428

BELL, WILLIAM WOODWARD, lawyer; b. Brownwood, Tex., May 15, 1938; s. Charles Smith and Jane Mae (Woodward) B.; B.B.A., Baylor U., 1960, J.D., 1965; m. Mary Elizabeth Beniteau, May 31, 1969; children—Susan Elizabeth, Carol Ann. Admitted to Tex. bar, 1965; partner firm Sleeper, Boynton, Burleson, Williams & Johnston, Waco, 1965-68, Holloway, Slagle & Bell, Brownwood, 1969-72, Johnson, Slagle & Bell, Brownwood, 1972-74; mcpl. judge City of Brownwood, 1968-80, city atty., 1980—; v.p. Bell Mortgage & Investment Co., Brownwood, 1962—; sec., dir. Mould-N-Mount, Inc., Brownwood. Chmn., Brownwood chpt. ARC, 1972-74, bd. dirs., 1972—; bd. dirs. Brownwood Indsl. Found., 1972-75, Brown County Water Improvement Dist., 1974—, Brown County Humane Soc., 1975—, Mental Health Mentally Retarded Workshop. Served as capt. USMCR, 1960-63. Mem. Am., Tex., Brown County bar assns., Am. Judicature Soc., Assn. Trial Lawyers Am., Brownwood C. of C. (dir. 1971-74), Phi Alpha Delta. Rotarian. Club: Knife and Fork (pres. 1973). Home: Old Lake Rd Brownwood TX 76801 Office: 109 N Fisk St Brownwood TX 76801

BELLAMY, DONALD GENE, JR., civil engr.; b. Chgo., Feb. 28, 1950; s. Donald Gene and Irene Margaret Mary (Van Pelt) B.; A.A., Edison Jr. Coll., 1971; B.S. in Engring., Fla. Technol. U., 1973; m. Sharon Lee Slonecker, Aug. 28, 1976. Civil engr. Bruce Green & Assos., Inc., Naples, Fla., 1973-78; partner Eagle Engring. & Testing, Inc., Marco Island, Fla., 1978-79; pres. Bellamy Engrs., Inc., Naples, Fla., 1979—. Registered profl. engr., Fla.; cert. gen. contractor, Fla. Mem. ASCE (founding sec. S.W. br. South Fla. sect. 1976-77, pres. 1978-79), Fla. Engring. Soc. (chmn. chpt. scholarship com. 1974-75), Nat. Soc. Profl. Engrs., Water Pollution Control Fedn., Kappa Sigma. Office: 852 1st Ave S Suite 101 Naples FL 33940

BELLAMY, JEANNE (MRS. JOHN TURNER BILLS), journalist, banker; b. Bklyn., Nov. 15, 1911; d. Donald Lamont and Ethel Park (Houston) Bellamy; student Barnard Coll., 1928-29; A.B., Rollins Coll., 1933; Ph.D. (hon.), Biscayne Coll., 1975; m. John Turner Bills, Jan. 30, 1942. Reporter, Miami (Fla.) Tribune, 1935-37; staff writer Miami Herald, 1937-58; sr. editorial writer, 1958-73; chmn. bd. Sun Bank Midtown, Miami; 1973-77; dir. Sun Bank of Miami, 1977—; commentator Sta. WGBS, 1962-63; moderator We Want to Know, Sta. WLBW-TV, 1961-63. Mem. Miami-Dade Water and Sewer Authority, 1975-80; mem. governing bd. So. Fla. Water Mgmt. Dist., 1979—; bd. dirs. Nat. Audubon Soc., 1963-71; trustee Biscayne Coll., Rollins Coll.; vestryman St. Stephen's Ch., 1975-78; trustee Fairchild Tropical Garden, Coral Gables, 1961—, pres., 1977—. Recipient ann. awards Fla. Bar, 1959, 62, Jose Marti Journalism award, 1966. Mem. Fla. Soc. Editors (pres. 1962), Hist. Assn. So. Fla., Greater Miami Opera Assn., Vizcayans, Women in Communications, Greater Miami C. of C. (pres. 1977-78), Kappa Alpha Theta. Episcopalian. Author: Taming the Everglades, 1947; Newspapers of America's Last Frontier, 1952; Communism: What It Means to You, 1961. Home: 2718 Segovia St Coral Gables FL 33134 Office: 1428 Brickell Ave Miami FL 33101

BELLE, JOSEPH VINCENT, environ. engr.; b. Medford, Mass., Apr. 14, 1920; s. John Dennis and Elena Frances (Lo Sciuto) B.; B.S. in Civil Engring. cum laude, Tufts U., 1943; m. Grace Marie Rando, Oct. 23, 1949; children—Joseph Michael, Margaret Elaine, Christine Ann. Engr., Bur. Aeronautics, Bur. Naval Weapons, Navy Dept., Washington, 1946-63, civil engr. Bur. Yards and Docks, Naval Facilities Engring. Command, 1963-73; environmental engr. ManTech of N.J. Corp., Washington, 1973-78, PA Engring., Corte Madera, Calif., 1978—; officer, dir. King Charles Apts., Ltd. Vice pres. Annandale Terrace Civic Assn., 1966. Served to lt. USNR, 1943-46. Registered profl. engr., Mass. Mem. Soc. Am. Mil. Engrs., Nat. Assn. Ret. Fed. Employees, Am. Concrete Inst. (hon.), Tau Beta Pi. Democrat. Roman Catholic. Club: K.C. Author govtl. publs. Home: 7452 Madeira Pl Annandale VA 22003 Office: 7452 Madeira Pl Annandale VA 22003

BELLINGHAUSEN, JAMES MICHAEL, ednl. adminstr.; b. Ponca City, Okla., Aug. 19, 1930; s. Louis Leonard and Martha Susan (Schiltz) B.; B.S., Okla. State U., 1956; M.A., St. Mary's U., San Antonio, 1974; m. Betty Ann Maher, Sept. 3, 1955; children—Mike, Karen, Danette, Tom, Linda, Lisa, Jeff, Katie, Terry. Auditor, Air Force Gen.'s Office, Ft. Worth, 1956-57; systems analyst IBM, Austin, Tex., 1957-60; mgmt. cons. Ernst & Ernst, San Antonio, 1960-64; asst. v.p. Nat. Bank of Commerce, San Antonio, 1964-68; v.p. for adminstrn. San Antonio Community Coll. Dist., 1968—; v.p. adminstrv. council Tex. State Coll. and Univ. Employees Uniform Ins. Act. Pres. home and sch. orgn., chmn. bd. edn. St. Pius X. Parochial Sch., San Antonio. Cert. in data processing Inst. Cert. Computer Profls. Mem. Nat. Office Mgrs. Assn. (treas. 1962-64), Nat. Assn. Accts. (dir., pres. 1966-67), Data Processing Mgmt. Assn. (dir., pres. 1968-69, internat. dir.), Tex. Assn. Ednl. Data Systems (past state dir.), San Antonio Bus. and Econ. Soc. Roman Catholic. Clubs: Rotary (San Antonio); Kiwanis, K.C. Home: 9715 Lantana St San Antonio TX 78217 Office: San Antonio Community Coll Dist 1300 San Pedro Ave San Antonio TX 78284

BELLMON, HENRY, U.S. senator; b. Tonkawa, Okla., Sept. 3, 1921; s. George and Edith (Caskey) B.; B.S. in Agr., Okla. State U., Stillwater, 1942; m. Shirley Osborn, Jan. 24, 1947; children—Patricia, Gail, Ann. Engaged in farming, Billings, Okla., 1946—; mem. Okla. Ho. of Reps. from Noble County, 1946-48; gov. State of Okla., 1962-66; mem. U.S. Senate from Okla., 1968—; past chmn. Interstate Oil Compact Commn.; past mem. exec. com. Nat. Gov.'s Conf. Chmn. Okla. Republican Com., 1960-62; past nat. chmn. Nixon-for-Pres. Com. Served with USMCR, 1942-46. Presbyterian. Home: Route 1 Red Rock OK 74651 Office: 125 Russell House Office Bldg Washington DC 20510

BELLOISE, JOSEPH, JR., engring. co. exec.; b. Bronx, N.Y., Oct. 6, 1942; s. Joseph and Phyllis Belloise; A.S. in Graphic Art Sci. Tech., Miami-Dade (Fla.) Community Coll., 1971, A.S. in Mktg. Mgmt., 1978; m. Joyce Ann Brower, Aug. 31, 1974; children—Mary, Danean, Christine. With Ryder Truck Rental Co., 1965-70; mgr. printing Printech Corp., 1970-71; dir. sales Acad. Lithographers, 1971-72; mgr. printing sers. Systems Engring. Lab., Ft. Lauderdale, Fla., 1972—; adv. bd. graphic art sci. Miami Dade Community Coll. Served with USAR, 1961-64. Mem. Inplant Printing Mgmt. Assn. (pres. S. Fla. chpt. 1978-80 regional v.p. 1980-82). Baptist. Author articles in field. Home: 2160 N 56th Terr Hollywood FL 33021 Office: 1700 NW 66th Ave Plantation FL 33313

BELLOS, JACK FRANK, dentist; b. San Antonio, Agu. 20, 1939; s. Photios Peter and Aphrodite (Varessis) B.; B.S., U. Tex. at Austin, 1962; D.D.S., U. Tex. at Houston, 1969; m. Mary Jane Beck, July 26, 1969; children—Gregory, Matthew, Amanda. Pharmacist, Sommers Drug Stores, San Antonio, 1962-63, Univ. Drug Store, San Antonio, 1963-65, practicing dentist, San Antonio, 1969—. Mem. ADA, Tex. Dental Assn., San Antonio Dist. Dental Soc., Psi Omega, Kappa Psi. Mem. Greek Orthodox Ch. Club: Order DeMolay. Home: 415 Rockhill St San Antonio TX 78209 Office: 7411 Broadway PO Box 6574 San Antonio TX 78209

BELLUS, DAN EDWARD, mgmt. sales mgmt.-motivation, personnel evaluation cons.; b. Williams, Calif., Oct. 11, 1920; s. Theron Forrest and Bessie Merle (Garst) B.; student Ottawa U., 1940-43, S.E. Mo. State Coll., 1943; m. M. Maurine Graper, Feb. 27, 1944; children—Robert Edward, Barbara Annette. Account exec. Sta. KFBC, Cheyenne, Wyo., 1946, Sta. KLO, Ogden, Utah, 1946-48; sales mgr. Sta. KXXX, Colby, Kans., 1948-49; gen. mgr. Sta. KNEX, Mc Pherson, Kans., 1949-50; sales mgr., asst. mgr. Nebr. Rural Radio Co., Lexington and Omaha, 1950-53; account exec. Sta. KFEQ-TV, St. Joseph, Mo., 1953-55; dir. sales devel., advt. and pub. relations Marietta Broadcasting Co., San Diego and Bakersfield, Calif. 1955-60; corporate dir. advt. promotion and pub. relations Transcontinent TV Corp., N.Y.C., 1960-64; pres., owner Human Devel. Unlimited, Inc., Dallas, 1964—; asso. dir. Profl. Devel. Inst., N. Tex. State Coll.; guest lectr. various univs. and colls. Certified reader Taping for the Blind, U.S. Library of Congress; mem. Mayor's Water Conservation Commn., San Diego, 1956-58; liaison 11th Naval Dist. Hdqrs.-City of San Diego, 1956-60; mem. Los Angeles Jr. Coll. Advisory Commn., 1965-67; bd. adminstrs. Richardson United Meth. Ch., 1973-76. Served in USNR, 1942-46; NATOUSA, PTO. Mem. Broadcasters Promotion Assn. (hon. life mem., nat. dir. 1960-63, nat. pres. 1963), Sales and Marketing Execs. Internat. (internat. dir. 1975-77), Sales and Mktg. Execs. Dallas (dir. 1972-76, pres. 1974-75), Nat. Speaker Assn. (trustee Speakers for Am.), Internat. Platform Assn., Broadcast Pioneers, Phi Sigma Epsilon. Republican. Methodist. Contbr. articles on free enterprise, sales and sales mgmt. to profl. publs. Home: 2505 Prairie Creek Dr W Richardson TX 75080 Office: 2997 LBJ Freeway Suite 231 Dallas TX 75234

BELTRAN-FORTUNY, RAFAEL, chemist; b. Jalapa, Veracruz, Mexico, Oct. 29, 1928; s. Jose M. Beltran and Carmen V. Fortuny, B.; B.S., U. Calif. at Berkeley, 1955; m. M. Cristina Rivera Ramírez, Feb. 14, 1959; children—Claudia Cristina, Rafael, Carlos, Luis Roberto. Trainee for research engr. Electric Auto-Lite Co., Oakland, Calif. and Owoosso, Mich., 1953-54; research chemist Cal. Packing Corp., San Francisco, 1955-57; research chemist Stauffer Chem. Co., Richmond, Calif., 1957-58; chief chemist Monsanto Mexicana SA, Lecheria, Mexico, 1958-63; quality control mgr. Avon Cosmetics SA Mexico City, 1963-64; with Uhthoff, Gomez Vega & Uhthoff, Mexico City, Mexico, 1964—, dir. internat. patent matters, 1968—. Mem. Asociacion Mexicana de la Propiedad Industrial AC (Mexican Assn. Indsl. Property) (v.p.), Association Internationale pour la Protection de la Propriete Industrielle, Instituto Mexicano de Ingenieros Quimicos AC (dir.), Asociacion Nacional de la Industria Quimica AC. Club: Reforma Athletic, Jr. SA. Home: 47 Juan Escutia Circuito Heroes Ciudad Satelite Edo de Mexico Mexico Office: 260 Hamburgo Mexico DF 6 Mexico

BENAVIDES, JAIME MIGUEL, physician; b. Chuquicamata, Chile, Oct. 20, 1923; s. Jaime and Elena (Spikula) B.; came to U.S., 1926, naturalized, 1934; A.B., Duke, 1943; M.D., U. Pa., 1947; m. Nela Montejo, May 14, 1947 children—Suzanne, Maria, Jaime Manuel. Intern, resident Lutheran Hosp., Cleve., 1947-49; resident orthopaedics U.S. Naval Hosp., Phila., 1953-55, asst. chief orthopedics, Newport, R.I., 1955-56; resident Newington (Conn.) Hosp. Crippled Children, 1957; asst. chief orthopedics U.S. Navy Hosp., Phila., 1958-61; chief orthopaedics U.S. Naval Hosp., Key West, Fla., 1961-66; ret. as capt. USN, 1966; chief of staff Monroe Gen. Hosp., Key West, 1966-70; chief staff, chief surgery Fla. Keys Meml. Hosp., 1971-73; chmn. bd. Lower Fla. Keys Hosp. Dist., 1970-71; mem. med. adv. council Fla. Easter Seal Soc., med. adv. com. Fla. Dept. Vocat. Rehab. Bd. dirs. Monroe County Health Planning Council. Diplomate Am. Bd. Orthopedic Surgeons. Fellow A.C.S., Am. Acad. Orthopedic Surgeons, Internat. Coll. Surgeons, Am. Orthopedic Foot Soc., N.Y. Acad. Scis., Internat. Soc. Orthopaedics and Traumatology; mem. Monroe County Med. Soc. (pres. 1971), Fla., Miami, Eastern orthopedic socs., AMA, Am. Orthopedic Soc. for Sports Medicine, So., Fla. med. assns., Coll. Sports Medicine, Am. Fracture Assn., U.S. Power Squadron, Greater Key West C. of C. (dir. 1970-73, 1st v.p. 1973-74, pres. 1975), Navy League (2d v.p. Key West chpt. 1977), Kappa Sigma, Phi Rho Sigma. Roman Catholic. Home: PO Box 1240/13 Hilton Haven Key West FL 33040 Office: 638 United St Key West FL 33040

BENDA, CHARLES JEFFERSON, JR., architect; b. Hilo, Hawaii, Feb. 16, 1927; s. Charles Jefferson and Eleanor (Rose) B.; B.A., Fla. State U., 1952; m. Nancy Carlton Tribble, Aug. 19, 1950. Cons., architect Fla. Dept. Edn., Tallahassee, 1960-66; architect firm Charles J. Benda, Tallahassee, 1966-69, Odom Benda Assos., Tallahassee, after 1969; now owner Charles Benda Assos., Tallahassee. Cons. architect U.S. AID, Survey of Njala U. Coll., Sierra Leone, West Africa. Mem. Council Ednl. Facility Planners, Internat., 1969. Served with AUS, 1945-47. Mem. Bldg. Research Inst., AIA, Sigma Nu. Democrat. Elk. Clubs: St. Mark's Yacht, Apalachee Bay Yacht. Home: 1700 Kathryn Dr Tallahassee FL 32303 Office: Charles Benda Assos Architects 2416 Old St Augustine Rd Tallahassee FL 32301

BENDELIUS, ARTHUR GEORGE, engr., cons. firm exec.; b. Passaic, N.J., May 21, 1936; s. Arthur Leopold and Lydia Ella (Flach) B.; B.E., Stevens Inst. Tech., 1958, M.M.S., 1966; m. Virginia Brown, June 21, 1958; children—Linda Ellen, Bonnie Sue, Heidi Ann. Engr. firm Syska & Hennessey, N.Y.C., 1958-60; engr. firm Parsons, Brinckerhoff, Quade & Douglas, Inc., N.Y.C., 1960-62, asst. dept. head, 1963-68, dept. head, 1968-70, project mgr., 1970-73, regional mgr., Atlanta, 1973-76, asst. v.p., 1976-78, v.p., 1978—; engr. Nat. Biscuit Co., N.Y.C., 1962-63; condr. seminars, moderator forums in computer usage and environ. design. Pres. Brookside Home Sch. Orgn., Westwood, N.J., 1972-73; co-v.p. Dunwoody (Ga.) Band Booster Club, 1975-76, co-pres., 1976-77. Named Atlanta Engr. of Yr. in Pvt. Practice, 1978; Harold R. Fee Alumni award, 1978; registered profl. engr., N.Y., N.J., Minn., Ga., Fla., Tex., Ala., Ky., N.C., S.C., Miss., Tenn., La.; lic. pilot. Mem. Nat., Ga. (dir. 1976-78) socs. profl. engrs., Nat. Council Engring. Examiners (certified), Ga. Engring. Found. (dir. 1977— sec. 1979, v.p. 1980), N.Y. Assn. Cons. Engrs. Computer Group Inc. (chmn. com. mech. advi. 1967-71), Stevens Alumni Assn. (fund agt. 1970—), ASME, Am. Soc. Heating, Refrigeration and Air Conditioning Engrs. (chmn. tech. com. 1975-79), Soc. Am. Mil. Engrs. (pres. Atlanta Post 1978-79), Soc. Automotive Engrs., Brit. Tunnelling Soc., Electric Railroaders Assn., Water Pollution Control Fedn., Aircraft Owners and Pilots Assn., Ga. Water Pollution Control Assn., Ga. Conservancy, Atlanta C. of C., Sigma Nu (pres. alumni assn. 1966-70, comdr. 1971-73). Lutheran. Club: Atlanta City, Atlanta Stevens (pres. 1974—). Contbr. articles to profl. jours. Home: 1220 Witham Dr Dunwoody GA 30338 Office: 400 Peachtree Broad Bldg Atlanta GA 30303

BENDURE, LEONA JENSEN, pianist, educator; b. Springtown, Tex., Sept. 27, 1912; d. James Daniel and Nettie Mae Folley Jensen; B.M. (Scholar), U. Kans., 1934, B.M.E. (Scholar), 1937; postgrad. Midwestern U., Wichita Falls, Tex., 1966-67; m. Lloyd Kenneth Bendure, Aug. 14, 1938 (dec. 1971); children—Lorene Joan Bendure Teed, Donald Wesley. Tchr. music edn., Gove, Kans., 1937-38; tchr. piano, Lawton, Okla., 1943—; bd. dirs. Lawton Symphony Soc., dir. childrens' concerts; pianist Meth. Youth camp, 1934-36. Mem. Citizens Edn. Council, Lawton, 1956-58; 3d v.p. Lawton's Woman's Forum, 1974-75, bd. dirs., 1976-79, 2d v.p., 1975-76, fine arts chmn., 1970-71. Friends in Council scholar, Theodore Presser scholar, Howard Taylor scholar. Mem. Nat. Piano Guild, AAUW, Okla. Music Tchrs. Assn. (pres. Lawton 1969-70), Nat. Assn. Music Tchrs., Mu Phi Epsilon (Scholar), Pi Kappa Lambda. Methodist. Club: Entre Nous.

BENEDETTO, ANTHONY RICHARD, med. physicist; b. El Paso, Tex., Dec. 19, 1946; s. Leo and Mabel (Kelly) B.; B.S., Tex. A&M U., 1968, M.Eng. in Nuclear Engring. (USPHS trainee), 1970; M.B.A., Sul Ross State U., 1976; grad. Command and Gen. Staff Coll.; m. Kathryn McAdams, May 23, 1970; children—Michele Eileen, Noel Kathryn. Commd. 2d lt. U.S. Army, 1970, advanced through grades to capt., 1974; served at Ft. Belvoir, Va., 1970-71; health physicist Walter Reed Army Med. Center, Washington, 1972-73; supervisory health physicist William Beaumont Army Med. Center, El Paso, Tex., 1973-79; asst. prof. radiology, div. nuclear medicine U. Tex. Health Sci. Center, San Antonio, 1979—; cons. comml. radiopharmacy. Decorated Army Commendation medal, Nat. Def. Service medal. Mem. Soc. Nuclear Medicine, Health Physics Soc., Am. Assn. Physicists in Medicine, Tex. Regional Med. Physicists, Bexar County (Tex.) Med. Soc. (affiliate). Methodist. Clubs: Masons, Shriners. Author, co-editor 4 books/chpts. in books; contbr. articles to profl. publs.; abstractor Physics in Medicine and Biology, 1978—. Home: 2906 Meadow Circle San Antonio TX 78231 Office: Dept Radiology U Tex Health Sci Center 7703 Floyd Curl Dr San Antonio TX 78284

BENEDICT, CHARLES EDWARD, engring. co. exec.; b. Tallahassee, Mar. 21, 1939; s. Charles William and Catherine B. (Grainger) B.; B.S. in Math., Fla. State U., 1963; B.S. in Mech. Engring., U. Fla., 1968, M.S. in Mech. Engring., 1969, Ph.D. in Mech. Engring. (NDEA Title IV fellow), 1971; m. Patricia Ann Casey, Aug. 26, 1962; 1 dau., Sharla Ruth. Engring. technician Barrett, Daffin & Coloney, Tallahassee, 1953-63; measurement technician Fla. Gas Transmission Co., Gainesville, 1964-67; mech. engring. cons. Wayne H. Coloney Co., Inc., Tallahassee, 1971-72, mgr. machine design div., 1972-73, v.p., 1973-77, pres., 1977—. Bd. dirs. Tallahassee Open, Springtime Tallahassee. Recipient award for outstanding tech. achievement Fla. Engring. Soc., 1977; Gen. Lewis Brereton award Air Force Assn., 1978; Jimmy Doolittle fellow, 1979. Fellow ASME, Fla. Engring. Soc.; mem. Nat. Soc. Profl. Engrs., Am. Soc. Value Engrs., Fla. Inst. Cons. Engrs., Water Pollution Control Fedn., Tau Beta Pi, Phi Kappa Phi, Pi Tau Sigma, Omicron Delta Kappa, Kappa Alpha. Episcopalian (vestryman, sr. warden). Clubs: Capital City Kiwanis; Tallahassee 100; Met. Dinner. Contbr. articles to various publs. Patentee in field. Home: 3114 Lakeshore Dr W Tallahassee FL 32312 Office: PO Drawer 5258 168 Blountstown Hwy Tallahassee FL 32301

BENEDICT, JAMES HUNT, advt. exec.; b. Buffalo, Sept. 9, 1947; s. James French and Alice (Hunt) B.; B.S., Ithaca Coll., 1969; m. Marguerite Elizabeth Prevatt, June 24, 1972; children—Tyler Hunt, Michael James, Jonathan Mark. News reporter WESH-TV, Daytona Beach, 1969-71; gen. mgr. WEKT-FM, Hammondsport, N.Y., 1971-72; creative dir. Keener & Assos., Advt., Daytona Beach, 1972-74; pres. Adcast, Inc., Daytona Beach, 1974—, Asso. Mktg., Inc., 1977-79. Trustee, Daytona Beach Mus. Arts and Scis., 1972—; mem. Volusia County Planning Bd., 1977-78. Recipient Silver medal Am. Advt. Fedn., 1978. Mem. Daytona Beach Advt. Fedn. (pres. 1975, 77). Republican. Methodist. Club: Kiwanis. Home: 200 Pelican Ave Daytona Beach FL 32018 Office: 218 Seabreeze Blvd Daytona Beach FL 32018

BENEDICT, JOHN LOUIS, elec. engr.; b. Miami, Fla., Oct. 28, 1952; s. Ralph Henry and Gloria Theresa (Garcia) B.; B.S. in Elec. Engring. cum laude, U. Miami, 1971; M.E.E., Rensselaer Poly. Inst., 1973; m. JoAnna E. Pozero, Nov. 5, 1976; children—Jason W., Jarret D. Asst. engr. Central Office equipment maintenance engring. So. Bell Tel. & Tel. Co., Miami, 1972-74, sr. engr., 1974-75, mgr. engring., 1975-76, mgr. minicomputer planning, 1976-78, mgr. fundamental planning, 1979—; instr. for profl. engr. examination rev. course U. Miami, part-time 1972-77. Mem. Fla. Engring. Soc. (pres. student chpt. 1969-70), IEEE, Am. Inst. Aeros. and Astronautics (treas. student chpt. 1971), Sch. Engring. and Environ. Design Alumni Assn. (sec. 1973-75, v.p. 1975-76, pres.-elect 1976-77, pres. 1977-78), Iron Arrow Honor Soc. (sec.-treas. 1973-74, pres. 1974-77, sec.-treas. 1978-79), Omicron Delta Kappa (alumni bd. mem. 1973-75, v.p. student chpt. 1976; charter mem. Miami Alumni Circle), Tau Beta Pi (pres. 1970, 71-72, v.p. 1970-71), Eta Kappa Nu (nat. corr. 1970-71, initiations dir. 1971-72), Phi Eta Sigma (sec. hist. 1969-70, sr. adviser 1970-71). K.C. (dist. Columbian Squires chmn. 1975-78, Circle Counsellor of Year 1974, 75, dep. grand knight council 1976-77, recorder 1977-78, co. chmn. ch. parish completion program 1979—). Home: 10901 SW 42 Pl Davie FL 33328 Office: 666 NW 79th Ave Miami FL 33126

BENEFIELD, CLYDE DEWAYNE, hosp. adminstr.; b. Haynesville, La., Jan. 28, 1948; s. Barney Lee and Grace Pauline (Martin) B.; B.S., La. Tech. U., 1970; m. Donna Sue Nichols, Nov. 30, 1968; children—Sabrina Michelle, Angelia Dawn. Auditor, Ernst & Ernst, C.P.A.'s, Shreveport, La., 1970-73; asst. controller Bossier Gen. Hosp., Bossier City, La., 1973-76; controller Good Shepherd Hosp., Longview, Tex., 1975, asst. adminstr., 1976—. Bd. dirs., treas. Montessori Sch., Shreveport; treas. Southside Day Care Center,

Longview, Tex.; dean, trustee, tchr. Sunday sch. Oakland Heights Baptist Ch. Mem. Tex. Hosp. Assn., Hosp. Fin. Mgmt. Assn., Soc. La. C.P.A.'s, Am. Inst. C.P.A.'s. Democrat. Home: 610 Sheffield Longview TX 75601 Office: 621 N 5th Longview TX 75601

BENELL, JULIE, newspaperwoman; d. Hollis Edmond and Nellie (Benell) Robb; student Pasadena Playhouse, 1932-34; m. C. Albert Minor (dec.). Various leading theatrical roles Broadway, 1936-40; various roles in soap operas NBC and CBS, N.Y.C., 1936-39; beauty cons. Walter Winchell, 1936-39; program dir. Sta. WKY, Oklahoma City, 1940-48; dir. Sta. WFAA radio, Dallas, 1948-51, Woman's dir. Sta. WFAA TV, 1951-66, food editor Dallas Morning News, 1952-75; mem. bd. chefs Braniff Internat.; freelance cons. newspaper, radio and TV; lectr. in field. Cons. with food cos. Mem. exec. com. Dallas Heart Assn., 1965; chmn. heart fund drive, 1972; dir. Multiple Sclerosis Assn., 1969. Bd. dirs. Nat. Found. Decorated in Le Confreie de la Chaine des Rotisseurs, 1961. Mem. S.W. Diabetic Assn. (dir. 1949), Dallas Fashion Group (dir.), Nat. Home Fashions League (v.p. hospitality). Author: Julie Benells Favorite Recipes, 1956, revised, 1966; Let's Eat At Home, 1972; Kitchen Magic, 1973. Home: 6630 Walnut Hill Ln Dallas TN 75230

BENEZECH, FRANCIS JAMES, trucking co. exec.; b. Lafayette, La., Sept. 12, 1929; s. Henry and Agnes (Boudreaux) B.; student public schs. Lafayette; m. Lou Ella Boudreaux, Apr. 1, 1951; children—Karen Benezech Kidder, James, Janice, Lou Ann Benezech Citron, Thomas, Phillip. Pres., part owner Lafayette Mack Sales, 1959—, B&M Trucking Co., Lafayette, 1972—, Internat. Services, Inc., 1979—; v.p., part owner Dependable Dodge Datsun Inc., 1963—. Mem. budget rev. com. Roman Catholic Diocese of Lafayette; mem. La. Tax Commn., 1976—. Served with USN, 1946-48, USAF, 1951-55. Mem. Lafayette C. of C. Club: Oakbourne Country. Office: PO Box 4629 Lafayette LA 70502

BENHAM, ANGELA GAIL, counselor; b. Cartersville, Ga., May 10, 1953; d. Robert Emory and Florence Henrietta Young; B.S. in Elementary Edn., Tuskegee (Ala.) Inst., 1974, M.S. in Student Personnel, 1976. Residence hall counselor Tuskegee Inst., 1976—, dir. programming residence life and devel., 1979-80, instr., facilitator freshmen orientation, 1979—. Mem. Am. Personnel and Guidance Assn., NEA, Kappa Delta Pi, Phi Delta Kappa, Delta Sigma Theta. Home and Office: Residence Life and Devel Tuskegee AL 36088

BENHAM, JACK EDWARD, marketing co. exec.; b. Cin., Nov. 18, 1925; s. Edward H. and Mary A. (Stanton) B.; Chem. Engring. Degree, U. Cin., 1948; m. June Gridley, Feb. 14, 1950 (dec. Dec. 1979); 1 dau., Cynthia Ann. Lab. technician Ault and Weborg, Cin., 1944; paint technician Interchem. Corp., Cin., 1945-46; tech. dir. So. Mfg. Co., Miami, Fla., 1950-54, Sun and Sea Paint and Varnish Co., Boca Raton, Fla., 1950-54, Bruning Paint Co., Boca Raton, 1954-64; v.p. Southseas Chem. Corp., Lake Worth, Fla., 1956; v.p. Graphic Arts Screen Process, Boca Raton, 1956, Palmer Supplies Co. Fla., 1964-71; chmn. JB Internat. Mktg. Corp., Miami, 1971—, v.p. SE sales div., 1971—; v.p. Billie Rose Dinner Theatre, St. Petersburg, Fla., 1969-71. Served with USNR, World War II. Fellow Am. Inst. Chemists; mem. N.Y. Acad. Sci., Am. Chem. Soc., Internat. Platform Assn., Boca Raton Jaycees, So. Soc. for Paint Tech., Fla. Paint and Coatings Assn. (past pres.), Nat. Assn. Chem. Distbrs. (past nat. pres.), Am. Security Council. Republican. Presbyterian. Clubs: Elks, Masons, Boca Lago Country. Author: Beings, Boundries and Beauty, 1967; Marcaronical, Metaphorical Montage, 1980; contbr. articles to profl. jours. Home: 558 NW 9th Ct Boca Raton FL 33423 Office: JB Internat Marketing Corp 5640 NW 35th Ct Miami FL 33142

BEN-MENACHEM, YORAM, radiologist; b. Jerusalem, Israel, Sept. 1, 1934; s. Haim and Eva (Beisem) Ben-M.; came to U.S., 1969; M.D., Hebrew U., Jerusalem, 1960; m. Sylvia Tizes, Dec. 24, 1957; children—Tamir, Gadi, Drory. Physician, Israel Def. Forces, 1960-63; med. supt. Lilongwe (Malawi) Gen. Hosp., 1963-66; fellow in vascular radiology Thomas Jefferson U., Phila., 1969-72; prof. radiology, dir. vascular radiology U. Tex. Med. Sch., Houston, 1977—. Diplomate Am. Bd. Radiology. Mem. Am. Coll. Radiology, Assn. Univ. Radiologists, Radiol. Soc. N.Am., AMA, Harris County Med. Soc., Houston Radiol. Soc., Tex. Med. Assn., Tex. Radiologic Soc. Jewish. Office: 6431 Fannin St Houston TX 77030

BENNETT, BETTY BESSE, librarian; b. Omaha, Feb. 18, 1921; d. Gordon Stanley and Besse Harriet (Amos) Bennett; B.A., Municipal U. Omaha, 1942; B.S. in L.S., U. Ill., 1943; M.A., U. Iowa, 1948; M.L.S., Tex. Woman's U., 1960. Asst. documents librarian U. Iowa Library, Iowa City, 1943-50; reference and documents librarian Kans. State Tchrs. Coll. Library, Pittsburg, 1950-57, reference librarian, archivist, 1957-67; reference and research librarian Stephen F. Austin State U. Library, Nacogdoches, Tex., 1967-72, govt. documents librarian, 1972—. Resource cons. Gov.'s Conf. on Libraries, Austin, Tex., 1974. Exec. dir. Westminster Presbyn. Ch. Telephone Reassurance Program for Elderly Shut-ins, 1977—. Mem. AAUW, AAUP, ALA (state document classification com. 1974-76, state documents task force), Tex. (chmn. govt. documents round table 1975-76), Southwestern library assns., Tex. Assn. Coll. Tchrs., Nacogdoches Friends of the Library, Alpha Xi Delta. Presbyn. (clk. of session 1967—, ruling elder 1975—). Home: 1525 Walnut St Nacogdoches TX 75961 Office: Stephen F Austin State U Library Nacogdoches TX 75962

BENNETT, BOBBIE JEAN, state ofcl.; b. Gwinnett County, Ga., July 13, 1940; d. William Claude and Clara Maude (Nichols) Holcome; B.B.A. magna cum laude, Ga. State U., 1973; 1 dau., Terri Lynne. With Ga. State Merit System, Atlanta, 1960—, sr. accountant, 1967, asst. div. dir., 1968-70, fiscal officer, 1970-74, div. dir., 1975-78, asst. dep. commr., 1978—. Mem. Internat. Personnel Mgmt. Assn., Ga. Fiscal Mgmt. Council, Ga. Council Personnel Adminstrn., Beta Gamma Sigma, Phi Kappa Phi, Beta Alpha Psi. Democrat. Home: 2072 Malabar Dr NE Atlanta GA 30345 Office: 244 Washington St SW Atlanta GA 30334

BENNETT, CHARLES DEAN, educator; b. Yuba, Okla., May 19, 1945; s. Charles Jennings and Melba Cloetta (Davidson) B.; B.S. in Edn., Southeastern Okla. State U., 1966; M.S. (grad. asst.), Okla. State U., 1967; m. Linda Kay Corbett, Mar. 25, 1967; children—Ruby Lynn, Rhonda Deann. Instr. bus. Tyler (Tex.) Jr. Coll., 1967—. Mem. Pi Omega Pi, Kappa Delta Pi, Delta Pi Epsilon. Democrat. Baptist. Home: Route 7 Box 987 Tyler TX 75707

BENNETT, CHARLES EDWARD, congressman; b. Canton, N.Y., Dec. 2, 1910; s. Walter James and Roberta Augusta (Broadhurst) B.; A.B., U. Fla., 1934, J.D., 1934; H.H.D. (hon.), U. Tampa, 1950; LL.D. (hon.), Jacksonville U., 1972; m. Jean Bennett; children—Bruce, James, Lucinda. Admitted to Fla. bar, 1934, practiced in Jacksonville, until 1949; mem. 81st-96th congresses from 3d Fla. Dist., mem. armed services com., chmn. seapower subcom. Mem. Fla. Ho. of Reps., 1941. Bd. dirs. Boys' Home, ARC, Tb Assn. Council Social Agys., Multiple Sclerosis Assn.; trustee Lynchburg Coll. Served from pvt. to capt., inf., AUS, 1942-47; New Guinea and Philippines, including guerrilla fighting in Luzon. Decorated Silver Star, Bronze Star; Philippine Legion of Honor and Gold Cross; French Legion of Honor; recipient Certificate of Merit, Freedoms Found., 1951, 56, Good Govt. award, Jr. C. of C., 1952, Good Citizenship gold medal Nat. S.A.R., 1959. Mem. DAV, VFW, Fla. Bar. Am. Legion, Fleet Res. Assn. (hon.), Jacksonville Bar Assn., Jr. C. of C. (pres. 1939). Democrat. Mem. Disciples of Christ Ch. (elder). Mason. Author: Laudonniere, 1964; Settlement of Florida, 1967; Congress and Conscience, 1970; Southernmost Battlefields of the Revolution, 1970; Three Voyages, 1974; also hist. papers. Home: 400 West Bay St Jacksonville FL 32204 Office: Rayburn House Office Bldg Washington DC 20515

BENNETT, HARRY JACKSON, biologist, ret. educator; b. Bernice, La., Aug. 1, 1904; s. Ernest Jerome and Alice Gertrude (Jones) B.; B.S., La. State U., 1926; M.S., U. Ill., 1928, Ph.D., 1935; m. Jane Tobie, Dec. 29, 1931; children—Carolyn (Mrs. C.D. Brown), Sarah Jane (Mrs. E. Brash), Katherine Ann (Mrs. J.G. May). Instr. La. State U., Baton Rouge, 1929-34, asst. prof., 1935-38, asso. prof., 1939-49, prof., 1950-74, prof. emeritus, 1975—, dir. Marine Lab., 1946-56, dir. sci. tng. programs office, 1969-74, asso. dean Grad. Sch., 1973-74, dir. Indsl. Research Lab., 1950-74, asst. dean Coll. Arts and Scis., 1938-42. Sr. scientist div. tropical diseases, USPHS, 1947-49. Decorated Bronze Star. Recipient Distinguished Service award Assn. Acads. Sci., 1969, La. Acad. Sci., 1973; named Distinguished Faculty fellow La. State U., 1968. Mem. AAAS, Am. Soc. Zoology, Am. Soc. Limnology and Oceanography, Am. Soc. Parasitology, Am. Micros. Soc., Gulf Estuarine Research Soc., Am. Soc. Systematic Zoology, Tenn., Miss. acads. sci., Am. Inst. Biol. Sci., Mil. Order World Wars, Assn. Acads. Sci., La. State Alumni Fedn., Sigma Xi, Phi Kappa Phi, Delta Sigma Phi. Democrat. Methodist. Kiwanian. Club: Faculty. Contbr. articles on marine zoology, parasitology and water pollution to sci. publs. Address: 4912 Tulane Dr Baton Rouge LA 70808

BENNETT, IVAN STANLEY, sch. adminstr.; b. Harrisburg, Pa., Jan. 27, 1949; s. Ivan Frank and Audrey (Poley) B.; student Butler U., 1967-69; B.A., Thomas More Coll., 1972; M.Ed., Xavier U., 1974; m. Susan Lee Elliott, Aug. 3, 1974; 1 son, Jonathan Lee. Tchr., Covington (Ky.) Ind. Sch. Dist., Job Preparation Center, 1973-75; coordinator Scott St. Job Preparation Center, Covington, 1975-76; mgr.-coordinator Greenup St. Job Preparation Center, Covington, 1976-77; mgr. Greenup St. Job Preparation Sch., 1977-78; dir. admissions and release No. Ky. State Vocat. Tech. Sch., Covington, 1978—; mem. tchr. adv. com. Dist. Speakers Bur. Chmn., Com. for Sch. Dropouts, 1974-75; chmn. Alternative Sch. Adv. Com., 1975-76; mem. Juvenile Delinquency Task Force, Ky. Adv. Commn., 1975-76, Regional Council on Substance Abuse, 1975-76, Kenton County Manpower Adv. Com., 1976-77, No. Ky. Adv. and Resources Council for Teenage Parents, 1975-78. Certified tchr. and guidance counselor, Ky., Ohio. Mem. Am. (So. Region Br. Assembly), Ky. (cert. of appreciation; pres. 1980), No. Ky. (cert. of appreciation) personnel and guidance assns., Ky. Assn. Sch. Adminstrs., Lambda Chi Alpha. Republican. Lutheran. Home: 2502 Belleview Rd Burlington KY 41005 Office: Amsterdam Rd Covington KY 41011

BENNETT, J. CLAUDE, med. educator; b. Birmingham, Ala., 1933; s. Claude and Lucille (Clark) B.; A.B., Samford U., 1954; M.D., Harvard U., 1958; m. Nancy Miller, June 17, 1958; children—Katherine Diane, Jennifer Miller, Clark Barton. Intern, Univ. Hosp., Birmingham, 1959-60; fellow arthritis unit Harvard Med. Sch., 1960-62; research asso. NIH, 1962-64; sr. research fellow Calif. Inst. Tech., 1964-65; asst. prof. U. Ala., Birmingham, 1965-66, asst. dir. div. clin. immunology and rheumatology, 1966-70, asso. prof. medicine and microbiology, 1966-70, prof. medicine, 1970—, dir. div. clin. immunology and rheumatology, 1970—, chmn. dept. microbiology, 1970—, sr. scientist cancer research and tng. program, 1972—, dir. Multipurpose Arthritis Center, 1977—, Disting. Faculty lectr., 1979; mem. nat. arthritis adv. bd. HEW, 1977-80. Diplomate Am. Bd. Internal Medicine. Fellow A.C.P.; mem. Am. Rheumatism Assn., Genetics Soc. Am., So. Soc. Clin. Investigation, Am. Fedn. Clin. Research, AAAS, N.Y. Acad. Sci., Am. Soc. Clin. Investigation, Am. Soc. Microbiology, Assn. Am. Physicians, Am. Soc. Biol. Chemists, Sigma Xi. Mem. Ch. of Christ. Editor-in-chief Arthritis and Rheumatism Jour., 1975—; author: Vistas in Connective Tissue Diseases, 1968. Home: 4236 Antietam Dr Birmingham AL 35216 Office: Univ Alabama University Station Birmingham AL 35294

BENNETT, JACOB TRAVIS, pediatrician; b. Smithville, Tex., Jan. 10, 1899; s. Wiley Oscar and Hester (Shaw) B.; B.A., U. Tex., 1922; M.D., Johns Hopkins U., 1926; m. Mabel Grace Snider, Mar. 27, 1930; children—Travis Hartley, Grace, Burgess. Intern, Union Meml. Hosp., Balt., 1926-27; resident in pediatrics Johns Hopkins Hosp., 1927-28; chief resident Hosp. for Sick Children, Toronto, Ont., Can., 1928-29; pvt. practice pediatrics, Albuquerque, 1929-31, El Paso, Tex., 1931—; chief staff Hotel Dieu Hosp., 1949. Recipient El Conquistador award El Paso, 1976; Diplomate Nat. Bd. Med. Examiners, Am. Bd. Pediatrics. Mem. Am. Acad. Pediatrics (life mem., pres. Tex. chpt. 1961-63), El Paso County Med. Soc. (pres. 1966), So., Tex. med. assns., Tex. Pediatric Soc., AMA, U. Tex. Alumni Assn., Phi Beta Kappa. Democrat. Episcopalian. Clubs: Kiwanis, Masons, Shriners. Home: 6229 Pino Real Dr El Paso TX 79912

BENNETT, JAMES BAXTER, geologist; b. Houston, Jan. 5, 1935; s. James Benjamin and Mary (Baxter) Mauldin; B.S., U. Tex., 1961; m. Kathryn Adele Giddens, Jan. 28, 1961; children—Kathryne Alison, Wiley Baxter. Oil scout Tex. Eastern Transmission Corp., Shreveport, La., 1960-63, exploration geologist, 1964-67; exploration petroleum geologist Skelly Oil Co., Shreveport, 1967-70; area geologist Champlin Petroleum Co., Shreveport, 1970, Houston, 1970-72; dist. geologist Belco Petroleum Corp., Houston, 1972—. Served with AUS, 1957-59. Mem. Am. Assn. Petroleum Geologists, Shreveport (2d. v.p. 1969-70), Houston geol. socs., Sigma Nu. Republican. Home: 10930 Burgoyne St Houston TX 77042 Office: 10000 Old Katy Rd Houston TX 77055

BENNETT, JAMES THOMAS, cons. statistician, educator; b. Memphis, Oct. 19, 1942; s. Louie Edward and Carrie (Tunnell) B.; B.S., Case Inst. Tech., 1964, M.S., 1966, Ph.D., 1970; m. Sara Ellen Dorman, Sept. 2, 1967. Operations research analyst, finance central staff Ford Motor Co., Dearborn, Mich., 1964-65; cons. econ. statistician Chesapeake & Ohio Ry. Co., 1966-70; research asso. Case Inst. Tech., 1965-67; asst. prof. indsl. mgmt. Cleve. State U., 1967-70; asst. prof. econs. George Washington U., 1970-77; prof. econs. George Mason U., Fairfax, Va., 1977—, also sr. staff scientist program in logistics; cons. Cleve. Transit System. Trustee Ohio Epsilon Corp. Research fellow Fed. Res. Bank Cleve., 1969-70. Mem. Contemporary Econs. and Bus. Assn. (sec.-treas.), Am. Econ. Assn., Am. Statis. Assn., Econometric Soc., Phi Kappa Psi, Tau Beta Pi. Democrat. Presbyn. Home: 5011 Gadsen Dr Fairfax VA 22032 Office: George Mason U Fairfax VA 22030

BENNETT, JERRY WAYNE, police officer; b. Virden, N.Mex., Aug. 24, 1941; s. Harley Ward and Mary (Givingo) B.; A.A., Golden West Coll., Costa Mesa, Calif., 1969; m. Terry Lynn Sanders, Apr. 18, 1962; children—Kristine Louise, Jerry Wayne. Patrolman, Tustin, Calif., 1967-70; chief of police, Converse, Tex., 1970-75; patrolman, crime prevention officer City of Selma, Tex., 1975-80; patrolman Castle Hills (Tex.) Police Dept., 1980—; law enforcement instr. State of Tex. Served with USMC, 1959-63. Awards Lions Club, 1973, Am. Legion, 1974-75, 78-79, VFW, 1976, Air Tng. Command, 1974; recipient award Air Force Sgts. Assn., 1973, named Outstanding Officer, 1973. Mem. Forgery Investigators Assn. Tex., Gualadupe County Police Officers Assn., Am. Legion. Baptist. Club: Lions. Home: 7613 Marigold Trace San Antonio TX 78233 Office: 6915 West Ave San Antonio TX 78213

BENNETT, JOHN CARLYLE, accountant; b. Doyle, Tenn., Sept. 11, 1910; s. John P. and Florence (Parker) B.; student Duke U., 1929-31, Cecil's Bus. Coll., Ashville, N.C., 1932-33, corr. course I.A.S., 1934-40; m. Betty E. Strunk, Dec. 1, 1943; children—Gloria Louise, John Richard, William Gordon, Charlotte Emily. Accountant, So. Dairies, Inc., Asheville, N.C., 1933-35; head accounting 15th Naval Dist., Panama C.Z., 1938-39, auditor Panama Canal, constrn. foreman Army Engrs., 1939-42; accountant, auditor, mem. staff Ernst & Ernst, C.P.A.'s, Detroit, 1943-45; chief accountant Alexander Tool & Mfg. Co., Detroit, 1945; internal revenue agt., 1945-48; practice as C.P.A., 1948—. Played with Ringling Bros. Circus Band; mem. Charlotte Symphony Orch.; bus. mgr. Charlotte Community Band Assn. Served with AUS, 1935-38, USNR, 1943. Mem. Am. Fedn. Musicians, Nat. Small Bus. Assn. Clubs: Masons (32 deg.), Shriners, Red Fez Country. Author: Book of Income Tax Rates, Federal Income Tax Calculator (pub. annually); Outlaws in Swivel Chairs, 1958; also articles and legal actions on polit sci. under Article III of Constn. Address: 2245 Chambwood Dr Charlotte NC 28205

BENNETT, MAX LEON, judge; b. Kingsville, Tex., May 6, 1938; s. Roy Chilton and Zachie Ford (Dunahay) B.; student Tex. A. and I. U., 1956-57; B.A., Baylor U., 1960, J.D., 1962; m. Betty Joyce Trapp, Dec. 23, 1961; children—Catherine, Susan. Admitted to Tex. bar, 1962; atty. Humble Oil and Refining Co., Corpus Christi, Tex., 1962-65; practiced in Corpus Christi, 1965—; partner firm Howard, McDowell, Bennett and Cartwright, 1973-75; judge Nueces County Ct. at Law, 1974-78, 319th Jud. Dist. Ct., 1979—; instr. in law adult edn. Del Mar Coll., Corpus Christi, 1971-72. Bd. dirs. Corpus Christi Boys Club, 1973—, pres., 1975—; mem. devel. council Baylor U., 1973—. Mem. Tex., Nueces County (pres. 1968-69) trial lawyers assns., Nueces County Bar Assn. (dir. 1972-74), Coastal Bend Baylor Alumni Club (pres. 1972-73), Baylor U. Alumni Assn. (dir. 1978—). Home: 13636 Smith Dr Corpus Christi TX 78410 Office: Nueces County Courthouse Corpus Christi TX 78401

BENNETT, RICHARD EDWIN, shopping center exec.; b. Oshkosh, Wis., July 29, 1943; s. Richard Howell, Jr. and Dorothy Coroline (Brain) B.; student U. Wis., 1961-63, 67-68; m. Priscilla Kowalski, Nov. 25, 1967; children—Richard Howell, Jean Ann, Carol Ann. Asst. mgr. Robert Hall Clothes, Janesville, Wis., 1968-69; v.p., gen. mgr. Bennett Industries, Inc., St. Petersburg, Fla., 1969-72, dir., 1969—; asst. mgr., then mgr. W.T. Grant Co., Mt. Dora, Fla., 1972-76; asst. gen. mgr. Rouse Co., Tampa (Fla.) Bay Center, 1976-78, v.p., gen. mgr. Charlottetown Mall, Charlotte, N.C., 1978—. Served with AUS, 1963-66. Mem. Greater Charlotte C. of C., Internat. Council Shopping Centers. Home: 5116 Chestnut Lake Dr Charlotte NC 28212 Office: 601 Charlottetown Mall Charlotte NC 28204

BENNETT, RICHARD HOWELL, JR., sales exec.; b. Chgo., Aug. 10, 1916; s. Richard Howell and Beatrice (Schieberl) B.; student U. Ill., 1935-37; m. Dorothy Caroline Brain, Dec. 28, 1940; children—Carol Ann Bennett Matenaer, Richard Edwin, Dorothy Marion Bennett Shope. Buyer coll. textbook dept. Wilcox & Follett, Chgo., 1937-42; salesman Bauer-Black, Oshkosh, Wis. and Detroit, 1942-47; salesman, dist. mgr., regional mgr., nat. sales mgr. U.S. Time Corp., N.Y.C., 1947-54; gen. sales mgr. Amity Leather Products, West Bend, Wis., 1954-64; mdse. coordinator Am. Optical Co., Boston, 1964-65; nat. sales mgr. Bentley Lighter Corp., N.Y.C., 1965-69; Fla. regional mgr. Garrity Industries, Inc., Stamford, Conn., 1969—; chmn. bd. Bennett Industries, Inc., Naples, Fla., 1969—; v.p., cons. Meeker Co., Joplin, Mo., 1976-77, Bruce Shope Enterprises, 1977—. Mem. Fed. Wholesale Druggists Assn., Nat. Assn. Tobacco Distbrs., Nat. Assn. Chain Drug Stores, Mawanda Assn. of U. Ill., Delta Alpha Epsilon. Clubs: Boston Skating, Glades Country (Naples). Home: 626 Park Shore Dr Naples FL 33940

BENNETT, ROBERT CHARLES, musician; b. Houston, Nov. 10, 1933; s. Charles Crane and Truman (Herring) B.; M.Ed., U. Houston, 1956; D.Music with honor, Southwestern U., 1979; m. Barbara Ann Wilhite, Nov. 12, 1954; children—Charles Gary, Robert Kerry. Fellow Trinity Coll. London, 1971; organist Riverside Bapt. Ch., 1947-52; music tchr. Kinkaid Pvt. Sch., 1952-54; organist-choirmaster St. Philip Presbyn. and St. Johns Meth. Chs., 1954; organ instr. St. Thomas U., Houston, 1974—; organist-choirmaster St. Luke's Meth. Ch., Houston, 1954—; organ cons. M.P. Moller Co., Hagerstown, Md. Recipient Music Leadership award Sigma Alpha Iota, 1979. Mem. Am. Guild Organists, Fellowship Meth. Musicians, Choristers Guild. Methodist. Contbr. articles to profl. jours. Home: 6004 Buffalo Speedway Houston TX 77005 Office: 3471 Westheimer St Houston TX 77027

BENNETT, ROBERT EARL, coll. adminstr.; b. Goldsboro, N.C., Aug. 26, 1932; s. Losker B. and Sarah H. (Herring) B.; A.B., Atlantic Christian Coll., 1957; M.Ed., Ohio U., 1958, Ph.D. (fellow), 1968; m. Carolyn Cherry, Aug. 27, 1955; children—Barbara, Robin. Head of residence Ohio U., Athens, 1957-58; dir. admissions Wesley Coll., Dover, Del., 1958-59; counselor, instr. Monmouth Coll., West Long Branch, N.J., 1959-61; teaching fellow Ohio U., 1961-63; dean of students Atlantic Christian Coll., Wilson, N.C., 1963-69; dir. freshman services U. S.C., 1969-72; asso. dir. student services Columbus (Ga.) Coll., 1972—; past pres. N.C. Coll. Personnel Assn. Served with USN, 1950-54; Korea. Eli Lilly Found. fellow, 1959. Mem. Am. Personnel and Guidance Assn., Am. Coll. Personnel Assn., Nat. Vocat. Guidance Assn., Nat. Assn. Student Personnel Adminstrs., Phi Delta Kappa. Mem. Disciples of Christ. Home: 3804 Wingate Dr Columbus GA 31904 Office: Columbus College Columbus GA 31907

BENNETT, ROBERT WILLIAM, drug co. exec.; b. N.Y.C., June 13, 1918; s. Robert William and Ruth Leslie (Valentine) B.; B.S., Alfred (N.Y.) U., 1941; m. Olga N. Salowich, Dec. 20, 1947; 1 dau., Susan Roberta. Design engr. James P. O'Donnell Engrs., N.Y.C., 1946-50; project engr., project mgr., mgr. projects Blaw-Knox Co., Pitts., 1950-69; capital projects coordinator, mgr. tech. services Tex. div. Hoffmann-LaRoche, Inc., Nutley, N.J., 1969-75, dir. tech. services Roche Products, Inc., Manati, P.R., 1975—; staff lectr. U. Pitts., 1966-68. Served with USNR, 1942-46. Decorated Bronze Star; registered profl. engr., Pa., N.Y. Mem. Am. Inst. Chem. Engrs., San Juan C. of C., San Juan Coll. Engrs., P.R. Wing CAP. Republican. Episcopalian. Club: Masons. Patentee concrete tank constrn. Home: 1503 Ashford Ave Santurce PR 00911 Office: PO Box 452 Manati PR 00701

BENNETT, SOLON ANTHONY, city ofcl.; b. Chgo., Sept. 21, 1922; s. Anthony Constantine and Anna C. (Damofli) B.; B.S., Ill. Inst. Tech., 1951, postgrad., 1951-52; postgrad. Ariz. State U., 1957-65; m. Loretta J. LaValley, June 3, 1958; children—Leslie Anne, Christopher Solon, Stephen Anthony. Mem. mfg. engring. staff Internat. Harvester Co., Chgo., 1945-52; mem. purchasing mgmt. staff Garrett Corp., Phoenix, 1952-67; dir. purchasing State of Ariz., Phoenix, 1967-68,

Overhead Door Corp., Dallas, 1968-71; dir. purchases and stores City of Austin (Tex.), 1971—; instr. U. Tex., 1974—, Austin Community Coll., 1975—; mem. Joint Fed., State and Local Govt. Adv. Panel on Procurement and Supply, 1975-77; mem. adv. com. on pub. purchasing and materials mgmt. U. Tex., 1974—; chmn. mktg. adv. com. Austin Community Coll., 1975—. Served with USAAF, 1944-45. Mem. Nat. Inst. Govtl. Purchasing (dir. 1975—, cert. public purchasing officer), Nat. Assn. Purchasing Mgmt. (Profl. Devel. Person of Yr. award 1979, cert.), Nat. Contract Mgmt. Assn. (cert.), Am. Prodn. and Inventory Control Soc. Club: Rotary. Sect. editor Purchasing Handbook, 4th edit., 1980. Home: 4201 Endcliffe Dr Austin TX 78731 Office: City of Austin 124 W 8th St Austin TX 78767

BENNETT, SYLVIA LOUISE, ins. co. exec.; b. Ft. Lauderdale, Fla., July 28, 1935; d. Harold Alton and Elsie N. (Graber) Hutcheson; student Hillsborough Community Coll., 1971-73; children—Robert Lee, Raymond Louis. With Liberty Mutual Ins. Co., Tampa, Fla., 1957-59, Stewart Ins. Agy., Tampa, 1959-60, Poe & Asso., Inc., Tampa, 1960-73, Benson Ins. Agy., Naples, Fla., 1973-74, Woodward-Crowder Co., Tampa, 1974-77, Best Insurers, Inc., Tampa, 1977-78, mktg. specialist W. T. Driscoll & Asso., Tampa, Fla., 1978-79; ins. instr. Metro. Property & Liability Ins. Co., Tampa, 1979—; instr. ins. U. Tampa, 1972-79, Chartered Property Underwriters, 1973—. Chartered property casualty underwriter; cert. profl. ins. woman. Mem. Chartered Property Casualty Underwriters, Ind. Ins. Agts. of Greater Tampa (edn. chmn. 1977-78), Ins. Women of Tampa. Democrat. Methodist. Club: Tampa Bay Mariners (pres. 1977-78). Home: PO Box 2148 Tampa FL 33601 Office: PO Box 25000 Tampa FL 33623

BENNETT, WILLIAM EVERETT, pub. co. exec.; b. Cumming, Ga., Apr. 16, 1933; s. Luther Leo and Mary Edith (Mangum) B.; B.A., Ga. State U., 1956, postgrad., 1967; m. Nancy Teresa Fowler, May 8, 1954; children—David William, Debra Teresa. Asst. treas., credit mgr. Tri-State Tractor Co., Atlanta, 1955-74; pres. Bennett Bros.; Doraville, Ga., 1968—, Life Enterprises, Inc.; vice chmn. bd. trustees Peachtree on Peachtree Inn. Mem. adv. council Hawaii Baptist Acad., Honolulu. Served with AUS, 1953-55. Baptist (chmn. bd., mem. exec. com. Atlanta Bapt. Assn. 1969—). Club: Northlake Rotary. Home: 2156 Saren Ct Tucker GA 30084 Office: 2930 Flowers Rd S Atlanta GA 30341

BENNIE, WILLIAM ANDREW, educator; b. Linton, Ind., Oct. 9, 1921; s. Andrew R. and Sylvia (Van Meter) B.; B.S. in Edn., Ind. State U., 1943, M.S., 1949; Ed.D., Ind. U., 1955; m. Betty Jean Burks, Jan. 31, 1944; children—James Andrew, Carol Ann. Tchr., Bloomfield (Ind.) Pub. Schs., 1946-49; asst. prof. Sch. Edn., then asso. prof., dir. student teaching Miami U., Oxford, Ohio, 1949-61; mem. faculty U. Tex., Austin, 1961—, dir. student teaching, 1961-65, dir. student field experience, 1965-73, prof., chmn. dept. curriculum and instrn., 1973-78, dir. edn. placement service, 1978—, asso. dir. research and devel. Center Tchr. Edn., 1965-68; regional coordinator Nat. Com. Edn. Family Fin., 1955-58; vis. prof. Eastern Mich. U., 1960, U. N.D., 1967, Wichita State U., 1970. Mem. Assn. Tchr. Educators (distinguished mem.), Nat. Soc. Study Edn., Assn. Supervision and Curriculum Devel., Nat. Student Teaching (exec. com. 1967-70), Tex. Assn. Student Teaching (pres. 1970-71), Phi Delta Kappa, Kappa Delta Pi, Phi Kappa Phi. Author: Cooperation for Better Student Teaching, 1966; Supervising Clinical Experiences in the Classroom, 1972; also articles. Address: 7205 Waterline Rd Austin TX 78731

BENOIT, ARTHUR JOSEPH, JR., air force officer; b. New Bedford, Mass., Sept. 12, 1934; s. Arthur Joseph and Elizabeth Alice (Stringer) B.; B.A. summa cum laude, St. Leo Coll., 1975; M.S., Troy State U., 1977; m. Dorothy Lee Pumphrey, Dec. 13, 1957; children—Vicki Ann, Brian Thomas. Joined U.S. Air Force, 1953, advanced through grades to chief master sgt., 1974; materiel control supt., Spangdahlem Air Base, Germany, 1975-77, materiel storage and distbn. officer, 1977, supt. mgmt. and procedures, 1977—; faculty Hartford Community Coll., 1975-78. Decorated Bronze Star medal, Air Force Commendation medal, Joint Service Commendation medal, Meritorious Service medal; recipient Distinguished Scholastic and Distinguished Edn. awards Tactical Air Command, 1975. Mem. Am. Personnel and Guidance Assn., Am. Legion, Noncommd. Officers Assn. Democrat. Roman Catholic. Clubs: Elks, Eifel Wanders Volksmarching (v.p. 1976-78). Address: 2214 Pavilion Pl Brandon FL 33511

BENOIT, CLARENCE JOHN, safety engr.; b. Port Sulphur, La., Dec. 20, 1944; s. Louis John and Eula Marie (Robichaux) B.; B.S., in Indsl. Tech., La. State U., Baton Rouge, 1970; m. Barbara Marie Mire, Mar. 4, 1967; children—Denise, Brian. Prodn. technician Union Carbide Corp., Taft, La., 1967-69; field rep., loss control and engring. dept. Continental Ins. Co., New Orleans, 1970-72; safety dir. Highline Constrn. Co., Westwego, La., 1973-74; sr. field safety engr. Dresser Industries, Houma, La., 1974-79; mgr. loss control and safety Newpark Marine Services, Inc., Morgan City, La., 1979—. Fireman, Thibodeux Vol. Fire Dept.; past pres. S. Central La. Safety Council. Cert. boiler inspector Nat. Bd. Boiler and Pressure Vessel Inspectors; cert. cardiopulmonary resusitation instr. Am. Heart Assn.; cert. safety profl. Mem. Am. Soc. Safety Engrs., S. Central La. (v.p., past pres.), Baton Rouge safety councils, La. Motor Transp. Assn., Terrebonne Parish Cardiopulmonary Resusitation Assn. Democrat. Roman Catholic. Club: K.C. Home: 1305 Park Dr Thibodaux LA 70301 Office: PO Box 976 Morgan City LA 70380

BENOWITZ, H(ERBERT) ALLEN, court reporter; b. Bklyn., Jan. 18, 1942; s. Isidore and Julia (Weisberg) B.; diploma Interboro Inst. Manhattan, 1961; children—Cheryl Lynn, Michael Craig. Hearing reporter N.Y. Dept. Motor Vehicles, N.Y.C., 1960-61; dep. ofcl. ct. reporter Jack W. Mallicoat, Circuit Ct., Miami, Fla., 1961-69; freelance ct. reproter, pres. H. Allen Benowitz & Assos., Inc., Miami, 1969—; videotape cons.; lectr. before profl. groups. Mem. Nat. (nat. video chmn., 1977—; recipient various awards), Fla. shorthand reporters assns., Dade County Freelance Reporters Assn. Home: 600 NE 36th St Miami FL 33137 Office: 720 Rivergate Plaza 444 Brickell Ave Miami FL 33131

BENSON, BETTY JONES, educator; b. Barrow County, Ga., Jan. 11, 1928; d. George C. and Bertha (Mobley) Jones; B.S. in Edn., N. Ga. U., Dahlonega, 1958; M.Ed. in Curriculum and Supervision, U. Ga., Athens, 1968, edn. specialist in Curriculum and Supervision, 1970; m. George T. Benson; children—George Steven, Elizabeth Gayle, James Claud, Robert Benjamin. Tchr. Forsyth County (Ga.) Bd. Edn., Cumming, 1956-66, curriculum dir., 1966—. Active Alpine Center for Disturbed Children; mem. N. Ga. Coll. Right-to-Read Adv. Com., Ga. Textbook Com.; adv. Boy Scouts; Sunday sch. tchr. 1st Baptist Ch. Cumming. Mem. NEA, Ga. Assn. Educators (dir.), Nat., Ga. (pres.) assns. supervision and curriculum devel., Assn. Childhood Edn. Internat., Bus. and Profl. Women's Club, Ga. Future Tchrs. Adv. Assn. (pres.), HeadStart Dirs. Assn., Forsyth County Hist. Soc. Home: Route 1 Box 12 Cumming GA 30130 Office: 101 School St Cumming GA 30130

BENSON, HARRY EDDIE, corp. ofcl.; b. Port Arthur, Tex., Dec. 13, 1925; s. William H. and Eddie Arkie (Rhea) B.; A.B.S., Lamar Jr. Coll., 1947; B.S., U. Houston, 1953; m. Mary Nell Harwell, Aug. 20, 1949; children—Elizabeth Ann Benson-Smith, David Harwell. Estimator prodn. man Gulf Printing Co., Houston, 1952-59, prodn. mgr., 1959; typographer Naylor Type and Mats, Houston, 1959-60; estimator prodn. man Webb Printing Co., Houston, 1960, Western Lithograph Co. Tex., Houston, 1960-61; buyer Tenneco Inc., Houston, 1961-67, purchasing rep., 1967-72, mgr. corp. procurement, 1972-75, mgr. purchasing and forms adminstrn., 1975—; instr. in forms adminstrn. N.Harris County; instr. in graphic communications Main Campus U. Houston. Pres. Oak Forest Civic Club, 1963-64; v.p. Nottingham Civic Club, 1965-66; precinct committeeman Harris County Rep. party, 1964, chmn. Neighbor to Neighbor fund drive, 1965-66, dir. public relations, 1966-69, mem. public relations com., 1969-70, del. county/dist. and state conv., 1962-78, alt. del. Rep. nat. conv., 1964; advisory com. Houston Ind. Sch. Dist. Office Edn., Printing Tech. Dept., San Jacinto Coll.; edn. com. Printing Industries of Gulf Coast; graphic communications career edn. council Tex. Edn. Agency; participant project bus. Jr. Achievement. Recipient Ben Franklin award, Houston Printing Week Com., 1974; named Graphic Communicator of Yr., Graphic Communication Council of Houston, 1979. Mem. Purchasing Mgmt. Assn. Houston (local bd. dirs. 1976-79, newsletter editor, co-chmn. publicity Dist. II), Bus. Forms Mgmt. Assn. Houston (pres. 1977-79, v.p. internat. of Dist. II, internat., Region II, local outstanding mem. of year 1976-77, outstanding mem. of year Dist. II 1977-78, internat., 1978-79), Houston Litho Club, Internat. Graphic Arts Edn. Assn., Graphic Arts Tech. Found., Nat. Assn. Printing Buyers (organizing dir.), Tex. Assn. Bus., Houston C. of C. Methodist. Clubs: Tennwood, Press Club of Houston, Masons, Scottish Rite. Contbr. articles in field to publs., 1951-79; conf. speaker, 1976. Home: 13930 Barryknoll Ln Houston TX 77079 Office: 1010 Milam St Suite 515 Houston TX 77002

BENSON, JAMES MICHAEL, mfg. cons. co. exec.; b. Tampa, Fla., Jan. 6, 1947; s. Hilton Rollin and Betty Jo (Alderman) B.; student Stetson U., 1965-67; B.A., U. South Fla., 1970; m. Connie Cope, Dec. 20, 1968; children—Michelle, Heather, James Michael. Mailroom clk. Systams Corp., Tampa, 1967-68, programmer, analyst, 1968-72, mgr. customer service dept., 1973; mgmt. analyst Hillsborough County Bd. County Commrs., Tampa, 1972; cons. Fails & Assos. of Tampa, Inc., 1973-77, v.p., mgr. cons., 1978-80; sr. v.p. W. Coast ops. Cheezem Devel. Corp., St. Petersburg, Fla., 1980—; dir. Sandak of Fla., Inc.; prof. bus. Fla. Coll., Temple Terrace, 1970-72. Pres., Fla. Coll. Athletic Boosters, 1973, chmn. bd., 1974. Named Falconeer of Yr., Fla. Coll. Athletic Boosters, 1974. Mem. Nat. Assn. Personnel Adminstrs. Republican. Mem. Ch. of Christ. Home: 9430 Channing Circle Apt 1701 Tampa FL 33617 Office: 7820 38 Ave N Saint Petersburg FL 33710

BENSON, MARY LOUISE BAKER, real estate broker; b. Wildwood, Fla., July 15, 1925; d. David Lewis and Gladys Pearl (Geiger) Baker; A.A. with honors, Brevard Community Coll., 1974; m. Richard Earl Benson, Mar. 7, 1943 (div. June 1971); children—Mary Virginia, Robert Howard, Ronald Gene. Sec., CSC, Washington, D.C., Dayton, Ohio, Cocoa Beach, Fla., 1962-73; asso. Gulf Atlantic Realty Inc., Wildwood, Fla., 1974-75; owner, mgr. Mary B. Benson Realty, Wildwood, 1976—; pres. Baker Properties, Inc., Wildwood. Camping cons., troop leader, dist. dir. Tex. Colo. council Girl Scouts U.S.A., Austin, Tex., 1957-59; mem. spl. gifts div. United Way Cocoa Beach, Fla., 1973-74; bd. dirs., sec. Brevard Assn. for Retarded Children, Rockledge, Fla., 1969-74, Fla. Assn. for Retarded Citizens, 1971—; pres. Sumter Assn. Retarded Citizens, 1979; vice chmn., sec. dist. 7 human rights adv. com. Sunland Hosp., Orlando, 1973-76. Recipient Thanks badge Tex. Colo. council Girl Scouts U.S.A., 1958; Appreciation award United Way Brevard County, 1974. Mem. Nat. Assn. Realtors, Federally Employed Women, Fla., Am. Nat. Cowbells Assn., Fedn. Women's Club, Phi Theta Kappa. Democrat. Clubs: Continental Country (Wildwood, Fla.); Order of Eastern Star (Cocoa Beach, Fla.). Home and Office: PO Box 1232 Wildwood FL 32785

BENSON, MELVIN LEE, equipment mfg. co. exec.; b. Marinette, Wis., Jan. 8, 1928; s. Melvin Edward and Bertha Marie (Linser) B.; student Engring. Ill. Inst. Tech., Rockford, 1948-50; B.S. in Chem. Engring., U. Wis.-Madison, 1953; m. Ann M. Lietz, Mar. 1, 1952; children—Sharon, James, Lynne, Scott. Asst. sales mgr. Eclipse Fuel Engring. Co., Rockford, 1955-60, Chattanooga, 1960-64; sales engr. Goslin-Birmingham (Ala.) Mfg. Co., 1964-65; regional mgr. air pollution control equipment Western Precipitation div. Joy Mfg. Co., Chgo., 1965-70, Atlanta, 1970-72; mfg. rep. air pollution control equipment Applied Engring. Co., Atlanta, 1972-75; v.p. Carotek Inc., Atlanta, 1975-80; pres. M. L. Benson & Assos., Inc., Atlanta, 1980—. Football ofcl. high schs., colls., 1955-70; swimming ofcl. high schs., YMCA, AAU, 1965-75; v.p. Dunwoody (Ga.) High Sch. P.T.S.A., 1973, pres., 1974; pres. Dunwoody High Sch. Swim Team Booster Club, 1974-75; vice chmn. swim com. Dunwoody Country Club, 1972-73. Served with USMC, 1946-48. Recipient Appreciation Plaque B.R. Ryall YMCA for orgn. swim team, 1970. Registered profl. engr., Ill., Tenn. Mem. Am. Inst. Chem. Engrs., Air Pollution Control Assn., TAPPI, Chem. Equipment Engring. Assn. Chgo., Chattanooga Engring. Club, Tenn. Soc. Profl. Engrs. (gen. chmn. engring. week 1963, sec. chpt. 1964-65). Club: Peachtree World of Tennis. Author: (with E. T. Blockley) ABC's of Dowtherm Engineering, 1962. Home: 1756 Tamworth Ct Dunwoody GA 30338 Office: PO Box 88296 Atlanta GA 30338

BENSON, PAUL HARRISON, JR., radio station exec.; b. Simpsonville, S.C., Apr. 18, 1915; s. Paul Harrison and Lucile (Woodside) B.; student U. S.C., 1932-33; A.A., Anderson Coll., 1934; student High Mus. Sch. Art (Atlanta), 1934-36; m. Sara D'Oyley Croft, Nov. 6, 1937; children—Paul Harrison III, George Laurence, Sara Legere (Mrs. Hugh B. Thomas), Peter Woodside. Mgr., partner Atlantic Outdoor Advt. Co., Florence, S.C., 1936-47; mng. dir. Radio Sta. WJMX, Florence, 1948—; pres., treas. Atlantic Broadcasting Co., 1947—; dir. Darlington Raceway Radio Network, 1952-77. Mem. Florence County Selective Service Bd., 1946-49, chmn. bd., 1948-49. Bd. dirs. Florence County chpt. ARC, 1974, Florence Boys Club, Florence County unit Am. Cancer Soc., 1977—; dir.-at-large Pee Dee council Boy Scouts Am., 1971-73. Served with USNR, 1945. Recipient Honor Certificate for editorial comment Freedoms Found. at Valley Forge, 1966; George Washington Honor medal, 1967, Honor certificate, 1968, 69; Paul Harris fellow, 1980. Mem. Florence C. of C. (dir. 1960-63), Assn. of Broadcasters (charter), S.C. Broadcasters Assn. (dir. 1970-72, 76-78). Rotarian (sec. Florence 1942-44, 77-78, pres. 1978-79, v.p. 1979-80, dir. 1974-76, treas. 1976-77). Home: McIver Rd Florence SC 29501 Office: PO Box F-21 Florence SC 29501

BENSON, STANLEY HUGH, librarian; b. Sparta, Ill., Oct. 1, 1930; s. Edward Hugh and Laurence (Sanders) B.; B.S., So. Ill. U., 1951; B.D., Southwestern Bapt. Theol. Sem., 1956, Th.D., 1964; M.L.S., U. Tex. at Austin, 1965; Ph.D., U. Okla., 1979; m. Sara Elizabeth Collins, Dec. 28, 1959; children—Andrew, Raymond. Library asst. Tex. Christian U., 1959-61; head librarian Ky. So. Coll., 1964-68, Gardner-Webb Coll., 1968-69, Berry Coll., 1969-71; head librarian Okla. Bapt. U., Shawnee, 1971—, dir. Mabee Learning Center, 1976—. Instr. library sci. and religion, part-time 1964—. Lilly Endowment fellow Am. Theol. Library Assn., 1963. Mem. ALA, Southwestern Library Assn., Okla. Library Assn. Baptist. Home: 234 E Pulaski Shawnee OK 74801 Office: Oklahoma Baptist University Mabee Learning Center Shawnee OK 74801

BENSON, WILLIAM DIXON, constrn. co. exec.; b. Dallas, Mar. 25, 1949; s. William Edward and Wilma Lee B.; B.A., U. Tex., Austin, 1973; m. Judith Lee Ryser, July 6, 1974; children—William Nicholas, Jeffrey Dixon. Reporter, Dallas Times Herald, 1974; project mgr. Gray-Gannaway Constrn., Austin, 1975-76; pres. Benson Gen. Contractors, Inc., Austin, 1976—; co-founder Guadalupe Entertainment Ventures. Bd. dirs. Austin YMCA. Mem. Asso. Builders and Contractors (dir.). Home: 709 Lost Canyon Austin TX 78746 Office: 1001 B West Austin TX 78701

BENT, DOROTHY FLORENCE (MRS. ALLEN EMERY BENT), realtor; b. Whitingham, Vt., June 1, 1920; d. Harold Edgar and Florence Vernette (Hicks) Plumb; B.S. (Cotting Meml. scholar), U. Mass., 1942; M.A. in Teaching, U. Vt., 1968; m. Allen Emery Bent, Nov. 11, 1944; children—Kim Allen, David Emery, Douglas Gene, Robert Arnold, Cynthia Lee. County 4-H club agt. Chittenden County, Burlington, Vt., 1942-43, Orange County, Middletown, N.Y., 1943-44; acting county club agt. Orange County, Chelsea, Vt., 1954; tchr. Whitcomb High Sch., Bethel, Vt., 1960-67; county extension agt. Windsor County, Woodstock, Vt., 1967-72; realtor Pyramid Realty & Mortgage Corp., Winter Haven, Fla., 1977—. Cons., instr. handicapped homemakers. Adviser Windsor, Springfield family centers; mem. tech. adv. com. Health Care and Rehab. Services Southeastern Vt., Inc., 1970-72; Orange County rep. to Vt. 4-H Club Found., 1952-53; mem. Orange County Extension Adv. Bd., 1965-67; mem. sub-com. on edn. Gov.'s Com. on Children and Youth, 1971-72; den. mother Cub Scouts, 1957-58; pres. Randolph Unit PTA, 1961-63; mem. Vt. Inter-Agy. Council on Smoking and Health, 1971-72, Vt. Preschool Planning Com., 1971-72; del. White House Conf. on Children, 1970. Town auditor Town of Braintree (Vt.), 1950-55; mem. Orange County Republican Com., 1961-62, Polk County Exec. Rep. Com., Winter Haven Tourist Com. Trustee Downer 4-H Camp; bd. dirs. Central Vt. Community Action Council, First Chance Project of Pre-Sch. Edn. Centers, Windsor County and Vt. Community Coordinated Child Care Com.; named Mrs. Vt. of 1963, Mrs. America Homemakers Council. Founder-fellow Internat. Inst. Community Service; mem. Nat. Congress Parents and Tchrs. (life mem.; mem. health and welfare commn. 1969-72, mem. nat. bd. mgrs. 1969-72), Vt. PTA (pres. 1969-73), Nat., Vt. (v.p. 1969-71), New Eng. (sec. 1969-71) assns extension home economists, Winter Haven Bd. Realtors (edn. and polit. action coms.), Nat., Fla. assns. realtors, Cert. Bus. Counselors Inst., Grad. Realtors Inst., Messiah Assn. of Winter Haven, Braintree Hist. Soc. (charter mem.), Vt. Hist. Soc., Orange County 4-H Leaders Assn. (pres. 1952-53), Vt. 4-H Hon. Soc., Mass. All-Stars 4-H Hon. Soc., Conglist. Home: 1310 Lake Elbert Dr SE Winter Haven FL 33880

BENTLEY, BERNARD FRANCIS, ceramic engr.; b. Wellsville, N.Y., Nov. 28, 1943; s. Arnold Albert and Margaret (Rouse) B.; B.S. in Ceramic Engring., Alfred U., 1965; m. Judith G. Wilson, Mar. 30, 1974. With Gen. Electric Co., various locations, 1965—, methods and work measurement, St. Petersburg, Fla., 1968-70, mfg. engr., Wilmington, N.C., 1971-72, sr. process control engr., 1973-76, mgr. powder prodn., 1976-78, mgr. fuel chem. ops., 1978—. Recipient Service to Youth award Clearwater (Fla.) YMCA, 1970. Mem. Am. Soc. Quality Control (certified quality engr.), Am. Ceramic Soc., Nat. Inst. Ceramic Engrs., Keramos. Democrat. Mem. 1st Christian Ch. Home: 1238 Kenningston St Wilmington NC 28401 Office: PO Box 780 MCO2 Wilmington NC 28405

BENTLEY, FRED DOUGLAS, lawyer; real estate investor; b. Marietta, Ga., Oct. 15, 1926; s. Oscar Andrew and Ima Irene (Prather) B.; J.D., Emory U., 1948; B.A., Presbyn. Coll., 1949; m. Sara Tom Moss, Dec. 26, 1953; children—Fred Douglas, Robert Randall. Admitted to Ga. bar, 1948; sr. mem. firm Bentley and Schindelar, and predecessors; sec.-treas. Town & Country Shopping Center, Marietta, 1956-71; pres. Community Investments, Inc., Marietta, 1968—, Market Sq., Inc., Marietta, 1969—; sec.-treas. Market Sq. of Cartersville, Inc., 1969-76, pres., 1976—; sec.-treas. Adirondack Investment Corp., Atlanta, 1969-76, pres., 1976—; founder, pres. Beneficial Investment Co., Marietta, 1970—; sec.-treas. Newmarket Mall, Inc., Marietta, 1972—; speaker, cons. Southeastern Electric Exchange, 1977, Southeastern Real Estate Appraisal Assn., 1976. Chmn., Grants Review Council for the Arts, Atlanta, 1975-77; trustee Kennesaw Coll. Found., 1975—; adv. bd. YWCA, Marietta, 1974—. Named Man of Year, Cobb C. of C., 1951. Mem. Cobb Landmarks Soc. (pres. 1976-77), Am., Ga. bar assns., Cobb County Bar Assn., Am. Trial Lawyers Assn., Am. Def. Lawyers Assn. Methodist. Clubs: Rotary, Gov.'s, Toastmasters (past pres.), Salmagundi. Home: 1441 Beaumont Dr Kennesaw GA 30144 Office: 272 Washington Ave Marietta GA 30060

BENTLEY, JAMES ROBERT, assn. curator; b. Louisville, Feb. 14, 1942; s. Francis Getty and Katharine Elizabeth (Wescott) B.; B.A., Centre Coll. Ky., 1964; M.A., Coll. William and Mary, 1971. Research asst. Colonial Williamsburg (Va.), 1966-68; asst. to curator Filson Club, Louisville, 1964-65, curator, 1968—, sec., 1972—; dir. G.R. Clark Press, Louisville; mem. advisory com. to photograph archives U. Louisville, 1971-72; mem. Hist. Zoning Task Force Louisville and Jefferson County, 1971-73; mem. hist. protection and preservation com. Bd. Aldermen Louisville, 1972-73; commr. Hist. Landmarks and Preservation Dists. Commn., Louisville, 1973-79. Mem. SAR (registrar 1970—, library com.), Ky. Soc. Mayflower Descs. (historian, librarian 1970-78, gov. 1978—, 5 generation project com. 1979—), Ky. Soc. Colonial Wars (councillor 1971-76, registrar 1976-78), Jeffersontown Hist. Soc. (dir. 1972-73, v.p. 1974-76, pres. 1976-78), Soc. Am. Archivists, Manuscript Soc., Hist. Homes Found. Louisville, Vt. Hist. Soc. (life), New Eng. Hist. Geneal. Soc., English Speaking Union, Nat. Geneal. Soc. (life), Vt. Geneal. Soc., Conn. Soc. Genealogists, Vt. Old Cemetery Assn., Alden Kindred Am., Soc. Stukely Westcott Descs., Edmund Rice 1638 Assn., Nat. Trust (Gt. Britain), Soc. Descs. Robert Bartlett of Plymouth Colony, Sigma Chi, Order Ky. Cols. Episcopalian. Club: Pendennis (Louisville). Editor, pub. Ky. Genealogist, 1979—. Home: 3621 Brownsboro Rd Louisville KY 40207 Office: 118 W Breckinridge St Louisville KY 40203

BENTLEY, KENTON EARL, chemist; b. Detroit, June 1, 1927; s. Kenneth and Marion (Tillman) B.; B.S., U. Mich., 1950; Ph.D., U. N.Mex., 1959; m. Elizabeth Montrose, Apr. 18, 1953. Research phys. chemist Consol. Electro-dynamics Corp., Pasadena, Calif., 1956-57; ind. cons. chemist, Albuquerque, 1957-59; vis. prof. Highlands U., Las Vegas, N.Mex., 1959; asst. prof. chemistry Am. U. Beirut, 1959-61; research scientist Lockheed Calif. Co., Burbank, 1962-63; scientist, task leader Jet Propulsion Lab., Calif. Inst. Tech., Pasadena, 1963-65; head electrochemistry group Hughes Aircraft Co., Culver City, Calif., 1965-67; dir. sci. and applications br., mgr. Iran earth resources contracts Lockheed Engring. & Mgmt. Services Co., Inc., Houston, 1967—. Served with USNR, 1945-46. Los Alamos research fellow, U. N.Mex., 1954-56. Mem. Am. Chem. Soc., AAAS (life), AAUP, Am. Astronautical Soc. (sr. mem., dir. 1969-73), Nat. Mgmt. Assn., Sigma Xi (life), Alpha Chi Sigma. Contbr. to profl. jours. Home: 15811

Dunmoor Dr Houston TX 77059 Office: 1830 NASA Rd 1 Houston TX 77058

BENTLEY, VIRGIL TEMPLE, clergyman; b. Kirkland, Tex., Apr. 19, 1919; s. James Thomas and Johnnie Anna (Green) B.; B.A., Harding Coll., 1943; M.Liberal Arts, So. Meth. U., 1971; M.A., North Tex. State U., 1975; m. Ann Ruth French, Sept. 7, 1943; children—Ann Hathaway (Mrs. Darryl Lee Tippens), John David. Ordained to ministry Ch. of Christ, 1941; minister chs., Rockingham, N.C., 1943-46, Flushing, N.Y., 1946, Humble, Tex., 1946-49, Cordell, Okla., 1949-56, Arlington, Va., 1956-57, Oklahoma City, 1957-67, Dallas, 1967—. Lectr. colls. and univs.; cons. pub. relations and pub. affairs to chambers commerce. Washita County (Okla.) chmn. March of Dimes, 1951-56; mem. Tex. Gov.'s Com. on Religious Responsibility in Aging, 1975; mem. exec. com. Tex. Alcohol Narcotics Edn., 1970—; Chs. of Christ rep. to Nat. Interfaith Coalition on Aging, 1974—. Mem. Nat. Gerontol. Soc. Kiwanian. Author: The Beauty of Age, 1975, Public Relations for Nursing Homes, 1975; editor Herald of Hope, 1970—; occasional guest editor 20th Century Christian, 1958—. Home: 10715 Wyatt Dallas TX 75218 Office: 1000 Wiggins Pkwy Dallas TX 75218

BENTLEY, WILLIAM GEORGE, economist; b. Pitts., Oct. 25, 1945; s. William Robert and Priscella Jean (Sweet) B.; B.A., Clemson U., 1968; M.A., Tex. Tech. U., 1969; Ph.D., Ga. State U., 1977; m. Sandra Sue Richardson, July 11, 1968; children—William Robert II, Ross Ashley. Asst. prof. of econs. DeKalb Coll., Atlanta, Ga., 1969-74; economist Office of the Gov., Atlanta, 1974-75, Fla. Power & Light Co., Miami, 1975—; adj. prof. Fla. Internal U., 1975—. Mem. Nat. Assn. Bus. Economists, So. Econs. Assn., Am. Statis. Assn. (award 1977), S. Fla. Econ. Soc. Republican. Contbr. articles on econs. to profl. jours. Home: 13381 SW 78th St Miami FL 33183 Office: PO Box 013100 Miami FL 33101

BENTON, EVELYN FLEMING, librarian; b. Ponchatoula, La., Aug. 10, 1921; d. Walter Raleigh and Mabel Magdalene (Varnado) Fleming; B.F.A. with high distinction and spl. mention in music, Okla. State U., 1943; student U. Tex. Grad. Sch. Library Sci., 1959-60; m. Douglas C. Benton, Aug. 25, 1942; children—Walter Bradford, Christopher Paul. Circulation asst. Tulsa Pub. Library, 1944, 1st asst. tech. dept., 1945; reference asst. Okla. State U., Stillwater, 1946-48, jr. reference librarian, 1948-50; piano tchr., Baytown, Tex., 1958-60; asst. librarian Lee Coll., Baytown, 1960-66; library dir. Deer Park (Tex.) Pub. Library, 1967—; chmn. long range planning com. Houston Area Library System, 1975-77, mem. automation and by-laws com., 1978—; mem. adv. council on public library curriculum Sam Houston State U. Sch. Library Sci., 1977—. Pres., San Jacinto Music Tchrs. Assn., 1960; chmn. Heritage '76 com. Deer Park Bicentennial Commn. Pres. Baytown Unitarian Fellowship, 1965. Mem. Am., Tex. (chmn. nominating com. 1971-72, chmn. reference roundtable 1972-73, sec. dist. V, 1969, treas. dist. VIII, 1971, mem. membership com. 1975-76), Southwestern (conf. program com. 1974, Tex. chmn. membership com. 1975-76), Pub. (editorial com.) library assns., Tex. Municipal Librarians Assn., Houston Library Club, Phi Kappa Phi, Sigma Alpha Iota (treas. Iota Alpha chpt. 1942-43). Unitarian. Contbr. articles to profl. jours.; co-author: An Introduction to the Houston Area Library System Computer Access Network, 1979. Home: 5874 Doliver Houston TX 77057 Office: 3009 Center St Deer Park TX 77536

BENTON, NICHOLAS, pub. exec.; b. Boston, Oct. 18, 1926; s. Jay Rogers and Frances (Hill) B.; grad. Phillips Exeter Acad., 1945; A.B., Harvard, 1951; m. Kate Lenthal Bigelow, June 5, 1954; children—Frances Hill, Kate, Emily Weld, Louisa Barclay. Promotion writer Life mag., N.Y.C., 1951-55; asst. to pub. Fortune mag., N.Y.C., 1955-57; advt. promotion mgr. Archtl. Forum, N.Y.C., 1957-64; gen. promotion mgr. Time-Life Books, N.Y.C., 1965-68, pub. relations dir., 1968—; v.p. Time-Life Books, Inc., Alexandria, Va., 1977. Mem. Nat. Book Awards Com., 1971, co-chmn. Nat. Book Awards week, 1974-79. Pres., E. 69th St. Assn., 1963-64; 1st v.p. Soc. Meml. Sloan-Kettering Cancer Center, 1963-64, asst. treas., 1964-66, treas., 1967-68. Served with AUS, 1945-46. Mem. Pubs. Publicity Assn. (pres. 1970-71), New Eng. Historic Geneal. Soc. (trustee 1979—), N.Y. Geneal. and Biog. Soc., Assn. Am. Publishers (Freedom to Read com. 1974-78, internat. freedom to publish com. 1979—). Clubs: Harvard (bd. mgrs. 1971-73) (N.Y.C.); Bourne Cove Yacht (Wareham, Mass.); Coffee House. Author: A Benton Heritage, 1964. Created musical revue Phoenix '55, 1955; co-producer musical Salad Days, 1958. Home: 1007 Turkey Run Rd McLean VA 22101 Office: Time-Life Books Inc Alexandria VA 22314

BENTSEN, LLOYD MILLARD, JR., U.S. senator; b. Mission, Tex., Feb. 11, 1921; s. Lloyd M. and Edna Ruth (Colbath) B.; LL.B., U. Tex., 1942; m. Beryl Ann Longino, Nov. 27, 1943; children—Lloyd M. III, Lan, Tina. Admitted to Tex. bar, 1942; practice law, McAllen, Tex., 1945-48; judge Hidalgo County (Tex.), hdqrs. Edinburg, 1946-48; mem. 80th to 83d congresses from 15th Tex. Dist.; pres. Lincoln Consol., Houston, 1955-70; U.S. senator from Tex., 1971—, mem. finance and pub. works coms., chmn. joint econ. com. Mem. Sam. Houston council Boy Scouts Am., U. Tex. Devel. Bd. Served to maj. USAAF, 1942-45; col. Res. ret. Decorated D.F.C., Air medal with 3 oak leaf clusters. Home: Houston TX Office: 515 Rusk Ave Suite 4026 Houston TX 77002 also Senate Office Bldg Washington DC 20510

BENYA, THEODORE JOHN, indsl. toxicologist; b. Cleve., Mar. 18, 1932; s. John H. and Emma Susan Banya; B.S. in Pharmacy, U. Mich., 1955, M.S. in Hosp. Pharmacy, 1958, M.S. in Pharm. Chemistry, 1973, Ph.D. in Pharmacy, 1974, M.S. in Public Health, 1977; children—Lauren E., Diana L., Sharon E. Asst. dir. pharmacy Harris Hosp., Ft. Worth, 1959-63; dir. pharm. services and central sterile supply U. Md. Hosp., Balt., 1963-69; asst. prof. pharmaceutics U. Ariz., Tucson, 1974-75, dir. clin. pharmacy, 1974-75; chmn. dept. pharmacy and health care adminstrn. Ohio No. U., Ada., 1975-76; toxicologist Ethyl Corp., Baton Rouge, 1977—; pharm. cons. Phoenix Hosp., 1974-75. Bd. dirs. March of Dimes, 1977—; mem. Baton Rouge Inter-Civic Council, 1979—. Upjohn fellow, 1956-58, Am. Found. Pharm. Edn. fellow, 1958-59; NIH grantee, 1969-74. Mem. Am. Public Health Assn., Am. Pharm. Assn., Am. Soc. Hosp. Pharmacists, Am. Indsl. Hygiene Assn. Republican. Methodist. Contbr. articles on clin. pharmacy, hosp. pharmacy adminstrn., toxicology to profl. jours. Home: 15411 Chickamauga Dr Baton Rouge LA 70816 Office: Ethyl Corp 451 Florida Ave Baton Rouge LA 70801

BENZ, GEORGE ALBERT, educator; b. St. Louis, Feb. 21, 1926; s. George and Genevieve B. (Klueg) B.; B.B.A., N. Tex. State U., 1953, M.S., 1955; Ph.D., U. Okla., 1969; m. D. Jean Tabor, Apr. 14, 1951; 1 dau., Lynda Kaye. Grad. asst. U. Okla., 1957-59; asst. prof. Central State U., 1959-66; prof., chmn. dept. econs. St. Mary's U., San Antonio, 1969-71, 78—, dir. U. Research Center, 1971—, chmn. urban studies dept., 1972—; cons. several poverty projects; econ. expert witness in loss of income and anti-trust cases, 1973—. Chmn., San Antonio Civil Liberties Union, 1970-71; mem. Tex. State adv. com. U.S. Civil Rights Comm., 1969-77. Served with Paratroops 11th Airborne Div., U.S. Army, 1943-49. Decorated Bronze Star medal. Mem. AAUP (v.p. Tex. chpt. 1970-71), Am., So. econ. assns., Southwest Social Science Assn., San Antonio Bus. and Econs. Soc. (v.p. 1975-77). Home: 206 E Sunshine Dr San Antonio TX 78228 Office: 2700 Cincinnati St San Antonio TX 78284

BERBARY, MAURICE SHEHADEH, physician, mil. officer, hosp. adminstr., educator; b. Beirut, Lebanon, Jan. 14, 1923; s. Shehadeh M. and Marie K. Berbary; came to U.S., 1945, naturalized, 1952; B.A., Am. U., Beirut, 1943; M.D., U. Tex., 1948; M.A. in Hosp. Adminstrn., Baylor U., 1970; diploma Army Command and Gen. Staff Coll., Leavenworth, Kan., 1963, Air Force Sch. Aerospace Medicine, 1964, Army War Coll., Carlisle, Pa., 1969; m. Bruennhild Hepp; children—Geoffrey Maurice, Laura Marie. Intern, Parkland Meml. Hosp., Dallas, 1948-49, resident in obstetrics and gynecology, gen. surgery and urology, 1949-53; resident in obstetrics and gynecology Walter Reed Army Hosp., Washington, 1955-57; fellow in obstetric and gynecologic pathology Armed Forces Inst. Pathology, Washington, 1959-60; practice clin. medicine in obstetrics and gynecology, 1953—; capt. M.C., U.S. Army, 1952, advanced through grades to col., 1968; chief dept. obstetrics and gynecology U.S. Army Hosp., Ft. Polk, La., 1957-59, Womack Army Hosp., Ft. Bragg, N.C., 1960-62; div. surgeon 1st. inf. div., Ft. Riley, Kans., 1963-64, 3d. Armored div., Germany, 1964-65; corps surgeon, V. Corps, Germany, 1965-67; corps surgeon 24th Army Corps, S. Vietnam Theater of Operation, 1970; comdr., hosp. adminstr. U.S. Army Hosp., Teheran, Iran, 1954-55; comdr. hosp. group complex, Vietnam, 1969-70; command surgeon U.S. Armed Forces Command and U.S. Army South, U.S. C.Z., Panama, 1970-73; comdr. 5th Gen. Hosp., U.S. Army, Stuttgart, West Germany, 1973-77, Munson Army Hosp., Ft. Leavenworth, Kans., 1977—. Vis. lectr. obstetrics and gynecology pathology Duke U. Med. Center, Durham, N.C., 1960-62; clin. instr. obstetrics and gynecology U. Kans. Med. Center, Kansas City, 1963-64; instr. 5th Army NCO Acad., Fort Riley, Kans., 1963-64. Decorated Legion of Merit with two oak leaf clusters, Bronze Star medal, Army Commendation medal. Diplomate Am. Bd. Obstetrics and Gynecology. Fellow A.C.S., Am. Coll. Obstetricians and Gynecologists; mem. AMA, Assn. of Mil. Surgeons, Soc. of U.S. Army Flight Surgeons, Am. Coll. Hosp. Adminstrs., Internat. Platform Assn., Am. Hosp. Assn., N.Y. Acad. Scis., Dallas County Med. Soc., Tex. State Med. Assn. Mason (32 deg.). Home: 6299 Martel Ave Dallas TX 75214 Office: Commander Munson Army Hosp Fort Leavenworth KS 66027

BERCAW, BEAUREGARD LEE, neurologist; b. Manila, May 30, 1938; s. Woodson Woods and Nancy Dunlap (Scott) B.; B.A., U. Va., 1959, M.D., 1964; m. Barbara Wynne Rixey, June 10, 1961; children—Nancy Stearns, Lee Rixey. Intern, U. Fla., Gainesville, 1964-65, resident in neurology, 1967-70; pvt. practice neurology, Huntsville, Ala., 1970-71, Clearwater, Fla., 1971—; founder, pres. Clin. Neurol. Splties., Clearwater, 1972-79; chief neurology and electroencephalography Morton Plant Hosp., Clearwater, 1971-79, Med. Center Hosp., Largo, Fla., 1979—; asst. clin. prof. neurology U. South Fla., 1975—. Served with USAF, 1965-67. Diplomate Am. Bd. Psychiatry and Neurology; certified Am. Assn. Electromyography and Electrodiagnosis. Fellow Stroke Council of Am. Heart Assn.; mem. Am. Electroencephalographic Soc., So. Med. Assn., So. Clin. Neurol. Soc. (sec. 1976-77, pres. 1978-80), Fla. Neurologic Soc. (sec. 1977-78). Episcopalian. Club: Rotary (dir. Clearwater 1977—). Home: 310 Harbor View Ln Largo FL 33540 Office: 1011 Jeffords St Clearwater FL 33516

BERCHTOLD, GLADYS BEAMAN, chemist; b. Keystone, W.Va., Aug. 1, 1922; s. Charles Bradshaw and Emma Rachel (Frye) Beaman; A.B. cum laude, Concord Coll., 1942; student U. Charleston; m. Paul R. Berchtold, Mar. 9, 1974; children from previous marriage—Troy Stallard, Susan Stallard Thomas, Catherine Stallard Hess. Chemist, Union Carbide, 1942-43; tchr. Beaver High Sch., 1944-45, Bluefield Coll., 1946-47; chemist Godwin Labs., 1947-49; founder, pres. Standard Labs. Ky., 1949—, Standard Labs. W.Va., Charleston, 1972—; v.p. Standard Enterprises, 1973—; sec. Standard Instrumentation, 1976—; v.p. Country Club Village, 1972—. Mem. ASTM (dir.), Am. Chem. Soc., Am. Council Ind. Labs. (chmn. energy com.), Republican. Presbyterian. Office: 3322 Pennsylvania Ave Charleston WV 25302

BERENGUER, JOHN, lawyer; b. Santiago, Cuba, Jan. 20, 1935; came to U.S., 1961, naturalized, 1966; s. Jose A. and Juana C. (Cancino) B.; B.A., U. Del., 1961; M.S.W., U. N.C., 1966; D.S.W., U. Costa Rica, 1969; LL.D. (hon.), Oriente U., 1971; m. Elba F. Martinez, July 22, 1972; children—Desiree, John Micah, George, Douglas. Exec. dir. Spanish Consultation Center, Spain, S. Am., Caribbean, 1965-75; consul of Costa Rica, 1976-78; pres. Lang. Bank Internat., Jacksonville, Fla., 1978—; cons. City of Jacksonville, 1975-78; cons. fgn. govts. Mem. U.S. Jaycees. Democrat. Methodist. Editor weekly newspaper OLA. Home: 3711 Riveredge Dr Jacksonville FL 32211 Office: 7530 Merrill Rd Suite 4 Jacksonville FL 32211 also 7825 Baymeadows Way Suite 103B Jacksonville FL

BERGAN, NORMAN ARNOLD, JR., design and mfg. exec., cons.; b. Buffalo, July 24, 1941; s. Norman Arnold and Ruth Elizabeth (Reisinger) B.; Asso. in Mech. Tech., Erie County Community Coll., 1963; B.S., Tri-State U., 1968; M.B.A., U. Dallas, 1974; m. Freda Lee Richards, Feb. 14, 1971. Plant engr. Wer Indsl. Corp., Buffalo, 1963-65, prodn. control mgr., 1965-66; mfg. engr. equipment div. Tex. Instruments, Inc., Dallas, 1968-70, producibility engr., 1970-74, program mgr., petroleum exploration div., 1974-76; dir. product engring. SMC Industries, Inc., Dallas, 1976-80; exec. dir. Indsl. Tech. Research and Devel. Found., Inc., Durant, Okla., 1980—. Recipient Incentive Compensation Plan award, 1972. Mem. IEEE, Soc. Tool and Mfg. Engrs., Soc. Automotive Engrs. Home: 5204 Creekwood Dr Durant OK 74701 Office: 1504 W Main St Durant OK 74701

BERGEAUX, PHILIP JAMES, educator; b. Eunice, La., May 1, 1918; s. Velmont Laurence and Lydia (Guillory) B.; B.S., Southwestern La. U., 1940; postgrad. N.C. State U., 1946-47; M.S., U. Ga., 1960, Ed.D., 1974; m. Gertrude Arlene Scholl, Jan. 15, 1943; children—Philip James, Lois Arlene. Sales agronomist Tenn. Corp., Atlanta, 1947-56; extension agronomist U. Ga., Athens, 1956-78; cons. agronomist Internat. Minerals & Chem. Corp., Atlanta, 1978—; cons. to Lowe & Stephens, Atlanta, 1966-70. Served to lt. comdr. USNR, 1944-46. Decorated Bronze Star. Mem. Am. Soc. Agronomy, County Agts. Assn., Ga. Plant Food Ednl. Soc. (hon. life; ednl. adviser), Phi Kappa Phi. Home: 125 Sharon Circle Athens GA 30601

BERGEN, HERBERT LOUIS, mgmt. analyst; b. Balt., Nov. 17, 1916; student U. Va., 1940-41, Del Mar Coll., 1948-49, U. Md., 1951, 59, Tulane U., 1954-56, Ohio State U., 1959; B.B.A., U. Miami, 1969; M.S. in Mgmt., Fla. Internat. U., 1974; m. Binnie Posner, Dec. 3, 1944; children—Mira Diana, Sally Ann. Served as enlisted man U.S. Army, 1942-43; commd. 2d lt. U.S. Army, 1943, advanced through grades to maj., 1959, discharged, 1963; stock control supr. 31 Air Def. Arty. Brigade, Homestead AFB, Fla., 1964-66, program analyst, 1966-74, mgmt. analyst, 1974-79; exec. officer 915 Tactical Fighter Group Homestead AFB, 1979—. Decorated Army Commendation medal with 2 oak leaf clusters. Recipient Sustained Superior Performance award, 1970, 76, 79; Outstanding Performance award, 1975; Outstanding Fed. Service award, 1975. Mem. Inst. for Mgmt. Scis., Ret. Officers Assn., Jewish War Vets. Democrat. Jewish. Club: Masons. Office: 915 Tactical Fighter Group Air Force Res Homestead Air Force Base FL 33039

BERGEN, HOWARD SILAS, JR., chem. and plastics co. exec.; b. St. Louis, Apr. 4, 1921; s. Howard S. and Marion Leonie (Broyer) B.; B.S. in Chem. Engring., Washington U., St. Louis, 1942; m. Joan Town, Apr. 27, 1963; children—Lisa T., Laurie A.; children by previous marriage—Bruce H., Patricia A. Engaged in plasticizer devel. Monsanto Co., St. Louis, 1946-55, field sales specialist, 1955-57, product mgr. plasticizers, 1957-64, dir. sales, 1964-67, sales dir. functional fluids, 1967-68, bus. dir. functional fluids, 1968-70, bus. dir. specialty products, 1970-76; pres. Shintech, Inc., Houston, 1976-77; gen. mgr. resins Ga.-Pacific Corp., Atlanta, 1978—. Served to capt. USAF, 1942-46. Mem. Am. Chem. Soc., Soc. Plastics Industry, Paper Industry Mgmt. Assn., Pulp Chem. Assn., Sigma Xi, Alpha Chi Sigma. Methodist. Clubs: Forest Hills Country (Chesterfield, Mo.); Atlanta Athletic; Pine Forest Country (Houston). Contbr. articles in plastic field, market research to profl. lit. Home: 1792 Castle Way NE Atlanta GA 30345

BERGEN, JUDY BERRY, pub. co. exec.; b. Dallas, Mar. 29, 1946; d. Ancel Lloyd and Carma Lee (Tidwell) Berry; student Dallas County Jr. Coll., 1971-73; m. John Fredric Whitaker, Dec. 23, 1977; children—Laurie Rae Tribble, Ted Lowrey Tribble. Mem. public relations staff Dallas C. of C. Conv. Bur., 1968-73; public affairs program producer Sta. KPBC, Dallas, 1973-74; pres. OK Street Ednl. Corp., Dallas, 1974—. Active worker Congressman Alan Steelman campaign. Mem. Am. Booksellers Assn., Am. Mgmt. Assn. Editor, pub.: Personal Marriage Contract, 1976; Unmask, 1978. Office: OK Street Ednl Corp 12800 Hillcrest Rd Suite 215 Dallas TX 75230

BERGER, GARY STERLING, physician; b. Rochester, N.Y., Oct. 19, 1942; s. Milton R. and Helen M. (Knopf) B.; A.B. cum laude, Harvard Coll., 1965; M.D., U. Rochester, 1969; M.S. in Public Health, U. N.C., 1976; m. Barbara Jean Mackenzie, Dec. 18, 1965. Intern, Duke U. Hosp., Durham, N.C., 1969-70; asst. resident ob-gyn Johns Hopkins Hosp., Balt., 1970-71; resident ob-gyn N.C. Meml. Hosp., Chapel Hill, 1973-76; practice medicine specializing in ob-gyn and public health, Chapel Hill, 1976-79, Raleigh, N.C., 1979—; asso. dir. research and tng. Internat. Fertility Research Program, Research Triangle Park, N.C., 1976-77; clin. asst. prof. dept. ob-gyn U. N.C., 1979—, dir. menstruation and reprodn. history program, 1978—; med. dir. Nat. Women's Health Orgn., N.Y.C., 1979—, Raleigh Women's Health Orgn., 1979—; bd. dirs. Charles A. Fields Found., Ltd., Madison, Wis., 1978—; pres. Center for Advancement of Reproductive Health, Raleigh, 1979—. Served with USPHS, 1971-73. Diplomate Am. Bd. Ob-Gyn, Am. Bd. Preventive Medicine. Fellow Am. Coll. Obstetricians and Gynecologists, Am. Coll. Preventive Medicine; mem. Am. Fertility Soc., Am. Assn. Gynecol. Laparoscopists, Robert A. Ross Obstet. and Gynecol. Soc., AAUP, AAAS, Assn. Planned Parenthood Physicians, Internat. Soc. for Twin Studies, AMA, N.C. Med. Assn., Am. Public Health Assn., Soc. Adolescent Medicine. Contbr. articles to med. jours.; contbg. author: Intrauterine Devices and Their Complications, 1979. Home: 3 Wolf's Rd Pond Chapel Hill NC 27514 Office: 917 W Morgan St Raleigh NC 27603

BERGER, HANNA LEONE, sch. counselor; b. Selma, Ala., Feb. 19, 1942; d. Hermann and Frieda (Kahn) B.; B.A., Ala. Coll., 1963; M.A. in English Edn., U. Ala., 1970, M.A. in Counseling and Guidance, 1978. Tchr. French and English, Baker High Sch., Columbus, Ga., 1963-68; resource tchr. with Fed. Project, Tuscaloosa, Ala., 1970-71; tchr. creative writing, humanities and lit. Druid High Sch., Tuscaloosa, 1971-76; tchr. English, Selma (Ala.) High Sch., 1976-78; counselor Westside Jr. High Sch., Selma, 1978—; participant psychology study group Centerpoint; vol. work with Crisis Center. Mem. NEA, Ala. Edn. Assn., Selma Edn. Assn., Am. Personnel and Guidance Assn., Assn. for Humanistic Psychology, Assn. for Humanistic Edn. and Devel., Am. Sch. Counselor Assn., AAUW. Jewish. Office: Westside Jr High Sch Summerfield Rd Selma AL 36701

BERGER, LEONARD, educator; b. Phila., June 15, 1947; s. Charles and Ethel B.; B.A., Temple U., 1968, M.A., 1970, Ph.D., 1972; m. Ellen Natalie Wesler, May 25, 1969. Asso. prof. psychology Clemson (S.C.) U., 1972—, asso. prof. profl. devel., 1973—, asso. prof. continuing edn., 1974—; vocational expert Bur. Hearing and Appeals, Social Security Adminstrn.; cons. to local industry and govt. Bd. dirs. Foothills Friends of Zoo. Named Outstanding Educator of Year, 1975, Personality of South, 1975, Men of Bicentennial Era, 1975, Best Tchr. dept. psychology Clemson U., 1974-75. Licensed indsl. psychologist, S.C. Mem. Am., Southeastern, S.C. psychol. assns., Internat. Applied Psychol. Assn., Psi Chi. Clubs: Sertoma (sec. 1975—); Sage (v.p. 1974—); Terpsichorean. Home: PO Box 1245 Clemson SC 29631 Office: Dept Psychology Clemson U Clemson SC 29632

BERGER, SIDNEY LOUIS, educator; b. N.Y.C., Jan. 25, 1936; s. Sam and Pauline (Schrank) B.; B.A., Bklyn. Coll., 1957; M.A., U. Kans., 1960, Ph.D., 1964; m. Helen Sandra Hopkins, Mar. 2, 1963; children—Jennifer Leslie, Erik William. Dir. grad. studies Mich. State U., 1964-69; chmn. dept. drama U. Houston, 1969—; Am. specialist in theatre dept. State, 1963-64; dir. USO Nat. Shows Com. Mem. cultural affairs com. Houston C. of C., 1969—; active Houston Cultural Affairs Council. Mem. Univ. Resident Theatre Assn., Am. Theatre Assn., Houston C. of C. (cultural affairs com. 1969—). Dir. prodns. for overseas touring Dept. Def., Am. Theatre Assn. and USO. Home: 4711 Imogene St Houston TX 77096 Office: Dept Drama U Houston Cullen Blvd Houston TX 77004

BERGER, STEVEN BARRY, physicist; b. N.Y.C., Dec. 1946; s. Bernard I. and Sylvia B.; B.S., M.I.T., 1967, Ph.D., 1973. Postdoctoral fellow Fight-For-Sight, Inc., Harvard-M.I.T. Program in Health Scis., 1974-76; sr. electro-optics scientist ITEK Corp., Lexington, Mass., 1976-77; asst. editor Am. Jour. Physics, Mass. Inst. Tech., 1975-78; sr. project engr. TRW, McLean, Va., 1978—. Mem. Am. Phys. Soc., Math. Assn. Am., IEEE, Optical Soc. Am., Acoustical Soc. Am., Ops. Research Soc. Am., Am. Math. Soc., N.Y. Acad. Scis., Am. Assn. Physics Tchrs., Sigma Xi. Home: 1-318 8350 Greensboro Dr McLean VA 22102 Office: TRW Systems Group 7600 Colshire Dr McLean VA 22102

BERGER, WALTER JASPER, JR., mfg. co. exec.; b. New Orleans, July 12, 1945; s. Walter J. and Jennie M. (Briguglio) B.; B.S., Loyola U., New Orleans, 1972, postgrad., 1973-74, 75-76; m. Sylvia Lee O'Brien, Apr. 2, 1966; children—Kristine Margarette, Walter Jasper. Dep. dir. fin. The Family Health Found., New Orleans, 1971-74; fin. cons. U.S. Dist. Ct. Eastern Dist. La. and State of La., 1974—; chief fin. officer, corp. controller The Laitram Corp., New Orleans, 1976—, Laitram Machinery, Inc., New Orleans, 1976—, Intralox, Inc., New Orleans, 1976—, Digicourse, Inc., New Orleans, 1976—, Tierra-Mar, Inc., New Orleans, 1976—. C.P.A., La. Mem. Nat. Assn. Accts., Am. Inst. C.P.A.'s, Soc. La. C.P.A.'s. Club: Pontchartrain, Inc. Home: 7030 Manchester St New Orleans LA 70126 Office: 220 Laitram Ln Harahan LA 70123

BERGER, WILLIAM ERNEST, newspaper pub.; b. Ferris, Ill., June 6, 1918; s. William George and Ethel (Nelson) B.; student Carthage Coll., 1935-38; m. Jerry June Barnes, Feb. 26, 1943; children—William Edward, Barbara, John Jeffrey. Newspaper editor and pub., Hondo, Tex., 1946-65; commr. Tex. Water Rights Commn., Austin, 1965-69; pres. Asso. Tex. Newspapers, Inc., 1957—; pres. S. Tex. Press, Inc., Hondo, 1979—; owner radio sta. KRME Hondo, 1969—. Treas., Medina Meml. Hosp., Hondo, 1962-64. Del., Tex. Democratic Conv., 1962, 64, 66, 68, Nat. Dem. Conv., 1968. Served with AUS, 1942-46. Mem. Tex. (pres. 1963), South Tex. (pres. 1954) press assns., Sigma Delta Chi (chpt. treas. 1967-69). Methodist. Lion (Hondo past pres.). Clubs: Headliners, Westwood Country (Austin). Home: 1801 Exposition Blvd Austin TX 78703 Office: 1801 Exposition Blvd Austin TX 78703

BERGERON, CLAUDE ERNEST, JR., acct.; b. New Orleans, July 16, 1941; s. Claude Ernest and Mary Lee (Richard) B.; B.S., Nicholls State U., 1963; M.S., La. State U., 1965; m. Kathleen Ann Noel, Jan. 29, 1966; children—Michael, Kristen, Mary Grace, Allison. With Peat, Marwick, Mitchell & Co., 1965-73, sr. acct. New Orleans, 1966-69, supr., 1969-70, mgr., Houston, 1970-73; partner firm Clement, Bergeron & Broussard, Houma, La., 1973-79; pres. Bergeron, Broussard & Co. P.C., 1979—. Mem. Bd. Tax Equalization in Water Dist. 91, 1973—; mem. St. Bernadette Cath. Sch. Bd., 1977—. C.P.A., La., Tex. Mem. Am. Inst. C.P.A.'s, Tex., La. pres. South Central chpt. 1977) socs. C.P.A.'s, Houma-Terrebonne C. of C., Phi Kappa Phi, Beta Gamma Sigma, Beta Alpha Psi. Club: Houma Rotary. Home: 305 Oak Alley Dr Houma LA 70360 Office: 720 E Main St Houma LA 70360

BERGERON, JIMMIE LEON, physician; b. Reardan, Wash., Nov. 1, 1932; s. Albert Ralph and Louise Marie (Brommer) B.; B.S. in Mech. Engring., B.S. in Indsl. Engring., U. Wash., 1955; postgrad. U. Fla., 1963; M.D., Emory U., 1968; m. Lynn Ann Peters, June 26, 1965; children—James Delbert, Michelle Ann. Mfg. engr. Aero div. Mpls. Honeywell Co., 1957, methods engr. pneumatic controls div., Morton Grove, Ill., 1957-58; with research and devel. staff Sperry Microwave Electronics Co., Clearwater, Fla., 1958-63; mech. engr. Electronic Communications, Inc., St. Petersburg, Fla., 1964; intern Emory U.-VA Hosp., 1968-69; resident in internal medicine Baylor U., Houston, 1969-71, fellow in nephrology, 1971-72; pvt. practice internal medicine, Houston, 1972—; pres. N. Houston Dialysis Center, Inc.; dir. A.R. Bergeron, Inc.; mem. staff Houston N.W. Hosp. Served with Transp. Corps, U.S. Army, 1955-57. Diplomate Am. Bd. Internal Medicine. Mem. A.C.P., Tex. Med. Assn., Harris County Med. Soc. Lutheran. Home: 1023 Maranon Ln Houston TX 77090 Office: 710 FM 1960 W Suite F Houston TX 77090

BERGGREN, GLENN MERRITT, tech. mktg. mgr.; b. Rochester, N.Y., June 3, 1928; s. Robert O. and Grace (Light) B.; B.S. in M.E., U. Rochester, 1950; M.B.A., U. Syracuse, 1962; student automotive engring. Chrysler Inst. Engring., 1950-52, profl. bus. mgmt., Gen. Elec. Co., 1957-58; m. Diane Hamp, June 27, 1953; 1 son, Bruce Robert. With Chrysler Corp., Detroit, 1950-52, Gen. Electric Co., Syracuse and Auburn, N.Y. and Decatur, Ill., 1955-62; theatre products mgr. Kollmorgen Corp., Northampton, Mass., 1962-68, 74-76; v.p., gen. mgr. Wil-Kin, Inc., Atlanta, 1968-74; v.p. cinema div. Schneider Corp., Mineola, N.Y., 1976-80; v.p. mktg. Optical Radiation Corp., Azusa, Calif., 1980—; cons. to motion picture theatre industry. Adult tchr. St. James Methodist Ch., Atlanta. Served with ordnance U.S. Army, 1953-55. Recipient Tech. Citation award Acad. Motion Picture Arts and Scis., 1968, 73, 76, 78. Hon. fellow Soc. Motion Picture and TV Engrs.; mem. Internat. Standards Orgn. Theatre Equipment Assn. N.Y. (bd. dirs.). Clubs: Rotary, Masons, Shriners. Contbr. articles to profl. jour., chpts. to books; regular contbr. to Boxoffice Mag. Developer high resolution projection system Ultravision, 1968-73. Home: 315 Westerhall Ct NE Atlanta GA 30328 Office: 6352 N Irwindale Ave Azusa CA 91702

BERGS, VICTOR VISVALDIS, biologist; b. Kuldiga, Latvia, Dec. 20, 1923; s. Augusts and Zenta (Veinbergs) B.; came to U.S., 1950, naturalized, 1955; A.M., Boston U., 1955; Ph.D. in Med. Microbiology, U. Pa., 1958; m. Maija Ducis, Aug. 20, 1960; 1 son, Alvis. Asst. prof. microbiology Rutgers U., 1958-62; research virologist Stanford Research Inst., Menlo Park, Calif., 1962-65; asst. prof. U. Miami (Fla.), 1965-69, asso. prof., 1969-73; asso. virologist, head virus diagnostic lab. Life Scis., Inc., St. Petersburg, Fla., 1973—; cons. Nat. Cancer Inst., 1972. Bd. dirs. Am. Cancer Soc., Dade County, Fla., 1969-71. NIH grantee, 1964-73. Fellow Am. Acad. Microbiology; mem. Am. Assn. Cancer Research, Am. Assn. Immunologists, Soc. Exptl. Biology and Medicine, Sigma Xi. Contbr. articles to profl. jours. Home: 14401 Tanglewood Dr N Largo FL 33540 Office: 2900 72d St N Saint Petersburg FL 33710

BERING, CONRAD, realtor; b. Houston, Dec. 20, 1895; s. August C. and Josephine (Pauska) B.; student U. Tex., 1914-17; m. Lorene Rogers, July 8, 1920 (dec. Nov. 1965); children—Conrad, Donald Rogers, Barbara Bering Dundas. Owner, operator Conrad Bering Co., Houston, 1922—; pres. Longwoods Corp., Houston, 1952-72, chmn. bd., 1972—; sec.-treas. Bering Realty Corp., Houston, 1952—, Rogers Investment, Inc., Austin, Tex. Life mem. bd. Methodist Hosp., Houston; founder mem. Naval War Coll. Found., Inc., U.S. Naval War Coll., Newport, R.I. Mem. Houston Bd. Realtors, Tex. Real Estate Assn., Navy League U.S. (hon. life pres. Houston council), Nat. Assn. Real Estate Bds., Houston C. of C. (mil. affairs com.). Methodist (mem. bd.). Clubs: Houston, Kiwanis (Houston). Home: 306 Fall River Ct Houston TX 77024 also Box 108 Route 5 Long Island Dr Lake Hamilton Hot Springs AR Office: Conrad Bering Co Suite 121 2221 S Voss Rd Houston TX 77027

BERKELEY, FRANCIS LEWIS, JR., ret. archivist; b. Albemarle County, Va., Apr. 9, 1911; s. Francis Lewis and Ethel (Crissey) B.; B.S., U. Va., 1934, M.A., 1940; m. Helen Wayland Sutherland, June 12, 1937. Tchr. Va. pub. schs., 1934-38; asst. curator manuscripts U. Va. Library, Charlottesville, 1938-41, curator and univ. archivist, 1946-63, asso. librarian, 1957-63, sec. of Rector and Visitors, 1953-58, exec. asst. to pres., 1963-74, archivist emeritus, prof. emeritus, 1974—; council Inst. Early Am. History and Culture. Fulbright research fellow U. Edinburgh, 1952-53; Guggenheim fellow U. London, 1961-62; sec. of navy adv. com. on naval history, 1958—. Trustee Thomas Jefferson Meml. Found.; mem. adv. com. Papers of Thomas Jefferson, Papers of James Madison, Papers of George Washington; mem. Va. Com. on Colonial Records, 1955-71, Va. Commn. on Hist. Records, 1976—. Served with USNR, 1942-46; capt. ret. Fellow Soc. Am. Archivists; mem. Am. Antiquarian Soc., Mass., Va., (v.p. 1970-78, trustee 1979—), other hist. socs., Colonial Soc. Mass., Walpole Soc., Raven Soc., Phi Beta Kappa, Omicron Delta Kappa. Democrat. Episcopalian. Clubs: Colonnade (Charlottesville); Century (N.Y.). Editor and compiler: Dunmore's Proclamation of Emancipation, 1941; Annual Reports on Historical Collections, University of Virginia Library, 1945-50, with cumulative indexes, 1945, 50; Jefferson Papers of the University of Virginia, 1950; Papers of John Randolph of Roanoke, 1950; John Rolfe's True Relation. 1951; Introduction to Thomas Jefferson's Farm Book, 1953. Editorial bd. Va. Quar. Rev., 1961-74. Contbr. to Dictionary of Biography, Ency. Brit., Collier's Nat. Am. Cyclopedia; and other reference works. Home: 1927 Thomson Rd Charlottesville VA 22903

BERKENKOTTER, MARY CARROLL, advt. agy. exec.; b. Fort Belvoir, Va., Apr. 29, 1948; d. Henry Stuart and Mary Story (Witham) Carroll; B.A. in English, U. Colo., 1970; m. Thomas E. Berkenkotter, Oct. 6, 1973; 1 dau., Anne Marie. Media planner Young & Rubicam, N.Y.C., 1970-73; sr. media planner Cunningham & Walsh, N.Y.C., 1973-74; media dir. James Gray Assos., Scranton, Pa., 1974-75, Weekley & Penny, Houston, 1975—. Regents scholar, 1966-70. Mem. Am. Advt. Fedn., Houston Advt. Fedn. (dir. 1979-81), Am. Mktg. Assn. (dir. 1979-80). Office: 3322 Richmond Ave Houston TX 77098

BERKEY, BARRY ROBERT, psychiatrist; b. New Kensington, Pa., Sept. 28, 1935; s. Saul M. and Esther F. (Freedlander) B.; A.B. magna cum laude, Washington and Jefferson Coll., 1957; M.D., U. Pitts., 1961; m. Velma A. Levin, June 23, 1960; children—Kent, Richard, Lori. Intern, Harrisburg Hosp., 1960-61; resident in neurology U. Wis.-Madison, 1961-62, resident in psychiatry, 1962-65; clin. dir. No. Va. Mental Health Inst., Fairfax, 1968; practice medicine specializing in psychiatry, Fairfax, 1968—; mem. staffs Fairfax Hosp., Alexandria (Va.) Hosp.; chmn. bd. dirs. Barry R. Berkey, M.D. Ltd.; cons. adv. bd. B'nai B'rith Career Counseling Service of Greater Washington, Human Resource Assos.; freelance writer. Served with M.C., AUS, 1965-67. Diplomate Am. Bd. Psychiatry and Neurology. Fellow Am. Psychiat. Assn., Am. Orthopsychiat. Soc.; mem. Washington Psychiat. Soc. (editor chpt. news honors, awards 1971-73), Am. Group Psychotherapy Assn., Phi Beta Kappa, Phi Delta Epsilon, Phi Sigma, Delta Phi Alpha, Chi Epsilon Mu. Club: B'nai B'rith. Author: Halfway through the Tunnel, 1972; (with V. Berkey) The Mind is a Funny Thing, 1973; (with V. Berkey, R. Berkey) Chincoteague for Children, 1975; Save Your Marriage, 1976; (with V. Berkey) The Guilty Book, 1977; (with V. Berkey and R. Berkey) Pioneer Decoy Carvers: A Biography of Lemuel and Stephen Ward, 1977; contbg. author: The Anatomy of a Prostitute, 1974; (with V. Berkey) Robbers, Bones and Mean Dogs, 1978; contbr. numerous articles to profl., popular publs. Office: 8301 Arlington Blvd Fairfax VA 22031

BERKEY, MAURICE EDWARD, JR., fin. exec.; b. Salem, Ind., Feb. 17, 1922; s. Maurice Edward and Ida Mae (Bush) B.; student Ind. Central Bus. Coll., 1940-41; 1 dau., Suzanne. Insp., Presto-lite Co., Inc., Speedway City, Ind., 1941, Union Carbide Co., Speedway City, 1941; with Internat. Harvester, San Antonio, 1946-59; with Roegelein Fed. Credit Union, San Antonio, 1960—, mgr., sec.-treas., dir.; acct. Roegelein Co. Served with inf. AUS, 1941-45. Mem. Smithsonian Inst., Hist. Preservation Soc., Audubon Soc., Nat. Hist. Soc. Mem. Christian Ch. Club: Masons. Office: Roegelein Co 1700 S Brazos St San Antonio TX

BERKLEY, FRED ALEXANDER, educator; b. Hobart, Okla., Nov. 4, 1908; s. Alexander and Maie (Webster) B.; A.B., Okla. U., 1930, M.S., 1932; Ph.D., Washington U., St. Louis, 1937; m. Elizabeth Anne Ducker, Aug. 14, 1930; children—Robert Wheeler, William Hugh, Anne (Mrs. Thomas J. Powers), Jorge Araque M. Prin. high sch., Mayesville, Okla., 1930-31; instr. botany U. Mont., 1937-42; tchr. biology Austin (Tex.) High Sch., 1942-43; instr. botany U. Tex., 1943-45, asst. prof., curator herbarium, 1945-47; State Dept. vis. prof., prof. jefe Faculted Nacional de Agonomia Medeilin, Colombia, 1947-49; prof. extraordianrio Fundacion Miguel Lillo, Nat. U. Tucuman (Argentina), 1949-51; virologist Hektoen inst., Chgo., 1951-52; dir. research microbiology Nepera Chem. Co., Yonkers, N.Y., 1952-57; sr. research asso. Warner Lambert Research Inst., Morris Plains, N.J., 1957-61; Fulbright prof. Coll. Agr., U. Baghdad (Iraq), 1961-65, chmn. dept. botany, 1963-65; prof. biology Northeastern U., Boston, 1965-74, prof. emeritus, 1977—, summer faculty, 1977, 79. Fulbright vis. prof. Jefe de Biologla y el Instituto de Investigaciones de Founa y Flora, Nat. U. Autonoma de Honduras, Tagucigalpa, 1969-70, 75-76. Mem. Phi Sigma (nat. vice chancellor 1939-47). Contbr. numerous articles to tech. jours. Bot. collections from U.S.A., Mexico, Colombia, Argentina, Iraq, Honduras. Home: 104 E Highland St Tecumseh OK 74873

BERKMAN, MONROE EUGENE, broadcasting exec.; b. Steubenville, Ohio, Nov. 13, 1939; s. Jack N. and Sybiel B.; B.A., U. Pa., 1962; m. Suzette C. McCune, Oct. 22, 1976; children—Eric Spencer, Paul Lawrence, Kirsten Sybiel. Gen. mgr. Sta. WRCP AM-FM, Phila., 1968-72; partner Berkman Equities, Stamford, Conn., 1972-75; gen. mgr. Sta. WSOL, Tampa, Fla., 1975—. Mem. Tampa C. of C. Club: Optimist. Home: 3926 Versailles Dr Tampa FL 33614 Office: 1711 W Kennedy Blvd Tampa FL 33606

BERKSTRESSER, GORDON ABBOTT, III, ret. textile co. exec.; b. Passaic, N.J., Dec. 23, 1930; s. Gordon Abbott, Jr. and Else (Pohlers) B.; grad. Phillips Acad., Andover, 1949; B.S., N.C. State U., 1954; M.B.A., Baruch Coll., N.Y.C., 1970; Ph.D., City U. N.Y., 1978; m. Elizabeth Ann Farquher, Oct. 29, 1955; children—Else, Susan, Mary, Gordon Abbott IV. Salesman, J.P. Stevens & Co., Inc., N.Y.C., Chgo., 1954-62; nat. sales mgr. Spring Air Co., Chgo., 1962-64; product mgr. Fieldcrest Mills, N.Y.C., 1964-67; dir. new products West Point Pepperell, Inc., N.Y.C., 1967-71, product mgr., 1971-72; asst. prof. marketing Stockton State Coll., Pomona, N.J., 1972-73, asso. prof., 1974-78; asso. prof. textile materials and mgmt. N.C. State U., Raleigh, 1978—. Mem. Phi Psi (treas. grand council), Alpha Tau Omega, Sigma Tau Sigma, Sigma Pi Alpha. Home: 1209 Brooks Ave Raleigh NC 27607

BERLIN, JEROME CLIFFORD, real estate devel. co. exec.; b. N.Y.C., Aug. 23, 1942; s. Benjamin R. and Muriel (Weintraub) B.; B.S. Bus. Adminstrn., U. Fla., 1964; J.D., U. Fla., 1968; m. Gwen Tischler, July 30, 1977; children—Bret Jason, Sharon Nichole, Ashley Lauren. Accountant, Peat, Marwick, Mitchell & Co., Houston, 1968-69; mem. law firm Jerome C. Berlin, Miami, Fla., 1969-71; pres. Sterling Capital Investments, Inc., Miami, 1971-74; pres., chief operating officer The Robino-Ladd Co., Miami, 1974-78; pres., chief operating officer Inprojet Corp., Miami, 1978-80; mem. firm Pallot, Stern, Pollack & Berlin, P.A., Miami, 1980—. Chmn. Dade County Zoning Appeals Bd., 1971-73; mem. exec. com. Anti-Defamation League; mem. State of Fla. Internat. Banking Com.; mem. planning bd. Variety Children's Hosp. C.P.A., Fla., Tex. Mem. Am., Fla. insts. C.P.A.'s, Tex. Soc. C.P.A.'s, Fla. Bar Assn., Am. Assn. Attys. and C.P.A.'s. Jewish. Home: 5425 SW 92d St Miami FL 33156

BERLIN, VIRGINIA LONG, univ. ofcl.; b. Macon, Ga., Dec. 20, 1938; d. Oscar Lee and Suellen (Walker) Long; B.A., Mercer U., 1960, M.Ed., 1974; postgrad. Fort Valley State Coll., 1977; m. Robert Allen Berlin, May 6, 1960; children—Robert Allen, Sarah Ellen, Alana Katherine. Tchr. social studies Bibb County (Ga.) Bd. Edn., 1961-66, SW High Sch., 1969-78, dir. student activities, 1975-78; dir. counseling Wesleyan Coll., Macon, 1978—. Residential co-chmn. Am. Cancer Soc.; Democratic candidate Macon City Council, 1975; pres.-elect Northside Neighborhood Assn. Mem. Central Ga. Speech and Hearing Assn. (v.p., dir.), Bibb County Assn. Edn., Ga. Assn. Edn., NEA, Nat. Assn. Activity Advisers, Am. Personnel and Guidance Assn., Ga. Assn. Women Deans, Adminstrs. and Counselors, Am. Coll. Personnel Assn., Middle Ga. Marriage and Family Therapy Assn., LWV, Phi Delta Kappa, Kappa Delta Epsilon. Methodist. Club, Macon Jr. Women's. Home: 1100 Hill Pl Macon GA 31210 Office: Wesleyan Coll Macon GA 31297

BERLS, FREDERICK EDWARD, SR., mech. engr.; b. Danbury, Conn., Apr. 18, 1945; s. Charles August and Lillian Augusta (Knerr) B.; student Wentworth Inst., 1963, 64, Waterbury State Tech. Inst., 1964-66; m. Lillian Tody Gavin, July 26, 1965; children—Julianne, Ricky. Mech. designer research and devel. Pitney Bowes, Stamford, Conn., 1971-73; indsl. engr. research and devel. Instapak Corp., Danbury, Conn., 1973-75; dir. bldg. ops. Southland Hosp., Mobile, Ala., 1975-77; mgr. bldg. ops. Country Club Mobile, 1977-78; mgr. bldg. ops. services Morrisons Inc., Mobile, 1978—. Asst. coach Mims Park Little League, 1977-79; den leader Cub Scouts Am., 1977-79. Mem. Am. Soc. Hosp. Engrs., Ala. Hosp. Engrs. Assn., Gulf Coast Hosp. Engrs. Soc., Nat. Fire Protection Assn., Mobile Assn. Purchasing Mgmt., Jr. C. of C. (sec. 1974-75). Methodist. Home: 2605 Shay Ct Mobile AL 36609 Office: 4721 Morrison Dr Mobile AL 36625

BERMAN, BENNY, composer, entertainment exec.; b. Netanya, Israel, Nov. 18, 1938; came to U.S., 1969, naturalized, 1969; s. Zvi and Hya (Biern) B.; student pub. schs., Israel; m. Linda Lee Earp, Nov. 17, 1972; 1 son by previous marriage, Ron. Pres., Harmony & Grits, Inc., Stuart, Fla., 1972—; singer, guitarist appearing at UCLA Coll. Concert, 1968, Carnegie Hall, 1971, Alice Tulley Hall, 1970, Shangri La Hotel, Singapore, 1970, Carlton Hotel, S. Africa, 1978-79, Dusit Thani, Bangkok, 1978, Cerromar Beach Hotel, P.R., 1973-77, Jerry Lewis Telethon, Las Vegas, 1976, Cruise Lines, 1976-79, Kid's Corner Children's Show, ABC-TV, Sioux City, Iowa, 1972-77. Served with Israeli Army, 1957-60. Recipient Gold Records, Israel, 1960, 61, 62, 63. Composer numerous songs including The Clown Song, 1960, Peace Song, 1971, Pegleg, 1961, The First, 1969, To See the World, 1972; composer musical scores: Emperor's New Clothes (Israel), Kofiko, Pinocchio (Israel), 1962. Address: 1724 Boatswain Pl Stuart FL 33494

BERMAN, RITA, writer; b. London, Eng., June 2, 1932; came to U.S., 1954, naturalized, 1976; d. Louis and Sophie (Mishkin) Castleman; student Pitman's Bus. Coll., London, 1947-49, Mich. State U., 1959-60, Colo. State U., 1967-68; m. Ezra Berman, Aug. 30, 1959; children—Jessica Rebecca. Officer mgr., bookkeeper A. Vogel Co. Ltd., London, 1949-53; officer mgr. Mutimer Sales Engring. Co., Phila., 1954-55, J. Toubkin Ltd., London, 1955-56; med. sec. Albany (N.Y.) Med. Coll., 1956-58, Hosp. for Spl. Surgery, N.Y.C., 1958-59; research asst. Office of Instl. Research, Mich. State U., Lansing, 1959-62; various secretarial positions in hosps., N.Y.C. and Cin., 1962-67; propr., secretarial positions in hosps., N.Y.C. and Cin., 1962-67; propr., secretarial service, Ft. Collins, Colo., 1967-68, Reston, Va., 1968-72; reporter Virginia Metro News, Reston, 1972-73; free lance writer, Chapel Hill, N.C., 1973—; editorial asst. (part-time) Pharmacology Revs., 1976—, Vitamins and Hormones, 1976—. Recipient Merit award Soc. for Tech. Communications, 1975, 80, Achievement award Soc. for Tech. Communications, 1977; Honorable Mention, Nat. Writers Club, 1975. Mem. Women in Communications (pres. N.C. Triangle chpt. 1980—, membership chmn. for So. Region 1979—), Chapel Hill Hist. Soc., Friends of U. Network TV. Democrat. Jewish. Contbr. feature articles to bus. and trade jours.; contbr. book revs. to lit. publs. Home: 316 Estes Dr Chapel Hill NC 27514 Office: Dept Pharmacology U NC Chapel Hill NC 27514

BERMELLO, GUILLERMO RUIZ, pub. co. exec.; b. Camaguey, Cuba, Apr. 16, 1918; s. Claudio C. and Amparo A. (Ruiz) B.; came to U.S., 1960, naturalized, 1969; Degree in Pub. Accounting, U. Havana (Cuba), 1949, D.Comml. Scis., 1952, Doctor in Laws, 1957; m. Martha Guarcia, Sept. 11, 1949; 1 son, Willy A. Pvt. practice accounting and law, Havana, 1949-58; justice Nat. Ct. of Accounts, Havana, 1959-60; pvt. practice accounting, Miami, Fla., 1961-65; exec. v.p., gen. mgr. Editorial Am., S.A., Virginia Gardens, Fla., 1966—; pres. Bermello Consulting Inc. Mem. Am. Accounting Assn. Roman Catholic. Club: Coral Gables Country. Home: 726 Santander Ave Coral Gables FL 33134 Office: 6355 NW 36th St Virginia Gardens FL 33166

BERNAL, JESUS RODRIGUEZ, ednl. adminstr.; b. Pearsall, Tex., Dec. 7, 1953; s. Jose B. and San Juana (Rodriguez) B.; B.A. in Bus. Edn. magna cum laude, St. Mary's U. of Tex., 1976; M.A., U. Tex., 1977, postgrad., 1978—. Library resource asst. St. Mary's U. Acad. Library, San Antonio, 1973-76; instr. acctg. N.E. Ind. Sch. Dist., San Antonio, 1976; librarian, media coordinator Antonio Olivares Elem. Sch., San Antonio, 1978; dir. bilingual edn. Pearsall Ind. Sch. Dist., 1978—; chmn. curriculum evaluation com. Bexar County Jail Detention Center Edn. Programs, San Antonio, 1977. U. Tex.-San Antonio State scholar, 1976-78, Nat. Hispanic scholar, 1977, 78; cert. tchr., Tex. Mem. Am. Assn. Personnel Adminstrn., Assn. for Supervision and Curriculum Devel., Nat. Assn. for Bilingual Edn., Tex. Assn. for Bilingual Edn., Tex. Bus. Edn. Assn., Tex. Tchrs. Assn., Pearsall Educators Assn. (Spl. Friend award 1980), AAUP, NEA, Phi Delta Kappa, Delta Epsilon Sigma, Delta Pi Epsilon, League of United Latin Am. Citizens. Roman Catholic. Home: 515 S Bernal St Pearsall TX 78061 Office: 522 E Florida St Pearsall TX 78061

BERNARD, SPENCER THOMAS, lt. gov. Okla.; b. Rush Springs, Okla., Feb. 5, 1918; s. Cicero Edgar and Helen (Sperling) B.; m. Vivian Dorman, Aug. 3, 1935; 1 dau., Kay Ann Bernard Jones. Rancher, farmer, Okla.; pres. Bernard Enterprises; partner Jones-Bernard Ins. Agy.; mem. Okla. Ho. of Reps. from 47th dist., 1960-78, chmn. soil and water resources com., 8 yrs., speaker pro tem, 1960-78; lt. gov. State of Okla., 1978—; vice chmn. State Bd. Equalization; vice chmn. Capitol Improvement Authority; chmn. Okla. Tourism and Recreation Commn.; chmn. Spl. Events Commn.; past pres. Fed. Land Bank; dir. 1st Nat. Bank, Rush Springs; v.p. Mid Continent Farmers Coop. Mem. Farmers Union, Cattlemen's Assn. Democrat. Club: Lions (past pres.). Office: 211 State Capitol Oklahoma City OK 73105

BERNARD, VINCENT EUGENE, food co. exec.; b. Waterloo, Iowa, Nov. 14, 1940; s. Vincent Leo and Evelyn Marie (Patava) B.; m. Nyleta Jean Nelson, Dec. 5, 1959; children—Christi (dec.), Kristin, Kraig, Brian (dec.), Perry. Tech. dir. Doerfer div. Container Corp. Am., Cedar Falls, Iowa, 1969-74; v.p. engring. Jimmy Dean Cos., Dallas, 1974-76, v.p. ops., 1976-77, pres., chief exec. officer, dir., 1977—. Served with USMC, 1958. Mem. Am. Meat Inst., Southwestern Meat Packers Assn., Pres.' Assn. Club: K.C. Patentee in field. Home: 422 Brook Glen Richardson TX 75080 Office: 1341 W Mockingbird Ln Suite 1100 E Dallas TX 75247

BERNEY, DAVID EUGENE, office machines sales and service co. exec.; b. Birmingham, Ala., Dec. 7, 1940; s. Alfred Eugene and Margaret (Lee) B.; student Tex. A&M U., 1959, Sam Houston State U., 1961, Alexander Hamilton Bus. Inst., 1964, U. Ala. Extension, 1965, Auburn U., 1966-73, Western Carolina U., 1978; m. Joyce Carrigan, Oct. 26, 1963; children—David Eugene, Michelle Renee. Machine operator Emory U. Computer Center, Atlanta, 1961; supr. Univac Computer Center, Remington-Rand Univac, Atlanta, 1961-62; exec. v.p., gen. mgr. Berney's Office Machines, Inc., Montgomery, Ala., 1962-74; gen. mgr. Lymberis & Wood, Inc., Panama City, Fla., 1974; pres., treas. Berney's, Inc., Asheville, N.C., 1974—. Team capt. United Appeal, 1966-68; bd. dirs. Retarded Children's Sch. Montgomery, 1966-69. Mem. C. of C. (membership com.), Southeastern Regional Office Machines Dealers Assn. (dir.

1968-73, sec. 1973-75, v.p. 1975-76, pres. 1976-77), Nat. Office Machines Dealers Assn. (dir. 1968-73, regent 1976-78). Mormon. Clubs: Jaycees (officer), Kiwanis (sec.), Masons, Shriners. Home: 8 Appian Way Arden NC 28704 Office: PO Box 15409 Asheville NC 28813

BERNI, RALPH JOHN, chemist; b. New Orleans, Nov. 1, 1931; s. Louis A. and Victorie (Parr) B.; B.S., La. State U., 1954; M.S., Tulane U., 1961, Ph.D., 1966; m. Joan McGuire, Oct. 17, 1957; children—Ann L., Ralph H., Erin E. Research chemist So. Regional Research Center, Agrl. Research SEA, U.S. Dept. Agr., New Orleans, 1955-75, research leader of spectroscopy, 1975-77, chief composition and properties lab., 1977—. Instr. chemistry Tulane U. 1960-68. Bd. dirs. Region 9 Sci. Fair. Served with AUS, 1955-57. Fellow Am. Inst. Chemists (chmn. La. chpt. 1970, 79); mem. Am. Chem. Soc. (treas. La. sect. 1969-70, chmn. 1974), Research Soc. Am. (chmn.-elect 1972), Am. Assn. Textile Chemists and Colorists, Orgn. Profl. Employees of Dept. Agr., AAAS, Sigma Xi (chmn. New Orleans chpt. 1973). Contbr. articles to profl. jours. Patentee in field. Home: 645 Aris Ave Metairie LA 70005 Office: PO Box 19687 New Orleans LA 70179

BERNINGER, JOAN A., physician; b. Bethlehem, Pa., July 12, 1944; d. Harold Henry and Ann Marie (Magyar) Berninger; B.S., U. Miami, 1966, M.D., 1970. Intern in obstetrics and gynecology Jackson Meml. Hosp., Miami, Fla., 1970-71; resident in psychiatry U. Miami Affiliated Hosps., 1971-74, chief resident, dept. psychiatry, 1973-74, asst. clin. instr., 1973-74; pvt. practice medicine specializing in psychiatry, Boca Raton, Fla., 1975—. Mem. Am. Women's med. assns., Alpha Lambda Delta. Home: PO Box 214 Boca Raton FL 33432 Office: 2200 N Federal Hwy Boca Raton FL 33431

BERNS, KENNETH IRA, educator; b. Cleve., June 14, 1938; s. Charles and Delnet (Cohn) B.; student Harvard, 1956-59; B.A., Johns Hopkins U., 1960, Ph.D. (Shell Oil fellow), 1964, M.D., 1966; m. Laura Louise Lawless, June 27, 1964; children—Jonathan, Deborah. Intern dept. pediatrics Johns Hopkins Hosp., Balt., 1966-67, fellow, 1966-67; staff asso., lab. biochemistry and metabolism Nat. Inst. Arthritis and Metabolic Diseases, NIH, Bethesda, Md., 1967-68, staff mem., lab. biology viruses Nat. Inst. Allergy and Infectious Diseases, 1968-70; asst. prof. microbiology Johns Hopkins U. Sch. Medicine, Balt., 1970-73, asso. prof., 1974-76, asst. prof. pediatrics, 1970-76, dir. year I program, 1973-76; prof., chmn. dept. immunology and med. microbiology U. Fla., Gainesville, 1976—, also prof. pediatrics. Served with USPHS, 1967-70. Research grantee USPHS, 1972, NSF, 1973, Am. Cancer Soc., 1970. Mem. Am. Soc. Biol. Chemists, Assn. Med. Sch. Microbiology Chmn. (chmn. com. pub. policy), Am. Soc. Microbiology, AAAS, Phi Beta Kappa, Sigma Xi. Home: 10921 NW 14th Ave Gainesville FL 32601 Office: Box J266 JHMHC Gainesville FL 32610

BERNSTEIN, DAVID ROBERT, accountant; b. N.Y.C., Sept. 26, 1950; s. George and Ethel (Klein) B.; B.B.A., Pace U., 1972; postgrad. in bus. adminstrn. U. Miami, 1980—. Intermediate clk. Westchester Library System, Yonkers, N.Y., 1967-72; accountant technician Milgo Electronic Corp., Miami, Fla., 1972-73, supr. accounts analysis group, 1973-75, sr. accountant, 1975-77, name changed to Racal-Milgo, Inc., mgr. gen. accounting dept., 1977-78, asst. controller, 1978—. Mem. Nat. Assn. Accountants. Home: 461 NW 107 Ave Apt 202 Miami FL 33172 Office: 8600 NW 41st St Miami FL 33166

BERNSTEIN, JOSEPH, lawyer; b. New Orleans, Feb. 12, 1930; s. Eugene Julian and Lola (Schlemoff) B.; B.S., U. Ala., 1952; LL.B., Tulane U., 1957; m. Phyllis Maxine Askanase, Sept. 4, 1955; children—Jill, Barbara, Elizabeth R, Jonathan Joseph. Clk. to Justice E. Howard McCaleb of La. Supreme Ct., 1957; admitted to La. bar, 1957; asso. firm Jones, Walker, Waechter, Poitevent, Carrere & Denegre, 1957-60, partner, 1960-65; gen. practice New Orleans, 1965—; pres. Turci's Inc., Mercury Prodns., Inc., pubs. of Figaro. Past pres. New Orleans Jewish Community Center; pres. Met. New Orleans chpt. March of Dimes. Trustee New Orleans Symphony Soc.; advisory council New Orleans Mus. Art; nat. exec. com. Am. Jewish Com. Served to 2d lt. AUS, 1952-54. Mem. Am., La., New Orleans bar assns., Phi Delta Phi, Zeta Beta Tau. Democrat. Jewish. Home: 3119 Prytania Ave New Orleans LA 70115

BERREY, BEDFORD HUDSON, physician; b. Carrollton, Mo., Apr. 20, 1922; s. Robert Wilson and Elizabeth Mary (Hudson) B.; student Kansas City (Mo.) Jr. Coll., 1939-40, U. Kans., 1940-42; B.S. in Medicine, U. Mo., 1943; M.D., U. Colo., 1945; M.A. in Internat. Relations, Am. U., 1969; m. Marcia Lois Bagley, May 22, 1943; children—Elizabeth, Barbara, B. Hudson, Christopher, Michael. Intern, Kansas City (Mo.) Gen. Hosp., 1945-46; resident in pediatrics Denver Children's Hosp., 1946-47; practice medicine specializing in pediatrics, Kansas City, Mo., 1947-48, Harlingen, Tex., 1950-51; fellow in pediatrics Ochsner Clinic, New Orleans, 1949; commd. capt. U.S. Army, 1951, advanced through grades to col., 1967, ret., 1976; dep. asst. chief med. dir. VA, Washington, 1976-77; asst. state health commr. Va. Health Dept., Richmond, 1977—. Pres. S. Tex. Amateur Athletic Union, 1962-63; pres. P.T.A., Berlin, 1954, Denver, 1952. Decorated Legion of Merit with 2 oak leaf clusters; diplomate Am. Bd. Pediatrics. Fellow Am. Acad. Pediatrics, A.C.P.; mem. Am. Acad. Med. Dirs., Med. Soc. Va., Richmond Acad. Medicine. Republican. Clubs: Army-Navy (Washington); Army and Navy Country (Arlington, Va.); Masons, Shriners. Home: 4431 Old Fox Trail Midlothian VA 23113 Office: Va Health Dept 109 Governor St Richmond VA 23219

BERRISFORD, THOMAS ROGERS, computer software co. exec.; b. Alton, Ill., June 13, 1944; s. Bertem Rogers and Edna Marie (Berry) B.; student U. Mo., 1962-63; B.S., Fla. State U., 1965; M.B.A. with honors, U. Houston, 1980; m. Maria C. Herrera, Apr. 5, 1974; 1 son by previous marriage—Thomas Rogers; 1 dau., Sally B. Programmer, Bellcomm, Washington, 1966-67; programmer, sr. programmer analyst Wolf Research & Devel. Corp., Riverdale, Md., 1967-69; systems analyst Computer Data Systems, Tallahassee, Fla., 1969-70, Systems Sci. Devel. Corp., Tallahassee, 1970; sr. systems analyst Humrro, Alexandria, Va. and Atlanta, 1972-74; sr. systems analyst Software AG of N. Am., Inc., Reston, Va., 1974-75, v.p. market devel., 1976-77, v.p. So. sales region, Houston, 1978—. Served with U.S. Army, 1970-71. Sangamo Electric Co. scholar, 1962-64. Mem. Am. Mgmt. Assn. Democrat. Club: Raveneaux Country. Office: Software AG of North America Inc 13231 Champiton Forest Dr Suite 403 Houston TX 77069

BERRY, BETTY LOUISE, nurse; b. Shreveport, La., Sept. 4, 1940; d. Martin Lawrence and Ethel Inez (Martin) Brown; B.S. in Nursing, Northwestern State U., Natchitoches, La., 1962; m. Charles Fred Berry, Nov. 15, 1968; stepchildren—Mary Katherine Berry Braswell, Charles Fred, Stephen Lee, Saundra Lynn Berry Cotton. Staff nurse pediatrics Confederate Meml. Med. Center (now La. State U. Med. Center), 1962, charge nurse, 1966-68, staff nurse, 1968-73, head nurse, 1973-75, supr. central med. supply, 1975—; staff nurse John Peter Smith Hosp., Ft. Worth, 1962-64; staff nurse Harris Hosp., Ft. Worth, 1964, charge nurse, 1964-65. Mem. Am. Nurses Assn., La. State Nurses Assn., Shreveport Dist. Nurses Assn., Internat. Assn. Hosp. Central Service Mgmt. Am. Soc. Hosp. Central Ser. Personnel, Am Hosp. Assn. Democrat. Baptist. Club: Order Eastern Star. Office: 1541 Kings Hwy Shreveport LA 71130

BERRY, CORRE IVEY, educator; b. Bastrop, Tex., Mar. 27, 1929; d. Leslie Dunn and Corre Christine (Ivey) Williams; B.A., Baylor U., 1950, M.A., 1952, Mus.B., 1953; Mus.M. (Brown scholar), New Eng. Conservatory, 1958; Ph.D. (fellow), N. Tex. State U., 1974. Asst. prof. music and/or physics Baylor U., 1955-56, 62-65, Northeastern U., Boston, 1957-61, Southwestern U., Georgetown, Tex., 1965-69, Sam Houston State U., 1972—. Danforth Tchr. Study grantee, 1956-57. Mem. Nat. Assn. Tchrs. Singing, Am. Musicological Soc., Mus. Library Assn., Alpha Chi, Pi Kappa Lambda, Pi Delta Phi, Mu Phi Epsilon. Contbr. articles to mus. jours. Baptist. Home: 1425 Ave O Huntsville TX 77340 Office: Music Building II Sam Houston State Univ Huntsville TX 77341

BERRY, DANIEL MCINTYRE, JR., assn. exec.; b. Augusta, Ga., Feb. 14, 1926; s. Daniel McIntyre and Miriam Lanham Berry; student Davidson Coll., 1943-44, Memphis State U., 1947; A.B., U. Ala., 1949, M.A., 1951; m. Mary Josephine Heuer, Aug. 28, 1948; 1 son, Daniel M. Instr., Ga. Mil. Acad., 1951-54; mem. faculty Oglethorpe U., Ga. State U., 1954-56; bus. rep., mgr. consumer div., asst. mgr. Better Bus. Bur. of Met. Atlanta, 1955-58; mgr. Better Bus. Bur. Greater Knoxville, 1958-61; gen. mgr., pres. Better Bus. Bur. of Nashville/Middle Tenn., Inc., 1961—; mem. mgmt. com., dist. gov. Council Better Bus. Burs., Inc., 1972-74. Pres. Consumer Credit Counseling Service of Met. Nashville, 1976-78; bd. dirs. Legal Services of Nashville, 1976-77. Mem. Nashville Advt. Fedn., Nashville Area C. of C., Phi Alpha Theta. Presbyterian. Club: Lions. Home: 2600 Hemingway Dr Nashville TN 37215 Office: 506 Nashville City Bank Bldg Nashville TN 37201

BERRY, EARL HADLEY, occupational therapist; b. Nashville, Oct. 2, 1913; s. Allen Benjamin and Lillie Bell (Wiggins) B.; B.S., Howard U., 1948; cert. occupational therapy, Wayne State U., Detroit, 1952; postgrad. U. Alaska, 1977-79; div.; 1 dau., Janice Lili. Staff occupational therapist Hines (Ill.) VA Hosp., 1952-53; asst. chief occupational therapist West Side VA Hosp., Chgo., 1953-56; sr. occupational therapist Highland View County Hosp., Cleve., 1956-57, Norristown (Pa.) Hosp., 1957-60; cons. Stephen Smith Home for Aged, Phila., 1957-69; supr. occupational therapy Coatesville (Pa.) Hosp., 1960-66; dir. dept. occupational therapy Polyclinic Hosp., Harrisburg, Pa., 1966-68, St. Joseph Hosp., Lancaster, Pa., 1968-69; supr. therapy Alaska Psychiat. Inst., Anchorage, 1969-77; rehab. counselor Anchorage Sch. Dist., 1977—. Served with AUS, 1942-46. Decorated Bronze Star. Mem. Am. Occupational Therapy Assn., Alaska Occupational Therapy Assn. (1st pres. 1969-70), Alaska Public Health Assn. Democrat. Address: 716 Myrtle St Nashville TN 37206

BERRY, HARDY DUANE, univ. exec.; b. Lenora, Kans., Mar. 17, 1926; s. Newell Hardy and Fern Marie Caroline (Georgeson) B.; B.S. in History and Govt., Kans. State U., 1950, B.S. in Journalism, 1951; m. Elizabeth Ann Thackrey, Jan. 27, 1950; children—Russell Stuart, Elizabeth Lee, John Newell. Editor Manhattan (Kans.) Tribune, 1951-52; editor Agrl. Expt. Sta. U. Maine, Orono, 1952-54; head dept. agrl. info. U. Conn., Storrs, 1954-57; dir. info., head dept. film, TV prodn. Mont. State U., Bozeman, 1957-62; dir. info. services N.C. State U., Raleigh, 1962-79, asst. vice chancellor, 1979—. Info. cons. Wash. State Study Commn. on Edn., 1960; dir. spl. projects Am. Assn. Higher Edn., Washington, 1962; co-dir. Sch. Bell award program Meet the Professor for ABC-TV. Mem. Greenway Commn., Raleigh, 1974-77. Served with USNR, 1944-46. Mem. Wake County (N.C.) Hist. Soc. (v.p. 1974-75, pres. 1975-77, Pub. Relations Soc. Am. (dir. chpt.), Council for Advancement, Support of Edn., Sigma Delta Chi, Tau Kappa Epsilon. Mason. Home: 2601 Wells St Raleigh NC 27608

BERRY, JULIA ELIZABETH, educator; b. Jones, Ala.; d. Charles Picton and Sarah Anne (Ousley) Berry; B.S., Central Mo. State U., 1943; A.M., U. Mich., 1948; Ph.D., Columbia U., 1955. Tchr., dept. head. Independence (Mo.) Pub. Schs., 1943-46; tchr., asst. in guidance Albuquerque (N.Mex.) Pub. Schs., 1946-57; guidance dir. Fort Lauderdale (Fla.) Pub. Schs., 1956-57; instr., coll. counselor Jr. Coll. Kansas City, Mo., 1957-69; pvt. practice counseling, Kansas City, Mo., 1969-71; asst. prof. City U. N.Y., 1971-72; asst. prof. U. Md., European div., 1973; asso. prof. edn. La. State U., Baton Rouge, 1975—; chmn. com. on Careers of English Majors study, Nat. Council Tchrs. English, 1960-65. Mem. Am. Personnel and Guidance Assn., Assn. for Counselor Educators and Suprs., Am. Coll. Personnel Assn., Nat. Council Tchrs. English (past bd. dirs.), Worldwide Acad. Scholars, Internat. Platform Assn. Methodist. Author: Guiding Students in the English Class, 1959, The Careers of English Majors, 1969. Contbg. author: An English Teacher's Reader, 1962. Contbr. articles to profl. jours. Home: 606 W Mechanic Harrisonville MO 64701 Office: PO Box 19545 Louisiana State U Baton Rouge LA 70893

BERRY, LAMAR DEVINE, food chain exec.; b. New Orleans, July 6, 1950; s. Jason F. and Mary Frances Berry; student U. New Orleans, U. Madrid, 1970. Field promotions Warner Bros. Pictures, New Orleans, 1970-71; account exec. Media Cons., Inc., New Orleans, 1971-72; v.p. Brown, Berry & Goodwin, 1972—; v.p. advt. Popeyes Famous Fried Chicken, Jefferson, La., 1975—. Recipient Gold Addy award, 1977, Silver Addt award, 1977, Silver award for excellence in advt., 1978. Mem. Nat. Restaurant Assn., La. Restaurant Assn. (dir.). Office: 700 Webb St Jefferson LA

BERRY, LEMUEL, JR., musician; b. Oneonta, N.Y., Oct. 11, 1946; s. Lemuel and Ethel (Flippen) B.; B.A., Livingstone Coll., 1969; M.A., Ph.D., U. Iowa, 1973; m. Christine Elizabeth Elliott, June 6, 1970; children—Lemuel III, Cyrus James. Chmn. dept. music Fayetteville (N.C.) State U., 1973-76, chmn. div. humanities, 1973-75; chmn. dept. music Langston (Okla.) U., 1976—; dir. black music program Sta. KOKC, Guthrie, Okla.; concert musician, U.S., Can., Mexico, Panama, Bahamas; music adjudicator and cons., brass clinician; radio and TV appearances. Mem. NAACP, Council for Research in Music Edn., Black Scholar Participants, Music Educators Nat. Conf., Nat. Assn. Jazz Educators, Nat. Black Music Colloquium (chmn. Okla.), Nat. Coll. Wind and Percussion Instrs., Assn. Concert Bands Am. (bd. govs.), Music Industry Council, Okla. Music Educators Assn., Assn. Coll., Univ. and Community Arts Adminstrs., Internat. Soc. Music Educators, Kappa Kappa Psi (gov. dist. VI). Mem. A.M.E. Zion Ch. Club: Lions. Author: Biog. Dictionary of Black Musicians and Black Educators, 1978; Afro-American Resource Guide and Dictionary: A Bibliographic Source Guide, 1978; African Instruments, 1980; contbr. articles to rpofl. jours. Home: 715 E Harrison St Guthrie OK 75050 Office: PO Box 120 Langston OK 73050

BERRY, MICHAEL ALDEN, physician; b. San Francisco, June 2, 1946; s. Charles Alden and Addella (Nance) B.; B.S., Tex. Christian U., 1968; M.D., U. Tex., Dallas, 1971; M.S. in Preventive Medicine, Ohio State U., 1977; m. Mary Frances Cauthen, Mar. 5, 1977; 1 dau., Jennifer Alice. Intern, Wilford Hall USAF Med. Center, San Antonio, 1971-72; resident in aerospace medicine Ohio State U., 1976-78; chief flight medicine NASA/Johnson Space Center, Houston, 1978—; adj. asso. prof. aerospace medicine U. Tex., Houston, 1979—; mem. staff USPHS Hosp., Houston, Clear Lake Hosp., Webster, Tex. Vice-pres. Am. Heart Assn., Clear Lake chpt., 1979-80, campaign chmn., 1979-80. Served to maj. M.C., USAF, 1970-76. Diplomate Am. Bd. Preventive Medicine. Fellow Am. Coll. Preventive Medicine; mem. Aerospace Med. Assn. (Julian Ward award, asso. fellow), AMA, Am. Coll. Emergency Physicians, Internat. Acad. Aviation and Space Medicine, Am. Public Health Assn., Tex. Med. Assn., Harris County Med. Soc., Soc. Air Force Flight Surgeons, Soc. NASA Flight Surgeons. Methodist. Office: Flight Med Clinic SD 24 NASA/JSC Houston TX 77058

BERRY, NANCY NELSON, art broker; b. Freer, Tex., Dec. 2, 1943; d. Thurman Wilbur and Florence Lila (Collinsworth) Nelson; student Nixon-Clay Coll., Abilene Christian Coll.; m. Bruce Carlton Berry, Apr. 26, 1962; children—Chaliise Alayn, Shanlii Dael. Stratigrapher, Shell Oil Co., 1964-65; land sec. Coastal States Oil Co., Abilene, Tex., 1966, product engr., 1968-69, accountant, 1968-72; art broker Kurt Schon Ltd., New Orleans, 1974—; pres. Berry-Nelson, Inc., 1979—. Vol. social worker Dallas Christian Services., Christ's Prison Fellowship; vol. chaplain Dallas County Jail, 1978—. Mem. Chs. of Christ. Home: 305 Northview St Richardson TX 75080 Office: 400 S Houston St PO Box 132 Dallas TX 75202

BERRY, OSCAR LEE, JR., obstetrician-gynecologist; b. Shreveport, La., Oct. 17, 1933; s. Oscar Lee and Mary Ellon (Skinner) B.; B.S., Tulane U., 1954, M.D., 1958; m. Joyce Ann Brugier, Aug. 11, 1955; children—Lianne, Susanne, Oscar Lee III. Intern, Confederate Meml. Med. Center, Shreveport, 1958-59, resident in obstetrics-gynecology, 1959-62, mem. vis. staff, 1964;, pres., 1975-76, mem. center bd. advisers, 1975-76; chief obstet.-gynecol. service Schumpert Meml. Med. Center, Shreveport, 1977-78; staff Physicians and Surgeons, Doctors hosps., Shreveport; asst. clin. prof. obstetrics-gynecology Med. Sch., La. State U., 1966—. Served to capt. M.C., U.S. Army Res., 1962-64. Diplomate Am. Bd. Obstetrics and Gynecology. Fellow Am. Coll. Obstetricians and Gynecologists; mem. AMA, So. Med. Assn., La., Shreveport med. socs. Democrat. Episcopalian. Clubs: Shreveport Country, Cotillion, Ambassadors, Pierremont Oaks Tennis, Elks. Home: 6444 Creswell Rd Shreveport LA 71106 Office: 865 Olive St Shreveport LA 71104

BERRY, WILLIAM RANDALL, retail exec.; b. Leesville, La., Apr. 30, 1954; s. Theodore Lloyd and Elenore Denise (West) B.; student Northwestern State U. La.; m. Virginia Louise Ball, Jan. 18, 1975. With West-Gibson, Inc., Leesville, La., 1974—, personnel mgr., asst. buyer, 1976-78, asst. gen. mgr., 1978—, also sec. treas.; sec. treas. Berry Realty Co. Treas. state rep. campaign Dist. 31, Republican Party, 1979, exec. committeeman, 1980-84. Mem. Leesville Jaycees (dir. 1978-79; external v.p., 1979, internal v.p. 1980; Outstanding project award 1977), Assn. U.S. Army, Leesville Vernon Parish C. of C. (retail mchts. com.), La. Lions League Crippled Children. Republican. Methodist. Club: Rotary (program chmn. 1979-80). Office: Hwy 171 N Leesville LA 71446

BERRYMAN, ROBERT LEE, drilling co. exec.; b. nr. Palestine, Tex., Oct. 11, 1899; s. Lee J. and Cora (Hathcock) B.; student Washington and Lee U., 1919-20, Tex. U., 1920-21; m. Juanita McPherson, Sept. 26, 1955; children—John Robert, Hugh Lee, Lee Howard. With Wheless Drilling Co., Shreveport, La., 1925—, sec.-treas., 1941—, dir., 1941—. Trustee, treas. Southfield Sch., Shreveport, 1936-46. Served with U.S. Army, 1918-19. Clubs: Shreveport, Shreveport Country. Home: 532 Monrovia St Shreveport LA 71106 Office: 920 Commercial Nat Bank Bldg Shreveport LA 71101

BERSCH, ROBERT SHERRILL, lawyer; b. Lynchburg, Va., Aug. 29, 1935; s. Benjamin Ernest and Mary Elizabeth (Dalton) B.; B.S. with distinction, U. Va., 1957, LL.B., 1960; M.Law and Taxation, Coll. William and Mary, 1961; m. Helen Kytha Padgett, June 18, 1960. Admitted to Va. bar, 1960, D.C. bar, 1965, U.S. Supreme Ct. bar, 1965; tax atty., office chief counsel IRS, Washington, 1961-65; tax atty. firm Haynes & Miller, Washington, 1965-70; partner firm Eggleston, Glenn & Bersch, Roanoke, 1970-78; owner, individual practice law Robert S. Bersch Law Offices, 1979—; tchr. income taxation Am. Coll. C.L.U.'s, Roanoke; tax aspects of real estate adult div. City Schs. Roanoke, 1971-75; pres. Roanoke Valley Estate Planning Council, 1978-79. Mem. Am. (mem. employee benefits com. of tax sect. 1975-77), Va., Roanoke, D.C., Fed. bar assns., Va. State Bar (gov. tax sect. 1971-76), Raven Soc., Beta Gamma Sigma, Phi Eta Sigma, Theta Delta Chi. Baptist (deacon). Clubs: Shenandoah, Nat. Lawyers, Lake of the Woods Golf and Country, Kiwanis. Home: 2360 Cantle Ln SW Roanoke VA 24018 Office: Suite 500 Shenandoah Bldg PO Box 1529 Roanoke VA 24007

BERT, CHARLES WESLEY, engring. educator; b. Chambersburg, Pa., Nov. 11, 1929; s. Charles Wesley and Gladys Adelle (Raff) B.; B.S. in Mech. Engring., Pa. State U., 1951, M.S. in Mech. Engring., 1956; Ph.D. in Engring. Mechanics, Ohio State U., 1961; m. Charlotte Elizabeth Davis, June 29, 1957; children—Charles Wesley IV, David Raff. Jr. design engr. Am. Flexible Coupling Co., State College, Pa., 1951-52; aero. design engr. Fairchild Aircraft div. Fairchild Engine and Airplane Corp., Hagerstown, Md., 1954-56; prin. mech. engr. Battelle Meml. Inst., Columbus, Ohio, 1956-61, sr. research engr., 1961-62, program dir., solid and structural mechanics research, 1962-63, cons., 1964-65; asso. prof. U. Okla., Norman, 1963-66, prof., 1966—, dir. Sch. Aerospace, Mech. and Nuclear Engring., 1972-77, Benjamin H. Perkinson prof. engring., 1978—; instr. engring. mechanics Ohio State U., Columbus, 1959-61; cons. various indsl. firms. Bd. dirs. Midwestern Mechanics Conf., 1971-79, chmn., 1973-75. Served from 2d lt. to 1st lt. USAF, 1952-54. Registered profl. engr., Pa., Okla. Asso. fellow AIAA (nat. tech. com. on structures 1969-72, vice chmn. Central Okla. sect. 1965-66, chmn. 1966-67); mem. Am. Acad. Mechanics (a founder, dir.), Am. Soc. Engring. Edn., ASME (Central Okla. sect. exec. com. 1973-78, Region X mech. engring. dept. heads com. 1972-77, chmn. 1975-77), Soc. Engring. Sci., N.Y., Okla. acads. scis., Nat., Okla. (chmn. engrs. in edn. 1979-80) socs. profl. engrs., Soc. Exptl. Stress Analysis (sec. mid-Ohio sect. 1958-59, chmn. 1959-60, adv. bd. mem. 1960-63), Scabbard and Blade, Sigma Xi, Sigma Tau, Pi Tau Sigma, Sigma Gamma Tau (Distinguished Engr. award), Tau Beta Pi (Distinguished Engr. award). Contbr. chpts. to books, articles and papers to profl. jours. and publs. Home: 2516 Butler Dr Norman OK 73069 Office: Sch Aerospace Mech and Nuclear Engring U Okla 865 Asp Ave Norman OK 73019

BERTANI, CHARLES LEONARD, labor assn. ofcl.; b. Houston, Tex., June 6, 1934; s. Tony and Lorraine O. (Davis) B.; student Houston Coll. Drafting, 1958-60, U. Mo., 1970; m. Lottie Mac Grigg, Nov. 10, 1956; children—Theresa Annette, Charles Leonard. Profl. boxer, Houston, 1957-58; welder Gen. Welding Works, Houston, 1958-59; constrn. foreman Brown & Root Co., Houston, 1959-62; maintenance welder Cameron Iron Works, Inc., Houston, 1962-65; pres. Internat. Assn. Machinists and Aerospace Workers, Lodge 15, AFL-CIO, Houston, 1965—, bus. rep., 1967-72, directing bus. rep., 1972—; v.p. Tex. AFL-CIO, 1971—, del. to ann. conv., 1968—, trustee, 1971—, chmn. trustees, 1977—, mem. appointments com., 1974—, chmn. fin. com., 1971—, mem. com. on polit. edn., 1971—; del. Tex. State Council Machinists Conv., 1968—, pres. council,

1968—; steering com. So. States Apprenticeship Conf., 1977—. Fund raising chmn. Tex. Machinists Non-Partisan Polit. League, 1968—; mem. adv. com. Tex. Constl. Revision Commn., 1973-74; del.-at-large Nat. Dem. Conv., 1978; mem. credentials com. Tex. Democratic State Conv., 1976, chmn. resolutions com., 1978; bd. dirs. Muscular Dystrophy Assn. Am., 1973—; trustee Houston and Harris County United Fund, 1969-74, mem. labor participation com., 1968—; condemnation commr. Harris County (Tex.), 1974—; labor rep. local steering com. Nat. Council on Alcoholism, 1976—; labor adv. com. Inst. Labor and Indsl. Relations, U. Houston, 1977—. Served to sgt. USAF, 1952-56. Recipient Outstanding Community Leadership award Houston and Harris County United Fund, 1970-78, Spl. Achievement award Machinists Non-Partisan League, 1972-76, Outstanding Service award Muscular Dystrophy Assn. Am., 1974-78. Mem. NAACP. Democrat. Roman Catholic. Club: K.C. Home: 1330 Del Norte Houston TX 77018 Office: 6640 Long Point Houston TX 77055

BERTINI, ALBERT JOSEPH, II, computer specialist; b. Chgo., Oct. 11, 1946; s. Albert Joseph and Isabel (Scinto) B.; grad. coll. with honors; m. Constance Josephine Leonard, Feb. 14, 1969; 1 son, Albert Joseph. Programmer, analyst Rydacom, Inc., Miami, Fla., 1971-74; sales rep., analyst min-computer applications Costal Data Service, Inc., Miami, 1974-76; regional mgr., analyst Datasaab Systems, Inc., Miami, 1976—; cons. in field. Head Zoning Campaign Miramar Township Com., 1976; active community activities, Miramar. Served with U.S. Army Security Agy., 1964-68. Recipient Presidential Medallion for support and protection Pres. Johnson on SE Asian Pacific tour, 1966. Democrat. Presbyterian. Contbr. articles to profl. jours. Creator computer programs for police, fire, and health services, 1975-76. Home: 6304 SW 30th St Miramar FL 33023 Office: 25 SE 2d Ave Miami FL 33131

BERTRAN, JORGE, mfg. co. exec.; b. Havana, Cuba, Aug. 4, 1955; came to U.S., 1961, naturalized, 1970; s. Enrique and Lydia Bertran-Guzman; B.S., Syracuse U., 1976; postgrad. Franklin Sch. of Transp. and Distbn. Mgmt., 1976, Inst. European Studies (Spain), 1977; M.B.A., World U. P.R., 1979; m. Mary Martha Llenza-Aponte, Jan. 5, 1980. Mgmt. trainee Internat. div. Gillette Co., San Juan, P.R., 1977-78; account exec. Bertran Internat. Graphics, Miami, Fla., 1978-79; product mgr. Nestle-Libby P.R., Inc., San Juan, 1979—; asst. prof. mktg. World U., San Juan, 1978-79. Mem. Am. Mktg. Assn., Sales and Mktg. Assn., Am. Mgmt. Assn. P.R. Republican. Club: Rotary. Contbr. articles to profl. jours. Home: 1052 Ashford Ave Condado PR 00907 Office: PO Box 4565 San Juan PR 00936

BERTRAND, RUSSELL EARL, retail grocery chain exec.; b. Houston, Aug. 4, 1948; s. Charles J. and Nancy M. (Hanks) B.; diploma Houston Fire Acad., 1967; B.S. in Edn., Howard Payne U., 1973; m. Katherine Ann Feuge, Aug. 15, 1970. With Kroger Co., Houston, 1976—, sr. personnel asst., 1977-78, personnel mgr., 1979—. Served to 2d lt. USAF, 1973-76. Mem. Am. Soc. Tng. and Devel., Alpha Phi Omega. Republican. Baptist. Home: 803 Fawn Circle Rt 2 Box 2870 Porter TX 77365 Office: 701 Gelhorn PO Box 1309 Houston TX 77001

BESHEAR, STEVEN L., atty. gen. Ky.; b. Dawson Springs, Ky., Sept. 21, 1944; A.B., U. Ky., 1966, J.D., 1968. Admitted to N.Y. bar, 1969, Ky. bar, 1971; asso. firm White and Case, N.Y.C., 1968-70, firm Harbison, Kessinger, Lisle & Bush, Lexington, Ky., 1971-75; partner firm Beshear, Meng and Green, Lexington, 1976-79; atty. gen. State of Ky., 1979—; mem. Ky. Ho. of Reps. from 76th dist., 1974-79. Mem. Fayette County Bar Assn., Ky. Bar Assn., Am. Bar Assn., Phi Beta Kappa, Phi Delta Phi, Omicron Delta Kappa, Order of Coif. Bd. editors Ky. Law Jour., 1967-68. Office: Office of Atty Gen State Capitol Frankfort KY 40601

BESS, SONJA HARTSELL, nurse; b. Statesville, N.C., Feb. 27, 1946; d. Walter Jackson and Sarah Ellen (Guy) Hartsell; nursing diploma Davis Hosp., Statesville, 1967; B.A., Pfeiffer Coll., Misenheimer, N.C., 1972; M.A., Appalachian State U., Boone, N.C., 1980; m. Donnie Pressly Bess, Aug. 26, 1967. Pediatric clinic nurse Davis Hosp., 1967-68, nursing instr., sch. health nurse Sch. Nursing, 1968—. Mem. Pfeiffer Coll. Circle of Faith Campaign, 1975. Mem. Nat., N.C. leagues nursing, Am. Personnel and Guidance Assn., Davis Hosp. Sch. Nursing Alumane Assn. (treas. 1970). Home: Route 8 Box 284 Statesville NC 28677 Office: PO Box 1780 Statesville NC 28677

BESSETTE, HENRY JOSEPH, psychologist; b. Pawtucket, R.I., July 2, 1921; s. Henry J. and Edna (Olson) B.; B.S., U. R.I., 1949; M.S., Purdue U., 1951, Ph.D., 1955; m. Frances Freeman Crowell, Oct. 26, 1946; children—Janice, Robert. Intern in clin. psychology VA Hosp., Marion, Ind., 1952-55, clin. psychologist, 1955-56; exec. dir. Henderson Clinic of Broward County, Fla., 1957-61; clin. prof. dept. psychology U. Miami (Fla.), 1960-62; pres. Bessette, Corlis & Assos., Ft. Lauderdale, Fla., 1969—. Pres., Broward County Community Mental Health Bd., 1974-75; bd. dirs. Crisis Intervention Center, pres., 1976-77. Served as 1st lt. USAF, 1941-46. Mem. Fla. Psychol. Assn. (pres. 1975-76), S.E. Psychol. Assn., Broward County Psychol. Assn. (pres. 1965). Clubs: Lauderdale Yacht, Gulfstream Sailing. Home: 2309 Desota Dr Fort Lauderdale FL 33301 Office: 1550 E Oakland Park Blvd Fort Lauderdale FL 33334

BESSONE, LUIS NESTOR, thoracic and cardiovascular surgeon; b. Rosario, Argentina, Jan. 23, 1936; s. Luis C. and Leonore F. (Jame) B.; came to U.S., 1962, naturalized, 1969; M.D., Universidad del Litoral, Rosario, 1959; m. Viviana Llorens, Dec. 22, 1962; children—Rosanna, Luis M., Marcello. Intern, Universidad del Litoral, 1958-59; resident in surgery Brit. Hosp., Rosario, 1960-62; intern in surgery Jewish Hosp. of St. Louis, 1962-63, resident in surgery, 1963-67; jr. fellow Washington U. Sch. Medicine-Barnes Hosp., St. Louis, 1967-68, sr. fellow, 1968-69; asst. in surgery Washington U., 1969-71; postgrad. fellow in cardiovascular surgery St. Luke's Episcopal Hosp., Houston, Tex. Children's Hosp. and Tex. Heart Inst., 1971; pvt. practice thoracic and cardiovascular surgery, Tampa, Fla., 1971—; mem. staff Tampa Gen. Hosp., St. Joseph's Hosp.; mem. courtesy staffs Univ. Community Hosp., Meml. Hosp., Centro Asturiano Hosp., Centro Espanol Hosp.; cons. staff All Children's Hosp., St. Petersburg, Fla., VA Hosp., Tampa; asst. clin. prof. surgery U. South Fla., 1975—. Recipient Sr. Clin. Trainee award USPHS, 1967-69; diplomate Am. Bd. Surgery, Am. Bd. Thoracic Surgery. Fellow Am. Coll. Cardiology; mem. Internat. Cardiovascular Soc., A.C.S., Am. Coll. Chest Physicians, Soc. Thoracic Surgeons, So. Thoracic Surg. Assn., AMA, Fla., Hillsborough County med. assns. Roman Catholic. Contbr. articles to med. jours. Home: 5137 San Jose St Tampa FL 33609 Office: One Davis Blvd Suite 703 Tampa FL 33606

BEST, RALPH LEE, JR., computer programmer; b. Tuscaloosa, Ala., Oct. 16, 1944; s. Ralph Lee and Rachel Ward (Browne) B.; B.S. in Chemistry and Physics, U. Ala., 1967, M.A. in Math., 1969; postgrad. U. Tex., 1971—. Teaching asst. in math. U. Ala., Tuscaloosa, 1967-68; instr. math. and chemistry Walker Coll., Jasper, Ala., 1968-71; teaching asst. in math. U. Tex., Austin, 1971-75, asst. instr., 1976-77; computer programmer Tex. Dept. Highways and Public Transp., Austin, 1977—. Mem. Am. Statis. Assn., Pi Mu Epsilon, Phi Kappa Phi. Presbyterian. Home: 407 W 18th St Apt 315 Austin TX 78701 Office: Dept Highways and Public Transportation Systems and Programming 38th and Jackson Sts Austin TX 78731

BEST, RAYMOND ARTHUR, mgmt. cons.; b. Troy, N.Y., Apr. 20, 1912; s. William Jacob and Claire Mary (Van Der Werken) B.; E.E., Rensselaer Poly. Inst., 1933; m. Ina Lorene Collinson, Apr. 16, 1938. With Montgomery Ward & Co., Albany, N.Y., 1935-48; with Spiegel Inc., Chgo., 1948-63, chain mgr., 1948-63, v.p., 1961-63; cons. bus. engring., fin., Eustis, Fla., 1979—. Capt., Democratic Precinct Com., Lake County, Fla., 1972. Mem. Rensselaer Alumni Club, Class of 1933 Club, Sigma Xi, Tau Beta Pi. Anglican. Clubs: Masons. Office: PO Box 547 Eustis FL 32726

BEST, RHYS JOHN, mgmt. cons.; b. Hartford, Conn., Sept. 14, 1946; s. Robert John and Eunice Marie (Spencer) B.; B.B.A., North Tex. State U., 1969; M.B.A., So. Meth. U., 1971; m. Sue Ewing, Apr. 18, 1969; children—Paul Spencer, Anne Elizabeth. Asst. v.p., asst. mgr. mcpl. investment div. 1st Nat. Bank in Dallas, 1968-73; regional mgr., v.p. S.W. region Mfrs. Hanover Leasing Corp. subs. Mfrs. Hanover Corp., Houston, 1973-80; v.p. Paul R. Ray Co., mgmt. cons., Dallas, 1980—. Mem. So. Meth. U. M.B.A. Assn. Office: 1201 Elm St Dallas TX 75270

BEST, WILLIE DEAN, architect; b. Goldsboro, N.C., Jan. 22, 1938; s. Cornelius Jackson and Wilda May (Bartlett) B.; B.Arch., N.C. State U., 1964; m. Anne Spencer, Aug. 3, 1958; children—Matthew Spencer, Melissa Noble. Chief designer, officer mgr. Simpson-Savage Architects, Raleigh, N.C., 1964-65; asso., project architect Leif-Valand & Assos., Raleigh, 1965-68; v.p., partner charhe archtl. preactice, also dir. Hakan-Best & Assos., Inc., Chapel Hill, N.C., 1968-71; pvt. archtl. practice, Raleigh, 1971-75; pres., dir. Best & Assos., Inc., architects-planners, Raleigh, 1975—; prin. works include Crabtree Valley Mall, Raleigh, NCNB Plaza, Chapel Hill. Mem. AIA (pres. Raleigh sect. 1974). Club: North Ridge Country (Raleigh). Home: 2200 White Oak Rd Raleigh NC 27608 Office: 3700 Computer Dr Raleigh NC 27609

BEST, WINFIELD JUDSON, writer, TV producer, public relations cons., ednl. agy. exec.; b. Dillon, Mont., Oct. 1919; s. Floyd and Margaret (Pearson) B.; B.S. summa cum laude, Northwestern U., 1943; m. Lois Gustafson, 1948; children—Charles, Mark, Constance. Editorial asso. Pub. Adminstrn. Clearing House, Chgo., 1946-48; dir. pub. relations Am. Municipal Assn., 1948-50; dir. research publs. HHFA, Washington, 1951-52; pub. relations dir. Planned Parenthood Fedn. Am., 1952-63; exec. v.p. Planned Parenthood-World Population, N.Y.C., 1963-69; exec. dir. Businessmen's Ednl. Fund, 1969-72; dir. communications and planning Carolina Population Center, U. N.C. at Chapel Hill, also lectr. population and ecology, 1972—; founder Winfield Best Communications, 1976; freelance writer; communications and TV producer, cons. Served with AUS, 1943-46. Mem. Nat. Assn. Sci. Writers, Am. Pub. Relations Soc., Population Assn. Am., other profl. socs., Phi Beta Kappa. Episcopalian. Author: (with Alan F. Guttmacher and Frederick S. Jaffe) The Complete Book of Birth Control, 1962, Planning Your Family, 1964; Birth Control and Love, 1969; (with Everett S. Lee and David L. Birch) America's Lands and Cities: Challenge of Transition, 1980. Contbr. numerous articles in fields of population, sex, conservation, social action in bus., problems of youth and old age to nat. mags.; contbr. to Ency. Brit. Home and Office: Box 148 Chapel Hill NC 27514

BETHEA, BARRON, lawyer, state legislator, elec. hardware mfr.; b. Birmingham, Ala., May 20, 1929; s. Malcolm and Wilma (Edwards) B.; student U. of South, 1948-50; B.S., U. Ala., 1952, LL.B., 1953. Admitted Ala. bar, 1953; practiced in Birmingham, 1953-54; founder Barron Bethea Co., Inc., elec. hardware mfrs., Birmingham, 1957, pres., sec., treas. 1957—. Mem. Ala. Democratic Exec. Com., 1958-62—; mem. Ala. Ho. of Reps., 1962—. Mem. mgmt. bd. Five Points YMCA, 1962—. Served as 1st lt. USAF, 1954-56. Mem. Ala. State Bar, Birmingham Bar Assn., Asso. Industries Ala., Birmingham C. of C., Scabbard and Blade, Phi Gamma Delta, Phi Alpha Delta. Methodist. Elk. Home: PO Box 2202 Birmingham AL 35201 Office: 1625 Carolina Ave Bessemer AL 35020

BETHEA, WILLIAM LAMAR, JR., lawyer; b. Dillon, S.C., June 2, 1940; s. William Lamar and Lillie Harding (Hotchkiss) B.; A.B. in English, Newberry Coll., 1962; J.D. magna cum laude, U. S.C., 1969; m. Paula M. Harper, Aug. 12, 1977; children—William Lamar III, Margaret Amanda. Admitted to S.C. bar, 1969; prin. firm Harvey, Battey & Bethea, P.A., Beaufort and Hilton Head Island, S.C., 1969—; dir. Island Investment Corp., Citizens and So. Corp., Citizens and So. Nat. Bank S.C., Harbour Town Clothiers, Ltd. Trustee Hilton Head Hosp., U. S.C. Served with USMC, 1962-66. Recipient Claud N. Sapp award for faculty and students U. S.C., 1969. Mem. Am., S.C., Beaufort County, Hilton Head bar assns., Phi Alpha Delta (Outstanding Scholastic Achievement award 1969), Order Wig and Robe. Episcopalian. Clubs: Masons, Lions (sec. 1973, dir. 1973-74). Editorial bd. S.C. Law Rev., 1968-69. Home: 3 Gray Fox Ln Hilton Head Plantation Hilton Head Island SC 29928 Office: C and S Bank Plaza Pope Ave Hilton Head Island SC 29928

BETHEL, SHELBA JEAN, physician; b. Gans, Okla., Sept. 8, 1937; d. Earl Wilson and Pearl Juanita (Brunk) Henry; B.S., Northeastern State Coll., Tahlequah, Okla., 1960; M.D., U. Okla., 1965; m. Lander Bethel, June 2, 1955; children—Lander Louis, Lesa Jean, Steven Henry, Scott Jonathan. Intern, St. Anthony Hosp., Oklahoma City, 1965-66, resident pathology, 1966-67, resident obstetrics and gynecology, 1967-70; practice medicine, specializing in obstetrics and gynecology, Norman, Okla., 1970—; mem. staff Norman Municipal Hosp.; cons. Purcell (Okla.) Hosp., Moorse (Okla.) Municipal Hosp., Cleveland County Health Dept. Jr. fellow Am. Fertility Soc., Am. Coll. Obstetrics and Gynecology; mem. Am. (Achievement award 1970), So., Okla. med. assns., Okla., Cleveland-McClain County med. socs., Oklahoma City Obstetrics and Gynecology Soc., Am. Med. Womens Assn., League Women Voters, Oklahoma U., Okla. U. Med. Sch. med. assns. Address: 500 E Robinson St Norman OK 73069

BETHUNE, EDWIN R., JR., Congressman; b. Pocahontas, Ark., Dec. 19, 1935; student Little Rock Jr. Coll., 1957-58; B.S., U. Ark., 1961, J.D., 1963; m. Lana Douthit, 1959; children—Paige, Sam. Admitted to Ark. bar, 1963, U.S. Supreme Ct. bar, 1972; practiced in Pocahontas, 1963; dep. pros. atty. Randolph County (Ark.), 1963-64; spl. agt. FBI, 1964-68; individual practice law, Searcy, Ark., 1968-78; pros. atty. 1st Jud. Dist. Ark., 1970-71; chmn. 9th dist. Fed. Home Loan Bank Bd., 1973-77; chmn. procedural com. Ark. Criminal Code Revision Commn., 1971-75; mem. 96th Congress from 2d Congl. Dist. Ark. Republican nominee for Ark. atty. gen., 1972. Recipient Disting. Service award Searcy Jaycees, 1971. Mem. Am. Bar Assn., Ark. Bar Assn., White County Bar Assn., C. of C. Methodist. Club: Rotary. Office: Room 1330 Longworth House Office Bldg Washington DC 20515

BETO, HELEN MAE, hosp. adminstr.; b. Buckhannon, W.Va., Nov. 20. 1929; d. George Luther and Anna Jane (Fox) Lowther; student Salem Coll., 1947-48, W.Va. U., 1948-49; m. Joseph Michael Beto, Nov. 14, 1976; children—Georgianna, Jonienne. Sec., R. D. Wilson Sons & Co., Clarksburg, W.Va., 1956-58, W.Va. Mine Supply Corp., Clarksburg, 1958-61; dir. community affairs, vol. services United Hosp. Center, Clarksburg, 1961—, dir. adv. bd. Fed. Credit Union, 1975-77. Mem. Nat. Secs. Assn. Internat. (pres. Clarksburg chpt.), Am. Soc. Dirs. Vol. Services, Nat. Assn. Hosp. Devel., W.Va. Soc. Dirs. Vol. Services, W.Va. Assn. Public Relations Dirs. Home: 512 Stanley Ave Clarksburg WV 26301 Office: 3 Hospital Plaza Clarksburg WV 26301

BETTERSWORTH, JOHN K(NOX), educator; b. Jackson, Miss., Oct. 4, 1909; s. Horace Greely and Annie McConnell (Murphey) B.; B.A. magna cum laude, Millsaps Coll., 1929; Ph.D. (grad. fellow), Duke, 1937; m. Ann L. Stephens, Oct. 28, 1943; 1 dau., Nancy B. Underwood. Tchr., Jackson Central High Sch., 1930-35; vis. instr. Asheville (N.C.) Normal, summer 1937; vis. prof. Duke, summer 1940; instr. history Miss. State U., 1937, asst. prof., 1938-42, asso. prof., 1945-48, prof. 1948—, head dept. history and govt., 1948-61, dir. Social Sci. Research Center, 1950-60, asso. dean liberal arts, Coll. Arts and Sci., 1956-61, acad. v.p., 1961-77, dean faculty, 1966-77, emeritus v.p., dean faculty and prof., 1977—; text editor Miss. Hist. Commn., 1948-68. Chmn. Miss. Research Clearing House, 1953-55; pres. Mississippians for Ednl. TV, 1971-72, bd. dirs., 1971—. Trustee, Miss. State Dept. Archives and History, 1955—; chmn. Miss. Hist. Preservation Rev. Bd., 1979—; founding pres. Friends of the Arts in Miss., 1978-80. Served as lt. (j.g.) USNR, 1942-45; instr. Naval Indoctrination Sch., Tucson. Mem. Miss. Hist. Soc. (dir. 1963-78, pres. 1963-64), Am., So. hist. assns., Phi Beta Kappa, Phi Kappa Phi, Phi Alpha Theta, Alpha Tau Omega, Omicron Delta Kappa. Democrat. Episcopalian. Rotarian (pres. Starkville 1951-52). Author: Confederate Mississippi, The People and Policies of a Cotton State in Wartime 1943; People's College: A History of Mississippi State, 1953; Mississippi: A History, 1959; Mississippi in the Confederacy, vol. 1, 1967; co-author South of Appomattox, 1959; Your Old World Past, 1961; Mississippi Yesterday and Today, 1964; This Country of Ours. 1965; New World Heritage, 1969; Your Mississippi, 1975; People's University: A Centennial History of M.S.U., 1980. Contbr. to A History of Mississippi, 1973; also articles to profl. publs. Home: 401 Broad St Starkville MS 39759 Office: Drawer B Mississippi State MS 39762

BETTERTON, ROBERT JERRY, savs. and loan exec.; b. Bruce, Miss., May 26, 1949; s. Robert L. and Wyneas J. B.; B.S., Millsaps Coll., 1971; m. Deboria L. Quinn, July 4, 1975; children—Brandi Leigh. Dir. field operations Geol. Labs., Inc., Jackson, Miss., 1971-73; credit mgr. mobile homes Bankers Trust Savings & Loan, Jackson, 1973-74; asst. v.p., asst. mgr. loan adminstr. dept., mgr. credit dept. and microfiche ops. Unifirst Fed. Savings & Loan, Jackson, 1974—. Mem. Inst. Fin. Edn. (chpt. treas.), Assn. Records Mgrs. and Adminstrs. (dir. Jackson chpt.), Kappa Sigma. Republican. Methodist. Home: Route 1 Box 675A Florence MS 39073 Office: PO Box 1818 Jackson MS 39205

BETTIS, DOROTHY DILLARD, educator; b. Mobile, Ala., Feb. 13, 1931; d. James Patrick and Inez Leslie (Holt) Dillard; B.S., Ala. State U. 1956; postgrad. U Kans. (NDEA fellowship), 1966; M.S. (NDEA Tchrs. fellow), Purdue U., 1968; A.A., U. So. Ala., 1976; 1 son, Victor Lomant Lett. Learning center tchr. Mobile County Pub. Schs., Ala., 1956—. Certified in elementary edn. supervision, library sci.; specialist in ednl. media; recipient 4 Human Relations awards; named Tchr. of Yr., Ed. A. Palmer Sch., 1966. Mem. Nat., Ala. edn. assns., Am. Library Assn., Educators Study. Mobile County Tchrs., Mo. Fedn. of Women, Nat. Congress of Colored Women, Delta Sigma Theta. Methodist. Clubs: Original Las Amigas, Nabers Dr. Civic Club. Home: 1861 Nabers Dr Mobile AL 36617 Office: 261 Rickarby St Mobile AL 36605

BETTS, EMMETT ALBERT, psychologist, educator; b. Elkhart, Iowa, Feb. 1, 1903; B.S., Des Moines U., 1925; M.A., U. Iowa, 1928, Ph.D., 1931; LL.D. (hon.), Sioux Falls Coll. Vocat. dir. Public Schs. Orient (Iowa), 1922-24; with dept. physics Public Schs. Northboro (Iowa), 1924-23, supt. schs., 1925-29; research asst. State U. Iowa, 1929-31; sch. psychologist Public Schs. Shaker Heights (Ohio), 1931-34, elem. prin., to 1934, dir. Reading Clinic; dir. tchr. edn. and summer sessions. dir. Reading Clinic, State Tchrs. Coll., Oswego, N.Y., 1934-37; research prof. and dir. Reading Clinic, Sch. Edn. Pa. State U., 1937-45; prof. psychology, dir. Reading Clinic, dept. psychology Temple U., 1945-54; dir. Betts Reading Clinic, Haverford, Pa., 1954-61; research prof. edn., adj. prof. psychology U. Miami, Coral Gables, Fla., 1961, now emeritus prof.; cons., adv. in field; trustee, mem. exec. com. Capital Yields Assets I Corp., Coral Gables, 1975—; lectr., demonstrator numerous schs., insts.; mem. Nat. Aerospace Edn. Council, 1971—; mem. adv. bd. CAP Acad., USAF, 1968—. Chmn. adv. bd. Winter Haven (Fla.) Lion's Research Found., Inc. Recipient numerous awards, including Apollo award, 1962, citation of merit Internat. Reading Assn., 1971, Crown Circle award Nat. Congress Aerospace Edn., 1979. Fellow Disting. Service Found. Optometry, Grad. Soc. Optometry; mem. numerous profl., social orgns. Clubs: Lake Region Yacht and Country (Winter Haven); Masons, Shriners. Author, editor numerous publs.

BETTS, JAMES FRANKLIN, ins. co. exec.; b. Cleve., Apr. 6, 1932; s. John W. and Lois Ann B.; B.S.B.A., Washington U., 1957; m. Martha Goebel, Dec. 29, 1956; children—Nancy, Susan, Liza. With New Eng. Life Ins. Co., 1950-72, gen. agt., Richmond, Va., 1966-69, home office v.p., 1959-72, sr. v.p., 1972; pres. Life Ins. Co. Va., Richmond, 1973—; dir. Va. Electric and Power Co., Central Nat. Bank, Central Fidelity Banks. Bd. dirs. United Way. Served with U.S. Army, 1954-56. Mem. Am. Soc. C.L.U.'s, Am. Council Life Ins. (com. field relations). Roman Catholic. Office: 6610 W Broad St Richmond VA 23261

BEVILL, TOM, lawyer, congressman; b. Townley, Ala., Mar. 27, 1921; s. Herman and Fannie Lou (Fike) B.; B.S., U. Ala., 1943, LL.B., 1948; m. Lou Betts, June 24, 1943; children—Susan B., Donald H., Patricia Lou. Admitted to Ala. bar, 1949; practiced in Jasper, Ala., 1949-1967; past mem. Ala. Ho. of Reps.; mem. 90th-96th congresses from 4th Ala. Dist. Mem. Am., Ala., Walker County (pres. 1954-55) bar assns., Am. Judicature Soc. Home: 1600 Alabama Ave Jasper AL 35501 Office: 2305 Rayburn House Office Bldg Washington DC 20515

BEVINS, THOMAS PETER, II, pump mfr.; b. Seneca Falls, N.Y., June 26, 1936; s. Thomas Peter and Louise Bernadette (Stapleton) B.; student U. Notre Dame, 1957-59; B.A. in English and History, Hobart Coll., Geneva, N.Y., 1962; M.A. in Mgmt., Claremont (Calif.) Grad. Sch., 1976; m. Joyce Ann Bertino, Apr. 23, 1960; children—Thomas Peter, Kimberly Ann, Kelly Elizabeth, Martin Joseph, Julibeth Stapleton, Mary Kathleen. Trainee, Goulds Pumps, Inc., Seneca Falls, 1963-65, asst. supt. water systems plant, 1965-67, asst. supt. engring. plant, 1967-68, mgr. mfg. Vertical Pump div., Industry, Calif., 1970-73, v.p., gen. mgr., 1973-76, pres. Tex. div., Lubbock, 1967-77; plant mgr. U.S. Pumps, Lubbock, 1968-70; pres. Hydr-O-Matic Pumps div. Wylan, Inc., Ashland, Ohio, 1977-78; pres. W.L. Somner Co., Shreveport, La., 1978—, also dir.; pres. TP Bevins Assos., mgmt. cons.; dir. G & H Castings Corp., Slaton, Tex. Served with USNR, 1954-57; ETO. Licensed community coll. tchr. bus. and indsl. mgmt., Calif.; notary pub., Tex. Mem. Tex. Mfrs. Assn., Sump Pump Mfrs. Assn., Submersible Waste Water Assn., Lone Star Water Well Assn.,

Soc. Metal Prodn. of World, Lubbock C. of C., Am. Mgmt. Assn., Am. Nuclear Soc. Home: 4833 Camillia Ln Shreveport LA 71106 Office: PO Box 82 Shreveport LA 71161

BEVIS, ROBERT ALLEN, cable TV exec.; b. Tallahassee, July 3, 1937; s. Albert Myers and Grace Vivian (Ellis) B.; student U. Fla., 1955-58; m. Jacqueline Mary Steiner, May 16, 1975; children—William Allen, Robert Jon Wayne Newell (stepson). Photo-optical engr. RCA Service Co., Cape Kennedy, Fla., 1958-68, Technicolor Corp., Cape Kennedy, 1968-69; chief engr. Communicable div. Southland Communications Inc., 1969-74, gen. mgr., 1974-79, dir. nat. ops., 1979—. Mem. City of Cocoa Beach (Fla.) Bus. Improvement Council, 1975—; treas. Cocoa Beach Police Cadets, 1976—. Mem. Soc. Cable TV Engrs. (sr.), Fla. Cable TV Assn. (pres. 1978—), Cape Kennedy Area C. of C. Republican. Methodist. Clubs: Optimists (life)(pres. chpt. 1976-77, disting. pres. 1977-78, Optimist of Year 1975-76), Elks (disting. citizen award 1976). Office: Southland Communications Inc 210 Center St Cape Canaveral FL 32920

BEWLEY, WESLEY LEON, supt. schs.; b. Kildare, Tex., Nov. 21, 1928; s. Archie and Genieve (Hogg) B.; B.S., East Tex. State U., 1950; M.Ed., U. Tex., Austin, 1956; Ph.D., U. Okla., 1975; m. Etta Estell Terrell, June 14, 1946; 1 son, Norlan Leon. Tchr. elementary schs. Kermit, Tex., 1950-59, prin. Purple Sage Elementary Sch., 1959-66; reading editor Economy Co., ednl. publs., 1966-68, mng. editor reading dept., 1968-73; adminstrv. officer curriculum sect. Okla. Dept. Edn., 1974-75; asst. supt. schs. for spl. programs Moore, Okla., 1975—. Recipient Tchr. of Year award Kermit C. of C., 1956. Mem. Tex. Tchrs. Assn. (life), NEA, Internat. Reading Assn., Assn. Supervision and Curriculum Devel., Phi Delta Kappa. Republican. Methodist. Club: Mason. Author: (with others) Words We Use: Books 1-4, 1976. Home: 2516 Highland Dr Moore OK 73160 Office: 400 Broadway N Moore OK 73160

BEYER, BRADLEY ARTHUR, printing co. exec.; b. Wichita Falls, Tex., Dec. 3, 1952; s. Arthur Frederick and Ruth Inez (Long) B.; B.A., Tex. Christian U., 1974; m. Echo Denise York, May 26, 1973; 1 son, Brandon York. Mktg. rep. Fed. Imports, Inc., Boca Raton, Fla., 1974-75; account mgr. Hallmark Cards, Inc., Wichita Falls, Tex., 1976-78, account exec., Arlington, Tex., 1979—. United Way rep., Wichita Falls, Tex., 1976-78; fund drive capt. YMCA, Wichita Falls, 1976-78; scoutmaster Boy Scouts Am., Wichita Falls, 1978. Served as 2d lt. USAF, 1974. Mem. Tex. Christian U. Alumni Assn., Air Force Assn. Mem. Christian Ch. (Disciples of Christ). Home and Office: 2000 Stacy St Arlington TX 76013

BEYER, GERALD, lawyer; b. N.Y.C., Oct. 30, 1936; s. Jack and Betty (Gorman) B.; A.B., N.Y. U., 1959; LL.B., Bklyn. Law Sch., 1962; LL.M., N.Y. U., 1964; m. Marilyn Goldstein, Aug. 19, 1961; children—Lauren, Russell, Kimberly. Admitted to N.Y. State bar, 1962, Fla. bar, 1970; asso. firm Riesner, Jawitz, & Holland, N.Y.C., 1964-67; sr. staff atty. SEC, Washington, 1967-69; asso. firm Stone, Bittel, Langer, Blass & Corrigan, Miami, Fla., 1969-71; partner firm Morse, Beyer, Moriner & Traver, Fort Lauderdale, Fla., 1971-72; prin. Gerald Beyer, Atty., Fort Lauderdale, 1972-78; partner Beyer & Lerner, P.A., 1978—; adj. prof. Nova Law Sch., 1976. Mem. Fla. Bar Assn. Club: Woodlands Country (Tamarac, Fla.). Home: 5912 Blue Beech Ct Tamarac FL 33319 Office: 2691 E Oakland Park Blvd Ft Lauderdale FL 33306

BEYER, KENNETH MAY, former naval officer, business mgmt. exec.; b. New Orleans, Aug. 14, 1920; s. Edward Flood and Nell Blanch (May) B.; B.S., Oreg. State U., 1950; M.B.A., Harvard U., 1955; m. Barbara Hale Hemphill, June 23, 1943; children—K. Kevin, Lisa. Commd. ensign U.S. Navy, 1941, advanced through grades to capt., 1959; comdg. officer Navy Electronics Supply Office, Great Lakes, Ill., 1964-65; dir. policy and programs div. Def. Logistics Agy., Alexandria, Va., 1966-68; ret., 1968; mem. ad hoc task force Office Asst. Sec. of Def., Washington, 1968-69; dir., group mgr. logistics Ingalls Shipbldg. div. Litton Systems, Pascagoula, Miss., 1969-79; gen. mgr. HBH Co., Royal Saudi Naval Supply Depot, Jidda Saudi Arabia, 1979—; v.p. Suburban Estates, Inc., Bay St. Louis, Miss., 1972—; lectr. bus. policy Carthage Coll., Kenosha, Wis., 1964. Decorated Legion of Merit. Mem. Am. Soc. Naval Engrs., Navy League. Republican. Roman Catholic. Club: Harvard of La. Contbr. reports, articles in field to profl. jours. Home: 80 Shore Dr Ocean Springs MS 39564 Office: Red Sea Area Office HBH USAED Jidda APO New York NY 09697

BEYER, PATRICK LEE, civil and environ. engr.; b. Norwalk, Ohio, Aug. 6, 1949; s. Harold Justice and Helen Irene (Gammill) B.; B.S. in Engring., U. S. Fla., 1972; postgrad. in Bus. Adminstrn., Nova U., 1977—; m. Kathy Ann Oehring, June 15, 1979. Research asst. Coll. Engring., U. South Fla., Tampa, 1970-72; project engr. Quentin Hampton & Assos., Daytona Beach, Fla., 1972-73; dir. dept. engring. City of Largo (Fla.), 1973-74; dir. engring. and constrn. estimating dept. Scarborough Corp., Clearwater, Fla., 1974-75; project mgr. Black, Crow & Eidsness, Inc., Clearwater, 1975-77; partner, corp. sec. Envisors, Inc., Tampa and Winter Haven, Fla., 1977-78; mgr. Tampa Bay regional office Dawkins & Assos., Inc., Clearwater, 1978—. Summer counselor Pinellas County (Fla.) Sci. Center, 1971-72; parade ofcl. St. Petersburg (Fla.) Festival of States, 1975-76; vol. Fla. Dept. Health and Rehab. Services, 1976—. Registered profl. engr., Fla.; recipient certificate of appreciation Fla. Dept. Health and Rehab. Services, 1976; certified scuba diver. Mem. Nat. Soc. Profl. Engrs. (sr.), Fla. Engring. Soc. (sr.; chmn. student profl. devel. com.), Water Pollution Control Fedn., Fla. Pollution Control Assn., Am. Water Works Assn., U. S. Fla. Alumni Assn., Alpha Tau Omega, Phi Theta Kappa. Democrat. Roman Catholic. Co-author tech. publs. in field of water resources. Home: 1401 Gulf Blvd #104 Clearwater FL 33515 Office: 1456 US 19 S Suite 319 Clearwater FL 33516

BEYERS, BERNICE WEST (MRS. ROBERT A. BEYERS), sculptor; b. N.Y.C., Apr. 26, 1906; d. E. Lovette and Bess (Palmer) West; A.A. in Fine Arts and Drama, Bennett Coll., 1925; pupil Alexander Archipenko, Edmond Amateis, Lu Duble, William Zorach, Winold Reiss, 1926-28, 1929, 1921-25, 1930; m. Robert A. Beyers, Mar. 2, 1940 (dec. Feb. 1962); children—Robert West, Arthur L. Exhibited one-woman shows Contemporary Arts Gallery, N.Y.C., 1931, Feragil Galleries, N.Y.C., 1933, Mid-Town Gallery, N.Y.C., 1932, Mint Mus., Charlotte, N.C., 1941, other galleries in South and Southwestern U.S.; group exhbns. include So. Vt. Art Center, Manchester, 1929-71, Mt. Dora (Fla.) Art League, 1935-40, Tex. Ann. and Dallas County Ann., 1946-67, Dallas Mus. Fine Arts, 1946-67, numerous others; represented in permanent collections including monument at Silver Springs, Fla., displays at Mead Bot. Gardens, Winter Park, Fla., Venice-Nokomis, Fla., Wadsworth Athenaeum, Hartford, Conn., Swarthmore Coll., Mint Mus. Mem. women's com. Dallas Theater Center; mem. Dallas Art Mus. League. Bd. dirs. Dallas Symphony Orch. League, Dallas Civic Opera Guild; trustee Dallas Civic Ballet Soc. (Trustee) Dallas Symphony Assn., Dallas Civic Opera, So. Vt. Artists, Inc. Awarded 1st prize sculpture So. States Art League, 1940, Conn. Acad. Fine Arts, 1943; recipient Medal of Honor Nat. Assn. Women Artists, 1932. Mem. Craft Guild Dallas, Print Soc. Dallas, Dallas Hist. Soc., Local History and Geneal. Soc., So. Vt. Artists, (dir.), D.A.R., Soc. Mayflower Descs., Nat. Soc. Magna Carta Dames, Colonial Order of Crown, Soc. Descs. Most Noble Order Knights of Garter, Plantegenet Soc., Sovereign Colonial Soc., Ams. Royal Descent, Nat. Soc. Women Descs. of Ancient and Hon. Arty. Co., Soc. Old Plymouth Colony Descendants, Nat. Soc. Colonial Dames Am., Nat. Soc. New Eng. Women, Order Descs. Colonial Govs., Nat. Soc. Daus. Am. Colonists, Nat. Soc. Daus. Founders and Patriots Am., Order of Washington, Soc. Daus. Colonial Wars. Episcopalian. Clubs: Garden, Woman's Brook Hollow Golf (Dallas); Pen and Brush (N.Y.C.); Ekwanok Country (Vt.). Address: 10008 Meadowbrook Dr Dallas TX 75229

BEYL, E(UGENE) GEORGE, JR., hosp. personnel adminstr.; b. Hammond, La., May 15, 1952; s. Eugene G. and Julia E. (Tanner) B.; B.A., Southeastern La. U., 1974; m. Catherine M. Ferrer, June 30, 1973; children—Brandon Geoffrey, Brittany Jordan. Personnel dir. St. Tammany Parish Hosp., Covington, La., 1974—. Treas., River Forest Homeowners Assn., Covington, 1978—. Mem. Greater New Orleans Soc. for Health Care Personnel Adminstrn., La. Soc. Personnel Dirs., La. Hosp. Assn., Am. Soc. Hosp. Personnel Adminstrn., Covington Athletic Assn. Home: 16 Karen Dr Covington LA 70433 Office: 1202 S Tyler St Covington LA 70433

BHAJAN, WILLIAM RUDOLPH, limnologist; b. Guyana, S. Am., Jan. 16, 1937; s. William Oswald and Lillian Irene (Baijnauth) B.; came to U.S., 1959; naturalized, 1976; B.A., InterAm. U., 1962; M.Sc., Mich. State U., 1966; Ph.D., U. Waterloo, 1970; m. Maria Magdalena Ortiz, Apr. 29, 1972; children—William Roshan, Indira Lymari. Tchr. pub. schs., Corentyne, Guyana, 1952-59; instr. InterAm. U., 1962-64, asst. prof., 1971-75; research fellow P.R. Nuclear Center, San Juan, summer, 1964; water pollution ecologist Dept. Health, State of P.R., San Juan, 1970-71; prof. ecology World U. P.R., San Juan, 1973-75; ecology external examiner U. Guyana (S. Am.), 1973-75; ecology cons. Environ. Research and Applications, San Juan, 1973—; limnologist CEER, San Juan, 1975—. Internat. scholar, 1960-62; Teaching fellow Mich. State U., 1964-66; teaching and research fellow U. Waterloo, 1966-70. Mem. P.R. Water Pollution Control Fedn., Internat. Water Resources Assn., Cousteau Soc., Ecol. Soc. Am., Beta Beta Beta. Contbr. articles in field to profl. jours. Home: 610 Dos Marinas Fajardo PR 00648 Office: CEER Caparra Heights Sta. San Juan PR 00935

BHATIA, DIL MOHAN SINGH, geologist, educator; b. Sialkot, India, Oct. 19, 1939; came to U.S., 1969, naturalized, 1978; s. Gian Singh and Jagjit Kaur (Sodhbans) B.; B.Sc., Jabalpur U., 1959; M.Tech., Saugar U., 1962; M.Sc., U. N.B. (Can.), 1970; Ph.D., U. Mo., Rolla, 1976; m. Rajinder Saluja, Aug. 26, 1973. Asst. prof. Coll. Engring. and Tech., Raipur U., 1963-66; geologist Dept. Natural Resources Province of N.B. (Can.), 1967; geologist, Brunswick exploration, geologist-geochemist New Ungava Iron Ore Co., Ungava, Que., Can. and Toronto, Ont., Can., 1970-72; geochemist Mo. Dept. Natural Resources, Rolla, 1973-77; cons. UN, 1976—, Phillips Petroleum Co., 1977, Internat. Oil & Gas Co., 1978—, Union Carbide Corp., 1980—; asso. prof. geology and geochemistry Austin Peay State U., Clarksville, Tenn., 1977—. Nat. Research Council Can. grantee, 1966-70; Geol. Survey Can. grantee, 1966-70; U.S. Geol. Survey grantee, 1975-76. Mem. AIME, Tenn. Acad. Sci., Assn. Mo. Geologists, Sigma Xi. Contbr. articles to profl. jours. Home: 2158 Michael Dr Clarksville TN 37040 Office: Dept Geology Austin Peay State U Box 8484 Clarksville TN 37040

BHATTACHARYYA, ASHIM KUMAR, physiologist; b. Kanpur, India, July 9, 1936; came to U.S., 1966; s. Viswanath and Asha B.; B.S. with honors, Presidency Coll., 1957, M.S., 1959; Ph.D., U. Calcutta, India, 1965; m. Bani Chatterjee, July 10, 1966; children—Rupa, Gopa. Research fellow dept. physiology and biochemistry Sarder Patel Med. Coll., Bikaner, Rajasthan, India, 1960-64; physiologist Himalayan Schoolhouse and Sci. Expedition, 1964; demonstrator in physiology Christian Med. Coll., Ludhiana, Punjab, India, 1965; lectr. in physiology Krishnath Coll., Berhampore, W.Bengal, India, 1966; postdoctoral fellow lab. physiol. hygiene U. Minn., Mpls., 1966-68, clin. research center U. Iowa, Iowa City, 1968-70, asso. research scientist, 1970-74, research scientist, 1974-75; asst. prof. pathology and physiology La. State U. Med. Center, New Orleans, 1975-80, asso. prof., 1980—. NIH project grantee, 1975—. Fellow Council on Arteriosclerosis, Am. Heart Assn. (council del. ann. del. assembly 1977, 78); mem. Am. Physiol. Soc., Am. Soc. Clin. Nutrition, Am. Inst. Nutrition, Am. Fedn. Clin. Research, Soc. Exptl. Biol. Medicine, N.Y. Acad. Scis., Am. Oil Chemists Soc., AAAS, Am. Heart Assn. La., Inc. (prin. investigator for grant 1976-78), Sigma Xi. Hindu. Clubs: India Assn. New Orleans, New Orleans Badminton. Contbr. chpt. to book, research articles and abstracts to profl. publs. Home: 1255 Orion Ave Metairie LA 70005 Office: Dept Pathology La State U Med Center 1542 Tulane Ave New Orleans LA 70112

BIBB, THOMAS CLIFFORD, educator; b. Montgomery, Ala., Oct. 29, 1938; s. Bennie Lee and Alma Lee B.; B.S., Ala. State U., 1960, M.Ed., 1961; Ph.D., Northwestern U., 1973; 1 dau., Tura Concetta. Asso. prof. English, Rust Coll., Holly Springs, Miss., 1961-65, Daniel Payne Coll., Birmingham, Ala., 1965-67; coordinator English program Miles Coll., Birmingham, 1967-71; asso. dir. project Upward Bound, Northwestern U., Evanston, Ill., 1971-73; asso. prof., chmn. dept. advancement studies Ala. State U., Montgomery, 1973—. Choir dir. Lilly Baptist Ch., Montgomery, 1975—. Mem. Nat. Council Tchrs. English, Ala. Council Tchrs. English, Ala. Coll. English Tchrs. Assn., MLA, Assn. Tchr. Educators, Conf. Coll. Composition and Communication, Coll. Lang. Assn., Phi Delta Kappa. Clubs: Masons, Shriners. Author: The Humanities: A Cross-Cultural Approach, 1979. Home: 5933 Provost Ave Montgomery AL 36111 Office: Alabama State University Montgomery AL 36111

BIBB, THOMAS FARRIS, mfg. co. exec.; b. Murfreesboro, Tenn., July 26, 1943; s. Charles McLean and Ann Larue (Farris) B.; B.S., La. State U. at New Orleans, 1964; m. Barbara Eliasen, Nov. 14, 1964; children—Patrick, Michael, John. Accountant, Ernst & Ernst, New Orleans, 1964-67, San Antonio, 1967-69; controller Conroy, Inc., San Antonio, 1969—, also v.p., 1975-78, v.p. fin., 1978-80, exec. v.p. adminstrn., 1980—. C.P.A., Tex., La. Mem. Am. Inst. C.P.A.'s, Fin. Execs. Inst. Democrat. Roman Catholic. Home: 3743 Chartwell St San Antonio TX 78230 Office: Suite 201 3355 Cherry Ridge Dr San Antonio TX 78230

BIBBY, WALTER BERRY, office supply mfg. co. exec.; b. Birmingham, Ala., Sept. 13, 1923; s. Walter James and Vira Rebecca (Berry) B.; B.Sc., Auburn U., 1948; m. Mary Ann Adams, Feb. 17, 1944; 1 child, Berry Adams. Agy. mgr. Smith Corona Marchant, San Antonio, 1948-54; gen. mgr. A.B. Dick AG, Switzerland, 1954-63; realtor, San Antonio, 1964-68; pres., chief exec. officer Liquid Paper Corp., Dallas, 1968—; dir. Greenville Ave. Bank and Trust, Liquid Paper Corp. Dir., Dallas Council on World Affairs, 1978—; dir. Dallas Symphony, 1978—; mem. nat. devel. com. Adventure/Unltd., 1977—. Served to capt. USAF, 1943-45. Decorated D.F.C., Air medal with 5 oak leaf clusters. Mem. Nat. Office Products Assn., Wholesale Stationers Assn., Internat. Trade Assn., Nat. Office Machine Dealers Assn., Dallas C. of C. Christian Scientist. Clubs: Lakewood Country, Brookhaven Country, Lancers, Chandlers Landing Yacht, Masons, Scottish Rite.

BICE, ERNEST GORDON, former meteorologist; b. Valley View, Tex., Dec. 10, 1906; s. John Robards and Sarah Elizabeth (Prather) B.; B.S., N. Tex. State U., 1931; M.S. (Weather Bur. fellow 1941), U. Chgo., 1944; postgrad. U. Miami, 1959; m. Emma Marie Henderson, May 29, 1934; 1 dau., Nancy Jean Bice McTaggert. Tchr. secondary schs., Tex., 1926-35; with Home Owners Loan Corp., Dallas, 1935-37; weather forecaster U.S. Weather Bur. (name changed to Nat. Oceanic and Atmospheric Adminstrn. Nat. Weather Service), 1937-44, analyst, 1944-47, meteorologist in charge, 1947-73, cons., 1973-77; ret., 1977. Pres. Brownsville (Tex.) Soc. Crippled Children, 1965-67; chmn. A.R.C., Brownsville, 1964. Dist. gov. Toastmasters Internat., 1963-64. Recipient U.S. Dept. Commerce gold medal, 1968, Meritorious Service award, City Brownsville, 1968; named Rotarian of year, Brownsville, 1968. Mem. Tex. State, Ft. Worth geneal. socs. Democrat. Methodist. Rotarian (dist. gov. Rotary Internat. 1969-70). Mason. Author: Hurricane Beulah Lashes the Lower Rio Grande Valley, 1968; Correlations of Isallobaric Patterns in the High Atmosphere with Surface, 1944; (with Gilley T. Stephens) Climatic Guide-The Lower Rio Grande Valley of Tex., 1967. Editor: Warning—A Call to Action (Bengamin F. McLuckie), 1974. Home: 8401 Bangor Dr Ft Worth TX 76116

BICEK, JEANETTE LYNNE, psychologist; b. Oklahoma City, Aug. 6, 1950; d. Lee A. and Violet M. (Benda) B.; B.A. cum laude, Oklahoma City U., 1972; M.S. in Clin. Psychology, Trinity U., 1973; cert. Central State U., 1973, postgrad., 1974—. Vol. probation officer Mcpl. Ct. of Oklahoma City, 1971-72; staff technician Robert B. Green Hosp., San Antonio, 1972-73; psychodiagnostician Community Guidance Center, San Antonio, 1972-73; psychometrist and counselor Sacred Heart Sch., Oklahoma City, 1973—; sch. psychologist Christ the King Sch., Oklahoma City, 1979—; tchr. social studies (part-time) St. Philip Neri Sch., Midwest City, Okla., 1974-75; counselor (part-time) Mt. St. Mary's High Sch., Oklahoma City, 1975-76; asst. librarian dept. libraries State of Okla., 1971-72. Jr. high youth dir. (part-time) Sacred Heart Ch., Oklahoma City, 1975-78. Cert. psychometrist, sch. counselor, sch. psychologist, Okla. Mem. Am. Personnel and Guidance Assn., Am. Sch. Counselor Assn., Okla. State Psychol. Assn., Okla. N.G. Assn., N.G. Assn., Okla. Sch. Psychol. Assn., Psychology Club of Oklahoma City U., Western Bohemian Fraternal Assn., Psi Chi, Delta Zeta. Democrat. Roman Catholic. Home: 7569 Embassy Terr Oklahoma City OK 73169 Office: Christ the King School 1900 Guilford Ln Oklahoma City OK 73120

BICKEL, CALDWELL CONRAD, JR., mech. engr.; b. Jefferson County, Ky., July 1, 1919; s. Caldwell Conrad and Anna Elizabeth (Meyer) B.; B.M.E., U. Ky., 1942; m. Flora Miller, Feb. 13, 1943; children—Sandra Joyce Bickel Martin, Paula Jo Bickel Angle. Mech. engr. Henry Vogt Machine Co., Louisville, 1945, Cin. Milling Machine Co., 1945-46, Curtiss-Wright Corp., Columbus, Ohio, 1946-47, Petroleum Exploration, Lexington, Ky., 1947-50, Army Q.M. Depot, Jeffersonville, Ind., 1950-54; hwy. engr. Materials Research Lab., U. Ky., Lexington, 1954-55; research engr. Wright-Patterson AFB, Dayton, Ohio, 1955-58; aerospace engr. Army Missile Materiel Readiness Command, Redstone Arsenal, Ala., 1958—. Served with USN, 1943-45. Registered profl. engr., Ky. So. Baptist. Home: 8808 Edgehill Dr SE Huntsville AL 35802

BICKNELL, KENT, financial service co. exec.; b. Atlanta, Ga., Nov. 17, 1945; s. Hunter and Martha Doris (Kent) B.; B.B.A., Baylor U., 1968; m. Carolyn Holloway, Apr. 24, 1976; children—Jordan Kent, Wilson Terrell. Salesman, Fidelity Union Life Ins. Co., Waco and Dallas, 1967-70; propr. Kent Bicknell & Assos., Dallas, 1972-73; founder, 1973, since chmn. and pres. Balanced Fin. Corp., Dallas; chmn., pres. BFC Planning Corp.; chmn. Balanced Fin. Securities Corp.; pioneer in devel. fee compensated objective fin. planning; tchr. financial seminars. Vol., Christian Citizens. Served with AUS, 1971. Certified financial planner. Mem. Internat. Assn. Financial Planners, Nat. Assn. Securities Dealers. Conservative. Evang. Christian. Club: E. Dallas Rotary (program chmn. 1977). Office: 6060 N Central Expressway Dallas TX 75206

BICOCCHI, JOAN LICHTENSTEIN, bottling co. exec.; b. New Orleans, Dec. 19, 1939; s. Edwin William and Beulah (Hart) Lichtenstein; student U. New Orleans, 1960-62; B.A., U. Tex., 1970; m. Louis Francis Bicocchi, May 20, 1977; children by previous marriage—Lisa Karen Dunn, Jodi Gail Dunn. Interviewer and employer relations rep. La. State Employment Service, New Orleans, 1967-69, supr. job tng., 1970-71; dir. personnel New Orleans Police Dept., 1971-73; asst. regional indsl. relations mgr. Hunt Wesson Foods, Gretna, La., 1973-78; mgr. corp. relations La. Coca-Cola Bottling Co., New Orleans, 1978—; info. panelist Tulane U., Nichols State U. Bd. dirs. S.E. council Girl Scouts U.S., 1980; bus.-sch. liaison Public Schs., 1979-80. Mem. Am. Soc. Personnel Adminstrn. (accredited personnel mgr.; nat. bd. dirs. 1979-80, Superior award 1977), Personnel Mgmt. Assn. (pres. 1976), Am. Soc. for Tng. and Devel., Am. Compensation Assn., Bocage Civic Assn. Presbyterian. Home: 3630 Rue Nichole New Orleans LA 70114 Office: PO Box 50400 New Orleans LA 70150

BIDEZ, THELMA CALHOUN (MRS. EARLE FELTON BIDEZ), club woman; b. Rockmart, Ga.; d. William Alexander and Eudora (Davitte) Calhoun; student pvt. schs.; m. Earle Felton Bidez, Sept. 4, 1916; children—Earle Calhoun (dec.), Miriam Elizabeth Bidez Clark, William Alexander. Vice pres. Froebel Circle, 1953-54, pres., 1954-56; awards chmn. Garden Club of Savannah, 1954-57; sec., 1957-58, 1st v.p., 1958-60; librarian Savannah chpt. DAR, 1957-58; adv. mem. M.B.L.S.; mem. Am. Bicentennial Research Inst. Mem. Ga., Polk County (charter mem.) hist. socs., Nat. Geneal. Soc., Daus. Am. Colonists (regent 1970), Magna Charta Dames, Plantagenet Soc., N.W. Ga. Hist. and Geneal. Soc., Ga. Geneal. Soc., Clan Colquhoun Soc. N.Am. Episcopalian (edited early marriage records of St. John's Ch.). Home: 116 E 53d St Savannah GA 31405

BIELEFELD, VERNON HAROLD, hosp. adminstr.; b. Auglaize County, Ohio, Dec. 4, 1917; s. John Alva and Freda May (Zorn) B.; diploma in Higher Acctg. and Bus. Adminstrn., Northwestern Sch. Commerce, Lima, Ohio, 1948; m. Ardythe June Huston, Aug. 21, 1942; children—Celeste Nadine, Dawne Colette. Acct., Goodyear Tire & Rubber Co., St. Mary's, Ohio, 1947-52; office mgr. St. Francis Hosp., Colorado Springs, 1952-54; comptroller Genesee Meml. Hosp., Batavia, N.Y., 1954-57; comptroller Lakeland (Fla) Gen. Hosp., 1957-70, adminstrv. asst., 1970-74; adminstr. Highlands Gen. Hosp., Sebring, Fla., 1974-78; adminstr. Good Samaritan Hosp. of Tampa (Fla.) Inc., 1978—; cons. in field. Served with AUS, 1942-46; ETO. Mem. Am. Coll. Hosp. Adminstrs., Hosp. Fin. Mgmt. Assn. (past pres.), W. Central Fla. Hosp. Council (pres.), Am. Hosp. Assn., Tampa Hosp. Council (sec.), Fla. Osteo. Hosp. Assn. (sec.), mem. small and rural hosp. com.). Republican. Methodist. Clubs: Rotary, Mason, Am. Legion. Home: 7817 N Cameron Ave Tampa FL 33614 Office: 7171 N Dale Mabry Hwy Tampa FL 33614

BIELEY, PEGGY MOSES, economist; b. N.Y.C., June 5, 1934; d. Louis and Bella (Kenarik) Moses; B.S. magna cum laude, N.Y. U. Sch. Commerce, 1950; M.A., Stanford U., 1953; student Columbia U., 1952-53; m. Alfred D. Bieley, Dec. 25, 1953 (div. Aug. 1977); children—Harlan C., Lily Beth. Economist, Nat. Indsl. Conf. Bd.,

N.Y.C., 1949, Jules Backman Asso., N.Y.C., 1949-50; teaching fellow Stanford U., 1950-51; economist Nat. Manpower Council, Columbia U., 1951-53; instr. econs. U. Miami, 1954-55; v.p., chief economist Julian Langner Research, Inc., Miami, 1955-60; pres., chief economist Bieley, Wagner & Assos., Miami, 1960-70, Econ. Data Bank, Inc., Miami, 1970-73; cons. economist Freedom Fed. Savs. and Loan Assn., Tampa, Fla., 1973-77; v.p. Am. Savs. & Loan Assn. Fla., Miami Beach, 1977—. Mem. Am. Econ. Assn., Am. Statis. Assn., Econ. Soc. So. Fla., Beta Gamma Sigma. Contbr. articles to tech. jours., nat. mags. Home: 11601 SW 64 Ave Miami FL 33156

BIENVENU, LIONEL JOSEPH, govt. park ofcl.; b. Opelousas, La., Mar. 9, 1931; s. Lionel Joseph and Carrie Gillis (Rogers) B.; student premed. Tulane U., 1948-51, postgrad., 1955; B.A., U. So. La., 1953; certificate humanities U. London (Eng.), 1953; postgrad. La. State U. Med. Sch., 1954; m. Patricia Collins, June 30, 1956; children—Patricia, Lionel, Louise, William. With Pan Am. Petroleum Co.- New Orleans, 1954-55, Sun Life Ins. Co. Can., New Orleans, 1956-58; with Nat. Park Service, various locations, 1958—, chief historian, Cabrillo and Channel Islands, Calif., 1964-67, supt. Pea Ridge (Ark.) Mil. Park, 1967-74, supt. Chalmette Nat. Hist. Park, Arabi, La., 1974—, also coordinator for State of La.; fed. rep. Dept. Interior for Youth Conservation Corps. Mem. Fed. Exec. Bd. New Orleans; St. Bernard Bicentennial Commn.; mem. fin. com., parish council Prince of Peace Roman Catholic Ch.; trustee Met. United Way. Mem. La., St. Bernard hist. socs., Pi Gamma Mu, Pi Alpha Theta. Club: Rotary. Address: PO Box 429 Arabi LA 70032

BIERLEY, JOHN CHARLES, lawyer; b. Portsmouth, O., Oct. 12, 1936; s. C. Harold and Mildred R. (Turner) B.; B.A., U. Fla., 1958, J.D. (Fla. Law Center Assn. scholar, 1961-63, Bigelow Meml. scholar, Am. Legion, 1961-63), 1963; m. Ruth Lykes Webb, Sept. 26, 1964; 1 son, John Charles. Admitted to Fla. bar, 1964, practiced in Tampa, 1964—; legal asso. firm Fowler, White, Gillen, Humpkey & Trenam, Tampa, 1964-66; legal partner Macfarlane, Ferguson, Allison & Kelly, Tampa, 1966—; pres. Internat. Cultural and Econ. Center, Inc., 1975-77; lectr. internat. studies U. South Fla., Tampa, 1964-72; dir. Cayman Nat. Bank & Trust Co., Ltd., 1973—; chmn. Fla. Council Internat. Devel., 1974-75; pres. Tampa World Trade Council, 1971-73; chmn. Fla. Gov.'s Conf. World Trade, 1980; chmn. Hurricane Disaster Com. ARC, 1958-61; sec. Tampa Bay Area Com. on Fgn. Relations, 1972—. Recipient Fla. Blue key award, Fla. Hall of Fame, 1958. Mem. Am. Soc. Internat. Law, Fla. (chmn. internat. law com. 1972-74), Am., Inter-Am., bar assns., Phi Delta Phi, Kappa Sigma. Democrat. Presbyn. Mem. Ye Mystic Krewe Gasparilla. Clubs: Univ., Tower, Merrymakers. Home: 4614 San Miguel St Tampa FL 33609 Office: 512 Florida Ave Tampa FL 33601

BIERMAN, DON EDWARD, educator; b. Kowel, Poland, July 24, 1931; s. Marion Chester and Natalja (Nikolajev-von Nolde) B.; came to U.S., 1949, naturalized, 1955; A.B. in Govt., George Washington U., 1963, M.A. in Geography, 1966; Ph.D. in Geography, Mich. State U., 1970; postgrad. in Transp. Northwestern U., Evanston, Ill., 1972; m. Marilyn Marie Brown, June 18, 1955. Asst. prof. geography U. Louisville, 1970-73, chmn. dept. geography, 1972-73, asso. prof., 1973-79, prof., 1979—, dir. Soviet studies, 1976—. Tutor St. Peter's Coll. U. Oxford (Eng.), 1974. Served with AUS, 1952-54; Korea. Decorated Bronze Star medal. Mem. Am. Assn. Advancement Slavic Studies, Assn. Am. Geographers, Am. Soc. Traffic and Transp. (examiner 1973—), Transp. Research Forum. Author: The Oder River: Transport and Economic Development, 1973. Contbr. articles to profl. jours. Home: 2134 Lowell Av Louisville KY 40205 Office: Geography Dept U of Louisville Louisville KY 40208

BIFERIE, DANIEL ANTHONY, JR., art gallery dir.; b. Miami, Dec. 17, 1950; s. Daniel A. and Ruth Teresa B.; Asso. Sci. with honors, Daytona Beach Community Coll., 1971; B.F.A. summa cum laude, Ohio U., 1972, M.F.A., 1974; m. Kathryn Louise Horn, June 10, 1973. Aerial photography lab. technician Rader & Assos., Miami, 1969-72; slide library photographer Ohio U., Athens, 1973-74; teaching asst., 1973-74; free-lance photographer, Mount Vernon, Ohio, 1974-75; dir. Daytona Beach (Fla.) Community Coll. Gallery Fine Arts, 1978—, instr., 1975—. Asst. scoutmaster Boy Scouts Am., 1973, scoutmaster, 1974. Mem. Soc. Photog. Edn. (pres. S.E. region), Fla. Profl. Photographers, Fla. U. Gallery Dirs. Assn., Daytona Beach Community Coll. Photog. Soc. (pres.). Exhibited artwork and photography, 1972—. Home: 22 Virginia Ave Deland FL 32720 Office: PO Box 1111 Daytona Beach FL 32015

BIFFLE, MORRIS SEARS, mech. research and mfg. co. exec.; b. Pauls Valley, Okla., Dec. 28, 1919; s. James Ethridge and Ruby Mae (Griffin) B.; grad. pub. schs.; m. Dorothy Carol Goad, June 23, 1940; children—Betty Sue (Mrs. Roger Billings), John Morris. Owner, mgr. Biffle Well Servicing Co., Farmington, N.Mex., 1959-61; pres. J & B Services, Farmington, also Lorain, Ohio, 1962-70; pres. DoBi Corp., Odessa, Tex., 1971-74; product mgr. Surface Pressure Control, Dresser-Swaco, Houston, 1974-76; pres. Indsl. Innovators, Inc., Midland, Tex., 1977—, also dir. Served with AUS, 1943-46, 50-52. Mem. Assn. Am. Inventors. Republican. Methodist. Mason. Patentee in field. Home: 2609 Country Club Dr Midland TX 79701 Office: 800 Front St Midland TX 79701

BIGBEE, ROSALYNN (LYNN), writer; b. Hot Springs, Ark., Mar. 31, 1931; d. Hervey Bowling and Lucille (Burns) B.; B.A. in Journalism, Memphis State U., 1953. Film editor Fotovox, Inc., 1953-55; film editor Motion Picture Labs., Inc., Memphis, 1955-57, film dept. supr. and customer service, 1957-73, asst. to pres., 1964—, publs. editor, 1973—; free-lance script writer Holiday Inns Am., 1960-66. Mem. Soc. Motion Picture and TV Engrs., Univ. Film Assn., Nat. League Am. Pen Women. Republican. Writer, editor MPL Recorder, 1959, MPL Table Talk, 1969; free-lance script writer for various orgns., 1960—. Home: 1623 Delmont Rd Memphis TN 38117 Office: 781 S Main St Memphis TN 38101

BIGBIE, CHARLES ROY, JR., estate planning and bus. cons.; b. Ardmore, Okla., Feb. 26, 1924; s. Charles R. and E. Geneva (Gauntt) B.; B.S. in Bus. Adminstrn., U. Okla., 1947; C.L.U., Am. Coll. Life Underwriters, 1958; m. Virginia Elizabeth Hittson, Sept. 22, 1950 (div. Jan. 1980); children—Charles R., III, Mary Elizabeth. Exec. trainee Carter Oil Co., Tulsa, 1947-51; agt. Mass. Mutual Ins. Co. Tulsa, 1951-62; gen. agt. New Eng. Life Ins. Co., Tulsa, 1962-76; pres. Employer Benefit Cons., Inc., Tulsa, 1962—; dir. Vulcan Mfg. and Spectron, Inc. Bd. dirs. Salvation Army Home, 1965—; pres. Tulsa Estate Planning Forum, 1962—. Mem. Tulsa Chartered Life Underwriters (pres. 1963), Tulsa Gen. Agts. Mgrs. Assn. (pres. 1966), Tulsa Assn. Life Underwriters (pres. 1976-77), Okla. Leaders Round Table (pres. 1976), Million Dollar Round Table (life, qualifing), Kappa Sigma Alumni (pres. 1960-63). Episcopalian (asso. vestryman). Clubs: So. Hills Country, Tulsa. Contbr. articles to profl. jours. Home: 1722 S Carson St Tulsa OK 74119 Office: 1722 S Carson St Suite 2700 Tulsa OK 74101

BIGELOW, MAURICE HUBBARD, research lab. exec.; b. New Haven, Oct. 25, 1903; s. Joseph Otis and Bertha Louise (Findeisen) B.; B.S. in Chem. Engring., Northeastern U., Boston, 1924; Ph.D., U. Pitts., 1935; m. Mary Graham Robbins, June 18, 1926; 1 son, John Hubbard. Chemist, Lever Bros. Soap Co., 1921-25; head sci. dept. Anatolia Coll., Salonica, Greece, 1925-28; research fellow Mellon Inst., 1933-35; research exec. Plaskon Co., Toledo, 1935-53; research v.p. Allied Chem. Corp., 1953-63; pres. Charlotte Biochem. Research Lab., Inc., Port Charlotte, Fla., 1970—; sec., dir. Health Service Agy. 6, HEW, Sarasota, Fla., 1975—. Marine officer Charlotte County, 1964—; chmn. Charlotte County Bd. Commrs., 1964-68; supr. Charlotte and Desoto County Deer Run Tax Dist., 1974-77; chmn. Charlotte County chpt. ARC. Served with AUS, 1942-46. Decorated Army Commendation medal. Mem. Am. Chem. Soc., Ret. Officers Assn., Res. Officers Assn., Boat Owners Assn., Internat. Oceanographic Found., Oceanic Soc., Marine Tech. Soc., Sigma Xi, Alpha Chi Sigma, Phi Lambda Upsilon. Republican. Co-author handbooks. Home: 115 Port Charlotte Village Port Charlotte FL 33952 Office: PO Box 2734 Port Charlotte FL 33952

BIGGERS, WILLIAM PAUL, surgeon; b. Charlotte, N.C., Sept. 15, 1937; s. William Carl and Mabel (Williams) B.; B.S., Davidson Coll., 1959; M.D., U. N.C., 1963; m. Joyce Wilson, Aug. 22, 1959; children—Machelle, Bill, Joy. Intern, N.C. Meml. Hosp., 1963-64, asst. resident gen. surgery, 1964-65, asst. resident otolaryngology, 1965-66, resident otolaryngology, 1966-67, chief resident, instr. otolaryngology, 1967-68, postgrad. fellow in allergy and immunology, 1969; dir. surgeons asst. program U. N.C. Sch. Medicine, Chapel Hill, 1968—; mem. N.C. Bd. Examiners in Lang. and Speech Pathology and Audiology; cons. Ft. Bragg Army Hosp. Recipient Roche award, 1963, Excellence in Teaching award U. N.C., 1975. Fellow A.C.S.; mem. AMA, Am. Acad. Ophthalmology and Otolaryngology, Am. Council Otolaryngology, Durham-Orange County Med. Soc., Alpha Omega Alpha. Clubs: Chapel Hill Tennis; U. N.C. Faculty. Contbr. articles to profl. jours. Home: Route 5 Box 184 Chapel Hill NC 27514

BIGHAM, WILLIAM STRICKLAND, ins. agy. exec.; b. Gatesville, Tex., Mar. 30, 1921; s. Madison C. and Tommie Clyde (Strickland) B.; B.B.A., Baylor U., 1947; grad. Inst. Ins. Mktg., So. Meth. U., 1947; m. Helen Marie Howard, Dec. 27, 1947; children—Elizabeth Ann (Mrs. Carey Blackstone), Mary Helen (Mrs. William P. Kliewer), Nancy Carol. Asst. store mgr. Montgomery Ward & Co., Brownwood, Tex., 1949; sec., asst. city mgr., tax assessor, collector City of Killeen (Tex.), 1951; agt. Gt. So. Life Ins. Co., Killeen, 1952—; gen. ins. agt., 1955—; partner Baumann & Bigham Ins. Agy., 1955-58, Killeen Ins. Agy., 1958-67; propr. Bigham Ins. & Real Estate, Killeen, 1967—; pres. Killeen Area Investment Corp., 1969—, Elm Grove Mobile Home Estates, Inc., 1970—. Mem. Tex. Gov.'s Hwy. Safety Com., 1958-59; 1st v.p. Killeen Welfare Agy., 1961-65, bd. dirs., 1961-67; mem. nat. council U.S.O., 1959; former chmn. Killeen Zoning Bd., Killeen Bd. Adjustments and Appeals; vice chmn. Killeen Bd. Econ. Devel., 1974—. Bd. dirs. Bell County chpt. ARC, 1954-60, Central Tex. Edn. Corp., 1973—, Research Inst. Advanced Tech., 1974—; pres. bd. dirs. Central Tex. Area Found., 1968—; mem. bd. Killeen Indsl. Found., 1966—, v.p., 1970; chmn. bd. trustees Central Tex. Coll., 1965—. Served with USAAF, 1941-45. Mem. Am. Legion (post comdr. 1954-55), V.F.W., Nat. Def. Transp. Assn. (dir. Central Tex. chpt. 1956), Killeen C. of C. (pres. 1956, bd. dirs. 1954-61, 69-71), Heart of Tex. Assn. Life Underwriters (pres. 1958, bd. dirs. 1957-60), Assn. U.S. Army (regional v.p. 1960, regional treas. 1965, state pres. 1961-62, mem. nat. resolutions com. 1961). Episcopalian (vestryman 1964-68, sr. warden 1965). Mason (Shriner), Lion (pres. Killeen 1959-60). Home: 800 Live Oak St Killeen TX 76541 Office: 807 N 8th St Killeen TX 76541

BIGLER, ERIN DAVID, neuropsychologist, educator; b. Los Angeles, July 9, 1949; s. Erin Boley and Natalie (Webb) B.; B.S., Brigham Young U., 1971, Ph.D., 1974; m. Janet Beckstrom, June 22, 1971; 1 dau., Alicia Suzanne. NIH fellow St. Joseph Hosp. and Med. Center, Phoenix, 1975-77; pvt. practice neuropsychology, Ariz., 1975-77, Austin, Tex., 1977—; chief psychologist Adolescent Unit, Austin State Hosp., 1977-78; asst. prof. psychology U. Tex., Austin, 1978—; staff psychologist Shoal Creek Hosp., Austin, 1978—. Mem. Am. Psychol. Assn., Soc. for Neurosci., N.Y. Acad. Sci., Internat. Soc. Neuropsychology, Nat. Acad. Neuropsychologists, Tex. Psychol. Assn., Sigma Xi. Democrat. Mem. Ch. of Jesus Christ of Latter Day Saints. Contbr. articles in field to profl. jours.; editor Tex. Psychologist, 1978-80; cons. editor Clin. Neuropsychology, 1978—. Home: Rural Route 1 Box 317 Buda TX 78610 Office: Austin Neurol Clinic Med Sci Center 711 W 38 St Bldg F Austin TX 78705

BILLINGS, HERBERT EDWARD, JR., inventory processor exec.; b. Memphis, Sept. 4, 1938; s. Herbert E. and Ileana (Guidi) B.; student Loyola U. (New Orleans), 1955-56; m. Linda A. Martin, Apr. 20, 1974; children—Herbert Edward III, Paul, Tammy, Scott. Regional mgr. Victor Comptometer Corp., Chgo., 1956-70; pres. Contract Dataflo, Inc., Dallas, 1970—. Recipient Outstanding Mem. award Nat. Assn. Accts., 1975, Hall of Fame Cert., 1979. Mem. Nat. Assn. Accts. (chpt. pres. 1977, pres. Tex. council 1980). Club: Lancers. Office: 1402 Elm St Suite 400 Dallas TX 75202

BILLINGS, KENNEY, business exec., profl. photographer; b. Boston, Nov. 26, 1933; s. A.W.K. and Doris (Colburn) B.; B.A. in Sociology, Stanford U., 1957; grad. in bus. law U. Hartford, 1959; m. Anne Price, Mar. 28, 1958; children—Richard K., David P. Mgr. spl. markets Howe Corp., New Britain, Conn., 1958-61; founder, pres. Billings Corp., Dallas, 1961—; founder Billings S.W., Inc., Houston, 1963-70; pres. Alexander Motor Parts, Dallas, 1961-69, ABC Sales, Inc., Dallas, 1974—; chmn. bd. Indsl. Truck Stop, Inc., Dallas, 1965—; freelance photographer, Dallas, 1975—. Mem. Dallas Citizens Council, Dallas Assembly. Bd. dirs. Constrn. Scis. Research Found., Washington; bd. dirs. Dallas Assn. Retarded Citizens, pres., 1973-74; bd. dirs., trustee Dallas Mus. Fine Arts. Served with AUS, 1970-75. Mem. Am. Soc. Archtl. Hardware Consultants, Constrn. Specifications Inst., Photog. Soc. Am., Dallas Profl. Photographers Assn., Phi Delta Theta. Clubs: Dallas Country (dir.), Salesmanship, Stanford Alumni. Home: 4211 Lorraine St Dallas TX 75205 Office: PO Box 1970 Dallas TX 75221

BILLINGSLEY, DAVID LEWIS, internat. petroleum cons.; co. exec.; b. Houston, Nov. 8, 1935; s. Louis Samuel and Mary Hazel (Bufkin) B.; B.S. in Petroleum Engring. (Socony Mobil scholar), U. Tex., 1957, M.S. in Petroleum Engring. (Pan Am. Petroleum Corp. fellow), 1958; m. Madora Mae Baker, Feb. 20, 1954; children—David Lewis, Carl Russ, John Thomas, Madora. Jr. petroleum engr. Pan Am. Petroleum Corp., Andrews, Tex., 1958-59; partner, cons. petroleum engr. Kirkpatrick & Assos., Shreveport, La., 1959; chief engr. Caddo Oil Co., Shreveport, 1959-63; organizer, owner Billingsley Engring. Co., Shreveport, 1963—; dir. Billingsley Engring. Co., Chapco, Inc. Co-chmn. area fund campaign Boy Scouts Am., 1965, 66; chmn. profl. petroleum engrs. div. United Fund Drive, 1972. Registered profl. engr., Ark., La., Okla., Tex. Mem. Am. Petroleum Inst., Am. Assn. Petroleum Engrs., Am. Assn. Petroleum Geologists, Internat. Oil Scouts Assn., Ind. Petroleum Assn. Am., Tex. Ex-Students Assn. (pres. N.W. La. chpt. 1969), Soc. Petroleum Engrs. (chmn. La.-Ark. sect. 1963-64, dir. 1964-65), Soc. Petroleum Evaluation Engrs., Nat. Soc. Petroleum Engrs., La. Engring. Soc., Shreveport Geol. Soc., Shreveport C. of C., Pub. Affairs Research Council La., Historic Preservation of Shreveport, La. Forestry Assn., Aircraft Owners and Pilots Assn., La. Quarter Horse Breeders Assn., La. Cattlemen's Assn., Am. Quarter Horse Assn., Am. Hereford Assn., Nat. Cutting Horse Assn., Nat. Rifle Assn., Sigma Gamma Epsilon, Tau Beta Pi. Episcopalian. Clubs: Petroleum of Shreveport, Shreveport Country, Ark-La.-Tex. Ambassadors, Gulf Coast Big Game Hunters, Safari Internat. Contbr. articles to profl. jours. Home: Route 3 Box 618A Keithville LA 71047 Office: 2000 Fairfield Ave Shreveport LA 71104

BILLINGTON, TED FRANKLIN, cons. engr.; b. Almo, Ky., Nov. 22, 1938; s. Eldred Guy and Lurline (Morris) B.; student Murray State U., 1956-59; B.S. in C.E., U. Ky., 1961; m. Joan Patricia Baker, Apr. 25, 1961; children—Julia Kathryn, Claudia Joan, Cheryl. Assn. resident engr. Ky. Dept. Hwy., Ashland, 1961-62; chief structural engr. Lee Potter Smith & Assos., architects, Paducah, Ky., 1962-67; cons. engr. Ted F. Billington, Murray, Ky., 1967—, prin. cons. services civil and structural engring., land surveying. Registered land surveyor, Ky., Tenn.; registered profl. engr., Tenn., Ky., Ind., Ill. Mem. ASCE, Nat. Soc. Profl. Engrs., ASTM, Am. Concrete Inst., Ky. Soc. Profl. Engrs./Profl. Engrs. in Pvt. Practice (chmn. 1978-79), Murray C. of C. Baptist. Club: Rotary (pres. Murray 1974-75). Home: 2014 Gatesborough Circle Murray KY 42071 Office: Johnson Blvd Box 422 Murray KY 42071

BILLIONS, NOVELLA STAFFORD, physicist; b. Huntsville, Ala., Nov. 30, 1930; d. Charlie Elmer and Rossie Beatrice (Woiaver) Stafford; student Detroit Bus. U., 1953-54; B.S., Athens (Ala.) Coll., 1958; postgrad. U. Ala., Huntsville, 1962-74; m. James Calvin Billions, Sept. 21, 1950. Meteorologist, USAF Air Weather Service, 1950-53, Army Ordnance Missile Labs., Redstone Arsenal, Ala., 1954-56; meteorologist Army Ballistic Missile Agy., 1956-58, physicist, 1958-60; research physicist U.S. Army Missile Command, 1960-77; ret., 1977; tech. supr., cons. Safeguard Systems Command and Kwajalein Missile Range, Marshall Islands, 1964-73; cons. RDT & E and Tactical Meteorol. Rocket Devel. Programs and to SAM-D Project Office. Recipient Letters of Commendation for contbns. and work Nike-X Project Office and KMR, 1965, 67, SAM-D Project mgr. for outstanding work, 1972-73, Certificate of Achievement award U.S. Army, 1968; 1st woman to fire missile Cape Canaveral, Fla., 1962. Mem. Am. Meteorol. Soc. (chmn. N.Ala. chpt. 1971-72), Assn. U.S. Army, Fed. Employed Women. Contbr. articles to profl. jours. Home: 707 Owens Dr SE Huntsville AL 35801

BILLS, THOMAS LOWERY, educator; b. Hillsboro, Tex., May 1, 1934; s. Furman Lowery and Gladys Pearl (Miles) B.; B.S. in Mech. Engring., Tex. Technol. U., 1955; m. Oma Nell Moore, Nov. 23, 1968; children—Keith Lowery, Kathryn Lanell. Design engr. Rocketdyne Inc., McGregor, Tex., 1963-65, Bell Helicopter Co., Ft. Worth, 1965-66; lead liaison engr. LTV Aerospace Corp., Dallas, 1967-70; program chmn. dept. applied physics Tex. State Tech. Inst., Waco, 1970—. Mem. Am. Vocat. Assn., Soc. Mfg. Engrs. Presbyterian. Home: Route 1 Box 126 Itasca TX 76055 Office: Tex State Tech Inst Waco TX 76705

BINDER, GARY, fin. exec.; b. Brookline, Mass., June 14, 1944; s. Jack and Rose (Tatelman) B.; B.S., Boston U., 1966; M.B.A., N.Y. U., 1968; m. Joan Golub, Oct. 1, 1967; children—Alan Jay, David Michael. Communications cons. Western Union Internat., N.Y.C., 1967-68; economist Gen. Motors Corp., N.Y.C., 1968-72; sr. fin. analyst McCall Pub. Co., N.Y.C., 1972-73; v.p. long range planning Foote & Davies, Inc., Atlanta, 1973—. Home: 1407 Lake Hearn Dr NE Atlanta GA 30319 Office: 3101 McCall Dr Doraville GA 30340

BINDER, ROBERT THOMAS, educator; b. Chgo., May 25, 1919; s. Robert E. and Theresa B.; B.S., E. Tex. State U., 1949, M.S., 1950; postgrad. various colls. and univs.; m. Betty Mason Lowery Corbiere, Dec. 29, 1975; 1 son, Robert Thomas. Commd. lt. C.E., U.S. Army, 1944, advanced through grades to lt. col., 1962, ret., 1967; writer Nat. Safety Council, 1946-48; with Sta. KFTV, Paris, Tex., after 1950; asst. prof. journalism and graphic arts East Tex. State U., Commerce, 1967—. Bd. dirs. Julien C. Hyer Youth Camp, Tex. Lions Camp for Crippled Children. Decorated Bronze Star, Commendation medal with oak leaf cluster. Mem. Public Relations Soc. Am. (accredited pub. relations counselor), Tex. Pub. Relations Assn. (past dir.), Public Relations Found. Tex. (charter life mem., trustee), Assn. of Educators of Journalism, Nat. Council Coll. Publs. Advs., Am. Philatelic Soc., Tex. Philatelic Soc., Am. Topical Assn., East Tex. State U. Quarterback Club, Tex. Assn. Coll. Tchrs., Splty. Advt. Assn., Internat., Am. Acad. Advt., Commerce C. of C. (pres. 1980), Lefthanders Internat., Blue and Gold Soc., Soc. Profl. Journalists/Sigma Delta Chi, Phi Delta Kappa. Clubs: Lions (dist. gov.), Masons (Commerce); Shriners, Am. Legion. Contbr. articles to various mags. Home: 2601 Campbell St Commerce TX 75428 Office: Dept Journalism and Graphic Arts E Tex State U Commerce TX 75428

BINE, PETER GEORGE, transp. industry exec.; b. Cleve., Nov. 1, 1941; s. William Joseph and Elsa Margaret (Wenck) B.; A.B. in Polit. Sci., Park Coll., Kansas City, Mo., 1964; M.P.A., U. Cin., 1965; postgrad. advanced mgmt. U. Ga., 1969; m. Deborah Ann Lazarus, Nov. 30, 1969; children—Peter George, Matthew Edward. Asst. city mgr. City of Durham (N.C.), 1965-70; mgr. Atlanta office Wilbur Smith & Assos., 1970-71, asso. in charge of S.E. Asia ops., Manila, Philippines, 1971-72, asso. dir. internat. ops., 1972-76; exec. dir. Pee Dee Regional Transp. Authority, Florence, S.C., 1976—. Chmn. Pee Dee Area Land Use Adv. Com., 1978—; mem. S.C. Transp. Policy Task Force, 1977; mem. oversight com. S.C. Statewide Transp. Coordination Study, 1977; U.S. rep. to UN meeting of Econ. Com. for Asia and Far East, 1972. Mem. Internat. City Mgmt. Assn., Am. Public Transit Assn. Author: Florida Urban Public Transit Needs Report, 1972; Georgia Manual C National Transportation Needs Study, 1971; Launching A Rural Transportation Program for the Disadvantaged, 1977.

BING, ROBERT KENDALL, univ. dean; b. Cambridge, Nebr., Mar. 2, 1929; s. Kenneth L. and Ruth (Thomas) B.; B.S. in Occupational Therapy, U. Ill., 1952; M.A., U. Md., College Park, 1954, Ed.D., 1961. Asst. prof. occupational therapy Richmond Profl. Inst. (now Va. Commonwealth U.), 1954-56; dir. indsl. therapy Norwich (Conn.) State Hosp., 1956-57; W.T. Grant Found. teaching fellow Inst. Child Study, U. Md., 1957-59; instr. in psychology Towson State Coll., 1959-60; asso. in psychiatry Nebr. Psychiat. Inst., U. Nebr., Omaha, 1960-61; asst. prof. occupational therapy U. Fla., 1961-63; dir. activity therapy Ill. State Psychiat. Inst., Chgo. and asst. prof. U. Ill. at Med. Center, Chgo., 1963-65; dir. occupational therapy univ. hosps. and planning dir. Sch. Allied Health Scis., U. Tex. Med. Br., Galveston, 1966-68, dean Sch. Allied Health Scis., 1968—; mem. adv. com. allied health coordinating bd. Tex. Colls. and Univs.; mem. adv. com. Tex. Mil. Experience Directed in Health Careers, 1969-72; bd. dirs. Nat. Rehab. Tng. Inst., Inc., 1974-76; mem. univ.'s faculty of research readers Walden U., 1976—. Chmn. commn. on missions Moody Meml. First Methodist Ch., Galveston, 1969-71; mem. exec. bd. Galveston County Area Soc. for Prevention Cruelty to Animals, Inc., 1974-75. Served with Med. Services Corps, U.S. Army, 1951-53. Named Hon. Citizen, City of Hidalgo (Tex.), 1977. Fellow Am. Occupational Therapy Assn. (cert. appreciation 1978, Eleanor Clarke Slagle lectr. 1981); mem. Am. Sch. Health Assn., Tex. Occupational Therapy Assn. (Tex. Occupational Therapist of Yr. 1974), Am. Soc. Allied Health Professions (editorial bd. Jour. Allied Health 1972-73), Tex. Hosp. Assn. Methodist. Club: Bob Smith Yacht. Author: William Rush Dunton, Jr., M.D.: American Psychiatrist, 1979; contbr. articles to profl. publs. Office: Sch Allied Health Scis U Tex Med Br Galveston TX 77550

BING, ROLAND EDWARD, JR., coll. adminstr.; b. Hempstead, Tex., Apr. 21, 1921; s. Roland Edward and Evelyn Ione (Winfree) B.; B.S., Tex. A&M U., 1942, M.Ed., 1952; Ph.D., U. Tex., 1953; m. Josephine Watts, Aug. 21, 1951; children—Donald Wayne, Jerry Ray. Mgr. student publs. Tex. A&M U., 1946-53; dir. publicity Victoria (Tex.) Coll., 1954-56, dir. evening sch., 1956-58, asst. dean, 1958-64, dean, 1964-75, pres., 1975—. Mem. United Fund Exec. Bd., 1975; bd. dirs. Victoria Regional Mus., 1976—; bd. trustees DeTar Hosp., 1979—. Served with U.S. Army, 1942-46. Mem. Tex. Jr. Coll. Tchrs. Assn., Tex. Assn. Coll. Tchrs., Phi Delta Kappa, Phi Kappa Phi. Presbyterian. Home: 1908 Loma Vista Victoria TX 77902

BINGHAM, BARRY, newspaper exec.; b. Louisville, Feb. 10, 1906; s. Robert Worth and Eleanor (Miller) B.; student Middlesex Sch., Concord, Mass., 1921-23; A.B. magna cum laude, Harvard U., 1928; LL.D., U. Ky., Kenyon Coll., Centre Coll.; Litt.D., U. Louisville, U. Cin., Edgecliff Coll., Alfred U., Berea Coll., Ind. U.; m. Mary Clifford Caperton, June 9, 1931; children—Worth (dec.), Barry, Sarah, Eleanor. With Courier-Jour. and Louisville Times Co., 1930—, reporter, sec., asso. pub., pub., 1930-45, editor, pub., until 1971, now chmn. bd.; chmn. bd. WHAS, Inc., Standard Gravure Corp. Chmn. bd. dirs. Historic Homes Found.; mem. Pres.'s Commn. on White House Fellowships; overseer Harvard U., U. Louisville; bd. dirs. Asia Found.; past chmn. Internat. Press Inst., Am. Press Inst. Chief of mission to France, ECA, 1949-50. Nat. chmn. Vols. for Stevenson-Kefauver, 1956. Served with USNR, 1941-45; comdr., 1945; ETO, PTO. Decorated comdr. Order Brit. Empire, comdr. Legion of Honor; recipient Sullivan award U. Ky. Mem. English Speaking Union U.S. (chmn. 1974-77), Sigma Delta Chi (hon. nat. chmn.). Democrat. Episcopalian. Clubs: Jefferson, River Valley, Wynn-Stay, Louisville Country (Louisville); Century Assn. Home: Glenview KY 40025 Office: Courier-Journal and Times Louisville KY 40202

BINGHAM, EDWARD CLARK, environ. engr.; b. Rutland, Vt., July 23, 1915; s. Edward Clark and Kathryn Maria (Niles) B.; B.S. in Chemistry, U. Vt., 1938; M.B.A. with distinction, U. Pa., 1952; m. Harriet Isabella Gile, Oct. 12, 1939; children—Robert Clark, John Edward. Research chemist Rutland Fire Clay Co. Specialty Products, 1938-41; commd. 2d lt. U.S. Army, 1938, advanced through grades to lt. col., 1954; head logistics acad. dept. Army Service Sch., 1960-63; home office mfg. mgr. various army ammunition plants, 1963-65; ret., 1965; dir. environ. and pub. affairs Farmers Chem. Assn., Chattanooga, 1965-73; sr. environmental engr. ICI Americas Inc., Chattanooga, 1973—. Selected as expert pollution control cons. for Fertilizer and Petrochem. Tech. div. UN Indsl. Devel. Orgn., Europe, 1974. Decorated Army Commendation medal with oak leaf cluster. Mem. Am. Inst. Chem. Engrs., Ret. Officers Assn., Res. Officers Assn. Presbyn. Mason (32 deg., Shriner). Contbr. articles to profl. jours. Home: 5840 Northshore Dr Hixson TN 37343 Office: ICI Americas Inc PO Box 6008 Chattanooga TN 37401

BINGHAM, JOHN JAY, assn. exec.; b. Vilas, N.C., Aug. 20, 1929; s. Thomas McCoy and Kenova Virginia (Morrell) B.; B.S., Appalachian State U., 1956; m. Joan Edna Phillips, May 21, 1954; children—Kirk, Brent. Phys. dir. Wilkes YMCA, North Wilkesboro, N.C., 1956-61; head phys. dept. Cannon Meml. YMCA, Kannapolis, N.C., 1961-68; exec. dir. Greater Clinton (S.C.) YMCA, 1968-76; mem. corp. staff Met. YMCA of Winston-Salem (N.C.) and Forsyth County assigned as exec. dir. East Forsythe Family YMCA, Kernersville, N.C., 1976—. Mem. YMCA Interstate Phys. Edn. Com., 1957-70, sec., 1958-61, pres., 1966-67. Mem. Carolinas Phys. Edn. Com., 1959-72; adviser to John R. Mott, Internat. Y's Mens Club, 1963-68. Served with AUS, 1951-53. Recipient Distinguished Service award Jr. C. of C., 1969, S.C. Phys. Fitness award, 1970. Mem. Assn. Profl. YMCA Dirs. (pres. S.C. chpt. 1971-72). Methodist. Rotarian. Home: 6210 Coltrane Dr Kernersville NC 27284 Office: PO Drawer Y Kernersville NC 27284

BINNING, BETTE FINESE (MRS. GENE HEDGCOCK BINNING), athletic assn. ofcl.; b. Brandon, Man., Can., Sept. 20, 1927 (father Am. citizen); d. Henry Josiah and Beatrice Victoria (Harrop) Ames; grad. Brandon Collegiate, 1944; student Brandon, U., 1944-46; m. Gene Hedgcock Binning, May 3, 1952; children—Gene Barton, Barbara Jo, Bradford Jay. Exec. sec. to mgr. Gardner-Denver Co., Denver, 1950-52; mem. age group swimming com. Amateur Athletic Union U.S., 1966-68, 70-72, women's swimming com., 1968-69, 72—, age group swimming objectives subcom., 1970-71, del. conv., 1971, 72, 73, 74, 75, 76, 77; Okla. state chmn. age group swimming Amateur Athletic Union, 1966-68, 70-72, chmn. women's swimming com., 1968-69, 72-79, mem. Okla. exec. bd. for all amateur sports, also registration com., 1971-79; mem. U.S. Olympic com., 1972—; nat. dir. swimming records, 1972—; U.S. rep. to records com. Amateur Swimming Assn. Ams., 1975—, dir. records com., 1975—; tech. ofcl. Pan Am. Games, Mexico City, 1975, San Juan, P.R., 1979; ofcl. XXI Olympiad, Montreal, Que., Can., 1976. Team capt. YMCA fund drives, 1966-78; active Community Chest, Cancer, Muscular Dystrophy fund drives, Okla. Horse Shows. Mem. Kiwanis Ladies, Youth Study Club (treas. 1971-72). Presbyn. Clubs: Kerr-Mcgee Swim (dir. 1968-75), Quail Creek Golf and Country, Oklahoma City Ski (Oklahoma City). Home: 3101 Rolling Stone Rd Oklahoma City OK 73120

BINNING, GENE HEDGCOCK, air conditioning co. exec.; b. Casper, Wyo., Oct. 28, 1927; s. Lloyd Cecil and Vera (Rhodes) B.; B.S., U. Wyo., 1949; postgrad. Oklahoma City U., 1959, U. Okla., 1963-64; m. Bette Fenis Ames, May 3, 1952; children—Gene Barton, Barbara Jo, Bradford Jay. Sales engr. Trane Co., Denver, 1950-58, mgr. Okla. dist., Oklahoma City, 1958—; pres. Gene H. Binning Co., Inc., Comml. Devel. Co.; mgr. Binning Oil & Gas Investment & Devel. Co. Served with AUS, 1946-47. Recipient Heating and Air Conditioning Seminar Course awards, 1966. Registered profl. engr., Okla. Mem. Am. Soc. Heating and Air Conditioning Engrs. (dir.), Oklahoma City C. of C., Sigma Nu. Presbyn. (elder). Mason (Shriner), Kiwanian. Club: Quail Creek Golf and Country (bd. dirs.). Home: 3101 Rolling Stone Rd Oklahoma City OK 73120 Office: 3800 Willowsprings Rd Oklahoma City OK 73112

BIRCH, FREDERICK TALBOT, computer programmer; b. Bridgeport, Conn., July 18, 1933; s. Charles R. E. and Anna F.; student U. Conn., 1952-55; B.A. in Mathematics, U. Bridgeport, 1964; M.S. in Ops. Research, N.Y. U., 1970; m. Maria Antonia van't Wout, Mar. 12, 1959 (dec.); children—Annelise C., Linda van't Wout, Yvette J.; m. 2d, Elsa Elisabeth Slamy, Jan. 1, 1979. Analytical chemist Escambia Chem. Corp., Wilton, Conn., 1958-65; ops. research analyst Warner Bros. Co., Bridgeport, 1965-66; sr. asso. programmer IBM, Mohansic, N.Y., 1966-72, staff programmer, East Fishkill, N.Y., 1972—, instr. in programming and simulation, 1972—. Mem. adminstrv. bd. First United Methodist Ch., Brewster, N.Y., 1977—, trustee, 1978—. Served with U.S. Army, 1958. Recipient informal awards IBM, 1968, 72. Mem. Am. Def. Preparedness Assn., Smithsonian Assos., Nat. Wildlife Fedn., U. Bridgeport Alumni Assn., Fedn. de L'Alliance Franciaise, Widow-Widowers Associated (v.p. chpt. 5, 1978), N.Y. U. Alumni Assn. Patentee in field. Home: 5816 Winthrop Dr Raleigh NC 27612 Office: Research Triangle Park NC

BIRCH, LARRY ARTHUR, psychologist, educator; b. Dayton, Ohio, Apr. 27, 1945; s. Marvin Orville and Garnet Evelyn (Slegal) B.; A.A., Pierce Coll., 1966; B.S., Wright State U., 1969; M.A., Calif. State U., 1971. Mem. staff Antioch Coll., Yellow Springs, Ohio, 1967-68; with U.S. Air Force Research Contract, Yellow Springs, 1968-69; with Nat. Cash Register Co., Dayton, 1969, Sears Roebuck & Co., Los Angeles, 1969-70; grad. asst. Calif. State U., Los Angeles, 1971-72; staff Wittenberg U., Springfield, Ohio, 1973-74; clin. supr. Dayton Mental Health Center, 1973-74; clin. supr. Mental Health Clinic, Jacksonville, Fla., 1975-79; adj. prof. psychology dept. U. N. Fla., Jacksonville, 1977—; cons. Sci. Mgmt. Corp., Washington, 1977—, Westinghouse Health Systems, Columbia, Md., 1977—, Eastern Area Alcohol Edn. and Tng. Program, Bloomfield, Conn., 1977-79. Chmn., N.E. Fla. Adv. Com. on Alcoholism, 1976—. Mem. Am., Midwestern, Fla. psychol. assns., Psi Chi. Democrat. Contbr. articles in field to profl. jours. Home: 2797 St Johns Ave Jacksonville FL 32205 Office: 2627 Riverside Ave Jacksonville FL 32204

BIRCH, WADE GORDON, educator; b. N.Y.C., Jan. 18, 1938; s. Clifton Charles and Ruth Elizabeth (Dehate) B.; B.S., U. Tampa, 1960; M.S., Fla. State U., 1963; M.S.Ed., Ind. U., 1968, Ed.D., 1970; m. Rita M. Marsh, Dec. 23, 1976; children—Dean Wade, Cynthia Clotiel. Tchr. social studies Meml. Jr. High Sch., Tampa, 1960-63; counselor Stranahan High Sch., Fort Lauderdale, 1963-65; counselor Reading and Study Skills Center, Ind. U., Bloomington, 1965-67, counseling psychologist Counseling and Psychol. Services Center, 1967-71, asst. prof. edn., 1970-71; dir. counseling, asst. prof. student personnel and guidance East Tex. State U., Commerce, 1971-74; dir. personal counseling service Tex. A. and M. U., 1974—. Mem. Am., Tex. psychol. assns., Am., Tex. personnel and guidance assns., Am. Coll. Personnel Assn., Assn. Counselor Edn. and Supervision, Pi Kappa Phi. Methodist. Contbr. articles to profl. jours. Home: 3109 Rolling Glen Dr Bryan TX 77801 Office: Personal Counseling Service YMCA Bldg Room 017 Tex A and M U College Station TX 77843

BIRCH, WILLIAM GARRY, physician; b. Janesville, Wis., July 8, 1909; s. Frank Earl and Lois Penina (Hill) B.; student U. Iowa, 1926-28; M.B., M.D., Northwestern U., 1933; LL.D., Western Mich. U., 1976; m. Vera Grace Anderson, June 3, 1936; children—Jae Anderson, Dawn Birch Sebek, William Garry II, James Devere. Intern, Evanston (Ill.) Hosp., Chgo. Maternity Center, 1932-34; resident in obstetrics and gynecology Chgo. Lying-In Hosp., 1934-37; pvt. practice obstetrics and gynecology, 1937-75; founding partner Sault Polyclinic, Sault Ste. Marie, Mich., 1937; obstetrician and gynecologist Birch, Peake & Gertner, Kalamazoo, 1945-75, also sr. partner, pres.; ind. cons., Largo, Fla., 1975—; clin. dir. physician's asst. program Western Mich. U., 1968-74, adj. prof. human and health services, 1968—. Chmn. Kalamazoo Symphony Soc., 1955; pres. Chamber Music Soc., 1955-65, S. Central Mich. Health Planning Council, 1969-74; mem. advisory council Gulf Health Systems Agency, 1977-78. Served to maj. M.C., U.S. Army, 1941-45; ETO; ret. col. Res., 1969. Decorated Bronze Star medal; recipient Outstanding Community Service award Kalamazoo, 1974, Distinguished Service award Mich. Med. Soc., 1973. Fellow A.C.S., Am. Coll. Obstetricians and Gynecologists (life); mem. AMA, Mich. Soc. Obstetrics and Gynecology, Kalamazoo Acad. Medicine (pres. 1965). Episcopalian. Clubs: Executives (pres. 1967), Rotary (pres. 1958), Elks. Author: A Doctor Discusses Pregnancy, 6th edit., 1976. Contbr. articles to profl. and lay jours., mags. Home: 62 Sabal Palm Dr Largo FL 33540

BIRCHUM, DONALD GENE, SR., supermarket chain exec.; b. Norman, Okla., Dec. 18, 1930; s. Joseph Wesley and Vada Lee (Southerland) B.; B.F.A. in Advt., Okla. U., 1953; m. Betty Marie Kegler, Nov. 10, 1961; 1 son, Donald Gene. Asst. advt. prodn. mgr. H.E. Butt Grocery Co., Corpus Christi, Tex., 1957-62, advt. mgr., family center div., 1969-71, corporate advt. mgr., 1971—; advt. mgr., grocery div. Gulf-Mart Inc., San Antonio, 1962-68. Mem. fin. com. troop 220 Boy Scouts Am. Served as 1st lt. USAF, 1954-56. Mem. Corpus Christi Advt. Fedn., S.Tex. Press Assn., Audit Bur. Circulation, U.S. Power Squadron (nat. com. audio visual aids 1978—, dist. 21 sec. 1980-81), Corpus Christi Power Squadron (sec. 1974-76, editor, art dir. Gulf Breeze 1974-78), N.Am. Cruiser Assn. (public relations chmn.), Am. Power Boat Assn., Alpha Delta Sigma, Phi Delta Theta. Club: Bay Yacht. Illustrator, cartoonist Ensign mag. U.S. Power Squadrons, 1975—. Home: 518 Evergreen Dr Corpus Christi TX 78412 Office: 807 N Upper Broadway Corpus Christi TX 78408

BIRD, DANIEL DAVID, constrn. co. exec.; b. Kansas City, Mo., Apr. 22, 1941; s. Charles Daniel and Mary (Gould) B.; B.S. in Civil Engring. (Kans. Contractors scholar), U. Kans., 1963; m. Mildred Louise Barr, Aug. 16, 1959; children—Cory David, Derek Daniel, Wendy Danielle. Engr., Martin K. Eby Constrn. Co., various locations, 1963-64, chief engr., 1964-66; chief engr. Henry C. Beck Co., Dallas, 1966, chief regional field engr., 1966-68, project mgr., supr., 1968; supt. projects Hensel Phelps Constrn. Co., Los Alamos, N.Mex., 1968-70; constrn. mgr. Forum Builders, Inc., Dallas, 1970-71; sr. project mgr. Charter Builders, Inc., Dallas, 1971-72; v.p. Cimarron Constrn. Co., Dallas, 1972; owner, mgr. Bird Constrn. Co., Dandan Engring., Dallas, 1972-78; owner, operator, pres. Daniel D. Bird Cos., Inc., 1978—. Registered profl. engr., Kans., Tex. Mem. Nat. Soc. Profl. Engrs., ASCE, Constrn. Specifications Inst. Home: 3137 Jubilee Trail Dallas TX 75229 Office: 11602 Reeder Rd Dallas TX 75229

BIRD, FRANCIS MARION, lawyer; b. Comer, Ga., Sept. 4, 1902; s. Henry Madison and Minnie Lee (McConnell) B.; A.B., U. Ga., 1922, LL.B., 1924; LL.M., George Washington U., 1925; m. Mary Adair Howell, Jan. 30, 1935; children—Francis Marion, Mary Adair, Elizabeth Howell, George Arthur. Admitted to Ga. bar, 1924, D.C. bar, 1925; since practiced in Atlanta, with U.S. Senator Hoke Smith, 1925, individual practice, 1930-45, Bird & Howell, 1945-59, now Jones, Bird & Howell; served as part-time U.S. referee in bankruptcy, 1945-54; spl. asst. to U.S. atty. gen. as hearings officer Nat. Selective Service Act; mem. commn. for preparation plan of govt. City of Atlanta and county in which located; mem. permanent rules com. Ga. Supreme Ct.; chmn. Ga. Bd. Bar Examiners, 1954-61; mem. Permanent Editorial Bd. Uniform Comml. Code, Fed. Jud. Conf., 5th Circuit; chmn. Met. Atlanta Commn. on Crime and Juvenile Delinquency, 1969-70. Former Ga. co-chmn. Tech-Ga. Devel. Fund; trustee Young Harris Coll., U. Ga. Found., Atlanta Lawyers Found., Interdenomnl. Theol. Center; trustee, past mem. exec. com. Emory U. Recipient Distinguished Service citation U. Ga. Law Sch., Alumni Achievement award George Washington U., 1965; Pres.'s award Assn. Pvt. Colls. and Univs. Ga., 1979. Fellow Am. Bar Found.; mem. Am. Judicature Soc. (past dir.) Am. Law Inst. (council 1949—), Am., Ga. (past pres.), Atlanta (past pres.; Distinguished Service award 1977), bar assns., Assn. Bar City N.Y., Atlanta C. of C. (past pres., Atlanta Civic Service award 1957), U. Ga. Alumni Assn. (past pres., certificate of merit 1952), Sigma Chi, Phi Kappa Phi, Phi Delta Phi. Methodist. Clubs: Peachtree Golf, Piedmont Driving, Capital City, Lawyers of Atlanta (past pres.), Atlanta Athletic (past pres.), Kiwanis (Atlanta); Augusta (Ga.) Nat. Golf. Home: 89 Brighton Rd NE Atlanta GA 30309 Office: Haas-Howell Bldg Atlanta GA 30303

BIRD, FRANCIS MARION, JR., lawyer; b. Atlanta, Apr. 14, 1938; s. Francis Marion and Mary Adair (Howell) B.; A.B., Princeton U., 1959; LL.B., Emory U., 1964; LL.M., Harvard U., 1966; m. Irene Woodruff Michael, July 18, 1962; children—Barbara, Michael. Admitted to Ga. bar, 1964; asso. firm Jones, Bird & Howell, Atlanta, 1964-65, 60-70, partner firm, 1970—. Bd. dirs. Southeastern Bankruptcy Law Inst., 1975-77; chmn. Ga. Health Laws Study Com., 1975. Served with USN, 1959-62. Mem. Ga. Soc. Hosp. Attys. (pres. 1976-77), Am. Bar Assn., Atlanta Bar Assn., State Bar Ga. (chmn. standing com. on publs. 1977-78), Comml. Law League Am., Phi Delta Phi, Omicron Delta Kappa. Club: Lawyers (Atlanta). Office: Haas-Howell Bldg Atlanta GA 30303

BIRD, FRANK EDWARD, JR., ednl. adminstr.; b. Netcong, N.J., Dec. 19, 1921; s. Frank Edward and Virginia (Goebel) B.; B.S., Albright Coll., 1950; postgrad. N.Y. U., 1956-57; m. Esther Savidge, Nov. 6, 1948; children—Frank Edward, Susan Bird Arnold, Billie Bird Baird, David, Johnny. Supr. safety Lukens Steel Co., Coatesville, Pa., 1953-68; dir. engring. services Ins. Co. N.Am., Phila., 1968-71; dir. Internat. Safety Acad., Macon, Ga., 1971-73; exec. dir. Internat. Loss Control Inst., Atlanta, 1973—; pres. Loss Control Mgmt. Coll., Loganville, Ga., 1976—; loss control adviser Ins. Inst. Am., Paoli, Pa. Chmn. safety com. Chester County council Boy Scouts Am., 1955-64; chmn. safety service Phila. regional office ARC, 1969-71; exec. sec. Chester County (Pa.) Safety Council, 1958-71. Served with USN, 1942-46. Recipient Gold award for Distinguished Service to Occupational Safety, Royal Soc. Prevention of Accidents (Eng.), 1976, Pub. Service award U.S. Dept. Interior, 1971, Spl. award St. Johns Ambulance Assn. Can.; Optimist of the Year award, 1967; registered profl. engr., Wis. Mem. Am. Soc. Safety Engrs., Systems Safety Soc., Vets. Safety Internat. Methodist. Author: Damage Control, 1966; Management Guide to Loss Control, 1974; Loss Control Management, 1976; contbr. articles in field to profl. jours.; inventor of metagard and Saf-T-Guider. Home: 1918 Fabersham Dr Snellville GA 30278 Office: PO Box 345 Hwy 78 Loganville GA 30249

BIRD, RALPH SIDNEY, ret. educator; b. Athens, W.Va., Aug. 1, 1913; s. Bluford Claude and Pinnie (Tolley) B.; B.S., Morris Harvey Coll., 1934; M.Ed., Duke, 1940; M.S., W.Va. U., 1962; postgrad. Tex. A & M U., 1969; m. Betty Lou Williams, June 1, 1942; children—Ralph S., David Noel, William, Richard. Tchr. Springton (W.Va.) Jr. High Sch., 1935-37; tchr. Matoaka (W.Va.) High Sch., 1937-42, 46, prin., 1947-65; prin. Spanishburg High Sch., 1946-47; asst. prof. math. Bluefield State Coll., 1965-67, asso. prof., 1967-74, dir. div. applied sci. and tech., 1968-74. Mem. Gov.'s Council Vocational Edn., 1969-71; exec. com. Mercer County March of Dimes, 1955-69; pres. Mercer County unit Am. Cancer Soc., 1954-60; active Boy Scouts Am., recipient Silver Beaver award; chmn. Mercer County Bicentennial Commn., 1974-77. Councilman, Town of Matoaka, 1973-75, recorder, 1975—; mem. Devel. Authority Mercer County, 1975—; mem. Mercer County Recreation Com., 1975—; chmn. Mercer County Emergency Med. Service Com., 1975-78. Served from pvt. to tech. sgt., AUS, 1942-45. Methodist (steward, treas.). Mason, Kiwanian (pres. local 1948, 73-74, dir. 1949—, dist. lt. gov. 1954, chmn. internat. com. on Key clubs 1954, dist. chmn. bicentennial com. 1975-76, adminstr. W.Va. Keywanetics 1978—). Clubs: Bluefield Automobile (dir.); Moose. Home: 121 Mercer Ave Matoaka WV 24736 Office: Box 346 Matoaka WV 24736

BIRDSALL, BRYAN EARL, guidance counselor; b. Gadsden, Ala., July 18, 1942; s. James Earl and Zerah Ruth (Edmondson) B.; B.S., Jacksonville State U., 1973; M.A., U. Ala., 1973, Ed.D., 1980. Tchr. public schs., Ala., 1965-77; counselor Miss. Band Choctaw Indians, Philadelphia, 1977-78; counselor spl. services program Livingston (Ala.) U.; 1978—; counselor freshman orientation U. Ala. Mem. NEA, Ala. Edn. Assn., Am. Personnel and Guidance Assn., Ala. Personnel and Guidance Assn. (parliamentarian 1979—), Jacksonville Jr. C. of C. (pres.), Capstone Coll. Edn. Soc., Kappa Delta Pi, Phi Delta Kappa, Phi Beta Lambda. Republican. Baptist. Home: PO Box 1012 Livingston AL 35470 Office: St 17 Livingston U Livingston AL 35470

BIRDWELL, JAMES EDWIN, JR., banker; b. Chuckey, Tenn., Apr. 22, 1924; s. James Edwin and Mary Eleanor (Earnest) B.; A.B., Tusculum Coll., 1948; M.A., Peabody Coll., 1951; m. Marilyn Margaretta Gibson, Dec. 20, 1949; children—James Edwin III, Amy Eleanor, Todd Gibson. Tchr., coach Doak High Sch., Greeneville, Tenn., 1948-50; field rep. Third Nat. Bank, Nashville, 1951-52; v.p. Va. Nat. Bank, Norfolk, 1957-73; pres. Union Peoples Bank, Clinton, Tenn., 1973—, chmn. bd., 1976—, also dir.; dir. Melton Hill Regional Indsl. Assn., Anderson County Indsl. Bd.; chmn., dir. Clinton Port Authority. Trustee, Daniel Arthur Rehab. Center, Oak Ridge, 1976—, Oak Ridge Hosp.; commr. Va. Beach Beach Bldg. and Grounds Commn., 1969-73, Clinton Recreation Commn., 1977—; mem. Smoky Mountain council Boy Scouts Am., 1975—. Served with USNR, 1943-46, 52-57; Korean. Mem. Am., Tenn. bankers assns., Roane-Anderson County Econ. Council, Clinton C. of C. (pres. 1977), Naval Res. Assn., Theta Chi, Phi Delta Kappa. Democrat. Methodist. Clubs: Oak Ridge Country; Clinton Civitan (Service award 1975); Le Conte (Knoxville). Home: 619 Woodland Dr Clinton TN 37716 Office: 245 N Main St Clinton TN 37716

BIRK, WILLIAM FRANK, real estate, oil exec., tobacco farmer; b. Owensboro, Ky., Sept. 28, 1904; s. George Washington and Dora (Baughman) B.; m. Daisy Smith, May 22, 1925; children—Anne Birk Stavis, Eleanor Birk Sutton. Farmer, Owensboro, Ky.; owner Birk Enterprises, Owensboro, 1960—; dir. Lincoln Income Life Ins. Co., Louisville, Central Bank & Trust Co., Owensboro. Home: 1911 Lexington Ave Owensboro KY 42301 Office: 1102 Triplett St Owensboro KY 42301

BIRKENWALD, EMIL S., civil engr.; b. Milw., May 30, 1901; s. Edward Bernard and Clara (Silber) B.; B.S. in Civil Engring., U. Wis., 1922; S.M., Mass. Inst. Tech., 1923; m. Edith Fauerbach, Sept. 29, 1925. With So. Ry. Co., various locations, 1924-67, bridge engr., 1946-64, asst. chief bridge engr., Atlanta, 1964-67; sole practice ry. bridge cons. engring., Atlanta, 1968—. Fellow Am. Soc. C.E. (life mem.); mem. Am. Ry. Engring. Assn. (life mem.), Am. Soc. Testing Materials. Republican. Episcopalian. Mason (32 deg.). Address: 3750 Peachtree Rd NE Apt 407 Atlanta GA 30319

BIRMINGHAM, EUGENE, food technologist; b. White Hall, Md., Aug. 29, 1927; s. Ralph and Hila Blanche (Gemmill) B.; B.S., U. Md., 1950; M.S., U. Mo., 1954, Ph.D., 1960; m. Barbara Ann Carpenter, Feb. 10, 1951; children—Hila Jean, Robert Meredith. Meat scientist U.S. Dept. Agr., Beltsville, Md., 1950-52; meat instr. U. Mo., Columbia, 1952-60; head cured meats research Swift & Co., Chgo., 1960-66; dir. research and devel./quality assurance Deltec Internat. Ltd., Coral Gables, Fla., 1966-77; self-employed internat. cons. sci. and tech. service to meat industry, Miami, 1977-78; v.p. tech. services Hebrew Nat. Kosher Foods, Inc., 1978-79; pvt. practice food tech. adviser, 1979—; mem. staff research to pres. Swift Argentina-Buenos Aires div. Deltec, 1968. Mem. Am. Meat Sci. Assn., AAAS, Am. Soc. Animal Sci., Am. Registry Certified Animal Scientists, Inst. Food Technologists, Am. Chem. Soc., Sigma Xi, Gamma Alpha, Gamma

Sigma Delta. Contbr. articles in field to profl. jours. Home: 7180 SW 64th St Miami FL 33143

BIRO, NICHOLAS GEORGE, pub. relations exec.; b. Budapest, Hungary, Nov. 30, 1929 (parents Am. citizens); s. Nicholar M. and Margaret M. (Mager) B.; B.S., U. Ill., 1952; student John Marshall Law Sch., 1955-57; m. Joan Brynda, Feb. 20, 1965; children—Michael, Nancy, David. Mgmt. trainee U.S. Steel Corp., Gary, Ind., 1952-57; sr. editor Billboard Publishing Co., Chgo., 1957-65; dir. pub. relations, promotions, and advertising WCFL Radio Sta., Chgo., 1965-66; v.p. pub. relations Martin E. Janis & Co., Inc., Chgo., 1966-69; dir. pub. relations Wilson Foods Corp., Chgo., Oklahoma City, Okla., 1969-77; group pub. relations dir. R.J. Reynolds Industries, Inc., Winston Salem, N.C., 1977-78; corp. v.p. pub. relations and communication Holiday Inns Inc., Memphis, 1978—; faculty adv. com. Okla. City U. Sch. Bus., 1973-77; mem. consumer affairs com. Nat. Pork Producers Council, 1976-77. Div. chmn. United Way Greater Memphis, 1979. Served with USMCR, 1952-54. Mem. Am. Meat Inst. (chmn. pub. relations com. 1975-77), Pub. Relations Soc. Am. (pres. Oklahoma City chpt. 1975-76, chmn. S.W. Dist. 1977-78), Soc. Profl. Journalists, Alpha Sigma Phi Alumni Soc. Home: 8218 Bryn Manor Ln Germantown TN 38138 Office: 3742 Lamar Memphis TN 38195

BIRZNIEKS, ILMARS, educator; b. Liepaja, Latvia, Aug. 16, 1932; s. Rudolfs and Alida (Stamers) B.; came to U.S., 1950, naturalized, 1954; A.B., Asbury Coll., 1958; Ph.D., Tulane U., 1968; postgrad. Goethe Inst. Tchrs. German, 1969; m. Faith Bell, Aug. 12, 1957; 1 dau., Laura Joy. Instr. German, U. N.C., Greensboro, 1965-66; asst. prof. U. Mo., Columbia, 1966-72; asst. prof. German and English Abendgymnasium der Stadt Bonn, Germany, 1972-74; asst. prof., chmn. German dept. Berea (Ky.) Coll., 1975-76, asso. prof., 1977—, chmn. dept. fgn. langs., 1976—. Served with AUS, 1953-55. U. Mo. Research Council grantee, 1970. Mem. Am. Assn. Tchrs. German, Modern Lang. Assn., AAUP, Assn. Advancement Baltic Studies, Delta Phi Alpha. Lutheran. Contbr. articles to prof. jours. Office: Berea Coll CPO 63 Berea KY 40403

BISBEE, CYNTHIA GAIL CARSON, psychologist; b. Savannah, Ga., Nov. 28, 1945; d. Edwin Williams and Lillie Corene (Smith) Carson; A.B., Ga. So. Coll., 1967; M.S. in Psychology (fellow) Auburn U., 1969, Ph.D., 1971; m. Paul Bisbee, Dec. 27, 1974. Grad. instr. psychology Auburn (Ala.) U., 1968-71; unit dir. E. Central Ala. unit Bryce Hosp., Tuscaloosa, 1973-75, clin. dir. Level II, 1975-76, chief psychologist admissions, 1975-76, asst. dir. psychology dept., 1977-78, dir. Psychol. Learning Center, 1977—. Charter mem. health professions adv. com. Sch. Arts and Scis., Auburn U., 1973—. NSF trainee, 1967-71. Mem. Am., Southeastern, Ala. psychol. assns., Assn. Advancement Behavior Therapy, Southeastern Assn. Behavior Therapy. Home: 49 Taylorwood Estates Tuscaloosa AL 35405 Office: Bryce Hosp Tuscaloosa AL 35403

BISHOP, CALVIN THOMAS, landscape architect; b. Alexander City, Ala., Oct. 11, 1929; s. Isaiah Washington and Flora Bernice (Carlton) B.; B.Landscape Architecture, Auburn U., 1951; m. Lenna Graves, Aug. 28, 1950; children—Leigh Carlton, Beverly Lynn, Lane Amanda. Landscape architect John F. Highberger, Memphis, 1949-51; planner Auburn Planning Bd., 1951; landscape architect, designer Ralph Ellis Gunn, Houston, 1952-53; partner Bishop & Walker, Houston, 1953—; asst. prof. landscape architecture La. State U., 1965-66. Post adviser Boy Scouts Am., 1971-73; chmn. Gov.'s Houston-Gulf Coast Region-10 year Goals For Tex. planning com., 1970; chmn. Houston-Am. Bicentennial Commn., 1973—; treas. Richmond Elementary P.T.O., 1975—. Mem. profl. adv. com. Sch. Environmental Design, Tex. A. and M. U. Recipient Houston Mcpl. Arts Environmental Distinguished Achievement awards, 1970-72. Mem. Am. Soc. Landscape Architects (v.p. 1973-74, 79-80, pres. S.W. chpt. 1970-71, Merit awards for design, Nat. Honor award for design), Houston C. of C., Houston-Auburn U. Alumni Assn. (pres. 1963-64), Pi Kappa Alpha. Baptist. Rotarian. Important works include Regency Sq. Fountain, FBI Tng. Acad., Houston Intercontinental Airport, Am. Rose Center, Shreveport, La. Home: 6103 Reamer St Houston TX 77036 Office: 3502 Roseland St Houston TX 77006

BISHOP, EDWIN LYMAN, priest; b. Seattle, Feb. 24, 1930; s. Edwin and Velma Marie (Spencer) B.; B.A., U. Wash., 1952; S.T.B., Gen. Theol. Sem., 1955; M.Ed., Va. Commonwealth U., 1977; M.A., Presbyn. Sch. Christian Edn., 1978; m. Joan Gail Avery, Aug. 11, 1956; children—Victoria Elizabeth, Antoinette Avery, Matthew Frederick Francis. Ordained Episcopal Ch. in USA, 1955; curate, St. Luke's Ch., Vancouver, Wash., also vicar St. Anne's Ch., Camas-Washougal, Wash., 1955-58; vicar St. Mark's Ch., Tonopah, Nev., 1958-60; rector All Saints' Ch., Hillsboro, Oreg., 1960-66; chaplain Oreg. Episcopal Schs., Portland, Oreg., 1966-67; staff asso. William Temple House, Portland, Oreg., 1967-68; chaplain St. Margaret's Sch., Tappahannock, Va., 1972—, pres. convocation Diocese of Olympia, 1956-58, liturg. cons. Diocese of Va., 1973-76, youth dir. Diocese of Nev., 1958-60. Dist. commnr. Boy Scouts Am., 1958-59; Nye County Democratic Com., 1958-59. Served with USNR, 1947-51, 68-72. Decorated Air medal. Mem. Nat. Assn. Episcopal Schs., Naval Reserve Assn., Am. Personnel and Guidance Assn., Clericus of Diocese of Va., Clergy Assn. Diocese of Oreg. Home: 3117 Skipwith Rd Richmond VA 23229

BISHOP, GEORGE WILLIAMS, III, bus. exec.; b. Williamson, W.Va., May 11, 1936; s. George W. and Dorothy Ann (Scott) B.; B.E.E., Va. Mil. Inst., 1958; postgrad. U. Va., 1959; m. Nancy Lee Long, Dec. 4, 1976; children—George, Angela, Brett, Dale Scott, Rebecca. Mgr. elec. div. Buchanan Williamson Supply Co., Grundy, Va., 1962-64, exec. v.p., 1964-77, pres., chmn. bd., 1977—; v.p., gen. mgr. Wingfield and Hundley, Inc., Richmond, Va., 1966-69, pres., 1969-72. Served to capt. USAF, 1959-62. Mem. Nat. Assn. Wholesalers, So. Indsl. Distbrs. Assn. Republican. Presbyn. Clubs: Brandermill Country, Jefferson, Rotary (past pres.). Home: 13600 Pebble Creek Ct Midlothian VA 23113 Office: BWS Co Grundy VA 24614

BISHOP, JOHN LARRY, hosp. adminstr.; b. Spartanburg, S.C., Jan. 13, 1943; s. John Baggott and Anna Mae (Dillard) B.; A.A., Wingate (N.C.) Coll., 1963; B.S., Appalachian State Tchrs. Coll., 1965; M.A., Appalachian State U., 1968; postgrad. U. N.C., 1970-72; m. Judith Carol Wilson, Oct. 11, 1969; children—Larry Michael, Jerry Bradford. Chmn. dept. bus. Lancaster (S.C.) Sr. High Sch., 1965-66; prof., chmn. dept. bus. Wingate Coll., 1966-77, dir. vocat. placement, 1968-77, dir. continuing edn., 1973-77; dir. edn. Eaton Home Study Course, Eaton Corp., Monroe, N.C., 1974-77; mgmt. cons., N.C. and S.C., 1966-77; v.p. adminstrn. Union Meml. Hosp., Monroe, N.C., 1977—. Mem. NEA, Am. Hosp. Assn., So. Fin. Assn., So. Mgmt. Assn., N.C. Hosp. Assn., N.C. Edn. Assn., Monroe-Union County C. of C. (chmn. traffic and safety com., named Outstanding Chmn.). Democrat. Baptist. Club: Kiwanis. Home: PO Box 83 Wingate NC 28174 Office: PO Box 130 Monroe NC 28110

BISHOP, JOHN OLLIE, orthopedic surgeon; b. Waco, Tex., Nov. 11, 1947; s. Leland Horace and Lois Lavelle (Polk) B.; B.A. in Chemistry, Baylor U., Waco, 1969, M.D., 1973; m. Peggy Breaux, Aug. 20, 1975; children—James, Kellie, Bonnie. Intern, Baylor U., 1973-74, resident in orthopedic surgery, 1974-77; Giannestras fellow in foot surgery U. Cin., 1977-78; asso. Cin. Orthopaedic Inst., 1978-79; practice medicine specializing in orthopedics and foot surgery, Houston, 1979—; asst. prof. orthopaedic surgery Baylor U., Clin. Inst. U. Tex. Med. Sch. at Houston. Diplomate Am. Bd. Orthopaedic Surgeons. Mem. AMA, Harris County Med. Soc. Republican. Methodist. Home: 2010 Dunstan St Houston TX 77005 Office: 6410 Fannin St Suite 305 Houston TX 77030

BISHOP, MINNIE SLADE (MRS. SANFORD DIXON BISHOP), former librarian; b. East Spencer, N.C., May 15, 1915; d. John Robert and Lossie Annie (Jones) Slade; A.B., Shaw U., 1936; postgrad. Columbia, summer 1937; B.S. in L.S., Hampton Inst., 1939; m. Sanford Dixon Bishop, Aug. 18, 1942; 1 son, Sanford Dixon. Tchr., librarian Ellerbe (N.C.) High Sch., 1936-38; librarian Cherry St. br. Evansville (Ind.) Pub. Library, 1939-40; librarian Ark. Agrl., Mech. and Normal Coll., Pine Bluff, 1940-43; organizer, librarian Mobile center Ala. State Coll., 1943-65, S.D. Bishop State Jr. Coll., Mobile, 1965-75; now ret. Bd. dirs. Culture in Black and White, Mobile County Mental Health Assn. Mem. Ala. Ret. Tchrs. Assn., Am. Southeastern, Ala., Bay Area library assns., Ala. Assn. Jr. Colls., Ala. Jr. Coll. Library Assn., Nat. Faculty Assn., Nat., Ala. edn. assns., Community Coll. Assn. Instrn. and Tech., League Women Voters, Nat. Ret. Tchrs. Assn., Assn. Coll. and Research Librarians. Delta Sigma Theta. Baptist. Mem. Order Eastern Star. Home: 2413 Ridge Rd Mobile AL 36617

BISHOP, SID GLENWOOD, union ofcl.; b. Gladehill, Va., Nov. 11, 1923; s. Clarence Glenwood and Lillian Helen (Onks) B.; grad. U.S. Naval Trade Sch., 1942; certificate in coll. labor relations Concord Coll., Athens, W.Va., 1961; m. Margaret Lucille Linkous, June 6, 1947. Telegraph operator Virginian R.R., 1946-47, C & O R.R., 1947-62; local chmn. Order R.R. Telegraphers, 1960-62, gen. chmn. C & O-Virginian R.R.'s, 1962-68; 2d v.p. Transp-Communication Employees Union, St. Louis, 1968-69; v.p. communication-transp. div. Brotherhood Ry. and Airline Clks., Rockville, Md., 1969-73, asst. internat. v.p., 1973—; mem. subcom. Labor Research Adv. Council, Dept. Labor, 1975, mem. com. on productivity, tech., growth Bur. Labor Statistics, 1975-77. Served with USN, 1941-46. Mem. AFL-CIO, Canadian Labor Congress, Greenbriar Civic Assn. Democrat. Clubs: Chantilly Nat. Golf and Country, VFW, Elks, Masons, Royal Arch Masons, K.T., Shriners. Home: 4414 Middle Ridge Dr Fairfax VA 22030 Office: 3 Research Pl Rockville MD 20850

BISHOP, TERRY NEAL, sch. adminstr.; b. Temple, Tex., Nov. 16, 1942; s. Clifford Andrew and Wilma Bessie (Riley) B.; B. S. in Edn., Abilene Christian Coll., 1965, M. Ed., 1969; Ph.D., U. Tex. at Austin, 1975; m. Barbara Kay Gill, May 25, 1968; children—Clifford Carl, Kevin Neal. Tchr., coach Abilene (Tex.) High Sch., 1965-69; research asst. N.E. Ind. Sch. Dist. San Antonio, 1970-71; dir. planning, programming Austin Ind. Sch. District, 1972—; cons. in field. Bd. dirs. Westover Hills Found., Brentwood Day Care Center Found. Founds. in Edn. Adminstrn. grantee, 1969-70. Mem. Am. Tex., assns. sch. adminstrs., NEA, Tex. State Tchrs. Assn., Tex. Assn. Ednl. Data Systems, Austin Assn. Pub. Sch. Adminstrs., Founds. in Ednl. Adminstrn. Assn. (pres. 1971-72), Tex. Assn. for Planning, Evaluation and Research, Tex. Assn. for Sch. Curriculum Devel., Capital Area Tennis Assn. Democrat. Mem. Ch. Christ. Club: Westover Hills. Author: Small Schools: A History of the Texas Small Schools Association and the Texas Small Schools Project, 1970; The Economic Development of San Antonio and of Bexar County School Districts, 1970; A Financial Projection and Analysis for Eanes Independent School District, 1972. Home: 12300 Mustang Chase Austin TX 78759 Office: 6100 Guadalupe St Austin TX 78752

BISHOP, THOMAS RAY, mech. engr.; b. Hutchinson, Kans., Oct. 26, 1925; s. Orren E. and Myrtle (Dale) Bish; student California (Pa.) State Tchrs. Coll., 1947-48; B.S., U. Houston, 1953; postgrad. U. Wash., 1960-61; grad. Alexander Hamilton Bus. Inst., 1972; m. Mary Lou Nesmith, Sept. 1, 1951 children—Thomas Ray II, Frances Joann. Research engr. Boeing Co., Seattle, 1953-64, research engr. Apollo program, 1964-69; asst. chief engr. Product div. Bowen Tools, Inc., Houston, 1969-75, chief engr., 1975-77, chief engr. research and devel., 1977—; asso. ABC Mech. Engr. Cons. Precinct committeeman King County (Wash.) Democratic Com., 1960. Served with USMCR, 1944-46. Decorated Purple Heart; named Engr. of Year, Boeing Aerospace Co., 1966; recipient Excellence in Engring. citation A.I.S.I., 1975. Registered profl. engr., Ala., La., Tex. Mem. Tex. Soc. Profl. Engrs. Democrat. Unitarian. Mason. Contbr. articles to profl. jours.; patentee oil field equipment field. Home: 8411 Delwin St Houston TX 77034 Office: 2429 Crockett St Houston TX 77001

BISHOP, WINFORD KENT, lawyer; b. Atlanta, Oct. 22, 1939; s. Winford R. and Virginia Sue (Spears) B.; A.B. in Econs. with distinction, Duke, 1961; J.D., Harvard, 1966; postgrad. Parker Sch. Fgn. and Comparative Law, Columbia, 1967; m. Caroline Sherman Howell, Mar. 30, 1968; children—Caroline Sherman Howell, Virginia Lindstrom Spears, Winford Kensington. Admitted to N.Y. bar, 1968, Ga. bar, 1971; law clk. to Griffin B. Bell, 5th Circuit U.S. Ct. Appeals, Atlanta, 1966-67; asso. firm Hill, Betts & Nash, N.Y.C., 1968-71; regional counsel Econ. Devel. Adminstrn., U.S. Dept. Commerce, Atlanta, 1972-73; gen. practice law, Atlanta, 1973—; dir. Bishop Industries Inc. Spl. lectr. econs. Ga. Inst. Tech., Atlanta, 1966. Chmn. bd. trustees Mt. Paran Area Civic Assn., Atlanta, 1975-76. Mem. Am., Ga., Atlanta bar assns., Assn. of Bar City N.Y., Alpha Kappa Psi, Kappa Alpha (corr. sec. 1960-61). Episcopalian. Clubs: Capital City, Harvard of Atlanta, Atlanta City. Home: 4670 Powers Ferry Rd NW Atlanta GA 30327 Office: 1835 First Nat Bank Tower 2 Peachtree St NW Atlanta GA 30383

BISK, NATHAN MARTIN, publisher; b. Maplewood, N.J., Mar. 16, 1940; s. Max David and Edith (Feldman) B.; A.B., Franklin and Marshall Coll., 1962; J.D., U. Fla., 1973; m. Barbara Engelhard, July 15, 1967; children—Michael David, Alison Lee. Admitted to Fla. bar, 1973; acct. Ernst and Ernst, and Arthur Andersen & Co., 1962-65; investment banker Merrill Lynch, Pierce, Fenner & Smith, Inc., 1965-71; individual practice law and acctg., 1971-75; pub., editor in chief Totaltape Pub., Inc., Gainesville, Fla., 1975—. Served with USAR, 1963-70. C.P.A., Fla. Mem. Fla. Inst. C.P.A.'s, Am. Inst. C.P.A.'s, Am. Acctg. Assn., Nat. Assn. Accts., Assn. Govt. Accts., Nat. Contract Mgmt. Assn., Am. Assn. Atty.-C.P.A.'s, Am. Bar Assn., Fla. Bar, Fla. Eighth Jud. Circuit Bar Assn. Editor in chief C.P.A. Rev., 1975—, Law Sch. Admission Test Rev., 1978—, Cost Acctg. Standards Rev., 1979—, Real Estate Rev., 1979—. Office: Robert Bisk Plaza 1505 NW 16th Ave Gainesville FL 32604

BISSET, NORMA BLAKELY, retail exec.; b. Joliet, Ill., Jan. 12, 1924; d. King and Florence (Samuelson) Salle; degree Joliet Jr. Coll., 1942, Northwestern Bus. Coll., 1944; 1 dau. (by previous marriage), Billie Blakely Fischer. Buyer, Davison Paxon Dept. Store, Atlanta, 1950-53; buyer, mgr. Boston Store, Joliet, 1953-56; owner Blakely's Dept. Stores, Taylorville, Ill. and Ft. Pierce, Fla., 1956-75; pres. Blakewood Realty Corp., Chgo., 1961—, also Blake-Bisset Corp., Chgo. Trustee George O. Blakely Trust. Mem. Beta Sigma Phi (past pres.). Episcopalian. Clubs: Order Eastern Star; Boca Raton (Fla.) Hotel. Home: 2204 Bay Dr Pompano Beach FL 33062

BISSETT, WILLIAM PAUL, JR., real estate broker, restaurant exec.; b. Tampa, Fla., Sept. 15, 1940; s. William Paul and Mary Elizabeth (Flournoy) B.; B.S. in Bus. Adminstrn., U. Fla., 1962; m. Pamela Kerr, Feb. 1, 1964; children—William Paul III, Courtney Patrica, Darby. Personnel supr. Anheuser-Busch, Inc., Tampa, Fla., 1964-65; v.p. D.G. Shults, Inc., Tampa, 1965-71; asso. William T. Young and Assos., Inc., Tampa, 1971-74; pres. Bissett & Co., Inc., Tampa, 1974— The Loading Dock, Inc., Tampa and Jacksonville, Fla., 1976—; instr. Bert Rodgers Sch. of Real Estate. Mem. Nat. Assn. Home Builders, Nat. Restaurant Assn., Aircraft Owners and Pilots Assn., Com. of 100 of C. of C. (vice chmn. urban planning council). Democrat. Presbyterian. Club: Tower (Tampa). Home: 1904 Cape Bend Ave Tampa FL 33612 Office: Suite 3018 First Fla Tower Tampa FL 33602

BITTEL, ANN BRAMWELL, librarian; b. Nashville, Aug. 9, 19Home: 607 Benham Ave Scottsboro AL 35768

BITTEL, LESTER ROBERT, educator; b. East Orange, N.J., Dec. 9, 1918; s. William Frederick and Helen Elsie (Korte) B.; B.S. in Indsl. Engring., Lehigh U., 1940; M.B.A., James Madison U., 1974; m. Muriel Albers Walcott, May 8, 1973; children—Bethel Leslie Bittel Breen, Martha Gilbert Bittel Dowdy, Amy Helen Calabrese. Instrument engr Leeds & Northrup Co., Phila., 1940-46; plant supt., training dir. Koppers Co., Inc., Pitts., 1946-54; editor, pub. Factory Mag., McGraw Hill Publs. Co., N.Y.C., 1954-70, dir. info. systems, 1970-72; asso. prof bus. James Madison U., Harrisonburg, Va., 1974—; exec. v.p. Chilton Meml. Hosp., Pompton Plains, N.J., 1960-72. Served to lt. USAAF, 1942-45. Recipient Jesse H. Neal award for outstanding bus. journalism, 1955, 57, 59, 62, 68. Fellow ASME (Henry Robinson Towne lectr. 1972); mem. Am. Soc. Tng. and Devel., Acad. Mgmt. Democrat. Unitarian Universalist. Club: Overseas Press. Co-author: Practical Automation, 1957; author: What Every Supervisor Should Know, 1974; Management by Exception, 1969; 9 Master Keys of Mangement, 1972; Improving Supervisory Performance, 1976; Shenandoah Management Games for Supervisors, 1977; editor: Encyclopedia of Professional Management, 1979. Home: 106 Breezewood Terr Bridgewater VA 22812 Office: James Madison U Harrisonburg VA 22801

BITTER, WILLIAM, JR., security services co. exec.; b. N.Y.C., Nov. 21, 1917; s. William and Lillian (Smith) B.; B.S.B.A., N.Y. U., 1947; M.Ed., U. Miami (Fla.), 1972; m. Doris M. Burgtorf, Sept. 4, 1943; children—Warren Alan, Ralph Edward. Personnel rep. Eastern Airlines, Miami, 1941-45, regional employment supr., 1945-46, asst. to v.p. indsl. and personnel relations, 1946-50; mgr. wage and salary adminstrn., 1950-53; personnel dir., corp. asst. sec. Maule Industries, Inc., Miami, 1953-61; personnel dir., v.p. personnel and adminstrn., v.p. labor relations Wackenhut Corp., Coral Gables, Fla., 1961—; mem. seminar panels Stetson U. Coll. Law, 1957-60. Chmn. personnel com. United Fund Dade County (Fla.), 1960. Served with U.S. Army, 1941. Recipient Accredited Personnel Diploma, Am. Soc. Personnel Adminstrn., 1976. Mem. Associated Industries Fla., Personnel Assn. Greater Miami, Am. Soc. Personnel Adminstrn., Am. Soc. Safety Engrs. Contbr. articles to profl. jours. Home: 991 Ibis Ave Miami Springs FL 33166 Office: 3280 Ponce de Leon Blvd Coral Gables FL 33134

BITTNER, DONALD FRANCIS, mil. officer, historian; b. Clayton, Mo., July 16, 1941; s. Francis Xavier and Agnes Shirley (Powers) B.; B.S. in Edn., U. Mo., 1963, M.A. in History, 1970, Ph.D. in History, 1974; m. Jean Elizabeth Crawford, Dec. 28, 1963; 1 dau., Sharon Lynne. Commd. 2d lt. U.S. Marine Corps, 1963, advanced through grades to maj., 1973; mil. historian Command and Staff Coll. Edn. Center, Marine Corps Devel. and Edn. Command, Quantico, Va., 1974—; lectr. in history No. Va. Community Coll., Woodbridge, 1976—. Am. Philos. Soc. grantee, 1975, 77. Fellow Inter-Univ. Seminar on Armed Forces and Soc.; mem. Royal United Services Inst. for Def. Studies, Soc. Army Hist. Res., Royal Marine Hist. Soc., Carolinas Symposium Brit. Studies, Am. Hist. Assn., Am. Mil. Inst., U.S. Com. Mil. History. Club: Army and Navy (Washington). Research Brit. officer corps pre-World War I. Home: 1225 Aquia Dr Aquia Harbour Stafford VA 22554 Office: Command and Staff College Education Center Marine Corps Development and Education Command Quantico VA 22134

BIUNDO, JOSEPH JAMES, JR., physician; b. Independence, La., Sept. 24, 1937; s. Joseph James and Ann Agnes (Dantone) B.; B.S. in Pharmacy, U. Houston, 1960; M.D., La. State U., 1964; m. Mary M. Cools, May 17, 1969; children—Elizabeth Ann, Brenda Marie, Jennifer Anne. Intern, then resident in internal medicine Charity Hosp., New Orleans, 1964-68; fellow in rheumatology Tulane U. Med. Sch.-VA Hosp. New Orleans, 1968-69; fellow rheumatology and immunology Georgetown U. Hosp., 1969-71; mem. faculty La. State U. Med. Center, 1971—, asso. prof. medicine, 1975—, chief sect. rheumatology and rehab., 1974—; dir. rehab. medicine and La. Rehab. Inst., Charity Hosp., 1975—; dir. arthritis unit Hotel Dieu Hosp., 1978; cons. spinal cord injury Emergency Med. Services Council, 1978. cons. Lafayette Charity, VA, Crippled Children's hosps.; mem. bd. dirs New Orleans Area Health Planning Council; dir. Community State Bank, Independence, La. Bd. dirs. Multipurpose Arthritis Center. Diplomate Am. Bd. Internal Medicine (rheumatology, allergy and immunology). Mem. Am. Rheumatism Assn., Am. Congress Rehab. Medicine, Internat. Rehab. Medicine Assn., La., Orleans Parish med. socs., New Orleans Acad. Internal Medicine, Nat. Rehab. Assn., La. Rheumatism Soc., Am. Med. Joggers Assn., Alpha Omega Alpha. Address: 1542 Tulane Ave New Orleans LA 70112

BIVINS, BRACK ALLEN, surgeon; b. Nashville, Nov. 28, 1943; s. Brack Amos and Marjorie (Belcher) B.; B.S., Western Ky. U., 1966; M.D., U. Ky., 1970; m. Brenda Kingston, Feb. 3, 1973; children—Brack David, Berkley Kingston. Intern and resident U. Ky. Med. Center, Lexington, 1970-73, asso. dir. emergency medicine, 1973-75, surg. resident, 1975-77, asst. prof. surgery, 1977—. Diplomate Am. Bd. Surgery. Am. Cancer Soc. clin. fellow, 1972-73. Mem. Lexington Surg. Soc., Ky. Med. Assn., Fayette County Med. Soc., Assn. Acad. Surgery, So. Med. Assn., Southeastern Surg. Soc., Am. Soc. Parenteral and Enteral Nutrition, Sigma Chi, Alpha Omega Alpha. Recipient Research award Am. Soc. Hosp. Pharmacists Research and Edn Found., 1976, Parenteral Drug Assn., 1976. Office: 800 Rose St Lexington KY 40536

BIZZELL, BOBBY GENE, educator; b. Frankston, Tex., Sept. 13, 1940; s. Ferrell Lawrence and Ruby LaVelle (Hanna) B.; B.B.A., U. Tex., Austin, 1963, M.B.A., 1964, Ph.D., 1971; children—Laurie Ann, Susan Leigh, Amy Rebecca. Mgr. mfg. Gen. Electric Co., Cin., 1964-65, Schenectady, 1965-67, adminstr. mfg. problems analysis, Oklahoma City, 1967-68; asst. dean Grad. Sch. Bus., U. Tex., Austin, 1968-71; instr. mgmt. Stephen F. Austin State U., Nacogdoches, 1971-80, prof., 1971—, dir. grad. programs, 1972—, acting chmn. dept. mgmt., 1979—; cons. to bus. Sec. bd. dirs. Nacogdoches Meml. Hosp.; mem. directing com. United Way, Nacogdoches. Stephen F. Austin State U. faculty research grantee, 1972, 79. Mem. Acad. Mgmt., Am. Inst. Decision Scis., So. Case Assn., Beta Gamma Sigma, Sigma Iota Epsilon, Phi Kappa Phi. Democrat. Mem. Chs. of Christ.

Home: 1524 Terracewood Ln Nacogdoches TX 75961 Office: PO Box 9070 Stephen F Austin State U Nacogdoches TX 75962

BJORLIN, DONALD LEROY, hosp. adminstr.; b. Donnelly, Minn., Feb. 19, 1932; s. Carl William and Emma Marie (Engel) B.; B.B.A., U. Minn., 1959, M.H.A., 1960; m. Carolyn L. Rogers, Nov. 27, 1971; children—Blair, Lynn, David. Adminstr., Waseca (Minn.) Meml. Hosp., 1960-64; exec. dir. District One Hosp., Faribault, Minn., 1964-74; pres. Union Meml. Hosp., Monroe, N.C., 1974—. Served with U.S. Army, 1952-54. Recipient Outstanding Young Man award Waseca Jaycees, 1963. Mem. Am. Coll. Hosp. Adminstrs., N.C. Hosp. Assn. (pres. dist. 3 1979-80). Lutheran. Office: Union Meml Hosp Box 130 Monroe NC 28110

BLACK, AUBREY KERMIT, JR., cons. chem. engr.; b. Vicksburg, Miss., Mar. 12, 1942; s. Aubrey Kermit and Minnie Allene (Downey) B.; B. Engring., Vanderbilt U., 1964, M.S. in Chem. Engring., 1966; children—Christopher Kermit, Jennifer Marie, Paul Michael. Engr., Exxon USA, Baton Rouge, 1965-71, Purvin & Gertz, Inc., Dallas, 1971-73; v.p. Pace Co., Cons. & Engrs., Houston, 1973-78; v.p. Pace Internat., Houston, 1978—. Registered profl. engr., Tex. Mem. Am. Inst. Chem. Engrs., Tau Beta Pi. Home: 9449 Briar Forest Dr Apt 2312 Houston TX 77063 Office: 3700 Buffalo Speedway Houston TX 77098

BLACK, CHARLES ALVIN, cons. engr.; b. Gainesville, Fla., July 7, 1920; s. Alvin Percy and Lillian Barnes (Russell) B.; B.S., U. Fla., 1947; m. Elizabeth Beck, Sept. 12, 1943; children—Charles Russell, Elizabeth Ann. Pres. Black, Crow and Eidsness of Ga.; sr. v.p. Black, Crow & Eidness, Inc., 1950—. San. engr. USPHS, 1959—; mem. Fla. Gov.'s Task Force for Water, Minerals and Solid Fuels for Civil. Served AUS, 1944-45. Recipient U.S.A. citation for outstanding pub. service. Registered profl. engr., Fla., Ga., S.C., Ala., Kans. Diplomate Am. Acad. Environmental Engrs. Mem. Am. Water Works Assn. (chmn. purification div. 1951, chmn. Fla. sect. 1962; George Warren Fuller award 1961, nat. dir. 1966—, nat. v.p. 1969-70, nat. pres. 1971-72), Cons. Engrs. Council, Cons. Engrs. Fla., ASCE, Royal Soc. Health, Nat. Soc. Profl. Engrs., Am. Pub. Health Assn., Internat. Water Supply Assn., Internat. Assn. Water Pollution Research, Fla. Pollution Control Assn., Soc. Am. Mil. Engrs., Alpha Tau Omega. Episcopalian. Elk. Contbr. articles to profl. jours. Home: 2941 NW 21st Ave Gainesville FL 32601 Office: SE 3d St Gainesville FL 32601

BLACK, CLARENCE ERVIN, radiologist; b. Bamberg, S.C., Sept. 25, 1915; s. Clarence Ervin and Leonard (Folk) B.; B.S., The Citadel, 1936; A.B., Mercer U., 1937; M.D., U. Ga., 1941; 1 dau., Carolyn Marie; m. Ruth Ann Marchbank, July 7, 1978. Intern, U.S. Marine Hosp., New Orleans, 1941-42; resident Ochsner Found., New Orleans, 1947-49, staff radiologist, 1949-60; practice medicine specializing in radiology, Marrero, La., 1960-79, Sarasota, Fla., 1979—; dir. dept. radiology and nuclear medicine West Jefferson Gen. Hosp., Marrero, La., 1960-76. Served as officer M.C., 1942-46. Mem. AMA, Am. Coll. Radiology, La. State Med. Soc. Episcopalian. Clubs: So. Yacht, Sarasota Yacht. Home and Office: 2344 Bee Ridge Rd Sarasota FL 33579

BLACK, DANIEL HUGH, educator; b. Arab, Ala., July 4, 1947; s. Lehmon Ray and Lillian Geneve (Divine) B.; B.S., U. Ala., Tuscaloosa, 1970; M.Ed., Ala. A. and M. U., 1976; postgrad. Vanderbilt U., 1978—. Social studies tchr. Grissom High Sch., Huntsville, Ala., 1970—. Mem. NEA, Ala. Edn. Assn., Huntsville Edn. Assn., Ala. Hist. Assn., Phi Delta Kappa. Baptist.

BLACK, DAVID LUTHER, research inst. exec.; b. Plainview, Tex., Apr. 3, 1934; s. Mac Truman and Wilma Louise (Bailey) B.; A.B., Baylor U., 1954; postgrad. U. Tex., 1956-59, Trinity U., 1977-78; m. Susana Soler Ahrens, 1977; stepchildren—Barry Snell, Whitfield Snell, Susana Haywood, Miguel Ahrens, Mario Ahrens; 1 son, David R. Asso. dir. exec. devel. program U. Tex., 1957-59; asst. dir. pub. relations S.W. Research Inst., San Antonio, 1959-64, dir. spl. programs, 1967-72, dir. spl. programs, asst. to pres., 1972—; dir. pub. relations HemisFair 1968, 1964-65; pres. David Black & Assos., 1965-67; cons. UN Indsl. Devel. Orgn., Vienna, Austria, 1971—, UNESCO, 1974—; mem. UN missions to Latin Am., 1972—; cons. UN Environ. Program, Nairobi, Kenya, 1975-76, Nat. Acad. Scis., 1975—. Bd. dirs. Planned Parenthood Assn., 1966-69; bd. dirs. San Antonio Chamber Music Soc., pres., 1972—; bd. dirs. Community Guidance Center, San Antonio. Mem. AAAS, Am. Soc. Metals (chmn. Latin Am. relations comm. 1975—), Nat. Assn. Sci. Writers. Episcopalian. Contbr. articles to profl. jours. Home: 432 Rittiman Rd San Antonio TX 78209 Office: Box 28510 San Antonio TX 78284

BLACK, DAVID R., acct.; b. Carthage, Miss., Nov. 19, 1952; s. W. Randolph and Bobbie B.; B.S., U. So. Miss., 1976; m. Penny B. Acct., asst. controller, McCarty Holman Co., Inc., Jackson, Miss., 1976-78, controller, 1978—. Mem. Nat. Assn. Accts. Republican. Baptist. Home: 345 Lakebend Dr Brandon MS 39042 Office: 453 N Mill St Jackson MS 39207

BLACK, DELIA WELLS, personnel specialist; b. Jackson, Miss., Feb. 18, 1936; d. James Madison and Sadie Lee (Clark) Wells; B.A., Blue Mountain Coll., 1958; postgrad. Nat. Autonomous U. Mex., 1958-59; M.Ed., U. Miss., 1964; M.P.A., Nova U., 1978, D.P.A., 1978; m. William Verbon Black, June 26, 1965. Program specialist Inst. Internat. Edn., N.Y.C., 1963-65; employee devel. specialist U.S. Army, Redstone Arsenal, Ala., 1965-70, 72-73, employee relations specialist, 1970-72, employee devel. specialist team leader, 1973-75, supr. employee devel. specialist, 1975-77, personnel mgmt. specialist, 1977—. Mem. credit adv. com. Redstone Fed. Credit Union. Recipient certificate of achievement Dept. Army, 1970, 72, Missile Command, 1972. Mem. Am. Soc. Pub. Adminstrn. (chpt. officer 1977-78, chpt. pres. 1979-80), Federally Employed Women (pres. N. Ala. chpt. 1973-74, nat. dir. 1973-74), Internat. Personnel Mgmt. Assn. (pres. Huntsville chpt. 1978-79, nat. fed. devel. com. 1979—), Nat. Trust Hist. Preservation, Ala. Hist. Assn. Address: DRSMI-PCTC Redstone Arsenal AL 35809

BLACK, ELDON LAVERNE, social worker; b. Beaumont, Miss., Nov. 7, 1933; s. William James and Martha Elizabeth (Kitterell) B.; B.S. in Social Sci., Livingston U., 1962; M.S.W., Fla. State U., 1968; m. JoAnn Coulter, Dec. 26, 1959; children—Mark, Melba, Martha, Michael. Social worker, Talladega, Ala., 1963-68; social work supr. Jefferson County (Ala.) Dept. Pensions and Security, Birmingham, 1968-70; psychiat. social worker NIMH Clin. Research Center, USPHS Hosp., Lexington, Ky., 1970-71; supr. Med. Rev. Team, State of Ala., 1971-72; adminstr., supr. Bur. Quality Control, Ala. Dept. Pension and Security, Montgomery, 1972—. Asst. scoutmaster Boy Scouts Am., 1971-76; recipient Order of Arrow. Served with U.S. Army, 1954-57, with USNR, 1962. Cert., Acad. Cert. Social Workers; lic. social worker, Ala. Mem. Nat. Assn. Social Workers, Ala. Employees Assn. (past chpt. pres., organizer). Baptist. Home: 224 Woodvale Rd Prattville AL 36067 Office: 64 N Union St Montgomery AL 36130

BLACK, ELDON UDELL, musician, educator; b. Spearman, Tex., Feb. 23, 1929; s. Walter Joseph and Myrtle Alice (Moddrell) B.; B.Music, N. Tex. State U., 1953, M.Music Edn., 1954; D.Musical Arts, U. Tex., Austin, 1976. Faculty San Angelo (Tex.) Coll. (now Angelo State U.), 1954-70, prof. music, 1973—; teaching asst. U. Tex., Austin, 1970-73. Mem. Tex. Assn. Coll. Tchrs., Tex. Music Educators Assn., Nat. Assn. Tchrs. of Singing. Mem. Christian Ch. (Disciples of Christ). Home: 624 Koberlin St San Angelo TX 76901 Office: PO Box 11000 Angelo State University San Angelo TX 76901

BLACK, HERBERT MALONE, physician; b. Walterboro, S.C., Jan. 19, 1909; s. David B. and Rosa (Ayer) B.; B.S. magna cum laude in Elec. Engring., U. S.C., 1930; grad. tng. course Westinghouse Electric Mfg. Co., East Pittsburgh, Pa., 1930-32; M.D., Med. Coll. S.C., 1937; m. Mae Martin Sprott, June 25, 1937; children—Jane Elizabeth, Barbara Anne, Nancy Mae. Intern, Met. Gen. Hosp., Cleve., 1937-38; surg. intern Med. Coll. Va., Richmond, 1938-39; asst. resident obstetrics and gynecology Louisville Gen. Hosp., 1939-40, resident, 1940-41; practice mecicine specializing in obstetrics and gynecology, Columbia, S.C., 1946-69, specializing in gynecology, 1969—; chief obstetrics and gynecology Columbia Hosp., 1956-58; chief of staff Providence Hosp., 1966-67; mem. cons. staff Baptist, Providence, Richland Meml. hosps. Served to comdr. M.C., USNR, 1941-46. Diplomate Am. Bd. Obstetrics and Gynecology. Mem. Am. Coll. Obstetricians and Gynecologists (founder, sect. chmn. 1963-66), AMA (Physicians Recognition award 1974-81), So. Med. Assn. (life), Columbia Med. Soc., S.Atlantic Assn. Obstetricians and Gynecologists, Am. Assn. Prolife Obstetricians and Gynecologists, S.C. Soc. Obstetricians and Gynecologists, Columbia Med. Jour. Club, S.C. Ob-Gyn Soc. (pres. 1963), Phi Beta Kappa, Omicron Delta Kappa, Tau Beta Pi, Sigma Chi, Phi Chi. Methodist. Clubs: Rotary of Columbia, Columbia Sailing. Home: 1518 Adger Rd Columbia SC 29205 Office: 1433 Gregg St Columbia SC 29201

BLACK, JAMES CALVIN, ins. co. exec.; b. Waco, Tex., Nov. 8, 1935; s. James Cecil and Juanita Mozell (Rogers) B.; B.B.A., Baylor U., 1957; postgrad. Tarleton State U., 1979; children—Craig Steven, Rebecca Renee. Field rep. Southwestern Investment Co., Houston, 1958; ins. investigator Retail Credit Co., Houston, 1958-59; acctg. mgr. So. Farm Bur. Casualty Ins. Co., Waco, 1959—; treas. Tex. Farm Bur. Fed. Credit Union, 1961-62; sec., treas. Liberty Bible Coll.; instr. McLennan Community Coll., part time. Treas., Tabernacle Baptist Ch., 1967-74; v.p. R.L. Smith PTA, 1973-74; active Waco United Fund, ARC. Served with U.S. Army, 1957-58. Recipient cert. in gen. ins. Ins. Inst. Am., 1968; Disting. Service award Liberty Bible Coll., 1977. Mem. Nat. Assn. Accountants (pres. Central Tex. chpt. 1974-75), Am. Acctg. Assn. Democrat. Baptist. Clubs: Waco Coin (pres. 1967), Civitan (Disting. Service award). Home: 618 Kipling Dr Waco TX 76710 Office: So Farm Bur Casualty Ins Co PO Box 489 Waco TX 76703

BLACK, JOHN CLINTON, aviation and mgmt. cons.; b. Basin, Wyo., Feb. 29, 1936; s. Clinton Melford and Rosa Vida (Bischoff) B.; student U. Utah, 1954-55, 60-62; B.S. in Design and Drafting Tech., Brigham Young U., 1965; M.B.A., U. Cin., 1970; m. Myrna Jean Murphy, June 15, 1961; children—Kevin John, Kelly Gene. Instr. Ohio Coll. Applied Sci., Cin., 1965-66; aviation planning cons. Landrum & Brown, Cin., 1966-70; aviation planning and engring. cons. Talbert, Cox & Assos., Columbia, S.C., 1970—; cons. mgmt. and aviation. Pres. Saluda River P.T.A., 1973-74, Parents, Tchrs. and Students Assn. of Northside Middle Sch., 1975-76. Served with AUS, 1959. Mem. Am. Soc. Planning Ofcls., Am. Planning Assn. Mem. Ch. of Jesus Christ of Latter-day Saints (area public relations coordinator 1973—). Designer airport master plans, 1966—, regional airport systems plans, 1967—. Home: 1840 Robin Crest Dr W Columbia SC 29169 Office: Columbia Met Airport Old Terminal Bldg W Columbia SC 29169

BLACK, KENNETH, JR., ednl. adminstr.; b. Norfolk, Va., Jan. 30, 1925; s. Kenneth and Margaret (Wolf) B.; B.A., U. N.C., 1948, M.A., 1951; Ph.D., U. Pa., 1953; m. Mabel Lewellyn Folger, Sept. 20, 1948; children—Kenneth, Kathryn Anne. Partner, Colonial Ins. Agy., Chapel Hill, N.C., 1948-50; instr. U. Pa., 1952-53; chmn. dept. ins. Ga. State U., Atlanta, 1953-69, regents prof. ins., 1959—, dean coll. bus. adminstrn., 1969—; pres., dir. gen. Internat. Ins. Seminars, Inc., 1975—; dir. N.Am. Reins. Corp., N.Am. Reassurance Co., USLIFE Corp., Haverty Furniture Stores, Computone Systems, Cousins Properties, Paul Manners & Assos., Inc. Trustee, Village of St. Joseph, Atlanta, 1972—. Served with USNR, 1944-46. Mem. Am. Soc. C.L.U.'s (Paul Speicher award 1958), Soc. C.P.C.U.'s, Am. Risk and Ins. Assn. (pres. 1964), So. Econ. Assn. Clubs: Capital City, Commerce. Author: Group Annuities, 1955; Cases in Life Insurance, 1965; Human Behavior in Business, 1972; (with S.S. Huebner) Life Insurance, 9th edit., 1976; (with others) Property and Liability Insurance, 2d edit., 1976. Home: 1762 Nancy Creek Bluff NW Atlanta GA 30327 Office: Coll Bus Adminstrn Ga State U University Plaza Atlanta GA 30303

BLACK, KENNETH ELDON, govt. ofcl.; b. Adrian, Mo., Feb. 2, 1922; s. Orville Vincent and Katherine (Trowbridge) B.; B.S. in Wildlife Mgmt., Wash. State U., 1949; m. Marjorie Jean Underwood, Nov. 3, 1944; children—Gerald L., Mark C. Waterfowl research U.S. Fish and Wildlife Service, Dept. Interior, 1951-54, various positions in water and resource devel., 1954-71, dep. asst., dir., 1971-73, asso. dir. environment, Washington, 1973-74, regional dir., Atlanta, 1974—; bd. dirs. Culebra Conservation and Devel. Authority, 1976—. Served with AUS, 1942-46. Congressional fellow Am. Polit. Sci. Assn. Mem. Wildlife Soc., Am. Fisheries Soc., Nat. Rifle Assn. (life). Club: Elks. Home: 2311 Castlewood Circle Lilburn GA 30247 Office: 75 Spring St SW Suite 1200 Atlanta GA 30303

BLACK, MINNIE LOU (ECHOLS), vocat. tng. coordinator, educator; b. Commerce, Ga., May 31, 1916; d. William Arthur and Minnie Lee (Tolbert) Echols; B.B.A., Atlanta div. U. Ga., 1950; M.S. in Bus. Edn., Ga. State U., 1972, postgrad. student, 1972-76; m. William Riddick Black, Mar. 3, 1951. Payroll supr. Blue Bell Mfg. Co., Commerce, Ga., 1933-34, 35-42; timekeeper, supr. Rich's Inc., Atlanta, 1942-47; sec. to regional mgr. Mut. of N.Y. Ins., Atlanta, 1947-56; co-owner, office mgr. Buckhead Furniture Mart, Atlanta, 1956-65; ind. furniture appraiser, 1965-66; office supr. Grady Prodn. Lab., Atlanta Schs., 1970-73; vocat. office tng. coordinator, tchr., chairperson dept. Henry Grady High Sch., Atlanta, 1973—; part-time instr. Ga. State U., 1954-57. Mem. Career Edn. Adv. Com., Atlanta Pub. Schs., 1977-79. Certified Profl. Sec. Mem. Am. Vocat. Assn., Ga. Vocat. Assn., 5th Dist. Bus. and Office Assn., Nat. Bus. Edn. Assn., So. Bus. Edn. Assn., Ga. Bus. Edn. Assn., Am. Soc. Tng. and Devel., AAUW, Beta Tau, Delta Pi Epsilon, Alpha Nu, Delta Kappa Gamma. Democrat. Baptist (past Sunday sch. tchr., young people leader, story hour dir.). Club: Pilot Internat. Home: 2520 Peachtree Rd NW #214 Atlanta GA 30305 Office: Henry Grady High Sch 929 Charles Allen Dr NE Atlanta GA 30309

BLACK, PATTI CARR, museum adminstr.; b. Sumner, Miss., May 18, 1934; d. Samuel Bismarck and Velma (Lewis) Carr; B.A., Miss. U. Women, 1955; M.A., Emory U., Atlanta, 1968; 1 dau., Elizabeth Lewis. From librarian to dir. library Miss. Dept. Archives and History, 1957-67; catalog and research librarian Met. Mus. Art, N.Y.C., 1968; research librarian Time mag., 1969; dir., exhibits designer Miss. State Hist. Mus., Jackson, 1976—; adv. bd. Center So. Folklore, Memphis, Center Study So. Culture, U. Miss.; founding mem., pres. bd. dirs. New Stage Theatre; mem. panel public program Nat. Endowment Humanities; cons. in field, 1977—. Fellow Nat. Endowment Arts, 1975. Mem. Am. Assn. Museums, Am. Assn. State and Local History, Miss. Folklore Soc., Miss. Hist. Soc. Democrat. Author: Mississippi Piney Woods, 2d edit., 1977. Home: 1157 Quinn St Jackson MS 39202 Office: 100 S State St Jackson MS 39205

BLACK, WILLIAM ELMER, economist; b. Moxahala, Ohio, June 3, 1915; s. Frank and Barbara (Komyate) B.; student Cleve. Coll., 1934; B.S., Ohio State U., 1938; M.S., Cornell U., 1940, Ph.D., 1942; m. Olive Rose Bischoff, June 26, 1948; children—Jeffrey, Jennifer, Randal, Renee. Gen. mgr. Cash Crops Coop., Wis., 1949-51; gen. mgr. Fla. Tomato Com., 1955-59; dir. econ. and mktg. research Fla. Citrus Commn., 1959-67; economist mktg. and policy Tex. Agr. Extension Service, Tex. A. and M. U., College Station, 1967—; asso. coordinator Tex. Agrl. Mktg. Research and Devel. Center; grad. faculty Tex. A. and M. U.; chmn. So. Extension mktg. com. Tex. Agrl. Extension Mktg. Staff, So. Regional Agrl. Outlook Workshop. Served to capt. AUS, World War II; to maj., Korean War. Recipient Nat. Coop. Edn. award, 1977. Danforth fellow, 1937. Mem. Am. Agrl. Economists Assn., So. Economists Assn., Am. Mktg. Assn., Found. Econ. Edn., Alpha Zeta, Gamma Sigma Delta, Phi Kappa Phi. Presbyterian (deacon, elder). Club: Sertoma (Lakeland, Fla.). Editor-in-chief Ag Student, 1937-38; contbg. author: Who Will Control U.S. Agriculture?; Food and Agricultural Legislation; Marketing Alternatives for Agriculture; contbr. articles to profl. jours. Home: 3805 Courtney Circle Bryan TX 77801 Office: 107B Agr Bldg Tex A and M U College Station TX 77843

BLACK, WILLIAM SCOTT, advt./mktg. co. exec.; b. Houston, Jan. 5, 1948; s. Albert Scott and Marilyn Patricia (Hammer) B.; B.B.A., Tex. A&M U., 1966; B.B.A., North Tex. State U., 1970; m. Mercedes F., Nov. 27, 1971; children—John Scott, Mercedes Magdalena. Account exec. First Mktg. Group, Inc., Houston, 1970-71, sr. v.p., 1975-77, exec. v.p., 1978—; dir. First Mktg. de Mexico, S.A., 1972-74. Bd. dirs. Nat. Kidney Found., 1979-80, Houston Achievement Pl., 1980-81. Recipient various local, regional and nat. advt. awards. Mem. Am. Advt. Fedn., Am. Mktg. Assn., Nat. Home Builders Assn., Theta Chi Alumni. Episcopalian. Clubs: Univ., Houston. Office: 2000 S Post Oak Suite 2100 Houston TX 77056

BLACK, WILLIAM VERBON, lawyer; b. Pell City, Ala., Sept. 18, 1931; s. William High and Ala Ray (Carter) B.; A.A., Snead Coll., 1951; A.B., Birmingham So. Coll., 1953; J.D., U. Ala., 1959; M.P.A. (Nat. Inst. Public Affairs fellow), Harvard U., 1965; m. Delia Leone Wells, June 26, 1965. Admitted to Ala. bar, 1959—; supervisiory atty. Dept. Army, 1959—, dep. chief counsel U.S. Army Missile Command, Redstone Arsenal, Ala., 1971—. Served U.S. Army, 1953-55. Fellow Nat. Inst. Public Affairs; mem. Ala. Bar Assn., Fed. Bar Assn., Farrah Order of Jurisprudence, Ala. Hist. Assn. Home: 1206 Chandler Rd Huntsville AL 35801 Office: US Army Missile Command Redstone Arsenal AL 25809

BLACKBURN, JAMES BERNARD, JR., environ. lawyer, educator; b. Alexandria, La., Sept. 17, 1947; s. James Bernard and Eleanor Eloise (Graves) B.; B.A. in History, U. Tex., Austin, 1969, J.D., 1972; M.S. in Environ. Sci. and Engring., Rice U., 1974; m. Garland Sorrells Kerr, Jan. 9, 1971. Environ. cons. Woodlands (Tex.) Devel. Corp., 1973-74; research asso. Rice Center, Houston, 1974-76; lectr. sch. architecture Rice U., Houston, 1975—; admitted to Tex. bar, 1972; individual practice law, Houston, 1976—; adj. asst. prof. Bates Sch. Law, U. Houston, 1979—. Exec. com. The Park People, Houston, 1978-79; bd. dirs. Armand Bayou Nature Center, 1975—, Houston Audubon Soc., 1975-78, Rice Design Alliance, 1977—, program chmn., 1979; mem. Houston-Galveston Area Council Water Quality Com., 1979, Area Growth Com., 1978, Harris County Flood Control Task Force, 1977—, City of Houston Urban Policy Task Force, 1978-79. Nat. winner Am. Trial Lawyers environ. law essay contest, 1972; EPA trainee, 1972-73. Mem. State Bar of Tex. Co-author: Principles for Local Environmental Management, 1978; author: Texas Law of Drainage with Case Study of Harris County, Tex., 1979; contbr. research studies on satellite power system, water quality, drainage and flooding, environ. law, energy systems to publs. Home: 2101 South Blvd Houston TX 77098 Office: 3417 Montrose #104 Houston TX 77006

BLACKBURN, JAMES ROSS, JR., oil co. exec., airline pilot; b. Lakeland, Fla., Feb. 28, 1930; s. James Ross and Esther Louise (Flagle) B.; student Davidson Coll., 1948-49; B.B.A., U. Miami, 1953, postgrad., 1968-69; m. Joyce Gaynelle Green, Aug. 29, 1960; children—Linda Marie, Lisa Joyce. Pilot, Eastern Air Lines, 1957—, capt., 1969—; mktg. cons. Comrex Corp., 1967-72; pres. Surete Ltd., 1973; pres. J.R. Blackburn & Assos., 1974-76; pres. Blackburn Assos., Inc., Miami, Fla., 1977—. Served with USAF, 1953-57. Mem. Air Line Pilots Assn., First Flight Soc., AMS/Oil Dealers Assn., Genealogical Soc. Greater Miami (past treas.), Am. Hall Aviation History (founding mem.) Quiet Birdmen, Soc. So. Families, Mil. Order Stars and Bars, Sigma Chi. Democrat. Baptist. Clubs: Masons, Country Club of Coral Gables. Home: 10745 S W 53d Ave Miami FL 33156

BLACKBURN, JEAN MC CONNELL, ednl. adminstr.; b. Gate City, Va., Sept. 3, 1924; d. Eugene Henry and Mary Ida (Whited) M.; B.S., Roanoke Coll., 1945; M.S., Radford Coll., 1972; m. Oran Lee Blackburn, Jr., June 21, 1960; children—Margery Sharon, Michael Jack. Office mgr. USO, Gate City, 1945-46; funeral dir. Mc Connell Funeral Service, Gate City, 1953-58; tchr. Scott County Schs., Gate City, 1954-67, guidance counselor, 1967—. Former chmn. Scott County Cancer Soc.; pres. Holson View Cemetery Devel. Co.; bd. dirs. Goodwill Industries Tenneva., Inc.; pres. Gate City High Sch. Aux.; adminstrv. bd. Gate City United Methodist Ch., chmn. comm. higher edn. Mem. Am., Va. personnel and guidance assns., Am., Va. sch. counselors, SW Personnel and Guidance Assn. (pres. 1979). Democrat. Home: 404 Cypress St Gate City VA 24251 Office: Gate City High Sch Gate City VA 24251

BLACKBURN, JOHN GILL, neurophysiologist; b. Lake Charles, La., June 25, 1935; s. Frank Canfield and Catherine Jewel (Gill) B.; B.S., Tulane U., 1959, Ph.D., 1965; m. Shirley Dee Bradford, June 29, 1956; children—John Bradford, Steven Canfield. Instr. in physiology Med. U. S.C., Charleston, 1964-67, asso. in physiology, 1967-68, asst. prof. physiology, 1968-75, asso. prof., 1975—. Committeeman, Boy Scouts Am., 1970-73; mem. CAP, 1967—. NIH pre-doctoral fellow, 1962-64; NSF summer fellow, 1967; recipient several research grants. Mem. AAAS, S.C. Acad. Sci., Digital Equipment Computers Users Soc., Am. Physiol. Soc., Soc. Neurosci., Internat. Soc. Oxygen Transport to Tissue, Sigma Xi. Episcopalian. Contbr. articles to sci. jours. Home: Rt 3 Box 367 Moncks Corner SC 29461

BLACKBURN, MARY MC WILLIAMS, educator; b. Steubenville, Ohio, Apr. 17, 1927; d. John William and Nelle (Wooley) Mc Williams; A.B., U. Ala., 1947; M.A., Columbia U., 1949; A.A., certification, U. Ala., 1965; m. Fleming Cocke Blackburn, Dec. 20, 1952 (div.); children—Fleming, Mary Ellen, Nancy. Instr. Livingston (Ala.) U., 1949-52; tchr. Mobile (Ala.) Pub. Schs., 1952-69; English fellow U. Ala., University, 1965; instr. U. South Ala., Mobile, 1970—. Mem. Nat. Soc. Lit. and the Arts, U. South Ala. Women Smithsonian

Assos., Phi Beta Kappa, Alpha Lambda Delta, Delta Gamma. Republican. Christian Scientist. Contbr. articles to profl. jours. Home: 428-4424 N Carlyle Way Mobile AL 36609 Office: English Dept U South Ala University Blvd Mobile AL 36688

BLACKMAN, BETTY LOU, hosp. social sers. dir.; b. Sarasota, Fla., Oct. 2, 1930; d. Jim and Ola Vastiah (Coker) Fowler; student Columbia (S.C.) Bible Coll., 1948-51, So. Bapt. Theol. Sem., 1964-65; B.A. in Sociology and Psychology, Ky. So. Coll./U. Louisville, 1968; M.S. in Social Work, Kent Sch. Social Work, U. Louisville, 1970; m. Frank Ogilvie Blackman, Aug. 26, 1951 (dec., 1964); children—Katherine Lynn Blackman Penick, Brenda Sue; m. 2d, John Quincy Woosley, Dec. 4, 1970 (div. 1978). Bank teller, Tex., Ky., Ga., 1951-66; child care nursery dir. Fowler's Toddler's Inn, Sarasota, Fla., 1968; social worker Ky. Dept. Child Welfare, Louisville, 1969, Family Relations Center, Louisville, 1970-72; sr. social worker River Region Mental Health-Mental Retardation, Louisville, 1972-78; clin. social worker, psychotherapist W. Central Fla. Human Resources Center, Ocala, 1978; treatment team Sarasota (Fla.) Palms Psychiat. Hosp., 1978-79; dir. social services Venice (Fla.) Hosp., 1979—; sec. to dir. Louisville and Jefferson County Children's Home, 1956-57; recreational dir. Perrine Bapt. Ch., Miami, Fla., 1965; condr. workshops, speaker churches, schs. Greater Louisville area; field instr. grad. sch. students U. Louisville. Chmn. Agencies United Appeal, 1974, 75; mem. Greater Louisville Area Mental Retardation Com.; active ch. activities, tchr., counselor, condr. workshops. Mem. Nat. Assn. Social Workers, Acad. Cert. Social Workers (certified), Nat. Assn. Hosp. Social Work Dirs., Fla. Assn. Hosp. Social Work Dirs., Fla. Chpt. Assn. Social Workers. Baptist. Home: 1323 Karen Dr Venice FL 33595 Office: Venice Hospital 540 The Rialto Venica FL 33595

BLACKMAN, BRUCE ALLEN, elec. engr.; b. Weleetka, Okla., Dec. 21, 1919; s. George C. and Ruby (Hamilton) B.; B.S., Okla. State U., 1941, M.S., 1955; m. Dorothy Atterberry, July 1, 1945; children—Barry, Susan. Instr. mech. engring. Okla. State U., Stillwater, 1946-48; research engr. Dowell Inc., Tulsa, 1948-53, Well Surveys, Inc., Tulsa, 1953-60; project engr. Otis Engring. Corp., Dallas, 1960-62; devel. engr., sect. leader Halliburton Co., Duncan, Okla., 1962-69, sect. supr., 1969—. Served to 1st lt. Signal Corps AUS, 1941-46, to capt., 1950-52. Registered profl. engr., Okla. Mem. IEEE, Soc. Petroleum Engrs., Eta Kappa Nu. Home: 1924 Parkview St Duncan OK 73533 Office: Research Center Duncan OK 73533

BLACKMAN, KENNETH EUGENE, microbiologist; b. Ilion, N.Y., June 30, 1938; s. Harold Scott and Ida Blackman LaFayette; B.S., Georgetown U., 1963; M.S., U. Cin., 1967, Ph.D., 1970; m. Doris Rowen, Apr. 20, 1963; children—Deborah, Colleen, Teresa. Research asso. with Dr. Albert Sabin, Children's Hosp. Research Found., Cin., 1963-65; instr. Coll. Medicine, U. Cin., 1967-70; scientist Meloy Labs., Inc. subs. Revlon Corp., Springfield, Va., 1970-71, tech. mgr. life scis. div., 1971-73, dir. life scis. div., 1973-76, v.p. life scis. div., 1976—. Served with USAF, 1956-60. Recipient Pres.'s award Am. Soc. Microbiology, 1969; spl. award Am. Cancer Soc., 1969; U. Cin. scholar, 1965-70; NIH summer fellow, 1961-63. Mem. Am. Soc. Microbiology, Tissue Culture Assn., Am. Assn. Lab. Animal Sci. Roman Catholic. Contbr. articles on virology and chem. carcinogenesis to profl. jours. Home: 3720 Prince William Dr Fairfax VA 22031 Office: Meloy Labs Inc 6715 Electronic Dr Springfield VA 22151

BLACKMAN, MURRAY, rabbi; b. N.Y.C., Nov. 18, 1920; s. Maxwell and Sarah (Levy) B.; B.S.S., Coll. City N.Y., 1940; B.H.L., Hebrew Union Coll., 1945, M.H.L., 1949, D.D., 1974; Ph.D., Walden U., 1975; m. Martha Dora Mecklenburger, Aug. 31, 1947; children—Michael Simon, Margaret Jo, Barbara Sarah. Rabbi, 1949; asst. rabbi Temple B'nai Jeshurun, Newark, 1949-50; rabbi Temple Concord, Binghamton, N.Y., 1950-51, Barnert Temple, Paterson, N.J., 1953-56; sr. rabbi Rockdale Temple, Cin., 1956-67; rabbi St. Thomas (V.I.) Synagogue, 1967-70, Temple Sinai, New Orleans, 1970—. Spl. lectr. edn. Hebrew Union Coll., Cin., 1962-67; instr. comparative religion Coll. of V.I., 1967-70; spl. lectr. history La. State U., Baton Rouge, 1971-75; asso. prof. U. New Orleans, 1974—. Chmn. Cin. Jewish Community Relations Com., 1966-67; interfaith chmn. Greater New Orleans United Fund, 1971; mem. adv. council New Orleans council Boy Scouts Am., 1971-73; mem. Mayor's Job Force for Vets. Com., 1970-72; mem. Am. Jewish Com., Central Conf. Am. Rabbis; chmn. community relations com. Jewish Welfare Fedn., New Orleans, 1971-79; pres. New Orleans Rabbinical Council, 1973-78; mem. exec. bd. Central Conf. Am. Rabbis, 1978—; mem. exec. bd. Nat. Jewish Community Relations Adv. Council, N.Y.C., 1975—, vice chmn., 1976—; exec. bd. La. State Com. for Humanities, 1975-80, Willowood Home for Jewish Aged, 1977—, La. Renaissance, Religion and the Arts, 1977—. Served with USNR, 1951-53. Mem. Adult Edn. Assn. U.S., Soc. Israel Philatelists, Southwest Assn. Reform Rabbis (pres. 1978-80), Phi Delta Kappa. Home: 1408 Frankfort St New Orleans LA 70122 Office: 6227 St Charles Ave New Orleans LA 70118

BLACKMON, FLOYD JACK, banker; b. Jersey City, July 18, 1940; s. Floyd Fletcher and Amy Elizabeth (Russell) B., Jr.; B.S. in Bus. Adminstrn., U. Conn., 1962; cert. S.C. Bankers Sch., 1975; postgrad. U. Wis. Bankers Sch., summers 1979—; m. Patricia Ann Pollock, July 28, 1962; 1 son, Floyd Jack. Indsl. engr. Warnaco, Inc., Hemingway, S.C., 1965, plant mgr., Bethune, S.C., 1965-69; chief engr. Campus Sportswear Co., LaCrosse, Va., 1970-71; system ops. dept. mgr. So. Bank & Trust Co., Columbia, S.C., 1971—. Team leader United Fund, 1972-73. Served with USAF, 1962-65. Mem. Am. Inst. Banking. Republican. Methodist. Club: Murraywood Swim and Racquet. Home: 136 Chillingham Rd Irmo SC 29063 Office: 3239 Sunset Blvd West Columbia SC 29169

BLACKMON, JACK RUSSELL, judge; b. Leesville, La., Feb. 5, 1918; s. Robert Franklin and Mamie Edna (Wisenbaker) B.; A.A., Wesley Coll., 1936; LL.B., So. Meth. U., 1939; m. Margaret Lucinda McGlaun, July 14, 1940; children—Robert M., Margaret Diane (Mrs. David Barfield), Deborah Claire (Mrs. A.E. Cox). Admitted to Tex. bar, 1939; partner firm Berger, Swearingen, Wade & Blackmon, Corpus Christi, Tex., 1946-49, North, Blackmon & White, Corpus Christi, 1949-72; dist. judge 117th Jud. Dist. Tex., Corpus Christi, 1973—. Sec.-treas. NBW Bldg. Corp., Corpus Christi, 1956—; pres. Municipal Gas Corp., Corpus Christi, 1967-71. Gen. chmn. Sister City Com. Corpus Christi, 1972-73. Mem. Tex. Democratic Exec. com., 1954-58; mem. City Council, Corpus Christi, 1963-65, mayor pro tem, 1965-67, mayor, 1967-71. Trustee U. Corpus Christi, 1969—, chmn. 1971—. Served with USNR, World War II. Named Outstanding Citizen Corpus Christi by Bd. Realtors, 1973. Mem. Nueces County Bar Assn. (past pres.), Res. Officers Assn. (past pres.), Naval Res. Lawyers Assn. (dir. 1972-73), Phi Alpha Delta. Mason (Shriner, 32 deg.). Club: Civitan Internat. (local past pres., past dist. gov., v.p. zone 8 1973-75). Home: 101 Alta Plaza Corpus Christi TX 78411 Office: Courthouse Corpus Christi TX 78401

BLACKMON, WILSON WHITAKER, petroleum co. exec.; b. Columbus, Ga., Nov. 7, 1930; s. Guy Rupert and Georgia Gaither (Whitaker) B.; B.S. in Engring., Clemson (S.C.) U., 1953; m. Martha Geraldine Dunn, Aug. 20, 1954; children—Susan Kay, Brian Whitaker. Engr., Lockheed Aircraft Corp., 1953-54; mgr. Guy Blackmon Inc., Columbus, 1956-62; pres. Blackmon Oil Co. Inc., Columbus, 1962—, also dir.; dir. GBInc., Blackmon Enterprises, G.O.A., Broadway Investment Co. Chmn. family ministries St. Luke Meth. Ch., also mem. ofcl. bd. stewards; bd. dirs. Open Door Community House. Served to 1st lt. AUS, 1954-56; Korea. Recipient Employer of Year for Hiring Vets. Am. Legion, 1977. Mem. Ga. Oilmens Assn. (v.p. 1977-79, pres. 1979-80), Petroleum Council Ga., Nat. Oil Jobbers Council, Clemson U. Alumni Assn. (pres.). Clubs: Kiwanis, Lions, Columbus Country, Atlanta Elks. Home: 2930 Averett Dr Columbus GA 31906 Office: PO Box 1336 Columbus GA 31902

BLACKMORE, JAMES DOUGLAS, pub. relations and advt. exec.; b. Acushnet, Mass., Dec. 7, 1946; s. James Howard and Clotilda (Perry-Ponte) B.; student Southeastern Mass. Technol. Inst., 1966, U. Tex., Austin, 1970-73; m. Sharon Cramer, Aug. 18, 1973. Pres., Blackmore Agy., Austin, 1969-73; announcer KTBC, Austin, 1970; exec. dir. Austin U.S.O., 1970-73; dir. pub. relat relations Tex. Pacific Oil Co., Inc., Dunigan Tool & Supply Co., Inc., Dallas, 1973—; vis. lectr. S.W. Tex. State U., 1975, U. Tex., Austin, Arlington, Dallas; mem. curriculum study com. public-relations and journalism Sch. Communication, U. Tex., Austin, 1980. Served with USAF, 1966-70. Recipient Excellence in Graphics award Ga.-Pacific, 1974, award of graphic recognition Internat. Papers, 1974, 75. Mem. Tex., La. Mid-Continent oil and gas assns., Okla. Petroleum Council, Aviation Space Writers Assn., Assn. Petroleum Writers (asso.), Internat. Assn. Bus. Communicators (Rookie Editor of Year 1974), Pub. Relations Soc. Am. (accredited mem.; accreditation chmn. North Tex. 1978, dir. 1979—, v.p. 1980, pres.-elect 1981). Clubs: Dallas Press (gen. chmn. Gridiron Show 1978), Lancer's (Dallas). Editor: TP Voice, Dunigan Diary, 1973—. Contbr. articles to profl. jours. Producer, NET-PBS TV Spl., Christmas Folk, 1971. Home: 2505 Pecan St Grand Prairie TX 75050 Office: 1700 One Main Pl Dallas TX 75250

BLACKSHEAR, AUGUSTUS TROY, JR., lawyer; b. Dallas, July 5, 1942; s. Augustus Troy and Janie Louise (Florey) B.; B.B.A. cum laude, Baylor U., 1964, LL.B. cum laude, 1968; m. Patty D. Milner, Aug. 9, 1973. With Arthur Andersen & Co., Dallas, 1964-66; admitted to Tex. bar, 1968; since practiced in Houston, partner firm Fulbright & Jaworski, 1975—; lectr. McLennan Community Coll., 1968-69. Mem. Am. Bar Assn. (tax sect.), State Bar Tex. (tax sect., chmn.). Home: 10631 N Evers Park Houston TX 77024 Office: 800 Bank Southwest Bldg Houston TX 77002

BLACKSTOCK, LEROY, lawyer; b. El Reno, Okla., Apr. 19, 1914; s. Herbert Austin and Ethel Mae (Gwin) B.; grad. Draughon's Bus. Inst., Tulsa, 1933; LL.B., U. Tulsa, 1938; m. Virginia Lee Lowman, Dec. 29, 1939; children—Craig, Priscilla, Birch, Lore, Trena. With Phillips Petroleum Co., Tulsa, 1933-41, asst. credit mgr., 1939-41; admitted to Okla. bar, 1938; practice law, Tulsa, 1941—; now of counsel firm Blackstock Joyce Pollard Blackstock & Montgomery; pres. Skelly Stadium Corp., 1964—; dir., gen. counsel Tulsa Home Builders Assn., 1959-68; pres., trustee Gt. Western Investment Trust; lectr. U. Tulsa Coll. Law, 1970—. Pres., Tulsa County Legal Aid Soc., 1961-62, bd. dirs. 1958-66; pres., bd. dirs. Tulsa County Bar Found., 1962-66; trustee Okla. Bar Found., 1966—; chmn. Citizen's Adv. Com. County Commrs., 1963-66; chmn. Okla. Supreme Ct. Bar Commn., 1966; pres. Tulsa Bapt. Laymen's Corp., 1962-66; mem. Gov.'s Acad. for State Govt., 1966-68; pres. Jud. Reform, Inc., 1966-70, Tulsa Sci. Center, 1968-73; chmn. law schs. com. Tulsa U., 1960; mem. Tulsa Mayor's Adv. Com. Community Problems; mem. nat. adv. com. Practising Law Inst., 1969—; chmn. Okla. Council on Jud. Complaints, 1974—; pres. Tulsa Campfire Council, 1971-72; bd. dirs. Tulsa County Mental Health Assn., 1963-70, Tulsa Psychiat. Found., 1964-67, Tulsa Downtown YMCA, 1974-77; chmn. U. Tulsa Loyalty Fund, 1969-70. Served with USNR, 1943-46. Recipient Distinguished Citizens award Okla. Psychol. Assn., 1963; Distinguished Alumni award U. Tulsa, 1969, 78; named Boss of Year Tulsa County Assn. Legal Secs., 1978. Fellow Am. Coll. Probate Counsel; mem. Am. (ho. dels. 1965-67, mem. com. on nat. coordination of disciplinary enforcement 1969-72, standing com. profl. discipline 1973-77), Okla. (pres. 1966, bd. govs. 1965-67), Tulsa County (pres. 1962; Outstanding Atty. award 1961) bar assns., Tulsa City Hist. Soc. (founding), Photog. Soc. Am., Soc. Amateur Cinematographers, World Assn. Lawyers (charter), Phi Alpha Delta. Republican. Baptist (chmn. deacons 1962, chmn. bldg. com. 1951-70). Club: Petroleum (dir. 1974—). Author: Paper Dolls; Lawyers' Fees; Managing Partner Approach. Home: 3740 Terwilleger St Tulsa OK 74105 Office: 515 S Main Mall Tulsa OK 74103

BLACKSTOCK, VIRGINIA LEE LOWMAN (MRS. LEROY BLACKSTOCK), civic worker; b. Bixby, Okla., July 2, 1917; d. Joseph Arthur and Winifred (Lundy) Lowman; student Tulsa Coll. Bus., 1935-37; m. Leroy Blackstock, Dec. 29, 1939; children—Vincent Craig, Priscilla Gay (Mrs. Richard S. Kurz), Birch Lee, Lore Anne (Mrs. Dwight Mitchell), Trena Jan (Mrs. Frank Dale). Legal sec. law firm, Tulsa, 1937-41. Chmn. program Internat. Students in Tulsa, 1955-65; mem. Tulsa Council Camp Fire Girls, 1963-66; mem. youth com. Tulsa Philharmonic Soc., 1969-70; now mem. women's assn.; pres. Eliot Elementary P.T.A., 1961-62, Edison High Sch. P.T.A., 1971-72; mem. Tulsa Opera Guild. Co-chmn. Democratic precinct No. 132, 1960-67. Mem. Tulsa County Bar Aux. (pres. 1954-55, sec. 1962-63, chaplain 1966-67). Baptist. Clubs: Summit, Petroleum. Home: 3740 Terwilleger Blvd Tulsa OK 74105

BLACKWELDER, RAMAH PENNY, dietary services coordinator; b. Centralia, Kans., Apr. 15, 1921; d. Charles William and Mary Elizabeth (Chamberlin) Gaston; B.A., U. Mont., 1943; postgrad. student Lenoir Rhyne Coll., 1956-57; m. Andrew Long Blackwelder, Oct. 19, 1945; children—Ramah Gaston (Mrs. Thomas H. Mackey), Andi Campbell (Mrs. Mitchell R. Setzer). Dietetics intern U. Okla. Med. Sch., 1943-44; sci. tchr. Hildebran (N.C.) High Sch., 1957-61; dir. dietary Catawba Meml. Hosp., Hickory, N.C., 1966-72; self-employed dietary cons. N.C. hosps., 1972-76; coordinator dietary services Eastern Region, Am. Med. Internat., Atlanta, 1976—. Pres., Viewmont Sch PTA, Hickory, 1957-58; treas. Hickory Sr. League, 1958-60. Mem. N.C. Dietetic Assn. (pres. 1975-76), Am. Dietetics Assn., Ga. Dietetics Assn., Am. Soc. Hosp. Food Service Adminstrs. Mem. United Ch. of Christ. Home: 2873 Torpeya Way Marietta GA 30067 Office: 6400 Powers Ferry Rd Suite 400 Atlanta GA 30339

BLACKWELL, ANNA MARGARET THOMPSON (MRS. DAMIAN LEE BLACKWELL, JR.), orgn. exec.; b. Ewing, Ill., Aug. 29, 1905; d. Edmund Lee and Effie (Moss) Thompson; student U. Ala., 1926, Watkins Inst., 1936-37, 38; m. Damian Lee Blackwell, Jr., May 22, 1926 (dec. Jan. 1967); children—Evelyn (Mrs. Marvin E. Loney), Sarah (Mrs. Bobby W. Johnson), Barbara (Mrs. Harold W. Atkinson). Recreation dir. Morgan County, Somerville, Ala., 1938-41; order office mgr. Sears, Roebuck & Co., Decatur, Ala., 1941-53; cashier White Way Pure Milk Co., Decatur, 1953-57; asso. dir. Morgan County United Fund, Decatur, 1957—. Mem. Community Services Planning Council, 1957—, pres., 1962-63, 67. Mem. Ala. Assn. Retarded Children, Morgan County Assn. for Mental Health, Morgan County Soc. Crippled Children and Adults, Internat. Platform Assn., Am. Bus. Women's Assn. (treas., pres. 1972-73), Wesleyan Service Guild (pres. 1964-68). Methodist. Club: Pilot (treas. Decatur 1971-72, pres. 1976-77), Opportunity Toastmistress (pres. 1977-78). Home: PO Box 213 Somerville AL 35670 Office: PO Box 1058 Decatur AL 35601

BLACKWELL, DOCTOR FREDERICK, JR., assn. mgmt. cons.; b. Kannapolis, N.C., Mar. 29, 1921; s. Doctor Frederick and Annie (Mc Intyre) B.; B.A., U. N.C., 1950; postgrad. Union Sem., 1960, Columbia Sem., 1961; m. Georgia Gibson, June 12, 1964. Asst. mgr. C. of C., Anderson, S.C., 1951-53; dist. mgr. U.S. C. of C., Roanoke, Va., 1953-54; exec. v.p. Nat. Wholesale Dry Goods Inst., N.Y.C., 1954-59; dir. Retail Merchants Assn., Greenville, S.C., 1962-63; v.p. Nat. Assn. Mfrs., N.Y.C., 1964-69; owner F 4 B Trucking Co., Hendersonville, Tenn., 1970-75; exec. dir. Tenn. Veterinary Med. Assn., Nashville, 1975-79; pres. Assn. Mgmt. Unltd., Charlotte, N.C., 1979—; adv. Tech. Exchange program U.S. Dept. State, 1956-58. Served with USN, 1942-45. Republican. Presbyn. Editor, Tenn. Veterinary Med. Assn. Newsletter, 1975—, Tenn. Veterinarian Mag., 1976-79. Office: PO Box 18543 Charlotte NC 28218

BLACKWELL, FLOYD ORIS, educator; b. Mayfield, Idaho, Feb. 27, 1925; s. Floyd Weaver and Mary Olive (Noel) B.; B.S., Wash. State U., 1950; M.S., U. Mass., 1954; M.P.H., U. Calif. at Berkeley, 1965, Dr.P.H., 1969; m. Eleanor Louise Edwards, May 5, 1951; children—Susan, Betsy, Mary, Stephen. Sanitarian, Dist. Health Dept., Pasco, Wash., 1950-53; health adviser Pakistan AID, 1954-59; asst. prof. Am. U. Beirut (Lebanon), 1959-64; asso. prof. Rutgers U., 1967-71; asso. prof. environmental health U. Vt., Burlington, 1971-74; prof. East Carolina U., 1974—. Mem. pub. health rev. com. Bur. Health Manpower, 1971-73; pres., East Brunswick Human Relations Council, N.J., 1970-71. Served with USNR, 1943-46. Recipient Certificate of Merit. Nat. Environmental Health Assn., 1970, H.R.H. Nicholas award N.J. Environmental Health Assn., 1970. Mem. Am. Acad. Certification Sanitarians (dir. 1973-77), Nat. Environ. Health Assn. (pres. 1975-76, vice chmn. instl. sect. 1979-80), Am. Pub. Health Assn., Nat. Health Council (consumer concerns com.). Mem. Religious Soc. of Friends. Book rev. editor Jour. Environ. Health, 1966-68. Home: 1210 E Rock Spring Rd Greenville NC 27834

BLACKWELL, HERMAN NEWMAN, accountant; b. Greenville, Ky., Aug. 26, 1917; s. Thomas Elliott and Eula (Newman) B.; A.B., Georgetown Coll., 1939; B.M.E., U. Louisville, 1939; postgrad. U. Ala., 1954-55; m. Floris E. Hurston, Dec. 18, 1945; 1 son, Thomas C. Instr., Barnes Sch. of Boys, Montgomery, Ala., 1939-42; owner, operator Herman N. Blackwell, C.P.A. and predecessors, Montgomery, 1946—, partner, 1956—; prof. mathematics U. S. Pacific, Noumea, New Caledonia, 1944-45. Served with AUS, 1942-45, USAR, 1946-70. C.P.A., Ala., 1956. Mem. Am. Inst. C.P.A.'s, CAP, Pi Kappa Alpha. Presbyterian. Clubs: Country, Kiwanis Internat. Home: 3637 Princeton Dr Montgomery AL 36111 Office: 240 Adams Ave Montgomery AL 36104

BLACKWELL, LEONARD DUNNAM, plastics mfg. co. exec.; b. Houston, Oct. 8, 1925; s. Leonard Alvin and Irene Rose (Petty) B.; m. Helen Marie Stroud, Apr. 24, 1948; 1 dau., Karen Marie. Pres. Blackwell Plastics, Inc., Houston, 1946—; dir. Fannin Bank; pres. Alvinne Devel. Corp. Served to 1st lt. USAAF, 1944-46. Mem. Houston Engring. and Scientific Soc., Modern Plastics Mgmt. Assn., Soc. Plastics Engrs., Houston C. of C. Presbyterian. Clubs: Mason, Shriner, Rotary. Home: 8103 Glencrest Houston TX 77061 Office: Blackwell Plastics Inc 5606 Cavanaugh Houston TX 77021

BLACKWELL, LUCY WHITE, ret. govt. ofcl.; b. Jackson, Tenn., Apr. 22, 1912; d. William Francis and Ethel (White) Blackwell; A.B., Lambuth Coll., 1933; postgrad. West Tenn. Bus. Coll., 1934-35. Stenographer Tenn. Emergency Relief Adminstrn., Jackson, 1935; accounting clk FSA, Jackson, Brownsville, Tenn., 1936-39; stenographer Tenn. Dept. Pub. Welfare, Jackson, 1939-40; clk., interviewer, local office mgr. Tenn. Dept. Employment Security, Jackson, 1940-73. Comdr. Am. Cancer Soc., Madison County, Tenn., 1943-54, dist. comdr. West Tenn., 1947-48; rec. sec. Tenn. div., 1954-56, bd. dirs., 1945—, organizer Madison County unit, 1954, pres., 1954-55; bd. dirs. Jackson Community Chest, 1955-57; pres. League Women Voters, 1951. Treas., chmn. bd. trustees Jackson Free Library, 1948-57. Recipient R.E. Womack Alumni Achievement award Lambuth Coll. Alumni Assn., 1956; named Jackson-Madison Woman of Year 1955. Mem. Internat. Assn. Personnel Emloyment Security (pres. Jackson 1956), Lambuth Coll. Alumni Assn. (pres. 1962-63). Presbyn. Clubs: Pilot (past pres. Jackson, dist. gov. Tenn., internat. dir. exec. com.), Altrusa (chmn.). Home: 45 Belle Haven Dr Jackson TN 38301

BLACKWELL, LYLE MARVIN, ednl. adminstr.; b. Charleston, W.Va., Jan. 29, 1932; s. James Elvin and Sarah Margaret (Ballard) B.; B.S. in Elec. Engring., W.Va. U., 1954; M.A. in Engring., Chrysler Inst., 1956; Ph.D. (NSF Sci. Faculty fellow), Ohio State U., 1966; m. Mary Jean Fitzgerald, June 20, 1953; children—James Lyle, Gerald Grant, Scott Allen, Mary Diane, Matthew Fitzgerald. Studio engr. Chrysler Corp., Detroit, 1954-59; chmn. dept. elec. engring. W.Va. Inst. Tech., 1960-64, dean Sch. Engring. and Phys. Sci., 1966—; research asst. Ohio State U., 1964-66. Mem. Soc. Automotive Engrs., IEEE, Am. Soc. Engring. Edn., Tau Beta Pi, Eta Kappa Nu. Baptist. Author: Gauley Bridge, 1960. Office: Sch Engring WVA Inst Tech Montgomery WV 25136

BLAIR, BOBBY CHARLES, chem. engr.; b. Arcadia, Kans., Sept. 21, 1941; s. Charles Warren and Hazel Louise (Wyckoff) B.; B.S. in Chem. Engring., Okla. State U., 1964; M.B.A., U. Tulsa, 1969. With Phillips Petroleum Co., 1964—, mktg. research engr., Bartlesville, Okla., 1974-77, mktg. and tech. analyst, 1977-80, mining chems. project dir., Bartlesville, 1980—. Wentz Found. Service scholar. Mem. Soc. Plastics Engrs., Phi Theta Kappa, Sigma Tau. Republican. Mem. Christian Ch. (Disciples of Christ). Co-inventor, patentee high speed fibrillation process. Home: 4200 Beacon Ct Bartlesville OK 74003 Office: 14 D2 Phillips Bldg Bartlesville OK 74004

BLAIR, DANNY LLOYD, mktg. services/petroleum co. ofcl.; b. Jackson, Tenn., Aug. 7, 1949; s. Lloyd Fred and Mary Morine (Young) B.; B.A. in Polit. Sci., Millsaps Coll., 1971; m. Carroll Tipton La Fleur, Nov. 26, 1973; 1 son, Parish Walker. Account rep., mgr. customer service, asst. to pres. and office mgr. Automated Bus. Systems, Inc., Memphis, 1972-74; data processing ops. coordinator, mgr. computer ops., asst. dir. info. services Mid Continent Systems, Inc., West Memphis, Ark., 1975-78, mgr. data processing adminstrn., planning and control, 1979—. Mem. Data Processing Mgmt. Assn., Pi Mu, Kappa Alpha. Home: 4863 Berrydale Ave Memphis TN 38118 Office: 310 Mid Continent Plaza West Memphis AR 72301

BLAIR, JOHN DOHERTY, JR., air force officer; b. Long Branch, N.J., Jan. 5, 1938; s. John Doherty and Gladys Harrington (Pearce) B.; B.A., W.Va. Wesleyan Coll., 1962; M.Ed., Springfield Coll., 1963; m. Sally Marie Schoening, June 25, 1972; children—Diane Kathleen, John Doherty III. Commd. lt. USAF, 1964, advanced through grades to lt. col., 1979; chief personnel quality control Robins AFB, Ga. and Tahkli Air Base, Thailand, 1964-68; chief Air Force career counseling programs Mil. Personnel Center, Randolph AFB, Tex., 1968-72; personnel staff officer Pentagon, Washington, 1972-76, dir. mil. personnel office, Carswell AFB, Tex., 1977—. Decorated Bronze Star medal, Meritorious service medals (2), Air Force Commendation medal, Vietnam Gallantry Cross; named Air Force Personnel Mgr. of Yr., 1978, numerous others. Mem. Am. Personnel and Guidance Assn., Nat. Vocat. Guidance Assn., Air Force Assn. Methodist. Club: Optimist. grad. Armed Forces Staff Coll. Va., 1977. Home: 3005 Mesa Rd Willow Park TX 76086 Office: 7th Combat Support Group DPM Carswell AFB TX 76127

BLAIR, MARIE LENORE, educator; b. Maramec, Okla., Jan. 9, 1931; d. Virgil Clement and Ella Catherine (Leen) Strode; B.S., Okla. A. and M. Coll., 1956; M.S., Okla. State U., 1961, postgrad., 1965-66; m. Freeman Joe Blair, Aug. 26, 1950; children—Elizabeth Ann Blair Stone, Roger Joe. Reading specialist, pub. schs. Stillwater, Okla., 1966—. Mem. state exec. com. Okla. Order Rainbow for Girls. Mem. Internat. Reading Assn., Okla., Cimarron reading assns., NEA, Okla. Edn. Assn. (dir.), Stillwater Edn. Assn., Cimarron Reading Council (pres.), Kappa Kappa Iota. Democrat. DeMolay Mothers Club, Rainbow Mothers Club, Lahoma, White Shrine Jerusalem; mem. Order Eastern Star (Grand Martha Okla.). Contbr. to Okla. Reader. Home: Route 1 Maramee OK 74045

BLAIR, R(ICHARD) CHARLES, coll. adminstr.; b. Los Angeles, Aug. 15, 1935; s. Ovid L. and Dorothy May (Blair) Lovell; student U. Wyo., 1952-53, So. Ill. U., 1954-56; B.A., Mid Continent Bapt. Bible Coll., 1960, postgrad.; postgrad. No. Bapt. Coll., 1961; B.A., Murray State U., 1965, M.A., 1974; m. Alma Grace Neace, July 12, 1956; children—Timothy Carl, Tina Carole, Terri Carletta. With various radio stas. including Sta. WDXR, Paducah, Ky.,1952-60; ordained to ministry, Bapt. Ch., 1959; minister 1st Bapt. Mission, Mayfield, Ky., Lakeview Bapt. Mission, Chgo., 1959-61; pastor Sedalia (Ky.) Bapt. Ch., 1962-65; acad. dean Mid-Continent Bapt. Bible Coll., Mayfield, Ky., 1966-76, v.p., 1976—. Mem. So. Assn. Bible Colls. (exec. com. 1971—), Bible Sci. Assn., Ky. Bapt. Hist. Soc. Republican. Baptist. Club: Rotary. Contbr. articles in field to profl. jours. Office: Route 2 Mayfield KY 42066

BLAIS, KIMBERLY RIDLEHUBER, dietitian; b. Austin, Tex., Nov. 1, 1947; d. Charles Henry and Eleanor Marie (Kornbacher) Ridlehuber; B.S. in Nutrition, Tex. Tech. U., 1970; M.S. in Health Adminstrn., S.W. Tex. State U., 1979. Dietetic intern Peter Bent Brigham Hosp., Boston, 1970-71; dietitian Med. Center Hosp. of Vt., Burlington, 1971-75; instr. nutrition U. Vt., Burlington, 1975-76; clin. dietitian St. David's Community Hosp., Austin, Tex., 1976; dir. dietetic sers. Shoal Creek Hosp., Austin, 1976—; corp. food service cons. Hosp. Affiliates Internat., Nashville. Sec. Pecan Springs Integrated Neighborhood Assn., 1977. Mem. Austin Dietetic Assn., Am. Dietetic Assn., Am. Soc. Hosp. Food Ser. Adminstrs. Episcopalian. Club: Austin Ski. Office: 3501 Mills Ave Austin TX 78731

BLAKE, FRANK, broadcasting co. exec.; b. Weston, W.Va., July 13, 1936; s. Gilbert and Wanda Grace (McCauley) B.; B.S. in Journalism, W.Va. U., 1962, M.S. in Journalism, 1965; m. Charlotte A. Francis, Dec. 29, 1956; children—Arlene, Yvonne, Aaron, Amber. Radio-TV editor W.Va. U. Coop. Extension Service; gen. mgr. Sta. WSWP-TV, Beckley, W.Va.; exec. sec. W.Va. Ednl. Broadcasting Authority, Charleston; pres. Kanawha Broadcasting Corp., Charleston. Chmn. bd. W.Va. div. Am. Cancer Soc., 1976-78. Served with USAF, 1956-60. Mem. Kappa Tau Alpha. Home: 1521 Summit Dr Charleston WV 25302 Office: 126 High St Charleston WV 25311

BLAKE, GEORGE BERNARD, mktg. cons.; b. Detroit, June 21, 1932; s. Francis Martin and Edna Loretta (VonMach) B.; B.S., Loyola U., Chgo., 1952. Pres., George Blake & Assos., Sarasota, Fla., 1965—; chmn. bd. Federated Chemicals, Inc., Sarasota, G & G Sales Co., Sarasota. Served with AUS, 1952-54; Korea. Named Farm Mktg. Man of Year, Nat. Assn. Agrl. Marketers, 1965. Republican. Roman Catholic. Home: 912 Magellan Dr Sarasota FL 33580 Office: Box 5975 Sarasota FL 33579

BLAKE, ILENE MILLS, county govt. exec.; b. Kegley, W.Va., Aug. 31, 1932; d. Ile Sheron and Okley Fay (Reid) Mills; student Concord Coll., 1950-51; B.B.A., George Washington U., 1967; m. Warren Porter Blake, May 24, 1951; children—Ile Wayne, Edward Dean. Adminstrv. asst. Arlington County, Arlington, Va., 1959-67; adminstrv. asst. Fairfax County, Fairfax, Va., 1967-71, budget analyst, 1971-72, budget officer, 1972-73, dir. Office Mgmt. and Budget, 1973—; founder, bd. dirs. Blake Pvt. Sch.; treas. Blake-Mills Ltd. Trustee, Sterling (Va.) Pub. Library, 1973—, treas., 1977. Mem. Municipal Fin. Officers Assn. Home: 125 Evergreen St Sterling VA 22170

BLAKE, LAMONT VINCENT, electronic scientist; b. Somerville, Mass., Nov. 7, 1913; s. Earl Clement and Mary Bella (Munro) B.; B.S., Mass. State Coll., 1935; M.S., U. Md., 1950, postgrad., 1950-53, 63-64; m. Charline Manees, July 16, 1938 (dec. 1956); children—Donald Earl, Barbara Jean; m. 2d, Elizabeth Hannah Cochran, June 17, 1957 (div. 1978); 1 son, David Munro. Radio interference investigator Ark. Power & Light Co., Little Rock, 1937-39, Pine Bluff, 1939-40; radar research scientist Naval Research Lab., Washington, 1940-69, head radar geophysics br., 1969-72, ret., 1972; sr. scientist Tech. Service Corp., Silver Spring, Md., 1972—. Recipient Applied Sci. award Naval Research Lab. chpt. Research Soc. Am., 1963; Superior Civilian Service award U.S. Navy, 1972. Fellow IEEE; mem. Am. Phys. Soc., AAAS, Internat. Sci. Radio Union (Commn. F), Sigma Xi, Sigma Pi Sigma. Author: Antennas, 1966; Transmission Lines and Waveguides, 1969; Radar Range-Performance Analysis, 1980. Home: 7814 Oaklawn Dr Alexandria VA 22306 Office: 8555 16th St Suite 300 Silver Spring MD 20910

BLAKE, WYATT HEFLIN, III, surgeon; b. Sheffield, Ala., Nov. 7, 1928; s. Wyatt Heflin and Rebecca Robertson (Stickney) B.; B.S., U. South, Sewanee, Tenn., 1950; M.D., Vanderbilt U., 1954; m. Jeanne Thomas, Nov. 22, 1957; children—Kelly Frances, Leslie Anne, Richard Wyatt. Intern U. Hosps. of Cleve., 1954-55, resident, 1955-56, 1958-59; resident Cleve. Metropolitan Gen. Hosp., 1959-61; practice medicine specializing in gen. surgery, Sheffield, Ala., 1961—; mem. staffs Shoals, Colbert County hosps. (both Sheffield); chief surgery Shoals Hosp., 1968, 69, 75, Colbert County (Ala.) Hosp., 1963, 66, 71. Trustee Sheffield Public Library. Served to lt., M.C., USNR, 1956-58. Recipient Physician's Recognition award AMA, 1973, 78. Diplomate Am. Bd. Surgery. Fellow A.C.S., Southeastern Surg. Congress, Internat. Coll. Surgeons; mem. Colbert County Med. Soc. (pres. 1969), Ala. Med. Assn. (chmn. dist. com. peer rev.), Am. Soc. Colon and Rectal Surgeons, Am. Soc. Gastrointestinal Endoscopy, Ala. Hist. Assn., Sigma Nu. Episcopalian. Home: 810 River Bluff Dr Sheffield AL 35660 Office: 323 N Montgomery Ave Sheffield AL 35660

BLAKELEY, ROBERT PHILIP, real estate co. exec.; b. Hampton, Ky., Jan. 3, 1917; s. William Roney and Gladys Mae (Styers) B.; student Dyke Sch. Commerce, 1936-38; m. Evelyn Diane White, Apr. 19, 1941; children—Brent Philip, Diana Gaye. Asst. office mgr. Chandler Products Co., Cleve., 1941-48; sec.-treas., gen. mgr. Plantation Farms, Inc. (Fla.), 1949—; pres., dir. Old Plantation Water Control Dist., 1958—; chmn. governing bd. Central & So. Fla. Flood Control Dist.; dir. Farsouth Growers Coop. Assn., Tropical Agr. Coop. Assn., Landmark Bank of Plantation, Landmark 1st Nat. Bank; chmn. bd. Landmark Bank West Broward. Fire chief Plantation Vol. Fire Dept., 1960-62; mem. Broward County Water Resources Adv. Bd.; bd. dirs. Broward County Indsl. Devel. Bd., 1965-66; co-trustee Plantation Land Trust, 1964-66; bd. dirs. Broward County chpt. ARC. Mem. C. of C. (dir. 1962-66, past pres.), Aquatic Weed Sci. Soc. (dir.), Hyacinth Control Soc. (dir.), Weed Sci. Soc. Am., So. Weed Soc. Club: Kiwanis. Home: 320 E Tropical Way Plantation FL 33314 Office: 7049 NW 4th St Plantation FL 33313

BLAKEMAN, ELEANOR MOSS, acct.; b. Letcher County, Blackey, Ky., Feb. 22, 1926; d. John Welsh and Lillie (Goldstein) Moss; B.Sec.Sci., Andrew Jackson U., 1945; m. Luther M. Blakeman, Dec. 14, 1948; children—John Wilson, Mary Elaine. With Central Exchange Bank, Lexington, Ky., 1945, Tafel Electric Co., Lexington, 1945-48, Yeary Lumber Co., Nicholasville, Ky., 1948-51, Sutherland Chevrolet Co., Nicholasville, 1955-58; dep. Jessamine County Ct. Clk.'s Office, Nicholasville, 1960-66; owner Blakeman Bookkeeping and Tax Service, Nicholasville, 1966—; stockholder Blakeman Oil Service, Inc., Nicholasville, 1977—. Mem. Jessamine County 4-H Council, 1964-74. Mem. Nat. Soc. Pub. Accts., Ky. Assn. Accts., Nat. Assn. Tax Consultors. Democrat. Christian Ch. Club: Lena Madesin Phillips Bus. and Profl. Women. Home: Route 4 Nicholasville KY 40356 Office: 200 W Maple St Nicholasville KY 40356

BLAKEMORE, TINA CROSS (HAMILTON), editor; b. Ocilla, Ga., Nov. 5, 1905; d. Walter Edmund and Ida E. (Bateman) Cross; student U. Fla., Stetson U., summers 1939, 40; m. Raymond Randall Hamilton, 1925 (dec. Jan. 1968); children—Raymond Randall and Waller E. (twins), James Polk; m. 2d, Watt Dodson Blakemore, Oct. 18, 1972. Journalist, Palmetto, Fla., 1926-28; sec. to pastor Orlando (Fla.) 1st Baptist Ch., 1930's; mem. staff Orange County (Fla.) Juvenile Ct. rehab. services, 1938-40; editor Iuka (Miss.) Vidette, 1941-50; journalist Daytona Beach (Fla.) News Jour., 1950; editor Millington-Shelby Star (formerly Millington Star), Millington, Tenn., 1953—. Active numerous ednl. and civic orgns. Mem. Nat., Tenn. press assns., C. of C. Baptist. Home: 8168 Wilkinsville Rd Millington TN 38053 Office: 5018 Navy Rd Millington TN 38053

BLAKENEY, ROGER NEAL, educator, psychologist; b. Deatur, Tex., Sept. 16, 1939; s. C.B. and Flora M. (McAnelly) B.; B.S. in Psychology, Tex. A. and M. U., 1964; M.A. in Indsl. Psychology, U. Houston, 1967, Ph.D. in Indsl. Psychology, 1969; children—Christopher Alan, Benjamin G. Teaching fellow dept. psychology U. Houston, 1965-68, instr. mgmt., 1968-69, asst. prof. behavioral mgmt. sci., 1969-72, dir. masters program, 1970, coordinator Human Resources Center, 1971-72, asso. prof. behavioral mgmt. sci., 1972-74, asso. prof. organizational behavior and mgmt. Coll. of Bus. Adminstrn., 1974—; adj. prof. Houston Bapt. U., 1978—; indsl. psychology intern Exxon U.S.A., 1967-68; pres. Organizational Tech., Inc., 1973-78; cons. to various govt., labor and bus. orgns. Served with AUS, 1960-62. Mem. Am., Southwestern, Tex., Houston psychol. assns., Am., Southwestern acads. mgmt., Internat. Transactional Analysis Assn., Sigma Xi, Beta Gamma Sigma, Alpha Kappa Delta, Alpha Zeta, Sigma Iota Epsilon. Author: (with E.C. Bell) Building Effective Local Unions; Course XV of the Labor Education Program of District 37 United Steelworkers of America, 1972, Advanced Leadership: Course XIII of the Labor Education Program of District 37 United Steelworkers of America, 1972; Introduction To Management By Objectives, 1974; Developmental Supervision: Performance Review and Career Planning. Editor: (with M.T. Matteson and D.R. Domm) Contemporary Personnel Management, 1972; (with D.R. Domm, R.W. Scofield and M.T. Matteson) The Individual and the Organization: A book of readings, 1971; Current Issues in Transactional Analysis, 1977; contbg. author: Certificate in Management Accounting Review, 1978. Contbr. articles to profl. publs. Home: 576 Warsaw Hitchcock TX 77563 Office: 2425 Underwood Blvd #151 Houston TX 77030

BLAKEY, HUBERT HIERONYMUS, psychiatrist; b. Beattyville, Ky., June 3, 1924; s. Hubert McGuire and Eva Edison (Hieronymus) B.; B.S., Mercer U., Macon, Ga., 1946; M.D., Vanderbilt U., 1949; m. Carole Anne Watson, June 12, 1965; children—Hubert Allen, Louise Becker, George Shaffer, Dennis Michael, Joel Patrick. Intern Vanderbilt U. Hosp., 1949-50, asst. resident internal medicine, 1952-53, asst. resident psychiatry, 1953-55, sr. resident, 1956, instr. psychiatry Sch. Medicine, 1956-57; practice medicine specializing in psychiatry, Nashville, 1957, Alexandria, Va., 1957—; mem. staff Alexandria Hosp.; psychiatrist Alexandria Mental Hygiene Clinic, 1957-62. Served with USNR, 1943-45, to capt., M.C., AUS, 1951-62. Fellow Am., So. psychiat. assns.; mem. Eastern Psychoanalytic Assn. (sec. 1973—), Washington Psychiat. Soc. (vice chmn. chpt. 1974—, exec. council chpt. 1968-70), Am. Soc. Physician Analysts (pres. 1979), Va. Assn. Professions (chmn. No. Va. region 1974-75, dir. 1975-76), Am. Orthopsychiat. Assn., Soc. for Gen. Systems Research, Blue Key, Alpha Tau Omega, Alpha Kappa Kappa. Presbyn. Club: Mansion House Yacht. Contbr. articles on psychiatry, neurology to profl. jours. Home: 9338 Old Mt Vernon Rd Alexandria VA 22309 Office: 1203 Quaker Ln Alexandria VA 22302

BLAKEY, REX HOWARD, assn. exec.; b. Tulsa, Mar. 19, 1929; s. Millard H. and Ruth A. B.; B.A., U. Tulsa, 1962, M.A., 1966; m. Ellen Sue Blakely; children—Patrick H., Kathleen D., Brian R., Darien R. Feature writer Tulsa World, 1958-61; sports editor Tulsa Tribune, 1961-62; dir. univ. relations U. Tulsa, 1968-79; communications dir. Am. Assn. Petroleum Geologists, Tulsa, 1979—. Served with USN, 1945-49. Mem. Assn. Petroleum Writers, Soc. Bus. Execs., Council for Advancement and Support of Edn. (past dist. officer), Public Relations Soc. Am., Internat. Bus. Communicators Am. Unitarian. Club: Tulsa Press. Home: 3531 S Yorktown St Tulsa OK 74105 Office: 1444 S Boulder St Tulsa OK 74101

BLAN, OLLIE LIONEL, JR., lawyer; b. Ft. Smith, Ark., May 22, 1931; s. Ollie Lionel and Eva Ocie (Cross) B.; A.A., Ft. Smith Jr. Coll., 1951; LL.B., U. Ark., 1954; m. Allen Conner Gillon, Aug. 19, 1960; children—Bradford Lionel, Elizabeth Ann, Cynthia Gillon. Admitted to Ark. bar, 1954, Ala. bar, 1959; research analyst Ark. Legis. Council, 1954-55; law clk. U.S. Dist. Judge No. Dist. Ala., 1959-60; asso. firm Spain, Gillon, Riley, Tate & Etheredge, Birmingham, Ala., 1960—, partner, 1965—. Tchr., Am. Inst. Banking, 1965-68. Treas., Jefferson County Hist. Commn., 1972—. Mem. Jefferson County Republican Exec. Com., 1973-76. Bd. dirs., sec. World Wide Jewish Missions. Served with USMCR, 1955-58. Mem. Am., Ark., Ala. (com. on admissions and legal edn. 1971-74, com. on jud. office 1972-76), Birmingham bar assns., Ala. Def. Lawyers Assn., Am. Life Ins. Assn. Republican. Baptist. Clubs: Birmingham Tip Off (charter), Relay House. Contbr. articles to legal jours. Home: 2100 22d Ave S Birmingham AL 35223 Office: 1700 John A Hand Bldg Birmingham AL 35203

BLANCHARD, CHARLES FULLER, lawyer; b. Hamlet, N.C., Oct. 3, 1923; s. Lawrence Eley and Anna Neal (Fuller) B.; A.B., Duke U., 1946, J.D., 1949; m. Bernard Manning Berkeley, Feb. 16, 1952; children—Lelia B., Anna Neal. Admitted to N.C. bar; individual practice law, Raleigh, N.C., 1950-52, 60-62; sr. partner firm Blanchard & Jordan, Raleigh, 1952-56, Blanchard & Farmer, Raleigh, 1958-60; partner firm Yarborough, Blanchard, Tucker & Denson, Raleigh, 1962-74; sr. partner firm Blanchard, Tucker, Twiggs & Denson, Raleigh, 1975—. Trustee St. Augustine's Coll., Raleigh, 1962-70; sr. warden St. Michael's Episcopal Ch., 1962-63; pres. Episc. Laymen of N.C., 1965-66; bd. dirs. Raleigh United Fund, 1970-74; pres. Kiwanis Found., Raleigh, 1972-73; mem. Duke U. Law Sch. Council, 1970-72. Served as lt. (j.g.) USNR, 1943-46. Nat. Endowment for Humanities fellow, 1977. Fellow Internat. Acad. Trial Lawyers; mem. Am., N.C., Wake County (pres. 1977) bar assns., N.C. State Bar (councilor 1980—), Assn. Trial Lawyers Am. (gov. 1966-69, 70-73), N.C. Acad. Trial Lawyers (pres. 1969-71), Phi Delta Phi. Democrat. Clubs: Kiwanis, Sphinx (Raleigh); Carolina Country. Home: 3343 Alamance Dr Raleigh NC 27609 Office: PO Drawer 30 Raleigh NC 27602

BLANCHARD, DANNY EDWARD, psychologist; b. San Francisco, Apr. 11, 1949; s. Shirley O. and Louise T. Blanchard; B.A., Oakwood Coll., Huntsville, Ala., 1970; M.A., Loma Linda (Calif.) U., 1973; Ed.S., George Peabody Coll., Nashville, 1976, Ed.D., 1979; m. Deborah Hamilton, Aug. 5, 1973; 1 dau., Cashanice Louise. Instr., Loma Linda U., 1973; psychologist Riverside County Probation Dept., Riverside, Calif., 1974; mem. faculty Oakwood Coll., 1974—, asst. prof. psychology, 1979—; cons. U.S. Army Cons. Personnel Dept.; mem. Ala. Human Relations Commn., 1978. Recipient Civilian Letter Commendation, U.S. Army, 1979. Mem. Adventist Psychol. Assn. (sec. 1978-81, Am. Psychol. Assn., Am. Personnel and Guidance Assn., Omega Sigma. Democrat. Seventh-day Adventist. Author articles in field. Home: 1107 Rockcliff Dr Huntsville AL 35804 Office: Oakwood Coll Huntsville AL 35801

BLANCHARD, GEORGIA ANN, utility exec.; b. Schulenburg, Tex., Apr. 15, 1949; d. Louis James and Stella Ann (Hrcek) Haba; student Houston Community Coll., 1973; m. Allen Ray Blanchard, Nov. 15, 1975. With Transcontinental Gas Pipe Line Corp., Houston, 1967—, contract adminstr., 1975-77, supr. contract adminstrn., 1977—. Named Outstanding Woman, YWCA, 1977. Cert. profl. sec. Mem. Nat. Secs. Assn. (asst. treas. 1980-81), Natural Gas Men Houston, Glencluster Community Assn. Roman Catholic. Club: Transco (Houston). Home: 10648 Bexley St Houston TX 77099 Office: 2700 S Post Oak St Houston TX 77056

BLAND, KIRBY ISAAC, surgeon; b. Dothan, Ala., Feb. 6, 1942; s. Howard Wilbur and Hazel (Gibbons) B.; B.S., Auburn U., 1964; M.D., U. Ala., 1968; m. Marilyn Alice Morton, July 16, 1966; children—Jonathan Boyette, Troy Howard, Jennifer Lynn. Intern, U. Fla., Gainesville, 1968-69, resident, 1969-70, resident in gen. surgery, 1972-76; fellow, clin. asso. surgery M.D. Anderson Hosp. and Tumor Inst., U. Tex., Houston, 1976-77; instr. surgery U. Louisville, 1977, asst. prof., 1978—, asso. in oncology, 1978—, chmn. breast cancer task force Sch. Medicine, 1978. Served with M.C., U.S. Army, 1970-72. Am. Cancer Soc. clin. fellow, 1974-75, 78—; diplomate Am. Bd. Surgery. Fellow Am. Coll. Emergency Physicians; mem. Ky. Med. Assn., Jefferson County Med. Soc., Ky. Cancer Commn., Assn. Acad. Surgery, Soc. Surg. Oncology, AMA, Southeastern Surg. Congress, Am. Assn. Cancer Edn., Louisville Surg. Soc., Ky. Surg. Soc., Southeastern Cancer Study Group, Alpha Epsilon Delta. Methodist. Contbr. articles in field to profl. jours. Home: 4019 Norbourne Blvd Louisville KY 40207 Office: Department of Surgery University of Louisville PO Box 35260 Louisville KY 40232

BLANFORD, IRVING IVEY, banker; b. Portsmouth, Va., Jan. 8, 1899; s. George Thomas and Claude Meredith (Sessoms) B.; student Va. Mil. Inst., 1918; m. Gladys Simmons Johnson, Sept. 7, 1935 (dec. 1966); children—Virginia Caroline Blanford Nicewander, Gladys Sessoms Blanford Godwin, Claudia Maria Blanford Hubbard. Radio operator Panama R.R., 1920; sec. Comml. Hardware Co., Norfolk, Va., 1922-25; salesman Chas. Syer & Co., Norfolk, 1926-28; food broker, New Bern, N.C., 1928-29; mfrs. rep. Nat. Sugar Refining Co., N.J., N.Y.C., 1930-41; exec. dir. pub. housing City of New Bern, 1945-69; chmn. exec. com. Bank of New Bern, 1959-63, pres., 1962-72, dir., 1957-72; dir. New Bern Morris Plan Co., 1943-57; chmn. local bd. N.C. Nat. Bank, New Bern, 1972—. Clubs: Elks (exalted ruler 1938), Masons, Shriners, Rotary (pres. 1928-29), Eastern Carolina Yacht (treas. 1956-57), Dunes. Home: 1604 Tryon Rd New Bern NC 28560 Office: 2119 Neuse Blvd New Bern NC 28560

BLANK, HORACE RICHARD, ret. educator; b. Phila., Aug. 8, 1898; s. David Jacob and Louisa Catherine (Rebholz) B.; B.S. in Chemistry, U. Pa., 1919, Ph.D., 1924; postgrad. U. Mich., 1925, Columbia, 1926-28; m. Marjorie Josephine Ferguson, Jan. 21, 1927; children—Emily Blank Bonwich, Horace Richard, Nancy Allen Kaesler. Instr. chemistry U. Pa., Phila., 1919-26; instr. mineralogy Columbia, 1926-29; asst. geologist Bd. Water Supply, N.Y.C., 1929-33; asst. geologist U.S. Geol. Survey, Jamaica, N.Y., 1934-35; asso. geologist U.S. Soil Conservation Service, Washington, also Waco, Tex., 1935-43; asso. prof. geology Southwestern U., Georgetown, Tex., 1943-49; prof. geology Tex. A. and M. U., College Station, 1949-66, prof. emeritus, 1966—. Research geologist Tex. Transp. Inst., 1966-68; cons. in field Brazos River Authority, also various comml. groups. Mem. charter commn. City of Bryan (Tex.), 1971. Bd. govs. Bryan Day Care Center, 1969-75, treas., 1970-72, 74-75. Served with Student Tng. Corps, AUS, 1918. Fellow Geol. Soc. Am., Mineral. Soc. Am., Tex. Acad. Sci. (v.p. earth scis. 1951, 58); mem. Am. Assn. Petroleum Geologists, Am. Geophys. Union. Methodist. Contbr. articles to profl. jours. Home: 719 Meadow Ln Bryan TX 77801 Office: Dept Geology Texas A and M Univ College Station TX 77843

BLANK, RALPH JOHN, JR., banker, lawyer; b. Lake City, Fla., Apr. 2, 1922; s. Ralph John and Stella Pauline (Kleinbeck) B.; B.S., B.A., U. Fla., 1942, J.D., 1948; m. Merry Lake, May 17, 1952; children—Pamela Hellin, Lisa Pauline, Michelle Susan. Admitted to Fla. bar, 1948; asso. mem. firm Moorehead, Pallot, Smith, Green & Phillips, Miami, 1948-49; home office counsel Am. Fire & Casualty Co., Orlando, Fla., 1950-51; individual practice law, West Palm Beach, Fla., 1952-72; sr. partner firm Blank, Williams & Benn, West Palm Beach, 1972—; chmn. bd. Citizens Bank Palm Beach County, West Palm Beach, 1962-80. Mem. Fla. Ho. of Reps., 1956-60, Fla. Senate, 1960-64; mem. Civil Service Bd. West Palm Beach, 1965-74. Bd. dirs. Fla. Atlantic U. Endowment Corp., Boca Raton, 1960—. Served with Arty., AUS, 1942-45; ETO; CIC, 1951-52; lt. col. Res. ret. Decorated Air medal with 5 oak leaf clusters. Presbyn. Home: 122 Forest Hill Blvd West Palm Beach FL 33405 Office: 1016 Clearwater Pl PO Box 2100 West Palm Beach FL 33402

BLANKENBAKER, RONALD GAIL, physician; b. Rensselaer, Ind., Dec. 1, 1941; s. Lloyd L. and Lovina (Anderson) B.; B.S. in Biology, Purdue U., 1963; M.D., Ind. U., 1968, M.S. in Pharmacology, 1970. Intern, Meth. Hosp. Grad. Med. Center, Indpls., 1968-69, resident in family practice, 1969-71; med. dir. Indpls. Home for Aged, 1971-77, Am. Mid-Town Nursing Center, Indpls., 1974-77; asst. prof. family practice Ind. U., Indpls., 1973-77, Home Assos., Tampa, Fla., 1977—; dir. family practice edn. Meth. Hosp. Grad. Med. Center, 1971-77; family practice editor Reference and Index Services, Inc., Indpls., 1976-77, sr. editor, 1977—; chmn., prof. dept. family medicine U. South Fla. Coll. Medicine, Tampa, 1977—; legis. lobbyist Ind. Acad. Family Physicians, 1973-77; med. advisor New Hope Found. of Am.,

Inc., 1974—. Bd. dirs. Meals on Wheels, Inc., Peoples Health Center Indpls., Marion County Cancer Soc. Served to maj. USAFR, 1971. Recipient Service to Mankind award Sertoma Club, 1976, Outstanding Alumnus award Mt. Ayr (Ind.) High Sch., 1976; diplomate Am. Bd. Family Practice. Fellow Am. Acad. Family Physicians, Soc. Prospective Medicine (pres. 1978—, dir.); mem. AMA, Ind. Acad. Family Physicians (v.p. 1977), Fla. Acad. Family Physicians (dir.), Ind. Allied Health Assn. (pres. 1973-74), Soc. Tchrs. Family Medicine, Ind. Arthritis Found. (dir.), Ind. Lung Assn. (dir.), Assn. Am. Med. Colls., Assn. Depts. Family Medicine. Republican. Home: 3104 Wesson Way Tampa FL 33618 Office: 12901 N 30 St Tampa FL 33612

BLANKENSHIP, DIANNA CHAMBERS, dietitian; b. San Antonio, Sept. 1, 1942; d. Norris R. and Ella M. (Sudderth) Chambers; B.S., Tex. Christian U., 1975; M.S., Tex. Womans U., 1977, postgrad., 1978—; m. William David Blankenship, Feb. 27, 1960; children—Sharenna Lynn, Lisa Dianna. Sec. legal firm Cantey, Hanger, Gooch, Cravens and Munn, Ft. Worth, 1964-69, McBryde, Bogle and Green, Ft. Worth, 1969-73; free lance exec. sec., 1971-74; teaching and research asst. Tex. Woman's U., Denton, 1976-77; clin. dietitian St. Joseph Hosp., Ft. Worth, 1977-78; clin. instr. coordinated undergrad. program in dietetics Tex. Woman's U., Denton, 1978—; cons. dietetian to various nursing homes, 1979—; guest lectr. various seminars and workshops in clin. dietetics, 1977—. Allsup Grad. fellow, 1978-79; State of Tex. doctoral fellow, 1978; cert. profl. sec., registered dietitian, Tex. Mem. Am. Dietetic Assn., Am. Home Econs. Assn., Tex. Home Econs. Assn., Tex. Ft. Worth Dietetic Assn., Soc. for Nutrition Edn., Nutrition Today Soc., Sigma Xi, Phi Theta Kappa, Phi Upsilon Omicron, Phi Delta Gamma. Baptist. Club: Order Eastern Star. Author: Nutritious Snacks for Children, 1977; Quantity Cooking Made Easy, 1978. Home: 1120 Irwin Dr Hurst TX 76053 Office: Dept Nutrition and Food Sciences Texas Woman's Univ TWU Campus Denton TX 76204

BLANKENSHIP, IRA, athletic dir.; b. Slab Fork, W.Va., Dec. 13, 1927; s. Noah and Pearl (Klug) B.; B.S. in Edn., Concord Coll., Athens, W.Va., 1952; M.A., W.Va. U., 1958; m. Duffie June Beane, Aug. 17, 1950; children—Dana Kee, Ira Neal. Tchr. high schs. in N.C., Va., 1952-58; football and basketball coach Davis and Elkins (W.Va.) Coll., 1958-62; coach basketball, golf, bowling, asst. coach football Concord Coll., 1962-79, athletic dir., 1973—; sports chmn. Partners for Am., 1972-79. Mem. town council, Athens, 1973-75. Served with USNR, 1946-48. Mem. Nat. Assn. Intercollegiate Athletics (nat. bowling chmn. 1972-74), W.Va. Intercolliagiate Athletic Conf. (sports chmn. for golf, tennis and basketball 1970-72), NEA, AAHPER. Republican. Author papers in field. Home: PO Box 607 State St Athens WV 24712 Office: Concord Coll Athens WV 24712

BLANKENSHIP, MAYME LEE, electron microscopist; b. Nashville, June 26, 1944; d. Ira Milton and Betty Christine (Hofstetter) B.; B.S., George Peabody Coll. for Tchrs., 1967; m. George Thomas Wood, May 6, 1978. Research technician George Peabody Coll., Nashville, 1966-72; research technician sr. Duke U., Zoology Dept., Durham, N.C., 1972-75; forensic chemist U.S. Army Criminal Investigation Lab., Ft. Gordon, Ga., 1975; research instr. Dept. Microbiology, Vanderbilt U. Med. Center, Nashville, 1976—. Mem. Sigma Xi. Presbyterian. Asso. editor Jour. of Tenn. Acad. Sci., 1969-72; contbr. articles in field to profl. jours. Home: 5012 Granny White Pike Nashville TN 37220 Office: Dept of Microbiology Vanderbilt Med Center Nashville TN 37232

BLANKENSHIP, SAMUEL MAX, physicist; b. Pulaski, Va., Aug. 3, 1943; s. William McKinley and Frances Adeline (Smythers) B.; B.S., U. S.C., 1965, Ph.D., 1975; postgrad. Case Inst. Tech., 1965-66; m. Arvila Anne Corwin, May 30, 1964 (div. Aug. 1973); 1 dau., Corwynn Alison; m. 2d, Brenda Dale Allen, Mar. 15, 1980. Instr., U. S.C., Columbia, 1971-75; research asso. U. Calif., Irvine, 1975-76; research scientist Ga. Inst. Tech., Atlanta, 1976-79, sr. research scientist, 1979—; cons. in field. Served with USAF, 1967-71. Mem. Am. Phys. Soc., AAAS, Phi Beta Kappa, Sigma Xi (pres. Kirtland chpt. Albuquerque 1969). Methodist. Author: A Backpacking Guide to the Southern Mountains, 1974, rev. edit., 1975; contbr. articles to profl. jours., also articles and poetry to popular mags. Office: Engring Experiment Sta Ga Inst Tech Atlanta GA 30332

BLANKS, DON HEWITT, oil pipeline engr.; b. Fairmont, W.Va., Oct. 13, 1920; s. Don Hewitt and Christine Blanks; student Union Coll., Schenectady, 1945. Field engr. Ingersoll Rand Co., 1946-48; automobile dealer, 1948-58; self-employed in vending sales, 1959-74; field engr. in oil field and pipeline constrn., 1974—; now with Sandbluff Gathering System and The Sterling Co. Home: Box 337 Sterling City TX 76951 Office: 600 Blanks Bldg Midland TX 79701

BLANNING, ROBERT BRESSLER, elec. engr.; b. Williamstown, Pa., Jan. 7, 1920; s. Charles Franklin and Carol Merle (Bressler) B.; B.S., Pa. State U., 1941; m. Estelle Marcelle Adams, Jan. 12, 1946; children—Kenneth, Virginia, Lisa, Linda. Engr., Gen. Electric Co., Schenectady, 1946-54; supervisory engr. Ordnance Dept., U.S. Army, WSPG, N.Mex., 1954-56; tech. specialist TEMCO, Dallas, 1956-61; prin. engr. Martin Marietta Corp., Orlando, Fla., 1961—. Served to capt. C.E., AUS, 1941-46. Registered profl. engr., N.Y., Fla. Asso. fellow Am. Inst. Aeros. and Astronautics; sr. mem. IEEE. Home: 5120 Dorian Ave Orlando FL 32812 Office: Sand Lake Rd Orlando FL 32805

BLANTON, FRED, JR., lawyer; b. Muscle Shoals, Ala., July 2, 1919; s. Fred and Mary (Covington) B.; A.B., Birmingham-So. Coll., 1939; J.D., U. Va., 1942; postgrad. U. Ala., summer 1946; postgrad. U. Mich., 1951; LL.M. in Taxation, U. Ala., 1979; m. Mercer Potts McAvoy, Aug. 11, 1962. Admitted to Ala. bar, 1946; pvt. practice law, Birmingham, Ala., 1946-48; prof. Dickinson Sch. Law, Carlisle, Pa., 1948-49; vis. prof. law U. Ala., Tuscaloosa, summer 1949; asst. prof. law U. Va., Charlottesville, 1949-51; asso. firm Martin & Blakey, Attys., Birmingham, 1951-54; pvt. practice law, Birmingham, 1954—. Served with USNR, 1942-46. Mem. Ala. Bar Assn. Republican. Episcopalian. Contbr. articles in field to profl. jours. Home: 1912 K C Dement Ave Fultondale AL 35068 Office: 3716 Fifth Ave S Birmingham AL 35222

BLANTON, HERBERT MILTON, real estate broker; b. Clearwater, Fla., Feb. 5, 1923; s. Herbert Milton and Bessie Carrie (Constantine) B.; student Emory U., 1941-42; m. Edwina L. Creech, July 7, 1946; children—Jane Blanton Deal, Carolyn Blanton Lawrence, James M. Minor partner Blanton Realty Co., Clearwater, 1946-50, sales mgr., 1950-56, sole owner, 1956—; dir. First Nat. Bank Clearwater. Chmn., Housing Bd. Adjustments, 1967-73; past chmn. Heart Fund drive, sustaining membership drive local Boy Scouts Am.; mem. adv. bd. Salvation Army; trustee Morton F. Plant Hosp., 1974-79, sec. bd., 1974-75. Served with C.E., AUS, 1943-46; ETO. Decorated Bronze Star medal; named Realtor of Year, Clearwater-Largo-Dunedin Bd. Realtors, 1966, Fla. Assn. Realtors, 1968; named Mr. Clearwater, 1977; recipient citation for pub. service City of Clearwater, 1970; cert. real estate appraiser. Mem. Clearwater-Largo-Dundein Bd. Realtors (pres. 1965), Nat. (dir. 1975-80), Fla. (treas. 1969, v.p. 1974, pres. Diamond Pin Club 1977) assns. realtors, Greater Clearwater C. of C. (v.p. 1968-69), Nat. Assn. Ind. Fee Appraisers (pres. Tampa Bay chpt. 1977). Methodist (treas. 1958-62, trustee 1966-71, 73-75, 77-80, chmn. adminstrv. bd. 1967-69). Club: Kiwanis (pres. Springtime City club 1969). Home: 738 Harbor Island Clearwater FL 33515 Office: 814 Chestnut St Clearwater FL 33516

BLANTON, HOOVER CLARENCE, lawyer; b. Green Sea, S.C., Oct. 13, 1925; s. Clarence Leo and Margaret (Hoover) S.; J.D., U. S.C., 1953; m. Cecilia Lopez, July 31, 1949; children—Lawson Hoover, Michael Lopez. Admitted to S.C. bar, 1953; since practiced in Columbia; mem. firm Whaley & McCutchen, 1953-66, Whaley, McCutchen, Blanton & Richardson, 1967-72, Whaley, McCutchen, Blanton & Dent, 1973-74, Whaley, McCutchen & Blanton, 1974—; bd. dirs. Legal Aid Service Agy., Columbia, chmn., 1972-73. Gen. counsel S.C. Republican Party, 1963-66; pres. Richland County Rep. Conv., 1962; del. Rep. State Convs., 1962, 64, 66, 68, 70, 74. Bd. dirs. Midlands Community Action Agy., Columbia, vice chmn., 1972-73; mem. Gov.'s Legal Services Adv. Council, 1976-77, Commn. on Continuing Legal Edn. for Judiciary, 1977—. Served with USNR, 1942-46, 50-52. Mem. S.C. Bar (mem. ho. of dels. 1975-76, chmn. fee disputes bd. 1977—), Am., Richland County (pres. 1980—) bar assns., S.C. Def. Trial Attys. Assn., Def. Research Inst., Assn. Ins. Attys. (state chmn. 1971-77, 80—, exec. council 1977-80), Phi Delta Phi. Baptist. Club: Toastmasters (pres. 1959). Home: 3655 Deerfield Dr Columbia SC 29204 Office: 1414 Lady St Columbia SC 29201

BLANTON, JEAN ANN SAIGE (MRS. STEWART BENNETT BLANTON), banker; b. Highland Springs, Va., Feb. 12, 1929; d. Walter Clair and Theresa (Coughlan) Saige; grad. high sch.; m. John Ruben Harrison, Jr., Aug. 3, 1947; children—Pamela Gayle, Michael Saige, m. 2d Stewart Bennett Blanton, Nov. 27, 1976. Accounting clk. Western Electric Co., Winston-Salem, N.C., 1947-49; accounting clk. Wachovia Bank & Trust Co., Winston-Salem, 1950-55, payroll clk., 1955-66, asst. sec., mgr., payroll, 1966-67, asst. v.p., 1967-69, v.p., 1969—. Active various community drives; treas. PTA; mem. Mayor's Com. Status Women. Mem. Nat. Assn. Bank Women (vice chmn. N.C. group 1969, chmn. 1970-71, mem. nat. editorial com. 1972, chmn. edn. com. S.E. region 1972-73), N.C. Bankers Assn. (v.p., women's dir. 1974-76, pres. 1976-77; county chmn. literacy project 1978-80), Altrusa (treas. 1974-77), Toastmasters Club. Am. Inst. Banking, Cath. Daus. Am. (N.C. state monitor 1960-66). Home: Box 662 Bermuda Run Advance NC 27006 Office: Wachovia Bldg Winston-Salem NC 27102

BLANTON, MILLY ALENA, hosp. central service dir.; b. Monroe, N.C., July 12, 1924; d. William Rowan and Effie Loutisha (Helms) Whitley; student Polk Community Coll., Winter Haven, Fla., 1964-68; m. Frank Stuart Blanton, Oct. 12, 1945; children—Kaye, Stuart. Supr. central service Winter Haven (Fla.) Hosp., 1955-71; asst. dir. materials mgmt. Richland Meml. Hosp., Columbia, S.C., 1971-72; dir. materials mgmt. Imperial Point Hosp., Ft. Lauderdale, Fla., 1972-74; dir. supply process and distbn. Indian River Meml. Hosp., Vero Beach, Fla., 1975-76; dir. materials mgmt. Brownsville (Tex.) Med. Center, 1976-77; supr. central service Naples (Fla.) Community Hosp., 1977; dir. central service Ochsner Found. Hosp., New Orleans, 1977—; cons. Medenco, Inc., 1976-77; dir. materials mgmt. Brownsville Med. Center. Recipient cert. of recognition Am. Hosp. Assn. Central Service Personnel. Mem. Am. Hosp. Assn. Central Service Personnel (dir. 1973, 74, 76, pres. 1978, del. conf. 1978; charter), Assn. Sterile Supply Adminstrs. (Eng.), Assn. Practitioners in Infection Control. Club: Eastern Star. Home: 117 Mark Twain Dr Apt 8 River Ridge LA 70123 Office: 1516 Jefferson Hwy New Orleans LA 70121

BLANTON, TERRELL DAVIS, otolaryngologist; b. Memphis, Apr. 18, 1938; s. George Terrell and Winona (Davis) B.; B.S., Milsaps Coll., 1959; M.D., U. Miss., 1962; m. Barbara Lene Yarbrough, Feb. 16, 1957; children—Douglas Terrell, Donna Michelle, Dianne Leigh. Commd. ensign USN, 1961, advanced through grade to comdr., 1974; intern U.S. Naval Hosp., Portsmouth, Va., 1962-63; resident in otolaryngology Nat. Naval Med. Center, Bethesda, Md., 1966-70; gen. med. officer, San Juan, P.R., 1963-66; chief ophthalmology and otolaryngology U.S. Naval Hosp., Camp Lejeune, N.C., 1970-73; resigned, 1974; practice medicine specializing in otolaryngology, Jackson, Miss., 1974—; faculty, cons. Sch. Medicine, U. Miss., 1974—. Diplomate Am. Bd. Otolaryngology. Fellow A.C.S., Am. Acad. Ophthalmology and Otolaryngology; mem. Soc. Mil. Otolaryngologists, AMA, Miss. Med. Assn., Miss.-La. Ophthal.-Otolaryngol. Assn. Home: 205 Hand Dr Brandon MS 39042 Office: 7 Lakeland Circle Jackson MS 39216

BLANTON, WYNDHAM BOLLING, JR., physician, farmer; b. Richmond, Va., Dec. 21, 1918; s. Wyndham Bolling and Natalie Friend (McFaden) B.; B.A. in Econs., U. Richmond, 1943; M.D., Med. Coll. Va., 1950, M.S. in Physiology, 1959; m. Lucy Jane Bowman, July 3, 1940; children—Wyndham Bolling, Jane Bowman. Traffic mgr. C & P Telephone Co., Richmond, 1940-44; intern Med. Coll. Va., 1950-51, resident, 1951-52; practice medicine specializing in internal medicine and allergy, Richmond, 1952—; mem. staff Stuart Circle Hosp., 1952—, chief of staff, 1969; v.p. med. affairs Charter Med. Corp., Macon, Ga., 1973—; asst. dean of medicine Med. Coll. Va., 1952-60, clin. prof., 1974—; owner, operator Cumva Farms, Farmville, Va., 1960—. Elder Presbyterian Ch.; bd. visitors Va. Commonwealth U., 1969—, rector bd. visitors, 1973—, exec. com. Atlantic Rural Expn. and Va. State Fair, Richmond, 1965—, v.p., 1970—; trustee Med. Coll. Va. Found., Richmond, 1973—, Richmond Profl. Inst. Found., Richmond, 1974—; mem. Nat. Profl. Standards Rev. Council, 1976-79; bd. dirs. Va. Council on Health and Med. Care, Va. Agribus. Council. Served to lt. (j.g.) USNR, 1945; PTO. Recipient award for greatest contbn. to dairy industry Va. Poly. Inst. Dairy Club, 1969. Mem. Va. (pres. 1976), Richmond, Am. socs. internal medicine, Richmond Acad. Medicine, AMA, So. Med. Assn., Am. Acad. Allergy, Va. Allergy Soc., Am. Coll. Chest Physicians, A.C.P., Am. Thoracic Soc., Med. Soc. Va., Med. Coll. Va. Alumni Assn. (trustee 1960-68), Royal Soc. Medicine, Am. Hosp. Assn. (council on patient services), Va. Hosp. Assn. (dir.), Fedn. Am. Hosps. (dir. 1975—), Assn. Am. Med. Colls., Am. Group Practice Assn., Va. Assn. Professions, Va. Hist. Soc., Soc. Colonial Wars, Soc. of Cincinnati, S.R., Richmond, Va. State chambers commerce, Alpha Omega Alpha, Sigma Zeta, Alpha Sigma Chi, Alpha Mu Omicron, Delta Kappa Epsilon. Presbyterian. Clubs: Commonwealth, Bull & Bear, Country of Va., Farmington Country. Contbr. articles to profl. publs. Home: 1 Roslyn Rd Richmond VA 23226 Office: 1526 West Ave Richmond VA 23220

BLASINGAME, EARL BENARD, glass co. exec.; b. Selmer, Tenn., Dec. 9, 1943; s. Leon Benard and Kathleen Mavoureen B.; B.S., Memphis State U., 1965; m. Lois Margaret Gooch, Jan. 24, 1971. Dist. mgr. sales Blue Cross & Blue Shield, Memphis, 1966-68; founder, pres. Aqua Glass Corp., Adamsville, Tenn., 1969—; pres., dir. Tombigbee Aviation, Inc., Pro-Con, Inc. Exec. dir. Boy Scouts Am.; chmn. Adamsville Planning Commn.; chmn. McNairy Airport Authority. Named Tenn. Businessman of Year SBA, 1977. Mem. Soc. Plastic Engrs., Acrylic Sanitary Ware Mfrs. Com. Baptist. Clubs: Adamsville Recreation, Memphis Racquet, Am. Tennis. Home: 600 Magnolia St Adamsville TN 38310 Office: PO Box 308 Adamsville TN 38310

BLASINGHAM, MARY CYNTHIA, physiologist; b. Indpls., Aug. 27, 1948; d. Harry Richard and Mary Ellen (Voyles) B.; B.A., Duke U., 1970; M.S. Ind. U., 1972; Ph.D., 1976. Research asso. in pharmacology U. Tenn. Center for Health Scis., Memphis, 1976—. Ind. U. fellow, 1971; NDEA fellow, 1971-72; NSF fellow, 1972-74; Kidney Found. W. Tenn. research fellow, 1978-79. Mem. English Speaking Union, Mensa, Am. Phsyiol. Soc., AAAS, Sigma Xi. Presbyterian. Clubs: Jr. League, Racquet of Memphis. Contbr. articles to profl. jours. Home: 5847 Park Ave Memphis TN 38138 Office: Dept Pharmacology Center Health Scis U Tenn Memphis TN 38163

BLASIUS, JACK MICHAEL, aluminum co. exec.; b. Atlanta, Feb. 29, 1932; s. Arthur George and Jessie Lee (Pate) B.; B.S. Indsl. Mgmt. and Accounting, U. Ala., 1954, M.B.A. in Mktg., 1957; m. Sybil Claire Watkins, Oct. 12 1957; children—Michael Stribling, Kimberly Anne. Successively indsl. salesman, area sales mgr., nat. mgr. foundry ingot products Kaiser Aluminum Corp.; pres., gen. mgr. Batchelder-Blasius, Inc., Spartanburg, S.C., 1966—, also dir.; dir. Charles Batchelder Co., Botsford, Conn., Statewide Waste Oil Chem. Corp., Evelyn Woods Reading Dynamics, Atlanta, 1st Nat. Bank, Spartanburg. Mem. Spartanburg City Council; exec. dir. Spartanburg YMCA; scholarship donor Clemson U.; bd. dirs. Spartanburg Girls' Home. Served with U.S. Army. Mem. Soc. Die Casting Engrs., Am. Foundryman Soc., Inst. Scrap Iron Steel, Aluminum Recycling Assn. (bd. dirs.), Spartanburg Devel. Assn., Spartanburg C. of C. (dir.), U. Ala. Alumni Assn. Republican. Presbyterian. Clubs: Spartanburg Country, Piedmont (Spartanburg); Atlanta Athletic, Ansley Golf (Atlanta); President's (Wofford Coll.); Founder's. Home: 1017 W O Ezell Blvd Spartanburg SC 29304 Office: Batchelder Blasius PO Box 5503 Spartanburg SC 29304

BLAYDES, DAVID FAIRCHILD, educator; b. Columbus, Ohio, Aug. 17, 1934; s. Glenn William and Bernice (Winstel) B.; B.S. cum laude, Ohio State U., 1956; M.S., U. Wis., 1957; Ph.D., Ind. U., 1962; m. Sophia Boyatzies, June 4, 1961; children—Stephanie Ann, Jeffrey Glenn. Postdoctoral work in plant physiology Mich. State U., 1962-65, NIH fellow, 1964-65; asst. prof. biology W.Va. U., Morgantown, 1965-69, asso. prof., 1969—. Fellow Ohio Acad. Sci.; mem. Bot. Soc. Am., Soc. Tissue Culture Assn., AAAS, N.Y. Acad. Scis., Am., Scandinavian, Japanese socs. plant physiology. Author: (with Frank Witham and Robert Devlin) Experiments in Plant Physiology, 1971. Contbr. numerous articles to profl. jours. Home: 652 Bellaire Dr Morgantown WV 26505

BLAYDES, JAMES ELLIOTT, JR., ophthalmologist; b. Bluefield, W.Va., Feb. 26, 1927; s. James Elliott and Mable (Hill) B.; A.B., Princeton U., 1950; M.D., U. Pa., 1954; postgrad. N.Y. U. Sch. Medicine, 1956; m. Anita G. Shrader, Sept. 25, 1976; children—James Elliott (dec.), William M., Stephen H., Elizabeth Boyd. Rotating intern Pa. Hosp., Phila., 1954-55; resident N.Y. Eye and Ear Infirmary, N.Y.C., 1955-58; practice medicine specializing in ophthalmology, Bluefield, 1958—; asso. prof. ophthalmology Marshall U. Sch. Medicine, 1977-78; mem. staff St. Luke's Hosp., 1978—, chief of ophthalmology, 1970—, chmn. bd. trustees, 1977; mem. staff Bluefield Community Hosp., Princeton (W.Va.) Community Hosp.; bd. dirs. Blaydes Found.; dir. First Nat. Bank Bluefield; cons. to industry, Norfolk and Western Ry., N.Am. Rockwell; speaker in field; mem. adv. bd. crippled children Dept. Welfare. Mem. Urban Renewal Commn., Bluefield, 1968-72; active Gt. Lakes to Fla Hwy. Assn.; mem. bd. deacons Westminister Presbyn. Ch., Bluefield, 1960-63, chmn., 1967-70, elder, 1970-73. Served with USN, 1945-46. Recipient certificate of appreciation Lions Club, 1966; Ethicon, Inc. grantee, 1967—. Diplomate Am. Bd. Ophthalmology. Fellow A.C.S.; mem. AMA, Mercer County (W.Va.) Med. Soc. (pres. 1967), W.Va. State, So. (asso. del 1960), Pan Am. med. assns., Am. Acad. Ophthalmology and Otolaryngology (adv. com. practitioners adv. faculty, award 1979), W.Va. Acad. Ophthalmology and Otolaryngology (sec.-treas. 1964-77), Pan Am. Assn. Ophthalmology, Am. Assn. Physicians and Surgeons (state del.), Soc. Eye Surgeons, Princeton U., U. Pa. and N.Y. Eye and Ear Infirmary alumni assns., Contact Lens Assn. of Ophthalmologists (indsl. safety com., dir.), Joint Commn. Allied Health Personnel in Ophthalmology, Bluefield C. of C., Bluefield Jr. C. of C. (dir.). Democrat. Clubs: Bluefield Country (v.p. 1972), Fincastle Country (dir.), Sedgewood Tennis, Triangle Gun, Mercer Anglers, Univ. Contbr. articles to profl. publs. Home: 2731 Marmount Dr Bluefield WV 24701 Office: Blaydes Clinic Frederick and Woodland Sts Bluefield WV 24701

BLAYDES, SOPHIA BOYATZIES, educator; b. Rochester, N.Y., Oct. 16, 1933; d. James George and Helene (Bougdanos) Boyatzies; B.A., U. Rochester, 1955; M.A., Ind. U., 1958, Ph.D., 1962; m. David Fairchild Blaydes, June 4, 1961; children—Stephanie Anne, Jeffrey Glenn. Instr. Am. thought and lang. Mich. State U., East Lansing, 1962-63, asst. prof., 1963-65; instr. English, W.Va. U., Morgantown, 1966-69, asst. prof., 1969-72, asso. prof., 1972-77, prof., 1977—. W.Va. U. Found. grantee, 1973-74. Mem. Am. Soc. 18th Century Studies, MLA, South Atlantic MLA, W.Va. Assn. Coll. English Tchrs. (pres. 1978), Renaissance and Shakespeare Soc. W.Va. (chmn. 1978). Author: Christopher Smart as a Poet of His Time (Distinguished Manuscript award Mich. State U. 1965), 1966; co-author: Sir William Davenant, 1981; editor: Selected Papers from the West Virginia Shakespeare and Renaissance Association, 1976; contbr. articles to profl. jours. Home: 652 Bellaire Dr Morgantown WV 26505 Office: 422 Stansbury Hall WVa U Morgantown WV 26506

BLAZER, DAN GERMAN, II, physician; b. Nashville, Feb. 23, 1944; s. Dan German and Mary Elizabeth (Owsley) B.; B.A., Vanderbilt U., 1965; postgrad. Harding Grad. Sch., 1966; M.D., U. Tenn., 1969; M.P.H. in Epidemiology, U. N.C., Chapel Hill, 1979; m. Sherrill Walls, Aug. 19, 1966; children—Dan German III, Natasha Leigh. Intern, City Memphis Hosps., 1970; med. dir. Christian Mobile Clinic, Kumba, United Republic Cameroon, 1971, 72; resident physician in psychiatry Duke U. Med. Center, Durham, N.C., 1973-75, teaching fellow dept. psychiatry, 1973-75, asst. prof. psychiatry, 1976-80, asso. prof., 1980—; fellow dept. psychiatry Montefiore Hosp. and Med. Center, Bronx, N.Y., 1975—; mem. staff Central State Psychiat. Hosp., Nashville, 1972—; asso. dir. programs Center for Study of Aging and Human Devel., 1976—. Bd. dirs. Concern, Inc., African Christian Hosps. Assn. Recipient Research Career Devel. award NIMH, 1977. Diplomate Am. Bd. Psychiatry and Neurology. Mem. Christian, So. med. socs., Am. Psychosomatic Soc., Gerontol. Soc., Geriatrics Soc., AAAS, Am., So. psychiat. assns., Alpha Phi Omega. Mem. Ch. of Christ (tchr. Bible sch. classes). Author: (with E.W. Busse) Handbook of Geriatric Psychiatry, 1979; Healing the Emotions, 1979; contbr. articles to sci. publs. Home: 408 Farmington Woods Dr Cary NC 27511 Office: Duke U Med Center Box 3003 Durham NC 27710

BLEDSOE, JOHN TRUETT, psychologist, educator; b. Arkadelphia, Ark., Oct. 10, 1908; s. John Dixon and Rosa Myrette (Terrell) B.; B.A., Henderson State Tchrs. Coll., 1934; M.S., U. Ark., 1940, postgrad., 1946-49; postgrad. George Peabody Coll., Nashville, 1953; m. Helen Gould Millen, Aug. 28, 1935; children—John Truett, Robert Terrell. Tchr., Sandyland High Sch., El Dorado, Ark., 1934-38; prin. Fairview High Sch., Camden, Ark., 1938-40; ednl. advisor Civilian Conservation Corps, Clarksville, Ark., 1940-43;

counseling psychologist VA, Little Rock, 1945—. Mem. evening faculty U. Ark., Little Rock, 1951-60. Served with USNR, 1943-45. Mem. Am., Ark. psychol. assns., Am. Legion, S.A.R. (chaplain 1973—), Ark., Va. geneal. socs., Nat. Hist. Soc., Early Am. Soc., Ark. Pioneers. Democrat. Baptist (deacon). Mason (Shriner), Rotarian, K.T. Author: The Bledsoe Family, 1973; The Bledsoe Family Supplement, 1976; A Family Story, 1979. Home: 7101 Hillwood Rd Little Rock AR 72207 Office: 700 W Capitol Ave Little Rock AR 72207

BLEDSOE, WILBERT EARL, assn. exec.; b. Falls County, Tex., Aug. 19, 1950; s. Wilbart and Daphinie (Shaw) B.; A.A., S. Plains Coll., 1970; B.A., W. Tex. State U., 1972; m. Barbara Ann Johnson, Oct. 15, 1968; children—Gregory Earl, Felicia Renee, Roderick Lynn. Program dir. N. Central YMCA, Amarillo, Tex., 1970-73, exec. dir., 1973-76; exec. dir. L.L. Melton Family YMCA, Beaumont, Tex., 1976—; grant panelist U.S. Office Edn., Washington, 1978-79. Lay minister United Meth. Ch.; v.p. bd. dirs. Carroll St. Nursery Inc. Cert. YMCA sr. dir. Mem. Nat. Soc. Fundraising Execs., Nat. Council YMCA's (dir.), Assn. Profl. Dirs. Home: 5290 Berard Circle Beaumont TX 77705 Office: 3455 Sarah St Beaumont TX 77705

BLEICH, ANNA LORETTA, nurse; b. Mineville, N.Y., Feb. 18, 1924; d. John Francis and Louise Marie (Fields) McKown; R.N., Champlain Balley Hosp., Plattsburg, N.Y., 1944; B.S. in Nursing, Northwestern State U., Shreveport, 1970; M.Ed., Northwestern State U., Natchitoches, La., 1971; M.S. in Nursing, U. Tex., 1973; m. LaMoyne Charles Bleich, May 6, 1946; children—Edward Joseph, John Francis, Anne Marie, Rebecca. Pvt. duty nurse, Washington, 1944; instr. Washington Vis. Nurse Soc., 1946-47; mem. nursing staff Park Ave. Hosp., Rochester, N.Y., 1947-48; vol. ARC, 1955-65; regional dir. continuing edn. in nursing Northwestern State U., 1971-72; instr. med.-surg. nursing Northeastern La. U., Monroe, 1972-73, asst. prof., then asso. prof., 1973-74; asso. prof. Northwestern State U., Shreveport, 1975-76; pvt. practice psychotherapy, Ruston, 1976—. Pres. Mental Health Assn. Lincoln Parish, 1978-79, chmn. edn. program, 1979—; bd. dirs. Ruston Emergency Pregnancy Service, Ruston Alcohol and Substance Abuse Clinic; past pres., disaster chmn. ARC, Lincoln Parish. Served to 1st lt. Army Nurse Corps, 1945-46. Mem. Am. Nurses Assn., Nat. League Nursing, Council Advanced Practitioners in Psychiat.-Mental Health Nursing, Am. Personnel and Guidance Assn., Am. Orthopsychiat. Assn., La. Nurses Assn., Nurses Coalition for Action in Politics, Ruston Dist. Nurses Assn., LWV, Ruston Bus. and Profl. Women, Phi Kappa Phi, Sigma Theta Tau. Republican. Roman Catholic. Home: 1004 D'Arbonne St Ruston LA 71270

BLEIMANN, KARL RICHARD, steel co. exec.; b. Siegen, W. Ger., Aug. 19, 1934; s. Friedrich and Irmgard (Kaufmann) B.; came to U.S., 1969; M.S. in Metall. Engring., U. Clausthal (W. Ger.), 1959; m. Rena J. Eggert, Aug. 21, 1964; children—Gregor, Joern, Tino. Asst. supt. meltshop Stahlwerke Bochum (W. Ger.), 1959-66; supt. meltshop Edelstahlwerke Witten (W. Ger.), 1967; supt. meltshop Georgetown Steel Corp. (S.C.), 1969-70, asst. v.p. engring., 1970-72, v.p. engring., 1972-74; v.p. engring. Korf Industries, Charlotte, N.C., 1974-78; exec. v.p. Korf Technologies, Inc., Charlotte, 1978-79; pres. Korf & Fuchs Systems, Inc., 1979—. Mem. Verein Deutscher Eisenhuettenleute, Am. Iron and Steel Engrs., Nat. Geog. Soc. Roman Catholic. Club: Raintree Country (Charlotte). Home: 8201 Eagles Point Matthews NC 28105 Office: 812 W Innes St Salisbury NC 28144

BLESSEY, WALTER JEROME, IV, investment co. exec.; b. Biloxi, Miss., Apr. 17, 1939; s. Walter James and Geraldine Ann (Fountain) B.; B.B.A. in Accounting, U. Miss., 1961, J.D., 1964; m. Mary Alice Wingo, Dec. 18, 1960 (div. Aug. 1968); children—Walter John V; m. 2d, Beverly Wartenbach Johnson, Sept. 29, 1968; stepchildren—Mitzi Lynn, Michael Louis. Instr. accounting U. Miss., 1962-64; admitted to Miss. bar, 1964; tax accountant Arthur Andersen & Co., Houston, 1966-69; controller, partner John E. Kilgore & Co., Houston, 1969—; v.p., dir. Indianola Co., Houston, 1971—; sec., treas., v.p., dir. Cambridge Royalty Co., Houston, 1970—; dir. Wicks-N-Sticks, Inc., Houston. Served to 1st lt., AUS, 1964-66. C.P.A., Tex. Mem. Am. Inst. C.P.A.'s, Am., Miss. bar assns., Tex. Soc. C.P.A.'s, Am. Legion, VFW, Delta Sigma Pi, Beta Alpha Psi, Phi Alpha Delta. Episcopalian (vestryman 1970-72, 77-79). Clubs: Plaza (Houston); Woodlands (Tex.). Home: 27222 Lana Ln Conroe TX 77302 Office: John E Kilgore & Co 1200 San Jacinto Bldg Houston TX 77002

BLESSING, JOHN EDD (JEDD), rehab. adminstr.; b. Amherst, Tex., Apr. 28, 1936; s. William Ray and Florice May (Garlington) B.; B.S., Tex. Tech. U., 1959, M.Ed., 1971; m. Shirley Gene Swart, May 25, 1958; children—William Eugene, Johnedda Elaine. Writer, editor, photographer various newspapers, Littlefield and Floydada, Tex., 1963-68; owner, editor Crosbyton (Tex.) Rev., 1966-68; tchr. Crosbyton Ind. Sch. Dist., 1968-69; dir. student life, dir. personnel, dir. staff tng., dir. rehab. services Lubbock (Tex.) State Sch., 1969-74; dir. personnel and staff devel. Fort Worth State Sch., 1974—; prof. Sch. Social Work, U. Tex., Arlington, 1975—; instr. Tarrant County Jr. Coll., Fort Worth, 1975—. Bd. dirs. Fort Worth Assn. Retarded Citizens, 1975-77. Served with AUS, 1955-57. Mem. Tex. Assn. Mental Deficiency, Am. Assn. Mental Deficiency, Fort Worth Assn. Retarded Citizens, Tex. Public Employees Assn. (pres. local chpt. 1970). Methodist. Home: 7320 Natalie Dr Fort Worth TX 76134 Office: 5000 Campus Dr Fort Worth TX 76119

BLESSINGTON, CLEMENT AUGUSTON, JR., chemist; b. Eagle Lake, Tex., Mar. 27, 1932; s. Clement Auguston and Florence (Smith) B.; B.A., Southwest Tex. State U., 1952, postgrad., 1956-57; m. Emmie Lou Nielsen, Dec. 31, 1959; 1 son, Kevin N. Tchr. chemistry Pub. Schs. Shiner (Tex.), 1952-54, Needville (Tex.), 1957-59; chemist Saybolt Lab., Houston, 1959-66; chemist Dresser Industries, Houston, 1966-71, project mgr. pollution control, 1971-74; supr. analytical sect. Halliburton Co., 1974-76; sr. devel. chemist Halliburton Co./IMCO Services, Houston, 1976-77; corp. mgr. research NCC, 1978; owner, pres. Blessington Research Labs., 1979—. Committeeman, scoutmaster Boy Scouts Am., 1958-77. Served with AUS, 1954-56. Fellow Am. Inst. Chemists; mem. Am. Chem. Soc., Soc. Applied Spectroscopy, Internat. Oceanographic Found., Instrument Soc. Am. AAAS. Republican. Lutheran. Contbr. articles to profl. jours. Patentee cleansing sytems for oil/water. Home: 9762 Woodwind Dr Houston TX 77025 Office: 7209 Stella Link Rd Houston TX 77025

BLEVINS, DALLAS RAY, educator; b. Muskogee, Okla., Dec. 22, 1938; s. Virgil James and Mary (Kessler) B.; B.E., U. Omaha, 1965; M.B.A., U. South Fla., 1967; D.B.A., Fla. State U., 1976. Instr. Fla. State U., part-time, 1969; asst. prof. Valdosta State Coll., 1970-74; mem. faculty U. Ala., Birmingham, 1976-79; asst. prof. fin. U. North Fla., 1979—. Bd. dirs. Health Systems Agy. N.E. Fla., 1980—. Served with USAF, 1958-69. Mem. Birmingham Regional Hosp. Council's Cost Containment Com., 1977-79. Contbr. articles to numerous publs. Home: 6663 Diane Rd Jacksonville FL 32211

BLEVINS, DAVID C., oil distbg. co. exec.; b. Oklahoma City, July 4, 1939; s. Ibera M. Blevins; B.S., U. Okla., 1962; m. Lynda Kay Bynum, July 29, 1961; children—David Todd, Timothy Bynum, Tricia Lynn, Laura Joy. Engr., Okla. Dept. Transp., Oklahoma City, 1963-73; tech. sales and other positions Exxon Co. U.S.A., rep. retail sales, region pres. Haywood Oil Co. Inc., Waynesville, N.C., 1973—, Gas 'N Groceries Convenience Stores, Waynesville, 1975—, Grandview Florists, Waynesville, 1978—; dir. Western Carolina Bank. Bd. dirs. Haywood County (N.C.) United Fund, Waynesville Little League, Tuscaloosa Activities. Mem. N.C. Oil Jobbers Assn., N.C. Convenience Store Assn., Nat. Convenience Store Assn., various trade assns. Mem. New Covenant Ch. Club: Appaloosa Horse. Home: PO Box 357 Waynesville NC 28786 Office: Haywood Oil Co Inc 2502 Asheville Rd Waynesville NC 28786

BLEVINS, EUGENE EDWARD, cons. co. exec.; b. Middletown, Ohio, Dec. 15, 1942; s. Thomas Edward and Mabel L. (Whisman) B.; B.S., Miami U., Oxford, Ohio, 1968; M.B.A., U. Dallas, 1976. Mem. sales staff Armco Steel Corp., Middletown, Ohio, 1961-68; new product planning mgr. Xerox Corp., Rochester, N.Y. and Dallas, 1968-78; pres. Blevins & Assos., Irving, Tex., 1978—. Mem. Internat. Word Processing Assn., Internat. Entrepreneurs Assn., Dallas Advt. League, Sigma Iota Epsilon. Contbr. articles to profl. jours. Office: 301 American Bank Bldg Irving TX 75062

BLEVINS, PHILLIP K., plastic surgeon; b. Parmleysville, Ky., Mar. 30, 1942; s. Guy Kimble and Marie (Guffey) B.; student Berea Coll., 1959-61; A.B., U. Ky., 1963, M.D., 1967; m. MaryJo McDaniel, July 2, 1977. Intern, Univ. Hosp., Lexington, Ky., 1967-68; resident in gen. surgery Harvard surg. service Boston City Hosp., 1968-75; resident in plastic surgery U. Miss., 1975-77; asst. prof. surgery U. Ky. A.B. Chandler Med. Center, Lexington, 1977—; mem. staff St. Joseph Hosp., Good Samaritan Hosp., VA Hosp., Shriner's Hosp., Univ. Hosp., dir. Peoples State Bank, Monticello, Ky. Served with M.C., USN, 1969-71. Decorated U.S. Navy Commendation medal with V; medal of honor 1st class (Republic of Vietnam); recipient cert. appreciation Vietnam Ministry of Health, 1970; diplomate Am. Bd. Surgery, Am. Bd. Plastic Surgery. Fellow Southeastern Surg. Soc.; mem. AMA, Fayette County Med. Soc., Ky. Med. Assn., Cleft Palate Assn., Ky. Soc. Plastic and Reconstructive Surgeons, Am. Burn Assn. Republican. Episcopalian. Club: Ky. Civil War Roundtable. Home: 1087 The Lane Lexington KY 40504 Office: 800 Rose St Univ Hosp Lexington KY 40536

BLEVINS, WILLIAM RUEL, coll. dean; b. Erwin, Tenn., Dec. 14, 1926; B.A., Johnson Bible Coll., Knoxville, Tenn., 1958; M.Div., Christian Theol. Sem., 1962; Ed.D., U. Tenn., 1967; m. Peggy Ann Meade, Mar. 29, 1947; children—Bonita Jane Blevins Pryor, Rhonda Susan Blevins Dunlap. Ordained to ministry Christian Ch., 1953; pastor chs. in Ky., Va., Tenn., Ind., 1953-62; prof. Bible edn. Johnson Bible Coll., 1963—, coach, 1965-68, athletic dir., 1965-79, adminstrv. asst. to pres., 1969-71, bus. mgr., 1972-74, acad. dean, 1974—. Served with USNR, 1944-46. Mem. Assn. Tchr. Educators, Johnson Bible Coll. Alumni Assn. (pres. 1961). Address: Johnson Bible Coll Kimberlin Heights Station Knoxville TN 37920

BLEWER, GLENDA GLORIA (MRS. ALTON GEORGE BLEWER), banker; b. Higgins, Tex.; Mar. 2, 1927; d. Lee Roy and Lillie Mae (Reimer) Goettsche; student Draughon's Bus. Coll., 1944-45, Tex. Tech U., 1952; m. Alton George Blewer, Apr. 7, 1946; 1 dau., Alison (Mrs. David Little King). Tchr. typing and machine practice Draughon's Bus. Coll., Lubbock, Tex., 1945; billing clerk Lubbock Sash and Door Co., 1946; bookkeeper First Nat. Bank, Lubbock, 1948-49, teller, 1950-55, asst. cashier, 1965-71, asst. v.p., 1972—. Vice pres. Lubbock P.T.A., 1957-58; electoral mem. YWCA, 1959—; life mem. Tex. Congress Parents and Tchrs., 1959—. Mem. Nat. Assn. Bank Women, Inc., Am. Inst. Banking (sec. 1965), Bank Adminstrn. Inst. Baptist. Home: 2308 53d St Lubbock TX 79412 Office: 1500 Broadway St Lubbock TX 79401

BLINCOE, GEORGE EARLY, JR., acct.; b. Charlottesville, Va., June 2, 1948; s. George Early and Charlotte Ettie (Cassell) B.; B.S., Va. Poly. Inst. and State U., 1971; m. Rita Jean Stanley, Sept. 12, 1970; children—Kelly Page, Drew Aaron. Asst. acct. Haskins & Sells, Richmond, Va., 1971-72, sr. asst. acct., 1972-74, sr. accountant, 1974-76, 77-78, mgr., 1978—. sr. acct. Armstrong & McMillan, 1976-77. C.P.A., Va. Mem. Chesterfield Jaycees (key man 1974-75, dir. 1975-76), Va. Soc. C.P.A.'s, Am. Inst. C.P.A.'s. Methodist. Home: 10015 Bayham Dr Richmond VA 23235 Office: 8th and Main Bldg 707 E Main St PO Box 2446 Richmond VA 23218

BLISS, H. PARRY, JR., ins. agy. exec.; b. Washington, Feb. 17, 1947; s. Henry P. and Joyce M. (Cancilla) B.; B.S. in Acctg. (Alpha Kappa Psi scholar, Ernst & Whinney scholar), U. N.C., Charlotte, 1969. With Ernst & Whinney, Charlotte, 1969-75; with Johnson & Higgins of Tex., Inc., Houston, 1975—, now chief fin. officer. Mem. Am. Mgmt. Assn., Am. Inst. C.P.A.'s, N.C. Assn. C.P.A.'s, Tex. Soc. C.P.A.'s, Nat. Assn. Accts., U. N.C. at Charlotte Alumni Assn. (past pres.), Alpha Kappa Psi Alumni Assn. Episcopalian. Home: 748 Augusta Dr Houston TX 77057 Office: Johnson & Higgins of Tex Inc 811 Dallas Ave Houston TX 77002

BLIZNAK, JOHNNY, physician; b. San Angelo, Tex., Oct. 26, 1940; s. Jameson Lee and Venita (Bratcher) B.; B.A., U. Tex. at Austin, 1963; M.D., Washington U., St. Louis, 1967; m. Carol Ann Hoajovsky, Aug. 8, 1965; children—John Houston, Leland Wade. Intern, Barnes Hosp., St. Louis, 1967-68; resident in radiology Mallinckrodt Inst. Radiology, St. Louis, 1968-69, 71-73, instr., 1973-74; radiologist Radiology Assos. Abilene, Tex., 1974—, dir. med. edn., 1974—; mem. staff Hendrick Meml. Hosp., West Tex. Med. Center (both Abilene). Served with USAF, 1969-71. Cancirco grantee, 1963, NIH grantee, 1965. Mem. Taylor Jones County Med. Soc., Tex. Med. Assn., AMA, Tex. Radiol. Soc., Radiol. Soc. N. Am., Am. Coll. Radiology, Am. Inst. Ultrasound in Medicine. Roman Catholic. Contbr. articles to profl. jours. Home: 3502 High Meadow St Abilene TX 79605 Office: 1101 19th St N Abilene TX 79601

BLIZZARD, BARRY EUGENE, athletic dir.; b. Coaldale, W.Va., June 15, 1951; s. Floyd Kermit and Wada Lucia Blizzard; B.S., Bluefield (W.Va.) State Coll., 1974; M.S., Radford (Va.) U., 1976. Asst. athletic dir. Bluefield State Coll., 1974-76, athletic dir., sports info. dir., coll. info. officer, 1976—. Mem. Coll. Sports Info. Dirs. Assn. (Nat. award publns. 1975), Nat. Assn. Intercollegiate Athletics (Nat. award publns. 1975, dist. exec. com. 1978—), W.Va. Intercollegiate Athletic Conf. Athletic Dirs. (vice chmn. 1978; named Info. Dir. of Year 1974, 75, 76), W.Va. Sports Writers Assn., Atlantic Coast Sports Writers Assn., U.S. Basketball Writers Assn., Nat. Assn. Collegiate Athletic Dirs. Home: General Delivery Coaldale WV 24717 Office: Bluefield State Coll Bluefield WV 24701

BLOCH, MILTON JOSEPH, mus. adminstr.; b. Bronx, N.Y., Apr. 1, 1937; s. Seymour Jerome and Evelyn Juliette (Foltz) B.; B.I.D., Pratt Inst., Bklyn., 1958; M.F.A., U. Fla., Gainesville, 1963; m. Mary Elizabeth Lynn, Feb. 14, 1976; 1 dau., Kimberly Dacia. Instr. art, chmn. dept. Lake Sumter Coll., Leesburg, Fla., 1961-63; dir. Pensacola (Fla.) Art Center, 1964-65; dir. Mus. Sci. and Natural History, Little Rock, 1965-68; dir. Monmouth Mus., Lincroft, N.J., 1968-76; dir. Mint Mus., Charlotte, N.C., 1976—; adj. prof. Brookdale Community Coll., Lincroft, 1970-76; instr. art Belmont (N.C.) Abbey Coll., 1977-78. Served with U.S. Army, 1958-61. Mem. Am. Assn. Mus., N.C. Arts Council, Southeastern Mus. Conf., Am. Assn. Mus. Dirs. Arts columnist Redbank (N.J.) Registar, 1974-76; guest columnist Charlotee News, 1978—. Contbr. articles in field to profl. jours. Office: 501 Hempstead Pl Charlotte NC 28207

BLOCK, (EDWARD) BATES, lawyer; b. Atlanta, Aug. 16, 1918; s. E. Bates and Julia (Porter) B.; A.B., Emory U., 1940, LL.B., U. Ga., 1942; m. Margaret Ann Davison, Dec. 18, 1956; foster children—Julia, Baxter, Douglas Jones. Admitted to Ga. bar, 1942; partner firm Hansell, Post, Brandon & Dorsey, Atlanta; sec., dir. So. Syndicate, Inc., 1962-73, Ga. Capital Corp., Peachtree Center, Inc.; pres., dir. Valley Devel. Corp., 1954-71, Investments Unlimited, Inc., 1975-76, Woodlands, Inc. Mem. Ga. Student Loan Commn., 1964-70; former instr. banking law Am. Inst. Banking. Trustee, Chi Phi Ednl. Trust; bd. dirs. Nat. Interfrat. Conf., 1978-81. Mem. Ga. Geneal. Soc. (pres. 1965-66), Atlanta Hist. Assn., Atlanta Art Assn., Ga., Atlanta (sec. 1943-49) bar assns., Atlanta Lawyers Club, Motor Carrier Lawyers Assn., Phi Beta Kappa, Omicron Delta Kappa, Chi Phi (nat. pres. 1979-81). Presbyn. (chmn. bd. deacons 1975). Clubs: Univ. Yacht; Capital City, Nine O'Clocks, Piedmont Driving (Atlanta). Editor: Atlanta Lawyer, 1956-62, Ga. Bar News, 1963-64. Contbr. articles to profl. and geneal. jours. Home: 25 Valley Rd NW Atlanta GA 30305 Office: 3300 First Nat Bank Tower Atlanta GA 30303

BLOCK, HAROLD MARTIN, lawyer; b. Thibodaux, La., July 24, 1945; s. Ferdinand H. and Ethel Marie (Rodrigue) B.; B.A., U. Va., 1968; J.D., Tulane U., 1971; m. Jane Ann Weihman, Aug. 24, 1968; children—Marjorie Elizabeth, Katherine Fernanda. Admitted to La. bar, 1971, U.S. Supreme Ct. bar, 1975; practice law, Thibodaux; dir. Block Furniture Stores, Inc., 1971—. Mem. La. Ednl. TV Authority, 1974—, treas., 1975-76, vice chmn., 1977—; mem. Tulane U. Planned Gifts Com., 1976—; co-chmn. Am. Cancer Soc., Thibodaux, 1972-76, v.p. Lafourche Parish Div., 1974-80, div. pres., 1980—; bd. dirs. La. Expo, Inc., 1977—. Mem. Am., La., Lafourche Parish (pres. 1976) bar assns. Clubs: Confrerie des Chevaliers du Tastevin, Chaine des Rotisseurs, Commanderie de Bordeaux; Shenorock Shore (Rye, N.Y.); Rotary, Bayou Country (Thibodaux). Office: 312 St Louis St Thibodaux LA 70301

BLOCK, JAMES HOWARD, veterinarian; b. Aurora, Ill., Aug. 5, 1946; s. Lee Ellis and Ruth Florence (Fisher) B.; B.S., U. Ill., 1968, B.S., 1970, D.V.M., 1972; m. Martha Jo Aiels, Jan. 30, 1972. Veterinarian, Glen Ellyn (Ill.) Animal Hosp., 1972-74, Knowles Animal Clinics, Miami, Fla., 1974—; dir. Snapper Creek Animal Clinic, Knowles Animal Clinic; mem. Ill. State Veterinary Medicine Polit. Action Com., 1972-74. Mem. Am. Animal Hosp. Assn., AVMA, Fla., South Fla. vet. med. assns., Soc. Aquatic Vet. Medicine, Internat. Oceanographic Found., Conservation, Ecology, Diving, Archaeology, Museums Internat., Fla. Underwater Council, Zool. Soc. Fla. Clubs: B'nai B'rith, Rotary. Office: 9933 Sunset Dr Miami FL 33173

BLOCK, JOHN BRADFORD, physician; b. Louisville, Ky., Oct. 27, 1933; s. Edward Joseph and Cecilia Ann (Ford) B.; A.B., Bellarmine Coll., 1955; M.S., U. Louisville, 1959, M.D., 1966; M.S., U. Cin., 1969; m. Mary Juanita Slack, June 11, 1960; children—John Gregory, Brian Christopher. Intern, Piedmont Hosp., Atlanta, 1966-67; resident in occupational medicine U. Cin., 1967-69; practice medicine specializing in occupational medicine; med. dir. Union Carbide, South Charleston, W.Va., 1969-71; med. cons. Ky. Dept. Health, 1971-73, Dept. Labor, 1973-79; corp. med. dir. Cin. Milacron, 1979—; asst. prof. U. Louisville, 1973—; guest faculty U. Ky., 1973—. Served with U.S. Army, 1955-57. Diplomate Am. Bd. Preventive Medicine. Recipient Norvin Green Meml. prize U. Louisville Med. Sch., 1966, Cleveland Acad. award, 1966; Distinguished Service award Ky. Dental Assn., 1977. Fellow Am. Acad. Occupational Medicine, Am. Coll. Preventive Medicine, Am. Occupational Med. Assn., So. Med. Assn., Royal Soc. Health; mem. Pan Am., Ky. Occupational med. assns., Alpha Epsilon Delta, Psi Chi. Democrat. Roman Catholic. Club: Filson. Contbr. articles to med. jours. Home: Route 1 Box 112 Bagdad KY 40003 Office: Cin Milacron 4701 Marburg Ave Cincinnati OH 45209

BLOCKER, LONNIE, space engr., mathematician; b. Arlington, Ga., Feb. 12, 1940; s. Charlie Luke and Dessie Mae (Wimes) B.; B.S. in Math. and Chemistry, Bethune-Cookman Coll., 1963; M.C.S. in Gen. Mgmt., Rollins Coll., 1969; m. Marion Catherine Pinkston, June 5, 1965; children—Michael Anthony, Eric Julian. AST tech. mgmt. NASA, John F. Kennedy Space Center, Fla., 1963-65, 70-71, prodn. controller, 1965-66, program specialist, 1966-70, AST exptl. facilities and equipment, 1971-76, AST tech. mgmt., 1977—. Co-founder New World Services Inc., Orlando, Fla., 1970, dir., 1970-71; broker-salesman real estate C.M. Darden & Assos., Titusville, Fla., 1973-78. Scoutmaster, Central Fla. council Boy Scouts Am., 1970—, mem. Order of Arrow, 1972—; pres. parents adv. council Head Start, Cocoa, Fla., 1973, v.p., 1972. Exec. bd. dirs. Brevard County (Fla.) Sickle Cell Anemia Found.; chief Calusa tribe YMCA Indian Guides, 1976; treas. Central Brevard YMCA Canaveral Nation Indian Guides. Recipient Scouts Key, Boy Scouts Am., 1974. Mem. Fla. State Registered Contractors Assn., Titusville Bd. Realtors (asso.), Alpha Phi Alpha (life mem., v.p. chpt. 1971, pres. 1972, 73, 75, 79, dir. edn. 1976, 77, 78, Man of Year 1973), Alpha Phi Omega, Alpha Kappa Mu. Baptist (trustee, tchr. Sunday Sch.). Club: Toastmasters Internat. (chpt. adminstrv. v.p. 1979). Home: 904 S Varr Ave Rockledge FL 32955 Office: NASA DF-MOO-1 John F Kennedy Space Center FL 32899

BLOCKWOOD, JAMES VERNON, air force officer; b. Lake Providence, La., Mar. 30, 1954; s. Benjamin and Elizabeth Louise (Brown) B.; B.A. (scholar 1971), Grambling State U., 1975; postgrad bus. adminstrn. Trinity U., San Antonio, 1976—; 1 son, James Brandon. Commd. 2d lt. USAF, 1975, advanced through grades to capt., 1979; exec. officer Hdqrs. Air Tng. Command, Randolph AFB, Tex., 1975-76, squadron comdr., 1976, exec. officer squadron sect., 1977—. Counselor, Big Bros., Randolph area, 1977. Am. Legion scholar, 1974. Mem. Air Force Assn., Omega Psi Phi. African Methodist Episcopalian. Office: ATC/CCQ Randolph AFB TX 78184

BLODGETT, BILLY PAUL, social worker; b. San Antonio, Mar. 8, 1952; s. Ollie Lee and Ruth May (Emsoff) B.; B.A., Oral Roberts U., 1974; M.S.S.W., U. Tex., Arlington, 1976. Psychiat. social worker Richard C. Bibb, M.D., Wichita Falls, Tex., 1976-79; chief social worker Wichita Falls (Tex.) StateHosp., 1979—; cons. Medicenter Psychiat. Hosp., Wichita Falls, 1977-80, North Tex. Easter Seal Rehab., Wichita Falls, 1979—. Bd. dirs. YMCA, 1977-79, chmn. youth com., 1977-79; mem. adminstrv. bd. Meth. Ch., 1977—, also council on ministries, mem. evangelism com., 1977—, chmn., 1978—. Mem. Nat. Assn. Social Workers (dir. Tex. chpt. 1978—), Acad. Cert. Social Workers, Nat. Assn. Christians in Social Work, Tex. Assn. Retarded Citizens, Tex. Public Employees Assn., Wichita Falls Jr. C. of C. Home: 4610 Spanish Trace 2A Wichita Falls TX 76310 Office: Box 300 Wichita Falls TX 76307

BLOMERTH, ELMER ALEXANDER, TV exec.; b. Melrose, Mass., Feb. 14, 1927; s. Elmer Alexander and Pearl Minnie (Blalock) B.; B.S. in Physics, Tex. A & M U., 1948; m. Jan Ardith Thompson, June 18, 1948; s. Todd, Kimberly Jan Blomerth Brunson. Geophysicist, Magnolia Petroleum Co., 1948-51; sr. geophysicist Gulf Oil Corp., 1951-54, Mene Grande Oil Co., 1954-61; div. chief Atmospheric Scis.

Lab. U.S. Army, White Sands, N.Mex., 1961-76; pres. Missionary Radio Evangel. Inc., El Paso, Tex., 1973—; v.p. InEn Corp., Stillwater, Okla.; v.p. Mision Compacion de Cristo, 1978—. Served with USNR, 1945-46. Mem. Nat. Religious Broadcasters, Community Antenna TV Assn. Contbr. articles in field to profl. jours. Office: 3100 N Stanton St El Paso TX 79902

BLOMGREN, PETER FREDERICK, physician; b. Mobile, Ala., Apr. 10, 1947; s. Holton Eugene and Bettee Elouise (Breckinridge) B.; student U. Wis., 1965-66; B.A. magna cum laude, Butler U., 1970; M.D., Ind. U., 1974; m. Rebecca Ann Frazier, May 27, 1973. Resident in family medicine Cone Meml. Hosp., Greensboro, N.C., 1974-77; practice family medicine Greensboro Family Practice Assos., 1977—; mem. staff Cone Meml. Hosp., Greensboro Hosp., Wesley Long Hosp.; cons., adv. bd. Upjohn Healthcare Services, Greensboro, 1978—; physician adv. N.C. PSRO, Wesley Long Hosp., 1979-80. Mem. fin. com. New Garden Friends Meeting, 1979-80. Diplomate Am. Bd. Family Practice. Mem. So. Med. Assn., Greensboro Acad. Medicine, Sierra Club, Nat. Wildlife Fedn., Cousteau Soc., Defenders of Wildlife, Humane Soc. U.S. and Guilford County, Nat. Parks and Conservation Assn., Wilderness Soc., Greenpeace, Animal Protection Inst., Fund for Animals, Whale Protection Fund, Nat. Resources Def. Council, Environ. Def. Fund, World Wildlife Fund. Democrat. Office: 1311 N Elm St Greensboro NC 27401

BLOMQVIST, CARL GUNNAR, cardiologist; b. Bararyd, Sweden, Dec. 31, 1931; s. Arvid Elias and Karin Johanna (Hullman) B.; B.M., U. Lund (Sweden), 1954, M.D., 1960; Ph.D., Karolinska Inst., Stockholm, 1967; m. Joan Barre Bakula, Aug. 5, 1961; children—Mary Jennifer, Peter Carl. Research fellow in cardiovascular epidemiology U. Minn., Mpls., 1960-61; resident Karolinska Inst., Stockholm, 1962-65; mem. faculty U. Tex. Health Sci. Center, Southwestern Med. Sch., Dallas, 1966—, prof. medicine and physiology, 1976—; mem. research study com. Am. Heart Assn., 1970-73, applied physiology study sect. NIH, 1974-78. Mem. Dallas Symphony Orch. Guild, 1975—. Grantee NIH, NASA; established investigator award Am. Heart Assn. Fellow Council Epidemiology Am. Heart Assn., Am. Coll. Cardiology; mem. Swedish Soc. Cardiology, Am. Fedn. Clin. Research, So. Soc. Clin. Research, Internat. Soc. Cardiology. Contbr. articles to profl. jours.; editorial bd. Circulation, 1969-73, Clin. Cardiology, 1978—, Medicine and Sci. in Sports, 1979—, Jour. Cardiac Rehab., 1979—. Office: Div Cardiology Southwestern Med Sch Dallas TX 75235

BLOMSTEDT, ROBERT KENT, educator; b. Kenedy, Tex., Feb. 17, 1931; s. Carl Gus and Laura (Gustafson) B.; B.S., Tex. Luth. Coll., 1952; postgrad. Washburn U., 1962; Reed Coll., 1965, M.Ed., U. Tex., Austin, 1967, Ph.D., 1974; m. Dona Linder, Mar. 6, 1959; children—J. Kirby, Russell D., Tarin Kay. Tchr., Kenedy (Tex.) Pub. Schs., 1952-54, 56-59, 67-68, Refugio (Tex.) Pub. Schs., 1959-62, Arlington (Tex.) Pub. Schs., 1963-66; dean admissions Tex. Luth. Coll., 1962-63; with Tex. A. & I. U., 1969—, asso. prof. edn., 1977—, dir. Tchr. Center, 1973-74, mem. doctoral faculty, 1979—. NSF grantee, 1966-67. Mem. Internat. Platform Assn., Tex. Assn. Coll. Tchrs., Tex. State Tchrs. Assn., Nat. Edn. Assn., Tex. Council Tchrs. Math., Tex. Assn. Tchr. Educators, Nat. Council Tchrs. of Math., Phi Delta Kappa. Democrat. Baptist (deacon vice-chmn. 1975-77, chmn. 1977-79). Clubs: Kingsville Rotary, Tex. Baptist Men (mem. exec. bd. 1976-77), Coastal Bend Bapt. Assn. Contbr. articles to profl. jours. Home: 901 S 23d St Kingsville TX 78363 Office: Tex A & I U Box 2153 Kingsville TX 78363

BLOOD, GORDON WILLIAM, speech and lang. pathologist; b. Jamestown, N.Y., Aug. 25, 1951; s. Gordon Patrick and Cathleen (Donovan) B.; B.S., SUNY, Buffalo, 1974; M.A. (U.S. Office of Edn. grantee 1975-76), Bowling Green State U., 1976, Ph.D. (teaching fellow 1977-78), 1978; m. Ingrid Maria Unczowsky, Dec. 27, 1975. Dir., Cleft Palate Rehab. Center, Toledo, 1975-77; laryngectomy therapist Mercy Hosp., Toledo, 1977-78; dir. Sandusky (Ohio) Speech and Hearing Clinic, 1977-78, Easter Seals Speech and Hearing Clinic, Napoleon, Ohio, 1977-78; asst. prof. communication disorders Radford (Va.) U., 1978—; cons. in field. Recipient Betty Gallagher award as outstanding clinician, 1974; Rotary scholar, W. Africa, 1973; lic. speech and hearing tchr., N.Y.; lic. speech and hearing pathologist, Va. Mem. Am. Speech and Hearing Assn. (lic. speech and lang. pathologist), Va. Speech and Hearing. Assn., Council of Univ. Practicum Suprs. in Speech Pathology and Audiology. Republican. Roman Catholic. Contbr. articles to profl. jours. Home: Route 2 Box 357 Radford VA 24141 Office: Dept Communication Disorders Radford U Radford VA 24142

BLOOD, INGRID MARIA, audiologist; b. Munich, Germany, Mar. 30, 1952; came to U.S., 1952, naturalized, 1959; d. Rudolph and Hildagarde Margaret (Schessler) Unczowsky; B.A., Montclair State U., 1974; M.A., Bowling Green State U., 1975, Ph.D. in Audiology, 1978; m. Gordon W. Blood, Dec. 27, 1975. Speech and hearing therapist Woodlane Sch. and Industry for Retarded, Bowling Green, Ohio, 1975, also audiologist Toledo Otolaryngology Clinic; asst. instr. Sch. Speech Communications, Bowling Green State U., 1976; dir. Wood County (Ohio) Nursing Home Speech and Hearing Program, 1977; therapist In Home Speech and Lang. Services, City of Toledo, 1977; asst. prof. communication disorders Radford (Va.) U., 1978—; cons. in field. Office of Edn. grantee, 1975. Mem. Am. Speech and Hearing Assn., Acoustical Soc. Am., Va. Speech and Hearing Assn., Am. Audiology Soc. Republican. Roman Catholic. Contbr. articles to profl. jours. Office: Dept Communication Disorders Radford U Radford VA 24141

BLOODWORTH, ALBERT WILLIAM FRANKLIN, lawyer; b. Atlanta, Sept. 23, 1935; s. James Morgan Bartow and Elizabeth Westfield (Dimmock) B.; A.B. in History, French, Davidson (N.C.) Coll., 1957; J.D. magna cum laude, U. Ga., 1963; m. Elizabeth Howell, Nov. 24, 1967; 1 dau., Elizabeth Howell. Asst. dir. alumni, pub. relations Davidson Coll.,. 1959-60; admitted to Ga. bar, 1962, U.S. Supreme Ct. bar, 1971; partner firm Hansell, Post, Brandon & Dorsey, Atlanta, 1963—. Mem. Vol. Counsel to organized crime com. Commn. on Crime, Juvenile Delinquency Metropolitan Atlanta, 1965-67; asst. sec., counsel Metropolitan Found. Atlanta, 1968-76. Bd. dirs. Atlanta Presbytery, Inc., 1974-78. Served to 1st lt., Intelligence Corps, AUS, 1957-59. Outstanding Student Leadership award Student Bar Assn. U. Ga., 1963; recipient Jessie, Dan MacDougal Scholarship award U. Ga. Found., 1963. Fellow Am. Coll. Probate Counsel; mem. Am., Atlanta bar assns., State Bar Ga., Lawyers' Club Atlanta, Atlanta Estate Planning Council, Phi Beta Kappa, Phi Kappa Phi, Omicron Delta Kappa, Alpha Tau Omega (chpt. pres. 1957), Phi Delta Phi (pres. chpt. 1963, Grad. of Year for S.E. award 1963). Presbyn. (elder). Clubs: Capital City, Sphinx, Gridiron. Home: 4110 Peachtree Dunwoody Rd NE Atlanta GA 30342 Office: 3300 First Nat Bank Tower Atlanta GA 30303

BLOODWORTH, JAMES NELSON, justice; b. Decatur, Ala., Jan 21, 1921; s. Benjamin M. and Marguerite (Nelson) B.; student Athens Coll., 1938-39; B.S., U. Ala. Sch. Commerce, 1942; LL.B., U. Ala., 1947; m. Mary Jean Gregg, Sept. 27, 1963; children—Catherine, Sandra, Jean Marguerite. Admitted to Ala. bar, 1947; mem. firm Calvin & Bloodworth, Decatur, 1947-58; judge, Recorder's Ct., Decatur, 1948-51; solicitor Morgan County, Decatur, 1951; judge Circuit Ct. Ala., 8th Jud. Circuit, Decatur, 1959-68; asso. justice Ala. Supreme Ct., 1968—. Co-chmn. Circuit Judges' Seminars Ala., 1960-66; lectr. before judges, solicitors assns., seminars, 1963—; chmn. Ala. Pattern Jury Instr. Com., 1966-68. Pres. Morgan County Jury Com., 1966-68. Pres. Decatur Boys Club, 1951; moderator North Ala. Presbytery, 1965; mem. bd. Morgan County chpt. A.R.C., 1959-60. Mem. Bd. Pardons and Paroles Ala., 1951-52; chmn. Ala. Democratic campaign steering com., 1961-63; faculty adviser Nat. Coll. State Trial Judges, 1967, 71; faculty Am. Acad. Jud. Edn., 1970-77; lectr. Ala. Police Acad., 1969-75. Served from pvt. to capt. U.S. Army. Decorated Bronze Star medal, Combat Infantry badge. Mem. Ala. Res. Officers Assn. (pres. chpt. 1959), Morgan County Bar Assn. (pres. 1955), Decatur C. of C., Ala. Bar Assn., Farrah Order of Jurisprudence, Phi Delta Phi, Kappa Alpha Order, Omicron Delta Kappa. Presbyn. (elder). Mason (K.T., Shriner), Rotarian (pres. 1953-54). Home: 3221 Bankhead Ave Montgomery AL 36106 Office: Judicial Bldg Capitol Montgomery AL 36104

BLOOM, HAROLD EDWARD, food co. exec.; b. N.Y.C., May 4, 1946; s. Sidney and Rose B.; B.B.A., U. Miami, 1968; M.B.A., City U. N.Y., 1971; m. Ellen T. Friedman, July 14, 1973; children—Allison, Robert. Project dir. Monar Market Planning, N.Y.C., 1968-71; asst. tech. dir. Grey Advt., N.Y.C., 1971-73; market research mgr. ITT Continental Baking, Rye, N.Y., 1973-74; mgr. consumer research Coca-Cola, Atlanta, 1973-78; dir. market research Pillsbury Co., Mpls., 1978-79; dir. market research STP Corp., Ft. Lauderdale, Fla., 1979—. Mem. Am. Mktg. Assn., Am. Mgmt. Assn. Home: 159 SW 101st Way Coral Springs FL 33065 Office: 1400 W Commercial Blvd Fort Lauderdale FL 33310

BLOOM, JEFFREY ALAN, data communications cons.; b. Bklyn., June 22, 1948; s. Herbert and Marion (Hittleman) B.; B.S.E.E., Rensselaer Poly. Inst., 1970, M.S.E.E., 1971, M.S. in Mgmt., 1972. Pres., Digital Devel. Corp., Troy, N.Y., 1971-73; corp. mgr. tech. services Budd Co., Troy, Mich., 1973-76; mem. tech. staff Network Analysis Corp., Vienna, Va., 1976-78, dir. info. systems studies, 1978—; speaker at confs. Mem. IEEE, Assn. for Computing Machinery, Soc. for Computer Simulation, IEEE Computer Soc. Office: Network Analysis Corp 301 Tower Bldg Vienna VA 22180

BLOOMQUIST, JAMES CLARENCE, electronic engr.; b. Jamestown, N.Y.; s. Melvin Axel and Ruby Florence (Wheelock) B.; B.E.E., Union Coll., Schenectady, 1949; M.S. in Physics, Fla. State U., 1964; m. Frances Napier, Nov. 11, 1950; children—James Clarence, Robert Alan. Electronic engr., radar devel. Rome Air Devel. Center (N.Y.), 1951-53; devel. engr. devel. and test bomb nav. systems Air Force Armament Center, Eglin AFB, Fla., 1953-57, devel. engr. devel. and test advanced scoring techniques, 1957-65; devel. engr. laser guided weapon devel. Air Force Armament Lab., 1965—. Served in USNR, 1943-45. Mem. IEEE, Am. Phys. Soc., Am. Def. Preparedness Assn., Sigma Pi Sigma. Republican. Methodist. Home: 5 Carl Brandt Dr Shalimar FL 32579 Office: Air Force Armament Lab Eglin AFB FL 32542

BLOSE, DONALD CURTIS, surgeon; b. Harrisonburg, Va., Mar. 31, 1933; s. Lloyd Curtis and Sylvia Graham (Myers) B.; B.A., Bridgewater Coll., 1954; M.D., Med. Coll. Va., 1958; m. Virginia Carroll Lutz, June 24, 1956; children—Dana Michelle, John Curtis, Beth Janine, Christopher Andrew. Intern, Med. Coll. Va. Hosps., Richmond, 1958-59, resident in surgery, 1959-63; practice medicine specializing in surgery, Galax, Va., 1964—; chief surg. service Twin County Community Hosp., Galax, 1973—. A.D. Williams scholar, 1957; diplomate Am. Bd. Surgery. Mem. Southwestern Va. Med. Soc., Med. Soc. Va., AMA, Va. Surg. Soc., Alpha Omega Alpha. Republican. Presbyterian. Club: Galax Country. Office: 199 Hospital Dr Galax VA 24333

BLOSKAS, JOHN D., editor, pub. relations dir.; b. Waco, Tex., July 13, 1928; s. George and Alvina (Schrader) B.; B.A., Baylor U., 1953; m. Anna Louise Nelson, Feb. 7, 1955; children—Suzanne (dec.), John D., Kenneth Douglas. Exec. sec. Waco Jr. C. of C., 1953-55; asso. editor Mexia (Tex.) Daily News, 1955-56; dir. publicity Valley C. of C., Weslaco, Tex., 1956-57; religion editor Houston Chronicle, 1957-58; v.p. pub. relations annuity bd. So. Bapt. Conv., Dallas, 1958—. Served with USNR, 1945-49, 50-51. Mem. So. Bapt. (past pres.), Tex. Bapt. (past pres.) pub. relations assns., Pub. Relations Soc. Am. (accredited), Religious Pub. Relations Council, Sales and Mktg. Execs., Fellowship of Christians in Arts, Media and Entertainment. Author: Staying in the Black Financially; Living Within Your Means (cassette). Editor: The Years Ahead. Home: 5816 Clendenin Dallas TX 75228 Office: 511 N Akard Bldg Dallas TX 75201

BLOSSER, DALE ALAN, architect; b. Brussels, Oct. 3, 1927; s. (father Am. citizen) Rolland Ernest Blosser and Josephine (My) B.; student Carnegie Inst. Tech., 1947-49; B.Arch., N.C. State Coll., 1956; m. Louise Ann Schultz Pinkerton, May 25, 1967; stepchildren—Stephen R., Susan L., Timothy J., Don Charles, Lizabeth Ann. Architect in tng. N.C. Div. Sch. Planning, Raleigh, 1954-55; draftsman William Moore Weber, architect, Raleigh, 1956; project mgr. Geodesics, Inc., Raleigh, 1957-60; project rep. John D. Latimer & Asso., Durham, N.C., 1960-62, Synergetics, Inc., Raleigh, 1962-65; architect Dale Blosser & Assos., constrn. contract administrn., Raleigh, 1966-72, prin., 1975—; partner Blosser, Boone & Assos., 1972-75; pres. Kimley-Horn, Blosser Assos., 1973—; lectr. profl. practice dept. architecture Sch. Design, N.C. State U., 1969—; constrn. contract adminstr. Electric Power & Light Exhbt., N.Y. World's Fair, 1962-64; manuscript reviewer for pub. tech. books. Alt. mem. Raleigh Bd. Adjustment, 1974-75, mem., vice chmn., 1975-78, chmn., 1978—; precinct officer Raleigh Democratic Com., 1972-74. Served with AUS, 1945-47. Registered architect, N.C., S.C., Va.; Honorable mention Carrier Weathermaker Home Competition, 1953, N.C. Concrete Masonry Assn. Modern Living Competition, 1954; co-winner logo design N.C. State Coll. Student Union Bldg., 1955. Mem. ASTM (councilor Carolinas dist., vice chmn. met. com. 1974—), AIA (office procedures com. N.C. 1966-72, govt. affairs com. 1974—, vice chmn. 1976, chmn. 1977, dir. 1978-79, sec. Raleigh sect. 1970-71, dir. chpt. 1974-79), Constrn. Specifications Inst. (Raleigh-Durham chpt. pres. 1967-68, tech. chmn. 1968-69, 73-74, dir. 1965-67, 74-77), Bldg. Research Inst. (chmn. sect 5.05 constrn. techniques subcom. of Div. V constrn. mgmt. 1969-71), N.C. Assn. Professions (dir. 1973-75, 76-78, 2d v.p. 1978, 1st v.p. 1979), Am. Concrete Inst., Am. Inst. Timber COnstrn., Am. Inst. Steel Constrn. Unitarian-Universalist (pres. Thomas Jefferson dist. 1968-69). Clubs: N.C. State U. Faculty, Capital City. Home: 3008 Ruffin St Raleigh NC 27607 Office: 2008 Hillsborough St Raleigh NC 27607

BLOUNT, FLOYD EUGENE, chem. engr.; b. Dallas, Dec. 11, 1922; s. Hal Holt and Ina Adelia (Fagala) B.; B.S. in Chemistry, East Tex. State U., 1943; postgrad. U. Tex., 1946-47; m. Ester Lue McGowan, Apr. 6, 1968. With Mobil Research and Devel. Corp., 1947—, research chemist, Paulsboro, N.J., 1947-52, sr. research chemist, Dallas, 1952-64, engring. asso., 1964—. Served with USNR, 1943-46, 1950-52. Decorated Navy Commendation medal. Mem. Soc. Petroleum Engrs., Nat. Assn. Corrosion Engrs., Am. Chem. Soc., Research Soc. Am., Am. Inst. Chem. Engrs. Patentee in field. Home: 5909 Burgundy St Dallas TX 75230 Office: 3600 Duncanville Rd Dallas TX 75211

BLUESTEIN, STEVEN MICHAEL, retail co. exec.; b. Charleston, S.C., Apr. 5, 1946; s. Melvin Harrison and Freda (Goldin) B.; student U. South Fla., Tampa, 1966-67; B.S. in Mgmt., U. S.C., Columbia, 1970; m. Robin Mimi Solomon, June 15, 1970 (div.); children—Gabrie Solomon Israel, Jessica Solomon. Gift buyer Sam Solomon Co., Inc., Charleston, 1970-71, asst. mdse. mgr., dir. research and devel., 1971-72, sec.-treas., 1972—, exec. v.p., 1973-79, chief operating officer, 1979—, also dir.; pres. Aviation Advt. subs., 1973—; pres. Rivers Import and Export Co. Mem. Jewish Community Center, Synagogue Emanu-El, Charleston, 1970—; mem. steering com. for mayor City of Charleston, 1975, for Charles Ravenel campaign for U.S. Senate; mem. fin. com. Riley for gov. Recipient Certificate of Distinction, 1974-77; named Brand Name Retailer of Year, Brand Names Found., 1974; recipient Outstanding Sales and Mdse. award Mor Music Co., 1974, $500,000 Vol. award Polaroid Co., 1974, Award of Excellence, Sunbeam Co., 1975, Mdse. Excellence award Regal Ware Co. 1974, Retailer of Yr. award, 1977-78. Mem. Merchandisers Assn., S.C., Charleston Trident chambers commerce, Nat. Assn. Catalog Showroom Mchts., Nat. Adv. Bd. Catalog Showroom Bus., Am. Mgmt. Assn., Audit Bur. of Circulation, U.S.C. Consumer Panel. Home: 12 Country Club Dr Charleston SC 29412 Office: 5000 LaCross Rd PO Box 10327 Charleston SC 29411

BLUM, GERALD SAMUEL, broadcasting co. exec.; B.S. in Psychology, Ariz. State U., 1954; m. Dorothy P. Blum. Nat. sales rep. Comml. Rec. Co., Dallas, 1959-60; sales mgr. Lee Broadcasting Co., Richmond, Va., 1960-62; now v.p., gen. mgr. Sta. WQXI-AM/FM, Atlanta. Served with USAF, 1954-56. Office: 3340 Peachtree Rd Suite 240 Atlanta GA 30326

BLUMAN, LOUIS DAVID, chem. co. exec.; b. Jersey City, Apr. 9, 1927; s. Isadore M. and Mollie (Monack) B.; student N.Y. U., 1947, Los Angeles City Coll., 1955-57; m. Bertha Zwerling, Feb. 7, 1960; children—Greg, Gary. Partner, Blumans Bakery, Jersey City, 1947-55; broker Bache & Co., Beverly Hills, Calif., 1955-58; partner Hirsch Shoes, Los Angeles, 1958-64; div. mgr. Nat. Chemsearch, Beverly Hills, 1964-77; exec. v.p. Selig Chem. Industries, Atlanta, 1977—. Served with U.S. Army, 1945-47. Club: Masons (32 deg.). Office: 840 Selig Dr SE Atlanta GA 30378

BLUMBERG, ALLEN, educator; b. Milw., Dec. 20, 1923; s. Nathan and Bella (Gaisenfield) B.; B.A., U. Wis., 1949; M.A., Wayne State U., 1952; Ed.D., Syracuse U., 1964; m. Barbara C. Griffiths, Nov. 23, 1960; stepchildren—David, Val. Dir. Commn. Mental Retardation, State of W.Va., 1965-68; prof. spl. edn. W.Va. U., 1968-71; prof. U. Hawaii, 1971-72; prof. spl. edn. W.Va. Coll. Grad. Studies, Institute, W.Va., 1972—, chmn. dept., 1976—; cons. W.Va. Dept. Mental Health. Named an Outstanding Educator in Spl. Edn., W.Va., 1975, Educator of Yr., Nat. Assn. Retarded Citizens, 1976; building named in his honor W.Va. U. 1974. Mem. Council Exceptional Children, Am. Assn. Mentally Disturbed, W.Va. Assn. Retarded Citizens. Democrat. Jewish. Home: 1422 Wilkie Dr Charleston WV 25314 Office: WVa Coll Grad Studies Institute WV 25112

BLUMENCRANZ, PETER WILLIAM, surgeon; b. N.Y.C., Mar. 8, 1946; s. Bernard and Evelyn (Guttman) B.; B.A., U. Pa., 1966; M.D., Cornell U., 1970; m. Ann Frances Garfes, June 6, 1970; children—Brett Michael, Lisa Eileen, Jennifer Leigh, Deborah Lynn. Intern, N.Y. Hosp.-Cornell Med. Center, N.Y.C., 1970-71, resident in surgery, 1971-72, 74-77; fellow in surg. oncology Meml. Hosp. Sloan Kettering Cancer Center, N.Y.C., 1976-77; practice medicine specializing in gen. and oncologic surgery, Belleair, Fla., 1977—; clin. asst. prof. U. South Fla., Tampa, 1979—; mem. staff Morton F. Plant Hosp., Clearwater Community Hosp. Served as lt. comdr. M.C., USN, 1972-74. Diplomate Am. Bd. Surgery. Fellow Southeastern Surg. Congress; mem. AMA, Fla. Med. Assn., Pinellas County Med. Soc., Am. Cancer Soc. Am. Cancer Soc. Office: 1016 Ponce de Leon Blvd Belleair Clearwater FL 33516

BLUMENTHAL, SIDNEY LEE, librarian; b. Sioux City, Iowa, Oct. 22, 1946; s. Ralph Abraham and Sylene Francis B.; B.S., SUNY, Oneonta, 1972; M.S. in Marine Sci., L.I. U., 1975, M.S. in L.S., 1976; m. Kathleen Lurana Knapp, July 3, 1973; children—Elizabeth, Rachael. Engring./geology librarian, asst. prof. U. Houston, 1977-78; librarian/tech. info specialist NL Petroleum Services/DST, NL Industries, Inc., Houston, 1978—. Pres., Friends of Aldine Br. Library, Houston, 1980. Served with USAR, 1965-68. Mem. Spl. Libraries Assn., Assn. Records Mgrs. and Adminstrs. Office: PO Box 60087 Houston TX 77205

BLUMENTRITT, CHARLES WAYNE, computer scientist; b. San Angelo, Tex., July 31, 1936; s. Samuel Albert and Edith Priscilla (Vogelsang) B.; B.S., Tex. Tech. Coll., 1962; M.S., Tex. A. and M. U., 1964. Field instrument operator Geophys. Integrators Inc., San Angelo, 1957-61; asst. research mathematician Tex. Transp. Inst., Tex. A. and M. U., College Station, 1964-66, sr. systems analyst, 1968-76, transp. systems analyst, 1976—; sci. programming analyst Lockheed Electronics Co., Houston Manned Space Craft Center, 1966-68; cons., lectr. in field. Pres., Post Oak Forest Home Owners Assn., College Station, 1976. Prin. investigator Nat. Coop. Hwy. Research Program, 1977. Nat. Acad. Scis. grantee. Mem. Assn. Computing Machinery, Inst. Transp. Engrs., Data Processing Mgmt. Assn., Soc. Computer Simulation, Instrument Soc. Am. Club: Tex. A. and M. U. Microcomputer. Designer first hierarchically structured computerized traffic control system in U.S., 1969-72. Home: 19 Forest Dr College Station TX 77840 Office: Tex A and M Univ College Station TX 77843

BLUNSON, SAMUEL JAMES, ins. broker; b. Houston, Dec. 8, 1931; s. Sam Thomas and Jessie Mae (Davis) B.; B.Th., Mt. Hope Bible Coll., 1972; B.A., Tex. So. U., 1977; m. Margaret Peterson, Feb. 12, 1968; children—Samuel James, Sebrena Joyce, Selina Jean, Stanford James, Sabenia Jos, Charlotte Jeanett, Chelah Jane. Dist. mgr. Am. Tchr. Mut. Ins. Co., 1964-65; investment and stock counselor Am. Capital Life Ins. Co., Houston, 1965-68; spl. agt. Bankers Life & Casualty Ins. Co., Houston, 1968-72; owner, broker Sunnyside Ins. Agy., Houston, 1972—; dir. Brotherhood Inc. Mem. Gov.'s Spl. Com. on Affairs, 1979—; mem. Nat. Com. on Human Resource Problems of Aging. Served with AUS, 1948-53. Mem. Prof. Ins. Agts. Am., Nat. Small Bus. Assn., Nat. Assn. Evangelicals, World Relief Commn. Democrat. Baptist. Clubs: Shriners. Home: 4522 Keystone St Houston TX 77021 Office: 4703 1/2 Sauer St Houston TX 77004

BLUNT, FRANK CHRISTOPHER, III, investment banker; b. Eng.; came to U.S., 1962, naturalized, 1975; gen. certificate Cambridge U., 1957; student C.P.A. Program, Sch. Commerce, McGill U., Can., 1959-62; m. Ann Wentworth Kerley, Dec. 1956; children—Gavin, Jason. Trainee, Touche, Ross & Co., 1959-62; account exec. Merrill Lynch et al, 1962-65; v.p. Shearson Loeb Rhoades & Co., 1966-72; pres., dir. Blunt Internat. Ltd., Hamilton, Bermuda, 1973—, exec. v.p.-fin. Mid Ocean Mgmt., Inc., Wilmington, Del., 1979—; dir. Enertek Oil & Gas Corp., Houston, 1979—, Clarendon Ins. Co. (Bermuda) Ltd., Hamilton, Clarendon Am. Ins. Co., Wilmington. Bd. dirs. Advocacy Internat. Ltd., Washington, 1980—. Served with RAF, 1956-59. Mem. Aircraft Owners and Pilots Assn. Clubs: Met. (N.Y.C.); Mid Ocean (Bermuda). Home: 3410 Galt

Ocean Dr Fort Lauderdale FL 33308 Office: Bank of Bermuda Bldg Hamilton Bermuda

BLYTHE, RICHARD MICHAEL, child care adminstr.; b. San Jose, Calif., Sept. 14, 1945; s. Dennis T. and Margie (Rohr) B.; student, Magic Valley Christian Coll., 1960-62, E. Tex. State U., 1963-65, Abilene Christian U., 1966-67; m. Sarah Oler, Aug. 25, 1964; children—Martha Ellen, John Michael, Michael Gayle. With Boles Home for Children, Quinlan, Tex., 1962-69; exec. dir. Foster Home for Children, Stephenville, Tex., 1970—. Bd. trustees Pecan Valley Mental Health Mental Retardation region, 1975—; elder Graham St. Ch. of Christ, Stephenville; chmn. U. Tex. Workshop for Personnel of Homes for Children, 1979; chmn. legis. liaison Washington, Nat. Assn. of Homes for Children, 1979. Mem. Tex. Assn. Lic. Children's Services (chmn. legis. com. 1978—), Tex. Assn. Exec. Homes for Children (chmn. legis. com. 1977—), Nat. Assn. Homes for Children, Southwestern Assn. Execs. of Homes for Children, Christian Child Care Conf., Stephenville C. of C., Erath County Assn. for Retarded Citizens. Club: Optimists. Home: 1776 N Graham St Stephenville TX 76401 Office: 1779 N Graham St Stephenville TX 76401

BOARDMAN, KATHERINE BAKER BLACKSHEAR, univ. counselor; b. Atlanta, May 15, 1929; d. Hinton Baker and Nora Katherine (Whitener) Blackshear; A.B., U. Ga., 1949; M.A., Duke U., 1951; M.Ed., U. Ga., 1974; m. William Kilbourne Boardman, III, July 24, 1951; children—William Hinton, David Robeson, Katherine Anne. Grad. asst. dept. romance langs. Duke U., 1949-51; community vol. Office Internat. Services and Programs, U. Ga., 1972-74, career planning adviser Office of Career Planning and Placement, 1974-76, career planning coordinator, 1976—, lectr. dept. counseling and human devel., 1977—. Den mother Atlanta Area council Boy Scouts Am., 1962-64, troop com. chmn. N.E. Ga. Area council, 1968-70; leader N.E. Ga. council Girl Scouts Am., 1969-71. Mem. Am. (mem. Commn. VI directorate 1978-81), Ga. (pres. 1979-80) coll. personnel assns., Am. Personnel and Guidance Assn., Ga., So. coll. placement assns., U. Ga. Student Personnel Assn., Mortar Bd., Phi Delta Kappa, Alpha Gamma Delta. Democrat. Presbyterian. Clubs: Emory U., U. Ga. woman's clubs, Belles of Meyerland Garden. Home: 590 Fortson Rd Athens GA 30606 Office: U Ga Career Planning and Placement Clark Howell Hall Athens GA 30602

BOATNER, FREDERICK LE ROI, photographer; b. Wellington, Kans., May 4, 1912; s. Lewis Jesse and Margaret Elizabeth (Grable) B.; grad. high sch.; m. Nila Avanelle Allen, Aug. 11, 1937; 1 son, Lynn Allen. Portrait photographer, Bonham, Tex., 1931, Clarkville, Tex., 1933-39, Texarkansas, Tex., 1943-47, Longview, Tex., 1948—; dir. Frederick-Nila Gallery, Longview, 1948—; also importer, speaker, lectr. and writer on photography, picture framing and decoration. Past pres., dir. Cherokee Water Corp. Bd. dirs., v.p. Longview Symphony. Recipient numerous awards for photography. Mem. Profl. Photographers Am. (masters degree), Am. Soc. Photographers, Tex. Profl. Photographers Assn. (past dir.). Episcopalian. Club: Knife and Fork (pres.). Photographs included in the Diamond Years of Texas Photography. Home: 1113 Pine Bluff Dr Longview TX 75601 Office: 306 N 4th St Longview TX 75601

BOATNER, ROY ALTON, state senator; b. Durant, Okla., Nov. 9, 1941; s. Frank and Minnie Ola B.; B.S., Southeastern Okla. State U., 1965, M.Ed., 1973; m. Winona Wlaker, Oct. 13, 1967; children—Rhonda, Alton. Office mgr. Smak Bar Inc., Dallas, 1964-65; credit rep. Ford Motor Credit Co., Dallas, 1965-66; adjustor Am. Road Ins. Co., Dallas, 1966-67; prin. Achille (Okla.) High Sch., 1967-70; mem. Okla. Ho. of Reps. 1970-74, Okla. Senate, 1974—. Democrat. Baptist. Office: 105 N 3d St Durant OK 74701

BOBO, BETTY RUTH GLASGOW, chemist, educator; b. Rector, Ark., Sept. 29, 1924; d. Alvin J. and Ivah (Campbell) Glasgow; B.S., U. Mo., 1946, M.S., 1950, Ph.D., 1953; m. William Benson Bobo, June 23, 1956; children—Todd C., Richard H., Malcolm, Rubb Glasgow. Research asst. agrl. chemistry U. Mo., Columbia, 1948-56; research asso. agrl. chemistry Sch. Medicine, Tulane U., also Alton Ochsner Med. Found. Endocrine Research Lab., New Orleans, 1953-56; instr. agrl. chemistry Coahoma Jr. Coll., Clarksdale, Miss., 1972-78. NSF grantee, 1979. M)em. Am. Chem. Soc., AAUW, Sigma Xi, Sigma Delta Epsilon, Kappa Epsilon Alpha. Presbyterian. Home: 1155 Oakhurst St Clarksdale MS 38614 Office: Coahoma Jr Coll RFD 1 Box 616 Clarksdale MS 38614

BOBULSKI, EDWARD S., graphic arts co. exec., artist; b. Peoria, Ill., Apr. 7, 1939; s. Stephen Jerome and Maureen Alice (O'Grady) B.; B.A., U. Ill., Champaign-Urbana, 1959; M.B.A., Loyola U., Chgo., 1961; m. Angela Marie Steffano, June 11, 1960; 1 son, Andre. Comml. artist Terra Arts, Inc., Chgo., 1961-63, creative dir., 1963-66, v.p. prodn., 1966-71; owner, pres. Dezign, Ltd., 1971—; instr. graphic design Northwestern Evening Div., Chgo., 1966—; exhibited in numerous one man and group shows. Democratic precinct capt., 1970-78; bd. dirs. D.A. Smythe Found., 1970—. Mem. Am. Assn. Graphic Artists. Democrat. Roman Catholic. Clubs: K.C., Rotary, Kiwanis, Ill. Athletic. Author: Graphic Design for the Novice, 1972. Home: 6121 N Sheridan Rd Chicago IL 60660

BOCK, BENNIE, II, state legislator Tex.; b. Lockhart, Tex., May 17, 1942; s. Bennie Walter and Ruth Margaret (Blackwell) B.; B.B.A., U. Tex., 1964; J.D., St. Mary's U., San Antonio, 1968; m. Kathy C. Holmberg, May 29, 1965; children—Suzanne Carterette, Lucretia Carole. Statistician, dir. air transp. Democratic Nat. Com., Washington, 1964; adminstrv. asst. to Congressman J.J. Pickle of Tex., 1968; admitted to Tex. bar, 1968; legis. counsel Tex. Senate, 1969-71; asst. atty. gen. Tex., 1969, 71; atty., New Braunfels, Tex., 1971—; mem. Tex. Ho. of Reps. from 38th Dist., 1972—, chmn. com. on liquor regulations, 1975-78, chmn. environ. affairs com., 1979-80, chmn. Sunset Commn. Mem. Am., Tex., Comal County bar assns., New Braunfels Jr. C. of C. (dir. 1971), S. Tex., New Braunfels chambers commerce, Delta Sigma Pi, Delta Theta Phi. Club: Lions (dir. New Braunfels 1971). Home: 402 Oakwood St New Braunfels TX 78130 Office: 340 N Seguin St New Braunfels TX 78130

BOCKIAN, HERBERT HAROLD, psychiatrist; b. Jersey City, Oct. 14, 1927; s. Abraham and Eva (Skner) B.; A.B., Columbia, 1950; M.A. in Modern Langs., U. Miami (Fla.), 1955; M.D., U. Tenn., 1960; m. Natalie Paula Fink, Aug. 15, 1958; children—Phyllis Ann, David Alan, Barry Israel, Steven Teo. Intern, St. Thomas Hosp., Nashville, 1960-61; resident adult psychiatry Vanderbilt U. Hosp., 1961-63, child psychiatry, 1963-65; dir. adolescent service Central State Hosp., Nashville, 1965-67; staff child psychiatrist Children's Psychiat. Center Miami, Inc., Coral Gables, Fla., 1967-73; practice medicine, specializing in psychiatry, Coral Gables, 1967-73; clin. dir. Bristol (Tenn.) Regional Mental Health Center, 1974—, coordinator psychiat. tng., 1975—; instr. modern langs. Memphis State U., 1956-60; instr. psychiatry Vanderbilt U., Nashville, 1962-65; clin. instr. psychiatry U. Miami, Coral Gables, 1967-70, clin. asst. prof., 1970-73; adj. clin. prof. psychopathology Grad. Sch. Social Work, Barry Coll., Miami Shores, Fla., 1972-73; clin. asso. prof. East Tenn. State U. Coll. Medicine, 1975—; mem. staff Jackson Meml. Hosp., Highland Park Gen. Hosp., Variety Children's Hosp., Miami, 1968-73, Bristol Meml. Hosp., 1973—. Mem. Children's Com., Nashville, 1965-67; chmn. small craft safety com., instr.-trainer water safety Dade County chpt. A.R.C., 1950-73. Served with USN, 1946-47. USPHS research fellow, 1958-59; recipient Charles C. Verstaendig award U. Tenn., 1960. Diplomate Am. Bd. Psychiatry and Neurology. Mem. Am. Psychiat. Assn., So., Tenn., S.W. Va., Sullivan-Johnson med. assns., Alpha Kappa Kappa. Jewish. Address: Bristol Regional Mental Health Center 26 Midway St Bristol TN 37620

BODDEKER, EDWARD WILLIAM, III, architect, govt. ofcl.; b. Houston, Mar. 22, 1929; s. Edward William and Ruth Margaret (Cook) B.; B.Arch., Tex. A. and M. U., 1951; m. Salee Boddeker; 1 son, Mark Montagne. Architect, MacKie & Kamrath, architects, Houston, 1960-63; architect Manned Spacecraft Center, NASA, Clear Lake, Tex., 1963—, project design mgr., 1963-65, master planner, 1965-67, head master planning sect., 1967-68, head archtl. civil sect., engring. div., 1968-76, head facilities programs sect., 1976-77, chief facilities planning office, 1977—. Bd. dirs., treas. Clear Creek Basin Authority, 1972-74. Served to 1st lt. Army Security Agy., AUS, 1953-54. Recipient Apollo and Skylab Achievement awards NASA, also NASA Gemini, Apollo, Skylab, Lunar Landing Team, Apollo Soyuz Test Project group achievement awards. Registered architect, Tex. Mem. AIA, Tex. Soc. Architects. Home: 13915 Grosvenor Houston TX 77034 Office: NASA Johnson Space Center Clear Lake TX 77058

BODDIE, ARTHUR WALKER, JR., surg. oncologist; b. Detroit, Dec. 21, 1941; s. Arthur Walker and Ellena Louise (Yerby) B.; B.A., Yale, 1963, M.D., 1967; m. Joy Marie Marchbanks, Aug. 20, 1966; children—Elise Catherine, Ellena Lois. Intern, Henry Ford Hosp., Detroit, 1967-68; resident in surgery David Grant USAF Med. Center, Fairfield, Calif., 1969-73; fellow in surg. oncology U. Calif. Sch. Medicine, Los Angeles, 1973-75; sr. fellow in surg. oncology U. Tex. System Cancer Center M.D. Anderson Hosp., Houston, 1975-76; chief surg. oncology service Willford Hall USAF Med. Center, San Antonio, 1976—, mem. jr. staff U. Calif. Sch. Medicine, Los Angeles, 1974-76; asst. clin. prof. Surgery U. Tex. at San Antonio, 1976-79. Diplomate Am. Bd. Surgery, Nat. Bd. Med. Examiners. Fellow A.C.S.; mem. Am. Radium Soc., Assn. for Academic Surgery, San Antonio Surg. Soc. Contbr. numerous articles to med. jours. Home: 110 Chimney Rock Ln San Antonio TX 78231

BODDIFORD, DYCHES V(ILLINES), corp. exec.; b. Lyons, Ga., May 4, 1949; s. Martin Dyches and Cinnie Samantha (Newsome) B.; B.S., Ga. Inst. Tech., 1971, M.S., 1972, postgrad., 1973. Prof. computer tech. DeVry Inst. Tech., Atlanta, 1971-73; with Taulman Co., Atlanta, 1973-77, asst. mgr. Analog and Standard Products Group, 1975, Turbitrol Systems mgr., 1976; dir. ops. Ace Industries, Inc. (formerly Ace Crane & Hoist, Inc.), Atlanta, 1977-79, exec. v.p., 1979—; owner Boddiford Co., Statesboro, Ga., 1979—. Ga. Power Tuition scholar, 1967-68. Mem. Nat. Space Inst. Club: Master 4-H. Home: 1495 Brandon Dr Marietta GA 30060 Office: 1616 Huber St NW Atlanta GA 30318

BODIN, BRUCE HAROLD, elec. engr., design exec.; b. Chgo., Sept. 15, 1932; s. Harold F. and Mable K. (Jacobsen) B.; B.S.E.E., Tri-State U., 1965; m. Marian Jean Robinson, Sept. 2, 1956; children—Hal, David, Lauri. Exptl. engr. Pratt Whitney Co., Palm Beach Gardens, Fla., 1965-67; tech. staff RCA Co., Palm Beach Gardens, 1967-72; sr. design mgr. GTE Automatic Elec. Labs., Huntsville, Ala., 1972—. Mem. planning/zoning bd., Jupiter, Fla., 1968-70; asst. dir. Little League Baseball, Jupiter, 1967-70; elder Christ the King Luth. Ch., Jupiter, 1966-67. Served with U.S. Army, 1952-54. Mem. IEEE. Lutheran. Contbr. article to profl. jour. Home: 309 Spring Valley Ct Huntsville AL 35802 Office: 13000 S Memorial Pkwy Huntsville AL 35803

BODINE, ASHBY BURGESS, dairy chemist, nutritional biochemist; b. Washington, June 24, 1947; s. Ashby Burgess and Frances Faye (Bohrer) B.; B.A. in Chemistry, Clemson U., 1969, M.S. in Nutrition, 1975, Ph.D., 1978; m. Linda Jean Sanders, July 12, 1968; children—Garrick Shannon, Keena Danielle. Research technologist, dept. dairy sci. Clemson (S.C.) U., 1970-78, asst. prof. dairy sci., 1978—; cons. mycotoxin analysis S.C. Dept. Agr., Dept. Health and Environ. Control. Mem. So. Assn. Agrl. Scientists, Sigma Xi, Gamma Sigma Delta. Contbr. articles to profl. jours. Home: 111 Scott Dr Seneca SC 29678 Office: 122 P&AS Bldg Clemson U Clemson SC 29631

BODLEY, DONALD ELWYN, educator; b. Monroe County, Mich., Feb. 3, 1929; s. Elwyn James and Grace Ellen (Quackenboss) B.; B.A., Eastern Mich. U., 1953, M.A. in Edn., 1965; Ph.D., Th.M., Internat. Free Protestant Episcopal U., (Eng.), 1960; children—Eric Scott, Elwyn James II. Ordained deacon Episcopal Ch., 1954, ordained priest, 1956; elementary sch. tchr., Mich., 1949-54; dir. leadership edn. Episcopal Diocese of Mich., 1954-63; v.p. mktg., nat. dir. rentals MULTICON, Columbus, Ohio, 1963-65; pres. Bodley Assos., Inc., Houston, 1965-75; prof. real estate, chmn. real estate studies Eastern Ky. U., Richmond, 1975—. Recipient outstanding teaching award Eastern Ky. U., 1976-77; cert. apt. mgr., cert. rev. appraiser. Fellow Mortgage Bankers Assn. Am.; mem. Am. Inst. Decision Scis., Nat. Assn. Realtors, Nat. Apt. Assn., Nat. Assn. Home Builders, Soc. Real Estate Appraisers, Urban Land Inst., Am. Soc. Tng. and Devel. Republican. Clubs: Rotary Internat., Masons, York Rite, Scottish Rite. Researcher multi-family housing for rent trends Central Ky. Service Area; contbr. reports, papers in field to instl. publs. Home: 236 Summit St Richmond KY 40475 Office: College of Business Eastern Kentucky University Richmond KY 40475

BODNAR, DONALD GEORGE, research elec. engr.; b. Fort William, Ont., Can., Apr. 30, 1941; came to U.S., 1951, naturalized, 1956; s. Steve and Daisy (Krelove) B.; B.E.E. with highest honors, Ga. Inst. Tech., 1963; M.S., M.I.T., 1964; Ph.D. in Elec. Engring. (NSF fellow), Ga. Inst. Tech., 1969; m. Judith Anne Boring, Sept. 14, 1964; children—David Stephen, Donald George. Mem. engring. staff microwave electronics div. Sperry Rand, Clearwater, Fla., 1969-70; research engr. Ga. Inst. Tech., Atlanta, 1970-73, sr. research engr., 1973—, mgr. electromagnetic programs office, 1973-75, sr. scientist antennas and countermeasures div., 1975-79, chief scientist systems and antennas br., 1979—, lectr. Sch. Elec. Engring., 1973—; cons. to industry and govt., 1974—. Vol. worker Grady Meml. Hosp., 1972-73; Sunday sch. tchr. Unitarian Universalist Ch., 1972-73. Mem. IEEE, Soc. of Antennas and Propagation (mem. standards com. 1979—), Sigma Xi, Phi Eta Sigma, Eta Kappa Nu, Tau Beta Pi, Phi Kappa Phi, Pi Mu Epsilon. Contbr. articles on radar, electromagnetic propagation and antenna design to profl. publs. Office: Systems and Techniques Lab Ga Inst Tech Atlanta GA 30332

BODTKE, SUSAN HERSHBERGER, nurse; b. Nappaunee, Ind., Dec. 26, 1934; d. Benjamin and Sarah (Borntreger) Hershberger; diploma Bethel Deaconess Hosp. Sch. Nursing, 1959; cert. nurse midwifery Frontier Nursing Service Sch., 1961; B.S., Bethany Nazarene Coll., 1970; postgrad Okla. U., 1979—; m. Clarence Bodtke, July 10, 1974. Midwife, Frontier Nursing Service, 1961-63; obstet. supr. Deaconess Hosp., Oklahoma City, 1964-70; devel., head prenatal clinic County Health Dept., Oklahoma City, 1970-73; inservice educator Midwest City (Okla.) Hosp., 1973-74; instr. maternal child health Okla. State U. Tech. Inst., Oklahoma City, 1975—, asst. prof., 1978—. Mem. Am. Coll. Nurse Widwives (sec. Okla.), Nurses Assn. Am. Coll. Ob-Gyn (nat. pres. 1972), Am. Nurses Assn., Okla. Nurses Assn. Lutheran. Mem. editorial bd. Jour. Ob-Gyn Neonatal Nursing, 1972-73. Home: 3217 N Wilburn St Bethany OK 73008 Office: 900 N Portland St Oklahoma City OK 73107

BOE, GERARD PATRICK, army officer, health care adminstr.; b. Washington, Jan. 20, 1936; s. Harold David and Bernice Virginia B.; B.S. in Biology, W.Va. Wesleyan Coll., 1958; M.T., U. Miami, 1959; M.S. in Clin. Pathology, Ohio State U., 1969; Ph.D. in Allied Health Edn. and Adminstrn., Tex. A&M U., 1976; m. Irene Margaret Dazevedo, Oct. 24, 1959; children—Steven Alan, Christine Ann. Commd. 1st lt. U.S. Marine Corps, 1960, transferred to U.S. Army as 1st lt., 1963, advanced through grades to lt. col., 1979; adminstrv. asst. to div. surgeon 3d inf. div., 1964-65; clin. lab. officer 33d Field Hosp., Wurzburg, Ger., 1965-67; officer-in-charge U.S. Army Vietnam Central Blood Bank, 1970-71; chief spl. subjects br. Acad. Health Scis., U.S. Army, 1971-72, chief hematology br., 1972-74; adminstrv. chief dept. pathology Dwight David Eisenhower Army Med. Center, Ft. Gordon, Ga., 1976—; asst. prof. health scis. Baylor U., 1971-74; chmn. div. med. tech. Incarnate Word Coll., 1972-74; mem. faculty S.W. Tex. State U., 1976; chmn. Brazos County (Tex.) Red Cross Blood Program, 1974-76; cons. lab. mgmt., gen. personnel mgmt. Decorated Bronze Star, Army Commendation medal with oak leaf cluster; recipient cert. appreciation ARC, 1976. Mem. Internat. Soc. Clin. Lab. Tech. (dir. 1974-78, pres. 1979—), Am. Soc. Allied Health Professions, Soc. Air Force Med. Lab. Scientists, Soc. Armed Forces Med. Lab. Scientists, Am. Soc. Clin. Pathologists (cert. med. tech.). Internat. Platform Assn., Am. Insts. Mgmt. (program contbg. editor 1978—), Beta Beta Beta. Contbr. articles to profl. jours. Home: 3601 Bimini Ct Augusta GA 30909 Office: Dept Pathology Eisenhower Army Med Center Fort Gordon GA 30905

BOEHLER, JACQUELINE BUNN, sch. adminstr.; b. Jonesboro, Ark., Aug. 1, 1927; d. S. Neal and Velma Iola (Freeze) Bunn; B.S.E., U. Tenn., 1965, M.A., 1971; Ed.S., Memphis State U., 1975; m. Albert F. Boehler, May 11, 1946; children—Cynthia, Michael, Jacquelynn, Albert F., William Mark. Tchr., 5th grade, pub. schs., Osceola, Iowa, 1965-68; tchr. 5th grade pub. schs., Milan, Tenn., 1968-70, elementary guidance counselor, 1970-74, supr. spl. edn., 1974—. Bd. dirs. Child Devel. Center, Trenton, Tenn., 1970-72, Paris Mental Health Center. Recipient Oriana B. Howley Tenn. State Guidance award, 1974. Mem. Am., West Tenn. personnel and guidance assns., NEA, Council Exceptional Children, DAR. Home: Route 5 Trenton TN 38382 Office: Box 528 Milan TN 38358

BOEHM, EDWARD GORDON, JR., univ. adminstr.; b. Washington, Jan. 30, 1942; s. Edward Gordon and Catherine A. (Murray) B.; B.S., Frostburg State Coll., 1964; M.Ed., Am. U., 1970, Ph.D., 1977; m. Regina Ellen Evans, June 25, 1966; children—Evan Arnold, Andrew Edward. Tchr., Montgomery County (Md.) Pub. Schs., 1964-68; instr., soccer coach Am. U., Washington, 1968-70, asst. dir. admissions, 1970-73, asso. dean freshman admissions, fin. aid, vet. affairs, programs and services, 1973-75, interim dean, 1978, dean students, 1975-77, dir. univ. devel., 1977-79; dean admissions, asst. prof. Sch. Edn., Tex. Christian U., Ft. Worth, 1979—; mem. Coll. Entrance Exam Bd., 1976—; exec. bd. Am. Coll. Test Program to Md./D.C., 1976-78. First nat. chmn. Washington Coll. Fair, 1974; bd. dirs. Project Open, Washington, 1971-75, Friends of Nat. Zoo, Washington, 1975—; v.p. Cashell Elem. Sch. PTA, 1979, Norbeck Meadows Civic Assn. Mem. Nat. Assn. Coll. Admissions Counselors (exec. bd. 1975-76), Am. Assn. Higher Edn., Am. Coll. Testing Program, Am. Personnel and Guidance Assn., Council Advancement and Support of Edn., Nat. Assn. Coll. Admissions Officers, Phi Gamma Mu. Democrat. Roman Catholic. Contbr. articles in field to profl. jours. Home: 7416 Fuller Circle Fort Worth TX 76133 Office: Office of Admissions Tex Christian U Fort Worth TX 76129

BOELCSKEVY, BENCE DAVID, physiologist; b. Gyongyos, Hungary, Oct. 1, 1944; s. Laudislaus Zoltan and Soja (Jovanovic) deB.; came to U.S., 1950, naturalized, 1956; B.S., W.Liberty State Coll., 1969; M.S., Ohio State U., 1971, Ph.D., 1976; m. Susan Patricia Metcalf, June 1, 1968. Quality assurance profl. Ross Labs., Columbus, Ohio, 1971-74; asst. prof. physiology W.Va. Sch. Osteopathic Medicine, Lewisburg, 1976-78, asst. dean clin. tng., 1978-79, asst. to pres., 1979—; pres. BDB Electronic Cons., 1979—. Mem. Soc. Tchrs. Family Medicine, Am. Soc. Quality Control, Digital Equipment Computer Users Soc., BMW Car Club Am. (nat. pres. 1978—). Episcopalian. Home: 17 Highland Circle Lewisburg WV 24901 Office: 400 N Lee St Lewisburg WV 24901

BOENIG, DAN LENNERT, seed co. ofcl.; b. San Antonio, June 8, 1953; s. Lennert Leslie and Edline Edna (Weyel) B.; B.S. in Agronomy, Tex. A&M U., 1975, M.Agr. in Agrl. Devel., 1977. Soil conservationist Soil Conservation Service USDA, Cuero, Tex., 1976; legis. asst. agr. and livestock com. Tex. Ho. of Reps., Austin, 1977; grad. asst. to dean of agr. Tex. A&M U., Coll. Sta., 1977; dist. sales mgr. La. Seed Co., Rosenberg, Tex., 1977—. State officer Tex. State Grange, 1972-74; pres. Area 7 Future Farmers Am., 1971-72, state v.p., 1972-73; active Tex. Farm Bur., Young Farmers Am. Coll. of Agr. scholar, 1971-72; Stiles Farm Found. scholar, 1973-75. Tex. Turfgrass Assn. scholar, 1972-73; recipient outstanding sr. in coll. agr. award, Tex. A&M U., 1975. Mem. Am. Soc. Agronomy (nat. pres. student div., 1973-74), Tex. Seed Trade Assn., Tex. A&M U. Assn. Former Students, Alpha Zeta. Mem. United Church of Christ. Clubs: Lions, Tex. Jaycees. Contbr. articles to publs. in field. Home and Office: PO Box 391 Rosenberg TX 77471

BÖER, GERMAIN BONIFACE, educator; b. Rockne, Tex., Nov. 19, 1937; s. August Henry and Lena (Bartsch) B.; B.S., St. Edward's U., Austin, Tex., 1960; M.B.A., Tex. Tech U., 1961; Ph.D., La. State U., 1964; m. Elinor Charles O'Brien, Jan. 25, 1964; children—Kathleen Marie, Robert James. Asso. prof. dept. acctg., acting asst. dean Coll. Bus. Adminstrn. Tex. Tech U., Lubbock, 1964-66; faculty resident Arthur Andersen & Co., Chgo., 1966-67; project mgr. Nat. Assn. Accts., N.Y.C., 1968-70; asso. prof. dept. acctg. Okla. State U., Stillwater, 1970-77; prof. Grad. Sch. Mgmt., Vanderbilt U., Nashville, 1977—. Cons. Nat. Assn. Accts., NIH, Hosp. Fin. Mgmt. Edn. Found. C.P.A., Tex. Mem. Am. Acctg. Assn. (chmn. com. on concepts and standards 1975-76), Nat. Assn. Accts. (nat. dir.), Am. Inst. C.P.A.'s, Beta Alpha Psi, Beta Gamma Sigma. Author: (with others) Automation and Management in the Clinical Laboratory, 1972; Direct Cost and Contribution Accounting, 1974; (with others) Financial Management of the Clinical Laboratory, 1975, Management and Cost Control Techniques for the Clinical Laboratory, 1977; editorial bd. The Acctg. Rev.; contbr. numerous articles in profl. jours. Home: 4519 Price Circle Dr Nashville TN 37205 Office: Owen Grad Sch Mgmt Vanderbilt U Nashville TN 37203

BOETTNER, JOHN L., JR., lawyer, state senator; b. Frostburg, Md., June 18, 1943; s. John Lewis and Grace Marie (Mitter) B.; A.B., W.Va. U., 1965, J.D., 1968; m. Mary Catherine Frerotte, 1968; children—John Lewis III, James Albert Theodore. Admitted to W.Va. bar, 1968; staff atty. Legal Aid Soc. of Charleston, W.Va., 1968-71; founder, directing atty. Appalachian Research and Def. Fund, 1971-73; partner firm Boettner, Campbell and Crane, Charleston;

mem. W.Va. Ho. of Dels., 1974-78; mem. W.Va. Senate, 1978—. Mem. Kanawha County Bar Assn., W.Va. State Bar, Am. Bar Assn., W.Va. Trial Lawyers Assn., Sierra Club. Democrat. Methodist. Club: Exchange. Home: 847 Edgewood Dr Charleston WV 25302 Office: 1115 Charleston National Plaza Charleston WV 25301

BOGAEV, LEONARD ROCKLIN, physician; b. Phila., Sept. 27, 1928; s. Harry A. and Vera Ethel (Rocklin) B.; B.A., Princeton, 1950; M.D., U. Pa., 1954; m. Rosa Lee Ayres, Oct. 1, 1957; children—Susan, Keith Richard, Douglas, Christopher. Intern U. Pa. Hosp., 1954-55; resident in urology, surgery U. Va. Hosp., Charlottesville, 1955-59; practice medicine specializing in urological surgery, Jonesboro, Ark., 1959—; chief of staff St. Bernard's Hosp., Jonesboro, 1974-76; pres. Bogaev & Williams Urology Clinic Profl. Assn., Jonesboro, 1972—; asst. clin. prof. U. Ark. Med. Center. Served with USNR, 1959-61. Diplomate Am. Bd. Urology. Fellow A.C.S.; mem. Am. Urol. Assn., Ark. Soc. Urologists (pres. 1975), Memphis-Shelby County (Tenn.) Urol. Soc., Ark. State Soc., AMA, Craighead-Poinsett Med. Soc., Phi Beta Kappa, Alpha Omega Alpha. Republican. Methodist. Elk. Home: 906 Pinecrest St Jonesboro AR 72401 Office: 812 Cobb St Jonesboro AR 72401

BOGAN, CARMEN PAGE, petroleum landman; b. Ballard County, Ky., June 4, 1918; d. Stanley Estes and Christina (Terrell) Page; student Murray State U., 1935-36, Draughon's Bus. Coll., Paducah, Ky., 1937; m. James Miller Bogan, Jan. 21, 1938; children—Carmen Bogan Murrey, James Miller. Sec., bookkeeper Paint and Glass Store, Paducah, 1937; sec., fin. adviser to ind. oil operator, 1957-61, asst. landman, fin. adviser, 1961-74; ind. petroleum landman, Shreveport, La., 1974—. Mem. Am., Ark-La-Tex assns. petroleum landmen. Republican. Methodist. Office: PO Box 5705 Shreveport LA 71105

BOGARDO, JEAN PAIVA, communications co. exec.; b. N.Y.C., Oct. 5, 1944; d. Thomas F. and Marie Daiva; student New Sch. Social Research, N.Y.C., 1960-63; m. Stephen L. Bogardo, Aug. 15, 1978. Co-owner, mng. editor Crawdaddy Mag., N.Y.C., 1969-72; free-lance writer, music and film columnist, N.Y.C., 1967-75; publicity dir., subsidiary rights mgr. Drake Pubs., N.Y.C., 1973-75; mktg. mgr. Am. Mgmt. Assn., N.Y.C., 1975-78; mktg. mgr. Birmingham Cable Communications, 1979—; mem. adv. bd. Birmingham Mag. (C. of C.). Mem. Am. Women in Radio and TV, Women in Communications, Birmingham Ad Club. Club: Riverchase Country. Home: 4425 Corinth Dr Birmingham AL 35213 Office: Birmingham Cable Communications 6429 1st Ave S Birmingham AL 35212

BOGART, DANIEL ROBERT, rehab. counselor, educator; b. Wilkes-Barre, Pa., Sept. 19, 1945; s. Harold William and Wilma Louise (Edwards) B.; B.A., Eastern Mich. U., 1968, M.A., 1970; postgrad. U. Fla., 1970—; m. Pamela Anne Parry, June 17, 1967; children—Laura Beth, Scott Daniel. Acad. cons. Correctional Tng. Inst., Fla. Div. Corrections, Raiford, 1973-74, asst. tng. dir. Fla. Dept. Offender Rehab., 1974-76; specialist rehab. therapy program standards N. Fla. Evaluation and Treatment Center, Gainesville, 1976-79, quality control dir., 1980—; nat. cons., lectr. in field. Chmn. Northwood Community Assn., 1972-74. Rehab. Services Adminstrn. doctoral fellow, 1970-73. Recipient Merit award Fla. Dept. Health and Rehabilitative Services, 1975. Certified correctional instr., Fla. Mem. Nat. (chpt. pres. 1971), Fla. (state sec. 1972) rehab. counselor assns., Am. Personnel and Guidance Assn., Assn. Counselor Edn. and Supervision (profl.), Am. Mental Health Counselor Assn. Home: 3239 NW 51st Pl Gainesville FL 32605 Office: PO Box N Fla Evaluation Treatment Center Gainesville FL 32601

BOGART, W(ILLIAM) HUMPHREY, banker; b. Toronto, Ont., Can., June 14, 1944; came to U.S., 1963; s. Ernest Charlton and Edith Mary (Clarkson) B.; B.A. in History and Polit. Sci., Trinity U., 1967; J.D., U. Tex., 1970; m. Jennifer Smith Josey, July 12, 1975; 1 son, Robert Clarkson. Trust intern Republic Nat. Bank, Dallas, 1970-71, trust adminstrv. officer, 1971-72, trust officer, 1972-73, asst. v.p., trust officer, 1973, v.p., trust officer, 1973-79, sr. v.p., trust officer, 1979—; mem. faculty Nat. Trust Sch./Nat. Grad. Trust Sch., Northwestern U., 1978—. Pres. bd. dirs. Big Bros. and Sisters of Met. Dallas, 1979-80; mem. design of city com. Goals for Dallas, 1979; bd. dirs. Hope Cottage Children's Bur., 1979—, also Dallas Rehab. Inst., Dallas Big Bros. Found. Mem. Am. Bankers Assn., S.W. Pension Conf. (dir.), Assn. Pvt. Pension and Welfare Plans. Episcopalian. Clubs: Calyx (past pres., gov.), Idlewild, Terpsichorean. Office: Republic Nat Bank PO Box 241 Dallas TX 75221

BOGEN, EUGENE MICHAEL, lawyer; b. Greenville, Miss., May 30, 1943; s. Edward Joshua and Mary Lee (Purtle) B.; B.A. in Polit. Sci., U. Va., 1965; J.D., U. Miss., 1968; postgrad. Labor Mgmt. Relations Program Harvard U., 1979; m. Eugenia Lanier Sykes, Aug. 13, 1966; children—Jane Conwell, Marian. Admitted to Miss. bar, 1968, since practiced in Greenville; asso. firm Bogen, Wilkes & McGough, 1968-69; partner firm Bogen, McGough & Bogen, 1970-71; partner firm Bogen & Bogen, 1972-76, Wynn & Bogen, 1977, Wynn, Bogen & Mitchell, 1978—. Atty. Greenville Mcpl. Separate Sch. Dist., 1970—. Pres. Washington County (Miss.) Mental Health Assn., 1970-72; chmn. Greenville United Fund Campaign, 1975, pres., 1977; chmn. adv. bd. Salvation Army, Greenville, 1975. Mem. Washington County Democratic Exec. Com., 1972-76. Bd. dirs. YMCA, Greenville, 1973-78, Greenville Council on Aging, 1978—. Recipient Spl. award Salvation Army, 1973. Mem. Am., Miss., Washington County (pres. young lawyers sect. 1974) bar assns., Am. Trial Lawyers Assn., Am. Judicature Soc. Home: 214 Taylor St Greenville MS 38701 Office: PO Box 1295 Greenville MS 38701

BOGGS, CORINNE C. (LINDY), congresswoman; b. Brunswick Plantation, La.; grad. Sophie Newcomb Coll.; m. Thomas Hale Boggs (dec.); children—Barbara (Mrs. Paul Sigmund), Thomas Hale, Corinne (Mrs. Steven V. Roberts). Active numerous civic activities; elected to 93d Congress from 2d La. dist. in spl. election to fill vacancy caused by death of husband, 1973, elected to 94th-96th congresses, chmn. joint com. Bicentennial arrangements, 1975-76, mem. com. on appropriations, 1977—, subcom. on energy and water devel., subcom. on housing and urban devel. and ind. agys. Past pres. Women's Nat. Democratic Club, Dem. Congl. Wives' Forum, Congl. Club; exec. com. Dem. Congl. Campaign Com., 1979—; active numerous Dem. events including inaugural balls Pres. Kennedy and Pres. Johnson; chairwoman Dem. Nat. Conv., 1976. Bd. regents Smithsonian Instn., 1976-77; bd. dirs. La. Council Music and Performing Arts, Am. Revolution Bicentennial Adminstrn. Mem. Nat. Soc. Colonial Dames, League Women Voters. Roman Catholic. Address: U S Congress Washington DC 20515

BOGGS, DOYLE WILLARD, educator; b. Charlotte, N.C., Sept. 20, 1948; s. Doyle W. and Carrie C. (Carroll) B.; B.A., Wofford Coll., 1970; M.A., U. S.C., 1973, Ph.D., 1977; m. Sara Nell Dalnodar, Mar. 15, 1975; 1 son, Jay William. Grad. teaching asst. U. S.C., Columbia, 1973-75; dir. info. services U.S.C., Spartanburg, 1975—, asst. prof. history, 1977—. Served with S.C. Army N.G. to capt., 1973—. Woodrow Wilson fellow, 1970-75. Mem. Coll. News Dirs. of the Carolinas, Carolinas Assn. Bus. Communicators, S.C. Hist. Assn., Council Advancement and Support Edn. Club: Sertoma (weekly bull. editor 1976-79). Home: 162 Cornelius Rd Spartanburg SC 29302 Office: Univ of SC Spartanburg SC 29303

BOGGS, J(AMES) PALMER, cons. structural engr.; b. Bartlesville, Okla., Apr. 21, 1906; s. James Francis and Mabel (Bailey); B.S., M.I.T., 1930; m. Virginia Underhill, Apr. 24, 1938; children—James P., Meredith, Jacqueline Jean. Prof. architecture Sch. Architecture U. Okla., 1951-66, chmn. Sch. Architecture, 1955-60; prof. architecture U. Ark., 1966-76, prof. emeritus, 1973—; cons. structural engr., Fayetteville, Ark., 1966—; Fulbright prof. Nat. Coll. Arts, Lahore, Pakistan, 1960-62. Mem. AIA, Am. Inst. Steel Constrn., Am. Concrete Inst., AAUP. Democrat. Episcopalian. Address: 1 Texas Way Fayetteville AR 72701

BOGGS, JAMES BISHOP, architect; b. Fort Worth, Jan. 21, 1936; s. Harry Hobart and W. Vera (Bishop) B.; student U. Miami (Fla.), 1954-55; B.Arch., Tex. Tech. U., 1962; m. Martha Juanita Dodson, Sept. 10, 1957; children—Pamela E., James Michael, Patricia Elaine, Paula Elisa. Designer firm Smyth & Smyth, architects, Corpus Christi, Tex., 1963-68; pvt. practice, Corpus Christi, 1968-70; prin. firm James B. Boggs, AIA, Corpus Christi, 1972-76; v.p. Total Design Four, 1976—; chmn. Callihan Land & Cattle Co., 1979—; dir. Omni-Tech of Am.; chmn. dept. architecture DelMar Coll., Corpus Christi, 1970-76. Chmn. Municipal Arts Commn., Corpus Christi, 1969-76. Founding mem. bd. dirs. Redevel. Assistance Center, 1970-72; bd. dirs Beautify Corpus Christi Assn., 1972-76; past pres. Community Devel. Corp.; mem. Corpus Christi Library Bd., 1977—. Served with USAF Res., 1954-62. Recipient certificate Nat. Council Archtl. Registration Bds., 1970; mem. 1st class Leadership Corpus Christi, 1973; Tex. Edn. Agy. grantee, 1971-72. Mem. AIA (corporate), Corpus Christi, Jr. (dir. 1967-72) chambers commerce, Tex. Tech. Ex-Students Assn. (dist. rep.), Tex. Soc. Architects, Theta Chi, Alpha Phi Omega. Methodist. Club: Conquistadors. Home: 4701 Donegal St Corpus Christi TX 78413 Office: Suite 300 101 N Shoreline Dr Corpus Christi TX 78401

BOHANNON, BILL, recording, publishing co. exec.; b. Mineral Springs, Ark., Nov. 28, 1939; s. Carl and Rebecca Sue (Walden) B.; student Ark. State U., Conway, 1965, Centenary Coll., Shreveport, La., 1966-68; 1 son, Jason Carl. Sr. clk. in planning dept. La. Army Ammunition Plant, Shreveport, 1963-70; ops. dir. Sta. KRMD-FM, Shreveport, 1970-71; dist. mgr. Savs. Life Ins. Co., Shreveport, 1971-72; staff announcer Sta. KWKH, Shreveport, 1972-75; pres. Bouquet Records-Orchid Pub. Co., Shreveport, 1972—; performer, singer, guitarist, Shreveport, 1965—, also rec. artist Paula Records and Bouquet Records, Shreveport. Mem. Am. Fedn. Musicians, Country Music Assn., Internat. Platform Assn., Democrat. Baptist. Composer: One More Trip, 1966, Tell Me the Truth, 1967, Shreveport, Louisiana, 1968, Remember My Darling, 1968, Gonna Be a Brighter Day Tomorrow, 1977. Home: 3020 Colquitt Rd Shreveport LA 71108 Office: PO Box 4220 Shreveport LA 71104

BOHANNON, JEAN LORRAINE, nurse; b. Blount County, Ala., Nov. 8, 1922; d. Fred Edward and Lila Gertrude (Ivey) Cleveland; R.N., South Highland Infirmary, Birmingham, Ala., 1944: m. James Bryce Bohannon, May 26, 1944; 1 dau., Penny Gail. Operating room supr. Children's Hosp., Birmingham, 1949-50, Blount Meml. Hosp., Oneonta, Ala., 1950-55; nursing service adminstr. Boaz (Ala.)-Albertville Hosp., 1956—. Sec. adv. com. Snead State Jr. Coll.; mem. admission com. Gadsden (Ala.) Tech. Inst.; mem. Ala. Commn. Higher Edn.; vice chair Marshall County Health Home Nursing Council, 1969—; bd. dirs. Marshall County Cancer Soc., 1975—; mem. North Ala. Health Planning Agy., 1971. Served to 2d lt. Nurse Corps, AUS, 1944-45; PTO. Named Woman of Yr., Boaz, 1976. Mem. Ala. Nurses Assn. (past pres. Dist.), Am. Nurses Assn. (conv. del.), Am. Hosp. Assn. (dir.), Ala. Council Nursing Service, Am. Soc. Hosp. Nursing Service Adminstrs., Am. Heart Assn., ARC, Am. Legion, Ala. Cattleman's Assn. Methodist. Club: Bus. and Profl. Women's. Office: Box 338 Boaz AL 35957

BOHANNON, MARY LEE, nurse; b. Akron, Ala., Dec. 28, 1920; d. Christopher Columbus and Zellia Mae (Ray) Gibson; b. grad. St. Vincent's Hosp. Sch. Nursing, 1943; m. Hagood Bohannon, May 21, 1946. With St. Vincent's Hosp., Birmingham, 1943—, mgr. operating room, 1970-76, mgr. recovery room, 1970-76, instr. hosp. edn., 1976—. Active Avondale United Meth. Ch., Birmingham. Lic. profl. nurse, Ala. Mem. Assn. Operating Room Nurses (past pres. Birmingham chpt.). Democrat. Home: 3809 4th Ave S Birmingham AL 35222 Office: 2701 9th Ct S Birmingham AL 35201

BOHANNON, RICHARD FREDERICK, psychiatrist; b. Oakland, Calif., Nov. 23, 1923; s. Joseph Altman and Dorothy Christina (Hoffman) DeGroodt; B.S., Abilene (Tex.) Christian U., 1950; M.D., Baylor Med. Coll., Houston, 1956; children—Sharlette Jayne, Shawn Eileen (Mrs. Wayne Snider), Richard Patrick, Paul Frederick, Kirk Ward Robinson, Sherra Lynn, Sarah Jane Cronin, Ann Michelle Cronin, Catherine Elizabeth Cronin. Intern, Jefferson Davis Hosp., Houston, 1956-57; practice gen. medicine, Pharr, Tex., and McAllen, Tex., 1957-64; mem. staffs McAllen Gen. Hosp., Grandview Hosp., Edinburg, Tex.; resident psychiatry Parkland Hosp., Dallas, 1964-67, Terrell (Tex.) State Hosp., 1967-69; practice medicine specializing in psychiatry, McAllen, 1969—. Psychiat. cons. Pan Am. U., Edinburg, Tex., 1969-75; founder, owner Pan Am. Aviation Ground Sch., McAllen, 1973—. Served to 1st lt., USAAF, 1942-47. Recipient citation as Unit Chief Terrell State Hosp., 1969, as dir. adolescent program, 1969, dir. deaf program, 1969; recipient plaque Helpline, 1972. Mem. Am. Psychiat. Assn., Am. Med. Assn., Tex. Med. Assn., Hidalgo-Starr (Tex.) Counties Med. Soc., Pan Am. Flying Club (pres., comml. instr. pilot), Aircraft Owners', Pilots' Assn. Alpha Chi. Founder Hidalgo County Council on Alcoholism, McAllen, 1969-70; founder Helpline, crisis telephone service, Edinburg, Tex., 1971-72. Home: 3200 S 2d St McAllen TX 78501 Office: 3200 S 2d St McAllen TX 78501

BOHLEN, JAMES ALBERT, chemist; b. Moweaqua, Ill., July 23, 1917; s. Martin Peter and Nellie Fern (Sanner) B.; B.S. in Chemistry, U. Ill., 1938; postgrad. in biochemistry U. Iowa, 1940; m. Betty Lou Holmquist, Dec. 7, 1941. Chemist, Jones-Dabney, Louisville, 1941-46, Am.-Marietta, Kankakee, Ill., 1946-52, Reliance Universal, Louisville, High Point, N.C., 1952-57, 61-67, DeSoto, Greensboro, 1957-61, Sherwin-Williams, Greensboro, 1967—; N.C. state liaison for nat. paint and coatings air quality, 1971-79. Usher, West Market Methodist Ch., pres. Couples Class, 1975-76. Mem. Am. Chem. Soc., Piedmont Soc. for Coatings Technology (council rep., 1973-79), Fedn. Socs. of Coatings Tech. (internat. bd. dirs., 1975-79). Home: 3817 Kirby Dr Greensboro NC 27403 Office: Box 8885 Greensboro NC 27410

BOHLER, CLORINDA SCARPA-SMITH (MRS. T. GORDON BOHLER), physician; b. Buenos Aires, Argentina; d. Jose and Maria (Smith) Scarpa; M. Teaching, Ministerio Nacional de Educacion de la Nacion (Buenos Aires), 1941, B.A., 1942; M.D., U. Buenos Aires, 1949; m. T. Gordon Bohler, Jan. 4, 1959. Intern, Hosp. Argerich Buenos Aires, 1946-47, resident, 1948-51; instr. anatomy U. Buenos Aires, 1946-47, asst. physician, dept. medicine, 1949-57; chief of colpocitology sect. Instituto Nacional de Endocrinologia, Nat. Ministry of Health, Buenos Aires, 1950-56; prof. spltys, of medicine Red Cross Sch. for Nurses, Buenos Aires, 1952-56; practice medicine, specializing in endocrinology, Buenos Aires, 1950-56; asst. physician Dr. Fred A. Simmons, Mass. Gen. Hosp., Harvard Med. Sch., Boston, 1957; clin. and research fellow Mass. Gen. Hosp., 1957; head sect. of Gonads and infertility NIH, Buenos Aires, Argentina, 1958; research fellow, dept. endocrinology Med. Coll. Ga., Augusta, 1958; cardiovascular research, 1959-60, research asso., 1960-63; research asso., dept. physiology and hemodynamic unit, dept. medicine Eugene Talmadge Meml. Hosp., Med. Coll. Ga., Augusta, 1963-65, asst. prof., dept. obstetrics-gynecology, instr. dept. physiology, 1965-70; research fellow endocrinology Med. Coll. Ga., 1970-71; practice medicine, specializing in endocrinology and metabolism, Augusta, 1971—; clin. tchr. Med. Coll. Ga., 1972—. NIH and Ga. Heart Assn. grantee, 1966-69. Fellow Am. Acad. Family Physicians; mem. AMA (Physicians Recognition award). Baptist. Author: Nociones de Especialidades Medicas para Enfermeras, 1954; (with others) Testicular Function in the Aging Male; Geriatric Endocrinology, Vol. 5, 1978. Contbr. articles in field to profl. jours. Home: 1337 Winter St Augusta GA 30904

BOHORFOUSH, JOSEPH GEORGE, physician; b. Birmingham, Ala., Dec. 20, 1907; s. George and Susan (Joseph) B.; A.B., Vanderbilt U., 1929, M.D., 1933; m. Bliss Page, Feb. 17, 1960; children—David, William, Eugenia Paige Hoffman (Mrs. R.S. Sayers). Intern Hillman Hosp., Birmingham, 1933-34; resident Waverly Hills (Ky.) Sanatorium, 1934-35; asst. med. dir. Lake View Sanatorium, Madison, Wis., 1936-41; med. dir. Jefferson Sanatorium, Birmingham, 1946-47; instr. medicine U. Ala. Med. Coll., 1946-48; chief profl. services VA Hosp., Memphis, 1947-51; asst. prof. medicine U. Tenn., Memphis, 1947, 51; clin. prof. medicine Med. Coll. Ga., 1951-60; chief medicine VA Hosp, Augusta, Ga., 1951-60; dir. phys. health services Central State Hosp., Milledgeville, Ga., 1960-69; dir. Jones Hosp., Milledgeville, 1969-72; dir. Bohorfoush Corp. Served as maj. M.C., AUS, 1941-45; col. M.C. ret. Diplomate Am. Bd. Internal Medicine, Am. Bd. Pulmonary Diseases. Fellow A.C.P., Am. Coll. Chest Physicians, Am. Fedn. Clin. Research; asso. Royal Soc. Medicine; mem. AMA, Med Assn. Ga., Baldwin County, 10th Dist. med. socs., Am., Ga. thoracic socs., Pan Am., So. med. assns., Ga. Acad. Sci., Ga. Heart Assn., Ret. Officers Assn., Internat. Soc. Internal Medicine. Kiwanian. Club: Milledgeville Country. Home: 1661 Stone Meadow Rd Milledgeville GA 31061

BOHORFOUSH, ROBERT LOUIS, real estate developer; b. Birmingham, Ala., Jan. 11, 1946; s. Louis Charles and Ruth (Davis) B.; B.A., Birmingham So. Coll., 1967; m. Martha Carol Minor, Dec. 20, 1969; 1 son, Robert Justin. Sales coordinator Saunders Leasing System, Inc., Birmingham, 1967-69; co-founder, adminstrv. v.p. Met. Properties, Inc., Birmingham, 1969—. Co-chmn. Downtown Birmingham Clear-Up Drive, 1970; mem. advisory com. Birmingham Regional Planning Commn.; mem. steering com. Met. Devel. Bd. Mem. Nat. Inst. Real Estate Bds. (certified comml. investment mem.) Birmingham Bd. Realtors (dir.), Nat. Inst. Real Estate Brokers, Birmingham Area C. of C. (chmn. steering com., mem. environmental econs. com.). Clubs: Vestavia Country, North River Yacht, The Club, Relay House (Birmingham). Home: 3405 Pine Ridge Rd Birmingham AL 35213 Office: 2 Metroplex Dr Birmingham AL 35209

BOHRMAN, JEFFREY STEPHEN, pharmacologist, physiologist; b. Easton, Pa., Jan. 19, 1944; s. Fred Berger and Rhoda Lucille (Claster) B.; B.S. in Biology, Dickinson Coll., 1967; B.S. in Pharmacy, U. Pitts., 1970; M.S in Pharmacology, U. Ill., 1972; Ph.D. in Pharmacology, U. Pacific, 1977; m. Evalyn Sue Rudman, Sept. 10, 1970; children—Rebecca Lyn, David Ryan. Pharmacy extern, intern Presbyterian Univ. Hosp., Pitts., 1968-70; teaching asst. U. Ill., 1970-72, U. Pacific, 1972-77; postdoctoral inYestigator Biology div. Oak Ridge Nat. Lab., 1977—. Me. Am. Pharm. Assn., AAAS, Rho Chi, Phi Kappa Phi. Democrat. Jewish. Home: 143 Cumberland View Dr Oak Ridge TN 37830 Office: PO Box Y Oak Ridge TN 37830

BOINODIRIS, STAVROS, electronic systems engr.; b. Drama, Greece, Nov. 15, 1943; s. Antonios and Elizabeth (Aslanoglou) B.; came to U.S., 1961; B.S., U. Fla., 1967, M.E., 1968; Ph.D. (IBM grantee), N.C. State U., Raleigh, 1979; m. Despina Kokinos, Sept. 2, 1967; children—Phaedra, Ismini. Jr. engr. IBM, Boca Raton, Fla., 1969, asso. engr., 1969-71, sr. asso. engr., 1971-74, staff engr., 1974—, also sub-system group leader. Recipient outstanding performance award IBM. Mem. Instrument Soc. Am., IEEE, Assn. Computing Machinery. Patentee isolated digital to analog converter. Home: 1417 Granada Dr Raleigh NC 27612 Office: IBM DPTE 76 Bldg 060 Research Triangle Park NC 27709

BOISSEAU, MARY LEIGH, educator; b. Danville, Va., Dec. 31, 1935; d. Jennings Kenneth and Nannie Leigh (Viar) Deane; B.A., Longwood Coll., 1958, M.A., 1972; postgrad. Va. State Coll., 1974-75; children—John Michael, Willie Edward III. Tchr. elem. schs., Danville, Va., 1958-65; tchr. English, George Washington High Sch., Danville, Va. 1965-70; instr. English, Southside Va. Community Coll., Alberta, 1970-75, asst. prof., 1975—. Mem. Assn. Tchrs. Tech. Writing, Southeastern Conf. on English in Two-Yr. Colls., Phi Delta Kappa. Home: 459 Brightwell Dr Danville VA 24541 Office: Southside Virginia Community College J H Daniel Campus Route 40 Keysville VA 23947

BOKESCH, CHARLES RICHARD, cardiologist; b. Youngstown, Ohio, Sept. 25, 1946; s. Elmer Richard and Jean (Kelso) B.; B.A., Johns Hopkins U., 1968; M.D., Emory U., 1973; m. Charlotte Louise Sykes, June 27, 1970 children—Charles Mark, Elizabeth Graves, Kimberly Louise. Med. intern N.C. Bapt. Hosp., 1973-74, resident in medicine, 1974-75, fellow in cardiology, 1975-77; pvt. practice medicine specializing in cardiology, Mount Airy, N.C., 1977—; chief of medicine, dir. coronary care unit and cardiovascular diagnostic unit No. Hosp. of Surry County, Mount Airy; sr. partner, founder No. Surrey Med.-Surg. Center, Mount Airy. Dir., N.C. Nat. Bank, Mount Airy. Bd. dirs. Surry County Heart Assn., Mount Airy, United Fund, Mount Airy; mem. physicians adv. com. Piedmont Med. Found., Winston-Salem, N.C. Diplomate Am. Bd. Internal Medicine. Asso. fellow Am. Coll. Cardiology; mem. A.C.P., AMA, N.C. Med. Soc., Surry County Med. Soc., Am. Soc. Internal Medicine, Ducks Unltd. (dir.). Methodist. Club: Rotary. Home: 851 Montclair Dr Mount Airy NC 27030 Office: 708 S South St Mount Airy NC 27030

BOLAN, ROBERT DAVID, accountant, state govt. exec.; b. Roanoke, Ala., Feb. 15, 1952; s. Robert Leroy and Alfie (Morris) B.; B.S. in Acctg., Troy State U., 1978, A.S. in Computer Sci., 1977. Account examiner Dept. Examiners of Public Accounts, State of Ala., Montgomery, 1978—. Lic. public accountant, Ala. Baptist. Home: Route 2 Box 162-S Eclectic AL 36024 Office: Examiners of Public Accounts State Capitol Montgomery AL 36130

BOLAN, ROBERT MOSIER, accountant; b. Topeka, July 3, 1940; s. Ralph William and Edith Charlotte (Riggs) B.; B.B.A. in Accounting and Econs., Washburn U., Topeka, 1962; grad. Southwestern Grad. Sch. Banking, So. Meth. U., Dallas, 1968; children—Brett Allen, Rebecca Jane. Sr. accountant firm Baird, Kurtz & Dobson, C.P.A.'s, Pine Bluff, Ark., 1971-73; sec.-treas. firm Smith, Bolan & Co. Ltd., C.P.A.'s, Pine Bluff, 1973-75; pres. firm Robert M. Bolan, Ltd. C.P.A., Pine Bluff, 1975—. Past mem. Pine Bluff Planning Commn., 1979; ad hoc revenue com. Mem. Am. Inst. C.P.A.'s, Ark. Soc. C.P.A.'s, Methodist (adv. bd., treas.). Club: Lions (dir.). Home: 521 Greenbriar

Pine Bluff AR 71603 Office: 720 Laurel St PO Box 8965 Pine Bluff AR 71611

BOLDING, LAURA HELEN BYRD (MRS. SAMUEL MCCONNELL BOLDING), librarian; b. Vimville, Miss., Sept. 8, 1913; d. Albert Sidney and Annie (Campbell) Byrd; B.A. cum laude, Millsaps Coll., 1935; certificate L.S., U. Ala., 1940; postgrad. Auburn U., 1958; m. Samuel McConnell Bolding, Aug. 21, 1939; 1 dau., Betty. Tchr. pub. high sch., Miss., 1936-37, librarian, 1937-38; librarian pub. high sch., Ala., 1939-42; asst. librarian U. Ala. Coll. Edn. Library, University, 1945-46; head popular lit. dept. Birmingham (Ala.) Pub. Library, 1948-50; reference librarian Montgomery (Ala.) Pub. Library, 1959-68, reader's adviser, supr. outreach to aging, 1968-79, dir. Normandale br., 1979—. Mem. Ala. Adv. Com. for Sch. Library Service, 1968-69. Mem. adv. com. Montgomery Area Commn. on Aging, 1972; mem. adminstrv. bd. 1st United Meth. Ch., Montgomery. Mem. Ala. Library Assn. (awards com. 1972-73, recruitment com. 1973-74, membership com. public library div. 1979-80), AAUW, Ala. Bus. and Profl. Women's Club (state exec. bd. 1950-51), Kappa Kappa Iota, Kappa Delta Pi, Beta Sigma Omicron. Methodist (librarian 1959-68, mem. commn. on edn. 1960-68). Clubs: Montgomery Music Study (pres. 1964-65); Soroptimist (Montgomery). Home: 620 Ponce De Leon Ave Montgomery AL 36106 Office: 135 Normandale Arcade Montgomery AL 36111

BOLDT, ALBERT WALTER, ret. govt. ofcl.; b. Altoona, Pa., Aug. 28, 1904; s. John Henry and Bertha (Seig) B.; B.S., Gettysburg Coll., 1927; M.A., Lehigh U., 1938; Ed.D., U. Fla., 1958; married; children—Jacqueline Boldt Poor, Sandra Boldt Bockman. Instr., Reading (Pa.) Sch. Dist., 1930-42; chief Vocat. Rehab. and Edn. div. VA, Reading, 1945-48; asst. dean men U. Fla., Gainesville, 1948-58; dean students Am U., Washington, 1958-60; dir. div. higher edn. HEW Region IV, U.S. Office Edn., Atlanta, 1960-74; cons. Bethune-Cookman Coll., Daytona Beach, Fla.; cons. evaluation sch. dists. Atlanta, Jacksonville, DeLand and Ocala, Fla., 1950-58. Served to lt. comdr. USNR, 1942-45. Mem. Am. Coll. Personnel Assn., Nat. Assn. Student Personnel Adminstrs., Nat. Assn. Sch. and Coll. Placement, NEA, Assn. Higher Edn., Nat. Assn. Deans and Advisers of Men, Phi Delta Kappa, Phi Kappa Phi, Kappa Delta Pi. Author: Objective Tests in American History, 1940; History of the Schools of Reading from 1748 to 1859, 1938; The Leadership Fraternity in American Society—A Study of the Florida Blue Key, 1956; editor: Gator Guide. Home: 5 Seafarers Dr Ormond Beach FL 32074

BOLEN, HELEN BUCKLER, charitable orgn. exec.; b. Lexington, Ky., Dec. 10, 1920; d. Carl William and Anna Katherine (Mikkelsen) Buckler; student Lassell Jr. Coll., 1937, Chouinard Art Inst., 1944, Pasadena Jr. Coll., 1944-45, Nat. Acad. Voluntarism, 1975, 77-78; m. Bennett Richard Bolen, Mar. 10, 1949; children—Bennett Richard, Wendy Anne. Jr. copywriter Dan B. Miner Advt. Agy., Los Angeles, 1944-45; chief communications dept. C.F. Braun & Co., Alhambra, Calif., 1946-49; staff mem. United Way, San Antonio, 1969-73, dir. Vol. Action Center, 1974-76; campaign div. dir., United Way of San Antonio and Bexar County, 1977—; cons. com. Spl. Olympics, Nat. Alliance Businessmen, New Horizons for Women Seminar, St Mary's U. Asso. mem. San Antonio Mayor's Commn. on Status of Women, 1974-79; vol. phone counselor San Antonio Crisis Center. Recipient awards San Antonio State Hosp., 1976, City of San Antonio Health Dept., 1976, S.W. Center for Hearing Impaired, 1976. Mem. San Antonio Assn. Vol. Services Dir., Bus. and Profl. Women's Assn. Home: 66 Brees Blvd Apt 106 San Antonio TX 78209 Office: 406 W Market St San Antonio TX 78205

BOLEN, WILLIAM HAROLD, educator, mktg. cons.; b. Savannah, Ga., Feb. 24, 1943; s. Harold Jean and Lucy Jane (Huggins) B.; B.S., Ga. So. Coll., 1964; M.B.A., U. Ark., 1966, Ph.D., 1972; m. Sheron Lee Smith, Dec. 21, 1968; children—William Harold, Charles Henry. Asst., Bur. of Bus. Research, U. Ark., 1964-65, instr. econs., 1965-66; asst. prof. mktg. Ga. Soc. Coll., Statesboro, 1966-73, asso. prof., 1973-79, prof., 1979—, head dept. mktg. and office adminstrn., 1973—. Mem. Am. Acad. Advt., Am. Collegiate Retailing Assn., Am. Mktg. Assn., So. Mktg. Assn., SW Mktg. Assn., Bulloch County C. of C., Pi Sigma Epsilon, Beta Gamma Sigma, Omicron Delta Epsilon, Pi Omega Pi, Delta Sigma Pi. Author: Contemporary Retailing, 1978; Introduction to Advertising, 1980; contbr. articles to profl. jours. Home: 18 Forest Pines Dr Statesboro GA 30458 Office: Dept Mktg Ga So Coll Statesboro GA 30458

BOLENE, MARGARET ROSALIE STEELE (MRS. ROBERT V. BOLENE), bacteriologist; b. Kingfisher, Okla., July 11, 1923; d. Clarence R. and Harriet (White) Steele; student Oreg. State U., 1943-44; B.S., U. Okla., 1946; m. Robert V. Bolene, Feb. 6, 1948; children—Judith Kay, John Eric, Sally Sue, Janice Lynn, Daniel William. Technician bacteriology dept. Okla. Dept. Health, Oklahoma City, 1946-48; asst. bacteriologist Henry Ford Hosp., Detroit, 1948-49; bacteriol. cons., also asst. bus. mgr. Ponca Gynecology and Obstetrics, Inc., Ponca City, Okla., 1956—. Organizing dir. Bi-Racial Council, 1963; lay adviser Home Nursing Service, 1967-68; mem. exec. bd. PTA, 1956-71; active various community drives including Ponca City HELPLINE, ARC Bloodmobile; sponsor Am. Field Service; patron Ponca Playhouse; precinct organizer Republican party, 1960. Mem. AAUW (treas. 1964-66), DAR (sec.-treas. 1961-67, 1st vice regent 1972-74, treas. 1974—); Kay-Noble County Med. Aux. (treas. 1957-58, 66-67), Pioneer Hist. Soc., Okla. Heritage Assn., Nat. Soc. Daus. Founders and Patriots, Nat. Huguenot Soc., Nat. Soc. Daus. Am. Colonists, Nat. Soc. Colonial Dames XVII Century. Ponca City Art Assn., Lambda Tau, Phi Sigma, Alpha Lambda Delta. Presbyterian. Clubs: Ponca City Country, Ponca City Music, Red Rose Garden. Home: 2116 Juanito St Ponca City OK 74601

BOLENE, ROBERT VICTOR, physician; b. Enid, Okla., Aug. 31, 1925; s. Victor Emanuel and Alna (Brown) B.; student Phillips U., 1942-43; Northwestern U., 1943, U. N.H., 1943-44; M.D., U. Okla., 1948; m. Margaret Rosalie Steele, Feb. 6, 1948; children—Judith Kay, John Eric, Sally Sue, Janice Lynn, Daniel William. Surg. intern Henry Ford Hosp., Detroit, 1948-49; county health dir. Garvin and Murray County, Okla., 1949-50; chief surgery VA Hosp., Sulphur, Okla. 1950, 1952-53; resident obstetrics and gynecology U. Okla. Med. Center, Oklahoma City, 1953-56, asso. instr., chief resident faculty Sch. Medicine, 1955-56; practice medicine specializing in obstetrics and gynecology, Ponca City, Okla., 1956—; mem. staff Ponca City Hosp., chief dept. obstetrics and gynecology, pres.-elect, 1971, chief staff, 1972; mem. staff Fairfax Hosp. Committeeman, Boy Scouts Am., patron Ponca City Playhouse; sponsor YMCA, 1960-61; rep. Cub Scouts Am., 1959-61. Served with Inf., U.S. Army, 1942-46; served from 1st lt. to capt. M.C., USAF, 1950-52. Diplomate Am. Bd. Obstetrics and Gynecology. Fellow A.C.S. (regional liaison officer for tumor registry), Am. Coll. Obstetricians and Gynecologists, Am. Geriatric Soc.; mem. Am. Soc. Study Sterility, Internat. Fertility Assn., Am. Assn. Colposcopy and Colpomicroscopy, Tulsa Obstetrics and Gynecology Soc., A.M.A., Okla., Kay Noble County (pres. 1969) med. socs., C. of C., New Hosp. Devel. Orgn., Phi Chi. Republican. Presbyn. Club: Ponca City Country. Home: 2116 Juanito St Ponca City OK 74601 Office: Ponca Med Arts 1215 E Hartford St Ponca City OK 74601

BOLES, PAUL DARCY, writer; b. Auburn, Ind., Mar. 5, 1916; m. Dorothy Kathleen Flory, Dec. 25, 1941; children—Shawn Michael, Terence Ross, Patric Laurence. Recipient Friends of Am. Writers Medal and $1,000 award, 1958; Freedoms Found. citation, 1958; fiction gold medal Ga. Writers Assn., 1969; award U. Ind., 1969; named Author of Year in Fiction, Dixie Council Authors and Journalists, 1976. Author: The Streak, 1953; The Beggars in The Sun, 1954; Glenport, Illinois, 1956; Deadline, 1957; Parton's Island, 1958; A Million Guitars, 1968 (Ind. U. Writers Distinguished Fiction award 1969); I Thought You Were a Unicorn, 1971; The Limner, 1975; The Mississippi Run, 1977; Glory Day, 1979. Contbr. to The Living Novel, 1957; also numerous short stories to maj. mags. Home: 40 Maddox Dr NE Ansley Park Atlanta GA 30309

BOLGER, ROBERT JOSEPH, trade assn. exec.; b. Phila., Aug. 9, 1922; s. Harold Stephen and Edna (Adams) B.; B.S., Villanova U., 1943; postgrad. Northwestern U., 1945-46, U. Pa., 1946-47, U. Geneva (Switzerland), 1948-49; m. Helen Siegfried, May 22, 1954; children—Robert, Mary T., Cynthia A., Ann M., Catherine B., David A. Salesman, Container Corp., Phila., 1946; sales supr. Kraft Food Co., Phila., 1949-52; overseas mgr., dir. retail relations Smith, Kline & French Labs., Phila., 1952-62; asst. to exec. v.p. Nat. Assn. Chain Drug Stores, Inc., Arlington, Va., 1962-72, pres., 1972—. Bd. dirs. Am. Found. Pharm. Edn.; bd. dirs. Nat. Drug Trade Conf., pres., 1974—. Served to lt. comdr., USNR; PTO. Decorated Air medal; named Man of Year Cosmetic and Toiletry sect. United Jewish Appeal, 1972; Chain Exec. of Year, Chain Drug Rev., 1979. Mem. Am. Pharm. Assn., Com. of 100, U.S. C. of C., Central Council Nat. Retail Assns. (chmn.), Am. Retail Fedn. (dir.), Nat. Assn. Retail Druggists. Clubs: Belle Haven Country (Alexandria); Metropolitan (N.Y.C.); Seaview Country (Absecon, N.J.). Contbr. articles to trade publs. Home: 7705 Maid Marian Ct Alexandria VA 22306 Office: 1911 Jefferson Davis Hwy Arlington VA 22202

BOLIN, DORSE LEON, petroleum landman; b. Dallas, Sept. 11, 1927; s. Claude Augusta and Evelyn (McFadden) B.; student Dallas pub. schs., 1941-45; m. Anna Lou Worley, Dec. 5, 1964; children—Terry Wayne, Donald Edward, Ronald Lee, Steven Morris. Radio announcer various stations, Tex. and Ark., 1947-49; traffic mgr. Trans Tex. Airways, Dallas and Houston, 1949-52; landman Texaco, Inc., Los Angeles, 1952-65; Atlantic Richfield Corp., Dallas, 1965-68; pvt. practice petroleum landman, Dallas, 1968—. Chief police, City of Star Harbor, Tex., 1976, tax assessor, collector, 1976. Served with USN, 1945-46. Mem. Am., Dallas assns. petroleum landmen Republican. Episcopalian. Home and office: 903 Agape Circle Rockwall TX 75087

BOLIN, SHIRLEY JUDITH, transformer mfg. co. exec.; b. Rolla, Mo., June 30, 1928; d. Abraham and Stella (Davidson) Wiseman; student pub. schs., St. Louis; m. Alpha E. Bolin, Jr., Jan. 6, 1956; children—Janis, Nancy Jo, Donald. Sec., Witte Hardware, St. Louis, 1947-51; sec. to exec. v.p. Wagner Electric Corp., St. Louis, 1951-57; sec.-treas. Vantran Electric Corp., Waco, Tex., 1963—. Area chmn. Girl Scouts St. Louis, county chmn., Fayette County, Ill. Mem. Nat. Trust Historic Preservation, Nat. Assn. Exec. Secs., Am. Mus. Natural History (asso.), Waco Art Center, Historic Waco Found., Beta Sigma Phi. Home: 425 Whitehall Rd Woodway Waco TX 76710 Office: 7711 Imperial Dr Waco TX 76710

BOLING, JEWELL, ret. govt. ofcl.; b. Randleman, N.C., Sept. 26, 1907; d. John Emmitt and Carrie (Ballard) Boling; student Women's Coll., U. N.C., 1926, Am. U., 1942, 51-52. Interviewer, N.C. Employment Service, Winston-Salem, Asheboro, 1937-41; occupational analyst U.S. Dept. Labor, Washington, 1943-57, placement officer, 1957-58, employment service adviser, 1959-61, occupational analyst, 1962, employment service specialist counseling and testing, 1963-69, manpower devel. specialist, from 1969. Recipient Meritorious Achievement award U.S. Dept. Labor, 1972. Mem. AAAS, Am. Personnel and Guidance Assn. (profl. mem. nat. vocat. guidance assn.), Am. Rehab. Counseling Assn. (archivist 1964-68), Assn. Measurement and Evaluation in Guidance, Assn. Humanistic Psychology, Smithsonians, Sierra Club, Internat. Platform Assn., Audubon Naturalist Soc., Nat. Capital Astronomers (editor Star Dust 1949-58), N.Y. Acad. Scis., Nature Conservancy. Author: Counselor's Handbook, 1967; Counselor's Desk Aid, Eighteen Basic Vocational Directions, 1967; Handbook for New Careerists in Employment Security, 1971. Contbr. articles to profl. pubs. Address: Route 2 Box 141 Randleman NC 27317

BOLLEY, JAMES ROBERT, mus. adminstr.; b. Topeka, Oct. 23, 1953; s. Donald William and Betty Ann (Fay) B.; student Washburn U., 1972, Oral Roberts U., 1972-74; m. Cristine Brenda, July 7, 1973. Office mgr. Osborn Found., Wellington, New Zealand, 1974-76; dir. World Mus. Art Centre, Tulsa, 1976—. Mem. Am. Assn. Mus., Okla. Mus. Assn., Am. Assn. State and Local History, Tulsa Press Club, Model T Ford Club Am., Model T Ford Club Tulsa (pres. 1979). Home: 825 W Waco St Broken Arrow OK 74012

BOLNER, CLIFTON JOSEPH, mfg. co. exec.; b. San Antonio, Tex., July 30, 1928; s. Joe and Josephine (Grandjean) B.; B.S., Tex. A. and M. U., 1949; m. Rosalie Richter, Jan. 20, 1949; children—Tim, Mike, Deb, Cindy, Bev, Chris, Mary. Partner, Bolner's Grocery & Meat Market, San Antonio, 1949-55; pres. Bolner's Fiesta Products, Inc., San Antonio, 1955—. Pres., Cath. Family and Children Services, San Antonio, 1968-69; chmn. fin. com. San Antonio Archdiocese, 1978-79; chmn. annual awards dinner NCCJ, 1974; bd. dirs. San Antonio Symphony Soc., 1973—, San Antonio Mus. Assn., 1973—, Opera Superman, 1975—, San Antonio Muscular Dystrophy Assn., 1975—; mem. devel. bd. Incarnate Word Coll., 1974—; San Antonio Cath. rep. NCCJ, 1978—. Served to 1st lt. USAF, 1950-52. Recipient Disting. Alumni award Central Cath. High Sch., 1979; Archbishop Furey Outstanding award medal, 1969. Mem. Oblate Asso., Assn. of Holy Family Guilds. Roman Catholic. Clubs: K.C., San Antonio Serra Vocation, Italo Am. Young Men's, St. Paul's Men's, Soc. of Mary Assos. Home: 110 W Lynwood St San Antonio TX 78212 Office: 426 Menchaca St San Antonio TX 78207

BOLNER, DEBBIE MARIE, advt. agy. exec.; b. San Antonio, Aug. 15, 1953; d. Clifton Joseph and Rosalie (Richter) B.; B.S. in Advt., Tex. Tech. U., 1975; M.B.A., U. Tex., 1979. Intern, J. Walter Thompson Advt. Agy., N.Y.C., 1974-75; with advt. display dept. San Antonio Express News, summer 1975; advt. rep. Univ. Daily, Tex. Tech. U., 1974-75; asst. account exec. Ed Yardang & Assos., San Antonio, 1975-76, account exec., 1976—, research project dir., 1976-78, research dir., 1978—, v.p. mktg. services, 1979—. Publicity chmn. Jr. Women's Com. San Antonio Symphony Orch., 1978, 79; vol. Cystic Fibrosis Found., 1976-79, recipient Outstanding Service citation, 1977. Recipient Meml. award Ed Yardang & Assos., 1977. Mem. Am. Advt. Fedn., Am. Mktg. Assn., Women in Communications (v.p. programs 1977-79), Leadership San Antonio, San Antonio C. of C., Alpha Delta Pi. Roman Catholic. Club: San Antonio Cotillion. Home: 618 Cobble St San Antonio TX 78216 Office: Ed Yardang & Assos 1 Romana Plaza Suite 301 San Antonio TX 78205

BOLOOKI, HOOSHANG, cardiovascular surgeon, educator; b. Langeh, Iran, Mar. 28, 1937; s. Hossein and Fatima (Arjomand) B.; came to U.S., 1961, naturalized, 1976; student Alborz Coll., Iran, 1952-54; M.D., Tehran U., 1961; m. C. Joanne McDonald; children—Hooshang Michael, Cyrus William. Intern Cambridge (Mass.) City Hosp., 1961; intern in surgery Kings County (N.Y.) Hosp., Bklyn., 1961-62, resident gen. surgery, 1962-67; resident in thoracic and cardiovascular surgery U. Miami Sch. of Medicine, 1967-69; resident Jackson Meml. Hosp., Miami, 1967-69, attending thoracic and cardiovascular surgeon, 1969—, lectr. nurses and physicians courses in coronary care unit, 1970—, practice medicine specializing in thoracic and cardiovascular surgery, Miami, Fla., 1969—; instr. surgery U. Miami, 1969-70, asst. prof. physiology, 1971-73, asst. prof. surgery, 1970-73, dir. research labs., div. thoracic and cardiovascular surgery, 1969—, asso. prof. surgery, 1973-77, prof., 1977—; cons. VA Hosp., Miami, 1977—; lectr. Sch. Biomed. Engring., 1971—. Diplomate Am. Bd. Surgery, Am. Bd. Thoracic Surgery Finalist Young Investigators award Am. Coll. Cardiology, 1968; fellow Council Cardiovascular Surgery Am. Heart Assn.; recipient Mead-Johnson Grand award, 1968, AMA cert. merit, 1970, Research Career Devel. award, Nat. Heart and Lung Inst., 1973-78. NIH grantee, 1971-75. Fellow A.C.S., Royal Coll. Surgeons of Can., Am. Coll. Cardiology, Am. Coll. Chest Physicians; mem. Am. Assn. for Thoracic Surgery, Am., Fla., Dade County, So. med. assns., Soc. of Thoracic Surgeons, Soc. U. Surgeons, Internat. Cardiovascular Soc., Am. Fedn. Clin. Research, Soc. Exptl. Biology and Medicine, N.Y. Acad. Scis., Assn. for Acad. Surgery, Heart Assn. of Greater Miami, Am., Fla. thoracic socs., So. Thoracic Assn., Soc. Vascular Surgery, Societe Internat. de Chir. Author: Clinical Application of Intra-aortic Balloon Pump; also Vol. 18 Thoracic Surgery, Med. Exam. Rev. Books. Contbr. numerous articles on cardiovascular surgery to profl. jours. Office: 1611 NW 12th Ave Miami FL 33136

BOLTON, ARTHUR KEY, state ofcl.; b. Griffin, Ga., May 14, 1922; s. Herbert Alfred and Eunice (Maddox) B.; grad. North Ga. Coll., 1941; LL.B., U. Ga., 1943; m. Marion Lee Cashen, Sept. 30, 1946; children—Arthur Key, Marion Lee. Judge Criminal Ct., Griffin, 1952-65; mem. Ga. Ho. of Reps., 1949-65, floor leader after 1963, chmn. tax equalization com.; individual practice law, Griffin, 1974—; atty. gen. State of Ga., Atlanta, 1965—. Served to capt. AUS; ETO. Decorated Silver Star, Purple Heart; recipient Statesmanship award Ga. Gen. Assembly, 1961-62, numerous other awards. Mem. Ga. State Bar (past gov.), C. of C., V.F.W., Am. Legion, Phi Delta Phi. Baptist. Elk. Home: PO Box 252 Griffin GA 30223 Office: State Judicial Bldg Room 132 Atlanta GA 30334*

BOLTON, JANET BLAIR, ednl. adminstr.; b. Danville, Ill., Jan. 20, 1934; d. Texas Eugene and Ardith L. (Fox) Davis; student Danville Jr. Coll., 1965-66, Ferris State Coll., 1966-68, extension U. Mich., Grand Rapids, 1968-69, paralegal program U. South Ala., Mobile, 1976-77; children—Candice Lyn, Tamara Lee, Richard David. With Nichols Loan Corp., Danville, 1955-57, William Davies Co., Danville, 1957-58, Lauhoff Grain Co., Danville, 1958-66, Ferris State Coll., Big Rapids, Mich., 1966-68, Lear Siegler, Inc., Grand Rapids, Mich., 1968-69, Hyster Co., Danville, 1969-70; adminstrv. asst. to dean of faculties U. South Ala., Mobile, 1970-78, to v.p. acad. affairs, 1978—. Hyster Co. advisor Danville Jr. Achievement, 1969-70; bd. dirs. Dixie Boys Baseball League, 1975-78, Dizzy Dean Baseball League, 1978-79. Mem. Nat. Fedn. Bus. and Profl. Women's Clubs, Ala. Fedn. Bus. and Profl. Women's Clubs, Mobile League Bus. and Profl. Women's Clubs (pres.), Exec. Women Internat. (rep.). Roman Catholic. Home: 1714 Dover St Mobile AL 36608 Office: 307 University Blvd AD 245 Mobile AL 36688

BOLTON, ROBERT HARVEY, banker; b. Alexandria, La., June 19, 1908; s. James Wade and Mary Esther (Calderwood) B.; B.S. in Econs., Wharton Sch. Finance and Commerce U. Pa., 1930; m. Elsie Elizabeth McLundie, Apr. 14, 1939; children—Robert Harvey, Jr., Elizabeth (Mrs. Robert C. Hassinger), Mary (Mrs. James K. Jennings, Jr.). Staff credit dept. Guaranty Trust Co., N.Y.C., 1930-32; asst. cashier Rapides Bank and Trust Co., Alexandria, La., 1932-36, cashier, 1936-43, v.p., 1943-47, exec. v.p., 1947-56, pres., 1956—, also dir.; dir. New Orleans br. Fed. Res. Bank of Atlanta Mem. Attakapas Council Boy Scouts Am., Alexandria, 1972—; mem. La. State U. Found., 1972—; pres. Indsl. Devel. Bd. of Rapides Parish; mem. Gov.'s Council of 100; bd. dirs. Rapides United Givers. Served with USNR, World War II. Mem. C. of C. of Alexandria (chmn. aviation com. 1972—; pres. 1965), La. Bankers Assn. (legis. study com. 1970—; pres. 1950), Am. Bankers Assn. (pres. state bank div. 1955), La. Mortgage Bankers Assn. (pres. 1952), Mortgage Bankers Assn. (legis. com.), Robert Morris Assos. (nat. dir. 1943-45, life mem.). Baptist. Clubs: Masons, Rotary (pres. 1942); Boston, Bienville (New Orleans); City (Baton Rouge); Golf and Country (Alexandria); Confrerie des Chevaliers du Tastevin. Home: 3200 Parkway Dr Alexandria LA 71301 Office: 400 Murray St Alexandria LA 71301

BOLTON, WADE EARL, educator; b. Galveston, Tex., Dec. 21, 1947; s. Alto James and Betty Jean (Leacroy) B.; B.S., U. Houston, 1970; postgrad. Med. Sch. U. Tex., 1976-77; m. Lois Joan Hanson, Oct. 15, 1976; 1 dau., Dawn Rachelle. Research technician U. Houston, 1968-69; research asst. Johnson Spacecraft Center, Houston, 1969-73; research asso. U. Tex. Med. Br., Galveston, 1973-78; research instr. in medicine Baylor Coll. of Medicine, Houston, 1978—, supr. endocrinology research lab. Pres. Young Republicans, 1965-66; ruling elder West Isle Presbyn. Ch., 1978-79. Recipient Apollo achievement award, 1969, Skylab achievement award, 1976. Mem. Tissue Culture Assn., Am. Soc. Human Genetics, Am. Soc. Cell Biology, Sigma Xi. Clubs: Northrop Mgmt., Cystic Fibrosis. Contbr. articles in field to profl. jours. Home: 2424 Perthuis Dr LaMarque TX 77568 Office: Dept of Medicine Baylor College of Medicine Texas Medical Center Houston TX 77030

BOLZ, SARAH DAVIS, curator; b. Saginaw, Mich., Mar. 14, 1945; d. Siegel Bloore and Kathleen Lydia (McGarvey) Davis; B.A. in Art and History, Albion (Mich.) Coll., 1967; M.A. in Art History, Mich. State U., East Lansing, 1970. Tchr. schs. in Saginaw and Albion, 1967-69; art tchr., Westville, Ill., 1969-71; curator O. Henry Mus., Austin, Tex., 1974—, Elisabet Ney Mus., Austin, 1974—; participant 13th ann. Woodlawn Conf. in Hist. Site Adminstrn., 1975. Drama coordinator Women's Art Festival, Austin, 1977; mem. statewide adv. bd. Tex. Circuit. Mem. Am. Assn. Museums, Nat. Trust Hist. Preservation, Tex. Assn. Museums. Home: 1606 Eva St Austin TX 78704 Office: 409 E 5th St Austin TX 78701

BOMAR, PORTIA HAMILTON, psychoanalyst, psychotherapist; b. Cleve., July 19; d. Charles Brooks and Marian (Clements) Goulder; B.A., U. Mich., 1923; M.A., Columbia U., 1932, Ph.D., 1940; postgrad. Oxford U., 1923-25; m. William P. Bomar, July 1, 1966. Pvt. practice pychoanalysis and psychotherapy, N.Y.C., 1930-58; dir. teaching clinic Columbia-Presbyn. Med. Center, 1942-50; asso. prof. psychology Univ. Coll., U. Richmond, 1964-66; mem. faculty Southwestern Grad. Sch. Banking, So. Meth. U., Dallas, 1975—; lectr. U. Tex., Austin, 1968—. Bd. dirs. Child Study Center, Ft. Worth, 1974—, Fort Worth Zool. Assn., 1974—, Tarrant County Mental Health Assn., 1974-76, Hist. Soc. Tarrant County, 1968—, Casa Manana, Fort Worth, 1975-76; mem. Human Relations Commn., Fort Worth, 1968-71. Fellow Am. Psychol. Assn.; mem. Psychical

Research Found. (bd. dirs.), Chi Omega. Home: 1503 Hillcrest Fort Worth TX 76107

BONAVENTURA, JOSEPH, biochemist; b. Oakland, Calif., Feb. 15, 1942; s. Filiberto Antonio and Corinne Van Lora (Fogarty) B.; B.A., San Diego State U., 1964; Ph.D., U. Tex., 1968; m. Celia Jean Taylor, Aug. 20, 1960; children—Marina Celeste, Michelle Celia. Postdoctoral fellow Calif. Inst. Tech., Pasadena, 1968-70; research fellow Regina Inst. Cancer Research, Rome, 1970-72; med. research asst. prof. biochemistry Duke U. Marine Lab., Beaufort, N.C., 1973-79, dir., med. research asst. prof. biochemistry Marine Biomed. Center, 1977—; pres. Biosponge Inc., Beaufort, 1978—. NIH grantee, 1971—, NSF grantee, 1971—, Office Naval Research grantee, 1971—, NATO grantee, 1972-74. Mem. AAAS, Am. Chem. Soc., Am. Soc. Biol. Chemists, Am. Soc. Zoologists, N.Y. Acad. Scis., Sigma Xi. Contbr. articles to profl. jours. Home: 127 Circle Dr Beaufort NC 28516 Office: Duke U Marine Biomed Center Beaufort NC 28516

BOND, BERNARD BATSON, materials engr.; b. Wiggins, Miss., Mar. 28, 1906; s. Willard Faroe and Susie (Graham) B.; B.A. in Chemistry, Miss. Coll., 1926; m. Laura Lee Traylor, Dec. 24, 1931 (div.); 1 dau., Myrna Rose; m. 2d, Elizabeth Elmore Fisher, July 17, 1953 (dec.); m. 3d, Sarah Conwell New, Jan. 31, 1976. Chemist testing div. Miss. Hwy. Dept., Jackson, 1936-42; materials engring. supt. overhaul and repair dept. U.S. Naval Air Sta., Pensacola, Fla., 1942-67, dir. materials engring. div. Naval Air Rework Facility, 1967-71; dir. Tech. Support Center, Dept. Def. Equipment Oil Analysis Program, 1971-72; cons. spectrometric wear metal analysis, Warrington, Fla., 1972—. Fellow Am. Inst. Chemists, AAAS; mem. N.Y. Acad. Scis., Am. Chem. Soc., Am. Inst. Aeros. and Astronautics, Navy League U.S., Am. Camelia Soc. Baptist. Clubs: Elks, Masons. Home: 308 E Sunset Ave Warrington FL 32507

BOND, GEORGE DOHERTY, educator; b. Hillsboro, Tex., Oct. 23, 1903; s. George Doherty and May (Wigley) B.; A.B., So. Meth. U., 1924, M.A., 1937; Ph.D., U. Mich., 1947; m. Mildred Elizabeth Martin, Sept. 6, 1922; children—Margaret Burke (Mrs. James T. Richmond), Robert Doherty. Instr. English, So. Meth. U., 1924-27, 35-41, asst. prof., 1941-47, asso. prof., 1947-50, prof., 1950-69, chmn. dept., 1953-57, chmn. faculty senate, 1957-58. Mem. MLA, Coll. English Assn., AAUP, Nat. Trust Hist. Preservation, Dallas County Heritage Soc., Tex. Conf. Coll. Tchrs. English (v.p. 1954, pres. 1965-66), Poetry Soc. Tex. (v.p. 1963-66), Tex. Inst. Letters, Phi Beta Kappa, Kappa Sigma. Methodist. Author: (with J.B. Hubbell and M.D. Hemke) Prairie Pegasus, 1924; (with J.W. Bowyer, J.L. Brooks and I.H. Herron) Better College English, 1950; (with Mildred Martin Bond) Alexander Carswell and Isabella Brown, Their Ancestors and Descendants, 1977. Editor: Inter-American Publs., 1941-45; Editor Southwest Rev., 1925-27, 44-45, contbg. editor, 1946-63. Home: 3460 Mockingbird Ln Dallas TX 75205

BOND, JULIAN, state senator, civil rights leader; b. Nashville, Jan. 14, 1940; s. Horace Mann and Julia Agnes (Washington) B.; B.A., Morehouse Coll., 1971; m. Alice Louise Clopton, July 28, 1961; children—Phyllis Jane, Horace Mann, Michael Julian, Jeffrey Alvin, Julia. A founder Com. Appeal for Human Rights, 1960, exec. sec., 1961; a founder Student Nonviolent Coordinating Com., 1960, communications dir., 1961-66; reporter, feature writer Atlanta Inquirer, 1960-61, mng. editor, 1963; mem. Ga. Ho. of Reps. from Fulton County, 1965-75, Ga. Senate, 1975—; barred from house because of Vietnam statements, 1966; U.S. Supreme Ct. ruled his Constl. rights were violated, 1966. Chmn. bd. So. Elections Fund; pres. So. Poverty Law Center. Bd. dirs. So. Conf. Edn. Fund, NAACP; mem. Robert Kennedy Meml. Fund, Highland Research and Edn. Center. Mem. So. Corr. Reporting Racial Equality Wars, Phi Kappa (hon.). Author poems, articles. Address: 361 West View Dr SW Atlanta GA 30310

BOND, LOUIS DEAN, accountant; b. Valliant, Okla., Jan. 26, 1940; s. Joe Wheeler and Dorothy Inez (Wiggington) B.; B.A., Harding Coll., 1967; m. Judith Maye Limburg, July 31, 1965; children—Shawn RaeAnn, Eric Scott. Sr. accountant Peat, Marwick, Mitchell & Co., Dallas, 1967-70, sr. auditor, Louisville, 1970-71; controller Servomation-Williams, Inc., Louisville, 1971-73; credit mgr., office mgr. Haas Cabinet Co., Inc., Sellersburg, Ind., 1973-75; pub. accountant in pvt. practice, Broken Bow, Okla., 1975—. Mem. pres.'s devel. council Harding Coll. Served with USN, 1959-63. C.P.A., Okla., Tex. Mem. Am. Inst. C.P.A.'s, Okla. Soc. C.P.A.'s, Broken Bow C. of C. (treas. 1977). Republican. Mem. Ch. of Christ (treas. 1971-75, 76—, deacon 1972-75, dir. adult edn. 1972-75, tchr. adult edn. 1976—, dir. edn. 1978—). Club: Lions (v.p. 1976-77, pres. 1977-78). Home: 400 Sunset Blvd Broken Bow OK 74728 Office: 10 N Broadway Broken Bow OK 74728

BOND, RONALD EUGENE, banker; b. Okemah, Okla., Sept. 7, 1945; s. Edgar Eugene and Irene (Montgomery) B.; B.S., Okla. State U., 1967; m. Mary Jon Garcia, Sept. 10, 1968; children—April Irene, Angela Marie. Bank examiner FDIC, Tulsa, 1968-70, Amarillo, Tex., 1970-72; v.p., dir. Citizens State Bank, Okemah, Okla., 1972-77; pres. Am. State Bank, Broken Bow, Okla., 1977—, also dir. Former pres. Broken Bow Indsl. Authority. Mem. Am. Bankers Assn., Okla. Bankers Assn., Broken Bow C. of C. (dir. 1977—). Democrat. Methodist. Club: Kiwanis. Home and Office: PO Box 280 Broken Bow OK 74728

BONDI, JAMES OLIVER, computer designer, elec. engr.; b. St. Louis, May 29, 1949; s. Oliver Joseph and Dorothy Eleanor (Kipp) B.; B.S., U. Mo.-Rolla, 1971, M.S., 1972, Ph.D., 1974; m. Judith Ann Sahaida, Aug. 8, 1970; 1 son, Robert James. Elec. design engr. Bussmann Mfg. Co., St. Louis, 1975; sr. engr. Burroughs Corp., Fed. & Spl. Systems Group, Advanced Devel. Orgn., Paoli, Pa., 1975-76, project engr., 1976-78; computer systems engr. Equipment group Tex. Instruments, Inc., Dallas, 1978—. NDEA fellow, 1971-74. Mem. U. Mo.-Rolla Alumni Assn., IEEE, Assn. Computing Machinery, Sigma Xi, Tau Beta Pi, Eta Kappa Nu, Phi Kappa Phi, Blue Key (life). Mem. United Ch. Christ. Author articles on hardware microcode optimization. Home: 10231 Echo Ridge Ct Dallas TX 75243 Office: PO Box 222013 Mail Sta 3407 Dallas TX 75222

BONDS, JOHN CLARK, mfg. co. exec.; b. Chgo., Feb. 6, 1933; s. John Phillips and Marion Veronica (Clark) B.; B.S., U. Ill., 1958; M.B.A., Loyola U., Chgo., 1973; m. Leora Ann Wittenberg, Nov. 25, 1967; 1 son, John Michael. Plant controller Dresser Industries, Chgo., 1968-70, mgr. planning, 1970-73, mktg. controller, 1973-76; mktg. controller Trailways Inc., Dallas, 1976-79; v.p.-controller Nat. Hand Tool Corp., Dallas, 1979—; lectr. in field. Served with U.S. Army, 1953-55; ETO. Mem. Planning Execs. Inst. Roman Catholic. Club: Dallas Athletic. Home: 10747 Lanett Circle Dallas TX 75238 Office: Nat Hand Tool Corp 12827 Valley Branch Ln Dallas TX 75234

BONDURANT, EDWARD JUSTINE, architect; b. Hunter, Mo., Oct. 31, 1929; s. Joseph Arthur and Alta Caroline (Bodamer) B.; B.Arch., Tulane U., 1952; m. Johnnie Louise Jenkins, June 2, 1952; children—Deborah Louise, Edward Bradford, Randall Joseph. Archtl. designer Clarence Fisher, Architect, Memphis, 1955-56, Rust Engring. Co., Inc., Birmingham, Ala., 1956-59; pvt. practice architecture, Birmingham, 1959-63; pres. Bondurant Entrekin & Assos., Inc., Architects, Birmingham, 1963-77; pres. Harmon, Collier, Bondurant, Assos., Inc., Birmingham, 1977—; ann. lectr. Freed-Hardeman Coll., 1977-79. Mem. adv. bd. Freed-Hardeman and Ala. Christian Colls.; trustee Childhaven, Inc. Served with USNR, 1952-55. Mem. AIA (pres. 1965). Mem. Ch. Christ. Home: 3773 Dunbarton Dr Birmingham AL 35223 Office: 1623 S 21st St Birmingham AL 35205

BONDURANT, GORDON EMERSON, sch. headmaster; b. Winston-Salem, N.C., Jan. 13, 1935; s. Stuart O. and Dorothy Louise (Siewers) B.; A.B., Davidson Coll.; postgrad. U. N.C.; M.A., U. Chattanooga; m. Linda Jane Reeves, Aug. 16, 1964; children—Robert Emerson, William Gordon. Tchr. McCallie Sch., Chattanooga, 1957-60, 62-66, asst. dean, 1964-66; dir. camps, confs. and youth work Moravian Ch. Am., Winston-Salem, 1960-62; dir. admissions and records U. Chattanooga, 1967-68, also chmn. scholarship com.; pres. Darlington Sch., Rome, Ga., 1968-79; headmaster Montgomery Bell Acad., Nashville, 1979—; dir. Home Federal Savs. and Loan. Vice pres. for adminstrn. N.W. Ga. council Boy Scouts Am. Past bd. dirs. United Fund; former lay v.p., bd. dirs. Am. Cancer Soc.; bd. dirs. Rome Community Concert Assn., Mid-South Assn. Ind. Schs., also treas., pres. Ga. Found. Ind. Schs. Mem. Nat., Ga., 7th Dist. assns. high sch. prins., Ga. (past pres.), Soc. (treas.) assns. ind. schs., Rome Area C. of C. (past dir.). Presbyn. (mem. ch. session). Clubs: Rotary (pres., trustee student fund), Coosa Country, Nine O'Clock Cotillion. Address: Montgomery Bell Acad 4001 Harding Rd Nashville TN 37205

BONDURANT, WILLIAM WALTON, JR., physician; b. Dallas, Tex., June 22, 1905; s. William W. and Lily Louise (Walton) B.; B.A., Austin Coll., 1925; M.D., U. Tex., 1929; m. Martha Nieminen, Mar. 6, 1931 (dec. 1964); children—Judith Elizabeth, William Walton, Edward Vaughan, Charles Julius; m. 2d, Katherine Carlisle, Aug. 11, 1965 (dec. 1977); stephchildren—Sandra Kay, Sherry, Katherine Rebecca, Debra Kim; m. 3d, Nina Jenkins Carr, May 3, 1979. Intern City Hosp. of Cleve., 1929-30, resident 1930-31; practice medicine, San Antonio, Tex., 1933—; mem. staff Bapt. Meml. Hosp., Santa Rosa Med. Center, Nix Meml. Hosp.; instr. in internal medicine U. Tex., Galveston, 1931-33; mem. bd. mgrs. Bexar County Hosp. Dist., Tex., 1958-60; pres. Community Nursing Service, San Antonio, 1952-54. Trustee Austin Coll., 1957-65. Served from maj. to lt. col., M.C., U.S. Army, 1943-46. Diplomate Am. Bd. Internal Medicine. Fellow A.C.P.; mem. Tex. Med. Assn., San Antonio Heart Assn., Tex. Rheumatism Assn. (pres. 1958), Bexar County Med. Soc. (pres. 1949-50), Tex. Club of Internists (pres. 1959-60). Presbyterian. Clubs: San Antonio Country (gov. 1954-57), Conopus. Home: 144 Wyckham Rise San Antonio TX 78209 Office: 414 Navarro St San Antonio TX 78205

BONE, EWELL OWEN, psychologist, ednl. adminstr; b. Izard County, Ark., Dec. 24, 1902; s. William Hollis and Arminta Melvina (McElmurry) B.; student Mt. Home, (Ark.) Jr. Coll., 1925; B.A., Hardin-Simmons U., 1929; M.Ed., U. Tex., 1950; M.S. in Psychology, East Tex. State U., 1958; m. Juanita Beatrice Cassle, May 30, 1932; children—Juanice (Mrs. Jerry Collins), Sylvia (Mrs. Howard Waldrop), Bobbye Bone Ferris. Tchr. pub. schs., Bear Creek, Ark., 1922-24; prin. elementary sch., Hamlin, Tex., 1930-33; prin. jr. high sch., Clarendon, Tex., 1934; prin. high sch., Tucumcari, N.M., 1934-39; dir. high sch. edn., Abilene, Tex., 1940-46; prin. high sch., Burnett, Tex., 1947-52; dir. spl. services, asst. supt., psychologist pub. schs., Texarkana, Tex., 1952-71; psychologist Texarkana Sheltered Workshop Tex. Rehab. Commn., 1971—;. Expert vocat. witness on social security HEW, 1956—; cons. Tex., Ark. vocat. rehab. offices, 1956—; psychol. examiner Texarkana Sheltered Workshop, 1963. Chmn. bd. dirs. Texarkana Mental Health-Mental Retardation Center, 1967; bd. dir. N.E. Tex. Mental Health-Mental Retardation Center, 1968. Named Citizen of Year Texarkana Civitans, 1968, Citizen of Day KATQ Radio, June 12, 1974. Mem. Texarkana Ret. Tchrs'. Assn. (pres. 1973-74), Tex. State Tchrs'. Assn., Tex., Am. psychol. assns., Phi Delta Kappa. Democrat. Baptist. Mason, Kiwanian (editor Ki-News 1969-75). Club: Texarkana Country. Home: 208 Wildwood Dr Texarkana TX 75501 Office: 1106 Whitaker St Texarkana TX 75501

BONER, MARIAN OLDFATHER, lawyer, law librarian; b. Cleburne, Tex., June 25, 1909; d. Henry Elwood and Berta Felicia (Clements) Oldfather; B.A., U. Tex. at Austin, 1930, M.A., 1931, LL.B., 1955; m. Charles Paul Boner, Sept. 9, 1930 (dec. Apr. 1979); children—Donald Stephen (dec. Jan. 1980), Charles Randal, Richard Elwood. Admitted to Tex. bar, 1955; research asso. Sch. Law U. Tex. at Austin, 1956-60, reference librarian, 1960-65, asso. librarian, asso. prof. law, 1965-72; dir. Tex. State Law Library, Austin, 1972—. Mem. Austin Pub. Library Commn., 1969-76. Bd. dirs. Univ. Coop. Soc., Austin, 1971-72. Mem. State Bar Tex., Southwestern (pres. 1969-70), Am. (pres. 1974-75) assns. law libraries, Order Coif, Phi Beta Kappa, Kappa Beta Pi. Episcopalian. Author: Reference Guide to Texas Law and Legal History, 1976. Home: 1508 Hardouin Ave Austin TX 78703 Office: PO Box 12367 Austin TX 78711

BONER, WILLIAM HILL, congressman; b. Nashville, Feb. 14, 1945; s. Dorris Elijah and Martha Mae B.; B.S., Middle Tenn. State U., 1967; M.A., Peabody Coll., 1969; J.D., Y.M.C.A. Night Law Sch., 1978; 1 dau., Christine Marie. Asst. prof. health and phys. edn. Trevecca Nazarene Coll., Nashville, 1969-71; sr. asst. to mayor Nashville Met. Govt., 1971-72; asst. v.p., dir. public relations First Am. Bank, 1972-75; law clk. Thompson & Crawford, 1976-77; mem. 96th Congress from Tenn. Bd. mgrs. East Nashville YMCA; trustee Middle Tenn. State U. Found.; bd. dirs. Hilltop House. Recipient Disting. Service award Franklin Rd. Jaycees, 1971; Outstanding Young Citizen award Music City Jaycees, 1975. Mem. Public Relations Soc. Am., Nashville Area C. of C. Office: 118 Cannon House Office Bldg Washington DC 20515

BONHAM, HOWARD BRYAN, JR., securities analyst; b. Tulsa, Dec. 21, 1928; s. Howard Bryan and Aubrey Estelle (Combs) B.; B.A. in Econs., U. Va., 1952; postgrad. Grad. Sch. Bus. U. Okla., 1955-57; m. Nancy Luella Furr, Aug. 23, 1958; children—Holly Adair, Howard Bryan, III, Alison York. With Shell Pipe Line Corp., Houston, 1957-60; pub. investment materials and editor Brookmire Investment Reports, Memphis, 1961-65; investment officer Life & Casualty Ins. Co. Tenn., Nashville, 1965-69; trust officer Republic Nat. Bank Dallas, 1969-73; v.p., sr. analyst Rauscher Pierce Securities Corp., Dallas, 1973—; pub. Oil Field Economic Report; lectr. in corporate finance Fisk U., Nashville. Bd. dirs. Good Shepherd Episcopal Sch., Dallas. Served with AUS, 1952-54. Recipient Graham-Dodd award Fin. Analyst Fedn., 1969. C.F.A. Mem. Inst. Chartered Fin. Analysts, Dallas Soc. Investment Analysts, Am. Fin. Assn., Am. Econ. Assn., Fin. Analysts Fedn., U. Va. Alumni Assn., Soc. Mayflower Descs., Sigma Nu. Episcopalian. Club: Dallas Athletic. Author: Ticker Talk, 1960. Contbr. to CFA Readings in Investment Analysis, Financial Analysts Jour., Stock Market Handbook. Home: 3544 McFarlin Blvd Dallas TX 75205 Office: 1200 Mercantile Dallas Bldg Dallas TX 75201

BONIFAZI, STEPHEN, chemist; b. Hartford, Conn., Oct. 31, 1924; s. Camillo and Carrie (Mortensen) B.; B.S., Trinity Coll., Hartford, 1947; postgrad. Okla. U., 1943-44, Rensselaer Poly. Inst., 1955-58; m. Joan Rose Dunlop, Dec. 19, 1959; 1 dau., Karen Stephanie. Sr. chemist Pratt & Whitney Aircraft Co., East Hartford, Conn., 1950-56, supr. chemistry, 1955-58, project chemist, West Palm Beach, Fla., 1958-63, gen. supr. chemistry, 1963—. Served with inf. AUS, 1943-45; ETO. Decorated Bronze Star medal. Mem. Am. Chem. Soc., Am. Soc. Lubrication Engrs., Internat. Assn. for Hydrogen Energy, ASTM, Sigma Pi Sigma. Contbr. articles to sci. jours. Home: 516 Kingfish Rd North Palm Beach FL 33408 Office: Box 2691 West Palm Beach FL 33402

BONILLA, EFRAIN SANTIAGO, mathematician; b. San Juan, P.R., Aug. 2, 1949; s. Benjamin Bonilla and Felicita Santiago (Gomez) Gonzalez; B.S., U. P.R., 1971, M.S. in Radiol. Physics, 1972; m. Luz S. Diaz Garcia, Oct. 6, 1973; children—Lucy Ivette, Efrain Antonio. Instr. math Cath U. P.R., Ponce, 1972, researcher, 1973-77, instr. math and biostatistics Med. Sch., 1978—, radiation safety officer, 1973—. Mem. P.R. Assn. Math Tchrs., P.R. Amateur Radio Club. Roman Catholic. Home: AC-20 41st St Los Caobos Ponce PR 00731 Office: Catholic U PR Ponce PR 00732

BONIN, JOSEPH MAURICE, univ. dean; b. LeRoy, La., Mar. 21, 1930; s. E. Whitney and Rita (Villien) B.; B.S., Spring Hill Coll., 1950; M.A., La. State U., 1952, Ph.D., 1960; m. Margie Ann Johnson, Dec. 22, 1956; children—Catherine, Theresa, Elizabeth, Susan, Judith, John, Rita. Instr., La. State U., 1957-58, asst. prof., 1959-60; asst. prof. U. Ark., 1958-59; assc. prof. Auburn U., 1960-63, prof., 1963-66; prof. econs. U. Ga., Athens, 1966-75; dean Coll. Bus. Adminstrn., Loyola U., New Orleans, 1975—. Research analyst Soc. Security Adminstrn., Washington, 1964-65. Trustee, treas. bd. New Orleans Mus. Art. Served to lt. (j.g.) USNR, 1952-55. Earhart Found. fellow, 1956-57; NSF grantee, 1969-71. Mem. Fin. Execs. Inst., Delta Sigma Pi, Pi Gamma Mu, Beta Gamma Sigma. Roman Catholic. Editor Jour. Bus. Research, 1972-74. Contbr. articles to profl. jours. Home: 4517 Chateau Dr Metairie LA 70002 Office: Loyola U 6363 St Charles Ave New Orleans LA 70163

BONIOL, EDDIE EUGENE, oil co. exec.; b. Port Arthur, Tex., Sept. 14, 1931; s. Willie Bernice and Leila Evelina (Chase) B.; diploma in acctg. Tyler Comml. Coll., 1949; student Baylor U., 1955-56, La. Coll., 1956; m. Margaret Faye Aguillard, Feb. 6, 1966; children—Joe Ed, Mark Eugene, Liesl Michelle. Various positions Comml. Credit Co., Bus. Services Group, Balt., 1959-73, area dir., 1970-73; freelance mgmt. cons. Dallas, 1973; v.p. Tex. Western Fin. Corp., Dallas, 1974-76; asst. v.p. Citicorp Bus. Credit Inc., Dallas, 1976-78; v.p. fin. and adminstrn., also chief fin. officer Superior Iron Works & Supply Co. Inc., Shreveport, La., 1978—; cons. in field. Served with USN, 1950-53. Cert. credit analyst, credit and fin. analyst. Republican. Baptist. Clubs: Lions (pres. LeCompte, La., 1959-60), Rotary, East Ridge Country, Petroleum of Shreveport. Home: 8606 Rampart Pl Shreveport LA 71106

BONNER, ALLAN BAKER, dentist; b. Aurora, N.C., Oct. 28, 1912; s. George Irving and Vesta Catherine (Mooring) B.; student U. N.C., 1933-36, 37-39; D.D.S., U. Tenn., 1943; m. Sally Ballou Jordan, Aug. 14, 1940; children—Allan Baker, Kathryn (Mrs. Robert Levin Reese), James J., Charles M. Pvt. practice dentistry, Hertford, N.C., 1943—. Chmn., Perquimans County Morehead Found.; chmn. Alcoholic Beverage Control Bd., Town of Hertford, 1961-63; chmn. Perquimans County Sch. Bd., 1963-69. Mem. Am., N.C. dental assns., Phi Chi. Democrat. Episcopalian (sr. warden 1965-66). Mason (Shriner), Rotarian (past pres.). Home: Route 1 510 Edenton Rd Hertford NC 27944 Office: 111 Market St Hertford NC 27944

BONNER, HUGH WARREN, educator; b. Chgo., Oct. 27, 1944; s. Hubert and Dorothea (Robinson) B.; B.S., U. Minn., 1967; M.S., Calif. State Coll., Hayward, 1970; Ph.D., U. Calif., Berkeley, 1972; m. Lynnette Nelson, Aug. 11, 1967; children—Matthew Nelson, Karin Robinson, Christopher Nelson. Tchr. English, coach Winona (Minn.) High Sch., 1967-68, Livermore (Calif.) High Sch., 1968-69; asst. prof. phys. edn.-exercise physiology U. Tex., Austin, 1972-77, asso. prof., 1977—, dir. exercise physiology labs., 1972-77. Mem. bd. of vestry All Sts. Episcopal Ch., Austin, 1974-78; bd. dirs. All Saints Episcopal Day Sch., 1977-78. Mem. AAAS, AAHPER, Am. Coll. Sports Medicine, Sigma Xi. Contbr. articles to profl. jours. Office: 222 Bellmont U Tex Austin TX 78712

BONNER, JACK WILBUR, III, psychiatrist; b. Corpus Christi, Tex., July 30, 1940; s. Jack Wilbur and Irldene (Turner) B.; A.A., Del Mar Coll., 1960; B.A. with honors U. Tex., 1961, M.D., U. Tex. S.W. Med. Sch., 1965; m. Myra Lynn Taylor; children—Jack Wilbur, IV, Katherine Lynn, Shelley Bliss. Intern, U. Ark. Med. Center, 1965-66; resident Duke U. Med. Center, 1966-69; asso. in psychiatry Highland Hosp. div. Duke U. Med. Center, Asheville, N.C., 1971, asst. prof. psychiatry, 1972—, dir. outpatient services, 1972-75, med. dir., 1975—; pres., bd dirs. The Highland Clinic, P.A., 1980—, The Highland Found., 1980—; bd. dirs. Western N.C. Med. Peer Rev. Found., 1975-78. Served to maj. M.C., USAF, 1969-71. Diplomate Am. Bd. Psychiatry, Neurology. Fellow Am. Psychiat. Assn., So. Psychiat. Assn., Am. Coll. Psychiatrists; mem. Am. Group Psychotherapy Assn., AMA, Buncombe County (N.C.) Med. Soc., N.C. Neuro-Psychiat. Assn., Nat. Anorexic Aid Soc. (nat. anorexia adv. council 1979—), So. Med. Assn. (sec. sect. on neurology, neurosurgery and psychiatry). Contbr. articles to profl. jours. Home: 27 Windsor Rd Asheville NC 28804 Office: PO Box 1101 Highland Hosp Asheville NC 28802

BONNER, MARK HERBERT, JR., journalist, utility exec.; b. Ft. Necessity, La., Aug. 5, 1918; s. Mark Herbert and Emma Dee (Johnson) B.; student La. Poly. Inst., 1938-41, La. State U., 1946-48; m. Janie Lee Coughran, Jan. 10, 1947; children—Janie Dee, Mark H. III. Reporter, Franklin Sun, Winnsboro, La., 1948-52, asso. editor, 1949-50, editor, 1950-52, editor Rural La. Opelousas, 1952-65, mgr. in charge publ., advt., pub. relations, legis. affairs, 1962; exec. v.p., gen. mgr. Assn. La. Electric Coops., 1967—. Pres. Nat. Rural Electric Consumer Publs., 1958-59, 64-65; dir. Central Area Data Processing Corp. Mem. exec. com. Franklin Library, 1948-51; mem. La. Superport Task Force Commn., 1972-74; mem. Gov.'s Tax Com., 1975—; mem. La. Com. Natural Resources, 1977—. Bd. dirs. local A.R.C. Served with USAAF, 1941-45; CBI. Recipient editorial award of year La. Press 1951, photography award, 1954, State Future Farmers Award, 1968, Newspaper Service award, 1968. Mem. Nat. Rural Electric Mgrs. Assn. (sec.-treas. 1971—), La. Partners Alliance (sec. 1967—), Am. Legion, V.F.W., Pub. Affairs Research Council, La. Wildlife Fedn. Opelousas C. of C., Soil Conservation Soc. (Conservationist of Year award 1974), Nat. State Mgrs. Assn. (pres. 1973-74), Internat. Platform Assn. Democrat. Methodist. Rotarian. Home: 1322 Casa Loma Dr Baton Rouge LA 70815 Office: 10725 Airline Hwy Baton Rouge LA 70816

BONNER, MURIEL DONNEICE, nurse; b. Littleton, N.C., Aug. 12, 1954; d. Donald Allen and Marion Verneice (Fitts) B.; B.S., Winston-Salem State U., 1976; postgrad. spl. edn. East Carolina U., 1979—. Head nurse Community Rehab. div. Murdoch Center, Butner, N.C., 1976-77; nurse Duke U. Med. Center, Durham, N.C.,

1977-78; med. nurse counsellor, mental retardation specialist N.C. Med. Peer Rev. Found., Raliegh, 1978-79; nurse orthopedic ward Pitt County Meml. Hosp., Greenville, 1979—. Mem. Am. Nurses Assn., Am. Assn. Mental Deficiency. Baptist. Home: 1900 S Charles Blvd Greenville NC 27834 Office: PO Box 19047 Raleigh NC 27609

BONNER, THOMAS, JR., hosp. adminstr.; b. Jackson, Miss., July 28, 1947; s. Thomas and Mildred Inez (Braxton) B.; student U. So. Miss., 1965-66; B.A. magna cum laude, Houston Bapt. U., 1969; M.M., Northwestern U., 1970; M.S. in Health Care Adminstrn., Trinity U., 1976; m. Kay Kepler, July 12, 1969; 1 dau., Kristin Day. Adminstrv. resident VA Hosp., Houston, 1975-76, program analyst, 1976; adminstrv. coordinator Meml. Hosp. System, Houston, 1976-77, adminstrv. asst., 1977-78, asst. v.p., 1978—. Mem. long-range planning com. Houston Bapt. U., 1977; organist Bapt. Temple, Houston, 1976—. Served with USAF, 1970-74. Houston Edn. Found. fellow, 1968. Mem. Am. Coll. Hosp. Adminstrs., Am. Hosp. Assn., Tex. Hosp. Assn., Young Hosp. Adminstrs. Houston, Alpha Tau Omega, Omicron Delta Kappa (award 1966), Pi Kappa Lambda (award 1966), Phi Eta Sigma. Baptist. Home: 11315 Burgoyne Dr Houston TX 77077 Office: 7600 Beechnut St Houston TX 77074

BONNESS, JOSEPH DENNY, JR., paving corp. exec.; b. Milw., Oct. 14, 1924; s. Joseph Denny and Margaret (Boylan) B.; B.S. in Mech. Engring., Marquette U., 1948; m. Virginia Mary Haas, Aug. 31, 1946; children—Margaret, Mary, Joseph, Theresa, Kathleen, Maureen, Eileen, Bridget, Patrice, Sharon. Pres., dir. Hwy. Pavers Inc., Milw., 1962—; sec., dir. Concrete Constrn. Inc., Milw., 1951-71; treas., dir. Joseph D. Bonness Inc., Milw., 1948—; sec., dir. Subdividers Inc., Elm Grove, 1954-71; pres., dir. Ochopee Rock, Inc., Naples, Fla. Bd. dirs. Collier County Water Mgmt. Advisory Bd., Cath. Ser. Bur. Inc. Mem. Wis. Rd. Builders Assn. (sec. 1956-57, pres. 1972-73), Wis. Asphalt Pavement Assn., Fla. Rd. Builders Assn., ASCE, Am. Road and Transp. Builders Assn. (pres. contractors div. 1978), Asphalt Contractors Assn. Fla., Fla. Transp. Builders Assn. (dir.), Cruising Club Am., Sigma Phi Delta, Pi Tau Sigma. K.C. Clubs: Milw. Athletic, Milw. Yacht; St. Petersburg Yacht; Naples Sailing and Yacht. Home: 1555 Ixora Dr Naples FL 33940 Office: PO Box 8809 Naples FL 33941

BONNET, JUAN AMÈDÉE, chem. and nuclear engr.; b. Santurce, P.R., Apr. 22, 1939; s. Juan A. and Josefa Luisa (Diez) B.; B.S. in Chem. Engring, U. Mich., 1960, Ph.D. in Nuclear Engring., 1971; M.S. in Nuclear Tech., U. P.R., 1961; m. Wally Vargas, Dec. 27, 1963; children—Juan, Carlos, Antonio, Luis, Gerardo, Gabriel. Safety and analysis engr. P.R. Water Resources Authority, 1962-67, head nuclear engring. dept., 1971-73, head environ. protection, quality assurance and nuclear divs., 1972-75, asst. exec. dir. planning and engring., 1975-77; dir. Center for Energy and Environment Research, U. P.R., San Juan, 1977—; adj. faculty P.R. Technol. U., 1973-77; adj. asso. prof. P.R. Sch. Medicine, San Juan, 1979—; adj. prof. Engring. Sch. Mayagüez (P.R.), 1979—; pres. Profl. Engrs., Architects and Surveyors Exam. Bd. of P.R., 1979—; cons. environ. and energy engring., 1971—. Dir., Rincon fund. dr. P.R. Soc. Mentally Retarded Children, 1967; mem. So. Interstate Nuclear Bd., 1975-77; bd. dirs. U. P.R., 1978—, So. Solar Energy Centers, 1979—; mem. UNESCO-U.S. Commn.: Man and Biosphere, 1979. Named Outstanding Young Scientist of P.R., Jaycees, 1978, Distinguished Engr., Tau Beta Pi, 1978; registered profl. engr., P.R. Mem. Am. Nuclear Soc., P.R. Inst. Chem. Engrs. (pres. 1977-78), Interam. Confedn. Chem. Engrs. (gen. sec. 1977-79), P.R. Chemists Soc., P.R. Assn. Engrs. and Surveyors (dir. 1967, 76-77), Internat. Solar Energy Soc., Internat. Assn. Hydrogen Energy, Pan Am. Union of Assns. of Engrs. (energy com. 1972—), Ateneo de P.R., P.R. Acad. Arts and Scis., N.Y. Acad. Sci., Caribbean Assn. Univ. and Research Insts. (chmn. energy com. 1980—), P.R. Inst. TV-Radio Ethics, Soc. Research Adminstrs., Sigma Xi, Phi Eta Mu. Roman Catholic. Contbr. articles on energy sources to profl. publs. Home: Calle 1 H-7 1 Los Frailes Norte Guaynabo PR 00657 Office: Caparra Heights Sta San Juan PR 00936

BONNEY, JOSEPH WAYNE, bus. exec.; b. Norfolk, Va., Oct. 27, 1941; s. William Kermit and Margaret Mary Frances (Shearer) B.; student Norfolk div. William and Mary Coll., 1960-61, 63-64, Norfolk Naval Shipyard, 1964; m. Wanda Nell Beersdorf, Jan. 27, 1969; children—Eunice Catherine, William Wayne, Mandi Brooke. Elec. engring. technician Norfolk Naval Shipyard, 1962-68; chief mech. engr. Tabet Mfg. Co., Inc., Norfolk, 1964-68, 68-69; program mgr. Ingalls Shipbldg. Co., Pascagoula, Miss., 1969-79; pres. Bonney Enterprises, Inc., 1978—; owner, operator Gen. Bus. Systems, Inc. Mem. Pas-Point Jaycees (dir. 1973-74; named Outstanding 1st Year Jaycee 1974). Presbyn. Mason (32 deg., Shriner). Home: 2908 Stratford Dr Chesapeake VA 23321

BONNIOL, THOMAS FRANCIS, purchasing exec.; b. Quincy, Ill., Mar. 2, 1933; s. Frank L. and Frances J. (Welch) B.; B.S. in Econs., Providence Coll., 1955; m. Betty Ann Bonniol; children—Noelle, Nicole. Sr. buyer foods div. Coca-Cola Co., Orlando, Fla., 1961-70; dir. purchasing Koscot Cosmetics, Inc., Orlando, 1970-74; v.p. Corp. Cons. Inc., Longwood, Fla., 1973-74; dir. purchasing STP Corp., Ft. Lauderdale, Fla., 1974—. Coach AAU and high sch. swim teams, Central and South Fla. Served as maj., USAR, 1973. Mem. Nat. Assn. Purchasing Mgmt. (cert. purchasing mgr.), Fla. Assn. Purchasing Mgmt., Met. Opera Guild, Smithsonian Assos. Roman Catholic. Club: K.C. Contbr. articles to Swimming World. Home: 1126 Vista Del Mar Delray Beach FL 33444 Office: 1400 W Commercial Blvd Fort Lauderdale FL 33310

BONSANGUE, NICHOLAS ANTHONY, state ofcl.; b. Englewood, N.J., Sept. 10, 1933; s. Anthony and Sarah (LaValle) B.; B.S. in Econs., Fairleigh Dickinson U., 1960; postgrad. U. Pa., 1962-63; M. in Urban Planning, N.Y. U., 1978; m. Dorothy Whitaker, Aug. 10, 1963; children—Jean, Laura. Jr. planner N.J. Div. State and Regional Planning, Trenton, 1961-63; planning dir. Cobb County-Marietta Planning Dept., Marietta, Ga., 1970-71; chief Office of Planning Assistance, Dept. Community Devel. State of Ga., Altanta, 1971—. Served with U.S. Army, 1954-56. Mem. Am. Inst. of Planners, Am. Soc. of Planning Ofcls. Home: 450 Burlington Rd NE Atlanta GA 30307 Office: Room 640 7 Martin Luther King Jr Dr Atlanta GA 30334

BONTOS, GEORGE EMMANUEL, physician; b. Alton, Ill., Dec. 7, 1924; s. Emmanuel Anthony and Lillian (Saris) Bontzolakis; B.A., U. Chgo., 1949; M.D., U. Athens (Greece), 1968; m. Athena M. Teregis, Sept. 21, 1952; children—E. Christopher, Elizabeth Ann. Research asso. Chgo. State Hosp., 1969; intern Wheeling (W.Va.) Hosp., 1970-71, resident, 1971-73; practice medicine specializing in family medicine, Wheeling, 1973—; sr. attending Wheeling Hosp., Ohio Valley Med. Center; plant physician Wheeling-Pitts. Steel Corp. Bd. dirs. Wheeling chpt. ARC, 1975, Vis. Nurses Assn. Ohio County, 1976. Served with U.S. Army, 1945-46; Korea. Diplomate Am. Bd. Family Practice. Fellow Am. Acad. Family Physicians, Am. Geriatrics Soc.; mem. AMA (Recognition award 1975, 78), So. Med. Assn., W.Va. Med. Assn., Ohio County Med. Assn., Ohio County Found. Med. Care, Pan-Cretan Assn. Republican. Greek Orthodox. Clubs: Masons, Shriners (Wheeling). Home: 160 Oakmont Rd Wheeling WV 26003 Office: 2427 Warwood Ave Wheeling WV 26003

BOOK, JOHN KENNETH, retail store owner; b. Hillsboro, Ill., June 26, 1950; s. Vern Ray and Pearl Iva (Foster) B.; Asso. Acctg., Ky. Bus. Coll., 1974. Laborer, Lexington Army Depot (Ky.), 1968-70; machine operator A.O. Smith, Mount Sterling, Ky., 1971-72; laborer Irvin Industries, Lexington, Ky., 1973-75; owner Kenny's Signs Unltd., Winchester, Ky., 1977—. Democrat.

BOOKER, CLARISSA GAMBLE, educator; b. Hubbard, Tex.; d. William Franklin and Georgia Lee (Sheppard) Gamble; B.S., Prairie View A&M Coll., 1968; M.A., U. No. Colo., 1969; Ed.D., U. Houston, 1977. Asst. prof. edn. Prairie View (Tex.) A&M U., 1969—; cons. sch. dists. Mem. Internat. Reading Assn., Tex. Assn. Improvement Reading, Greater Houston Area Reading Council, Phi Delta Kappa, Kappa Delta Pi, Delta Sigma Theta. Office: Sch Edn Prairview A&M Coll Prairie View TX 77445

BOOKER, DORIS EDWINIA WOODARD, educator; b. Portsmouth, Va., Dec. 13, 1936; d. Edward Delma and Clarine (Jones) W.; A.B. in English, Va. State Coll., 1959, M.A. in English, 1970; postgrad. in English Edn. (fellow), U. Va., 1973-76; div.; 1 dau., Angela Denise. Tchr. English and history Russell Grove High Sch., Amelia, Va., 1959-61, Central High Sch. and Northumberland High Sch., Heathsville, Va., 1961-70; instr. English Va. State Coll., Petersburg, 1970-73, asst. prof. English, 1976—; lectr. dept. humanities Piedmont Community Coll., Charlottesville, Va., 1973-74; instr., supr. student tchrs. U. Va., Charlottesville, 1973-75; coordinator reading program Albemarle High Sch., Charlottesville, 1975-76. Mem. Va. Assn. Tchrs. of English, Conf. English Educators, Nat. Council Tchrs. of English, Phi Delta Kappa, Delta Sigma Theta. Baptist. Home: 8637 Aldershot Dr Richmond VA 23229 Office: 219 Vawter Hall Va State U Petersburg VA 23803

BOOKER, WILMA ROWE, nurse, hosp. adminstr.; b. Washington, Ark., June 14, 1924; d. James Russell and Willie Mavous (Nannie) Rowe; R.N., Leo N. Levi Meml. Hosp., 1946; m. Joe Charles Booker, Oct. 8, 1947; children—Joe Lester, Wilma LaNelle. Staff nurse Julia Chester Hosp., Hope, Ark., 1946-47, Texarkana (Tex.) Hosp., 1947-48, DeQueen (Ark.) Gen. Hosp., 1947-50; dir. nursing Polk County Hosp., Mena, Ark., 1950-51, Dickinson Hosp., DeQueen, 1951-54; staff, asst. nursing Hempstead County Hosp., Hope, 1955-77, dir. nursing, 1977—; cons. in field. Mem. Dist. 16 Nurses Assn. (pres. 1967-69), Ark. League of Nursing, Assn. Practitioners in Infection Control, Hempstead County Hist. Soc. (charter). Methodist. Club: Order of Eastern Star. Office: Hempstead County Hosp 1900 S Main St Hope AR 71801

BOOKOUT, JOHN FRANK, JR., oil co. exec.; b. Shreveport, La., Dec. 31, 1922; s. John Frank and Lena (Hagen) B.; student Iowa Wesleyan Coll., 1943, Centenary Coll., 1946-47; B.Sc., U. Tex., 1949, M.A., 1950; m. Mary Carolyn Cook, Dec. 21, 1946; children—Beverly Carolyn, Mary Adair and John Frank (twins). Geologist, Shell Oil Co., Tulsa, 1950-59, div. exploration mgr., 1959-61, area exploration mgr., Denver, 1961-63, The Hague, Netherlands, 1963-64, exploration mgr., New Orleans, 1964, mgr. exploration and prodn. econs. dept., N.Y.C., 1965, v.p. Denver exploration and prodn. area, 1966, v.p. Southeastern exploration and prodn. region, New Orleans, 1967-70, pres., chief exec. officer, dir. Shell Can. Ltd., Toronto, Ont., 1970-74, exec. v.p., dir. Shell Oil Co., Houston, 1974-76, pres., chief exec. officer, dir., 1976—; dir. Safeway Stores, Inc., Irving Trust Co. Bd. dirs. Meth. Hosp., Houston; trustee Found. Bus., Politics and Econs.; mem. so. regional adv. bd. Inst. Internat. Edn., Inc.; mem. Houston Regional Minority Purchasing Council; mem. adv. council U. Tex., Austin; bd. visitors Tulane U. Served with USAAF, 1942-46. Decorated Air medal with 3 oak leaf clusters. Mem. Am. Petroleum Inst. (dir.), Am. Assn. Petroleum Geologists, Nat. Petroleum Council, Conf. Bd., All-Am. Wildcatters Assn., Houston C. of C. (dir.), Internat. C. of C. (trustee U.S. council), Twenty-Five Year Club of Petroleum Industry (bd. govs. southwest dist.), Bus. Roundtable (policy com.). Home: PO Box 13614 Houston TX 77019 Office: Shell Oil Co PO Box 2463 Houston TX 77001

BOOKS, EARL JAMES EUGENE, editor; b. Carlisle, Pa., June 22, 1942; s. Cleo Earl and Ruth Kathleen (Little) B.; student Thiel Coll., 1960-63; B.A., U. Md., 1970, M.Ed., 1974; m. Hiroko Miyaguni, May 16, 1969; 1 dau., Julita Nona. Vice pres., dir., Gt. Eastern Corp., Naha, Japan, 1968-69; budget analyst U.S. Govt., Japan, 1969-73; mental health counselor Camp Kue Army Hosp., Japan, 1973-74; writer/editor (scientific), career counselor U.S. Govt., Ft. Belvoir, Va., 1974—. Served in USN, 1964-68. Mem. Nat. Assn. Govt. Communicators, Am. Personnel and Guidance Assn., Am. Coll. Personnel Assn., Assn. for Counselor Edn. and Supervision, Nat. Vocat. Guidance Assn., Assn. for Humanistic Edn. and Devel., Am. Sch. Counselor Assn., Am. Rehab. Counseling Assn., Assn. for Measurement and Evaluation in Guidance, Nat. Employment Counselors Assn., VFW, Am. Legion. Lutheran. Home: 8202 Martha St Alexandria VA 22309 Office: US Army Engr Topographic Labs Fort Belvoir VA 22060

BOOKSTAVER, ALEXANDER, fin. cons.; b. Sag Harbor, N.Y., Apr. 11, 1911; s. Samuel and Jennie (Lekus) B.; student Coll. City N.Y., 1929-32; student bus. adminstrn., N.Y.U., 1933-34; grad. Am. Inst. Banking, 1936; m. Dorothy Ravitt, Sept. 3, 1936; 1 son, Richard. With trust dept. Hanover Bank, N.Y.C., 1930-41; with comptroller's dept. Schroder Trust Co., N.Y.C., 1941-46; v.p., comptroller Amalgamated Bank N.Y., 1946-56; controller, dir. investment dept. Internat. Ladies Garment Workers Union, N.Y.C., 1956-61; dir. investment dept. AFL-CIO, Washington, 1961-68; v.p. instl. relations Anchor Corp., Elizabeth, N.J., 1968-71; sr. v.p. investor liasion Heritage Corp. South Fla., Miami, 1971-73; v.p., sr. mortgage loan officer Midwest Mortgage Co., Miami, 1973-75; fin. cons., 1976—; dir. Peoples Nat. Bank of Md., Suitland. Mem. adv. com. housing and urban devel. AID, 1963-68; mem. adv. bd. Nat. Found. Health, Welfare and Pension Plans, 1963-68. Bd. dirs. Hebrew Inst. of L.I. Editorial adv. bd. Pension World. Home: 20 Island Ave Belle Isle Miami Beach FL 33139

BOONE, BETTY JANE PRATT, realtor; b. Chgo.; d. William Everett and Betty L. (Wright) Pratt; student pub. schs.; m. George C. Boone, May 16, 1932 (div. June 1950); children—Betty Lee (Mrs. Jack Schram), George C. Owner, Betty Jane Boone, Realtor, Daytona Beach, Fla. Mem. adv. council Fla. Indsl. Commn., 1962-63; chmn. Multiple Listing Service Daytona Beach area Bd. Realtors, 1965—, dir., 1964—. Mem. steering com. Volusia County chpt. ARC, 1965; founding mem. Daytona Beach Area Com. of 100, treas., 1961-62. City commr., Daytona Beach, Fla., 1966-67. Bd. dirs. Volusia County Mental Health Assn., 1961-62. Named Realtor of the Year, 1957, 60, 61, 65. Mem. Daytona Beach Area Bd. Realtors (hon. life mem., pres. 1960-61), Nat. (nat. dir. 1976-78), Fla. (v.p. 1951, 59, corp. sec. 1952-56, 57, mem. speakers bur., pres. diamond pin club 1975, life mem. polit. action com.) assns. realtors, Nat. Brokers Council (nat. sec.-treas., dir. 1965—), Nat. Assn. Real Estate Bds. (gov. women's council nat. assn. realtors 1959-60, regional v.p. 1961-62, pres. 1966—, nat. dir. 1968-70, 76-78), Nat. Inst. Real Estate Brokers, Nat. Inst. Farm and Land Brokers (regional v.p.), Internat. Traders Club, Daytona Beach C. of C. (bd. govs. 1961-63). Club: Pilot (pres. 1958-59, 1st lt. gov. 1962). Editor: What Women Realtors Are Doing, 1965. Home: Bayshore Bath and Tennis Club Unit 1109 925 N Halifax Ave Daytona Beach FL 32018 Office: 402 Seabreeze Blvd Daytona Beach FL 32018

BOONE, HARRY LINDSAY, JR., wholesale distbr.; b. Portsmouth, Va., Feb. 5, 1950; s. Harry Lindsay and Martha Elizabeth (Richardson) B.; A.A.S., Tidewater Community Coll., 1976; m. Ann Candler Cardwell, Aug. 4, 1979. With Boon Distributing Co., Inc./Pet Supplies, Inc., Portsmouth, Va., 1969—, v.p., office mgr., 1976—. Mem. Portsmouth Democratic Exec. Com., 1975-77. Served with USMCR, 1969-75. Recipient Recognition award, Portsmouth Clean Community Commn., 1979. Mem. Nat. Food Delaers Assn., Tidewater Food Dealers Assn., Sons Confederate Vets. (comdr. camp), Nat. Rifle Assn., N-S Skirmish Assn., Mil. Order Stars and Bars. Episcopalian. Club: K.P. Home: Route 1 PO Box 426 Carrollton VA 23314 Office: 2030 Ponderosa St Portsmouth VA 23701

BOONE, MARSHALL NOLAN, JR., physician; b. Langdale, Ala., Oct. 18, 1942; s. Marshall Nolan and Daisy (Zeiger) B.; B.S., Samford U., 1964; Ph.D., U. Ala., 1972, M.D. cum laude, 1975; m. Carla Wallace, Sept. 20, 1964; children—Jonathan Michael, Ashley Rebecca. Research asso. physiology and biophysics U. Ala., Birmingham, 1969-72, resident in family medicine, Huntsville, 1975-78; emergency room physician Shelby Meml. Hosp., Alabaster, Ala., 1978—, chief emergency med. services, 1979—; exec. dir. Double Oak Emergency Med. Assn., Birmingham, 1979—; clin. asst. prof. family practice U. Ala. Med. Sch., 1978—. Diplomate Am. Bd. Family Practice. Mem. Am. Acad. Family Physicians, Am. Physiol. Soc., Ala. Acad. Sci., Am. Heart Assn., Sigma Xi, Alpha Omega Alpha, Alpha Epsilon Delta. Baptist. Home: 5120 Shadowbrook Trail Birmingham AL 35244 Office: Shelby Meml Hosp Box 488 Alabaster AL 35007

BOORMAN, HOWARD LYON, educator; b. Chgo., Sept. 11, 1920; s. William Ryland and Verna (Lyon) Boorman; B.A., U. Wis., Madison, 1941; postgrad. Yale, 1946-47; m. Mary Houghton, Jan. 20, 1972; 1 son by previous marriage, Scott A. Divisional asst. Div. Def. Materials, Dept. State, Washington, 1942-43; fgn. service officer, Peking, Hong Kong, 1947-54; research asso. Sch. Internat. Affairs Columbia U., N.Y.C., 1955-67; prof. history Vanderbilt U., Nashville, 1967—; mem. Nat. Com. on U.S.-China Relations, 1966—. Served to lt. USN, 1943-46. Recipient Rockefeller Pub. Service award, 1954-55; vis. scholar U. Center Va., 1963. Mem. Am., Tenn. hist. socs., Am. Polit. Sci. Assn., Assn. Asian Studies, Council Fgn. Relations. Club: University (Nashville). Gen. editor: Biographical Dictionary of Republican China, 1967-71. Contbr. articles to profl. jours. Home: 3603 Hoods Hill Rd Nashville TN 37215 Office: Dept History Vanderbilt U Nashville TN 37235

BOOTH, DONALD JAMES, surgeon; b. Wisconsin Rapids, Wis., Mar. 12, 1935; s. Conrad and Doris Marie (Bever) B.; B.A., Marquette U., Milw., 1958, M.D., 1963; children—Lynne Therese, Mark Daniel. Intern, USAF Med. Center, San Antonio, 1963-64; resident in surgery Wilford Hall USAF Med. Center, San Antonio, 1964-69; fellow in surgery Johns Hopkins U. Hosp., Balt., 1969-70; practice medicine specializing in surgery, Ocean Springs, Miss.; surgeon-in-chief Gulf Coast Surgical and Diagnostic Center, Ocean Springs, 1972—, also pres., chmn. bd.; asso. dir. So. Nat. Bank, Ocean Springs; chmn. bd. Southland Devel. Co. Bd. dirs. Gulf Coast YMCA. Served as officer M.C., USAF, 1963-72. Mem. AMA, Miss. Med. Assn., A.C.S., Assn. Acad. Surgery. Office: Medical Plaza Van Cleave Rd Ocean Springs MS 39564

BOOTH, EDEN COMFORT, former exec.; b. Cedar Springs, Mich., Feb. 21, 1900; s. Fremont D. and Ida Jane (Gates) B.; LL.B., Peoples Coll., Ft. Scott, Kan., 1922; m. Lucy C. Temple, May 2, 1922 (dec. Mar. 1966); 1 dau., Elizabeth Jane (Mrs. William L. Frakes); m. 2d Mozelle Murray, Jan. 13, 1968. Founder, chmn. bd. Colonial Poultry Farms, Inc., Pleasant Hill, Mo., 1922-55; pres. Mo. Poultry Expt. Sta., Mt. Grove, 1934-43; pres. Pleasant Hill Bank, 1940-51. Pres. bd. edn., Pleasant Hill, 1930-48, mayor, 1956-58. Trustee Patriotic Edn., Inc., 1963—. Mem. S.A.R. (pres. DeLand chpt. 1962-63, state registrar 1963-68). Democrat. Presbyn. Mason (Shriner), Lion, Odd Fellow. Club: University (Winter Park, Fla.). Publisher: Standard Poultry Jour., 1925-31; Genealogy of the Booth Family, 1956. Home and Office: 806 W Howry Ave DeLand FL 32720

BOOTH, GORDON DEAN, JR., lawyer; b. Columbus, Ga., June 25, 1939; s. Gordon Dean and Lois Mildred (Bray) B.; B.A., Emory U., 1961, J.D., 1964, LL.M., 1973; m. Katherine Morris Campbell, June 17, 1961; children—Mary Katherine, Abigail Kilgore, Sarah Elizabeth, Margaret Campbell. Admitted to Ga. bar, 1964, U.S. Supreme Ct. bar, 1973; practiced in Atlanta, 1964-68; partner firm Troutman, Sanders, Lockerman & Ashmore, 1967-77, Seward and Kissel, 1978—; dir., v.p. Stallion Music, Inc., Nashville, Tenn. Trustee Met. Atlanta Crime Commn., 1977—, chmn., 1979—; mem. assembly for arts and scis. Emory Coll., 1974—. Mem. Atlanta, Internat. (mem. council, sect. on bus. law 1974—, chmn. aeronaut. law com. 1971—), Am. bar assns., Am. Soc. Internat. Law, Assn. Bar City N.Y., State Bar of Ga., Lawyers Club of Atlanta, Sigma Chi. Clubs: Capital City, Lawyers, University (N.Y.C.). Contbr. articles to profl. jours. Home: 580 Old Harbor Dr Atlanta GA 30328 Office: 500 Candler Bldg Atlanta GA 30303 also 63 Wall St New York NY 10005

BOOTH, MARY JEAN, speech pathologist; b. Baton Rouge, Jan. 27, 1942; d. Marion Albert and Rebecca Charlotte (Brandau) Young; B.S., U. Miss. for Women, 1964; M.Communication Disorders, La. State U. Med. Center, 1978; m. Robert Allen Booth, Jr., July 25, 1964; children—Christopher Lee, Virginia Elizabeth, Mary Catherine. Speech and lang. clinician Caddo Found. Exceptional Children, Shreveport, La., 1964-67; itinerant speech clinician Caddo Parish Sch. Bd., Shreveport, 1967-69, Bossier Parish Sch. Bd., Bossier City, La., 1969-72; speech and lang. pathologist DeSoto Parish Sch. Bd., Mansfield, La., 1977-79; speech and hearing cons. II, N.W. La. State Sch., Bossier City, 1979—; pvt. practice, 1979—. Mem. Am. Speech, Lang. and Hearing Assn., La. Speech and Hearing Assn., La. Assn. Educators, NEA, Shreve-Bossier Speech and Hearing Assn., La. State

U. Alumni Assn. Episcopalian. Home: 3533 LaNell St Bossier City LA 71112 Office: 5401 Shed Rd Bossier City LA 71010

BOOTH, RALPH RAY, chemist; b. Pickens, W.Va., May 22, 1928; s. Harry Barnhart and Myrtle (Tenney) B.; B.S. Davis and Elkins Coll., 1949, M.H.L., 1972; M.S., W.Va. U., 1951; m. Edith Mae Reid, Jan. 28, 1950; children—Janet Lynn, Harry Allen, Joyce Marie, David Reid. Chief chemist Honeggers & Co., Fairbury, Ill., 1953; asso. prof. chemistry Davis & Elkins Coll., 1953-56, 67—, chmn. dept., 1968—, registrar, 1970-76; chemist Hercules Inc., Wilmington, Del., 1956-57; asst. prof. Grove City (Pa.) Coll., 1957-61; asso. prof. Indiana (Pa.) State Coll., 1961-63; asso. editor Chem. Abstracts Service, Columbus, Ohio, 1963-67. Served with USN 1945-46. Mem. Am. Chem. Soc. (chmn. 1973-74, councilor 1975—). Presbyterian. Home: 106 Guy St Elkins WV 26241 Office: Davis and Elkins Coll Dept Chemistry Elkins WV 26241

BOOTHBY, MARY CAROLYN GIBBS, landscape designer, horticulturist; b. Birmingham, Ala., June 24, 1932; d. Elbert Ward and Mary (Brinskelle) Gibbs; student Randolph-Macon Women's Coll., 1949-50, 50-51, U. Ala., 1951; A.B., Birmingham So. U., 1953; A.S., Jefferson State U., 1977, m. Wallace Johnson Boothby, Jr., Sept. 19, 1952; children—Wallace Johnson III, Elbert Ward Gibbs, Mary Katharine. Freelance Landscape designer and hort. cons., Birmingham, 1977—; lectr. hort. subjects. Pres. jr. women's com. Birmingham Symphony, 1957; pres. Vis. Nurses Assn., 1980; v.p. Red Mountain Museum Soc., 1980; sec. bd. trustees Highlands Day Sch., 1979-80; bd. dirs. Children's Aid Soc., Ala. Symphony. Mem. Am. Hort. Soc., Royal Hort. Soc., Birmingham Bot. Soc. Congregationalist. Home and Office: 1994 Shades Crest Rd Birmingham AL 35216

BOOTON, JOHN ROLLER, engring. co. exec., thoroughbred horse breeder; b. Luray, Va., Jan. 1, 1910; s. John H. and Pearl (Roller) B.; B.S., Va. Mil. Inst., 1930; m. Mary Daniel, Sept. 20, 1948. Structural engr., Am. Bridge Co., Ambridge, Pa., 1930-33; county engr. Civil Works Authority, Shenandoah, Va., 1933-34; works engr. E. I. DuPont de Nemours & Co. Inc., Richmond, Va., 1934-59; sr. v.p. Wiley & Wilson Inc., Richmond, 1960—. Registered profl. engr., Md., N.C., Ohio, Va. Fellow ASCE, ASME (policy bd. profl. and public affairs, profl. affairs and ethics com.), Va. Assn. Professions, Nat. Soc. Profl. Engrs., Soc. Am. Mil. Engrs. Presbyterian. Clubs: Engrs. Richmond, Commonwealth. Home: Long Meadow Farm Chester VA 23831 Office: 100 E Main St Richmond VA 23219

BOOZER, ALBERT MARION, physician; b. Newberry, S.C., July 24, 1920; s. Alonzo Pinkney and Rhoda (Boozer) B.; B.S. magna cum laude, Newberry Coll., 1942; M.D., U. Tenn., 1945; m. Virginia Ellen Baker, June 20, 1946; children—Albert Marion, Russell Whitman, Lou Ann. Intern, Denver Gen. Hosp., 1945-46; resident in surgery City Hosp., Winston-Salem, N.C., 1948-49; gen. practice medicine and surgery, Dalton, Ga., 1949—; mem. staff Hamilton Meml. Hosp., Dalton, 1949—, pres., 1956, 61, v.p., 1960, dir. tumor clinic, 1958-59. Served to capt. AUS, 1946-48. Mem. AMA, Med. Assn. Ga., Am. Geriatrics Soc., Am. Acad. Gen. Practice, Whitfield County Med. Soc. (pres. 1953, 67-68), Alpha Omega Alpha, Alpha Kappa Kappa, Theta Nu Epsilon. Clubs: Lions, Elks. Home: 603 Valley Dr Dalton GA 30720 Office: Dalton Med Arts Bldg 1109 Burleyson Dr Dalton GA 30720

BOOZER, HOWARD RAI, state ednl. ofcl.; b. Monterey, Ky., Aug. 14, 1923; s. Claud Dow and Harriet Ruth (Foster) B.; A.B., Howard Coll., 1946; B.S., Washington U., St. Louis, 1950, M.A. in Edn., 1948, Ph.D., 1960; LL.D. (hon.), Baptist Coll. at Charleston (S.C.), 1976; m. Frances Alleen Kintner, Aug. 23, 1946; children—Claudia Ruth, Margaret Ann, Catherine Mae, Barbara Frances. High sch. tchr., Webster Groves, Mo., 1949-51; staff asso. Am. Council Edn., Washington, 1954-61; asst. dir., then dir. N.C. Bd. Higher Edn., Raleigh, 1961-68; v.p. Nat. Lab. Higher Edn., Durham, N.C., 1968-70, also adj. prof. edn. Duke U.; dir. Ednl. Devel. Adminstrn., RCA Corp., 1970-73; exec. dir. S.C. Commn. Higher Edn., Columbia, 1973—; bd. dirs. N.C. League Nursing, 1964-66, pres., 1969-70; mem. rev. panel constrn. nurse tng. facilities USPHS, 1965-69; bd. dirs. N.J. League Nursing, 1972-73; mem. task force implications of report of nat. commn. study nursing and nursing edn. Nat. League Nursing, 1971-72, mem. nat. bd. dirs., 1973-77, mem. appeal panel diploma programs, 1975—; trustee Meredith Coll., Raleigh, N.C., 1963-66, Wingate (N.C.) Coll., 1967-70; bd. dirs. Learning Inst. N.C., 1965-68, Nat. Lab. Higher Edn., 1966-68; devel. bd. Lenoir Rhyne Coll., Hickory, N.C., 1968-73, Cumberland (Ky.) Coll., 1970—; S.C. del. Edn. Commn. States, 1973-79, mem. task force state, instl. and fed. responsiblities in providing postsecondary ednl. opportunity service personnel, 1975-76; State Higher Edn. Exec. Officers Assn., 1965-68, 73—, exec. com., 1974-75; S.C. del. So. Regional Edn. Bd., 1974—, exec. com., 1974-75; mem. S.C. Com. Humanities, 1975—; adv. bd. Servicemen's Opportunity Coll., 1976—. Served to lt. USNR, 1943-46, 51-54, capt. Res. Mem. So. Assn. Coll. Schs. (higher edn. adv. bd. 1976—), Am. Assn. Higher Edn., Newcomen Soc. N.Am., Phi Delta Kappa, Kappa Delta Pi. Democrat. Club: Torch. Contbr. articles to profl. jours. Office: SC Commn Higher Edn 1429 Senate St Columbia SC 29201

BOOZER, SIMON DAVID, architect; b. Anniston, Ala., Jan. 12, 1936; s. David Leon and Ruby Margaret (Kyle) B.; B.Arch., Washington U., 1959; m. Doris Ann Sweet, Jan. 28, 1961; children—Margaret Ann, David Edward. Archtl. designer, delineator Bank Bldg. Corp., St. Louis, 1960; architect William B. Ittner Architects & Engrs., St. Louis, 1961, James M. Hoffman Architect, Anniston, 1962, Hofferbert & Ellis, Gadsden, Ala., 1963-66; partner Christian, Boozer, Jenkins, Anniston, 1966-78; pvt. practice architecture as S. David Boozer AIA P.C., 1978—; dir. Guaranty Fed. Savs. & Loan Assn. of Calhoun County (Ala.). Mem. bd. advisers Salvation Army, Anniston, 1970—; bd. dirs. YMCA. Served with AUS, 1959-60. Mem. AIA, Nat. Council Archtl. Registration Bd., Anniston C. of C. (v.p. 1974). Methodist (bd. dirs.). Mason, Rotarian. Clubs: Anniston Country; The Club (Birmingham). Author: Solar Engineering News, 1977. Office: Broadcasting Central Bldg 1115 Leighton Ave Anniston AL 36201

BORCHARDT, LOVIE LEE MCBRAYER, educator; b. Draketown, Ga.; d. William Arthur and Dona Leo (Vaughan) McBrayer; A.B. (Rosenwald Scholar), Shorer Coll., 1955; M.Ed., U. Ga., 1961, Ed.S., 1970; postgrad. U. Ala., 1977, U. S.C., 1978—; m. Raphael David Borchardt, June 9, 1946 (dec.); children—Donna Rebecca Borchardt Cox, Millie Lee. Tchr., Brunswick (Ga.) City Schs., 1948-72; instr. reading Ga. So. Coll., Statesboro, 1970-71; asso. prof. edn. and reading Floyd Jr. Coll., Rome, Ga., 1972—; speaker to various ednl. groups. Mem. Internat. Reading Assn., AAUP, Ga. Assn. Educators, Am. Assn. Early Childhood Internat., NEA, Alpha Delta Kappa (past chpt. pres.), Delta Kappa Phi. Baptist. Home: 27 Berkshire Dr Rome GA 30161 Office: Floyd Jr Coll PO Box 1864 Rome GA 30161

BORCHERS, KAREN LILY, social work adminstr.; b. Detroit, Apr. 4, 1940; d. Albert Oscar and Lily Louise (Denzler) Borchers; student U. Chgo., 1957-59, M.A. in Social Service Adminstrn., 1964; B.A. magna cum laude in Psychology and Sociology, Mich. State U., 1961; M.S. in Edn., No. Ill. U., 1976. Child welfare worker Ill. Dept. Children and Family Services, Rockford, 1962-65; sch. social worker Komarek Schs., North Riverside, Ill., 1965-67; exec. dir. Seguin Sch., Berwyn, Ill., 1967-72, Seguin Tng. Center, Cicero, Ill., 1967-72; adminstr. Orchard Hill, Madison, Wis., 1972-76; adminstrv. dir. Children's Home Soc. Fla., West Palm Beach, 1976—; mem. Fla. Human Rights Advocacy Com. for Mentally Retarded. Pres., United Way Council of Agencies, Palm Beach Country; pres. Palm Beach Regional Achievement Center for Retarded Citizens; pres. Masterworks Chorus of Palm Beaches. Named Woman of Yr. in Social Services, Palm Beach County, 1979. Mem. Acad. Certified Social Workers, Nat. Assn. Social Workers (chmn. Gulfstream Unit), Am. Assn. on Mental Deficiency, Nat., Palm Beach County (dir.) assns. for retarded citizens, Mensa. Club: Soroptomists. Home: 5791 S Rue Rd West Palm Beach FL 33406 Office: 3600 Broadway West Palm Beach FL 33407

BORDERS, BEN, clergyman, lawyer; b. Springfield, Ky., Aug. 23, 1906; s. Frank and Nettie (Lyddane) B.; diploma Christian tng. New Orleans Bapt. Theol. Sem., 1952; student LaSalle U., Chgo., 1927, Jefferson Sch. Law U. Louisville, 1930; m. Clarissa Lasseter, May 30, 1947; 1 son, Bruce. Shorthand expert firm Carter, Schindler & Guthrie, Attys., Louisville, 1925-27; with firm John Bold, Atty. at Law, Evansville, Ind., 1937-45; founder, pres. Automotive Bur. Credits, Louisville, 1927-37; accountant payroll City Mech. Co., Miami, Fla., 1946-50; ordained to ministry Bapt. Ch., 1950; pastor Ruth (Miss.) Baptist Ch., 1950-52, First Baptist Ch., Branford, Fla., 1953-54, Mt. Pisgah Baptist Ch., McAlpin, Fla., 1955-64, North Pleasant Grove Ch., Santa Fe, Fla., 1967-70, First Baptist Ch., Micanopy, Fla., 1970-73; evangelist, Branford, Fla., 1954-67. Columnist Fla. Bapt. Witness, Jacksonville, 1970-71; tchr. vocat. tech. Morgan Coll., Louisville, 1929-30; founder, tchr. Franklin Coll., Louisville, 1932-33. Mem. Louisville Jr. C. of C. (editor Barker 1940-41), Fla. Accountants Assn., Nat. Soc. Pub. Accountants, Miami (Fla.) Gideons (pres. 1949). Clubs: Optimist, K.C. (editor Compass 1944-45). Author: 40 Years in the Wilderness, 1951; Conversion, 1957. Editor Behold, 1958-59. Co-founder Northeast Baptist Ch., Miami, 1948; founder Cross Creek Baptist Ch., Hawthorne, Fla., 1971; collector flags of all nations, lent to U.S. Govt. for P.O. dedications, to cities, states for vis. dignitaries. Address: PO Box 516 Branford FL 32008

BOREK, JOHN MICHAEL, JR., educator; b. Anniston, Ala., June 29, 1943; s. John Michael and Dorothy Lois (Waldrep) B.; B.B.A., Ga. State U., 1968, M.B.A., 1970, Ph.D., 1974; m. Lois Brewer, Mar. 14, 1964; children—Rebecca, Catherine, Jennifer. Computer operator The Kroger Co., E. Point, Ga., 1962-66; systems analyst So. Bell Tel. & Tel. Co., Atlanta, 1966-69; comptroller, asst. prof. mgmt., acting dir. Office Ednl. Media, Ga. State U., Atlanta, 1969—; instr. Atlanta Area Tech. Sch., part-time, 1968-69; dir. Ga. Med. Plan, Inc., 1979—; cons., lectr. in field. Officer, Blessed Sacrament Ch. Sch. bd., 1974-76, pres. exec. council, 1974-75, treas. exec. council, 1973-74; pres. Ga. State U. Doctoral Fellows, 1972-73. Served to capt., USAR, 1963—. Mem. Acad. Mgmt., Adminstrv. Mgmt. Soc., Inst. Mgmt. Acctg., Coll. and Univ. Personnel Officers Assn., Nat. Assn. Coll. and Univ. Bus. Officers, Purchasing Mgmt. Assn. Ga., Nat. Assn. Purchasing Mgrs. (cert.), Nat. Micrographics Assn., Ga. State U. Alumni Assn., Tau Kappa Epsilon, Sigma Iota Epsilon. Clubs: Rotary, Masons (32 deg.). Home: 5923 Four Winds Dr Lilburn GA 30247 Office: Ga State Univ University Plaza Atlanta GA 30303

BOREN, DAVID LYLE, U.S. Senator; b. Washington, Apr. 21, 1941; s. Lyle H. and Christine (McKown) B.; B.A. summa cum laude, Yale, 1963; M.A. (Rhodes scholar), Oxford (Eng.) U., 1965; J.D. with honors, U. Okla. 1968; m. Molly W. Shi, Nov. 1977; children—Carrie Christine, David Daniel. Resident counsellor U. Okla., Norman, 1965-66; practiced in Wewoka and Seminole, Okla., 1968-73; prof. polit. sci., chmn. div. social scis. Okla. Baptist U., Shawnee, 1969-74; mem. Okla. Ho. of Reps. 1966-74; gov. Okla., 1975-79; mem. U.S. Senate from Okla., 1979—; propaganda analyst USIA, Washington, 1962—; asst. to liaison dir. OCDM, Washington, 1961. Mem. Okla. Gov.'s Task Force on Tech. Edn., 1967-73. Mem. Am., Okla. bar assns., Am. Assn. Rhodes Scholars, Order of Coif, Phi Beta Kappa, Phi Delta Phi. Democrat. Methodist. Club: Yale (Western Okla.). Home: 2369 S Queen St Arlington VA 22202 Office: 440 Russell Senate Office Bldg Washington DC 20510

BOREN, JOHN ALLEN, pharmacist; b. Anadarko, Okla., Apr. 4, 1948; s. Jasper Coy and Naomi Bernice (Byrd) B.; B.S. in Pharmacy, Southwestern Okla. State U., 1971; m. Joy Lynn Cobb, June 4, 1970; children—Jason Allen, Jared Ian. Pharmacist, AMC Drug, Oklahoma City, 1971; dep. chief pharmacist USPHS Indian Hosp., Crow Agency, Mont., 1971-72, chief pharmacist, 1972-73; chief pharmacist USPHS W.W. Hastings Indian Hosp., Tahlequah, Okla., 1973—; clin. pharmacy instr. Coll. Pharmacy, S.W. Okla. State U. Recipient Outstanding Service plaque USPHS, 1975. Mem. Am. Soc. Hosp. Pharmacists, Okla. Pharmacy Assn., Okla. Soc. Hosp. Pharmacists, Rho Chi. Democrat. Baptist. Office: USPHS W W Hastings Indian Hosp 1120 N Grand Ave Tahlequah OK 74464

BORG, HARRY THEODORE (TED), photographer; b. Mobile, Ala., Oct. 15, 1937; s. Harry Theodore and Emma Victoria (Calloway) B.; student Germain Sch. Photography, 1962; m. Virginia Dale Webster, July 21, 1961; 1 dau., Melanie Leigh. Office asst., clk. Gulf, Mobile & Ohio R.R., Mobile, 1955-60; photographer Mobile Press-Register, 1960-62; owner, photographer Ted's Studio of Photography, Sheffield, Ala., 1963; photographer Mgmt. Services Inc., Marshall Space Flight Center, Huntsville, Ala., 1963-66; photographer Wylie Testing Labs., Huntsville, 1966-67; chief photographer Ga. Game and Fish Commn., Atlanta, 1967-71; chief photographer S.C. Wildlife Mag. and S.C. Wildlife and Marine Resources Dept., Columbia, 1971—. Served with Ala. Army N.G., 1955-62. Recipient 1st place awards S.C. Profl. Photographers Assn., Am. Assn. Conservation Info. Photography, Southeastern Game and Fish Commn. Mem. Profl. Photographers Am., Southeastern, S.C. (bd. dirs.) profl. photographers assns., Outdoor Writers Assn. Am., Am. Assn. Conservation Info. Baptist. Home: 232 Stirlington Rd Columbia SC 29210 Office: PO Box 167 Columbia SC 29202

BORICK, STEVEN JAMES, oil and gas co. exec.; b. St. Paul, July 8, 1952; s. Louis L. and Nita B. (Byers) B.; A.A., Ariz. State U., 1972; B.A. in Fin. and Econs., Western State Coll., Gunnison, Colo., 1975; Supr., Superior Industries Internat., Van Nuys, Calif., 1968-70; asst. prodn. supt. Texakota, Inc., Houston, 1975-76, sec., treas., 1976-78, exec. v.p., 1978—, also dir. Mem. Am. Mgmt. Assn., Am. Petroleum Inst., Mid-Continent Oil and Gas Assn., Ind. Petroleum Assn. Am. Republican. Office: 6315 Gulfton St Suite 3 Houston TX 77081

BORING, JOHN WAYNE, physicist, educator; b. Reidsville, N.C., Oct. 9, 1929; s. Robert Lee and Eunice Violet (Clapp) B.; B.S., U. Ky., 1952, M.S., 1954, Ph.D., 1961; m. Ethel Belle Watts, Aug. 17, 1957; children—Rebecca, Pamela, Judith. Ordnance engr., U.S. Naval Proving Ground, Dahlgren, Va., 1951-52; devel. engr., AEC, Oak Ridge, 1953; research asst. Los Alamos Sci. Lab., 1955; sr. scientist U. Va., Charlottesville, 1960-67, prof. engring. physics, 1971—; vis. prof. U. Aarhus (Denmark), 1974-75; cons. Internat. Commn. on Radiation Units. Ky. Research Found. fellow, 1956; Sesquicentennial asso. U. Va., 1974-75. Mem. Am. Phys. Soc., Tau Beta Pi, Pi Tau Sigma. Presbyterian. Club: Keswick. Home: 3510 W Monacan Dr Charlottesville VA 22901 Office: Dept Nuclear Engring and Engring Physics Univ Va Charlottesville VA 22901

BORKAN, WILLIAM NOAH, biomed. electronics co. exec.; b. Miami Beach, Fla., Apr. 29, 1956; s. Martin Solomon and Annabelle (Hoffman) B.; B.S.E.E., Carnegie Mellon U., 1977; Ph.D., Sussex Coll. Tech., 1979. Tech., Dominicks' Radio & TV Co., Miami Beach, 1971-74; computer programmer Mt. Sinai Hosp., Miami Beach, 1973-74; chief studio engr. WGMA, Hollywood, Fla., 1973-74; disc. jockey WBUS-FM, Miami Beach, 1974; chief recording engr. Dukoff Recording Studios, Miami, 1974-75; rec. studio design and constrn. TSI, Hollywood, Fla., 1975-77; chief design engr. Lumonics Co., Miami, 1974; service mgr. 21st. Century Electronics Co., Miami, 1975; lab. tech. Carnegie-Mellon U.; mgr. Tech. Electronics Co., Pitts., 1976; pres. Borktronics Co. Miami, 1974—; cons. specialist in neurobiometrics St. Barnabas Hosp., N.Y.C., 1978—; v.p. Electronic Diagnostics, Inc., 1978—; mem. coll. curricular coms. E.E. Dept. Grantee Carnegie Corp., Carnegie Mellon U. Mem. Am. Soc. Heating, Refrigeration and Air Conditioning Engrs., Assn. Energy Engrs., Soc. Automotive Engrs., Assn. for Advancement Med. Instrumentation, AAAS, N.Y. Acad. Scis., Audio Engring. Soc. Author publs. in field; patentee. Home: 3031 Prairie Ave Miami Beach FL 33140 Office: 2398 Oceanview Miami Beach FL 33140

BORLAUG, NORMAN ERNEST, agrl. scientist; b. Cresco, Iowa, Mar. 25, 1914; s. Henry O. and Clara (Vaala) B.; B.S. in Forestry, U. Minn., 1937, M.S. in Plant Pathology, 1940, Ph.D. in Plant Pathology, 1941; Sc.D. (honoris causa), Punjab (India) Agrl. U., 1969, Royal Norwegian Agrl. Coll. 1970, Luther Coll., 1970, Kanpur U. (India), 1970, Uttar Pradesh Agrl. U. (India), 1971, Mich. State U., 1971, Universidad de la Plata (Argentina), 1971, U. Ariz., 1972, U. Fla., 1973, Universidad Católica de Chile, 1974, Universität Hohenheim, Germany, 1976, U. Agrl. Lyallpur, Pakistan, 1978; L.H.D., Gustavus Adolphus Coll., 1971 LL.D. (hon.), N.Mex. State U., 1973; m. Margaret G. Gibson, Sept. 24, 1937; children—Norma Jean (Mrs. Richard H. Rhoda), William Gibson. With U.S. Forest Service, 1935-36, 37, 38; instr. U. Minn., 1941; microbiologist E.I. DuPont de Nemours, 1942-44; research scientist in charge wheat improvement Coop. Mexican Agrl. Program, Mexican Ministry Agr.-Rockefeller Found., Mexico, 1944-50; asso. dir. assigned to Inter-Am. Food Crop Program, Rockefeller Found., 1960-63; dir. wheat research and prodn. program Internat. Maize and Wheat Improvement Center, 1964-79, asso. dir. Rockefeller Found., 1964—; cons., collaborator Instituto Nacional de Investigationes Agricolas, Mexican Ministry Agr., 1960-64; cons. FAO, North Africa and Asia, 1960; ex-officio cons. wheat research and prodn. problems to govts. in Latin Am., Africa, Asia. Mem. Citizen's Commn. on Sci., Law and Food Supply, 1973-74, Commn. Critical Choices for Am., 1973—, Council Agr. Sci. and Tech., 1973—; dir. Population Crisis Com., 1971; asesor especial Fundacion para Estudios de la Poblacion A.C., Mexico, 1971—; mem. adv. council Renewable Natural Resources Found., 1973—; Presdl. commn. World Hunger, 1978-79. Recipient Distinguished Service awards Wheat Producers Assns., and state govts. Mexican States of Guanajuato, Queretaro, Sonora, Tlaxcala and Zactecas, 1954-60; Recognition award Agrl. Inst. Can., 1966, Instituto Nacional de Tecnologia Agropecuaria de Marcos Juarez, Argentina, 1968; Sci. Service award El Colegio de Ingenieros Agronomos de Mexico, 1970; Outstanding Achievement award U. Minn., 1959, E.C. Stakman award, 1961, named Uncle of Paul Bunyan, 1969; recipient Distinguished Citizen award Cresco Centennial Com., 1966; Nat. Distinguished Service award Am. Agrl. Editors Assn., 1967; Genetics and Plant Breeding award Nat. Council Comml. Plant Breeders, 1968; Star of Distinction, Govt. of Pakistan, 1968; citation and street named in honor Citizens of Sonora and Rotary Club, 1968; Internat. Agronomy award Am. Soc. Agronomy, 1968; Distinguished Service award Wheat Farmers of Punjab, Haryana and Himachal Pradesh, 1969; Nobel Peace prize, 1970, 79; Diploma de Merito, El Instituto Tecnologico y de Estudios Superiores de Monterrey (Mexico), 1971; medalla y Diploma de Merito Antonio Narro, Escuela Superior de Agricultura de la U de Coahuila (Mexico), 1971; Diploma de Merito, Escuela Superior de Agricultura Hermanos Escobar (Mexico), 1973; award for service to agr. Am. Farm Bur. Fedn., 1971; Outstanding Agrl. Achievement award World Farm Found., 1971; Medal of Merit, Italian Wheat Scientists, 1971; Service award for outstanding contbn. to alleviation of world hunger 8th Latin Am. Food Prodn. Conf., 1972; Bernardo O'Higgins award Govt. Chile, 1974; Presdl. medal of Freedom (U.S.), 1977; Hilal-I-Imtiaz award, Pakistan, 1978; numerous other honors and awards from govts. ednl. instns., citizens groups. Hon. fellow Indian Soc. Genetics and Plant Breeding; mem. Nat. Acad. Sci., Am. Soc. Agronomy (1st Internat. Service award 1960, 1st hon. life mem.), Am. Assn. Cereal Chemists (hon. life mem., meritorious service award 1969), Crop Sci. Soc. Am. (hon. life mem.), Soil Sci. Soc. Am. (hon. life mem.), Sociedad de Agronomia do Rio Grande do Sul Brazil (hon.), India Nat. Sci. Acad. (fgn.), Royal Swedish Acad. Agr. and Forestry (fgn.), Academia Nacional de Agronomia y Veterinaria (Argentina); hon. academician N.I. Vavilov Acad. Agrl. Scis. Lenin Order (USSR.). Address: Centro Internacional de Mejoramiento de Maiz y de Trigo Apartado Postal 6-641 Londres 40 Mexico City 6 Mexico

BOROCHOFF, CHARLES ZACHARY, mfg. co. owner; b. Atlanta, Apr. 11, 1921; s. Isadore and Pauline (Reisman) B.; LL.B., Atlanta Law Sch., 1941; m. Ida Dorothy Sloan, Jan. 11, 1942; children—Lynn (Mrs. Myles Jarrett Gould), Toby Ann (Mrs. Jeffrey Bernstein), Jean Sue (Mrs. Mark Shapiro), Lance Mark. Exec. v.p. So. Wire & Iron Works, Atlanta, 1956-63; pres. Borochoff Properties, Inc., real estate, Atlanta, 1954—, Designs Unlimited, Inc., Atlanta, 1964—, Scottdale Enterprises, Atlanta, 1972—. Mem. High Museum of Art, 1955—, NCCJ, 1967—, Planned Parenthood, 1970—; mem. Nat. UN Day Program Com., 1977, 78, 79; trustee Atlanta Playhouse, 1971—, A.A. Synagogue; lt. col. a.d.c. Gov.'s Staff, 1975-80. Mem. Dekalb C. of C. (mem. exec. devel. com. 1975), Nat. Retail Wholesale Furniture Assn., Internat. Home and Furniture Reps. Assn., UN Assn. U.S.A., Nu Beta Epsilon. Mason (Shriner, 32 deg.); mem. B'nai B'rith. Clubs: Atlanta Music, Progressive, Jockey. Home: 3450 Old Plantation Rd NW Atlanta GA 30327 Office: 3451 Church Scottdale GA 30079

BOROCHOFF, IDA SLOAN (MRS. CHARLES Z. BOROCHOFF), real estate exec., artist; July 29, 1922; d. Louis and Eva (Bistrick) Sloan; ed. U. Ga., 1939-40, Ga. State U., 1940, Chgo. Sch. Interior Decorating, 1966, Allegro Sch. Ballet, Chgo., Atlanta Ballet, 1948-54, Emory U., 1971-72; m. Charles Zachary Borochoff, Jan. 11, 1942; children—Lynn (Mrs. Myles J. Gould), Jean Sue (Mrs. Mark Shapiro), Toby Ann (Mrs. Jeffrey Bernstein), Lance Mark. Investor and owner real estate, 1941—; v.p. Designs Unltd., Inc., Atlanta, 1964—; pres. Sloan Borochoff Gallery, Atlanta, 1970—; art lectr. Met. Ednl. Service; tchr. Ga. Inst. Tech.-Free U.; exhibited several one-woman shows, 1961-71, one-woman show Lovett Sch., 1972, 75, Ga. Inst. Tech., 1972, 75. Bd. dirs. Atlanta Ballet, 1950-57; bd. dirs. Atlanta Music Club, also co-editor Newsletter; hostess Altanta Arts Festival, Columnist Profile, Neighborhood Newspaper, area chmn. Heart Fund Drive; active various multi-media groups; artistic dir. Atlanta Playhouse Theatre; active Dogwood Festival; chmn., trustees Atlanta Playhouse Theatre. Recipient several art awards; named hon. alumnus Atlanta Art Inst., 1968, One of 10 Atlanta Leading Ladies, J.C. Singles, 1976. Mem. Atlanta Press Club,

Atlanta Writers Club (membership com.), Atlanta Artists Club, League Women Voters, High Mus. Art, Ga. Writers Assn., Atlanta Women's C. of C. (chmn. fine arts com. 1977-78), Am. Fedn. of Arts. Mem. B'nai B'rith Women (pres. chpt. 1975, Southeast regional editor, dir. 1976-78, editor Atlanta council 1978—). Clubs: Jockey, Progressive. Author-artist Images of Woman, WGTV presentation, Atlanta, Georgia Girl, 1977. Home: 3450 Old Plantation Rd NW Atlanta GA 30327 Office: 3451 Church St Scottdale GA 30079

BOROUGHS, MARY FRANCES, mental health facility adminstr.; b. Pickens, S.C., July 23, 1939; d. Paul Bryan and Lena Rae (Cavenaugh) B.; student Anderson Coll., 1961-62, Central Wesleyan Coll., Central, S.C., 1971. With Anderson County Health Dept., Anderson, S.C., 1963-70, E.J. Daniels Evangelistic Assn., Orlando, Fla., 1970-71; bus. adminstr. Anderson-Oconee-Pickens Mental Health Center, S.C. Dept. Mental Health, Anderson, 1972—. Vol. youth worker various churches, 1958-75. Mem. S.C. State Employees Assn. Democrat. Baptist. Home: 2702 Lane Ave Anderson SC 29621 Office: Anderson-Oconee-Pickens Mental Health Center 200 McGee Rd Anderson SC 29621

BORRAS, JAIME ANDRES, elec. engr.; b. Sagua La Grande, Cuba, July 3, 1951; s. Jaime and Carmen Emelina (Parayuelos) B.; A.A., Miami Dade Community Coll., 1972; B.S. in Elec. Engring., Fla. Atlantic U., 1974, B.S. in Physics, 1974; m. Maria Leon, Dec. 21, 1974; 1 dau., Emily Maria. Devel. engr. Motorola Inc. Fort Lauderdale, Fla., 1974-76, sr. devel. engr., 1976-78, tech. specialists engr., 1978-79, staff engr., 1979—. Selby fellow, 1972-74. Mem. IEEE, Soc. Students of Physics. Home: 8545 NW 177th St Hialeah FL 33015 Office: 8000 W Sunrise Blvd Fort Lauderdale FL 33322

BORSCHOW, RON CLARKE, statis. cons.; b. Houston, Feb. 8, 1933; s. Reuben and Hazel I. (Beatty) B.; B.B.A., U. Houston, 1958 M.B.A., So. Methodist U., 1960; postgrad. Ohio State U., 1958, U. Chgo., 1960-61, U. Houston, 1964—. Market research analyst Toni Co., Chgo., 1960-61; research mgr. Product Acceptance & Research, Evansville, Ind., 1961-63; founder, pres. R. Borschow & Assos., statis. and market research consultants, Houston, 1963—; statis. cons. Houston Health Dept., 1964—. Mem. Am. Mktg. Assn., Am. Statis. Assn., Tex. Pub. Health Assn., Houston Symphony Soc., Houston Grand Opera Assn., Phi Theta Kappa. Home: 2422 Albans St Houston TX 77005 Office: 1115 N MacGregor St Houston TX 77025

BORSELLINO, CONCETTA ANN, educator; b. Beaumont, Tex., Sept. 12, 1945; d. James Frank and Josephine Mary (Coco) Messina; B.B.A., Lamar U., Beaumont, Tex., 1967; m. Paul Don Borsellino, Aug. 27, 1967; children—Jamie Charles, Tammy Jo. Part-time staff White House Dry Goods, Beaumont, 1963-67, Eiband's Dept. Store, Galveston, Tex., 1969; part-time tchr. Emmett Owem Sch., Galveston, 1970-71; part-time bookkeeper Walgreen Drug Store, Galveston, 1970-71; part-time tax preparer H & R Block, Galveston, 1973; coop. tchr. office edn., coordinator Ball High Sch., Galveston, 1973—; res. instr. office occupations Galveston Coll., 1978—. Cert. tchr. vocat. office edn., Tex. Mem. Tex. Tchrs. Assn. (life), Tex. Bus. Edn. Assn. Roman Catholic. Home: 7710 Beaudelaire Circle Galveston TX 77551 Office: Ball High Sch 4115 Ave O Galveston TX 77550

BORTHICK, MAVIS ARY, counselor; b. Perry County, Tenn., Nov. 21, 1914; d. Elbert and Eugenia (Harder) Ary; B.S., Middle Tenn. State U., 1939; M.A., Peabody Coll., 1956; specialist in edn. U. Tenn., Nashville, 1970; m. Joseph William Borthick, June 29, 1942 (dec. 1974); children—Joary Borthick Hampton, Alice Faye. Tchr. pub. schs., Perry County, 1935-37, Marshall County, 1939, Robertson County, 1944-65; reading specialist, 1966-70; counselor Greenbier Elementary Schs., Robertson County, 1971—; rep. Field Enterprises Ednl. Corp., 1963-68. Tchr., Sunday Sch., Springfield Bapt. Ch., 1965-67. Mem. Robertson County (pres. 1976-77), Tenn. (pres. 1977—) sch. counselor assns., NEA, Tenn. (pres. guidance sect. 1979-80), Middle Tenn. edn. assn., Am., Tenn., Middle Tenn. (award 1979) personnel and guidance assns., Bus. and Profl. Womens Club (Woman of Year 1977), Am. Sch. Counselors Assn. Baptist. Home: 613 Crestview Dr Springfield TN 37172 Office: Greenbier Elementary Sch Greenbrier TN 37073

BORUM, OLIN HENRY, realtor, former govt. adminstr.; b. Spencer, N.C., Nov. 3, 1917; s. Oscar Henry and Marjorie Mae (Leigh) B.; B.S., U. N.C., 1938, M.A., 1947, Ph.D., 1949; postgrad., teaching fellow U. Md., 1940-41; m. Beatrice Star Comulada, Nov. 14, 1944; children—Pamela Leigh, Robin Olin, Denis Richard. Research chemist E.I. duPont de Nemours & Co., Phila. Lab., 1949-50; interim research asst. prof. Cancer Research Lab., U. Fla., 1950; instr., asst. prof. chemistry U.S. Mil. Acad., 1952-55; research adminstr. U.S. Army Chem. Corps Research and Devel. Command, Washington, 1956-60; research adminstr. U.S. Army Materiel Command (now Army Materiel Devel. and Readiness Command), Washington, 1964-76; realtor asso. Unique Properties, Alexandria, Va., 1974-79; realtor The J. Edwards Co., Inc., Alexandria, 1979—; tchr. chemistry U. Va., Arlington, 1966-68; teaching fellow U. Md., 1940-41; grad. asst., teaching fellow U. N.C., 1946-49. Adult scouter Nat. Capital Area council Boy Scouts Am., 1964-75, unit commr., 1968-75; sec. Mt. Vernon (Va.) Civic Assn., 1965-66; mem. Com. of 33 (nat. adv. group Nat. Sojourners, Inc.), 1962-71, chmn., 1969-71. Nat. trustee Nat. Sojourners, Inc., 1971-73. Served from 2d lt. to maj. AUS, 1941-46; as maj. USAF, 1951-56, lt. col., 1960-64. Recipient Certificate of Achievement Dept. Army, 1971. Fellow Am. Inst. Chemists; mem. Am. Chem. Soc., Phi Beta Kappa, Sigma Xi. Presbyn. Mason (K.T., Shriner). Contbr. articles to profl. jours. Home: 9002 Volunteer Dr Alexandria VA 22309 Office: 8747 Cooper Rd Alexandria VA 22309

BOSCHMA, WILLIAM JOSEPH, retail exec.; b. Vincennes, Ind., Oct. 30, 1936; s. Riniji Dootsie and Dorothy Evelyn (Case) B.; B.A., Mich. State U., 1962; m. Betty Louise De Hart, Sept. 11, 1964; children—Bradley, Brett. Staff accountant Price Waterhouse & Co., C.P.A.'s, Houston, 1962-65, mgr. audit, 1969-73; controller Steve Kruchko Co. mech. contractor, Drayton Plains, Mich., 1965-69; v.p. finance Wicks N Sticks Inc., candle retailers, Houston, 1973—. Mem. Am. Inst. C.P.A.'s, Tex. Soc. C.P.A.'s, Nat. Assn. Accountants. Home: 13923 Britoak St Houston TX 77079 Office: Wicks N Sticks PO Box 40307 Houston TX 77040

BOSE, ORU, architect, urban planner; b. Bombay, India, Feb. 7, 1944; came to U.S., naturalized, 1978; s. Abinash Chandra and Amita Kumari (Chanda) B.; B.Arch., U. Delhi, India, (Merit scholar), 1966; M.S. in Architecture, Pratt Inst. and Columbia U., 1970; postgrad. N.Y. Sch. of Visual Arts, 1970; m. Patricia Kathleen Dessert, Apr. 22, 1978. Architect and planner Chem. and Metall. Design Co., New Delhi, India, 1966-69, archtl. designer for various indsl. plants in Asia, 1966-67, Cuba, 1968; sr. urban planner N.Y. Hudson River Valley Commn., 1970-71; architect/planner N.Y. State Urban Devel. Corp., N.Y.C., 1971-72; architect/planner Buena Vista Land Co., Fla., 1972-73, also Walt Disney Productions, 1972-73; sr. architect Hart, Krivatsy and Stubee, N.Y.C., 1973-75; partner Lewis, Burke and Bose Associates, Orlando, Fla., 1975-76, partner in-charge of architecture and planning Central Fla. area, 1975-76; pvt. practice architecture and urban planning Winter Park, Fla., Washington and N.Y.C., 1976—; adj. prof. Fordham U., 1971-72; vis. lectr. various colls. and univs., 1973-76; free lance profl. photographer, 1967—; major works include: downtown devel. plan, Albany, N.Y., 1971-72; master plan Lake Buena Vista, Disney World, Fla., 1972-73; various condominium projects, residences and comml. devels., solar energy community. landscaping and site planning for various urban areas in Ill., Ark., Tenn., Ga., P.R.; Recipient Engring. News Record award, 1978; registered architect, Fla., Md., N.Y. Henry Luce Found. fellow, 1970 Mem. AIA, Royal Inst. Brit. Architects, Indian Inst. Architects, Nat. Pilots Assn., Canadian Automobile Sports Club, Aircraft Owners and Pilots Assn. Hindu. Club: Citrus. Home: 200 Maitland Ave Altamonte Springs FL 32701 Office: 180 Park Ave North Winter Park FL 32789

BOSHELL, BURIS RAYE, physician, educator; b. nr. Phil Campbell, Ala., Oct. 9, 1926; s. Harvey M. and Lela (Alexander) B.; B.S., Ala. Polytech. Inst., 1947, postgrad., 1947-49; postgrad. Med. Coll. Ala., 1949-51; M.D., Harvard, 1953; m. Martha Sue Johnson, June 4, 1951; children—Patty, Thomas Eppinger. Intern, Peter Bent Brigham Hosp., Boston, 1953-54, resident, 1954-59; practice medicine, specializing in internal medicine, Birmingham, Ala., 1959; mem. staff U. Ala. Hosps. and Clinics; instr. Harvard, 1956-58, asst. in medicine, 1958-59; asst. prof. medicine Med. Coll. Ala, 1959-62, asso. prof., 1962-64, prof., 1964-67, Ruth Lawson Hanson prof. medicine, 1967—, asst. dir., dept. medicine, 1963-69, dir. div. diabetes, endocrinology and related disorders, 1970—; med. dir. Diabetes Research and Edn. Hosp.; dir. div. endocrinology and metabolism U. Ala. Sch. Medicine, Birmingham; vis. prof. U. Mexico, 1975, U. Witwaterstrand, Johannesburg, S. Africa, 1975; dir. Central Bank Birmingham. Mem. Nat. Com. on Diabetes. Pres. bd. dirs. Diabetes Trust Fund of Ala.; bd. dirs. Diabetes Research Lab. Recipient Sr. U.S. Scientist award Alexander von Humboldt Found., West Germany. Diplomate Am. Bd. Internal Medicine. Fellow A.C.P., Am. Coll. Clin. Pharmacology and Chemotherapy; mem. A.M.A., Ala., Jefferson County med. assns., A.A.U.P., Birmingham Acad. Medicine, Am. Soc. for Clin. Pharmacology and Therapeutics (mem. com.), Ala. Acad. Sci., Am., New Eng., N.Y., Ala. diabetes assns., Endocrine Soc., Am. Fedn. for Clin. Research, So. Soc. for Clin. Investigation, Sigma Xi, Omicron Delta Kappa, Phi Kappa Phi, Gamma Sigma Delta, Tau Kappa, Alpha Omega Alpha. Contbr. articles to profl. jours. Home: 3017 Old Ivy Rd Birmingham AL 35210 Office: 1808 7th Ave S PO Box 3371-A Birmingham AL 35294

BOSHER, WILLIAM CLEVELAND, JR., ednl. adminstr.; b. Richmond, Va., Jan. 21, 1946; s. William Cleveland and Miriam Mae (Trainum) B.; B.A. in English, U. Richmond, 1968; M.Ed. in Counseling, Va. Commonwealth U., 1969; Ed.D. in Ednl. Adminstrn., U. Va., 1974; m. Jo Anne Tucker, July 29, 1967; children—William Cleveland, Matthew Paul, Jocelyn Tucker. Tchr., English and humanities J.R. Tucker High Sch., Richmond, 1968-71; supr. English, Henrico County Schs., Richmond, 1971-73; prin. Highland Springs High Sch., Henrico, Va., 1974-77; dir. Va. Dept. Edn., Richmond, 1978—; adj. prof. U. Va., U. Richmond. Dist. chmn. Boy Scouts Am., 1978—; mem. Police Promotion Bd. Henrico County, 1976; trustee Eastern Christian Coll.; bd. dirs. Christ Ch. at Va. Poly. Inst. and State U., 1978-79; elder Fairmount Christian Ch. Old Dominion Found. fellow, 1970. Mem. Am. Assn. Sch. Adminstrs., Assn. Supervision and Curriculum Devel., Va. Assn. Tchrs. of English (past pres.), Va. Evangelizing Fellowship (past pres.), Phi Delta Kappa, Kappa Delta Pi. Club: Rotary (dir. Sandston chpt.). Contbr. articles to profl. jours. Office: Va Dept Edn PO Box 6-Q Richmond VA 23216

BOSLEY, DAVID EMERSON, textile co. chemist; b. Lundale, W. Va., Dec. 16, 1927; s. Thomas Richard and Bess Dale (Corey) B.; B.S. in Chemistry, W. Va. U., 1950; Ph.D. in Phys. Chemistry, Mass. Inst. Tech., 1954; m. Ann Wheeler, May 31, 1952; children—Rebecca, Matthew, Linus, Patience. Research asso. Dacron tech. sect. E. I. du Pont de Nemours & Co., Kinston, N.C., 1956—. Commr. Grifton, N. C., 1967-69; mayor, Grifton, 1969—. Served with AUS, 1954-56. Mem. Phi Beta Kappa, Sigma Xi. Home: PO Box 531 Grifton NC 28530

BOSS, BARBARA JANET, educator; b. Balt., Jan. 24, 1947; d. George Adam and Regina Charlotte (Seitz) B.; B.S. in Nursing, Georgetown U., 1969; M.Nursing, U. Fla., 1970, Ph.D., 1979. Staff nurse New Eng. Med. Center Hosps., Boston, 1969; charge nurse Shands Teaching Hosp., Gainesville, Fla., 1970-71; nursing supr, 1971; instr. Coll. Nursing U. Fla., Gainesville, 1971-73, asst. prof., 1973-77; asst. prof. Sch. Nursing, U. Miss. Med. Center, Jackson, 1979—. Recipient Tchr. of Year award U. Fla., 1974-75. Mem. Am. Nurses Assn., Am. Assn. Critical Care Nurses, Am. Ednl. Research Assn., Nat. Council Measurement in Edn., Miss. Nurses Assn., Phi Kappa Phi, Pi Lambda Theta, Kappa Delta Pi, Sigma Theta Tau (research grantee 1978). Democrat. Roman Catholic. Home: 23 Old Mill Pl Brandon MS 39042 Office: Sch Nursing U Miss Med Center 2500 N State St Jackson MS 39216

BOST, HOWARD WILLIAM, petroleum co. exec.; b. Robstown, Tex., Sept. 29, 1924; s. Harold Alphonse and Ora Pearl (Jones) B.; B.S., SW Tex. State Coll., 1948; M.A., U. Tex., Austin, 1950, Ph.D., 1955; m. Theda Ruth Kerby, Sept. 10, 1940; children—Janet E. Bost Gruel, Barbara S., Carol A. Research chemist Phillips Petroleum Co., Bartlesville, Okla., 1950-51, 54-55, group leader chem. research, 1955-74, tech. recruitment rep., 1974—; mem. Joint Army-Navy-Air Force Com. on Liquid Propellant Test Methods, 1959. Pres., Wesley Found., San Marcos, Tex., 1948, Will Rogers PTA, Bartlesville, 1964; chmn. council on ministries 1st United Methodist Ch., Bartlesville, 1969-72 bd. dirs. Bartlesville Community Concert Assn., 1979; mem. Allied Arts and Humanities Council of Bartlesville. Served with USNR, 1943-46. Mem. Am. Chem. Soc. (chmn. NE Okla. sect. 1960), Midwest Coll. Placement Assn., Sigma Xi, Alpha Chi, Phi Lambda Upsilon. Patentee in fields of petrochems., rocket propellants, adhesives. Home: 1334 Quail Dr Bartlesville OK 74003 Office: Phillips Research Center Bartlesville OK 74004

BOSTIC, STEPHEN JULIAN, govt. ofcl.; b. Christiansted, V.I., Sept. 17, 1932; s. Theodore William and Ilma Maria (Joseph) B.; B.S. in Music Edn., Hampton Inst., 1955; M.A. in Music Theory, Eastman Sch. Music, U. Rochester, 1959; certificate (Fulbright scholar), Hochschule fuer Musik, Stuttgart, Germany, 1961; m. Evelin Dagma Karla Beulke, Feb. 7, 1963; children—Daniela Anita, Melanie Ann. Chmn. music dept. Christiansted High Sch., 1959-61; edn. adviser Gen. Edn. Devel. Agy., Def. Dept., Bad Kissingen, Germany, 1966-67; exec. dir. V.I. Council on Arts, Christiansted, 1967—; minister music, vestryman St. Johns Anglican Ch.; pvt. music tchr. piano. Treas., St. Croix chpt. ARC, 1969-75, St. Croix Forum, 1973—; bd. dirs. Human Resources, Inc., W.I. Lab. of Fairleigh Dickinson U., 1972-75, St. Croix chpt. Opportunities Industrialization Center, St. Dunstan's Episcopal Sch., 1972-77. Served to 1st lt. AUS, 1955-57. Richard Wagner Verband scholar to Bayreuth Festival, 1962, scholar to Darmstatt Summer Festival from Baden-Wurtemburg for study with Stockhausen and Boulez, 1963. Mem. Gesellschaft fuer Musikalishe Auffuhrungs and mechanische Verfulfaltigungsrechte, V.I. Acad. Arts and Letters, Alpha Phi Alpha, Alpha Kappa Mu. Rotarian (pres. St. Croix 1973). Home: 27 Orange Grove Christiansted St Croix VI 00820 Office: VI Council on the Arts Caravelle Arcade Christiansted VI 00820

BOSTON, JOHN ARMISTEAD, JR., psychiatrist; b. Arlington, Va., July 3, 1924; s. John Armistead and Edith (Hill) B.; student Va. Mil. Inst., 1942-43, Duke U., 1943-44, U. Ga. Sch. Medicine, 1944-46; M.D., Temple U., 1948; m. Louise Morgan, Oct. 1950 (div. 1970); children—Paula Alice Boston Hopkins, Diane Edith Boston Goldberg, David Morgan, Gail Louise. Intern, Bryn Mawr (Pa.) Hosp., 1948-49; resident in psychiatry Phila. VA Program, 1949-50, 52-53; fellow in child psychiatry Phila. Child Guidance Clinic, 1954-56; dir. Austin Community Guidance Center, (Tex.), 1956-63; practice medicine, specializing in psychiatry, Austin, 1964—; asst. prof. State U. Iowa Sch. Medicine, 1963-64. Past v.p. Travis County Mental Health and Mental Retardation Bd.; bd. dirs. Catholic Charities of Austin, John A. Boston Jr. Found., Hospice. Served to lt. j.g., M.C., USNR, 1950-52. Fellow Am. Psychiat. Assn., Acad. Child Psychiatry; mem. Am., Tex. med. assns., Travis County Med. Soc., Tex. Soc. Child Psychiatry (past sec./treas., v.p., pres.), Austin Psychiat. Soc. (past pres.), Central Neuropsychiat. Assn., Alpha Tau Omega, Phi Rho Sigma. Clubs: Austin Woods and Waters; Headliners. Contbr. articles to med. jours. Address: 500 W 15 th St Austin TX 78701

BOSTON, WILLIAM CLAYTON, JR., lawyer; b. Hobart, Okla., Nov. 29, 1934; s. William Clayton and Dollie Jane (Gibbs) B.; B.S., Okla. State U., 1958; LL.B., U. Okla., 1961; LL.M., N.Y. U., 1967; m. Billie Gail Long, Jan. 20, 1962; children—Kathryn Gray and William Clayton. Admitted to Okla. bar, 1961; asso. firm Mosteller, Fellers, Andrews, Snider & Baggett, Oklahoma City, 1962-64; partner firm Feller, Snider, Baggett Blankenship & Boston, 1968-69; partner firm Andrews, Davis, Legg, Bixler, Milsten & Murrah, Oklahoma City, 1969—. Bd. dirs. Nichols Hills Meth. Ch., 1976—; pres. Ballet Oklahoma Inc., 1975, 76, trustee, 1975-80; v.p., dir. Art Council Oklahoma City, 1977-80. Served with U.S. Army, 1954-56. Mem. Fed., Am., Okla., Oklahoma County bar assns., Phi Kappa Tau, Delta Theta Phi. Republican. Methodist. Club: Rotary. Contbr. articles to profl. publs. Home: 1701 Camden Way Nichols Hills OK 73116 Office: 1600 Midland Center Oklahoma City OK 73102

BOSWELL, EVERETT WHITMIRE, lumber co. exec.; b. Travellers Rest, S.C., Sept. 14, 1914; s. Clyde Charles and Allie Eugenia (Whitmire) B.; student U. Chattanooga, 1932-33, Edmondson Bus. Coll., 1934; m. Emma Jean Hinkle, May 31, 1966; children—Everett, Rita (Mrs. James Nabors, Jr.). Sales mgr. Cash & Carry Lumber Co., Chattanooga, 1936-71; v.p., sales mgr. Archtl. Millwork & Lumber Co., Chattanooga, 1971—. Served with USAAF, 1942-45. Mem. Nat. Assn. Home Builders, Chattanooga Contractors Assn. (pres. 1965), Constrn. Specifications Inst., Am. Legion. Democrat. Baptist. Clubs: Spike (life); City Salesman (pres. 1966). Home: 3505 Valley Trail Chattanooga TN 37415 Office: PO Box 2758 Chattanooga TN 37407

BOSWELL, GARY TAGGART, electronics co. exec.; b. Ft. Worth, Dec. 24, 1937; s. David W. and Marjory (Taggart) B.; B.A., Tex. Christian U., 1958, M.S., 1965; postgrad. San Diego State Coll., 1960-61; m. Margaret Ruth Yelvington, Sept. 8, 1957; children—Michael David, Margaret McQuiston, Susannah Ruth. Scientist U.S. Govt., White Sands (N.M.) Missile Range, 1958-59; research engr. Gen. Dynamics, San Diego, 1959-60; programmer Bell Helicopter, Hurst, Tex., 1960-63; sect. head Collins Radio Co., Dallas, 1963-68; mgr. software devel. Tex. Instruments, Inc., Austin, 1968-72; mgr. ASC (Advanced Sci. Computer) Marketing, 1973-75, mgr. ASC div., 1975-76, mgr. computer systems, 1976—. Mem. Am. Nat. Fortran Standards Com., 1970-74. Mem. Assn. Computing Machinery, Snipe Class Internat. Racing Assn. Club: White Rock Sailing. Designer several Fortran Compliers. Winner Western Hemisphere Snipe championship, 1970, also other maj. regattas. Home: 9221 Clover Valley Dr Dallas TX 75243 Office: PO Box 6015 Dallas TX 75222

BOSWELL, GEORGE MARION, JR., surgeon; b. Grand Prairie, Tex., May 12, 1920; s. George Marion and Viola (Scarbrough) B.; B.S., Tex. Tech. Coll., 1940; M.D., U. Tex., 1950; m. Veta M. Fuller, Oct. 30, 1958; children—Brianna Fuller, Kama, Maia. Intern, Parkland Hosp., Dallas, 1950-51; resident surgery and orthopaedic surgery Parkland, Baylor U. Med. Center, and Scottish Rite Hosps., Dallas, 1950-55; practice medicine specializing in surgery, Dallas, 1955—; instr. anatomy U. Tex. Southwestern Med. Sch., 1955—; chief surg. service Garland Hosp., 1960-61; attending staff Baylor U. Med. Center and Doctors Hosp., 1955—. Served from ensign to lt. comdr., USNR, 1940-45. Diplomate Am. Bd. Orthopaedic Surgery. Fellow A.C.S.; mem. Tex., Western orthopaedic assns., Am. Acad. Orthopaedic Surgeons, Tex., Dallas County med. assns., Am. Coll. Traumatology, Tex. Soc. Traumatology, Flying Physicians Assn. (pres. Tex. chpt. 1959, nat. dir.), U. Tex. Southwestern Med. Sch. Alumni Assn. (pres.), Phi Chi. Republican. Methodist (chmn. ofcl. bd., charge lay leader, trustee, del. Gen. Conf. Home: 7249 Wabash St Dallas TX 75214 Office: 4849 W Lawther Dr Dallas TX 75218

BOTHFELD, ROBERT, former automotive engr.; b. Sherborn, Mass., Sept. 26, 1920; s. Theodore and Viola May (Clark) B.; B.S.M.E., Tufts Coll., 1943; M.S. Engring. in Mech. Engring., U. Mich., 1947; m. Helen Audrey Marsh, Apr. 21, 1946; children—Robert, Bronwyn Lee, Holly Marsh. With Gen. Motors Co., 1947-78, buyer, methods supr., developmental engr. truck and coach dept., Pontiac, Mich., 1950-55, prodn. engr. gen. offices Fisher Body div., Warren, Mich., 1955-78, supr. prodn. engring., 1972-78. Active Boy Scouts Am., 1949-57. Served with USN, 1943-46. Registered profl. engr., Ohio. Mem. Soc. Automotive Engrs., Exec. Club Pensacola, Nat. Soc. Profl. Engrs. Republican. Presbyterian. Club: Otsego-Hidden Valley Ski. Home: 421 Kenilworth Gulf Breeze FL 32561

BOTIK, ROBERT FRANK, broadcasting co. exec.; b. Ft. Worth, Jan. 23, 1944; s. Charles Jerry and Gertrude Francis (Houzvicka) B.; student Tex. Christian U., 1962-65; m. Theresa Ann Schexnayder, June 24, 1978; 1 dau. by previous marriage, Kathleen. With Wendell Mayes Broadcast Stas., Austin, Tex., 1962-79; pres. Botik Broadcast Services, Austin, 1979—. Mem. Nat. Assn. Broadcasters. Roman Catholic.

BOTT, HARVEY JOHN, artist; b. Greeley, Colo., Dec. 28, 1933; s. John J. and Linda O. (Dill) B.; student Art Center Sch. of Los Angeles, 1952-53, U. So. Calif., 1952-53, Kans. State U., 1953-54, Inst. Fine Arts, N.Y. U., 1954, 56, 58, 60; postgrad. Art Academie, Dusseldorf, Germany, 1955; m. Margaret Jane Deats, May 27, 1970; 1 dau. by previous marriage—Gretchen LaVonna. One man shows of sculpture and paintings include: Dusseldorf Kunsthalle, 1956, Madison Gallery, N.Y.C., 1962, ADG Arts, Inc., N.Y.C., 1964, St. Mary's U., San Antonio, 1966, 69, U. Mo., Columbia, 1977, Bienville Gallery, New Orleans, 1977, 79, WORKS, San Jose, Calif., 1977, Beaumont (Tex.) Art Mus., 1974, Tex. A. and I. U., Kingsville, 1967, 78, Barnwell Mus. and Sculpture Garden, Shreveport, La., 1975; group shows include: Columbia U., N.Y.C., 1954, U. Heidelberg (Germany), 1954, Guild Hall, L.I., N.Y., 1959, 60, 62, 65, Alessandra Gallery, N.Y.C., 1977, Denver Arts Mus., 1959, 60, 66, Calif. Palace of the Legion of Honor, San Francisco, 1960, 63, Minn. Mus. Fine Arts, Mpls., 1962, 67, Contemporary Arts Mus., Houston, 1979, San Diego Fine Arts Gallery, Calif., 1963, Pa. Acad. Fine Arts, Phila., 1966, Roots Art Center, Clinton, N.Y., 1979; represented in permanent collections:

Southland Corp. Dallas, U. Houston, U. St. Thomas, Houston, City of Honolulu, New Orleans Mus. Fine Arts, Abilene (Tex.) Fine Arts Mus., Rice U., Houston, USAF Acad., Colo., Anglo-Texas Soc., London, also pvt. collections; artist-in-residence Joint Art Ventures Group, Loft-on-Strand, Galveston, Tex., 1969-78. Served with U.S. Army, 1953-56. Recipient Premier les plus Sculpture, Prix de Paris, 1965, U.S. Presdl. citation, 1968, Tex. Gov.'s citation, 1967, 68, Wis. Gov.'s citation, 1967, numerous internat., nat. and regional awards in sculpture and painting. Author: The Letters of Yevvah T. Tob, 1968-77, 1977. Home: 5400 Memorial Dr Apt 703 Houston TX 77007

BOTTA, JOSE ANGEL, JR., engring. co. exec.; b. Santiago de Cuba, Cuba, Aug. 27, 1937; came to U.S., 1961, naturalized, 1966; s. Jose Angel and Carmen Rosa (Llarch) B.; B.S. in Metall. Engring., Mo. Sch. Mines and Metallurgy, 1965; m. Maria Del Carmen Alvarez, May 11, 1961; children—Maria Del Carmen, Jose Angel. Cadet engr. Koppers Co., Inc., Pitts., 1965-66, engr., 1966-67, sr. staff engr., 1967-74; gen. mgr. Complejo Metalurgico Dominicano, Santo Domingo, 1974-76; export mgr. S.A. Person, Inc., Pitts., 1976; pres. Siderurgical Services Corp., Miami, Fla., 1976—. Mem. Am. Iron and Steel Engrs., Am. Soc. Metals. Roman Catholic. Contbr. articles to profl. jours.; patentee continuous casting of steel. Home and Office: 1733 SW 103d Pl Miami FL 33165

BOTTOMS, KENNETH RILEY, elec. engr.; b. Longview, Tex., Oct. 1, 1945; s. Johnny Harvey and Emma Jo (Copeland) B.; student Kilgore Jr. Coll., 1963-65; B.S. in Elec. Engring., Tex. Tech U., 1968; postgrad. Oklahoma City U., 1969-70, Abilene Christian U., 1979—; m. Harriet Anne Kelley, June 29, 1968; children—David Carl, Karen Michelle. Engr., Southwestern Bell Telephone Co., Dallas, 1968, 72-73, engr. toll facilities, 1973-74, sr. engr. spl. services, 1974, sr. engr. metro facilities, 1974-75, engring. project supr., 1975-78, staff mgr. tng., 1978—. Adviser, Jr. Achievement, Dallas, 1973-74. Served to capt. USAF, 1968-72. Decorated Air Force Commendation medal. Registered profl. engr. Mem. Nat., Tex. socs. profl. engrs., Phi Theta Kappa, Eta Kappa Nu. Mem. Ch. of Christ (deacon 1973—, chmn. youth com. 1972-73, bus. ministry dir. 1974—). Home: 4427 Image Circle Dallas TX 75211 Office: Southwestern Bell Telephone Co 6631 Larmanda St Dallas TX 75231

BOTTS, WILLIAM HAROLD, hosp. adminstr.; b. Abbeville, S.C., Nov. 6, 1924; s. William D. and Marzette (Anderson) B.; B.A., Furman U., 1949; postgrad. U. S.C., U. N.C., U. Chgo., Cornell U.; m. Jeanette Anderson, Sept. 4, 1954; children—Jean, William Harold, Hayne A. Agt. Prudential Ins. Co., Greenville, S.C., 1949; field rep. Gen. Motors Acceptance Corp., Greenville, also Columbia, S.C., 1950-55; adminstr. Allen Bennett Meml. Hosp., Greer, S.C., 1955-67, Roger Huntington Nursing Center, Greer, 1967; dir. planning and devel. Greenville Hosp. System, 1968-71, dir. staff services, 1972, dir. adminstrn., 1973, adminstr. suburban div., 1974-77, dir. facilities devel. and constrn., 1977—. 1st vice chmn. adv. council S.C. Comprehensive Health Planning, Columbia, 1967-75; mem. facilities com. Applachia Health Planning Council, Greenville. Bd. dirs. YMCA, 1972-74, pres. 1972-73; bd. dirs., pres. S.C. Peach Festival, 1964, 65, 67; bd. dirs. United Way of Greenville County, 1975—, Piedmont Schs. Project, 1974-77; chmn. bd. dirs. S.C. Health and Sci. Fair, 1967-69; trustee H. Carl Rowland Meml. Library, 1970-75; chmn. S.C. Bd. Examiners for Nursing Home Adminstrs., 1969-75. Served with USNR, 1943-46. Recipient Distinguished Service award Greer Jr. C. of C., 1963; named Citizen of Year, Kiwanis Club, 1966; award of Honor, S.C. Health and Sci. Fair, 1971. Fellow Am. Coll. Nursing Home Adminstrs.; mem. Am. Coll. Hosp. Adminstrs., S.C. Hosp. Assn. (trustee 1963, pres. 1967), S.C. Nursing Home Assn. (mem. bd. trustees, 1st v.p. 1963-65), Carolinas-Virginias Hosp. Assn. (dir. 1968), Greer C. of C. (dir., pres. 1968). Methodist (chmn. bd. trustees 1970-73, adminstrv. bd. 1973). Lion (pres., dir. Greer 1962). Home: 309 Hillside Dr Greer SC 29651 Office: 705 Grove Rd Greenville SC 29652 Died Feb. 9, 1980.

BOUCHER, FREDERICK CARLYLE, lawyer, state senator; b. Abingdon, Va., Aug. 1, 1946; s. Ralph Emerson and Dorothy Boucher (Buck) B.; B.A., Roanoke Coll., 1968; J.D., U. Va., 1971. Admitted to Va. bar, 1971, N.Y. State bar, 1973; with firm Milbank, Tweed, Hadley & McCloy, N.Y.C., 1971-73, Penn, Stuart, Eskridge & Jones, Abingdon, Va., 1973-78; mem. firm Boucher & Boucher, Abingdon, 1978—; mem. Va. Senate, 1975—, mem. Democratic caucus policy com., 1980—; dir. Bank of Damascus; mem. Va. Coal and Energy Commn., Va. Crime Commn.; mem. Va. Coastal Erosion Abatement Study Commn.; mem. Gov.'s Overall Adv. Council on the Needs of Handicapped Children and Adults; bd. dirs. Odyssey, Inc., Client Centered Legal Sers. SW Va., Inc.; asst. majority whip, Va. Senate, 1976—. Mem. Washington County Democratic Com., 1974—; del. Democratic Nat. Issues and Policies Conv., 1974. Recipient award for Outstanding Young Businessman, Abingdon Jaycees, 1975. Mem. Assn. Bar of City of N.Y., Am. Bar Assn., Washington County Bar Assn., Va. State Bar Assn., Am. Judicature Soc., Phi Alpha Delta, Kappa Alpha. Methodist. Clubs: Jaycees, Kiwanis. Office: 188 E Main St Abingdon VA 24210

BOUCK, DAVID WILLIAM, cons. civil and environ. engr.; b. Corning, N.Y., Sept. 26, 1949; s. Harold Jacob and Frances Lorraine (Barker) B.; student U. Tenn., 1967-69; B.S., U. Central Fla., 1971, M.S. in Environ. Systems Mgmt., 1973. Student engr. Martin Marietta Corp., Orlando, Fla., 1968-69; project engr./mgr. Dawkins & Assos., Inc., cons. engrs., Orlando, 1971—. Registered profl. engr., Fla., Ga. Mem. Nat. Soc. Profl. Engrs., ASCE, Fla. Engring. Soc., Fla. Pollution Control Assn., Water Pollution Control Fedn., Orlando Area C. of C. (leadership council). Contbr. to tech. jours. Office: PO Drawer 14024 Orlando FL 32807

BOUDREAUX, EDWARD ANTHONY, educator; b. New Orleans, Oct. 30, 1933; s. Frank Anthony and Marguerite Ann (Robert) B.; B.S., Loyola at New Orleans, 1956; M.S., Tulane, 1959, Ph.D., 1962; m. Carolyn Rose Amato, Feb. 19, 1955; children—Edward Anthony, Margret, Yvette, Robert. Research scientist Kalvar Corp., New Orleans, 1956-62, cons., 1962-64; asst. prof. chemistry La. State U., New Orleans, 1962-64, asso. prof., 1964—. Cons., U.S. Dept. Agr., New Orleans, 1968-70. Treas., Cub Scouts, New Orleans, 1963-72. Served to capt. Signal Corps, AUS, 1962-63. Fulbright fellow, 1970-71; recipient research grants Petroleum Research Fund, 1964-66, Greater New Orleans Cancer Assn., 1966, 77, 78, NSF, 1967. Fellow Chem. Soc. London; mem. Am. Chem. Soc. (mem. com. for edn. in inorganic chemistry), Creation Research Soc., Sigma Xi. Author: Noble-Gas Compounds, 1963; Modern Aspects of Diffuse Reflectance Spectroscopy, 1968; Numerical Tables of Two—Center Overlap Integrals, 1970; Elementary Aspects of Chemical Periodicity, 1977. Editor: Theory, Principles and Application of Magnetochemistry, 2 vols., 1976; editorial adv. bd. Inorganica Chimica Acta, 1967, Inorganica Chimica Acta Revs., 1967. Contbr. articles to profl. jours. Home: 432 12th St New Orleans LA 70124

BOUDREAUX, WARREN LOUIS, bishop; b. Berwick, La., Jan. 25, 1918; s. Alphonse Louis and Loretta Marie (Senac) B.; student St. Joseph's Sem., Benedict, La., 1931-36; student Notre Dame Sem., New Orleans, 1937, 42, LL.D., 1963; student Grand Sem. de St. Sulpice, Paris, 1938-39; J.C.D., Catholic U. Am., 1946; D.D., Pope John XXIII, 1962. Ordained priest Roman Cath. Ch., 1942; asst. pastor, Crowley, La., 1942-43; vice chancellor Diocese Lafayette (La.), 1946-54, officialis, 1949-54; pastor St. Peter's Ch., New Iberia, La., 1954-71; vicar gen. Diocese Lafayette, 1957-71, also diocesan consultor; dean New Iberia Deanery, 1954-71; apptd. aux. bishop Diocese of Lafayette, 1962, bishop Diocese of Beaumont (Tex.), 1971-77, Diocese of Houma-Thibodaux (La.), 1977—. Mem. Bishops Com. on Liturgy, Nat. Conf. of Cath. Bishops, 1966-70, mem. Louvain com., 1971-75; mem. U.S. Cath. Conf. Adv. Council, 1969-73; chmn. liaison com. Nat. Conf. Cath. Bishops-U.S. Cath. Conf., 1972-75, mem. liturgy commn., 1975—, mem. canon law com., 1975—; nat. Episcopal moderator Marriage Encounter, 1974-77. Vice pres. S.W. La. Register Newspaper, 1957—; mem. New Iberia Community Relations Council, 1963-71; bd. dirs. Iberia Paris Youth Home, Consolata Home for Aged, New Iberia, S.W. Ednl. Devel. Lab.; pres. Archdiocesan Conf. Chancery Ofcls., Archdiocese New Orleans, 1950-51, bd. dirs., 1952-55. Club: K.C. (Tex. state chaplain 1975-77). Address: 1220 Aycock St PO Box 9077 Houma LA 70361

BOUGHTON, JAMES KENNETH, instrument engr., educator; b. Akron, Ohio, Mar. 22, 1922; s. James Arthur and Louise (Smith) B.; student U. Akron, 1940-42; B.S. in Elec. Engring., Ill. Inst. Tech., 1944; M.S., Lamar Coll. Tech., 1968; m. Evelyn Frances Robottom, Feb. 10, 1945; children—Steven Kent, Susan Lynn, Lisa Jean, Jeffrey Leigh. With Goodyear Tire and Rubber Co., 1942-77, machine designer, Akron, 1951, atomic supt. elec. and instrument maintenance, 1953-60, mgr. engring., Beaumont, Tex., 1960-77; sr. instrument engr. Stubbs Overbeck & Assos., Beaumont, 1977—; asso. prof. Lamar U., Beaumont, 1977—; instr. U. Akron, 1947-49. Mem. cultural affairs com. Lamar U., 1968—; active Beaumont Symphony, Lamar Philharmonic Orch. Served to lt. comdr. USNR, 1942-45, 51-53; PTO. Recipient Goodyear Patent award, 1974. Registered profl. engr., Ohio. Mem. I.E.E.E., Beaumont C. of C. Republican. Episcopalian (sr. warden 1970-71). Club: Pinewood Country (Pinewood Estates, Tex.). Patentee tire bldg. machines, prodn. counters and controls. Home: Route 9 Box 485 Sour Lake TX 77659 Office: Lamar Univ Beaumont TX 77710

BOUKNIGHT, HUEY RANDALL, ednl. adminstr.; b. Lexington, S.C., Oct. 11, 1947; s. Simon Dewey and Laverne (Greer) B.; A.A., Panola Coll., 1967; B.S., Northwestern State U., 1970, M.A. (dir. grad. student housing), 1972; m. Patricia Tynes, Dec. 19, 1970; children—Nathan Randall, Patrick Ryan. Asst. dean students Lander Coll., Greenwood, S.C., 1972-74, dean student affairs, 1974-78, v.p. student affairs, 1978—. Mem. Nat. Assn. Student Personnel Adminstrs., S.C. Coll. Personnel Assn., Kappa Sigma. Methodist. Clubs: Greenwood Rotary, Greenwood Sertoma (v.p. membership 1974-75), Lander Coll. Athletic (dir. 1974-76). Home: Rumford Ct Greenwood SC 29646 Office: Lander Coll Stanley Ave Greenwood SC 29646

BOULDIN, ERNEST FLOYD, carpet mill exec.; b. Dekalb County, Ala., July 23, 1936; s. Virgle Simmie and Flonnie Pearl B.; A.B., Snead State Coll., 1957; postgrad. U. Ala., 1958; m. Barbara Parker, June 1, 1958; 1 dau., Marsha Ann. Gen. mgr. Redford's Sales Co., Boaz and Guntersville, Ala., 1957-74, owner dept. stores, 1974—; personnel mgr. Standard-Coosa-Thatcher Co., Boaz, 1978—; pres. Famous Shoetique, Boaz, 1971-80. Pres., Downtown Action Com., 1977. Mem. Boaz C. of C. (pres. 1975-76, 77-78). Democrat. Baptist. Clubs: Lions, Masons. Home: PO Box 145 Boaz AL 35957 Office: PO Box 457 Boaz AL 35957

BOULTINGHOUSE, DANIEL FRANK, architect; b. Corpus Christi, Jan. 3, 1944; s. Avery Leland and Alma Lefay (Martin) B.; A.A., Del Mar Coll., 1964; B. Arch., U. Tex., 1969; m. Nancy Sharon Miller, June 8, 1968; 1 dau., Wanza Lefay. Mem. staff Brooks, Barr, Graeber & White, Austin, Tex., 1968-69, Jack Rice Turner & Assos., Corpus Christi, 1969-72; asso. Turner, Rome, Cotten & Assos., Corpus Christi, 1972-76; v.p. Turner, Rome, Boultinghouse, Inc., McAllen, Corpus Christi and Laredo, Tex., 1976—, also dir. Mem. adv. com. Tex. State Tech. Inst.; mem. City of McAllen Housing Bd. of Appeals, 1977—; bd. dirs. McAllen Housing Services Inc. Recipient Featherlite Design Competition award, 1968. Mem. Tex. Soc. Architects, AIA, Am. Planning Assn., Sphinx. Methodist. Club: Rotary. Home: 2208 Westway St McAllen TX 78501 Office: Turner Rome Boultinghouse Inc 1418 Beech St McAllen TX 78501

BOUNDS, LAURENCE HAROLD, gas co. exec.; b. Newcastle, Wyo., Feb. 15, 1922; s. James Henry and Blanche Agnes (McKay) B.; B.S., Simpson Coll., 1943; postgrad. Columbia, 1943; m. Dorothy May Bostrom, Nov. 20, 1965. With comptroller dept. Kemper Ins., Chgo., 1947-51; sec.-treas. W & J Constrn. Co., 1951-64; auditor Roosevelt Hotel, Jacksonville, Fla., 1964-66; v.p., sec., dir. Western Natural Gas Co., Jacksonville, 1966—. Served to lt. USNR, 1942-46. Mem. Navy League, Jacksonville Symphony Assn., Alpha Tau Omega. Episcopalian. Clubs: St. Simons Island, Willow Lakes Golf and Country; Tournament Players (Ponte Vedra, Fla.). Home: 6926 Bakersfield Dr Jacksonville FL 32210 Office: 2960 Strickland St Jacksonville FL 32205

BOUNDS, SARAH ETHELINE, historian; b. Huntsville, Ala., Nov. 5, 1942; d. Leo Deltis and Alice Etheline (Boone) B.; A.B., Birmingham-So. Coll., 1963; M.A., U. Ala., 1965, Ed.S., 1971, Ph.D., 1977. Tchr. social studies Huntsville City Schs., 1963, 65-66, 71-74; instr. history N.E. State Jr. Coll., Rainsville, Ala., 1966-68; instr. history U. Ala., Huntsville, 1975, 78—; asst. prof., supr. student tchrs. U. North Ala., Florence, 1978; residence hall advisor, dir. univ. housing U. Ala., 1963-65, 68-71. Mem. Huntsville Hist. Soc., Ala. Hist. Assn., Ala. Assn. Historians, Assn. Tchr. Educators, Ala. Assn. Tchr. Educators, Nat. Council Tchrs. Social Studies, Ala. Personnel and Guidance Assn., NEA, Huntsville Edn. Assn., AAUW, Alpha Delta Kappa, Kappa Delta Pi, Phi Alpha Theta. Methodist. Home: 1100 Bob Wallace Ave SE Huntsville AL 35801

BOUQUARD, MARILYN LLOYD, congresswoman; b. Ft. Smith, Ark., Jan. 3, 1929; d. James E. and Iva Laird; ed. Shorter Coll.; m. Joseph P. Bouquard; 8 children. Mem. 94th-96th Congresses from 3d Tenn. dist. Mem. Asso. Women for Boyd-Buchanan Sch.; active civic and profl. clubs and orgns. Mem. Tenn. Fedn. Bus. and Profl. Women's Clubs. Mem. Ch. of Christ. Office: 208 Cannon House Office Bldg Washington DC 20515*

BOURG, BONNIE JEAN, univ. adminstr.; b. New Orleans, Feb. 17, 1927; d. Francis Floyd and Malvin Marguerite (Boudreaux) Bourg; student H. Sophie Newcomb Coll., 1943-47; B.A., Tulane U., 1947; M.S., La. State U., 1948, Ph.D., 1979. Instr. in health and phys. edn. F.T. Nicholls Jr. Coll., La. State U. (name later changed to Nicholls State U.), 1947-50, head dept. women's health and phys. edn. 1950-63, dean women, 1963-77, dean student devel., 1977, asst. v.p. student affairs, 1977—; cons. in human relations devel. La. Bur. Vocat. Edn., 1976. Mem. City of Thibodaux (La.) Planning Commn., 1967-75. Recipient Pre's. award Nicholls State U., 1975, named Hon. Alumna, 1975; Delta Kappa Gamma Soc. Internat. Epsilon State scholar, 1975-76, Internat. scholar, 1978-79; certified tchr., counselor, La. Mem. Nat., La. assns. women deans, adminstrs. and counselors Am., La. personnel and guidance assns., Am. Coll. Personnel Assn. La. Sch. Counselors Assn., La. Folklore Soc., Terrebonne Hist. Soc., Delta Kappa Gamma, Phi Delta Kappa, Phi Mu, Delta Psi Kappa, Alpha Psi Omega. Democrat. Roman Catholic. Club: Thibodaux Music. Home: 306 Cherokee Ave Thibodaux LA 70301 Office: Box 2008 Nicholls State U Thibodaux LA 70301

BOURGEOIS, ALBERT JOSEPH, radio engr.; b. White Castle, La., Sept. 10, 1905; s. John Felix and Helen Marie (Daigle) B.; student U. Dayton, 1942, Capitol Engring. Inst., 1945; m. Ella G. Gaspard, Dec. 6, 1941; children—Dana J., Jane M. Chief radio on shipboard for several cos., 1927-39, staff research and devel. Aircraft Radio Lab., Wright Field, Dayton, Ohio, 1942-44; chief engr. Sta. WNOE, New Orleans, 1944-62, Sta WSMB, New Orleans, 1962—. Mem. Internat. Brotherhood of Elec. Workers. Democrat. Home: 212 Bordeaux St Metairie LA 70005 Office: Sta WSMB Maison Blanche Bldg New Orleans LA 70112

BOURGEOIS, RUDOLPH JOHN, JR., surgeon; b. New Orleans, Feb. 23, 1929; s. Rudolph John and Marie (Huguet) B.; student Loyola U., New Orleans, 1947-50; M.D., La. State U., 1954; m. Ritarose Hoover, July 30, 1955; children—John Rupert, Mary Mildred. Intern, Charity Hosp., New Orleans, 1954-55, resident, 1955-59; practice medicine, specializing in surgery, New Orleans, 1962—; co-founder Surg. Clinic of East New Orleans, 1962, Med. Center of East New Orleans, 1973; chief of staff, mem. bd. Methodist Hosp., New Orleans, 1970-72; clin. asso. prof. surgery La. State U. Sch. Medicine, 1962—. Served to capt., M.C., U.S. Army, 1959-62. Recipient Gold medal in excellence Jesuit High Sch., 1946. Mem. AMA, So., La., Orleans Parish med. socs., La. New Orleans surg. socs., Alpha Omega Alpha, Phi Kappa Kappa. Democrat. Roman Catholic. Clubs: Exchange of New Orleans. Home: 2326 Lake Oaks Pkwy New Orleans LA 70122 Office: 5640 Read Blvd New Orleans LA 70127

BOURNE, RUSSELL AMERICUS, JR., psychologist; b. Harrisonburg, Va., Apr. 7, 1951; s. Russell Americus and Anne Bernice (Browning) B.; B.A., U. Va., 1973, M.S., 1974, Ph.D., 1979; m. Anna Blanche Duke, June 22, 1974; children—Russell Americus III. Asst. dir. admissions Randolph Macon Coll., Ashland, Va., 1974-76, adj. faculty, 1976—, dir. Counseling Center, 1976—; adj. faculty U. Va., 1978—; clin. staff Commonwealth Psychiat. Center, Richmond, Va., 1978—; cons. Waynesboro (Va.) Sch. System. Mem. adv. com. Capitol Area Health Systems, Hanover County Health Dept.; mem. Va Commn. for Visually Handicapped, Randolph Macon Parents Adv. Council. U. Va. fellow, 1977-78; Zeta Psi Found. scholar, 1971-72. Mem. AAUP, Am. Psychol. Assn., Va. Psychol. Assn., Va. Assn. Student Personnel Adminstrs., U. Va. Alumni Assn., Phi Delta Kappa, Kappa Delta Pi, Chi Psi, Zeta Psi. Democrat. Methodist. Club: Ashland Randolph Macon Running. Home: 127 Hanover Ave Ashland VA 23005 Office: Counseling Center Randolph Macon Coll Ashland VA 23005

BOURQUE, ROBERT MARTIN, educator; b. Farmville, Va., June 1, 1953; s. Robert Joseph and Mae Ellen (Martin) B.; A.A.S., Southside Va. Community Coll., 1973; B.S. Engring. Tech., Va. Poly. Inst. and State U., 1978; m. Dixie Lee Higdon, Mar. 23, 1974. Technician, Smith TV and Appliance, Victoria, Va., 1968-73; asst. prof. electronics servicing Southside Va. Community Coll., Alberta, 1973—. Mem. Phi Kappa Phi. Author: (with Clarence Green) The Theory and Servicing of AM, FM and FM Stereo Receivers, 1979. Home: PO Box 148 Kenbridge VA 23944 Office: Southside VA Community Coll Alberta VA 23821

BOUSQUET, THOMAS GOURRIER, lawyer; b. Houston, Oct. 18, 1934; s. John A. and Ophelia Ann (Tucker) B.; B.A., U. Tex. at Austin, 1956, J.D., 1958; m. Katherine Lynn Cummings, Aug. 22, 1959 (div. Feb. 1970); children—Thomas Gourrier, Robert Brant, Katherine Lynn; m. 2d, Duke Ellen Taylor, Nov. 27, 1970 (div. Feb. 1973). Admitted to Tex. bar, 1958, U.S. Supreme Ct. bar, 1971; practiced in Houston, 1958—; partner firm Bousquet & Assos.; judge 165th Dist. Ct., 1980—; dir. Electronic Data Labs., Inc., Houston, Figure World Internat., Houston. Served to maj. USAF, 1958-64; maj. Res. Cert. civil trial lawyer, Tex. Mem. Houston Bar Assn. (sec. 1960, v.p. 1961), Lawyers Soc. Houston (pres. 1973), Tex. Assn. Def. Counsel, Order Stars and Bars, Gulf Coast Family Law Specialists Assn. (sec. 1975-78, v.p. 1978-79), Tex. Assn. Cert. Trial Lawyers (pres. 1979-80), Houston Family Law Forum, S.A.R. (chancellor 1966), Sons Confederate Vets, Houston Heritage Soc., Spain and Tex. Soc., Phi Alpha Delta. Clubs: Cadre (pres. 1975), Houston. Author: Become an Effective Player at Casino Craps, 1973. Home: 4606 Richmond Ave Houston TX 77027 Office: Suite 480 2500 W Loop South Houston TX 77027

BOUTWELL, MARY FRANCES, educator; b. Eufaula, Ala., Oct. 31, 1921; d. Emmett Tyler and Frances Perry (Warr) Brown; B.S., Troy State U., 1962; M.S., Auburn U., 1964, postgrad., 1972-73; postgrad. Ga. State U., 1979; 1 son, William Henry Askew, IV; m. 2d, Archie Lee Boutwell, Jan. 1, 1978. Tchr. Ft. Rucker (Ala.) Elem. Sch., 1963-69; tchr. Ft. Benning (Ga.) Dependents' Schs., 1969-72, reading specialist, 1979—. Night Circle pres. Women of the Ch., First Presbyterian Ch., Phenix City, Ala.; den mother Cub Scouts, Eufala and Ft. Benning; 1st v.p. Ft. Benning PTA, 1977-78; pres. Barbour County Dist. PTA Eufala PTA. Mem. Ala. Hist. Assn., Ga. Hist. Soc., NEA, Ga. Assn. Educators, Benning Edn. Assn. (pres. 1976-77), Internat. Reading Assn. (pres. Muscogee County Reading Council 1978-79), Ga. Reading Assn., Ala. Reading Assn., East Ala. Geneal. Soc., Old Muscogee Geneal. Soc., Russell County Hist. Commn., Eufaula Heritage Assn., Phenix City Preservation Soc., Chattahoochee Valley Assn. Children with Learning Disabilities, Ga. Assn. Children with Learning Disabilities (local dir.), Nat. Assn. Children with Learning Disabilities, Nat. Registrar Children of Confederacy, L.S. Raiford Soc. (organizer, pres. 1973-79), Children Am. Revolution, Daus. Am. Colonists, D.A.R., Children of Confederacy (Ala. dir.), UDC (pres. Russell County 1977-81), Eufaula Bus. and Profl. Women's Assn. (pres.), Kappa Delta Pi. Editor profl. studies. Home: 212 N Randolph Ave Eufaula AL 36027 Office: 300 First Division Rd Fort Benning GA 31905

BOUVIER, HELEN SCHAEFER (MRS. JOHN A. BOUVIER, JR.), leasing co. exec.; b. McAlester, Okla., Sept. 11, 1910; d. William John and Anna (Perrin) Schaefer; student U. Fla., 1928-29, Northwestern U., 1929-30; m. John A. Bouvier, Jr., June 6, 1928; children—Elizabeth Bouvier Spencer, John A., Thomas R. Sec., Sunset Rock & Sand Co., Miami, Fla., 1939-45, Coral Rock & Sand Co., 1945-48; now chmn. Nat. Leasing, Inc.; pres., dir. Knight Manor, Inc., Miami, Miami Service Co., S. Central Manor Inc. West Kingsway, Inc., Miami, East Kingsway, Inc., Miami, South Kingsway, Inc., Miami, Karen Garden, Inc., Ft. Lauderway, Inc., 50th St. Heights, Inc., Miami and N.Y.C.; mgmt. cons., Miami and N.Y.C., 1945—. Bd. dirs., v.p. Ella R. Bouvier Found. Presbyterian (pres. women's aux., pres. women's aux. synod). Clubs: Corinthian (Syracuse, N.Y.); Skaneateles (N.Y.) Country; Riveria County (Coral Gables, Fla.); Beach Colony (Miami Beach, Fla.). Home: 2756 NE 17th St Fort Lauderdale FL 33305 Office: Blowing Rock NC also 6888 NW 7th Ave Miami FL 33150

BOUVIER, JOHN ANDRE, JR., lawyer, investment counselor, corp. exec.; b. nr. Ocala, Fla., May 16, 1903; s. John Andre and Ella (Richardson) B.; student Davidson Coll., 1922-24; A.B., U. Fla., 1926,

J.D., 1929; M.B.A., Northwestern U., 1930; D.Litt., Windham Coll., 1977; m. Helen A. Schaefer, June 6, 1928; children—Helen Elizabeth (Mrs. William Spencer), John Andre III, Thomas Richardson. Admitted to Fla. bar, 1929, pvt. practice, Gainesville, 1929, Miami, 1930—, specialist corp., real estate, probate law, cons.; gen. counsel Patterson & Maloney, Ft. Lauderdale; chmn. bd., pres. Pantex Mfg. Corp. (Delaware), 1958-60; pres. Pantex Mfg. Corp. (Can.), 1958-60; chmn. exec. com. Permutit Co.; chmn. bd. Prosperity Co. div., vice chmn. bd. Ward Industries Corp.; pres. Nat. Leasing Inc., Miami; pres. West Kingsway, Inc., 1952-73, East Kingsway, Inc., 1952-73, South Kingsway, Inc., 1952-73; now pres. Knight Manor #1, Inc., Knight Manor #2, Inc., South Central Manor, Inc.; pres. Knaust Bros., Inc., West Coxsackie, N.Y., 1960-64, chmn., 1964-65; pres. K-B Products Corp., Hudson, N.Y., 1960-64, chmn., 1960-65; pres. Farm Industries, Inc., Iron Mtn. Atomic Storage Vaults, Inc.; v.p., sec. Miami Service Co., 1956-73, pres., chmn., 1973—; sec. 50th St. Heights, Inc., Dade Constrn. Co., Miami, Karen Club Apt. Hotel, Ft. Lauderdale, 1951-67; dir. Ocean 1st Nat. Bank, Landmark Banking. Commr. Dade County council Boy Scouts Am.; chmn. Malecon Com. Dade County; dir. Syracuse Govtl. Research Bur., Inc.; mem. Nat. Def. Exec. Res. Planning council Zoning Bd. Miami. Bd. trustees Parkinson Rehab., Diagnostic and Research Inst.; vice chmn. Nat. Parkinson Found.; pres. Ella R. Bouvier Fund; bd. dirs. Boys Club. Mem. Internat. Platform Assn., Am. Ordnance Assn., Am. Judicature Soc., Am., Florida, Dade County, Broward County bar assns., N.A.M. (conservation of renewable natural resources com.), Mfrs. Assn. of Syracuse (dir.), Miami, Auburn civic music assns., Cayuga Mus. History and Art, Am. Acad. Polit. Sci., C. of C., Sigma Chi. Presbyn. (trustee, chmn., elder). Mason (Shriner), Elk, Rotarian. Clubs: Civitan (dir.), Miami Beach Rod and Reel, Surf, Riviera Country, Skaneatcles Country; Tower; Ponte Vedra; Washington Lawyers, Capitol Hill. Author monographs, newspaper articles in field. Home: 2756 N E 17th St Fort Lauderdale FL 33305 also Lenoir Rd Blowing Rock NC 28605 Office: PO Box 11297 Fort Lauderdale FL 33339

BOVA, PAUL DAVID, food chain exec.; b. Roanoke, Va., Nov. 20, 1953; s. Joseph Paul Bova; student public schs., Roanoke; m. Carol Gay Tilley, Aug. 17, 1974. With Hop-In Food Stores Inc., 1970—, supr., Roanoke, 1976-79, dist. mgr., Knoxville, Tenn., 1980—. Recipient Disting. Salesman's award Sales and Mktg. Assn. Roanoke Valley, 1980, Supr. of Yr. award Hop-In Food Stores, 1979. Home: 721 Walker Springs Rd Apt K-5 Knoxville TN 37923 Office: 7009 Kingston Pike Knoxville TN 37919

BOW, DAVID CARL, athletic dir.; b. Jamestown, Tenn., Mar. 21, 1949; s. Ward Carl and Lorene Kate (Peters) B.; B.S., Tenn. Tech. U., 1972, M.A., 1975; D.Arts, (fellow 1975-76), Middle Tenn. State U., 1977; m. Patsy Ann Tinch, Mar. 17, 1972. Tchr., coach Allard Elementary Sch., Fentress County, Tenn., 1972-73; dir. athletics, asst. prof. phys. edn. Tusculum Coll., Greeneville, Tenn., 1977—. Chmn. water safety Green County, 1979—. Mem. AAHPER, Tenn. Assn. Health, Phys. Edn. and Recreation, Am. Coll. Sports Medicine. Baptist. Address: Tusculum Coll Box 92 Greeneville TN 37743

BOWARD, ROBERT JAMES, bus. cons.; b. San Antonio, Tex., Oct. 29, 1934; s. Richard Carl and Nettie Greene (Turnage) B.; B.S., Trinity U., San Antonio, 1957; postgrad. St. Mary's Coll., San Antonio, 1959; M.S., Reach Inst. Tulsa, 1974; m. Esther Faye Denson, Aug. 1, 1959; 1 dau., Kimberly Anne. Investigator Retail Credit Co., 1957-59; mgr. Retailers Comml. Agy., San Antonio, 1959-62, dir. operating and sales div., Atlanta, 1962-64, mgr. retailers, N.Y.C., 1964-67; div. mgr. CBR, Inc., Tulsa, Okla., 1967-77; owner, mgr. Boward Enterprises, Tulsa, 1972—. Chief inspector Modified and Antique Auto Inspections State of Okla. Named Tulsa Boss of the Year, Am. Businesswomen Assn., 1971; recipient key to City of Tulsa, 1976. Mem. Internat. Consumer Credit Assn., Tulsa Consumer Credit Assn., Tulsa Credit and Fin. Mgmt. Assn., Antique Car Club Am., Model A Ford Club Am., Model T. Ford Club Am., Tulsa Roadsters, Blue Key (hon.), SAR. Republican. Methodist. Club: Masons. Research in hypnosis as applied clinically in habit control, regression therapy and pain control. Contbr. articles to Rod Action Mag., The Vintage Ford, Rod and Machine Gazzette and others. Home: 3241 S 82d Ave E Tulsa OK 74145 Office: 6111 E Skelly Dr Suite 327 Tulsa OK 74135

BOWDEN, BOBBY G., ednl. adminstr.; b. Altha, Fla., Aug. 24, 1929; s. C. B. and Mamie (Walker) B.; m. Ethel Marie Vickery; children—Nancy, Deborah, Bobby. B.S. in Bus. Adminstrn., Fla. State U., Tallahassee, 1951. Dir. fed. programs Bay County (Fla.) Sch. Dist., Panama City, 1960—. Bd. dirs. Am. Cancer Soc., 1974—, chmn. public edn. com., 1980. Recipient Lucille Moore award Am. Cancer Soc., 1979. Mem. Fla., Am. assns. sch. bus. ofcls., Fla. Sch. Finance Officers Assn. Home: 1608 W 22nd St Panama City FL 32401 Office: PO Drawer 820 Panama City FL 32401

BOWDEN, CHARLES MALCOLM, research physicist; b. Richmond, Va., Dec. 31, 1933; s. Charles Edward and Emma Stevens (Hoover) B.; B.S., U. Richmond, 1956; M.S., U. Va., 1959; Ph.D., Clemson U., 1967; m. Lou Marguerite Tolbert, Oct. 1, 1960; children—David Malcolm, Steven Mark, Melissa Gail. Research physicist U.S. Naval Research Lab., Washington, 1959-61; mem. faculty physics U. Richmond, 1961-64; research physicist Redstone Arsenal, Ala., 1967—; mem. physics faculty U. Ala., Huntsville, 1971—. Active Boy Scouts Am. Recipient Paul A. Siple award, 1978, others. NASA fellow, 1965-67. Mem. Am. Phys. Soc., N.Y. Acad. Scis., Sigma Xi, Sigma Pi Sigma. Baptist (adult tng. tchr., deacon). Club: Huntsville Athletic. Editor books in field; contbr. articles to profl. jours. Research solid state physics and quantum optics. Home: 716 Versailles Dr Huntsville AL 35803 Office: Quantum Physics Bldg 7770 Redstone Arsenal AL 35809

BOWDEN, OSSIE HANSON, corp. exec.; b. Cullman, Ala., Jan 1, 1918; s. Richard E. and Stella (Allgood) B.; grad. with honors Auburn U., 1941; m. Julia Batastini, Dec. 20, 1941; 1 dau., Sara Beatrice. County agt. Ala. Agrl. Extension Service, 1941-44; farm products marketing agt. T.C.I. div. U.S. Steel Corp., Birmingham, Ala., 1944-54; gen. mgr. Farmers Marketing and Exchange Assn., Montgomery, Ala., 1954-60; v.p. Gold Kist, Inc. (formerly Cotton Producers Assn.), Atlanta, 1960—. Distinguished lectr. Practitioner Coll. Bus. U. Ga. Bd. govs. St. Bernard Coll.; vice chmn. bd. Agrl. Coop. Devel. Internat.; bd. dirs. Asso. Coops., Ala. Farmers Coop., Vol. Devel. Corps; mem. Adv. Com. on Overseas Coop. Devel.; pres. Ga. Council of Farmers Coop. Adv. bd. Coll. Bus., U. Ga. Atlanta C. of C., Am. Inst. Coops. (chmn. bd. trustees), Ga. Bus. and Industry Assn. (bd. govs.), Internat. Platform Assn., Nat. Coop. Council, Phi Kappa Phi, Gamma Sigma Delta, Kappa Delta Phi. Baptist. Mason, Kiwanian. Clubs: Commerce, Chattahoochee Plantation. Home: 4686 Brinkley Ln NE Atlanta GA 30342 Office: 242 Perimeter Pkwy Center W Atlanta GA 30346

BOWEN, A'DELBERT, judge; b. Tuscumbia, Ala., Nov. 13, 1919; s. A'Delbert and Gertrude (Willett) B.; student State Tchrs. Coll., Florence, Ala., 1936-38; LL.B., Atlanta Law Sch., 1954; m. Rebecca Montez Proctor, July 27, 1945; children—A'Delbert III, Lanny Proctor, Montez Elizabeth. Gen. ins. agt. Proctor Ins. Agy., Cuthbert, Ga., 1950—; admitted to Ga. bar, 1954, since practiced in Cuthbert; atty. City of Shellman (Ga.), 1961-78, City of Georgetown (Ga.), 1966-78, City of Lumpkin (Ga.), 1974-78, City of Coleman (Ga.), 1968-78; county atty. Randolph County, Ga., 1960-71, Quitman County, Ga., 1966-78, Stewart County, Ga., 1974-78; judge Superior Cts. of Pataula Jud. Circuit, Cuthbert, 1978—. Mem. Ga. Gen. Assembly, 1959-64. Bd. dirs. Randolph Devel. Corp.; trustee Andrew Coll. Served to maj. USAAF, 1941-47. Decorated Air medal with five oak leaf clusters. Mem. Am., Ga. bar assns., Council of Superior Ct. Judges, Am. Legion. Methodist (trustee). Mason. Home: 118 W Harris St Cuthbert GA 31740 Office: Randolph County Courthouse Cuthbert GA 31740

BOWEN, (ALFRED) DALE, newspaper exec.; b. Suffolk, Va., Dec. 10, 1940; s. Alfred Dale and Ruth (Peale) B.; student Va. Commonwealth U., 1961-63, Old Dominion U., 1971-72. Advt. mgr. Virginian Pilot and Ledger Star (Landmark Communications), Virginia Beach, Va., 1963-68, mktg. rep. key accounts, Norfolk, Va., 1969-72, nat. advt. mgr., 1972—; advt. dir. Virginia Beach Beacon, No. Va. Sun, Arlington, 1968-69; cons. So. Living mag., Birmingham, Ala., 1973—, Williamsburg (Va.) Hotel-Motel Assn., 1978—; pres. Twinkle Toes, Inc., 1978—. Mem. North End Virginia Beach Civic League, 1974—; cons. numerous civic, polit. groups, 1968—. Recipient award Advt. Club of Tidewater, 1974. Mem. Internat. Newspaper Advt. Exec. Assn., Sales and Mktg. Execs. Inst. (award 1975), Va. Press Assn. (award 1973), Newspaper Advt. Bur., Norfolk C. of C. (award 1970). Methodist. Clubs: Racquet of Miami; Toastmasters. Writer, designer program So. Living Cooking Schools, 1975. Home: 225 64th St Virginia Beach VA 23451 Office: Virginian Pilot & Ledger Star 150 W Brambleton Ave Norfolk VA 23501

BOWEN, DAVID REECE, congressman; b. Houston, Miss., Oct. 21, 1932; s. David Reece and Lera (Pinnix) B.; student U. Mo., 1950-52; A.B., Harvard, 1954; M.A., Oxford U.; postgrad. U. Chgo., 1965-66. Instr., Am. Sch. in London, 1956-57; asst. prof. polit sci. and history Miss. Coll., 1958-59; asst. prof. polit. sci. Millsaps Coll., 1959-64; instr. English, U. Mo., 1964-65; coordinator S.E. region OEO, Washington, 1966-67; staff asso. for edn. U.S. C. of C., Washington, 1967-68; spl. asst. to gov., coordinator Fed.-State programs State of Miss., 1968-72; mem. 93d-96th Congresses from Miss. Trustee William H. Donner Found. Served with AUS, 1957-58. Mem. Kappa Alpha Order. Democrat. Home: 512 Hillcrest Circle Cleveland MS 38732 Office: 2421 Rayburn House Office Bldg Washington DC 20515

BOWEN, FRANK WESTON, physician; b. Memphis, May 5, 1921; s. George Samuel and Virgie (Hamill) B.; B.A., U., Miss., 1948, B.S. 1949; M.D., U. Tenn., 1951; m. Bobbie Elizabeth McPhail, May 1, 1943; 1 son, Frank Weston. Intern, Methodist Hosp., Memphis, 1951-52; practice family medicine, Walnut Grove, Miss., 1952-57, Carthage, Miss., 1957—; chief of staff Leake County Meml. Hosp., Carthage, 1961, 72; clin. instr. U. Miss. Sch. Medicine, 1977—. Served from pvt. to 2d lt. MAC, AUS, 1942-46. Diplomate Am. Bd. Family Practice. Fellow Am. Geriatrics Soc.; mem. Am. Heart Assn., A.M.A., Am. Acad. Family Practice, Miss. Med. Assn., Central Med. Soc. (pres. 1969), Leake County C. of C. (pres. 1975), U. Miss. Alumni Assn. (pres. med. chpt. 1974), Leake County Hist. Soc., Phi Chi. Methodist. Home: 514 Woodland Hills Carthage MS 39051 Office: 303 W Franklin St Carthage MS 39051

BOWEN, JUDY WILLIAMS, speech and lang. pathologist; b. Atlanta, Mar. 30, 1939; s. Leslie Spencer and Jewell Winifred (Ivey) Williams; B.A., Mercer U., 1961; M.Ed., Emory U., 1964; m. Henry Horace Bowen, Feb. 21, 1965; children—Susan Elizabeth, Sally Winifred. Speech pathologist DeKalb County Bd. Edn., Decatur, Ga., 1963-65, Atlanta Speech Sch., 1963-65, Central State Hosp., Milledgeville, Ga., summer 1966, Clarke County Bd. Edn., Athens, Ga., 1966-68, Wilkes County Bd. Edn., Washington, Ga., 1977—. cons. in field. Mem. Title 1 adv. council Washington-Wilkes Middle Sch., 1979—; bd. dirs. Friends of Savannah River, 1976-78; v.p. prodns. Washington Little Theater Co., 1977, bd. dirs., 1977—; v.p. Fidelis Sunday Sch. class, 1st. Baptist Ch., Washington, 1979—; pres. Washington-Wilkes Primary Sch. Parent-Tchr. Group, 1977-78. Cert. speech/lang. pathologist Ga. Mem. Am. Speech and Hearing Assn. (cert. clin. competence), Ga. Speech and Hearing Assn. (sec. 1967-68), DAR, Phi Mu. Home: 202 Water St Washington GA 30673 Office: Wilkes County Bd Edn PO Box 279 Washington GA 30673

BOWEN, KATHERINE MARY RICCHETTI, speech pathologist; b. Cleve., May 11, 1953; d. Carmine Carl and Margaret (Miko) Ricchetti; B.S. Ed. summa cum laude, Kent State U., 1974; M.S., U. South Fla., 1978; m. Gary Thomas Bowen, Apr. 12, 1975. Speech pathologist Stark County Bd. Mental Retardation, Canton, Ohio, 1974-75; speech pathologist Sch. Bd. Sarasota County (Fla.), 1975—. Mem. Am. Speech and Hearing Assn. (cert.). Home: 2879 Dueby St Sarasota FL 33581 Office: 3550 Wilkinson Rd Sarasota FL 33581

BOWEN, RALEIGH L., Democratic nat. committeeman, ret. soldier; b. Sherman, Tex., Dec. 27, 1911; s. Alexander A. and Dixe Lee (Powel) B.; student Wiley Coll., 1932-35, U. Md., 1952-62; B.A., Northeastern Okla. State U., now postgrad.; m. Pearl E. Soloman, Aug. 21, 1941. Enlisted as pvt. U.S. Army, 1942, advanced through grades to master sgt., 1962; with 92d Inf. Div., Italy, World War II, later served in Korea, ret., 1962; food service dir. U. Md., Princess Anne, 1962-73; now with Leake Industries, Inc., Tulsa. Steward, trustee, treas. Bee Be C.M.E. Ch., Muskogee, Okla.; mem. Westsiders Community Action Bd. Muskogee; mem. Democrat Nat. Com., 1955—; sec. Muskogee County Bicentennial Com., 1975-76. Mem. Internat. Platform Assn., Northeastern Okla. State U. Alumni Assn., Lost Bridge Village Community Assn., Am. Assn. Ret. Persons, Md. Classified Employees Assn., Pacific Twelve Emergency Club, Am. Legion, Armed Forces Communications and Electronics Assn., C. of C., Kappa Alpha Psi (life). Methodist. Mason (32 deg., Shriner), Elk. Home: 2705 W Broadway Muskogee OK 74401

BOWEN, ROBERT CALLENDER, savs. and loan exec.; b. State College, Miss., Aug. 12, 1925; s. James Vance and Albye (Callender) B.; B.S., Auburn U., 1948; M.S., Pa. State U., 1952, postgrad., 1953; m. Doris Katherine Lee, Nov. 26, 1964. So. regional dir. Student Mktg. Inst., N.Y.C., 1953-56; asst. project dir. Crossley S-O Surveys, Inc., N.Y.C., 1956-57; mktg. and econ. research asso. N.Y. Stock Exchange, 1958-59; mktg. specialist Am. Bankers Assn., N.Y.C., 1959-62; mgt. dev. mktg. officer Chem. Bank, N.Y.C., 1962-65; mktg. officer Franklin Nat. Bank, N.Y.C., 1965-66; pres. Lee/Bowen, Inc., N.Y.C., 1967, pres., Cleve., 1973-74; v.p., dir. mktg. research Cleve. Trust Co., 1968-72; v.p. mktg. First Fed. Savs. & Loan Assn. of Orlando, Fla., 1974—. Chmn. buyers'-sellers' guide com., chmn. research council Greater Cleve. Growth Assn., Cleve., 1970-74; trustee John Young Mus. and Planetarium, 1975-79, chmn. membership drive, 1976, treas., 1978; bd. dirs. Central Fla. Boys' Club, 1976—, Council Arts and Scis. for Central Fla. chmn. Local Pub. Broadcasting Service Nat. and Local Gifts Campaign, 1977. Served with inf. AUS, 1943-46, 50-52. Mem. Am. Mktg. Assn. (chmn. finance sect. consumer div. 1964-66, publicity chmn. Cleve. chpt. 1968, chmn. attendance and hospitality Cleve. chpt. 1969, exec. v.p., pres. Cleve. chpt. 1970-72), Bank Mktg. and Pub. Relations Assn., Cleve. Advt. Club, Am. Mgmt. Assn. (chmn. modern practice in bank mktg. 1965-67), Am. Bankers Assn. (mem. edn. and tng. com. mktg./savs. div. 1969-70), Auburn U. Alumni Club (dir. 1977—), Orlando Area C. of C. (chmn. promotion com. 1975), Theta Chi, Phi Delta Kappa, Pi Gamma Mu. Clubs: Citrus; Univ. of Winter Park, Winter Park Racquet. Author: Customer Analysis-A Profit Building Tool, 1961; Bank Holding Company Reporter, 1973. Editorial bd. Finance Mag., 1967, mktg. editor, 1968. Contbr. articles to profl. jours. Home: 801 Pine Tree Rd Winter Park FL 32789 Office: PO Box 2073 Orlando FL 32802

BOWEN, ROBERT KLIEN, JR., surgeon; b. Birmingham, Ala., Dec. 10, 1939; s. Robert Klien and Martha (McGill) B.; M.D., U. Ala., 1965; m. Anne Barham Jones, Apr. 10, 1960; children—Leigh Anne, Karen Lane, Robert K. III. Intern, Carraway Meth. Med. Center, Birmingham, 1966-67, resident in surgery, 1967-70; pvt. practice surgery, Sheffield, Ala., 1972-75, Orlando, Fla., 1975—; chief surgeon Shoals Hosp., 1973-75; staff surgeon Orange Meml., Holiday, Lucerne Gen. hosps., Orlando, 1975—. Served to maj., M.C., USAF, 1970-72. Diplomate Am. Bd. Surgery. Fellow A.C.S., Internat. Coll. Surgery, Am. Trauma Soc., Soc. Abdominal Surgery; mem. Fla. Assn. Gen. Surgeons, AMA, Fla., Orange County med. socs. Republican. Methodist. Home: 118 Live Oak Ln Altamonte Springs FL 32701 Office: 515 S Orange Ave Orlando FL 32801

BOWEN, TED, hosp. adminstr.; b. Alto, Tex., Nov. 4, 1921; B.S., Stephen F. Austin Coll., 1941; M.A., Washington U. Sch. Medicine, Sch. Hosp. Adminstrn., St. Louis, 1948; L.H.D. (hon.), Southwestern U., 1967; m. Roberta June Clendenin, Aug. 20, 1948; children—Rebecca Jane, Robert Ted. Intern in hosp. adminstrn. Barnes Hosp., St. Louis, 1947-48; asst. adminstr. Methodist Hosp., Houston, 1948-53, adminstr., 1953-70, exec. v.p., 1970-72, pres., 1972—; mem. Nat. Adv. Research Resources Council NIH; cons. USPHS; mem. adv. com. on nursing edn. Tex. Coll. and Univ. System. Vice chmn. bd. regents Stephen F. Austin State U. Served to sgt. AUS05 1942-46. Fellow Am. Coll. Hosp. Adminstrs. (Ted Bowen Ednl. Fund); mem. Am. Hosp. Assn. (alt. del.), Council Teaching Hosps., Tex. Hosp. Assn. (Earl M. Collier award 1968, chmn. study com. on health careers). Methodist. Clubs: River Oaks Country, Doctors. Contbr. articles to profl. jours. Home: 2510 Avalon Pl Houston TX 77019 Office: 6565 Fannin St Houston TX 77030

BOWER, FREDERICK JOHN, food co. exec.; b. Waukeegan, Ill., Dec. 17, 1936; s. Frederick Clarence and Jewel Elisabeth (Farmer) B.; B.S., Calif. State U., 1960; grad. Am. Inst. Baking, 1961; m. JoAnna Davis, June 21, 1958; children—Frederick Mark, Diana Lyn. Regional ops. supr. ITT Continental Baking Co., Washington, 1967-71; v.p. mfg. F.R. Lepage Baking Co., Lewiston, Maine, 1971-76; dir. ops. bakery div. Beatrice Food Co., Winston Salem, N.C., 1976-78, pres., gen. mgr. Krispy Kreme div., 1978—. Office: Beatrice Foods Co 514 S Stratford Rd Winston Salem NC 27103

BOWER, KENNETH LEE, ednl. adminstr.; b. Waco, Tex., Feb. 11, 1943; s. James Lee and Clara Mae (Madden) B.; B.S., Stephen F. Austin U., 1966; M.Ed., Loyola U., New Orleans, 1970; Ed.D., U. Houston, 1977; m. Linda Kay Lambert, Sept. 4, 1965; 1 son, Todd Allen. Tchr. biology East Jefferson High Sch., Metairie, La., 1966-70; tchr. English, Alief (Tex.) High Sch., 1970-71, guidance counselor, 1971-74; dir. data processing Alief Ind. Sch. Dist., 1974-76, spl. projects coordinator, 1976-77, dir. research devel. and evaluation, 1977-79, dir. curriculum and research, 1979—. Mem. Am. Personnel and Guidance Assn., Am. Sch. Counselors Assn., Tex. Assn. Ednl. Data Systems, Tex. Assn. Planning, Evaluation and Research, Assn. Supervision and Curriculum Devel., Tex. Assn. Supervision and Curriculum Devel., Kappa Delta Pi, Phi Delta Kappa. Methodist. Home: 11218 Montverde Ln Houston TX 77099 Office: Box 68 Alief Ind Sch Dist Alief TX 77411

BOWERS, CHARLES MICHAEL, banker; b. Jonesboro, Ark., Aug. 8, 1947; s. Charles M. and Kathleen F. (Davidson) B.; B.S. in Bus. Adminstrn., La. State U., 1970; m. Norma S. McDonald, Aug. 7, 1976; 1 son, Michael. Asst. v.p. First Tenn. Corp., Memphis, 1970-73; asst. v.p. Union Commerce Leasing Corp., Memphis, 1973-75; v.p. nat. accounts Union Nat. Bank, Little Rock, 1975—. Mem. Sales and Mktg. Execs. Assn. (dir. 1979-80). Club: Kiwanis. Office: Union Nat Bank 1 Union Nat Plaza Little Rock AR 72203

BOWERS, EDWARD SAVANNAH, elec. engr.; b. Nashville, Oct. 27, 1947; s. Edgar S. and Julia Mae (Wilson) B.; B.S. in Elec. Engring., Tenn. State U., 1973; m. Janie Latrelle Nesbitt, Dec. 30, 1974. Elec. engr., Boston, then field engr., Sandwich, Mass. for Stone and Webster Engring. Corp., 1973-75; elec. engr. quality control and insp., elec. and instrumentation sect. TVA, Sequoyah Nuclear plant, Daisy, Tenn., 1975-77, system engr., instrumentation engring. unit, 1977-78, elec. engr. TVA material mgmt., Chattanooga, 1978—. Chmn. Innovators, civic orgn., 1977—. Mem. IEEE, NAACP. Baptist. Home: 4008-B Morrison Springs Rd Chattanooga TN 37415

BOWERS, S(ANFORD) DEAN, energy cons.; b. Alice, Tex., July 14, 1931; s. Frame John and Mignon (Brock) B.; B.S. in Chem. Engring., Tex. A&M U., 1952; m. Judith Ann McCoy, June 30, 1956; children—Keith Douglas, Ann Mignon, Douglas Warren, Carrie Dean. Process engr. Mobil Oil Corp., Dallas, 1952-57; refinery engr. Pontiac Refining Corp., Corpus Christi, 1957-59; process econs. cons., v.p., dir. Purvin & Gertz, Inc., Dallas, 1959-73; cons. H. Zinder & Assos., Inc., also sr. v.p., dir., Dallas, 1973-78; cons. to energy industries, pres. S. Dean Bowers, Inc., Dallas, 1978—; gas contract seminar panelist. Bd. dirs. Dallas Civic Opera, Dallas Civic Opera Guild, Dallas Mus. Fine Arts; civic and polit. fund raiser. Registered profl. engr., Tex. Mem. Am. Petroleum Inst., Am. Inst. Chem. Engrs., Tex. Ind. Producers and Royalty Owners Assn., Mid-Continent Oil and Gas Assn., Gas Processors Assn., L.P. Gas Assn., Natural Gas Soc. N. Tex., Houston Natural Gas Men's Soc., Dallas Petroleum Club. Republican. Episcopalian. Home: 5366 Nakoma Dr Dallas TX 75209 Office: 210 Meadows Bldg Dallas TX 75206

BOWERSOCK, ROGER BATES, psychologist; b. Lima, Ohio, Apr. 5, 1940; s. Martin Bates and Grace Edna (Rogers) B.; B.S., Xavier U., Cin., 1962, M.S., 1966; Ph.D., Fla. State U., 1970; m. Suellen Delores Weis, June 19, 1965; children—Paul, Timothy, Amy. Tchr., McNicholas High Sch., Cin., 1962-66; psychologist U.S.C. Counseling Center, Columbia, 1970-74, asso. dir., 1974-76, coordinator, 1976—, also adj. prof. psychology; pvt. practice psychology, 1976—; cons. to edn., govt. and industry. Licensed psychologist, S.C. Mem. Am. Psychol. Assn., Am., S.C. personnel and guidance assns., S.C. Psychol. Assn., Nat. Rehab. Assn., Kappa Delta Pi. Roman Catholic. Contbr. articles to Jour. Counseling Psychology, Jour. Counseling and Values, Jour. Counseling Services, Jour. Counseling and Values, Jour. Counseling Services, Jour. Elementary Sch. Counseling and Guidance. Home: 455 Brookshire Dr Columbia SC 29210 Office: 1321 Pendleton St Columbia SC 29208

BOWES, KENNETH EBERLE, advt. agy. exec.; b. Montreal, Que., Can., May 16, 1937; s. David Proctor and Corine (Eberle) B.; came to U.S., 1943, naturalized, 1955; B.S., Fla. State U., 1959; m. Mary Priscilla Mohlhenrich, Aug. 10, 1958; children—Kenneth William, Douglas Proctor, Ann Eberle. Advt. writer Atlanta Gas Light Co., 1959-66; with Liller Neal Battle & Lindsey, Atlanta, 1966-72, v.p., 1969-72; pres. Bowes/Hanlon Advt., Atlanta, 1972—; bd. govs. Trans-World Advt. Agy. Network. Bd. dirs. Kidney Found. Ga.,

Atlanta Area council Boy Scouts Am., Hub Family Crisis Center; pres. Ga. Youth and Family Network. Mem. Ga. C. of C., Cobb County C. of C., Friends of the Alphabet. Republican. Mem. Moravian Ch. Clubs: Druid Hills Golf, Toastmasters. Home: 5290 Antelope Ln Stone Mountain GA 30087 Office: 550 Pharr Rd NE Atlanta GA 30305

BOWLING, ANDREW CHARLES, educator; b. Booneville, Ky., June 16, 1936; s. Chester and Mary (Amis) B.; B.A. with High Honors, U. Cin., 1957; M.A., Brandeis U., 1960, Ph.D., 1962; m. Donna Jeane Weathers, Aug. 18, 1958; children—David Andrew, Stephen Jonathan, Mark Daniel. Asso. prof. religion, history, philosophy Haigazian Coll., Beirut, Lebanon, 1962-68; asst. prof. world history Am. U. Beirut, 1968-69; prof. Bibl. studies John Brown U., Siloam Springs, Ark., 1969—; lectr. in field. Chmn. Benton County (Ark.) Republican com., 1973-74. Bd. dirs. Benton County Assn. Land Use Planning by Landowners, Benton County Christian Schs. NDEA fgn. lang. fellow Arabic, 1960-62. Mem. Soc. Bibl. Lit., Am. Acad. Religion, Evang. Theol. Soc. (pres. Southwest sect. 1978-79), Phi Beta Kappa. Ranger Christian Service brigade. Contbr. articles to profl. publs. Home: 612 S Oak Hill St Siloam Springs AR 72761 Office: John Brown U Siloam Springs AR 72761

BOWLING, CAROLYN SUE, social worker; b. Lynchburg, Va., Feb. 6, 1951; d. Cleveland Leonard and Hettie Angus B.; B.A., Lynchburg Coll., 1973; M.S., Va. Commonwealth U., 1975. Team leader, Lynchburg Tng. Sch. and Hosp., 1974-78, social worker, 1978—. Crisis intervention worker Help Hotline, United Way, 1974-76. Recipient Vibro Stimulation grant, 1975-76. Mem. Am. Assn. Mental Deficiencies. Democrat. Home: Route 3 Box 91B Madison Heights VA 24572 Office: Box 1098 Lynchburg VA 24505

BOWLING, ROBERT EDWARD, JR., microbiologist, educator; b. Pauls Valley, Okla., Aug. 9, 1926; s. Robert Edward and Clara Ellen (Merkle) B.; B.S., U. Okla., 1948, M.S., 1950, Ph.D., 1957; m. Dorothy Ann Clark, Mar. 12, 1955; children—Ann Elizabeth, John Robert, Susan Ellen, Mary Merkle, Paul Edward. Asst. microbiologist Okla. Health Dept., 1950-51; instr. dept. microbiology U. Ark. Med. Center, Little Rock, 1957-59, asst. prof., 1959-68, asso. prof. microbiology, 1968—, asst. dean Sch. Medicine, 1973—. Mem. Am. Soc. Microbiology, Soc. for Gen. Microbiology (Gt. Britain), Am. Inst. Biol. Scis., Soc. for Cryobiology, Soc. for Exptl. Biology and Medicine, Ark. Acad. Sci., Sigma Xi. Episcopalian. Home: 4400 I St Little Rock AR 72205

BOWLING, WILLIAM EDGAR, elec. engr.; b. Dunbar, W.Va., Sept. 25, 1941; s. William Green and Pearl (Hartley) B., Jr.; B.S. in Elec. Engring., W.Va. U., 1964; postgrad U. Ala., 1965-71; m. Katherine Ann Erwin, Aug. 21, 1965; 1 dau., Karen Ann. Jr. engr. IBM, Owego, N.Y., 1964-65, asso. engr., Huntsville, Ala., 1966-68, sr. asso. engr., 1968-71, staff engr., 1971-75, staff engr., Lexington, Ky., 1975-77, Austin, Tex., 1977—. Instr. IBM Vol. Edn. Program, Huntsville, 1973-74. Registered profl. engr. Mem. IEEE, Eta Kappa Nu, Pi Kappa Alpha. Baptist. Club: Balcones Country. Home: 9803 Bordeaux Ln Austin TX 78750 Office: IBM Corp 11400 Burnet Rd Austin TX 78759

BOWMAN, HAL LAMAR, retail co. exec.; b. Hardeeville, S.C., Nov. 23, 1941; s. William Abbot and Eula (Barker) B.; student public schs., Hardeeville; m. Kathryn Joyce Crawford, June 23, 1961; children—Donna Jeanne, Hal Lamar, Angelia Rene. Display trimmer Levy's of Savannah (Ga.), 1962-66; display dir. Leggett Stores, Inc., Charlottesville, Va., 1966-69, regional display dir., 1969-73, corp. visual merchandising mgr., 1973-77, sales promotion dir., Lynchburg, Va., 1977—; bd. dirs. Belk/Leggett Advt. Display Assn., 1971-77, pres. 1975-76. Deacon, Ch. of Christ, Lynchburg, 1975-79, elder, 1979—. Recipient 1st Place award visual merchandising contest, 1972; Nat. Retail Mchts. Assn. award, 1979; Award of Excellence in TV Prodn., Knoxville Ad Club, 1979. Mem. Lynchburg Ad Club. Home: 1413 Ramsgate Ln Lynchburg VA 24501 Office: 11 Pittman Plaza Lynchburg VA 24501

BOWMAN, JEFFERY SCOTT, hosp. adminstr.; b. Albany, Ky., Jan. 20, 1947; s. Ray Lee and Hattie Mae Bowman; B.S., Tenn. Wesleyan Coll., 1975; m. Sherry Ann Corn, Aug. 28, 1972; children—Chris, Michael. Chief med. technologist Woods Meml. Hosp., Etowah, Tenn., 1965-74; med. technologist Athens Community Hosp., Athens, Tenn., 1974-76; asst. adminstr., controller Sweetwater (Tenn.) Hosp. Assn., 1976-77, adminstr., 1977—. Bd. dirs. Coordinated Hosp. Services, Monroe County Health Improvement Council. Mem. Monroe County C. of C., Tenn. Hosp. Assn., Am. Hosp. Assn., Hosp. Fin. Mgmt. Assn., Coll. Hosp. Adminstrs. Baptist. Club: Kiwanis. Home: Oakland Rt Sweetwater TN 37874 Office: PO Box 312 Sweetwater TN 37874

BOWMAN, NED DAVID, med. adminstr.; b. Chattanooga, July 15, 1948; s. Ned Turner and Ernie June White; B.S., U. Tenn., 1971, postgrad., 1971—; m. Linda Carol Eggers, Sept. 18, 1970; children—Bob, Jean, Beth, Scott, Ben. Adminstr., pres. Ancillary Physicians Services, Oak Ridge, 1971—; cons. med. adminstrn. Mem. Oak Ridge Human Resources Bd., 1975; co-chmn. substance abuse com. Anderson County Health Council, pres., 1980; adv. com. vocat. edn. Oak Ridge city schs., 1977; treas. UN Com. Oak Ridge, 1977. Recipient certs. of appreciation City of Oak Ridge, Oak Ridge City Schs. Mem. AAAS, UN Assn. U.S., Soc. Advancement Mgmt. (certificate appreciation 1975, v.p. 1975), Oak Ridge C. of C. (past dir.), Med. Group Mgmt. Assn. (pres. Tenn. chpt.), Am. Coll. Med. Group Adminstrs., Tenn. Med. Group Mgmt. Assn. Mormon. Club: Rotary. Home: 502 Delaware Ave Oak Ridge TN 37830

BOWMAN, SAMUEL LEONARDO, clergyman; b. Benton, Miss., Feb. 19, 1933; s. Warren and Nora (Johnson) B.; B.S., Natchez (Miss.) Coll., 1950, Th.D. (hon.), 1972; Th.B., Miss. Baptist Sem., 1960, L.H.D. (hon.), 1977, Th.M., 1979; m. Willie M. Jackson, June 30, 1957; children—Gwendolyn, Jacqueline. Ordained to ministry Bapt. Ch., 1952; pastor, Mt. Olive, Miss., 1956-65, Greater Clark St. Bapt. Ch., Jackson, Miss., 1965—; prof. O.T., Miss. Bapt. Sem., 1961—. Bd. dirs. Jackson Urban League, 1969-72; chmn. bd. mgrs. Farish St. br. YMCA, Jackson, 1970-72. Recipient Outstanding Citizenship award Mich. State Legislature, 1972. Mem. Bapt. Ministers Union Jackson (pres. 1968—), Phi Delta Kappa. Mason. Author: Black Sons of Thunder, 1973. Home: 3761 Terrell Ave Jackson MS 39213 Office: 415 N Gallatin St Jackson MS 39203

BOWMER, JIM DEWITT, lawyer; b. Temple, Tex., May 4, 1919; s. DeWitt and Linnie B. (Morgan) B.; A.A., Temple Jr. Coll., 1938; B.A. cum laude, Baylor U., 1940, LL.B. cum laude, 1942; m. Daurice Spoonts, Mar. 26, 1961; children—Bonnie Nell (Mrs. Larry Neal), Mary Helen (Mrs. Charles Schreiner IV). Admitted to Tex. bar, 1942; county atty. Bell County, Tex., 1946-47; lectr. law Baylor U. Law Sch., 1949-50, 56-57; mem. firm Bowmer, Courtney, Burleson & Pemberton, 1964—. Bd. dirs. Nat. Park Found., 1968-69. Served with AUS, 1942-46. Mem. Am. Law Inst., Am. Judicature Soc., Tex. Assn. Def. Counsel, Temple C. of C. (past pres.), Baylor Law Alumni Assn. (past pres.), Bell-Lampasas-Mills Counties Bar Assn. (past pres.), State Bar Tex. (dir. 1968-71, chmn. bd. 1970-71, pres. 1972-73), Phi Alpha Delta. Democrat. Baptist. Mason (K.T.), K.P. (past grand chancellor Tex.), Kiwanian. Contbr. articles to profl. jours. Home: Bowmer's Ranch Route 2 Killeen TX 76541 Office: First Fed Savings & Loan Bldg Temple TX 76501

BOWMER, WILLIAM JACKSON, agronomist; b. Bertram, Tex., Apr. 29, 1937; s. Charlie Burket and Susie Mildred (Boyce) B.; B.S., Tex. A. and M. U., 1960, M.S., 1967; m. Mona Louise Dodd, Sept. 1, 1956; children—Jacquelyn, William Jay. Farm foreman, Van Horn, Tex., 1960; range conservationist U.S. Dept. Agr. Soil Conservation Service, Midland, Tex., 1961-63; research asso. Tex. Transp. Inst., Tex. A. and M. U., College Station, 1963-70; agronomist Tex. Dept. Agr., Austin, 1970—. Served with USAR, 1960-61. Mem. Weed Sci. Soc. Am., Indsl. Weed Control Conf. Tex., Soc. Range Mgmt., Sigma Xi. Mem. Ch. of Christ. Club: Woodman of the World. Contbr. articles to profl. jours. Home: Route 2 Box 90 Bertram TX 78605 Office: PO Box 12847 Austin TX 78711

BOYAJIAN, GREGORY KARNIG, dental technologist; b. Kounie, Syria, Mar. 3, 1949; came to U.S., 1971, naturalized, 1979; s. Karnig Benjamin and Zahour Ibrahim (Ghraibi) B.; B.S. in Chemistry, Salem (W.Va.) Coll., 1975; m. Jessica Bond, July 25, 1979. Designer, mfr. dental fixed prostheses, 1975—; owner, dir. Boyajian Dental Lab., Clarksburg, W.Va., 1975—. Cert. dental technician. Mem. Nat. Assn. Dental Labs. Home: 216 Buchanan Ave Clarksburg WV 26301 Office: Gore Bldg Clarksburg WV 26301

BOYCE, BETTY JEAN, ednl. adminstr.; b. Greenville, Tex., July 10, 1929; married, 2 children; R.N., St. Paul Hosp., Dallas, 1949. Nurse, Mesquite (Tex.) Ind. Sch. Dist., 1961-64, dir. health services, 1964—. Bd. dirs. Mesquite Social Services, 1965-69, local chpt. Am. Cancer Soc., 1979—. Mem. Tex., Mesquite edn. assns., Tex. State Tchrs. Assn., Am. Sch. Health Assn., Tex. Sch. Health Assn., Dallas Area Sch. Health Assn., Tex. Nurses Assn., Dallas County Child Welfare Assn. Home: 524 Riggs Circle Mesquite TX 75149 Office: 405 E Davis St Mesquite TX 75149

BOYCE, EDWARD WAYNE, JR., lawyer; b. Tuckerman, Ark., June 20, 1926; s. Edward Wayne and Sylla (Harvey) B.; student The Citadel, 1943-44; A.B., U. Ark., 1950, LL.B., 1951; m. Phyllis Elayne Williams, Oct. 29, 1951; children—Martha Elayne, Edward Wayne III. Admitted to Ark. bar, 1951; asso. firm Pickens & Pickens, 1951-54; practiced law, 1954-59; mem. firm Pickens, Boyce, McLarty & Watson, and predecessor, Newport, Ark., 1959—. Dep. pros. atty., 1951-56, pros. atty., 3d Jud. Circuit, 1957-60. Mem. Ark. Penitentiary Study Commn. Chmn., Jackson County chpt. Nat. Found., 1965-69. Served with 31st Inf. Div., AUS, 1944-47. Mem. Am. (bd. gen. practice sect.), Ark. (exec. com. 1968-71, 74-77, pres. 1978-79), Jackson County (pres. 1954, 62), 8th Chancery (v.p. 1973) bar assns., Ark. Legal Edn. Council, Am. Law Inst., Am. Judicature Soc., Phi Alpha Theta, Phi Delta Theta. Episcopalian (mem. exec. council Diocese of Ark. 1970-73, mem. diocesan standing com. 1975-78). Chmn. editorial adv. bd. Law Notes for the general practitioner. Home: 7 Pickens St Newport AR 72112 Office: 209 Walnut St Newport AR 72112

BOYCE, ERNEST FREDRICK, retail food chain exec.; b. Somerville, Mass., 1916; B.A., Boston U.; postgrad. in Bus. Adminstrn., Harvard U., 1947. Various positions in testing, tng. mgmt., devel., and lab. relations Stop & Shop, Inc., 1929-46, divisional mgr., 1940-44, personnel dir., 1944-46; in corp. relations Liggett Drug Co., Inc., Stamford, Conn., 1946-64, dir. of personnel, 1946-49, v.p. indsl. relations, 1949-64; with Colonial Stores Inc., East Point, Ga., 1964—, chmn. bd., chief exec. officer, 1976—, also dir.; dir. Coastal States Corp., Fulton Nat. Bank, Associated Distributors. Mem. Phoenix Soc. Club: Rotary. Office: Colonial Stores Inc 2251 N Sylvan Rd East Point GA 30344*

BOYCE, MEHERWAN PHIROZ, cons. engr.; b. Poona, India, July 25, 1942; came to U.S., 1960, naturalized, 1971; s. Phiroz H. and Nergesh Phiroz (Colabawalla) B.; B.S.M.E., S.D. Sch. Mines and Tech., 1962; M.S., SUNY, Buffalo, 1964; Ph.D., U. Okla., 1969; m. Zarine Cowas Dubash, June 28, 1977; children—Phiroz, Anita. Devel. engr. Joy Mfg., 1962-64; group leader compressor div. Curtiss Wright, 1964-66; group leader aerodynamics Fairchild Hiller Corp., 1966-69; prof. mech. engring., dir. gas turbine lab. Tex. A. & M. U., 1969-79; pres. Boyce Engring., Houston. 1977—; chmn. Turbomachinery Symposium; cons. major petrochem. and utilities cos. Mem. ASME (Herbert Allen award), Soc. Automotive Engrs. (Ralph Tector award), Am. Soc. Engring. Edn., Nat. Soc. Profl. Engrs., Sigma Xi, Phi Kappa Phi, Tau Beta Phi, Pi Tau Sigma. Zorastrian. Author: Gas Turbine Handbook, 1980; contbr. articles tech. jours. Home: 10959 Beinhorn St Houston TX 77024 Office: 10555 Rockley Rd Houston TX 77099

BOYD, CLARENCE ELMO, surgeon; b. Leesville, La., Nov. 2, 1911; s. Isaac C. and Ada Lee (Stakes) B.; B.A., U. Tex., 1932, M.D., 1935; m. Emma Sims, Aug. 13, 1937; children—Charles E., Marjorie E., Frances A., James E. Intern, Charity Hosp., New Orleans, 1935-36; resident North La. San. (now Doctors Hosp.), Shreveport, La., 1936-37; gen. practice medicine, Shreveport, 1937-42, specializing in gen. surgery, 1942—; founder, sr. mem. C.E. Boyd Clinic, Shreveport, 1942—; vis. surgeon Doctors Hosp., Shreveport, 1937—, founding dir., 1959, chmn. bd., 1959-80, med. dir., 1959—; sr. vis. surgeon Charity Hosp. (now Confederate Meml. Hosp.), 1937-42; sr. vis. surgeon Confederate Meml. Hosp., Shreveport, 1942—; clin. asst. prof. surgery La. State U. Postgrad. Sch. Medicine, 1957-67, La. State U. Sch. of Medicine, Shreveport, 1967—; teaching faculty Am. Bd. Abdominal Surgeons, 1967; chief surgeon La. and Ark. Ry. Co. Employees' Hosp. Assn. to 1967; founding dir., chmn. bd. Dr.'s Hosp., Shreveport, 1959; vis. surgeon, 1937—; also lectr. Founding dir. Shreveport Bank & Trust Co., 1954—, chmn. investment com., 1954-78, chmn. bd. dirs., 1961—. Sponsors com. Shreveport United Fund, 1962-66. Dir. Vols. Am., 1950-58, pres. bd., 1955-57; trustee Pub. Affairs Rev. Council, Shreveport, 1959-79; nat. adv. bd. We the People, 1964—. Diplomate Internat. Bd. Proctology. Fellow A.C.S., Internat. Coll. Surgs., Southwestern Surg. Congress, Am. Soc. Abdominal Surgeons (founder 1959, pres. 1966-67, chmn. com. preparing audio-visual postgrad. program on diseases of gall bladder, teaching faculty 1962, Gold medal 1962), mem. AMA (mem. surg. sect. 1969-71, chmn. 1964, alt. del. sect. council on surgery 1972-78, mem. surg. council 1972-78, del. 1978, Recognition award 1966-69, 70-72, 73-78, 79-81), La. (chmn. pub. policy and legislative com. 1954-57, 4th dist. councilor 1959-66, del. 1945-59, v.p. 1967-68), Shreveport (pres. 1956, 1st chmn. med. progress 1957-59, Gold medal 1956-57), med. socs., Am. Cancer Soc. (dir. Caddo br. 1952-59, vice chmn. bd. 1957-58), Surg. Assn. La., So. Med. Assn. (asso. Councilor 1959-68), Pan Pacific Surg. Assn., Am. Assn. Physicians and Surgeons (del., mem. chmn. 1950-72, pres. La. chpt. 1972). Episcopalian (vestryman, Gold Medal Bible Class 1965). Rotarian (pres. Cedar Grove, Shreveport, 1940-41, founder, 1941 and chmn. com. of student loan fund), Mason (32 deg., Shriner). Contbr. articles to profl. jours. Research on operative cholangiography, local hernioplasty with immediate ambulation; producer color film on cholangiogram, 1954, 60. Home: 401 Delaware St Shreveport LA 71106 Office: 1128 Louisiana Ave Shreveport LA 71101

BOYD, DANNY DOUGLASS, marriage, family, fin. counselor; b. Olustee, Okla., Oct. 18, 1933; s. Robert and Juanita Henrietta (Crawford) B.; B.A. magna cum laude, Abilene Christian U., 1954; M.A. in Linguistics, U. Tex., Arlington, 1976; m. Mary Ann Thomas, Jan. 25, 1953; children—Robert Lee, Rebecca Dyann Boyd McCully, Scott Thomas, Douglas Dean. Minister Churches of Christ, Ardmore, Okla., 1954-56, Velma, Okla., 1956-57, Cisco, Tex., 1958-60, Utrecht, Netherlands, 1960-65. Wilmington, Del., 1965-69, Dallas, 1969-71; v.p. Nat. Comp Assos., Dallas, 1972-77; marriage and family counselor Adaptive Counseling Assos., Dallas, 1977—; fin. counselor Conn. Gen. Life Ins. Co., 1979—; founder Chair of Bible, Cisco Jr. Coll., 1959. Bd. dirs. Skyline High Sch. PTA, 1971; intervenor for integrated neighborhoods fed. dist. ct. desegregation suit, Dallas, 1977. Mem. Dallas Assn. Life Underwriters, Am. Personnel and Guidance Assn. Republican. Office: Pkwy Central Plaza 611 Ryan Plaza Dr Suite 940 Arlington TX 76011

BOYD, HELEN MCPHERSON (MRS. DEWARD GASTON BOYD, JR.), mathematician; b. Marks, Miss., Jan. 27, 1937; d. William Joseph and Miriam (Till) McPherson; student Miss. State Coll. Women, 1954-55; B.A. with distinction, U. Miss., 1958, M.A., 1959; postgrad. U. Ala., 1967-74; m. Deward Gaston Boyd, Jr., June 1, 1963. Instr. math Miss. State U., State College, 1959-64; asst. prof., 1964-65; release chemist Baxter Labs, Mountain Home, Ark., 1965; mathematician Army Missile Research and Devel. Command, Redstone Arsenal, Ala., 1967—. Mem. Southeast Huntsville Civic Assn., 1972-77; vol. mem. Madison County Local Govt. Study Commn., 1972-74. Recipient Taylor medal math. U. Miss., 1958; So. Fellowships Fund fellow, 1958-59. Mem. Math. Assn. Am., Am. Math. Soc., AAAS, Am. Fedn. Govt. Employees, Assn. U.S. Army, Assn. Women in Math., Federally Employed Women (treas. chpt. 1975-76, v.p. 1976-77, parliamentarian 1977-79), Phi Kappa Phi, Gamma Sigma Epsilon. Presbyn. Toastmistress. Home: 703 Dellwood Rd SE Huntsville AL 35802 Office: US Army Missile Command DRSMI-TRA Redstone Arsenal AL 35809

BOYD, HOWARD TANEY, lawyer, gas co exec.; b. Woodside, Md., June 5, 1909; s. Howard and Mary Violet (Stewart) B.; A.B. magna cum laude, Georgetown U., 1932, J.D., 1935, LL.D., 1977; m. Lucille A. Belhumeur, June 15, 1935; children—Dennis Brooke, Sharon Ann Boyd Rodriguez, Deborah Boyd Fitch. Admitted to D.C. bar, 1934, Tex. bar, 1953; sec. to atty. gen. U.S., 1934; spl. atty. U.S. Dept. Justice, 1935; asst. U.S. atty. in and for D.C., 1935-39; former prof. Nat. Law Sch., also Washington Coll. Law; partner law firm Hogan & Hartson, Washington, 1939-52; v.p., asst. gen. counsel El Paso Natural Gas Co., 1952-57, exec. v.p., 1957-60, pres. 1960-65, chmn. bd., chief policy officer El Paso Co., 1965-79, chmn. exec. com., 1979—; partner firm Liddell, Sapp, Zivley & Brown, 1979—; pres. Groupe Internat. des Importateurs de Gaz Naturel Liquefie; dir. Greyhound Corp., Tex. Commerce Bank, N.A., Armour and Co.; mem. bd. dirs. U.S.-USSR Trade and Econ. Council, U.S. Nat. Com.-World Energy Conf. Bd. dirs. Tex. Research League, regent emeritus Georgetown U.; trustee U. So. Calif., Center Internat. Bus. Research fellow Southwestern Legal Found.; decorated chevalier French legion of Honor; recipient Golden Plate award, 1977. Mem. Am., Tex., D.C. (dir. 1950) bar assns., Nat. Petroleum Council, Am. Gas Assn., Interstate Natural Gas Assn. (pres. 1968), Am. Soc. French Legion of Honor. Clubs: Barrister, Chevy Chase, Columbia Country, Met., Burning Tree, Georgetown (Washington); Petroleum, Ramada, River Oaks Country, Houston Country (Houston); Links, Wall St. (N.Y.C.). Home: 6042 Crab Orchard Houston TX 77057 Office: 2727 Allen Pkwy Houston TX 77019

BOYD, JOHN HAMILTON, osteo. physician; b. Wharton County, Tex., Sept. 20, 1924; s. John Hamilton and Grace Laura (Smith) B.; B.A., Tex. Tech., 1949; D.O., Kirksville Coll. Osteo. Medicine, 1955; m. Myrtle Juanita Ferguson, Feb. 21, 1970. Individual practice osteo. medicine, Louise, Tex., 1955-70, Silverton, Tex., 1971-74, Eden, Tex., 1974—. County health officer, Wharton County, Tex., 1961-65, Briscoe County, Tex., 1971-74; city health officer, Eden, 1974—. Mem. local bd. SSS, 1967-70; v.p. Tex. Inst. Med. Assessment, 1974-76, pres., 1977-79; bd. dirs. Concho County Hosp. Dist., 1975—, Tex. Med. Found., 1976-77, Wharton County Jr. Coll., 1961-70. Served with USAAF, 1942-46. Mem. Civil Aviation Med. Assn. (dir. 1978—), Am. Osteo. Assn., Aerospace Med. Assn., Am. Coll. Utilization Rev. Physicians, Am. Osteo. Acad. Public Health and Preventive Medicine, La Asociacion Latino Americano de Aviacion y del Espacio, Mensa, Nat. Rifle Assn. (life), Tex. Rifle Assn. (life), Am. Acad. Osteopathy, Tex. Osteo. Med. Assn. (pres. 1973-74). Home: Drawer W Eden TX 76837 Office: Drawer G Eden TX 76837

BOYD, JOSEPH ARTHUR, JR., justice Fla. Supreme Ct.; b. Hoschton, Ga., Nov. 16, 1916; s. Joseph Arthur and Esther (Puckett) B.; grad. Piedmont Coll., LL.D., 1963; J.D., U. Miami, 1948; m. Ann Stripling, June 6, 1938 children—Joanne (Mrs. Robert Goldman), Betty Jean (Mrs. David Jala), Joseph, James, Jane. City atty., Hialeah, Fla., 1951-58; commr. Dade County, 1958-68, vice mayor, 1967; chmn. Dade County Commn., 1963; dir. Fla. Assn. County Commrs., 1964-68; justice Fla. Supreme Ct., Tallahassee, 1969—. Trustee Piedmont Coll. Served with USMCR, 1943-46; PTO. Decorated Japanese Occupation medal with one star; recipient Top Hat award for advancing status of women Nat. Bus. and Profl. Women's Clubs, 1967. Mem. Am. Fla., D.C., Hialeah-Miami Springs (pres. 1955), Tallahassee bar assns., Hialeah-Miami Springs (pres. 1956), Tallahassee chambers commerce, Am. Legion (state comdr. 1953), V.F.W., Soc. of Wig and Robe, Pi Kappa Psi, Phi Alpha Delta. Baptist. Mason (Shriner), Lion, Elk, Moose. Club: Tallahassee Shrine. Home: 2210 Monaghan Dr Tallahassee FL 32308 Office: Supreme Ct Bldg Tallahassee FL 32304

BOYD, LINDA GAIL, broadcasting co. exec.; b. Duncan, Okla., Sept. 22, 1952; d. Lloyd Elbert and Oneida (Ahart) B.; B.S., Murray State U., 1974. Bus. analyst Dun & Bradstreet, Louisville, 1974; mktg. rep., 1974; account exec. Sta. WAKY Radio, Inc., Louisville, 1974-79; field mktg. rep. Burger Queen Enterprises, Louisville, 1979-80; account exec. Sta. WAVE, Louisville, 1980—. Mem. retail devel. task force Louisville C. of C., 1977. Mem. Am. Women in Radio and TV (bd. dirs., pres. 1978). Democrat. Baptist. Home: 2505 Brownsboro Rd Louisville KY 40206 Office: 725 S Floyd St Louisville KY

BOYD, LOUIS JEFFERSON, educator; b. Lynn Grove, Ky., Mar. 14, 1928; s. Bernice B. and Ethel Belle (Turnbow) B.; B.S., U. Ky., 1950, M.S., 1951; Ph.D., U. Ill., 1956; m. Rebecca Charlotte Conner, June 12, 1948; children—Beverly (Mrs. Timothy T. Gallagher), Beda (Mrs. Steven F. Smith), Garth, Bettina (Mrs. Curtis G. Mize). Extension specialist U. Ky., Lexington, 1951-53; research asso. U. Ill., Urbana, 1953-56; assoc. prof. U. Tenn., Knoxville, 1956-62; prof. Mich. State U., East Lansing, 1963-72; prof., chmn. div. animal sci. U. Ga., Athens, 1972-79, head animal and dairy sci. dept., 1974-79. Researcher, Inst. Research on Animal Diseases, Agrl. Research Council, Compton, Eng., 1970-71; dir. Coble Dairy Products Coop., Inc., 1976—. Served with AUS, 1946-47. Recipient Outstanding Adviser award Am. Dairy Sci. Assn., 1966, Outstanding Extension Specialist award Mich. State U., 1971, NSF travel grant, France, 1968. Mem. Soc. Study Reproduction, Am. Soc. Animal Sci., Am. Dairy Sci. Assn. (dir. 1973-76), Soc. Study Fertility, A.A.A.S., Farm House (nat. dir. 1960-64), Dairy Shrine Club, Sigma Xi, Gamma

Sigma Delta, Sigma Phi, Phi Zeta. Presbyn. (elder). Optimist (v.p. 1961). Breeding columnist Hoard's Dairyman mag., 1967-72. Patentee process to improve fertility of animal semen. Home: 106 St James Ct Athens GA 30606 Office: Coll Agr Univ Georgia Athens GA 30602

BOYD, ROBERT EDWARD LEE, II, ret. mech. engr.; b. Wheeling, W.Va., Nov. 12, 1914; s. Robert E. Lee and Mary (Bachtler) B.; A.B. in Physics, Kenyon Coll., 1936; m. Julia Eleanor Beal, Jan. 1, 1938; children—Mary Eleanor Boyd Eads, Barbara Ann Boyd Hall, Robert E. Lee, III. With Airtemp Co., 1948-51, field service engr., Dallas, 1948-49, engr., Houston, 1950-51; with Westinghouse Co., 1937-38; tech. dir. Edwin L. Wiegand Co., Pitts., 1957-66; engring. cons. climate control div. Singer Co., Auburn, N.Y., 1966-71; asso. prof. air-conditioning tech. State U. N.Y. Coll., Alfred, 1971-74; asso. tech. dir. Sheet Metal and Air Conditioning Contractors' Nat. Assn., Vienna, Va., 1974-76; sr. mech. engr. NAHB (Nat. Assn. Home Builders) Research Found., Inc., Rockville, Md., 1976-78, ret., 1978; v.p. Bayley, Boyd, Childs, Hungerford, Jones, P.C. and Assos., Wellsville, N.Y., 1973—. Served to 1st lt. C.E. AUS, 1942-46. Fellow Am. Soc. Heating, Refrigerating and Air Conditioning Engrs.; mem. Engrs. Joint Council Engrs. of Distinction, Phi Beta Kappa, Tau Kappa Alpha. Club: Masons. Contbr. numerous articles on heating and air conditioning application engring. to trade and profl. pubs.; patentee in field. Home: 413 Brewers Creek Ln Carrollton VA 23314

BOYD, ROBERT FRIEND, lawyer; b. Richmond, Va., May 11, 1927; s. Oscar L. and Ruby (Friend) B.; A.B., Coll. William and Mary, 1950, J.D., 1952; m. Sara Grace Miller, Sept. 20, 1952; children—Robert Friend, David Miller, Mary Elizabeth, James Matheson. Admitted to Va. bar, 1952; practiced in Norfolk, 1955—; sr. partner firm Boyd, Payne Gates & Farthing, 1957—; commr. Chancery for Circuit Ct., Norfolk, Circuit Ct., Chesapeake, Va., 1967—; dir. Dundee Cement Co. (Mich.); chmn. bd. Holly Hill Lumber Co. (S.C.); v.p. fin., dir. Stewart Sandwiches, Inc. (Va.). Mem. adv. com. Norfolk city council, 1966-71. Trustee, vice chmn., mem. exec. com. Va. Wesleyan Coll.; trustee, v.p. Randolph-Macon Acad.; bd. dirs. Coll. William and Mary Law Sch., Norfolk Mcpl. Hosp.; chmn. bd. Va. Cultural Found.; trustee Coll. William and Mary; bd. dirs. Union Mission, Am. Heart Assn.; chmn. bd. trustees local Methodist Ch. Served to capt. USMC, 1952-54. Named Outstanding Young Man of City, Norfolk Jr. C. of C., 1958. Mem. Va. State Bar (chmn. judiciary com.), Nat. Assn. Coll. and U. Attys., Va. Trial Lawyers Assn. (v.p.), Tau Kappa Alpha. Clubs: Masons, Shriners, Kiwanis (dir., pres. Norfolk), Harbor, Norfolk Yacht and Country. Home: 3199 Adam Keeling Rd Great Neck Point Virginia Beach VA 23454 Office: Suite 1240 Va Nat Bank Bldg Norfolk VA 23510

BOYD, RONALD LEE, absorbent clay processing mgr.; b. Paris, Tenn., Oct. 21, 1946; s. Luther Leon and Jewel Estelle (Dowdy) B.; student U. Tenn., Martin, 1969; m. Glenda Gayle Douglas, Feb. 24, 1968; 1 son, Russell Wayne. With Lowe's Inc., 1969—, packaging and shipping mgr., 1972-75, plant mgr., Paris, 1975—. Clubs: Rotary, Elks. Address: Lowe's Inc Box 819 Paris TN 38242

BOYD, SPENCER WALLACE, cons. elec. engr.; b. Atlanta, Oct. 14, 1904; s. Warren N. and Emma L. (Garrett) B.; B.S. in Elec. Engring., Ga. Inst. Tech., 1926; m. Verdery Rosenbusch, Oct. 25, 1930; children—Spencer Wallace, George V., Verdery D. Test engr. Gen. Electric Co., Schenectady, 1926-27; cons. engr. Newcomb & Boyd Co., Atlanta, 1928—. Mem. City of Atlanta Bldg. Code Com., 1946. Served to lt. comdr. USN, 1943-45. Registered profl. engr., Ga., N.C., S.C., Ala., Tenn., Ky. Fellow Am. Soc. Heating, Refrigeration and Air Conditioning Engrs. (life); mem. IEEE (life). Presbyterian. Clubs: Capital City, Atlanta Yacht, Commerce. Home: 2690 Habersham Rd NW Atlanta GA 30305 Office: One Northside 75 Suite 200 Alpha Bldg Atlanta GA 30318

BOYD, THOMAS, univ. adminstr.; b. Rocky Mount, N.C., Dec. 27, 1946; s. William and Henrietta (Bynum) B.; B.S., N.C. A&T U., 1969; M.B.A., U. Bridgeport, 1973. Opns. mgmt. trainee AVCO-Lycoming, Stratford, Conn., 1969-71, performance measurement control specialist, 1971-73; programmer analyst PPG Industries Inc., Pitts., 1976; asst. prof. N.C. A&T State U., Greensboro, 1973-77, budget officer, 1978—; material planner specialist Western Electric Co., Greensboro, 1977-78; pvt. mgmt. cons., Greensboro, 1976—. Vol., United Way, 1977-78; bd. dirs. N.C. Fellows Program, 1976—. Mem. Nat. Assn. Coll. and Univ. Bus. Officers, N.C. A&T State U. Alumni Assn. (v.p. 1977-79), NAACP, Omega Psi Phi. Democrat. Baptist. Club: Masons. Home: 412-K E Montcastle Dr Greensboro NC 27406 Office: 312 N Dudley St Greensboro NC 27411

BOYD, WAYMON LEWIS, pipeline constrn. co. exec.; b. nr. Port Lavaca, Tex., Sept. 2, 1933; s. Arbie Lewis and Ruby (Elswick) B.; grad. pub. high sch.; m. Ann Fisher, July 8, 1956; children—Wayne Allen, Randy Lynn. With King Fisher Marine Service, Inc., Port Lavaca, 1956—, pipeline foreman, 1958-67, v.p. constrn., 1967—; pres. Bafco, Inc., Port Lavaca, 1971—. Leader 4-H Club, Port Lavaca, 1969—. Served with AUS, 1954-56. Mem. Calhoun County C. of C. (dir. 1977). Home: 2304 Larry St Port Lavaca TX 77979 Office: PO Box 108 Port Lavaca TX 77979

BOYDSTON, CAROL ANN, advt. agency exec.; b. Mt. Clemons, Mich., Dec. 21, 1939; d. Cecil James and Barbara Helen (Edwards) Colwell; student Fla. State U., 1957-59, Jacksonville Jr. Coll., 1966-67; m. William Cliff Boydston, June 13, 1959; children—Susie Cliff, Cynthia Ann, David Alan, Christopher William. Mgr. Alhambra Dinner Theater, Jacksonville, Fla., 1972; communications technician Seaboard Coastline R.R., Jacksonville, 1973-74; right-of-way technician Dept. Transp., Tallahassee, 1974-75; mgr. Fla. office of Fla. Bar Review, Tallahassee, 1975-76; account. exec. Pruitt, Davis & Cuneo Advt., Tallahassee, 1976-77; pres. Boydston Advt. & Creative Services, Inc., Tallahassee, 1977—. Mem. Mayor's Adv. Com., Tallahassee, 1977. Mem. Am. Advt. Fedn. (state legis. liaison, 1978—, numerous Addy awards 1977—), Tallahassee Advt. Fedn. (pres. 1978-79, membership chmn. 1977-78, dir. 1978-79), Fla. Public Relations Assn. Democrat. Presbyterian. Home: 2022 Greenwood Dr Tallahassee FL 32303 Office: 211 Delta Ct Tallahassee FL 32303

BOYDSTUN, JACKSON BENJAMIN, architect; b. Natchitoches, La., Feb. 5, 1908; s. Benjamin Kendall and Eunice Augusta (Hargis) B.; grad. high sch.; m. Bernice Erline Hill, Apr. 19, 1930; children—Nelwyn (Mrs. Dan W. Poole, Jr.), Betty Sue (Mrs. Stuart Carpenter), Jackson Benjamin, David H. Constrn. supervising engr. constrn. firms, 1936-46; archtl. asso. Barron, Hienberg & Brocato, architects, Alexandria, La., 1947-50; self-employed as architect, Natchitoches, 1960—; dir., chmn. bd. J. B. Boydstun & Assos., Inc. Mem. Constrn. Legislative Council La., 1970-72; trustee First Meth. Ch., Natchitoches. Served with AUS, World War II. Mem. AIA, Am. Legion (comdr. 1945-46), La. Architects Assn. Democrat. Mason (Shriner). Prin. archtl. works include Marthaville Phys. Edn. and Auditorium, St. Matthew High Sch., Elementary Sch. Library, Allen High Sch. Classroom Bldg., Goldonna High Sch. Auditorium and Classroom Bldg., Robeline Phys. Edn. and Classroom Bldg., Conv. Center-Hodges Garden, ch. bldg. for Ch. of Nazarene, Natchitoches, La., apt. bldg. and two shopping centers, Natchitoches. Author: (novel) On the Wings of Truth. Home and Office: 410 Stephens Ave Natchitoches LA 71457

BOYENGA, PAUL DOUGLAS, elec. products co. exec.; b. Ashton, Ill., Feb. 27, 1936; s. A.M. and Julia (Sweiter) B.; student pub. schs., Ashton; m. Josie Talton, Feb. 26, 1971; children—Jerome I., Mark L. Field engr. Gilfillan Bros. Inc., Turkey, Spain, Germany, 1960-64; mktg. mgr. ITT Gilfillan, Europe, 1964-67, Washington, 1967-69; dir. field mktg. Emerson Electric Co., St. Louis, 1969-70, Washington, 1970-76; group v.p. mktg. Gould Inc., Washington, 1976-79; pres. DSP Inc., 1979—. Served in USAF, 1956-60. Mem. Am. Def. Preparedness Assn. (pres. Washington chpt.), Nat. Security Indsl. Assn., Navy League, Air Force Assn., Assn. U.S. Army, U.S. Coast Guard Aux. Republican. Home: 2691 Treehouse Dr Woodbridge VA 22192 Office: 1111 Army Navy Dr Arlington VA 22202

BOYER, JOHN CLOYD, plastic co. exec.; b. Littlefield, Tex., Oct. 20, 1929; s. Robert McKinley and Viola Ann (Aucutt) B.; grad. high sch.; m. Imogene Alsup, June 3, 1949; children—John Larry, Patricia Boyer Neal. Pres., Thermo Plastics Corp., Ft. Worth, 1964—. Mem. Soc. Plastic Engrs. Republican. Methodist. Home: 3501 N Beach St Fort Worth TX 76111 Office: 4101 Hahn St Haltom City TX 76117

BOYER, LESTER LEROY, JR., archtl. engr., educator; b. Hanover, Pa., Apr. 6, 1937; s. Lester Leroy and Ruth Florence (Kessler) B.; B. Archtl. Engring., Pa. State U., 1960, M.S., 1964; Ph.D. in Architecture, U. Calif. at Berkeley, 1976; m. Patricia Barbara Hayes, Dec. 28, 1958; children—Douglas Lester, Blane Edward, Darla Mae. Instr. archtl. engring. Pa. State U., 1960-64; research engr. Armstrong Cork Co., Lancaster, Pa., 1964-68; sr. cons. acoustics and noise control Bolt Beranek and Newman, Inc., Cambridge, Mass., 1968-70; asso. prof. architecture Okla. State U., Stillwater, 1970-78, prof., 1979—; cons. acoustics and environ. comfort, 1970—. Active Will Rogers council Boy Scouts Am.; pres. Zion Luth. Ch., 1977-78. Named Explorer Adviser of Year, Lancaster (Pa.) Council, 1967. Registered profl. engr., Pa., Mass., Okla. Am. Iron and Steel Inst. grantee, 1972. Mem. Acoustical Soc. Am., Illuminating Engring. Soc., ASHRAE, Human Factors Soc., Nat. Soc. Profl. Engrs. (course dir. 1964—), Am. Soc. Engring. Edn., Sigma Tau, Scarab, Tau Beta Pi, Alpha Rho Chi, Theta Xi. Democrat. Lutheran. Editor: Design for Environmental Hazards (Dept. of Defense), 1973. Author articles on comfort, acoustics, lighting, thermal control, to tech. jours. Home: Meadowbrook 8 Route #1 Stillwater OK 74074 Office: School of Architecture Oklahoma State University Stillwater OK 74074

BOYETT, GEORGE EDWARD, JR., furniture mfg. co. exec.; b. Niles, Mich., Jan. 2, 1947; s. George Edward and Eva Louise B.; student Internat. Corrs. Schs.; m. Linda M. Phillips, June 30, 1965; children—Kenneth, Shelley. Raw material coordinator Samsonite Corp., Denver, 1965-74; landscape cons., Denver, 1974-76; prodn. supr. Kroehler Mfg. Co., Dallas, 1976-77; prodn. control and quality control mgr. Okla. Furniture Co., Guthrie, Okla., 1977-79, plant supt. night shift, 1979—. Active youth sports. Mem. Am. Prodn. and Inventory Control Soc. Democrat. Baptist. Clubs: Masons, Moose (Guthrie). Home: 702 E Mansur Guthrie OK 73044 Office: Okla Furniture Co 304 E College St Guthrie OK 73044

BOYKIN, GERALDINE MONSEES, social worker, health center adminstr.; b. Columbus, Ga., Feb. 17, 1919; d. John F.W. and Irma Rebecca (Redmond) M.; B.S.H.E., U. Ga., 1940; m. Roscoe R. Boykin, June 7, 1941; children—Linda Boykin Marshall, Bonnie Boykin Cooper, John W. Home supr. Farm Security Adminstrn., Millen and Staterboro, Ga., 1940-41; tchr. sci. public schs., Thomson, Ga., 1941-42; tchr. health public schs., Nashville, 1942-44; social worker Dept. Public Welfare, Rockingham, N.C., 1957-58; social worker Meml. Med. Center, Savannah, Ga., 1961-67, dir. social services, 1967-78, dir. eligibility screening, 1978—; mem. Sr. Citizens Bd., Mental Health Bd., Protective Services Family and Children's Adv. Bd.; mem. Ga. Gov.'s Adv. Council on Mental Health and Retardation. Mem. Ga. Soc. Hosp. Social Workers (Disting. Service award 1977, award name changed to Geraldine Boykin award 1979), Ga. Hosp. Assn., Am. Soc. Hosp. Social Work Dirs., Am. Hosp. Assn., Ga. Gerontology Assn., Ga. Conf. Social Welfare, Nat. Assn. Social Workers, Nat. Council on Aging, Nat. Rehab. Assn., Nat. Mental Health Assn., Ga. Mental Health Assn., Mental Health Assn. Savannah (pres. 1976-78). Lutheran. Club: Soroptimist (pres. local club 1972-74) (Savannah). Home: 231 Dyches Dr Savannah GA 31406 Office: Meml Med Center PO Box 23089 Savannah GA 31403

BOYKIN, JOHN CLAUDE, business exec.; b. Crandall, Tex., Jan. 24, 1935; s. Allie C. and Agnes (Henery) B.; student St. Benedicts Coll., 1953-54, Arlington State Coll., 1954-56, So. Meth. U., 1956-57, 63-66; m. Beverley Jo Stillings, Sept. 4, 1954; children—Shean, Kevin, Shannon, Colleen. Mem. engring. staff Gen. Electric Co., Dallas, 1954-56; football coach Jesuit High Sch., Dallas, 1956-57; with Space Corp., Garland, 1957-58; with Geotech, Teledyne Co., Garland, 1959-70, mgr. marketing of instruments, 1966-70; pres., dir. Calcite Crystal Corp., 1966-67; v.p., mem. bd. Rare Minerals Corp., 1967; v.p. Copper-Pitt-Copper Corp., 1967; pres., chief exec. officer Technitron Internat., Inc., Dallas, 1970-72; exec. v.p., dir. Electronic Flo-Meters, Inc., Garland, Tex., 1974-78, pres., 1978—; pres. CSC Instruments, Houston, 1977—. Athletic dir. Dallas-Ft. Worth Diocesan Catholic Youth Orgn., 1967-68; mem. adult bd. dirs. Cath. Youth Orgn., 1967-68; pres. alumni Jesuit Coll. Prep., 1975-76, bd. advisers, 1975-76, bd. dirs., 1976. Mem. Petroleum Electric Supply Assn., Am. Geophys. Union, Internat. Union Geodesy and Geophysics, Instrument Soc. Am., Dallas Geophys. Soc., Tex. Gas Assn. Democrat. Roman Catholic. KC. Home: 2420 El Cerrito Dr Dallas TX 75228 Office: 1621 Jupiter Rd Garland TX 75042

BOYLAN, HUNTER REED, coll. adminstr.; b. Cleve., Apr. 3, 1945; s. Chester Reed and Dorothy Virginia (Hunter) B.; B.A., Miami U., Oxford, Ohio, 1967; M.Ed., Temple U., 1970; Ph.D. (NEA fellow), Bowling Green U., 1977; m. Gwendolyn Anne Workman, Aug. 17, 1968; 1 dau., Heather Marie. Asst. dir. residence, adviser to fraternities Temple U., 1967-69; hall dir., research asst. Bowling Green State U., 1969-71, acad. adviser, 1971-72, asst. dir. for acad. services and research, student devel. program, 1972-73, acting dir. modular achievement center, 1973, coordinator acad. devel. and instrn., 1973-78, coordinator acad. intervention, 1978-80; dir. Kellogg Inst. Developmental Edn., Appalachian State U., 1980—; cons. instructional devel. Served with USAF, 1967. Recipient Outstanding adviser award Temple U., 1969, Outstanding Hall Dir. award Bowling Green State U., 1971; Office Edn. grantee, 1975; Bowling Green State U. grantee, 1976. Mem. Nat. Assn. Student Personnel Adminstrs., Am. Personnel, Guidance Assn. (dir. Commn. XVI), Am. Coll. Personnel Assn., Ohi Developmental Edn. Assn., Sigma Nu. Presbyterian. Contbr. articles on instructional devel. and individualized learning systems to profl. jours.; editor Am. Coll. Personnel Assn. Commn. Newsletter, 1977—; editorial bd. Jour. Devel. and Remedial Edn. Office: Center for Developmental Edn Appalachian State U Boone NC 28608

BOYLE, STEPHEN WILLIAM, data processing co. exec.; b. Coffeyville, Kans., Mar. 4, 1946; s. Author William and Lois Nadine (Malicoat) B.; student Coffeyville Coll., 1963-64, Grayson County Coll., 1966-67; m. Ladine Ann Barnett, Oct. 28, 1978; children—Mark, Lorie, John, Randy, Danny. Programmer/analyst Sinclair Pipeline Co., Independence, Kans., 1969; mgr. terminal systems Tulsatronics Computing Corp., Tulsa, 1969-70; v.p. info. services Ednl. Devel. Corp., Tulsa, 1970-77; owner Boyle & Assos., data processing cons., Tulsa, 1977—. Treas. Union Sch. PTA, Tulsa, 1974-75, 76-77, pres., 1975-76; coach Girls Softball, Tulsa, 1974, Boys Baseball, 1975-79, Boys Soccer, 1976; active Boy Scouts Am. Served in USAF, 1964-68. Mem. Data Processing Mgmt. Assn. Republican. Presbyterian. Home: 1520 W Nashville Broken Arrow OK 74012 Office: PO Box 35752 Tulsa OK 74145

BOYLES, HARLAN EDWARD, SR., state ofcl.; b. Vale, N.C., May 6, 1929; s. Curtis E. and Kate (Scronce) B.; student U. Ga., 1947-48; B.S., U. N.C., 1951; m. Frances Wilder, Feb. 29, 1928; children—Lynn, Harlan Edward. Auditor, N.C. Dept. Revenue, 1951-56; exec. sec. N.C. Tax Rev. Bd., 1956-60; dep. treas. State of N.C., Raleigh, 1960-77, state treas., 1977—, sec. N.C. Local Govt. Commn., 1960-77. Mem. municipal securities rulemaking bd. U.S. Securities and Exchange Commn., 1975-77. C.P.A., N.C. Mem. N.C. Assn. C.P.A.'s. Presbyn. (elder). Rotarian. Home: 1924 Fairfield Dr Raleigh NC 27608 Office: Albemarle Bldg Raleigh NC 27611

BOYLES, JAMES EDWARD, indsl. engr.; b. Houston, Aug. 15, 1929; s. Lester Tucker and Hazel Viola (Montgomery) B.; B.S., Tex. A. and M. U., 1951; m. Martha Faye Brannen, Oct. 20, 1957; children—William, Johnna. Home builder, Houston, 1955; indsl. engr. Reed Roller Bit Co., 1956-60; indsl. engr. W.K.M. Valve div. A.C.F. Industries, Houston, 1960-66, head indsl. engring. dept., 1966-69, mgr. indsl. engring., 1970-73, mgr. mfg. engring., 1973-74; mgr. indsl. engring. and prodn. planning and control, casting facility TRW/Mission Mfg. Co., Houston, 1974-76, mgr. mfg. casting facility, 1976-77, prodn. supt., 1977-79, plant mgr. casting facility, 1979-80; mgr. indsl. engring. Fluid Control div. F.M.C. Corp., Houston, 1980—; lectr. U. Houston. Served from lt. to capt. USAF, 1952-54, now lt. col. Res. Registered profl. engr., Tex. Mem. Am. Inst. Indsl. Engrs. (pres.; nat. gen. conf. chmn. 1969), Res. Officers Assn., Air Force Assn., Armed Forces Communications and Electronics Assn., Tex. Soc. Profl. Engrs., Nat. Mgmt. Assn. Home: 2923 Shadowdale St Houston TX 77043 Office: PO Box 40402 Houston TX 77040

BRABBAN, MAYLENE MAGERS, counselor; b. Baldwyn, Miss., Jan. 2, 1922; d. Herbert Moses and Minnie Mae (Burns) Magers; A.B., Marshall U., 1944, M.A., 1960, postgrad., 1962-73; m. Ralph J. Brabban, Nov. 22, 1944; children—Linda Gay, Ralph J. II. Tchr. sci. Marmet (W.Va.) Jr. High Sch., 1944-45; tchr. Village Elementary Sch., South Charleston, W.Va., 1953-54; tchr. sci. St. Albans (W.Va.) Jr. High Sch., 1954-62, counselor, 1954-62, counselor high sch., 1964—. Sec., Lupus Found. Am., Kanawha Valley, 1977—; trustee Alderson-Broaddus Coll., 1980—. Mem. Kanawha County Classroom Tchrs. Assn., W.Va. Edn. Assn., NEA, Kanawha County, W.Va., Am. personnel and guidance assns., Nat., W.Va. (sec. 1975-76) sch. counselors assns., Delta Kappa Gamma. Baptist. Club: Order Eastern Star. Democrat. Home: 684 Forest Circle South Charleston WV 25303 Office: Kanawha Terr at Hudson St St Albans WV 25177

BRABSTON, BRYAN WILLIS, JR., chem. co. exec.; b. Vicksburg, Miss., July 20, 1933; s. Bryan Willis and Sarah Natalie (Newell) B.; B.S. in C.E., Miss. State U., 1959; m. Helen Joy Banks, Aug. 27, 1955; children—Barbara Ellen, Bryan Willis III, Maura Agnes. With Exxon Chem. Co., Baton Rouge, 1959—, sect. supr., 1969-74, sr. sect. supr., 1974—. Mem. Zachary (La.) City Council, 1971-78; dir. Lane Meml. Hosp., 1979—. Served with U.S. Army, 1952-55. Recipient Outstanding City Award La. Mcpl. Assn., 1973. Mem. ASCE. Democrat. Episcopalian. Clubs: Fennwood Hills Country, Camelot. Home: 6718 Fennwood Dr Zachary LA 70791 Office: PO Box 241 Baton Rouge LA 70821

BRACE, RICHARD CULVER, air force officer; b. Randolph, N.Y., Aug. 13, 1934; s. Eddy J. and Gretchen L. Brace; B.A., U. Buffalo, 1957; B.S. in Elec. Engring., Armed Forces Inst. Tech., 1964; M.S. in Systems Engring., U. So. Calif., 1967; Ed.D., Lehigh U., 1974; grad. Air Force Command and Staff Coll., Air Force War Coll.; m. Jeanette L. Warning, Apr. 19, 1958; children—Richard R., Kimberly J., Randall R., Kristen L. Commd. 2d lt. U.S. Air Force, 1958, advanced through grades to lt. col., 1975; ground environment Air Def. officer NATO, 6th Allied Tactical Air Force, Turkey, 1968-70; asst. prof. aerospace studies Lehigh U., Bethlehem, Pa., 1970-74; cmdr. 3270th Tech. Tng. Group, Lackland AFB, Tex., 1974-76; dean academics Def. Lang. Inst., Lackland AFB, 1976—. Hon. bd. dirs. ARC, 1976-79. Mem. Tchrs. of English to Speakers of Other Langs., Air Force Assn., Ret. Officers Assn., Mensa, Phi Delta Kappa, Theta Chi. Club: Masons. Home: 5639 Sir Gareth St San Antonio TX 78218 Office: Def Lang Inst Lackland AFB TX 78236

BRACEWELL, THOMAS FREDERICK, clin. psychologist, pastoral counselor; b. Columbus, Ga., Aug. 19, 1944; s. Walter Jefferson and Frances Ruth (Pritchett) B.; B.A., Troy State U., 1973; M.A., George Washington U., 1978; children—Paul Wesley, Jeremy Sean. News dir. WDHN-TV, Dothan, Ala., 1969-72; prodn. mgr., radio sports dir. WTVY-TV and Radio, Dothan, 1972-75; sports dir. WJHG-TV, Panama City, Fla., 1977-78; Houston County dir. Wiregrass Comprehensive Mental Health Center, Dothan, 1978—; cons. psychologist United Meth. Ch. Family Counseling Center, 1976—; asso. pastor singles ministry First Presbyterian Ch., 1979—. Served with U.S. Army, 1963-67, 75-77. Decorated Bronze Star medal, Air medal with V, Army Commendation medal. Mem. Assn. U.S. Army, Jr. C. of C., Am. Personnel and Guidance Assn., Am. Assn. Religious Counselors, Armed Forces Chaplains Assn., Res. Officers Assn. of U.S. Army. Methodist. Clubs: Olympia Spa/Country, Elks. Address: Fieldcrest Apts Apt 109 Dothan AL 36301

BRACHMAN, LEON HAROLD, chem. mfg. co. exec.; b. Marietta, Ohio, July 21, 1920; s. Elias and Ella Leah (Beren) B.; B.S., Harvard, 1942; m. Fay Rosenthal, Aug. 10, 1941; children—Deborah Ray, Ellen Bari, Marshall Aaron, Wendy Susan. Teaching fellow Harvard, 1942-44; radar engr. Consol. Vultee Aircraft, Ft. Worth, 1944-46; sec.-treas. Marco Chem. Co., Ft. Worth, 1946-60, pres., 1960—; pres. Petrochems. Co., Inc., Ft. Worth, 1968-79; dir. Chattem Drug and Chem. Co., Chattanooga, Elba Oil Corp., Ft. Worth. Pres., Casa Manana Mus. Theater and Sch., 1973-76; treas. All Saints Episcopal Hosp., 1965—; pres. Ft. Worth Symphony Orch. Assn., 1978—. Mem. Am. Chem. Soc., Am. Oil Chemists Soc., TAPPI, Soaring Soc. Am. Republican. Jewish religion. Mem. B'nai B'rith. Club: Fort Worth. Home: 3720 Autumn Dr Fort Worth TX 76109 Office: 2626 B W Freeway Suite 107 Fort Worth TX 76102

BRACHMAN, MARSHALL AARON, computer co. exec.; b. Fort Worth, July 6, 1950; s. Leon Harold and Fay (Rosenthal) B.; student Brandeis U., 1968-70; B.B.A., U. Tex., Austin, 1973, M.B.A., 1975; m. Karen Lee Bishop, May 21, 1972; children—Amy Lynn, Ellis Andrew. Cost analyst Gen. Dynamics Corp, Fort Worth, 1976-77; v.p. Huileries Caraibes S.A., Fort Worth, 1973-76; exec. v.p. Marco Chem. Co., 1977—; pres. Computerized Bus. Systems, Inc., 1978—. Pres. Dan Danciger Jewish Community Center, Fort Worth, 1977—; v.p. Fort Worth Hebrew Day Sch., 1976—; treas. Ft. Worth Art Assn., 1977—; regional chmn., exec. com. nat. young leadership cabinet

United Jewish Appeal, 1977—; mem. allocation subcom., speakers bur. United Way Fort Worth 1977—; bd. dirs. Jewish Nat. Fund, Fort Worth. Recipient Young Leadership award Jewish Fedn. Ft. Worth, 1977. Mem. Air Force Assn., Nat. Mgmt. Assn., Phi Kappa Phi. Republican. Jewish. Clubs: B'nai B'rith, Fort Worth, Colonial Country, Forum (treas.) (Fort Worth); Petionville (Port-au-Prince, Haiti). Home: 2000 Pembroke Dr Fort Worth TX 76110 Office: PO Box 8 Fort Worth TX 76101

BRACKIN, HENRY BRYAN, JR., psychiatrist; b. Raleigh, N.C., Nov. 3, 1924; s. Henry Bryan and Rachel Pauline (Luker) B.; B.A., Vanderbilt U., 1944, M.D., 1947; m. Eva Drucilla Cato, Oct. 15, 1948; children—Henry Bryan III, John Curtis and Robert Lewis (twins). Intern surgery St. Thomas Hosp., Nashville, 1947-48; resident in surgery Nashville Gen. Hosp., 1948-49; resident in psychiatry Perry Point VA Hosp., 1950, U.S. Naval Hosp., Oakland, Calif., 1951-52, Hosp. U. Pa., 1952-54; practice medicine specializing in psychiatry, Nashville, 1954—; mem. staff Vanderbilt U. Hosp., Park View Hosp., Bapt. Hosp., St. Thomas Hosp., Met. Gen. Hosp.; asst. clin. prof. psychiatry Vanderbilt U., Nashville. Mem. Met. Bd. Hosp., 1963-75; trustee Park View Hosp., 1973—. Served with USNR, 1943-45; lt. M.C., USNR, 1950-52. Diplomate Am. Bd. Psychiatry and Neurology. Fellow Am. Psychiat. Assn. (pres. Tenn. dist. br. 1970, pres. Middle Tenn. chpt. 1976, trustee 1977-81), So. Psychiat. Assn.; mem. AMA, Tenn. Med. Assn., Nashville Acad. Medicine. Phi Beta Kappa, Kappa Alpha, Alpha Kappa Kappa. Republican. Methodist. Club: Richland Country. Home: 616 Timber Ln Nashville TN 37215 Office: 2012 West End Ave Nashville TN 37203

BRACKMEYER, SHIRLEY ANN, nurse; b. Bryan, Tex., Aug. 9, 1938; d. E.J. and Rosa Lee (Rhudy) Malone; R.N., Brackenridge Hosp., Austin, Tex., 1959; A.A., Blinn Jr. Coll., 1958; m. William L. Brackmeyer, May 23, 1959 (dec. Nov. 1978); 1 son, William Kevin. Staff nurse Harlingen (Tex.) State Chest Hosp., 1959-62, asst. dir, 1962-64, dir. nurses, 1964—. Mem. adv. bd. Tex. Southmost Coll. Cert. in CPR. Mem. Tex. Nurses Assn. (past sec.-treas.), Tex. Public Employees Assn. (past pres.), Nurses Council (v.p., dir.), Am. Nurses Assn. Democrat. Mem. Christian Ch. Home: 2007 E Washington St Harlingen TX 78550 Office: PO Box 592 Harlingen TX 78550

BRADBURY, ROSANNE BROWN, speech pathologist; b. Norfolk, Va., Jan. 10, 1944; d. Melvin Dillard and Mattye Marie (Cox) Brown; B.S., U. Ga., 1968, M.Ed., 1971; m. Luke Lindley Bradbury, Dec. 13, 1974; children—Steve, Amy. Speech pathologist Barrow County Schs., Winder, Ga., 1968-69, Madison County schs., Danielsville, Ga., 1969-70, Hall County Schs., Gainesville, Ga., 1971-72, Hope Haven Sch. for Retarded Children, Athens, Ga., 1972-73, Buford (Ga.) City Schs., 1973-75, Duval County Bd. Pub. Instrn., Jacksonville, Fla., 1975-79, Orange County Public Schs., Orlando, Fla., 1979—. Sallie Maude Jones scholar, U. Ga., 1966-68; U.S. Public Health grad. fellow, 1970-71. Mem. Am. Speech and Hearing Assn. (cert. of clin. competence), Duval Tchrs. United (faculty rep. 1977-79), Delta Zeta, Zeta Phi Eta, Kappa Delta Pi, Phi Kappa Phi. Mem. Disciples of Christ. Clubs: Order Eastern Star, U.S.S. Yosemite Wives (pres. 1977), U.S.S. Sarsfield Wives (pres. 1975). Home: 606 David St Winter Springs FL 32707 Office: 800 S Delaney Ave Orlando FL 32801

BRADDOCK, GROVER HOLMES, ins. co. exec.; b. Forsyth, Ga., July 23, 1925; s. George Holmes and Maud Marie (Abernathy) B.; A.B. in Journalism, U. Miami (Fla.), 1949, M.Ed. in Human Relations, 1953; m. Ruth Gene Fenner, Nov. 18, 1945; children—George Holmes II, James A., Rebecca G., Robert A. Asst. dir. admissions U. Miami, 1950-51, mgr. student union, 1951-54; mgr. Miami Shores (Fla.) Country Club, 1954-55; agt. Mass. Mut. Life Ins. Co., Miami, Fla., 1955-57, agt., asst. gen. agt., 1957-61; gen. agt. Midland Mut. Life Ins. Co., Miami, 1961-67, agt., 1967-75; resident mgr. Pilot Life Ins. Co., 1975—; dir. Capital Bank, Miami. Mem. Dade County (Fla.) Sch. bd., 1962—, chmn., 1969-71, 72-74, vice-chmn., 1971-72; mgr. baseball Khoury League, 1959-71; coach Am. Legion Baseball, 1974; pres. Miami Touchdown Club, 1963-64. Bd. dirs. Wesley Found., U. Miami. Served with AUS, 1944-46. Recipient Human Relations award Am. Jewish Com., 1970, Whitney M. Young Meml. Humanitarian award Greater Miami Urban League, 1971, Sch. Bell award for Outstanding Citizen of Fla., Fla. Edn. Assn., 1971. Mem. Nat. Sch. Bds. Assn. (chmn. council big city bds. 1972-73), Nat. Assn. Life Underwriters, Am. Soc. C.L.U.'s, Million Dollar Round Table, Sigma Alpha Epsilon. Democrat. Methodist. Home: 7801 SW 134th St Miami FL 33156 Office: PO Box 561134 Miami FL 33156

BRADEN, JEFFREY STEPHEN, systems corp. exec.; b. Belleville, Ill., Nov. 10, 1952; s. Jerome Curtis and Regina Ellen (Soller) B.; B.S. in Elec. Engring. (Univ. Scholar, 1970), Miss. State U., 1975. Pres., chief design engr., Digital and Analog Systems, Inc., Pensacola, Fla., 1975—; chmn. bd. Digital and Analog Systems; pres. Braden-Ham Industries, Inc.; v.p. System Software Internat., Inc.; cons. engr. C. R. Bender Co. Designer, developer electronic systems and circuits; research in solar energy. Home: 600 Scenic Hwy Apt 203 Pensacola FL 32503 Office: 2181 N Guillemard St Pensacola FL 32503

BRADEN, WALDO W., educator; b. Ottumwa, Iowa, Mar. 7, 1911; s. Wilbern C. and Stella (Warder) B.; B.A., Penn Coll., 1932; M.A., U. Iowa, 1938, Ph.D., 1942; m. Dana Crane, Aug. 18, 1938; 1 dau., Helen Dana. Tchr., Fremont (Iowa) High Sch., 1933-35, Mt. Pleasant High Sch., 1935-38; tchr. speech Iowa Wesleyan Coll., 1938-40, dean of students, 1942-43, 45-46; asso. prof. speech La. State U., Baton Rouge, U., 1946-51, prof., 1951-73, Boyd prof., 1973—, chmn., 1958-76. Vis. prof. Washington U., summer 1952, Mich. State U., summer 1953, U. Pacific, summer 1965, Calif. State Coll., Fullerton, summer 1969. Served with AUS, 1943-45. Mem. Speech Assn. Am. (council 1954—, exec. sec. 1954-57, pres. 1962), So. Speech Assn. (pres. 1969-70), Pi Kappa Delta, Delta Sigma Rho-Tau Kappa Alpha, Omicron Delta Kappa. Methodist. Author: (with Gray) Public Speaking, 1951, rev. 1963; (with Brandenburg) Oral Decision-Making, 1955; (with Gehring) Speech Practices, 1958; Public Speaking: Essentials, 1966; (with Pennybacker) Broadcasting and the Public Interest, 1969; (with Thonssen and Baird) Speech Criticism, 1970. Editor: Speech Methods and Resources, 1961; revised, 1972; The Speech Teacher, 1967-69; Oratory in the Old South, 1970; Representative American Speeches, 1971-79; Oratory in the New South, 1979. Contbr. articles speech, hist. jours. Home: 535 Ursuline Dr Baton Rouge LA 70808

BRADEN, WILLIAM BERNARD, JR., chem. engr.; b. Waco, Tex., Nov. 22, 1937; s. William Bernard and Lydia (Wokaty) B.; B.A., Rice U., 1959, B.S. in Chem. Engring., 1960. Chem. engr. chems. research Texaco Inc., Port Arthur, Tex., 1959, chem. engr. fuels research, 1960, chem. engr. oil prodn. research, Bellaire, Tex., 1963-74, asst. to mgmt. dept. petrochems., N.Y.C., 1974, sr. project engr. dept. petrochems., Houston, 1975-79, sr. staff asso. dept. petrochems., 1979—; mem. tech. adv. com. Petroleum Recovery Research Inst. Alta. (Can.), 1972-74. Served with C.E., AUS, 1961-63; Germany. Mem. Soc. Petroleum Engrs. Patentee in field. Home: 2229 W Alabama Houston TX 77098 Office: PO Box 430 Bellaire TX 77401

BRADFORD, M(ELVIN) E(USTACE ADONIS), educator; b. Fort Worth, May 8, 1934; s. E.A. and Ruby M. (Hunter) B.; B.A., U. Okla., 1955, M.A., 1956; Ph.D., Vanderbilt U., 1968; m. Marie Jones, 1955; 1 son, Douglas. Instr. in English, U.S. Naval Acad., 1957-59, Vanderbilt U., 1959-62; asso. prof. English, chmn. dept. Hardin-Simmons U., 1962-64; asst. prof. English, Northwestern Coll. of La., 1964-67; faculty English, U. Dallas, 1967—, prof. English, Am. studies, 1978—. State Democratic committeeman for Dallas County, Tex., 1972-74; chmn. Am. party, Dallas County, 1968-70. Served to lt. (j.g.) USNR, 1956-59. Nat. Endowment for Humanities summer fellow, 1970, sr. research fellow, spring 1977. Mem. MLA Am., S. Central MLA, Southwestern Am. Lit. Assn. (pres. 1974—), Philadelphia Soc., SCV, Mil. Order Stars and Bars (Tex. comdr. 1979). Baptist. Co-editor: The Southern Tradition at Bay (Richard Weaver), 1968; editor The Form Discovered - Esseys in the Achievement of Andrew Lytle, 1973, Arator (John Taylor of Carolina), 1977; author: A Better Guide than Reason: Studies in the American Revolution, 1979; asso. editor Modern Age, 1978—. Home: 1106 S Edwards Ct Irving TX 75062 Office: Box 457 Dept English U Dallas Sta Irving TX 75061

BRADFORD, MICHAEL EDWARD, ribbon co. exec.; b. Newark, Sept. 14, 1944; s. David and Ruth (Chekofsky) B.; student Newark Coll. Engring., 1962-64, Upsala Coll., summer 1967, Seton Hall U., summer 1968; B.A. in Bus., Bloomfield (N.J.) Coll., 1968; postgrad. mktg. Rutgers U., 1966-69, U. Calif., Los Angeles, 1970, internat. mktg. U. Tex., Dallas, 1977—. Chem. lab. technician E.I. duPont Co., Newark, 1964-68; field sales rep. Gubelman Chart div. Nashua Corp., Compton, Calif., 1968-71; product mgr. Univ. Computing Co., Bus. Supplies div., Dallas, 1971-72; spl. products rep. Control Data Corp. (merged with Univ. Computing Co. 1972), Dallas, 1972-73; gen. mgr. Fine Line Ribbon Co., Inc., Ennis, Tex., 1973, v.p., 1974-76, pres., 1976—, also dir. Scoutmaster S. Bay council Boy Scouts Am., 1969, Circle Ten council Explorer Scouts, 1976; founder 1st coednl. Sea Scout Troop, 1969-70. Mem. U.S. Power Squadron. Home: 15725 Mapleview Circle Dallas TX 75248 Office: 2405 N Preston St Ennis TX 75119

BRADFORD, THOMAS LEONARD (BRAD), III, ins. agy. exec.; b. Los Angeles, Apr. 5, 1945; s. Joseph Reichman and Tommie Bradford Reichman; student bus. adminstrn. U. Okla., 1963-65, U. Tex., Austin, 1965-68, also So. Meth. U.; m. Charlotte Ann McGuire, Apr. 10, 1976. Exec. v.p. Mgmt. Jets Internat., Dallas, 1968-71; mgr. adminstrn., sec. LTV Jet Fleet Corp., Dallas, 1971-74; pres. ANCO-Dallas, property and casualty ins. agy., Dallas, 1976-78, also dir.; pres. Bradford & Assos., Inc., 1978—. Mem. Ind. Ins. Agts. Dallas, Ind. Ins. Agts. Tex., Ind. Ins. Agts. Am., Profl. Ins. Agts. Dallas, Profl. Ins. Agts. Tex., Nat. Bus. Aircraft Assn. Clubs: Brook Hollow Golf, Dallas Gun, T Bar M Racquet. Home: 9221 Sunnybrook Ln Dallas TX 75220 Office: 2930 Turtle Creek Plaza Dallas TX 75219

BRADFORD, TUTT S., publisher; b. Columbia, S.C., Apr. 30, 1917; s. Tutt S. and Zula (Bowen) B.; student Wofford Coll., 1934; m. Elizabeth Hendley, June 30, 1941; children—Nancy, Debbie. Pub. Cleve. Daily Banner, 1948-51; asst. to pres. Gen. Newspapers, 1951; pub. Bristol (Va.) Herald Courier, 1951-55, Maryville (Tenn.) Alcoa Daily Times, 1955—. Pres. Blount County Indsl. Devel. Bd., 1970-72. Mem. bd. Audit Bur. Circulations, 1967-72. Bd. dirs. Maryville Coll., 1974-79. Served with AUS, 1943-45; ETO. Recipient Distinguished Service award Bristol Jr. C. of C., 1952, Maryville-Alcoa Jr. C. of C., 1958, 73. Mem. So. Newspaper Pubs. Assn. (dir. 1968-70), Blount County C. of C. (pres. 1960), Sigma Delta Chi. Kiwanian (pres. Maryville 1967). Home: 1901 Westwood St W Maryville TN 37801 Office: 307 E Harper St Maryville TN 37801

BRADFORD, WILLIAM EDWARD, petroleum mfg. co. exec.; b. Dallas, Jan. 8, 1935; B.S., Centenary Coll., 1958; m. Jo Deane Browning, Aug. 18, 1955; children—William B., Kathleen A., Jon E. Sales, Hycalog, Inc., 1958-61; gen. partner, v.p., Analytical Logging, Inc., Oklahoma City, 1961-70; product mgr. data systems Swaco div. Dresser Industries, Houston, 1970-72, area mgr. Mid-Continent area, Oilfield Products Group, Houston, 1972-75, ops. mgr., Europe, Africa, and Middle East, 1975-76, v.p. U.S. and Can. ops. Security div., 1976-78, pres. div., 1978-79, pres. group, 1979—. Mem. bd. equalization, Tomball Sch. Dist., Houston, 1979—. Mem. Soc. Petroleum Engrs., AIME, Am. Assn. Petroleum Geologists, Petroleum Equipment Suppliers Assn., AAAS, Assn. Oilwell Drilling Contractors, Internat. Petroleum Assn., Tex. Mid-Continent Oil and Gas Assn. Republican. Presbyterian. Clubs: Petroleum of Houston, Champions Country. Home: 15218 Rainhollow Dr Houston TX 77070 Office: Dresser Industries Inc 601 Jefferson St Suite 3408 Houston TX 77002

BRADLEY, BRAD, rancher, bus. exec.; b. Del Rio, Tex., Jan. 20, 1947; s. Robert Bruce and Johnnie B. (Reynolds) B.; student S.W. Tex. Jr. Coll., Uvalde, 1966-67, Sul Ross State U., Alpine, 1967-68; m. Jo Marie Stark, June 5, 1968; children—Heath Lee, Chanc Ray. Credit officer Farm Credit Banks Tex., Llano; wagon boss W. Tex. Boys Ranch, San Angelo. Mem. Llano C. of C. (dir.), Hill Country Livestock Raisers Assn., Independent Cattleman's Assn., Hill Country Pork Producers Assn., Tex. Pork Producers Assn. Office: PO Box 398 Llano TX 78643

BRADLEY, JOHN DANIEL, III, lawyer, state legislator; b. Atlanta, May 26, 1946; s. John Daniel and Dorothy Page (Jones) B.; B.A., The Citadel, 1968; J.D., U. S.C., 1971; m. Beverly Rae Cox, Aug. 15, 1970; children—John Daniel, David Charles, Michael Edwin. Admitted to S.C. bar, 1971, U.S. Ct. Appeals bar, 1974, U.S. Dist. Ct., 1974; practice law, Charleston, S.C., 1972—; mem. S.C. Ho. of Reps., 1974—. Vice-chmn. Charleston County Republican Party., 1974-75. Served with U.S. Army, 1971. Mem. S.C. Bar Assn., Charleston County Bar Assn., Am. Bar Assn. So. Baptist. Clubs: Optimist, Sons Confederate Veterans, Washington Light Infantry. Office: PO Box 10814 North Charleston SC 29411

BRADLEY, MARTHA WASHINGTON NUTTER (MRS. GEORGE WASHINGTON BRADLEY), educator; b. East St. Louis, Ill.; d. Cecil Grafton and Mabel (Hunt) Nutter; B.S. in Edn., U. Va., 1951, M.Ed., 1960; diplome de la langue Francaise, Alliance Francaise, Paris, 1958; Ph.D. (NDEA fellow), Syracuse U., 1967; m. George Washington Bradley, Feb. 20, 1960. Tchr. elementary sch., East St. Louis, 1951-53, Long Beach, Calif., 1953-54, U.S. Army Dependent Schs., Europe, 1954-59, 60-61; reading cons. pub. schs., Fredericksburg, Va., 1961-62; instr. U. Va. Sch. Gen. Studies, 1962-63; asst. prof. edn. East Tenn. State U., Johnson City, 1967-70, asso. prof. edn., 1970-76, prof., 1976—, bd. dirs. Christian Student Fellowship, 1978—; faculty adviser Student NEA, 1968-71. Trustee George and Martha Washington Bradley Found., Johnson City; bd. dirs. Sister City Town Affiliation, Johnson City, 1971—, 2d v.p., 1972-76; mem. Robert Young Cabin com. City of Johnson City, 1975—; vol. service nat. appointee VA, 1973—; bd. dirs. Appalachian Dist. Council Girl Scouts U.S., 1978-79. Mem. Nat. (life), Tenn., East Tenn. (pres. East Tenn. State U. unit 1977-78) edn. assns., Conf. English Edn. evaluator com. to evaluate documents 1968—), Nat. Council Tchrs. English, D.A.R. (chmn. service for vet. patients Tenn. 1971-74, 76-77, chpt. vice regent 1974-77, regent 1977-80, pres. Tenn. regents' club 1978-79), Daus. Am. Colonists (rec. sec. 1973-76, 1st vice regent 1976-79), Internat. Reading Assn. (upper East Tenn. council research chmn. 1969-70), Bus. and Profl. Womens Club (chmn. nominating com. Tenn. fedn. 1972-73; dist. dir. 1974-75, finance chmn. 1976-77, treas. 1977-78, local chmn. personal devel. com. 1969-70, local pres. 1971-72, 2d v.p. 1972-73; local chmn. by-laws com. 1973-75, chmn. young careerist com. 1975-76, legis. com. 1976-79), Am. Ednl. Research Assn., Nat. Soc. Study of Edn., AAUW (publicity chmn. 1968-70, corp. del. 1976-79, br. pres. 1976-80), Unaka Rock and Mineral Soc. (pres. 1969-70), Friends of the Reece Mus. (mem. edn. com. 1973-75), Assn. for Preservation Tenn. Antiquities, Mensa (East Tenn. proctor 1975-79), Phi Kappa Phi (life, charter pres East Tenn. State U. chpt. 1970-72), Kappa Delta Pi (life, counselor Zeta Iota chpt. 1968—), Delta Kappa Gamma (1st v.p. 1972-74), Phi Delta Kappa (life). Mem. Christian Ch. (pres. Women's council 1970-72, edn. com. 1970—, dir. Bible sch. 1971-73). Clubs: Wednesday Morning Music (yearbook com. 1971-74, chmn. Music Week com 1974—), East Tenn. State U. Women's Faculty (co-chmn. book com. 1969-70), v.p. 1971-72, pres. 1972-73). Office: Box 20110A East Tenn State U Johnson City TN 37601

BRADLEY, MATTHEW HENRY, III, cardiologist; b. Akron, Ohio, Aug. 7, 1926; s. Matthew Henry and Margot (Williams) B.; B.S., Kent State U., 1947; M.D., Ohio State U., 1951; m. Marian Young, July 1, 1950; children—Sandra Baden, Matthew, Kathleen, Laura. Intern, U.S. Naval Hosp., Pensacola, Fla., 1951-52; resident VA Hosp., Milw., 1955-58, U.S. Naval Sch. Aviation Medicine, Pensacola, 1952-53; practice medicine specializing in internal medicine and cardiology, Miami, 1958—; pres. med. staff, dir. Miami Heart Inst., also v.p., trustee; FAA med. examiner. Served with USNR, 1951-55. Fellow A.C.P., Am. Coll. Cardiology, Am. Coll. Chest Physicians; mem. AMA, Fla. Med. Assn., Dade County Med. Assn., Flying Physicians Assn., Vol. Physicians Vietnam. Contbr. articles to profl. jours. Home: 184 Park Dr Bal Harbour FL 33154 Office: 1160 Kane Concourse Miami Beach FL 33154

BRADLEY, NOLEN EUGENE, JR., coll. ofcl.; b. Memphis, Nov. 29, 1925; s. Nolen Eugene and Anice Pearl (Luther) B.; B.S., Memphis State U., 1951, M.A., 1952; Ed.D., U. Tenn., 1966; m. Eloise Mullins, Jan. 7, 1947; children—Sharon (Mrs. Brabson), Diana (Mrs. Wiley M. Rutledge), Nolen Eugene III, David Lee. Instr. polit. sci. Memphis State U., 1951-52; tchr. English, Messick High Sch., Memphis, 1952-56; asst. dean admissions Memphis State U., 1956-64; dir. State Agy. for Title I, Higher Edn. Act 1965, Div. Continuing Edn., U. Tenn., 1966-70; dean instrn. Vol. State Community Coll., Gallatin, Tenn., 1970-78, tutor, cons., 1979—. Served with AUS, 1944-46. Mem. Am. Assn. Sch. Adminstrs., Tenn. Adult Edn. Assn., Tenn. Edn. Assn., Omicron Delta Kappa, Phi Delta Epsilon, Phi Delta Kappa, Phi Kappa Phi. Baptist (deacon 1966—). Lion. Home: 907 Harris Dr Gallatin TN 37066

BRADLEY, RONALD JAMES, educator; b. Enniskillen, No. Ireland, Feb. 17, 1943; s. Samuel John and Mary Elizabeth (Irvine) B.; came to U.S., 1967; B.Sc., Queens U., Belfast, No. Ireland, 1965; Ph.D., U. Edinburgh (Scotland), 1967; m. Doris Maud Brown, Mar. 5, 1966; children—Nicola May, Jason Samuel. Postdoctoral fellow in psychiatry Yale, 1967-69; sr. research asso. in psychology U. N.Mex., Albuquerque, 1970-71; asst. prof. psychiatry U. Ala. Med. Sch., Birmingham, 1972-74 asso. prof., 1974-76, prof., 1976—, dir. Neuroscis. Program, 1974-77. Mem. AAAS, Biophys. Soc., Soc. Biol. Psychiatry (A.E. Bennett award 1967). Methodist. Club: Altadena Valley Country (Birmingham). Co-editor Internat. Rev. of Neurobiology, 1975—. Contbr. articles to profl. jours. Home: 2644 Butte Woods Dr Birmingham AL 35243

BRADSHAW, CHARLES MARSHALL, physician; b. Springtown, Tex., Dec. 14, 1938; s. Joseph Kenton and Iris (Carter) B.; B.A., Tex. Tech U., 1961; M.D., U. Tex., 1965; m. Judy Cole, Nov. 22, 1966; children—Damon Robert, Lloyd Kenton. Intern, Meth. Hosp. of Dallas; gen. practice medicine, Crosbyton, Tex., 1966-69, Lubbock, Tex., 1969-70; resident dept. neurology, psychiatry U. Tex. Med. Br., Galveston, 1970-72; pvt. practice medicine specializing in psychiatry, neurology and clin. EEG, Fort Worth, 1970—; pres., co-dir. EEG Services, Inc., 1975—; mem. staffs various hosps.; guest lectr. neuropharmacology Tex. Coll. Osteo. Medicine, Fort Worth. Served with USAF. Diplomate Am. Bd. Psychiatry and Neurology. Mem. AMA, Am. Med. EEG Assn., Tex. Med. Assn., So. EEG Soc., Tarrant County Med. Soc., Central Neuropsychiat. Assn. Club Fort Worth Internists. Office: Suite 722 1550 W Rosedale St Fort Worth TX 76104

BRADSHAW, EARL RATHBUN, public relations exec.; b. Geneva, Ill., June 8, 1923; s. Hugh and Irene L. (Rathbun) B.; student various univ. courses, 1947-69; m. Loretta Cox, Mar. 5, 1955; 1 dau. by previous marriage, Katherine Ann. Editor, Aetna Ins. Co., Park Ridge, Ill., 1949; supr. coding and keypunch dept. Nat. Fire Ins. Co., Chgo., 1950-53; news dir. WMRO Radio, Elgin, Ill., 1960-62, KKAM, Pueblo, Colo., 1963-66, KTLN, Denver, 1967-69; dir. public relations Barry Coll., Miami Fla., 1978—; public relations cons., Glen Ellyn, Ill., 1954-59; bus. editor Sun Sentinel, Ft. Lauderdale, Fla., 1971-79. Served as radio officer U.S. Maritime Service, 1942-45. Author numerous by-line stories, Colo. Springs Sun, 1970-71, Sun Sentinel of Ft. Lauderdale, 1971-78. Home: 609 S State Rd 7 Margate FL 33068 Office: 11300 NE 2nd Ave Miami FL 33161

BRADSHAW, HERMAN LUTHER, JR., coll. adminstr.; b. Rome, Ga., July 22, 1942 s. Herman L. and Daisy M. (Waters) B.; B.A., Shorter Coll., 1964; M.A. in Teaching, Emory U., 1969, postgrad., 1972-73; postgrad. W. Ga. Coll., 1973-74; m. Carol Braden, Dec. 18, 1966; 1 son, Jason Todd. Tchr. math. Pepperell High Sch., Lindale, Ga., 1964-73; resource tchr. for gifted Floyd County Schs., Rome, Ga., 1973-74; registrar, dir. admissions Floyd Jr. Coll., Rome, 1974—; real estate agt. Smith Real Estate, Rome, 1977. Mem. advisory bd. Coosa Valley Area Mental Health Center. Mem. Am., Ga. assns. coll. registrars and admissions officers, Nat., Ga. assns. student fin. aid adminstrs., Ga. Council Tchrs. Math. (pres. 1974), Rome Bd. Realtors. Democrat. Baptist. Home: Route 2 Old Rockmart Rd Silver Creek GA 30173 Office: PO Box 1864 Rome GA 30161

BRADSHAW, LILLIAN MOORE, librarian; b. Hagerstown, Md., Jan. 10, 1915; d. Harry M. and Mabel E. (Kretzer) Moore; B.A., Western Md. Coll. 1937; B.L.S., Drexel U., 1938, D.H.L. (hon.), 1978; m. William Theodore Bradshaw, May 19, 1946. Asst. adult circulation dept. Utica (N.Y.) Pub. Library 1938-41, asst. head, 1941-43; adult librarian Enoch Pratt Free Library, Balt., 1943-44, asst. coordinator work with young adults, 1944-46; br. librarian Dallas Pub. Library, 1946-47, readers adviser, 1947-52, head dept. circulation, 1952-55, coordinator work with adults, 1955-58, asst. dir., 1958-62, dir., 1962—; del. White House Conf. on Library and Info. Services, Washington, 1979; mem. adv. group on libraries Library of Congress, 1976-77. Conferee, asst. task force leader Goals for Dallas, 1966-69, chmn. citizen info. and participation com., 1976-77, trustee, exec. com., sec., 1977—, treas., 1979—; mem. So. Methodist U. Bd. Publs., 1970-78, vice chmn. goals achievement com. for continuing edn., 1971, chmn., 1972; mem. Com. to Plan Future of Goals for Dallas, 1973-74; mem. Gov.'s Commn. on Status of Women, 1970-72; mem. U.S. Com. for Am. Library in Paris, 1970-71; mem. friendship mission to France, 1970; mem. Nat. Reading Council, Washington, 1970-73;

adv. com. Leadership Dallas, 1978-80, curriculum com., 1978-79. Bd. dirs. Hoblitzelle Found., 1971—; trustee Lamplighter Sch., 1974—, Dallas Am. Revolution Bicentennial Com., 1976. Named Tex. Librarian of Year, 1961; recipient Distinguished Alumnus award Drexel Library Sch., 1970, Titche's Arete award, 1970; Distinguished Service award Tex. Library Assn., 1975. Mem. ALA (pres. adult services div. 1967-68, mem. council 1968-69, pres. 1970-71, trustee Freedom To Read Found. 1969-71), Internat. Fedn. Library Assns. (rep. to revise standards for pub. libraries 1970-72), Tex. Library Assn. (pres. 1964-65, chmn. pub. libraries div. 1955-56, chmn. awards com. 1973-74, 79-80, Library Systems Act adv. bd. 1974-77), Public Library Assn. (legis. com. 1979-81), Central Bus. Dist. Assn. (quality of life com. 1977—), League Women Voters, Beta Phi Mu. Club: Zonta of Dallas I (pres. 1976-77). Home: 6318 E Lovers Ln Dallas TX 75214 Office: 1954 Commerce St Dallas TX 75201

BRADSHAW, ROBERT JOHN, JR., mfg. exec.; b. Chattanooga, May 29, 1921; s. Robert John and Hattie Pauline (Copeland) B.; B.S., U. of Chattanooga, 1950. Instr. engring. U. of Chattanooga 1950-51; design engr. Indsl. Research Inst., Chattanooga, 1951-56; indsl. cons. Rudisill Foundry, Sylacauga, Ala., 1956-57; owner, operator Mech. Industries, Chattanooga 1957—; v.p., sec. Energy Converters, Inc., Chattanooga 1973—, also dir.; insp. Underwriters Labs, Chattanooga 1952-68. Deacon 1st Baptist Ch., Chattanooga 1964—; bd. dirs., sec.-treas. Chattanooga-Hamilton County Law Enforcement Commn., 1961-71; dir. Chattanooga-Hamilton County CD, 1964-75. Served with AUS 1942-46; ETO. Decorated 2 battle stars. Fellow Tenn. Acad. of Sci.; hon. mem. Chattanooga Engrs. Club, Order of the Engr.; mem. Am. Phys. Soc., Internat. Solar Energy Soc., Blue Key, Alpha Phi Omega (life, mem. nat. exec. bd. 1954-60), Lambda Chi Alpha. Baptist. Clubs: Rotary, Am. Legion, K.P. Home: 2209 Vance Ave Chattanooga TN 37404 Office: 2501 N Orchard Knob PO Box 5245 Chattanooga TN 37406

BRADY, DALE EUGENE, computer scientist; b. Anaheim, Calif., Jan. 27, 1943; s. Eugene Dewitt and Lillie (Matthews) B.; B.S. in Computer Sci., Mo. Sch. Mines, 1966; M.S. in Indsl. Engring., U. Tenn., 1972; postgrad. Vanderbilt U., 1973; m. Phyllis Fern Tracy, Sept. 7, 1963; children—Tracy Lynn, Matthew Allen, Sharon Maeve. Systems analyst E.I. duPont, Old Hickory, Tenn., 1966-69; mgr. systems and programming, Met. Govt., Nashville, 1969-73; asst. dir. data base adminstrn. State of Tenn., Nashville, 1973-78, EDP security officer, 1979—; participant intergovtl. teaching. Founder, pres. El Bus, 1973—; dir. Church Bus Ministry, deacon, youth leader, Temple Baptist Ch., 1970—. Mem. IEEE, Am. Inst. Indsl. Engrs., Assn. Systems Mgmt., Computer Security Inst. Democrat. Research in cooperation with U.S. Geog. Survey on computer based mapping to engring. specifications, 1973. Home: 1248 Neelys Bend Rd Madison TN 37115 Office: 10th Floor One Commerce Pl Nashville TN 37219

BRADY, SHEILA ANN, mfg. co. exec.; b. Connersville, Ind., Dec. 11, 1935; d. Francis Elmer and Mary (Underwood) B.; student Ind. U., 1954-55; B.S., Ball State U., 1959; postgrad. Rutgers U., 1959-60. Tchr. art N. Plainfield (N.J.) High Sch., 1959-65, Bound Brook (N.J.) High Sch., 1965-66, Warren Twp. Sch. System, Warrenville, N.J., 1966-68; head dept. art Wardlaw Pvt. Boys Sch., Edison, N.J., 1968-72; asst. to pres. F.E. Brady Products, Clearwater, Fla., 1972-73, pres., chmn. bd., treas., dir., 1973—; treas. Brady Air Controls, Muncie, Ind., 1973, pres., 1975—, also dir., chmn. bd., 1976—; miniature horse breeder, Tarpon Springs, Fla. Mem. Am. Mgmt. Assn., Fla. C. of C., Nat. Water Well Assn., Water Systems Council, Water Suppliers Council. Club: Innisbrook Resort and Country (Tarpon Springs, Fla.). Paintings displayed in pvt. galleries. Home: 1331 Appaloosa Rd Tarpon Springs FL 3358 Office: PO Box 5304 Clearwater FL 33518

BRAENDER, BROOKS HENRY DAVID, III (PEN NAME BROOKS BRENDER), writer, photographer, lectr.; b. Spring Lake, N.J., Aug. 1, 1941; s. Henry Braender and Maria Jeanne Christina (de Cendoya) Braender McCahill; student Daytona Beach (Fla.) Jr. Coll., 1961-62, Mary Karl Vocat. Sch., 1966-68. Pres., Tom McCahill Reports, Inc., Ormond Beach, Fla., 1975—; writer monthly mail column Mechanix Illustrated, 1974—; part-time salesman for Mid-Fla. (East Coast) Aston Martin Lagonda, New Rochelle, N.Y.; substitute tchr. English and power mechanics Volusia County Jr.-Sr. High Sch.; automobile tester. Spl. lay minister of the eucharist Roman Catholic Ch.; high sch. tchr. religion; ambassador of Holy Rosary of Pilgrim Virgin. Served with USNR, 1961-64. Mem. Am. Def. Preparedness Assn., Nat. Rifle Assn. (life), Fla. Sheriffs Assn. (life), Ducks Unltd. Clubs: Rolls Royce Owners, Southeastern R.R. Owners, Internat. Motor Press Assn. Home: 373 S Halifax Dr Box 2206 Ormond Beach FL 32074 Office: Box 2206 373 S Halifax Dr Ormond Beach FL 32074

BRAGG, RAY EDWARD, bus. services co. exec.; b. Waynesboro, Va., May 18, 1950; s. Raymond Wallace and Mary Francis B.; A.B.A., Blue Ridge Community Coll., 1969; m. Mary Christine Bragg, Dec. 13, 1979. Auditor, area mgr., dist. supr. Walden Inventory Service, Columbus, Ohio, 1969-73; store mgr. BeLo Markets, Norfolk, Va., 1973; dist. supr., sr. v.p. Accurate Inventory Service Co., Virginia Beach, Va., 1973—. Mem. Am. Mgmt. Assn. Democrat. Presbyterian. Home: 5001 Mosby Rd Virginia Beach VA 23455 Office: 4991 Cleveland St Virginia Beach VA 23462

BRAID, MALCOLM ROSS, biologist, educator; b. Balt., June 7, 1947; s. Robert Bruce and Elva Dawn (Outland) B.; B.S., U. Montevallo, Ala., 1969; M.S., Auburn U., Ala., 1974, Ph.D., 1977; m. Linda Lee Grimm, Jan. 22, 1972. Research biologist ecology sect. U.S. Army, Edgewood Arsenal, Md., 1972; grad. research asst. biology Auburn (Ala.) U., 1972-77; asst. prof. biology U. Montevallo (Ala.), 1977—; research asst. Nat. Marine Fisheries Service, 1973-77. Served with Chem. Corp, U.S. Army, 1970-72. Mem. Ala. Conservancy, Ala. Acad. Sci., Auburn Alumni Assn., Bass Anglers Sportmen's Soc., Sigma Xi, Beta Beta Beta, Gamma Sigma Delta. Republican. Baptist. Home: 89 Comanche St Montevallo AL 35115

BRAID, MICHAEL HERBERT, indsl. engr.; b. Charleston, S.C., May 29, 1947; s. Herbert Cordes and Grace Margaret (Duc) B.; B.S. in Indsl. Engring., Ga. Inst. Tech., 1970; M.B.A., Fla. Internat. U., 1973; m. Linda Ford Story, Mar. 30, 1971. Planning engr. Fla. Power & Light Co., Sarasota, 1970-72, systems analyst, Miami, 1972, sr. mgmt. analyst, 1972-77, coordinator comml., indsl. energy conservation, 1978—; adj. instr. Miami-Dade Community Coll. Registered profl. engr., Fla. Mem. Nat. Soc. Profl. Engrs., Fla. Engring. Soc., Am. Inst. Indsl. Engrs. (v.p. programs 1979-80, v.p. chpt. affairs 1978-79; recipient Internat. Community Affairs award 1979), Assn. Energy Engrs. Home: 10475 SW 78th St Miami FL 33173 Office: PO Box 529100 Miami FL 33152

BRAINARD, JAYNE DAWSON (MRS. ERNEST SCOTT BRAINARD), club woman; b. Amarillo, Tex., Nov. 1; d. Bill Cross and Evelyn (McLane) Dawson; A.B., Oklahoma City U., 1950; m. Ernest Scott Brainard, Nov. 26, 1950; children—Sydney Jane, Bill Dawson. Guardian Camp Fire Assn., 1960-65; vol. N.W. Tex. Hosp. Aux., 1960-63; state chmn. Am. heritage D.A.R., 1963-67, vice regent chpt., 1963-66, regent, 1966-68, state historian Tex. soc., 1967-70, state chmn. marshalls Tex. soc., 1967-70, 73-76, nat. vice chmn. marshal com., 1969-79, Tex. rec. sec., 1970-73, vice regent Tex. soc., 1976-79, state regent Tex. Soc., 1979-82, mem. state organizing com., 1967-70, mem. by-law revision com., 1974-75, Tex. conf. chmn., 1975, 78, nat. vice chmn. motion picture commn., 1971-74, Tex. chmn. State Regents Project, 1973-76, mem. state speakers staff, 1973—, pres. chpt. Regents' club, 1974, state vice chmn. nat. def., 1973-76, state mem. fin. com., pres. Nat. Vice Regents Club, 1977-78, mem. Nat. Officers' Club, 1979—, area rep. nat. speakers staff, 1977—, organizing pres. Children of Am. Revolution, 1963-66, state chmn.; organizing regent Daus. Am. Colonists, 1972-75, state chmn. radio-TV com., 1975—; bd. pres. A.A.U.W., 1963-65, mem. state library com., 1967-69; sec.-treas. group League of Democratic Women, 1964; pres. Amarillo Rep. Women's Club, 1968, v.p., 1972, pres., 1973; pres. Panhandle Geol. Soc. Aux., 1959; pres. Speaking of Living Study Club, 1962-63, 77-78, sec., 1974-75; pres. Starlighters Dance Club, 1963-64; bd. dirs., chmn. pub. relations Amarillo Little Theater; chmn. leaders assn. Amarillo Camp Fire Council, Inc., 1964-69, 75—, pres. bd. dirs., 1977-78; mem. steering com. Nat. Library Week, Amarillo, 1964-68; bd. dirs. Amarillo Fine Arts Council, 1966-68, Amarillo Heart Assn., 1972-73; pres. Amarillo Little Theatre, 1968-69; mem. Revitalize Amarillo Com. Recipient medal of appreciation S.A.R., 1975. Profl. registered parliamentarian. Mem. U.D.C., United Daus. of 1812 (regent 1979), Nat. Assn. Parliamentarians, Daus. Colonial Wars, Internat. Platform Assn., Amarillo Art Alliance, Nat. Soc. So. Dames. Editor: Texas Society D.A.R. Cookbook, 1972; Texas Daughters Revolutionary Ancestors, 4 vols., 1975. Home: 2119 S Lipscomb St Amarillo TX 79109 Office: Box 1101 Amarillo TX 79105

BRAINARD, JEFFREY MICHAEL, mfg. co. exec.; b. Peekskill, N.Y., Oct. 3, 1954; s. Alexander Nash and Suzanne (Alderman) B.; B.A., St. Lawrence U., 1976. Sales rep. Gillette Co., Buffalo, 1976-77, account mgr., Washington, 1977-78, key account mgr., 1978-79, dist. tng. supr., 1979-80, dist. supr., Dallas, 1980—. Little League coach, Cheektowaga, N.Y., 1977. Recipient William DiSantis award Interfrat. Council, 1976; named Dist. Salesman of the Yr., Gillette Co., 1978. Mem. St. Lawrence U. Alumni Assn., Outward Bound Alumni, Beta Theta Pi. Republican. Roman Catholic. Clubs: Am. Yacht, Key Service. Home: 9513 Blake St T9 Fairfax VA 22031 Office: 6350 LBJ Freeway 223 Dallas TX 75240

BRAM, MARJORIE, orch. condr., author, performer, educator; b. Phila., June 28, 1919; d. Israel and Frances (Silver) Bram; B.S., Temple U., 1940; postgrad. Juillard Sch. Music, summer 1945, Tanglewood, 1950; M.A., Columbia, 1951; certificate in conducting Internat. Acad. of Mozarteum, Salzburg, Austria, 1957. Instr. instrumental music South Orange (N.J.) Maplewood Sch. Dist., 1942-74; condr. South Orange Community Orch., 1949-69. Founder, musical dir. Friends Early Music (N.J.), 1964-74, Fla. Friends of Early Music, 1975—; 1st desk viola N.J. Symphony Orch., 1945-48; 1st chair viola Am. Symphony Orch. League Workshop for Condrs. and Composers, Asilomar, Calif., 1959, condr., Sewanee, Tenn., 1959. Adv. mem. M.B.L.S. Mem. Am. Symphony Orch. League, Internat. Soc. Music Educators, Music Educators Nat. Conf., Am. String Tchrs. Assn. (chamber music coach Pa. chpt. 1962-63), N.E.A., Brit. Gamba Soc., Viola da Gamba Soc. Am. (dir. 1966—, pres. 1970-72), N.J. Music Educators Assn. (hon. life mem.), Dolmetsch Found. Author instrumental program Sound Dimensions for New Players, 1971. Contbr. articles to profl. publs. Home: 3611 22d Ave W Bradenton FL 33505 Office: Music Dept Manatee Jr Coll Bradenton FL 33505

BRAME, DURWARD BELMONT, gen. engr.; b. Sherman, Tex., Apr. 20, 1914; s. James Richard and Mary Ann (Fields) B.; student U. Tulsa, 1935-36, So. Meth. U., 1941-42, various service schs.; m. Doris June Hibbard, Sept. 1, 1967; children by previous marriage—Dulcie Anne (Mrs. Lyndell N. Sumner), Nancy Lynn (Mrs. Richard D. Landes). Inspection and quality engr. USAF, 1941-57; aerospace engr. NASA, 1961-67; developer quality systems, mgr. quality programs for Apollo/Saturn hardware Dept. of Def., Tulsa, 1967-71; mgr. indsl. resources services div. Def. Contract Adminstrn., Dallas, 1971-75; mgr. petroleum exploration services Autodyne, Arlington, Tex., 1975—. Mem. Stone Ridge Home Owners Assn., Irving Fire Fighters, Internat. Circus Fund Underprivileged Children, Tarrant County Police Benefit Assn. Mem. Am. Soc. Metals, Am. Soc. Quality Control. Republican. Presbyn. Mason (32 deg., Shriner). Author: Quality Assurance Familiarization Manual, 1943; Instruction Manual Midwestern Procurement District Functions, 1944. Home and office: 2510 Richmond Dr Arlington TX 76014

BRAME, MYRNA MARSHALL, counselor; b. Louisville, Dec. 5, 1949; d. LeRoy Vance and Qumiller (Pearson) Marshall; B.S., Western Ky. U., 1971, M.A., 1973; m. Lawrence Ray Brame, Sept. 16, 1970; 1 dau., Monique Desha. Tchr., West End Cath. Elem. Sch., Louisville, 1972-74; counselor Bowling Green (Ky.) Area Vocat. Sch. and Mammoth Cave Job Corps, summer 1973; chief counselor, project rebound NAACP, Louisville, 1974-76; employment specialist, creative employment project YWCA, 1976-78; asst. dir. Female Offender Resource Center, 1978, dir., 1978—; sr. counselor Kentuckiana Metrovesity Ednl. Opportunity Center, 1978—. Mem. Louisville and Jefferson County Female Offender Task Force, 1978—; sec. Louisville Male High Sch. P.T.A., 1979—. Mem. NAACP, Am. Personnel and Guidance Assn., Am. Correctional Assn., Ky. Council on Crime and Delinquency, Ky. Council for the Blind, Alpha Kappa Alpha. Baptist. Home: 1516 Olive Louisville KY 40210 Office: 1018 S 7th St Louisville KY 40203

BRAMLETT, EDWIN CHANDLER, JR., hosp. adminstr.; b. Mobile, Ala., Sept. 13, 1942; B.S., U. Ala., 1964; M. Hosp. Adminstrn., U. Fla., 1966. Adminstrv. resident Shands Teaching Hosp. and Clinics, Gainesville, Fla., 1966; adminstrv. resident Baptist Hosp., Pensacola, Fla., 1966, adminstrv. asst., 1966; cons. USPHS Region 4, Atlanta, 1966-68; v.p. No. Miss. Med. Center, Tupelo, 1968-72; adminstr. Jackson County Hosp., Scottsboro, Ala., 1972-76; v.p. Mobile (Ala.) Infirmary, 1976—. Fellow Am. Coll. Hosp. Adminstrs.; mem. Am., Ala. (dir. 1976) hosp. assns., S.E. Hosp. Conf. Office: Louiselle St Box 2144 Mobile AL 36601

BRAMLETT, LARRY WILLIAM, real estate salvage co. exec.; b. Athens, Ga., Dec. 30, 1943; s. D.B. and Cammie Lois (Doster) B.; B.S. in Agrl. Engring., U. Ga., 1970; children—Lisa LuAnne, Jon Dewel. With Ga. Power Co., Hoschton, 1970—, indsl. sales engr. (real estate), 1972—, named Outstanding Salesman of Year, 1971; pres. I-85 Corp., 1972—; v.p. I-85 Investments, 1972—, I-85 Properties, 1972—; pres. Madison Timber Co., 1975—. Served with USNR, 1962-66. Mem. Am. Soc. Agrl. Engrs., Am. Motorcycle Assn., U. Ga. Alumni Assn. Baptist. Address: Rural Route 1 Box 404 Oakwood GA 30566

BRAMMER, KARL EDMUND, purchasing agt.; b. Lake Charles, La., Sept. 5, 1920; s. Peter Bernhardt and Edith Martha (Bailey) B.; ed. Vincent Bus. Coll., Sowela Tech. Sch., Lake Charles, U. Fla., Gainesville; m. Janice Normand, Dec. 19, 1945; children—Cynthia Hughes, Martha, Peter, Elizabeth. Purchasing agt. Olin Mathieson Chem. Corp., Lake Charles, 1945-57; purchasing agt., traffic mgr. Ormet Corp., Burnside, La., 1957—. Served with AUS, 1938-45. Cert. purchasing mgr. Lutheran. Home: Route 5 Box 96 Gonzales LA 70737 Office: PO Box 15 Burnside LA 70738

BRAMS, EUGENE ARNOLD, soil scientist; b. Milw., July 6, 1923; s. Morris and Bell B.; B.S., U. Wis., 1948, M.S., 1949; Ph.D., U. Fla., 1967; m. Patricia Craig, Aug. 13, 1950; children—Jolie, Craig, Matthew, Andrew. Instr. soils U. Miami (Fla.), 1950-52; owner, mgr. Gen. Chem. Co., Miami, 1953-64; asst. prof. U. Ill., Urbana, 1967-71, also Njala U Coll., Sierra Leone, 1967-71; asso. prof. soils Prairie View (Tex.) A&M U., 1971—. Served with USN, 1943-46; PTO. Grantee USDA, NASA, AID. Mem. AAAS, Am. Soc. Agronomy, Internat. Soil Sci. Soc., Council Agr. Sci. and Tech. Sigma Xi. Democrat. Research: effect of large cities on soil pollution and quality of food chain, cropping systems in internat. agronomy. Home: 9718 Clanton St Houston TX 77080 Office: Coll Agr Prairie View A&M U Prairie View TX 77445

BRANCH, ALFRED LEE, JR., civil engr.; b. Houston, July 31, 1948; s. Alfred Lee and Mattie Mae (Pence) B.; student San Jacinto Jr. Coll., 1966-68, U. Houston, 1968-70; B.S. in Civil Engring., Tex. A. and M. U., 1971; M.S. in Civil Engring., U. Tex. at Arlington, 1978; m. Janice Lorene Barrett, Nov. 15, 1968; children—Lori Ann, Alfred Lee III, Matthew Parker, Amber Michelle. Civil engr. U.S. Army C.E., Ft. Worth, 1971—. Registered profl. engr., Tex. Mem. ASCE, Soc. Am. Mil. Engrs., Tau Beta Pi, Phi Kappa Phi, Chi Epsilon. Mem. Ch. of Christ. Home: 533 NW Mound St Burleson TX 76028 Office: US Army CE USAED Fort Worth TX 76102

BRANCH, CHARLES HERBERT, advt. agency exec.; b. Chgo., Mar. 30, 1926; s. Harold Francis and Margaret Cowenhoven (Brokaw) B.; B.A., U. Wis., Madison, 1949; m. Marguerite Ann Hendrix, June 24, 1950; children—Laura Hendrix, Steven Hendrix, Patricia Alison. Sunday feature writer Kansas City (Mo.) Star, 1944, 45; asst. editor Wis. Alumnus, Madison, 1947-49; mgr. publicity Abingdon Press, Nashville, 1949-53; copywriter, account exec. Noble-Dury & Assos., Inc., Nashville, 1953-56; copywriter Stockton-West-Burkhart Inc., Cin., 1956-58, Maurice Mullay Inc., Columbus, Ohio, 1958-60; copywriter, account exec. Greenhaw & Rush Inc., Memphis, 1961-72, v.p., 1971-72; founder, pres. Branch Advt. Inc., Memphis, 1972-73, v.p. John Malmo Advt. Inc. (merged with Branch Advt. Inc.), Memphis, 1973—; instr. advt. Memphis State U., 1964-67; lectr. Inst. Fin. Devel., 1966-67, Nat. Planned Giving Inst., Memphis, 1968—; area dir. campaign Radio Free Europe, 1965-73; lectr. Nat. Fund Raising Council, N.Y.C., 1970; humor columnist Memphis Press-Scimitar, 1971; area cons. pub. relations Muscular Dystrophy Assn., 1972-77; freelance writer. Bd. dirs. Josephine Lewis Sr. Citizens' Center; trustee Memphis and Shelby County Public Library and Info. Center, 1979—. Served to 1st lt. AC, AUS, 1944-45, AUS, 1950-52. Recipient Williams Jennings Bryan Polit. Sci. Writing award U. Wis., 1949. Mem. Memphis, Am. advt. fedns., Pub. Relations Soc. Am. (chpt. treas. 1973-74), Iron Cross Honor Soc., Sigma Delta Chi (Best News Story of Yr. award 1949, Outstanding Journalism Grad. 1949). Clubs: Delta, Petroleum (Memphis). Contbr. articles to popular mags. Home: 4526 Charleswood Rd Memphis TN 38117 Office: John Malmo Advt 1500 Commerce Title Bldg Memphis TN 38103

BRANCH, CHARLES WILLIAM, coll. pres.; b. Gaffney, S.C., Dec. 22, 1930; s. Amos Oren and Velma Louise (Kimbrell) B.; A.A., Spartanburg Jr. Coll., 1951; A.B., Wofford Coll., 1953; M.Ed., U. S.C., 1958; Ed.D., U. Ala., 1971; m. Barbara Jean Collins, July 8, 1951; children—Teresa Elaine Branch Matthews, Vicki Jean. Tchr., coach Gaffney (S.C.) High Sch., 1953-55, others, to 1960; asst. prin. Dreher High Sch., Columbia, S.C., 1960-63; asso. dir. Midland Tech. Edn. Center, Columbia, 1963-71; dir. career edn. Columbia City Schs., 1971-72; asst. exec. sec., commn. on colls. So. Assn. Colls., Atlanta, 1972-74; pres. Chattanooga State Tech. Community Coll., 1974—. Former trustee Erskine Coll.; bd. dirs. Chattanooga Conv. and Tourism Bur., Team Evaluation Center, S.E. Tenn. Area Health Edn. Council; former mem. Chattanooga-Hamilton County Planning Commn.; mem. allocations com. United Fund. Mem. Am. Vocat. Assn., Am. Mgmt. Assn., Tenn. Conf. Aerospace Edn., Tenn. Personnel and Guidance Assn., Tenn. Conf. Social Welfare, E. Tenn. Edn. Assn., Phi Delta Kappa, Phi Theta Kappa (named Disting. Alumni 1975). Baptist. Clubs: Kiwanis (Chattanooga); Masons. Home: Signal Mountain TN 37377

BRANCH, HARLLEE, JR., ret. public utility exec.; b. Atlanta, June 21, 1906; s. Harllee and Bernice (Simpson) B.; A.B., Davidson Coll., 1927, LL.D., 1962; LL.B., Emory U., 1931, LL.D., 1965; L.H.D., Howard Coll. (now Samford U.), 1965; m. Katherine Quintard Hunter, June 8, 1932; children—Harllee III, Katherine B. McKenzie, Barrington Heath, David Stuart. Reporter Atlanta Jour., 1929-31; admitted to Ga. bar, 1931; publicity dir., radio sta. WSB, 1930-32; lectr. Emory U., 1931-36, U. Ga. Evening Coll., 1929-34, Atlanta Law Sch., 1936-40; asso. firm Colquitt, MacDougald, Troutman & Arkwright, 1931-35; mem. firm MacDougald, Troutman Sams & Branch, 1936-49; v.p., gen. mgr., dir. Ga. Power Co., 1949-50, pres. 1951-56; pres., dir. So. Co. (parent firm Ala., Ga., Gulf and Miss. power cos.), 1957-69, chmn. bd., dir., 1969-71; chmn., dir., chmn. exec. com. So. Services, Inc., 1969-71; v.p., dir. Ala., Ga., Gulf, Miss. power cos., 1951-68; dir., dep. chmn. Fed. Res. Bank of Atlanta, 1953-59. Hon. mem. Bus. Council; mem. Ga. Sci. and Tech. Commn., 1956-71; mem. president's adv. council Agnes Scott Coll.; mem. Atlanta Found. Mem. Pres.'s Nat. Center for Vol. Action, 1970-71, Pres.'s Commn. on Productivity, 1969-71. Trustee emeritus Davidson Coll.; Emory U.; past trustee Ga. Tech. Research Inst., Tax Found., Inc.; past dir. Ga. 4-H Club, State YMCA Ga.; trustee United Student Aid Funds, Inc., 1963-71; hon. trustee Ga. Coll. at Milledgeville; bd. visitors Davidson Coll., 1973—; Sr. fellow Woodrow Wilson Found., 1973-74. Served as lt. (jg.) USNR, 1944-45. Mem. Ga. Bar Assn., Beta Theta Pi, Omicron Delta Kappa, Phi Delta Phi, Alpha Kappa Psi. Independent. Presbyn. (elder). Clubs: Piedmont Driving, Capital City, Terminus Racquet; Highlands (N.C.) Country; Kingwood Country. Author: The Crowd and the Commonplace and Other Addresses, 1971; Georgia - The Reluctant Rebel, 1975; Populism in Georgia, 1976. Home: 3106 Nancy's Creek Rd NW Atlanta GA 30327 also Lakemont GA 30552

BRANCH, JOHN ELLISON, lawyer; b. Atlanta, Sept. 17, 1915; s. William Harllee and Bernice (Simpson) B.; B.S., Davidson Coll., 1937; J.D., Emory U., 1940; m. Jean I. McKay, Nov. 19, 1938; children—Jean Elizabeth, Barbara Ann, Patricia Elaine, John Ellison. Sr. partner firm Branch and Swann, Atlanta, 1970—; employer advisor U.S. delegation Internat. Labor Orgn., Geneva, 1962-63. Bd. dirs. Ga. Hospitality and Travel Assn., 1977—. Served to maj. U.S. Army, 1943-45. Mem. Nat. Council State Chambers Commerce (chmn. employee relations com. 1968-78), Ga. C. of C. (dir. 1972—, chmn. indsl. relations council 1964-71), Atlanta C. of C. (dir. 1962-65, chmn. govt. affairs dept. 1960-62), Am. Bar Assn., Ga. State Bar, Atlanta Bar Assn., Lawyers Club of Atlanta, Am. Judicature Soc., Corp. Counsel Assn., Phi Beta Kappa, Omicron Delta Kappa, Phi Delta Phi, Phi Delta Theta. Presbyterian. Clubs: Capital City, Cherokee, Commerce, Atlanta Athletic, Univ. Yacht, Amelia Island Plantation. Author: (with J. P. Swann) The Wage and Hour Law Handbook, 1978; contbr. articles to profl. jours. Home: 8945 River Run Atlanta GA 30338 Office: Suite 1701 3400 Peachtree Rd NE Atlanta GA 30326

BRANCH, JOHN RUSSELL, geologist; b. Los Angeles, Dec. 9, 1914; s. John Shubael and Mabel Elizabeth (Richardson) B.; B.A., U. Cin., 1940; M.A. in Geology, U. Cin., 1946; m. Dorothy C. Lebedczewski, Nov. 2, 1942; children—Barbara (Mrs. Barbara Branch Whorton), John M., Marjorie (Mrs. Marjorie Branch Wiles). Teaching fellow geology U. Mich., 1946-49; with Shell Oil Co., 1949—, supr. exploration, prodn. lab., New Orleans, 1974—; lectr. High Sch. Career Days, New Orleans area, 1970—. Judge, New Orleans Sci. Fair, 1970—; chmn. judges Internat. Sci. Fair, New Orleans, 1973; chmn. judges sr. div. Natural and Phys. Scis., 1973—; pres. Shell Employees Credit Union-So. Region. Served to comdr. USNR, 1941-46. Mem. AAAS, Am. Assn. Petroleum Geologists, Marine Tech. Soc. (pres. New Orleans chpt. 1973-74), New Orleans Geol. Soc. (sec. 1973-74), Soc. Exploration Geophysicists, Sigma Xi. Home: 4454 Fiesta Dr New Orleans LA 70114 Office: Shell Oil Co 2483 One Shell Sq New Orleans LA 70160

BRANCH, WILLIAM TERRELL, urologist; b. Paragould, Ark., Dec. 7, 1937; s. William Owen and Mary Rose (Dempsey) B.; B.S. (hon.), Ark. State U., 1963; B.S., U. Ark., Little Rock, 1966, M.D., 1971; m. Mary Fletcher Cox, Dec. 11, 1965; 1 dau., Ashley Tucker. Adminstrv. asst. mental retardation planning State Ark., Little Rock, 1964-66; intern U. So. Fla. Sch. Medicine, Tampa, 1971-72, surg. resident, 1972-73, urology resident, 1973-76; practice medicine specializing in urology, Tampa, 1976—; clin. asst. prof. U. S. Fla. Sch. Medicine, Tampa, 1976—; cons. urology Tampa VA Hosp., 1977—; co-chmn. surgery, mem. exec. com. Meml. Hosp., Tampa, 1978-80; vice-chief urology Tampa Gen. Hosp., 1978-80; mem. Profl. Health Care Found., Tampa, 1978—; Named Outstanding Intern, U. S. Fla. Sch. Medicine, 1971-72. Diplomate Am. Bd. Urology. Fellow A.C.S.; mem. Am. Urol. Assn., AMA (Physicians Recognition award 1977, 80), Fla. Urol. Soc. (Milton Copeland award 1976, mem. exec. council 1979-81), Hillsborough County Med. Assn. (mem. exec. council 1979-81). Club: Yacht and Country (Tampa, Fla.). Home: 909 Golfview St Tampa FL 33609 Office: 2919 Swann St Suite 303 Tampa FL 33609

BRAND, JOHN, state ofcl.; b. St. Louis, Apr. 30, 1923; s. William Herman and Mabel Edith (Wimbush) B.; B.S. in Mech. Engring., Mo. Sch. Mines and Metallurgy, 1944; M.Div., Louisville Presbyn. Theol. Sem., 1964; postgrad. U. Ky., 1969-70; m. Virginia May Haggard, Dec. 24, 1970; children—Christy (Mrs. Ghary Akers), Ronald C. Rainey, Donald C., Stephanie Rainey, Virginia, Robin Rainey, Elizabeth Carol. Plant engr. Krummrick plant Monsanto Chem. Corp., East St. Louis, Ill., 1944-46, Queeny plant, St. Louis, 1946-53, mech. standards engr. organic div., St. Louis, 1953-55, mgr. mech. standardization, research and engring. div., world hgqrs., St. Louis, 1955-58; ordained to ministry Presbyn. Ch. U.S., 1964 (transferred to Christian Ch. 1970); pastor South Louisville Presbyn. Ch., 1958-60, Eastminister Presbyn. Ch., Lexington, Ky., 1960-69; cons. services adminstr. Ky. Dept. Child Welfare, Frankfort, 1970-72; asst. dir. office occupational programs, bur. health services Dept. for Human Resources, Frankfort, 1972-74, dir., 1974—. Part time pastor Berea Christian Ch., Henry County, Ky., 1970—. Bd. deacons Westminister Presbyn. Ch., St. Louis. Mem. Mfg. Chemists Assn. (chmn. mech. tech. com.), Am. Standards Assn., Lexington Assn. Social Professions, Lexington Ministers Assn., Engrs. Club St. Louis, Kappa Sigma. Rotarian. Home: 3500 Tates Creek Rd Lexington KY 40502 Office: Dept for Human Resources Bldg Frankfort KY 40601

BRANDAU, ADAM GORDON, JR., cardiologist; b. Balt., Jan. 11, 1938; s. Adam G. and Frances N. Brandau; B.A. in Chemistry, U. Pa., 1960; M.D., Thomas Jefferson U., 1964; m. Dorothy J. Richardson, June 17, 1961; children—Dorothy, Kathleen, Adam III, J. Matthew, Amanda. Intern, U.S. Naval Hosp., Portsmouth, Va., 1964-65; resident in internal medicine Thomas Jefferson U. Hosp., 1969-71; fellow in cardiology Sch. of Medicine, Emory U., Atlanta, 1971-73, asst. prof. medicine (cardiology), 1973-74, clin. asst. prof. medicine (cardiology), 1974—; practice medicine specializing in internal medicine and cardiology, Tucker, Ga., 1974—; mem. staff DeKalb Gen. Hosp. Served from lt. to lt. comdr. M.C., USN, 1964-69. Diplomate Am. Bd. Internal Medicine. Fellow Am. Coll. Cardiology; mem. DeKalb County Med. Soc. Home: 5740 Musket Ln Stone Mountain GA 30087 Office: Bldg 11 Suite 21 LaVista Perimeter Office Park Tucker GA 30084

BRANDENBERGER, STANLEY GEORGE, research chemist; b. Houston, Jan. 18, 1930; s. Stanley Sylvester and Evelyn Ella (Duke) B.; B.A., Rice U., 1952; Ph.D., U. Tex., 1956; m. Betty Lea McCauley, June 17, 1967; 1 son by previous marriage, Joel Harris; 1 dau., Evelyn Lea. Research chemist Houston Research Lab., Shell Oil Co., 1956-64, supr., 1964-68, 69-72, sect. head Royal Dutch Shell Lab., Amsterdam, 1968-69; staff research chemist Shell Devel. Co., 1972—. Mem. Am. Chem. Soc., Catalysis Soc. Am., S.W. Catalysis Soc., Sigma Xi, Phi Lambda Upsilon, Alpha Chi Sigma. Presbyterian (deacon, elder). Contbr. articles to profl. jours. Patentee in field. Home: 5726 Kuldell St Houston TX 77096 Office: PO Box 1380 Houston TX 77001

BRANDINO, THOMAS FRANCIS, JR., pharm. co. exec.; b. Jamaica, N.Y., Dec. 30, 1944; s. Thomas Francis and Marguriete Virginia (DeLorenzo) B.; B.B.A., U. Houston, 1969; m. Rosalie Montalbano, June 22, 1969; 1 son, Thomas III. With Comatic Labs., Inc., 1963—, plant mgr. charge packaging and related ops., 1968-72, pres., 1972—; mem. regulatory and tech. com. Nat. Pharm. Alliance, 1975—; participant Nat. Pharm. Packaging Conf. N.Y.U., 1974. Club: University (Houston). Home: 11838 Westmere Dr Houston TX 77077 Office: PO Box 42300 Houston TX 77032

BRANDON, ALFRED NORTHRUP, med. librarian; b. Ogden, Utah, Sept. 10, 1922; s. Abraham Alfred and Anna Margaret (Northrup) B.; Th.B., Atlantic Union Coll., 1945; B.S., Syracuse U., 1948; M.S. in L.S., U. Ill., 1951; M.A. in History, U. Mich., 1956; m. Mabel Louise Pomeroy, May 27, 1945 (dec. May 1966); children—Robert Alfred, Sharon Ann. Asst. librarian Atlantic Union Coll., South Lancaster, Mass., 1946-48, head librarian, 1948-52; head librarian U. Mich. Transp. Library, Ann Arbor, 1952-53; Loma Linda (Calif.) U., 1953-57, U. Ky. Med. Center, Lexington, 1957-63; dir. Welch Med. Library Johns Hopkins U., Balt., 1963-69; prof. library sci., chmn. dept. Mt. Sinai Sch. Medicine, N.Y.C., 1969-73, Janet Doe lectr., 1969; librarian N.Y. Acad. Medicine, N.Y.C., 1973-78; med. library cons., 1979—; vis. lectr. Syracuse U. Library Sch., summers 1950, 52-55, U. Md. Sch. Library and Informational Scis., summer 1966. Recipient Ida and George Eliot Prize Essay award, 1972, Marcia C. Noyes award, 1977. Mem. ALA, Spl. Libraries Assn., Med. Libraries Assn. (pres. 1965-66, editor Jour. 1961-69), Beta Phi Mu, Pi Lambda Sigma. Contbr. articles to profl. jours. Home: 10639 Regency Ct Orlando FL 32817

BRANDON, DALE EDWARD, oceanographer; b. Canonsburg, Pa., Sept. 22, 1938; s. George Edward and Mabel Elizabeth (Pugh) B.; B.S. in Geology, Wayne State U., 1965; M.S., Ph.C. in Oceanography, U. Mich., 1967, Ph.D. in Phys. Oceanography, 1970; postgrad. (Fulbright fellow) U. Sydney (Australia), 1967-69. Sr. research oceanographer Esso Production Research Co., Houston, 1970-73; environ. adminstr. Alyeska Pipeline Service Co., Anchorage, 1973-76; environ. coordinator Exxon Minerals Co., Houston, 1976-78; sr. program mgr. Environ. Research & Tech., Houston, 1978—. Served with USN, 1955-59. NSF fellow, 1965, 66, 67, 69, 70. Mem. AAAS, Am. Geophys. Union, Soc. Econ. Paleontologists and Mineralogists, Sigma Xi. Home: 10931 Britoak Ln Houston TX 77079 Office: 6630 Harwin Dr Houston TX 77036

BRANDON, MARK EDWARD, lawyer; b. Augusta, Ga., July 14, 1954; s. Frank Thomas, Jr., and Myra Patricia (Alexander) B.; B.A., U. Montevallo, 1975; J.D., U. Ala., 1978. Admitted to Ala. bar, 1978; asst. atty. gen., Ala. Atty. Gen's. Office, Montgomery, 1978—. Mem. Ala. Conservancy. Mem. Am. Bar Assn., Ala. Bar Assn., Am. Judicature Soc., Assn. Trial Lawyers Am., Ala. Trial Lawyers Assn., Ala. Hist. Assn., ACLU. Editor, co-author Alabama Environmental Enforcement Handbook for Citizens and Public Officials, 1978. Home: 331 Cloverdale Rd Montgomery AL 36104 Office: 250 Administrative Bldg Montgomery AL 36130

BRANDON, STEPHEN ARTHUR, agribusiness trade exec.; b. Helena, Ark., Oct. 4, 1950; s. Willard C. and Dorothy E. (Gladin) B.; B.S., Miss. State U., 1972, M.S. in Agr., 1973; m. Anita Lynn Warren, Oct. 24, 1975; 1 son, Warren. Gen. mgr. Garden Center, Helena, 1973-75; treas. West Acres Farm Store, Inc., W. Helena, Ark., 1975-76, pres., 1976—, gen. mgr., 1976—; partner S-S Cattle Co., 1980—; instr. community service and continuing edn. program Phillips Coll., Helena, 1976-78, bd. dirs., 1975—, chmn. adv. bd., 1976-79; guest columnist Twin City Tribune. Bd. dirs. Phillips County Fair, 1975-77, v.p., 1979—; bd. dirs. Serendipity Festival, 1976, United Fund, 1980—. Recipient Sales Achievement award McCulloch Corp., 1978, 79; subject of Phillips County Father's Day feature Twin City Tribune, 1977; Outstanding Young Man of Ark., Jaycees, Outstanding Young Man of Am., 1976. Mem. So., Miss. turfgrass assns., Phillips C. of C. (dir. 1979), West Helena Promotional Assn. (treas. 1978). Miss. State U. Alumni Assn., Sigma Phi Epsilon. Democrat. Methodist. Clubs: Lions (dir. 1976-77, v.p. 1979-80), Homelite 100. Contbr. articles on agr. to profl. publs. Home: Route 2 Box 572 West Helena AR 72390 Office: Route 2 Box 542 West Helena AR 72390

BRANDON, WILLIAM HOUSTON, JR., physician; b. Cartersville, Ga., Mar. 27, 1943; s. William Houston and Lois (Daniel) B.; B.S. in Polit Sci., U. Tenn., 1965; B.S. in Biology and Chemistry, Memphis State U., 1968; M.D., Creighton U., 1974; m. Donna Meyer, July 14, 1973; children—Daniel, Michael. Intern, Mayo Clinic, Rochester, Minn., 1974-75, resident in internal medicine, 1974-78; practice medicine specializing in internal medicine, Clearwater, Fla., 1978—; mem. staff Morton Plant Hosp., Clearwater, 1978—. Served with USAR, 1966-72. Diplomate Am. Bd. Internal Medicine. Mem. AMA, Am. Soc. Internal Medicine, Pinellas County Med. Soc., Mayo Clinic Alumni Soc. Office: 300 Jefford St Clearwater FL 33516

BRANDSTETTER, LAWRENCE WILLIAM, architect; b. Cin., Oct. 13, 1949; s. Lawrence Francis and Elaine Laverne (Dwertman) B.; B.S. in Architecture, Ohio State U., 1971, M.Arch., 1974, now postgrad in city planning; m. Susan Annette Koelliker, Sept. 16, 1972; 1 son, Benjamin Ernest. Designer, Brubaker/Brandt, Inc., Columbus, Ohio, 1972-75; asst. mgr., then dir. client devel. Raike Assos., Inc., Ashland, Ohio, 1975-79; prin. works include Bellevue Community Center, Tri-State Airport Terminal; prin. Brandstetter/Carroll & Assos., LeXington, Ky., 1979—; v.p. Main Properties Ohio; condr. seminars. Mem. AIA, Soc. Mktg. Profl. Services, Am. Assn. Airport Execs. Club: Lexington Rotary. Home: 225 Whitfield Dr Lexington KY 40503 Office: 359 Waller Ave Lexington KY 40504

BRANDT, ALVA ESMOND, statistician; b. Larchwood, Iowa, Nov. 13, 1892; s. Charles August and Arvetta (Blue) B.; B.S. in Engring., Iowa State Coll., 1917, M.S., 1927, Ph.D. in Genetics and Statistics, 1932; m. Lula Litten May, July 2, 1921; children—Jane Brandt McGee-Russell, Peter Blue. Extension specialist U. Ill., 1917; asst. prof. farm mechanics Oreg. State Coll., Corvallis, 1919-23; asst. prof. math. Iowa State Coll., Ames, 1924-37, research asst. prof. statistics, 1924-37; sr. math. statis. analyst of research div. Soil Conservation Service, U.S. Dept. Agr., Washington, 1937-40, prin. soil conservationist, 1940-43, research specialist, 1945-46; statis. cons. to tech. dir. Naval Ordnance Lab., White Oaks, Md., 1946-48; biometrician in health and safety div. of AEC, N.Y. Ops. Office, 1948-58; biometric cons. to Atomic Bomb Casualty Commn., Japan, 1951, 53-54; statistician Agrl. Expt. Station, U. Fla., Gainesville, 1958-63, also head dept. statistics Coll. of Agr., prof. emeritus; vol. statis. cons. Served with USNR, 1917-19; served to lt. col. USAAF, 1943-45; ETO. Post-doctoral fellow, 1934-35; recipient Pres.'s medallion U. Fla. Fellow Am. Statis. Assn.; mem. Radiation Research Soc., Inst. Math. Statistics, Biometric Soc., Am. Genetic Assn., AAAS, Sigma Xi, Tau Beta Pi, Gamma Sigma Delta, Pi Mu Epsilon. Contbr. articles on applications of statis. analysis to biol. research, genetics and conservation to sci. jours.; chmn. com. for establishing dept. statistics in Coll. of Agr. at U. Fla. Address: 2009 NW 14th Ave Gainesville FL 32605

BRANDT, ISAAC DAVID, III, mgmt. exec.; b. Lebanon, Pa., June 12, 1934; s. Isaac David, Jr., and Irene May (Plantz) B.; B.A. in Polit. Sci. and History, Fla. Tech. U., 1971; M.P.A., Fla. Atlantic U., 1974; m. Charmaine Faye Long, Dec. 27, 1952; 1 dau., Denise Faye. Ops. systems engr. Grumman Engring. Corp., Kennedy Space Center, Fla., 1965-69; adminstrv. asst. City of Deerfield Beach (Fla.), 1971-72; asst. city mgr. City of Coral Springs (Fla.), 1972-74; city mgr. City of DeLand (Fla.), 1974-75; dir. bus. devel. and pub. relations Smith & Gillespie Engrs., Inc., Jacksonville, Fla., 1975-80; dir. bldg. ops. Blue Cross-Blue Shield, Jacksonville, 1980—; cons. Rep. from Coral Springs to N.W. Broward County Council Mayors, 1974, Volusia County Council Govts., 1974-75; mem. DeLand (Fla.) Council of 100. Served with USN, 1952-56. Mem. Fla. Pub. Relations Assn., Internat. City Mgmt. Assn., Nat. Rifle Assn. (life). Republican. Methodist. Clubs: Masons, Shriners, Kiwanis (dir. 1979—). Home: 8000 Baymeadows Circle E 22 Jacksonville FL 32216 Office: PO Box 1798 Jacksonville FL 32231

BRANNON, PAUL WHITING, mfg. co. exec.; b. Douglas, N.D., June 19, 1908; s. Lonnie Martin and Ardus Gay (Moffett) B.; m. Jane Anne Buening, Oct. 1, 1949. Machine operator to gen. foreman Internat. Harvester Co., 1927-37; chief engr. Milw. Gear Co., 1937-41; works mgr. B.W. Supercharger div. Borg-Warner, Milw., 1941-46; works mgr. Wayne Pump Co., Ft. Wayne, Ind., 1946-52; v.p. mfg. Pesco Products Co. div. Borg Warner, Cleve., 1952-55; v.p. mfg. and engring. Cloyes Gear Works, Cleve., 1955-56; works mgr. Brad Foote Gear Works, Chgo., 1956-60; mgr. rep. spl. gears and speed reducers N.E. Ohio, 1960-70; pres., owner Magnolia Mobile Manor, St. Petersburg, Fla., 1970—. Mem. Fla. Mobile Home Assn. Pinellas County (v.p. 1975). Republican. Methodist. Clubs: Masons, Shriners, Seminole Lake Country. Home and Office: 4190 71st St N Saint Petersburg FL 33709

BRANNON, RUSSELL HERBERT, agrl. economist; b. Bartlesville, Okla., Aug. 25, 1931; s. Luther Herbert and Pauline Frances (South) B.; B.S., Okla. State U., 1954; M.A., George Washington U., 1958; M.S., U. Wis., 1965, Ph.D., 1967; m. Janice Lee McElfresh, Feb. 9, 1957; children—Shaun Russell, Paula Lou, Scot Alan. Agronomy advisor USAID, Thailand, 1958-63, econs. advisor, chief of party, 1971-74; research asso. Land Tenure Center, U. Wis., 1963-65; research asso. Ford Found., Uruguay, Paraguay, Argentina, 1965-67; asst. prof. agrl. econs., U. Ky., 1967-69, asso. prof., 1969-72, prof., 1972—, asso. dir. Center for Devel. Change, 1969-71; cons. in field. Served with U.S. Army, 1954-56. Mem. Am., So., agrl. econs. assns., Internat. Assn. Agrl. Economists, Gamma Sigma Delta, Phi Eta Sigma. Author: The Agricultural Development of Uruguay, 1968; The Agricultural Development of Argentina, 1969. Editor: Agricultural Cooperatives and Markets in Developing Countries, 1969; Social and Economic Issues Confronting the Tobacco Industry in the Seventies, 1972. Home: 3307 Roxburg Dr E Lexington KY 40503 Office: Dept Agricultural Economics U Kentucky Lexington KY 40503

BRANNON, STEVE FRANKLIN, educator; b. Greeneville, Tenn., Apr. 9, 1943; s. Clarence Earl and Ona Marie (Lowe) B.; A.A., Warren Wilson Coll., 1963; B.A., Tusculum Coll., 1966; M.A., E. Tenn. State U., 1969; postgrad. Middlebury Coll., 1972, U. S.C., 1978, Converse Coll., 1979; m. Doris Ann Barb, May 29, 1965; 1 dau., Sabra Sarah Marie. English instr. Chuckey-Doak High Sch., Afton, Tenn., 1966-68; prof. English, speech and drama Chowan Coll., Murfreesboro, N.C., 1969-73; asso. charitable endowments So. Life Ins. Co., Norfolk, Va., 1973-74; instr. English, speech and drama, dir. humanities Spartanburg (S.C.) Meth. Coll., 1974—; humanities cons. Juvenile Justice Collaboration Spartanburg Council on Aging. Recipient A. V. Huff faculty award Spartanburg Meth. Coll., 1978. Mem. Southeastern Council on English in Two-Year Colls., Southeastern Theatre Conf., S.C. Artists Registry, S.C. Theatre Assn. Democrat. Presbyterian. Home and Office: Spartanburg Meth Coll Spartanburg SC 29301

BRANNON, TERENCE C., banker; b. Mobile, Jan. 1, 1938; A.B., Birmingham (Ala.) So. Coll., 1960; m. Sybil Brown, June 7, 1958; 1 son, J. Michael. Mortgage loan officer Prudential Ins. Co. in Fla., Va. and N.C., 1960-65; with real estate dept. Southwestern Life Ins. Co. in N.C. and Va., 1965-68; with Central Bank Birmingham, from 1968, sr. v.p., sr. loan officer, 1974; sr. v.p. loan adminstrn., then exec. v.p. asset and liability mgmt. Central Bancshares of South, Birmingham, 1975-77, pres., chief operating officer, 1977— also dir.; dir. Central Bank Mobile, N.A., Central Computer Services, Inc., Central Corr. Services, Inc., Central Ins. Co. Mem. Young Pres.'s Orgn. Methodist. Clubs: The Club, Mountain Brook Swim and Tennis (Birmingham). Office: 701 S 20th St Birmingham AL 35296

BRANSON, ROBERT EARL, market research economist; b. Dallas, Dec. 3, 1918; s. Earl and Gertrude (Smith) B.; B.S. in Bus. Adminstrn., So. Meth. U., 1941; M.A. in Econs., Harvard, 1949, M.A. in Pub. Adminstrn., 1948, Ph.D. in Econs., 1954; m. Ruth Parker, May 18, 1945; children—Donald Elliott, Richard Parker. Economist, U.S. Dept. Agr., 1941-47; asso. dir. market research U. P.R., 1949-50; statistician U.S. Dept. Agr., 1950, economist, 1951-54; prof. econs., chmn. market devel. research, dept. agrl. econs and sociology Tex. A and M. U., also dir. consumer market research Tex. Agrl. Expt. Sta., 1954-69, coordinator Tex. Agrl. Market Research and Devel. Center, 1969—; pres. Branson & Assos., Inc.; cons. economist U.S. AID, Argentina, 1962. Chmn. Bryan City Planning Commn., 1970-72. Served as economist OSS, Hdqr. Detachment, U.S. Army, Washington, World War II. Mem. Am. Mktg. Assn., Am. Econ. Assn., Am. Agrl. Econs. Assn. Democrat. Methodist (bd. dirs). Kiwanian. Author: (with others) Marketing Efficiency in Puerto Rico, 1955. Contbr. articles on consumer marketing. Home: 2511 Broadmoor St Bryan TX 77801 Office: Agrl Market Research and Devel Center Tex A and M Univ College Station TX 77840

BRANTLEY, ALICE VIRGINIA SINGER (MRS. EDWARD FITZROY BRANTLEY), civic worker; b. Muncie, Ind.; d. Harry Dwight and Dessa (Slater) Singer; student Muncie Conservatory Music, 1912-20, Met. Sch. Music, 1920-22; studied harp with Louise Schelschmidt Koehne, Indpls., 1917-22, Henriette Renie, Paris, France, 1922-26, 50; m. Edward Fitzroy Brantley, Sept. 19, 1956. Concert debut, Paris, 1925; mem. Septuor Renie, 1923-26; concerts in Paris, N.Y.C., Chgo., Ft. Wayne, Indpls., St. Petersburg, Fla., 1920-63, with Alice Singer Trio, St. Petersburg, 1933-56; performed with St. Petersburg Symphony, Jacksonville (Fla.) Symphony, Tampa (Fla.) Philharmonic, Fla. Philharmonic, 1950-66; radio program WSUN, St. Petersburg, 1933. Ambassador, People-to-People Goodwill Mission from St. Petersburg to Europe and Middle East, 1960, to Soviet Union and satellites, 1965; mem. Fla. Art Commn., 1964-67; v.p. Suncoast Goodwill Industries, 1965-69, v.p. Aux. Guild, 1965-66; mem. St. Anthony's Hosp. Guild, 1961—, Children's Home Soc., 1963—, Suncoast Heart Assn., 1966; chmn. Queen of Hearts Ball, St. Petersburg, 1968; Heart Sunday chmn., 1963. Bd. dirs. Pinellas County Mental Health Assn., Mound Park Hosp. Aux., All Children's Hosp. Guild. Recipient Renie Harp award Paris, 1926, citation Radio Sta. WDAE, Tampa, 1965; named Princess of Royal Ct., St. Petersburg Heart Assn., 1963, Queen of Hearts, 1967; Contessa of Yr., Suncoast Opera Guild, 1970. Mem. Fla. Philharmonic Soc. (charter pres. 1954), Chamber Music Soc. (charter pres. 1966-68), Bel Canto (charter 1956), St. Petersburg opera assns., Fla. Art Council (charter 1963), Lions Club Aux. (past pres.), Soroptimist Internat. (pres. St. Petersburg 1962-63), St. Petersburg Hist. Soc., Mus. Fine Arts.

BRANTLEY, JOHN CROFT, psychologist, educator; b. Nashville, Apr. 7, 1938; s. John McKinley and Winnie (Croft) B.; B.S., U. Miami, 1960; M.S., Fla. State U., 1962, Ph.D., 1965; m. Helen Louise Thomas, June 15, 1963; children—Elizabeth Ann, John Thomas. Fellow Devereux Found., Devon, Pa., 1965-66; asst. prof. edn., U. N.C., Chapel Hill, 1967-71, asso. prof., 1971—, coordinator sch. psychology program, 1976—. Mem. Nat. Assn. Sch. Psychologists (pres. 1976-77), Am. Psychol. Assn., Southeastern Psychol. Assn., Inst. Research in Social Sci., Nat. Council Accreditation Tchr. Edn. (rep. 1978—). Guest editor: School Psychology Digest, 1977. Mem. editorial bd. Psychology in the Schools, 1974—, School Psychology Digest, 1974—. Office: 107 Peabody Hall University of North Carolina Chapel Hill NC 27514

BRANTLEY, MARGARET MARY, nurse, hosp. ofcl.; b. New Castle, Pa., Feb. 27, 1920; d. Thomas Francis and Mary Theresa (Heinrich) Maher; R.N., St. Francis Hosp. Sch. Nursing, Pitts., 1943; m. James Wallace Brantley, May 30, 1949; children—Mary Evelyn, James Wallace, Edward Gilmore. Newborn nursery nurse St. Francis Hosp., Pitts., 1943-44; pvt. duty nurse New Castle, 1951-52; gen. duty and pvt. duty nurse Amory, Miss., 1952-64; dir. nursing Gilmore Meml. Hosp., Amory, 1964—. Adv. com. nursing Miss. U. for Women; adv. com. Sch. Practical Nursing, Itawamba Jr. Coll.; active Miss. Heart Assn. Served with Nurse Corps, U.S. Army, 1944-50. Mem. Dist. 25 Miss. Nurses Assn., Miss. Nurses Assn., Am. Nurses Assn., Miss. Hosp. Assn. Nursing Service Adminstrn. Roman Catholic. Home: 100 S 4th St Amory MS 38821 Office: Gilmore Meml Hosp S Boulevard Dr Amory MS 38821

BRANUM, FRED ALLEN, telecommunications exec.; b. Chattanooga, Nov. 6, 1940; s. Franklin Jewell and Etta B. (Clift) B.; grad. Southeastern Inst. Electronics, 1960; A.A. in Acctg., U. S.C., 1978, also postgrad.; m. Barbara Ann Akins, Aug. 5, 1962; children—Jeff, Kim, Teresa. With Chattanooga Warehouse & Cold

Storage, 1958-59, Cowan Boze Co., Atlanta, 1959, Vitro Weapons Service, Eglin AFB, Fla., 1959-60, Am. Tel. & Tel., Chattanooga, 1960-63; staff asst. Am. Tel. & Tel., Nashville, 1964, instr., Birmingham, Ala., 1964, Atlanta, 1964-66, ops. supr., Knoxville, Tenn., 1966-68, ops. mgr., Knoxville, 1968-69, staff supr., N.Y.C., 1969-70, sales supr., Charlotte, N.C., 1970-72, S.C. sales/service mgr., Columbia, 1972-74; telecommunications mgr. Springs Mills, Inc., Lancaster, S.C., 1974, asst. dir. office services, 1974, dir. office services, 1975—. Scoutmaster, Boy Scouts Am., 1961-63; advisor Jr. Achievement, 1965-66; Dixie Youth Baseball coach, 1973-78, dir., 1978-79, pres., 1979—; Sun. sch. tchr., Bapt. Ch., 1959-64, 75-77, Sunday sch. dept. supt., 1977-78. Named Atlanta S.W. Jr. Achievement Advisor of the Yr., 1966; Lancaster's Nat. Sectl. Assn. Boss of the Yr., 1979. Mem. Am. Textile Mfrs. Inst., Am. Mgmt. Assn., Internat. Communications Assn., S.C. Telecommunications Mgrs. Assn. Baptist. Contbr. articles to profl. jours. Home: 205 Edgemont Dr E Lancaster SC 29720 Office: PO Box 111 Lancaster SC 29720

BRANUM, JEAN PRYOR, ednl. adminstr.; b. Louisville, Nov. 10, 1940; d. Sherman Guy and Alvina Ella (Pryor) B.; B.Mus.Edn., Western Ky. U., 1962, M.A., 1969; postgrad. Xavier U., 1977. Elem. music tchr. Jefferson County (Ky.) Public Schs., 1962-68; social service supr. Central Ky. Reception Center, Louisville, 1969-72; dir. edn. No. Ky. Treatment Center, Crittenden, 1972-79, supr. secondary edn., 1979—; cons. and condr. workshops on behavioral disorders Kenton County Sch. System, 1978-79. Mem. Council for Exceptional Children, Am. Personnel and Guidance Assn., Ky. Assn. Sch. Adminstrs., No. Ky. Assn. Sch. Adminstrs., Ky. Assn. Ednl. Suprs., No. Ky. Assn. Ednl. Suprs., Kenton County Adminstrv. Assn., Phi Delta Kappa. Republican. Mem. United Ch. of Christ. Home: 8333 Sunnybrook Dr Florence KY 41042 Office: 5533 Madison Pike Independence KY 41051

BRAREN, SUSAN LOUISE, guidance counselor; b. Jacksonville, Fla., Sept. 5, 1954; d. Frederick Ingwert and Helen (Ahern) B.: B.A. in English, U. Fla., 1977; M.A. in Guidance Counseling and Edn., U. N. Fla., 1979. Counselor, Alpha IV Program, Orange Park, Fla., 1979; vocat. rehab. counselor Fla. State Health Rehab. Program, 1979—. Mem. Am. Personnel and Guidance Assn., Fla. Personnel and Guidance Assn. Roman Catholic. Address: 333 San Juan Dr Ponte Vedra Beach FL 32082

BRASFIELD, MILTON STANHOPE, III, pediatrician; b. Demopolis, Ala., Feb. 16, 1937; s. Milton Stanhope and Laura Francis (Kirven) B.; A.B., Birmingham So. Coll., 1959; M.D., U. Ala., 1964; m. Lois Martin Neely, June 14, 1959; children—Milton Stanhope, Martin Neely, Lois Christiana, Martha Leigh, David Anthony. Intern, Lloyd Noland Hosp., Fairfield, Ala., 1964-65; resident, 1965-67; practice medicine specializing in pediatrics, 1968—; mem. staff Craddock Clinic, Sylacduga, Ala., 1969-70; private practice, Alexander City, Ala., 1970—. Served with MC, USN, 1967-69. Diplomate Am. Bd. Pediatrics. Fellow Am. Acad. Pediatrics; mem. Ala. Med. Assn., Tallapoosa County Med. Soc., A.C.S. Contbr. articles in field to med. jours. Home: River Bend Alexander City AL 35010 Office: PO Box 255 Alexander City AL 35010

BRASHER, SAM EARL, building materials mfg. co. exec.; b. Birmingham, Ala., Nov. 5, 1934; s. W. F. and Lucile C. Brasher; B.S. in Mktg., U. Ala., 1957; m. Jewell Waldrop, Sept. 3, 1954; children—Russell, Richard, Christopher. Sales rep. Gen. Electric Co., 1957-58, Chrysler Airtemp Co., 1958-60; partner, mgr. Brasher Hardware, Birmingham, 1960-61; sales rep. Barret div. Allied Chem. Co., Memphis, 1961-65, field sales mgr., Birmingham, 1965-66, field product mgr., N.Y.C., 1966-67; with Celotex Corp., Tampa, 1967—, v.p., 1976-77, pres. Roofing Products div., 1980—, pres., dir. Celotex-Marley, Inc., 1980—. Served with USAR, 1955-63. Republican. Methodist. Clubs: Bardmoor Country, Masons. Office: 1500 N Dale Mabry Tampa FL 33607

BRASWELL, DENTON GRAHAM, JR., mental health exec.; b. Meridian, Miss., July 7, 1949; s. Denton Graham and Monecha Platt (Braswell); A.A., Meridian Jr. Coll., 1969; B.S., U. So. Miss., 1971; M.Ed., Miss. State U., 1974; postgrad. U. Ala., 1976-78; m. Deborah Ann Smith, Dec. 24, 1971; 1 dau., Ashley Shea. Tchr., Meridian public schs., 1971-72; tchr. West Ala. Mental Health Center, Demopolis, 1974-75, tchr./coordinator, 1975-77, dir. mental retardation services, 1977-79; dir. Clarke County Assn. for Retarded Citizens Activity Center, 1979—; chmn. Region VIII Title XX Adv. Com., 1979-80. Served with USAF, 1972-73. U. So. Miss. fellow, 1970-71. Mem. Am. Assn. Mental Deficiency, Nat. Assn. Retarded Citizens, Ala. Assn. Mental Health, Air Force Assn., N.G. Assn. U.S. Baptist. Club: Jackson Civitan. Home: 150 Chesley Ave Jackson AL 36545 Office: PO Box 553 Jackson AL 36545

BRASWELL, J(AMES) RANDALL, civic leader, ret. chemist, environ. engr.; b. Columbus, Ga., July 7, 1926; s. James Allen and Irma (Pierson) B.; A.B. in Chemistry, Emory U., 1948; B.S. summa cum laude in Biology, Columbus Coll., 1972; M.S. in Environ. Engring., U. Fla., 1974. Mem. lab. staff Royal Crown Cola Co., Columbus, 1946-49, mem. tech. services dept., 1949-65, dir. quality control, 1965-68, mgr. quality control services, 1968-71. Pres. United Cerebral Palsy of Muscogee County (Ga.), 1976-78; bd. dirs. Cerebral Palsy and Rehab. Center, 1971—, recipient citation, 1978; adult adv. Jr. Achievement, Inc., 1956-58; group capt. United Givers Campaign, 1957; trustee Empty Stocking Fund, Inc., 1958-59; bd. dirs. Community Safety Council, 1959-61, Youth Craft Shop, Inc., 1959-61, Greater Little League Baseball Columbus, 1962-63; bd. dirs. Goodwill Industries Chattahoochee Valley, 1976—; active numerous civic orgns. Served with USN, 1944-46. Recipient Key Man award Columbus Jaycees, 1957, named Young Man of Year, 1959. Mem. Am. Inst. Biol. Scis., Am. Chem. Soc., Am. Water Works Assn., AAAS, Water Pollution Control Fedn., Ga. Acad. Sci., Ga. Water Pollution Control Assn., Columbus Jaycees (pres. 1961-62), Columbus Coll. Alumni Assn. (dir. 1976-78, citation 1978), Ga. Jaycees (dir. 1961-62), Columbus C. of C. (dir. 1961-62), Phi Kappa Phi. Democrat. Baptist. Club: Kiwanis (past dir.). Author: Manual on Quality Control, 1967, Royal Crown Cola Co. Plant Operations Manual, 1968; Water and Water Treatment, 1968; contbr. articles on water treatment and plant sanitation to profl. jours. Address: 4205 17th Ave Columbus GA 31904

BRASWELL, JACK GUY, dentist; b. Mitchell County, N.C., Sept. 14, 1928; s. Ted R. and Pearl Lula (Gunter) B.; B.S., Berea Coll., 1949; D.M.D., U. Louisville, 1956; Certificate in Orthodontics, Dewey Sch. Orthodontics, 1965; postgrad. Eastern Ky. U., 1950, Wheaton Coll., 1952, U. Ill., 1952, U. Ark., 1952; m. Pauline Ledbetter, June 3, 1950. Tchr., pub. schs., Spruce Pine, N.C., 1949-51, Paw Paw, Ill., 1951-52; dental surg. intern Corona, Calif., 1957; pvt. practice dentistry, Spruce Pine, N.C., 1960—; v.p. Kings Mountain (N.C.) Brick, 1967—. Scoutmaster, Boy Scouts Am., Spruce Pine, 1949-51. Served with Dental Corps, USN, 1956, comdr. Res. Named hon. Ky. col. Licensed pilot, N.C., 1962, instrument and comml. pilot, 1974; licensed dentist, N.C., 1956. Fellow Acad. Gen. Dentistry, Royal Soc. Health. Home: Spruce Pine NC 28777 Office: PO Box 77 Penland NC 28765

BRASWELL, L. RENDER, surgeon; b. Adrian, Ga., Oct. 26, 1907; s. Timothy J. and Diva (Dewberry) B.; Ph.G. in Pharmacy, U. Ga., 1925, B.S., 1929; M.D., Emory U., 1932; m. Lillian Cox, Nov. 1974; children from previous marriage—Stephen R., Elizabeth Anne, Thomas S.; 1 stepdau., Rhonda Dawes. Extern, Grady Meml. Hosp., Atlanta, 1931-32, intern, 1932-33; commd. 1st lt., U.S. Army, 1933, advanced through grades to maj. gen. USAF, 1961; chief gen. surgery sect. Walter Reed Army Gen. Hosp., Washington, 1940-42; comdr., chief surgery USAF Hosp., Big Springs, Tex., 1942-43; comdr. Lackland Hosp., Tex., 1943-44; command surgeon VII Fighter Command, Iwo Jima, 1944, command air surgeon 20th Air Force, Guam, 1945; comdr., chief of surgery Kessler Field Hosp., Miss., 1946-47; hosp. comdr. chief surgery Maxwell AFB, Ala., 1947-52; chief med. officer Am. Mil. Forces, London, Eng., 1952-55; command surgeon Mil. Air Transport Service, 1955-59; command surgeon, adviser to comdr. Air Force Logistics Command, Wright-Patterson AFB, Ohio, 1959-62; ret., 1962; med. dir. Chevrolet div. Gen. Motors Corp., Altanta, 1962-72. Decorated Legion of Merit with oak leaf cluster, D.S.M. Diplomate Am. Bd. Preventive Medicine. Fellow A.C.S., Am. Coll. Preventive Medicine; mem. Assn. Mil. Surgeons U.S., Aerospace Med. Assn., Soc. Air Force Clin. Surgeons, AMA, Sigma Alpha Epsilon, Alpha Kappa Kappa. Club: Masons. Home: 143 W Paces Ferry Rd NW Atlanta GA 30305

BRATAGER, PETE (ELLSWORTH), newspaper exec.; b. Miami, Fla., Oct. 11, 1928; s. Ellsworth Victor and Garnet (Severin) B.; B.A., U. Miami, 1951; m. Alicia Helen Radulski, Jan. 10, 1953; children—Stephen Ellis, Daniel Victor, Donald Pete, James Edward, Reid Thomas. Sports writer Miami Herald, 1946-59, night sports slot, 1959-64, Fla. state news editor, 1964-69, photo editor, 1969—. Served with AUS, 1951-53. Home: 245 E 34th St Hialeah FL 33013 Office: 1 Herald Plaza Miami FL 33101

BRATT, JAMES HOWARD, counselor; b. Teaneck, N.J., Aug. 27, 1944; s. Joseph Frederick and Martha (Kroner) B.; student Trenton State U., 1964-66, U. Md., 1967-69, Washburn U., 1971, Marymount Coll., 1975-76; B.A. in Psychology and Social Work, U. Tampa, 1978, M.Ed. in Adminstrn. and Supervision, 1979; postgrad. Southeastern U., 1978—; m. Carol Ann Scheibler, June 14, 1975; children—Michael, Patrick, Kevin, Maureen. Psychiat. orderly Asburry Hosp., Salina, Kans., 1975; psychiat. counselor Medfield Center Psychiat. Hosp., Clearwater, Fla., 1976-77, Morton Plant Hosp., Clearwater, 1977-79; dir. family and marriage counseling services Comprehensive Counseling Center, Seminole, Fla., 1979—; cons. inservice edn. services. Served with USAF, 1963-71. Mem. Am. Personnel and Guidance Assn. Club: Golden Rule Lodge. Research on attitude change in mental health workers. Home: 8717 78th Ave N Seminole FL 33542 Office: 8950 Seminole Blvd Seminole FL 33542

BRATTON, ALVIS TRUMON, educator; b. De Leon, Tex., Apr. 28, 1915; B.S., Tex. A&M U., 1937; M.Ed., Howard Payne U., 1956; doctoral candidate N.D. State U., 1960-67; m. Capitola Robertson, Feb. 17, 1940; children—Jackson, Clementine, Bonnie, Charles, Stanley. Prof., head agr. dept. Howard Payne U., Brownwood, Tex., 1955-65; prof. botany Tarleton State U., Stephenville, Tex., 1965-66; high sch. sci. tchr., Bangs, Tex., 1967-68; math. tchr., Brownsville, Tex., 1970—. Mem. NEA (del. 1974—), Tex. State Tchrs. Assn. (del. 1974—), Brownsville Educators Assn. (chmn. ins. com. 1972-77, faculty rep. 1970-77, consultation com. 1973-77, pres. 1978-79), Brown County Farm Bur., Sigma Xi. Democrat. Baptist. Lic. real estate broker, Tex. Home: 239 Hibiscus Ct Brownsville TX 78520 Office: 1102 E Madison St Brownsville TX 78520

BRATTON, JAMES HENRY, JR., lawyer; b. Pulaski, Tenn., Oct. 9, 1931; s. James Henry and Mabel (Shelley) B.; B.A., U. of South, 1952 B.A. Oxford U. (Eng.), 1954, M.A., 1978; LL.B., Yale U., 1956; m. Alleen Sharp Davis, Oct. 15, 1960; children—Susan Shelley, James Henry III, Margaret Alleen. Admitted to Tenn. bar, 1956, Ga. bar, 1957; practice in Atlanta, 1956—; mem. firm Gambrell, Russell & Forbes, 1956—; vis. lectr. law U. Ga., 1967—. Bd. dirs. Churches Homes for Bus. Girls, 1970—, Protestant Welfare and Social Service, Atlanta, 1960—; mem. council Christian Council of Met. Atlanta, 1966—. Mem. Am. Law Inst., Am. (chmn. standing com. on aero. law 1977-79), Ga. (founding chmn. environ. law sect. 1970-71), Atlanta, Internat. bar assns., Am. Judicature Soc., Gridiron Secret Soc., Phi Beta Kappa. Democrat. Methodist. Clubs: Lawyers, Burns (both Atlanta). Contbr. articles to profl. jours. Home: 63 N Muscogee Ave NW Atlanta GA 30305 Office: 1st Nat Bank Tower Atlanta GA 30303

BRAUN, GARWOOD ABBOTT, ednl. adminstr.; b. Zion, Ill., June 21, 1920; s. Frank Garwood and Dorothy Abbott (Taylor) B.; B.S., Eureka Coll., 1942; M.S., U. Ill., 1949; postgrad. Duke U., 1949, Ind. U., 1960, Ohio State U., 1952; m. Mary Jane Tewes, Aug. 28, 1943; 1 son, Geoffrey David. Ednl. cons. Ford Found., Ankara, Turkey, 1963-64; prin. high sch. Am. Community Sch., Beirut, 1967-69; ednl. mgr. Raytheon Service Co., Iran, Saudi Arabia and Kenya, 1969-74; dir. corp and found. relations Fla. State U., Tallahassee, 1974—. Trustee, Village of Lake Bluff (Ill.), 1963, Am. Community Sch., 1965-69, Beirut Coll. Women, 1965-69. Served with USN, 1942-45. Decorated Air medal with oak leaf cluster; NSF grantee, 1960. Mem. U. Ill. Alumni Assn., Eureka Coll. Alumni Assn., Sigma Xi. Presbyterian. Clubs: Royal Nairobi (Kenya) Golf, Pan Am. Clipper, Illearn Golf and Country.

BRAUN, WARREN L(OYD), communications engr.; b. Postville, Iowa, Aug. 11, 1922; s. Karl William and Cornelia (Muller) B.; student Valparaiso Tech. Inst., 1940-41, Capitol Radio Engring. Inst., 1953; m. Lillian Carol Stone, May 24, 1942; children—Warren (dec.), Dikki Carol. Chief engr. WKEY, 1941, WSVA, 1941; E.S.M.W.T.P. sect. head, 1942-45; charge installation stas. WSIR, WTON, WJMA, WSVA-FM, WJZ-TV, WSVA-TV, Blue Ridge TV cable facilities, 1945-55; gen. mgr. WSVA-AM-FM-TV, 1964-65; pres. Com Sonics, Inc., Research and Devel. Labs., Warren Braun, cons. engrs., Shenandoah Devel. Corp. Panel 4 mem. TV allocations study orgn.; mem. FCC coms., 1961-63; del. Internat. Deliberations at Interim Conf. of CCIR, 1962; mem. FCC-C-TAC Com., panels 1 and 8; v.p. Market Dimensions, Inc., 1965-71. Bd. dirs. Salvation Army, 1961-73. Chmn. Harrisonburg-Rockingham County Recreation Study Commn., 1963-66; mem. Va. Air Pollution Control Bd., 1966-73, mem. Va. State Water Bd., 1974—, chmn., 1977-78; mem. Va. Citizens Com. for Outdoor Planning, 1964-69; chmn. Upper Valley Regional Park Authority, 1966-69, dir., 1969—; mem. Regional Export Expansion Council, Air Pollution Control Task Force; mem. Va. Far East Trade Mission, 1972, 77; mem. Ohio River Sanitation Commn., 1974—, chmn., 1978-80; mem. bd. Tb and Thoracic Soc., Va. state seal chmn., 1967—. Bd. dirs. Va. Cultural Laureate Found., 1976—. Registered profl. engr. Va., S.C. Recipient Jefferson Davis medal U.D.C., 1961; named outstanding engr. of year Va. Soc. Profl. Engrs., 1965; man of year Harrisonburg and Rockingham County, 1965; Internat. award Am. Soc. Engring., 1969; Rietzke Nat. award, 1972. Fellow Audio Engring. Soc. (bd. dirs. 1962), Internat. Consular Acad.; mem. IEEE, Soc. Motion Picture and TV Engrs., Acoustical Soc. Am., Nat. Soc. Profl. Engrs., Va. Soc. Profl. Engrs. (mem. bd. and exec. com. 1964-65, chpt. pres. 1963-64, Distinguished Service award 1973), Va. Assn. Professions (charter, regional v.p. 1970-73, pres. 1974—), Va. C. of C. (chmn. world trade com. 1968—, dir. 1973—, v.p. 1975—), Harrisonburg C. of C. (chmn. bus. relations com. 1959-61, mem. bd. 1961-66, pres. 1964), ESOP Assn. Am. (dir. 1979—), Soc. Cable Television Engrs. (chpt. pres. 1973, nat. dir. 1972), Internat. Broadcaster Soc. (corp. mem.), ASTM. Lutheran. Club: Elks. Address: PO Box 1106 Harrisonburg VA 22801

BRAWNER, LEE BASIL, librarian; b. Seguin, Tex., May 1, 1935; s. Lee Basil and Thelma (Davenport) B.; student Tex. A. and M. U., 1953-55; B.A., N. Tex. State U., 1957; M.A., George Peabody Coll. Tchrs., 1960; m. Nancy Jayne Wallis, Dec. 6, 1958; children—Betsy Lynn, Allen Lee. Head popular library and circulation dept. Dallas Pub. Library, 1958-60, head Lakewood br., 1961-62, chief br. services, 1964-67; dir. Waco (Tex.) Pub. Library, 1962-64; asst. state librarian Tex. State Library, 1967-71; dir. Met. Library System, Oklahoma City, 1971—; library bldg. cons. Mem. Okla. Humanities Com., 1975-78; adv. bd. Oklahoma City Literacy Council; mem. Intellectual Freedom Com., 1979—; adv. task force ALA/Nat. Endowment Humanities courses by newspaper project, 1979-80. Served with AUS, 1957-58. Mem. ALA (chmn. nominating com. 1975-76, legislation com. 1975-77, chmn. intellectual freedom round table 1978-79, council 1978—), Okla. (exec. bd. 1977-78), Southwestern (pres. 1971-72, adv. bd. oral history-humanities planning grant 1978-79) library assns., Am. Library Trustee Assn. (2d v.p. 1973-74), Assn. Specialized and Coop. Agys. (dir. 1977-80), ACLU, Freedom to Read Found., Okla. C. of C., Sigma Phi Epsilon. Contbr. articles to profl. jours. Home: 5013 NW 61st Pl Oklahoma City OK 73122 Office: 131 McGee Ave Oklahoma City OK 73102

BRAXTON, GLORIA JENNIEN, educator; b. Lynchburg, Va., July 11, 1946; d. James Fredinand and Myrtle Virginia (Wood) B.; B.A. in History, Va. State Coll., 1969; M.Ed. in Social Studies, U. Va., 1969-70; M.A. in Polit. Sci. (Ford Found. fellow), Atlanta U., 1974, Ph.D. in Polit. Sci. (AAUW fellow), 1978. Tchr., James Monroe High Sch., Fredericksburg, Va., 1970-71; asso. prof. polit. sci. So. U., Baton Rouge, 1974—. Mem. exec. bd., corr. sec. La. Lupus Found., 1978-79. Phelps-Stokes study grantee, summer 1979; Dept. State scholar-diplomat, April 1980. Mem. Nat. Conf. Black Polit. Sci., Am. Polit. Sci. Assn., African Studies Assn., So. Polit. Sci. Assn., Phi Delta Kappa, Pi Gamma Mu. Editor Lupus Newsletter, 1978-79. Office: Box 10321 So U Baton Rouge LA 70813

BRAXTON, HERMAN HARRISON, physician; b. Almanance County, N.C., Nov. 13, 1906; s. James Guy and Nette E. (Guthrie) B.; A.B., U. N.C., 1928; M.D., Johns Hopkins, 1932; m. Anne Norfolk Grimm, June 22, 1935; children—Herman Harrison II, Elizabeth Anne. Mem. house staff Duke Hosp., 1932-33, White Plains (N.Y.) Hosp., 1933-34; gen. practice medicine, Chase City, Va., 1934—; mem. staffs Community Meml. Hosp., South Hill, Va., Southside Community Hosp. Farmville, Va., local med. dir. Nat. Found.; med. examiner Mecklenburg County, 1947—; surgeon So. R.R. Bd. dirs. Chase City Indsl. Devel. Corp.; mem. adv. bd. Fidelity Nat. Bank. Mem. local bi-racial commn., 1965—. Mem. Chase City Town Council, 1955-63. Recipient Outstanding Citizenship award Chase City Jaycees, 1968; Service to Mankind award Mecklenberg Sertoma Club, 1975. Fellow Am. Acad. Family Practice (charter); mem. Va. Med. Soc., A.M.A., Chase City C. of C. (past pres.), Phi Beta Kappa. Episcopalian. Clubs: Lions (past pres., zone chmn.); Mecklenburg Country (past pres.). Home: 440 Walker St Chase City VA 23924 Office: Chase City Med Clinic 946 N Main St Chase City VA 23924

BRAXTON, HERMAN HARRISON, JR., lawyer; b. Durham, N.C., May 15, 1936; s. Herman Harrison and Anne (Grimm) B.; A.B. in Polit. Sci., U. N.C., 1958; J.D., U. Va., 1961; m. Patricia Gail Galway, June 26, 1965; children—Herman Harrison III, Grace Anne, William Marshall. Admitted to Va. bar, 1961; partner firm Willis, Garnett, Braxton & Ashby, Fredericksburg, 1965—; commonwealth atty. City Fredericksburg, 1974—. Pres. Fredericksburg chpt. Va. Mus. Fine Arts, 1970-72. Served to capt. Judge Advocate Gen. Corps, USAF, 1961-64. Recipient distinguished service award Fredericksburg Jr. C. of C. Mem. Fredericksburg C. of C. (pres. 1972-73), Va., 15th Judicial Circuit, Fredericksburg Area (pres. 1980) bar assns., Pi Kappa Alpha, Phi Alpha Delta. Episcopalian. Home: 1204 Charles St Fredericksburg VA 22401 Office: 315 William St Fredericksburg VA 22401

BRAY, CHARLENA HARRIS, educator; b. Birmingham, Ala., Apr. 11, 1945; d. Charlie and Maggie (Green) Harris; B.A., Miles Coll., 1965; M.A., U. Ala., Birmingham, 1971, class AA certificate, 1977. Tchr. high sch. math. Jefferson County Bd. Edn., 1965-72; project dir. human resources program Ala. Center for Higher Edn., Birmingham, 1977—, adminstrv. asst. to exec. dir., 1975—, coordinator gerontology tng. program, 1976—; broadcaster Vet. Affairs Information program WBUL, 1974—. Bd. dirs. Cooper Green Hosp., 1977—, Jefferson County Area Agy. on Aging, 1976-77, Regional Office of Edn. Spl. Programs, 1974-76; sec., chmn. standing com. Birmingham Area Manpower Consortium's Advisory Council, 1974—; sec. Vol. Bur., 1974—; mem. staff spl. programs U. Ala., Birmingham, 1976-78. Recipient Recognition award Spl. Program Regional Advisory Bd., 1976. Mem. Am. Personnel and Guidance Assn., NAACP, Jefferson County Mental Health Assn., Rho Nu Tau (pres. grad. chpt. 1975-77). Baptist. Office: 2121 8th Av N Suite 1520 Birmingham AL 35203

BRAY, JUANITA PHIPPS, microbiologist; b. Galveston, Tex., Feb. 20, 1931; d. James Hansen and Juanita (Fountain) Phipps; student Ward-Belmont Coll., 1947-49; B.A., U. Tex., 1952; M.A., U. Tex. Med. Br., 1965, Ph.D., 1968. Lab. dir. Northwestern U. Med. Sch., San Fernando, Trinidad, W.I., 1968-69; asst. prof. U. Tex. Med. Br., Galveston, 1969-76, U. Houston at Clear Lake City, 1978-79; mgmt. cons. Parker Assos., Metairie, La., 1979—. McLaughlin fellow, 1965-68; NIH tng. grantee, 1964-65; Med. Found. Tex. grantee, 1970-71; McLaughlin grantee, 1971-72. Mem. Am. Soc. for Microbiology, Sigma Xi. Episcopalian. Contbr. articles to profl. jours. Home: 4011 Alberta St Metairie LA 70001

BRAY, NANCY ANN, educator; b. El Paso, Tex., Aug. 3, 1947; d. Otis Kyle and Helen Marjorie (Wilson) Moreland, B.S. with honors, E. Tex. State U., 1968, M.Ed., 1969, Ed.D., 1973; m. Gary G. Bray, Sept. 23, 1972; 1 dau., Laura Elisabeth. Instr. dept. pediatrics U. Tex. Health Sci. Center, 1970-75; asst. prof. U. Tex., Dallas, 1975—; cons. Project Kids Early Childhood Spl. Edn. program Dallas Independent Sch. Dist. Mem. Am. Personnel and Guidance Assn., Council for Exceptional Children Assn., Dallas Assn. Children Learning Disabilities (recording sec. 1974-75), Tex. Psychol. Assn., Alpha Delta Pi. Presbyterian. Contbr. articles in field to prof. jours. Home: 7138 Lavendale St Dallas TX 75230 Office: Green 4 1 Box 688 Richardson TX 75080

BRAZDA, FREDERICK WICKS, pathologist; b. New Orleans, Dec. 17, 1945; s. Fred George and Helen Josephine (Wicks) B.; B.S. cum laude, Tulane U., 1966; M.D., La. State U., 1970; m. Margaret Mary Hubbell, Sept. 8, 1973; 1 son, Geoffrey Frederick. Intern, then resident in pathology Charity Hosp., New Orleans, 1970-75; pathologist Hotel Dieu Hosp., New Orleans, 1975—, dir. sch. med. tech., 1976—; cons. St. Tammany Parish Hosp., Covington, La., Riverside Hosp., Franklinton, La.; asst. clin. prof. La. State U. Med. Center. Diplomate Am. Bd. Pathology. Mem. AMA, Am. Soc. Clin.

Pathologists, Coll. Am. Pathologists, Am. Assn. Clin. Chemistry, So. Med. Assn., La. Med. Soc., La. Pathology Soc., Orleans Parish Med. Soc., New Orleans Grad. Med. Assembly, Phi Beta Kappa, Alpha Omega Alpha, Phi Beta Pi. Democrat. Roman Catholic. Home: 6525 Argonne Blvd New Orleans LA 70124 Office: 2021 Perdido St Hotel Dieu Hosp Lab New Orleans LA 70112

BRAZZELL, EMMA ANN, dietitian; b. Escambia, Fla., Apr. 3, 1953; d. Louis Clark and Annie Pearl B.; B.S., Tenn. State U., 1975; cert. Dietetic Internship Tuskegee Inst., 1976, postgrad., 1977—. Dietary aide Vanderbilt U. Med. Center, Nashville, 1975; dietetic intern Tuskegee Inst., 1975-76; now adj. prof. dept. home econs.; adminstrv. dietitian John A. Andrew Meml. Hosp., Tuskegee Inst., Ala., 1976—; cons. Macon County (Ala.) Sheriffs Dept. Leader Carver dist. Tukabatchee Council Boy Scouts Am., Tuskegee Inst., 1978—. Mem. Am. Dietetic Assn., Ala. Dietetic Assn., Tuskegee Dist. Dietetic Assn., AAUW. Baptist. Home: PO Box 543 Tuskegee Institute AL 36088 Office: Dietary Department Andrew Hospital Tuskegee Institute AL 36088

BREAUX, JOHN BERLINGER, Congressman; b. Crowley, La., Mar. 1, 1944; s. Ezra H., Jr. and Katherine (Berlinger) B.; B.A. in Polit. Sci., U. Southwestern La., 1964; J.D., La. State U., 1967; m. Lois Gail Daigle, Aug. 1, 1964; children—John Berlinger, William Lloyd, Elizabeth Andre, Julia Agnes. Admitted to La. bar, 1967; partner Brown, McKernan, Ingram & Breaux, 1967-68; legislative asst. to Congressman Edwin W. Edwards, 1968-69, dist. asst., 1969-72; mem. 92d-96th Congresses from 7th Dist. La., mem. select com. on outer continental shelf, mem. com. on mcht. marine and fisheries, com. on pub. works and transp.; mem. select com. on coms., Dem. policy and steering com.; chmn. subcom. on fisheries and wildlife conservation and environ. Mem. Dem. Research Orgn. Recipient Am. Legion award. Moot Ct. finalist La. State U., 1966. Mem. La., Acadia Parish bar assns., Internat. Rice Festival Assn. (dir.), Crowley Jr. C. of C., La. Jr. C. of C., Nat. Blue Key Honor Soc., Pi Lambda Beta, Phi Alpha Delta, Lambda Chi Alpha. Democrat. Office: 2159 Rayburn House Office Bldg Washington DC 20515

BREAUX, PAUL WHITNEY, chem. engr.; b. Kaplan, La., Oct. 5, 1934; s. Yves and Isabelle (Vidalier) B.; B.S. in Chem. Engring., La. State U., 1956; m. Vashti Cuevattus Carter, June 4, 1955; children—Janice Gale, Angela Paulette. With Olin Corp., 1956—, shift supr., Niagara Falls, N.Y., 1956-61, chem. supt., McIntosh, Ala., 1961-67; tech. mgr., Saltville, Va., 1967-69, sect. mgr., Charleston, Tenn., 1969-77, mgr. chlor-alkali process tech., 1977—. Mem. Am. Inst. Chem. Engrs. (sec.-treas., v. chmn. Chattanooga sec.). Republican. Roman Catholic. Club: Cleveland Country. Patentee preparation pentachloronitrobenzene, 1977. Home: 3825 Jill St Cleveland TN 37311 Office: PO Box 248 Charleston TN 37310

BREAZEALE, ROSCOE JEFFERSON, chem. co. exec.; b. Salem, S.C., July 27, 1916; s. Ed Thomas and Doshia Marie (Chappell) B.; B.S., U. S.C., 1938, M.S., 1949; m. Rachael Rankin, May 7, 1941; children—Ronald, Jeffrey. Research chemist Am. Enka Corp., 1950-52; prof. organic chemistry Clemson U., 1952-56; tech. sales chem. rep. Sun Chem. Corp., 1956-62, So. sales mgr., Chester, S.C., 1962-72, v.p. sales devel., 1972—; pres. Tenco, Inc., Chester, 1975—; vis. lectr. Clemson U., 1973—. Chmn. bd. Chester County unit Am. Cancer Soc., 1973—; v.p. S.C. div. Am. Cancer Soc., 1977—; deacon Presbyn. Ch., 1975-79. Served with U.S. Army, 1941-42; served to lt. col. USAAF, 1942-47. Mem. Am. Assn. Textile Chemists and Colorists (chmn. Palmetto sect. 1966), S.C. Acad. Sci. Presbyterian. Clubs: Rotary, Moose, Masons, Wildcat Cliffs Country. Home: McLure Woods Dr Chester SC 29706 Office: PO Box 70 Chester SC 29706

BRECHIN, JOHN BRYCE, III, oil co. exec.; b. Beaumont, Tex., Dec. 3, 1926; s. John Bryce and Carlyse (Bliss) B.; B.B.A., U. Tex., 1951; postgrad. U. Houston, 1952-53, Lamar U. Continuing Edn. Program, 1972-74; m. Jane Alice Hodges, Apr. 8, 1951; children—John B. IV, Heidi Lynn (Mrs. Gatlin W. Edwards II), Jamie Leigh, Mark Andrew. Solicitor, Newtex S.S. Lines, Houston, 1951; traffic mgr. oil tool div. Cameron Iron Works, Houston, 1951-54; traffic mgr., mfg. plant buyer Moncrief-Lenoir Mfg. Co., Houston, 1954-57; gen. mgr. Rioco Oil Co., Beaumont, 1957-60; pres. Ranger Ind. Oil Corp., Winnie, Tex., 1960—. Lectr. drilling fluids Lamar U. Oil and Gas Drilling Inst., 1975. Active Boy Scouts Am., 1967—, camping chmn., 1969—, mem. council com., 1964—, recipient Dist. Merit award, 1973, Vigil of Honor, 1977, Silver Beaver award, 1979. Mem. Soc. Petroleum Engrs., Am. Inst. Mining and Metall. Engrs., Optimists. Episcopalian (tchr. 1966-68, mem. bishop's com. 1967). Club: Lions. Patentee drilling fluids additives. Home: 213 Westview Dr Sealy TX 77474 Office: PO Drawer A Sealy TX 77474

BRECK, LOUIS WILLIAM, physician, orthopaedic surgeon; b. El Paso, Mar. 24, 1909; s. Louis M. and Olive Jane (Roblee) B.; B.S., Northwestern U., 1930, M.D., 1933; m. Julia S. North, June 11, 1932; children—Louis W., Julia A., Alan N., Susan M. Rotating intern Mary's Help Hosp., 1932-33, gen. resident, 1933-35; spl. tng. orthopaedic surgery Mayo Clinic, 1935-37; practice medicine, specializing in orthopaedic surgery, El Paso, 1937—; clin. prof. orthopaedic surgery Tex. Tech. U. Sch. Medicine; mem. staff Hotel Dieu Sisters Hosp., chief of staff, 1955; cons. Thomason Gen. Hosp., Carrie Tingley Hosp. for Crippled Children; civilian cons. to William Beaumont Gen. Hosp.; orthopaedic cons. M.P. R.R., Tex. Crippled Children's Div.; sr. cons. med. consultation com. Tex. Rehab. Commn. Trustee Clin. Orthopaedics and Related Research. Served from capt. to lt. col. AUS, 1942-46; chief orthopaedic sect. Regional Hosp., Camp Swift, Tex. Recipient Legion of Honor Order of DeMolay, 1953; Outstanding Civilian Service award Dept. Army, 1970; Order of Phoenix, others; Physician's award of year Tex. Rehab. Assn., 1966; Nicolas Andry award Assn. Bone and Joint Surgeons, 1965. Diplomate Am. Bd. Orthopaedic Surgery. Fellow A.C.S., AAAS, Am. Writers Assn.; mem. Am., Tex. State, med. assns., El Paso County Med. Soc. (pres. 1961), Am. Acad. Orthopaedic Surgeons, Assn. Bone and Joint Surgeons (pres. 1955, Distinguished Service award 1977), Western (pres. N.Mex. chpt. 1958), Texas (pres. 1950) orthopaedic assns., Societe Internationale de Chirurgie et de Traumatologie, Tex. Soc. Athletic Team Physicians (pres. 1965), Tex. Traumatic Surg. Soc. (pres. 1967), Tex. Rehab. Assn. (pres. 1968), Sigma Alpha Epsilon, Phi Beta Pi (Arnold-Surman lectr. U. Tex. 1951). Mason (32 deg., Shriner), Kiwanian. Author: Atlas of the Osteochondroses. Editorial bd., trustee Clin. Orthopaedics. Contbr. articles to profl. jours. Home: 1207 N Kansas St El Paso TX 79902 Office: 1209 N Kansas St El Paso TX 79902

BRECKINRIDGE, CHARLES EDWARD, JR., educator; b. Louisville, June 21, 1923; s. Charles Edward and Elizabeth Clark (Kendall) B.; B.S. with distinction, U. Ky., 1953; M.S., Purdue U., 1959, Ph.D. (NIH fellow), 1960; m. Doris Jean Smith, June 25, 1955; children—Charles Edward III, Debbie Jean, Richard Glenn. Instr., U. Ky., Lexington, 1954-57; instr. Purdue U., Lafayette, Ind., 1957-59, prof., 1964; sr. health physicist Oak Ridge Nat. Lab., 1960-63; sr. scientist Hanford Labs., Richland, Wash., 1963; prof. environ. health scis. Sch. Pharmacy, U. Ark. Med. Center, Little Rock, 1965-75, chmn. dept., 1965-75, dir. radiol. health tng. program, 1965-75, prof. clin. pharmacy, chmn. dept. clin. pharmacy, 1975-76, prof., chmn. dept. nuclear pharmacy Coll. of Pharmacy, 1976—. Mem. Am. Pharm. Assn., AAAS, Am. Assn. Colls. of Pharmacy, Ark. Pharm. Assn., Pulaski County Pharm. Assn., Sigma Xi, Rho Chi, Phi Delta Chi. Asst. editor: Nuclear Safety, 1962-63. Contbr. articles to profl. jours. Home: Route 6 Box 202-G Benton AR 72015

BREDAL, ROY HENRY, JR., mech. engr.; b. Spartanburg, S.C., Aug. 7, 1946; s. Roy Henry and Mildred Lois (McBride) B.; B.S. in Mech. Engring., Clemson U., 1968; m. Monte Peeples, Oct. 30, 1976; 1 dau., Monica Anne. Project engr. Hercules Inc., Spartanburg, and Wilmington, N.C., 1968-75; project engr. Agrico, Inc., Lakeland, Fla., 1975-76; resident engr. Constrn. Mgmt. Div., J.E. Sirrine Co., Greenville, S.C., 1976-77; project engr. Internat. Mineral & Chem. Co., Bartow, Fla., 1977—. Served with USNR, 1970-72. Decorated Navy Commendation medal. Mem. ASME, Am. Mgmt. Assn., Kappa Sigma. Methodist. Home: 1361 Summit Chase Dr W Lakeland FL 33803 Office: PO Box 867 Bartow FL 33830

BREELAND, GELENE ELIZABETH WALLACE, nurse; b. Birmingham, Ala., Mar. 22, 1951; d. Charles Edward and Betty (Reese) Wallace; student Jefferson State Jr. Coll., 1969-71; diploma Carraway Methodist Med. Center Sch. Nursing, Birmingham, 1971-73; m. Stanley David Breeland, July 1, 1977; stepchildren—Stanley David, Phillip Jason. Nursing asst. Carraway Meth. Med. Center, 1969-73, staff nurse, 1973-74, head nurse emergency dept., 1975—; nurse, night supr. Lakeshore Hosp., Homewood, Ala., 1974. Mem. Emergency Dept. Nurses Assn. Baptist. Office: 1615 25th St N Birmingham AL 35234

BREELAND, SALLY ANN, found. exec.; b. Jacksonville, Fla., Oct. 31, 1944; s. William N. and Ellen Rose (Smith) Case; student U. Md., 1964-65, Tarleton State U. Extension, 1976-80; m. Allan H. Breeland, Jr., Sept. 20, 1977; children—William Joseph Lacher, Christopher Brian Lacher, Sarah Ellen. Counselor, Evins Personnel Consultants, Temple, Waco, Tex., 1972-74; tech. writer and counselor Office Community Devel., City of Waco, 1975-76; coordinator student activities Tex. State Tech. Inst., Waco, 1976-80; exec. dir. March of Dimes Birth Defects Found., Waco, 1980—. Bd. dirs. ARC, Waco, 1974-75. Named Evins Counselor of Yr., 1972, 73. Mem. Tex. Assn. Coll. and Univ. Personnel Adminstrs., Jr. Coll. Student Personnel Assn. Tex., Tex. Tech. Soc., Tex. Jr. Coll. Press Assn., Nat. Fedn. Bus. and Profl. Women's Clubs. Republican. Episcopalian. Home: 507 Travis Mart TX 76664 Office: 534-A New Rd Waco TX 76710

BREEN, JOSEPH WILLIAM, chem. co. exec.; b. Phila., Aug. 4, 1945; s. Joseph James and Bertha (Popowsky) B.; student Muskingum Coll., 1963-64; B.A., U. Del., 1968, B.Chem. Engring., 1968; M.B.A., U. Pa., 1971; m. Linda Jean Miller, Sept. 2, 1967; children—Tara Leigh, William Ryan. Mktg. asso. Westvaco Corp., Charleston, S.C., 1971-73, product mgr. new ventures, 1973-74, dist. sales mgr. custom chem. dept., Mulberry, Fla., 1974-75, ops. mgr. custom chem. dept., 1975-76, mktg. mgr. carbon dept., Covington, Va., 1976-78, gen. mktg. mgr. oleochem. dept., Charleston, S.C., 1978-79, gen. mgr., 1979—; vis. lectr. Coll. Charleston. Served with U.S. Army Res., 1968-74. Mem. Am. Inst. Chem. Engrs., AIME, Am. Chem. Soc. Republican. Presbyterian. Club: Snee Farm Country. Home: 1080 Deleisseline Blvd Snee Farm Mount Pleasant SC 29464 Office: PO Box 70848 Charleston Heights SC 29405

BREESKIN, BARNETT, orch. condr.; b. N.Y.C., Feb. 20, 1914; s. Saul and Sadye (Koonin) B.; student L.I. U., 1931-32, Bklyn. City Coll., 1932-34; m. Annette Lager, June 6, 1962. Mem. violin sect. Nat. Orch., Washington, 1939-45; pvt. instr., Washington and Md., 1945-55; condr., mgr. Miami Beach (Fla.) Symphony Orch., 1955—, lifetime contract, 1977—. Chmn. Miami Beach Social Sgrvice Advisory Bd. Mem. Cultural Execs. Council of Dade County (Fla.). Office: 420 Lincoln Rd Miami Beach FL 33139

BREITHAUPT, THOMAS BROWN, biochemist; b. Gatesville, Tex., Apr. 13, 1946; s. Claude Vernon and Francis (Brown) B.; B.S., U. Tex., Arlington, 1969; M.A. in Teaching, Tex. Christian U., 1975, Ph.D. in Chemistry, 1977; m. Barbara Janine Zaker, Apr. 1, 1972; 1 son, August Thomas. Research asso. in biochemistry Med. U. S.C., Charleston, 1977-78, Fla. State U. Tallahassee, 1978-80; asst. prof. chemistry Fla. A&M U., Tallahassee, 1980—. Served with Hosp. Corps, USNR, 1969-73. Welch fellow, 1973-77. Mem. Sigma Xi. Home: 124 Westridge Dr Tallahassee FL 32304 Office: Dept Chemistry Fla A&M U Tallahassee FL 32306

BRELAND, LOIS TRUE, humanist, educator; b. Lumberton, Miss., Apr. 5, 1915; d. George William and Della (Bufkin) T.; B.S., U. So. Miss., with highest honors, 1958; M.S., U. So. Miss., 1963; m. Roland Woodruff Breland, Jan. 10, 1940; children—Elizabeth Adele Clark, Carol Lynne Lancaster. Tchr. English, Petal (Miss.) High Sch., 1958-63; part-time instr. English methods U. So. Miss., Hattiesburg, 1958-63, instr. English, also dir. English proficiency tests, 1963-65, asst. prof., dir. freshman English, 1965-74, asst. prof., univ. editor, 1974—. Mem. Miss. Assn. Educators, U. So. Miss. Alumni Assn., Pi Kappa Pi, Lambda Iota Tau, Kappa Delta Pi. Republican. Baptist. Club: Order of Eastern Star. Home: 221 N 20th Ave Hattiesburg MS 39401 Office: Dept English U So Miss So Sta Box 8188 Hattiesburg MS 39401

BRELSFORD, ALLEN KENT, mfg. co. exec.; b. Dayton, Ohio, May 4, 1947; s. Edwin Allen and Lillian (Urban) B.; B.B.A., Eastern Ky. U., 1969; m. Patricia Bailey, June 7, 1969. Market analyst Delco Products div. Gen. Motors Corp., Dayton, 1969-72; research asst. Colo. State U., Ft. Collins, 1973; buyer, asst. store mgr. Denver Dry Goods Co., 1973-77; mktg. mgr. Koehring Atomaster, Bowling Green, Ky., 1979—; part-time instr. Western Ky. U. Adv. local Jr. Achievement. Served with U.S. Army, 1970-71; Vietnam. Decorated Bronze Star; recipient Siccardi award Longmont Jaycees, 1977. Mem. Western Ky. Mktg. Club, Bowling Green Jaycees. Republican. Methodist. Club: Western Ky. Fencers. Address: Route 13 Box 200 Minnie Way Bowling Green KY 42101

BRELSFORD, GEORGE WILLIAM, V, fiberglass co. exec.; b. Bridgeton, N.J., Oct. 5, 1927; s. George William and Jeanette (Brockway) B.; A.B., Vanderbilt U., 1949; m. Patricia Murphy, Oct. 15, 1949; children—George William VI, Kathleen, Robin, Jean Ann, Debbie. Personnel staff asst. Owens-Ill., Bridgeton, N.J., 1949-59, employment mgr., Barrington, N.J., 1959-60, corporate communications supr., Toledo, 1960-63; personnel dir. Owens-Corning Fiberglas Corp., Aiken, S.C., 1963—; adj. prof. U. S.C., Columbia, 1971—. Pres. Aiken County United Fund, 1970. Adv. bd. Salvation Army; bd. dirs. Aiken County Public Service Authority. Recipient communications award for mgmt. publs. Internat. Council Indsl. Editors, 1961, 62. Mem. Am. Assn. Indsl. Editors (dir. 1962, 63), Am. Soc. Personnel Adminstrn., Am. Soc. Tng. and Devel., S.C. (chmn. human relations com.), Aiken (dir.) chambers commerce. Kiwanian (pres. 1974). Clubs: Pinnacle (Augusta, Ga.); Palmetto Golf, Midland Valley Country, Green Boundary (Aiken). Home: 807 Calhoun St Aiken SC 29801 Office: PO Box 499 Aiken SC 29801

BRELSFORD, JEANNE KAYE, criminologist; b. Freer, Tex., Oct. 28, 1943; B.S., Sam Houston State U., 1967, M.A., 1974. Unit counselor and psychometrist Tex. Dept. Corrections, 1967-70; diagnostician Edn. Service Center, Region VI, 1970-72; psychometrist Harris County Dept. Edn., 1972-73; dept. Harris County Sheriff's Dept., Houston, 1973-74; instr. Harris County Sheriff's Acad., Humble, Tex., 1973—; program dir., instr. criminal justice Abilene Christian U., Metrocenter, Houston, 1974-75; instr., chmn. div. criminal justice U. Houston, Downtown Coll., 1975—; cons. learning disabilities in delinquent children and youth. Mem. Acad. Criminal Justice Scis., AAUP, Internat. Platform Assn., Tex. Corrections Assn. Home: 8103 Ivan Reid Dr Houston TX 77040 Office: 1 Main Houston TX 77002

BREMMER, JOSEPH PAUL, elec. design engr.; b. Kansas City, Mo., Dec. 3, 1946; s. Paul and Dorothy May (Monger) B.; A.A., Los Angeles Harbor Coll., 1971; B.S. in Engring. Tech., Calif. State Poly. U., 1973; M.S.E.E. (Hughes Aircraft Co. fellow), U. Calif. at Los Angeles, 1976; M.B.A., U. Dallas, 1979; m. Margaret Cecelia Pope, Sept. 4, 1971. Tech. staff Hughes Aircraft Co., Culver City, Calif., 1973-76; design engr. Tex. Instruments, Inc., Dallas, 1977-78; product mgr. Harris Data Communications, Dallas, 1978—. Served with U.S. Army, 1966-68. Recipient Outstanding Scholar award Calif. Poly. U., 1973; Achievement award Bank of Am., Los Angeles, 1971; Leon Heseman scholarship, 1972, scholarship Lomita Rotary Club, 1971. Mem. Sigma Iota Epsilon, Tau Alpha Pi, Alpha Sigma Epsilon, Alpha Gamma Sigma. Republican. Roman Catholic. Inventor in field. Home: 6409 Green Oaks Ct Plano TX 75023 Office: 16001 Dallas Pkwy Dallas TX 75240

BRENAN, RICHARD LEE, oil co. exec.; b. Burbank, Calif., June 13, 1930; s. Jack R. and Ruth Oretta (Oppe) B.; A.A., Palomar Coll., 1949; B.S., U. Redlands, 1953; postgrad. U. Calif. at Los Angeles, 1953-54; m. June Howells, Haviland, Nov. 20, 1971; children—Cathleen Gale, Cynthia Lee. Geophysicist, United Geophys. Corp., Pasadena, Calif., 1954-63; geophysicist Union Oil Co., Calif., Bakersfield, 1963-64, Olympia, Wash., 1964-65, Santa Fe Springs, Calif., 1965-66, div. geophysicist, Los Angeles, 1966, dist. exploration mgr., Santa Fe Springs, 1966-71, Casper, Wyo., 1971-76, sr. geophysicist, Houston, 1977-79, regional geophysicist, 1979—. Served with U.S. Army, 1950-52. Registered geologist, Calif. Mem. Am. Girls Sports Assn. (pres. 1971), Soc. Exploration Geophysicists, Casper Geophys. Soc., Pacific Coast Soc. Exploration Geophysicists, Wyo. Geol. Assn., Am. Petroleum Inst. Republican. Clubs: Briar, Kingwood Country. Home: 3414 Fawn Creek Dr Kingwood TX 77339 Office: 4635 SW Freeway Houston TX 77027

BRENNAN, CLAYTON PAUL, plastic mfg. co. exec.; b. San Antonio, Jan. 2, 1932; s. George and Leola Alberta (Wetzel) Brennan; B.A., Marietta (Ohio) Coll., 1953; B.S., U. Calif., Santa Barbara, 1954; M.B.A., N.Y. U., 1964; m. Dolores Burks, July 14, 1956; children—Terrise Ann, Christopher Mark. Mktg. exec. Am. Can Co., various locations, 1960-70; mktg. dir. Van Leer U.S.A., Houston, 1970-75; v.p. Texcon Products, Inc., Houston, 1975—. Mem. adv. panel to Tex. State Rep. Milton Fox and U.S. Rep. John Archer, congressional adv. com. on consumer safety in packaging. Served with USMC, 1954-60. Mem. Houston C. of C., Nat. Flexible Packaging Assn. (past dir.). Soc. Plastics Industries, Soc. Packaging and Handling Engrs., Packaging Inst., Marine Corps Res. Officers Assn., Marine Corps Aviation Assn. Episcopalian. Office: 3301 Sherman St Houston TX 77003

BRENNAN, SISTER FLORA, artist, educator; b. Toledo, Ohio, Sept. 12, 1918; d. Andrew Philip and Clara Viola (Hartley) B.; B.A., Marygrove Coll., Detroit, 1952; M.E. in Art Edn., Wayne State U., 1961; M.F.A., U. Notre Dame, 1970. Joined Sisters of the Immaculate Heart of Mary, 1935; tchr. Mich. pvt. schs., 1940-53; tchr. fine arts and crafts St. Mary High Sch., Akron, Ohio, 1953-58, St. John High Sch., Jackson, Mich., 1958-62; founder dept. fine arts Cath. U. P.R., Ponce, 1962, chmn., 1962-71, instr. fine arts, 1971—; exhibited in various shows, including Wayne State U. Alumni Show, 1962, Ponce Art Mus., 1970, 71, 73, U. P.R. Gallery, Mayaguez, 1970, Biblioteca Encarnacion Valdes of Cath. U., Ponce, 1975; paintings and ceramics in numerous collections in U.S. and P.R.; art dir. Charismatic Renewal Services, Aguas Buenas, P.R., 1975-78; organizer, dir. Apostolate of the Sick, Ponce, 1973. Recipient Tchr. of Tchrs. plaque Ponce Dept. Public Instrn., 1978. Mem. Ponce Museum Club. Art editor Alabare, 1974-78; contbr. articles to profl. jours.

BRENNAN, RICHARD OLIVER, physician; b. Maplehill, Kans., Feb. 25, 1916; s. William M. and Cor A. (Sawyer) B.; grad. jr. coll., Kansas City, Mo., 1928; Ph.G., Mo. Coll. Pharmacy, 1925; D.O., Kansas City Coll. Osteo. Medicine, 1936; M.D., D.P.H., Kansas City U. Physicians and Surgeons, 1939; m. Gloria Wild, 1975; children—Phyllis, Patricia, Michael, June, Patrick. Intern, Bush Hosp., Harper, Kans., 1937, Lakeside Hosp., Kansas City, Mo., 1937; resident Urol. Clinic and Presbyn. Hosp., Phila., 1940-41; preceptee Warren Urol. Clinic, Kansas City, 1941; practice medicine specializing in preventive medicine, Houston, 1948—; instr. medicine and toxicology Kansas City Coll. Osteo. Medicine, 1941-47, instr. urology and proctology, 1941-47; instr. medicine and toxicology Kansas City U. Physicians and Surgeons, 1938-39; dir. Bellevue Metabolic Clinic, 1948-79; chief of staff Houston Osteo. Med. Hosp., 1952-53; vis. prof. preventive medicine Okla. Coll. Osteo. Medicine, 1975—; pres. Internat. Preventive Medicine Found., 1978-79, Brennan Preventive Medicine Center, 1979—; co-founder Nat. Child Health Conf., Kansas City, Mo., 1940; guest lectr. preventive medicine and nutrition to various profl. and lay groups, 1960—; guest appearances numerous radio and TV shows, 1960—. Recipient Miller Biomed. award, 1972; Appreciation award Internat. Preventive Medicine Found., 1975; Alumnus of Yr. award Kansas City Coll. of Osteo. Medicine, 1976. Fellow Internat. Acad. Preventive Medicine (Founders award 1970), Internat. Coll. Applied Nutrition, Am. Coll. Gen. Practitioners (hon.); mem. Tex. Soc. Gen. Practitioners (founder, pres. 1965), Am. Osteo. Assn., World Med. Assn., Am. Public Health Assn., Am. Osteo. Coll. Preventive Medicine (pres. 1970), Internat. Acad. Preventive Medicine (chmn. bd. 1970-78), Am. Clin. Soc. Arthritis, Orthomolecular Psychiat. Soc., Am. Med. Writers Assn., Tex. Soc. Osteo. Radiologists (founder, pres. 1965), Harris County Soc. Osteo. Medicine, Am. Geriatric Soc., Internat. Metabolic Soc. (dir. 1950-61), Authors Guild, Psi Sigma Alpha. Club: Rotary. Author: Become Nutrition Wise, 1970; Help for the Loser, 1972; Nutrigenetics, 1975; Treasury of Diet Menus, 1979; Diabetes and Hypoglycemia Handbook, 1979; Coronary? Cancer? God's Answer: Prevent It, 1979; contbr. articles to med. jours.; editorial bd. NW Acad. Preventive Medicine, 1970—. Address: 5615 Richmond Suite 151 Houston TX 77057

BRENNER, JOANN FISHMAN, speech and lang. pathologist; b. Atlanta, Ga., Apr. 17, 1953; d. Herman and Nina Jane (Bloch) Fishman; B.S. in Edn. (Z Soc. Shannon scholar 1975), U. Va., 1975, M.Ed. in Speech Pathology, 1977; m. Theodore Ira Brenner, Dec. 26, 1976. Unit. head, supr. counselor's activities RJCC Camps, Richmond, Va., 1977; speech and lang. pathologist Hanover County schs., Ashland, Va. 1977—; recreation leader Summer Recreation for Mentally Retarded, Henrico County, Richmond, 1978—. Mem. Am. Speech-Lang. Hearing Assn. (cert. of clin. competence), Speech and Hearing Assn. Va., Alpha Lambda Delta (past v.p.). Home: 2306 Thousand Oaks Dr Richmond VA 23229 Office: 200 Berkley St Ashland VA 23005

BRENNER, WILLIAM GERARD, constrn. equipment mfg. co. exec.; b. Dusseldorf, Ger., Jan. 21, 1929; came to U.S., 1957, naturalized, 1963; s. Guillermo E. and Agnes M. (Priemer) B.; A.S. in Bus. Adminstrn., Dusseldorfer Beruf Akademi (W.Ger.), 1946; grad. Nat. Corr. Sch., 1953; m. Maxi E. Priemer, Sept. 11, 1970; children—Christel D., Rebecca M., Michelle E. With contrn. equipment importers, Peru, 1947-57, Internat. sales Huber Corp., Marion, Ohio, 1957-63, Galion Mfg. Div., internat. sales rep. to asst. v.p. internat. Constrn. Equipment div., Galion, Ohio, 1963-77, gen. sales mgr. internat. ops. A-T-O Constrn. Equipment div., Charleston, S.C., 1977—. Republican. Roman Catholic.

BRENT, ADALIE JOLEENE, painter, mus. dir.; b. Dallas, Nov. 27, 1920; d. Joseph and Bertha (Raphiel) Margules; B.A. UCLA, 1941, postgrad 1943-44, La. State U., 1956-57; m. Allan R. Brent, Dec. 19, 1941; 1 dau., Joanna Raphiel. One man shows: UCLA Grad. Student Show, 1941, La. Art Commn., 1965; two-man show Baton Rouge Gallery, 1979; group shows include Dallas Mus. Fine Arts, Witte Mus., La. Art Commn., Ark. Art Mus., PanAm. Exhn.; represented in permanent collections: WAFB Broadcasting Co., Vincent Price Collection, firm Kantrow, Spant, Weaver and Walter, Am. Bank, Cath. Life Center, La. State U. Law Center, various chs.; works include leaded and faceted windows, murals; tchr. art, supr. Calif. Public Schs., 1941-42; instr. art La. State U., 1947-51, instr. landscape architecture, 1980; tchr. St. Joseph Acad., Baton Rouge, 1955-63; dir. La. Arts and Sci. Center, Baton Rouge, 1963—. Mem. Am. Assn. Mus., Am. Assn. Youth Mus. (past sec., treas., v.p.), Delta Kappa Gamma, Kappa Delta. Office: 100 S River Rd Baton Rouge LA 70801

BRERETON, THOMAS FRANCIS, educator, urban planner; b. N.Y.C., May 21, 1945; s. John T. and Lucy G. (Moore) B.; B.S. in Fgn. Service cum laude, Georgetown U., 1967; M.R.P., Syracuse U., 1970, Ph.D., 1973. Cons. Nat. Capital Planning Commn., Washington, 1969, 71-72; city planner Fayette, Miss., 1970; asst. prof. urban studies Trinity U., San Antonio, 1972-79, asso. prof., 1979—, dir. univ.-municipal league joint project on urban mgmt. edn., 1975-77. Mem. San Antonio Citizens' Advisory Com., Tex. Constl. Revision Commn., Austin, 1973-74, active in pvt. groups, 1973-75. Herbert H. Lehman fellow, Syracuse U., 1967-71; recipient distinguished service award Tex. Chpt., Am. Inst. Planners, 1975. Mem. Am. Inst. Cert. Planners (chmn. legislative affairs, San Antonio section, 1977—, vice chmn. awards, Tex. chpt. 1974-75, chmn. speaker arrangements nat. conf. 1975), AAUP, Am. Soc. Public Adminstrn., Am. Soc. Planning Ofcls., Council Univ. Insts. for Urban Affairs, Internat. Platform Assn., Nat. Assn. Schs. of Pub. Affairs and Admnstrn. (program and research section rep. 1975—), Nat. Municipal League. Author, editor in fields of city planning, ednl. finance, comparative local govt., and urban mgmt. edn. Home: 112 Lindell Pl San Antonio TX 78212 Office: Dept of Urban Studies Trinity U San Antonio TX 78284

BRES, PHILIP WAYNE, automobile mktg. co. exec.; b. Beaumont, Tex., Mar. 6, 1950; s. DeFrance R. and Edna Gene (Griffith) B.; B.B.A. with honors, Lamar U., 1972; M.B.A., Stephen F. Austin State U., 1973; m. Kathryn Anne Perkins, Sept. 8, 1973. Distbn. mgr., bus. mgmt. mgr. Mazda Motors Am., Houston, 1973-75; analyst cons. C.H. McCormack & Assos., Houston, 1975-76; asso. Frank Gillman Pontiac Co., Houston, 1976-79; sales rep. David Taylor Cadillac Co., Houston, 1979—. Mem. Am. Mktg. Assn., Phi Kappa Phi, Phi Eta Sigma. Home: 13032 Clarewood Dr Houston TX 77072

BRESSLER, BERNARD, psychiatrist; b. Milan, Mich., May 22, 1917; s. Sam and Rose (Grossman) B.; A.B., Washington U., St. Louis, 1938, M.D., 1942; grad. Chgo. Psychoanalytic Inst., 1951. Intern, St. Louis City Hosp., 1942-43; resident in psychiatry St. Louis City Sanitarium, 1943, Michael Reese Hosp., Chgo., 1943-45; practice medicine specializing in psychiatry, Chgo., 1946-53; mem. faculty Duke U. Med. Center, Durham, N.C., 1955—, prof. psychiatry, 1962—; asst. dir. U. N.C.-Duke Psychoanalytic Inst., also tng. analyst. Served with U.S. Army, 1953-55. Fellow Am. Psychiat. Assn. (life); mem. AMA, Am. Psychoanalytic Assn., Am. Psychometric Soc., Pan Am. Med. Assn. Unitarian. Home: 4001 Cheyenne Rd Richmond VA 23231 Office: 106 N Thompson St Richmond VA 23221

BRETT, CLAUDE WILLIAM, hosp. adminstr.; b. Richmond, Va., Oct. 14, 1942; s. Claude W. and Gloria Esther (Penny) B.; B.S. in Psychology, Old Dominion U., 1971, cum laude; M.S. in Psychology, Va. Poly. Inst. and State U., 1973, Ph.D., 1977; m. Mary Elaine Diddle, Nov. 27, 1962; children—Adam William, Paige Elaine. Psychologist, div. of corrections Southampton Correctional Farm, Va., 1973; lectr. Wytheville (Va.) Community Coll., 1973-78; clin. psychologist Southwestern State Hosp., Marion, Va., 1973-76, dir. tng. and research, 1976-77; clin. dir. Mount Rogers Community Mental Health and Mental Retardation Services Bd., 1977-78; dir. Southwestern State Hosp., Marion, 1978-80; dep. commr. Dept. Mental Health and Mental Retardation, Richmond, 1980—. Bd. dirs. YMCA, 1978—. Served with USAF, 1963-68; Vietnam. Mem. Am. Psychol. Assn. Assn. of Mental Health Adminstrs. Contbr. articles on physiol. psychology to profl. publs. Office: Drawer 670 Marion VA 24354

BREUER, BRADFORD ROBERT, banker; b. San Antonio, Aug. 9, 1946; s. Alfred and Harriet Isabell (Kingsbacker) B; B.A. in Govt., Austin Coll., 1968. Mgr. credit card ops. Alamo Nat. Bank, San Antonio, 1969-70, asst. cashier comml. credit dept., 1970-71, asst. v.p. comml. loan dept., 1971-73, v.p. comml. loans, 1973, v.p. banking services dept., 1973-78, sr. v.p., mgr. banking services div., 1978—. Bd. dirs. Friends of McNay Art Inst., 1975-79, pres., 1978; bd. dirs. San Antonio Livestock Expn., 1973—; pres. San Antonio River Assn., 1977—; trustee Amon Carter Mus. Western Art, 1978—; vice-chmn. City of San Antonio Conv. and Visitors Commn., 1978—. Mem. Am. Mktg. Assn., Am. Inst. Banking, Austin Coll. Alumni Assn. (dir. 1977—), Order of Alamo (dir. 1969-77, pres. 1977). Episcopalian. Clubs: Argyle, San Antonio German, Oak Hills Country, Conopus. Home: 403 Madison St Apt 2 San Antonio TX 78204 Office: Alamo Nat Bank 154 E Commerce St San Antonio TX 78205

BREWER, CHARLES EUGENE, purchasing agt.; b. Knoxville, Tenn., Jan. 29, 1934; s. Maurice Jackson and Gladys Louise (Whaley) B.; B.S., U. Tenn., 1956; M.B.A., U. Ala., 1966; m. Betty Carolyn Skelton. Procurement analyst Army Ballistics Missile Agency, Redstone Arsenal, Ala., 1958-60; contract negotiator NASA, Huntsville, Ala., 1960-67, chief mgmt. support office, 1967-74; staff purchasing agent TVA, Chattanooga, Tenn., 1974—; instr. staff Army Logistics Mgmt. Center, Ft. Lee, Va., 1974—. Served with U.S. Army, 1956-58. Certified profl. contracts mgr. and purchasing mgr. Mem. Nat. Mgmt. Assn., U. Tenn. Alumni Club (pres. N. Ala. chpt. 1960-63, 66-67), Delta Sigma Pi. Baptist. Home: 8921 Villa Rica Circle Chattanooga TN 37421 Office: 6700 Commerce Union Bank Bldg Chattanooga TN 37401

BREWER, CLYDE WESLEY, mfg. co. exec.; b. Mineral Wells, Tex., Aug. 31, 1930; s. Clyde Alfred and Maezelle Hayes (Rike) B.; M.S. in Bus., U. Dallas, 1977; m. Norma Dean Maxey, June 23, 1960; children—Elizabeth Sue, Brenda Gail, Kerry, Laurie Kai, David Wesley, Lisa Karen, Leah Kim. With dept. quality mgmt. Vought Corp., Dallas, 1951-78; dir. quality Otis Engring. Co., Dallas, 1978—; owner Creative Visability Systems, Grand Prairie, Tex., 1978—. Mem. adv. bd. Dallas Jr. Coll., 1980—. Served with U.S. Navy, 1948-51. Recipient Spl. Apollo Commendation, NASA, 1977. Registered profl. quality engr., Calif. Mem. Am. Soc. Quality Control, Am. Mgmt. Assn., Mensa, Sigma Iota Epsilon. Author: (with Tom Frongillo) Assurance Costing For Profit, 1977. Home: 2505 Locksley St Grand Prairie TX 75050 Office: PO Box 34380 Dallas TX 75234

BREWER, GORDON MORGAN, investment co. exec.; b. New Orleans, Mar. 8, 1946; s. Marion Chester and Elizabeth Joyce (Morgan) B.; B.S., McNeese State U., 1969; M.S., Ga. Inst. Tech., 1977; m. Susan Virginia Davis, Nov. 23, 1973; children—Andrew Morgan, Elizabeth Anne. Mgr., Airborne Freight Corp., Atlanta, 1972-73; accountant Shallowford Hosp., Atlanta, 1973-76; prodn. supt. Country Pride Foods, Ltd., Natchitoches, La., 1978-80; gen. mgr. Atchafalaya Investment Co., Inc., New Orleans, 1980—. Served as capt. Ordnance Corps, U.S. Army, 1969-72. Decorated Army Commendation medal, Bronze Star with oak leaf cluster. Mem. Assn. M.B.A. Execs., Ga. Tech. Alumni Assn., N.G. Assn. U.S., Kappa Sigma. Democrat. Methodist. Home: 84 Lisa Ave Kenner LA 70062 Office: 6944 Canal Blvd New Orleans LA 70124

BREWER, ROSE MARIE, sociologist; b. Tulsa, Oct. 30, 1947; d. Wilson and Cloviece R. B.; B.A. with honors magna cum laude, Northeastern State Coll., 1969; M.A., Ind. U., 1971, Ph.D. (fellow), 1976. Asso. instr. sociology Ind. U., Bloomington, 1971-73; vis. lectr., asst. prof. Rice U., Houston, 1974-77; asst. prof. U. Tex. Austin, 1977—; cons. Nat. Endowment for Humanities project Women in Tex. History. Bd. dirs. Big Bros. and Big Sisters, Austin. Mem. Assn. Black Sociologists (exec. bd. 1977—, sec.-treas.), Black Women for Social Change, Sociologists for Women in Soc., Am. Sociol. Assn., Phi Gamma Mu, Alpha Chi, Rho Theta Sigma. Office: Dept Sociology U Texas Burdine Hall 468 Austin TX 78712

BREWSTER, ROBERT GENE, concert singer, educator; b. Pinson, Ala., July 7, 1938; s. Hubert and Chrisella (Ayers) B.; B.Mus., Wheaton Coll., 1958; M.M., Ind. U., 1961; Ph.D., Washington U., St. Louis, 1967, Konzertreife Diploma, Stuttgart Musikhochschule, 1970; diplom. Mozarteum Salzburg, 1969. Tchr. music and French, Westfield (Ala.) High Sch., 1959-60; chmn. dept. music Miles Coll., Birmingham, Ala., 1960-62; chmn. area fine arts Jackson (Miss.) Coll., 1962-63; chmn. dept. music Dillard U., New Orleans, 1974; chmn. dept. voice U. Miami, Coral Gables, Fla., 1974—; guest lectr. Stanford U. in Germany, Beutelsbach, 1968-70; dozent fur gesang Berliner Kirchenmusikschule, 1970-72; consert tours throughout Europe, Asia and The Ams. Seely Mudd fellow, 1964-66; Fulbright fellow, 1966-68; Deutsche Akademische Austausch Dienst award, 1968-70. Mem. Nat. Assn. Tchrs. of Singing, Coll. Music Soc., AAUP, Nat. Assn. Schs. of Music, Phi Mu Alpha. Recs. include I See the Stars, 1961. Home: 125 San Sebastian Ave Coral Gables FL 33134 Office: U Miami Sch Music Coral Gables FL 33124

BRIAN, ALEXIS MORGAN, JR., lawyer; b. New Orleans, Oct. 4, 1928; s. Alexis Morgan and Evelyn (Thibaut) B.; B.A. in Sociology, La. State U., 1949, J.D., 1956; M.S. in Psychology, Trinity U., 1954; m. Elizabeth Louise Graham, Mar. 17, 1951; children—Robert Morgan, Ellen Graham. Admitted to La. bar, 1956; asso. firm Deutsch, Kerrigan & Stiles, New Orleans, 1956-60, partner, 1961-79; sr. partner firm Brian, Simon, Peragine, Smith & Redfearn, New Orleans, 1979—; mem. legal adv. council Ams. United for Separation Ch. and State, 1977—. Mem. com. on bds. So. Bapt. Conv., 1969, mem. exec. bd. New Orleans Bapt. Assn., 1958-63, sec. trustees, 1967-70. Asst. scoutmaster local troop Boy Scouts Am., 1963-72. Trustee New Orleans Bapt. Theol. Sem., 1961-74, v.p., 1966-68, pres., 1968-74; bd. dirs. Goodwill Industries, 1968-77, 79—, v.p., mem. exec. com., 1975-77, mem. adv. bd., 1978; bd. dirs. New Orleans Bapt. Theol. Sem. Found., 1972—, Inter-Varsity Christian Fellowship, 1974—; bd. dirs. Trinity Christian Community, 1970-78, treas., 1977-78. Served with USAF, 1951-55. Named Boss of Year, New Orleans Legal Secs. Assn., 1966. Mem. Am. (constrn. industry forum and fidelity and surety coms.), La. (asst. examiner admissions com.), New Orleans bar assns., Internat. Assn. Ins. Counsel (fidelity and surety com.), La. Assn. Def. Counsel, Def. Research Inst., Am. Arbitration Assn. (panel of arbitrators 1970—), Internat. House, La. Civil Service League, La. State U. Found., Upper Carrollton Neighborhood Assn. (v.p. 1976-77), Phi Delta Phi, Theta Xi. Baptist (deacon; trustee; tchr.; lay preacher). Home: 1738 S Carrollton Ave New Orleans LA 70118 Office: 4300 One Shell Sq New Orleans LA 70139

BRICE, JAMES ALFORD, oil co. exec.; b. Watha, N.C., Nov. 19, 1916; s. Roscoe Preston and Annie Irene B.; student Alexander Hamilton Inst., 1950; m. Ruth Virginia Norris, Jan. 8, 1942; children—James Alford, Russell P., Jeffrey L., Gayle. Mgr., Eastern Carolina Lumber Co., Tabor City, N.C., 1950-57, Tabor City Wood Yard, 1958-60; sec., treas., mgr. Tabor City Oil Co., 1960—. Mem. Tabor City C. of C. (dir. 1974). Clubs: Booster (past pres.), Civitan (past pres.). Home: 704 Anderson St Tabor City NC 28463 Office: PO Box 576 Tabor City NC 28463

BRICE, MARGARET HEMMINGER, civic worker; b. Willington, S.C., July 28, 1919; d. James Morrow, Sr., and Margaret Josephine (LeRoy) Hemminger; A.B., Lander Coll., Greenwood, S.C., 1939; m. Laurie Simonton Brice, Sept. 7, 1943; children—Laurie Simonton, James Douglas, Carolyn Ann. Elementary tchr. Calhoun Falls (S.C.) Pub. Schs., 1939-42, 45, Ware Shoals (S.C.) Pub. Schs., 1942-43; librarian's aide Carnegie Library, Pitts., 1943-44; mem. McCormick County (S.C.) Social Services Bd., 1966—; foreman McCormick County Grand Jury, 1971. Sec.-historian Women of Ch., Willington Presbyterian Ch., 1957—; chmn. annuities, relief Women of Ch., S.C. Presbytery, 1962-66, v.p., 1966-67, chmn. nominating com., 1968-69, hon. life mem. Women of Ch., 1974—. Mem. S.C., McCormick County (charter) hist. socs. Club: McCormick Study. Home: Route 1 McCormick SC 29835

BRICKER, DONALD LEE, surgeon; b. Denver, Jan. 7, 1935; s. J.F. and Marjorie Ellen (Mahon) B.; B.S., Colo. State U., 1956; M.D., Cornell U., 1959; children—Donald Lee II, Alex (dec.), Adam. Intern, N.Y. Hosp., N.Y.C., 1959-60, resident, 1960-61; resident Baylor U. Affiliated Hosps., Houston, 1961-65, resident in thoracic surgery, 1967-68; practice medicine specializing in thoracic surgery, Houston, 1968-70, Lubbock, Tex., 1970—; mem. staff St. Luke's Hosp., Tex. Inst. for Rehab. and Research, Bellaire Gen. Hosp., Methodist Hosp., Ben Taub Gen. Hosp., St. Mary of the Plains Hosp., West Tex. Hosp.; asst. instr. dept. surgery Baylor U. Coll. Medicine, Houston, 1961-65, instr., 1967-68, asst. prof. surgery, 1968-70; acting chief surgery Ben Taub Gen. Hosp., 1968-70; clin. prof. surgery and dir. div. cardiovascular surgery Tex. Tech U. Sch. Medicine, Lubbock, 1972—; pres. Heart Inst. of South West, 1972—. Served to capt. USAF, 1965-67; maj. Res., 1968-70. Diplomate Am. Bd. Surgery, Am. Bd. Thoracic Surgery. Fellow A.C.S., Am. Coll. Chest Physicians, Am. Coll. Cardiology, Am. Assn. Thoracic Surgery, Am. Assn. Surgery of Trauma, Tex. Surg. Soc.; mem. So. Thoracic Surg. Assn. (pres.'s award for best sci. paper 1973), Soc. Thoracic Surgeons, Tex. Med. Assn., Houston, Lubbock surg. socs., Internat. Cardiovascular Surg. Soc., Denton A. Cooley Cardiovascular Surg. Soc. Republican. Methodist. Contbr. numerous articles on cardiovascular surgery to profl. jours. Home: 3314A 74th St Lubbock TX 79423 Office: 3420 22d Pl Lubbock TX 79410

BRICKLE, JUDITH HERRMANN, copywriter; b. Evansville, Ind., Nov. 19, 1940; d. Edwin Frederick and Anna Zerilda (Fridy) Herrmann; B.S., Northwestern U., 1962; 1 dau., Anne Elizabeth. Asst. to advt. mgr. Fortune Mag., Boston, 1962; editorial asst. Am. Pharm. Assn., Washington, 1962; asst. editor Nat. Def. Transp. Assn., Washington, 1962-63; freelance writer, Washington, 1963-70; womens editor No. Va. Sun, Arlington, 1970-71; copy editor Evansville (Ind.) Courier, 1971-72; sr. writer Keller Crescent Co., Evansville, 1972-77; copy dir. Gen. Electric Advt., Louisville, 1977—. Mem. Advt. Club Louisville, Am. Mensa Soc. Home: 10604 Linn Station Rd Louisville KY 40223 Office: 2100 Gardiner Ln 301 Louisville KY 40205

BRIDENBAUGH, EDWIN REDMOND, electronics engr.; b. San Antonio, July 23, 1934; s. Edwin Ray and Nettie Mae (Smith) B.; A.S. in Electronic Engring., So. Inst. Tech., 1954; B.E.E., Ga. Inst. Tech., 1962; m. Brenda Gail Eason, Sept. 15, 1961; children—David Neil, Robert Edwin. Engr., North Electric Co., Galion, Ohio, 1954-55; sr. engr. Dynatronics, Inc., Orlando, Fla., 1962-64; sr. project engr. Vitro Services, Huntsville, Ala., 1964-71; supr. electronic devel., apparatus div. ITT Telecommunications, Corinth, Miss., 1971-77, product mgr., 1977—. Mem. adminstrv. bd. Meth. Ch. Served with U.S. Army, 1955-58. Mem. Am. Mgmt. Assn., IEEE, Electronic Industries Assn. (chmn. standards for key systems). Club: Kiwanis. Patentee in field of electronics. Home: 1005 E 6th St Corinth MS 38834 Office: Fulton Dr Corinth MS 38834

BRIDGEMAN, DENNIS PATRICK, hosp. adminstr.; b. Milw., Apr. 14, 1946; s. Maurice James and Laura Honora (Alt) B.; B.S. in Bus., Miami U., Oxford, Ohio, 1968; M.P.A. with cert. in hosp. adminstrn., Cornell U., 1972; m. Elizabeth Amick Skaggs, Sept. 10, 1977. Systems analyst A.O. Smith Corp., Milw., 1970; USPHS trainee Cornell U., 1970-72; adminstrv. asst. to clin. dir. Weston (W.Va.) Hosp., 1972-78; supt. Huntington (W.Va.) State Hosp., 1978—; mem. W.Va. Mental Health Adv. Council; mem. adv. bd. on med. edn. Marshall U. Sch. Medicine. Served with U.S. Army, 1968-70. Decorated Army Commendation medal with V device. Mem. Assn. Mental Health Adminstrs., W.Va. Assn. Health Services Execs. (sec.). Democrat. Roman Catholic. Home: 417 W Ninth Ave Huntington WV 25701 Office: 1530 Norway Ave Huntington WV 25709

BRIDGER, GALE WESSON, educator; b. Minden, La., Jan. 15, 1939; d. George Dudney and Corrie Ethel (Bennett) Wesson; B.A. cum laude, La. Tech. U., 1960, M.A., 1965; Ed.D., U. Miss., 1974; m. Robert Dixon Bridger, Dec. 26, 1956; 1 son, Robert Jeffrey. Tchr. English, Caddo Parish (La.) Schs., 1960-70, curriculum coordinator, 1970-72; supr. lang. arts-social studies Holly Springs (Miss.) Schs., 1972-73; adminstrv. coordinator Caddo Parish Schs., 1973-75; asso. prof., dir. profl. lab. experience, coordinator grad. studies La. State U., Shreveport, 1975—. Mem. Caddo Parish Sch. Bd., 1977. Mem. Assn. Tchr. Educators, Assn. Supervision and Curriculum Devel., Midsouth Ednl. Research Assn., NEA, La. Assn. Educators, S.E. Regional Assn. Tchr. Educators, La. Assn. Tchr. Educators, Kappa Delta Pi, Sigma Kappa. Methodist. Home: 244 Roma Dr Shreveport LA 71105 Office: 8515 Youree Dr Shreveport LA 71115

BRIDGERS, THOMAS FLEMING, JR., research and devel. co. exec.; b. Wilson, N.C., Oct. 17, 1941; s. Thomas Fleming and Mary Louise (Anderson) B.; B.S., N.C. State U., 1967; M.B.A., U. N.C., 1969; m. Lynda J. Forrest, Dec. 31, 1977; 1 dau. by previous marriage—Mary Clyde. Bus. mgr. Smith Richardson Found., Inc., Greensboro, N.C., 1969-71; sec., treas. Center for Creative Leadership, Greensboro, 1971—. Treas., bd. dirs. Chesterfield Manor Assn., Inc., 1974—; keyman United Way, 1969—; adviser Jr. Achievement, 1976. Served with AUS, 1960-62. Recipient Outstanding Sr. award Wall St. Jour., 1967. Beta Gamma Sigma/Bus. Found. scholar, 1967-69. Mem. Am. Mgmt. Assn., Personnel Assn. Greensboro Area, Blue Key, Golden Chain, Phi Kappa Phi, Gamma Sigma Delta, Alpha Zeta. Democrat. Methodist. Clubs: Toastmasters (past pres., Toastmaster of Yr. 1978). Elks. Home: 1107 W Bessemer Ave Greensboro NC 27408 Office: PO Box P-1 Greensboro NC 27402

BRIDGES, GILBERT SADLER, economist; b. Stanton, Tex., Aug. 19, 1934; s. Cecil and Sarah E. (Sadler) B.; B.B.A., Tex. A&M U., 1958, M.S. in Econs., 1960; postgrad. So. Meth. U., 1960-63; m. Angie Lou Chesser, Feb. 25, 1956; children—Amy Elizabeth, Steven T. Asst. prof. dept. econs. Tex. Tex. A&M U., College Station, 1964-66; asso. research economist Tex. Transp. Inst., 1967-68, 71-74, v.p. Tele-data Systems Corp., Dallas, 1969-70, head econs. and planning div., 1975—. Mem. Soc. Govt. Economists, Delta Nu Alpha, Phi Kappa Phi, Omicron Delta Epsilon. Democrat. Methodist. Contbr. articles on transp. systems to profl. publs. Home: 2510 Memorial Dr Bryan TX 77801 Office: Tex Transportation Inst Tex A&M Univ College Station TX 77843

BRIDGES, JAMES EDWARD, JR., state ofcl.; b. Catherine, Ala., Dec. 17, 1946; s. James Edward and Ethel Mae (Dees) B.; B.S., U. Ala., 1970; M.S., Troy State U., 1973; M. Adminstrv. Sci., U. Ala., Huntsville, 1979. Quality control technician Ala. Metall. Corp., Selma, 1966-67; statistician Ala. Dept. Pensions and Security, Montgomery, 1970-72; employment counselor Ala. Employment Service, Birmingham, 1972-73, supr. employment counseling, Huntsville, 1973-79; asst. mgr., Birmingham, 1979—; instr. bus. Calhoun Community Coll. (Ala.), 1974-79, U. Montevallo (Ala.), 1974-77, U. Ala., Huntsville, 1979—. Mem. Employment Com., Council of Aging Huntsville-Madison County, 1979—. Mem. Am. Personnel and Guidance Assn., Nat. Employment Counselors Assn., Nat. Vocat. Guidance Assn., Ala. Personnel and Guidance Assn., Ala. Vocat. Guidance Assn., Am. Soc. for Personnel Adminstrn., Am. Mgmt. Assn., Internat. Assn. Personnel in Employment Security. Presbyterian. Home: 4935 Caldwell Mill Ln Birmingham AL 35243 Office: PO Box 2414 Birmingham AL 35202

BRIDGES, JULIAN CURTIS, sociologist, educator; b. Miami, Fla., Apr. 3, 1931; s. Clyde Clifton and Bessie Myrtle (Williams) B.; A.B., U. Fla., 1952, M.A., 1969, Ph.D. (NDEA Title VI fellow, 1969-70), 1973; B.D., Southwestern Bapt. Theol. Sem., 1956, Th.D. (Lilly Found. fellow, 1957-58), 1961; m. Charlotte Annelle Martin, Aug. 25, 1954; children—Rebecca Ann, Deborah Lea, Esther Marelyn. Nuclear tech. analyst Convair, Ft. Worth, 1953; ordained to ministry Baptist Church, 1954; pastor English and Spanish speaking congregations, Dallas-Ft. Worth, 1953-59; Bapt. rep. to Mex., Fgn. Mission Bd., So. Bapt. Conv., San Jose, Costa Rica, and Mexico City, 1959-73; asso. prof. sociology, head dept. sociology and social work Hardin-Simmons U., Abilene, Tex., 1973-77, prof., 1978—; interim and supply pastor English and Spanish-speaking chs.; leader marriage enrichment retreats. Active, Community Relations Com., City of Abilene, 1974-78, chmn. Community Devel. Com.; del. Dem. Conv. of Tex., 1978-79. Mem. Southwestern Sociol. Assn., Southwestern Social Sci. Assn., Southwestern Council Latin Am. Studies, Nat. Council Family Relations, Tex. Council Family Relations, Latin Am. Studies Assn., Population Assn. Am., Phi Kappa Phi, Alpha Kappa Delta, Pi Gamma Mu. Contbr. articles to profl. publs. Home: 1526 N

Pioneer Dr Abilene TX 79603 Office: Dept Sociology and Social Work Hardin-Simmons U Abilene TX 79698

BRIDGES, LEON GERALD, mortgage banker; b. Dublin, Ga., Jan. 28, 1943; s. Rowie Alexander and Lola Moye B.; B.B.A., U. Ga., 1968; postgrad. Woodrow Wilson Law Sch., 1970-72; m. Elizabeth E. Bridges, Dec. 27, 1969; children—Andrew, Denae. With Lockheed Engring. Co., Marietta, Ga., 1968-71; v.p., br. mgr. L.F.A. Mortgage Co., Marietta, 1972-74; owner, pres. Mortgage Alliance Corp., Atlanta, 1974—; sr. exec. v.p. Mortgage Title and Escrow Corp., Marietta, 1976-79; v.p. Alliance Ins. Agency, Marietta, 1979—. Served with USAF, 1961-65. Lic. real estate agt., Ga. Mem. Ga. Assn. Realtors, Cobb County Bd. Realtors, Cobb County C. of C., Clayton County C. of C., Atlanta Mortgage Bankers Assn. Republican. Baptist.

BRIDGMAN, MARSHALL BRUCE, mfg. co. exec.; b. Belton, S.C., July 21, 1931; s. Bruce Byron and Lois Sue (Clodfelter) B.; B.S. in Textile Engring., Clemson U., 1953; m. Peggy Janet Kelly, June 1, 1952 (div. June 1972); children—Michael K., Kelli Sue, Laird P.; m. 2d, Kathy Griffitts, Dec. 15, 1979. Process and product devel. supr. Celanese Corp., Charlotte, N.C., 1956-59; sr. research chemist Hercules, Inc., Covington, Va., 1960-64, sr. tech. sales, Charlotte, N.C., 1964-68, process control supr., Covington, Ga., 1969-71, quality assurance supt., 1972—. Active Am. Cancer Soc., United Fund, Boy Scouts Am. Served to 1st lt. U.S. Army, 1953-56. Democrat. Methodist. Clubs: Masons, Elks. Home: Route 5 Box 232 Covington GA 30209 Office: PO Box 8 Oxford GA 30267

BRIETZ, ROBERT JAMES, securities co. exec.; b. Charlotte, N.C., July 21, 1943; s. Edwin Raymond and Marie Louise (Wilkinson) B.; B.S. in Acctg., Pfeiffer Coll., 1965; m. Jane A. Cashion, May 25, 1967; children—Robert James, Rex D. Staff acct. Coopers & Lybrand, Charlotte, 1965-68; sr. v.p., controller Interstate Securities Corp., Charlotte, 1968—. Mem. Nat. Assn. Accts., N.C. Assn. C.P.A.'s. Methodist. Office: 2700 NCNB Plaza Charlotte NC 28211

BRIGGS, GARRETT, geologist, ednl. adminstr.; b. Dallas, Dec. 31, 1934; s. Albert Sidney and Margaret Campbell (Garrett) B.; B.S. in Geology, So. Meth. U., 1958, M.S. in Geology, 1959; Ph.D. in Geology, U Wis., Madison, 1962; m. Susan Lynn Walters; children—Doug, Jim, Paul, Molly. Geologist Chevron Oil Co., New Orleans, 1962-65; asst. prof. geology Tulane U., 1965-68; asst. prof. U. Tenn., 1968-69, asso. prof., 1969-74, prof., 1974—, interim head dept. geology, 1972-74, head dept., 1974—, asso. dean for research and adminstrn. Coll. Liberal Arts, 1977—; cons. in field. ERDA grantee, 1975-77. Fellow Geol. Soc. Am.; mem. Soc. Econ. Paleontologists and Mineralogists, Am. Assn. Petroleum Geologists. Contbr. articles on sedimentology to profl. publs. Home: 7141 Cheshire Dr Knoxville TN 37919 Office: Coll Liberal Arts U Tenn 226 Ayres Hall Knoxville TN 37916

BRIGGS, PHILIP HENRY, educator; b. Ponca City, Okla., Feb. 26, 1933; s. Henry E. and Lillie T. (Strain) B.; student U. Tex., U. Mo.; B.A., Hardin-Simmons U., 1955; M.R.E., Southwestern Sem., 1957, D.R.E., 1964, Ed.D., 1971; m. Jennette C. Crouch, July 24, 1953; children—Philip Henry, Randall C., Brenda. Prof., Midwestern Sem., Kansas City, Mo., 1965-71, Southwestern Sem., Ft. Worth, 1971—; guest prof. U. Ark., Little Rock, 1965, Midwestern Sem., 1977, 80. Mem. Religious Edn. Assn., So. Bapt. Religious Edn. Assn. Contbr. chpts. to books, articles to denominational periodicals. Home: 3920 Wedgworth Rd S Fort Worth TX 76133 Office: Box 22328 Fort Worth TX 76122

BRIGGS, RANDY R., radio and TV ratings co. exec.; b. Berea, Ohio, June 18, 1949; s. Walter William and Anne Louise B.; B.S. in Mktg., Bowling Green U., 1971; m. Donna J. Hjortsberg, June 18, 1977. Account exec. radio advt. sales WIXY/WDOK, Cleve., 1972-74, WSPD-TV, Toledo and WAGA-TV, Atlanta, 1974-78; southeastern mgr. Arbitron Co., Atlanta, 1978—. Mem. Atlanta Broadcast Advt. Club. Home: 1427 Woodwind Ct Marietta GA 30067 Office: 5775 Peachtree-Dunwoody Rd Suite 210D Atlanta GA 30342

BRIGHAM, ELBERT ORAN, engring. exec.; b. Stamford, Tex., Sept. 13, 1940; s. Elbert Oran and Evelyn Marie (Hargrove) B.; B.S. in Elec. Engring., U. Tex., 1963, M.S. in Elec. Engring., 1964, Ph.D. (Ford Found. fellow), 1967; M.S. in Engring. Mgmt., George Washington U., 1971; m. Evangeline Rushing, June 12, 1965; 1 dau., Cami. Teaching asso. U. Tex., 1964-67; cons. Greenville (Tex.) div. LTV Electrosystems, Inc., 1966-67, supr. information scis., 1967-69, div. tech. coordinator, 1971-73; with Nat. Security Agy., Ft. Meade, Md., 1969-71; asst. dir. signal intelligence systems Office of Asst. Sec. Def. (intelligence), Washington, 1973-75, dir. for reconnaissance and surveillance, 1975-76; v.p. engring. E-Systems, Inc., Melpar div., Falls Church, Va., 1976-78, v.p., gen. mgr., 1978—; cons. Dept. Def., 1971-73; adviser, engring. devel. program George Mason U. Mem. IEEE, Assn. Old Crows, Assn. U.S. Army, Am. Def. Preparedness Assn., Tau Beta Pi, Eta Kappa Nu, Phi Eta Sigma. Author: The Fast Fourier Transform, 1974. Contbr. articles in field to profl. jours. Office: 7700 Arlington Blvd Falls Church VA 22046

BRIGHT, JERLENE ANN, info. systems programs dir.; b. Norman, Okla., July 4, 1942; d. Hoyt David and Pearl Jerlene Little; Asso. in Bus., Oklahoma City Coll., 1964; student U. Okla., 1974-76; m. James Bright, July 25, 1959; children—Bridget, Michelle, Ericka. Project coordinator U. Okla. Computing Center, 1965-68, U. Okla. Research Inst./Oil Info. Center, 1968-74; dir. U. Okla. Info. Systems Programs, Norman, 1974—. Mem. Soc. Petroleum Engrs. Maj. presentations annually before large profl. energy oriented orgns. Home: PO Box 1370 Norman OK 73070 Office: U Okla Info Systems Programs PO Box 3030 Norman OK 73070

BRIGHTWELL, JUANITA SUMNER (MRS. LOUIE BRIGHTWELL), librarian; b. Sylvester, Ga., Jan. 4, 1918; d. Robert Beauregard and Lottie (Davis) Sumner; grad. Ga. Southwestern Jr. Coll., Americus, 1936; B.S. in Edn., Woman's Coll. Ga., 1938; M.Librarianship, Emory U., 1965; m. Louie Brightwell, June 30, 1938; 1 dau., Claire (Mrs. Charles W. Shaeffer, Jr.). Elementary tchr. Weston (Ga.) High Sch., 1937-38; tchr. English, also librarian Smithville (Ga.) High Sch., 1941-42, Americus High Sch., 1942-43; operator Brightwell's Nursery, Americus, 1946-52; asst. librarian Lake Blackshear Regional Library (formerly Americus Carnegie Library), 1953-56; tchr. New Era Elementary Sch., Americus, 1956-57; tchr. English, also library asst. Americus High Sch., 1957-62; dir. Lake Blackshear Regional Library, 1962—. Tchr. Merit scholar program Ga. Dept. Edn., 1962-65. Recipient Outstanding Pub. Servant award Civitan, 1973. Mem. ALA, Southeastern Library Assn., Ga. Library Assn. (chmn. pub. library sect. 1969-71) D.A.R., Azalea Garden Club (pres. 1955), U.D.C., Nat. Soc. Magna Charta Dames, Bus. and Profl. Woman's Club (pres. 1968-69; Woman of Year 1968), Alpha Chi Omega, Delta Kappa Gamma. Baptist. Author: The Organization of the Americus Library Association, 1965. Home: 1307 Hancock Dr Americus GA 31709 Office: 307 E Lamar St Americus GA 31709

BRILLHART, DAVID WINTHROP, bank exec.; b. Bethlehem, Pa., Jan. 9, 1925; s. David H. and Elizabeth L. (Lehr) B.; B.S., U.S. Mil. Acad., 1946; M.B.A., N.Y. U., 1960; m. Joan Jeffris, Mar. 5, 1948; children—Jeff, Sally, Jon. Vice pres. Morgan Guaranty Trust Co., N.Y.C., 1954-72; exec. v.p. S.E. First Nat. Bank of Miami (Fla.), 1972-76; pres., chief exec. officer 1st Bancshares of Fla., Inc., Boca Raton, 1977-79; chmn. David Brillhart and Assos., Miami, 1979—; dir. Union Bank & Trust Co. Eastern Pa., Bethlehem. Served to capt. AUS, 1946-54. Mem. N.Y. Soc. Security Analysts, AIM, Am. Mgmt. Assn., Econ. Council Palm Beach County. Clubs: Standard, Miami (Miami); Royal Palm Yacht and Country (Boca Raton). Home: 780 NE 37th St Boca Raton FL 33431 Office: 150 E Palmetto Park Rd Boca Raton FL 33432

BRIMER, TERRY MIKE, pharmacist; b. Morristown, Tenn., Dec. 17, 1947; s. Robert Leland and Texie (Fox) B.; student Tenn. Technol. U., 1965-67; B.S. with honors in Pharmacy, U. Tenn., 1970, Pharm.D., 1971; m. Cheryl Rae Bailey, Oct. 1, 1971; children—Allen Clark, Robert Andrew. Registered pharmacist Katz Drug Co. and Walgreen's Drug Co., Memphis, 1970-71; co-owner, v.p., dir. pharmacy services Doctor's Hosp. Pharmacy, Inc., Morristown, Tenn., 1971—; co-owner The Prescription Shop, Morristown, 1975—; partner Phys. Therapy & Convalescent Aids Center, Morristown, 1979—; cons. pharmacist Lifecare Center of Morristown, 1973—, Ridgeview Terrace Convalescent & Nursing Home, Rutledge, Tenn., 1979—, Regency Health Care Center, Rogersville, Tenn., 1980—; mem. Tenn. Med. Malpractice Rev. Bd., 1975-77; clin. instr. dept. pharmacy practice U. Tenn. Coll. Pharmacy, 1976—; dir. Jefferson Fed. Savs. & Loan. Elder, St. Paul Presbyterian Ch. Recipient Bob and Lorene Walker award U. Tenn. Coll. Pharmacy, 1969, Dean's Spl. Recognition award, 1970. Fellow Am. Soc. Cons. Pharmacists, Am. Coll. Apothecaries (instl. practice com. 1978—); mem. Am. Pharm. Assn., Acad. Gen. Practice Pharmacy, Am. Soc. Hosp. Pharmacists, Tenn. Pharm. Assn. (profl. relations com. 1977), Tenn. Soc. Hosp. Pharmacists, Lakeway Pharmacists Assn. (charter mem., pres. 1977-78), U. Tenn. Alumni Assn. (chpt. dir. 1974). Home: 805 Drinnon Dr Morristown TN 37814 Office: Doctor's Hosp Pharmacy Inc 726 McFarland Ave Morristown TN 37814

BRINDLEY, JOSEPH DURWOOD, univ. adminstr.; b. Blountsville, Ala., Aug. 23, 1939; s. Van Buren and Betty Lou (Harris) B.; B.S., Jacksonville State U., 1964; M.A., U. Ala., 1966, Ed.D., 1974; m. Syble Delean Hazelrig, Aug. 12, 1961; children—Patrick Andrew, Elizabeth Anne. Tchr., Susan Moore High Sch., Clarence, Ala., 1960-61, J.B. Pennington High Sch., Blountsville, 1963-64, tchr., coach, adminstr. Oneonta (Ala.) High Sch., 1964-71: dir. community services Snead State Jr. Coll., Boaz, Ala., 1971-75; asst. dir. jr. colls. Ala. Dept. Edn., Montgomery, 1975-77; exec. asst. to pres. and dir. public affairs U. Montevallo (Ala.), 1977—, prof., 1978—; mem. Ala. Ho. of Reps., 1974-78. Mem. Ala. adv. reading commn., 1976-77; mem. Ala. Dem. Exec. Com., 1974-78. Named Alumnus of Year, Jacksonville State U., 1976; Kellogg fellow, Mich. State U., 1971. Mem. Ala. Hist. Assn., Council of Univ. Pres.'s (adv. com. 1977), Phi Delta Kappa. Baptist. Club: Civitan. Home: 282 Cardinal Crest Rd Montevallo AL 35115 Office: Calkins Hall U Montevallo Montevallo AL 35115

BRINGARDNER, THELMA LOIS, accountant; b. Parkersburg, W.Va., Dec. 1, 1928; d. Everett Bernard and Leona May (Hendershott) Marshall; grad. Bur. Better Bus. Exec. Women's Workshop, 1975; m. Mar. 27, 1956 (div. Sept. 1977); children—Diana Jean, Linda Ruth, Candice Marie. Sec., bookkeeper Marcy Enterprises, Inc., Columbus, Ohio, 1972-75; rep. Wilma Boyd Airline & Travel Career Sch., Pitts., 1976; bookkeeper Aerospace Materials, Inc., Columbus, 1977; controller Formitex, Inc., Columbus, 1978-79; acctg. liaison Jones Electric Supply Co., Sanford, Fla., 1979—. Active PTA, Whitehall, Ohio, 1960-74; leader Ohio Trefoil council Girl Scouts U.S., 1959-62. Recipient award Norfolk (Va.) Naval Supply Center, 1952. Mem. Blennerhassett Dental Asst. Soc. (charter mem.; sec. 1947), Nat. Assn. Accountants, Am. Bus. Women Assn. Democrat. Mem. Assemblies of God Ch. Home: 136 Bedford Ct Sanford FL 32771 Office: Jones Electric Supply Co 401 S Laurel Ave Sanford FL 32771

BRINK, GERALD ROLLA, hosp. exec.; b. Muskegon, Mich., June 25, 1938; s. Ivan William and Marguerite Elizabeth (Wood) B.; B.A., Western Mich. U., 1964; M.H.A., Med. Coll. Va., 1966; m. Madonna Carol Jones, June 19, 1964; children—Valerie Dawn, Ivanessa Carol. Served as hosp. corpsman USNR, 1957-60; med. technologist Hackley Hosp., Muskegon, 1959-64; adminstrv. resident Riverside Hosp., Newport News, Va., 1965-66, asst. adminstr., 1966—, exec. v.p.-adminstr., 1976—; rep. Health Systems Agy. Found. Com.; chmn. funding devel. com. Tidewater Health Edn. Com. II; bd. dirs. chpt. X, Mental Health and Mental Retardation Bd., 1968-77, chmn. budget com., 1972; bd. dirs. Hampton Roads chpt. ARC, 1971-76, 79—; pres. Peninsula Health Careers Com., 1966-72. Bd. dirs. United Way Va. Peninsula, 1977—, chmn. hosp. div. drive, 1971-78, chmn. profl. div., 1979; past pres. Wendwood Recreation Assn. Fellow Am. Coll. Hosp. Adminstrs.; mem. Am. Hosp. Assn., Va. Hosp. Assn. (chmn. coms.), Tidewater Hosp. Council (pres. 1979), Am. Mgmt. Assn., Va. Council Health and Med. Care (chmn. health careers com. 1975, 77), Tidewater Health Care Forum. Club: Warwick Rotary (pres. 1976). Author papers in field. Home: 314 Dominion Dr Newport News VA 23601 Office: 500 J Clyde Morris Blvd Newport News VA 23601

BRINKLEY, CHARLES ALEXANDER, geologist; b. Moody, Tex., Oct. 3, 1929; s. Jess Daniel and Vera Allene (Anderson) B.; student Temple Jr. Coll., 1947-48; B.S. in Geology, Midwestern U., 1957; M.S. in Geology, Pa. State U., 1960; m. Jeraldine Athalene Skeeter, June 18, 1952. Checker, stock mgr. A & P Tea Co., Temple and Waco, Tex., 1947-50; office asst. John M. Mouser, ind. oil operator, Wichita Falls, Tex., 1957; grad. asst. Pa. State U., 1957-59; geologist Texaco, Inc., New Orleans and Jackson, Miss., 1959-70, dist. geologist, 1970-72, dist. stratigrapher, 1972-75; regional geologist Gen. Crude Oil Co., Houston, 1975-77, exploration mgr. W. Gulf dist., 1977-79; exploration mgr. Maralo, Inc., Houston, 1979—. Served with USN, 1950-54. Fellow AAAS; mem. Am. Assn. Petroleum Geologists (cert.), Am. Soc. Photogrammetry, Soc. Econ. Paleontologists and Mineralogists, Assn. Profl. Geol. Scientists (cert.), New Orleans Geol. Soc., Houston Geol. Soc., Miss. Geol. Soc., West Tex. Geol. Soc., Airline Passengers Assn. Baptist. Club: Houston. Home: 3015 Redwood Lodge Dr Kingwood TX 77339 Office: 4600 Post Oak Pl Suite 307 Houston TX 77027

BRINKLEY, JACK THOMAS, congressman, lawyer; b. Faceville, Ga., Dec. 22, 1930; s. Lonnie Elester and Pauline (Spearman) B.; student Young Harris Coll., 1947-49, Okla. A. and M. U., 1952; LL.B. cum laude, U. Ga., 1959; m. Alma Lois Kite, May 29, 1955; children—Jack Thomas, Fred Alen II. Admitted to Ga. bar, 1958; asso. mem. firm Young, Hollis and Moseley, 1959-61; partner Coffin and Brinkley, 1961-66; part-time tchr. Columbus Coll., 1964; mem. Ga. Ho. of Reps., 1965-66; mem. 90th-96th congresses from 3d Ga. Dist., mem. armed service com., vets. affairs com. Pres., Reese Rd. PTA, 1963-64. Chmn. fund raising and Ga. state chmn. Nat. Found., 1966. Judge adv. South Ga. Dist. Civitan Internat., 1964-65. Served to 1st lt., pilot, USAF, 1951-56. Mem. Am., Ga., Columbus bar assns., Am. Legion, Blue Key, Phi Alpha Delta. Democrat. Baptist (supt. Sunday Sch. 1962-64). Mason. Home: 4108 Appalachian Way Columbus GA 31907 Office: 2412 Rayburn House Office Bldg Washington DC 20515

BRINKMAN, FRANK PETER, III, surgeon; b. Jacksonville, Tex., Feb. 20, 1947; s. Frank Peter and Jeanne Travis (Brandenberger) B.; B.S., Tulane U., 1969; M.D., La. State U., Shreveport, 1973; m. Mary Beth Dabbs, Nov. 18, 1972; children—Sean Michael, Patricia Carol, Christopher Ryan. Intern, Madigan Army Med. Center, Tacoma, 1973-74, resident in surgery, 1974-78; chief dept. gen. surgery, Ft. Polk, La., 1978—. Active, Am. Cancer Soc. Served as maj. U.S. Army, 1978-80. Diplomate Am. Bd. Surgery. Mem. Am. Owners and Pilots Assn., La. Med. Soc. Republican. Roman Catholic. Home: 42 Birch St DeRidder LA 70634 Office: PO Box 122 MEDDAC Fort Polk LA 71459

BRINKMAN, MARILYN JOAN, nurse; b. Villisca, Iowa, May 25, 1931; d. Henry F. and Ethelda (Armstrong) Tyler; B.S.N., State U. Iowa, 1953; M.S., East Tex. State U., 1974; m. Frank P. Brinkman, Jr., July 20, 1976; children—Denise Michel, Amy Michel, Brenda Muller, Karen Michel. Instr., Tex. Eastern Sch. Nursing, Tyler, Tex., 1970-73; inservice coordinator Med. Center Hosp., Tyler, 1972-73, dir. nursing service, 1979—; pres. Lone Star Distbg. Co., Tyler, 1979—. Mem. Planning and Zoning Commn., Sac City, Iowa, 1963-69; circle chmn. Presbyn. Ch., Sac City, 1963-69. Mem. Dist. Nurses Assn., Nat. League for Nursing, P.E.O. Republican. Methodist. Club: Order Eastern Star. Home: 8242 Purdue St Tyler TX 75703 Office: 1851 Gentry St Tyler TX 75702

BRINSMADE, LYON LOUIS, lawyer; b. Mexico City, Feb. 24, 1924 (parents Am. citizens); s. Robert Bruce and Helen (Steenbock) B.; student U. Wis., 1940-43; B.S., Mich. Coll. Mining and Tech., 1944; J.D., Harvard, 1950; m. Susannah Tucker, June 9, 1956 (div. 1978); children—Christine Fairchild Brinsmade Pedersen, Louisa Calvert; m. 2d, Carolyn Hartman Lister, Sept. 22, 1979. Admitted to Tex. bar, 1951; asso. Butler, Binion, Rice, Cook & Knapp, Houston, 1950-58, partner in charge internat. dept., 1958—. Bd. dirs. Houston br. English-Speaking Union of U.S., 1972-75. Served with AUS, 1946-47. Mem. Am. (chmn. com. on internat. investment and devel. 1970-76, mem. council 1972-76, vice chmn. 1976-79, chmn.-elect 1979-80), Internat., Inter-Am. (co-chmn. sect. on oil and gas laws, com. on natural resources 1973-76), Houston bar assns., State Bar Tex. (chmn. internat. law com. 1970-74, mem. council sect. internat. law 1975-78), Am. Soc. Internat. Law, Houston World Trade Assn. (sec., dir. 1967-70, chmn. legis. com.), Houston C. of C. (chmn. legis. subcom. internat. business com. 1970-72), Houston Com. on Fgn. Relations, S.A.R., Allegro of Houston, Sigma Alpha Epsilon. Episcopalian. Clubs: Houston, Houston Athletic Harvard (Houston). Home: 1700 Main The Beaconsfield Houston TX 77002 Office: 1100 Esperson Bldg Houston TX 77002

BRINSON, DONALD EDWARD, data processing mgr.; b. Ponca City, Okla., Sept. 6, 1953; s. Merwyn Glen and Mildred Colleen (Good) B.; student U. Okla., 1970—. With Sta. KGOU, Norman, Okla., 1971-73; lab. instr. ELS Lang. Center, Norman, 1972-74; computer programmer Oscar Rose Jr. Coll. Midwest City, Okla., 1974-78; systems programmer Okla. Tax Commn., Oklahoma City, 1978-80; dir. computer center Oscar Rose Jr. Coll., 1980—; cons. Organizer, activities coordinator Single Adult Persons, 1977-79. Mem. Assn. Computing Machinery. Methodist. Club: Order of Foresters. Home 303 Draper Dr Midwest City OK 73110 Office: 6420 SE 15th Midwest City OK 73110

BRINSON, WOODROW WILSON, JR., town adminstr.; b. Kinston, N.C., Dec. 3, 1947; s. Woodrow Wilson and Nannie (Pollock) B.; student Wake Forest U., 1966-69; B.B.A., Campbell Coll., 1971; m. Gail LaRue Swinson, Aug. 16, 1970; children—Karen LaRue, Kevin Ryan. Tchr., Duplin County Schs., Albertson, N.C., 1969-70; acct. Quinn Wholesale Co., Warsaw, N.C., 1971-74; employment interviewer N.C. Employment Security Commn., Kenansville, 1974-76; mayor Town of Kenansville, 1973-76, town adminstr., 1976—; planner towns of Magnolia and Rose Hill (N.C.), 1978—. Democratic precinct chmn., Kenansville, 1976—. Mem. Kenansville C. of C. (exec. dir. 1975-76), Kenansville Jaycees (charter pres. 1972-73), Internat. City Mgmt. Assn., N.C. City and County Mgrs. Assn., Delta Sigma Pi. Democrat. Baptist. Home: Grove Circle Kenansville NC 28349 Office: Town of Kenansville Hill St Kenansville NC 28349

BRISLEY, QUENTIN LEE EDWARD, investment exec.; b. Frederick, Okla., Dec. 24, 1910; s. Benjamin Eugene and Flossie Lee (Storm) B.; B.A., U. Okla., 1933; postgrad. Santa Monica Tech. Inst., 1941-42; m. Geraldine Rae Johnson, Oct. 2, 1935; children—Melissa Ann, Bruce Edward. Field rep. Okla. Tax Commn., 1935-39; exptl. mechanic Douglas Aircraft, Santa Monica, Calif., 1941-50, Boeing Co., Renton, Wash., 1953; mgr., co-owner Family Portfolio, Frederick, Okla. 1953—. Mem. Am. Numis. Assn., Delta Chi. Democrat. Methodist. Clubs: Masons, Shriners. Home: 800 12th St Frederick OK 73542 Office: PO Box 974 Frederick OK 73542

BRISOLARA, ASHTON, alcoholism and drug abuse com. exec.; b. New Orleans, Sept. 14, 1924; B.S. Maxima cum laude, Springhill (Ala.) Coll., 1952; M Ed., Loyola U., New Orleans, 1960; certificate Yale, 1961, Columbia, 1961; m. Geri Martin, Mar. 12, 1961; children—Sharon, Anne Marie, Joanne, Janet. Tchr., St. Joseph's High Sch., Metuchen, N.J., 1943-46, St. Joseph's Novitiate, Metuchen, 1946-47, St. Willibrord High Sch., Montreal, Que., Can., 1947-48, McGill Inst., Mobile, Ala., 1948-50, St. Joseph High Sch., 1950-52, St. Stanislaus Coll., Bay St. Louis, Miss., 1952-54, St. Francis de Sales High Sch., Houma, La., 1954-55, Cor Jesu High Sch., New Orleans, 1954-55, St. Aloysius High Sch., Vicksburg, Miss., 1957-59, St. Aloysius High Sch., New Orleans, 1959-61; vocat. counselor high schs. and colls. in La., Miss., Ala. and Fla., 1955-57; exec. dir. Com. on Alcoholism and Drug Abuse for Greater New Orelans, Inc., 1961—; cons. VA Hosp., New Orleans, 1978—. Spl. lectr. dept. health and phys. edn. La. State U., New Orleans, 1961-74; pres. faculty La. Inst. Alcohol Studies, Baton Rouge, 1964-67, spl. lectr., 1966—, faculty, 1972—; faculty New Orleans Police Acad., 1961-74; lectr. So. U. of New Orleans, 1962—, Charity Hosp. Sch. Nursing, 1963-75; staff Alcoholism Treatment Service, S.E. La. Hosp., Mandeville, 1965—; lectr., faculty Jefferson Parish (La.) Tng. Acad., Sheriff Dept., 1973; lectr. div. continuing edn. U. Miss., 1974; mem. exec. com. Blue Ridge (N.C.) Inst. So. Community Service Execs., 1964—, pres., 1975; lectr., group discussion leader Southeastern Alcoholism Clinic, 1965-73; faculty S.C. Sch. Alcohol Studies, 1975; faculty Fla. State Sch. Alcohol Studies, U. Miami, Fla. Technol. Inst., Orlando, 1965-73; hon. capt. New Orleans Police Dept., 1964, spl. officer, 1969—; dep. sheriff Hancock County, Miss., 1969-72; faculty Southeastern Sch. Alcohol Studies, U. Ga., Athens, 1966—; faculty dept. psychiatry and neurology Tulane U. Sch. Medicine, 1968—, adj. asso. prof. dept. health services adminstrn., 1971—; faculty, sect. leader Utah Sch. on Alcoholism and other Drug Dependencies, U. Utah, 1971—; vis. prof., cons. U. So. Miss., 1973—; faculty Southwestern Sch. Alcohol Studies, U. Ariz., 1975—; asso. dir., faculty Deep South Sch. Alcohol and Drug Studies, Centenary Coll., Shreveport, La., 1974, dir., 1975—; cons. DePaul Community Mental Health Center, New Orleans, 1969-72, N.I.A.A.A. occupational br., 1972-73, N.W. Fla. Mental Health Center, Panama City, Fla., 1972-75, Gulf Coast Mental Health Center, Gulfport, Miss., 1973—, S.W. La. Edn. and Referral Center, Inc., Lafayette, 1963; bd. mem. La. Inst. Alcohol Studies, 1964-67; staff Mid-South Exec. Devel.

Program, 1972—; mem. council of agencies bd. mgmt. Alcohol and Drug Problems Assn. N. Am.; community cons. Nat. Council on Alcoholism, N.Y.C. Mem. profl. advisory com. Social Welfare Planning Council, New Orleans; speaker, lectr. various univs. and orgns. Author: Handbook for Handling the Alcoholic Employee, 1978. Contbr. articles to profl. publs. Home: 4013 Cleary Ave Metairie LA 70002 Office: 3314 Conti St 2d floor New Orleans LA 70119

BRISTER, COMMODORE WEBSTER, theologian, educator; b. Pineville, La., Jan. 15, 1926; s. Elaine (Holmes) B.; M.Div., New Orleans Baptist Sem., 1952; Ph.D., Southwestern Bapt. Sem., 1957; also postdoctoral study; m. Gloria Nugent, Mar. 28, 1946; 1 son, Mark Allen. News editor Sta. KALB, Alexandria, La., 1946-47; alumni sec. La. Coll., 1947-48; teaching fellow in econs. La. State U., Baton Rouge, 1948-49; ordained minister Bapt. Ch.; pastor Folsom (La.) Bapt. Ch., 1950-52, Ethel (La.) Bapt. Ch., 1952-53, Haltom Bd. Bapt. Ch., Fort Worth, 1954-57; prof. pastoral theology Southwestern Bapt. Sem., Fort Worth, 1957—; internat. lectr., 1966, 68, 75, 80; cons. Clin. Pastoral Edn. and Counseling Centers, Tex. Served with Armed Forces, World War II. Fellow Assn. Theol. Schs.; mem. Assn. Clin. Pastoral Edn. (supr.). Assn. Profl. Edn. for Ministry. Author: Pastoral Care in the Church, 1964; People Who Care, 1967; Dealing with Doubt, 1970; It's Tough Growing Up, 1971; El Ciudad Pastoral en la Iglesia, 1974; Life Under Pressure: Dealing with Stress in Marriage, 1976; The Promise of Counseling, 1978; Take Care, 1978; Becoming You, 1980; Beginning Your Ministry, 1981. Home: 3705 Wedghill Way Fort Worth TX 76133 Office: PO Box 22036 Fort Worth TX 76122

BRISTOW, THOMAS COLE, JR., hosp. ofcl.; b. Orangeburg, S.C., Sept. 4, 1939; s. Thomas Cole and Naomi (Whittington) B.; B.S., Wofford Coll., 1961; M.S., U. Tenn., 1966; Ph.D., U. S.C., 1977; m. Elizabeth Jane Elwood, July 1, 1967; children—Thomas Cole, Christopher Francis. Supr. protective services Greenville County (S.C.) Dept. Social Services, 1966-67; psychiatric social worker Greenville Mental Health Center, 1967-70; asst. prof. U. S.C., Columbia, 1970-73; coordinator staff devel. S.C. State Hosp., Columbia, 1973-75, unit chief of social services, 1975—; partner, counselor Irmo (S.C.) Family Counseling Clinic, 1978—. Served with U.S. Army, 1964-77. Mem. Nat. Assn. Social Workers, S.C. Mental Health Counselors Assn., Phi Alpha. Baptist. Home: 208 Middlesex Rd Columbia SC 29210 Office: South Carolina State Hospital Bull St Columbia SC 29202

BRITT, CHESTER OLEN, elec. engr.; b. Hughes Springs, Tex., July 2, 1920; s. Beverly A. and Ida Emma (Martin) B.; student Texarkana Jr. Coll., 1938-40; B.S., U. Tex., 1949, M.S., 1951; Ph.D., 1962; m. Patricia Ashworth, Jan. 4, 1946. Research engr. Elec. Engring. Research Lab., Austin, Tex., 1951-56, systems devel. specialist, 1956-61; systems devel. specialist U. Tex. at Austin, 1961-62, research scientist dept. chemistry, 1962—. Served with USAAF, 1941-46. Decorated D.F.C., Air Medal with oak leaf clusters. Registered profl. engr., Tex. Mem. I.E.E.E. (sr.), A.A.A.S., Am. Phys. Soc. Home: 2708 Rae Dell Ave Austin TX 78704

BRITT, DAVID MAXWELL, justice N.C. Supreme Ct.; b. McDonald, N.C., Jan. 2, 1917; s. Dudley H. and Martha Mae (Hall) B.; m. Louise Teague, July 16, 1941; children—Nancy Britt Stud, Martha Britt Grun, Mary Louise Britt Hayes. Admitted to N.C. bar; individual practice law, Fairmont, N.C., 1938-67; mem. N.C. Ho. of Reps., 1958-67, speaker, 1967; judge N.C. Ct. Appeals, 1967-78; asso. justice N.C. Supreme Ct., 1978—. Mem. Am. Bar Assn., N.C. Bar Assn., Wake County Bar Assn. Democrat. Baptist. Club: Rotary. Office: Justice Bldg Raleigh NC 27602

BRITT, JOHN EDWARD, civil engr.; b. Ninety Six, S.C., Sept. 23, 1939; s. James Boggs and Martha Louisa (McCracken) B.; B.S. in Civil Engring., Clemson U., 1961; m. Claire Turk, May 12, 1963; children—John Robert, Alice Marie. Jr. hwy. engr. Ga. Hwy. Dept., 1961-63, 66; design engr. Gifford Hill Concrete Co., Atlanta, 1966-68; co-founder, owner Guillebeau, Britt & Waldrop, Inc., Decatur, Ga. and Greenville, S.C., 1968—, pres., 1979—. Chmn. ednl. commn. Allgood Road United Methodist Ch., 1967-69, ch. sch. supt., 1970-71, chmn. council on ministries, 1973-74, mem. fin. commn., 1976, mem. bldg. com., 1978; fin. chmn. PTA, 1972; neighborhood commr. Boy Scouts Am., Atlanta, 1973-75; Republican candidate for Ga. Ho. of Reps., 1970; mem. County Rep. Exec. Com., 1968-76, Dist. Rep. Exec. Com., 1968-76. Served with U.S. Army, 1963-65. Mem. ASCE, Prestressed Concrete Inst., Post Tension Concrete Inst., Nat. Soc. Profl. Engrs., Ga. Soc. Profl. Engrs., Cons. Engrs. Council. Home: 103 Ashton Ct Easley SC 29640 Office: Box 453 Greenville SC 29607 also 4277-D Memorial Dr Decatur GA 30032

BRITT, MORRIS FRANKLIN, psychologist; b. Robeson County, N.C., Jan. 26, 1936; s. Douglas Greenwood and Goldie Mae (Davis) B.; B.A., Wake Forest U., 1958; M.S.W., U. N.C., Chapel Hill, 1960; M.A., U. N.C., Greensboro, 1968, Ed.D., 1971; m. Ann Robertson, Apr. 24, 1976; children by previous marriage—Leslie Morris, Andrew Carlyle. Chief psychiat. social worker Guilford County Mental Health Center, Greensboro, 1960-65; research psychologist Smith Richard Found., Greensboro, 1966-69; psychol cons. to mgmt. James N. Farr Assos. and Patric B. Comer Assos., Greensboro, 1969-75; asso. prof. psychology High Point (N.C.) Coll., 1970-75; clin. psychologist Durham, 1975—; dir. psychol. services Lenox Baker Children's Hosp., Durham, 1975—; adj. prof. Sch. Social Work, U. N.C., Chapel Hill, 1976-77; instr. genealogy U. N.C., Greensboro, 1974-75; cons. psychiat. social worker Patrick Henry Mental Hygiene Clinic, Martinsville, Va., 1962-67. Pres., Guilford County Geneal. Soc., 1974-75. Mem. Am., N.C. psychol. assns., Soc. Pediatric Psychology. Humanist. Author: Bibliography of Behavior Modification, 1924-75, 1975; contbr. articles to profl. jours.; editor Guilford County Genealogist, 1974-75. Home: 704 Constitution Dr Durham NC 27705 Office: Northgate Mall Area 2 Suite 224 Durham NC 27701

BRITTAIN, THOMAS HERSCHELL, JR., indsl. and organizational psychologist; b. Lake Charles, La., July 13, 1942; s. Thomas Herschell and Billie Gladys (Welborn) B.; B.S. in Psychology, La. Tech. U., 1964; M.S.W. in Psychiat. Social Work, La. State U., 1966, Ph.D. in Psychology, 1973; m. Mary Annette Sowers, Aug. 14, 1964; children—Thomas Herschell, Brandi. Oil refinery operator Cities Service Oil Co., Lake Charles, summers 1961, 62; pastoral counselor Tex. Dept. Corrections, Huntsville, 1964; sales agt. United Cos. Life Ins. Co., 1968-69; psychotherapist Mental Health Center, Baton Rouge, 1966-68, adminstr. community program, 1969-73; asso. prof. Purdue U.-Ind. U., Indpls., 1973-74; corp. psychologist Eli Lilly Pharms. Co., Indpls., 1973-74; mgr. orgn. and mgmt. devel. Borg-Warner Corp., Chgo., 1974-76; dir. mgmt. devel. and tng. Frito Lay, Inc., Dallas, 1976—; pres. Brittain & Assos., Inc., Dallas, 1977—. Recipient Vol. award Baton Rouge Area Mchts., 1971-72, Businessman's Employment Com. for Mental Patients, 1973, Dallas Soc. Advancement of Mgmt., 1976. Mem. Am. Psychol. Assn., Am. Soc. Tng. Dirs., Am. Mgmt. Assn., Nat. Assn. Social Workers, Acad. Cert. Social Workers, Southwestern Psychol. Assn., Internat. Psychol. Assn., Am. Assn. Vol. Action Scholars. Democrat. Baptist. Office: PO Box 45133 Dallas TX 75245

BRITTIN, DOROTHY HELEN CLARK, educator; b. Gadsden County, Fla., June 27, 1938; d. Herbert Hampton and Lucy Virginia (Stokes) C.; B.S. cum laude, Fla. State U., 1960; M.S., Tex. Tech. U., 1965; postgrad. N.Y. U., 1973, Wash. State U., 1973; Ph.D., Tex. Tech. U., 1974; m. Anthony Norman Brittin, Jan. 23, 1960; children—Ruth Virginia, Clark Norman, Carol Jeanette. Tchr., Mobile (Ala.) Public Schs., 1960; asst. county home demonstration agt., Nassau County, N.Y., 1961-63; research and teaching asst. Tex. Tech. U., Lubbock, 1963-65, instr., 1965-70, asst. prof., 1970-78, asso. prof. dept. food and nutrition, 1978—; cons. nat. textbook pub. cos., Presbyn. Center, Tex. Tech. U.; faculty research fellow Tex. Tech. U., 1972. Named Woman of Yr., Tex. Tech. U., 1978; Jonnie McCerie Michie grad. food and nutrition fellow, 1964-65. Mem. Am. Dietetic Assn. (mem. scholarship com. 1979-82), Am. Home Econs. Assn. (mem. world food supply com. 1975-78), Am. Meat Sci. Assn. (mem. resolutions com. 1977), Am. Soc. Animal Sci., Inst. Food Technologists, Soc. Nutrition Edn., Tex. Dietetic Assn. (pres. 1978-79), Sigma Xi, Phi Kappa Phi, Omicron Nu, Kappa Delta Pi, Phi Upsilon Omicron, Tau Beta Pi. Presbyterian. Contbr. articles in field to profl. jours. Home: 5220 15th St Lubbock TX 79416 Office: Dept Food and Nutrition Tex Tech U Lubbock TX 79409

BRITTON, BRUCE KEENE, psychologist; b. Nyack, N.Y., Mar. 19, 1944; s. Hugh Willoughby and Christine (Stehelin) B.; B.A., Goddard Coll., 1967; M.S., Boston U., 1969; M.A., U. Iowa, 1972, Ph.D., 1973. Mem. faculty Coe Coll., Cedar Rapids, Iowa, 1974, Iowa State U., Ames, Iowa, 1974-75; asst. prof. U. Ga., Athens, 1975—. NSF fellow, 1967-68; USPHS fellow, 1969-73; Law Enforcement Assistance Adminstrn. grantee, 1974-75. Mem. AAAS, Am., Midwestern, Southeastern psychol. assns., Iowa Acad. Sci., So. Soc. for Philosophy and Psychology, Sigma Xi. Editorial reviewer Memory and Cognition, Jour. Exptl. Psychology: Human Learning and Memory; contbr. articles to profl. jours.; author research reports. Home: Route 2 Box 36B Hull GA 30646 Office: Dept Psychology U Ga Athens GA 30602

BRITTON, JOHNNIE WILLIAM, JR., army officer; b. San Francisco, Feb. 28, 1936; s. Johnnie William and Ruby Del (Tomer) B.; grad. Officer Candidate Sch., 1960; B.A., U. Nebr., 1969, M.B.A., Claremont (Calif.) Grad. Sch., 1974, M.A. in Urban Studies, 1975; m. Jay Eckhardt, June 30, 1963; children—Johnny W., Jeffrey Jay. Commd. officer U.S. Army, advanced through grades to lt. col., 1976; asst. dir. Mil. Personnel Policy, Manpower and Res. Affairs, Dept. Def., 1976-78; commanding officer Army Officer Candidate Sch., Ft. Benning, Ga., 1979—. Asst. scoutmaster Nat. Capital Area council Boy Scouts Am., Dept. Def. rep. ARC, Washington, 1977-78. Decorated Silver Star, Bronze Star with 3V clusters, Purple Heart. Mem. Am. Mgmt. Assn., Assn. U.S. Army (bd. govs. 1978-79), Assn. M.B.A.'s. Home: 308 Miller Loop Fort Benning GA 31905

BRITTON, VICKI WELLS, banker; b. Mt. Sterling, Ky., July 21, 1950; d. William Kenneth and Helen Clay (Moore) W.; B.S. with honors, U. Tenn., 1975; m. William Turner Britton, Dec. 9, 1978; children—Grady L. Sain III, Kenneth Wells Sain. Teller, bookkeeper Peoples Bank, Carrollton, Ga., 1969-70; teller Park Bank, Knoxville, Tenn., 1970-72; tchr. Mt. Sterling High Sch., 1975-76; internat. rep. United Am. Bank, Knoxville, 1976, corporate accounts rep., 1977, asst. v.p., 1978, v.p., 1979—, nat. mgr. cash mgmt. and nat. accounts, 1979—. Mem. Exec. Women Am., Female Execs. Am. Episcopalian. Home: 9524 W Aiken Ln Knoxville TN 37922 Office: 800 S Gay St Knoxville TN 37901

BRITTON, W(ILLIAM) TURNER, banker; b. Atlanta, Nov. 30, 1951; s. Taylor Woodyard and Margaret Virginia (Turner) B.; B.S. in Bus. Adminstrn., U. Tenn., 1974, postgrad. in bus. adminstrn., 1975-77; m. Vicki Wells Sain, Dec. 9, 1978; stepchildren—Grady Sain, Kenneth Sain. Internat. cons. to Govt. of Nicaragua, Central Am., 1975-76; corp. accounts officer United Am. Bank, Knoxville, Tenn., 1976-78, real estate loan officer, 1978—; instr. cash mgmt. seminar, 1977. Mem. Am. Mgmt. Assn., State of Tenn. Affiliated Real Estate Brokers, Tenn. Assn. of Bank Credit and Lending. Episcopalian. Club: Men's Cotillion (sec., treas. 1977-78). Office: PO Box 280 Knoxville TN 37901

BRIXIUS, WILLIAM HENRY, materials engr.; b. Wilson Boro, Pa., May 8, 1950; s. John William and Alice Martha (Heger) B.; B.S. in Materials Engring., N.C. State U., 1972; M.S. in Engring. Sci.-Metallurgy, Rensselaer Poly. Inst., Troy, N.Y., 1976; m. Theresa Helen Scalf, July 27, 1973. Spl. tech. asst. Western Electric Co., Greensboro, N.C., 1969-72; process devel. engr. Pratt & Whitney Aircraft Co., East Hartford, Conn., 1973-78; scientist Poco Graphite Inc., Decatur, Tex., 1978—, materials engr., 1978—; cons. in field. Mem. Am. Ceramic Soc., Am. Carbon Soc., ASTM, Internat. Metallographic Soc., Am. Powder Metallurgy Inst., Am. Soc. Metals, Alpha Sigma Mu. Author papers in field. Home: 1912 Lariat Rd Denton TX 76201 Office: 1601 S State St Decatur TX 76234

BROADHURST, NORMAN NEIL, foods co. exec.; b. Chico, Calif., Dec. 17, 1946; s. Frank Spencer and Dorothy Mae (Conrad) B.; B.S., Calif. State U., 1969; M.B.A., Golden Gate U., 1975; m. Victoria Rose Thomson, Aug. 7, 1976; 1 son, Scott Andrew. With Del Monte Corp., San Francisco, 1969-76, product mgr., 1973-76; product mgr. Riviana Foods, Inc., div. Colgate Palmolive, Houston, 1976-78; new products brand devel. mgr. foods div. Coca Cola Co., Houston, 1978-79, brand mgr., 1979—. Mem. Am. Mktg. Assn. Clubs: Toastmasters Internat. (past chpt. pres.), Houston Met. Racquet. Home: 3914 Mayfield Oaks Houston TX 77088 Office: 7105 Old Katy Rd Houston TX 77005

BROADNAX, FRANK, wood refinishing products co. exec.; b. Glascock County, Ga., Apr. 5, 1931; s. Earnest Brookins and Susie (Johnson) B.; student Augusta Jr. Coll., 1953-55, Ga. Southwestern Tech. Inst., 1962-63; m. Rhonda Smith, June 11, 1961; children—Mark Stephen, Barry Maxwell, Erica Rae. Lab. technician Gen. Refractories, 1956-66; quality control supr. Life of Ga. Ins., 1966-70; pres. Broadnax Refinishing Products, Inc., Ila, Ga., 1970—; lectr. wood refinishing, restoration. Served with USAF, 1950-53. Mem. Soc. for Preservation and Encouragement Barber Shop Quartet Singing in Am. Baptist. Author: Restore, 1972; Good News for Antiques and Fine Furniture, 1974. Contbr. articles to Old House Jour. Home: PO Box 196 Ila GA 30647 Office: Sewell Mill Rd Ila GA 30647

BROADWAY, CHARLES EDWARD, textile co. exec.; b. Bishopville, S.C., Nov. 26, 1941; s. Ollie Austin and Lettie Idell (Hodge) B.; A.A., Wingate Coll., 1962; B.A. in Math., Pembroke State U., 1964; postgrad. U. S.C., 1968, U. N.C., 1969; m. Mary Frances Flynn, Apr. 14, 1963; children—Charles Jeffrey, Alicia Ann, David Duane. Tchr. pub. schs., Md., 1963-67, N.C., 1967-69; tng. specialist in data processing Springs Mills, Inc., Lancaster, S.C., 1969-77; supr. human resources J.P. Stevens & Co., Inc., Charlotte, N.C., 1977—; instr. Lancaster Vocat. Sch.; cons. data processing dept. U. S.C. Com. chmn. Boy Scouts Am., 1972—; mem. data processing adv. bd. York Tech. Coll., Rock Hill, S.C.; dean Presbyterian Ch., 1968-76, elder, 1977—. NSF fellow, 1968. Mem. Am. Soc. Tng. and Devel., Carolina Large Users Group for Data Processing, Guide Internat. Democrat. Home: Route 2 Box 95 Waxhaw NC 28173 Office: J P Stevens & Co Inc PO Box 31426 6300 Fairview Rd Charlotte NC 28231

BROBST, GLENDA ELAINE ALLEN, speech pathologist; b. Longview, Tex., Nov. 25, 1953; d. Forest Delma and Malinda Elaine (Rogers) Allen; B.S. summa cum laude in Secondary Edn., N. Tex. State U., 1977, M.S. summa cum laude in Communication Disorders, 1978; m. Gary Garth Brobst, June 23, 1979. Research analyst Deep East Tex. Council of Govts., Jasper, 1972-73; clk./typist Def. Civil Preparedness Agy., Denton, Tex., 1974-76; transcriptionist, oral history collection N. Tex. State U., Denton, 1976-78, grad. asst., 1977-78; speech pathologist Plano (Tex.) Ind. Sch. Dist., 1979-80. Mem. Am. Speech and Hearing Assn., Dallas Assn. Speech Pathologists, Stardusters of Kappa Sigma. Baptist. Home: 2514 Wamath Dr Charlotte NC 28210

BROCK, DAN MORGAN, hosp. adminstr.; b. Tarrant County, Tex., Aug. 15, 1924; s. William Elmer and Lillie Marie (Tomlinson) B.; student N. Tex. State U., 1941; B.A., U. Tex., Austin, 1949; m. Winona Bickley, June 5, 1948; children—Sharon Lynn, Dan Morgan Jr. Corp. sec., gen. mgr. Bickley Bros. Inc., Houston, 1949-60; field engr. J.E. Sjostrom Co. Inc., Phila., 1960-62; dir. purchasing-City of Houston, 1962-72; dir. procurement St. Luke's Episcopal and Tex. Children's Hosps. and Tex. Heart Inst., Houston, 1972—. Del. Harris County, Tex. Republican state convs., 1972—. Served with USNR, 1942-46. Mem. Nat. Purchasing Inst. (cert. purchasing officer)(nat. pres. 1971), Purchasing Mgmt. Assn. Houston (pres. 1972-73), Nat. Purchasing Mgmt. Assn. (cert. purchasing mgr.; nat. v.p. 1978-79), Am. Soc. Hosp. Purchasing and Materials Mgmt., Tex. Soc. Hosp. Purchasing Mgrs. Methodist. Home: 5003 Shady Nook Ct Houston TX 77018

BROCK, JACKIE EDWARDS, biologist, educator; b. Bon Secour, Ala., Dec. 4, 1932; d. Albert Gabriel and Catherine Dafina (Matika) Edwards; B.S., U. Ala., 1959, M.S., 1961; m. Martin Pearson Brock, Dec. 12, 1966. Instr. biology Middle Tenn. Coll., Murfreesboro, 1962-65; instr. biology Jefferson Davis State Jr. Coll., Brewton, Ala., 1966—. NDEA scholar, 1959-62. Mem. Assn. Southeastern Biologists, Sigma Xi (asso.). Methodist. Discoverer new genus of algae Chlorospirulina, 1959-61. Office: Drawer N Jefferson Davis Jr Coll Brewton AL 36426

BROCK, JAMES STANLEY, civil engr.; b. Bessemer, Ala., Sept. 15, 1928; s. James Sinyard and Jessie (Bailey) B.; B.S. in Civil Engring., U. Ala., 1957; m. Mae Will Bruce, Mar. 12, 1949; children—Elizabeth, Bruce, Bradley. Engr., sr. engr., sect. engr. Gulf States Paper Co., Tuscaloosa, 1957-63; staff, project engr. Olinkraft, Inc., West Monroe, La., 1963-66; project engr., lead project engr. Rust Engring. Co., Birmingham, Ala., 1966-68; engring. supt. MacMillan Bloedel Inc., Pine Hill, Ala., 1968-70; engring. and constrn. supt. Olinkraft, Inc., West Monroe, 1970-73; mgr., dir. Ford Bacon e Davis Ltda, Sao Paulo, Brazil, 1973-75; mgr. bus. devel. Ford, Bacon & Davis, Monroe, La., 1975-79, v.p. bus. devel., 1979—. Served with USAF, 1948-52, USAFR, 1952-56; Korea, Japan. Registered profl. engr., Ala., Tex., Miss., La., Okla., Ark., Tenn. Mem. Nat. Soc. Profl. Engrs., TAPPI, La. Engring. Soc., Paper Industry Mgmt. Assn., ASME, Soc. Mktg. Profl. Services. Baptist. Home: 3109 River Oaks Dr Monroe LA 71203 Office: PO Box 1762 Monroe LA 71201

BROCK, LOUISE MURPHY, former ednl. adminstr., artist; b. Jackson County, Ga., May 20, 1913; d. Andrew E. and Nora (Foster) Murphy; A.B. in English, Piedmont Coll., Demorest, Ga., 1945; M.A. in Elementary Edn., U. Ga., Athens, 1957, Edn. Specialist in Elementary Edn., 1962; m. Telford Carroll Brock (dec.); children—Telford Carroll, Benny Murphy. Tchr. Jackson County (Ga.) Bd. Edn., 1933-50; tchr. Hall County (Ga.) Bd. Edn., Gainesville, 1950-66, cons. reading, 1967-74, dir. remedial reading, 1974-79; oil painter. Mem. NEA, Hall County, Ga. assns. educators, Internat. Reading Assn., Chattahoochee Reading Council, Assn. Childhood Edn., AAUW, Delta Kappa Gamma, Kappa Delta Pi. Baptist. Patentee reading device. Home: Route 3 Box 128 Gainesville GA 30501

BROCK, LUTHER AMOS, JR., educator; b. Bridgeport, Tex., Mar. 23, 1931; s. Luther Amos and Velma Abbie (Anderson) B.; B.B.A., N. Tex. State U., 1952, M.B.A., 1954; Ph.D., La. State U., 1963; m. Linda Joanne Miller, Aug. 26, 1967; 1 son, Darren Keith. Instr. bus. communications W. Tex. State U., Canyon, 1954-56; asst. prof. U. Southwestern La., 1957-60; mem. faculty dept. bus. communications N. Tex. State U., Denton, 1961—, prof., 1968—; cons. direct mail advt. and bus. communications. Mem. Direct Mail/Mktg. Assn., Am. Bus. Communication Assn., Tex. Assn. Coll. Tchrs. Methodist. Author 4 books in field; contbr. articles to profl. jours. Home: 2911 Nottingham Dr Denton TX 76201 Office: Coll Bus North Tex State Univ Denton TX 76203

BROCKWAY, RICHARD STUART, former ins. co. exec.; b. Ripley, N.Y., Mar. 21, 1917: s. Frederick Bourbon and Annie Campbell (MacNee) B.; B.A., Cornell U., 1939; m. Margaret Bishop, July 10, 1943; children—Carol Anne and Susan Jane (twins). With Hurdman & Cranstoun, 1939-41; with U.S. Aviation Underwriters, N.Y.C., 1941-78, sr. v.p. fin., dir., 1971-78; pres., dir. Aerospace Mgmt. Services Internat. (Can.) Ltd. Mem. Drug and Chem. Club N.Y. (pres. 1974-75), Gen. Soc. Mayflower Descs., Gen. Soc. Colonial Wars. Soc. Ins. Accountants (exec. com.), Delta Chi. Republican. Presbyterian. Home: 32 Harleston Green Hilton Head Island SC 29928

BROCKWELL, PAUL ANTHONY, III, accountant, welding co. exec.; b. Tulsa, Feb. 11, 1946; s. Paul Anthony and Betty Lou (Page) B., Jr.; B.B.A., U. Okla., 1969. Accountant, Arthur Young & Co., Tulsa, 1969-74; v.p., dir. The Jimmie Jones Co., Tulsa, 1974—; gen. mgr. C&E Leasing Co., Tulsa, 1974—; pres. Sunrise Properties. C.P.A., Okla. Mem. Am. Inst. C.P.A.'s, Okla. Soc. C.P.A.'s, Am. Mgmt. Assn., Sigma Chi. Republican. Roman Catholic. Club: Tulsa Country. Home: 3470 S Zunis St Tulsa OK 74105 Office: PO Box 1152 Tulsa OK 74101

BRODERMANN, NOHELY SÁNCHEZ, educator; b. Guane, Pinar del Río, Cuba, Nov. 28, 1923; came to U.S., 1960, naturalized, 1970; d. Francisco and Blanca (Parra) Sánchez; teaching degree Normal Sch. for Tchrs., Pinar del Río, 1943; M.A. in Polit. Scis., Northwestern State U., 1969; M.A. in Spanish, Stephen F. Austin U., 1972; m. R. E. Brodermann, Nov. 8, 1953; 1 dau., María Cristina. Asst. prof. Northwestern State U., Natchitoches, La., 1969—, advisor fgn. students. Mem. AAUP, Assn. Profs. of Spanish and Portuguese. Republican. Roman Catholic. Club: Cosmopolitan. Contbr. writings in field to profl. publs. Home: 847 Parkway Dr Natchitoches LA 71457 Office: Kyser Bldg Northwestern State U Langs Dept Natchitoches LA 71457

BRODNAX, CHARLES TEDDY, educator, ins. exec.; b. Bastrop, La., Mar. 30, 1931; s. Clarence Eugene and Ethel Pernice (Smith) B.; B.S., La. State U., 1952; M.R.E., SW Baptist Theol. Sem., 1959; m. Mary Margaret O'Bryan, Sept. 1, 1956; children—Mary Margaret, Faulkner Eugene. Asst. in employee relations United Gas Co., Monroe, La., 1954-57; minister of edn., business adminstr. Second Baptist Ch., Lubbock, Tex., 1959-60, First Baptist Ch., Bastrop, La., 1960-62; field underwriter life ins. Mut. of N.Y., Monroe, La., 1962-69; regional v.p. Protective Life, Birmingham, Ala., 1969—; adjunct prof. life ins. salesmanship NE U. of La., 1966-68, U. of Ala.,

Tuscaloosa, 1971-72. Served with U.S. Army, 1952-54. Chartered life underwriter, The Am. Coll., 1968. Mem. NE La. Chartered Life Underwriters (charter pres. 1969), Ala. Advisory Bd. on Commerce & Indsl. Development (subcom. chmn., 1973, indsl. tng. development program, 1972-77), Birmingham, Ala., Nat. assns. of life underwriters, Birmingham, Am. socs. of chartered life underwriters, Ala., Am. socs. for tng. and development (sales tng. div.). Democrat. Episcopalian. Clubs: The Club, Rotary, Green Valley Country. Editor Protective Life Ratebook, 1976; contbr. presentation, articles in field. Home: 1801 Winchester Circle Birmingham AL 35226 Office: 2801 Highway 280-S Birmingham AL 35223

BRODY, AARON LEO, packaging co. exec.; b. Boston, Aug. 23, 1930; s. Nathan and Lillian (Gorman) B.; B.S., Mass. Inst. Tech., 1951, Ph.D. (William Underwood fellow 1955-56), 1957; M.B.A., Northeastern U., 1970; m. Carolyn Goldstein, Apr. 11, 1953; children—Stephen, Glen, Robyn. Head food research labs Whirlpool Corp., St. Joseph, Mich., 1957-61; packaging and product devel. mgr. Mars, Inc., Hackettstown, N.J., 1961-66; packaging coordinator Arthur D. Little, Inc., Cambridge, Mass., 1967-73; new ventures mgr. Mead Packaging, Atlanta, 1973—. Course dir. Mich. State U., East Lansing, 1959-61; instr. Emory U., 1979. Mem. optimal program for edn. DeKalb County (Ga.), 1975, sec., 1975; mem. food service adv. com. U.S. Navy, 1958-62; active Kerry for Congress campaign, 1972; mem. legis. subcom. on spl. edn. State of Ga., 1974; mem. Nat. Def. Exec. Res., 1978—. Served with AUS, 1952-54. Recipient Willis H. Carrier award Am. Soc. Heating, Refrigerating and Air Conditioning Engrs., 1960; Indsl. Achievement award Inst. Food Technologists, 1964; TOP award of excellence, Packaging Inst. U.S.A., 1972; Braverman Meml. award Israel Inst. Tech., 1976. Fellow AAAS, Packaging Inst. U.S.A.; mem. Packaging Inst. (v.p. 1979), Inst. Food Technologists (sci. lectr. 1972-74), Planning Execs. Inst., N.Y. Acad. Scis., Am. Assn. Candy Technologists, Food Distbrs. Research Soc., Nat. Council of Distbn., Sigma Xi. Clubs: Mass. Inst. Tech. (pres. 1977-79) (Atlanta); Toastmasters. Inventor in field. Contbr. articles to profl. jours. Home: 1101 Wynterhall Lane Dunwoody GA 30338 Office: PO Box 4417 Atlanta GA 30302

BRODY, ERWIN WILLIAM, pub. relations exec.; b. N.Y.C., Feb. 10, 1933; s. Joseph and Sophie (Barish) B.; student Memphis State U., 1961-63; B.A., Eastern Ill. U., 1977; M.A., Calif. State U., 1978; m. Sandra Gail Williams, June 9, 1972. Journalist, Daytona Beach (Fla.) Evening News, 1956-69; dir. advt. and pub. relations Ellinor Village Resort, Daytona Beach, 1959-61; journalist The Comml. Appeal, Memphis, 1961-63; editor Memphis Sunday Times, 1964-65; info. officer Memphis Housing Authority, 1965-66; pres. Communications Group Inc., Memphis, 1966—; founder Inst. Continuing Edn., 1977; instr. Center for Govt. Tng., U. Tenn. Bd. dirs. Memphis Boys Town, 1968-70, Family Service Assn. Memphis, 1968—. Mem. Pub. Relations Soc. Am. (accredited), Internat. Assn. Bus. Communicators (accredited), Internat. Public Relations Assn., Am. Hosp. Assn. Republican. Author: Model Supervisory Manual for Hospitals, 1977. Home: 2196 Cornwall St Memphis TN 38138 Office: 2277 West St Memphis TN 38138

BROEKER, ANNIE BARR, chem. engr.; b. Columbia, S.C., Dec. 20, 1951; d. Decania Dowling and Norma Tallon (Galloway) Barr; B.S. in Chem. Engring., U. S.C., 1973; postgrad. in bus. U. Houston, 1976—; m. Roger John Broeker, Jr., Oct. 11, 1975. With Badische Corp., 1973—, spl. assignments engr., Anderson, S.C., 1973-74, subs. Castlecreek Fabrics, Washington, N.J., 1974, environ. engr. Tombigbee plant, 1974-75, environ. engr., Freeport, Tex., 1975-76, prodn. engr., 1976-78, econ. evaluator, 1978—. Mem. local Republican orgn. Mem. Nat. Assn. Female Execs., Nat., Tex. (Young Engr. of Yr. Gulf Coast chpt. 1978-79) socs. profl. engrs., Am. Inst. Chem. Engrs., Soc. Women Engrs. Presbyterian. Home: 113 N Cay Ct Angleton TX 77515 Office: 602 Copper Rd Freeport TX 77541

BROHAMER, RICHARD FREDERIC, psychiatrist; b. Rockford, Ill., Nov. 9, 1934; s. Joseph C. and Marthe Marie (Ringuette) B.; Ph.B., U. Detroit, 1960; M.D., U. Fla., 1964; postgrad. Basic Tng. Diving Medicine Internat. Underwater Explorers Soc., 1973, Advanced Tng. Diving Medicine, 1974; m. Shirley Ruth Noble, June 22, 1956; children—Richard Frederic II, Renee Marie, Rory Christopher. Intern Duval Med. Center, Jacksonville, Fla., 1964-65; resident psychiatry U. Fla., 1965-68; practice medicine specializing in psychiatry, Fort Lauderdale, Fla., 1968—; mem. staffs Broward Gen., Coral Ridge, Holy Cross, North Beach, North Ridge hosps.; chmn. dept. psychiatry Imperial Point Hosp., 1975—. Research fellow Tropical medicine La. State U., Costa Rica, 1963, Central Am., 1968. Served with USAF, 1954-58; Korea. Diplomate Am. Bd. Psychiatry and Neurology. Mem. Am. (pres. student chpt. 1961-64), So. Fla., Broward County (Fla.) med. assns., Am., Fla., Broward County psychiat. socs., Undersea Adventurers, Internat. Soc. Diving Medicine. Republican. Roman Catholic. Home: 3200 NE 38th St Fort Lauderdale FL 33308 Office: 2340 NE 53d St Fort Lauderdale FL 33308

BROHARD, ELLEN BRADY, educator; b. Ashland, Va., Aug. 11, 1942; d. Patrick L. and Effie B. Brady; B.S. in Bus. Edn., Longwood Coll., 1963; M.S. in Vocat. Tech. Edn., Va. Poly. Inst./State U., 1975; m. Thomas L. Brohard, Feb. 10, 1967; children—Bill, Mark. Bus. edn. tchr. Fairfax County Schs., George Marshall High Sch., Falls Church, Va., 1963-68; bus. edn. tchr., coordinator Fairfax County Adult Edn., Falls Church, 1969-74; secretarial sci. program coordinator, asst. prof. No. Va. Community Coll., Loudoun Campus, 1974—; supr. Shaklee Corp., 1979—. Asst. soccer coach; mem. PTA, 1978—; sec. Cub Scouts, 1978—; mem. fund raising com. Soccer League, 1979, Pee Wee League, 1979. Mem. Bus. and Profl. Women's Club, Longwood Coll. Alumni Assn. (sec.). Baptist. Home: Route 2 Box 218F Leesburg VA 22075 Office: 1000 H F Byrd Hwy Sterling VA 22170

BROILES, BARNES HOOVER, ret. pub. co. exec.; b. Belton, Tex., Oct. 5, 1897; s. Hiram Stokey and Ama (Yarbrough) B.; student So. Jr. Coll., 1918; m. Mary Louise Reed, June 30, 1921; children—Barnes W., Mary Joan Broiles Payne. Reporter, Los Angeles Record, 1919, San Bernadino (Calif.) Telegram, 1920, Houston Post, 1923-24; mng. editor El Centro Valley Press, 1921-22; editor Mexia (Tex.) Daily News, 1924-36, also pub. Gladewater (Tex.) Times-Tribune, 1936-49, Jacksonville (Tex.) Daliy Progress, 1951-78. Del. Democratic Conv., 1960. Bd. dirs. Jacksonville Indsl. Found.; pres. East Tex. Med. Edn. Research Found., Travis Clinic Found. Recipient distinguished service award Cherokee County Soil Conservation Dist., 1965; Sam Holloway Meml. award North and East Tex. Press, 1974; Alexander award Lon Morris Coll. Rotary Paul Harris fellow. Mem. Tex. Press Assn. (50 Year Certificate 1971), Tex. Daily Newspaper Assn., Jacksonville C. of C. (pres. 1968, named Man of Year 1971), Sigma Delta Chi. Mem. Christian Ch. (elder). Club: Rotary. Author: Small Town Editor, 59 Years in Journalism. Home: 811 Circle Dr Jacksonville TX 75766

BROKAW, MARVIN JAY, JR., bank mktg. exec.; b. Kansas City, Mo., Nov. 14, 1938; s. Marvin J. and Eleanor Marie (Chitty) B.; B.A. in Market Research, Mich. State U., 1960; m. Charlotte Rosalie Carpenter, Jan. 20, 1968; 1 dau., Leslie Diane. Reporter, F. W. Dodge div. McGraw-Hill, Inc., Kalamazoo, 1960-61, dist. salesman, Mpls., 1964-69; sec.-treas. Compos-it, Inc., Montgomery, Ala., 1969-77; asst. mktg. officer First Ala. Bank, Montgomery, 1977—; mem. Ala. Gov.'s Conf. on Library and Info. Services, 1979—, mem. exec. com., 1979—; mem. Citizens Adv. Com. on Public TV. Served with U.S. Army, 1961-64. Mem. Am. Inst. Banking, Advt. Club Montgomery (Silver Medal award 1978), Bank Mktg. Assn., Sales and Mktg. Execs. Club Montgomery. Club: Kiwanis. Home: 3010 Merrimac Dr Montgomery AL 36111 Office: PO Box 511 Montgomery AL 36101

BROKHOFF, JOHN RUDOLPH, clergyman; b. Pottsville, Pa., Dec. 19, 1913; s. John Henry and Gertrude Amanda (Heiser) B.; A.B., Muhlenberg Coll., 1935, D.D. (hon.), 1951; M.A., U. Pa., 1938; M.Div., Phila. Luth. Sem., 1938; m. Barbara Jean MacFarland; children—Wendy, Helen, Virginia, John, Jodi. Ordained to ministry Lutheran Ch., 1938; pastor Ebenezer Luth. Ch., Marion, Va., 1940-42, Christ Luth. Ch., Roanoke, Va., 1942-45, Luth. Ch. of the Redeemer, Atlanta, 1945-55, St. Mark's Luth. Ch., Charlotte, N.C., 1955-62, Trinity Luth. Ch., Lansdale, Pa., 1962-65; prof. homiletics Candler Sch. Theology, Emory U., Atlanta, 1965-78, prof. emeritus, 1979—; pres. Atlanta Christian Council, Mecklenberg Ministers (Charlotte). Named one of Atlanta's leaders of tomorrow Atlanta C. of C. and Time Mag., 1953; recipient George Washington medal Freedom Found., 1966, certificate of merit Charlotte Jr. Women's Club, 1961. Mem. Omicron Delta Kappa, Tau Kappa Alpha, Alpha Kappa Alpha, Sigma Phi Epsilon. Author: This Is Life, 1959; Table for Lovers, 1974; If Your Dearest Should Die, 1975; Wrinkled Wrappings, 1975; Cross Purposes, 1976; Jesus...Who?, 1977; (with B. Brokhoff) Faith Alive!, 1978; Lectionary Preaching Workbook, 1979; contbg. editor Pulpit Digest, 1977—; contbr. column to Charlotte Observer, 1960-62, North Penn Reporter, 1962-65. Home: 6 Belleview Blvd Apt A/501 Clearwater FL 33516

BROMBERG, ALAN ROBERT, lawyer, educator, writer; b. Dallas, Nov. 24, 1928; s. Alfred L. and Juanita (Kramer) B.; A.B., Harvard, 1949; J.D., Yale, 1952; m. Anne Ruggles, July 26, 1959. Admitted to Tex. bar, 1952, U.S. Tax Ct. bar, 1959; asso. firm Carrington, Gowan, Johnson, Bromberg and Leeds, Dallas, 1952-56; atty. and cons., 1956-76; of counsel Jenkens & Gilchrist, 1976—; part-time lectr. Law Sch., So. Methodist U., Dallas, 1955-56, vis. asst. prof. law, 1956-57, asst. prof. law, 1957-58, asso. prof., 1958-62, prof. law, 1962—, chmn. law curriculum com., 1961-72, trustee retirement plan, 1967-70, faculty rep. bd. trustees, 1969-70, 74, mem. exec. com. faculty senate, 1968-70, mem. presdl. search group, 1971-72; faculty adviser Southwestern Law Jour., 1958-65; sr. fellow Yale U. Law Faculty, 1966-67; vis. prof. Stanford U. Law Sch., 1972-73; lectr. in field; adv. bd. U. Calif. Securities Regulation Inst. Counsel Internat. Data Sytems, Inc., 1961-65, sec., dir. 1963-65; mem. Tex. Legis. Council Bus. and Commerce Code Adv. Com., 1966-67. Sec., mem. bd. dirs. Community Arts Fund, 1963-73; gen. atty. Dallas Mus. Contemporary Arts, 1956-63. Bd. dirs. Dallas Theater Center, 1955—, sec., 1957-66, finance com., 1957-65, mem. exec. com., 1957-70, life mem., 1973—, v.p., trustee endowment fund, 1974—. Served as cpl. M.I., AUS, 1952-54. Mem. Am. Bar Assn. (mem. com. commodities, com. partnerships; mem. com. fed. regulation of securities), Dallas Bar Assn. (chmn. com. on uniform partnership act 1959-61), State Bar Tex. (mem. com. on corporate law revision, 1957—, mem. com. on securities and investment banking 1957—, chmn. 1965-69, mem. com. on information of corp. banking and bus. law sect. 1961-69, mem. council of sect. 1963-69, vice chmn. 1965-67, chmn. 1967-68, reporter com. on revision of penal code 1967-70, com. on partnership 1974—), Am. Law Inst., Southwestern Legal Found., Am., Assn. U. Profs. (exec. com. So. Methodist U. chpt. 1962-63; chmn. acad. freedom and tenure com. 1968-70, 71-72). Author: (with Byron D. Sher) Cases and Materials on Texas Partnerships, 1958, supplemented 1960; Supplementary Materials on Texas Corporations, 1959, rev. 1965, 71; Partnership Primer-Problems and Planning, 1961; Materials on Corporate Securities and Finance—A Growing Company's Search for Funds, 1962, rev. 1965; Securities Law-Fraud-SEC Rule 10b-5, Vol. 1, 1967, Vol. 2, 1970, Vol. 3, 1973, Vol. 4, 1977, supplements pub. annually; Crane and Bromberg on Partnership, 1968; Corporate Organizational Documents and Securities—Forms and Comments, rev. edit., 1976. Contbr. numerous articles and revs. to law and bar jours. Adv. editor Rev. Securities Regulation, 1969—, Securities Regulation Law Jour., 1973—, Jour. Corp. Law, 1976—; ednl. publs. adv. bd. Matthew Bender & Co., 1977—. Office: So Meth U Law Sch Dallas TX 75275 also 2200 First Nat Bank Bldg Dallas TX 75202

BROMLEY, HAWORTH PEERY, coll. adminstr.; b. Washington, Aug. 5, 1947; s. Haworth and Frances Elizabeth (Peery) B.; student Va. Commonwealth U. Music Sch., Richmond, 1965-68; Asso. Sci., No. Va. Community Coll., 1972. coordinator bus. labs. No. Va. Community Coll., Alexandria, 1972-74, supr. ops. TICCIT Computer Center, 1974—; cons. in field. Served with U.S. Army, 1968-70. Decorated Bronze Star Medal. Mem. Am. Guild Organists, Data Processing Mgmt. Assn. Episcopalian. Home: 302 Mansion Dr Alexandria VA 22302 Office: 3001 N Beauregard St Alexandria VA 22311

BRONG, ROSCO, coll. dean, clergyman; b. Monroe County, Pa., Mar. 16, 1908; s. Francis Samuel and Jennie (Erwin) B.; A.B., Georgetown Coll., 1950; M.A., U. Ky., 1952; postgrad. U. Mich., summer, 1952; m. Virginia Conley, Oct. 5, 1930; 1 adopted dau., Edna May Davis. Ordained to ministry Baptist Ch., 1934; pastor various Bapt. churches in Ky., 1934-72; instr. Lexington (Ky.) Bapt. Coll., 1952-79, dean, 1954-79. Mem. Am. Philol. Assn. Democrat. Club: Masons. Author: Love Builds Up, 1962; Better Than the Angels, 1963; For His Name's Sake, 1963; Following Holiness, 1973; Christ's Church and Baptism, 1977. Home: PO Box 5675 Lexington KY 40555

BRONITSKY, GORDON JAY, archeologist, educator; b. Hagerstown, Md., June 17, 1949; s. Jacob and Hedwig (Alexander) B.; B.A., U. N.Mex., 1971; M.A., U. Ariz., 1972, Ph.D., 1977; m. Janet Lisa Shafton, June 6, 1976; 1 son, Micah Ari. Lectr., Rutgers U., New Brunswick, N.J., 1976-77; lithics analyst Eastern N.Mex. U. San Juan Valley Project, 1977; asst. prof. U. Tex. of the Permian Basin, Odessa, 1977—; with Cozumel Archeol. Project, 1973, Grasshopper Field Sch., 1974; resident scholar Sch. Am. Research, 1975; dir. modern material culture field sch., 1979. Nat. Endowment for Humanities summer seminar in archeology, 1978. Mem. Am. Anthropol. Assn., Soc. Am. Archeology, Council Tex. Archeologists, Tex. Archeol. Soc., Midland Archeol. Soc. (v.p., 1978), ACLU. Jewish. Club: B'nai B'rith. Contbr. articles to profl. publs. Home: 3939 Tanglewood #206 Odessa TX 79762 Office: Dept Anthropology Univ Texas of the Permian Basin Odessa TX 79762

BRONOCCO, TERRI LYNN, editor; b. San Antonio, Jan. 7, 1953; d. Lawrence and Jimmie (Mears) B.; student U. Tex., Austin, 1970-73. Public relations liaison U. Tex. Health Sci. Center, Dallas, 1974-75; editorial asst. Nat. Assn. Retarded Citizens, Arlington, Tex., 1975-76; public relations asst. Assos. Corp. N.Am., Dallas, 1976-77; editor, 1977-78, public relations mgr., 1978-79; editor-in-chief Nat. Tax Shelter Digest, Dallas, 1979-80; fin. editor Dallas/Fort Worth Bus., Dallas, 1980—. Mem. Dallas County Democratic Party. Recipient Outstanding Service award Dallas C. of C., 1978. Mem. Internat. Assn. Bus. Communicators, Am. Mgmt. Assn., Women in Communications, Am. Soc. Mag. Editors. Roman Catholic. Home: 6630 Eastridge #127 Dallas TX 75231 Office: 11300 N Central Suite 417 Dallas TX 75243

BRONSON, WILLIAM HOWARD, JR., newspaper pub.; b. Crowley, La., Nov. 16, 1936; s. William Howard and Lillian (Francez) B.; B.S. in Indsl. Mgmt., Ga. Tech. U., 1958; m. Dorsey Ann Ebarb, Oct. 18, 1968; children—Dana Carol, Howard Zachary, Kathryn Sinclair, William Howard. Rate engr. United Gas, Shreveport, 1958-60; prodn. engr. Newspaper Prodn. Co., Shreveport, 1960-68, prodn. mgr., 1968-72 pres., gen. mgr., 1972—; pres. The Shreveport Times, 1976—, pub., 1977—. Bd. dirs. YMCA Shreveport, 1964—; pres. Shreveport Bossier Econ. Devel. Found., 1974—; bd. dirs. Council for a Better La., 1978—. Mem. So. Newspaper Pubs. Assn., Am. Newspaper Pubs. Assn., Tex. Daily Newspaper Assn., Shreveport C. of C. (dir. 1978—). Democrat. Roman Catholic. Clubs: Pierremont Oaks Tennis, Petroleum. Office: 222 Lake St Shreveport LA 71130

BROOKFIELD, H. MORGAN, III, banker; b. N.Y.C., June 1, 1941; s. Henry Morgan and Elisabeth Scott (Bradley) B.; B.S.B.A., U. Tenn., 1968; m. Judith Ann Hitchings, Aug. 24, 1974; children—Henry Morgan IV, Rowe Bradley, Kathryn Elizabeth. Mgmt. trainee Morgan Guaranty Bank, N.Y.C., 1967-68; mgr. br. bank 1st Tenn. Nat. Bank, Memphis, 1968-72; mgr. comml. loans Comml. & Indsl. Bank, Memphis, 1972-74; mgr. comml. fin. dept. Union Planters Nat. Bank of Memphis, 1974—. Mem. Tenn. Gov.'s Task Force on Fin. Resources, 1979—; sr. warden St. Elisabeth's Episcopal Ch., Memphis, 1978—; sec. Vollintine Boys' Club, 1978—, also bd. dirs. Served with paratroops U.S. Army, 1961-64. Mem. Nat. Mortgage Bankers Assn., Nat. Comml. Fin. Conf., Water Resources Congress. Home: 3121 Dumbarton Ave Memphis TN 38128 Office: Union Planters Nat Bank of Memphis 67 Madison Ave Memphis TN 38103

BROOKS, BARBARA TAIT, investment and real estate devel. co. exec.; b. Springfield, Mass.; d. James C. and Mary Emily (Dana) Tait; student LaSalle Seminary, 1927, Skidmore Coll., 1929; m. J. Loring Brooks, Oct. 10, 1930 1 dau., Grace (Mrs. Robert I. Knibb). Owner, dir. Brookmont Farms, Lebanon, Tenn., 1950—; treas., dir. Brookmont Assos., Wilmington, Del., 1975—. Chmn. Well Child Clinic, Wilbraham, Mass., 1950-58, Wilbraham Horse Show, 1938-55, Eastern States Horse Show, 1960-71; corporator Vis. Nurse Assn., 1959-65. Bd. dirs. Mass Horse Show Council, 1939-50; trustee J. Loring Brooks Found. 1950—. Recipient 7 World Championships, 2 World Grand Championships, Ky. State Fair World Championship Horse Show, Louisville. Mem. Am. Horse Shows Assn. (life), Am. Hackney Horse Soc. (life). Republican. Congregationalist. Clubs: Lebanon Golf and Country; Ocean of Fla. Composer: Million Yards of Ribbon, 1954; Why Does Santa Have a Red, Red Nose, 1960; Greetings from the Moon, 1960; The Legend of the Red Bird, 1969; A Little Christmas Shop, 1969; Wishes, 1972; Ode to the Christmas Spirit, 1975; Sing Heigh-Heigh-Heigh, 1978; Thank Heaven for Christmas, 1979.

BROOKS, CHARLES GORDON, editorial cartoonist; b. Andalusia, Ala., Nov. 22, 1920; s. Gordie Motts and Emily Elizabeth (Smith) B.; student Birmingham So. Coll., 1940-41, Chgo. Acad. Fine Arts, 1941-42; m. Virginia Ruth Matson, Sept. 4, 1943; children—Barbara Jean (Mrs. Michael Lee Hynds), Charles Gordon. Editorial cartoonist Birmingham (Ala.) News, 1948—. Served with C.E., AUS, 1942-45. Recipient Sigma Delta Chi Service award and Bronze medallion, 1960, Vigilant Patriot award D.A.V., 1968, 13 Freedom Found. awards, 1960-73; 1st ann. Grover C. Hall award Troy State U., 1974. Mem. Assn. Am. Editorial Cartoonists (pres. 1969-70), Birmingham Press Club (pres. 1968-69), Ala. Library Assn., Sigma Delta Chi (pres. Ala. profl. chpt. 1968) Methodist. Clubs: Friends of German Lang. and Culture; Birmingham Sailing. Editor: Best Editorial Cartoons of the Year, 1972— Illustrator: Real Spiro Agnew, 1970. Contbr. cartoons to textbooks, encys., yearbooks. Home: 1612 Cresthill Rd Birmingham AL 35213 Office: 2200 4th Ave N Birmingham AL 35202

BROOKS, DAVID KENDRICK, JR., profl. counselor; b. Jackson, Miss., Mar. 20, 1944; s. David Kendrick and Marguerite Rhodes (Hamilton) B.; B.A. (Wilkins scholar), U. South, 1968; M.A. in Edn., E. Carolina U., 1971; m. Polly Elizabeth Walston, July 31, 1971; children—Laurel Elizabeth, Caroline Rebecca. Tchr. social studies Goldsboro (N.C.) High Sch., 1969-70; counselor Dudley High Sch., Greensboro, N.C., 1971-78; human relations trainer U. Ga., 1978—; mem. various profl. coms. Del., N.C. State Democratic Convs., 1974, 76, 168th Annual Conv., Episcopal Diocese N.C., 1978; chmn. Young Dems. of N.C., 6th congressional dist., 1974; pres. Guilford County Young Dems., 1975; vestryman Holy Trinity Episcopal Ch., Greensboro, 1977-78. Mem. Am. Personnel and Guidance Assn. (senator 1979—), N.C. Personnel and Guidance Assn. (pres. 1976-77), Am. Sch. Counselors Assn. (chairperson licensure com. 1977-80), N.C. Sch. Counselors Assn., Nat. Vocat. Guidance Assn., Kappa Delta Pi, Phi Delta Kappa. Author: (with Richard W. Warner, Jr., Jean A. Thompson) Counselor Licensure: Issues and Perspectives, 1980; editor: Licensure Educational Package for Professional Counselors, 1978. Home: 184 Stafford Dr Athens GA 30605 Office: 402 Aderhold Hall Univ Ga Athens GA 30602

BROOKS, FREDERIC LENNOX, broadcasting exec.; b. Bemis, Tenn., June 10, 1935; s. Roy Lennox and Mable (Mullis) B.; student Pathfinder Radio and TV Sch., Washington, 1953-54; m. Delois Earlene Bell, Oct. 13, 1962; children—Frederic Glenn, Freida Dawn; m. 2d, Darnanne Herron, Apr. 4, 1980. Newscaster dir. news dept. KFDX-TV, Wichita Falls, Tex., 1959-64; reporter, newscaster KPRC-TV, Houston, 1964-65; spl. projects dir., newscaster WBRZ-TV, Baton Rouge, La., 1966—; freelance film producer. Recipient Best Newsfilm award U.P.I.-Tex., 1964; Merit citation La. Bar Assn., 1972; News Media award La. Tchrs. Assn., 1973; Community Service award, 1974; Best Documentary award UPI, 1980; others. Mem. Radio-TV News Dirs. Assn., Nat. Rifle Assn., Pelican Arms Collectors Assn. (dir. pub. relations), S.C.V. Clubs: Baton Rouge Pistol, Civil War Roundtable Baton Rouge Press (Baton Rouge). Home: 10615 Airline Hwy #34 Baton Rouge LA 70816 Office: 1650 Highland Rd Box 2906 Baton Rouge LA 70821

BROOKS, JACK BASCOM, congressman; b. Dec. 18, 1922; s. Edward Chachere and Grace Marie (Pipes) B.; m. Charlotte Collins; children—Jack Edward, Katherine Inez, Kimberly Grace. Admitted to Tex. bar, 1949; mem. Tex. Legislature, 1946-50; mem. 83d-96th Congresses from 9th Tex. dist. Col. USMCR ret. Home: 1029 East Dr Beaumont TX 77706 Office: House Office Bldg Washington DC 20515

BROOKS, JAMES GORDON, JR., physician; b. Bainbridge, Ga., May 14, 1947; s. James Gordon and Miriam Imogene (Powell) B.; B.S., U. Ala., 1969, M.D., 1973; m. Suanne Kaye Touchstone, Aug. 15, 1970; children—James Gordon III, Christopher Charles. Intern in surgery Parkland Meml Hosp., Dallas, 1973-74; resident orthopedic surgery U. Tex. Health Sci. Center, 1974-78; pvt. practice orthopedic surgery Dallas Bone and Joint Clinic, 1978—. Diplomate Am. Bd. Orthopedic Surgery Mem. AMA, Texas Med. Assn., So. Med. Assn., Dallas County Med Soc., Alpha Epsilon Delta. Office: 9201 Garland Rd Dallas TX 75218

BROOKS, JERRY CLAUDE, food co. exec.; b. College Park, Ga., Apr. 23, 1936; s. John Bennett and Mattie Mae (Timms) B.; B.S., Ga. Inst. Tech., 1958; m. Peggy Sue Thornton, Feb. 26, 1961; children—Apryll Denise, Jerry Claude, Susan Vereen. Safety engr. Cotton Producers Assn., Atlanta, Ga., 1959-64, dir. safety and loss control, 1964-70; dir. corporate protection Gold Kist, Inc., Atlanta, 1970—. Instr., Ga. Safety Inst., Athens, Ga., 1971—. Bd. dirs. Ga. Safety Council, Ga. Soc. Prevention of Blindness. Served with AUS, 1958-59. Mem. Am. Soc. Safety Engrs. (chpt. pres. 1968-69, regional v.p. 1974-76), Nat. Safety Council (gen. chmn. fertilizer sect. 1969-70), So. Safety Conf. (pres. 1973), Am. Soc. Indsl. Security, Ga. Bus. and Industry Assn. (bd. govs.). Mason, Rosicrucian. Club: Exchange (pres. 1969-70) (Lithonia, Ga.). Home: 6411 Evans Mill Way Lithonia GA 30058 Office: 244 Perimeter Center Pkwy Atlanta GA 30346

BROOKS, JOHN, elec. engr.; b. Harrogate, Tenn., Sept. 7, 1940; s. Roscoe M. and Mamie L. (Carmack) B.; B.S. in Engring., U. Tenn., 1967; m. Virginia Sue Cashion, Dec. 14, 1968. Elec. engr. Alcoa Co. (Tenn.), 1967-70; plant elec. engr. Western Electric Co., Aurora, Ill., 1970-75; project engr. mgr. Abbott Labs., Rocky Mounty, N.C., 1975—. Served with USAF, 1960-64. Registered profl. engr., Ill., N.C. Mem. IEEE, Nat. Soc. of Profl. Engrs. (pres. East Carolina chpt. 1979-80). Republican. Baptist. Home: 3005 Wellington Dr Rocky Mount NC 27801 Office: Abbott Labs PO Box 2226 Rocky Mount NC 27801

BROOKS, MORRIS ALAN, ins. co. exec.; b. Lubbock, Tex., Aug. 9, 1951; s. Raymond Morris and Helen Marie (Collins) B.; B.A., Tex. Technol. U., 1974; m. Marilynn Davis, May 19, 1973; 1 dau., Amanda Leigh. Mgr., El Chico Restaurant, Lubbock, 1974-75; agt. Southland Life Ins. Co., Lubbock, 1975-77, field sales mgr., 1977-79; gen. agt. Security Mut. Life Ins. Co., Lubbock, from 1979; agy. supr. Am. Nat. Life, Lubbock, 1980—. Vol., team capt. United Way, 1975-79. Recipient presdl. citation for mgmt. excellence Southland Life Ins. Co., 1979. Mem. Gen. Agts. and Mgrs. Assn., Lubbock Area Assn. Life Underwriters, Phi Kappa Psi. Home: 8203 Belmont Lubbock TX 79424 Office: Am Nat Life 6500 Slide Rd #306 Lubbock TX 79424

BROOKS, NANCY LEE, holistic counselor; b. Charlotte, N.C., Jan. 23, 1938; d. Julian Allen and Ruby Evelyn (Caudle) B.; B.A., Wake Forest U., 1961; M.Ed. in Counseling, U. N.C., Greensboro, 1975; adopted dau., Julia Yolanda; 1 foster dau., Soledad Irene Paredes. Social worker N.C. Dept. Social Services, Winston-Salem and Charlotte, 1961-65; rehab. counselor N.C. Dept. Vocat. Rehab., 1968-79; pvt. practice as holistic counselor, Winston-Salem, 1979—. Recipient Most Outstanding Rehab. Case in N.C., 1970, citation of merit for exceptional contbns. to handicapped in N.C., 1974, cert. of merit for outstanding contbns. to rehab. counseling services in N.C., 1974. Mem. Am. Rehab. Counseling Assn., Am. Personnel and Guidance Assn., Am. Fedn. Astrologers, Edgar Cayce Research and Enlightenment Assn. Mem. Nat. Spiritual Frontiers Fellowship. Editor Impact, Jour. N.C. Rehab. Counseling Assn., 1972-76.

BROOKS, RICHARD O., indsl. relations mgr.; b. Birmingham, Ala., Sept. 7, 1938; s. Joseph M., Sr., and Faye D. B.; B.S. in Indsl. Mgmt., Auburn U., 1960; m. Norma Ann Williams, Dec. 23, 1961; children—Richard O., Mark, Lisa. Personnel mgr. Beloit Woodlands, Birmingham, 1965-68, Altec, Inc., Birmingham, 1968-69, The Ceco Corp., Birmingham, 1969-74; mgr. indsl. relations Jim Walter Resources, Inc., Birmingham, 1974—. Advisor Walker State Tech. Coll.; mem. W. Ala. Health Council; troop committeeman, counselor Boy Scouts Am.; pres. PTA, 1977-78. Served with AUS, 1960-61, 61-62. Mem. AIME, Am. Soc. Personnel Adminstrs. Democrat. Methodist. Clubs: Altadena Valley Country, Elks. Office: PO Box C79 Birmingham AL 35283

BROOKS, (PATRICIA) SUANNE, govt. ofcl.; b. Syracuse, N.Y., Jan. 23, 1945; d. Roger Berton and Patricia Louise (Deady) B.; B.A., Salem Coll., 1967; postgrad. U. Ga., 1979, U. Madrid, 1965-66. Sr. counselor Grow, Inc., Raleigh, N.C., 1967; confdl. asst. to dir. Head Start, HEW, Washington, 1968-71; program info. specialist HEW, Atlanta, 1971-73, planning and evaluation specialist, 1973-77, sr. program analyst Office Prin. Regional Ofcl., 1977-80, regional dir. Office Refugee Affairs, Atlanta, 1980—; mem. Nat. Acad. Scis./Engring., Commn. Sociotech. Systems, Transp. Research Bd. com. public transp. planning and devel., 1978-81; resource asso. Met. Atlanta Rapid Transit Authority Adv. Com. Elderly and Handicapped, 1978-80; mem. Barrier Free Adv. Com., Hartsfield Internat. Airport Adv. Com., 1978-79. Mem. Atlanta Symphony Jr. Women's Com., 1977-79. Mem. Atlanta Mental Health Assn., Salem Alumnae Assn. (treas. Washington area 1971-72). Presbyterian. Author: (with others) Transportation Authorities in Federal Human Services Programs, 1976; others. Home: 2083 Golf View Dr NW Atlanta GA 30309 Office: Suite 1403 101 Marietta Tower Atlanta GA 30323

BROSCHART, GEORGE BERNART, audiovisual co. exec.; b. Phila., July 1, 1934; s. Charles Bernart and Anna Gertute (McGovern) B.; B.A. in Bus., Drexel Inst., 1959; M.A., Temple U., 1961; m. Lydia Schlucter, June 10, 1957; children—Robert, Charles, Lisa, George, Meg. Mem. sales staff Borg Warner Co., 1971-72, McGraw Hill Co., N.Y.C., 1972-73, EAC Corp., Waco, Tex., 1973-74; pres. C.S.I., Orlando, Fla., 1974—. Pres. Bristol PTA, 1960, Pine Hills Civic Assn., 1974. Served with U.S. Army, 1954-57. Mem. Nat. Audio-Visual Assn. Republican. Roman Catholic. Clubs: Elks, K.C. (Phila.). Office: C S I PO Box 15262 Orlando FL 32808

BROUHARD, BEN HERMAN, pediatrician; b. Indpls., Oct. 30, 1946; s. Elton Edgar and Emma Jean B.; B.A., Wabash Coll., 1968; M.D., Ind. U., 1972; m. Julia Ranney, June 12, 1970; 1 dau., Katherine Jean. Resident in pediatrics Duke U., Durham, N.C., 1972-74; fellow in pediatric nephrology Tex. Med. Br., Galveston, 1974-76, asst. prof. pediatrics, 1976-79, asso. prof., 1979—. Diplomate Am. Bd. Pediatrics; Am. Heart Assn. grantee. Mem. Am. Acad. Pediatrics, Am. Soc. Neprhology, Internat. Soc. Nephrology, Am. Fedn. Clin. Research, Soc. Pediatric Research, So. Soc. Pediatric Research, Am. Soc. Pediatric Nephrology, Internat. Soc. Pediatric Neprhology, So. Med. Assn., Bay Area Pediatric Soc. (sec. 1978-79), Phi Beta Kappa, Alpha Omega Alpha. Contbr. articles to profl. jours. Home: 4817 Ave O Galveston TX 77550 Office: Child Health Center Room C-221 Galveston TX 77550

BROUILLETTE, ALBERT CLARENCE, painter; b. Holyoke, Mass., Jan. 9, 1924; s. Eugene and Leona (Spinks) B.; student Okla. A. and M. Tech. Coll., 1948-49, Am. Sch. Comml. Art, 1950-51; m. Mary Kathleen Ross, June 3, 1946; children—Maureen Green, Michael Anthony, Andrew Thomas, Ann Elizabeth Merett. With Parker-Willson Advt. Agy., Ft. Worth, 1951-56, Robbins-Caver-Page Advt. Co., Dallas, 1957-59, Worrell-Ericson Advt. Agy., Ft. Worth, 1960-71, Balcom & Asso. Advt. Co., 1971-75; art tchr., painter, Arlington, Tex., 1968—; instr. Ft. Worth Art Mus. Sch., 1971. Served with AUS, 1943-45. Decorated Purple Heart; recipient Paton award Nat. Acad. Ann., 1975, Hearsay award Tex. Watercolor Soc., 1975, CFS award Am. Watercolor Soc., 1975, Mary Little medal, 1976, Antoinette Graves Goetz Award, 1977; Colo. Water Media award Rocky Mountain Nat., 1975. Mem. Am., Nat., Southwestern (dir.), So., Tex. (dir. at large) watercolor socs., Audubon Artists, Rockport Art Assn., Allied Artists Am. Roman Catholic. Pub. in art mags., books. Home: 1300 Sunset Ct Arlington TX 76013

BROUILLETTE, LYNN JOSEPH, physician; b. Marksville, La., Mar. 25, 1945; s. Amabe Joseph and Florence Rose (Borell) B.; B.S. in Zoology, Northwestern State Coll., Natchitoches, La., 1966; M.D., La. State U., 1970; m. Karen Bearden, Aug. 6, 1966; children—David, John. Intern, Confederate Meml. Med. Center, 1970-71, resident in Ob-Gyn, 1973-76; practice medicine specializing in Ob-Gyn, Natchitoches, 1976—. Served with M.C., USN, 1971-73. Fellow Am. Coll. Obstetrics and Gynecology; mem. La. State Med. Soc., Natchitoches Parish Med. Soc. Republican. Roman Catholic. Office: 215 Hwy 1 S Natchitoches LA 71457

BROUILLETTE, MARY JOAN, med. technologist; b. Church Point, La., Apr. 14, 1942; d. Ewel George and Elizabeth Jean (Hornsby) B.; B.S., U. Southwestern La., 1964; M.Ed., U. Houston, 1976. Lab. technologist Ochsner Found. Hosp., New Orleans, 1965-66; lab. technologist Diagnostic Clinic of Houston, 1966, head chemistry dept., 1966-69, asst. chief technologist, 1967-76, asst. adminstrv. technologist, 1973-76; asst. prof. med. tech. U. Fla., 1976-78; sr. asso. in pathology Vanderbilt U. Med. Center, 1978—; constructed proficiency exam. questions in clin. chemistry for profl. exam. service, contracted by HEW. Registered clin. technologist, clin. chemist, Am. Soc. Clin. Pathologists, Nat. Registry in Clin. Chemistry. Mem. Am. Soc. for Med. Tech. (chmn. state biochemistry sci. assembly), Am. Soc. Allied Health Professions. Roman Catholic. Home: PO Box 178 Church Point LA 70525 Office: Dept Pathology Vanderbilt U Med Center Room 3306 21st Ave at Garland Nashville TN 37232

BROUSSARD, NORMAJ (MRS. LEE R. BROUSSARD), artist, journalist; b. Lake Providence, La., Aug. 28, 1931; d. C. Thomas and Hazel Valli (Ainsworth) Edwards; student Stephen F. Austin State Coll., 1951-52, U. Tex., 1973—; mem. Internat. Workshop Danish Sch. Design, Copenhagen, 1973; m. Lee R. Broussard, Dec. 31, 1958; 1 dau., Cherie Antoinette; children from previous marriage—Bonnie Greening (Mrs. Allen P. Bennett), Billy E. Greening. Owner, The Chateau, Port Arthur, Tex., 1968—, Broussard's Mobile Villages, Port Arthur, 1960—, Studio Normaj, 1972—; pres. Travel Magic Corp., Broussard Enterprises; organizer, sponsor Gulf Coast Arts and Crafts Festival, 1970, Jefferson County (Tex.) Arts and Crafts Festival, 1972, Diamond Jubilee Fine Arts Show, 1973; tchr., lectr. in field; art dir. City of Port Arthur. Founder, Tex. Artists Mus. Soc., 1972, pres., 1973-74; mem. com. Tex. Constl. Rev. Commn., 1973—; pres. Am. Cancer Soc.; mem. Port Arthur Bicentennial Commn. Recipient numerous awards local and state art competitions including La. Art and Folk Festival, 1970-73, Sabine Area Art Show, 1972. Mem. Port Arthur Art Assn. Fine Arts Guild (pres. 1971), Diocesan Council Cath. Women (pres. 1965), Noon Bus. and Profl. Women's Club, Internat. Platform Assn., Tex. Fedn. Women's Clubs, Tex. Poetry South and Major Poets Club, S.E. Tex. Arts Council, Port Arthur C. of C., Zeta Phi Delphians (pres. 1967), Beta Sigma Phi, Roman Catholic (pres. altar soc. 1965, 66). Club: Heritage Antique Study (pres. 1973-74). Address: 101 Dryden Pl Port Arthur TX 77640

BROWDER, JOHNIE MAE GOMILLION, ednl. adminstr.; b. McKenzie, Ala., Oct. 2, 1919; d. Thad Jackson and Irene (Lee) Gomillion; B.S., Troy State U., 1949; M.Ed., Auburn U., 1956; m. Ralph J. Browder, Dec. 15, 1939; children—Ralph Thaddeus, Tempie Leah. Tchr. pub. schs., 1943-46; tchr., guidance counselor McKenzie High Sch., 1946-65; supr. guidance and evaluation Butler County Pub. Schs., 1965-71; prin. W. O. Parmer Elementary Sch., Greenville, Ala., 1971—. Mem. Ala., Nat. edn. assns., Ala. Dept. Elementary Prins. Assn., Butler County Edn. Assn. (pres. 1973-74), Internat. Platform Assn. Delta Kappa Gamma, Kappa Delta Pi. Baptist. Home: Route 1 McKenzie AL 36456 Office: Parmer School Butler St Greenville AL 36037

BROWER, WALTER JORDAN, physician; b. Birmingham, Ala., Feb. 5, 1921; s. Walter Scott and Elizabeth (Jordan) B.; B.A., U. Ala., 1942; M.D., Duke, 1947; m. Miriam Timmons, Jan. 20, 1949; children—William Jordan, Carl Timmons, Caroline Elizabeth, Franklin Perry. Rotating intern Jefferson-Hillman Hosp., 1947-48, resident in radiology, 1948-51; instr. radiology Med. Coll. Ala., 1948-51; practice medicine specializing in radiology, Birmingham, 1955—; dir. dept. radiology VA Hosp., 1956-57; radiologist Doctors Hosp., Cullman, Ala.; cons. radiologist Cullman, Blount Meml. hosps.; clin. asst. prof. Med. Coll. Ala., 1957—. Served with Med. Dept., AUS, 1944-46; from lt. to capt. M.C., USAF, 1951-55. Fellow Am. Coll. Radiology (chpt. pres. 1969-70; councillor 1971-77), Am. Coll. Nuclear Medicine; mem. Radiol. Soc. N.Am., So. Radiol. Conf. (charter; chmn. 1974-75), Am., So. med. assns., Ala., Cullman County (chmn. bd. censors 1977, chmn. bd. health 1977) med. socs., Ala. Cattleman's Assn., Internat. Arabian Horse Assn., Nat. Skeet Shooting Assn. (life), Arlington Hist. Assn., So. Commemorative Soc., SCV, Soc. War 1812, Nat. Rifle Assn., Delta Kappa Epsilon, Alpha Kappa Kappa. Episcopalian. Mason (Shriner). Address: PO Box 1053 Cullman AL 35055

BROWN, ALBERT BELMONT, physician; b. Kingston, Ont., Can., June 27, 1918; s. Charles Henry Penton and Charlotte Elizabeth (Gunning) B.; came to U.S., 1967, naturalized, 1973; M.D., Queens U., Kingston, 1943; m. Margaret Estella Moore, Feb. 18, 1944; children—Pamela, Sheila, Albert, Lauraine, Maynard, Charles. Intern, Kingston Gen. Hosp., 1943; gen. practice medicine, Kingston, 1946-48; resident Johns Hopkins Hosp., 1948-54; prof., chmn. dept. obstetrics and gynecology U. Sask. (Can.), 1954-67; pvt. practice obstetrics and gynecology, Wilmington, N.C., 1967—; clin. asso. prof. U. N.C., 1976—. Served to capt. M.C., Canadian Army, 1943-46. Mem. Am. Coll. Obstetricians and Gynecologists, AMA, Am. Assn. Gynecol. Laparoscopists, Am. Soc. Abdominal Surgeons. Republican. Episcopalian. Home: 1223 Windsor Dr Wilmington NC 28401 Office: 1415 Medical Center Dr Wilmington NC 28401

BROWN, ALFRED WILLIAM, educator; b. Muse, Okla., June 19, 1932; s. Arthur Willie and Lela Mae B.; B.S. in Edn., E. Central State Coll., Ada, Okla., 1968; postgrad. in Corrections, Okla. State U., 1979; LL.B., LaSalle Extension U., 1979; m. Margie Nell Bohanan, July 22, 1961; 1 dau., Winifred Nell. Counselor, tchr., Tununak, Alaska, 1964-65; with Head Start program, Tununak, 1968-69; counselor, Shonto, Ariz., 1970-71; counselor, tchr. spl. learning problems, Kayenta, Ariz., 1971-72; prin., Barter Island, Alaska, 1971-72; dir. community health reps. Choctaw Nation, Talihina, Okla., 1972; prin. Paden (Okla.) Elem. Sch., 1973-74, Panama (Okla.) Public Schs., 1975; tchr. spl. reading problems Okla. State Reformatory, Granite, Okla., 1975—. Served with AUS, 1951-55; Korea. Recipient spl. recognition award Center Internat. Security Studies, 1979. Mem. Okla. Edn. Assn., NEA. Democrat. Club: Masons. Research on vocat. rehab. counseling. Home: Box 505 Talihina OK 74571

BROWN, ALTON RIVES, III, real estate broker; b. Columbus, Ga., Jan. 28, 1953; s. Alton Rives, Jr., and Mary Katherine (Thomason) B.; student U. Ala., 1971-73; B.A., U. So. Ala., 1976, M.A., 1978; m. Toni Goubil, Sept. 18, 1976; 1 son, Alton Rives, IV. Real estate broker Herman Maisel & Co., Inc., Mobile, Ala., 1978—. Active, Mobile Area council Boy Scouts Am. Mem. Mobile Area C. of C., Mobile County Bd. Realtors, Nat. Assn. Realtors, Realtors Nat. Mktg. Inst. Methodist. Club: Kiwanis. Home: 2358 Taylor Ave Mobile AL 36606 Office: PO Box 160247 Mobile AL 36616

BROWN, ANNE WARWICK, med. center exec.; b. Galveston, Tex., Sept. 4, 1945; d. Clovis Auteen and Marjorie (McCullough) Brown; B.B.A., U. Tex., Austin, 1967; M.S.A., U. Houston, Baylor Coll. Medicine, 1976. Research asst. U. Tex., Austin, 1967-69; personnel clk. Dallas Morning News, 1969-70; tng. specialist U. Tex. Med. Br., Galveston, 1970-72; dir. personnel Sharpstown Gen. Hosp., Houston, 1972-76; dir. personnel Med. Center Del Oro Hosp., Houston, 1976-77, asst. adminstr., 1977-79, asso. adminstr., 1979—. Mem. profl. steering com. Jr. League of Houston, 1975; vol. juvenile probation counselor, 1975-76. Mem. Am. Soc. Personnel Adminstrn., Tex. Hosp. Assn., Am. Coll. Hosp. Adminstrs., Young Hosp. Adminstrs. Presbyterian. Home: 6623 Burning Tree Houston TX 77036 Office: 8081 Greenbriar Houston TX 77054

BROWN, ARTHUR DIXON, SR., agrl. ext. agent; b. Vildo, Tenn., Mar. 16, 1915; s. Washington and Neely Cornelius (Franklin) B.; B.S., Tenn. State U., 1948; postgrad. Prairie View A. and M. U., 1957; m. Alice Arlisadine Winrow, Aug. 13, 1941; children—Arthur D., John Edward, Thomas Joseph. Vocat. agrl. tchr. Douglass Jr. High Sch., Stanton, Tenn., 1948-50; agrl. extension agt. U. Tenn. Agrl. Ext. Service, Knoxville, 1950—. Pres. Edgehill Neighbors Orgn., 1974-76. Served with AUS, 1940-45. Mem. Nat. Assn. County Agrl. Agents, Tenn. Agrl. Agents Assn. and Specialists (past v.p. Dist. II), Tenn. Assn. Chs. (mem. exec. com., treas.), Epsilon Sigma Phi. Mem. Christian Meth. Episcopal Ch. Club: Century, Masons. Home: 1703 Villa Pl Nashville TN 37212 Office: 701 Jefferson St Nashville TN 37208

BROWN, BAILEY, fed. judge; b. Memphis, 1917; s. Joshua Goodlett and Lillian (Pearcy) B.; A.B., U. Mich., 1939; LL.B., Harvard U., 1942; m. Doris Frances Lawhorn, Dec. 24, 1964; 1 son, Bailey Brown. Admitted to Tenn. bar; partner Burch, Porter, Johnson & Brown, Memphis; judge U.S. Dist. Ct., Western Dist. of Tenn., Memphis, now chief judge. Guest lectr. Southwestern U., Memphis. Pres., Memphis Symphony, 1958-60, Memphis Pub. Affairs Forum, 1955. Served to lt. USNR, 1942-46. Episcopalian (Vestryman). Home: 115 Morningside Park Memphis TN 38104 Office: Federal Bldg 167 N Maine St Memphis TN 38103*

BROWN, BENNETT A., banker; b. 1929; B.S., Presbyn. Coll., 1950; postgrad. La. State U. Sch. Banking of South; postgrad. advanced mgmt. program Harvard U.; married. With Chem. Corn Exchange Bank, N.Y.C., before 1953, Fed. Res. Bank Atlanta, 1953-55; with Citizens & So. Nat. Bank, Savannah, Ga., 1955—, asst. cashier, 1957-59, asst. v.p., 1959-60, v.p., 1960-68, exec. v.p. Augusta brs., 1968-71, asst. prosecutor, Savannah, 1971-78, pres., chief exec. officer, 1978—, also dir., chmn. bd., 1979—; pres., chmn., chief exec. officer Citizens & So. Holding Co. Office: Citizens & So Nat Bank 99 Annex Atlanta GA 30399

BROWN, BERNARD LOAM, JR., hosp. adminstr.; b. Metter, Ga., Nov. 27, 1939; s. Bernard Loam and Elizabeth (Jones) B.; B.S., Valdosta State Coll., 1961; M.B.A., George Washington U., 1964; m. Annette Bradford Rigdon, June 17, 1962; children—Jennifer, Jeffrey, Amanda. Asst. adminstr. Meml. Hosp., Gulfport, Miss., 1964-67; asst. dir. N.C. Meml. Hosp., Chapel Hill, 1967-68; asst. adminstr. Univ. Hosp., Augusta, Ga., 1968-71; adminstr. Kennestone Hosp., Marietta, Ga., 1971—; preceptor in hosp. adminstrn. Ga. State U., 1971—, George Washington U., 1978—. Bd. dirs. Atlanta-Cobb County Emergency Aid Assn.; div. chmn. United Way, 1978. Fellow Am. Coll. Hosp. Adminstrs.; mem. Ga. Hosp. Assn. (pres. 1980), Am. Hosp. Assn., George Washington U. Alumni Assn., Valdosta State Coll. Alumni Assn. (dir.). Methodist. Author: Risk Management for Hospitals, 1979. Home: 1486 Longwood Dr Marietta GA 30060 Office: 677 Church Marietta GA 30060

BROWN, BETTY JANE, nurse; b. Carlisle, Pa., Mar. 27, 1922; d. Albert Elsworth and Ann Mae (Gibbs) Brown; R.N., South Balt. Gen. Hosp., 1943; B.S., U. Pa., 1950. Head nurse, supr. VA Hosps., Martinsburg, W.Va., and Clarksburg, W.Va., 1950-56; asst. dir. nursing service Miners Meml. Hosp., Beckley, W.Va., 1957-64; dir. nursing services Appalachian Regional Hosp., Beckley, 1965—. Served with Nurse Corps, AUS, 1943-48; PTO. Ky. col. Mem. Am. Soc. Hosp. Nursing Service Adminstrs., Am. Hosp. Assn., Am. Heart Assn. Home: 103 Glenn Ave Beckley WV 25801 Office: Appalachian Regional Hospital Box 1149 Beckley WV 25801

BROWN, CAROLYN SCURRY, biochemist, educator; b. Greenwood, S.C., June 13, 1942; d. Grady Bullock and Rosa Beatrice (Hellams) Scurry; B.A. cum laude, Winthrop Coll., 1964; Ph.D., Vanderbilt U., 1969; m. William P. Brown, Sept. 12, 1965; children—William Scott, Mary Diana. Postdoctoral research asso. biochemistry Dept. Microbiology, Vanderbilt U., Nashville, 1969-71; postdoctoral research asso. biochemistry dept. biol. sci. Purdue U., Lafayette, Ind., 1971-74, dept. biochemistry, 1974-75, vis. asst. prof. dept. chemistry, summer 1973; vis. asst. prof. dept. biochemistry Clemson (S.C.) U., 1975-77, asst. prof., 1977—. NIH postdoctoral fellow, 1969-71, predoctoral tng. grantee, 1964-69; NIH biomed. research sci. grantee, 1979-80, Clemson U. faculty research grantee, 1976-80. Mem. Am. Soc. Microbiology, AAAS, Sigma Xi, Sigma Delta Epsilon. lMethodist. Contbr. articles to profl. publs. Home: 407 Shorecrest Dr Clemson SC 29631

BROWN, CARSON LEE, safety and welding supply co. exec.; b. Sugar Grove, N.C., May 6, 1927; s. Stewart Barton and Annie (Vines) B.; student Hobart Welding Tng. Schs., intermittently, 1956-64; m. Georgia Lee Scott, June 27, 1953; children—Tracy Leigh, Kelly Dawn. Farmer, Boone, S.C., 1946-49; sales rep. Edmac, Inc., Winston-Salem, N.C., 1952-62, sales mgr., 1962-64, also dir.; pres., chmn. bd., founder AIRWELD, Inc., Winston-Salem, 1964—. Bd. dirs. Pop Warner Little League Football, Pfafftown, N.C., 1978-79, Pfafftown Tiny Packers, 1978-79; deacon, mem. choir, tchr. Pfafftown Baptist Ch. Served with U.S. Army, 1945-47; Japan. Recipient Disting. Salesman's award Sales and Mktg. Execs. Internat., 1962; Outstanding Sales Performance award Lehigh Safety Shoe, 1976. Mem. Vets. of Safety, Nat. Fedn. Ind. Businessmen, Winston-Salem C. of C., Nat. Welders Supply Assn., Am. Welding Supply Assn. Democrat. Club: Lions (dir. 1978-79). Office: PO Box 50 Winston-Salem NC 27102

BROWN, CHARLES LESLIE, ins. agt.; b. Centerton, Ark., Mar. 8, 1927; s. Leslie Nelson and Frances Willard (McCumber) B.; B.S. in Agr., U. Ark., Fayetteville, 1951; m. Ethel Jean Wiseman, May 25, 1947; children—James L., Charles E., Lydia Jean. Tchr., Bentonville and Pea Ridge, Ark., 1951-55; life ins. agt., Fayetteville, Ark., 1953-60; agy. tng. dir. Preferred Risk Life Assurance Co. Fayetteville, 1960-62; mgr. gen. ins. agencies Rogers and Siloam Springs, Ark., 1962-75; pres., mgr. The Ins. Office div. Centair Corp., Siloam Springs, 1975—; instr. life ins., Fayetteville, 1962-63. Mayor Centerton, Ark., 1962-66; mem. city council Siloam Springs, 1966-70. Served with U.S. Army, 1945-47. Mem. Ark. Assn. Life Underwriters, Nat. Assn. Life Underwriters, N.W. Ark. Assn. Life Underwriters (pres., 1953-54), Ind. Ins. Agts. Am., Ind. Ins. Agts. Ark., Profl. Ins. Agts. Assn. Democrat. Baptist. Club: Kiwanis (pres. Siloam Springs, 1973-74). Home: PO Drawer E Siloam Springs AR 72761 Office: 225 N Mt Olive Siloam Springs AR 72761

BROWN, CLAYTON, educator; b. Houston, Apr. 12, 1941; s. William O. and Ruvena (Dillehay) B.; B.A., Nest Tex. State U., 1965, M.A., 1966; Ph.D., UCLA, 1970; m. Cynthia Kay Brown, Apr. 12, 1941; children—Carolyn Renee, Richard Douglass. Tchr., Westlake Sch., Los Angeles, 1968-70; asst. prof. E. Tex. State U., Commerce, 1971; asst. prof. history Tex. Christian U., Fort Worth, 1972-76, asso. prof., 1976—. Mem. Am. Assn. for History of Medicine, Tex. Hist. Assn., Agrl. History Soc. Methodist. Home: 5305 Westminster Court Fort Worth TX 76133 Office: History Dept Texas Christian University Fort Worth TX 76129

BROWN, CONNY RAY, mech. engr.; b. Bryan, Tex., Oct. 21, 1947; s. Charlie Ray and Helen Victoria (Kosh) B.; B.M.E., Tex. A. and M. U., 1970; m. Nancy Faith Toups, Jan. 6, 1978. With Caudill Rowlett Scott, Houston, 1970—, design engr., 1970-76, project engr., 1976—, asso., 1977—. Served to capt. USAR, 1970-78. Registered profl. engr., Ill., Ky., Tex. Mem. Am. Soc. Heating, Refrigerating and Air Conditioning Engrs. (gov. Houston chpt.), ASME. Roman Catholic. Home: 701 Bering St #1503 Houston TX 77057 Office: 1111 West Loop S Houston TX 77027

BROWN, CONSTANT CLEMENT, counselor; b. Paris, Aug. 30, 1933; s. Frank Arthur and Gabrielle Angela (Vuillaumie) B.; B.S., E. Tenn. State U., 1959, M.A., 1965; Ed.S., U. Ga., 1976; m. Janice Maxine Brown, Feb. 8, 1958; 1 dau., Collette. Tchr., bd. edn., Atlanta, 1959-65, counselor, 1965-74; dir. guidance and Title I programs, Rockdale County, Ga., 1974-75; counselor pub. schs., Conyers, Ga., 1976-78, Richmond County Public Schs., 1978—. Vice pres. Collins Band Parents Assn., 1975-76; treas. Therrell High Sch. PTA, 1969-72. Served to maj. U.S. Army. Mem. Atlanta Assn. Educators (v.p. 1969-72), NEA, Ga. Assn. Educators, Ga. Assn. Sch. Counselors, Assn. Supervision and Curriculum Devel., Kappa Phi Kappa. Roman Catholic. Club: Civitan (dir.). Home: PO Box 617 Conyers GA 30207 Office: 2400 Granade Rd Conyers GA 30207

BROWN, DALE, physician; b. Mosheim, Tenn., Jan. 26, 1915; s. Walter C. and Matilda (Hartman) B.; B.A., B.S., Carson-Newman Coll., 1937; M.D., U. Tenn., 1941; m. Kathryn Jones, June 14, 1942; children—Gale Ann (Mrs. Lynn Baumgartner), Dale. Intern, Nashville Gen. Hosp., 1942; practice medicine, Mosheim, 1943—; mem. staff Greeneville, Laughlin, Takoma hosps.; also lectr., geographer, photographer, explorer. Mem. Am. Acad. Family Physicians, AMA, World, So., Tenn., Greene County (pres. 1944-52) med. assns. Republican. Mason (32 deg., Shriner). Address: Box 38 Mosheim TN 37818

BROWN, DALE PATRICK, advt. agy. exec.; b. Richmond, Va., Aug. 11, 1947; d. Thomas Windom and Helen Mae (Curtis) P.; B.A. in Journalism, U. Richmond, 1968, M.A. in English, 1978; m. William Melville Brown, III, Jan. 1, 1977. City news reporter Richmond Times-Dispatch, 1968-71; free-lance writer, 1971-73; public relations account exec. Martin Agy., Richmond, 1973-76, v.p. public relations, 1976-78, v.p., advt. account supr., 1978—. Publicity chmn. Richmond Friendship Force, 1977-78; public relations chmn. Richmond-First Club, 1978-79. Recipient Nat. award for outstanding collegiate journalism Pi Delta Epsilon, 1968, various awards for advt. and public relations campaigns, including Addy award Advt. Club of Richmond, 1975, Effie award Am. Mktg. Assn., 1979. Mem. Richmond Public Relations Soc., Public Relations Soc. Am., Nat. Agri-Mktg. Assn., Am. soc. Hosp. Public Relations. Baptist. Club: Country of Va. Editor-in-chief The Messenger, 1966-67, The Collegian newspaper, 1967-68. Home: 4201 Hanover Ave Richmond VA 23221 Office: 500 N Allen Ave Richmond VA 23220

BROWN, DENNIS LEROY, indsl. engr.; b. Onawa, Iowa, Feb. 6, 1949; s. Philip Buster and Shirley Mae Brown; M.E., Purdue U., 1967; student Manatee Jr. Coll., 1974—; m. Sharon Louise Hartman, Sept. 23, 1967; children—Brian, Denise, Michael. Detailer, Wabash (Ind.) Magnetics Co., 1968-70; designer Magnavox Corp., Ft. Wayne, Ind., 1970-71; package designer Honeywell Corp., St. Petersburg, Fla., 1971-72, Electro Corp., Sarasota, Fla., 1972-76; indsl. engr. Tropicana Products Ind., Bradenton, Fla., from 1976, now prodn. supr. Active, Boy Scouts Am. Mem. Am. Inst. Indsl. Engrs., Am. Engring. Model Soc. Republican. Baptist. Home: 2516 30th Ave Dr E Bradenton FL 33508 Office: Tropicana Products Inc PO Box 338 Bradenton FL 33505

BROWN, DICK CODY, acct.; b. Dante, Va., Oct. 11, 1928; s. Pat Abernathy and Zelma Clara (Cassell) B.; student E. Tenn. State Coll., 1945-46; m. Lucille Jones, May 6, 1950; children—Cynthia Ellen Brown Farris, Sharon Elaine Brown Lin. Various clerical positions Clinchfield R.R. Co., Erwin, Tenn., 1948-52, head tabulating clk., 1952-54, staff asst., 1954-56, mgr. machine acctg., 1956-61, asst. auditor, 1961-63; asso. to comptroller Louisville & Nashville R.R. Co., Louisville, 1963-66, mgr. acctg. systems and procedures, 1966-77; staff acct. Seaboard Coast Line Industries, Louisville, 1977—; co-owner The Money Tree, Louisville. Chmn. bd. mgrs. St. Matthews YMCA, 1970-71; pres. L & N Employees Fed. Credit Union, 1970—, pres. Family Lines Credit Union Assn., 1975-79; deacon Broadway Baptist Ch., Louisville, 1967—. Served with U.S. Army, 1952-54. Recipient Silver Beaver award Boy Scouts Am. Mem. Assn. Am. Railroads, E. Tenn. Data Processing Assn. (pres. 1960-61), Am. Numis. Assn. (dist. rep. 1977—), Louisville Coin Club (past pres.), Ky. State Numis. Assn., Central States Numis. Assn. Home: 7327 Maria Ave Louisville KY 40222 Office: Room 617 908 W Broadway Louisville KY 40232

BROWN, DONNA MARIE, speech pathologist; b. Morgantown, W.Va., Aug. 29, 1951; d. Donald Painter and Yvonne (Gallaher) B.; B.S. in Speech Pathology and Audiology, W.Va. U., Morgantown, 1973; M.S., U. Southwestern La., Lafayette, 1975. Trainee, VA, 1973; asst. La. Dept. Hosps., 1974; grad. asst. U. Southwestern La., 1975; speech and hearing cons. dept. spl. edn. Nicholls State U., Thibodaux, La., 1975-79; speech and lang. specialist developmental evaluation center State of N.C., Hickory, 1979—; mem. Catawba County Child Abuse Task Force, Alexander County Case Mgmt. Council. Lic. in N.C., La. Mem. Am. Speech and Hearing Assn., Council Exceptional Children, N.C. Speech, Lang. and Hearing Assn., N.C. Public Health Assn. Democrat. Presbyterian. Home: 818 2d St Pl NE Hickory NC 28601 Office: Devel Evaluation Center Route 3 Box 338 Hickory NC 28601

BROWN, EARL FELTON, govt. ofcl.; b. Jacksonville, Fla., Apr. 20, 1932; s. Felton and Frances (Wilkerson) B.; B.S., Savannah State Coll., 1956; A.B., Benedict Coll., 1966; M. Devel. Adminstrn., Duke U., 1970; M.B.A., Harvard U., 1971; M.Criminal Justice, U. S.C., 1977; children—Earl Felton, Kim Lanette. Ins. rep. Afro-Am. Ins. Co., Jacksonville, Fla., 1958-62; asst. dean of men Cheyney (Pa.) State Coll., 1967; public sch. tchr., Columbia, S.C., 1966-67; probation counselor Richland County (S.C.) Family Ct., 1967-69; dir. devel. Vorhees Coll., Denmark, S.C., 1970-71, dir. spl. projects and fed. relations, 1971-72; dir. tng. coordination center for displaced educators Tenn. State U., Nashville, 1972-73; dir. div. compliance and investigation State Human Affairs Commn., Columbia, S.C., 1973-75, dir. community relations div., 1975—. Mem. Dist. 1 Ednl. Adv. Com., Richland County, Columbia; pres. St. Andres Middle Sch. PTA, Columbia, 1970-71; bd. dirs. Midlands Youth Homes, 1974-75, Scampa, 1974-75, A.F.R.O., Inc., 1971-75. Served to 1st lt. AUS, 1953-56. Cert. labor arbitrator. Mem. NAACP, Columbia Urban League, Columbia Pan-Hellenic Council, Savannah State Coll. Nat. Alumni (pres. 1977), Nat. Juvenile Corrections Assn., Am. Coll. Pub. Relations Assn., Am. Council on Edn., Nat. Tchrs. Assn., Kappa Alpha Psi. Democrat. Mason, Elk. Home: 15 Grand Court Columbia SC 29203 Office: 2611 Forest Dr Columbia SC 29203

BROWN, EARL J., elec. engr.; b. Omaha, Jan. 1, 1928; s. Earl Jefferson and Daisy Mae (Ritter) B.; B.S., U. Nebr., 1953; M.S., U. Mo., 1973, postgrad., 1973-74; postgrad. Washington U., St. Louis, 1959-60, Calif. State U. at Fullerton, 1976-77; m. Mary Helen Peterson, Mar. 5, 1947; children—Jolene Joyce Ellebracht, Barbara Lyne Dunn. Test engr. Collins Radio Corp., Cedar Rapids, Iowa, 1953; devel. engr. instrumentation McDonnell Douglas Corp., St. Louis, 1953-65, flight test engr. new programs, 1966-70, advanced programs and theoretical studies, 1970-74; teaching asst. U. Mo.-Rolla, 1974; research electronics engr. Chevron Oil Field Research Co., La Habra, Calif., 1975-78; registered profl. engr., engring. dept. Standard Oil Co. Calif., San Francisco, 1978—; cons. in field. Vice-pres. Pkwy PTA, Creve Coeur, Mo., 1972. pres., 1973; elder Presbyn. Ch., 1960—. Served with USN, 1946-47. Registered profl. engr., Calif., Tex., La. Mem. IEEE (editor publ. St. Louis 1973-74), Republican. Club: Masons. Contbr. tech. papers to profl. pubis. Developer biomed. instrumentation for astronauts, primates on Project Mercury, 1961; inventor in field. Home: 12 Heritage Ln 46 New Orleans LA 70114 Office: 555 Market St San Francisco CA 94105

BROWN, EDWARD MCLAIN, JR., lawyer; b. Balt., Apr. 26, 1929; s. Edward McLain and Rita Virginia (House) B.; student U. Pa., 1946-47; B.B.A., U. Tex., 1958, LL.B., 1960; m. Patsy Sue Millikan, Jan. 28, 1956; children—Carol Lorraine, Ruth Virginia, David William. Admitted to Tex. bar, 1960; practiced in Lamesa, 1960-62, Dallas, 1962—; asso. firm Karl Cayton, 1960-62, Lyne, Blanchette, Smith and Shelton, 1962-65; mem. firm Brown, Elliott, Brown, 1965-70, Brown & Moore, 1970-75, Brown, Moore & Lee, 1975-79, Brown & Walker, 1980—; sec., dir. Fas-Pak, Inc., 1971—, Pat Jetton, Inc., 1971—; pres., dir. Joppe Co., 1972-74; sec., dir. Vari-Universal, Inc., 1974-77; dir. Constellation Prodns., Inc., Ranchmen Mfg. Co., Inc. Mem. Dallas Estate Planning Council, Greater Dallas Planning Council, 1965-69, Farmers Branch Charter Com., 1967-70, chmn. 1969-70; mem. Farmers Branch Indsl. Devel. Com., 1971. Bd. dirs. Farmers Branch Library, 1964-67, chmn., 1967-68. Served with USAF, 1950-56. Mem. Lamesa (sec. treas. 1961-62), Dallas (legal ethics com. 1972-73) bar assns., State Bar Tex. (mem. admissions com.), Farmers Branch-Carrollton Lawyers Assn. (pres. 1973). Episcopalian (sr. warden 1967). Lion (treas. 1961-62), Rotarian. Home: 3212 Rolling Knoll Pl Dallas TX 75234 Office: 2711 Valley View Ln Suite 101 Dallas TX 75234

BROWN, ELEANOR JEAN, hosp. adminstr.; b. Piqua, Ohio, Dec. 28, 1921; d. Hugo Batista and Sarah Lucille (Offenbacher) Comolli; grad. Christ Hosp. Sch. Nursing, Cin., 1944; B.S., Southeastern U., 1975, M. Bus. and Pub. Adminstrn., 1977; m. Byron Winfield Brown, Dec. 7, 1944; children—Byron Craig, Bruce Allen, Gary Lee. Staff nurse numerous hosps., 1944-47; pvt. duty nursing mil. hosps., Germany, 1949-52, Japan, 1957-59; mem. Vis. Nurse Service, Fairfax County, Va., 1960-62; asst. exec. dir. Potomac Lung Assn., Fairfax, 1962-66; dir. social work Prince Georges Gen. Hosp., Cheverly, Md., 1966-72, dir. admissions 1972-75; asst. adminstr. Doctors Hosp. of Prince Georges County, 1975—. Trustee, Southeastern U. Mem. Md., Va., Am. nurses assns. Methodist. Home: 5616 Fillmore Ave Alexandria VA 22311

BROWN, ERIC THOMAS, physician; b. New Orleans, June 22, 1924; s. Edwin Madison and Floy Katherine (Phillips) B.; M.D., La. State U., 1952; m. Marie Claire Foerster, Sept. 3, 1945; children—Sandra (Mrs. Robert Lapp), Barbara (Mrs. Mercer Whitson, Jr.). Intern, So. Baptist Hosp., New Orleans, 1952-53, resident, 1955; gen. practice medicine, Ferriday, La., 1953-55; resident Charity Hosp. New Orleans, 1956-58; practice medicine specializing in pediatrics and pediatric allergy, New Orleans, 1958-60, Arabi, La., 1960-65; practice medicine specializing in pediatric allergy, Metairie, La., 1965—; clin. asst. prof. pediatrics, allergy div. La. State U. Sch. Medicine, 1963—; vis. physician Charity Hosp., New Orleans, 1960—. Served with USNR, 1942-45; PTO. Diplomate Am. Bd. Allergy and Immunology. Fellow Am. Coll. Allergists, Am. Assn. Clin. Immunology and Allergy. Contbr. articles to profl. lit. Home: 5617 David Dr Kenner LA 70062 Office: 1431 Veterans Memorial Blvd Metairie LA 70005

BROWN, ERNEST JAMES, JR., pianist, educator; b. Chesapeake, Va., Jan. 12, 1938; s. Ernest James and Minnie Lee (Williams) B.; B.A., U. Md., 1959; M.Mus., Peabody Conservatory Music, 1966; D.Mus. Arts, U. Md., 1976; m. Annie Elaine Wood, Aug. 12, 1961; children—Ernesto James, Keith Lafayette. Organist, dir. music Dept. Army, Edgewood Arsenal, Md., 1963-67; asst. prof. music Del. State Coll., Dover, 1967-70; asst. prof. music Hartford Community Coll., Bel Air, Md., 1970-73; asso. prof. music Norfolk (Va.) State U., 1973—. Bd. dirs. music dept. Cecil Community Coll., North East, Md., 1976—; bd. dirs. Norfolk Com. for Improvement Edn., 1979—. Nat. Endowment Arts grantee, 1973-75. Mem. Coll. Music Soc., Nat. Assn. Negro Musicians, Am. Choral Dirs. Assn., Inter-Collegiate Music Assn., AAUP, Alpha Kappa Mu, Alpha Phi Alpha. African Meth. Episcopalian. Home: 2308 Rock Creek Dr Chesapeake VA 23325 Office: Norfolk State Univ Norfolk VA 23504

BROWN, FRANK DOUGLAS, univ. adminstr.; b. Century, Fla., Jan. 18, 1941; s. Jesse Frank and Mildred Lucile (McKibben) B.; A.B., N.W. Miss. Jr. Coll., 1961; B.S., U. So. Miss., 1963; M.B.A., U. Ala., 1969; Ph.D., Fla. State U., 1974; m. Jo Ann Nichols, Apr. 29, 1967; children—Jo April, Jay Douglas. Systems analyst VF Corp., Monroeville, Ala., 1964-66; dir. data processing Livingston U. (Ala.), 1966-69; mktg. rep. IBM, 1969-72; asso. exec. dir. Ala. Commn. on Higher Edn., 1974-79; asst. vice chancellor fin. and ops. U. Houston, 1979—. Kellogg fellow, 1972-74. Mem. So. Higher Edn. Fin. Officers Assn. (founding chmn. 1977), Assn. Instnl. Research, Nat. Assn. Coll. and Univ. Bus. Officers, Assn. Study of Higher Edn. Baptist. Home: 12502 Deep Spring Ln Houston TX 77077 Office: 408 E Cullen Bldg 4800 Calhoun Houston TX 77004

BROWN, GEORGE WAYNE, state ofcl.; b. Union City, Tenn., Nov. 27, 1939; s. George Leon and Hattie Lou (Stubblefield) B.; B.S., Union U., 1961; M.S. in Physics, U. Fla., 1963, Ph.D. in Radio Astronomy, 1970; m. Bonnie Baker, Aug. 20, 1961; children—Tambi, Tifni, Todd, Trev. Acting dean men Union U., 1963-64, dir. men's dormitory, 1963-65, academic dean, 1968-72, v.p. academic affairs, 1972-75; exec. dir. Tenn. Higher Edn. Commn., Nashville, 1975—; ex-officio mem. Tenn. Bd. Edn., Tenn. Bd. Regents; trustee U. Tenn. Mem. exec. com. So. Baptist Sunday Sch. Bd. Mem. So. Assn. Colls and Sch., Am. Phys. Soc., Am. Astron. Soc., Am. Assn. Physics Tchrs., Sigma Xi, Kappa Mu Epsilon, Alpha Psi Omega, Sigma Pi Sigma, Alpha Chi, Alpha Tau Omega. Contbr. articles to profl. jours. Office: 501 Union Bldg Suite 300 Nashville TN 37219

BROWN, GERARD JAMES, hosp. engr.; b. Cleve., Feb. 18, 1934; s. Warner James and Victoria Katherine (Manzell) B.; B.S. in Mech. Engring., Fenn Engring. Coll., 1955; m. Majorie I. Van Nostrand, Mar. 26, 1956 children—Darlene Aune, Gerard James. With Eveready Batteries, Cleve., 1955-61; mech. design engr. Firestone Tire & Rubber Co., Akron, Ohio, 1961-66, Taylor Instruments, Akron, 1966-68; machine design engr. Sensormatic Electronics, Akron and Hollywood, Fla., 1969-70; chief mech. design engr. Coulter Electronics, Hialeah, Fla., 1970-72; chief engr. Key Marine Products, Hialeah, 1972-74; chief mech. design engr. Sunair Electronics, Ft. Lauderdale, Fla., 1974-75; dir. engring. Plantation (Fla.) Gen. Hosp., 1975-78; dir. plant and facilities Palmetto Gen. Hosp., Hialeah, 1978—. Served with U.S. Army, 1956-58. Mem. Nat. Fire Protection Assn., Am. Inst. Indsl. Engrs., Nat. Assn. Power Engrs., Am. Hosp. Engrs. Assn., S. Fla. Soc. Hosp. Engrs. (pres. 1978-79). Inventor original pulsor used in shower heads and of chem. descaling process for stainless steel castings. Home: 5261 SW 3rd Ct Plantation FL 33317 Office: Palmetto General Hospital 2001 W 68th St Hialeah FL 33010

BROWN, GREGG CARROL, comml. systems corp. ofcl.; b. Marion, Ky., Apr. 23, 1953; s. Charles Ray and Ellen Louise (Ramage) B.; student Paducah Community Coll., 1971-72; m. Debbie L. Colson, June 29, 1972 (div.); 1 dau., Shannon Michelle. Computer operator Comml. Systems. Inc., Paducah, Ky., 1972-75, dir. customer support, 1975-76, customer services rep., 1976-77, ops. mgr., 1977-79, customer services rep., 1979—; part-time real estate salesman Cardinal Realtors. Active Khoury League baseball program. Recipient Edwin Gunter academic/athletic award, 1971. Lic. real estate salesman. Democrat. Methodist. Home: 2839 Alabama St Paducah KY 42001 Office: 1632 Kentucky Ave Paducah KY 42001

BROWN, HARLAN JAMES, acquistion search, acquisition study exec.; b. Altoona, Pa., Dec. 16, 1933; s. Lindsey Andrew and Emma Grace (Ackerman) B.; M.Engring. (Sch. grantee-in-aid), Colo. Sch. Mines, 1957; M.B.A., George Washington U., 1969; m. Judith Lynn Wix, Oct. 17, 1964 (div.); 1 son, Harlan James II. Field engr. Beckman Instruments Co., Arlington, Va., 1957-59; partner Shaheen, Brown & Day, Denver, Colo., 1959-60; v.p. Nat. Engring. Service subsidiary NESINC, Washington, 1960-63; pres. NSC Internat. Inc., engring. recruitment, pub. Washington, 1963-67; pres. Harlan Brown & Co., Inc., acquistion search, Acquistion study, McLean, Va., 1967—; cons. in field. Guest lectr. George Washington U., Washington, 1969, 70, 71, 75, FRS, 1975; lectr. sem. U. Toronto (Ont., Can.), 1970; cons., lectr. Nat. Congress Community Devel., Washington, 1975. Mem. IEEE, Am. Soc. Metall. Engrs., Am. Chem. Soc., Am. Mgmt. Assn., M-Club, Blue Key, Theta Tau, Sigma Delta Psi (pres. 1956-57), Alpha Tau Omega. Clubs: Washington Athletic, Regency Racquet. Author: (with Shuckett, Mock) Financing For Growth, 1971. Produced nation's first merger center expt., Cherry Hill, N.J., 1969. Home: 1800 Old Meadow Rd McLean VA 22102 Office: 1307 Dolley Madison Blvd McLean VA 22101

BROWN, HARVEY THOMAS, II, business ofcl.; b. Little Rock, Nov. 11, 1945; s. Harvey Thomas and Betty L. (Becknell) B.; B.S., Memphis State U., 1969, M.Ed., 1973. Mem. quality control staff Chapman Chemicals Co., Memphis, 1970-71; counselor alcoholism program HEW, Memphis, 1970-73; probation and parole counselor Tenn. Dept. Corrections, Memphis, 1974—, dir. project 1st offender, 1974-76, coordinator volunteer services, 1976-78; exec. dir. Sr. Citizen Center, Memphis, 1979; salesman Volkswagen cars, Ams/Oil dealership, Memphis, 1980—. Bd. dirs. Memphis House Drug Treatment Facility. Served with AUS, 1967-68. Mem. Am. Personnel and Guidance Assn., Assn. Group Specialists, Assn. Offender Correction, Tenn Correctional Assn., Sr. Citizens Adv. Council, Tenn. Conf. Social Welfare, Thresholds Inc. Club: Masons. Home: 5720 Sycamore Ridge Rd Memphis TN 38134 Office: 2509 Summer Ave Memphis TN 38112

BROWN, HENRY ARTHUR, III, sign supply mfg. co. exec.; b. Columbia, S.C., Nov. 18, 1951; s. Henry Arthur and Dorothy Ann (White) B.; B.B.A., U. Notre Dame, 1974. Staff acct. Clarkson, Harden & Gantt, C.P.A., Columbia, 1975-77; purchasing agt. Colite Industries, Inc., W. Columbia, S.C., 1977-78, controller, 1978-79; pres. Transco, Inc., W. Columbia, 1979—. Republican. Roman Catholic. Address 229 Parsons St West Columbia SC 29169

BROWN, HYDER JOSEPH, JR., architect; b. Hillsboro, Tex., Oct. 16, 1925; s. Hyder Joseph and Rosalie (Wilkinson) B.; B.Arch., U. Tex., 1951. Cons. sch. architecture Tex. Edn. Agy., Austin, 1951-57; with Paderewski, Dean & Assos., architects, San Diego, 1957-62; architect partner Livingstone & Brown, La Jolla, Calif., 1962-67; staff architect Brooks, Barr, Graeber, White, Inc., Austin, 1967-68; project architect firm Jessen Assos., Inc., Architects and Planners, Austin, 1968-72, sr. asso., dir. programming and devel., 1972-78; prin. Hyder Joe Brown, architect, 1978—; now dir. profl. affairs Sch. Architecture, U. Tex. at Austin. Mem. adv. bd. Austin (Tex.) Pre-Sch. Hearing Center, 1955-56; mem. Council Ednl. Facility Planning, 1954-74; mem. Planning and Zoning Commn., West Lake Hills, Tex., 1971-72, chmn., 1972-73; mem. adv. com. The Wild Basin Wilderness Com., Inc., Travis County, Tex., 1974-79, bd. dirs., 1979—; trustee Woodall-Bowden Trusts 1 and 2; mem. Laguna Gloria Art Museum, Austin; mem. Austin Citizens' Com. for Landscape Ordinance, 1978-79; mem. dean's council U. Tex. Sch. Architecture; panelist Am. Arbitration Assn. Served with USNR, 1943-46. Mem. Tex. Soc. Architects (chmn. resolutions com. 1979, honors com. 1976, design awards com. 1978, pub. relations com. 1978, environ. resources and urban planning 1979-80, pres.'s 1981 planning com.), AIA (chpt. chmn. commn. on edn. and research 1966; chmn. chpt. activities 1971, chpt. chmn. pub. affairs commn. 1972-73, mem. exec. com. 1974-76, pres. chpt. 1975; recipient outstanding service award San Diego chpt. 1962, mem. nat. jud. bd. 1977—; co-chmn. Austin downtown revitalization com. 1978), Austin Symphony Soc., Tex. Fine Arts Assn., English Speaking Union, Austin Natural Sci. Assn., Heritage Soc. Austin. Episcopalian (former lay reader). Contbr. to profl. jours.; editorial cons. Tex. Architect Mag. Prin. works include schs., pub. housing, residences, instns., apts., comml. bldgs.; mem. constrn. drawing team Lyndon B. Johnson Library, Austin, 1967-68. Home: 1512 Hardouin Ave Austin TX 78703 Office: Sch Architecture U Tex Austin TX 78712

BROWN, J. AL, constrn. co. exec.; b. Grapeland, Tex., Dec. 23, 1935; s. Joe Al and Velma B.; B.S., Tex. A&M U., 1958; m. Jo Beth Serres, June 14, 1957; children—Jeffrey Al, Jon Derek, Joseph Damon, Lane Antoinette, Berri Nicolette. Vice-pres. constrn. Am. Devel. Systems, Inc., Houston, 1978—. Home: 4810 Wedgewood Cibolo TX 78108 Office: 50 Briar Hollow Ln Suite 425E Houston TX 77027

BROWN, JAMES, educator; b. Boston, May 1, 1934; s. Gus and Sophia (Lucas) B. student U. Tex., Austin, 1952-54; B.A., Tex. Christian U., 1960; M.A., SUNY, Buffalo, 1969, Ph.D., 1971; m. Bonnie Jo Russell, Nov. 25, 1964; 1 dau., Shannon Sophia. Instr. polit.

sci. So. Meth. U., Dallas, 1962-67, 69-70, asst. prof., 1970-74, asso. prof. polit. sci., 1974—, mem. faculty senate, 1977—, S.W. regional coordinator for Inter-Univ. Seminar on Armed Forces and Soc., 1976—, chmn. fellows selection com, dir. grad. program and minors and internship program dept. polit. sci., dir. Inst. of Internat. Edn. Fgn. Student Devel. Seminars, 1966-68, S.W. area mgr., regional dir. News Election Service, 1972-78, state mgr. Tex. and N.Y., 1964-70; polit. cons. Grove & Assos., Dallas; organizer, chmn. U.S. Mil. in Fgn. Policy in the 1980's Conf. Served with U.S. Army, 1954-57. Ames Lab. NASA research grantee, 1974-78; Dept. State scholar-diplomat program grantee, 1971, 75; Arnold Found. research grantee, 1971, 73; So. Meth. U. faculty fellow, 1971; NSF grantee, 1971, 73. Mem. Inter-Univ. Seminar on Armed Forces and Soc., Am. Polit. Sci. Assn., AAUP, So. Polit. Sci. Assn., Southwestern Polit. Sci. Assn., Modern Greek Studies Assn., Pi Sigma Alpha. Clubs: Masons, Scottish Rite. Speaker profl. confs.; contbr. articles in field to publs. in field. Home: 2733 Rosedale St Dallas TX 75205 Office: Southern Methodist University Story Hall Room 34 Dallas TX 75275

BROWN, JAMES HARVEY, state ofcl.; b. Kansas City, Mo., May 6, 1945; s. James Harvey and Helen (Gentry) B.; B.A., U. N.C., 1962; LL.B., Tulane U., 1966; m. Alma Dale Campbell; children—Cami, Meredith, Gentry. Admitted to La. bar, 1967; mem. La. Senate, 1972-79, chmn. jud. com., 1976-79, chmn. joint legis. com. on pub. works, 1972-79; sec. of state, State of La., 1979—; del. La. Constl. Conv., 1973. Bd. dirs. Ouachita Valley council Boy Scouts Am. Mem. La. Jaycees (past regional v.p.), Am. Legion (past post comdr.), Concordia Parish Farm Bur., Concordia Parish Cattlemen's Assn. Democrat. Clubs: Lions, Rotary. Address: PO Box 797 Ferriday LA 71334

BROWN, JAMES POPE, ret. savs. and loan exec.; b. Hawkinsville, Ga., Sept. 1, 1911; s. Stephen William and Elizabeth Calhoun (Bivins) B.; diploma Ga. Mil. Coll., 1930; cert. Grad. Sch. Savs. and Loan, Ind. U., 1961; m. Josephine Sibley Jennings, June 17, 1939; 1 son, James Pope. With Rankin-Whitten Realty Co., Atlanta, 1937-41, Fulton Fed. Savs. & Loan Assn., Atlanta, 1947-60; sr. v.p. public relations Ga. Fed. Savs. & Loan Assn., 1960-76; tchr. Am. Savs. and Loan Inst., 1960-65. Mem. Atlanta Citizens Crime Com., 1958-61, Atlanta Civic Design Com., 1969-72; pres. Grand Jurors Assn. Fulton County, 1967; treas. Met. Atlanta Rapid Transit Authority, 1970-72. Served as lt. col. C.E., AUS, 1941-46. Mem. Am. Legion, Grand Jurors Assn. Fulton County, Dixie Council Authors and Journalists, Atlanta Writers Club. Presbyterian (elder). Contbr. articles to profl. jours. Home: 33 Beverly Rd NE Atlanta GA 30309

BROWN, JERRY DALE, health care adminstr.; b. Vernon, Tex., Sept. 21, 1943; s. Emmitt Elwood and Edythe Louise (Cooksey) B.; B.S., Tex. Tech. U., 1977, M.P.A., 1980; m. Norma Brunett, June 16, 1973; children—Angela, Kimberly. Adminstrv. asst. Wichita Gen. Hosp., Wichita Falls, Tex., 1967-68; adminstr. Wilbarger Gen. Hosp., Vernon, 1968-70; hosp. systems cons. Moore Bus. Forms, Denton, Tex., 1970-72; asst. dir. public health City of Lubbock, Tex. Vice pres. bd. dirs. Family Services Assn., 1979-80. Served with USAF, 1963-67. Mem. Am. Coll. Hosp. Adminstrs., Am. Public Health Assn., Tex. Public Health Assn., Tex. Hosp. Assn. Club: Optimist. Office: PO Box 2548 Lubbock TX 79408

BROWN, JERRY HOUSTON, tng. and mgmt. resources co. exec.; b. South Pittsburgh, Tenn., Feb. 19, 1933; s. Claude Andrew and Lula Eunice (Hampton) B.; various courses U. Tenn., U. Miami (Fla.), and Air Force U., 1952-70; m. Billie Gragg, May 24, 1957; 1 son, David Andrew. Instructional systems technologist, liaison govt. and bus., 1961-68; cons. social devel. programs OEO and Dept. Labor, Washington, 1968-72; pres. Universal Resource Inst., nat. cons. co., Ocean Springs, Miss., 1972—; owner, operator Tng. & Mgmt. Resources Corp., Inc., Atlanta, 1977—; cons. in field. Adv. bds. mil. credit unions. Served with USAF, 1951-61. Clubs: Order of Ky. Cols., Masons (32 deg.), Shriners. Home: Gulf Park Estates PO Box 599 Ocean Springs MS 39564 Office: Tng & Mgmt Resources Inc 14 Perimeter Center E Suite 1402 Atlanta GA 30346

BROWN, JESSIE MINNETTE, business exec.; b. Okomulgee, Okla., Nov. 18, 1939; d. Hubert H. and Ruby L. (Carter) Loyd; student Okla. Bapt. U., 1959-60; m. Earnest M. Brown, Nov. 8, 1971; 1 dau., Dawn Betryce. Sec., Johnson Controls, Inc., Tulsa, 1970—, clerical supr. br. office, 1977—; sec.-treas., office supr. Brown Mech. Services Inc., Tulsa, 1979—. Mem. Nat. Assn. for Female Execs. Republican. Home: 8423 S 36 W Ave Tulsa OK 74132 Office: 822 E 6th St Tulsa OK 74120

BROWN, JIMMIE LEE, clergyman, police officer; b. Mariana, Fla., Aug. 19, 1944; s. Willie Henry and Ida Mae (Timmons) B.; A.S. in Police Sci., Miami-Dade Community Coll., 1971; B.A. in Public Adminstrn., Biscayne Coll., 1973, M.S., 1979; student Emory U., 1976-79, Candler Sch. Theology, 1976-77; m. Alma Jane Thomas, June 16, 1963; children—Gregory Vincent, Darryl Lamont. Lic. to preach United Methodist Ch., 1969; mem. Dade County Public Safety Dept., Miami, Fla., 1969—, police sgt., 1974—; pastor St. Paul United Meth. Ch., Deerfield Beach, Fla., 1974, Mt. Sinai United Meth. Ch., Hallandale, Fla., 1974—; asso. cons. Internat. Assn. Chiefs of Police. Served with USAF, 1962-69. Decorated Bronze Star. Mem. Dade County Police Benevolent Assn. (chaplain, exec. com.), Ministerial Alliance of Deerfield Beach, Jaycees. Democrat. United Methodist. Home: 10241 SW 152d St Miami FL 33157

BROWN, JOHN ALLEN, mfg. co. exec.; b. Denham Springs, La., May 25, 1920; s. John Allen and Eula (Hones) B.; student La. State U., 1939-40; m. Lucille Campbell, Jan. 13, 1940; 1 son, John Thomas. Pres., W. F. Brown & Sons, Denham Springs, La., 1940—. Served with U.S. Navy, 1944-45. Democrat. Baptist. Inventor fiberglass foam filled boat oar and canoe paddle. Home: 406 Centerville St Denham Springs LA 70726 Office: PO Box 356 Denham Springs LA 70726

BROWN, JOHN ROBERT, power co. exec.; b. Harrisburg, Pa., July 7, 1917; s. Robert and Ruth Alberta (Dimm) B.; B.A., Swarthmore (Pa.) Coll., 1939; postgrad. Fla. State U., Tallahassee, 1950; m. Katherine Simon Cooper, May 1, 1959; children by previous marriage—Robert W., James M. Salesman, Allied Asphalt & Mineral Corp., N.Y.C., 1939-42, Colgate-Palmolive-Peet Co., Jersey City, 1942-43; instr., night prin. Pinellas County Bd. Public Instrn., Clearwater, Fla., 1946-51; supr. employee devel. services Fla. Power Corp., St. Petersburg, 1951—. Chmn. media adv. com. and gen. adv. com. St. Petersburg Vocat. Tech. Inst., 1975—; mem. disadvantaged adv. com. Nat. Alliance Bus., 1976—. Served with USN, 1943-46, U.S. Army, 1943; PTO. Decorated Bronze Star (2). Mem. Am. Soc. Tng. and Devel. (pres. Fla. chpt. 1960-61), Fla. Power Club (bd. dirs. 1959-61), Girard Coll. Alumni Assn. (pres. Fla. chpt. 1963-70), Coop. Edn. Assn., Iota Lambda Sigma. Democrat. Presbyterian. Club: St. Petersburg Yacht. Home: 4904 38th Way S Saint Petersburg FL 33711 Office: PO Box 14042 Saint Petersburg FL 33733

BROWN, JOHN ROBERT, fed. judge; b. Funk, Nebr., Dec. 10, 1909; s. E.E. and Elvira (Carney) B.; A.B., U. Nebr., 1930, LL.D., 1965; J.D., U. Mich., 1932, LL.D., 1959; m. Mary Lou Murray, May 30, 1936; 1 son, John R. Admitted to Tex. bar, 1932; mem. firm Royston & Rayzor, 1932-55; judge U.S. Ct. Appeals, 5th circuit, 1955—, chief judge, 1967—. Chmn., Harris County (Tex.) Republican Party, 1953-55. Served to maj. Transp. Corps, USAAF, 1942-46. Mem. Am., Tex., Houston bar assns., Am. Judicature Soc., Am. Law Inst., Maritime Law Assn. U.S., Assn. ICC Practitioners, Order Coif, Phi Delta Phi, Sigma Chi. Presbyterian (elder). Clubs: Houston, Houston Country; Boston (New Orleans). Office: 11 501 US Court House Houston TX 77002*

BROWN, JOHN WILLIAM HARRELL, bus. cons.; b. Paris, Tenn., May 7, 1933; s. Jessie T. and Eunice Martha (McClain) B.; B.S., U. Tenn., 1956; postgrad. U. Md., 1957-60, U. Tenn., 1966-69; m. Mary Lou Smith, Nov. 13, 1960; children—Abby Lee, Dixie Ann. Economist, Econ. Research Service, Washington, 1957-62; project leader Spindeltop Research Inst., Lexington, Ky., 1962-64; economist Econ. Research Service, 1964-66; instr. econs. U. Tenn., Knoxville, 1966-69; bus. cons., Concord, Tenn., 1969—; dir. Asso. Housing, Intime Advt. Chmn., Dem. party Concord, 1972-78, exec. com. Knox County, 1972-78, pres. Dems. W. Club, 1977—. Served with U.S. Army, 1956-57. Recipient outstanding service award Gov. Tenn., 1975, community service award Mayor Knoxville, 1976. Mem. Tenn. Hosp. Assn., Bldg. Owners and Mgrs. Assn., Orgn. Profl. Employees Dept. Agr., Alpha Gamma Rho. Baptist. Kiwanian. Home: 620 Fox Rd Concord TN 37922 Office: PO Box 1 Concord TN 37922

BROWN, JOHN Y., gov. Ky.; grad. law sch. U. Ky., 1960; m. 2d, Phyllis George, Mar. 17, 1979; 3 children by previous marriage. Pres., Ky. Fried Chicken, to 1971, chmn. bd., 1971-74; owner Lums Restaurants and Ollie's Trolley, Inc., Louisville, Buffalo Braves, profl. basketball; gov. Ky., 1979—; bd. govs. Nat. Basketball Assn.; chmn. Ky. Gov.'s Econ. Devel. Com. Nat. chmn. Democratic Nat. Telethon, 1972-73, Nat. Young Leadership Council. Recipient Spl. Service to Am. award Lions Am. Bowl, 1974. Address: Office of Governor State Capitol Frankfort KY 40601

BROWN, JOHNNIE WAYNE, elec. engr.; b. Providence, Ky., June 19, 1936; s. John Lee and Inez (Wood) B.; B.E.E., Ga. Inst. Tech., 1959; M.B.A., Middle Tenn. State U., 1973; M.S., U. Tenn., 1979; m. Ruby Irene Headrick, Nov. 26, 1958; children—David Earl, Donna Elaine. Coop. engr. Cin. Gas & Elec. Co., 1955-58; engr. Firestone Tire & Rubber Co., Akron, Ohio, 1959-61, Sverdrup/Aro, Arnold AF Sta., Tenn., 1961-76, engring. supr., 1977—. Pres. local PTA, 1967; deacon, treas. Westwood Baptist Ch. Served to capt. Signal Corps, USAR, 1960-68. Registered profl. engr., Tenn. Mem. Nat. Soc. Profl. Engrs., Nat. Mgmt. Assn., Tenn. Soc. Profl. Engrs. Home: 301 Oakdale St Manchester TN 37355 Office: Arnold Air Force Station ETF TI TN 37389

BROWN, KAREN RENE', interior decorator, real estate sales exec.; b. Bartlesville, Okla., Apr. 23, 1945; d. Conrad Nagel and Lelah Lucille (Lawless) Brown; B.S. in Bus. Edn., Central State U., 1968; postgrad. U. Calif., Sacramento, 1968-72; stude nt Prep Real Estate Sch., 1978, other profl. tng. courses. With Plaza Pharmacy, Bartlesville, Okla., 1962-63, Brown-Thomas Jewelers, Bartlesville, 1963-64, Nat. Chemsearch, Irving, Tex., 1965; sec. to chmn. Bus. Dept. Southwestern State Coll., Weatherford, Okla., 1965-66; sec. Central State U., Edmond, Okla., 1966-67; with Aetna Life & Casualty, Sacramento, 1968-73, Oakland, Calif., 1973-74; adminstrv. asst. to pres. and sec/treas. Curtis Fin. Corp./Mitchell T. Curtis, Inc., San Francisco, 1974; owner, mgr. From the Ground Up, Bartlesville, 1974—. Instr. Cantonese cooking YWCA Ladies' Day Out program, Bartlesville, 1975. Lic. real estate asso., Okla.; lic. life, health, variable annuity and mut. funds agt., Calif.; recipient Nat. Bull. award Life Ins. Cashiers' and Office Mgrs. Assn., 1972. Mem. Bartlesville Art Assn. (pres. 1975-76), AAUW, Nat. Trust for Historic Preservation, Life Ins. Cashiers' and Office Mgrs. Assn. (nat. first v.p. 1970-71, chpt. pres. 1972-73), Oakland-E. Bay Life Underwriters Assn., Gen. Agts. and Mgrs. Assn., Pi Omega Pi, Gamma Delta Kappa. Address: 2208 Tuxedo Blvd Bartlesville OK 74003

BROWN, KENNETH FRANCIS, communications co. exec.; b. Pacific Grove, Calif., Nov. 27, 1946; s. Charles Howard and Elizabeth Helen Brown; student U. Ariz., 1964-66, N.Mex. State U., 1966-67, U. Tex., 1967-69; m. Janice Hilburn, June 29, 1974. Salesman, Wall St. Jour., Chgo., 1970; Midwest dir. research and promotion Dow Jones Inc., Chgo., 1971-73; research dir. Dallas Times Herald, 1973-75; dir. mktg. research Progressive Farmer Co., Birmingham, Ala., 1975-79; So. mgr. Telmar Communications Corp., Atlanta, 1979—. Bd. dirs. Shades Valley YMCA, Birmingham, 1978-79. Mem. Sales and Mktg. Execs., Am. Mktg. Assn. Democrat. Roman Catholice. Office: 3955 Pleasantdale Rd Suite 101 Atlanta GA 30340

BROWN, KENNETH HUGH, JR., health care co. exec.; b. Corpus Christi, Tex., Oct. 15, 1948; s. Kenneth Hugh and Louise (Soulier) B.; B.A., La. State U., 1971. Asst. personnel dir. Our Lady of the Lake Hosp., Baton Rouge, 1972-73; personnel dir. Drs. Meml. Hosp., Baton Rouge, 1973-75, Delta Med. Center, Greenville, Miss., 1975-76; dir. human resources Bapt. Med. Center, Birmingham, Ala., 1976-79; employee relations mgr. Touro Infirmary, New Orleans, 1979—. Mem. Am. Mgmt. Assn., Am. Hosp. Assn. Democrat. Roman Catholic. Office: Touro Infirmary 1401 Foucher St New Orleans LA 70115

BROWN, LOUISE SCOTT, pulpwood co. exec.; b. Greenwood, S.C., Jan. 26, 1923; d. James William and Ivey Bell (Davis) Scott; grad. Greenwood Coll. Commerce, 1940; m. William Kenneth Brown, Feb. 14, 1942; children—Sandra Brown Nickles, Connie Brown Babb, Brenda Faye. Clk. tpyist, 1941-46; mgr., grocery store, Hodges, S.C., 1950-60; bookkeeper, Brown's Pulpwood, Hodges, 1960-73; v.p., sec. W.K. Brown Pulpwood Corp., Hodges, 1974—. Methodist. Club: Order Eastern Star. Home: Route 1 Hodges SC 29653 Office: Route 1 Box 170 Hodges SC 29653

BROWN, LYNNE ROMINGER, food co. exec.; b. Del Norte, Colo., Aug. 5, 1954; d. R. Vernon and Caroline Ann (Chenoweth) Rominger; B.S. in food sci. and Nutrition, Colo. State U., 1976; m. Tyler Jay Brown, June 5, 1976. Dietetic intern Presbyn., Hosp., Dallas, 1977; dietary dir. Mesquite Meml. Hosp., Mesquite, Tex., 1977-79; coordinator mfrs. specifications Anderson Clayton Foods, W.L. Clayton Research Center, Richardson, Tex., 1979—. Registered dietitian. Mem. Am. Dietetic Assn., Tex. Dietetic Assn., Dallas Dietetic Assn. Home: 6814 Royal Ln Dallas TX 75230 Office: Anderson Clayton Foods 3333 N Central Expressway Richardson TX 75080

BROWN, MARCUS GORDON, educator; b. Miami, Fla., Mar. 14, 1908; s. David Chappel and Lula (Bell) B.; A.B., Columbia Union Coll., 1927; M.A., Emory U., 1936; Docteur ès Lettres, U. Dijon (France), 1939; Doctor en Filosofía y Letras, U. Madrid (Spain), 1940. Tchr. fgn. langs. high sch., Jacksonville, Fla., 1927-30, Boys' High Sch., Atlanta, 1930-36; instr. English and French, U. Fla., 1936-38; asst. prof. fgn. langs. Ga. Inst. Tech., Atlanta, 1940-42, asso. prof., 1942-43, prof., 1943-50; specialist U.S. Office Edn., 1944-46; cultural attache Am. embassy, Bogota, Colombia, 1950-52, Rio de Janeiro, Brazil, 1952-54; asst. chancellor Univ. System Ga., Atlanta, 1954-57; fgn. lang. coordinator Ga. State Dept. Edn., Atlanta, 1957-62; asso. prof. Romance langs. Memphis State U., 1963-67, prof., 1967-71, prof. modern langs., 1971-73; summer vis. prof. Duke U., 1941-44, U. Havana, 1943, U. Ga., 1947, U. Mont., 1948; vis. prof. Ft. Lewis Coll., 1975, Henderson State U., 1976-77; lectr. U.S. Dept. State, Latin Am., 1948-49, Spain and Portugal, 1957-58; lectr. numerous instns. and orgns. U.S. and abroad. Recipient Anchieta medal Municipality of Rio de Janeiro, Brazil, 1954; medals for excellence in French lang. and lit. French Govt., 1936. Mem. Sociedad Bolivariana de Colombia, Am. Assn. Tchrs. Spanish and Portuguese, Am. Assn. Tchrs. French, Am. Assn. Tchrs. Italian, Am. Assn. Tchrs. German, AAUP, Modern Lang. Assn. Am., S. Central Modern Lang. Assn., Phi Sigma Iota, Sigma Delta Pi, Pi Delta Phi, Delta Phi Alpha. Author: Les Idées Politiques et Religieuses de Stendhal, 1939; La Vida y Las Novelas de Emilia Pardo Bazán, 1940; (with J. Russell) Bibliography for the Teaching of English to Foreigners, 1947; also translations, articles, condensations of Brazilian novels. Address: 2765 Ketchum Pl Apt 8 Memphis TN 38114

BROWN, MARGARET CANNON BOYCE, civic worker; b. Amarillo, Tex., Dec. 13, 1922; d. John Kirkpatrick and Margaret Owen (Curtis) Boyce; B.S., Tex. U., Austin, 1944; M.A., Columbia U., 1945; m. Shepherd Spencer Neville Brown, Mar. 31, 1951; children—Spencer, Margaret, Maria Stanton, Boyce. Instr. home econs. U. Tex., Austin, 1946-51; pres. Waco (Tex.) Jr. League, 1959; founder St. Paul's Episcopal Day Sch., Waco, 1956—, pres. sch. bd., 1960-61; pres. St. Paul's Asso. Women, 1968-70; pres. Waco Symphony Women's Assn., 1964; founding chmn. Waco Cotton Palace Pageant, 1971-74, pres. corp. bd., 1970-78; pres. Tex. Women's Assn. Symphony Orch., 1972-73; pres. Tex. Soc. Nat. Soc. Colonial Dames Am., 1974-78; bd. trustees Hockaday Sch., Dallas, 1977—; youth protection com. Waco PTA City Council, 1968; pres. Crestview Sch. PTA, 1968; pres. Kappa Alpha Theta Alumnae Club, 1972-74. Recipient Liberty Bell award Waco Jr. Bar, 1972; named Woman of Year, Baylor U. Mortar Bd., 1974. Mem. Daus. Republic Texas, Waco Woman's Club, Thursday Lit. Club, Pi Lambda Theta (Theta of Yr. award Austin alumnae chpt. 1978), Omicron Nu, Dallas Woman's Club. Republican. Episcopalian. Club: Ridgewood Country. Home: Stanton Hall 2620 MacArthur Dr Waco TX 76708

BROWN, MARY HILDA RUSHING, educator; b. San Francisco, June 29, 1945; d. Marvin Henry and Hazel (Gann) Rushing; B.S. in Nursing, U. Miss., 1967, M.Nursing, 1976; m. John Milton Brown, Aug. 18, 1968; children—Jay Milton, John Coleman. Staff nurse pediatrics Univ. Hosp., Jackson, Miss., 1967-68; staff nurse, charge nurse med. unit Hinds Gen. Hosp., Jackson, 1968-69; public health nurse Child Devel. Clinic, Univ. Hosp., Jackson, 1970; asst. head nurse Psychiatric Unit, Forrest Gen. Hosp., Hattisburg, Miss., 1971-72; clin. asst. instr. Sch. Nursing, Miss. U. for Women, Columbus, 1973-76, asst. prof. asso. degree program, 1976—. Mem. Nat. League for Nursing, Am. Nurses Assn., Miss. Nurses Assn. (mem. pres.'s adv. council, regional coordinator for task force open hearings, dist. 17 pres. 1978-79, Health Ednl. Media Assn., Nursing Honor Soc. Baptist. Home: 100 Petersburg Rd Columbus MS 39701 Office: Sch of Nursing Miss Univ for Women Columbus MS 39701

BROWN, MICHAEL JOHN, accountant; b. Chgo., June 25, 1941; s. John William and Christina Margarite (Roule) B.; B.B.A. in Acctg., Loyola U., Chgo., 1963; m. Dolores Jean Gwozdz, Feb. 2, 1963; children—Janet, Jeffrey, Kathleen, Thomas, Nancy, John, Mary. With Touche Ross & Co., Miami, Fla., 1974—, partner, dir. profl. standards, Miami office, 1975—. Vice pres. fin. Clearbrook Center for Retarded, Rollings Meadows, Ill., 1969-73; mem. Securities Law Adv. Council, State of Fla., 1978—; adviser Friends of Sch. Vols., Dade County public schs., 1976—; Dade partner rep. Dade County public schs., 1978—; bd. dirs., classroom cons. Project Bus., Jr. Achievement, 1978—. Mem. Am. Inst. C.P.A.'s, Fla. Inst. C.P.A.'s, Mcpl. Fin. Officers Am., Beta Alpha Psi. Club: Serra. Office: 444 Brickell St Miami FL 33131

BROWN, NATHANIEL BAKER, JR., agrl. scientist, natural resources mgmt. cons.; b. Greensboro, N.C., Dec. 18, 1947; s. Nathaniel B. and Lydia M. (Martin) B.; B.S., N.C. Central U., Durham, N.C., 1970, M.S., 1972; Ph.D., Sch. Natural Resources, U. Mich., 1978; m. Fredrena Burgess, June 7, 1969; children—Kenneth Bernard, Kysha Naetta, Kimberly Bernetta. Med. lab. technician Duke U. Hosp. and Med. Center, Durham, 1968-72; instr. biology Ft. Valley (Ga.) State Coll., 1972-74, research asso., div. of agr., 1978—; resident dir., student housing office U. Mich., Ann Arbor, 1975-76, spl. student asst. to dir. minority affairs Sch. Natural Resources, 1977-78; community devel. dir. City of Ft. Valley, 1976-77. Asst. scout master Boy Scouts Am.; usher Temple Christian Methodist Episcopal Ch., Ft. Valley, 1978—; chmn. acad. com. Citizens Orgn. for Public Edn., Ft. Valley, 1979. Nat. Urban League faculty research fellow, summers 1973, 74. Mem. Nat. Inst. Sci., Orgn. Black Scientists, AAUP, Ga. Vegetable Growers Assn., So. Assn. Agrl. Scientists, Am. Assn. for Evolutionary Econs., NAACP. Democrat. Office: Fort Valley State Coll PO Box 5236 Fort Valley GA 31030

BROWN, PATRICIA CYNTHIA, home care services exec.; b. Daytona Beach, Fla., Apr. 21, 1936: d. William Vann and Willie Lee (Brown) Daughtry; B.S. in Nursing, Tuskegee Inst., 1958; M.Adminstrn. and Supervision Public Health Nursing, Columbia U., 1966; m. Bobby Lee Brown, Dec. 26, 1958; children—Beverley, Michael, Tempie. Staff nurse St. Mary's Hosp., West Palm Beach, Fla., 1958, N.Y. Hosp., N.Y.C., 1958-59; staff nurse Palm Beach Regional Vis. Nurse Assn., 1960-63, ednl. dir., 1963-79, dir. profl. services, 1979—: cons., tchr. Palm Beach Jr. Coll. Corr. sec. Palm Beach County Kidney Assn.; active Cancer Soc., S.E. Fla. Lung Assn. Mem. Am. Public Health Assn., Nat. League Nursing, Fla. League Nursing, Delta Sigma Theta. Democrat. Baptist. Club: Zonta of Palm Beaches (v.p. 1979—). Office: 5601 Corporate Way Suite 400 West Palm Beach FL 33407

BROWN, RICHARD HAIL, motel exec.; b. Greensboro, Ala., Mar. 21, 1903; s. Edward Lamar and Frances (Hail) B.; A.B., U. Ala., 1927, LL.B., 1929; m. Anita Washington Shepard, June 12, 1932; children—Anita Brown Cowart, Brownie Brown Barker, Barbara Brown Evans. Admitted to Ala. bar, 1929; owner Hiway Host Motel. Jr. warden, vestryman St. Mary's Episcopal Ch.; trustee Webb Sch., Tenn., 1959—. Served to lt. comdr. USN, 1942-47. Mem. Nat. Assn. Homebuilders (v.p., exec. com. 1950-53), Ala. Motel Assn., Birmingham Motel Assn., Birmingham Assn. Homebuilders (pres. 1949, 56-57), Birmingham Bar Assn., Phi Alpha Delta, SAR. Republican. Presbyterian. Clubs: Mountain Brook Country, The Club. Home: 6 Rockledge Rd Birmingham AL 35213 Office: 4301 Bessemer Superhwy Bessemer AL 35020

BROWN, ROBERT STANLEY, psychiatrist, psychologist, educator; b. Norfolk, Va.; s. George Stanley and Louise (Beale) B.; B.A. in Biology, U. Va., 1953, M.Ed. in Ednl. Psychology, 1958, Ph.D. in Edn., 1963, M.D., 1967; m. Dorothy Ann Hinkle, Feb. 6, 1954; children—Robert Stanley, David, Nancy, Clinton. Sec., Boys Work, Norfolk, 1954-55; bacteriologist Norfolk Health Dept., 1955-56; tchr. Norfolk Acad., 1956-58; prin. Blue Ridge Sch., Dyke, Va., 1958-59; exec. dir. Hillside Cottages, Atlanta, 1959-61; intern U. Va. Hosp., Charlottesville, 1967-68, resident, 1968-71; practice medicine specializing in psychiatry, Charlottesville, Va., 1971—; mem. staff U. Va., Martha Jefferson Hosp., David C. Wilson Hosp.; vis. prof. edn. and clin. asso. prof. behavioral medicine and psychiatry U. Va.; cons.

Inst. Textile Tech., Charlottesville, 1977—. Mem. Albemarle County (Va.) Democratic Com., 1971-73; pres. Woodbrook PTA, Charlottesville, 1974-75. Served to 1st lt., inf., USAR, 1954-62. Recipient James Research prize U. Va., 1971. Fellow Am. Psychiat. Assn., Royal Soc. Medicine; mem. AMA, Am. Psychol. Assn., Med. Soc. Va., Neuropsychiat. Soc., N.Y. Acad. Sci. Episcopalian. Contbr. numerous articles to profl. jours. Office: 1400 Jefferson Park Ave Charlottesville VA 22903

BROWN, RON, real estate broker; b. Victoria B.C., Can., July 10, 1922; s. William Harry and Maud Marjorie (Hirst) B.; came to U.S., 1923, naturalized, 1947; student San Jose State Coll., 1939-42; m. Celeste Hopkins, Oct. 24, 1945; children—Charlotte, Michael, Rawley. With Prudential Ins., Victoria, Tex., 1947-50; with Victoria Real Estate Co., 1950-53; owner The Ron Brown Co., Victoria, 1953-75, sr. v.p., 1975—. Mem. City of Victoria Planning Commn., 1961-69. Accredited appraiser Canadian Inst. Mem. Victoria C. of C. (v.p. 1968-70, pres. 1970-71, dir. 1971-72), Am. Inst. Real Estate Appraisers, Nat., Tex. bds. realtors, Soc. Real Estate Counselors, Soc. Real Estate Appraisers, Am. Arbitration Assn. Contbr. articles to profl. jours. Home: 6012 Country Club Dr Victoria TX 77901 Office: Drawer B Victoria TX 77901

BROWN, SCOTT NEWTON, real estate, ins. cons.; b. Chattanooga, May 3, 1909; s. C. Victor and Catherine (Colburn) B.; student Davidson Coll., 1926-28; B.S. in Commerce, U. Tenn., 1930; student Am. Inst. Banking, 1931; spl. courses Am. Inst. Real Estate Appraisers, 1947, 68; grad. Law Sch., LaSalle Extension U.; m. Margaret Frierson Williamson, Dec. 2, 1939; children—Scott Newton, George W. propr., Scott N. Brown Co.; exec. v.p. N.Am. Capital Corp. Real estate commr. State of Tenn., 1959-62. Vice chmn. City Planning Commn., 1940-42; dir. Chattanooga Safety Council, 1950-51; commr. Walden's Ridge Utility Dist., 1948-53, Chattanooga-Hamilton County Hist. Commn., 1953. Trustee, sec. McCallie Sch. Alumni Endowment Fund, Inc.; trustee Brown Found. Mem. Am. Finance Assn., Nat. Assn. Real Estate Appraisers, Nat. Assn. Rev. Appraisers, Am. Coll. Real Estate Cons. Nat. Apt. Assn., Chattanooga Bd. Realtors (pres. 1948, 62), Chattanooga C. of C. (pres. 1958), Insurors of Chattanooga (pres. 1949), Delta Sigma Pi, Pi Kappa Phi. Presbyn. (past elder, trustee). Lion (past sec. Chattanooga; Lion of Year). Home: 401 Crewdson Ave Chattanooga TN 37405 Office: James Bldg Chattanooga TN 37402

BROWN, TED LEWIS, mech./structural engr.: b. Haughton, La., Jan. 22, 1936; s. Harry Lewis and Margy (Stinson) B.; student Centenary Coll., 1954-56, U. Tex., Arlington, 1963-66; m. Jo Ann Dunaway; children—Michael Douglas, Patrick Kent. Design draftsman Thiokol Corp., Marshall, Tex., 1956-61, sr. mech. designer, Brigham City, Utah, 1961-63; project engr. Tex. Industries, Inc., Dallas, 1963-72, corp. constrn. adminstrn., 1972-74, corp. chief engr., 1974—. Scoutmaster, Longhorn council Boy Scouts Am., 1975—, dist. commr., 1978—, sustaining membership chmn., 1977. Mem. Order of Arrow. Republican. Baptist. Club: Masons (32 deg.). Office: 8100 Carpenter Freeway Dallas TX 75247

BROWN, THELMA BARNES, hosp. nursing adminstr.; b. Durham, N.C., Nov. 25, 1939; d. William Wesley Barnes and Elizabeth Barnes Toran; A.B.A., Durham Bus. Coll., 1968; B.S., N.C. Central U., Durham, 1973; M.P.H., U. N.C., Chapel Hill, 1974; cert. health adminstrn. Duke U., 1979; m. Oliver Ezekiel Brown, Aug. 23, 1958; children—Dona Venice, Oliver Ezekiel. Nurse, Duke U. Med. Center, 1963-65, Durham Nurses Registry, 1965-68; tchr. aide Durham City Schs., 1966-67; technician cardiac catherization lab. Duke U., 1968-69, inhalation therapy technician, 1969-72; asst. dir. nursing Lincoln Hosp., Durham, 1974-75, dir. nursing, 1975-76; asso. dir. nursing service Durham County Gen. Hosp., 1976—; bd. dirs. Research Triangle div. Am. Lung Assn. Mem. exec. com. Durham Com. on Affairs for Black People, 1978—; co-chmn. health com. Durham Com. Black Affairs, 1978—; chmn. young adults First Calvary Bapt. Ch., Durham; v.p. Hillside Band Parents Orgn., Durham. Recipient 3 Yrs. Service award Durham County Gen. Hosp., 1975. Mem. Black Women's Polit. Caucus, Vocat. Student Devel. for 57 Club (hon.), Chi Eta Phi (pres. Pi Beta chpt. 1972-73, corr. sec. 1972—), Delta Sigma Theta. Home: 2923 Cedarwood Dr Durham NC 27707 Office: 3643 N Roxboro St Durham NC 27704

BROWN, THOMAS LORENZO, civil engr.; b. Hampton, Va., June 10, 1948; s. John Thomas and Katie Louise (Price) B.; B.S. in Civil Engring., Howard U., 1971; M.S. in Civil Engring., MIT, 1973; postgrad. UCLA, summer 1975. Engr. in tng. Soil Conservation Ser. USDA, Md., Va., Pa., 1967-73; project engr. Soil Testing Sers., Merrifield, Va., 1973-74; asst. project engr. Delon Hampton & Assos., Washington, 1973, project engr. on loan Alyeska Pipeline Service Co., Anchorage, 1975-77; project engr. Woodward Clyde Cons., Rockville, Md., 1977-80; v.p. Hardin Assos. Inc., Pasadena, Md., 1980—; instr. civil engring. Howard U., Washington, 1974—. ALCOA scholar, 1970; Sloan trainee, 1973; registered prof. engr., Va., Md., Washington. Mem. ASCE, Nat. Soc. Profl. Engrs., Soc. Am. Mil. Engrs., Internat. Soc. Soil Mechanics and Found. Engrs., Sigma Xi, Tau Beta Pi, Alpha Phi Omega. Roman Catholic. Home: 1015 N Pegram St Alexandria VA 22304 Office: PO Box 163 Gov Ritchie Hwy Pasadena MD 21122

BROWN, THOMAS PATRICK, educator; b. Jacksonville, Fla., July 29, 1945; s. John William and Modestine (Singletary) S.; B.Sc., Fla. A&M U., 1968; Mus.M., So. Ill. U., 1973. Dir. bands Cairo (Ill.) Jr.-Sr. High Schs., 1970-71, Avona Park (Fla.) Middle Sch., 1969-70; percussionist Jacksonville Symphony Orch., 1971-74; instr. percussion, asst. dir. bands Valley State U., Itta Bena, Miss., 1974-75; asst. band dir., instr. percussion Prairie View (Tex.) A&M U., 1975-76; instr. percussion, asst. band dir., coordinator music merchandising Bethune Cookman Coll., Daytona Beach, Fla., 1978—; founder, mgr. Sesaun Experience Music Prodns., 1973—. Fla. A&M scholar, 1964-68. Mem. Percussive Arts Soc., ASCAP, Am. Fedn. Musicians, NAACP, Kappa Kappa Psi. Methodist. Composer songs. Home: PO Box 41425 Jacksonville FL 32203 Office: Dept Music Bethune Cookman Coll Daytona FL 32015

BROWN, THOMAS TOWNSEND, educator; b. Zanesville, Ohio, Mar. 18, 1905; s. Lewis K. and Mary (Townsend) B.; student Calif. Inst. Tech., 1922-23, Kenyon Coll., 1923-24, Denison U., 1924-25, Bowdoin Coll., 1941; m. Josephine Alberta Beale, Sept. 8, 1927; children—Joseph Townsend, Linda Ann. Lab. asst. electronics research dept. physics Denison U., Granville, Ohio, 1924-25; mem. staff astrophysics research lab. Swazey Obs., Granville, 1926-30; jr. physicist radiation and spectroscopy Naval Research Lab., Washington, 1930-33; state erosion engr. Fed. Emergency Relief Adminstrn., Columbus, Ohio, 1934; asst. adminstr. relief Ohio, dir. fed. student aid, dir. selection CCC, Ohio, 1934-35; research cosmic radiation observations Townsend Brown Found., Zanesville, Ohio, Laguna Beach, Calif., 1936-37; material and process engr. Glenn L. Martin Co., Balt., 1939-40; officer in charge magnetic and acoustic minesweeping research and devel. Bur. Ships, Navy Dept., Washington, 1940-41; radar cons. advanced design sect. Lockheed Aircraft Corp., Burbank, Calif., 1944-45; individual research biophysics, plant growth Island Kauai, Hawaii, 1948-52; cons. physicist Société Nationale Construction Aeronautique, Paris, France, 1955-56; chief cons. research and devel. Whitehall-Rand project Bahnson Co., Winston-Salem, N.C., 1957-58; pres. RAND Internat., Ltd., Nassau, Bahamas, 1958-74, Energy Resources Group, Ltd., Honolulu, 1974-79; with dept. physics U. N.C., Chapel Hill, 1979—. Staff physicist Navy-Princeton Gravity Expdn., W.I., Navy Dept., 1932; physicist Johnson-Smithsonian deep sea expdn., Smithsonian 1933; cons. physicist Pearl Harbor Navy Yard, Honolulu, 1950; cons. Clevite-Brush Electronics Co., Cleve., 1954. Served to lt. comdr. USNR, 1933-43. Fellow AAAS; mem. Soc. Naval Engrs., Physics Soc., Geophys. Union. Address: Dept Physics U NC Chapel Hill NC 28514

BROWN, TRAVIS WALTER, oil drilling equipment co. exec.; b. Oklahoma City, June 18, 1934; s. H. Travis and Una Irene (Robison) B.; B.B.A., Okla. U., 1956; J.D., Oklahoma City U., 1962; m. Marilynn Davis, June 1, 1957; children—Deborah Sue, Travis Carson, Thomas Walter, Darla Lynn. With Geolograph Co., Oklahoma City, 1948—, dir., 1960—, pres., 1963—; pres., gen. mgr. drilling equipment and services div. parent co. Geosource Inc., 1979—; admitted to Okla. bar, 1962; practiced in Oklahoma City, 1962—; pres., dir. Medearis Oil Well Supply Corp.; chmn. bd. Bowman Printing Co., 1977-79; v.p., dir. Geolograph Service Ltd. (Can.); sec., dir. Robinwood Farms Ltd.; dir. Okla. Beef Inc., chmn. bd. Geolograph Medearis Service (U.K.) Ltd., London, Aberdeen and Singapore. Pres., Oakdale Sch. Assn., 1975-77. Served to lt. (j.g.) USNR, 1956-58. Named to Am. Cattleman's Hall of Fame, 1979. Mem. Okla. County Cattlemans Assn. (pres. 1975), Palomino Horse Breeders Am. (nat. v.p. 1977—, nat. youth dir. 1973-78), Okla. Palomino Exhibitors Assn. (state youth dir., v.p. 1972-79, pres. 1979—), Internat., Okla. (sec. 1979) brangus breeders assns., Am., Okla. quarter horse assns., Am. Petroleum Inst., Internat. Assn. Drilling Contractors, Am. Inst. Mining, Metall. and Petroleum Engrs., Soc. Petroleum Engrs., Canadian Diamond Drilling Assn., Am. Mining Congress, Canadian Inst. Mining, Nat. Water Well Assn., Ind. Petroleum Assn. Am., Am., Okla. bar assns., Okla. Poultry Fedn., World Cochin Family. Clubs: Cosmopolitan Internat. Civic (internat. pres. 1972-73, Distinguished Service awards 1963-64, 66-67), Oklahoma City U. Alumni (dir.). Co-author: Subsurface Geology, 1976. Contbr. articles to profl. jours. Home: Route 1 Box 154 Oklahoma City OK 73131 Office: PO Box 25246 Oklahoma City OK 73125

BROWN, W(ILLIAM) RAY, city ofcl.; b. Dillon, S.C., July 2, 1948; s. Ernest and Lilly Kate (Ray) McKenzie; B.A., U. S.C., 1972, M.P.A., 1974; m. Elaine Ann Wheeler, Mar. 19, 1977. Dir. govtl. mgmt. Santee-Lynches Council for Govt., Sumter, S.C., 1975-76; classification and compensation analyst S.C. State Personnel Div., Columbia, S.C., 1976-77; adminstr. Clarendon County, Manning, S.C., 1977-78, City of Manning, 1978—. Mem. Santee Lynches region 208 Water Quality Adv. Com., 1978—. Treas. bd. dirs. Salvation Army, 1979. Served with USNR, 1965-71, 74-76; with USMCR, 1971-72, 79-80. Recipient Young Man of Am. award U.S. Jaycees, 1978, Presdl. cert. for community achievement to Vietnam era vet., 1979. Mem. Internat. City Mgmt. Assn., Am. Soc. for Public Adminstrn., Academy Polit. Sci. Presbyterian. Clubs: Masons, Rotary. Home: 611 Major Dr Manning SC 29102 Office: City Hall PO Box 546 N Brooks ST Manning SC 29102

BROWN, WALTER JACK, hosp. adminstr.; b. Andersonville, Ga., Mar. 3, 1941; s. Gordon Lee and Irene (Ferguson) B.; diploma Ga. Mil. Coll., 1961; B.B.A., Auburn U., 1963; grad. Dale Carnegie Course, 1972; m. Gail Sterne Hendry, Dec. 27, 1969; children—Anthony Jack, Kristin Gail. Dept. purchasing supr. Westinghouse Electric Corp., Athens, Ga., 1966-74, Bloomington, Ind., 1974-75; dir. procurement services Richland Meml. Hosp., Columbia, S.C., 1975-78; purchasing mgr. Look Products, Millen, Ga., 1978-80; materials mgr. Our Lady of Lourdes Hosp., Lafayette, La., 1980—; grad. asst. Dale Carnegie Course, 1973; regional dir. Carolinas Affiliated Purchasing Program. Served with U.S. Army, 1963-66. Mem. Am. Hosp. Assn., Purchasing-Mgmt. Assn. Carolinas-Va., S.C. Hosp. Assn. Methodist. Home: 155 Mimosa Pl Lafayette LA 70506

BROWN, WARREN JOSEPH, physician; b. Bklyn., July 17, 1924; s. Benjamin Oscar and Angela Marie (Cahill) B.; student Ursinus Coll., 1942-43; B.S., Bethany Coll., 1945; M.D., Ohio State U., 1949; m. Greet Roos, July 3, 1969; children—Warren James, Robert E., Suzanne J., Annemarie, Eric Jan. Reporter, Pottstown (Pa.) Mercury, 1942-43; intern U.S. Naval Hosp., Long Beach, Calif., Oceanside, Calif.; resident Pottstown Hosp., 1950-51; asso. Roos Loos Med. Group, Alhambra, Calif., 1951 pvt. family practice, Largo, Fla., 1953—; sr. civilian flight surgeon FAA, 1964—; pres. Aero-Med. Consultants, Inc., Largo, 1969—. Historian, Fla. Aviation Hist. Soc., 1978-80, St. Petersburg-Clearwater-Tampa Hangar, Order of Quiet Birdmen, 1969-80. Served with USN, 1943-45, 49-50, 51-53. Diplomate Am. Bd. Family Practice. Fellow Am. Acad. Family Physicians; mem. Pinellas County Med. Assn., Fla. Med. Assn., Fla. Pilots Assn., Aircraft Owners and Pilots Assn. Christian. Author: Florida's Aviation History, 1983; Child Yank Over the Rainbow, 1977; Patients' Guide to Medicine, 8th edit., 1978. Home: 14607 Brewster Dr Largo FL 33540 Office: 10912 Hamlin Blvd Largo FL 33540

BROWN, WENDELL WELLS, elec. engr.; b. E. Smithfield, Pa., Sept. 3, 1934; s. Francis Gardener and Threse Anna (Bailey) B.; A.A.S., SUNY, Alfred, 1960; B.S., Tri-State U., Angola, Ind., 1962; M.S., Mich. State U., 1966; m. Marylyn Sue Landon, June 25, 1960; children—Diane, Donna, Doris, Dawn. Elec. technician Westinghouse Corp., Elmira, N.Y., 1960; with IBM, 1962—, successively jr. engr., asso. engr., sr. asso. engr., Endicott, N.Y., 1962-67, staff engr., E. Fishkill, N.Y., 1967-69, adv. engr., devel. engr., Boca Raton, Fla., 1969-79, sr. engr., mgr. new systems architecture advanced devel., 1979—. Bd. dirs. Bibletown Community Ch., Boca Raton, 1975-76. Served with U.S. Army, 1954-56. NSF fellow, 1965. Mem. IEEE. Republican. Patentee in field. Home: 830 NW 6th Dr Boca Raton FL 33432 Office: IBM 51st St Boca Raton FL 33432

BROWN, WILLARD RICHARD, lawyer, banker; b. Scipio, Utah, July 25, 1909; s. George Ernest and Susan (Yates) B.; A.B., U. Utah, 1934; LL.B., Columbia, 1937; m. Mary Scull Jacoby, Nov. 24, 1948; children—Bowman, Barton, James Ralph, John Scull, Katharine Creevey. Admitted to N.Y. bar, 1938, Fla. bar, 1950; asso. Shearman & Sterling, N.Y.C., 1939-44; trust officer Chem. Bank & Trust Co., N.Y.C., 1944-50; v.p., sr. trust officer First Nat. Bank, Miami, Fla., 1950-61; partner Shutts & Bowen, attys., Miami, 1961—. Pres., S.E. Fla. Estate Planning Council, 1959-60. Trustee J.D. Shatford Meml. Trust Assn., Halifax, N.S., Can. Mem. Am., Fla., bar assns., Corp. Fiduciaries Assn. (pres. S.E. Fla. 1957), Fla. Bankers Assn. (past chmn. trust div., founder, trustee, instr. trust tng. sch.), Kappa Sigma, Phi Alpha Delta. Episcopalian. Kiwanian. Clubs: Church, The Pilgrims (N.Y.C.); Riviera Country, Century (Coral Gables, Fla); Ocean Reef (Key Largo, Fla.). Contbr. articles to law jours. Home: 3720 Harlano St Coral Gables FL 33134 Office: Southeast First Nat Bank Bldg Miami FL 33131

BROWN, WILLIAM CRAWFORD, educator; b. Charles City County, Va., June 3, 1930; s. Michael and Lena Brown; B.S., Hampton Inst., 1950; M.A., N.Y. U., 1952, Ed.D., 1960; postgrad. (Econs. in Action fellow), Case-Western Res., summer 1961, William and Mary Coll. Grad. Sch. Bus., 1973-75; m. Jessie Lemon, Dec. 9, 1950; Tchr. public schs., Balt., 1951-52, Newport News, Va., 1952-55; mem. faculty Hampton (Va.) Inst., 1955-65, 66—, prof., 1966—, dir. Project Step, 1966-75, dir. Small Bus. Devel. Center, 1976—; dir. Sch. Bus. Prairie View (Tex.) A&M U., 1965-66. Pres., Peninsula Pan Hellenic. Mem. Nat. Bus. League (Peninsula cons., chmn. Peninsula chpt. 1962-65), Am. Mktg. Assn., So. Mktg. Assn., AAUP, Peninsula Bus. League, Smithsonian Instn., Peninsula C. of C. (adv. com. on consumer affairs), Alpha Phi Alpha (fin. sec. Delta Beta Lambda chpt.), Kappa Delta Pi, Phi Delta Kappa, Delta Pi Epsilon. Author: Building a Model Academic Business Program at Hampton Institute, 1980. Office: Sch Bus Hampton Institute Hampton VA 23668

BROWN, WILLIAM DAVID, educator; b. Shreveport, La., Dec. 26, 1922; s. Percy Edgerton and Dulcie (Mobley) B.; B.A., La. Poly. U., 1943; M.A., La. State U., 1948; postgrad. Amherst Coll., 1943-44, Morehead State U., 1969; m. Susan Harte, June 5, 1949; children—Elizabeth, William David, Rebecca, Sarah, Louise, Philip, Ellen. State editor Delta Democrat Times, Greenville, Miss., 1947-52, mng. editor, 1952-60, asso. editor, 1960-62; mng. editor Pascagoula (Miss.) Chronicle, 1962-63, editor, 1963-64; copy editor Louisville Times, 1964-66; asst. prof. journalism Morehead (Ky.) State U., 1966-76, asso. prof., 1976—, coordinator journalism program, 1967—; Time, Inc., UPI, 1951-64. Served with U.S. Army, World War II. Mem. Lambda Chi Alpha, Sigma Tau Delta, Sigma Delta Chi. Democrat. Presbyterian. Editor Miss. sect. Colliers Ency., 1966. Home: Route 5 Box 384 Morehead KY 40351 Office: Morehead State U Morehead KY 40351

BROWN, WILLIAM KNOX, physician; b. Austin, Tex., July 31, 1920; s. Joseph Chenoweth and Elva (Trueheart) B.; B.A., Rice U., 1943; M.D., U. Va., 1947; m. Eleanor Randolph Brooks, Jan. 13, 1952; children—Armstead Brooks, Polly Randolph, Philip Minor. Postgrad. fellow, instr. Southwestern Med. Sch. of U. Tex., Dallas, 1947-52; practice medicine specializing in internal medicine, Houston, 1954—; asso. clin. prof. internal medicine Baylor Coll. Medicine, 1972—; cons. to dept. ophthalmology, 1956-71; mem. staff Meth. Hosp. Served to capt. M.C., U.S. Army, 1952-54; Korea. Diplomate Am. Bd. Internal Medicine. Mem. AMA, A.C.P., Tex., So. med. assns., Am. Soc. Internal Medicine. Republican. Episcopalian. Club: Bayou (Houston). Home: 30 Saddlebrook Houston TX 77024 Office: 340 Hermann Profl Bldg Houston TX 77030

BROWN, WILLIAM RUSSELL, lawyer; b. Holly Springs, Miss., July 5, 1914; s. Horace Brightberry and Aileen (Blackburn) B.; B.B.A., LL.B., U. Tex., 1937; m. Ruth Cunningham, Apr. 19, 1941; children—Betsy (Mrs. Thomas M. Smith III), Virginia, Russell. Admitted to Tex. bar, 1937, since practiced in Houston; asso. firm Baker, Botts, Andrews & Wharton (now Baker & Botts), 1937—, partner, 1948—; gen. counsel, dir. Houston Industries Inc., Houston Lighting & Power Co.; dir. Primary Fuels, Inc., Utility Fuels, Inc. Served to lt. USNR, 1943-45. Decorated Bronze Star. Fellow Tex. Bar Found.; mem. Am. (mem. council pub. utility sect. 1974-77), Tex. (mem. council pub. utility sect. 1976-77), Houston bar assns. Democrat. Episcopalian. Clubs: Houston, Houston Country. Home: 5816 Bayou Glen Rd Houston TX 77057 Office: 29th Floor One Shell Plaza Houston TX 77002

BROWN, WILLIS ELLSWORTH, JR., neurosurgeon, educator; b. Ann Arbor, Mich., Dec. 12, 1938; s. Willis Ellsworth and Dorothy Ethel (Anderson) B.; B.A., Vanderbilt U., 1960, M.D., 1963; m. Elizabeth Ann Bliedung, Dec. 28, 1960; children—Willis Ellsworth III, Lisa Ann. Intern Vanderbilt U. Hosp., Nashville, 1963-64, resident in gen. surgery, 1964-65; resident, fellow in neurosurgery U. Minn. Hosp., Mpls., 1968-73; instr. neurosurgery U. Minn., 1973-74; asst. prof. neurosurgery Med. Sch., U. Tex., San Antonio, 1974-80, asso. prof., 1980—; chief neurosurgery Audie Murphy VA Hosp., San Antonio, 1974—. Vestry, St. Luke's Episcopal Parish, San Antonio, 1977—, sr. warden, 1979, bd. dirs. parish sch., 1977—, pres.-elect sch., 1979; bd. dirs. Good Samaritan Center, San Antonio, 1977—; trustee Tex. Mil. Inst., San Antonio, 1980—. Served as sr. asst. surgeon USPHS, 1965-68. Recipient Roche award, 1961, Founders medal Vanderbilt U., 1963. Diplomate Am. Bd. Neurol. Surgery. Fellow A.C.S., William T. Peyton Soc.; mem. Bexar County (Tex.) Med. Soc., Tex. Med. Assn., AMA, San Antonio Surg. Soc., Tex. Assn. Neurol. Surgeons, Congress Neurol. Surgeons, Am. Assn. Neurol. Surgeons, Soc. Univ. Neurosurgeons, Am. Neurosurg. Soc., So. Neurosurg. Soc., Phi Beta Kappa, Alpha Omega Alpha. Episcopalian. Club: Oak Hills Country. Asso. editor Clinical Neurosurgery, Vols. 24 and 25. Research on brain tumors, cerebrovascular disease. Home: 7523 Shady Ln San Antonio TX 78209 Office: 7703 Floyd Curl Dr San Antonio TX 78284

BROWN, WILSON GORDON, physician, educator; b. Bosworth, Mo., Jan. 18, 1914; s. Arthur Grannison and Clemma (Frock) B.; A.B., William Jewell Coll., 1935; M.D., Washington U., St. Louis, 1939; m. Anne Buckalew, Oct. 25, 1940; 1 son, Gordon Alan. Intern pathology Barnes Hosp., St. Louis, Mo., 1939-40; resident pathology St. Louis City Hosp., 1940-41; instr. pathology Washington U., 1945-51; clin. asso. prof. Baylor U. Coll. Medicine, Houston, 1951—; clin. prof. U. Tex. Med. Sch. at Houston, 1972—. Pathologist, dir. labs. Hermann Hosp., Houston, 1951-71; dir. labs. Twelve Oaks Hosp., Houston, 1965—, Polly Ryon Hosp., Richmond, Tex., 1954—, Park Plaza Hosp., Houston, 1975—; partner Brown & Assos. Med. Labs., Houston, 1954—. Mem. adv. bd. Living Bank, Houston, 1968—; founding mem. Mus. Med. Sci., Houston, 1969—, trustee, 1969—, pres. bd. trustees, 1974-75. Bd. dirs. Ewing Center Inc., Am. Cancer Soc. Harris County (Tex.) Br., 1952, pres., 1967-68. Served to maj., M.C., AUS, 1942-46. ETO, MTO. Decorated Bronze Star medal. Diplomate Am. Bd. Clin. Pathology, Am. Bd. Anatomic Pathology. Mem. Am., Tex. med. assns., Harris County Med. Soc., Coll. Am. Pathologists, Am. Soc. Clin. Pathology, Houston, Tex. socs. pathologists, Sigma Xi, Beta Beta Beta, Theta Chi Delta, Aeons, Phi Gamma Delta. Club: Warwick (Houston). Contbr. articles to various med. publs. Home: 3518 Westridge St Houston TX 77025 Office: 165 Hermann Profl Bldg Houston TX 77025

BROWNE, ALICE PAULINE, accountant; b. Topeka, June 26, 1918; d. James Paul and Alice Bertha (Crabb) Sweeney; B.B.A., U. Miami, (Fla.), 1975; student Atlanta Law Sch.; m. Raymond Smetzer, Jan. 4, 1948; children—Gerald E. Smetzer, Raymond Smetzer, Jonathan Smetzer, Patricia Alice Smetzer Gibson. Owner, operator Smetzer Airport and Restaurant, Castalia, Ohio, 1948-58; legal sec. 3d Dist., Appellate Ct., Toledo, 1958-63; legal sec. firm Nat Williams and Marx Faber, Miami 1963-73; med. transcriber Drs. Hosp., Miami, 1973-75; pvt. practice tax cons., Miami, 1948—; instr. in field; treas. Lucas County Credit Union, Toledo, 1962-63. Deaconess Coral Congregational Ch., 1963-69. Mem. Christian Pilots Assn., Ga. Trial Lawyers Assn., Delta Theta Phi, Phi Lambda Pi. Democrat. Contbr. articles to profl. jours. Home and office: 2025 Peachtree Rd NE Apt 539 Atlanta GA 30309

BROWNE, HENRY JAMES, architect; b. Hamden, Conn., Apr. 28, 1932; s. Henry Alexander and Alice (Lord) B.; B.S. in Arch., U. Va., 1955; m. Ellen Adelaide Allison Browne, Dec. 19, 1957; children—Tracy Allison, Leslie Lord, Kari Alexander. Mem. firm Granger & Gillespie, Syracuse, N.Y., 1957-58, Milton L. Grigg, Charlottesville, Va., 1958-63, Grigg, Wood & Browne, Charlottesville, 1963-75; partner Grigg, Wood, Browne, Eichman & Dalgliesh, Charlottesville, 1975—; dir. Guarantee Savs. & Loan Assn., 1978—; cons. U.S. Banknote Corp., 1973—, U.S. Tech. Devel. Sales Co., 1973—, Holywell Corp., Washington, 1976—. Bd. dirs. Downtown Charlottesville, Inc., 1970-75, pres., 1973-75; dist. adv. council SBA, 1970-72; co-founder Citizens for Albemarle, 1973. Served to 1st lt. C.E., U.S. Army, 1955-57. Recipient Gold medal in arch. Alpha Rho Chi, 1955. Mem. Albemarle County Hist. Soc., Assn. of Preservation Tech., Soc. Archtl. Historians, AIA (chpt. treas. 1970-71, pres. 1973-74), Nat. Com. Hist. Resources, Nat. Archtl. Accreditation Bd., U. Va. Alumni Assn. Republican. Christian Scientist. Clubs: Farmington Country, Torch, Redlands. Home: 2 Oak Circle Charlottesville VA 22901 Office: 206 5th St NE Charlottesville VA 22901

BROWNE, JAMES HOUSTON, chem. mfg. co. exec.; b. El Paso, Tex., Oct. 13, 1928; s. Lewis Edwin Joel and Jean Houston (Lindsey) B.; B.S.Ch.E., U. Colo., 1950, B.S. in Bus., 1950; m. Jane Whistler, June 10, 1950; children—James Marquiss, Roxanne. Plant supr. Monsanto Co., Texas City, Tex., 1951-56, plant tech. service, engr., 1958-65, project mgmt. process design, St. Louis, 1965-74; regional mgr. process engring. Olin Corp., Lake Charles, La., 1974-78, regional mgr. project engring. and constrn., 1978—. Registered profl. engr., Tex., La. Mem. Am. Inst. Chem. Engrs., La. Engring. Soc. Episcopalian. Club: Lake Charles Country. Home: 28 Riverridge Rd Lake Charles LA 70605 Office: Olin Corp Box 2896 Lake Charles LA 70602

BROWNE, WALTER BROACH, motivational communications co. exec.; b. St. Louis, Feb. 26, 1938; s. Henry Silas and Willie Myers B.; A.A. with high distinction (English scholar), Mesa Community Coll., 1968; B.A. (Rotary student), Grand Canyon Coll., 1970; M.S.L.S., U, Ky., 1971; m. Virginia Starr Lund, Dec. 30, 1959; children—William Henry, Michael Myers, Joly Starr, Elizabeth Starr. Asst. dir. Pike-Amite Library System, McComb, Miss., 1971-73; dir. NE Regional Library, Corinth, Miss. 1973-79; pres. Nat. Growth Industries, Memphis, 1979—; motivational speaker; condr. success seminars, personality devel., sales tng. Treas. Corinth Theatre Arts, 1975-77; pres. Presbyn. Men's Group, 1979; state coordinator Spl. Arts Fair, 1978; bd. dirs. United Way. Served with U.S. Army, 1958-60. Named outstanding librarian in Miss., 1973. Mem. ALA, Miss. Library Assn. (treas. 1974), Miss. Public Library Assn. (pres. 1975), C. of C. Clubs: Rotary (state highway com.), Toastmasters, Mensa Rosicrucians. Home: 1504 Cruise St Corinth MS 38834 Office: 1133 Wheaton St Memphis TN 38117

BROWNING, CARROLL WELLES, ophthalmologist; b. Springfield, Ill., Sept. 2, 1916; s. Cornelius Alfred and Mabel Clifton (Welles) B.; student U. Chgo., 1938-40; B.S., U. Ill., 1940, M.D., 1943; children—Ronald, Betty, Kathy. Intern, Garfield Meml. Hosp., Chgo., 1944; resident U. Ill. Eye and Ear Infirmary, Chgo., 1947-50; chmn., prof. dept. ophthalmology U. Tex. Med. Sch., Dallas, 1953-63, clin. prof., 1963—; adminstr. Oak Cliff Eye Center, Dallas, 1970—; chief dept. ophthalmology Parkland City-County Hosp., Dallas, 1953-63. Served to capt. M.C., U.S. Army, 1944-46. Mem. Am. Acad. Ophthalmology, AMA, A.C.S., Tex. Med. Assn., Tex. Assn. Ophthalmology, Dallas Acad. Ophthalmology, Dallas County Med. Soc. Home: 4242 Shorecrest Dr Dallas TX 75209 Office: 836 N Zang Blvd Dallas TX 75208

BROWNING, CHAUNCEY H., JR., state ofcl.; b. Charleston, W.Va., Nov. 21, 1934; s. Chauncey H. and Evelyn (Mahone) B.; A.B., W.Va. U., 1956, LL.B., 1958; children—Chauncey H. III, Charles Preston, Steven Thomas; m. Patricia Ann Lewis. Law clk. U.S. Dist. Ct. for So. Dist. W.Va., 1958; atty.-in-charge Legal Aid Soc. Kanawha and Putnam Counties, 1959-60; practiced in Charleston, 1958-62; commr. pub. instns. State of W.Va., 1962-68; atty. gen. State of W.Va., 1968—; mem. Presdl. Commn. for Rev. Antitrust Laws and Procedures. Mem. Nat. Assn. Attys. Gen. (pres. 1978-79), Am., W.Va., Kanawha County bar assns., W.Va. State Bar, W.Va. Trial Lawyers Assn., Order of Coif, Phi Delta Phi, Kappa Sigma. Former editor W.Va. Law Quar. Office: Capitol Bldg Charleston WV 25305

BROWNING, DAVID E., JR., physician; b. Texarkana, Tex., June 18, 1935; s. David and Lamena (Nichols) B.; A.B., Princeton U., 1957; M.D., Baylor U., 1961; m. Ann Lynn Harvey, Nov. 18, 1961; children—Lynnley Elisabeth, David Mark, Jared Jonathan. Intern, Jefferson Davis Hosp., Houston, 1961-62; resident Baylor U., Houston, 1965-67; practice medicine specializing in internal medicine, Tulsa, 1968—; pres. Diagnostic Physicians of Tulsa, Inc., 1972—. Served with M.C., USNR, 1962-65. Diplomate Am. Bd. Internal Medicine. Mem. Tulsa County Med. Soc. (pres. 1980), Am. Soc. Artificial Internal Organs, Am. Soc. Nephrology, A.C.P. Republican. Episcopalian. Club: Tulsa. Home: 1103 E 19th St Tulsa OK 74120 Office: 820 Kelly Bldg 6565 S Yale St Tulsa OK 74177

BROWNLEE, BOBBY GENE, mech. engr.; b. W. Monroe, La., Jan. 8, 1932; s. Henry Grady and Anna Mae (Hammond) B.; B.S.M.E., Tri-State U., 1957; m. Gail Church Habley, Jan. 28, 1961; children—Sarah Megan, Elizabeth Gail. Design engr. Ex-Cell-O Corp., Costa Mesa, Calif., 1958-60; test engr. Lockheed Missiles and Space Co., Sunnyvale, Calif., 1961-67, quality assurance specialist, 1967-69, supr., 1970-76, mgr. quality engring. Polaris Missile Facility, Goose Creek, S.C., 1976—. Served with USN, 1951-55. Mem. Am. Soc. Quality Control, Nat. Mgmt. Assn. Republican. Episcopalian. Home: 12 Sabina Ct Hanahan SC 29405

BROWNSON, CHARLES BRUCE, editor, publisher, govt. relations exec.; b. Jackson, Mich., Feb. 5, 1914; s. Charles Matthew and Helen Gray (Oxby) B.; A.B., U. Mich., 1935; LL.B., Butler U., 1955; m. Christine Phyllis Augspurger, Oct. 22, 1938; children—Nancy Gray Corazzo, Judith Anne Garrelts, Charles Christopher; m. 2d, Anna Louise Harshman, Nov. 23, 1966; children—Dwight C., Bruce B., Guy David, Catharine Andrea Lunsford, Scott Malcolm. Pres., Central Wallpaper & Paint Corp., Indpls., 1936-59; mem. 82d-85th Congresses from 11th Dist. Ind.; asst. commr. pub. affairs and congl. liaison Housing and Home Finance Agy., Washington, 1959-60; founder, editor, publisher Congl. Staff Directory, Washington, 1959—; prin. Charles Brownson Assos. pub. and govt. relations, 1960—; profl. asso. East-West Center Seminar Pacific Prospects in Global Perspective, 1978, Energy and Growth Problems, 1978; participant Johnson Found. Seminars U.S. and UN, Racine, Wis., 1977; accredited observer Zimbabwe-Rhodesian elections, 1979. Served to lt. col. AUS, 1941-45, col. USAR. Decorated Legion Merit, Medaille de Reconnaissance (France); recipient Outstanding Young Man award Indpls. Jr. C. of C., 1947. Mem. Former Mems. Congress (pres. 1978-79), Pub. Relations Soc. Am., Fusaliers (charter pres. 1972-77), Internat. Oceanographic Found., Fairchild Tropical Gardens Assn., Nat. Trust Historic Preservation, Washington Direct Mktg. Assn. (dir. 1973-75), Smithsonian Assos., Assn. Corcoran Galleries, Gunston Hall Neighbors Assn., Am. Film Inst., Indiana Soc. Washington, Fla. State Soc. Washington, Sigma Nu. Republican. Presbyterian. Clubs: Masons, Indpls. Athletic. Home: 4748 Neptune Dr Yacht Haven Alexandria VA 22309 also 1261 S Alhambra Circle Coral Gables FL 33146 Office: 6911 Richmond Hwy Alexandria VA 22306

BROWNSON, ROBERT HENRY, med. edn. research; b. Evanston, Ill., Mar. 14, 1925; s. Walter Converse and Martha Virginia (White) B.; B.S., John Carroll U., 1948; M.S., George Washington U., 1950, Ph.D., 1953; m. Carol Ann Priestaf, June 15, 1957; children—Michael R., Patrick S., Barbara L., Timothy T. Instr. anatomy U. So. Calif. Med. Sch., 1952-54; asst. prof. anatomy Med. Coll. Va., 1954-62, asso. prof., 1962-64, prof., 1966-67, prof., chmn. dept., 1967-68; vis. prof., postdoctoral NIH fellow Donner Lab., Lawrence Radiation Lab., U. Calif., Berkeley, 1964-66; prof., vice-chmn. human anatomy Sch. Medicine, U. Calif., Davis, 1968-78; prof., chmn. dept. human anatomy Eastern Va. Sch. Medicine, Norfolk, 1978—; vis. prof. dept. anatomy U. Helsinki (Finland), 1974. Served with USNR, 1943-46; capt. Res., comdt.'s rep. Med. Sch., 11th Naval Dist., 1955—. Mem. Am. Assn. Anatomists, Am. Assn. Neuropathologists, Am. Acad. Neurology, Radiation Research Soc., Electron Microscopy Soc. Am., Sigma Xi, Phi Chi. Author articles in field. Home: 2417 Trant Lake Dr Virginia Beach VA 23454 Office: PO Box 1980 Norfolk VA 23501

BROXSON, JOHN RAY, ins. agt., real estate broker; b. Holley, Fla., June 10, 1932; s. Bart Dell and Annie Rachel (Gordon) B.; B.S., S.W. Assemblies of God Coll., 1954; M.A., U. W. Fla., 1974; m. Christina Rose Cissna, June 4, 1954; children—Sylvia June, John Robert, Cheryl Rose, Bart James, Angela Christina. Owner, founder John Broxson & Assos., Gulf Breeze, Fla., 1964—; sheriff, Santa Rosa County, Fla., 1959-61; mem. Fla. Ho. of Reps., 1962-64; mem. Fla. Senate, 1966-72. Chmn. Gov.'s Adv. Council on Criminal Justice, Region 1; v.p. U. W. Fla. Found.; bd. dirs. Southeastern Coll. Assemblies of God Coll. Mem. Pensacola Bd. Realtors (pres. 1978, dir.), Pensacola Assn. Life Underwriters. Home: 2655 Delmar St Gulf Breeze FL 32561 Office: 31 Hoffman Dr Gulf Breeze FL 32561

BROYLES, ROBERT GEORGE, town ofcl.; b. Onalinda, Pa., June 21, 1930; s. George Warren and Mary Jane (Hale) B.; A.A., Am. U., 1961, B.S. in Pub. Adminstrn., 1965; m. Donna Elizabeth Boland, Nov. 24, 1950; children—James, Beth Ann, Donya Rae. Mem. Police Dept., Altoona, Pa., 1954-56, Arlington County, Va., 1956-66; public safety adviser to Republic of South Vietnam, 1966-68; chief of police, Williamsburg, Pa., 1969, South Whitehall Twp., Pa., 1969-74, Town of Blacksburg (Va.), 1974—; lectr. police sci. New River Community Coll., Dublin, Va. Served with USN, 1952-54. Recipient Vietnamese Police Medal of Honor, 1968; medal for Civilian Ser. in Vietnam, U.S. Govt., 1968. Mem. Internat. Assn. Chiefs of Police, Va. Assn. Chiefs of Police, Nat. Assn. Chiefs of Police. Methodist. Club: Masons. Home: 1107 Golfview Dr Blacksburg VA 24060 Office: Town of Blacksburg 300 S Main St Blacksburg VA 24060

BRUBAKER, LOWELL LEE, educator; b. Johnstown, Pa., Feb. 15, 1943; s. Richard C. and Gladys M. (Blough) B.; B.S., Juniata Coll., 1965; M.S., Western Reserve U., 1967; Ph.D., U. Tex., 1970; m. Susan Elizabeth Bruell, June 14, 1969. Programmer asso. Devereux Found., Devon, Pa., 1964-65; teaching asst. Case Western Res. U., Cleve., 1967; asst. prof. Tenn. Wesleyan Coll., Athens, 1970-73, asso. prof., 1973-77, prof., chmn. Dept. Behavioral Scis., 1977—; vis. scientist Tenn. Acad. Sci., 1976-79; dir. training McMinn-Meigs Contact, 1976—. Mem. McMinn-Meigs Multi-Disciplinary Child Abuse team, 1978—; mem. Tenn. task force on drug and alcohol abuse, 1973-74. NDEA fellow, 1965-67; Russell Sage Found. fellow, 1968-70; USPHS research grantee, 1976. Mem. Am. Psychol. Assn., Southeastern Psychol. Assn., Soc. for Study of Evolution, Behavior Genetics Assn. Ch. of the Brethren. Contbr. articles in field to profl. jours. Home: 511 Guille St Athens TN 37303 Office: PO Box 40 Tenn Wesleyan College Athens TN 37303

BRUCE, PATRICIA ELLEN, educator; b. Roanoke Rapids, N.C., June 26, 1940: d. Shirrell Houston and Dorothy Elizabeth (Fadeley) Norton; student Old Dominion U., 1975; div.; children—Regina Lynn, Cynthia Louise, James Crandall. Vocat. tchr. Wards Corner Beauty Acad., Norfolk, Va., 1966-72; cosmetologist spl. services Little Creek Amphibious Base, Norfolk, 1973-75; retarded children's tchr. A, Southeastern Va. Tng. Center, Chesapeake, 1975—. Mem. Am. Assn. Mental Deficiencies, Tidewater Council for Learning Disabilities. Home: 1617 Janke Rd Virginia Beach VA 23455 Office: 2100 Steppingstone Sq Chesapeake VA 23320

BRUCE, RUFUS ELBRIDGE, JR., physicist, educator; b. New Orleans, Mar. 20, 1966; s. Rufus E. and Lucy A. (Salles) B.; B.S., La. State U., 1949; M.S., Okla. State U., 1962, Ph.D., 1966; m. Beverly F. Bond, Oct. 6, 1951; children—Rebecca F., Allison, Lucy A., Annadora Safety engr. Liberty Mut. Ins. Co., New Orleans, 1951-52, Jackson, Miss., 1952-53, sales rep., 1953-55, resident mgr., Shreveport, La., 1955-58; ind. sales ins., Monroe, La., 1958-59; instr. math. N.E. La. State U., Monroe, 1959-60; research asst. physics Okla. State U., Stillwater, 1960-65; head dept. math. and physics Ark. State U., Jonesboro, 1965-66; faculty U. Tex., El Paso, 1966—, prof. physics, 1976—; research physicist Electronics Command, U.S. Army, 1967-69; cons. in field. Exec. com. El Paso County Republican party, Tex., 1970-79, precinct chmn., 1970-72; mem. liaison com. Mayor of City of El Paso, 1975-77; bd. dirs. United Way of El Paso, 1976-79, El Paso chpt. NCCJ, 1977—. Served with USNR, 1943-45. NASA fellow, 1964, 70. Mem. Sigma Xi, Phi Delta Theta, Epsilon Pi. Roman Catholic. Research on radioactive transfer, planetary atmospheres, interferomatric optical techniques, atmospheric remote probing. Office: Physics Dept U Tex at El Paso El Paso TX 79969

BRUCE, WILLIAM RANKIN, ins. co. exec.; b. Columbia, S.C., Oct. 18, 1915; s. Charles Joy and Anna (Rankin) B.; B.S. in Commerce, U. S.C., 1937; m. Jane Parsley Emerson, Jan. 12, 1946; children—William Rankin, Jane Emerson, Charles Joy. With Seibels Bruce & Co., Columbia, 1937—, v.p., 1958-66, pres., 1966—, also dir.; pres., dir. S.C. Ins. Co., Consol. Am. Ins. Co., Catawba Ins. Co., Argus Life Ins. Co., Investors Nat. Life Ins. Co., Premium Service Corp. Columbia, 1966—; pres., chief exec. officer Seibels Bruce Group Inc.; dir. Am. Agy. Inc., Louisville, Ky. Ins. Co., Louisville, Seibels, Bruce Policy Mgmt. Systems Ltd. Toronto, S.C. Fed. Savs. and Loan Assn., Columbia, First Service Corp. S.C., Service Mortgage Corp., S.C. Electric & Gas Co.; mem. Columbia adv. bd. S.C. Nat. Bank. Served to lt. comdr. USNR, 1941-45. Mem. Nat. Assn. Mng. Gen. Agts. (pres. 1966-67), Columbia C. of C., Columbia Ball Soc. (pres. 1963). Clubs: Forest Lake (pres. 1967-68), Palmetto, Summit. Home: 4367 Chicora St Columbia SC 29206 Office: 1501 Lady St Columbia SC 29201 also PO Box 1 Columbia SC 29202

BRUENE, WARREN BENZ, electronics engr.; b. Beaman, Iowa, Nov. 1, 1916; s. Fred K. and Luella L. (Benz) B.; B.S., Iowa State U., 1938; m. Mildred Clare Meyer, July 13, 1941; children—Julia Beth Bruene Thomas, Jo Carol Bruene Lilley. Design engr. Collins Radio Co. (became div. Rockwell Internat. Co. 1971), Cedar Rapids, Iowa, 1939-64, Richardson, Tex., 1964—, group head, 1953-58, div. tech. cons., 1958-60, asst. div. dir., 1960-61, sr. tech. cons., 1961-64, Dallas div., 1964—, sr. engring. tech. staff Collins Telecommunications Systems div., 1964—; dir. Taxlogic Corp. Mem. Richardson Community Concert Bd., 1970-74. Named Engr. of Year, Tex. Soc. Profl. Engrs., 1975. Registered profl. engr., Tex. Fellow IEEE (chmn. sect. 1958, dir. region 1962), Nat., Tex. (dir. Preston Trails chpt. 1975-77) socs. profl. engrs., Nat. Mgmt. Assn., Armed Forces Communication and Electronics Assn. Republican. Methodist. Author: Single-band Principles and Circuits, 1964; contbg. author to handbooks. Patentee in field. Home: 7805 Chattington Dr Dallas TX 75248 Office: 1200 N Alma Rd MS 401-132 Richardson TX 75080

BRUFF, BEVERLY OLIVE, assn. adminstr.; b. San Antonio, Dec. 15, 1926; d. Albert Griffith and Hazel Olive (Smith) Bruff; B.A., H. Sophie Newcomb Coll., 1948; postgrad. Our Lady of the Lake Coll., 1956, Okla. Center for Continuing Edn., 1960-70. Asst. dir. New Orleans Theatre Guild, 1948-50; dist. dir. San Antonio Area Council, Girl Scouts U.S.A., 1958-70, pub. relations dir., 1970—. Mem. Council of Presidents, 1971, Council of Internat. Relations, 1971—. Zoning commr. Hill Country Village, Tex., 1973—. Mem. Assn. Girl Scout Profl. Workers (mem. exec. bd. 1963-72, pub. relations chmn. 1964-69, v.p. 1969-72, mem. nat. bd. dirs. 1972—, communications chmn. 1972), Tex. Pub. Relations Assn. (Silver Spur award), Women in Communications (historian 1969-70, v.p. 1970-71, treas. 1971-73), Tex. Press Women (recipient state writing contest awards 1971, 72, 73, 74, 77, dist. treas. 1972-73, state exec. bd. 1970-71, 73-74, dist. v.p. 1973-76), San Antonio Soc. Fund Raising Execs., Nat. Fedn. Press Women, Internat. Assn. Bus. Communicators, Speech Arts of San Antonio (v.p. 1963-64, pres. 1964-66, 70-72, dir. 1964-72, chmn. bd. dirs. 1966-69), Am. Women in Radio and TV (chpt. dir. 1975, sec. 1976, pres.-elect 1978-79, pres. 1979-80). Home: 508 Tomahawk Trail San Antonio TX 78232 Office: 335 King William St San Antonio TX 78204

BRUMBACK, CLARENCE LANDEN, physician; b. Denver, Apr. 19, 1914; s. Carl Alvin and Hildur Athelia (Landen) B.; A.B., U. Kans., 1936, M.D., 1943; M.P.H., U. Mich., 1948; m. Lucile Leslie Gillie, June 17, 1943; children—Richard Alvin, Carl Frederick. Intern, U.S. Marine Hosp., San Francisco, 1943-44; resident U. Mich., Ann Arbor, 1947-48; dir. Laclede County (Mo.) Health Dept., Lebanon, 1947; dir. pub. health AEC, Oak Ridge, 1948-50; dir. Palm Beach County Health Dept., W. Palm Beach, Fla., 1950—; clin. prof. U. Miami, 1975—; adj. prof. Fla. Atlantic U., Boca Raton, 1974—. Served with U.S. Army, 1944-47. Recipient Physician of Yr. award Am. Assn. Pub. Health Physicians, 1975; State of Fla. merit award, 1972; Meritorious Service award Fla. Public Health Assn., 1968; Meritorious award So. br. Am. Pub. Health Assn., 1978; diplomate Am. Bd. Preventive Medicine (trustee 1969-78). Fellow Am. Coll. Preventive Medicine, Royal Soc. Health, Am. Pub. Health Assn. (pres. So. br. 1975-76); mem. Fla. Pub. Health Assn. (pres. 1965), AMA, Fla. Med. Assn., Palm Beach County Med. Soc. Lutheran. Clubs: Rotary, Elks, Mayacoo Country. Contbr. articles to profl. jours. Home: 7405 S Flagler Dr West Palm Beach FL 33405 Office: 826 Evernia St West Palm Beach FL 33402

BRUMBELOE, WALTER ALVIN, radio sta. exec.; b. Augusta, Ga., Feb. 18, 1941; s. Howell and Elsie (Burch) B.; ed. public schs.; m. Shelor N. Barron, Oct. 14, 1962; children—Lynda, Angela, Frank, June. With Sta. WGAC, Augusta, 1959, Sta. WBIA, Augusta, 1960-64; engr. Brumbeloe Engring. Service, North Augusta, S.C., 1964-68; owner/mgr. Delta Airlines, Atlanta, 1968-69; engr. Stas. WZZW/WTHB, Augusta, 1969-74, gen. mgr., 1974—. Served in U.S. Army, 1959-60, 61-62. Mem. Am. Bonanza Soc., Nat. Rifle Assn. (life). Baptist. Home: 1711 Apple Valley Dr Augusta GA 30906 Office: Rt 3 Box 75 North Augusta SC 29841

BRUMBELOW, CHARLES WESLEY, broadcasting exec.; b. Sheffield, Ala., Dec. 28, 1940; s. Wesley O'Dell and May Ola (Watson) B.; student David Lipscomb Coll., 1958-61; B.S., U. Tenn., 1963; M.S., U. Tenn., 1964; m. Dorothy Pearl Handley, Mar. 9, 1961; children—Jacynthia Marie, Charles Scott. Instr. acctg. Tenn. Tech. U., Cookeville, 1964-66, asst. prof., 1966-67; staff acct. Price Waterhouse & Co., Nashville, 1967-70; systems analyst Syercon Corp., Nashville, 1970-72; dir. adminstrn. Synerconsultants Corp., Nashville, 1972-74; asst. to gen. mgr. WDCN-TC (public TV), Nashville, 1974—; sec. publs. Mid South Live Steamers, 1972-73. C.P.A., Tenn.; Tenn. Soc. C.P.A.'s scholar, 1963. Mem. Am. Inst. C.P.A.'s, Tenn. Soc. C.P.A.'s, Am. Numismatic Assn., Nat. Rifle Assn., Train Collectors Assn. Mem. Ch. of Christ. Home: 271 Cathy Jo Dr Nashville TN 37211 Office: PO Box 120609 Nashville TN 37212

BRUMFIELD, DEBORAH JAGERS, sociologist; b. McComb, Miss., Sept. 16, 1954; d. Hugh Fitzgerald and Mary Francelia (Moore) Jagers; B.S. in Sociology, U. So. Miss., 1975, M.A. in Sociology, 1980; 1 dau., Autumn Richelle. Med. sociologist, dir. public relations S.W. Med. Center, McComb; mem. Miss. Welfare Adv. Bd. County demographic cons. state senatorial campaign Thad Cochran, 1978. Mem. NOW, Am. Assn. Hosp. Public Relations Dirs., Assn. Employed Women Profls. (pres.), Women in Communications. Methodist. Home: 513 Caston St McComb MS 39648 Office: 215 Marion St McComb MS 39648

BRUMFIELD, GLENN ALTON, rehab. center exec.; b. Yazoo City, Miss., Oct. 8, 1940; s. Aubrey Manor and Earline Willard (O'Neal) B.; B.S., Miss. State U., 1962; M.S. (U.S. Office Edn. fellow), U. So. Miss., 1966; m. Jima Carter Schaen, Dec. 20, 1966; children—Leah, Adam, David. Social worker Miss. Dept. Public Welfare, 1963-65; sch. speech pathologist McComb (Miss.) public schs., 1966-68; dir., then program dir. Mont. Easter Seal Soc., 1968-70; dir. Spartanburg (S.C.) Speech and Hearing Clinic, 1970-78; exec. dir. Charles Lea Center, Spartanburg, 1978—; instr. U. S.C.; adminstrv. survey cons. Commn. Accreditation Rehab. Facilities. Mem. Nat. Rehab. Assn., Am. Speech and Hearing Assn. Episcopalian. Club: N. Spartanburg Rotary. Home: 617 Sharondale Ct Spartanburg SC 29303 Office: 195 Burdette St Spartanburg SC 29302

BRUMFIELD, JOE LAMAR, phys. sci. adminstr.; b. McComb, Miss., July 12, 1938; s. Joe Reid and Ouida Belle (Varnado) B.; student Miss. State U., 1956-58; B.S., Miss. Coll., 1960; postgrad. U. Miss. Med. Center, 1962-63; M.A., U. No. Colo., 1975; m. Cherryl Pauline Wells, Aug. 4, 1967; children—Jennifer, Amy. Research asso. dept. pediatrics U. Miss. Med. Center, Jackson, 1960-64; research chemist Naval Weapons Lab., Dahlgren, Va., 1964-74; adminstr. environ. scis. br. Naval Surface Weapons Center, Dahlgren, 1974—; chmn. Joint Army, Navy, Air Force, NASA Environ. Protection Com., 1976—, nat. tech. steering com., 1979—. Research grantee Dept. Navy, 1965; recipient Outstanding Performance award Dept. Navy, 1972, 74. Inventor atmospheric monitor. Home: 106 Kinloch Dr Fredericksburg VA 22401 Office: Code G-51 NSWC/DL Dahlgren VA 22448

BRUMFIELD, SHANNON MAUREEN, speech and lang. pathologist; b. New Orleans, Sept. 14, 1946; d. Dr. Fred Orlan and Mary Kathleen (Maloney) B.; B.A., La. State U., 1968; M.A., Temple U., 1970; Ph.D., U. Fla., 1978. Speech therapist Sch. Dist. Upper Darby (Pa.), 1970-71; tchr. of deaf, rank tchr. Jefferson Parish Sch. Bd., La., 1971-74; instr. Holy Cross Coll., summer 1974; grad. asst. U. Fla., 1977; pvt. practice speech and lang. pathology, New Orleans, 1979—; lectr. La. Med. Sch. Sec., Les Amies Ensembles, 1979; active

La. Council Performing Arts. Lic. speech pathologist, La.; cert. Council on Edn. of Deaf; cert. tchr. of speech and hearing handicapped (cert.), La. Mem. Am. Speech and Hearing Assn. (cert.), La. Speech and Hearing Assn., Fla. Speech and Hearing Assn., Am. Educators of Deaf, Internat. Assn. Logopedics and Phoniatrics, Alliance for Good Govt., Kappa Kappa Gamma. Clubs: Orleans, Jeunesse d'Orleans. Home: 1416 Killdeer St New Orleans LA 70122

BRUMLEY, JOHN DAVID, discount chain exec.; b. Walnut, Miss., Nov. 8, 1942; s. Rufus Leroy and Edith B.; A.A., Northeast Miss. Jr. Coll., Booneville, 1962; m. Beverly A., Jan. 4, 1980; 1 son by previous marriage, Jason Darren. With High's Ice Cream Co., Memphis, 1964-65; with Baddour, Inc., Memphis, 1965—, graphic communications dir., 1973—. Mem. In Plant Printing Mgmt. Assn., Jaycees, Internat. Assn. Printing House Craftsmen. Republican. Ch. Christ. Home: 6232 Bent Birch Cove Germantown TN 38138 Office: 4300 New Getwell Rd Memphis TN 38118

BRUMMER, LYDIA SAMMON, savs. and loan assn. exec.; b. Tasmania, Fla., Aug. 3, 1920; d. Thomas John and Dellzell (Johnson) Sammon; grad. C.F. Young's Bus. Coll., 1940; m. C. William Brummer, June 5, 1954. Dep. clk. Clk. of Circuit Ct., Desoto County, Arcadia, Fla., 1941-42; office mgr. Riddle Aero. Inst., Arcadia, 1942-45; sec. Lanier Wholesale Candy Co., Arcadia, 1945-50; legal sec. Rosin and Paderewski, Sarasota, Fla., 1950-52; v.p. Coast Fed. Savs. and Loan Assn., Sarasota, 1942—. Bd. dirs. United Way, v.p., 1976, pres., 1977; pres., bd. dirs. Girls Clubs, 1974-76, recipient disting. service award; bd. dirs. Sarasota County ARC, Sarasota-Manatee chpt. NCCJ. Recipient Service to Mankind award Sarasota Sertoma Clubs, 1979, SW Fla. Dist. Sertoma Internat., 1979; Key to Sarasota. Mem. Inst. Fin. Edn., Mental Health Assn., Women's Council Sarasota Bd. Realtors, Sarasota C. of C. (bd. dirs.), Altrusa. Democrat. Clubs: Sarasota Yacht, Forest Lakes Country. Home: Harbor House W Apt 64 226 Golden Gate Point Sarasota FL 33577 Office: PO Box 2199 1777 Main St Sarasota FL 33578

BRUMMETT, CLAUDIA MAE, steel co. exec.; b. Amarillo, Tex., Feb. 28, 1927; d. Claude Jamieson and Mae (Kight) Brummett; student Amarillo Coll., 1944-46, U. Colo., 1946-48. Chief diversion and tracer clk. Santa Fe Rwy. Co., 1948-68; partner, JAL Co., JAL Ranch, Alvarado, Tex., 1968—; corp. sec., J & M Steel Co., Inc., Fort Worth, 1971—; v.p., corp. sec. Western Tool & Mfg. Co., Alvarado, Tex.; silversmith one-man shows at Simpson Gallery, Amarillo, Tex., Square House Mus., Panhandle, Tex.; exhibited in group shows at Tex. Tech. Mus., Wichita Falls, Tex. Mus., Pan-Am. Mus., McAllen, Tex.; represented in permanent collection Carlin Gallery, Ft. Worth. Mem. State Democratic Exec. Com., 1962-70, mem. dist. exec. com., 1962-70; del. Dem. Nat. Conv., 1964, 68, 74, mem. rules com., 1964, mem. credentials com., 1968, 72; mem. del. selection commn. Dem. Nat. Com., 1973-74; Dem. nat. committeewoman, Tex., 1975-76; co-chmn. Briscoe Campaign for Gov., 1972; pres. Johnson County Human Guidance Assn. Mem. Tex. Designer Craftsman, Tex. Artist, Craftsman Guild, W. Tex. C. of C., Tex. Exec. Club, Nat. Fedn. Democratic Women (dir. S. Central region 1976—). Baptist. Address: JAL Ranch Box 308 Alvarado TX 76009

BRUNEAU, ROBERT WILLIAM, marine cons.; b. Fall River, Mass., Aug. 6, 1936; s. William and Lumina (Dorilda) B.; student Delgardo Coll.; children—Kim Corrine, Joann, Scott Allen, Stacy Ann. Enlisted in U.S. Navy, 1953; deep sea diver, 1960-73; ret., 1973; diving supr. Taylor Diving, 1973-76, Ocean Systems, Inc., 1976—; tng. dir. Comml. Diving Center, Wilmington, Calif., 1976-78; hyperbaric welding supr. Odd Berg, Tronso, Norway, 1978-79; marine cons. saturation diving and hyperbaric welding, New Orleans, 1976—; pres. R.M.C. Marine, Inc., 1979—. Mem. Am. Welding Soc., Profl. Assn. Diving Instrs., Mensa, Nat. Assn. Uniformed Services. Republican. Roman Catholic. Club: Elks. Home: 1620 Newport Pl Kenner LA 70062 Office: 4700 Canal St New Orleans LA 70119

BRUNEGRAFF, JANE BURGESS, banker; b. Brunswick, Ga., Dec. 26, 1939; d. Carlton D. and Alberta C. (Kinstle) Burgess; student pub. schs., Brunswick, Ga.; children—Karen, Cynthia, Dana. With Coastal Chevrolet Corp., Brunswick, Ga., 1957-58; with First Nat. Bank of Brunswick, 1958—, banking officer, asst. br. mgr. Island br., St. Simons Island, 1972—. Active fund raising Am. Cancer Soc., 1969-79, Mother's March, 1966-70, Muscular Dystrophy, 1966-71; mem. St. Francis Xavier Sch. Bd. Edn., 1972-73, 75-77, chmn. bd., 1976, vice chmn., 1977; mem. St. Francis Xavier Parish Bd., 1975-76; pollworker city commn. elections. Mem. Beta Sigma Phi. Roman Catholic. Home: 804 Avoca Villa Rd Brunswick GA 31520 Office: 2203 Demere Rd Saint Simons Island GA 31522

BRUNER, RAYMOND RUSSELL, county ofcl.; b. Bascom, Fla., Nov. 19, 1930; s. Hershel Lee and Minnie L. (Ray) B.; B.S., Fla. State U.; m. Virginia Stephenson, Sept. 5, 1950; children—Robert, Carol Bruner Clark. Clk., Jackson County Circuit Ct., Marianna, Fla., 1961—, Jackson County Ct., 1972—; clk. Bd. Jackson County Commrs., 1961—; mem. Jackson County Bd. Public Instruction, 1960-61. Pres., Jackson County Conservation Club; sec., recorder Jackson County Hist. Commn.; chmn. Jackson County March of Dimes, also Christmas Seal chmn.; bd. dirs. Jackson County Cancer Soc., Chipola dist. Boy Scouts Am.; pres. Jackson County unit Am. Cancer Soc.; sec. brotherhood 1st Bapt. Ch., Marianna. Recipient awards Marianna C. of C., 1966, Am. Cancer Soc., 1967-76, Jackson County Devel. Council, 1972, Tb and Respiratory Disease Assn., 1975, 76, March of Dimes, 1977. Mem. Fla. Assn. Ct. Clks. (pres. 1971-72, Outstanding Service citation, 1971, 72), Farm Bur., Jackson County Cattlemen's Assn. Clubs: Marianna Quarterback, Century (Marianna); Jackson County Sportsmen, Kiwanis (interclub com.), West Fla. Shrine (past treas. and pres., now v.p.). Home and Office: PO Drawer 510 Marianna FL 32446

BRUNI, BRUNELLA LINDA, broadcasting co. exec.; b. Tacoma, Wash., Jan. 28, 1956; d. Edward Raymond and Anna Maria (Tafi) B.; A.A.S., San Antonio (Tex.) Coll., 1976; B.A. in Radio, TV and Film, Trinity U., Sa Antonio, 1979. Sta. mgr. Sta. KSYM-FM, San Antonio, 1976; prodn. asst. TV unit U. Tex. Health Sci. Center, San Antonio, 1977-78; gen. mgr. Sta. KRTU-FM, San Antonio, 1978-79; prodn. mgr. Tex. Nat. Prodns., Inc., San Antonio, 1978—; project dir. San Antonio Community Radio Corp., San Antonio, 1979—. Nat. youth com. rep. Muscular Dystrophy Assn., Tex., 1976-79. Mem. Tex. Assn. Independent Film Producers. Office: 543 Brooklyn Ave San Antonio TX 78209

BRUNI, EILEEN MARY, ednl. adminstr.; b. Bklyn., Mar. 25, 1928; d. John Paul and Helen Agatha (McDonald) Bree; B.S. in Secondary Edn., U. Dayton, 1951; M.A. in English, Villanova U., 1957; M.S. in Religious Edn., U. Detroit, 1972; m. John Pius Bruni, July 29, 1972. Secondary and coll. tchr., Pa., 1951-65; adult leadership trainer, Asheville, N.C., 1965-66; adult educator, Denton, Tex., 1972-73, Shelby, Ohio, 1970-71, Athens, Ga., 1966-70; dir. religious edn. St. Francis Ch., Metuchen, N.J., 1971-72; dir. vols. Denton State Sch., 1973-79; dir. edn. Genetics Screening and Counseling Service, Tex. Dept. Mental Health and Mental Retardation, Denton, 1979—. Pres., Ret. Sr. Vol. Program, Denton, 1976-78; adv. com. adult edn. Denton Ind. Sch. Dist., 1973-74; religious edn. adv. bd. Diocese Atlanta, 1966-70. Recipient Outstanding Service award Ret. Sr. Vol. Program, 1978. Mem. Am. Assn. Mental Deficiency, Tex. Public Employees Assn. Democrat. Roman Catholic. Club: Pecan Plantation Country (Granbury, Tex.). Home: 4228 Buckthorn St Box 40906 Lewisville TX 75028 Office: 404 W Oak St Denton TX 76201

BRUNI, ROBERT JOSEPH, investor real estate, oil; b. Laredo, Tex., Oct. 26, 1933; s. Leo Ed and Feliz (Rodriguez) B.; B.S., Tex. A. and M., 1954; postgrad. Fordham U., 1959-60. Owner, operator R.J. Bruni Investment Co., San Antonio, 1961—, Bruni Mineral Trust, San Antonio, 1939—; owner ranch, Zapata and Webb Counties, Tex., 1940—. Mem. finance com. Bexar County (Tex.) Dem. Club, 1975—. Served with C.I.C., U.S. Army, 1956-57. Roman Catholic. Office: Century Bldg 121 E 84 NE Loop 410 San Antonio TX 78216

BRUNINI, JOSEPH BERNARD, bishop; b. Vicksburg, Miss., July 24, 1909; s. John and Blanche (Stein) B.; A.B., Georgetown U., 1930, LL.D., 1957; S.T.B., North Am. Coll., Rome, 1933; J.C.D., Cath. U., Washington, 1937. Ordained priest Roman Catholic Ch., 1933; rector Cathedral, Natchez, Miss., 1943-44; chancellor Natchez Diocese, 1941-49; pastor St. Peter's Co-Cathedral, Jackson, Miss., 1949-62; vicar gen. of Diocese, 1951-66, aux. bishop Natchez-Jackson Diocese, 1957-66, apostolic adminstr., 1966-67, bishop, 1967-79; bishop Jackson Diocese, 1979—. Recipient John Carroll award Georgetown U. Mem. Cath. Hosp. Assn. U.S. and Can. (past pres.), Fed. Hosp. Council, Am. Hosp. Assn. (trustee). K.C. (4 deg.). Home: 123 N West St Jackson MS 39201 Office: Box 2248 Jackson MS 39205

BRUNS, ARCHIE THEODORE, hosp. adminstr.; b. Porter, Minn., July 8, 1930; s. Theodore J. and Susie J. (Benson) B.; B.B.A., Old Dominion U., 1958; M.H.A., Va. Commonwealth U., 1973; m. Dorothy Wright, Nov. 29, 1952; children—Rhonda Bruns Alvarez, Archie Theodore, Scott G. Asst. dir. fin. City of Virginia Beach (Va.), 1963-67; controller Leigh Meml. Hosp., Norfolk, Va., 1967-70; asst. adminstr. Rockingham Meml. Hosp., Harrisonburg, Va., 1973-77; asst. adminstr. Blue Ridge Hosp.-Monticello, Charlottesville, Va., 1977-79, acting adminstr., 1979—. Served with USNR, 1948-52. Mem. Old Dominion U. Alumni Assn. (pres. 1962-63), Am. Coll. Hosp. Adminstrs., Am. Hosp. Assn., Va. Hosp. Assn. Presbyterian. Clubs: Rotary (dir. Harrisonburg 1976-77), Lions (sec.-treas. Kempsville, Va., 1968-70. Home and office: Blue Ridge Hosp-Monticello Charlottesville VA 22901

BRUNSON, CHARLES MACK, steel co. exec.; b. Canton, Tex., Feb. 14, 1937; s. Charley Lender and Maxine (Remola) B.; student Draughans Bus. Coll., 1956-57; m. Kathryn A. Bruton, Sept. 20, 1958; children—Dudley C., Kirk M., Surett, Carla. Shop clk., asst. plant supt., draftsman, sales estimator Delta Steel Bldg. Co., Dallas, 1960-65; with Star Mfg. Co., Oklahoma City, 1965—, mgr. sales service, 1972-77, mgr. mktg. services, 1977-79, dir. agrl. sales, 1979—. Mem. Businessmen's Profl. Advt. Assn. (dir.), Am. Mgmt. Assn. Republican. Baptist. Club: Willow Pine Country. Home: 9613 Allen Dr Oklahoma City OK 73139 Office: 8600 Interstate Hwy 35 Oklahoma City OK 73143

BRYAN, BARBARA NORRIS, nurse; b. Aberdeen, Miss., June 21, 1947; d. Thomas Avery and Gertrude (Hurst) Norris; student in edn. Miss. State U., 1965-69; B.S. in Nursing (Pres.'s scholar), Miss. U. for Women, 1974; m. Thomas Drayton Bryan, Dec. 20, 1970. Staff nurse Ivy Meml. Hosp., West Point, Miss., 1972, inservice edn. dir., 1974-75, dir. nursing services, 1975—; indsl. nurse Babcock & Wilcox Co., West Point, 1972-74; mem. adv. bd. Miss. U. for Women Sch. Nursing; mem. Adv. Bd. for Vo-Tech. Health Occupations; adv. Council Regional Mental Health Complex, 1975-76. Bd. dirs., 1st v.p. Clay County (Miss.) Assn. Retarded Children, 1976-77; mem. adv. com. Vols. in Public Schs., West Point, 1978-79; co-chmn. fund-raising dr. Miss. affiliate Am. Heart Assn., 1979. Recipient cert. appreciation Miss. Heart Assn., 1979; named Outstanding Young Women in Am., Jaycees, 1977. Mem. Miss. Nurses Assn. (Nurse of Yr. Dist. 18 1977), Am. Nurses Assn., Miss. Hosp. Assn., Soc. Nursing Service Adminstrs. Methodist. Clubs: West Point Music Coterie 2d v.p. 1977. West Point Home and Garden. Office: Ivy Meml Hosp 217 W Broad St West Point MS 39773

BRYAN, BART EBERT, assn. exec.; b. Johnstown, Pa., May 5, 1894; s. Bart and Carrie (Ebert) B.; student U. Mass., 1913-14, Cornell U., 1914-15; m. Marie Elizabeth Genung, Mar. 28, 1921; children—John B., William Joseph. Directory pub., Asbury Park, N.J., 1923-24; salesman display advt. St. Petersburg (Fla.) Times, 1927-34, advt. mgr., 1934-44, pub. relation dir., 1944-59; pub. St. Petersburg Visitors News, 1944-46; pres. St. Petersburg Motor Club (A.A.A.), 1960-65, treas., 1965-70, dir., 1947—. Pres. St. Petersburg Inter Civic Council, 1942; chief fire watcher Civilian Def., 1943; treas. St. Petersburg Civic Music Assn., 1962-69; treas. Religion United in Action for Community for Pinellas County, 1975—; life mem. bd. Pinellas Area council Boy Scouts Am. Served with AEF, 1917-19. Recipient Mr. Citizen award, 1958; Silver citation First Fed. Savs. & Loan Assn., 1958; Ann. Advt. Silver medal St. Petersburg Advt. Fedn., 1975; mem. Silver Key club Times Pub. Co., 1977. Mem. Am. Legion, VFW. Episcopalian (sec. vestry 1960-62). Clubs: St. Petersburg Yacht, Advertising (life mem.) (St. Petersburg). Editor: You Can Sell Newspaper Advertising, 1941. Address: 6020 Shore Blvd S Apt 405 Windsor Bldg Saint Petersburg FL 33707

BRYAN, CAROL BARCLAY LINDSAY, govt. ofcl.; b. Atlanta, Oct. 17, 1922; d. John Samuel and Florence Gertrude (Hand) Lindsay; student U. Ala., 1952; m. Francis Aaron Smelley, June 30, 1948; children—Dorothy Ann Echols Raymond, Susan Grace Smelley Milewicz; m. 2d, Colgan Hobson Bryan, July 14, 1979. With Social Security Adminstrn., HEW, Tuscaloosa, Ala., 1946—, claims rep., 1947-55, field rep., 1955-75, ops. analyst, 1975—. Neighborhood chmn. Tombigbee council Girl Scouts U.S.A., 1959-62. Named 1st honoree Tuscaloosa area Internat. Women's Year, 1975. Mem. Tuscaloosa County Preservation Soc. (trustee 1969—, rec. sec. 1970-74), Tuscaloosa C. of C. (women's div.), Tuscaloosa Arts and Humanities Council, Birmingham Geneal. Soc., Tuscaloosa County Geneal. Soc. Methodist. Clubs: Altrusa (dir. 1968-73, 1st v.p. 1970-71, pres. 1971-72); Woodland Hills Garden (pres. 1964-65), North River Yacht (Tuscaloosa); Univ. Women's. Contbr. to Coll. Poetry Anthology. Home: 171 Woodland Hills Tuscaloosa AL 35405 Office: 1118 Greensboro Ave Tuscaloosa AL 35401

BRYAN, DAVID TENNANT, newspaper publisher; b. Richmond, Va., Aug. 3, 1906; s. John Stewart and Anne Eliza (Tennant) B.; student U. Va., 1925-28; LL.D., U. Richmond, 1973; m. Mary Harkness Davidson, May 11, 1932. Chmn. bd., dir. Media Gen., Inc.; chmn. bd. Tribune Co., Tampa; dir. So. Ry. Co. Vice chmn., trustee Richmond Meml. Hosp.; bd. assos. U. Richmond; bd. overseers Hoover Instn. War, Revolution and Peace. Served with USNR, 1942-46. Mem. Am. Newspaper Pubs. Assn. (pres. 1958-60), Soc. of Cincinnati, SAR, SR, Va. Hist. Soc. (pres. 1978-80), Soc. Colonial Wars, Sigma Delta Chi. Clubs: Commonwealth, Country of Va. (Richmond); Farmington Country (Charlottesville); St. Anthony, Union (N.Y.C.); Nat. Press, Alfalfa (Washington); Bohemian (San Francisco). Home: Ampthill Rd Richmond VA 23226 Office: 333 E Grace St Richmond VA 23219

BRYAN, EDWARD RAYMOND, flow meter co. exec.; b. Llano, Tex., Apr. 4, 1935; s. Eldon Raymond and Helen Estelle (Ewing) B.; student Okla. State U., 1957-59; B.S., E. Central U., Ada, Okla., 1962; postgrad. So. Meth. U., 1968; m. Ella Mae Swadley, Aug. 8, 1955; children—Terri Lynn, Edward Raymond, Patrick Loyd. Owner, pres. Bryan Electric Co., Wetumka, Okla., 1959-62; geophys. engr. Geotech, Inc., Garland, Tex., 1962-64; geophys. project engr. Geotech/Teledyne, Inc., Garland, 1964-68, sales engr., 1968, internat. mktg. mgr., 1968-70; pres., chmn. bd. Electronic Flo-Meters, Inc., Dallas, 1970—; chmn. bd., pres. Tecnitron Internat., Inc., Dallas, 1969, dir., cons., 1969—. Active Republican Party. Served in USNR, 1952-56. Decorated Purple Heart. Mem. Instrument Soc. Am. (sr.), Am. Mgmt. Assn., So. Gas Assn., Internat. Trade Assn. Dallas, Internat. Union Geodesy and Geophysics, Am., Dallas geophys. socs. Baptist. Club: Elks. Contbr. articles on geophysics and control instrumentation to profl. jours. Home: PO Box 2227 Garland TX 75041 also Route 1 Wylie TX 75098 Office: 6121 Jupiter Rd Garland TX 75042

BRYAN, J(OSEPH) KENT, elec. engr.; b. Fulton, Mo., June 1, 1943; s. F. Martin and Ruby Rae (Renner) B.; B.S.E.E., U. Mo., Columbia, 1966, M.S.E.E. (NDEA Title IV fellow), 1968, Ph.D. (NDEA Title IV fellow), 1971; children by previous marriage—Jerry Joseph, James William. Research asst. dept. elec. engring. U. Mo., Columbia, 1968-71; asst. prof. engring. U. Mo., Kansas City, 1971-73; asst. prof. elec. and computer engring. Clemson U., 1973-76, asso. prof., 1976—; reviewer NSF; faculty fellow Auburn U., 1975. Recipient Curator's award U. Mo., Columbia, 1961-62; USAF grantee, 1976-77; Dept. Energy grantee, 1977-78; Los Alamos grantee, 1978-79. Mem. IEEE, Pattern Recognition Soc., Tau Beta Pi, Eta Kappa Nu, Pi Mu Epsilon. Baptist. Contbr. articles to profl. jours.; paper reviewer IEEE Transactions on Pattern Analysis and Machine Intelligence. Home: 22-A Barre St Clemson SC 29631 Office: Dept Elec and Computer Engring Clemson U Clemson SC 29631

BRYAN, JACOB FRANKLIN, III, ins. co. exec.; b. Jacksonville, Fla., Feb. 26, 1908; s. Jacob Franklin and Olive Julia (Gibson) B. II; grad. Fla. Bus. U., 1932; LL.D. (hon.), Bethune-Cookman Coll., 1965; m. Josephine Christian Hendley, May 25, 1935; children—Jacob Franklin IV, Carter Byrd, Kendall Gibson. With Ind. Life & Accident Ins. Co., Jacksonville, Fla., 1927—, exec. v.p., 1954-56, chmn. bd., pres., 1957-79, chmn. bd., chief exec. officer, 1979—; chmn. bd., pres. Herald Life Ins. Co., Jacksonville, 1960-79, chmn. bd., chief exec. officer, 1979—; dir., mem. trust com. Fla. 1st Nat. Bank, Jacksonville, 1957—; dir. Fla. Fed. Savs. & Loan, Jacksonville, 1955—, v.p., 1974—; dir. S.C. Life & Health Inst. Guaranty Assn. Columbia, S.C., 1972—. Mem. White House Com. Fund Raising Fed. Employees, 1953-61, White House Com. Employment Handicapped, 1962—; pres. Jacksonville Symphony Assn., 1969-70, now bd. dirs.; state chmn. fund dr. Fla. Heart Assn., 1970, Fla. Arts Commn., 1961-65, Health Planning Council Jacksonville Area, 1964-70; v.p. Fla. div. Am. Cancer Soc.; state v.p., mem. exec. com., bd. dirs. U.S. Indsl. Council, 1970—; mem. advisory bd., bd. dirs. Children's Mus.; v.p. Cathedral Found. Jacksonville, 1963-72; exec. adviser N. Fla. council Boy Scouts Am., 1961—; former chmn. Citizens Com. Juvenile Ct., sec., mem. bd. dirs Fla. Devel. Commn., 1961-65; mem. Fla. Council 100, 1967—; State Ins. Advisory Com., 1960-70, program com. Bold New Jacksonville, 1968, contact com. HUD, 1970—, advisory bd. Jacksonville Art Mus., 1959, nat. advisory council SBA, 1970, Commn. Quality Edn., 1967, lay advisory bd. St. Vincent's Med. Center, 1972—, Historic St. Augustine Preservation Bd.; mem. fin. com. Am. Bicentennial Commn. Jacksonville. Mem. Fla. Pub. Sch. Bd., 1968-69; chmn. 3d Congl. Dist., Nixon-Agnew campaign, 1972. Bd. dirs. Indsl. Am. Corp., Jacksonville, Jr. Achievement, March Dimes, Girls' Club Jacksonville, Child Guidance Clinic, Childrens Home Soc. Fla., Jacksonville Downtown Devel. Authority, United Way Jacksonville, Community Planning Council Jacksonville Area, Inc., United Negro Coll. Fund, and several others; trustee Jacksonville U. (also mem. ops. com., bd. devel.), Bapt. Meml. Hosp., Bethune-Cookman Coll.; founding trustee Jacksonville Episcopal High Sch.; nat. trustee Life Underwriters Tng. Council, Washington, mem. bd. fellow U. Tampa (Fla.). Recipient Champions Higher Ind. Edn. Fla. award Ind. Colls., Univs. Fla. Assn., 1971; spl. award for outstanding service to cancer Fla. Cancer Soc.; Ted Arnold award for outstanding service and civic accomplishment Jacksonville Jaycees; named Boss of Year Arlington Jaycees, 1960, Am. Bus. Women's Assn., 1965; Man of Year Fla. Assn. Life Underwriters, 1960, others. Fellow Royal Hort. Soc. (Eng.); mem. Am. Life Ins. Assn. (Fla. v.p. 1975), Fla. (dir.-at-large), Jacksonville Area (past gov., mem. advisory com. Com. 100) chambers commerce, Nat. Over the Counter Cos. (advisory bd. 1973—), Internat. Platform Assn., N.A.M. (pub. affairs com., edn. com.), Fla. Life Ins. Cos. Assn. (pres.), Life Insurers Conf. (past bd. mem.), Newcomen Soc. Fla., Nat. Orchid Soc. (past v.p.), S.A.R., Huxford Genealogical Soc. Inc., Jacksonville Genealogical Soc., Fla., Jacksonville hist. socs., Nat. Trust Hist. Preservation, Order Stars and Bars, English Speaking Union (dir.), sons Am. Revolution, Sons Confederate Vets., Alpha Kappa Psi (hon., life). Episcopalian (vestry 1959-61, 63-65, 67-69, sr. warden 1964-65, 67-68). Clubs: Florida Yacht, Timuquana Country, River, Seminole, Ye Majestic Reveliers (all Jacksonville). Home: 4255 Yacht Club Rd Jacksonville FL 32210 Office: 1 Independent Dr Jacksonville FL 32276

BRYAN, JAMES NELSON, JR., lawyer; b. Nashville, July 12, 1947; s. James Nelson and Dorethy Hope (Tharp) B.; B.S., Auburn U., 1969; J.D., Vanderbilt U., 1973; m. Patricia Ann Lavorini, Oct. 17, 1975; children—Dawn, Amy, John. Admitted to Tenn. bar, 1973, U.S. Supreme Ct. bar, 1976; asso. firm Woods, Bryan & Thomas, P.A., and predecessor firm, Nashville, 1973-76, mem. firm, 1976—. Pres., Vol. in Tenn. Corrections, Inc.; bd. dirs. Middle Tenn. Civil Liberties Union, 1972-79, pres., 1975-77; sec., treas. Tenn. Young Democrats, 1971-72; bd. dirs. Tennesseans for Handgun Control, 1978-79; v.p. Home and Sch. Assn. Christ the King Sch., Nashville. Mem. Am. Bar Assn., Tenn. Bar Assn., Nashville Bar Assn., Nat. Assn. Criminal Def. Lawyers, Tenn. Assn. Criminal Def. Lawyers, Tenn. Trial Lawyers Assn., Tenn. Trails Assn., Tenn. Scenic Rivers Assn., ACLU, Omicron Delta Kappa. Roman Catholic. Club: K.C. Home: 3505 Amanda Ave Nashville TN 37215 Office: 121 17th Ave S Nashville TN 37203

BRYAN, JANE CAMPBELL, ins. exec.; b. Covington, Va., Sept. 29, 1925; d. Charles Langdon and Rhoda Elizabeth (Trego) Campbell; student Marshall U. 1942-44, Temple U., 1954-55, Elec. Computer Programming Inst., 1966-67; A.B. in Psychology, Case-Western Reserve U., 1947, A.B. in Art, 1947; children—Elizabeth, Carolyn, James. Portrait painter, Summit, N.J. 1958-67; registrar Summit Art Center, 1964-67; methods examiner Prudential Ins. Co., Houston, 1968-69, programmer, 1969-76, programming analyst, 1976—. Officer, trustee Summit Art Center, 1962-65; trustee Union County (N.J.) Psychiat. Clinic, 1966-67. Recipient various art awards state and local shows. Certified life underwriter, 1975, cert. data processor, 1976. Fellow Life Office Mgmt. Assn. Inst.; mem. Life Office Mgmt. Assn., Mensa, Soc. Certified Data Processors, Chi Beta Phi. Presbyterian. Home: 14460 Misty Meadow Houston TX 77079 Office: 6500 W Loop S Bellaire TX 77401

BRYAN, JOHN BAYNE, III, state ofcl.; b. Geneva, N.Y., Nov. 22, 1947; s. John B. and Clara (Flick) B.; B.A. in Polit. Sci., State U. N.Y., 1973; M.Librarianship, U. S.C., 1974. Warehouse mgr. United Overton Corp., Albany, N.Y., 1967-70; law librarian S.C. Atty. Gen.'s Office, Columbia, 1973-74, dir. adminstrn., 1975—. Coordinator, Easter Seal campaign for state govt. employees, 1976, 77. Mem. Nat. Orgn. of Attys. Gen. (office rep. mgmt. sect. 1975—), U. S.C. Grad. Library Sch. Alumni Assn. (exec. bd. 1979—), AA Law Librarians. Home: 2604 Kiawah Ave Columbia SC 29205 Office: PO Box 11549 Columbia SC 29211

BRYAN, JOHN STEWART, III, newspaper pub.; b. Richmond, Va., May 4, 1938; s. David Tennant and Mary Harkness (Davidson) B.; B.A., U. Va., 1960; postgrad. U. Va. Law Sch., 1962-63; m. Alice Pyle Zimmer, June 15, 1963; children—Elizabeth Talbott, Anna Saulsbury. Advt. salesman, reporter Burlington (Vt.) Free Press, 1963-65; bus. editor, polit. reporter The Tampa (Fla.) Times, 1965-67; v.p. The Tribune Co., Tampa, 1968-70, exec. v.p., 1970-77, pub., 1976-77; pub. Richmond Times-Dispatch, Richmond News Leader, 1978—. Trustee U. Tampa, 1972-78; mem. council of advisors U. South Fla., 1975-77; pres. Tampa Bay Art Center, 1970; pres. Fla. Gulf Coast Symphony, 1977; pres. Tampa Citizens Safety Council, 1971-72; pres. Tampa United Way, 1974; bd. dirs. Richmond Symphony, Va. Council on Health and Med. Care, Goodwill Industries, Salvation Army, Richmond. Served with USMC, 1960-62. Recipient Disting. Service award Fla. Press Assn., 1976. Mem. So. Newspapers Pubs. Assn. (dir. 1973-74, found. chmn. 1978-79), Newspaper Advt. Bur. (dir.), Fla. Press Assn. (pres. 1971-72), Am. Newspaper Pubs. Assn., Young Presidents Assn. Sigma Delta Chi. Episcopalian. Clubs: Country of Va., Commonwealth, Tampa Yacht and Country, Univ. (Tampa). Home: 4608 Sulgrave Rd Richmond VA 23221 Office: 333 E Grace St Richmond VA 23219

BRYAN, JOHN THOMAS, JR., steel co. exec.; b. Memphis, Nov. 20, 1944; s. John Thomas and Carrie Elizabeth (Jackson) B.; B.A., U. Miss., 1965; m. Melanie Kaye Hunter, Feb. 9, 1969; children—John Thomas, Todd Hunter. Sales rep. lock, hardware div. Eaton, Yale & Towne, Rye, N.Y., 1968-71; sales engr. Lamson & Sessions Co., Birmingham, Ala., 1971-74, group sales engr., 1974-75, dist. sales mgr., 1975-76, regional sales mgr., 1976-77, gen. sales mgr., 1977—. Served with USAR, 1965-73. Mem. Am. Soc. Machine Mfg. Assn., Tex. Wholesale Hardware Assn., Pi Kappa Alpha. Republican. Methodist. Clubs: Young Exec. of Am. Office: 1327 27th Ave N Birmingham AL 35201

BRYAN, ONELL CORNELIUS, lab. technician; b. Blount County, Ala., Feb. 26, 1923; d. Zion Alvie and Fannie Mae (Gibson) Cornelius; student public schs., Ala.; children—Vernell, E.J. and Derf. Practical nurse Blount Meml. Hosp., Oneonta, Ala., 1956-63; lab. and x-ray technician Wittmeier Clinic, Oneonta, 1962—. Cert. lic. practical nurse. Mem. Lic. Practical Nurses Assn., Nat. Assn. Practical Nurse Edn., Ala. Hist. Assn. Baptist. Club: Order Eastern Star. Home: Route 1 Cleveland AL 35049 Office: Wittmeir Clinic 112 First Ave E Oneonta AL 35121

BRYAN, THORNTON EMBRY, JR., physician; b. Frankfort, Ky., Mar. 16, 1927; s. Thornton Embry and Mary Ellen (Stivers) B.; B.S., U. Ky., 1949; M.D., U. Louisville, 1954; 1 son, Thornton Embry III. Instr. dept. anatomy U. Louisville Med. Sch., 1950-52; intern Phila. Gen. Hosp., 1954-55; gen. practice medicine, Cadiz, Ky., 1955-71; coordinator residency program, asso. prof., dept. family practice U. Iowa Coll. Medicine, Iowa City, 1971-74; prof., chmn. dept. family medicine U. Tenn. Center for Health Scis., Memphis, 1974—; mem. staff St. Joseph Hosp.-East. Served with USNR, 1945-46. Diplomate Am. Bd. Family Practice. Fellow Am. Acad. Family Physicians (charter); mem. AMA, Assn. Departmental Chmn. Family Medicine (dir. 1979—), Tenn. Med. Assn., Shelby County Med. Soc., Soc. Tchrs. of Family Medicine. Office: 66 N Pauline St Suite 233 Memphis TN 38105

BRYANT, BRITAIN HAMILTON, polit. party ofcl.; b. Louisville, Mar. 21, 1940; s. William Hamilton and Virginia (Throgmorton) B.; student Centre Coll. Ky., 1958-59; B.S. in Law, U. Louisville, 1962, J.D., 1964; student Sch. Law, Washington and Lee U., 1963; m. Peyton Gresham, Apr. 24, 1965; children—Anne Hamilton, Stewart Wells. Admitted to Ky. bar, 1965, V.I. bar, 1965, U.S. Supreme Ct. bar, 1972; partner firm Bryant, Costello, Burke & Scott, Christiansted, St. Croix, V.I., 1970—; mem. V.I. Senate, 1973-79, v.p., 1975-79; chmn. Dem. Party of V.I., 1979—. Mem. Law Enforcement Assistance Commn., V.I. Am. Bicentennial Commn. Bd. dirs. St. Croix chpt. A.R.C. Mem. V.I. (sec. 1969-71, v.p. 1972), Am. bar assns., St. Croix C. of C. (sec. 1969-72), Am. Trial Lawyers Assn., World Peace through Law Assn., V.I. Jud. Council (permanent mem. 3d circuit jud. conf.), Am. Law Inst., Beta Theta Pi, Phi Delta Phi. Home: 3 Betsy's Jewel Christiansted St Croix VI 00820 Office: 7 King St Christiansted St Croix VI 00820

BRYANT, DENNIS MICHAEL, bus. exec.; b. Austin, Tex., June 30, 1947; s. L.D. and Mildred Virginia B.; B.S., Trinity U., 1970; m. Nancy Louthan, Apr. 17, 1976; children—Dennis Michael, Sarah Elizabeth. With Briggs-Weaver, 1974—, now mgr. San Antonio ops. Served with U.S. Army, 1971-73. Presbyterian. Club: Tex. Flying. Home: 14315 Ben Brush Dr San Antonio TX 78248 Office: 1014 Paulson San Antonio TX 78219

BRYANT, DONALD EUGENE, oil co. exec.; b. Shawnee, Okla., Mar. 26, 1933; s. Jacob Calvin and Ruby Jane (Smith) B.; B.B.A. with distinction, U. Okla., 1958, M.B.A. (Humble Oil and Refining Fellow in Accounting, 1958-59), 1960, grad. Sch. Banking (Am. Bankers Assn. Harold Stonier Fellow, 1972-73), 1973; m. Susan Elizabeth Epperson, Apr. 26, 1973. Accountant, Peat Marwick Mitchell and Co., Oklahoma City, 1959-60; asst. prof. econs., U. SW La., Lafayette, 1960-63; executor estate, Shawnee, Okla., 1963-65; sec. South Gulf Oil Co., 1962-65; asso. prof. accounting, Bentley Coll., Boston, 1965-66; research asso., Bus. Sch., Harvard U., Cambridge, Mass., 1967-68, 71-73; asst. prof. adminstrn., Wichita (Kans.) State U., 1969-71, asso. prof. accounting, 1973-75; asst. to pres., Alpha Exploration, Inc., Midland, Tex., 1975-76; v.p., Veritas Exploration, Inc., Midland, 1976—; controller RPM Energy, Inc., 1979—; lectr. U. Tex. of Permian Basin, 1975. C.P.A., Okla. Mem. Midland Bd. Realtors, Omicron Delta Kappa, Beta Gamma Sigma. Democrat. Episcopalian. Clubs: Harvard (Boston), Moose, Kappa Sigma Alumni (sec., Wichita 1970, v.p. 1973). Contbr. to books on corp. fin and fin. mgmt. Home: 1 Linda Court Midland TX 79701 Office: 228 Comml Bank Tower Midland TX 79702

BRYANT, DONALD GRANT, funeral dir.; b. Greenville, S.C., Apr. 10, 1923; s. James Robert and Lillian Grant (Cameron) B.; B.S., Davidson Coll., 1948; m. Frances Vinson, Aug. 28, 1948; children—Lillian Melissa Bryant Graeber, Frances Cameron. Vice pres. J.M. Harry & Bryant Co., Inc., Charlotte, N.C.; dir. Southeastern Savs. & Loan Co.; past chmn. bd. dirs. 1st Union Nat. Bank, Charlotte. Pres., United Community Services, Charlotte, 1970, bd. dirs., 1960-73; chmn. govt. task force Charlotte-Mecklenburg Dimensions Program, 1974; chmn. human services delivery study Social Planning Council, 1974-75; mem. city council, Charlotte, 1961-65; chmn. bd. dirs. Central br. Charlotte YMCA, 1977; pres. Charlotte Speech and Hearing Center; trustee N.C. Baptist Children's Homes, Davidson Coll.; life trustee, chmn. bd. Nat. Found. Funeral Service; bd. dirs. Carolina Internat. Tennis Found.; trustee Charlotte Nature Mus., Mercy Hosp.; deacon Myers Park Bapt. Ch. Served with USAAF, 1943-45. Recipient Distinguished Citizenship award Charlotte Civitan Club, 1971. Mem. N.C. Funeral Dirs. Assn., Nat. Selected Morticians, Davidson Coll. Alumni Assn. (nat. pres. 1974). Republican. Clubs: Charlotte City (pres. 1978, dir.), Charlotte Country (pres. 1967-68), Charlotte Sportsman's, Davidson Wildcat (dir., pres. 1965), U.S. Golf Assn. (sectional affairs com., nat. amateur tournament chmn. 1972). Home: 2327 Forest Dr Charlotte NC 28211 Office: 500 Providence Rd PO Box 6054 Charlotte NC 28207

BRYANT, DONALD WAYNE, ednl. adminstr.; b. Winston-Salem, N.C., Apr. 24, 1941; s. George Robert and Lucy Eugenia (Gardner) B.; A.A., Presbyn. Jr. Coll., 1961; B.A., Wake Forest U., 1963; M.A., U. Ga., 1965; Ed.D., N.C. State U., 1971; m. Martha Ann Wooten, Sept. 28, 1968; children—Tiffany Lynn, Tyler Wayne. Chmn. bus. dept. Martin Tech. Inst., Williamston, N.C., 1968-69; intern Fayetteville (N.C.) Tech. Inst., 1969-71; dean instrn. Sampson Tech. Inst., Clinton, N.C., 1971-73; pres. Carteret Tech. Coll., Morehead City, N.C., 1973—. Mem. N.C. Assn. Public Community Coll. Presidents, Community Coll. Adv. Council. Presbyterian. Home: Route 2 Box 287A Morehead City NC 28557 Office: Carteret Technical College 3505 Arendell St Morehead City NC 28557

BRYANT, EDWARD JOE, govt. ofcl.; b. Shreveport, La., Sept. 19, 1947; s. Moses Boyd and Ester Lee (Harper) B.; diploma Chanute Tech. Tng. Sch., 1966; grad. ANG and NCO Acad., 1973; A.A. in Gen. Edn., Palmer Coll., 1975; B.S., Bapt. Coll., 1978. With Sperry-Rand Corp., Doyline, La., 1969-71; with La. Army Ammunition Plant, Shreveport, from 1972, now power plant specialist, Charleston, S.C. Served with USAF, 1965-69. Cert. counselor, S.C. Mem. S.C. Personnel and Guidance Assn., Air Force Assn. Democrat. Methodist. Club: Sound Wave Unltd. (pres. 1978-80). Address: 7356 Stall Rd N Charleston SC 29405

BRYANT, ELIZABETH ANN, counselor; b. Mobile, Ala., Feb. 28, 1950; d. Percy Ausphera and Claire Howze (Kimbrough) Bryant; B.A., U. Ala., 1972, M.A., 1974. Counselor, U. Ala., 1974; psychometrist Tuscaloosa County Bd. Edn., 1974; placement coordinator, counselor Tri County Youth Porgram, Montgomery, Ala., 1974-75; equal opportunity officer Montgomery Community Action Agy. (Ala.), 1975—. Mem. Ala. Equal Opportunity Officers Assn. (v.p. 1978-79), Ala., Am. (v.p. chpt. 1974) personnel and guidance assns., Ala., Nat. vocational guidance assns. Methodist. Home: 1152 Lombard Dr Montgomery AL 36109 Office: 1066 Adams Ave Montgomery AL 36104

BRYANT, HARRY JOHN, III, real estate exec.; b. Fort Worth, Tex., June 26, 1924; s. Harry John and Mamie Clacke B.; B.S., Tex. Christian U., 1950; children—Marilou Stovall, Becky Sue Bryant, John Mark. Vice-pres. Richland Realty Co., Inc., Fort Worth, 1952-62; pres. Harry J. Bryant & Co., Inc., Fort Worth, 1954-79; pres. Anderson & Assos., Inc., Fort Worth, 1970-73; pres. Alliance Properties, Inc., Alliance Property Mgmt., Ft. Worth, 1977-80. Bd. stewarts Richland Hills Meth. Ch., 1955-69. Served with USNR, 1943-46. Mem. Fort Worth Bd. Realtors (v.p. 1968), Fort Worth and Tarrant County Home Builders Assn. (bd. dirs. 1965-69), Apartment Assn. Tarrant County. Democrat. Club: Masons. Home: 4104 Eldridge Fort Worth TX 76107 Office: 1024 Currie Fort Worth TX 76107

BRYANT, HOWARD LOUIS, real estate appraiser, farmer; b. Drewryville, Va., Dec. 7, 1921; s. Lewis Harum and Bessie Elizabeth (Vick) B.; student U. Va., Va. Commonwealth U.; m. Maude Gertrude Bryant, June 5, 1942; children—Stephen L., Robyn Denise. Owner, operator Merrydale Farm, Boykins, Va., 1941—, Boykins Hardware Co., also Boykins Tractor & Implement Co., 1947-50; contractor, real estate developer, 1950-62; dist. appraiser Va. Dept. Hwys., 1963—; guest lectr. Mem. Am. Soc. Appraisers (sr., pres. Richmond chpt.), Assn. Fed. Appraisers, Am. Right of Way Assn., Nat. Assn. Review Appraisers. Baptist. Lion (dir.), Mason (Shriner); mem. Order Eastern Star. Home: 300 Nottingham Dr Colonial Heights VA 23834 Office: Virginia Dept of Highways PO Box 391 Petersburg VA 23803

BRYANT, JACK DEAN, sales exec.; b. Ringling, Okla., Nov. 22, 1934; s. Carmen E. and Beatrice J. (Tucker) B.; student public schs., Healdton, Okla.; m. Anne Mobley, Mar. 22, 1978; children—Stephen Ray, Jeffrey Don. With Western Co., Shreveport, La., 1956—, sales and service supr., Woodward, Okla., 1960-65, regional sales rep., Oklahoma City, 1965-76, city sales mgr., Shreveport, La., 1978-79, regional sales rep., Shreveport, 1979—. Served with Army N.G., 1952-55. Recipient Meritorious award Am. Petroleum Inst., 1971. Mem. AIME, Shreveport C. of C. Republican. Baptist. Clubs: E. Ridge Country, Shreveport Petroleum, Univ. Office: 1012 Mid South Towers Shreveport LA 71101

BRYANT, LELAND MARSHAL, accountant; b. Gainesville, Ga., Apr. 28, 1950; s. William Marcus and Perrie Lou (Milner) B.; student (Alfred P. Sloan fellow) Vanderbilt U., 1968-70; B.B.A. with honors, U. Tex., Austin, 1972; M.B.A. (William E. Newcomb fellow), Wharton Sch., U. Pa., 1978; m. Rebecca Lea Biegert, Sept. 2, 1973; children—Shauna Rebecca, Natalie Anne. Staff asst. Southwestern Life Ins. Co., Dallas, 1973; comml. real estate salesman, Dallas, 1974; mgr. Southwestern Life Ins. Co., Dallas, 1975-76; accountant Arthur Andersen & Co., Dallas, 1978—. Mem. membership com. Dallas C. of C., 1974; team capt. United Way Fund drives, Dallas, 1973, 75, 76; vol. fund drive Am. Cancer Soc., Dallas, 1973, 75, Bishop Coll. Operating Fund, Dallas, 1976. Mem. Am. Inst. C.P.A.'s, Tex. Soc. of C.P.A.'s. Home: 9836 Estate Ln Dallas TX 75238 Office: Suite 2200 1201 Elm St Dallas TX 75270

BRYANT, RONALD DALE, indsl. rep.; b. Huntsville, Ala., July 27, 1948; s. Roy Lee and Evelyn Henrietta (Craig) B.; B.B.A., U. Tex., Arlington, 1970; m. Marva Ann Polley, Aug. 21, 1970; 1 son, Ross David. Accounts mgr. Swift & Co., 1971-72; regional mgr. U.S. Envelope Co., Dallas, 1972-73, Edmont-Wilson Co., Dallas, 1973-75; sales mgr. Tarvin & Son, Dallas, 1975—. Named Vendor of Month, Gen. Electric Co., Tyler, Tex., 1975. Lic. broker, Tex. Real Estate Commn., 1976. Mem. Am. Soc. Safety Engrs., Delta Sigma Pi (dist. dir.). Democrat. Baptist. Club: Toastmasters Internat. Home: 613 Trailview Garland TX 75043 Office: 11151 Denton Dr Dallas TX 75229

BRYANT, TALBERT CHALMER, JR., auto club exec.; b. Durham, N.C., Dec. 5, 1942; s. T. Chalmer and Sarah Edna (Sockwell) B.; B.A. in Econs., Davidson Coll., 1964; M.B.A., Ga. State U., 1969; m. Leslie Johnsen, Oct. 21, 1979; children—Ashley Elizabeth, Robert Scott. Vice pres. Nat. Automobile Assn., Inc., Atlanta, 1970-75, pres., 1975—; pres. DeSoto Hilton, hotel, Savannah, Ga.; gen. partner Hyatt Regency Hotel, Nashville. Scoutmaster Troop 212 council Boy Scouts Am., 1972-74; chmn. Atlanta Community Relations Commn., 1976; mem. mgmt. conf. bd. Emory U. Bus. Sch., Atlanta, 1975—; chmn. alumni fund drive Westminster Sch., 1973; elder Trinity Presbyn. Ch., 1973—; trustee Galloway Schs., Atlanta, 1974-77; chmn. young businessmen Atlanta Com. to Re-elect Pres., 1972; co-chmn. fin. com. Atlantans for Maynard Jackson, 1973. Served to 1st. lt., Intelligence Corps., U.S. Army, 1965-67; Vietnam. Mem. Am. Automobile Touring Alliance (exec. v.p. 1976—), Alliance Internat. de Tourisme, Atlanta C. of C. (dir. 1971-72), Beta Gamma Sigma. Club: Capital City. Office: 1730 Northeast Expy Atlanta GA 30359

BRYANT, THOMAS CORWIN, athletic dir.; b. Chillicothe, Ohio, May 31, 1933; s. Dennis and Bess Mae (Watts) B.; B.S., Miami U., Oxford, Ohio, 1955; M.Ed., Xavier U., Cin., 1963; m. Jeralyn Thomas, Dec. 22, 1963; children—Todd, Jeff, Scott. Coach, then athletic dir. high schs. in Ohio, 1956-68; dir. athletics, chmn. phys. edn. dept., head basketball coach Centre Coll., Danville, Ky., 1968—. Mem. All-Am. Selection Com. for Basketball, South Region NCAA Div. III, also selection com. for playoffs. Named to Ohio Coaches Basketball Hall of Fame; holder winning basketball coaching record Centre Coll. Mem. Nat. Basketball Coaches Assn. (div. Coach of Year award 1979), Nat. Dirs. Athletics Assn., Nat. Softball Umpires Assn., Coll. Athletic Conf. (past pres. exec. com.), Ky. Phys. Edn. Assn. Democrat. Methodist. Club: Kiwanis. Address: Centre Coll College St Danville KY 40422

BRYANT, THOMAS FLOYD, JR., physician; b. Wellington, Tex., July 17, 1937; s. Thomas Floyd and Tiny Willie (Glasgow) B.; B.A., North Tex. State U., 1959; M.D., U. Tex., 1963; m. Beryl U. Dickens, Aug. 15, 1970; children (by previous marriage)—Thomas Floyd III, Enid Tina. Intern St. Joseph Hosp., Ft. Worth, 1963-64; resident U. Tex. Med. Br. Hosps., 1966-68; resident in pediatric anesthesiology Children's Hosp., Los Angeles, 1968-69; practice medicine specializing in anesthesiology, Galveston, Tex., 1969—; former mem. faculty U. Tex. Med. Br. Hosps., now asso. prof. clin. anesthesiology, Galveston; former faculty John Sealy Hosp.; asst. prof. anesthesiology U. Tex. Med. Br., Galveston, 1971—; asso. clin. prof. anesthesiology Tex. Tech U. Sch. Medicine. Served with AUS, 1964-66. Diplomate Am. Bd. Anesthesiology. Fellow Am. Coll. Anesthesiologists; affiliate fellow Am. Acad. Pediatrics; mem. AMA, Am., Atlantic (hon.), Tex. socs. anesthesiologists, Lamar-Delta County Med. Soc. Home: 695 SE 33d St Paris TX 75460 Office: 130 SE 8th St Paris TX 75460

BRYANT, THOMAS LEE, educator; b. Enid, Okla., Feb. 28, 1929; s. Tom E. and Cleo Jean Smyer; B.S. in Bus. Mgmt., Okla. State U., 1949; M.A. in Geography, U. Okla., 1963, postgrad., 1979; m. Mariann Mitchell, May 29, 1949; children—Sue Ann, Tamie Lee. Commd. 2d lt. USAF, 1949, advanced through grades to lt. col., 1972; chief safety adv. Republic Vietnam, 1971-72; instr. geography and econs., dir. internat. travel study programs No. Okla. Coll., Tonkawa, 1973—. Flotilla comdr. USCG Aux., 1977-78. Decorated Bronze Star, Air medal with 3 oak leaf clusters. Fellow Royal Geog. Soc.; mem. Assn. Am. Geographers, Nat. Council Geographic Edn., Middle East Inst., Oceanic Soc., Am. Geog. Soc., Am. Legion, VFW, Ret. Officers Assn., Sigma Xi, Phi Kappa Phi. Presbyterian. Contbr. articles to profl. jours. Home: PO Box 1293 Ponca City OK 74601 Office: No Okla Coll Tonkawa OK 74653

BRYARS, WILLIAM CARTER, JR., otolaryngologist; b. Mobile, Ala., June 28, 1946; s. William Carter and Mary Kathryn (Compton) B.; B.S., U. Ala., 1968; M.D., U. Ala., 1972; m. Kay Galbraith, Oct. 30, 1970; children—William Carter, Kathryn Galbraith. Intern, U. Va., Charlottesville, 1972-73; resident eye, ear, nose throat U. Ala., Birmingham, 1973-76; practice medicine specializing in otolaryngology Mobile Eye Ear Nose and Throat Center, 1976—; instr. U. So. Ala. Med. Center. Diplomate Am. Bd. otolaryngology. Mem. AMA, A.C.S., Med. Assn. Ala., Am. Acad. Ophthalmology and Otolaryngology. Presbyterian. Club: Mobile Country. Home: 134 Eaton Sq Mobile AL 36608 Office: 1359 Springhill Ave Mobile AL 36604

BRZEZICKI, MICHAEL JOSEPH, hosp. adminstrn. exec.; b. Bristol, Conn., May 19, 1949; s. Stanley Walter and Elizabeth (Neidzwicki) B.; A.A., Northwestern Conn. Community Coll., 1969; student Central Conn. State Coll., 1969-70, Queens Coll., 1972-73; m. Anne Mather, May 11, 1973. Mgr. operating room instrument div. U. Conn. Health Center, Farmington, 1975; coordinator materials processing St. Thomas Hosp., Nashville, 1976-79; dir. materials mgmt. Blount Meml. Hosp., Maryville, Tenn., 1979—; staff cons. BRS Healthcare Cons., 1977—. Cert. profl. health care material mgr. Served with USN, 1971-74; Vietnam. Mem. Tenn. Hosp. Assn., Internat. Materials Mgmt. Soc. (mem. hosp. sect.), Am. Soc. Hosp. Central Service Personnel, Tenn. Soc. for Central Service Personnel (pres. 1978-79). Roman Catholic. Office: Blount Memorial Hosp New Walland Hwy Maryville TN 37801

BUCHANAN, ARTHUR E., JR., systems analyst; b. Nashville, Apr. 23, 1925; s. Arthur E. and Bertha Jane (Graves) B.; LL.B., YMCA Law Sch., Nashville, 1950, J.D., 1971; m. Jerry Davis, Feb. 4, 1950; children—Alice Lynn, Nancy Carol. Admitted to Tenn. bar, 1950; mem. firm Buchanan & Harvey, Nashville, 1950-55; pres. Jetbec Investors, Inc., St. Petersburg, 1957-60, St. Petersburg Title Corp. (Fla.) 1960-65; mgr. data processing Holsum Baking Co., Miami, 1966—; lectr. Fla. title ins. and bus. law. Served with AUS, 1943-45. Aide de camp Gov. Staff Tenn. Mem. Tenn. Bar Assn., Nashville Bar Assn., Univac Users Assn. Am., Roller Skating Operators Am. (internat. judge). Democrat. Methodist. Clubs: Mason, Rotary. Home: 8270 163d St SW Miami FL 33157 Office: Sunset Dr and Red Rd South Miami FL 33143

BUCHANAN, D. JEAN, accountant; b. Prescott, Ark., July 22, 1944; d. Albert Vernon and Pauline Iris (Simpson) B.; student U. Ark., 1962-65, 67-68; B.S. in Bus. Adminstrn., Tulsa U., 1973. Photographer, Pine Bluff (Ark.) Comml., 1966-67; photo lab technician Photo Services Internat., Tulsa, 1969-72, lab mgr., 1973; acct. Bareco div. Petrolite Corp., Tulsa, 1974-78, plant controller, office mgr., Kilgore, Tex., 1978—. Presbyterian. Office: PO Box 390 Kilgore TX 75662

BUCHANAN, HARRY WINTERS, III, chem. co. exec.; b. Bklyn., Nov. 9, 1923; s. Harry W. and Eugenie Marie (O'Brien) B.; B.S., Rensselaer Poly. Inst., 1947; postgrad. (Sloan fellow) M.I.T., 1956; m. Barbara Combes, Oct. 30, 1951; children—Harry W., Cathleen, Joan, Bruce Stewart, Virginia Gail, Brien Combes, Mary Ann. With Metal and Thermit Corp. (name changed to M&T Chems. 1962), 1947-66, group v.p., 1962-65, pres. M&T Products of Can. Ltd., 1965-66; chief exec. officer, pres. Va. Chems., Inc., Portsmouth, Va., 1966—, chmn., chief exec. officer, 1970—; dir. Crompton & Knowles, United Va. Bank, Seaboard Nat., United Va. Bankshares, N, F & D. Ry. Trustee Colgate Darden Sch. Bus., U. Va., trustee Va. Ind. Coll. Fund; bd. assos. U. Richmond. Served with U.S. Army, 1944-46. Mem. Mfg. Chemists Assn. (past bd. dirs.), Va. Mfrs. Assn. (chmn. 1976-78), Am. Chem. Soc., Am. Electroplaters Soc. Roman Catholic. Clubs: Augusta Nat. Golf, Commonwealth, Union League, Pinnacle, Sky, Cedar Point, Chemists. Office: 3340 W Norfolk Rd Portsmouth VA 23703

BUCHANAN, JOHN HALL, JR., congressman; b. Paris, Tenn., Mar. 19, 1928; s. John Hall and Ruby (Lowrey) B.; A.B., Howard Coll., 1949; grad. student U. Va., 1950-51; Th.B., So. Bapt. Theol. Sem., 1957; LL.D., Samford U., 1967; m. 2d, Elizabeth Moore, May 9, 1961; children—Elizabeth Jakes, Lynn Lowrey. Ordained to ministry Baptist Ch., 1952; pastor in Glasgow, Va., 1952-53,

Hartsville, Tenn., 1955-56, Birmingham, Ala., 1957-62; minister edn. Southside Bapt. Ch., Birmingham, 1953-54; speaker, lectr. in Ala., also interim and supply pastor, 1962-64; mem. 89th-96th Congresses from 6th Dist. Ala. Mem. U.S. delegation to UN, 1973, also spl. session, 1974; U.S. del. to Belgrade Conf., 1977, to UN Human Rights Commn., 1978; ex-officio mem. Pres.'s Commn. on Coal, 1978-79; mem. Commn. on Security and Cooperation in Europe; bd. selectors Am. Inst. Public Service; co-founder, vice chmn. Congressional Steel Caucus. Chmn. Jefferson County Republican Com., 1964—; pres. Rep. Workshops Ala., 1963-64; mem. exec. com., dir. finance Ala. Rep. Com., 1963-64; bd. dirs. Gallaudet Coll. Served with USNR, 1945-46. Mem. Pi Kappa Alpha. Mason, Kiwanian. Office: Rayburn House Office Bldg Washington DC 20515

BUCHANAN, ROBERT BYRON, service co. exec.; b. Omaha, Dec. 2, 1941; s. Howard Byron and Verna Evelyn (Boyer) B.; B.S. in Elec. Engring., Wichita State U., 1963; M.S. in Elec. Engring., Okla. State U., also Ph.D.; m. Roberta Walters, June 8, 1968; children—Stephen Bradley, Paul Robert. Engr. King Radio Corp., Wichita, Kans., 1963; sr. research engr. N. Am. Aviation Co., Tulsa, Okla., 1964-68; supr. GTE Sylvania, Mountain View, Calif., 1968-69; dir. ops. BDM Corp., Albuquerque, 1969-73, v.p. western operations, 1973-75, group v.p., McLean, Va., 1975—. Served with USMC, 1971. Mem. IEEE (vice chmn. nuclear and space radiation effects steering group 1973-76), Am. Mgmt. Assn. Club: Internat. (Washington). Home: 2404 Black Cap Ln Reston VA 22091 Office: 7915 Jones Branch Dr McLean VA 22091

BUCHANAN, ROBERT STEPHEN, hosp. supply adminstr.; b. Charleroi, Pa., Apr. 2, 1948; s. Robert R. and Betty Lou (Duvuvuei) B.; student Steed Coll., 1974-79, U.S. Army Med. Sch., 1967, Ohio Labor and Tng. Sch., 1971; m. Vivian Dianne Buchanan, Sept. 24, 1966; children—Chris (dec.), Stephen Wayne. Foreman, Labor Local 860, Cleve., 1970-71, steward, 1971-72; foreman Carpenter's Local, Ft. Lauderdale, Fla., 1972-74; central service mgr. Holston Valley Community Hosp., Kingsport, Tenn., 1974—. Served with U.S. Army, 1967-70. Recipient numerous awards and trophys for karate, including 4th Pl. All Canadian Karate Championship, 1966, 3 Master's Ratings, 1978-79, Black Belt in 5 Styles of Karate, 1965-79. Mem. Internat. Assn. Hosp. Central Service Mgrs., Am. Hosp. Assn., Eastern Tenn. Regional Central Supply (founder 1979, pres. 1979-80), Tenn. Central Service Assn. (chmn. bd. 1979-80), East Tenn. Infectious Disease Study Group, Elite Fighting Arts Soc. (v.p.), World Sholin Kung Fu Assn. (Ohio rep. 1970-72). Baptist. Home: 119 Kindrick St Kingsport TN 37660 Office: West Ravine St Kingsport TN 37662

BUCHANAN, THOMAS LOUIS, physician, surgeon; b. Wynne, Ark., Feb. 7, 1942; s. James Graydon and Anabell Elizabeth (Koonce) B.; student Memphis State U., 1960-63; B.S., U. Ark., 1967, M.D., 1967; m. Vickie Lee Bradshaw, June 12, 1967; children—Thomas Martin, Andrew Morgan. Intern, U.S. Naval Hosp., N.Y.C., 1968, resident, Orlando, Fla.; practice medicine specilaizing in family practice and surgery, Morrilton, Ark., 1970—; mem. staff Conway County Hosp.; instr. Petit Jean Vocat. LPN Sch. Bd. dirs. Ark. River Valley Area Council Day Care Center. Served with USN, 1967-70. Mem. County Med. Soc. (sec.), Ark. Med. Soc., Am. Med. Assn., Am. Acad. Family Physicians, Chi Beta Phi. Home: Cedar Crest Dr Morrilton AR 72110 Office: 200 S Moose St Morrilton AR 72110

BUCHER, MURIEL MOWEN, ceramic co. exec.; b. Plainfield, N.J., Dec. 29, 1913; d. Waldo Recher and Sarah Augusta (Hand) Mowen; m. Bruce S. Bucher, June 30, 1934; children—Joan Muriel Bucher Gowell, W. Kenneth. Sec., John Day Pub. Co., N.Y.C., 1931, Standard Oil Co., Calif., N.Y.C., 1932-34; pres. Ceramic Enterprises of Fla., Inc., Winter Park, 1969—; tchr. ceramics for handicapped. Mem. Roselle (N.J.) Bd. Edn., 1948-53, pres., 1950-53; vol. Winter Park Meml. Hosp., 1955-63; pres. Winter Park Welcome Wagon Club, 1954-55; local precinct election ofcl.; bd. dirs. Winter Park Day Nursery, 1968—, past pres. Mem. Central Fla. Ceramic Soc. (pres.). Republican. Congregationalist. Club: Forrest Hills Garden (past pres.). Address: 270 W Reading Way Winter Park FL 32789

BUCHMAN, BILL, mfg. co. exec.; b. Tampa, Fla., Nov. 15, 1940; s. Manuel Jacob and Ruth (Weber) B.; B.S. in Civil Engring., Ga. Inst. Tech., 1962; m. Joyce Stone, June 10, 1962; children—Richard, Lauri, Marty, Wendy. Materials testing specialist Lockheed Aircraft Co., Marietta, Ga., 1962-63; sales staff Atlanta Envelope Co., 1963; sales Zep Mfg. Co., 1963—, dir. sales, 1971—. Mem. Camp Barney Medintz com. Jewish Welfare Assn.; bd. dirs. Atlanta Jewish Community Center. Mem. Am. Mgmt. Assn., Internat. Entrepeneurs Assn. Home: 7485 Old Maine Trail Atlanta GA 30328 Office: 1310 Seaboard Industrial Blvd Atlanta GA 30318

BUCK, CREED, JR., clergyman; b. Madison County, Miss., Jan. 14, 1933; s. Creed and Alma (Crowmwell) B.; B.S., Jackson State U., 1955, M.S., 1965; Ed.S. in Adminstrn. and Supervision, Miss. State U., 1975; D.D., Am. Bible Sch., Kansas City, Mo., 1966; m. Novella Shelby, Dec. 25, 1956; children—Angela, Kenneth, Gregory. Student prin. lab. sch. Jackson State U., 1956; ordained to ministry Nat. Baptist Conv., 1956; pastor Chapel Hill Starkville (Miss.) Ch., 1956-66; coach, then prin. elem. schs. in Miss., 1957-71; prin. Motley Attendance Center, also pastor Missionary Union Bapt. Ch., Columbus, Miss., 1971—; exec. dir., pres. N.E. Regional Community Devel., 1975-79; exec. sec. N.E. Miss. Bapt. Conv., 1979; dir. gen. Mt. Olivet Congress, 1979. Mem. Miss. Edn. Assn., Miss. Assn. Adminstrs., Lowndes County Assn. Educators NAACP, Operation Push, Lowndes County Voters League. Democrat. Club: Masons. Home: PO Box 1754 Columbus MS 39701 Office: Route 3 Box 301 Columbus MS 39701

BUCK, HARVEY SHARPE, judge; b. Tchula, Miss., July 19, 1921; s. George Thad and Florence (Baine) B.; B.S., Miss. State U., 1942; LL.B., U. Miss., 1956, J.D., 1968; m. Helen Eugenia Poirier, July 20, 1946; children—Brenda Poirier Buck Moore, George Thad II, Janis Parrish Buck Smith. Admitted to Miss. bar, 1955; practiced in West Point, 1956—; city judge, West Point, 1958-60; dist. atty. 16th Jud. Dist. Miss., West Point, 1960-76, circuit judge, 1976—; preceptor clin. legal edn. program U. Miss. Law Sch., 1971—. Mem. Gov.'s Commn. Criminal Justice Standards, 1974-75. Served to maj. AUS, 1955. Mem. Am., Miss., Clay County (pres. 1966-68) bar assns., Nat. Dist. Attys. Assn. (dir.), Miss. Prosecutors Assn. (pres. 1971-72), Miss. Circuit Judges Assn. (v.p. 1980, pres.-elect 1980), Clay County C. of C. (pres. 1968). Presbyn. (elder). Clubs: Masons, Shriners (Meridian). Home: Old Waverly Rd West Point MS 39773 Office: 203 Jordan S West Point MS 39773

BUCK, PEGGY SULLIVAN, educator; b. North Augusta, S.C., Aug. 3, 1930; d. Charles Edmund and Ethlene Amanda (Peacock) Sullivan; A.B., Coker Coll., 1961; M.A., Appalachian State U., 1976; m. William D. Buck, Oct. 18, 1954; (div.); children—Wilson E., Deborah Ann. Tchr., Smith's Elementary Sch., Lumberton, N.C., 1964, Butner Elementary Sch., Fort Bragg, N.C., 1965—. Fellow Anglo-Am. Acad. (Cambridge; hon.), Internat. Biog. Assn. (Cambridge); mem. NEA, N.C. Assn. Educators, Internat. Platform Assn. Episcopalian. Author: I'm Divorced—are you listening, Lord?, 1976; I'm Depressed-are you listening, Lord?, 1978; It's So Lovely Here Now, Lord-But Not Always, 1980. Home: 210 13th St E Lumberton NC 28358 Office: Drawer A Fort Bragg Dependents Schs Fort Bragg NC 28307

BUCK, RICHARD EDWARD, III, banker; b. Fayetteville, Ark., July 19, 1952; s. Richard Edward and Frances Elizabeth (Glass) B.; B.S., U. Ark., 1974; postgrad. U. Wis. Grad. Sch. Banking; m. Jan Garner, July 28, 1973; 1 dau., Susan Emily. Asst. cashier Bank of Pea Ridge, (Ark.), 1974-75, v.p., cashier, 1975-76, pres., chief exec. officer, dir., 1976—. Mem. adv. bd. Ozark Guidance Center, 1976—; mem. Benton County Com. Ark. Ednl. Goals. Mem. Ark. Bankers Assn., Washington-Benton County Bankers Group (chmn. 1977). Clubs: Prairie Creek Country, Kiwanis (pres. club). Home: 76 Brush Creek Hills Rogers AR 72756 Office: Box 5 Pea Ridge AR 72751

BUCKALEW, LOUIS WALTER, III, behavioral scientist; b. Bloomsburg, Pa., Apr. 21, 1944; s. Louis W. and Maryruth (Rishe) B.; B.A., Ga. So. Coll., 1967; M.S., U. So. Miss., 1969; postgrad. Howard U., 1978-79. Instr. psychology S.C. State Coll., Orangeburg, 1970-73; sr. partner Buckalew & Davis Asso., Orangeburg, S.C., 1973-75; NSF faculty fellow Howard U., Washington, 1978-79; asst. prof. psychology and dir. Inst. for Alcohol Research, Ala. A. and M. U., Normal, 1975—; dir. NSF pre-coll. tchr. devel. in sci. program, 1978-79; cons. N. Ala. Drug Edn. program, 1979—. Dir., moderator PBS TV series on applied psychology, 1977-78, series on drug edn., 1979—. Served with U.S. Army, 1969-70. Decorated Bronze Star medal, Army Commendation medal. NSF fellow, 1978-79. Mem. Am. Orthopsychiatric Assn., Nat. Inst. Sci., Southeastern Psychol. Assn., So. Assn. for Counselor Edn. and Supervision, Ala. Psychol. Assn., Ala. Personnel and Guidance Assn., Psi Chi, Kappa Delta Pi. Republican. Episcopalian. Author 3 books; contbr. numerous articles to profl. jours. Office: Dept Psychology Ala A and M Univ Normal AL 35762

BUCKELEW, MORRIS THOMAS, computer co. exec.; b. Cleveland, Tenn., Oct. 24, 1918; s. Robert G. and Harris (McDaris) B.; student U. Va., 1936-37, Nat. U., Washington, 1938-41; m. Patricia June Few, Aug. 16, 1941; children—Roger G., Bruce N., Daniel V. Jr. engr. U. Calif., Los Alamos Sci. Lab., also Sandia Labs., Albuquerque, 1945-49; mem. staff Applied Physics Lab., John Hopkins U., 1949-52; ordnance projects mgr. Corvey Engring. Co., Washington, 1952-56; asst. to v.p. engring. AMF Co., Washington, 1956-62; v.p. Specialties Inc., aircraft instrumentation, Charlottesville, Va., 1962-66; dist. mgr. Rosemont Engring., then United Control Co., Washington, 1966-72; v.p. SAID, Inc., computer research and services, Falls Church, Va., 1972—; mem. Radio Tech. Com. Aeros., 1963-64. Served with AUS, 1941-43, USAAF, 1943-45. Rated Comml. pilot. Mem. Am. Soc. Quality Control, Data Processing Mgrs. Assn., Soc. Wireless Pioneers, Am. Radio Relay League, Rho Epsilon, Sigma Nu Phi. Episcopalian. Home: PO Box 10 Falls Church VA 22046 Office: 417 W Broad St Falls Church VA 22046

BUCKLEY, EMERSON, music dir., condr.; b. N.Y.C., Apr. 14, 1916; s. Wendell and Minnie (Buckley) B.; B.A., Columbia, 1936; L.H.D., U. Denver, 1959; m. Mary Henderson, May 27, 1948; children—Robert Allen, Richard Edward. Music dir. Columbia Grand Opera, 1936-38, Palm Beach (Fla.) Symphony and Chorus, 1938-41, N.Y.C. Symphony, 1941-42, San Carlo Opera, 1943-45, WOR-MBS, N.Y.C., 1945-54, Marquis de Cuevas Ballet, 1950, Mendelssohn Glee Club, N.Y.C., 1954-63, P.R. Opera Festival, 1954-58, Symphony of the Air, also Empire State Mus. Festival, 1955, Chgo. Opera, 1956, Tagarazuka Dance Theatre, also Greek Theatre, Los Angeles, 1958, Chautauqua Festival, N.Y., 1960, Temple U. Music Festival and Inst., 1970; music dir. Miami (Fla.) Opera Guild, 1950—; artistic dir. Greater Miami Opera Assn., 1973—; music dir. Central City (Colo.) Opera, 1956-69, Ft. Lauderdale (Fla.) Symphony, 1963—, Seattle Opera, 1964—; condr. N.Y.C. Opera, 1955-69, Chgo., Milw., New Orleans, Balt., Cin., Duluth (Minn.) operas, 1970—, San Francisco, Houston, Phila., Tulsa operas, 1975—, Opera Metropolitana, Caracas, Venezuela, 1977. Guest appearances with various orchs., including Toronto (Ont., Can.) Philharmonic, Mpls. Symphony, Miami Symphony; mem. faculty U. Denver, 1956, Columbia, 1957-58, Manhattan Sch. Music, 1958-70, Temple U., 1970, N.C. Sch. Arts, 1971; dir. world premiers of Am. operas including The Ballad of Baby Doe, 1956, Gallantry, 1958, He Who Gets Slapped, 1959, The Crucible, 1961, Gentlemen Be Seated, 1963, Lady from Colorado, 1964; recordings for Deutsche Grammophon, M-G-M, Columbia, Composers Records Inc., Heliodor. Recipient Fox prize Columbia Coll., 1936; Alice M. Ditson Conductor's award, 1964; Colo. Ambassadors Sash, 1965; Gold Chair award Central City Opera, 1965; Am. Patriot award state of Fla., 1971; decorated Chevalier de l'Ordre des Arts et Lettres (France). Mem. Nat. Assn. Am. Composers and Condrs. Mason (Shriner). Home: 19640 NE 20th Ave North Miami Beach FL 33179 Office: 1430 N Federal Hwy Fort Lauderdale FL 33304 also 1200 Coral Way Miami FL 33145

BUCKLEY, JACK BOYD, mech./elec. engr.; b. Fort Wayne, Ind., Feb. 6, 1926; s. Chauncey Jason and Ruth W. (Boyd) B.; student Ind. State U., 1944, Kan. State U., 1944-45, Purdue, 1947; B.S. in C.E., Rice Inst., 1948; postgrad. U. Houston, 1948-49; m. Helen C. Sartwelle, Jan. 18, 1952; children—Elizabeth Ann (Mrs. Christopher Till), James S., Steven B., William H. Exec. v.p. I. A. Naman & Assos. and I. A. Naman & Assos. West, Inc., Houston, 1949—, also dir.; pres. Internat. Engrs., Inc., Houston, dir. Port City Stockyard, Tex. Agribus. Co., Inc. Mem. Houston Air Conditioning Bd., 1974-78, Houston Gen. Appeals Bd., 1978—. Mem. Aldine (Ind.) Sch. Bd., 1954-55; adv. council Am. Arbitration Assn. Served with USNR, 1944-46. Registered profl. engr., Tex. Mem. Am. Soc. Heating, Refrigerating and Air Conditioning Engrs. (chpt. pres. 1961), Constrn. Specifications Inst. (chpt. pres. 1973-74), Nat., Tex. socs. profl. engrs., Am. Hosp. Assn., Nat. Fire Protection Assn., Illuminating Engring. Soc., Smoke Control Assos., Am. Cons. Engr. Council, Houston Livestock Show and Rodeo (life), Nat. Rifle Assn., Am. Forestry Assn., Am. Mgmt. Assn., Constrn. Industry Council Houston, Houston Zool. Soc. (dir. 1969-73). Rotarian. Club: 100 (life, dir. 1975) (Houston). Cons. editor Specifying Engr. Mag., 1974—. Contbr. articles to profl. jours. Home: 10047 Del Monte Dr Houston TX 77042 Office: 2 Greenway Plaza E No 520 Houston TX 77046

BUCKLEY, THOMAS HUGH, historian, educator; b. Elkhart, Ind., Sept. 11, 1932; s. Bernard L. and Martha B. (Swoveland) B.; student Northwestern U., 1950-53; A.B., Ind. U., 1955, M.A., 1956, Ph.D., 1961; postgrad. Stanford, 1968; m. Patricia Cox, 1968; children—Christopher, Kathryn, Elizabeth, Thomas, Barbara. Instr. history U. S.D., Vermillion, 1961, asst. prof., 1961-64, asso. prof., 1964-68, prof., 1968-69; vis. prof. Ind. U., Bloomington, 1969-71; prof. history U. Tulsa, 1971—, chmn. dept., 1971—. Recipient citation for Best First Book by Historian, Phi Alpha Theta, 1971. Fulbright fellow, 1962. Mem. Orgn. Am. Historians, Phi Alpha Theta. Author: The United States and the Washington Conference, 1921-22, 1970; Challenge Was My Master, 1979; also chpt. in book. Home: 7951 B S Yale St Tulsa OK 74136

BUCKLEY, WILLIAM STUART, real estate appraiser; b. Chester, Pa., Nov. 10, 1943; s. Leslie Stuart and Helen (Boluck) B.; B.S. in Econs., Widener U., 1965; m. Jean Campbell Carr, Sept. 24, 1966; children—Kevin, Brian, Heather. Right-of-way negotiator, rev. appraiser N.J. Dept. Transp., 1965-72; sec., mng. officer Beckett Bldg. & Loan Assn. of Camden (N.J.), 1969-72; rev. and staff appraiser coordinator Fla. Dept. Transp., 1972-73; staff appraiser Wheeler & Klusza Realty, Inc., Lakeland, Fla., 1974-75; pres., mgr., appraiser, real estate broker W.S. Buckley Appraisal Services, Inc., Tampa, 1975—. Mem. Hillsborough County Zoning Task Force Com.; pres. Forest Hills Youth Soccer League, 1979-80. Named An Outstanding Young Man of Am., U.S. Jaycees, 1977. Mem. Am. Soc. Appraisers, Nat., Fla. assns. realtors, Tampa Bd. Realtors, Soc. Real Estate Appraisers (dir., chmn. edn. Fla. West Coast chpt.; Fla. regional chmn. market data center), Tampa C. of C. (urban planning council, com. of 100, state and local govt. council). Rotarian (editor newsletter). Home: 11812 Lipsey Rd Tampa FL 33618 Office: 2004 W Busch Blvd Tampa FL 33612

BUCKNAM, HOWARD VICTOR, club exec.; b. Berlin, N.H., July 16, 1936; s. James Romeo and Adrienne (Meteyer) B.; A.B., Dartmouth Coll., 1958; m. Muriel Rose Carignan, July 19, 1958; children—Lisa, Steven, Jennifer, Christopher. Commd. 2d lt. USMC, 1958, advanced through grades to lt. col., 1978; dir. Basic Sch. Officers Club, Quantico Va., 1970-72; dir. Marine Corps Club System, Washington, 1976-78; clubs dir. USMC Base, Quantico, Va., 1978—. Pres., Eastern Prince William County Citizens Assn., 1973. Decorated Bronze Star. Mem. Nat. Restaurant Assn., Internat. Mil. Club Execs. Assn. (pres. 1980-81). Republican. Roman Catholic. Home: 14819 Elmwood Dr Woodbridge VA 22193 Office: Clubs Director MCDEC Quantico VA 22134

BUCKNER, GERALDINE LAREE, nurse; b. Dallas, Jan. 11, 1924; d. Avery Manual and Geraldine Kinney (Macon) Millican; A.D. in Nursing, El Centro Jr. Coll., Dallas, 1974; B.S. in Health Care Adminstrn., E. Tex. State U., 1979; m. Leonard Cooke Buckner, Aug. 11, 1942 (dec. 1967); children—Janet Laree, Rebecca Sue, Joni Kay. Supr. emergency room East Town Osteo. Hosp., Dallas, from 1966, now dir. nursing. Mem. Am., Tex., Emergency Dept. nurses assns., Am. Nat. Red Cross. Democrat. Baptist. Club: Eastern Star. Home: 7515 Lovett St Dallas TX 75227

BUCKNER, JOHN KENDRICK, aero. engr.; b. Indpls., June 13, 1936; s. Roland Kendrick and Lucille (Cave) B.; B.A., De Pauw U., 1958; M.S. in Aero. Engring., Stanford U., 1960; m. Nancy Ann Smith, June 13, 1974; children—James Kendrick, Bari Kay. Aerodynamics engr. Gen. Dynamics Corp., Ft. Worth, Tex., 1960-64, sr. aerodynamics engr., 1964-68, project aerodynamics, engr., 1968-69, group supr. aerodynamics, 1969-75, mem. aerospace tech. staff of advanced programs, 1975-77, engring. mgr., 1977—. Asso. fellow Am. Inst. Aeros. and Astronautics (advisory bd. N. Tex. sect. 1973-76, atmospheric flight mechanics tech. com. 1979). Club: Rivercrest Country. Contbr. articles on aerodynamics to tech. publs. Home: 5408 Berbridge Dr Ft Worth TX 76107 Office: PO Box 748 Ft Worth TX 76101

BUCKNER, MARY JO, dietitian; b. Cleburne, Tex., Jan. 7, 1946; d. Joe C. and Mary J. (Coody) Glover; B.S. magna cum laude, Tex. Wesleyan Coll., 1968; postgrad. Tex. Christian U., 1969, Tex. Women's U., 1971-77; m. Thomas J. Pruitt, July 13, 1964 (div. 1970); children—Karen A., Michael D., Patti Jo; m. 2nd Charles E. Buckner, Apr. 29, 1972 (div. 1978). Adminstrv. dietitian Tarrant County Hosp. Dist., Ft. Worth, Tex., 1969-75; dir. nutritional service Great SW Gen. Hosp. Grand Prairie, Tex., also Arlington (Tex.) Community Hosp., 1975-77; corporate cons. dietitian Jewell Enterprises, Inc., Arlington, 1977-79; dir. dietary service The Meadow Green, Dallas, 1979—; regional supervising dietitian ARA Services Inc.; instr. Tarrant County Jr. Coll., part-time, 1977, Tex. Christian U., 1974, Ft. Worth Pub. Sch. Adult Edn., 1974-76; long term care facilities dietary cons., 1973-78. Mem. Am. Dietetic Assn., Tex. Dietetic Assn., Ft. Worth Dietetic Assn., Gamma Omicron, Alpha Chi. Home: 5201 Gibbons St Fort Worth TX 76118

BUCUR, JOHN CHARLES, neurol. surgeon; b. Youngstown, Ohio, Mar. 5, 1925; s. John and Victoria (Marginean) B.; B.S., Ohio U., 1947; postgrad. U. Biarritz (France), 1946; M.D., U. Pitts., 1951, M.Surgery, 1952; m. Anna Jane Alberson, July 12, 1951; children—John Ellsworth, Dean Charles, Victoria Ann. Intern, Western Pa. Hosp., Pitts., 1951-52; resident in neurosurgery Long Beach (Calif.) VA Hosp., 1953-56, staff neurosurgeon, 1956-57; neurosurg. cons. Harbor Gen. Hosp., Torrance, Calif., 1956-57; practice medicine specializing in neurol. surgery, Falls Church, Va., 1957—; chief staff Nat. Orthopedic and Rehab. Hosp., Arlington, Va., 1973; chief neurol. surgery Fairfax Hosp., Falls Church, 1961-75, Nat. Orthopedic and Rehab. Hosp., Arlington, Va., 1957-79, No. Va. Drs. Hosp., Arlington, 1963—, Arlington Hosp., 1977—; sr. attending neurosurgeon Alexandria Hosp., 1959—, Circle Terrace Hosp., Alexandria, Va., 1962—; sec., dir. 7 Corners Med. Bldgs., Inc., Falls Church, 1958—; partner Edward R. Lang M.D., Falls Church, 1969—. Mem. Va. Gov.'s Com. for Regional Med. Program, dir. regional med. program, 1969-77. Served with U.S. Army, 1943-45; ETO. Diplomate Am. Bd. Neurol. Surgery. Fellow ACS; mem. Am. Assn. Neurol. Surgeons, Mid-Atlantic Neurosurgery Soc., Washington Acad. Neurosurgery, Neurosurg. Soc. Vas., No. Va. Acad. Surgery, Congress Neurol. Surgeons, Pan Am. Med. Assn., So. Med. Assn., Arlington County Med. Soc., Fairfax County Med. Soc., Am. Legion. Methodist. Club: Masons. Office: 6305 Castle Pl Falls Church VA 22044

BUCY, J. FRED, electronics co. exec.; b. Tahoka, Tex., July 29, 1928; s. J. Fred and Ethel (Montgomery) B.; B.A. in Physics, Tex. Tech. U., 1951; M.A. in Physics, U. Tex., 1953; m. Odetta Greer, Jan. 25, 1947; children—J. Fred III Roxanne, Diane. With Tex. Instruments Inc., Dallas, 1953—, gen. mgr. apparatus div., corp. v.p. 1963-67, corp. group v.p. components group, 1967-72, exec. v.p., 1972-75, exec. v.p., chief operating officer, 1975—, pres., 1976—. also dir. Bd. regents Tex. Tech U.; mem. bd. devel. U. Tex., Dallas. Recipient Distinguished Engr. award Tex. Tech U., 1972. Fellow IEEE (USAC adv. com.); mem. Nat. Acad. Engring., AAAS, Soc. Exploration Geophysicists, Navy League, Sigma Pi Sigma, Tau Beta Pi. Clubs: Petroleum (Dallas); Cosmos (Washington); Northwood Country (Dallas). Office: PO Box 225424 Dallas TX 75265

BUDA, JOSEPH GEORGE, univ. ofcl.; b. Rochester, N.Y., Mar. 27, 1917; s. August and Grace (Alafaci) B.; student pub. schs., Rochester, 1923-35; m. Grace Benfante, Apr. 1, 1944; children—Julianne, Susan, Doreen. Truck driver McCurdy & Co., Rochester, 1937-42; letter carrier U.S. Post Office, Rochester, 1942-74; campus postmaster U. South Fla. Med. Center, Tampa, 1975—. Mem. Sons of Italy. Club: Moose. Home: 2229 Keyes Ave Spring Hill FL 33526 Office: U South Fla Med Center 12901 N 30th St Tampa FL 33612

BUDALUR, THYAGARAJAN SUBBANARAYAN, educator, univ. adminstr.; b. Tiruvarur, India, July 14, 1929; s. Subbanarayan Subbuswamy and Paravatham (Copalakrishnan) B.; came to U.S., 1969, natrualized 1977; M.A., U. Madras, 1951, M.Sc., 1954, Ph.D., 1956; children—Chitra, Poorna, Kartik. Reader organic chemistry U. Madras, 1960-68 prof. chemistry U. Idaho, Mosow, 1968-74; prof. chemistry, dir. div. earth phys. sci. U. Tex., San Antonio, 1974—; lectr. in field. Mem. Idaho Research Found. Recipient Intra Sci. Research award, 1966. Fellow Am. Chem. Soc., Am. Inst. Chemists; mem. Chem. Soc. London, N.Y. Acad. Sci., Nat. Commn. Cert.

Chemists, Sigma Xi. Club: Lions. Author: Mechanisms of Molecular Migrations; Selective Organic Transfomations. Editorial bd. chem. jours.; contbr. articles to profl. jours. Home: 4518 Maybrook Woods San Antonio TX 78249 Office: San Antonio TX 78285

BUDD, JOSEPH EDWARD, utilities exec.; b. Houston, Aug. 25, 1947; s. Kline Fischer and Margaret Edna (Underwood) B.; student Lamar U., 1979; m. Deborah Gail Howell, June 12, 1970; children—Julie Carol, Jamie Leigh Anne. With Gulf States Utilities, Beaumont, Tex., 1969—, sr. engr., 1973-78, real estate rep., 1978—. Active Jr. Cardinal Football, Beaumont, 1971-78. Served with USMC, 1966-70. Decorated Purple Heart, Silver Star. Mem. Am. Right of Way Assn., Am. Cattlemen's Assn., Am. Quarterhorse Assn. Democrat. Baptist. Home: 272 Rosine St Beaumont TX 77707 Office: PO Box 2951 Beaumont TX 77704

BUDD, LOUIS JOHN, educator; b. St. Louis, Aug. 26, 1921; s. Vincent and Sophia (Kajszo) Budrewicz; B.A., U. Mo., 1941, M.A., 1942; Ph.D., U. Wis., 1949; m. Isabelle Amelia Marx, Mar. 3, 1945; children—Catherine Lou, David Harry. Instr., U. Mo., Columbia, 1941, 46; instr. dept. English, U. Ky., Lexington, 1949-52, asst. prof., 1952; asst. prof. dept. English, Duke U., Durham, N.C., 1952-60, prof., 1966—, chmn. dept. English, 1973-79; mem. vis. faculty Washington U., St. Louis, summer 1954, Northwestern U., Evanston, Ill., 1961; Fulbright lectr., India, 1967, 72, U. Damascus, Syria, 1978; lectr. seminar Kraft div. Internat. Paper Co., summer 1959. Served to 2d lt. USAF, 1942-45. Guggenheim fellow, 1965-66; Am. Philos. Soc. grantee, 1956, 70, 73; sr. fellow Nat. Endowment for Humanities, 1979-80. Mem. Modern Lang. Assn., AAUP (pres. Duke chpt. 1971-72), Internat. Assn. Univ. Profs. English, Soc. Study of So. Lit. (exec. com. 1973-77), Phi Beta Kappa, Phi Eta Sigma. Author: Mark Twain: Social Philosopher, 1962; Robert Herrick, 1971; (with others) Literature and Society, 1956; A Listing of and Selection from Newspaper and Magazine Interviews with Mark Twain, 1977; mng. editor: American Literature, 1979—; contbr. numerous articles on lit. history and criticism to lit. jours. Home: 2753 McDowell St Durham NC 27705 Office: 325 Allen Bldg Dept English Duke U Durham NC 27706

BUDIG, GENE ARTHUR, ednl. adminstr.; b. McCook, Nebr., May 25, 1939; s. Arthur G. and Angela B. (Schaaf) B.; B.S., U. Nebr., 1962, M.Ed., 1963; Ed.D., 1967; m. Gretchen Van Bloom, Nov. 30, 1963; children—Christopher, Mary Frances. Exec. asst. to gov. Nebr., Lincoln, 1964-67; adminstrv. asst. to chancellor, asst. prof. ednl. adminstrn. U. Nebr., Lincoln, 1967-70, asst. vice chancellor of academic affairs, prof. ednl. adminstrn., 1970, asst. v.p., dir. public affairs, 1971; v.p., dean univ. Ill. State U., Normal, 1972, pres., 1973-77; pres. W.Va. U., Morgantown, 1977—; dir. W.Va. Council Econ. Edn., 1977. Bd. dirs. W.Va. U. Found., 1977; chmn. State Com. Coal and Energy Research, 1977—. Recipient Disting. Service award Univ. and Coll. Women Ill., 1975; named one of 100 top leaders in Am. higher edn. Chance mag., 1978. Mem. Council Public Coll. and Univ. Pres.'s, Nat. Assn. State Univs. and Land-Grant Colls. Author: (with Stanley G. Rives) Academic Quicksand: Expectations of the Administrator, 1973; editor: Preceptions in Public Higher Education, 1970; Dollars and Sense: Budgeting for Today's Campus, 1972; editorial cons. Phi Delta Kappa, 1976—; contbr. articles to profl. jours. Home: 948 Riverview Dr Morgantown WV 26505 Office: Office of President WVa Univ Morgantown WV 26506

BUDINGER, JEAN-PAUL, architect, engr.; b. Chgo., May 6, 1939; s. Peter W. and Pauline (Pond) B.; student Purdue U., 1957-58; B.A. in Architecture, U. Ill., 1963; postgrad. Entwickiung Statte fur den Lichtbau (West Berlin, Fed. Rep. Germany), 1963-64; m. Patricia Ann Plaza, June 10, 1961; children—Melinda Jean, Michelle Patricia. Apprentice architect, engr. firm R. Swanson, Evanston, Ill., 1964-65, with firm Stanley D. Anderson, Lake Forest, Ill., 1965-67; chief architect. engr. for 24 state region Dept. Agr., Mpls., 1967-69; pres. Jean-Paul Budinger, Inc., Wayzata, Minn., and Austin, Tex., 1969—; v.p. Internat. Diversified Corp., Austin. Recipient award merit Ill. Sesquicentennial Stamp Design Contest, 1959. Registered profl. architect, Ill., Minn., N.D., Ariz., Wis., Tex., Fla., Iowa, Colo., registered profl. engr., Minn., Tex. Mem. Nat. Council Archtl. Registration Bds., A.I.A., Minn. Soc. Profl. Engrs. Designer, engr. for Bentonshire Apts., St. Cloud, Minn., 1972, Ramada Motor Inn, Moorhead, Minn., 1971; designer, partner Angushire Apts., St. Cloud, 1973, Crossroads Apts., 1975; v.p. T.J.J. Inc., gen. contractors, St. Cloud, 1976—; designer Tantara, Menominie, Wis., 1976, Park Pl., Hibbing, Minn., 1976. Address: 3805 Greentrails N Austin TX 78731

BUDWIG, IRA ADOLPH, JR., pediatrician; b. Chgo., June 9, 1923; s. Ira A. and Ida G. Budwig; B.S. with honors, U. Ill., 1944, M.D. with honors, 1946; children—Sandra, I. Andrew, Ralph S. Intern, Cook County Hosp., Chgo., 1946-47, resident in pediatrics, 1949-51; practice medicine specializing in pediatrics El Paso (Tex.) Pediatric Assos. P.A., 1951—; med. dir. El Paso Rehab. Center, 1964—, El Paso Genetic Counseling Clinic, 1976—, Trans Pecos Health Plan, 1979—; chmn. W. Tex. Health Systems Agy., 1976-78, chmn. project rev. com., 1978—; bd. mgrs. R.E. Thomason Gen. Hosp., 1975—. Bd. dirs. El Paso Symphony Orch., 1977—. Served to lt. (j.g.) M.C., USN, 1947-49. Recipient Vol. of Yr. award Tex. Assn. for Retarded Citizens, 1973. Mem. Am. Acad. Pediatrics, Am. Acad. Cerebral Palsy and Devel. Medicine, AMA, Tex. Med. Assn., Tex. Pediatric Soc., El Paso County Med. Soc., El Paso C. of C. (Merit award 1974, dir. 1975—), Alpha Omega Alpha. Republican. Club: Coronado Country. Office: El Paso Pediatric Assos PA P-120 1501 Arizona St El Paso TX 79902

BUE, CARL OLAF, JR., fed. judge Tex.; b. Chgo., Mar. 27, 1922; s. Carl Olaf and Mabel Port (Shollar) B.; A.A., U. Chgo., 1942; student U. Rome, 1945; Ph.B., Northwestern U., 1951; LL.B., U. Tex., 1954; m. Mary Kathryn Waring, Dec. 27, 1948; children—Kathryn Anne, Richard Charles. Admitted to Tex. bar, 1954; with firm Royston, Rayzor & Cook, Houston, 1954-70, partner, 1958-70; U.S. dist. judge for So. Dist. Tex., Houston div., 1970—. Lectr. admiralty seminars, 1960-70. Served to capt. AUS, 1942-46. Mem. Am., Fed., Houston bar assns., State Bar Tex., Maritime Law Assn. U.S., Am. Judicature Soc., Alpha Delta Phi, Phi Alpha Delta. Republican. Lutheran. Contbr. articles to law revs. Home: 338 Knipp Rd Houston TX 77024 Office: 9134 US Courthouse 515 Rusk St Houston TX 77002

BUERGER, DAVID CHARLES, broadcasting co. exec.; b. Pitts., Dec. 5, 1949; s. David Bernard and Anne Marie (Fortun) B.; B.A., Davis and Elkins Coll., 1971; m. Diane Weese, July 3, 1971. Pres., Vantage Broadcasting Co., Winter Haven, Fla., 1972—, gen. mgr. Sta. WZNG-Radio, 1972—; mem. exec. com. Fla. West Coast Broadcast Skills Bank. Served with U.S. Army, 1971-72. Mem. Fla. Assn. Broadcasters, Nat. Assn. Broadcasters, Polk Advt. Fedn. (past dir.), Am. Contemporary Radio Affiliates Council. Republican. Club: Civitan Internat. Home: 2020 Leisure Dr Winter Haven FL 33880 Office: 1505 Dundee Rd Winter Haven FL 33880

BUESCHEN, ANTON JOSLYN, urologist; b. Toledo, June 7, 1940; s. Robert F. and Mary Julia (Joslyn) B.; student Va. Mil. Inst., 1958-61; M.D., U. Va., 1965; m. Norma Jean McClanahan, Sept. 5, 1964; children—Anton, Elaine. Intern surgery Vanderbilt U., Nashville, 1965-66, asst. resident surgery, 1966-67; resident in urology Ind. U., Indpls., 1969-72; instr. urology Tulane U., New Orleans 1972-73; vis. surgeon Charity Hosp. La., New Orleans, 1972-73; asst. prof., acting dir. div. urology U. Ala. Med. Center, Birmingham, 1973-75, asso. prof., 1975-79, prof., 1979—, dir. div., 1975—; chief urology Children's Hosp., Birmingham, 1977—. Served with M.C., U.S. Army, 1967-69. Recipient Carmichael award Va. Mil. Inst., 1960, Leavell Hematology award U. Va., 1965, McCaskey award Ind. chpt. A.C.S., 1970. Mem. A.C.S., Soc. Pediatric Urology, AMA (Billings Gold medal 1978), Am. Urol. Assn., Soc. Univ. Urologists. Home: 3512 Mill Run Rd Birmingham AL 35223 Office: 1813 6th Ave S Birmingham AL 35294

BUETTGENS, ROBERT MARIO, investigator; b. Syracuse, N.Y., Dec. 7, 1947; s. Frederick and Mary (Angeli) B.; B.A. in Sociology, U. Buffalo, 1969; M.S. in Mgmt., Rollins Coll., 1977, M.S. in Criminal Justice, 1979; m. Patricia Jane Seibel, June 14, 1969; 1 son, Matthew Robert. Tchr., counselor West Senaca (N.Y.) State Instn. for Retarded and Emotionally Disturbed, 1969; tchr. social sci. Canajoharie (N.Y.) public schs., 1969-71; with Orlando (Fla.) Police Dept., 1973-77; spl. agt. Naval Investigative Service, Orlando, 1977—; forensic hypnotist. Served with USN, 1972-73. Mem. Nat. Forensic Hypnosis Soc. (co-founder, sec. 1978-79), Fed. Law Enforcement Agts. Assn. Republican. Methodist. Club: United Meth. Men's. Author: The Use of Hypnosis in Law Enforcement, 1978.

BUFFA, PATRICK JOSEPH, fin. exec.; b. Hollywood, Calif, May 5, 1944; s. Edwin Joseph and Marie Theresa (Fawsett) B.; B.S., W.Va. U., 1967; m. Deborah Lynn Hinds, Mar. 31, 1973; 1 son, Alexander P. Co. rep. Kanawha Valley Data Control, Wheeling, W.Va., 1970-71; self-employed fund raiser, Wheeling, 1971-73; account exec. Smith, Barney, Harris, Upham, Charleston, W.Va., 1973—. Vice chmn. Kanawha Valley Youth Services Council, 1975—; mem. Kanawha Valley Community Schs. Council, 1973—, Salvation Army Boy Club Council, 1974—. Served with U.S. Army, 1967-70. Decorated Bronze Star medal, Army Commendation medal. Mem. Charleston Area C. of C. Democrat. Roman Catholic. Club: Rotary. Home: 208 Shellar Dr Charleston WV 25314 Office: PO Box 671 Charleston WV 25323

BUFFINGTON, JESSE LEE, economist; b. Chriesman, Tex., July 13, 1929; s. Lee Roy and Ila Fae Buffington; student S.W. Tex. State U., 1947-49; B.S. in Agrl. Edn., Tex. A&M U., 1951, M.S., 1958, Ph.D., 1973; m. Rosalie Wheeler, Sept. 3, 1955; children—Jesse Damon, Lanette Rose, Ruth Ann. Tchr., Wharton (Tex.) Ind. Sch. Dist., 1951-52; research asst. agrl. econs. Tex. A&M U., College Station, 1956-58, research asst. Tex. Transp. Inst., 1958-62, asst. research economist, 1962-73, asso. research economist, 1973-79, research economist, 1979—. Mem. Nat. Acad. Scis. Transp. Research Bd. Com., 1976—. Active PTA, Boy Scouts Am. Served with USAF, 1952-56. Mem. AAAS, Sigma Xi. Mem. Ch. of Christ. Contbr. articles to profl. jours. Home: 1809 Lawyer Pl College Station TX 77840 Office: Tex Transp Inst Tex A and M U College Station TX 77843

BUFFLER, PATRICIA ANNE HAPP, epidemiologist; b. Doylestown, Pa., Aug. 1, 1938; d. Edward M. and Evelyn G. (Axenroth) Happ; B.S.N., Cath. U. Am., 1960; M.P.H., U. Calif., Berkeley, 1965, Ph.D., 1973; m. Richard T. Buffler, Jan. 20, 1962; children—Martyn, Monique. Asst. prof. epidemiology U. Tex., Houston, 1970-72; lectr. U. Alaska, U. Wash., 1972-74; asst. prof. health scis., coordinator Center for Health Scis., Alaska Meth. U., 1973; asst. prof. preventive medicine U. Tex. Med. Br., Galveston, 1974-78; asso. prof. U. Tex. Health Scis. Center Sch. of Public Health, Houston, 1978—; med. adv. panel Tex. Air Control Bd., 1977-79; reviewer NIH; cons. in field. Mem. Soc. Epidemiologic Research (mem. exec. com.), Am. Public Health Assn. (chairperson sect. epidemiology), Am. Soc. Preventive Oncology, Assn. Tchrs. Preventive Medicine, Internat. Epidemiol. Assn., Soc. Occupational and Environ. Health, Tex. Public Health Assn. Unitarian. Contbr. articles to profl. jours. Home: 2875 Dominique Circle Galveston TX 77551 Office: Univ of Tex Health Scis Center Sch of Public Health PO Box 20186 Houston TX 77025

BUFORD, MARK WAYNE, communications co. exec.; b. Pittsburg, Kans., Apr. 14, 1954; s. William Edward and Mary Eudella (Long) B.; student Pittsburg State U., 1972-75; m. Andrea Buford, Sept. 23, 1978. Asst. sports editor Pittsburg (Kan.) Pub. Co., 1972-76; sports writer/copy editor Okla. Pub. Co., Oklahoma City, 1976; sales/mktg. adminstr. Computype, Inc., Ann Arbor, Mich., 1976-78; product mktg. mgr. Harris Composition Systems, Melbourne, Fla., 1978-79, mgr. office systems market requirements, 1979—. Recipient Cert. of Achievement, Am. Legion Boys State of Kans., 1971; Cert. of Merit, State of Kans. Scholarship Program Competition, 1971-72. Mem. Quill and Scroll, Sigma Tau Delta. Home: 199 Hwy AIA Satellite Beach FL 32937 Office: PO Box 2080 Melbourne FL 32901

BUICE, PATTERSON NALL, counselor; b. Atlanta, Mar. 2, 1934; d. Andrew Walton and Elizabeth (Merritt) Nall; B.A., Peabody Coll., Oglethorpe U., 1956; M.Ed., Ga. State U., 1975; postgrad. U. Notre Dame, 1974-75, Ga. State U., 1976-79; Advanced Standing, Emory U., 1979; m. Bonnie Carl, Dec. 14, 1957; children—Merrianne Dyer, Shannon, Sam, Bill, Chris. Tchr., Atlanta Public Schs., 1956-58, Brenau Coll., Gainesville, Ga., 1972; instr. Tom Gordon's Parent Effectiveness Tng., 1972-73; counselor Holy Trinity Counseling Center, Decatur, Ga., 1976-78; pvt. practice counseling, Tucker, Ga., 1978-79, Macon, Ga., 1979—. Pres. Episcopal Churchwomen, Grace Ch., Gainesville, 1964-65, sr. warden, 1970-71; pres. Churchwomen United, Gainesville, 1965-67; bd. dirs. Yonah council Girl Scouts U.S.A., 1962-65, Gainesville Girls Club, 1968-73, pres. bd., 1971-73; bd. dirs. Gainesville Christian Study Center, 1970-72. Recipient Sidney-Sullivan award Peabody Coll., 1955; named Young Woman of Year, Gainesville, 1970. Mem. Internat. Transactional Analysis Assn., Am. Assn. Marriage and Family Therapists, Am. Personnel and Guidance Assn. Democrat. Home and Office: PO Box 207 LWW 785 Will Scarlet St Macon GA 31210

BUIE, JANET PAULINE, speech pathologist; b. Independence, Mo., Feb. 16, 1947; d. John Albert and Pauline M. (Campbell) B.; B.S., Central Mo. State U., 1968, M.S., 1970. Tchr., Independence Public Sch., 1968; asst. dir. lang. devel. program Central Mo. State U., Warrensburg, 1969; dir. children's speech and lang. services U. Mo. Med. Center, Columbia, 1970-73; coordinator, early edn. for speech and hearing handicapped program S.C. Region V Ednl. Services Center, Lancaster, 1973-79; owner, speech pathologist Communication and Exercise, Lancaster, 1979—. Mem. Am. Speech, Lang. and Hearing Assn. Democrat. Author: Articulation and Language Learning, 1978; Action, Objects and Space: 3 Keys to Success of Children's Programs, 1979; How to Develop Speech, Language and Hearing Programs for Children, 1979. Home: Route 6 Box 379-A Lancaster SC 29720 Office: Communication and Exercise Incline Bldg Hwy 9 Bypass Lancaster SC 29720

BUIST, WILLIAM EDWARD, III, sales engr.; b. Greenville, S.C., July 16, 1945; s. William Edward and Roberta (Cecil) B.; B.S. in M.E., Vanderbilt U., 1967; m. Velvet Anne Foss, Dec. 13, 1969; children—William Edward, Keri Lynn. Proposition engr. Gen. Electric Co., Lynn, Mass., 1967-69, Schenectady, 1969-70, San Jose, Calif., 1970-71, sales engr., Raleigh, N.C., 1971-74, Chattanooga, 1974—. Recipient Sales Engr. of Yr. award in power generation Gen. Electric Co., 1976. Mem. Am. Nuclear Soc. (sec.-1978, treas. 1979), ASME, Chattanooga Engrs. Soc., Tau Beta Pi. Republican. Office: 832 Georgia Ave Chattanooga TN 37402

BULL, HELEN MAY, artist, author; b. Sweet Springs, Mo., Apr. 20, 1920; d. John Theodore and Ethel Henrietta (Butemeyer) Langewisch; student Washington U., St. Louis, 1941-47, U. Calif. Los Angeles, 1972; B.F.A., Otis Art Inst., Los Angeles, 1971; m. William Emerson Bull, Sept. 15, 1945 (dec.); children—Jan Emerson, Guy William. Canvas and ceramic sculpture exhibited juried show Moorpark (Calif.) Coll. Festival of the Arts, 1972, Hill Country Arts Found., Ingram, Tex., 1979; spl. exhibit Vista Room of Faculty Center, U. Calif. Los Angeles, 1973; exhibitor B.F.A Show, Otis Art Inst., Los Angeles, 1971; portrait painter; asst. in presentation of Brazilian Primitive Painting Exhibit, Dept. Spanish and Portuguese and Latin Am. Center, Plenary Session of U. Calif. Los Angeles Semana de Arte Moderna Symposium, 1972; cons. art and color for hosp. patients; author monograph: Widowhood, A Way Out of the Maze, for People In Transition, 1975. Pres. Bay West Assn. of Community Assistance for Homeless Youngsters, 1973; moderator, panelist seminar of Inst. for Study of Women in Transition, Manchester, N.H., 1976; mem. career devel. com. nursing service Audie Murphy Meml. VA Hosp., 1979. Recipient Certificate of Merit, Juried Faculty Art Exhibit, U. Calif. Los Angeles, 1960; Certificate Outstanding Service, Audie Murphy Meml. VA Hosp., 1976. Mem. Portrait Club N.Y., Hill Country Arts Found., Newspaper Inst. Am. Lutheran. Home: 9104 Dartbrook Apt 2 San Antonio TX 78240

BULL, ROBERT FRANCIS, ins. co. exec.; b. Alton, Ill., Sept. 1, 1934; s. William Frederick and Velmya Irene (Gelvin) B.; B.S. in Bus. Adminstrn., So. Ill. U., 1956; m. Judith Ann Green, June 23, 1956; children—Robert Frederick, Julie Ann, Ann Renee, Diana Michelle. With trust dept. First Nat. Bank & Trust Co., Alton, 1955-56; claims supr., adminstrv. asst. Gen. Am. Life Ins. Co., 1956-66; mgr. group and credit claims Fed. Life & Casualty Co., 1966-67; with Republic Nat. Life Ins. Co., Dallas, 1967—, v.p. charge policy benefit div., 1971—; dir. C, Lone Star Life Ins. Co., Dallas, 1975—; cons. Life Ins. C. SW-Halliburton, 1977. Chmn. Civic Award Com., Alton, 1962-66. Served with USMCR, 1951-55. Mem. Dallas Soc. Claimsmen (past pres., chmn.), S.W. Ins. Assn. (past chmn. bd.), Tex. Osteopathic Ins. Assn. (v.p.), Health Ins. Assn. Am., Alpha Phi Omega. Methodist. Home: 3431 Chaparral Dr Farmers Branch TX 75234 Office: 200 Treadway Dallas TX 75235

BULLARD, BOBBY GERALD, educator; b. Dardanelle, Ark., July 2, 1939; s. Gerald Lavern and Mary Elizabeth (Dean) B.; B.A. in Music, Harding Coll., 1962; M.Music Edn., Tex. Tech. U., 1965; postgrad. Sam Houston State U., 1967; m. Treva Lou DaVee, Sept. 8, 1961; children—Britt William, Ashlea Elaine. County music supr., Scurry County, Tex., 1962-64; choral dir. Seagraves (Tex.) Ind. Sch. Dist., 1964-66; prof. music Blinn Coll., Brenham, Tex., 1966—; bd. dirs. Festival Hill, Round Top, Tex., 1971—. Mem. NEA, Music Educators Nat. Conf., Tex. Jr. Coll. Tchrs. Assn., Tex. State Tchrs. Assn., Tex. Music Educators Assn. Democrat. Mem. Ch. of Christ. Home: 205 Meadow Ln Brenham TX 77833 Office: 903 College St Brenham TX 77833

BULLARD, BYRON LUTHER, hosp. adminstr.; b. Lumberton, N.C., Nov. 30, 1927; s. Byron Luther and Anna Britt B.; B.A., Wake Forest U., 1951; Master's Cert. in Hosp. Adminstrn., Presbyn. Hosp., 1953; m. Carolyn Timberlake, Aug. 2, 1952; children—Byron Luther, Leigh Timberlake. With Presbyn. Hosp., Charlotte, N.C., 1953—, asso. dir., 1969-71, exec. v.p., 1971-77, pres., 1977—; bd. dirs. N.C. Blue Cross/Blue Shield, 1978—. Treas. Am. Heart Assn., 1962-72; bd. dirs. Am. Cancer Soc. Served with USAF, 1946-48. Fellow Am. Coll. Hosp. Adminstrs.; mem. N.C. Hosp. Assn. (bd. dirs.), Charlotte C. of C. Baptist. Office: PO Box 33549 Charlotte NC 28233

BULLARD, EDGAR JOHN, III, museum dir.; b. Los Angeles, Sept. 15, 1942; s. Edgar John and Katherine Elizabeth (Dreisbach) B.; B.A., U. Calif. at Los Angeles, 1965, M.A., 1968. Asst. to dir., curator spl. projects Nat. Gallery Art, Washington, 1968-73; dir. New Orleans Mus. Art, 1973—; alt. mem. Citizens Stamp Adv. Com., 1969-71; mem. mus. adv. panel Nat. Endowment for Arts, 1974-77. Trustee Ga. Mus. Art, U. Ga., Athens. Decorated Order of Republic (Egypt); Samuel H. Kress Found. fellow, 1967-68. Mem. Assn. Art Mus. Dirs. Internat. Council Museums, Am. Assn. Museums, Coll. Art Assn. Democrat. Episcopalian. Club: Nat. Arts (N.Y.C.). Author: Edgar Degas, 1971; John Sloan 1871-1951, 1971; Mary Cassatti: Oils and Pastels, 1972; A Panorama of American Painting, 1975. Home: 1031 Peniston St New Orleans LA 70115 also Greenleaf Deer Island ME 04627 Office: New Orleans Mus Art PO Box 19123 New Orleans LA 70179

BULLARD, K(ENNEDY) C(ORNELIUS), state ofcl.; b. Palatka, Fla., Dec. 9, 1917; s. George Frank and Eva Marie (Mealor) B.; student U. Fla., 1935-37, Bus. U. Tampa, 1938; m. Carmen Martha Valdespino, Dec. 14, 1941; children—Patricia Bullard Willis, Timothy Bruce. Accountant, Hillsborough County Tax Collector's Office, Tampa, Fla., 1946-52, exec. asst. to tax collector, 1952-68, county tax collector, 1968-75; adj. gen. State of Fla., St. Augustine, Fla., 1975—. Served with U.S. Army, 1940-45; maj. gen. Fla. N.G., 1975—. Decorated Bronze Star, Purple Heart. Mem. Fla. N.G. Officers Assn. (past pres.), Delta Tau Delta. Democrat. Methodist. Home: 86 Marine St Saint Augustine FL 32084 Office: Office of the Adj Gen State Arsenal Saint Augustine FL 32084

BULLEN, ADELAIDE KENDALL (MRS. RIPLEY PIERCE BULLEN), anthropologist; b. Worcester, Mass., Jan. 12, 1908; d. Oliver Sawyer and Grace (Marble) Kendall, III; A.B. cum laude, Radcliffe Coll., 1943; grad. study Harvard, 1943-48, 50; m. Ripley Pierce Bullen, July 25, 1929; children—Dana Ripley II, Pierce Kendall. Research anthropologist Health Center, Radcliffe Coll., 1943-44, Fatigue Lab., Harvard Grad. Sch. Bus. Adminstrn., 1944-46; civilian cons. in anthropology U.S. War Dept., 1946; anthropologist dept. anthropology, Peabody Mus., Harvard U., 1946-48, Fla. State Mus., 1949—. Fellow Am. Anthrop. Assn., A.A.A.S., Royal Anthrop. Inst., London, Soc. Applied Anthropology; mem. Am. Assn. Phys. Anthropologists, Am. Psychosomatic Soc., Am. Acad. Social and Polit. Sci., Soc. Research in Child Devel., World Fedn. for Mental Health, Sigma Xi. Clubs: Gainesville Garden, Gainesville Golf and Country, University Women's, Gainesville Woman's. Author: New Answers to the Fatigue Problem, 1956; also articles in field. Contbg. editor anthropology Handbook of Latin Am. Studies, Library of Congress, 1969-71. Home: 2720 SW 8th Dr Gainesville FL 32601 Office: Fla State Mus Univ Fla Gainesville FL 32611

BULLOCK, BOB, state govt. ofcl.; b. Hillsboro, Tex., July 10, 1929; s. Thomas A. and Ruth M. Bullock; B.A., Tex. Technol. U., 1955; LL.B., Baylor U., 1958; children by previous marriage—Lindy, Bob. Admitted to Tex. bar, 1957; individual practice law, Hillsboro, 1957-59, Tyler, Tex., 1960-61, Austin, Tex., 1961-67; mem. Tex. Ho. of Reps., 1956-59; asst. atty. gen., Tex., 1967-68; legal counsel Office of Gov., State of Tex., 1969-71; sec. of state, Tex., 1971-73; comptroller of public accounts, Tex., 1975—. Alt. del. Democratic Nat. Conv., 1976. Served with USAF, 1951-54; Korea. Recipient Louisville Gold Medal award Mcpl. Fin. Officers Assn., 1978. Mem.

Nat. Assn. State Auditors, Nat. Tax Assn., Nat. Assn. Tax Adminstrs., Fedn. Tax Adminstrs., N. Am. Gasoline Assn. Democrat. Home: PO Box 2243 Austin TX 78767 Office: LBJ Bldg 111 E 17th St Austin TX 78774

BULLOCK, ELLIS WAY, JR., architect; b. Birmingham, Ala., Sept. 11, 1928; s. Ellis Way and Martha (Alexander) B.; student Marion Mil. Inst., 1945-48; B.Arch., Auburn U., 1954; student U. Wis. Extension, 1972-74, Harvard Grad. Sch. Design, 1976; m. Ann Pope, Nov. 23, 1951; children—Ellis Way III, Elbert Pope, John Howard Keith, William Frank. Apprentice architect Yonge, Look & Morrison, Pensacola, Fla., 1954-57; asso. firm Look & Morrison, 1957-59; practice architecture, Pensacola, 1959-73; pres., chmn. bd. Bullock/Graves & Assos., Pensacola, 1973—; guest lectr. Auburn U., 1976-78. Mem. City of Pensacola Zoning Bd., 1968-72, Bd. Adjustment, 1968-72; chmn. Pensacola Bldg. Bd. Appeals, 1970—, Pensacola Archtl. Rev. Bd., 1971-72. Served to 1st lt. C.E., AUS, 1950-52. Mem. AIA (nat. dir. 1979—, Community Service award Fla. chpt. 1974, pres. 1977, Community Service award Fla. N.W. chpt. 1974), Pensacola C. of C. (v.p. 1969-71). Episcopalian. Clubs: Pensacola Country, Pensacola Sports Assn., Saints and Sinners, Rebellaires, Courts of Deluna, Order of Tristan, Hit and Miss Hunting. Archtl. works include: Century Bank and Office Tower, Pensacola, 1974, Regional Service Center, Pensacola, 1979, Ednl. Research and Devel. Center, U. W. Fla., Pensacola, 1980, Pensacola Jr. Coll. Library, 1978, Woodham High Sch., 1967. Home: 2 Hyde Park Rd Pensacola FL 32503 Office: Bullock/Graves & Assos 1823 N 9th Ave Pensacola FL 32503

BULLOCK, NELLE SPAHN, social worker; b. Poughkeepsie, N.Y., Nov. 18, 1937; d. Otto Joseph and Nell Maude (Mitchell) Spahn; B.Social Welfare, U. Ala., 1972; M.S.W., U. Ga., 1974; student Cornell U., 1955-57, U. North Ala., 1958, Brevard Jr. Coll., 1968-69; m. Paul Bullock, Nov. 23, 1956; children—Paul Joseph, Mitchell Dockstader. Dir. social services dept. Martin Meml. Hosp., Stuart, Fla., 1974—. Pres. Martin County Interagy. Com., 1978—. Mem. Nat. Assn. Social Workers, Nat. Assn. Hosp. Social Workers, Fla. Assn. Hosp. Social Workers (dir.), Acad. Cert. Social Workers. Home: 529 Palm Beach Rd Stuart FL 33494 Office: PO Bin 2396 Stuart FL 33494

BULLOCK, ROBERT EDWARD, ins. co. exec.: b. Meridian, Miss., Feb. 21, 1941; s. Edward N. and Axeth (Hodge) B.; B.S. in Bus. Adminstrn., Miss. State U., 1963; grad. Aetna Life Estate Control Plan Sch., 1966; m. Margene Ann Dement, June 28, 1962; children—Robert Edward, Jamie H. Ins. agt. Greater Miss. Life Ins. Co., Meridian, 1963-66; v.p. sales Meyer & Rosenbaum, Inc., Meridian, 1966—. C.L.U. Mem. Ind. Ins. Agts. Assn. Am., Am. Coll. C.L.U.'s, Nat. Assn. Life Underwriters (Nat. Quality award 1969-78, Nat. Sales Achievement award 1978), Miss. Assn. Life Underwriters (v.p. 1969-70, chmn. state law and legis. 1972-79), Meridian Assn. Life Underwriters (pres. 1967-68, Outstanding Achievement award 1968). Roman Catholic. Clubs: Moose (Meridian); Northwood Country. Developed means by which Miss. ins. assn. can present views in state legis. Office: PO Box 1729 Meridian MS 39301

BULLOCK, SANDRA LEE, parasitologist; b. Chester, Pa., Feb. 6, 1943; d. William Ellis and Melceina Mae (Gerwick) B.; B.S. in Med. Tech., U. Fla., 1966, M.Ed., 1968; M.P.H., U. N.C., 1975, Dr.P.H., 1977. Med. technologist Emory U. Hosp., Atlanta, 1968-71; microbiologist, instr. Parasitology Training Br., Bur. Labs., Center for Disease Control, Atlanta, 1971—; cons. in field. Registered med. tech.: HEW grantee, 1967-68. Mem. Am. Soc. Trop. Medicine and Hygiene, Am. Soc. Parasitologists, Am. Soc. Clin. Pathologists, Sigma Xi. Contbr. articles to profl. jours. Home: 819 Heritage Sq Decatur GA 30033 Office: Center for Disease Control Bldg 1 Rm SB 215 1600 Clifton Rd Atlanta GA 30333

BUMBAUGH, MARY KAY (MICKEY), community coll. adminstr.; b. Clinton, Iowa, July 25, 1942; d. Richard F. and Virginia E. Kelly; A.A., Cottey Coll., Nevada, Mo., 1962; B.A., U. Wyo., 1964; M.Ed., Fla. Atlantic U., 1968; m. Jon Charles Bumbaugh, Aug. 30, 1975. Asst. prof. psychology Marymount Coll., Boca Raton, Fla., 1968-72; adminstrv. and clin. dir. Boca Raton Drug Abuse Found., 1973-75; adminstrv. asst., counselor Jacksonville (Fla.) physician, 1974-75; pvt. practice counseling, Jacksonville, 1975-77; equal access-equal opportunity officer Valencia Community Coll., Orlando, Fla., 1977—; founder Equal Employment Opportunity Specialists of Central Fla., 1978; pub. Network News. Bd. dirs. Center Continuing Edn. for Women, Met. Orlando Urban League, Profl. Community Service League; mem. affirmative action task force Citrus council Girl Scouts U.S.A., U. Central Fla.; adv. bd. Center Ind. Living. Recipient vol. cert. Center Ind. Tng. and Edn., 1978. Mem. Am. Assn. Affirmative Action, Am. Personnel and Guidance Assn., Assn. Specialists in Group Work, Fla. Assn. Children with Learning Disabilities (charter). Mem. pit crew for Class E Hydro Plane. Office: 1 W Church St Orlando FL 32802

BUMBREY, JOSEPH LOUIS, oil co. exec.; b. Caroline County, Va., Jan. 10, 1938; s. George and Ellen B.; B.S. in Bus. Adminstrn., Winston-Salem State U., 1972; postgrad. Wake Forest U., 1975; m. Frances E. Williams, Aug. 13, 1977; children—Joseph Louis, Pamela, Michelle. Computer operator Wachovia Bank & Trust Co., Winston-Salem, N.C., 1969-72; placement and career devel. dir. Wake Forest U., Winston-Salem, 1972-76; corp. recruiter Ashland Oil, Inc. (Ky.), 1976-78, corp. coll. relations coordinator, 1978—. Served with USAF, 1958-69. Named Outstanding Vet., Winston-Salem State U., 1971. Mem. So. Coll. Placement Assn. (dir.), N.C. Placement Assn. (dir.), Ky. Coll. Placement Assn. (dir.), Coll. Placement Council (communications com.), NAACP (pres. local br. 1978—). Clubs: Vets. (pres. 1970-72), Kiwanis. Office: PO Box 391 Ashland KY 41101

BUMGARNER, JOHN WESLEY, JR., constrn. engr.; b. Newport, Tenn., Mar. 24, 1942; s. John Wesley and Maudie Lee B.; Asso. Sci. in Archtl. Tech., Walters State Community Coll., 1973; B.S., U. Tenn., Knoxville, 1978; m. Nancy Lee Harris, Jan. 24, 1962; children—Kimberly Faye, Donna Elaine. Quality control lab. technician Chemetron Corp., Newport, 1962-71, environ. control technician, 1971-73; engring. designer Arapahoe Chems., Newport, 1973-78, maintenance planner, estimator, scheduler, 1978-79, asso. engr., 1979—. Served with U.S. Army, 1966-68. Mem. Am. Mgmt. Assn. Democrat. Home: Route 4 Newport TN 37821 Office: PO Box 480 Newport TN 37821

BUMPAS, GILES ANTHONY, purchasing exec.; b. Los Angeles, Oct. 28, 1941; s. Carl Leonard and Virginia Elizabeth (Waldo) B.; B.A. in Econs., Rice U., 1963; J.D., U. Tex., Austin, 1967. Buyer, Tex. Instruments, Dallas, 1969-74; dir. purchasing Seaco Computer Display, Garland, Tex., 1974-75; purchasing agt. Atlas Powder Co., Dallas, 1975—. Bd. dirs. Dallas Met. Ballet, 1975-78; sponsor 500, Inc., Dallas, 1978; bd. dirs. Dallas Dance Council. Served with C.E., U.S. Army, 1967-69. Republican. Methodist. Home: 4517 W Amherst St Dallas TX 75209 Office: 12700 Park Central Suite 1700 Dallas TX 75251

BUMPERS, DALE LEON, U.S. senator; b. Charleston, Ark., Aug. 12, 1925; ed. U. Ark.; LL.B., Northwestern U., 1951; m. Betty Flanagan; children—Brent, Bill, Brooke. Owner Charleston Hardware and Furniture Co., 1951-66; admitted to Ark. bar, practiced in Charleston, 1951-70; owner cattle breeding farm, 1966-70; gov. Ark., 1971-75; U.S. senator from Ark., 1975—. Past chmn. United Fund, Boy Scouts Am. Fund, Cancer Fund. Former city atty., Charleston; past pres. Charleston Sch. Bd. Served with USMC, World War II. Recipient C. of C. Citizen's award. Democrat. United Methodist. Office: 3229 New Senate Office Bldg Washington DC 20510

BUNCH, DEAN BOGGS, lawyer; b. Jacksonville, Fla., Aug. 17, 1948; s. Franklin Swope and Virginia B.; B.S. in Polit. Sci., Stetson U., 1968; B.S. in Journalism, U. Fla., 1969, J.D., 1973; m. Martha Lynn Williams, Aug. 26, 1972; 1 dau., Lynn Jennifer. Admitted to Fla. bar, 1974; asst. dean U. Fla. Coll. Law, Gainesville, 1974-76; asso. firm Ervin, Varn, Jacobs, Odom & Kitchen, Tallahassee, 1976-79, partner, 1979—; chmn. council U. Fla. Law Center. Served to 1st lt., Signal Corps, AUS, 1969-71. Decorated Bronze Star. Mem. Tallahassee Bar Assn. Democrat. Methodist. Editor Tallahassee Bar Bull., 1979-80. Home: 3037 Stillwood Ct Tallahassee FL 32312 Office: 305 S Gadsden St Tallahassee FL 32301

BUNCH, FRANKLIN SWOPE, architect; b. Madison, Ind., Jan. 4, 1913; s. Walker Franklin and Susan Beatrice (Swope) B.; B.S. in Architecture, U. Fla., 1934; m. Virginia Aurelia Boggs, June 8, 1937; children—Franklin Swope, Dean Boggs. Draftsman, designer, architect and constrn. supr. various Fla. architects, 1934-41; archtl. engr. U.S. Engrs. Dist. Office, Jacksonville, Fla., 1942-43, Jacksonville Naval Air Sta., 1944-45; partner Kemp, Bunch & Jackson, Architects, Inc., Jacksonville, 1946-69, sr. v.p., 1970—. Pres. Fla. Bd. Architecture, 1959-61; mem. com. on exams. Nat. Council Archtl. Registration Bds., 1961-62; pres. Bldg. Code Adv. Bd., Jacksonville, 1949-68; mem. examining com. Jacksonville, 1949—; chmn. bldg. codes adjustment bd. Jacksonville Consol. Govt.; mem. housing com. Jacksonville Council on Aging, 1962. Pres., Little Theatre of Jacksonville, 1952-53. Fellow AIA; mem. Fla. Assn. Architects (pres. 1947-48), Area C. of C., Phi Kappa Tau. Methodist. Clubs: San Jose Country (sec. 1964, gov. 1964-67), River (Jacksonville). Home: 4300 Gadsden Ct Jacksonville FL 32207 Office: Kemp Bunch & Jackson Architects Inc Coast Line Bldg Jacksonville FL 32202

BUNDY, MICHAEL LYMAN, sch. counselor; b. Laurens, S.C., Sept. 4, 1947; s. Dwight Lyman and Ella Mae Bundy; B.S., Milligan Coll., 1969; M.S., U. Tenn., 1973, postgrad., 1973—; m. Barbara Lynn Gresham, Aug. 1, 1970; 1 son, Adrian Michael. Secondary sch. counselor Parrottsville (Tenn.) High Sch., 1969-72; elem. sch. counselor Lincoln Hts. Elem. Sch., Morristown, Tenn., 1972—. Mem. Morristown Edn. Assn. (pres. 1979-80, Human Relations award 1978), Tenn. Edn. Assn., NEA, East Tenn. Personnel and Guidance Assn. (Oriana B. Howley award 1977), Tenn. Personnel and Guidance Assn., Am. Personnel and Guidance Assn., Tenn. Sch. Counselor Assn., Am. Sch. Counselor Assn. Christian. Mem. editorial bd. Elem. Sch. Guidance and Counseling Jour., 1980—; contbr. articles to profl. jours. Home: PO Box 1691 Morristown TN 37814 Office: Lincoln Elem Sch 215 Lincoln Ave Morristown TN 37814

BUNN, CHARLES IVY, JR., accountant; b. Rocky Mount, N.C., July 14, 1951; s. Charles Ivy and Florence Craig B.; A.B. in Mgmt. Scis. and Acctg., Duke U., 1973; m. Catherine Barnes, Nov. 20, 1976. Staff acct. Price Waterhouse & Co., Charlotte, N.C., 1973-74, Raleigh, N.C., 1974-76, sr. acct., 1976-78; individual practice acctg., Rocky Mount, 1978—; co-discussion leader nonprofit acctg. seminar Grad. Sch. Bus., Duke U., 1976; instr. N.C. Wesleyan Coll. and NASH Tech. Inst., Rocky Mount, 1978-79; notary public, N.C., 1972—. C.P.A., N.C. Sec., Young Democrats of Nash County, 1971-72, pres., 1975-76, 79-80; exec. com. Young Dems. N.C., 1975-77, chmn. 2d congl. dist., 1976-77; exec. com. Nash County Dem. Party, 1975-76, 79-80; budget com. United Community Services of Rocky Mount, 1979. Mem. Am. Inst. C.P.A.'s, N.C. Assn. C.P.A.'s (leader nonprofit acctg. seminar 1977, mem. com. on govtl. affairs and legislation 1977-80, com. public and community relations 1979-80), Am. Acctg. Assn., E. Carolina Estate Planning Council, Rocky Mount Area C. of C. (council on area devel. and legis. 1979, small bus. adv. council), N.C. Student Legislature Alumni Assn. (sec. 1974, pres. 1975, dir. 1976—), Lambda Chi Alpha. Methodist. Clubs: Twin County Jaycees (treas. 1979-80, fin. v.p. 1980—), Rocky Mount Breakfast Optimists (sec.-treas. 1979-80, dir. 1980—), Iron Dukes. Office: 3709 Westridge Circle Dr Rocky Mount NC 27801

BUNN, EDWARD DEVERE, lawyer; b. Miami Beach, July 26, 1936; s. Everett Duane and Alma K. (Hill) B.; LL.B., Stetson U., 1965; LL.M., George Washington U., 1970; m. Sandra N. Harris, Sept. 19, 1961; children—Edward, Jr., Sheri K., Robert. Admitted to U.S. Supreme Ct. bar, 1977, Fla. bar, 1966, Va. bar, 1975, Supreme Ct. of Fla. bar, 1965, Supreme Ct. bar of Va., 1975, U.S. Ct. of Claims bar, 1972, U.S. Ct. of Mil. Appeals bar, 1968, D.C. Ct. of Appeals bar, 1966, U.S. Ct. of Appeals, 1968, U.S. Dist. Ct. bar of D.C., 1966; spl. asst. to Atty. Gen. Fla., 1965; legis. advisor U.S. Dept. Justice, Washington D.C. 1965-68; individual practice law, Washington, Fla. and Va., 1968—. Author: Presidential War Powers, 1972. Address: Skyline Office 5707 Seminary Rd Bailey's Crossroads VA 22041

BUNTING, DOUGLAS, plastic surgeon; b. Roanoke, Va., Oct. 9, 1944; s. Douglas and Martha Virginia (Clarke) B.; B.A., Birmingham So. Coll., 1966; M.D., U. Ala., 1970; m. Derry Brice, July 10, 1971; children—Elizabeth Derry, Virginia Louise. Intern, Mass. Gen. Hosp., Boston, 1970-71, resident in surgery, 1971-74, chief resident in plastic surgery, 1974-76; fellow in surgery Harvard U., 1975-76; practice medicine specializing in plastic and reconstructive surgery, Birmingham, Ala., 1978—; mem. staff U. Ala., Baptist-Montclair, Children's, Brookwood hosps.; mem. faculty U. Ala. Med. Sch., Birmingham, 1978—. Alumni bd. dirs. Birmingham So. Coll., 1979—; adv. bd. Boy Scouts Am., 1979—. Served to maj. USAF, 1976-78. Diplomate Am. Bd. Surgery, Am. Bd. Plastic and Reconstructive Surgery. Mem. Am. Soc. Plastic and Reconstructive Surgery, Jefferson County Med. Soc., Med. Soc. Ala., Birmingham Acad. Medicine, Alpha Omega Alpha. Presbyterian. Home: 2957 Pine Haven Dr Birmingham AL 35223 Office: 3940 Montclair Rd Suite 210 Birmingham AL 35223

BURAN, WALLACE PAGE, mgmt. cons.; b. Atlanta, May 11, 1953; s. McDaniel and Josephine Buran Hopkins; B. Indsl. and Systems Engring., Ga. Inst. Tech., 1975, M. Indsl. Engring., 1978. With Delco Moraine div. Gen. Motors Corp., Dayton, 1975-76, Avon Products Co., Cin., 1976-77; asso. Theodore Barry and Assos., mgmt. cons., Atlanta, 1978—. Mem. Am. Inst. Indsl. Engrs. Home: 1805 Roswell Rd Marietta GA 30062 Office: Theodore Barry and Assos 229 Peachtree St Atlanta GA 30303

BURBANK, DORIS ANN DEATS, coll. adminstr.; b. Houston, May 25, 1940; d. Wilson Sparkman and Phraulene Hamilton Deats; B.Mus.Edn., Southwestern U., 1962; M.Ed., U. Houston, 1976; m. Philip Francis Burbank, June 23, 1962; children—Phyllis Ann, George Deats. Music tchr. Alvin (Tex.) Public Schs., 1962-65; pvt. piano tchr., Alvin, Tex., 1965-68; music instr. Alvin Community Coll., 1968-76, choral dir., 1976—; dir. music First United Meth. Ch., Alvin, Tex., 1978—; Alvin rep. Gulf Coast Intercollegiate Conf., 1976—. Mem. AAUW, Tex. Jr. Coll. Tchrs. Assn. (pres. 1980), Alvin Coll. Tchrs. Assn. (pres. 1976), Phi Mu, Delta Omicron, Alvin Aglaian Study Club. Democrat. Methodist. Home: 1726 Glennview St Alvin TX 77511 Office: Alvin Community Coll Mustang Rd Music Dept Alvin TX 77511

BURBO, JAMES HOWARD, electro-optical engr.; b. Burlington, Vt., Jan. 25, 1932; s. Howard Louis and Viola Ruth (Houde) B.; B.S. in Elec. Engring., U. Vt., 1956, M.S. in Physics, 1958; m. Marguerite Ann Herrera, Aug. 23, 1958; children—Michael J., Gregory F., Andrew H., Thomas W. Staff engr., group leader Instrumentation Lab., Mass. Inst. Tech., 1958-66; mem. tech. staff Sanders Assos., Inc., Nashua, N.H., 1966-72; tech. specialist electro-optics ITT Electro-Optics Products Div., Roanoke, Va., 1972—. Mem. Republican Town Com., Bedford, Mass., 1964-72; mem. Bd. Pub. Welfare, 1966-70. Served with USMCR, 1950-52. Recipient IR-100 Design award Indsl. Research Mag., 1975. Registered profl. engr., Mass., N.H. Mem. IEEE, Soc. Photo-Optical Inst. Engrs., Nat. Rifle Assn. (life), Va. Archeol. Soc., Tau Beta Pi. Home: 5109 Falcon Ridge Rd SW Roanoke VA 24014 Office: PO Box 7065 Roanoke VA 24019

BURBY, RAYMOND JOSEPH, III, educator; b. Los Angeles, June 26, 1942; s. Raymond and Carolyn Barbara (Del Pino) B.; student U. Wash., 1960-62; A.B., George Washington U., 1964; M.R.P., U. N.C., Chapel Hill, 1966, Ph.D., 1969; m. Nannie Pearl Harbour, Dec. 27, 1965; children—Barbara Derina, Raymond Joseph. Research asso. Center for Urban and Regional Studies, U. N.C., Chapel Hill, 1968-76, asst. prof. planning, 1969-72, asst. dir. for research Center for Urban and Regional Studies, 1976—. Vice chmn. Chapel Hill Parks and Recreation Commn., 1979—; mem Orange County Energy Conservation Commn., 1979—; pres. Village W. Homeowners Assn., 1975-77. Mem. Am. Planning Assn., Am. Inst. Cert. Planners, Regional Sci. Assn. Democrat. Presbyterian. Author: Recreation and Leisure in New Communities, 1976; co-author: New Communities U.S.A., 1976, Health Care in New Communities, 1976; Schools in New Communities, 1976; co-editor: Energy and the Community, 1978, Energy and Housing, 1980; book rev. editor Jour. Am. Planning Assn., 1980—. Home: 315 Granville Rd Chapel Hill NC 27514 Office: 108 Battle Ln Chapel Hill NC 27514

BURCH, LARRY EUGENE, delivery service exec.; b. Mt. Holly, N.C., Feb. 13, 1947; s. Earl and Katie B.; B.A. in History, Barber-Scotia Coll., 1969; m. Dottie McGimpsey; children—Lamone, Janté. With United Parcel Service, Charlotte, N.C., 1966—, center mgr., 1973-76, div. mgr., 1976—. Served with U.S. Army, 1970-72. Mem. Omega Psi Phi. Roman Catholic. Home: 2125 Lawton Bluff Rd Matthews NC 28105 Office: United Parcel Service 1514 N Graham St Charlotte NC 28206

BURCHAM, GWENDOLYN FRANCES PARKER (MRS. RALPH JACK BURCHAM), home economist; b. Drakes Creek, Ark., June 11, 1932; d. Nolan Henry and Leta Clair (Drake) Parker; student John Brown U., 1949-51; B.S., U. Ark., 1953, M.S., 1957, postgrad., 1961-62; postgrad. Wichita State U., 1957-58; m. Ralph Jack Burcham, Apr. 9, 1955; 1 dau., Thresa Clair. Tchr. home econs. high schs. in Mabelvale, Elkins and Decatur, Ark., Wichita, Kans., 1953-61; extension home economist Pulaski County, Ark., 1961-62; dir. pub. relations Am. Dairy Assn., Ark., 1962-65; dir. Ark. Milk Promotion Com. Little Rock, 1965-66; exec. dir. Dairy Council Ark., Little Rock, 1966-68; program coordinator Dairy Council, Inc., Little Rock, 1968-77; mgr. hobbies, arts and crafts Ark. State Fair, 1977—. Cons. TV stas. in Little Rock, 1961-76. Recipient Outstanding Service award Ark. Extension Homemakers Council, 1968; Alumni awards Pulaski County 4-H, 1974, Ark. 4-H, 1974. Mem. Am. (chmn. state pres. unit 1972, dir. 1972-73), Ark. (v.p. 1968-69, pres. 1971-72, membership chmn. 1967—) home econs. assns., Ark. Pub. Health Assn., Am. Bus. Women's Assn., Am., Ark. (chmn. 1975-76) home economists in bus., Ark. Women's Com. on Pub. Affairs (past pres.), Nutrition Today Soc. (charter), Ark. Interagy. Nutrition Com. (past chmn.), Pulaski County 4-H Clubs (hon.), Ark. Arts Center, Quapaw Quarter Assn., Ark. Geneal. Soc., Gamma Sigma Delta (hon.). Baptist. Clubs: Ark. Kennel (past sec. Little Rock), German Shepherd Dog of Little Rock (dir. 1972), Lakeside Country. Home: 3924 Base Line Rd Little Rock AR 72209 Office: PO Box 907 Little Rock AR 72203

BURCHAM, JAMES EDWARD, educator; b. Cleve., Sept. 1, 1941; s. Lester Arthur and Zora (Gray) B.; B.A., Parsons Coll., Fairfield, Iowa, 1963; postgrad. Sch. Bus. Adminstrn., U. N.C., Chapel Hill, 1963-64. Savs. mgr. Home Savs. & Loan Assn., Phoenix, 1964-65; dir. coll. relations Motorola, Inc., Phoenix, 1965-67; sec. Blair Acad., Blairstown, N.J., 1967-71; prin. Burcham Realty & Investment Co., Berryville, Ark. 1971-77; asst. headmaster external affairs and planning Asheville (N.C.) Sch., 1977—, also project instr. Mem. Council Advancement Edn. Republican. Presbyterian. Home: 63 Maple Ridge Ln Asheville NC 28806 Office: Asheville Sch Asheville NC 28806

BURCHAM, RALPH JACK, civil engr.; b. Ft. Scott, Kans., Feb. 13, 1931; s. Ralph and Ruby (Hays) B.; student Ft. Scott Jr. Coll., 1949-51; B.S., U. Ark., 1957; m. Gwendolyn Francaes Parker, Apr. 9, 1955; 1 dau., Thresa Clair. Stress analyst Boeing Airplane Co., Wichita, Kans., 1957-59; sr. resident engr. Ark. Hwy. Dept., Little Rock, 1959-63; owner Ralph J. Burcham, cons. engrs., Little Rock, 1963-70; pres. Found. Explorations, Inc., Little Rock, 1965-70; partner Assos. Engrs. & Land Surveyors, Little Rock, 1967-70; engr. Granite Mountain Quarries, Sweet Home, Ark., 1970—. Served to capt. AUS, 1951-53. Decorated Bronze Star medal. Mem. Central Ark., Am., Ark. socs. profl. engrs., Ark. Kennel Club (dir. 1966-70), German Shepherd Dog Club Little Rock (pres. 1972), Ark. Arts Center, Quapaw Quarter Assn., Am. Legion. Baptist. Eagle. Club: Lakeside Country. Home: 3924 Base Line Rd Little Rock AR 72209 Office: Shamburger Ln Sweet Home AR 72206

BURCHARD, JOHN KENNETH, scientist; b. St. Louis, May 12, 1936; s. Kenneth Reginald and Vernora Emma (Angell) B.; B.S., Carnegie Mellon U., 1957, M.S., 1959, Ph.D., 1962; m. Elizabeth Lee Suesserott, Aug. 23, 1958; children—John Christopher, Gregory Charles. Head vehicle analysis group United Tech. Center, Sunnyvale, Calif., 1961-68; chief scientist Combustion Power Co., Menlo Park, Calif., 1968-70; lab. dir. EPA, Research Triangle Park, N.C., 1970—. Served with Chem. Corps U.S. Army, 1963-64. NSF fellow, 1959-61, Standard Oil Co. fellow, 1957-58, Shell Oil Co. fellow, 1958-59. Mem. Am. Inst. Chem. Engrs., Sigma Xi, Tau Beta Pi, Phi Sigma Phi. Club: Chapel Hill Country. Contbr. articles to profl. publs Home: 22 Kendall Dr Chapel Hill NC 27514 Office: MD-60 (IERL) EPA Research Triangle Park NC 27711

BURDEN, THOMAS EARL, equipment mfg. exec.; b. Knoxville, Tenn., May 11, 1943; s. Jess W. and Alva Leona (Patterson) B.; B.S. in Indsl. Tech., Tenn. Technol. U., 1965; M.B.A., Samford U., 1976; m. Sandra Carol Crawford, Dec. 17, 1964; children—Christopher Lee, Monica Leigh. Foundry supt. Birmingham (Ala.) Stove and Range, 1965-71; materials mgr. Hackney Corp., Birmingham, 1971-74; foundry mgr. Cole Mfg. Co., Charlotte, N.C., 1974-77; plant mgr. Clow Corp., Birmingham, 1977—. Bd. dirs. Asso. Industries Ala.,

1979—. Foundry Ednl. Found. scholar, 1962. Mem. Am. Foundrymen's Soc. (bd. dirs., chpt. pres., 1964-65), Am. Mgmt. Assn. Club: Relay House. Patentee fine particle recycling method and apparatus. Home: 1613 Gentilly Dr Birmingham AL 35226 Office: PO Box 6226 Tarrant AL 35217

BURDETTE, EVERETTE CLIFTON, microwave engr., electrophysiologist; b. Charleston, W.Va., June 26, 1950; s. Orral Lorain and Helen Grace (Gaal) B.; student Palm Beach Coll., 1968-69; B.S., Ga. Inst. Tech., 1973; M.S., Ga. Tech. U., 1976, postgrad., 1976-77; postgrad. (tuition fellow) Emory U., 1977—; m. Sheila Sue Lafon, Feb. 16, 1971; children—Michelle Lorraine, Christa Ann, Jennifer Renee. Announcer, engr. Daytona Broadcasting Co., Sta. WJNO, 1967-69; co-op. trainee Ga. Inst. Tech., Atlanta, 1970-73, grad. research asst., 1973, asst. research scientist, 1973-76, research scientist, 1976-79, research scientist II, 1979—; design engr. Zepaf Electronics and Controls Co., Atlanta, 1972-73; v.p. engring. Tech. Assos., Inc., Atlanta, 1973-75; clin. asst. prof. dept. medicine Emory U., Atlanta, 1979—; dir. Tech. Assos., Inc., 1974—, Microwave Inc., 1978—; cons. in field; lectr. tech. schs. Named Outstanding Engr. in Research, State of Ga., 1979; grantee Nat. Cancer Inst., 1977—, NSF and NATO, 1979—. Mem. IEEE (co-founder recognition award Atlanta chpt. 1977), Antenna and Propagation Soc., Engring. in Medicine and Biology Soc., Microwave Theory and Techniques Soc., Soc. for Cryobiology, Bioelectromagnetics Soc., N.Y. Acad. Scis., Atlanta Engring. in Medicine and Biology Soc. (co-founder 1977, vice-chmn. 1977-78, chmn. 1978-79), Sigma Xi. Club: Tender Heart. Contbr. numerous articles to profl. publs. Home: 2860 Windfield Circle Tucker GA 30084 Office: Engring Experiment Sta Ga Inst Tech Atlanta GA 30332

BURDICK, EVERETTE MARSHALL, cons. chemist; b. Champaign, Ill., Aug. 9, 1913; s. Pearl Oscar and Margaret Alice (Hyde) B.; B.S. cum laude, U. Miami, 1935; M.S., Purdue U., 1937, Ph.D., 1943; m. Lois Aline Enyart, Nov. 13, 1937. Research chemist U.S. Dept. Agr., Northern Regional Research Lab., Peoria, Ill., 1941-45, U.S. Fruit & Vegetable Products Lab., Weslaco, Tex., 1945-46; dir. research Texsum Citrus Exchange, Weslaco, 1946-52; tech. cons. Rio Farms, Inc., Edcouch, Tex., 1949-52; tech. dir. Am. Chlorophyll, 1952-53; dir. labs. Am. Chlorophyll div. Strong-Cobb & Co., 1953; v.p., dir. research Strong Cobb & Co., Inc., 1953-54; pres. Am. Papain & Chem. Co., Inc., 1954-57; cons. Florida Citrus Mutual, 1957-58, Wallerstein Labs., Baxter Labs., Arbee Biochem. Corp., Resources Research, 1959-64; dir. research and devel. True Taste Corp., 1961-63. Fellow Am. Inst. Chemists (chmn. Fla. sect. 1962-63), AAAS; mem. Am. Chem. Soc. (emeritus), Fla. Hort. Soc., Inst. Food Technologists (emeritus), N.Y. Acad Scis., Sigma Xi, Phi Lambda Upsilon. Methodist. Mason. Co-author: Modern Chemical Processes, vols. I and IV; Fruit and Vegetable Juice Production. Contbr. to profl. jours. Patentee in field. Home: 4821 Ronda St Coral Gables FL 33146 Office: Coral Gables FL 33146

BURDICK, HAROLD EUGENE, publisher; b. Enid, Okla., Dec. 11, 1924; s. Jesse Leroy and Maude Elizabeth (Koch) B.; B.S. in Journalism, Okla. U., 1938; m. Lillian C. Lopp, Dec. 23, 1970; children—Robin, Steve, Leah, Cynthia, Kelly, Robert Michael. Advt. salesman Banner, Duncan, Okla., Times Gazette, Ashland, Ohio; advt. dir. publ. Alliance, Ohio, bus. mgr., then gen. mgr.; gen. mgr., pub. Public Opinion, Chambersburg, Pa.; pres., pub. Huntington (W.Va.) Pub. Co. Adv., council Boy Scouts Am.; bd. dirs. Huntington C. of C., YWCA, YMCA, Huntington, ARC; chmn. Tri-State Metro Nat. Alliance Bus., Inc., 1978; bd. dirs. United Way, 1979-80. Served to sgt. USAAF; ETO. Decorated Air Force medal with 3 clusters. Recipient award Nat. Alliance Bus., United Way, YMCA, ARC, Boy Scouts Am., Huntington Jaycees. Mem. Am. Newspaper Pubs. Assn., Newspaper Enterprise Assn., So. Newspubs. Assn., W.Va. Press Assn. Office: 946 Fifth Ave Huntington WV 25701

BURES, PAUL LESLIE, JR., television exec.; b. Cleve., Apr. 19, 1933; s. Paul Leslie and Margaret Elizabeth (Tompkins) B.; B.S., Miami U., Oxford, Ohio; m. Felicia M. Visconti, Sept. 26, 1966; children—Kristen Lee, Heather Elizabeth. Media supr. oil account J. Walter Thompson, Inc., N.Y.C., 1957-60; account, mktg. exec. Ogilvy & Mather, Inc., N.Y.C., 1960-66; sales exec. ABC-TV, N.Y.C., 1966-71; gen. sales mgr. KTRK-TV (Capital Cities Communications), Houston, 1971—; exec. com. TvB Sales Adv. Com., 1977—. Served with USCG, 1952-55. Mem. Nat. Acad. TV Arts and Scis., Houston C. of C. Republican. Episcopalian. Script editor: Your Competitive Medium, 1979, The Sum of the Alternatives, 1978, Television: The Persuasive Medium, 1980. Home: 10810 Idlebrook St Houston TX 77070 Office: KTRK-TV 3310 Bissonnet St Houston TX 77001

BURFORD, ALEXANDER MITCHELL, JR., physician; b. Memphis, Mar. 21, 1929; s. Alexander Mitchell and Mary Young (Tittle) B.; B.S., Florence (Ala.) State Coll., 1951; M.D., U. Tenn., Memphis, 1957. Intern, U. Tenn., Knoxville, 1957-58, resident in pathology, Memphis, 1958-62; asso. pathologist Eliza Coffee Meml. Hosp., Florence, Ala., 1962-73, dir. lab., chief pathology, 1973—; practice medicine specializing in pathology, 1958—, Florence Pathologists P.C., 1977—. Mem. Ala. Assn. Pathologists (pres. 1974-75), Coll. Am. Pathologists (del. 1972—), Am. Soc. Microbiology, Am. Soc. Clin. Pathologists, Am. Assn. Blood Banks, Alpha Kappa Kappa, Kappa Mu Epsilon, Alpha Phi Omega. Home: 652 Howell St Florence AL 35630 Office: Eliza Coffee Meml Hosp 600 W Alabama St Florence AL 35631

BURFORD, ANNA MARIE, educator; b. Glasgow, Ky., May 3, 1927; d. Ollis Bernard and Pearlie (Quinn) B.; A.A., Freed Hardeman Coll., Henderson, Tenn., 1947; B.S., Western Ky. U., Bowling Green, 1964, M.A., 1967; Ph.D., Ohio State U., 1979. Sec., underwriter Continental Ins. Cos., 1951-63; acad. adviser Western Ky. U., 1963-67; asst. prof. bus. Morehead (Ky.) State U., 1967-75, asso. prof., 1976—; condr. secretarial seminars and discussion groups at nat., state and local levels. Cert. in secondary teaching, Ky. Mem. Nat. Bus. Edn. Assn., Am. Vocat. Assn., Ky. Bus. Edn. Assn., Eastern Ky. Bus. Tchrs. Edn. Assn. (past pres., dir.), Phi Kappa Phi, Delta Pi Epsilon, Phi Delta Kappa. Mem. Ch. of Christ. Contbr. articles to profl. jours. Office: Combs Bldg Morehead State U Morehead KY 40351

BURGAN, WILLIAM MICHAEL, counselor; b. Harlan, Ky., June 15; s. Donald Edwin and Doris Hilda (Robinson) B.; B.S., U. Montevallo, 1971; M.A., U. Ala., 1973; A.A., U. Ala. in Birmingham, 1977; m. Debra Sue Pitts, May 31, 1970; children—Emily Michelle, William Michael. Counselor guidance South Girard High Sch., Phenix City, Ala., 1972-74, Mountain Brook (Ala.) Jr. High Sch., 1974—. Mem. Am. (govtl. relations chmn. 1977, pres. 1978), Ala. sch. counselor assns., Nat. (chmn. Uniserv Dist. VIII adv. council 1977—), Mountain Brook (chmn. polit. action 1976-77, pres. 1977—), Ala. edn. assns., Am., Ala. personnel and guidance assns. Presbyterian. Home: 4329 Mountaindale Rd Birmingham AL 35213 Office: 205 Overbrook Rd Birmingham AL 35213

BURGESS, ARTHUR HARRY, accountant; b. Sharon, S.C., Oct. 25, 1903; s. Arthur Calhoun and Mary (Love) B.; student Furman U., 1921-23; m. Sara Elizabeth Doll, Nov. 30, 1933; children—Sara Elizabeth (Mrs. John Sidney Frazer), Arthur Harry. Public accountant, Hickory, N.C., 1928—; chmn. bd. Arthur H. Burgess and Co., Hickory; dir. Maxwell Royal Chair Co. Mem. adv. bd. trustees Queens Coll.; pres. Sharon Found. C.P.A., N.C. Mem. Am. Inst. C.P.A.'s, N.C. Assn. C.P.A.'s. Presbyn. Rotarian. Clubs: Catawba (Newton, N.C.); Lake Hickory Country (Hickory); Charlotte (N.C.) City. Home: 322 3d Ave NE Hickory NC 28601 Office: First Security Bldg Hickory NC 28601

BURGESS, DEBRON RAY, ins. co. exec.; b. Wendall, Idaho, Feb. 28, 1947; s. Delbert R. and Jeanette Burgess; B.B.A., Boise State U., 1969; postgrad. Ga. State U., 1979—; m. Beverly Drummond, May 20, 1967; 1 dau., Stacy. Supr., Equitable Life Ins. Co., Sacramento, 1971-73; sr. supr., Newark, 1973-74, stock trader, N.Y.C., 1974-76, asst. treas., Atlanta, 1976—. Mem. Nat. Assn. Securities Dealers, Atlanta Cash Mgmt. Assn. (pres. 1979-80). Republican. Methodist. Club: Pinetree Country (dir. 1980—) (Kennesaw, Ga.). Home: 2361 Cajun Dr Marietta GA 30066 Office: 100 Peachtree St Suite 2327 Atlanta GA 30303

BURGESS, MARY JOHANNAH, ednl. adminstr.; b. Pensacola, Fla., Dec. 29, 1925, Student Liberal Arts, David Lipscomb Coll., Nashville, 1945; B.A. in Fine Arts and Edn., George Peabody Coll., Nashville, 1947; M.A. in Elementary Edn., U. W. Fla., Pensacola, 1970. Tchr. art Anderson County (Tenn.) schs. Oak Ridge, 1947-51, Escambia County Sch. Dist. 27, Pensacola, 1951-66, supr. art edn., 1966—. Trustee Pensacola Art Center Bd., 1972-75, Pensacola Mus. Art, 1972-79. Mem. Nat., Fla. art edn. assn., Fla. Assn. Supervision and Curriculum Devel., Delta Kappa Gamma. Contbr. articles to profl. jours. Certified in art edn., elementary edn., supervision, Fla. Home: 1310 N 18th Ave Pensacola FL 32503 Office: 5402 Lillian Hwy Pensacola FL 32506

BURGESS, OLIVER TAYLOR, hairstylist, cosmetologist; b. Dendron, Va., Aug. 29, 1918; s. Herman Oliver and Virginia (Trueheart) B.; student Kirby's Beauty Sch., Norfolk, Va., 1948, Robert Fiance Hair Design Inst., N.Y.C., 1949;; m. Ida Madjestic Chester, Dec. 17, 1941; 1 son, Oliver Taylor. Owner beauty salon, Wakefield, Va., 1948-50; owner beauty salons, Norfolk, 1950—, as owner Taylor Burgess Hairstyling Salons, Inc., 1962—; guest stylist John H. Breck Co., in U.S. and Europe, 1957—; pres. Taylor Burgess HairKare Products, Ltd., 1975—. Cons. com. cosmetology Norfolk Tech. Vocat. Center, Norfolk. Served as cpl. 116th Inf., AUS, 1941-45; ETO. Decorated Purle Heart, Bronze Star. Mem. Nat. (hair fashion com.), Norfolk hairdressers assns., Internat. Platform Assn., Intercoiffure U.S. (parliamentarian 1977), Va. Hairdressers and Cosmetologists Assn. (pres. 1965-66), Norfolk C. of C., Wards Corner Bus. Men's Assn. Baptist (trustee). Mason (Shriner), Lion. Club: Oceans (Virginia Beach, Va.). Home: 6435 Newport Ave Norfolk VA 23505 Office: 7500 Granby St Wards Corner Norfolk VA 23505

BURGESS, REMBERT OLIVER, physician; b. Spartanburg, S.C., Sept. 3, 1922; s. Rembert Bennett and Marie (Blair) B.; B.S., Wofford Coll., 1943; M.D., Vanderbilt U., 1946; m. Margaret Smith Burgess, Apr. 12, 1952 (dec.); children—Mary Emily, Marie Blair, James Madison, Charles Rembert. Intern Vanderbilt U., 1946-47, resident in medicine, 1949-52; practice medicine specializing in internal medicine, Spartanburg, 1953—; mem. staff Spartanburg Gen. Hosp., Mary Black Meml. Hosp.; asso. clin. prof. Med. U. S.C., 1973—. Served to capt. U.S. Army, 1947-49. Diplomate Am. Bd. Internal Medicine. Fellow A.C.P, Am. Coll. Chest Physicians, Am. Coll. Cardiology; mem. S.C., Spartanburg County med. socs., Phi Beta Kappa. Methodist. Club: Kiwanis. Home: 106 Rosewood Ln Spartanburg SC 29302 Office: 210 Catawba St Spartanburg SC 29303

BURGESS, SHIRLEY H., cosmetologist; b. Ashland, W.Va., June 5, 1937; d. Zachariah and Alma Ardelia (Walker) Harman; m. Herman T. Burgess, July 31, 1966. Co-owner, cosmetologist The House of Burgesses Beauty Salon, Petersburg, Va., 1966—; sec., co-owner Burgess Shopping Center, 1973—; sec., co-owner Burgess Enterprises, Inc. Chmn., Tri-County Vocat. Edn. Adv. Council. Mem. Va. State Hairdressers and Cosmetologist Assn. (pres. 1973-75), Nat. Hairdressers and Cosmetologist Assn. (5th v.p.). Republican. Baptist. Home: 2490 Poe Ln Petersburg VA 23803 Office: 2557 B S Crater Rd Petersburg VA 23803

BURGESS, WALTER JACKSON, educator; b. Colquitt County, Ga., Nov. 14, 1933; s. James R. and Autrey B.; B.S., Fla. State U., 1959; M.Bus. Edn., Ga. State U., 1967, Ph.D., 1972; m. Joyce H. Hart, May 2, 1953; children—Walter J., Catherine. Supr. acctg. data processing Lockheed Aircraft Corp., Marietta, Ga., 1961-67; prof. bus. Abraham Baldwin Coll., Tifton, Ga., 1967-72; prof. Madison U., Harrisonburg, Va., 1972-74; prof., chmn. div. bus. Albany State Coll. (Ga.), 1974—; mgmt. cons. data processing systems. Served with USN, 1952-56. Mem. NEA, Nat. Bus. Edn. Assn., Nat. Assn. Accts., Nat. Mgmt. Assn., Data Processing Mgmt. Assn. Baptist. Clubs: Kiwanis, Toastmasters. Contbr. articles to profl. jours. Home: 1900 Broach Ave Albany GA 31705 Office: Sch Bus Albany State Coll Albany GA 31705

BURGHARDT, THEODORE AUGUST, space systems engr.; b. Bronx, N.Y., Oct. 3, 1940; s. Frederic Charles and Dorothy Ethel (Aldridge) B.; A.A.S., SUNY, Farmingdale, 1966; B.S., U. Central Fla., Orlando, 1973; m. Judith Marie Hamilton, Feb. 20, 1965; children—Patrick Charles, Robert Andrew (dec.), William Richard. Electronic technician Intercontinental Electronics Corp., Westbury, N.Y., summers 1958-59; jr. electronics engr. Radio Recepter Co., Inc., Hicksville, N.Y., 1960-61; engr. field site ops. Raytheon Co., Kennedy Space Center, Fla., 1965-69, field engr., systems support engr., Sudbury, Mass., 1969-70; investigator computer applications study group Wuesthoff Meml. Hosp., Rockledge, Fla., 1970-72; master scheduler Harris Controls, Palm Bay, Fla., 1972-79; engr. Rockwell Internat., Kennedy Space Center, Fla., 1979—. Crew chief, driver, maintenance officer Harbor City Vol. Ambulance Squad, 1975—; dist. chmn. South Brevard dist. Cub Scouts, 1975-76; lic. lay reader Episcopal Ch. Diocese of Central Fla. Served with USAF, 1961-65. Registered emergency med. technician, Fla. Mem. Am. Prodn. Control Soc. Investigator integration flow-charting. Home: 2420 Dakota Dr Melbourne FL 32935 Office: PO Box 21105 Kennedy Space Center FL 32815

BURING, DAVID MYRON, obstetrician, gynecologist; b. Memphis, July 2, 1940; s. Louis and Julia S. (Lehman) B.; B.A., U. Tex., El Paso, 1961; M.D., Southwestern Med. Sch., 1965; m. Ann Lovin, Sept. 18, 1965; children—Bram, Joel, Benjamin. Intern, Jackson Meml. Hosp., Miami, Fla., 1965-66; resident Baylor Med. Center, Dallas, 1968-71; practice medicine specializing in Ob-Gyn, Corpus Christi, Tex., 1971-72, Denison, Tex., 1972—; chief obstetrics Texoma Med. Center; pres. Gate City Bldg. Co. Served with USN, 1966-68. Recipient Physicians Recognition award AMA, 1979; diplomate Am. Bd. Ob-Gyn. Mem. AMA, Am. Coll. Obstetricians and Gynecologists, Am. Fertility Soc., Am. Assn. Gynecol. Laparoscopists, Tex. Med. Assn., Acad. Polit. Sci., Flying Physicians Assn., Mensa, Ob-Gyn. Assn. (pres.), C. of C. Republican. Jewish. Clubs: Texoma Racquet, Denison Rod and Gun, B'nai Brith. Home: 11 Spring Creek St Denison TX 75020 Office: 100 Memorial Dr Denison TX 75020

BURK, SYLVIA JOAN, petroleum landman; b. Dallas, Oct. 16, 1928; d. Guy Thomas and Sylvia (Herrin) Ricketts; B.A., So. Meth. U., 1950, M.L.A., 1974; postgrad. U. So. Calif., 1973; children by previous marriage—Jeffery Randolph Murray, Brian BeVaughn Murray; m. 2d, Sam Bryan Burk, Jr., Apr. 26, 1973. Sec. to pres. Magna Oil Corp., Dallas, 1962-70; petroleum landman E.B. Germany & Sons., Dallas, 1970-73; asst. mgr. hdqrs. real estate dept. Atlantic Richfield Co., Los Angeles, 1973-74; office mgr., petroleum landman Gold King Prodn. Co., Houston, 1974-77; pvt. practice petroleum landman, Houston, 1977—. Tchr. Highland Park Meth. Ch., Dallas, 1958-70, mem. women's assn., 1962-70. Semi-finalist Mrs. Dallas Contest, 1957. Mem. Dallas Assn. Mental Health, Am. Assn. Petroleum Landmen (regional chmn. tax and legis. com. 1976-78, dir. 1978-80), Houston Assn. Petroleum Landmen (dir. 1977), Los Angeles, Dallas assns. petroleum landmen, Houston Opera Guild, Young Women of the Arts, Houston Rose Soc., River Oaks Bus. Women's Assn., Chi Omega, Sigma Delta Pi. Republican. Presbyterian. Clubs: Petroleum (Houston); Sugar Creek Country. Home: 3110 Country Club Blvd Sugar Land TX 77478 Office: 1111 S Post Oak Rd Suite 307 Houston TX 77056

BURKE, CAROL ELIZABETH, lawyer; b. Gt. Bend, Kans., June 23, 1946; d. Robert M. and Virginia (Jaworski) Burk; B.A. with highest distinction, State U. N.Y., 1971, J.D., 1974; 1 dau., Gina Faye. Admitted to Tex. bar, 1974, since practiced privately in Houston; faculty Bryant Stratton Bus. Coll., Buffalo, 1972. Dir. research and evaluation Mayor's Summer Youth Program, Buffalo, 1971. Jaeckle-Abrams research grantee, 1973. Mem. Tex. Trial Lawyers Assn., Am., N.Y. State, Tex. bar assns., AAUW. Club: Toastmasters. Contbr. articles to profl. jours. Office: 744 Augusta St Houston TX 77057

BURKE, FRANKLIN LEIGH, banker; b. Appomattox, Va., Apr. 20, 1941; s. William Wood and Mary Emily (Harvey) B.; student U. Va., 1959-62; B.A. magna cum laude, Oglethorpe U., 1966; m. Eleanor Dawson Sledge, Nov. 24, 1962; children—Eleanor Hallowell, Richard Cobb. With Bank of Va., Richmond, 1962-64; mgmt. trainee, broker Norris & Hirschberg, Atlanta, 1966; with Fulton Nat. Bank Atlanta, 1967—, sr. v.p., 1976—, sec., 1977—; sec. Fulton Nat. Corp., 1977—, v.p., 1979—. Bd. dirs. Central Atlanta Civic Devel., Inc., Park Central Communities, Inc.; mem. exec. com. Atlanta Steeplechase, 1966—; chmn. Ga. Multiple Sclerosis Soc., 1974-75; chmn. Oglethorpe U. Alumni Assn., 1971; mem. Leadership Atlanta. Mem. Am. Inst. Banking, Robert Morris Assos., Phi Delta Theta, Omicron Delta Kappa. Baptist. Clubs: Highlands Country, Piedmont Driving, Benedicts of Atlanta. Home: 3495 Ridgewood Rd NW Atlanta GA 30327 Office: 55 Marietta St NW PO Box 4387 Atlanta GA 30302

BURKE, HELEN RUTH CHRISTIE, guidance counselor; b. Dallas, Jan. 29; d. William Preston and Ruth (Harris) Christie; student Tex. Women's U., 1944-45, Tex. Christian U., 1945-47; B.S. in Edn., U. Houston, 1961, M.Ed., 1971; m. Jack Ray Burke, June 1, 1947 (dec. Jan. 1976); children—Barbara Suzanne (Mrs. M.A. Kennedy), Glenn Richard. Co-owner, operator Tyler County Motor Co., Woodville, Tex., 1956-57; co-owner, operator Jack Burke Co., Houston, 1962-69; tchr. history Houston Ind. Sch. Dist., 1970-77; counselor Lamar Sr. High Sch., 1977—; counselor Houston Ednl. Excellence Program, 1977-78. Active, Jr. League of Houston, United Fund, 1955-56, S.W. Cub Scouts, 1959-60, Houston Grand Opera, 1962-63, Hermann Hosp. Vols., 1964—, Delta Gamma Gulf Coast Charity Arabian Horse Show, 1971-72; exhibitor Houston Garden Club Assn., 1954-56. Lifetime profl. counselor cert.; Exxon grantee; Shell grantee. Mem. Am. Personnel and Guidance Assn., Tex. Personnel and Guidance Assn., Houston Personnel and Guidance Assn., Assn. for Humanistic Edn. and Devel., Am. Sch. Counselors Assn., Houston Sch. Counselors Assn., Tex. Christian U. Alumni Assn., Epsilon Sigma Alpha. Episcopalian. Clubs: Houston Tex. Christian U. Womens (past pres.), Delphian Past Pres.'s. Home: 2421 Westcreek St Apt 103 Houston TX 77027 Office: Lamar Sr High Sch 3325 Westheimer St Houston TX 77098

BURKE, MARY THOMAS, educator; b. Westport, Ireland, Nov. 28, 1930; d. Thomas J. and Annie (McGuire) Burke; B.A., Belmont Abbey Coll., 1955; M.A., Georgetown U., 1965; Ph.D., U. N.C., Chapel Hill, 1968. Tchr. elem. and secondary schs., Gastonia, Salisbury and Charlotte, N.C., Greenport, N.Y., 1952-64; asso. prof. human devel. Sacred Heart Coll., Belmont, N.C., 1968-71, acad. dean, 1968-70; asso. prof. U. N.C., Charlotte, 1970-76, prof., 1976—, head support services, chmn. spl. programs, counselor edn. program; cons. Duke Power Co., Meth. Counseling Center; dir. Nat. Bus. Firms, Inc. Pres., Open House Counseling Service, 1975-76; co-chmn. NCCJ, 1978—; exec. com. Am. Cancer Soc. Recipient Human Relations award Assn. Non-White Concerns, 1978, Anti-Defamation award, 1978. Mem. N.C. Personnel and Guidance Assn., N.C. Assn. Counselor Educators (named Counselor Educator of Yr. 1976), So. Regional Assn. Counselor Edn., Am. Personnel and Guidance Assn., Am. Counselor Edn. Assn., Am. Assn. Religious Values, Phi Delta Kappa. Republican. Roman Catholic. Home: Main St Belmont NC 28012 Office: Coll Human Devel U NC Charlotte NC 28223

BURKES, BOBBY, biochemist; b. New Orleans, Sept. 25, 1951; s. Joseph W. and Lucille (Addison) B.; B.S. in Chemistry, Xavier U., La., 1973; M.S. in Biochemistry, Atlanta U., 1975; m. Augusta Baudy, Dec. 30, 1973; children—Bobby, Brittany Ann. Research and devel. chemist Dow Chem. Co., 1975-77; research asso. dept. orthopaedics La. State U. Med. Center, New Orleans, 1977—; cons. in field. Mem. Am. Chem. Soc., NAACP, Beta Kappa Chi, Omega Psi Phi. Democrat. Author papers in field. Home: 41 Christy Ln New Orleans LA 70127

BURKETT, BENJAMIN CLINTON, II, oil and gas co. exec.; b. Amarillo, Tex., Jan. 22, 1936; s. Benjamin Clinton and Ione Mary (Braudt) B.; B.B.A., U. Tex., 1958; postgrad. N.Y.U., 1958-60; m. Janice Carole Oliver, Mar. 1, 1968; children—Benjamin, Bob, Mike, David. Security analyst Dominick & Dominick, N.Y.C., 1958-61; asst. to fin. v.p., asst. treas. Shamrock Oil & Gas Corp., Amarillo, Tex., 1961-66; asst. to pres. Mesa Petroleum, Amarillo, Tex., 1966-69; rep. Schneider, Bernet & Hickman, Amarillo, 1970-71; v.p. Lear Petroleum Corp., Dallas, 1971—, also dir.; dir. Dacresa Corp., Producer's Gas Co., Rael Gas Co. Mem. Petroleum Accountants Soc. Dallas, Fin. Execs. Inst., Ind. Petroleum Assn. Am. Clubs: Royal Oaks Country, Brookhaven Golf. Home: 5905 Haraby Ct Dallas TX 75248 Office: 950 One Energy Sq Dallas TX 75206

BURKETT, DAVID YOUNG, III, educator; b. Pitts., July 7, 1934; s. David Young and Faith Virginia (Espy) B.; B.S.J., Medill Sch. Journalism, Northwestern U., 1956, M.S.J., 1957; m. Lynnell Jackson, May 31, 1979. Reporter, Valley Daily News, Tarentum, Pa., 1956-57; writer Black Diamond mag., Chgo., 1957; news editor, newscaster Sta.-KITE and Sta.-KEXL, San Antonio, 1965-69; public relations agt. Trinity U., 1960-70, instr. in journalism, 1960-70, asst. prof. journalism, broadcasting and film, 1970-75, asso. prof., 1975—, gen. mgr. Sta.-KRTU-FM, 1979—; dir. Trinity U. High Sch. Journalism Inst., 1978—. Served with USAF, 1957-60. Decorated Air Force Commendation medal with oak leaf cluster. Recipient Bastian Honor award Northwestern U., 1957; named Res. Info. Office of Yr. in U.S., USAF, 1973. Mem. Internat. Assn. Bus. Communicators (pres. San

Antonio chpt. 1966-67, Chpt. Communicator of Yr., 1975), Assn. Edn. in Journalism, Internat. Communication Assn., Radio-TV News Dirs. Assn., Internat. Soc. Gen. Semantics, Acad. Para-psychology and Medicine, Armadillo Breeders Assn., Armed Forces Info. Council (v.p. San Antonio council 1977-78), Sigma Delta Chi (pres. San Antonio chpt. 1973-74, Harrington Meml. award 1957), Kappa Tau Alpha. Lutheran. Author: (with John Narciso) Declare Yourself: Discovering The Me In Relationships, 1975; Reserve Forces Information Handbook, 1978. Home: 1235 E Mulberry St San Antonio TX 78209 Office: 715 Stadium Dr San Antonio TX 78284

BURKETT, HELEN ROSE (MRS. CHARLES WILLIAM BURKETT, JR.), co. exec.; b. Cleve., Dec. 22, 1903; d. Frederick Holland and Mary Chloe (Upson) Rose; B.A., Mt. Holyoke Coll., 1925; m. Charles Willliam Burkett, Jr., Feb. 12, 1927 (dec. 1975); children—Charles William, Diana Rose Burkett Brewer, Helen Upson Burkett Stevens. Sec., treas. Burkett Assos., Miami, Fla., 1951-76, pres., 1976—. Chmn. communications Dept. Nat. Def., Harrison, N.Y., 1941-45, chief block leader service, 1943-45; mem. Harrison War Council, 1941-45, Service Corps ARC, 1945-47; mem. Harrison Republican Town Com., 1946-47; mem. Dade County Rep. Exec. Com., Fla., 1956-58. Mem. DAR (Fla. chmn. radio and TV 1954-56, rec. sec. 1958-60, regent Biscayne chpt. 1956-58, regents' council 1956-60), Children Am. Revolution (sr. pres. Golden Sands soc. 1960-63, 70-74, sr. state v.p. 1972-76, sr. state pres. 1976-78, hon. life pres. 1978—), Colonial Dames XVII Century (Fla. sec. 1957-59, treas. 1959-61, librarian gen. 1959-61, state 1st v.p. 1961-63, state pres. 1963-65, nat. curator gen. 1965-67, nat. pres.-gen. 1967-69, hon. life pres.-gen. 1969—), Colonial Dames Am. (chpt. scholarship com. 1959-61, dir. 1969-71), Cleve. Apt. Owners Assn., Nat. Assn. Parliamentarians, Daus. Am. Colonists (chpt. v.p. 1961-64), Women Descs. Ancient and Honorable Arty. Co., Daus. of 1812 (chpt. v.p. 1961-63), N.Y. Geneal. and Biog. Soc., N.E. Hist. and Geneal. Soc., Nat. Geneal. Soc., Ams. Royal Descent, Magna Charta Dames Fla. (corr. sec. 1960—). Clubs: La Gorce Country, Surf, Indian Creek Country, Bath (Miami Beach, Fla.); Bankers (Miami). Home: 5800 N Bay Rd Miami FL 33140 Office: 8080 NE 2d Ave Miami FL 33138

BURKETT, NORMAN D., hosp. adminstr.; b. Okeechobee, Fla., June 20, 1925; s. Sanford B. and Lillian E. (Littleton) B.; B.S., U. Ga., 1950; postgrad. Cornell U., 1964; m. Bobbie Penn, Feb. 18, 1953; children—Norman D., Timothy Eugene. Med. rep. Sharp & Dohme, Inc., 1950-53; adminstr. Rockmart-Aragon Hosp., Rockmart, Ga., 1953-54; faculty Ga. State U., 1954-62; now pres., chief exec. officer Hamilton Meml. Hosp., Dalton, Ga.; dir. Hardwick Bank and Trust Co., Dalton, Blue Cross of Ga.-Atlanta; mem. Ga. Comprehensive Health Planning Adv. Council, 1967-74, chmn., 1971-74; chmn. hosp. adv. council State of Ga., 1969-70, mem., 1965-71; mem. Ga. State Commn. on Aging, 1965-67. Trustee, Shorter Coll., Rome, Ga. Served with M.C., USN, 1943-46, USAF Res., 1951-66. Named Man of Yr., Dalton, 1959; recipient citation for meritorious service Am. Hosp. Assn., 1979; Gold honor award of excellence Ga. Hosp. Assn., 1979. Fellow Royal Soc. Arts, London, Am. Coll. Hosp. Adminstrs. (past chmn.); mem. Ga. Hosp. Assn. (past trustee, pres.), Am. Hosp. Assn. (ho. of dels., past trustee), Dalton-Whitfield C. of C. (past pres.). Baptist. Clubs: Dalton Golf and Country, Rotary, Elks. Home: 2209 Rocky Face Circle Dalton GA 30720 Office: Hamilton Meml Hosp Dalton GA 30720

BURKETT, WARREN LEVI, JR., mfg. co. exec.; b. Winter Park, Fla., Nov. 2, 1926; s. Warren Levi and Nuna (Boatwright) B.; B.S., Sam Houston State Coll., 1949; m. Mary Alice Bibey, Feb. 4, 1954; children—Warren Levi III, Kathy Ann. Data process account mgr. Humble Oil Co., Baytown, Tex., 1951-52; dir. data processing Publix Supermarkets Inc., Lakeland, Fla., 1954-58; dir. mgmt. info. services Tropicana Products Inc., Bradenton, Fla., 1958—. Instr. Manatee Jr. Coll., 1965-66. Served with USAF, 1945-46. Mem. Data Processing Mgrs. Assn. Democrat. Lutheran. Home: 1016 51st W Bradenton FL 33505 Office: PO Box 338 Bradenton FL 33505

BURKHARDT, MARY ELIZABETH, mktg. exec.; b. Paterson, N.J., Feb. 21, 1945; d. Andrew and Betty M. Mitchell; B.A. (Nat. Merit scholar), Trenton State Coll., 1966; M.S., Montclair State Coll., 1969; M.B.A., U. Dallas, 1979; m. Douglas A. Hellman, Apr. 15, 1976. Fin. analyst Thomas J. Lipton, Englewood Cliffs, N.J., 1969-71, mktg. research analyst, 1971-74; mktg. research mgr. Coca-Cola U.S.A., Dallas, 1974-76; product mgr. Frito-Lay, Inc., Dallas, 1976-78; mktg. dir. The Drawing Board, Inc., Dallas, 1978-79; mktg. mgr. GTE Service Corp, Irving, Tex., 1979—; guest lectr. U. Colo., So. Meth. U., Tex. Tech. U.; profl. Grad. Sch. Bus., Fairleigh-Dickinson U., 1969-74. Active Am. Cancer Crusade, United Fund, Girl Scouts U.S.A. Mem. Nat. Assn. Univ. and Coll. Instrn., Am. Mgmt. Assn. (local pres.), Am. Mktg. Assn. (local pres., nat. dir.), Market Research Assn. (nat. sec.), Soc. Advancement Mgmt. Author articles. Home: 3147 Golden Oak Dallas TX 75234 Office: 4500 Fuller Dr Irving TX 75062

BURKHARDT, WILLIAM CHRISTIAN, food co. exec.; b. Cleve., Nov. 29, 1937; s. Chris and Willma (Turbott) B.; B.S., Fla. State U., 1960; m. Joan Harmon, Jan. 31, 1959; children—Robert Christian, Thomas Christian, David Christian. With ITT Continental Baking Co., 1960-73, asst. regional v.p., dir. sales, Rye, N.Y., 1972-73; exec. v.p., chief operating officer, dir. Nat. Continental Corp., Kingston, Jamaica, 1973-76; pres. splty. bakery group Beatrice Foods Co., Chgo., 1976-77, pres. bakery div., Winston-Salem, N.C., 1977—; dir. Bahamas Bakeries Ltd., Nassau, Société Haitian de Biscuitiere, Port au Prince. Mem. Am. Bakers Assn. (bd. govs.), Biscuit and Cracker Mfrs. Assn., Am. Soc. Bakery Engrs., So. Bakers Assn. Republican. Episcopalian. Clubs: Rotary, Masons, Shriners. Home: 632 Hertford Rd Winston-Salem SC 27104 Office: 514 S Stratford Rd Suite 404 Winston Salem NC 27103

BURKIG, THOMAS ORLANDO, psychologist; b. Seattle, July 25, 1948; s. Arthur Ralph and Virginia May B.; B.A. in Psychology and Sociology, Tex. A&I U., 1975, M.A. in Psychology, 1978; m. Gloria Perez, May 2, 1969; children—Celeste Michelle, Heather Kristin; permanent foster son, Jesse Ponce. Psychologist, Corpus Christi (Tex.) State Sch. for Mentally Retarded, 1973—; chmn. Council on Adoptable Children, Corpus Christi. Served with U.S. Army, 1967-71. Project VOICE grantee, 1979—. Mem. Am. Assn. on Mental Deficiency, Alpha Chi. Author: On the Inside-Looking Out, 1979; contbr. papers in field to profl. confs. Home: 333 Stages Dr Corpus Christi TX 78412 Office: 902 Airport Rd Corpus Christi TX 78408

BURKS, LINDA KAYE, psychologist; b. Stillwater, Okla., Jan. 2, 1944; d. Floyd Alley and Elvia Opal (Morris) Gantt; B.S., Okla. State U., 1974, M.S., 1976; m. Sterling Leon Burks, July 30, 1972; children—Tracey Lynn McCauley, Glynn Wayne McCauley. Clin. intern, Bi-State Mental Health Clinic, Ponca City, Okla., 1976; staff psychologist Psychol. Services Center, Okla. State U., Stillwater, 1976—; cons. in field. Mem. Council for Exceptional Children, Okla. Psychol. Assn., Am. Mental Health Counselors Assn., Am. Personnel and Guidance Assn., Beta Sigma Phi. Democrat. Club: Order of Eastern Star. Office: 118 N Murray Hall Okla State U Stillwater OK 74074

BURKS, MACK SKAGGS, business cons.; b. Dallas, May 14, 1924; s. Joseph Cooper and Grace (Skaggs) B.; student U. Okla., 1942-43; Ph.D. in Bus. Adminstrn., Colo. State Christian Coll., 1973; m. Peggy Crosswhite, Sept. 14, 1946; children—Cynthia (Mrs. John Starling), Susan, Carol (Mrs. Michael Hawk). Sec.-treas. Connolly's Inc., 1947-52; partner Burks & Smartt, 1952-56; pres. Burks, Inc., 1956-61; account exec. Glenn Advt., Inc., 1962-64; v.p., sec.-treas. Keystone Industries, 1965-67; v.p. mktg. Harter Concrete Products Inc., 1967-74 (all Oklahoma City); pres. Heritage Concrete Products, Inc., 1971-74; dir. Ims, Inc. Chmn., Okla. Plan and Resources Bd., 1959-63, mem. bd., 1963-65; mem. Okla. Lakes Redevel. Authority, 1961-63; chmn. pub. relations Govs. Com. on Pub. Safety, 1962-63; mem. Oklahoma City Community Council. Chmn., 5th Congl. Dist. Democratic Party Okla. Bd. dirs. Traveler's Aid Soc., 1964-65, 72—, v.p., 1965, treas., 1967. Served with USNR, 1943-46. Mem. Nat. Concrete Masonry Assn. (chmn. mktg. com.), C. of C. (vice chmn. tourist and conv. div.), Phi Gamma Delta. Methodist. Home: 1712 Guilford Ln Oklahoma City OK 73120 Office: 1260 First Nat Center E Oklahoma City OK 73102

BURLEIGH, BRUCE DANIEL, JR., biochemist; b. Augusta, Ga., June 23, 1942; s. Bruce Daniel and Billie Ann (Carter) B.; B.S., Carnegie-Mellon U., 1964; M.S., U. Mich., 1967, Ph.D., 1970; m. Dorothy Jean Roskos, Sept. 4, 1962; 1 son, Michael Eugene. Predoctoral teaching fellow in biochemistry U. Mich., Ann Arbor, 1966-70; vis. scholar MRC Lab. of Molecular Biology, Cambridge, Eng., 1970-72, mem. research staff, 1973; asst. prof. biochemistry U. Tex. System Cancer Center, M.D. Anderson Hosp., Houston, 1974—. NIH fellow, 1967-70; Am. Cancer Soc. fellow, 1970-72. Mem. AAAS, Am. Chem. Soc., Endocrine Soc., Sigma Xi, Tau Beta Pi, Phi Lambda Upsilon. Episcopalian. Contbr. numerous articles to profl. jours. Home: 5707 Creekbend Houston TX 77096 Office: Biochemistry Dept MD Anderson Hosp and Tumor Inst Tex Med Center Houston TX 77030

BURLESON, ROBERT JOE, orthopedic surgeon; b. Birmingham, Ala., Oct. 20, 1918; s. Daniel Downs and Stella Lee (Collins) B.; A.B., U. Ala., Tuscaloosa, 1939; M.D., U. Louisville, 1943; M.S. in Orthopedic Surgery, U. Minn., 1954; m. Mary Beth Hall, Mar. 29, 1943; children—Carol Jo, Genabeth, Robert Mark. Intern, USPHS-U.S. Marine Hosp., Stapleton, N.Y., 1943-44; surg. service U.S. Marine Hosp., Buffalo, 1944-46; fellow in orthopedic surgery Mayo Clinic, 1951-54; gen. practice medicine and surgery, Decatur, Ala., 1946-51, specializing in orthopedic surgery, Asheville, N.C., 1954-74; orthopedics sports medicine Univ. Health Service, U. Ala., University, 1974-76, asso. prof. surgery, dir. surg. edn. Coll. Community Health Scis., 1977—; mem. staff Tuscaloosa Orthopedic Clinic, 1976-77, Ala. Crippled Children Program, Student Health Center, U. Ala.; courtesy staff Druid City Hosp., Tuscaloosa; cons. Vets. Hosp., Tuscaloosa; past pres. N.C. Orthopedic Assn. Deacon, elder, trustee, chmn. congregation First Christian Ch., Asheville, 1954-74; bd. dirs. Asheville Orthopedic Hosp., Asheville Lions Club Workshop for Blind. Diplomate Am. Bd. Orthopedic Surgery. Fellow Am. Acad. Orthopedic Surgery; mem. Am. Orthopedic Soc. for Sports Medicine, So., Ala. med. assns., Tuscaloosa County Med. Soc., Eastern Orthopedic Assn. (past pres.), Ala. Orthopedic Soc., Mayo Clinic Alumni Assn., Mayo Orthopedic Alumni Club, N.C. Commn. for Blind (life), Phi Chi, Phi Delta Theta. Republican. Presbyn. Clubs: Lions (pres. 1966, zone chmn. Internat. Dist. 31-A 1967); University. Contbr. articles to med. jours. Home: 180 Woodland Hills Tuscaloosa AL 35405 Office: Box 6291 U Ala University AL 35486

BURLINGAME, JAMES MONTGOMERY, lawyer; b. Great Falls, Mont., Dec. 25, 1926; s. James Montgomery and Eloise (Corbin) B.; B.A., Tulane U., 1949, J.D., 1950; m. Joella Claire Blache, June 15, 1950; children—James Montgomery IV, Ann Blache, John Marshall. Admitted to La. bar, 1950, U.S. Supreme Ct bar, 1961 practiced in Washington, 1950; partner Jones, Walker, Waechter, Poitevent, Carrere and Denegre, New Orleans, 1953—. Served to ensign U.S. Maritime Service, 1945-46; to capt. AUS, 1950-52. Trustee, St. Martin's Protestant Episcopal Sch., 1968—, pres. bd. trustees, 1976-79. Mem. Am., Fed., La. (chmn. mineral sect. 1971-72), New Orleans bar assns., Am. Judicature Soc., Beta Theta Pi. Episcopalian. Club: Petroleum, New Orleans Country, Pickwick, Stratford, International House (New Orleans). Home: 433 Iona St Metairie LA 70005 Office: 225 Baronne St 28th Floor New Orleans LA 70112

BURLISON, PAT ED, plastic surgeon; b. Hornersville, Mo., Dec. 24, 1935; s. Pat and Eula Mae (Ferguson) B.; B.S., Memphis State U., 1957; M.D., U. Tenn., 1960; m. Robbie Jane Baskin, Mar. 15, 1969; 1 dau., Lauren. Intern City of Memphis Hosps., 1960-61; resident in gen. surgery U. Tenn., 1963-67, resident in plastic and reconstructive surgery, 1967-69; practice medicine specializing in plastic and reconstructive surgery, Huntsville Ala., 1969—; mem. faculty U. Ala. Sch. Primary Med. Care. Served with USPHS, 1961-63. Diplomate Am. Bd. Surgery, Am. Bd. Plastic Surgery. Fellow ACS; mem. Huntsville Acad. Medicine (pres. 1977-78), Madison County Med. Soc., Med. Assn. Ala., AMA, Am., Ala. (pres. 1977-78), Southeastern socs. plastics and reconstructive surgeons. Methodist. Home: 2710 Westminster Way SE Huntsville AL 35801 Office: 303 Williams Suite 1321 Huntsville AL 35801

BURLONE, DOMINICK ANTHONY, JR., research chemist; b. Pittston, Pa., Dec. 30, 1948; s. Dominick Amedeo and Constance (DiCio) B.; B.S., King's Coll., 1970; M.S., Pa. State U., 1975, Ph.D., 1975; m. Joyce Ann Rother, May 4, 1974; children—Karen, Suzanne. Research chemist Badische Corp., Anderson, S.C., 1976—; instr. chemistry Pa. State U., 1971-75. Served with U.S. Army, 1970. NSF fellow, 1972-75. Mem. Am. Chem. Soc. Contbr. articles to profl. jours. Home: Route 2 Stagecoach Dr Anderson SC 29621 Office: Box 3025 Anderson SC 29621

BURMAHLN, ELIZABETH LEONA BUTLER, ret. high sch. tchr. and adminstr.; b. Seymour, Iowa, June 9, 1900; d. Jesse Elroy and Mae Bell (White) Butler; A.B., Des Moines U., 1926; M.Ed., Boston U., 1930; postgrad. N.Y. U., Wayne U., U. Va.; m. Elmer F. Burmahln, Apr. 3, 1931. Sec., Coll. Edn., Des Moines U., 1918-23; legal sec. J.F. Page, Des Moines, 1923-26; tchr. bus. edn. Des Moines Pub. High Sch., 1926-30, Detroit Pub. High Sch., 1930-37; instr. secretarial scis. Radford (Va.) State Coll., 1940-41; tchr. E.C. Glass High Sch., Lynchburg, Va., 1941-67, prin. Evening Sch., 1942-67, asst. accountant Sr. High Sch., 1954-67; ret., 1967; chmn. Iowa Com. Bus. English, 1928-30; mem. Va. Tchr. Certification Com.; lectr. in field. Recipient Most Outstanding Student award Detroit Advt. Club, 1933; Tchr. of Month award. Mem. Va. Bus. Edn. Assn. (pres., dir.), NEA, AAUW, P.E.O., Delta Chi Delta, Delta Kappa Gamma. Club: Lynchburg Woman's. Contbr. articles to Am. Vocat. Assn. Jour. Home: 3716 Manton Dr Lynchburg VA 24503

BURMAHLN, ELMER FRED, bus. cons., ret. ednl. adminstr.; b. Kiel, Wis., Oct. 6, 1897; s. John Henry and Emma H. (Klopfer) B.; student U. Wis.-Whitewater, 1916-17; summer student Tchrs. Coll., Columbia U., 1920, U. Calif., Berkeley, 1921, U. Chgo., 1922, U. Wash., 1923, Harvard U., 1924; B.S. in Accounting and Bus. Edn., Boston U., 1930; M.A. in Bus. Edn., N.Y. U., 1934; postgrad. U. Va. Extension, 1941-43; spl. edn. Gregg Coll., 1914; diploma Stenotype Sch., 1917; tchr.'s certificate Tulloss Sch., Springfield, Ohio, 1918, Zanerian Coll. Penmanship, Columbus, Ohio, 1919; diploma in bus. adminstrn. LaSalle Extension U., 1921; diploma Sheldon Sch. Salesmanship, Chgo., 1922, Knox Sch. Salesmanship, Chgo., 1923; accounting and auditing diploma South-Western Pub. Co., Cin., 1923; m. Elizabeth L. Butler, Apr. 3, 1931. Head of comml. dept. Escanaba (Mich.) High Sch., 1917-18, Lead (S.D.) High Sch., 1918-22; supr. comml. edn. Houston pub. schs., 1922-23; dir. bus. edn. E.C. Glass High Sch., Lynchburg, Va., 1923-67, also tchr. accounting and bus. law, controller high sch. finances, 1923-67; cons. and adviser to Today's Bus. Law, Fitman Pub. Corp., N.Y.C., 1956-76; Va. State comml. contest mgr. of typewriting, bookkeeping and shorthand, 1926-29; chmn. Va. State Prodn. Com. in Bus. Edn., 1931-34; local and state ofcl. Va. State High Sch. Track Meet, Lynchburg, 1934-38; chmn. Lynchburg Gasoline Rationing, 1941-45; condr. Olson Travel Orgn. tours in Eng., Holland, Germany, Italy, France and Switzerland, summer 1936; moderator Indsl. Council Panel Confs., Rensselaer Poly. Inst., Troy, N.Y., 1952-56; lectr. Columbia U., 1936, Washington and Lee U., 1937, U. Minn., 1938, Nat. Scholastic Press Assns. Recipient certificates of appreciation Va. Bus. Edn. Assn., 1963, Lynchburg Bd. Edn., 1967; Hon. Legion of Honor, Internat. Supreme Council Order of De Molay, 1974; Collegiate Profl. teaching certificate, Va. Named Tchr. of Month, E.C. Glass High Sch., 1935. Mem. Internat. Soc. Bus. Edn., Nat. Assn. Accountants (v.p. 1960-61), NEA, Va. Edn. Assn., Nat., So. Va. (pres., chmn. bd. dirs. 1930-33) bus. edn. assns., Am. Accounting Assn., Va. Ret. Tchrs. Assn., Boston U. Alumni Assn., N.Y. U. Alumni Fedn., Houston C. of C. Clubs: Houston U.; University (Seattle); Masons (Shriner, K.T., 32 deg.). Cons. and contbg. editor Sch. Feeding Mgmt. Mag. (name changed to Catering World of Mgmt. Mags., Inc.), 1926-32. Contbr. numerous articles on bus. edn. and sch. adminstrn. to profl. publs. Home: 3716 Manton Dr Lynchburg VA 24503

BURNER, MARY LIPPITT, mfg. co. exec.; b. New Haven, Aug. 22, 1945; d. Gordon Leslie and Phyllis (Parker) Lippitt; m. June 1966 (div. 1975); 1 dau., Julie Lynn. Personnel specialist, also coordinator mgmt. devel. Met. Dade County, Fla., 1974-79; coordinator mgmt. devel. Racal-Milgo Co., Miami, 1979—; adj. prof. Fla. Internat. U., Miami, 1979—. Active Big Bros./Big Sisters Greater Miami. Mem. Am. Soc. Tng. and Devel. (pres. Miami chpt. 1978—), Am. Soc. Public Adminstrn. (dir. 1979—), Am. Soc. Personnel Adminstrn., Greater Miami C. of C., Personnel Assn. Greater Miami. Methodist. Office: Racal-Milgo Co 8600 NW 41st St Miami FL 33166

BURNET, THORNTON WEST, marketing exec.; b. Cin., Aug. 27, 1917; s. David and Agnes McClung (West) B.; B.S. in Commerce, U. Va., 1940; m. Mary Elizabeth Charlton, Aug. 14, 1948; 1 son, Thornton West. Asst. treas. Lincoln Service Corp., Washington, 1941-50, v.p., sec., 1950-59; v.p. marketing Am. Finance Mgmt. Corp., Silver Spring, Md., 1959-77; v.p. marketing ADS Agy., 1977—; v.p., treas., dir. Monet Constrn. Co., Fairfax, Va., 1962—; sec., dir. Worldwide Yellow Pages Service Co., 1979—. Committeeman, Boy Scouts Am., 1945—. Pres. bd. trustees Fletcher Meml. Library. Served with AUS, 1940-43. Mem. Alpha Kappa Psi. Republican. Episcopalian (vestryman, past sr. warden). Home: 10800 Hunters Valley Rd Vienna VA 22180 Office: 10 Post Office Rd Silver Spring MD 20910

BURNETT, HARRY, III, public relations, advt. exec.; b. Staunton, Va., Nov. 17, 1946; s. Harry Burnett, Jr. and Pearl I. (Alexander) Cuyler; student U. Tex., 1965-68, Harvard U., 1967; B.A., George Washington U., 1970; m. Rae Garber, Oct. 4, 1975; children—Peyton Blackburn, Caroline Marquis; stepchildren—Jean Melton Lane, Edward Emerson Lane III. Curator artmobile program Va. Mus. Fine Arts, Richmond, 1972-74; pvt. investor, Charlottesville, Va., 1974-76; asst. to pres. Christian Aid Mission, Charlottesville, 1976-77; dir. public relations PTL-TV Network, Charlotte, N.C., 1977-79; mgr. Focus Advt., James Robison Evangelism Assn., Hurst, Tex., 1979—. Advt. chmn. Greater Episcopal Fellowship, Charlotte, 1978-79; publicity chmn. Mecklenburg County (N.C.) Rep. ann. fund raiser, 1979; active Mecklenburg County Young Republicans Club.

BURNETT, THOMAS DOUGLASS, III, engring. co. exec.; b. Balt., Nov. 22, 1950; s. Thomas Douglass and Doris Virginia (Eiford) B.; B.S. in Marine Engring., U.S. Mcht. Marine Acad., 1973; m. Cheryl Ann Giroir, Oct. 17, 1978. Field service engr. Combustion Engring. Inc., Windsor, Conn., 1973-75, field service engr. II, Houston, 1975-77, resident service engr., 1977-79; system boiler maintenance supr. Gulf States Utilities Co., 1979—. Mem. ASME, Nat., Tex. socs. profl. engrs. Democrat. Roman Catholic. Home: 560 25th St Beaumont TX 77706 Office: Gulf States Utilities Co PO Box 2951 Beaumont TX 77704

BURNETT, THOMAS J., toiletries mfg. co. exec.; b. Ft. Worth, Sept. 24, 1950; s. Jack and Mary Jean B.; student U. Tex., Arlington, 1969-71; m. Patty Ann Harrison, Nov. 24, 1970; 1 son, Thomas J. With Maybelline Sales Corp., 1973-79, dist. mgr., Memphis, 1978-79; dist. mgr. Tex., Alberto-Culver Co., Hurst, 1979—. Treas., Hurst-Bedford Jaycees, 1975-76. Mem. Am. Mktg. Assn. Address: 2033 Normandy Dr Hurst TX 76053

BURNETT, WILBUR WEEDEN (BILL), bus. cons.; b. Kansas City, Mo., May 10, 1927; s. Emery and Vivian (Weeden) B.; B.S. in Physicis, U. Denver, 1950; m. Dolores Mae Hough, Oct. 17, 1953; children—Gary Michael, Sherri Lynn. Resident engring. rep. Ampex Corp., 1959-61; sales mgr. research and devel. Martin Co., Denver, 1961-64; dir. mktg. Tyco Labs., Inc. Waltham, Mass., 1964-66; mgr. Melpar, Inc. Space Scis. Labs., Natick, Mass., 1966-67, product mgr., 1967; rep. Bendix Corp., Washington, 1967-69; pres. Burnett & Assos., Inc., Reston, Va., 1969—; pres., treas., dir. Sentor Security Group of Va., Inc., 1973-75; bd. advisors Services Nat. Bank, Arlington, Va.; sec.-treas., dir. Mandex, Inc. Research adv. bd. U. Detroit, 1971-74. Served with USCG, 1943-46. Decorated Purple Heart. Mem. U.S. Naval Inst., Navy League, Am. Oceanic Orgn., Assn. Old Crows. Club: Reston Golf and Country (dir.). Patentee electronic devices. Home and office: 2506 Goldcup Ln Reston VA 22091

BURNETTE, BETTY DAVENPORT, health care adminstr.; b. Chowan County, N.C., Oct. 25, 1928; d. James Alton and Mary Eliza (Brickhouse) Davenport; m. Robert Hugh Burnette, Mar. 31, 1949; children—Mary Gray, Frances Rebecca, Betsy Cherlyn. Nurse's aide Chowan Hosp., 1945-47, floor mgr. Variety Store, 1947-50; clk. Davenport's Meat Market, Chowan County, 1951-56; owner, operator The Remnant Shop, Louisburg, N.C. and Nashville, 1968—; adminstr. Burnettes Rest Home, Louisburg, N.C., 1968—; owner Stage Coast Manor Rest Home, Angier, N.C., 1978—, Melody Manor Rest Home, Boydton, Va., 1978—. Mem. N.C. Homes for the Aging (dir. 1977—, recipient award for outstanding and dedicated services, 1977), N.C. Long Term Care Facility (dir. 1977—, dist. v.p. 1978-80). Home: Rex Heights Louisburg NC 27549 Office: Route 2 Louisburg NC 27549

BURNEY, BEN RICHARD, mfg. co. exec.; b. Crystal Springs, Miss., July 30, 1926; s. Ben Isaac and Velma Faye (McCoy) B.; diploma Copiah-Lincoln Jr. Coll., 1948; B.B.A., U. Miss., 1949; postgrad. in traffic and transp. Tulane U., 1951-52; m. Catherine Wilson, May 30, 1949; children—Glynn, Janice, Virginia. Gen. agt., br. mgr. New

Orleans div. office and warehouse Weil Bros., cotton mchts. 1949-56; pvt. practice water well drilling, 1956-58; purchasing agt., prodn. controller Kuhlman Electric Co., Crystal Springs, 1958-63; with Royal Maid Co., Hazlehurst, Miss., 1963-73, chief accountant and controller, 1967-71, plant mgr., 1971-73; asst. exec. dir., sales mgr. Miss. Industries for Blind, Jackson, 1973—. Mem. Copiah County (Miss.) Democratic Exec. Com. Served with USN, 1944-46. Methodist. Club: Lake Copiah (Crystal Springs). Home: Burney Rd Crystal Springs MS 39059

BURNHAM, CHARLES JOSEPH, ophthalmologist; b. Bay Springs, Miss., May 19, 1919; s. Charles Edney and Zenobia (Blankenship) B.; B.A. magna cum laude, Miss. Coll., 1940; M.D., Tulane U., 1944; m. Mary Nicholl, Aug. 21, 1951; children—Charles Edney, Thomas Nicholl, John Kirk. Intern, Jefferson Hillman Hosp., Birmingham, Ala., 1944-45, resident in ophthalmology, 1945-47, practice medicine specializing in ophthalmology, Birmingham, 1947—; chief ophthalmology Norwood Clinic, Carraway Meth. Med. Center, 1947—; past pres. Carraway Meth. Hosp. staff; asso. prof. ophthalmology U. Ala., Birmingham. Bd. dirs. Eye Found. Hosp., Birmingham; bd. dirs. exec. com. Carraway Meth. Med. Center. Served with USNR, 1947-48, 54-55. Diplomate Am. Bd. Ophthalmology. Fellow A.C.S., Am. Acad. Ophthalmology; mem. Jefferson County, Ala. State med. assns., AMA, Ala. Acad. Ophthalmology (pres.), Contact Lens Assn., Am. Introcular Implant Soc., Am. Contract Bridge League (past pres. So. div., life master), Ala. Bridge Assn. (past pres.), Alpha Omega Alpha. Republican. Baptist. Home: 212 Fairmont Dr Birmingham AL 35213 Office: 1529 N 25th St Birmingham AL 35234

BURNHAM, J. V., printing co. exec.; b. Pascagoula, Miss., May 23, 1923; s. George Luther and Eli Vashti (Hough) B.; A.A., Jones Jr. Coll., Ellisville, Miss., 1946; A.S., Rochester Inst. Tech., 1948; B.S., U. Houston, 1951, M.Ed., 1953; m. Patti Lauri Latham, May 18, 1946; children—James Steven, Jon Douglas, Richard Scott, Bruce Edward, Vernon Alan. Mgr., Progress-Item, Ellisville, 1948-51; asst. prof. graphic arts and journalism and asst. dir. printing dept. U. Houston, 1951-57; with Fidelity Printing Co., Houston, 1957—, estimator, prodn. supt., purchasing dir., 1957-67, asst. sec.-treas., 1967-69, v.p., 1969—; pres. Printing Industries of Gulf Coast, 1971-73, chmn. edn. com., 1960-70. Served to lt. (j.g.) USN, 1943-46. Named Houston Graphics Man of Year, 1968; named Man of Year, Printing Industries of Gulf Coast, 1970; recipient Scouter award Boy Scouts Am., 1966, Scoutmaster award, 1968; Benjamin Franklin award Houston Craftsmen's Club, 1971. Mem. Houston Advt. Fedn. Bus. and Profl. Advt. Assn., Nat. Eagle Scout Assn., Houston Litho Club, Houston Club of Printing House Craftsmen, Houston C. of C. (edn. com. 1970—), Nat. Rifle Assn., Phi Delta Kappa. Methodist. Clubs: Braeburn Country, Newport Country. Asso. editor Am. Oceanography, 1968-71; S.W. corr. Inland Printer, 1952-60. Home: 7403 Beechnut St Houston TX 77074 Office: 1801 Walker St Houston TX 77003

BURNS, CORNELIUS, mgmt. cons.; b. L.I., N.Y., Jan. 11, 1951; s. Warren Harding and Martha Jesus (Payen) B.; I.B.A., U. de Mexico, 1973; instructional cert. U. of the Ams., 1972-73. Investments cons. Olavaretta-Ortiz, S.A., Mexico City, 1968-73; bus./fin. mgr., spl. cons. Salas Estrade, Mexico City, 1969-77; master instr. internat. bus. mgmt. U. of the Ams., Mexico City, 1972-73; chief cons. Cornelius Burns & Assos., El Paso, Tex., 1976—; exec. trustee/adminstrv. coordinator Garcia Internacional, S.A., 1978—. Staff dir. Goodwill Industries of El Paso, 1977; student adv. com., dept. fin. and econs. U. Tex., El Paso, 1973-74. Recipient Cert. of Appreciation, Dept. Commerce, Mexico, 1975; U. de Las Americas teaching fellow, 1971-74. Mem. Am. Mgmt. Assn., Ind. Businessmen of Am., Internat. Assn. Profl. Adminstrs., Am. Mgmt. Soc. Roman Catholic. Clubs: Internat. Skyriders of Am., Lulac. Home: 7736 Phoenix Ave El Paso TX 79915 Office: 7736 Phoenix Ave B Level El Paso TX 79915

BURNS, DANNY KAYE, auctioneer; b. Pittsburg, Tex., Apr. 12, 1949; s. Sam Joe and Mildred Katherine (Henderson) B.; B.S. in Agr. Bus., Sam Houston State U., 1971; m. Jamie Lou Henderson, Aug. 15, 1970; children—Tausha Rene, Blake Daryn. Mktg. asso. Tex. Dept. Agr., Austin, 1970-71; nat. account rep. Elanco Products Co., Dallas, 1971-76; partner, auctioneer Herb Henderson Auctioneers, Wolfforth, Tex., 1976—; founder West Tex. Agr. Publishers; partner Richardson Oil & Gas Investments; also speaker. Named Outstanding Agr.-Businessman, Tex. Young Farmers, 1978. Mem. Nat. Auctioneers Assn., Tex. Auctioneers Assn. Democrat. Baptist. Club: Lions. Cons. gen. mgr. South Plains Agr mag., 1979—. Home: 600 6th St Wolfforth TX 79382 Office: Borwnfield Hwy Wolfforth TX 79382

BURNS, DENNIS PATRICK, pub. accountant; b. Appleton, Wis., Nov. 17, 1942; s. Patrick L. and Helen E. (Steinhoff) B.; B.S. in Math. and Bus., Mich. Tech. U., 1965; M.B.A., State U. N.Y. at Buffalo, 1971; m. Anne H. Hayward, May 26, 1966; 1 son, Nicholas F. Profl. football player Hamilton Tiger-Cats, 1965; asst. v.p., asst. dir. mgmt. sci. Mellon Bank, N.A., Pitts., 1971-73; sr. mgr. accounting and audit Arthur Young & Co., Washington, 1973-77; pres. N.A.D.M., Ltd., Merrifield, Va., 1977—; mng. dir. D.P. Burns, Chartered, Washington, 1976—; cons. fed. funding and bank ops. to FRS and U.S. Treasury. Trustee Fairfax Supplemental Retirement System, Fairfax County, Va. Served to capt. USMC, 1965-69; Vietnam. Mem. Inst. Mgmt. Sci., Ops. Research Soc. Am., Acad. Polit. Sci., Am. Bankers Assn., Am. Econometric Soc., Nat. Soc. Public Accts., Bank Adminstrn. Inst., Econ. Soc., Assn. Govt. Accountants, Aircraft Owners and Pilots Assn., Airline Transp. Pilots Assn. Democrat. Roman Catholic. Home: 3711 Whispering Ln Falls Church VA 22041 Office: PO Box 1280 Falls Church VA 22041

BURNS, DEWAYNE LLOYD, semiconductor accessories hardware mfg. co. exec.; b. Dallas, July 31, 1942; s. Earl L. and Evelyn Josephine (Arendall) B.; A.A.S. in Quality Control Tech., Richland Coll., 1978; postgrad. U. Dallas, 1979—; m. Austena Williams, Dec. 19, 1975; children—Bobby Johns, Elaine Christina. Chief inspector Summit, Inc., Garland, Tex., 1966-67; sr. inspector Unitron, Inc., Garland, 1967-70; quality assurance mgr. Thermalloy Inc., Dallas, 1970—. Served with USMC, 1961-64. Mem. Am. Soc. for Quality Control. Baptist. Home: 3519 Case Verde Apt 169 Dallas TX 75234 Office: 2021 W Valley View Ln Dallas TX 75234

BURNS, GARY MICHAEL, ins. co. exec.; b. Steubenville, Ohio, May 26, 1953; s. Robert Michael and Eileen Elizabeth (Barnett) B.; student Okla. State U., 1971-74; m. Debbie Ann Horton, July 9, 1976. Polit. cons. Ron Platt/Assos., Oklahoma City, 1974-75; with Office of Clk., U.S. Ho. of Reps., Washington, 1975; regional advance rep. U.S. Senator Lloyd Bentsen presdl. campaign, 1975-76; public affairs rep. Cities Service Gas Co., Oklahoma City, 1976-77; asst. v.p., dir. public relations United Founders Life Ins. Co., Oklahoma City, 1977—. Jr. Achievement bus. cons., 1977-79; chmn. Nesbitt for U.S. Senate, Okla. state, 1974. Mem. Life Ins. Advertisers Assn., Mass Mktg. Ins. Inst., Okla. Real Estate Assn. (sales asso.), Nat. Rifle Assn. Democrat. Roman Catholic. Clubs: Posse Club (Okla. State U.), Oklahoma City All Sports Assn. (dir.), K.C. Office: 5900 Mosteller Dr Oklahoma City OK 73116

BURNS, GEORGE FRANK, educator; b. Milan, Tenn., Aug. 17, 1921; s. George Frank and Katherine Pearle (Barbee) B.; B.A., Cumberland U., 1942, J.D., 1944; M.A., George Peabody Coll., 1967; Ph.D., Vanderbilt U., 1973; postgrad. Brit. Univs. Summer Sch., 1970, 72, 75, 77; m. Mary John Wade, Aug. 24, 1968; 1 step-son, William Scott Lockwood, II. Reporter, Wilson County News, Lebanon, Tenn., 1942-43; asso. editor Lebanon Democrat, 1943-66, acting editor, 1943-45, 64, editorial columnist, 1968—; pub. relations dir. Cumberland Coll., Lebanon, 1959-63, 66-74, prof. English, 1967-74; asst. prof. English, Tenn. Technol. U., Cookeville, 1974-79, asso. prof., 1979—; reviewer lit. page Nashville Tennessean, 1962—; mem. Nat. Jr. Coll. English Study, 1969. Founder, Vol. State Athletic Conf., 1947; sec. Lebanon Mcpl. and Regional Planning Commn., 1950-60; sec. Tenn. Jr. C. of C., 1950, Distinguished Service award, 1952; chmn. Wilson County Library Bd., 1956; chmn. Wilson County Civil War Centennial Commn., 1961-65; heritage theme chmn. Wilson County Am. Revolution Bicentennial Commn., 1975-76; pres. History Assos. Wilson County, 1970-72. Recipient Service award Lebanon and Wilson County C. of C., 1958; named Outstanding Educator of Am., 1973. Mem. Modern Lang. Assn., Nat. Council Tchrs. of English, Coll. English Assn., Soc. for Study So. Lit., Tenn. Philol. Assn. Democrat. Presbyn. Clubs: Rotary, Torch. Author: (with Dixon Merritt and others) The History of Wilson County, 1961. Editor: Tenn. Coll. English Assn. Newsletter, 1969-71. Contbr. book revs. to various publs. Home: 406 S Tarver Ave Lebanon TN 37087 Office: Box 5053 Tenn Technol U Cookeville TN 38501

BURNS, GROVER PRESTON, physicist, mathematician; b. nr. Hurricane, W.Va., Apr. 25, 1918; s. Joshua Alexander and Virgie (Meadows) B.; A.B., Marshall U., 1937; M.S., W.Va. U., 1941; student Duke, 1939-40, U. Md., 1946; D.Sc., Colo. State Christian Coll., 1973; m. Julia Belle Foster, Nov. 4, 1941; children—Julia Corinne, Grover Preston. Tchr. high sch., W.Va., 1937-40; fellow W.Va., U., 1940-41; instr. physics U. Conn., 1941-42; asst. prof. Miss State Coll., 1942-44, acting head physics dept., 1944-45; asst. prof. physics Tex. Tech. Coll., 1946; asso. prof. math. Marshall U., 1946-47; research physicist Naval Research Lab., Washington, 1947-48; asst. prof., chmn. physics dept. Mary Washington Coll., 1948-68, asso. prof., chmn., 1968-69; quality control supr. Am. Viscose div. FMC Corp., 1950-67; pres. Burns Enterprises, Inc., Fredericksburg, Va., 1958—; mathematician Naval Surface Weapons Center, 1967—. Served with AUS, 1945-46. Mem. Am. Phys. Soc., Am. Assn. Physics Tchrs., Fed. Profl. Assn., AAUP, N.Y. Acad. Sci. Reviewer, Am. Jour. Physics; contbr. articles to profl. jours. Patentee in field of thermometers, conductivity testers, star finders. Research in fields of superconductivity, synthetic div., thermoelectricity, numerical integration, exterior ballistics. Home: 600 Virginia Ave Fredericksburg VA 22401 Office: Naval Surface Weapons Center Dahlgren VA 22448

BURNS, HERBERT INCE, architect, educator; b. Lexington, Ky., Aug. 27, 1948; s. Herbert Ince and Anna Rebecca (Burner) B.; A.A., Lee's Jr. Coll., 1971; B.Arch., U. Ky., 1975; m. Susan Jane Seiler, June 12, 1971; children—Herbert Ince, David Edward. Archtl. intern Housing Aid Corp., Lexington, 1973-74; estimator E. H. Straus Co., Lexington, 1974; pres. Triad Resdl. Planning Services, Kernersville, N.C., 1977-78; pres. H. B. and Assos., Winston-Salem, N.C., 1978—; architect-in-tng. Newman, Calloway, Johnson, Van Etten, Winfree, Architects, Winston-Salem, 1979—; chmn. dept. architecture Forsyth Tech. Inst., Winston-Salem, 1975—. Recipient The Joseph D. Hall Scholarship award; St. Martin's League Design award. Mem. AIA (asso. mem. Winston-Salem sect. N.C. chpt.). Democrat. Baptist. Club: Atelier. Home: 332 Keating Dr Winston-Salem NC 27104 Office: 6213 2100 Silas Creek Pkwy Winston-Salem NC 27103

BURNS, LARRY DEMONT, controller; b. Greenville, S.C., June 20, 1945; s. John Baylus Alston and Isabel Myrtle (Davis) B.; A.A., North Greenville Coll., 1965; B.A., William Carey Coll., 1967, B.S., 1970; postgrad. LaSalle Extension U., 1973—; m. Norma Elaine Mills, Mar. 2, 1968; children—Rachelle DeLaine, Ashley DeMont. Tchr. Am. govt. and econs. Picayune (Miss.) Meml. High Sch., 1967-70; claims adjuster, claims adjuster trainer Nationwide Mut. Ins. Co., Greenville, 1970-72; accountant Lackey, Ferrell & Harris, C.P.A.'s, Greenville, 1972-73; div. controller Jim Pinnix Homes, S.C. div. Pinnix Corp., Greenville, 1973-75; internal auditor, fin. analyst Pinnix Corp., Greensboro, N.C., 1975-76, asst. to controller, corp. accountant, 1976-77, controller, asst. to pres., asst. treas., 1977-78; sec., treas. Addison Industries, Inc. (Ala.), 1977-78, B.C.H., Inc., Danville, Va., 1977-78; controller, sec., treas. High Point Sprinkler Co. (N.C.), 1978—. Bd. dirs., treas. Battle Forest Village Townhouse Assn., 1976-79. Mem. Nat. Assn. Accts. (chpt. dir. 1980-81), Am. Accounting Assn., Am. Soc. Notaries, Alpha Psi Omega, Phi Beta Lambda. Republican. Methodist. Home: 500 Hayworth Circle High Point NC 27262 Office: US Hwy 29-70S PO Box 2478 High Point NC 27261

BURNS, RALPH EDWARD, educator; b. Jackson, Miss., Aug. 16, 1941; s. Emmett Carl and Clara Ruth B.; B.S., Jackson State U., 1962, M.S., 1973; Ed.D., E. Tex. State U., 1976. Athletic dir., coach high schs. in Miss. and Ill., 1964-65, 67-72; asst. football coach E. Tex. State U., 1973-76; chmn. dept. health and phys. edn. Ky. State U., Frankfort, 1976—; bd. dirs. Gov. Ky. Council Phys. Fitness; cons. in field. Bd. dirs. Frankfort chpt. Big Bros.-Big Sisters Am.; mem. Frankfort Community Relations Com. Served with USAR, 1965-67. Recipient Community Service award City of Frankfort, Vol. Service award. Mem. AAHPER (chmn. aquatic com. 1974), Am. Coaches Assn., Nat. Assn. Coll. Dirs. Athletics, AAUP, Ky. Assn. Health, Edn. and Phys. Edn., NAACP, Kappa Alpha Psi. Democrat. Mem. Ch. of God and Christ. Clubs: Rotary, Masons, Elks. Home: 408 Raven Crest Frankfort KY 40601 Office: Box 182 Ky State Univ E Main St Frankfort KY 40601

BURNS, ROBERT LEROY, engr.; b. Wall, S.D., Aug. 28, 1929; s. Erwin Leroy and Mary Alice (Creighton) B.; B.S., S.D. Sch. Mines and Tech., 1950; M.B.A., Tex. Christian U., 1965; postgrad. in bus. adminstrn. U. Tex., Arlington, 1971—; m. Barbara Ann Gildersleeve, Dec. 22, 1962; children—Kimberly Ann, Robin Lea. Jr. engr. Consol.-Vultec Aircraft, Inc., Ft. Worth, 1950-52; service engr. Convair Aerospace, Inc., Ft. Worth, 1952-54; design engr. Gen. Dynamics Corp., Ft. Worth, 1958-60, sr. design engr., 1960-66, project design engr., 1966-77, asst. project engr., 1977—. Served with USN, 1954-58. Mem. Nat. Mgmt. Assn., Beta Gamma Sigma, Sigma Tau, Theta Tau. Republican. Club: Masons. Home: 4321 Miraloma Dr Fort Worth TX 76126 Office: Gen Dynamics Corp PO Box 748 Fort Worth TX 76101

BURNS, WILLIAM GOODYKOONTZ, mktg. communications co. exec.; b. Vandalia, Ill., Aug. 23, 1935; s. Farrell Francis and Sarah J. (Goodykoontz) B.; B.A., Washington and Lee U., 1957; postgrad. U. Colo., U. Chgo.; m. Lorraine Kay Olsen, Mar. 21, 1980; children—Janean Mary, Pamela Ann. Grocery products promotion mgr. Wilson & Co., Inc., Chgo., 1957-67; dir. merchandising and sales tng. Blue-Cross-Blue Shield, 1967-71; v.p. mktg. Sammons Enterprises Inc., Dallas, 1971-74; owner, pres. William G. Burns Mktg. Communications Co., Bus. Express Press, Pigments of the Imagination, and Aqua Mart, Dallas, 1974—. Mem. Sales and Mktg. Execs. (past dir.), Sales Promotion Execs. (past pres.), Dallas Advt. League, Assn. Broadcasting Execs., Mktg. Communications Execs. Internat. Assn. (past dir.), Dallas 40. Republican. Episcopalian. Club: Masons. Home: 1605 S Alamo Rockwall TX 75087 Office: 13601 Preston Rd Dallas TX 75240

BURNSIDE, HAMILTON STANLEY NATHANIEL, life underwriter; b. Nassau, New Providence, Bahamas, Nov. 22, 1899; s. Herbert Nathaniel and Caroline (Poitier) B.; student Cambridge U.; m. Mary Elizabeth Haynes, July 6, 1940; 1 dau., Florence Caroline (Mrs. Mays). Baggage and checking room Fla. East Coast R.R., 1922-25; also part-time sales Afro-Am. Life Ins. Co., 1922-25; agt., asst. mgr., mgr., agy. asst. Nat. Benefit Life Ins. Co., 1925-33; organized Columbia Life Ins. Co., 1933-35; field supr., mgr. Pilgrim Health & Life Ins. Co., 1935-45, mgr., 1954-69, cons., 1969—; mgr., supr. Guaranty Life Ins. Co., 1945-50; mgr. Mammoth Life Ins. Co., 1951-54. Divisional chmn. Cherokee div. N.E. Ga. Boy Scouts Am., 1942-69; chmn. bd. mgmt. Samuel F. Harris YMCA, Athens, 1956-69, chmn. emeritus, 1969—; chmn. co-chmn. campaigns A.R.C., Community Services, and others. Served as cpl. Brit. Army, 1916-19. Recipient Silver Beaver Award Boy Scouts Am., 1950. Episcopalian. Home: 191 Chicamauga Ave SW Atlanta GA 30314 Office: 181 W Washington St Athens GA 30601

BURNSIDE, MARY ELIZABETH HAYNES, educator; b. Athens, Ga., July 24; d. Christopher Stephen and Florence Mayfield (Gary) Haynes; A.B., Talladega Coll., 1929; M.A. (NSF fellow), Atlanta U., 1963; NSF grantee Atlanta U., summers 1958-59, U. Ill., summers 1963-65, Ga. Inst. Tech., summer 1972; postgrad. U. Ga.; m. H.S.N. Burnside, July 6, 1940; 1 dau., Florence Caroline Burnside Mays. Tchr. math. Atlanta Pub. Schs.; now ednl. and bus. cons. Adviser sr. troop N.W. Ga. council Girls Scouts U.S.A., 1955-75, adviser sr. senate, 1964-75; mem. troop com. Boy Scouts Am.; chmn. alumni cruise com. Talladega Coll., 1972-76; chmn. supervisory com. bd. dirs. Atlanta Tchrs. Fed. Credit Union. Recipient Thanks badge Girl Scouts U.S.A. Mem. NEA, Ga., Atlanta edn. assns., Nat. Soc. Public Accts., Nat. Council Negro Women, Talladega Coll. Alumni Assn., NAACP, Alpha Kappa Alpha (Gold Medallion). Episcopalian (vestrywoman). Clubs: Saturday Bridge; Chicamauga Community. Home and Office: 191 Chicamauga Ave SW Atlanta GA 30314

BURNSIDE-FISHER, JANET RAE, advt. agy. exec.; b. Fargo, N.D., May 12, 1943; d. Roy E. and Beatrice I. (Kloustad) Palmer; student U. South Fla., 1961-62, U. Fla., 1970-72, Richland Coll., 1973-74; B.A. summa cum laude, N. Tex. State U., 1976. With Gen. Telephone Co. of Fla., Tampa, 1962-70; free lance writer, 1974-76; account exec. Alexander Warnock Advt., Inc., Dallas, 1976—; lectr. in field. Named Outstanding Ad Student, N. Tex. State U., 1976. Mem. Dallas Ad League, Bus. and Profl. Women (pres. 1967-68), Dallas Mus. Fine Arts, Kappa Tau Alpha, Alpha Delta Sigma. Clubs: Ad, Public Relations, 500 Inc. Office: 2995 LBJ Freeway Suite 233 Dallas TX 75234

BURR, DAVID ANTHONY, univ. adminstr.; b. Columbus, Kans., Apr. 19, 1925; s. Hugh Henry and Grace Elizabeth (Mitchell) B.; A.A., Northeastern Agrl. and Mech. Coll., Miami, Okla., 1948; B.A., U. Okla., 1952; m. Carol Jean Robinson, Nov. 18, 1962; children—Michael James, Kathleen Elizabeth, Thaddeus Mitchell. Editor, Sooner Mag., U. Okla., Norman, 1950-57; asst. to pres. U. Okla., 1957-59, asst. to pres. and dir. Univ. relations and devel., 1959-68, v.p. dir. univ. community, 1968-71, v.p. devel., 1971-77, v.p. univ. relations and devel., 1977-79, v.p. univ. affairs, 1979—; coordinator, dir. U. Okla. leadership program, 1961; dir. Editorial Projects for Edn., Inc. Dir., Okla. Gov.'s Opportunity Porgram, 1964; mem. Civic Improvement Council, Norman, 1965; deacon 1st Presbyn. Ch., Norman, 1968-69, now elder. Served to lt. U.S. Army, 1944-46. Recipient Sibley award, 1956; named Outstanding Alumnus Northeastern Agrl. and Mech. U., 1971. Mem. Council Advancement and Support of Edn., Okla. Higher Edn. Alumni Council, U. Okla. Assn., Norman C. of C. (dir. 1968-70), Lambda Chi Alpha. Democrat. Home: 1409 Brookdale St Norman OK 73069 Office: 900 Asp Ave Norman OK 73019

BURR, HORACE, educator; b. New Castle, Ind., Feb. 9, 1912; s. Horace Lychurgas and Grace (Peirce) B.; A.B., DePauw U., Greencastle, Ind., 1934; fellow Am. Drama League, Central Sch. Speech, London, also Univ. Coll., Oxford (Eng.) U., 1935; M.A., U. So. Calif., 1939; fellow Acad. Fine Arts, Florence, Italy, 1953; m. Helen Gunderson, July 24, 1954; 1 son, David Stanford. Instr., DePauw U., 1934; dir. Muncie (Ind.) Civic Theatre, 1939-51; mem. art faculty N.Y.U., 1941-42; dir. Punch and Julip, U. Va., Charlottesville, 1954-55; asso. prof. drama, dir. theatre Madison Coll., Harrisonburg, Va., 1960-74; prof. communication arts James Madison U., Harrisonburg, 1974-77, curator fine arts, art cons., 1977—; bd. dirs. New Castle Civic Theatre, 1947-51, Randolph County (Ind.) Little Theatre, 1947-51, Vagabond Players, Hendersonville, N.C., 1948-49; co-dir. Arena Theatre, Studio 17, Met. Opera House, 1950; editorial staff Cinema Progress, Am. Inst. Cinematography, 1936; del. Internat. Pan-Pacific Conf. Cultural and Ednl. Relations, Honolulu, 1929; vice chmn. Am. Theatre Wing, War Services Inc., 1942-46; pres. Albemarle Art Assn., Charlottesville, 1955-66, Va. Hearing and Speech Found., 1961-71, Va. Speech and Drama Assn., 1976—; sculptor with over 100 exhbns. in 12 states and 53 cities, 1952—. Recipient Internat. Cultural medal Kokusai Bunka Shinkokai, Tokyo, 1941; Gold Cup Exhbn. winner U. Va., 1960-76; recipient Best of Show award Contemporary So. Arts Exhbn., 1965. Mem. Actors Equity, Sigma Delta Chi, Pi Epsilon Delta, Kappa Pi. Clubs: Colonnade (U. Va.); Torch. Author, narrator: (documentary film) The Ancient City, 1957. Author numerous articles. Home: Carrsgrove Stribling Ave Charlottesville VA 22902 Office: 8 Wellington James Madison Univ Harrisonburg VA 22801

BURR, RICHARD MELVIN, educator, bus. adminstr.; b. Denton, Tex., Mar. 21, 1939; s. Charles Edward and Frances Agnes (Hoey) B., Jr.; A.B., Huntingdon Coll., 1961; M.A., U. Ala., Ph.D., 1972; m. Patricia Ann LeMay, June 5, 1965; 1 child, Ashley LeMay. Asst. prof. bus. statistics N. Tex. State U., Denton, 1965-72; asst. prof. statistics and mktg. research Trinity U., San Antonio, 1972-75, dir. grad. studies bus. adminstrn., 1974-76, asso. prof., 1975—, dean Faculty Bus. and Mgmt. Studies, 1976-78, chmn. dept. bus. adminstrn., 1980—; vis. prof. Am. U., Washington, 1978-79; on leave as Am. Assembly Collegiate Schs. Bus.-Sears Found. fed. faculty fellow, spl. asst. to dir. Sci. and Tech. Info. Office, NASA, Washington, 1977-78; cons. NASA, Washington, 1978—; cons. for numerous firms, San Antonio area, 1973—. Mem. Greater San Antonio C. of C. (bus. outlook com., 1973, 76), San Antonio Advt. Fedn. scholarship com. 1976-1977), Am. Mktg. Assn., Am. Inst. Decision Scis., Am. Statis. Assn. Democrat. Presbyterian. Contbr. numerous articles to profl. jours. Home: 119 Park Dr San Antonio TX 78212 Office: Trinity Univ 715 Stadium Dr San Antonio TX 78284

BURR, THOMAS SHEPARD, accountant; b. Columbia, Mo., Feb. 26, 1943; s. Arthur H. and Phyllis I. (Carter) B.; B.S., Cornell U., 1969; M.B.A., Drexel U., 1973; m. Lois Susan Cohen, Apr. 8, 1967; children—Daniel G., Deborah E. Accountant, Laventhol & Horwath, accountants, Phila., 1969-72, Orlando, Fla., 1972-73, Alexander Grant & Co., Orlando, 1973-74; partner and accountant Watsky & Burr Co., Orlando, 1974-75; cons. in investment planning and accounting systems, 1969—; owner T. Shepard Burr, C.P.A., Winter

Park, Fla., 1975—. Guest panelist, Arthritis Found. estate planning seminars, 1976, 77; mem. arena task force Speakers Bur., Orlando Civic Center, 1973. Served to lt., arty., U.S. Army, 1965-68. C.P.A., Fla., Pa., Ala., Ga. Mem. Am., Fla., Pa. insts. C.P.A.'s, Orlando C. of C. (chmn. conv. com. 1975), Cornell Soc. Hotelmen (treas. 1976—, pres. 1975-76). Jewish. Club: Cornell of Central Fla. (treas.). Home: 1182A Paseo del Mar Casselberry FL 32707 Office: 1400 S Orlando Ave Winter Park FL 32789

BURRIS, JOHN CARROLL, physician; b. Warren County, Ky., Dec. 26, 1927; s. John Anderson and Sophia Isabell (Crews) B.; B.S., Western Ky. U., 1952; M.D., U. Louisville, 1956; m. Nadine Miller, Dec. 26, 1948; 1 son, Robyn Blaine. Intern, Good Samaritan Hosp., Lexington, Ky., 1956-57; rural family med. practice, Butler County, Ky., 1957-65; resident in radiology U. Louisville Hosp., 1965-68; asso. radiologist Lourdes Hosp., Paducah, Ky., 1968-70, dir. dept. radiology, 1970—. Served with USN, 1946-48, Diplomate Am. Bd. Radiology, Am. Bd. Nuclear Medicine. Recipient Physician's Recognition award, AMA, 1977. Mem. Am., Ky., So. med. assns., Am. Coll. Radiology, Radiol. Soc. N.Am., Am. Coll. Nuclear Physicians. Protestant. Home: 4333 Saint Charles Ct Paducah KY 42001 Office: 1530 Lone Oak Rd Paducah KY 42001

BURROW, JAMES GORDON, educator; b. Bandana, Ky., May 2, 1922; s. Gupton Burns and Mary Bishop (Northington) B.; B.A., U. Mo., 1943; M.A., U. S.C., 1947; Ph.D. in Am. History, U. Ill., 1956; m. Robin Graeme Smith, June 21, 1952; children—Robin Rutledge, James Shannon, Rachel Northington. Instr. Am. history U. S.C., 1946-47, Harding Coll., Searcy, Ark., 1954-57; asst. prof. Memphis State U., 1957-62; asso. prof. Middle Tenn. State U., Murfreesboro, 1963-66, Ind. State U., 1966-69; prof. Abilene (Tex.) Christian U., 1969—. Chmn. public responsibilities com. to supervise implementation of Mentally Retarded Persons Act of 1977; past pres. Abilene Assn. Retarded Citizens. Am. Philos. Soc. grantee. Mem. Am. Hist. Assn., Orgn. Am. Historians, AAUP, Phi Alpha Theta. Democrat. Mem. Ch. of Christ. Author: AMA: Voice of American Medicine, 1963; Organized Medicine in the Progressive Era: The Move Toward Monopoly, 1977; contbr. Ency. Bioethics, 1978; others. Home: 2516 Garfield St Abilene TX 79601 Office: Box 8057 Sta ACC Abilene TX 79699

BURROW, MARY BIRCHETT, social worker; b. Henderson County, Tenn., Dec. 13, 1916; d. Thomas D. and Claudia Estes (Wilson) B.; B.A., Union U., Tenn., 1937; M.S.W., U. Chgo., 1947; m. Floyd Leon Burrow, Oct. 7, 1934; 1 son, Floyd Leon. Tchr. public schs., Gibson County, Tenn., 1937-47; with Gibson County Dept. Public Welfare, Trenton, Tenn., 1947-74; exec. dir. Mental Retardation Agy., Lexington, Tenn., 1974—; State pres. Democratic Women's Clubs, 1971-72; pres. Tenn. PTA, 1950-51; tchr. Sunday sch. Bapt. Ch., 1952—. Social Services scholar, 1952-53. Mem. Tenn. Fedn. Public Relations (state treas.; budget dir.), Am. Assn. Mental Deficiency (pres. state dirs. mental deficiency; West Tenn. dir. 1978-79), Am. Bus. Women, Tenn. Fedn. Bus. Women. Club: Order Eastern Star (grand marshal, grand Esther). Home: Rt 1 Box 16 Milan TN 38358 Office: PO Box 703 Lexington TN 38351

BURRUS, JOHN NEWELL, educator; b. Gilmer, Tex., Jan. 23, 1920; s. Herman Clifford and Beulah (Blalack) B.; A.B., U. Miss., 1942; M.A., La. State U., 1944, Ph.D., 1950; postgrad. U. Minn., 1945-47, Vanderbilt U., 1948. Grad. fellow La. State U. 1942-44, 48-49, research asso., 1949-50; teaching fellow U. Minn., 1945-47; faculty U. Miss., 1943-45, Vanderbilt U., 1947-48, U. Fla., 1950-51; faculty, chmn. dept. sociology U. So. Miss., Hattiesburg, 1951-70, 78-80, prof., 1957-70, Distinguished U. prof., 1970—, mem. Council U. Honors Program, 1959-67. Past bd. dirs. ARC. Mem. So. Sociol. Soc., So. (nomination com. 1966-68, sect. chmn. 1968, mem. exec. com. 1955-58, awards 1976-78), Rural sociol. socs., Sigma Chi, Alpha Kappa Delta, Pi Gamma Mu, Phi Kappa Phi, Omicron Delta Kappa. Kiwanian (bd. dirs. 1975—). Author: Life Opportunities: Differential Mortality in Mississippi, 1951; (with C.A. McMahan, R.H. Bradford) Manual to Accompany the Sociology of Urban Life, 1952; (with H.A. Pedersen, M.B. King) Mississippi Life Tables, 1954; Mississippi's People, 1950; (with others) Social Problems, 1955. Mem. editorial bd. So. Quar., 1962-70, 76—, chmn., 1967-68. Contbr. chpt. to A History of Mississippi, 1973; contbr. to Ency. Brit., also articles, book revs. to profl. publs. Home: 213 Arlington Loop Hattiesburg MS 39401

BURRUSS, ROYCE ALLEN, pharmacist, hosp. ofcl.; b. Richmond, Va., Nov. 15, 1946; s. Frederick Ralph and Margaret Lee (Ammons) B.; student Richmond Profl. Inst., 1966-67; B.S., Va. Commonwealth U., 1971; m. Sandra Lee Keene, Nov. 12, 1966; 1 dau., Nikole Renee. Clin. pharmacist St. Mary's Hosp. Richmond, Inc., 1971-74, asst. dir. pharmacy, devel. and control, 1974-76, dir. pharmacy, 1976—; clin. instr. pharmacy Med. Coll. Va., Va. Commonwealth U., 1972—; cons. instl. pharmacy practice. Chmn. Richmond Met. Area Cardiac Emergency Med. Technician Drug Box Com., 1976-78. Grantee Meade-Johnson Labs., 1970-71. Mem. Am. Pharm. Assn., Va. Pharm. Assn., Am. Soc. Cons. Pharmacists, Am. Soc. Hosp. Pharmacists, Va. Soc. Hosp. Pharmacists (sec.). Baptist. Home: 6011 Quailfield Rd Mechanicsville VA 23111 Office: St Mary's Hosp of Richmond Inc 5801 Bremo Rd Richmond VA 23226

BURSTEIN, ALVIN GEORGE, psychologist; b. Omaha, Mar. 31, 1931; s. Harry and Jennie Zelda (Gerstein) B.; B.A., U. Chgo., 1950, M.A. (USPHS fellow), 1957, Ph.D., 1959; m. Sandra Loucks, Apr. 15, 1978; children—Jessica Lee, Daniel James. Psychology intern Billings Hosp., Chgo., 1959-60; asst. prof. dept. psychology U. Mich., Ann Arbor, 1960-63; asso. prof. psychology div., dept. psychiatry U. Ill. Med. Sch., Chgo., 1963-70; prof., chief div. psychology, dept. psychiatry U. Tex. Health Sci. Center, San Antonio, 1970—; adj. prof. Trinity U., 1973—; dir. NIMH grant, 1964-70, 71—. Bd. dirs. Halfway House, 1975-76; mem. profl. bd. San Antonio Mental Health Assn., 1976-77. Served with U.S. Army, 1954-56. Lic. psychologist, Tex., Ill.; diplomate Am. Bd. Profl. Psychology. Mem. Southwestern Psychol. Assn. (pres. 1977-78), Tex. Psychol. Assn. (pres. 1974-75), Sigma Xi. Author: Psychosocial Basis of Medical Practice, rev. edit., 1979; editorial cons. Jour. Abnormal Psychology, 1971-73, Psychiatry and Medicine, 1975—, Contemporary Psychology, 1977—, Jour. Sch. Psychology, 1976—. Office: U Tex Health Sci Center Psychiatry Dept 7703 Floyd Curl Dr San Antonio TX 78284

BURSTEN, MARTIN A., publisher; b. Bialystok, Poland, July 6, 1911; s. Samuel and Miriam (Applebaum) B.; B.S., Syracuse U., 1935; m. Ellen Joan Newman, June 20, 1937; children—Steven K., Barbara Bursten Hanover, William C. Reporter, columnist Syracuse (N.Y.) jour.-Am., 1931-40; news editor Civic Broadcasting Corp., Syracuse, and bur. chief Internat. News Service, Central N.Y., 1940-42; combat corr. ETO, 1943-45; news commentator U.S. Voice Am., N.Y.C., 1945-46; dir. press, pub. relations United Hias Service, global migration agy., roving fgn. corr. Parade Mag., Graphic News Features Syndicate, and various other publs., Europe, N. Africa, Mid-East, Latin Am., 1946-68; v.p. Community Bank L.I., 1965-70; pres. Bursten Whitford & Newman, Inc., Advt., Pub. Affairs, Publ., N.Y.C., 1958-66; pub., prin. officer Graphic News Features Syndicate, N.Y.C., 1958—; spl. asst. to Gov. Nelson A. Rockefeller of N.Y., 1966-74; lectr. geo-politics. Mem. Nassau County (N.Y.) Republican Com., 1960-75; dir. Hope for Youth Inc., Tranquillity Inc.; pres. Happy Landing Police Fund, Nassau County. Served with Intelligence, USAF, 1942-43. Decorated Hon. Croix de Guerre (France); recipient Syracusan Cum Laude award Syracuse U., 1968; certificates of honor U.S. Olympics Com., 1972, 76, CARE, 1960. Mem. Nat. Press Club, Overseas Press Club Am., N.Y. Clubs: Gov's, Elks (hon. life). Author: Escape from Fear, 1958; (with others) Off the Record, 1949; I Can Tell It Now, 1964; How I Got That Story, 1967. Home: 3051 Palm Aire Dr S Pompano Beach FL 33060 Office: 741 W Oakland Park Blvd Fort Lauderdale FL 33311

BURT, ALLEN DANIEL, artist; b. Owensboro, Ky., Aug. 17, 1930; s. Harold Allan and Catherine Eleanor (Coulter) B.; student Kans. State U., 1949-50, Trinity U., San Antonio, 1955; m. Anne Warren, Jan. 18, 1964; 1 dau., Barbara Anne. Vice-pres. Coppini Acad. Fine Arts, San Antonio, 1971-72, pres., 1973-74; one-man shows: Kendall Gallery, San Angelo, Tex., 1968-70, 76, McNamara-O'Conner Mus., Victoria, Tex., 1969, Bee County Coll., 1969-72, San Antonio Main Library, 1969; group shows: Am. Artists Profl. League, N.Y.C., 1974, 75, 76, 79, Allied Artists Am., N.Y.C., 1975, Coppini Acad. Fine Arts, San Antonio, 1967-77, U. Tex., Austin, 1968, Hudson Valley Art Assn., White Plains, N.Y., 1979, Salmagundi Club, N.Y.C., 1979, Knickerbocker Artists Am., N.Y.C., 1979, others; represented in permanent collections; tchr. oil landscape painting Hill Country Arts Found., Ingram, Tex., 1976, San Angelo Art Group, 1977. Served with U.S. Army, 1951-54. Recipient best of show award, 3d. best, 1st pl. oil Central Park Invitational, San Antonio, 1975; gold medal Coppini Acad. Fine Arts, 1976. Mem. Artists and Craftsmen Asso. Dallas (2d prize opaque painting 1972, 2d prize landscape exhibit 1974, merit award 1977, 79), Hill Country Arts Found., Southwestern Watercolor Soc. Dallas, San Antonio Watercolor Group, Am. Artists Profl. League. Republican. Episcopalian. Home: 1304 Ford St Kerrville TX 78028

BURT, ALVIN MILLER, III, anatomist; b. Bridgeport, Conn., Aug. 14, 1935; s. Alvin Miller and Esther Louise (Carey) B.; B.A., Amherst Coll., 1957; Ph.D. (USPHS fellow), U. Kans., 1962; m. Dorothy Hanlin, July 15, 1961; children—Constance Walker, Carolyn Marie. Asst. prof. anatomy Med. Coll. Va., 1962-63; instr. Yale U. Sch. Medicine, 1963-66; asst. prof. Vanderbilt U., 1966-69, asso. prof., 1969-74, prof., 1974—; vis. scientist Agrl. Research Council Inst. Animal Physiology, Babraham, Cambridge, Eng., 1972-73; research grant reviewer and cons. NIH, NSF. Recipient Research Career Devel. award USPHS, 1968-73. Mem. Am. Assn. Anatomists, Am. Soc. Neurochemistry, AAAS, Internat. Soc. Neurochemistry, Internat. Brain Research Orgn., Soc. Neurosci. Episcopalian. Research on devel. neurochemistry, anat. localization of neurotransmitter systems. Home: 8108 Devens Dr Brentwood TN 37027 Office: Dept Anatomy Vanderbilt U Nashville TN 37232

BURTCH, SUSAN THIELEMANN, copywriter, calligrapher; b. Washington, Oct. 9, 1946; d. Leland James and Marjorie Houghton Thielemann; student Colo. Coll., 1964-66; B.A., Smith Coll., 1968; m. Jack W. Burtch, Jr., June 21, 1969; children—Anson James, Douglas Robinson. Editorial asst. New Yorker mag., N.Y.C., 1968-69; editor in-house publs. Holder & Kenndy Public Relations, Nashville, 1969-71; copywriter, prodn. mgr. Buntin & Assos. Advt., Nashville, 1971-72; copywriter Jackson & Kline Advt., Richmond, Va., 1973; free-lance copywriter, calligrapher, Richmond, 1974—; contbr. articles Richmond Lifestyle mag., 1973—; syndicated newspaper columnist Bridal Lines, 1977—. Mem. Soc. Italic Handwriting, Washington Calligraphers Guild. Contbr. articles to various newspapers, nat. and local mags. Home: 3504 Moss Side Ave Richmond VA 23222

BURTON, ALLEN DUANE, gas co. exec.; b. Mount Vernon, Ill., Oct. 4, 1942; s. Elvin and Sue (Webb) B.; student public schs. Mount Vernon, Ill.; m. Darlene Rae Hindahl, Sept. 23, 1970; children—Mark Allen, Scott Anthony. Billing and shipping clk. Vernois, Inc., Mt. Vernon, Ill., 1960-63; parts and service mgr. Locke Stove Co., Kansas City, Mo., 1963-67; dist. sales mgr. Midland Sales Co., Kansas City, 1967-68; div. sales rep. No. Propane Gas Co., Des Moines, 1968-72, asst. div. mgr., 1972-73, div. mgr., Paragould, Ark., 1973—. Mem. Ark. Liquid Propane Gas Assn., Tenn. Liquid Propane Gas Assn., Miss. Liquid Propane Gas Assn., Nat. Liquid Propane Gas Assn. Episcopalian. Home: 104 Keasler Dr Paragould AR 72450 Office: Suite 2 Paragould Plaza Park Paragould AR 72450

BURTON, CURTBERT, coll. adminstr.; b. Orlando, Fla., Jan. 4, 1947; s. Lewis Cleveland and Dorothy Mae (Bell) W.; B.S., Savannah State Coll., 1973; m. Carol J. Chambers, June 28, 1975; 1 son, Cornelius. Program dir. Boy Scouts Am., Cimmaron, N. MeX., 1970-72; dir. student housing Savannah (Ga.) State Coll., 1973-76, dir. residence hall life, 1976—; cons. So. Regional Press Inst., 1973-78. Bd. dirs. Boy Scouts Am. camps, Atlanta, 1972-73. Recipient Sidney A. Jones Human Relations awards, Savannah State Coll., 1972; Silver Star award, So. Region Press Inst., 1976. Mem. Assn. Coll. and Univ. Housing Officers, Ga. Coll. Personnel Assn., So. Coll. Personnel Assn., Nat. Soc. for Collegiate Journalists, Nat. Assn. Coll. and Univ. Residence Halls, NAACP, YMCA, Phi Beta Sigma, Alpha Phi Omega. Democrat. Baptist. Home: 1600 Cresthaven St Orlando FL 32805 Office: PO Box 20373-SSC Savannah GA 31404

BURTON, DAVID JAMES, land devel. co. exec.; b. Columbia, S.C., Mar. 1, 1945; s. William Henry and Carinne (Bailey) B.; B.S., Morgan State U., 1967; M.City Planning, U. Pa., 1969; postgrad. George Washington U., 1973; m. Beryl Michelle Dakers, Nov. 27, 1973; 1 son, Jared Dakers. Instr. urban planning/adminstrn. Howard U., Washington, 1971-73; dir. planning Bldg. Systems Internat., Washington, 1971-73; v.p. Harbison Devel. Corp., Columbia, S.C., 1973—. Bd. dirs. Children Unltd., 1977-80, Columbia Urban Lending Project, 1977-80; vice chmn. Three Rivers Health Systems Assn.; mem. Columbia Urban League Guild. Served to capt. U.S. Army, 1967-72. Decorated Army Commendation medal, Bronze Star; recipient various awards. Mem. Am. Inst. Cert Planners, Am. Planning Assn., Urban Land Inst., Community Assn. Inst., Alpha Phi Alpha. Democrat. Episcopalian. Home: 17 Woodpine Ct Columbia SC 29210 Office: 1 Harbison Way Columbia SC 29210

BURTON, DOLORES WEST, sch. psychologist; b. Selma, Ala., Mar. 21, 1936; d. Joseph Clark and Vera Frances (Hiatt) West; B.S., Auburn U., 1957; M.A., U. Ala., 1961, advanced profl. diploma, 1963; m. Jack Raymond Burton, Apr. 18, 1958; children—Marna, Ginger Lynn. Tchr., Dallas County (Ala.), 1957-58, Birmingham City Schs., 1958-63; girls' adviser Woodlawn High Sch., Birmingham, Ala., 1963-68; guidance dir. Dallas County Schs., 1968-77, sch. psychologist-psychometrist, from 1977; part time psychometrist West Central Ala. Vocat. Rehab. Center, from 1974; part time instr. George C. Wallace Jr. Coll., 1975, 77, U. Montevallo, from 1975, Troy State U., from 1975; now sch. psychologist Montgomery (Ala.) Public Schs. Mem. NEA, Dallas County Profl. Edn. Assn. (pres. 1973-74), Am., Ala. (historian 1975-76) personnel and guidance assns., Dallas County Assn. Retarded Citizens (past sec.), Delta Kappa Gamma (past sec.). Presbyterian. Club: Pilot of Montgomery. Home: 208 Busch Hill Dr Wetumpka AL 36092 Office: 1153 S Lawrence St Montgomery AL 36104

BURTON, GEORGE WASHINGTON, ret. educator; b. Brosville, Va., July 4, 1908; s. John William and Annie (Harvey) B.; B.S., U. Va., 1929, M.A., 1942; m. Sarah Dudley, Mar. 24, 1945; children—Sarah Elizabeth, Brown Dudley. Tchr. high sch., Henry County, Va., 1930-32, prin., 1932-42; supt. schs., Clarke County, Va., 1946-66; state dir. secondary edn. Dept. Edn., Richmond, Va., 1966-68, asst. state supt. for instrn., Richmond, 1968-72, asst. state supt. adminstrv. field services, 1972-75; dir. Bank of Clarke County. Served with AUS, 1942-46. Mem. Am., Va. assns. sch. adminstrs., Va. Edn. Assn., C. of C. (pres. 1957-58), Clarke County Hist. Assn. (pres. 1975-80). Lion (pres. 1960-61). Home: Route 1 Berryville VA 22611

BURTON, HARRY ROSS, chemist; b. Westernport, Md., Jan. 14, 1932; s. Ross Edward and Ida Agnes (Baer) B.; B.S. in Biol. Sci., Shepherd Coll., 1960; m. Jean Frances Nofsinger, Aug. 1, 1959; 1 son, Clifford Ross. Scheduling expeditor Westvaco Corp., Luke, Md., 1960-61, office services coordinator, 1964-67; quality control insp., asst. shift supr., Allegheny Ballistics Lab., Rocket Center, W.Va., 1961-64; chief chemist Va. Electric & Power Co., Mt. Storm, W.Va., 1967-77; pres. Burton Lab., Inc., Keyser, W.Va., 1976—. Served with U.S. Army, 1951-54. Mem. Am. Council Ind. Labs., ASTM, VFW, Cumberland Valley Firemen's Vol. Assn. Republican. Methodist. Clubs: Lions, Masons. Home: 210 Baker St Keyser WV 26726 Office: Burton Lab Inc 375 W Piedmont St Keyser WV 26726

BURTON, HUNTER DURWOOD, oil co. exec.; b. Mercer County, Ky., Sept. 24, 1915; s. James Edgar and Hallie (Brewer) B.; student pub. schs., Harrodsburg, Ky., 1922-33; m. Mary Zella Smith, Feb. 2, 1946; children—Mary Sue, Ann Hunter, Edgar Smith, Stella Louise. With So. R.R., Louisville, 1936-39, brakeman, 1939-46; with Marathon Oil Co., Harrodsburg, Ky., 1947-73; pres. Burton Oil Co., Harrodsburg, 1973—; v.p. H. & B. Sanitation, Harrodsburg, 1976—. Exec. dir. Housing Authority, Harrodsburg, 1962—. Served with U.S. Army, 1942-45. Decorated Bronze Star (6). Mem. Mercer C. of C. (pres. 1956-57), Ky. Housing Assn. (pres. 1974-75), Ky. Housing and Community Devel., Am. Legion, VFW. Republican. Clubs: Rotary, Danville Country. Address: PO Box 385 Harrodsburg KY 40330

BURTON, RONNIE ALLAN, chem. tech. services mgr.; b. Loudon County, Tenn., Feb. 6, 1940; s. Joe Henry and Nettie Elizabeth (Tutterrow) B.; B.S. in Chem. Engring., U. Tenn., 1963, M.S. in Engring. Adminstrn., 1974; m. Marcena Horton, Sept. 27, 1963; children—Pamela Marcena, Ronnie Allan. Jr. engr. E.I. duPont de Nemours, Inc., Chattanooga, 1959-63, research engr., 1963-65; process engr. Velsicol Chem. Corp., Chattanooga, 1965-73, sr. engr., 1972-77, tech. services mgr., El Dorado, Ark., 1977—. Chmn. Chattanooga Regional Sci. and Engring. Fair, Inc., 1976-77. Mem. Am. Inst. Chem. Engrs. (chmn. Chattanooga chpt. 1976-77), Order of Engrs. of Am., Tau Beta Pi, Alpha Chi Sigma. Republican. Baptist. Club: Chattanooga Engrs. Home: Route 1 611 Oak Manor Dr El Dorado AR 71730 Office: Route 2 Box 162X El Dorado AR 71730

BURTON, STEVEN MICHAEL, savs. and loan exec.; b. Tulsa, Apr. 6, 1954; s. Herman Otto and Fern L. (Hogan) B.; B.B.A. in Mgmt., Pan Am. U., 1976; m. Geraldene Elane Davis, Apr. 7, 1977. Sales rep. Xerox Corp., Houston and the Rio Grande Valley, Tex., 1976-78; br. mgr., mortgage loan officer Valley Fed. Savs. and Loan Assn., McAllen, Tex. 1978—, asst. v.p. Edinburg (Tex.) br., 1978—. Republican. Mem. Churches of Christ. Club: Kiwanis (Edinburg). Home: 2400 Willow St Mission TX 78572 Office: Valley Fed Savs and Loan Assn of McAllen 400 S Closner St Edinburg TX 78539

BURTON, TOM L., advt. and pub. relations exec., mgmt. exec., journalist; b. Shreveport, La., Sept. 9, 1947; s. Jeff Adams and Hattie Elizabeth (Smart) B.; B.A., Centenary Coll. La., 1971; postgrad. La. Tech. U., 1973; m. Judy Margaret Kinnebrew, Dec. 20, 1973; 1 son, Jason Adams. Adminstrv. asst. to commr. pub. works City of Shreveport, 1970-71; legis. campaign dir. City of Shreveport, 1971; sr. sales rep. Singer Bus. Machines, Shreveport, 1971-73; police reporter The Shreveport Times 1973-75; dir. mktg. The Bossier Press and Unicom Ltd., 1975-76; gen. mgr. La. Housing Devel. Corp., housing cons., mgmt. and pub. relations specialists, 1976-78; gen. mgr. Residential Mgmt. Corp., 1978—; lectr. journalism Caddo Parish Schs., Shreveport, 1974-75. Active Centenary Coll. Great Tchrs.-Scholars drive, Shreveport, 1972-73, Jr. Achievement drive, Shreveport, 1973 chmn. bd. Open Ear, Inc., telephone crisis-intervention service; elem. coordinator Noel United Methodist Ch., 1978-80. Named Outstanding First Year Jaycee, Shreveport Jaycees, 1971; Key-man award; Exchange Club of Shreveport, 1972-73, Outstanding Exchangite, 1974; meritorious service award, La. Am. Revolution-Bicentennial Commn., 1975. Mem. Shreveport Jaycees, Alpha Phi Omega. Democrat. Clubs: Elks, Exchange (dir. 1973-75, pres. 1975-76) (Shreveport). Contbr. articles to profl. jours. Home: 10116 Salinas Dr Shreveport LA 71115 Office: 10100 Youree Shreveport LA 71115

BURTON, WILLIAM EARL, mfg. co. exec.; b. Poteau, Okla., Dec. 28, 1944; s. Buford Earl and Francis Virginia (Hardy) B.; B.S. in Math., Mo. So. State U., 1969; postgrad U. Tex., Arlington, 1975-76; children—Jeffery Scott, John Kevin, Kimberly Rachele. Research chemist Eagle Picher Industry, Joplin, Mo., 1968; ops. research analyst Continental Oil Co., Ponca City, Okla., 1969-71; mgr. ops. Champlin Petroleum Co., Enid, Okla., 1971—; cons. v.p. C.S.I. Inc., Oklahoma City. Mem. Bd. Adjustment and Appeals White Settlement (Tex.), 1975-76, Planning and Zoning Commn., 1975-76. Mem. Am. Mgmt. Assn., Am. Soc. Indsl. Security, Nat. Assn. Chiefs Police, Am. Petroleum Inst. Club: Oakwood Country. Home: 2009 Buggywhip Ln Enid OK 73701 Office: PO Box 552 Enid OK 73701

BURWELL, (GEORGE) ERNEST, ret. automobile dealer; b. Tarboro, N.C., July 22, 1897; s. George Ernest and Lilla Pugh (Bell) B.; ed. pub. schs., spl. courses; H.H.D. (hon.), Wofford Coll., 1978; m. Ethel Marie McMurray, Mar. 4, 1946; children—Ernest Burwell III, Faith Burwell Stewart-Gordon. Owner, partner Burwell-Parker Motor Co., Gastonia, N.C., 1920-22; owner, pres. Ernest Burwell, Inc., Spartanburg, S.C., 1922-27, 27-32, 32—; owner, pres. Burwell Chevrolet, Inc.; owner Burwell Ins., Ernest Burwell, Inc. Organizer Spartanburg Naval Armory, 1946; dir. Kiyosato Ednl. Expt. Project, Japan, 1950—. Bd. dirs. Mchts. Bur., United Fund, Salvation Army, Mental Health Clinic, Polk County Found., KEEP Found.; active Spartanburg Found.; mem. council assos. Wofford Coll., sponsored Burwell Campus Center at coll., 1968. Served to comdr. USNR, 1940-46. Decorated Navy Commendation award; recipient Dealer award for S.C., Time mag., 1970. Mem. Nat. (S.C. dir. 1937-53), S.C. (dir.) automobile dealers assns., Am. Camellia Soc., S.C. Camellia Soc. (exec. v.p., dir.), Spartanburg C. of C., Am. Legion (life), Res. Officers Assn. U.S. (life). Episcopalian (vestryman). Clubs: Red Fox Country, Tryon Riding and Hunt; Piedmont (Spartanburg). Home: Red Fox Country Club Route 1 Tryon NC 28782 Office: 265 N Church St Spartanburg SC 29301

BURWELL, SOPHRONIA WEST, hosp. adminstr.; b. Newport News, Va., Aug. 14, 1924; d. Joseph Logan and Rebecca Williams West; asso. degree N.C. Central U., 1945; m. W. Alvin Burwell, Sept. 22, 1974; 1 son, George Andrew White II. Adminstrv. sec. Whittaker Meml. Hosp., Newport News, Va., 1945-74, adminstrv. asst., 1974—, acting asst. adminstr., 1979—. Dir. public relations Sickle Cell

Anemia Bd. Dirs. Recipient Outstanding Community Service award Masonic Order; longevity service award Whittaker Hosp. Mem. Am. Soc. Hosp. Public Relations, Va. Soc. Hosp. Public Relations, Tidewater Hosp. Council Public Relations, Continental Socs. Inc., Iota Phi Lambda. Democrat. Baptist. Clubs: Dochiki Wives, Peninsula Vocation. Home: 1324 Hampton Dr Newport News VA 23607 Office: Whittaker Meml Hosp 1003 28th St Newport News VA 23607

BURZYNSKI, STANISLAW RAJMUND, internist; b. Lublin, Poland, Jan. 23, 1943; s. Grzegorz and Zofia Miroslawa (Radzikowski) B.; came to U.S., 1970; M.D. with distinction, Med. Acad., Lublin, 1967, Ph.D., 1968. Teaching asst. Med. Acad. Lublin, 1962-67; intern, resident in internal medicine, Med. Acad., 1967-70; research asso. Baylor U., 1970-72, asst. prof., 1972-77; pvt. practice specializing in internal medicine, Houston, 1977—; dir. Burzynski Research Lab. Nat. Cancer Inst. grantee, 1974 West Found. grantee, 1975. Mem. Am. Heart Assn., AAAS, Am. Assn. for Cancer Research, AMA, Fedn. Am. Scientists, Harris County Med. Soc., Polish Nat. Alliance (pres. Houston chpt. 1974-75), Soc. Neurosci., Tex. Med. Assn., Sigma Xi. Roman Catholic. Contbr. articles profl. jours. Discoverer of antineoplastons components of biochem. def. system against cancer; described structure of Ameletin, 1st substance known to be responsible for remembering sound in animal's brain. Home: 5 Concord Cr Houston TX 77024 Office: 1213 Hermann Houston TX 77004

BUSBEE, CYRIL B., state supt. edn. S.C.; b. Wagener, S.C., Dec. 17, 1908; s. William J. and Minnie (Toole) B.; B.A., U. S.C., 1928, M.A., 1938, LL.D., 1969; LL.D., Wofford Coll., 1970; m. Thelma Ecord, July 20, 1929; children—Carolyn Busbee Carpenter, Cyril B. Tchr., coach, supt. schs., Aiken, Kershaw and Lexington counties, S.C.; supt. Brookland Gayce schs., 1943-67; state supt. edn. S.C., 1967—; ex-officio S.C. Ednl. TV Commn., S.C. Tech. and Comprehensive Edn. Bd.; mem. steering com. Edn. Commn. States. Dir. Citizens and So. Bank. Trustee U. S.C., The Citadel, Winthrop Coll.; bd. dirs. Agy. Instrnl. TV. Served with USNR, World War II. Mem. Nat. Council Chief Sch. Officers (dir.), Nat., S.C. edn. assns., Am. Assn. Sch. Adminstrs., U. S.C. Alumni Assn. (pres. 1955). Methodist. Kiwanian (pres. Camden, S.C.), Lion (pres.). Office: 1006 Rutledge Bldg Columbia SC 29201

BUSBEE, GEORGE DEKLE, gov. Ga.; b. Vienna, Ga., Aug. 7, 1927; s. Perry Green and Nell (Dekle) B.; B.B.A., U. Ga., 1949, LL.B., 1952; m. Mary Elizabeth Talbot, Sept. 5, 1949; children—Beth Talbot, Jan Guest, George Dekle, Jeff Talbot. Admitted to Ga. bar, practice in Albany; gov. Ga., 1975—; chmn. Nat. Govs. Assn., 1980—. Mem. Ga. Ho. of Reps., 1957-75, majority leader. Served with USNR, World War II. Baptist. Home: Governor's Mansion 391 W Paces Ferry Rd Atlanta GA 30339 Office: Office of the Governor State Capitol Atlanta GA 30334

BUSCHE, FREDERICK DAVIS, geologist; b. Elkhart, Ind., Oct. 20, 1943; s. Henry Edward and Dorothy Isabelle B.; B.S., U. Ill., 1965; M.S., U. Hawaii, 1968; Ph.D. in Geochemistry, U. N.Mex., 1975; m. Diane Harrison, June 11, 1966; children—Justin, Amber. Geologist, Ranchers Exploration & Devel., Albuquerque, 1973-75; sr. metall. engr. Wyo. Mineral Corp., Lakewood, Colo., 1975-79; sr. geologist Shell Oil Co., Houston, 1979—. Sec.-treas. Malcomson Rd. Utility Dist., 1979—. Mem. AIME, Am. Inst. Profl. Geologists, Sigma Xi. Methodist. Home: 11602 Gatesden Dr Tomball TX 77375 Office: Two Shell Plaza Houston TX 77001

BUSE, RAYMOND LEO, JR., liquor co. exec.; b. Cin., Apr. 5, 1925; s. Raymond Leo and Jane Frances (Barrett) B.; B.S.S.S., Georgetown U., 1948; m. Marjorie Pahls, Aug. 28, 1948; children—Barbara B. Vollmer, Jane, Raymond L. III. Pres., R.L. Buse Co., Cin., 1955—; pres. Old Boone Distillery Co., Meadowlawn, Ky., 1959-70, chmn. bd., 1970—; dir. Fasig Tipton Co. Ky., Lexington, Covington Trust & Banking Co. (Ky.), Citizens Bank, Dry Ridge, Ky., Mid Am. Ins. Agy., Cin., Cin. Bengals, Inc., Ohio Valley Sports, Inc., Cin. Commr., Boone County Planning Commn., Florence, Ky.; vice chmn., trustee Thomas More Coll., Ft. Mitchell, Ky. Served with AUS, 1943-45. Decorated Knight comdr. Equestrian Order Holy Sepulchre Jerusalem. Mem. Ohio Thoroughbred Breeders Owners (dir. emeritus), Ind. Am. Whiskey Assn., Cin. C. of C., Thoroughbred Club Am., Bankers Club Cin. Roman Catholic. Home: Rte 2 Box 40 Walton KY 41094 Office: 2600 Care Tower Cincinnati OH 45202

BUSE, SYLVIA TWEEDT, educator; b. San Francisco, Oct. 8, 1926; d. Lloyd Milton and Pearl (Carlson) Tweedt; B.A., U. Calif. at Berkeley, 1948, M.S., 1961; doctoral student Okla. State U., 1977—; m. Donald Eugene Buse, June 26, 1948; children—Charles Tweedt, Deborah Elizabeth, Sarah Christine, John Thorvold. Grad. research psychologist Inst. Human Devel., U. Calif., 1959-62; psychometrist, birth defects Clinic Children's Hosp., San Francisco, 1961-62, 64-65; research psychologist Inst. Neurol. Scis., Pacific Med. Center, San Francisco, 1962-70; co supr. diagnostic clinic, instr. psychologic processes, Sch. Med. Scis., U. Pacific, San Francisco, 1970-74; instr. psychology of learning disabilities and child devel. Southwest Mo. State U., Springfield, 1975—. USPHS grantee Mem. Am., Mo. psychol. assns., Jean Piaget Soc., Mo. Assn. Children with Learning Disabilities, Sigma Xi. Republican. Lutheran. Home: 2318 Dorchester Dr Bartlesville OK 74003 Office: Southwest Mo State Univ Springfield MO 65802

BUSER, SAMUEL JACKSON, mental health counselor; b. Henderson, Tex., Dec. 1, 1950; s. Clement Joseph and Virginia (Jackson) B.; B.S. in Psychology summa cum laude, Tex. A&M U., 1973; M.Ed. in Counseling, U. Md., 1977; m. Sarah Snavely, June 8, 1974; 1 dau., Mariko Gene. Casework supr. Falfurrias (Tex.)/Freer Mental Health-Mental Retardation Centers, 1978-79; asst. adminstr. Rio Grande State Center Sch. for Mentally Retarded, Harlingen, Tex., 1979—. Served to capt. U.S. Army, 1973-77. Decorated Army Commendation medal. Mem. Am. Personnel and Guidance Assn., Am. Specialists in Group Work, Jaycees (individual devel. v.p. Falfurrias 1978-79, Harlingen 1980—; state dir. Falfurrias 1979; various state and regional awards), Phi Kappa Phi, Psi Chi. Home: 2505 S Parkwood Harlingen TX 78550 Office: PO Box 2668 Harlingen TX 78550

BUSFIELD, ROGER MELVIL, JR., trade assn. exec.; b. Ft. Worth, Feb. 4, 1926; s. Roger Melvil and Julia Mabel (Clark) B.; student U. Tex., spring 1943, summer 1946; B.A., Southwestern U., 1947, M.A., 1948; Ph.D., Fla. State U., 1954; m. Jean Wilson, Mar. 26, 1948 (div. Oct. 1960); children—Terry Jean, Roger Melvil III, Timothy Clark; m. 2d, Virginia Bailey, Dec. 1, 1962; 1 dau., Julia Lucille. Asst. prof. Southwestern U., 1947-49; instr. U. Ala., 1949-50, Fla. State U., 1950-54; asst. prof. speech Mich. State U., 1954-60; editorial services specialist Oldsmobile div. Gen. Motors Corp., Lansing, Mich., 1960; gen. publs. supr. Consumers Power Co., Jackson, Mich., 1960-61; asso. dir.Mich. Hosp. Assn., Lansing, 1961-73; exec. dir. Ark. Hosp. Assn., Little Rock, 1973—. Trustee, Central Mich. U., 1967-73, chmn., 1970; mem. Mich. Gov.'s Commn. on Higher Edn., 1972-74; mem. Ark. Gov.'s Emergency Med. Services Adv. Council, 1975—, chmn., 1978-80. Served with USMC, 1943-46. Named Tex. Outstanding Author, Theta Sigma Phi, 1958; recipient Disting. Alumnus award Southwestern U., 1971; Senate-House Concurrent Resolution of Tribute, Mich. Legis., 1973. Mem. Am. Soc. Assn. Execs., Ark. Soc. Assn. Execs., Public Relations Assn. Mich. (pres. 1966), Speech Communication Assn., Am. Coll. Hosp. Adminstrs., State Hosp. Assn. Exec. Forum, Am. Hosp. Assn. (council on legislation 1975-77), Am. Theatre Assn. Methodist. Club: Rotary (Little Rock). Author: The Playwright's Art, 1958, Arabic transl., 1964; (with others) The Children's Theatre, 1960; editor Theatre Arts Bibliography, 1964; constbr. articles to profl. jours.; author profl. motion picture scenarios. Office: 1501 N University Suite 400 Little Rock AR 72207

BUSH, ALFRED KYLE, surgeon; b. Glenville, W.Va., Dec. 18, 1914; s. Ivan H. and Meta M. (Hays) B.; A.B., Glenville State Coll., 1935; B.S., W.Va. U., 1940; M.D., U. Pa., 1942; m. Elizabeth Eleanor Mockler, Apr. 17, 1943; children—Robert Kyle, Eleanor Caroline Esposito. Instr. chemistry Tanner (W.Va.) High Sch., 1935-38; intern Receiving Hosp., Detroit, 1942-43; resident in surgery Myers Clinic, Philippi, W.Va., 1946-48, surgeon, 1948—, chief surgery, 1974—, partner, 1948—; instr. surgery Alderson-Broaddus Coll., 1948. County chmn. Better Schs. Philippi, 1960; mem. Gov.'s Statewide Drug Porgram W.Va., 1970; trustee Broaddus Hosp., Phillipi, 1955—. Served to lt. M.C., USNR, 1943-46. Diplomate Am. Bd. Surgery. Mem. Tyagart's Valley Med. Soc. (pres. 1955, pres. 1960—), W.Va. Med. Assn. (council 1967-72), A.C.S., Southeastern Surg. Congress, Alpha Omega Alpha. Democrat. Methodist. Clubs: Kiwanis, Masons (32 deg.). Contbr. articles to profl. publs. Home: 5 Bush Ave Philippi WV 26416 Office: Myers Clinic 112 N Wood St Philippi WV 26416

BUSH, CARMEL CORRIVEAU, librarian; b. Salem, Kans., Nov. 15, 1949; d. Martial P. and Juliette A. Corriveau; B.S., Coll. St. Catherine, 1971; M.S., Grad. Sch. Library Sci., U. Ill., 1972; m. Steve Bush, Feb. 14, 1976. Librarian, Life Scis. Research Library, U. Notre Dame, South Bend, Ind., 1973-74; media coordinator U. Ark. for Med. Scis., Little Rock, 1974-76; program coordinator Talon Regional Med. Library program U. Tex. Health Scis. Center, Dallas, 1976—. USPHS fellow, 1971-73. Mem. Med. Library Assn. (cert. level II), Health Scis. Communications Assn., Metroplex Council Health Sci. Librarians, Blacklands Div. Hosp. Educators, Beta Beta Beta, Beta Phi Mu. Asso. editor for abstracts Jour. of Biocommunication, 1975-79. Office: 5323 Harry Hines Blvd Dallas TX 75235

BUSH, ELEANOR MOCKLER, civic worker; b. Mannington, W.Va., July 1, 1913; d. Robert Emmett and Alberta (Baumgartner) Mockler; A.B., W.Va. U., 1935, B.S., 1937; A.M., Ohio State U., 1942; m. John Alfred Kyle Bush, Apr. 17, 1943; children—Robert Kyle, Carolina Bush Esposito. Research chemist Frederick Stearns Drug Co., Detroit, 1942-43; biology asst. Alderson-Broaddus Coll., Philippi, W.Va., 1959-60; substitute tchr. Barbour County Sch., Philippi, 1966-72; chmn. W.Va. chpt. The Nature Conservancy, 1976-80; chmn. Barbour County (W.Va.) Easter Seal Soc., Philippi, 1965—; publicity chmn. Barbour County Clean Streams Project, 1970—; mem. Philippi and Barbour County Bicentennial Commns., 1975-76; nat. accredited flower show judge; lectr. in slide programs on wildflowers, conservation to various schs., civic groups, 4-H Club, others, 1966—. Chmn., Philippi Civic Improvement Com., 1968-72; mem. Philippi Bridge Commn., Philippi, 1970-74. Named State Conservationist of the Year, W.Va. Garden Club, 1975; recipient Conservationist award AAUW of W.Va., 1975; winner prize Morgantown Poetry Soc., 1975. Mem. AAUW (pres. Philippi br. 1955-57), Barbour County Med. Aux. (pres. 1958-59), D.A.R. (regent Philippi chpt. 1960-62), W.Va. Highlands Concervancy (sec. 1971-72, dir. 1974-75), Am. Soc. Plant Taxonomists, Bot. Soc. Am., Soc. Appalachian Bot. Club, Wilderness Soc., Wildlife Fedn., P.E.O. (pres. chpt. C. 1978—), Pi Beta Phi Alumni Club. Republican. Methodist. Clubs: Daus. of 1812, Philippi Garden (Pres. 1970-74), Order of Eastern Star. Home: 5 Bush Ave Philippi WV 26416

BUSH, FRANK WILLIAM, indsl. relations exec.; b. Jefferson County, Ky., Feb. 22, 1938; s. Shelby Thomas and Yvonne Mae (Barnes) B.; ed. U. Ky., 1972-77; m. Carolyn Clemmons, Apr. 15, 1961. Instr. barbering Tri City Barber Coll., 1958-65; owner, mgr. Lexington (Ky.) Barber Coll., 1958-69; supr. Gates Rubber Co., Elizabethtown, Ky., 1969-75, indsl. relations specialist, 1976—; exec. dir. ARC, Hardin County, Ky., 1975-76. Bd. dirs. ARC; campaign chmn. Mayors race, 1977; mem. nat. adv. bd. Am. Security Council, 1977-80; sustaining mem. Republican Nat. Com., 1975-79. Served with Army N.G., 1954-61. Mem. Nat. Mgmt. Assn. (mgmt. devel. chmn. 1978), Research Inst. Am., Inst. Cert. Mgrs. (speaker), C. of C. Republican. Baptist. Clubs: Lions, Masons. Author: Successful Supervision, 1976. Home: Route 2 Box 145 Sonora KY 42776 Office: PO Box 40 Elizabethtown KY 42701

BUSH, GLADYCE KING, educator; b. Smith County, Miss., Mar. 13, 1926; d. John O'Flynn and Lucy Ola (McLeod) King; B.S. in Bus. Edn., William Carey Coll., Hattiesburg, Miss., 1956, M.Ed. in Bus. Edn., U. So. Miss., Hattiesburg, 1969; m. James Hildred Bush; children—James Donald, Janice Carol. Tchr. Smith County (Miss.) Schs., Taylorsville, 1956-72, coordinator vocat., 1972—. Mem. Miss., Nat. Bus., Smith County edn. assns., Miss., Nat. bus. edn. assns., Am. Vocat. Assn., Miss. Dept. Classroom Tchrs., Delta Kappa Gamma, DAR. Club: Green Sprouts Garden. Home: PO Box 158 Taylorsville MS 39168

BUSH, KATHERYN BISHOP, speech pathologist; b. Enfield, N.C., Sept. 19, 1939; d. Jesse, Jr. and Carrie B. Whitaker; B.S. in Edn. with honors, Hampton Inst., 1961; M.Ed. in Speech Pathology and Audiology with honors, U. Ga., 1968; postgrad., Woodrow Wilson Coll. Law, 1977—. Speech pathologist pub. schs. and clinics, Atlanta and Augusta, Ga., 1965-71; cons. speech impaired program Ga. Dept. Edn., Atlanta, 1971-74, coordinator Ga. Learning Resources System, 1974—. Mem. marketing task force Bur. Edn. for Handicapped, U.S. Office Edn., 1977-79. U.S. Office Edn. fellow U. Ga., 1963-65; certified speech pathologist, Ga. Mem. Am. Speech and Hearing Assn. (certificate of clin. competence), Ga. Speech and Hearing Assn. (past pres.), Ga. Fedn. Council for Exceptional Children (pres. elect), Zeta Phi Beta, Kappa Delta Pi. Baptist (sec. bd. trustees). Author: A Program of Sex Education for the Pre-Adolescent Deaf, 1968, The Merry Sounds of Speech, 1970. Home: 974 Veltre Circle SW Atlanta GA 30311 Office: Program for Exceptional Children Ga Dept Edn Atlanta GA 30334

BUSH, NANCY JANE WAGONER, ednl. adminstr.; b. Malvern, Pa., Aug. 6, 1934; d. George S. and Alverda (Kennedy) Wagoner; B.S., West Chester State Coll., 1953; M.S., Fla. State U., 1963, Ad. M.S., 1969, Ph.D., 1972. Reporter and feature writer The Archive, Downington, Pa., 1947-49; art and copy expeditor N.W. Ayer, Phila., 1953; instr. English and polit. sci. Warwick Sch., Pottstown, Pa., 1953-55; instr. emotional problem children Biddle Sch., West Chester, Pa., 1955-56; br. librarian Miami (Fla.) Public Library, 1960-66; chief of circulation and collection bldg. Jacksonville (Fla.) Public Library, 1966-68; lectr. Sch. Library Sci., Fla. State U., Tallahassee, summer, 1969, asst. prof. non-print media research, 1971-72; dir. community coll. librarian program, asso. prof. Appalachian State U., Boone, N.C., 1972-75, asst. to vice chancellor acad. affairs, 1975-76; head dept. ednl. media Auburn U., Auburn, Ala., 1976—; vis. asso. prof. Sch. Library Sci., U. N.C., summer 1973. William Morris Phillips scholar, 1949-53; Harvard fellow, 1972-73. Mem. ALA, NEA, Southeastern Library Assn., Spl. Libraries Assn., Nat. Assn. for Women Deans, Adminstrs. and Counselors, Ala. Assn. for Women Deans, Adminstrs. and Counselors, Am. Assn. Library Schs., Ala. Instructional Media Assn., Ala. Library Assn., AAUP, Assn. for Ednl. Communications and Tech. Contbr. articles to profl. publs., editor The Pilot Light, 1966-68. Home: PO Box 970 Auburn AL 36830 Office: Haley Center 3064 Auburn Univ Auburn AL 36830

BUSH, POWELL DANIEL, JR., educator; b. Athens, Ga., Oct. 2, 1924; s. Powell Daniel and Rosamond (Epps) B.; student Ga. Inst. Tech., 1942-43, 46; B.S. in Medicine, Emory U., 1948, M.A. in Physics, 1951; postgrad. Vanderbilt U., summers 1958-60, U. Ga., summer 1962; m. Edwina Johnston, Sept. 15, 1970; children—Katherine Marion, Isabelle Rosamond. Instr. physics Morehouse Coll., Atlanta, 1951-52; engr. Lockheed Aircraft, Marietta, Ga., 1952-58; asst. prof. physics Mercer U., Macon, Ga., 1958—, acting chmn. physics dept., 1958-78; cons. two cases Dist. Atty's. Office. Served with USAAF, 1943-45. Carnegie Found. grantee, 1952; Franklin Found. grantee, 1967; Pitts. Spectroscopic Soc. grantee, 1979. Mem. Am. Assn. Physics Tchrs., Am. Phys. Soc., Sigma Xi, Sigma Pi Sigma. Republican. Club: Masons (Legion of Honor comdr. 1971, master Wolihin lodge 1972, high priest Constantine chpt. 1972, master Washington, Ill. council 1972, comdr. St. Omar commandary 1971-72). Contbr. abstracts to profl. publs. Home: 205 Angus Blvd Warner Robins GA 31093 Office: Mercer U Macon GA 31207 Mailing Address: PO Box 816 Warner Robins GA 31099

BUSH, RALPH EVERETT, builder, developer; b. Lenior, N.C., Aug. 26, 1903; s. Robert Burkhead and Siddie Anna (Underdown) B.; B.S., U. Va., 1925; m. Louise Cecilia Trice, Sept. 3, 1932; children—Mary Cuthbert Bush Digges, Nancy Louise Bush Lawson. Bldg. contractor, Miami, Fla., 1925-27, Washington, 1927-28, Norfolk, Va., 1928-42; owner Bush Constrn. Co., Norfolk, Washington and Balt., 1946—, also pres. subs. corps.; dir. emeritus Dominion Nat. Bank, Norfolk., Med. Center Hosps., Norfolk; bd. dirs. Inst. Govt. Assisted Housing, Washington; mem. devel. com. Norfolk State Coll. Found. Served from capt. to maj. C.E., U.S. Army, 1942-46. Mem. Soc. Am. Mil. Engrs., Nat. Assn. Homebuilders, Norfolk C. of C. Clubs: Norfolk Yacht and Country; Va.; Harbor; Univ. (Washington); Farmington Country (Charlottesville, Va.); Commonwealth (Richmond, Va.). Home: 601 Pembroke Ave Norfolk VA 23507 Office: 5532 Raby Rd Norfolk VA 23502

BUSH, WENDELL EARL, lawyer, govt. ofcl.; b. Little Rock, Dec. 10, 1943; s. David J. and Annie O. (Hamilton) B.; A.B., Philander Smith Coll., Little Rock; postgrad. Atlanta U.; J.D., Emory U.; postgrad. (Reginald Heber Smith fellow) U. Pa. Law Sch. Admitted to bar; staff Emory U. Community Law Clinic, Indpls. Legal Services Orgn.; dist. counsel Memphis dist. office EEO Commn., now sr. trial atty. H. Sol Clark fellow. Mem. Am., Nat. bar assns. Home: 3685 Winchester Park Circle Memphis TN 38118 Office: 1407 Union Ave Suite 502 Memphis TN 38103

BUSHNELL, DENNIS MEYER, research exec.; b. New Haven, May 10, 1941; s. Jordan L. and Anna M. B.; B.S. in Mech. Engring. with distinction (univ. scholar), U. Conn., 1963; M.S. in Mech. Engring., U. Va., 1967; m. Judith Anne Simoni, June 8, 1963; 1 son, Matthew Gregory. Research scientist fluid and flight mechanics NASA, Langley Research Centre, Hampton, Va., 1963-69, sect. head viscous flows research, 1969-73, br. chief fluid mechanics, 1973—; cons. Air Force Rocket Propulsion Lab., Brookhaven Nat. Lab., Army Ballistic Missle Def. Command, Office Naval Research. Vice pres. Vol. Rescue Squad; scoutmaster Boy Scouts Am. Recipient Hamilton and Pi Tau Sigma awards U. Conn. Asso. fellow AIAA (Lawrence Sperry award); mem. ASME, Sigma Xi, Pi Tau Sigma, Phi Kappa Phi, Tau Beta Pi. Home: PO Box 176 Hayes VA 23072 Office: 163 NASA Langley Research Center Langley AFB VA 23369

BUSHNELL, FRANK FROST, botanist; b. DeLand, Fla., Dec. 19, 1932; s. Roswell Sauls and Pearl Craig B.; A.B., Stetson U., 1958; M.A., Appalachian U., 1965; m. Elizabeth Dell, July 4, 1969; 1 dau., Jennifer Elizabeth. Tchr., Boca Ciega High Sch., St. Petersburg, Fla., 1958-65; instr. div. sci. St. Petersburg Jr. Coll., 1965-78, prof., 1978—; cons. ecol. and environ. problems; lectr. Fla. archeology, bot. ecology. Served with AUS, 1950-53. Mem. Fla. Anthropol. Soc., St. Petersburg C. of C., St. Petersburg Jr. Coll. Roundtable of Scholars, Phi Delta Kappa. Contbr. articles to profl. jours. Office: Div Sci St Petersburg Jr Coll St Petersburg FL 33710

BUSK, ROBERT SCHOLLEY, metallurgist; b. Bklyn., Dec. 13, 1915; s. Anthony Soren and Marion Alida (Ingrahan) B.; B.A., Colgate U., 1937; D.Eng., Yale U., 1940; m. Evelyn M. Busk, June 7, 1941; children—Theodore A., Robert L., Ralph I., M. Kristin. Metallurgist, Dow Chem. Co., Midland, Mich., 1940-55, lab. dir., 1955-65, asst. dir. research, 1968-72; pres. R.S. Busk, Inc., Midland, 1972—. Fellow Am. Soc. Metals; mem. Internat. Magnesium Assn. (dir. 1976—), ASTM, AIME, AAAS, Sigma Chi. Contbr. articles to profl. jours. Patentee in field. Address: PO Box 3174 Hilton Head SC 29928

BUSKEY, FRANCES WECHSLER, nurse, family and marriage counselor, sex therapist; b. Bronx, N.Y., Feb. 22, 1942; d. Samuel and Clara Sybil (Steckler) Wechsler; A.S. in Nursing with honors, Miami Dade Community Coll., 1974; postgrad. Fla. Internat. U., 1977—; children—Debra Jeanne, Jeffrey Grant, Heidi Lin. With check clearance dept. Mfrs. Hanover Trust, N.Y.C., 1959; pre and post abortion counselor Atlantic Med. Clinic, S. Miami, Fla., 1973; birth control and venereal disease counselor Planned Parenthood, Opa Locka, Fla., 1974; head nurse oncology Mt. Sinai Med. Center, Miami Beach, Fla., 1974-77; co-planner Found. for Human Sexual Dysfunction, Dade County, 1978—; now rehab. nurse for cardiologist, Miami Beach; dir. Jackard and Jaffarud Realty Corp., N.Y. Pres. local chpt. PTA, 1971-72; life mem. state PTA; sponsor B'nai B'rith Yough Group. Recipient certificate of appreciation Family Health Centers of Miami, 1973. Republican. Jewish. Speaker in field med. conf., 1978.

BUSLIG, BELA STEPHEN, biochemist; b. Budapest, Hungary, Aug. 27, 1938; naturalized Can. citizen; s. Gyula Alajos and Ilona Anna (Balazsy) B.; B.A., Queen's U., Kingston, Ont., Can., 1962; postgrad. Western Res. U., 1962-63; M.S., Fla. State U., 1967; Ph.D., U. Fla., 1970; m. Bertha Joanne Horsfall, Aug. 27, 1964; children—Aileen Laura Susanne, Bela Stephen. Clin. chemist Northwestern Gen. Hosp., Toronto, Ont., Can., 1957-59, 60, 62; research fellow in microbiology Western Res. U., Cleve., 1962-63; research and teaching asst. biochemistry Fla. State U., Tallahassee, 1963-67; chemist, research biochemist Fla. Dept. Citrus, Lake Alfred, 1967-77, research scientist, 1977—. NIH fellow, 1962-63. Mem. Am. Chem. Soc. (chmn. Fla. sect. 1980), AAAS, Can. Soc. Plant Physiologists, Am. Soc. Plant Physiologists, Genetics Soc. Am. Office: Fla Dept Citrus PO Box 1909 Winter Haven FL 33880

BUSQUETS, FRANCISCO, counselor; b. Ciales, P.R., July 9, 1927; s. Pelegrin and Isabel (Arce) B.; B.A., Inter Am. U. P.R., 1974, M.A. in Edn., 1975; m. Carmen Barrientos, Sept. 6, 1952; children—Anita Isabel, Francisco R. Enlisted in U.S. Air Force, 1952, advanced through grades to master sgt., 1968; adv. Vietnam Air Force, 1972; ret., 1972; counselor Inter Am. U. P.R., San German, 1975—, dir. counseling services San German campus, 1977—. Decorated Bronze Star; Vietnam Honor medal of combat. Mem. Am. Personnel and Guidance Assn., Nat. Employment Counselors Assn. Democrat. Roman Catholic. Home: 170 E St Aquadilla PR 00603 Office: Inter Am U San German PR 00753

BUSSEY, MALCOLM L., gas co. exec.; b. Timpson, Tex., Aug. 1, 1918; s. Charlie Ray and Maggie L. (Finigan) B.; m. Mattie Lou Steele, July 8, 1936; children—Charlie Mac, Barbara Lois, Mary Lou. With Bu-Pane Gas Co., Inc., Center, 1945—, owner, pres., to 1965; owner La.-Tex. LP Gas Inc., La., to 1965; owner M.L. Bussey Investments. Mem. Tex. (dir. 1956-58, v.p. 1958, outstanding dealer of year award 1968), La. (dir. 1961-64, outstanding dealer of year award 1968) liquified petroleum gas assns., Center C. of C. (dir. 1954—, pres. 1961-62). Democrat. Mem. Christian Ch. Contbr. articles to profl. jours. Home and office: Tenah Rd Box 648 Center TX 75935

BUSTAMANTE, CLEO, JR., retail grocer; b. Carrizo Springs, Tex., July 29, 1952; s. Cleo and Martha (Aguirre) B.; student S.W. Tex. Jr. Coll., 1972; B.B.A., St. Mary's U., 1975; M.B.A., U. Tex., 1977. With Bustamante Enterprises, Inc., Carrizo Springs, 1977—, v.p., 1977—; dir. First Nat. Bank of Dimmit County, 1977—. Mem. Carrizo Springs Planning and Zoning Commn., 1977—, vice chmn., 1977-80; del. to Tex. Dem. Conv., 1978. Recipient Appreciation award Vocat. Indsl. Clubs of Am., 1977. Mem. Pizza Inn Franchise Assn., Nat. Assn. Convenience Stores, Tex. Retail Grocers Assn., Dimmit County C. of C. (dir. 1979-80). Roman Catholic. Club: Kiwanis (dir. 1979-80). Address: 1003 9th St Carrizo Springs TX 78834

BUSTAMANTE, ROBERT J., med. research adminstr.; b. Havana, Cuba, July 24, 1954; came to U.S., 1960; s. Luis and Mayda Bustamante; A.A., Miami-Dade Community Coll., 1974; B.S. in Psychology and Bus. Adminstrn., Fla. Internat. U., 1976; m. Mitzi A. Gimenez, Apr. 22, 1977. Mgr. sporting goods J & S, 1974-75; pres., owner RJB Sportswear, Inc., 1975-76; sales rep. Star Pharm., Inc., 1976-77; asst. adminstr. Howard Hughes Med. Inst., Miami, Fla., 1977—. Mem. Soc. Research Adminstrs. (editorial bd.). Roman Catholic. Club: Miami Rotary (pres.-elect 1980). Home: 7277 Sunset Dr Miami FL 33143 Office: PO Box 330837 Coconut Grove FL 33133

BUSTAMANTE-SUGG, JORGE ROLANDO, engring. cons.; b. Valdivia, Chile, July 21, 1937; came to U.S., 1966, naturalized, 1974; s. Clodomiro Segundo and Elena (Sugg-Soto) Bustamante-Acuna; Engring. deg., Academia Politecnica Aeronautica, 1962; M.Sc., U. Tex., 1972; m. Dorothy W. Watkins, Oct. 17, 1970; children—Melitta Oriana, Mireya Amparo, Monika Valeska. Performance analyst Boeing Co., Phila., 1968-70; mktg. rep. Burroughs Corp., Mexico City and Houston, 1971-74; sr. process engr. Biles & Assos., Houston, 1975-76; proposal mgr. TRW Controls, Houston, 1977-78; engring. cons. Intercomp, Houston, 1978—; teaching asst. U. Tex., Austin, 1966-68. Served to 2d lt. Chilean Air Force, 1957-62. Nat. fellow Barros Arana Inst., 1952-55; Chile research fellow U. Tex., Austin, 1967-68. Mem. Colegio de Ingenieros, Chile, Am. Mgmt. Assn. Democrat. Author: Chile, 1962; short stories, essays pub. Chile Aviation Gasolines, 1953-62. Home: 2101 Hayes Rd Apt 1002 Houston TX 77077 Office: 1201 Dairy Ashford Houston TX 77079

BUTALA, MAHENDRA BHOGILAL, structural engr.; b. Modasa, India, Aug. 9, 1945; came to U.S., 1970, naturalized, 1978; s. Bhogilal G. and Suryankanta B.; B.S., Baroda Coll., 1966, M.E., 1969; M.S., Brigham Young U., Provo, Utah, 1971; m. Kalpana N. Shodhan, Oct. 18, 1973. Structural engr. J.N. Pease Assos., Charlotte, N.C., 1972-74; design engr. Catalytic Inc., Charlotte, 1974-75, United Engrs., Knoxville, 1975-76; lead structural engr. Russell & Axon Co., Knoxville, 1977—. Registered profl. engr., Tenn.; M.S.U. scholar, India, 1966-69. Mem. Am. Concrete Inst. Democrat. Hindu. Home: 1900 Plumb Creek Circle Knoxville TN 37922 Office: Russell & Axon Engrs 1801 United American Plaza Knoxville TN 37929

BUTAUD, LOUIS CLARENCE, JR., air force officer; b. Rayne, La., July 4, 1937; s. Louis Clarence and Louetta Josephine (Gossen) B.; B.S. in Bus. Adminstrn., U. Southwestern La., 1959; m. Constance Marie Devillier, May 30, 1959; children—Marla, Lisa, Mark, Nadine. Commd. 2d lt. U.S. Air Force, 1959, advanced through grades to lt. col., 1975; personnel officer, Williams AFB, Ariz., 1959-62; adminstrv. officer, Phoenix, 1962; adminstrv. officer, Salt Lake City, 1962-64; automated systems designer Randolph AFB, Tex., 1964-67, chief requirements analysis Air Force Personnel Center, 1972-76, chief info. systems planning group Air Force Manpower and Personnel Center, 1978-80; personnel officer Phan Rang, Vietnam, 1967-68; chief budget and statistics systems, Washington, 1968-72; dir. personnel, England AFB, La., 1976-78; guest lectr. Dept. Def. Computer Inst., Washington. Decorated Bronze Star. Roman Catholic. Club: K.C. Home: 12207 Las Nubes San Antonio TX 78233 Office: 6800 Park Ten Blvd Suite 140E San Antonio TX 78213

BUTCALIS, MARY LOUISE, nurse; b. Shreveport, La., Mar. 26, 1931; d. Henry Louis and Rosemary (Anderson) Riley; R.N., Schumpert Sch. Nursing, 1953; B.S., Northwestern State U., 1968, M.S., 1974; m. Steven T. Butcalis, Nov. 24, 1954; children—Stephen Anthony, Mary Annette. Nurse, Davis Hosp., Pine Bluff, Ark., 1954-55, VA Hosp., Shreveport, La., 1955-56, Schumpert Hosp., Shreveport, 1958; occupational health nurse Brewster County, Shreveport, 1963-66; nurse Confederate Meml. Med. Center, Shreveport, 1966-67; nurse adminstr. Family Health Found., Shreveport, 1968-72; instr. nursing Northwestern State U., Natchitoches, La., 1972-75; dir. nursing service, asst. prof. La. State U., Shreveport, 1976—. Mem. Am. Nurses Assn., Am. Soc. Nursing Service Adminstrs., La. Soc. Nursing Service Adminstrs., La. Hosp. Assn., Phi Kappa Phi, Sigma Theta Tau. Home: 533 E Southfield Rd Shreveport LA 71105 Office: La State U Med Center 1541 Kings Hwy Shreveport LA 71130

BUTCHER, DONALD FRANKLIN, statistician, computer scientist; b. Parkerburg, W.Va., June 29, 1937; s. John Franklin and Anna Pearl (Herschman) B.; B.S., W.Va. U., 1960, M.S., 1962; Ph.D., Iowa State U., 1965; m. Alice Adelia Rosier, July 24, 1959; children—Dianna Lynn, Daniel Bruce, Damon Scott. Mem. faculty W.Va. U., 1965—, prof. statistics, 1974—, chmn. dept. stats. and computer sci., 1972—; cons. to govt., 1971—; asst. prof. Kans. State U., 1969-70. Mem. Biometrics Soc., Am. Statis. Assn., Assn. Computing Machinery, Sigma Xi, Gamma Sigma Delta. Republican. Methodist. Contbr. articles to profl. jours. Home: Route 7 Box 464 Morgantown WV 26505 Office: Hodges Hall West Va Univ Morgantown WV 26506

BUTLER, BENNIS GLENN, land devel. exec.; b. San Augustine, Tex., Sept. 21, 1942; s. Bennie Lee and Lela May (Thacker) B.; B.S., Stephen F. Austin U., 1964; m. Janet Tee Leisk, Dec. 11, 1963; children—Bennie Wardell, Laura Michelle. Vice pres., dir. 1st Gen. Realty Corp., Houston, 1970-77; pres. Stuckey, Pace & Butler, Inc., Houston, 1977—, also dir.; dir. Westhollow Nat. Bank. Bd. dirs. Boys Country, Inc. Mem. Greater Houston Builders Assn., Tex. Assn. Builders, Nat. Assn. Home Builders. Baptist. Club: River Oaks Country.

BUTLER, FARLEY PORTER, SR., hosp. exec.; b. Beaver Dam, Ky., June 15, 1922; s. Arthur George and Henrye Arnold (Porter) B.; student Miss. Coll., 1939, U. Md., 1949-59; m. Helen G. Edwards, Feb. 14, 1943; children—Farley Porter, Sharon Diane. Commd. officer U.S. Army, 1940, advanced through grades to lt. col., 1961; staff Adj. Gen. Office, Washington, 1946-56; staff officer Supreme Hdqrs. Allied Powers Europe, 1951-54; chief personnel assignments U.S. Army Forces Far East, 1958-59; post adj. gen. Fort Leonard Wood, Mo., 1959-61, ret., 1961; asst. adminstr. Alachua Gen. Hosp., Gainesville, Fla., 1969-76, v.p., 1976—. Baptist. Clubs: Rotary, Civitan (treas. Fla. dist. 1967-68) (Gainesville). Home: 803 NW 36th Ave Gainesville FL 32601 Office: 801 SW 2d Ave Gainesville FL 32602

BUTLER, FRANCIS ANDREW, educator; b. Memphis, July 12, 1920; s. William Andrew and Addie Iola (Jamison) B.; A.S., Marion Inst., 1939; B.S. in Marine Engring., U.S. Naval Acad., 1942; M.S. in Adult Edn., Va. Poly. Inst. and State U., 1978; m. Mary Helen Broughton, Apr. 20, 1943; children—John Andrew, Mary Jalene Butler King, Rosanna Lynn Butler Currie, Lucia Ann Butler Hertsburg, Claudia Gail Butler Mayberry, Carla June Robin Sue, Robert Stewart, Rebecca Joyce, Christy Jo. Commd. ensign, U.S. Navy, 1942, advanced through grades to capt., 1961; gunnery officer U.S.S. Trathen, 1942-44; exec. officer U.S.S. Brush, 1946-48; asst. prof. naval sci. U. Wash., 1948-51; comdg. officer U.S.S. Kleinsmith, 1951-53; ops. officer Amphibious Group 4, 1953-56; logistic plans NATO, 1956-59; comdg. officer U.S.S. Putnam, 1959-61; ops. officer Amphibious Force Atlantic, 1961-63; chief staff for tng. Amphibious Tng. Command, 1963-64; comdg. officer U.S.S. Uvalde, 1964-65; chief staff Amphibious Group 4, 1965-67; dir. joint ops. U.S. Atlantic Command, 1967-69; ret., 1969; coordinator tng. Babcock & Wilcox, 1969-76, mgr. employee edn. and devel. Naval Nuclear Fuel Div., Lynchburg, Va., 1976—; lectr. U.S. Mil. Acad., U.S. War Coll.; U.S. rep. for transfer of floating drydock to Republic of China; mem. Korean Patrol; ops. officer Invasion Force, Cuban Missile Crisis; task group comdr. Dominican Rep. Crisis and Landing. Mem. ch. bd. United Methodist Ch., 1955-61; mem. adv. com. supr. program Central Va. Community Coll., 1974-75. Mem. Am. Mgmt. Assn., Soc. Advancement Mgmt. (chpt. v.p. 1978). Republican. Research on group effectiveness; developer data-based program for personal growth, 1978. Home: 219 Windsor Rd Lynchburg VA 24502 Office: Babcock & Wilcox Co Naval Nuclear Fuel Div PO Box 85 Lynchburg VA 24505

BUTLER, JACK LAWRENCE, newspaper editor; b. Seymour, Tex., Oct. 21, 1917; s. Wash Cain and Margaret (Lawrence) B.; B.J., U. Tex., 1939; m. Mary Louise Ford, Oct. 26, 1940; children—Lawrence Ford, Helen Lynn (Mrs. David Hays). Mng. editor Tyler (Tex.) Morning Telegraph, 1940, Gladewater (Tex.) Tribune, 1940-41; news editor Austin (Tex.) Tribune, 1942-43; with Ft. Worth Star-Telegram, 1943—, city editor, 1951-54, news editor, 1954-58, asst. mng. editor, 1958-63, editor, 1963—; Disting. lectr. journalism Tex. Christian U., Ft. Worth, 1978—. Bd. dirs. Tex. Christian U. Research Found. Served with USNR, 1944-45. Mem. Am. Soc. Newspaper Editors, Sigma Delta Chi (pres. Tex. Assn. 1956). Home: 1613 Scenery Hill Rd Fort Worth TX 76103 Office: 400 W 7th St Fort Worth TX 76102

BUTLER, JACK SCOTT, life ins. co. exec.; b. Lamar County, Ala., Oct. 26, 1918; s. Waller Edward and Naomi Jane (Caine) B.; B.S. in Agri-Bus., Auburn U., 1942; m. Phyllis Maxine Hill, Dec. 21, 1941; children—William Hill, Jack Scott, Thomas Albert. Farmer, founder Fairview Seed Co., 1946-60; mgr. Fayette (Ala.) Seed Co., 1960-70; agt., mgr., v.p., state mgr. for Ala., dir. Paramount Life Ins. Co., Fayette, 1970—. Lay leader Bethlehem United Methodist Ch. Served to capt. U.S. Army, 1942-46. Decorated Purple Heart, Bronze Star. Mem. Nat. Assn. Life Underwriters, Ala. Cattle Assn., Fayette County Cattle Assn. Clubs: Lions Internat., Ala. Methodists, Alpha Gamma Rho. Home and Office: 1807 Griffin St Fayette AL 35555

BUTLER, JAMES HANSEL, dentist, periodontist; b. Canton, Ohio, Dec. 7, 1936; s. Hansel Harmon and Mary Frances (Kelley) B.; B.A., Denison U., 1958; D.D.S., Ohio State U., 1962; M.S., U. Rochester Sch. Medicine and Dentistry, 1967; cert. in periodontics Eastman Dental Center, Rochester, N.Y., 1967; m. Carol Teegardin, July 29, 1961; children—Catherine J., Matthew T., Sarah A. Asso. prof. periodontics U. Minn., 1970-74; asso. prof., chmn. div. occlusion Va. Commonwealth U. med. Coll. Va. Sch. Dentistry, 1974—; cons. in field. Served with USAF, 1962-64. Fellow Internat. Coll. Dentists; mem. ADA, Va. Dental Assn., Richmond Dental Soc., Am. Acad. Periodontology, Va. Soc. Periodontology, Internat. Assn. Dental Research, Am. Assn. Dental Research, Periodontal Research Group, Sigma Xi, Omicron Kappa Upsilon. Republican. Lutheran. Contbr. articles to profl. publs. Home: 10612 Harborough Rd Richmond VA 23233 Office: 520 N 12th St Richmond VA 23298

BUTLER, JO ANN TABOR, coll. adminstr.; b. Madison County, Ala., Sept. 16, 1931; s. Joe Ben and Laura B. (Craft) Tabor; grad. N. Ala. Coll. Commerce, 1969; B.S., Athens State Coll., 1977; m. John G. Butler, Sept. 9, 1948; children—Laura Butler, Conwell, Henri Butler McDaniel, John G. Sec., N. Ala. Coll. Commerce, Huntsville, Ala., 1969-71, dir. adminstrn., 1977—; sr. sec. U. Ala., Huntsville, 1971-72, sec. to pres., 1972-77. Mem. Madison County (Ala.) Elected Ofcls. Salary Study Commn., 1975; mem. Madison County Jud. Commn., 1976—. Named Most Courteous Sec., Huntsville-Madison County C. of C., 1971, Sec. of Yr., 1977. Cert. profl. sec., 1977. Mem. Nat. Secs. Assn., Nat. Assn. Exec. Secs. Mem. Ch. of Christ. Club: Altrusa. Home: 190 Pine St New Hope AL 35760 Office: N Ala Coll of Commerce 528 Madison St S Huntsville AL 35801

BUTLER, JOHN HARRISON, educator; b. Mpls., July 14, 1932; s. Benjamin Joseph and Olive Ann (Wood) B.; B.Mus.Edn., W. Tex. State U., 1955; M.F.A., U. Ga., 1960, Ed.D., 1968. Band dir. high schs., Vega, Tex., 1951-55, Tulia, Tex., 1957-59; faculty Clemson (S.C.) U., 1960—, dir. bands, prof. music and chmn. Music Dept., 1969—; clinician and adjudicator for high sch. bands; condr., performer, actor little theatre work, Clemson, 1966—, Greenville, S.C., 1972, Anderson, S.C., 1974—. Served with USN, 1955-57. Recipient Best Actor award Greenville Little Theatre, 1972, Clemson Little Theatre, 1974, 75; U. Ga. Alumni fellow, 1966-67. Mem. Music Educators Nat. Conf., Coll. Band Dirs. Nat. Assn. (So. div. pres. 1966-68), Kappa Kappa Psi, Mu Beta Psi, Phi Beta Mu, Phi Kappa Phi. Contbr. articles to profl. jours; composer opera The Outcasts of Poker Flat, 1959. Home: PO Box 2355 University Sta Clemson SC 29632 Office: Dept Music Clemson Univ Clemson SC 29631

BUTLER, JOHN WILLIAM, meat packing co. exec.; b. Maben, Miss., June 3, 1919; s. Joyce Preston and Sarah (Hannah) B.; student Tex. Christian U. 1940, Tex. Tech U., 1941; m. Daisy Marie Murray, Jan. 1, 1940; children—Beverly Janice, John William, Catherine Ann. With Leonard Bros., Ft. Worth, Tex., 1937-40, Swift & Co., Ft. Worth, 1940-56; gen. sales supr. Armstrong Packing Div., Ft. Worth, 1950-56; with John Morrell & Co., Ft. Worth, 1956—, dist. sales mgr., 1969—; dir., sec.-treas. John Butler Cos., Inc., Ft. Worth, 1977—. Bd. dirs. Hurst (Tex.) Parks and Recreation Bd., 1974—; councilman City of Haltom City (Tex.), 1954; mem. Hurst Citizens Capital Improvements adv. com., 1974-79. Served with USN, 1944-46. Recipient Commodore Club award, 1974; Certificate of Appreciation, City of Hurst, 1977; Pres.'s Club award, John Morrell & Co., 1969. Democrat. Baptist. Club: Masons (excellent high priest 1979-80). Home: 408 Carnation Ln Hurst TX 76053 Office: 1244 Karla Dr Hurst TX 76053

BUTLER, LEWELL COLBERT, JR., plastic surgeon; b. Shreveport, La., Mar. 6, 1922; s. Lewell Colbert and Mary Lou (Doll) B.; student Centenary Coll., 1938, U. Mich., 1939, Tulane U., 1940-41; M.D., La. State U., 1946; M.S., U. Minn., 1956; children—Lewell Stephen, Bradley Wayne. Intern, Highland Hosp., Shreveport, 1946-47; resident Princeton (N.J.) Hosp., 1947; fellow in surgery Grad. Sch., Tulane U., New Orleans, 1948; resident in surgery Scott and White Hosp., Temple, Tex., 1949-51; fellow in surgery Grad. Sch., U. Tex., 1949-51; fellow in plastic surgery Mayo Found., Rochester, Minn., 1953-56; pvt. practice plastic surgery, Shreveport, 1956—; mem. staff Schumpert Med. Center, Willis-Knighton, Doctors, Highland, Bossier hosps. Served with M.C., USNR, 1951-53. Diplomate Am. Bd. Plastic Surgery. Mem. Am., La. socs. (1st pres.) plastic and reconstructive surgery, Tex. socs. plastic surgeons, Am. Assn. Hand Surgery, La., Shreveport med. socs. Home: 429 Lowell Ct Shreveport LA 71115 Office: 865 Margaret Pl Shreveport LA 71101

BUTLER, MANLEY CALDWELL, congressman, lawyer; b. Roanoke, Va., June 2, 1925; s. W.W.S. Butler; A.B., U. Richmond (Va.), 1948; LL.B., U. Va., 1950; m. June Nolde; children—Manley, Jimmy, Henry, Marshall. Chmn. Roanoke City Rep. party, 1960-61; mem. Va. Ho. of Dels., 1962-72, minority leader, 1966-72; mem. 92d-96th Congresses from 6th Dist. Va., 1972—, mem. coms. on judiciary and govt. ops. Mem. Va. State Bar, Am., Roanoke bar assns., Raven Soc., Order of the Coif, Phi Beta Kappa, Tau Kappa Alpha, Omicron Delta Kappa, Phi Gamma Delta. Episcopalian (former vestryman). Office: Cannon House Office Bldg Washington DC 20515

BUTLER, MARILYN, med. technologist, educator; b. Champaign, Ill., June 12, 1941; d. Lloyd Sheldon and Norma Augusta (Seider) B.; B.S., Ariz. State U., 1963; M.S., U. So. Calif., 1965; Ph.D., U. Calif., Davis, 1975; m. James Alan Subach. Instr. div. med. tech. W.Va. U., Morgantown, 1966-67; tchr. Elk Grove (Calif.) Unified Sch. Dist., 1968-71; asso. in anatomy, dept. human anatomy U. Calif., Davis, 1973; instr. anatomy, sci. depts. Mesa (Ariz.) Community Coll., 1976; asst. prof., asso. program dir., med. tech. program U. Ariz., Tucson, 1976-78; asst. prof. U. Tex., San Antonio, 1978—. VA grantee, 1977—. Jr. coll. teaching certification, Calif., Ariz.; secondary teaching certificate, Calif. Mem. Am. Soc. Clin. Pathologists (certified in med. technology), Am. Soc. Med. Technologists, AAUP, Am. Assn. Anatomists, Tex. Soc. Med. Tech., Sigma Xi, Alpha Sigma Alpha, Beta Beta Beta, Gamma Phi Omega, Presbyterian. Clubs: Tucson Athletic, Racquetball and Handball (San Antonio). Home: 16240 N San Pedro Apt 254 San Antonio TX 78232 Office: Div Allied Health and Life Scis U Tex San Antonio TX

BUTLER, MILTON LEE, med. technologist; b. Dilworth, Ala., Aug. 2, 1939; s. Kressor Burl and Verla (Brock) B.; B.S., Samford U., 1967; m. Helen Morrell Smith, Aug. 16, 1963; children—Milton L., Misty Lynn, Marc Thomas. Med. technologist Lloyd Noland Hosp., Fairfield, Ala., 1960-67; evening supr. Druid City Hosp., Tuscaloosa, Ala., 1968-69; asst. supt. chemistry Baptist Med. Center, Birmingham, 1969-72; supr. blood bank Cooper Green Hosp., Birmingham, 1972-73, chief med. technologist, 1973—. Served with USNR, 1958-60. Mem. Ala. Assn. Lab. Mgmt. (co-founder, 1st pres., treas. 1978-80), Am. Soc. Clin. Pathologists. Baptist. Office: 1515 6th Ave S Birmingham AL 35233

BUTLER, NED NILE, state adminstr.; b. Fayette, Ala., Jan. 28, 1928; s. Charlie L and Maude Louise (Clements) B.; student Cook's Radio Engring. Sch., 1949, Capitol Advanced Radio Engring. Sch., 1952; m. Elizabeth Joy Slaughter, Oct. 31, 1948; children—Ned N., Steve, Robin. Owner, operator Sta. WTLS, Tallassee, Ala., Sta. WLVN, Laverne, Ala.; adminstr. Office Opportunity State of Ala., dir. Office Telecommunications; pres. Ala. ETV Commn. Served with U.S. Navy. Mem. Tallassee Jaycees (pres.), Tallassee C. of C. Baptist. Club: Lions. Designer radio telephone switch sta., 1977. Office: 3734 Atlanta Hwy Montgomery AL 36120

BUTLER, PAMELA JEAN, govt. contracting co. exec.; b. Amarillo, Tex., May 3, 1947; d. Ervin Vancil and Betty Joan (Banister) Stone; student Amarillo Coll., 1975; m. Royce Elmo Butler, June 26, 1965; children—Royce Lynn, Vincent Alexander, Katrina D'Ann. Clk., Amarillo Hardware Co., 1967; sec. Am. Quarter Horse Assn., Amarillo, 1968; with Mason & Hanger Co.-Silas Mason Co., Amarillo, 1968—, engring. asst., 1974-77, quality analyst, 1977—. Mem. Am. Soc. Quality Control Am. Def. Preparedness Assn. Republican. Baptist. Mem. Order Eastern Star. Home: 3609 Atkinsen St Amarillo TX 79109 Office: PO Box 30020 Amarillo TX 79177

BUTLER, ROY FRANCIS, educator; b. Atlanta, May 4, 1914; s. Roy Edward and Mae Ellison (Kenner) B.; A.B. (Chattanooga Times scholar), U. Chattanooga, 1935; M.A., U. Tenn., 1938; PH.D. (Univ. scholar), Ohio State U., 1942; m. Barbara Goehring Scott, Nov. 17, 1943; children—Roy Francis, John Scott. Instr., U. Tenn., 1946, asst. prof. classics, 1947-48; instr. Ohio State U., 1946-47; asst. prof. classics Baylor U., 1947-49, asso. prof., 1949-52, prof., 1952—, chmn. dept. classics, 1958—. Served with USAAF, 1942-45. Mem. Am. Philol. Assn., Oriental Soc. Am., Linguistic Soc. Am., Classical Assn. Middle West and South, Classical Assn. Southwestern U.S., AAAS. Author: Handbook of Medical Terminology, 1958, rev. 2d edit., 1972; The Meaning of Agapao and Phileo in the Greek New Testament, 1977; The Roman Numina, 1979; Sources of the Medical Vocabulary, 1980. Home: 2613 Starr Dr Waco TX 76710 Office: Baylor U Waco TX 76703

BUTLER, WILLIAM THOMAS, physician, univ. adminstr.; b. Boston, Aug. 10, 1932; s. Albert Quigg and Elizabeth West (Visknisski) B.; A.B., Oberlin Coll., 1954; M.D., Western Res. U., 1958; grad. Program for Health Systems Mgmt., Harvard Bus. Sch., 1974, grad. Advanced Mgmt. Program, 1979; m. Marilou Beutel, Apr. 26, 1957; children—Marilyn West, Thomas Charles, Robin Eileen; m. 2d, Carol Ann Pike, Nov. 23, 1977. Intern, resident in medicine Mass. Gen. Hosp., Boston, 1958-61; clin. asso., chief clin. asso., clin. investigator, acting head clin. immunology sect. Lab. Clin. Investigations Nat. Inst. Allergy and Infectious Diseases, NIH, 1961-66; asst. prof. Baylor Coll. Medicine, Houston, 1966-68, asso.

prof., 1968-71, prof. microbiology and immunology and internal medicine, 1971—, asso. dean, 1973-74, dean admissions, 1974-77, acting exec. v.p., 1976-77, exec. v.p., dean, 1977-79, pres., 1979—. Mem. Am. Assn. Immunologists, Am. Soc. Clin. Investigation, Am. Soc. Microbiology, Infectious Diseases Soc. Am., So. Soc. Clin. Investigation, Transplantation Soc., Assn. Acad. Health Centers, Assn. Am. Med. Colls., Council of Deans, AMA, Harris County Med. Soc., Houston Acad. Medicine, Tex. Med. Assn., Sigma Xi, Alpha Omega Alpha. Methodist. Club: Sugar Creek. Contbr. articles to med. jours. Office: 1200 Moursund St Houston TX 77030

BUTTS, JANE ESTHER DICKSON, comml. real estate broker; b. Washington, Apr. 3, 1920; d. Walter Stone and Helene Marguerite (Guerdrum) Dickson; student Lamar Coll. 1964; grad. Tex. A. and M. U., 1979; m. Jack Rockward Butts, Mar. 25, 1952; children—Victor Stone, Raymond Carl, Lawrence Lee, Loretta Ann. Operator pvt. dancing sch. Savannah, Ga., from 1936; traveling producer Empire Producers, Washington, 1937; singer, dancer various night clubs, Washington and Cleve. 1938; mem., dancer Roxyettes, Gay Foster Dancers, N.Y.C., Atlanta, Balt. 1939; instr. dancing, N.Y.C., 1940-41, Washington, 1941-43, Hawaii, 1946-47, Fla., 1947-54, Beaumont, Tex. 1954-63; real estate salesman, Beaumont, 1964-66; broker Butts Real Estate Co., Port Arthur, Tex. 1966—; cons. comml. real estate, specializing in shopping center leasing and mgmt. Mem. Greater Port Arthur C. of C. 1968-78; mem. Pride in Port Arthur 1971-76, chmn., 1976. Recipient numerous letters of appreciation. Democrat. Christian Scientist and Methodist. Writer 57 songs 1950—. Home: 2312 Procter St Port Arthur TX 77640 Office: 4349 Procter St Port Arthur TX 77640

BUTTS, KENNETH EUGENE, dietitian; b. Milledgeville, Ga., Feb. 25, 1954; s. George and Eliza Bell (Williams) B.; B.S., Auburn U., 1976; m. July 3, 1979. Staff nutritionist, research, div. preventive medicine U. Ala., 1976-77; patient service mgr. Saga Food Corp., Evansville, Ind., 1978-79; dietitian Central State Hosp., Milledgeville, Ga., 1979. food service dir. Ga. Regional Hosp., Atlanta, 1979—. Tchr. Bible class Washington Rehab. Center; v.p. Friends in Christ, Christian Teaching Fellowship. Served with USAR, 1977. Mem. Am. Dietetic Assn. (asso.), Am. Soc. Hosp. Food Service Adminstrs. Home: 847 N Clark St Milledgeville GA 31061

BUTTS, MICHELE TUCKER, educator; b. Clarksville, Tenn., Dec. 23, 1952; d. Ray Runyon and Ruth (Bumpus) B.; B.A., Austin Peay State U., 1973, M.A., 1974; postgrad. U. Ky., 1975, U. N.Mex., 1976-79. Asst. editor, bus. mgr., advt. mgr. Austin Peay State U. student newspaper, 1971-72; tchr. Houston County (Tenn.) Schs., 1974-75; instr. Prestonsburg Community Coll., 1975-79, asst. prof. history and journalism, 1979—; speaker on Indian lore and U.S. western history. Mem. Big Sandy Area Devel. Dist. Environ. Quality Com.; cons. on Indian lore Lonesome Pine council Order of Arrow Boy Scouts Am. Recipient Halbert Harvill Citizenship award Austin Peay State U., 1973, Service award Lonesome Pine council Order of Arrow Boy Scouts Am., 1977. Mem. Orgn. Am. Historians, Am. Hist. Assn., Ky. Assn. Tchrs. History, Ky. Hist. Soc., Ky. Assn. Community and Jr. Coll. Profs., Anthropologists and Sociologists Ky., Sierra Club, Wilderness Soc., Environ. Action Ky. Conservation Com., Order Indian Wars, Alpha Mu Gamma, Phi Alpha Theta. Baptist. Home: 118 Westminister St Prestonsburg KY 41653 Office: Prestonsburg Community Coll Prestonsburg KY 41653

BUXEDA, ROBERTO, ophthalmologist; b. Arecibo, P.R., Jan. 4, 1916; s. Miguel and Ambrosina (Velez) B.; student U. P.R., 1933-36; M.D., Hahnemann Med. Coll., 1940; M.Sc., U. Pa., Phila., 1951; m. Helen Dolores Dacri, Apr. 17, 1941; children—Roberto Miguel, Adriano Roberto. Intern, Woman's Hosp., Phila., 1940; resident Ophthlamic Inst. P.R., San Juan, 1948-49, McGuire VA Hosp., Richmond, Va., 1949-51; co. physician South P.R. Sugar Co., Guanica, 1941-43; physician VA Hosp., New Castle, Del., 1946-47; practice medicine specializing in ophthalmology, San Juan, 1951—; clin. prof. ophthalmology U. P.R., 1952—; advisor Eye Bank P.R., 1954—. Pres. fin. campaign P.R. chpt. Am. Cancer Soc., 1961; dir. glaucoma clinics Lions Club P.R., 1960. Served with M.C., U.S. Army, 1943-46. Recipient Certificate of Admiration for treatment of physically handicapped Antilles Command Personnel, 1964; Recognition award Italian Am. Club P.R., 1967; diplomate Am. Bd. Ophthalmology. Fellow Am. Acad. Ophthalmology and Otolaryngology, A.C.S.; mem. Pan. Am. Assn. Ophthalmology, Barraquer Inst., P.R. Ophthalmol. Soc. (pres. 1953). Club: Lions. Contbr. articles on ophthalmology to med. jours. Home: 52 King's Ct San Juan PR 00911 Office: Ashford Med Center San Juan PR 00907

BUXTON, RONALD LOWELL, chem. co. exec.; b. St. Louis, Nov. 13, 1942; s. Orville Horace and Lillian Faye (Long) B.; B.S., Washington U., St. Louis, 1969; m. Roberta Ruth Boettger, Sept. 9, 1968; children—Amanda Ruth, Heather Faye. Chemist, Monsanto Co., St. Louis, 1969-72, mktg. tech. service rep., Springfield, Mass., 1974-77, sr. sales rep., Monroe, La., 1977—; mktg. specialist Rohm & Haas Pty. Ltd., Melbourne, Australia, 1972-74. Mem. Am. Chem. Soc., TAPPI. Episcopalian. Home: 16 Fair Oaks Dr Monroe LA 71203 Office: 1300 Post Oak Tower 5051 Westheimer St Houston TX 77056

BUYAMA, EDWARD T., JR., gen. contractor; b. Miami, Fla., Feb. 1, 1933; s. Edward T. and Gloria B.; student Furman U., 1951-52; m. Sandra Kay Mandeville, July 30, 1954; children—Jeannie Sue, Carol Lynn, Helen Kay, Patricia Ann, Susan Edwina. Bldg. insp. Met. Dade County (Fla.), 1960-62; sec., treas., co-owner Buyama Airconditioning Co., Miami, 1962—; owner, mgr. Miami Shores Electric Co., 1968—; sec.-treas. Bama Constrn. Co., Miami, 1978—. Bd. dirs. Ronald McDonald House South Fla., also gen. contractor-constrn. mgmt. cons. Served with USAF, 1951-53. Mem. Associated Builders and Contractors, Refrigeration Service Engrs. Soc. (past pres.), Am. Soc. Heating and Air Conditioning Engrs., Master Electricians Soc. (state v.p.), Vintage Automobile Club of Miami, Elec. Council Fla., Am. Legion. Democrat. Baptist. Clubs: Optimists, Old Glory Bass Anglers, Spot Lite, Everglades Sportsmen and Conservation. Home: 11611 W Biscayne Canal Rd Miami FL 33161 Office: 651 NW 106th St Miami FL 33150

BUZDAR, AMAN ULLAH, physician; b. M. Garh, Pakistan, Jan. 1, 1945; s. Nabi Bakhash and Bakhat Sawai Buzdar; came to U.S., 1968, naturalized, 1975; M.B.B.S., U. Punjab, 1967, F.Sc., B.Sc., 1962; m. Barbara Anne Whaley, Aug. 22, 1970; children—Aaron, Ben, Sarah. Intern, Kaukini Hosp., Honolulu, 1968-69; resident in gen. practice Maryview Hosp., Portsmouth, Va., 1969-70; resident in medicine Luth. Hosp., Cleve., 1971-72, Lakewood (Ohio) Hosp., 1970-71; sr. resident in medicine Norwalk (Conn.) Hosp., 1972-73, fellow in hematology-oncology, 1973-74; fellow in oncology U. Tex. System Cancer Center, M.D. Anderson Hosp. and Tumor Inst., Houston, 1974-75, faculty asso. in medicine (med. breast service), 1975-76, asst. internist, instr. medicine, 1976-77, asst. prof., internist medicine, 1977—. Diplomate Am. Bd. Internal Medicine (Oncology). Fellow A.C.P.; mem. AMA, Tex. Med. Assn., Am. Soc. Clin. Oncology, Am. Assn. Cancer Research, Harris County Med. Assn. Contbr. numerous articles, abstracts to profl. jours. Muslim. Home: 2642 Hodges Bend Sugarland TX 77478 Office: M D Anderson Hosp U Tex 6723 Bertner Ave Houston TX 77030

BYARS, EDWARD FORD, educator; b. Lincolnton, N.C., Mar. 22, 1925; s. Edward Hayes and Lois (Ford) B.; B.S. in Mech. Engring., Clemson U., 1946, M.C.E., 1950; Ph.D., U. Ill., 1957; m. Betsy Alice Cromer, June 25, 1950; children—Laurie, Betsy, Nan, Guy, Instr., Clemson U., 1947-53, asst. prof., 1953-55, asso. prof., 1957-60; instr. U. Ill., Champaign-Urbana, 1955-57; prof., chmn. dept. mech. engring. and mechanics W.Va. U., Morgantown, 1960-79, acting dean Coll. Engring., 1979—; cons. in field. Served with Signal Corps, U.S. Army, 1946-47. Mem. ASME, Soc. Exptl. Stress Analysis, Am. Acad. Mechanics, Am. Soc. Engring. Edn., Soaring Soc. Am., Sigma Xi, Tau Beta Pi, Pi Tau Sigma. Author: Engineering Mechanics of Deformable Bodies, 1963. Contbr. articles to profl. jours. Patentee in field. Home: 641 Vista Pl Morgantown WV 26505

BYARS, ILA PEARL, orgn. exec., civic worker; b. Travis, Tex., June 25, 1908; d. William Lafayette and Sibyl Allen (Massey) Byars; student pub. schs. With Mid-west States Telephone Co., Blanco, 1924-53; with Bigden Ins. and Real Estate, Tex., 1953-55; pvt. kindergarten tchr., Blanco, 1955-56; waitress various restaurants, 1956-62, 63-65; with Wall Furniture, also Wall Funeral Home, Blanco, 1952-53, 65-66; staff food dept. Blanco Mill Nursing Home, 1966—. County chmn. Am. Heart Assn., 1957-72, meml. and campaign mgr., 1957-72. Bd. dirs. Blanco County unit Am. Cancer Soc., 1959-72, unit sec., 1971-74, pres., 1974-76; trustee Blanco Library, 1950-53, librarian, 1952-53; bd. dirs. Blanco County Tb Assn., 1951-53. Recipient Achievement citations Am. Heart Assn., 1970, 71, 73, Am. Cancer Soc., 1971. Mem. Blanco C. of C. (sec. 1967-72, dir. 1967-71), Daus. of Nile, Wesleyan Service Guild (co-founder 1952, pres. 1968—), Order Eastern Star (past matron, sec.). Methodist. (dir. vacation Bible sch. 1968—, Sunday sch. tchr. 1949—, mem. pastoral com. 1972-75, chmn. commn. on elderly 1974—, sec. council on ministries 1977—, chmn. night circle 1979—). Home: PO Box 246 Blanco TX 78606

BYERLEY, WILLIAM MUELLER, accountant; b. Wichita, Kans., Nov. 5, 1953; s. William A. and Jennie E. (Mueller) B.; B.B.A., So. Meth. U., 1975, M.B.A., 1976. Mem. audit staff Price Waterhouse & Co., Dallas, 1976—, mem. sr. audit staff, 1979—. Mem. Tex. Soc. C.P.A.'s, So. Meth. U. M.B.A. Alumni Assn., So. Meth. U. Alumni Assn. Republican. Presbyterian. Office: Price Waterhouse & Co 4500 First International Bldg Dallas TX 75270

BYERS, BRENT EUGENE, architect; b. Hoisington, Kans., Sept. 17, 1950; s. Neal Eugene and Mary Nell (Bertles) B.; B.Arch., Okla. State U., 1973. Project architect Jack Corgan and Assos., Dallas, 1973-74; project architect Corgan Assos., Inc., Dallas, 1975-77, asso., 1977-78, v.p., 1978—. Mem. Dallas C. of C. Career Adv. Bd., 1977. Mem. AIA (chmn. adv. com. to Skyline High Sch., Dallas; chmn. adv. com. to El Centro Community Coll.; certificate of merit 1974, delineation citation 1974, 80, delineation honor award 1975, 78, 80), Tau Sigma Delta, Sigma Tau. Mem. Christian Ch. (Disciples of Christ). Home: 3623 Routh St Unit 3 Dallas TX 75219 Office: 1509 Main St Suite 1600 Dallas TX 75201

BYERS, WILLIAM SEWELL, elec. engr., educator; b. Ironton, Ohio, Oct. 3, 1925; s. William T. and Anna M. (Sewell) B.; B.E.E., Ohio State U., 1951; M.B.A., Rollins Coll., 1966; M.Eng., Pa. State U., 1969, M.Ed., 1972; Ed.D., Nova U., 1976; B.A., U. State N.Y., 1977; D.Eng., Clayton U., 1978; m. Marjorie E. Reidel, Dec. 28, 1946; children—Thomas William, Robert M., Catherine G. Broadcast engr. Crosley Broadcasting Corp., Columbus, Ohio, 1949-51; dist. engr. Gen. Elec. Co., Syracuse, N.Y., 1951-55; staff engr., engring. mgr. Martin Marietta Aerospace Corp., Orlando, Fla., 1955-75; asso. prof. elec. engring. tech. U. Ala., Tuscaloosa, 1975—; academic advisor tech. Institut National d'Electricitie et d'Electronique at Boumerdes, Algeria, 1977-78. Adj. faculty Seminole Jr. Coll., Fla. So. Coll., Valencia Community Coll. Trustee Atlantic States U. Amateur radio operator. Nat. Sci. Found. grantee, 1968-69. Registered profl. engr., Fla., Ala. Mem. Soc. Wireless Pioneers, AAUP, Am. Soc. for Engring. Edn., Nat., Ala. socs. profl. engrs., Mensa (proctor for Western Ala.), IEEE (sr.), Capstone Engring. Soc., Pa. State Amateur Radio Club (hon. life), Tau Alpha Pi, Eta Kappa Nu. Home: 28L Northwood Lake Northport AL 35476 Office: Box 1941 University AL 35486

BYRD, CHATTIE PRICE, biol. supply co. exec.; b. Union County, N.C., Oct. 10, 1929; d. John Henry and Bertha Isabel (Chaney) Price; B.S. in Home Econs., U. N.C., Greensboro, 1951, postgrad. in edn., 1966; m., Feb. 18, 1951; children—Brenda Faye, Carol Lynette. Office worker Kayser-Roth Co., Burlington, N.C., 1951-55; public relations dir. Ewing Motors, Lincoln-Mercury dealer, Burlington, 1960-64; public sch. tchr. Alamance County Sch. System, Burlington, 1966-69; office mgr. Bobbitt Labs., Burlington, 1969-74; adminstrv. asst. Caroling Biol. Supply Co., Burlington, 1974—. Mem. Am. Bus. Women's Assn., U. N.C. Alumni Assn., Am. Home Econs. Assn. for Profls. Democrat. Presbyterian. Home: 1609 Inglewood Dr Burlington NC 27215 Office: Caroling Biol Supply Co 2700 York Rd Burlington NC 27215

BYRD, DANIEL MADISON, III, pharmacologist; b. Detroit, Dec. 30, 1940; s. Daniel Madison and Mary Jeanne (McKay) B.; B.A. with honors, Yale U., 1963, Ph.D., 1971; m. Jan. 26, 1963 (div. 1978); children—Mary Katherine, Laura McKay, Daniel Madison IV. Research asso. U. Md., Balt., 1970; vis. scientist Nat. Cancer Inst., Balt., 1971; research asso., oncology div. Johns Hopkins Med. Sch., Balt., 1971-72; cancer research scientist Roswell Park Meml. Inst., Buffalo, 1972-75; asst. prof. dept. pharmacology Coll. Medicine, U. Okla., Oklahoma City, 1975—. Mem. Am. Chem. Soc., Am. Soc. Microbiology, Am. Contract Bridge League, Les Amis du Vin, Sigma Xi. Methodist. Home: 6412 Urschel Ct NW Oklahoma City OK 73132 Office: Dept Pharmacology Okla U Health Scis Center PO Box 26901 Oklahoma City OK 73190

BYRD, GARY JEFFERSON, psychiatrist; b. San Saba, Tex., Dec. 31, 1941; s. James Jefferson and Grace Maurine (Rogers) B.; B.A. in Math., U. Tex., 1963, B.S. in Chemistry, 1963; M.D., Baylor Coll. Medicine, 1967; m. Mary Eugenia Pettigrove, June 28, 1969; children—John Jefferson, Lisa Ann. Intern, Ben Taub Gen. Hosp., 1967-68; resident, Baylor affiliated program, 1968-71; practice medicine, specializing in psychiatry and legal medicine, Houston, 1971—; staff Meth., St. Lukes, Tex. Children's hosps. (all Houston); instr. psychiatry Baylor Coll. Medicine, Houston, 1971, asst. prof. psychiatry, 1973-78; vis. lectr. Tex. Woman's U., Denton, 1973-75. Served to maj., M.C., USAF, 1971-73. Mem. Harris County Med. Soc., Houston Acad. Medicine, Am., Tex. med. assns., Houston Group Psychotherapy Assn. (pres. 1979-81), Southwestern Group Psychotherapy Soc., Am. Group Psychotherapy Soc., Am. Psychiatric Assn., Houston Soc. Adolescent Psychiatry, Phi Beta Pi. Republican. Episcopalian. Home: PO Box 42496 Houston TX 77042 Office: Suite 112 Plaza Level Lifemark Bldg 3800 Buffalo Speedway Houston TX 77098

BYRD, HARRY FLOOD, JR., newspaper editor, U.S. senator; b. Winchester, Va., Dec. 20, 1914; s. Harry F. and Anne Douglas (Beverley) B.; student Va. Mil. Inst., 1931-33, U. Va., 1933-35; numerous hon. degrees; m. Gretchen B. Thomson, August 9, 1941; children—Harry Flood III, Thomas Thomson, Beverley Bigelow (Mrs. G. P. Greenhaigh III). Editor Winchester (Va.) Evening Star, 1935—; pub. Harrisonburg (Va.) Daily News-Record, 1937—; pres., dir. Rockingham Pub. Co., 1946—; dir. H. F. Byrd, Inc., 1948—; dir. Asso. Press, 1950-59, 61-66, v.p., mem. exec. com.; mem. U.S. Senate from Va., 1965—; mem. Va. Senate, 1947-65, author state automatic tax reduction law. Mem. State Democratic Central Com., 1940-66. Served as lt. comdr. USNR, 1942-46, exec. officer Patrol bombing squadron, Pacific. Recipient Honor Medal Freedoms Found. Mem. VFW, Am. Legion. Clubs: Rotary (pres. Winchester 1940-41); Nat. Press, Army-Navy (Washington). Home: 411 Tennyson Ave Winchester VA 22601 Office: Senate Office Bldg Washington DC 20510

BYRD, LANIER ELDRIDGE, educator; b. San Antonio, Aug. 3, 1946; s. Napoleon P. and Gwendolyn Lorraine (Sandles) B.; A.A., St. Philip's Coll., 1966; B.S., Prairie View A & M U., 1969, M.S., 1973; m. Deborah Elaine Jones, Apr. 9, 1976; children—Shanna Lorraine, Sean Lanier. Exec. trainee Joske's of Tex., 1967-69; tchr. physics and biology San Antonio Ind. Sch. Dist., 1969-72; instr. biology St. Philips Coll., San Antonio, 1972-76, asst. prof., 1976—, chmn. dept. biology, 1975—; lab. worker San Antonio State Hosp., 1966-67, 69; cons. San Antonio Ind. Sch. Dist., 1978, NSF Resource Center for Sci. and Engring., 1978, Acad. Health Scis., Fort Sam Houston, Tex., 1979. Mem. AAUP (v.p. St. Philip's Coll. chpt. 1975-77), S.W. Football Assn., S.W. Basketball Assn., Tex. Jr. Coll. Tchrs. Assn., Beta Beta Beta, Kappa Kappa Psi, Alpha Phi Alpha. Mem. Pentecostal Ch. Home: 5907 Woodgreen St San Antonio TX 78218 Office: 2111 Nevada St San Antonio TX 78203

BYRD, LAWRENCE HERMAN, oil co. exec.; b. Jacksonville, Tex., May 22, 1915; s. Herman Decalb and Bonnie Inez (Boaz) B.; B.S. in Chem. Engring., Tex. A. and M. U., 1937; m. Elsie Lee Carter, Oct. 24, 1937; 1 dau., Linda Lee. With Exxon Co., U.S.A., 1937—, asst. dist. supt., New London, Tex., 1948-52, area supt., Los Angeles, 1952-54, asst. div. supt., Midland, Tex., 1954-59, prodn. operations mgr., Houston, 1959-61, area prodn. mgr., Dallas, 1961-63, area mgr., Dallas, 1963-65, div. prodn. mgr., Midland, 1965—. Pres. bd. trustees Midland Meml. Hosp., 1975-76; pres. Permian Basin Oil Show, 1977, 78, Jr. Achievement of Midland, 1967-68. Served with C.W.S., AUS, 1942-45. Mem. Am. Inst. Mining Engrs., Am. Petroleum Inst., N.Mex., Tex. Mid-Continent oil and gas assns., Okla. Petroleum Council, W. Tex. C. of C., Midland Petroleum Club. Home: 15 Bristol Ct Midland TX 79701 Office: PO Box 1600 Midland TX 79702

BYRD, RICHARD EARL, educator; b. Houston, July 22, 1927; s. B.M. and Pansy (Borders) B.; B.S., U. Houston, 1965; M.Ed., Sam Houston State U., 1976; m. Laque Yeager, June 10, 1973; children—Charles Edgar, Sharon Elaine, David Lee. Acct., Braden Steel Corp., 1949-52; carpenter, operator, tng. supr. Shell Chem. Co., Deer Park, Tex., 1952-76; instr. instrument tech. San Jacinto Coll., 1973—, chmn. dept., 1976—; owner, mgr. Instrument Service Co., Deer Park, 1975—; cargo agt. Internat. Shipping Co., 1975—. Chmn., Bd. Parks and Recreation Deer Park, 1960, asst. chmn., 1961; bus. mgr. Little League, Teenage League Deer Park, 1963, 64; dir. Royal Ambassadors, 1st Bapt. Ch., 1962-64, tchr. Sunday sch., 1958-61. Served with USN, 1945-46. Mem. Instrument Soc. Am. (sr.), Phi Delta Kappa. Democrat. Home: 127 W 6th St Deer Park TX 77536 Office: 8060 Spencer Hwy Pasadena TX 77505

BYRD, ROBERT CARLYLE, U.S. senator; b. North Wilkesboro, N.C., Nov. 20, 1917; s. Cornelius Sale and Ada (Kirby) B.; student Beckley Coll., Concord Coll., Morris Harvey Coll., 1950-51, Marshall U., 1951-52; J.D., Am. U., 1963; m. Erma Ora James, May 29, 1937; children—Mona Carole, Marjorie Ellen. Mem. W.Va. Ho. of Dels., 1946-50, W.Va. Senate, 1950-52; mem. 83d-85th Congresses, 6th Dist. W.Va.; U.S. senator from W.Va., 1959—. Democrat. Baptist. Office: 133 Senate Office Bldg Washington DC 20510*

BYRD, TYRONE, banker; b. Coweta County, Ga., Feb. 21, 1944; s. Otis B. and Lois B.; B.B.A., U. Ga., 1966, M.B.A., 1976; postgrad. Columbia U., 1972; m. Sylvia R. Boyd, Sept. 29, 1968. Tchr., coach Coweta County (Ga.) Bd. Edn., 1967; dist. accounting supr. Ga. Power Co., Hartwell, 1970-71; accounts exec., bond trader Merrill Lynch Pierce Fenner & Smith, Athens, Ga., 1971-75; exec. v.p., corp. sec. Mchts. & Farmers Bank, Comer, Ga., 1976—; fin. and investment counselor. Group leader Heart Fund; chmn. fin. area United Way. Served to capt. Med. Service Corps U.S. Army, 1967-70. Decorated Bronze Star, Air medal. Callaway fellow, 1964-66; recipient certificate of merit State of Ga., 1962. Mem. Young Bankers Assn., Bank Adminstrn. Inst., Jaycees (bd. dirs., 1974, chmn. various projects, Athens, man of yr. award, 1975). Beta Gamma Sigma, Sigma Iota Epsilon. Republican. Baptist. Home: 188 Dunwoody Dr Athens GA 30605 Office: Sunset Ave Comer GA 30629

BYRDSONG, NAPOLEON GOODWIN, educator; b. Carthage, Tex., Mar. 24, 1934; s. Napoleon and Roberta Hortense (Goodwin) B.; B.S., Bishop Coll., 1954; M.Ed., Prairie View A. and M. U., 1963; Ed.D., East Tex. State U., 1980; m. Ruth Marie Hunter, June 10, 1960; children—Napoleon Goodwin III, Lissa Hortense. Tchr., band dir. Mary Brown High Sch., Smithville, Tex., 1954-57; tchr. spl. edn. Longview (Tex.) Public Schs., 1960-69; rep. N.Y. Life Ins. Co., 1970-73; asst. prof. edn. Jarvis Christian Coll., Hawkins, Tex., 1974—. Served with U.S. Army, 1957-59. Mem. NEA, Tex. Soc. Coll. Tchrs. Edn., Tex. State Tchrs. Assn., Tex. Assn. Tchr. Educators, Phi Delta Kappa, Kappa Delta Pi. Democrat. Baptist. Clubs: Masons. Home: 8 Carver Longview TX 75601 Office: Jarvis Christian Coll Hawkins TX 75765

BYRNE, IRENE HART, city ofcl.; b. Brookhaven, Miss., Sept. 8, 1917; d. Judge L. and Ethel Belle (Roberts) Hart; A.A., Copiah Lincoln Jr. Coll., 1938; student Whitworth Coll., 1968-69; postgrad. Miss. State U., also certified as city clk., tax collector and assessor; m. Tommie C. Byrne, Sept. 23, 1939; children—Patricia (Mrs. Frank Emerson), Tim, Kathy (Mrs. Gary Nix). Tchr., basketball coach Fair Oak-Springs Sch., Brookhaven, 1938-39; bookkeeper Office of County Supt. Edn., Brookhaven, 1949-52; dep. chancery clk. Lincoln County, Brookhaven, 1952-68; with Office of Sheriff, Brookhaven, 1968, First Fed. Savs. & Loan Assn., Brookhaven, 1968-69, mcpl. clk., treas. City of Brookhaven, 1969—. Mem. Internat. Inst. Municipal Clks. (mem. election adminstrn. com., cert.), Mcpl. Treas.'s Assn. U.S. and Can., Internat. City Clks. Assn., Miss. Municipal City Clks., Tax Assessors and Tax Collectors Assn. (treas. 1978-79, cert.), Brookhaven Bus. and Profl. Womens Club, Beta Sigma Phi. Club: Camellia (Brookhaven). Home: 1051 S Church St Brookhaven MS 39601 Office: S Whitworth Ave PO Box 560 Brookhaven MS 39601

BYRNE, WILLIAM JOSEPH, real estate exec.; b. N.Y.C., Nov. 19, 1940; s. Michael Joseph and Helen (O'Niell) B.; B.S., Boston Coll., 1962; m. Mary Katherine Burnett, June 23, 1974; children—Tara, Erin, Moire. Project gen. mgr. Boise Cascade, Lake Ariel, Pa., 1968-72; regional dir. sales and mktg. Larwin Devel., 1973-74; v.p. mktg. and real estate Palmetto Dunes Resort, Inc., Hilton Head Island, S.C., 1976-77; pres. Dunes Mktg. Group, Hilton Head Island, 1978—. Mem. Am. Land Devel. Assn. Republican. Roman Catholic. Club: N.Y. Athletic. Home: 125 Walker Dr Hilton Head Island SC 29928 Office: PO Box 5628 Hilton Head Island SC 29928

CABASSO, ISRAEL, polymer scientist; b. Jerusalem, Nov. 17, 1942; came to U.S., 1973, naturalized, 1975; B.S. in Chemistry and Physics, Hebrew U., Jerusalem, 1966, M.S. in Polymer Chemistry with distinction, 1968; Ph.D., Weizmann Inst. Sci., 1972. Research asso. plastics Weizman Inst., 1973; research asst., instr. chemistry Profl. Sci. and Tech. Sch., Hebrew U., 1973-78; sr. investigator polymer dept., then group leader Gulf South Research Inst., New Orleans, 1974-76, mgr. polymer dept., 1976—; clin. asso. prof. La. State U. Med. Center; adj. prof. U. Miss. Served to capt. Israeli Army, 1961-71. Mem. Am. Chem. Soc. Israeli Chem. Soc. Author papers in field; also books; patentee. Office: PO Box 26518 New Orleans LA 70186

CABE, ROBERT DUDLEY, lawyer; b. Little Rock, June 25, 1942; s. Robert Lee and Dorris Lucille (Saugey) C.; B.A., Hendrix Coll., 1963; LL.B., Duke, 1966; m. Gloria Sue Burford, Aug. 18, 1963; children—Meredith Elizabeth, Matthew Robert. Admitted to Ark. bar, 1966, since practiced in Little Rock; with firm Wright, Lindsey & Jennings, 1966—, partner, 1970—. Chmn. bd. trustees Hendrix Coll. Mem. Am., Ark., Pulaski County bar assns. Club: Little Rock (v.p.), Capital. Home: 415 Colonial Ct Little Rock AR 72205 Office: 2200 Worthen Bank Bldg Little Rock AR 72201

CABLER, FLOSSIE CRUM, nurse, hosp. ofcl.; b. Sopchoppy, Fla., Mar. 27, 1929; d. Hardy A. and Rosa Lee (Stephens) C.; diploma Fla. State Hosp. Sch. Nursing, 1951; student St. Joseph's Coll., North Windham, Maine, 1977—; m. Wiley F. Cabler, Mar. 14, 1953 (dec.); children—Ronald Wiley, Donald Franklin. Staff nurse Tallahassee Meml. Hosp., 1952-53; head nurse admissions, supr. evening shift W.T. Edwards Tb Hosp., Tallahassee, 1953-61; supr. night shift N.E. Fla. State Hosp., Macclenny, 1961-63, asst. dir. nursing, 1963-66, dir. nursing, 1966-79, specialist nursing standards, 1979—. Adv. council Coll. Nursing, Lake City (Fla.) Community Coll. Mem. Am. Nurses Assn., Fla. Nurses Assn. Democrat. Mem. Ch. of Christ. Home: 232 Denise St Jacksonville FL 32218 Office: NE Fla State Hosp Hwy 121 Macclenny FL 32063

CABRAL, GUY ANTONY, virologist, educator; b. Azores, Portugal, Dec. 15, 1938; s. Antonio and Mary (Andrade) C.; came to U.S., 1948; B.A. (Univ. scholar), U. Mass., 1967; M.S. (NSF fellow), U. Conn., 1970, Ph.D. (NSF fellow), 1973; m. Francine Marciano, Aug. 31, 1969; children—Beth Anne, Wayne Anthony, Allison Marie. Postdoctoral fellow Baylor Coll. Medicine, Houston, 1974, research asso., 1974-75, viral immunologist, 1974—, asst. prof., 1976-78; asst. prof. Med. Coll. Va., Va. Commonwealth U., Richmond, 1978—; cons. in field. Served with AUS, 1964-67; Vietnam. Recipient German prize German Consulate, Boston, 1967; NIH fellow, 1975, 76. Mem. Am. Electron Microscopy Soc., Am. Soc. Microbiology, AAAS, Am. Soc. Parasitology, Phi Eta Sigma, Phi Kappa Phi. Roman Catholic. Research in hepatitis type B components for vaccines, virus induced cell transformation. Home: 1500 Elmart Ln Richmond VA 23235

CABRERA, LANDELINO CESAR, physician; b. Matanzas, Cuba, Sept. 25, 1923; came to U.S., 1956, naturalized, 1975; s. Antonio Abad and Matilde de la Caridad (Hernandez) C.; B.S., Inst. Secondary Instrn. of La Vibora (Cuba), 1947; M.D., U. Havana, 1956; m. Melba Virginia Xiques, July 25, 1956; 1 dau., Mary Elizabeth. Intern, Ky. Bapt. Hosp., Louisville, 1956-58; resident Michael Reese Hosp., Chgo., 1958-59; fellow Am. Arias Maternity Hosp., Havana, 1959-60; resident in pediatrics Jackson Meml. Hosp., Variety Children's Hosp., Miami, Fla., 1960-61; practice medicine specializing in pediatrics, Camaguey, Cuba 1961-67; mem. staff Mann (W.Va.) Appalachian Regional Hosp., 1968-69, N.J. State Hosp., Greystone Park, 1970-73; chief of pediatrics Holden (W.Va.) Hosp., 1969-70; med. dir. Sunland Tng. Center, Marianna, Fla., 1973-76; practice medicine specializing in pediatrics, Marianna, Fla., 1976—; mem. staff Jackson Hosp., 1976—. Diplomate Am. Bd. Family Practice. Mem. Am. Acad. Family Physicians, AMA (Physician Recognition award 1977-80), Fla. Med. Assn., Cuban Med. Assn. in Exile, Panhandle Med. Soc. (v.p. 1975), Fla. Acad. Family Physicians. Republican. Roman Catholic. Club: Rotary. Home: 700 College St Marianna FL 32446 Office: 802 4th St Marianna FL 32446

CABRI, PHILIP EUGENE, sales and mktg. exec.; b. Manorville, L.I., N.Y., Apr. 1, 1940; s. Eugene and Eleanor (Dittmeier) C.; student St. Bernard Coll., 1958-60; m. Gloria Jane Thomas, June 20, 1959; children—D'ete, Gina. Fingerprint clk. FBI, Washington, 1959-60; produce mgr. A & P Tea Co., Huntsville, Ala., 1960-63; asst. mgr. Bruno Foods, Cullman, Ala., 1963-65; store mgr. Sears, Roebuck & Co., Cordele, Ga., 1965-68; with Redman Industries, Americus, Ga., 1968-71; with Winston Industries, Double Springs, Ala., 1971—, v.p. sales and mktg., 1976—. Mem. Ala. Mobile Home Inst. (dir. 1977), S. Central Mfd. Housing Inst. (chmn. show com. 1978-79). Roman Catholic. Clubs: Larkwood, Elks. Home: 1469 Longbrook Dr Cullman AL 35055 Office: PO Box 347 Double Springs AL 35553

CACCAMISE, GENEVRA LOUISE BALL, librarian; b. Mayville, N.Y., July 22, 1934; d. Herbert Oscar and Genevra (Green) Ball; B.S., Stetson U., DeLand, Fla., 1956; M.L.S., Syracuse U., 1967; m. Alfred Edward Caccamise, July 7, 1974. Tchr. grammar sch., Sanford, Fla., 1956-57, elementary sch., Longwood, Fla., 1957-58; tchr., librarian Enterprise (Fla.) Sch., 1958-63; librarian, media specialist Boston Ave. Sch., DeLand, 1963—; area dir. for Volusia County (Fla.) Edn. Assn., 1963-65. Charter mem. West Volusia Meml. Hosp. Aux., DeLand, 1962-80; Girl Scout leader, 1955-56; bd. dirs. Alhambra Villas Home Owners Assn., 1972-76; trustee DeLand Pub. Library, 1977—, also sec., v.p.; pres. Violet Garden Circle, 1975-77. Mem. AAUW (2d v.p. chpt. 1965-67, rec. sec. 1961-65, 78-80, 1st v.p. 1980—), Assn. Childhood Edn. (1st v.p. 1965-66, corr. sec. 1963-65), DAR (chpt. registrar 1969-80; asst. chief page Continental Congress, Washington 1962-65), Bus. and Profl. Women's Club (corr. sec. DeLand 1968-71, 2d v.p. 1969-70), Stetson U. Alumni Assn. (class chmn. for ann. fund drive 1968—), Magna Charta Dames, Soc. Mayflower Desc., Colonial Dames XVII Century, Delta Kappa Gamma. Democrat. Episcopalian. An author Volusia County manual Instructing the Library Assistant, 1965. Home: PO Box 241 DeLand FL 32720

CACCIATORE, RONALD KEITH, lawyer; b. Donalsonville, Ga., Feb. 5, 1937; s. Angelo Dino and Myrtice Evelyn (Williams) C.; student Spring Hill Coll., 1955-56; B.A., U. Fla., 1960, J.D., 1963; m. Jean Jewell, Jan. 12, 1973; children—Rhonda, Cynthia, Sabina, Donna, Rex. Admitted to Fla. bar, 1963; asst. state atty., Tampa, Fla., 1963-65; asso. firm Yado, Keel & Nelson, Tampa, 1965-67; pvt. practice law, Tampa, 1967—. Lectr. criminal law continuing legal edn. Fla. bar; mem. adv. com. to Supreme Ct. Fla. on Criminal Justice, 1975. Trustee Hillsborough Community Coll., 1979—. Mem. Am., Hillsborough County (pres., dir.) bar assns., Fla. Bar (chmn. criminal law sect. 1977-78, chmn. 13th jud. circuit nominating commn. 1979-80), Am. Judicature Soc., Nat. Assn. Criminal Def. Lawyers, Acad. Fla. Trial Lawyers, Pi Kappa Phi, Tau Kappa Alpha, Delta Theta Phi. Club: Palma Ceia Golf and Country. Home: 2308 S Hesperides St Tampa FL 33609 Office: 725 E Kennedy Blvd Tampa FL 33602

CADDESS, JAMES HARVEY, engr. cons., ret. educator; b. Winona, Miss., Apr. 4, 1911; s. Leonard Taylor and Dora Alice (Townsend) C.; B.S., Tex. A. and M. U., 1932, M.M.E., 1934; m. Patti Orlie Minkert, June 21, 1935; 1 son, Hugh Neil. Jr. engr. Gulf Oil Corp., Port Arthur, Tex., 1934-35; sr. engr. George J. Fix Co., Dallas, 1937; pvt. practice engring. and surveying, Bryan, Tex., 1939-40; with Tex. A. and M. U., College Station, 1940—, asst. prof. mech. engring., 1947-53, asso. prof., 1953-76, prof. emeritus, 1976—; vis. prof. Bangladesh U. for Engring. and Tech., 1954-58; tchr. metallurgy Kelly AFB, Tex., 1969-76; cons. engring., 1965—. Bd. dirs. Easter Seal campaign, 1975. Served with U.S. Army, W.W. II. Recipient Distinguished Faculty award Tex. A. and M. U., 1966; registered profl. engr., Tex. Mem. Nat., Tex. socs. profl. engrs., Am. Soc. Engring. Edn., Am. Soc. Metals, Am. Powder Metals Inst., Ret. Officers Assn., Am. Def. Preparedness Assn., Nat. Ret. Tchrs. Assn., Res. Officers Assn., ASTM, Pi Tau Sigma, Tau Beta Sigma. Baptist. Club: Kiwanis (pres. College Station 1970-71, lt. gov. div. 9 1976-77). Author: (with Virgil M. Faires and Sherman D. Chambers) Analytic Mechanics, 1952, Engineering Problems, 1957, 66. Home and Office: 707 S Haswell Dr Bryan TX 77801

CADDY, MICHAEL DOUGLAS, lawyer; b. Long Beach, Calif., Mar. 23, 1938; s. Frank Edward and Tabitha (Miles) C.; B.S. in Fgn. Service, Georgetown U., 1960; J.D., N.Y. U., 1966. Admitted to D.C. bar, 1970, since practiced in Washington and Tex.; exec. dir. Com. on Pub. Affairs, McGraw-Edison Co., N.Y.C., 1960-61; asst. to lt. gov. N.Y., 1962-65; asst. to exec. v.p. N.A.M., N.Y.C., 1966-67; Washington liaison Gen. Foods Corp., 1968-70; asso. firm Gail, Lane, Powell & Kilcullen, 1970-74; legis. counsel Nat. Assn. Realtors, Washington, 1975-76; pres. Consumers Energy Found., Inc., Houston; exec. dir. Freedom Internat. Found., Inc., Washington; corp. sec. Am. Tax Reduction Found. Mem. Republican County Com., N.Y.C., 1965-66. Scholar, Intercollegiate Studies Inst., 1957-59. Mem. Am., D.C., Fed., Tex. bar assns., Am. Judicature Soc., Am. Econ. Assn., Am. Acad. Polit. and Social Sci., Internat. Platform Assn., Nat. Council Crime and Delinquency, Supreme Ct. Hist. Soc. Clubs: Union League (N.Y.C.); Capitol Hill, Nat. Economists (Washington). Author: The Hundred Million Dollar Payoff, 1974; How They Rig Our Elections, 1975. Home: 745 W Creekside Dr Houston TX 77024

CADENA, MARIO ANTONIO, health care adminstr.; b. Monterrey, Mex., Mar. 9, 1939; came to U.S., 1952, naturalized, 1963; s. Mario Jesus and Virginia (Davalos) C.; student El Centro Coll.; M.P.H., U. Mich., 1978; m. Consuelo Diaz, May 29, 1961; children—Virginia Eileen, Teresa J., Mario A. II, Marcos A., Frances A., Rita A., Rebecca E. Commd. 2d lt., USMC, 1957, advanced through grades to capt., 1968; pres. Aztec Airways, Ft. Worth, 1969-72; spl. rep. Southwestern Bell Telephone Co., Dallas, 1972-73; exec. dir. Los Barrios Unidos Community Clinic, Dallas, 1973-78; exec. dir. Community Health Centers of Dallas, 1978—; chmn. Rio Grande Fedn. Health Centers, Inc., San Antonio, 1978—. Pres. Dallas chpt. Mex. Am. Republicans of Tex., 1978—; pres. Tex. Assn. Mex. Am. C.'s of C., 1975-76, Bus. Hispanic Hall of Fame award, 1979; pres. Dallas Mex. C. of C., 1974-75; v.p. Dallas Mex. Am. Polit. Caucus, 1979; co-chmn. Mex. Am. Assembly for Civic Involvement, 1978—. Decorated 3 D.F.C.'s, 19 Air Medals. Mem. Am. Public Health Assn. (Presdl. award Latino Caucus 1978), Tex. Public Health Assn., Roman Catholic. Home: 3969 Lost Creek St Dallas TX 75224 Office: 912 Commerce St Suite 202 Dallas TX 75202

CADLE, DEAN, librarian, educator; b. Middlesboro, Ky., Jan. 16, 1920; s. David Bert and Dora (Brooks) C.; B.A., Berea Coll., 1947; postgrad. Columbia U., 1946, 64, Stanford, 1947-49, U. Kans., 1949; M.A., U. Iowa, 1950; postgrad. U. Tenn., 1951; M.S., U. Ky., 1957; m. Jo Lee Dannel, May 28, 1952. Lit. tchr. Union Coll., Barbourville, Ky., 1950-53, Detroit Inst. Tech., 1954-55; librarian Ky. Dept. Libraries, Frankfort, 1957-59, U. Ky., Lexington, 1959-60, U. Ky. S.E. Community Coll., Cumberland, 1960-66; asso. librarian, asso. prof. U. N.C., Asheville, 1966—. Bus. mgr. Western Review, Iowa City, 1949-50. Served with USAAF, 1942-46. Winner short story contest Tomorrow mag. and Creative Age Press, 1947. Wallace Stegner Creative Writing fellow Stanford U., 1947-48. Mem. Southeastern, N.C. library assns., Profl. Photographers Am. Editor: High Cost of Writing (Rebecca Caudill), 1965. Asst. editor Wilson Library Bull., N.Y.C., 1958, Gambit, 1950-53, Images, 1966-74; adv. and contbg. editor Appalachian Heritage, 1972—. Contbr. fiction and criticism to mags. including Yale Rev., Southwest Rev., Carolina Quar., Today, others. Home: 30 Valle Vista Dr Asheville NC 28804 Office: U NC Asheville NC 28804

CADY, CHARLES BERNARD, airline co. exec.; b. Crossett, Ark., Sept. 17, 1931; s. Clifton Lee and Vene Elvira (McPherson) C.; B.S. in B.A., Memphis State U., 1957; m. Clara Frances Clark, Aug. 9, 1953; children—Charles Lee, Beverly Claire, Roy Allen. With Gordons Transports, Inc., Memphis, 1956-57; housing mgmt. asst. Public Housing Adminstrn., Memphis, 1957-65; asst. mgr. Bus. Mgmt. Dept., Cessna Aircraft Co., Atlanta, 1965-69; controller Gen. Corrosion Service, Inc., Atlanta, 1969-70, Hangar One, Inc., Atlanta, 1971-76; v.p. Mackey Internat., Inc., Ft. Lauderdale, Fla., 1978—, Sunny South Aircraft Service, Inc., Ft. Lauderdale, 1977—, Charter Air Center, Inc., Ft. Lauderdale, 1976—. Co-founder Civil Def. Para-rescue team, Tenn., 1961; mem. Civil Air Patrol. Served with USMC, 1950-52. Decorated Purple Heart. Methodist. Club: Optimist. Home: 8407 SW 26 St Davie FL 33324 Office: 3116 S Andrews Ave Fort Lauderdale FL 33316

CADY, DAVID CHRISTIAN, structural engr.; b. Birmingham, Mich., May 7, 1931; s. Leonard A. and Alma C. Cady; B.S., Mich. Technol. U., 1957; m. Barbara Lee Brown, Nov. 20, 1950; children—Charlene, David Christian, Rosanna Lyn, Phillip Lee, Brenda Jean. Sr. design engr. Gen. Dynamics, San Diego, 1961-68; design engr. LTV Aerospace Corp., Dallas, 1968-70; systems engr. McDonnel Aircraft Co., St. Louis, 1971-73; machine operator, product engr. Gardner Denver, Reed City, Mich., 1973-75; mine supt., chief engr. Gold Bond Bldg. Products (Va.), 1976-78; structural design contract engr., Brunswick and Marion, Va., 1978-79, Nordam and Tulsa, Okla., 1979; aircraft structural design contract engr. Swearingon Aircraft Co., San Antonio, 1979—. Served with USAF, 1951-52.

CAFFEY, WILLIAM STEWART, educator; b. Gorman, Tex., Dec. 10, 1939; s. William Burton and Ina (Stewart) C.; B.A., Howard Payne Coll., 1962, M.Ed., 1965; m. Donajean Smith, July 20, 1963; children—Shana Marie, Terri Leigh, Michael David. Ordained to ministry Methodist Ch., 1963; tchr. Peace Corps, Morocco, 1962-63; minister Comanche Circuit, Methodist Ch., Comanche, Tex., 1963-65; tchr. Abernathy (Tex.) Jr. High Sch., 1965-74, Adult Edn. Program, Abernathy, 1968-72, Comanche Sch. Dist. Jr. High Sch., 1974—; lay pastor Fairy (Tex.) Meth. Ch., 1974-76. Vice pres. Abernathy Community Action Program, 1969-70; sch. rep. Dist. 17 Drug Edn. Program, 1971-72; mem. heritage com. Comanche County Bicentennial Celebration; bd. dirs. Central Plains Community Action Program, Inc., Hale County, 1970-73, Comanche County Hist. Soc. and Mus., 1974-77, Comanche Pub. Library, 1976—. Mem. Tex. State Tchrs. Assn. (life; chmn. Dist XVII necrology com. 1971-72), Tex. (charter life), Comanche (pres. 1977—) classroom tchrs. assns., NEA, Tex. Farm Bur. Democrat. Methodist. Author: Dialogs and Drills for Intermediate Students in English As a Foreign Language, 1963; Abernathy-Now and Then, 1969; The Sidney Community, Vol. 1; A Football Scoresheet 1940-70, 1971. Home: Sidney TX 76474

CAFFREY, WILLIAM DANIEL, lawyer; b. Morehead City, N.C., Nov. 5, 1928; s. Daniel F. and Audrey (Phillips) C.; B.S., Ind. State U., 1950; M.A., George Washington U., 1954; postgrad. U. N.C., 1954; J.D., Duke U., 1958; m. Ona Faye Willis, June 3, 1952; children—William Daniel, Russell Howard. Tchr., asst. prin. Aycock Jr. High Sch., Greensboro, N.C., 1950-54; prin. David Caldwell Sch., 1954-55; admitted to N.C. bar, 1958; mem. firm Nichols, Caffrey, Hill, Evans & Murrelle, and predecessor, 1958—; instr. Greensboro div. Guilford Coll., 1959—; adj. prof. civil trial practice and ins. Duke Sch. Law, 1969-78; mem. faculty Nat. Inst. Trial Advocacy Am. Bar Assn., 1973, 74, 79; past state chmn. Def. Research Inst. Past pres. Greensboro Sports Council; chmn. United Forces for Edn.; trustee Greensboro Coll., emeritus trustee Meth. Children's Home; bd. visitors High Point Coll. Served with USAAF, 1946-48. Mem. Am., N.C., Greensboro bar assns., 4th Circuit Judical Conf., Am. Judicature Soc., Internat. Assn. Ins. Counsel, Duke Law Alumni Assn. (past nat. pres.), Order of Coif, Blue Key, Phi Delta Phi, Pi Gamma Mu, Kappa Delta Pi. Democrat. Methodist (bishop's lay adv. com., chancellor, past parliamentarian West N.C. Conf.). Club: Civitan. Home: 2902 Round Hill Rd Greensboro NC 27408 Office: 500 W Friendly Ave Bldg Greensboro NC 27402

CAGLE, GORDON WAYNE, JR., chemist; b. Clark County, Ark., July 23, 1943; s. Gordon Wayne and Mildred Joy (Dawson) C.; B.S. in Chemistry, Ouachita Bapt U., 1965; Ph.D. in Chemistry, U. Ark., 1970; m. Carolyn Jane Berry; children—Dawson Wayne, Davilyn Ruth. Tech. info dept. supt., uranium resource evaluation project chemist, microanalysis group leader, nuclear div. Union Carbide Corp., Oak Ridge, 1969—. Mem. Am. Chem. Soc. Baptist. Club: Photography. Contbr. articles to profl. jours. Home: Route 3 Box 355 Clinton TN 37716 Office: Union Carbide Corp Nuclear Div Oak Ridge TN 37830

CAHOON, JACK, JR., mech. engr.; b. Quincy, Fla., July 11, 1925; s. Jack and Mattie Lee (Cox) C.; B.S.M.E., Auburn U., 1948; M.S.M.E., U. Okla., 1958; m. Patty Sue Moore, Mar. 2, 1952; children—Douglas Mark, Jamie Carol. Combustion engr. Republic Steel, Gadsden, Ala., 1948-50; commd. 2d lt. USAF, 1950, advanced through grades to lt. col., 1968; various positions research and devel., to 1972; ret., 1972; sr. systems engr. Teledyne Brown, Huntsville, Ala., 1972-74, cons. engr., pres. sub. co., 1974-76; tech. dir. ITT Henze Service, Mobile, Ala., 1977—. Served with U.S. Army, 1946-47. Decorated Meritorious Service medal, various others. Mem. Am. Soc. Non-Destructive Testing (level III examiner penetrant testing 1978—), Am. Welding Soc., ASME, Ret. Officers Assn. Home: 6055 Highland Circle S Mobile AL 36608 Office: 3100 Cottage Hill Rd Mobile AL 36606

CAHOON, KARL GLEN, JR., banker; b. Greenville, N.C., Nov. 27, 1947; s. Karl Glen and Frances (Jones) C.; B.S., East Carolina U., 1971; m. Christine Catherine Sharick, Jan. 23, 1971; 1 dau., Krista Grace. Field rep. Wachovia Bank & Trust Co., Williamston, N.C., 1971-73, credit mgr., Fayetteville, N.C., 1974-76; br. mgr. First Citizens Bank & Trust Co., Fayetteville, 1976—, asst. v.p., 1979—. Asst. chmn. small bus. div. Cumberland County United Way, 1977-78. Democrat. Mem. Disciples of Christ. Club: Moose. Home: 1442 Duncan St Fayetteville NC 28303 Office: First Citizens Bank & Trust Co PO Box 789 Fayetteville NC 28301

CAHOON, STUART NEWTON, physician, health adminstr., educator; b. Avalon, Pa., Dec. 9, 1916; s. Reno McCune and Belle Elizabeth (Newton) C.; B.A., Oberlin Coll., 1939; M.D., Temple U., 1943; postgrad. in psychoanalysis William-Alanson-White Inst., 1946-53; m. Myrtle Katherine Opdyke, Sept. 19, 1942; children—Elizabeth (Mrs. David Knickerbocker), Sandra (Mrs. Harry Anderson). Intern, Wilmington (Del.) Gen. Hosp., 1943-44; resident N.J. State Hosp., Greystone Park, 1944-47; clin. dir. N.J. State Hosp., Skillman, 1949-50; practice medicine specializing in psychoanalysis, Newark, 1950-56, Miami, Fla., 1957-60, also mem. staff Jackson Meml. Hosp., Miami; chief Mental Health Clinics, also mem. staff Leahi Hosp., Honolulu, 1961-64, clin. dir. Community Mental Health Center, also mem. staff Halifax Dist. Hosp., Daytona Beach, Fla., 1964-68; asso. prof. psychiatry U. Fla., Gainesville, 1968-71, asso. clin. prof. 1972-74, clin. prof., 1974—; dir. Community Mental Health, Tallahassee, 1971-74; dir. Fla. Div. Mental Health, Tallahassee, 1974-76; supr. Mental Health Program, Dist. 8, Ft. Myers, Fla., 1976—. Mem. adv. com. on library service To State Instns. Fla., 1974—. Fellow Royal Soc. Health; mem. Mental Health Assn. Fla., Hawaii Psychiat. Soc. (past pres.), Am. Psychiat. Assn. (life), Am. Acad. Psychotherapists, AAAS, Fla. Med. Assn. Fla. Psychiat. Soc., AMA. Contbr. articles to profl. jours. Home: 511 El Dorado W Cape Coral FL 33904 Office: PO Box 2258 Fort Myers FL 33902

CAHUE, ANTONIO, physician; b. Ciego de Avila, Cuba, Mar. 9, 1926; s. Antonio Vicente and Gertrudis Engracia (Romero) C.; B.S. cum laude, Inst. Secondary Instruction, Ciego de Avila, Cuba, 1944; M.D., Havana U. Med. Sch., 1951; m. Candelaria Bernardo, May 11, 1957; children—Monica Gertrudis, Claudina Veronica, Antonio Bernardo, Judith Lilliane, Teodoro Eugenio. Came to U.S., 1953, naturalized, 1961. Intern internal medicine U. Hosp., Calixto Garcia, Havana, Cuba, 1951-53; rotating intern Michael Reese Hosp., Chgo., 1953-54, fellow cardiovascular disease, 1954-55, resident internal medicine, 1956-57, clin. asst. thoracic medicine, 1958-61; resident VA Research Hosp., Chgo., 1957; med. dir. dept. inhalation therapy and pulmonary function lab. Methodist Hosp., Gary, Ind., 1965-68; practice medicine specializing in internal medicine and cardiology, Maitland, Fla., 1970—; mem. staff, chief of cardiology Mercy Hosp., Orlando, Fla.; mem. active staff Fla. Hosp., Orlando; clin. asst. prof. medicine U. South Fla., Tampa. Diplomate Am. Bd. Internal Medicine. Fellow Am. Coll. Chest Physicians, Am. Coll. Cardiology, A.C.P.; mem. A.M.A., Fla. Med. Assn., Orange County Med. Soc., Am. Heart Assn. (fellow Council Clin. Cardiology), Am. Thoracic Soc. Home: 1141 Covewood Trail Maitland FL 32751 Office: 331 N Maitland Ave Maitland FL 32751

CAIN, DONALD EZELL, judge; b. San Marcos, Tex., Oct. 8, 1921; s. Erie Montclair and Betty (Howell) C.; Asso. Sci., North Tex. Agrl. Coll., 1941; B.B.A., U. Tex., 1943, LL.B., 1948; m. Betty Anne Culberson, June 14, 1952; children—David, Dale, Donald Ezell, Randolph C. With contracts dept. Convair, 1948-50; admitted to Tex. bar, 1948; pvt. practice, Pampa, 1951-76; county atty. Gray County, 1955-69, county judge, 1971-77; dist. judge, 1977—. Bd. dirs. United Fund, 1956-60; pres. Adobe Walls council Boy Scouts Am. 1957-60. Served from ensign to lt. USNR, 1943-46, lt. 1950-51. Recipient Silver Beaver award Boy Scouts Am., 1958. Mem. Am., Gray County (pres. 1968) bar assns., State Bar Tex., C. of C. (dir. 1959-60), Am. Judicature Soc., Phi Alpha Delta. Democrat. Baptist. Rotarian (pres. 1958-59). Home: 1826 Williston St Pampa TX 79065 Office: Court House PO Box 2160 Pampa TX 79065

CAIN, LAURENCE SUTHERLAND, physicist; b. Washington, Feb. 4, 1946; s. Leighton Aubrey and Beatrice (Sutherland) C.; B.S., Wake Forest U., 1968; M.S., U. Va., 1970, Ph.D., 1973; m. Mary Jane

Dimmock, Aug. 21, 1971; 1 dau., Rebecca Anne. Research asso. U. N.C., Chapel Hill, 1973-76, lectr., 1976-78; asst. prof. physics Davidson Coll., 1978—. Recipient Scholar-Athlete award Atlantic Coast Conf., 1968; Va. Gov.'s fellow, 1972-73; DuPont fellow, 1971-72; Center Advanced Studies fellow 1970-71; U. Va. fellow, 1968-69. Mem. Am. Phys. Soc., Am. Assn. Physics Tchrs., AAAS, Phi Beta Kappa, Sigma Xi, Kappa Mu Epsilon. Democrat. Presbyterian. Research in elastic, mech. and defect properties of solids; contbr. articles to profl. jours. Office: Dept Physics Davidson Coll Davidson NC 28036

CAIN, WILLIAM ALLEN, lawyer; b. Chgo., Nov. 9, 1924; s. Albert Paul and May (Gainer) C.; LL.B., DePaul U., 1946, J.D., 1971; m. Audrey Helene Rosin, Nov. 28, 1953; children—May Lydia, Jordan Scott. Admitted to Ill. bar, 1947, Fla. bar, 1978; former partner law firm Cain & Cernek, Chgo.; adj. prof. law U. Miami Sch. Law, 1979-80. Pest mem. caucus com. Sch. Dist. 108, Highland Park, Ill.; counsel Skokie Police Patrolmen's Assn., North Suburban Police Patrolmen's Assn. Commr. Sheriff Lake County Commn. Narcotics and Drug Abuse, 1972-73. Past pres. S.E. Clavey Homeowners Assn., Highland Park, Ill.; flotilla staff officer USCG Aux., 1974-75, North Miami, Fla., 1980—. Mem. bd. assos. DePaul U., 1972-73. Mem. Am. (com. criminal law, mem. speakers bur.), Ill. (Am. citizenship com., com. on fair trial-free press 1977—), Fla. (com. on internat. law, unauthorized practice of law com., agr. com.), Dade County (com. on criminal law and ethics), Chgo. (past chmn. def. of prisoners com.; chmn. com. narcotics and drug abuse 1972) bar assns., Chgo. Trial Lawyers Club, Assn. Def. Lawyers, Internat. Platform Assn., Am. Guild Variety Artists (mem. Chgo. br. exec. com., chmn. 1968), Nat. Assn. Def. Lawyers in Criminal Cases (Ill. chmn. strike force 1976-77), Am. Judicature Soc., Assn. Trial Lawyers Am., Nat. Geog. Soc., Vol. Talent Pool Highland Park, Ill. Mem. B'nai B'rith (dir. Lincolnwood 1974-75). Club: Belmont Yacht (dir. 1977-78). Profl. hypnotist, lectr. Starred on Pantomine Party, WBKB-TV, Chgo., 1953. Home: 1940 NE 119th Rd North Miami FL 33181 Office: 1795 NE 164th St North Miami Beach FL 33162

CAINE, NORA COOK, public relations exec.; b. Savannah, Ga., Mar. 17, 1949; d. Ellison Richards and Helen Brown Cook; B.A. in Journalism, U. Ga.; m. Martin Squier Caine, Nov. 27, 1976. Girl Friday, receptionist WSGA Radio, Savannah, Ga., 1971; feature writer Savannah Morning News and Evening Press, 1971-73; asst. dir. community relations Candler Gen. Hosp., Savannah, 1973-74; communications dir. S.C. Hosp. Assn., Columbia, 1974-76; asst. public relations dir. Providence Hosp., Washington, 1976-77; asst. public relations dir. Suburban Hosp., Bethesda, Md., 1977-78; dir. public relations St. Joseph Hosp., Memphis, 1978—. Mem. Am. Hosp. Assn., Am. Soc. Hosp. Public Relations Dirs., Tenn. Hosp. Assn. (public relations council), Tenn. Soc. Hosp. Public Relations Dirs. Office: 220 Overton Ave Memphis TN 38105

CAIRNES, WILLIAM ELLIOTT, elec. engr.; b. Chgo., July 22, 1909; s. Chauncey Edison and Ethel May (McConnell) C.; student U. of Ill., 1929-30; m. Rose Irma Pratscher, Nov. 6, 1937; children—Nancy Rose Cairnes McBurney, Donna Gail Cairnes Mannon. Radio engr. Sentinel Radio Co., Chgo., 1936-37; chief engr. Motorola, Inc., Chgo., 1937-47; pres., gen. mgr. Radio Cores, Inc., Oak Lawn, Ill., 1947-72; chmn. bd. dirs. Am. Bank of Oak Lawn, 1960-63; pres., chmn. 94th & Cicero Bldg. Corp., Oak Lawn, 1960-63; dir. Shelco Enterprises, Inc., S. Holland, Ill., 1976—, Shelco Steel Works, S. Holland, 1968—; dir. Metal Powder Industries Fed., N.Y.C., 1950-60, v.p., 1950-60, div. chmn., 1950-60, chmn. bd., 1954-55; dean Fla. Faculty for Interim Business Seminar, Buena Vista Coll., Sarasota, Fla., 1976—. Republican committeeman, Palos (Ill.) Township, 1970, 1974; pres. Oak Lawn C. of C., 1959, dir., 1950-70; chmn. bd. dirs. S.W. YMCA, Oak Lawn, 1952-58, 1963-67, dir., 1952-73; chmn. Palos Orland YMCA, 1958-59, dir., 1958-64; gov. Bird Key Improvement Assn., Sarasota, Fla., 1977-80; del. Fla. Council Yacht Clubs, 1977-78, 80-81; trustee Buena Vista Coll., Storm Lake, Iowa, 1965, treas., chmn. bus. affairs, 1972—. Registered profl. engr., Ill. Mem. IEEE (sr.), Nat., Ill. socs. of profl. engrs., USCG Aux. (flotilla staff officer for public edn.), U.S. Power Squadron (sr.), U.S. Navy League (1st v.p. Sarasota-Manatee council 1979-80, pres. 1980-81). Republican. Presbyterian. Clubs: Bird Key Yacht (asst. sec., chmn. food com. 1977-78, gov. 1977-81, commodore 1978-80), Elks, Lions (pres. Oak Lawn, 1952-53). Patentee in field. Home: 263 Robin Dr Sarasota FL 33577

CALATAYUD, JUAN BAUTISTA, physician; b. Valencia, Spain, May 17, 1928; s. Agustin and Carmen (Llobat C.; M.D., U. Valencia (Spain), 1952; m. Helen T. Lupton, July 2, 1960; children—Mary Carmen, Juan Cesar. Intern, Alexian Bros. Hosp., Elizabeth, N.J., 1955; resident St. Pauls Hosp., Dallas, 1956-57; fellow in medicine George Washington U. Hosp.; asso. dir. med. edn. Doctors Hosp., Washington , 1970—, dir. heart sta. and exercise EKG Lab., 1974—, sec. profl. staff, 1973, also dir.; dir. continuing med. edn. Capitol Hill Hosp., Washington, 1980—; research asst. U. Montreal (Que., Can.), Sch., 1974-75, Guggenheim fellow medicine Montreal Gen. physician Deborah Hosp., Browns Mills, N.J., 1961-62; practice medicine specializing in cardiology, Washington, 1962—; cons. VA Center, Martinsburg, W.Va., 1965—. Fellow Am. Coll. Angiology; mem. A.M.A., Am., Washington heart assns., Am. Fedn. Clin. Research (v.p. 1966-67, pres. 1967-68), Am. Coll. Angiology (gov. 1979—), D.C. Med. Soc., A.A.A.S., Pan Am. Med. Assn. (pres. 1979-80), Peruvian Cardiac Soc. (hon.), Peruvian Angiology Soc. (hon.). Contbr. articles in field to profl. jours. Home: 6217 Cheryl Dr Falls Church VA 22044 Office: 1835 I St NW Washington DC 20006

CALBETO, GABRIEL ANTHONY, appraiser; b. Barcelona, Spain, May 6, 1925; s. Gabriel and Josephine (DeGrau) C.; came to P.R., 1955; B.A., Barcelona U., 1944; B.S., Santiago (Spain) U., 1947; Licentiate in Pharmacy, Ofcl. Coll., Barcelona, 1949; B.A., U. P.R., 1958; postgrad. courses, Chgo., Cin., Washington; m. Carmen Iriarte, July 30, 1953; children—Gabriel E., Joseph M., James J., Francis J. Owner, operator Bonanova, Barcelona, 1948-55; owner, operator Verdaguer & Calbeto, transp. co., Barcelona, 1951-55; owner, operator G. Calbeto, Inc., San Juan, P.R., 1955-73, pres., 1962-72; pvt. appraiser personal property, collector's items, coins, Santurce, P.R., 1968—; lectr. in fine arts and personal property; lectr. U. P.R., Rio Piedras, 1966-73; cons. in field. Mem. Pharmacy Coll. Bd., Barcelona, Pharmacy Bd. Del. Auctioneer charity activities. Served with Spanish Army, 1946-49. Recipient diploma of merit P.R. Med. Assn., 1966, award Soc. Internat. Numismatics, 1971, honor diploma Assn. Numismatica Espanola, 1971, Gold medal P.R. Numis. Soc., 1973. Mem. Am. Numis. Assn., Numis. Lit. Guild (life), Am. Soc. Appraisers (sr. mem., dir. P.R. chpt. 1969-76, dir. Orlando chpt. 1977—, pres. 1973-74, appreciation award 1974), Soc. Real Estate Appraisers P.R. (dir. 1969-71), Assn. Grads. Spanish Univs. (dir. 1956-58). Club: Santurce Rotary (dir. 1959-61). Author: The VIII Reales Compendium, 1970. Contbr. articles to profl. jours. Address: 211 Timbercove Circle Longwood FL 32750

CALDERON SERRANO, ALFREDO, chemist; b. N.Y.C., Jan. 11, 1952; s. Nicolas Calderon and Milagros Rodriguez (Serrano); B.S., U. P.R., 1975. Research asso. U. P.R. Nuclear Center, Mayaguez, 1976; tchr. Colegio del la Milagrosa, Mayaguez, P.R., 1976-77, instr., 1977—; tchr. Colegiodela Milagrosa, Mayaguez, 1977—. Searle fellow, 1977, 78. Mem. Nat. Geog. Soc., Am. Chem. Soc., Nat. Sci. Tchrs. Assn., N.Y. Acad. Scis., Associaon Alunmi del Colegio de Agriculture, Artes Mechanicas de Mayaguez, Colegio de Quimicos de P.R. Roman Catholic. Home: Cond El Residencial Apt 201 Luna 67 Mayaguez PR 00708 Office: Chemistry Dept Univ PR Mayaguez PR 00708

CALDWELL, ANNIS LEE, machinist, mfg. co. exec.; b. Tulsa, Oct. 4, 1936; s. Lee Oren and Marie Remmel (Kesseler) C.; grad. high sch., Tulsa, 1955; m. Ina Mae Bumgardner, June 23, 1956; children—Patricia, Rebecca, James, Lora, Jane, Steven. With Ramsey Winch Co., Tulsa, 1953—, mfg. mgr., 1975—. Mem. Soc. Mfg. Engrs., Am. Mgmt. Assn. Democrat. Methodist. Home: Rural Route 3 Box 2965 Owasso OK 74055 Office: PO Box 15829 Tulsa OK 74112

CALDWELL, BENJAMIN EARL, mfg. co. exec.; b. Washington, May 7, 1940; s. Benjamin Franklin and Mary Nell (Willis) C.; B.S, Auburn U., 1962; M.B.A., U. West Fla., 1978; m. Donnacella Morgan, Sept. 6, 1969; children—Kimberly Ann, Benjamin Albert, Stacey Elizabeth. Systems engr. IBM, Pensacola, Fla., 1967-70; systems analyst Escambia Treating Co., Pensacola, 1970-74; computer specialist Monsanto Co., Pensacola, 1974—. Served with USN, 1962-67. Decorated D.F.C., Air medal (21), Navy Commendation medal. Mem. Phi Kappa Phi. Home: 2460 Bayou Blvd Pensacola FL 32503 Office: PO Box 12830 Pensacola FL 32575

CALDWELL, CLAUD REID, lawyer; b. Augusta, Ga., Sept. 18, 1909; s. John Mars and Ethel (Bennett) C.; student Acad. Richmond County, 1922-26; m. Josephine F. Clarke, June 30, 1940; children—Claud R., Kathryn C., James W. Admitted to Ga. bar, 1932, practiced in Augusta, 1934—; judge Municipal Ct., City of Augusta, 1948-49. Pres., Richmond County Independent Party, 1950-51; bd. dirs. Augusta chpt. ARC, YMCA; chmn. Augusta council Boy Scouts Am., 1949-50. Served with AUS, 1941-45; ETO. Recipient Distinguished Pistol Marksman award U.S. Army, 1965. Mem. Am., Ga., Augusta bar assns., Ga. Sport Shooting Assn. (dir., past pres.), U.S. Power Squadron, Augusta Amateur Radio Club, Ret. Officers Assn. (Augusta chpt.), Am. Legion, Sons of Confederacy, Assn. U.S. Army, Am. Radio Relay League, Hephzibah Agrl. Club. Presbyn. (deacon). Mason (32 deg., Shriner). Clubs: Augusta Country, Augusta Sailing, Sudlow-Silver Bluff Rifle and Skeet. Home: 343 Hemlock Hill Rd Augusta GA 30904 Office: Southern Finance Bldg Augusta GA 30902

CALDWELL, DAVID LEON, electronic systems engr.; b. Arcadia, Kans., Sept. 23, 1934; s. Virgil Scott and Denia Doyle (Crays) C.; B.E.E., George Washington, U., 1964; M.S., U. So. Miss., 1978; m. Dolores Caldwell; children—John, Barbara, Sharon. Instr., Philco Corp., El Paso, Tex., 1958-59; computer engr. UNIVAC div. Remington Rand Corp., Alexandria, Va., 1959-61; engr. Atlantic Research Corp., Gainesville, Va., 1961-65, 68-70; electronic systems engr. Gen. Electric Co., Bay St. Louis, Miss., 1965-68, 71-76; elctronic networks engr. Space div. Rockwell Internat., Bay St. Louis, 1976—; owner cons. co. Digital Computer Systems, Bay St. Louis, 1973—. Served in U.S. Army, 1954-56. Mem. IEEE, Miss. Acad. Scis., Nat. Geog. Soc., Nat. Mgmt. Assn. Home: 216 Main St Bay Saint Louis MS 39520 Office: NSTL Bldg 4210 Bay Saint Louis MS 39520

CALDWELL, HAROLD LEROY, petroleum engr.; b. Pawnee, Okla., Aug. 14, 1925; s. Harold Ralph and Eula P. (Buckner) C.; B.S. in Petroleum Engring., U. Tulsa, 1951; m. Patricia T. Poorman, Dec. 24, 1948; children—Michael Alan, Douglas Owen. Exploitation engr. Sunray Oil Co., 1951-55; chief engr. Keener Oil Co., Tulsa, 1955-59, gen. supt. prodn., 1959-62; cons. engr., 1962-63; drilling engr. Fenix & Scisson, Inc., Tulsa, 1963-65; gen. prodn. supt. K.W.B. Oil Property Mgmt., Inc., 1965—; engr. Williams Bros. Engring. Co., 1967-74; mgr. Perrault-Caldwell, Inc., Tulsa, 1974-75; petroleum cons. Caldwell and Assos., Inc., 1975—. Served with AUS, 1943-46. Registered profl. engr., Okla. Mem. Am. Inst. Mining Engrs., Am. Petroleum Inst., Okla. State Profl. Engrs. Republican. Mem. Reorganized Ch. of Jesus Christ of Latter-day Saints. Home: 5129 S Richmond Tulsa OK 74135 Office: Suite 305 7030 S Yale St Tulsa OK 74177

CALDWELL, HENRY STEPHEN, clin. psychologist; b. Cin., June 17, 1941; s. Henry Charles and Pat (Rothhaas) C.; B.A., Hanover Coll., 1963; M.S., DePauw U., 1964; Ph.D., Purdue U., 1969; children—Kevin Lee, Timothy Lynn, Annelise Jean. Staff psychologist Ind. Dept. Corrections, Pendleton, 1964-65; coordinator inpatient psychol. services Children's Meml. Hosp., U. Okla. Health Scis. Center, Oklahoma City, 1969-71; pvt. practice clin. psychology, Stillwater, Okla., 1971—; asso. prof. dept. psychology Okla. State U., Stillwater, 1974—, coordinator psychol. Services Center, field services, 1976—. Mem. Okla. Gov.'s Com. on Children and Youth, 1970; bd. dirs. Community Sheltered Workshop, 1972-74. Recipient Outstanding Instr. award Okla. State U., 1974; licensed clin. psychologist, Okla. Mem. Am., Southwestern Okla. psychol. assns., Am. Assn. Child Care in Hosps. Contbr. articles in field to profl. jours. Home: Route 2 Box 96 Perkins OK 74059 Office: 2324 W 7th Pl Stillwater OK 74074

CALDWELL, LEONA IOLA WILL (MRS. OLIVER CROMWELL CALDWELL), clergyman, writer; b. Sabina, Ohio, Apr. 13, 1903; d. Silas Joseph and Luella Marie (Reed) Will; B.S., Ohio State U., 1925; M.A., Columbia, 1933; D.H.L., Capitol Coll., 1965; m. Oliver Cromwell Caldwell, June 20, 1938. Ordained to ministry Methodist Ch., 1954; lectr. Swarthmore (Pa.) Chautauqua, 1925-29; tchr. speech Sabina High Sch., 1930-34; minister, Franklin Square (Ohio) Meth. Ch., 1957-58; minister, Leetonia, Ohio, 1959—; spiritual dir. Hospitality House, Tampa, Fla., 1959-61. County v.p. ARC, Lisbon, Ohio, 1940-44; vol. St. Stephens (Wyo.) Indian Sch., Wind River Indian Reservation, 1972-79; bd. dirs. County Health, Lisbon, 1943-47. Mem. Internat. Platform Assn. (hon. life; bd. govs. 1950-65, 68-69), Am. Assn. Women Ministers, AAUW, Nat. League Am. Pen Women (pres. br., state chaplain), Internat. Poetry Assn., Am. Poetry League, London Poetry Soc., Versewriters Guild Ohio, Epsilon Sigma Alpha. Methodist. Club: Order Eastern Star (past matron). Author: (poetry) To You From Me; Reflections. Address: 11 Terrace Gardens Lakeland FL 33801

CALHOUN, EVELYN WILLIAMS, social worker; b. Tyler, Tex., Sept. 12, 1921; d. James Stanley and Norma (Skelton) Williams; B.A., Baylor U., 1941; M.S.W., Worden Sch. Social Work, 1960; postgrad. U. Chgo., 1955-56; m. William Benjamin Calhoun, Jr., Mar. 15, 1942 (div. Mar. 1949); children—William Benjamin III, Anne Stanley (Mrs. Donald Elliot Loyd). Field worker Tex. Dept. Pub. Welfare, Tyler, 1953-55; field placement Salvation Army Family Service, Chgo., 1955-56; child welfare worker Tyler-Smith County Child Welfare Unit, 1957-59; field placement Tex. Inst. Rehab. and Research, Baylor U., Houston, 1959-60, med. social worker, 1960-64; research social worker pre-natal research project dept. obstetrics and gynecology U. Tex. Med. Br. at Galveston, 1964-66, supr. social service dept. obstetrics and gynecology, 1966-74, cons. satellite clinics, 1967-74, cons. family planning project, 1969-74, cons., supr. head and neck cancer service, ear, nose and throat, chest surgery and neurosurgery, 1974-78, cons., supr. plastic surgery and oral surgery service, 1975-78, supr. internal medicine services, otolaryngology, ophthalmology and dermatology, 1978—; field instr. U. Houston Grad. Sch. Social Work, 1968—. Bd. dirs. Galveston County Community Action Council, 1966-68, Galveston chpt. Am. Cancer Soc., 1974—; trustee Houston Intergroup Assn., 1974-76. Lic. social psychotherapist, Tex. Mem. Nat. Assn. Social Workers (chmn. research council San Jacinto chpt. 1963-64, dir. chpt. 1964-67, chmn. Galveston br. 1964-67, sec. 1967-68; group leader so. regional inst. 1966, alt. Tex. del. 1969-71, Tex. del. 1971-73, dir. 1969-73; alt. del. Tex. state council 1967), Acad. Cert. Social Workers, Galveston County Soc. Social Service Dirs. (sec. 1979-80), AAUW, Baylor Alumnae Assn., Daus. King (pres. 1976-78), Order De Moley, Delta Alpha Pi. Episcopalian. Toastmistress. Home: 2408 Ave O Galveston TX 77550

CALHOUN, FRANK WAYNE, lawyer, state legislator; b. Houston, Apr. 15, 1933; s. Wilmer Cecil and Ruby Edith (Willis) C.; B.A., Tex. Tech U., 1956; J.D. U. Tex., 1959; m. Susan Fortescue Ripley, June 24, 1978; children by previous marriage—Michael, David. Admitted to Tex. bar, 1959, U.S. Supreme Ct. bar, 1965; partner firm Byrd, Shaw, Weeks & Calhoun, Abilene, Tex., 1959-73; partner firm Liddell, Sapp, Zivley & Brown, Houston, 1974—; mem. Tex. Ho. of Reps., 1966-75. Del. Tex. Constl. Conv., 1974. Mem. exec. bd. Chisholm Trail council Boy Scouts Am.; mem. exec. com. Tex. Film Commn., 1979—; bd. dirs. Abilene YMCA; trustee Tex. Tech Law Sch. Found.; bd. govs. S.W. Outward Bound Sch. Served with USNR, 1951-53. Named Abilene's Outstanding Young Man, Jaycees, 1968; Distinguished Service award State Bar Tex., 1969, 71, 73. Mem. Am., Tex. (past com. chmn.) bar assns., Am. Judicature Soc., Abilene C. of C. (past dir.), Tex. Tech U. Ex-Students Assn. (past pres.), Nat. Soc. State Legislators (bd. govs., past program chmn., exec. com.), Tex. Archeol. Soc., Sierra Club, Nat. Audubon Soc., Nat. Trust for Hist. Preservation, Houston Fine Arts Mus., Sigma Alpha Epsilon, Alpha Kappa Psi. Democrat. Methodist. Clubs: Rotary, Houston, Austin. Contbg. editor Tex. Lawyers Weekly Letter, 1964. Home: 12917 Trail Hollow Houston TX 77079 Office: 500 Gulf Bldg Houston TX 77002

CALHOUN, JACK ROWLAND, electric utility exec.; b. Poplar, N.C., Oct. 21, 1919; s. Glenn David and Pearl Wanda (Willis) C.; B.E.E., Tenn. Tech. U., 1949; m. Jacqueline Capps, Sept. 23, 1944; children—Carol, Patrick, Janice, Susan. With TVA, 1954—, elec. maintenance supr. Johnsonville Steam plant, 1958-60, asst. supt. Shawnee steam plant, Paducah, Ky., 1960-64, asst. project mgr., gas-cooled reactor, Oak Ridge, 1964-68, asst. chief maintenance br., Chattanooga, 1968-71, supt. Brown Ferry nuclear plant, Decatur Ala., 1971-77, chief nuclear generation br., Chattanooga, 1977-79, dir. div. nuclear power, 1979—. Served in USN, 1938-45. Mem. Am. Nuclear Soc. (nat. chmn. reactor ops. div. 1977). Methodist. Home: 4106 Oakmont St Chattanooga TN 37415 Office: 716 Edney Bldg Chattanooga TN 37401

CALHOUN, MALCOLM DONALD, elec. engr., educator; b. Eddyville, Ky., Nov. 13, 1931; s. Russell Garland and Charlene Elizabeth (Duncan) C.; B.S.E.E., Purdue U., 1965; M.S.E.E., Memphis State U., 1968; Ph.D., Miss. State U., 1976. Served as enlisted man U.S. Navy, 1949-69, ret., 1969; instr. elec. engring. Memphis State U., 1969-74; research asst. Miss. State U., 1974-76, asst. prof. elec. engring., 1977—; asst. prof. Va. Mil. Inst., 1976-77. NSF fellow, summer 1972; NASA-Am. Soc. Engring. Edn. fellow, summers 1977-78. Mem. IEEE, Sigma Xi, Phi Kappa Phi, Eta Kappa Nu, Tau Beta Pi. Research on digital holographic filter generation, NASA, 1976. Home: PO Box 382 Mississippi State MS 39762 Office: Drawer EE Mississippi State MS 39762

CALI, PAUL VINCENT, real estate cons.; b. Jamestown, N.Y., July 25, 1942; s. John Michael and Mary Helen (Salamone) C.; B.S. in Econs., St. Bonaventure U., Olean, N.Y., 1964; M.B.A. in Real Estate and Urban Devel., Am. U., 1972; m. Judith Ann Smisko, June 8, 1968; children—Jason Paul, Damon Michael. Real estate broker, 1967-68; pres. Ratcliffe, Cali & Co., real estate valuation and investment counselors, Arlington, Va., 1968—, also dir.; sec., dir. Resort Realties, Inc.; dir. First Fin. Service Corp. Va. Served to capt. USMCR, 1964-67, Vietnam. Decorated Bronze Star with combat V, Purple Heart. Mem. Am. Inst. Real Estate Appraisers, Am. Soc. Appraisers, No. Va. Bd. Realtors (asso.). Republican. Roman Catholic. Home: 6202 Vernon Palmer Ct McLean VA 22101 Office: 1600 Wilson Blvd Arlington VA 22209

CALLAHAN, ERRETT HARGROVE, JR., archeologist; b. Lynchburg, Va., Dec. 17, 1937; s. Errett Hargrove and Mary (Ingraham) C.; B.A. cum laude, Hampden-Sydney Coll., 1960; M.F.A., Va. Commonwealth U., 1973; M.A., Cath. U. Am., 1978, Ph.D., 1980; m. Linda Abbey, Oct. 29, 1978; 1 son by previous marriage, Timothy McFarland. Freelance artist, East Africa and U.S., 1964-67; founder, head art dept. Blue Ridge Sch., Dyke, Va., 1967-69; instr. anthropology and art depts. Va. Commonwealth U., Richmond, 1971-77; research asso., instr. anthropology Cath. U., Washington, 1976—; dir. Piltdown Prodns., King William, Va., 1978—; founder, dir. Pamunkey Research Center, Pamunkey Indian Reservation, 1977—; cons. Pamunkey Indian Mus., 1978-80. Served with U.S. Army N.G., 1960-61. Pamunkey Indian Nation grantee, 1977. Mem. Am. Anthrop. Assn., Soc. Am. Archeology, Council Va. Archeologists, Eastern States Archeol. Fedn., Archeol. Soc. Va., Sigma Xi. Author: The Basics of Flintknapping in the Eastern Fluted Point Tradition, 1979; founder, co-editor Flintknappers Exchange, 1978—; editor Exptl. Archeology Papers, 1971-76. Home: Route 1 Box 210A King William VA 23086 Office: Pamunkey Research Center Route 1 Box 217-AA King William VA 23086

CALLAHAN, VINCENT FRANCIS, JR., publisher, state legislator; b. Washington, Oct. 30, 1931; s. Vincent Francis and Anita (Hawkins) C.; B.S. in Fgn. Service, Georgetown U., 1957; m. Dorothy Helen Budge, Aug. 27, 1960; children—Vincent Francis III, Elizabeth Lauren, Anita Marie, Cynthia Helen, Robert Bruce, Became partner Callahan Publs., 1957, pres., editor numerous publs., 1957—; v.p., dir. McLean Savs. and Loan Assn.; past pres. Ind. Newsletters Assn., Washington; mem. Va. Ho. of Dels., 1968—. Candidate for lt. gov. Va., 1965; state fin. chmn. Rep. Party of Va., 1966-68; dir. Washington Met. Council Govts. Served with USMC, 1950-53; as lt. USCGR, 1959-63. Mem. U.S. Naval Inst., Marine Tech. Soc., Am. Def. Preparedness Assn. Republican. Roman Catholic. Clubs: Nat. Press; Kiwanis (past pres.) (McLean, Va.); Bull and Bear (Richmond, Va.). Author eight books including; Missile Contracts Guide, 1958; Space Guide, 1959; Underwater Defense Handbook, 1963; Military Research Handbook, 1963. Home: 6220 Nelway Dr McLean VA 22101 Office: 6631 Old Dominion Dr McLean VA 22101

CALLAN, PATRICK JOSEPH, mktg. exec.; b. Washington, Mar. 2, 1937; s. John L. and Rose (Goodwin) C.; B.S., U. Fla., 1965; m. Sylvia Crusoe, May 27, 1978; children—Patricia Lee, Patrick Clark. Dir. public relations Fla. Cypress Gardens, 1962-72; dir. mktg., 1972-75, v.p. corp. mktg., 1975-78; pres. Mktg. Group Suncoast, Sarasota, Fla., 1978—. Mem. Fla. Tourism Council. Mem. Public Relations Soc. Am. (pres. Fla. dist. 1972), Fla. Attraction Assn. (pres. 1976-78), Sigma Delta Chi. Republican. Roman Catholic. Club: Elks. Contbr. articles to profl. jours. Home: 4318 Rockefeller Ave Sarasota FL 33579 Office: 3800 S Tamiami Trail Sarasota FL 33579

CALLARMAN, WILLIAM GLEN, educator; b. Corvallis, Oreg., May 3, 1943; s. C.C. and Cora May (Humphrey) C.; B.B.A., W. Tex. State U., 1965; M.B.A., Ariz. State U., 1967, D.B.A., 1972; m. Mary Helen Ayres, Aug. 28, 1965; children—Julia Ayres, Michel William. Asst. prof. dept. bus. adminstrn. U. Central Fla., Orlando, 1972-78, asso. prof. mgmt., 1978—, chmn. mgmt. dept., 1974-77, dir. Mgmt. Inst., 1976—; cons. to state, local and nat. orgns. Served to capt. Adj. Gen. Corps, U.S. Army, 1970-71. Decorated Army Commendation medal. Mem. Acad. Mgmt., So. Mgmt. Assn., Southwestern Mktg. Assn., Am. Soc. Tng. Dirs., Sigma Iota Epsilon, Alpha Kappa Psi, Beta Gamma Sigma. Democrat. Methodist. Club: Econs. (Orlando). Contbr. articles to various jours. Home: 110 Park Ave Casselberry FL 32707 Office: Coll Bus Adminstrn U Central Fla Box 25000 Orlando FL 32816

CALLAWAY, CAREY ANN SKINNER, biologist; b. Birmingham, Ala., Nov. 22, 1929; d. Charles William and Janice Margaret (Young) Skinner; B.S. in Edn., U. Ala., Tuscaloosa, 2952. Tchr. biology and phys. edn. Peperell High Sch., Rome, Ga., 1952-58; dance supr. recreation dept. City of Atlanta, 1958; instr. Atlanta YMCA, 1959; research asso. N.Y. Hosp., 1960; research asso. elctron microscopy Emory U., 1961-65; biologist, electron microscopist Center Disease Control, USPHS, Atlanta, 1965—; mem. faculty Ga. State U., 1968-69. Mem. Electron Microscopy Soc. Am. (cert. electron microscopy technician), S.E. Electron Microscopy Soc. (founding mem.), Am. Soc. for Microbiology, N.Y. Acad. Scis., Internat. Platform Assn., Sigma Xi, Delta Zeta. Roman Catholic. Co-author: Laboratory Methods in Medical Mycology; author articles in field. Home: 1015 Shepherds Ln Altanta GA 30324 Office: CDC Room 2315 Bldg 1 1600 Clifton Rd Atlanta GA 30333

CALLAWAY, JOHN WILSON, real estate and ins. exec.; b. Penfield, Ga., Nov. 6, 1915; s. John Sanders and Frances Mae (Wilson) C.; B.S., U.S. Mil. Acad., 1941; grad. various mil. schs.; m. Lillian Madeleine Sohlstrom, Sept. 27, 1944; children—Francis Fielding, II, John Wilson. Commd. 2d lt. U.S. Army, 1941; advanced through grades to col., 1961; service in Australia, New Guinea, Korea, France; ret., 1971; broker life ins. Bennington and Assos., Atlanta; salesman comml. real estate Georgetown Properties, Inc. Vice pres. USO, Atlanta, 1974-79; chmn. Ft. McPherson Army Retiree Council, 1974-79; chmn. service to mil. families com. Atlanta chpt. ARC, 1968-74; mem. Atlanta Area council Boy Scouts Am., 1970-79, dist. chmn., 1970-71; trustee Ga. Rotary Student Fund, 1972-77; ruling elder Columbia Presbyn. Ch., Decatur. Decorated Silver Star (4), Legion of Merit (2), Bronze Star (2), Commendation medal, Combat Inf. badge with star; Greek Distinguished Service medal; recipient Silver Beaver award Boy Scouts Am., 1971. Mem. Assn. U.S. Army, Am. Def. Preparedness Assn., Nat. Assn. Life Underwriters, Ret. Officers Assn. Club: West End Rotary (pres.) (Atlanta). Home: 165 Rue Fontaine Decatur GA 30038 Office: 2630 Tower Pl Atlanta GA 30326

CALLEN, IRWIN R., physician; b. Chgo., May 3, 1919; s. Harry and Esther (Levey) C.; student U. Chgo., 1936-39; B.S., U. Ill., 1941, M.D., 1943; M.S., 1949; m. Rose P. Cohen, Aug. 10, 1941; children—Jeffrey P., James Jay. Intern, Ill. Research and Ednl. Hosps., U. Ill., 1943, fellowship dept. internal medicine, 1946-47, electrocardiographer, asso. attending physician, 1948-51; practice medicine specializing in internal medicine and cardiology, Chgo., 1947—; asso. attending physician Cook County Hosp., Chgo., 1951-57, attending physician dept. internal medicine, 1958—, prof. medicine and cardiology grad. sch., 1958—; instr. dept. medicine U. Health Scis., Chgo. Med. Sch., 1951-56, asso. dept. internal medicine, 1956-66, asso. prof. medicine, 1966-72, prof. clin. medicine, 1972—; chmn. dept. internal medicine Edgewater Hosp., Chgo., 1964-68, v.p. med. staff, 1967, dir. cardiology, 1964—, pres. med. staff, 1968, 69, bd. dirs., 1968—; attending physician, Louis A. Weiss Meml. Hosp., Chgo., 1952-72; hon. med. staff in cardiology and internal medicine Miami Heart Inst., Miami Beach, Fla., 1976—, bd. dirs., 1976—. Served as capt., M.C., AUS, 1944-45. Diplomate Am. Bd. Internal Medicine (Subsplty. in cardiovascular diseases). Fellow Am. Coll. Cardiology (sec. Chgo. roundtable 1963), A.C.P., Am. Coll. Chest Physicians, Am. Assn. Bioanalysts; mem. Ill. Soc. for Med. Research, Am. Heart Assn. (dir. Fla. 1977—, dir. Greater Miami 1975—, chmn. speakers bur. 1975—), Am., Fla., Chgo., Dade County med. assns., N.Y. Acad. Scis., Am., Fla. socs. internal medicine, AAAS, Brain Research Found. Contbr. numerous articles to profl. jours.; book reviewer Jour. AMA, Jour. Chest. Address: 800 NE 195th St North Miami FL 33179

CALLEN, JEFFREY P., dermatologist; b. Chgo., May 30, 1947; s. Irwin R. and Rose P. (Cohen) C.; B.S., U. Wis., 1969; M.D., U. Mich., 1972; m. Susan Beth Manis, Dec. 21, 1968; children—Amy, David. Intern, U. Mich. Affiliated Hosps., Ann Arbor, 1972-73, resident in internal medicine, 1972-75, resident in dermatology, 1975-77; practice medicine specializing in dermatology and internal medicine, Louisville, 1977—; asst. prof. Dept. Medicine, U. Louisville, 1977—; attending physician Louisville VA Hosp., 1977—. Recipient Award of Excellence for Sci. Exhibit, Ky. Med. Assn., 1978; diplomate Am. Bd. Internal Medicine, Am. Bd. Dermatology. Fellow A.C.P.; mem. Ky. Med. Assn., AMA, Soc. Investigative Dermatology, Dermatology Found., Am. Acad. Dermatology, Galens Hon. Med. Soc. Author: Dermatology: A Teaching Manual, 1977, 78; Manual of Dermatology, 1980 Yearbook; editor: Cutaneous Aspects of Internal Disease, 1980; editor spl. issue of Cutis, 1978, 79; contbg. editor Internat. Jour. Dermatology, 1979—; editor Cutis, 1980—. Office: 554 Med Towers S Louisville KY 40202

CALLENDER, MARTHA V. LINDER (MRS. RICHARD ERVIN CALLENDER), club woman, genealogist, artist, musician; b. Prairie Dell, Tex.; d. Franklin Trimmier and Adeline (Hunter) Linder; student Baylor Coll., 1914-16; grad. Sam Houston State Tchrs. Coll., Huntsville, Tex., 1916; m. Richard Ervin Callender, children—Catherine V. (Mrs. Merrill Smith), Richard Ervin (dec. 1963). Tchr. pub. schs., Rosenberg, Tex., 1917-18; sec. Gulf Oil Co., Houston 1918-19; exec. sec. Fed. Farm Loan Assn., Lockhart, Tex., 1925-30. Recipient various awards for artwork. Corr. sec. A. and M. Garden Club, 1968-69; mem. A. and M. Mother's Club, A. and M. Social Club, Extension Service Club; mem. A. and M. Fine Arts and Crafts Group, v.p., 1976-77. Mem. Tex. Hist. Assn., Tex. Fine Arts Assns., D.A.R. (chpt. corr. sec. 1952-54, librarian 1948-50; nat. vice chmn. scholarships com. 1960-63, Tex. chmn. geneal. records com. 1952-58, chpt. registrar 1950-52, 60-62, 71-74, chpt. regent 1965-67), Daus. Am. Colonists (Tex. chmn. colonial and geneal. records 1957-59, regent Louis Guion chpt. 1961-63, hon. regent, Tex. parliamentarian 1959-61, state registrar 1963-65, chmn. our colonial heritage com. 1965-67, 2d vice regent chpt. 1967-71), U.D.C. (pres. L.S. Ross chpt. 1961-63, chpt. registrar 1963-65 dist. chmn. 1964-66, historian 1977—), Children Am. Colonists (nat. chaplain, sr. adv. council 1964-66, v.p. So. sect. 1971-73, historian 1975—), Brazos County Bar Assn. Aux., Pan-Am. Round Table (treas. 1975-76), United Daus. 1812 (state chmn. 1971-74), Tex. State Geneal. Soc., So. Linder Family Assn. (1st pres.), Tex. Folklore Soc., Brazos Valley Art Council, Art Gallery League, Opera and Performing Arts Soc. (charter), Tex. Hist. Assn., Tex. Folklore Soc. Club: Bryan College Station Art (charter). Home: 209 Lee Ave College Station TX 77840

CALLEY, DAVID JEFFERSON, indsl. health cons.; b. Sherwood, Tex., Mar. 18, 1930; s. Clive Raymond and Ida Cora C.; B.S. in Zoology, Tex. Tech U., 1952; M.S. in Toxicology, U. Tex., Austin, 1967; Ph.D. in Preventive Medicine, U. Tex., Galveston, 1979; m. Minta Adele Bowen, Sept. 7, 1949; children—Stanla Jean, David Jefferson II, Lisa Ann. With Tex. State Health Dept., 1952-54; tchr. Midland (Tex.) Public Schs., 1954-55; research asso. U. Tex., Austin, 1955-56; bioecologist Tex. Game and Fish Commn., 1956-62; research asso. U. Tex., Austin, 1962-67; indsl. hygienist, toxicologist Dow Chem. Co., Freeport, Tex., 1967-68; bioenviron. scientist Kelsey Seybold Clinic, NASA, Houston, 1968-73; indsl. health cons., 1973—; prof. allied health scis. U. Houston, Clear Lake City, Tex., 1979—. Served with USAR, 1947-49. Cert. occupational hearing conservationist, audiometrist, hazard controlmgr., basic radiol. health, basic safety mgmt. and total loss control in industry. Mem. Am. Indsl. Hygiene Assn., Air Pollution Control Assn., Tex. Water Pollution Control Assn., Sigma Xi. Democrat. Methodist. Clubs: Masons, Rotary. Contbr. articles to profl. jours. Home: PO Box 721 Friendswood TX 77546 Office: U Houston 2700 Bay Area Blvd Houston TX 77058

CALLIGAS, GARY LAZAROS, assn. exec.; b. Shreveport, La., Mar. 8, 1950; s. Lazaros G. and Pyra A. (Asimakis) C.; B.S. in Elec. Engring., La. Tech. U., Ruston, 1972; m. Katina M. Miaoulis, Apr. 28, 1974; children—Louis Michael, Jason Patrick. Communications engr. Tex. Eastern Gas Pipeline Co., Shreveport, 1973-77; exec. dir. North La. Med. Rev. Assn., Shreveport, 1977—; dir. Health Info. Corp. La., 1978-80. Vice-pres. St. George Greek Orthodox Ch., Shreveport, 1979-80. Mem. Am. Hellenic Ednl. Progressive Assn. (pres. Shreveport chpt.), Am. Assn. Profl. Standards Rev. Orgns. (dir. exec. dirs. sect.), Am. Mgmt. Assn. IEEE, Sigma Pi. Greek Orthodox. Editor Skepsou, 1973—. Home: 304 Medallion Circle Shreveport LA 71119 Office: 1612 Fairfield Ave Suite 210 Shreveport LA 71101

CALLOWAY, MARY CAMPBELL, speech and lang. pathologist; b. Forrest City, Ark., May 25, 1950; d. Ossie and Helen Sue Campbell; B.S.E., Ark. State U., Jonesboro, 1972; M.A., U. Tenn., Knoxville, 1973; postgrad. Memphis State U., Memphis, 1979—; m. William Bennett Calloway, Nov. 23, 1975; 1 dau., Kendra Malaka. Student clinician Ark. Children's Speech and Hearing Center, Little Rock, 1972-74; dir. Radford (Va.) U. Speech and Hearing Clinic, 1974-78, coordinator communications disorders area, dept. theater, speech and communication disorders, 1974-77, instr. communication disorders, 1973-76, asst. prof., 1977—, dir. speech and hearing clinic, 1974-79, acting-chairperson, 1979—. Mem. New River (Va.) Community Action Health Adv. Bd., 1977-79; sec. bd. dirs. Christiansburg (Va.) Community Center, 1978-79. Warwick Electronics scholar, 1968-72; lic. speech pathologist, Va. Mem. Am. Speech and Hearing Assn. (cert. clin. competence), Speech and Hearing Assn. Va. AAUP, Alpha Kappa Alpha. Democrat. Methodist. Home: 630 Stuart St Christiansburg VA 24073 Office: Dept Communications Disorders Radford U Box 5776 Radford VA 24142

CALOGERO, PASCAL FRANK, JR., state justice; b. New Orleans, Nov. 9, 1931; s. Pascal Frank and Louise (Moore) C.; student Loyola U. La., 1949-51, J.D., 1954; m. Geraldine James, June 18, 1955; children—Deborah Ann, David, Pascall, Elizabeth, Thomas, Michael, Stephen, Gerald. Admitted to La. bar; partner firm Landrieu, Calogero & Kronlage, 1958-69, Calogero & Kronlage, 1969-73; gen. counsel La. Stadium and Exposition Dist., 1970-73; asso. justice La. Supreme Ct., New Orleans, 1973—. Del., Dem. Nat. Conv., 1968. Served to capt. U.S. Army, 1954-57. Mem. Am. Bar Assn., La. Bar Assn., New Orleans Bar Assn., Greater New Orleans Trial Lawyers Assn. (v.p. 1967-69). Office: 301 Loyola Ave New Orleans LA 70112

CALONJE, MARIO ARNOLDO, radiologist; b. New Orleans, Mar. 12, 1931; s. Cesar Esteban and Virginia Amelia (Mayeur) C.; student Tulane U., 1952-55; M.D., La. State U., 1959; m. Geraldine Ann Parrino, Apr. 29, 1963; 1 son, Paul Stephen. Intern, Cambridge (Mass.) City Hosp., 1959-60; resident in radiology Charity Hosp., New Orleans, 1960-63; staff radiologist Mercy Hosp., New Orleans, 1963-65, Ochsner Clinic, New Orleans, 1965-73, New Orleans Radiol. Group, 1978, Hotel Dieu Hosp., 1978; staff radiologist East Jefferson Hosp., New Orleans, 1973-78, head dept., 1975—; clin. asso. prof. radiology Tulane U., New Orleans. Served in USAF, 1948-52. Mem. AMA, So. Med. Assn. (chmn. radiology sec. 1974), Radiol. Soc. N.Am., Am. Coll. Radiology, Roentgen Ray Soc., La., Jefferson Parish med. socs., La. (sec.-treas. 1979), New Orleans (pres. 1972) radiol. socs., Am. Inst. Ultrasound in Medicine. Democrat. Roman Catholic. Club: Bayou Teal and Trout. Contbr. articles to med. jours. Home: 1834 Upperline St New Orleans LA 70115 Office: 4200 Houma Blvd Metairie LA 70011

CALUB, ALFONSO DE GUZMAN, plant breeder; b. Aringay, La Union, Philippines, Aug. 1, 1938; s. Eduardo and Juana (de Guzman) C.; Ph.D., U. N.H., 1972; m. Laura Vivas Norcio, June 19, 1967; children—Janice Fides, Florence. Grad. research asst. U. Philippines, 1960-62, research asst., 1962-64, research instr., 1964-67, instr., 1967-68; grad. research asst. U. Ky., 1968-69, U. N.H., 1969-72; post-doctoral fellow U. Nebr., 1972-74; dir. research, sr. plant breeder Alexandria (La.) Seed Co., 1974—. Mem. Am. Soc. Agronomy, Crop Sci. Soc. Am., Soil Sci. Soc. Am., Council Agrl. Sci. and Tech., Am. Registry Cert. Profls. in Agronomy, Crops and Soils, Sigma Xi, Phi Sigma. Roman Catholic. Contbr. articles to profl. jours. Home: 5811 Skylark Dr Alexandria LA 71301 Office: PO Box 1830 Alexandria LA 71301

CALVER, RICHARD ALLEN, coll. dean; b. Chillicothe, Ohio, Feb. 16, 1939; s. Katherine Mae (Roush) Bryan; student U. Hawaii, 1959-61; B.S. in Bus. Adminstrn., W.Va. U., 1963; M.S. in Bus., Va. Commonwealth U., 1970; postgrad. U. Va., Va. Tech. U., 1979—; m. Glenda Leigh Davidson, Mar. 13, 1965. Mgmt. trainee Sears Roebuck & Co., 1963; mgmt. trainee Reuben H. Donnelley Corp., 1963-64, state publs. and customer relations mgr., 1964-68; state job analyst Va. Div. Personnel, Richmond, 1968-70; dean adminstrv. services S.W. Va. Community Coll., Richlands, 1970—; mem. accreditation team So. Assn. Colls. and Schs. Mem. Lebanon (Va.) Town Council, 1978—. Served with USAF, 1957-61. Mem. Russell County (Va.) C. of C. (pres. 1975-76), Delta Tau Delta. Methodist. Clubs: Lions (pres. Lebanon club 1976-77), Shriners (pres. club 1974-75), Masons. Home: Lebanon Manor Lebanon VA 24266 Office: PO Box SVCC Richlands VA 24641

CALVERT, JON CHANNING, educator; b. Sonora, Calif., May 17, 1941; s. Floyd Raymond and Aloha Jean (Fernandes) C.; A.B., Stanford U., 1963; M.S., Baylor U., 1968, M.D., 1968, Ph.D., 1970; m. Lynnette Laurene Jacobson, June 6, 1970; children—Joshua and Stephen (twins). Intern, Meth. Hosp., Houston, 1970-71; pvt. practice family medicine, Houston, 1971-73; asst. prof. dept. anatomy and cell biology Baylor Coll. Medicine, Houston, 1971-73; asst. prof. dept. family practice Med. Coll. Ga., Augusta, 1973-75, asso. prof., 1975-77, prof., 1977—, chmn. dept. family practice, 1976—; mem. Gov.'s Joint Bd. Family Practice, 1976—; pres. Ga. Fed. Family Practice Residency Programs, 1976-77; mem. Ga. Dept. Human Resources Adv. Council on Phys. Health Needs of Children and Youth, 1977-78. Deacon, Covenant Presbyn. Ch., 1978—. Diplomate Am. Bd. Family Practice. Fellow Am. Acad. Family Physicians; mem. AMA, AAAS, So. Soc. Anatomists, Ga. Acad. Family Physicians (Disting. Service award 1975), Christian Med. Soc., Sci. Research Soc. N.Am., Richmond County Med. Soc. Home: PO Box 320 Evans GA 30809 Office: Med Coll Ga Augusta GA 30912

CALVERT, RICHARD L., security systems co. exec.; b. Hackensack, N.J., Jan. 15, 1932; s. Thomas and Jean M. (Griffiths) C.; B.S., Fairleigh Dickinson U., 1958; M.B.A., Ark. State U., 1971; m. Carolyn Lavin, Sept. 12, 1977; children—E. Scott, Chris. With Huffman-Koos, Hackensack, 1957; sales mgr. Leonard Motors, New Milford, N.J., 1957-59; prodn. engr., buyer A.D.T. Security Systems, Clifton, N.J., 1959-65, plant mgr., Jonesboro, Ark., 1965—; guest speaker Memphis State U., 1972-73, Ark. State U., 1974-75, 80—. Bd. dirs. United Way Jonesboro, 1972-73. Mem. Am. Soc. Personnel Adminstrs., N.E. Ark. Personnel Mgmt. Assn. (pres.), Greater Jonesboro C. of C. (dir. 1970-73), Ark. C. of C., New Industry Commn. C. of C. (dir.), Ark. Indsl. Devel. Commn. Republican. Episcopalian. Clubs: Jonesboro Country, Paragould Country, Stonebridge Country, Elks. Home: 2300 Redbud Dr Jonesboro AR 72401 Office: 3506 Airport Dr Jonesboro AR 72401

CALVERT, WILLIAM PRESTON, radiologist; b. Warrensburg, Mo., July 2, 1934; s. William Geery and Elizabeth (Spaulding) C.; B.S., Mass. Inst. Tech., 1956; M.D., U. Pa., 1960; m. Mary Kay Kersh, Apr. 4, 1976. Intern, Pa. Hosp., Phila., 1960-61, resident in medicine, 1961-62, 64-66, chief med. resident, chief resident physician, 1965-66; resident in gastroenterology Jackson Meml. Hosp., U. Miami (Fla.), 1966-67, NIH fellow in gastroenterology, 1967-68, resident in radiology, 1968-71; radiologist Meml. Hosp., Hollywood, Fla., 1971-72; chief dept. radiology Larkin Gen. Hosp., South Miami, Fla., 1972—; clin. instr. radiology U. Miami Sch. Medicine, 1971-76. Served with M.C., USAF, 1962-64. Diplomate Am. Bd. Nuclear Medicine, Am. Bd. Radiology. Mem. AMA, Fla. Med. Assn., Fla., Greater Miami radiol. socs., Soc. Nuclear Medicine, Radiol. Soc. N.Am. Home: 6851 SW 106th St Miami FL 33156 Office: 7031 SW 62d Ave South Miami FL 33143

CALVIN, LARRY O., zoo adminstr.; married; 1 son. Formerly curator Dallas Zoo, now dir. Mem. Am. Assn. Zool. Parks and Aquariums, Nat. Recreation and Park Assn. Kiwanian. Office: 621 Clarendon Dr Dallas TX 75203*

CAMACHO, REMEDIOS MONAHAN, chem. engr.; b. Manila, Oct. 13, 1939; s. Martin Pinalosa and Rafaela Sanchez (Monahan) C.; B.S. in Chem. Engring., Mapua Inst. Tech., 1961; postgrad. Stevens Inst. Tech., 1971-72. Research asst. Rockefeller U., N.Y.C., 1968-69; biochemist Merck & Co., Rahway, N.J., 1969-74; process engr. Calgon Corp., Catlettsburg, Ky., 1975-77, Allied Chem. Co., Ashland, Ky., 1977—. Mem. Philippine Inst. Chem. Engrs., Women Chem. Engrs. Philippines Roman Catholic. Home: 614 LaGar St Flatwoods KY 41139 Office: PO Box 111 Ashland KY 41101

CAMBLIN, MARK LESTER EBERLEIN, microbiologist; b. Stevens Point, Wis., Nov. 3, 1941; s. Lester Brazil and Marian Elizabeth (Marty) Eberlein; student Wabash Coll., 1960-62; B.A., Ind. U., 1964; M.S., U. Tenn., 1967, Ph.D., 1971. Program dir. splty. microbiology trainee program dept. pathology St. Mary's Meml. Hosp., Knoxville, Tenn., 1971-77, faculty Sch. Med. Tech., 1971-77; partner Cons. Assos., Knoxville, 1974—; lectr. dept. microbiology U. Tenn., 1974—. Mem. Am. Bd. Bioanalysts, Am. Soc. Microbiology, AAAS, Tenn. Soc. Clin. Microbiology (pres. 1975), South Central Assn. Clin. Microbiology, Sigma Xi, Phi Sigma, Tau Kappa Epsilon, Nat. Wildlife Fedn. Presbyn. Contbr. articles to profl. jours. Home: 5421 Yosemite Trail Knoxville TN 37919 Office: Dept Pathology St Mary's Med Center Knoxville TN 37917

CAMBRON, ALBERT MOSELEY, retail car agy. exec.; b. Hartford, Ky., Oct. 28, 1908; s. John Payton and Rena Jane (Moseley) C.; student Western Ky. Tchrs. Coll., 1929-32, U. Ky., 1946; m. Emma Lee Hinton, Aug. 14, 1928; children—Margaret Ann (Mrs. Thomas Y. Catron), Max Gordon, Gary Dale. Tchr. Whitesville (Ky.) High Sch., farmer, Whitesville, 1945-51; mgr. Farmers Coop. Store, Owensboro, Ky., 1951-53, salesman Short Bros., Owensboro, 1953-58; gen. mgr. Ohio Motor Co., Hawesville, Ky., 1958-69; pres. Cambron Chevrolet, Inc., Hawesville, 1969—. Mem. Hawesville C. of C. (pres. 1968), Internat. Platform Assn., Dale Carnegie Alumni Assn. (pres. Owensboro chpt. 1966). Baptist (chmn. bd. deacons 1971-72, 74-76, 78-79, dir. lay team 1978-80). Mason, Lion (pres. 1964). Contbr. articles to profl. publs. Home: Box 295 Hawesville KY 42348 Office: Hwy 60 E Hawesville KY 42348

CAMERON, C. ARNOLD, lawyer; b. Cookeville, Tenn., Apr. 5, 1916; s. Orren Edward and Bessie (Arnold) C.; B.S., Tenn. Technol. U., 1937; LL.B., Andrew Jackson U., 1940; M.A. in Econs. and Bus. Adminstrn., Vanderbilt U., 1953; m. Billie Scott, June 26, 1938; children—William A., Anne E. Admitted to Tenn. bar, 1946, since practiced in Cookeville; sr. partner Cameron & Madewell, attys.; city judge, Cookeville, 1947-50; county atty. Putnam County, 1948-49; dir. Cookeville Fed. Savs. & Loan Assn. Vice pres., fin. chmn. Middle Tenn. council Boy Scouts Am., 1963-78, pres., 1978-80. Served with USNR, 1943-45. Recipient Silver Beaver award Boy Scouts Am., 1963. Mem. Putnam County, Tenn., Am. bar assns. Democrat. Presbyterian. Rotarian. Lion. Club: Golf and Country (Cookeville). Home and office: PO Box 529 Cookeville TN 38501

CAMERON, DON ROYCE, real estate broker; b. Jefferson City, Tenn., July 8, 1947; s. Simmie E. and Farris Joy (Thorpe) C.; B.S. in Agr., U. Tenn., 1975, M.B.A. in Real Estate and Fin., 1976; m. Sharon Lynn Blakley, June 15, 1974. Rep. Xerox Corp., Kingsport, Tenn., 1971-74; affiliate broker Zirkle-Rainwater Auction Co., Dandridge, Tenn., 1974-77; v.p. fin. Publix Oil Co., Morristown, Tenn., 1977-78; pres. Pegasus Corp., Knoxville, 1978—; pres. Cameron, Downing & Co., Knoxville, 1979—; appraisal cons. City of White Pine (Tenn.). Served with U.S. Army, 1966-69. Lic. real estate broker, Tenn. Real Estate Commn. Mem. Am. Soc. Farm Mgrs. and Rural Appraisers (asso.), Tenn. Soc. Farm Mgrs. and Rural Appraisers, Tenn. Hotel/Motel Assn., Knoxville Apt. Council. Mem. Ch. of Brethren. Home: Route 2 Box 305 White Pine TN 37890 Office: Suite 1018 Park Bank Tower Knoxville TN 37902

CAMMACK, JACK BEASLEY, JR., home furnishings co. exec.; b. New Orleans, Mar 10, 1950; s. Jack Beasley and Lois (Valadie) C.; B.B.A. magna cum laude, Ga. State U., 1972; children—Christopher, Michael. Store controller Sears, Roebuck & Co., Atlanta, 1971-73, Tallahassee, Fla., 1973-76, Atlanta, 1976-77; comptroller Warehouse Home Furnishings Distbrs., Inc., Dublin, Ga., 1977-78, v.p. fin., sec., treas., 1978—, also dir. Mem. Fin. Execs. Inst. Roman Catholic. Clubs: Dublin Country. Elks. Home: 301 Ridgecrest Dr Dublin GA 31021 Office: PO Box 1140 Industrial Blvd Dublin GA 31021

CAMMARATTA, DOMENIC PHILLIP (DON), educator; b. Tampa, Fla., Mar. 26, 1926; s. Phillip and Mary (Pendino) C.; B.A., Fla. State U., 1950, M.A., 1955; Ed.S., U. South Fla., 1971, Ph.D., 1975; m. Margaret Agnes O'Rourke Nogueira, Apr. 26, 1949; children—Patricia Lorraine, Frances Marie, Peggy Lynn, Don Patrick. Tchr., Hillsborough County Sch. Bd., Tampa, 1950-62, prin., 1962-64, supr., 1964-66, dir., 1966-74, gen. dir. vocat. tech. adult edn.,

1974-76, 78—, asst. supt. schs., 1976-78; prof. U. Tampa, 1957-58; adj. prof. U. South Fla., 1967-74; also cons. Chmn. Manpower Area Planning Council, 1977-79. Served with coast arty. U.S. Army, 1944-46. Mott Found. grantee, 1970-71. Mem. Am. Vocat. Assn., Am. Tech. Edn. Assn., Nat. Council Local Adminstrs., Fla. Vocat. Assn., Fla. Adult Edn. Assn. (pres.), Hillsborough County Ednl. Assn. (pres.), Phi Delta Kappa (pres.). Roman Catholic. Home: 3414 14th St Tampa FL 33605 Office: Hillsborough County Sch Bd 6410 Orient Rd Tampa FL 33610

CAMMENGA, JOHN ALDEN, furniture mfg. co. exec.; b. Rock Valley, Ia., Nov. 6, 1932; s. Andrew and Tillie (Visser) C.; student Davenport Inst. (Grand Rapids, Mich.), 1955-56; m. Esther Ellen Hoolsema, Mar. 18, 1955; children—Elizabeth M., Sarah L., John A., Anna K., Mary E. Vice pres., mgr. Drapery House Inc., Grand Rapids, 1955-60; adminstrv. head mfg. Furniture City Upholstery Co., Grand Rapids, 1960-66; v.p. mfg. La-Z-Boy Chair Co., Monroe, Mich., 1966-72, Dayton, Tenn., 1972— chmn. bd. Tenn. Consol. Industries Inc., Dayton, 1973—, also dir.; chmn. bd. 1st Nat. County Bank of Rhea County (Tenn.), 1977—, also dir.; dir. Am. Warehouse Inc., Civic Credit Corp. Mem. budget com. Mich. chpt. United Fund, 1958-59; chmn. bd. Monroe County United Fund, 1971-72, campaign mgr., 1971; mem. adv. bd. Bryan Coll., 1974, also trustee. Served with M.P., AUS, 1953-55; Korea. Mem. Dayton C. of C., Gideons Internat. (dir.). Mem. Christian Ref. Ch. (past elder). Kiwanian. Clubs: Dayton Golf and Country (dir.), Middlemans (dir.). Home: Rural Route 1 Dayton TN 37321 Office: Walnut Grove and Broadway Sts Dayton TN 37321

CAMP, BEN HERMAN, wholesale distbn. co. exec.; b. Toccoa, Ga., June 30, 1935; s. John Earl and Florence Lucille (Thomas) C.; student LaSalle Extension U., 1958; m. Joyce Evelyn Bryson, June 19, 1954; children—Barrey Stanton, Lynda Joyce, Terri Layne. Supr. accounts receivable-statis. Crane Co., Atlanta, 1955-57, salesman, 1958-62; salesman Atlas Supply Co., Atlanta, 1962-66; chief exec. officer Hub, Inc., Tucker, Ga., 1966—, also dir.; chmn. bd. Piping Products, Bedard Corp. Mem. So. Wholesalers Assn., Am. Supply Assn. Republican. Baptist. Club: Druid Hills Golf and Country. Home: 5464 Silver Ridge Dr Stone Mountain GA 30087 Office: 2146 Flintstone Dr Tucker GA 30084

CAMP, EHNEY ADDISON, JR., former ins. co. exec.; b. Maylene, Ala., May 9, 1907; B.S. in Commerce and Bus., U. Ala., 1928, LL.D., 1979; m. Mildred Fletcher Tillman, Feb. 25, 1933; children—Patricia Alice Camp Faulkner, Mary Gene Camp Boulware, Ehney A. III. With Ward, Sterne & Co., investment bankers, Birmingham, Ala., 1928-29, Banker's Mortgage Bond Co., Birmingham, 1929-32; mgr. loan dept. Liberty Nat. Life Ins. Co., Birmingham, 1932-34, asst. treas., 1934-35, treas., 1935-43, v.p., treas., 1943-60, exec. v.p., treas., 1960-73, dir., 1940-78, dir. emeritus, 1978—; past treas. and dir. Liberty Nat. Fire Ins. Co.; past pres. and dir. First Nat. Bank, Columbiana, Ala.; past mem. Nat. Com. Voluntary Home Mortgage Credit Program. Mem. Pres. Eisenhower's Spl. Adv. Com. on Govt. Housing Policies and Programs, 1953; past mem. adv. com. to fed. housing commrs.; past chmn. Jefferson County Air Pollution Adv. Com.; mem. alumni council U. Ala., trustee, 1959-79, life trustee, 1979—; bd. dirs., mem. exec. com. U. Ala. in Birmingham Med. and Ednl. Found.; mem. adminstrv. bd., vice chmn., past chmn. bd. trustees 1st United Methodist Ch., Birmingham; pres. Anti-Tb Assn. Jefferson County, 1954, trustee Campaign against TB, 1955—. Named to Ala. Acad. of Honor, 1976. Mem. Newcomen Soc. N. Am., Ala. Ins. Soc. (hon.), Am. Life Conv. (past chmn. fin. sect.), Mortgage Bankers Assn. Am. (past gov.), Mortgage Bankers Assn. Ala. (past pres.), U. Ala. Alumni Assn. (past nat. pres.), Jefferson County Alumni Assn. U Ala. (Disting. Alumni award 1974, past treas.), Phi Beta Kappa, Beta Gamma Sigma, Sigma Nu, Omicron Delta Kappa. Clubs: Kiwanis (past pres.), Mountain Brook Country (past gov.), Birmingham Country, The Club, Relay House (Birmingham).

CAMP, EHNEY ADDISON, III, mortgage banker; b. Birmingham, Ala., June 28, 1942; s. Ehney Addison and Mildred Fletcher (Tillman) C.; B.A., Dartmouth Coll., 1964; m. Patricia Jane Hough, Sept. 17, 1966; children—Ehney Addison, Margaret Strader. Sr. v.p. Cobbs, Allen & Hall Mortgage Co., Inc., Birmingham, 1965-72; v.p., gen. mgr. The Rime Cos., Birmingham, 1972-75; pres. Camp & Co., Birmingham, 1975—. Bd. dirs. Community Chest/United Way Jefferson, Walker and Shelby Counties. Served with USAF, 1965, Ala. Air N.G., 1966. Mem. Am., Ala. mortgage bankers assns., Birmingham Real Estate Bd. Methodist. Clubs: Kiwanis (dir. 1977-78), Mountain Brook (bd. govs. 1976-77), Birmingham Country, The Club, Downtown, Ponte Vedra. Home: 3621 Rockhill Rd Birmingham AL 35223 Office: 3940 Montclair Rd Suite 502 Birmingham AL 35213

CAMP, JAMES VERNON, assn. exec.; b. Union, S.C., Aug. 8, 1924; s. Thomas Franklin and Agnes Mae (Davis) C.; student Randolph Macon Coll., 1942-43; B.A., U. N.C., 1947, M.A. in Edn., 1948; m. Carol Enloe Cantrell, Aug. 9, 1952; children—Carey, Sara Carver, Cantrell, James Vernon. Profl. football player Bklyn. Dodgers, 1948; varsity football coach U. N.C., 1949-53; asst. football coach Miss. State U., 1953-54, U. Minn., 1954-61; head football coach George Washington U., Washington, 1961-67; asst. football coach UCLA, 1967-70; econ. devel. dir. Durham (N.C.) C. of C., 1970—. Mem. adminstrv. bd. Trinity United Meth. Ch., 1973-75; mem. alumni bd. dirs. and athletic council U. N.C., 1979-80. Served with USMC, 1943-45. Mem. So. Indsl. Devel. Council, N.C. Indsl. Developers Assn. (bd. dirs. 1971-72). Methodist. Clubs: Masons, Rotary, Hope Valley Country, Croasdaile Country. Home: 3748 St Marks Rd Durham NC 27707 Office: NW-Bank 201 N Roxboro C of C Durham NC 27701

CAMP, JOHN L., lawyer; b. Sparta, Tenn., Dec. 22, 1939; s. Lucius H. and Eloise C. (Cheatham) C.; student U. Tenn., 1957-59, Middle Tenn. State U., 1959-60; J.D., YMCA Law Sch., 1969; m. Angela Ellen Ashe; children—William, Richard, Ethan. Adjuster, U.S.F. & G. Ins. Co., Nashville, 1962-69; admitted to Tenn. bar, 1969; asso. firm Camp & Camp, Attys., Carthage, Tenn., 1969-70, partner, Sparta, 1970—. City judge, Carthage, 1969-70; mem. White County (Tenn.) Quar. Ct., 1972-74; mem., presiding officer Tenn. Med. Malpractice Rev. Bd., 1975—; del. Tenn. Constl. Conv., 1977; mem. Tenn. Dem. Exec. Com., 1978—. Mem. Tenn. (gov. 1971—), White County (pres. 1971-74), Am. bar assns., Tenn. Def. Lawyers Assn., Am. Judicature Soc., Lambda Chi Alpha. Democrat. Clubs: Sparta Country, Capitol Hill. Home: 1 Rosebud Ln Hickory Hills Sparta TN 38583 Office: 11 Rhea St Sparta TN 38583

CAMP, N. HARRY, JR., clin. psychologist; b. Des Moines, Mar. 28, 1918; s. N. Harry and Hazel Grace (Hohl) C.; B.A., U. Chgo., 1940, M.A., 1941; D.Ed., U. Calif., Los Angeles, 1948; postgrad. Johns Hopkins U., 1963-65. Sch. prin., Sigourney, Iowa, 1941-42; teaching asst. U. Calif., Los Angeles, 1946-48; prof. edn. Bklyn. Coll., 1948-49; prof. edn. and guidance Bucknell U., 1949-53; dir. guidance and clin. services Balt. County Schs., 1953-56; dir. psychiat. clinic Sch. for Boys, Marianna, Fla., 1956-58; dir. guidance and clin. services Brevard County, Fla., 1958-60; vis. prof. U. Miami, Fla., 1957-60, Pa. State U., 1960-65, Hunter Coll., N.Y., 1974-76; pvt. practice clin. psychology, 1961—; speaker on learning disabilities. Served to ensign, USNR, 1942-45. Editor Edn. Mag., 1949-53, The School Counselor, 1953-58. Address: 7520 SW 105th Terr Kendall FL 33156

CAMPBELL, AGNES KNIGHT (MRS. JOHN FRANKLIN CAMPBELL), ret. social agy. exec.; b. Boom, Tenn.; d. George Allen and Nora (Clark) Knight; B.S., Tenn. Tech. U., 1934; postgrad. Vanderbilt U., 1935, U. Chgo. Sch. Social Service Adminstrn., 1942, 46; M.S. in Social Work, U. Tenn., 1953; m. John Franklin Campbell, June 20, 1942. Regional dir. Tenn. Dept. Pub. Welfare, Nashville, 1942-55; social worker Youth Service, Child and Family Service, Knoxville, Tenn., 1955-58; exec. dir. Knoxville Travelers Aid Soc., 1958-79. Bd. dirs. Knoxville Legal Aid Soc., 1967-70, Workmen's, Inc., 1975-78, Turn Around, 1975-78, Greater Knoxville Nutritional Council, 1975—, Knox County Assn. on Alcoholism, 1974—; planning council United Community Services Greater Knoxville, 1967-69; nat. council Travelers Aid Internat. Social Service Am., 1973—. Recipient Distinguished Alumni award Tenn. Tech. U., 1977. Mem. Nat. Assn. Social Workers (chpt. pres. 1951-53, chpt. sec. 1966-68, editor chpt. newsletter 1971-73, bd. mem. at large 1973-76; mem. nat. nominating com. 1974—, named social worker of year Knox area chpt. 1976), Acad. Certified Social Workers, Tenn. Conf. Social Welfare (state sec. 1955), Nat. Travelers Aid Assn., Profl. Execs. Council Knoxville (pres. 1967-68), Social Service Club Knoxville (pres. 1958-59, 62-63). Author script: Some of Those We Help, 1962; play: Trouble Away From Home, 1964. Home: 6515 Sherwood Dr Knoxville TN 37919

CAMPBELL, ARCHIBALD ALGERNON, lawyer, state legislator; b. Wytheville, Va., July 23, 1921; s. P. Fitzgerald and Mary (Austin) C.; B.S., Va. Mil. Inst., 1943; LL.B., U. Va., 1949; m. Eloise Richberg, Feb. 19, 1950; children—Donald Richberg, Marenda Ann, Florence Weed. Admitted to Va. bar, 1948; temporary fgn. service officer Amfoge II, Greece, 1946; partner Woods & Campbell, attys., Wytheville; mem. Va. Ho. Dels., 1966—, chmn. fin. com., 1974—; adv. bd. First Nat. Exchange Bank Va., Wytheville; dir., treas. Tourists, Inc., Wytheville, 1960—. Mem. exec. com. Va. State Tb Assn., 1958-63; sec. Smyth-Wythe Joint Airport Commn., 1958-69; chmn. Wythe County Economy Commn., 1962-63. Served with USMCR, 1943-46. Decorated D.F.C. Mem. Am., Va. (v.p. 1962-63, exec. com. 1976-79) bar assns., Southwest Va. Horsemen's Assn. Democrat. Presbyn. Club: Rotary (local pres. 1958-59). Home: Pine Ridge Wytheville VA 24382 Office: 340 W Monroe St Wytheville VA 24382

CAMPBELL, BERTHA JOYCE, speech-lang. pathologist; b. Temple, Tex., Mar. 28, 1945; d. Clyde Edward and Roxie Mae (Flakes) Moore; A.A. with honors (scholar), Temple Jr. Coll., 1965; B.A., N.Tex. State U., 1967, M.A., 1970; postgrad. Lamar U., 1973, Ariz. State U., 1973-75, U. Houston, Clear Lake City, 1979; m. James Harold Campbell, Dec. 29, 1968; 1 child, Turik Kyle. Speech-lang. pathologist LaMarque (Tex.) Sch. Dist., 1968-71, Texas City (Tex.) Sch. Dist., 1972-73, Tempe (Ariz.) Elem. Sch. Dist., 1973-75; speech-lang. pathologist for early childhood and spl. edn. Clear Creek Sch. Dist., Houston, 1975—; instr. Sch. Communications, Tex. So. U., Houston, 1980; speech-lang. pathologist U. Tex. Moody Sch. Cerebral Palsy, summer 1971, Ariz. Children's Hosp., summers 1974, 75; pvt. practice speech, hearing and lang. therapy, Houston, 1971-72. Vice pres. Mainland Council of Children with Learning Disabilities, 1970-71. Grad. fellowship trainee, research asst., 1967-68; named outstanding student in dept. speech pathology and audiology, 1967. Mem. Am. Speech Lang. and Hearing Assn. (cert. clin. competency), Tex. Speech, Lang. and Hearing Assn., Houston Area Assn. for Communicative Disorders, Tex. Classroom Tchrs. Assn., Delta Sigma Theta (pres. LaMarque chpt. 1971-72), Phi Theta Kappa. Democrat. Methodist. Club: Sisters of Calanthe. Home: 16434 Havenpark Dr Houston TX 77059 Office: Webster Primary School S Austin St Webster TX 77058

CAMPBELL, CAREY WALTON, neurol. surgeon; b. Hattiesburg, Miss., Oct. 24, 1937; s. Brutus Randolph and Maggie Corin (Smith) C.; B.S., Miss. So. U., 1960; M.D., U. Miss., 1964; 1 dau. by previous marriage, Phyllis Catherine. Surg. intern Ochsner Found. Hosp., New Orleans, 1964-65; resident in neurosurgery U. Miss. Med. Center, Jackson, 1965-66, Walter Reed Army Hosp., Washington, 1968-69, George Washington U. Med. Center, 1969-71; practice neurosurgery, Paducah, Ky., 1975—; neurol. surgeon dept. neurosurgery George Washington U. Med. Center, Washington, 1971-74; instr. neurol. surgery George Washington U., 1971-74. Served to maj., M.C., U.S. Army, 1967-69; Vietnam. Diplomate Am. Bd. Neurol. Surgeons. Mem. Am. Assn. Neurol. Surgeons, Internat. Soc. Study of Lumbar Spine, Congress Neruol. Surgeons, Pi Kappa Alpha. Democrat. Club: Masons. Contbr. articles to profl. jours. Office: 1532 Lone Oak Rd Paducah KY 42001

CAMPBELL, CARROLL ASHMORE, JR., congressman; b. Greenville, S.C., July 24, 1940; student U. S.C.; m. Iris Rhodes, 1959; children—Carroll Ashmore III, Richard Michael. Farmer; pres. Handy Park Co., 1962-78; v.p. Rex Enterprises, operators Burger King Restaurants in Fla. and Ga., Tallahassee, 1967-78; mem. S.C. Ho. of Reps., 1970, 72, asst. minority leader; exec. asst. to Gov. of S.C., 1975; mem. S.C. Senate, 1976; mem. 96th Congress from 4th Congressional Dist. S.C.; participant Nat. Fgn. Policy Conf., 1972, 77. Govtl. rep. Med. U. S.C., 1975-76; del. Republican Nat. Conv., 1976, alt. del., 1972; former mem. S.C. Developmental Disabilities Council, S.C. Gov.'s Com. on Employment of Handicapped, Am. Legis. Exchange Council, S.C. Health Coordinating Council; past mem. adv. council White House Conf. on Handicapped Individuals. Recipient Disting. Service award Jaycees, award K.C., Citizenship award Rehab. Assn. Clubs: Sertoma (life), Masons, Shriners. Office: Room 1723 Longworth House Office Bldg Washington DC 20515

CAMPBELL, CHARLIE ROBERT, airport exec.; b. Elk Garden, Va., June 13, 1946; s. Edward Milton and Lucille Virginia (Warner) C.; student public schs., Lebanon, Va.; m. Doris Marie Switzer, Mar. 27, 1969. Craftsman, Radford (Va.) Army Ammunition Plant, 1967-69; asst. to airport mgr. New River Valley Airport, Dublin, Va., 1969-72; airport supt. Roanoke (Va.) Mcpl. Airport, 1972-74, ops. supr. safety and security, 1974—. Served with USAF, 1963-67. Mem. DAV. Home: Route 2 Box 43 Fincastle VA 24090 Office: Roanoke Municipal Airport Airport Operations Office Roanoke VA 24012

CAMPBELL, DAVID GWYNNE, petroleum exec., geologist; b. Oklahoma City, May 2, 1930; s. Lois Raymond Henager and LaVada (Ray) Henager Campbell; B.S., Tulsa U., 1953; M.S., U. Okla., 1957; m. Janet Gay Newland, Mar. 1, 1958; 1 son, Carl David. Geologist, Lone Star Producing Co., Oklahoma City, 1957-65; dist. geologist and geol. cons. Mid-Continent div. Tenneco Oil Co., Oklahoma City, 1965-77; exploration mgr. Leede Exploration, Oklahoma City, 1977—. Active Last Frontier council Boys Scouts Am., 1960-65; Oklahoma City rep. to Cherokee Nation, 1976-78. Served with U.S. Army, 1953-55. Mem. Am. Petroleum Inst., Am. Assn. Petroleum Geologists (field trip chmn. 1978 conv.), Oklahoma City Geol. Soc. (chmn. Speakers bur. 1963-64, chmn. stratigraphic code com. 1967-68, presdl. appointee 1969-70), Tulsa Geol. Soc., Am. Assn. Petroleum Landmen, Oklahoma City Geol. Discussion Group (pres. 1975-76), Oklahoma City Petroleum Club, Sigma Xi, Pi Kappa Alpha. Home: 6109 Woodbridge Rd Oklahoma City OK 73132 Office: 1515 Liberty Tower Oklahoma City OK 73102

CAMPBELL, DEANNA LYNN, newspaper exec.; b. San Angelo, Tex., Sept. 17, 1954; d. Elo Frank and Mary Patricia (Jansa) Schwertner; B.S. in Distributive Edn/Bus. Adminstrn., Angelo State U., San Angelo, 1978; m. Scott Edward Campbell, Nov. 13, 1976. With San Angelo Standard-Times, Inc., 1974—, personnel coordinator, 1978—. Millard Cope journalism scholar, 1974; vocat. edn. scholar, 1977. Mem. San Angelo Personnel Assn. (sec. 1980), Am. Soc. Personnel Adminstrn., Newspaper Personnel Relations Assn. Roman Catholic. Club: San Angelo Jr. Women's (treas. 1979-80, reporter 1980-81). Office: PO Box 5111 34 W Harris St San Angelo TX 76903

CAMPBELL, DONALD RICHARD, chem. co. exec.; b. Portsmouth, Va., Dec. 4, 1928; s. Donald Gregory and Macel Lola (Rollyson) C.; B.S. in Chemistry, U. Va., 1956; M.S. in Chemistry, Brown U., 1958; m. Dorothy Dolores Mroz, May 6, 1955; children—Cheryl Susan, Dorothy Cassandra. With E.I. du Pont Co., Florence, S.C., 1958—, research chemist, 1958-59, devel. supt., 1960-71, staff chemist, 1971—, tech. coordinator Mylar mfg. facilities expansion. Pres. Lake Oakdale Assn., 1978, bd. dirs., 1972-78; v.p. Colonial Forest Civic Assn., 1969. Served with U.S. Army, 1951-52. NSF fellow, 1957-58; recipient Atlas Powder Co. award, 1956. Mem. Nat. Speleol. Soc., Mythopoeic Soc., Alpha Chi Sigma. Baptist. Contbr. articles to profl. publs. Office: EI du Pont Co PO Box 3000 Florence SC 29501

CAMPBELL, EDDIE RAY, univ. dean; b. Roaring Springs, Tex., Sept. 8, 1931; s. John K. and Vada B. (Bearden) C.; B.A., Harding Coll., 1959, M.A., 1961; m. Martha Kathryn Roberts, Sept. 7, 1951; children—David, Linda K., Danny, Julie. Ordained to ministry Churches of Christ; minister chs., Palatka, Fla., 1954-58, St. Augustine, Fla., 1952-54; dean of students Ga. Christian Sch., 1960-64; asst. dir. admissions, admissions counselor Harding Coll., Searcy, Ark., 1965-71, dean of men, 1969—. Vice chmn. White County chpt. ARC, 1974. Mem. Am. Personnel and Guidance Assn., Nat. Assn. Student Personnel Adminstrs., S.W. Assn. Student Personnel Adminstrs. (program chmn. 1973), Phi Delta Kappa. Home and Office: PO Box 673 Station A Searcy AR 72145

CAMPBELL, EWING, author; b. Alice, Tex., Dec. 26, 1940; s. James Vernon and Marie (Crofford) C.; B.B.A., N.Tex. State U., 1968; M.A., U. So. Miss., 1972; Ph.D., Okla. State U., 1980; m. Lois R. Glenn, Apr., 1972. Author: (novel) Weave it Like Nightfall, 1977; contbr. short stories to various lit. jours.; translator; Tierra en el dia (Julio Ortega), 1978. Served with U.S. Army, 1959-62. Mem. Authors Guild, Am. Lit. Translators Assn., S. Central MLA, Phi Kappa Phi. Address: 2612-A Audubon Pl Austin TX 78741

CAMPBELL, GEORGE EMERSON, lawyer; b. Piggott, Ark., Sept. 23, 1932; s. Sid A. and Mae (Harris) C.; J.D., U. Ark., 1955; m. Joan Stafford Rule, Apr. 9, 1973; children—Dianne, Carole. Admitted to Ark. bar, 1955, U.S. Supreme Ct. bar, 1971; asso. firm Kirsch, Cathey & Brown, Paragould, Ark., 1955; law clk. Asso. Justice Ark. Supreme Ct., 1959-60; mem. firm Rose, Nash, Williamson, Carroll, Clay & Giroir and predecessors, Little Rock, 1960—; spl. chief justice Ark. Supreme Ct., 1977. Mem. Ark. Ednl. TV Commn., 1976—, vice chmn., 1978—; exec. sec. Ark. Constl. Revision Study Commn., 1967-68; chmn. Ark. Constl. Conv. Prep. Commn., 1968-69; del. Seventh Ark. Constl. Conv., 1969-70. Served with USNR, 1955-59. Recipient Distinguished Citizen award, Nat. Municipal League, 1973. Fellow Ark. Bar Found.; mem. Am., Ark., Pulaski County bar assns., Am. Law Inst., Nat. Municipal League. Presbyterian. Club: Country Club of Little Rock. Home: 4 Kingston Dr Little Rock AR 72207 Office: 720 W 3d St Little Rock AR 77201

CAMPBELL, HAROLD MONROE, govt. ofcl.; b. Monahans, Tex., Aug. 18, 1933; s. Alva Lee and Elisabeth Estelle (Kemp) C.; B.S., Sam Houston State U., 1967; grad. Command and Gen. Staff Coll., Fort Leavenworth, Kans., 1977, Indsl. Coll. Armed Forces, Washington, 1977; m. Diane Denise Luther, Mar. 19, 1976; children—William, Charles, Karen. Sgt. detective El Paso (Tex.) Police Dept., 1955-63; with Fed. Narcotics Bur., Houston, 1963-65; with intelligence div. IRS, San Antonio, 1967-68; with Bur. Alcohol, Tobacco and Firearms, Dept. Treasury, 1968—, resident agt. in charge, Muskogee, Okla., 1974-76, New Orleans, 1976-78, rep. to Dept. Justice Organized Crime Strike Force, New Orleans, 78; spl. agy., 1978—. Served with USN, 1951-54; lt. col. U.S. Army Res. Mem. Fed. Investigators Assn., Tex. Police Officers Assn., Res. Officers Assn., Civil Affairs Assn., Okla. Sheriffs and Peace Officers Assn. Baptist. Club: Masons, Optimists. Home: 3232 Flowerdale Ln Dallas TX 75229 Office: 1100 Commerce St Room 12C52 Dallas TX 75242

CAMPBELL, J. THOMAS, statistician, real estate exec.; b. Michigan City, Ind., Feb. 19, 1938; s. James P. and Marie H. (Schultz) C.; B.S., U. Bridgeport, 1962; M.B.A., U. Hartford, 1969; m. Diane Patricia Campbell, Feb. 10, 1979; 1 son, Jonathan Scott. Sr. statistician United Technologies Corp., Hartford, Conn., 1962-72; mgr. corp. planning Gen. Devel. Corp., Miami, Fla., 1972-76, dir. planning, budgeting and control, 1976—. Mem. Planning Exec. Inst., Nat. Assn. Bus. Economists, Am. Real Estate and Urban Econs. Assn., Am. Statis. Assn. Republican. Methodist. Contbr. research in field; editor handbook. Home: 2105 Brickell Ave Miami FL 33129 Office: 1111 S Bayshore Dr Miami FL 33131

CAMPBELL, JAMES LEE, motor mfg. co. exec.; b. Des Moines, Apr. 23, 1923; s. James Edward and Jessie E. (Allen) C.; student U. Notre Dame, 1941-43; B.S. in Mech. Engring., U. Tenn., 1948; m. Margaret A. Heffernan, May 14, 1946; children—Elyse A., James Lee, John W., David R. Inspection test supr. Crosley div. Avco, Richmond, Ind., 1952-55; mgr. product reliability elec. products div. Ambac Industries, Columbus, Miss., 1955—. Served with U.S. Army, 1943-46, USAF, 1951-52. Registered profl. engr., Calif. Mem. Am. Soc. Quality Control (past. chmn. N.E. Miss. sect.), Columbus C. of C. Roman Catholic. Clubs: Rotary (pres. 1967), Columbus Country (pres. 1962). Home: 1100 Southdown Pkwy Columbus MS 39701 Office: McCrary Rd Columbus MS 39701

CAMPBELL, JOHN ASA LEWIS, coal co. exec.; b. Petrolia, Pa., Apr. 9, 1938; s. Asa L. and Betty A. (King) C.; B.S. in Chemistry, Pa. State U., 1960, M.S. in Mineral Processing, 1963, Ph.D., 1969; m. Donna Lee Lease, Jan. 11, 1963; children—Ann Kristine, John A. Lease, Donalei Kelly, Famie King. Engr. scientist coal mining research N.J. Zinc Co., Central Lab., Palmerton, Pa., 1967-71; sr. project engr. coal mining research Kennecott Copper Co., Ledgemont Lab., Lexington, Mass., 1971-75; dir. tech. support Peabody Coal Co., Belleville, Ill., 1975-79; dir engring. and tech. support Kerr McGee Coal Corp., Oklahoma City, 1979—. Mem. AIME, Am. Chem. Soc., Sigma Xi, Alpha Chi Sigma, Phi Lambda Upsilon. Lutheran. Home: 11816 Bevenshire Oklahoma City OK 73132 Office: Kerr McGee Center Oklahoma City OK 73125

CAMPBELL, JOHN ESKEW, interior designer; b. Alexandria, La., Sept. 26, 1945; s. Forrest Leroy and Laura Elizabeth (Eskew) C.; cert. U. Bordeau and Toulouse (France), 1962; B.A., La. Polt. Inst., 1968,

B.A., 1969. Pres., John Campbell Design Assos., Inc., interior designers, Alexandria, 1969—; mem. adv. com. dept. interior design Delgado Coll., New Orleans, 1976—. Mem. Am. Soc. Interior Designers (pres. La. chpt. 1978, 79, dir. 1980-81); asso. mem. Asso. Gen. Contractors La., La. Assn. Home Builders. Democrat. Roman Catholic. Mem. adv. panel Interior Design mag., 1977. Home: Route 1 Gardner Hwy Alexandria LA 71301 Office: PO Drawer 7087 Alexandria LA 71306

CAMPBELL, JOHN HOWARD, minister; b. Rutherfordton, N.C., Jan. 27, 1947; s. Wayne Edward and Mary Willie (Norville) C.; B.A., Mars Hill Coll., 1969; M.Div., So. Bapt. Theol. Sem., 1973; M.S.S.W., U. Louisville, 1974; m. Shirley June Brazeal, Sept. 28, 1969; children—Brian Scott, Chelsy Camille. Ordained to ministry So. Baptist Ch., 1968; pastor Mountain Rd. Bapt. Ch., Statesville, N.C., 1967-69; dir. vol. aftercure program Ormsby Village Treatment Center, Louisville, 1972-73; ch. project dir. So. Bapt. Theol. Sem., Louisville, 1974; dir. Bapt. Friendship House, New Orleans, 1975—. Bd. dirs. New Orleans Food Bank. Mem. Nat. Assn. Social Workers, So. Bapt. Social Service Assn. Democrat. Office: Baptist Friendship House 813 Elysian Fields Ave New Orleans LA 70117

CAMPBELL, LESLIE CAINE, educator; Prof. history, journalism Auburn (Ala.) U., asso. dean Sch. Arts and Scis., dir. honors program, chmn. univ. disciplinary com.; exec. com. Council of Deans of Arts and Scis., Commn. on Higher Edn.; mem. Joint Com. for Off-Campus Grad. Instruction in Ala. Recipient Am. Inst. History Pharmacy Commendation award, 1977; NSF fellow. Pres., Auburn United Fund; commr. public info. City of Auburn. Mem. Am. Assn. Univ. Adminstrs. (pres., founder Ala. chpt., nat. membership chmn.). Club: Rotary (pres. Auburn chpt., dist. chmn. internat. service, chmn. dist. ednl. awards Rotary Found.). Author: History of the Mississippi State Pharmaceutical Association, 1964; Two Hundred Years of Pharmacy in Mississippi, 1974; editor Alpha Jour., 1974—. Office: Sch Arts and Scis Auburn U Auburn AL 36830

CAMPBELL, LLOYD TYE, JR., elec. engr.; b. Athens, Tenn., Oct. 12, 1947; s. Lloyd Tye and Virginia Doris (Wade) C.; Asso. Sci., Middle Ga. Coll., 1968; B.S. in Elec. Engring., La. Inst. Tech., 1971; M.S. in E.E. (Tex. Instruments fellow) So. Meth. U., 1978; m. Cheryl Renee Camp, Aug. 24, 1974. Elec. engr. Spurling Fire Alarm Co., Athens, 1972; project engr. 3 M Co., Chattanooga, 1973; project engr. Container Corp. Am., Chattanooga, 1974-76; elec. engr. Tex. Instruments, Dallas, 1976—. Served to 1st lt. USAR, 1971—. Registered profl. engr., Tex. Mem. IEEE, Kappa Epsilon Sigma. Baptist. Home: 7003 Sable Ln Wylie TX 75098 Office: PO Box 225303 M/S 3176 Dallas TX 75267

CAMPBELL, LUCY BARNES (MRS. ALFONSO L. CAMPBELL), librarian; b. Windsor, N.C., Oct. 30; d. Eley and Frankie Elizabeth (Carter) Barnes; B.A., N.C. Central U., 1941, B.L.S., 1942, M.L.S., 1960; m. Alfonso L. Campbell, Sr., May 4, 1946; children—Alfonso L., Sharon I. Librarian, Darden High Sch., Wilson, N.C., 1942-45; asst. librarian Ala. State U., Montgomery, 1945-63; circulation librarian Hampton Inst., Huntington Library, Hampton, Va., 1963, acting dir., coordinator student activities, 1964, asst. reference librarian, 1964-65, asst. prof./head periodicals dept., 1966—, coordinator residence hall reading rooms, 1967-73; participant Inst. Black Studies Librarianship, Fisk U., summer 1970. Solicitor, United Negro Coll. Fund, 1964-70, Hampton Inst. Peninsula Ann. Fund Campaign, 1972-78. Recipient citation for service and leadership Ala. State U., 1962; certificate of merit Women's Senate, 1965, named Mother of Yr., 1965, Mother of Men of Hampton, 1968 (all Hampton Inst.). Mem. ALA, Assn. Coll. and Research Libraries, Southeastern, Va. library assns., Assn. Study of Afro-Am. Life and History, YWCA, Black Caucus, NAACP (life), Alpha Kappa Alpha. Baptist. Clubs: Women's Service League, Order Eastern Star. Author: Black Librarians in Virginia, 1976; The Story of the Hampton Institute Library School, 1925-39, 1976. Home: 819 Lincoln St Portsmouth VA 23704 Office: Box 6003 Hampton Inst Hampton VA 23668

CAMPBELL, MARGARET FOOTE, speech pathologist; b. Gadsden, Ala., Mar. 9, 1949; d. Gurnie Hershel and Sarah Lois (Osborne) Foote; B.S., Auburn U., 1971, M.Speech Communication, 1972; m. William Edward Campbell, Jr., Dec. 26, 1972; 1 son, Joshua William. With Tenn. Valley Rehab. Center, Decatur, Ala., 1972, Comprehensive Mental Health Center, Paris, Ky., 1973-74, Partlow State Hosp., Tuscaloosa, Ala., 1974, Hale County Bd. Edn., Greensboro, Ala., 1974-75, Mobile Head Start Program, 1977, Mobile Rehab. Rotary Center, 1977, Mobile County Bd. Edn., 1977-78; speech pathologist Etowah County Bd. Edn., Gadsden, Ala., 1978—. Clin. competence cert. Mem. Am. Speech and Hearing Assn., Speech and Hearing Assn. Ala., Kappa Delta Pi. Home: 124 Monroe Circle Gadsden AL 35904 Office: Attala City Spl Edn Attalla AL 35901

CAMPBELL, MARY HOLMES, guidance counselor; b. St. Louis; d. Claude Norman and Alice Mooney (Gorsuch) Holmes; B.S. in Psychology summa cum laude, Troy (Ala.) State U., 1978; m. Schaffner Carl Campbell, II, Aug. 7, 1955; 1 dau., Sydney Cay. Successively youth counselor, coordinator youth, dir. youth Shalimar (Fla.) United Methodist Ch., 1973-76; chem. abuse counselor Hurlburt Field, Fla., 1977-78; counselor Human Growth and Devel., Ft. Walton Beach, Fla., 1978—; cons. Center for Rational Behavior Edn., Ft. Walton Beach. Mem. Internat. Transactional Analysis Assn., Nat. Vocat. Guidance Assn., Am. Rehab. Counseling Assn., Am. Personnel and Guidance Assn., Am. Mental Health Counselors Assn. Democrat. Address: 22 Windsor Ln Fort Walton Beach FL 32548

CAMPBELL, MARY MCCRACKEN, counselor; b. Savannah, Ga., Jan. 28, 1935; d. John and Estelle Theresa (Powers) McC.; B.A., Mt. St. Agnes Coll., 1957; M.A., Ga. So. Coll., 1974; m. Thomas Kelly Campbell, Aug. 16, 1974. Mem. Sisters of Mercy, Roman Catholic Ch., 1952-67; houseparent, counselor Villa Marie Orphanage, Balt., 1960-63; tchr. elem. schs., Savannah, Ga., 1963-73, counselor, 1975—. Chmn. 2d Dist. Republican. Com., 1979—. Office Edn. grantee, 1973-74. Mem. Am. Personnel and Guidance Assn., Am. Sch. Counselors Assn., Ga. Sch. Counselors Assn., Navy League. Roman Catholic. Home: 1 Bishop Ct Savannah GA 31401 Office: 50 Byck Ave Savannah GA 31408

CAMPBELL, MYERS DALLAS, III, banker; b. Kansas City, Mo., July 14, 1929; s. Myers Dallas and Wilma (Morris) C.; B.S. in Bus. Adminstrn., NE Mo. State U., 1954; m. Patricia Maureen Mogg, May 24, 1953; children—Myers, IV, John, Susan, Matthew. Regional credit mgr. Citcorp., Oklahoma City, 1957-63; pres. Am. Nat. Bank, Midwest City, Okla., 1963-75, chmn. bd., chief exec. officer, 1975—; pres., dir. Am. Nat. Bancshares, Inc., 1975—. Bd. dirs. Tinker Area br. YMCA; mem. met. bd. dirs. YMCA. Served with USAF, 1951-52. Mem. Midwest City C. of C. (past dir., v.p.). Office: Am Nat Bank 1500 S Midwest Blvd Midwest City OK 73110

CAMPBELL, NANCY CAROL, audiologist; b. Ft. Belvoir, Va., Oct. 21, 1954; d. Robert Asbury and Anne F. C.; B.S., Madison Coll., Harrisonburg, Va., 1976; M.Ed. in Audiology, U. Va., 1977. Chief audiologist with pvt. physician, Winchester, Va., 1977—; mem. Warren County Spl. Edn. Adv. Com.; adv. bd. Easter Seal Soc. Pilot Club scholar, 1972; summer fellow U. Va., 1977; recipient Daniel Coulter award Madison Coll., 1976. Mem. Council Exceptional Children (pres. Blue Ridge chpt. 1979-80), A.G. Bell Children's Assn. Deaf, Am. Speech and Hearing Assn., Sigma Alpha Eta (past officer). Roman Catholic. Club: Winchester Quota (chmn. public hearing screening com. 1978, chmn. aid to hard hearing com. 1979). Home: 1201 Whittier Ave Winchester VA 22601 Office: 125 Medical Circle Winchester VA 22601

CAMPBELL, P. M., govt. ofcl.; b. Washington, Sept. 13, 1941; d. R. Patrick and Margaret A. (Murray) McFerren; student George Washington U., 1960, U.S. Army Adj. Gen. Sch., 1969-75, Marywood Coll., 1977-79, Center for Degree Studies, 1979-80; m. Ellis C. Campbell, Sept. 25, 1972; children—Sharon P.H., Dorothy E.H., Ellis C. With U.S. Dept. State, Washington, 1959-63, ACDA, 1963-64, Mil. Dist. Washington Commissary Office, U.S. Army, Alexandria, Va., 1965-67, U.S. Army Petroleum Center, Alexandria, 1967-69; adminstrv. officer Def. Supply Agy., Alexandria, 1969-74; mgmt. analyst Defense Logistics Agy., Alexandria, 1974—, participant in establishment of over 30 nation-wide word processing centers, 1976-80. Recipient Meritorious Civilian Service award Defense Logistics Agy., 1979, Hon. Mention award Pres.'s Con. for Hiring Handicapped, 1959. Mem. Internat. Word Processing Assn., Fed. Govt. Word Processing Council. Baptist. Home: Route 7 Box 260 Stafford VA 22554 Office: DLA-XWP Cameron Station Alexandria VA 22314

CAMPBELL, RONALD ANTHONY, lawyer; b. Tulsa, July 13, 1951; s. Parris Clifford and Mabel Ellen Campbell; B.A. in Polit. Sci. and Spanish, Fisk U., 1973; J.D. (Earl Warren scholar), U. Ky., 1977. Admitted to Ky. bar, 1979; analyst Standard Oil Co., 1973-74; analyst, investigator Lexington (Ky.) Human Rights Commn., 1975; coordinator Bluegrass Employment and Tng. Summer Youth Program, 1976-77; securities atty. Capital Holding Corp., Louisville, 1977—. Bd. dirs. Miles Meml. Community Center, 1979—; active NAACP. Mem. Ky. Bar Assn. Democrat. Methodist. Home: 1242 S 2d St Louisville KY 40203 Office: Capital Holding Corp PO Box 32830 Louisville KY 40232

CAMPBELL, SELMA RONALD, obstetrician and gynecologist; b. Lake Wales, Fla., Mar. 1, 1933; s. Selma Buford and Nina Elizabeth (Callahan) C.; A.A., U. Fla., 1953; M.D., U. Miami, 1960; children—Valerie, Devonie, Alandrea, Steven, Michael; m. Carol Wilson, July 7, 1978. Commd. 1st lt. M.C., U.S. Army, 1960, advanced through grades to maj., 1965; intern Martin Army Hosp., Ft. Benning, Ga., 1960-61; resident in obstetrics and gynecology Tripler Gen. Hosp., Honolulu, 1962-65; chief obstetric-gynecol. service Ft. Jackson (S.C.) Army Hosp., 1965-68; practice medicine specializing in obstetrics and gynecology, Georgetown, S.C., 1968, Lake Wales, 1969—; mem. staff Lake Wales Hosp., 1969—, chief of staff, 1975-76. Chmn. bd. dirs. Lake Wales YMCA; bd. dirs. Lake Wales Little League, Lake Wales Band Assn. Diplomate Am. Bd. Obstetrics and Gynecology. Fellow Internat., Am. colls. obstetricians and gynecologists; mem. AMA, Fla., Polk County, Christian med. assns., Am. Fertility Soc., Fla. Obstet.—Gynecol. Soc. Baptist. Club: Kiwanis. Home: Crooked Lake Lake Wales FL 33853 Office: 415 S 11th St Lake Wales FL 33853

CAMPBELL, VIRGINIA PATRICE, social worker; b. Winston-Salem, N.C., Aug. 14, 1946; d. John Webster and Virginia (Thomas) C.; B.A., Mary Baldwin Coll., 1968; M.Ed., U. Va., 1972; M.S.W., Va. Commonwealth U., 1979. Social service aide DeJarnette Center, Staunton, Va., 1968-72, rehab. counselor, 1972-73, dir. admissions, 1973-76; with People Places, Inc., Staunton, 1973—, program supr., 1977—, bd. dirs., pres., 1977-78, treas., 1978—. Lic. counselor, Va.; cert. rehab. counselor. Mem. Assn. for Advancement of Behavior Therapy, Nat. Assn. Social Workers, Council for Exceptional Children, Am. Personnel and Guidance Assn., Am. Rehab. Counselor Assn. Home: PO Box 42 New Hope VA 24469 Office: 24 W Beverly St Staunton VA 24401

CAMPBELL, WILLIAM J., judge; b. Chgo., Mar. 19, 1905; s. John and Christina (Larsen) C.; grad. St. Rita Coll. Prep. Sch., 1922; J.D., Loyola U., 1926, LL.M., 1928, LL.D., 1955, Litt.D., 1965, J.C.D., 1967; m. Marie Agnes Cloherty, 1937; children—Marie Agnes (Mrs. Walter J. Cummings), Karen (Mrs. James T. Reid), Heather (Mrs. Patrick Henry), Patti (Mrs. Peter V. Fazio, Jr.), Roxane (Mrs. Wesley Sedlacek), William J., Christian, Thomas. Admitted to Ill. bar, 1927; Ill. adminstr. Nat. Youth Adminstrn., 1935-38; U.S. dist. atty. No. Dist. of Ill., 1938-40; judge U.S. Dist. Ct., 1940—, chief judge, 1959-70; asst. dir. Fed. Jud. Center, Washington, 1974—. Citizens bd. U. Chgo., Loyola U., Barat Coll. of Sacred Heart; bd. dirs. Catholic Charities Chgo.; co-founder Cath. Youth Orgn. Chgo., 1930; mem. exec. bd. Chgo. council, also nat. exec. bd. Boy Scouts Am. Mem. Am., Ill., Chgo., Fed. bar assns., Jud. Conf. U.S. (chmn. com. on budget 1955-69). Clubs: Law, Ill. Athletic, Union League, Standard (Chgo.); La Coquille (Manalapan, Fla.). Home: 400 S Ocean Blvd Villa 305-A Manalapan FL 33462 Office: 401 Fed Bldg 701 Clematis St West Palm Beach FL 33401

CAMPBELL, WILLIAM RANSOM, JR., architect; b. Durham, N.C., Feb. 6, 1920; s. William Ransom and Flossie Love (Mann) C.; B.Arch., N.C. State U., 1954; student E. Central State Coll., 1946-47, Tulane U., 1947-51; m. Ola Adelle Stearns, Mar. 3, 1945; children—Barclay William, Kelly Sue. Designer, draftsman Louis Asbury & Son, Charlotte, N.C., 1954-56, Albert C. Woodroof, Architect, Greensboro, N.C., 1956-57; archtl. designer Harris & Pine, Durham, N.C., 1957-59; coordinator new constrn. U. Ark., Fayetteville, 1959-65; dir. campus devel. U. Hawaii, Honolulu, 1966-68; dir. facilities planning, univ. architect U. Okla., Norman, 1968-73; exec. v.p. Binnicker Assos., Oklahoma City, 1973—; v.p. Gralla Assos., Oklahoma City, 1979—; asso. prof. architecture U. Okla., Norman, 1968-73; adj. asso. prof. community health U. Okla. Health Scis. Center, Oklahoma City, 1968-73; lectr. Internat. Coll. and Univ. Conf. and Exposition, Atlantic City, 1970, Council of Ednl. Facility Planners, Las Vegas, 1971, Am. Inst. Architects Nat. Conv., Houston, 1972; photographer exhibiting Future of Architecture in Am., Mus. of Modern Art, N.Y.C., 1953. Exec. sec. archtl. adv. commn. to Duke Endowment, N.C. Meth. Conf., 1957-59. Mem. adminstrv. officers council U. Okla., 1969-73. Served with USNR, 1942-45. Mem. Tulane Archtl. Soc. (pres. 1949-50), AIA (Tulane student chpt. pres. 1950-51, bd. dirs. Okla. chpt. 1972-73), Assn. Univ. Architects (pres. 1971-72, bd. dirs. 1972-73), Soc. for Coll. and Univ. Planning, Norman C. of C., Council of Ednl. Facility Planners. Club: Sertoma (organizer, charter mem.) (Chapel Hill, N.C.). Author: Long Range Development Plan, 1969; Guide and General Program to Consultants, 1971. Cons. editor to Coll. and Univ. Bus., pubs., 1974. Home: 810 Jona Kay Norman OK 73069 Office: Suite 1330 50 Penn Pl Oklahoma City OK 73118

CAMPBELL, WILLIAM ROCKWELL, concrete co. exec.; b. Cleve., Dec. 3, 1926; s. Frank William and Ollie (Rockwell) C.; student Ohio U., 1946-48; B.S.I., Cleve. Coll., 1950; m. Doris Prestwood Holloway, May 5, 1950; 1 dau., Susan Nanette. Chief design engr. Cleve. Lathe & Machine Co., 1950-52; dir. human resources Rinker Materials Corp., West Palm Beach, Fla., 1952—. Sec., West Palm Beach Camp Gideons, 1965. Served with USNR, 1944-45. Mem. Am. Inst. Indsl. Engrs. (chpt. v.p. 1965), Christian Bus. Men's Com. (sec.-treas. 1965; dir. S.Am. mission), Nat. Concrete Masonry Assn. (tech. com., chmn. prodn. sub-com.), Fla. Engring. Soc., Am. Mgmt. Assn., Am. Concrete Inst., Fla. Concrete and Products Assn. (tech. com., jr. coll. com.), SAR (sec. 1968, 1st v.p. 1969). Presbyterian (deacon 1966-69, elder 1969—). Clubs: Atlantis Golf, Lago Mar Country. Home: 230 NW 130th Ave Lago Mar Colony Plantation FL 33325 Office: 431 7th St West Palm Beach FL 33401

CAMPION, EILEEN, lawyer; b. Great River, N.Y., d. Patrick and Mary (Gaughan) C.; J.D., U. Miami (Fla.), 1961. Admitted to Fla. bar, 1962; individual practice law, Miami, 1962-64; law editor Lawyers Co-op. Pub. Co., Rochester, N.Y., 1964-65; atty. U.S. Treasury Dept., Miami, 1965—; editor Fed. Exec. Bd. publ. The Short End, 1976-77. Founding pres. Women's Com. of One Hundred, Miami, 1970-73; mem. fed. exec. bd. Miami Consumers Com., 1972-77, chmn., 1974-77; mem. Metro Dade County Water and Sewer Bd., 1973-75; city rep. Bd. Legal Services Greater Miami, 1974—. Recipient Outstanding Service award Fed. Bar Assn., 1968, 69; award for untiring efforts for community betterment Women's Com. of One Hundred, 1973; Internat. award in legal writing Phi Delta Delta, 1963, AAUW fellow, 1976. Mem. Am., Dade County (Outstanding Service award 1971) bar assns., Fla. Bar, AAUW, Am. Arbitration Assn. (panel arbitrator), UN Assn. (chmn. speakers bur. Miami-Coral Gables chpt. 1977-73), Bus. and Profl. Women's Club. Home: 453 Brickell Ave Miami FL 33131 Office: 51 SW 1st Ave Miami FL 33130

CANAAN, GERSHON, architect; b. Berlin, Jan. 19, 1917; s. Ernst and Hedwig (Davidson) Kortner; B.A., Technion (Haifa, Israel), 1937; M.A., U. Tex., 1952, B.A. in City Planning, 1954; m. Doris Smith, May 23, 1954; 1 son, Robert Ernst. Apprentice Erick Mendelsohn, Israel, 1950-51, Frank Lloyd Wright, U.S.A., 1947; instr. archtl. design U. Tex., 1950-51; prin. architecture and planning, Dallas, 1958-62; spl. archtl. adviser PHA, 1962-65, nat. design cons., 1965-68; v.p. design J.L. Williams & Co., Dallas, 1978-80, sr. v.p., 1980—. Consul of Fed. Rep. Germany, 1962; initiator Ann. Celebration of Germany Day in Tex., 1963; mem. Am. Council on Germany; found chmn. Tex. German Day Council, 1963—; founder, pres. Dallas Goethe Center, 1964—. Served to capt. Garrison Engr., Royal Engrs., Brit. Army, 1942-45; served as field comdr., staff officer Israel Def. Army 1948. Recipient Presdl. Citation, 1964; medal of merit German Inst. Fgn. Relations, 1967; Officers Cross of Order of Merit, Germany, 1968; Fighters Decoration Volunteerism medal, Israel, 1969; named Ambassador of Goodwill, Gov. Tex., 1965, 76; recipient Consul of Year award Consular Corps Acad., 1974; Honor medal City of Frankfurt, 1972; Liberty Bell, City of Berlin, 1976; recognition Tex. Senate, 1977, 79. Mem. AIA, Dallas Consular Corps, C. of C., Tex. Soc. Architects. Author: Rebuilding the Land of Israel, 1954; Design of Memorials, 1960; co-author: German Days in Texas. Home: 4700 St Johns Dr Dallas TX 75205 Office: Simons Bldg Dallas TX 75201

CANADA, ALONZO FRANKLIN, III, mfrs. rep.; b. Tulsa, Jan. 15, 1937; s. Alonzo Franklin, Jr. and Edythe (Blackmer) C.; B.S. in Mech. Engring., Okla. State U., 1960; m. Bonnie Jean Hoeft, Nov. 24, 1964; children—Lonnie, Deke, Cami. Sales engr. Elliot Co., Los Angeles, 1960-66; sales mgr. Arduser & Co., Tulsa, 1966-73; pres. Canada Co., Tulsa, 1973—. Served as officer AUS, 1960-61. Sr. mem. ASME, Instrument Soc. Am. (past officer); mem. Pipe Liners Tulsa, Gas Processors Suppliers Assn. Republican. Mormon. Club: Tulsa. Home: 5201 S Irvington St Tulsa OK 74135 Office: 4145 S 87th E Ave Tulsa OK 74145

CANALIZO, ALBERT EUGENE, fin. corp. exec.; b. St. Augustine, Fla., Dec. 26, 1943; s. Albert Eugene and Aline (McElroy) C.; B.S. in Bus., La. State U., 1964; m. Marilyn Suzanne Belanger, Sept. 19, 1964; 1 dau., Donna Lynn. Mgr., All-State Credit Plan, Inc. div. U.S. Industries, New Orleans, 1964-78, v.p., dir. advertisement, dir. bus., 1979—. Co-founder, treas. Lakeshore Hebrew Day Sch., 1970—; mem. Jewish Burial Soc., 1970—. Named Businessman of Year, Better Bus. Bur., 1973; Salesman of Year, All-State Credit Plan, 1976; Leader of Year, C. of C., 1972 Mem. Am. Mgmt. Assn., Nat. Consumer Fin. Assn., La. Consumer Fin. Assn. Republican. Pub. Jewish religious guides, 1974—, Notes of Credit, 1979—. Home: 6578 Louis XIV St New Orleans LA 70124 Office: All-State Credit Plan Inc 1201 Saint Charles Ave New Orleans LA 70124

CANAN, HOWARD VOORHEIS, cons. engr., author; b. Omaha, Aug. 6, 1894; s. Clarence John and E. Lizette (Voorheis) C.; B.S., U.S. Mil. Acad., 1918; postgrad. U.S. Army Engring. Sch., 1921, Command and Gen. Staff Coll., 1939, Naval War Coll., 1942. Commd. 2d lt. U.S. Army, 1918, advanced through grades to col.; with C.E., 1921-28; asst. prof. mil. sci. and tactics Colo. Sch. Mines, Golden, 1928-32; asst. dist. engr. Duluth, 1932-34; dist. engr. U.S. Lake Survey, 1934-36; gen. staff M.I. Div. War Dept., 1939-41; G-2 sec. GHQ, 1941-42; duty with Amphibious Corps and Force, Pacific Fleet, 1942-43; asst. to engr. ETO, 1943-46; dist. engr. Nashville, 1946-49; engr. 2d Army, Ft. Meade, Md., 1949-52; engring. insp. gen., 1952-53; asst. chief engrs. for real estate, 1953-54; ret., 1954; cons. practice, 1954-56; cons. civil engr. Melpar, Inc., Alexandria, 1956-60; cons. engr., 1960—. Trustee Patriotic Edn., Inc. Decorated Legion of Merit, Bronze Star (U.S.); Croix Guerre (France). Fellow ASCE Am. Geog. Soc.; mem. Mil. Inst., Soc. Am. Mil. Engrs., SAR, Civil War Round Table. Clubs: Cosmos, Army and Navy. Co-author book on bass fishing. Contbr. articles to profl. and hist. jours. Home: Apt 522 1200 S Washington St Alexandria VA 22314

CANDLER, JOHN SLAUGHTER, II, lawyer; b. Atlanta, Nov. 30, 1908; s. Asa Warren and Harriet Lee (West) C.; A.B. magna cum laude, U. Ga., 1929; J.D., Emory U., 1931; m. Dorothy Bruce Warthen, June 13, 1933; children—Dorothy Warthen (Mrs. Joseph W. Hamilton, Jr.), John Slaughter. Admitted Ga. bar, 1931, partner Candler, Cox, Andrews & Hansen and other firms, 1931—; dir. Leon Propane, Inc., Weatherly Corp., Propane Gas Service, Inc., D.M. Weatherly Co., Sungas, Inc., Equipment Sales Co., Ga. Motor Club Inc., others; dep. asst. atty. gen. State of Ga., 1951-68. Mem. Greater Atlanta Council USO, 1969—, exec. com., 1970-79, pres., 1974-75. Trustee Ga. Student Ednl. Fund; trustee Kappa Alpha Scholarship Fund, pres., 1970-72; trustee Northside Atlanta Kiwanis Found., chmn., 1962-79. Served from capt. to col. AUS, 1941-46. Decorated Commendation Ribbon. Fellow Am. Coll. Probate Counsel (regent 1968-74), Internat. Acad. Law and Sci.; mem. Nat. Tax Assn.-Tax Inst. Am. (Tax Inst. Am. adv. council 1969-72), Newcomen Soc., Am. Judicature Soc., State Bar Ga. (chmn. sect. on fiduciary law 1964-65), Am., Atlanta bar assns., Internat. Platform Assn., Atlanta Estate Planning Council (pres. 1963-64), Lawyers Club Atlanta, Am. Legion (post comdr. 1949-50), Res. Officers Assn. (state pres. 1946, nat. exec. com. 1947), Mil Order World Wars, English-Speaking Union, U.S. Power Squadrons, Phi Beta Kappa, Phi Kappa Phi, Phi Delta Phi, Kappa Alpha Order, Sigma Delta Chi. Episcopalian (vestryman 1953-56, sr. warden, 1955, cathedral trustee 1957-67, Lay reader 1971—). Clubs: Masons, Kiwanis, Atlanta Touchdown, Piedmont Driving, Capital City, Commerce, Peachtree Racket; Ft. McPherson Officers; Oglethorpe (Savannah); Army-Navy (Washington). Home: 413 Manor Ridge Dr NW Atlanta GA 30305 Office: 2400 Gas Light Tower Atlanta GA 30303

CANEY, LOUIS LINCOLN, service co. exec.; b. West Springfield, Mass., Feb. 12, 1936; s. Randolph Elliott and Lena Louise (Gagnon) C.; grad. high sch., 1952; divorced; children—Louis Lincoln (dec.), Kevin Michael. Sales mgr. Standard Food Service, Springfield, 1959-62, Lustra Corp., Boston, 1962-64; sales dir. Standard Uniform Serviced, Springfield, 1964-68; regional mgr. Servisco, Dallas, 1968—, adviser to bd. dirs., 1972—. Served with US Army, 1952-53. Named Regional Mgr. of Year, Servisco, 1974, 75, 76, 77, 78, recipient award for plant of year, 1970, 71, 72. Mem. Inst. Indsl. Launderers, Linen Suppliers Assn. Am. Clubs: Masons, Shriners. Home: 3009 Country Club Rd Garland TX 75043 Office: 1703 Chestnut St Dallas TX 75226

CANFIELD, BOURBON ELLIS, surgeon; b. Berea, Ky., Aug. 16, 1924; s. Maurice Maxwell and Leila Bourbon (Current) C.; student Eastern Ky. State Teacher's Coll., 1942-43; M.D., U. Louisville Med. Sch., 1946; m. Lois Tipton, June 23, 1946 (dec. Sept. 1968); m. 2d, Linda Chinn, Sept. 6, 1969; 1 son, David A. Intern, Louisville Gen. Hosp., 1947-48, grad. research asst. physiology, 1949; resident Louisville Gen. Hosp., 1949-53; asst. clin. prof. surgery U. Louisville, 1962—; pvt. practice surgery, Louisville, Ky., 1956—; mem. staff St. Joseph's Infirmary and Methodist Evangelical, Ky. Bapt. Hosps., Suburban Hosp., St. Anthony Hosp.; Jewish Hosp., Sts. Mary and Elizabeth Hosp., Norton-Childrens Hosp., Kosair Crippled Childrens Hosp. Served with AUS, 1950-55. Diplomate Am. Bd. Surgery. Fellow Am. Coll. Surgeons, Southeastern Surg. Congress. Mem. Am., Ky. med. assns., Jefferson County Med. Soc., Ky., Louisville surg. socs. Bapt. (deacon 1959—). Club: Glendale Flying Club of Louisville (sec.). Home: 5401 Hempstead Rd Louisville KY 40207 Office: 308 Medical Towers North Louisville KY 40202

CANFIELD, NOAH LA MAR, motel broker and cons.; b. Buchanan, Mich., May 20, 1931; s. Robert Noah and Mable (Moon) C.; student U. Mich., 1967-69; m. Treva Delores Swift, Oct. 6, 1956; 1 son, Steven Robert. Owner, operator Capitol City Speed Shop, Lansing, Mich., 1959-67, Colonial House Motel, Clearwater, Fla., 1970-74; asso. All Star Realty Co., Lansing, Mich., 1967-70; pres. Am. Motel Brokers, Inc., Clearwater, Fla., 1974—. Served with USNR, 1951-54. Mem. Motel Brokers Assn. Am. (pres.), Clearwater-Largo-Dunedin Bd. Realtors (dir.), Cert. Rev. Appraisers Assn., Soc. Real Estate Appraisers (asso.). Roman Catholic. Home: 2117 Keene Rd N Clearwater FL 33515 Office: 1441-A Court St Clearwater FL 33516

CANGELOSI, ANTHONY, ins. co. exec.; b. New Orleans, Sept. 15, 1923; s. Donato A. and Virginia (Cangelosi) C.; B.A., Tex. A&M U., 1947; m. Anthonette Scardino, Oct. 15, 1944; children—Virginia, Don, Samuel, Carol Anne, Anthony, Victor. Office clk. Anderson, Clayton & Co., Houston, 1947-49; ind. ins. agt., San Antonio, 1949—; asst. mgr. M.O.N.Y., San Antonio, 1961-62; pres., owner Regal Life Am. Ins. Co., San Antonio, 1973—, Pan Am. Acceptance Corp., 1971—, Internat. Bankers Ins. Agy., Inc.; v.p. Valls-Laurel Ins. Agy., Laredo, Tex.; owner Internat. Ins. Services, Granada Ins. Agy. Mem. State of Tex. Joint Interim Study Com. on Small Bus., 1975—, Tex. State Metric System Adv. Council, 1977; chmn. bd. dirs. Burke Found.'s Darden Hill Ranch Sch. Served with AUS, 1943-46. Mem. Internat. Good Neighbor Councils Tex. (pres. 1975-76, sec. 1976—), San Antonio Council Pres.'s. Democrat. Roman Catholic. Clubs: Italo-Am., Oak Hills Country (San Antonio). Home: 101 Tamworth St San Antonio TX 78213 Office: 924 Camaron St San Antonio TX 78212

CANIZARO, BENNY LEE, architect; b. San Antonio, Jan. 6, 1945; s. Bennett G. and Doris Ray (Grosdidier) C.; B.Arch., U. Tex., Austin, 1969; m. Mary Avis Votaw, Aug. 27, 1965; children—Christine Michelle, David Ryan, Anne Elizabeth. Architect intern O'Connell & Probst Architects, 1969-70, 71-72; partner Environetics, Austin, 1972-74; asso. Wukasch Assos., Architects, Austin, 1975-76; prin. Lasseter Assos. Architects, Austin, 1976-78; partner Canizaro/Holeman Architects, Austin, 1978-80, Canizaro-Roccaforte Assos., Wimberley, Tex., 1980—; vocat. drafting instr. Round Rock Vocat. Sch., 1974-75. Mem. City of West Lake Hills Zoning and Planning Commn., 1979; mem. Master Planning Com. West Lake Hills, 1976-79. Mem. AIA (treas. Austin chpt. 1979), Constrn. Specifications Inst., Tex. Soc. Architects. Baptist. Clubs: Kiwanis (v.p. 1979-80), Lions. Home: Route 1 Box 330 F Wimberley TX 78676 Office: PO Box 636 Wimberley TX 78676

CANIZARO, JOSEPH CORTE, real estate developer; b. Balt., Mar. 1, 1937; s. Vito J. and Gilda M. (Melone) C.; student Spring Hill Coll., Miss. State U.; m. Sue Ellen Mettina, June 16, 1961; children—Joellen Theresa, Jill Suzanne. Appraiser, Standard Mortgage Co., New Orleans, 1963-65; pres., chief exec. officer Joseph C. Canizaro Interests, New Orleans, 1965—. Pres. bd. commrs. Downtown Devel. Dist., 1977-78; mem. med. bd. govs. Tulane U., 1975—. Named Italian-Am. of the Yr., 1978; Outstanding Young Man of Yr., New Orleans Jaycees, 1973; one of 10 Outstanding Persons of Yr., Inst. Human Understanding, 1977; recipient St. Louis medal, 1978. Mem. Nat. Assn. Office and Indsl. Parks (past pres. La. chpt.), Urban Land Inst., Inst. Real Estate Mgmt., Internat. Council Shopping Centers, Young Pres.'s Orgn, Internat. House, New Orleans Area C. of C. (dir., exec. com.). Roman Catholic. Clubs: Sch. of Design (New Orleans); Beau Chene Country, Plimsoll. Hon. mem. editorial bd. Nat. Mall Monitor. Home: 516 Northline St Metairie LA 70005 Office: 300 Poydras St Suite 2201 New Orleans LA 70130

CANN, RAYFORD EARL, transp. co. exec.; b. Abbeville, S.C., Apr. 16, 1945; s. Thomas Talmadge and Vessie Aline (Wallace) C.; A.S., DeKalb Coll., 1966, A.A. in Bus. Adminstrn., 1973; B.B.A. cum laude, Ga. State U., 1976; m. Brenda Joyce Maxwell, Nov. 29, 1968; children—Stephanie Renea, Jeffery Chandler. Computer operator Emory U. Hosp., Atlanta, 1963-66, computer programmer, 1966-68; programmer DeKalb Bd. Edn., Clarkston, Ga., 1968-70, computer systems analyst, 1970-73; systems analyst Tenneco Oil Co., Atlanta, 1974-76; data processing mgr. Brown Transport Corp., Elberton, Ga., 1976—; cons. Elberton High Sch., 1977-78. Served with USN, 1966-67. Methodist. Home: Route 1 PO Box 46 Dewy Rose GA 30634 Office: PO Box 460 Clairmont Ave Elberton GA 30635

CANNEDY, LLOYD LON, hosp. adminstr.; b. Wichita Falls, Tex., Sept. 13, 1943; s. Glen C. and Mammie B. (Reid) C.; B.B.A., Midwestern U., 1966; M.B.A., Samford U., 1968; M.S. in Hosp. Adminstrn., U. Ala., 1968; Ph.D., U. Iowa, 1971; m. Bobbie Lurene Ledbetter, Aug. 27, 1964; children—Nolan Dean, Norene Boyce, Janell Lurene. Adminstrv. resident U. Ala. Hosp. and Clinics, Birmingham, 1968; adminstrv. asst. U. Iowa Hosps. and Clinics, Iowa City, 1968-69; instr. U. Iowa grad. program hosp. adminstrn., Iowa City, 1970-71; adminstr. Bradford (Pa.) Hosp., 1971-74; exec. dir. Amarillo (Tex.) Hosp. Dist., 1974—; cons. health facility to U.S. Govt. Overseas Private Investment Corp., Latin Am. div., 1973-74; preceptor adminstrv. residency program City U. N.Y., 1971-74; mem. state adv. com. on family practice residency Tex. Coll. and U. System Coordinating Bd., 1977—. Chmn. profl. div. Amarillo United Way, 1978-79; bd. dirs. Amarillo Area Acad. Health Center Corp., 1974—, Amarillo Found. for Health and Sci. Edn., 1974—, Potter-Randall Counties Tex. Child Welfare, 1974—, chmn. fin. com., 1975-79. Fellow Am. Coll. Hosp. Adminstrs. (Robert S. Hudgens award 1979), Royal Soc. Health; mem. Am. Acad. Med. Adminstrs., Tex. Hosp. Assn., Am. Hosp. Assn., Assn. of Mental Health Adminstrs. Clubs: Rotary, Masons. Office: 2200 W 7th St Amarillo TX 79175

CANNING, HAROLD MOOD, assn. exec.; b. New Hope, Pa., Nov. 13, 1904; s. Albert Hibbs and Margaret Thornton (Conover) C.; B.A. in Bus., Rider Coll., 1934; m. Edna Mary Prigge, Nov. 2, 1931; children—Cynthia (Mrs. Fred Leslie Smith), Patricia (Mrs. Ronald Carney). Advt. dir. Asbury Park (N.J.) Press, 1934-52, Wilmington (Del.) Sunday Star, 1952-55; mgr. N.Y.C. office, Lancaster (Pa.) Newspapers, 1955; nat. advt. dir. St. Petersburg (Fla.) Times and Evening Independent, 1955-75; exec. dir. St. Petersburg Sales and Mktg. Execs., 1974—, also past pres. Pres., Shore Community Chest, 1947-48; bd. dirs. Salvation Army, 1972—. Served with USCGR, 1944-45. Recipient Spl. Plaque, St. Petersburg, 1962—; award Salvation Army, 1968—. Mem. St. Petersburg Advt. Fedn. (past pres.), Fla. Newspaper Advt. Execs. (past pres.), Am. Advt. Fedn. (recipient silver medal for distinguished service to advt. 1963), C. of C. Presbyn. (elder). Mason, Kiwanian (past pres.). Club: Bath. Home and office: 6229 13th Ave N St Petersburg FL 33710

CANNIZZARO, KENNETH PETER, bus. equipment sales exec.; b. Bronx, N.Y., Dec. 27, 1944; s. Anthony Joseph and Rae Maria (Licitra) C.; B.S. cum laude in Computer Sci., N.Y. Inst. Tech., 1970; M.B.A., L.I. U., 1973; m. Roma M. Maniaci, Oct. 30, 1971; 1 dau., Tristen Ann. Asst. dir. data processing N.Y. Inst. Tech., Old Westbury, 1968-74; systems analyst Xerox Data Systems, N.Y.C., 1974-75; with Digital Equip. Corp., 1975—, sales group mgr., Dallas, 1979—; cons. in field. Served with USN, 1965-67. Mem. Digital Computer User Soc. Office: 12100 Ford Rd Suite 200 Dallas TX 75234

CANNON, CHARLES DALE, educator; b. Bruce, Miss., May 27, 1928; s. Walter Dale and Eunice Kate (Johnson) C.; B.A., U. Miss., 1951, M.A., 1952; Ph.D., U. Mo., Columbia, 1964; m. Patricia Faye Capwell, Dec. 25, 1952; children—Patricia Dianne, Charles Dale. Instr. English, Copiah Lincoln Jr. Coll., Wesson, Miss., 1953-55, U. Mo., Columbia, 1955-56; investigator U.S. CSC, Dallas, 1956-57; asst. prof. Miss. Coll., Clinton, 1957-59; instr. U. Mo., 1960-64; asst. prof. Southeast Mo. State Coll., Cape Girardeau, 1965-66; asst. prof. U. Miss., University, 1964-65, 1966-68, asso. prof., 1968-71, prof., 1971—, acting chmn. dept., 1976-77. Served with U.S. Army, 1946-49. Mem. MLA, Malone Soc., Eta Sigma Phi, Delta Phi Alpha, Pi Kappa Pi, Phi Kappa Phi, Sigma Tau Delta. Democrat. Baptist. Club: Oxford Music. Author: A Warning for Fair Women: A Critical Edition, 1975. Home: 1101 S 14th St Oxford MS 38655 Office: Dept English U Miss University MS 38677

CANNON, HARRY RICHARD, clergyman; b. Asheville, N.C., Oct. 13, 1932; s. Horace Rufus and Glovene (Hart) C.; B.A., Columbia Bible Coll., 1956; lic. vocat. nurse, missionary med. cert. Bible Inst. Los Angeles, 1957; m. Carol Lee Kretzler, June 9, 1956; children—Kimberly Anne, Kevin Lee, Christina Lyn. Ordained to ministry Evangelical Synod Reformed Presbyterian Ch., 1965; asst. pastor South Hollywood (Calif.) Presbyn. Ch., 1957-59; missionary Dutch New Guinea, 1959-63; missions exec. Evang. Alliance Mission, Wheaton, Ill., 1966-72; pastor, Calvary Presbyn. Ch., Fort Lauderdale, Fla., 1972-77; pres. French Camp (Miss.) Acad., 1977—; tchr. missions Miami Christian Coll., 1975-76, trustee, 1975-76. Contbr. articles to mission mags. Address: French Camp Acad French Camp MS 39745

CANNON, HUGH, lawyer; b. Albemarle, N.C., Oct. 11, 1931; s. Hubert Napoleon and Nettie (Harris) C.; A.B., Davidson Coll., 1953; B.A. (Rhodes scholar) Oxford U., 1955, M.A., 1960; LL.B., Harvard, 1958; m. Lorrie Clark, July 17, 1979; children by previous marriage—John Stuart, Marshall, Martha Janet. Admitted to N.C. bar, 1958, S.C. bar, 1979; mem. staff U. N.C. Inst. Govt., Chapel Hill, 1959; atty. Sanford, Phillips, McCoy & Weaver, Fayetteville, 1960; asst. to Gov. of N.C., Raleigh, 1961; dir. adminstrn. State of N.C., 1962-65, state budget officer, 1963; mem. firm Sanford, Cannon, Adams & McCullough, Raleigh, 1965-79; individual practice law, Charleston, S.C., 1979—. Parliamentarian NEA, 1965—; lectr. N.C. State U., Raleigh, part-time, 1965, 66. State dir. N.C. Emergency Resources Planning Com., 1962-65; pres. Friends of Coll., Raleigh, 1963; alt. del. Democratic Nat. Conv., 1964; chief parliamentarian, 1976; bd. govs. U. N.C.; trustee Davidson Coll., 1966-74. Mem. Phi Beta Kappa, Omicron Delta Kappa, Phi Gamma Delta. Democrat. Methodist. Home: 25 State St Charleston SC 29401 Office: 995 Morrison Dr Charleston SC 29402

CANNON, JOHN LAWRENCE, accountant, county ofcl.; b. Orangeburg, S.C., July 18, 1950; s. Riddick Ackerman and Doris A. (Livingston) Proveaux; B.S., Baptist Coll. at Charleston, 1972; m. Linda Susan Byrd, May 26, 1973; 1 dau., Lawra Susan. Office mgr., tax cons. Marcoin Mgmt. Services, Charleston, S.C., 1973-74; accountant, fin. supr. Charleston County Dept. Social Services, Charleston, S.C., 1974—. Recipient Leadership Devel. Achievement award Charleston Trident C. of C., 1977. Mem. Baptist Coll. Alumni Assn. (pres. 1979), S.C. State Employees Assn., S.C. Assn. Govtl. Purchasing Ofcls., S.C. Dept. Social Services Dirs. and Suprs. Assn. Republican. Baptist. Club: Civitan (pres.-elect W. Ashley 1979). Home: 2142 Church Creek Dr Charleston SC 29407 Office: 409 The Center Charleston County Dept Social Services Charleston SC 25403

CANNON, LEE FERRARA, home economist; b. Morgantown, W.Va., Oct. 12, 1918; B.A. in Home Econs., W.Va. U., 1940, M.S. in Home Econs., 1944; postgrad. U. Wis., 1944-48; m. Robert Y. Cannon, June 10, 1948; children—Emilie Cannon Johnson, Robert Y., Leigh. High sch. home econs. tchr., Osage, W.Va., 1941-44; nutrition researcher Sch. Home Econs., U. Wis., Madison, 1944-48; asst. prof. Sch. Home Econs. Auburn (Ala.) U., 1948-70, home econs. specialist Ala. Coop. Extension Service, 1970—; asso. producer, hostess Ala. Public TV, Auburn, 1955—. Mem. Gov.'s Commn. on Aging. Mem. Am. Home Econs. Assn., Am. Women in Radio and TV, Women in Communications, Ala. Home Econs. Assn. (v.p.), Ala. Dairy Products Assn. (past pres. women's div.), Phi Upsilon Omicron. Clubs: Auburn U. (pres. 1977-78), Auburn U. Faculty (bd. dirs.). Author: Southern Living's Quick and Easy Cookbook; Today's Home Idea Book, 3 vols., 1972-75. Home: 525 Forestdale Dr Auburn AL 36830 Office: Auburn TV Auburn U Auburn AL 36830

CANON, ROBERT MORRIS, arts adminstr.; b. Winona, Miss., July 26, 1941; s. Booma Sharp and Elizabeth Pauline (Harrison) C.; B.A., U. Miss., 1964, M.A., 1967. Instr. opera theatre U. Miss., 1964-66, coordinator performing and fine arts, 1966-72; program dir., cons. Miss. Arts Commn., Jackson, 1967-72; dir. Galveston (Tex.) Arts Center, 1972-74; exec. dir. Arts Council of San Antonio (Tex.), 1975—; artistic dir. Panola Playhouse, 1962-70; guest lectr. U. Va., 1972; dir. The Joffrey Workshop, 1973-74, 78—. U.S. del. AITA-UNESCO Conf., Monaco, 1969; cons. Nat. Endowment Arts, 1976—. Bd. dirs. Tex. Assembly Arts Councils, 1976-79; mem. urban affairs com. Tex. Arts Commn. Mem. Miss. Theatre Assn. (pres. 1966-68), Southeastern Theatre Conf. (dir. 1967-72), Am. Community Theatre Assn. (bd. govs. 1969-72), Am. Council Arts, Am. Theatre Assn., Assn. Am. Dance Companies (mem. exec. com. 1975-77), Soc. for Performing Arts (dir. 1978—). Contbr. articles to arts jours. Home: 310 E Mistletoe San Antonio TX 78212 Office: 201 N St Marys San Antonio TX 78205

CANSLER, DOROTHY PHILLIPS, social worker; b. Bonlee, N.C., Sept. 12, 1925; d. Diffie Cummings and Martha (Speas) Phillips; A.B., U. N.C., 1946, M.S.W., 1966; postgrad. Duke U., 1947-49, U. N.C., 1961-63; m. James Olin Cansler, Sept. 7, 1947; children—Linda Carol, David Clay, Martha Karen. Dir. girls and women's activities YMCA, Petersburg, Va., 1946-47; psychologist Murdock Center, Butner, N.C., 1963-64; counselor Family Counseling Service, Durham, N.C., 1966-70; mental retardation div. coordinator Durham Mental Health Center, 1972-73; family coordinator Chapel Hill (N.C.) Tng. Outreach Project, 1973—; cons. in field. Chmn., Y-Teen Bd., 1966-67; deacon Binkley Bapt. Ch., 1970-73; mem. U. N.C. Univ. Women's Bd. (v.p. 1972-73), Children's 100 Com. N.C., 1974-76; mem. Orange County Bd. of N.C. Symphony, Chapel Hill, 1977—, pres., 1979—; mem. Am. Dance Festival Assn., 1979—. AAUW fellow, 1962-63; NIMH grantee, 1964-66. Mem. Acad. Cert. Social Workers, Nat. Assn. Social Workers, Am. Assn. Mental Deficiency, Council Exceptional Children, Nat. Assn. Retarded Citizens. Democrat. Contbr. articles to profl. jours. Home: 716 Caswell Rd Chapel Hill NC 27514 Office: Lincoln Center Merritt Mill Rd Chapel Hill NC 27514

CANTEY, WILLIAM CHILDS, surgeon; b. Columbia, S.C., May 16, 1910; s. John Manning and Elizabeth (Childs) C.; B.S., U. S.C., 1933; M.D. with honors, Med. U. S.C., 1936; m. Blanche Moorer Dennis, Aug. 27, 1938; children—William Childs, Blanche Dennis Cantey Foster. Intern, resident Episcopal Hosp., Phila., 1936-42; fellow in surgery Lahey Clinic, Boston, 1942—; practice medicine specializing in surgery, Columbia, 1946-76; med. dir. S.C. Med. Care Found., Columbia, 1976—; cons. surgery Barnwell and Kershaw County hosps., VA Hosp.; sr. surgeon Richland Meml., Baptist, Providence hosps.; dean com. Med. Sch. U. S.C., also clin. prof. surgery; dir. First Carolina Savs. & Loan, C & S Nat. Bank, Columbia Outdoor Advt. Co. Pres. S.C. State Fair, 1969-80; chmn. Columbia Met. Airport Authority, 1978; mem. Columbia Planning Commn., 1951-57; active Am. Cancer Soc.; vestry Episc. Ch. Served to maj. U.S. Army, 1942-46. Named Distinguished Alumni Med. U.S.C., 1974; City of Columbia Ambassador of Year, 1976. Diplomate Am. Bd. Surgery. Mem. A.C.S. (pres. S.C. chpt., gov. for S.C.), AMA, S.C. Med. Assn. (Outstanding Community Service award 1975), So. Surg. Assn. (v.p. 1978), So. Soc. Clin. Surgeons (pres.), Southeastern Surg. Congress (pres.), S.C. Surg. Soc. (pres.), Med. Jour. Club (pres.). Democrat. Clubs: Cotillion, Centurion, Pine Tree Hunt, Kiwanis. Author: My Health Record, 1955; contbr. numerous articles to med. jours. Home: 3605 Chateau Dr Columbia SC 29204 Office: 3325 Med Park Rd Columbia SC 29203

CANTINE, CLIFFORD CHARLES, SR., golf course equipment distbg. co. exec.; b. New Orleans, July 2, 1931; s. Clarence Conrad and Helen Margarite (Fuselier) C.; student Loyola U., New Orleans, 1950-53; m. Shirley Mae Maillian, Apr. 29, 1951; children—Clifford Charles, James Matthew, Gayle Marie. Sugar weighter R. H. Keen & Co., New Orleans, 1949; sales clk. Western Auto Store, New Orleans, 1949; parts clk. So. Specialty Sales Co., Inc., New Orleans, 1949-50, warehouse mgr., 1950-51, parts mgr., 1951-67, customer service mgr., 1967-72, sales mgr., 1972-75, v.p., gen. mgr., 1975—; mem. service adv. council Jacobsen-Textron div., Racine, Wis., 1978-80. Served with U.S. Army, 1954-61. Mem. So. Turf Grass Assn., Miss. Turf Grass Assn. Democrat. Roman Catholic. Clubs: Hank Stramm Racquet and Health, Elks. Home: 2220 Taft Park Metairie LA 70001 Office: 617 N Broad Ave New Orleans LA 70119

CANTOR, ROBERT LEONARD, leasing co. exec.; b. N.Y.C., Apr. 30, 1928; s. Saul and Blanche (Bursutsky) C.; B.S., N.Y. U., 1952, M.A., 1953; m. Myra Werner, Dec. 8, 1966; children—Scott Howard, Nina Gail. In investment banking, 1955-60; exec. v.p., dir. C.F. Kirk Labs., N.Y.C., 1960-62; exec. v.p. Dragor Shipping Corp., N.Y.C., 1964-67; v.p. Am. Export Industries, N.Y.C., 1967-68; sr. v.p. Nat. Equipment Rental, Ltd., N.Y.C., 1965-68, pres., chmn. 1968-69; chmn. exec. com., dir. Detroit Steel Corp., N.Y.C., 1969-71; fin. cons., 1971-72; pres., dir. Barnett Leasing Co. subs. Barnett Banks Fla. Inc., Ft. Lauderdale, Fla., 1973—; dir. Barnett Bank of Port Everglades, Ft. Lauderdale, Barnett Bank Broward County. Served with USN, 1946-48. Home: 2009 St Andrews Rd Hollywood FL 33021 Office: 1 Financial Plaza Ft Lauderdale FL 33394

CANTRELL, ELROY TAYLOR, pharmacologist; b. Mobile, Ala., May 10, 1943; s. William Vernon and Thelma Charlotte (Taylor) C.; B.S. in Biology, Ark. State U., 1965; M.S. in Pharmacology, U. Tenn., 1968; Ph.D. in Pharmacology, Baylor Coll. Medicine, 1972; m. Carlene Hannis, Mar. 31, 1967; children—Melissa Kaye, William Floyd II. NIH postdoctoral fellow Baylor Coll. Medicine, Houston, 1971-72; research asso. M.D. Anderson Hosp., Houston, 1972-73; chmn. dept. pharmacology Tex. Coll. Osteopathic Medicine, Ft. Worth, 1973—; cons. Becton, Dickinson Research Center. Named Outstanding Young Man Am., U.S. Jaycees, 1979. Mem. Am. Soc. Pharmacology and Exptl. Therapeutics, Am. Thoracic Soc., Soc. Analytical Cytology, Tex. Pharmacologists. Mem. Chs. of Christ. Club: Kiwanis (sec.-treas. 1974-77). Author numerous articles on carcinogen metabolism in human and rodent tissues and methods devel. for assessment of cancer risk. Home: 1812 Rockmoor Fort Worth TX 76134 Office: Tex Coll Osteopathic Medicine Camp Bowie at Montgomery Fort Worth TX 76107

CANTRELL, JAMES CURTIS, speech and lang. pathologist; b. Hampton, Va., Oct. 15, 1951; s. Bruce Head and Elizabeth (Colvard) C.; A.B., Catawba Coll., 1973; M.A., Marshall U., 1975, 77; m. Bonnie Sue Cunningham, Dec. 19, 1975; 1 dau., Rachel Cunningham. Teaching asst. speech Marshall U., Huntington, W.Va., 1974-75; counselor for mentally and physically disabled Glen, W.Va., 1975; speech and lang. pathologist Easter Seal Soc., Gt. Falls, Mont., 1977-78, Albemarle Regional Center for Communication Disorders, Elizabeth City, N.C., 1978—; intern speech pathology W.Va. Rehab. Center, Institute, W.Va., 1977. Grad. fellow Marshall U., 1977. Mem. Am. Speech-Lang. and Hearing Assn. (cert. clin. competence in speech pathology). Episcopalian. Home: 713 Greenleaf St Elizabeth City NC 27909 Office: PPCC Health Dept Box 189 Elizabeth City NC 27909

CANTRELL, JOHN HARRIS, JR., physicist; b. Memphis, June 24, 1943; s. John Harris and Dorothy Marie (McDaniel) C.; B.S., U. Tenn., 1965, Ph.D., 1976; m. Davie Sue Wykle, Sept. 2, 1967. Cons. physics Oak Ridge Nat. Lab., 1975-77; research asso. NRC, Washington, 1977-79; physicist NASA Langley Research Center, Hampton, Va., 1979—. Recipient Indsl. Research IR-100 award, 1978; NIH radiol. health physics fellow, 1973-75. Mem. Am. Phys. Soc., Acoustical Soc. Am., AAAS, Sigma Xi, Sigma Pi Sigma, Phi Kappa Phi. Contbr. articles to profl. jours.; patentee in field. Home: 1013 Willow Green Dr Newport News VA 23602 Office: NASA Langley Research Center Hampton VA 23665

CANTRELL, KIZZIE ANN, counselor; b. London, Ky., Sept. 17, 1935; d. Robert E. and Maud M. (Estep) Sasser; B.S., U. Louisville, 1964; M.A. in Edn., Murray (Ky.) State U., 1970; m. Grady L. Cantrell, Sept. 17, 1954; 1 son, Randall. Public sch. tchr. in Ky. and

Ohio, 1955-73; counselor, coordinator spl. programs Murray State U., 1974—, also tchr. career and self devel. Del., Internat. Women's Year, Houston, 1977; mem. steering com. Pro-ERA Alliance, 1979; chmn. Murray Women's Agenda Coalition, 1979. Cert. tchr., Ky. Mem. Am. Personnel and Guidance Assn., Southeastern Assn. Spl. Edn. Programs, NOW, Nat. Women's Polit. Caucus, Ind. Judo Assn. Democrat. Home: Box 3120 University Station Murray KY 42071 Office: Box 3278 University Station Murray KY 42071

CANTRELL, WILLIAM ALLEN, educator; b. Everton, Ark., Nov. 6, 1920; s. William E. and Vida (Vinson) C.; B.S., McMurry Coll., 1940; M.D., U. Tex., 1943; m. Joyce LaRee Hobbs, Jan. 17, 1945; children—Mary Elizabeth, William Robert. Rotating intern U.S. Naval Hosp., Corona, Calif., 1943-44; resident neuropsychiatry U. Tex. Med. Br. Hosps., 1947-49; asst. prof. neuropsychiatry U. Tex. Med. Br., 1949-54; practice medicine, specializing in psychiatry, Houston, 1951-63; prof. psychiatry Baylor Coll. Medicine, Houston, 1963—; chief psychiatry service Meth. Hosp., Houston, 1966-73. Mem. med. adv. com. Tex. Bd. Mental Health and Mental Retardation, 1965-73, chmn., 1965-69, 72-73; bd. dirs. Tex. Assn. Mental Health, 1965-72. Served to lt. M.C., USNR, 1944-47. Fellow Am. Psychiat. Assn. (br. pres. 1958-59), Am. Coll. Psychiatrists; mem. Tex. Med. Assn., Tex. (v.p. 1958-59), Central (v.p. 1974-75, pres. 1976-77) neuropsychiat. assns., Houston Psychiat. Soc. (pres. 1956). Home: 5018 Loch Lomond St Houston TX 77096

CANTU, BLAS, JR., hosp. adminstr.; b. Laredo, Tex., Aug. 11, 1938; s. Blas and Alicia (Hinojosa) C.; B.B.A., N. Tex. State U., 1960; M.S.W., Our Lady of the Lake Coll., 1966; m. Melinda I. Garza, Aug. 25, 1961; children—Rebecca M., Daniel B. Child welfare worker Tex. Dept. Public Welfare, Laredo, 1962-64, supr., 1966-68, regional dir., 1968-69; unit dir. Laredo Community Mental Health Outreach Center, 1969-71; chief of staff services Rio Grande State Center for Mental Health and Mental Retardation, Harlingen, Tex., 1971, supt., 1972—; commr. Epilepsy Assn. Tex. Mem. Nat. Assn. Social Workers, Acad. Cert. Social Workers, S. Tex. Health Systems Agy., Am. Legion. Club: Civitan. Office: 2115 N 28th St Harlingen TX 78550

CAPEHART, BARNEY LEE, educator; b. Galena, Kans., Aug. 20, 1940; s. Samual Alfred and Mary Jane (Bliss) C.; B.S.E.E., U. Okla., Norman, 1961, M.E.E., 1962, Ph.D., 1967; m. Lynne Carol Fowler, Sept. 2, 1961; children—Thomas David, Jeffrey Donald, Cynthia Diane. Grad. asst. elec. engring. U. Okla., Norman, 1961-62, U. Ariz., Tucson, 1962-63; instr. elec. engring. U. Okla., Norman, 1965-67; mem. tech. staff Aerospace Corp., San Bernardino, Calif., 1967-68; asst. prof. indsl. and systems engring. dept. U. Fla., Orlando, 1968-72; asso. prof. indsl. engring. dept. U. Tenn., Knoxville, 1972-73; asso. prof. indsl. and systems engring. dept. U. Fla. Grad. Engring. Center, Elgin AFB, 1973-74; coordinator student affairs Coll. Engring. U. Fla., Gainesville, 1974-75, asso. prof. indsl. and systems engring. dept., 1974-79, prof., 1979—; cons. Martin-Marietta Corp., Orlando, Fla., 1971, 69, Naval Tng. Device Center, Orlando, 1970-71; chmn. region III Regional Energy Action Com., Fla. State Energy Office, 1977-79; mem. tech. task force Gainesville Regional utilities Bd., 1978—; mem. dept. energy region IV adv. group on appropriate tech., 1979—. Served to lt. USAF, 1963-65. Fellow AAAS; mem. Am. Inst. Indsl. Engrs., IEEE, Soc. Computer Simulation, Sigma Xi, Sigma Tau, Alpha Pi Mu, Tau Beta Pi. Contbr. articles to profl. jours. Home: 1601 NW 35th Way Gainesville FL 32605 Office: Dept Indsl and Systems Engring 303 Weil Hall U Fla Gainesville FL 32611

CAPELL, ANNIE HALL, supermarket exec.; b. Anson County, N.C., Sept. 20, 1913; d. Walter Cleveland and Mary Ella (Bowman) Hall; student E. Carolina U., 1933-34; m. Herman Ross Capell, Apr. 4, 1935; 1 dau., Carroll Anne. Mem. sales staff, buyer J.E. Moore Co., Wadesboro, N.C., 1936-41; cashier, office clk., buyer Carl's Food Center, Wadesboro, 1955-65, v.p., 1965-75, pres., 1975—, also dir.; mgr. Wadesboro Cash and Carry Subs. Carl's Food Center, 1970-73. Troop leader Girl Scouts U.S.A., 1960-63; active Anson County Hosp. Aux. Recipient Service award Distributive Edn. Clubs Am., 1975; Career Exploration award Anson Jr. High Sch., 1977; Service award Shrine Crippled Children's Hosp., 1977. Mem. Associated Grocers Mut. Carolinas, Inc., N.C. Food Dealers Assn., Anson County C. of C. Democrat. Methodist. Clubs: Okala Garden, Twin Valley Country. Home: 400 Eastview St Wadesboro NC 28170 Office: 805 Camden Rd Wadesboro NC 28170

CAPELL, ROBERT DONALD, physician; b. Easley, S.C., Feb. 14, 1941; s. William Bruce and Fleda Frances (Findley) C.; B.S., Wofford Coll., 1963; M.D., Med. Coll. S.C., 1967; m. Mary Ellen Johnson; children—Bob, Lisa, Jennifer, Jacob. Intern, U.S. Naval Hosp., Newport, R.I., resident in radiology U.S. Naval Hosp., Oakland, Calif., 1974-76; chmn. dept. emergency medicine York Gen. Hosp., Rock Hill, S.C., 1977—. Pres., Am. Heart Assn., Rock Hill. Diplomate Am. Bd. Family Practice. Mem. Am. Coll. Radiology, Am. Coll. Emergency Physicians, Am. Assn. Family Practitioners. Club: Gamecock. Home: 1497 Alexander Rd Rock Hill SC 29730 Office: PO Box 3056 Rock Hill SC 29730

CAPERTON, CHARLES LEE, lawyer; b. N.Y.C., Dec. 25, 1937; s. Albert Helvey and Loraine (Ellston) C.; B.B.A., So. Methodist U., 1961, J.D., 1964; m. Frances Ann McNatt, Dec. 23, 1963 (div.); children—Kelly Conder, Charles Lee II; m. 2d, Marilyn Graves, Apr. 14, 1979. Admitted to Tex. bar, 1964, U.S. Supreme Ct. bar, 1967; asst. dist. atty. Dallas County, 1964-68; partner Akin, Steinberg & Stanford, 1968-71; pvt. practice law, Dallas, 1971—. Mem. citizen's adv. com. Tex. Constl. Revision Commn., 1973—. Served with AUS, 1964. Mem. Tex. Criminal Def. Lawyers Assn. (charter), Am. (criminal law editor Trial Lawyers Forum mag.), Dallas (sec. treas. 1973, v.p., 1974, pres. 1975), Tex. (state dir.) trial lawyers assns., Dallas (chmn. criminal law sect. 1973) bar assns., State Bar Tex. (speaker criminal law skills course 1973—), Am. Coll. Legal Medicine (state committeeman 1976-77), Kappa Alpha, Phi Alpha Delta, Alpha Kappa Psi. Democrat. Methodist (dir.). Mason (32 deg.), Contbr. articles to profl. jours. Office: 2823 Routh St Dallas TX 75201

CAPLAN, FRED HARRY, state justice; b. Clarksburg, W.Va., Dec. 3, 1914; s. Henry A. and Hannah (Siegelman) C.; A.B., W.Va. U., 1939; LL.B., U. Richmond, 1941, LL.D., 1971; m. Miriam Kessler, Nov. 12, 1941; 1 dau., Betty Lee. Admitted to W.Va. bar, 1941; practice in Clarksburg, 1946-53; asst. atty. gen. W.Va., 1953-61; chmn. Pub. Service Commn. W.Va., 1961-62; judge Supreme Ct. Appeals W.Va., Charleston, 1962—, pres., 1966, 71, chief justice, 1977—. Mem. W.Va. Legislature from Harrison County, 1949-51. Served with AUS, 1941-46; PTO. Mem. Am., W.Va., Harrison County bar assns., W.Va. State Bar, W.Va. Jud. Assn. Democrat. Jewish. Mem. B'nai B'rith. Home: 4218 Noyes Ave SE Charleston WV 25304 Office: Supreme Ct Appeals Charleston WV 25305

CAPLAN, SYLVIA DAVIS, audio/visual producer, writer public relations cons., sculptor; b. Mexico City, Nov. 21, 1936 (parents Am. citizens); d. Irving and Bertha (German) Davis; student U. Mex., Houston Mus. Fine Art; m. Arthur Morris Caplan, Oct. 12, 1952; children—Curtis Ray, Marcia Dianne, Mark David. Owner, pres. Media Masters, Inc., InterMedia Corp., Executrend Internat., Houston and Dallas; on-air personality and writer stas. KRIO, McAllen, Tex., KURV, Edinburg, Tex. and KPAB, Laredo, Tex.; feature editor, columnist Edinburg Daily Rev.; free-lance writer Women in Business, Audio-Visual Ind. Producers; ghost writer, polit. speech writer. Active March of Dimes. Recipient award March of Dimes, 1963, 65, Am. Heart Assn., 1969, Tex. B'nai B'rith, 1967, Am. Legion of Tex., nat. Am. Legion. Mem. Am. Soc. Tng. and Devel., Assn. Multi-Images, Contemporary Women in Am. Art, Artes Internacionales de las Americas, Houston Art League, Houston C. of C., Am. Women in Radio and TV, Am. Public Relations Assn., Nat. Assn. Women Bus. Owners, B'nai B'rith Women, Am. Film Inst., Motion Picture Council Houston. Jewish. Home: 5630 Grape St Houston TX 77096 Office: 2640 Fountainview Suite 228 Houston TX 77057

CAPOZZOLI, PATRICIA KATHERINE, educator; b. Steubenville, Ohio, Sept. 4, 1934; d. Daniel Thomas and Mary Magdalene (Fullen) Wylie; B.A. in English, Coll. Steubenville, 1968; M.A. in Ednl. Adminstrn., W.Va. U., 1974; M.S. in Guidance and Counseling, Dayton (Ohio) U., 1976, Ed.S., 1978; m. William N. Capozzoli, 5 children. Secondary sch. tchr., 1968-69; spl. edn. tchr., 1969-74; ednl. cons. Psychol. Services, Inc., Steubenville, 1974; asst. prof. edn. spl. edn. div., supr. student tchrs. Coll. Steubenville, 1974—, dir. spl. edn. program, 1978; cons. in field. Named Outstanding Spl. Edn. Tchr., W.Va. Jr. Women's Club, 1971. Mem. Assn. Curriculum and Instrn. for Adminstrs., Internat. Reading Assn., Piaget Soc., Assn. Childhood Edn. Internat., W.Va. Women's Club (chmn. No. dist. 1959), W.Va. Fedn. Women's Club (chmn. state com. 1958), Sigma Tau Delta, Delta Kappa Gamma. Club: Wierton Jr. Women's (pres. 1957). Office: Coll Steubenville Edn Dept Steubenville OH 43952

CAPPEL, KLAUS LEO, design engr.; b. Wuppertal, W. Ger., Mar. 18, 1920; came to U.S., 1938, naturalized, 1944; s. Adolf and Else Cappel; student U. London, 1937-38; B.S., U. Calif., Berkeley, 1940; postgrad. Columbia U., 1953-54, U. Del., 1954-55, Stevens Inst. Tech., 1951; 1 dau., Susan. In shipbldg. and design field, San Francisco, 1941-46; pvt. practice patent devel., San Francisco, 1946-49; engr. specialist M.L. Bayard & Co., Phila., 1949-52; from design engr. to prin. engr. Franklin Inst. Research Labs., Phila., 1952-70; chief design engr. Wyle Sci. Services & Systems Group, Huntsville, Ala., 1970—; cons. machine design and dynamics to railroads and mfrs., NSF. Registered profl. engr., Pa. Mem. ASME, AAAS, Soc. Naval Architects and Marine Engrs. (asso.), Sigma Xi. Patentee gravity davit, flight simulator, vibration tables. Home: PO Box 87 Madison AL 35758 Office: 7800 Governors Dr W Huntsville AL 35807

CAPPS, JAMES BARRI, mortgage banker; b. Paterson, N.J., Jan. 31, 1946; s. Aaron and Mae (Joel) C.; B.A. in Sociology, N.C. State U., 1971; m. Katherine Lawing, Oct. 10, 1970; 1 dau., Holly Elizabeth. Mgr., asst. v.p. Cameron Brown Co., Arlington, Va., 1971-74; loan officer, asst. v.p., Colonial Mortgage Service Co., Annandale, Va., 1974-76; mgr., v.p., 1977—; mgr., parnter, asst. v.p. Baker Mortgage Co., Fairfax, 1976-77. Mem. No. Va. Bd. Realtors, Mortgage Bankers Assn., No. Va. Builders Assn., Kappa Alpha. Club: Country (Fairfax). Home: 1310 Timberly Ln McLean VA 22102 Office: 7700 Little River Turnpike Annandale VA 22003

CAPPS, MILTON FEREBEE, advt. agy. exec.; b. Charleston, S.C., Oct. 6, 1948; s. Harris Milton and Doris Ferebee (Traxler) C.; B.A. in Journalism, U. S.C., 1970; m. Vivian Frances Cooper, Oct. 20, 1977; 1 dau. by previous marriage, Channing Nicole. Mgr. communications div. S.C. State Devel. Bd., Columbia, 1974-75; dir. communications Blue Cross-Blue Shield S.C., Columbia, 1975-76; dir. public affairs Winthrop Coll., Rock Hill, S.C., 1976-77; account exec. Cook, Ruef, Spann & Weiser, Inc., Columbia and Washington, 1977-79; dir. communications and mktg. Harbison Devel. Corp., Columbia, 1979; account supr. Eric Ericson & Assos., Nashville, 1979—. Served to capt. USAF, 1970-74. Mem. Am. Assn. Public Opinion Research, Southeastern Assn. Public Opinion Research, Public Relations Soc. Am., Soc. Profl. Journalists, Internat. Assn. Bus. Communicators, Omicron Delta Kappa, Kappa Tau Alpha. Home: 145 Kenner Ave Nashville TN 37205

CAPRAUN, LYNN WALTER, respiratory therapist, educator; b. Kane, Pa., Feb. 12, 1948; s. Claire Laverne and Gwendolyn Gladys C.; A.A., Orlando Jr. Coll., 1968; B.S. in Biol. Scis., Fla. Tech. U., 1970, B.S. in Respiratory Therapy, 1972, M.S. in Biol. Scis., 1978; m. Leeane Jean Pendley, Apr. 24, 1970; children—Erick Lynn, Jeffrey Russell. Respiratory therapy technician Orlando (Fla.) Regional Med. Center, 1970, shift supr. respiratory therapy, 1970, chief therapist, 1970-73, dir. inservice edn., 1973-74; instr. respiratory therapy Valencia Community Coll., Orlando, 1973-74, program dir. respiratory therapy, 1974—; instr. med. pharmacology U. Central Fla. Instr. drummers Shriner's Drum & Bugle Corps; lectr. sr. citizens groups on care of respiratory disorders. Served with U.S. Army, 1970-71. Registered respiratory therapist; cert. respiratory therapy technician. Mem. Am. Assn. Respiratory Therapy, Fla. Soc. Respiratory Therapy, Nat. Bd. Respiratory Therapy, Am. Lung Assn., Am. Heart Assn., Am. Thoracic Soc., Alpha Eta. Republican. Roman Catholic. Club: Am. Legion (Pinecastle, Fla.). Home: 125 Sweetbay Ln Orlando FL 32811 Office: 1800 S Kirkman Rd Orlando FL 32811

CAPRITA, BARBARA JEAN, oil co. exec.; b. Argentia, Nfld., Aug. 10, 1949; d. Charles and Janet C.; ed. Pensacola Jr. Coll., 1968-70, Tulane U., 1977. Drafter, Texaco, Inc., New Orleans, 1970-75; mem. geophys. survey crew Chevron Oil, New Orleans, 1975-76; chem. operator Am. Cyanamid, Westwego, La., 1976-77, engring. technician, 1977-79; engring. technician, offshore engring. div., energy conservation coordinator Shell Oil Co., New Orleans, 1979—. Office: One Shell Sq Poydras St New Orleans LA 70153

CAPULONG, RENE ABRERA, surgeon; b. Tarlac, Philippines, Feb. 24, 1940; s. Pedro R. and Maria S. (Abrera) C.; M.D., U. St. Tomas, 1963; married; children—Rachelle Angelie, Rene Aldrin, Regina Aine. Intern, Coney Island Hosp., Bklyn., 1965; resident Maimonidies Hosp., Bklyn., 1965-66, Bklyn. Jewish Hosp. and Med. Center, 1966-69; practice medicine specializing in thoracic and gen. surgery, DeLand, Fla.; mem. staff West Volusia Meml. Hosp., Fish Meml. Hosp. Mem. AMA, Internat. Coll. Surgeons, Soc. Clin. Vascular Surgeons, Am. Coll. Chest Physicians, A.C.S., Fla. Med. Assn., Am. Coll. Angiology, Pan Am. Med. Assn., Volusia County Med. Assn. Home: 120 E New York St DeLand FL 32720

CAPUTO, RAYMOND VINCENT, dermatologist; b. Bridgeport, Conn., Oct. 17, 1947; s. Sebastian L. and Sadie V. (Pirrello) C.; A.S., Jr. Coll. of Broward County (Fla.), 1967; student Fla. Atlantic U., 1969; M.D., U. Miami, 1973; m. Janet Tringali, June 14, 1975. Intern, Jackson Meml. Hosp., Miami, Fla., 1973-74, resident, 1974-75; resident Mt. Sinai Hosp., Miami Beach, Fla.; fellow in dermatology U. Ill. Hosp., Chgo., 1977-78; practice medicine, specializing in dermatology, Atlanta, 1979—; mem. staff St. Joseph Hosp., Scottish Rete Children's Hosp., Northside Hosp., Emory Hosp. Mem. AMA, So. Med. Assn., Soc. for Pediatric Dermatology, Internat. Soc. Pediatric Dermatology, Atlanta Dermatol. Assn., Med. Assn. Atlanta, Ga. Med. Assn., Alpha Omega Alpha. Democrat. Roman Catholic. Author: (with L. Solomon) chpt. in Textbook of Adolescent Dermatology, 1978. Home: 2062 Pernoshal Ct Dunwoody GA 30338 Office: 960 Johnson Ferry Rd NE Atlanta GA 30342

CARALIS, PANAGIOTA VIRGINIA, physician; b. Miami, Fla., June 17, 1951; d. Theodore and Athina C.; B.S. cum laude, U. Miami, 1971, M.D., 1975. Intern, U. Miami Affiliated Hosps., 1975-76, resident, 1976-78 chief med. resident U. Miami-VA Hosps., 1978-79; asst. prof. medicine, dept. internal medicine U. Miami Sch. Medicine, 1979—; mem. staffs VA, Jackson Meml., Nat. Children's Cardiac hosps. Recipient Achievement award Alpha Epsilon Delta, 1970; Alpha Lambda Delta scholar, 1971; Woods Johnson Found. scholar, 1972; Am. Bus. Women's Assn. scholar, 1973. Mem. AMA, Am. Med. Women's Assn., A.C.P. (diplomate), Am. Bus. Women's Assn., U. Miami Med. Alumnae Assn., Alpha Omega Alpha, Phi Kappa Phi, Delta Theta Mu (U. Miami pres. 1970-71). Greek Orthodox. Home: 708 NE 24th St Miami FL 33137 Office: Med Service Office 1201 NW a6th St Miami FL 33125

CARAMEROS, GEORGE DEMITRIUS, JR., natural gas co. exec.; b. El Paso, Mar. 1 1924; s. George Demitrius and Esperanza (Purdy) C.; B.A., U. Tex. at El Paso, 1947; m. Verna Narcissus Easterling, May 26, 1944; children—Cecille (Mrs. George Shannon), Cynthia (Mrs. John Blevins), Cathy (Mrs. David Patton), George Demitrius III, Carl. With El Paso Natural Gas Co., 1948—, mgr. new projects devel. of subsidiary El Paso Products Co., 1957-60, mng. dir. El Paso Europe-Afrique, Paris, France, 1960-65, adminstrv. asst. to chmn. bd., N.Y.C., 1965-66, asst. v.p., 1966-70, v.p., 1970-73, exec. v.p., 1973-75, dir., 1973—; dir. El Paso Co., 1974—, exec. v.p., 1975-78, vice chmn., 1978—; pres. El Paso LNG Co., Houston, 1975-78, chmn. bd., 1978—, also dir.; dir. El Paso Products Co., Tex. Commerce Med. Bank, Houston. Served with AUS, World War II. Decorated Bronze Star, Combat Inf. badge. Methodist. Clubs: Ramada, Houston, Lakeside Country Houston Racquet (Houston). Home: 660 Shartle Circle Houston TX 77024 Office: 2727 Allen Pkwy Houston TX 77019

CARATTINI, LUIS CESAR, mfg. co. exec.; b. Cayey, P.R., Oct. 24, 1949; s. Victor and Providencia (Melendez) C.; B.A., U. P.R., 1973; m. Neyzza O'Farrill, Apr. 4, 1975; children—Victor C., Luis M. Faculty, U. P.R., Rio Piedras, 1973-74; materials analyst Baxter Labs., Carolina, P.R., 1974-76, materials supt., 1976-79; materials mgr. Travenol Labs., Inc., Carolina, 1979—; cons. in field. Served with U.S. Army, 1968-70. Mem. Am. Mgmt. Assn. Roman Catholic. Club: Am. Mgmt. Assn. Gunners. Home: Calle 73 Bldg 116 #28 Villa Carolina Carolina PR 00630 Office: PO Box 678 Carlina PR 00630

CARAVATI, CHARLES MARTIN, JR., dermatologist; b. Richmond, Va., May 9 1937; s. Charles M. and Mary Virginia (Dore) C.; B.A., U. Va., 1959, M.D., 1963; m. Betty Noland, Aug. 31, 1963; children—Charles M. III, Elizabeth Noland, Nancy Caroline. Intern, Barnes Hosp., St. Louis, 1963-64; resident in dermatology U. Va. Hosp., Charlottesville, 1966-69; practice medicine specializing in dermatology, Richmond, Va., 1969—; mem. staff Johnston-Willis, Chippenham, St. Mary's, Retreat, Stuart Circle Richmond Meml., Henrico Doctors hosps.; clin. instr. dermatology Med. Coll. Va., 1969-75, clin. asst. prof., 1975-79, clin. asso. prof., 1979—; dir. Investors Savs. and Loan Assn. Bd. dirs. Richmond chpt. ARC, 1972-78, Am. Cancer Soc., 1972-76; co-organizer, bd. dirs. Richmond Met. Blood Service, 1974-76; bd. dirs. Central Va. Health Systems Agy., 1977—. Served with USPHS, 1964-66. Diplomate Am. Bd. Dermatology. Fellow Am. Acad. Dermatology; mem. AMA, So. Med. Assn., Va., Richmond dermatological socs., Med. Soc. Va. (councilor 1975—), Richmond Acad. Medicine (trustee 1975, 2d v.p. 1979, pres.-elect 1980), Phi Beta Kappa, Alpha Omega Alpha, Omicron Delta Kappa. Contbr. articles to So. Med. Jour., Archives of Dermatology. Home: Shallobro Farm Route 250 Box 200 Manakin-Sabot VA 23103 Office: 5600 Grove Ave Richmond VA 23226

CARBAUGH, ROBERT GARY, anesthesiologist; b. Chambersburg, Pa., Dec. 4, 1938; s. Robert Kaufman and Elsie Catherine C.; B.S., Fla. So. Coll., 1962; M.D., U. Miami, 1966; m. Katherine Maude Bryan, July 11, 1964; children—Anne, Robert, Christopher, Jennifer. Intern, Tampa (Fla.) Gen. Hosp., 1966-67, resident in anesthesiology, 1967-69; practice medicine specializing in anesthesiology, Waycross, Ga., 1971—; mem. med. staff Waycross Meml. Hosp. Served as maj. U.S. Army, 1969-71. Decorated Army Commendation medal; diplomate Am. Bd. Anesthesiology. Fellow Am. Coll. Anesthesiologists; mem. Am. Soc. Anesthesiologists, Ga. Soc. Anesthesiologists, Ware County Med. Soc., Rosicrucian Order. Republican. Methodist Home: 914 Carrie Dr Waycross GA 31501 Office: 1908 Allice St Waycross GA 31501

CARBON, FRANK HENRY, JR., accountant; b. New Orleans, Aug. 17, 1948; s. Frank Henry and Beatrice (Jacobs) C.; B.B.A., Loyola U. of the South, 1970; m. Janice Brown, June 23, 1973; children—Stephanie Anne, Courtney Marie. Staff acct. Laporte, Senrt, Romig & Hand, C.P.A.'s, New Orleans, 1971-73, partner, 1973—. Mem. fin. planning com. La. Supreme Ct., 1979—; mem. fin. com. Big Bros. Greater New Orleans. Served with USMC, 1971-77. Mem. Am. Inst. C.P.A.'s, La. Soc. C.P.A.'s, Young Men's Bus. Club Greater New Orleans, Alpha Sigma Nu, Beta Alpha Psi, Beta Gamma Sigma. Republican. Roman Catholic. Home: 3716 Tolmas Dr Metairie LA 70002 Office: 2475 Canal St New Orleans LA 70119

CARBONE, NICHOLAS, hosp. adminstr.; b. N.Y.C., June 23, 1941; s. Joseph and Teresa (Petracca) C.; B.B.A. in Acctg., Fla. Atlantic U., 1975; m.; children—Nicholas, Lisa Ann. Mgr., Diplomat Hotel, Hollywood, Fla., 1964-68; bus. office mgr. Plantation Gen. Hosp., Ft. Lauderdale, Fla., 1968-72, controller, 1970-75; asst. v.p., regional controller Hosp. Corp. Am., Dallas, 1973-78; adminstr. Okaloosa Meml. Hosp., Crestview, Fla., 1978—. Served with U.S. Army, 1959-62. Mem. Am. Coll. Hosp. Adminstrs., Am. Hosp. Assn., Fedn. Am. Hosps., Hosp. Fin. Mgmt. Assn., Fla. Hosp. Assn., Fla. League Hosps. Crestview C. of C. (dir. 1979). Roman Catholic. Club: Crestview Kiwanis (dir. 1979). Office: 601 N Pearl St Crestview FL 32536

CARDELLI, GIOVANNI GUIDO CARLO, architect, producer; b. London, Eng., Oct. 2, 1910; s. Count Giovanni and Ruth (Lamson) C.; M.A. Scis. Politiques, Lycee Jansen, Paris, France, 1928; m. Jacqueline Stewart, Nov. 22, 1931; children—Diane (Mrs. Lawrence O. Houghon), Giola. Came to U.S., 1933, naturalized, 1941. Naval architect, designer, Chgo., N.Y.C., Southampton, N.Y., Westport, Conn., 1932-64; head design dept. Lyon & Barney, Yachts, Greenwich, Conn., 1952-62; resident naval architect Rybovich & Sons Boat Works Inc., West Palm Beach, Fla. 1964-70; exec. v.p. John H. Witman Interiors, Palm Beach, 1970-72; dir. interior design Outcalt Environment, Stuart, Fla., 1972-73; pres. By Design, Inc., Jupiter, Fla., 1973—; asst. to pres. Chgo. Opera Co., 1938-40; gen. mgr. Opera Theater, Chgo., 1940-49; producer Rape of Lucretia, Chgo., N.Y.C., 1948-49; gen. mgr. Dallas Symphony, 1949-52. Clubs: River, N.Y. Yacht (N.Y.C.); Seawanhaka Yacht (Center Island, N.Y.), Arts Club (Chgo.); Westhampton Yacht, Delray Beach Yacht; Coral Harbor Yacht (Nassau); Sag Harbor Yacht (Long Island). Translator operas, 1939-54. Home: 100-C Vision Ct Palm Beach Gardens FL 33410 Office: 1620 US Hwy No 1 Jupiter FL 33458

CARDEN, BRADLEY LAMAR, physician; b. Phenix City, Ala., Jan. 1, 1948; s. Samuel Bradley and Jane Leola (Wallin) C.; B.S., U. Ala., Tuscaloosa, 1970, M.D., Birmingham, 1974; m. Helen Jean Snow, June 3, 1972; 1 dau., Jennifer Marie. Intern, Med. Center, Columbus, Ga., 1974-75, resident in family medicine, 1975-77; practice family medicine, Phenix City, 1978—; mem. staff Cobb Hosp., Phenix City, Med. Center Dr.'s Hosp., Columbus; asso. instr. Auburn U. Sch. Pharmacy, 1979—; instr. Med. Center Columbus, 1979—. Chmn., Russell County March of Dimes, 1979; adv. bd. Chattanoochee Valley Community Coll., 1979-80; deacon Baptist Ch., 1978—. Diplomate Am. Bd. Family Practice. Mem. Russell County C. of C., AMA, Am. Acad. Family Physicians. Office: Cobb Med Park Suite 401 Phenix City AL 36867

CARDEN, HOOVER, ednl. adminstr.; b. Fairfield, Tex., July 5, 1930; s. Isiah and Anner (Dickens) C.; B.S., Prairie View A&M U., 1954, M.S., 1964, postgrad., 1972-74; postgrad. Lamar U., 1970-72; m. Rena Mae Denson, Dec. 20, 1954; children—Cassandra, Aretta, Helen, Diana, Lila. Tchr. vocat. agr., Burton (Tex.) High Sch., 1960-61; county/agrl. extension agt., Beaumont, Tex., 1961-72; adminstr. Prairie View (Tex.) A. and M. U. Coop. Extension Program, also asso. dean agr., 1972—; cons. for internat. devel. AID, Washington. Chmn. adminstrv. bd., trustee Bethlehem United Meth. Ch. Served with U.S. Army, 1954-59. Mem. Tex. State Tchrs. Assn., Nat. Agrl. Extension Workers Assn., Tex. Agrl. Extension Workers Assn., Extension Com. on Orgn. and Policy, Washington, Prairie View A. and M. U. Nat. Alumni Assn. (treas.), Tex. Alumni Assn. (v.p. Beaumont), Epsilon Sigma Phi, Omega Psi Phi (keeper of fin., 1970). Club: Masons. Contbr. articles to profl. publs. Home: PO Box 2423 Prairie View TX 77445 Office: PO Drawer B Prairie View TX 77445

CARDENAS, PORFIRIO GUS, mktg. exec.; b. San Antonio, Aug. 21, 1932; s. Edmundo and Frances (Urdiales) C.; B.B.A., St. Mary's U. of Tex., 1955, M.A., 1962; m. Dolores Garza, Sept. 17, 1955; children—Gus Thomas, Adele, Esther. Sales rep. Litton Industries, San Antonio, 1958-64; mktg. rep. Xerox Corp., San Antonio, 1964-69, area sales mgr./N.Mex. and West Tex., El Paso, 1969-71, Corpus Christi, Tex., 1971-72, account exec., San Antonio, 1972-78, br. mktg. exec., 1978—; instr. econs. San Antonio Coll., 1964—, Incarnate Word Coll., 1976-78; mgmt. cons. Internat. Trainers Educators and Cons. Corp., 1976—, U.S. Civil Service Commn., 1972—. Mem. nat. bd. Child Welfare League Am., N.Y.C., 1978—; chmn. alumni placement-bd. St. Mary's U. Tex. Alumni Bd., 1977-79, pres.-elect, past chmn. 1979—; San Antonio Nat. Econ. Devel. Assn., 1973-75; commr., vice chmn. City of San Antonio Planning Commn., 1976-77; pres. Cath. Family and Children's Service of San Antonio, 1972-78. Served to 1st lt., U.S. Army, 1956-58. Mem. San Antonio C. of C. (econ. and devel. adv. council 1978—), Assn. for Social Econs. Democrat. Roman Catholic. Home: 3430 Triola St San Antonio TX 78230 Office: One Park Ten S 6800 Park Ten Blvd San Antonio TX 78213

CARDENAS, RAMIRO I., chem. engr.; b. Harlingen, Tex., Mar. 13, 1949; s. Frank Hart and Maria (Trevino) C.; student Del Mar Coll., 1967-69; B.S. in Chem. Engring., Tex. A. and I. U., 1971; m. Diana Laura Torres, Feb. 5, 1976. Metall. trainee Asarco, Inc., Corpus Christi, 1971-73, supt. pilot plant ops., 1973;. Mem. Air Pollution Control Assn. (treas. S.W. sect., sec.-treas. Corpus Christi chpt.), Tex. Soc. Profl. Engrs., Am. Inst. Chem. Engrs., Metall. and Petroleum Engrs. Republican. Roman Catholic. Office: PO Box 810 Corpus Christi TX 78403

CARDINALE, MARIAN FRANCES, med. technologist; b. Independence, La., June 21, 1933; d. Isadore Thomas and Rosalie Marietta Cardinale; B.S. in Zoology and Chemistry with honors, Southeastern La. U., 1955; M.B.A., U. New Orleans, 1977. Staff technologist Charity Hosp., New Orleans, 1955-56, chemistry supr., 1956-62; chemistry supr. Mercy Hosp., New Orleans, 1962-68; chief med. technologist Pendleton Meml. Meth. Hosp., New Orleans, 1968—. Mem. Am. Soc. Med. Tech., La. (pres. 1969-70), New Orleans socs. med. tech., Am. Assn. Blood Banks, Sierra Club. Democrat. Roman Catholic. Home: 2708 Whitney Pl Apt 702 Metairie LA 70002 Office: Pendleton Meml Methodist Hosp 5620 Read Blvd New Orleans LA 70127

CARDOSO, ANTHONY ANTONIO, artist, educator; b. Tampa, Fla., Sept. 13, 1930; s. Frank T. and Nancy (Messina) C.; B.S. in Art Edn., U. Tampa, 1954; B.F.A., Minn. Art Inst., 1965; M.A., U. So. Fla., 1975; m. Martha Rodriguez, July 27, 1954; children—Michele Denise, Toni Lynn. Art instr., head fine arts dept. Jefferson High Sch., Tampa, 1952-67, Leto High Sch., Tampa, 1967—, instr. adult art edn., 1965—; dir. summer program center Hillsboro County Schs.; rep. Tampa Art Council; painter, 1952—; one-man shows include Warren's Gallery, Tampa, 1974, 75, 76, Tampa Realist Gallery, Tampa, 1975; group shows include Rotunda Gallery, London, Eng., 1973, Raymon Duncan Galleries, Paris, France, 1973, Brussells (Belgium) Internat., 1973; represented in permanent collections Minn. Museum, St. Paul, Tampa Sports Authority Rep. Tchrs.' Art Council, Tampa, 1971—, Tampa Arts' Council, 1978—; mem. Latin Quarter Art Gallery, Tampa, 1970—. Recipient Prix de Paris Art award Raymon Duncan Galleries, 1970, Salon of 50 States award Ligoa Duncan Gallery, N.Y.C., 1970, Latham Found. Internat. Art award, 1964, XXII Bienniel Traveling award Smithsonian Instn., 1968-69, Purchase award Minn. Mus., 1971, First award Fla. State Fair, 1967. Mem. East Tampa Civic Club (sec. 1957), Hillsborough County Tchrs. Assn., Rho Nu Delta. Democrat. Roman Catholic. Executed murals at Suncoast Credit Union Bldg., Tampa, 1975, Tampa Sports Authority Stadium, 1972. Home: 3208 Nassau St Tampa FL 33607 Office: 4409 W Sligh Ave Tampa FL 33614

CARDWELL, BILLIE JO, counseling psychologist; b. Angelina County, Tex., Jan. 12, 1931; d. Andrew Jackson and Rosa America (Murphy) Jumper; B.B.A., Stephen F. Austin State U., 1958, M.Ed., 1964; Ed.D., East Tex. State U., 1971; m. Horace Milton Cardwell, Sept. 14, 1957. Asst. supt. Angelina County schs., Lufkin, 1959-62, counselor-supr., 1962-67; counselor East Tex. Center Ednl. Services, Nacogdoches, 1967-69; spl. edn. counselor Region VII Ednl. Service Center, Kilgore, Tex., 1971-73; counseling psychologist, Lufkin, 1973—; seminar leader Okla.-Tex. Tng. Tchrs. of Tchrs. Project. Mem. Am., Tex., Southwestern psychol. assns., Council Exceptional Children. Home: Route 5 Box 217X Lufkin TX 75901 Office: 1121 Ellis Ave Lufkin TX 75901

CARDWELL, HORACE MILTON, hosp. adminstr.; b. Oklahoma City, Feb. 3, 1919; s. Horace M. and Lona (Bridges) C.; B.S. in Econs., Tex. A. and M. Coll., 1941; m. 2d, Billie Jo Cardwell; children (by previous marriage)—Barbara Ann, Beverly Kay, Horace Milton III. Asst. adminstr. Herman Hosp., Houston, 1946-48; adminstr. Meml. Hosp., Lufkin, Tex., 1948—. Chmn. Hosp.-Ins.-Physicians Joint Adv. Com. Tex., 1954—; mem. Tex. Commn. Patient Care, 1957-61; pres. State Bd. Vocat. Nurse Examiners, 1962-68; dir. Med. Info., 1968—; bd. dirs. Blue Cross Tex., 1962—; commr. Joint Commn. Accreditation Hosps., 1975—; cons. Coll. Am. Pathologists, 1976—. Chmn. Lufkin United Fund, 1961, 76; med. adv. com. State Dept. Pub. Welfare, 1968-70. Served with AUS, 1941-46; ETO, PTO. Fellow Am. Coll. Hosp. Adminstrs.; mem. Am. (ho. dels. 1956-68, speaker 1975; mem. council govt. relations 1966-68, mem. council on adminstrv. practice 1957-61, trustee 1968-71, chmn. bd. trustees 1974), Tex. (pres. 1956-57, chmn. council govt. relations 1958-69, chmn. bldg. com. 1965-76, Earl M. Collier award 1970) hosp. assns., AMA (com. allied health and accreditation 1975—), Tex. Assn. Hosp. Accountants (pres. 1953-54), C. of C. Rotarian (local pres. 1969-70). Address: PO Box 1447 Lufkin TX 75902

CARELOCK, TED LEE, radiologist; b. Douglas, Ga., Sept. 15, 1936; s. Claude Lee and Vallie (Lewis) C.; student S. Ga. Jr. Coll., 1958-59, U. Ga., 1959-62; M.D., Med. Coll. Ga., 1966; married; children—Lee Ann, Victoria Margaret, Teresa Lynn, Cynthia Allen. Intern, Baylor U. Med. Center, Waco, Tex., Tex., 1966-67, resident in radiology, 1967-70; staff radiologist Meml. Hosp. of Garland (Tex.), 1970-73, chief radiologist, 1973—; counselor Med. Coll. Radiology. Served with USAF, 1954-58. Mem. AMA, Am. Coll. Radiology, Radiol. Soc. N.Am., Soc. Nuclear Medicine, Tex. Med. Assn., Tex. Radiol. Soc., Dallas County Med. Soc. Home: 1917 Nancy Jane Circle Garland TX 75043 Office: 2300 Marie Curie St Garland TX 75042

CAREW, GLENN STRATTON, accountant; b. New Bedford, Mass., Aug. 21, 1942; s. John Edwin and Elizabeth Grace (Stratton) C.; B.S., Piedmont Coll., 1968; M.Accounting (NDEA fellow), U. Ga., 1970; m. Frances Carol Tisdale, Jan. 23, 1970; children—Brien, Cheryl. Asst. prof. bus. adminstrn. Francis Marion Coll., Florence, S.C., 1971-74; staff accountant, data processing mgr. Yochum, Oxner & Co., C.P.A.'s, Florence, 1974-76; asst. prof. accounting and fin. Clemson (S.C.) U., 1976—; cons. bus. computer systems design, 1976—. Treas., 6th Congl. dist. S.C. Republican party, 1975, del. S.C. Rep. Conv., 1974, 76. Served with AUS, 1962-64. C.P.A., S.C.; cert. in data processing; cert. in mgmt. acctg. Mem. Am. Inst. C.P.A.'s, Nat. Assn. Accountants, Am. Accounting Assn., Data Processing Mgmt. Assn., S.C. Assn. C.P.A.'s. Congregationalist. Clubs: Lions, Mason (32 deg.). Home: PO Box 1627 Clemson SC 29631 Office: Dept Accounting and Fin Clemson U Clemson SC 29632

CAREY, GERALDINE, educator; b. Nashville, Oct. 25, 1924; d. Samuel K. and Ivey (Dillehay) C.; B.S., George Peabody Coll. for Tchrs., 1969, postgrad., 1977—; M.S., Vanderbilt U., 1970. Itinerant lang.-speech pathologist Met. Public Schs., Nashville, 1970-72; lang.-speech pathologist for behavior disordered and learning disabled children, Nashville, 1972-73; speech pathologist pilot program for children with auditory disorders Norman Binkley Elem. Sch., Nashville, 1974-76, prin. program developer, 1976-79, comprehensive devel. tchr., 1974—; in-service leader Davidson County and Williamson County schs., 1972-79. Cert. speech pathologist, elem. tchr., Tenn. Mem. Am. Speech and Hearing Assn., Tenn. Speech and Hearing Assn., NEA, Met. Nashville Edn. Assn., Assn. for Supervision and Curriculum Devel., Tenn. Edn. Assn. Mem. Ch. of Christ. Contbg. author: a Language Reference Manual for Children with Communicative Disorders, 1974. Home: 1608 Green Hills Dr Nashville TN 37215 Office: 4700 W Longdale St Nashville TN 37211

CAREY, JOHN THOMAS, art historian; b. Wilmont, Minn., Aug. 23, 1915; s. Thomas and Elizabeth Cecilia (McMahon) C.; B.A., Milw. State Coll., 1946; M.S., U. Wis., 1947; Ph.D., Ohio State U., 1954; m. Eileen Francis Schumann, Sept. 23, 1948; children—Thomas George, Michael John. Mem. faculty U. Wis., 1947-48, Ill. State U., 1949-51, Ohio State U., 1953-54, Bowling Green (Ohio) State U., 1954-56; prof., chmn. art dept. No. Ill. State U., 1956-66; vis. prof. Rollins Coll., Winter Park, Fla., 1966-67; prof. art, chmn. dept. U. W. Fla., Pensacola, 1967—; vis. prof. World Campus Afloat, springs 1969, 73, U. Hawaii, spring 1977. Served to capt. C.E., AUS, 1941-46. Grantee Pacific Cultural Found., spring 1977. Mem. Nat. Coll. Art Assn., Southeastern Coll. Art Assn. (pres. 1975). Contbr. articles to profl. publs. Home: 2320 Risen Dr Cantonment FL 32533 Office: Art Dept Univ West Fla Pensacola FL 32504

CAREY, ROBERT PAUL, railroad exec.; b. Bronxville, N.Y., Mar. 1, 1949; s. Frederick Stanton and Dorothy Marie (Fitzgerald) G.; A.B., Colgate U., 1971; postgrad. Boston U. Grad. Sch. Bus., 1973-74. Dist. mgr. ops., maintenance Amtrak, St. Louis, 1975-76, mgr. route planning, Washington, 1976, mgr. schedule, consist planning, 1976-77; v.p. and gen. mgr. Va. & Md. R.R. Co., Cape Charles, Va., 1977-79, pres., 1979—; mgr. ops. improvement Conrail, 1979—; dir., sec.-treas. Va. & Md. R.R. Co., Md. & Del. R.R. Co., Del-Md.-Va. Co., 1977-79. Mem. Kappa Delta Rho. Republican. Roman Catholic. Clubs: Northampton Country, Rotary. Home: Oak Grove Farm Eastville VA 23347 Office: PO Box 439 Eastville VA 23347

CARGILE, DAVID LEE, reins. brokerage co. exec.; b. Marietta, Ga., Feb. 7, 1946; s. Elzie Lee and Allie Louise (Cochran) C.; student St. Mary's U., 1966-67, Kennesaw Coll., 1968-70; m. Georgia Ann Morton, Mar. 1, 1974; children—Kristopher Lee, Stacey Amanda. Spl. agt. Gt. Am. Ins. Co., Atlanta, 1969-72; reins. underwriter Internat. Facultative Co., Atlanta, 1972-74; reins. broker RFC Intermediaries Corp., Atlanta, 1974-75, Atlanta br. mgr., 1975-78, regional mgr., 1978—; sr. v.p. Reins. Facilities Corp., Los Angeles, 1978—; asst. v.p. RFC Bermuda, Ltd., Hamilton, 1977—. Served with USAF, 1964-68; Vietnam. Decorated Air Force Commendation medal. Mem. Southeastern Underwriters Assn. Clubs: Willow Springs Country, Holly Springs. Home: 2579 Spencers Trace Marietta GA 30062 Office: 219 Perimeter Center Pkwy Suite 402 Atlanta GA 30346

CARGILL, OTTO ARTHUR, JR., lawyer; b. Oklahoma City, May 30, 1914; s. Otto Arthur and Delia Ann (Arnold) C.; LL.B., Cumberland U., 1934; m. Rebecca Kay; children—Otto Arthur III, Carole Sue Cargill Lash, Henson, Christina Cargill Best, John Russell, Angela Beth, Kima Leigh, Jennifer Ann. Admitted to Okla. bar, 1935; U.S. Dist. Cts., Western, No., Eastern dists. Okla., U.S. Ct. of Appeals, 10th Circuit, U.S. Supreme Ct.; practiced in Oklahoma City, 1935—. Pres., Buffalo Breeders of Am., Inc. Served with U.S. Army, 1943. Fellow Internat. Acad. Trial Lawyers; mem. Oklahoma City C. of C., Am., Okla., Oklahoma County bar assns., Assn. Trial Lawyers Am., Okla. Trial Lawyers Assn. (pres. 1947, 63), Nat. Assn. Criminal Def. Lawyers (co-chmn. membership com. 1971), Am. Judicature Soc., Law-Sci. Acad. Am. (founding mem., Gold Medal award 1969). Democrat. Baptist. Home: 6305 Northwest 83 Oklahoma City OK 73132 Office: Park-Harvey Center Oklahoma City OK 73102

CARIS, JOHN CLAYTON, business cons.; b. Cleve., Sept. 5, 1929; s. Alfred Clayton and Mildred Winifred (Hooper) C.; B.S. in Physics, Case Inst. Tech., 1951; Ph.D. in Physics, U. Calif., Berkeley, 1960; children—Wendy Lee, John Randolph. Asst. venture mgr. E.I. duPont Co., Wilmington, Del., 1960-68; sr. investment analyst Laird, Bissell & Needs, Inc., Wilmington, 1968-69; dir. corp. devel. planning Univ. Computing Co., Dallas, 1969-72; strategist, mktg. mgr. Tex. Instruments Inc., Dallas, 1972-75; pres. Devel. Inst. Southwest Inc., Dallas, 1977—, Southwest Cons. Group, Inc., 1975—; pres., chmn. ISIS Corp., Dallas, 1978—. Bd. dirs. New Arts Theater, Dallas, 1979; mem. Circle 10 council Boy Scouts Am. Served with USAF, 1952-56. Lic. real estate broker, Tex. Mem. World Future Soc. (pres. N. Tex. chpt.), Entrepreneurship Inst., N.Am. Soc. Corp. Planning. Club: Brookhaven Country. Patentee in phys. optics. Home: 3553 Granada St Dallas TX 75205 Office: 5315 Preston Rd Dallas TX 75205

CARL, ROBERT E., mktg. co. exec.; b. Independence, Mo., Sept. 1, 1927; s. Elmer T. Carl and Marion R. (Pack) G.; B.S., U. Kans., 1950; certificate in real estate So. Meth. U., 1965; certificate in investment analysis N.Y. Inst. Fin., 1967; m. Linda Arlene Sutton, Aug. 30, 1967; children—Melanie Ruth, Robert Brady. Vice pres. sales promotion Riverside Press, Inc., Dallas, 1951-54; pres., chief operating officer Jones-Carl, Inc., Dallas, 1954-62; v.p. mktg. communications Modern Am. Corp., Dallas, 1962-70; v.p. sales Dunn Properties of Tex., Inc., Dallas, 1970-71; sr. v.p. mktg. services Vantage Cos., Dallas, 1971—. Recipient legion of honor degree Internat. Supreme Council of Order of De Molay, 1957; Silver Anvil award Pub. Relations Soc. Am., 1958. Mem. Sales and Mktg. Execs. Internat. Assn. (sr. v.p.), Sales and Mktg. Execs. Dallas (pres. 1976-77, Distinguished Salesman's award 1954), S.W. Found. Free Enterprise (pres. 1975-76), Tex., So. indstl. devel. councils. Republican. Methodist. Clubs: Big D. Toastmaster (pres. 1966), Press, Dallas, Masons, Shriners. Contbr. articles to profl. jours. Home: 4209 Gloster Rd Dallas TX 75220 Office: 2525 Stemmons Freeway Dallas TX 75207

CARLETON, ROBERT L., truck trailer co. exec.; b. Fremont, Nebr., Sept. 4, 1940; s. Paul J. and Isabel Caryl (Lewis) C.; B.S. in Bus. Adminstrn. summa cum laude, U. Denver, 1962; m. Daughn Alene Dalrymple, July 8, 1961; children—Robin Caryl, Michael Robert. Accountant, Arthur Young & Co., Denver, 1962-63, tax mgr., 1966-69; partner Kring, Tietz, Carleton & Co., Denver, 1963-66; v.p., treas. Timpte, Inc., Denver, 1969-70, v.p. mktg., 1970-72, pres., 1972-75, also dir.; v.p. fin. PepsiCo Transport, Inc., Tulsa, 1975-77; v.p. Timpte Industries, Denver, 1972-75; v.p. ops. Lee Way Motor Freight Inc. subs. Pepsi Co Transport, Inc., Oklahoma City, 1977-78, pres., 1978—; regional dir. Truck Trailer Mfrs. Assn. Am., 1973-74. Recipient gold medal for highest score on C.P.A. exam., Nov. 1963; C.P.A., Colo. Mem. Am. Inst. C.P.A.'s, Colo. Soc. C.P.A.'s, Beta Gamma Sigma, Beta Alpha Psi, Omicron Delta Kappa. Home: 1820 Garrett Dr Edmond OK 73034 Office: 3000 N Reno St Oklahoma City OK

CARLEY, JAMES REA, JR., educator; b. Hillsboro, N.D., May 17, 1909; s. James Rea and Anne Moore (Sutton) C.; B.A., U. N.D., 1931; M.Mus., Northwestern U., 1943; D.Sacred Mus., Union Theol. Sem., 1952; m. Isabel McNeill, June 28, 1943; children—Elizabeth Carley Hebert, John McNeill, Anne McNeill. Asst. prof. music Pacific U., Forest Grove, Oreg., 1946-49, N. Tex. State U., Denton, 1949-53; prof. ch. music Christian Theol. Sem., Indpls., 1953-73; lectr. Tri-County Tech. Inst., Murphy, N.C., 1974—; dir. Carley Singers (chamber group), Indpls., 1958-63, Carley Consort, Indpls., 1965-73, Brasstown, N.C., 1974—; organizer, dir. Children's Choir Festivals, Central Ind., 1958-74; dir. music United Meth. Ch., Murphy, 1975—; dir. Community Choir, 1975—. Served with USAAF, 1943-45. Mem. Assn. Disciples Musicians (pres. 1971-73), Nat. Assn. Tchrs. Singing, Brasstown Concert Assn. (pres. 1974-77), Viola da Gamba Soc. Am., Country Dance and Song Soc., Phi Beta Kappa, Alpha Tau Omega. Composer Fresh Airs/Old Songs Retuned, 1970. Address: Brasstown NC 28902

CARLIN, FRANK JOSEPH, paint co. exec.; b. Phila., Sept. 21, 1913; s. Francis Joseph and Kathryn Elizabeth (Walker) C.; student Drexel Inst. Tech., 1931-32, Temple U., 1936-39, U. Chgo., 1940-42; m. May P. Peterson, Dec. 20, 1943; children—Nancy May Carlin Figel, James H. Asst. chemist Rohm & Haas Co., Phila., 1934-39; chemist Sherwin-William Co., Chgo., 1939-43; group leader polymer devel. Am. Cyanamid Co., Stamford, Conn., 1943-44; group leader polymer applications research U.S. Rubber Co., Passaic, N.J., 1944-48; owner, pres. Worth Chem. Paint Co., Lake Worth, Fla., 1952—. Named Man of the Year Lake Worth C. of C., 1964. Mem. Am. Chem. Soc., Soc. Coatings Tech., Fla. Paint and Coatings Assn. C. of C. Clubs: Rotary (dir. 1974-75), K.C. (grand knight 1963-64), Notre Dame, Serra (pres. 1975-76), (Palm Beach, Fla). Patentee in field. Home: 400 Beach Curve Lantana FL 33460 Office: 1800 10th Ave N Lake Worth FL 33460

CARLIN, JAMES BOYCE, educator; b. Paducah, Ky., June 19, 1932; s. L.W. and Flora Lee (Newton) C.; A.A., Paducah Jr. Coll., 1952; A.B., Murray State U., 1954; M.A., George Peabody Coll., 1957; Ed.D., U. Miss., 1969; m. Hellon Lillian Upchurch, June 22, 1968; children—Rhonda Hope. Tchr., McCracken County Public Schs., Paducah, 1954-63; asst. prof. edn. Middle Tenn. State U., 1964-67; supr. reading instrn. Meridian (Miss.) Public Schs., 1967-68; asst. prof. U. Miss., 1968-69; prof. Murray (Ky.) State U., 1969—: reading, lang. arts cons. Mem. Ky. Assn. Childhood Edn. (state pres. 1979—), Internat. Reading Assn., NEA, Phi Delta Kappa, Kappa Delta Pi. Democrat. Baptist. Club: Rotary (program chmn. 1977-78). Author: Vowel Word Attack: 4 Step Process, 1976; contbr. articles to profl. jours. Office: Dept Spl Edn Murray State U Murray KY 42071

CARLISLE, JOHNNIE, educator; b. Wedowee, Ala., Sept. 14, 1921; d. John William and Hattie (Burrow) Carlisle; B.S., Ala. Coll., 1942; M.S., Columbus U., 1949; Ph.D., U. Tenn., 1975; m. Gordon Lee Carlisle, Oct. 15, 1950. Vocat. home econs. tchr. Gordo (Ala.) High Sch., 1942-43; supervisory tchr. vocat. home econs. Montevallo (Ala.) High Sch., 1943-45; supervisory tchr. home econs. and sci. Memphis State Tng. Sch., 1945-46; tchr. home econs. Miami Beach (Fla.) High Sch., 1946-50; asst. prof. home econs. Ala. Coll., Montevallo, 1950-57; tchr. Larrymore Elem. Sch., Norfolk, Va., 1958-59; substitute tchr. Oceanside (Calif.) Jr.-Sr. High Sch., 1960-61; tchr. biology, physics and gen. sci. Randolph County High Sch., Wedowee, Ala., 1961-62; asst. prof. home econs. U. Montevallo (Ala.), 1965—, asso. prof., 1973—; state advisor Coll. Home Econs. Clubs, 1954-55; mem. Ala. Nutrition Council, 1971-74, Birmingham Regional Nutrition Com., Inc., 1977—; area worker March of Dimes, 1964-65. Recipient Disting. Service award for Grey Lady activities Kennedy Gen. Hosp., 1946; Nat. Teaching Fellowship grantee, 1967-68. Mem. Ala. Home Econs. Assn. (panel participant), Am. Home Econs. Assn., Nutrition Today Soc., Soc. for Nutrition Edn., Joint Legis. Council of Ala., Omicron Nu. Democrat. Baptist. Contbr. articles to profl. jours. Home: 365 Nabors St N Montevallo AL 35115 Office: 102 Bloch Hall Sta 101 Univ of Montevallo Montevallo AL 35115

CARLISLE, WILLARD ROGER, physician; b. Los Angeles, Aug. 6, 1945; student Westminster Coll., Fulton, Mo.; M.D., Baylor U., 1971; married. Intern, resident in internal medicine Baylor U. Coll. of Medicine, Houston, 1971-73; resident U. Ala. Med. Center, Birmingham, 1975-76; fellow in digestive diseases Emory U. Affiliated Hosps., Atlanta, 1976-78; practice medicine specializing in gastroenterology, Birmingham, 1978—. Served to maj. M.C., U.S. Army, 1973-75. Diplomate Am. Bd. Internal Medicine. Office: Brookwood Profl Bldg Suite 303 2018 Brookwood Medical Center Dr Birmingham AL 35209

CARLISLE, WILLIAM EDGAR, physician; b. Montgomery, Ala., Dec. 8, 1927; s. Edgar and Hattie Elva (Watson) C.; B.S., Tulane U., 1950, M.D., 1953; m. Mary Elizabeth Jackson, June 11, 1951; children—William Gregory, Sara Elizabeth. Intern, Charity Hosp. of La., New Orleans, 1953-54; med. officer USAF, 1953-56; resident in obstetrics and gynecology Ochsner Clinic and Found. Hops., New Orleans, 1956-59; practice obstetrics and gynecology, Tuscaloosa, Ala., 1960—; cons. Bryce Hosp., Tuscaloosa. Diplomate Am. Bd. Obstetrics and Gynecology. Fellow Am. Coll. Obstetrics and

Gynecology; mem. Am., Ala., So. med. assns., Tuscaloosa Surg. Soc. Presbyterian. Clubs: Indian Hills Country, North River Yacht, Millwood Hunt. Home: 44 High Forest Tuscaloosa AL 35401 Office: 1788 McFarland Blvd N Tuscaloosa AL 35401

CARLO, MICHAEL JOHN, chemist, educator; b. Hammond, Ind., Dec. 27, 1937; s. Joseph F. and Anne H. Carlo; B.S. in Chemistry, Tex. A&M U., 1961, B.A. in Math., 1961, M.S. in Chemistry, 1962, Ph.D. in Chemistry, 1970; m. Mary L. Carlisle, Feb. 3, 1978; children—Michael, Laura, Meredith. Instr. chemistry Tex. So. U., Houston, 1963, Tarleton State Coll., Stephenville, Tex., 1963-64, asst. prof., 1965-67; spl. research fellow Tex. Christian U., Ft. Worth, 1964-65; asst. prof. chemistry Angelo State Coll., San Angelo, Tex., 1967-68, prof. chemistry, 1970—; research asso. Tex. A&M U., Thermodynamic Research Center, 1968-70; cons. toxicologist to various govt. agys., 1972—. Baseball coach YMCA, 1971-74; pres. Holy Angels Cath. Sch. Bd. Edn., 1972-74; mem. Diocese of San Angelo Bd. Edn., 1971-73; bd. dirs. San Angelo Council on Alcoholism, 1976-79, San Angelo ARC, 1977—, San Angelo Civic Theater, 1977—, Halfway House, 1976—, pres., 1977-79; bd. dirs. San Angelo Planned Parenthood, 1978—; bd. dirs. San Angelo Alcohol Detox, 1977—, pres., 1978-79. NSF grantee, 1967; San Angelo Drug Central Research grantee, 1972. Fellow Tex. Acad. Sci.; mem. Am. Chem. Soc., Fedn. Am. Scientists, Am. Acad. Forensic Scis., Tex. Assn. Coll. Tchrs., Instrument Soc. Am., AAUP (dir. 1973-76), AAAS, Alpha Phi Omega, Lambda Chi Alpha. Roman Catholic. Club: Lions (Lion of Yr. award 1974-75, pres. 1976-77). Author: (with D.G. Tarter) General Chemistry: First Semester Laboratory, 1972; Elements of Chemistry: A Laboratory Manual, 1976; A Study Guide to Accompany Basic Chemistry for the Life Sciences, 1977; editor Texas Jour. Sci., 1973—. Home: 3217 Sierra Dr San Angelo TX 76901 Office: PO Box 10986 Angelo State Univ Station San Angelo TX 76901

CARLOS, EDWARD, artist, gallery exec.; b. Kingsville, Pa., Nov. 8, 1937; s. James Brian and Josephine Gladys (Aaron) C.; B.S., Indiana U. of Pa., 1959; M.F.A., Catholic U. Am., 1963; Ph.D., Ohio U., 1969; m. Sarah Ann McPherson, July 11, 1964; children—Aaron Edward, Adam William, Malia Elizabeth. Prof., Ohio U., 1963-64, 66-69, Western Ill. U., 1965-66, Portland State Coll., summer 1965, U. Hawaii, 1964-65; chmn. fine arts dept. U. of South, Sewanee, Tenn., 1969—, gallery dir. Mus. Fine Arts, 1969—; exhibited in one man show at Edinburgh Internat. Festival, 1976, also numerous group shows. Ford Found. grantee, 1973, 75. Mem. Nat. Art Adminstrs. Am., So. Watercolor Soc., Coll. Art Assn., Delta Phi Delta. Contbr. poetry to Mountain Summer, 1975, 76, 78, 79, The Dixie Rev., 1976. Home: 71 Tennessee Ave Sewanee TN 37375

CARLSON, JAMES GORDON, zoologist, educator; b. Port Allegany, Pa., Jan. 24, 1908; s. James August and Mabel (Johns) C.; B.A., U. Pa., 1930, Ph.D., 1935; m. Elizabeth Shirley, Dec. 24, 1936; children—Shirley Carlson Bowen, Bette Carlson Schrader, James Marvin. Asst. in zoology U. Pa., Phila., 1929-30; demonstrator in biology Bryn Mawr (Pa.) Coll., 1930-31, instr. biology, 1931-35; instr. zoology U. Ala., Tuscaloosa, 1935-39, asst. prof., 1939-45, asso. prof., 1945-46; sr. biologist NIH, Bethesda, Md., 1946-47; head dept. zoology and entomology U. Tenn., Knoxville, 1947-67, prof. zoology, 1947-78, dir. Inst. Radiation Biology, 1955-75, Alumni Disting. Service prof., 1962-78, prof. emeritus, 1978—; instr. cytology Mt. Lake Biol. Sta., U. Va., summer, 1936; guest investigator Carnegie Inst. of Washington, Cold Spring Harbor, summers, 1937, 38, 40; Rockefeller fellow in natural sci. Genetics Lab., U. Mo., 1940-41; asso. biologist USPHS, 1945-46, spl. cons. in biology, 1943-46, 47-48; cons. biology Oak Ridge Nat. Lab., 1947-78. USPHS spl. fellow U. Heidelberg, Germany, 1964-65; Pa. State scholar, 1925-29; Pa. Senatorial scholar, 1926-29. Fellow AAAS (v.p. 1955); mem. Am. Inst. Biol. Scis., Am. Soc. for Cell Biology, Assn. Southeastern Biologists, Radiation Research Soc. (bd. editors of radiation research 1972-74), Tenn. Acad. Sci. (pres. 1961). Republican. Presbyterian. Contbr. articles to profl. jours. Home: 2134 Island Home Blvd Knoxville TN 37920 Office: Dept Zoology U Tenn Knoxville TN 37916

CARLSON, MAURICE IRWIN, educator, editor; b. Fulton, Ky., July 26, 1914; s. Peter Arvid and Della Elizabeth (Irwin) C.; B.A. with honors, Southwestern Coll., Memphis, 1936; M.A., Vanderbilt U., 1937; postgrad. Brown U., La. State U., 1938-39; m. Martha Elizabeth Deniger, Jan. 13, 1939; children—Martha Ann, Martha Elizabeth Carlson Crain. Agt., br. mgr. Acacia Mut. Life Ins. Co., Memphis, New Orleans, field supr., Washington, 1941-47; mgr. N.Tex. dept. Reliance Life Ins. Co. Pitts., Dallas, then supt. agys., Pitts., 1947-51; v.p. Universal Life and Accident Ins. Co., Dallas, 1951-59; with Life Ins. Co. N.Am., Tex., 1959; pres., dir. Reliance Life and Accident Ins. Co. Am., Dallas, 1959-65; mem. English and Greek faculties U. Tex., Arlington, 1966—, editor Arlington Quar., 1967—; guest lectr. So. Meth. U., U. Tex., Arlington; a founder weekly newspaper Hudkins Jour. (now Dallas County Jour.), 1962. Gen. chmn. Dallas County Cancer Crusade, 1954, Dallas County chpt. Nat. Kidney Disease Found., 1960; organizer Greater Dallas Citizens Com. for Old-Time Celebration Am. Ind. Day, 1961, chmn. adv. bd., 1961-67; pres. Bible class Park Cities Baptist Ch., Dallas, 1977; chmn. adv. bd. Operation LIFT, 1962-65; pres. Dads' Club So. Meth. U., 1963-64; exec. v.p. Dallas Am. Revolution Bicentennial Corp., 1975-76; chmn. Dallas County Republican Exec. Com., 1958-60; co-founder Dallas Charter League, 1961, exec. com., 1961-65, pres., 1965; bd. dirs. Dallas Council on World Affairs, also 1st v.p., chmn. exec. com., 1977; bd. dirs. Dallas UN Assn. U.S. C.L.U. Mem. Dallas Forum, Tex. Bur. Econ. Understanding (pres. 1971). Author: Aubrey Beardsley: A Study in Decadence, 1937; book reviewer Dallas Times-Herald, 1950—. Home: 3520 Centenary Dr Dallas TX 75225 Office: Box 366 Univ Station U Tex at Arlington Arlington TX 76010

CARLSON, MERLE THOMAS, phys. therapy co. exec.; b. Lodgepole, Nebr., Nov. 28, 1932; s. Merle Dixon and Helen (Rubado) C.; B.B.A., U. Nebr., 1957; M.A., George Washington U., 1963; M.A., Am. U., 1963; certified Hermann Hosp. Sch. Phys. Therapy, 1964; m. Jacqueline Elizabeth Viau, Sept. 2, 1961; children—Thomas David, John Joseph, Deborah Anne, Nancy Catherine. Tchr., Lisco (Nebr.) Pub. Schs., 1951-52; computer systems analyst Statis. div. IRS, Washington, 1957-58; internat. economist Office of Econ. Analysis, Bur. Fgn. Commerce, Washington, 1958-62; partner pvt. phys. therapy practice, Houston, 1963-64; exec. v.p. Phys. Therapy Assos. Inc., Houston, 1964-69, pres., Wharton, Tex., 1969—; chmn. bd. dirs., pres. Tocar Inc., Wharton, 1967—; chmn. bd. Carlson Builders, Inc., Wharton Health Center, Inc.; owner Carlson Devel. Co. Scoutmaster, Boy Scouts Am., 1968-71. Served with U.S. Army, 1953-55. Mem. Am. Phys. Therapy Assn., Am. Registry of Phys. Therapists, Am. Econ. Assn., Am. Mgmt. Assn., Wharton C. of C. (pres., dir.), Omicron Delta Epsilon. Republican. Roman Catholic. Clubs: Lions, K.C., Toastmasters. Patentee Swim-Trainer, 1967. Home: Rural Route 2 Box 148B Wharton TX 77488 Office: 301 W Milam Wharton TX 77488

CARLSTON, ROBERT ALFRED, elec. co. exec.; b. Honolulu, Mar. 15, 1930; s. Alfred George and Helen Marie Carlston; B.S. in Engring., U.S. Coast Guard Acad., 1952; M.S. in Indsl. Adminstrn. (Krannert scholar), Purdue U., 1964; m. Rosalie E. Montaleone, Feb. 24, 1951; children—Deborah G., Robert L., Richard G., Christopher S., Gail L. Carlston Fucci, Julie. Commd. ensign U.S. C.G., 1952, advanced through grades to comdr., 1967; gunnery officer U.S.C.G. cutter Falgout, 1952-54; aviator C.G. Air Sta., Salem, Mass., 1955-59; aviator, engr. C.G. Air Sta., Barbers Point, Hawaii, 1960-63; aviator, chief tech. research, chief mgmt. systems, C.G. Aircraft Repair and Supply Center, Elizabeth City, N.C., 1964-67; mgr. mgmt. info. systems office Sec. Dept. Transp., Washington, 1967-70; v.p. Consad Research Corp., Pitts., 1970-72; regional mgr. Westinghouse Electric Corp. pub. mgmt. systems, Dayton, Ohio, 1972-74, mgr. Urban Systems Center, Washington, 1975-76, dir. Nat. Issues Center, 1976—; professorial lectr. Am. U., 1967-70. Chmn. fund raising Harrison Twp. Republican Com., 1972-73. Mem. Nat. Aviation Club. Roman Catholic. Home: 2071 Bingham Ct Reston VA 22091 Office: 2341 Jefferson Davis Hwy Suite 1111 Arlington VA 22202

CARLTON, ALWIN HORATIO, mech. engr.; b. Birmingham, Ala., Feb. 24, 1933; s. Basil Brown and Nannie Hope (Lee) C.; B.S., Auburn U., 1960; postgrad. U. Tenn., 1965-67; m. Dorothy Emma Bowles, Sept. 16, 1952; children—Patricia Ann, Linda Jane, James Alwin, Robert Duane. Mech. engr. Holston Def. Corp., Kingsport, Tenn., 1960-72, chief engr., 1972-79, supt. utilities, 1979—. Bd. dirs. Community Chest Kingsport, 1974—. Registered profl. engr., Tenn. Mem. ASME, Tenn. Soc. Profl. Engrs. (dir. Upper East Tenn. chpt. 1978-79). Baptist (deacon). Clubs: Bays Mountain Flying, Elks. Home: 1308 Dupont Dr Kingsport TN 37664 Office: Holston Def Corp Kingsport TN 37660

CARLTON, JEDFREY MICHAEL, botanist; b. Gainesville, Fla., Sept. 22, 1947; s. Loran Veirs and Lucille (Burzenski) C.; A.A., Manatee Jr. Coll., 1968; B.S., Fla. State U., 1969; M.A., U. South Fla., 1974. Instr. gen. sci. Ketterlinus Jr. High Sch., St. Augustine, Fla., 1969-70; marine biologist Marine Lab., Fla. Dept. Natural Resources, St. Petersburg, 1972-78, botanist C.E., U.S. Army, New Orleans dist., 1978—; guest lectr. dept. botany U. Natal, Durban, S. Africa, 1978. Haydon Burns scholar, 1965-67; Fla.-Colombia Alliance grantee, 1966; NSF grantee, 1971. Mem. Am. Bot. Soc., Gulf Estuarine Research Soc., Am. Littoral Soc., Soc. Econ. Botany, Internat. Oceanographic Found. Democrat. Mem. Christian Ch. (Disciples of Christ). Author: Land-building and Stabilization by Mangroves, 1974; A Guide to Common Florida Salt Marsh and Mangrove Vegetation, 1975; Techniques for Coastal Restoration and Fishery Enhancement in Florida, 1975; A Survey of Selected Coastal Vegetation Communities of Florida, 1977. Home: PO Box 15826 New Orleans LA 70175 Office: Environ Analysis Br US Army Dist New Orleans PO Box 60267 New Orleans LA 70160

CARLTON, THOMAS MABRY, county ofcl., agrl. co. exec.; b. Wauchula, Fla., July 2, 1901; s. Thomas Newton and Ada (Altman) C.; LL.B., Stetson U., 1929; m. Septa Virginia Savell, June 12, 1931; children—Thomas Mabry, Ben Savell, Winston Cambron. Admitted to Fla. bar, 1929; practiced in Wauchula, 1929-36; county tax assessor Hardee County, 1937-50; pres. Mabry Carlton & Sons Citrus Groves, Inc., Wauchula, 1959—, Mabry Carlton & Sons Ranch, Inc., Wauchula, 1959—. Chmn. Hardee County Park Bd., 1962-75; mem. exec. com. Agri-Civic Center, 1974-76; bd. dirs. Hardee County Property Owners' Assn.; vice chmn. Wauchula Mus. Assn. Recipient award for service to industry Fla. Cattleman's Assn., 1970. Mem. Am. Bar Assn., Fla. Farm Bur., Fla. Citrus Mut., Fla. Cattleman's Assn. (hon. life dir. 1968—), Peace River Valley Hist. Soc. (pres. 1970-75), SAR, Sigma Nu Phi, Pi Gamma Mu, Delta Sigma Phi. Baptist (bd. deacons 1958-65, 67-77, 78-80, chmn. 1967-73). Address: 1100 Magnolia Ln Wauchula FL 33873

CARMACK, HAROLD DEAN, coll. adminstr.; b. Macon County, Ala., Sept. 3, 1937; s. James Leo and Gertrude (Craft) C.; B.S. in Bus. Adminstrn., Jacksonville U., 1961; M.A., U. Ala., Ed.S., 1968; grad. Southeastern Sch. Alcohol Studies, U. Ga., 1968, Rutgers U. Summer Sch. Alcohol Studies, 1969, Utah Sch. Alcoholism and other Drug Dependencies, U. Utah, 1971; m. Jackie Sue Moore, Aug. 3, 1961; children—Joey Dean, Carol Ann. Supr., Goodyear Tire & Rubber Co., Gadsden, Ala., 1961-66, credit sales mgr. Goodyear Service Store, 1966-67; intern alcohol unit Bryce State Mental Instn., 1967-68; counselor Ala. Vocat. Rehab. Service, Gadsden, 1968; evaluator for handicapped Darden Rehab. Center, 1966-67; dir. mental health Gadsden State Jr. Coll., 1969—. Bd. mem. Cherokee-Etowah-Dekalb Fellowship House, 1967—, Serenity Home, 1979—. Mem. Nat. Council Alcoholism, Nat. Mental Health Assn., NEA, Ala. Edn. Assn., Regional Council Alcoholism (mem. exec. bd.). Baptist. Home: 705 Crestview Dr Gadsden AL 35903 Office: Dept Mental Health Gadsden State Jr Coll Gadsden AL 35903

CARMAN, THOMAS WILSON, health planner; b. Ithaca, N.Y., Aug. 1, 1951; s. Samuel L. and Elizabeth Ann (Wilson) C.; B.A., Antioch Coll., 1973; M.S.W., Tulane U., 1976. Exec. dir. Open Door, Inc., New Orleans, 1976-79; sr. health planner div. of data mgmt. and analysis Health Systems Agy., Inc., New Orleans, 1979—; pvt. practice psychotherapy, 1976—; mem. faculty Tulane U. Continuing Edn., Sch. Social Work, New Orleans, 1979—. Cert. social worker, La. Mem. Nat. Assn. Social Workers, Am. Orthopsychiat. Assn. Author: (manual) Multi Family Groups for Adolescents and Parents, 1978. Office: 333 St Charles Ave New Orleans LA 70130

CARMEAN, JAMES LIGGETT, JR., data processing exec.; b. Dallas, Aug. 1, 1950; s. James Liggett and Marian Carmean (Howard) C.; student So. Meth. U., 1968-71; B.A., N. Tex. State U., 1975, postgrad., 1975; m. Sandra Sue Milliner, June 17, 1972; children—Christopher, Andrea. Mgr., 7-11 Grocery, Denton, Tex., 1971-73; communications officer N. Tex. State U. Police Dept., Denton, 1974-76; computer correlator Horchow Collection, Dallas, 1976-77; computer operator customer service ops. Electronic Data Systems, Inc., Dallas, 1977-78; programer, systems analyst Info. Retrieval Methods, Inc., Dallas, 1978—. Bd. dirs. Irving Community Concerts Assn., 1977-78. Mem. N. Tex. State U. Policy Activity Assn. (sec.-treas. 1975-76). Methodist. Clubs: N. Tex. Sky-Diving, N. Tex. Radio-TV-Film. Home: 510 E 2d St Irving TX 75060 Office: 2925 LBJ Suite 140 Dallas TX 75234

CARMICHAEL, EMMETT BRYAN, biochemist; b. Shelbyville, Mo., Sept. 4, 1895; s. George Frank and Amelia Grant (Tingle) C.; B.A., U. Colo., 1918, M.S., 1922; Ph.D., U. Cin., 1927, D.Sc. (hon.), Central Meth. Coll., 1979; m. Lelah Marie Van Hook, Nov. 23, 1921. Instr. chemistry U. Colo., 1919-24; instr. biochemistry U. Cin., 1924-26; bacteriologist W.S. Merrill Co., 1926-27; asst. prof. head dept. physiol. chemistry Sch. Medicine, U. Ala., Tuscaloosa, 1927-28, asso. prof., 1928-32, prof., 1932-45; prof., head dept. biochemistry Med. Coll., U. Ala., Birmingham, 1945-60, prof., head dept. biochemistry Sch. Dentistry, 1948-60, asst. dean Med. Coll. and Sch. Dentistry, 1959-66, prof. emeritus biochemistry, 1966—. Chmn., N. Central Ala. Regional Sci. Fairs, 1954-57; trustee Gorgas Scholarship Found. Inc., 1947—, chmn., 1957-73, hon. chmn., 1973—. Served with U.S. Army, 1918-19. Recipient W.C. Gorgas award, 1966; Service award Alpha Epsilon Delta, 1966; Gold medal Am. Inst. Chemists, 1971; Order of Golden Heart, Sigma Phi Epsilon, 1973; named to Ala. Acad. Honor, 1973. Mem. Am. Chem. Soc., AAAS, Am. Inst. Chemists, Soc. Exptl. Biology and Medicine, Am. Assn. Clin. chemists, Internat. Coll. Anesthetists, Am. Soc. Biol. Chemists, Am. Physiol. Soc., Am. Assn. History of Medicine, Ala. Acad. Sci., AMA (affiliate), Acacia Frat., Sigma Xi. Club: Masons. Contbr. articles to profl. jours. Home: 3501 Redmont Rd Birmingham AL 35213 Office: Univ Sta U Ala Birmingham AL 35294

CARMICHAEL, JERRY HARRIS, math. geophysicist; b. Brownfield, Tex., Nov. 23, 1938; s. William Harris and Mary Lois (White) C.; B.S., U. Tex., 1962; postgrad. (spl. math scholar 1964), Tex. Technol. Coll., 1962-64, U. Houston, 1968-69; m. Anna Jean Parker, June 9, 1962; children—Angela, Jeffrey, Joseph. Teaching fellow Tex. Technol. Coll., 1962-64; seismologist Geophys. Service, Inc., Dallas, 1964-66; programmer Chevron Oil Co., Houston, 1966-69; sr. analyst (geophysics) Permian Information & Computing Center, Midland, Tex., 1969; project engr. Tex. Instruments, Inc., Houston, 1970; geophys. analyst Geospace Corp., Houston, 1971-74; sr. research mathematician Dresser Olympic Ops., Houston, 1974-77; sr. project engr. Dresser Atlas, 1977—. Finalist, Nat. Merit Award Scholarships, 1957. Mem. Soc. Exploration Geophysicists, Geophys. Soc. Houston. Republican. Meth. Mason. Home: 4306 Oxhill Rd Spring TX 77373 Office: PO Box 1407 Houston TX 77001

CARMICHAEL, JOHN LESLIE, physician; b. Goodwater, Ala., May 22, 1897; s. Daniel Monroe and Amanda (Lessley) C.; A.B., U. Ala., 1916; M.D., Tulane U., 1924; m. Grace Donald, Apr. 28, 1928; children—John L., Jr., Daniel Erskine, James Donald, Robert Glenn, Grace Amanda Carmichael Finkel. Attending surgeon Birmingham Baptist Hosp., 1927—, St. Vincent's Hosp., 1934—; asso. attending surgeon Hillman Hosp., 1934-41, attending surgeon, 1941-45; asst. prof. surgery Med. Coll. of Ala., 1945-52, asso. prof., 1952-55, prof. clin. surgery, 1955—. Chmn. city council, Fairfield, Ala., 1932-36. Diplomate Am. Bd. Surgery. Fellow ACS, Southeastern Surg. Congress; mem. Birmingham Clin. Club, Birmingham Surg. Soc., Jefferson County Med. Soc., Ala. State Med. Assn., So., Am. med. assns., Phi Beta Kappa, Alpha Omega Alpha. Clubs: The Country, Birmingham, the Club. Home: 3803 Glencoe Dr Birmingham AL 35213 Office: 2011 9th Ave S Birmingham AL 35205

CARMICHAEL, MIRIAM WILLENA, neurologist; b. Birmingham, Ala., Oct. 21, 1925; d. Patrick Henry and Mary McPhail (Partridge) C.; B.A., Converse Coll., 1946; postgrad. U. Richmond, 1946-47; M.D., Med. Coll. Va., 1951; m. S. P. Lingo, Apr. 22, 1960; 1 son, Stuart Patrick. Intern, U. Wis. Hosp., Madison, 1951-52; jr. asst. resident Med. Coll. Va., 1952-53, asst. resident in internal medicine, 1953-54; jr. asst. resident in neurology Neurol. Inst. N.Y., N.Y.C., 1954-55; asst. resident in neurology Mass. Gen. Hosp., Boston, 1955-57; teaching fellow in neuropathology Harvard U.-Mass. Gen. Hosp., 1955-57; asst. prof. neurology Med. Coll. Va., 1957-58; research fellow in neuropharmacology Coll. Physicians and Surgeons N.Y., N.Y.C., 1959-60; practice medicine specializing in neurology, Richmond, 1960—; mem. staff Richmond Meml., St. Mary's hosps.; asst. clin. prof. neurology U. Va., 1961-71, asso. clin. prof., 1971—; mem. teaching staff Richmond Meml. Hosp., 1960—; mem. adv. med. bd. Chesterfield County (Va.) Diagnostic Center, 1960—. Mem. Beford Acad. Sch Bd., Richmond, 1960-70. Mem. Assn. Childhood Edn., AMA, Va. Med. Soc., Am. Acad. Neurology, Richmond Acad. Medicine, Va. Neurol. Soc., Am. Epilepsy Soc., Assn. Research in Nervous and Mental Diseases. Presbyterian. Home: 3919 Seminary Ave Richmond VA 23227 Office: 1400 Westwood Ave Richmond VA 23227

CARMODY, ARTHUR RODERICK, JR., lawyer; b. Shreveport, La., Feb. 19, 1928; s. Arthur R. and Caroline (Gaughan) C.; B.S., Fordham U., 1949; LL.B., La. State U., 1952; m. Renee Aubry, Jan. 26, 1952; children—Helen Bragg, Renee, Arthur Roderick III, Patrick, Timothy, Mary, Virginia, Joseph. Admitted to La. bar, 1952; mem. firm Wilkinson, Carmody Peatross & Caverlee, Shreveport, 1952—; dir. Kansas City So. Transport Co., Kansas City, Shreveport and Gulf Terminal Co., Shreveport Captains Baseball Club. Chmn. Met. Shreveport Zoning Bd. Appeals, 1959-72; bd. dirs. Caddo Democratic Assn., Shreveport, 1966—; pres. bd. trustees Jesuit High Sch., Shreveport; trustee Schumpert Med. Center, Shreveport; bd. dirs. La. State U. Found., Baton Rouge, Agnew Day Sch., Shreveport, Ridgewood Montessori Sch., Shreveport; nat. bd. dirs. N.Mex. Mil. Inst., Roswell, 1967—. Fellow Am. Coll. Trial Lawyers; mem. Am., Fed., La., Shreveport bar assns., Am. Judicature Soc., La. Law Inst., Nat. Assn. R.R. Trial Counsel, La. Assn. Def. Counsel, Nat. Acad. Law and Medicine, Tarshar Soc., Shreveport C. of C. (bd. dirs. 1967—), Soc. Hosp. Council, La. Civil Service League, Phi Delta Phi, Kappa Alpha. Roman Catholic. Clubs: Shreveport, Petroleum (Shreveport); Pierremont Oaks Tennis. Home: Box 1707 Shreveport LA 71166 Office: Beck Bldg Shreveport LA 71166

CARNAHAN, ADELE CHERRY, guidance counselor; b. Ark., Dec. 1, 1916; d. Jess A. and Cellie Mae (Hobbs) Cherry; B.S. Nursing Ed., St. Joseph's Hosp. Hot Springs, Ark., 1938; B.S., Incarnate Word Coll., 1960; M.Ed. Trinity U., 1967; M.S., Our Lady of Lake Coll., 1970; m. Richard Henry Carnahan, Nov. 26, 1940; children—Richard Jr., Susie Carnahan Hawthorne, Peggy Carnahan Hawthorne. Nurse, anesthesist Army-Navy Hosp., Hot Springs, Ark. and Ft. Sill. Okla., 1939-40; tchr. Middle Sch. San Antonio, 1959-68, guidance counselor, 1968—. Mem. Women Deans and Counselors Assn. San Antonio Area (pres. 1974-75), San Antonio Counselors Assn. (pres. 1976-77), Women's Aux. San Antonio Dental Soc. (past v.p.), Tex., S. Tex., Am. personnel and guidance assns., San Antonio Ind. Sch. Dist. Counselors Assn. Episcopalian. Home: 130 Melrose Pl San Antonio TX 78212 Office: 2411 San Pedro Ave San Antonio TX 78212

CARNAHAN, ROBERT NARVELL, lawyer; b. Littlefield, Tex., Nov. 22, 1928; s. Clarence D. and Wilma L. (Hartness) C.; B.A., Tex. Technol. Coll., 1950; J.D., U. Tex., Austin, 1957; m. Betty L. Stewart, Mar. 25, 1952; children—Cynthia Lou, Michael S., Christopher Kelly. Admitted to Tex. bar, 1957; asst. county atty., Potter County, 1957; practice law, Amarillo, 1958—. Pres., Amarillo Little Theatre, Inc. Served as 1st lt. USAF, Korean War. Named Outstanding Young Lawyer, Amarillo Jr. Bar Assn., 1964. Mem. Am. Judicature Soc., Tex. Assn. Def. Counsel, Tex., Amarillo bar assns., Alpha Tau Omega, Phi Alpha Delta. Mem. Christian Ch. (dir.). Lion. Club: Amarillo Country. Home: 105 Palomino St Amarillo TX 79106 Office: Plaza One Amarillo TX 79101

CARNELL, CLAUDE MITCHELL, JR., speech and hearing clinic exec.; b. Woodruff, S.C., Apr. 27, 1934; s. Claude Mitchell and Edith Iler (Gossett) C.; A.A., Mars Hill Coll., 1954; B.A., Furman U., 1956; M.A., U. Ala., 1958; Ph.D., La. State U., 1972; m. Elizabeth Jean Frei, July 6, 1957; children—Elizabeth Suzanne, Claude Michael. Instr., Furman U., Greenville, S.C., 1958-59; speech pathologist Wheeling (W.Va.) Soc. for Crippled Children, 1959-60; chief speech pathologist Cerebral Palsy Center of Greater Baton Rouge, 1960-64; with Charleston (S.C.) Speech & Hearing Center, 1964—, exec. dir., 1964—; adj. asso. prof. The Citadel, 1972—; asst. clin. prof. otolaryngology Med. U S.C., 1973-77; cons. VA Hosp., Columbia, S.C., 1973—; partner Health Mgmt. Center, 1979—. Pres., St. Andrews Elementary Sch. PTA, Charleston, 1970-72; mem. mayors com. Employment of Handicapped, 1972-76; chmn. adv. com. Charleston Home Health Services, 1974-75; mem. Charleston County Health Adv. Com., 1973-79. Mem. adv. bd. Charleston Council for

Deaf, 1964-75; bd. dirs. United Cerebral Palsy Carolina Low Country, 1964-66, Council for Retarded Child of Charleston County, 1965-68, S.C. Orgn. for Hearing Impaired, 1972-76, Assn. Service Programs in Communicative Disorders, 1974—, Commn. Accreditation Rehab. Facilities, 1976-78, Charleston Sr. Citizens Center, 1979—, Sea Island Comprehensive Health Center, 1978—; Pulmetto Low Country Health Systems Agy., 1980—, Charleston very Spl. Arts Program, 1979—; bd. dirs. S.C. Adv. Council for the Deaf/Blind, 1972—, chmn., 1973—; vice chmn. S.C. Bd. Examiners in Audiology and Speech Pathology, 1973-77: bd. dirs. Hope Center for Retarded, 1968-72, 75-80; trustee First Bapt. of Charleston Day Sch., 1969-72. Fellow Am. Speech and Hearing Assn. (mem. subcom. on evaluation for regional confs. 1973-75); mem. Nat. Assn. Execs. of Hearing and Speech Action, S.C. Speech and Hearing Assn. (pres. 1969-71, chmn. govtl. affairs com. 1971-75), Council for Exceptional Children (dir. 1961-64, chpt. pres. 1968-69), Internat. Platform Assn. Baptist. Author: Development, Management and Evaluation of Community Speech and Hearing Centers, 1976. Contbr. articles to profl. and popular jours. Home: 2444 Birkenhead Dr Charleston SC 29407 Office: 30 Lockwood Dr Charleston SC 29401

CARNES, JAMES OLIVER, gas co. exec.; b. Winnsboro, Tex., Apr. 11, 1927; s. Dolphus C. and Julia C. (Hanson) C.; ed. mgmt. courses U. N.M., 1958, Harvard, 1971; m. Joyce F. Smith, Dec. 26, 1947; children—Ned C., Kenneth E. Road and equipment accountant Tex. & Pacific Ry., Dallas, 1946-48, treas., gen. mgr. employee fed. credit union, 1948-50; office mgr. So. Union Gas Co., Galveston, Tex., 1952-55, office mgr., asst. dist. mgr., Albuquerque, dist. mgr., Farmington, N.Mex., 1955-63, v.p., dist. mgr., Flagstaff, Ariz., 1963-73, sr. v.p., Dallas, 1973—; pres. So. Union Realty Co., Dallas, 1975—. Chmn. industry legis. com. utility taxation State of Ariz., 1967; mem. bd. adv. council State of Ariz. Tech. Services, 1963; mem. Coconino County Air Pollution Adv. Council, 1968-73; mem. personnel bd. City of Flagstaff, 1971-73; mem. exec. adv. com. to dean Coll. Bus. of No. Ariz. U., 1965-73. Bd. dirs. Ariz. Dept. Econ. Planning and Devel., 1969-73. Served with AUS, 1944-46, 50-52; PTO, CBI. Mem. Am., So. gas assns., Dallas Petroleum Club, Beta Gamma. Republican. Baptist. Mason. Club: Royal Oaks Country (Dallas). Home: 9616 Orchard Hill Ct Dallas TX 75243 Office: Suite 1800 First Internat Bldg Dallas TX 75270

CARNES, JESS GALE, ret. educator; b. Tolono, Ill., Aug. 9, 1913; s. Jess Gale and Eva Duckett (Pratt) C.; B.A., U. Ill., 1940, M.A., 1942; Ph.D., Cornell U., 1949; m. Cornelia Schlorff, Oct. 4, 1942; 1 son, Jess Gale, Jr. Instr., U. Mass. at Amherst, 1949-52; asso. prof. Trinity U., 1952-59, prof., 1959-79. Served with AUS, 1941-46. Decorated Bronze Star. Mem. Phi Beta Kappa, Phi Kappa Phi, Alpha Chi (nat. v.p. 1967-75, nat. council 1967-79, editor Recorder 1967-75, editor Newsletter 1970-75). Meth. Home: 311 Burnside Dr San Antonio TX 78209

CARNEVALE, DARIO, petroleum and petrochem. co. exec.; b. Paola, Cosenza, Italy, Jan. 11, 1935; s. Emilio and Olinda (Marcelli) C.; came to U.S., 1968, naturalized, 1974; D.Eng., U. Rome, 1960; m. Franca Nelken, Feb. 28, 1959; children—Daniela, Flavia, Fulvia, Dario. Project mgr. compagnia Tecnica Industrie Petroli, Italy, Egypt, Lebanon and France, 1960-65; project dir. process div. Universal Oil Products Co., Rumania, 1966-67, Colombia, 1968-71, project. dir., mktg. dist. mgr., gen. mgr., Colombia, Venezuela, Panama, Netherlands Antilles, Trinidad and Tobago, 1972-77, gen. mgr. UOP Processes Internat., Bogota, Colombia, 1977—. Mem. Am. Inst. Chem. Engrs., Am. Mgmt. Assn. Roman Catholic. Home: 1325 NE 138th St North Miami FL 33101 Office: 20 UOP Plaza Des Plaines IL 60016

CARNEY, ROBERT STEPHEN, personnel firm exec.; b. Columbia, S.C., Aug. 9, 1943; s. George Marion and Iris (Booker) C.; B.B.A. in Fin., B.B.A. in Mktg.-Mgmt., Armstrong State Coll., 1976; m. Olivia Koon, July 15, 1966; children—Ashley Kevin, Eric Joel. Personnel cons. Continental Cons., Inc., Columbia, 1967-71, v.p., 1969-71; personnel cons., v.p. Atlantic States Personnel Cons., Inc., Savannah, Ga., 1971-77, pres., 1977—. Served with USNR, 1961-64. Mem. Nat. Assn. Personnel Consultants, First Internat. Group Personnel Consultants, Ga. Assn. Personnel Services. Methodist. Clubs: Masons (32 deg.), Shriner, Rotary. Home: 12507 Kingwood Dr Savannah GA 31406 Office: Atlantic States Personnel Consultants Inc PO Box 9928 31 W Congress St Savannah GA 31412

CARNLEY, SAMUEL FLEETWOOD, judge; b. Elba, Ala., Nov. 13, 1918; s. Jefferson A. and Mary (Ray) C.; B.A., U. Ala., 1939, LL.B., 1941; m. Mary Magdalene Talbot, Mar. 21, 1939; children—Nancy Hart Carnley Morrow, Mary Oliver Carnley Brown, Terry David, Samuel Fleetwood, Melanie Carnley Jones. Admitted to Ala. bar, 1941; practice law, Elba, 1941-44, 46, 53—; dir. indsl. relations State of Ala., Montgomery, 1947-50; judge 12th Jud. Circuit Ala., Elba and Troy, 1950-52, Inferior Ct. Coffee County (Ala.), 1969-74. Mem. Interstate Conf. Employment Security Agys., 1947-50, mem. exec. com., dist. pres., 1948; mem. Elba Bd. Edn., 1953-58; pageant dir., master ceremonies Elba Centennial, 1953; mem. exec. com. Elba PTA, 1960-63, pres., 1966-68; chpt. chmn. ARC, 1966-68; program chmn. Elba Halloween Carnival, 1960-63; pres. Elba Little Theater, 1964-65; moderator Coffee County Bapt. Assn., 1967-68; mem. Ala. Bapt. Commn. on Higher Edn., 1967-76; trustee Judson Coll., 1960—, v.p. bd., 1964-67, pres. bd., 1967-78, acting pres. coll., 1969-70. Served with AUS, 1944-45. Recipient Algernon Sidney Sullivan award Judson Coll., 1970. Mem. Am. Judicature Soc., Am., Coffee County (past pres.) bar assns., Ala. State Bar, Elba C. of C., Pi Kappa Phi (past pres.). Democrat. Baptist (chmn. bd. deacons, Sunday sch. tchr., trustee state pres. brotherhood). Club: Elba Country. Home: 416 W Collier St Elba AL 36323 Office: 463 Carnley Ave Elba AL 36323

CARNS, MARY LOUISE, polit. scientist; b. Salem, Ohio, Mar. 10, 1939; d. Richard M. and Dorothy M. (Stanley) C.; B.A., Hiram (Ohio) Coll., 1961; M.A., Case-Western Res. U., 1965; postgrad. U. Nebr., 1964-67. Tchr. history Mineral Ridge (Ohio) High Sch., 1962-64; Congl. intern U.S. Ho. of Reps., summer 1965; teaching asst. U. Nebr., 1964-67; asst. prof. polit. sci. Stephen F. Austin State Coll., Nacogdoches, Tex., 1967—. Election clk., Nacogdoches, 1971-78; chmn. Nacogdoches Democratic Precinct Conv., 1976; del. Dem. County Conv., 1976. Mem. Tex. Assn. Coll. Tchrs., Pi Sigma Alpha. Presbyterian. Clubs: Univ. Women's, Stephen F. Austin Profl. Women's. Home: 3321 Pearl St Nacogdoches TX 75961 Office: Box 3045 Stephen F Austin State Univ Nacogdoches TX 75962

CARO, RICHARD HARVEY, indsl. process control computers and instruments mfg. co. exec.; b. N.Y.C., Sept. 30, 1936; s. Marshall Harry and Mildred (Miller) C.; B.S., U. Fla., 1957; M.S., La. State U., 1964; m. Patricia Ann McCallum, Aug. 3, 1958; children—James Richard, Annette Louise, Debora Lynn. Process engr. Ethyl Corp., Baton Rouge, 1957-62; project leader Union Camp Corp., Savannah, Ga., 1962-70; product mgr., mktg. mgr. The Foxboro (Mass.) Co., 1970-76, research mgr., 1976-78; mktg. mgr. Modular Computer Systems, Ft. Lauderdale, Fla., 1978—. Chmn. Am. region Internat. Purdue Workshop on Indsl. Computer Systems, 1977—; mem. PL/I lang. com. and alt. to FORTRAN lang. com. Am. Nat. Standards Inst. Mem. Am. Inst. Chem. Engrs., Instrument Soc. Am. (mem. indsl. FORTRAN standards com.), IEEE. Mem. Evang. Covenant Ch. (deacon 1971-74, mem. steering com. 1974-77, treas. 1977-78). Home: 2320 Cypress Bend Dr Apt 405 Pompano Beach FL 33060 Office: Modular Computer Systems 1650 W McNab Rd Fort Lauderdale FL 33310

CARPENTER, BARBARA LYNETTE, mgmt. cons. co. exec.; b. Milw., May 1, 1947; d. Earl Ernest and Viola Anna (Zinda) Bethke; B.F.A., U. Wis., 1970; postgrad. St. Edward's U., 1978—; m. Ted Galen Carpenter, May 11, 1968; children—Lara Michele, Amber Janell. Personnel asst. Dayton Hudson Corp., Milw., 1970-73; employment counselor Dynamic Personnel, Austin, Tex., 1973-74; asst. personnel dir., job analysis and tng. dir. Tex. Bd. Ins., Austin, 1974—; owner, mng. cons. Profl. Mgmt. Systems, Austin, 1979—. Mem. Am. Soc. for Tng. and Devel. (chpt. pres. 1980), Austin Area Intergovernmental Tng. Council.

CARPENTER, CARLTON LANIER, JR., dermatologist; b. Starville, Miss., Aug. 11, 1930; s. Carlton Lanier and Ruth (Deloach) C.; B.S., Miss. State U., 1951; M.D., Tulane U., 1955; m. Lynda Moss, Dec. 27, 1963; children—Will Moss, Michael Edward, Laura Elizabeth. Intern, Phila. Gen. Hosp., 1955-56; resident Charity Hosp., New Orleans, 1958-62; practice medicine specializing in dermatology, Baton Rouge, 1962—; mem. staff Our Lady of Lake Hosp.; clin. prof. La. State U. Sch. Medicine, 1970—; dir. Citizens Savs. & Loan, Baton Rouge. Pres. bd. dirs. Baton Rouge Speech and Hearing Found., 1977—. Served to capt. USAF, 1956-58. Fellow A.C.P.; mem. Am. Acad. Dermatology, Am. Dermatol. Assn., La. Dermatol. Soc. (pres. 1975-76), So. Med. Assn. (sec. dermatology sect. 1972-75, chmn. 1976-77), East Baton Rouge Parish Med. Soc. (pres. 1974-75), Baton Rouge C. of C., Baton Rouge Round Table, SAR. Rotarian. Home: 1151 S Cloverdale Baton Rouge LA 70808 Office: 1415 Main St Baton Rouge LA 70802

CARPENTER, CHARLES LEE, air force officer; b. Appleton City, Mo., June 12, 1939; s. Forrest Lee and Julia Mildred (Ledbetter) C.; B.S., Central Mo. State U., 1965, M.A. in History, 1965; m. Phyllis Ruth Beard, Sept. 1, 1962; children—Travis Charles, Stacy Michelle, Matthew Forrest. Served as enlisted man U.S. Air Force, 1957-61, commd. lt., 1966, advanced through grades to maj., 1977; underwriter Farmers Ins. Group, Mission, Kans., 1965-66; personnel officer McCoy AFB, Orlando, Fla., 1966-68; intelligence officer Goodfellow AFB, San Angelo, Tex., 1968-69, Korat Royal AFB, Thailand, 1969-70, Kelly AFB, Tex., 1974-77; assigned to postgrad. intelligence course Anacostia Naval Sta., Washington, 1977-78, research programming officer, 1978-79; exec. officer, dep. chief staff plans Hdqrs. Electronic Security Command, Kelly AFB, 1978—; asst. prof. dept. history Far East div. U. Md., 1969-70. Deacon, Marbach Christian Ch., San Antonio, 1976-77. Decorated D.F.C. with oak leaf cluster, Meritorious Service medal with oak leaf cluster, Commendation medal with oak leaf cluster. Mem. Air Force Assn., Acad. Polit. Sci. Democrat. Home: 2019 Wilsons Creek San Antonio TX 78245 Office: Hdqrs Electronic Security Command/XP Kelly AFB TX 78243

CARPENTER, CLARENCE WILLARD, JR., petroleum exploration scientist; b. Woodbury, N.J., Feb. 12, 1922; s. Clarence Willard and Bertha E. (Cox) C.; B.S., Oreg. State U., 1949; M.S., U. Minn., 1952; m. Marie Ethyl Baker, May 22, 1921; 1 dau., Shari Lynn. Research engr. Carter Oil Co., Tulsa, 1952-60; research engr. Jersey Production Research Co., Tulsa, 1960-64; sr. research engr. Esso Production Research Co., Houston, 1964-73; research specialist Exxon Production Research Co., Houston, 1973—. Served with U.S. Army, 1942-46. Mem. Soc. Petroleum Engrs., Internat. Assn. Hydraulic Research. Contbr. articles in field to profl. jours. Home: 8610 Cedarbrake Dr Houston TX 77055 Office: Box 2189 Houston TX 77001

CARPENTER, CLAYTON DUFFEY, oil co. exec.; b. Denver, Aug. 6, 1940; s. Everett Knowlton and Mary Janet (Duffey) C.; B.S., U. Colo., 1963; M.B.A., U. So. Calif., 1970; m. Patricia Joyce Jones, May 25, 1974; children—Robyn Diane, Michael Scott. Mktg. rep. for computers IBM, San Francisco, 1966-69; prin. Cresap, McCormick & Paget Inc., Melbourne, Australia, 1970-77; mgr. acctg. services Aramco Services Co., Houston, 1977—. Served with USN, 1963-66; Vietnam. Mem. Delta Sigma Phi, Beta Gamma Sigma, Kappa Sigma. Methodist. Club: Royal Automobile of Victoria. Home: 3523 Oak Lake Dr Kingwood TX 77339 Office: Suite 4000 1100 Milam St Houston TX 77002

CARPENTER, JAMES MAXWELL, chem. co. exec.; b. Throckmorton County, Tex., May 23, 1918; s. Jacob Leslie and Lydia Margaret (Cole) C.; B.S. in Agrl. Edn., Tex. A&M U., 1942; m. Mildred Evelyn Ableson, June 2, 1946; children—Cynthia Ann, Cherrie Margaret. Asst. county agrl. agt. Wichita County (Tex.), 1946; county agrl. agt. Knox County (Tex.), 1946-48, Wichita County, 1948-51; mgr. Hamilton T-Bone Ranches, Wichita Falls, 1951-63; with Am. Cyanamid Co., Amarillo, Tex., 1963—, dist. mgr. Feedlot div., 1963—. Mem. Plains Nutrition Council, 1970—. Bd. dirs. Tex. Okla. Fair, 1949-53. Served to capt. U.S. Army, 1942-46; ETO. Decorated Bronze Star. Mem. Tex. Cattle Feeders Assn., Nat. Cattlemen's Assn., Panhandle Livestock Assn. Tex. Democrat. Baptist. Club: T-Bone (Amarillo). Home: 6109 Elmhurst Rd Amarillo TX 79106

CARPENTER, LINDA LEE, counselor; b. Houston, Tex., Feb. 3, 1948; d. Pierce Fleming and Dorothy (Rayburn) C.; B.A. in Psychology, Centre Coll. Ky., 1970; M.S. in Clin. Psychology, Eastern Ky. U., 1972; postgrad. Walden U., Fla., 1977—. Psychology technician VA Hosp., Lexington, Ky., 1970; grad. asst. dept. psychology Eastern Ky. U., Richmond, 1971-74; research asst. dept. psychiatry Sch. Medicine, U. Ky., Lexington, 1972, coordinator rational behavior therapy sect., 1973-77, program devel. specialist, 1977-78, coordinator Rational Behavior Therapy Center, 1978—; condr. various workshops on counseling and therapy various schs. and community orgns., 1972—. Vol., Big Sister for Juvenile Deliquents, 1970-72. Mem. Am. Personnel and Guidance Assn., Nat. Assn. of Alcohol Counselors, Internat. Assn. for Clear Thinking (exec. dir. 1977—), Am. Assn. for Sex Educators, Counselors and Therapists, Am. Assn. Mental Health Counselors, U.S. Combined Tng. Assn. Contbr. articles on counseling to profl. jours. Home: 106 Delmont St Lexington KY 40504 Office: Rational Behavior Therapy Center Univ Kentucky Lexington KY 40536

CARPENTER, MICHAEL KENNETH, computer mfg. co. exec.; b. Jacksonville, Fla., Feb. 2, 1941; s. Eldridge Kenneth and Mary Nell (Pendery) C.; student Ga. Inst. Tech., 1959-61; B.S.E.E., U. Ala., 1968; m. Ann Carroll Livingston, Mar. 16, 1968. Acting lead engr. RCA Service Co., Atlantic Missile Range, Patrick AFB, Fla, 1961-64; lead engr. LTV Aerospace Co., Dallas, 1968-71; pres. Ammic Assos., Dallas, 1971-72; pres. Scientific Machines Corp., Dallas, 1974—; cons. Digitest Corp. and other cos. Contbr. papers in field. Home: 1219 Oak Meadows Dallas TX 75232 Office: 2636 Walnut Hill Ln Dallas TX 75229

CARPENTER, ROBERT DURWARD, mortician; b. Huntington, W.Va., Sept. 8, 1932; s. Veri S. and Zelma (Wagstaff) C.; A.B.S., Marshall U., 1952; grad. Cin. Coll. Mortuary Sci., 1953; Ph.D. (hon.), Marlow U., 1956; m. Grace Evelyn Edwards, May 28, 1954; children—Robert David, Timothy Durward. Pres., Klingel-Carpenter Mortuary, Inc., Huntington, W.Va., 1964—; mem. staff Marshall U. Med. Sch., Huntington, 1977—, dir. mortuary services, 1978-79; dir. Chesapeake (Ohio) area Bd. Trade, 1970-75. Mem. Civic Center Adv. Bd., City of Huntington, 1975-76, pres. Huntington Econ. Devel. Bd., 1972-73; chmn. Huntington Fire Dept. Adv. Bd., 1962-65; campaign chmn. United Fund and Red Cross Drive, 1968-69; mem. bd. deacons Presbyn. Ch., 1956-65, 69-75, co-chmn. World Wide Missions, 1958, chmn. property com., 1958-60; bd. dirs. Nat. council Boy Scouts Am., 1976-77; bd. dirs. Civil Emergency Def., 1954-79, chmn., 1959-60, mem. adv. com. for County and City, 1973-76; bd. dirs. Tri-State Fire Sch., 1958-79, chmn., 1962-76; bd. dirs. ARC, 1956-58; bd. dirs. March of Dimes, 1964-77, v.p., 1969; bd. dirs. Stella Fuller Settlement, 1959-77, pres., 1962-64; bd. dirs. Cin. Found. Mortuary Sci., 1977-81, W.Va. Heart Assn., 1972-73, Cabell Area Heart Assn., 1969-77, United Comml. Travelers Tri State Council, 1967-68. Recipient March of Dimes Service award, 1976, Mayor's award, Huntington, W.Va., 1972, Outstanding Service award Tri State Execs. Club, 1969; named Hon. W.Va. Fire Marshall, 1968, Ky. Col., 1970. Fellow Royal Soc. Health of London; mem. Huntington C. of C. (dir. 1969-71, chmn. crime prevention com. 1974-75), Navy League (pres. Tri-State area 1975), Jr. C. of C., U.S. C. of C., Presidents Assn., Fla. Land Owners League, Internat. Platform Assn., Internat. Assn. of Fire Fighters (hon. mem.), Tri-State Audubon Soc., SAR, Central Ohio Valley Indsl. Council, Marshall U. Alumni Assn., Asso. Funeral Dirs. Service Internat. (pres. 1979-80), W.Va. Funeral Dirs. Assn. (pres. 1962-63), So. W.Va. Funeral Dirs. Assn. (pres. 1955-58), Internat. Thanatopractic Assn., Ohio Funeral Dirs. Assn., W.Va. Hist. Soc., Nat. Hist. Soc., U.S. Naval Inst., Pi Sigma Eta. Clubs: Elks, Big Green, Rotary (pres. Huntington 1977, dist. gov. 1980-81). Address: PO Box 2125 328 6th Ave Huntington WV 25721

CARPENTER, ROBERT HUNT, veterinarian, air force officer; b. Kenedy, Tex., Mar. 22, 1948; s. William Henry and Leora (Hunt) C.; student Baylor U., 1966-68; B.S., Tex. A. and M. U., 1970, D.V.M., 1971, M.S., 1972; m. Betsy Doylene Owens, June 13, 1970; children—Robert Owens, Erin Elizabeth. Grad. asst. Tex. A. and M. U., College Station, 1971; chief surgeon Mil. Working Dog Sect., Wilford Hall, USAF Med. Center, Lackland AFB, San Antonio, 1972; base veterinarian Brooks AFB, Tex., 1974; chief disaster medicine sect. Disaster Medicine Survival Tng. Br., USAF Sch. Aerospace Medicine, Brooks AFB, 1975-76; asst. prof. vet. medicine and surgery U. Tex. System Cancer Center, M.D. Anderson Hosp. and Tumor Inst., Houston, 1976-77; asst. prof. vet. medicine and surgery vet. resources div. U. Tex. System Cancer Center Sci. Park, Bastrop, Tex., 1977—. Scoutmaster, Boy Scouts Am., 1973-74. Cons. Emergency Animal Clinic, Inc., San Antonio, 1974-75. Mem. Am., Tex. vet. med. assns. Baptist. Mason. Home: 1303 Pecan St Bastrop TX 78602 Office: Route 2 Box 151 B1 Bastrop TX 78602

CARPENTER, STANLEY HAMMACK, engring. research and devel. co. exec.; b. Hattiesburg, Miss., Jan. 21, 1926; s. Henry Herbert and Esther Mae (Cooper) C.; B.S., Tulane U., 1946; U.S. Naval Postgrad. Sch., 1956; Aero. Engr., Calif. Inst. Tech., 1957; m. Catherine Jane Sadler, Nov. 29, 1946; children—Stanley Hammack, Louise N., Catherine D., Mary C. Enlisted USN, 1944, commd. 2d lt. USMC, 1946, advanced through grades to col., 1968; liaison officer Naval Weapons Center, China Lake, Calif., 1959-62; comdg. officer 1st Marine Corps A4E Squadron, 1963-65; aide to asst. sec. navy for research devel., 1965-68; Viet Nam combat tour officer in charge Chu-Lai Air Base, commdg. officer Marine Wing Support Group, 1968-69; staff officer, dir. def. research engring., asst. chief of staff and div. chief Marine Corps Devel. Center, Quantico, Va., 1971-74; ret., 1974; aero. engr., project mgr. Unified Industries, Inc., Alexandria, Va., 1975—. Decorated Legion of Merit, Air medal. Mem. Marine Corps Aviation Assn., Marine Corps Assn., Assn. Naval Aviators, Ret. Officers Assn., Am. Def. Preparedness Assn., Tulane U., Calif. Inst. Tech. alumni assns., Phi Beta Kappa, Omicron Delta Kappa, Kappa Sigma, Kappa Delta Phi. Roman Catholic. Home: 8404 Boundbrook Ln Alexandria VA 22309 Office: 5400 Cherokee Ave Alexandria VA 22312

CARPENTER, VIRGINIA FAY LEWIS, educator; b. Chgo., Sept. 11, 1929; d. James Dewey and Anna Frederika (Stahl) Lewis; A.B., Washington U., St. Louis, 1951, M.A. in Edn. (Heermans fellow), 1958, Ph.D., 1967; m. Jack Carpenter, Feb. 12, 1954 (dec. Oct. 12, 1974). Mus. docent Mo. Hist. Soc., St. Louis, 1954-57; tchr. social sci. Kirkwood (Mo.) High Sch., 1958-61; instr., research asst. Washington U., 1961-67; asst. prof. psychology, asso. prof. edn. Lindenwood Coll., St. Charles, Mo., 1967-76, chmn. dept. edn., 1973-76; asso. prof. edn. psychology Corpus Christi (Tex.) State U., 1976—; instr. So. Ill. U., Edwardsville, 1968. Mem. Am., Southwestern psychol. assns., Am. Ednl. Research Assn., Am. Assn. U. Profs., Soc. Psychol. Study Social Issues, Assn. Supervision and Curriculum Devel., Assn. Tchr. Educators, Urban League, Freedom of Residence, Am. Civil Liberties Union, Friends of Art Mus., Phi Delta Kappa (chpt. pres.), Kappa Delta Pi. Contbr. articles to profl. jours. Home: 20 Lakeshore Dr Corpus Christi TX 78413 Office: Coll Edn Corpus Christi State U Corpus Christi TX 78411

CARPER, HARRY ELWAINE, banker; b. Mount Hope, W.Va., Aug. 29, 1916; s. Harry Allen and Adena Blanche (Leffel) C.; cert. in bookkeeping and acctg. Beckley Coll., 1935; m. Margaret Hudson Secrest, Nov. 11, 1936; children—Harry Hudson, Robert Allen. Credit mgr. Appalachian Electric Power Co., 1935-40; sales rep. Burroughs Adding Machine Co., 1940-42; indsl. engr. Union Carbide Co., 1943-62; sales rep. Equitable Life Assurance Soc., 1962-65; asst. agy. mgr. Mut. of N.Y., 1965-68; exec. dir. Downtown Bus. Council, Oak Ridge, 1967-68; with United Am. Bank, Knoxville, 1968—, asst. v.p., 1972—. Treas. Knoxville Area Communication Center for Deaf, 1976-80; pres. Oak Ridge Community Chest, 1954; v.p. Friends of Oak Ridge Library, 1964-66; active Boy Scouts Am., 1930—. Recipient Disting. Service award Gt. Smoky Mountain council Boy Scouts Am., 1950, Jaycees, Oak Ridge, 1950. Clubs: Lions (pres. South Charleston, W.Va. 1944-45, pres. Oak Ridge 1947-48), Kiwanis (pres. 1966-67), Masons. Home: 159 Outer Dr Oak Ridge TN 37830 Office: PO Box 280 Knoxville TN 37901

CARPER, WILLIAM GRADY, ins. agt., former motel exec.; b. Pearisburg, Va., Sept. 8, 1906; s. William O. and Harriet Lou Ella (Kinzie) C.; student Union U., 1926, Emory and Henry Coll., 1927-28; m. Ruth P. Morris, Oct. 26, 1929; children—Carolyn C., Jenny Lou, William Grady. Tchr. math. Pocahontas (Va.) High Sch., 1927-29; ins. agt. Metropolitan Life Ins. Co., Welch, W.Va., 1927-37, asst. mgr., 1937-40; gen. agt. Atlantic Life Ins. Co., Bluefield, W.Va., 1940-79; gen. agt. Combined Ins. Co., Princeton, W.Va., 1945-70; partner Mercer Gen. Ins. Agy., Princeton, 1950-77; partner Turnpike Motel, Oakwood Motor Court, Princeton, 1945-78; dir. Princeton Bank & Trust Co., 1958—. Pres. Appalachian council Boy Scouts Am., 1958—, Youth, Inc., 1948-70; chmn. Mercer County Heart Fund, 1962-63, Princeton (W.Va.) Red Cross Blood Program, 1957-72; pres. Princeton Community Chest, 1963-64, Princeton Park and Recreation Assn., 1948-66; mem. Mercer County Bd. Health, 1974-80; bd. dirs. Concord Coll. Found., 1978—, Princeton Community Hosp., 1950-76, hon. dir., 1976—; bd. dirs. Mercer County Cancer Assn., pres., 1958—; mem. nat. council USO,

1976-79; bd. dirs., treas. Mercer County Bicentennial Commn., 1974-77. Recipient Silver Beaver award Boy Scouts Am., 1955; Award of Merit, Princeton C. of C., 1957; named Man of Yr., Princeton Lions, 1951. Mem. W.Va. Motel Assn. v.p. 1965-66), W.Va. Assn. of Accident and Health Underwriters (pres. 1955), Mountainaire Travel Council (dir. 1967-79, treas. 1967-77), Princeton C. of C. (pres. 1957). Methodist. Clubs: Rotary (dist. gov. 1958-59), Elks (spl. citation 1970-71, state pres. W.Va. 1960-61, dist. dep. 1966-67), Bluefield Automobile (dir. 1959—, pres. 1968-70), Met. Dinner (pres. 1972-75). Address: 1008 Henry St Princeton WV 24740

CARR, BEAUCHAMP COPPEDGE, arts adminstr.; b. Atlanta, July 31; s. Julian Shakespeare and Anne (Coppedge) C.; B.A., U. N.C., 1970; m. Kimberly Ann Kyser, Nov. 13, 1970; 1 son, Trevor Beauchamp. Pres., Atlanta Landmarks, Inc., 1977—; v.p. Atlanta Arts Alliance, 1978—. Former mem. bd. sponsors Atlanta Symphony Orch.; trustee Neighborhood Arts Center. Served to 1st lt. U.S. Army, 1967-69; Vietnam. Decorated Bronze Star with oak leaf cluster. Christian Scientist. Clubs: Atlanta Rotary, Piedmont Driving, Nine O'Clocks. Office: 1280 Peachtree St NE Atlanta GA 30309

CARR, DANIEL PHILLIPS, real estate co. exec.; b. Atlanta, Oct. 29, 1938; s. Daniel Pitts and Erline (Rogers) C.; student Vanderbilt U., 1956-57; B.S., U. Ala., 1961; m. Anne Ross Dee, Sept. 19, 1964; children—Katherine Searcy, Anne Phillips. City planner Ala. Planning and Indsl. Devel. Bd., Montgomery, 1962-65; exec. trainee dept. mortgage loans Guaranty Savs. Life Ins. Co., Montgomery, 1965-67; v.p. real estate E.B. Joseph Co., Montgomery, 1967-76; pres. Phillip Carr & Co., Inc., Montgomery, 1976—; dir. Home Protection Inc. Bd. dirs. Montgomery Mental Health Assn., 1967-71, Montgomery Civic Ballet, 1963-67, Montgomery Community Council, Vol. Action Center, Montgomery Little Theatre, Montgomery br. English Speaking Union, Montgomery Community Concerts Assn., Montgomery and Ala. units Cystic Fibrosis Found.; trustee, v.p. Tumbling Waters Mus.; bd. dirs. Friends Montgomery City-County Pub. Library, 1971-75, pres., 1975—. Mem. Blue and Gray Cols., Old South Hist. Soc., Phi Delta Theta. Episcopalian. Rotarian. Club: Montgomery Country. Home: 3391 Warrenton Rd Montgomery AL 36111 Office: 492 S Court St PO Box 2446 Montgomery AL 36103

CARR, HAROLD NOFLET, airlines exec.; b. Kansas City, Kans., Mar. 14, 1921; s. Noflet B. and Mildred (Addison) C.; B.S., Tex. A. and M. U., 1943; postgrad. Am. U., 1944-45; m. Mary Elizabeth Smith, Aug. 5, 1944; children—Steven Addison, Hal Douglas, James Taylor, Scott Noflet. Asst. dir. route devel. Trans World Airlines, Inc., 1943-47; exec. v.p. Wis. Central Airlines, Inc., 1947-52; mem. firm McKinsey & Co., 1952-54; dir. Republic Airlines, Inc., 1952—, chmn. bd., 1979—; pres. N. Central Airlines, Inc., 1954-69, chmn. bd., 1965-79; professorial lectr. mgmt. engring. Am. U., 1952-62; dir. Detection Scis., Inc., Ross Industries, Inc., Stange Co., Cayman Water Co., Governor's Sound, Ltd., Westland Capital Corp.; mem. adv. com. Tex. Transp. Inst., Tex. A&M U. System. Trustee, Tex. A&M Research Found.; bd. nominations Nat. Aviation Hall Fame; bd. dirs. Minn. Safety Council. Served with AUS, 1942-43. Mem. World Bus. Council, Smithsonian Assos., Am. Mgmt. Assn., Air Transport Assn., Assn. Local Transport Airlines, Minn. Execs. Orgn., Tex. A. and M. Century Club and Former Students Assn., Nat. Aero. Assn. (Washington), Am. Assn. Airport Execs., Nat. Def. Transp. Assn., Am. Econ. Assn., Greater Mpls., St. Paul Area chambers commerce, Stearman Alumnus Club, Pine Beach Peninsula Assn. Episcopalian. Clubs: Nat. Aviation, Aero (Washington); Wings (N.Y.C.); Aggie (dir.), Briarcrest Country (Bryan, Tex.); Racquet (Miami); Gull Lake Yacht (Brainerd, Minn.); Minneapolis. Home: PO Box H Bryan TX 77801 Office: 4103 S Texas Ave Bryan TX 77801

CARR, HOWARD ERNEST, ret. ins. agy. exec.; b. Johnson City, Tenn., Oct. 4, 1908; s. William Alexander and Gertrude (Feathers) C.; B.S., E. Tenn. State U., 1929; M.Ed., Duke, 1935; postgrad. U. N.C., 1938-39; m. Thelma Northcutt, June 11, 1937 (dec. Oct., 1972); 1 son, Howard Ernest. Supt., Washington Coll. (Tenn.), 1929-35; ednl. advisor U.S. Office Edn., Ft. Oglethorpe, Ga., 1935-37; prin. Greensboro (N.C.) city schs., 1937-42; dir. activities First Presbyn. Ch., Greensboro, 1946-47; with Jefferson Standard Life Ins. Co., Greensboro, 1947-77, spl. rep., 1947-54, supr. agy. Greensboro, 1964, mgr., 1964-67; pres. Everett's Lake Corp. Chmn. Guilford County Bd. Edn., 1950-77; vice chmn. N.C. Gov's Com. Edn., 1956-60; N.C. rep. White House Conf. Edn., 1955. Mem. adv. com. Greensboro div. Guilford Coll., 1958—; head Guilford County Cancer Drive, 1956, bd. dirs. Cancer Soc., 1956—; v.p. N.C. State Sch. Bds. Assn., 1959-61; bd. dirs. Greensboro Jr. Mus., 1956-62, Sternberger Found. Served to lt. with USNR, 1942-46, asst. head motion picture dept., Washington; to capt., 1951-54, as head motion picture dept; ret. as capt., 1968. Recipient Nat. Quality award, Nat. Assn. Life Underwriters, 1948—; named Boss of the Year, Lou-Ellin chpt. Am. Bus. Woman's Assn., 1967. Mem. Nat., N.C. (pres. 1964-65; Man of Year award 1969), Greensboro (pres. 1956-57) assns. life underwriters, N.C. Leaders Club, Greensboro C. of C. (chmn. edn. com. 1960-62). Presbyn. (elder). Mason (32 deg.), Kiwanian (pres. Greensboro 1951). Author: History of Higher Education in East Tennessee, 1935. Home: 3927 Madison Ave Greensboro NC 27410 Office: Jefferson Sq Greensboro NC 27401

CARR, JEFFREY ROLAND, univ. exec.; b. Mt. Vernon, N.Y., Mar. 21, 1941; s. Roland Provoost and Beulah (Mott) C.; B.A., U. Chattanooga, 1963; LL.B., Vanderbilt U., 1966; m. Anne Allen Oglesby, Dec. 20, 1968; children—Ellen Oglesby, Anna Meredith. Admitted to Tenn. bar, 1966; asso. dir. devel. Vanderbilt U., 1966-69, univ. legal officer, 1969-76, vice chancellor for govt. relations gen. counsel, 1976-79, v.p. univ. relations, gen. counsel, sec., 1979—; mem. Dickson County (Tenn.) Quar. Ct., 1972-78. Bd. dirs. Tenn. Spl. Olympics, 1977-79; mem. Leadership Nashville, 1978-79. Served to lt. comdr. Judge Adv. Gen. Corps., USNR, 1967. Mem. Nat. Assn. Coll. and Univ. Attys., Am. Bar Assn., Tenn. Bar Assn., Nashville Bar Assn., Dickson Bar Assn. Club: Univ. of Nashville. Office: Box 506 Peabody Vanderbilt U Nashville TN 37203

CARR, JOHN CURTIS, editor, author; b. Lexington, Miss., Apr. 8, 1942; s. Curtis Washington and Marybelle (Anderson) C.; B.A., U. Miss., 1964; postgrad. (Ford Found. fellow, Mark Etheridge fellow) U. N.C., 1968; M.A., Hollins (Va.) Coll., 1969; m. Patricia Gayle Sims, Apr. 9, 1977. Editor, Webster Progress, Eupora, Miss., 1966, Clarksdale (Miss.) Press-Register, 1966; writer, sports editor, asst. mng. editor Greenville (Miss.) Delta Democrat-Times, 1966-68; instr. U. N.C., Charlotte, 1969-70, Loyola U., also Dillard U., New Orleans, 1977-78; editor Richmond (Va.) Mercury, 1973-74; freelance writer, tchr. fiction New Orleans Center Ctreative Arts, 1979—; leader workshops, 1970—. Charter mem., officer Young Democrats Miss., 1965; mem. Uptown Dem. Assn., New Orleans, 1972; mem. investigating commn. Nat. Caucus Labor Coms., 1974. Gordon Bennett fellow, 1970-71. Mem. Am. Hist. Assn., Sigma Delta Chi, Delta Psi. Episcopalian. Club: St. Anthony (N.Y.C.). Author: Kite-Flying and Other Irrational Acts: Interviews with Twelve Southern Writers, 1972; co-author: Teaching in the Dark, 1973; editorial bd. Red Clay Reader, 1970; asso. editor Contempora, 1971-73; contbr. non-fiction, fiction and poetry to mags. and newspapers. Address: 1527 Burdette St New Orleans LA 70118

CARR, LEO CARLTON, geophysicist; b. Port Neches, Tex., May 22, 1933; s. Joseph Columbus and Agnes Mae (Fruzia) C.; B.S., U. Ark., 1960, M.S., 1963; m. Judith Mae Warren, Feb. 4, 1956; children—Joe Carlton, Mark Clinton, Matt Cullen. With Exxon Co. U.S.A., Midland, Tex., 1962-78, sr. geophysicist, 1971-72, sr. petroleum geophysicist, 1972-78, exploration geophysicist, 1978; dist. geophysicist Oxy Petroleum, Inc., Midland, 1978-79; cons. geophysicist, Midland, 1979—. Bd. dirs. Tri-County Foster Home, 1968—; trustee Tex. Tech. Dads' Assn., 1975-77. Served with USN, 1951-54. Mem. Soc. Exploration Geophysicists, Soc. Ind. Profl. Earth Scientists, U. Ark. Alumni Assn. (life mem.). Democrat. Baptist (deacon). Club: High Sky Bass. Home: 1604 N C St Midland TX 79701 Office: Suite 418 Bldg of SW Midland TX 79701

CARR, LOUIE WOODS, ednl. adminstr.; b. Milledgeville, Ga., Apr. 28, 1931; s. Iverson Curry and Ruth Aurilla (Hardie) C.; B.S., Augusta Coll., 1967; M.Ed., Ga. Coll. 1971; m. Argent Sue Herrington, Nov. 13, 1949; children—Patricia Suzan, Mary Ivy, Argent Sue. Computer programmer E.I. Du Pont de Nemours & Co. Inc., Aiken, S.C., 1951-67; tchr. math., coordinator adult edn. Richmond County Bd. Edn., Augusta, Ga., 1967-71; headmaster John Milledge Acad., Milledgeville, Ga., 1972—. Exec. bd. Southeastern Assn. Ind. Schs., 1974—. NSF grantee, 1969. Mem. Fellowship Christian Athletes (pres. 1976—), Nat., Ga. assns. secondary sch. prins., Nat. Beta Club (permanent state council 1975—). Baptist. Club: Rotary (dir. club service Milledgeville 1976—, pres. 1978—). Home: Route 5 Box 63 Milledgeville GA 31061 Office: Route 5 Box 220X Milledgeville GA 31061

CARR, MAXINE FAGAN, psychotherapist; b. Spartanburg, S.C., Jan. 20, 1941; d. Mack D. and Sybil (Cromer) Fagan; A.B., Newberry (S.C.) Coll., 1962; M.A., Appalachian State U., Boone, N.C., 1966; Ph.D., Nova U., Fla., 1975. Asst. prof. behavioral sci. U. Central Fla., Orlando, 1970-73; dir. career edn. project Fla. Dept. Edn., Tallahassee, 1972-73; research asso. Fla. State U., Tallahassee, 1974-75; vis. asst. prof. U. Central Fla., 1975-77; pvt. practice marriage and family therapy, Winter Park, Fla., 1977—. Mem. Am. Personnel and Guidance Assn., Fla. Assn. Mental Health Counselors, Fla. Assn. Counselor Educators, Phi Delta Kappa. Author: Gaining the Realities of Work, 1975; also articles. Office: Suite 450 New England Bldg Winter Park FL 32789

CARR, ROBERT LON, pediatrician; b. Farlie, Tex., Aug. 16, 1925; s. Vincent and Ruth (Warlick) C.; B.A., Tex. Tech. U., 1949; M.D., Southwestern Med. Sch., U. Tex., 1951; m. Betty Jean Sullivan, June 18, 1949; children—Robert Vincent, Brian David, Julie Beth. Intern, Colo. Gen. Hosp., Denver, 1951-52; resident Tex. Children's Hosp., Dallas, 1952-54; practice medicine specializing in pediatrics, Lubbock, Tex., 1954—; chief staff, chmn. pediatric dept. St. Mary's Hosp.; chmn. pediatric dept. Meth. Hosp.; chief of staff W.Tex. Hosp.; chmn. Family Service, Lubbock. Served with USNR, 1949-51. Mead Johnson fellow, 1952; diplomate Am. Bd. Pediatrics. Fellow Am. Acad. Pediatrics; mem. Soc. Adolescent Medicine (charter), Lubbock Crosby Garza County Med. Soc. (pres.), AMA, Tex. Med. Assn. Home: 3212 56th St Lubbock TX 79413 Office: 2602 Ave Q Lubbock TX 79405

CARR, WILLIAM FRANCIS, advt. cons.; b. Cin., Mar. 4, 1910; s. Alvin Henry and Anna Helen (Schemann) C.; student William and Mary Coll., 1930-33; m. Romaine Meyer, June 9, 1936; children—William Francis, Richard R., David B., Thomas N., Mary C. Advt. salesman Cin. Post, 1933-36; with Cin. Enquirer, 1936-40, retail salesman, 1940-42, classified advt. mgr., 1944-49; salesman La Boiteaux Co., Cin., 1942-44; classified advt. mgr. Phila. Bull., 1949-62, nat. advt. dir., 1962-72; prin. William F. Carr Equities, Longboat Key, Fla., 1972—; v.p. Carr Ford Inc., Carr Constrn. Inc.; chmn. action com. Newspaper Advt. Bur., 1959-62; chmn. profl. seminars. Mem. Pa. Newspaper Pubs. Assn., Assn. Newspaper Classified Mgrs., Poor Richard Club, Phila. Auto Trade Assn., Phila. Bd. Realtors, Cin. Advt. Club (dir.), Assn. Newspaper Advt. Mgrs. (pres. 1957-58), Assn. Advt. Mgrs. (Disting. Service award 1960, permanent life mem. 1962—), Pa. Acad. Fine Arts. Roman Catholic. Clubs: Republican, Aronimink Country, Overbrook Golf, Union League of Phila., Peale, K.C. Home and Office: 4825 Gulf of Mexico Dr Longboat Key FL 33548

CARRABBA, MICHAEL PAUL, aircraft components mfg. co. exec.; b. Dayton, Ohio, Jan. 31, 1945; s. Paul G. and Margie (Nichols) C.; student Miami Dade Jr. Coll., 1964—; m. Carol Frances Young, Nov. 1, 1968. Gen. mgr. D&C—Airparts Corp., Hialeah, Fla., 1969-70, pres., owner, 1970—, also chmn. bd.; pres. D.C. A/P Battery Co., 1974—, D.C. A/P Battery of Europe, D.C. Battery Exide div., Indsl. Air Service of Ga. Served with USMCR, 1962-66. Mem. Nat. Pilots Assn., Profl. Aviation Maintenance Assn., Nat. Air Transp. Conf., Nat. Bus. Aircraft Assn., Am. Helicopter Soc., Aviation Maintenance Found. Home: 10175 SW 53d St Cooper City FL 33055 Office: 485 W 27th St Hialeah FL 33010

CARRELL, HILMA BARTLETT, counselor; b. Lamesa, Tex., Nov. 11, 1911; d. Homer T. and Lois Irma (Hill) Bartlett; B.A., Tex. Tech U., 1932; M.A., Tex. A. and I. U., 1953; Ed.D., U. Wyo., 1969; m. S. M. Carell, May 25, 1934; 1 dau., D'Aun Carrell Altom. Secondary tchr. pub. schs., Dimmitt, 1932-48, Mercedes, Tex., 1949-51, Weslaco, Tex., 1951-58; counselor Tivy High Sch., Kerrville, Tex., 1958-61, Comfort and Boerne Schs., 1961-69; dir. counseling and guidance dept. Amarillo Coll., 1969-75; pvt. practice counseling, Dimmitt, 1975—. Recipient award of Merit, Tex. Researchers Assn., 1974. Mem. Tex. Library Assn., Tex. State Tchrs. Assn., Tex., Am. (life), Wyo. personnel and guidance assns., Am. Sch. Counselors Assn., Castro County (Tex.) Museum Assn., Castro County Library Assn., Southwestern Scholarship and Grants, Delta Kappa Gamma (life mem.; state certificate of merit and distinction 1974). Clubs: Study, Book. Author: Exploratory Study of Guidance Practices and Policies in Selected European Countries, 1968; research, publs. on counseling, guidance. Home and office: PO Box 51 Dimmitt TX 79027

CARRERAS, FRANCISCO JOSE, univ. adminstr.; b. San Juan, P.R., May 13, 1932; s. Francisco and Antonia (Muriente) C.; student Instituto Superior de Estudios Clasicos, Havana, Cuba, 1957; B.A., U. Pontificia de Comillas, Santander, Spain, 1959; M.A., Fordham U., 1960; Ph.D., Universidad Pontificia Gregoriana, Rome, 1966; m. Ana Elisa Carreras, Mar. 29, 1964; children—Ines Maria, Maria Soledad, Irene Maria, Marianne, Francisco Jose. Mem. faculty U. P.R., Humacao Regional Coll., 1962-69, acad. asst. to dir., 1967-69, dir. humanities dept., 1967-68; pres. Cath. U. P.R., Ponce, 1969—; pres. P.R. Found. for the Humanities. Bd. dirs. Angel Ramos Found., 1977, Damas Hosp., 1978, Banco Popular de P.R., 1979. Mem. P.R. Acad. Arts and Scis. Roman Catholic. Clubs: Rotary, Lions. Office: Cath Univ of PR Ponce PR 00731

CARRERE, CHARLES SCOTT, judge; b. Dublin, Ga., Sept. 26, 1937; B.A., U. Ga., 1959; LL.B., Stetson U., 1961. Admitted to Fla. bar, 1961, Ga. bar, 1960; law clk. to U.S. Dist. judge, Orlando, 1962-63; asst. U.S. atty. Middle Dist. Fla., 1963-66, chief trial atty., 1965-66, spl. asst. to U.S. atty., 1966-67; partner firm Harrison, Greene, Mann, Rowe & Stanton, St. Petersburg, 1970-80; county judge Pinellas County (Fla.), 1980—. Served with inf. AUS. Mem. Am., Fla., St. Petersburg bar assns., Stetson Lawyers Assn. (dir. 1968), Phi Beta Kappa, Phi Delta Phi. Home: 115 17th Ave NE Saint Petersburg FL 33704

CARRIER, GERALD OLIVER, pharmacologist, educator; b. Charleston, S.C, Dec. 12, 1944; s. Oliver and Mary Frances (Malone) C.; B.S. in Math., Belhaven Coll., 1966; M.S. in Pharmacology, U. Miss., 1968; Ph.D., U. Tex., San Antonio, 1972; m. Jutta Evelyn Charlotte Ehler, Dec. 21, 1973. Asst. prof. pharmacology U. Kiel, W. Ger., 1972-73; instr. pharmacology Med. Coll. Ga., Augusta, 1974-76, asst. prof., 1976-78, asso. prof., 1978—. Bd. dirs. Central Savannah River Area Sci. Fair, 1978—. Ga. Heart Assn. research grantee, 1976-79. Fellow Am. Coll. Clin. Pharmacology; mem. Am. Soc. for Pharmacology and Exptl. Therapeutics, Soc. for Neurosci., Ga. Heart Assn. (dir. Richmond County unit 1976—), Am. Heart Assn., Soc. Exptl. Biology and Medicine, Am. Pharm. Assn., Sigma Xi (treas. 1978-79). Episcopalian. Contbr. articles to pharmacology jours. Home: 362 Habersham Rd Augusta GA 30907 Office: Dept Pharmacology Med Coll Ga Augusta GA 30912

CARRIERE, CHARLES PIERRE, III, ins. agt., lawyer; b. Meridan, Miss., July 16, 1940; s. Charles Pierre and Charlotte Eggleston (Wilbourn) C.; student Yale U., 1958-59; B.A., Tulane U., 1963, J.D., 1965; m. Cynthia Vaughn Doyle, Dec. 21, 1965; children—Charles Pierre, Elizabeth Vaughn, Cynthia Doyle, Michael Guibet. Admitted to La. bar, 1965, U.S. Ct. Mil. Appeals, 1966; v.p. Charles P. Carriere & Co., Inc., New Orleans, 1968-71, 73—; fin. planner Walton Miller Cos., New Orleans, 1971-73; speaker in field. Served to lt. USNR, 1965-68. Mem. La. Bar Assn., Am. Bar Assn., Am. Soc. C.L.U.'s, C.P.C.U.'s. Roman Catholic. Home: 3408 Nashville New Orleans LA 70125 Office: 629 Baronne St New Orleans LA 70113

CARRIGAN, NORMA LEE SHEWMAKER, speech pathologist; b. New Albany, Ind., Sept. 27, 1945; d. William Henry and Lois Marie (Backherms) Shewmaker; B.A., Ursuline Coll., Louisville, 1968; M.A., Western Ky. U., Bowling Green, 1977; m. John Edward Carrigan, Sept. 3, 1970; 1 dau., Cathie Marie. Tchr. 1st grade Holy Rosary Sch., Evansville, Ind., 1968-69; speech clinician Ky. Commn. Handicapped Children, Bowling Green, 1969-74; speech correctionist Warren County Bd. Edn., Bowling Green, 1974—; lectr. in field, student tchr. supr. Named Ky. col., 1970. Mem. Am. Speech, Lang. and Hearing Assn., NEA, Ky. Edn. Assn. Home: 1017 Blake Way Bowling Green KY 42101 Office: 806 Kenton St Bowling Green KY 42101

CARRIGAN, ROBERT EDWARD, lawyer; b. Worcester, Mass., Aug. 1, 1944; s. James F. and Frances (O'Sheasy) C.; B.S., Emerson Coll., 1966; J.D. U. Fla., 1972. Admitted to Fla. bar, 1973; producer, newsman Sta. WKOX AM-FM, Framingham, Mass., 1966-68; program producer Sta. WCOA-AM, Pensacola, Fla., 1968-70; individual practice law, Gainesville, Fla., 1973-76; founder, pres. Am. Legal Research Corp., Gainesville, 1971—. Del. state bd. ACLU, 1975, 79, pres. Fla., 1980; vice-chmn. Gainesville Housing Bd., 1979-80; legal editor, announcer Tel-Consumer tel. consumer assistance program. Served with U.S. Army, 1966-72. Mem. Fla. Bar, Am. Bar Assn., Asso. Info. Mgrs., Alpha Epsilon Rho. Home: 2516 NW 55th Blvd Gainesville FL 32601 Office: 3450 SW 24th Ave Gainesville FL 32608

CARRINGTON, FREDRICK MURRAY, psychologist; b. Paris, Tex., July 19, 1948; s. Murray and Martha Eugenia (Coston) C.; student Kilgore Jr. Coll., 1966-67; B.S., E. Tex. State U., 1970, M.S., 1971; Ph.D., U. Ga., 1973; m. Emma Feliz Berry, Feb. 14, 1970; children—Cristi Rose, Sunny Bianca. Psychologist, asst. supt. Dept. Corrections, Jackson, Ga., 1972-73; coordinator psychology services Bur. Prisons, Texarkana, Tex., 1973—; pvt. practice as psychologist, Texarkana, 1975—; adj. asst. prof. E. Tex. State U., Texarkana, 1974—. Bd. dirs. Red River Regional Council on Alcoholism, Texarkana, 1974—. Licensed psychologist, Tex. Mem. Am., Tex. correctional assns., Am., Tex., Southwestern psychol. assns., Am. Personnel and Guidance Assn., Kappa Alpha, Kappa Delta Pi. Democrat. Methodist. Home: 13 Cerrato Ln Texarkana TX 75503 Office: 2605 Texas Blvd Texarkana TX 75501

CARRINGTON, HENRY AL (PETE), mining and mfg. co. exec.; b. Bay City, Tex., Feb. 23, 1929; s. Alfred Frederick and Josephine Anna (Matthews) C.; B.S. in Math., Trinity U., 1954; m. Geraldine Z. Richardson, Jan. 26, 1951; children—John Fredrick, Merry Kathryn. With Uvalde Rock Asphalt Co., San Antonio, 1950—, div. sales mgr. Azrock Floor Products div., 1968-78, asst. to pres., 1978—. Served with USMC, 1945-49. Mem. San Antonio Charter Producer's Council (pres. 1964-65), Constrn. Specification Inst. Methodist. Club: Masons. Patentee in field. Home: 415 Gettysburg Rd San Antonio TX 78228 Office: 480W Century Bldg 84 NW Loop 410 San Antonio TX 78216

CARRIS, PAUL NICHOLAS, Realtor, ins. agt., developer; b. McAlester, Okla., June 11, 1927; s. John Nicholas and Viola (Anderson) C.; B.A., U. Okla., 1950; m. A. Jeannine Kelley, June 28, 1959; 1 son, Paul Nicholas. Partner, Chapman-Carris Agy., McAlester, 1959-69; pres. Carris Agy. Inc., McAlester, 1969—; dir. Hatter Farms, Nat. Bank of McAlester. Pres. McAlester Found., 1973—; chmn. Okla. Indsl. Commn., 1979—. Served with USN, 1945-46; PTO. Mem Ind. Ins. Agts. Okla. (v.p. 1979—), Okla. C. of C. (dir. 1974—), McAlester C. of C. (pres. 1968-69), McAlester Urban Renewal (chmn. 1968-70), Nat. Assn. Realtors. Democrat. Methodist. Clubs: McAlester Country (pres. 1969-70), Elks, Masons, Shriners. Office: 1st and Carl Albert Pkwy McAlester OK 74501

CARRITHERS, PAUL NORMAN, realtor, clergyman; b. Hindman, Ky., Apr. 16, 1923; s. Oliver Roy and Leah (Wiseman) C.; student N.C. State Coll., Raleigh, 1940-41, Coll. William and Mary, 1949—, Assn. Unity Chs. Sch. Ministerial and Religious Studies, 1973-74; m. Marie Brown, July 20, 1944; children—Faye Jeanette, Kaye Louise, Gaye Elizabeth. Realtor Fidelity Real Estate Service, Newport News, Va., 1947—, mgr., 1950—; a founder 1st Peninsula Bank & Trust Co. of Hampton (Va.), 1970; minister Unity Ch., Christ Ch. of Truth, Williamsburg, Va. Chmn. adv. bd. Salvation Army, 1965-68; bd. pres. Peninsula Family Counseling Agy., Newport News, 1956-60. Served with USAAF, 1944-46. Mem. Nat. Assn. Real Estate Bds., Nat. Inst. Real Estate Brokers, Va. Assn. Realtors, Newport News-Hampton Bd. Realtors, Peninsula C. of C. Mason. Home: 898 Cloverleaf Ln Newport News VA 23601 Office: 99 28th St Newport News VA 23607

CARROLL, CHARLES LEMUEL, III, hospitality industry exec.; b. Durham, N.C., Oct. 29, 1952; s. Charles Lemuel and Geraldine (Budd) C.; B. Indsl. Engring., Ga. Inst. Tech. 1974, M.S., 1976, postgrad., 1976-77; m. Mary Lou Donaldson, Sept. 10, 1977. Research asst. in applied stats., Ga. Inst. Tech., Atlanta, 1974-77; dir. communications Days Inns of Am., Inc., Atlanta, 1977—. Mem. Southeastern Telecommunication Assn., Alpha Pi Mu. Republican. Presbyterian. Office: 2751 Buford Hwy Atlanta GA 30324

CARROLL, CHARLES MICHAEL, educator; b. Otterbein, Ind., Mar. 5, 1921; s. James William and Catherine Doretta (Bohan) C.; B.M., Ind. U. at Bloomington, 1949; M.M., Fla. State U., Tallahassee, 1951, Ph.D., 1950; m. Mary Lipford Rosenbush, Sept. 4, 1951;

children—Charles Michael, Mary Catherine, Theresa Jane, William Rosenbush. Asst. coordinator music services Ind. U., 1949-50; instr. music Fla. State U., 1950-53; concert mgr. symphony orchs. Toledo, Washington, Savannah, Ga., 1953-58; prof. music Pensacola (Fla.) Jr. Coll., 1960-64; prof. St. Petersburg (Fla.) Jr. Coll., 1964— music critic Tallahassee Democrat, 1950-53, St. Petersburg Evening Independent, 1976—. Served to capt., AUS, 1942-46; ETO. Mem. Am. Symphony Orch. League (v.p. 1955-56), Am. Musicol. Soc. (nat. council 1974-77, chmn. chpt. 1974-76), Am. Soc. Eighteenth-Century Studies (exec. bd. region 1974-77, regional pres. 1979—), Coll. Music Soc. (editor 1979—, nat. council 1978—, chmn. chpt. 1979—). Author: The Great Chess Automaton, 1975. Contbr. articles to profl. jours. Home: 1701 80th St N St Petersburg FL 33710

CARROLL, DEWITT EDWARD, public relations co. exec.; b. Gastonia, N.C., Oct. 4, 1914; s. Wiley Tot and Constance (Hege) C.; student U. N.C., 1932-36; m. Marguerite Elizabeth Bishop, Apr. 8, 1943; 1 dau., Betsy Bishop Carroll Forrest. With U.P.I., 1936; with Raleigh (N.C.) Times, 1936-40, city editor, 1939-40; asst. city editor Greensboro Record, 1951-52; asst. city editor Greensboro Daily News, 1952-53; exec. sec. Piedmont Asso. Industries, 1953-60; v.p., sec. John Harden Assos., Greensboro, 1960-72; sr. partner DeWitt Carroll/Pub. Relations, 1972—; exec. dir. Guilford County (N.C.) Bicentennial Commn., 1970-72. Cons. bus. letter and report writing, speech writing, pub. relations, co. publs., 1955—, lectr. in field. Exec. committeeman, pub. relations chmn. Carolinas United, 1966-67; mem. budget com., Greensboro United Fund, 1953-54; mem. adv. bd. Greensboro div. Guilford Coll., 1954-64, Guilford Tech. Inst., 1956-60. Served to capt. USAAF, 1942-45, USAF, 1950-52; Korea. Mem. Charlotte (N.C.) Pub. Relations Soc. (pres. 1968), Pub. Relations Soc. Am. (accredited; pres. N.C. chpt. 1969, counselors and corps sects). Episcopalian (vestryman, lay reader 1969—). Home and office: 1503 Seminole Dr Greensboro NC 27408

CARROLL, EDWARD PERRY, educator; b. Sarasota, Fla., Dec. 17, 1934; s. Oliver Henry Perry and Sarah Theodoshia (Amsden) C.; B.M., Baylor U., 1957; M.C.M., So. Bapt. Theol. Sem., 1970; Ed.D. in Ch. Music Edn., New Orleans Bapt. Theol. Sem., 1979; m. Rosa Marion Harvey, Dec. 30, 1965; 1 dau., Kathryn Susan. Instr., So. Bapt. Theol. Sem., Louisville, 1968-70; prof. music Brewton Parker Coll., Mt. Vernon, Ga., 1970-73; instr. New Orleans Bapt. Theol. Sem., 1973-75; prof. music Anderson (S.C.) Coll., 1975, chmn. Fine Arts Div. and Dept. Music, 1975—; co-condr. Anderson Symphony Orch., 1975—. Served with USAF, 1957-66. Recipient Outstanding Trombone Performance award, So. Bapt. Theol. Sem., 1969. Mem. Music Educators Nat. Conf., Arnold Air Soc., Coll. Band Dirs. Assn., Am. Musicological Soc., Nat. Assn. Schs. Music, Hymn Soc., Phi Mu Alpha, Kappa Kappa Psi. Republican. Baptist. Club: Lions. Home: 106 McGee Ct Anderson SC 29621 Office: 316 Boulevard Box 337C Anderson SC 29621

CARROLL, FRANCES LAVERNE, librarian; b. Scammon, Kans., Dec. 6, 1925; d. Robert Allen and Truda Hilda (Flanagan) Carroll; B.S., Kans. State Tchrs. Coll., 1948; M.A., U. Denver, 1956; postgrad. Western Res. U., 1957; Ph.D., U. Okla., 1970. Bookkeeper, Baxter Springs Bank (Kans.), 1944; high sch. tchr., Caney, Kans., 1947-49; tchr. English and journalism, librarian Field Kindley Meml. High Sch., Coffeyville, Kans., 1949-54; librarian Coffeyville Jr. Coll., 1954-62, supr. elementary sch. libraries, 1957-62; mem. faculty U. Okla., Norman, 1962—, prof. library scis., 1975—, acting dir. Sch. Library Sci., 1974, dir. U.S. Office Edn. insts., 1966, 67, 69; sr. lectr., head dept. library studies Nedlands Coll. Advanced Edn., Perth, Australia, 1977—; guest lectr. Drexel Inst. Tech., Phila., 1964, U. London, 1972, Pahlavi U., Shiraz, Iran, 1976. Grantee U.S. Office Edn., 1969. Mem. AAUW, AAUP, Internat. Relations Round Table (chmn. membership 1970—), Internat. Fedn. Library Assns. (chmn. planning group sch. libraries 1973-77), Am., Southwestern, Okla. library assns., Delta Kappa Gamma, Phi Delta Kappa, Beta Phi Mu. Contbr. profl. jours. Address: Room 115 401 W Brooks St Norman OK 73019

CARROLL, GEORGE JOSEPH, physician; b. Gardner, Mass., Oct. 14, 1917; s. George J. and Kathryn (O'Hearn) C.; A.B., Clark U., 1939; M.D., George Washington U., 1944. Intern, Worcester (Mass.) City Hosp., 1944-45; resident Doctors Hosp., 1945-46, Sibley Hosp., 1948-49, VA Hosp., 1949-50, all Washington; asst. pathologist D.C. Gen. Hosp., 1950-51, pathologist, 1951-52; practice medicine, specializing in pathology, Suffolk and Franklin, Va., 1952—; pathologist Louise Obili Meml. Hosp., Suffolk, Southampton Meml. Hosp., Franklin, Greensville Meml. Hosp., Emporia, Va., all 1952—; instr. pathology Med. Sch., Georgetown U., Washington, 1950-52; instr. clin. micrology Am. U., Washington, 1950-51; asso. clin. prof. pathology Med. Coll. Va., Richmond, 1968—; clin. prof. pathology Health Sci. Center, Va. Commonwealth U., Richmond, 1970—. Mem. Va. Bd. Med. Examiners, 1967—, sec., treas., 1970—. Bd. dirs. Va. div. Am. Cancer Soc., 1955-62, Va. Med. Service Assn., 1960-71. Diplomate Am. Bd. Pathology. Fellow Am. Soc. Clin. Pathologists (dir. 1969-75, 1st v.p. 1974-75, pres. 1976-77), Coll. Am. Pathologists, A.C.P.; mem. Am. Assn. Blood Banks, Va. Soc. Pathology (sec., treas. 1954-68, pres. 1973-74, mem. council), Va. Med. Soc. (mem. ho. of dels. 1960-80), Med. Soc. Va., So. Med. Assn. (councillor from Va. 1965-70, chmn. council 1969-70, 1st v.p. 1971-72, pres. 1973-74), 4th Dist. Med. Soc. Va. (pres. 1968), Internat. Acad. Pathology, AMA, George Washington, D.C. (asso.), Seaboard (past pres.) med. socs., Am. Soc. Clin. Pharmacy and Therapeutics, Soc. Nuclear Medicine. Rotarian. Home: 219 Northbrook Av Suffolk VA 23434 Office: Louise Obici Meml Hosp Suffolk VA 23434

CARROLL, HOWARD LAWRENCE, accountant; b. N.Y.C., Dec. 24, 1944; s. Jacob and Dorothy Rosalind (Scheir) C.; A.A., Miami-Dade Community Coll., 1965; B.B.A., U. Miami, 1968; m. Shirley Ann Culp, Dec. 21, 1967; 1 dau., Cynthia Louise. Staff accountant Price Waterhouse & Co., Miami, Fla., 1970-71; asst. controller Hardwicke Cos., Miami, 1971-73; partner Lexow Brackins & Carroll, C.P.A.'s, Miami, 1973-76; individual practice accounting, Pembroke Pines, Fla., 1976—; community prof. Nova U., 1973—. Served to 1st lt. U.S. Army, 1968-70. Mem. Am. Inst. C.P.A.'s, Fla. Inst. C.P.A.'s, Nat. Assn. Accountants. Club: Rotary. Home: 10631 NW 21st Ct Pembroke Pines FL 33026 Office: 7752 Taft St Pembroke Pines FL 33024

CARROLL, JULIAN MORTON, lawyer; b. Paducah, Ky., Apr. 16, 1931; s. Elvie B. and Eva (Heady) C.; A.A., Paducah Jr. Coll., 1952; A.B., U. Ky., 1954, LL.B., 1956; m. Charlann Harting, July 22, 1951; children—Kenneth Morton, Iva Patrice, Bradley Harting, Ellynn Kriston. Admitted to Ky. bar, 1956; mem. Ky. Ho. of Reps., 1962-71, speaker of ho., 1968-71; lt. gov. of Ky., 1971-74, gov., 1974-79; practice law, Frankfurt, 1979—. Trustee Paducah (Ky.) Jr. Coll. Recipient Minerva award U. Louisville, 1977; Man of Yr. award Advt. Club Louisville, 1978. Mem. Am., Ky., Paducah bar assns., Nat. Govs. Assn. (chmn. 1978-79), Phi Delta. Clubs: Optimists, Masons. Home: 218 Raintree Rd Frankfort KY 40601 Office: Frankfort KY 40601

CARROLL, KENNETH LANE, educator; b. Easton, Md., May 8, 1924; s. Albert Raymond and Mary Ethel (Lane) C.; B.A., Duke U., 1946, B.D., 1949, Ph.D., 1953. Mem. faculty So. Methodist U., 1952—, prof. religious studies, 1960—. T. Wistar Brown fellow Haverford (Pa.) Coll., 1969-70. Life mem. Soc. Bibl. Lit., Friends Hist. Assn., Md. Hist. Soc., U.K. Friends Hist. Soc.; mem. Friends World Com. Consultation, Am. Friends Service Com., S.Central Yearly Meeting Friends. Club: Penn (life) (London). Author: Joseph Nichols and the Nicholites, 1962, Quakerism on the Eastern Shore, 1970, John Perrot: Early Quaker Schismatic, 1970; editor: The Creative Centre of Quakerism, 1965; contbr. religious and hist. articles Am. and fgn. jours. Home: 3212 C Daniels St Dallas TX 75205 Office: Box 202 So Methodist Univ Dallas TX 75275

CARROLL, NAOMI ELETA, army nurse; b. Owatonna, Minn., Nov. 15, 1946; d. Harold Everett and Mary Ramona (Wise) White; B.S. in Nursing, Calif. State U., Bakersfield, 1974; M.Nursing, UCLA, 1976; m. John Thomas Kimbrough Carroll, Aug. 20, 1976; children—Kristopher Nolan and Kevin Nicholas (twins). Instr., Long Beach (Calif.) Med. Coll., 1971-72; nurse Meml. Hosp. Med. Center, Long Beach, 1974-75; commd. 1st lt. Nurse Corps, U.S. Army, 1974; advanced through grades to capt., 1976; chief nursing edn. and tng. U.S. Army Hosp., Ft. Campbell, Ky., 1979—. Decorated Army Commendation medal. Mem. Am. Nurses Assn., Tenn. Nurses Assn. (trustee dist. 13, ednl. adv.). Republican. Author nursing attitudes study. Home: 803 Alton Dr Clarksville TN 37040 Office: US Army MEDDAC Fort Campbell KY 42223

CARROLL, RICHARD SCOTT, museum dir.; b. Greenwich, Conn., Feb. 4, 1929; s. Richard Augustine Valentine and Eva Virginia (Howell) C.; B.F.A., Yale U., 1953, M.F.A. (Rabinowitz fellow 1953-55), 1955; Ed.D. in Art Edn., N.Y. U., 1955; m. Mary Lou Bush, Apr. 21, 1951; children—Jan, Suzanne, Ann. Dir. Wonder Workshop, Jr. Mus., Bridgeport, Conn., 1955-59; asst. dir., supr. edn. Mus. Art and Sci., Columbia, S.C., 1959-66; asst. dir., curator edn. Norfolk (Va.) Mus. Arts and Scis., 1966-70; dir. galleries Lowe Art Center, Syracuse (N.Y.) U., 1970-73; dir. John and Mable Ringling Mus. Art, Sarasota, Fla., 1973—. Served with AUS, 1946-47. Mem. Am. Assn. Museums, Southeastern Art Mus. Dirs. Assn., Southeastern Museums Conf., Internat. Inst. Conservation. Home: 6216 Ravenwood Dr Sarasota FL 33580 Office: PO Box 1838 Sarasota FL 33578

CARROLL, ROBERT CLINTON, JR., elec. engr.; b. Florence, S.C., June 11, 1930; s. Robert Clinton and Harriet (Holland) C.; B.S., Clemson U., 1953; m. Helen White, Aug. 29, 1954; children—Robert F., Helen Haynsworth. Sr. elec. engr. Broad River Elec. Coop, Gaffney, S.C., 1956-57; extension engr. Clemson U., 1957-58; engr. Horry Elec. Coop, Conway, S.C., 1958-60; mgr. bd. pub. works Water Power & Sewer Utility, Gaffney, 1960-65; elec. engr. Harwood Beebe Co., Cons. Engrs., Spartanburg, S.C., 1965-73, dirs., 1971-73; mgr. Broad River Electric Coop., 1973—; pres. S.C. Electric Coop. Mgrs. Assn. Dist. chmn. Boy Scouts Am.; clk. of session Limestone Presbyn. Ch. Served with AUS, 1953-55. Mem. Spartanburg Soc. Profl. Engrs. (pres. 1968-69), S.C. Pollution Control Assn. (pres. 1965-66), Am. Water Works Assn., IEEE. Club: Rotary (pres. Gaffney 1975-76). Home: 119 Hillside Dr Gaffney SC 29340 Office: PO Box 790 Gaffney SC 29340

CARROLL, ROBROY CHARLES, real estate mgmt. co. exec.; b. Houston, Nov. 18, 1910; s. I.C. and Hattie (Rotten) C.; B.A. in Bus. Adminstrn., Rice U., 1934, B.S. in Architecture, 1935; m. Ilma Wilday, May 10, 1938. Sec.-treas. Tanglewood Corp., Houston, 1945-70, pres., 1970—, also pres. affiliated cos., 1970—; dir. Greenway Bank & Trust. Mem. City of Houston Planning Commn., 1975—. Served to maj. USAAF, 1942-45. Mem. Houston Builders Assn. (dir.), Nat. Assn. Home Builders (dir.). Clubs: Kiwanis (pres. 1961), Briar (pres. 1965), (Houston). Home: 6239 Sugar Hill Houston TX 77057 Office: 1661 Tanglewood St Houston TX 77056

CARROLL, STEPHEN DOUGLAS, chemist; b. Clarendon, Ark., Nov. 2, 1943; s. Albert Genson and Wilma Mae (Hill) C.; B.A., Hendrix Coll., 1965; M.S., U. Ark., 1968; m. Sharon K. Hooten, Jan. 10, 1969; 1 son, Geoffrey Genson. Developmental chemist Chicopee Mfg. Co., North Little Rock, Ark., 1969-73, mgr. quality assurance, 1973—. Mem. Am. Chem. Soc., Am. Soc. Quality Control, AAAS. Democrat. Methodist.

CARROLL, THOMAS CHARLES, lawyer; b. Louisville, Sept. 1, 1921; s. Tarlton Combs and Irene (Crutcher) C.; B.A., Harvard U., 1942; J.D., U. Ky., 1948; m. Julianne Kirk, Apr. 23, 1959. Admitted to Ky. bar, 1948; partner firm Carroll, Chauvin, Miller & Conliffe, Louisville, 1967—; dir. Brokerage, Inc., Roads and Rivers Transport, Inc. Legal counsel Ky. Democratic Com., 1964-75; parliamentarian Dem. Nat. Com., 1973-75; mem. Dem. Charter Com., 1973—; mem. Dem. Exec. Com., 1964-75. Served from pvt. to capt. AUS, 1942-46. Mem. Louisville, Ky., Am. bar assns., Assn. Trial Lawyers Am., Phi Delta Phi. Clubs: Hasty Pudding, Pendennis, Harvard of N.Y.C., Nat. Dem., Jefferson. Home: 1603 Evergreen Rd Anchorage KY 40223 Office: 2720 Citizens Plaza Louisville KY 40202

CARRUTHERS, G. THOMAS, design engr.; b. Lake Charles, La., Nov. 26, 1935; s. David H. and Vena Elaine (Hutchins) C.; B.S. in Civil Engring., Lamar U., 1964; m. Mary Beth Furches, Aug. 30, 1959; children—John Alfred, Jeffrey Daniel. Engr. asst. Tex. Hwy. Dept., Nederland, 1964-65; project mgr. Chas. R. Haile Assos., Inc., Houston, 1965-70; city engr. City of League City (Tex.), 1968-70; sr. design engr. CRS, Inc., Houston, 1970-71, Community Program Cons., Inc., Pacudah, Ky., 1971-79; asso. dir. for bldg. maintenance, phys. plant Murray (Ky.) State U., 1979—. Dir. tng. union First Bapt. Ch., 1974-76; asst. scoutmaster Troop 77, Boy Scouts Am., Murray, Ky. Served in U.S. Army, 1957-58. Registered profl. engr., Tex. Club: Masons (Houston). Home: Route 4 Box 135A Murray KY 42071 Office: Murray State U Murray KY 42071

CARRUTHERS, JAMES DONALD, educator; b. Liverpool, Eng., Nov. 10, 1942; s. James Henry and Eunice Margaret (Burns) C.; came to U.S., 1969; B.Sc. with honors, Liverpool Poly. U., 1965; Ph.D., Brunel U., 1968; m. Janet Margaret Copland, Sept. 1, 1965; children—Paul James, Jacqueline Eunice, Susan Rose. Instr. chemistry Ambassador Coll., Bricket Wood, Eng., 1968-70; asso. prof. chemistry Ambassador Coll., Pasadena, Calif., 1970-75, prof., 1975-78; sr. research chemist Ashland Oil Co. (Ky.), 1978—. Mem. Am. Chem. Soc., Royal Inst. Chemistry. Home: Route 4 Box 249M Briarwood Estates Catlettsburg KY 41101 Office: Research and Devel Dept Ashland Oil Co Catlettsburg KY 41101

CARSON, CARL THOMAS, leasing co. exec.; b. Chattanooga, Aug. 11, 1907; s. Joseph Andrew and Florence (Lerch) C.; Tulane U., 1933-34, Southwestern U., 1935-36, Memphis State U., 1937-38, U. Tenn., 1939-41; m. Emma Winifred Stewart, Feb. 5, 1937; children—Judith Elizabeth, Karen Jean, Carl Joseph. Asst. mgr. Saunders Drive-It Yourself, Chattanooga, 1925-30; v.p. Dixie Drive-It Yourself, New Orleans and Memphis, 1930-35, 35-57; pres. Carl Carson Car & Truck Rental Co., Inc., Memphis, 1957-72, Carl Carson Leasing Corp., Memphis, 1957-72; v.p. Saunders Leasing System, Inc., Memphis, 1972-79, Carl Carson & Asso., Memphis, 1979—; dir. Leader Fed. Savs. & Loan, Memphis. Mem. adv. com. Memphis Cotton Carnival Assn., 1935—; dir., mem. exec. com. Future Memphis, 1965-67; dir. Memphis-Shelby County Safety Council, 1967-69, Goodwill Boys' Club, 1968-70, WDIA Found., 1970—; charter mem. Liberty Bowl Festival com., 1967—; v.p. Memphis Transit Authority, 1960-66; pres. Memphis council Navy League U.S., 1976-77; chmn., bd. dirs. Memphis roundtable NCCJ, 1970-71; pres., dir. Memphis Area Better Bus. Bur., 1955-56; v.p., mem. exec. com. Downtown Assn. Memphis, 1953-55; dir. United Service Orgn., 1953-54; bd. dirs. Arthritis Found., 1954-55; mem. Tenn. Gov.'s Commn. for Human Devel., 1968-70; mem. Pres. Lyndon Johnson's Citizens Com. on Community Relations, 1965-66; v.p. Memphis Com. on Community Relations, 1956-66; mem. Tenn. Gov.'s Adv. com. on minority econ. devel., 1970-71; adv. com. Chickasaw council Boy Scouts Am., 1969—; chmn. Memphis Indsl. Devel. and Pollution Control, 1975—; bd. dirs. YMCA, 1955-57; chpt. chmn. ARC; crusade chmn. Am. Cancer Soc., Memphis and Shelby County Unit, 1969 fund dr.; active Jr. Achievement, recipient Master of Free Enterprise award, 1979. Recipient Outstanding Citizen award Civitan Club, 1961; Outstanding Community Sales award Memphis Sales Execs. Club, 1966; Most Outstanding Civic Leader award Al Chymia Temple of the Shrine, 1967; Transp. Man of Year, Traffic Club Memphis, 1969; Disting. Service award Nat. Conv. of Nat. Def. Transp. Assn., 1969; Outstanding Exec. Car and Truck Renting and Leasing Industry, 1969; Outstanding Boss of Year award Jr. C. of C., 1953, 69; Human Relations award Memphis roundtable NCCJ, 1971; C. of C. Disting. Service award, 1966. Mem. Tennesseans for Better Transp. (v.p., exec. com. 1977-79), Am. Truck Hist. Soc., Pvt. Truck Council Am., Nat. Def. Transp. Assn. (pres. 1957-58), Asso. Transp. Club Memphis (pres. 1935-36), Car and Truck Renting and Leasing Assn. (pres. 1967-69), Tenn. Motor Transport Assn. (dir. 1945-49), Ark. Bus. and Truck Assn., Miss. Bus. and Truck Assn.; Nat. Speakers Assn., Public Relations Soc. Am., C. of C. (v.p.), Pi Sigma Epsilon, Delta Sigma Pi, Delta Nu Alpha. Republican. Episcopalian. Clubs: Memphis Sales Execs. (pres. 1954-55), Memphis Speakers (pres. 1971-72), Memphis Traffic (dir. 1937-39), Masons, Shriners, Univ., Petroleum (v.p. 1959—), Rotary (dir. Memphis 1969, 71-77, sec. 1963, pres. 1970, dist. gov. 1973, Paul Harris fellow 1974), Summit, Rivermont. Home: 475 N Highland St 11J Memphis TN 38122 Office: 644 Madison Ave Memphis TN 38103

CARSON, DALE, city ofcl.; grad. Ohio State U., 1949; m. Doris N. Carson; children—Dale, Chris, Cynthia. Formerly with FBI; sheriff, Jacksonville, Fla., 1958—, police chief, 1968—; lectr. polit. sci. various colls. and univs.; mem. Fla. Police Standards Council, Fla. Gov.'s Council on Criminal Justice. Mem. Nat., Fla. (past pres.), sheriffs assns., Internat. Assn. Chiefs of Police. Home: 1671 Woodmere Dr Jacksonville FL 32205 Office: Duval County Courthouse Jacksonville FL 32202

CARSON, GEORGE JOHN, lawyer; b. San Antonio, Nov. 12, 1936; s. John Chris and Sophia (Couloheras) C.; grad. Tex. Mil. Inst., 1954; B.S., Tex. A. and M. U., 1959; J.D., Tex. U., 1963; m. Georgia Williams, Nov. 26, 1971; children—John George, Penelope G., Philip George. Admitted to Tex. bar, 1963; partner Morrison, Dittmar, Dahlgren & Kaine, San Antonio, 1964—. Dir. State Jr. Bar of Tex., 1968-70; pres. San Antonio Jr. Bar, 1967. Mem. Am., Tex., San Antonio bar assns. Greek Orthodox (pres. ch. bd. trustees, mem. archdiocesan council). Home: 11426 Whisper Breeze San Antonio TX 78230 Office: Milam Bldg San Antonio TX 78205

CARSON, LEONARD ALLEN, lawyer; b. Lorain, Ohio, Nov. 6, 1940; s. Frank and Josephine (Suleski) Guzewicz; B.S. in Bus. Adminstrn., U. Fla., 1963, J.D., 1966; m. Rosa Nelson Houston, Nov. 27, 1976. Staff accountant Peat, Marwick, Mitchell & Co., N.Y.C., 1963-64; admitted to Fla. bar, 1967; mem. firm Kates and Ress, P.A., Miami, Fla., 1967-70; corp. counsel, asst. to exec. v.p. and treas. Cordis Corp., Miami, 1970-73; judge Indsl. Claims Ct., Ft. Lauderdale, Fla., 1973; mem. Fla. Indsl. Relations Commn., Tallahassee, 1973-74, chmn., 1974-76; chmn. Fla. Public Employees Relations Commn., Tallahassee, 1976-80; of counsel firm Seyfarth, Shaw, Fairweather & Geraldson, Tallahassee and Miami, 1980—; mem. Fla. Law Revision Council, 1976-77; mem. Internat. Assn. Indsl. Accident Bds. and Commns., 1974-76; Served with USMCR, 1960. Mem. Am., Dade County, Tallahassee, Fla. Govt., Fla. bar assns., Am. Arbitration Assn. (nat. panel 1968-73), Democrat. Roman Catholic. Club: Capital Tiger Bay. Home: 3128 Blair Stone Ct Tallahassee FL 32301 Office: One Biscayne Tower 2 S Biscayne Blvd Suite 2950 Miami FL 33131

CARSON, STANLEY FREDERICK, biol. research cons.; b. San Francisco, Oct. 4, 1912; s. David S. and Erma (Simon) C.; A.B., Stanford, 1934, Ph.D., 1941; m. Dorothy M. Wieser, Apr. 22, 1944; children—Suzanne, Scott, Wendy. Sr. microbiologist Merck & Co., Rahway, N.J., 1942-45; with Wyeth Inst., Phila., 1945-46; with biology div. Oak Ridge Nat. Lab., 1947—, now dep. dir. emeritus; prof. biomed. sci. U. Tenn., 1967-79, emeritus, 1979—; mem. adv. panel molecular biology NSF, 1955-57, adv. panel spl. facilities and programs, 1961-68; v.p. microbial metabolism div. Internat. Congress Microbiology, Rome, Italy, 1953; E.R. Squibb lectr. Rutgers U., 1958; hon. prof. U. Ga., 1960—. Haskins lab fellow, Stanford, 1941-42. Fellow AAAS; mem. Am. Chem. Soc., Am. Soc. Biol. Chemists, Am. Soc. Microbiology, Asso. editor Jour. Bacteriology, 1951-56, Bacteriology, Revs., 1958-64; editorial com. Ann. Rev. Microbiology, 1965-69; editorial bd. Grants Mag., 1977—. Contbr. numerous articles to profl. jours. Patentee in field. Pioneer research with radioactive isotopes on role of carbon dioxide in cellular biochemistry. Home: 109 Pleasant Rd Oak Ridge TN 37830 Office: Biology Div ORNL PO Box Y Oak Ridge TN 37830

CARSON, THOMAS MOORE, librarian; b. Pecos, Tex., June 5, 1917; s. Robert Kimbrough and Ruby Alice (Moore) C.; B.S. in Edn. with honors, U. Tex., El Paso, 1971, M.L.S., 1971; m. Lois Violet Luce, July 24, 1937; children—Patricia Kay, Pamela Lee, Thomas Moore. Toolmaker, Corona Clipper Co. (Calif.), 1937-41, plant insp., 1946; edn. counselor, Ft. Bliss, Tex., 1972-74; dir. El Paso County Library, Fabens, Tex., 1975—; cons. Am. Research Corp. (El Paso). Bd. dirs. Allied Mil. Host Family Program, 1972—. Served with U.S. Army, 1934-36, 41-45, 46-68. Decorated Army Commendation medal. Mem. ALA, Tex. Library Assn., S.W. Library Assn., Border Regional Library Assn., El Paso Public Library Assn., Ret. Officers Assn., Mil. Order World Wars, Council Abandoned Mil. Posts Dept. of the Rio Grande (past pres.). Baptist. Clubs: Masons, Nat. Sojourners. Home: 8719 Marble Dr El Paso TX 79904 Office: 601 NE 10th St Fabens TX 79838

CARSON, WILLIAM EDWARDS, nuclear engr., automobile broker; b. Danville, Va., July 31, 1930; s. Joseph Edwin and Elinor (Edwards) C.; B.S., Va. Poly. Inst., 1952, M.S., 1959; children—Kathryn Elise, William Edwards, John Edwin. Test engr. ERCO div. ACF Industries, Inc., Riverdale, Md., 1952-53, field engr., Tex., Fla., N.C., 1953-56; nuclear engr. Babcock & Wilcox Co., Lynchburg, Va., 1957-71; sr. elec. engr. Burns & Roe, Inc., Oradell, N.J., 1971; staff engr. So. Nuclear Engring., Inc., Dunedin, Fla., 1971-73; prin. engr., project mgr. nuclear power projects NUS Corp., Clearwater, Fla., 1973—; owner Prime Auto Brokers, Inc. State chmn. Young Republican Fedn. Va., 1965-67; mem. Va. Rep. Central Com., 1965-67. Registered profl. engr., Calif. Mem. IEEE (sr.), Am. Nuclear Soc., Sigma Xi. Methodist. Club: Sertoma. Home: PO Box 111 Dunedin FL 33528 Office: 2536 Countryside Blvd Clearwater FL 33515

CARSTEA, DUMITRU DUMITRU, research hydrologist, environ. scientist; b. Paduroiu, Rumania, Mar. 22, 1930; s. Dumitru Marian and Teodora (Soare) C.; B.S., M.S. in Agrl. Engring. Soils, Agrl. Inst. (Bucharest, Romania), 1954; M.S., Ore. State U., 1966, Ph.D., 1967; m. Eleanor Tolci, Nov. 14, 1956; children—Julius, Eugene, Virgil, Adina. Came to U.S., 1961, naturalized, 1965. Research scientist (project chief) Rumanian Acad. Sci., Bucharest, 1954-60; research asst. dept. soils sci. Ore. State U., Corvallis, 1961-66; research scientist (project chief) Canadian Dept. Agr., Vancouver, B.C., 1966-67; with U.S. Geol. Survey, Phila. and Arlington, Va., 1967-70, hydrologist chemist, 1967-68; project chief hydrology, 1968-74; tech. staff (project leader) Mitre Corp., McLean, Va., 1974-76, group leader environ. chemistry/toxic substances, 1976-79; project dir. environ. Union Oil Products/System Devel. Corp., McLean, 1980—; cons. environ. field; mem. B.C. Com. Soil Testing and Fertility, 1966-67; mem. Soil Conf. FAO, 1966, Internat. Soil Sci. Conf., Bucharest, 1958. Mem. Greenbriar Civic Assn., Fairfax, Va., 1969—. Mem. Internat., Am. soil sci. socs., Western Soil Soc., Am. Geophus. Union, Internat. Assn. Study Clays, Am. Soc. Agronomy, Clay Minerals Soc. (mem. program quality com. 1971), A.A.A.S., Sigma Xi, Phi Kappa Phi. Contbr. articles to profl. jours. Home: 13563 Point Pleasant Dr Chantilly VA 22021

CARSTENS, KENNETH CHARLES, anthropologist, educator; b. Bay City, Mich., Feb. 12, 1949; s. Calvin Zeno and Dorothy Marie (Ranney) C.; B.S., Central Mich. U., 1971; student Western Mich. U., 1971-72; A.M., Washington U., St. Louis, 1974, Ph.D., 1978; m. Katherine Ann Dunkelberg, Mar. 24, 1974 (div. 1978); 1 son, Jason L. Substitute tchr. secondary and elem. schs., Pinconning Mich. Area Schs., 1970-73; asst. dir. Archeol. Field Sch., Central Mich. U., 1970; archeol. lab. supr. dept. anthropology Washington U., St. Louis, 1974-76; instr. anthropology N. Ky. U., 1976-78, also curator Mus. Anthropology, 1976-78; asst. prof. anthropology Murray (Ky.) State U., 1978—; prin. investigator for contract archeol. projects, 1977—; participant various archeol. expdns. in midwestern U.S., 1970—; mem. task force for planning of site preservation Ky. Office of State Archeology, 1979—. Served with Air N.G., 1973. Cave research Found. grantee, 1974; Nat. Endowment Humanities co-grantee, 1977. Mem. Am. Anthrop. Soc., Soc. Profl. Archeology, Ky. Archeol. Soc., Mich. Archeol. Soc., Assn. Field Archaeology, Plains Anthrop. Orgn., AAAS, Sigma Xi. Lutheran. Contbr. articles on archeol. surveys to profl. jours. Office: Archeology Lab Murray State Univ Murray KY 42071

CARSTETTER, DAVID WILSON, lawyer; b. Lewistown, Pa., Dec. 5, 1937; s. Fred R. and Ruth L. (Minton) C.; B.A., Pa. State U., 1960; J.D., Duke U., 1968; m. Joy Ann Thompson, Jan. 28, 1961; children—David, Mary, John, Laura. Admitted to Fla. bar, 1968; asso. firm Mahoney, Hadlow, Chambers & Adams, Jacksonville, Fla., 1968-70, Sears, Dunlap & Sears, Jacksonville, 1970-73; partner firm Kent, Watts, Durden, Kent & Mickler, Jacksonville, 1973—. Served with USNR, 1960-65. Mem. Am., Fla., Jacksonville bar assns., Lawyers-Pilots Bar Assn. Presbyterian. Home: 8040 Holiday Rd S Jacksonville FL 32216 Office: 870 Florida Nat Bank Bldg Jacksonville FL 32202

CARSWELL, ELBA WILSON, journalist; b. nr. Bonifay, Fla., Jan. 4, 1916; s. John Robert and Victoria (Judah) C.; A.B., La. Poly. Inst., 1946; m. Mabel Bagley, Apr. 5, 1947 (dec. Jan. 1953); children—Carol, David Clements; m. 2d, Catherine Powell, Apr. 4, 1958; 1 dau., Catherine Melody. Exec. sec. Santa Rosa County C. of C., also asso. editor The Milton (Fla.) Gazette, 1946; asst. dir. publicity, asst. prof. journalism La. Poly. Inst., Ruston, 1947-49; editor The Milton Gazette, 1949-53, Graceville (Fla.) News, Washington County News, Chipley, Fla., 1953-61; staff writer Pensacola News Jour.; editor, co-founder The Tri-County Gazette, Jay, Fla., 1951-53; staff writer Pensacola News-Jour., Chipley, 1961—; pres. Central Office Supply and Pub. Co., Bonifay, Fla., 1963-71; founding dir., chmn. bd. First Bank Holmes County, Bonifay. Mem. N.W. Fla. Regional Housing Authority, Citizens' Tax Council; chmn. Washington County Rural Area Devel. Council, 1961-66; chmn. Fla. adv. com. Farmers Home Adminstrn.; mem. regional adv. com. Fla. Dept. Recreation and Parks, 1972—; adv. com. on pub. relations Fla. State Welfare Bd., 1960-71; mem. Fla. Bd. Parks and Historic Memls., 1966-69, chmn., 1969; chmn. Washington County Hist. Commn., 1965-66; bd. dirs. Children's Home Soc. Fla. Mayor, Chipley, Fla. 1963-67; chmn. Washington County Democratic Com., 1958-62. Adv. bd. Washington-Holmes Area Vocational-Tech. Sch., Chipley, Fla.; founder Carswell Found., pres. 1972; mem. U. West Fla. adv. council. Recipient Florida Forestry editorial award, 1956, 57, 58, Fla. State U. editorial award, 1958, Fla. Gov.'s Festival of Fla. Products award, weekly newspaper div., 1958; Fla. Press Assn. editorial oscar, 1959; Fla. Outdoor Writers award, 1960; Fla. Outstanding Conservationist award Soil Conservation Soc. Am.; Fla. Man of Year for Agr., Fla. Assn. Agrl. Agts., 1966; Gov.'s appreciation award outstanding contbns. to State of Fla., 1969, named Fla. Patriot, recipient Silver Medallion Patriot award Fla. Bicentennial Commn., 1976. Served with AUS, 1942-45. Mem. Fla. Municipal Judges Assn., Washington County C. of C. (pres. 1961-62), Fla. Hist. Soc., Washington County League Municipalities (pres. 1967), Carswell Assn. (pres. 1970), SAR, VFW, Am. Legion, Alpha Lambda Tau, Sigma Tau Delta. Tau Kappa Epsilon. Democrat. Methodist. Mason, Kiwanian (Chipley pres. 1960). Author: Among These Hills, 1968; Holmes Valley, 1969; Tempestuous Triangle. Editor: The Carswell Chronicle, 1972. Contbr. numerous hist. articles. Home: Dekle St at Forest Ave Chipley FL 32428 Office: PO Box 584 Chipley FL 32428

CARSWELL, RONALD VICTOR, educator; b. Houston, Nov. 28, 1941; s. Ralph Victor and Dolores Evelyn (Kerr) C.; student Delmar Jr. Coll., 1960-61, S.W. Tex. State Coll., 1961-62; B.B.A., U. Tex., 1965; M.B.A., Baylor U., 1971; m. Mary Helen Jones, Oct. 17, 1970; children—Angela Gail, Randall Vincent. Quality control engr. Gen. Tire & Rubber Co., Waco, Tex., 1965-68; asst. prof. James Connally Tech. Inst., Waco, 1969; asso. prof., program chmn. Tex. State Tech. Inst., Waco, 1970-76, prof., program chmn. computer sci. tech., 1976—; owner, operator Computer Software Assos., cons., Waco. Vice pres. Tex. State Tech. Inst. Booster Club, 1978-79. Named Boss of Year, Indian Springs chpt. Am. Businesswomen's Assn., 1979. Mem. Data Processing Mgmt. Assn. (cert. data processing), Tex. Tech. Soc. (charter and life mem.), Gamma Sigma Tau, Epsilon Delta Pi. Baptist. Home: 912 Melrose St Waco TX 76710 Office: Tex State Tech Inst Computer Sci Tech Bldg 23-13 Waco TX 76705

CARTER, ALBERT HOWARD, III, coll. dean; b. Washington, Mar. 14, 1943; s. Albert Howard and Marjorie Dargan C.; student Fla. Presbyn. Coll., 1960-61; A.B., U. Chgo., 1965; M.A. (NDEA fellow), U. Iowa, 1967, M.A., 1969, Ph.D., 1971; m. Nancy Corson, Aug. 26, 1967; 1 dau., Rebecca Alice. Presbyn. grad. fellow, Florence, Italy, 1969-70; postdoctoral fellow Soc. for Value in Higher Edn., 1973; asst. prof. lit. Tarkio (Mo.) Coll., 1970-71; asst. prof. comparative lit. Eckerd Coll. (formerly Fla. Presbyn. Coll.), St. Petersburg, 1971-77, asso. prof., 1977—, asso. dean faculty for gen. edn., 1979—, chmn. Foundations Collegium, 1979—, dir. Eckerd London Study Center, 1976. Danforth Asso., 1975; Nat. Endowment Humanities fellow, 1977; Inst. Ecumenical and Cultural Research fellow, 1977. Mem. MLA, Am. Assn. Higher Edn., AAUP. Presbyterian. Contbr. articles to profl. jours. Home: 4201 Narvarez Way S Saint Petersburg FL 33712

CARTER, BETTY LOU (MRS. CHARLES E. CARTER), ret. educator; b. Collierville, Tenn., July 6, 1907; d. Claude Marcellus and Eloise (Neville) Ballard; B.A. magna cum laude, Lambuth Coll., 1928; M.A., La. State U., 1935; m. Charles E. Carter, Sept. 6, 1930; 1 son, Charles Ballard. Tchr. French, Medina (Tenn.) High Sch., 1928-29; tchr. English, Pope (Miss.) High Sch., 1929-30; instr. French, Belhaven Coll., Jackson, Miss., 1940; instr. English, Southwestern Coll., Memphis, 1943-44; tchr. English, St. Mary's Episcopal Sch., Memphis, 1944-45; prof. French, Texarkana (Tex.) Coll., 1953-70. Bd. dirs. local chpt. ARC, 1950; mem. Community Service Council, 1949-50; active Heart Fund, 1957-60; trustee Texarkana Coll. Named Tchr. of Year, Texarkana Coll., 1962; R.E. Womack award Lambuth Coll., 1969. Mem. Am. Assn. Tchrs. French, Modern Lang. Assn., S. Central Modern Lang. Assn., Coll. English Assn., AAUW, AAUP, Tex. Tchrs. Assn., Tex. Jr. Coll. Tchrs., P.E.O. (pres. chpt. 1960-61, 67-68), Delta Kappa Gamma. Methodist. Home: 2801 Stillwell Dr Texarkana TX 75501

CARTER, BETTY WERLEIN (MRS. HODDING CARTER), journalist; b. New Orleans; d. Philip and Elizebeth (Thomas) Werlein; B.A., Newcomb Coll., 1931; Litt.D. (hon.), Bowdoin Coll., 1979; m. Hodding Carter, Oct. 14, 1931; children—Hodding III, Philip Dutartre Carter. Newspaper reporter Daily Courier, Hammond, La., 1932-36, Delta Star, Greenville, Miss., 1936-38; reporter Delta Democrat-Times, 1938-40, 45-72, pub., 1972-80; researcher O.W.I., 1942-45; freelance writer. Mem. So. dist. Marshall Scholarship Com., 1961-69, Gulf Regional Rhodes Scholarship Com.; vestry St. James Episcopal Ch.; mem. corp. U.S. Com. for UNICEF; pres. Mississippians for Ednl. TV. Mem. Nat. Assn. Ednl. Broadcasters (dir.). Author: (with husband) So Great a Good, A History of the Episcopal Church in Louisiana, 1805-1955, 1955, Doomed Road of Empire, 1962.

CARTER, CHARLES FINLEY, county planner; b. Potsdam, N.Y., Oct. 17, 1949; s. Everett Finley and Ann (Terriberry) C.; B.A., Lehigh U., 1972; m. Robin Lee Ahrens. Jr. layout engr. Pa. Electric Co., Towanda, 1968-69; planning intern Mpls. Planning & Devel., 1971; planning cons. Urban Research & Devel. Corp., Bethlehem, Pa., 1972-76; planning dir. County of Culpeper (Va.), 1976—. Chmn., Culpeper Mental Health Adv. Bd., 1977-79; mem. governing bd. Rappahannock-Rapidan Community Services, 1978-79. Mem. Am. Planning Assn., Va. Citizens Planning Assn., Urban Land Inst., Kappa Sigma. Home: Boston VA 22713 Office: 135 W Cameron St Culpeper VA 22701

CARTER, CHARLES FLOYD, hosp. housekeeper; b. Meridian, Miss., Sept. 14, 1938; s. Charles Floyd and Ruth Boone C.; student E. Central Jr. Coll., 1959-61; m. Johnnie Katherine Chapman, May 5, 1961; children—Robert Carlton, Katherine Ruth, Charles Kevin. Asst. dir. bldg. service dept. Miss. Bapt. Hosp., Jackson, 1964-66; dir. bldg. service dept. Miss. Bapt. Med. Center, Jackson, 1966—; disaster coordinator Hinds/Rankin/Warren County Hosps., 1978—; mem. faculty Hinds Jr. Coll.; bd. dirs. Miss. Bapt. Hosp. Fed. Credit Union; housekeeping cons. Served with USN, 1956-59. Mem. Nat. Exec. Housekeepers Assn. (charter pres. Natchez trace chpt. 1969-71; cert.), Miss. Assn. Hosp. Housekeeping (pres. 1968), Southeastern Assn. Hosp. Housekeepers (pres. 1972). Baptist. Club: Masons. Home: 84 Terrapin Dr Brandon MS 39042 Office: Miss Bapt Med Center 1225 N State St Jackson MS 39201

CARTER, CHARLES LESLIE, JR., mgmt. cons.; b. Newark, May 26, 1926; s. Charles Leslie and Isabelle May (Frazee) C.; diploma Newark Coll. Engring., 1955; M.A., Nat. Christian U., Dallas, 1969, Ph.D., 1970; B.A., Thomas A. Edison Coll., Princeton, N.J., 1981; m. Gladys M. Craig, July 3, 1948; children—Charles Leslie, Susan Jane. Prodn. supt. Electro-Mech. Research, Inc., Sarasota, Fla., 1957-60; supr. quality and safety planning Martin-Marietta Co., Cape Canaveral, Fla., 1960-61; mgr. quality engring. div. Collins Radio Co., Dallas, 1961-64; dir., exec. cons. C.L. Carter Jr. & Assos., Inc., Richardson, Tex., 1964-76; mgr. quality, reliability and safety Action Communication Systems Inc., Dallas, 1976-79; dir. quality, reliability and safety Rath & Strong Inc., Dallas, 1979—. Served with USNR, 1943-46; PTO. Registered profl. engr., Calif., Can.; cert. quality engr., reliability engr., mfg. engr.; certified profl. mgr., profl. mgmt. cons.; certified counseling psychologist. Fellow Am. Soc. Quality Control; mem. Nat. Mgmt. Assn., Adminstrv. Mgmt. Soc., Am. Soc. Tng. and Devel., Am. Personnel and Guidance Assn., Internat. Assn. Counseling Services, Am. Soc. Safety Engrs., Vets of Safety, Soc. Mfg. Engrs., Nat. Psychol. Assn., others. Baptist. Club: Kiwanis (pres. Richardson 1977). Author: Quality Assurance Workmanship Standards and Training Manual, 1967, 70, 78; The Control and Assurance of Quality, Reliability and Safety, 2d edit., 1978; Quality Assurance, Quality Control and Inspection Handbook, 3d edit., 1979; Workmanship Standards in Color, 1966, 68, 77; also profl. papers, tng. and motivation films in fields quality, reliability and safety; develops and conducts mgmt. tng. and devel. seminars in U.S., Can. and Mex. Home: 1211 Glen Cove Dr Richardson TX 75080

CARTER, CLARICE GRAHAM, educator; b. Winston-Salem, N.C., Dec. 2, 1933; 1 child. B.S. in Elem. Edn., Winston-Salem State U., 1955; M.S. in Elem. Edn., Agrl. and Tech. State U., Greensboro, N.C., 1965. Tchr. Diggs Sch., Winston-Salem, 1955-57, 67-69, tchr. academically talented classes, 1959-66; tchr. spl. reading Latham Sch., Winston-Salem, 1970-74, tchr. reading lab., 1975—. Mem. NEA, N.C. Assn. Educators, N.C. Poetry Soc., Assn. Classroom Tchrs., Council Exceptional Children, Internat. Reading Assn., Alpha Kappa Mu. Author: I Can Keep You In My Heart, 1975; A Bit of Care, 1976. Authored filmstrip and tape, 1969. Home: 2909 Teresa Ave Winston-Salem NC 27105 Office: 986 Hutton St Winston-Salem NC 27101

CARTER, DAVID EDWARD, communications exec.; b. Ashland, Ky., Nov. 24, 1942; s. Victor Byron and Lillie Elzena (Clarke) C.; A.B., U. Ky., 1965; M.S., Ohio U., 1967; m. Linda Louise Gibson, May 31, 1969; children—Christa Ann, Lauren Louise. Dir. advt. Wheeler & Williams Co., Ashland, 1965-66; instr. U. Ky., 1967-70; dir. communications Ky. Electric Steel Co., Ashland, 1970-77; pres. David E. Carter Corporate Communications, Inc., Ashland, 1977—; dir. Home Fed. Savs. & Loan Assn., Ashland, Decathlon Corp. Scoutmaster, Tri-State Area Council Boy Scouts Am., 1970-77, dist. commr., 1977-78, recipient dist. award of merit, 1975. Mem. Am. Inst. Graphic Arts. Republican. Presbyterian. Author: It's Not the Money—It's The Principle, 1975; Book of American Trade Marks, 7 vols., 1972-79; Designing Corporate Symbols, 1975; Corporate Identify Manuals, 1976; Letterheads/1, 1977; Ideas for Editors, 1977; Letterheads/2, 1979; Best Financial Advertising, 1979. Home: 2350 Hickory Ridge Dr Ashland KY 41101 Office: 1500 Carter Ave Ashland KY 41101

CARTER, DEAN, sculptor, educator; b. Henderson, N.C., Apr. 24, 1922; s. Clement Dean and Mary Clegg (Goodrich) C.; student Corcoran Sch. Art, 1940-43; A.B., American U., 1947; M.F.A. Ind. U., 1948; postgrad. Studio of Zadkine, Paris, 1948-49; m. Rosina McDonnell, Aug. 8, 1950; children—Frances, Katharine, Clement Dean, James Thomas, Mary. Mem. faculty Coll. Architecture, Va. Inst. Tech., Blacksburg, 1950-75; prof. dept. art Coll. Arts and Scis., Va. Poly. Inst. and State U., Blacksburg, 1975—, head dept. art, 1967-79; guest lectr. to various community and art groups, 1950-79; one-man shows include: Schneider Gallery, Rome, Italy, 1955, Weatherspoon Gallery, Greensboro, N.C., 1956, The Contemporaries, Inc., N.Y.C., 1956, U. Va., Charlottesville, 1959, The Artists Mart, Washington, 1960, 64, 71, Washington and Lee U., Lexington, Va., 1962, Mary Baldwin Coll., Staunton, Va., 19—, Randolph Macon Woman's Coll., Lynchburg, 1960, Va. Mus. Fine Arts, Richmond, 1960, Hollins Coll., Roanoke, Va., 1978, Danville (Va.) Mus. Fine Arts and History, 19—, Nat. Bank of Blacksburg, 1978, Lynwood Community Center, Martinsville, Va., 1978, Roanoke Fine Arts Center, 1978; numerous group shows including: Pa. Acad. Fine Arts, Phila., 195 , Boston Mus., 1955, Corcoran Gallery Art, Washington, 19‑0, Art Inst. Detroit, 1949, Sculpture Center, N.Y.C., 1950-56, John Herron Mus., Indpls., 1948, Carnegie Inst. for Peace, N.Y.C., 1955, N.C. Mus. Fine Arts, Raleigh, 1960, Winston-Salem (N.C.) Gallery, 1971; represented in numerous permanent collections including: U. Ind., Bloomington, Mary Baldwin Coll., Washington and Lee U., Wesley Found. Bldg., Blacksburg, Roanoke Meml. Hosp., 1st Colony Ins. Co. Lynchburg, Cranbrook Mus. Art. Bloomfield Hills, Mich., also pvt. collections. Served with USAAF, 1943-46; PTO. Recipient numerous awards including: Sidney Sculpture award Festival in the Park, 1975, Sculpture award, 1976, 78; 1st prize Festival of Arts, Radford, 1979; cert. of distinction Roanoke Fine Arts Center, 1979; purchase award Bank of Va., Roanoke, 1979. Mem. Coll. Art Assn. Am., Am. Fedn. Art, Va. Arts Council, So. Sculptors Assn., So. Highlands Handicraft Guild, Blacksburg Regional Art Assn., Am. Crafts Council, Washington Soc. Arts. Home: 1011 Highland Circle Blacksburg VA 24060 Office: Art Dept 21-B Owens Hall Virginia Polytechnic Inst & State University Blacksburg VA 24061

CARTER, DONALD CLAYTON, psychiatrist; b. Blair, Nebr., July 30, 1922; s. Earl Dion and Josephine Emma (Romanowski) C.; student pre-med. SE Mo. State Tchrs. Coll. Cape Girardeau, 1943-45; M.D., U. Nebr., 1950; m. Selma Louise Smith, July 21, 1946; children—Gregory, Donna, Jeffrey, Theodore. Rotating intern Lincoln (Neb.) Gen. Hosp., 1953-54; resident in internal medicine Riverside Hosp., Newport News, Va., 1950-51, in psychiatry Duke Med. Center, 1957-60; practice medicine specializing in family medicine Beaver City, Nebr., 1954-57; asst. div. chief psychiatry VA Hosp., Durham, N.C., 1960-62; med. dir. Central Minn. Mental Health Center, St. Cloud, Minn., 1962-67; asst. prof. psychiatry U. Mo., Columbia, 1967-68; practice medicine specializing in psychiatry Morgantown, 1968—; asso. prof. psychiatry, chief psychiatry outpatient clinic W. Va. U. Hosp. and Med. Sch. Morgantown, 1968-73, prof., chief psychosomatic consultative service, hosp. sch. medicine, 1973—, prof., dir. undergrad. edn. in psychiatry. Served to lt. (j.g.), USNR, Hosp. Corps, 1942-46, capt. M.C., 1951-53. Decorated Bronze Star. Diplomate Am. Bd. Psychiatry and Neurology. Fellow Am. Psychiat. Assn. (pres. W. Va. dist. br. 1977-79, W.Va. rep. to assembly 1977—), mem. Am. Acad. Psychiatry and Law Monongalia County Med. Soc., W.Va. Med. Assn., AMA, Am. Philatelic Soc. Republican. Methodist. Club: Masons. Contbr. articles to profl. jours. Home: 217 S Walnut St Morgantown WV 26505

CARTER, EMMETT DALE, ins. co. exec.; b. San Diego, July 7, 1945; B.S. in Acctg., Okla. State U., 1967; married; 2 children. Staff accountant Haskins & Sells C.P.A.'s, Tulsa, 1967-71, Stephenson Flow & Co., C.P.A.'s, Norman, Okla., 1971-72; treas. Mark Twain Life Ins. Corp., Oklahoma City, 1972-77, v.p., 1976-78, adminstrv. v.p., 1978—. Served to capt. U.S. Army, 1968-70; Korea. C.P.A., Okla. Fellow Life Mgmt. Inst.; mem. Am. Inst. C.P.A.'s, Okla. Soc. C.P.A.'s. Methodist. Club: Kiwanis (dir.). Office: 4400 N Lincoln Blvd Oklahoma City OK 73105

CARTER, ERNEST EUGENE, vending co. exec.; b. Rutledge, Ga., Jan. 18, 1918; s. William G. Grant, Sr., and Elizabeth (Morris) C.; ed. spl. courses Jacksonville Jr. Coll., Ga. Evening Sch.; m. Sarah Mae Guice, Apr. 18, 1948; children—Patricia Carter Patterson, Barbara. With Sands & Co., Inc., Atlanta, 1938—, gen. auditor, 1946-54, office mgr., gen. auditor, 1954-60, asst. sec., office mgr., 1960—. Officer Belvedere Civic Club, 1965; bd. stewards Decatur 1st United Methodist Ch. Served with USNR, 1942-46. Mem. Adminstrv. Mgmt. Soc. (treas., Merit award 1974). Democrat. Club: Snapfinger Country. Home: 3329 York Pl Decatur GA 30032 Office: 1735 DeFoor Pl NW Atlanta GA 30318

CARTER, EUGENE BLALOCK, educator; b. Woodlawn, Tex., Nov. 17, 1917; s. John Issaic and Fannie Deva (Dillard) C.; cert. BMI Bus. Coll., 1948; B.S., Southwest Tex. State U., 1976; m. Nellie G. Haney, May 22, 1937 (dec. 1977); 5 children; m. 2d, B. Lorene Flanery, June 14, 1978. With U.S. Civil Service, San Antonio, 1949-70; electronics technician St. Philips Coll., San Antonio, 1971-72, instr., 1972-73, instr., 1973—, chmn. electronic dept., 1973—. Lic. to ministry Baptist Ch., 1972. Served with AUS, 1945. Mem. Tex. Tech. Soc., Tex. Jr. Coll. Assn. Tchrs., Southwest Tex. State U. Alumni Assn. Republican. Clubs: Masons, Lions. Home: 7811 Rimfire Dr San Antonio TX 78227 Office: 2111 Nevada St Box 13 Campus San Antonio TX 78203

CARTER, FRANCES TUNNELL (MRS. JOHN T. CARTER), educator; b. Springville, Miss., May 21; d. David Atmond and Mary Annie (McCutcheon) Tunnell; A.A., Wood Jr. Coll., 1942; B.S., U. So. Miss., 1946; M.S., U. Tenn., 1948; Ed.D., U. Ill., 1954; postgrad. Ursuline Coll., 1961, Dayton U., 1963, Fla. State U., 1970, Sanford U., 1975-76, U. Ala., Birmingham, 1976-77; m. John T. Carter, Mar. 16, 1946; children—John Wayne, Frankye Nell. Tchr. elementary schs., Thaxton, Miss., 1942-43, Cumberland, Miss., 1943-44; tchr. home econs. high schs., Randolph and Maben, Miss., 1944-47, Wood Jr. Coll., Mathiston, Miss., 1948; head dept. home econs. E. Central Jr. Coll., 1948-49, Clarke Coll., 1950-56; mem. faculty Samford U., Birmingham, Ala., 1956—, prof., 1963—; vis. prof. Hong Kong Baptist Coll., 1965-66; dir., cons. summer workshops for tchrs., 1962—; mem. supervisory panel Tri-State Project in Early Childhood Edn., 1972-74, Ala. Advisory Com. Early Childhood Edn., 1974—. Mem. Ala. Gov.'s Commn. on Status of Women, 1964-68, advisory bd. Dairy Council Ala., 1966-74; active Girl Scouts U.S.A., 1963—. Recipient Spl. Service award ARC, 1962; named Woman of Year City of Birmingham, 1977. Mem. Internat. Council on Edn. for Teaching, Ala. Acad. Sci., Nat. Assn. for Edn. Young Children, Nat. Aerospace Edn. Assn., CAP (lt. col., state info. officer 1973-79, internal dir. aerospace edn. 1975—), Assn. for Childhood Edn. (state pres. 1970-72), Internat. Council Women, Internat. Reading Assn., D.A.R., Ala. Writers Conclave (corr. sec. 1975-76, pres. 1978-79), Ala. Poetry Soc. (pres. 1979-80), Ala. Assn. Young Children, Birmingham Story League (co-founder), Nat. League Am. Penwomen (state exec. bd., pres. Birmingham br. 1968, 76-78), Ala. Assn. Tchr. Educators, Birmingham Women's C. of C. (pres. 1975-76, dir. 1976-78), Kappa Delta Epsilon (nat. 1st v.p. 1978—), Alpha Delta Kappa, Kappa Delta Pi, Kappa Omicron Phi, Pi Gamma Mu. Baptist. Author: Sammy in the Country, 1960; Teachers Guide for Missions Books, 1969; 'Tween-Age Ambassadors, 1970; co-author: Sharing Times Seven, 1971; Ching Fu and Jim, 1977; contbr. articles, poems to religious and profl. jours.; author curriculum unites for denominational work.

Home: 2561 Rocky Ridge Rd Birmingham AL 35243 Office: Sch Edn Samford U Birmingham AL 35209

CARTER, GEORGE FRANKLIN, educator; b. Bowie, Tex., Feb. 22, 1922; s. George Franklin and Mary Agnes (Blakney) C.; B.A., Abilene Christian U., 1950; M.A., N.Tex. State U., 1968; Ed.D., E. Tex. State U., 1978; m. Marjorie Lucile Beck, Nov. 23, 1946; children—David Landon, Wendell Glen, Judith Anne. Asst. to pres., instr. English, S.W. Christian Coll., 1950-51; evangelist Central Ch. of Christ, Ardmore, Okla., 1951-53, Oklahoma City, 1953-56, San Benito, Tex., 1956-59, Texarkana, Tex., 1959-64, Weatherford, Tex., 1964-68; asst. prof. English and linguistics Abilene (Tex.) Christian U., 1968-73, asso. prof., 1973—. Served with U.S. Army, 1938-47. Office: ACU Sta Box 8064 Abilene TX 79699

CARTER, GRADY LEE, III, physician, ret. air force officer; b. Fort Worth, Apr. 25, 1945; s. Grady Lee and Ora Natalie (Bailey) C.; B.A., Tex. Christian U., 1968; D.O., Coll. Osteopathic Medicine and Surgery, 1972; m. Lucy Devereaux Swanson, Aug. 10, 1974; children—Grady Lee IV, Ashley Mason, Christopher Randolph. Commd. capt. USAF, 1971, advanced through grades to maj., 1975; intern Wilford Hall USAF Med. Center, Lackland AFB, San Antonio, 1972-73, resident anesthesiology, 1973-74, mem. staff, 1974-76; ret., 1976; resident in anesthesiology U. Ala. at Birmingham, 1976-77; mem. staff Harris Hosp.-Ft. Worth Med. Center, Ft. Worth-Cook Children's Hosp. Fellow Am. Coll. Anesthesiologists; mem. Internat. Anesthesiology Research Soc., Am., Tex. med. assns., Am. Soc. Anesthesiology, Tarrant County Med. Assn., Sigma Alpha Epsilon, Sigma Sigma Phi. Office: Dept Anesthesiology Harris Hosp Fort Worth TX

CARTER, JAMES BYARS, allergist; b. Dallas, July 15, 1934; s. Algie Billie and Naomi (Byars) C.; B.A., U. Tex., 1956, M.D., 1959; M.S., U. Minn., 1966; m. Jean Foxhall Clement, Apr. 4, 1970; children—Gregory James, Kathleen Jo, William Adam, John Gregory. Intern, Letterman Gen. Hosp., San Francisco, 1959-60; resident internal medicine Mayo Grad. Med. Sch., Rochester, Minn., 1963-66; practice medicine, specializing in internal medicine, partner Capital Med. Clinic, Austin, 1967-71; resident allergy and immunology Kaiser Found. Hosp., San Francisco, 1971-73; asso. Allergy Assos., Austin, 1973—; pres. staff Seton, St. David's, Shoal Creek, Brackenridge hosps., Austin, 1973—. Cub scout den leader Boy Scouts Am., Austin, 1974-75, asst. scoutmaster, 1974-75, scoutmaster, 1976—. Served with USAF, 1959-63. Mead Johnson scholar, 1965-66; Am. Coll. Allergists and Am. Acad. Allergy grantee, 1971-72. Diplomate Am. Bd. Internal Medicine, Am. Bd. Allergy and Immunology. Fellow Am. Coll. Allergists, A.C.P., Am. Acad. Allergy, Am. Coll. Chest Physicians; mem. Travis County Med. Soc., Tex. Med. Assn., Am. Assn. Certified Allergists, AMA, Am. Tb Soc. (dir. 1967-70), Southwest Allergy Forum. Episcopalian (asst. Sunday sch. supt. 1973-74, lay reader 1977—). Contbr. articles to profl. jours. Office: Suite 107 1301 W 38th St Austin TX 78705

CARTER, JAMES EARL, JR. (JIMMY), Pres. U.S.; b. Plains, Ga., Oct. 1, 1924; s. James Earl and Lillian (Gordy) C.; student Ga. Southwestern Coll., 1941-42, Ga. Inst. Tech., 1942-43; B.S., U.S. Naval Acad., 1946; postgrad. Union Coll., 1952; LL.D., Morehouse Coll., 1972, U. Notre Dame, 1977, Emory U., 1979; D.E. (hon.), Ga. Inst. Tech., 1979; m. Rosalynn Smith, July 7, 1946; children—John William, James Earl III, Donnel Jeffrey, Amy Lynn. Peanut farmer, warehouseman, Plains, 1953-77; mem. Ga. Senate, 1963-67; gov. Ga., 1971-75; Pres. U.S., 1977—. Chmn. congressional campaign com. Democratic Nat. Com., 1974; candidate Dem. nomination Pres. U.S., 1976. Mem. Sumter County (Ga.) Sch. Bd., 1955-62, chmn., 1960-62; mem. Americus and Sumter County Hosp. Authority, 1956-70; bd. dirs. Ga. Crop Improvement Assn., 1957-63, pres., 1961; mem. Sumter County Library Bd., 1961; pres. Plains Devel. Corp., 1963; chmn. W. Central Ga. Area Planning and Devel. Commn., 1964; pres. Ga. Planning Assn., 1968; state chmn. March of Dimes, 1968-70. Served with U.S. Navy, 1946-53. Club: Lions (dist. gov. 1968-69). Author: Why Not the Best?, 1975; A Government as Good as Its People, 1977. Home: 1 Woodland Dr Plains GA 31780 Office: White House 1600 Pennsylvania Ave NW Washington DC 20500

CARTER, JAMES EDWARD, JR., dentist, assn. ofcl.; b. Augusta, Ga., July 1, 1906; s. James Edward and Emma (Barnett) C.; D.D.S., Howard U., 1930; postgrad. Haines Normal and Indsl. Inst., 1920-24; m. Marjorie Butler, Jan. 7, 1928; 1 son, James Edward III. Pvt. practice dentistry, Augusta, 1930—. Mem. Nat. Council YMCA, 1958-64, 67-69; chmn. 9th St. YMCA, Augusta, 1950-57; active United Coll. Fund, Cancer Dr., United Chest Fund, Boy Scouts Am. Del. Republican Nat. Conv., 1960. Bd. dirs. Augusta-Richmond County Library. Recipient Achievement award in pub. service Upsilon Sigma chpt. Omega Psi Phi, 1949; award of merit Georgia Dental Soc., 1961; 55 Year award Thankful Bapt. Ch., 1973. Fellow Am. Coll. Dentists, Royal Soc. Health, Acad. Gen. Dentistry, World Wide Acad. Scholars, Acad. Dentistry Internat.; mem. Nat. (life; past pres.; mem. exec. bd. 1940-52), Am. (life), Ga., (life, pres. 1940-41, 35-year service plaque) dental assns., Stoney-Med. and Dental Soc. (pres. 1961-63), Acad. Gen. Dentistry, John A. Andrew Clin. Soc. (pres. dental sect. 1947), Fedn. Dentaire Internationale, Omega Psi Phi (past basilius Psi Omega chpt. 1936-37, treas. 7th dist. 1943-75; recipient achievement award human relations Psi Omega chpt. 1963, 50 Year Pin), Sigma Pi Phi. Republican. Baptist (chmn. bd. trustees 1937-77, deacon 1961—). Clubs: Frontiers (Augusta, Ga.); Optimist Internat. Home: 2347 Fitten St Augusta GA 30904 Office: 1141 12th St Augusta GA 30901

CARTER, JAMES HARVEY, physician; b. Maysville, N.C., May 11, 1934; s. Thomas and Irene (Barber) C.; B.S., N.C. Central U., 1956; M.D., Howard U., 1966; m. Jettie Lucille Strayhorn, Oct. 21, 1957; 1 son, James Harvey. Intern, Walter Reed Army Hosp., Washington, 1966-67; resident in psychiatry Dorothea Dix Hosp., Raleigh, N.C., 1967-70; psychiat. research fellow Duke U. Med. Center, Durham, N.C., 1970-71, asso. prof. psychiatry, 1971—; mem. staff Duke Hosp., Lincoln Hosp., Durham. Mem. Senate Adv. Com. on Aging and Aged Blacks, 1973—. Served to capt. MC AUS, 1966-67, col. Res. Falk fellow Am. Psychiat. Assn., 1968-69; Macy Faculty fellow, 1971-74. Diplomate Am. Bd. Psychiatry and Neurology. Fellow Am. Psychiatric Assn. (observer, cons. 1974-76); mem. Nat. Med. Assn. Home: 3310 Pine Grove Rd Raleigh NC 27610 Office: Box 3106 NP Duke U Med Center Durham NC 27710

CARTER, JAMES JOHNSTON, lawyer; b. Samson, Ala., Apr. 13, 1913; s. Castilla L. and Mary Ann (Smith) C.; LL.B., Jones Law Sch., 1934, grad. law study, U. Mich., 1940, U. Va., 1941; m. Eva Jane Edwards, Sept. 6, 1947; children—Harold M., David E. (stepsons), James M., Kathy Jane. Admitted to Ala. bar, 1934; atty. Montgomery County Probate Ct., 1935-38; law clk., sec. U.S. Circuit Judge Leon McCord, Montgomery, Ala. and New Orleans, 1938-47; mem. firm Hill, Hill, Carter, Franco, Cole & Black, Montgomery, 1947—; apptd. spl. judge 15th Jud. Circuit Ala., 1949, 51, 55, 60, Judge Ala. Ct. of Judiciary, 1974—; pres. Jones Law Sch. 1963-72. Served from pvt. to 1st lt. AUS, 1943-46; spl. agt. criminal investigation div. S.W. Pacific, and pros. officer legal sect. H.Q. Supreme Comdr. for Allied Powers, Tokyo, Japan, 1945-46. Recipient Distinguished Service award U.S. Jr. C. of C. 1937. Mem. (hon.) Circuit Conf. U.S. Circuit and Dist. Judges, 5th Circuit. Fellow Am. Bar Found., Am. Coll. Trial Lawyers; mem. Jud. Conf. Ala., Ala. State Bar (bd. bar examiners 1969-77, pres. 1962-63), Am., Fed., Montgomery County (pres. 1957), Tenn. (hon.) bar assns., Ala. Law Inst. (mem. council 1970-75), Fedn. Ins. Counsel, Sigma Delta Kappa. Presbyn. (moderator E. Ala. Presbytery 1965). Clubs: Country, Beauvoir. Home: 2602 Wildwood Dr Montgomery AL 36111 Office: Hill Bldg PO Box 116 Montgomery AL 36101

CARTER, JIMMY. see Carter, James Earl, Jr.

CARTER, JOHN EDWARD, med. adminstr.; b. Galveston, Tex., Sept. 19, 1950; s. Arthur James and Edna Jane (Starnes) C.; B.B.A., Tex. Tech. U., 1973; postgrad. U. Mich., 1976; m. Linda Kaye Forest, Feb. 18, 1978. Asst. mgr. Flagship Hotel, Galveston, 1973-75; budget officer City of Galveston, 1975-77; dir. fin. Gulf Coast Mental Health-Mental Retardation, Galveston, 1977—. City councilman of Galveston, 1979—; mem. human devel. com. Nat. League of Cities, 1979—. Mem. Inst. Internal Auditors, Mcpl. Fin. Officers Assn., Am. Contract Bridge League (dir. unit 124 1976—), Tex. Mental Health-Mental Retardation Fiscal Officers. Home: 18 Back Bay Circle E Galveston TX 77551 Office: Gulf Coast Mental Health-Mental Retardation 507 Tremont St Galveston TX 77550

CARTER, JOHN MARSHALL, JR., stockbroker; b. Beckley, W.Va., Oct. 30, 1943; s. J. Marshall and Kushleen Anne (Maguire) C.; B.A., Duquesne U., 1966. Rep., Harris Upham & Co., Inc., Huntington, 1967-76, Smith Barney, Harris Upham, Inc., 1976; account exec. E.F. Hutton, Huntington, W.Va., 1976—. Republican. Roman Catholic. Clubs: Guyan Golf and Country, Serra (dist. gov.). Home: 1569 Upland Rd Huntington WV 25701 Office: Frederick Bldg Huntington WV 25701

CARTER, JOSEPH CARLYLE, JR., lawyer; b. Mayfield, Ky., June 3, 1927; s. Joseph Carlyle and Cynthia Elizabeth (Stokes) C.; B.A., U. Va., 1948, LL.B., 1951; m. Dianne C. Dinwiddie, July 15, 1949; children—Joseph Carlyle, Hugh D., William H., Henry S., Dianne C. Admitted to Va. bar, 1951, since practiced in Richmond; asso. firm Hunton & Williams, 1951-58, partner, 1958—, mgn. partner, 1972—; dir. Gen. Med. Corp.; Garfinckel, Brooks Bros., Miller & Rhoads, Inc. Active elder 2d Presbyn. Ch., Richmond, 1962—; chmn. Richmond Pub. Library Bd., 1967-77; trustee Colonial Williamsburg Found., 1977—, Med. Coll. Va. Found., 1976—, U. Va. Patent Found. and Steward Sch., 1975—. Recipient Algernon Sidney Sullivan award, 1948. Mem. Am., Va., Richmond bar assns., Am. Law Inst., Am. Judicature Soc., Newcomen Soc. Presbyterian. Clubs: Commonwealth, Country of Va., Downtown (Richmond); Union League (N.Y.C.). Home: 6102 St Andrew Ln Richmond VA 23226 Office: PO Box 1535 Richmond VA 23212

CARTER, JOSEPH COLEMAN, III, engr.; b. Woodford, Ky., Sept. 28, 1910; s. Joseph Coleman and Caroline Dupree (Steele) C.; B.S., U.S. Naval Acad., 1934; M.S., Columbia U., 1937; m. Mary Rodes Leaphart, July 1, 1938; children—Joseph, Mary, William, John. Mech. engr. Foster Wheeler Corp., N.Y.C., 1937-41; nuclear engr. Manhattan Project, 1941-47, Naval Reactor div. Oak Ridge Nat. Lab., 1947-50; sr. nuclear engr. Argonne (Ill.) Nat. Lab., 1950-75; prof. Coll. Engring., U. Ky., 1975—; cons. engr., 1975—; pres. Carter Farms, Inc. Registered profl. engr. Mem. Am. Nuclear Soc., ASME, Soc. Naval Architects. Contbr. articles to tech. jours. Patentee nuclear reactors. Home: 110 Morgan St Versailles KY 40383

CARTER, LAMORE JOSEPH, ednl. adminstr.; b. Carthage, Tex., Apr. 18, 1925; s. Peter and Nancy (Fite) C.; student Wiley Coll., 1946-47; A.B., Fisk U. 1950; M.S., U. Wis., 1952; Ph.D., State U. Iowa, 1958; postgrad. U. Chgo., summer 1954, U. Tex., summer 1966, Columbia U., summer 1967, Emory U. summer 1970, Harvard U., summer 1976; m. Lena Mae Jones, Aug. 18, 1957; children—Greta Lisa, Kris-Lana. Tchr. Union High Sch., Gallatin, Tenn., 1950-51; asso. prof. edn. and psychology, dir. spl. edn. center Grambling Coll. (La.), 1958-61, asso. dean of coll., 1971-76, v.p. acad. affairs, 1977—, prof. edn. and psychology, dir. spl. edn. center, 1961-66, adminstr. Instl. Research, 1966-69; dean of faculties Tex. So. U., Houston, 1970-71; research asst. State U. Iowa, 1956-58; licensed to practice psychology La. 1965—. Cons. Social Security Adminstrn. Bd. Hearings and Appeals, 1965—, U.S. Office Edn., 1967—, Peace Corps, 1970-72, Commn. Colls., So. Assn. Colls. and Schs., 1970—. Served with AUS, 1943-46. Decorated Bronze Service Star medal; Distinguished prof. psychology Morehouse Coll., Atlanta, 1970; Nat. Edn. Research fellow U.S. Office Edn., 1969-70; Am. Council Edn. fellow, 1976-77. Diplomate Am. Bd. Profl. Psychology. Mem. AAUP (chpt. pres. 1960-63), Am., Southwestern, La. psychol. assns., Nat. Council Univ. Research Adminstrs., Assn. for Instl. Research, Am. Ednl. Research Assn., Assn. for Higher Edn., Nat. Soc. for Study Edn., Am. Assn. on Mental Deficiency, N.Y. Acad. Sci., La. Assn. Mental Health, N.E.A., Council Exceptional Children, Internat. Platform Assn., Phi Beta Sigma, Phi Delta Kappa. Democrat. Methodist. Mason (32 deg.). Contbr. articles to profl. jours., monographs, books. Home: 110 Richmond Dr Grambling LA 71245

CARTER, LAURENCE STROUD, urban planner; b. Newtown, Pa., Nov. 2, 1928; s. Charles Franklin and Helen Eyre (Stroud) C.; B. Gen. Studies, U. Nebr., 1967; M. Tech. Internat. Devel., N.C. State U., 1974; m. Mary Margaret Steele, Aug. 10, 1963; children—Thomas P.G. Franklin, Corrine B., Laurence Stroud. Commd. 2d lt. U.S. Army, 1951, advanced through grades to lt. col., 1965; served with C.E.; ret., 1971; sr. planner Cumberland County Joint Planning Bd., Fayetteville, N.C., 1974—; adj. instr. polit. sci. Fayetteville State U., 1975-78. Mem. Am. Inst. Planners, Nat., N.C. recreation and parks socs. Democrat. Episcopalian. Home: 2718 Fordham Dr Fayetteville NC 28304 Office: 801 Arsenal Ave Fayetteville AR 28305

CARTER, MARY EDDIE, chemist; b. Americus, Ga.; d. Walker G. and Esther (Stewart) C.; B.A., LaGrange (Ga.) Coll., 1946; M.S., U. Fla., 1949; Ph.D., U. Edinburgh (Scotland), 1956. Instr. chemistry LaGrange Coll., 1946-47; chemist Callaway Mills, LaGrange, 1947-48; microscopist So. Research Inst., Birmingham, Ala., 1949-51; chemist West Point Mfg. Co., Shawmut, Ala., 1951-53; research asso. FMC Corp., Marcus Hook, Pa., 1956-71; lab. chief textiles and clothing lab. U.S. Dept. Agr., Knoxville, Tenn., 1971-73, dir. So. Regional Research Center, Sci. and Edn. Adminstrn., New Orleans, 1973—. Mem. Am. Chem. Soc., Am. Assn. Textile Chemists and Colorists, Inter-Soc. Color Council, Fiber Soc., Inst. Food Technologists, Am. Assn. Cereal Chemists, Sigma Xi. Contbr. articles to profl. jours. Patentee in field. Office: PO Box 19687 New Orleans LA 70179

CARTER, PRENTISS HENSON, JR., ins. co. exec.; b. Greensburg, La., May 29, 1931; s. Prentiss Henson and Rebecca (Matthews) C.; B.A., Southeastern La. U., 1952; M.Ed., La. State U., 1954; m. Sadie W. Carter, Apr. 5, 1969; children—Karlette, Kevin, Rhenette. Tchr. pub. schs., Greensburg, La., 1952-55, asst. prin. Greensburg, 1955-73; pres. Carter Ins. Agy., Greensburg, 1953—, Carter Real Estate Agy.; 1963—, Carter Mobile Homes Inc., Greensburg, La., 1970—; v.p. St. Helena Acceptance Corp., Greensburg, 1963—. Mem. La. Manufactured Housing Assn. (past pres., dir.). Democrat. Baptist. Contbr. articles to profl. jours. Home: Tall Timber Sub Greensburg LA 70441 Office: S Main St Greensburg LA 70441

CARTER, PURVIS MELVIN, historian, educator; b. Columbus, Tex., Nov. 22, 1925; s. Earnest and Daisy Sammie (Jones) C.; A.B., Tillotson Coll., 1948; M.A., Howard U., 1950; postgrad. U. Denver, 1954, 55; Ph.D., U. Colo., 1970; m. Gwendolyn M. Burns, June 1, 1956; children—Purvis Melvin, Frederick Earl, Burnest Denise. Tchr.-coach Harlingen (Tex.) Ind. Sch. Dist., 1950-55; instr. dept. history Prairie View A. and M. U., 1956-60, asst. prof., 1960-66, asso. prof., 1966—; cons., lectr. race relation activities; cons. Fgn. Relations series U.S., Office Historian, U.S. Dept. State; tchr. Bethlehem Study course Bethlehem Meth. Women Soc. Christian Service. Mem. Tex. Hist. Commn.; active Waller High Sch. Tex. Booster Club, Sam Houston Area council Boy Scouts Am. Served with USMCR, 1944-46. Recipient Social Sci. Found. scholarship, 1954; U. Colo. fellowships, 1968-70. Mem. So., Tex., Waller County hist. socs., Orgn. Am. Historians, Western History Assn., Assn. Study Negro Life and History, AAUP, Phi Epsilon chpt. Phi Alpha Theta. Methodist (lay leader 1970-72). Author: Congressional and Public Reaction to Wilson's Caribbean Policy 1913-1917, 1977; The Black Press and Its Counterparts: Reaction to the Application to Wilson's Caribbean Policy in Haiti; compiler index Jour. Negro History, Vols. 1-54; compiler The Negro in Periodical Literature 1970-72, 73-76, Jour. Negro History, 1978-79. Contbr. articles to profl. publs. Home: PO Box 2243 Prairie View TX 77445 Office: Dept History Prairie View A and M U Prairie View TX 77445

CARTER, REX LYLE, lawyer; b. Honea Path, S.C., June 20, 1925; s. D. B. and Eunice Y. C.; A.B., Erskine Coll., 1950, LL.D. (hon.), 1974; LL.B., U. S.C., 1952; LL.D. (hon.), The Citadel, 1977; m. Floride Gulledge; children—Lucy Coulter, Kimberly Lyle, Rex Lyle. Partner firm Carter, Philpot, Johnson and Smith, Greenville, S.C.; mem. S.C. Ho. of Reps., 1973—, also speaker. Served with AUS, 1943-46. Office: 123 Broadus Ave Greenville SC 29601

CARTER, RICHARD TRAVIS, investment exec.; b. Corpus Christi, Tex., Feb. 12, 1944; s. Samuel Tobe and Bobbie Jo (McLemore) C.; student S. Tex. Jr. Coll., 1962-64, U. Houston, 1964-66, Northwestern U., 1966-70; m. Judith Marie Franck, July 25, 1964; children—Melanie Judith, Richard Travis. Data processing specialist A. C. Nielsen/FBS Data Processing, Chgo., 1966-72; pvt. investment exec., Mt. Prospect, Ill., 1972-74; mem. floor broker Chgo. Mercantile Exchange, 1974-78; account exec. Bache Halsey Stuart Shields, Corpus Christi, 1978—. Mem. sch. bd. River Trails Dist., Mt. Prospect, 1977; cub scouts packmaster Boy Scouts Am., Corpus Christi, 1979—. Office: 105 Guaranty Bank Plaza Corpus Christi TX 78475

CARTER, ROBERT KENT, drilling co. exec.; b. Crystal City, Tex., June 19, 1944; s. Frank Ardary and Evelyn (Moore) C.; B.B.A., Tex. A. and I. U., 1967; postgrad. U. Tex., Austin, 1968-69; m. Dorothy Ann Fulkerson, Feb. 14, 1975; 1 dau., Ann Crockett. Tchr., Asherton (Tex.) High Sch., 1969-70; engr., IMC Drilling Co., Carrizo Springs, Tex., 1970-76; owner, Winter Garden Theater, Crystal City, Tex., 1972—; pres. Dimmit Drilling Mud Co., Carrizo Springs, 1976—; dir. 1st Nat. Bank Dimmit. Mem. Carrizo Springs Zoning Bd.; mem. Tax Grievance Com.; sr. warden Holy Trinity Episcopal Ch., also mem. bishops com. Served with USMC, 1962-63. Mem. Nat. Assn. Theater Owners, Carrizo Springs C. of C. (dir., 1st v.p.). Republican. Club: Lions (dir.). Home: 209 S 19th St Carrizo Springs TX 78834 Office: PO Box 829 Carrizo Springs TX 78834

CARTER, TIM LEE, physician, congressman; b. Tompkinsville, Ky., Sept. 2, 1910; s. James Clark and Idru (Tucker) C.; A.B., Western Ky. U., 1934; M.D., U. Tenn., 1937; m. Kathleen Bradshaw, Nov. 13, 1931. Gen. practice medicine, Tompkinsville, 1937—; mem. 89th to 96th congresses from 5th Ky. Dist., mem. interstate and fgn. commerce com., also com. on small bus.; dir. Deposit Bank of Monroe County, Tompkinsville. Mem. staff Monroe County War Meml. Hosp. Served to capt., inf. AUS, World War II. Decorated Combat Med. Badge, Bronze Star. Mem. AMA (Dr. Benjamin Rush Bicentennial award 1978), Ky. Med. Assn., Am., Ky. acads. gen. practice, Am. Legion, VFW, Alpha Omega Alpha. Republican. Mason (33 deg., Shriner). Home: 701 N Main St Tompkinsville KY 42167 Office: Rayburn Office Bldg Washington DC 20515

CARTER, TOM HOWELL, mortgage banker; b. Orange, Tex., Jan. 19, 1946; s. Abe Presley and Thomasine Mary (Howell) C.; B.B.A., Stephen F. Austin State U., 1968; m. Jenny Amelia Roberts, Sept. 4, 1971. With Gen. Motors Acceptance Corp., Lufkin, Tex., 1968-70; asst. br. mgr. Ben Gordon Fin., Houston, 1970-71, Avco Fin. Services, Houston, 1971-72; asst. v.p. in charge of tax dept. Lomas & Nettleton Co., Houston, 1972—. Chmn., Willowood Civic Assn., 1975—; chmn. fin. com. Terlingua Ranch Assn., 1976— vice chmn. Lomas & Nettleton Employees Credit Union, 1977—. Mem. Houston Mortgage Bankers Assn. (planning com. 1977—), Nat. Mortgage Bankers Assn., Houston Jaycees, Nat. Rifle Assn. Democrat. Methodist. Club: Terlingua Ranch Hunt. Home: 7807 Lawnwood Ln Houston TX 77086 Office: 201 Main St Houston TX 77001

CARTER, VERNON HENRY, JR., physician; b. Ft. Smith, Ark., May 22, 1929; s. Vernon H. and Helen Florence (Stewart) C.; M.D., U. Ark., 1959; m. Kathryn LaRa Brown, Dec. 12, 1964; children—Robert Stewart, Barbara Ann, Cynthia Louise, Kenneth Owen. Intern, St. Vincents Infirmary, Little Rock, 1959-60; resident in dermatology U. Ala. Med. Center, 1965-68, resident in pathology, 1966-68, instr. dermatology, 1968; practice medicine specializing in dermatology and cosmetic surgery, Boca Raton, Fla., 1968-76, Fayetteville, Ark., 1977-78, Rogers, Ark., 1978—; cons. Rogers Meml. Hosp., 1978—, Washington Regional Hosp., Fayetteville, 1977—, Springdale (Ark.) Meml. Hosp., 1978-79. Diplomate Am. Bd. Dermatology. Mem. Am. Acad. Dermatology, Am. Soc. of Dermatol. Surgery, N.Am. Clin. Dermatol. Soc., Ark. Dermatol. Soc., Benton County Med. Soc., Ark. Med. Assn., So. Med. Assn. Contbr. articles to med. jours. Home: PO Box 95 Pinnacle Star Route Elkins AR 72727

CARTER, VERTIE LEE, educator; b. Hope, Ark.; B.S. in Elementary Edn., Pine Bluff (Ark.) A.M. and N. Coll., 1949; M.S. in Secondary Edn., U. Ark., Fayetteville, 1954; Ed.D., N. Tex. State U., Denton, 1970; children—Larry Darnell, Michael Rovine. Elementary tchr., then high sch. English tchr. in Ark.; prof. edn., dir. elementary and secondary student tchrs., chmn. div. edn. Philander Smith Coll., Little Rock, 1964—; dean instrn. Ark. Baptist Coll., Little Rock, 1970-73; edn. cons. Ford Found. chmn. council Ark. Merit System, 1969, 72, 75. So. Edn. fellow, 1960; IBM Corp. fellow, 1969; grantee Ford Found., 1968; named Female Faculty Mem. of Year, Philander Smith Coll., 1970. Mem. AAUP, Ark. Assn. Tchr. Edn. (dir. 1973-75), Urban League, Alpha Chi, Phi Delta Kappa. Baptist. Club: Order Eastern Star. Author: How to Get a Career Job, 1979. Address: 1621 E 38th St Little Rock AR 72206

CARTER, VIRGINIA MILNER, financial mgmt. exec.; b. Atlanta, July 1, 1919; d. Willis Justus and Virginia Amanda (Cohen) Milner; B.A., Agnes Scott Coll., 1940; student Smith Coll., 1943, Radcliffe Coll., 1944, So. Methodist U., 1959-60, Wharton Bus. Sch., 1978; children—Alverson, Ida Richards (Mrs. Joseph N. Consola, Jr.), Virginia Seixas (Mrs. J.R. Cissell), Robert Milner. Dist. mgr. Prestige Silver Co., Atlanta, Charlotte, N.C. and Richmond, Va., 1947-58; agt.

Ga. Internat. Life Ins. Co. and predecessor co., Atlanta, 1959-61, agy. dir., 1961-69, asst. corp. sec., 1965-69; v.p. Employee Benefit Plans, Rome, Ga., 1969; acct. exec. Planned Equity, Atlanta, 1971; v.p. Profl. Investment Counselors, Atlanta, 1970; div. mgr. Waddell & Reed, Atlanta 1972-76; v.p. A.L. Williams & Assos., Tucker, Ga., 1976—, also dir.; dir. Mario's Ristorantes, Inc., Nelco Enterprises. Bd. dirs. Atlanta YWCA, 1966-69; trustee N. Atlanta Presbyterian Ch., 1978-79. Served to lt. USNR, 1942-45. Mem. AAUW, LWV, Bus. and Profl. Women, D.A.R., Internat. Assn. Fin. Planners, Nat. Assn. Life Underwriters, Cert. Fin. Planners. Republican. Clubs: Dunwoody Country, Horseshoe Bend Country, West Paces Racquet. Home: 1786 Trapnall Dr Dunwoody GA 30338 Office: 2260 Northlake Pkwy Suite 100 Tucker GA 30084

CARTER, WILLIAM BAILEY, advt. and mktg. co. exec.; b. Shreveport, La., Sept. 30, 1951; s. Edward Lynn and Sybil Rowena (Brown) C.; B.A., Northwestern State U., 1973; m. Catherine Murrell, Mar. 19, 1977; 1 son, W. Stinson. Account exec. Jack Hodges III Communications Inc., Shreveport, 1973-76, Glenn Mason & Assos., Shreveport, 1976-77; pres., owner Carter Advt. Inc., Shreveport, 1977—; instr. advt. Centenary Coll. La., Shreveport, since 1978—. Bd. dirs. Shreveport/Bossier Assn. Retarded Citizens. Mem. Shreveport Advt. Fedn., Am. Mktg. Assn., Bus./Profl. Advt. Assn., S.W. Assn. Advt. Agys. Democrat. Methodist. Office: Carter Advt Inc 1810 Elizabeth Ave Shreveport LA 71101

CARTER, WILLIAM CAUSEY, educator; b. Jesup, Ga., Mar. 28, 1941; s. William Lafayette and Sarah Elsie (Causey) C.; A.B., U. Ga., 1963, M.A., 1967; postgrad. (Fulbright scholar) U. Strasbourg (France), 1965-66; Ph.D., Ind. U., 1971; m. Lynn Marie Goudreau, Aug. 7, 1967; children—Josephine Marie, Sarah Lynn, Susanna Ellen. Asst. prof. French, Ohio U., Athens, 1971-75, dir. Ohio U.-Bowling Green U. Jr. Year Abroad Program, Tours, France, 1973-74; asst. prof. U. Ala., Birmingham, 1975-79, asso. prof., chmn. dept. fgn. langs. and lits., 1979—. Mem. Modern Lang. Assn., Soc. des Amis de Marcel Proust et de Combray, Phi Beta Kappa, Phi Kappa Phi. Author: Concordance to the Complete Works of Arthur Rimbaud, 1977. Home: 604 Warwick Rd Birmingham AL 35209 Office: Univ Coll 3 U Ala Birmingham AL 35205

CARTER, WILLIAM CHESTER, JR., legislator Tenn.; b. Chattanooga, Nov. 12, 1926; s. William C. and Marjorie Taylor (Slaughter) C.; student Tenn. Wesleyan Coll., 1946-47; B.B.A., U. Tenn., 1949; m. Carol Sharpe, Dec. 1, 1967; 1 son, William Chester, III. Mgr. Bill Brock for Congress campaign, 3d Dist. Tenn., 1964; mem. staff Congressman Bill Brock, 1965; dir. orgn. Tenn. Republican Party, exec. dir., 1967-68; mem. Tenn. Ho. of Reps., 1967-68, 73—, vice chmn. Ho. caucus, 1968—, minority whip, 1973-76, minority floor leader, 1979-80. Mem. Tenn. Fiscal Rev. Com., 1967-68. State pres. Tenn. Young Republican Fedn., 1956-57; del. Rep. Nat. Conv., 1976. Served with AC, USNR, 1944-45. Mem. Nat. Office Mgmt. Assn. (dir. 1960—), Am. Legion. Methodist. Club: Lions. Home: 24 Tennessee Ave Spring City TN 37381 Office: Post Office Bldg Dayton TN 37321

CARTER, WILLIAM JOSEPH, hosp. ofcl.; b. Dallas, Mar. 28, 1920; s. William Franklin and Annie Leah (Janes) C.; student Tex. A & M U., 1937-39, So. Methodist U., 1939-41; A.B. in Accounting, George Washington U., 1949, postgrad., 1949-51; m. Lucille Orr, June 6, 1954. Pub. accountant Luke B. Garvin & Co., Dallas, 1939-41; systems supr. Dallas County, Dallas, 1957-62; asst. comptroller Dallas County Hosp. Dist., 1962-67; comptroller Meml. Hosp. of Garland (Tex.), 1967-79, budget dir., 1979—. Served with USAAF, 1941-47, USAF, 1950-57; lt. col. Res. ret. C.P.A., Tex., D.C. Mem. Tex. Hosp. Assn., Tex. Assn. Hosp. Accountants, Hosp. Fin. Mgmt. Assn. Baptist. Home: 1506 Hiawatha Way Garland TX 75043 Office: 2300 Marie Curie St Garland TX 75042

CARTER, WILLIAM PRICE, JR., mech. equipment sales engr.; b. Bluefield, Va., Nov. 3, 1926; s. William Price and Lolita Sue (Peck) C.; B.S.M.E., Va. Poly. Inst., 1949; m. Phyllis Jean Alley, June 16, 1951; children—Leslie Jean, William David, Randolph Price. Safety engr. Liberty Mut. Ins. Co., Roanoke, Va., High Point, N.C. and Richmond, Va., 1949-54; sales engr. Tidewater Machinery & Machine Tool Co., Roanoke, 1954-78; partner Capital Equipment Sales, Inc., Salem, Va., 1978—. Served to 1st lt. arty. USAR, 1949-54. Recipient awards for engring. and sales performance. Mem. ASME, Soc. Mfg. Engrs. Republican. Presbyterian (elder, deacon). Club: Masons. Home: 2315 Circle Dr SW Roanoke VA 24018 Office: 1435 Lakeside Circle Suite 2A Salem VA 24153

CARTWRIGHT, CHARLES NELSON, lawyer; b. Ft. Worth, July 22, 1933; s. Charles L. and Mildred (Epperson) C.; student, U. Houston, 1952; B.A., U. Tex., 1956, J.D., 1960; m. Suzanne Oberwetter, Sept. 5, 1956; 1 son, Charles Rea. Admitted to Tex. bar, 1960; asst. city atty., Corpus Christi, Tex., 1960-63; asso. firm Utter & Chase, Corpus Christi, 1964-67, partner, 1967-73; mem. firm Howard, McDowell & Cartwright, Corpus Christi, 1973-76, Prichard, Peeler, Cartwright & Hall, Corpus Christi, 1976—; instr. real estate law Del Mar Coll., Corpus Christi, 1965-68, guest lectr., 1968-70. Mem. City Zoning and Planning Commn., Corpus Christi, 1970-76, chmn., 1973-76; bd. dirs. Municipal Legal Studies Center, research fellow, 1978—; mem. Southwestern Legal Found., Dallas, 1973—. Served to 2d lt. AUS, 1957. Mem. Am., Nueces County (pres. 1975-76) bar assns., State Bar Tex., Nueces County Trial Lawyers Assn. (dir. 1970-71), Am. Soc. Hosp. Attys., Corpus Christi C. of C., Leadership Corpus Christi. Clubs: Town, Masons, Kiwanis. Home: 934 Barracuda Corpus Christi TX 78411 Office: Guaranty Bank Plaza Corpus Christi TX 78475

CARUSO, SALVATORE ANTHONY, social worker, city ofcl.; b. New Orleans, Aug. 25, 1941; s. Frank Salvatore and Josephine Delores (Vitale) C.; B.A., La. State U., 1965; M.S.W. (Public Health scholar), Tulane U., 1971; m. Mary Martha Joachim, Jan. 21, 1967; children—Salvatore Anthony, Mary Martha. Employment interviewer La. Employment Service, New Orleans, 1965-67, employment technician, 1967-69; dist. exec. Boy Scouts Am., New Orleans, 1967; employment counselor Holman Vocat. Center, New Orleans, 1969-70; chief social worker, behavioral sci. coordinator children and youth project Driscoll Children's Hosp., Corpus Christi, Tex., 1972-73; exec. dir. Big Bros. of Greater New Orleans, 1973-75; faculty mem. La. State U. Med. Center, New Orleans, 1975—; pvt. practice social work, New Orleans and Slidell, La., 1973—. Bd. dirs. Youth Services, New Orleans, 1976-78; mem. Slidell City Council, 1978—, v.p., 1979-80; Named hon. dep. atty. gen. State of La., hon. dep. civil sheriff Orleans Parish; recipient Outstanding Service award Big Bros. Greater New Orleans, 1975; cert. social worker, La. Mem. Nat. Assn. Social Workers, Acad. Cert. Social Workers. Democrat. Roman Catholic. Home: 3842 Brookwood Dr Slidell LA 70458 Office: Bldg 138 1100 Florida Ave New Orleans LA 70119

CARUSO, VINCENT GEORGE, otolaryngologist; b. Bklyn., May 28, 1941; s. Antohny and Annette Caroline (Eyer) C.; B.S., Dickinson Coll., 1963; M.D., Jefferson Med. Coll., 1967; m. Marylynne Aldridge, July 10, 1965; children—Christine Elizabeth, Annette Elizabeth, Michelle Lynne. Intern, Geisinger Med. Center, Danville, Pa., 1967-68; resident in otolaryngology Thomas Jefferson U. Hosp., Phila., 1968-72; asst. prof. otolaryngology U. Tex. Med. Br., Galveston, 1974-77, clin. asst. prof., 1977—; pvt. practice medicine specializing in otolaryngology, Beaumont, Tex., 1977—; mem. staffs St. Elizabeth's, Bapt., Beaumont Med. Surg. hosps.; cons. otolaryngology USPHS Hosp., Galveston. Served to lt. comdr. USNR, 1972-74. Diplomate Am. Bd. Otolaryngology. Fellow Am. Acad. Ophthalmology and Otolaryngology, ACS, Am. Acad. Facial Plastic and Reconstructive Surgery; mem. Underwater Med. Soc., Soc. Univ. Otolaryngologists, Sigma Xi. Contbr. articles to med. jours., chpts. to books. Home: 48 Ave of Oaks Beaumont TX 77706 Office: 2780 Eastex Freeway Beaumont TX 77703

CARVAJAL, RICHARD DEANE, real estate appraiser; b. Mission, Tex., Nov. 4, 1933; s. Joseph Manuel and Marda Ree (Walker) C.; student U. Tex., Austin, 1952-53, Arlington State Coll., 1953, Hillsborough County Community Coll., 1975-76; m. Barbara E. Mott, May 9, 1959; children—Marta E., Teresa M. Enlisted in U.S. Marine Corps, 1953, advanced through grades to sgt., 1957, discharged, 1962; real estate salesman James D. Mott Realtors, Tampa, 1962-63, real estate salesman, appraiser, 1975—; sr. abstractor Office of Hillsborough County Property Appraiser, Tampa, Fla., 1963-71; adminstrv. asst. to pres., real estate salesman, appraiser ad valorem tax cons. Realty Exchange, Inc., Tampa, Fla., 1971-75. Asst. scout master Boy Scouts Am., 1974—; instr. State Hunting and Firearms Safety Course. Mem. Nat. Assn. Ind. Fee Appraisers (certified), Fla. Assn. Realtors, Nat. Rifle Assn. (life; pres. 1978-79), Suncoast Hunters Assn. Inc., Tampa Bd. Realtors, Tampa Bay Arms Collectors Assn. Democrat. Roman Catholic. Office: 5409 N Miami Ave Tampa FL 33604

CARVAJAL-ULLOA, HUGO FRANCISCO, physician; b. Cartago, Costa Rica, Jan. 9, 1941; s. Hugo Carvajal-Castro and Delia Ulloa; came to U.S., 1964; M.D., Nat. U. Mex., 1962; div.; children—Karina Kay, Hugo Francisco III. Intern, San Juan de Dios Hosp., U. Costa Rica Sch. Medicine, San Juan, 1963; pediatric intern Genesee Hosp., Rochester, N.Y., 1964-65; resident in pediatrics U. Tex. Med. Br., John Sealy Hosp., Galveston, 1965-67, fellow in pediatric nephrology and metabolism, 1967-69; asso. prof. pediatrics U. Tex. Med. Br., 1975—; chief pediatrics Shriner Burn Inst., 1975—; cons. in nephrology Brooke Army Med. Center, 1976—; pres. Pedi-Care Inc., Galveston, 1977—. Served as maj. U.S. Army, 1969-71. Am. Acad. Pediatrics fellow, 1966-67; Nat. Inst. Child Health and Human Devel. spl. research fellow, 1968-69. Fellow Am. Acad. Pediatrics; mem. Galveston Research Club, Soc. for Pediatric Research, So. Soc. for Pediatric Research, Am. Soc. Pediatric Nephrology, Tex. Diabetes Assn., Internat., Am. burn assns., AMA, Tex. Med. Assn., Galveston County Med. Soc., Am. Soc. Nephrology, Soc. for Exptl. Biology and Medicine, Sigma Xi. Club: Galveston Racquet. Contbr. articles to profl. jours. Home: 3205 Pine St Galveston TX 77550 Office: Shriners Burn Inst 610 Texas Ave Galveston TX 77550

CARVELL, RICHARD ALLEN, broadcaster, educator; b. Brinkley, Ark., Dec. 18, 1943; s. Robert and Charlotte Amelia (Allen) C.; student Hendrix Coll., 1962-64; B.S., Ark. State U., 1966; M.S., U. Ill., 1971; m. Linda Sue Collins, Sept. 3, 1977; children by previous marriage—Richard, David; 1 stepson, Dean. News dir. Sta. KASU, Jonesboro, Ark., 1971-72, mgr., 1976—; instr. radio-television Ark. State U., 1972-76. Mem. fin. com. Jonesboro United Way; mem. adminstrv. bd. Huntington Ave. United Meth. Ch. Served to capt. USAF, 1967-71. Decorated Bronze star. Mem. So. Ednl. Communications Assn. (sec. radio div.), Nat. Assn. Ednl. Broadcasters, Sigma Delta Chi, Alpha Epsilon Rho. Clubs: Lions (2d v.p.). Home: 4214 Brenda Dr Jonesboro AR 72401 Office: PO Box 4B State University AR 72467

CARY, BOYD BALFORD, physicist; b. Enid, Okla., Oct. 29, 1923; d. S. Boyd Balford and Margaret Grace (McLaughlin) C.; student Princeton, 1943-44; B.S., U. Md., 1947, M.S., 1948, Ph.D., 1954; m. Emily Marshall Pritchard, Sept. 28, 1957; children—Roger, Roland. Research asso. Inst. Fluid Dynamics and Applied Math., U. Md., 1954-56; specialist physicist Gen. Electric Co. Missile and Space Sci. Lab., King-of-Prussia, Pa., 1956-64; mem. sr. research staff Gen. Dynamics Electronics, Rochester, N.Y., 1964-71; lead scientist Tracor, Inc., East Orange, N.J., 1971-74; ind. physics cons., Short Hills, N.J., 1975-78; dir. research and devel. Parmetic Filter Corp., Livingston, N.J., 1976—; sr. analyst EDMAC Assos., Inc., Falls Church, Va., 1978—; sr. scientist EG&G, Riverdale, Md., 1979—. Served to lt. (j.g.) USNR, 1943-46. Named Inventor of Year, Gen. Dynamics Corp., 1968. Mem. Am. Phys. Soc., Sigma Xi, Phi Kappa Phi. Democrat. Episcopalian. Patentee in field. Address: 12013 Gary Hill Dr Colchester Hunt Fairfax VA 22030

CARY, TRACY GLEN, ins. co. exec.; b. Pampa, Tex., Apr. 29, 1929; s. J. Tracy and Leta Irene (Gillham) C.; student LaSalle Extension U. Sch. Law, 1948-52; B.B.A., Tex. Tech U., 1956; postgrad. So. Methodist U., 1960; m. Shirley Ann Hamlett, Aug. 24, 1957; children—Lance Hamleft, Shelley Ann. Mgmt. trainee Citizens Nat. Bank, Lubbock, Tex., 1956-57, new bus. devel. officer, 1957; agt. Gt. So. Life Ins. Co., 1957-58; v.p., dir. agys., exec. v.p., chmn. exec. com. Preferred Risk Life Assurance Co., 1958-62; pres. Glen Cary & Assos., 1966-67; asst. dir. agys., dir. agys., chief agy. officer Union Life Ins. Co., 1962-66; field v.p., v.p., v.p. and dir. gen. agys., v.p., dir. agys. and spl. markets, v.p., dir. agys. Gt. Am. Res. Ins. Co., Dallas, 1967-79; exec. v.p., mem. investment com., mem. exec. com. First Pyramid Life Ins., 1979—; chmn. bd. First Pyramid Mktg. Co., 1979—; dir. Computronics, Football coach YMCA, 1969-71, also bd. govs.; mem. Mayor's Com. Citizens Ballot, Lubbock, 1957; trustee Tex. Tech U. Loyalty Fund; bd. dirs. Tex. Tech U. Found., 1976—; mem. fin. adv. council Tex. Tech U., 1977—; mem. adv. com. Cotton Bowl, 1960-62. Served with AUS, 1948-52. Decorated Silver Star, Bronze Star, Army Commendation medal with pendant, Purple Heart, Combat Inf. badge, Legion of Merit; C.L.U. Mem. Nat. Assn. Life Underwriters, Sales and Mktg. Execs. Internat. (chmn. distinguished sales award com. 1961, dir. 1962), Internat. Platform Assn., Tex. Tech U. Ex-Students Assn. (nat. pres. 1975, pres. Old Red Club 1974—, internat. pres. 1975—), Phi Delta Theta (internat. gov., internat. pres.), Delta Sigma Pi, Pi Sigma Epsilon. Elk. Clubs: Brookhaven Country, Insurance (dir.) (Dallas). Office: PO Box 2941 Little Rock AR 72201

CASARIEGO, JORGE ISAAC, psychiatrist; b. Havana, Cuba, Apr. 25, 1945; came to U.S., 1960, naturalized, 1970; s. Isaac Alberto Casariego and Elena Mercedes Portela de Casariego; B.S., U. New Orleans, 1967; M.D., La. State U., 1969. Med. intern Jewish Hosp. Bklyn., N.Y.C., 1969-70; psychiat. resident N.Y. Med. Coll., N.Y.C., 1970-71, Walter Reed Army Hosp., Washington, 1971-73; chief psychiatry clinic U.S. Army Hosp., Heidelberg, W. Ger., 1973-75; clin. instr. dept. psychiatry Sch. Medicine U. Miami (Fla.), 1976-78, asst. prof. psychiatry, 1978—; practice medicine specializing in psychiatry, Miami, 1976—; med. dir. drug dependence outpatient unit VA Med. Center, Miami, 1976, dir. crisis intervention program, 1976—, attending psychiatrist, 1978—; attending psychiatrist Jackson Meml. Hosp., 1978—; cons. Cedars of Lebanon Hosp., Miami; invited examiner Am. Bd. Psychiatry. Served with M.C., U.S. Army, 1971-74. Diplomate Am. Bd. Psychiatry and Neurology. NIH Tropical Medicine fellow, U. Recife (Brazil), 1968; recipient Physician's award, AMA, 1977. Mem. Am. Psychiat. Assn. (observer-cons. Council on Internal Orgn.), S. Fla. Psychiat. Soc. (chmn. membership com., 1978-80), Dade County Med. Assn., Com. of 1000 (Washington), Aesculapians. Editor-in-chief The Tiger Rag, La. State U., 1968-69; reviewer, contbr. articles Am. Jour. Psychiatry; contbr. articles to profl. publs. Home: 1225 La Mancha Ave Coral Gables FL 33134 Office: Dept Psychiatry D-29 U Miami Sch Medicine PO Box 016960 Miami FL 33101

CASCIANO, DANIEL ANTHONY, biologist; b. Buffalo, Mar. 1, 1941; s. Frederick James and Rose Ann C.; B.S., Canisius Coll., 1962; Ph.D., Purdue U., 1971; m. Gertrude Ann Tara, Aug. 22, 1964; children—Anne, Jonathan. Research asst. Roswell Park Meml. Inst., Buffalo, 1963-64; research asst. dept. biol. scis. Purdue U., Lafayette, Ind., 1965-66, teaching asst., 1969, research trainee, 1966-71; postdoctoral investigator U. Tenn., Oak Ridge Nat. Labs., 1971-73; research biologist Nat. Center Toxicol. Research, Jefferson, Ark., 1973—, program dir. div. mutagenesis research, 1976-78, dir. div. mutagenesis research, 1978—; asst. prof. U. Ark. Med. Scis., Little Rock, 1974— trainee NIH, 1966-71. Mem. Tissue Culture Assn., Environ. Mutagen Soc., AAAS, Beta Beta Beta. Contbr. articles to profl. jours. Home: 1921 Romine Rd Little Rock AR 72205 Office: Nat Center Toxicological Research Jefferson AR 72099

CASDORPH, PAUL DOUGLAS, educator; b. Charleston, W.Va., Sept. 5, 1932; s. Newell Douglas and Virginia Elizabeth (Miller) C.; A.A., Victoria Coll., 1958; B.A., U. Tex., 1960, M.A., 1961; Ed.D., U. Ky., 1970; m. Patricia Ilene Barker, July 22, 1972. Social worker Tex. Dept. Pub. Welfare, 1962-66; instr. history W.Va., State Coll., Institute, 1966-71 asst. prof., 1971-72, asso. prof., 1972-77, prof., 1977—. Mem. Orgn. Am. Historians, Am. Radio Relay League, Tex., So. hist. assns., W.Va. History Assn., Phi Theta Kappa, Phi Delta Kappa, Phi Alpha Theta. Republican. Presbyn. Author: A History of the Republican Party in Texas 1865-1965, 1966; Youth Education in West Virginia: A Bicentennial View, 1975. Contbr. articles to profl. jours. Home: 1413 Alexandria Pl Charleston WV 25314 Office: WVa State Coll Institute WV 25112

CASE, CAROL BAKER, photographer, journalist; b. Pa., July 10, 1940; d. John and Mildred R. Baker; student Stevens Coll., Wilkes Coll., N.C. Tech. Sch.; m. Larry Case (dec. Sept. 1979); children—Suzette, Lawrence. Successively society editor Cape Cod Illustrated, Hyannis, Mass.; pres. N.Mex. Illustrated, Taos; v.p. Coastal Illustrated, Sea Island, Ga.; also pres., photographer Larry Case Photography Sea Island; lectr., photography instr.; resident Mt. Crested Butte Resort, Crested Butte, Colo. Mem. Profl. Photographers Am., Ga. Profl. Photographers Assn., Photo Mktg. Assn., Am. Soc. Profl. and Exec. Women. Home: 102 Cater St Saint Simons Island GA 31522 also Taos Ski Valley Taos NM 87571 Office: 4th and Hudson Pl Sea Island GA 31561

CASE, GERALD CLARENCE, ins. co. exec.; b. Peoria, Ill., Aug. 10, 1937; s. Clarence A. and Edna B. Case; B.S. in Polit. Sci. and Mktg., U. Mo., 1959; m. Janet Marie Dunagan, Nov. 28, 1959; children—Kimberly Marie, Gregory Gerald, Bradley Gerald. Area sales rep. Proctor & Gamble Distbg. Co., Dade and Monroe counties, Fla., 1959-62, office head salesman, 1962-64, unit mgr. for Pitts. and Charleston, W.Va., 1964-65; exec. v.p. Scope Co., Miami, Fla., 1965-68; spl. agt. Mass. Mut., Fla., 1968-71, asst. to gen. agt. Miami area, 1971-72; asso. Hale & Jones, Inc., Miami, 1970-72; agy. mgr. Bankers Life Co. of Des Moines, Miami, 1972—; dir. Community Bank of Homestead, chmn. exec. com., 1975-78. Mem. Dade County (Fla.) Transp. Adv. Com., 1974-75; chmn. com. fin. Silver Palm Meth. Ch., 1974-78. Served with U.S. Army, 1956-58. Mem. Miami Assn. Life Underwriters (v.p. 1973-78), Gen. Agts. and Mgrs. Miami (dir. 1973—, pres. 1979), Greater Homestead Motel Assn. (pres. 1970-72), Redlands Citizen Assn., Homestead South Dade C. of C. (dir. 1974-78), Phi Delta Theta. Democrat. Clubs: Elks, Rotary (pres. 1976-78) (Homestead); Miami Dolphin Booster; Redlands Golf and Country. Home: 14925 SW 232d St Goulds FL 33170 Office: 10621 SW 88th St Miami FL 33176

CASE, JACK WILLIAM, govt. ofcl.; b. Muskogee, Okla., Apr. 5, 1931; s. John Wardrobe and Delia Belle (Baker) C.; A.A., Central Christian Coll., 1952; B.S. in B.A., Harding Coll., 1960; student Tulsa U., 1955-58; m. Janece Morgan, Nov. 15, 1952; children—Michael Lawrence, Susan Ellayne Case Armstrong. Security patrolman E.I. Du Pont De Nemours & Co., Inc., Aiken, S.C., 1953; revenue officer IRS, Little Rock, 1960-67, personnel mgmt. specialist, 1967-77; personnel officer VA Regional Office, Little Rock, 1977—; classroom instr. IRS, 1970-76; chmn. Govt. Recruiting Council Ark., 1980. Mem. adv. council Central Ark. Consortium, 1978-79, Central Ark. Pvt. Industry Council, 1979—; mem. admissions com. Ark. Enterprises for the Blind, 1968—. Served with U.S. Army, 1953-55. Recipient Spl. Achievement award IRS, 1970; Outstanding Performance award VA Regional Office, 1979. Mem. Ch. of Christ. Home: 8201 Alvin Ln Little Rock AR 72207 Office: 1200 W Third St Little Rock AR 72201

CASELLA, SANTO, urban planner; b. N.Y.C., Nov. 5, 1944; s. James Anthony and Marie (Geraci) C.; B.A., L.I. U., 1967; M. Urban Planning, Hunter Coll., 1973; m. Laura Ann Hicks, July 12, 1969; children—Chloe Jean, Sam. Social worker N.Y. Dept. Social Services, 1968-71; urban planner Charlotte Mecklenburg Planning Commn. (N.C.), 1973-75, City of Clearwater (Fla.), 1975-77; exec. dir. Clearwater Downtown Devel. Bd., 1977—. Regents scholar, 1961-65. Mem. Am. Inst. Cert. Planners, Internat. Downtown Execs. Assn., Am. Planning Assn., Urban Land Inst. Home: 310 Overbrook Dr Belleair FL 33516 Office: 600 Cleveland St Suite 1100 Clearwater FL 33515

CASELLAS, ELIZABETH REED (BRANNON), library adminstr., educator, writer; b. New Orleans, Jan. 7, 1925; d. Dallie Reed and Elizabeth (Robinson) Brannon; B.M., Chgo. Mus. Coll., 1948; M.A., Columbia U., 1949, Profl. Diploma, 1950; student U. Paris (Sorbonne), 1953-54; M.S., Columbia U. Sch. Library Service, 1964; m. Joaquin Casellas, Mar. 16, 1954. Instr., Valparaiso U., 1946-47; asst. librarian J. M. Mathes, Inc., N.Y.C., 1955-57; librarian Communications Counselors, Inc., N.Y.C., 1957-59; head librarian, mgmt. cons. Cresap, McCormick & Paget, Inc., N.Y.C., 1959-60; head librarian, marketing mgmt. cons. Stewart, Dougall & Assos., N.Y.C., 1960-65; asst. prof. Grad. Sch. Library Studies, bibliographer in bus. U. Hawaii, Honolulu, 1965-66; head bus., sci. and tech. dept. Orlando (Fla.) Pub. Library, 1966-69; asso. prof., dir. library Grad. Sch. Bus. Adminstrn., Tulane U., New Orleans, 1969—; writer, 1977—. Recipient Composition award for Piano Sonata, No. 2, Phi Mu Gamma, 1948. Mem. Spl. Libraries Assn. (pres. La. chpt. 1974-75, founder Fla. chpt. 1968, past lectr. N.Y. group Advt. div., rep. McKinsey Found. mgmt. book awards com.), A.L.A., La. library assns., Am. Assn. U. Women, Beta Gamma Sigma, Kappa Delta Pi, Phi Mu Gamma. Republican. Episcopalian. Author: Guide to Basic Information Sources in Business Administration, 1974. Contbr. articles on bus. librarianship and classification to profl. jours. Home: 2442 Dauphine St New Orleans LA 70117

CASEY, ALBERT E(UGENE), pathologist; b. N.Y.C., Mar. 13, 1903; s. Eugene Joseph and Anna Alma (Powell) C.; A.B., Spring Hill Coll., 1922; M.D., St. Louis U., 1927; m. Bourdon Eason Veazey, Apr.

19, 1928; children—Anna Elizabeth Casey Kent, Bourdon Irene Casey Payne, Albert Eugene; m. 2d, Joanne Gunn, Nov. 8, 1952; 1 son, Paul Travis. Intern, St. Louis U. Hosp., 1926-27; asst. anatomy St. Louis U., 1924-27, asso. prof. pathology, 1936-38; asst. and asso. in pathology and bacteriology Rockefeller Inst., 1927-34; asso. prof. pathology U. Va., 1934-36; sr. asst. prof. pathology and bacteriology La. State U., 1938-42; sr. vis. pathologist Charity Hosp. of La., New Orleans, 1938-42; pathologist, dir. labs. Birmingham Bapt. Hosps., 1942-72, pres. staff, 1956, chmn. exec. com., 1958; prof. pathology U. Ala., 1953—, dir. Meml. Inst. Pathology, 1961—; pathologist Eye Found. Hosp., 1972-79, hon., 1979; cons. pathologist Children's Hosp., 1943-72, hon., 1972—, pres. staff, 1947; pathologist Univ. Hosp., Hillcrest Hosp.; pathologist to coroner, 1942-67, Domestic Relations Ct., 1942-72; field epidemiologist Nat. Found. Infantile Paralysis, 1941-42, 45-50, mem. sci. adv. com., 1948-51. Bd. dirs. Blue Cross, Blue Shield of Ala., 1957-60. Diplomate Am. Bd. Pathology. Mem. Coll. Am. Pathologists (chmn. S.E. regional com. 1954-57), Ala. Assn. Pathologists (pres. 1947), Soc. Exptl. Biology and Medicine (council 1941-43), Am. Soc. Clin. Pathology, (counselor 1947-50), Am. Soc. Exptl. Pathology, Am. Inst. Chemists, Internat. Acad. Pathology, Internat. Cancer Congress, Am. Soc. Phys. Anthropology, Harvey Soc. Am. Assn. Anatomists, Am. Assn. Cancer Research, N.Y. Acad. Sci., AAAS, Am. Assn. Blood Banks (Ala. rep. 1959-67), Am. Assn. Pathology and Bacteriology, Am. Pub. Health Assn., Am., So. (chmn. sect. pathology 1955-56) med. assns., Miss. Geneal. and Hist. Soc. (hon.), Am. Irish Hist. Soc. (v.p., life member), Sigma Xi, Phi Beta Pi, Alpha Omega Alpha. Democrat. Baptist. Clubs: Masons, Shriners, Clin., The Club, Exchange (Birmingham). Author: (with others) Amite County, Miss. History, 4 vols., 1948, 52, 57, 68; Slieve Lougher and Upper Blackwater in Ireland, 15 vols., 1954, 58, 59, 60, 62, 63, 64, 65, 66, 67, 68, 70, 72; Encyclopedia of Pathologists Southern U.S.A., 1963; Host Reaction and Cancer, 1962; Compilation of Common Physical Measurements on Adult Males of Various Races, 1969; articles on enhancement of malignancy, specific mammalian tumor antigens, poliomyelitis, encephalitis, metabolic profile, sta-tens, med. edn., anthropology in profl. jours.; editor Jefferson County Med. Soc. Bull., 1956-59. Home: 2011 Southwood Rd Birmingham AL 35216 Office: 1025 18th St S Birmingham AL 35205

CASEY, CHRISTOPHER ALAN, communications co. exec.; b. Whittier, Calif., Apr. 11, 1955; s. Dennis Roger and Ingrid (Krumm) C.; student Ithaca Coll., 1973-74. Audio visual technician Gen. Tel. & Electronics, Stamford, Conn., 1973-74; tech. dir. Spotlight Presents Inc., N.Y.C., 1974-76; dir. prodn. Greyhound AudioVisual, Atlanta, 1976; dir. prodn. TCG Corp., Atlanta, 1977; pres. Communication Techniques, Inc., Atlanta, 1977—; dir. prodn., corp. sec. 20/20 Media Communications, Inc., Atlanta, 1978—. Mem. Assn. Multi Image. Office: 3355 Lenox Rd Suite 1160 Atlanta GA 30326

CASEY, JACK MOORE, pvt. social club owner; b. Boston, June 22, 1937; s. John and Christine (Moore) C.; student Boston Coll., 1959. Served as enlisted man U.S. Marine Corps, 1953-61; gen. mgr. Cape Resort Hotels, Inc., Cape Cod, Mass., 1961-66; resident mgr. Surf Club, Miami Beach, Fla., 1966-68; owner, operator Brendans Restaurant, N.Y.C., 1968-71; regional dir. sales Restaurant Assn. Industries, Inc., Miami, Fla., 1971-79; dir. sales and mktg. Menage, Miami, 1979-80; pres. Biltmore Mgmt. Corp., Inc., Coral Gables, Fla., 1980—. Founder, co-chmn. St. Patrick's Day Parade Com., Miami; vice chmn. U.S. Marine Corps Com. of South Fla. Recipient cert. of appreciation U.S. Marine Corps, 1976, 77, 78, 79; award Am. Soc. Public Adminstrn., 1974; award Boy Scouts Am., 1977; nat. award Dept. Alcohol, Tobacco and Firearms, 1975; award Va. Crime Commn., 1976; Internat. Toastmasters award, 1976. Mem. Nat. Restaurant Assn., Emerald Soc. (pres. S. Fla.), Marine Corps Commn. S. Fla., Marine Corps Assn., Marine Corps League (sr. vice comdr.), Miami Police Benevolent Assn. (hon. life). Democrat. Roman Catholic. Clubs: Marina Bay, Top Draw, Racquet (Miami Beach); Menage (Miami); Marines Memorial (San Francisco). Home: 3195 Foxcroft Rd Miramar FL 33025 Office: The Biltmore 1208 Anastasia Ave Coral Gables FL 33134

CASEY, MARY FRANCES YODER (MRS. TIMOTHY DENNIS CASEY), actress; b. South Bend, Ind., Nov. 14, 1944; foster dau. Gladys Pearl Yoder; grad. with honors (Greenleaf scholar) Interlochen (Mich.) Nat. Music Camp; B.S., Western Mich. U., 1967; M.A., S.W. Mo. State U., 1971; m. Timothy Dennis Casey, Sept. 16, 1972; 1 son, Matthew Gerald. Profl. actress appearing as Marifran Casey; appeared in Harvey, Kansas City; nat. tour as Ado Annie in Oklahoma; appeared in Music Man, South Pacific, Damn Yankees, Sunday in New York, Sunshine Boys, Accommodations, Oklahoma, Fiddler on Roof, Sound of Music; mus. dir. Asolo State Theatre prodn. Oh, Coward; participant USO tour to Orient, 1968; tchr. music Northside Jr. High Sch., Elkhart, Ind., 1967-68; publicity, box office theatre mgr. S.W. Mo. State U., 1969-71; with Alley Theatre Co., Houston, 1971; women's editor, entertainment editor, reviewer Naples (Fla.) Daily News, 1972-73; 1st v.p., treas. Sunshine Promotions, Inc., Sarasota, Fla.; guest musical condr. Sarasota Players prodn. Applause, 1978; dir. music Out-of-Door Acad., 1979-80. Mem. fine arts com. Edison Community Coll., Ft. Myers, Fla., 1972-73; organist, choir dir. St. Mary's Star of the Sea Ch., 1978-79. Mem. Actors' Equity Assn., Theta Alpha Phi, Alpha Psi Omega. Roman Catholic. Home: 1002 S Orange Ave PO Box 3544 Sarasota FL 33578

CASEY, OFFA LUNSFORD, state legislator, lawyer; b. Mobile, Ala., Apr. 22, 1912; s. Benjamin Dudley and Ethel Lou (Shivers) C.; student Jones County Jr. Coll., 1929-30; B.A., U. Miss., 1935, J.D., 1936; m. Muriel Elizabeth Terry, Nov. 21, 1936 (dec. Feb. 1973); children—Thomas Lunsford, Michael Reynolds; m. 2d, Naomi Knight, Nov. 22, 1973. Admitted to Miss. bar, 1936; pvt. practice, Laurel, 1936-38, 46-48; atty. lands div. Dept. Justice, Washington, 1938-40; asst. to gen. counsel Adminstr. of Export Control, Washington, 1940-42; judge City Ct., Laurel, 1947-48; asst. U.S. dist. atty. So. Dist. Miss., 1949; judge county and youth cts., Laurel, 1951-55; circuit ct. judge 18th Dist., Laurel, 1955-70; mem. firm Maxey, Clark & Casey, 1971-76, Casey & Casey, 1977-78; mem. Miss. Ho. of Reps., 1980—; mem. adv. com. on rules of civil practice and procedure Miss. Supreme Ct., 1975—. Pres. Miss. Assn. Crime and Delinquency, 1953-55; chmn. Easter Seal Soc., Jones County, 1959-61. Served from 2d lt. to lt. col. AUS, 1942-46, PTO; now col. Res. ret. Mem. Miss., Jones County (v.p. 1973-74, pres. 1974-75) bar assns., Miss. State Bar (jud. adminstrn. com. chmn. 1969-70, commr. 1971-72, bar com. 1971-72, 74-75), Miss. Circuit Judges Assn. (chmn. 1969-70), Jones County Bapt. Assn. (moderator 1957-58), Pi Kappa Phi, Phi Alpha Delta. Democrat. Baptist. Mason, K.P., Rotarian (pres. Laurel 1967-68). Home: 1006 Broadway Laurel MS 39440 Office: PO Box 185 Laurel MS 39440

CASEY, STEPHEN HUNTLEY, ins. agy. exec.; b. Anderson, S.C., Feb. 20, 1939; s. David Gordon and Lucy Marguerite (Leverett) C.; A.B., Duke, 1960; M.B.A., So. Meth. U., 1968; m. Terry Pearlstone, Jan. 31, 1961; children—Karen Elizabeth, Stephen Huntley. Partner, Pearlstone-Casey Agy., Inc., Dallas, 1964-70, pres., 1970—; dir. Tex. Commerce Bank, Dallas. Pres. 500, Inc., 1971-72; bd. dirs. Dallas Civic Opera Guild, 1968-69, Dallas Civic Opera, 1972-73, Dallas Arts Found., Inc., 1972—, Theatre Three, 1975-79, Dallas Theatre Center, 1979—; trustee Dallas Community Chest Trust Fund; bd. dirs. U.S.A. Film Festival, 1972—, pres., 1975-76, chmn., 1976-77. Served with USNR, 1960-64. Mem. Nat., Tex., Dallas (dir., chmn. bus. practices com., sec.-treas. 1979-80, Life Underwriter of Yr. 1978) assns. life underwriters, Am. Soc. C.L.U.'s (dir. Dallas chpt. 1971-72, sec.-treas. 1972-73, pres. 1974-75, nat. dir. 1977—, now also nat. v.p.), Assn. Advanced Life Underwriting, Dallas Assn. Ins. Agts., Dallas Estate Council (trustee 1977-79), Tex. Leaders Roundtable, Dallas Jr. C. of C. (dir. 1967), Dallas Duke U. Alumni Assn. (pres. 1971-79). Club: City. Home: 4211 Arcady St Dallas TX 75205 Office: 3624 Oaklawn #110 Dallas TX 75219

CASH, DEWEY BYRON, educator; b. Wadley, Ala., Dec. 22, 1930; s. Joe Jackson and Iola (McCormick) C.; Asso. Sci., So. Union Coll., 1950; B.S., Auburn U., 1955, M.Ed., 1957, M.S., 1964; m. Louise Hammock, Dec. 18, 1954; children—Paul, Sally. Tchr. pub. high sch., Fla., 1955-56, Ga., 1956-58; asso. prof. math. Columbus (Ga.) Coll., 1958-77, prof., 1977—. Served with AUS, 1951-54. Mem. Math. Assn. Am. Home: 3317 Mustang Dr Columbus GA 31904

CASH, JAMES TIMOTHY, state govt. social worker; b. Spartanburg, S.C., Jan. 11, 1949; s. James William and Margaret Ann (Martin) C.; B.A. cum laude, Wofford Coll., 1971; cert. addiction studies U. S.C., 1974, M.S.W., 1976; cert. mgmt. objectives Greenville Tech. Coll., 1977. Caseworker, Spartanburg County (S.C.) Dept. Social Services, 1972-75; caseworker II Sumter County (S.C.) Dept. Social Services, 1975-76; program coordinator Medicaid div. S.C. State Dept. Social Services, Columbia, 1976-77, state program dir. for adult protective services, 1977—. Recipient God and Country award S.C. Alumni chpt. Boy Scouts Am., 1967; cert. appreciation Dentsville Optimist Club, 1979; named an Outstanding Young Man in S.C., U.S. Jr. C. of C., 1979. Mem. Nat. Assn. Social Workers (sec. S.C. chpt. 1977-79), Am. Public Welfare Assn., S.C. State Employees Assn., S.C. Mental Health Assn., Palmetto Alumni Assn. Schs. of Addiction Studies, Phi Beta Kappa. Home: Apt 210 Granby Oaks West Columbia SC 29169 Office: SC State Dept Social Services PO Box 1520 Columbia SC 29202

CASHMAN, CHAPPELL FRANCIS, stock broker; b. Joyce, La., Jan. 16, 1923; s. Robert and Zelma Anna (Chappell) C.; student Denison U., 1942-43, 45-48, U. Houston, 1970-71; m. Colleen Belle Sherman, children—Sally Lu, Cathy Ann, Laurie Colleen. Accountant, Rohm & Haas Co., Deer Park, Tex., 1948-54; pres. Ark. Land Mgmt. Inc., Houston, 1969—, also Little Rock; pres. Gas Products Inc., Houston, 1969-70; asst. v.p., co-mgr. Dominick & Dominick Inc., Houston br. office, 1970-72; v.p. sales, investment exec. Underwood, Neuhaus & Co. Inc., Houston, 1972—. Mem. City Charter Study Com. City of Pasadena (Tex.), 1970; precinct chmn., mem. finance com. Republican party Harris County, 1973; chmn. bd. stewards Sunset United Meth. Ch., Pasadena, 1976—. Served with U.S. Army, 1942-46; ETO. Decorated Combat Inf. Badge. Recipient Citizenship award Am. Legion, Chgo., 1940, Pres.'s award Putnam Orgn., 1976. Mem. Houston Security Dealers Assn., Tex. Municipal League, Securities Industry Assn., Am. Assn. Mgmt., Houston Rose Soc., Am. Rose Soc., Phi Gamma Delta. Clubs: Houston Stock and Bond, Bayshore Country, Rotary, SAR, Am. Legion. Home: 2514 San Jacinto St Pasadena TX 77502 Office: 724 Travis St Houston TX 77002

CASHMAN, EUGENE K., JR., hosp. adminstr.; b. Savannah, Ga., Nov. 12, 1941; s. Eugene K. and Isobel Grace (McRaw) C.; B.S., Auburn U., 1964; M.S., Am. U., 1974; m. Kathleen Mary Gilmore, Dec. 19, 1964; children—Elizabeth McRae, Catherine Lynn, Eugene K., III. Mem. staff Computer Sci. Center, Auburn U., 1964-66; computer analyst Office of Surgeon Gen., Dept. Army, 1966-69; dir. mgmt. info. systems Children's Hosp. Nat. Med. Center, Washington, 1969-73, asst. adminstr., 1973-75, asso. adminstr., 1975-77; pres. LeBonheur Children's Hosp., Memphis, 1977—; instr. No. Va. Community Coll., Annandale, 1974-77. Served to capt. U.S. Army, 1966-69. Mem. Am. Coll. Hosp. Adminstrs., Hosp. Mgmt. Systems Soc., Am. Hosp. Assn. Club: Kiwanis. Home: 160 Lombardy Rd Memphis TN 38111 Office: 848 Adams Ave Memphis TN 38103

CASHWELL, PAMELA KLUTTZ, food service exec.; b. Albemarle, N.C., Apr. 15, 1948; d. Warren Keith and Verna Bost Kluttz; B.S.H.E., U. N.C., Greensboro, 1970; m. John C. Cashwell, July 7, 1977. Dietetic intern Duke Med. Center, Durham, N.C., 1971; clin. dietitian Wake County Med. Center, Raleigh, N.C., 1971-74, asst. food service dir., 1974-75, asso. food service dir., 1975-79, food service dir., 1979—; staff dietitian Rex Hosp., Raleigh, 1974. Recipient Mead Johnson award, 1971; Danforth scholar, 1968. Mem. Am. Soc. Hosp. Food Service Adminstrs. (dir. N.C.), Am. Dietetic Assn., N.C. Dietetic Assn., Raleigh Dietetic Assn., Beta Sigma Phi, Alpha Zeta, Eta Chi, Omicron Nu. Democrat. Lutheran. Home: Route 2 137 Winchester Dr Wendell NC 27591 Office: 3000 New Bern Ave Raleigh NC 27610

CASKEY, JEFFERSON DIXON, librarian, educator; b. Lancaster, S.C., July 31, 1922; s. John Lathan and Lessie (Helms) C.; A.B., Erskine Coll., 1948; M.S.L.S., Syracuse U., 1953; M.A., U. Houston, 1966, Ed.D., 1972; m. Louise Huffaker, June 14, 1957; children—Nora Constance, Gretchen Louise. Tchr. English pub. schs., S.C., 1948-52; catalog librarian, asst. reference librarian Auburn U., 1953-54; asso. librarian, asst. prof. library sci. Shepherd Coll., 1954-56; head librarian, asso. prof. Pfeiffer Coll., 1956-60; head librarian, asst. prof. library sci. U. Ark., Little Rock, 1960-63; head librarian, asso. prof. Houston Baptist U., 1963-70, asso. prof., dir. library sci. program Tex. A. and I. U., 1970-74; asso. prof. library sci. Western Ky. U., Bowling Green, 1974-77, prof., 1977—. Served with USN, 1943-45. Mem. ALA, Ky. Library Assn., Nat. Council Tchrs. English, Ky. Sch. Media Assn., Southeastern Library Assn., Ch. and Synagogue Library Assn., Phi Delta Kappa. Democrat. Baptist. Editor: Samuel Taylor Coleridge: A Selective Bibliography of Criticism, 1935-77, 1978; contbr. articles to profl. jours., children's mags. Home: 1016 Meadowwood Bowling Green KY 42101 Office: Dept Library Sci Western Ky U Bowling Green KY 42101

CASOLA, THOMAS, mgmt. info. systems specialist; b. Cuba, Dec. 21, 1948; s. Eulogio R. and Maria V. C.; diploma Fort Lauderdale Tech. Coll., 1969; M.I.S. certificate, Fla. Internat. U., 1973; m. Donna Lynn Brown, Dec. 17, 1968. Computer operator XIOX Internat., Inc., 1969-70; sr. computer operator SPS, Inc., 1970-71; data processing mgr. August Bros. Bakery, 1971-72; programmer analyst Royal Palm Beach Colony, Inc., 1973-74; systems analyst City of Miami Beach (Fla.), 1974-78, dir. mgmt. info. systems, 1978—. Mem. Urban and Regional Info. Systems Assn. Office: 1700 Convention Center Dr Miami Beach FL 33139

CASON, CLEO STARGEL (MRS. CHARLES MONROE CASON, JR.), librarian; b. Dahlonega, Ga., June 24, 1910; d. John Jones and Georgia (Jones) Stargel; student North Ga. Coll., 1926-28; LL.B., Am. Sch. Law, 1949; postgrad. U. Ala., 1951-53, U. Chgo., 1954-55; m. Charles Monroe Cason, Jr., Mar. 8, 1930; 1 son, Charles Monroe III. Adminstrv. asst. to comdr. Redstone Arsenal, Ala., 1944-47, chief office service br., 1947-49, tech. librarian, 1949-74; chief librarian Madison County Pub. Law Library, Huntsville, Ala., 1974—. Recipient Meritorious Civilian award Dept. Army, 1970, citation of Merit for outstanding service Madison County Ala., 1971. Mem. Spl. Libraries Assn. (pres. Ala. chpt. 1955-56), Southeastern, Ala. (pres. coll., univ. and spl. libraries div. 1959-60) library assns., Bus. and Profl. Women's Club (chpt. pres. 1950-51). Club: Aladdin (pres. 1958, 67) (Huntsville). Home: 700 Watts Dr SE Huntsville AL 35801 Office: Madison County Pub Law Library 205 East Side Sq Huntsville AL 35801

CASON, DICK KENDALL, physician; b. Beaumont, Tex., June 27, 1922; s. Dick Kendall and Maurine (Mills) C.; B.A., Rice U., 1945; M.D., U. Tex., 1945; m. Maxine Skocdopole, Apr. 4, 1946; children—Dick Mills, Alma Christine. Intern, Kings County Hosp. Bklyn., 1945-46; med. resident Meth. Hosp., Dallas, 1948-49; gen. practice medicine, Hillsboro, Tex., 1949—; staff mem. Grant-Buie Hosp.; charter mem. Am. Bd. Family Practice. Pres. Hillsboro Indsl. Devel. Found., 1955-60; mem. regional adv. com. Dallas Civic Opera Co., 1960—. Served from 1st lt. to capt., AUS, 1946-48. Fellow Royal Soc. Health (Eng.); mem. Hill County Med. Soc. (pres. 1951), Tex. Med. Assn., Am. Acad. Gen. Practice, N.Y. Acad. Sci., C. of C., Hill County Soc. Crippled Children, Royal Soc. Medicine (affiliate). Presbyterian (elder). Clubs: Hillsboro Country, Rotary (pres. Hillsboro 1955). Contbr. articles to profl. jours. Home: 1303 Park Dr Hillsboro TX 76645 Office: 150 Circle Dr Hillsboro TX 76645

CASON, JOEL MALCOLM, JR., container co. exec.; b. Fernandina Beach, Fla., June 17, 1949; s. Joel Malcolm and Betty Elmira (Kaney) C.; B.S. in Pulp and Paper Engring. and Tech., Internat. Corr. Schs., 1971; m. Deborah Rhodes Cason, Aug. 12, 1978; stepchildren—Ronald Carter, James Carter. Quality control technician Container Corp. of Am., Fernandina Beach, 1967-72, environ. technician, 1972-74, process engr.-environ., 1974-77, paper mill tour foreman, 1977—. Home: PO Box 81 Fernandina Beach FL 32034 Office: Container Corp Am N 8th St Fernandina Beach FL 32034

CASSANOVA, LAWRENCE JOSEPH, III, telephone co. engr.; b. New Orleans, Jan. 13, 1948; s. Lawrence Joseph, Jr., and Catherine Josephine (Cousans) C.; B.S. in Math., La. State U., Baton Rouge, 1972; m. Donna Carol Ezell, July 17, 1972. Research statistician La. State U., Baton Rouge, 1973; legis. liaison La. State U. Student body and La. Constl. Conv., 1973; asst. engr. South Central Bell Telephone Co., New Orleans, 1973-75, asso. engr. spl. services circuit design, 1975-76, engr. customer services, spl. projects and designs, 1976-77, project engr.-switching, 1977-79, project engr.-trunking, 1979-80, staff engr.-fundamental planning, 1980—; tutor math. U. New Orleans. Recipient Centennial Honor award, La. State U., 1965. Mem. IEEE. Democrat. Home: 3425 Ridgelake Apt 107 Metairie LA 70002 Office: Canal Place One 365 Canal St Room 1140 New Orleans LA 70140

CASSATA, JOHN T., bishop, Roman Cath. Ch. Ordained priest Roman Catholic Ch., 1932; consecrated bishop, 1968; titular bishop of Bida, aux. bishop of Dallas-Ft. Worth, 1968; bishop of Ft. Worth, 1969—. Address: 1206 Throckmorton St Fort Worth TX 76102*

CASSEL, CHESTER, physician; b. N.Y.C., Feb. 23, 1918; s. Lionel and Florence (Dannenberg) C.; B.S. with high honors, U. Fla., 1939; M.D., Columbia, 1943; m. Carol Isaacson, Dec. 17, 1947; children—Karen, Laurie, Claudia, Juliet. Intern, Mt. Sinai Hosp., N.Y.C., 1943, resident, 1947-49; resident Bellevue Hosp., N.Y.C., 1946, Duke Hosp., Durham, N.C., 1949-51; practice medicine specializing in gastroenterology, Miami, Fla., 1951—; mem. staffs Cedars of Lebanon Hosp., Jackson Meml. Hosp., Miami; cons. VA Hosp., Victoria, Mercy hosps., Miami; clin. prof. medicine U. Miami Sch. Medicine, 1951—. Served to maj. AUS, 1944-46. Diplomate Am. Bd. Internal Medicine. Fellow A.C.P. (state gov. 1971-75); mem. Am. Gastroent. Assn. (councillor governing bd. 1975-78), Am. Soc. Gastrointestinal Endoscopy, Fla. Gastroent. Soc. (pres. 1971), Phi Beta Kappa, Alpha Omega Alpha. Home: 260 Shore Dr E Miami FL 33133 Office: 1150 NW 14th St Miami FL 33136

CASSEL, JOHN ELDEN, accountant; b. Verden, Okla., Apr. 24, 1934; s. Elbert Emery and Erma Ruth (McDowell) C.; m. Mary Lou Malcom, June 3, 1953; children—John Elden, James Edward, Jerald Eugene. Plant mgr., also asst. gen. mgr. Baker and Taylor Co., Oklahoma City, 1966-71; paymaster, office mgr. Robberson Steel Co., Oklahoma City, 1971-76; pvt. investor, 1976—. Democrat. Methodist. Home: 2332 NW 118th St Oklahoma City OK 73120

CASSELBERRY, RICHARD SHANNON, civil engr.; b. Orlando, Fla., Sept. 28, 1948; s. Leonard and Margaret Jane (Williams) C.; A.A., Orlando Jr. Coll., 1968; B.S. in Engring., U. Central Fla. (formerly Fla. Technol. U.), 1971; 1 dau., Lesley Shannon. Staff engr. Glace & Radcliffe, Inc., Winter Park, Fla., 1971—. Mem. adminstrv. bd. Community United Meth. Ch., Casselberry, Fla. Mem. ASCE, Nat. Soc. Profl. Engrs., Fla. Engring. Soc. (sr.), U. Central Fla. Alumni, Casselberry Jaycees (charter; past v.p., past treas.). Republican. Home: PO Box 595 Casselberry FL 32707 Office: PO Box 731 Winter Park FL 32790

CASSELS, GORDON BERRY, accountant; b. Pensacola, Fla., Sept. 1, 1942; s. Gordon Berry and Lois (Huff) C.; A.A., Pensacola Jr. Coll., 1964; B.S., Fla. State U., 1966; m. Faye; children—Mark Jeffrey, Donna Sue, Christopher Lee, Sandra. Semi-sr. accountant Peat, Marwick, Mitchell & Co., Houston, 1967; sr. accountant Saltmarsh, Cleaveland & Gund, Pensacola, 1967-69; dir. fin. and accounting div. comml. devel. Fla. Dept. Commerce, Tallahassee, 1969-71, dir. fin. and accounting div. vocat. rehab. Dept. Health and Rehab., 1971-72, chief bur. auditing, beverage div. Dept. Bus. Regulation, 1972-74; sec. Robert A. Benz & Co., pub. accountants and C.P.A.'s, Pensacola, 1974-76; sec.-treas. Cassels & McMillan, C.P.A.'s, Pensacola, 1976—. Bd. dirs., treas. Fla. Jr. Miss Pageant. C.P.A., Tex., Fla. Mem. Am., Fla. insts. C.P.A.'s, Am. Accounting Assn., Fla. State U. Alumni Assn. Democrat. Baptist. Club: Suburban W. Rotary. Home: Route 5 Box 91-C Cantonment FL 32533 Office: 3250 Navy Blvd Suite 220 Pensacola FL 32505

CASSIDY, DENNIS STEPHEN, coll. adminstr.; b. Kansas City, Mo., Aug. 24, 1933; s. William Paul and Donna Elizabeth (Davis) C.; B.A. in Geology, Fla. State U., 1962; m. Fabiola Bustamante, Oct. 15, 1966; children—Maria Angelica, Patrick Michael Pantelis. Geophysicist, Texaco, Inc., Lafayette, La. and New Orleans, 1962-63; asst. dir. sedimentology research lab., dept. geology Fla. State U., 1963-68, asso. curator Antarctic Marine Geology Research Facility and Core Library, 1968-75, curator, 1975—, research asso., 1972—. Served with U.S. Army, 1953-55. Mem. Paleont. Research Inst., Soc. Econ. Paleontologists, and Mineralogists. Contbr. articles in field to profl. jours. Home: 718 W Pensacola St Tallahassee FL 32304 Office: Dept Geology Fla State U Tallahassee FL 32306

CASSIDY, PATRICK EDWARD, educator; b. East Moline, Ill., Nov. 8, 1937; s. Bert Garfield and Ilene Vertha (Anderson) C.; B.S., U. Ill., 1959; M.S., U. Iowa, 1962, Ph.D., 1963; 1 son, Andrew Patrick. Fellow, U. Ariz., Tucson, 1963-64; staff mem. Sandia Corp., Albuquerque, 1964-66; sect. mgr. Tracor, Inc., Austin, Tex., 1966-71; asst. prof. chemistry S.W. Tex. State U., San Marcos, 1971-76, asso. prof., 1976—; v.p. Tex. Research Inst., Austin, 1975—. Pres., Austin (Tex.) Skiers, Inc., 1972-73. DuPont fellow, 1962-63. Fellow Tex.

Acad. Sci., Am. Inst. Chemists; mem. Am. Chem. Soc. (chmn. 1969, councillor 1975—, co-chmn. membership polymer div. 1973), Sigma Xi, Phi Lambda Upsilon. Presbyn. (elder 1973, 78-79, chmn. bd. deacons 1972, 76). Club: Town Lake Breakfast (pres. 1970) (Austin). Asst. editor Polymer Preprints, 1976—. Contbr. articles in field to profl. jours. Home: 6006 Shadow Valley Cove Austin TX 78731 Office: Dept Chemistry Southwest Texas State University San Marcos TX 78666 also Tex Research Inst 5902 W Bee Cave Rd Austin TX 78746

CASSIDY, ROBERT GORDON, elec. engr.; b. West Baden, Ind., Mar. 15, 1917; s. Elza and Alta (Wininger) C.; B.S. in Elec. Engring., Rose Poly. Inst., 1950; m. Lilah Beryl Pinnick, Jan. 31, 1946; children—Daniel G., Marcia G. (Mrs. Jimmy Fletcher), Mary D. (Mrs. Larry Bass), Christine M. Various positions including auto mechanic, store clk., 1934-42; elec. engr. Hill AFB, Utah, 1951-53; elec. engr. U.S.Army C.E., 1953—, chief, elec. sect. engring. div., Jacksonville Fla., 1967-73, elec. engr. constrn. div., 1973—. Served with AUS, 1942-45. Registered profl. engr., Fla., Ind. Methodist. Home: 5514 Norde Dr Jacksonville FL 32210 Office: 400 W Bay St Jacksonville FL 32201

CASSIDY, THEODORE VINCENT, data systems analyst; b. Montclair, N.J., Sept. 5, 1934; s. Thomas Joseph and and Helen Mary (Gleason) C.; B.S., St. Peter's Coll., 1956; m. Patricia Ann Paterson, June 28, 1958; children—Dawn, Sean, Jennifer. Commd. 2d lt. U.S. Marine Corps, 1956, advanced through grades to maj., 1976; supply officer, 1962-68, data systems analyst, 1968-76; ret., 1976; data systems analyst Duke U., 1976-78; dir. automated services County of Durham, 1978—; instr. data processing dept. Coastal Carolina Community Coll., Jacksonville, N.C., 1975-76. Dist. commr. Boy Scout Am., Okinawa, 1967-74, Mawat-Durham dist. Occoneechee council. Mem. Marine Corps Assn., N.C. Telecom Assn., N.C. Local Govt. Info. Systems Assn., S.E. Area Regional Interest Group, Data Processing Mgmt. Assn., VFW, Am. Legion. Democrat. Roman Catholic. Club: K.C. Home: 49 Buckhorn Rd R1 Hillsborough NC 27278 Office: 255 Computer Center Duke U Durham NC 27706

CASSIL, DONALD RODNEY, advt. agy. exec.; b. Little Rock, Feb. 12, 1945; s. James Edwin and Nancy Black C.; B.S., U. Ark., 1967; m. Gloria Howell, Apr. 16, 1977; children—Brad, Kyle. Dir. advt. Ark. Ind. Devel. Commn.; div. mktg. Twin City Bank; v.p. Union Nat. Bank of Little Rock; v.p. Holland and Assos., Little Rock; pres. Don R. Cassil and Assos., Little Rock. Mem. Ark. Advt. Fedn. (past pres.), Am. Advt. Fedn. (past dist. dir.), Public Relations Soc. Am., Ark. Assn. Communicators and Editors (past pres.). Methodist. Clubs: Jaycees (state dir.), Maumelle Golf and Country (v.p.). Home: 8 Portia Little Rock AR 72212 Office: 1001 W Markham Suite 200 Little Rock AR 72201

CASSIN, WILLIAM BOURKE, lawyer, energy resources co. exec.; b. Mexico City, Sept. 11, 1931 (parents Am. citizens); s. William Michael and Elouise (Hall) C.; A.B., Princeton U., 1953; J.D., U. Tex., 1959; m. Kristi Shipnes, July 15, 1961; children—Clay Brian, Michael Bourke, Macy Armstrong. Admitted to Tex. bar, 1959; clk. to Judge Warren L. Jones, 5th U.S. Circuit Ct., 1959-60; asso. firm Baker & Botts, Houston, 1960-70; v.p., gen. atty. United Gas Pipe Line Co., Houston, 1970-73, sr. v.p., gen. atty., 1973, group v.p., gen. counsel, dir., exec. com., 1974: exec. v.p., gen. counsel, dir., exec. com. United Energy Resources, Inc. and United Gas Pipe Line Co., Houston, 1976—; dir. Cotton Petroleum Corp. Gen. counsel Harris County Republican Party, 1963-64, 67-68, Houston Grand Opera Assn., 1961-70; vestryman Christ Ch. Cathedral, Houston, 1971-73, 80—. Served to lt., arty., AUS, 1953-57, capt. USA ret. Fellow Tex. Bar Found.; mem. Am., Tex., Houston, Fed., Fed. Energy bar assns., Order of Coif, Phi Delta Phi. Republican. Clubs: Houston Country, Bayou, Ramada, Athletic (Houston); Army and Navy (Washington); Princeton (N.Y.C.); Princeton Terr. Home: 1 S Wynden Dr Houston TX 77056 Office: PO Box 1478 Houston TX 77001

CASSON, GARRY ALVIN, educator; b. Dayton, Ky., Nov. 23, 1945; s. Charles Albert and Hilda (Plummer) C.; student No. Community Coll., 1965-68, U. Ky., 1968-69; B.S., U. Cin., 1972, Ed.D. candidate, 1979—; M.B.A., Xavier U. 1974; m. Linda Marie Shoptaugh, June 28, 1969; children—Amy Lynn, Adam Matthew. Computer operator Am. Computer Leasing Corp., Cin., 1965-67; engr. asst. Gen. Electric Corp., Evandale, Ohio, 1967; dept. head data processing No. Ky. Vocat. Sch., Highland Heights, 1968-74, dir. computer services, asst. prof. computer sci., 1974—. Recipient cert. of appreciation No. Ky. U., 1977. Mem. Digital Equipment Users Soc. (adv. com. for guidance counselors N. Ky. Vocat. Region), Ky. Info. Processing Assn., Ky. Acad. Computer Uses Group, Computer Services Policy Com. Republican. Baptist. Clubs: Campbell County Game and Fish Protective Assn., Elks. Home: 736 Carol Dr Taylor Mill KY 41015 Office: Nunn Dr Highland Heights KY 41076

CASSON, WALTER ANDREW, JR., civil engr.; b. Jacksonville, Fla., Nov. 11, 1933; s. Walter A. and Alice S. (Coney) C.; B.E., Vanderbilt U., 1956; m. Lauzanne D. Sims, Dec. 25, 1955; 1 son, Leonard Walter. Mgr. br. office C. Fred Deuel & Assos., 1956-62; pres. Casson Engring. Co., New Port Richey, Fla., 1963—; city engr. City of New Port Richey, 1963-71; dir. First Nat. Bank of New Port Richey, Meadowlawn Meml. Gardens, Inc. Sec. Pithlachascotee water bd. S.W. Fla. Water Mgmt. Bd., 1962-66; bd. dirs. Fla. Internat. Students. Served to 1st lt. AUS, 1956-57. Registered profl. engr., Fla. Mem. ASCE, Fla., Tampa Bay socs. profl. land surveyors, Fla. Sheriffs Assn., Greater New Port Richey C. of C. (Citizen of Yr. award 1976). Club: Rotary (pres. 1966-67, dir.). Home: 406 Carlton Rd New Port Richey FL 33552 Office: 106 N Boulevard St PO Box 1348 New Port Richey FL 33552

CASSUTO, JERRY, physician, corporate med. dir.; b. N.Y.C., Nov. 30, 1931; s. Louis and Celia (Nahmias) C.; B.S., Coll. City N.Y., 1952; M.D., State U. N.Y., 1956; M.S., U. Rochester, 1961; m. Ingrid Kurz, Sept. 10, 1967. Intern, Bronx Municipal Hosp., N.Y.C., 1956-57; resident in occupational medicine Strong Meml. Hosp., Rochester, N.Y., 1959-61; med. dir. Aerojet Gen. Corp., Azusa, Calif., 1961-64; med. dir. Western Electric Co., Newark, 1964, staff med. dir., N.Y.C., 1965-69, gen. med. dir., Greensboro, N.C., 1969—. Served with M.C., USNR, 1957-58. AEC fellow in indsl. medicine, 1959-61; diplomate Am. Bd. Preventive Medicine. Mem. AMA, Am. Acad. Occupational Medicine (pres. 1979-80), Am. Coll. Preventive Medicine (v.p. 1973-74), N.Y. Soc. Indsl. Medicine (pres. 1976), N.Y., Greensboro acads. medicine, N.C. Med. Soc., Am. Occupational Medicine Assn., Alph Omega Alpha. Asso. editor Jour. Occupational Medicine, 1968-79. Home: 5308 Mecklenburg Rd Greensboro NC 27407 Office: Guilford Center PO Box 25000 Greensboro NC 27420

CASTELLANO, CHARLES NICHOLAS, mgmt. cons.; b. Bklyn., Feb. 16, 1944; s. Angelo Charles and Ann (Picollo) C.; B.B.A., N. Tex. State U., 1970, M.B.A., 1974; m. Carol Foster, Aug. 30, 1970; children—Anthony, Carrie. Electro-mech. draftsman Teledyne-Geotech., Garland, Tex., 1967-71; methods analyst Neiman-Marcus, Dallas, 1971-74; mgr., asso. v.p. methods and procedures Fidelity Union Life, Dallas, 1974-78; 2d v.p., mgr. corp. methods USLIFE Systems Corp., Dallas, 1978—. Advisor, Jr. Achievement, Dallas, 1976-77. Served with U.S. Army, 1964-66. Fellow Life Mgmt. Inst.; mem. Form Mgmt. Assn. (pres. 1974-75), Life Office Mgmt. Inst., Adminstrv. Mgmt. Soc. Republican. Roman Catholic. Office: Frito-Lay Tower Suite 1020 Dallas TX 75235

CASTELLO, JAMES E., JR., advt. agency exec.; b. Jacksonville, Fla., Oct. 19, 1941; s. James E. and Mildred R. (Raulerson) C.; B.S. in Journalism with honors, U. Fla., 1964, M.A. (teaching asst.), 1965; m. Maridell Walters, Aug. 30, 1963; children—Derek Charles, Anne Carol. Presentations editor Martin Marietta Corp., Orlando, Fla., 1965-69; account exec. Dave Chapman Advt., Orlando, 1969-71, partner, 1971-72; v.p., partner Chapman and Castello Advt., Orlando, 1972-75, pres., 1975—, also dir. Vice-chmn. zone commn., City of Orlando, chmn. munic. planning bd.; mem. Indsl. Devel. Commn. Mid-Fla. dir. We Care Suicide Prevention, Orlando, Intercom-Crisis Intervention, Orlando; chmn. pub. relations Rotary, First Baptist Ch. Served with USNG, 1965-71. Recipient various advt. Fedn. awards. Mem. Assn. Direct Mktg. Agencies, Direct Mail Mktg. Assn., Fla. Direct Mktg. Assn. (exec. com. 1978—), Orlando Area C. of C., Orlando Area Advt. Fedn. Democrat. Baptist. Office: 924 N Magnolia Ave Suite 303 Orlando FL 32803

CASTELLOW, BEN LAYMAN, mfg. co. exec.; b. Windsor, N.C., Dec. 4, 1954; s. William Layman and Margaret Lucille (Harden) C.; student U. N.C., Chapel Hill, 1973-75; B.S. in Bus. Adminstrn., E. Carolina U., 1977; postgrad. U. S.C. Control edit clk. Wachovia Bank & Trust, Greenville, N.C., 1977; mem. audit staff Arthur Andersen & Co., Columbia, S.C., 1977-79; budget analyst Homelite div. Textron Industries, Gastonia, N.C., 1979—. Mem. Nat. Assn. Accts., N.C. Assn. C.P.A.'s (asso.), Beta Gamma Sigma, Phi Sigma Pi, Omicron Delta Epsilon. Republican. Episcopalian. Home: Woodwinds Apt 6619-H Charlotte NC 28210 Office: PO Box 1788 Little Mountain Rd Gastonia NC 28052

CASTILLO, PROBO HERRERA, physician; b. Manila, Jan. 12, 1944; s. Pablito Abriol-Santos and Pura Almonte (Herrera) C.; student U. Santo Tomas, Philippines, 1960-63; M.D., U. East Ramon Magsaysay Meml. Med. Center, Philippines, 1968; m. Maryann R. Guanzon. Intern, U. East Ramon Magsaysay Meml. Med. Center, 1967-68, Mercy Hosp., Buffalo, 1969-70; pediatric resident Beth Israel Med. Center, N.Y.C., 1970-73, chief resident, 1972-73; chief service, pediatrician Children's Phys. Habilitation Service, Newark Developmental Center, Newark, N.Y., 1973-76; practice medicine specializing in pediatrics, Pikeville, Ky., 1976-77; dir. emergency dept. Clinch Valley Community Hosp., Richlands, Va., 1977—. Lic. physician, N.Y., N.J., Ky., Pa., Va. Diplomate Am. Bd. Pediatrics, Am. Bd. Family Practice. Fellow Am. Acad. Family Physicians; mem. Am. Acad. Pediatrics, Am. Coll. Emergency Physicians, Drs. Alumni Assn. Beth Israel Med. Center, Med. Soc. Va., Tazewell County Med. Soc. Roman Catholic. Home: PO Box 38-A Richlands VA 24641 Office: Clinch Valley Community Hospital Richlands VA 24641

CASTILLO-BERNAL, ISMAEL, mfg. co. exec.; b. San Sebastian, P.R., Feb. 22, 1939; s. Ismael and Maria (Bernal) Castillo-Gandulla; B.S. in I.E., U. P.R., 1962; m. Agnes M. Castillo, Feb. 20, 1965; children—Javier I, Hector J. Sales engr. Minn. Mining Co., San Juan, P.R., 1962-65; staff engr. Econ. Devel. Adminstrn., San Juan, 1966-67; prodn. dept. head Eli Lilly & Co., Inc., Carolina, P.R., 1967-72; mgr. prodn. sect. Abbott Pharm., Inc., Barceloneta, P.R., 1972-77; mgr. training sect. Abbott Hosps., Inc., Barceloneta, 1977—; cons. in field. Served with U.S. Army, 1964. Recipient Instructional Ability award, P.R. N.G. Mil. Acad., 1965. Mem. Am. Inst. Indsl. Engrs., Am. Mgmt. Assn., Am. Soc. for Tng. and Devel. Roman Catholic. Club: Rotary. Home: 13 AL Susoni St Arecibo PR 00612 Office: PO Box 278 Barceloneta PR 00617

CASTLE, FRANK ELLES, elec. mfg. co. exec.; b. Chgo., Nov. 12, 1932; s. Albert J. and Edna E. Castle; B.A., U. Ill., 1957; m. Pauline Richards, July 31, 1954; children—Nancy, Janet. Regional mgr. CBS Electronics, Houston, 1958-61; Westinghouse Electric, Atlanta, 1961-65; regional distbr. mgr. Motorola Semicondrs., Dallas, 1965-69; distbr. mktg. mgr. Tex. Instruments, Dallas, 1969-70; dir. indsl. mktg. Sterling Electric, Houston, 1971-76, pres. indsl. mktg., 1976—. Office: 4201 SW Freeway Houston TX 77027

CASTLE, WILLIAM GRAVES, JR., real estate exec., oil and gas co. exec.; b. Lake Charles, La., Jan. 6, 1940; s. William Graves and Marguerite (Wheeler) C.; student Tex. A. and M. U., 1958-59; B.S., La. State U., 1962; m. Linda Morris, Mar. 26, 1960; children—William Graves, III, Kevin Morris. Pres., Castle Properties, Inc., Lake Charles, 1967—; notary pub., Calcasieu Parish, La., 1976—. Mem. La. Expressway Authority, 1973-77, Lake Charles Planning and Zoning Commn., 1967-71, Natural Resources Study Com., 1977—; trustee Boys Club of Lake Charles, 1979; campaign mgr. U.S. Congressman John Breaux, La., 1972—. Licensed real estate broker, licensed gen. contractor, La. Mem. Soc. Advancemnt Mgmt., Am. Assn. Petroleum Landmen, La. Assn. Ind. Producers and Royalty Owners, Delta Sigma Pi, Sigma Alpha Epsilon. Methodist. Club: Young Men's Bus. Home: 7 Little Dr Lake Charles LA 70605 Office: 303 Magnolia Life Bldg Lake Charles LA 70601

CASTLEBERRY, DONALD GRANT, state legislator Ga.; b. Stewart County, Ga., Mar. 23, 1929; s. James Homer and Alberta (Wood) C.; degree Gupton-Jones Sch. Mortuary Sci., 1949; m. Maryneil Stephens, Mar. 15, 1953; children—Eddie Stephens, James Clinton. Mgr., H.L. Moore Co., Richland, Ga., 1951-61; gen. mgr. Campbell Funeral Home, Richland, 1961-66; owner Castleberry Ins. Agy., Richland, 1961—; owner, mgr. J.H. Castleberry Inc., Richland, 1966—; mem. Ga. Ho. of Reps., 1973—. Served with U.S. Army, 1950-51. Democrat. Methodist. Home: RFD Richland GA 31825 Office: PO Box 377 Richland GA 31825

CASTLEBERRY, GEORGE ALFRED, real estate broker; b. Nashville, Ark., June 28, 1928; s. Bathus E. and Berdie (Trott) C.; A.Sci., Ark. Tech. Coll., 1949; children—Debra Adele, George Stanley, Rodney Lynn. Tchr., Nashville, Ark., 1949-51; office mgr. Massey Pulpwood Co., Nashville, 1952-61; pvt. practice pub. accounting, Nashville, Ark., 1961—; real estate broker, Nashville, 1970—. Served with U.S. Army, 1951-52. Licensed pub. accountant, real estate broker, Ark. Mem. Nat. Geog. Soc., Nat. Assn. Tax Consultors, Nat. Soc. Pub. Accountants, Ark. Future Farmers Assn. (pres., parliamentarian 1947-48). Home: PO Box 152 Nashville AR 71852 Office: 516 N Main St Nashville AR 71852

CASTRO, ALBERT, scientist, educator; b. San Salvador, El Salvador, Nov. 15, 1933; s. Alberto Lemus and Maria Emma (de la Cotera) C.; B.S., U. Houston, 1958; postgrad. Baylor U., 1958; Ph.D., U. El Salvador, 1962; m. Jeris Adelle Goldsmith, Oct. 19, 1956; children—Stewart, Sandra, Alberto, Juan, Richard. Came to U.S., 1952. Asst. prof. microbiology and biochemistry U. El Salvador, San Salvador, 1958-60, asso. prof. dental and med. sch., 1960-63, prof., head dept. basic sci., 1965-68, dir. research in basic sci. dental sch., 1964-68, co-dir. grad. research, 1965-66, bd. dirs. dental sch., 1961-66, mem. research and scholarship com., 1964-65; asst. prof. pediatrics, co-dir. pediatrics metalobic lab. U. Oreg., Portland, 1969-73; dir. endocrinological dept. and research unit United Med. Lab., Portland, 1970-73; sr. scientist Papanicolaou Cancer Research Inst., Miami, Fla., 1973-75; asso. prof. pathology and medicine U. Miami, 1973-77, prof. pathology, medicine and microbiology, 1977—; coordinator Inter Am. Tech. Transfer and Tng. Program, 1976—. NIH postdoctoral fellow, 1966-70; U. Oreg. Med. Sch. grantee, 1966-69; Northwest Pediatric Research fellow, 1971. Fellow Am. Inst. Chemists, Royal Soc. Tropical Med. and Hygiene; mem. N.Y. Acad. Scis., Am. Chem. Assn. Am. Assn. Microbiology, AAAS, Tooth and Bone Research Soc., Acad. Sci. El Salvador. Roman Catholic. Contbr. over 150 publs. to nat. and internat. sci. jours.; basic research in diabetes, hypertension and immunochemistry. Home: 6275 SW 123d Terr Miami FL 33156 Office: Univ of Miami Sch Medicine Dept Pathology PO Box 520875 Biscayne Annex Miami FL 33152

CASTRO, ESTEFANA VILLARREAL, dietitian; b. Holtville, Calif., Mar. 17, 1934; d. Felipe Preciado and Estefana Diaz (Calderon) Villarreal; A.A., East Los Angeles Coll., 1960; B.A., Calif. State U., Los Angeles, 1963; postgrad. Imperial Valley Coll., Calif. State U. (San Diego), UCLA; 1 son, Phillip Paul. Typist, Imperial (Calif.) Irrigation Dist. 1953-57; gen. office asst. Arco Ins. Service, Inc., Los Angeles, 1957-63; dir. food service Pioneers Meml. Hosp., Brawley, Calif., 1963-76 dir. dietary Mercy Hosp. of Laredo (Tex.), 1976—; mem. Laredo resource com. Tex. Agr. Extension Service; cons. dietitian Laredo Artificial Kidney Center. Registered dietitian. Mem. Am. Soc. Parenteral and Enteral Nutrition, Am. Dietetic Assn., Tex. Dietetic Assn., Soc. Nutrition Edn., San Antonio Dist. Dietetic Assn., Am. Home Econs. Assn., Laredo Diabetes Assn. (chmn.). Roman Catholic. Home: 206 W Oak Circle Laredo TX 78041 Office: 1515 Logan St Laredo TX 78040

CASTRO, JOHN GONZALES, clergyman, educator; b. San Antonio, Nov. 18, 1935; s. John Riojas and Elvira (Medrano) Gonzales C.; B.A. in Philosophy, Oblate Coll. S.W., 1959, M. Div. (equivalent), 1963; Ph.D. in Counseling Psychology, Mich. State U., 1975. Joined Missionary Oblates of Mary Immaculate, 1956; ordained priest Roman Catholic Ch., 1962; tchr. Spanish, St. Anthony High Sch. Sem., San Antonio, 1972; grad. asst. Mich. State U., East Lansing, 1973-75, coordinator Chicano program com. Coll. Edn., 1972-73; asso. pastor Our Lady of Guadalupe, Austin, Tex., 1975-78; prof. Mexican Am. psychodynamics, counseling psychology and homiletics, dir. dept. cultural awareness and devel. Oblate Coll. S.W., San Antonio, 1978—; mem. diaconate program teaching staff Archdiocese of San Antonio, 1978—; trustee El Visitante Dominical, nat. weekly newspaper, 1978—; co-dir. undergrad. coll. program Missionary Oblates of Mary Immaculate, Austin, 1975-76; coordinator master's program Antioch Juarez Lincoln U., Austin, 1976-77; program dir. Mexican Am. Center for Econ. Devel., Austin, 1978-79; psychologist Diocese of Austin, 1975-78. Charter mem. Juvenile Rev. Bd. Brownsville (Tex.), 1971-72; mem. central council Mental Health and Mental Retardation Adv. Bd., Austin, 1976-77; chmn. adv. bd. Drug Abuse Mental Health and Mental Retardation, Austin, 1976-78; chmn. adv. bd. VISTA, Austin, 1976-77. Mem. Am. Personnel and Guidance Assn., Priests Organized for Religious, Econ. and Social Rights, Mich. State U. Alumni Assn. Democrat. Club: K.C. Home: 10311 Willowick San Antonio TX 78217 Office: 285 Oblate Dr San Antonio TX 78216

CASWELL, GREGORY KELTON, engr., scientist; b. Somerville, N.J., June 13, 1947; s. Stanley Kelton and Barbara Jean C.; student Newark Coll. Engring., 1965-68, Rutgers U., 1969-77; m. Joyce Ann Reilly, Aug. 31, 1969; children—Christopher, Kelly. Sr. technician Burroughs Corp., Piscataway, N.J., 1967-73; tech. specialist RCA Solid State Tech. Center, Somerville, N.J., 1973-77; reliability engr. Tracor Inc., Austin, Tex., 1977-78, engr./scientist, 1978—. Mem. Am. Soc. Quality Control. Republican. Roman Catholic. Contbr. articles to profl. jours. Home: 2303 Monaco Dr Cedar Park TX 78613 Office: 6500 Tracor Ln Austin TX 78721

CATE, BYRON LEE, state senator; b. Norman, Okla., Jan. 18, 1942; s. Roscoe S. and Frances (Mitchell) C.; J.D., U. Okla., 1972; m. Sylvia S. Martin, June 15, 1963; children—Christie Lee, Byron Lee, Chad Mitchell. Justice of peace, Norman, 1964-66; mem. Okla. Ho. of Reps. from 44th Dist., 1966-73, Okla. Senate from 16th Dist., 1973—; admitted to Okla. bar, 1972, since practiced in Norman as partner firm Lucas & Cate; pres. Cleveland County Publishing Co., 1977—. Mem. Okla. Bar Assn., Okla. Trial Lawyers Assn., Cleveland County Bar Assn., Norman C. of C. (past dir.), Phi Gamma Delta. Democrat. Presbyterian. Club: Kiwanis. Home: 1519 Magnolia St Norman OK 73069 Office: 231 S Peters St Norman OK 73069

CATECHIS, SPYROS, psychologist; b. Port Arthur, Tex., Nov. 29, 1945; s. Anastasios Spero and Grace (Manos) C.; B.S., Stephen F. Austin U., 1968; M.S., E. Tex. State U., 1969; Ed.D., U. Houston, 1978; m. Marian E. Graham, May 19, 1979; children—Christopher, Nicholas. Psychologist Tex. Research Inst. Mental Scis., Houston, 1974-77; dir. Spring Branch Acad., Houston, 1978-79; psychologist Houston Psychotherapy Assos., 1979—; mem. faculty U. Houston Downtown, 1975-77. Bd. dirs. Mental Health Assn. Harris County, 1977-78. Mem. Am. Group Psychotherapy Assn., Am. Psychol. Assn., Houston Group Psychotherapy Soc., Am. Soc. Clin. Hypnosis, Am. Hellenic Edn. Progressive Assn. Greek Orthodox. Home: 5720 Rampart #268 Houston TX 77081 Office: 6900 Fannin Suite 360 Houston TX 77030

CATER, ROBERT JOSEPH, physician; b. Meridian, Miss., Jan. 6, 1945; s. Eugene Felix and Mary Ellen (Legget) C.; M.D., U. Miss., 1970; m. Barbara Kay Coltharp, June 14, 1969; children—Amy, Megan, Robert. Intern, Univ. Med. Center, Jackson, Miss., 1970-71, resident gen. surgery, 1971-72, resident in otolaryngology, 1972-75; practice medicine specializing in otolaryngology, Meridian; mem. staffs Jeff Anderson Meml., F.G. Riley Meml. hosps. Diplomate Am. Bd. Otolaryngology. Fellow A.C.S., Am. Acad. Facial Plastic and Reconstructive Surgeons; mem. AMA. Presbyterian. Home: 4935 Country Club Place Meridian MS 39301 Office: 1516 23rd Ave Meridian MS 39301

CATES, CURTIS ANTHONY, ednl. adminstr., evangelist; b. Phenix City, Ala., Feb. 8, 1941; s. Curtis C. and Margaret Anthony C.; A.A., Ala. Christian Coll., 1961, B.S., 1962; B.S., Livingston U., 1965; M.S., Samford U., 1969; M.R.E., Ala. Christian Grad. Sch. of Religion, 1973, M.Th., 1978; Ed.D., U. Ala., 1977; m. Annette Riley Bingham, Oct. 29, 1960; children—Curtis Anthony, Daniel Frazier. Evangelist, Church of Christ, 1960—, Columbiana (Ala.) Ch. of Christ, 1976—; tchr. Escambia Christian Sch., Pensacola, Fla., 1965-66, Ala. Christian High Sch., Montgomery, 1970-71; prof. Bible and English, Ala. Christian Coll., Montgomery, 1971-73; prof. Bible, English, apologetics and Christian doctrine Ala. Christian Sch. of Religion, Montgomery, 1971—, dir. extensions, 1973-74, asst. to pres., 1974-76, dean acad. affairs, 1976-78, v.p. in charge acad. affairs, 1978—; lectr. in field; speaker youth and evangelistic meetings. Mem. Internat. Platform Assn., Pi Tau Chi, Phi Delta Kappa, Kappa Delta Pi. Club: Optimists. News editor Sound Doctrine, 1975—; contbr. articles to profl. jours. and newspapers. Home: 4461 Blackwood Dr Montgomery AL 36109 Office: 6020 Atlanta Hwy Montgomery AL 36117

CATES, GERALD LEE, educator; b. Burlington, N.C., June 16, 1941; s. Boyd Lee and Dorothy Naomi (Kelley) C.; A.B., Elon Coll., 1966; M.A., U. Ga., 1968, Ph.D., 1976; m. Nancy Channel Hobart, Jan. 29, 1966. Tchr. U.S. history and polit. sci. Madison County High Sch., Danielsville, Ga., 1975-77; history faculty, chmn. div. social scis. Truett-McConnell Coll., Cleveland, Ga., 1977—, acad. dean, 1979—, chmn. steering com., dir. Truett-McDonnell Coll. Self Study for So. Assn. Colls. and Schs., 1978-79. Named Tchr. of Year, Madison County High Sch., 1978. Mem. Am. Hist. Assn., Ga. Hist. Assn., Orgn. Am. Historians, So. Hist. Assn., Phi Alpha Theta, Phi Kappa Phi. Methodist. Contbr. articles to med., hist. publs. Home: Route 1 Box 157-10 Valley Court Oakwood GA 30566 Office: Miller Building Truett-McConnell College Cleveland GA 30528

CATHEY, RONALD RAY, ins. broker; b. Lubbock, Tex., Nov. 20, 1944; s. B.M. and L.P. Cathey; student Tex. Tech U., 1964-69; m. Nancy Northcutt, Aug. 15, 1969; children—Robert Northcutt, Caroline Roberts, Thomas Graham. Vice pres. Edwards-Northcutt-Locke, Dallas, 1978—. Mem. Ind. Agts. Assn. Republican. Presbyterian. Home: 3615 Bryn Mawr St Dallas TX 75205 Office: 5011 McKinney St Dallas TX 75205

CATLEDGE, GRIER MOEN, educator; b. Boston, Feb. 6, 1936; d. Rene Moen and Jean (Grier) Smith; student Sorbonne, Paris, 1956-57; B.A., Hollins Coll., Va., 1958; postgrad. in occupational therapy U. Pa., 1958-60; M.Ed., U. Fla., 1972; certificate in neurodevel. treatment for cerebral palsy Marymount Coll., 1977; m. Donald A. Nelson, Aug. 27, 1960 (div. 1970); children—Brigetta Grier, Caswell Moen, Keith Greycloud, Ruckman Greycloud (adopted Sioux Indians); m. 2d, Norman W. Catledge, June 11, 1977. Occupational therapist Jefferson Meml. Coll. Hosp., Phila., 1960-61, Kings Park State Hosp., 1962-63, Hillside Hosp., Glen Oaks, N.Y., 1963-65, Rehab. Inst., Mineola, N.Y., 1965-66; dir. occupational therapy Dixmont State Hosp., Sewickley, Pa., 1967-70; occupational therapist VA Hosp., Gainesville, Fla., 1970-72; asst. prof. occupational therapy Med. Coll. Ga. Augusta, 1972-77; dir. occupational therapy Duval County (Fla.) Public Schs., 1977-80; pvt. practice occupational therapy, 1977—; cons. psychiat. occupational therapy programs Talmadge VA Hosp. and Regional Hosp.; supr. students, cons. residential Easter Seal Camp for Multi-handicapped children, summer 1974, Montessori Sch. for learning disabilities program, summer 1975. Active, Augusta and Jacksonville Mental Health Assn., 1972—, Richmond County Youth Council, 1974—; mem. parent adv. com. Boy Scouts Am., 1975—; tchr. Sunday Sch.; exec. bd. Richmond County Learning Disabilities Sch. and Day Camp Program, 1976; dir. United Cerebral Palsy Summer Day Camp, 1978. Mem. Am. Acad. Cerebral Palsy, Am., Ga. occupational therapy assn., Council for Exceptional Children, Ga., Augusta assns. for children with learning disabilities, Center for Study Sensory Integration Dysfunction (pres.-elect), Alpha Eta. Author: Joey Can't Read, 1975. Home: 4355 Coquina Dr Jacksonville Beach FL 32250

CATON, HARDY MORRIS, electronics co. exec.; b. Dallas, July 27, 1937; s. Walter Augusta and Evelyn (Morris) C.; B.S. in Mech. Engring., Tex. A. and M. U., 1960; postgrad. in Bus. Adminstrn., Baylor U., 1966; m. Sarah Irene Mathis, Aug. 16, 1956; children—Jay Lynn, Gregory Glen, Melissa Jane. Engr. Martin Co., Orlando, Fla., 1960; devel. test engr. Mason & Hanger Silas Mason Co. Inc., Amarillo, Tex., 1961-62; sr. engr. Rocketdyne Solid Rocket Div., McGregory, Tex., 1962-67; engr./scientist Tracor Inc., Austin, Tex., 1967-71, dir. for countermeasures and avionics, 1971-75, v.p., gen. mgr., 1975—, group v.p. Tracor Aerospace Group, 1979—. Mem. Inst. Environ. Scis. (sec. 1965-66), Am. Mgmt. Assn., Assn. Old Crows, Armed Forces Communication and Electronics Assn., Wild Goose Assn., Air Force Assn., Soc. Logistics Engrs., Am. Def. Preparedness Assn., Tex. Assn. for Minorities in Engring. (chmn. Austin chpt.). Home: 3901 Silverspring St Austin TX 78759 Office: 6500 Tracor Ln Austin TX 78721

CATON, JAMES WILLIAM, real estate exec.; b. Washington, Oct. 17, 1939; s. Howard Leslie and Katherine Elizabeth (Sinclair) C.; student extension U. Colo., 1959; student U. Md. Far East, 1960-61; A.A., Montgomery Jr. Coll., 1964; B.S., U. Md., 1967; postgrad. George Washington U., Washington, 1968-71; m. Shirley Ann Scales, Mar. 24, 1968; children—Patrick Evan, Frank Gordon. Clk.-cashier, asst. mgr. Giant Food Inc., Washington and Rockville, Md., 1962-67; prin. market analyst Morton Hoffman & Co., Urban and Econ. Cons., Balt., 1967-71; mktg. coordinator Ryland Group Home Builders, Columbia, Md., 1971-73; v.p., mktg. mgr. GreenMark Inc., residential div. Gerald D. Hines Interests, Houston, 1973-75; owner, pres. Realty Mktg. Assos., Houston, also RMA Communications Group, advt. agy., Houston, 1976—. Served with USAF, 1957-62. Decorated Air Force Commendation medal. Lic. real estate broker Tex. Mem. Am. Mktg. Assn., Sales and Mktg. Council of Nat. Assn. Homebuilders (Million Dollar Circle award 1978), Greater Houston Builders Assn. (sales and mktg. council), Tex. Assn. Builders, Houston C. of C. Republican.

CATRON, MICHAEL STANLEY, electronic mfg. co. exec.; b. Montgomery, Ala., Mar. 19, 1947; s. Evorit Leroy and Jacqueline Jean (Ingels) C.; B.S. in Metall. Engring., Auburn U., 1970; M.B.A. cum laude in fin., U. Louisville, 1975; m. Mary Ann Zoeller, Mar. 23, 1978; children—Jennifer Leigh, James Crawford. Prodn. supr., process engr. Union Carbide Co., Sheffield, Ala., 1970-71; field sales engr. Tex. Instruments, Louisville, 1972-75, field sales engr., Dallas, 1976-77, product mgr., 1977, purchasing supr., 1977-78; area mgr. Aero-Go, Louisville, 1975-76; regional mgr., U.S. direct mktg. mgr., export mgr. Tex. Instruments Supply, Inc., Dallas, 1978-80; product mgr. Harris Corp., Dallas, 1980—. Mem. Am. Mgmt. Assn. Republican. Episcopalian. Club: Brookhaven Country. Office: Harris Corp 16001 Dallas Pkwy Dallas TX 75248

CATURANO, CARLO, interior designer; b. N.Y.C., June 26, 1939; s. Vincent and Mary (Marano) C.; certificate Parson Sch. Design, 1958-63; 1 dau., Ann Marie. Homefurnishing coordinator Woodward & Lothrop, Washington, 1966-68; interior designer, Kennebunk, Maine, 1968-71; interior designer Archtl. Interiors Unitd., Holyoke, Mass., 1971—. Served with AUS, 1964-66. Mem. Inst. Bus. Designers. Republican. Roman Catholic. Home: Route 3 PO Box 560 RR Silver Spring FL 32688

CAUDELL, JOY LARAINE, hosp. ofcl.; b. Toccoa, Ga., Aug. 14, 1948; d. Dwain and Nell Marie (Smith) C.; B.S. in Home Econs., U. Ga., 1970; M.B.A., U. South Ala., 1979. Tng. instr. Davis Bros., Inc., Atlanta, 1970-72; asst. to food service dir. West Paces Ferry Hosp., Atlanta, 1972-74; dir. food services Drs. Hosp., Mobile, Ala., 1974-79; adminstrv. asst. Indian Path Hosp., Kingsport, Tenn., 1979—; food service cons. Sunday sch. tchr. Dauphin Way Baptist Ch.; adv. Experience Based Career Edn. Program, Murphy High Sch., 1977-79. Mem. Nutrition Today Soc., Am. Soc. Hosp. Food Service Adminstrs., Christian Med. Soc., Assn. Bus. Grad. Students (dir. 1978-79). Home: Route 11 Box 335 Johnson City TN 37615 Office: Indian Path Hosp 2000 Brookside Rd Kingsport TN 37660

CAUDILL, ESTILL LEFTRAGE, JR., surgeon, textile exec.; b. Narrows, Va., Aug. 21, 1916; s. Estill Leftrage and Flora (Weatherly) C.; student U. Tenn., East Tenn. State U., Va. Poly. Inst., 1934-37; M.D., Med. Coll. Va., 1941; m. Lucy Denny Bolton, Nov. 25, 1939; children—Estill L. III, Anne (Mrs. Clifton Reginald Lewis, Jr.), Lucy (Mrs. John Newby Austin, Jr.). Intern, Baroness Erlanger Hosp., Chattanooga, 1941-42; individual practice gen. surgery, Elizabethton, Tenn., 1946-66; med. dir. Beaunit Corp., Elizabethton, 1966—; dir. Elizabethton Security Fed. Savs. and Loan Assn., Citizens Bank; med. examiner Carter County, 1961—. Mem. Tenn. Bd. Med. Examiners, 1964-71; mem. Carter County Bd. Health, 1946—; a founder Appalachian Regional Center for Healing Arts, 1968, bd. dirs.; sec.-treas. Elizabethton Airport Commn., 1972-73, chmn., 1973—. Served with M.C., AUS, 1942-46, USPHS Res., 1960—. Decorated Bronze Star, Combat Med. badge. Past Pres. Tenn. Acad. Gen. Practice, 1960. Mem. Tenn. Med. Assn. (trustee 1963-66), Am. Soc. Abdominal Surgeons, AMA, Phi Gamma Delta, Theta Kappa Psi. Rotarian (pres. 1950), Mason (32 deg.). Home: PO Box 551 Elizabethton TN 37643 Office: Beaunit Fibers Elizabethton TN 37643

CAUDILL, JOHN, agriculturist; b. Blackey, Ky., May 28, 1927; s. George Matt and Dora Alice (Fields) C.; B.S. in Agr., U. Ky., 1953, M.S., 1962, postgrad., 1968, 72; m. Alma Florence Lane, June 11, 1949; children—Aaron Mark, John Maurice. Asst. county agrl. extension agt. U. Ky. Coll. Agr., Whitley and Perry Counties, Ky., 1953, county agrl. extension agt. Owsley and Wolfe Counties (Ky.), 1954-66, area extension resource devel. specialist, Quicksand Area, 1967-68, county extension agt. for agr. Wolfe County, 1962—. Bd. dirs. vol. fire depts., Hazel Green and Campton, Ky., 1968—. Served with AUS, 1945-47. Recipient award Ky. Div. Natural Resources, 1968, Ky. Service to Agr. citation, 1971, Distinguished Service award Nat. Assn. County Agrl. Agts., 1971. Mem. Nat. Assn. County Agrl. Agts., Community Devel. Soc., Epsilon Sigma Phi. Club: Kiwanis (pres. Wolfe County 1965, dir. 1965—). Instrumental in mobilizing and organizing local leaders to bring improvements to area, including new electronics plant, pub. library, city water and sewer systems, 2 vol. fire depts., other. Home: PO Box 61 Hazel Green KY 41332 Office: PO Box 146 Campton KY 41301

CAUDILL, WILLIAM NEVILLE, physician; b. Boston, Nov. 28, 1933; s. Fred Welden and Edna Frank (Snyder) C.; A.B., U. Louisville, 1955, M.D., 1959; m. Eleanor Ann McFarland, Dec. 22, 1956; children—Catherine Lynne, Eleanor McFarland, Fred W., William N., Hendricks M. Intern, USPHS Hops., Balt., 1959-60; practice medicine USPHS Indian Hosp., Cherokee, N.C., 1960-61, resident urology USPHS Hosp., S.I., N.Y., 1961-65, chief of urology USPHS Hosp., New Orleans, 1965-68; pvt. practice medicine, specializing in urology, Louisville, 1968—; mem. attending staff La. State U. Med. Sch., New Orleans, 1966-68; vis. surgeon Charity Hosp., New Orleans, 1966-68; asst. clin. prof. surgery U. Louisville, 1968—; mem. staff Louisville Bapt. Hosp., Suburban Hosp. Chmn. utilization review com. Ky. Med. Assn., 1972-75; pres., dir. Ky. Peer Review Orgn., 1974-78. Vice-pres., bd. dirs. Ky. Found. for Med. Care. Diplomate Am. Bd. Urololgy. Mem. Jefferson County Med. Soc., AMA, Ky., So. med. assn., Southeastern sect. Am. Urologic Assn., Am. Assn. Profl. Service Review Orgns., Alpha Omega Alpha. Republican. Home: 2130 Douglass Blvd Louisville KY 40205 Office: 3950 Kresge Way Louisville KY 40207

CAULKINS, CHARLES WHITNEY, JR., surgeon; b. Whitemarsh Twp., Pa., Dec. 18, 1923; s. Charles Whitney and Eunice Adnah (Field) C.; student U. Richmond, 1941-43; M.D., Med. Coll. Va., 1947; m. Jennie Kennedy, Dec. 22, 1946; children—David Whitney, Michael Kennedy. Intern surgery Vanderbilt U. Hosp., Nashville, 1947-48; resident surgery Med. Coll. Va., Richmond, 1948-50, 52-55; practice medicine specializing in surgery Waynesboro, Va., 1955—; mem. staff Waynesboro Community Hosp., pres. staff 1961, chief surgery 1972-73; mem. courtesy staff King's Daus. Hosp., Stauton, Va.; football team physician Waynesboro High Sch., 1955—; lectr. in field. Chmn. United Fund, 1959; bd. dirs. Cancer Soc., 1957-59, Waynesboro YMCA, 1957-59, Community Concerts, 1957-59. Served with USN 1950-52. Named outstanding man, Jaycees, 1959. Diplomate Am. Bd. Surgeons. Fellow A.C.S.; mem. So., Am. med. assns., Augusta County, Va. med. socs., Va. Surg. Soc., Pi Kappa Alpha, Phi Beta Pi. Presby. (trustee, elder). Rotarian. Club: Waynesboro Country. Home: 622 Northgate Ave Waynesboro VA 22980 Office: 220 Rosser Ave Waynesboro VA 22980

CAUSEY, JACK QUIN, physician; b. Liberty, Miss., Sept. 29, 1932; s. Jack and Marguerite Eva (Quin) C.; B.S., Miss. Coll., 1953; M.D., Tulane U., 1957; m. Lillian Ruth Hatcher Wills, Mar. 5, 1977; children by previous marriage—Jack Quin II, Edward Bruce, William David. Intern, Confederate Meml. Med. Center, Shreveport, La., 1957-58; resident medicine Charity Hosp., New Orleans, 1960-61, 63-65; clin. dir. medicine Lallie Kemp Hosp., Independence, La., 1965-66; practice medicine specializing in internal medicine, Baton Rouge and Centreville, Miss., 1966—; chief staff Field Meml. Hosp., Centreville, 1969-70, 74-75, chief medicine, 1969—; instr. Tulane U. Sch. Medicine, 1960-66; clin. instr. La. State U. Sch. Medicine, 1968—; adv. bd. Farmers Exchange Bank. Served with AUS, 1961-63. Diplomate Am. Bd. Internal Medicine. Fellow A.C.P.; mem. Am. Soc. Internal Medicine, AMA, So., Miss. med. assns., Amite Wilkinson Med. Soc. (pres. 1969-70, 74-75), Centreville C. of C. (pres. 1970), Alpha Omega Alpha. Home: Centreville MS 39631 Office: Field Clinic Centreville MS 39631

CAUTHEN, WILEY MITCHELL, pipe line co. engr.; b. Montgomery, Ala., Aug. 27, 1935; s. George Ernest and Lois Ilean (Mitchell) C.; Asso. Sci. (Nat. LP Gas Assn. scholar), So. Tech. Inst., 1955; B.S., Auburn U., 1962; M.B.A., Rollins Coll., 1965; m. Jo Ann Watkins, Mar. 23, 1957; children—Wade Nelson, LoisAnn, Carol Rene. Asso. engr. Martin Marietta Corp., Orlando, Fla., 1962; staff engr., v.p. sales Fla. Gas Transmission Co., Winter Park, 1962-63, distbn. sales engr., 1963-64, mgr. indsl. sales, 1964-73, project engr., 1973-74, mgr. indsl. sales, 1974-75, sr. engr., 1975-77, sr. engr. products pipeline, 1977—, project coordinator coal slurry pipeline, 1978—. Bd. mgmt. Central Fla. YMCA, Orlando. Served to lt. (j.g.) USNR, 1957-59. Registered profl. engr., Fla. Mem. Am. Soc. Heating, Refrigerating and Air-Conditioning Engrs. (chpt. pres. 1972-73), Nat. Soc. Profl. Engrs., Fla. Engring. Soc., ASME, Associated Industries Fla., Fla. Natural Gas Assn., Res. Officers Assn., Naval Res. Assn. Baptist. Home: 508 Harbour Island Rd Orlando FL 32809 Office: PO Box 44 Winter Park FL 32790

CAVALLARO, JOSEPH JOHN, microbiologist; b. Lawrence, Mass., Mar. 18, 1932; s. John and Salvatrice (Zappala) C.; B.S., Tufts U., 1952; M.S., U. Mass., 1954; Ph.D., U. Mich., 1966; m. Kathleen Frances Kraus, Dec. 2, 1972; children—Theresa Margaret, Sandra Marie, Elizabeth Camille, Danielle Kay. Pub. health sanitarian Hartford (Conn.) Health Dept., 1954-55, 57-61; teaching asso. dept. microbiology U. Mass., Amherst, 1961-62; research virologist Med. Research Labs., Charles Pfizer & Co., Groton, Conn., 1966-67; research asso. dept. epidemiology Sch. Pub. Health, U. Mich., Ann Arbor, 1967-70; microbiologist, diagnostic immunology tng. br. Center for Disease Control, Atlanta, 1971—; lectr. resident pathologists Grady Meml. Hosp., Atlanta, 1975. Served with M.C., AUS, 1955-57. Registered specialist microbiologist Nat. Registry Microbiologists, Am. Acad. Microbiology. Mem. Am. Soc. Microbiology, Am. Assn. Immunologists, N.Y. Acad. Scis., Sigma Xi. Democrat. Roman Catholic. K.C. Contbr. articles to profl. jours. Home: 1325 Balsam Dr Decatur GA 30033 Office: 1600 Clifton Rd Atlanta GA 30333

CAVANAUGH, CHARLES WILLIAM, profl. ice skater; b. Freeport, Ill., Oct. 7, 1919; s. Charles Lawrence and Laura Henrietta (Holsinger) C.; student public schs., Rockford, Ill.; m. Lucille Jeannette Risch, Apr. 12, 1947; children—Dennis Alan, Martin Del. Mem. acrobatic adagio ice skating team (with Lucille Jeannette Cavanaugh), 1947-77; appeared in various ice skating shows and at various hotels and theaters, 1947-77, with Barry Ashton's French Style Revuew, 1959-70, S.S. Leonardo Da Vinci, Italian ship and other ships, 1970-73, Americana Hotel, San Juan, P.R., 1974-75; on tour of Southwestern U.S. with plastic ice, 1976-77; cons. U.S. amateur skaters. Active campaign John B. Anderson for Pres. Mem. AGVA. Lutheran. Office: 2817 S Ocean Dr Jacksonville Beach FL 32250

CAVANAUGH, LUCILLE JEANNETTE, profl. ice skater; b. Hackensack, N.J., Oct. 25, 1927; s. Charles F. and Thelma Rosemond (King) Risch; grad. Tutoring Sch. N.Y., N.Y.C., 1944; m. Charles William Cavanaugh, Apr. 12, 1947; children—Dennis Alan, Martin Del. Mem. acrobatic adagio ice skating team (with Charles William Cavanaugh), 1947-77; appeared in various ice skating shows and at various hotels and theaters, 1947-77, with Barry Ashton's French Style Revue, 1959-70, S.S. Leonardo Da Vinci, Italian ship, and other ships, 1970-73, Americana Hotel, San Juan, P.R., 1973-75; on tour of Southwestern U.S. with plastic ice, 1976-77; cons. U.S. amateur skaters. Active campaign John B. Anderson for Pres. Mem. AGVA. Lutheran. Office: 2817 S Ocean Dr Jacksonville Beach FL 32250

CAVE, MAC DONALD, anatomist, educator; b. Phila., May 14, 1939; s. Edward Joseph and Adeline Roberta (MacDonald) C.; B.A., Susquehanna U., Selinsgrove, Pa., 1961; M.S., U. Ill., 1963, Ph.D., 1965; div.; children—Eric MacDonald, Heidi Lee. Instr. dept. anatomy U. Ill. Coll. Medicine, Chgo., 1964-65; asst. prof. U. Pitts. Sch. Medicine, 1967-72; asso. prof. anatomy U. Ark. Med. Center, Little Rock, 1972-79, prof. anatomy, 1979—. Am. Cancer Soc.-Swedish Am. exchange fellow, 1966; USPHS postdoctoral fellow Max Planch Inst., Tubingen, West Germany, 1966-67. Mem. Am. Assn. Anatomists, Am. Soc. Cell Biology, AAAS, Sigma Xi, Pi Gamma Mu. Contbr. numerous articles to profl. jours. Home: 801 S Rodney Parham Little Rock AR 72205 Office: Dept Anatomy Univ Ark Med Scis 4301 W Markham Little Rock AR 72201

CAVIN, BRUCE WAYNE, acct.; b. Longview, Tex., Aug. 4, 1949; s. David Wayne and Stella Lucille (Hill) C.; B.B.A. in Econs., Stephen F. Austin U., 1975, M.B.A. in Acctg., 1979; m. Barbara Lynn Lewis, May 15, 1971; 1 son, Jeffrey Wayne. Regional planner housing and community devel. E. Tex. Council Govts., Kilgore, 1975-78; cost acct. Harris Corp., Kilgore, 1978, supr. cost acctg. dept., 1979; cost acct. Marathon-Letourneau Corp., Longview, 1980—; mgmt. cons. William M. Slay and Assos., 1980—. Served with U.S. Army, 1972-74. Mem. Western Econ. Assn., Am. Mgmt. Assn., Omicron Delta Epsilon. Democrat. Methodist. Home: 127 Rawley Cts Longview TX 75601 Office: 1613 Pineland St Longview TX 75604

CAVIN, ODIS BURL, metallurgist; b. Hancock County, Tenn., Jan. 22, 1929; s. Joseph Herbert and Mossie Emily (Pauley) C.; B.S., Lincoln Meml. U., 1953; M.S., U. Tenn., 1960; m. Mable Jeanette Smith, Apr. 17, 1954; children—Margaret Carole, Mary Ruth, David Burl. Tchr. math Lee County Schs., Jonesville, Va., 1953-55; metallurgist, research staff mem. Oak Ridge Nat. Lab., Nuclear div. Union Carbide Corp., 1958—. Supt. Christian edn. Assemblies of God Ch., 1957-76, chmn. bd. trustees, 1970-76, lay minister, 1976—. Mem. Am. Crystallographic Assn. Co-inventor improved boron nitride insulators. Home: 3501 Cunningham Dr Knoxville TN 37918 Office: PO Box X Oak Ridge National Lab Oak Ridge TN 37830

CAVINESS, GREGORY DON, ins. agt.; b. Oklahoma City, Mar. 14, 1946; s. Don Malcolm and Jo (Willey) C.; B.B.A. in Mktg., U. Tex., El Paso, 1972; m. Lori D. Childress, Oct. 11, 1968; 1 son, Eric Dawson. Br. mgr. Southland Life Ins. Co., Austin, Tex., 1972-74; v.p., gen. mgr. Mulder Corp., Austin, 1974-75; gen. agt. Am. Nat. Ins. Co., Denver, 1975-79, overall responsibility for N.Mex. and West Tex., El Paso, 1979—; pres. Caviness Co., Denver, 1977—; founder, mng. gen. partner Project Child Indemnity. Active United Way; co-chmn. ball com. Children's Diabetes Found. at Denver, 1978. Served to 1st lt. U.S. Army, 1966-70. Decorated Army Commendation medal. Mem. Nat. Assn. Life Underwriters, Gen. Agts. and Mgrs. Assn. (dir.). C.L.U. Soc. Republican. Baptist. Club: Lions (Denver). Home: 7001 Granero Ct El Paso TX 79112 Office: 1170 Westmoreland Suite 306 El Paso TX 79925

CAVINESS, VERNE STRUDWICK, physician; b. Hillsborough, N.C., Feb. 9, 1895; s. Newby and Nora (Cummings) C.; A.B., Trinity Coll., 1915; student U. N.C., 1916-19; M.D., Jefferson Med. Coll., 1921; postgrad. McGill U., 1936; m. Alice Webb, Oct. 14, 1933; children—Verne Strudwick Jr., Elizabeth (Mrs. George E. Levings III), Alice (Mrs. Richard Hardy). Intern, Jefferson Med. Coll., 1921-22, resident, 1922-23; pvt. practice medicine specializing in internal medicine and cardiology, Raleigh, N.C., 1923—; chief cardiovascular medicine Rex Hosp., Raleigh, 1937-65; med. dir. Occidental Life Ins. Co., Raleigh, 1926-52; asso. prof. clin. medicine U. N.C., 1952-67, prof. emeritus, 1967—; cons. physician Methodist Home for Children, Raleigh, 1923—. Pres. Travelers Aid, 1928-29, Raleigh Salvation Army, 1938-39, Broughton High Sch. PTA, 1951-52, Daniels Jr. High Sch. PTA, 1960-61. Served with U.S. Army, 1918. Fellow A.C.P.; mem. Am., Raleigh (past pres., dir.) heart assns., Am., N.C., Wake County (past pres.) med. assns., Raleigh Acad. Medicine (past pres.), Raleigh Med. Writers Soc. (past pres.), Am. Diabetes Assn., Phi Alpha Sigma. Democrat. Methodist. Mason (Shriner). Home: 913 Vance St Raleigh NC 27608 Office: 109 N Boylan Ave Raleigh NC 27603

CAWOOD, CHARLES DAVID, JR., urologist; b. Lexington, Ky., May 22, 1937; s. Charles David and Helen Elizabeth (Rinke) C.; B.S. cum laude, U. Ky., 1957; M.D., U. Louisville, 1961; m. Susan Ruth O'Dell, June 3, 1958; children—Todd Christopher, Amy Elizabeth. Intern, St. Joseph's Infirmary, Louisville, 1961-62; resident Baylor Coll. Medicine, 1964-68; practice medicine specializing in urology, 1968—; asso. chief urology service Ben Taub Gen. Hosp., Houston, 1968-72; asst. prof. urology Baylor Coll. Medicine, 1971—; asso. chief urology St. Lukes Episcopal Hosp., Houston, 1975—. Served as capt. M.C., USAF, 1962-64. Diplomate Am. Bd. Urology. Mem. Houston (pres. 1972), Am. (chmn. exhibits com. South-Central sect. 1972-75) urol. assns., AMA, Harris County Med. Soc., Phi Beta Kappa. Presbyterian. Club: Doctors (pres. 1976). Contbr. articles to med. jours. Home: 11527 N Lou-Al Houston TX 77024 Office: 2210 Maroneal Houston TX 77030

CAWTHON, PETER WILLIS, JR., petroleum cons.; b. Mexia, Tex., Aug. 26, 1921; s. Peter Willis and Virginia (Smith) C.; B.S. in Petroleum Engring., U. Okla., 1947, M.Petroleum Engring. (Amoco Prodn. Co. fellow), 1949; grad. Columbia U. Exec. Program in Bus. Adminstrn., 1970; m. Charlsie Elaine McLaughlin, Jan. 23, 1947; children—Peter Willis III, Mark McLaughlin, David Kelly. Petroleum prodn. employee Exxon, U.S.A., Wink, Tex., 1947; petroleum engr. Phillips Petroleum Co., Eureka Kans., 1948-49, Midland, Tex., 1949-50; with First City Nat. Bank of Houston, 1950—, sr. v.p., mgr. petroleum and minerals dept., 1973-77; sr. v.p. petroleum and minerals First City Bancorp. Tex., Inc., 1977-78; petroleum cons., 1979—. Served to 1st lt. Ordnance Corps, AUS, 1943-46; ETO. Registered profl. engr., Tex. Mem. Soc. Petroleum Engrs. of Am. Inst. Mining, Metall. and Petroleum Engrs. (chmn. Gulf Coast sect. 1960, nat. dir. 1965-67), Tau Beta Pi, Sigma Tau, Sigma Gamma Epsilon, Phi Delta Theta. Methodist. Club: Petroleum (dir., pres. 1975-76), Houston, Ramada. Home: 13152 Trail Hollow Houston TX 77079 Office: 10575 Katy Freeway Suite 130 Houston TX 77024

CAWTHON, WILLIAM CONNELL, communications mfg. co. exec.; b. Roxton, Tex., Sept. 1, 1922; s. William Arthur and Lura (Denton) C.; B.M.E., Cornell U., 1944; M.S. in M.E., Tex. U., 1947; M.Auto Engring., Chrysler Inst. Tech., Detroit, 1949; m. Flora Keith Campbell, May 31, 1947; children—William Connell, Clark Campbell, Flora Keith. Ops. exec. Chrysler Corp., Detroit, 1947-62; v.p. mfg. Am. Standard, N.Y.C., 1962-66; v.p., dir. indsl. engring. and mfg. ITT Corp., N.Y.C., 1966-68; exec. v.p. Weatherhead Co., Cleve., 1968-70; owner, mgr. William Cawthon Cons., Hudson, Ohio, 1970-72; v.p., gen. mgr. parts div. textile machinery Rockwell Internat., Hopedale, Mass., 1972-73; v.p. mfg. No. Telecom Ltd., Montreal, Que., Can., 1973-77, v.p. ops., Nashville, 1973—. Served with USN, 1945-46, 51-53. Mem. Newcomen Soc. Republican. Mem. Ch. of Christ. Club: Cornell of N.Y. Home: 1024 Lynwood Blvd Nashville TN 37215 Office: 2 International Plaza Nashville TN 37217

CAYCE, ROBERT CLINTON, wholesale distbn. co. exec.; b. Hopkinsville, Ky., Oct. 25, 1929; s. Granville L. and Sara Elizabeth (Gary) C.; B.S., U. Ky., 1952; m. Ruth Cornelius Winn, May 29, 1954; children—Dorothy Elizabeth, Susan Winn, Nancy Ruth. Mem. sales dept. Cayce Mill Supply Co., Hopkinsville, 1952-54, sales mgr., 1954-56, v.p. sales, 1956—, exec. v.p., 1978—. dir. First Federal Savs. & Loan Assn. Active Audubon council Boy Scouts Am., Owensboro, Ky.; bd. dirs. Jennie Stuart Meml. Hosp., Hopkinsville, Christian Ch. Homes of Ky., 1965—, Hopkinsville-Christian County Indsl. Found.; elder First Christian Ch.; pres. Salvation Army Adv. Bd., Hopkinsville. Recipient Silver Beaver award Boy Scouts Am., 1960. Mem. Hopkinsville C. of C. (past pres.), Am. Supply Assn., Ky. C. of C., Penny Royal Homebuilders Assn. Clubs: Elks, Hopkinsville Golf and Country, Kiwanis (lt. gov. dist. 1970-71). Home: 2608 Cayce Meade St Hopkinsville KY 42240 Office: 505 E 1st St Drawer 689 Hopkinsville KY 42240

CAZALAS, MARY REBECCA WILLIAMS, lawyer; b. Atlanta, Nov. 11, 1927; d. George Edgar and Mary Annie (Slappey) Williams; R.N., St. Joseph's Infirmary Sch. Nursing, 1948; postgrad. Vanderbilt U., 1950-51, U. Ga., 1951-52; B.S., Ogelthorpe U., 1954; M.S. in Anatomy, Emory U., 1960; J.D., Loyola U., 1967; m. Albert Joseph Cazalas. Gen. duty nurse St. Joseph's Infirmary, Atlanta, 1948-50, Vanderbilt U. Hosp., Nashville, Tenn., 1950-51, Johns Hopkins Hosp., Balt., 1953; instr. maternity nursing St. Joseph's Infirmary Sch. Nursing, Atlanta, 1954-59; med. researcher urology Tulane U. Sch. Medicine, New Orleans, 1961-65; legal researcher Fourth Circuit Ct. Appeals, New Orleans, 1965-71; admitted to La. bar, 1967, practiced in New Orleans, 1967-71; asst. U.S. atty., New Orleans, 1971-79; trial atty. Equal Employment Opportunity Commn., 1979—. Mem. New Orleans Mayor's Drug Abuse Adv. Com., 1976-79; mem. Task Force Area Agency on Aging, 1976-78. Recipient awards Am. Jurisprudence, 1963, Loyola Law Rev., 1967; 1st place for oil painting Fed. Bus. Assn., 1973; Superior Performance award U.S. Dept. Justice, 1974; cert. of appreciation Fed. Exec. Bd., 1975, 76, 77, 78; Outstanding Cardinal Key Rev. E. A. Doyle award, 1976. Mem. D.A.R., Fed. Bus. Assn. (dir. 1972-76, sec. 1976, v.p. 1976—, pres. 1976-78), Fed. (pres. New Orleans chpt. 1974-75, mem. nat. council 1974—, chmn. nat. drug abuse com. 1976—), Am., La., New Orleans bar assns., Nat. Assn. Women Lawyers, Nat. Health Lawyers Assn., Am. Judicature Soc., New Orleans Art Assn., Federally Employed Women (chmn. fed. women's program 1976-78), New Orleans Bus. and Profl. Women's Club (dir. 1979—), Emory U., Ogelthorpe U., Loyola U. alumni assns., Loyola Law Alumni (v.p. 1975-76, bd. dirs. 1974-75, 77), Cardinal Key, Leconte, Phi Sigma, Alpha Epsilon Delta, Phi Delta Delta, Phi Alpha Delta (vice justice New Orleans 1974-76, justice 1976—). Democrat. Roman Catholic. Author textbook; contbr. articles to profl. jours. Home: 1116 City Park Ave New Orleans LA 70119 Office: 600 South St New Orleans LA 70130

CAZAUBON, MARILYN SEHRT, coll. purchasing ofcl.; b. New Orleans, Dec. 13, 1923; d. William August and Juliet Josephine (Lecourt) Sehrt; student Delgado Coll., 1967-73; m. Maurice S. Cazaubon, Sr., Jan. 2, 1941; children—Maurice S., Caren H., Patrice E. Asst. to buyers City of New Orleans, 1964-69; supr. sales tax office City of New Orleans, 1969; buyer I Delgado Coll. Purchasing Office, New Orleans, 1969-76, buyer II spl. mgmt. service, 1976-79, purchasing supr., 1979—. Mem. Nat. Inst. Govtl. Purchasing. Democrat. Presbyterian. Club: Order Eastern Star. Office: 615 City Park Ave New Orleans LA 70119

CAZEL, HUGH ALLEN, indsl. engr.; b. Asheville, N.C., Aug. 6, 1923; s. Fred Augustus and Agnes (Petrie) C.; B.S. in Indsl. Engring., N.C. State U., 1948, M. Indsl. Engring., 1972; m. Edna Faye Hawkins, Sept. 2, 1944; children—Audre Elizabeth, Hugh Petrie, Susan Margaret, Steven Sidney. Service mgr. Cazel Auto Service Co., Asheville, 1948-51; sales rep. Snap-On Tools Corps., Kenosha, Wis., 1951; estimator, cost accountant Standard Designers Inc., Asheville, 1951-52; designer Robotyper Corp., Hendersonville, N.C., 1952-53; engr. Western Electric Co., Burlington, N.C., 1953-74; engr. So. Bell Telephone Co., Atlanta, 1974-79; instr. Elon (N.C.) Coll., 1956-59; instr. Ga. Inst. Tech., 1977—. Served with U.S. Army, 1943-46. Registered profl. engr., Ga., N.C. Mem. Am. Inst. Indsl. Engrs., Nat., N.C., Ga. (dir., named Ga. Engr. of Year in Industry 1976) socs. profl. engrs., Ga. Profl. Engrs. in Industry (chmn. 1976), AAAS. Republican. Methodist. Club: Odd Fellows, Home: 218-K Forkner Dr Decatur GA 30030 Office: 249 Mason Bldg Sch Civil Engring Ga Inst Tech Atlanta GA 30332

CEBALLOS, LEONARDO MIGUEL, engring. co. exec.; b. Havana, Cuba, June 4, 1953; s. Leonardo Antonio and Concepcion (Roldan) C.; B.S., B.A., Swarthmore Coll., 1975; m. Maria M., Nov. 21, 1975. Salesman Structural Steel System-Cuprioc1, Inc., San Juan, P.R., 1972-75, mgr. constrn., 1975-77, v.p., 1977—; asso. Morales & Ceballos, Engrs. Walter M. and Florence Schirra scholar, Soc. Am. Mil. Engrs., 1974-75. Mem. ASCE, Colegio de Ingenieros & Agrimensores de Puerto Rico, P.R. C. of C., Sigma Xi. Roman Catholic. Club: Casade España. Home: 61-63 Apt 501 Santiago Iglesias Santurce PR 00901 Office: G P O Box 1366 San Juan PR 00936

CECIL, ALLAN VAUGHN, petroleum co. exec.; b. Bristow, Okla., Mar. 16, 1941; s. Laymond Bud and Mary Eleanor Cecil; B.A. in Journalism, U. Okla., 1963, postgrad., 1963-64; m. Ellen Kay Jones, Feb. 1, 1964; children—Jill Maureen, Sarah Ellen, Molly Kate. Communications services coordinator Kerr-McGee Corp., Oklahoma City, 1969-72; field account exec. N.W. Ayer & Son, Inc., Phila., 1972-74; mktg. mgr. Starline Creative Printing, Albuquerque, 1974-76; mgr. corp. communications, Mesa Petroleum Co., Amarillo, Tex., 1976—. Mem. central com. Bernallilo County Republican Party, Albuquerque, 1975. Served to capt. USAF, 1964-69. Decorated Bronze Star. Presbyterian. Club: Amarillo. Home: 3900 Danbury St Amarillo TX 79109 Office: PO Box 2009 Amarillo TX 79189

CECIL, DAVID ROLF, educator; b. Tulsa, July 12, 1935; s. Neil McKinley and Ola Ethel (Turner) C.; student Carnegie Inst. Tech., 1954-55, Okla. A. and M. U., 1955-56; B.A., Tulsa U., 1958; postgrad. Tulane U., 1958-59; M.S., Okla. State U., 1960, Ph.D., 1962; m. Betty Lou Poe, June 14, 1958; 1 son, Eric Alan. Asst. prof. math. N. Tex. State U., 1962-67, asso. prof., 1967-69; prof. math. Butler U., 1969-70; asso. prof. mathematics Tex. A. and I. U., 1970-73, prof., 1973—, acting chmn. dept., summers 1974, 75, 77—; cons. magnetic div. Vero, Inc., Region I Edn. Service Center, Edinburg, Tex., Region II Edn. Service Center, Corpus Christi, Eagle Pass Ind. Sch. Dist.; lectr. Mem. supervisory com. Denton County Tchrs. Credit Union, 1968-69. Research fellow Tulane U., 1958-59; NSF summer fellow, 1960, 61; grantee North Tex. State U., 1968-69, Tex. A. and I. U., 1971, 72, 73. Fellow Tex. Acad. Sci. (chmn. math. scis. sect.); mem. Am. Math. Soc., N.Y. Acad. Scis., Tex. Assn. Children Learning Disabilities, Kingsville Amateur Radio Club (pres.), Sigma Xi. Methodist. Contbr. articles to profl. jours. Home: PO Box 1484 1921 S Park Dr Kingsville TX 78363

CELAURO, FRANCIS PAUL, civil engr.; b. Syracuse, N.Y., Dec. 10, 1943; s. Francis L. and Lillian U. C.; B.S.C.E., Vanderbilt U., 1965; m. Sibylle Neumann; children—Charles, Nicholas, Rebecca, Stuart. Civil engr. Brown & Root, Inc., Houston, 1969-71; asso., partner Dannenbaum Engring. Corp., Houston, 1972—. Served with C.E., U.S. Army, 1966-69; ETO. Registered profl. engr., Tex. Mem. ASCE, Nat. Soc. Profl. Engrs., Tex. Soc. Profl. Engrs. (treas. 1979-80, R. S. Guinn award 1976-77 Young Engr. of Yr. 1978, Houston C. of C. (flood control and water supply coms. 1976-79). Office: PO Box 22292 Houston TX 77027

CELLINI, WILLIAM QUIRINO, JR., elec. engr.; b. Ardmore, Pa., Mar. 12, 1951; s. Quirino and Clara (Ricciardi) C.; B.S. in E.E., Drexel U., 1974; M.B.A., U. Pitts., 1975. Intern in radiation physics Phila. Gen. Hosp., 1971, 72; research asst., energy systems Franklin Inst. Research Labs., Phila., 1973; systems analyst, elec. engr. Advanced Marine Enterprises, Arlington, Va., 1977-79; asso. solar thermal power systems PRC Energy Analysis Co., McLean, Va., 1979—. Mem. IEEE, Nat. Soc. Profl. Engrs., Pa. Soc. Profl. Engrs., Am. Soc. Engring. Edn., Soc. Am. Mil. Engrs., Assn. U.S. Army, Assn. M.B.A. Execs., Alpha Phi Omega. Home: 2111 Jefferson Davis Hwy Apt 1012-S Arlington VA 22202 Office: 7600 Old Springhouse Rd McLean VA 22102

CENTER, DANIEL HAYDN, JR., computer processing co. exec.; b. Campton, Ky., Aug. 5, 1930; s. Daniel Haydn and Ruth (Tutt) C.; B.S., Ohio State U., 1961, M.S., 1961; student Berea Coll., 1947-48, 50-51, Am. U., 1953, George Washington U., 1953-55; m. Barbara Ann Willis, Feb. 10, 1973; children—Timothy Joseph, Brendan Dale. Supr., Communications Center CIA, Washington, 1951-56; research asst. Ohio State U., 1960-61; maj. projects mgr. Gen. Telephone of Fla., Tampa, 1961-66; statis. dir. Gen. Telephone of Calif., Santa Monica, 1967-69; dir. mgmt. services dept. GTE Data Services, Tampa, 1969-74, v.p. field ops., 1974—. Served with AUS, 1948-49. Named Ky. Col.; registered profl. engr., Ohio, Fla., Calif. Mem. Am. Inst. Indsl. Engrs., Nat., Fla. socs. profl. engrs., Am. Statis. Assn., Am. Inst. Indsl. Engrs. (sec. 1973, pres. elect 1974, pres. 1975), Am. Statis. Assn., Com. of 100, Tampa C. of C. (chmn. research com. 1962-63), Am. Mktg. Assn. (v.p. 1962, 64, pres. 1965), Tau Beta Pi, Alpha Pi Mu. Home: 2419 Carolina Tampa FL 33609 Office: Box 1548 First Financial Tower Tampa FL 33601

CENTIFANTO, YSOLINA MEJIA, microbiologist; b. Panama City, Panama, Sept. 12, 1928; d. J. and Benelda (Paneda) Mejia; B.S., U. Panama, 1951; M.S., Western Res. U., 1954; Ph.D., U. Fla., 1964; div.; children—Loraine, James, Anthony, Matthew. Came to U.S., 1951, naturalized, 1960. Asst. prof. U. Panama, 1955-56, physiology asst. Sch. Medicine, 1955-56; instr. E.Carolina Coll., 1958; research technologist Kodak Tropical Research Lab., Panama City, 1956-58, Eastman Kodak Research Lab., Rochester, N.Y., 1958-61; abstractor Chem. Abstracts, Rochester, 1960-61; research asst. dept. ophthalmology Coll. Medicine, U. Fla., Gainesville, 1964-65, instr., 1965-66, asst. prof., 1966-72, asso. prof. ophthalmology, immunology and med. microbiology, 1972—; prof. microbiology and opthalmology La. State Med. Coll., New Orleans. Mem. Am. Chem. Soc., Am. Soc. Microbiology, AAAS, Assn. Research in Ophthalmology, N.Y. Acad. Scis., Sigma Xi. Contbr. articles to profl. jours. Home: 852 Wilshire Blvd Metairie LA 70005 Office: La State Univ Eye Center 136 S Roman St New Orleans LA 70112

CERALDI, ATTILO ANTONIO, surgeon; b. Mondragone, Italy, Jan. 17, 1928; s. Michael and Concetta (Conte) G.; came to U.S., 1953, naturalized, 1961; M.D., Rome Med. U., 1951; m. Evelyn Sizemore, May 21, 1958; children—Christopher, Mark, Katherine. Intern, St. Francis Hosp., Jersey City, 1954-56; surg. resident Ft. Howard (Md.) Vets. Hosp., 1962-67; staff surgeon Vets. Hosp., Columbia, S.C., 1967-70; med. officer Frankford Arsenal, Phila., 1958-62; practice medicine specializing in gen. surgery, Abbeville, S.C., 1970-79; attending surgeon Abbeville County Meml. Hosp., 1970-79; mem. courtesy staff Self Meml. Hosp., Greenwood, S.C.; surgeon VA Med. Center, Salisbury, N.C., 1979—. Served to lt., M.C., Italian Army, 1952-53. Diplomate Am. Bd. Gen. Surgery. Fellow Internat. Coll. Surgeons, A.C.S.: mem. Assn. Mil. Surgeons U.S. Roman Catholic. Home: Woodbridge Run Candlewick St Route 2 Salisbury NC 28144 Office: VA Med Center Salisbury NC 28144

CERNAK, STEPHEN MICHAEL, personnel agy. exec.; b. Cumberland, Md., Dec. 29, 1947; s. Steve and Ann Margaret (Healy) C.; student So. Meth. U. Data processing trainee Bank of Va., Richmond, 1970; adminstrv. asst. Dept. Corrections, State of Va., Richmond, 1970; field supr. Universal Mgmt., Virginia Beach, Va., 1971-75; owner, pres. United Personnel Services, Dallas, 1975—. Served with USMC, 1967-69; Vietnam. Decorated Purple Heart. Cert. personnel cons. Mem. Dallas Assn. Personnel Consultants, Tex. Assn. Personnel Consultants, Nat. Personnel Assos., Nat. Assn. Personnel Consultants, Dallas C. of C. (services com. 1978—). Roman Catholic. Home: 2617 Walnut Hill Ln 115 Irving TX 75062 Office: 13612 Midway Rd Suite 100 Dallas TX 75234

CERNUDA, CHARLES EVELIO, physician; b. Tampa, Fla., June 19, 1941; s. Evelio Perez and Angelina (Leto) C.; B.A., Emory U., 1963, M.D., 1968; m. Mary Margaret McElory, Nov. 24, 1967; children—Mary Robin and Meredith Lynley (twins), Lindsey Elizabeth. Intern, Emory U. Affiliated Hosps., Atlanta, 1968-69, resident in internal medicine, 1969-70, fellow in pulmonary disease, 1970-72; practice medicine specializing in internal medicine and pulmonary disease, Tampa, 1974—; med. dir. intensive care unit, pulmonary lab. and respiratory therapy depts. St. Josephs Hosp., 1974—, sec. treas., 1977-81; med. dir. pulmonary lab. and respiratory therapy depts. Centro Asturiano Hosp., 1974, vice chief med. staff, 1975-78. Served with M.C., USAF, 1972-73. Diplomate Am. Bd. Internal Medicine. Fellow Am. Coll. Chest Physicians; mem. A.C.P., Nat. Assn. Med. Dirs. Respiratory Care, So. Med. Assn., Fla. Med. Assn., AMA, Am., Fla. thoracic socs., Fla. Soc. Internal Medicine, Hillsborough County Med. Assn. (bd. censors 1979—), West Coast Acad. Medicine, Am. Soc. Internal Medicine. Democrat. Episcopalian. Clubs: Tampa Yacht and Country; Rotary of Ybor City (Tampa). Home: 4930 Andros Dr Tampa FL 33609 Office: 4900 N Habana Ave Tampa FL 33614

CERRA, JOSÉ JOAQUIN, surgeon; b. Fajardo, P.R., Dec. 6, 1938; s. José and Sara (Diaz) C.; B.S., U. P.R., 1959, M.D., 1963; m. Ines Maria Castaner, Apr. 20, 1968; children—Maria Ines, Jose Joaquin Alfredo, Maria del Pilar. Intern, resident U. P.R., 1966-70; chief surgery Caguas Subregional Hosp., Caguas, 1971-75; pvt. practice surgery, San Juan, 1975—; chief surgery Tchrs. Hosp., 1977—; attending in surgery Auxilio Muto Hosp., San Juan. Served to capt. AUS, 1964-66. Diplomate Am. Bd. Surgery. Fellow Am. Cancer Soc., A.C.S.; mem. Phi Sigma Alpha. Roman Catholic. Home: 1801 Diamela Santa Maria Rio Piedras PR 00927 Office: 500 Domenech St Hato Rey PR 00918

CERRONE, KENT MARVIN, mgmt. cons.; b. St. Charles, Ill., Jan. 19, 1949; s. Carmen Anthony and LaVerne Minetta (Boulter) C.; B.S., Iowa State U., 1971; m. Lynne Barbara Dozer, Nov. 1, 1975. Mgmt. analyst Sci. Mgmt. Corp., Moorestown, N.J., 1971-73; asst. v.p. materials mgmt. I.C.N. Pharmaceuticsl, Cin., 1973-74; sr. mgmt. analyst, project mgr. Sci. Mgmt. Corp., Moorestown, 1974-76; dir. edn. and mgmt. sers. Ky. Hosp. Assn., Louisville, 1976-79; v.p. health care sers. Opns Mgmt. Group, Inc., Atlanta, 1979—; cons. mem. Ky. Dept. Energy Planning Com. Mem. Hosp. Mgmt. Systems Soc. (pres. Appalachian chpt.), Eastern Jaguar Group N. Am. Republican. Lutheran. Home: Rt 1 Box 106 Union KY 41091 Office: 3300 Buckeye Rd Suite 264 Atlanta GA 30341

CERRUTI, RICHARD JOSEPH, bus. service exec.; b. N.Y.C., Mar. 31, 1939; s. Eligo and Laura Francesca (Grasso) C.; B.A., Colby Coll., 1961; postgrad Russian Lang. Sch., 1964-65, Am. U., 1969-70; m. Dianne Jean Spooner, Dec. 1, 1963; children—Michael, Laura, Eric. Pres., Nationwide Resumes of Am., Virginia Beach, Va., 1970—; mem. faculty Tidewater Community Coll., Portsmouth, Va., 1975-78. Bd. dirs. Big Bros. of Tidewater, 1979—. Served to lt. comdr. USN, 1962-70; Vietnam. Mem. Air Force Sgts. Assn. (cons. 1976—), Army Sgts. Assn. (cons. 1979—). Club: Cardinal Racquetball Assn. Author: The Career Search as a Science, 1978. Home: 504 Edwin Dr Virginia Beach VA 23462 Office: Suite 206 3500 Virginia Beach Blvd Virginia Beach VA 23452

CESAR, THOMAS EUGENE, health services center exec.; b. Riverside, Calif., Aug. 25, 1944; s. Edmund Broadman and Annette (Thomas) C.; A.A., Santa Monica City Coll., 1965; B.S., Calif. State U., Los Angeles, 1969; M.A., Boston State Coll., 1976; m. Amber Henson, Aug. 24, 1968; children—Todd Alan, Eric Thomas. Tchr. Pilgrim Sch., Los Angeles, 1971-73; staff asst. Mass. Bd. Regional Community Colls., Boston, 1974-75; unit mgr. Mt. Auburn Hosp., Cambridge, Mass., 1976-78; exec. dir. Rehab. and Cerebral Palsy Center, Raleigh, N.C., 1978—. Served with USAF, 1965-68. Mem. Assn. Med. Rehab. Dirs. and Coordinators, Am. Hosp. Assn., Assn. Retarded Citizens, Wake County Child Advocacy Council, Nat. Rehab. Assn. Mem. Christian Ch. Office: Rehab and Cerebral Palsy Center of Wake County 3004 New Bern Ave Raleigh NC 27610

CESSNA, PHYLLIS KESSEL, counselor; b. Petersburg, W.Va., Oct. 9, 1938; d. Leo Clyde and Lettie Marie (Evans) Sites; B.S., W.Va. U., 1966, M.A., 1971; postgrad. Math. Inst., 1970, Coll. of Grad. Studies, 1973-74, Marshall U., 1974-75; children—Maria, Michael, Todd. Tchr., Maysville (W.Va.) Elementary Sch., 1957-58, spl. edn. tchr., 1958-59; tchr Petersburg (W.Va.) Elementary Sch., 1960-71, guidance counselor, 1971-72, curriculum specialist, 1972-75; tchr. adult edn. Berkeley County (W.Va.), 1974-75; coordinator Nat. Inst. Edn. research project Berkeley County Schs., 1975-76; asso. ednl. specialist Appalachia Ednl. Lab., Charleston, W.Va., 1976-77; counselor Berkeley County Schs., Martinsburg, W.Va., 1977—; cons. to various colls. and secondary schs., 1971—. Named Regional Tchr. of the Year, W.Va. Edn. Assn., 1965; Benedum scholar, 1966. Mem. Am. Personnel and Guidance Assn., NEA, Assn. Supervision and Curriculum Devel., W.Va. Vocat. Guidance Assn., W.Va. Edn. Assn., W.Va. U. Alumni Assn. Baptist. Author: Student Career Guide, 1976; (with others) Career Education: A Structured Intervention Curriculum for Appalachian Youth, 1974; editor: English/Communications Cross Reference Catalog, 1976; (videotape and discussion presentation) Title IX: What Does It Mean to You?, 1976. Home: 3017 Tonbridge Martinsburg WV 25401 Office: Tuscarora Elementary School Martinsburg WV 25401

CETRULO, ROBERT CAMILLUS, lawyer; b. Covington, Ky., Feb. 13, 1935; s. Camillo D. and Estelle (McGrath) C.; student Xavier U., 1952-54; J.D., U. Ky. Coll. Law, 1958; m. Elaine E. Poage, Nov. 22, 1956; children—Cathleen, Robert, Nancy, Michael, Carol, Daniel, Lynn, Amy, Cara. Admitted to Ky. bar, 1958, since practiced in Covington; part-time U.S. magistrate Eastern Jud. Dist. Ky., 1960-75; lectr. polit. sci. and constl. law U. Ky. No. Community Coll., 1957-67; lectr. Salmon P. Chase Coll. Law, No. Ky. U. Bd. dirs. No. Ky. Community Action Commn., No. Ky. Assn. for Retarded, No. Ky. Area Devel. Dist. Human Resources Com. Mem. Ky., Am., Kenton County (pres. 1968) bar assns., No. Ky. Legal Aid Soc. (pres. 1967), Ky. Assn. Def. Counsel (dir.), Nat. Council U.S. Magistrates (2d v.p. 1974). Mem. law jour. editorial bd. U. Ky. Coll. Law. Home: 1716 Mt Vernon Dr Fort Wright KY 41011 Office: 303 Greenup St Covington KY 41011

CHABLE, E(UGENE) ROBERT, clergyman; b. Cleve., June 7, 1920; s. Eugene Ray and Marion Margaret (Skym) C.; B.B.A., Cleve. State U., 1944 M.Div., Colgate Rochester Div. Sch., 1946; M.A., U. Rochester, 1948; Ph.D., Columbia, 1955; postgrad. Union Theol. Sem., 1951-54, Princeton, 1952; D.D., Piedmont Coll., 1975; m. Marion Hayes Boynton, Oct. 26, 1946. With Elizabeth Jones Studios, Cleve., summer 1938, Gage Gallery, part-time 1939-40, Fed. Res. Bank, 1940-41, Crane Co., 1941-44; ordained to ministry Bapt. Ch., 1946; asso. minister Brighton Presbyn. Ch., Rochester, N.Y., 1944-45; minister 1st Bapt. Ch., Palmyra, N.Y., 1945-51; interim minister Wyckoff (N.J.) Reformed Ch., 1951-53; asso. minister Park Av. Meth. Ch., N.Y.C., 1954; dir. student personnel, dean of men, asso. prof. history Hillsdale Coll., 1954-57; dean of student personnel, acting registrar, prof. philosophy and religion Rio Grande Coll., 1957-59; incorporator, mem. exec. com. New Coll., Inc., Sarasota, Fla., 1959-62; v.p., bus. rep. Venice-Nokomis Bank, Venice, Fla., 1959-63; minister Venice United Ch. of Christ, 1963—. First v.p. Fla. Migrant Ministry, 1967-68; pres. Manatee-Sarasota Guidance Center, 1961-66. Vice pres. Sarasota County Community Health and Welfare Council, 1968-70. Bd. dirs. S. Sarasota County Retarded Children's Assn., 1961-63, Venice-Nokomis Art Assn., 1961-63; bd. dirs. Venice Little Theatre, 1962-65, treas., 1963-64, 64-66; bd. dirs. Family Service Assn., Sarasota County, 1963-65, Venice Civic Center, 1971-77; trustee New Coll., Sarasota, Fla., 1968-74; gov. Manatee-Sarasota chpt. NCCJ; mem. S. Sarasota County Meml. Hosp. Assn., chmn. nominating com. 1962, co-chmn. major gifts, 1973-75; adv. bd. South Sarasota County YMCA; sponsoring com. Venice br. Manatee Jr. Coll. Mem. Venice Area Ministerial Assn.

(pres. 1967-69, 77-78), Soc. Bibl. Lit. and Exegesis, Am. Council Learned Socs., Fla. Conf. United Ch. of Christ (moderator 1972-73), Audubon Soc., Nat. Geog. Soc., Sarasota County Mental Health Assn., Ringling Mus. Art (mem.'s council), Delta Sigma Phi. Mason (33 deg., K.T., Shriner); mem. Order DeMolay. Club: Venice Yacht. Contbr. articles to profl. jours. Home: 104 Alba St W Venice FL 33595 Office: PO Drawer 998 Venice FL 33595

CHACE, WILLIAM GEORGE, research lab. tech. cons.; b. Stamford, Conn., Dec. 10, 1904; s. William Weld and Katherine Louise (George) C.; Ph.B., Brown U., 1926; M.S., Lowell Tech. Inst., 1942; postgrad. Mass. Inst. Tech., 1948; m. Helen Myra Sheldon, Nov. 19, 1926; children—William George, Stephen Sheldon. Instr. in math. and physics Lowell (Mass.) Textile Sch., 1926-28; asst. prof. chemistry Lowell Tech. Inst., 1929-42, prof., 1947-56, also dir. libraries, 1948-56; research physicist Cambridge Research Labs., USAF, Bedford, Mass., 1956-67, tech. cons., 1968—; instr. Photodata Inst., Neenah, Wis., 1969-71; chmn. Internat. Conf. on Exploding Conductors, Boston, 1959, 61, 64, 67.; U.S. del. Internat. Symposium on Impulse Generators, Warsaw, Poland, 1966; H. W. Gould lectr., No. Ill. U., DeKalb, 1965. Mem. Mass. War Ration Bd., 1942-44; mem. Vets. Housing Bd., 1948. Served to comdr. USNR, 1942-46. Textile Found. Edn. grantee, 1947-49. Mem. Am. Phys. Soc., Soc. Motion Picture and TV Engrs., Am. Chem. Soc., IEEE, U.S. Power Squadrons (comdr. Boston chpt. 1965), Ret. Officers Assn., Am. Radio Relay League, U.S. Coast Guard Aux., Sigma Xi. Clubs: Appalachian Mountain, Boston Navigators (life), Wally Byam Caravan (pres. Everglades chpt. 1975). Author: (with H. K. Moore) Exploding Wires, vols. 1-4, 1959-68; (with E. M. Watson) Bibliography of Exploding Conductors, 1962. Editor: (with W. G. Hyzer) Procs. of 9th Internat. Congress on High Speed Photography, 1970. Home: 381 Delido Ct Punta Gorda FL 33950

CHACKO, JOHN KABZEEL YESUDAS, surgeon; b. Kerala, India, Sept. 14, 1941; s. John C. and Mariam P. Chacko; M.D., U. Kerala (India), 1964, M.Surgery, 1969; m. Jeanne Marie Hyde, June 26, 1977; came to U.S., 1970, naturalized, 1979. Intern, N.Y. Infirmary, N.Y. U., 1970-71; resident Mt. Sinai Hosp., N.Y.C., 1971-72, Westchester County Med. Center, Columbia U., 1972-75; surgeon Fellowship Hosp., Oddamchathram, Madras, India, 1969-70; fellow vascular surgery Mt. Sinai Sch. Medicine, N.Y.C., 1975-76; asst. chief surgery VA Med. Center, Lake City, Fla., 1976—; clin. asst. prof. surgery U. Fla., Gainesville, 1977—. Exec. dir. Evangelical Social Services, Gainesville. Fellow A.C.S., Internat. Coll. Surgeons; mem. Internat. Acad. Proctolgy, Am. Coll. Quality Assurance and Utilization Rev., Am. Geriatric Soc., Assn. Mil. Surgeons, Peripheral Vascular Surgery Club. Home: 5610 NW 28th Terrace Gainesville FL 32601 Office: VA Med Center Lake City FL 32055

CHACKO, MATHEWS, univ. registrar; b. Tiruvella, India, Apr. 7, 1939; came to U.S., 1965, naturalized, 1972; s. Gee Varghese and Mary (Kuruvella) C.; B.Th., So. Asia Bible Coll., Bangalore, India, 1965; B.A., So. Calif. Coll., 1967; M.Div. cum laude, Oral Roberts U., 1970; m. Rachel John, May 6, 1965; children—James, Elizabeth, Mary Sheba. Asst. registrar Oral Roberts U., Tulsa, 1969—; founder India Practical Missions, Tulsa, 1978—. Mem. Okla. Assn. Collegiate Registrars and Admissions Officers, Am. Assn. Collegiate Registrars and Admissions Officers, Am. Mgmt. Assn. Mem. Pentecostal Ch. Home: PO Box 425 Jenks OK 74037 Office: 7777 S Lewis St Tulsa OK 74171

CHADICK, T. C., state supreme ct. justice; b. Winnsboro, Tex., Sept. 21, 1910; s. Walter Martin and Carrie (Mars) C.; LL.B., Cumberland U., 1933;; m. Doris Adlyne Scruggs, Apr. 14, 1941; children—Mary Susan, Nancy Doris. Admitted to Tex. bar, 1933; pvt. law practice, 1934-40; county atty., Wood County, Tex., 1939-40; state senator, 1941-49; dist. judge, Quitman, Tex., 1949-56; chief justice Ct. of Civil Appeals, Texarkana, Tex., 1956-77; asso. justice Supreme Ct. Tex., 1977—. Mem. Tex. Constl. Revision Commn. Pres. Tex. Civil Jud. Council, 1961-64. Democrat. Methodist. Mason (Shriner). Home: 4017 Potomac St Texarkana TX 75501

CHADWICK, CHARLES ROBERT, JR., communications engr.; b. Atlanta, Jan. 14, 1943; s. Charles Robert and Katherine Eleanor (Hunt) C.; student Old Dominion Coll., 1965, U. Wis., 1967; m. Julaine Mary Hendricks, May 11, 1973; children—Philip Austin, Kevin Patrick, Paul Robert, Jennifer Lynn. Quality control supr. Admiral Corp., Harvard, Ill., 1966-69; field tech. rep. Motorola C. & E., Schaumburg, Ill., 1969-73, sr. internat. tech. rep., 1973-76, mgr. engring. field services, Latin Am., 1976-79, mgr. spl. products, Ft. Lauderdale, Fla., 1979—. Pres., Town of Delavan Fire Dept., 1968-72. Served with USNR, 1962-65. Roman Catholic. Home: 1144 SW 23d Ave Boynton Beach FL 33435 Office: 8000 W Sunrise Blvd Fort Lauderdale FL 33322

CHADWICK, CHARLES WILLIAM, veterinarian; b. Jackson, Miss., Mar. 8, 1912; s. Hudson and Anne Louise (Eley) C.; student Hinds Jr. Coll., 1933; D.V.M., Tex. A. and M. Coll., 1938; m. Evelyn Elizabeth Clark, June 14, 1938; children—Charles Eley, Martha Ann, Evelyn Elizabeth, William Lyon, Hudson Barnett, Clara Gene. With U.S. Bur. Animal Industry, Jacksonville, Fla., 1938-42; practice vet. medicine, Jackson, Miss., 1946—. Cons., veterinarian Union Stock Yards, Jackson, 1946-76. Vice pres. S.W. Jackson Improvement Assn.; mem. Jackson Pub. Schs. Survey Com., 1961; parent council Wilkins Sch., 1963-69; trustee Forest Hill Sch., 1955, Forest Hill United Meth. Ch., also adminstrv. bd.; bd. dirs. YMCA. Served as officer Vet. Corps, AUS, World War II. Col. Gov.'s Staff, State of Miss., 1960-72. Mem. Am., Miss. vet. medicine assns., Miss. Cattlemen's Assn., Farm Bur., Tex. A. and M. Former Students Assn., SCV. Clubs: Masons, Shriners. Contbr. cartoons, articles vet. publs. Home: 1426 Raymond Rd Jackson MS 39204

CHADWICK, ROBERT WILLIAM, toxicologist; b. Buffalo, Mar. 16, 1930; s. Elihu Clair and Helen (Murray) C.; B.A., Western Res. U., 1957, M.S., 1962; Ph.D., Utah State U., 1967; m. Claire Jeannette Crisp, Aug. 20, 1966; 1 dau., Natanya Laurel. Electrician apprentice Doan Electric Co., Cleve., 1950-51; chemist Republic Steel Research Center, Cleve., 1957-62; toxicologist EPA Primate and Pesticide Effects Lab., Perrine, Fla., 1966-73, Research Triangle Park, N.C., 1973—. Served with AUS, 1951-53. Recipient certificate for outstanding vol. service in field recreation Coral Gables (Fla.) Recreation Dept., 1973. Mem. Soc. Toxicology, AAAS, Am. Chem. Soc., N.Y. Acad. Scis., Fla. Chess Assn. (pres. 1972-73), U.S. Chess Fedn., Miami Chess Internat. (v.p.), Sigma Xi, Pi Delta Epsilon. Democrat. Club: Coral Gables Chess (pres. 1969-73). Contbr. articles to profl. jours. Home: Route 2 Box 56-A Apex NC 27502 Office: US Environmental Protection Agy Environmental Research Center Research Triangle Park NC 27711

CHAFIN, TROY ED, coal co. exec.; b. New Town, W.Va., Aug. 20, 1945; s. Troy and Alice C.; student Berea Coll., 1962, 65; m. Nancy Lambert Chafin, Oct. 16, 1965; children—Anita, Allison. News asst. Wall St. Jour., Cleve., 1963-64; news dir. Radio Sta. WBTH, Williamson, W.Va., 1965; engring. party chief Island Creek Coal Co., Holden, W.Va., 1966-70; resident engr. Royalty Smokeless Coal Co., Premier, W.Va., 1970-73; dir. safety and tng. Martin County Coal Corp., Inez, Ky., 1973—. Mem. Tng. and Edn. Assn. for Mining (v.p.), Nat. Mine Rescue Assn., AIME, Nat. Registry EMT's, Nat. Safety Mgmt. Soc., Ky. Mining Inst., Big Sandy-Elkhorn Coal Mining Inst. Democrat. Home: Box 132 Kermit WV 25674 Office: Route 40 Box 82A Inez KY 41224

CHAGY, JOHN, musician; b. Russia, Dec. 6, 1912; s. Berele and Esther (Fienstein) C.; Artist diploma Juilliard Grad. Sch., N.Y.C., 1936; came to U.S., 1912, naturalized; m. Etta Cohen, June 15, 1937; children—Linda, Alan. Piano fellow with Carl Friedberg Juillard Grad. Sch., 1932-36; debut pianist Carnegie Recital Hall, N.Y.C.; numerous concerts, 1930-65; tchr. piano, West Orange, N.J., 1937-72, Atlanta, 1972—; composer March of Atlanta, 1972, Peachtree St. Rag, 1977, Atlanta Sonatina, 1977, Ga. Rag, 1979, Atlanta Ragtime Blues, 1979, numerous other work for piano, 1958—; music critic So. Israelite, newspaper, Atlanta. Mem. Met. Atlanta Music Tchrs. Assn. (v.p. 1974-76), Am. Fedn. Musicians. Home: 77 E Andrews Dr Atlanta GA 30305

CHAHINE, ROBERT ANTOINE, cardiologist; b. Lebanon, Feb. 8, 1941; s. Antoine H. ahd Jamileh A. (Sfeir) C.; B.S., Am. U., Beirut, Lebanon, 1962, M.D., 1966. Asst. prof. medicine Sch. Medicine U. Calif., Los Angeles, 1972; asst. prof. medicine Baylor Coll. Medicine, Houston, 1972-76, asso. prof., 1976—; chief of cardiology VA Hosp., Houston, 1974—. Fellow Am. Coll. Cardiology, ACP, Am. Heart Assn. (dir. Houston chpt. 1975, chmn. physician edn. com. 1977). Contbr. numerous articles on coronary spasm, hypertrophic cardiomyo[pathy and other topics in cardiology to med. jours. Home: 2504 Bering Dr Houston TX 77057 Office: VA Hospital 2002 Holcombe Blvd Houston TX 77211

CHAIN, BOBBY LEE, elec. contractor; b. Hattiesburg, Miss., Sept. 19, 1929; s. Zollie Lee and Grace (Sellers) C.; B.S., U. So. Miss., Hattiesburg, 1974; m. Betty Sue Green, June 30, 1967; children—Robin Ann, Laura Grace, Bobby Lee, John Webster. Chief electrician Miss. Power & Light Co., Natchez, 1950-53; asst. to gen. supt. atomic energy plant Allegany Electric Co., Oak Ridge, 1954-55; owner, chmn. bd. Chain Electric Co., Hattiesburg, 1957—, Chain Lighting & Appliance Co., Hattiesburg, 1957—; owner, pres. Chainco, Inc., oil properties, Hattiesburg, 1974—; dir. Deposit Guaranty Nat. Bank, Jackson; mem. Interstate Oil Compact Commn., 1972—; nat. adv. council SBA, 1966-67. Pres. Miss. Trustees Instns. Higher Learning, 1972—; alt. del. Democratic Nat. Conv., 1964. Served with AUS, 1950. Recipient Albert Gallatin award Zurich Am. Ins. Co., 1975; Distinguished Service award U. So. Miss., 1976; Recognition plaque City of Hattiesburg, 1961-68. Mem. Newcomen Soc. N.Am., U. So. Miss. Alumni Assn. (Outstanding Service award 1972), Hattiesburg C. of C. (past dir.), Omicron Delta Kappa. Baptist. Clubs: Kiwanis, Hattiesburg Country, U. So. Miss. Century, Shriners, Elks; Univ., Capitol City (Jackson, Miss.). Home: 312 6th Ave Hattiesburg MS 39401 Office: PO Box 2058 Hattiesburg MS 39401

CHAKRABORTY, PRABIR KUMAR, educator; b. Calcutta, India, Jan. 1, 1936; s. Manindra Nath and Rama C.; came to U.S., 1967; B.S., Calcutta U., 1955; dairy diploma Nat. Dairy Research Inst., India, 1957; M.S., Oreg. State U., 1969, Ph.D., 1971; m. Purnima Chatterjee, Feb. 25, 1963; children—Sulagna, Sayan, Simanta. Research asst. Oreg. State U., Corvallis, 1967-71; research asso. Wash. State U., Pullman, 1971-74; asst. prof. U. Oreg. Health Sci. Center, Portland, 1974-76; asst. prof. cell biology, head of endocrinology Inst. Comparative Medicine Baylor Coll. Medicine, Houston, 1976; vis. prof. Tex. A. and M. U., College Sta., 1976-79; staff endocrinologist Vet. Resources br. NIH, Bethesda, Md., 1979—. NIH fellow, 1971-74. Mem. Am. Soc. Animal Sci., Am. Soc. Vet. Physiology and Pharmacology, Endocrine Soc., Soc. for Study of Reproduction, N.Y. Acad. Scis., Sigma Chi, Phi Kappa Phi, Phi Sigma. Contbr. articles in field to profl. jours. Home: 19821 Westerly Ave Poolesville MD 20837 Office: Vet Resources Br NIH Bethesda MD 20205

CHALKLEY, BLANTON ROLFE, printing co. exec.; b. Richmond, Va., Apr. 29, 1932; s. Bernard Elmore and Phyllis Lorean (Griffin) C.; student U. Richmond Evening Sch.; m. Patsy Bowles, May 11, 1973; 1 dau., Jane Elizabeth. With So. States Coop., 1952-65, Satterwhite Printing Co., 1965-70; with Custom Mailers & Cons., Inc., Richmond, 1970—, exec. v.p. prodn., 1972—, also dir.; adv. printing Va. State Coll.; cons. Inst. Continuing Edn.; chmn. Internat. Printing Week in Va., 1976, 78, 80. Adv. bd. Christ Ch. Sch. Mem. Richmond Printers Assn., Printing House Craftsmen (past pres. Richmond), Mechanicsville Civic Assn. Democrat. Baptist. Club: Masons. Home: 293 Crocus Ct Mechanicsville VA 23111 Office: 2400 Westwood Ave Richmond VA 23230

CHAMBERLAIN, CHARLES DEVERE, JR., physician; b. San Antonio, Apr. 26, 1928; s. Charles Devere and Opal Esteleene (Scott) C.; A.B., U. Tex., Austin, 1950, M.D., Galveston, 1954; m. Nancy Cravens (div.); children—Anne Wesley, Mary Cravens, Laura Roberts, Charles Devere; m. 2d, Kae Sandifer Chamberlain. Intern, U. Pa., 1954, resident in surgery, 1955-61, instr. surgery, 1960-61; practice medicine specializing in surgery Surg. Clinic Houston, 1963—, dir., 1974—; clin. asso. prof. U. Tex. Health Scis. Center, Houston, 1972—. Bd. dirs. Am. Cancer Soc., Am. Diabetes Soc., Houston. Served to capt. AUS, 1956-58; Japan. Mem. AMA, Tex., Harris County med. assns., Houston Surg. Soc., A.C.S., Tex. Traumatic Surg. Soc., Pan Am., So. med. assns., Am. Coll. Angiology, Am. Soc. Abdominal Surgeons, Am. Cancer Soc., Am. Diabetes Assn., Am. Geriatric Soc., Post Grad Med. Assembly S. Tex., Doctors Club Houston, Washington County C. of C., Sigma Alpha Epsilon, Phi Chi. Republican. Episcopalian. Clubs: Tejas, Allegro, Bayou Houston Polo. Contbr. articles to profl. jours. Home: 2601 Augusta 16 Houston TX 77057 Office: Surgical Clinic Houston 1005 Hermann Profl Bldg Houston TX 77030

CHAMBERLAIN, CLINTON JOHNSON, recreation industry mgmt. cons. co. exec.; b. Chgo., Oct. 9, 1924; s. Clinton Goodloe and Olivia Langdon J.; B.S.M.E., Oreg. State Coll., 1945; B.S., Ga. Inst. Tech., 1948; M.S., U. Mo., 1951; m. Dorothy Lyle Jones, June 12, 1948; children—Langdon, Lowry, Paul, Olivia, Nancy, Helen, Gilmer. Instr. physics Ga. Inst. Tech., 1946-48; instr. So. Tech. Inst., 1948-50, Kans. State Coll., 1951-52; grad. instr. U. Mo., Rolla, 1950-51; specialist in control and flight test monitoring instrumentation Boeing Aircraft, Seattle, 1952-56; Gen. Electric Co., Ithaca, N.Y., 1956-59; dir. research Nat. Rejectors, Inc., St. Louis, 1959-62; dir. research and engring. Northeast Corridor Project, Dept. Commerce, 1962-64; head quality engring. sect. NASA-Goddard, 1965-67; mgr. tech. applications group N. Am. Aviation Corp., Washington, 1967-68; mng. asso. Arthur Young & Co., Bethesda, Md., 1969-71; owner, mgr. Buoy 22 Marina, Gloucester, Va., 1971-74; owner, mgr. The Sailing Shop, Newport News, Va., 1974-76; cons. C.A. Chaney & Assos., also Lorenzi, Dodds & Gunnill, Pitts., also Washington, 1971-76; dir. grants and research contracts Coll. William and Mary, 1976; pres. C.A. Chaney Inc., Hayes, Va., 1976—. Served with U.S. Army, World War II. Decorated Purple Heart. Mem. Nat. Recreation and Parks Assn., Va. Assn. Marine Industries, Sigma Xi. Home: PO Box 120 Hayes VA 23072 Office: Tidemill Shopping Center Hayes VA 23072

CHAMBERLAIN, NUGENT FRANCIS, chem. researcher; b. Henderson, Tex., Mar. 10, 1916; s. Hubbard Bailey and Emmie (Chamberlin) C.; student N. Tex. Agrl. Coll., 1933-35; B.S., Tex. A. and M. U., 1938; m. Barbara Wilsdon Hall, Oct. 2, 1943; children—John Harold, Scott Nugent, David Alan. Trainee Humble Oil & Refining Co., 1938, jr. chemist, 1939-41, research chemist, 1941-50, sr. research chemist, 1950-61, research specialist, 1961-63; research asso. Esso Research & Engring. Co., Baytown, Tex., 1963-69, sr. research asso., 1969—. Mem. bd. reviewers Thermodynamics Research Center of Tex. A. and M. U.; mem. NMR subcom. and adv. com. Nat. Bur. Standards, 1970-73; vis. scientist Tex. Acad. Sci., 1959-67; seminar leader; speaker. Served to maj. C.W.S., AUS, 1942-46. Decorated Legion of Merit; recipient profl. progress award Soc. Profl. Chemists and Engrs., 1961, Southeastern Tex. sect. award, S.W. regional award Am. Chem. Soc., 1969. Mem. Am. Chem. Soc. (councillor 1972, dir. 1973, 75), Am. Inst. Chemists, Tex. Inst. Chemists (honor scroll 1977), ASTM (com. E13, subcom. NMR), Am. Def. Preparedness Assn., Electron Microscopy Soc. Am., Tex. Soc. Electron Microscopy, Microbeam Analysis Soc. Republican. Presbyterian (elder). Author: A Catalog of the Nuclear Magnetic Resonance Spectra of Hydrogen in Hydrocarbons and Their Derivatives, 1958; Chemical Shift and Spin Coupling Data, 1963; Nuclear Magnetic Resonance Data for Hydrogen, 1965, Nuclear Magnetic Resonance Data for Sulphur Compounds, 1971; The Practice of NMR Spectroscopy, 1974. Contbr. articles profl. jours. Patentee in field. Home: 209 Edgewood St Baytown TX 77520 Office: PO Box 4255 Baytown TX 77520

CHAMBERLIN, DONALD LESLIE, state senator; b. Dunedin, Fla., Dec. 13, 1935; s. James Graham and Mary Ruth (Bruce) C.; B.S., Fla. State U., 1959, M.A., 1968; s. Therese Elizabeth McBride, July 1, 1961; children—Karen Leslie, Jeffrey Drake. Tchr., Pinellas (Fla.) County Sch. Bd., 1964—; mem. Fla. Senate from 19th Dist., 1976—; mem. Edn. Commn. States, 1979. Mem. NEA, Nat. Council Social Studies, Fla. Council Social Studies, Fla. Teaching Profession (exec. com. 1975-76), Pinellas Classroom Tchrs. Assn. (past pres.), Phi Delta Kappa. Democrat. Home: 2256 Curtis Dr S Clearwater FL 33516 Office: 307 S Osceola Ave Clearwater FL 33516

CHAMBERS, BILLY J., chem. co. exec.; b. Feb. 22, 1952; s. William j. and Marjorie (Lannom) C.; B.S. in Criminal Law, S.W. Tex. State U., 1973, postgrad., 1974-79. Gen. mgr. Lannom Property Co., Seguin, Tex., 1975-77; sales rep. Puritan Churchill Chem. Co., Atlanta, 1977—; instr. S.W. Tex. State U. Vol. Softball Assn., Seguin. Mem. Seguin C. of C., Tau Kappa Epsilon, Kappa Chi Lambda. Methodist. Home: PO Box 527 Seguin TX 78155

CHAMBERS, CARL DEAN, social and health research assn. exec.; b. Miami, Okla., Oct. 30, 1934; s. Lowell Andrew and Clella Elizabeth (Lewis) C.; B.A., Okla. State U., 1960; M.S., Kan. State Coll., 1961; Ph.D., U. Colo., 1966; m. Kathryn Mae Keplar, Nov. 1, 1968; 1 dau., Christine Elise. Dir. Personal Devel. Inst., Geneva, Fla., 1973—; exec. v.p. Resource Planning Corp., Washington, 1971-76; pres. RPC Found., N.Y.C., 1973-76; asso. prof. U. Miami Sch. Medicine, 1971-73; prof. dir. Inst. for Pub. Health Research, Antioch Coll.; advisor NIMH, 1971-74, FDA, 1977—, U.S. Drug Enforcement Adminstrn., Nat. Acad. Scis.; mem. Pres.'s Nat. Adv. Council for Drug Abuse Prevention, 1971—. Served with USAF, 1953-57. Recipient 9 NIMH fellowships and grants, 1962-74. Mem. Am. Soc. Criminology (mem. exec. council), Am. Sociol. Soc. Author: Epidemiology of Opiate Addiction in U.S., 1970; Employee Drug Abuse, 1972; Methadone: Experiences and Issues, 1972; Drugs and The Criminal Justice System, 1974; Chemical Coping, 1975; Heroin Epidemics, 1976. Contbr. numerous articles to profl. jours. Editor: Internat. Jour. of Chem. Dependencies, 1973—. Home: 17345 SW 112th Ave Miami FL 33157 Office: Sandy Grove Farm Lake Geneva Dr Geneva FL 32732

CHAMBERS, FRANCIS EUGENE, priest; b. Phila., Oct. 12, 1949; s. Frank Warren and Rita Geraldine (Fearn) C.; B.A., Villanova U., 1973, M.A., 1977; postgrad. Washington Theol. Union, 1974-78. Ordained priest Roman Catholic Ch., 1978; dir. student activities Biscayne Coll., Miami, Fla., 1978—. Mem. Cath. Campus Ministry Assn., Am. Personnel and Guidance Assn., Kappa Delta Pi. Address: 16400 NW 32d Ave Miami FL 33054

CHAMBERS, JAMES DOUGLAS, farmer; b. Jones County, Ga., Sept. 25, 1948; s. William Harris and Sara Elizabeth (Napier) C.; student Middle Ga. Coll., 1977; B.S., U. Ga., 1970; m. Mary Foster, Dec. 20, 1969; children—James Douglas, Jennifer Gwen, Casey Clinton. Mgr. dairy farm, Jones County, 1970-73; owner, operator dairy farm, Macon, Ga., 1973—. Named Man of Yr. in Soil and Water Conservation, Piedmont Soil and Water Conservation Dist., 1979. Mem. Ga. Farm Bur., Southeastern United Dairy Industry Assn., Ga. Agrl. Commodity Commn. Methodist. Home and Office: Route 6 Macon GA 31201

CHAMBERS, JANICE ELAINE JOHNSON, toxicologist; b. Oakland, Calif., Sept. 2, 1947; d. Giles Weston and Eva Marie (Fehr) Johnson; B.S., U. San Francisco, 1969; Ph.D., Miss. State U., 1973; m. Howard Wayne Chambers, June 14, 1969. Lab. technician U. Calif., Berkeley, 1964-68; grad. teaching asst. zoology dept. Miss. State U., Mississippi State, 1969-70, 71, NSF fellow, zoology dept., 1970-72, postdoctoral fellow, 1973-76, research zoologist, dept. biol. scis., 1976-79, asst. prof., 1980—; co-investigator/prin. investigator various grants. Recipient Outstanding Young Woman of Starkville award Jaycettes, 1978; named one of Three Outstanding Young Women in Miss., 1979; Outstanding Woman at Miss. State U. award Miss. State U. Pres.'s Commn. on Status of Women, 1979. Mem. Am. Physiol. Soc., Am. Coll. Toxicology, Am. Chem. Soc., Miss. Acad. Scis., Starkville Area Bus. and Profl. Women's Club (1st v.p. 1979-80), Sigma Xi (research award 1980, sec. Mississippi State chpt. 1978, pres. elect 1980), Phi Kappa Phi. Contbr. articles to sci. jours. Home: Route 5 Box 3 Starkville MS 39759 Office: Miss State U PO Drawer GY Mississippi State MS 39762

CHAMBERS, LESLIE ADDISON, educator; b. Mystic, Iowa, Oct. 11, 1905; s. Clarence Edwin and Bertha Alice (Lang) C.; B.S., Tex. Christian U., 1927, M.S., 1928; Ph.D., Princeton, 1930; m. Ione Lee Way, May 30, 1930; children—Sabra Lee (Mrs. Herbert H. Henke), John Leslie, Linda Jean (Mrs. Victor Caldwell), Alys Ione (Mrs. James Cameron). Asst. prof. biology Tex. Christian U., 1930-32; fellow med. physics Johnson Found., instr. pediatrics Sch. Medicine, U. Pa., 1932-36, asst. prof. biophysics, 1942-45, asso. prof., 1945-46; chief phys. def. div. Biol. Labs., Chem. Corps, 1946-51; dir. research R.A. Taft San. Engring. Center, USPHS, 1951-56; dir. research Los Angeles Air Pollution Control Dist., 1956-60; dir. Allan Hancock Found., U. S.C., 1960-68; dir. Inst. Environ. Health, U. Tex. Sch. Pub. Health, Houston, 1968-70, prof. environ. sci., 1970—, dir. South-North Center, 1977—; cons. USPHS, NSF; mem. emergency action com. Los Angeles County Air Pollution Control Dist.; cons. McNeese State U., 1974-75, Pan Am. Health Orgn., 1974—; adj. prof. Rice U., 1974—. Mem. Surgeon Gen.'s Com. on Environmental Health, 1961-62; pres. Los Angeles County Tb Assn., 1964-65; mem. Nat. Air Conservation Commn., 1966-72; chmn. Tex. Air Conservation Com., 1971-73; mem. tech. adv. com. Tex. Air Control Bd., 1972-74. Served with OSRD, 1943-45; col. USAF Res., 1949-50,

USPHS, 1950-51. Recipient Distinguished Alumnus award Tex. Christian U., 1957. Fellow AAAS, Am. Pub. Health Assn. (com. chmn.), N.Y. Acad. Scis., Am. Chem. Soc.; mem. Soc. Immunologists, Am. Physiol. Soc., Am. Soc. Microbiologists, Air Pollution Control Assn. Club: Princeton (Houston). Contbr. articles to profl. jours. Home: 502 Walnut Bend Ln Houston TX 77042 Office: PO Box 20186 Houston TX 77025

CHAMBERS, MARVIN DEAN, mfg. co. exec.; b. Asheville, N.C., Dec. 15, 1941; s. Marion Thomas and Edith Viola C.; student N.C. A. and T. U., 1960-61; student Asheville-Buncombe Tech. Inst., 1961-63, 1966-67, A.A.S. in Mech. Engring. Tech., 1975; m. Cordelia Pedew, May 19, 1962; children—Marvin D., Alethea Jeanette; stepchildren—Victor R., Ricardo L. Draftsman Am. Enka Corp., Enka, N.C., 1963-67; draftsman Rondesics Co., Asheville, N.C., 1967-68, Stencel Aero Engring., Arden, N.C., 1968-69, C.P. Clare Co., Fairview, N.C., 1969-70; draftsman Taylor Instrument Co., Arden, N.C., 1970-74, layout designer, 1974-80; designer Stencel Aero Engring., Arden, 1980—. Bd. dirs. Buncombe County (N.C.) Assn. Retarded Citizens, 1968-71; bd. mgrs. Asheville YMCA, 1970-76; pres. local PTA, Asheville, 1975-76; Vice chmn. Asheville City Sch. Adv. Council, 1976-77, chmn., 1977-79; mem. Asheville Civic Center Commn., 1977—; 2d vice chmn. Buncombe County Democratic Com., 1977—. Cert. mfg. technologist. Mem. Engrs. Soc. Western N.C., Soc. Mfg. Engrs. Democrat. Baptist. Clubs: Optimists, Toastmasters, Masons. Home: 2 Lakewood Dr Asheville NC 28803 Office: Airport Rd Arden NC 28704

CHAMBERS, RAYMOND LEE, polit. scientist, educator; b. Detroit, Jan. 17, 1947; s. Binning Pearce and Victoria Ada (Nye) C.; student Montgomery Coll., 1964-65; A.B., U. Mich., 1969; M.A., Emory U., 1971, Ph.D., 1975; postgrad. Ga. State U., 1973, Fla. State U., 1976-79; m. Paula Marilyn Haver, Aug. 13, 1972; 1 son, Herschel Benjamin. Asst., Sci. Info. Exchange, Washington, 1965-66; instr. West Ga. Coll., Carrolton, 1970-71, Ga. State U., Atlanta, 1971-72, Dalton (Ga.) Jr. Coll., 1972-73; asst. prof., acting chmn. dept. social scis. Bainbridge (Ga.) Jr. Coll., 1973-75, asso. prof. polit. sci., 1975—, chmn. div. social sci. and phys. edn., 1976—; elections cons., 1978—; mem. adv. com. Ga. Consumers' Utility Counsel, 1977—. Founder Bainbridge-Decatur County Citizens Council on Crime, 1974. Inst. of Life Ins. grantee, 1976; Nat. Endowment Humanities Summer grantee, 1976. Mem. Am. Polit. Sci. Assn., So. Polit. Sci. Assn., Ga. Polit. Sci. Assn. (v.p. 1979-80, pres. 1980-81), Am. Council Consumer Interests, Soc. Research Adminstrs., Am. Soc. Criminology, League Women Voters, Community Coll. Social Sci. Assn., Presidency Research Group, Acad. Criminal Justice Scis., Am. Assn. U. Adminstrs., Bainbridge-Decatur County C. of C. (dir. 1976-77), Decatur County Hist. Soc. Democrat. Jewish. Club: Kiwanis (dist. coordinator 1979—). Author: Buyer's Handbook, 1976; contbr. articles to jours. in field; editor Readings in Am. Govt., 1973-76. Office: Div of Social Science Bainbridge Jr College Hwy 84E Bainbridge GA 31717

CHAMBLISS, JOE PRESTON, thermal analysis engr.; b. Kerrville, Tex., Nov. 5, 1947; s. Preston Ray and Marian Joyce (Ganz) C.; student Tex. A. and M. U., 1966-68; B.S. in Aerospace Engring., U. Tex., Austin, 1970; M.S. in Mech. and Aerospace Engring. (Univ. fellow), Rice U., 1972, M.S. in Space Physics and Astronomy, 1975. Engr., McDonnell Douglas Aircraft, St. Louis, 1970, Lockheed Eelctronics Co. Inc., Houston, 1974-76, Rockwell Internat., Houston, 1976-79, McDonnell Douglas Tech. Services Corp., 1979—. NSF fellow, 1972-73. Mem. Am. Astron. Soc., Fedn. Am. Scientists, L-5 Soc., Am. Phys. Soc., Aircraft Owners and Pilots Assn., Am. Inst. Aeros. and Astronautics, ACLU, Environ. Def. Fund. Club: Rockwell Flying. Contbr. articles to tech. jours. Home: 15030 St Cloud Houston TX 77062

CHAMBLISS, MARCIA JEANELLE, speech pathologist; b. Pasadena, Tex., Sept. 29, 1950; d. Duke Thorpe and Maxie Bell (McNair) Jeanes; B.S., U. Tex., 1972; M.A., U. Houston, 1973; m. Joe Preston Chambliss, Aug. 19, 1978. Speech pathologist, lang./learning disabilities specialist, ednl. diagnostician Clear Creek Ind. Sch. Dist., 1973—; pvt. practice speech pathologist, Houston, 1976—. Mem. Am. Speech and Hearing Assn., Am. Instrs. of the Deaf, Tex. Speech and Hearing Assn., Houston Assn. for Communication Disorders, Council for Exceptional Children. Methodist. Home: 15030 St Cloud St Houston TX 77062 Office: Clear Creek Independent School District 2301 E Main League City TX 77573

CHAMBLISS, MELETTE MELOY, audiologist; b. Independence, Mo., May 18, 1954; d. Nott Samuel and Ruby Grace (Stephens) Meloy; student Central Mo. State U., 1972-73; B.S. with high honors, So. Meth. U., 1975, M.S., 1976; m. Larry Lee Chambliss, Mar. 31, 1979. Ednl. audiologist Richardson (Tex.) Ind. Sch. Dist., 1976—; dir. hearing screening Richardson Pre-Sch. PTA, 1978-80. Bur. Educationally Handicapped grantee, 1975. Mem. Am. Speech Lang. and Hearing Assn., Dallas Speech Pathologist and Audiologists. Home: 1001 Longhorn Dr Plano TX 75023 Office: 1301 N Custer St Richardson TX 75080

CHAMPAGNE, JOEL JOHN, hosp. adminstr.; b. Raceland, La., Jan. 2, 1929; s. Alcide Joseph and Hedwige (Folse) C.; B.A., Southwestern La. Inst., 1949; M.Ed., La. State U., 1952; postgrad. health services adminstr. devel. program U. Ala., 1970; m. Mae Lou Cortez, June 1, 1952; children—Don, Brian, Joellyn, Brad. Tchr., Raceland Elem. Sch., 1949-54; tchr. English, Raceland High Sch., 1958-59; adminstrv. asst. Freeport Sulphur Co., 1959-62; purchasing agt. St. Joseph Hosp., Thibodaux, La., 1962-65, asst. adminstr., 1965-71, adminstr., 1971-75; adminstr. Thibodaux Gen. Hosp., 1975—. Bd. dirs. Lafourche Cancer Soc., Cath. Charities. Served with USAF, 1954-58. Named Boss of Yr., Bus. and Profl. Womens Club, 1975. Mem. Am. Acad. Med. Adminstrs. (state dir.), La. Soc. Hosp. Purchasing Agts. (organizing chmn., 1st pres. 1966-67), La. Hosp. Assn. (dir. and past pres. S.E. dist.), Thibodaux C. of C. (dir. 1973-75). Democrat. Roman Catholic. Clubs: Century (Nicholls State U.); Lions (pres. 1971-72). Home: 108 Garden Circle Thibodaux LA 70301 Office: 602 N Acadia Rd Thibodaux LA 70301

CHAMPION, PAUL HENRI, nat. bank examiner; b. Orlando, Fla., Dec. 24, 1945; s. Paul Henri and Marion Alice (Joyce) C.; B.S., U. West Fla., 1968; M.B.A., Stetson U., 1970. Asst. trust examiner Regional Adminstr. of Nat. Banks, Atlanta, 1971-74, nat. trust examiner, 1974-78, examiner-in-charge Atlanta Trust Subregion, 1976, nat. bank examiner, 1978—; tech. edn. specialist Comptroller of Currency, Washington, 1976-78; instr. mgmt. techniques Fed. Fin. Instns. Council, 1977—. Recipient Spl. Achievement award Dept. Treasury, 1978; Comptroller of Currency Spl. Recognition award Comptroller of Currency, 1978. Mem. Am. Mgmt. Assn., Soc. for Advancement Mgmt. Republican. Roman Catholic. Clubs: Sweetwater Country; Elks. Home: 603 Fox Valley Dr Longwood FL 32750 Office: 229 Peachtree St Atlanta GA 30303

CHAMPLIN, HERBERT HIRAM, rancher, oil co. exec. b. Lawton, Okla., Jan. 1, 1912; s. Roy Frank and Frances (Cobb) C.; student U. Okla., 1929-33. Pvt. practice oil landman, Okla., Tex., 1933-35; finance clk. U.S. Army, 1936-40, commd. 2d. lt., 1933, advanced through grades to col., 1962; ret., 1967; rancher, Lawton, 1967—; with Champ Resources Inc., Lawton, 1972—, chief exec. officer, pres., chmn. bd., 1976—. Precinct chmn. Republican party, 1968-76. Decorated Legion Merit. Mem. Ind. Oil Operators Assn., Phi Delta Theta. Home and office: 505 NW Gore Blvd Lawton OK 73501

CHAMPLIN, WILLIAM GLEN, clin. microbiologist; b. Rogers, Ark., Sept. 10, 1923; s. Glen and Anna (Boatright) C.; B.S., Northeastern State U., 1948; M.S., U. Ark., 1965, Ph.D., 1971; m. Helen Elizabeth Garner, Feb. 2, 1951; 1 son, Steven Glen. Med. technologist VA Hosp., Muskogee, Okla., 1951-55; supervisory microbiologist VA Hosp., Fayetteville, Ark., 1955—; cons. Washington Regional Med. Center, Fayetteville City Hosp., 1964—; guest lectr. immunology U. Ark., 1971-77. Served with AUS, 1943-45. Mem. Sigma Xi, Phi Sigma Epsilon (pres. 1945-46, 47-48). Home: 3018 Sheryl Ave Fayetteville AR 72701 Office: VA Hosp Fayetteville AR 72701

CHAN, RAFAEL CAMACHO, radiation oncologist; b. Manila, Philippines, Apr. 19, 1945; s. Enrique O. and Jovita Velasquez (Camacho) C.; came to U.S., 1971; m. Christina V. Garcia, Apr. 6, 1969; children—Alfonso, Anna Maria Rita, Rafael Honorio, Joseph Francis. Intern, Hosp. St. Raphael, New Haven, 1971-72; resident in gen. radiology Monmouth Med. Center, Long Branch, N.J., 1972-73; resident in radiotherapy U. Tex. System Cancer Center, M.D. Anderson Hosp., Houston, 1973-76, asst. prof. radiotherapy, 1976-79; asst. prof. U. Tex. Med. Sch., Houston, 1978-79; clin. asso. prof. radiotherapy U. Tex. Health Sci. Center, Dallas, 1979—; practice medicine specializing in radiation oncology Radiation and Chemotherapy Assos., Fort Worth, 1979—; cons. staff Hermann Hosp., Houston, 1976—. Mem. AMA, Tex. Med. Assn., Harris County Med. Soc., Tarrant County Med. Soc., Am. Coll. Radiology, Am. Radium Soc., Am. Soc. Clin. Oncologists, Am. Soc. Therapeutic Radiologists, Gilbert Fletcher Soc., S.W. Oncology Group, Philippine Coll. Radiology, Tex. Assn. Philippine Physicians. Roman Catholic. Contbr. articles in field to profl. jours. Office: Suite 319 800 5th Ave Fort Worth TX 76104

CHANDA, JOSEPH JOHN, dermatologist; b. Passaic, N.J., Feb. 20, 1946; s. George and Mary Anna Chanda; M.D., Georgetown U., 1971; m. Marilyn Joan Brunda, Aug. 3, 1968; children—Joseph Michael, Michelle Marie. Intern, Cornell Hosps., N.Y.C., 1971-72; resident in internal medicine Georgetown U. Hosp., Washington, 1972-73; resident in dermatology U. Mich., Ann Arbor, 1975-78; practice medicine specializing in dermatology Melbourne, Fla., 1978—; cons. physician James E. Holmes Regional Med. Center, 1978—. Served with USN, 1973-75. Diplomate Am. Bd. Dermatology. Fellow Am. Acad. Dermatology; mem. AMA, So. Med. Assn., Dermtology Found. Roman Catholic. Contbr. articles to profl. jours. Home: 353 Amberjack Pl Melbourne Beach FL 32951 Office: 1327 S Oak St Melbourne FL 32901

CHANDLER, ALBERT GALLATIN, oil equipment co. exec., rancher; b. McKinney, Tex., Sept. 21, 1913; s. James Throckmartin and Eva Grace (Hartin) C.; m. Oletha A. Hollingsworth, Oct. 23, 1950; children—James Albert, John Emmet. Service engr. John Deere Tractor Co., Houston, 1934-36; service engr., dist. sales mgr. then div. mgr. Reed Roller Bit Co., Houston, 1936-56; mgr. Eastern hemisphere Security Engring. Corp., London, 1956-57; pres. Petroleum & Mining Equipment Co., Geneva, Switzerland, 1957—; owner, pres. Chandler Ranch & Petroleum Services, Inc., Bastrop, Tex., 1967—. Mem. Soc. Petroleum Engrs., Am. Inst. Mech. Engrs., Am. Petroleum Inst. Clubs: Nomads, Houston, Pine Forest Racquet. Home: Route 1 Box 62A Bastrop TX 78602 Office: 1249 Soral Geneva Switzerland

CHANDLER, DAVID WAYNE, audiologist, army officer; b. Columbus, Ga., Mar. 21, 1952; s. Johnny Wilburn and Wanna Lee (Batts) C.; B.A. in Communication Disorders, Columbus Coll., 1976; M.S. in Audiology, Fla. State U., 1977; m. Virginia Frances Farrell, Mar. 19, 1977. With pub. relations Visa dept. Columbus Bank & Trust Co., 1973-76; grad. asst. Fla. State U., Tallahassee, 1977; commd. 1st lt. Med. Ser. Corps, U.S. Army, 1978; audiologist U.S. Army Hosp., Ft. Campbell, Ky., 1978—; chief of audiology, hearing conservation officer, Ft. Campbell. Com. chmn. Baptist Student Union, Columbus Coll., 1972-74; scoutmaster Troop 533 Boy Scouts Am., Ft. Campbell, 1978—. Cert. audiologist. Mem. Am. Speech and Hearing Assn., Assn. Mil. Audiologists and Speech Pathologists. Home: 538 Briarwood Dr Clarksville TN 37040 Office: ENT Audiology Dept US Army Hosp Fort Campbell KY 42223

CHANDLER, DENVIL FORD, mfg. co. exec.; b. Charley, Ky., June 29, 1912; s. John Henry and Nora (Hayes) C.; student Washburn Elec. Sch., Chgo., 1931; m. Sarah Louise Walters, Sept. 13, 1935; children—Nora Ann (Mrs. Terry Thornburg), Mary Jo (Mrs. Richard Thompson), Peggy Jewell (Mrs. Raymond Pollard III), Henry Phillip, Denvil Ford II. Formerly short order cook, restaurant mgr., shipping clk.; asst. mgr. Wholesale Grocery Co., Huntington, W.Va., 1939-43; owner Chandler's Plywood Products, Huntington, 1935-49, pres., 1949—; pres. Cabinet Supplier, Inc., Huntington, 1953—. Mem. Tri-State Airport Authority, 1961-67, pres., 1961-64; mem. Wayne County (W.Va.) Vocational Council, 1970—. Councilman, Huntington, 1957-61, asst. mayor, 1960-61. Named Boss of Year Am. Bus. Women's Assn., 1963. Mem. Nat. Assn. Plastic Fabricators (charter, pres. 1962-63), Am. Inst. Kitchen Dealers, Nat. Assn. Home Builders, Wholesale Kitchen Distbrs. Assn. (gov.), United Comml. Travelers, W.Va. C. of C., Hon. Order Ky. Cols., Huntington Mfrs. Club, Engrs. Club Huntington. Rotarian (pres. 1968-69). Home: 3717 Brandon Rd Huntington WV 25704 Office: 3716 Waverly Rd Huntington WV 25722

CHANDLER, EDWARD LEE, chem. co. exec.; b. Kansas City, Kans., Dec. 25, 1926; s. Joseph Penn and Catherine Rose (Bauer) C.; B.S., Kans. State U., 1949; Ph.D., Mich. State U., 1953. Buyer, dir. garden shops J.L. Hudson Co., Detroit, 1953-55; tech. mgr. agr. Diamond Shamrock Corp., Cleve., 1955-68; dir. research F. A. Bartlett Tree Co., Charlotte, N.C., 1968-74; mgr. tech. sers. and micronutrients Mineral Research and Devel. Corp., Charlotte, 1974—; owner, operator real estate co. Served with USNR, 1945-46. Roses Inc. fellow, Mich. State U., 1949-53. Mem. Nat. Agrl. Chem. Assn. (chmn. granular pesticide com. 1965-68), Nat. Fertilizer Sci. Assn., Agronomy Soc., Am. Assn. Hort. Sci., Sigma Xi, Pi Alpha Xi. Contbg. author Time-Life Trees book, 1972. Home: 1000 Rocky Ridge Dr Charlotte NC 28210 Office: 4 Woodlawn Green Suite 232 Mineral Research and Devel Corp Charlotte NC 28210

CHANDLER, JAMES THOMAS, ins. co. exec.; b. Nashville, Jan. 28, 1899; s. Samuel Jones and Elizabeth (Bonner) C.; student Tenn. State U., 1914-15, Meharry Med. Coll., 1918; m. Helen Lucile Howard, Aug. 1918 (dec.); children—James Thomas, Helen Chandler Shelby, Howard B., Erdyne A., Horace L. Agt., Life & Casualty Ins. Co., Nashville, 1918-21; dist. mgr. Miss. Life Ins. Co., Ft. Worth, 1921-25; agy. organizer Nat. Benefit Ins. Co., Tex., La., Ala., 1925-26; spl. agt. Atlanta Life Ins. Co., 1927-28; auditor, chief auditor, personnel dir., supr. records retention Universal Life Ins. Co., Memphis, 1928—; pres. Memphis Area Transit Authority, 1972-76; treas. Memphis Health Systems Mgmt., Inc. Vice pres. Memphis Met. YMCA; mem. Memphis ahd Shelby County Bd. Health, 1969-76; mem. exec. bd. Chickasaw council Boy Scouts Am.; elder, treas. Mississippi Blvd. Christian Ch. Recipient Silver Beaver award Boy Scouts, 1962; plaques Chmn. Abe Scharff br. YMCA, 1968, Christian Men's Fellowship, Christian Ch. in Tenn., 1973, Memphis Area Assn. Christian Chs., 1973, Memphis Area Transit Authority, 1976, award of merit City of Memphis, 1976. Democrat. Club: Masons. Home: 1047 McDowell St Memphis TN 38126 Office: 480 Linden Ave Memphis TN 38126

CHANDLER, JOHN BRANDON, JR., lawyer; b. Boston, Sept. 25, 1939; s. John Brandon and Juliette (Blackburn) C.; diploma Ga. Mil. Acad., 1957; B.A., Vanderbilt U., 1961, J.D., 1964; student Instituto Technilogico y Estudios Superiores de Monterrey, 1959; 1 son, John Brandon III. Admitted to Tenn. bar, 1964, Fla. bar, 1967, U.S. Supreme Ct. bar, 1971; asso. Rogers, Towers, Bailey, Jones & Gay, Jacksonville, Fla., 1966-73, partner, 1973—. Panel mem. Am. Arbitration Assn. Pres. Jacksonville Beach Young Republican Club, 1967. Served to capt. AUS, 1964-66. Mem. Am., Fla., Tenn., Jacksonville (gov. 1975—) bar assns., Phi Delta Phi (pres. Malone Inn 1964), Kappa Alpha Order. Clubs: Jacksonville Vanderbilt (pres.), Fla. Yacht, Sawgrass, Seminole, Ponte Vedra, University, Friars, Ye Mystic Revelers. Contbr. articles profl. jours. Home: 2025 Oceanfront Atlantic Beach FL 32233 Office: The 1300 Bldg Jacksonville FL 32207

CHANDLER, JOSEPH LUCK, mfg. co. ofcl.; b. Athens, Ga., Jan. 20, 1933; s. Joel Ira, Jr., and Nell Wells (Luck) C.; B.S. in Indsl. Mgmt., Ga. Inst. Tech., 1960; m. Nancy Helen Jones, Aug. 25, 1962; children—Joseph Luck, Leslie Ann. Prodn. control supr. Westinghouse Corp., South Boston, Va., 1969-72, indsl. engring. supr., 1972-73, mgr. mfg. unit, 1973-74, mgr. prodn. planning and systems, indsl. engr., from 1974, now mgr. prodn. resources. Scoutmaster Boy Scouts Am., 1963-68. Served with USAF, 1951-55. Mem. Am. Inst. Indsl. Engrs., Am. Legion (post comdr. 1964). Methodist. Clubs: Turbeville Ruritan (pres. 1963-64, 80), Shriners, Masons. Home: PO Box 325 Alton VA 24520 Office: PO Box 920 South Boston VA 24520

CHANDLER, THERESA BILODEAU, educator; b. Nashua, N.H., Mar. 11, 1931; d. John and Eva (Richard) Bilodeau; student Keene (N.H.) State Col., 1950-53; B.A. in Elem. Edn., Rollins Coll., 1974, M.A. in Guidance and Counseling, 1978; children—Michael, Jonathan, Lisa, Stephen. Tchr. various Catholic schs., 1963-69; sec./bookkeeper Nidy constrn. Co., Winter Park, Fla., 1969-72; columnist Winter Park Sun Herald, 1966; fin. counselor Orthopaedic Clinic, Winter Park, 1972; sec., receptionist Superior GMC, Orlando, Fla., 1973-74; tchr. Webster Adult Edn. Center, Winter Park, 1974—. Mem. Am. Personnel and Guidance Assn., Fla. Adult Edn. Assn., Nat. Wildlife Fedn., Fla. Audubon Soc., Fla. Fgn. Lang. Assn., Am. Coll. Personnel Assn., Nat. Employment Counselors Assn. Republican. Roman Catholic. Club: Orlando Bridge. Home: 5218 Lake Howell Rd Winter Park FL 32792 Office: Webster Adult Edn Center 901 Webster Ave Winter Park FL 32789

CHANDLER, THOMAS WALTER, JR., librarian; b. Carrollton, Ga., Nov 12, 1924; s. Thomas Walter and Florence (Pope) C.; student West Ga. Coll., 1942-43, 46-47; B.A., Emory U., 1949, M.L.S., 1951. With Ga. State Coll., 1951-61, beginning as book order librarian, 1951-57, head acquisitions dept., 1957-61; head librarian Oglethorpe U., Atlanta, 1961—. Served AUS, 1943-45. Decorated Purple Heart. Mem. Ga. Library Assn. Address: 2873 Hermance Dr NE Atlanta GA 30319

CHANDLER, WINSTON GRIGGS, transp. corp. exec.; b. Clinton, Ark., Oct. 9, 1919; s. Lester W. and Mattie (Griggs) C.; student Coll. Ozarks, 1940; LL.B., Ark. Law Sch., 1951, J.D., 1979; m. Ouida G. Hunnicutt, Sept. 16, 1942; children—Winston Griggs, Michael Lee, Jeffrey Scott. Owner Chandler 5 and 10, Clinton, Ark., 1946-48; safety insp. Ark. Pub. Service Commn., Little Rock, 1949-53; chmn. bd. Chandler Trailer Convoy, Inc., Little Rock, 1953—, dir., 1963-67; v.p. Razorback Realty; dir. Safety Boom, Inc. Mem. Ark. Athletic Commn., 1954-56; formerly chmn. Sch. Bd., Pulaski County; mem., chmn. Ark. State History Commn., Little Rock, 1957-67; mem. pres. devel. council Harding Coll., Searcy, Ark.; mem. fin. com. Democratic Nat. Com., 1974 also mem. exec. com.; chmn. So. div. Dem. Fin. Council, 1975—. Served to maj. USAAF, 1941-45. Mem. Am. Legion, Ark. Pioneers, Air Force Assn. (charter), Ark. Truck and Bus. Assn., Tenn. Walking Horse Assn., Internat. Platform Assn. Mem. Ch. of Christ (deacon, elder). Lion. Home: 24 4 Arrowbrook Ct Little Rock AR 72207 Office: 8828 N Benton Hwy Little Rock AR 72204

CHANDLER, WYETH, mayor Memphis; s. Walter C.; grad. Memphis State U.; J.D., U. Tenn.; 4 children. Admitted to Tenn. bar, practice in Memphis; spl. judge City Memphis; mem. Memphis City Council, 1967-71, chmn., 1971; mayor, Memphis, 1972—. Del. Tenn. Constl. Conv., 1959, 65. Bd. dirs. Memphis and Shelby County Youth Guidance Commn., Boys' Club Memphis; citizens' adv. bd. Juvenile Ct. Served with USMC, Korean conflict. Mem. Tenn., Memphis bar assns. Club: Phoenix. Office: Office of Mayor 125 N Main St Memphis TN 38103*

CHANDWANI, ARJAN DHALUMAL, airport exec.; b. Umarkot, Sind, Pakistan, June 15, 1936; s. Dhalumal Santdas and Gyanidevi D. C.; came to U.S., 1966, naturalized, 1974; M.S. in Civil Engring., U. Cin., 1968; m Meera M. Nebhrajani, July 21, 1969; children—Alpana Sunita, Sanjay, Shalni. Gazetted officer Central Designs Orgn., Ahemdabad, India, 1961-66; project mgr. Dade County Aviation Dept., Miami, Fla., 1972-80; project mgmt. specialist Rapid Transit System, Dade County Office of Transp., Miami, 1980—; pvt. practice cons. transp. engring., Pembroke Pines, Fla., 1980—; adj. faculty mem. Broward Community Coll., Embry Riddle Aero. U. Mem. Am. Concrete Inst., Am. Mgmt. Assn., India Assn. of U. Detroit, India Club. Met. Dayton, Am. Assn. Airport Execs., India Assn. Greater Miami (pres. 1978-79). Democrat. Hindu. Club: Kiwanis (pres. club 1979-80). Contbr. articles to profl. jours. Home: 18805 W Lake Dr Country Club of Miami Miami FL 33015 Office: Dade County Office of Transp 44 W Flaglar Miami FL 33130

CHANEY, BETTY BAKER, educator; b. Washington, Nov. 21, 1929; d. S. Harry and Margaret (Walters) Baker; A.B., U. Md., 1951; student U. Ill., 1948-49, U. Miami, 1966, U. Pitts., 1969; M.A., Fla. Atlantic U., 1968; Ed.D., Nova U., 1975; m. Alvan C. Chaney, Aug. 26, 1950; now single; 2 sons, Stephen C., Bruce H. Tchr. elementary schs., Balt., 1951-54, Dade County, Fla., 1961-68, coordinator Head Start, 1966-69, dir. career devel., 1967-69; asst. prof. Coll. Edn., Fla. Atlantic U., Boca Raton, 1969—; task force leader Office Child Devel. Broward County, 1972; chmn. S. Fla. Child Devel. Consortium, 1974-76; cons. HEW and Office of Edn. Actice Community Concert Assn., Mus. Arts, Focus, speaker, children's counselor, arts dir. cruise ships Queen Elizabeth II, Fairwind, Federico C, Cunard Countees, Cunard Princess. Mem. Nat. Assn. Edn. Young Children, So., Fla. assns. children under six, So. Assn. Colls. and Schs., Assn. for Childhood Internat., Fla. Assn. Supervision and Curriculum Devel., United Faculty Fla., Phi Delta Kappa, Delta Kappa Gamma, Gamma Phi Beta. Methodist. Clubs: Viscaya (Dade County). Author text: Stimulating Language Development in Early Childhood, 1976; contbr. curriculum guide, article in field to profl. jour. Home: Royal

Ambassador Apt 1514 3700 Galt Ocean Dr Fort Lauderdale FL 33308 Office: Florida Atlantic Univ Boca Raton FL 33431

CHANEY, CHARLES BUREN, JR. (DICK), ins. agt.; b. Birmingham, Ala., June 6, 1937; s. Charles Buren and Mildred Myra (Herrin) C.; student Ga. So. Coll., 1955-57, U. Ala., 1960-61, Jones Law Sch., 1969-71; m. Carole Wilson, Feb. 11, 1967; children—William Scott, Christen Lane, Charles Grant. Scout exec. Boy Scouts Am., Montgomery, Ala., 1963-67; ins. adjuster Ala. Farm Bur., Montgomery, 1967-72; owner ins. agy., Monroeville, Ala., 1972—; real estate appraiser. County chmn. ARC, 1971—; chmn. United Fund campaign, 1972, pres., 1973; chmn. Vanity Fair Golf Com., 1971—; co-chmn. Monroe County Republican party, 1972—. Served with USMC, 1957-60. Mem. Monroeville Jr. C. of C. (pres. 1969). Methodist. Kiwanian. Home: Longleaf Circle Monroeville AL 36460 Office: 721 S Alabama Ave Monroeville AL 36460

CHANEY, ELMER LEE, JR., psychologist; b. Charlotte, N.C., Apr. 6, 1934; s. Elmer Lee and Moselle Virginia (Redfearn) C.; student Davidson Coll., 1952-55; B.A. in English, Elon Coll., 1956; M.Ed. in Counseling, U. N.C., 1962; m. Mary Marshalene McCants, Dec. 27, 1958; 1 son, John David. English and French tchr. Bethany High Sch., Reidsville, N.C., 1956-58, Wadesboro (N.C.) High Sch., 1958-61; prof. psychology Jacksonville (Ala.) State U., 1962—; dir. guidance Project Head Start, Anniston, Ala., 1966; guest prof. Mil. Police Sch., Ft. McClellan, Anniston, Ala., 1976, Gadsden (Ala.) State Jr. Coll., 1977; guest speaker. Mem. vestry Episcopal Ch. St. Michael and All Angels. Cert. counselor, Ala. Contbr. articles to profl. jours. including N.C. English Tchr., Anniston Star. Home: 906 4th Ave Jacksonville AL 36265 Office: Suite DI Ramona Wood Bldg Jacksonville State University Jacksonville AL 36265

CHANEY, WARREN HERBERT, educator; b. Louisville, Nov. 3, 1942; s. Herbert R. and Izetta May (Farmer) C.; B.S., Austin Peay State U., 1964; M.B.A., St. Mary's U., 1969; Ph.D., N. Tex. State U., 1974; m. Harriett Suzanne Doebele, Sept. 18, 1968; 1 dau., Lesley Lane. Profl. ventriloquist, 1961-65; nat. dir. sales tng. Frito Lay, Inc., Dallas, 1970-72; nat. dir. orgnl. devel. World Trade Imports, Inc., Dallas, 1972-74, The Western Co. N. Am., Ft. Worth, 1974-75; prof. mgmt. and health care adminstrn. U. Houston, 1975—; mgmt. cons.; owner, mgr. Syndicate Films, Inc., Dallas, 1974—. Bd. dirs. Vent Haven, Inc., Covington, Ky., 1974—. Served with U.S. Army, 1965-70. Decorated Legion of Merit, Army Commendation medal with oak leaf cluster. Mem. Internat. Ventriloquists Assn. (bd. dirs. 1973—), Nat. Acad. Mgmt., Southwestern Fedn. Acad. Disciplines, So. Mgmt. Assn., Internat. Transactional Analysis Assn., Internat. Brotherhood of Magicians. Christian Ch. Author: The Union Epidemic: Prescription for Supervisors, 1976; contbr. articles to profl. jours. Home: 2101 Pine Dr Friendswood TX 77546 Office: 2700 Bay Area Blvd Suite 3 514 Houston TX 77058

CHANG, DAVID CHUAN-WEN, mfg. co. exec.; b. Chungking, China, May 20, 1941; came to U.S., 1967, naturalized, 1975; s. Su-tze and I-Hsien (Yen) C.; M.B.A., St. Mary's U., 1971; m. Doris C. Liang, July 21, 1968; children—Susan, Tony, Lisa. Assistance mgr. Taiwan Nav. Co., Ltd., Taipei, 1967-68; staff accountant McDonough Bros., Inc., San Antonio, 1972-78; controller Manufactured Concrete Inc., San Antonio, 1978-79, Manco Prestress Co., 1979—; cons. in field. Served with Chinese Army, 1964-65. Mem. Chinese Community of San Antonio (cons. 1979—). Baptist. Home: 6330 Sunview Dr San Antonio TX 78238 Office: Route 2 PO Box 223 San Antonio TX 78229

CHANG, FENG-CHENG, elec. engr.; b. Taipei, Taiwan, Mar. 18, 1935; s. Ting-yao and Song-chu (Chen) C.; came to U.S., 1966, naturalized, 1979; B.E.S.S., Nat. Taiwan U., 1958; M.S.E.E. Nat. Chao Tung U., 1962; Ph.D., U. Ala., 1972; m. Juey-ching Chien, Mar. 29, 1964; children—Key Chang, Judy. Jr. engr. Broadcasting Corp. China, Taiwan, 1961-64; instr. elec. engring. Nat. Chao Tung U., China, 1964-66; research asso. elec. engring. NASA Marshall Space Flight Center, Huntsville, Ala., 1972-74; acad. asso. IBM Research Lab., San Jose, Calif., 1976-77; asst. prof. elec. engring. Ala. A&M U., Normal, 1974-78; project engr. ITT Electro Optical Products div., Roanoke, Va., 1978—. NASA Internat. U. fellow, 1966-67. Mem. IEEE, Optical Soc. Am., Sigma Xi, Eta Kappa Nu. Contbr. articles to tech. jours., presenter papers at nat., internat. confs. Home: 3924 Blandfield Dr Vinton VA 24179 Office: 7635 Plantation Rd Roanoke VA 24019

CHANG, HENRY CHUNG-LIEN, library adminstr.; b. Canton, China, Sept. 15, 1941; s. Ih-ming and Lily (Lin) C.; LL.B., Nat. Chengchi U., 1962; M.A., U. Mo., 1966; M.L.S., U. Minn., 1968, Ph.D., 1974; m. Marjorie Li, Oct. 29, 1966; 1 dau., Michelle. Book selector Braille Inst. Am., Los Angeles, 1965-67; reference librarian U. Minn. Libraries, Mpls., 1968-70, instr., librarian, 1970-72, asst. head govt. document div., 1972-74; library dir., lectr. social scis. Coll. of V.I., St. Croix, 1974-75; dir. libraries, museums and archaeol. services, state librarian Govt. V.I., 1975—; dir. Library Tng. Inst., V.I., 1975-76; adv. mem. com. on research tng. Caribbean Research Inst., 1974-75. Served to 2d lt. Taiwan Army, 1962-63. Recipient Library Adminstrs. Devel. Program fellowship award, 1972; Certificate of Appreciation award Fort Frederik Commn. V.I., 1978, Am. Bicentennial Commn. V.I., 1977; named mem. Staff of Year, Coll. V.I., 1974-75. Mem. ALA, AAUP, Population Assn. Am., Am. Sociol. Assn., Assn. Caribbean Univ. and Research Libraries, V.I. Library Assn. Club: Rotary. Author: A Bibliography of Presidential Commissions, Committees, Councils, Panels and Task Forces, 1961-72, 1973; Taiwan Demography, 1964-71: A Selected Annotated Bibliography of Government Documents, 1973; A Selected Annotated Bibliography of Caribbean Bibliographies in English, 1975; contbr. numerous articles and book revs. on library sci. to profl. jours. Home: PO Box 818 Kingshill Saint Croix VI 00850 Office: PO Box 390 Saint Thomas VI 00801

CHANG, HOU-MIN, wood and paper scientist, educator; b. Chiayi, Taiwan, Aug. 29, 1938; came to U.S., 1963, naturalized, 1972; s. Li-Sho and Fun (Lee) C.; B.A., Nat. Taiwan U., 1962; M.S., U. Wash., 1966, Ph.D., 1968; m. Anne Han-Ming, Mar. 18, 1966; children—Lisa I., Christopher H. Research asso. forest sci. N.C. State U., Raleigh, 1968-69, asst. prof., 1969-73, asso. prof., 1973-77, prof., 1977—; cons. paper industry. Mem. Am. Chem. Soc., TAPPI, Co-editor book; contbr. articles to profl. publs. Patentee in field. Home: 3410 Redbud Ln Raleigh NC 27607 Office: Dept Wood and Paper Sci NC State U PO Box 5516 Raleigh NC 27650

CHANG, JEFFREY CHIT-FU, mathematician; b. Canton, China, Jan. 10, 1928; s. Chih-mao and Jui-ying (Chih) C.; came to U.S., 1963, naturalized, 1973; Ph.D., U. Ga., 1974; m. Frances Hung-Wen Lin, Aug. 22, 1946; children—Paul, Margaret, John. Sect. chief Taiwan Food Bureau, Taipei, 1952-63; specialist Central Statis. Bureau, Taipei, 1961-63; asst. prof. math., stats. and computer sci. Gardner-Webb Coll., Boiling Springs, N.C., 1966-74, asso. prof., 1974—. Served with Chinese Army, 1946-49. Certified data educator. Mem. Am., Chinese statis. assns., Inst. Math. Statistics, Soc. Data Educators, Phi Kappa Phi. Baptist. Contbr. articles to econ. and statis. jours. in Taiwan. Research internal multi-dimensional scaling of categorical variables, pattern recognition. Home: PO Box 307 Woodhill Dr Boiling Springs NC 28017 Office: Dept Math Gardner Webb Coll Boiling Springs NC 28017

CHANG, JEFFREY P., research scientist, educator; b. Changteh, Hunan, China; came to U.S., naturalized; grad. Nat. Central U. China; M.S., U. Ill., 1946, Ph.D., 1949; m. Sulaine Tang; children—Betty, Kaidy, Joann, Landy, Peter. Acting chief, sect. exptl. pathology U. Tex. M.D. Anderson Hosp., Houston, until 1964, prof. biology, also mem. faculty Grad. Sch. Biomed. Scis., 1964-72; prof. cellular biology U. Tex. Med. Br., Galveston, 1972—. Formerly cons. NIH, USAF Sch. Aerospace Medicine, Brooks AFB, Tex.; chmn. Symposium Preparative Histochemistry, 1961, 1st Internat. Congress Histochemistry and Cytochemistry, Paris, session chmn. 4th congress, Japan, 1972; also Internat. Cancer Congress, Japan, 1961, U.S., 1970; vis. prof., lectr. Vanderbilt U., U. Kans. Sch. Medicine, U. Taiwan, Chin Hwa U., Med. Coll. of Dept. Def., Republic of China, others. Academician, Academia Sinica. Contbr. articles to profl. publs. Developer open-top cryostat, sect. freeze substitution; research tumors, electron microscopy, histochemistry, reproductive biology. Office: Div Cell Biology U Tex Med Branch Galveston TX 77550

CHAPIN, CAROL LYNNE, oil co. exec.; b. Tulsa, Aug. 1, 1946; d. Robert Riley and Margaret Adelle C.; student Okla. State U., 1964-65, Tulsa U., 1970—. With Cities Service Co., Tulsa, 1966—, sec. to purchasing agt., 1966-68, sec. to mgr. purchasing, 1968-73, staff asst., 1973-77, office supplies buyer, 1977-79, material handling equipment buyer, 1979—. Mem. Purchasing Mgmt. Assn. Tulsa. Democrat. Home: 17596 N Peoria Skiatook OK 74070 Office: 110 W 7th St Tulsa OK 74145

CHAPLIN, GERVASE MICHAEL, aluminum co. exec.; b. Cape Town, S. Africa, Oct. 4, 1936; s. Leonard Frank and Mercia (Varkevisser) C.; came to U.S., 1965, naturalized, 1970; B.Sc. in Chemistry, U. Cape Town, 1955, B.Sc. in Geology, 1955; B.S. in Metallurgy, U. Ariz., 1958, Ph.D. (fellow) in Chem. Engring., 1972; m. Eleanor Louise Sanders, Jan. 26, 1958; children—Michael Bradley, Catherine Gaye. Metallurgist, plant supt. Tsumeb Corp. Ltd., S.W. Africa, 1958-60, tech. mgr., 1961-64; sr. research engr. Exxon Prodn. Research Co., Houston, 1972-75; mgr. process devel. div. Toth Aluminum Corp., New Orleans, 1976-77; v.p. engring. and tech. Toth Aluminum, 1978—; cons. in field. NDEA grantee Krebs Engring., 1968, Wilson Found., 1971. Mem. Am. Inst. Chem. Engrs., Oceanographic Found., Am. Chem. Soc., Am. Inst. Mining and Metall. Engrs., Tau Beta Pi, Phi Kappa Phi, Phi Lambda Upsilon, Pi Mu Epsilon. Republican. Presbyterian. Patentee in field. Home: 812 Holyoke Pl Gretna LA 70053 Office: 5010 LeRoy Johnson Dr New Orleans LA 70182

CHAPMAN, A. JAY, forensic pathologist; b. Covington, Ky., Jan. 1, 1939; s. Jay P. and Thelma (Sipple) C.; B.S., Carson-Newman Coll., 1960; M.D., Wake Forest U., 1964. Intern, N.C. Bapt. Hosp., Winston-Salem, 1964-65; resident in pathology Baylor U. Med. Center, Dallas, 1965-68, Am. Cancer Soc. fellow, 1966-67; fellow in legal medicine and forensic pathology Office of Chief Med. Examiner and Med. Coll. Va., Richmond, 1968-70; lectr.-registrar in forensic medicine St. George's Hosp. Med. Sch., London, 1969; pathologist, Ft. Worth, 1970-71; chief med. examiner State of Okla., Oklahoma City, 1971—; clin. prof. forensic pathology U. Okla. Health Scis. Center, Oklahoma City, 1971—. Diplomate Am. Bd. Pathology. Mem. Am. Acad. Forensic Scis., Nat. Assn. Med. Examiners, Internat. Acad. Pathology, Okla. Assn. Pathologists, Canterbury Soc., Alpha Omega Alpha. Contbr. articles to profl. jours.; editor Okla. Jour. Forensic Medicine, 1972-75, assoc. editor, 1975—. Home: 2115 Bandit Point Edmond OK 73034 Office: PO Box 26901 Oklahoma City OK 73190

CHAPMAN, ALVAH HERMAN, JR., newspaper exec.; b. Columbus, Ga., Mar. 21, 1921; s. Alvah Hermann and Wyline (Page) C.; B.S., The Citadel, 1942; m. Betty Bateman, Mar. 22, 1943; children—Dale Page (Mrs. Dennis Webb), Chris Ann (Mrs. Robert Hilton). Bus. mgr. Columbus Ledger, 1945-53; v.p., gen. mgr. St. Petersburg (Fla.) Times, 1955-57; pres., pub. Morning News and Evening Press, Savannah, Ga., 1957-60; pres. Savannah News-Press, Inc., 1957-60; exec. Knight-Ridder Newspapers, Inc., Miami, Fla., 1960—, exec. com., 1960—, exec. v.p., 1967-73, pres., 1973—, chief exec. officer, 1976—; v.p., gen. mgr. Miami Herald, 1962-70, pres., 1970—; lectr. Am. Press Insts., Columbia. Served from 2d lt. to maj. USAAF, World War II. Decorated D.F.C. with 2 oak leaf clusters, Air medal with 5 clusters (U.S.); Croix de Guerre; named one of five outstanding young men in Ga., 1951, Outstanding Young Man, Columbus Jr. C. of C., 1952, Dade County's Outstanding Citizen of 1968-69. Mem. Am., So. newspapers pubs. assn. Methodist. Home: 4255 Lake Rd Miami FL 33137 Office: Miami Herald 1 Herald Plaza Miami FL 33101

CHAPMAN, ANTHONY BRADLEY, psychiatrist; b. Salem, Mass., Aug. 22, 1938; s. Anthony Bredick and Gladys Gwendolyn (Poole) C.; B.S., Northeastern U., 1961; M.D., Stanford U., 1966; m. Ella Muller, June 30, 1963; children—Bradley Johann, Jeffrey Anthony. Intern in pediatrics Cleve. Met. Gen. Hosp., 1966-67; resident in psychiatry Johns Hopkins Hosp., Balt., 1967-69; fellow in child psychiatry Phila. Child Guidance Clinic, 1969-71; pvt. practice child and adolescent psychiatry, Alexandria, Va., 1973—; cons. in field. Served to maj. U.S. Army, 1971-73. Diplomate Nat. Bd. Med. Examiners, Am. Bd. Psychiatry and Neurology. Mem. Va., Alexand0ia med. socs., AMA, Mt. Vernon Park Assn. Club: Army-Navy Country. Editor: The Hyperactive Child Newsletter, 1976—. Home: 1106 Morningside Ln Alexandria VA 22308 Office: 2059 Huntington Ave Alexandria VA 22303

CHAPMAN, ARTHUR EDWARD, county ofcl.; b. Miami, Fla., Sept. 11, 1943; s. Lawrence Vihlen and Thelma Endoa (Goodson) C.; A.A., Miami-Dade Community Coll., 1972; B.A., Fla. Internat. U., 1973, M.B.A., 1974; M.A. in History, U. Miami, 1977, postgrad., 1977-79; m. Antonietta Bizzarro, Oct. 7, 1967; 1 son, John Edward. Various positions Western Elec. Co., Inc., Miami, 1962-77; free-lance researcher, Miami, 1976-78; teaching asst. U. Miami, 1978-79; adminstrv. officer I, Met. Dade County Seaport Dept., Port of Miami, 1978-79, adminstv. officer II, 1979—. Served with NG, 1965-69. Recipient Tebeau prize U. Miami, 1978-79; named Outstanding Scholar Delta-Alpha chpt. Phi Alpha Theta, 1978-79. Mem. Soc. Mayflower Descs., SAR, Phi Alpha Theta. Democrat. Baptist. Home: 11942 N E 8th Ave Biscayne Park FL 33161 Office: Met Dade County Seaport Dept 1015 N America Way Room 210 Miami FL 33023

CHAPMAN, EDWIN ROBERT, coll. adminstr.; b. Asheville, N.C., May 24, 1927; s. Ernest E. and Dorothy E. (Stephens) C.; B.A., Lenoir-Rhyne Coll., 1951, B.A. in Biology, 1958; M.A. in Biology, Appalachian State U., 1964; Ed.D., U. Fla., 1969; m. Martha Lou Sigmon, Oct. 7, 1961; children—Edwin Robert II, Gregory Scott. Office and traffic mgr. Poteat Motor Lines, Hickory, N.C., 1951-56; pres., gen. mgr. Wilder Transfer Co., Greensboro, N.C., 1956-60; asst. to pres. G&W Transfer Co., Hickory, 1956-60, gen. mgr., 1960-62; acct. and auditor S.E. Dist. Luth. Ch., Washington, 1962-63; prof. biology and chemistry Gaston (N.C.) Coll., 1964-67; acad. dean Western Piedmont Community Coll., Morganton, N.C., 1969-75, dean of planning and devel., 1975—, dir. research, 1971—. Mem. troop com. Piedmont council Boy Scouts Am., 1972—. Served with USN, 1945-48; PTO; to col. USAR, 1955—. Kellogg fellow, 1967-68; Ednl. Satellite grantee, 1977-79. Mem. N.C. Acad. Sci., N.C. Assn. Acad. Deans (pres. 1972-73), Assn. for Institutional Research, Am. Legion. Democrat. Lutheran. Clubs: Rotary, Ski, Masons. Author: Biology Laboratory Manual, 1967. Home: 202 Davis Dr Morgantown NC 28655 Office: 1001 Burkemont Ave Morgantown NC 28655

CHAPMAN, GEORGE CAYWOOD, coll. adminstr., biologist; b. Worth County, Ga., Nov. 29, 1943; s. George Daniel and Ruby LaVert (Culpepper) C.; B.S., Valdosta State Coll., 1965; M.S., U. Ga., 1970, Ph.D. in Botany, 1973; m. Ella Janet Wilder, Dec. 26, 1965; children—Amanda Lynn, George Caywood. Tchr. sci. public high schs., Ga., 1965-67; instr. biology Norman Jr. Coll., 1967-68; asst. prof. biology Gordon Jr. Coll., 1973-74, asso. prof., dean of students, 1974—. NSF travel grantee, 1971-72. Mem. So. Coll. Personnel Assn., Ga. Coll. Personnel Assn., So. Appalachian Bot. Club, Sigma Xi. Baptist. Club: Optimist (sec.-treas. local club 1977-78, v.p. 1978-79). Home: PO Box 181 Orchard Hill GA 32266 Office: Gordon Jr Coll Barnesville GA 30204

CHAPMAN, JOSEPH, carpet co. exec.; b. Saltville, Va., June 15, 1936; s. Lawrence Allen and Kansas Sarah Chapman; m. Wanda Faye Barnett, Dec. 20, 1957; 1 dau., Donna Jo. Artist, Newspaper Agy. Corp., Charleston, W.Va., 1959-60; pictorial artist, designer Stanford Signs Inc., Bluefield, W.Va., 1960-67; elec. sign designer Allen Displays, Inc., Greensboro, N.C., 1967-72; prodn. artist Allen Wendt & Assos., Charlotte, N.C., 1972-73; advt. dir. retail div. Salem Carpets, Winston-Salem, N.C., 1973-79; advt. coordinator N.Y. Carpet World, Winston-Salem, 1979—. adv. com. comml. art Guilford Tech. Inst., 1970-72. Served with U.S. Army, 1957-59. Mem. Piedmont Triad Advt. Fedn. (treas. 1977-79, dir. 1979). Office: 3435 Myer Lee Dr Winston-Salem NC 27107

CHAPMAN, MARY LUCILE, educator; b. Louisa, Ky.; d. Napoleon Bonaparte and Ida Belle (Porter) Chapman; A.B., U. Ky., 1929; A.M., 1937; Ph.D., 1945. Tchr. pub. schs., Ashland, Ky., 1922-40, supr., 1940-56; asst. prof., history Marshall Coll., Huntington, W.Va., 1946-48; asso. prof. history E. Tenn. State Coll., Johnson City. 1948-55; prof. social studies Jr. Coll., 1955-57; prof. history Ashland Center U. Ky., 1957-59; head dept. history Piedmont Coll., Demorest, Ga., 1959-62; asso. prof. history Jacksonville (Ala.) State U., 1962-65, prof., 1965—, chmn. div. social studies, 1959-62. Mem. Nat. Council Social Studies, Am., So., Ala. hist. assns., Nat., Ga. hist. socs., AAUW (pres. Anniston br. 1967-69, mem. Ala. div. bd.), Internat. Fedn. U. Women, AAUP, Calhoun County Hist. Assn., Orgn. Am. Historians, Atlantic Council of U.S., Nat., Ala. edn. assns., Acad. Polit. Sci., So. Polit. Sci. Assn., Friends of Library, Fgn. Affairs Assn., Am. Heritage Assn., Nat. Soc. Lit. and Arts, Coalition for Better Edn. in Ala., Ala. Woman's Civil Def. Orgn., Polit. Sci. Soc., Council So. Life and Work, Internat. Platform Assn., Am. Acad. Polit. and Social Sci., U.D.C., Intercontinental Biog. Assn., D.A.R., Marquis Library Soc., Trust for Hist. Preservation, Smithsonian Instn. (asso.), Alpha Phi Theta, Kappa Delta Pi. Democrat. Methodist. Clubs: Jacksonville State College Faculty, Garden. Home: 703 12th Ave Jacksonville AL 36265

CHAPPELL, BUFORD SOUTER, physician; b. Bookman, S.C., July 28, 1914; s. Oscar and Belva (Lever) C.; M.D., Med. Coll. S.C., 1938; m. Mary Marjorie Cooper, Nov. 8, 1940; children—Buford Souter, Mary (Mrs. Charles F. Mills), Richard F., Pamela A. Intern, St. Francis Infirmary, Charleston, S.C., 1937-38, U. Kans. Hosp., Kansas City, 1938-39; asst. resident urology U. Va., 1945-46, resident urology, 1947; sr. resident urology VA Hosp., Columbia, S.C., 1948-49, cons. urology, 1949—; practice medicine specializing in urology Columbia, 1949—; chief urology service Columbia Hosp., 1950-60; active urology staff Providence Hosp., Columbia, Bapt. Hosp. Served from capt. to lt. col. M.C., AUS, 1942-46. Mem. AMA, Am. Urol. Assn. Author: The Chappell Family in Early South Carolina; The Winns of Fairfield County. Home: 1373 Kathwood Rd Columbia SC 29206 Office: 2011 Hampton St Columbia SC 29204

CHAPPELL, EUGENE WATSON, JR., mgmt. cons.; b. Newport News, Va., Jan. 1, 1945; s. Eugene Watson and Virginia Lee (Cathell) C.; B.E.E. (Navy scholar), U. Va., 1967. Asst. to gen. mgr. Northrop Services Inc., Arlington, Va., 1972-74; project dir. Sci., Engring. & Analysis, Inc., Arlington, 1974-77; pres., chmn. bd. Fiscal Assos. Inc., Alexandria, Va., 1977—; dir. Omnetics Inc.; sr. partner CAMS Enterprises, 1977—, The Company, 1976—. Served with USN, 1967-72. Mem. IEEE, Data Processing Mgmt. Assn., Sigma Pi. Baptist. Clubs: Army Navy Country (Arlington); Shirley Racquet (Fairfax, Va.). Home: 6101 Edsall Rd W Apt 1107 Alexandria VA 22304 Office: 5911 Edsall Rd Suite 1213 Alexandria VA 22304

CHAPPELL, FRANK BENJAMIN, JR., food chain exec.; b. Washington, July 14, 1948; s. Frank B. and Eloise (Martin) C.; B.S., Auburn U., 1970; M.B.A., Am. U., 1972; m. Jean S. Crump, Aug. 30, 1969; children—Benjamin Stott, Martin Patrick. Asst. merchandising mgr. E-Z Shops div. Grand Union Co., Elmwood Park, N.J., 1972-74; merchandising mgr. Village Mkts., Inc., Gallatin, Tenn., 1974-77, dir. mktg., 1977, gen. mgr., 1977—. Vestryman, treas. Episcopal Ch. So. Rys. fellow, 1970-72. Mem. Greater Nashville Auburn Alumni Assn. (dir. 1977-79, treas. 1979), Theta Chi. Home: 1045 Woodmont Dr Gallatin TN 37066 Office: PO Box 711 Gallatin TN 37066

CHAPPELL, ROBERT HARVEY, JR., lawyer; b. Clarksville, Va., Nov. 28, 1926; s. Robert Harvey and Edna Kathryn (Lumpkin) C.; B.A., Coll. William and Mary, 1948, B.C.L., 1950; m. Ann Marie Callahan, Nov. 25, 1950; 1 son, Robert Harvey, III. Admitted to Va. bar, 1949, since practiced in Richmond as partner firm Christian, Barton, Epps, Brent & Chappell; dir., gen. counsel Thalhimer Bros., Inc., Richmond. Mem. Richmond Ind. Bicentennial Commn., 1971; mem. Richmond Community Facilities Adv. Bd., 1974-77; past rector, bd. visitors Coll. William and Mary; past pres., exec. com. bd. trustees Crippled Children's Hosp., Richmond; bd. dirs. Richmond Eye Hosp. Served with USAAF, 1944-46. Fellow Am. Bar Found., Am. Coll. Trial Lawyers (bd. regents 1979—); mem. Am. Bar Assn. (bd. govs. 1978—, chmn. standing com. on fed. judiciary 1977-78), Va. Bar Assn. (exec. com.), Richmond Bar Assn. (past pres.), Va. State Bar (pres. 1977-78), Internat. Assn. Ins. Counsel (past exec. com.), S.R. (past pres. Va.), Soc. Alumni William and Mary Coll. (past pres.; Alumni medallion 1968), William and Mary Law Sch. Assn. (past pres.), Phi Beta Kappa (pres. chpt. 1978—), Omicron Delta Kappa. Democrat. Episcopalian. Clubs: Downtown (pres. 1976-77), Country of Va., Commonwealth. Editor Ins. Counsel Jour., 1963-72. Home: 4607 Menokin Rd Richmond VA 23225 Office: 1200 Mutual Bldg Richmond VA 23219

CHAPPELL, WILLIAM VENROE, JR., congressman; b. Kendrick, Fla., Feb. 3, 1922; s. William Venroe and Laura (Kemp) C.; B.A., U. Fla., 1947, LL.B., 1949, J.D., 1967; m. Marguerite Gutshall, Mar. 26, 1944; children—Judith Jane (Mrs. Gadd), Deborah Kay (Mrs. Bond), William Venroe III, Christopher Clyde. Admitted to Fla. bar, 1949; mem. firm Sturgis and Chappell, and predecessors, Ocala, Fla., 1949—; pros. atty. Marion County, 1950-54; mem. Fla. Ho. of Reps. from Marion and other counties, 1954-64, 66-68, speaker, 1961-63; mem. 91st-96th congresses from 4th Dist. Fla. Served with USNR,

1942-46. Named Most Valuable Mem. Fla. Ho. Reps., 1967, Most Effective in Debate, 1967. Mem. Am., Fla., Marion County, Inter-Am. bar assns., Am. Trial Lawyers Assn., Acad. Fla. Trial Lawyers, Am. Legion. Democrat. Methodist. Mason (Shriner), Lion, Elk. Office: 2353 Rayburn House Office Bldg Washington DC 20515

CHARBONNEAU, JOSEPH JOHN, bus. exec.; b. Superior, Wis., July 8, 1940; s. Emery Earl and Marion Nell (Milroy) C.; m. Dawn Elaine Allen, Mar. 10, 1973; children—Joseph John, Charles Allen. Owner, Charbonneau Ins. Agy., Superior, Wis., 1961-69; pres. Personal and Profl. Devel. Inst., Mpls., 1969-76; v.p. Learning Dynamics, Inc., Boston, 1976-77; pres. Performance Group, Inc., Dallas, 1977—, Kangaroo Press, 1979—; chief exec. officer Info Systems, 1979—. Chmn. March of Dimes Nat. Found., 1965-66. Served with USNR, 1958-61. Mem. Am. Mgmt. Assn., Dallas C. of C. Clubs: Masons, Shriners. Home: 6403 Genstar Ln Dallas TX 75252 Office: 13507 Branch View Ln Dallas TX 75234

CHARGOIS, DEBORAH MAJEAU (MRS. ASHTON JOSEPH CHARGOIS), neurophysiologist, educator; b. New Orleans, Nov. 8, 1940; d. John Ashton and Marie Antoinette (Barbot) Majeau; B.A., St. Mary's Coll., 1963; M.S. (NIH fellow), La. State U., 1967, Ph.D. (Bio-space Tech. Tng. Program fellow), 1969; M.D., United Am. Med. Coll., 1976; m. Ashton Joseph Chargois, Sept. 6, 1969. Instr., La. State U. Med. Center, New Orleans, 1968-69; asst. prof. physiology, 1969-71, clin. asst. prof. physiology and biochemistry, 1971-74, asst. prof. physiology, 1974-75, dir. dental physiology, 1975—. Cons., lectr. Marshall Space Flight Center Miss. Test Facility, 1969-71. Recipient First award for Sci. Merit, Am. Speech and Hearing Assn., 1970. NIH fellow in tropical medicine, 1973; Deafness Research Found. grantee, 1970-71. Mem. AAAS, Am. Inst. Biol. Sci., Am. Physiol. Soc., Soc. Neurosci., USCG Aux., Internat. Platform Assn., N.Y. Acad. Scis., Sigma Xi. Contbr. articles to profl. jours. Home: 2339 Palmer Ave New Orleans LA 70118 Office: Dept Physiology La State U Med Center 1100 Florida Av New Orleans LA 70119

CHARLES, REID SHAVER, urban planner, adminstr.; b. Wichita, Kans., Sept. 16, 1940; s. Harry Lytton and Margaret Virginia (Shaver) C.; B.A., U. Wichita, 1964, postgrad., 1964-65; postgrad. Tulane U., 1968-69; M.A., Wichita State U., 1970; m. Mary Elizabeth Rouland, June 1, 1963; children—Reid Shaver II, Rouland Shannon. Grad. fellow Wichita State U., 1965; adminstrv. asst. to city mgr. Newton (Kans.), 1965-66; planning asso., New Orleans, 1966-69; adminstrv. asst. to exec. sec. devel. Town of Brookline (Mass.), 1969-73; chief systems planning City of Kansas City (Mo.), 1973-74, acting dep. dir. city devel., 1974-75; prin. CHJ Assos., Kansas City, Mo., 1975-78; adminstrv. dir. City of Lincoln (Nebr.), 1976-79; chief adminstrv. officer City of Shreveport (La.), 1979—; lectr., cons. in field; participant Nat. Urban Policy Roundtable IV, 1977; mem. tech. adv. group Urban Econ. Policy and Mgmt. Group, U.S. Conf. Mayors-Nat. League Cities, 1977—. Served with USAAF, 1961. Mem. Am. Polit. Sci. Assn., Am. Inst. Cert. Planners, Am. Acad. Polit. and Social Scis., Internat. City Mgmt. Assn., Am. Planning Assn., Am. Soc. Pub. Adminstrn., Pi Sigma Alpha. Mem. Soc. of Friends. Author municipal budgeting manuals. Home: 9480 Shartel Dr Shreveport LA 71108 Office: 1234 Texas Ave PO Box 31109 Shreveport LA 71130

CHARLES, ROBERT ALAN, educator; b. Harrisburg, Pa., Apr. 5, 1924; s. John Riley and Harriet Jane (Dietz) C.; B.A., Gettysburg Coll., 1948; M.A., U. Wis., 1949; diploma U. Toulouse, France, 1950; Ph.D., Pa. State U., 1952; m. Jean Catherine Cassell, Dec. 25, 1946 (div.); children—David Laird, Stephen Paul-Andre, Robert Alan, Michael James, Peter Joel. Instr., Pa. State U., 1950-52; asst. prof. Coll. William and Mary, 1952-55; asst. prof. U. Mont., 1955-60; prof., chmn. humanities Alaska Meth. U., 1960-66, Parsons Coll., 1966-71; prof., chmn. div. lang. and lit. Morehead (Ky.) State U., 1971—. Served to sgt. maj., USAAF, 1943-46. Recipient award Alaska Eng. Council, 1967, Alaska Gov.'s award, 1964. Mem. Nat. Council Tchrs. English, Coll. English Assn. (chmn. Ky.), Modern Lang. Assn., AAUP, Conf. Coll. Composition Communication. Author: Anglo-German Cross-Currents, 1956; Literature Beyond the Horizon, 1965. Contbr. articles to periodicals and profl. jours. Home: 933 N Wilson St Morehead KY 40351

CHARLTON, JESSE MELVIN, JR., educator; b. Livonia, La., May 12, 1916; s. Jesse Melvin and Anna Lela (Medlin) C.; B.S., La. State U., 1937, M.B.A., 1938; J.D., Harvard U., 1951; m. Mary Camp, Oct. 4, 1941; children—Jesse Melvin, Frances Anne. Instr. U. Ala., University, 1938-40; commd. 2nd. lt., inf., U.S. Army, 1940, advanced through grades to col., Judge Advocate Gen.'s Corps, 1962, ret. 1964; dep. comdr. Judge Advocate Gen.'s Sch., Charlottesville, Va., 1962-64; asst. prof., asst. dean Coll. Bus., U. New Orleans, 1964-71, prof. mgmt., dean Grad. Sch., 1979—. Admitted to practice Ct. Mil. Appeals, 1952, U.S. Dist. Ct., 1951, U.S. Ct. Appeals D.C., 1951, U.S. Supreme Ct., 1963. Decorated Bronze Star medal, Army Commendation medal. Mem. So. Bus. Law Assn. (pres. 1969-70), AAUP, Lambda Chi Alpha. Author: Staff Judge Advocate Handbook, 1962. Editor: (with James R. Bobo) Statis. Abstract of La., 5th edit., 1974. Home: 5401 Bancroft Dr New Orleans LA 70122

CHARLTON, MARGARET ELLEN JONSSON, civic worker; b. Dallas, Aug. 7, 1938; d. John Erik and Margaret Elizabeth (Fonde) Jonsson; student Skidmore Coll., 1956-57, So. Meth. U., 1957-60; m. George Volk Charlton, Jan. 23, 1960; children—Laura, Emily, Erik. Dir. KRLD radio, Dallas, 1970-74; 1st woman dir. First Nat. Bank Dallas, 1976—. First woman trustee Meth. Hosp., 1972—, mem. exec. com., 1977—; bd. dirs., chmn. exec. com. Lamplighter Sch., 1967—; bd. dirs. Winston Sch., 1973—; bd. dirs., mem. exec. com. Episcopal Sch. Dallas, 1976—; bd. dirs. Callier Center for Communications Disorders, 1967—, v.p., 1974—; mem. vis. com. dept. psychology M.I.T., 1978—; past chmn. Crystal Charity Ball; past bd. dirs. Children's Med. Center, Hope Cottage, Children's Bur., Baylor Dental Sch., Dallas Health and Sci. Mus., Dallas YWCA, Dallas Day Nursery Assn. Margaret Jonsson Charlton Hosp. named in her honor, Dallas, 1973. Republican. Club: Dallas Woman's.

CHARLTON, NINA, petroleum landman; b. Hopkins County, Tex., Aug. 21, 1932; d. Dave E. and Lela May (Wofford) Charlton; ed. Sulphur Springs (Tex.) pub. schs. Cashier, bookkeeper, Bealls Dept. Store, Sulphur Springs, 1949-52, clerk Lone Star Gas, Sulphur Springs, 1952-62; bookkeeper, teller, The City Nat. Bank, Sulphur Springs, 1962-70, receptionist, sec. to pres., 1965-70; credit clk. Portland Gen. Electric, Oregon City, Oregon, 1970; bookkeeper C.E. Wingo Feed Mill, Sulphur Springs, 1970-72; machine operator H.D. Lee Mfg. Co., Sulphur Springs, 1972; typist, clerk, sec. M.C. Bailey Abstract Co., Sulphur Springs, 1972-74; abstracter Morris Abstract Co., Sulphur Springs, 1974-75; independent landman for energy co., Sulphur Springs, 1975—. Mem. Am., E. Tex. assns. of petroleum landmen. Baptist. Address: 231 Rogers St PO Box 654 Sulphur Springs TX 75482

CHARNOV, CRAIG STEPHEN, communications co. exec.; b. Grand Rapids, Mich., May 23, 1949; s. Abraham and Winona Charnov; student U. Mich., 1968-69, Ind. U. Normal Coll., 1967-71; 1 son, Jason Tyler. With Motorola Co., 1976—, communications rep., New Castle, Ind., 1977—. Chmn. Henry County (Ind.) Heart Assn., 1978-79. Republican. Jewish. Home: 6721 NW 28th Ave Fort Lauderdale FL 33308 Office: PO Box 454 New Castle IN 47262

CHARRY, MICHAEL, orch. condr.; b. N.Y.C., Aug. 28, 1933; s. Harold Paul and Sylvia Charry; B.S. in Orch. Conducting, Juilliard Sch. Music, N.Y.C., 1956, M.S., 1956; m. Jane Thoms, Mar. 31, 1956; children—Stephen Walter, Barbara. Condr., pianist Jose Limon Modern Dance Co. tours of Europe, 1957, S. and C. Am., 1960, Far East, 1963; asst. condr., prin. oboist R.I. Philharm., 1960-61; music dir., condr. Canton (Ohio) Symphony Orch., 1961-74; apprentice condr., then asst. condr. Cleve. Orch., 1961-72; music dir., condr. Nashville Symphony Orch., 1976—, Peninsula Music Festival, 1978—; chmn. Music Consortium Nashville, 1977-79, Nashville Inst. Arts, 1979—; also guest condr. in U.S. and abroad. Served with AUS, 1958-60. Fulbright scholar, 1956-57; apprentice condr. Kulas Found., 1961-65; Martha Baird Rockefeller grantee, 1973. Mem. Am. Symphony Orch. League, Musicians Union. Office: 1805 West End Ave Nashville TN 37203

CHARTER, JODY B., educator, librarian; b. Tulsa, July 18, 1943; d. Joe Burnett and Margaret (Wann) Beckley; B.S., Okla. State U., 1967; M.L.S., U. Okla., 1972; postgrad. Fla. State U., 1979; m. Jerald O. Charter, Dec. 30, 1969. Tchr. public schs., Bartlesville, Okla., 1966-67, Wichita, Kans., 1968-71; instr. instructional resources U. Ark., Fayetteville, 1972-76, asst. prof., 1976—; mem. Task Force Certification Revision for Sch. Media Personnel in Ark., 1976-78. Madge Hutcherson scholar; Delta Kappa Gamma scholar, 1979. Mem. N.W. Ark. Library Assn. (pres. 1975-76), Ark. Council Library Edn. (chairperson 1976-78), AIA, Am. Assn. Sch. Librarians Edn. Com., Assn. Ednl. Communications and Tech., Ark. Edn. Assn. (v.p. U. Ark. unit 1975-76), Ark. Audio Visual Assn., NEA, Southwestern Library Assn., Delta Kappa Gamma, Kappa Delta Pi. Democrat. Baptist. Contbr. articles to profl. jours. Home: 1974 Fox Hunter Rd Fayetteville AR 72701 Office: 201 Peabody Hall Coll of Edn Univ of Ark Fayetteville AR 72701

CHASE, GAYLORD RICHARD, otologist; b. Salt Lake City, Sept. 6, 1909; s. Alphonso and Grace Marguerite (Gaylord) Snow; Geol. Engr., Colo. Sch. Mines, 1932; M.D., U. Colo., 1939; m. Frances Lorraine Schaer, June 15, 1945; children—Jon Gaylord, Anne Schaer Chase, Julia Frances, Gaylord Richard. Geologist, mine supt. Royal Consol. Silver Mine, Georgetown, Colo., 1933-35; intern U. Colo. Sch. Medicine, 1939-40; gen. practice medicine Longmont, Colo., 1940-41; resident in otolaryngology U. Tex. John Sealy Hosp., Galveston, 1946-48; clin. asst. Temple U., 1947; instr. otolaryngology U. Tex., 1947-48; pvt. practice otolaryngology, Amarillo, Tex., 1948—; asso. clin. prof. surgery Tex. Tech. Sch. Medicine, Amarillo, 1977—. Pres. Amarillo Speech and Hearing Found., 1972-76. Served with U.S. Army, 1941-42, USAAF, 1942-46. Diplomate Am. Bd. Otolaryngology. Fellow Am. Acad. Otolaryngology, ACS, mem. Potter-Randall County Med. Soc. (pres. 1952-53), AMA, Pan-Am. Assn. Otolaryngology, Tex. Otolaryngological Assn., Tex. Soc. Ophthalmology and Otolaryngology. Republican. Roman Catholic. Home: 3201 S Bowie St Amarillo TX 79109 Office: 2306 Line Ave Amarillo TX 79106

CHASE, JAMES STATON, educator; b. Richmond, Va., July 2, 1932; s. Francis Seabury and Sue Wilbourne (Elder) C.; A.B., Coll. William and Mary, 1953; M.A., U. Chgo., 1957, Ph.D., 1962. Instr., U. Tex. at Austin, 1961-64, asst. prof., 1964-68; asso. prof. history U. Ark., 1968-73, prof., 1973—, chmn. dept. history, 1970-76. Mem. Ark. Am. Revolution Bicentennial Commn., 1972-76; mem. Ark. State Com., Ark. Humanities Program, 1973-76; mem. Washington County Dem. Central Com., 1970—. Served with AUS, 1954-55. Mem. Ark. Assn. Coll. History Tchrs. (pres. 1974-76), Am., So., Ark. hist. assns., Orgn. Am. Historians, Southwestern Social Sci. Assn., Phi Alpha Theta, Omicron Delta Kappa, Kappa Delta Pi. Author: Emergence of the Presidential Nominating Convention, 1789-1832, 1973. Home: 1606 W Center St Fayetteville AR 72701 Office: Dept History U Ark Fayetteville AR 72701

CHASE, JOANNA BARINEAU, speech pathologist; b. McRae, Ga., Aug. 23, 1926; d. Walter Edward and Margaret Marjorie (Cook) Barineau; B.B.A., U. Ga., 1947; M.A., U. Houston, 1970; m. Henry Hughes Chase, Nov. 16, 1946; children—Henry, Michael, Jeffrey. Speech pathologist Houston Ind. Sch. Dist., 1970-71, Rosewood Gen. Hosp., Houston, 1970-72, dir. speech pathology, 1972-76; pvt. practice speech pathology, Houston, 1976—. Vol. therapy aid Houston Speech and Hearing Clinic, 1962-67. Mem. Am. Speech, Lang. and Hearing Assn., Tex. Speech, Lang. and Hearing Assn., Houston Area Assn. for Communication Disorders, Internat. Assn. Laryngectomees Directory. Contbr.: Basic Rehabilitation Techniques, 1977. Address: 11602 Green Oaks Houston TX 77024

CHASE, RAMON LEROY, aero-space engring. exec.; b. Crosswell, Mich., June 19, 1933; s. Victor John and Alma Leona (Gardner) C.; A.A., Graceland Coll., 1953; B.S.E., U. Mich., 1956; M.B.A., U. Calif., 1975; m. Arlene Hazel Torsch, July 27, 1957; children—Kirt Alan, Diane Rene, Rodney Ramon. Supr. trajectory analysis group Chrysler Missile div., 1957-63; supr. performance analysis group LTV Mich. Div., 1963-65; mem. tech. staff Aerospace Corp., 1965-71; registrar Riverside Community Coll., 1971-73; mem. tech. staff Jet Propulsion Lab., Calif. Inst. Tech., 1973-76; mem. tech. staff Analytic Services, Inc., Herndon, Va., 1976—; bd. dirs. Zionic Enterprises, Inc.; cons. in field. Mem. Am. Astron. Soc., AIAA, Am. Mgmt. Assn., N.Y. Acad. Scis. Contbr. articles to profl. jours. Home: 12605 Denmark Dr Herndon VA 22070 Office: 400 Army-Navy Dr Arlington VA 22202

CHASTAIN, CECIL PYRON, safety engr.; b. Atlanta, Nov. 10, 1935; s. Cecil P. and Lois Louise C.; B.S. in Engring. Tech., U. Tenn., Nashville, 1974; m. Mar. 9, 1974; children—Cecilia, Suzanne, Andrea. Sr. engring. mgr. CNA Ins. Cos., 1967-75; profl. engring. cons., safety and health Fred S. James, Tulsa, 1975-77; profl. engr., dir. ops. Cannon-Cochran Inc., Danville, Ill., 1977-78; profl. engr., dir., cons. Fla. Commerce and Constrn. Self Insurers Fund, Sarasota, 1978-79; pres. Cannon-Cochran of Fla., Sarasota Ins. and Engring. Cons., 1979—. Served with USN, 1953-59. Registered profl. engr., Calif., Ill. Mem. ASCE, Am. Soc. Safety Engrs. Clubs: Masons (Chambleee, Ga.); Shriners (Atlanta). Home: PO Box 446 Laurel FL 33545

CHASTAIN, DOYLE EDWARD, physician; b. Lakes Wales, Fla., Oct. 29, 1936; s. Johnson E. and Lucille (Mullins) C.; A.A., U. Fla., 1956; M.D., U. Miami, 1960; m. Jacqulyn Smith, Jan. 30, 1965; children—John, David. Intern, Brooke Army Hosp., San Antonio, 1960-61; resident in internal medicine U. Ala. Sch. Medicine, Birmingham, 1963-65, U. Fla. Teaching Hosp., Gainesville, 1965-66; practice specializing in internal medicine, Titusville, Fla., 1966—; mem. staff Jess Parrish Meml. Hosp.; dir. Fla. Nat. Bank of Titusville, 1974—. Served with M.C., USAF, 1960-63. Diplomate Am. Bd. Internal Medicine. Mem. Fla. Coll. Physicians, A.C.P., AMA, So., Fla., Brevard County med. assns., Am., Fla. socs. internal medicine. Republican. Presbyterian. Home: 3200 Royal Oak Dr Titusville FL 32780 Office: 1309 Garden St Titusville FL 32780

CHATMAN, ALEX, educator, magistrate; b. Greeleyville, S.C., Oct. 7, 1943; s. Alex Oscar and Alma Virginia (Montgomery) C.; B.S. (United Negro Fund scholar), Benedict Coll., 1965; Ed.M., S.C. State Coll., 1973. Tchr. pub. schs. S.C., 1965—; tchr. Williamsburg High Sch., Greeleyville, 1971—; magistrate City of Greeleyville, 1972—. Chmn. Greeleyville Precinct, 1966—, adviser registrants, 1970—; mem. credentials com. State Democratic Conv., 1972, 74; chmn. 6th Congl. Dist. polit. action com. edn., 1974—; chmn. Williamsburg County Grassroots Citizens Adv. Com.; adv. bd. S.C. Human Affairs Commn. Mem. Nat. (ofcl. black caucus 1974—), Williamsburg County (pres. 1974-75) edn. assns., S.C. Magistrate Assn., NAACP, Welfare Rights Orgn., Nat. Bus. League (pres. Greeleyville br. 1966—), Phi Beta Sigma (award 1973). Club: Masons. Contbr. to publ. South Carolina Blacks and Native Americans, 1776-1976. Home: Route 2 Box 203 Greeleyville SC 29056

CHATTIN, GILBERT MARSHALL, state ofcl.; b. Decherd, Tenn., Jan. 13, 1914; s. Murrell Emmett and Lena Catherine (Jones) C.; B.A., U. South, Sewanee, 1937; LL.B., Blackstone Sch. Law, 1965, J.D., 1971; m. Hester Stroud, June 18, 1938; 1 dau., Marsha Jane. Credit analyst, chief, mgr. Dun and Bradstreet, Inc., Knoxville, 1938-43; partner, A & A Service & Supply Co., wholesale and retail chain, Atlanta, 1946-70; chief auditor Ga. Dept. Health, 1963-72; chief auditor, audit mgr. Ga. Dept. Human Resources, 1972—; corp. auditor Ga. Dept. Revenue, 1955-63; fin. analyst, investor, cons., 1955—; dir. Ga. Dept. Human Resources Credit Union. Served with AUS, 1943-46: ETO. Mem. Ch. of Christ. Home: 1068 Reeder Circle Atlanta GA 30306 Office: 1256 Briarcliff Rd Atlanta GA 30306

CHAUDHURI, TAPAN KUMAR, physician; b. India, Nov. 25, 1944; s. Taposh Kumar and Bulu Rani (Chowdhury) C.; came to U.S., 1967; M.B., B.S., Calcutta U., 1966; m. Chhanda; 1 dau., Lakshmi Rani. Intern, South Side Hosp., Pitts., 1968-69; research asso. nuclear medicine Yale U., 1967-68; resident W.Va. U., 1969-70; research cons. physiology and biophysics U. Okla., 1970; clin. asso. nuclear medicine U. Iowa, 1970-71; vis. research asst. prof. U. Okla., 1971; asst. prof. nuclear medicine U. Iowa, 1971-74; chief nuclear medicine VA Center, Hampton, Va., 1974—; asso. prof. nuclear medicine Eastern Va. Med Sch., Norfolk, 1974-79, prof., 1979—. Diplomate Am. Bd. Nuclear Medicine. Fellow Am. Coll. Gastroenterologists, ACP; mem. Soc. Nuclear Medicine, Biophys. Soc., N.Y. Acad. Scis., Am. Physiol. Soc., AMA, AAAS, Am. Fedn. Clin. Research, Am. Coll. Nuclear Physicians, Radiol. Soc. N.Am., Am. Geriatric Soc. Contbr. articles to med. jours, chpts. to textbooks. Home: 304 Rudisill Rd Hampton VA 23669 Office: VA Hosp Hampton VA 23667

CHAVERS, DEAN, coll. pres.; b. Pembroke, N.C., Feb. 4, 1941; s. Luther C. and Dorothy M. (Godwin) C.; B.A., U. Calif. at Berkeley, 1970; M.A., Stanford U., 1973, Ph.D., 1976; m. Antonia Navarro, Apr. 26, 1970; children—Cynthia Christine, Monica Lynn, Celia Ricarda. Asst. prof. Calif. State U., Hayward, 1972-74; pres. Indian Edn. Assos., Palo Alto, Calif., 1975-77, Native Am. Scholarship Fund, Palo Alto, 1977-78; pres. Bacone Coll., Muskogee, Okla., 1978—. Mem. com. on equal ednl. opportunity Calif. Postsecondary Edn. Commn., 1977-78. Served to capt. USAF, 1963-68. Decorated D.F.C., Air medal. Ford Found. fellow. Mem. Nat. Congress Am. Indians, Internat. Communication Assn. Democrat. Baptist. Club: Rotary Internat. Mng. editor Indian Voice, 1971-73; contbr. articles to profl. jours. Address: Bacone College Muskogee OK 74401

CHEA, FRANCISCO, mech. engr.; b. Nassau, Bahamas, June 23, 1927; s. Louis and Maria Josepha (Wong) C.; came to U.S., 1951, naturalized, 1954; B.S., U. Miami, 1959; m. Mavis Audrey Chin, Nov. 5, 1959; children—Francis Edward, Maria Aoling, Alicia Christina. Project engr. Ship Machinery Design div. N.Y. Naval Shipyard, Bklyn., 1960-65, research and tech. dept. Naval Tng. Equipment Center, Orlando, Fla., 1966—. Treas., Central Fla. Boy Scout Troop, 1976-79. Served with AUS, 1951-54. Mem. Cousteau Soc., Chinese Am. Assn. Central Fla. Democrat. Roman Catholic. Contbr. articles profl. jours. Home: 2773 Vine St Orlando FL 32806 Office: Naval Training Equipment Center Orlando FL 32813

CHEAH, KEONG-CHYE, psychiatrist; b. Penang, W. Malaysia, Mar. 15, 1939; s. Thean-Hoe and Hun-Kin (Keong) C.; came to U.S., 1959, naturalized, 1973; B.A. in Psychology, U. Ark., 1962, M.D., 1967, M.S., 1968; m. Sandra Fern Massey, June 10, 1968; children—Chylynn, Maylynn. Intern, U. Ark. Med. Center, Little Rock, 1967-68, resident, 1969-72; geriatric fellow VA Hosp., Tacoma, and U. Wash., Seattle, 1974; practice medicine specializing in psychiatry, Little Rock, 1972—; chief addiction sect. VA Med. Center, Little Rock, 1972-73, staff physician in psychiatry, 1973-74, staff physician in geriatrics-psychiatry, 1974—; asst. clin. prof. psychiatry U. Ark. for Med. Scis., 1972-75, asst. prof. psychiatry, 1975—, asst. prof. medicine, 1975—; mem. med. care evaluation com. Ark. Found. for Med. Care, 1978—; mem. spl. com. on drug abuse study Pulaski County Health and Welfare Dept., 1972-73. Bd. dirs. Crisis Center Ark., 1974-79, vice chmn., 1977; mem. adv. council Ark. State Plan Comprehensive Mental Health Services, chmn., 1979-81. Recipient State of Ark. Cert. of Merit, 1973; diplomate Am. Bd. Psychiatry and Neurology. Mem. Am. Psychiat. Assn., Ark. Psychiat. Soc. (pres. 1980-81), Mid-Continent Psychiat. Soc. (pres. 1979-80), Am. Geriatrics Soc., Am. Group Psychotherapy Assn., Ark. Group Psychotherapy Soc. (past pres.), Gerontology Soc., Am. Assn. for Geriatric Psychiatry, Internat. Transactional Analysis Assn., Pulaski County Council for Aging, Ark. Gerontology Soc., Chinese Assn. Ark. (sec. 1978-80), Chinese Assn. of Central Ark. (pres. 1977). Club: Arkansas Caduceus. Contbr. articles on geriatrics and psychiatry to profl. jours. Home: 410 Sierra Madre North Little Rock AR 72118 Office: VA Medical Center 300 E Roosevelt Rd Little Rock AR 72206

CHEARY, BRIAN SIDNEY, chem. co. exec.; b. Durban, South Africa, May 25, 1936; came to U.S., 1961, naturalized, 1967; s. Sidney Eric and Esther (Shrives) C.; B.S., Calif. Poly. Inst., Pomona, 1967; Ph.D. (USPHS fellow), U. Calif., Riverside, 1971; m. Elisabeth Ann Wilkinson, Oct. 25, 1958; children—Kelly, Craig Alan, Stacey Lynn. Adminstrv. and exec. officer Dept. Native Affairs, South Rhodesia Civil Service, 1954-57; asst. public service attache Diplomatic Service Fedn. Rhodesia and Nyasaland, 1957-60; yacht broker, Vancouver, B.C., Can., 1960-61; sales staff Pan Am. Airways, 1962-64; asst. dir., ecologist Wau Ecology Inst., New Guinea, 1971-73, also ecologist, Bishop Mus., Honolulu; product specialist Union Carbide Agrl. Products Co., Inc., Salinas, Calif., 1973-74, new products devel. specialist, 1974-77, area product devel. mgr. Africa and Middle East, 1977-79, product devel. mgr. new products, Jacksonville, Fla., 1979—. Mem. tech. service adv. bd. Am. Cotton Grower, 1976-78. Nat. Acad. Scis. research grantee, 1971-73. Mem. Entomol. Soc. Am., Entomol. Soc. Can., Pacific Coast Entomol. Soc., Assn. Tropical Biology, Coleopterists Soc., Orgn. Tropical Am. Nematologists, Am. Registry Profl. Entomologists, Soc. Nematology, Sigma Xi. Republican. Club: Woods Racquet. Contbr. articles to profl. pubs. Home: 2276 The Woods Dr Jacksonville FL 32216 Office: PO Box 17610 Jacksonville FL 32216

CHEATHAM, DAVID ALAN, internist; b. Amarillo, Tex., Jan. 10, 1949; s. Roy Francis and Nell (Spann) C.; B.A. with honors, Tex. Tech. U., 1971; M.D. with honors, U. Tex. Med. Br., Galveston, 1975;

m. Barbara Elise Beckmann, July 31, 1970; children—Jeffrey David, Christopher Alan. Intern, U. Tex. Med. Br., 1975-76, resident in internal medicine, 1976-78; practice medicine specializing in internal medicine, Dallas, 1978—. Mem. A.C.P., AMA, Dallas County Med. Soc., Tex. Med. Assn., Alpha Omega Alpha, Theta Kappa Psi, Beta Beta Beta, Alpha Epsilon Delta, Mu Delta. Mem. Reformed Ch. in Am. Office: 8220 Walnut Hill Ln Suite 514 Dallas TX 75231

CHEATHAM, REBECCA AULTMAN, speech pathologist; b. Albany, Ga., Aug. 7, 1948; d. Forrest Earl and Helen Alicia (Evanoff) Aultman; B.S. in Edn., U. Ga., 1970, M.Ed. in Speech Pathology, 1972; m. Frank Sellers Cheatham, Jr., Oct. 9, 1976; 1 dau., Lara Rebecca. Speech pathologist Savannah (Ga.) Speech and Hearing Center, 1972-74, Ga. Regional Hosp., Savannah, 1974-77; instr. Armstrong State Coll., Savannah, 1977-78; part-time speech pathologist in pvt. practice with Home Health Services, Savannah, 1979—. Vice pres. auction Savannah Symphony Women's Guild, 1979, v.p. season tickets, 1980; chmn. adv. bd. Ga. Advocacy Office, 1979; bd. dirs. Parent and Child Devel. Services, 1980, Girl Scouts U.S., 1980. Mem. Council Exceptional Children (chpt. pres. 1979), Am. Speech and Hearing Assn., Ga. Speech and Hearing Assn., Zeta Phi Eta. Episcopalian. Clubs: Chatham, Savannah Yacht. Address: 2 Sandy Point Rd Savannah GA 31404

CHEATUM, DON ELWOOD, rheumatologist; b. Dallas, Aug. 11, 1939; s. Elmer Phillip and Edith Isabel (Deck) C.; B.A., So. Meth. U., 1960; M.D., George Washington U., St. Louis, 1964; m. Lori Ellen Young, Mar. 9, 1978; children—Kathleen Kay, Melissa Lynn, Christopher Don, Joseph Raymond. Intern, Dallas VA Hosp., 1964-65; resident in internal medicine, also fellow in rheumatology Southwestern Med. Sch., U. Tex., 1964-68, 71-73; rheumatologist Dallas Med. and Surg. Clinic, also Baylor Hosp., Dallas, 1973—, dir. rheumatology Baylor U. Med. Center, 1973-79; sr. attending physician Parkland Meml. Hosp., Dallas, 1973—; clin. asst. prof. medicine U. Tex. Southwestern Health Sci. Center, Dallas, 1975—. Bd. dirs. Richardson (Tex.) Symphony Orch., 1974-76; sci. bd. dirs. N.Tex. chpt. Arthritis Found., 1975—; bd. govs. Tex. Rheumatism Assn., 1978—. USPHS fellow, 1971-73. Diplomate Am. Bd. Internal Medicine. Served to maj., M.C., U.S. Army, 1968-71. Fellow A.C.P.; mem. Dallas County Med. Soc., So. Clin. Med. Soc., Tex. Med. Assn., AMA, Dallas Acad. Internal Medicine, Tex. Rheumatism Assn., Am. Rheumatism Assn., Pi Kappa Alpha, Phi Beta Pi. Republican. Presbyterian. Clin. investigator drug cos., 1971-74, contbr. articles to med. publs., 1973-78. Office: Dallas Med and Surg Clinic 4105 Live Oak St PO Box 28 Dallas TX 75221

CHEE, ANTHONY NGIK CHOONG, scientist, educator; b. Taiping, Malaysia, Feb. 9, 1942; came to U.S., 1962, naturalized, 1972; s. Fook On and Ah Yin (Lau) C.; B.S. (scholar), St. Edward's U., 1966; M.A., U. Mass., 1968; Ed.D., U. Houston, 1979; m. Ann Ping Sze, Dec. 27, 1969; 1 son, Andy. Lab. asst. Coll. Physicians and Surgeons Columbia U., N.Y.C., 1964; teaching fellow dept. zoology U. Mass., Amherst, 1966-68, NIH fellow, 1969; research asso. Baylor Coll. Medicine, Houston, 1972-75; head biology faculty Houston Community Coll., 1975—; biomed. researcher Tex. Med. Center, Houston, 1971-78; sci. Fair judge, guest lectr. schs. and colls. USPHS scholar U. Tex., 1970. Mem. AAAS, Nat. Sci. Tchrs. Assn., AAUP, Am. Assn. Clin. Chemists, Tex. Acad. Sci., Sigma Xi. Roman Catholic. Club: Chinese Profl. Author: (with others) Biology, A Laboratory Experience, 1978; Anatomy and Physiology—A Dynamic Approach, 1979; contbr. articles in field to profl. jours. Home: 8914 Sterlingame St Houston TX 77031 Office: 22 Waugh Dr Houston TX 77007

CHEEK, ALTON LEONARD, ednl. adminstr.; b. Durham, N.C., June 21, 1943; s. Otis Isaac and Mary (Perry) C.; B.S., Elizabeth City State Coll., 1966; postgrad. Wake Forrest U., 1966-67; M.A., N.C. Central U., 1973; postgrad. U. N.C., Chapel Hill, 1978-79; children—Jacqueline Nichelle, Ainee Lynette. Tchr., Grady Brown Elementary Sch., Hillsborough, N.C., 1968-72, vice-prin., 1973-75; vice-prin. Central Elementary Sch., Hillsborough, 1975-77; prin. Elfland-Cheeks Elementary Sch., Elfland, N.C., 1977—. Active Democratic party, Boy Scouts Am., Girl Scouts U.S., 4-H. Named outstanding young educator N.C. Jaycees, 1974. Mem. Orange County Prins. Assn. (pres.), N.C. Assn. Educators (pres. dist. 9 1977-78), NEA, Am. Assn. Elementary Sch. Adminstrs., N.C. Assn. Sch. Adminstrs., Omega Psi Phi. Democrat. Baptist. Club: Elks. Home: 3547 Mayfair St Apt 107 Durham NC 27707 Office: Elfland-Cheeks Elementary Sch PO Box 298 Hy 70 Elfland NC 27243

CHEEK, TOM FRANK, JR., adminstrv. elec. engr.; b. Bowling Green, Ky., Sept. 10, 1938; s. Tom F. and Katie N. (Romans) C.; B.S.E.E., U. Tenn., 1961, M.S.E.E., 1966, Ph.D. (NDEA fellow), 1969; m. Judith M. Scott, Aug. 7, 1966. Mem. tech. staff Advanced Tech. Lab., Tex. Instruments Inc., Dallas, 1968-73, mgr. processor devel. br., 1974—; vis. indsl. prof. So. Meth. U., U. Tex., Arlington, U. Tenn., Knoxville. Mem. IEEE, U. Tenn. Gen. Alumni Assn. (bd. govs. 1971-74, past pres. Dallas/Ft. Worth), Sigma Xi. Club: Toastmasters (ednl. v.p.). Author papers on charge-coupled device and surface acoustic wave technolgies; patentee in field. Home: 3422 Castle Rock Ln Garland TX 75042 Office: PO Box 225936 M/134 Texas Instruments Dallas TX 75222

CHEESEMAN, CHARLES EDWARD, JR., systems engr.; b. Portersville, Pa., Aug. 3, 1940; s. Charles Edward and Madelyn Elizabeth (Oliver) C.; B.S. in Engring. Sci., U.S. Air Force Acad., 1962; Ph.D. in Systems Engring., U. Pa., 1973. Project engr. ARO Inc., Arnold Engring. Devel. Center, Tullahoma, Tenn., 1962-64; weapon effects test dir. re-entry systems div. Gen. Electric Co., Phila., 1964-66, systems engr. manned orbiting lab., space div., Valley Forge, Pa., 1966-69, Skylab expt., 1969-71, mgr. mission applications programs, 1971-76, space shuttle payload programs, 1976-78, mgr. digital control systems, Daytona Beach, Fla., 1978—; lectr. U. Pa. Counsellor in engring. to high sch. students, 1975. Served with USAF, 1958-62. Recipient Danforth Leadership award, 1957. Asso. fellow Am. Inst. Aeros. and Astronautics (mem. editorial com. 1964-66); mem. U.S. Naval Inst., Soc. Naval Architects and Marine Engrs., Air Force Hist. Found. Presbyterian. Asso. editor Jour. Spacecraft and Rockets, 1977; contbr. articles to profl. jours. Office: Electronic Systems Div Gen Electric Co PO Box 2500 Daytona Beach FL 32015

CHEESEMAN, JERRY WILLIAM, civil engr.; b. Pitts., Sept. 9, 1942; s. Cyril Edward and Helen Wilhelmina (Francis) C.; B.S., Pa. State U., 1964; m. Georgia Ann Cole, June 12, 1965; children—Richard Edward, Shannon Elizabeth, Marc Albert. Staff engr. IBM Corp., Rochester, Minn. and Boca Raton, Fla., 1968—. Served to capt. USAF, 1964-68; maj. Res. Registered profl. engr., Fla. Mem. ASCE, Nat. Hist. Soc., Pa. State U. Alumni Assn. (life), IBM Club (dir. 1974). Episcopalian. Home: 1102 N Swinton Ave Delray Beach FL 33444 Office: 2000 NW 51st St Boca Raton FL 33432

CHELTON, LOUIS GUY, JR., physician; b. Balt., May 14, 1925; s. Louis Guy and Anna Bowie (Shaw) C.; student Springfield Coll., Gettysburg Coll., 1942-45; M.D. summa cum laude, U. Md., 1950; M.S. in Internal Medicine, U. Minn., 1955; m. Alice Katherine Graybill, Sept. 15, 1945 (div. 1979); children—Louis Guy, Susanna, Katharine; m. 2d, Barbara Terrien Schell, Mar. 15, 1980; stepchildren—Jennifer, John, Margaret. Intern, USPHS Marine Hosp., Balt., 1950-51; resident Mayo Clinic, Mayo Found., U. Minn. Extension, Rochester, 1951-55; practice medicine specializing in internal medicine, Atlanta, 1955-65; dir. internal medicine Peachtree Parkwood Hosp., 1968-72; gen. dir. Peachtree Parkwood Mental Health Center and Hosps., Altanta, 1972—; internal medicine and psychiatry faculty Sch. Medicine, Emory U. Chmn. governing bd. Peachtree Parkwood Hosps. Served in USNR, 1944-46, USPHS, 1950-51. Diplomate Am. Bd. Internal Medicine. Mem. AMA, Am. Soc. Internal Medicine, Ga. Soc. Internal Medicine, Ga., Atlanta med. assns., Ga. Heart Assn., Am. Acad. Med. Dirs. Home: 7955 Spalding Hills Dr Atlanta GA 30338 Office: 1999 Cliff Valley Way NE Atlanta GA 30329

CHELTON, ROBERT GUSTAVE, corp. exec.; b. Cleve., May 19, 1924; s. Gustave A. and Julia B. (Eisner) C.; B.S. in Indsl. Engring., Case Western Res. U., 1945; LL.D., U. of the Andes, 1956; m. Pasty Jo Irby, Sept. 20, 1958; children—Kimberley Watt, Michelle Whitney. Indsl. engr., Republic Steel Corp., Cleve., 1946-48; asst. dist. mgr., Acme Cleve Corp., 1948-54; with R. Barroco and Cie, Bolivia, 1954-59; market devel. mgr., White Consolidated Industries, Cleve., 1959-65, Curtiss Wright Corp., Cleve., 1965-70; pres. Marietta Internat. Corp., Ft. Lauderdale, Fla., 1970-77; pres. Chelcher Inc., Ft. Lauderdale, 1977—; dir. Asso. Swimming Pool Industries, Chelmac Industries, A.G.F. Constructors. Served with USMC, 1943-45. Clubs: Boca Yacht and Racquet (dir.). Home: 1323 Sycamore Terr Boca Raton FL 33432 Office: Chelcher Inc 2662 N Dixie Hwy Fort Lauderdale FL 33334

CHEN, BILL CHUNG-MOON, engr.; b. Taiwan, Apr. 25, 1942; s. Noon-shieu and King-may (Huang) C.; came to U.S., 1967, naturalized, 1975; B.S. in Marine Engring., Provincial Coll. Marine Tech. (Taiwan), 1967; M.S. in Aero. Engring., Wichita State U., 1970; Ph.D. in Engring. Sci., U. Ark., 1974; m. Judy Boyd, Dec. 26, 1971; children—William Boyd, James Thomas. Research asst. U. Ark., Fayetteville, 1970-73; systems design engr. Avondale Shipyards Inc., New Orleans, 1973-79; sr. engr. Brown & Root Inc., Houston, 1979—. Lic. marine engr., Taiwan. Mem. Chs. of Christ. Contbr. articles to profl. jours. Home: 4718 Sabrina Houston TX 77066

CHEN, FONG HSIUNG, physician; b. Taitung, Taiwan, June 7, 1941; came to U.S., 1972, naturalized, 1979; s. Swei Moo and Long Mai (Lee) C.; M.D., Taipei (Taiwan) Med. Coll., 1970; m. Helen S.F. Chiou, Jan. 23, 1973; 1 son, Sing Ming. Intern, Vets. Gen. Hosp., Taipei, 1969-70, resident in medicine, 1971-72; intern in surgery Watts Hosp., Durham, N.C., 1972-73; resident in surgery Huron Rd. Hosp., Clev., 1973-77; practice medicine specializing in surgery, Woodward, Okla., 1977—; staff surgeon Woodward Meml. Hosp., 1977—. Served as 2d lt. M.C., Republic of China Air Force, 1970-71. Diplomate Am. Bd. Surgery. Fellow Am. Soc. Abdominal Surgeons; mem. AMA, A.C.S., Okla. Med. Assn. Roman Catholic. Home: 2419 Maple Ave Woodward OK 73801 Office: 1103 Hillcrest St Woodward OK 73801

CHEN, JAMES PAI-FUN, biochemist; b. Fengyuan, Taichung, Taiwan, May 1, 1929; s. Chuan and Su-Wuo (Lin) C.; came to U.S., 1952, naturalized, 1969; student Nat. Taiwan U., 1949-51, U. Pa., 1952-53; B.S., Houghton (N.Y.) Coll., 1955; M.S., St. Lawrence U., 1957; Ph.D., Pa. State U., 1962; m. Metis Hsiu-chun Lin, Dec. 19, 1964; children—Mark H., Eunice H., Jeremy H. Instr. chemistry Houghton Coll., N.Y., 1960-62, asso. prof., 1962-64; research asso. in immunology U. Vt., Burlington, 1964-65, SUNY, Buffalo, 1965-68; research asst. prof. internal medicine U. Tex. Med. Br., Galveston, 1968-70, asst. prof. human genetics 1970-75; sr. research asso. NASA Johnson Space Center, Houston, 1975-76; asso. prof. med. biology U. Tenn. Center for Health Scis., Knoxville unit, 1976—. Vt. Heart Assn. postdoctoral fellow, 1964-65, NIH postdoctoral fellow, 1965-68; sr. research asso. NRC, 1975-76. Mem. Am. Soc. Biol. Chemists, Am. Assn. Immunologists, AAAS, Am. Soc. Human Genetics. Presbyterian. Researcher coagulation and fibrinolysis. Home: 1225 Southbreeze Circle Knoxville TN 37919 Office: U Tenn Meml Research Center 1924 Alcoa Hwy Knoxville TN 37920

CHEN, JAMES TSUNG-TSUN, radiologist; b. Shantung, China, Jan. 11, 1924; s. Yi and Chung-yu (Wang) C.; came to U.S., 1959, naturalized, 1971; M.D., Nat. Def. Med. Center, Taiwan, 1950; m. Alice Wu, June 29, 1963. Intern, Presbyn. Hosp., Phila., 1962-63, resident Hosp. U. Pa., 1955-57, 60-62, St. Christopher Hosp. for Children, Phila., 1963-64; asst. instr. radiology U. Pa., 1956-57; instr. radiology Nat. Def. Med. Center, Taipei, China, 1957-59; asso. in radiology Duke U. Med. Sch., Durham, N.C., 1965-68, asst. prof. radiology, 1968-71, asso. prof., 1971-75, prof., 1975—, dir. cardiopulmonary radiology, 1976—. Named Tchr. of Year, Dept. Radiology, Duke U., 1974. Fellow Am. Coll. Cardiology, Am. Coll. Radiology, Am. Heart Assn.; mem. Radiol. Soc. N.Am., Am. Roentgen Ray Soc., Assn. Univ. Radiologists, N.Am. Soc. Cardiac Radiology. Presbyterian. Office: Dept Radiology Duke Hosp Durham NC 27710

CHEN, PING-FAN, geologist; b. Kiangyin, Kiangsu, China, May 13, 1917; s. Mou-Chu and Lan-yin (Men) C.; B.S., Nat. Central U. China, 1938; M.S., U. Cin. (fellow), 1956; Ph.D. (fellow) Va. Poly. Inst. and State U., 1959; m. Tsing-fang Tsao, Jan. 1, 1947 (dec.); children—Jane, June, Julia. Came to U.S., 1956, naturalized, 1969. Petroleum geologist Nat. Geol. Survey China, 1938-46; sr. petroleum geologist Chinese Petroleum Corp., Taiwan, 1946-55; stratigrapher, W.Va. Geol. Survey, Morgantown, 1960—; adj. prof. W.Va. U., 1975—. Adviser W.Va. U. Chinese Student Assn., 1962. Mem. Geol. Soc. China, Chinese Engrs. Assn., Chinese Assn. Advancement Scis., Sigma Xi, Sigma Gamma Epsilon. Author: Mineral Resources of China, 1954; New Outlook for the Oil Fields of Taiwan, 1949; Tectonic Analogies and Antitheses between Taiwan and the Appalachians, 1976; Lower Paleozoic Stratigraphy in the Central Appalachians, 1978. Home: 1277 Dogwood Ave Morgantown WV 26505 Office: PO Box 879 Morgantown WV 26505

CHEN, REX LONG-SHUNG, educator; b. Taiwan, Aug. 25, 1942; came to U.S., 1968, naturalized, 1978; s. Pau and Lin Chen; M.S., U. Wis., 1971, Ph.D., 1974; m. Phoebe F. Chen, Sept. 25, 1972; children—Celena, Eric. Research asst. U. Wis., Madison, 1968-74, research asso., 1974-76; asst. prof. soil chemistry La. State U., Baton Rouge, 1976-79; water chemist Waterways Expt. Sta., U.S. Army C.E., Vicksburg, Miss., 1979—. Mem. Am. Soc. Agronomy, AAAS, Soil Sci. Soc. Am., Council for Agr. and Tech., Sigma Xi. Contbr. articles to profl. jours. Home: 1107 River Bend Rd Vicksburg MS 39180 Office: Environ Lab Waterways Expt Sta Vicksburg MS 39180

CHEN, WAYNE H., elec. engr., ednl. adminstr.; b. Soochow, China, Dec. 13, 1922; s. Ting Li and Yung-Chin (Hu) C.; came to U.S., 1947, naturalized, 1957; B.S. in Elec. Engring., Nat. Chiao Tung U., China, 1944; M.S., U. Wash., 1949, Ph.D., 1952; m. Dorothy Teh Hou, June 7, 1957; children—Avis Shirley and Benjamin Timothy (twins). Electronic engr. cyclotron project Applied Physics Lab., U. Wash., 1949-50, asso. in math., 1950-52; mem. faculty U. Fla., Gainesville, 1952—, prof. elec. engring., 1957—, chmn. dept., from 1965, dean Coll. Engring., dir. Engring. and Indsl. Expt. Sta., 1973—; vis. prof. Nat. Chiao Tung U., also Nat. Taiwan U., spring 1964; vis. scientist Nat. Acad. Scis. to USSR, 1967; mem. tech. staff Bell Telephone Labs., summers 1953, 54, cons., 1955-60; mem. tech. staff Hughes Aircraft Co., summer 1962; vis. prof. U. Carabobo, Venezuela, summer 1972. Recipient Fla. Blue Key Outstanding Faculty award, 1960; Outstanding Publ. award Chia Hsin Cement Co. Cultural Fund, Taiwan, 1964; Tchr.-Scholar award U. Fla., 1971; registered profl. engr., Fla. Fellow IEEE; mem. AAUP, Am. Soc. Engring. Edn., Nat. Soc. Profl. Engrs., Fla. Engring. Soc., Sigma Xi (pres. U. Fla. chpt. 1967-68), Sigma Tau, Eta Kappa Nu, Epsilon Lambda Chi, Omicron Delta Kappa, Phi Tau Phi. Club: Rotary. Author: The Analysis of Linear Systems, 1963; Linear Network Design and Synthesis, 1964; patentee in field. Home: 2065 NW 19th Ln Gainesville FL 32605 Office: Coll Engring Univ Fla Gainesville FL 32611

CHENAULT, WILLIAM BLEWETT, JR., chem. engr., plant utilities cons.; b. Beaumont, Tex., Oct. 27, 1917; s. William Blewett and Clara Brandon (Russell) C.; student Rice Inst., 1936-38, Alfred U., 1938-40; B.A. in Chemistry, U. Houston, 1941; m. Rebecca Frances Burrell, July 23, 1940; children—William B. III, Charles Bruce, Harriot Elizabeth. Chem. engr. Sinclair Refining Co., Houston, 1941-44, Ford, Bacon & Davis Co., Oak Ridge, Tenn., 1944; research chemist Sinclair Refining Co., East Chicago, Ind., 1945-46; chem. engr. Sinclair Rubber Inc., Houston, 1946-47; spectroscopist Sinclair Refining Co., Houston, 1947-50; chem. engr. Sinclair Rubber Inc., Houston, 1950-52, asst. purchasing agt., 1952-54, chem. engr., 1954-55; chem. engr. Petro-Tex Chem. Co., Houston, 1955-62, utilities supr., 1962-77; plant utilities cons., Houston, 1977—. Civil Def. worker, World War II; merit badge counselor Boy Scouts Am., 1953-65; lay reader Episcopal Ch., Houston, 1963—; active various polit. campaigns, civic orgns. Served alt. mil. duty Manhattan project, Oak Ridge, 1944. Licensed stationary engr., Tex. Mem. Cooling Tower Inst. (com. chmn. 1961-71), Air Pollution Control Assn. (chmn. S.W. sect. 1961-63, vice chmn. nat. program com. 1964), Am. Chem. Soc., Am. Inst. Chem. Engrs., Water Pollution Control Fed., Nat. Assn. Corrosion Engrs., Sam Houston Water Utilities Assn., Houston C. of C., Huguenot Soc., Delta Sigma Phi. Republican. Episcopalian. Clubs: Brotherhood of St. Andrew, Southwest Civic, Toastmasters, Houston Lodge (past master), Masons (32 deg.), Shriners, K.T., Order Eastern Star (past patron), Tex. Lodge of Research. Contbr. article, research papers in field. Address: 3715 Dumbarton St Houston TX 77025

CHENG, AYLMER PAO-SHENG, civil engr.; b. Hankou, China, Sept. 4, 1936; s. Shao Liang and Hui Lien (Liang) C.; came to U.S., 1961, naturalized, 1971; B.S., Nat. Taiwan U., 1959; M.S., U. Mo.-Rolla, 1962; Ph.D., Tex. A. and M. U., 1967; m. Mary Jo Wen-ying Ting, Sept. 2, 1967; children—Julie, Kelly. Sr. structural engr. Brown & Root, Inc., Houston, 1963-65, chief structural dynamist, 1965-66; mech. engr. Shell Devel. Co., Houston, 1966-70; adj. lectr. U. Houston, 1968-69; sr. petroleum engr. Amoco Internat. Oil Co., Chgo., 1970-73, staff engr. sr. grade, 1973-75, engring. group leader, Chgo., 1975-78, engring. group supr., Houston, 1979—. Mem. spl. com. on single point moorings and offshore fixed platforms Am. Bur. Shipping. 1974—; mem. Oil Industry Internat. Exploration and Prodn. Forum, 1978—. Mem. ASCE, Soc. Petroleum Engrs., Sigma Xi, Kappa Mu Epsilon. Contbr. articles to profl. jours.; editorial adv. bd. Ocean Engring. mag., 1976—. Home: 15715 TC Jester St Houston TX 77068 Office: PO Box 4381 Houston TX 77210

CHENG, BIN-LUH, elec. engr., educator; b. Kwangtung, China, June 6, 1941; came to U.S., 1967, naturalized, 1976; s. Hai-Chu and Shu-Tsan (Lo) C.; B.S. in Elec. Engring., Nat. Taiwan U., 1964; M.S. in Computer Sci., Nat. Chiao-Tung U., 1967; M.S. in Elec. Engring., Colo. State U., 1968; Ph.D. in Elec. Engring., Mich. State U., 1972; m. Vera Pi-Nan Chu, Dec. 30, 1972; children—Jimming V., Winston. Instr., Detroit Inst. Tech., 1971-72; asst. prof. Fla. A. and M. U., Tallahassee, 1972-76; chmn., asso. prof. dept. elec. engring. tech., 1977—. Registered profl. engr., Fla. Mem. IEEE (sec. Tallahassee subsect.), Am. Soc. Engring. Edn., Fla. Tech. Edn. Assn. Home: 2041 Doomar Tallahassee FL 32308 Office: Fla A and M U Tallahassee FL 32307

CHENOWETH, PETER JOHN, veterinarian, educator; b. Melbourne, Australia, June 24, 1946; came to U.S., 1975; s. Ian Harold and Ruth (Farrer) C.; B Vet. Sci. with honors, U. Queensland, Australia, 1968, Ph.D., 1979; m. Leonie Mary Byrne, May 24, 1969. Research asst. U. Queensland, 1968-72; pvt. practice vet. medicine, Mackay, Queensland, Australia, 1972-74; external lectr. James Cook U., N. Queensland, 1972-74; vis. asst. prof. dept. physiology and biophysics Colo. State U., Ft. Collins, 1975, asst. prof., 1975-78, adv. grad. students, 1976-79, acting dir. Animal Reprodn. Lab., summers 1976, 77; asso. prof. theriogenology dept. vet. large animal medicine and surgery Tex. A. and M. U., College Station, 1978—. Mem. Am. Soc. Animal Sci., Am. Soc. Theriogenology, Am. Assn. Bovine Practitioners, AVMA, Australian Vet. Assn., Royal Coll. Vet. Surgeons, Tex. Vet. Med. Assn., Assn. Am. Vet. Med. Colls., Sigma Xi, Phi Zeta. Methodist. Contbg. author books on animal sci.; also articles on theriogenology. Office: Dept Veterinary Large Animal Medicine and Surgery Tex A and M Univ College Station TX 77843

CHEROFF, IRVING SHERWIN, educator; b. Bklyn., Aug. 11, 1914; s. Max and Bertha (Matz) C.; B.S., Bklyn. Coll., 1935; M.A., Columbia U., 1936; student Jewish Welfare Bd. Sch. for Execs., 1947; M.A. in Social Adminstrn., Ohio State U., 1949, postgrad, 1946-49; postgrad. N.Y. U., Boston U., Hunter Coll.; LL.D., Burton Coll. & Sem., 1958; D.Litt (hon.), William Carter Bible Sch., 1959; m. Isabelle Rosenbloom, Aug., 1940; 1 son, Richard. Dir., Schonthal Center and Camp Schonthal, Columbus, Ohio, 1946-50; exec. dir. Jewish Community Center, Jewish Youth Center, Worcester, Mass., 1950-52; area dir. U.S.O., Inc., Nat. Jewish Welfare Bd. for N.C., 1952-64, chmn. area staff tng. conf., 1953—; co-chmn. dept. sociology and social work Fayetteville (N.C.) State U., 1970—; adj. prof. N.C. State U.; field instr. Ohio State U. Sch. Social Work; instr. NCCJ, 1953; pvt. practice social work cons.; bd. dirs. Anti-Defamation League B'nai B'rith. Treas., Council Social Service Agys., Cumberland County, 1952—; active Boy Scouts Am.; publicity chmn., mem. steering com. Bicentennial Celebration, Cumberland County; mem. Fort Bragg-Fayetteville Mil. Affairs Com. and 3d Army adv. com., 1953—; parade chmn. United Services Fund Cumberland City and Ft. Bragg (N.C.), 1957—. Served with U.S. Army, 1943-46. Decorated Commendation medal with pendant; Tercenternary medal Am. Jewish Tercentenary Commn., 1954; named Man of the Year, Fayetteville, 1960; recipient Award of Honor, State of Israel. Mem. Acad. Cert. Social Workers, Nat. Assn. Social Workers (chpt. founder and v.p.), Acad. Polit. and Social Sci. Assn., Assn. U.S. Army, Fayette- ville C. of C. (co-chmn. civil affairs), N.C. Assn. Jewish Men, Women, Youth (dir. 1955), Am. Camp Dirs., AAUP, NEA, B'nai B'rith (N.C. exec. com. 1954—, chmn. public relations and program com. N.C.). Clubs: Ft. Bragg Officers, Execs., Masons, Shriners. Feature writer Am. Jewish Times-Outlook mag., 1952—; book reviewer, contbg. editor Fayetteville Observer. Office: Dept Social/Sociology Fayetteville State U Fayetteville NC 28301

CHERRY, CHARLES LOUIS, stockbroker; b. Jacksonville, Fla., Mar. 8, 1936; s. Sam and Gussie (Rabinowich) C.; B.S. in Bus., U. Fla., 1959; postgrad. Sch. of Banking of South, 1963-65, Am. Inst. Banking, 1966; m. Carole Safer, Dec. 29, 1957; children—Brian Howard, Amy

Frances. Asst. cashier First Nat. Bank of Orlando (Fla.), 1960-63, trust investment officer, 1963-67; registered rep., stockbroker Smith Barney, Harris Upham & Co., Tampa, Fla., 1967—, v.p. sales, 1975—. Mem. sales council Jewish Community Center, Tampa, 1967—. Served with USNR, 1955-57. Recipient Wall St. Jour., Mrs. Charles Ulrick Bay awards in fin., 1959. Mem. Inst. Chartered Fin. Analysts, Am., So. fin. assns., U. Fla. Alumni Assn., Central Fla. Analysts Soc. (dir. 1973-76). Jewish. Clubs: Lions (pres. Orlando 1967); University, Tampa Airport Racquet (Tampa); River (Jacksonville); Bankers (Miami). Home: 4402 Brookwood Dr Tampa FL 33609 Office: Smith Barney Harris Upham & Co 610 Florida Ave Tampa FL 33602

CHERRY, DAVID EARL, lawyer; b. Fort Worth, Sept. 10, 1944; s. Leonard Earl and Dorothy (Brown) C.; B.B.A., Tex. Christian U., 1967, J.D., Baylor U., 1968; m. Katherine Ann Yarbrough, Dec. 23, 1967; children—Lisa Michelle, Craig David. Admitted to Tex. bar, 1968; asso. firm Pakis, Cherry, Beard & Giotes, Inc., and predecessor firms, Waco, 1969-71, partner, 1971-72, v.p., 1972—. Mem. Planning, Zoning Commn. Woodway, Tex., 1972-79, chmn., 1975-76; mem. City Charter Commn., 1973. Voter's rights chmn. Com. to Re-elect Pres., Tex. Region V, 1972; bd. dirs. Waco Lighthouse for Blind, 1971-74, Waco-McLennan County Legal Aid Soc., 1970-72, YMCA, 1976—; bd. devel. Tex. Baptist Children's Home, 1975-80; mem. nat. exploring com. Boy Scouts Am., 1976—. Served with Tex. Army N.G., 1968. Mem. Waco-McLennan County Young Lawyers Assn. (pres. 1974-75, named outstanding young lawyer of year 1977), Am., Waco-McLennan County (treas. 1974-75, dir. 1979—) bar assns., State Young Lawyers Assn. Am. Judicature Soc., Delta Sigma Pi, Phi Alpha Delta. Methodist. Republican. Club: Founders Lions of Waco (dir. 1974-79, sec. 1975-78). Office: 800 1st Nat Bldg Waco TX 76701

CHERRY, FRANCES REESE, nursing adminstr.; b. Freeport, Fla., Apr. 15, 1922; d. Edward Horace and Evelyn (Jernigan) Reese; grad. Carraway Methodist Hosp. Sch. of Nursing, 1968; m. Robert Edward Cherry, Dec. 6, 1942 (div. 1975); children—Frances Cherry Scott, Cecile, Harriet Robin. Supr., Carraway Meth. Med. Center, Birmingham, Ala., 1968-70, asst. dir. nursing service, 1970—; health nurse Birmingham So. Coll., 1977-78. Recipient Ola Mabry Collins award, 1968; Faculty award, 1968. Mem. Nat. League Nursing, Am. Nurses Assn. Methodist. Home: 1825 Fultondale Apt Rd Fultondale AL 35068 Office: 1615 N 25th St Birmingham AL 35234

CHERTOK, WILLIAM MICHAEL, JR., ednl. adminstr.; b. Spartanburg, S.C., Aug. 6, 1938; s. William Michael and Maude Mae (McCall) C.; A.B., U. S.C., 1960; M.Div., Southeastern Bapt. Theol. Sem., 1964; grad. student Boston U., 1964-65; m. Nancy Katrina Mullins, Sept. 30, 1967. Asso. dir. univ. relations Furman U., 1965-68; dir. devel. U. S.C., 1969-71; v.p. for devel. Stetson U., 1971-78; asst. v.p. for devel. U. Louisville, 1978—. Bd. dirs. West Volusia County chpt. ARC, 1974-78, West Volusia Humane Soc., House Next Door, 1977-78. Mem. DeLand Area C. of C. (dir. 1974-77, pres. 1976), Council for Advancement and Support Edn., Public Relations Soc. Am. Rotarian (chmn. internat. youth activities 1973-74, program chmn. 1974-75, dir. 1975-77). Home: 10709 Sunderland Pl Middletown KY 40243 Office: Devel Programs U Louisville Louisville KY 40208

CHESLEY, WILLIAM RORAH, advt. agy. exec.; b. Pitts., Dec. 24, 1928; s. John Osborne and Eugenia Rorah C.; B.A., U. Pitts., 1951; m. Shirley Ann Tanner, Sept. 10, 1955; children—John Osborne II, Janet Tanner, Mary Ellen. Account asst. Ketchum, McLeod & Grove, Pitts., 1951-53; advt. mgr. tar products div. Koppers Co., Pitts., 1955-57; account exec. Fuller & Smith & Ross, Pitts., 1957-60; mgr. advt. and sales promotion Corry Jamestown Corp., Corry, Pa., 1960-63; account exec. Jayme Orgn., Cleve., 1963-66; copy dir. Griswold-Eshleman, Pitts., 1966-68; prin. Creative Bus. Communications, Pitts. and Miami Shores, Fla., 1968—. Served to 1st lt. arty. U.S. Army, 1953-55. Recipient 1st award, div. 1 TF Club of Cleve., 1961. Republican. Presbyterian. Home and Office: 10920 N Miami Ave Miami Shores FL 33168

CHESNUTT, EDWIN LEE, JR., mfg. co. exec.; b. Atlanta, Mar. 4, 1940; s. Edwin Lee and Mary Ellen (Bell) C.; B.S. in Engring., Duke U., 1963; M.B.A., U. N.C., 1964; m. Ann Tanner, Nov. 17, 1977; 1 son, Edwin Lee III; 1 stepson, James Herold Mason III. With Cryovac div. W.R. Grace Co., Duncan, S.C., 1964—, dir. mktg., 1975-77, v.p. mktg. and planning, 1977—. Mem. Greenville County (S.C.) Devel. Bd., 1971-74, chmn., 1974; trustee United Way of Greenville, 1969-76; pres. Jr. Achievement of Greenville, 1975-76; mem. Greenville County Planning Commn., 1976—, vice chmn., 1977; bd. dirs. Am. Cancer Soc., Greenville, 1975. Named Boss of Yr., Nat. Secs. Assn., Greenville, 1974, Young Man of Yr., Greenville Jaycees, 1973; S.C. Young Man of Yr. S.C. Jaycees, 1974. Mem. Soc. Plastics Engrs., Am. Mgmt. Assn. Republican. Episcopalian. Office: PO Box 464 Duncan SC 29334

CHESSER, ROBERT EPPS, home builder and designer; b. Houston, Sept. 8, 1951; s. Jesse Willard and Lenny Soffie (Goodwynn) C.; student Tex. A&I U., 1971, San Jacinto Coll., 1972, Angelo State U., 1978; m. Karen Patricia Killian, Aug. 20, 1971; 1 dau., Patricia Lynn. Supt., Allen Watts Co. Inc., Houston, 1971-72; home designer, builder Stein Lumber Co., Fredericksburg, Tex., 1972-75; owner Chesser Insulation Co., 1972-75; constrn. mgr. Builders Service Co., San Angelo, Tex., 1975-76; owner, bldg. engr. B.C. Designs Co., San Angelo, 1972—; home builder Chapple Bryan Inc., San Angelo, 1977—. Mem. San Angelo Jaycees (v.p. 1976-78). Democrat. Methodist. Home: 23 W 31st St San Angelo TX 76903 Office: 325 N Main St San Angelo TX 76901

CHESTER, EDWARD WILLIAM, author, educator: b. Richmond, Va., Nov. 9, 1935; s. Edward William and Mary Elizabeth (Lewis) C.; A.B. summa cum laude, Morris Harvey Coll., 1956; M.A., U. Pitts., 1958, Ph.D., 1961. Asst. prof. history Lambuth Coll., Jackson, Tenn., 1961; instr. history U. Ky., Covington, from 1962; asst. prof. history Inter-Am. U., P.R., Hato Rey, 1964; asst. prof. history U. Tex., Arlington, 1965-68, asso. prof., 1968—. Earhart Found. summer research grantee, 1977, 78. Mem. Am., So. hist. assns., Orgn. Am. Historians, Soc. for Historians of American Fgn. Relations, AAUP, Am. Assn. for State and Local History. Republican. Methodist. Author: Radio, Television and American Politics, 1968; Clash of Titans: Africa and U.S. Foreign Policy, 1974; A Guide to Political Platforms, 1977, others. Home: 708 W Main St Apt E Arlington TX 76013 Office: Dept History U Tex Arlington TX 76019

CHESTER, ROBERT ANSON, JR., mental health adminstr.; b. Rochville Center, N.Y., Aug. 15, 1945; s. Robert A. and Florence I. (Harwood) C.; B.S., Rollins Coll., 1969. Asst. dir. drug abuse dept. Brevard County Mental Health Center, Rockledge, Fla., 1972-73, dir. emergency services, 1974—; grants coordinator Office Drug Abuse, Fla. Dept. Health and Rehab. Services, Tallahassee, 1973-74; lectr. Sch. Nursing, Fla. State U., Tallahassee, 1973-74. Mem. Young Democrats of Brevard County, 1974-77; bd. dirs. Family Aid Soc. of Brevard Runaway Center, Inc. Recipient award Am. Legion Boy's State Program, Fla., 1962, award Colgate U., Hamilton, N.Y., 1962; N.Y. State Regents scholar. Mem. Am. Pub. Health Assn., Fla. Council for Community Mental Health. Episcopalian. Home: 164 Dover St Satellite Beach FL 32937 Office: 1770 Cedar St Rockledge FL 32955

CHEVES, HARRY LANGDON, JR., physician; b. Birmingham, Ala., Oct. 17, 1924; s. Harry Langdon and Myrtle (Churchill) C.; A.B., Mercer U., 1949; M.D., Med. Coll. Ga., 1953; m. Lois Rebecca Corry, Dec. 25, 1949; children—Rebecca Churchill, Harry Langdon III; m. 2d, Mary Agnes Moon; 1 son, Harry Michael. Intern, Univ. Hosp., Augusta, Ga., 1953-54; practice medicine, East Point, Ga.; mem. staff S. Fulton Hosp., chief of staff, 1980—. Served with USAAF, 1942-46. Fellow Internat., Am. colls. angiology; mem. Royal Soc. Health, AMA, So. Med. Assn., Med. Assn. Atlanta, Atlanta, So. Dist. (pres.) med. socs., Am. Geriatric Soc., Med. Assn. Ga., Ga. Heart Assn., Phi Delta Theta. Clubs: Am. Antique Automobile, Classic Car Club Am., Packard Automobile Classics, Rolls-Royce Am., Rolls-Royce Owners, Model A, Chrysler Restorers, Lakeside Country. Home: 333 Plantation Circle Riverdale GA 30296 Office: 2726 Felton Dr East Point GA 30344

CHI, LOTTA C(HAI) J(UI) LI, research and devel. co. exec.; b. N.Y.C., Dec. 5, 1930; d. Chen Pien and Han Chih (Tang) Li; B.S., Heidelberg Coll., Tiffin, Ohio, 1953; M.S., Rutgers U., 1955; m. Michael Chi, June 15, 1957; children—Loretta, Maxwell. Virologist NIH, Bethesda, Md., 1956-63; sec., treas. Chi Assos., Inc., Arlington, Va., 1975—, contract mgr., 1975—, office mgr., 1976—; pres. L Chi Assos., 1979—; cons. in field. Mem. Am. Soc. Microbiology, N.Y. Acad. Scis., Nat. Assn. Women Bus. Owners, Orgn. Chinese Am. Women (nat. soc.), Sigma Xi, Sigma Delta Epsilon. Democrat. Home: 2721 N 24th St Arlington VA 22207 Office: 1011 Arlington Blvd Arlington VA 22209

CHIAPPINI, CLAIRE PHELPS, real estate co. exec.; b. St. Louis, Dec. 23, 1926; d. Harold Raymond and Lillian (Shultz) Phelps; student public schs., Melrose, Fla.; m. Francis D. Chiappini, Dec. 29, 1947; children—Heidi, David, Nick, Robin, Mark, Lily. Sec. depts. of anesthesiology and ophthalmology Coll. Medicine, U. Fla., Gainesville, 1964-69, dean's sec. Coll. Arts and Scis., 1970; v.p. Chiappini, Inc., Melrose, 1976—. Mem. Nat. Assn. Realtors, Fla. Assn. Realtors, Gainesville Bd. Realtors, Putnam County Bd. Realtors (dir.). Democrat. Episcopalian. Club: Jr. Woman's of Melrose (organizer, pres.). Home: PO Box 170 State Rd 21 and Pine St Melrose FL 32666 Office: Chiappini Inc PO Box 182 N State Rd 21 and State Rd 26 Melrose FL 32666

CHIERI, PERICLE ADRIANO C., educator, cons. mech. and aero. engr., naval architect; b. Mokanshan, Chekiang, China, Sept. 6, 1905; s. Virginio and Luisa (Fabbri) C.; Dr. Engring., U. Genoa, Italy, 1927; M.E., U. Naples, Italy, 1927; Dr. Aero. Engring., U. Rome, 1928; m. Helen Etheredge, Aug. 1, 1938. Came to U.S., 1938, naturalized, 1952. Naval architect, mech. engr. research and exptl. divs., submarines and internal combustion engines, Italian Navy, Spezia, 1929-31; naval architect, marine supt. Navigazione Libera Triestina Shipping Corp., Libera Lines, Trieste, Italy, 1931-32, Genoa, 1933-35; aero. engr., tech. adviser Chinese Govt. commn. aero. affairs, Nat. Govt. Republic of China, Nanchang and Loyang, 1935-37; engring. exec., dir. aircraft materials test lab., supt. factory's tech. vocat. instrn., SINAW Nat. Aircraft Works, Nanchang, Kiangsi, China, 1937-39; aero. engr. FIAT aircraft factory, Turin, Italy, 1939; aero. engr. and tech. sec. Office; Air Attache, Italian Embassy, Washington, 1939-41; prof. aero. engring. Tri-State Coll., Angola, Ind., 1942; aero. engr., helicopter design Aero. Products, Inc., Detroit, 1943-44; sr. aero. engr. ERCO Engring. & Research Corp., Riverdale, Md., 1944-46; asso. prof. mech. engring. U. Toledo, 1946-47; asso. prof. mech. engring., faculty grad. div. Newark (N.J.) Coll. Engring., 1947-52; prof., head dept. mech. engring. U. Southwestern La., Lafayette, La., 1952-72; cons. engr., Lafayette, 1972—; research engr., advanced devel. sect., aviation gas turbine div., Westinghouse Electric Corp., South Philadelphia, Pa., 1953; exec. dir. Council on Environment, Lafayette, 1975—. Instr. water safety ARC Nat. Aquatic Schs., summers 1958-67. Bd. dirs. Lafayette Parish chpt. ARC. Registered profl. engr., Italy, N.J., La., S.C.; chartered engr., U.K. Fellow Royal Instn. Naval Architects London (life); asso. fellow Am. Inst. Aeronautics and Astronautics; mem. Soc. Naval Architects and Marine Engrs., AAAS, AAUP (emeritus), Am. Soc. Engring. Edn. (life), ASME, Soc. Automotive Engrs., Instrument Soc. Am., Soc. Exptl. Stress Analysis, Nat. Soc. Profl. Engrs., N.Y. Acad. Scis., La. Engring. Soc., La. Tchrs. Assn., AAHPER, La. Acad. Scis., Commodore Longfellow Soc., Cons. Engrs. Council La., Phi Kappa Phi, Pi Tau Sigma (hon.). Home: 142 Oak Crest Dr Lafayette LA 70503 Office: PO Box 52923 OCS Lafayette LA 70505

CHILCOAT, BETTY JACKSON, nursing home adminstr.; b. Jackson, Miss., Aug. 28, 1936; d. Paul Lee and Audrey I. (Bulice) Jackson; grad. Oklahoma City Vocat. Sch. Practical Nursing, 1967; student Okla. U., 1970, No. Okla. Coll., 1977—; m. Charles Cecil Chilcoat, Jan. 22, 1952; children—Janet Lynne, Charles Neil, Howard Kent, Karl Alan. Nursing supr. Golden Age Nursing Home, Guthrie, Okla., 1967-69; nursing personnel dir. Four Season Nursing Center, Guthrie, 1969-70; adminstr. Guthrie Nursing Center, 1970; adminstr., owner Green Valley Convalescent Center, Perry, Okla., 1970-77; co-owner, asst. adminstr. Chilcoat Nursing Center, Tonkawa, Okla., 1977—. Treas. Noble County Republican Women, 1974-75, del. state conv., 1974, 76. Mem. Okla. State Nursing Home Assn., Am. Coll. Nursing Home Adminstrs. Baptist. Home: 202 Carousel Dr Tokawa OK 74653 Office: 1301 N 5th St Tonkawa OK 74653

CHILD, ROBERT DANVERS, agrl. cons.; b. El Dorado, Ark., Sept. 21, 1927; s. Thomas Harold and Sarah (Wallace) C.; B.S., U. Ark., 1950, M.S., 1966; m. Wanda Gay Daniel, May 3, 1951; children—Lisa Gay, Robert Danvers, Jr. Research and teaching asst. U. Ark., 1962-65; div. mgr. Carlisle div. Winrock Farms, Carlisle, Ark., 1965-67, ops. mgr., Morrilton, Ark., 1967-69, gen. mgr., 1969-75; pres. Child and Assos., agrl. cons., 1976—; dir. Riceland Foods, Inc. Bd. govs. Livestock Merchandising Inst. Served with USNR, 1944-46. Mem. Nat. Livestock and Meat Bd. (dir.), Am. Nat. Cattlemen's Assn. (regional v.p.), Santa Gertrudis Breeders Internat. (mem. exec. com.), Ark. Cattlemen's Assn. (past pres.), Alpha Zeta, Gama Sigma Delta. Club: Farm and Ranch of Arkansas (pres.). Contbr. articles to farm jours. Address: Route 3 Morrilton AR 72110

CHILDERS, PERRY ROBERT, govt. ofcl.; b. Monticello, Ky., July 17, 1932; s. Charles T. and Leva M. (Spradlin) C.; B.A., U. Ky., 1958; M.A. (Grad. fellow), U. Ga., 1961, Ed.D., 1963; m. Wanda Faye Argo, Sept. 26, 1967; children—William Charles, Richard Calvin, Linda Louise, Leva Catherine. Asst. prof. psychology U. Ky., 1963-65; mgmt. psychologist Rohrer, Hibler & Replogle, Atlanta, 1966-67; asso. prof. psychology U. Fla., 1967-68, U. Wis., 1968-73; dep. supt. edn. State of La., 1973; dir. evaluation and monitoring, social and rehab. service HEW, Atlanta, 1974—; dir. quality control Social Security Adminstrn., 1977—; psychol. cons. to bus. mgmt. Recipient Spl. Achievement award HEW, 1976; Outstanding Performance award, 1977; licensed psychologist, Wis. Author publs. in field. Home: 119 Robin Hood Rd NE Atlanta GA 30309 Office: 101 Marietta St Atlanta GA 30323

CHILDERS, ROY EUGENE, JR., agrl. engr.; b. Big Springs, Tex., Sept. 14, 1947; s. Roy Eugene and Marcella (Rogers) C.; B.S., Tex. A. and M. U., 1970, M.S., 1972; children—Roy Dale, Michael Rogers, David Raymond. Research asso. Tex. Agrl. Experiment Sta., College Station, 1970-72; agrl. engr. Tex. Agrl. Extension Service, Lubbock, 1972-74, U.S. Dept. Agr., Lubbock, 1974-78; agrl. engr., state cotton ginning and mechanization specialist Tex. Agrl. Extension Service, College Station, 1978—. Served with U.S. Army, 1972. NDEA fellow, 1970. Mem. Am. Soc Agrl. Engrs., Reserve Officers Assn. Methodist. Home: 3102 Blue Stem College Station TX 77840 Office: 303 Scoates Hall Tex A&M U College Station TX 77843

CHILDERS, TERRY RANDALL, food co. exec.; b. Tulsa, July 26, 1947; s. Thomas B. and Evarae (Nordstrom) C.; student Okla. State U., 1965-66, Purdue U., 1966-69; m. Cherry Rae Hurley, Sept. 16, 1967; children—Todd Randall, Shelley Anne. Prodn. supr. Holloway House div. Green Giant Corp., Lafayette, Ind., 1967-69; ops. mgr. So. div. Ice Cream Specialties Co., Marietta, Ga., 1969-77; v.p. ops. Eastern Foods Inc., College Park, Ga., 1977—, also dir. Candidate for College Park City Council, 1979. Served with USMC, 1966-72. Named Marine of Yr., 1968. Mem. Ga. Dairy Tech. Soc. (past pres.). Republican. Mem. Christian Ch. (Disciples of Christ). Inventor branding iron code dater. Office: PO Box Drawer L College Park GA 30337

CHILDRESS, GEORGE RODNEY, ins. co. exec.; b. Richmond, Va., May 2, 1953; s. Henry T. and Catherine B. Childress; B.S., Va. Poly. Inst. and State U., 1975; m. Kathryn Lou Jenkins, June 28, 1975; 1 dau., Kristina Reagan. Mgmt. trainee Blue Cross of Va./Blue Shield of Va., Richmond, 1975-76, unit head, 1976-78, supr. hosp. claims, 1978-79, supr. Federal Employee program, 1979—. Mem. Va. Poly. Inst. and State U. Alumni Assn., West End Jaycees. Baptist. Home: 2906 Putney Rd Richmond VA 23228 Office: 2015 Staples Mill Rd Richmond VA 23279

CHILDRESS, THOMAS CLINTON, basketball coach; b. Mt. Airy, N.C., June 13, 1942; s. Clinton Alfred and Ruth Alma (Tatum) C.; B.A., Catawba Coll., Salisbury, N.C., 1964; postgrad. Appalachian State U., Boone, N.C., 1968-69; m. Judy Hollar, Dec. 19, 1964; children—Jeff, Brad, Paul, Beth. Basketball coach, phys. edn. instr. East Surry High Sch., Pilot Mountain, N.C., 1964-67; asst. basketball coach, phys. edn. instr. Appalachian State U., 1967-69; head basketball coach Pfeiffer Coll., Misenheimer, N.C., 1969—, asst. prof. phys. edn., 1973—, dir. athletics, 1977—. Named Coach of Year, Carolinas Basketball Conf., 1975, 77, 79. Mem. N.C. High Sch. Coaches Assn., Nat. Assn. Intercollegiate Athletics Athletic Dirs. Assn., Pfeiffer Coll. Alumni Assn. (hon.). Address: Athletic Dept Pfeiffer Coll Misenheimer NC 28109

CHILES, LAWTON MAINOR, U.S. senator; b. Lakeland, Fla., Apr. 3, 1930; B.S., U. Fla., 1952, LL.B., 1955; m. Rhea Grafton; children—Tandy, Lawton III, Edward G., Rhea Gay. Admitted to Fla. bar, practiced in Lakeland; mem. Fla. Ho. of Reps., 1958-66; mem. Fla. Senate, 1966-70; U.S. Senator from Fla., 1971—. Served with AUS; Korea. Democrat. Home: Lakeland FL 33801 also 1800 Old Meadow Rd McLean VA 22101

CHILTON, HORACE THOMAS, pipeline co. exec.; b. San Antonio, June 18, 1923; s. Horace Thomas and Lear Isabel (Word) C.; B.S. in Mech. Engring., U. Tex., 1947, B.A. in Bus. Adminstrn., 1947; grad. Advanced Mgmt Program, Harvard, 1958; m. Betty Jane Gray, Oct. 18, 1947; children—Thomas G., William D. Engr., Stanolind Pipe Line Co., Tulsa, 1947; div. chief engr. Service Pipe Line Co., Lubbock, Tex., 1950-52, supt. maintenance and constrn., 1956-60, asst. gen. mgr., 1950; mil. pipe line cons. U.S. Govt., Paris, France, 1955; mgr. products pipelines, lake tankers and barges Chgo. Amoco Oil Co., 1963-68; mgr. transp. ops., v.p. Amoco Pipeline, Amoco Oil Co., Chgo., 1969-71, gen. mgr. transp., pres. Amoco Pipeline, 1971-74; pres., chief exec. officer Colonial Pipeline, Atlanta, 1974—. Mem. U. Tex. Engring. Adv. Found. Bd., 1977—. Served with USNR, 1944-46. Mem. Assn. Oil Pipe Lines, Am. Petroleum Inst. (mem. gen. com. div. transp. 1971—, mem. coordinating com. central pipeline com. 1971—, dir. 1975—), Transp. Assn. Am. (dir. 1975—, pipeline panel 1971—, dir. 1975—), Beta Theta Pi. Presbyn. Club: Cherokee Town and Country (Atlanta). Home: 8920 River Landing Way Atlanta GA 30338 Office: 3390 Peachtree Rd NE Lenox Towers PO Box 18855 Atlanta GA 30326

CHILTON, ROBERT ELWOOD, ednl. adminstr.; b. Forsyth County, N.C., Feb. 6, 1926; married, 5 children. B.S. in English, Social Studies, Appalachian State U., Boone, N.C., 1950; M.Ed. in Ednl. Adminstrn., U. N.C., Greensboro, 1955; postgrad. in Ednl. Adminstrn., U. N.C., Chapel Hill, 1965. Dean Surry Community Coll., Dobson, N.C., 1965-67; pres. Glade Valley (N.C.) Sch., 1967-71; asst. supt. Mt. Airy (N.C.) City schs., 1972-75, supt., 1975—. Mem. NEA, N.C. Assn. Educators. Recipient Distinguished Service award Jaycees, Mt. Airy. Office: Drawer 710 Mount Airy NC 27030

CHINNOV, IGOR, educator, author; b. Tukum, Latvia, Sept. 25, 1909; s. Vladimir A. and Alexandra D. (von Zweygberg) C.; ed. U. Latvia, The Sorbonne, U. Munich. Came to U.S., 1962, naturalized, 1967. Asst. lawyer Riga; interned World War II; tchr. German, Russian Lyceum, Paris, 1947-50; lectr. Christian Assn. Russian Students, 1947-50, L'Institut des Statistiques, Paris, 1951; news writer, then sr. news editor Radio Liberty, Munich, 1953-62; asso. prof. Russian, U. Kan., 1962-69; vis. asso. prof. U. Pitts., 1969-70; prof. Russian lit. Vanderbilt U., Nashville, 1970-77, prof. emeritus, 1977—. Mem. Am. Assn. Advancement Slavic Studies, Am. Assn. Tchrs. Slavic and East European Langs., L'association des ecrivains russes Paris, Assn. Writers in Exile. Author: (poetry) Monologue, 1950, Lines, 1960, Metaphors, 1968, Partitura, 1970, Composition, 1972, Pastorals, 1976, Antithese, 1978. Home: 1224 S Peninsula Dr Daytona Beach FL 32018

CHIOU, CHUNG YIH, educator; b. Hsinchu, Taiwan, July 11, 1934; s. Chang and Mei (Wei) C.; B.S. in Pharmacy, Nat. Taiwan U., 1957, M.S. in Pharmacology, 1960; Ph.D. in Pharmacology (Research fellow Mead Johnson & Co. 1964-67), Vanderbilt U., 1967; m. Tricia T.S. Tsen, Sept. 23, 1961; children—Linda, Faye. Came to U.S., 1964, naturalized, 1973. Pharmacist William Pharm. Works, Hsinchu, Taiwan, 1960-61; instr. China Med. Coll., Taichung, Taiwan, 1962-64; research asst. pharmacology Vanderbilt U., Nashville, 1964-67, research asso. pharmacology, 1967-68; postdoctoral fellow pharmacology U. Iowa, Iowa City, 1968-69; asst. prof. pharmacology U. Fla., Gainesville, 1969-73, asso. prof., 1973-77, prof., 1977-78; prof., head pharmacology Tex. A&M U., College Station, 1978—; chmn. sci. session Fedn. Am. Socs. for Exptl. Biology, 1974, 77. Served to 2d. lt. Chinese Air Force, 1961-62. Recipient Health Scis. Advanced award NIH, 1967-68; research grantee, 1969-71; research grantee Nat. Inst. Neurol. Diseases and Stroke, 1971-74, Nat. Cancer Inst., 1975-77, Nat. Eye Inst., 1976-78, Am. Cancer Soc., 1977-79. Mem. N.Y. Acad. Scis., Am. Soc. Pharmacology and Exptl. Therapeutics (chmn. sci. session 1976). Sigma Xi. Contbr. articles to profl. jours. Home: 1019 Rose Circle College Station TX 77840

CHIPMAN, DENNIS CLARENCE, psychiatrist; b. Seattle, Jan. 7, 1934; s. Dennis Clarence and Esther Ronghild (Lund) C.; student U. Wash., 1952-55, M.D., 1959; m. Karen Ekern, Mar. 17, 1968; children—Kimberly Maria, Jason, Carolyn. Intern, U. Nebr. Hosp., Omaha, 1959-60; resident U. Wash. Hosp. System, 1960-63; pvt. practice, Seattle, 1963-66; dir. Kingsport (Tenn.) Mental Health Center, 1969-73; pvt. practice, Kingsport, 1973—; mem. staff Holston Valley Community Hosp., Indian Path Hosp.; dir. Kingsport Mental Health Center, Kingsport Center Opportunity; clin. instr. psychiatry U. Wash. Sch. Medicine, 1963-69; asso. prof. dept. family practice East Tenn. State U. Sch. Medicine, also clin. asso. prof. psychiatry. Served with M.C., AUS, 1966-68. Diplomate Am. Bd. Psychiatry and Neurology. Mem. Am. Psychiat. Assn., AMA, Kappa Sigma. Episcopalian. Clubs: Kingsport Dinner, Ridgefields Country (Kingsport). Home: 516 Forestdale Rd Kingsport TN 37660 Office: 1920 Brookside Dr Kingsport TN 38664

CHIQUIAR-ARIAS, VICTOR, contactologist; b. Mexico City, Feb. 19, 1925; s. Salomon Chiquiar and Mathilda Arias; O.D., Mex. Sch. Optometry, 1943; postgrad. Cambridge U., 1948, U. Mich., 1953, U. Houston, 1959, Ind. U., 1963; m. Dora Rabinovich, June 12, 1960; children—Maty, Salomon. Gen. practice optometry, Mexico City, 1943-54; practice optometry specializing in contact lenses and subnormal vision, Mexico City, 1954—; sci. dir. Plastic Contact Lenses de Mexico, Mexico City, 1959-66, chmn. bd., pres., 1967—; prof. geometrical and phys. optics Escuela de Optometria de Mexico, Mexico City, 1943-50; chmn. sci. sessions XIX Internat. Contact Lens Congress, Las Vegas, 1973; prof. contact lens fitting Gen. Hosp., Nat. Med. Center, Mexico City; prof. contactology Escuela Superior Medicina IPN and UNAM, 1965-66; guest faculty Shands Teaching Hosp., U. Fla., 1972, Ill. Coll. Optometry, So. Coll. Optometry, Escuela Optom. Colombia. Fellow Am. Soc. Ophthalmology and Optometry, Internat. Soc. Contact Lens Specialists; mem. Mex. Optometric Soc., Sociedad Mexicana de Contactología (charter mem. and fellow contact research study group), Internat. Soc. Orthokeratology, Contact Lens Assn. for Optometry, Contact Lens Specialists (Europe), Distinguished Service Found. Optometry, Asociación de Optometristas de Ecuador, Sociedad Venezolana de Contactología, Mex. Soc. Contactology (pres. 1964—), Nat. Eye Research Found. (Internat. Contact Lens award 1966), Jewish Sports Center. Jewish. Clubs: B'nai B'rith (past pres.), Masons, Shriners. Author: A New Technique of Fitting Contact Lenses in Keratoconus, 1962; Adaptacion del Lente Durasoft: Guia Del Especialista, 1975; contbr. chpts. to books, articles to profl. jours. Office: 107 Insurgentes Sur Mexico City 6 Mexico

CHIRANJEEVI, SIRAM, chem. co. exec.; b. Rajahmundry, India, June 25, 1937; s. Venkataraju and Subbamma Siram; came to U.S., 1964, naturalized, 1968; M.S., E. Tex. State U., 1967; m. Sujatha Chiranjeevi, Feb. 2, 1960; children—Laxmi, Sunitha. Sci. asst. Nat. Chem. Lab., Poona, India, 1958-59; sci. officer Indian AEC, Bombay, 1960-64; research fellow Tex. Christian U., Ft. Worth, 1964-66; teaching asst. chemistry E. Tex. State U., Commerce, 1966-67; instr. chemistry Navarro Coll., Corsicana, Tex., 1967-70; chief chemist Jetco Chems. Inc., Corsicana, 1970—. Tex. Christian U. research fellow, 1964-66. Mem. Am. Chem. Soc. Home: 500 Oakridge Corsicana TX 75110 Office: Box 1898 Hwy 31E Corsicana TX 75110

CHIRON, HARLAN SCOTT, orthopaedic surgeon; b. N.Y.C., Oct. 24, 1941; s. Albert E. and Rose L. (Levine) C.; B.A. in Chemistry, Lafayette Coll., 1962; M.D., Chgo. Med. Sch., 1966; m. Adrienne I. Silverman, Sept. 10, 1967; children—Stewart T., Pamela F., Diana B. Intern, Hosp. for Joint Diseases, N.Y.C., 1966-67, resident in gen. surgery, 1967-68, resident in orthopaedic surgery, 1970-72; practice medicine specializing in orthopaedic surgery, Coral Gables, Fla., 1973—; mem. staff Victoria Hosp., mem. corp., chief orthopedic surgery, 1978—; mem. staff Cedars Hosp., Baptist Hosp., South Miami Hosp., Mercy Hsop.; clin. instr. dept. orthopaedics U. Miami, 1974-79, asst. clin. prof., 1979—; cons. USPHS, Fla. Vocat. Rehab. Dept. Served to capt. M.C., USAF, 1968-70. Diplomate Am. Bd. Orthopaedic Surgery; Frauenthal travelling fellow, 1972-73. Fellow ACS, Am. Coll. Orthopaedic Surgeons; mem. AMA, Fla., Dade County med. assns., Fla., Miami orthopaedic socs., Eastern Orthopaedic Assn., Miami Zool. Soc. Clubs: Men's of Temple Judea; Rotary. Office: 2695 Lejeune Rd Coral Gables FL 33134

CHISHOLM, TOMMY, utilities exec.; b. Baldwyn, Miss., Apr. 14, 1941; s. Thomas Vaniver and Ruby (Duncan) C.; B.S. in Civil Engring., Tenn. Tech. U., 1963; J.D., Samford U., 1969; m. Janice McClanahan, June 20, 1964; children—Mark Alan (dec.), Andrea, Stephen Thomas, Patrick Ervin. Civil engr. TVA, Knoxville, Tenn., 1963-64; with So. Services, Inc., 1963-73, coordinator spl. projects, Atlanta, 1971-73; admitted to Ala. bar, 1969; asst. to pres. So. Co., Atlanta, 1973-75; mgr. adminstrv. services dept. Gulf Power Co., Pensacola, Fla., 1975-77; sec., asst. treas. So. Co., Atlanta, 1977—; sec., house counsel So. Co. Services Inc., Atlanta, 1977—. Active local United Appeal fund drives, 1967, 68, 72, 75, 78, 79. Registered profl. engr., Ala., Fla., Ga., Miss. Mem. Am. Bar Assn., Ala. State Bar, ASCE, Am. Soc. Corp. Secs., Phi Alpha Delta. Club: Rotary. Home: 1611 Bryn Mawr Circle Marietta GA 30067 Office: PO Box 720071 Atlanta GA 30346

CHISMAN, JAMES ALLEN, educator; b. Ravenna, Ohio, Mar. 4, 1935; s. Wallace Forbray and Marthalee (Wood) C.; B.S. in Elec. Engring., Akron U., 1958; M.S. in Indsl. Engring., Iowa U., 1960, Ph.D. in Mgmt. Engring., 1963; m. Elaine Cromer; Devel. engr. Def. Research Div. Firestone, Akron, Ohio, 1958-59; mem. faculty Clemson (S.C.) U., 1963—, prof. systems engring. and engring. tech., 1976—, dir. engring. tech. program, 1974—, dir. engring. graphics program, 1976—, mem. faculty senate, 1974-77; pres. Clemson Investment & Devel. Co., 1963—; owner antique shop, 1978—; mgmt. cons. Consumers Power Co., Jackson, Mich., 1963-73, various other industries. Chmn. troop com. Boy Scouts Am., Clemson, 1968-70; pres. Clemson Arts Council, 1972-74; dir. Clemson Youth Theater, 1972-75. Mem. Am. Inst. Indsl. Engrs. (sr.), Am. Soc. Engring. Edn., Ops. Research Soc. Am., Inst. Mgmt. Scis., Sigma Xi, Tau Beta Pi, Tau Alpha Pi, Omega Rho, Tau Kappa Epsilon. Mem. editorial bd. Am. Inst. Indsl. Engrs. Trans., 1969-78. Contbr. articles to profl. jours. Home: PO Box 1111 Clemson SC 29631

CHISMAN, THOMAS PESCUD, broadcasting co. exec.; b. Hampton, Va., Dec. 8, 1921; s. Samuel Reade and Mary Lee (Cannon) C.; B.A., U. Va., 1943; m. Martha Pamela Merritt, Oct. 2, 1943; children—Thomas Pescud IV, Martha Pamela, Lila Elizabeth, Anne Meriwether Michie. Mgr., Fuel Co., Hampton, 1946-47; pres., gen. mgr. Corp., Hampton, 1947—; pres. PBK Ltd., Peninsula Cable Corp., Multra-Guard, Inc.; dir. Va. Nat. Mem. Peninsula Port and Indsl. Authority, 1956-65; chmn. Peninsula Stadium Authority, 1963-64; mem. Hampton Rds. Area Cooperation Com., 1961-65; mem. Adv. Com. on Naval Affairs, 1959-65; chmn. Old Hampton Redevel. Com. 1963-65; chmn. Citizens Adv. Com. for Community Improvement, 1964-65; exec. producer Bicentennial Radio Network. Trustee Old Dominion U. Found., Am. Women in Radio and TV Ednl. Found.; bd. visitors Old Dominion U.; bd. dirs. Va. Peninsula Symphony Orch., Va. Opera Assn., Eastern Va. Med. Found., Chrysler Mus., Norfolk, Va., mem., chmn. promotion and publicity Yorktown Bicentennial Com. Served to lt. (j.g.) USNR, 1943-46, to capt. AUS, 1947-52. Mem. Va. Assn. Broadcasters (dir. 1955-63, pres. 1960-61), Nat. Assn. Broadcasters, Radio and TV Execs. Assn. N.Y., ABC Affiliates Assn. (chmn. bd. govs. 1962-64), Am. Peninsula C. of C. (dir. 1953-64). Episcopalian. Clubs: Huntington (chmn. bd.); Harbor; James River Country. Hampton Roads German; Broadcasters (Washington). Home: 2300 Chesapeake Ave Hampton VA 23361 Office: 1930 E Pembroke Ave Hampton VA 23363

CHISOLM, CHARLES SMITH, foundry exec.; b. Selma, Ala., Sept. 10, 1916; s. James Satterfield and Ernestine (Smith) C.; B.S. in Chem. Engring., Auburn (Ala.) U., 1938, M.S., 1939; postgrad. Birmingham So. Coll., 1940; m. Martha Elizabeth Gilbert, Nov. 6, 1942; children—Betsy Chisolm Silberman, John Grier, Catherine. Instr. chemistry Auburn U., 1939; with metall. dept. U.S. Steel Corp., 1939-41; supt. metallurgy and quality control Wheland Foundry div. N.Am. Royalties, Chattanooga, 1946-56, gen. mgr., 1956—; pres. Valley Farms, Selma, 1950—, Chisolm Corp., Selma, 1969—, Satterfield Co., Selma, 1970—, Peter Pan Industries, Lookout Mountain, Tenn., 1954—. Vice chmn. Lookout Mountain Planning Bd., 1968—. Served to lt. col. AUS, 1941-45. Registered profl. engr., Tenn.; registered asso. real estate broker, Tenn. Mem. Am. Soc. Metals, Am. Foundrymen's Soc. (nat. dir. 1973-77), ASTM, Omicrom Delta Kappa, Spades, Kappa Alpha. Presbyterian (ruling elder). Clubs: Mountain City (Chattanooga); Fairyland (Lookout Mountain) (dir.). Home: 1213 Peter Pan Rd Lookout Mountain TN 37350 Office: 1800 S Broad St Chattanooga TN 37401

CHISOLM, JACK TAYLOR, physician; b. Birmingham, Ala., July 27, 1923; s. Joseph James and Lillie Tom (Thomasson) C.; student Samford U., 1941-43, Stanford U., 1944; M.D., Med. Coll. Ala., 1947; m. Martha Lee Hatcher, Feb. 7, 1953; children—James Edward, John Craig, Patrick Taylor. Intern, St. Louis City Hosp., 1947-48; resident in surgery Hackensack (N.J.) Hosp., 1948-49, Scott & White Clinic, Temple, Tex., 1949-50, 53-55; pvt. practice medicine, specializing in surgery, Dallas, 1955—; mem. med. staff St. Paul Hosp., Presbyn. Hosp., both Dallas; med. dir. Employers Nat. Life Ins. Co.; med. advisor Employers Casualty Co. Served with AUS, 1943-44, USNR, 1951-53. Diplomate Am. Bd. Surgery. Mem. Am., Tex., So. med. assns., Dallas County Med. Soc. (pres. 1972), Am. Coll. Surgeons. Baptist. Home: 6531 Prestonshire St Dallas TX 75225 Office: 8210 Walnut Hill Ln Dallas TX 75231

CHITTENDEN, DAVID MORSE, II, nuclear chemist; b. Buffalo, Apr. 7, 1936; s. David Morse and Roberta (Young) C.; B.S., Rensselaer Poly. Inst., Troy, N.Y., 1958; M.S., U. Ark., 1960, Ph.D., 1966; m. Ruby Carol Lucas, Jan. 17, 1970; children—Jennifer Lynn, Julie Diane. Research, teaching postdoctoral fellow Rensselaer Poly. Inst., 1966; asst. prof. chemistry Hudson Valley Community Coll., Troy, 1966-67; asst. prof. chemistry Ark. State U., State University, 1967-70, asso. prof., 1970—. Pres. Jonesboro (Ark.) Fine Arts Council, 1975-76, treas., 1976-79. Mem. Am. Chem. Soc., AAUP, Ark. Acad. Scis., Sigma Xi. Elk. Researcher neutron-induced fission thorium, radioisotopes in liquid effluents from power reactors, neutron-induced reactions of iron isotopes, noble gases in granites and minerals. Home: 1710 S Church St Jonesboro AR 72401 Office: PO Box 837 State University AR 72467

CHITTENDEN, STANLEY MATTHEW, city ofcl.; b. Hays City, Kans., July 24, 1922; s. Stanley Stewart and Myrtle Helen (Truan) C.; B.S., Fort Hays (Kans.) State Coll., 1948; student Washburn Law Sch., 1959-61; m. Louise Stillwell, Nov. 30, 1947; children—John Stanley, Jill Lynn, Kimberly Kay. Cost supr. Brown & Root Constrn. Co., Pampa, Tex., 1951-53; accountant Celanese Chem. Corp., Pampa, 1953-59; adminstrv. asst. operation and prodn. Hill Packing Co., Topeka, Kan., 1959-63; asst. city mgr., dir. finance, sec.-treas. City of Pampa, 1963—. Scoutmaster, Adobe Walls Area council Boy Scouts Am., 1959-72. Served with USNR, 1941-44. Mem. Internat. City Mgmt. Assn., Municipal Fin. Officer Assn. U.S. and Can., Nat. Purchasing Inst., Phi Mu Alpha Sinfonia. Presbyn. Mason (Shriner). Home: 2540 Christine St Pampa TX 79065 Office: PO Box 2499 Pampa TX 79065

CHITTY, (MARY) ELIZABETH NICKINSON, univ. adminstr.; b. Balt., Apr. 27, 1920; d. Edward Phillips and Em Turner (Merritt) Nickinson; B.A. cum laude, Fla. State U., 1941, M.A., 1942; postgrad. Middle Tenn. State U., 1970, 71; m. Arthur Benjamin Chitty, June 16, 1946; children—Arthur Benjamin, John Abercrombie, Em Turner, Nathan Harsh Brown. Tchr., Fla. Indsl. Sch. for Girls, Ocala, 1942-43; psychometrist neuropsychiat. dept. Sch. Aviation Medicine, Pensacola (Fla.) Naval Air Sta., 1943-46; asso. editor Sewanee Alumni News, U. of the South, Sewanee, Tenn., 1946-62, bus. mgr. and mng. editor Sewanee Rev., 1962-65, dir. Fin. aid and career services, 1970-80; free-lance editor. Bd. dirs. Sewanee Civic Assn., 1979-80. Mem. Nat. Coll. Placement and Student Fin. Aid Assn., Tenn. Coll. Placement and Student Fin. Aid Assn., Assn. Preservation Tenn. Antiquities, AAUW (pres. Sewanee br. 1975-77), Fla. State U. Alumni Assn. (dir.), Mortar Bd., Phi Beta Kappa, Phi Kappa Phi, Phi Alpha Theta. Democrat. Episcopalian. Club: EQB Faculty (sec. 1975-76). Editor: (with H.A. Petry) Sewanee Centennial Alumni Directory, 1954-62; Centennial Report of the Registrar of the University of the South, 1959; (with Arthur Ben Chitty) Too Black, Too White (Ely Green), 1970. Home: 100 SC Ave Sewanee TN 37375 Office: U of the South Sewanee TN 37375

CHITWOOD, ROBERT HODSON, oil co. exec.; b. Pratt, Kans., Oct. 2, 1930; s. Joe Vern and Blanche Katherine (Hodson) C.; B.B.A., Okla. State U., 1952; grad. exec. devel. program Cornell U., 1970; m. Barbara Ann Johnson, Mar. 10, 1952; children—Catherine Chitwood Hurst, Thomas, Nancy Chitwood Ryan, Amalie. With Cities Service Co., Tulsa, 1952—, v.p. supply and transp., 1970-74, pres., dir. Cities Services Gas Co., 1974-76, exec. v.p. parent co., pres., petroleum products group, 1976—; pres. Cities Service Mid-East, Inc., Cities Service Mid-East Trading Co., Cities Service S&T Europe-Africa Co., Cities Service Trading Co., Grand Bassa Tankers Inc.; v.p., dir. Cities Service Internat., Inc.; dir. Cities Service Gas Co., CSG Exploration Co., First Nat. Bank and Trust Co., Oklahoma City. Bd. dirs. Industries for Tulsa, Inc.; trustee Philbrook Art Center. Served with AUS, 1952-53. Mem. Okla., Tulas chambers commerce, Nat. Petroleum Refiners Assn. (dir.), Am. Petroleum Inst., Mid-Continent Oil and Gas Assn., Okla. Petroleum Council. Republican. Episcopalian. Clubs: Internat. (Washington); Tulsa, So. Hills Country, Petroleum (Tulsa); Beacon (Oklahoma City). Home: 2108 E 29th St Tulsa OK 74114 Office: PO Box 300 Tulsa OK 74102

CHITWOOD, THOMAS EDWARD, JR., systems analyst; b. Seattle, Aug. 7, 1931; s. Thomas Edward and Vera A. (McCauly) C.; B.A., U. Wash., 1954; M.A., U. Wyo., 1966; M.P.A., Golden Gate U., 1977; m. Margaret Irene Zander, June 13, 1954; children—Scott A., Connie E., Allan T., Carrie I. Commd. 2d lt. U.S. Army, 1954, advanced through grades to lt. col., 1975; asst. prof. mil. sci. U. Wyo., 1961-64; ops. analyst Hdqrs. Dept. Army, Washington, 1968-70; asst. plans officer Joint Chiefs of Staff, Washington, 1970-71; ret., 1975; systems analyst Litton Industries, Springfield, Va., 1977-79; sr. systems analyst McLean Research (Va.), 1979—. Decorated Legion of Merit, Bronze Star, Meritorious Service medal; chevalier Legion of Honor. Mem. Am. Def. Preparedness Assn., Am. Soc. Pub. Adminstrn., Am. Polit. Sci. Assn., Am. Acad. Polit. and Social Sciences, Ret. Officer Assn., Lake Ridge Civic Assn., Order of DeMolay. Republican. Presbyterian. Club: Masons (Seattle). Home: 509 N Roosevelt Blvd Apt D220 Falls Church VA 22044 Office: 6870 Elm St McLean VA 22101

CHOI, JUNHO, elec. engr.; b. Seoul, Korea, Apr. 19, 1941; came to U.S., 1970; s. Kwonsik and Chaugnyer (Yoo) C.; B.S.E.E. (Univ. Alumni scholar), Seoul Nat. U., 1964; M.S.E.E. (Univ. scholar), SUNY, Buffalo, 1972; Ph.D. in Elec. Engring. (NIH Trainee fellow), Duke U., 1978; m. Seungyun Ham, June 8, 1970; children—Charles D., John D. Lead engr. Internat. Electric Enterprise Co., Ltd., Seoul, 1966-69; sales engr. M-C Internat., Seoul, 1969-70; digital systems engr. Planning Research Corp. at Kennedy Space Center, Fla., 1978-79; asst. prof. dept. elec. and computer engring. Fla. Inst. Tech., Melbourne, 1979—. Served with Korean Army, 1964-66. Mem. IEEE, AAAS, Korean Scientist and Engrs. Assn., Sigma Xi. Home: 121 Bristol Ln Melbourne FL 32935 Office: Fla Inst Tech Country Club Rd Melbourne FL 32901

CHOISSER, ROBERT WILLIAM, systems engr.; b. Harrisburg, Ill., July 21, 1930; s. Robert Edmund and Sarah Elizabeth (Grace) C.; B.S., UCLA, 1951, M.S., 1960; m. Suzanne Keller, June 2, 1979; children by previous marriage—Janis Elaine, Catherine Louise. Engr., Douglas Aircraft Co., Santa Monica, Calif., 1951-56; chief weapons employment sect. System Devel. Corp., Santa Monica, 1957-59; chief analysis dept. Pneumodynamics Co., El Segundo, Calif., 1959-60; supr. opns. research sect. Philco Ford Aeronutronic div., Newport Beach, Calif., 1960-63; tech. adv. to opns. analysis br. N.Am. Rockwell, Anaheim, Calif., 1963-70; chief systems analysis br. Def. Communications Agy., Reston, Va., 1970—; also cons. ops. research; mem. ops. analysis panel Def. Sci. Bd., 1966-69. Bd. dirs. World Unity Forum, 1976—. Mem. Ops. Research Soc. Am., Washington Ops. Research Council, Smithsonian Assos. Republican. Presbyterian. Clubs: Lions (treas. 1973-74), Ski of Washington). Home: 3705 S George Mason Dr Falls Church VA 22041 Office: 1860 Wiehle Ave Reston VA 22090

CHOUDHURY, SANTOSH KUMAR, educator; b. Jhalda, India, Sept. 9, 1933; s. Debendra Nath and Bela Rani (Roy) C.; B. Commerce, St. Xavier's Coll. (India), 1956; M. Commerce, Patna U. (India), 1958; Ph.D., Northwestern U., 1972; student Grad. Sch. Banking, U. Wis., summer 1975; m. Ruby Dey, Apr. 29, 1959; children—Arindam, Devasmita. Came to U.S., 1967. Asst. prof. bus. Ramananda Coll., Bishnupur, India, 1958-64, Panjab U., Chandigarh, India, 1964-67; instr. bus. adminstrn. Northwestern U., Evanston, Ill., 1969-70; asst. prof. bus. adminstrn. U. Wis., Milw., 1970-72; asso. prof. fin. U. Pacific, Stockton, Calif., 1972-74; prof. fin. Norfolk (Va.) State U., 1974—, head dept. bus. adminstrn., 1979—; cons. HEW, 1971-72, Nat. Bus. League, 1971; mem. World Trade Com., 1972-74. Mem. Am., So., Western fin. assns., Fin. Mgmt. Assn. Author: Lectures on Transport, 1967. Editor: Econ. Ambassador, 1960-63. Contbr. articles to profl. jours. Home: 4761 Cranbrook Ct Virginia Beach VA 23462

CHOVNICK, STANLEY DAVIS, urologist; b. N.Y.C., Apr. 13, 1930; s. Herman and Florence (Hutkins) C.; B.A., N.Y.U., 1951; M.D. State U. N.Y., 1956; m. Cherry Ann Webber; children—Carin, Bruce, Josh, Pamela. Intern, Upstate Med. Center Hosps., Syracuse, N.Y., 1956-57; resident in surgery Bronx Municipal Hosp. Center, Albert Einstein Coll. Hosps., 1957-58, resident in urology, 1958-61; pvt. practice urology, N.Y.C., 1961-72, New Port Richey, Fla., 1972—; asst. prof. urology Albert Einstein Coll. Medicine, N.Y.C., 1967-72; chief surgery, chief staff Community Hosp.; bd. dirs. Health System Agency. Served with U.S. Army, 1956-59. Diplomate Am. Bd. Urology. Fellow ACS; mem. AMA, Fla., Pasco County (del.) med. assns., Am., Southeastern urol. assns., Phi Beta Kappa. Contbr. articles to med. jours. Home: 1105 Mandy Ln New Port Richey FL 33552 Office: 310 High St New Port Richey FL 33552

CHRISTENSEN, EVERETT M., savs. and loan exec.; b. New Ulm, Minn., Mar. 15, 1935; s. Everett M. and Hildegard F. (Amann) C.; B.A. in Econs., Mich. State U., 1957; M.A. in Indsl. Psychology, U. Minn., 1965; m. Sybil Burreson, May 5, 1962; children—Brent, Dawn, Glenn, Sue. With Jostens, Inc., Owatonna, Minn., 1960-61; personnel adminstr. Honeywell, Inc., Mpls., 1961-65; personnel dir. F & M Savs. Bank, Mpls., 1965-72; pres. PPSD, Inc., personnel cons., Mpls. and Ft. Lauderdale, Fla., 1972—; sr. v.p., dir. human resources First Fed. of Broward Savs. & Loan, Ft. Lauderdale, 1978—; dir. Madelia Telephone Co. (Minn.). Bd. dirs. Greater Mpls. Jr. Achievement, 1971-72. Served with USAF, 1957-59. Mem. Am. Soc. Personnel Adminstrn., Am. Soc. for Tng. and Devel. Roman Catholic. Author: Dynamic Supervision, 1971. Home: 2024 NW 86th Terr Coral Springs FL 33065 Office: 350 SE 2d St Fort Lauderdale FL 33301

CHRISTENSEN, JOHN, chemist; b. Mahtowa, Minn., June 19, 1908; s. Christ E. and Dorothy M. (Christensen) C.; B.A., Union Coll., 1939; M.A., U. Nebr., 1946; Ph.D., Mich. State U., 1956; m. Caroline B. Lord, June 1, 1964; children—John Eric, Fern Adelle; children by previous marriage—Clarice Christensen Papendick, Eunice Christensen Morton. Tchr., Shelton Acad., Shelton, Nebr., 1939-41; instr. Union Coll., Lincoln, Nebr., 1941-45; asst. prof. Emmanuel Missionary Coll., Berrien Springs, Mich., 1945-55; prof. chemistry So. Missionary Coll., Collegedale, Tenn., 1955-74, prof. emeritus, 1974—. Mem. Am. Chem. Soc. (chmn. Chattanooga sect. 1961, recipient sect. pub. service award 1968, chmn. exams. subcom. on inorganic-organic-biol. chemistry 1968-76, rep. on nat. council 1971-77). Seventh Day Adventist. Research on periodic acid oxidation of organic compounds. Home: Box 507 Collegedale TN 37315 Office: So Missionary Coll Collegedale TN 37315

CHRISTENSEN, PATRICIA M. BARNETT, nurse, educator; b. Augusta, Ga., July 14, 1944; d. Leonard L. and Martha (Gilstrap) Barnett; B.S. in Nursing, Med. Coll. Ga., 1973, M.S., 1974; m. William F. Christensen, Dec. 11, 1964; children—Sean, Katie. Team leader surg., maternal-child nursing, staff nurse St. Joseph's and E. Talmadge Meml. hosps., Augusta, 1972-73, Med. Coll. Ga., Augusta, 1973-74; asst. prof. nursing U. S.C., Aiken, 1973-80, asso. prof., 1980—; cons. fed. Head Start programs; cons. sex edn., early mother-infant attachment. Recipient Sister Mary Herman nursing award Augusta Coll., 1972. Mem. Am. Nurses Assn., NOW, Sigma Theta Tau. Author, producer film, Assessment of the Newborn, 1979. Home: 1867 Lodgepole Ave North Augusta SC 29841 Office: Dept Nursing U SC Aiken SC 29801

CHRISTIAN, ALMERIC LEANDER, chief fed. judge; b. Christiansted, St. Croix, V.I., Nov. 23, 1919; s. Adam Emmanuel and Elena (Davis) C.; student U. P.R., 1937-38; A.B., Columbia U., 1941, LL.B., 1947; m. Virginia Cecilia Sterling, Sept. 13, 1943 (div. Sept. 1962); 1 dau., Donna Marie; m. 2d, Shirley Camille Frorue, Aug. 31, 1963; children—Adam, Rebecca Therese. Admitted to V.I. bar, 1947; pvt. practice V.I., 1947-62; U.S. dist. atty. V.I., St. Thomas, 1962-69; judge U.S. Dist. Ct. for V.I., St. Thomas, 1969-70, chief judge, 1970—. Mem. bd. adv. St. Dunstan's Episcopal Sch., St. Croix. Mem. Bd. Edn., V.I., 1961. Served to 1st lt. AUS, 1942-46; ETO, PTO. Mem. Bar V.I. Democrat. Office: PO Box 1441 St Thomas VI 00801*

CHRISTIAN, ARTHUR CARL, educator; b. Cleveland, Tenn., July 11, 1941; student Okla. Southwestern State U., 1960-67; B.B.A., Okla. State U., 1975, M.A. in Public Adminstrn., 1978; m. Linda M. Dick; children—Wayne, Jeffrery. Joined USAF, 1960, advanced through grades to sr. master sgt., 1976; dir. profl. mil. edn. Tinker AFB, Okla., 1978, instr. leadership mgmt., 1979—; instr. Okla. State U., 1976—; ops. mgr. Apcoa, Oklahoma City, 1980—; family fin. cons. Mem. Air Force Sgts. Assn., Tinker Mgmt. Club, Air Force Assn. Democrat. Home: 4929 Beacon Hill Rd Oklahoma City OK 73135 Office: Tinker AFB OK 73145

CHRISTIAN, BEVERLY MELBALYN JONES, pianist-organist; b. Bonham, Tex., Sept. 16, 1927; d. Alvres and Hazel (Armstrong) Jones; student East Tex. State U., Commerce, U. Tex., Dallas, Richland Coll., Dallas; m. J.C. Christian, Aug. 2, 1947; 1 adopted son. Tchr., piano, organ Bonham, Garland and Plano, Tex., 1947—; organist, 1st Christian Ch., Bonham, 1953, summer 75, Clark Meml. Meth. Ch., Bonham, 1954-55, Axe Meml. Ch., Garland, 1955-59, 1st Bapt. Ch., Bonham, 1959-70, 1st United Meth. Ch., Plano, 1974-75, Briarwood United Meth. Ch., Plano, 1977—; organist meml. service Rep. Sam Rayburn, 1961, Bonham; organist-accompanist Bonham Community Choirs, 1966-69; piano accompanist Plano Civic Chorus, 1968. Home: PO Box 1227 Plano TX 75074

CHRISTIAN, CARLE ERNEST, clergyman; b. Perry, Ohio, Jan. 24, 1935; s. Lloyd Pitcher and Esther Grace (Ernst) C.; B.A., Furman U., 1960; M.Div., Midwestern Baptist Theol. Seminary, 1963; D.Min., New Orleans Baptist Theol. Seminary, 1975; m. Grace Esther Henck, Nov. 28, 1957; children—Paul Kevin, Heidi Nanette. Ordained to ministry So. Baptist Conv., 1960; pastor First Baptist Ch., Independence, Mo., 1963-65; So. Bapt. missionary, San Jose, Costa Rica, 1965-69; pastor First Baptist Ch., Bushnell, Fla., 1971-72; chaplain N.C. Baptist Hosps., Winston-Salem, 1972-74; dir. Christian Counseling Center, Tampa, Fla., 1974—. Served with U.S. Army, 1955-57. Mem. Am. Personnel and Guidance Assn., Am. Assn. Marriage and Family Therapists, Am. Assn. Pastoral Counselors, Tampa Ministers Assn., Assn. Couples for Marriage Enrichment. Republican. Home: 511 Julie Ln Brandon FL 33511 Office: 5109 Nebraska Ave Tampa FL 33603

CHRISTIAN, JOHN CATLETT, JR., lawyer; b. Springfield, Mo., Sept. 12, 1929; s. John Catlett and Alice Odelle (Milling) C.; A.B., Drury Coll., 1951; LL.B., Tulane U., 1956; m. Peggy Jeanne Cain, Apr. 12, 1953; children—Cathleen Marie, John Catlett III, Alice Cain. Admitted to La. bar, 1956, Mo. bar, 1956, to practice before Supreme Ct. U.S., Fifth Circuit Ct. Appeals, Western and Eastern Dists. Fed. Cts. La.; asso. Porter & Stewart, Lake Charles, La., 1956-58; asso. to partner Wilkinson, Lewis, Wilkinson & Madison, Shreveport, La., 1958-64; partner Milling, Benson, Woodward, Hillyer & Pierson, New Orleans, 1964—; pres. Sherburne Land Co., 1974—. Pres. Kathleen Elizabeth O'Brien Found., 1963—. Served with USMC, 1951-53. Fellow Am. Coll. Trial Lawyers; mem. Am., Mo., Fed., La. bar assns., Am. Judicature Soc., Omicron Delta Kappa, Phi Delta Phi, Kappa Alpha Order. Clubs: Boston, Essex, Plimsoll, Petroleum (New Orleans), Timberlane Country. Home: 5 Fernwood St Gretna LA 70053 Office: Whitney Bank Bldg New Orleans LA 70130

CHRISTIAN, JOSEPH ROY, oil co. exec.; b. Tenaha, Tex., June 20, 1927; s. Joseph Richard and Irene Elizabeth (Brown) C.; student Tex. Tech. Coll., 1944, N.Mex. A&M Coll., 1944-45; B.S., La. State U., 1949; m. Mary Delores Dooley, Nov. 16, 1951; children—Randall Allen, Marc Richard. Geologist, Shell Oil Co., Hobbs, N.Mex., 1949-57; petroleum engr. DeGolyer & MacNaughton, Dallas, 1957-59; area engr., chief engr. Stekoll Petroleum Corp., Dallas, 1959-61; sr. engr. Colo. Interstate Gas Co., Colorado Springs, 1961-62; petroleum engr. R.F. Kravis Assos., Tulsa, 1962-63; v.p. Oliver & West Inc., Dallas, 1963-65; v.p. trusts First Nat. Bank Dallas, 1965-74, sr. v.p., 1974-77; pres. Petroleum Exploration and Devel. Funds, Inc., Midland, Tex., 1977—, also dir.; pres., dir. Exploration and Devel. Corp. Group chmn. Dallas County United Fund, 1970, 71. Served with U.S. Army, 1945-47. Mem. AIME Soc. Petroleum Engrs., Ind. Petroleum Assn. Am., Mid Continent Oil and Gas Assn., Am. Petroleum Inst., West Tex. Geol. Soc., Tex. Mid Continent Oil and Gas Assn., Petroleum Club Midland. Home: 9011 Maple Glen Dr Dallas TX 75231 Office: 8350 N Central Expressway Suite 744 Dallas TX 75206

CHRISTIAN, MARILYN JEANNE, nurse, hosp. assn. exec.; b. Harvey, Ill., Mar. 15, 1930; d. Arthur E. and Mildred A. Christian; diploma Wesley Meml. Hosp. Sch. Nursing, Chgo., 1951; B.S. in Nursing, Northwestern U., 1958; M.S. in Nursing Service Adminstrn., DePaul U., 1964; student MacMurray Coll., 1955-57. Staff nurse Wesley Meml. Hosp., Chgo., 1951-53, head nurse, 1953-55, 57-58; instr. Presbyn.-St. Luke's Hosp., Chgo., 1959-63, asst. dir. Sch. Nursing, 1962-64, asst. chmn. div. nursing, 1965-68; dir. nursing Ingalls Meml. Hosp., Harvey, Ill., 1969-73, v.p. patient care, 1973-74; dir. nursing U. Community Hosp., Tampa, Fla., 1975-79; prof. community health scis. Govs. State U., Park Forest, Ill., 1972; field rep. Joint Commn. on Accreditation of Hosps., Chgo., 1979—; guest speaker various civic and profl. orgns. Mem. Nat. League Nursing, Am. Soc. Hosp. Nursing Service Adminstrs., Fla. Soc. Hosp. Nursing Service Adminstrs. Republican. Mem. Disciples of Christ Ch. Home: 10378 Carrollwood Ln Tampa FL 33618

CHRISTIANSEN, PAUL BENJAMINE, safety cons.; b. Helena, Mont., June 27, 1926; s. Clarence O. and Janette M. (Christison) C.; A.A., Chaffey Coll., 1948, Calif. Poly. Inst., 1950; m. Mary Jo Briscoe, Jan. 16, 1974; 1 son, Rex B. Corp. loss prevention supr. Signal Oil & Gas Co., Houston, 1953-73; safety dir. Pride Refining Co., Abilene, Tex., 1974-75, 77-79; cons. for safety on site of oil storage for Dept. Energy, Strategic Petroleum Res. Program, West Hackberry, La., 1979—; loss control dir. Crystal Oil Co., Shreveport, 1975-77. Served with USN, 1944-46; PTO. Certified safety profl. Mem. Am. Soc. Safety Engrs., Nat. Fire Protection Assn. Lutheran. Home: 9323 Leader Houston TX 77036 Office: Box 273 Hackberry LA

CHRISTIANSEN, WILLIAM EARL SMITH, materials handling equipment mfg. co. exec.; b. River Forest, Ill., Oct. 25, 1944; s. Soren Edward Smith and Mary Catherine (Badger) C.; B.S., M.I.T., 1967, M.S. in Indsl. Mgmt., 1969; m. Theresa Roff Burke, June 1, 1974; children—Brian E., Lynley M., William E. With Equipment Co. of Am., Hialeah, Fla., 1967—, exec. v.p., 1970—, also dir.; pres. William Earl & Assos., Inc.; dir. ECOA Internat., Inc. Mem. Com. of 100, Miami Beach, Fla., 1970—. Served with AUS, 1969-71. Mem. SAR, Sigma Xi, Tau Beta Pi, Eta Kappa Nu. Clubs: 200 (Miami); Coral Reef Yacht. Home: 7431 Monaco St Coral Gables FL 33143 Office: 1075 Hialeah Dr Hialeah FL 33010

CHRISTIE, LAURENCE GLENN, JR., surgeon; b. Houston, May 13, 1930; s. Laurence Glenn and Tommie Katherine (Myers) C.; B.S., Washington and Lee U., 1953; M.D., Med. Coll. Va., 1957; m. Constance Graham Kelsey, Sept. 15, 1973; 1 dau. Susan Elizabeth. Intern surgery Med. Coll. Va., 1957-58, resident surgery, 1957-62; practice medicine specializing in gen. and vascular surgery, Ft. Smith, Ark., 1962-63, Richmond, Va., 1963—; clin. instr. Med. Coll. Va., Richmond, 1963—; mem. active staff Retreat Hosp., Henrico Doctors Hosp.; attending staff Sheltering Arms Hosp.; courtesy staff Stuart Circle Hosp., Grace Hosp., St. Mary's Hosp., Richmond Meml. Hosp., St. Luke's Hosp.; chmn. dept. surgery chmn. med. exec. com., med. dir. Henrico Doctors Hosp.; pres. Med. Planning Corp. Mem. sci. adv. bd. Richmond chpt. Nat. Found. for Ileitis and Colitis, Inc. Diplomate Am. Bd. Surgery. Fellow A.C.S.; mem. Southeastern Surg. Congress, So. Med. Assn., Richmond Acad. Medicine, Richmond Surg. and Gynecol. Soc., Med. Soc. Va., AMA, Humera Soc. Episcopalian. Clubs: Bull and Bear, Irish Setter of Greater Richmond, Irish Setter of Am. Contbr. articles to profl. jours. Home: Killagay Crozier VA 23039 Office: Suite 115 Doctors Office Bldg 7601 Forest Ave Richmond VA 23229

CHRISTIE, MARY LOU BRANDON, educator; b. Waverly, Iowa, Nov. 7, 1917; d. William Lewis and Mary Wilson (Cooke) Brandon; A.B., John B. Stetson U., 1942; M.S., Fla. State U., 1969, doctoral studies, 1969-71; m. William Traugott Christie, Jr., May 2, 1942 (div. Oct. 1970), remarried May 18, 1974; children—Mary Elizabeth, Lewis Traugott, Terris Jean. Tchr., Orange City (Fla.) Elementary Sch., 1939-43; tchr., dir. girls phys. edn. Leon High Sch., Tallahassee, 1943-45; owner, mgr. Christie's Kiddie Kottage-Juvenile Retail Store, Tallahassee, 1948-61; tchr. Fed. Correctional Instn., Tallahassee, 1966-67; counselor Leon County Juvenile Ct., Tallahassee, 1969-70, supr. tng., 1970-71; dir. tng., youth counselor supr. Bur. Field Services, Fla. Div. Youth Services, Tallahassee, 1971—, dist. coordinator vol. programs, 1972—, acting regional dir. Bur. Community Service, 1975—, vol. program specialist, 1975-76; instr. Lively Vocat. Tech. Center, 1976—; tchr. piano, Tallahassee, 1934-48, 62—; guest lectr. Fla. State U., also Fla. A. and M. U., 1967-71. Mem. Leon County Sch. Bd., 1965-69, chmn. bd., 1968; mem. Fla. Gov.'s Task Force on Standards. Chmn. adv. com. Sunland Hosp., Tallahassee, 1969-70; sec., dir. Leon Assn. for Retarded Children, 1969-70; mem. Leon County Assn. Community Services. Bd. dirs. Easter Seal Rehab. Center, 1953—, sec., 1955-65; bd. dirs. Vol. Action Center of Leon County; adv. bd. Supplementary Assistance Center Leon County, Fla. Assn. Health and Social Services, Inc. Mem. NEA, Fla. Teaching Profession Assn., Leon County Tchrs. Assn., Tallahassee Music Tchrs. Assn., D.A.R. (regent 1959-61), Fla. Council on Crime and Delinquency, Lambda Alpha Epsilon. Baptist. Club: Tallahassee Womans. Author: A Model for the Training of Interns in Juvenile Corrections, 1974; Informational Manual for Full-time Vocational Training, 1977. Home: 1437 Chowkeebin Nene Tallahassee FL 32301 Office: 500 Appleyard Dr Tallahassee FL 32301

CHRISTIE, WESLEY REN, educator; b. Parrott, Ga., Jan. 13, 1918; s. Dudley Whaley and Mary Byrd (Kirksey) C.; B.S. in Edn., U. Ga., 1942, M.Ed., 1963, Ed.S., 1971, Ed.D., 1971; m. Connie Kinsler, Mar. 18, 1962; children—Wesley Renijah, Ricky Ralph. Served as enlisted man U.S. Marine Corps, 1936-40, 42, commd. 2d. lt., 1942, advanced through grades to lt. col., 1954, served World War II and Korea, comdr. infantry squads, platoons, cos., battalions, ret., 1961; grad. asst. U. Ga., Athens, 1963-64; prof. dept. speech and drama, 1964-67, head dept. speech and drama, prof., 1967-78, acting dir. div. fine arts, 1978-79; head dept. speech and drama Valdosta (Ga.) State Coll., 1979—. Bd. dirs. Ga. Lung Assn., active Community Concerts, Valdosta High Sch. Band Boosters, parliamentarian; Sunday Sch. tchr. First United Meth. Ch. Decorated 2 Bronze Stars; recipient Man of Year Black Key award, Valdosta State Coll., 1967. Mem. Ga. Speech Communication Assn. (v.p. 1972 sec.-treas. 1980), Speech Communication Assn. Am., So. Speech Communication Assn., AAUP, Ga. Theatre Conf., Speech Communication Adminstrs. Assn., Ret. Officers Assn. (Valdosta chpt.), Omicron Delta Kappa. Clubs: Moody AFB Officer's, So. Pines Dinner (pres., 1968-69), Rotary (sec., pres.-elect). Author: playbook Historical Moments in Georgia Methodism, 1976; actor, dir. 6 vignettes S.Ga. Conf. of Meth. Ch., 1976; actor plays; producer, dir. ann. play First United Meth. Ch., Valdosta, 1964-78. Home: 1211 Dellwood Dr Valdosta GA 31601 Office: Dept Speech and Drama Valdosta State College Valdosta GA 31601

CHRISTOPHER, CLYDE, educator; b. Jacksonville, Tex., Oct. 26, 1929; s. William Vanus and Ora (Hancock) C.; B.S., Prairie View A. and M. Coll., 1950; M.A., Tex. So. U., 1960; postgrad. U. Kans., 1960-61, U. Mo., Rolla, 1066-68, Tex. A. and M. U., 1968-74; m. Joyce Mae Guinn, June 13, 1953; children—Gerald Allen, Mitchell Claude, Michael Clyde. Tchr., Tyler (Tex.) Ind. Sch. Dist., 1953-54, Troup (Tex.) Ind. Sch. Dist., 1954-55, Palestine (Tex.) Ind. Sch. Dist., 1955-56, Jacksonville (Tex.) Ind. Sch. Dist., 1956-60, Kansas City (Mo.) Ind. Sch. Dist., 1961-63; prof. dept. math. Prairie View (Tex.) A. and M. U., 1963—, head dept. computer sci., 1976—. Bd. trustees Waller (Tex.) Ind. Sch. Dist., 1974—; chmn. bd. trustees, chmn. finance com. Bethlehem United Meth. Ch., Hempstead, Tex., 1972—; Cubmaster, Hempstead, Tex., 1977—. Served to 1st lt. inf. U.S. Army, 1951-53. NSF study grantee, 1959, 60-61, 65, 66, 68, Ford Found. grantee, 1968-69. Mem. Math. Assn. Am., Assn. Computing Machinery. Democrat. Methodist. Home: PO Box 2782 Prairie View TX 77445 Office: Prairie View A and M U Prairie View TX 77445

CHRISTOPHER, E. WAYNE, hosp. adminstr.; b. Genesee County, Mich., Apr. 6, 1925; s. Carl C. and Estelle Christopher; B.S., Ferris State Coll., 1949; M.S., U. Tenn., 1951; postgrad. U. Mich., 1966; m. Katherine Mary Kuipers, June 29, 1946; children—Edward Wayne, Michael Paul, Mark Allen, Carla Jean, Craig Scott. Instr. bus. Acme Bus. Coll., Lansing, Mich., 1949-50; accountant TVA, 1951-52; instr. acctg. Bus. Inst., Pontiac, Mich., 1952-54; central adminstrv. aide Ferris State Coll., Big Rapids, Mich., 1954-60; asst. divisional accountant Kroger Co., Grand Rapids, Mich., 1960-61; exec. v.p. Fund Fulfillment Corp., Chgo., 1961-63; dir. devel. Sisters of Mary Provincialate, Farmington, Mich., 1963-66; adminstr. Mercy Community Hosp., Manistee, Mich., 1966-69; cons. and adminstr. West Shore Hosp., Manistee, 1967-70; v.p. adminstrn. Ravenswood Hosp. Med. Center, Chgo., 1970-74; exec. dir. Parkway Gen. Hosp., N. Miami Beach, Fla., 1974—. Chmn. Citizens for Schs., Manistee, Mich.; co-chmn. United Way Campaign, 1977; mem. bd. canvassors Farmington Sch. Dist., Farmington Twp. Planning Commn.; bd. dirs. Ravenswood Conservation Comm., v.p., 1972-73. Served with USMC, 1942-46. Recipient citation Ravenswood Conservation Commn. Mem. Am. Hosp. Assn., Am. Acad. Med. Adminstrs., Am. Coll. Hosp. Adminstrs., Fla. Hosp. Assn. (mem. legis. com. 1978-79), Fedn. Am. Hosps., Fla. League Hosps. (pres. 1979), S. Fla. Hosp. Assn. (trustee 1976-79), S. Fla. Hosp. Council (sec. treas. 1979—). Club: Rotary (program chmn.). Office: 160 NW 170th St North Miami Beach FL 33169 .

CHRISTY, AUDREY B., public relations cons.; b. N.Y.C., Mar. 11, 1933; d. Mathias J. and Harriet Meyer; B.A., U. Buffalo, 1967; m. James R. Christy, Apr. 19, 1952; children—James R., III, Kathryn M., John T., Alysia A., William J. Public relations officer Turgeon Bros., Buffalo, 1968-69; mem. public relations staff Sch. Fine Arts, U. Nebr., Omaha, 1972; public relations exec. Mathews & Clark Advt., Sarasota, Fla., 1974-75; profiles editor Tampa Bay mag., Tampa, Fla., 1972; public relations cons. Bildex Corp., 1973-79; owner, operator Christy & Assos., Venice, Fla., 1976—. Vice chmn. Erie County March of Dimes, 1970. Recipient various advt. awards. Mem. Public Relations Soc. Am., Am. Soc. Hosp. Public Relations, Fla. Public Relations Assn., Fla. Hosp. Assn., Sarasota Manatee Press Club, LWV (editor Sarasota publn. 1978-79).

CHU, SZE-FOO MADELINE, architect; b. Shensi, China, May 1, 1942; came to U.S., 1961, naturalized, 1973; d. Yen-Chen and Er-Ying (Chi) Yen; student Cheng-Kung U. (Taiwan), 1959-61; B.Arch., Ohio State U., 1965; m. Chueng Chu, Aug. 1, 1964; children—Yvonne, Albert. Draftsperson, Brooks & Coddington, Architects, Columbus, Ohio, 1965, LWKH Architects, Houston, 1972-73, Simmons, Cavitt, McKnight, Weymouth, Architects, Houston, 1973-74; project mgr., designer Cavitt, McKnight & Weymouth, Architects, Houston, 1975-78, v.p., 1979—. Mem. AIA. Club: Plaza Oaks Civic. Office: 4600 Post Oak Pl Houston TX 77027

CHU, TIEN-YUNG JULIAN, environ. engr.; b. Chengtu, Szuchuan, China, Sept. 1, 1946; s. Chien-Chiu Chu and Chien-I Wong; came to U.S., 1972, naturalized, 1976; B.S., Nat. Cheng-Kung U., Taiwan, 1969, M.S., 1971; M.S. in Civil and Environ. Engring. (EPA fellow), U. Ill., Urbana, 1974; m. Ling Shirley Hsia, Aug. 8, 1972. Environ. engr. div. water resources TVA, Chattanooga, 1974—. Mem. Am. Inst. Chem. Engrs., Am. Water Pollution Fedn., ASCE, Phi Tau Phi. Contbr. articles on water pollution control tech. to profl. jours. Home: 7823 Celeste Ln Hixon TN 37343 Office: 401 Chestnut St Chattanooga TN 37401

CHUITES, PAUL EDWARD, govt. ofcl., logistics mgmt. specialist; b. Pensacola, Fla. Nov. 19, 1930; s. Joseph Risdon and Etta Lee (Campbell) C.; grad. Pensacola Jr. Coll., 1958; student Macon Jr. Coll., 1970; m. Frances Susan Whiddon, Dec. 17, 1950; children—Susan Lee, Paul W., Michael E. Electronics mechanic Dept. of Navy, Pensacola, Fla., 1955-59; electronics technician Gen. Electric Co., Syracuse, N.Y., 1959-62; field engr. Acoustica Associates, Inc., Los Angeles, 1962; supervisory quality control specialist Gen. Electric Co., Syracuse, 1962-64; quality control specialist NASA, Houston, Tex., 1964-67; supervisory quality assurance specialist Dept. Air Force, Clark AB, Philippines, 1967-69, Robins AFB, Ga., 1969-71; supervisory equipment specialist Dept. Air Force, St. Louis, 1971-73; supervisory quality assurance specialist Dept. Air Force, Bien Hoa AB, Vietnam, 1973-74; supervisory logistics specialist Dept. Air Force, Robins AFB, 1974-75, supervisory quality assurance specialist, 1975-79, supervisory logistics mgmt. specialist, 1979—. Served with USAF, 1951-54. Recipient Superior Performance award Dept. Air Force, 1967, Air Force Organizational Excellence award 1959-72, Vietnam Air Service medal, 1973-74. Mem. Soc. Quality Assurance, Air Force Assn. Home: 101-B Westcliff Circle Warner Robins GA 31093 Office: WR-ALC/MMRMS Robins AFV GA 31098

CHUMBLEY, ROBERT EMMETT, III, educator; b. Covington, Va., Feb. 29, 1944; s. Robert Emmett and Bessie Rinehart (Stokes) C.; A.B., Davidson Coll., 1965; Diplome, U. Aix-Marseille (France), 1964; Ph.D., Yale U., 1972; m. Premila Irene Burns, Aug. 15, 1970. Teaching asso., instr. Summer Lang. Inst., Yale U., 1967-69; instr. French, La. State U., Baton Rouge, 1969-72, asst. prof., 1973-77, asso. prof., head French sect., 1978—. Woodrow Wilson fellow, 1965-66; Yale fellow, 1966-69; La. State U. travel grantee, Budapest, Hungary, 1976. Mem. Modern Lang. Assn., Internat. Assn. Comparative Lit., Internat. Fedn. for Modern Langs. and Lits., Semiotics Soc. Am., Assn. for Univs. Partially or Entirely of the French Lang., Phi Beta Kappa, Omicron Delta Kappa. Democrat. Presbyterian. Contbr. articles to profl. jours. Home: 2100 College Dr 170 Baton Rouge LA 70808 Office: Dept Fgn Langs La State U Baton Rouge LA 70803

CHUN, THOMAS HWA-YOUNG, physician; b. Sari Won, Korea, July 3, 1927; s. Chang Soo and Suck Chin (Kim-Chun) C.; came to U.S., 1953, naturalized, 1968; student N.Y. U., 1955; M.D., Seoul Nat. U. Med. Coll., 1952, postgrad., 1953; m. Lucia Soon-Dong Lee-Chun, June 20, 1955; children—Helen M., Joseph T., Grace M., Juliana M., Daniel T. Intern, N.Y.C., Harlem hosps., 1954; resident Bronx Municipal Hosp. Center, 1955-57; instr. dept. anesthesia Albert Einstein Med. Coll., 1957-60; asst. prof. dept. anesthesia Med. Coll. Va., 1964-68, assc. prof., 1968-69; chmn. dept. anesthesia St. Mary's Hosp., Richmond Va., 1969—; pres. West End Anesthesia Group, Inc., Richmond, 1969—; clin. prof. dept. anesthesia Med. Coll. Va., 1977—. Diplomate Am. Bd. Anesthesiology. Fellow Am. Coll. Anesthesiologists; mem. Korean Med. Assn. Va., Md. and D.C., Med. Council Can., AMA, Va. Med. Soc., Am., Va. socs. anesthesiologists, Richmond Acad. Medicine. Home: 1200 Loch Lomond Ct Richmond VA 23221 Office: 5801 Bremo Rd Richmond VA 23226

CHUNG, T. J., mech. engr.; b. Korea, May 20, 1929; came to U.S., 1960, naturalized, 1971; s. Kutaek and Inah (Kim) C.; M.S., Okla. State U., 1961, Ph.D., 1964; m. Wharan Kim, June 24, 1964; children—Arleen, Jason. Asst. prof. civil engring. Tenn. Tech. U., 1964-68, asso. prof., 1968-70; asso. prof. engring. mechanics U. Ala., Huntsville, 1970-75, prof. mech. engring., 1975—, chmn. dept. mech. engring., 1978—. Mem. ASCE, ASME, AIAA. Author: Finite Element Analysis in Fluid Dynamics, 1978. Home: 2702 Garth Rd Huntsville AL 35801 Office: U Ala in Huntsville Huntsville AL 35807

CHURCH, DOUGLAS HAROLD, business exec.; b. Fort Hood, Tex., Aug. 18, 1953; s. Richard Leonard and Geraldine Ethelle (Harden) C.; student Augusta Coll., 1972-78; m. Roxann Alden, Dec. 14, 1974; 1 son, Brian Douglas. Lab. technician Babcock & Wilcox Co., Augusta, Ga., 1975-77, inventory control analyst, 1977, sales corr., 1977-78, capital equipment buyer, 1978-80; buyer Gen. Electric Co., Waynesboro, Va. 1980—. Mem. Am. Nuclear Soc. Presbyterian. Club: Kiwanis. Home: 413 Elmwood Ave Lynchburg VA 24503 Office: G E Rd Waynesboro VA 22980

CHURCH, HARRIETT GREEN, counselor; b. Durham, N.C.; d. Donarell Rhea, Jr., and Marian Kathleen (Williams) Green; student Howard U., Washington, 1961-63; B.A., Livingstone Coll., Salisbury, N.C., 1965; M.S., Ft. Valley State Coll., 1969. Second grade tchr., Athens, Ga., 1965-66; asst. dir. recreation Morris Brown Coll., Atlanta, 1969-70; counselor, counseling coordinator, 1970-79, asst. dir., counseling coordinator spl. programs, 1979—. Active NAACP, YWCA. Recipient Spl. Services Students Outstanding Services award Morris Brown Coll., 1974, Spl. Programs Outstanding Services award, 1976, 77; named Outstanding Female Staff Person, Alpha Phi Alpha, 1976. Mem. Am. Personnel and Guidance Assn., Southwestern Assn. Ednl. Opportunity Program Personnel, Ga. Assn. Ednl. Opportunity Program Personnel. Mem. A.M.E. Ch. Home: 680 W Hancock Ave Athens GA 30601 Office: 643 M L King Jr Dr NW Atlanta GA 30314

CHURCHWELL, ROBERT LANE, chem. engr.; b. Del Rio, Tex., Aug. 10, 1924; s. William Cleveland and Effie Lelia (Wilkinson) C.; B.S., U. Tex., 1950; postgrad. U. Houston, 1962-63; m. Myrtle Pauline Wise, June 17, 1950; children—Thomas, Carl, William, Pamela, Brenda. Constrn. engr. Tenn. Gas Pipeline, 1950-52, dehydration engr., 1952, div. measurement engr., Houston, 1953-58; research engr. Tenneco Chems. Inc., Pasadena, Tex., 1958-62, lab. supr., 1962-68, environ. and utility engr., 1968-74, mgr. environ. and utility engring., 1975—. Served with USAAF, 1942-45. Recipient T.L. Satterwhite award Tex. Water Pollution Control Fedn., 1974, 78; registered profl. engr., Tex. Mem. Am. Inst. Chem. Engrs., Water Pollution Control Fedn., Air Pollution Control Assn. Methodist. Home: 1216 Wirt Rd Houston TX 77055 Office: Tenneco Chems Inc PO Box 849 Pasadena TX 77501

CHVALA, WILLIAM JAMES, beverage equipment mfg. co. exec.; b. Chgo., Apr. 16, 1943; s. James V. and Rosalia P. (Roth) C.; B.M.E., Gen. Motors Inst., 1967; M.B.A., Ga. State U., 1971; m. Judy A. Herring, Mar. 13, 1969; children—Kristin, Erika, Amanda. Reliability engr. Oldsmobile div. Gen. Motors Corp., Lansing, Mich., 1962-67; systems engr. data processing IBM Corp., Lansing, 1967-68; project engr., group mgr. distbn. Coca-Cola U.S.A., Atlanta, 1968-73; dir. distbn. Pepsi-Cola Co., Purchase, N.Y., 1973-76; exec. v.p. Swan, Inc., Powhatan, Va., 1976—, also dir.; dir. Distbn. Systems Internat., Brevet, Inc., Merritt Metals, Inc., Media Masters, Inc., Jefferson Assos. Mem. Soc. Soft Drink Technologists, Nat. Council Phys. Distbn. Mgmt., Truck Body and Equipment Mfrs. Assn. Republican. Roman Catholic. Patentee distbn. equipment. Home: 2900 Vistapoint Rd Midlothian VA 23113 Office: Route 711 at Route 522 Powhatan VA 23139

CHVATAL, SARAH CURTIS, speech pathologist; b. Eufaula, Ala., Feb. 23, 1949; d. John Warner and Mazie (Sims) Curtis; student Huntingdon Coll., 1967-68; B.S., Auburn U., 1971; M.S., Vanderbilt U., 1973; m. Robert Carlton, Chvatal, Jan. 30, 1976. Speech pathologist Anderson County Schs., Knoxville, 1973-74, Jefferson County Schs., Louisville, 1974-76; speech pathologist-cons. Head Start Programs, Monroe, La., 1977; speech-lang. pathologist Strauss Rehab. Center, Monroe, 1977-79, chief speech-lang. pathologist, 1978-79; speech pathologist, cons., curriculum writer, asst. adminstr. to tchrs. of severely and profoundly retarded children Ouachita Parish Schs., 1979—. Mem. Little Theater of Monroe, 1977-80, chorus mem. various prodns., 1978, 79. Lic. speech pathologist, La. Mem. La. Speech and Hearing Assn., Am. Speech-Lang.-Hearing Assn. (cert. clin. competence), Sigma Alpha Eta, Kappa Delta Pi. Presbyterian. Club: New Voice. Home: 1401 Erin St Monroe LA 71201 Office: GB Cooley Hosp Whites Ferry Rd West Monroe LA

CHYTIL, FRANK, educator; b. Prague, Czechoslovakia, Aug. 28, 1924; s. Frantisek and Ruzena (Vitouskova) C.; M.S., Sch. Chem. Tech., Prague, 1949, Ph.D., 1952; C.Sc., Czechoslovak Acad. Sci., Prague, 1956; m. Lucie Scheinost, Nov. 26, 1949; children—Frank, Anna, Helena. Came to U.S., 1965, naturalized, 1971. Research biochemist Charles U., Prague, Czechslovakia, 1949-51; research fellow Inst. Human Research, Prague, 1952-63; sr. scientist Czechoslovakia Acad. Sci., Prague, 1956-64; sr. research fellow Brandeis U., Waltham, Mass., 1964—, sr. research asso., 1965-66; head sect. enzymology S.W. Found. Research and Edn., San Antonio, 1966-69; mem. faculty Vanderbilt U., Nashville, 1969—, asso. prof. biochemistry, 1972-75, prof., 1975—; adj. asso. prof. U. Tex., San Antonio, 1968-69. USPHS grantee, 1967—. Mem. Am. Chem. Soc., Am. Soc. Biol. Chemists, Am. Inst. Nutrition, Endocrine Soc., Sigma Xi. Contbr. to profl. jours., books. Home: 914 Lynnwood Blvd Nashville TN 37205

CICALA, JOHN ANTHONY, counseling therapist; b. Norristown, Pa., July 14, 1944; s. John J. and Beatrice (Salerio) C.; B.S., U. Nev., Reno, 1974; M.S. in Psychology, Pittsburg (Kans.) State U., 1977; m. Maxine Cicala. Veteran's counselor U. Nev., Reno, 1975; family counseling Pittsburg State U., 1976, grad. asst., 1976—. Served with USAF, 1962-67. Included among 50 Outstanding Am. Poets, J. Mark Press. Mem. Nutrition Today Soc., Am. Personnel and Guidance Assn., Nat. Vocational Guidance Assn., Nat. Council on Family Relations, New Writers Club, Alpha Epsilon Delta, Phi Delta Kappa. Contbr. poetry to popular mags. and small press publs.

CIECHALSKI, JOSEPH CHARLES, sch. counselor; b. Bklyn., Feb. 18, 1946; s. Charles and Olga (Musnicky) C.; B.Ed., U. Miami, 1967; M.Ed., Fla. Atlantic U., 1973, Ed.S., 1977; postgrad. N.C. State U., Raleigh. Tchr. biology St. Thomas Aquinas High Sch., Ft. Lauderdale, Fla., 1971-72; tchr. math. and sci. Imperial Point Sch., Ft. Lauderdale, 1973-74; guidance counselor Rickards Middle Sch., Ft. Lauderdale, 1974—. Served with USN, 1967-71. Decorated Letter of Commendation, Comdg. Officer U.S.S. John F. Kennedy for services; recipient Outstanding Grad. Student Teaching Asst. award N.C. State U., 1979. Mem. Am., Fla. personnel and guidance assns., Am., Fla. measurement and evaluation in guidance assns., Am., Fla. sch. counselors assns., Am. Ednl. Research Assn., VFW, Am. Legion, Phi Delta Kappa. Republican. Russian Orthodox. Home: 3925 NW 19th Ave Oakland Park FL 33309 Office: Rickards Middle Sch 6000 NE 9th Ave Fort Lauderdale FL 33334

CIMIJOTTI, LEW F., architect; b. Mason City, Iowa, May 18, 1931; s. Leo M. and Mary E. (Pedelty) C.; A.A., Mason City Jr. Coll., 1951; B.S., Iowa State U., 1958; m. Patricia J. Kennedy, Sept. 17, 1956; children—Mark Trenton, Bruce Trenton, Laura Denise (dec.). Practice architecture, Chgo., 1960-65, Fairborn, Ohio, 1965-68; with HUD, 1968—; prodn. mgr. Space Jour. mag., Huntsville, Ala., 1958. Served with AUS, 1956-58. Recipient Lincoln Arc Welding Found. award, 1958. Mem. Ill. Soc. Architects, Am. Registered Architects, AIA, Toastmasters Internat. Home: 963 Parkridge Circle W Jacksonville FL 32211

CIMINO, LOUIS EUGENE, physician; b. Tampa, Fla., Sept. 9, 1926; s. Peter S. and Cecelia (Justen) C.; B.S., Spring Hill Coll., Mobile, Ala., 1946; M.D., St. Louis U., 1950; m. Jo Ann Haskins, Aug. 21, 1952; children—Louis Eugene, Michael, Patrick, Catherine, Cecelia, Thomas, Joseph, Steven. Intern, St. John's Hosp., St. Louis, 1950-51; resident in pediatrics Children's Hosp., Cin., 1951-53; instr. pediatrics U. Cin., 1952-55; asst. med. dir. outpatient dept. Children's Hosp., Cin., 1952-53; fellow in cardiology, 1953-55; chief pediatrics Tampa Gen. Hosp., 1963-66; asst. prof. pediatrics (cardiology) U. So. Fla., Tampa, 1973—; pvt. practice medicine specializing in pediatrics, Tampa, 1957—; dir. cardiology All Children's Hosp., St. Petersburg, Fla., 1970—; program supr., med. dir. children's med. services Dept. Health and Rehab., Dist. V, State of Fla. Pres., Acad. of Holy Name Found., Tampa, 1979—; v.p. Jesuit High Sch. Found., Tampa, 1978—. Served with USAF, 1955-56. Mem. AMA, Hillsborough County (pres. 1973-74), Fla. med. assns., Am. Acad. Pediatrics (cardiology sect.), Am. Coll. Cardiology, Fla., Southeastern assns. pediatric cardiologists, Am. Heart Assn. (council cardiovascular disease in young), Alpha Omega Alpha. Club: Rotary. Home: 10109 N Willow Ave Tampa FL 83603 Office: 801 W Buffalo Ave Tampa FL 33603

CINTRÓN, REINALDO, chem. engr.; b. Rio Piedras, P.R., Jan. 5, 1942; s. Domingo V. and Ledia (Cordero) C.; B.S. in Chem. Engring., U. P.R., Mayaguez, 1964; M.E., Stevens Inst., 1967, Ph.D., 1971; m. Evelyn J. Sepulveda, Nov. 1, 1975; children—Odlanier, René. Asst. chemist P.R. Water and Sewage Authority, Puerto Nuevo, 1963; computer programmer P.R. Water Resources, Santurce, 1964-65; asst. prof. chem. engring. U. P.R., Mayaguez, 1968-69, 71-76, asso. prof., 1976—; research engr. Celanese Plastics Corp., 1974; vis. prof. Union Carbide-Caribe, Peñuelas, P.R., 1972-74, Stevens Inst., 1977-78; systems engr., designer NASA, Tex. and Ala., 1976-77; chmn. com. on tech. transfer and chem. industry Instituto de Ingenieros Quimicos de P.R., 1973. Bd. dirs. Mayaguez YMCA, 1972-73; mem. citizens adv. bd. to P.R. supt. pub. edn., Mayaguez, 1971-72. Served with U.S. Army NG, 1964-70. Recipient Monzon medal U. PR., 1964; P.R. Econ. Devel. Adminstrn. grad. fellow, 1965-68; U. P.R. and PIA grad. fellow, 1969-71; registered profl. engr., P.R. Mem. AAUP, Am. Inst. Chem. Engrs., Am. Soc. Engring. Edn., Asociacion Puertorriquena de Profesores Universitarios (chmn.), Colegio de Ingenieros, Arquitectos y Agrmensores de P.R., Soc. Plastics Engrs., Rho Omicron Rho. Contbr. articles to tech. jours. Home: E-32 Yaurel Mayaguez PR 00708 Office: Depto INQU-RUM Mayaguez PR 00708

CISNE, MAXWELL GERARD, accountant; b. Champaign, Ill., Dec. 28, 1936; s. Richard Gerard and Margaret (Maxwell) C.; B.S., U. Ill., 1958; M.S., U. Richmond, 1964; m. Mary Ann Inwood, Aug. 27, 1960; children—Katrin Neill, Mary Megan. Staff accountant Reynolds Metals Co., Richmond, Va., 1960-65; mgr. Peat, Marwick, Mitchell & Co., C.P.A.'s, 1965-72; mgr. Arthur Young & Co., C.P.A.'s, Richmond, 1972-79; partner Kuehl & Cisne, C.P.A.'s, Richmond, 1973-79, Cary, Stosch, Walls & Co., 1979—; instr. acctg. U. Richmond, 1970-71, Richmond chpt. Am. Inst. Banking, 1971-72, Va. Commonwealth U., 1971—; treas., dir. Hope Housing, Inc., Hope Village, Inc., 1969-76. Account exec. United Givers Fund, 1972-74, group chmn., 1974—; bd. dirs. Southampton Citizens Assn., 1972-74; mem. adv. services bd. Richmond Mental Health and Mental Retardation; deacon, treas. Presbyterian Ch., 1972-75, elder, 1976—, supt. Sunday sch., 1977—. Served to lt. USNR, 1958-60. C.P.A., Va. Mem. Am. Inst. C.P.A.'s, Nat. Assn. Accts. (v.p. Richmond chpt. 1976-80), Va. Soc. C.P.A.'s (pres. Richmond chpt. 1976), Va. Jr. (life), Richmond Jr. (v.p. 1972-73, Sparkplug of Year 1971-72, Key Man Club 1973) chambers commerce, Phi Delta Theta. Clubs: U. Richmond Alumni (pres. 1972-73), Richmond First (pres. 1976-77). Home: 4601 Butte Rd Richmond VA 23235 Office: 1001 Main St Richmond VA 23219

CISSEL, NORMAN RALPH, ret. acct.; b. Washington, Dec. 9, 1911; s. William and Emma (Pearson) C.; B.C.S., Benjamin Franklin U., 1935; m. Dorothy E. Fleming, Sept. 14, 1940 (div.); 1 son, William F. With V.I. Corp. (formerly V.I. Co.), Christiansted, 1936-51, comptroller, 1940-51; territorial acctg. exec. OPS, Charlotte Amalie, V.I., 1952-53; supervisory auditor, asst. comptroller Govt. Comptroller of V.I., Charlotte Amalie, 1957-61; pvt. practice as C.P.A., St. Croix, V.I. 1952-66; sr. partner Cissel & Ellis, C.P.A.'s, 1966-71 (merged with Seidman & Seidman, C.P.A.'s, 1971); cons. partner Seidman & Seidman, C.P.A.'s, 1971-74. Mem. Food Commn. Municipality of St. Croix, 1946-49; mem. Banking Bd. V.I., 1949-72, 77-79, chmn., 1949-54; mem. Tax Exemption Bd. Municipality of St. Croix, 1951-55; pres. V.I. Bd. Public Accountancy, 1957-72; mem. investment bd. V.I. Unemployment Compensation, 1963—; mem. V.I. Bd. Tax Rev., 1977—. C.P.A., V.I. Mem. Nat. Assn. State Bds. Accountancy, Am. Inst. C.P.A.'s (council 1960-67), V.I. Soc. C.P.A.'s (pres. 1952-72), Inst. Internal Auditors, Nat. Assn. Accts., Am. Acctg. Assn., Mcpl. Fin. Officers Assn. Home: Estate La Reine Box C Kingshill PO St Croix VI 00850

CITTONE, HENRY ARON, hotel exec.; b. Istanbul, Turkey, May 15, 1937; s. Joseph and Debrah (Benbanaste) C.; B.A., Coll. St. Michel, 1956; student Los Angeles Trade and Tech. Coll., 1971; m. Liliane Robert, Oct. 2, 1965; children—Henry Joseph, Marc Ely. Food service mgr. U. So. Calif., Los Angeles, 1971; mgr. food and beverages Sheraton Poste Inn, Cherry Hill, N.J., 1972-73; resident mgr. Aruba Caribbean Hotel (Netherlands Antilles), 1973-74; dir. food and beverage Lima Sheraton Hotel, (Peru), 1974-76, Bahia Mar Hotel, Fort Lauderdale, 1978-79, Maison Dupuy Hotel, New Orleans, 1979—; cons. govt. owned hotels Curacao, Netherlands Antilles., Hotel and Restaurant Internat. Food and Beverage Cons. Served with Israeli Army, 1956-59. Mem. Internat. Food Service Execs. Assn., Internat. Hotel Sales Mgmt. Assn., Am. Hotel and Motel Assn. Home: 6462 Park Manor Dr Metairie LA 70003

CIVEY, GEORGE ARNOTT, III, art historian, critic; b. Des Moines, Jan. 20, 1944; s. George Arnott and Annette Newcomer (Foley) C.; B.A., Transylvania U., Lexington, Ky., with distinction, 1966; M.A., U. Iowa, Iowa City, 1971; postgrad. U. N.C., Chapel Hill, 1974—; m. Mary Janet Eberwein, Aug. 22, 1969; 1 dau., Jorgianne Irene. Research asst. art history U. Iowa, Iowa City, 1970-71; instr. art history and criticism Memphis State U., 1971-74; teaching asst. art history U. N.C., Chapel Hill, 1974-75; asst. prof. art Eastern Ky. U., Richmond, 1975—; cons. in field. Served with USAF, 1966-68. Recipient Excellence in Teaching award Coll. Arts and Scis., Eastern Ky. U., 1977-78; Transylvania U. acad. scholar, 1962-66; NDEA fellow U. Iowa, 1968-70. Mem. Coll. Art Assn. Am., SE Coll. Art Conf., South Central Renaissance Conf., Southeastern Medieval Assn., AAUP (sec. chpt. 1978-80), Arlington Assn., Delta Sigma Phi. Democrat. Presbyterian. Club: Lions. Author: Selected Aspects of the History of French Painting During the Bourbon Restoration 1814-1830, 1975—. Contbr. to Goldsmith's Jour. Home: 253 Sunset Ave Richmond KY 40475 Office: 425 Jane Campbell Fine Arts Complex Eastern Ky U Richmond KY 40475

CLAGETT, ARTHUR F(RANK), JR., sociologist, educator; b. Little Rock, Dec. 3, 1916; s. A.F. and Mary Gertrude (Bell) C.; B.A. in Chemistry, Baylor U., 1943; M.A. in Psychology, U. Ark., 1957; Ph.D. in Sociology, La. State U., 1968; m. Dorothy Ruth Pinckard, Dec. 23, 1954. Shift chemist Celanese Corp., Cumberland, Md., 1942-44; shift supr. penicillin prodn. Comml. Sovents Corp., Terre Haute, Ind., 1944-45; research supr. streptomycin pilot plant, Schenley Labs., Lawrenceburg, Ind., 1945-48; asst. mgr. Clagett's Feed and Seed Store, Donna, Tex., 1948-50; grad. teaching asst. in psychology U. Ark., Fayetteville, 1950-51; med. service rep. Blue Line Chem. Co., St. Louis, 1952-56; prison classification officer La. State Penitentiary, 1956-59, classification supr. of new admissions, 1959-60; counseling psychologist, Baker, La., 1960-64; asst. prof. sociology Lamar State Coll. Tech., Beaumont, Tex., 1964-66; asso. prof. sociology Stephen F. Austin State U., Nacogdoches, Tex., 1968—, library rep. of sociology dept., 1973-76, mem. Univ. Research Council, 1973-75. Certified rehab. counselor, vocat. guidance counselor. Mem. Am., Southwestern sociol. assns., AAUP, Am. Personnel and Guidance Assn., Mid-South Sociol. Assn., Internat. Platform Assn. Clubs: Masons (32 deg.), Kiwanis Internat. Contbr. articles on social psychology and sociology, book revs. to profl. publs. Developed theory of relative involvement in delinquency and criminality. Home: 609 Egret Dr Nacogdoches TX 75961 Office: PO Box 6173 Stephen F Austin Station Nacogdoches TX 75962

CLANTON, WAYNE ALLEN, color co. exec.; b. Ingalls, Ark., May 25, 1932; s. Joseph Clifton and Reba A. (Nutt) C.; B.S. in Chemistry, U. Ark., Monticello, 1956; M.S. in Bus. Mgmt., Washington U., St. Louis, 1959; m. Martha Ora King, Feb. 14, 1952; children—Timothy D., David A., Mark A., Cathy C. Sci. instr. Walnut Ridge (Ark.) High Sch., 1956; chief chemist Monsanto Chem. Co., St. Louis, 1957-59; sales Inmont Corp., N.Y.C., 1958-68; tech. sales rep. Sun Chem. Corp., N.Y.C., 1968-76; v.p. mktg. Spartan Color Co., Houston, 1976—. Asst. dir. Khory League Ohio, 1966-68. Served in USN, 1950-53; to capt. Mo. N.G., 1957-59. Mem. Am. Chem. Soc., Paint, Varnish and Lacquer Assn., Am. Ink Makers. Republican. So. Baptist. Home: Rt 1 Box 279 Warren AR 71671 Office: 5803 Northdale St Houston TX 77087

CLAPPER, GEORGE KNIGHT, JR., mfg. engr.; b. Bessemer, Ala., Oct. 20, 1940; s. George Knight and Wilma (Jackson) C.; B.S., Miss. State U., 1974; m. Betty Jo Gregg, May 29, 1962; children—Ginger, Lee, George-Paul. Spar-cap former Lockheed Aircraft Co., Marietta, Ga., 1962-65; indsl. engr. Atkins Saw Co., Greenville, Miss., 1968-69; indsl. engr. Sperry-Vickers Corp., Jackson, Miss., 1969-77, sr. mfg. engr., 1977—. Registered profl. engr., Calif. Mem. Am. Inst. Indsl. Engrs. (bd. dirs. Miss. chpt.). Republican. Mem. Christian Ch. Home: Route 8 Box 403 Jackson MS 39213 Office: 5353 Highland Dr Jackson MS 39206

CLARIDGE, ELMOND LOWELL, chem. engr.; b. Delaplaine, Ark., June 5, 1917; s. Elmond Lee and Irene Cynthia(Gates) C.; B.S. in Chem. Engring., U. Mo., Rolla, 1939, M.S. in Chem. Engring., 1941; Ph.D. in Chem. Engring., U. Houston, 1979; m. Zola Ruth McDowell, Jan. 1, 1939; children—David Elmond, Jonathan McDowell. With Shell Oil Co., 1941-64, Shell Devel. Co., 1964-79; asso. prof. chem. engring., dir. petroleum engring. grad. program U. Houston, 1979—; also cons. Registered profl. engr., Tex. Mem. Am. Inst. Chem. Engrs., Soc. Petroleum Engrs., Am. Chem. Soc., AAAS, S.W. Catalysis Soc., Sigma Xi, Alpha Chi Sigma. Methodist. Home: 5439 Paisley Ln Houston TX 77096 Office: Chem Engring Dept U Houston Houston TX 77004

CLARIDGE, RICHARD ALLEN, civil engr.; b. Chgo., Feb. 22, 1932; s. Dalbert Otis and Lucille Alma Marion (Lindquist) C.; B.S.B.A., Fla. State U., 1953; B.C.E., U. Fla., 1959; m. Joan Elaine Powell, June 12, 1952; children—Cathy, Richard Allen, Jaylynn Powell. With McDonnell Douglas Astronautics Co., various locations, 1959—, sr. engr. mech. sect. Cape Canaveral Air Force Sta., 1974—, sr. engr. designer Kennedy Space Center, 1969—; structural, environ. and civil engr.; pres. Atlantic Cons. Inc. Served with USNR, 1953-57. Registered profl. engr., Fla., S.C. Mem. ASCE, Fla. Engring. Soc. Home: 1713 Guldahl Dr Titusville FL 32780 Office: Box 21007 Kennedy Space Center FL 32815

CLARK, ALVIN WALLACE, gas co. exec.; b. McAlester, Okla., June 26, 1949; s. Floyd Karlton and Edriss Ann (Dutton) C.; B.A. magna cum laude, Okla. Baptist U., 1971; M.A. in Econs., U. Okla., 1974. Analyst, El Paso Natural Gas Co. (Tex.), 1974-75, coordinator regulatory affairs, 1976-78, adminstr. regulatory affairs, 1978-79, mgr. regulatory affairs, 1980—; lectr. dept. econs. and fin. U. Tex., El Paso, 1975-76. Deacon 1st Baptist Ch., El Paso. Club: Rio Grande Econs. Home: 7317 Cerro Negro Dr El Paso TX 79912 Office: PO Box 1492 El Paso TX 79978

CLARK, BARBARA ANN RANDALL, educator; b. Macon, Ga., July 18, 1937; d. LeRoy and Lillian Evelyn (Battle) Randall; B.S., Morgan State U., 1959; M.S., S.C. State Coll., 1976; m. Carl Oliver Clark, June 11, 1966; children—Carl Robert, Angela Teresa. Research chemist NIH-City Hosps., Balt., 1959-66; instr. chemistry S.C. State Coll., Orangeburg, 1966-67; testing evaluator Orangeburg City Sch. Dist. 1976; in-sch. suspension coordinator, counselor Belleville Jr. High Sch., 1976-77; instr. edn. Claflin Coll., Orangeburg, 1977—; pres. Felton Lab. Sch. Parent Tchr. Orgn., 1976-78. Mem. Am. Tchrs. Assn., AAUW, NEA, Am., S.C. (treas.-elect) personnel and guidance assns., NAACP, Women's Internat. Bowling Congress, Am. Sch. Counselor Assn., S.C. Edn. Assn., S.C. Assn. Non-White Concerns, Neferdames (pres. 1970-71), Alphabettes, Phi Delta Kappa, Delta Sigma Theta (pres. 1977-79). Democrat. Roman Catholic. Home: Box 1632 SC State College Orangeburg SC 29117

CLARK, BILLY LEWIS, entomologist; b. Ben Wheeler, Tex., Apr. 29, 1933; s. Curtis Lee and Eunice (Lewis) C.; B.S., Tex. A&M U., 1958; m. Kay Constance Roscoe, Mar. 9, 1969; children—Keven, Shannon, Shawn, Jonna, Cullen, Chase. Partner, Stroope Pest Control Co., Tex., 1958-65, mng. partner, Beaumont br., 1958-65; pres. Bill Clark Pest Control, Inc., Beaumont, 1965—. Pres., Better Bus. Bur. S.E. Tex., 1967-68; pres. Beaumont Internat. Seaman's Center, 1974; active United Appeals, Boys Club, YMCA. Served with USN, 1951-54. Mem. Nat. Pest Control Assn. (regional v.p.), Entomol. Soc. Am., Tex. Pest Control Assn. (pres. 1977), Tex. Restaurants Assn., Tex. Homebuilder's Assn., Tex. Apts. Assn., C. of C., Pi Chi Omega. Republican. Presbyterian. Clubs: Beaumont Profl. Men's, Pinewood Country, Beaumont Rotary, Beaumont Downtown Lions (pres. 1966), Beaumont A&M (pres. 1965). Contbr. articles in field to profl. jours. Home: 84 Ave of the Oaks Beaumont TX 77707 Office: PO Box 5511 Beaumont TX 77706

CLARK, BILLY PAT, physicist; b. Bartlesville, Okla., May 15, 1939; s. Lloyd A. and Ruby Laura (Holcomb) C.; B.S., Okla. State U., 1961, M.S., 1964, Ph.D., 1968. Grad. asst. dept. physics Okla. State U., 1961-68; postdoctoral research fellow dept. theoretical physics U. Warwick, Coventry, Eng., 1968-69; sr. mem. tech. staff Booz-Allen Applied Research, 1969-70; sr. mem. tech. staff field services div. Computer Scis. Corp., Leavenworth, Kans., 1970-73, sr. mem. tech. staff, field services div., Hampton, Va., 1973-76; head quality assurance engring. Landsat project applied tech. div. Computer Scis. Corp., 1976-77, mgr. data quality assurance, 1977-79, sr. system scientist, 1979—. Recipient undergrad. scholarships Phillips Petroleum Co., 1957-61, Am. Legion, 1957-58, Okla. State U., 1957-58. Mem. Am. Acad. Polit. and Social Sci., Internat. Platform Assn., Am. Phys. Soc., AAAS, N.Y. Acad. Scis., Pi Mu Epsilon, Sigma Pi Sigma. Club: Victory Hills Golf and Country (Kansas City, Kans.). Author or co-author tech. publs. Home: 502 S Hamilton St Dewey OK 74029

CLARK, CARL OLIVER, physicist; b. Savannah, Ga., June 19, 1936; s. William Eagar and Susan Ann (Dowse) C.; B.S., Morgan State U., 1959; M.S., Howard U., 1961; Ph.D., U. S.C., 1976; m. Barbara Ann Randall, June 11, 1966; children—Carl R., Angela T. Asst. prof. physics S.C. State Coll., Orangeburg, 1960-61, asso. prof., 1961-77, prof., 1977—; cons. Howard Coop. Physics Project. NSF faculty fellow, 1964; U.S. Dept. Agr. grantee, 1977—. Mem. Am. Phys. Soc. (divs. chem. physics, solid state physics and biophysics, Apker awards com. 1979-80), Am. Assn. Physics Tchrs. (com. on physics in minority edn. 1978—). Democrat. Roman Catholic. Contbr. articles to profl. jours. Home: PO Box 1632 SCSC Orangeburg SC 29117 Office: Room 210 Hodge Hall SCSC Orangeburg SC 29117

CLARK, CHARLES DANIEL, automobile dealer; b. Peoria, Ill., May 28, 1917; s. Richard Fardon and Melba Iona (Kirkpatrick) C.; B.A., U. Mich., Ann Arbor, 1939; m. Dorothy Elizabeth Van Gelder, Jan. 3, 1942; children—Kirk Allen, Robin Anne. Apprentice purser S.S. Santa Lucia, Grace Lines, N.Y.C., 1939-40; sales mgr. Carpenter Chevrolet Co., McAllen, Tex., 1940-41, v.p., 1945-50; pres. Charles Clark Chevrolet Co., McAllen, 1951—; dir. McAllen State Bank. City commr. City of McAllen, 1950-52. Served to maj., USAAF, 1941-45. Decorated D.F.C., Air Medal with oak leaf clusters. Nat. com. Univ. Art Mus., U. Calif. at Berkeley, 1969-70; Council of Friends U. Mich. Mus. Art, 1972-78; mem. Coll. Fine Arts Found. adv. council U. Tex. at Austin, 1972—; mem. mus. adv. panel Tex. Commn. Arts and Humanities, 1972-74. Mem. McAllen C. of C. (pres. 1957, outstanding citizen 1958). Tex. Automobile Dealer Assn. (award personnel relations 1963, v.p. 1965-66), Delta Upsilon. Episcopalian. Home: 404 Lindberg Ave McAllen TX 78501 Office: PO Box 938 McAllen TX 78501

CLARK, CHARLES RODNEY, univ. adminstr.; b. Birmingham, Ala., Feb. 23, 1947; s. Cynthia Hammond O'Neal; student Jefferson State Jr. Coll., Birmingham, 1970-71; B.S., Auburn U., 1973; M.S., U. So. Miss., 1975; m. Sandra Pederson Clark, Sept. 2, 1972. Transp. planner Gulf Regional Planning Commn., Gulfport, Miss., 1975-76;

project devel. officer Center for Urban Affairs U. Ala., Birmingham, 1976—, instr. urban studies, 1979—. Scoutmaster Birmingham Area council Boy Scouts Am. Served with U.S. Navy, 1965-69. Mem. Assn. Am. Geographers, Am. Planning Assn., Am. Soc. Photogrammetry, Am. Congress Surveying and Mapping, Alpha Phi Omega. Home: 5139 Cornell Dr Birmingham AL 35210 Office: 901 S 15th St #249 Birmingham AL 35294

CLARK, DANNY MILES, obstetrician, gynecologist; b. Paris, Ky., July 8, 1937; s. Daniel Pepper and Lelia Bell (Whittington) C.; A.B., Transylvania U., 1958; M.D., U. Cin., 1962; m. Joyce Carew, July 6, 1957; children—Joyce Ann, James Michael, Mark Edward, Patrick Ward, William Miles. Intern, Los Angeles County Gen. Hosp., 1962-63, resident in obstetrics-gynecology, 1963-67; partner Betts, Clark & Ellis, Somerset, Ky., 1969—; pvt. practice medicine specializing in obstetrics and gynecology, Somerset, 1969—; pres. med. staff Lake Cumberland Med. Center, 1976—. Elder 1st. Christian Ch. Somerset, 1975—; bd. dirs. Somerset YMCA. Served with USAF, 1967-69. Mem. Pulaski County Med. Soc. (pres. 1974), Ky., Am. med. assns., Am. Coll. Obstetrics-Gynecology, Am. Fertility Soc., Ky. Obstetrics-Gynecology Soc. Republican. Mem. Disciples Christ. Home: 314 Robin Dr Somerset KY 42501 Office: 401 Bogle St Somerset KY 42501

CLARK, DONALD HAMILTON, lawyer; b. Washington, Jan. 29, 1937; s. Cecil Hamilton and Virginia (Miller) C.; B.S., U.S. Naval Acad., 1959; J.D., George Washington U., 1968; m. Faye Blanton Pratt, Feb. 22, 1962; children—Julia Lynn, Donald Hamilton. Admitted to Va. bar, 1968, U.S. Supreme Ct. bar, 1974; individual practice law, Virginia Beach and Norfolk, Va., 1968-72; pres. firm Clark and Stant, Virginia Beach and Norfolk, 1972—; gen. counsel Tidewater Transp. Dist. Commn., 1976—; instr. Old Dominion U. Inst. Mgmt., 1974-75. Pres. Chesopeian Colony Civic League, 1970; legal counsel Virginia Beach Jaycees, 1971-72; vestryman Eastern Shore Episcopal Chapel, 1973-75, sr. warden, 1974. Served with USN, 1959-65. Mem. Va. State Bar (2d Dist. ethics com. 1974-77, chmn. 1977—) Am., Virginia Beach (chmn. spl. com. jud. endorsements 1976, treas. 1979, sec. 1980), Norfolk-Portsmouth bar assns. Clubs: Virginia Beach Racquet, Harbor. First place award ASCAP, for essay, 1966. Home: 1312 W Little Neck Rd Virginia Beach VA 23452 Office: 211 Pembroke Three Bldg Virginia Beach VA 23462

CLARK, DOUGLAS ADRON, accountant; b. Wallace, N.C., June 27, 1944; s. Adron Emmett and Evelyn Grace (Sandlin) C.; A.B. in Bus., U. N.C., Wilmington, 1969. Asst. state auditor State of N.C., Raleigh, 1969-72; pvt. practice acctg., Kenansville, N.C., 1972—. Treas. N.C. Young Democrats, 1975; chmn. Duplin County (N.C.) Dem. Party, 1975-78; mem. N.C. Ho. of Reps., 1978-80. Served with Mil. Police Corps, U.S. Army, 1966-68. Presbyterian. Club: Masons.

CLARK, EMORY EUGENE, ins. agy. exec.; b. Opelika, Ala., Jan. 24, 1931; s. Bunk Henry and Dorothy (Bolt) C.; grad. pub. schs.; m. Jean F. Reed, Sept. 30, 1951; children—Steven E., Michael E. With Mgrs. Life Ins. Co., 1956-74, agt., supr., Los Angeles, 1956-60, mgr. Hawaii br., 1960-65, Pitts. br., 1965-68, Houston br., 1968-74; with Jefferson Standard Life Ins. Co., Fort Worth, 1974—. Served with AUS, 1950-56. Mem. Fort Worth Life Underwriters Assn., Am. Soc. Life Underwriters, Fort Worth Gen. Agts. and Mgrs. Assn. Home: 8109 Meadowbrook Dr Fort Worth TX 76112 Office: 2001 Beach St Suite 516 Fort Worth TX 76103

CLARK, EUGENE CORRY, ceramic engr.; b. Washington, Ga., Oct. 18, 1941; s. Walter Nathaniel and Mary Helen (Corry) C.; B.S., Ga. Inst. Tech., 1964, M.S., 1968; m. Mary Elizabeth Adams, Apr. 27, 1963; children—Mary Corry, Walter Emmett. Research engr. Pemco div. Glidden Co., Balt., 1963-64, sr. ceramic engr., 1968-70; processing gen. foreman Am. Standards, New Orleans and Torrence, Calif., 1970-72; plant ceramic engr. Lapp Insulation div. Interpace Corp., Sandersville, Ga., 1972-74; fabrication plant supr. Glasrock Products Inc., Calhoun, Ga., 1974-75; mgr. plant Isolantite Mfg. Co., Sterling, N.J., 1974-75; quality control mgr. Am. Feldmuelhe Corp., Hendersonville, N.C., 1976-77, head prodn. mfg., 1977-78, corp. quality control mgr., 1978—. Chmn., Great Locomotive Chase Festival, 1974; dist. commr. Echota dist. Boy Scouts Am., 1978—; sec. Smith for State N.C., 1977. Served to 1st lt. Inf., AUS, 1964-66. Mem. Am. Ceramic Soc., Nat. Inst. Ceramic Engrs., Alumnia Mfg. Assn., Keramos. Democrat. Presbyterian. Club: Lions. Home: 703 Orchard St Hendersonville NC 28739 Office: AFC PO Box 2090 Hendersonville NC 28739

CLARK, FAYE LOUISE, educator; b. La., Oct. 9, 1936; student Centenary Coll., 1954-55; B.A. with honor, U. Southwestern La., 1962; M.A., U. Ga., 1966; m. Warren James Clark, Aug. 8, 1969; children—Roy, Kay Natalie. Tchr., Nova Exptl. Schs., Fort Lauderdale, Fla., 1963-65; faculty dept. drama and speech DeKalb Community Coll., Atlanta, 1967—, chmn. dept., 1977—. Mem. Southeastern Theatre Conf., Ga. Theatre Conf. (sec. 1968-69, rep. to Southeastern Theatre Conf. 1969), Ga. Psychol. Assn., Ga. Speech Assn., Atlanta Ballet Guild, Young Women of the Arts, Phi Kappa Phi, Pi Kappa Delta, Sigma Delta Pi, Kappa Delta Pi, Thalian-Blackfriars. Presbyterian. Clubs: Atlanta Artists, Lake Lanier Sailing. Home: 2521 Melinda Dr NE Atlanta GA 30345 Office: Dept Drama and Speech DeKalb Community College Clarkston GA 30021

CLARK, FRANCES JANETTE, counselor; b. Kinston, Ala., Mar. 20, 1938; d. Curry Franklin and Emma (Cole) C.; B.A. in Religious Edn., Central Bible Coll., 1969; M.Ed. in Counselor Edn., U. South Ala., 1978. With So. Bell Telephone Co., Mobile, Ala., 1960-66; tchr. Crichton Acad., Mobile, 1970-75; detention officer Mobile County Youth Center, 1976-78, dentention officer supr., counselor, 1978—. Mem. Am. Personnel and Guidance Assn., Ala. Personnel and Guidance Assn. Mem. Assembly of God Ch. Home: 100 Burtonwood Dr Mobile AL 36608 Office: 2315 Costarides St Mobile AL 36617

CLARK, FRANKLIN JACOB, JR., architect; b. Anderson, S.C., Dec. 7, 1937; s. Franklin Jacob and Corrie Elizabeth (Watson) C.; B.Arch., Clemson U., 1962; m. Beverly Thornton Bowie, Nov. 19, 1960; 1 son, Franklin Jacob. Designer, A.G. Odell, Jr. & Assos., 1966, Ledbetter & Earle Architects, 1966-67; dir., asso. architect, v.p. Odell Assos., Inc., Charlotte, N.C., 1967—; dir. Clark Tribble Harris & Li, Architects, Charlotte, 1973—; pres., chmn. bd. Clark Assos., Inc., Anderson, 1977—. Served to lt. USAF, 1962-66. Registered architect, S.C., Ga., N.C., Tenn.; certified Nat. Council Archtl. Registration Bds. Mem. AIA (Design Honor awards), Anderson, Charlotte chambers commerce, Anderson Council Architects. Presbyterian (elder 1971-73). Clubs: Charlotte City, Anderson Country, Cobb's Glen Country. Works include Cedar Forest Racquet Club, Charlotte, N.C. State Govt. Office Bldg., Raleigh, Mecklenburg County Parking Facility, Charlotte, U. N.C. Phys. Plant Bldg., Charlotte. Mem. Mint Mus. Art. Home: Route 10 Williamsburg Dr Anderson SC 29621 Office: 126 N McDuffie St Anderson SC 29621

CLARK, FRED STEPHEN, lawyer; b. Savannah, Ga., July 10, 1936; s. H. Sol and Matilda (Shapiro) C.; B.A., Cornell U., 1958; LL.B., U. Ga., 1961; m. Nancie K. Meddin, Dec. 27, 1970; children—Jonathan A., Alison P. Admitted to Ga. bar, 1960; practiced in Savannah, 1960—; asso. firm Brannen, Clark and Hester, 1961-64; asst. U.S. Atty., So. Dist. of Ga., 1964-66; partner firm Brannen, Clark and Hester, 1966-71, Lee and Clark, Profl. Corp., 1972—; part owner Quality Motel Airport, Quality Motel Oasis Village. Asst. city atty. and police ct. judge pro tem, Savannah, 1968-70; asst. town atty, police judge pro tem., Thunderbolt, Ga., 1971-73; city atty., police ct. judge, City of Savannah Beach, 1973-74; founder Athens Legal Aid Soc., 1961; pres. Legal Aid Soc. of Savannah, 1969. Pres. R.J. Nunn Trust Fund, 1972-79; chmn. Urban Renewal Adv. Com., Savannah, 1968; chmn. 1st Community Support Program, Savannah State Coll., 1970; mem. U. Ga. Fund Drive, 1971; mem. State Democratic Exec. Com., 1971-74; chmn. First Senatorial Dist. Dem. Com. Conv., 1970; bd. dirs. Jewish Ednl. Alliance, 1964-67, pres. men's club, 1967-68; bd. govs. Savannah Jewish Council, 1962-63; bd. dirs. Parent and Child Devel. Services, 1976-79, pres. 1980-81; bd. dirs. Leadership Savannah. Named Outstanding Young Man of Savannah, 1968. Recipient 5 Outstanding Young Man of Ga. awards, 1968. Mem. State Bar Ga. (mem. exec. council young lawyers sect. 1964-67), Internat. Acad. Trial Lawyers (dir. 1979—), Fedn. of Ins. Counsel, Savannah Jaycees, Am., Fed. (pres. Savannah chpt. 1967), Savannah (pres. 1979-80) bar assns., Maritime Law Assn. U.S., Coastal Empire Law Enforcement Officers Assn., Benedictine Mil. Sch. Alumni Assn. (pres. 1967). Clubs: Masons (Shriner), Elks, B'nai B'rith. Contbr. articles to profl. jours. Home: 318 Early St Savannah GA 31405 Office: 711 C & S Bank Bldg Savannah GA 31401

CLARK, GAIL DAVIS, accountant; b. St. Petersburg, Fla., Sept. 16, 1942; d. Robert Clarence and Mary Lu (Smith) Davis. A.A., St. Petersburg Jr. Coll., 1971; B.A., U. South Fla., 1973; M.B.A., Fla. Inst. Tech., 1978; m. Donald Jan Clark, Nov. 25, 1960; children—Donald Jan, Carrie. Accountant, Tornwall Lang & Lee, C.P.A.'s, St. Petersburg, 1973-75; controller Gary Froid & Asso., Northwestern Mutual Life Ins., St. Petersburg, 1975-76; acctg. systems analyst, fin. E-Systems Inc. div. ECI, St. Petersburg, 1979—. C.P.A., Fla. Mem. Am. Inst. C.P.A.'s, Fla. Inst. C.P.A.'s, Contract Mgmt. Assn., Phi Kappa Phi, Beta Alpha Psi, Beta Gamma Sigma. Baptist. Home: 811-40th Ave NE Saint Petersburg FL 33703 Office: 1501 72nd St N Saint Petersburg FL 33710

CLARK, ISAAC EDGAR, publisher; b. Schulenburg, Tex., Dec. 9, 1919; s. Harvey Robert and Annie Ruby (Miekow) C.; B.A., U. Tex. at Austin, 1941, M.A., 1945; m. Lila Rhea Norwood, Sept. 1, 1945; children—Candace Ann, Robin Rhea. Rancher, 1945—; tchr., theatre dir., publs. dir., lang. arts coordinator Schulenburg Pub. Schs., 1945-77; founder, owner I.E. Clark, Inc., Pub., Band Magic Halftime Shows and Stage Magic Plays, 1959—; tchr. Newspaper Fund seminars U. Tex. at Austin, summers 1961-66; regional observer for Nat. Observer, 1961; mem. Tex. Edn. Agy. Commn. for Lang. Arts Curriculum Revision, 1958-59, State Com. Devel. of Speech-Drama Publ. of Tex. Edn. Agy., 1960-61. Mem. Fayette County His. Survey Com., 1969—; founder, artistic dir., bd. dirs., officer Backstage, Inc., Fine Arts Council for South Central Tex., 1969—; adv. dir. 1st Nat. Bank of Schulenburg, 1974—. Democratic precinct chmn., Fayette County Dem. Exec. Com., 1955—; county campaign chmn. Lyndon B. Johnson, 1949, 55; area campaign chmn. Tex. Lt. Gov. Bill Hobby, 1972. Bd. dirs. Schulenburg Hist. Soc. Recipient Finest Journalism Tchr. in Tex. award U. Tex. Interscholastic League, 1967; Order Golden Quill, 1977; named Hon. State Farmer, Future Farmers Am., 1956; Newspaper Fund fellow, 1959. Mem. Am. Theatre Assn. (nat. chmn. play publishers panel 1977), Am. Community Theatre Assn., Childrens Theatre Assn., Tex. Secondary Theatre Conf. (dir., Newsletter editor, 1966-69, mem. Interscholastic League adv. com.), Tex. Ednl. Theatre Assn., Modern Music Masters (hon. life), English Speaking Union, Farm Bur., Phi Beta Kappa, Delta Tau Delta, Sigma Delta Chi, Phi Eta Sigma. Methodist. Mason (Shriner). Author: (plays) Twelve Dancing Princesses, 1969; Hansel and Gretel, 1970; It's A Dungaree World, 1974; also several one-act plays including The Christmas Dream, transl. into Spanish, produced TV, Ecuador, 1973. Home: Bermuda Valley Farm Schulenburg TX 78956 Office: PO Box 246 Schulenburg TX 78956

CLARK, JACK CROWLEY, physician; b. Whitleyville, Tenn., Feb. 24, 1936; s. Cordell Hull and Clio Elizabeth (Cassetty) C.; student Vanderbilt U., 1954-57; M.D., U. Tenn., 1961; m. Donna Jefferson, Oct. 24, 1976; children—Jack Crowley, Christopher David, Julie Elizabeth. Intern, Nashville Gen. Hosp., 1961-62; gen. practice medicine, Lafayette, Tenn., 1962-71; resident in radiology U. Tenn., 1972-74, chief resident, 1974-75; mem. staff Smith-Chitwood Hosp., Lafayette, 1962-71; radiologist Cumberland Med. Center, Crossville, Tenn., 1975—, also White County Hosp., Sparta, Tenn., Chamberlain Meml. Hosp., Rockwood, Tenn., Fentress County Hosp., Jamestown, Tenn.; med. dir. Cordell Hull Econ. Opportunity Corp., Lafayette, 1967-71; former dir. Citizens Bank, Lafayette, Tenn.; mem. Gov's. Adv. Bd. on Mental Retardation, 1969-72. Mem. City Council Lafayette, 1964-68, Macon County Election Commn., 1968-70; bd. dirs. Macon County Cancer Soc.; trustee Tenn. Dept. Mental Health and Mental Retardation, 1971—; chmn. bd. trustees Arlington Devel. Center, 1972-76, Clover Bottom Developmental Center, Nashville, 1975—. Served in Tenn. Army N.G., 1966—, state surgeon, 1976—. Mem. Am. Acad. Gen. Practice, So., Memphis, Cumberland County, Tenn. med. assns., Radiol. Soc. N.Am., Phi Chi, Pi Kappa Alpha. Democrat. Methodist. Home: 30 Roma Dr Crossville TN 38555 Office: Cumberland Med Center 811 S Main St Crossville TN 38555

CLARK, JACK LEWIS, educator; b. Moultrie, Ga., Sept. 24, 1924; s. Homer Lee and Ellen (Reaves) C.; B.Arch., U. Fla., 1955; M.S., Bradley U., 1968, M.A., 1969; Ph.D., Laurence U., 1971; m. Hilda M. Coletrain, Feb. 20, 1943; children—Ronnie R., Marc L., Kim M. Contractor, Contemporary Homes Ltd., Gainesville, Fla., 1947-67; faculty U. Fla., Gainesville, 1955-67; prof. Bradley U., Peoria, Ill., 1967-71, Clemson (S.C.) U., 1971-74; prof., chmn. dept. constrn. Fla. Internat. U., Miami, 1975—. Served with USMC, 1942-45. Decorated Purple Heart. Mem. Am. Inst. Constructors, Asso. Schs. Constrn. Home: 9633 SW 20th Terrace Miami FL 33165 Office: Dept Construction Florida International University Miami FL 33199

CLARK, JAMES STEVEN, veterinarian; b. Indpls., Oct. 11, 1942; s. James Shortridge and Frances Estelle (Harris) C.; D.V.M., Purdue U., 1966; children—Danielle Kathleen, Melissa Ellen, Leslie Suzanne. Intern, Meyers & Green, vets., Sheridan, Ind., 1966-67; pvt. vet. practice Brunswick, Ga., 1967—; dir. Sea Circus, 1974—. Mem. Am., Ga. vet. med. assns., C. of C., Phi Delta Theta. Office: 2719 Glynn Ave Brunswick GA 31520

CLARK, JOHN MARTIN, JR., research engr.; b. San Antonio, Oct. 5, 1916; s. John Martin and Dorothy (Hilgers) C.; B.M.E., Rice Inst., Tech., 1940, M.S., Mass. Inst. Tech., 1941; m. Mary Frances Dittmar, Aug. 23, 1941 (div. July 1975); children—Anne Clark Johnson, Marsha Clark Page, John Martin; m. 2d, Betty Jean Talley Shwiff, Aug. 26, 1976; stepchildren—Danean Flurry Brody, Brad Flurry, Denise Flurry. Powerplant designer, test engr. Douglas Aircraft, Santa Monica, Calif., 1941-47; pres. John Clark Industries, San Marcos, Tex., 1947-55; sr. research engr. S.W. Research Inst., San Antonio, 1955-58, dir. dept. automotive research, 1958—, tech. v.p., 1972-74, v.p., 1974—. Mem. Soc. Automotive Engrs., Sci. Research Soc. Am. Republican. Episcopalian. Contbr. articles to profl. jours.; author book on emergency driving techniques. Patentee in field. Home: 11103 Whisper Meadow San Antonio TX 78230 Office: 8500 Culebra Rd San Antonio TX 78206

CLARK, KARL BENTON, mgmt. cons. exec.; b. Coshocton, Ohio, Jan. 18, 1942; s. William Henderson and Suzanne (Bachert) C.; student Ohio Wesleyan U., 1960-62; A.A.S., Capital Inst. Tech., 1965; postgrad. U. Md., 1965; B.S. in Elec. Engring., U. South Fla., 1971, M.B.A., 1973; m. Pamela Jane Lombardi, Jan. 20, 1968; 1 dau., Karla Suzanne. Mgmt. asso. C & S Nat. Bank, Atlanta, 1973; support services supr. Dade County Public Schs., Miami, Fla., 1973-77; dir. planning and analysis New Eng. Oyster House, Ft. Lauderdale, Fla., 1977; mgmt. cons Brisch, Birn & Partners Ft. Lauderdale, 1978; project dir. Sperry-Bocm, Tampa, Fla., 1979—. Mem. adv. bd. Nat. Tax Limitation Com., 1979; mem. adv. com. Am. Security Council, 1978. Served with U.S. Army, 1966-68. Mem. IEEE, Assn. M.B.A. Execs., Am. Inst. Banking, Gold Key, AAUP, AAAS, Fla. Engring. Soc., Am. Mgmt. Assn., Tau Beta Pi, Phi Kappa Phi, Omicron Delta Kappa, Beta Gamma Sigma, Sigma Phi Epsilon, Tau Alpha Pi. Republican. Methodist. Home: 10112 12th Way N 201 Saint Petersburg FL 33702 Office: 730 S Sterling Ave Tampa FL 33609

CLARK, LORRAINE HOWARD (MRS. BANKS WORTH CLARK), gerontologist; b. Knoxville, Tenn., Dec. 1, 1924; d. Thomas Oliver and Mary Agnes (Smith) Howard; B.A., Duke U., 1948; M.S., East Tex. State U., 1966, Ph.D. (Teaching fellow), 1969; m. Banks Worth Clark, Sept. 4, 1943; children—Banks Jefferson, Roderic Howard, Victoria Jean. Adminstrv. dir. Bur. Testing and Guidance, Duke U., 1948-50; girl's Work sec. Cone Meml. YMCA, Greensboro, N.C., 1950-52; adj. prof. edn. research and counseling East Tex. State U., Dallas, 1968—; cons. adult edn., 1967—, preretirement edn., 1969—. Pres., W.E. Truax Scholarship Found., 1971, 74. Mem. Am. (chmn. com. on aging 1975-77), Tex. (chmn. commn. on middle age and aging 1975-77) personnel and guidance assns., Adult Edn. Assn. (sec. sect. on aging 1977-78, regional rep. 1977-79), Am. Psychol. Assn., Gerontol. Soc., Nat. Ret. Tchrs. Assn. (asst. area rep. 1972—). Research in life-styles ret. tchrs., needs older Ams., psychophysiol. aspects of empathy. Home: 5338 Drane St Dallas TX 75209

CLARK, MARK ANDREW, mfg. co. exec.; b. Leary, Ga., Mar. 4, 1951; s. Mark Andrew and Annie (George) C.; B.A. in Math., Carleton Coll., 1973; m. Ada King, June 28, 1975; 1 dau., Melise. Warehouse ops. mgr. Procter & Gamble, Albany, Ga., 1973-75, indsl. engr., 1975-77, warehouse dept. mgr., 1977-78, employee relations dept. mgr., 1978-80, personnel mgr., 1980—. Mem. Dougherty County Aviation Commn., 1978—; sect. head Ga. Heart Assn., 1975—; dist. capt. United Way Campaign, 1976—; bd. dirs. Carleton Coll., 1980—. Recipient several awards. Mormon. Home: 1713 Pine Knoll Ln Albany GA 31707 Office: PO Box 1747 Albany GA 31702

CLARK, MARVIN RAY, desk mfg. co. exec.; b. Brownfield, Tex., Dec. 6, 1942; s. Theodore Roosevelt and Lola Carmen (Wyly) C.; B.A. in English and Math., U. Houston, 1967; m. Carol Ann Little, Nov. 19, 1966; children—Tonya Michelle, Tammy Renee. Prodn. planner Larkin div. Joy Mfg. Co., Waxachachie, Tex., 1967-70, supr. data processing, 1970-72, mgr. systems and data processing Deco div., Colorado Springs, Colo., 1973-75; mgr. mgmt. info. systems Am. Desk Mfg. Co., Temple, Tex., 1975—. Active 1st Baptist Ch., Temple. Mem. Data Processing Mgmt. Assn. (internat. dir. 1978—). Home: 206 Ruggles St Temple TX 76501 Office: PO Box 429 Temple TX 76501

CLARK, MELVIN EUGENE, chem. co. exec.; b. Ord, Nebr., Oct. 2, 1916; s. Ansel B. and Ruth J. (Bullock) C.; B.S. in Chem. Engring., U. Colo., 1937; postgrad. Columbia U., 1952; Harvard U., 1961; m. Virginia M. Hiller, Sept. 16, 1938; children—John Robert, Walter Clayton, Dale Eugene, Merry Sue. Asst. editor McGraw-Hill Pub. Co., N.Y.C., 1937-41; chief program br., chem. bur. War Prodn. Bd., Washington, 1941-44; mgr. alkali sales Wayandotte Chem. Corp. (Mich.), 1944-53; v.p. mktg. Frontier Chem. Co. div. Vulcan Materials Co., Wichita, Kans., 1953-65, asst. gen. mgr., v.p. chem. div., 1965-69, exec. v.p. chem. div., 1969—, Birmingham, Ala., 1975—. Mem. Chem. Mktg. Research Assn. (Man of Year 1962), Am. Inst. Chem. Engrs., Chlorine Inst. (dir., officer). Republican. Mem. Christian Ch. Clubs: Inverness Country, Wichita Country, Relay House. Contbr. articles to tech. jours. Home: 3200 Kiltie Ln Birmingham AL 35243 Office: PO Box 7689 Birmingham AL 35223

CLARK, PHILIP HART, urban and regional planner; b. Hartford, Conn., May 23, 1938; s. Raymond Gilbert and Phyllis Angeline (Hart) C.; B.Arch. (Univ. scholar, Gannett Found. scholar, United Aircraft Corp. scholar, Mellon fellow, Kellogg fellow), Cornell U., 1961, M.Regional Planning, 1968. Asst. project mgr. W. R. Grimshaw Co., Denver, 1964-65; project coordinator U. Pa., 1968-69; sr. planner County of Fairfax (Va.), 1969-72; urban planner Hellmuth, Obata & Kassabaum, architects, Washington, 1972-73; chief air transp. planning Met. Washington Council of Govts., 1973-77; urban planning cons., Reston, Va., 1977-78; with Gordian Assos., Washington, 1978-79; program mgr. base comprehensive planning USAF Engring. and Services Center, Tyndall AFB, Fla., 1979—; vis. lectr., George Washington U., 1975, Am. U., 1976-77, Air Force Inst. Tech., 1979-80; speaker aviation assn. meetings. Mem. Paul Hill Chorale, 1970-76. Served with USAF, 1961-64. Mem. Am. Inst. Cert. Planners, Am. Planning Assn., Urban Land Inst., Choral Arts Soc. Washington, Theta Chi. Home: 7517 Coleridge Rd Panama City FL 32401 Office: HQ AFESC/DEVC Tyndall AFB FL 32403

CLARK, REBA M., ednl. adminstr.; b. Marion County, Ala., Aug. 25, 1929; d. J. Morgan and Edna E. (Chastain) Mays; B.S. in Speech, U. Ala., Tuscaloosa, 1955, M.A. in Guidance, Counseling, 1962, Edn. Specialist in Guidance and Counseling, 1964; m. James R. Clark; children—Debra, Stanley. Tchr. Birmingham (Ala.) Bd. Edn., 1957-60, counselor, 1960-70; dir. guidance, counseling Vestavia Hills (Ala.) Bd. Edn., 1970-76, dir. instrn. and guidance, 1976—; mem. Am. U. curriculum devel. team, Egypt, summer 1979. Mem. NEA, Ala. Edn. Assn., Am., Ala. personnel and guidance assns., Am. Sch. Counselors Assn., Ala. Assn. Counselor Edn. and Supervision, Phi Delta Kappa, Kappa Delta Pi. Recipient Distinguished Service award Ala. Personnel and Guidance Assn., 1974. Certified psychometrist, Ala. Home: 3215 Cornwall Dr Birmingham AL 35226 Office: 1204 Montgomery Hwy Vestavia Hills AL 35216

CLARK, RICHARD, wholesale swimming pool equipment co. exec.; b. Tampa, Fla., Aug. 20, 1927; s. Charles C. and Rhetta (Lang) C.; student Fla. Mil. Acad., St. Petersburg; grad. Royal Sch. Work Study, Portsmouth, Eng., 1950; m. Patricia Anne Gay, Sept. 23, 1966; 1 dau., Gayle Margarite; children by previous marriage—Betty Jo, Sandra Jean, Beverly Ann. Served as enlisted man U.S. Navy, 1945-66; indsl. engr. Stanwick Corp., Norfolk, Va., 1966-67; photographer Meml. Hosp., Sarasota, Fla., 1967-68; office mgr. sales Esquire Pools, Sarasota, 1968-69; field engr. Ionics Inc., Boston, 1969-70; br. mgr. Nor-Cal Engring. Co., Sarasota, 1970-77; v.p. purchasing Outdoor World/Nor-Cal Distributing Co. Inc., Bradenton, Fla., 1977—. Recipient various mgmt. awards. Mem. Nat. Swimming Pool Inst., Am. Mgmt. Assn., C. of C. Republican. Club: Masons (New Orleans). Home: 4409 S Lockwoodridge Rd Sarasota FL 33581 Office: 1023 Manatee Ave W Suite 4_3 Bradenton FL 33505

CLARK, RICHARD JOE ALLERTON, ins. exec.; b. Toledo, Mar. 23, 1934; s. Melvin H. and Ruth Marion (Williams) C.; student Ohio Wesleyan U., 1952-54; B.A., B.S., Ohio No. U., 1956; m. Janet Ellen Wert, Dec. 17, 1955; children—Richard Lee, Katherine Elaine, Debra Leah, Linda Anne, Lorie June. Asst. personnel mgr. Union Carbide Corp., Columbia, Tenn., 1956-57; agt., asst. mgr. Combined Ins. Co. Am., Chgo., 1958-59; agt., adminstrv. asst., dist. sales mgr., adminstrv. sales mgr., field sales mgr. Allstate Ins. Cos., Midwestern U.S., 1959-73; v.p., officer Total Ins. Planning Systems, Calif., 1973-76; partner, officer Risk Mktg. Corp., Dallas, 1976—; pres., chmn. bd. dirs. various ins. agencies western U.S. Recipient various sales and mktg. awards. Mem. Ind. Ins. Agts., Sales and Mktg. Execs. of Dallas, Dallas C. of C. Republican. Club: Spring Park Racquet (dir.). Office: 4099 McEwen Rd Suite 200 Dallas TX 75234

CLARK, RICHARD LEE, radiologist; b. Mt. Vernon, N.Y., June 1, 1940; s. Kenneth Fenton and Gertrude Lathrop (Dezendorf) C.; B.A. magna cum laude, Oberlin Coll., 1962; M.D., Johns Hopkins U., 1966; m. Linda Lenore Horne, Aug. 27, 1963; children—Jonathan Kenneth, Jennifer Lee. Intern, U. Ky. Med. Center, Lexington, 1966-67; resident in radiology Johns Hopkins Hosp., Balt., 1967-70, chief resident, instr., 1970-71; asso. prof. radiology U. N.C., Chapel Hill, 1973—, dir. diagnostic radiol. research, 1973—, dir. div. gen. radiology, 1979—, advisor to med. class of 1981; cons. to Chief Med. Examiner, N.C., 1973—. Bd. dirs. Chapel Hill Chamber Players. Served with USPHS, 1971-73. Recipient Henry Strong Denison award Johns Hopkins U., 1965-66; faculty research grantee N.C., 1974-75; NIH research grantee, 1976-79, James Picker Found. scholar 1975-79. Diplomate Am. Bd. Radiology. Mem. Assn. Univ. Radiologists, Am. Coll. Radiology, Radiol. Soc. N.Am., N.C. Med. Soc., Johns Hopkins Med. Assn., Johns Hopkins U. Alumni Assn., Durham Orange County Med. Soc., Sigma Xi. Unitarian-Universalist. Clubs: Oberlin Alumni of N.C. (pres. 1975-77), Chapel Hill Music Tchrs. Contbr. numerous articles to profl. jours. Home: 994 Cleland Dr Chapel Hill NC 27514 Office: Dept Radiology U NC Sch Med Chapel Hill NC 27514

CLARK, RICHARD PATTERSON, physician; b. Eatontown, N.J., Jan. 28, 1946; s. John Simpson and Winifred Drake (Feurst) C.; B.S., Memphis State U., 1968; M.D., U. Tenn., 1972. Intern, Long Beach (Calif.) Hosp., 1972-73; emergency physician San Francisco Bay Area, 1973-75; gen. practice medicine, Telluride, Colo., 1977-78; resident in otolaryngology and maxillofacial surgery U. Tenn., Memphis, 1978—; instr. advanced emergency medicine Nat. Ski Patrol. Bd. dirs. Berkeley (Calif.) Free Clinic, 1973-75. Served as maj. Navajo Indian Health Service, USPHS, 1975-77. Diplomate Am. Bd. Family Practice. Mem. Am. Acad. Emergency Physicians (charter), Am. Acad. Family Physicians, Sigma Alpha Epsilon, Omicron Delta Kappa. Home: 224 Hawthorne St Memphis TN 38112

CLARK, ROY THOMAS, JR., educator; b. Lockhart, Tex., Feb. 22, 1922; s. Roy Thomas and Ada Louise (Masur) C.; B.S. in Chemistry, S.W. Tex. State Coll., 1947, M.A. in Chemistry, 1950; m. Lavanie Anne Busby, Jan. 3, 1948; 1 son, Thomas David. Commd. 2d lt. USAAF, 1943; advanced through grades to lt. col. USAF, 1966; various assignments U.S., 1943-59; project officer propulsion br. Agena div. Directorate Space Systems, Air Force Ballistic Missile Div., Los Angeles, 1959-60; chief propulsion sect., astrovehicle br. Agena div. Office Dep. Comdr. Satellite Systems, Space Systems Div., Los Angeles, 1960-61; asst. prof. chemistry USAF Acad., Colo., 1961-63, asso. prof., 1963-64; student Air Force Inst. Tech., Edn.-with-Industry Program, Aerojet Gen. Corp., Sacramento, 1964-65; project officer 6595th Aerospace Test Wing, Vandenberg AFB, Calif., 1965-66; chief Titan Launched Satellite Systems Office, 1966-69; ret., 1969; adminstrv. officer dept. chemistry U. Tex. at Austin, 1969—. Decorated Air medal, Air Force Commendation medal, Meritorious Service medal. Mem. Am. Chem. Soc. Episcopalian. Home: 7711 Shadyrock Dr Austin TX 78731

CLARK, STANLEY EUGENE, oil co. exec.; b. Baytown, Tex., Oct. 1, 1949; s. Arthur and Geneva C.; ed. Lee Coll., 1972; m. Gloria Jena Abraham, Jan. 18, 1976; children by previous marriage—Dianna, Stanley Eugene, Sherlyn, Kelvin. Chem. technician Exxon Co., Baytown, 1969-73, process technician, 1974-78, chem. technician, 1969—; real estate salesman Pyramid Corp., Houston, 1973-75; sales mgr. Universal Life Ins., Houston, 1975-76; sales mgr. Custom Carpet Cleaners, LaPorte, 1977—; now with Dupont Syngas Plant, Deer Park, Tex.; sales rep. Tex. Refinery Corp., Ft. Worth. Mem. Full Gospel Bus. Men's Fellowship Internat. Democrat. Baptist. Club: Blackwood Sportsman. Home: 1020 Dailey St Baytown TX 77520 Office: PO Box 681 LaPorte TX 77571

CLARK, THOMAS GATES, cons. forester, state legislator, b. Uniontown, Pa., May 10, 1920; s. Guy Moser and Mildred (Gates) C.; B.S., W.Va. U., 1942; M.F., U. Mich., 1946; postgrad. U. Miami, 1943—; m. Rhode Mildred Shortridge, Jan. 19, 1944; children—Conrad W., Timothy Ritner, Guy Alan, Bruce Shortridge, Daniel Quentin. With U.S. Forest Service, W.Va., Pa., Vt., Va., 1946-52; self-employed cons. forester, Morgantown, W.Va., 1953—; partner Arkley Forest Lands, 1965—; pres. Upper Elk Coal Corp., Elkins, W.Va., 1971—; sec.-treas. Krakrow Corp., oil and gas producers, 1974—; mem. W.Va. Ho. of Dels., 1979—. Served with A.C., USNR, 1942-45. Decorated D.F.C. Mem. Assn. Cons. Foresters (nat. pres. 1963-64), Soc. Am. Foresters, Forest Farmers Assn. (dir.), Wildlife Soc. Home: 436 Callen Ave Morgantown WV 26505 Office: 432 Callen Ave PO Box 1046 Morgantown WV 26505

CLARK, VERNON RAY, petroleum engr.; b. McPherson, Kans., May 5, 1932; s. Martin Joel and Laura (Wann) C.; student McPherson Coll., 1955-56; B.S., Kans. State U., 1959; m. Donna Marlene Alexander, May 5, 1955; children—Kyanna Kay, Kevin Ray, Keith Warren, Kayla Ann. Asso. engr. Nortronics Inc., Hawthorne, Calif., 1959-61; design engr. Gen. Dynamics Astronautics, Salina, Kans., 1961-62; sr. engr. Chrysler Space Div., Huntsville, Ala., 1962-65; project engr. Applied Automation, Bartlesville, Okla., 1965—. Served with AUS, 1953-55. Registered profl. engr., Ala. Mem. Kesed Ch. (deacon 1977—). Research, devel. latest state-of-the art computerized process control systems. Patentee in field. Home: 3308 Nowata Rd Bartlesville OK 74003 Office: 221C RB2 PRC Pawhuska Rd Bartlesville OK 74003

CLARK, WESLEY GLEASON, educator; b. Wadsworth, Ohio, July 1, 1933; s. Alfred William and Mary June (Starn) C.; B.A., U. Colo., 1955, M.S., 1958; Ph.D. (USPHS predoctoral research fellow 1958-61, USPHS trainee 1961-62), U. Utah, 1962; m. Yvonne Lee Stanfield, Apr. 16, 1965; children—David Lee, Rebecca Lynne, Roger Dale. Instr., U. Tex. Southwestern Med. Sch., Dallas, 1962-63, asst. prof., 1963-72, asso. prof. pharmacology, 1972—. NIH research grantee USPHS, 1964-66, 70—. Mem. AAAS, Am. Soc. Pharmacology and Exptl. Therapeutics, Soc. Exptl. Biology and Medicine, Soc. for Neurosci., N.Y. Acad. Scis., Am. Physiol. Soc., Phi Lambda Upsilon. Home: 1334 Carriage Dr Irving TX 75062 Office: 5323 Harry Hines Blvd Dallas TX 75235

CLARK, WILLIAM DALLAS, physician; b. Waynesville, N.C., May 5, 1943; s. Grover Cleveland and Bonnie (Morrow) C.; B.S., U. N.C., Chapel Hill, 1965; M.D., N.C. Sch. Medicine, 1969; m. Linda G. Adams, Apr. 14, 1979. Intern, N.C. Meml. Hosp., Chapel Hill, 1969-70, resident in pathology 1970-71; resident in pathology Med. Coll. Va., Richmond, 1973-75; mem. faculty surg. pathology M.D. Anderson Hosp., Houston, 1976; pres. Physicians Lab. Service, Inc., Franklin, N.C., 1977—. Diplomate Am. Bd. Pathology. Fellow Coll. Am. Pathologist; mem. Am. Soc. Clin. Pathology. Democrat. Baptist. Clubs: Rotary, Mason. Home: 150 Porter St Franklin NC 27834 Office: Profl Bldg Oak St Franklin NC 28734

CLARK, WILLIAM HENRY, III, lawyer; b. Dallas, Dec. 11, 1930; s. William Henry Clark Jr. and Martha Mildred (Harral) C.; B.A., U. Tex., 1952, LL.B., 1955; m. Anne Kerby Williams, Jan. 28, 1955; children—Kimberly Ann, William H. IV, James Littlefield. Admitted to Tex. bar, 1955, U.S. Supreme Ct. bar; asst. atty. gen. State of Tex., 1955-56; mem. firm Clark, West, Keller, Sanders & Butler, Dallas, 1956—. Trustee Greenhill Sch., Dallas, 1972-75; chmn. bd. Dallas County Cerebral Palsy Assn., 1962-64; chmn. Dallas County Democratic Exec. Com, 1963-66, State Dem. Exec. Com., 1966-70. Mem. Tex., Dallas bar assns., Phi Delta Theta. Methodist. Clubs: City of Dallas, Brookhollow Golf, Dallas Petroleum. Home: 6116 Westwick St Dallas TX 75205 Office: 4949 First Internat Bldg Dallas TX 75270

CLARK, WILLIAM KEMP, physician, educator; b. Dallas, Sept. 2, 1925; s. James and Florine (Kemp) C.; B.A., U. Tex., 1945, M.D., 1948; m. Fern Blair, Mar. 30, 1952; children—Elizabeth, Sarah, Florine, Blair, Peter, Jonathan. Intern, Ind. U., 1948-49; resident Neurol. Inst. N.Y., 1953-56; practice medicine specializing in neurosurgery, Dallas, 1956—; prof. div. neurosurgery Southwestern Med. Sch., Dallas, 1956—; dir. neurosurg. service Parkland Meml., Children's Med. Center hosps., 1956—; cons. VA Hosp., 1956—, St. Paul Hosp., 1960—; nat. cons. surgeon gen. U.S. Navy, 1977—; mem. nat. adv. council for neurol. surgery VA, 1974—; mem. Linz Award Com., 1972; mem. Am. Bd. Med. Specialists, 1972—; mem. Residency Rev. Com. for Neurol. Surgery, 1972-78, chmn., 1978—. Mem. lay adv. bd. St. Michael's Sch., Dallas, 1973—. Bd. dirs. Tex. div. Am. Cancer Soc. Served to capt. USAF, 1950-52. Diplomate Am. Bd. Neurol. Surgery (mem. bd., sec. 1972-74, chmn. 1974-78). Mem. Soc. Neurol. Surgeons (sec. 1979—), Am. Assn. Neurol. Surgeons (bd. dirs. 1978—), Am. Neurol. Assn. Clubs: Brookhollow Golf, City (Dallas). Home: 3909 Euclid St Dallas TX 75205 Office: 5323 Harry Hines Dallas TX 75235

CLARK, YVONNE DIANE, retail store exec.; b. Monroe, Ga., Oct. 23, 1947; d. Troy Edward and Betty Ernestine Dotson; Asso. in Bus., Truett McConnell Coll., 1967; B.S., Presbyn. Coll., 1969; m. Michael L. Clark, Sept. 25, 1976. Staff accountant Carborundum Co., Niagara Falls, N.Y., 1969-71, supr. accounting, 1971-73; staff asst. to controller Rich's Dept. Stores div. Federated Dept. Stores, Atlanta, 1973-74, mgr. credit authorization, 1974-76, mgr. accounts receivable, 1976-78, mgr. corp. customer services, 1978—. Home: 4198 Oak Crest Dr Tucker GA 30084 Office: Rich's Dept Stores PO Box 4539 Atlanta GA 30302

CLARKE, ANN NEISTADT, environ. engr.; b. Phila., July 27, 1946; d. Donald B. and Besse (Levinson) Neistadt; B.S., Drexel U., 1968; M.A. in Chemistry, Johns Hopkins U., 1970, M.A. in Geology, 1971; Ph.D. in Chemistry, Vanderbilt U., 1975; m. James Harold Clarke, June 18, 1972. Chemist, U.S. Dept. Agr., Wyndmoor, Pa., 1964-68; cons. engr. Sheppard T. Powell Assos., Balt., 1971-72; reseach asst. prof. Center Environ. Quality Mgmt., Vanderbilt U., Nashville, 1974—, asst. prof. environ. and water resources engring., 1975—; project mgr. Resources Mgmt. div. AWARE, Inc., Nashville, 1977—. Blum scholar, Lindbach scholar, 1962-68; Gilman fellow, 1968-70. Mem. Water Pollution Control Fedn., Am. Chem. Soc., ASTM, Sigma Xi. Home: 1109 Twin Springs Dr Brentwood TN 37027 Office: AWARE Inc PO Box 40284 Nashville TN 37204

CLARKE, ANNE GREER, educator; b. Asheville, N.C., May 6, 1920; d. Allen M. and Betty H. Greer; student Livingston Coll., 1935-38, Atlanta U., 1942, 45, Cin. U., 1951; A.B., N.Y. U., 1961; grad. Columbus Coll., 1977; m. Morris Clarke, Jan. 4, 1942; children—Morris Otis, George Allen, Betty Anne Clark Tinsley. Tchr. Talbatton (Ga.) High Sch., 1941-43, Eddy High Sch., Milledgeville, Ga., 1943-45, Carver High Sch., Milledgeville, 1945-46, Risley High Sch., Brunswick, Ga., 1946-47, Carver High Sch., Douglas, Ga., 1947-50, Fifth Ave. Pub. Schs., Columbus, Ga., 1950-52, Davis Elementary Sch., Columbus, 1952-67, Winterfield Elem. Sch., Columbus, 1968-79. Mem. Democratic Com. Recipient various certificates and plaques in field; also Outstanding tchr. award Winterfield Sch., 1979. Mem. NEA, Ga. Assn. Educators, Muscogee Edn. Assn., AAUW, Delta Sigma Theta. Presbyterian. Clubs: Woodmen; Matrons, Phi Beta Sigma Shadows. Home: 1483 Brazie Ave Columbus GA 31903

CLARKE, CLIFFORD MONTREVILLE, assn. exec.; b. Ludowici, Ga., July 20, 1925; s. Clifford Montreville and Lella Bertrue (Hightower) C.; A.B. in Polit. Sci., Emory U., 1951. Radio engr., announcer Sta. WSAV, Savannah, 1941-43; pub. relations dir. Dept. Ga., Am. Legion, 1945-47; instr. Armstrong Coll., Savannah, 1947-48; asst. supt. Savannah Park and Tree Commn., 1951; instr., then supr. tng. dept. Lockheed Aircraft Corp., Marietta, Ga., 1951-52, mgr. employee services dept., 1952-53; exec. v.p. Asso. Industries, Ga., 1953-67; pres. Ga. Bus. and Industry Assn., 1968-73; exec. dir. Bicentennial Council Thirteen Original States, 1973-74; pres. Arthritis Found., Atlanta, 1975—; mem. Am. Soc. Assn. Execs., 1955—, bd. dirs., 1958-67, mem. exec. com., 1960-67, treas., 1962-64, sr. v.p., 1964-65, pres., 1965-66; pres. Ga. Soc. Assn. Execs., 1958-60; v.p., chmn. state group Nat. Indsl. Council, 1966-68; mem. Ga. Urban and Tchr. Assistance Adv. Council, 1965-68, Ga. Intergovtl. Relations Commn., 1966; mem. Ga. Ednl. Improvement Council, 1964-69, chmn., 1967-69; mem. Forward Ga. Commn., 1969-72, Ga. Commn. for Nat. Bicentennial Celebration, 1969-73, chmn., 1973-74; chmn. Chartered Assn. Exec. Chartering Bd., 1969-73; exec. com. Conf. State Mfrs. Assns., 1969-73. Bd. dirs. Atlanta Conv. Bur., 1968-72; mem. policy com. Grad. Sch. Bus., U. Ga., 1968-72; adv. bd. Ga. Vocat. Rehab., 1962-68; bd. dirs. Arthritis Found. Ga., 1965-71, Atlanta Community Services to Blind, 1965-72, Coop. Services for Blind, 1962-70, Atlanta Sch. Art. Served with inf. AUS, World War II. Decorated Purple Heart with 2 oak leaf clusters. Home: 2 Lullwater Pl NE Atlanta GA 30307 Office: 3400 Peachtree Rd NE Suite 1100 Atlanta GA 30326

CLARKE, JACK WELLS, corp. exec.; b. Abingdon, Va., June 26, 1914; s. James Sydnor and Ottie B. (Wells) C.; A.B., Williams Coll., 1935; postgrad. N.Y. U., 1935-37; grad. Real Estate Inst. La., 1971; m. Dorothy Irelan, Mar. 24, 1938. Bond analyst, statistician, N.Y.C., 1935-37; asst., later mgr., budget and statis. dept. Lion Oil Co., 1938-41, asst. to pres., asst. to chmn. bd., 1947-51; dir. pub. relations Tex. Eastern Transmission Corp., 1951-55; exec. v.p. Freestate Indsl. Devel. Co., 1955-56, pres., dir., 1956-68; pres., dir. North Shreveport Devel. Co., 1956-68; now ind. investor developer. Dir. Holiday in Dixie. Past chmn. Caddo Parish Dem. Assn. Served from ensign to lt. USNR, 1942-45. Mem. Shreveport C. of C., Am. Ordnance Assn., Urban Land Inst., Pub. Affairs Research Council La., Navy League, Am. Indsl. Devel. Council, Shreveport Com. of 100, Internat. Council Shopping Centers, Ret. Officers Assn., Phi Delta Theta. Episcopalian. Clubs: Shreveport, Shreveport Country (La.); El Dorado Country (Indian Wells, Calif.). Home: 708 Azelea Dr Shreveport LA 71106 Office: PO Box 6 Shreveport LA 71161

CLARKE, JESSE EDWARD, engring. corp. exec.; b. Louisville, Aug. 3, 1914; s. Edward Hokar and Jesse (Miles) C.; student U. Louisville, 1936; m. Marie Dorothy Kornacki, Jan. 1, 1946; children—Richard S., Virginia L. Clarke Betts, Betty J. Clarke Shultz, David E., Philip J., Rose M. Clarke Harbour, Bonnie M. Clarke Kingsbury, Deborah Clarke del Junco. Supr. elec. power wiring Jeffersonville Boat Works, 1941-43; tech. sales and service Rotating Parts Co., 1945-46, v.p., 1946-47; pres. Autoquip Corp., 1948—, chmn. bd., 1970—. Mem. Nat. Right to Work Com. Served as pvt. USMC, 1943-45. Mem. AIM (mem. pres.'s council), Ill. C. of C., U.S. C. of C., Nat. Mfrs. Assn., Chgo. Commerce Assn. Patentee in field. Home: 1276 Laurel Ct Marco Island FL 33937 Office: 2872 Davis Blvd Naples FL 33940

CLARKSON, CHARLES ANDREW, real estate investment exec.; b. Grove City, Pa., Sept. 1, 1945; s. Harold William and Jean Henrietta (Jaxtheimer) C.; A.B., Princeton U., 1967; J.D., George Washington U., 1972; m. Patricia Holt, June 14, 1969; children—Thomas Byerly, Blair Elizabeth. Real estate negotiator Safeway Stores, Washington, 1968-69; mortgage banker J.W. Rouse Co., Washington, 1970-73; pres. Alex Brown Realty, Balt., 1973-76; founder, pres. Charles A. Clarkson, Inc., Balt. and Jacksonville, Fla., 1976—. Clubs: Sawgrass, River. Home: 5201 Atlantic Blvd Jacksonville FL 32207 Office: 3205 Independent Sq Jacksonville FL 32202

CLARKSON, LAWRENCE WILLIAM, aircraft co. exec.; b. Grove City, Pa., Apr. 29, 1938; s. Harold William and Jean Henrietta (Jaxtheimer) C.; A.B., DePauw U., 1960; J.D., U. Fla., 1962; m. Barbara Louise Stevenson, Aug. 20, 1960; children—Michael, Elizabeth, Jennifer. Admitted to Fla. bar, 1963; mem. firm, Caldwell, Pacetti, Barrow, Palm Beach, Fla., 1965-67; dept. counsel Pratt & Whitney Aircraft, Fla. Research and Devel. Center, West Palm Beach, 1967-69, mgr. contract adminstrn., 1969-72, program mgr. F100/F401 Engine Program, 1972-74, F100/F-16 engine program dir., 1974-75, mng. dir. NATO F100 program, 1975-77, v.p. internat., 1977; v.p. United Technologies (Europe), 1975—; asst. sec. United Aircraft, 1971-75; v.p. mktg. Pratt & Whitney Aircraft, govt. products div., West Palm Beach, 1978—. Musical dir. North County Choral Soc., 1968-74; mem. nat. council Met. Opera. Mgr., Leroy Collins campaign U.S. Senate, Palm Beach County, 1968; mem. Palm Beach County Democratic Exec. Com., 1967-68; town counsel, Town of Haverhill, Fla., 1968-72, pres. town counsel, 1971-72, judge, 1970-72. Bd. dirs. Palm Beach County Goodwill Industries, 1966-68, Palm Beach County chpt. Am. Cancer Soc.; chmn. Palm Beach County Cancer Crusade, 1973-74. Served to capt. USAF, 1962-66. Mem. Am. Bar Assn., Fla. Bar, Am. Judicature Soc., Phi Delta Phi, Delta Chi, Phi Mu Alpha. Episcopalian (vestryman). Clubs: LaCoquille (Palm Beach, Fla.); Cercle des Nations. Home: 272 Via Marila Palm Beach FL 33480 Office: Box 2691 West Palm Beach FL 33402

CLAUSER, MICHAEL CHARLES, educator; b. Detroit, Apr. 19, 1944; s. Robert Charles and Lillian Elaine (Thompson) C.; B.S.D., U. Mich., 1967, M.A., M.F.A. (Rackham grantee, 1973, Rackham fellow, 1973-74), 1974; m. Christine A. Momet, Oct. 28, 1977. Art dir. Donald Landy Advt., Inc., Southfield, Mich., 1969-72; asst. prof. art U. Tenn., Knoxville, 1974—; dir. Headlights Studio, Knoxville; design cons. Tau Beta Pi. Video tape grantee dept. art, U. Tenn., 1978. Mem. AAUP, Indsl. Graphics Internat. (award of appreciation, 1978). Designer trademark dept. of art U. Tenn. Home: 2515 S Haven St Knoxville TN 37920 Office: 927 Volunteer Blvd Knoxville TN 37916

CLAUSTRO, LUDGERIO ZABALA, physician; b. Philippines, Dec. 16, 1940; came to U.S., 1968; s. Luis B. and Cladia Z. Claustro; A.A., Ateneo de Manila (Philippines), 1961; M.D., U. Santo Tomas (Manila), 1966; m. Minda Pacifico, Mar. 1, 1969; children—Alvin, Ricky, Loreto. Intern, South Side Hosp., Pitts., 1968-69; resident, Hamot Med. Center, Erie, Pa., 1969-72; med. staff Mattie Williams Hosp., Richlands, Va., 1973-79; active staff Clinch Valley Community Hosp., Richlands, 1979—; practice family medicine, SW Va. Med. Center, Cedar Bluff, 1979—. Mem. Richlands Investment Group. Diplomate Am. Bd. Family Practice. Fellow Am. Acad. Family Practice; mem. Va. Acad. Family Practice (Highland chpt.), Va. Med. Soc., Tazewell County Med. Assn., SW Va. Assn. Philippine Practitioners Am. (co-organizer), Richlands C. of C. Co-author papers in field. Office: PO Box 37 Cedar Valley Dr Cedar Bluff VA 24609

CLAWSON, HARRY QUINTARD MOORE, bus. exec.; b. N.Y.C., Aug. 8, 1924; s. Harry Marshall and Marguerite H. (Burgoyne) C.; grad. Staunton Mil. Acad., 1943; student N.Y. U., 1951-52, New Sch. for Social Research, 1953; m. (div. June 1964); m. 2d, Annemarie Korntner Thinnes, Dec. 1967. Supr. transp. responsible adminstrn. and liaison with U.S. Army for ARC overseas, 1945-46; asst. to dir. personnel UNESCO, Paris, France, 1947; resident rep. Texas Co., Douala, French Cameroun, West Africa, 1948-50; asst. dir. overseas bus. service McGraw-Hill Pub. Co., 1951-58; dir. client service Internat. Research Assos., N.Y.C., 1958-61; v.p., sec., dir. Frasch Whiton Boats, Inc., gen. mgr. sailboat tng. facility; pres. Harry Q.M. Clawson & Co., Inc., 1961-76; dir. planning and adminstrn., splty. chems. div. Essex Chem. Corp., 1976—. Pres., Centre Island Assn., 1974-76. Chmn. planning bd. Village of Centre Island (N.Y.). Served with inf., AUS, 1943-45, ETO. Decorated Bronze Star medal. Mem. Ex-Mems. Assn. Squadron A. Clubs: Seawanhaka Corinthian Yacht (Oyster Bay); N.Y. Yacht (N.Y.C). Contbr. articles to profl. jours. Home: 1 King St Charleston SC 29401

CLAY, HARRIS AUBREY, chem. engr.; b. Hartley, Tex., Dec. 28, 1911; s. John David and Alberta (Harris) C.; B.S., U. Tulsa, 1933; Ch.E., Columbia U., 1939; m. Violette Frances Mills, June 19, 1948 (dec. June 1972); m. 2d, Garvice Stuart Shotwell, Apr. 28, 1973. Pilot plant operator Phillips Petroleum Co., Burbank, Okla., 1939-42, resident supr. Burbank pilot plants, 1942-44, process design engr., Bartlesville, Okla., 1944-45, process engring. supr. Philtex Plant, Phillips, Tex., 1946-56, tech. adviser to pilot plant mgr., Bartlesville, 1957-61, chem. engring. asso., 1961-74; cons. engr., 1974—; chmn. tech. com. Fractionation Research, Inc., 1966-71, mem. tech. com., 1972-73. Fellow Am. Inst. Chem. Engrs.; mem. Am. Chem. Soc., Electrochem. Soc. Presbyterian. Clubs: Elks, Lions. Contbr. articles to profl. jours. Patentee in field. Home: 1723 Church Ct Bartlesville OK 74003

CLAY, ORSON C., ins. co. exec.; b. 1930; B.S., Brigham Young U., 1955; M.B.A., Harvard, 1959; married. Dir. econ. div. Continental Oil Co. Ltd., London, 1964, gen. mgr. adminstrn. and ops., 1965, asst. mgr. marine transp., N.Y.C., 1966-68; exec. asst. fin. Pennzoil United Inc., Houston, 1968-70; exec. v.p. fin., treas. Am. Nat. Ins. Co. Galveston, 1970-73, sr. exec. v.p., treas., 1973-77, pres., 1977—, pres., chief exec. officer, dir., 1978—; chmn., dir. Am. Nat. Life Ins. Co. Tex., Am. Nat. Property & Casualty, Standard Life & Accident Ins. Co., Am. Printing Co.; v.p., dir. Am. Nat. Real Estate Mgmt. Corp.; dir. Am. Nat. Income Fund, Commonwealth Life & Accident Ins. Co., Dillard Dept. Stores, Inc., Am. Nat. Growth Fund, Am. Nat. Bond Fund; dir., mem. exec. com. Securities Mgmt. & Research, Inc., Trans World Life Ins. Co. of N.Y. Trustee, mem. fin. com. William Temple

Found.; mem. investment adv. com. for permanent univ. fund U. Tex. System. Mem. Tex. Research League (dir.), Tex. Guaranty Assn. (dir.), Tex. Life Ins. Assn. (dir.). Served to lt. USMCR, 1955-57. Office: 1 Moody Plaza Galveston TX 77550

CLAY, WILLIAM CALDWELL, JR., lawyer, corp. exec.; b. Mt. Sterling, Ky., Dec. 28, 1915; s. William Caldwell and Kathryn (Greene) C.; A.B., Dartmouth, 1937; J.D., Yale, 1940; LL.D., Transylvania Coll., 1973; m. Esther Briggs, Apr. 13, 1946; children—Jeanette Dobbs, Sally Sue, Kathryn Caldwell. Admitted to Ky. bar, 1939, since practiced in Mt. Sterling and Lexington; with Anti-trust div. Dept. Justice, 1938-40; counsel pub. relations Burley Auction Warehouse Assn., 1946-56; chmn. bd. Exchange Bank of Ky.; v.p., dir. Mt. Sterling Broadcasting Co.; pres., dir. Ky. Pub. Co.; sec., dir. Cowden Enterprises, Inc., Top Yield Industries, Inc., Hwy. Concrete Pipe, Inc. Mem. bd. curators, mem. exec. com. Transylvania Coll. Mem. Am., Ky. bar assns., C. of C., Sigma Alpha Epsilon. Mem. Christian Ch. Clubs: Odd Fellows, Masons, Rotary. Author: Farmers Tax Manual, 1943; How to Read and Understand the Bible, 1974; The Dow Jones-Irwin Guide to Estate Planning, 1976; Estate Planning and Administration, 1977; How to Win Maximum Awards for Lost Earnings, 1980. Office: 50 Broadway Mount Sterling KY 40353

CLAYTON, BILLY WAYNE, state legislator Tex.; b. Olney, Tex., Sept. 11, 1928; s. William and Myrtle Clayton; B.S. in Agrl. Econs., Tex. A & M U., 1950; m. Delma Jean Dennis; children—Brenda Jean (Mrs. Chuck Smith), Thomas Wayne. Engaged in farming and ranching, Springlake, Tex., 1950—; exec. dir. Water, Inc., Lubbock, Tex., 1968-72; pres. Springlake Enterprises, Inc., Texhold, Inc.; mem. Tex. Ho. of Reps. from 74th Dist., 1962—, speaker of house, 1975—, chmn. aero. com., counties com., livestock com., interim water com., vice chmn. banks and banking com. Mem. W. Tex. adv. com. Water Devel. Bd.; chmn. Interstate Conf. Water Problems, 1973; exec. bd. W. Tex. Water Inst.; past chmn. exec. com. So. Environ. Resources Conf., 1973-74; chmn. intergovtl. relations com. Nat. Legis. Conf., 1973; mem. for Tex., Nat. Water Congress; chmn. Council of State Govts., 1978, also mem. exec. com.; chmn. exec. com. So. Legis. Conf., 1973-74, chmn., 1975-76; chmn. So. States Speakers Conf., 1975-76. Mem. adv. bd. Young Americans for Freedom; trustee High Plains Research Found. Named Outstanding Farmer in Lamb County, Hon. Water Well Digger; recipient Distinguished Service to People of Tex. award, 1967, Outstanding Service to Farmers in Lamb County award, Distinguished Service award Democratic Party Tex., commendation Tex. Water Rights Commn., Outstanding Service award in water conservation Ft. Worth Press Club, 1972, 1st award W. Tex. Water Inst., 1971; named May of Yr. in Service to Agr., Farmers mag., 1975; recipient Disting. Alumnus award Tex. A & M U., 1979. Mem. W. Tex. C. of C. (exec. com. water resources com.), W. Tex. Water Inst. (exec. bd.). Baptist (deacon). Club: Lions (past pres. Springlake). Home: PO Box 38 Springlake TX 79082 Office: PO Box 2910 Austin TX 78767

CLAYTON, JOHN MARK, drugs and cosmetics mfg. exec.; b. Kevil, Ky., Aug. 6, 1945; s. Hubert F. and Mary L. (Brooks) C.; B.S., Tenn. Tech. U., 1968; Ph.D., U. Tenn., 1971; m. Doris Jeffers, Aug. 14, 1970; children—Mark, Stephanie, Beth. Insts. Health predoctoral fellow, grad. research asst. U. Tenn. Med. Units, 1969-71; postdoctoral research asso. Pomona Coll., Claremont, Calif., 1971-72; research biologist FDA, Jefferson, Ark., 1972-73; asst. prof. drug design div. U. Tenn. Center Health Scis., 1974; clin. research asso. med. dept. Plough, Inc., Memphis, 1974-75, dir. clin. and regulatory services, 1975-78, v.p. quality control and clin. and regulatory services, 1978—; asst. prof. U. Ark. Med. Sch., 1972-74. Mem. Acad. Pharm. Scis., Am. Chem. Soc., AAAS, N.Y. Acad. Scis., Regulatory Affairs Profls. Soc., Am. Soc. Quality Control, Rho Chi. Methodist. Author: (with W.P. Purcell and G.E. Bass) Strategy of Drug Design: A Molecular Guide to Biological Activity, 1973; contbr. articles profl. jours. Home: 8657 Wine Leaf Cove Germantown TN 38138 Office: 3030 Jackson Ave Memphis TN 38151

CLAYTON, REBECCA KILGO, educator; b. Givhans, S.C., Sept. 25, 1916; d. Middleton Samuel and Catherine Rebecca (Green) Clayton; B.S., Coll. Charleston, 1944; M.A., U. Mich., 1959; postgrad. Pa. State U., The Citadel, U. N.C., U. S.C., LaVerne Coll., U. Ala. Elementary tchr., Dorchester County, S.C., 1939-43, Charleston County, S.C., 1944-53; tchr., prin. 1st Orthopedic Sch., Charleston, 1953-55; spl. tchr. U.S.Army Schs., Verdun, France, Frankfurt and Munich, Germany, 1955-59; tchr. class for retarded Mitchell Elementary Sch., Charleston, 1959-60; elementary tchr., spl. tchr., remedial instr. Panama Canal Co., Balboa, C.Z., 1960—; prin. migrant summer sch. program. Devotions chmn. Fellowship of the Concerned; jr. dept. pianist Balboa Union Ch., Pedregal Meth. Mission Ch. (Panama). Mem. NEA, Council Exceptional Children (treas. C.Z. br.), Internat. Reading Assn., Nat. League Am. Pen Women, Japan Internat. Christian Univ. Found. (women's com.), Nat. Trust Hist. Preservation, Nat. Hist. Soc., Internat. Soc. Artists, AAUW, Phi Delta Kappa. Club: Interam. Womens. Artist, works exhibited in galleries in C.Z. and Panama. Home: RFD Givhans Ridgeville SC 29472 Office: PSC Box 1117 APO Miami FL 34002

CLAYTON, ROBERT LOUIS, ednl. cons., clergyman; b. Pensacola, Fla., Feb. 25, 1934; A.B., Talladega Coll., 1955; B.D., Hood Sem., 1959; S.T.M., Interdenom. Theological Center, 1965; m. Minnie Harris, June 22, 1957; children—Robert Joel, III, Myrna Audenise. Ordained to ministry African Methodist Episcopal Zion Ch., 1955; coll. chaplain, chmn. dept. sociology Ala. A. and M. Coll., 1959-63; asso. minister Shaw Temple AME Zion Ch., Atlanta; instr., dir. publicity Interdenom. Theological Center, 1964-65; chmn. dept. sociology, placement dir. Livingstone Coll., 1965-68; coll. minister Spelman Coll., 1968-69; nat. dir. Black Coll. Placement Dirs., Atlanta, 1968-72; regional dir. Am. Coll. Testing Program, Atlanta, 1972-75, dir. spl. services, Atlanta, 1975—, dir. minority programs, 1976—; Danforth Found. Sem. Intern Dillard U., New Orleans, 1957-58; pres., exec. dir. C.E.S.H.E.P.; cons. Office Edn. Bd. dirs. W. J. Walls Found., N.Y.C.; 1st v.p. Concerned Citizens of S.W. Atlanta. Danforth Campus Ministers grantee, 1963-64. Mem. Am. Personnel, Guidance Assn., Am. Sch. Counselors Assn., Am. Coll. Pres. Assn., Assn. Measurement and Evaluation in Guidance, Assn. for Non-White Concerns in Personnel and Guidance (past pres.), Nat. Vocat. Guidance Assn., Nat. Assn. of Coll. and Univ. Chaplains, Alpha Phi Alpha. Democrat. Author: Counseling Non-White Students; contbr. numerous articles on counseling, minority student needs, career edn. to profl. jours. Home: 668 Waterford Rd NW Atlanta GA 30318 Office: 4480 Shallowford Rd Atlanta GA 30338

CLAYTON, RONNIE WAYNE, educator; b. Alexandria, La., Jan. 16, 1942; s. Harry D. and Anabell (Stracener) C.; B.A., La. Coll., 1964; M.A., Northwestern State U. La., 1968; Ph.D., La. State U., 1974; m. Sharon Ann Williams, June 2, 1967; children—Ronnie Wayne, Jonathan Randall, James William. History instr. La. Coll., Pineville, 1967-68, dean students, 1968-69; grad. asst. La. State U., Baton Rouge, 1969-74; chmn. div. social scis. Meridian (Miss.) Jr. Coll., 1975-78, history instr., 1974—; pres. Clayton Research Assos., Inc., Meridian, 1979—. Served with U.S. Army, 1960. Mem. Orgn. Am. Historians, Am. Hist. Assn., Acad. Polit. Sci., So. Hist. Assn., Miss. Hist. Assn., La. Hist. Assn., Greater Meridian C. of C., Phi Alpha Theta, Phi Delta Kappa. Democrat. Baptist. Club: Dimension 80. Home: 3714 40th Ave Meridian MS 39301 Office: 5500 Hwy 19 N Meridian MS 39301

CLAYTOR, JOANN IRWIN, psychologist; b. Pineville, Ky., July 24, 1934; d. Albert Austin and B. Carolyn (York) Irwin; diploma nursing Berea Coll., 1957, B.A., 1972; M.Ed., Okla. U., 1973, Ph.D., 1979; m. Robert B. Claytor, Aug. 19, 1956; children—Lynn, Suzanne. Nurse, Duke U. Med. Center, Durham, N.C., 1959-68; nursing supr. John Umstead Mental Health Center, Butner, N.C., 1958-59; dir. in-service Central Okla. Community Mental Health Center, Norman, Okla., 1975-77; instr. in-service edn. Spartanburg (S.C.) Gen. Hosp., 1968-70; psychologist, counseling center St. Andrews Presbyn. Coll., Laurinburg, N.C., 1978—. HEW fellow, 1973-74. Mem. AAUW (pres. 1979-80), Southeastern Psychol. Assn., N.C. Psychol. Assn., So. Coll. Personnel Assn., Am. Personnel and Guidance Assn., Council Exceptional Children, Phi Delta Kappa. Methodist. Home: 603 Graham Ct Laurinburg NC 28352 Office: Counseling Center St Andrews Presbyn Coll Laurinburg NC 28352

CLEARY, JOHN BENJAMIN, radio sta. exec.; b. Birmingham, Ala., July 15, 1953; s. John Leroy and Doris Ann (Whitley) C.; B.A. in Broadcast Journalism, Samford U., 1979. Newscaster, announcer, disc jockey Sta. WDJC-FM, Crawford Broadcasting Co., Birmingham, 1972-75, asst. program dir., music dir., 1975-77, program dir., 1979—; engr. Sta. WSGN, Birmingham, 1977-78; master of ceremonies various social functions. Mem. Aircraft Owners and Pilots Assn., Mensa, Gospel Music Assn., Alpha Phi Omega. Baptist. Club: Birmingham Press. Home: 733 G Sunhill Rd Birmingham AL 35215 Office: WDJC-FM PO Box 58021 Birmingham AL 35209

CLEEK, JO BEATRICE, educator; b. Gate City, Va., Dec. 20, 1926; d. Charles Robert and Esther Ernestine Tipton C.; B.S., E. Tenn. State U., 1964, Ed.D., 1976; M.S., U. Tenn., 1967. Clk., Agr. Stblzn. and Conservation Service, Gate City, 1945-61; extension home economist Va. Poly. Inst. Coop. Extension Service, Wise, 1964-66; human devel. specialist Fla. Coop. Extension Service, Gainesville, 1968-69; kindergarten tchr. Washington County Public Schs., Glade Springs, Va., 1969-71; asst. prof. edn. Clinch Valley Coll., U. Va., Wise, 1974—; cons. Head Start, 1972-73, 79, Scott County Vocat. Center Day Care, Buchanan County Elem. Sch. Psychomotor Program, 1978-80. E. Tenn. State U. doctoral fellow, 1971-74. Mem. Am. Home Econs. Assn., NEA, Nat. Assn. Edn. Young Children, AAUP, Phi Delta Kappa. Home and Office: PO Box 1082 Clinch Valley Coll Wise VA 24293

CLELAND, DAVID HILL, state ofcl.; b. Charleston, W.Va., Oct. 14, 1929; s. Ronald Stewart and Dorothy Catherine (Leslie) C.; student Ga. Inst. Tech., 1948; A.B. in Econs., Morris Harvey Coll., 1951; M.A. in Social Service Adminstrn., U. Chgo., 1955; m. Lois Ann Andrews, Sept. 10, 1954; children—Eudora Catherine, Ann Carden, Robert Carl Andrews. Asst. exec. dir. United Fund of Kanawha Valley, Charleston, W.Va., 1956-60; exec. dir. Kanawha-Clay chpt. ARC, Charleston, 1960-64; asst. exec. dir. Action for Appalachian Youth, Charleston, 1964-67; asst. chief casework services W.Va. Div. Vocat. Rehab., Charleston, 1965—; del. dir. Nat. Mental Health Assn., Alexandria, Va., 1979—; dir. Eastern Area Alcoholism Edn. and Tng., Bloomfield, Conn., 1974—; pres., W.Va. Welfare Conf., Charleston, 1960-62. Mem. Kanawha County Planning and Zoning Commn., Charleston, 1961-70. Mem. Assn. Cert. Social Workers, Nat. Assn. Social Workers, Nat. Rehab. Adminstrs. Assn. (profl. mem.), Internat. Assn. Psycho-Social Rehab. Programs, Sigma Nu. Democrat. Presbyterian. Clubs: Univ. (Charleston); Lake Chaweva. Home: 2410 Kanawha Blvd E Charleston WV 25311 Office: P & P Bldg State Capitol Charleston WV 25305

CLEM, HOWARD DOUGLAS, JR., hosp. ofcl.; b. Chambers County, Ala., Mar. 23, 1954; s. Howard Douglas and Billie Jeanne (Williams) C.; B.S. in Bus. Adminstrn. (Nat. Merit Scholar), Auburn U., 1972. With George H. Lanier Meml. Hosp., Langdale, Ala., 1968-70, supr. environ. sers. dept., 1972-76, asst. dir. dept., 1976-78, dir. central supply, 1978-79, dir. material services, 1979—; final product insp. Langdale div. West Point Pepperell, 1970-72; asst. dir. environ. sers. dept. Jackson Hosp., Montgomery, Ala., 1976. Mem. Am. Soc. for Hosp. Central Service Personnel, Am. Soc. for Hosp. Purchasing and Materials Mgrs., Ala. Soc. for Hosp. Purchasing and Materials Mgrs. Baptist. Club: Kiwanis. Home: Route 3 Box 176 Lanett AL 36863 Office: George H Lanier Meml Hosp 4800 48th St Langdale AL 36864

CLEMENT, JOHN ROBERTS, psychologist; b. Roanoke, Va., May 14, 1950; s. John Roop and Jacqueline Irene (Aldworth) C.; B.A. in Psychology, U. S.C., 1972; M.A. with honors in Psychology, West Ga. Coll., 1977. Group leader Village System Pilot Project, William S. Hall Psychiat. Inst., Columbia, S.C., 1972-75; grad. asst. psychology W. Ga. Coll., 1976; psychologist Blue Ridge Community Mental Health Center, Asheville, N.C., 1977—; coordinator psychiat. inpatient services St. Joseph's Hosp.; cons. instr. allied health services Mountain Area Health Edn. Center of U. N.C.-Chapel Hill Med. Sch.; pvt. practice cons. psychology. Recipient cert. of Recognition Highland Acad. Soc., 1979; lic. psychol. examiner, N.C. Mem. Am. Mental Health Counselors Assn., Assn. Humanistic Psychologists, Assn. Humanistic Edn., Ga. Psychol. Assn., N.C. Mental Health Counselors Assn., Phi Kappa Sigma. Home: 148 Spooks Branch Rd Asheville NC 28804 Office: 356 Biltmore Ave Asheville NC 28801

CLEMENTS, B. GILL, corp. exec.; b. 1941; B.B.A., So. Meth. U., 1963; married. Loan officer 1st Nat. Bank Dallas, 1963-68; treas. Sedco Inc., Dallas, 1968-73, pres., 1973—, chief exec. officer, 1973-77, also dir. Office: Sedco Inc 1901 N Akard St Dallas TX 75201*

CLEMENTS, JAMES DAVID, retardation center exec.; b. Pineview, Ga., May 7, 1931; s. Marcus Monroe and Dewey Thelma (Gammage) C.; B.A., Emory U., 1952; M.D., Med. Coll. Ga., 1956; m. Janet Collier Swan, Aug. 25, 1952; children—Leiliar Ann, David Marcus. Intern, Temple U. Med. Sch., Phila., 1956-57, resident pediatrics, 1957-59; fellow in mental retardation Yale, 1959-60; med. dir. Gracewood (Ga.) State Sch., Hosp., 1960-63, asst. supt., 1963-64; dir. Ga. Planning for Mental Retardation, 1964-65; asst. clin. prof. pediatrics and psychiatry Emory U., Atlanta, 1964; asso. clin. prof. neurology and pediatrics Med. Coll. Ga. Augusta, 1970; mem. Pres.'s Com. on Mental Retardation; mem. council on mental retardation and other developmental disabilities Joint Commn. on Accreditation Hosps.; state med. cons. in mental retardation State of Ga., 1979—; asst. med. dir. div. mental health and mental retardation Ga. Dept. Human Resources, 1980—. Mem. adv. bd. Arbor Acad., De Kalb County Dept. Edn., 1973—; trustee Gatchell Sch., 1969, Mental Health Law Project. Fellow Am. Geriatrics Soc., Pan Am. Med. Assn., Am. Acad. Pediatrics; mem. Am. Assn. Mental Deficiency (pres. 1974-75, Leadership award 1980), Am. Bar Assn. (commn. on mental disabilities 1977—), Nat. Assn. Retarded Citizens (legal adv. com. 1975—), Ga. Pediatric Soc., Nat. Assn. Supts. Pub. Residential Facilities for Mentally Retarded. Contbr. articles to profl. jours. Home: 1247 Mt Vernon Rd Dunwoody GA 30338 Office: 4770 N Peachtree Rd Chamblee GA 30341 also 2 World Trade Center New York NY 10047

CLEMENTS, SAM ALLEN, JR., wholesale co. exec.; b. Harrisburg, Ark., May 11, 1903; s. Sam A. and Annie Elizabeth (Akin) C.; student Bus. Coll., Memphis, 1922-23; m. Gladys Mayes Baldwin, Aug. 21, 1941. Asst. mgr., Ford dealership, Harrisburg, 1925-33; in cotton gin mgmt., 1935-41; partner cotton gin, 1942-44; asst. mgr. several cotton gins, 1944-45; with Lummus Cotton Gin Co., 1945-47; owner, pres. Sam Clements buying, selling cotton gin machinery, West Memphis, Ark., 1947—. Mem. So. Cotton Ginners Assn., Tex. Cotton Ginners Assn. Presbyterian. Home and Office: 216 W Barton St West Memphis AR 72301

CLEMENTS, WILLIAM P., JR., gov. Tex.; b. Dallas, Apr. 13, 1917; grad. So. Meth. U., 1937; m. Rita Clements; 2 children. Former oil field worker and driller on drilling rigs; founder SEDCO, Inc., 1947; dep. sec. Dept. Def., Washington, 1973-77, also past mem. Blue Ribbon Def. Panel; gov. State of Tex., Austin, 1979—. Trustee, bd. govs. So. Meth. U., former chmn. bd. govs.; mem. nat. exec. bd. Boy Scouts Am. Decorated Disting. Public Service medal Dept. Def., 1975, Bronze Palm (Pres. Ford), 1976. Mem. Am. Assn. Oil Well Drilling Contractors (past pres.), Ind. Petroleum Assn. Am. (past dir.). Republican. Episcopalian. Office: Office of Governor State Capitol Bldg Austin TX 78701*

CLEMMONS, FRANCES ANNE MANSELL (MRS. SLATON CLEMMONS), gov. ofcl.; b. Camden, Miss., Dec. 21, 1915; d. Otho Franklin and Pearl (Dunlap) Mansell; B.S., Belhaven Coll., 1937, Mus.B., 1937; m. Rowe Sanders Crowder, Dec. 17, 1938 (div. Mar. 1954); children—Rowe Sanders, Frances Elizabeth; m. 2d, Slaton Clemmons, Nov. 21 1955. Owner, operator Crowder Art Gallery, Jackson, Miss., 1946-50; dept. mgr., buyer Valley Dry Goods Co., Vicksburg, 1954-56; with Social Security Adminstrn., 1956—, asst. dist. mgr., Rome, Ga., 1962—. Mem. Rome-Floyd County Interagy. Council. Mem. Rome Community Concert Assn., Rome Little Theatre, Rome C. of C. Democrat. Presbyterian. Club: Quota Internat. (pres. 1974-75, 75-76; dist. lt. gov. 1979-80) (Rome). Home: 412 E 3d Ave Rome GA 30161 Office: Federal Bldg Rome GA 30161

CLEMMONS, SLATON, lawyer; b. Rome, Ga., July 19, 1909; s. Thomas Edmondson and Annie Ross (Slaton) C.; student Davidson Coll., 1926-27; J.D., U. Ga., 1929; postgrad. U. Pa., 1929-30; m. Starr Reynolds Quigg, 1939 (div. 1957); children—Diana Edmondson, Byard Quigg, Thomas Slaton; m. 2d, Frances Mansell Crowder, Nov. 1965. Admitted to Ga. bar, 1929, U.S. Supreme Ct. bar, 1937; practiced in Rome, 1930-35, 46-54; spl. atty. U.S. Dept. Justice, 1935-37, 42-46; spl. atty. gen. Ga., 1938-39; spl. asst. to atty. gen. U.S., 1940-41; asst. U.S. atty. No. dist. Ga., 1954-62; 1st asst. U.S. atty., 1962-70, ret., 1970. Served as lt. (j.g.) USNR, 1942. Mem. Ga., Rome (past pres.) bar assns., Am. Legion, Mil. Order World Wars, Phi Delta Phi, Sigma Alpha Epsilon. Democrat. Presbyn. Mason. Clubs: Coosa Country, Nine O'clock Cotillion (Rome, Ga.). Home: 412 E 3d Ave Rome GA 30161

CLENDENIN, RICHARD BLAINE, guidance counselor; b. Peytona, W.Va., July 22, 1945; s. Blaine Homer and Lillian Carmen (Vickers) C.; B.A. in English and Speech, Morris Harvey Coll., 1968; M.A. in Counseling and Guidance, W.Va. U., 1976; cert. adminstrn. W.Va. Coll. Grad. Studies; m. Virginia Lynn Ferrell, Sept. 28, 1968; 1 dau., Kimberly Paige. Tchr., Stonewall Jackson High Sch., Charleston, W.Va., 1968-75, guidance counselor, 1975-79; vice prin. Scott High Sch., Madison, W.Va., 1979—; adj. instr. English grammar, report writing Am. Inst. Banking, Union Carbide. Mem. Am., W.Va., Kanawha County (pres. 1978) personnel and guidance assns., Kanawha County Assn. Tchrs. of English (pres. 1974), Am. Sch. Counselors Assn. Home: 203 56th St Charleston WV 25304 Office: 404 Riverside Dr Madison WV 25130

CLEVELAND, ARTHUR GORDON, educator; b. Granbury, Tex., Aug. 17, 1940; s. Henry Earl and Doris Lorraine (James) C.; B.S. in Biology and Chemistry, Arlington State Coll., 1962; M.A. in Ecology, N.Tex. State U., 1965, Ph.D. in Mammalogy and Vertebrate Biology, 1971; m. Patricia Lee Malone, May 23, 1974; children—Robert Earl, Marcelle Lynn. Prof. biology, dept. chmn. Tex. Wesleyan Coll., Ft. Worth, 1965—; adj. prof. biology and environ. sci., Tex. Christian U., Served to capt. Chem. Corps U.S. Army, 1962-65. Fellow Welder Wildlife Found.; mem. Southwestern Assn. Naturalists (officer), Am. Soc. Mammalogists (life), Tex. Acad. Sci., N.Tex. Biol. Soc. (pres., 1977-78), Tex. Assn. for Environ. Edn., Sigma Xi. Author: A Manual of Vertebrate Natural History, 1977; contbr. research articles to profl. publs. Office: Texas Wesleyan Coll Fort Worth TX 76105

CLEVELAND, GENE RICKEY (MRS. CROMWELL COOK CLEVELAND), type setter; b. Dayton, Ohio, Oct. 22, 1914; d. Homer Herron and Ruth Victoria (Nystrom) Rickey; student U. Chgo., 1938-39, Moser Bus. Coll., Chgo., 1936, Art Inst. Chgo.; m. Cromwell Cook Cleveland, Nov. 26, 1947; 1 son, Cromwell Cook. With Am.-Fore Ins. Co., 1934-37; sec. athletic dept. U. Chgo., 1937-43; adminstrv. asst. to field dir. ARC Hosp. Service, 1943-45; exec. sec. Argonne Nat. Lab., Chgo., 1947-48; sec. Howard K. Bell, Cons. Engrs., Inc., Lexington, Ky., 1965-73; type setter printing dept. U. Ky., 1974—. Co-chmn. Lexington fund raising U. Chgo. Alumni, 1968; del. World Conv. Christian Chs., Edinburgh, 1960. Notary pub., Ky. Mem. Internat. Conv Ministers Wives, Internat. Platform Assn., Women's Club Central Ky. Republican. Mem. Christian Ch. Home: 3564 Lansdowne Dr Lexington KY 40503 Office: Printing Dept U Ky Lexington KY 40506

CLEVELAND, RAYMOND ELLSWORTH, univ. chancellor; b. Sulphur, Okla., Mar. 8, 1928; s. James E. and Edna A. (Runyan) C.; B.A., E. Central U., Okla. 1952, also B.S.; M.S., Okla. State U., 1959, Ed.D., 1967; m. Mary Virginia Warren, Dec. 9, 1949; children—Mark Warren, John David, Gregory Lynn, Valerie Ann, Jeffrey Ray. Tchr. public schs. in Okla., N.Mex. and Tex.; pres. Pratt (Kans.) Community Coll., 1962-64, Lee Coll., Baytown, Tex., 1965-72; prof. Tex. A&M U., College Station, 1972-76; prof. La. State U. System, Alexandria, 1976-79, chancellor, 1979—. Dist. committeeman local council Boy Scouts Am., 1962. Served with USAF, 1949-53. NSF fellow, 1968. Mem. Am. Assn. Higher Edn., Council of Univs. and Colls., Am. Assn. Univ. Adminstrs., Am. Acad. Arts and Scis., Tex. Assn. of Community Colls. (named Outstanding Adminstr. 1972), Aircraft Owners and Pilots Assn., Phi Theta Kappa, Phi Delta Kappa, Kappa Delta Pi. Democrat. Baptist. Club: Rotary (v.p. 1976-79). Author: (with Allan Ornstein and Steven Miller) Policy Issues in Education, 1976; A History of Baptists in Colonial America, 1976; contbr. articles on edn. to profl. pubs. Home: 5233 Argonne Blvd Alexandria LA 71301 Office: Louisiana State Univ Alexandria LA 71301

CLEVELAND, SCOTT J., clin. social worker; b. Belding, Mich., Oct. 26, 1940; s. Russell and Tressa A. (Bera) Belfield; B.A., Kalamazoo Coll., 1962; M.S.W., Fla. State U., 1964; m. Janice K. Harper, Oct. 5, 1968; children—Kelly Glenn, Randall Adam. Caseworker, Family and Children's Services, Battle Creek, Mich., 1964-65; asst. prof. grad. dept. social work Fla. State U., Tallahassee, 1965-70; asst. prof. dept. sociology Central Fla. U. Orlando, 1970-71; chief psychiat. worker Jacksonville (Fla.) Mental Health Center, Marion-Citrus Mental Health Center, Ocala, Fla., 1971-74; pvt. practice marriage and family counseling, Ocala, 1974—; guest lectr. Central Fla. Community Coll., 1978—; cons. to several social agys., 1975—. Fellow Fla. Fedn. Clin.

Social Workers; mem. Nat. Assn. Social Workers (treas. Tampa chpt. 1968-69, chmn. various coms. 1966-69, exec. bd. 1968-69), Nat. Registry of Health Care Providers in Clin. Social Work, Am. Assn. Marriage and Family Therapists (clin.). Office: 2 S W 12th St Ocala FL 32670

CLEVENGER, ERNEST ALLEN, JR., clergyman, sch. adminstr.; b. Chattanooga, Christ, Chattanooga, 1979—; Oct. 30, 1929; s. Ernest Allen and Mary Ellen (Fridell) C.; B.A., David Lipscomb Coll., 1951; M.A., Harding Grad. Sch., 1967; B.Th., Ala. Christian Sch. Religion, 1971, M.R.E., 1974, M.Th., 1975; S.L.D., Berean Christian Coll. and Sem., 1971; m. Glenda Willoughby, Dec. 17, 1950; children—Ernest Allen III, Elisabeth Anne Loyd. Entered ministry Ch. of Christ, 1949; minister Ohio Av. Ch. of Christ, Athens, Tenn., 1951-53, Univ. Ch. of Christ, Murray, Ky., 1953-57, North Highlands Ch. of Christ, Russellville, Ala., 1957-63, West End Ch. of Christ, Birmingham, Ala., 1963-76, Hunter Sta. Ch. of Christ, Montgomery, Ala., 1976-79, Brainerd Ch. of Christ, Chattanooga, 1979—; tchr. gen. and phys. sci. Russellville High Sch., 1959-63; prof. bible Ala. Christian Sch. Religion, Montgomery, 1968-73, dir., 1969-73; lectr. David Lipscomb Coll., Abilene Christian Coll.; pres. Ala. Christian Coll. Bibl. Studies, Birmingham, 1973-76; minister, acad. dean Ala. Christian Coll., Montgomery, 1976-79; pres. Boyd-Buchanan Sch., Chattanooga, 1979—. Owner, Parchment Press; exec. v.p. Bible Learning Materials, Inc., Honolulu. Founder, pres. Franklin County Conservation Club, 1958-60. Bd. dirs., trustee Central Ala. Christian Youth Camp; trustee Childhaven, Inc. Recipient research grant Ala. sect. Am. Chem. Soc., 1962; named Franklin County Sportsman of Year, 1959. Mem. Am. Schs. Oriental Research, Creation Research Soc., Am. Sci. Affiliation, S.A.R. Clubs: Oak Mountain Hunting (pres.), Rotary. Author: The Bible, 1960; Lesson Commentary Index, 1963, rev., 1968, 73; The History of God's People, 1963; Leadership Training Course, 1964; A Condensed Harmony of the Gospels, 1964; Bible Geography, 1965; Jesus of the Bible, 1965, rev., 1972; Wisdom Books of the Bible, 1966; Bible Doctrine, 1967; The Church Usher's Guide, 1967, rev. The Art of Greeting and Seating, 1970; Bible Evidences, 1968; Bible Survey, 1969; Bible Characters, 1970; Psychology of Jesus, 1975; Men's Leadership Training Course, 1975; Parchment Notes on the New Testament, 1976. Weekly columnist The Ledger and Times, 1954-58, Franklin County Times, 1958-63. Editor high sch. sect. Christian Bible Tchr. mag., 1970—; monthly columnist The World Evangelist. Composer: (hymn) He Is My Everything, 1968. Contbr. articles profl. jours. Home: 8617 Clearwood Rd Chattanooga TN 37421 Office: 4626 Bonnieway Dr Chattanooga TN 37411

CLEVENGER, WILLIAM THOMAS, elec. engr.; b. Chattanooga, Nov. 6, 1950; s. Asa Ralph and Effie Clarine (Harris) C.; B.S., David Lipscomb Coll., 1972; B.S. in Elec. Engring., U. Tenn., 1973; m. Mary Elizabeth Carman, Sept. 12, 1970; children—Elizabeth Eve, Emily Anne. Design engr. TVA, Chattanooga, 1973-74; elec. engr. Smith Seckman Reid, Inc., Nashville, 1974—, sec. bd. dirs., 1980—. Registered profl. engr., Tenn., Nev., N.J. Mem. SAR, IEEE, Constrn. Specifications Inst., Illuminating Engring. Soc. (sec.-treas., pres.), Tenn. Soc. Profl. Engrs., Nat. Soc. Profl. Engrs. Mem. Ch. of Christ. Club: Civitan. Home: 4305 Dale Ave Nashville TN 37204 Office: 2135 Blakemore Ave Nashville TN 37212

CLIBURN, CECIL DEBERRY, mathematician; b. Hazlehurst, Miss., Jan. 13, 1927; s. Charles Inge and Addie Ruth (Bufkin) C.; B.S., U. So. Miss., 1950; postgrad. New Orleans Baptist Theol. Sem., 1955-57; B.D., Emory U., 1964; M.Combined Scis., U. Miss., 1968; m. Dorothy Nell Stovall, Aug. 23, 1949; children—Charles William, Robert Rynearson, Cecilia Nell. Geophysicist aide Continental Oil Co., 1953-55; tchr. math. and sci., Stonewall, Miss., 1957-59; ordained elder Methodist Ch., 1964; minister Meth. Chs. in So. Miss., 1959-68; computer programmer, Eglin AFB, Fla., 1968—; pastor Alaqua-Wesley Meml. United Methodist Chs., DeFuniak Springs, Fla., 1977-78, Portland Meth. Ch., Freeport, Fla., 1978—. Served with USNR, 1945-46, to lt. AUS, 1949-50, 51-53. NSF grantee, 1967-68. Mem. Quarter Century Wireless Assn., Mensa, Kappa Mu Epsilon. Mason. Author article. Home: 219 Staff Dr Fort Walton Beach FL 32548 Office: ADTC/ADAB Eglin AFB FL 32542

CLIFFORD, MARGARET LOUISE, psychologist; b. Lakeland, Fla., Dec. 13, 1920; d. Thomas Saxon and Beatrice (Tillie) C.; A.B., Chapman Coll., 1950; M.S., San Diego State U., 1972; Ph.D., Union Grad. Sch., Yellow Springs, Ohio, 1976; m. Charles Robert Davis, Apr. 4, 1950; children—Daniel Thomas, Kelly Owen. Elem. sch. tchr., Hanford, Cuyama, Blythe, and La Mesa-Spring Valley, Calif., 1950-68; columnist Daily Midway Driller, Taft, Calif., 1955; owner/operator Marge Davis Sch. Dance, Blythe, 1961-64; counselor Family Services Assn., San Diego, 1971-72; dir. Child Guidance Clinic, psychologist Belleview Psychiat. Hosp., dance instr. Jamaica Public Schs., U.S. Peace Corps, Kingston, Jamaica, W.I., 1973-76; psychologist Apalachee Community Mental Health Services, Quincy, Fla., 1977—. Pres., Women's Soc. Christian Service, Methodist. Ch., Blythe, 1962-64. Served with WAVES, USN, 1943-45. Mem. Fla. Council Community Mental Health (chpt. pres. 1979-80).

CLIFFORD, PAUL INGRAHAM, psychologist, assn. exec.; b. Martinsburg, W.Va., Jan. 22, 1914; s. J. Paul and Mabel (Douglass) C.; B.S., State Tchrs. Coll., Shippensburg, Pa., 1938; A.M., Atlanta U., 1948; Ph.D., U. Chgo., 1953; m. Elizabeth Edith Sterrs, Jan. 21, 1950 (dec.); m. 2d, Margaret Washington Cabiness, Nov. 26, 1975. Civilian adminstrv. asst. USAAF, 1941-46; prof. chemistry Paine Coll., Augusta, Ga., 1947-48; instr. in edn. Atlanta U., 1948-51, asst. prof., 1952-54, asso. prof., 1954-57, prof., 1957-68, registrar, 1954-66, dir. admissions, 1954-66, dir. summer sch., 1957-68; staff psychologist Am. Mgmt. Psychologists, Inc., 1966—, v.p., dir., 1969—, nat. dir. profl. services, 1969-71; prof., chmn. dept. psychology S.C. State Coll., 1971-76; psychologist Career Mgmt. Atlanta, Inc., 1976—. Cons. U.S. Office Edn., 1961—; vis. prof. edn. U. Calif. at Berkeley, 1968-69; cons. psychologist various indsl. orgns. Bd. dirs. So. Fellowships Fund, Nat. Fellowships Fund; trustee Zale Found., Dallas. Licensed psychologist, Ga., Ill. Fellow A.A.A.S., Ga., Pa. psychol. assns.; mem. Am., Southeastern, S.C., Ill. psychol. assns., Soc. for Psychol. Study Social Issues, Nat. Soc. Study Edn., Am. Assn. U. Profs., Assn. for Higher Edn., N.E.A., Am. Ednl. Research Assn., Am. Personnel and Guidance Assn., Nat. Vocational Guidance Assn., Nat. Assn. Guidance Suprs., Assn. Counselor Edn. and Supervision, Assn. Measurement Edn. and Guidance, Nat. Council on Measurement in Edn., Am. Acad. Polit. and Social Scis., N.Y. Acad. Scis., Internat. Platform Assn., Phi Delta Kappa, Omega Psi Phi. Episcopalian. Author monograph, articles for ednl. and psychol. jours. Home: 859 Woodmere Dr NW Atlanta GA 30318

CLIFT, ALLEN RAY, mfg. co. exec.; b. Knoxville, Nov. 10, 1940; s. Edward Burchell and Ceora Patricia (Loy) C.; B.S., U. Tenn., 1962, M.S., 1966, postgrad., 1971—; m. Carol A. Bishop; 1 dau., Suzanne Dow. Tchr. graphics, Knoxville Sch. System, 1963-65; chmn. dept. graphic arts DeKalb Coll. & Tech. Sch., Clarksville, Ga., 1966; tng. dir. Rohm & Haas Inc., Bristol, Pa., 1969-70, Louisville, 1970-71, coordinator personnel benefits and tng., Knoxville, 1974—. Served with USAF, 1962-68. HEW fellow, 1973-74. Mem. Tenn. Valley Personnel Assn. (pres. 1980-81), Soc. Advancement Mgmt. (v.p. Knoxville 1980-81, pres.-elect 1981-82), Iota Lambda Sigma. Baptist. Home: 6541 Vestine Dr Corryton TN 37721 Office: PO Box 591 Knoxville TN 37901

CLIFT, ANNIE SUE, nursing educator; b. Newbern, Tenn., Nov. 29, 1931; d. James L. and Mollie Sue (Gelzer) C.; B.S.N., U. Tenn. Sch. Nursing, 1954; cert. Tokyo Sch. Japanese Lang., 1964; M.R.E., Southwestern Bapt. Theol. Sem., 1967; student Union U. Extension, 1955-56, Memphis State Coll., 1956; M.N. in Rehab., Emory U., 1969. Gen. duty staff nurse John Gaston Hosp., Memphis, 1954-55; staff nurse Memphis and Shelby County Public Health Dept., Memphis, 1955-56; supr., asst. dir. nurses Parkview Hosp., Dyersburg, Tenn., 1956-59, acting dir. nurses, 1958; charge nurse (part-time) Harris Hosp., Fort Worth, 1959-60, W.I. Cook Meml. Hosp. Center for Children, Fort Worth, 1960; missionary nurse, fgn. mission bd. So. Bapt. Conv., Richmond, Va., 1961-75; gen. duty nurse Japan Bapt. Hosp., Kyoto, 1964-66, ednl. dir., 1966-67; instr. (part-time) Japan Bapt. Sch. Nursing, Kyoto, 1966-67; charge nurse, in-service dir. Jibla (Yemen) Bapt. Hosp., 1969-71; clin. instr. ob-gyn. Japan Bapt. Sch. Nursing, Kyoto, 1971-72, exec. dir., 1971-75; asst. prof. nursing U. Tenn., Martin, 1973—. Missionary, Fujisawa (Japan) Bapt. Ch., 1962-64; youth dir. Kyohoku Bapt. Mission, Kyoto, 1964-67; ednl. dir. Kitayama Bapt. Ch., Kyoto, 1971-72; instr. English as second lang. various schs. and hosps. in Japan, 1962-66, 71-72. Children's Sunday sch. tchr. Emmaus Bapt. Ch., 1972-77; dir. Acteens Dyer Bapt. Assn., 1976-77. Mem. Am. Nurses Assn., Tenn. Nurses Assn. (chmn. fin. com. 1974-77, pres. dist. 12 1959, treas. and sec. dist. 12, dir. 1957-58, 74-77), Assn. Rehab. Nurses, Am. Congress Rehab. Medicine, AAUP. Baptist. Contbr. book revs. on rehab. and phys. medicine to profl. publs. Home: Route 2 Newbern TN 38059 Office: School of Nursing U Tenn Martin TN 38238

CLIFTON, GLENN ALVIN, respiratory therapist; b. Lincoln, Nebr., Feb. 17, 1945; s. Glenn Alvin and Grace Adeline (Carey) C.; A.A., St. Petersburg Jr. Coll., 1975; m. Edna Brady, Dec. 17, 1973; 1 dau., Laura Marie. Chief respiratory therapist Apollo Med. Center, St. Petersburg, Fla., 1970-71; ednl. dir. respiratory therapy dept. Jackson Meml. Hosp., Miami, 1971-72; clin. coordinator respiratory therapy program St. Petersburg Jr. Coll., Clearwater, Fla., 1972-76; tech. dir. respiratory services Tampa (Fla.) Gen. Hosp., 1976—; cons. St. Petersburg Vocat. Tech. Inst., 1976—, Appleton-Century-Crafts, Med. Pub. Div., 1978—; affiliate faculty mem. St. Petersburg Jr. Coll., Clearwater, Fla., 1976—, St. Petersburg Vocat. Tech. Inst., 1976—. Mem. Am. Assn. Respiratory Therapy (pres. Central Fla. chpt.), Nat. Bd. Respiratory Therapy, Am. Heart Assn., Fla. Heart Assn., Gulf Coast Lung Assn. Democrat. Home: 7000 52d Ln Pinellas Park FL 33565 Office: Tampa Gen Hosp Davis Islands Tampa FL 33606

CLIFTON, YERGER HUNT, educator; b. Jackson, Miss., July 26, 1930; s. Yerger Hunt and Sudie Cocke (Wilson) C.; B.A., Duke U., 1952; student law Washington and Lee U., 1952-53; M.A., U. Va., 1958; Ph.D., Trinity Coll., Dublin, Ireland, 1962; postgrad. Oxford U., U. Munich. Instr., Coll. William and Mary, Williamsburg, Va., 1958-59, U. Ky., Lexington, 1962-65; vis. lectr. Youngstown (Ohio) U., 1964-65; lectr. humanities Memphis Acad. Arts, 1966-69; asst. prof. English lit. Southwestern U., Memphis, 1965-70, asso. prof., 1970-77, prof., 1977—; dean Brit. Studies at Oxford, Univ. Coll. of Oxford U., 1970-79, St. John's Coll., 1980, So. Coll. Univ. Union, (including Birmingham-So. Coll., Centenary Coll. La., Centre Coll. Ky., Fisk U., Millsaps Coll., U. of South, Vanderbilt U.); pres. 26th So. Lit. Festival, 1967, trustee, 1967-70. Served to lt. USNR, 1953-56. Menkenmeller fellow, 1952-53. Mem. AAUP, Modern Lang. Assn., Oxford Soc., Monteagle (Tenn.) Assembly, Green Ribbon Soc., Phi Kappa Sigma. Republican. Episcopalian. Clubs: Oxford and Cambridge Univs. (London). Author: Angelic Knowledge in Paradise Lost, 1958; Milton and the Fall of Man, 1962. Home: 1539 North Pkwy Memphis TN 38112 Office: 2000 North Pkwy Memphis TN 38112

CLINE, BOBBY JAMES, ins. co. exec.; b. Floydada, Tex., Mar. 12, 1932; s. Howard O. and Carrie T. C.; B.B.A., U. Tex., Austin, 1954; m. Martha Nolan, May 29, 1954; children—Carolyn, Pamela, Millie, Robert, Sean. Casualty underwriter Ins. Co. N. Am., Dallas, 1956-59; account exec./partner Munger-Moore & Assos., Dallas, 1959-68; partner Harris-Moore & Assos., Dallas, 1968-70; sr. v.p. Alexander & Alexander of Tex., Inc., Dallas, 1970-72, exec. v.p., 1972-77, pres., regional dir., 1977—; dir. Prestonwood Nat. Bank, Dallas. Dir., pres. Young Life Dallas. Served with USN, 1954-56. Mem. Soc. C.P.C.U.'s (dir.), Dallas Assn. Ins. Agts. (dir.), Tex. U. Ex-Students Assn. (past pres.). Baptist. Clubs: Salesmanship, Preston Trails Golf, Dallas, Dallas Athletic, Garland Toastmasters, Riverhill Country. Office: Alexander & Alexander of Tex 2001 Bryan Tower Dallas TX 75201

CLINE, CHERYL KAY, retail trade co. exec.; b. Evansville, Ind., July 27, 1949; d. Herschel Estel and Bettye L. (Blaksley) C.; student U. Nev., 1967-69; U. Nev., Las Vegas, 1970-71. Sec. phys. plant U. Nev., Reno, 1967-68; acctg. clk. Julies, Inc., Las Vegas, Nev., 1969-70, asst. mgr., 1970-71, mgr., 1971-72, dist. mgr., Houston, Tex., 1971-72, Dallas, Tex., 1973-74, asst. gen. mgr., Las Vegas, Nev., 1974-75, southwest regional mgr., Houston, Tex., 1975—; salesperson Joseph Magnin Store, Las Vegas, 1972-73. Mem. Ladies Go-Tex. Com. Mem. Galleria Center Assn. (mem. marketing com. 1978-79, dir. 1978-80), Blvd. Mchts. Assn. (dir.). Office: 5015 Westheimer 2430 Galleria Mall Houston TX 77056

CLINE, JEWELL ALLEN, educator; b. Printer, Ky., Mar. 7, 1921; d. Henry H. and Elizabeth (Frasure) Allen; B.S. cum laude, Pikeville Coll., 1969; M.A. in Edn., Morehead State U., 1974, Ed.S., 1977; m. Jacob P. Cline, Jr., Oct. 4, 1944; children—Karen, Jacob P. Tchr. various schs., 1941-44, 54-66; supr. Headstart tchrs. and aides Pike County (Ky.), 1966-69; co-dir., career coordinator Career Edn. Program, Eastern Ky. U., Richmond, 1970-73; instr., community coordinator Tchr. Corps Program, Pikeville (Ky.) Coll., 1973-77, asst. prof., chmn. dept. edn., 1977—; career edn. cons.; cons. Pike County Headstart and Kindergarten Programs, Model Cities Day Care. Mem. Headstart Adv. Council, 1975—, vice chmn., 1975-76; mem. Friend's Bd. Dirs. Ky. Ednl. TV, 1976—, pres.-elect, 1980—. Recipient Outstanding Faculty award Student Govt. Assn. Pikeville Coll., 1977-78. Mem. So. Assn. Children Under Six, Ky. Assn. Children Under Six, Nat. Sch. Vols., Inc., AAUW, Ky. Assn. Tchr. Educators, Assn. Supervision and Curriculum Devel. Democrat. Presbyterian. Home: 104 Mt Martha Dr Pikeville KY 41501 Office: Pikeville Coll Pikeville KY 41501

CLINE, RUTH LAYNE, assn. exec.; b. Charleston, W.Va., Apr. 22, 1935; d. Arvel and Beulah Ethel (Coulter) Layne; B.S. in Edn., U. Charleston, 1958; M.A. in Counseling and Rehab., Marshall U., 1966; children—Sandra Lynn, Philip Andrew, Holly Leeann. Tchr. Man High Sch., Logan County Bd. Edn., Logan, W.Va., 1958-59; circulation supr. James Morrow Library, Marshall U., Huntington, W.Va., 1962-63; counselor Family Service, Inc., Huntington 1974-77, exec. dir. Family Service, 1977-79; exec. dir. Cabell-Wayne United Way, 1980—; pres. Consumer Credit Counseling of Huntington, 1975-78. Pres., Fifth Ave. Bapt. Ch. Women, Huntington, 1968-70, Greater Huntington Church Women United, 1972-74; treas. Community Service Roundtable, 1977-79, program chmn., 1978-79; pres. United Way Exec. Dirs., 1979. Named Outstanding Woman of Huntington, 1978. Mem. Am. Personnel and Guidance Assn., W.Va. Personnel and Guidance Assn., W.Va. Public Health Assn., AAUW, Marshall U. Alumni Assn., YWCA. Regular contbg. editor to Mid-day Mag., sta. WOWK-TV. Home: 11 Parkway Dr Huntington WV 25705 Office: 1111 Veterans Memorial Blvd Huntington WV 25701

CLINGAN, FRANK HARRINGTON, elec. engr.; b. El Cajon, Calif., Sept. 6, 1902; s. Robert Lee and Elva Jane (Richey) C.; grad. Westminster Jr. Coll., 1924; B.S. in Elec. Engring., U. Mich., 1929, postgrad., 1929, 32; m. Elnora S. Clingan, June 4, 1938. With Utah Power & Light Co., Salt Lake City, 1924, Chevrolet Gear & Axle Div., Detroit, 1925; maintenance supr. Chevrolet and Chrysler Corp., 1926-29; apprentice electrician Detroit Bd. Edn., 1929-35, elec. journeyman, 1935-37, asst. foreman, 1937-38, foreman, 1938-42, gen. foreman, 1942-44, asso. elec. engr., 1944-52, sr. asso. elec. engr., 1952-62; asst. elec. engr. Kaislrik, Snell & Whitehead, Sarasota, Fla., 1962-63; asso., Kaisrlik, Snell & Assos., 1963-66; owner Clingan & Assos., Inc., Bradenton, Fla., 1966-67; sr. elec. engr. Watson & Co., architects, engrs., planners, Tampa, Fla., 1967-69, asst. dept. head elec. engring. dept., 1969-71; chief elec. engr. Rowe-Paras & Assos., Tampa, Fla., 1971-72, Lanbanque Engring., Holiday, Fla., 1972-73; elec. engr. Edward Dean Wyke, architect, Bradenton, 1974—. Registered profl. engr., Fla.; Design Affiliation Architecture, Jacksonville, Fla., 1977—. Mem. Nat. Soc. Profl. Engrs., Fla. Engring. Soc., Illuminating Engring. Soc., Aircraft Owners and Pilots Assn., Nat. Pilots Assn. Baptist. Club: Schoolmen's (Detroit). Patentee in field. Address: Regency House 33 W Adams St Jacksonville FL 32202

CLINGERMAN, EDGAR ALLEN, business exec.; b. Wolf Lake, Ind., Dec. 27, 1934; s. Virgil Wilson and Jessie Pauline (Miller) C.; B.S. in Bus. Adminstrn., Ball State U., 1960; postgrad. Ball State U., Purdue U.; grad. Advanced Mgmt. Program, Harvard, 1974; m. Betty Gean White, Dec. 9, 1966; children—Tamera, Sarah, Johnny, Edgar Allen. Sr., Cooper Lybrand, Ft. Wayne, Ind., 1960-63; controller Monteith Bros. Co., Elkhart, Ind., 1963-66; plant controller Joy Mfg. Co., Michigan City, Ind., 1966-68; v.p. fin., treas., controller, pres. Ophthalmic Group, Milton Roy Co., St. Petersburg, Fla., 1968-69, v.p. fin., 1979—; dir. E-C Apparatus Corp. Active local Boy Scouts Am. Served with USN, 1952-55. Mem. Nat. Assn. Accountants, Am. Mgmt. Assn., Corporate Controllers Assn., Sci. Apparatus Mfg. Assn. (chmn. fin. execs. group 1973-74), Contact Lens Mfg. Assn. (dir.). Mem. Christian Ch. (deacon, dir.). Mason, Rotarian (pres. local group 1963). Home: 2534 Heron Ln N Clearwater FL 33520 Office: One Plaza Pl NE Saint Petersburg FL 33701

CLINGMAN, WILLIAM HERBERT, JR., mgmt. cons.; b. Grand Rapids, Mich., May 5, 1929; s. William Herbert and Elizabeth (Davis) C.; B.S. with distinction and honors in Chemistry, U. Mich., 1951; M.A., Princeton U., 1954, Ph.D., 1954; m. Mary Jane Wheeler, Feb. 6, 1951; children—Mary Constance, James Wheeler. Chemist, Am. Oil Co., Texas City, Tex., 1954-57, group leader, 1957-59; head thermoelectric sect. Tex. Instruments, Inc., Dallas, 1959-61, dir. energy research lab., 1961-62, mgr. corporate research and devel. mktg. dept., 1962-67; pres. W.H. Clingman Co., Inc., Dallas, 1967—; dir. Graham Magnetics Inc., 1974-77; speaker, cons. SBA, 1967-70; mem. adv. com. on sci., tech. and economy Nat. Planning Assn., 1966-67. Mem. Am. Chem. Soc., IEEE, Assn. Computing Machinery, Sigma Xi. Club: Brook Hollow Golf (Dallas). Mem. editorial adv. bd. Jour. Advanced Energy Conversion, 1961-66. Home: 4416 McFarlin St Dallas TX 75205 Office: 2001 Bryan St Dallas TX 75201

CLINTON, ROBERT L., coll. pres.; b. Putnam, Tex., Nov. 27, 1923; s. Robert Lovett and Eva Frances (Park) C.; B.M., N. Tex. State U., 1948, M.M., 1950; Ed.D., Tex. Tech. U., 1962; m. Wanda Merle Lowry, Oct. 14, 1944; children—Robert Lowry, David Reagan, Ronald Dale. Dir. music Cisco Jr. Coll., 1949-53; music dir. Snyder (Tex.) Public Schs., 1953-60, prin. high sch., 1961-63, supt. of schs., 1964-67; asst. commr. for jr. colls. Coll. Coordinating Bd., Tex. Coll. and Univ. System, 1967-70; pres. Western Tex. Coll., Snyder, 1970—. Mem. Gov.'s Com. for re-codification of Tex. Public Sch. Law. Served with USAAF, 1943-46. Mem. Tex. Assn. Community Colls. (dir.), So. Assn. Colls. and Schs., Phi Mu Alpha, Alpha Chi, Phi Delta Kappa. Methodist. Club: Rotary. Home: 2905 Westridge Snyder TX 79549

CLINTON, WILLIAM JEFFERSON, gov. of Ark.; b. Hope, Ark., Aug. 19, 1946; B.S. in Internat. Affairs, Sch. Fgn. Service, Georgetown U., 1968; postgrad. (Rhodes scholar), Univ. Coll., Oxford (Eng.) U., 1968-70; J.D., Yale U., 1973. Admitted to Ark. bar, 1973; individual practice law, Fayetteville, Ark., 1973-76; atty. gen. State of Ark., Little Rock, 1977-79; gov. of Ark., 1979—; instr. U. Ark., Little Rock, 1975-76, asst. prof. law, Fayetteville, 1976-77; chmn. bd. Ark. Housing Devel. Corp. Candidate for U.S. Congress from Ark. 3d Congl. Dist., 1974; Ark. coordinator Carter for Pres. campaign, 1976. Mem. Ark., Am. bar assns., Nat. Assn. Attys. Gen., Phi Beta Kappa. Democrat. Baptist. Office: Room 250 State Capitol Bldg Little Rock AR 72201

CLIPPARD, EURAL DAY, textile co. exec.; b. Alexis, N.C., July 12, 1927; s. Fred Roe and Noveda Randall C.; m. Odessa M. Coley, Sept. 3, 1948; 1 dau., Janice Euralene. Mem. dept. maintenance J. P. Stevens Co., Stanley, N.C., 1948-54; supr. Templon Spinning Mills, Inc., Mooresville, N.C., 1954-55, mem. dept. purchasing, 1957-67, now plant mgr., v.p., Wytheville, Va.; supr. Chemspan Yarns Ltd., Mooresville, 1956-57. Chmn. bd. Eye Bank of Va., Roanoke, 1974-75. Served with U.S. Army, 1946-47. Republican. Presbyterian. Club: Lions (pres. 1971-72). Home: 510 Withers Rd Wytheville VA 24382 Office: 1150 S 3d St Wytheville VA 24382

CLOGAN, PAUL MAURICE, educator; b. Boston, July 9, 1934; s. Michael J. and Agnes J. (Murphy) C.; B.A., Boston Coll., 1956, M.A., 1957; Ph.D., U. Ill., 1961; F.A.A.R., Am. Acad. in Rome, 1966; m. Julie Sydney Davis, June 27, 1972; children—Michael Rodger, Patrick Terence, Margaret Murphy. Asst. prof. Duke U., 1961-65; asso. prof. Case Western Reserve U., Cleve., 1965-72; prof. English, N. Tex. State U., Denton, 1972—; vis. prof. U. Keele (Eng.), 1965, U. Pisa (Italy), 1966, U. Tours (France), 1978; vis. mem. Inst. Advanced Study, Princeton, N.J., 1970, 77; cons. Library of Congress, Ednl. Testing Service, Nat. Endowment Humanities, Nat. Acad. Scis., NRC Commn. Human Resources, Am. Council Learned Socs., Nat. Enquiry into Scholarly Communication, Chilton Research Services, Am. Arts Assn. Duke Endowment grantee, 1961-62; Am. Council of Learned Socs. grantee, 1963-64, 70-71; Philos. Soc. grantee, 1964-69; sr. Fulbright-Hays Postdoctoral Research fellow, Italy, 1965-66, Research grantee, France, 1978; Prix de Rome fellow, 1966-67; Bollingen Found. fellow, 1966; Nat. Endowment Humanities fellow, 1969-70; N. Tex. State U. Faculty grantee, 1972-75. Mem. Internat. Assn. Univ. Profs. of English, MLA, Mediaeval Acad. Am., Internat. Comparative Lit. Assn., Internat. Arthurian Soc., Modern Humanities Research Assn. Democrat. Roman Catholic. Author: The Medieval Achilleid of Statius, 1968; Social Dimensions in Medieval and Renaissance Studies, 1972; In Honor of S. Harrison Thomson, 1970; Medieval and Renaissance Studies in Review, 1971; Medieval and Renaissance Spirituality, 1973; Medieval Historiography, 1974; Medieval Hagiography and Romance, 1975; Medieval Poetics, 1976; Transformation and Continuity, 1977; Innovation and Tradition, 1978; editor Medievalia et Humanistica: Studies in Medieval and

Renaissance Culture, 1970—; contbr. articles to profl. jours. Office: PO Box 13348 North Texas Station Denton TX 76203

CLOSSER, PATRICK DENTON, artist; b. San Diego, Apr. 27, 1945; s. Daniel Penn and Helen Marjorie Closser; diploma, Am. Schs. of Cinema, 1970. Artist, Sta. KBFI-TV, Dallas, 1972-73; with radio Stas. KVTT and Sta. KDTX, Dallas, 1976-77; one man shows include: First Bapt. Ch., Chula Vista, Calif.; worked on TV commls. for Dr. Pepper, Am. Chiropractic Assn., feature movies Operation Red Star, Mars Needs Women, show Comment on Our Times, Bible's Forecast; evangelist Stas. KDTX-FM, KVTT-FM; worked on theatre trailers, network TV shows, Nelson Golf Classic, Operation Entertainment. Mem. Internat. Christian Broadcasters Assn., Soc. Motion Picture and TV Engrs. Home: 3875 Dunhaven St Dallas TX 75220

CLOUDT, FLORENCE RICKER, archtl. accents co. exec.; b. Houston, Tex., July 12, 1925; d. Norman Hurd and Sallie Lee (St. Louis) Ricker; B.F.A., Sophie Newcomb Coll., Tulane U., 1946; m. Frank Winfield Cloudt, Aug. 12, 1977; children by previous marriage—Norman Sandford Pottinger, Margaret Halliday Pottinger. Tchr. kindergarten Montgomery County Sch. System, Md., 1956-60, Nat. Cathedral Sch., Washington, 1960-62; founder Florence Pottinger Interiors, 1963, mgr., 1963-78; co-founder, v.p. Focal Point Inc., Smyrna, Ga., 1970-78, pres., 1978—, gen. mgr., 1970—; dir. public relations Theater Atlanta, 1966; pres. Young Matrons Circle, Tallulah Falls Sch., 1951-52. Bd. dirs. Charlotte (N.C.) Jr. League, 1953-55; trustee Atlanta Landmarks, 1974—; mem. 50th Anniversary Celebration Com., Fox Theater, 1979. Mem. Sales and Mktg. Execs. Internat. Republican. Episcopalian. Producer, writer TV Show: 25th Hour, Washington, 1958. Office: 2005 Marietta Rd NW Atlanta GA 30318

CLOUSE, CLYDE, accountant; b. Knox County, Ky., Aug. 8, 1921; s. Lee and Fannie (Hubbard) C.; grad. Perry Bus. Coll., 1941; student U. S.D., 1943-44; m. Ruth Gover, Nov. 29, 1947; children—Michael, William, James, Thomas. Accountant, VA, 1946-47, Jellico Grocery Co., 1947-48, Time Finance Co., 1948-50, Dill Scott & Assos., 1950-51, Harold Kennedy, 1951-54, Eagle Express Co., 1954-57; cost accountant and plant mgr. Diamond Nat. Corp., Burnside, Ky., 1958-60; pvt. accounting firm, Somerset, Ky., 1961—. Vice pres. Clouse-Wesley Co., 1969-72; dir. Standard Armature & Electric Co., 1970-75. Pres., Somerset Babe Ruth Baseball League, 1968, 75-76, Somerset Little League Baseball, 1960-79, Somerset Little League Basketball, 1972-75. Served with AUS, 1942-46. Mem. Nat. Soc. Pub. Accountants, Ky. Assn. Methodist (mem. ch. bd. 1955-75). Club: Somerset Country. Home: 416 Holmes Ave Somerset KY 42501 Office: 116 N Main St Somerset KY 42501

CLOWER, DANIEL CLANTON, III, physician; b. Troy, Ala., Sept. 5, 1946; s. Daniel Clanton and Cupiedeen (Rogers) C.; B.S. in Pharmacy, Auburn U., 1969; M.D., U. Ala., 1973; m. Elizabeth Ruth Edwards, Sept. 6, 1975; 1 dau., Amy Elizabeth. Resident in internal medicine Carraway Med. Center, Birmingham, Ala., 1973-76; pvt. practice medicine specializing in internal medicine, Selma, Ala., 1976—; instr. in medicine family practice program Selma Med. Center, 1977—, also chmn. internal medicine. Diplomate Am. Bd. Internal Medicine. Mem. A.C.P., AMA, Ala. Med. Assn. Methodist. Club: Selma Country. Home: 1908 Laforet Selma AL 36701 Office: 509 Parkman Selma AL 36701

CLOYD, HELEN MARY, educator, acct.; b. Austria-Hungary, 1918; d. Valentine and Elizabeth (Kretschmar von Kienbusch) Yuhasz; came to U.S. 1922, naturalized, 1928; B.S., Eastern Mich. U., 1953; M.A., Wayne State U., 1956; Ph.D., Mich. State U., 1963; m. George S. Smith, Mar. 4, 1939 (dec.); children—George, Nora; m. Chester L. Cloyd, Apr. 16, 1960 (dec.). Pub. accounting Haskins & Sells, Detroit, 1945-53; tchr. Marine City (Mich.) High Sch., 1954-59; instr. acctg. Central Mich. U., Mt. Pleasant, 1959-60; asst. prof. Wayne State U., Detroit, 1960-61; tchr. Grosse Pointe (Mich.) High Sch., 1961-64; asso. prof. acctg. Ball State U., Muncie, Ind., 1964-71; prof. Shepherd Coll., Shepherdstown, W.Va., from 1971; now asso. prof. George Mason U., Fairfax, Va. Recipient McClintock Writing award C.P.A., Mich., Ind., W.Va. Mem. Am. Inst. C.P.A.'s, Am. Acctg. Assn., Am. Econs. Assn., AAAS, Assn. Sch. Bus. Ofcls., Delta Pi Epsilon, Pi Omega Pi, Pi Gamma Mu. Clubs: Order Eastern Star, White Shrine. Contbr. numerous articles to pubs. Home: PO Box 186 Inwood WV 25428 Office: George Mason U Fairfax VA 22030

CLUM, DENNIS PATRICK, city ofcl.; b. Poughkeepsie, N.Y., May 1, 1925; s. Frederick J. and Margaret M. (Murphy) C.; B.A., Union Coll., Schenectady, 1947; LL.B., Fordham U., 1951; m. Dorothy M. Diederichs, Oct. 14, 1953 (div. Oct. 1973); children—Dennis Patrick, Robert, Laura; m. 2d, Lucille Michaud, Sept. 5, 1975. Sr. v.p., trust officer, dir. Miami Beach, First Nat. Bank (Fla.), 1954-71; sr. v.p., dir. United Bancshares of Fla., Inc., 1965-71; exec. v.p., trust officer First State Bank of Miami (Fla.), 1972, also dir. Past pres. Estate Planning Council Dade County; bd. dirs. Miami Heart Inst., Miami Opera Guild, Com. of 100 Miami Beach, Dade Found.; mem. adminstrv. bd. Biscayne Coll.; mem. devel. fund bd. Barry Coll.; chmn. endowment fund com. U. Miami. Served to lt. USNR, 1943-46, 51-54. Mem. Miami Shores C. of C. (v.p., dir.), Corporate Fiduciaries Assn. Clubs: Surf, La Gorce, Miami Shores Country, Rod and Reel, Miami, Racquet, Standard, Beach Colony, Army and Navy. Home: 1430 NE 102d St Miami Shores FL 33138 Office: 7900 NE 2d Ave Miami FL 33138

CLYDE, GERARD ANTHONY, educator, ret. army officer; b. Phila., Nov. 1, 1938; s. Frank Foote and Mary Margaret (Gormley) C.; B.A., Okla. Coll. Liberal Arts, 1973; M.A., Boston U., 1977; m. Barbara Vallaint, July 29, 1967; children—Gerard Anthony, Angela M., Gregory N. Enlisted in U.S. Army, 1958, commd. 2d lt., 1966, advanced through grades to capt., 1976; service in Germany, Vietnam; systems analyst Tacfire Software Support Center, 1976-79; instr. social sci., 1979—. Decorated Bronze Star, Army Commendation medal. Mem. Am. Personnel and Guidance Assn. Democrat. Roman Catholic. Club: K.C. Home: 321 NW 63d St Lawton OK 73505

CMELIK, HELMUT RUDOLF MAX, wireline services co. exec.; b. Hermsdorf, Germany, Mar. 20, 1938; came to U.S., 1976; s. Rudolf and Margarete C.; grad. Trade Sch., Hannover, Germany, 1959; m. Mercedes Maria Ibarra, Sept. 7, 1968. With Telefunken A.G. (Germany), 1956-64; field engr. Tri-Can, Trinidad and Venezuela, 1964-69; mng. dir. Pro-Data C.A., Venezuela, 1969-76; mgr. prodn. logging G0 Wireline Services, Fort Worth, 1976—. Mem. Soc. Petroleum Engrs. of AIME, Am. Mgmt. Assn. Lutheran. Club: Ridglea Country (Ft. Worth). Contbr. articles to profl. jours. Home: 4354 Salix Ct Fort Worth TX 76109 Office: 1100 Everman Rd Fort Worth TX 76140

COAN, JOHN DAVID, physician; b. Norfolk, Va., Sept. 28, 1941; s. Nahum Edward and Elizabeth Lee (Sommers) C.; A.B., U. N.C., 1963; M.D., Med. Coll. Va., 1968; m. Sharon Pasternak, May 18, 1975. Intern, N.C. Meml. Hosp., Chapel Hill, 1968-69, resident Duke U. Med. Center, Durham, N.C., 1969-72; staff radiologist Hermann Hosp., Houston, 1974-75, Med. Center Hosp., Norfolk, Va., 1975-76, Med. Center Del Oro Hosp., Houston, 1976—; asst. prof. U. Tex. Med. Sch., Houston, 1974-75, M.D. Anderson Hosp. and Tumor Inst., Houston, 1974-75. Served to maj. AUS, 1972-74. Recipient Aaron Brown scholarship award, 1968. Diplomate Am. Bd. Radiology. Mem. Radiol. Soc. N.Am., Am. Coll. Radiology, Harris County, Tex. med. assns., Phi Delta Epsilon. Contbr. articles in field to profl. jours. Home: 2519 Bellefontaine Houston TX 77030 Office: Radiology Dept Med Center Del Oro Hospital Houston TX 77054

COATES, FREDERICK ROSS, lawyer; b. Madison, Va., June 27, 1933; s. Fred I. and Sarah C. (Hale) C.; B.A., U. Richmond, 1954; J.D., T.C. Williams Sch. Law, 1959; m. Rebecca C. White, Nov. 25, 1959; children—Stephanie Renee, Susan Cecilia. Admitted to Va. bar, 1959; partner firm Coates & Province, Madison, Va., 1959—. Adv. bd. Nat. Bank and Trust Co., Madison, 1973-77. Commr. accounts Madison County, Va., 1974-77, mem. sch. bd., 1970-76, mem. planning commn., 1969-71; sr. legal officer Madison (Va.) Rescue Squad, 1964—; vice chmn. Madison County (Va.) Republican Party, 1969-70. Served with AUS, 1954-57. Mem. Am., Va. Madison-Greene County bar assns., Sigma Alpha Epsilon, Phi Alpha Delta. Baptist (deacon 1959-62, trustee 1965—). Lion (pres. 1968-69), Mason (Shriner). Club: Greene Hills (v.p. 1967-68). Home: PO Box 328 Madison VA 22727

COATS, MARY LOUISE (COLEMAN), architect; b. Mckenzie, Tenn., July 24, 1919; d. Mort Dormer and Julia May (King) Coleman; student Washington U. Sch. Architecture, St. Louis, 1951-60; B.Arch., U. Tex., Austin, 1966; m. Cletus Benton Coats, June 16, 1940. Partner, Coats Constrn. Co., Jackson, Tenn., 1946—; zoning and codes coordinator City of Jackson, 1970—; with Haywood Smith, Architect, Jackson, 1970-72, John Skelton, Architect, Jackson, Dallas, 1972-74; pvt. practice architecture, Jackson, 1974—; mem. Goals for Jackson, 1970—. Cert. Nat. Council Archtl. Registration Bds. Mem. AIA (sec.-treas. Memphis chpt.), Tenn. Soc. Architects. Baptist. Residential designer, 1946—; designer Coats Bldg., Jackson, 1976-77. Home: 640 N Russell Rd Jackson TN 38301 Office: Coats Bldg 1903 N Highland Jackson TN 38301

COBB, GLYNDA HAWKINS, recreation assn. adminstr.; b. Houston, Mar. 10, 1930; d. Douglas Harris and Leonora Elizabeth (Sherrill) Hawkins; grad. Edgewood Park Jr. Coll., 1947; B.A., So. Meth. U., 1949; postgrad. in Bus. Adminstrn., U. Tex., 1949-50, U. Tex. Sch. Law, 1952-53; m. Carroll Cobb, Sept. 5, 1950; children—Carolynn Elizabeth, Martha Anne. Sec. to public relations and press dir. Tex. Ins. Adv. Assn., Austin, 1953-55; supr. check violations Lubbock County (Tex.) Atty.'s Office, 1956-58; public relations dir., sec. Malouf's Men's Store, Lubbock, 1973-74; exec. dir. Camp Fire Council of Lubbock, 1974—. Pres., Jr. League of Lubbock, 1965-66; chmn. Jr. League Follies, 1964-65; mem. City Youth Council Bd., Lubbock, 1968-71; bd. dirs. South Plains Guidance Center, 1963-66; bd. dirs. Am. Lung Assn., Lubbock, 1958-74, pres., 1964-65; bd. dirs. Lubbock Cancer Soc., 1968-71, chmn. fund drive, 1968-71; bd. dirs. Edna Gladney Home, Ft. Worth, 1968—, Children's Protective Services, Lubbock County, 1978—, Treehouse Village Inc., 1979—. Named Lubbock's Woman of Yr. Altrusa Club of Lubbock, 1966. Mem. Nat. Assn. of Camp Fire Profls. (sec. 1978—), Lubbock Bd. Realtors, Delta Delta Delta. Office: PO Box 5630 Lubbock TX 79417

COBB, JOHN PHILLIP, accountant, lawyer; b. Evanston, Ill., Feb. 17, 1940; s. Osro and Audrey (Umsted) C.; student Okla. U., 1958-59; B.S.B.A. in Accounting, U. Ark., 1963, LL.B., 1966; m. Cita Elizabeth Gracie Rogers, June 1, 1962; children—Elizabeth, Lallie, Mary Melissa. Admitted to Ark. bar, 1966; staff accountant Russell Brown & Co., Little Rock, 1966-70; practice accounting, Little Rock, 1970-73; prin. Cobb, Engstrom & Co. Ltd., profl. C.P.A. corp., Little Rock, 1973-76; tax mgr. Gaddy & Co., C.P.A.'s, 1977, partner, 1978-79; cons. Brown, Rogers & Brietz, C.P.A.'s, Little Rock, 1980—. Mem. exec. budget com. United Way, Little Rock, 1973-77, bd. dirs., 1976-77; bd. dirs. Ada Thompson Meml. Home. Served with U.S. Army, 1960. Mem. Am. Inst. C.P.A.'s., Am. Bar Assn., Am. Assn. Atty.-C.P.A.'s. Clubs: Capital, Little Rock, Country of Little Rock. Office: 1690 Worthen Bank Bldg Little Rock AR 72201

COBB, RON LAVELL, Realtor, builder, state ofcl.; b. Greenville, S.C., Nov. 8, 1948; s. J.W. and Edna Kelly C.; m. Diane Granger, Nov. 25, 1967; children—Christopher Jay, Amanda Diane. Pres., Cobb Builders Inc., Greenville, 1976—; pres. Ron Cobb Co., Greenville, 1975—, Hydrotex Corp., Greenville, 1978—; mem. S.C. Ho. of Reps., 1977—. Mem. S.C. Housing Authority Commn. Mem. Nat. Home Builders Assn., Greenville Home Builders Assn., Greenville Bd. Realtors, Greenville C. of C. Democrat. Baptist. Clubs: Rotary, Masons, Shriners. Office: PO Box 8538 Greenville SC 29604

COBB, WILLIAM CHARLES, mgmt. cons.; b. St. Louis, Apr. 5, 1943; s. James and Eileen (Provost) C.; B.S. in Aerospace Engring., U. Tex., Austin, 1966; M.B.A., Ohio State U., 1970; m. Nancy Hale, June 25, 1966; children—Marlo Jane, Haley Tribble. Mgmt. cons. Touche Ross & Co., Houston, 1970-73; exec. dir. law firm Bracewell & Patterson, Houston, 1973-77; mgmt. cons., Houston, 1977—; lectr. meetings Am. Bar Assn., 1975, 77, nat. conf. on law firm mgmt., 1976—; mem. faculty Practising Law Inst., 1975—. Mem. exec. bd. and adminstrv. bd. St. Luke's United Meth. Ch., Houston, 1976-77, 80—. Served with USAF, 1966-70. Mem. Houston C. of C. (transp. com. 1973—), Am. Inst. C.P.A.'s, Tex. Soc. C.P.A.'s, AIAA. Clubs: Athletic, Houstonian (Houston), Ducks Unltd. Author Law Firm Planning Workbook, 1977. Home: 6150 Holly Springs Houston TX 77057 Office: Suite 4720 1100 Milam Bldg Houston TX 77002

COBBS, JAMES HAROLD, petroleum engr.; b. Bristow, Okla., Aug. 25, 1928; s. Harold M. and Ella (Rouintree) C.; B.S., U. Okla., 1949, postgrad., 1949-51; postgrad. U. Tulsa, 1955-67; m. Charlotte Marie Fisher, Aug. 16, 1953; children—James Harold, David C., Gregory L., Matthew L. Grad. asst. U. Okla., 1949-51; asso. engr. Tidewater Oil Co., Midland, Tex., 1951-52, reservoir engr., Houston, 1952-55, div. reservoir engr., Tulsa, 1955-59; pvt. practice engring., Tulsa, 1959-63, 69—; pres. Cobbs Engring. Inc.; partner Rock Store Test; sr. engr. Fenix & Scisson, Inc., Tulsa, 1963-69. Com. chmn., asst. scoutmaster Indian Nations council Boy Scouts Am., 1962—; instr. first aid A.R.C., 1969—. Precinct chmn. Republican party, 1961-62. Fellow A.A.A.S.; mem. Soc. Petroleum Engrs., Nat., Okla. socs. profl. engrs., Am., Okla. cons. engrs. councils, Vols. in Tech. Assistance, Sigma Phi Epsilon. Mem. Christian Ch. (elder, chmn. bd. 1971-72, 79). Contbr. articles to profl. jours. Patentee in field. Home: 5144 S New Haven St Tulsa OK 74135 Office: 5021 S Fulton St Tulsa OK 74135

COBERLY, SAMMIE LEE, hosp. exec.; b. Borger, Tex., Oct. 29, 1930; d. William Samuel and Mary Lee (Freeman) Shipley; student Ark. Poly. Coll., 1949-51; m. Bill S. Coberly, Dec. 13, 1952; 1 son. Office mgr., Ozark Supply Co., Rogers, Ark., 1965-69; dir. purchasing Rogers Meml. Hosp., 1970-72; dir. purchasing and materials mgmt. Highland Gen. Hosp., Pampa, Tex., 1977—. Mem. Internat. Material Mgmt. Soc., Nat. Assn. Hosp. Purchasing Mgmt., Soc. Ark. Hosp. Purchasing Agts., Tex. Hosp. Assn., Tex. Soc. Hosp. Purchasing Mgrs., Beta Sigma Phi. Home: 1827 Williston St Pampa TX 79065 Office: 1224 N Hobart St Pampa TX 79065

COBEY, WILLIAM WILFRED, JR., athletic dir.; b. Washington, May 13, 1939; s. William Wilfred and Mary Gray (Munroe) C.; B.A., Emory U., Atlanta, 1962; M.B.A., U. Pitts., 1964, M.Ed., 1968; m. Nancy Lee, Feb. 20, 1965; children—Catherine Gray, William Wilfred IV. Adminstrv. asst. Suburban Trust Co., Hyattsville, Md., 1964-65; salesman Dow Chem. Co., 1965-66; instr. phys. edn. sch. dists. outside Pitts., 1967-68; successively acad. counselor, asst. bus. mgr., asst. athletic dir. U. N.C., Chapel Hill, 1968-76, dir. athletics, 1976—; mem. Chapel Hill adv. bd. Home Savs. & Loan Assn. Bd. dirs. Happenings, Inc.; past pres., past bd. dirs. Chapel Hill-Charboro YMCA, 1975-76; active Chapel Hill-Charboro United Fund. Served with AUS, summer 1957. Recipient Disting. Service award Chapel Hill Jaycees, 1976. Mem. Nat. Assn. Collegiate Athletic Dirs. Republican. Mem. Bible Ch. Clubs: E. Chapel Rotary, Chapel Hill Country. Home: 617 Greenwood Rd Chapel Hill NC 27514 Office: PO Box 3000 Chapel Hill NC 27514

COBURN, DAVID THAYER, automotive service cons.; b. Boston, Aug. 2, 1938; s. William and Glayds Louise (Thayer) C.; B.S. in Bus. Adminstrn., Tulane U., 1961; M.B.A., Columbia U., 1963. Sales and gen. mgmt. positions automobile retail stores, 1963-72; pvt. practice automobile service cons., 1972-76; with Nat. Automobile Dealers Assn., McLean, Va., 1976—, service problems cons. to new car dealers, 1977—; service system cons. to various orgns. Served with USAF, 1955-57. Mem. Am. Mgmt. Assn. Club: Antique Automobile of America. Home: 108 S Columbus St Arlington VA 22204

COCHRAN, BENJAMIN PORTER, ins. co. exec.; b. Dallas, Dec. 2, 1913; s. Barksdale Porter and Harriet Catherine (Keefer) C.; student U. Tex., Arlington, 1933; postgrad. in bus. adminstrn., Am. Inst. Banking, 1935; m. Billie June Mitchell, Dec. 28, 1959; children—Benjamin Porter, Anita Cay Cochran Lacey. Asst. sec.-treas. Roswell Ins. & Surety Co. and Roswell Bldg. and Loan Assn. (N.Mex.), 1934-39; ins. mgr. and safety dir. Am. Liberty Oil Co., Dallas, 1944-47; casualty supt. U.S. Fidelity & Guaranty Co., Dallas, 1947-51; asst. v.p. Traders & Gen. Ins. Co., Dallas, 1951-58; resident v.p. Pacific Employers Ins. Co., Dallas, 1958-65, Chubb/Pacific Indemnity Ins. Co., Dallas, 1965-72; pres. ProTexn, Inc., Dallas, 1972—; resident sec. N.H. Ins. Co., Dallas, 1972—; atty.-in-fact A.I. Lloyd's Ins. Co., 1973—; cons. in field. Pres.-elect Southwest Ins. Info. Service, 1969; bd. dirs. Greater Dallas Crime Commn. Recipient Dir.'s Cup, Pacific Indemnity Co., 1966, Pres.'s Award, N.H. Ins. Co., 1978. Mem. Blue Goose. Republican. Methodist. Clubs: Pioneer of Dallas, Brookhaven Country, Ins. of Dallas (pres. 1973-74). Home: 4232 Boca Bay Dr Dallas TX 75234 Office: NH Ins Co 2001 Bryan Tower Suite 2115 Dallas TX 75201

COCHRAN, GEORGE MOFFETT, judge; b. Staunton, Va., Apr. 20, 1912; s. Peyton and Susie (Robertson) C.; grad. Episcopal High Sch., Alexandria, Va., 1930; B.A., U. Va., 1934, LL.B., 1936; m. Marion Lee Stuart, May 1, 1948; children—George Moffett, Harry Carter Stuart. Admitted to Md. bar, 1936, Va. bar, 1935; asso. firm Balt., 1936-38; partner firm Peyton Cochran and George M. Cochran, Staunton, 1938-64, Cochran, Lotz & Black, Staunton, 1964-69; justice Supreme Ct. Va., Richmond 1969—. Pres, Planters Bank & Trust Co., Staunton, 1963-69. Chmn. Woodrow Wilson Centennial Commn. of Va., 1952-58, Va. Cultural Devel. Study Commn., 1966-68; mem. Va. Commn. on Constl. Revision, 1968-69, Jud. Council of Va., 1963-69. Mem. Va. Ho. of Dels., 1948-66, Va. Senate, 1966-68. Chmn. bd. dirs. Stuart Hall; bd. visitors Va. Poly. Inst., 1960-68; trustee Mary Baldwin Coll. Served to lt. comdr. USNR, 1942-46. Mem. Am. Bar Assn., Va. Bar Assn. (pres. 1965-66), Raven Soc., Phi Beta Kappa, Phi Delta Phi, Beta Theta Pi. Episcopalian. Clubs: Staunton Country; Commonwealth (Richmond). Office: Masonic Temple Bldg Staunton VA 24401 also Supreme Ct Bldg Richmond VA 23210

COCHRAN, JOHN DICKINSON, minister, ch. adminstr.; b. Washington, June 2, 1932; s. Frank M. and Lucy (Dickinson) C.; B.S. in Bus. Adminstrn., Carson-Newman Coll., 1954; M.Religious Edn., Southwestern Bapt. Theol. Sem., 1956; m. Mable Wynn Kirkland, June 10, 1955; children—John Andrew, Stephen Paul, Jenni Lynn. Minister of edn. Fountain Meml. Bapt. Ch., Washington, 1956-59; minister to youth Capitol Hill-Metro. Bapt. Ch., Washington, 1959-66; minister of edn. First Bapt. Ch., Alexandria, Va., 1966-69, First Bapt. Ch., Roanoke, Va., 1969—; conf. leader, tchr. various states. Mem. Va. Bapt. Religious Edn. Assn. (pres. 1970-72), So. Bapt. Religious Edn. Assn., Downtown Ministers of Edn. Assn. Co-author: Working With Single Adults in Sunday School; contbr. articles in field to profl. jours. Home: 917 Charnwood Circle NW Roanoke VA 24012 Office: 515 3d St SW Box 2799 Roanoke VA 24001

COCHRAN, JOHN HENRY, JR., photographer, educator; b. Greeleyville, S.C., July 23, 1929; s. John H. and Dora Jessie (Reid) C.; B.A., Paine Coll., 1952; M.A., Atlanta U., 1962; Ed.D., U. Ga., 1972; m. Hattie Burton, Mar. 28, 1976; children—John Henry III, Donald Jerome, Christopher Oscar. Spl. counselor N.C. Mutual Life Ins. Co., 1955-57; tchr. elem. schs. Fulton County Bd. Edn., 1957-66, Atlanta City schs., 1966-71; instr. U. Ga., Athens, 1969-71; asso. prof. edn. Savannah (Ga.) State Coll., 1971-79, asst. to dean, 1977-78; asso. prof. edn. Armstrong State Coll., Savannah, 1979—; cons. for So. Assn. of Colls. and Univs., State Dept. Edn., 1973—; dir. workshops in human relations and curriculum devel., 1973—. One-man shows of photographs and/or paintings include: Ch. of the Covenent, Savannah, 1979, Savannah State Coll., 1979, Ft. Stewart Army Base, 1979; group shows include: Savannah State Coll., 1977-80, Hunter AFB and Fort Stewart, 1978, Macon (Ga.) Jr. Coll., 1980, Savannah State Coll., 1980; represented in permanent collections Dusable Mus., Chgo., numerous pvt. collections. Chmn. various civic projects in Atlanta, 1956-69, Savannah, 1973-78; bd. dirs. Butler YMCA, 1962-70. Served with U.S. Army, 1952-54; Korea. Recipient numerous civic work awards, 1957-70; NSF fellow, summer 1963, NDEA fellow, summer 1967, So. Fellowships Fund fellow, 1969-71. Mem. Nat. Alliance Black Sch. Educators, Nat. Soc. Study of Edn., Nat. Council for Basic Edn., Assn. Supervision and Curriculum Devel., Assn. Tchr. Educators, Ga. Coalition Higher Edn., Assn. for Study Afro Life and History, Nat. Conf. Artists, Ga. Assn. Tchr. Educators, Phi Delta Kappa, Kappa Delta Pi. Clubs: Elks, Masons. Author: (with others) Curriculum Guide for Elementary Teachers, 1960; Opinions About Economically Deprived Children, 1971; Opinionnaire on Curriculum Development, 1971; contbr. articles on edn. to profl. publs. Office: School of Education Armstrong State College Abercorn Extension Savannah GA 31406

COCHRAN, JUDITH ANN, educator; b. Hannibal, Mo., Sept. 11, 1944; d. Joseph H. and Dorothy E. C.; B.A., U. Colo., 1966; M. Ed., UCLA, 1970; Ph.D., Ariz. State U. State U., 1974. Tchr. English, Riggetti and Santa Maria High Schs., Santa Maria, Calif., 1966-69; supr. basic edn. Camp Fenner Canyon, Lancaster, Calif., 1970-71; tchr. English, Foothills Jr. High Sch., Arcadia, Calif., 1971; asst. dean, student advisement, Ariz. State U., Tempe, 1972-75; asst. prof. secondary edn. N. Tex. State U., Denton, 1975—; cons. in field. Adv. bd. 8th. Pl., halfway house for delinquents; precinct chmn. Republican party, Denton, 1976—. Recipient Elks Leadership award, 1962; U. Colo. Joint Honor scholar, 1962-66; Ariz. State U. grad. fellow, 1969-73; research grantee. Mem. Assn. Ednl. Motivation (dir. 1978—), Internat. Reading Assn., Nat.Reading Assn., Am. Ednl.

Research Assn. Republican. Methodist. Home: 2224 Georgetown St Denton TX 76201

COCHRAN, MARY JO, educator; b. Marshall County, Ala., June 12, 1928; d. Haden Paul and Jimmie Alice (Bodine) Copeland; B.S., Auburn U., 1949, M.S., 1970; m. Walter Livingston Cochran, June 11, 1950; children—Walter Livingston, Joseph Lynn, Charles Lee. Home economist, Ala. Gas Co., Montgomery, 1949; caseworker Tenn. Dept. Public Welfare, Harriman, 1950-52; instr. U. Chattanooga, 1964-70; head dept. home econs. and asst. prof., U. Tenn., Chattanooga, 1970—. Active, Missionery Ridge PTA, 1960-66, Senter Sch. Parents Assn., 1967-70. U. Chattanooga Found. grantee, 1978-79. Mem. Am. Home Econ. Assn., Tenn. Home Econ. Assn., Chattanooga Nutritional Council, Southeastern Regional Assn. of Home Mgmt.-Family Economics, Tenn. U. Home Econ. Adminstrs., Coll. Educators in Household Equip., Am. Council on Consumer Interests, Inst. Food Technologists, Elec. Women's Round Table, Am. Assn. Housing Educators, Hamilton County Pharm. Soc. Aux. (v.p. 1961), Omicron Nu, Kappa Omicron Phi. Methodist. Clubs: Missionary Ridge Garden, Kosmos Woman's. Home: 82 S Crest Rd Chattanooga TN 37404 Office: 105 Hunter Hall Univ of Tenn Chattanooga TN 37402

COCHRAN, MCKENDREE THOMAS, JR., dairy co. exec.; b. Altus, Okla., May 24, 1918; s. McKendree Thomas and Ray (Wheeler) C.; Asso. B.A., Kemper Mil. Sch., 1937; B.A., U. Okla., 1939; m. Mary Delores Coleman, June 22, 1940; children—Mary Chris (Mrs. Alexander Pryor Murray), McKendree Thomas, III, William Chesley, James Coleman. Asst. to pres. Eskimo Pie Corp., Bloomfield, N.J., 1940-52; gen. mgr. ice cream div. DCA Food Industries, N.Y.C., 1952-57; v.p., gen. mgr. dairies group Southland Corp., Dallas, 1957—. Served to lt. USNR, 1943-46. Mem. Nat. Dairy Council (dir.), Dairy Products Inst. Tex. (pres. 1966-67), Internat. Assn. Ice Cream Mfrs. (dir. 1968—), So. Assn. Dairy Food Mfrs. (pres. 1971-72), Kappa Alpha. Presbyn. Club: Northwood Country (Dallas). Home: 6440 Northport Dr Dallas TX 75230 Office: 2828 N Haskell St Dallas TX 75230

COCHRAN, SAMUEL LYNN, electronics engr.; b. Crab Orchard, W.Va., Sept. 30, 1949; s. Ray Samuel and Nellie Mae (Harris) C.; grad. with honors Raleigh County Vocat. Tech. Center, Beckley, W.Va., 1968; B.E.E., W.Va. Inst. Tech., 1972; m. Debra Lynne Garrett, Apr. 10, 1976. Electronics engr. Naval Air Rework Facility, Jacksonville, Fla., 1972-73, Naval Surface Weapons Center, Dahlgren, Va., 1973—; lectr. Counselor, Rappahannock Drug Abuse and Crisis Intervention Center, Fredericksburg, Va., 1975—. Recipient awards for directing little theatre plays. Democrat. Baptist. Clubs: Masons, Shriners, Moose. Home: PO Box 701 Dahlgren VA 22448 Office: Naval Surface Weapons Center Mail Code DF-11 Dahlgren VA 22448

COCHRAN, THAD, U.S. Senator; b. Pontotoc, Miss., Dec. 7, 1937; s. William Holmes and Emma Grace (Berry) C.; B.A., U. Miss., 1959, J.D. cum laude, 1965; postgrad. (Rotary Found. fellow), U. Dublin (Ireland), 1963-64; m. Rose Clayton, June 6, 1964; children—Thaddeus Clayton, Katherine Holmes. Admitted to Miss. bar, 1965, practiced in Jackson, 1965-72; asso. firm Watkins & Eager, 1965-72; mem. 93d-95th congresses from Miss.; mem. U.S. Senate from Miss., 1980—. Mem. exec. bd. Andrew Jackson council Boy Scouts Am., 1973—. Served to lt. USNR, 1959-61. Named Outstanding Young Man of Jackson, 1971, One of Three Outstanding Young Men of Miss., 1971. Mem. Am., Miss. (pres. young lawyers sect.) bar assns., Omicron Delta Kappa, Phi Kappa Phi, Pi Kappa Alpha. Republican. Baptist. Club: Rotary. Office: 212 Cannon House Office Bldg Washington DC 20515

COCKE, WILLIAM MARVIN, JR., physician; b. Balt., Aug. 2, 1934; s. William M. and Clara E. (Bosley) C.; B.S., Tex. A&M Coll., 1956; M.D., Baylor U., 1960; children—William Marvin III, Catherine Lynn, Deborah Kay, Brian Thomas. Intern, Vanderbilt U. Hosp., Nashville, 1960-61; fellow gen. surgery Ochsner Clinic and Found. Hosp., New Orleans, 1961-64; Am. Cancer Soc. clin. research fellow surgery Ochsner Clinic, 1962-63; chief resident surgery, clin. dir. Monroe (La.) Charity Hosp., 1963-64; resident head and neck surgery Roswell Park Inst., Buffalo, 1965; resident in plastic surgery N.Y. Hosp.-Cornell Med. Center, 1964-66; practice medicine specializing in plastic surgery; clin. instr. plastic surgery U. Tex. Med. Sch., San Antonio, 1968; asst. prof. surgery Vanderbilt U. Sch. Medicine, Nashville, 1968-69, developer div. plastic surgery, 1969, asst. clin. prof. plastic surgery, 1969-75; asso. prof. surgery Ind. U. Sch. Medicine, Indpls., 1975-76; chief plastic surgery Wishard Meml. Hosp., Ind. U. Med. Center, Indpls., 1975-76; asso. prof. surgery U. Calif., Davis, 1976-79, chmn. dept. plastic surgery, 1976-79; mem. staff Kaiser Found. Hosp., Sacramento, 1976-79; cons. plastic surgery VA Hosp., Martinez, Calif., 1976-79; prof. surgery, chief div. plastic surgery Tex. Tech. U. Sch. Medicine, 1979—; mem. staff Health Scis. Center, St. Mary's of the Plains Hosp. Served with USAF, 1966-68. Diplomate Am. Bd. Plastic Surgery. Fellow A.C.S.; mem. Am. Assn. Plastic Surgeons, Am. Soc. Plastic and Reconstructive Surgery, Am. Cleft Palate Assn., Am. Burn Assn., Southeastern Soc. Plastic Surgeons, Pan Am. Med. Soc., Assn. Acad. Surgery, Soc. Head and Neck Surgeons, Internat. Soc. Aesthetic Plastic Surgeons, Alton Oshsner Surg. Soc., Tex. Med. Assn., AMA, Lubbock County (Tex.) Med. Soc., Herbert Conway Soc. Author: Breast Reconstruction Following Mastectomy for Carcinoma, 1977; (with John S. Silverton and R.McShane) Basic Plastic Surgery, 1979; contbr. articles on reconstructive surgery to jours. in medicine. Office: Div Plastic Surgery Room 3A-144 Health Scis Center Lubbock TX 79430

COCKRELL, BILLY HUGH, JR., computer scientist; b. Corpus Christi, Tex., Mar. 25, 1948; s. Billy Hugh and Edith Blanch (Koepf) C.; A.S. in Computer Sci., San Antonio Coll., 1969; postgrad. Eastfield Jr. Coll., U. Tex., Arlington. Journeyman aircraft machinest Air Force Logistics Command, Kelly AFB, Tex., 1966-69; with Tex. Instruments Co., Dallas, 1969-75, mgr. postprocessor devel. and maintenance-N/C programming dept., 1973-75; sr. postprocessor analyst Univ. Computing Co., Dallas, 1975-78, lead postprocessor analyst, 1978-79, supr. postprocessor devel. Computer Aided Mfg., 1979—; APT part programming instr. Tex. Edn. Agy., 1978—. Mem. Computer and Automated Systems Assn. (charter). Office: 1930 Hi Line Dr Dallas TX 75207

COCKRELL, CLAUDE O'FLYNN, JR., container co. exec.; b. Memphis, May 10, 1937; s. Claude O'Flynn and Audrey (Roberts) C.; student Memphis State U., 1955, U. Miami, 1955-57; div.; children—Cana Lynn, Claude O'Flynn III. Pres., Shelby Paper Box Co., Memphis, 1952-56; pres.-owner Memphis Corrugated Container Co., 1956-61; adminstr., owner Cockrell Container Co., Memphis, 1961—; owner West Corp., Memphis, 1971—, Diamond Bar Ranch, Memphis, 1972—; pres. Tenn. Aviation, 1970—, Am. Divers, 1972—, Great Am. Container Corp., 1975—, Nashville Corrugated Box Inc., 1975—, West Prodns., 1977—, Photo-Finish Inc., 1978—, TVC Internat., Inc., 1979—; dir. So. Corrugated Box, Inc. State marshall Freedom Trail Found. Tenn., 1973—. Head campaign George Wallace for Pres., Memphis and Tri-state area, 1968. Mem. Tenn. Thoroughbred Breeders and Racers Assn. (chmn. 1978, pres. 1980), Pi Kappa Alpha. Presbyn. Moose. Home: 111 Old Hickory Blvd SW Apt 361 Nashville TN 37221 Office: PO Box 90387 Nashville TN 37209

COCKRILL, CHARLES BERTON, coll. adminstr.; b. Stringtown, Okla., Feb. 7, 1935; s. Clive Bakerand Thelma Lou (Pierce) C.; Asso. B.S., Eastern A&M Jr. Coll., 1953; B.S., Southeastern State Coll., 1955, masters degree, 1963; m. Barbara Joyce Collins, July 3, 1969; children—Steve, Shari, Chris, Cheryl, Collin. Coach, tchr. Putnam City High Sch., Oklahoma City, 1955-57; coach, tchr., chmn. dept. LaMarque (Tex.) High Sch., 1957-69; dir., sales mgr. Acad. Computer Tech., Dallas, 1969-70; dir., gen. mgr. Allstate Bus. Coll., Dallas, 1971—, Four-C Coll., Waco, Tex., 1971—; pres. Tex. Assn. Pvt. Schs., 1976, chmn. fin. aid com., 1977—; mem. Tex. Adv. Council for Tech.-Vocat. Edn., 1976. Mem. Gov.'s Adv. Council (1202 Commn), 1976. Served with USAR, 1953-61. Coe Found. fellow, summer 1969. Mem. Nat. Assn. Fin. Aid Adminstrs., Tex. Rehab. Assn., Assn. Ind. Colls. and Schs., Dallas C. of C. Presbyterian. Home: 1808 E Grauwyler Rd Irving TX 75061 Office: Allstate Bus Coll 2909 Oaklawn Dallas TX 75219

CODDING, FREDERICK HAYDEN, lawyer; b. Hopewell, Va., Dec. 13, 1938; s. Francis Chadwick and Ruthcille Sharon (Craven) C.; A.B., Coll. William and Mary, 1962; J.D., Georgetown U., 1966; m. Judith Willis Hawkins, Apr. 30, 1966; children—Forrest Hayden, Judith Chadwick, Cally Willis, Clare Catharine. Legal asst. VA, Washington, 1963-65; Capitol Hill reporter, editor Congl. Monitor, Washington, 1966; admitted to Va. bar, 1966, D.C. bar, 1968; law clk. to chief judge D.C. Ct. Appeals, 1966-68; individual practice law, Va. and Washington; v.p., counsel Nat. Assn. Miscellaneous, Ornamental and Archtl. Products Contractors, Fairfax, 1970—; counsel, dir. Nat. Assn. Reinforcing Steel Contractors, Fairfax, 1970—. Mem. federally established rev. bds. for constrn. industry, N.Y.C. Bldg. Standards Com. Counsel, Fairfax County Youth Club. Mem. Am., D.C., Va., Fairfax bar assns., Nat. Council Erectors, Fabricators and Riggers, Sigma Nu. Editor, pub. legislative, adminstrv., bldg. and constrn. industry newsletters, reports. Office: 10382 Main St Fairfax VA 22030

COE, MIRIAM, writer, librarian, artist; b. Liverpool, Eng., July 1, 1902; d. David Avrom and Shaynah Froma (Lippsman) Cohen; honors diploma, Oulton Coll.; diploma, Skerry's Coll.; student Liverpool U., Liverpool City Sch. Art, U. Rochester (N.Y.), Columbia U., N.Y. Sch. Theatre, Carnegie Hall Studios, Sch. Chinese Brushwork, N.Y.C., L.I. U., George Peabody Coll. for Tchrs., Utah, Fla. univs.; B.F.A., La. State U. Sec., J. Ogden Co., shipbrokers, Liverpool, Eng., 1916-19; tchr. violin, 1924-29; article writer Liverpool Express, 1928; lectr. on psychology of music Sta. WHAM, Stromberg Carlson Telephone Co., Hotel Sagamore, Rochester, 1929-30; writer children's stories, 1938; comml. artist, N.Y.C., 1944-48; coach in English lang.; librarian, Baton Rouge, 1961-63; one-woman shows, Baton Rouge; exhibitor paintings, N.Y., La. Mem. Greater Baton Rouge Council Arts and Humanities, La. Arts and Scis. Center. Recipient various awards and prizes. Mem. A.L.A. (coll. and research div.), Roundtable for the Blind, La., Southwestern library assns., La. Library Assn., Am. Assn. Sch. Librarians, Am. Assn. State Librarians, Am. Assn. Polit. and Social Scis., Friends of La. State U. Library, Am. Hist. Soc., Am. Sociol. Assn., Am. Assn. for Natural History, Am. Judicature Soc., Am. Pub. Health Assn., Am. Soc. Photogrammetry, Smithsonian Assos., Alumni Palmer Grad. Sch. L.S., Am. Assn. Museums, La. Water-color Soc., La. Art and Artists Guild, Greater Nat. Soc. Poets, Am. Dickens League (hon.), Acad. Am. Poets, Am. Vegetarian Union, Nat. Soc. Lit. and Arts, Alumni La. State U., Southwestern Poetry Soc., La. Soc. Poets, Nat. Soc. Published Poets, Mystery Club N.Y., Assn. La. Arts and Artists, Alpha Beta Alpha. Author: Librarians Manual; Librarianship as a Career Field; The Psychology of Music; Development of Education in England; Careers in Art; Dictionary and Handbook of Photogrammetry and Related Terms; Poems for the Young; Poets, Portraits, Poems & Paintings; Man's Struggle for Survival Against Disaster—Natural and Man-Made; also miscellaneous poems, children's story books. Editor: Anthology of World Literature, A Sociological Cyclopedia; Pitirim Sorokin: His Life and His Work; Haiku, East/West: Ancient/Modern Illustrated. Composer: Our Land; I'm Praying for Him. Developed original color system for teaching typewriting; inventor spectrum color system for teaching theory of music; inventor type-face, adjuncts for mechanism in constructing typewriters. Home: Apt 29 839 Azalea Baton Rouge LA 70802 Office: Box 18184 La State U Baton Rouge LA 70893

COE, ROBERT STANFORD, educator; b. Cin., July 9, 1919; s. Louis Herman and Alma Mary (Jenkins) C.; B.S., Miami U., Oxford, Ohio, 1941; M.S., U. Houston, 1948, Ph.D., 1957; m. Nancy Jean Ayres, Oct. 28, 1950; children—Carolyn Lee, William Ayres, Jon Bruce. Asst. to v.p. Dresser Industries, Dallas, 1956-58; personnel adminstr. Ling-Temco-Vought, Dallas, 1958-64; prof., grad. adviser Stephen F. Austin State U., Tex., 1964-69; prof., chmn. dept. mgmt. Angelo State U., San Angelo, 1969—; lectr. U. Tex. at Arlington, 1960-64; pres. Mgmt. Resources Assos., San Angelo, 1970—. Mem. Gov.'s Com. on Goals for Tex., 1970. Served with USNR, 1941-45. Mem. AAUP, Am. Psychol. Assn., Acad. Mgmt., Am. Inst. Decision Scis., Alpha Kappa Psi, Phi Kappa Phi, Pi Kappa Alpha. Presbyterian. Clubs: Rotary, San Angelo Country, Rolling Hills Country. Contbr. articles to profl. jours. Home: 3223 Trinity St San Angelo TX 76901 Office: Angelo State U San Angelo TX 76901

COE, WILLIAM CLITUS, JR., accountant; b. Swifton, Ark., Sept. 18, 1941; s. William Clitus and Mary Inez (McCall) C.; B.S. in Bus. Adminstrn., U. Ark., 1963; M.B.A., Wharton Grad. Sch. Finance, 1965; m. Yvonne Marie Ross, Nov. 16, 1968; children—Mary, Rebeccka. Office mgr. Frank Whitbeck for Gov., Little Rock, 1968; partner Ernst & Whinny, New Orleans, C.P.A.'s, 1968—. Adviser Jr. Achievement, New Orleans, 1971-72; mem. Spring Festa Assn. Bd. dirs. Jefferson Place Civic Assn., New Orleans, 1971-74, pres., 1972-73, v.p., 1973-74; bd. dirs., treas. Community Service Center, 1976—; bd. dirs., 1st v.p. Tall Timbers Improvement Assn.; bd. dirs., v.p. New Orleans Floral Trail, 1973-74, 3d v.p., 1976. Served to 1st lt. Finance Corps, AUS, 1966-68. C.P.A., La., Ark. Mem. Goals to Grow Found., Am. Inst. C.P.A.'s, New Orleans, La. socs. C.P.A.'s, Financial Analyst Soc., New Orleans Jaycees (dir. 1972-73, state dir. 1972-73), C. of C. (ambassador's com.), Mus. Art, Internat. Platform Assn., Phi Eta Sigma, Alpha Kappa Psi, Phi Delta Theta, Omicron Delta Kappa. Republican. Methodist. Clubs: Variety (dir. 1973-78), Young Men's Business (dir. 1971-73, 76—, treas., program chmn. 1977, pres. 1979) (New Orleans). Editor: Action, 1972-73, 75; Friends of Cabildo. Home: 3708 Post Oak Ave New Orleans LA 70114 Office: 920 One Shell Sq New Orleans LA 70139

COFFEE, JAMES MADISON, JR., educator; b. Douglas, Ga., Nov. 18, 1918; s. James Madison and Bessie (Hatfield) C.; B.A. in History, Duke, 1949; M.A. in History, Cornell U., 1950; Ed.D. in Guidance and Counselling, Harvard, 1957. Mem. faculty Clark U., Worcester, Mass., 1954-68, asso. prof. edn., 1962-68, acting chmn. dept., 1967-68, dir. guidance and placement, 1954-67; prof. edn. Jacksonville (Fla.) U., 1968-75, dir. tchr. edn., 1970-75, dir. M.A. in Teaching program, 1972-75, chmn. div. edn., 1968-75; prof. edn. Stetson U., DeLand, Fla., 1975—, dir. tchr. edn., 1975—. Mem. Fla. Council on Tchr. Edn., 1975-77. Co-chmn. edn. com. Jacksonville Sesquicentennial Com., 1971-72. Served to 2d lt. USAAF, World War II. Named Man of Year, Clark U. chpt. Lambda Chi Alpha, 1957. Mem. Am. Personnel and Guidance Assn., Am. Psychol. Assn., Am. Ednl. Research Assn., Fla. Council Deans and Dirs. Tchrs. Edn. (pres. 1978-79), Phi Beta Kappa, Phi Delta Kappa, Kappa Delta Phi. Baptist. Home: 5903 Woodside Dr Jacksonville FL 32210

COFFEY, JACK LEROY, pharmacist; b. Vanoss, Okla., May 20, 1935; s. Woodrow and Alice Mae (Cranford) C.; B.S., U. Okla., 1957; m. Frances Davis, Aug. 11, 1956; children—Allyson, Catherine. Practice pharmacy Owl Drug, Shawnee, Okla., then Richards Drug, Shawnee; partner, mgr. Shawnee Med. Center Pharmacy and Clinic Pharmacy, 1963—; adj. clin. instr. U. Okla., mem. Okla. State Bd. Pharmacy. Commr. at large City of Shawnee, 1972-74. Served to capt. USAF, 1958-63. Fellow Am. Coll. Apothecaries; mem. Nat. Assn. Retail Druggists, Am. Pharm. Assn., Nat. Assn. Bd. Pharmacy, Soc. Hosp. Pharmacists, Okla. Pharm. Assn. Democrat. Methodist. Clubs: Rotary, Mason, Elks. Home: 1917 N Minnesota St Shawnee OK 74801 Office: 2803 N Seratoga St Shawnee OK 74801

COFFIN, EDWARD RAY, airline exec.; b. Clinton, Ind., June 23, 1937; s. Eugene A. and Ruth M. (Davies) C.; student U. Colo., 1954-55, Ind. State U., 1955-58; G.E.E., USAF Inst. Tech., 1959-60; m. DeAnn Kay St. Clair, Aug. 26, 1961; children—Christopher, Cynthia. Radar installation chief USAF, 1960-62; field engr. Burroughs Corp., 1962-63; with AVCO Corp., 1964-65; programmer Mutual Omaha, 1965-66; program analyst CBS, Inc., 1967; corp. systems analyst Rath Packing, 1967-70; systems project mgr. Massey-Ferguson, Inc., Des Moines, 1970-76; head comml. data processing tng. Am. Airlines, Tulsa, 1976—. Counselor, Des Moines Jr. Achievement, 1971. Served with USAF, 1958-62. Mem. Am. Mgmt. Assn., Nat. Mgmt. Assn. (nat. dir.), Assn. Systems Mgmt., U.S. Golf Assn., Am. Airlines Golf Assn. (v.p.), Waterloo Data Processing Mgmt. Assn., Iowa Council Mgmt. Clubs, Am. Airlines Adminstrn. Assn. Clubs: Indian Springs Country; Indianola Country. Home: 909 W Glendale St Broken Arrow OK 74012 Office: MD355 American Airlines Box 51330 Tulsa OK 74151

COFFIN, MILLER GERARD, geophysicist; b. Mathis, Tex., May 11, 1917; s. Arthur Benjamin and Zenna Hortense (Miller) C.; B.S. in Physics, Tex. Coll. Arts and Industries, 1939; m. Florence Asenath Miller, Sept. 14, 1919; children—Peggy (Mrs. Michael D. Peters), Linda (Mrs. Donald D. Lofland), James. With Central Power & Light Co., Corpus Christi, Tex., 1939-42; electric instrument instr., mechanic Air Service Command Kelly Field, San Antonio, 1942-45; with Atlantic Refining Co., 1945-60, seismograph observer, 1945-50, seismograph computer, 1950-52, seismologist, 1952-60; geophys. cons. in Corpus Christi, Tex., 1960—. Mem. Coastal Bend Geophys. Soc., Corpus Christi Geol. Soc., Soc. Exploration Geophysicists, Soc. Independent Profl. Earth Scientists. Home: 238 Cape Hatteras Corpus Christi TX 78412 Office: 1728 Guaranty Bank Plaza Corpus Christi TX 78475

COFFMAN, BARRY PRESTON, broadcast co. exec.; b. Harrisonburg, Va., Dec. 20, 1947; s. Carr Preston and Kathleen (Kiracofe) C.; A.B., Coll. William and Mary, 1970. Account exec., writer Martin/Remick/Moore Advt. Co., Richmond, Va., 1972-73; pres., gen. mgr. Sta. WGOE, Inc., Richmond, 1975—. Campaign chmn. Va. Capital Area March of Dimes, 1978; treas. The Daily Planet, Inc., Community Counseling Center, Richmond, 1978—. Served with U.S. Army, 1970-72. Mem. Greater Richmond Broadcasters (past pres.), Richmond Advt. Club, Nat. Assn. Broadcasters, Greater Richmond C. of C. Office: 3122 W Gary St Richmond VA 23221

COFFMAN, CLAUDE T., lawyer; b. Robinsonville, Miss., Jan. 20, 1916; s. Tulus Jackson and Addie (Mick) C.; A.B., U. Miss., 1938, LL.B., 1938; postgrad. Harvard U., 1938-39; m. Ninna Carr Bailey, July 15, 1940; children—Mary Coffman Tilton, Margaret Coffman Noll. Admitted to Miss. bar, 1938; atty. U.S. Dept. Agr., Washington, 1939-51, dep. gen. counsel, 1968-74; asst. legal counsel Tech. Cooperation Adminstrn., Washington, 1951-53; prof. law faculty Memphis State U., 1974—. Home: 5439 Glenwild Rd Memphis TN 38117

COFFMAN, JOHN EDWIN, geographer, educator; b. Robstown, Tex., Feb. 17, 1942; s. Carl Simeon and Zada Lee (White) C.; A.A., Del Mar Coll., 1960; B.A., U. Calif. at Los Angeles, 1967, M.A., 1968, C.Phil., 1970, Ph.D., 1972. Tech. pubs. and media display cons., N.Y. and Calif., 1960-65; instr. geography Calif. State U. at Fullerton, 1970, Calif. State Coll. at Dominguez Hills, 1970; from instr. to asso. prof. U. Houston, 1970—. Mem. regional selection com. Office of Edn., 1970—. Mem. Nat. Council Geog. Edn. (exec. bd.), Assn. Am. Geographers (com. on geography and bus.), Am. Geog. Soc., Internat. Geog. Congress, Assn. Pacific Coast Geographers, Southwestern Social Sci. Assn. (nominating com.), Southwest Conf. on Asian Studies (sec.-treas., editor newsletter), Nat., Tex. councils for social studies, Calif. Council Geography Tchrs., Assn. Asian Studies, Western Social Sci. Assn., Conf. Latin Am. Geographers, Geographic Educators of Tex. (founder), AAUP (pres. U. Houston chpt.), AAAS, Soc. Econ. Botany, Alaska Geog. Soc., Sigma Xi, Phi Theta Kappa, Gamma Theta Upsilon; fellow Royal Geog. Soc. (London), U.S. Naval Inst., Omicron Delta Kappa. Author coll. textbooks; contbr. articles to profl. jours., World Book Ency. Home: Route 3 Box 692 Porter TX 77365 Office: Dept Geography U Houston Houston TX 77004

COFFMAN, WESLEY LAVON, employment ser. counselor; b. Oil City, La., Feb. 6, 1932; s. S.K. and Ruby Lee (Mears) C.; B.A., Northwestern State U., 1955, M.Rehab. Counseling, 1979; m. Marion Estelle Whitley, Aug. 1, 1953; children—Steve W., Guy M., Jeffery D., Beverly C. Enlisted U.S. Army, 1953, advanced through grades to master sgt., 1969, served career counselor supr., 1953-74, ret., 1974; employment ser. counselor La. Dept. Employment Security, Dept. Labor, Leesville, 1974—; instr. personal fin. Northwestern State U. Ops. dir. Vernon Youth Services, 1978—; chmn. awards com. Human Resources Council, 1976—; mem. Tri-Community Council, 1977—; deacon, Sunday Sch. tchr. Bapt. Ch., dir. weekly TV program. Decorated Nat. Defense ser. medal. Mem. Am. Personnel and Guidance Assn., La. Personnel and Guidance Assn., La. Employment Counselors Assn., Nat. Employment Counselors Assn. Democrat. Clubs: VFW, Am. Legion, Masons, Shrine. Home: PO Box 1167 Leesville LA 71446 Office: PO Box 1547 Leesville LA 71446

COFFMAN, WESLEY SURBER, musician; b. Ardmore, Okla., June 17, 1927; s. George Wesley and Mayme Rebecca (Surber) C.; B. Mus., No. Tex. State U., 1950, M.Mus. in Edn., 1953; Ph.D., Fla. State U., 1968; m. Patricia Elaine Russell, Dec. 27, 1949; children—Russell Surber, Nancy Catherine, Rebecca Leone. Choral dir. Sherman (Tex.) High Sch., 1950-58; organist, minister of music 1st Baptist Ch., Sherman, 1949-58; minister of music 2d Bapt. Ch., Houston, 1958-66; choral asst. Fla. State U., 1966-68; prof. music Dallas Bapt. Coll., 1968—, chmn. dept. music, 1968-74, chmn. arts div., 1974—; mem. Oak Cliff bd. Dallas Symphony, 1976—; mem. Oak Cliff Fine Arts Festival Bd., 1975-76. Served with USN, 1945-46. Mem. Am. Guild Organists (exec. com. Dallas, 1970-73), Tex. Choral Dirs. Assn. (dir. 1954-56), Music Educators Nat. Conf., Tex. Music Educators Assn., Pi Kappa Lambda, Alpha Chi, Phi Mu Alpha. Baptist. Home: 607

Little Creek Duncanville TX 75116 Office: 7007 W Kiest St Dallas TX 75211

COFFMAN, WILLIAM THOMAS, lawyer; b. Alva, Okla., Nov. 10, 1940; s. Harry R. and Wilma Coffman Lee (Hellman) C.; B.S. in Bus. Adminstrn., U. Tulsa, 1963, J.D., 1966; postgrad. U. Okla., 1963-64; m. Sharon D. Jones, June 12, 1965; children—Scott Gregory, Kendra Lynn. Admitted to Okla. bar, 1966; asso. firm Gable, Gotwals, Rubin, Fox, Johnson & Baker, Tulsa, 1966-72, mem. firm, 1972—. Bd. dirs. Magic Empire council Girl Scouts U.S.A., 1976-79. Served to lt. comdr. Judge Adv. Gen. Corp., USNR. Fellow Am. Coll. Probate Counsel; mem. Am., Okla. (chmn. probate and trust law sect. 1974), Tulsa County (outstanding jr. mem. 1972), bar assns., Am. Judicature Soc., Tulsa Estate Planning Forum (pres. 1976-77), Tulsa Title and Probate Lawyers Assn. (pres. 1979). Club: Kiwanis. Home: 6601 S Florence St Tulsa OK 74136 Office: 20th Floor 4th Nat Bank Bldg Tulsa OK 74119

COFRAN, GEORGE LEE, mgmt. cons.; b. Buffalo, Sept. 30, 1945; s. Louis Lee and Virginia Carolyn (Breneman) C.; B.S.E.E., Purdue U., 1967; M.B.A., Dartmouth Coll., 1969; m. Jane Ann Kimsey, Apr. 24, 1969; children—Jeffrey Todd, Jennifer Rene. Systems analyst Burlington Mgmt. Services, Greensboro, N.C., 1969-70; mgmt. cons. Arthur Young & Co., Houston, 1971-77; pres. Cofran & Assos., Inc., Houston, 1977—; comml. arbitrator Am. Arbitration Assn.; speaker, lectr. Bd. dirs. Huntwick Civic Assn., Houston, 1979; charter v.p. Active Corps of Execs., SBA, 1974, 75. Served to 1st lt., AUS, 1970-71. Decorated Army Commendation medal; C.P.A., Tex.; cert. data processing Data Processing Mgmt. Assn. Mem. Am. Inst. C.P.A.'s, IEEE, Assn. Systems Mgmt. (past pres., dir. Houston chpt., Outstanding Service award Houston chpt. 1978-79), Tau Beta Pi. Club: Huntwick Racquet (Houston). Home: 5610 Ascalon Circle Houston TX 77069 Office: 500 Champions Bank Bldg 5625 FM 1960 W Houston TX 77069

COGAN, DENNIS B., psychologist; b. Chgo., Aug. 24, 1943; s. Abe and Dorothy (Lewis) C.; B.A., Calif. State U., Los Angeles, 1970, M.S., 1973; Ph.D., Ariz. State U., 1977. Elem. tchr. Claremont (Calif.) Unified Sch. Dist., 1971-73, Dept. of Def., Okinawa, 1973-74; cons. psychologist Maricopa County (Ariz.) Headstart, 1975-77; asst. prof. psychology, coordinator human services program U. Miami, Coral Gables, 1977—; vol. supr. Ednl. Parcipation in the Community, 1969; supr. East Valley Free Clinic, LaPuente, Calif., 1970-73; adminstr., supr. South Mountain Free Clinic, Phoenix, 1974-77, Open Door Counseling Center, Okinawa, 1973-74. Served with USNR, 1962-64. HEW Rehab. fellow, 1971-73. Mem. Am. Psychol. Assn., Am. Personnel and Guidance Assn., Fla. Personnel and Guidance Assn., Am. Assn. Marriage and Family Therapists, Nat. Orgn. Human Service Educators, Assn. Non-White Concerns. Home: 10985 SW 107th St #102 Miami FL 33176 Office: Dept of Educational Psychology University of Miami Coral Gables FL 33124

COGAN, FELICIA HENDERSON, humanist, educator; b. DeQueen, Ark., May 1, 1932; d. Edward Cooke and Marguerite (Lee) Henderson; B.A., U. Tulsa, 1954; M.A., Trinity U., San Antonio, 1965; postgrad. U. Oreg., 1954-55, So. Meth. U., 1967-70; m. Myles I.C. Cogan, Oct. 15, 1960; 1 dau., Courtenay. Feature writer Tulsa Daily World, 1956-60, San Antonio Light, 1962-64; mem. faculty So. Meth. U., Dallas, 1965-70, Tarrant County Jr. Coll., Ft. Worth, 1970-71; mem. faculty Lord Fairfax Coll., Middletown, Va., 1971—, asst. prof. English, 1974—. Founder, faculty dir. Shenandoah Valley Writers' Guild, 1977—. Recipient Achievement award Tarrant County Jr. Coll., 1971, Lord Fairfax Coll., 1979. Mem. AAUW, DAR, Daus. of Republic of Tex., Mortar Bd., Theta Sigma Phi, Kappa Kappa Gamma. Episcopalian. Home: Oaklee PO Box K Shepherdstown WV 25433 Office: Dept English Lord Fairfax Coll Middletown VA 22645

COGAN, MYLES IRVING COURTENAY, oral and maxillofacial surgeon; b. Tampico, Mexico, June 3, 1929; came to U.S., 1940, naturalized, 1943; s. Myles H.R. and Ruth Lillian (Sessoms) C.; D.D.S., U. Tex., 1953; M.P.H., U. Mich., 1958; M.S.D., Baylor U., 1966; m. Felicia Lee Henderson, Oct. 15, 1960; 1 dau., Courtenay. Clin. instr. restorative dentistry U. Tex. Dental Br., Houston, 1956-57; pvt. practice gen. dentistry, Houston, 1958-62; research asso. in dentistry VA Med. Center, Dallas, 1966-67, chief oral surgery sect., 1967-70; staff oral surgeon VA Med. Center, Martinsburg, W.Va., 1970-73, chief dental service, 1973—; asst. prof. dept. oral surgery Baylor U. Coll. Dentistry, Dallas, 1967-70; clin. instr. oral surgery W.Va. U. Sch. Dentistry, Morgantown, 1976—. Served to capt. Dental Corps, USAF, 1953-55. Diplomate Am. Bd. Oral and Maxillofacial Surgery, Pan Am. Med. Assn. Fellow Royal Soc. Health, Am. Coll. Oral and Maxillofacial Surgeons, Am. Coll. Dentists; mem. Eastern Panhandle Dental Soc. of W.Va. (v.p. 1972-74), Am. Assn. Hosp. Dentists (sec. Southeastern Regional conf. 1975-76, chmn. W.Va. sect. 1979—), ADA, Tex. Dental Assn., Am. Assn. Oral and Maxillofacial Surgeons, Internat. Assn. Oral Surgeons, Southeastern and S.W. Soc. Oral Surgeons, W.Va. Soc. Oral and Maxillofacial Surgeons, Am. Assn. Public Health Dentists, Am. Public Health Assn., Am. Dental Soc. of Anesthesiology, Am. Acad. Dental Radiology, Assn. Mil. Surgeons of U.S., Sigma Xi, Omicron Kappa Upsilon. Episcopalian. Clubs: Rotary, Men's of Shepherdstown. Contbr. articles in field to profl. jours. Home: PO Box K Shepherdstown WV 25443 Office: Dental Service VA Med Center Martinsburg WV 25401

COGGESHALL, ROBERT WALDEN, ret. govt. ofcl.; b. Darlington, S.C., Sept. 11, 1912; s. Robert Werner and Beulah (Walden) C.; B.S., U. S.C., 1932; M.A., George Washington U., 1964; postgrad. Am. U., 1964-69; m. Ellie Mason Thomas, Sept. 3, 1934; children—Peter Collin V., John Pennington. Administrv. analyst Home Owners Loan Corp., Washington, 1934-41; budget analyst Fed. Works Agy., 1941-43; asst. dep. adminstr. for rent control OPA, 1943-46; chief systems and procedures Bur. Reclamation, 1946-53; editor Postal Manual, Office Postmaster Gen., 1954; chief mgmt. analysis Bur. Indian Affairs, 1954-57; chief div. mgmt. sci. Office of Sec., Dept. Interior, 1957-68; fellow Brookings Instn., 1968-69; mem. faculty U.S. Dept. Agr. Grad. Sch., 1959-65. Mem. Common Cause (S.C. chmn. 1974-75), Alpha Tau Omega. Episcopalian. Author: Administrative Functions of the Fish and Wildlife Service, 1958; Coordination of Federal Oceanography, 1963. Home: Shaggy Acres Ballentine SC 29002

COHEN, AVRUM ISAAC, social services adminstr.; b. Chgo., Nov. 11, 1941; s. Ben and Sarah (Gutter) C.; B.A., U. Ill., 1963, M.S.W., 1966; D.S.W., Tulane U., 1971; m. Susan Barbara Singer, Oct. 2, 1963; children—Jordan Samuel, Jonathan Matthew. Social work aide Jewish Community Centers of Chgo., 1963-64, social group worker and head children's div., 1966-68; asst. exec. dir. Jewish Community Center of New Orleans, 1971-73, exec. dir., 1973—; instr. Sch. of Social Work, Tulane U., New Orleans, 1970-71; instr. seminar on community Urban League St. Acad. of New Orleans, 1975, 76. Chmn., Conf. of Agy. Execs. of United Way of Met. New Orleans, 1976—; trainer and lectr. group process and mgmt. Girl Scouts U.S., New Orleans, 1972; vice chmn. Audubon dist. Boy Scouts Am., 1978; mem. bd. advs. De Paul Hosp. of New Orleans, 1973—; mem. profl. scholarship com. Jewish Welfare Bd., 1978; bd. dirs. Commn. on Jewish Edn. of New Orleans, 1975—, Conservative Congregation of New Orleans, 1972-74. Recipient Louis Kraft award, 1972; cert. social worker Ill., La.; cert. tchr., Ill. Mem. Nat. Assn. of Social Workers (chmn. com. on inquiry 1977-78), Assn. of Jewish Center Workers (nat. v.p. 1974-76, pres. so. region chpt. 1972-74, mem. editorial adv. com. 1975), Council on Social Work Edn. Jewish. Contbr. articles on social work to profl. jours. Home: 7921 Burthe St New Orleans LA 70118 Office: 5342 St Charles Ave New Orleans LA 70115

COHEN, BARRY MENDEL, historian; b. Dallas, Feb. 1, 1939; s. Ben and Marjorie Joyce (Novich) C.; B.A., Rice U., 1960; M.A., U. Tex., 1964, postgrad., 1971-72, 74—; postgrad. (fellow) U. Ill., summer 1974; m. Rosalee Valent-Torres, July 30, 1967. Instr. history Tex. Arts and Industries U., Kingsville, 1965-67; prof. social sci. Chowan Coll., Murfreesboro, N.C., 1969-73; exec. Cohen Candy Co., Dallas, 1973—; lectr. Richland Coll., Dallas, 1976-77, Mountain View Coll., Dallas, spring 1977, U. Tex. at Dallas, summer 1977; symposium speaker 14th Internat. Genetics Congress, Moscow, 1978. Mem. nat. bd. advisers Ad Hoc Com. for Intellectual Freedom. Bd. dirs. Kleberg County Community Action, 1966-67, Chowanoke Area Devel. Assn., 1971. Mem. Am. Hist. Assn., Am. Assn. for Advancement Slavic Studies, A.A.U.P. Democrat. Jewish religion. Contbr. articles to profl. jours. and newspapers. Office: 171 Howell St Dallas TX 75207

COHEN, DAVID MICHAEL, pharm. co. exec.; b. Bklyn., Dec. 5, 1940; s. Teddy and Anne Helene (Katz) C.; B.S., Poly. Inst. Bklyn., 1962, Ph.D., 1972; m. Carole Lee Miller, Apr. 24, 1965; children—Stacey Ann, Matthew Robert, Mark Steven. Supr. quality control Pfizer Inc., Bklyn., 1962-65, supr. oral products release, 1965-67, supr. sterile products release, 1967-69, sr. supr. oral products release, 1969-71, mgr. quality control research labs., 1971-76; dir. quality assurance and drug regulatory affairs Key Pharms. Inc., Miami, 1977-80, v.p., 1980—. Mem. Am. Chem. Soc., Nat. Mgmt. Assn., Am. Soc. Quality Control, Am. Assn. Clin. Chemistry, Phi Lambda Upsilon. Contbr. articles to profl. publs. Home: 1921 SW 67th Terr Plantation FL 33317 Office: 50 NW 176th St Miami FL 33169

COHEN, EUGENE ERWIN, univ., health inst. adminstr.; b. Johnstown, Pa., Nov. 1, 1917; s. Leroy Samuel and Ann (Aronson) C.; B.B.A., U. Miami (Fla.), 1941, M.B.A., 1951; postgrad. Wayne State U., 1944-45, U. N.C., 1951-52; m. Lee Woodard Edmundson, Dec. 31, 1944; children—William Palmer, Margaret Gene, Ann Woodard. Mem. faculty U. Miami, 1945—, asso. prof. acctg., 1954-67, prof. acctg., 1967—, treas., 1957-79, v.p., 1958-79, v.p. emeritus, 1979—; treas. Howard Hughes Med. Inst., 1979—; also treas. univ. Research Found.; v.p., dir. Dormitory Housing Assn., Inc.; chmn., pres. Laurel Corp., 1971-73; dir. Am. Bankers Ins. Co. Fla., Am. Laser Corp., Garrett & Co., Consortium Investors Corp., Univ. Fed. Savs. and Loan Assn. Cons. Greyhound Corp., Plastetics, Inc., Reynolds & Co., NSF, NIH, U.S. Office Edn., So. Assn. Colls. and Schs.; stockholders agent Garrett Inst.; rep. Univ. Corp. for Atmospheric Research, 1969-73; mem. com. taxation Am. Council Edn.; rep. Univ. Corp. Atmospheric Research. Pres. Orange Bowl Com.; asso. mem. Internat. Center Coral Gables, 1973—, also New World Center at Miami Com.; mem. Miami Mayor's Spl. Adv. Com. on Interama, 1969-72; bd. dirs. Miami Goodwill Industries, Miamians, Dade County Citizens Safety Council, Greater Miami Indsl. Commn.; chmn. Dade County Higher Edn. Facilities Authority, 1969—, Jackson Found., 1972—; v.p., dir. Nat. Children's Cardiac Hosp.; mem. Health Systems Agency of South Fla., Family Services, Miami, 1968-74; bd. dirs. Heart Learning Resources Center; trustee United Way Dade County. Served with AUS, 1941-45. Mem. Dade County C. of C., Am. Mgmt. Assn., Nat. (dir.), So. (pres. 1963) assns. coll. and univ. bus. officers, Coll. and U. Personnel Assn., Coll. and U. Housing Officers Assn., Nat. Assn. Cost Accts., Fin. Execs. Inst. (founder mem. Fla. chpt., chpt. pres. 1963), Fin. Analysts Soc. Miami, Econ. Soc. S. Fla., Miami Beach Com. of 100, Hist. Assn. So. Fla. (dir.), Coral Gables Com. of 21, Friends of Univ. Library, Newcomen Soc., Iron Arrow, Omicron Delta Kappa, Alpha Phi Omega, Phi Mu Alpha, Alpha Kappa Psi, Beta Gamma Sigma. Clubs: Univ. Yacht, Miami (v.p.); Ocean Reef Yacht and Country (Key Largo, Fla.). Cons. editor Coll. and Univ. Bus. Mag., 1963-68. Author articles in field. Home: 6700 SW 117th St Miami FL 33156 Office: Howard Hughes Med Inst PO Box 330837 Coconut Grove FL 33133

COHEN, FRANK, pediatrician; b. Dallas, Aug. 10, 1913; s. Mendel Beryl and Fannie (Schemer) C.; B.A., Baylor U., 1937, M.D., 1937; m. Helen Markusfeld, Dec. 17, 1939 (dec. July 1975); children—Susan Cohen Grodsky, Burton Irwin; m. 2d, Sara Elizabeth Goldblatt, May 22, 1976. Intern, Baylor U. Hosp., Dallas, 1937; resident Bradford Hosp., Dallas, 1938-39, Cook County Hosp., Chgo., 1940, Contagious Disease Hosp., Chgo., 1941; pvt. practice pediatrics, Fort Worth, 1946—; chief staff Petersmith Hosp., 1966; chief pediatrics Harris Hosp., 1970-73. Pres. Jewish Fedn., 1959-60. Served to lt. col. U.S. Army, 1941-46. Decorated Bronze Star; named Jewish Man of Year, B'nai B'rith, 1962. Mem. Tarrant County Med. Soc. (pres. 1977; Goldheaded Cane award 1975), AMA, Tex., So., World med. assns., Am. Acad. Pediatrics, Tex. Pediatric Soc. Democrat. Clubs: Kiwanis (pres. Fort Worth 1972-73), Columbian Country of Dallas, Masons, Shriners. Home: 3728 Echo Trail Fort Worth TX 76109 Office: 1009 Pennsylvania St Fort Worth TX 76104

COHEN, FRANK BURTON, wholesale novelty co. exec.; b. Miami, Fla., Dec. 18, 1927; s. Herman and Helen Florence (Rudich) C.; B.S., Emory U., 1948; m. Janis E. Stewart, Sept. 23, 1971; children—Ilene Michele, Mona Helene. With Tampa Novelty Co., Inc. (Fla.), 1948—, partner, 1953-72, owner, pres., 1972—. Officer, Rodeph Sholom Synagogue, Tampa. Mem. Tampa C. of C., Eagle Squadron CB Club, Classic Cadillac Convertible Club Am., Classic Thunderbird Club Am. Democrat. Clubs: B'nai B'rith, Masons, Moose, Rodeph Sholom Men's (officer). Patentee center seat car tray. Home: 4934 San Rafael St Tampa FL 33609 Office: 501-07 S Florida Ave Tampa FL 33602

COHEN, JOEL STEVEN, ophthalmologist; b. Lawrence, Mass., Mar. 9, 1944; s. Morris and Rose Cohen; B.S. in Elec. Engring., Northeastern U., 1966, M.S., 1969; M.D., Tulane U., 1973; m. Louise Lepie, Dec. 30, 1972; children—David Adam, Ethan Oren. Jr. engr. RCA, 1962, Gen. Electric Co., 1963; systems engr. Sylvania Electronic Corp., 1964-65; research asst. biomed. engring. Northeastern U., Boston, 1966-69; intern, Charity Hosp., New Orleans, 1973-74; resident in ophthalmology Baylor Coll. Medicine, Houston, 1974-77, fellow in ophthalmic pathology, 1977-78; practice medicine specializing in ophthalmology, Houston, 1978—; instr. ophthalmic pathology Baylor Coll. Medicine, 1978—; mem. staff Methodist Hosp., Spring Branch Meml. Hosp. Commonwealth of Mass. Bd. Higher Edn. scholar, 1971-72; diplomate Am. Bd. Ophthalmology. Mem. Am. Assn. Ophthalmology, Am. Acad. Ophthalmology, Tex. Med. Assn., Eta Kappa Nu, Phi Sigma. Contbr. articles to med. jours.; contbg. editor The New Physician, 1977.

COHEN, LOIS MIRIAM, real estate broker; b. Tuscola, Ill., Jan. 1, 1926; d. William F. and Ruth (Monger) Weiler; grad. Tex. Real Estate Inst., 1963; m. Harry E. Cohen, June 16, 1944; children—Gary Lynn, Lynda Gail Cohen Wright. Teletype operator Western Union, Tex., 1943; partner, mgr. Cinderella Shop, Mineral Wells, Tex., 1945-60; founder Western Realty, Mineral Wells, 1961, owner, 1961-66; owner Lois Cohen Realtors, Mineral Wells, 1969-80, Possum Kingdom Real Estate, 1976, Lois Cohen Decorating Service, Graford, Tex., 1978—. Sec., Mineral Wells Tax Equalization Bd., 1966; sec. City Housing Authority Com., 1966-67. Cert. residential broker. Mem. Realtors Nat. Mktg. Inst., Farm and Land Inst., Mineral Wells Bd. Realtors (sec. 1964, 66, pres. 1965, 76), Nat. Assn. Real Estate Bds., Tex. Assn. Realtors (dir. 1965-73), Internat. Real Estate Fedn., DAR, C. of C. Club: Zonta (charter mem., past pres.). Home: 408 NW 7th Ave Mineral Wells TX 76067 Office: 102 NE 6th Ave Mineral Wells TX 76067 or PO Box 1189 Mineral Wells TX 76067

COHEN, MATTHEW MICHAEL, physician; b. Bklyn., May 8, 1949; s. Stanley Leon and Sonia (Auerbach) C.; M.D., U. Miami (Fla.), 1975; m. Leslie Ann Slade, June 18, 1972; children—Jessica Sheryl, Gabriel Aaron. Resident in family practice Tallahassee Meml. Hosp., 1975-78; practice medicine specializing in family medicine, Tallahassee, 1978—; mem. staff Tallahassee Meml. Regional Med. Center. Bd. dirs. Big Bend br. Fla. Lung Assn., Planned Parenthood Tallahassee. Diplomate Am. Bd. Family Practice. Fellow Am. Acad. Family Physicians; mem. Fla. Acad. Family Physicians, Capital Med. Soc., AMA, Fla. Med. Assn., Am. Orchid Soc. Author: Instructions for Parents, 1979; The Family Doctor's Answer Book: A Total Guide to Your Child's Health, 1980. Office: 1616 Riggins Rd Tallahassee FL 32308

COHEN, RICHARD DAVID, physician; b. Tifton, Ga., Aug. 31, 1943; s. Louis and Evelyn B. C.; B.A., Emory U., 1964, M.D., 1968; children—Natalie Fraser, Angela Lynn. Intern, Emory U. Affiliated Hosps., Atlanta, 1968-69, resident, 1969-70, 73-75; practice medicine specializing in internal medicine and pulmonary diseases, Tampa, Fla., 1975—; asst. dir. intensive care unit and respiratory therapy St Joseph's Hosp., Tampa, 1975—. Bd. dirs., chmn. fund raising com. Tampa Ballet, 1978—. Served with M.C., USAF, 1970-73. Diplomate Am. Bd. Internal Medicine. Mem. AMA, A.C.P., Am. Thoracic Soc., Hillsborough County Med. Assn., Phi Beta Kappa, Alpha Omega Alpha, Phi Sigma, Alpha Epsilon Delta, Alpha Epsilon Upsilon. Home: 13913 Hayward Pl Tampa FL 33624 Office: 4900 N Habana St Tampa FL 33614

COHENOUR, FRANCIS DALE, health care facility adminstr.; b. Muskogee, Okla., July 11, 1917; s. Ira Scott and Ruby Bennett C.; B.B.A., Okla. State U., 1939, B.S., 1948, M.S., 1948; Ph.D., Miss. State U., 1966; m. Janet Steward, July 22, 1944; children—Dale, Chad, Gretchen. With Armour & Co., Chgo., 1948-55; mem. faculty Iowa State U., Ames, 1955-61, Miss. State U., Starkville, 1961-68, Union Coll., Barbourville, Ky., 1968-74; regional dir. research and evaluation Cumberland River Comprehensive Care Center, Corbin, Ky., 1974—; adj. prof. biology Union Coll., Barbourville. Served with USNR, 1940-47. Mem. AAAS, So. Regional Assn. Mental Health Statisticians, Am. Legion, Lambda Chi Alpha. Republican. Methodist. Sigma Xi. Clubs: Masons, Shriners. Office: Cumberland River Comprehensive Care Center Box 568 Corbin KY 40701

COHORN, RON L., clin. psychologist; b. Lamesa, Tex., Oct. 24, 1943; s. Alvin B. and Ruby M. (Galaway) C.; B.A., Tex. Tech U., 1966, M.A., 1969, Ph.D., 1972; m. Martha L. Whiddon, 1976. Staff psychologist Big Spring (Tex.) State Hosp., 1968-69; psychol. cons. Dawson County (Tex.) Mental Health Clinic, 1969-71; exec. dir. outpatient services Big Spring (Tex.) State Hosp., 1972-77; mem. staff Malone and Hogan Clinic, 1977—; cons. Andrews Ind. Sch. Dist., 1977—, Permian Basin Rehab. Center, 1977—, Ector County Ind. Sch. Dist., 1978—. Dir., founder Hideaway Village Halfway House, Lamesa, Tex., 1973-75; dir. Big Spring Halfway House, 1973-75. Adj. prof. dept. of psychology Tex. Tech. U., 1973—. Bd. dirs. Howard County (Tex.) Family Service Center, Am. Cancer Soc.; mem. Health Systems Agy. Mem. Am. Psychol. Assn., Big Spring C. of C. (ambassador). Club: Rotary. Home: 1300 Douglas St Big Spring TX 79720 Office: 1501 W 11th Pl Big Spring TX 79720

COIT, ROBERT DANIEL, lawyer; b. Enterprise, Miss., Mar. 31, 1930; s. Robert Edwin and Faye (Armstrong) C.; student Meridian Jr. Coll., 1947-49; B.S., Miss. State Coll., 1952; LL.B., U. Miss., 1956; m. Elna Faye Haden, Aug. 2, 1959; children—Lauren Faye, Linda Ann, Nancy Margaret, Edwin Daniel. Admitted to Miss. bar, 1956; since practiced in Meridian, mem. firm Huff & Williams, 1956-62, gen. practice, 1962—. Mem. Selective Service Bd., 1965-75; incorporator, pres. Lamar Sch. Found., 1964-72; trustee Beauvoir, 1976-78, bd. dirs., 1979—, pres., 1979—; bd. dirs. Beauvoir Devel. Found. Served to lt. AUS, 1952-54; capt. Res. Col. on Gov.'s Staff, 1972-76. Mem. Miss. State, Lauderdale County bar assns., Miss. Forestry Assn., Phi Alpha Delta, SCV (comdr. Miss. div. 1976-78), Miss. Pvt. Sch. Assn. (dir. 1965-77), Miss. Hist. Soc., Am. Legion (judge adv.), Am. Right of Way Assn. Presbyterian (deacon). Mason. Home: 2305 36th Ave Meridian MS 39301 Office: Lamar Bldg Meridian MS 39301

COKE, C(HAUNCEY) EUGENE, cons. co. exec.; b. Toronto, Ont., Can.; s. Chauncey Eugene and Edith May (Redman) C.; B.Sc., U. Man., also M.Sc. magna cum laude; M.A., U. Toronto; postgrad. Yale U.; Ph.D., U. Leeds, Eng., 1938; m. Sally B. Tolmie, June 12, 1941. Dir. research Courtaulds (Can.) Ltd., 1939-42; dir. research and devel. Guaranty Dyeing & Finishing Co., St. Catharines, Ont., 1946-48; various exec. research and devel. positions Courtaulds (Can.) Ltd., Montreal, 1948-59; dir. research and devel., mem. exec. com. Hart-Fibres Co., 1959-62; tech. dir. textile chem. dept. Drew Chem. Corp., 1962-63; dir. new products fibers div. Am. Cyanamid Co., 1963-68, dir. application devel., 1968-70; pres. Coke & Asso. Consultants, 1970-78, chmn., 1978—; pres. Aqua Vista Corp. Inc., 1971-74; vis. research prof. Stetson U., 1979—. Vice chmn. North Peninsula adv. bd. Volusia County Council, 1975-78. Bd. dirs. Council of Assns. of North Peninsula, 1972-74, 76-77. Served from 2d lt. to maj. RCAF, 1942-46. Recipient bronze medal Canadian Assn. Textile Colourists and Chemists, 1963. Fellow Royal Inst. Chemistry (life) Gt. Britain), Textile Inst. (Gt. Britain), Soc. Dyers and Colourists (Gt. Britain), Inst. Textile Sci. (co-founder, 3d pres.), Chem. Inst. Can. (life), AAAS, N.J. Acad. Sci.; mem. Am. Assn. Textile Technologists (life, past pres., recipient Bronze medal 1971), Canadian Assn. Textile Colourists and Chemists (past pres., hon. life), N.Y. Acad. Scis. (life), Fla. Acad. Scis., Internat. Platform Assn. Clubs: Greater Daytona Beach Republican Men's (pres. 1972-75), Rep. Pres.'s Forum (pres. 1976-78), The Chemist's. Author articles in field. Home: 26 Aqua Vista Dr Ormond by the Sea FL 32074 Office: Ormond Beach FL 32074

COKER, DENTON REUBEN, coll. pres.; b. Waco, Tex., Nov. 21, 1920; s. Samuel E. and Corinne Adell (Daughtry) C.; B.A., U. Houston, 1941; B.D., So. Bapt. Theol. Sem., 1948, Ph.D., 1950; postgrad. (fellow) Harvard U., 1959-60; m. Octavia Langley McGeachy, May 31, 1944; 1 dau., Anne Langley Coker Nelson. Asst. prof. religious edn. So. Bapt. Theol. Sem., Louisville, 1950-54; prof. religious edn. Southeastern Bapt. Theol. Sem., Wake Forest, N.C., 1954-64; acad. dean Brunswick (Ga.) Jr. Coll., 1965-68; pres. South Ga. Coll., Douglas, 1968—. Served with USNR, 1942-45. Mem. Am. Council on Edn., Am. Assn. Community and Jr. Coll., Ga. Assn. Jr. Colls. (pres. 1979-80), So. Assn. Colls., C. of C. (dir.). Democrat. Baptist. Club: Rotary (past pres.). Office: S Ga Coll Douglas GA 31533

COKER, LILLIAN JOHNSON, club ofcl., former educator; b. Georgiana, Ala., June 29, 1906; d. John Bomar and Emma Mae (Avant) Johnson; A.B., Judson Coll., 1927; postgrad. Troy State Coll., 1953, Auburn U., 1959-60; m. Albert Steinhart Coker, June 18, 1928; children—Marjorie Coker Lee, Albert Steinhart. English tchr. McKenzie (Ala.) High Sch., 1927-28; prin. Liberty Sch., Greenville, Ala., 1928-29; tchr. W.O. Parmer Sch., Greenville, 1929-35, 53-60; jr. high sch. tchr., 1942-44, 60-69; mem. curriculum visitation team, Butler County, Ala., 1966-68; sec.-treas. Anti-Litter campaign, 1972-73; pres. Pilot Club of Greenville, Ala., 1966-67; pres. Greenville Fedn. Garden Clubs, 1977—; chmn. artistic arrangements Camellia Show, 1977—; chmn. Butler County Fair Flower Show, 1979—. Mem. NEA, Ala. Edn. Assn., Ala. Hist. Assn., Butler County Hist. Soc., Landmarks, Delta Kappa Gamma (treas. 1943-60). Baptist. Clubs: Camellia City Garden, Nat. Camellia, Camellia of Greenville, Greenville Country, Pilot. Home: 326 Fort Dale St Greenville AL 36037

COKER, ROBERT ULYSSES, vocat. edn. adminstr.; b. La Follette, Tenn., Aug. 8, 1943; s. Ulysses and Bernice C.; B.A. in Sociology, Georgetown (Ky.) Coll., 1965; M.A. in Distributive Edn. and Ednl. Adminstrn., U. Tenn., Knoxville, 1971, postgrad. in Curriculum, 1975; Ph.D. in Vocat. Edn. and Adminstrn., Ohio State U., 1974; m. Brenda Terry, May 25, 1969; 1 dau., Amanda Paige. Operator, Citco Service Sta., Harrogate, Tenn., 1963-64; field rep. Agrl. Stblzn. Conservation Office, Jacksboro, Tenn., summers 1965-67; tchr. Norris (Tenn.) High Sch., 1965-67; salesman Sears Roebuck & Co., Knoxville, 1967-68; coordinator distributive edn. program South High Sch., Knoxville, 1967-68, Morristown, Tenn., 1968-70; research asso. Center for Vocat. and Tech. Edn., Columbus, Ohio, 1972-73; coordinator product utilization State Research Coordinating Unit Tenn., Knoxville, 1973-74, research asso., 1974-75; dir. vocat. edn. Bainbridge (Ga.) Jr. Coll., 1975—; cons. U.S. Dept. Labor, Saudia Arabia, 1979. Mem. Am. Vocat. Assn., Ga. Vocat. Edn. Assn., Am. Vocat. Research Assn., Phi Delta Kappa, Delta Pi Epsilon. Republican. Baptist. Author: (with Garry R. Bice) Your Key to Easier Research, 1971; (with Daniel E. Koble, Jr.) Demographic Characteristics of State Level Vocational Education Agencies, 1973; editor: (with Daniel E. Koble, Jr.) Improving Administrative Activities in State Vocational Education Agencies, 1974, The Role of Vocational Education in Career Education, 1973; contbr. articles to profl. jours. Home: 2205 Twin Lake Bainbridge GA 31717 Office: US Hwy 84 East Bainbridge GA 31717

COKER, ROY AKINYELE, entomologist; b. Lagos, Nigeria, Apr. 14, 1940; came to U.S., 1964; s. Jonathan Kusimo and Comfort Lolade (Ajayi) C.; B.S., Calif. State U., Long Beach, 1968, M.S., 1970; Ph.D., U. Calif., Riverside, 1973; m. Sheila Clark, Apr. 12, 1969; 1 son, Che Nathaniel. Entomologist, CIBA-Geigy, Lagos, Nigeria, 1973-74, Internat. Inst. Trop. Agr., Nigeria, 1974-77, Stauffer Chem. Co., Raleigh, N.C., 1977—. Served with Royal Air Force, 1962-64. Ford Found. fellow, 1971-73. Mem. Entomol. Soc. Am., Weed Sci. Soc. Am., Nat. Geographic Soc., Sigma Xi. Christian Ch. Home: 4405 Old Colony Rd Raleigh NC 27612 Office: PO Box 30383 Raleigh NC 27622

COKINOS, GENEOS PETE, petroleum engr.; b. Beaumont, Tex., Jan. 7, 1919; s. Panayotis Demetrios and Elizabeth (Vellianitis) C.; B.S., Tex. A. and M. U., 1939; m. Lola Pellas, Dec. 10, 1946; children—Peter, Elizabeth, Natalia, Nena, Katie. Roustabout, roughneck Stanolind Oil & Gas Co., 1937; engring. trainee Hamman Oil & Gas Co., 1939-40, petroleum engr. oil and gas conservation dept., Beaumont, Tex., 1946-62; dir. Orange Nat. Bank (Tex.); guest lectr. Served with USAAF, 1941-44. Mem. Soc. Petroleum Engrs. (pres. Beaumont chpt. 1958), Tex. Mid-Continent Oil & Gas Assn. Greek Orthodox (pres. Port Arthur). Contbr. articles to tech. jours. Home: 4675 Gladys St Beaumont TX 77706 Office: 947 Hazel St Beaumont TX 77701

COLBURN, KATHLEEN GRAHAM, univ. adminstr.; b. Decatur, Tex., Aug. 10, 1945; d. Richard Walker and Ayleen (Barrett) Graham; B.S., North Tex. State U., 1968; postgrad. U. Tex. at Arlington, 1974—; children—Jimaleen, Richard. Dir. Denton County (Tex.) Mental Health Clinic, 1970-72; asst. to dean edn. N. Tex. State U., Denton, 1972-74; dir. continuing edn. U. Tex. at Arlington, 1974-78, coordinator insts. energy devel. and Tex. Paralegal insts., 1975-78; program dir. div. public service Office Continuing Edn., Lamar U., Beaumont, Tex., 1979—. Mem. Ft. Worth Regional Council on Alcoholism, 1972-74; pres. Denton County Council on Alcoholism, 1972-74; adv. council Denton (Tex.) City Day Nursery, 1971-74; active Vol. Service Council, Beaumont. Danforth awardee, 1963. Mem. Arlington (ambassador 1974—), Arlington Women's (v.p. 1975-76), chambers commerce, Am. Bus. Women's Assn., Am., Tex. med. records assns., Tex. Tchrs. Assn., Tex. Assn. Community Service and Continuing Edn., Beta Sigma Phi. Republican. Methodist. Club: Altrusa. Home: 8715 Manion Dr Beaumont TX 77707 Office: PO Box 11061 Lamar U Beaumont TX 77710

COLDEN, WILLIAM HENRY, electronics engr.; b. Abington, Pa., Feb. 27, 1924; s. Harry Richard and Anna Rita (Montague) C.; student Wright Jr. Coll., Chgo., 1943, Grove City (Pa) Coll., 1944; B.S.E.E., Va. Poly. Inst. and State U., 1962; m. Marie Boogades, Oct. 15, 1949; children—William Henry, Damian Andrew, Susan Marie, Ann Margaret. Field engr. Burroughs Corp., Norfolk, Va., Detroit, 1949-57, Westinghouse Corp., Balt., 1962-66; supervisory electronic engr. Naval Electronics Systems Engring. Center, Portsmouth, Va., 1966—, head planning and analysis div., 1975—. Served with USMCR, 1943-46. Mem. IEEE (chmn. chpt. 1977). Roman Catholic. Home: 4616 Curtiss Dr Virginia Beach VA 23455 Office: Naval Electronics Systems Engring Center PO Box 55 Portsmouth VA 23705

COLDEWAY, WILLIAM GUS, JR., businessman; b. Floresville, Tex., Nov. 20, 1920; s. William Gus and Emily (Stoltze) C.; m. Dorothy Strozier, Dec. 20, 1941 (dec.); children—Dian Beverly, Paula Mae, Mary Kay. Rt. mgr., asst. gen. mgr. Nat. Linen Service, Houston, 1946-53, gen. mgr., Lubbock, Tex., 1953-55, San Antonio, 1955-68, Houston, 1968-71; v.p., gen. mgr. Guess Towel and Uniform Supply, San Antonio, 1971—; dir. Mission Fed. Savs. and Loan Assn. Served with AUS, 1942-46. Mem. San Antonio Mfg. Assn. (bd. dirs.), S.W. Linen and Indsl. Assn. (past v.p., dir.). Republican. Presbyterian. Clubs: Lions (past pres., past dep. dist. gov.), Masons, Shriners. Office: 541 Roosevelt San Antonio TX 78210

COLE, FRANK W., energy co. exec.; b. Connerville, Okla., Aug. 14, 1925; s. Fred W. and E. Velma (Ingram) C.; B.S., U. Okla., 1948, M.S., 1949; m. Martha Barton, Feb. 7, 1968; 1 son, Frank Warren. Petroleum engr. Humble Oil & Refining Co., Houston, 1949-51, 53-55; asso. prof. petroleum engring. U. Okla., 1955-63; pres. Frank W. Cole Engring. Co., Dallas, 1963-73, Amcole Energy Corp., Dallas. Served with USNR, 1943-46, 51-53. Author: (with A.W. McCray) Oil Well Drilling Technology, 1959; Reservoir Engineering Manual, 1961; Well Spacing in the Aneth Reservoir, 1962; Basic Principles of Reservoir Engineering, 1963; (with P.L. Moore) Drilling Operations Manual, 1964. Contbr. papers to tech. lit. Home: 6130 Spring Valley Dallas TX 75240 Office: 4825 LBJ Freeway Suite 110 Dallas TX 75234

COLE, HARPER LEROY, JR., educator; b. Pasadena, Calif., Dec. 5, 1921; s. Harper Leroy and Maidie Belle (McBride) C.; A.B., Bethany (Okla.) Nazarene Coll., 1965; M.A., U. Okla., 1970; Ed.D., Okla. State U., 1978; m. Pearl Mae Cook, Aug. 2, 1942; children—Stephen Leroy, Myrla Dawn Cole Cook. Ordained to ministry Nazarene Ch., 1945; minister Christian edn. Ch. of Nazarene, Bethany, 1945-48, Kansas City, Mo., 1949-51, Oklahoma City, 1953-56; asst. to gen. treas. Ch. of Nazarene, Kansas City, Mo., 1951-53, 56-66; administrv. asst., asst. prof. bus. Bethany Nazarene Coll., 1966-72, dir. data processing, 1966-73, asso. prof., 1973-74; exec. v.p. Trevecca Nazarene Coll., Nashville, 1974-77; prof. mgmt. and computer sci., chmn. dept. adminstrv. services Bethany Nazarene Coll., 1977—. Recipient B award Bethany Nazarene Coll. Alumni, 1979. Mem. Soc. Advancement Mgmt., Acad. Mgmt., Data Processing Mgmt. Assn., Phi Delta Lambda, Beta Gamma Sigma, Delta Pi Epsilon, Delta Mu Delta. Author: Unified Treasury System, Church of the Nazarene Handling Finance in the Local Church. Home: 6502 NW 31 St Bethany OK 73008 Office: Bethany Nazarene Coll Bethany OK 73008

COLE, JIM C., ednl. adminstr.; b. Paragould, Ark., May 19, 1932; m. Freda; 6 children. B.S. in Edn., Ark. State U., Jonesboro, 1963, M.S. in Edn., 1965, edn. specialist in Elem. Adminstrn., 1975. Elem. supr. Hayti (Mo.) Consol. Schs. R-1, 1961-64; prin. Trumann (Ark.) Elem. Sch., 1964-70, E. Elem. Sch., Jonesboro, 1970—. Past officer Trumann Youth Commn.; pres. Jonesboro Adminstrv. Council, 1977-78; mem. Ark. State Council Econ. Edn., 1978—; deacon Walnut St. Baptist Ch. Mem. Ark. Elem. Prins. Assn. (pres.), Nat. Elem. Sch. Prins. Assn. Named Outstanding Young Educator Trumann Jaycees. Club: Trumann Jaycees (past officer). Certified in elementary and secondary edn., elementary adminstrn., as supt. Home: Route 4 Jonesboro AR 72401 Office: 1218 Cobb St Jonesboro AR 72401

COLE, LOUISE, artist; b. Eagle City, Okla., Aug. 8, 1913; d. Francis Marion and Lucy Evelyn (Wright) Miller; B.A., Williams Coll., Boise, Idaho, 1943; m. Cloyse Charles Cole, Feb. 23, 1940; children—Cheri Christine Cole Massey, Curtis Craig. Office mgr. Oklahoma City Postal Telegraph, 1934-40; owner, operator two sundries stores, 1945-60; gen. illustrator Tinker AFB, 1957-58; advt. artist, editor in-house publ. Okla. Press Assn., 1958-60, Mut. Fed. Savs. & Loan Assn., 1960-64; reading editor, in-house publ. editor Economy Co., 1964-66; with Learning Lab., Guthrie (Okla.) Job Corps Center, 1966-69; tchr. tng., artist, cons., in-house mag. editor Central Amids, govt. agy., Oklahoma City, 1969-73; artist, editor Finders Seekers mag., Oklahoma City, 1973-75; tchr. trainer Manpower div. Okla. State Dept. Vocat.-Tech. Edn., Stillwater, 1975—. Tchr. arts and crafts Mission Ch. Recipient Oklahoma City Writers award, 1978; named Indsl. Editor of Year, 1964. Mem. Indsl. Editors Central Okla. (pres. 1960, Outstanding Achievement with Okla. Manpower Devel. and Tng. 1969), Art Dirs. Club Oklahoma City, Okla. Mus. Art (treas., pub. 1963), Theta Sigma Phi. Presbyterian. Author: Meat Substitutes for Meatless Meals, 1973; editor: Oklahoma Publisher, 1957-58, Oklahoma Nurse, 1960-65, Mutual-ly Speaking, 1960-64, Key Notes, 1964-66, Sooner Sashay, 1964-66, Oklahoma Oil Jobber, 1964-66, Admidsview, 1969-73. Home: 3900 NW 60th St Oklahoma City OK 73112

COLE, NORMAN MOORE, plastic surgeon; b. Prairie City, Oreg., Mar. 3, 1936; s. William J. and Dorothy (Moore) C.; student U. Oreg., 1954, 55; B.A., Pacific Union Coll., 1958; M.D., Loma Linda U., 1962; m. Patricia Rowena Palmer, Jan. 13, 1973; children—Cheryl, Michelle, Cameron, Mark, Palmer. Intern Los Angeles County Gen. Hosp., Los Angeles, 1962-63, resident in gen. surgery, 1963-67; resident in plastic and reconstructive surgery Duke U. Med. Center, 1970-73; pvt. practice plastic and reconstructive surgery, Louisville, 1973—; clin. instr. surgery Sch. Medicine, U. Louisville, 1973—. Served to maj. U.S. Army, 1967-69. Decorated Army Commendation medal, 1969; diplomate Am. Bd. Surgery, Am. Bd. Plastic Surgery. Mem. A.C.S., Am. Soc. Plastic and Reconstructive Surgeons, Am. Soc. Aesthetic Plastic Surgery, Am. Cleft Palate Assn., Southeastern Soc. Plastic and Reconstructive Surgeons, Ohio Valley Soc. Plastic and Reconstructive Surgery (past pres.), Ky. Surg. Soc., Jefferson County Med. Soc., Ky. Med. Assn., AMA (Physician's Recognition award 1976, 79). Republican. Club: Jefferson. Contbr. articles to profl. jours. Office: 4001 Dutchmans Ln Louisville KY 40207

COLE, RICHARD RAY, journalist, educator; b. Forney, Tex., Apr. 20, 1942; s. Richard W. and G. Gladys C.; B.Journalism, U. Tex., Austin, 1964, M.A., 1966; Ph.D., U. Minn., 1971; m. Lynda F. Painter, May 31, 1968. Asst. city editor The News, Mexico City, 1966-67; free lance writer, 1966-67; reporter The Harrow Observer, Harrow on the Hill, Eng., 1968; asst. prof. W.Va. U., 1967-68; instr. U. Minn., 1968-71; asst. prof. journalism U. N.C., Chapel Hill, 1971-76, asso. prof., 1976—, dir. grad. studies, 1977-79, dean Sch. of Journalism, 1979—. Mem. N.C. Scholastic Press Assn. (dir.), Assn. Edn. in Journalism (mem. exec. com., chmn. standing com. research), Internat. Assn. Mass Communication Research, Inter Am. Press Assn., Sigma Delta Chi, Kappa Tau Alpha. Co-author: Gathering and Writing News: Selected Readings, 1975. Contbr. articles to profl. jours. Home: 402 Lake Shore Ln Chapel Hill NC 27514 Office: Howell Hall Sch Journalism Univ of NC Chapel Hill NC 27514

COLE, STEPHEN VAN, constrn. engr.; b. Amarillo, Tex., June 21, 1951; s. Richard Shively and Eleanor Ruth (Van Valkenburg) C.; B.S. in Civil Engring., Tex. Tech. U., 1975; m. Leanna Margaret Williams, Sept. 17, 1977. Transmission engr. Pioneer Corp., Amarillo, 1976—; partner J.P. Publs., Amarillo, 1974-77, Task Force Games, Amarillo, 1978—. Registered profl. engr., Tex. Mem. Tex. Soc. Profl. Engrs., Game Mfrs. Assn., Hobby Industry Am., Game Designers Guild. Republican. Methodist. Designer, publisher simulation games including Starfire, Zeppelin, Marine!, Fall of Bataan, Asteroid, Cerberus. Office: PO Box 511 Amarillo TX 79163

COLE, THOMAS WINSTON, JR., chemist, univ. ofcl.; b. Vernon, Tex., Jan. 11, 1941; s. Thomas Winston and Eva Mae (Sharp) C.; B.S., Wiley Coll., Marshall, Tex.; 1961; Ph.D., U. Chgo., 1966; m. Brenda S. Hill, June 14, 1964; children—Kelley S., Thomas Winston. Mem. faculty Atlanta U., 1966—, prof. chemistry, chmn. dept., 1971—, Fuller E. Callaway prof., 1969—, project dir. Resource Center for Sci. and Engring., 1979—, univ. provost, v.p. for acad. affairs, 1979—; vis. prof. U. Ill., summer 1972, Mass. Inst. Tech., 1973-74; summer chemist Miami Valley Lab., Procter and Gamble Co., 1967, Celanese Corp., Charlotte, N.C., 1974; UNCF lectr., 1975—. Scoutmaster local troop Boy Scouts Am.; chmn. environ. protection com. Neighborhood Planning Inst. So. Regional fellow, summer 1961; Woodrow Wilson fellow, 1961-62; Allied Chem. fellow, 1963; Danforth asso., 1971—; Mem. Am. Chem. Soc., AAAS, Nat. Inst. Sci., Ga. Acad. Sci., Nat. Orgn. Profl. Advancement Black Chemists and Chem. Engrs., NAACP, Sigma Xi, Alpha Phi Alpha. Methodist. Contbr. articles to profl. jours. Home: 1669 Laurens Dr SW Atlanta GA 30311 Office: Atlanta U Atlanta GA 30314

COLEMAN, CATHERINE TOWNE, educator, counselor; b. Marvell, Ark., Oct. 12, 1940; s. Aaron and Irene (McCreary) Towne; B.S., U. Ark., 1965; M.S. in Edn., Ark. State U., 1972; m. Willie Alexander Coleman, Sept. 15, 1957; children—Cyrus B., C. Denisho, Michael G. Tchr., Forrest City (Ark.) Schs., 1965-71, counselor, 1971-73; dir. Emergency Sch. Aid Act program Cotton Plant (Ark.) Schs., 1973-74; counselor, coordinator testing and evaluation E. Ark. Community Coll., Forrest City, 1974—. Bd. dirs. Sch. for Exceptional Children, Forrest City, 1973-75, v.p. bd., 1975—). Mem. Am. Personnel and Guidance Assn., Am. Coll. Personnel Assn., Ark. Assn. Counselor Edn. and Supervision. Home: 515 D St Forrest City AR 72335 Office: PO Box 1039 Forrest City AR 72335

COLEMAN, FRANK CARTER, physician, pathology and lab. mgmt. cons.; b. Jackson, Miss., May 14, 1915; s. Francis Marion and Emma (Carter) C.; B.A., Miss. Coll., 1935; M.D., Tulane U., 1941; m. Ruth Yvonne Ellzey, Sept. 2, 1937; children—Nancy Ruth (Mrs. James Lujan), Stephen Carter, John Timothy, Jeanne Laurie. Intern Touro Infirmary, New Orleans, 1941-42, resident in pathology, 1942-45, asst. dir. pathology, 1945; practice medicine specializing in pathology, Des Moines, 1945-64, Tampa, Fla., 1964—; dir. labs. Mercy Hosp., Des Moines, 1945-64, Patterson Coleman Labs., Tampa, 1964-77; dir. dept. pathology Centro Asturiano Hosp., Tampa, 1964—, Citrus Meml. Hosp., Inverness, Fla., 1964—, Hillsborough County Hosp., Tampa, 1964—, Jackson Meml. Hosp., Dade City, 1965—, Hardee Meml. Hosp., Wauchula, Fla., 1970—, Centro Espanol Hosp., Tampa, 1967—, DeSoto Meml. Hosp., Arcadia, Fla., 1969—, Community Hosp., New Port Richey, 1971—, Tarpon Springs (Fla.) Gen. Hosp., 1967—, West Pasco Hosp., New Port Richey, 1966—, G. Pierce Wood Meml. Hosp., Arcadia, 1971—; resident asst. in pathology Sch. Medicine Tulane U., 1942-44, instr. pathology, 1944-45; asst. clin. prof. dept. pathology Coll. Medicine U. Nebr., 1951-64; clin. prof. pathology U. South Fla., Tampa, 1972—; cons. Tampa Gen. Hosp., 1964—, dept. pathology residency program St. Joseph's Hosp., Tampa, 1967—; med. dir. SW Fla. Blood Bank, 1971-75. Mem. Pres.'s Com. Health Services Industry, 1972-73, Gov.'s Community Hosp. Edn. Council, 1971—; mem. subcom. profl., sci. and tech. manpower Nat. Manpower Adv. Com. Dept. Labor, 1973-74; mem. spl. com. nation's health care needs C. of C. U.S., 1977-79. Pres. Gulf Coast Symphony, 1975-76, chmn. Master Bd., 1978-79; bd. dirs. Blue Shield of Fla., 1967-70; bd. dirs. Am. Med. Polit. Action Com., 1960-69, chmn., 1965-67; pres. Fla. Med. Polit. Action Com., 1980—. Recipient award of merit Iowa Med. Soc., 1957; Sci. Products Found. award for outstanding service to pathology and medicine, 1965; Disting. Service award Am. Soc. Clin. Pathologists and Coll. Am. Pathologists, 1978; spl. award for contbns. and activities in fostering pvt. practice pathology Am. Pathology Found., 1979; diplomate Am. Bd. Pathology (life trustee). Fellow Am. Soc. Clin. Pathologists, Coll. Am. Pathologists (bd. govs. 1953-58, pres. 1960-61, mem. nat. legis. com. 1966—, chmn. council on govt. affairs 1971-78, archivist, historian 1979—), A.C.P., Am. Coll. Chest Physicians; mem. AMA (chmn. council legislative activities 1963-64, chmn. council health manpower 1972-74, profl. standards rev. orgns. adv. com. 1973-74, awards 1974), Fla. Med. Assn. (chmn. council on legislation and regulations 1979-80), Hillsborough County Med. Soc. (pres. 1979-80, chmn. membership com. 1966-67, 69, mem. exec. council 1967-70, chmn. pub. service com. 1970-73, del. to Fla. Med. Assn.), Am. Assn. Pathologists and Bacteriologists, Am. Assn. Blood Banks (pres. 1968-69, dir.), N.Y. Acad. Scis., Fla. Soc. Pathologists (chmn. ins. com. 1966-68, chmn. com. contractual and profl. ethics 1968-69), Soc. Nuclear Medicine, Am. Therapeutic Soc., AAAS, Am. Soc. Cytology, Fla. Assn. Blood Banks (pres. 1970-71), Internat. Acad. Pathologists, Am. Pub. Health Assn., Tampa C. of C. (chmn. air pollution task force 1971-72, chmn. med. sch. com. 1966-67, chmn. health care com. 1969-74, gov. 1974-77), Theta Kappa Psi, Alpha Omega Alpha. Presbyterian. Clubs: Krewe of Venus, University, Carrollwood Golf and Tennis, Avila Golf and Country, Rotary. Contbr. articles to profl. jours. Contbg. editor Recent Advances in Clinical Pathology, 1971. Home: 16407 Zurraquin Ct Tampa FL 33612 Office: 4600 N Habana Ave Suite 21 Tampa FL 33614

COLEMAN, HENRIETTA JOLLY, educator; b. Claymont, Del., Dec. 3, 1934; s. Elton and Ozella Louise (Jones) Jolly; M.Ed., Boston U., 1969; B.S., St. Pauls Coll., 1956; postgrad. U. Wis., U. Va.; m. Clarence W. Coleman, Apr. 8, 1958; children—Tori Andrewa, Clarence Webster. Sec., Patent Office, Washington, 1956-59; tchr. bus. Brunswick County (Va.) Public Schs., 1959-71; tchr. secretarial sci. Southside Va. Community Coll., Christanna Campus, 1971—, asst. prof., 1972-73, asso. prof., 1974—. Leader Girl Scouts, 1971-76; adviser Youth Ch., Union Bethel Reform Union Zion Apostolic Ch., 1970—, ch. clk., 1970-79; mem. evaluation com. Sturgeon Elemen. Sch., textbook selection com. Brunswick County. Named Tchr. of Year Brunswick County Tchrs. Assn., 1970. Mem. Christanna Edn. Assn., Nat. Bus. Edn. Assn., Va. Bus. Edn. Assn., NEA, Va. Edn. Assn., Delta Sigma Theta (pres. chpt. 1979-81). Democrat. Home: Rt 1 Box 118 Freeman VA 23856 Office: Dept Secretarial Sci Southside Va Community Coll Alberta VA 23821

COLEMAN, JAMES EDWIN, JR., lawyer; b. Atlanta, May 23, 1923; s. James Edwin and Demis Cecelia (Thrower) C.; B.S., Ga. Inst. Tech., 1948; LL.B., U. Va., 1951; m. Margaret Copeland Sutherland, June 24, 1947; children—J. Hamilton, Margaret S., Sarah C., James Edwin III. Admitted to Ga. bar, 1952, Tex. bar, 1954; mem. firm Carrington, Gowan, Johnson, Bromberg & Leeds, Dallas, 1953-58; partner firm Carrington, Johnson & Stephens, Dallas, 1958-70, firm Carrington, Coleman, Sloman & Blumenthal, Dallas, 1970—. Pres. Dallas Sch. Lunch Assn., 1967; bd. dirs., chmn. legal com. Dallas Community Chest, 1957; bd. dirs., research fellow Southwestern Legal Found., Dallas. Served to 1st lt. AUS, 1943-46. Decorated Silver Star. Fellow Am. Bar Found., Am. Bar Assn., Tex. Bar Found., Am. Coll. Trial Lawyers; mem. State Bar Tex., Dallas Bar Assn. (v.p. 1965-66), Am. Law Inst., Am. Bd. Trial Advocates (pres. Dallas chpt. 1976-77), Tex., Dallas assns. def. counsel, Sigma Alpha Epsilon, Phi Delta Phi. Methodist (mem. ofcl. bd. 1965-66, 68-71, chmn. bd. trustees 1967). Club: City. Home: 4420 Fairfax St Dallas TX 75205 Office: 2500 South Tower Plaza of Americas Dallas TX 75201

COLEMAN, JOHN MARSHALL, state govt. ofcl.; b. Staunton, Va., June 8, 1942; s. William W. and Marguerite B. Coleman; B.A. with high honours, U. Va., 1964, J.D., 1970; m. Nicols Compton Fox, July 9, 1977; children—Sean Kelly, William Phillip. Admitted to Va. bar, 1970; partner firm Lotz, Black, Coleman & Gudal, Staunton, 1970-77; U.S. magistrate Western Dist. Va., 1971-72; mem. Va. Ho. of Del. from 15th Dist., 1972-75, Va. Senate from 24th Dist., 1975-77; atty. gen. State of Va., 1977—; mem. Va. Commn. to Study Needs of Elderly, 1973-77; mem. food supply and agr. task force Nat. Conf. State Legislators, 1975-78. Bd. visitors James Madison U., Harrisonburg, Va., 1972; chmn. Staunton Augusta United Find drive, 1973. Served to 1st lt. USMCR, 1966-69. Mem. Nat. Assn. Attys. Gen., Am. Bar Assn., Phi Beta Kappa, Omicron Delta Kappa. Republican. Episcopalian. Clubs: Raven Soc., Thirteen Soc. Office: Supreme Ct Bldg 1101 E Broad St Richmond VA 23219

COLEMAN, MARION LESLIE, ins. co. exec.; b. Mobile, Ala., Mar. 20, 1925; s. Luther Woodward and Carrie (Lockler) Coleman; student pub. schs.; m. Joyce Kelley, Aug. 29, 1944; children—Connie, Woodward L. and Franklin M. (twins). Agt., Life Ins. Co. of Ga., Mobile, 1946-53, staff mgr., Texarkana, Ark., 1953-55, dist. mgr., El Dorado, Ark., 1955-56, Hattlesburg, Miss., 1957-60, Meridian, Miss.,

1957-60, Meridian, Miss., 1960-64; v.p., agy. dir. Nat. Preferred Life Ins. Co., Atlanta, 1964-65; v.p. tng. Found. Life Ins. Co., Atlanta, 1965-67; v.p., dir. agys. Tenn. Nat. Life Ins. Co., Nashville, 1967—, also dir.; v.p. Kelley Blakeley Land Co., Inc., Mobile, Ala.; owner Meridian Sportarama, Inc. Yamaha Sports World, B & J Motors, Mel co Ltd., Fashion Tailors (all Meridian); v.p., dir. Merchandisers Inc., Meridian. Served with USNR, 1943-46. Mem. Life Underwriters Assn., Sales and Marketing Execs. Club, Civitan Club (pres. Meridian). Home and Office: 2100 23d Ave Meridian MS 39301

COLEMAN, MARY KATHRYN, dietitian, hosp. ofcl.; b. Shamrock, Okla., Oct. 21, 1923; d. Robert Kenner and Victoria Emma (Martin) Forester; ed. high sch.; m. Theodore Harrison, May 4, 1941; children—Linda Victoria, Teddy Lowell, Bobby Dave, Kathy Lanette. Mem. staff dietary dept. Dr. Gray's Hosp., Batesville, Ark., 1969—, Supr., 1974-79, dir. dietary dept., 1979—. Mem. Nat. Hosp. Instn. and Ednl. Food Service Soc. (cert.), N. Central Ark. Dist. Hosp. Instn. and Ednl. Food Service Soc. (pres. 1978-79). Democrat. Presbyterian. Address: Dr Gray's Hosp Box 2437 Batesville AR 72501

COLEMAN, MICHAEL DORTCH, physician; b. Jackson, Tenn., June 16, 1944; s. Ivery R. and Kathleen (Campbell) C.; B.A. in Chemistry, U. Ark., 1966; M.D., Duke U., 1970; children by previous marriage—Michael Dortch, Christopher Mathew. Intern, Duke U. Med. Sch., Durham, N.C., 1970-71, resident internal medicine, 1971-72, nephrology fellow, 1972-74; practice medicine specializing in nephrology, Durham, 1972-74, Kannapolis, N.C., 1973-74, Ft. Smith, Ark., 1974—; nephrology cons. Cabarras County Hosp., Kannapolis, 1973; chief dept. nephrology Holt Krock Clinic, Ft. Smith, 1974—, dir. dialysis Holt Krock Dialysis Center, 1974—, Sparks Regional Med. Center, Ft. Smith, 1974—, St. Edwards Mercy Med. Center, Ft. Smith, 1980—; asso. prof. medicine U. Ark., Ft. Smith, 1976—; mem. med. rev. bd. Ark. Kidney Disease Commn., 1974—; nephrology cons., 1974—; mem. exec. com. and med. rev. bd. Ark.-Okla. Endstage Renal Disease Council, 1977—. Diplomate Am. Bd. Internal Medicine. Mem. Internat. Soc. Nephrology, Renal Physician Assn., Am. Soc. Nephrology, Am. Heart Assn., AMA, Ark. Med. Assn., Sebastian County Med. Assn., Alpha Omega Alpha. Clubs: Ft. Smith Racquet, Hardscrabble Country. Contbr. articles to med. jours. Office: 1500 Dodson St Fort Smith AR 72901

COLEMAN, RICHARD HARVEY, computer services co. exec.; b. Savannah, Ga., Dec. 7, 1937; s. Sidney Macon and Helen Carol (Harvey) C.; B.E.E., Ga. Inst. Tech., 1960; M.B.A., So. Meth. U., 1970; m. Linda Bump, June 2, 1962; children—Cara, Alana, Peter. With tech. areas, computer div. Gen. Electric Co., Ariz., N.C., Calif., 1960-65, sales rep., Dallas, 1966-68; mktg. div., University Computing Co., Dallas, 1968-71; v.p. market area Utility Network Am., Dallas, 1972-76; v.p. mktg. Itel-Utility Data Service Divs., Dallas, 1977—. Republican. Methodist. Home: 7019 Spanky Branch Dr Dallas TX 75248 Office: 14838 Venture Dallas TX 75234

COLEMAN, ROBERT BOISSEAU, JR., lawyer; b. Birmingham, Ala., Mar. 15, 1916; s. Robert Boisseau and Jessie (Wheeler) C.; B.S., N.C. State U., 1939; postgrad. Mass. Inst. Tech., 1940; LL.B., Birmingham Sch. Law, 1952; m. Ann Alderson, Mar. 16, 1956; children—Clayton L. Campbell, Claire Campbell Lindberg, Mary Virginia, Robert Boisseau III, Barbara Anne, Caroline. Metall. engr. Am. Cast Iron Pipe Co., Birmingham, 1940-41; acid plant supr. E.I. duPont de Nemours & Co., Inc., Kankakee Ordnance Plant, 1941-42, metall. engr. Kings Mills Ordnance Plant, 1942-43, chem. engr. ammonia dept., Charleston, W.Va., 1943-44; tech. asst. to plant mgr. Indsl. Rayon Co., Covington, 1944-48; research engr. So. Research Co., Birmingham, 1948-50, So. Cement Co., Birmingham, 1948-53; admitted to Ala. bar, 1952; Okla. bar, 1953; patent atty. Phillips Petroleum Co., Bartlesville Okla., 1953-59; real estate, ins. broker Alderson Coleman Agy., Ada, Okla., 1959-64; supr. patents and trademarks Continental Oil Co., Ponca City, Okla., 1964—; partner Coleman Bros. Investments; dir. Investors Security. Past pres. Ada Boys Club. Registered profl. engr., Ala., Okla. Mem. Am. Inst. Chem. Engrs., Am. Patent Law Assn. (past com. chmn.), Am., Okla., Kay County bar assns. Episcopalian. Mason, Rotarian. Home: 2513 Mockingbird Ln Ponca City OK 74601 Office: 1000 S Pine St Ponca City OK 74601

COLEMAN, RONALD D'EMORY, state legislator Tex.; b. El Paso, Tex., Nov. 29, 1941; s. Ralph Monroe and Louise Virginia (Hooper) C.; B.A. (Stevens Estate scholar), U. Tex. at El Paso, 1963; J.D. U. Tex. at Austin, 1967; m. Jacquelyn Mowbray, Sept. 1, 1964; 1 dau., Kimberly Michelle. Admitted to Tex. bar, 1969; asst. county atty. El Paso County, 1969-70, 1st asst. county atty., 1970-72; mem. Tex. Ho. of Reps. from 72d Dist., 1972—. Served to capt. AUS, 1967-69. Decorated Army Commendation medal; recipient H.L. Smith Price award U. Tex. Law Sch., 1966. Mem. Tex., El Paso (chmn. membership com. 1973—) bar assns., Lambda Chi Alpha. Home: 1101 Robinson St El Paso TX 79902 Office: 1551 Montana St El Paso TX 79902

COLEMAN, SYLVIA ETHEL, microbiologist; b. Gainesville, Fla., Mar. 23, 1933; d. John Melton and Jessie Lee (Coleman) C.; B.S., U. Fla., 1955, M.S., 1956, Ph.D., 1972; m. Henry Carl Aldrich, Jan. 1, 1978. Grad. asst. U. Fla., 1955-56, 67-69, 70-72, electron microscopy technician, 1972, adj. asst. prof. dept. microbiology, 1976—; research microbiologist VA Center, Bay Pines, Fla., 1960-67; research biologist VA Med. Center, Gainesville, 1972—. NDEA fellow, 1969-70. Mem. Am. Soc. for Cell Biology, Am. Soc. for Microbiology (chmn. morphology and ultrastructure sect.), Am. Assn. Pathologists, Electron Microscopy Soc. Am., Southeastern Electron Microscopy Soc., AAAS, NY. Acad. Scis., Fla. Acad. Sci., Sigma Xi. Contbr. articles to sci. jours. Home: 122 NW 28th Terr Gainesville FL 32707 Office: Research Service 151 VA Med Center Gainesville FL 32602

COLEMAN, TERRY LEWIS, state legislator Ga.; b. Dodge County, Ga., Dec. 5, 1943; s. Lewis Warren and Mary Ruth (Shiver) C.; A.A., Reinhardt Coll., 1977; B.S., Brenan Coll. Criminal Justice, 1978; m. Carol Cofield, Jan. 31, 1969; children—Tracy Lewis, Brett Terry. Mem. Ga. Ho. of Reps. from 102-1 Dist., 1972-76, from 118th Dist., 1976—, chmn. public safety com. Mem. Ga. Democratic Exec. Com., 1969-74; mem. State Crime Commn., 1971-75. Served with Ga. N.G. Mem. Eastman C. of C. (dir.). Clubs: Moose. Lions. Home: 1201 4th Ave Eastman GA 31023 Office: PO Box 157 Eastman GA 31023

COLEMAN, THALIA JEAN, speech pathologist, educator; b. Mullins, S.C., Dec. 20, 1948; d. Rudolph and Lily Mae (Ford) C.; B.A., S.C. State Coll., 1970; M.S., Pa. State U., 1971; postgrad. U. Ill., 1977. Speech clinician Coastal Habilitation Center, Lodson, S.C., 1970; instr., speech clinician S.C. State Coll., Orangeburg, 1971-72, supr. directed teaching speech pathology, 1973-75, asst. prof. speech pathology, supr. Speech and Hearing Clinic, 1976—; cons. St. Luke Headstart Center, 1977, Sr. partner Orangeburg County Partners Program for Juvenile Delinquents, 1973-76; guest lectr. Orangeburg County Foster Parents Assn., 1976-77; vol. mgr. Faith Christian Bookstore, 1977-79. Recipient Oscar for Best Actress, Henderson-Davis Players Internat. Tour Group, 1969; Rehab. Services Adminstrn. fellow, 1970; lic. speech pathologist, S.C. Mem. Am. Speech and Hearing Assn., S.C. Speech and Hearing Assn., Black Caucus, Zeta Phi Beta, Delta Psi Omega. Club: Criterion Social. Home: Route 1 1101 Cherry Ln Orangeburg SC 29115 Office: Box 1661 SC State Coll Orangeburg SC 29117

COLEMAN, WILLIAM BALLIN, III, textile co. exec.; b. New Orleans, Oct. 8, 1943; s. William Ballin Jr. and Stella (Sherer) C.; B.S., Trinity U., 1967, M.S. in Econs. and Bus. Adminstrn., 1969; m. Cynthia Anna Groos, May 12, 1973. With William B. Coleman Co., Inc., New Orleans, 1969—, v.p., 1971-73, pres., 1973—; pres. Joint Enterprises, Inc., New Orleans, 1971—. Pres., trustee Three CCC Found. Recipient Triniteer of Year award Trinity U., 1967, Triniteer Outstanding Service award, 1966, 67. Mem. Young Pres. Orgn. Am., Nat. Branded Distbrs. Assn. (dir.), New Orleans C. of C., Trinity U. Alumni Assn. (bd. dirs.). Christian Scientist. Home: 530 Woodvine Ave Metairie LA 70005 Office: PO Box 61004 New Orleans LA 70161

COLEMAN, WILLIAM PATRICK, JR., physician; b. Lynchburg, Va., Aug. 5, 1925; s. William Patrick and Agatha (Stanislaus Doherty) C.; A.B., Duke U., 1949; M.D., U. Va., 1953; m. Barbara Grant, Sept. 20, 1947; children—William Patrick, James Grant. Intern, U. Va. Hosp., Charlottesville, 1953-54, resident in internal medicine, 1954-55, 56-57; resident Dartmouth Med. Sch. Group Hosps., Hanover, N.H., 1955-56; practice medicine specializing in allergy, Charlotte, N.C., 1957-58, Lynchburg, Va., 1958-60; chief allergy dept. Ochsner Clinic and Ochsner Found. Hosp., New Orleans, 1960-78; clin. prof. medicine Tulane Med. Sch., 1974—; charter mem. adv. com. U. Va. Med. Sch. Served with AUS, 1943-45. Decorated Air medal with 4 oak leaf clusters. Fellow A.C.P., Am. Acad. Allergy; mem. Southeastern Allergy Assn. (pres. 1966-67, chmn. continuing edn. com. 1973-78), La. Allergy Soc. (sec.-treas. 1979-80), Brit. Soc. Allergy and Clin. Immunology, Am. Soc. Internal Medicine, Am. Heart Assn., Internat. Soc. Tropical Dermatology, So. Med. Assn., others. Roman Catholic. Contbr. articles to profl. jours. Home: 3908 Edenborn Ave Metairie LA 70002 Office: 3100 Houma Blvd Metairie LA 70002

COLES, WILLIAM HENRY, ophthalmologist; b. Rochester, N.Y., Mar. 2, 1937; s. Morris J. and Mary Louise A. Coles; M.D., Emory U., 1962; M.S. in Physiology, La. State U., 1970; m. Caroline Evans, June 25, 1960; 1 dau., Claudia Sarah. Intern, Grady Meml. Hosp., Atlanta, 1962-63; resident Charity Hosp. of La., New Orleans, 1966-69; instr. La. State U. Med. Center, 1969, asst. prof. ophthalmology, 1970; asst. prof. Med. Univ. of S.C., 1971-73, asso. prof., 1973—, dir. residency program, dir. out-patient clinic, 1971—. Bd. dirs. Gibbes Art Gallery, Charleston, 1974—. Served with USAF, 1963-66. Diplomate Am. Bd. Ophthalmology. Fellow ACS; mem. Am., S.C. med. assns., Charleston County Med. Soc., Am. Acad. Ophthalmology and Otolaryngology (lectr.), Research to Prevent Blindness, AAUP, Charleston Ophthalmol. Soc., Pan-Am. Assn. Ophthalmology, So. Med. Assn. (sec. sect. ophthalmology), Trident C. of C., Charleston Preservation Soc., Hist. Charleston Found. Tours, S.C. Hist. Soc. Author: Intraocular Injuries, 1972. Home: 1 Philadelphia Alley Charleston SC 29401 Office: Dept of Ophthalmology Med Univ of SC 171 Ashley Ave Charleston SC 29403

COLEY, BETTY ANN, librarian; b. Corrigan, Tex., Aug. 4, 1933; d. Bennie Boyd and Louise (Long) Gilbert; B.S., Sam Houston State U., 1953; M.Ed., E. Tex. State U., 1961; m. Kenneth Coley, Jan. 27, 1951; 1 dau., Carol Ann. With register's office Tex. A. and M. U., 1954; tchr. Mesquite (Tex.) Ind. Sch. Dist., 1957-64, elementary librarian, 1964-67, dir. central processing center, 1964-66; elementary librarian Aldine Ind. Sch. Dist., Houston, 1967-69; law librarian firm Fulbright & Jaworski, 1969-72; librarian Armstrong Browning Library, Baylor U., 1972—. Pres. Mesquite Jr. Woman's Study Club, 1966-67; rec. sec. Florence Black Elem. PTA, 1965-67. Mem. AAUW (past chpt. sec., pres., state historian, dist. coordinator, Outstanding Mem. Waco br. 1980, named gift given to Ednl. Found. 1979), Am., Tex. (dist. chmn. 1979-80), Southwestern library assns., Spl. Libraries Assn., Baylor U. Round Table (rec. sec. 1976, publs. coordinator 1977-78), Sam Houston State U. Ex-Students Assn., Delta Kappa Gamma (Zeta scholar 1977). Baptist. Editor: My Browning Family Album (by Vivienne Browning), 1979; contbr. to Studies in Robert Browning and His Circle 1976. Office: Armstrong Browning Libary PO Box 6336 Waco TX 76706

COLEY, CLINTON JACKSON, banker; b. Alexander City, Ala., June 17, 1902; s. Eugene A. and Nannie (Sandlin) C.; student U. Ala., 1921-24; LL.D. (hon.), Troy U., 1979; m. Evelyn McCord, Oct. 15, 1923; children—Clinton Jackson, Evelyn Forrest. With First Nat. Bank, City of Alexander, Ala., 1925-45, 1960—, cashier, 1935-45, dir., 1940-45; chief exec. officer, pres. Alexander City Bank, 1960-78, chmn. bd., 1975—; judge of probate Tallapoosa County, Ala., 1946-60; hon. pres. Troy State U., 1977—. Pres. Tukabatchee area council Boy Scouts Am., 1964-65, Ala. 4-H Club Found., Inc., 1950-60; mem. adv. bd. U. Ala., Birmingham, 1950-70; elder First Presbyn. Ch., Alexander City, 1935—; mem. Ala. Commn. of Higher Edn., 1965-66; chmn. Alexander City Centennial Celebration, 1973; trustee Lyman Ward Mil. Acad., 1954; chmn. bd. Dept. Archives and History, State of Ala., 1965. Recipient Silver Beaver award Boy Scouts Am., 1972; named Man of the Year of Alexander City, 1965. Mem. Ala. Hist. Assn. (pres., mem. exec. com. 1973), Newcomen Soc. N.Am., Alexander City C. of C. (pres. 1963-64), U. Ala. Nat. Alumni Assn. (pres. 1968-69). Democrat. Presbyterian. Clubs: Lions, Masons. Contbr. articles on history of Ala. to scholarly publs. Home: 509 Circle Dr Alexander City AL 35010 Office: Alexander City Bank Alexander City AL 35010

COLEY, SILAS BODIE, JR., psychiatrist; b. Raleigh, N.C., Jan. 14, 1934; s. Silas B. and Pearl (Denny) C.; B.S. in Bus. Econs., U. N.C., 1956, M.D., 1965; B.A. in Chemistry, U. Miami, 1961; m. Rachel N. Brooks, Sept. 28, 1956; children—Silas Bodie, Mary Lyle. Intern, N.C. Meml. Hosp., Chapel Hill, 1965-66, resident in psychiatry, 1966-69; practice medicine specializing in psychiatry, Chapel Hill, 1969—; dir. Orange-Person-Chatham Mental Health Center, Chapel Hill, 1971—; asst. prof. psychiatry U. N.C. Sch. Medicine, Chapel Hill, 1971-77, asso. prof., 1977—; mem. staff N.C. Meml. Hosp., 1969—. Served with USN, 1956-59. Recipient Merck award, 1965. Diplomate Am. Bd. Psychiatry and Neurology. Mem. Am. Psychiat. Assn., AMA, N.C. Neuropsychiat. Assn., N.C., Durham, Orange County med. socs., Am. Soc. Clin. Hypnosis, Am. Assn. Sex Educators and Counselors (cert. sex educator and sex therapist), Nat. Council Family Relations, N.C. Group Behavior Soc., Alpha Omega Alpha, Chi Psi. Contbr. articles to profl. jours. Home: 815 Kenmore Rd Chapel Hill NC 27514 Office: Suite 110 400 Eastoune Office Park Chapel Hill NC 27514

COLIGADO, EDUARDO YLANAN, internist; b. Cebu City, P.I., Apr. 18, 1936; came to U.S., 1963, naturalized, 1976; s. Jose B. and Pacita E. (Ylanan) C.; M.D., U. Philippines, Manila, 1962; m. Eladia A. Clemente, June 29, 1963; children—Eric, Edwin, Edward, Emy Lee. Intern, Phila. Gen. Hosp., 1961-62; resident in medicine St. Vincent Charity Hsp., 1963-64, Cleve. Metro-Luth. Hosp., 1964-65; resident in gastroenterology Cleve. Metro Gen. Hosp., 1965-67; house physician Shaker Med. Center, Cleve., 1967-68; demonstrator medicine Highland View Hosp., Case Western Res. U., 1968-70; practice medicine specializing in internal medicine, Geneva, Ohio, 1970-76, Borger, Tex., 1976—; cert. examiner Tex. Rehab. Commn. Mem. Borger C. of C. Roman Catholic. Author: (with B. Fleshler) Neutral Amino Acid Absorption in Humans, 1967. Home: 7 Altamira St Borger TX 79007 Office: 202 S McGee St Borger TX 79007

COLINS, CHRISTOPHER, social worker; b. Lynn, Mass., Sept. 3, 1925; s. James and Pota (Scipitari) Kolinites; B.A., U. Mass.; M.S.W., U. Pa., 1950, postgrad., 1955-56; m. Christine Maynard, Aug. 3, 1953. Social worker VA Regional Office, Roanoke, Va., 1952-56; dir. social services Embreeville (Pa.) State Hosp., 1956-60; program adminstr. Piedmont Mental Health Complex, Concord, N.C., 1960-70; clin. social worker Lenoir County Mental Health Clinic, Kinston, N.C., 1970—. Mental health cons. various community resources. Served with USAAF, 1943-46. Recipient certificate for dedicated service Pa. Mental Health Assn., 1960. Methodist (chmn. social concerns com.). Home: 108 Park Ave Kinston NC 28501 Office: 1007 N College St Kinston NC 28501

COLLARD, ROBERT EUGENE, state edn. cons.; b. Marion, Ill., June 5, 1919; s. Earl Sam and Myrtle Ethel (Carmichael) C.; B.Ed., So. Ill. U., 1940, M.S., 1948; postgrad. U. Ill., 1948-50; m. Virginia Nell Witacre, Nov. 21, 1940; children—Robert Michael, Susan Elizabeth, Robert Andrew, Robert Stephen. Rural sch. tchr., So. Ill., 1940-41; tchr. indsl. arts, Williamston, N.C., 1941-42; draftsman Pines Engring. Co., Aurora, Ill., 1942-43, Am. Well Works, Aurora, 1943; tchr. Milw. Sch. Engring., 1946-47; halftime tchr. indsl. arts Univ. High Sch., Carbondale, Ill., 1947-48, U. Ill., 1948-50; prin. Pesotum (Ill.) Elem. Sch., 1950-51; engr.'s aide F.H. McGraw & Co., Paducah, Ky., 1951-53, estimator, 1953-55; estimator Rust Engring. Co., Birmingham, Ala., 1955; ter. mgr., sales engr. Lennox Industries, Inc., Decatur, Ga., 1955-59; sales rep. Steel City Supply Co. subs. Wimberly & Thomas Howe Co., Inc., Birmingham, 1959; ter. mgr., sales engr. G.M. Harper Co., Avondale Estates, Ga., 1959, Am. Furnace Co., St. Louis, 1959-66; dir. Manpower Devel. Tng. Act Youth project Center for Adult Studies, Pensacola (Fla.) Jr. Coll., 1966-67; dir. George Stone Vocat.-Tech. Center, Pensacola, 1967-70; cons. Fla. Dept. Edn., Tallahassee, 1970—; cons. on career/indsl. edn., adminstrn., planning, Fed. funding to local ednl. agys., 1975—; tchr. Fla. State U., Tallahassee, spring 1975. Mem. Tallahassee Little Theater, 1970—. Served to lt. (j.g.) USNR, 1953-46. Recipient various ednl. certs. Mem. Am. Vocat. Assn., Fla. Vocat. Assn., Nat. Local Adminstrs. Assn., Fla. Assn. Local Adminstrs., Nat. Assn. State Suprs. Trade and Indsl. Edn., World Future Soc., Iota Lambda Sigma, Phi Delta Kappa. Democrat. Episcopalian. Home: 810 Watt Dr Tallahassee FL 32303 Office: Dept Edn Knott Bldg Tallahassee FL 32304

COLLE, JOSEPHINE BURNS, speech pathologist; b. Union, Miss., Mar. 27, 1943; d. William Vernon and Lillie Ruth (Miles) Burns; B.S., Miss. State Coll. for Women, 1964; M.S. in Speech Pathology, La. State U., 1966; m. Herman Beauchamp Colle, Jr., Dec. 23, 1966; children—Kimber, Holly Adana, Trace. Diagnostician, clinician N. Tex. Rehab. Center, Wichita Falls, 1967-71; pvt. practice, Alexandria, La., 1974—; cons. home health service Rapides Gen. Hosp., 1976—, cons. in-patient, out-patient clinic, 1979. Mem. day sch. com. 1st Baptist Ch., Pineville, La., 1979, ensemble dir., 1978-79, dir. children's choir, 1976—; spl. worker La. Bapt. Conv., 1976-78. Lic. speech pathologist, La. Mem. La. Speech and Hearing Assn. (mem. elections com. 1973, mem. pvt. practice com. 1979), Am. Speech., Lang. and Hearing Assn., Myofunctional Therapy Assn. Am. Author: (with Beau Colle) CB for Christians. Home: 409 Holiday Circle Pineville LA 71360 Office: 1758 Elliott St Alexandria LA 71301

COLLETT, HENRY AUGUSTUS, dentist, lawyer; b. Phila., May 19, 1914; s. Henry A. and Nettie Jean (Morris) C.; D.D.S., Temple U., 1939; J.D., U. Miami, 1962; m. Virginia Houston, Sept. 11, 1959. Commd. lt. (j.g.) USN, 1940, advanced through grades to capt. Dental Corps, 1955, ret., 1960 head partial denture dept. Navy Grad. Sch. Dentistry, 1943; instr. postgrad. prosthodontics Navy dental intern program, 1947-50; cons. instr. advanced prosthodontics Navy residency program, 1954-58; pvt. practice dentistry, Phila., 1939-40, Jacksonville, Fla., 1962—; prof. restorative dentistry N.J. Coll. Medicine and Dentistry, 1968-69; prof. prosthodontics, chmn. fixed sect., dir. grad. prosthodontics Fairleigh Dickinson U. Sch. Dentistry, Hackensack, N.J., 1974-75; mem. staff Univ. Hosp., Jacksonville; courtesy staff Bapt. Med. Center, Jacksonville; cons. in prosthodontics VA. Admitted to Fla. bar, 1962; individual practice law, Jacksonville, 1962—. Diplomate Am. Bd. Prosthodontics. Fellow Acad. Denture Prosthetics (life); mem. Am., Fla. dental assns., Jacksonville Dental Soc., Fla. Prosthodontic Assn. (pres. 1972), Fedn. Prosthetic Orgns., Ret. Officers Assn., Nat. Sojourners (pres. 1972-73). Democrat. Episcopalian. Clubs: Masons, Shriners. Contbr. articles to dental jours. Address: 2251 Post St Jacksonville FL 32204

COLLETT, LOUISA BARRY, petroleum co. exec.; b. San Antonio, Aug. 31, 1931; d. Charles Drew and Louise Antoinette (Burton) C.; B.A., Centenary Coll., 1953. Continuity dir. Sta. KTBS, Shreveport, La., 1953-54; with Cities Service Co., 1954—, editorial asst. Ark. Fuel Oil Corp., Shreveport, 1954-60, editor parent co., N.Y.C., 1960-62, Tulsa, 1962-70, coordinator spl. services pub. relations div., Tulsa, 1970-75, spl. services mgr. pub. affairs div., Tulsa, 1975-76, mgr. publs., public affairs, 1976-78, mgr. speaker services, public affairs, 1978—; lectr. consumer affairs U. Tulsa, 1969—, also various trade groups. Mem. Pub. Relations Soc. Am. (accredited), Am. Mktg. Assn. (former chpt. pres.), Am. Women in Radio and TV, Internat. Assn. Bus. Communicators, Okla. Petroleum Council, Am. Petroleum Inst. (consumer affairs com. 1970-74), Okla. Lung Assn. (chmn. public relations com.). Home 3215 S Yorktown Tulsa OK 74105 Office: Cities Service Box 300 Tulsa OK 74102

COLLEY, JESSE OTTIS, JR., lawyer, business exec.; b. Temple, Tex., Aug. 15, 1944; s. Jessie O. and Maude (Whitelow) C.; A.A., Temple Jr. Coll., 1964; B.S., Abilene Christian U., 1966; J.D., U. Tex., 1970; m. Jan Stewart, May 14, 1971; children—Jon Douglas, Jill Renee. Admitted to Tex. bar, 1970; tax supr. Ernst & Whinney (formerly Ernst & Ernst), Houston, 1970-73; tax sr. Seidman & Seidman, Houston 1973-74; tax mgr. and pension plan coordinator Tracor, Inc., Austin, Tex., 1974—. Vice pres. Home Help Resources, Austin, 1976—; fund raising coordinator Hensel Meml. Encampment, 1978—; deacon Southside Ch. of Christ, 1976-79, v.p., 1978-79, chmn. fin. com., 1975-79. Served with USMC, 1969-75. C.P.A., Tex. Mem. Tex. Bar Assn., Tex Soc. of C.P.A.'s, Am. Inst. of C.P.A.'s, Republican. Mem. Ch. of Christ. Home: 4905 Buckskin Pass Austin TX 78745 Office: 5500 Tracor Ln Austin TX 78721

COLLIER, COURTLAND ALDEN, civil engr.; b. Buffalo, July 29, 1925; s. Leo Robert and Marcheniel Overton (Bass) C.; B.E. in Civil Engring., Yale U., 1949; grad. Canadian Summer Inst. Linguistics, Carenport, Sask., 1955; M.E., U. Fla., 1963; m. Albertine Elizabeth Taylor, Aug. 8, 1946 (div. Feb. 1963); children—Deborah Elizabeth, Nathan Stafford, Dennis Brainerd; m. 2d, Marian Fryer Legate, Feb. 22, 1971; stepchildren—Alexis Arthur, Amy Alice, Michael Fryer, Becky Marie. Jr. civil engr. Calif. Div. Hwys., 1950-51; office engr. Western Contracting Corp., 1951; asst. city engr. Dodge City, Kan., 1951-52; asso. resident engr. Tex. Hwy. Dept., Pharr, 1952-55; instr. mechanics div. Coll. Engring., Lehigh U., 1955-56; field engr. Raymond Conc. Pile Co., Havana, Cuba, 1956-57; design engr.

Lummus Co., Edmonton, Alta. and Maracaibo, Venezuela, 1957-59; design engr. D.E. Britt & Assos., Ft. Lauderdale, Fla., 1960-61; cons. engr., asso. prof. Coll. Engring., U. Fla., 1961—; v.p. C.A.V. Inversiones Zulianas, Maracaibo. Mem. Gainesville (Fla.) City Commn., 1967-73, 79—; chmn. Pub. Works Commn. Gainesville, 1967-73, 79—, chmn. pub. safety commn., 1971-73. Mem. ASCE (pres. Gainesville br. 1966-67), Fla. Engring. Soc., Am. Assn. Cost Engrs., Am. Arbitration Assn. Club: 300 (Gainesville). Author: Engineering Cost Analysis, 1975. Home: 2620 NW 4th Ave Gainesville FL 32607

COLLIER, DWIGHT AUSTIN, telemetry electronics engr.; b. Silverhill, Ala., May 2, 1932; s. William Presley and Mollie King (Gregg) C.; diploma gen. and analytical chemistry Internat. Corr. Schs. Ship's instrumentation engr. RCA Internat. Service Corp., Patrick AFB, Fla., 1954—, sect. leader missile tracking ship, since 1967. Served with USN, 1950-54. Registered profl. engr., Fla. Mem. Locksmithing Inst., Nat. Soc. Profl. Engrs., Assn. Research and Enlightment, Pyrotechnics Guild Internat., Internat. Platform Assn., Internat. Graphoanalysis Soc., Nat. Locksmith Assn., Am. Def. Preparedness Assn., Nat. Rifle Assn. Republican. Baptist. Author: Kathy's Visit to Mars, 1955; The Little Girl Who Gould Perform Miracles, 1959. Home: 108 S Magnolia St Loxley AL 36551 Office: USNS Redstone T-AGM-20 Patrick AFB FL 32925

COLLIER, GAYLAN JANE, educator; b. Fluvanna, Tex.; d. Ben V. and Narcis N. (Smith) Collier; B.A., Abilene Christian Coll., 1946; M.A., U. Iowa, 1949; Ph.D., U. Denver, 1957. Instr., U. N.C., Greensboro, 1946-47; asst. prof., acting chmn. dept. speech and drama Greensboro Coll., 1949-50; asst. prof., dir. theatre Abilene Christian Coll., 1950-57, asso. prof., dir. theatre, 1957-60; asso. prof., chmn. acting studies Idaho State U., 1960-63; asso. prof. drama Sam Houston State U., 1963-65, prof., 1965-67; prof., chmn. acting studies Tex. Christian U., Ft. Worth, 1967—; dir. summer theatre programs Parkway Playhouse, Greensboro, 1951; guest dir. Ft. Worth Community Theatre, summer, 1976; guest lectr. Idaho State U., summers 1958, 59, Wis. State U., Whitewater, 1965; staff dir. Scott Actors Repertory Co., Ft. Worth, summers 1968, 69; guest dir. U. Denver Theatre Festival, 1962; dir. Ft. Worth Repertory Co., 1972; dir. The Imaginary Invalid, rep. U.S. at Am. Festival in Britain, 1970. Named Best Actress, Abilene Christian Coll., 1944, 45, 46. Mem. Am. Theatre Assn., Children's Theatre Assn., S.W. Theatre Conf., Tex. Ednl. Theatre Conf., AAUP, Alpha Psi Omega, Zeta Phi Eta. Democrat. Mem. Ch. of Christ. Author: Assignments on Acting, 1966; also articles on theatre. Home: 2616 S University Dr Fort Worth TX 76109 Office: Tex Christian Univ Fort Worth TX 76129

COLLIER, HENRY MORGAN, JR., physician, surgeon; b. Savannah, Ga., Aug. 7, 1916; s. Henry M. and Annie B. (Gilliard) C.; A.B. cum laude, Savannah State Coll., 1935; M.D., Meharry Med. Coll., Nashville, 1942; m. Mozella B. Gaither, June 22, 1943; children—Vincent Louis, Roberle E., Henry M. III. Resident, Kate Bitting Reynolds Meml. Hosp., Winston-Salem, N.C., 1942-43; practice medicine, Savannah, 1943-52, 55—; treas., chief staff Charity Hosp., 1959-64; asso. staff St. Joseph's Hosp., Warren A. Candler Hosp.; pres. bd. dirs. William A. Harris Hosp. and Nursing Home; active staff Meml. Hosp. Chatham County (Ga.); treas. Seaside Devel. Corp., Hilton Head, S.C.; owner, operator Collier Meml. Beach, Hilton Head. Mem. Savannah Port Authority, 1970-73, Savannah Devel. Authority, 1971-73. Vice pres. Coastal Empire council Boy Scouts Am., 1972-73; chmn. Savannah State Coll. Found., 1973—. Trustee W. Broad St. YMCA; past pres. Savannah chpt. Nat. Guardsmens, Inc. Served to capt. USAF, 1952-55. Recipient Silver Beaver award Boy Scouts Am., 1970; Man of Year award Mut. Benevolent Soc., 1977. Fellow Am. Soc. Abdominal Surgeons; mem. AMA, Ga. Med. Soc., Med. Assn. Ga., Nat., Ga. (pres. 1961-62) med. assns., South Atlantic Med. Soc. (past pres.), Mid Town C. of C. of Savannah (pres. 1956-69), NAACP, Savannah State Coll. Nat. Alumni Assn. (exec. v.p.), Alpha Phi Alpha (Greene award 1974). Democrat. Eqiscopalian. Club: Hub Bus. and Profl. Men's (pres. 1961-62). Home: 1827 Mills B Lane Blvd Savannah GA 31405 Office: Collier Profl Bldg 900 W Broad St Savannah GA 31401

COLLIER, LOUIS MALCOLM, physicist, community service worker, educator; b. Little Rock, May 19, 1919; s. Albert and Ludia (Lewis) C.; B.S. (La. Legis. scholar), Grambling State U., 1954; M.S., Okla. State U., 1960, postgrad., 1962-64; postgrad. Cornell U., 1961; m. Pearlie B. May, June 6, 1947; children—James Bernard, Irving Orlando, Albert Jerome, Phillip Louis, Eric Wayne. Tchr., chmn. sci. and math. dept. Central High Sch., Calhoun, La., 1955-62; instr. physics and math. So. U., New Orleans, 1962-64, asst. prof., 1964-66, asso. prof. physics, Shreveport, La., 1967-75, chmn. dept. physics, 1975-77; formerly chmn. sci. and math. dept. Hopewell High Sch., Dubach, La.; mem. Caddo-Bossier Community Council, Shreveport, 1972—, mem. exec. com., 1975-77; v.p. Newton Smith PTA, 1973-74, pres., 1975-77; pres. Cooper Rd. Area PTA, 1975-77; v.p. 7th Dist. Bicentennial Com.; mem. Caddo Parish (La.) Bicentennial Commn, 1973-76, also Shreveport Regional Bicentennial Commn., serving on Art and Cultural Task Force and on Black Cultural Com., 1975-76; bd. dirs. Shreveport Performing Arts Council, 1975-77, treas., 1976-77; mem. Shreveport's Mayor's Com. on Youth Services, 1974; bd. dirs. Caddo chpt. ARC; bd. dirs. George Washington Carver br. YWCA, 1972, sec. bd., 1972-76, dir. publicity, 1976—, chmn. bd. mgmt., 1978-79; program dir. Sunday Morning radio program Youth Wants to Know, 1972-77, bus. mgr., Shreveport, 1972-77; v.p. Shreveport chpt. Nat. Pan Hellenic Council, Inc., 1972-74, pres., 1974-79; v.p. Caddo Community Action Agy., 1972-77, chmn. fin. com., 1972-77; pres. Cooper Road Health Club, 1973-77, Cooper Rd. Med. Bd., 1975-77; chmn. edn. com. Cooper Road Adv. Council, 1974-77; mem. Cooper Road Vol. Fireman's Assn., 1971-77, sec., 1972-73; sec. Cooper Road Adv. Council, 1976-77; vol. counselor Caddo Parish Juvenile Ct., 1972-77; adv. Caddo Parish 4-H Club, 1975-77. Served to sgt. U.S. Army, world War II. Recipient Ednl. Leadership award Ouachita Parish (La.), 1959, NSF award, 1970, Urban League award Dept. Commerce, 1975, Community Leadership and Service award George Washington Carver br. YMCA Bd., 1975, Bicentennial Commn. award City of Shreveport, 1976, Leadership and Service award Nat. Pan Hellenic Council, 1976, Top Citizens award Caddo Edn. Assn. and Caddo Tchrs. Assn., 1977, Found. for Econ. edn. award, 1978, Citizenship award Shreveport chpt. NAACP., 1978; award for dedicated service to community Cooper Road Adv. Council of Caddo Community Action Agy., 1978, Disting. and Outstanding Community Service award Caddo Community Action Agy., Inc., 1979; named Tchr. of Yr., Freedom Found., 1962, recipient Freedom Found. award, 1977; Shell Merit fellow, 1962. Mem. AAAS (research participation award 1961, Fellowship award 1962-64), Nat. Assn. Mathematicians, AAUP, Nat. Council Tchrs. Math., Nat. Sci. Tchrs. Assn., La. Acad. Sci., La. Edn. Assn. (Ednl. Leadership award 1973, Sci. Edn. award 1976, program coordinator 1976-77), NEA, La. Assn. Educators, Am. Legion (post child welfare officer 1975-77, adv. Sons of Am. Legion 1976-77, Leadership, Scholarship and Service award, post Meritorious Service award 1978, Area Meritorious Service award 1979), Sigma Phi Sigma (hon. award 1975), Phi Beta Sigma (Community Service award 1976, Meritorious Service award Gulf Coast region 1977, Appreciation award Epsilon Eta chpt. 1977, Disting. Service award Gulf Coast Region 1978, Appreciation award Epsilon Eta chpt. 1978, regional dir. 1979—), Alpha Xi Sigma. Club: Kiwanis (pres. club 1974-75, Outstanding Club Leadership award 1975). Home: 3031 Oak Forest St Shreveport LA 71107 Office: So U 3050 Cooper Rd Shreveport LA 71107

COLLIER, SAVANNAH MARIE, educator; b. Haughton, La., Dec. 20, 1926; d. Thomas and Celia Ann Jones; B.S., Prairie View A&M U., 1946, M.S., 1965; postgrad. U. Houston; m. Frank Collier, Nov. 16, 1953 (dec.); 1 son, John Henry Thomas. Clk.-typist Ct. of Calanthes, Houston, 1949-50; clk.-typist, sec. Houston Informer Newspaper, 1950-56; bus. edn. tchr. Cy-Fair Sch. Dist., Houston, 1956-68; tchr., supr. dept. bus. edn. Prairie View (Tex.) A&M U., 1968—; guest lectr., cons. Recipient E.B. Gee Community Relations award, 1968. Mem. Tex. Bus. Edn. Assn., Tex. Bus. Edn. Tchr. Council, Nat. Bus. Edn. Assn., Am. Bus. Communication Assn., Friend of Youth Soc. (bus. mgr., scholarship sec. 1958—), Delta Pi Epsilon, Iota Phi Lambda, Sigma Gamma Rho, Pi Omega Pi. Baptist. Savannah J. Collier Library, Houston, dedicated in her honor, 1969. Home: 10114 Algiers St Houston TX 77041 Office: Coll of Bus Prairie View A&M U Prairie View TX 77445

COLLIN, EVERETT EATON, packaging machinery mfg. co. exec.; b. Arthur, Iowa, Dec. 2, 1938; s. Burdette Gibson and Myrtle Margaret (Neal) C.; B.S., Syracuse U., 1962; m. Nancy Marble, Jan. 1, 1977. Drafting and design mgr. Onondaga Assos., Syracuse, N.Y., 1960-64; engr. Valcar Sheet Metal Corp., Syracuse, 1964-67; designer Cleminshaw Design, Syracuse, 1967-74; div. engring. mgr. Ampak div. Nordson Corp., Greenville, S.C., 1974—. Republican. Methodist. Home: Route 2 Box 19 Gray Court SC 29645 Office: PO Box 878 Anderson SC 29622

COLLINS, ALVIN OAKLEY, clergyman, educator; b. Myrtle, Miss., Aug. 5, 1921; s. Charles Graham and Rose Alice (Oakley) C.; B.A., Miss. Coll., 1942; Th.M., So. Baptist Theol. Sem., 1945, Ph.D., 1952; postdoctoral Cambridge U.; m. Margaret Gordon, May 28, 1953; children—Gordon Wayne, Robert Graham. Ordained to ministry So. Bapt. Conv., 1942; pastor 1st Bapt. Ch., Booneville, Miss., 1955-60, Fifteenth Ave. Bapt. Ch., Meridian, Miss., 1960-63; prof. dept. Christianity, Houston Bapt. U., 1963—, chmn. dept., 1978—. Mem. AAUP, Am. Schs. Oriental Research, Soc. Bibl. Lit., Assn. Bapt. Tchrs. Religion, Omicron Delta Kappa. Author: The Story of Moses Collins and His Descendants; contbr. articles in field to religious jours. Home: 7902 Edgemoor St Houston TX 77036 Office: 7502 Fondren Rd Houston TX 77074

COLLINS, ARLEE GENE, geochemist; b. Forest City, Iowa, Dec. 20, 1927; s. Paul Wilbur and Esther E. (Matson) C.; B.A., Kletzing Coll., 1951; M.S. in Chemistry, Kans. State Coll., 1955; M.S. in Petroleum Geology, Tulsa U., 1972; postgrad. Drake, 1951-52, George Washington U., 1969-70; m. Barbara Joan Howard, Sept. 1, 1961; children—Michael Gene, Sandra Diane. Chemist Howard Moffit, Cons. Chemist, Des Moines, 1951-52, Spencer Chem. Co., Pittsburg, Kans., 1952-55; asst. chief chemist Co-op. Refinery Assn., Phillipsburg, Kans., 1955-56; chemist, project leader Bur. Mines, U.S. Dept. Interior, Bartlesville, Okla., 1956-75, ERDA, Bartlesville, Okla., 1975-77; sect. chief U.S. Dept. Energy, Bartlesville, 1977—. Served with AUS, 1946-47. Mem. ASTM (vice chmn. subcom.), Petroleum Data System (chmn. subcom.), Am. Chem. Soc., Geochem. Soc. Am., Internat. Assn. Geochemistry and Cosmochemistry, Soc. Petroleum Engrs. Elk (officer). Author: Geochemistry of Oilfield Waters. Contbr. articles to tech. publs. Home: 228 SE Roselawn Bartlesville OK 74003 Office: Bartlesville Energy Tech Center US Dept Energy PO Box 1398 Bartlesville OK 74003

COLLINS, DANIEL ROY, JR., hosp. exec.; b. Tupelo, Miss., Dec. 31, 1914; s. Daniel Roy and Lou Winston (Cavett) C.; student U. Miss., 1933-35; m. Rose Catherine Willkom Meindl, Sept. 6, 1968. Office mgr. OK Storage & Transfer Co., Memphis, 1935-43; partner Watson & Ragsdale, C.P.A.'s, Memphis, 1946-54; regional supervising auditor Standard Oil Co. N.J., N.Y.C., 1954-65; v.p. fin. services Meml. Med. Center, Corpus Christi, Tex., 1965—. Served with AUS, 1943-46; ETO. Decorated Bronze Star. C.P.A., Tenn. Mem. Tex. Assn. Hosp. Accts. (past pres.), Hosp. Fin. Mgmt. Assn., Tenn. Soc. C.P.A.'s, Am. Inst. C.P.A.'s. Roman Catholic. Club: Petroleum of Corpus Christi. Home: 625 Gregory Dr Apt 2 Corpus Christi TX 78412 Office: 2606 Hospital Blvd Corpus Christi TX 78405

COLLINS, DON ELMO, product engr.; b. Kansas City, Mo., Sept. 1, 1937; s. Robert Elmo and Ida Marie (Wortman) C.; student Santa Monica City Coll., 1961-62, El Camino Coll., 1959-60; A.A., Los Angeles Trade-Tech. Coll., 1961; B.S.E.E., U. So. Calif., 1965; postgrad., 1965; postgrad. U. Del., 1966-67, m. Naomi Ruth Bennett, Dec. 24, 1966; children—David Michael, Steven Anthony, Kevin Patrick. With Hughes Aircraft Co., Culver City, Calif., 1958-62, student engr., 1962-65, mem. tech. staff, 1965-66; engring. specialist Martin-Marietta Corp., Balt., 1966-67; project mgr. Rockwell Internat., Anaheim, Calif., 1967-72; dir. process control systems Texfi Industries, Inc., Greensboro, N.C., 1972-78; cons. engr. Process Systems, Inc., Charlotte, N.C., 1978; mgr. product engring. Camsco Inc., Richardson, Tex., 1978—; tchr. vocat. edn., asst. simulation lab. U. So. Calif., Los Angeles, 1962-65. Pres. Grade Sch. YMCA, Anaheim, 1972, bd. dirs., 1972, sec., 1971-72; bd. dirs. Plano Youth Soccer Assn., 1979—. Served with USN, 1955-58. Hughes Aircraft Co. work-study fellow, 1962-65; registered profl. engr., Tex. Mem. IEEE. Republican. Lutheran. Patentee in field. Home: 2831 Biscayne Dr Plano TX 75075 Office: PO Box 1328 Richardson TX 75081

COLLINS, GALEN FRANKLIN, pharm. chemist; b. Winona Lake, Ind., Dec 29, 1927; s. Harry Franklin and Elsie (Bahney) C.; B.S., Purdue U., 1949, M.S., 1952, Ph.D., 1954; m. Ann Elizabeth Averitt, Sept. 30, 1956; children—Galen Robert, Amelia Lynn, Scott Franklin, Daniel Chancelor. Grad. asst. Purdue U., 1949-52, research fellow, 1952-53; pharm. chemist Miles Labs., Inc., Elkart, Ind., 1953-58, asst. to dir. Miles-Ames pharm. research lab., 1958-59, sr. research scientist, sect. head Ames Products, 1959-60; sect. chief Norwich Products Devel., Norwich Pharmacal Co. (N.Y.), 1960-63; mgr. research div. S.E. Massengill Co., Bristol, Tenn., 1963-67, dir. research, 1967-71; v.p. research and devel. Dade div. Am. Hosp. Supply Corp., Miami, Fla., 1971-75, v.p., sci. dir., 1975—. Bd. dirs. Bristol unit Am. Heart Assn., 1967-71, pres., 1969-71. Fellow AAAS, Am. Inst. Chemists; mem. Am. Assn. Clin. Chemists, Assn. Clin. Scientists, Am. Chem. Soc., Am. Pharm. Assn., Acad. of Pharm. Scis., Sigma Xi, Rho Chi, Phi Lambda Upsilon. Mem. United Ch. of Christ. Patentee in field. Home: 10800 SW 69th Ave Miami FL 33156 Office: PO Box 520 672 Miami FL 33152

COLLINS, GLENN ROGER, hosp. adminstr.; b. Metter, Ga., Nov. 5, 1939; s. Irvin and Nellie C.; B.S., Ga. So. Coll., 1965; LL.B., Atlanta Law Sch., 1968; M.B.A., Ga. State U., 1971; m. Judi M. Roberts, Dec. 18, 1965. Adminstr., Tattnall Meml. Hosp., Reidsville, Ga., 1972-76, St. Lukes Hosp., Bluefield, W.Va., 1976-77; exec. dir. Bayside Hosp., Virginia Beach, Va., 1977-78; exec. dir. Suburban Hosp., Louisville, Ky., 1978—. Bd. dirs. Health Systems Agy., 1975-76; county chmn. ARC, 1974-76, mem. exec. bd., 1976. Served with U.S. Army, 1960-62. Mem. Hosp. Council So. W.Va. (sec. 1976-77), Am. Coll. Hosp. Adminstrs. Baptist. Home: 6019 Innes Trac Louisville KY 40222 Office: 4001 Dutchmans Ln Louisville KY 40207

COLLINS, HARRY DAVID, mech. engr., ret. army officer; b. Brownsville, Pa., Nov. 18, 1931; s. Harry Alonzo and Cecelia Victoria (Morris) C.; B.S. in Mech. Engring., Carnegie Mellon U., 1954; M.S., U.S. Naval Postgrad. Sch., 1961; m. Suzanne Dylong, May 11, 1956; children—Cynthia L., Gerard P. Commd. 2d lt. C.E., U.S. Army, 1954, advanced through grades to lt. col. 1969; comdr. 802d Heavy Engr. Constrn. Bn., Korea, 1972-73; dep. dist. engr. Army Engr. Dist., New Orleans, 1973-75; ret., 1975; v.p. deLaureal Engrs., Inc., New Orleans, 1975-78; v.p. Near East mktg. Kidde Consultants, Inc., 1978—. Decorated Legion of Merit, Bronze Star, meritorious Service medal; registered profl. engr., La. Mem. ASME, Am. Soc. Mil. Engrs., La. Engring. Soc., Sigma Xi. Home: 2024 Audubon St New Orleans LA 70118

COLLINS, JAMES MITCHELL, congressman; b. Hallsville, Tex., Apr. 29, 1916; s. Carr P. and Ruth (Woodall) C.; B.S.C., So. Meth. U., 1937; M.B.A., Northwestern U., 1938; M.B.A., Harvard, 1943; m. Dorothy Dann, Sept. 16, 1942; children—Michael James, Dorothy Colville Collins Weaver, Nancy Miles Collins Fisher. Pres. Consol. Industries, Inc., 1954-66, Internat. Industries, Inc., 1954-66, Fidelity Union Life Ins. Co., 1954-65; mem. 90th-96th Congresses 3d Dist. Tex. Chmn. White House Conf. Youth. Vice chmn. Nat. Republican Congl. Com., 1974—. Bd. dirs. Greater Dallas Planning Council, Heart Assn., TB Assn., Dallas Assembly, Big Bros., United Fund; trustee So. Meth. U., Salvation Army; pres. Dallas Council World Affairs. Served to capt. C.E., U.S. Army, 1943-45. Named Distinguished Alumnus, So. Meth. U., 1971, Man of Year, Fedn. Ind. Bus., 1971; Legislator of Year, Mexican Am. C. of C., 1974; Watchdog of Treasury, Nat. Assn. Businessmen, 1968-79. C.L.U. Mem. Am. Legion, Young Pres.'s Orgn., Mil. Order World Wars, VFW, Cycen Fjodr, Blue Key, Phi Delta Theta, Psi Chi, Alpha Kappa Psi. Republican. Baptist. Elk. Home: 10311 Gaywood Rd Dallas TX 75229 Office: 2419 Rayburn House Office Bldg Washington DC 20515

COLLINS, JAMES WILLIAM, mining co. exec.; b. Amarillo, Tex., Mar. 26, 1953; s. J.W. and LaVerne A. (McMurtry) C.; B.B.A. cum laude, So. Meth. U., 1975, M.B.A., 1977; postgrad. Chgo. Bd. Trade Inst., 1977; m. Kathleen Cook, June 11, 1977. With Anspacher & Assos., Chgo., 1977; investment analyst Hunt Internat. Resources, Dallas, 1977-78; fin. analyst Sunshine Mining Co., Dallas, 1977-78, asst. v.p. ops., 1978—, corp. sec., 1979—, asst. v.p. ops., fin. analyst, 1979—; pres., dir., Lajana Corp., Amarillo, 1978—. Active Vols. for Clements for Gov., 1978, Connally for Pres., 1979. Mem. So. Meth. U. Alumni Assn., So. Meth. U. M.B.A. Assn., Phi Delta Theta. Methodist. Home: 6055 Norway Rd Dallas TX 75230 Office: 3633 First Internat Bldg Dallas TX 75270

COLLINS, KATHLEEN MORRIS EUDY, educator; b. Oakboro, N.C., Oct. 19, 1921; d. Thomas Seymour and Cora Alice (Morris) Eudy; B.S. in Edn., Asheville (N.C.) Coll., 1942; M.A. in Edn., Columbia U., 1951; divorced; 1 son, Carleton Ray. Tchr., Brunswick County schs., Shallotte, N.C., 1942-44; tchr. Asheville city schs., 1944-69, coordinator elementary and secondary edn., 1969—. Vice chmn. troop com. local Boy Scouts Am., 1977—. Mem. NEA, N.C. Assn. Educators, N.C. Assn. Compensatory Educators, Alpha Delta Kappa, Pi Kappa Delta. Baptist. Author children's plays for radio. Home: 105 Cranford Rd Asheville NC 28806 Office: PO Box 7347 Asheville NC 28807

COLLINS, KIMBALL ALBERT, accountant; b. High Point, N.C., Apr. 15, 1951; s. William Wesley and Estelle Cekan C.; B.B.A. in Acctg., Columbus Coll., 1977; m. Sybil Benelia Collins, May 20, 1978; stepchildren—Debbie, Winston, Tamatha. Traffic controller Burnham Van Service, Columbus, Ga., 1974-76; acct. Ga. Power Plant Mitchell, Albany, Ga., 1977—. Republican. Methodist. Office: Ga Power Plant Mitchell PO Box 386 Route 6 Albany GA 31705

COLLINS, MARTHA LAYNE, lt. gov. Ky.; b. Shelby County, Ky., Dec. 7, 1936; d. Everett Larkin and Mary Lorena (Taylor) Hall; student Lindenwood Coll., St. Charles, Mo., 1955-56; B.S., U. Ky., 1959; m. Bill Collins, July 3, 1959; children—Stephen Louis, Marla Ann. Tchr. public schs., Ky., 1959-63; lt. gov. State of Ky., 1979—. Mem. Woodford County (Ky.) Democratic Exec. Com., 1963; mem. Dem. Nat. Com., 1972-76; del. Dem. Nat. Conv., 1972; chair-woman Ky. Com. for Carter, 1976; mem. Ky. State Dem. Central Exec. Com., 1972-79, sec., 1974-79; clk. Ct. of Appeals, 1975; clk. Supreme Ct. of Ky., 1975-79; mem. Ky. Commn. on Women; exec. dir. The Friendship Force, Ky., 1977. Mem. U. Ky. Alumni Assn. Baptist. Clubs: Jaycee-ettes (past pres. Woodford County), Bus. and Profl. Women's, Order of Eastern Star. Office: Lieutenant Gov's Office State Capitol Frankfort KY 40601

COLLINS, OBERT DALE, hosp. adminstr.; b. Guntersville, Ala., Aug. 13, 1946; s. Willard and Eunice Letha (Hunt) C.; A.D., Snead Jr. Coll., 1966; B.S., Samford U., 1968; M.B.A., George Washington U., 1971; m. Barbara Ann Medlen, June 15, 1968; children—Jason Patrick, Lara Katherine. Asst. in adminstrn. Baptist Med. Center-Princeton, Birmingham, Ala., 1971-72, v.p., 1972-75, asso. adminstr., 1974-75, exec. v.p. corp. services Baptist Med. Centers, Birmingham, 1975-77; pres. Walker County Med. Center, Inc., Jasper, Ala., 1977—; adj. asst. prof. U. Ala., Birmingham, 1977—. Chmn. manpower resources Mountain dist. Boy Scouts Am., 1977—; mem. adv. bd. Ida V. Moffett Sch. Nursing, 1977—, Ret. Sr. Vol. program, 1978—. USPHS fellow, 1969-70. Mem. Jasper Area C. of C. (dir. 1979—), Birmingham Area C. of C. (life), Am. Coll. Hosp. Adminstrs., Ala. Assn. Hosp. Execs., Hosp. Fin. Mgmt. Assn. (advanced), Am. Health Planning Assn., Am. Hosp. Assn., Ala. Hosp. Assn., Birmingham Regional Hosp. Council. Baptist. Clubs: Birmingham Breakfast Sertoma (pres. 1976-77), Rotary (v.p. Jasper 1978—), Jasper Quarterback, Walker Coll. Blue Tie, Sertoma Silver Honor (pres. 1976-77). Home: 1902 Pawnee Circle Jasper AL 35501 Office: Walker County Med Center Inc 201 E 18th St Jasper AL 35501

COLLINS, ROBERT FREDERICK, fed. judge; b. New Orleans, Jan. 27, 1931; s. Frederick and Irma V. (Anderson) C.; B.A. cum laude, Dillard U., 1951, LL.D., 1979; J.D., La. State U., 1954; grad. spl. summer course Nat. Jud. Coll., U. Nev., 1973; m. Aloha Collins, Dec. 28, 1957; children—Francesca Collins McManus, Lisa Ann, Nanette C., Robert A. Admitted to La. bar, 1954; mem. firm Augustine, Collins, Smith & Warren, New Orleans, 1956-59; instr. law So. U., 1959-61; sr. partner firm Collins, Douglas & Elie, New Orleans, 1960-72; asst. city atty.-legal adv. New Orleans Police Dept., 1967-69; judge ad hoc Traffic Ct., New Orleans, 1969-72; atty. Housing Authority New Orleans, 1971-72; judge magistrate sect. Criminal Dist. Ct., Orleans Parish, La., 1971-78; judge U.S. Dist. Ct., Eastern Dist. La., 1978—; asst. bar examiner State of La., 1970-78. Bd. dirs. New Orleans Housing Council, 1962-64, Social Welfare Planning Council, New Orleans, 1965-67, Dryades St. YMCA, New Orleans, 1963-65, New Orleans Urban League, 1970-72, 75; mem. La. State Welfare Bd., 1970-72; trustee Loyola U., New Orleans, 1977—. Served with U.S. Army, 1954-56. Mem. La. State Bar Assn., Nat. Bar Assn. (regional dir. 1964-65), Am. Bar Assn., Louis A. Martinet Legal Soc. (pres. 1959-60), Nat. Conf. State Trial Judges, La. Dist. Judges Assn., Am. Judicature Soc., Fifth Circuit Dist. Judges Assn.

Democrat. Roman Catholic. Office: 500 Camp St Suite 465 New Orleans LA 70130

COLLINS, ROBERT IRA, entertainment mktg. exec.; b. Cleve., Aug. 8, 1948; s. Philip Gilbert and Dorothy (LaVetter) C.; B.S. in Speech, Northwestern U., 1970; M.S. in Public Relations, Am. U., 1974. Prodn. asst. Sta WBBM-TV, Chgo., 1968; asso. dir. Sta. WKYC-TV, Cleve., 1969; regional mktg. dir. Ringling Bros. and Barnum & Bailey Circus, Washington, 1974-78; nat. dir. advt. and promotion Clyde Beatty-Cole Bros. Circus, Winter Park, Fla., 1979-80; promotion dir. Ice Capades, Hollywood, Calif., 1980—. Served with USCG, 1970-74. Recipient Broadcasting award for public service program with Sta. KGO, Lighthouse for Blind and Ringling Bros. Circus, Ohio State U., 1975; Found. for Public Relations Research and Edn. grantee, 1974. Mem. Public Relations Soc. Am. (asso.). Contbr. articles in entertainment mktg. and marine safety to publs. Home: 1704 Pelican Cove Rd Sarasota FL 33581 Office: 6121 Santa Monica Blvd Hollywood CA 90038

COLLINS, STEPHEN BARKSDALE, hosp. adminstr.; b. Houston, Mar. 14, 1932; s. Ray George and Ruth Ella (Davis) C.; B.A., Baylor U., 1954; M.H.A., Washington U., St. Louis, 1956; m. Katherine Jane Justice, June 6, 1955; children—Nancy Catherine, Rebecca Jane, Ruth Anne, Stephen Barksdale, Cynthia Marye. Asst. adminstr. Good Samaritan Hosp., Vincennes, Inc., 1959-61, adminstr., 1961-65; adminstr. Rosewood Gen. Hosp., Houston, 1965-72; chief exec. officer Lake Charles (La.) Meml. Hosp., 1972—. Bd. dirs. Better Bus. Bur., Lake Charles, Lake Charles C. of C. Served with USAF, 1956-59. Decorated Air Force Commendation medal. Fellow Am. Coll. Hosp. Adminstrs.; mem. Am. Hosp. Assn., La. Hosp. Assn. (dir.). Baptist. Club: Rotary (dir. club). Office: 1701 Oak Park Blvd Lake Charles LA 70601

COLLINS, WARREN EUGENE, physicist; b. Memphis, Jan. 26, 1947; s. Joe Lee and Gertrude (Cochran) C.; B.S., Christian Bros. Coll., 1968; M.S., Vanderbilt U., 1970, Ph.D., 1972; m. Joyce Ann Powell, Sept. 4, 1971; 1 dau., Evangeline. Faculty, So. U., Baton Rouge, 1972-73, Fisk U., Nashville, 1973-77; research asso. Vanderbilt U., Nashville, 1974-77; prof., chmn. Dept. Physics So. U., Baton Rouge, 1977—; cons. in field. Supporter, YMCA, United Givers. Served with U.S. Army, 1973. Danforth fellow, 1968-70; NSF grantee, 1976-77. Mem. ACLU, Am. Assn. Physics Tchrs., Assn. Black Physicists, Am. Phys. Soc., AAAS, AAUP, Nat. Inst. Sci., Sigma Xi, Sigma Pi Sigma, Beta Kappa Chi. Baptist. Contbr. articles to profl. jours. Home: 11336 Perkins Rd Baton Rouge LA 70810 Office: PO Box 10554 Baton Rouge LA 70813

COLLINS, WILLIAM SEELEY, JR., coll. adminstr., basketball coach; b. Williamsport, Pa., Aug. 5, 1946; s. William Seeley and Shirley Jean (Leidhecker) C.; A.S., Williamsport Area Community Coll., 1967; B.A., Millersville State Coll., 1969; M.S., Shippensburg State Coll., 1975. Tchr., Frederick County (Va.) Schs., 1969-71; asst. basketball coach Shenandoah Coll. and Conservatory of Music, Winchester, Va., 1969-70, head baseball coach, 1969-70, dir. admissions, 1972-73, dir. intramural athletics, 1969-72, residence hall supr., 1969—, asst. dean students, 1973—, dir. housing, 1975—; sportscaster Sta. WINC, 1973—. Vice-pres. Shenandoah Apple Blossom Festival. Mem. Va. Assn. Coll. Housing Officers, S.E. Assn. Coll. Housing Officers, Assn. Coll. and Univ. Housing Officers, Va. Assn. Student Personnel Adminstrs., Am. Personnel and Guidance Assn., Am. Counseling and Personnel Assn. Republican. Lutheran. Home: 1816 Valley Ave Winchester VA 22601 Office: Shenandoah Coll Winchester VA 22601

COLLURA, JAMES GERARD, quality control adminstr.; b. Rockville Center, L.I., N.Y., Feb. 18, 1947; s. Frank Leonard and Florence Marie (Seaman) C.; diploma Burlington County Vocat. Tech. Sch., 1966; student U.S. Govt. Pkg. Sch., Aberdeen, Md., 1974; student Rider Coll., 1975—; m. Frances Elaine Heydorn, Oct. 7, 1967; children—James Gerard, Michele Lynn, Melanie Ann. Chuck turret operator De-Laval Turbine Inc., Trenton, N.J., 1968-69, insp. quality control, 1969-74, quality control supr., 1974—, staff writer DeLaval Digest. Served with Seabees, USN, 1966-68. Mem. Atco Dragracing Assn., Drag Bike Racing Assn. Roman Catholic. Home: Oakdale Subdiv Route 2 Box 874F Monroe NC 28110 Office: IMO Pump Div DeLaval Turbine Inc Airport Rd Monroe NC 28110

COLN, CHARLES DALE, surgeon, educator; b. Dallas, Dec. 23, 1934; s. Charlie Edward and Jessie Ruth (Enix) C.; A.B., Baylor U., 1957, M.D., 1961; m. Shirley Jane Kindberg, May 12, 1962; children—Sara, Eric, Lois, Ruth, Mary. Intern Jefferson Davis Hosp., Houston, 1961-62; NIH research fellow in surgery U. Tex. Southwestern Med. Sch., Dallas, 1962-63, asst. prof. surgery, 1969-74, chmn. div. pediatric surgery, 1972—, asso. prof., 1975—. resident in surgery Parkland Meml. Hosp., Dallas, 1963-67, chief pediatric surgery, 1972—; chief of surgery Children's Med. Center, Dallas, 1972—; Lectr., U. Capetown (South Africa), 1971-72; cons. Red Cross War Meml., Children's Hosp., Capetown, 1971-72. Served with USPHS, 1967-69. Diplomate Am. Bd. Surgery. Fellow A.C.S.; mem. Tex. Pediatric Surg. Soc., A.M.A., Am. Acad. Pediatrics, Am. Trauma Soc., Southwestern Surg. Assn., Fellowship Christian Athletes. Baptist. Research, publs. on shock, fluid and electrolyte therapy, trauma, transplantation of pancreas, pediatric surgery. Home: 3712 Stratford St Dallas TX 75205

COLON, DORIS E., biologist; b. Lares, P.R., June 9, 1930; d. Vicente E. and Elmina (Gonzalez) C.; B.S., U. P.R., 1950; M.S., U. Pa., 1953; Ph.D., U. Okla., 1963; married; 1 dau., Mayra Yudex Colon. Mem. faculty U. P.R., Mayaguez, 1956—, asso. prof. biology Med. Sch., 1954-56, prof., 1970—. Mem. AAUP, Am. Inst. Biol. Scis., Sigma Xi, Beta Beta Beta, Gamma Sigma Delta, Phi Sigma, Alpha Delta Kappa. Home: 63 Galicia St Mayaguez PR 00708 Office: Dept Biology U PR College Station Mayaguez PR 00708

COLON, GUSTAVO ALBERTO, plastic surgeon; b. Ponce, P.R., June 14, 1938; s. Gustavo Enrique and Araceli (de Ramery) C.; B.A., Johns Hopkins U., 1960; M.D., U. Md., 1964; m. Nairda Muniz, June 23, 1962; children—Gene, Albert, Lisa, Nairda. Intern, USPHS Hosp., Balt., 1964-65; resident in surgery USPHS Hosp., New Orleans, 1965-69; resident in plastic surgery Tulane U., New Orleans, 1969-71, asso. prof. plastic surgery, 1972—; chief plastic surgery USPHS Hosp., New Orleans, 1971-72; pvt. practice plastic surgery, Metairie, La., 1972—; mem. staff East Jefferson Gen. Hosp., Touro Infirmary, Lakeside Hosp. Served with USPHS, 1964-71. Diplomate Am. Bd. Plastic Surgery. Decorated U.S. Coast Guard Commendation Ribbon. Fellow A.C.S.; mem. Am. Soc. Plastic and Reconstructive Surgery, AMA, A.C.S., Am. Burn Assn., Am. Soc. Aesthetic Surgery, Am. Cleft Palate Assn., New Orleans Surg. Soc. Roman Catholic. Home: 4801 Hessmer Ave Metairie LA 70002 Office: 4330 Loveland St Metairie LA 70002

COLONEY, WAYNE HERNDON, civil engr.; b. Bradenton, Fla., Mar. 15, 1925; s. Herndon Percival and Mary Adore (Cramer) C.; B.C.E. summa cum laude, Ga. Inst. Tech., 1950; m. Anne Elizabeth Benedict, June 21, 1950; 1 dau., Mary Adore. Project engr. Constructora General, S.A., Venezuela, 1948-49, Fla. Rd. Dept., Tallahassee, 1950-55; hwy. engr. Gibbs & Hill, Inc., Guatemala, 1955-57, project engr., Tampa, Fla., 1957-59; prject engr. J.E. Greiner Co., Tampa, 1959-62, asso., 1962-63; partner Barrett, Daffin & Coloney, Tallahassee, 1963-70; pres. Wayne H. Coloney Co., Inc., Tallahassee, 1970-77, chmn., chief exec. officer, 1977—; pres., sec. Tesseract Corp., 1975—; chmn., chief exec. officer Coloney Co. Cons. Engrs., Inc., Tallahassee, 1978—; dir. Internat. Enterprises, Inc. Pres. United Fund of Leon County, 1971-72; chmn. adv. com. Area Vocational Tech. Sch., 1965-78. Bd. dirs. Springtime Tallahassee, 1970-72; bd. dirs. Heritage Found., 1965-71, pres., 1967; bd. dirs. LeMoyne Art Found., 1973, v.p., 1974-75; bd. dirs. Goodwill Industries, 1972-73; mem. Tallahassee-Popoyan Friendship Commn., 1968-73; mem. Adv. Com. for Hist. Cultural Preservation, 1969-71; mem. selection com. Fla. So. U., 1969-71; mem. Pres.'s Adv. Council on Indsl. Innovation, 1978-79. Served with AUS, 1943-46. Recipient citation of excellence in water pollution control field, 1972. Registered profl. engr. and land surveyor, Fla., Ga., Ala., N.C.; registered gen. contractor, Fla. Fellow ASCE; mem. Nat. Soc. Profl. Engrs., Fla. Engring. Soc. (sr.), Am. Water Works Assn., Fla. Inst. Cons. Engrs., Fla. Soc. Profl. Land Surveyors, C. of C., Anak, Koseme Soc., Phi Kappa Phi, Omicron Delta Kappa, Sigma Alha Epsilon, Tau Beta Pi. Episcopalian. Club: Metropolitan Dinner (dir., v.p., later pres.). Contbr. articles to profl. jours. Patentee roof framing system, tile mounting structure, curler rotating device, bracket system for roof framing. Home: Argyle House 2540 Marston Rd Tallahassee FL 32312 Office: PO Box 5258 Tallahassee FL 32301

COLQUITT, JOHN ORVILLE, JR., beverage co. exec.; b. Macon, Ga., June 11, 1923; s. John Orville and Isabel Harris (Denham) C.; A.A., Wentworth Mil. Acad., 1941; student W. Tex. State Coll., 1941, U. Tex., 1941-42; m. Margaret Jane Jones, Oct. 18, 1944; children—R. Jeff, John Orville 3d, James M. With Dalhart Coca-Cola Bottling Co. (Tex.), 1947—, pres., 1969—; dir. First Nat. Bank, Dalhart. Mem. Dalhart Ind. Sch. Dist., 1963-69, pres., 1967-69; mem. Dalhart City Council, 1971—; mayor pro-tem of Dalhart, 1972, mayor, 1973-79; chmn. Panhandle Regional Planning Commn., 1973. Trustee Coon Meml. Hosp., Dalhart. Served to 1st lt. USAAF, 1942-45. Recipient Most Outstanding Citizen award Dallam-Hartley County C. of C., 1958, Man With A Heart award Community Services Bur., 1958, Silver Beaver award Llano Estacado council Boy Scouts Am., 1964. Mem. Tex. Municipal League (dist. pres. 1973). Methodist (chmn. ofcl. bd. 1972). Mason (32 deg., Shriner). Home: 1323 Rock Island St Dalhart TX 79022 Office: 819 Chicago St Dalhart TX 79022

COLSKY, JACOB, physician; b. Memphis, Dec. 5, 1921; s. Abraham Samuel and Jennie (Shefsky) C.; student Memphis State Coll., 1938-40; M.D., U. Tenn., 1944; m. Irene Vivian Belen, July 26, 1953; children—Liane Caryl, Arthur Spencer, Andrew Evan. Intern, Jackson Meml. Hosp., Miami, Fla., 1944-45; fellow dept. preventive medicine Johns Hopkins Med. Sch., 1947-50, instr. dept. preventive medicine, 1950-51; asst. chief clin. research unit Nat. Cancer Inst., Balt., 1951-52; asst. physician, out-patients Johns Hopkins Hosp., 1947-52; asso. dir. medicine Maimonides Hosp., Bklyn., 1952-57; asso. attending physician Kings County Hosp. Med. Center, 1955-57; instr. medicine State U. N.Y. Coll. Medicine, N.Y.C., 1952-54, asst. prof. medicine, 1954-55, asso. prof. 1955-57; pvt. practice medicine, specializing in internal medicine and med. oncology, Miami, Fla., 1957—; mem. staffs Cedars of Lebanon, Jackson Meml. hosps., Miami; cons. Bapt., Mount Sinai, VA hosps., Miami; asso. prof. medicine U. Miami Sch. Medicine, 1957-66, clin. asso. prof., 1966-74, clin. prof. medicine, 1973—, prof. oncology, 1975—; dir. med. oncology sect. dept. medicine U. Miami and Jackson Meml. Hosp., 1960-70; chief med. oncology sect. Cedars Lebanon Hosp., 1972—, chief medicine, 1977-78; sr. investigator Eastern Coop. Oncology Group, 1960—, mem. exec. com. 1971-73; pres. Med. Oncology and Chemotherapy Found. Miami, Inc., 1970-73. Bd. dirs. Papanicolaou Cancer Research Inst., 1969—. Served to capt. M.C., AUS, 1945-47. Diplomate Am. Bd. Internal Medicine, Am. Bd. Med. Oncology. Fellow N.Y. Acad. Medicine, A.C.P.; mem. N.Y. Acad. Sci., AAAS, Am. Fedn. Clin. Research, Am. Assn. Cancer Research, Am. Geriatrics Soc., Leukemia Soc. (state bd. dirs. 1970—), Am. Cancer Soc. (county bd. dirs. 1968-71), Fla. Med. Soc. (vol. health agy. com. 1971—), Internat. Soc. Lung Cancer (founding mem.), Am. Soc. Clin. Oncology (founding mem.). Contbr. articles to profl. jours. Home: 1150 NW 14th St Suite 310 Miami FL 33136 Office: 1150 NW 14th St Miami FL 33136

COLTHARP, LELAND HOMER, JR., judge; b. Maringouin, La., Mar. 8, 1926; s. Leland Homer and Una Mae (Lefeaux) C.; student McNeese State Coll., 1946-47; LL.B., La. State U., 1950; m. Barbara Anne Bennett, Aug. 16, 1947 (div. Aug. 1974); children—Karen L., Debra J., Pamela A.; m. 2d, Laura Ray Seals, Sept. 14, 1974. Admitted to La. bar, 1950, practiced in DeRidder, 1950-51, 53-76; asst. U.S. atty. Western Dist. La., 1951-53; partner LeCompte, Hall & Coltharp, DeRidder, La., 1953-60, Hall & Coltharp, DeRidder, 1960-74, Hall, Coltharp & Lestage, DeRidder, 1974-76; asst. dist. atty. 30th Dist. of La., 1955-64; city atty. City of DeRidder, 1960-70; gen. counsel So. Casualty Ins. Co., 1963-76; judge 30th Jud. Dist. La., 1976-78, 36th Jud. Dist. La., 1979—. Mem. bd. control Beauregard Parish Public Library, 1964-76, pres., 1968-76; mem. Library Devel. Com. La., 1968-76, chmn., 1970-73; mem. La. State Adv. Council on Libraries, 1971-74. Trustee Beauregard Meml. Bapt. Hosp., 1954-66, chmn. bd., 1958-59. Served with USNR, 1944-46. Recipient Modisette award La. Library Assn., 1972. Mem. Am., La. bar assns., ALA (intellectual freedom com. 1973-75), La. Library Assn. Methodist. Home: 611 Davella St DeRidder LA 70634 Office: Beauregard Parish Courthouse DeRidder LA 70634

COLVIN, (OTIS) HERBERT, JR., musician, educator; b. El Dorado, Ark., Mar. 18, 1923; s. Otis Herbert and Irene (Hammons) C.; B.A., Baylor U., 1944, M.B., 1948; Mus.M., U. Colo., 1950; Ph.D., U. Rochester (N.Y.), 1957; m. Mary Ila Ullom, June 18, 1948; children—Carol Kay (Mrs. James Lee Smith), Mary Edith (Mrs. George M. Reitmeier), Susan Elizabeth. Instr. music Tex. Technol. Coll., 1950-55; chmn. piano dept. Baylor U., Waco, Tex., 1957-62, chmn. dept. theory and composition, 1962-76, coordinator theory div., 1976—; teaching asst. Eastman Sch. Music, Rochester, 1955-57; organist 7th and James Baptist Ch., 1960—. Served USNR, 1944-46; PTO. Mem. Music Tchrs. Nat. Assn., Am. Guild Organists (dean Waco chpt. 1958-60, 68-69, 79-80), Phi Mu Alpha. Baptist. Mason (32 deg.). Composer: Organ Voluntaries Based on Early American Hymn Tunes; Short Pieces for Organ; For Sunday (6 organ pieces based on modal melodies), also Vol. Two; Nine Hymn Settings for Organ; Gloria (for accompanied 8 part mixed chorus); Four Madrigals (texts by A.E. Housman); Surely the Lord is in This Place; Sheep May Safely Graze (6 organ-piano duet arrangements by J.S. Bach and William Billings); (with Kurt Kaiser) two vols. organ-piano duet arrangements hymns and gospel melodies. Editor choral compositions. Contbr. articles to profl. publs. Home: 80 Cottonwood St Waco TX 76706 Office: Sch Music Baylor U Waco TX 76703

COLVIN, JAMES MICHAEL, constrn. co. ofcl.; b. Shreveport, La., Mar. 21, 1952; s. James Henry and L'Marie (Bayles) C.; student La. Tech. U., 1970-71; B.S., N.E. La. U., 1974, postgrad. in bus. adminstrn., 1974-76; m. Judy Kay Coon, Aug. 10, 1974. Constrn. materials buyer Craft Corp., 1974; cost and schedule analyst Ford, Bacon & Davis Constrn. Corp., Monroe, La., 1974-75, chief cost and schedule analyst, 1975-76, asst. to mgr. projects, 1978, proposals mgr., 1979—; lectr. local univs., 1975—; cons. on project mgmt. and control methods to local firms, 1975—. Mem. N.E. La. U. Sch. Constrn. Found.; bd. dirs. Indsl. Devel. Bd. N.E. La.; loaned exec. 1977 campaign United Way. Mem. Am. Assn. Cost Engrs. (charter sec.-treas. No. La. sect.), Project Mgmt. Inst., Am. Inst. Constructors, West Monroe Jaycees (treas. 1976-78, Key Man award 1977, 78), Sigma Lambda Chi. Republican. Baptist. Club: Masons. Home: 207 Dupont Dr West Monroe LA 71291 Office: 3901 Jackson St PO Box 1762 Monroe LA 71201

COLVIN, MARY ILA, voice tchr.; b. El Paso, Tex., Feb. 26, 1927; d. Pliny Leroy and Gladys Evelyn (Johnson) Ullom; B.A., Baylor U., 1948; postgrad. Colo. U., Juilliard Sch., U. Rochester; m. Otis Herbert Colvin, Jr., June 18, 1948; children—Carol Kay Colvin Smith, Mary Edith Colvin Reitmeier, Susan Elizabeth. Dir. children's choirs, soloist First Presbyterian Ch., Boulder, Colo., 1949-50; pvt. voice studio tchr., Lubbock, Tex., 1950-55; soloist, dir. children's choirs Centenary Methodist Ch., Rochester, N.Y., 1955-57; instr. voice Baylor U., 1957-74, lectr. in voice, 1974—; choral, vocal clinician Baptist Gen. Conv. of Tex., 1962—, Ga. Bapt. Conv., 1968—. Mem. Nat. Assn. Tchrs. of Singing, P.E.O., Delta Kappa Gamma, Mu Phi Epsilon, Alpha Chi, Phi Gamma Nu. Home: 80 Cottonwood St Waco TX 76706 Office: Sch Music Baylor U Waco TX 76703

COLWELL, GENE THOMAS, educator; b. Chattanooga, Aug. 3, 1937; s. William Clarence and Mary Virginia (Smith) C.; B.S., U. Tenn., 1959, M.S., 1962, Ph.D., 1966; m. Peggy Ann Fletcher, June 1, 1973. Research engr. Oak Ridge Nat. Lab., 1959-62, design specialist, 1965-66; instr. U. Tenn., Knoxville, 1962-65; asst. prof. Sch. Mech. Engring. Ga. Inst. Tech., Atlanta, 1966-71, asso. prof., 1971-76, prof., 1976—. Postgrad. prof. U. Carabobo, Valencia, Venezuela, 1971; cons. various indsl., govt. orgns. Registered profl. engr., Ga. Mem. Am. Soc. M.E., Sigma Xi, Pi Tau Sigma. Contbr. articles to profl. jours. Patentee gas turbine engine, 1973. Home: 4011 Gunnin Rd Norcross GA 30071 Office: Sch Mech Engring Ga Inst Tech Atlanta GA 30332

COLWELL, JAMES LEE, educator; b. Brush, Colo., Aug. 31, 1926; s. Francis Joseph and Alice (Bleasdale) C.; B.A., U. Denver, 1949; M.A., U. No. Colo., 1951; Certificate, Sorbonne, 1956; Diploma, U. Heidelberg (Germany), 1957; A.M. (Univ. fellow), Yale, 1959, Ph.D. (Hale-Kilborn fellow) 1961; m. Claudia Alsleben, Dec. 27, 1957; children—John Francis, Alice Anne. Tchr. high sch., Snyder and Sterling, Colo., 1948-52; civilian edn. adviser U.S. Air Force, Japan, 1952-56; asso. dir. Yale Fgn. Student Inst., summers 1959-60; asst. dir. European div. U. Md., Heidelberg, 1961-65; dir. Office Internat. Edn., asso. prof. Am. lit. U. Colo., Boulder, 1965-72; prof. Am. studies, chmn. lit. U. Tex. Permian Basin, Odessa, 1977—, dean Coll. Arts and Edn., 1972-77. Mem. nat. adv. council Inst. Internat. Edn., 1969-75. Vice pres. Ector County chpt. ARC, 1974-76; mem. Ector County Hist. Commn. 1973-75. Served with USAAF, 1945; brig. gen. USAF Res. Mem. AAUP, Am. Studies Assn., Western Social Sci. Assn. (life mem. pres. 1974-75), MLA, NEA (life), Orgn. Am. Historians (life), South Central Modern Lang Assn., Permian Basin Hist. Soc., Air Force Assn., Air Force Hist. Found. (life), Res. Officers Assn. (life), Ret. Officers Assn. (life), Phi Beta Kappa. Unitarian-Universalist. Contbr. articles to learned jours. Home: 1501 Westbrook Ave Odessa TX 79761

COLYER, GEORGE EDWARD, educator; b. Dinorwic, Ont., Can., Feb. 7, 1921; s. Walter and Nellie (Back) C.; B.S., Western Mich. U., 1963, M.A., 1965, Ed.S., 1967; m. Alice LaVoy, Feb. 7, 1940; children—Alyce, William, Paul, George, Walter. Tchr. handicapped children Vicksburg (Mich.) Community Schs., 1962-67; asst. prof. edn. W. Ga. Coll., Carrollton, 1967-68, acting coordinator spl. edn., 1968-70, prof. edn., 1971—. Mem. Vicksburg Village Council, 1967; mem. Sand Hill Reactivation Com., 1979. Served with USN, 1944-46. Educable Mentally Retarded vocat. tng. fellow, 1964. Mem. Council Exceptional Children, Assn. Talented and Gifted, Am. Legion. Methodist. Club: Moose. Home: 22 Sage Dr Carrollton GA 30117 Office: W Ga Coll Carrollton GA 30117

COLYER, JULIAN S., chem. cons.; b. Jersey City, Mar. 11, 1896; s. Benno and Nina (Seeman) Cohen; B. Chemistry, Cornell U., 1919; m. Ruth Lachman, June 25, 1936; children—Robert J., Jean R. Colyer Harper. Chemist, Am. Apple Products Co., N.Y.C., 1919-20, Sigmund Ullman Co., N.Y.C., 1920-22, A.C. Horn Co., N.Y.C., 1922-24; owner, mgr Colyer Pectin Co., N.Y.C., 1922-71, BarCol Labs., N.Y.C., 1939-46; chem. cons., St. Petersburg, Fla., 1971—; cons. cholesterol project U. Fla. Sch. Medicine. Mem. Mayor's Com. Larchmont, N.Y. 1959-62. Served with U.S. Army, 1917-18. Mem. Inst. Food Technologists, AAAS, Sigma Xi. Club: Cornell. Developer first comml. powdered pectin, 1919, first oral penicillin, 1942. Home: 4822 B Coquina Key Dr SE Saint Petersburg FL 33705

COLYER, RICHARD ALLEN, fund raiser; b. Cin., July 20, 1946; s. Bethel Floyd and Neva Ethel (Morrow) C.; B.B.A. (J.C. Aspley scholar 1968), Stetson U., DeLand, Fla., 1968; M.B.A., Fla. State U., 1970. Asst. dir. mktg. Life Care Am., Inc. and Baptist Village Retirement Center, Pompano Beach, Fla., 1972-73; fin. planning cons. Conn. Gen. Life Ins. Co., 1973-74; dir. devel. Evangelism Explosion III Internat., Ft. Lauderdale, Fla., 1974—; mem. faculty Devel. Assn. Christian Instns. Ann. Insts., Tulsa, 1978-80. Mem. Broward Citizens for Community Standards. Served with AUS, 1971-72. Decorated Army Commendation medal. Mem. Am. Mgmt. Assn., Alpha Kappa Psi. Republican. Presbyterian. Home: 258 Neptune Ave Lauderdale-By-The-Sea FL 33308 Office: PO Box 23820 Fort Lauderdale FL 33307

COLYER, VERA ESTELLE, ins. co. exec.; b. Tishomingo, Okla., Apr. 18, 1914; d. Henry Clay and Emily Elizabeth (Emerson) Sellars; student public schs., Grandfield, Okla.; m. Glen Gillis Colyer, Dec. 21, 1945 (dec.); dau., Glenna Kay Colyer Wirz. Bookkeeper, First State Bank, Grandfield, Okla., 1931-36; sec., bookkeeper for various businessmen, 1936-71; farmer nr. Grandfield, Okla., 1964-73; owner, pres. Colyer Ins. Agency, Inc., Grandfield, 1936—; co-founder Center Internat. Securities Studies. Co-chmn., Okla. Democratic Party, state conv. del.; rep. to Pres.'s Hiring of Handicapped Bd., Washington. Mem. Internat. Ins. Women's Assn., Nat. Ins. Women's Assn., Nat. Assn. Ins. Agts., Profl. Ins. Agts. Assn., Am. Bus. Womens Assn., Nat. Fedn. Ind. Bus. Assn., Internat. Platform Assn., Inter-Am. Soc. Am. Security Council Nat. Tax Counselors Assn., C. of C. (past pres., ins. legis. com.). Democrat. Mem. Ch. of Christ. Clubs: Am. Legion Aux., Great Plains Country, Presidents, Grandfield Bearcat. Hon. mem. editorial adv. bd. Am. Biog. Inst. Home: 1001 W 1st St Grandfield OK 73546 Office: Colyer Insurance Agency Inc 123 W 2nd St Grandfield OK 73546

COMBS, DOUGLAS LEE, publishing co. exec.; b. Cin., Dec. 16, 1946; s. Francis G. and Nellie Marie (Lauterwasser) C.; B.S. with honors, U. Fla., 1972 M.B.A., U. Ala., 1978; m. Sonya Rea Horowitz, July 17, 1969. Dir., Combs & Assoc., Gainesville, Fla., 1971; communication dir. Gainesville C. of C., 1972; pub. relations dir. Blount Bros. Corp., Montgomery, Ala., 1973-77; circulation promotion dir. So. Living Mag., Birmingham, Ala., 1977—. Bd. dirs. Montgomery United Appeal, 1975-76. Served with Intelligence Corps, U.S. Army, 1964-68. Decorated Army Commendation medal;

recipient Outstanding Indsl. Photography award Montgomery Advt. Club, 1976. Mem. Pub. Relations Soc. Am., Pub. Relations Council Ala. (dir. 1975-76), Soc. Profl. Journalists, Am. Soc. Personnel Adminstrn., Alpha Delta Sigma. Clubs: Montgomery Ad (dir. 1976), Toastmasters (pres. 1976). Editor The Blount Banner, 1973-77. Home: 3101 Lorna Rd Suite 1224 Vestavia Hills AL 35216 Office: 820 Shades Creek Pkwy Birmingham AL 35209

COMBS, JOSEPH FRANKLIN, author, columnist; b. Center, Tex., Nov. 23, 1892; s. Frank and Annie Mae (Beck) C.; student Tex. A. and M. Coll., 1917; m. Addie Laura Brittain, Sept. 8, 1912 (dec.); children—Talmage Franklin, Doris, Addie Mae Combs Bedford, Thomas Buchanan, Jo Ruth Combs Arriola. Rural sch. tchr., Shelby County, Tex., 1910-17; agrl. agt. Tex. A. and M. U. Extension Service, Montgomery County, 1917-27; county agrl. agt., Beaumont, Tex., 1927-55; farm editor Beaumont Enterprise, 1955-58, farm columnist, 1958—. Adminstr., New Deal Agrl. Acts, Jefferson County, Tex., 1933-38; operator German Prisoner of War Farm Labor Camp, Jefferson County, 1944-45; pres. Montgomery County Fair, 1923-27. Bd. dirs. Houston Fair and Exposition, 1923, Camp Fire Girls. Served with Tex. State Guard, 1941-47; mem. Res. Mem. Am. Mus. Natural History, Smithsonian Assos., Tex. Guard Assn., Tex. and Southwestern Cattle Raisers Assn. (dir. Ft. Worth 1948-55). Baptist. Club: Masons. Author: Growing Pastures in the South, 1936; Farm Corner, Nature Stories, 1963; Legends of the Pineys, 1965; Gunsmoke in the Redlands, 1968; Kudjo Quatterman, 1972. Discoverer grass species. Home: 5635 Duff Ave Beaumont TX 77706

COMBS, LARRY LEE, coal co. exec.; b. Louisville, Feb. 25, 1948; s. Tolbert and Aileen (Ballard) C.; B.C.E., U. Ky., 1971; m. Susan Margaret Griffin, Dec. 11, 1971; 1 son, Damon Bryce. Mining engr. TVA, Chattanooga, 1971-72; sect. foreman Peabody Coal Co., Madisonville, Ky., 1972-74, mining engr., 1974; dir. mining tech. program Madisonville Community Coll., 1974-76; dir. tng. Western Ky. div. Island Creek Coal Co., Madisonville, 1976—; mem. Ky. Bd. Miner Tng., Edn. and Certification, 1978—; adv. com. indsl. tech. Murray State U.; chmn. mine occupations program Madisonville Area State Vocat.-Tech. Sch. Com. mem. United Way, 1976; mem. sub-area health council Pennyrile Area Devel. Dist., 1978—. Mem. Ky. Soc. Profl. Engrs., Am. Inst. Mining, Metall. and Petroleum Engrs., Ky. Mining Inst., West Ky. Mining Inst. (program and fin. coms.), U. Ky. Alumni Assn. Mem. Christian Ch. Club: Jaycees (pres. 1975-76, sec. 1974-75, dir. 1973-74), Kiwanis (key club com. 1977—). Home: 3080 Buffalo Trace Madisonville KY 42431 Office: S Main St Madisonville KY 42431

COMBS, ROBERT HEARIN, utilities exec.; b. El Dorado, Ark., Feb. 11, 1923; s. John Hearin and Estelle (Hammons) C.; student U. Ark., 1940-43, 47, U. Okla., 1958, Okla. State U., 1959, U. Tex., 1961; m. Toni Louise Rogers, June 12, 1945; children—Gary L., William Bryce. Sales mgr. Ark.-La. Gas Co., 1947-56; dist. sales mgr. Okla. Natural Gas Co., Tulsa, 1956-63; dir. sales, promotion Am. Gas Assn., N.Y.C., 1963-65; v.p. marketing Western Ky. Gas Co., Owensboro, 1965—. Pres. Audubon council Boy Scouts Am., 1969-71, exec. bd., 1966—, mem. Region II exec. bd., v.p. Ky. area, 1975-78. Chmn. bd. dirs., trustee Ky. Ind. Coll. Found., life trustee award 1980; bd. dirs. Owensboro United Fund. Served to maj. USAF, 1943-47, 51-52. Recipient Gas Industries Hall of Flame award, 1959, Silver Beaver award Boy Scouts Am., 1971, Silver Antelope award, 1977; named Boss of Year, Am. Bus. Womens Assn., 1968. Mem. Tulsa Exec. Assn. (past pres.), Am., So. (sect. chmn.), Ky. (past pres.) gas assns., Sales and Marketing Exec. Internat., Tulsa (life), Ky. (past dir., pres.), Owensboro-Daviess County chambers commerce. Baptist. Mason (32 deg., Shriner), Rotarian (dir. Owensboro), Kiwanian (past pres.). Home: 2169 N Stratford Dr Owensboro KY 42301 Office: 311 W 7th St Owensboro KY 42301

COMBS, WALTER HARRISON, data processing exec.; b. Jackson, Ky., Feb. 4, 1913; s. John Sidney and Laura (Patton) C.; A.B. in Math., Berea Coll., 1934; certificate LaSalle Extension U., 1942; postgrad., U. Mich., 1961; m. Nancy Katherine Gott, June 6, 1935; children—Walter Kent, James Carl, Linda Carol McCall. Tchr. math. Perry County (Ky.) High Sch., 1934-35; supr. customer accounting Kentucky Power Co., 1935-58; supr. data processing Appalachian Power Co., Roanoke, Va., 1958—. Instr. A.R.C., Hazard, Ky., 1941-46. Mem. adv. bd. Roanoke County Bd. of Edn., 1964—. Kiwanian (dir. 1970-72). Home: 2736 Avenel Ave SW Roanoke VA 24015 Office: 40 Franklin Rd SW Roanoke VA 24009

COMER, DONALD, III, textile products co. exec.; b. N.Y.C., June 23, 1938; s. Donald and Isabel (Anderson) C.; B.S., U. Ala., 1962; m. Jane Stephens Comer, May 4, 1962; children—Jason Legare, Luke McDonald, Carrie St. George. Pres., treas. Avondale Mills, Sylacauga, Ala., also dir.; dir. Techsonic Industries, Eufaula; adv. dir. Southeast div. Am. Mut. Ins. Cos., Boston. Bd. dirs. Ala. Safety Council; trustee Avondale Ednl. and Charitable Found., Inc., Sylacauga; bd. dirs. Choccolocco council Boy Scouts Am., Anniston, Ala. Served with USAF, 1961-64. Named Boss of Year Jr. C. of C., 1972; Citizen of Year, Kiwanis, 1966. Mem. Ala. Textile Mfrs. Assn. (pres., dir.), Am. Textile Mfrs. Inst., Ga. Textile Mfrs. Assn. Clubs: Country (Sylacauga, Ala.); Mountain Brook Country (Birmingham). Home: 1500 Stone Hill Rd Sylacauga AL 35150 Office: Avondale Mills Sylacauga AL 35150

COMKOWYCZ, SHARON MCMANUS, lang. and speech pathologist; b. Bridgeport, Conn., Nov. 7, 1953; d. Thomas William and Dolores Wood (Brewster) McManus; B.A., So. Conn. State Coll., 1975, M.S., 1977; m. Paul Comkowycz, Jan. 9, 1976. Clerical asst. circuit ct. State of Conn. Jud. System, Bridgeport, 1971-75; lang. and speech pathologist Bristol (Conn.) Bd. Edn., 1977; lang./speech pathologist, diagnostician Polk County (Fla.) Sch. Bd., 1977—; cons. in field; pvt. practice speech-lang. pathology, Winter Haven, Fla., 1977—; instr. speech-lang. pathology Fla. So. Coll., 1979—. Active Spl. Olympics, 1978—. Lic. lang./speech pathologist, Fla. Mem. Am. Speech and Hearing Assn. (cert. clin. competence), Fla. Lang. and Speech and Hearing Assn. (chmn. membership com. 1978—), Nat. Blissymbolics Assn. (cert. instr.), Council for Exceptional Children, NEA, Fla. Ednl. Assn., Polk County Ednl. Assn., Fla. Cleft Palate Assn. Winter Haven Soccer Club. Home: 200 Shore Dr SE Winter Haven FL 33880

COMM, EDWARD DANIEL, engring. exec.; b. Fargo, N.D., Jan. 10, 1912; s. Otto Ben and Emily (Riebhoff) C.; B.S., N.D. State U., 1933; grad. U.S. Army War Coll., 1953. Practice civil engring., N.D., 1933-40; commd. 1st lt. C.E., U.S. Army, 1940, advanced through grades to col., 1944, ret. due to phys. disability, 1967; served N. Africa, Italy, France, Germany, 1942-45; exec. asst. to Q.M. Gen. and dir. logistics, Washington, 1946-52; asst. chief of staff logistics, France, 1953-56; engr. U.S. Army Engr. Dist., Louisville, 1956-58; mem. Joint Chiefs Staff, Washington, 1958-60; comdg. officer Advanced Individual Tng. Regiment, Ft. Leonard Wood, Mo., 1960-62; spl. asst. to dep. chief staff for logistics Dept. Army, Washington, 1962-67; dir. Washington operations Howard Needles Tammen & Bergendoff, cons. Engrs., 1968—; cons. to Dept. Def., Washington, 1967-69. Mem. directorate Presdl. Task Force on Structure SSS, 1967. Decorated D.S.M., Legion of Merit with two oak leaf clusters, Bronze Star, Army Commendation medal, officer Order Brit. Empire; Legion of Honor, Croix de Guerre (France) comdr. Crown of Italy Medahla de Guerra (Brazil). Fellow Am. Soc. C.E.; mem. Soc. Am. Mil Engrs., Amateur Trapshooting Assn., Phi Kappa Phi, Tau Beta Pi. Clubs: Army and Navy (Washington); Army-Navy Country (Arlington, Va.). Address: 1111 Army Navy Dr Arlington VA 22202

COMOLA, JAMES PAUL, govt. ofcl.; b. Leland, Miss., Nov. 16, 1931; s. Wilson and Freda (Saba) C.; student Hinds Jr. Coll., 1950; B.A., Millsaps Coll., 1957; profl. social worker Fla. State U., 1958; postgrad. U. Miss., 1959-62; M.A. in Urban Planning, U. Tex. at Arlington, 1975; children—James Paul, Jon Ronald. Asst. buyer Kennington's, 1954-57; dir. Miss. Dept. Pub. Welfare, Yazoo County, 1957-59; tech. liasion Commn. Small Watersheds, U.S. Ho. of Reps., 1959-60; exec. v.p. Miss. Rivers and Harbors Assn., 1960-62; asst. gen. mgr. Trinity Improvement Assn., Arlington, Tex., 1962-66, gen. mgr., 1967-70; asst. regional adminstr. EPA, Dallas, 1970-77; EPA liaison to SW Fed. Regional Council, 1977—; clin. instr. community medicine U. Tex. Southwestern Med. Sch., Dallas; cons., 1970—. Mem. Bedford City Council, Tex., 1963-65, chmn. mid-cities adv. council, 1963-66. Served with USN, 1950-54. Recipient award Rivers and Harbors Assn. Miss., 1962; Appreciation award Bedford Council Good Govt., Bedford, 1966. Mem. Am. Inst. Planners (asso.), Urban Land Inst., Assn. Tchrs. Preventive Medicine, Soil Conservation Soc. Am., Audubon Soc., Ducks Unltd., Okla. Coalition for Clean Air. Club: Lions (dir. Bedford). Editor Trinity Valley Progress, 1963-67. Contbr. articles to profl. jours. Home: 5105 Vandelia Dallas TX 75235 Office: 1201 Elm St Dallas TX 75270

COMPTON, ASBURY CHRISTIAN, state justice; b. Portsmouth, Va., Oct. 24, 1929; s. George Pierce and Edyth Gordon (Christian) C.; B.A., Washington and Lee U., Lexington, Va., 1950, LL.B., 1953, LL.D. (hon.), 1975; m. Betty Stephenson, Nov. 17, 1953; children—Leigh Christian, Mary Bryan, Melissa Anne. Admitted to Va. bar, 1957; partner firm May, Garrett, Miller, Newman & Compton, Richmond, 1957-66; judge Richmond City Law and Equity Ct., 1966-74; justice Supreme Ct. Va., 1974—; trustee Collegiate Schs., Richmond, 1972—, chmn., 1978—; mem. adminstrv. bd. Trinity United Methodist Ch., Richmond, 1974—; trustee Washington and Lee U., 1978—. Served as officer USNR, 1953-56. Recipient Letter of Commendation. Mem. Va. Bar Assn., Va. State Bar, Bar Assn. Richmond, Washington and Lee U. Alumni Assn. (past pres., dir.), Omicron Delta Kappa, Phi Kappa Sigma, Phi Alpha Delta. Club: Country of Va. Home: 5508 Queensbury Rd Richmond VA 23226 Office: PO Box 1315 Richmond VA 23210

COMPTON, HENRY TAYLOE, JR., savs. and loan assn. exec.; b. Savannah, Ga., June 5, 1925; s. Henry Tayloe and Sarah Millward (Walthour) C.; B.S. in Commerce, U. N.C., 1948; divorced; children—Randall Adams, Cameron Walthour, Tayloe Bond. Staff accountant D.F. Stewart, C.P.A., Savannah, 1948-51; partner William Lattimore, realtor, Savannah, 1951-66; with First Fed. Savs. & Loan Assn., Savannah, 1966—, mgr. data processing, 1967—, v.p., 1972—. Bd. dirs. May River Acad., Bluffton, S.C.; mem. vestry Ch. of the Cross, Bluffton, 1976—. Served with USNR, 1943-46. Mem. Data Processing Mgmt. Assn., Controllers Soc. Savs. Instns. (chmn. off-line computer com. 1972, chmn. regional conf. 1974), Soc. Colonial Wars (sec. 1978—). Clubs: Oglethorpe, Cotillion, Century, Exchange (dir. 1972-73) (Savannah). Home: Star Route Box 50R Bluffton SC 29910 Office: PO Box 8206 Savannah GA 31402

COMPTON, SUSAN LANELL, ret. librarian; b. Batesville, Ark., Aug. 20, 1917; d. Thomas Smith and Susan (Whitlow) Compton; B.S. in Edn., Ark. State Tchrs. Coll., 1939; B.S. in L.S., Peabody Coll. Tchrs., 1948. Asst. cataloger U. Ark. Gen. Library, Fayetteville, 1948-49; head catalog dept. Ark. Library Commn., Little Rock, 1949-77, chief cataloger, bibliographer, indexer, 1977-79. Free lance writer. Mem. Nat. League Am. Pen Women (v.p., program chmn. Ark. Pioneer br. 1972-74, pres. 1974-76), Ark. Choral Soc., AAUW, Ark. Hist. Assn., Ark. Fedn. Women's Clubs. Christadelphian. Author: Beauty Transient & Other Poems, 1969. Contbr. to Collier's Ency., 1970-76; editor quar. library bull. Ark. Libraries, 1949-74. Home: 620 N Oak St Little Rock AR 72205

COMPTON, WILLIAM SHANNON, elec. equipment co. exec.; b. Louisa, Ky., Aug. 22, 1937; s. Thomas Shannon and Claudia Mae (Ellis) C.; B.S. in Elec. Engring., U. Ky., 1960; m. Sue Ellen McElhinny, Apr. 2, 1977; children—Thomas Mitchell, John Lawrence, Janet Marie. Sales engr. Gen. Electric Co., 1960-68; v.p. Compton Power Equipment Corp., Cleve., 1968-69; pres. Compton Elec. Equipment Corp., Huntington, W.Va., 1969—. Mem. Am. Fedn. Ind. Bus. (v.p. 1977-79), Am. Mining Congress, Elec. Apparatus Service Assn., W.Va. Mfrs. Assn. Republican. Baptist. Club: Masons. Office: 720 15th St W Huntington WV 25776

CONAGHAN, DOROTHY DELL, state legislator; b. Oklahoma City, Sept. 24, 1930; d. John Joseph and Wilhelamina Elizabeth (Boyer) Miller; student U. Okla., 1949-51; m. Brian Francis Conaghan, June 10, 1951; (dec. Apr. 1973); children—Joseph Lee, Charles Alan, Roger Lloyd. Mem. Okla. Legislature, 1973—; vice chmn. Kay County (Okla.) Republicans, 1961-64, 6th Congl. Dist. Rep. Party, 1967-69; del. Rep. Nat. Conv., 1968. Bd. dirs. United Fund, 1966-69. Named Woman of Year, Soroptimists Internat. of Ponca City., 1975. Mem. Tonkawa C. of C., Am. Legion Aux., Orgn. Women Legislators, P.E.O., Beta Sigma Phi, Theta Chi. Mem. Christian Ch. Clubs: Order Eastern Star, Soroptimists (hon. Ponca City), Delphi Study, Tonkawa Rep. Women's. Home: 904 E Grand St Tonkawa OK 74653 Office: Ho of Reps State Capitol Bldg Oklahoma City OK 74653

CONARD, VIRGIL WARREN, fast food entreprenuer; b. Topeka, Nov. 24, 1921; s. Oscar Clyde and Ella Marie (Pfister) C.; A.B., Washburn U., Topeka, 1947, B.B.A., 1948; m. Rene Ann Reeves, Dec. 11, 1971; children—Rocky Lee, Ricki Lou, Cindy Sue Conard Bailey. With Southwestern Bell Telephone Co., 1947-65, traffic supt., Topeka, 1954-65; pres., chief exec. officer, dir. Conard Corp., Corpus Christi, Tex., 1974—, Conard Pizza Corp., 1975—, Hutco, Inc., 1973—, Krebcon Corp., 1974—, Statewide Foods, Inc., 1973—. Chmn. spl. events United Way Coastal Bend, 1976-77; bd. dirs. Corpus Christi Symphony Soc., 1978—, Corpus Christi chpt. NCCJ, 1978—, Art Museum S. Tex., Corpus Christi, 1978—. Served with USNR, 1942-46. Recipient Cosmopolitan Internat.-Unity Service award, 1964. Mem. Internat. Pizza Hut Franchise Holders Assn., Tex. Restaurant Assn. (v.p. 1978), Tex. Hotel-Motel Assn., Corpus Christi C. of C., ACLU, Common Cause, NAACP, Washburn U. Alumni Assn., Tues. Luncheon Group. Democrat. Clubs: Corpus Christi Country, Santa Fe Swim. Office: PO Box 3610 403 N Shoreline St Corpus Christi TX 78404

CONDE, CESAR AUGUSTO, physician; b. Lima, Peru, Oct. 31, 1942; s. Aurelio Vicente and Mercedes (Portocarrero) C.; M.D., San Marcos U. (Lima, Peru), 1967; m. Maria C. Perez-Teran, Sept. 8, 1972; children—Cesar R., Jorge C., Enrique A. Intern, Phila. Gen. Hosp., U. Pa., 1968-69; resident Henry Ford Hosp., Detroit, 1969-71; resident cardiology Mt. Sinai Hosp. and Mt. Sinai Sch. Medicine, 1971-73, asst. prof. medicine and cardiology, 1973-74; asst. clin. prof. medicine and cardiology U. Miami, 1974-78, asso. clin. prof., 1978—, chief div. cardiology Parkway Gen. Hosp., Miami, Fla., 1977—. Fellow Am. Coll. Cardiology, A.C.P., Nat. Council Clin. Cardiology; mem. Am., Miami heart assns. Roman Catholic. Club: Big Five (Miami). Home: 8100 Los Pinos Blvd Miami FL 33143 Office: 16800 NW 2d Ave North Miami Beach FL 33169 also 1295 NW 14th St Miami FL 33139

CONDOM, JAIME ERNESTO, hosp. adminstr., physician; b. Mariel, Cuba, Feb. 27, 1932; s. Jaime Simeon and Maria Matilde (Valera) C.; B.S., U. Havana, 1957; M.D., U. Madrid, 1962; m. Kathryn Du Cloux, Dec. 5, 1974; children—Marie Elizabeth, Kathryn Leigh, Valerie DuCloux. Came to U.S., 1960, naturalized, 1966. Intern, Mobile (Ala.) Gen. Hosp., 1962-63; staff physician Searcy State Hosp., Mt. Vernon, Ala., 1963-68, acting clin. dir., 1968-69, clin. dir., 1969-70, acting supt., clin. dir., 1970, supt., 1970—; supt. Thomasville, Andalusia and Eufaula Adjustment Centers, 1975—; asso. prof. psychiatry U. South Ala. Sch. Medicine, 1977—; supt. Bryce Hosp., Tuscaloosa, Ala., 1979. Bd. dirs. Mobile Mental Health Assn. Recipient Physician's Recognition award AMA, 1970. Mem. Assn. Med. Supts. Mental Hosps., Med. Assn. State Ala., Mobile County Med. Soc., Gulf Coast Soc. Neurology, Psychiatry, Neurosurgery and Psychology. Address: Searcy Hosp PO Box 23 Mount Vernon AL 36560

CONDRON, STEWART LEWIS, accountant; b. Elgin, Tex., Oct. 17, 1919; s. Harvey Elmo and Ruth (Carter) C.; B.S., Bowling Green Coll. Commerce, 1942; M.B.A., Harvard Bus. Sch., 1947; m. Helen Johnson, Sept. 24, 1943; 1 dau., Helen Ruth (Mrs. John M. Balentine, Jr.). With Ernst & Whinney, Greenville, S.C., 1947—, partner, 1958—. Adj. prof. bus. adminstrn. U. S.C., Columbia, 1972-73. Pres. United Fund Greenville County, 1961, Little Theatre, Greenville, S.C., 1962, 64. Chmn. Greenville County Found., 1967, Greenville Hosp. System, 1971. Served with USNR, 1942-46. Recipient Diamond Merit award Adminstrv. Mgmt. Soc., 1960; named Outstanding Boss Greenville Jr. C. of C., 1961. C.P.A., S.C., Tex. Mem. Greater Greenville C. of C. (dir. 1963-66), S.C. Assn. C.P.A.'s (pres. 1964), Am. Inst. C.P.A.'s (mem. council 1964). Kiwanian (pres. 1964). Clubs: Poinsett, Green Valley Country, Country (all Greenville, S.C.); Biltmore Forest Country (Asheville, N.C.). Home: 11 Indian Spring Greenville SC 29615 Office: 1814 Daniel Bldg Greenville SC 29602

CONDRY, CARSON EMMITT, mech. engr.; b. Liberal, Kans., July 12, 1923; s. Sterling H. and Gladys B. (Carson) C.; B.S., Kans. State U., 1948; m. Martha Elizabeth Baker, July 9, 1944. Prodn. draftsman, design engr., asst. chief engr. The J.B. Ehrsam & Son Mfg. Co., Enterprise, Kans., 1948-50; chief engr. Hamilton Constrn. Co., Salina, Kans., 1950-51; with A.J. Boynton & Co. of Tex., Dallas, 1951-66, successively draftsman, design engr., project engr., asst. chief engr., 1951-61, chief engr., 1961-66; v.p., dir. Zetterlund-Boynton-Condry & Assos., engrs. and tech. counselors, 1966-67; pres. Condry, Cayton, Burford & Assos., cons. engrs., indsl. specialists, Dallas, 1967—. Served from pvt. 1st class to 1st lt. A.C., AUS, 1941-45; ETO. Decorated Air medal. Registered profl. engr., Tex., Okla., Kans. Mem. Am. Soc. M.E., Nat., Tex. socs. profl. engrs., Alumni Assn. Kans. State U., Nat. Geog. Soc., Cons. Engrs. Soc., Profl. Engrs. in Pvt. Practice, Joint Engrs. Council, Greater Dallas Planning Council, White Rock YMCA, Nat Wildlife Fedn. Democrat. Methodist. Home: 2216 Longwood Ln Dallas TX 75228 Office: 10901 Garland Rd Dallas TX 75218

CONE, CARL BRUCE, historian; b. Davenport, Iowa, Feb. 22, 1916; s. Carl S. and Lena (Petersen) C.; B.A., U. Iowa, 1936, M.A., 1937, Ph.D., 1940; m. Mary Louise Regan, Dec. 20, 1942; 1 son, Carl Timothy. Instr. history Allegheny Coll., Meadville, Pa., 1940-41; asst. prof. history La. State U., Baton Rouge, 1942-47; asst. prof. U. Ky., Lexington, 1947-49, asso. prof., 1949-56, prof., 1956—, chmn. dept., 1965-70. Mem. Lexington Civil Service Commn., 1958-68; mem. Lexington Library Bd., 1978—. Guggenheim Found. fellow, 1963-64. Mem. So. Hist. Assn. (mem. exec. council), So. Conf. Brit. Studies (chmn. 1972). Republican. Roman Catholic. Author: Torchbearer of Freedom, 1952; Burke and the Nature of Politics, Vol. I, 1957, Vol. 2, 1964; The English Jacobins, 1968. Home: 203 Sycamore Rd Lexington KY 40502 Office: Dept History U of Ky Lexington KY 40506

CONE, JOHN CHARLES, ednl. adminstr.; b. Geneva, Ill., June 6, 1941; married, 2 children. B.A. in English, Clemson (S.C.) U., 1965. Staff writer Christian Sci. Monitor, Boston, 1965-67; account exec. Corrigan & Co. Advt., Charleston, S.C., 1967-69; dir. infor. services Charleston County Pub. Schs., 1969-77; exec. dir. S.C. Sch. Bds. Assn., Columbia, 1977—. Dist. commr. Mt. Pleasant Boy Scouts Am., 1973—; bd. dirs. S.C. Kidney Found.; mem. adv. bd. S.C. Dept. Youth Services. Recipient Disting. Service award Charleston Mental Health Assn. Mem. Charleston Mental Health Assn. (pres. 1972-74), Nat. Sch. Pub. Relations Assn. (pres. S.C. chpt. 1976-77, chmn. electronic media com. 1977-78), Public Relations Soc. Am. (pres. S.C. chpt. 1978-79), Am. Assn. Sch. Adminstrs. Author tng. modules, articles, reports. Named Outstanding Young Man of Year S.C. Jaycees, 1974. Home: 6217 Westshore Columbia SC 29206 Office: 1706 Senate St Columbia SC 29201

CONE, THOMAS FITE, SR., oil co. exec.; b. Nashville, June 15, 1938; s. Clarence William and Sue Gran (Fite) C.; B.A. in Bus. Adminstrn., Vanderbilt U., 1960; LL.B., YMCA Law Sch., 1964, J.D., 1971; m. Charlotte Ladell Huskey, June 5, 1965; children—Susan Ladell, Thomas Fite. Vice pres. Cone Oil Co., Inc., Nashville, 1958-69, pres., 1969—; chmn. bd. Cone Solvents, Inc., Tenn Adhesives & Chem. Corp. Mem. devel. council David Lipscomb Coll. Served in U.S. Army, 1956-57. Mem. Tenn. Oil & Gas Assn., Tenn Bar Assn., Nashville C. of C. Baptist. Club: Richland Country. Home: 825 N Curtiswood Ln Nashville TN 37204 Office: 195 N 1st St Nashville TN 37213

CONGLETON, CONLEY COLE, III, lawyer; b. N.Y.C., Sept. 17, 1945; s. Conley Cole and Gladys Hale Congleton; B.A., Eastern Ky. U., 1968; J.D., U. Ky., 1971; m. Brenda Kay Cromer, June 26, 1979. Admitted to Ky. bar, 1973; practice law, Lexington, Ky., 1974-76; corp. counsel Begley Drug Co., Richmond, Ky., 1976—. Bd. dirs., treas. Bluegrass Boys' Ranch, Lexington, 1975—. Served to capt. U.S. Army, 1968-76. Mem. Nat. Assn. Chain Drug Stores (mem. com. human resources devel.), Madison County Bar Assn., Ky. Bar Assn., Fayette County Bar Assn. Republican. Home: 203 Leimaur Dr Richmond KY 40475 Office: PO Box 1000 Eastern Ky U By-Pass Richmond KY 40475

CONGLETON, JAMES CLEVELAND, JR., ednl. adminstr.; b. Parkersburg, W.Va., Jan. 24, 1921; s. James Cleveland and Bessie (Sprout) C.; student Carson-Newman Coll., 1938-40; B.S. in Advt., U. Fla., 1970; m. Dorothy Louise Satterfield, Apr. 29, 1942; children—Bruce Arthur, James Patrick. Engaged in retail music bus., W. Va., Fla., 1947-69; mem. faculty Seminole Community Coll., Sanford, Fla., 1971—, info. dir. Served with USAF, 1941-45. Decorated Air medal, Group Citation with two clusters. Mem. Fla. Assn. Community Colls., Kappa Tau Alpha. Presbyn. Home: 801 W 18th St Sanford FL 32771 Office: Seminole Community Coll Sanford FL 32771

CONGRAM, GARY EUGENE, engring. co. exec.; b. Houston, Mar. 18, 1941; s. Jennings William and Helen Lorene (Breidenbach) C.; B.S., Okla. State U., 1963; M.S., U. Houston, 1966; m. Fern Marie Overholt, June 18, 1961; children—Jeffrey, Steven, Becky. Corrosion engr. Continental Oil Co., Ponca City, Okla., 1964-68; refinery engr. Petrolite Corp., Tulsa, 1968-74; pipeline engring. editor Oil and Gas Jour., Houston, 1974-78; mgr. processing plants Ventech Engrs., Inc., Houston, 1978—. Mem. Am. Inst. Chem. Engrs., Am. Welding Soc., Am. Soc. Nondestructive Testing, Houston Engrs. Sci. Soc., Am. Chem. Soc., Nat. Assn. Corrosion Engrs., Radio Emergency Orgn. (pres. 1975-76), Traffic Assistance Control Team, Jaycees (v.p. 1965), Sigma Alpha Upsilon (Speakers award 1970). Democrat. Clubs: Toastmasters, Kiwanis. Author tech. articles. Home: 2207 Mission Mill Circle Houston TX 77084 Office: PO Box 4261 Pasadena TX 77502

CONKLIN, DEBORAH JEANNE, child devel. specialist; b. Richmond, Va., Sept. 26, 1950; d. Edward Gordon and Jeanne Manson (Clayton) C.; B.A. in Psychology, East Carolina U., 1972, M.S. in Child Devel. and Family Relations, 1973. Daycare dir. Winterville-Ayden-Grifton Child Devel. Center, Ayden, N.C., 1973-75; area mental retardation specialist Pitt County Mental Health Center, Greenville, N.C., 1975—. Mem. Am. Assn. Mental Deficiency, Nat. Assn. for Retarded Citizens, N.C. Assn. for Retarded Citizens, Pitt County Assn. for Retarded Citizens. Democrat. Baptist. Home: Rawlwood Arms Apt 1-F Greenville NC 27834 Office: Pitt County Mental Health Center 306 Stantonsburg Rd Greenville NC 27834

CONLEY, JAMES MONROE, ednl. adminstr.; b. Livingston, Ala., Aug. 18, 1915; s. D.L. and Nancy (Lowe) C.; Inst., 1941; M.Ed., Tenn. State U., 1963; m. Ellie M. Banks, Nov. 21, 1945; children—Eddie Roy, Judy Lenee, James Randy, Janie Evette. Commd. 2d. lt. U.S. Army Air Force, 1942, advanced through grades to maj., 1956; served as adminstrv. officer, personnel officer, statis. services officer, unit comdr., asst. prof. air sci. U.S. Army Air Force and U.S. Air Force, 1942-63, ret., 1963; counselor Tenn. State U., Nashville, 1963-69; guidance counselor Met. Nashville Public Schs., 1970-72, vocat. edn. program leader, 1972—. Ordained deacon Mt. Olive Bapt. Ch., ch. clk., 1966-76; active NAACP. Mem. NEA, Tenn. Edn. Assn., Met. Nashville Edn. Assn., Ret. Officers Assn., Omega Psi Phi (life, chpt. basileus 1974-76, 1st vice dir. 5th Dist. 1977-78). Club: Optimists (v.p. Central Nashville chpt.). Home: 912 38th Ave N Nashville TN 37209 Office: 700 Broadway Nashville TN 37203

CONLEY, MABEL, biologist, educator; b. Ringgold, La., Sept. 9, 1940; d. Verlis and Annie (Lloyd) Conley; B.S., Grambling (La.) State Coll., 1962; M.S. in Teaching, So. U., Baton Rouge, 1967. Instr. biology and gen. sci. DeSoto Parish Sch. Bd., Mansfield, La., 1962-67; mem. faculty So. U., 1967—, asst. prof. biology; sci. fair judge and cons.; participant NSF summer insts; vis. scientist fellow Lawrence Livermore Lab., Livermore, Calif., 1974; faculty research fellow Argonne (Ill.) Nat. Lab., 1975. Lay speaker Evergreen Baptist Ch., also Pilgrim Rest Bapt. Ch. Mem. Nat. Sci. Tchrs. Assn., Nat. Assn. Biology Tchrs., La. Assn. Mental Health, Am. Fedn. Tchrs., Grambling State U., So. U. alumni assns., Cooper Rd Civic Assn., Alpha Kappa Alpha, Phi Delta Kappa, Kappa Delta Pi. Home: 4028 Powell St Shreveport LA 71109 Office: 3050 Cooper Rd Shreveport LA 71107

CONN, JACK TRAMMELL, banker, lawyer; b. Ada, Okla., Nov. 19, 1909; s. Jared Trammell and Carrie (Cahplin) C.; grad. East Central U., Okla., 1931; LL.B., U. Okla., 1940, Ph.D. (hon.), Oklahoma City U., 1968; m. Mary Gillett Massey, Sept. 1, 1937. Admitted to Okla. bar, 1940; practice law, Ada and Oklahoma City, 1940-46; mem. firm Conn, Mayhue & Kerr, Ada, 1947-64; pres., chmn. bd. Okla. State Bank, Ada, 1951-64; chmn., chief exec. officer Fidelity Bank Nat. Assn., Oklahoma City, 1964-79, vice chmn., 1979—; chmn. bd. Fidelity of Okla., Inc. Pres. Okla. Hist. Soc. Named to Okla. Hall of Fame; recipient Distinguished Alumnus award E. Central U., Ada, 1972; Distinguished Service citation U. Okla., 1978. Mem. Okla. (past pres.), Am. (past pres.) bankers assns., Res. City Bankers Assn., Order of Coif, Phi Delta Phi, Sigma Nu. Democrat. Presbyterian. Home: 7202 Waverly St Oklahoma City OK 73120 Office: Fidelity Bank Box 24128 Oklahoma City OK 73124

CONNALLY, HERSCHEL JOSEPH, judge; b. San Angelo, Tex., July 15, 1935; s. Herschel Christian and Hazel Corinne (Faris) C.; student Southwestern U., 1953-54, 1957, San Angelo Coll., 1955-56, U. Tex., 1960-61; J.D., U. Tex. Law Sch., 1964; m. Lanita Connally; children—Vella Katherine, Jennifer Robin, Matthew Caleb. Admitted to Tex. bar, 1964; practiced in Abilene, Tex., 1964, Odessa, 1964—; mem. firms Jackson & Jackson, Abilene, 1964; mem. firm Turpin, Smith, Dyer, Harman & Dawson, Odessa, Tex., 1964-74, partner, 1967-74; individual practice law, 1974—; county judge, Ector County, Tex., 1975-77; judge 244th Dist. Ct., 1977—. Chmn. zoning bd. adjustment City Odessa, Tex., 1972-74; mem. Tex. Bd. Pvt. Investigators and Pvt. Security Agys., 1973-77, chmn., 1975-77; v.p. Presidential Mus. Odessa, Tex., 1971—, bd. trustees, 1969—. Tex. Dem. Exec. Com., 1972—; campaign mgr. U.S. Senator Lloyd Bentsen, 1970, Gov. Dolph Briscoe, 1972. Served with AUS, 1958-60. Mem. State Bar Tex., Ector County Bar Assn. (chmn. grievance com. 1972, v.p. 1976), Kappa Sigma, Phi Alpha Delta. Democrat. Methodist. Club: Exchange (Odessa, Tex.). Home: 4214 Clover Odessa TX 79760 Office: Room 300 Ector County Ct House Odessa TX 79761

CONNELL, SUZANNE (SPARKS) MCLAURIN, ret. librarian; b. Bennettsville, S.C., Sept. 12, 1917; d. John Bethea and Aleine (McLeod) McLaurin; A.B., Woman's Coll. of U. N.C., 1938; A.B. in L.S., U. N.C., 1940; 1 son, John Alexander (dec.). Library asst. Mt. Pleasant br. D.C. Pub. Library, Washington, 1940-41; post librarian Camp Sutton, N.C., 1943-44; post librarian McGuire Gen. Hosp., Richmond, Va., 1945-46, chief librarian McGuire VA Hosp., 1946-52, 59-62; chief librarian VA Hosp., Lake City, Fla., 1952-56; cataloger, chief books acquisitions, chief books circulation, asst. chief documents acquisitions Air U. Library, Maxwell AFB, Ala., 1956-59; head extension, head circulation Greensboro (N.C.) Pub. Library, 1962-63; reference librarian, asst. and acting base librarian Marine Corps Base, Camp Lejeune, N.C., 1963-66; part time cataloger Wilmington (N.C.) Pub. Library, 1967-75. Past vol., ARC; now vol. local hosp. Mem. ALA (pres. assn. hosp. and instn. libraries 1955-56), N.C., Southeastern library assns., Phi Beta Kappa. Contbr. articles to Brit. and Am. periodicals. Home: 502 Brunswick St Southport NC 28461

CONNELLY, ROBERT JOSEPH, educator; b. Greeley, Nebr., Aug. 17, 1939; s. Gerald Charles and Anna Lorine (Lee) C.; B.A. magna cum laude, Regis Coll., 1961; M.A., St. Louis U., 1965, Ph.D., 1970; m. Gail Ann Winchester, June 4, 1966; children—Kimberly Ann, Corin James. Instr., St. Louis U., 1962-68; asst. prof. Fontbonne Coll., St. Louis, 1968-72; asso. prof. Incarnate Word Coll., San Antonio, 1972-78, prof. philosophy, 1978—, Moody prof., 1979-80, Mini Stevens Piper prof., 1980, chmn. dept. philosophy, 1968-72, dir. Change in Liberal Edn. program, 1975-76; lectr. in field; mem. Commn. on Coll. Planning, 1974—; instr. 4 continuing edn. programs, 1977-79, coordinator 6 other programs, 1974-79. New Curriculum Cons. grantee, 1977; NSF-AAAS grantee, 1977-79; Danforth asso., 1979-85. Mem. Nat. Jesuit Honor Soc., Internat. Social Sci. Honor Soc., Am. Philosophical Assn., Am. Cath. Philosophical Assn., Inst. of Soc., Ethics and the Life Scis. Contbr. articles in field to profl. jours. Home: 227 Arcadia Pl San Antonio TX 78209 Office: 4301 Broadway San Antonio TX 78209

CONNER, J(AMES) ERNEST, automobile agy. exec.; b. Wichita Falls, Tex., Mar. 14, 1943; s. James D. and N. Graham C.; B.B.A., U. Tex., 1965; m. Glenda Williams, Aug. 3, 1979. Asst. sales mgr. D-FW Chrysler-Plymouth, Ft. Worth, 1975; fin. mgr. Jet Port Chrysler-Dodge, Irving, Tex., 1975-76; bus. mgr. Mid City Chrysler-Plymouth Co., Arlington, Tex., 1976-79; bus. mgr. George Grubbs Datsun Inc., Bedford, Tex., 1979—. Bd. dirs. Dallas Vocal Arts Ensemble, Arlington Fine Arts League. Served with U.S. Army, 1965-67; Vietnam. Decorated Purple Heart. Republican. Baptist. Home: PO Box 682 Bedford TX 76021 Office: George Grubbs Datsun Inc PO Box 845 Bedford TX 76021

CONNER, JAMES TILLAR, newspaper exec.; b. Newport, Ark., June 6, 1930; s. Jake W. and Annie Lou (Wilbourn) C.; B.A., La. State U., 1951; student Am. Press Inst., 1967, 75; m. Nancy Robert, Oct. 28, 1951; children—Robert, John, Holly, Scott. Mgr. trainee J.C. Penney & Co., Inc., Baton Rouge, La., 1951-53; ad salesman Sta. WAFB, Baton Rouge, 1953-57; display ad salesman Advocate & State-Times, Baton Rouge, 1957-66, asst. classified ad mgr., 1966-73, classified ad mgr., 1973—; classified advt. cons. La. Press Assn. Bd. dirs. Better Bus. Bur., 1977—; chmn. bus. II, United Way Drive, 1976, chmn. bus. I, 1977. Served with USNR, 1948-49. Mem. Internat. Newspaper Advt. Execs. Assn., Assn. Newspaper Classified Advt. Mgrs. (dir. 1976-78), So. Classified Advt. Mgrs. Assn. (pres. 1978-79), Baton Rouge C. of C. Home: 9140 Ventura Dr Baton Rouge LA 70815 Office: 525 Lafayette St Baton Rouge LA 70821

CONNER, WILLIAM MICHAEL, tire co. exec.; b. Chattanooga, Feb. 16, 1941; s. William Ray and Mary Jane (Sands) C.; student Bryan Coll., 1964, Tenn. Technol. U., 1964, LaSalle U., 1967; m. Jane Blevins, Mar. 21, 1965; 1 son, Scott. Credit mgr. Goodyear Tire & Rubber Co., Sweetwater, Tenn., 1964-65, credit mgr., Fayetteville, Tenn., 1965-67, territory sales mgr., Johnson City, Tenn., 1975-77; owner Sparta (Tenn.) Men's Shop, 1967-69; mgr. Poes Men's Shop, Florence, Ala., 1969; credit mgr., budget mgr., asst. store mgr., various locations, Tenn., 1969-74; mgr. Free Service Tire Co., Knoxville, Tenn., 1977-80; pres., treas. Conner Tire Co., Knoxville, 1980—. Served with USMC, 1959-63. Democrat. Baptist. Club: Masons. Home: 8710 Vultee Lane Knoxville TN 37919 Office: Conner Tire Co PO Box 10471 Knoxville TN 37919

CONNER, WILLIAM SAMUEL, naval nuclear mfg. co. exec.; b. Chillicothe, Ohio, Jan. 20, 1930; s. Samuel Danuel and Alice Blanche (Rakes) C.; student Va. Tech. U., 1947-49; degree in mech. engring. Detroit Tech. U., 1959; m. Catherine Willia McGraw, Feb. 14, 1976; children—Barry Kent Martin, Kathy Darnell Wright, James Thomas Conner. Gear specialist Western Electric Co., Greensboro, N.C., 1949-51; quality controll staff mem. Lennox Tool & Die Co., Lima, Ohio, 1951-52; mem. process engring. staff Excello Corp., Lima, 1952-64; project engring. mgr. Babcock & Wilcox, Lynchburg, Va., 1964—; welding cons. Chmn. spl. projects Parkview Methodist Ch., Lynchburg, 1976—. Recipient Boss of Yr. award Appomattox Jr. C. of C., 1973. Mem. Lynchburg Soc. Engring. and Sci. Club: Ruritan (pres. 1976) (Lynchburg). Home: 529 Fox Hall Rd Lynchburg VA 24551 Office: PO Box 785 Lynchburg VA 24505

CONNETT, ROBERT PAUL, mfg. co. exec.; b. Wymore, Nebr., Aug. 3, 1917; s. Myron Smith and Bessie May (Salisbury) C.; student U. Nebr., 1935-39; B.Sc., Mo. Sch. Mines, 1946; m. Janice Marie Brugh, Feb. 20, 1942; children—Richard James, Charles Robert, Catherine Ann. Mine engr. Fredericktown Lead Co. (Mo.), 1946-49; quarry engr., operating supt. U.S. Gypsum Co., Alabaster, Mich., 1949-53, works mgr. Plasterco plant, 1960—; asst. works mgr. Canadian Gypsum Co., Windsor, N.S., 1953-54; mng. dir. Jamaica (W.I.) Gypsum Co., 1954-60. Chmn. Washington County Bd. Zoning Appeals, 1972—; mem. Washington County Planning Commn., 1964—, vice chmn., 1977—; trustee Meth. Ch., 1970—; bd. dirs. Johnson Meml. Hosp., 1977—. Served with C.E., U.S. Army, 1941-46. Mem. Am. Soc. Mining Engrs., Am. Mgmt. Assn., Va. Safety Assn., Va. Mfg. Assn., Va. C. of C., Washington County C. of C. Republican. Club: Kiwanis. Home: Route 1 Saltville VA 24370 Office: US Gypsum Co Saltville VA 24370

CONNIN, JOHN LYMAN, office bus. systems equipment co. exec.; b. Defiance, Ohio, Dec. 31, 1941; s. Carson H. and Lucille M. (Grime) C.; B.S. in Elec. Engring., Ohio U., Athens, 1964; M.S. in Elec. Engring., U. Rochester (N.Y.), 1967; children—Sean L., Lance B. With Eastman Kodak Co., Rochester, 1964-78, advanced systems specialist, 1976-78; dir. QWIP Systems Co. div. Exxon Enterprises Inc., Orlando, Fla., 1978-79, v.p., 1979—. Mem. Am. Mgmt. Assn., Tau Beta Pi, Eta Kappa Nu. Home: 105 Red Cedar St Longwood FL 32750 Office: 5551 Vanguard Rd Orlando FL 32806

CONNOLLY, VINCENT HAROLD, educator; b. Lyndhurst, N.J., Apr. 4, 1925; s. Vincent Paul and Mildred Olga (Barringer) C.; student Drew U., 1941-42; B.A., Rutgers U., 1950; M.Ed., U. N.C., Raleigh, 1970; m. Laura Joyce Morgenson, June 25, 1950; children—Kathleen Joy, Nancy Louise. Acct., Shell Oil Co., Sewaren, N.J., 1951-58; supr. data processing SE & M Vernow Co., Elizabeth, N.J., 1958-60; supr. data processing Vulcan Materials Co., Sewaren, N.J., 1960-62; mg. info. services J. P. Stevens Co., Aberdeen, N.C., 1962-67; instr. bus. and econs. Sandhills Community Coll., Carthage, N.C., 1967—; bus. and tax cons. Bass baritone ch. choirs, 1950—; deacon, elder Reformed Ch. in Am., Presbyterian Ch., 1950—. Served with USN, 1943-46. Mem. Data Processing Mgmt. Assn., Mensa, Theta Chi. Republican. Clubs: Elks, So. Pines Country. Home: 1115 E Massachusetts Ave Southern Pines NC 28387 Office: Rt 3 Box 182C Carthage NC 28327

CONNOR, SEYMOUR VAUGHAN, educator; historian; b. Paris, Tex., Mar. 4, 1923; s. Aikin Beard and Gladys (Vaughan) C.; B.A., U. Tex., 1948, M.A., 1949, Ph.D., 1952; 1 son, Charles Seymour. Archivist, W. Tex. State U., 1952-53, Tex. State Library, 1953-55; prof. history, dir. S.W. collection Tex. Tech. U., Lubbock, 1955-63, prof. history, 1965-79, prof. emeritus, 1979—. Served with AUS, 1943-45; ETO. Fellow Tex. State Hist. Assn. (mem. exec. council 1957-71, pres. 1967-68); mem. Panhandle-Plains Hist. Soc. (editor Rev. 1954-59; life mem.), W. Tex. Hist. Assn. (exec. council 1960-63), W. Tex. Mus. Assn. (exec. council 1956-62), Tex. Inst. Letters, Phi Kappa Tau, Phi Kappa Psi, Phi Alpha Theta. Author: Preliminary Guide to Texas Archives, 1956: Peters Colony of Texas, 1959; A Biggers Chronicle, 1961; Adventure in Glory, 1965; Texas: A History, 1971; (with Odie Faulk) North America Divided, 1971; (with W.C. Pool) Texas, the 28th state, 1971; Texas in 1776, 1975; (with J.M. Skaggs) Broadcloth and Britches, 1977. Editor: Texas Treasury Papers (3 vols.), 1955; The West Is for Us, 1957; Builders of the Southwest, 1959; Saga of Texas (6 vols.), 1965; Dear America, 1971; (with Odie Faulk) Politics in the American West, 1975. Contbr. articles to profl. jours. Home: 3503 45th St Lubbock TX 79413

CONNORS, JOHN KEITH, substance abuse counselor; b. Memphis, Mar. 5, 1952; s. William Keith and Margaret Jane (Gilmer) C.; B.S. (duPont scholar 1970-74), U. Va., 1974, M.Ed., 1979. Counselor, Alcoholism Treatment Center, Charlottesville, Va., 1973-78; dir. Charlottesville Honor Ct., 1974-78; substance abuse specialist Valley Mental Health Services, Staunton, Va., 1978—; instr. alcohol safety action project, 1975—; cons. in field. Publicity dir. Planned Parenthood, Charlottesville, 1976. Mem. Nat. Assn. Alcoholism Counselors, Am. Personnel and Guidance Assn., Substance Abuse Program Dirs. Assn., Va. Assn. Alcoholism Counselors, Jefferson Lit. and Debating Soc., Phi Delta Kappa. Author papers in field. Home: PO Box 48 Batesville VA 22924 Office: 19 S Coalter St Staunton VA 24401

CONOLE, RICHARD CLEMENT, mgmt. exec.; b. Binghamton, N.Y., Dec. 7, 1936; s. Clement V. and Marjorie E. (Anable) C.; student U. Pa., 1955, 1960, Clarkson Coll., 1956-57; children—Margaret Ann, Linda Elizabeth; m. Sharyn Stafford, Apr. 18, 1969; 1 dau., Samantha Erin. Data processing dept. Campbell Soup Co., Inc., Camden, N.J., 1954; draftsman Gannett, Fleming, Corddry & Carpenter, Inc., Ardmore, Pa., 1955-56; plant mgr., office mgr. Tabulating Card Co., Inc., Princeton, N.J., 1957-59, asst. to pres., asst. sec.-treas., sec. 1959; pres., dir. Data Processing Supplies Co., Inc., Princeton, 1959; sec., dir. Whiting Paper Co., Inc., Princeton, 1959, pres. 1961-62; pres., dir. Mercer-Princeton Realty Co., Inc., Princeton, 1959-61; pres. Am. Bus. Investment Co., Inc., Princeton, 1960; pres., dir. Business Supplies Corp. Am., Skytop, Pa., 1962-65, Gen. Bus. Supplies Corp., Ardmore, 1965-71; chmn. bd. Nat. Productive Machines, Inc., Elkridge, Md., 1965-71; v.p., chmn. finance com., dir. Pocono Internat. Raceway Inc., 1964-74; pres. Gen. Automotive Supplies Co., 1971-72; pres., dir. Autoberfest, Inc., 1973—. Promotional Printing Ltd., 1973; pres. The World Series of Auto Racing Corp., 1973-78, Tex. World Speedway Inc., 1976—, Speedway Mgmt. Corp., 1978—; sales cons. Hess & Barker, 1972-76; mem. competition com. U.S. Auto Club, 1976—. Clubs: Skytop (Skytop, Pa.); Phila. Country, Merion Cricket (Haverford, Pa.); Manor (Pocono Manor, Pa.). Home: Box 9191 College Station TX 77840 Office: Box A. College Station TX 77840

CONOLLY, RICHARD NOBLE, machine mfg. co. exec.; b. Athens, Ga., May 2, 1913; s. Paul Hybart and Dixie (Lawhead) C.; B.S. (Danforth fellow, Cotton Tour fellow), Tex. A. and M. U., 1937; m. Virginia Rainey, Dec. 14, 1940 (dec.); children—Richard Noble, Dana Wingfield Taggart III, Ann Brown, Timothy Noble; m. 2d, Marca Bailey Spence July 15, 1978. Dist. mgr. Stewart & Stevenson Services, Inc., Corpus Christi, 1946-64, v.p. branches and dealers, 1964—; v.p., dir. Machinery Acceptance Corp., Houston, 1956—, Rocky Mountain Power, Inc., Denver, Internat. Switchboard Co., Houston, 1971—; dir. Stewart & Stevenson Co. de Venezuela, S. Am., Goldetron Co., Corpus Christi; pres., dir. Corpus Christi Airport Devel. Corp., 1972—. Chmn. Corpus Christi Indsl. Commn., 1976—. Pres. Coastal Bend Youth City, 1972-73; trustee Corpus Christi Indsl. Found. Served to lt. col., USAAF, 1941-45; PTO. Decorated six Bronze Star medals. Mem. Tex. Energy Council, Tex. Motor Transp. Assn., Sprinkler Irrigation Assn., Assn. Former Students Tex. A. and M. U. (pres. 1958-59), Corpus Christi C. of C. (pres. 1971-72), Navy League, Def. Orientation Conf. Assn. Episcopalian. Rotarian. Clubs: Dallas Petroleum; Corpus Christi Yacht, Corpus Christi Country, Corpus Christi Town. Home: 3535 Santa Fe No 41 Corpus Christi TX 78411 Office: PO Box 4975 Corpus Christi TX 78408

CONOVER, ARTHUR VERNER, III, fin. exec.; b. Washington, June 25, 1942; s. Arthur Verner and Alma Irene (Van Sciver) C.; student Strayer Bus. Coll., 1960-62, U.S. Dept. Agr. Grad. Sch., 1963-64; m. Betty Jane Compton, June 4, 1966; 1 son, Michael Wayne. Cost accountant County of Fairfax (Va.), 1961-65; acctg. mgr. ARIES Corp., McLean, Va., 1965-67; controller Williams Ents., Inc., Merrifield, Va., 1967-73; v.p. Sonny Hylton Cos., Woodbridge, Va., 1973; chief fin. officer Williams Industries, Inc., Merrifield, 1973—, also dir.; dir. Williams Steel Erection Co., Inc., Cranes Unltd., Inc., S.I.P., Inc., Bridge & Paving Services, Inc., Comml. Mfg. and Repair Co., Inc., Dominion Ceisson Corp., others. Mem. Washington Bd. Trade, 1974—, task force on workmen's compensation, 1974-78, task force on unemployment compensation, 1974-78. Served with USAF, 1960-61. Mem. Am Mgmt. Assn., Nat. Assn. Accountants, Nat. Assn. Purchasing Mgmt., Am. Arbitration Assn., Nat. Fedn. Ind. Bus. Club: Lions. Home: 12320 Old Yates Ford Rd Clifton VA 22024 Office: 2931 Gallows Rd Merrifield VA 22116

CONRAD, RALPH, retail exec.; b. Columbus, Ohio, June 14, 1928; s. Glen Bryan and Ada Faith (Dillie) C.; student U. Md., Far East div., 1959-60; m. Irene B. Almeida, Oct. 5, 1962. Joined U.S. Navy, 1946, advanced through grades to lt. comdr., 1969; comdr. USS Ajax, 1965-67, U.S. Navy Ships Parts Control Center, Mechanicsburg, Pa., 1967-70, USS Wasp, 1970-72, ret., 1973; mgr. Coll. of Charleston Bookstore, 1973—. Mem. Nat. Assn. Coll. Stores, S.C. Assn. Coll. Stores. Club: Masons. Home: 2 Brook Hollow Ct Charleston SC 29407 Office: 181 Calhoun St Charleston SC 29401

CONRADY, DENIS ANTHONY, computer engr.; b. Cin., Dec. 1, 1930; s. John August and Elvira Rose (Frey) C.; B.S., U.S. Naval Acad., 1954; M.S. in Elec. Engring., Mass. Inst. Tech., 1958; Ph.D., Case Inst. Tech., 1966; m. Catherine M. Frisz, Dec. 27, 1954; children—Denise Rose, David Paul. Commd. 2d lt. U.S. Air Force, 1954, advanced through grades to lt. col., 1959; asso. prof. computer sci. USAF Acad., 1965-71; computer researcher Hanscom (Mass.) AFB, 1971-74, ret., 1974; asso. prof. computer sci. N. Tex. State U., Denton, 1974-78, vis. asso. prof., 1979—; sr. engr. Tech. Devel. Corp., Arlington, Tex., 1978—; cons. IRS, 1978. Mem. Assn. Computer Machinery, Internat. Soc. Preservation and Encouragement Barbershop Quartet Singing in Am. (cert. nat. judge), Champion Chorus, Vocal Majority, Sigma Xi, Tau Beta Pi. Home: 2024 Kendolph Dr Denton TX 76201 Office: 624 Six Flags Dr Arlington TX 76011

CONROY, DAVID JEROME, lawyer; b. New Orleans, Dec. 27, 1929; s. George E. and Lilyon (Bowling) C.; B.A., Tulane U., 1950, J.D., 1952; m. Ann Kathryn Gunderson, May 15, 1954; children—Kathryn Ann, David Michael, Elizabeth Helen, Mary Daire, Peter George Edward, Patrick Frank. Admitted to La. bar, 1952; partner firm Milling, Benson, Woodward, Hillyer, Pierson & Miller, New Orleans, 1956—, mng. partner, 1974—; sec. Jahncke Service Inc., New Orleans, 1961-69, Pub. Grain Elevator New Orleans, 1964—; sec., dir. C.B. Fox Co., New Orleans, 1965—. Del., La. Constl. Conv., 1973; mem. planning com. Tulane Tax Inst., 1975-79. Bd. dirs. New Orleans Speech and Hearing Center, 1968-74, pres., 1970-72; bd. dirs. Family Service Soc., 1972-77; bd. dirs. Council for a Better La., 1975—, mem. exec. com., 1976—; bd. dirs. Louise S. McGehee Sch., 1970-77, pres., 1975-77; trustee United Way Greater New Orleans, 1974-80; bd. dirs. Pub. Affairs Research Council La., Inc., 1974—. Served with AUS, 1952-54. Mem. Am., La. (chmn. sect. corp. law 1968-69, chmn. com. law reform 1977—), New Orleans bar assns., Internat. House (dir. 1978—), St. Thomas More Cath. Lawyers Assn. (bd. govs. 1969-73, 78—, 1st v.p. 1972-73). Roman Catholic. Clubs: Pickwick, New Orleans Country, Plimsoll, Essex. Home: 437 Dorrington Dr Metairie LA 70005 Office: Whitney Bldg New Orleans LA 70130

CONROY, JOHN ALBERT, ret. psychiatrist; b. Bound Brook, N.J., Jan. 31, 1906; s. Dennis Martin and Mary Ellen (Cusick) C.; student Middlesex U., Waltham, Mass., 1927-29; M.D., Kans. City U., 1933; m. Rita Margaret Ginty, Oct. 25, 1934. Intern Broad St. Hosp., N.Y.C., 1933-34; resident St. Mary's Meml. Hosp., Knoxville, Tenn., 1934-35; gen. practice, Gatlinburg, Tenn., 1935-40, Newton Centre, Mass., 1940-57; staff psychiatrist VA Hosp., Murfreesboro, Tenn., 1958-71, acting chief psychiatry, 1971-75. Served with USPHS-USCGR, 1942-45. Mem. Mass. Med. Soc., Assn. Mil. Surgeons, Assn. Res. Officers USPHS, V.F.W., Am. Legion, Am. Radio Relay League, Nat. Assn. Ret. Fed. Employees (pres. Murfreesboro chpt. 1975-76). Republican. Roman Catholic. Elk. Home: 1003 Elliott Dr Murfreesboro TN 37130

CONROY, JOHN JEFFREY, architect; b. Chgo., May 20, 1947; s. John Francis and Lucille Claire (Racette) C.; B.Arch., U. Ill., 1970, M.Arch., 1972; m. Luan Joyce Eberhardt, Sept. 30, 1978. Part-time instr. architecture U. Ill., Champaign, 1972-74; sr. design architect Skidmore, Owings & Merrill, Chgo., 1972-77; asso. Caudill, Rowlett, Scott, Houston, 1977—; lectr. in field. Mem. archtl. awards jury Am. Assn. Sch. Adminstrs., 1979. Recipient Bradley & Bradley award U. Ill., 1969; Allerton Traveling fellow, 1968. Mem. Council of Ednl. Facility Planners (disting. service award 1976), AIA (com. architecture for edn.), Soc. Coll. and Univ. Planning. Author: (with William Caudill and Charles Schorre) From Infancy to Infinity, 1977. Office: Caudill Rowlett Scott 1111 W Loop St S Houston TX 77027

CONROY, THOMAS JOHN, oil co. exec.; b. Astoria, N.Y., Jan. 7, 1939; s. Oliver and Louise Madeline (Neubauer) C.; B.S.M.E., Clarkson Coll. of Tech., 1960; M.S. in Indsl. Mgmt., Poly. Inst. Bklyn., 1966; m. Barbara J. Arnett, June 15, 1963; children—Kathryn, Kevin, Brian. Maintenance engr. Grumman Aircraft Engring. Corp., Bethpage, N.Y., 1960-65; with Mobil Oil Corp., 1966—, mgr. product exchanges, N.Y.C., 1978-79, mgr. crude oil trading, Dallas, 1979—. Mem. vestry St. John's Ch., Stamford, Conn., 1975-78. Registered profl. engr., N.Y. Mem. ASME, Am. Soc. Lubrication Engrs. (course lectr.), Omicron Pi Omicron. Episcopalian. Office: Mobil Oil Corp 1201 Elm St Dallas TX 75220

CONSTANT, CLINTON, chem. engr.; b. Nelson, B.C., Can., Mar. 20, 1912; s. Vasile and Annie (Hunt) C.; B.Sc. with honors, U. Alta., 1935, postgrad., 1935-36; Ph.D., Western Res. U., 1939; m. Margie Robbel, Dec. 5, 1965. Came to U.S., 1936, naturalized, 1942. Devel. engr. Harshaw Chem. Co., Cleve., 1936-38, mfg. foreman, 1938-43, sr. engr. semi-works dept., 1948-50; supt. hydrofluoric acid dept. Nyotex Chems., Inc., Houston, 1943-47, chief devel. engr., 1947-48; mgr. engring. Ferro Chem. Co., Bedford, Ohio, 1950-52; tech. asst. mfg. dept. Armour Agrl. Chem. Co. (formerly Armour Fertilizer Works), Bartow, Fla., 1952-61, mgr. research and devel. div., 1961-63, mgr. spl. projects, research div. (co. name changed to USS Agri-Chems, 1968), 1963-65, project mgr., 1965-70; chem. adviser Robert & Co. Assos., Atlanta, 1970-79; chief engr. Almon & Assos., Inc., Atlanta, 1979—. Registered profl. engr. Fellow AAAS, Am. Inst. Chemists, Am. Inst. Chem. Engrs., AIAA (asso.); mem. Am. Chem. Soc., Am. Astron. Soc., Astron. Soc. Pacific, Royal Astron. Soc. Can., N.Y. Acad. Scis., Am. Water Works Assn., Ga. Water and Pollution Control Assn., Ala. Assn. for Water Pollution Control, Soc. Mfg. Engrs. Author tech. reports, sci. fiction. Patentee in field. Home: PO Box 1221 Atlanta GA 30301 Office: Almon & Assos Inc 1800 Water Pl Suite 200 Atlanta GA 30339

CONSTANT, ERIC LARSEN, mfg. co. exec.; b. Kingston, N.Y., Oct. 27, 1941; s. LeRoy Andrew and Wilhelmina Bahr (Simmons) C.; Electronic Engr., Ind. Inst. Tech., 1961; B.B.A., Augusta Coll., 1969; m. Kathleen Lee Darrow, Apr. 17, 1965; children—Eric Larsen, Jeffrey Andrew, Christopher Duane. Acctg. clk. Cox Newsprint, Inc., Augusta, Ga., 1966-68; cost accountant Kimberly-Clark Corp., Beech Island, S.C., 1968-73; cost and pricing analyst ITT Semiconductors, West Palm Beach, Fla., 1973-74; mgr. acctg./EDP, Waynesboro Industries, Inc. (Ga.), 1974-80; comptroller Goldberg Bros. Inc., Augusta, 1980—. Weblos leader Cub Scouts, 1978-79; active YMCA Indian Guides; advisor Jr. Achievement, 1968-74, Future Bus. Leaders Am., 1975-79. Served with U.S. Army, 1961-64. Home: 2013 Jeffrey Ave North Augusta SC 29841 Office: 241 Dan Bowles Rd Augusta GA 30901

CONSTANT, RUTH LAVERN, nurse, educator; b. Port Arthur, Tex., Jan. 14, 1932; d. Carl Leon and Mary (O'Grady) Ellerbee; B.S. in Nursing, U. Tex., 1966, M.S. in Nursing, 1972; postgrad. Tex. A and M U.; m. George A. Constant, Apr. 16, 1971; children—Melinda, Jame Dewit, Rebecca. Exec. dir. Schlesingers Home Health Service, Beaumont, Tex., 1964-65; exec. v.p. Beaumont Home Health, Inc., 1969—, Port Authur Home Health, 1969—; v.p., adminstrv. cons. Wichita Home Health, Wichita Falls, Tex., 1969; bus. mgr. Constant Clinic, Victoria, Tex., 1973—; dir. asso. degree nursing program Victoria (Tex.) Coll., 1975—. Fellow Am. Coll. Nursing Home Adminstrs.; mem. Nat. (dir. 1970-77), Tex. (pres. 1970) assns. home health agencies, Am. Nurses Assn., Nat. League for Nursing, Nat. Nursing Forum Adminstrs., Tex. Nursing Home Assn., Am. Acad. Med. Adminstrs., Nat. Pub. Relations Assn. Democrat. Methodist. Club: Pilot. Home: 2206 E Loma Vista Victoria TX 77901 Office: 2710 Hospital Dr Suite 206 Victoria TX 77901

CONSTANTIN, JAMES ALFORD, educator; b. Tulsa, June 15, 1922; s. Jules Joseph and Nelle (Alford) C.; B.B.A., U. Tex., 1943, M.B.A., 1944, Ph.D., 1950; m. Wanda Anita Moyer, May 18, 1941; children—Nina Katherine Constantin Beaird, James Alford, Jules Joseph, Anne Constantin Calinsky. Instr., U. Tex., 1946-47; asst. prof., asso. prof., asst. dir. Bur. Bus. Research, U. Ala., Tuscaloosa, 1947-52; asso. prof. U. Wash., 1952-53; prof. mktg. and transp. U. Okla., Norman, 1953-69, David Ross Boyd prof. bus. adminstrn., 1969—. Served with USAAF, 1942-43. Mem. Am. Mktg. Assn., Transp. Research Forum, Am. Soc. Traffic and Transp. Author: (with W.J. Hudson) Motor Transportation, 1958, Principles of Logistics Management, 1966; (with W.N. Peach) Zimmermann's World Resources and Industries, 1972; (with R.E. Evans and M.L. Morris) Marketing Strategy and Management, 1976. Home: 2708 Meadowbrook Dr Norman OK 73069

CONTRERAS, FERMIN M., banker; b. Santurce, P.R., Jan. 20, 1944; s. Benigno and Argelia (Bordallo) C.; B.B.A. cum laude, U. P.R., 1965; M.B.A., Inter-Am. U., 1971; m. Gisela Gómez, Sept. 3, 1965; children—Fermin, Omar, Gisela, Mariana. Trainee, Chase Manhattan Bank, San Juan, 1965-66, credit analyst, credit officer, 1966-67; asst. mgr. Banco Economias, San German, P.R., 1967-68, asst. v.p. in charge of operations and personnel, 1968-69, v.p. in charge of S.W. credit ops., 1969-72, sr. v.p. in charge bank credit adminstrn., 1972—; sr. v.p., dir. S.W. ops. Banco Central y Economias, 1979—. Certified comml. lender. Mem. Am. Banking Assn., Am. Inst. Banking, Robert Morris Assos. Clubs: Mayaguez (P.R.) Hilton Tennis and Swimming, Deportivo del Oeste, Casino de Mayaguez. Home: Rd 108 K3-5 Mayaguez PR 00708 Office: Box 146 San German PR 00753

CONVERSE, PHILIP RAY, lawyer, finance co. exec.; b. Oklahoma City, Sept. 7, 1942; s. Ray Bozell and Melrose Elizabeth (Wheeler) C.; student Millsaps Coll., Jackson, Miss., 1964; LL.B., Miss. Coll., 1966; m. Minna Cheryl Barrett, Dec. 21, 1968. Admitted to Miss. bar, 1967, Tenn. bar, 1969; asso. dir. devel. Millsaps Coll., 1966-69; dir. estate planning, deferred gifts U. Tenn., Knoxville, 1969-72; exec. v.p., Robert F. Sharpe & Co., Inc., Memphis, 1972—, asso. dir. Nat. Planned Giving Inst., 1972—; cons., lectr. in field. Mem. alumni bd. Millsaps Coll., 1977. Mem. Tenn., Miss. bar assns., Nat. Cath. Devel. Conf., Council Advancement and Support Edn., Kappa Alpha, Sigma Delta Kappa. Author booklets tax implications charitable gifts, 1972—; co-author: Guide to Administration of Charitable Trusts 1970. Contbr. articles to nat. mags. Home: 2312 Howard St Germantown TN 38138 Office: 5050 Poplar St Memphis TN 38138

CONWAY, FRENCH HOGE, lawyer; b. Danville, Va., June 11, 1918; s. Lysander Broadus and Mildred (Hoge) C.; B.S., U. Va., 1942, LL.B., 1946; m. Louise Throckmorton, Feb. 3, 1961; children—French Hoge, William Chenery, Helen (Mrs. Carlton Bedsole), Donna (Mrs. D. L. Starnes). Admitted to Va. bar, 1942, since practiced in Danville; mem. firm Clement, Conway & Winston, 1950-60. Dir., Danville Industries (Va.). Sec. Danville Election Bd., 1969—, v.p. Va. Election Bd. Assn., 1974. Served with USNR, 1942-46. Mem. Am., Va., Danville bar assns., Am. Trial Lawyers Assn., Va. Trial Lawyers Assn., Soc. Cincinnati in State of Va., Ret. Officers Assn., Boat Owners Assn. U.S. Kiwanian, Mason. Home: 912 Main St Danville VA 24541 Office: 105 S Union St Danville VA 24541

CONWAY, SYLAS PAUL, plastics mfg. co. exec.; b. Little Rock, Sept. 4, 1951; s. Sylas Paul and Billie Sue (Stewart) C.; B.S., Ark. Tech. U., 1973; m. Janice Renee Finchum, June 29, 1974. Cost acct., office mgr. Jackson Cookie Co., West Memphis, North Little Rock, Ark., 1974-75; acct., cost acct. Williams Plastics Co., Inc., North Little Rock, 1975, office mgr., 1976, controller, 1976-78, v.p. adminstrn., 1978—, also dir. Coach, Babe Ruth League Baseball Team, Vestal Ball Park, North Little Rock, 1975-79; youth sponsor First Assembly of God Ch., North Little Rock, 1978—, pre-sch. children's dir., 1976—, coach men's softball team, 1978—. Mem. North Little Rock C. of C. Club: Optimist (North Little Rock, Ark.). Home: 510 Beaconsfield St Sherwood AR 72116 Office: 309 Phillips Rd North Little Rock AR 72118

CONWELL, HALFORD ROGER, physician; b. Cin., Jan. 28, 1924; s. Halford Fredrick and Erma Pearl (Cornelius) C.; B.A., U. Wooster, 1948; M.A., U. Louisville, 1950; M.D., U. Cin., 1955; m. Margaret Ann King, Dec. 15, 1965; 1 son, Mark A. Intern, Christ Hosp., Cin., 1955-56; resident Maumee Valley Hosp., Toledo, 1956-57, Baylor U. Hosp., Houston, 1957-58; gen. practice medicine and aviation medicine, Huntsville, Tex., 1959—; mem. staff Huntsville (Tex.) Meml. Hosp., chief of staff, 1974-75, chief medicine, 1976—; cons. Tex. Dept. Corrections, 1970—; U.S. med. advisor Brit. Caledonian Airline; mem. Walker County Hosp. Dist., 1975—, chmn., 1976—; med. dir. Planned Parenthood Assn., Huntsville, 1975-77; asst. dean of men, instr. psychology Heidelberg U., Tiffin, Ohio, 1950-51; instr. psychology Cin. Coll.; sr. med. examiner FAA. Trustee Biol. Analysis and Research Found., Sam Houston U. Served to lt. USNR, 1942-46. Fellow Am. Soc. Abdominal Surgeons, Airline Med. Dirs. Assn., Aerospace Med. Assn. (asso.); mem. Am., Tex. med. assns., Walker-Madison-Trinity Med. Soc. (pres. 1974-75), Civil Aviation Med. Assn. (v.p. 1968—, dir. 1968—), Mitchell Pediatric Soc., Confederate Air Force, Friends of RAF Mus., Order Ky. Cols., Psi Chi. Mem. Christian Ch. Clubs: Masons, Rotary. Home: 825 Cherry Hills Elkins Lake TX 77340 Office: 2800 Lake Rd Huntsville TX 77340

CONWELL, JOSEPH THOMAS, lawyer; b. Oakman, Ala., Nov. 9, 1914; s. Joe D. and Elma Pettus (Wells) C.; student Transylvania Coll., 1934-35; B.A., U. Ala., 1937, LL.B., 1940; m. Winifred Maxwell, June 25, 1946; 1 son, Joseph Thomas. Admitted to Ala. bar, 1940; pvt. practice law, Jasper, Ala., 1940-42, Birmingham, Ala., 1946-48, Huntsville, Ala., 1955—; atty. ICC, Atlanta, 1948-49; claim and ins. investigator, San Francisco, 1949-54. Mem. nat. honor sec. Walker County High Sch.; mem. Madison County Democratic exec. com. Served with AUS, World War II. Mem. Am., Ala., Huntsville-Madison County (meml. com.) bar assns., Am. Judicature Soc., Ala. Trial Lawyers Assn. (gov.), Farrah Law Soc., Civitan Club, Am. Legion. Episcopalian. Mem. Woodmen of World. Contbr. articles to profl. publs. Home: 7118 Chadwell Rd SW Huntsville AL 35802 Office: Conwell Legal Bldg 607 Madison St Huntsville AL 35801

CONYERS, J. C., drilling engr.; b. Saint Jo, Tex., Oct. 31, 1937; s. Joe Crump and Ellie Evelyn (Ray) C.; student (Alfred P. Sloan scholar), Dartmouth Coll., 1956-58; B.S. in Geology (Am. Petroleum Inst. scholar), Tex. Technol. U., 1962; m. Dinah Gunter, Sept. 3, 1960. Cons. geologist, Dallas, 1962-63; logging supr. Monarch Logging Co., Aransas Pass, Tex., 1963-68; data engr. Dresser-Magcobar, Houston, 1969-70, data supr. Dresser Internat., Singapore, 1971-73, devel. engr., tech. services engr., tng. coordinator, tng. mgr., div. tech. services mgr., div. products applications mgr. Dresser-Swaco, Houston, 1973—; guest lectr. various univs. Mem. Soc. Petroleum Engrs., Am. Assn. Petroleum Geologists, ASME, Houston Geol. Soc. Baptist. Home: 14115 Kingsride Ln Houston TX 77079 Office: Dresser Industries Inc 10201 Westheimer Rd PO Box 1407 DC2 Houston TX 77001

COOK, AUGUST JOSEPH, pub. accountant; b. Devine, Tex., Sept. 25, 1926; s. August E. and Mary H. (Schmidt) C.; B.S., Trinity U., 1949; B.B.A., U. Tex., 1954; LL.B., St. Mary's U., San Antonio, 1960; m. Matie M. Brangan, July 12, 1952; children—Lisa Ann, Mary Beth, John Joseph. Staff accountant Ernst & Ernst, C.P.A.'s, San Antonio, 1949-50; bus. mgr., sec., dir. Life Enterprises, Inc., Beverly Studios, Inc., Castle Land Co., Inc., Randolph Studios, Inc., San Antonio, 1950-58; admitted to Tex. bar, 1960; with Ernst & Ernst, 1960—, mgr., Memphis, 1969-70, partner, Memphis, 1970—. Vice pres. Tex. Municipal League, 1968-69. Alderman, Castle Hills, Tex., 1961-63, mayor, 1963-69; chmn. Bexar County Council Mayors, 1967-69. Bd. dirs. Met. YMCA San Antonio. Served with AUS, 1945-46. C.P.A., Tex. Mem. Am. Inst. C.P.A.'s, Tex. Soc. C.P.A.'s, Tex. Bar Assn., Estates Planners Council San Antonio (pres. 1967), Delta Theta Phi, Kappa Pi Sigma. Clubs: Optimist (dir.), Toastmasters (pres. San Antonio 1963). Home: 6785 Slash Pine Ct Memphis TN 38138 Office: Sterick Bldg Memphis TN 38103

COOK, CHARLES DEVERE, JR., accountant; b. Waco, Tex., Mar. 5, 1943; s. Charles DeVere and Wanda Elizabeth (Maedgen) C.; B.B.A., U. Tex., 1964; M.B.A., Baylor U., 1970; m. Ann Elizabeth Stephani, Mar. 9, 1968. C.P.A., Wilcox, Pattillo, Brown & Hill, Waco, Tex., 1970-72, Main Lafrentz & Co., Waco, 1972-74; resident controller Tex. Plant E-Z Packaging div. Gulf States Paper Corp., Waco, 1974-75; chief fin. officer, controller Mosley Machinery Co., Inc. subs. Elcor Corp., Midland, Tex., 1975-78; individual practice acctg., 1978—. Bd. dirs. Friends of Waco-McLennan County Pub. Library, Waco, 1972-77, pres., 1977. Served with USNR, 1964-69. Decorated Army Commendation medal, Navy Commendation medal with Combat V. C.P.A., Tex. Mem. Naval Reserve Assn. (chpt. sec., treas. 1971-73), Navy Supply Corps Alumnai Assn. (life) (area adminstr. 1971-73), Tex. Soc. C.P.A.'s, Am. Inst. C.P.A.'s, Beta Gamma Sigma. Club: Kiwanis (bd. dirs. 1971-79), K.P. Home: 2111 Wooded Acres Waco TX 76710 Office: 401 Precision Dr Waco TX 76703

COOK, CLARENCE SHARP, physicist, educator; b. St. Louis Crossing, Ind., Aug. 18, 1918; s. Clarence C. and Musa Gladys (Sharp) C.; A.B., DePauw U., 1940; M.A., Ind. U., 1942, Ph.D., 1948; m. Marian Norma Waring, June 19, 1943; children—Sherma Louise, Wayne William. Asst. prof. physics Washington U., St. Louis, 1948-53; br. head U.S. Naval Radiol. Def. Lab., San Francisco, 1953-60, head nucleonics div., 1960-61; physics cons. to sci. dir., 1962-65, head radiation physics div., 1965-69; lectr. U. Santa Clara (Calif.), 1969-70; prof. physics U. Tex., El Paso, 1970—, chmn. physics dept., 1970-71. Bd. dirs. El Paso Radiation Center Found., 1971—, El Paso Public TV Found., 1972—; chmn. Energy Task Force, Goals for El Paso Program, 1976-78. Served to capt. U.S. Army, 1942-46. Fulbright research scholar, 1961-62. Fellow Am. Phys. Soc., Calif. Acad. Scis.; mem. Am. Geophys. Union, Health Physics Soc. (mem. history com. 1979—), Am. Assn. of Physics Tchrs., AAAS, Meteoritical Soc., Sigma Xi (pres. U. Tex. chpt. 1973-74, 75-76, regional lectr. 1973-75), Phi Beta Kappa. Club: Explorers (fellow 1978—). Author: Modern Atomic and Nuclear Physics, 1961; Structure of Atomic Nuclei, 1964; contbr. articles to sci. jours. Home: 285 Maricopa El Paso TX 79912 Office: Univ of Texas El Paso TX 79968

COOK, CLAYTON HENRY, rancher; b. Moundridge, Kans., Apr. 21, 1912; s. Herbert and Bertha (Wilkening) C.; student pub. schs., Moundridge; m. Margery Maxine Manning, Apr. 13, 1941; children—Larry Clayton, Ronald Leigh, Michael Craig, Melanie Beth. Engaged in ranching. Vega, Tex. Mem. Tex. Econ. Commn., 1950-57-59, 62—; mem. Gov.'s Com. on Aging; mem. Tex. Constn. Revision Com.; profl. actor; play critic, judge Tex. U. Interscholastic League. Past mem. governing bd. Amarillo Little Theatre; mem. governing bd. High Plains Center of Performing Arts; bd. dirs. Friends of Fine Arts West Tex. State U. Chmn. Oldham County Democratic Exec. Com. Mem. Internat. Platform Assn. (chmn.). Methodist. Mason, Kiwanian (lt. gov. Tex.-Okla. dist. 1959, chmn. new club bldg. 1960, chmn. past lt. govs. 1967). Club: Amarillo Knife and Fork (dir.). Home: Box 57 Vega TX 79092

COOK, CLIFFORD CARROLL, oil co. exec.; b. Battle Creek, Mich., Jan. 25, 1946; s. Clinton Clifford and Edna Marguerite (Bauer) C.; student (Math. Competition scholar), Mich. Tech. U., 1964-67; B.Ch.E., U. Detroit, 1969, M.Ch.E., 1970; m. Maureen Ellen O'Connor, July 25, 1970; children—Carolyn Denise, Colleen Michelle. Asso. refinery engr. Mich. Refining div. Marathon Oil Co., Detroit, 1969-71, refinery engr. Tex. Refining div., Texas City, 1975-76, environ. coordinator, 1976-78, crude oil trading rep., 1978—. Chmn. com. environ. affairs Texas City Port Safety and Adv. Council, 1976-77; advisor Jr. Achievement, 1975-76, project bus. tchr., 1977-78; mem. Environ. Concern Com., Texas City, 1976-78. Served to lt. USN, 1971-75. Named Texas City Jaycee Dir. of Quarter, 1976-77. Mem. Water Pollution Control Fedn., Am. Inst. Chem. Engrs., Tex. Chem. Council, Texas City Jaycees (treas. 1976-78), La Marque C. of C., U. Detroit Alumni Assn., Omega Chi Epsilon, Tau Beta Phi. Republican. Roman Catholic. Home: 2034 Masters Missouri City TX 77459 Office: PO Box 3128 Houston TX 77001

COOK, DONALD LEON, chemist; b. Pampa, Tex., Mar. 26, 1936; s. Leon Marvin and June Madeline (Converse) C.; B.A., McMurry Coll., 1959; student Tex. Tech. U., 1965-67, Tex. Eastern U., 1978-79; m. Lou Ann Smith, Apr. 4, 1958; children—Terrel Lee, Donna Michelle. Plant chemist Reef Corp., Big Spring, Tex., 1959-65; teaching asst. Tex. Tech. U., 1965-67; analyt. chemist Anderson Clayton Foods, Dallas, 1967-70, supr. analyt. labs., 1970-74; with Prudential Ins. Co., Dallas, 1974-75; with Acromatic Industries, Dallas, 1975; chemist, lab. supr. Tyler Pipe Industries (Tex.), 1975—. Cubmaster, Circle Ten council Boy Scouts Am., 1967-69, scoutmaster, 1969-72, Explorer Post advisor, 1973-75. Mem. Am. Chem. Soc. Methodist (mem. choir, tchr. Sunday sch.). Club: Masons. Home: 421 Wilma St Tyler TX 75701 Office: PO Box 2027 Tyler TX 75710

COOK, DORIS, artist; b. Clinton, Iowa; d. Daniel and Martha (Narber) Holland; student Chgo. Acad. Fine Arts, 1921, Chgo. Art Inst., 1923, 65, Paul Wieghardt, 1965-66; m. Harold J. Cook, Sept. 24, 1934 (dec. Feb. 1977); 1 son, Jeffrey Holland. Operator, Glimpse Hill Studio, Chgo., 1926; owner, operator studio, Chgo., 1927; advt. illustrator, Lane Bryant Co., Chgo., 1928-34, advt. mgr., 1934; free-lance illustrator Chgo. stores and studios, 1935-42; operator Harding Balcony Gallery, Chgo., 1960-61; one-person shows: 9th Profl. Art Exbn., Springfield, Ill., 1955, Madison Art Directions Gallery, N.Y.C., 1963, Ill. Festival Art, McCormick Pl., Chgo., 1964, Paul Theobald Gallery, Chgo., 1965, 71, Robert Paul Gallery, Chgo., 1971; represented in permanent collection Art Inst. Chgo., 1962-76. Recipient 1st award All Ill. Soc. Fine Arts, 1950, N. Shore Art Guild, 1954; Dingle award Nat. League Am. Women Profl. Artists, 1956-75, 2d award, Salt Lake City, 1970. Mem. N. Shore Art Guild, Nat. League Am. Pen Women, All-Ill. Soc. Artists, Chgo. New Art Assn. Home: 9 Forbes Pl Apt 205 Dunedin FL 33528

COOK, DORIS MARIE, educator; b. Fayetteville, Ark., June 11, 1924; d. Ira and Mettie Jewell (Dorman) C.; B.B.A., U. Ark., 1946, M.S., 1949; Ph.D., U. Tex., 1968; Staff accountant, Haskins & Sells Tulsa, 1946-47; instr. accounting U. Ark., Fayetteville, 1947-52, asst. prof., 1952-62, asso. prof., 1962-69, prof., 1969—. C.P.A., Okla., Ark. Mem. Fayetteville Bus. and Profl. Women's Club (pres. 1973-74, 75-76), Ark. Fedn. Bus. and Profl. Women's Clubs (chmn. found. com. 1975-77, treas. 1979-80), Ark. Soc. C.P.A.'s (v.p., 1975-76), Am. Accounting Assn., Am. Inst. C.P.A.'s, Am. Woman's Soc. C.P.A.'s, Mortar Bd., Beta Gamma Sigma, Beta Alpha Psi (pres. nat. council 1977-78, editor newsletter 1973-77), Phi Gamma Nu, Alpha Lambda Delta, Delta Kappa Gamma (sec. 1976-78, pres. 1978-80), Phi Kappa Phi. Contbr. to profl. jours. Home: 1115 Leverett St Fayetteville AR 72701 Office: Dept Accounting U Ark Fayetteville AR 72701

COOK, EDWARD WILLINGHAM, diversified industry exec.; b. Memphis, June 19, 1922; s. Everett Richard and Phoebe (Willingham) C.; grad. Hotchkiss Sch., 1940; A.B., Yale U., 1944; m. Patricia L. Weaver, Mar. 17, 1973; 1 dau., Patricia Kendall children by previous marriage—Edward Willingham, Everett Richard II, Barbera Moore (Mrs. Steven Brooks). Chmn. bd., chief exec. officer Cook Industries, Inc., Memphis; dir. First Tenn. Corp., Memphis. Mem. Cotton Adv. Commn., 1964-68; mem. exec. com. Nat. Council U.S.-China Trade, 1973-78, Pres.'s Export Council, 1973-79; dir. Chgo. Bd. Trade, 1974-77. Squire, Shelby County Ct., 1948-66; chmn. Memphis-Shelby County Airport Authority, 1968—. Served to maj. USAAF, 1943-45; MTO. Decorated D.F.C., Bronze Star, Air medal with six oak leaf clusters. Mem. Am. Cotton Shippers Assn. (pres. 1966-67), So. Cotton Assn. (past pres.), Cotton Council Am. (dir. 1962-65), Cotton Council Internat. (dir. 1964-65), Memphis Area C. of C. (dir.), Tenn. Taxpayers Assn. (dir.). Democrat. Episcopalian. Clubs: Memphis Country, Memphis Hunt and Polo; Links (N.Y.C.); Everglades (Palm Beach, Fla.); Island (Hobe Sound, Fla.); Old Baldy (Saratoga, Wyo.). Office: 855 Ridge Lake Blvd Memphis TN 38138

COOK, ERNEST EWART, oil exploration co. exec.; b. Wiltshire, Eng., Mar. 23, 1926; s. Edgar John and Dorothy May (Wiltshire) C.; B.A. in Natural Scis., Cambridge (Eng.) U., 1946, M.A., 1950; m. Nina Cairo, Sept. 23, 1953; 1 dau., Julia Ann. Came to U.S., 1946. Geophysicist, Cia Shell de Venezuela, Maracaibo, 1947-56; chief geophysicist Pakistan Shell Oil Co., Karachi, 1956-57; with Signal Oil & Gas Co., 1957-67, internat. exploration mgr., Los Angeles, 1966-67; v.p. Seismic Computing Corp., Houston, 1968-70; chmn. Invent Inc., Houston, 1971-78; pres. Zenith Exploration Co. Inc., Houston, 1978—; dir. Triton Oil and Gas Corp., Dallas, Invent Energy Ltd., Tanks Oil & Gas Ltd., London, Eng. Fellow Geol. Soc. London; mem. Soc. Exploration Geophysicist, Seismological Soc. Am., Marine Tech. Soc., Am. Geophys. Union, Am. Assn. Petroleum Geologists. Home: 624 Hedwig Rd Houston TX 77024 Office: Suite 320 9111 Katy Freeway Houston TX 77024

COOK, GEORGE GLENN, landscape architect; b. Port Arthur, Tex., June 20, 1940; s. James Dykes and Clairbell (Creswell) C.; student McNeese State Coll., 1961; B.S. in Landscape Architecture, La. State U., 1964; m. Wanda Guidry, June 3, 1961; children—Stephen Keith, Gary Paul. Landscape architect Stewart E. King & Asso., San Antonio, 1966-70; owner Glenn Cook, Landscape Architect, San Antonio, 1970-78; asso. prof. landscape architecture Miss. State U., 1978—; owner Glenn Cook, Landscape Architect and Planning Cons., Starkville, Miss., 1979—. Mem. Old Spanish Missions Restoration Com., San Antonio, 1970-78; v.p. San Antonio Bd. Rev. Hist. Dists., 1974-78; rep. N. Side Ind. Sch. Dist., Council PTA's, 1977; mem. troop com. Boy Scouts Am., 1976-78. Served to 1st lt. C.E., AUS, 1964-66; capt. Res. ret. Mem. Am. Soc. Landscape Architects (pres. Tex. chpt. 1976-77). Club: Toastmaster Internat. (San Antonio). Home: PO Box 4206 Mississippi State MS 39762 Office: PO Drawer MQ Mississippi State MS 39762

COOK, JAMES JOSEPH, city ofcl.; b. El Dorado, Kans., Aug. 22, 1934; s. Roy Andrew and Ada Josephine (Jones) C.; B.A. (honors scholar), Yale, 1956; postgrad. (grad. fellow) Kans. U., 1956-58; M.A. in Pub. Adminstrn. (HUD scholar 1971-73), Okla. U., 1975; student program for sr. mgrs. in govt. Harvard Bus. Sch., 1978; m. Martha Ann Saunders, Dec. 8, 1961; children—David Johnston, James Lloyd. Asst. city mgr., El Dorado, Kans., 1957-58; budget analyst, Cin., 1959-61; budget dir., asst. city mgr., Winston-Salem, N.C., 1961-64; village mgr., Northfield, Ill., 1964-69; city mgr., Ada, Okla., 1969-74; asst. city mgr. Oklahoma City, 1974-76, city mgr., 1976—; cons. fin. Okla. State U., 1973—. Trustee, treas. Okla. Municipal Retirement Fund, 1970-74; trustee Municipal Improvement Authority, 1976—, Oklahoma City Airport Trust, 1976—, Myriad Gardens Trust, 1976—, Youth Park Authority, 1976—, Devel. Trust, 1976—, State Fair Bd., 1976—, Oklahoma City Zoo Trust, 1976—. Mem. Am. Soc. Pub. Adminstrn., Internat., Oklahoma (dir. 1973-76, pres. 1978-79) city mgmt. assns., Oklahoma City C. of C. (dir., Man of Yr. 1978). Clubs: Lions (pres. 1974); Yale (Tulsa, Oklahoma City). Home: 425 NW 33d St Oklahoma City OK 73118 Office: Office City Mgr 200 N Walker St Oklahoma City OK 73102

COOK, JENNINGS BRYAN, JR., oil co. exec.; b. Waco, Tex., Apr. 10, 1941; s. Jennings Bryan and Ruth Marie (Taylor) C.; B.B.A., U. Tex. at Austin, 1964; m. Mildred Emelene Keilers, July 17, 1959; children—Barsa Sue, Carmen Rene, Kendra Lynn, Dawn Rachelle. Accountant, Texaco Inc., Houston, 1964-66; accountant Texas City Refining Inc., (Tex.), 1966-68, systems analyst, 1968-71, asst. controller, mgr. budgets and systems, 1971-77; asst. treas., 1977—. Pres., Dickinson Girls Softball, 1976, 77; v.p. Dickinson Soccer Club, 1976. Mem. Assn. Systems Mgmt., Bay Area Soccer Referees Assn. (pres. 1977—), South Tex. Soccer Referees Assn. (pres. 1978—). Republican. Baptist. Clubs: Mason, Shriners. Home: 5108 Bayou E Dr Dickinson TX 77539 Office: PO Box 1271 Texas City TX 77590

COOK, LYNN SCOTT, clin. pharmacologist; b. Searcy, Ark., Dec. 6, 1948; d. Joseph Edgar and Virginia Evelyn (Smith) C.; A.A., Ark. State U., 1968; B.S., U. Central Ark., 1970, M.S., 1972; Ph.D., U. Tenn., 1978; M.D., U. Ark., 1981. Teaching fellow U. Central Ark., Conway, 1970-72, Center for Health Sci., U. Tenn., Memphis, 1974-78, cons. pharmacology, 1979—. Served to 2d. lt., U.S. Army, 1972-73, NIH postdoctoral fellow Med. Coll. S.C., Charleston, 1978. Mem. Memphis Heart Assn., Tenn. Acad. Sci., Basic Sci. Council Am. Heart Assn., AAAS, Sigma Xi, Sigma Tau Gamma, Cardiovascular Jour. Club (pres. 1976-77). Home: Route 1 McRae AR 72102

COOK, MARIAN ALICE, educator; b. Louisville, Aug. 4, 1928; d. Clarence Frederick and Aline (Swisher) C.; B.Mus., Ohio Wesleyan U., 1950; M.Ed., Miami U., Oxford, Ohio, 1955. Music tchr. Hamilton (Ohio) Bd. Edn., 1951-58; cons. Clearwater (Fla.) Bd. Pub. Instruction, 1959-71, music specialist, 1971—; chmn. textbook evaluation and recommendations Fla. Com. on Facilities; cons. workshops, supr. student tchrs. Mem. Pinellas Youth Symphony Bd., 1976—. Recipient recognition awards West Coast Profl. Pan-Hellenic, St. Petersburg Boychoir. Mem. Am. Recorder Soc., Pinellas County Music Educators Assn. (sec.-treas. 1963-71, pres. 1974-75), Music Educators Nat. Conf., Delta Kappa Gamma (pres. Beta Iota chpt. 1972-74, chmn. Tri-county coordinating council 1974—), Mu Phi Epsilon (sec. St. Petersburg alumnae chpt. 1967), Alpha Delta Kappa (sec. 1964). Methodist (music com.). Home: 4210 24th Ave N Saint Petersburg FL 33713

COOK, PAUL JONATHAN, broadcasting co. exec.; b. Ann Arbor, Mich., Mar. 12, 1942; s. Paul and Carmen C.; student Southeastern La. State U., 1967, La. Tech. U., 1968; Nicholls State U., 1972; m. Linda M. Devine, Nov. 5, 1977; children—Paul L., Christa C. Asst. mgr. sta. WTGI, 1966; news dir. sta. KRUS, 1968; gen. mgr. sta. KVFG, Thibodaux, La., 1970; news dir. sta. KMRC, Morgan City, La., 1972, public info. officer, 1973; owner, gen. mgr. sta. KQKI, Morgan City, La., 1976—; pres. Teche Broadcasting, Morgan City, 1976—. Mem. Nat. Assn. Broadcasters, Internat. Narcotics Officers Assn., Am. Law Enforcement Officers Assn., La. Assn. Broadcasters, La. Peace Officers Assn. Republican. Methodist. Clubs: Krewe of Adonis, Krewe of Janius. Office: 10 Pluto St Morgan City LA 70380

COOK, ROGER ADDISON, clin. audiologist; b. Fulton, N.Y., July 3, 1946; s. Carlon Addison and Marjorie (Sylvester) C.; B.S., The Citadel, 1969; M.A., East Carolina U., 1971; M.Ed., U. S.C., 1973; m. Nancy Cassity, May 19, 1973. Instr. otolaryngology Med. U. S.C., Charleston, 1973-74; asst. prof. audiology S.C. State Coll., Orangeburg, 1974-77; clin. audiologist, adj. prof. Western Carolina U., Cullowhee, 1977—; clin. instr. otolaryngology Med. U. S.C., Charleston, 1976—. Served with Med. Service Corps, U.S. Army, 1977-79. Recipient Prof. of Year award Western Carolina U., 1979. Mem. Am. Speech and Hearing Assn., Soc. for Ear, Nose and Throat Advancements in Children, Soc. Craniofacial Genetics, Sigma Xi. Mem. Ch. of Christ. Office: Killian Annex Cullowhee NC 28723

COOK, WAYNE RALPH, lawyer, state ofcl.; b. Danville, Ill., Aug. 13, 1912; s. Charles A. and Grace (Massey) C.; A.B., U. Ill., 1934; LL.B., Ind. U., 1944; J.D., 1945; M.A., Georgetown U., 1946; m. Maryla Karpin, June 4, 1934 (dec. Dec. 1969); 1 dau., Bonnie Karen (Mrs. Herbert L. Tallitsch); m. 2d, Irene G. Samuel, Apr. 17, 1976. Admitted to Ill. bar, 1945, Ind. bar, Ark. bar, 1977, U.S. Supreme Ct.; practiced in Danville, 1947-51, St. Charles, Ill., 1970-78; asst. Ill. atty. gen., Springfield, 1949-53; mem. firm Hubachek & Kelly, Chgo., 1953-59; spl. counsel Bankers Life & Casualty Co., Chgo., 1959-69; past pres., dir. Okla. Oil Co., Denver; former v.p., dir. Nat. Drilling Co., Inc., Property Investment Co., Inc., Ponderosa Paper Products, Inc., Ariz.; past dir. Forum Record Sales Corp., N.Y., Artia Records Corp., N.Y., Home Lockers, Inc., Parliament Records Corp.; asst. U.S. atty., No. dist. Ill., Chgo., 1969-70; dep. atty. gen. State of Ind., 1970-71, asst. atty. gen. in charge environ. law, 1971-73, chief counsel depts., 1973-77; appeals referee Bd. of Rev., State of Ark., 1977—. Served to lt. col. AUS, 1941-43, 45-47. Decorated Purple Heart, Bronze Star medals. Mem. Am., Ill., Ind., Ark., 7th Fed. Circuit, Chgo. (chmn. judiciary com. 1966-67), Indpls., Pulaski County bar assns., Am. Soc. Internat. Law, Am. Judicature Soc., Selden Soc., U.S. Armor Assn., 1st Armored Div. Assn. (pres. 1970-71), Sigma Delta Kappa. Clubs: Army and Navy (Washington); Ill. Athletic (Chgo.); Capitol (Little Rock). Home: 8 Pinnacle Point Little Rock AR 72205 Office: 436 National Old Line Bldg Little Rock AR 72201

COOK, WILLIAM WILBER, advt. agy. exec.; b. Evansville, Ind., Apr. 23, 1921; s. Wilburn Frederick and Mabel (Brookins) C.; student UCLA, 1940-42; B.A. in Bus., Evansville Coll., 1947; LL.D. (hon.), Bethune-Cookman Coll., 1976; m. Mary Andross Brewster, Nov. 2, 1963; children—William F., Constance C., Betty B., Jane R., Robert B. Sales rep. Sta. WIKY, Evansville, 1947-49, WMBR Radio and TV, Jacksonville, Fla., 1949-55; v.p. Dennis, Parsons & Cook Advt. Agy., Jacksonville, 1955-65; pres. William Cook Advt., Inc., Jacksonville, 1965-77, chmn. bd., 1977—. Former chmn. United Negro Coll. Fund; mem. lay adv. com. St. Vincent's Med. Center; trustee Jacksonville Symphony; former vestryman Episcopal Ch. Served as aviator USNR, 1942-46. Recipient CHIEF award Fla. Pvt. Higher Edn. Assn., 1977. Mem. Jacksonville C. of C. (gov., Com. of 100), Am. Assn. Advt. Agencies (vice chmn. S.E. Council), Am. Advt. Fedn. (Silver medal), Fla. Public Relations Assn., Sales and Mktg. Execs. Assn. (Top Mgmt. award). Clubs: River, Univ., Selva Marina Country, Hidden Hills Country, Waynesville (N.C.) Country, Rotary, Masons. Home: 1325 Beach Ave Atlantic Beach FL 32233 Office: American Heritage Life Bldg Jacksonville FL 32202

COOKE, CARROLL GENE, ins. co. exec.; b. Salisbury, N.C., Nov. 17, 1940; s. Norman Willie and Vera Annabell (Mauldin) C.; student public schs., Granite Quarry, N.C.; m. Brenda Kaye Heglar, June 20, 1964; 1 son, Brent Lee. With Rowan Printing Co., Salisbury, 1958-70, supr. sheet dept., 1967-70; asst. printing supr. Integon Corp., Winston-Salem, N.C., 1970-72, supr. printing, 1972-75, forms adminstr., 1975—. Mem. In Plant Printing Mgmt. Assn. (chpt. pres. 1978—), Winston-Salem Assn. Purchasing Agts. (chpt. pres. 1980), Bus. Forms Mgmt. Assn. Democrat. Lutheran. Clubs: Civitan, Jaycees, Moose. Home: Route 2 Box 164 Gold Hill NC 28071 Office: Integon Corp 420 N Spruce St Winston-Salem NC 27101

COOKE, HELEN HEMLIN, editor, writer; b. N.Y.C.; d. Valentine and Katherine (Fischer) Hemlin; student U. N.Mex., 1925-26, Columbia, 1927-29; m. Charles Cooke, Jan. 29, 1931 (div. Sept. 1955); 1 son, Harris Craig. Mem. staff writers Lowell Thomas, 1929-33; reporter New Yorker Mag., N.Y.C., 1933-35; publicity dir. Douglas Leigh, Inc., N.Y.C., 1938-45; publicity dir. Monroe Dreher Advt. Agy., N.Y.C., 1941-45; free-lance editor, writer, Washington, 1948—; asst. to exec. v.p. Aerospace Med. Assn., Washington, 1960-61. Clubs: Am. Newspaper Womens, Nat. Press (Washington). Author: (with Evelyn D. Boyer) Distinguished Women of Washington, D.C., 1964. Contbr. articles to various newspapers, mags. including Washington Star Sunday mag., Balt. Sun, Aerospace Medicine, Cue mag., others. Patentee in field of toys. Home: 2244 N Nottingham St Arlington VA 22205

COOKE, JACK KENT, bus. exec., publisher; b. Hamilton, Ont., Can., Oct. 25, 1912; s. Ralph Ercil and Nancy (Jacobs) C.; student Malvern Collegiate; m. Barbara Jean Carnegie, May 5, 1934 (div.); children—John Kent. Joined No. Broadcasting and Pub. Ltd., Can., 1937; partner Thomson Cooke Newspapers, 1937-52; pres. Sta. CKEY, Toronto, Ont., 1944-61; pres. Liberty of Can., Ltd., 1947-61, Toronto Maple Leaf Baseball Club Ltd., 1951-64, Micro Plastics, Ltd., Acton, Ont., 1955-60, Robinson Indsl. Crafts, Ltd., London, Ont., 1957-63, Precision Die Casting Ltd., Toronto, 1955-60, Consol. Frybrook Industries, Ltd., 1952-61, Aubyn Investments, Ltd., 1961-68, Continental Cablevision, Inc., 1965-68; chmn. Jack Kent Cooke Inc. (JKC Realty Inc. and Am. Cable TV Co.), 1964—; chmn. bd. Transm. Microwave, Inc., 1965-69; chmn., chief exec. officer Pro-Football, Inc. (Washington Redskins, Nat. Football League), Washington, 1960; pres. Calif. Sports, Inc. (Los Angeles Lakers, Nat. Basketball Assn., Los Angeles Kings, Nat. Hockey League), 1965-79; pres. The Forum of Inglewood, Inc., 1966-79; dir., chmn. exec. com. H & B Am. Corp., 1969-70; chmn., chief exec. officer Teleprompter Corp., 1974—, also dir. Pres., Boxing Forum, 1972-79; chmn. bd. pres. The Raljon Corp. (Nev.), The Ercil Corp. (Nev.), The JKC Corp. (Nev.); pres. JRT Inc. (Nev.). Trustee Little League Found., City of Hope; bd. govs. Arthritis Found.; bd. dirs. Nat. Athletic Inst. Home: Fallingbrook Route 1 Box 72 Upperville VA 22176

COOKE, JERRY (GERALD) NICHOLS, antique co. exec.; b. Shelby, N.C., Nov. 25, 1935; s. Robert Hoyle and Christine (Nichols) C.; student pub. schs.; m. Shirley Virginia Holland, Dec. 25, 1964; children—Jeri Catherine, Sara Eyvette, Gerald Nichols, June Christine. Owner, mgr., pres. Cooke Enterprises, Shelby, 1970—; editor Wheelchair Rev., 1954—; owner Obsolete Autos & Parts Co., Nostalgia Unlimited, Hobby House; pres. Carolina Licence Plate Collectors. Mem. Am. Numismatic Assn., Nat. Hist. Soc., Auto Licence Plate Collectors Am., Nat. Rifle Assn. Republican. Methodist. Home: 837 W Marion St Shelby NC 28150 Office: 11900 E Independence Blvd PO Box 1391 Matthews NC 28105

COOKSEY, EDWARD DALE, petroleum and roofing materials mfg. co. exec.; b. Wichita Falls, Tex., Dec. 14, 1935; s. Bennie Edward and Gladys Elizabeth (Rutledge) C.; B.B.A., Tex. A&M U., 1959; M.B.A., Central State U., Edmond, Okla., 1976; m. Marian Dee Miller, Aug. 30, 1975; children—Ronnie Ann, Elizabeth Denise, Patricia Edrea. With Aetna Casualty & Surety Co., Dallas, 1959-60, engring. rep., Denver, 1962-66; chief safety engr. RMK-BRJ, South Vietnam, 1966-67; supr. safety and security A.O. Smith Corp. of Tex., Waco, 1968-70; div. mgr. safety and security Rockwell Internat, Bethany, Okla., 1970-75; sr. safety engr. Xerox Corp., Oklahoma City, 1975-77; corporate dir. safety Allied Materials Corp., Oklahoma City, 1977—. Precinct chmn. Republican Party, 1977, mem. candidate selection com., 1977-78. Served with U.S. Army, 1958, 61-62. Cert. safety profl. Mem. Am. Soc. Safety Engrs., Nat. Safety Mgmt. Soc., Vets. of Safety. Baptist. Club: Masons (Oklahoma City). Office: PO Box 12340 5101 N Pennsylvania St Oklahoma City OK 73112

COOKSEY, WILLIAM TRAVIS, bus. exec.; b. Phenix City, Ala., Mar. 20, 1915; s. Samuel Hill and Verna (Brodnax) C.; student pub. schs.; m. Mildred Alice Jenkins, May 16, 1936. Accounting dept. Tom Huston Peanut Co., Columbus, Ga., 1931-39; salesman Liley Ames Corp., Columbus, Ohio, 1939-40; chief clk. supply Q.M.C., Ft. Benning, Ga., 1940-44; gen. mgr. Blue Springs Farms-Cason J. Callaway, Hamilton, Ga., 1944-60; sec. Ida Cason Callaway Found., Pine Mountain, Ga., 1951—, treas., 1960—, exec. sec., 1964—. Instl. rep. Boy Scouts. Chmn. Harris County (Ga.) Planning Commn. Bd. dirs. Harris County Mental Health Assn.; bd. dirs. Harris County chpt. ARC, chmn. fin. com., 1963—; life bd. dirs., past pres. Ga. Lions Lighthouse Found.; bd. dirs., past pres., treas. Peach Bowl, Inc. Mem. U.S. Hwy. 27 of Ga. (dir., past pres.). Methodist. (steward, chmn. ofcl. bd., lay speaker). Clubs: Masons, K.T., Lions (past pres., zone chmn., dep. dist. gov.). Home: Blue Springs Rd Hamilton GA 31811 Office: Pine Mountain GA 31822

COOLEY, JAMES FRANKLIN, clergyman, educator, civic worker; b. Rowland, N.C., Jan. 11, 1926; s. James F. and Martha (Buie) C.; A.B. in Social Sci. Johnson C. Smith U., 1953, B.D., 1956, M.Div., 1973; M.A. in Sociology, Eastern Nebr. Christian Coll., 1972, D.C.L. (hon.), 1972; D.D. (hon.), Shorter Coll., 1971, D.D. (hon.), Illinois Coll., 1971; m. Carolyn Ann Butler, Mar. 23, 1976; children—Virginia M. Cooley Lewis, James F., Gladys M. Cooley Taylor, Franklin D., Stephen Lamar. Ordained to ministry Presbyterian Ch., 1956; minister Grant Chapel Presbyn. Ch., Darien, Ga., 1956-57, St. Andrews Presbyn. Ch., Forrest City, Ark., 1957-69; tchr. Forrest City Spl. Sch. Dist. 7, 1957-69; juvenile probation officer St. Francis County, Ark., 1959-68; asso. juvenile judge St. Francis County, 1963-64; minister of service Shorter Coll., North Little Rock, Ark., 1969-71, dean of men, acad. dean, 1971-73; chaplain Tucker Intermediate Reformatory, 1971-72; public relations officer Ark. Bapt. Coll., 1972-77; pastor West End Presbyn. Ch., Arkedelphia, 1975-76, Allen Temple A.M.E. Ch., W. Helena, Ark., 1976; chaplain Corps of the Pulaski County (Ark.) Correctional Facilities, 1977—; hon. dep. sheriff St. Francis County, 1962; justice of the peace, Little Rock, 1973-76; 1st. lt. North Little Rock (Ark.) Police Dept., 1975-77, capt., 1977—; dep. sheriff Pulaski County, 1978; constable Dist. 3A. Founder Cooley's Athletic and Teenage Club, Inc., Forrest City, 1956, Day Care Centers 1955-72, Forrest City Council on Human Relations, Ark., 1967. Served with U.S. Army, 1944-46; ETO, PTO. Recipient numerous trophies and plaques for promoting recreational activities for young people, 1963—, cert. of Recognition from various orgns., 1968—; named Hon. Citizen of North Little Rock, Ark., 1977; cert. law enforcement officer Commn. on Law Enforcement Standards Ark. Mem. Am. Security Council, Welfare Rights Orgn., Early Am. Soc., Ministerial Alliance of Greater Little Rock, Nat. Hist. Soc. (cert. recognition 1973, 74), Urban League, Ark. Tchrs. Assn. (award 1968), Nat. Sheriff's Assn., Juvenile Correctional Assn., NCCJ, NAACP, Ark. Law Enforcement Assn., Ark. Council on Human Relations, Internat. Platform Assn., Vets Orgn., Omega Psi Phi (Named Citizen of the Year 1971). Democrat. Weekly columnist State Weekly News, 1975-77; asso. editor Bapt. Vanguard mag. and newspaper, 1972-77; founder, owner, editor Ark. Weekly Sentinal, 1978 instrumental in establishing a college program for prison inmates of State of Ark.; Dr. J.F. Cooley week proclaimed in his honor in North Little Rock. Address: PO Box 4520 Little Rock AR 72202

COOMBES, DAVID HARRISON, hosp. adminstr.; b. Washington, Apr. 14, 1939; s. David Russell and Christine (Spignul) C.; B.A., Duke U., 1962; M.H.A., U. Minn., 1969; m. Mary Dee Gaasterland, June 9, 1962; children—Karen Marie, David. Adminstrv. asst. Bapt. Meml. Hosp., Memphis, 1969-73; exec. dir. Tenn. Health Facilities Commn., Nashville, 1973-75; exec. dir. hosps. and clinics U. of Tenn., Memphis, 1975—, asst. prof. coll. of Community and Allied Health, U. Tenn., 1978—. Bd. dirs. Vis. Nurse Assn., Memphis. Mem. Memphis Hosp. Council (pres.), Am. Coll. Hosp. Adminstrs., Tenn. Hosp. Assn., Am. Hosp. Assn. Clubs: Colonial Country. Home: 2086 Pine Valley Cove Germantown TN 38138 Office: 951 Court Ave Memphis TN 38103

COOPER, AGNES PEARSON (MRS. DAVID ACRON COOPER), educator; b. Bonner Springs, Kans., Oct. 18, 1910; d. James P. and May B. (Luther) Pearson; B.S., Pittsburg (Kans.) State U., 1932; M.S., U. Denver, 1938; postgrad. Harvard, 1939, 40; m. David Acron Cooper, Oct. 15, 1941 (dec. 1974); 1 son, David Acron. Tchr. high schs., Kans., Mo., 1929-37; tchr. Wyandotte High Sch., Kansas City, Kans., 1937-39; instr. secretarial sci. Alfred U., 1939-41; instr. U. Tenn., 1941-42; dir. edn. and placement Knoxville (Tenn.) Bus. Coll., 1942-48; sec.-treas. Cooper Inst., Inc., Knoxville, 1948—. Mem. Knox County adv. com. Tenn. Welfare Dept., Knoxville, 1955—, chmn. 1959; mem. East Tenn. Community Improvement Central Com., 1952—, pres., 1968; mem. Knox County Citizens Adv. Com. on Human Resources, 1970—; chmn. Knox County citizens adv. com. Dept. Human Resources, 1975-76; mem. Emergency Energy Conservation Policy Adv. Com., 1975-78. Mem. nat. bd. Woman's Med. Coll. of Pa. Mem. East Tenn. Edn. Assn. (chmn. bus. sect. 1958, sec. 1957), Am. Mgmt. Assn., AAUW, Am. Bus. Women's Assn., Better Bus. Bur. Baptist. Club: Quota (gov. 23d dist. 1956-57, gov. 8th dist. 1949-51 trustee ednl. revolving fund Knoxville 1962-63, 77—, internat. pres. 1965-66). Home: Route 2 Kodak TN 37764 Office: PO Box 3369 724 N 5th Ave NE Knoxville TN 37917

COOPER, BERNARD LABE, owner retail clothing store; b. Hampton, Va., Sept. 27, 1922; s. Morris Samuel and Rose Mary (Harris) C.; student U. Va., 1939-41; m. Pearl Strauss, Nov. 23, 1947; children—Sharman Fae (Mrs. Joseph Jeffrey Leinwand), Wayne, Marla Sue. With Coopers Dept. Store, Hampton, Va., 1937-39, 1946—, partner, 1948-64, owner, 1964—; mem. adv. bd. Va. Nat. Bank, Hampton. Treas. Phoebus Civic Assn., Hampton, 1959-63, pres., 1964; mem. Hampton citizens adv. council of Housing and Community Devel. Act.; pres. B'nai Israel Cong. and Synagogue, Hampton, Va., 1968-69. Commr., Hampton Redevel. and Housing Authority. Served with A.C. AUS, 1943-46. Recipient Outstanding Community Service award Phoebus Civic Assn., 1975. Mem. Hampton Retail Mchts. Assn. (dir. 1949-50), Peninsula Retail Mchts. Assn. (dir. 1973—, treas. 1980—), Am. Legion, AUS Assn. Elk, Mason (Shriner). Home: 104 Eggleston Ave Hampton VA 23669 Office: 14-16 E Mellen St Hampton VA 23663

COOPER, BOBBY GENE, coll. adminstr.; b. Bolton, Miss., Nov. 3, 1938; s. Willie and Lucile (Ross) C.; B.S., Tougaloo Coll., 1961; M.S., U. Ill., 1970; Ed.S., U. Colo., 1972, Ed.D., 1977; m. Della M. Larkin, June 8, 1970; children—Christopher Marc, Demetria Lysandra, LaCarole Maria. Tchr., Hawkins High Sch., Forest, Miss., 1961-68; adminstrv. asst. Bromley Hall, U. Ill., Urbana, 1969-70; music counselor Camp Tree Tops, Lake Placid, N.Y., 1968-69; chmn. humanities div. Utica (Miss.) Jr. Coll., 1972—, instr. music, 1972—; dir. Community Chorus Bolton. Bd. dirs. Opera South. Ford Found. fellow, 1968-69; U. Ill. Music Sch. fellow, 1969-70; U.S. Office Edn. grantee, 1971; U. Colo. fellow, 1972. Mem. Music Educators Nat. Conf., Am. Choral Dirs. Assn., Phi Delta Kappa. Methodist. Home: 270 Somerset Dr Jackson MS 39206 Office: Utica Jr Coll Utica MS 39175

COOPER, CARL RICHARD, mfg. co. exec.; b. Bklyn., Dec. 12, 1933; s. H. William and Molly Cooper; B.S., L.I. U., 1964; M.B.A., C.W. Post Coll., 1966; postgrad. bus. adminstrn. Nova U., 1977—; m. Jacqueline Sklare, Oct. 2, 1976; children—Michael, Michelle, Jennifer. Dir. ops. Condec/Conavco, Westbury, N.Y., 1956-68; dir. materials, contracts Litton Communications Co., Melville, N.Y., 1968-69; dir. materials, adminstrn. Norelco, Montvale, N.J., 1969-73; dir. materials Visual Graphics Corp., Tamarac, Fla., 1973-77; mgr. purchasing and inventory Motorola Inc., Fort Lauderdale, Fla., 1977—. adj. prof. Nova U., 1977—, Broward Community Coll., 1977—; mem. industry adv. council County Exec. Suffolk County,

N.Y. Mem. Am. Prodn. and Inventory Control Soc., Purchasing Mgmt. Assn., Internat. Materials Mgmt. Assn., Acad. Mgmt., Am. Mgmt. Assn. Contbr. articles to profl. jours. Home: 300 East Dr North Miami Beach FL 33162 Office: 8000 W Sunrise Blvd Fort Lauderdale FL 33322

COOPER, CHARLES HOWARD, photo-journalist, newspaper pub. co. exec.; b. Clinton, N.C., July 17, 1920; s. John Howard and Ella Jane (Bass) C.; grad. USAF Sch. Photography; m. Nell Elizabeth Slaughter, Jan. 2, 1943; children—Charles Howard II, John Phillip. Chief photographer, mgr. photo dept. Durham (N.C.) Herald Co., pub. Durham Morning Herald and Durham Sun, 1945—. Chmn. Miss Nat. Press Photographer Pageant, 1952, 53, 55. Mem. citizen's safety com., Durham, 1961-71. Served with USAAF, 1942-45; ETO. Mem. Nat. (exec. sec. 1963—, Fellowship award 1958, Joseph A. Sprague award 1961, Pres's. medals (2), 1964, 67, Merit award 1965, Joseph Costa award 1977, life mem.), Carolinas (pres. 1952-54) press photographers assns. Democrat. Baptist. Home: Box 1146 Durham NC 27702 Office: 115 Market St Durham NC 27702

COOPER, CHARLOTTE MALISSA, civic worker; b. Bristol, Conn., July 3, 1943; d. Herbert Auvin and Marie (Cochran) Hervey; B.A., U. Ark., 1965; postgrad. N. Tex. State U., 1965-67; m. James N. Cooper, Dec. 29, 1964. Tchr. speech and English, Richardson (Tex.) Public Schs., 1965-69, head English dept., 1968-69; interior designer, Arlington, Tex., 1977—. Founder Arlington Girls Club, 1976, pres. bd., 1976-77, fund raising chmn., 1978-79, 1st v.p., 1979-80; bd. dirs. Nat. Girls Club Am., 1979—; sec. Newcomers Club, 1972, pres., 1973; mem. style show com. Big Sisters, 1974; team capt. United Way, 1976, mem. allocations com., 1978-80; youth coordinator First United Methodist Ch., Arlington, 1972; active Boys Club Aux., 1973—, YMCA Aux., 1976—, Fine Arts League, 1976—, Service League; bd. dirs. Arlington Gymnastics Club; chmn. bd. U. Tex. Arlington Curtain Call Assn., 1980—. Named Newsmaker of Year, Arlington Citizen-Jour., 1977; recipient award merit Arlington Girls Club, 1977, 79. Mem. AAUW, Good Times Corp. (charter), Arlington Hist. Soc., Zeta Tau Alpha (province pres. 1973-77, nat. v.p. 1978—, cert. of merit 1975, honor ring 1978). Clubs: Jr. Women's (pres. 1978-79, parliamentarian 1979-80), Scotswood Garden (pres. 1974), Encore (v.p. 1975), Bailando Dance (sec. 1976). Home: 3016 Glasgow Dr Arlington TX 76015

COOPER, CLAUDE GEORGE, county ofcl.; b. Buffalo, June 16, 1940; s. Paul Andrew and Elsbeth Julia (Schuler) C.; B.C.E., Clarkson Coll. Tech., 1963; m. Elma May Triebel, Aug. 18, 1962; children—Timothy Alan, Kyryn Linda. With Va. Dept. Hwys., Richmond, 1963-72; dir. inspection service County of Fairfax (Va.), Fairfax 1972—; chmn. region 3 tech. com. Va. Bd. Housing, 1973. Mem. edn. adv. bd. on bldg. No. Va. Community Coll., 1974—. Registered profl. engr., Va. Mem. Nat. Soc. Profl. Engrs., Am. Concrete Inst. (chmn. com. 437), ASCE, Met. Washington Council Govts. (chmn. codes and regulations com. 1973-74). Clubs: Masons, Fairfax Rod and Gun. Home: 5554 Ann Peake Dr Fairfax VA 22032 Office: 10555 Main St Fairfax VA 22030

COOPER, CURTIS VICTOR, med. care adminstr.; b. Savannah, Ga., Sept. 22, 1932; s. Joshua and Clara (Baxley) C.; B.S., Savannah State Coll., 1955; M.P.H., U. Mich., 1977; m. Constance Y. Hartwell, Apr. 8, 1956; children—Curtis Victor, Constance Allyson. Debit mgr. Guaranty Life Ins. Co., Savannah, 1955, Afro Am. Life Ins. Co., Savannah, 1956; mgr. of rents Toomer Realty Co., Savannah, 1957-59; research asst. U.S. Dept. Agr., Savannah, 1959-71; exec. dir. Westside Comprehensive Health Center, Inc., Savannah, 1971—. Bd. dirs. Greenbriar Children's Center, Hodge Day Care Center, Savannah Port Authority; del. White House Conf. on Families, 1980; mem. Chatham County Hosp. Authority; mem. blood services com. Savannah chpt. ARC. Recipient Outstanding Service award Future Farmers Am., 1964, 67, Community Service award Jack and Jill, Inc., 1974, Man of Yr. award Alpha Phi Alpha, 1975; Community Service award Iota Phi Lambda, 1980. Mem. Am. Public Health Assn., Nat. Assn. Community Health Centers, Ga. Primary Care Assn., Savannah Health Care Assn., So. Assn. of Community Health Centers. Baptist. Clubs: Masons (Outstanding Community Service award 1969, 74), Shriners. Home: 1470 Chevy Chase Rd Savannah GA 31401 Office: PO Box 2024 #2 Roberts Savannah GA 31402

COOPER, DAVID ACRON, JR., coll. pres.; b. Knoxville, Oct. 4, 1947; s. David Acron and Agnes (Pearson) C.; B.S., U. Tenn., 1968, M.S., 1969, postgrad., 1970. Instr., Cooper Inst., Knoxville, 1967-70; sci. programmer Tennecomp Systems Inc., Oak Ridge, 1973-76; pres. Cooper Inst., Inc., Knoxville, 1974—; pres. Knoxville Bus. Coll., 1979—. Served to lt. USNR, 1970—. Mem. Internat. Platform Assn., Am. Mgmt. Assn., Am. Soc. Naval Engrs., Res. Officers Assn. U.S. Better Bus. Bur., C. of C., Sigma Pi Sigma, Phi Kappa Phi. Home: 5112 Catalina Dr Knoxville TN 37918 Office: PO Box 3369 720-24 N 5th Ave Knoxville TN 37917

COOPER, EUGENE BRUCE, speech-lang. pathologist, educator; b. Utica, N.Y., Dec. 20, 1933; s. Clements E. and Beulah (Wetzel) C.; B.S., State U. N.Y. at Geneseo, 1955; M.Ed., Pa. State U., 1957, Ed.D., 1962; m. Crystal Silverman, Sept. 12, 1965; children—Philip Adam, Ivan Bruce. Asst. prof. Ohio U., 1962-64, Pa. State U., 1964-66; program specialist Bur. Edn. Handicapped, U.S. Office Edn., 1966; exec. sec. sensory study sect., research and demonstrations div. Rehab. Services Adminstrn., Dept. HEW, 1966-67; prof., chmn. dept. communicative disorders, dir. Speech and Hearing Center, U. Ala., 1967—; cons. in field. Mem. Gov. Ala. Adv. Council Devel. Disabilities Services Act, 1972-75; Mem. Ala. Bd. Examiners in Speech Pathology and Audiology, 1976—, chmn., 1978-79. Bd. dirs. Tuscaloosa County Crippled Children and Adults Assn., chmn., 1974-75; bd. dirs. United Cerebral Palsy West Ala., Ala. Soc. for Crippled Children and Adults; acting chmn. Nat. Council on Communicative Disorders, 1979-80; pres. Nat. Council State Bds. Examiners in Speech-Lang. Pathology and Audiology, 1980. pres. Nat. Council Grad. Programs in Speech and Lang. Pathology and Audiology, 1978-80. Fellow Am. Speech and Hearing Assn. (legis. councilor 1971-73; asso. editor jour.); mem. Assn. Advancement Behavior Therapies, Council Exceptional Children (pres. div. for children with communicative disorders), Nat. Assn. Speech and Hearing Action, Nat. Rehab. Assn., Speech and Hearing Assn. Ala., Sigma Xi, Kappa Delta Pi. Author: Personalized Fluency Control Therapy, 1976; Understanding Stuttering: Information for Parents, 1979. Contbr. profl. jours. Authority on stuttering. Home: 117 Woodland Forrest Sect 3 Tuscaloosa AL 35405 Office: PO Box 1903 University AL 35486

COOPER, FRANKLIN DIXON, JR., civil engr., land surveyor; b. Binghampton, N.Y., Aug. 3, 1939; s. Franklin Dixon and Evelyn (Dotson) C.; B.S., The Citadel, 1961; student Command and Gen. Staff Coll., 1976, Indsl. Coll. Armed Forces, 1977; m. Judith Lynn Robbins, Dec. 4, 1970; children—Franklin Dixon III, Gregory Curtis, Brian Ashley. Civil engr. U.S. Dept. Agr., Soil Conservation Service, Syracuse, N.Y., 1964-67; naval architect structures Dept. Navy, Charleston Naval Shipyard (S.C.), 1967-69, nuclear welding engr., 1969-71; master planning engr., directorate facilities engring., Dept. Army, Ft. Jackson, S.C., 1971—; owner, operator F.D. Cooper Jr., cons. engr. and land surveyor, Columbia, S.C., 1971—. Served to lt., U.S. Army, 1962-64, lt. col. Res. Registered profl. engr., land surveyor N.Y. State, S.C., Ga. Mem. Nat. Soc. Profl. Engrs., Soc. Am. Mil. Engrs., ASCE, Am. Congress Surveying and Mapping, S.C. Soc. Land Surveyors, Res. Officers Assn., Assn. U.S. Army. Episcopalian. Clubs: Columbia Citadel, Masons, Shriners. Home: 3208 Berkeley Forest Dr Columbia SC 29209 Office: DFAE Master Planning Div Ft Jackson SC 29207

COOPER, HAROLD HOMER, JR., lawyer; b. Tulsa, Aug. 3, 1940; s. Harold Homer and Marjorie (Burkett) C.; B.A., U. Tulsa, 1962, J.D., 1966; postgrad. So. Methodist U., 1958-60; div.; 1 son, Christopher Lee. Admitted to Tex. bar, 1968; corp. sec., gen. counsel Linbeck Constrn. Corp., Houston, 1967-72; asso. gen. counsel Mitchell Energy & Devel. Corp., Houston, 1972-74; v.p., sec., gen. counsel 1st Constrn. Group, Inc., Houston, 1974-77, Vantage Cos., Houston, 1978—. Bd. dirs. Houston Grand Opera Assn. Mem. Am., Okla. bar assns., State Bar Tex., Kappa Alpha, Phi Alpha Delta. Home: 7703 Bobbitt Ln Houston TX 77055 Office: 4635 Southwest Freeway Houston TX 77027

COOPER, HARRY EZEKIEL, educator; b. Kansas City, Mo., Dec. 10, 1897; s. Ezekiel and Helen (Moore) C.; Mus.B., Horner Inst. Fine Arts, 1920; Mus.D., Bush Conservatory, 1923; A.B., Ottawa U., 1937; m. Agnes Bickford, Nov. 18, 1926; children—Robert Ezekiel, Alice Caroline (Mrs. Theo Robert Potter). Supt. music Liberty (Mo.) Schs., 1917-19; prof. music, chmn. dept. William Jewell Coll., 1919-28; dean music Ottawa U., 1928-37; chmn. dept. music, prof. music Meredith Coll., 1937—. Organist, choirmaster Kansas City (Mo.) Chs., 1911-37, Christ Ch., Raleigh, N.C., 1937-47, 1st Bapt. Ch., 1948—; organist N.C. Symphony Orch., 1949. Condr., Raleigh Oratorio Soc., 1940-48. Fellow Am. Guild Organists; mem. N.C. Music Tchrs. Assn. (pres. 1943-44), Raleigh Chamber Music Guild (pres. 1942-43). Writer musical articles, various songs, others. Home: 3 Henderson St Raleigh NC 27607

COOPER, HOWARD LEE, SR., hosp. food adminstr.; b. St. Louis, Feb. 22, 1930; s. Levi and Phillippa Lane (Roberts) C.; student Ala. State U., 1950-51, Tuskegee Inst., Ala., 1953-55, Ga. State U., 1975, Massey Bus. Coll., 1975-76; B.S., N.Mex. State U., 1971; M.A., Central Mich. U., 1979; grad. course U.S. Army Q.M.C. Sch.; married; children—Alice Cooper, Elizabeth J. Cooper, Valencia D., Howard L., Theodore P. Ritchey. Mem. staff VA Med. Center, Amarillo, Tex., 1961-62, Amarillo AFB Hosp., 1962-67; dir. food service Holliman AFB (N.Mex.) Hosp., 1967-72; chief food prodn. and service VA Med. Center, Decatur, Ga., 1973—. Active Boy Scouts Am., 1962-71; pres. Concerned Citizens of DeKalb County, 1975-76, DeKalb Families in Action, 1977-78; bd. dirs. East Lake Ch. of Christ, Decatur, 1973—. Served with U.S. Army, 1951-53, USAF, 1955-60; Korea; USAFR, 1961-73, USAR, 1973—. Cert. food exec. Ga. Mem. Hosp. Instl. and Ednl. Soc., Am. Soc. for Hosp. Food Service Adminstrs. (pres. Atlanta chpt.), Internat. Food Service Execs. Assn. (pres. elect Atlanta chpt.). Republican. Club: Kiwanis (dir. chpt. 1969-71). Home: 2327 Springside Way Decatur GA 30032 Office: VA Med Center 1670 Clairmont Rd Decatur GA 30033

COOPER, JEROME MAURICE, architect; b. Memphis, Jan. 24, 1930; s. Samuel and Bessie (Phillips) C.; B.S., Ga. Inst. Tech., 1952, B. Arch., 1955; postgrad. Universita di Roma, Rome, Italy, 1956-57; m. Jean Kanter Cooper, Dec. 29, 1957; children—David Franklin, Samuel Randolph, Beth Lauren. Draftsman Willner & Millkey, Atlanta, 1955-56; Fulbright fellow Rome, Italy, 1956-57; designer Abreu & Robeson, Atlanta, 1957-59, Heery & Heery, Atlanta 1959-60; pres. Cooper, Salzman & Carry, 1960—. Past chmn. citizens adv. bd. for urban devel. City of Atlanta. Served to lt. (j.g.) USNR, 1952-54. Fellow A.I.A. (past pres. Atlanta chpt., regional dir.). Prin. archtl. works include: addition to architecture bldg. Ga. Tech., Atlanta, Cross Creek Mall, Greenwood, S.C., United Am. Bank Plaza, Knoxville, Tenn., Hickory Hollow Mall Shopping Center, Nashville, Riverbend Apts., Atlanta, Landmark Interchange Office Bldg., Atlanta, Gen. Motors Regional Hdqrs., Atlanta, also elem. and secondary schs. Home: 1070 Judith Way NE Atlanta GA 30324 Office: 1819 Peachtree St NW Atlanta GA 30309

COOPER, JIMMY LEE, pharmacist; b. Kirbyville, Tex., Mar. 22, 1942; s. Mitchell and Ocella (Simmons) C.; B.S. in Pharmacy, Tex. So. U., 1965; m. Diana Hightower, July 16, 1966; 1 son, James Sebestian Cabot. With Walgreen Drugs, Houston, 1962—, pharmacist, 1965—, store mgr., 1967—. Trustee, Variety Boys' Club; pres. Tex. So. Alumni Found., Inc. Mem. Nat., Houston pharm. assns., Am. Mgmt. Assn., Houston Jaycees, Chi Delta Mu. Baptist. Club: Rotary. Address: 9413 Bertwood St Houston TX 77016 Office: 9410 Cullen St Houston TX 77051

COOPER, KATHIE PITTS, fin. exec.; b. Greenwood, Miss., Mar. 25, 1948; d. James Jefferson and Katharine Brenda (Smith) Pitts; B.S. in Bus. Adminstrn., U. S.C., 1970; m. N.L. Cooper, Oct. 11, 1975; 1 son, Jonathan Travis. Tax auditor U.S. Treasury Dept., Greenville, S.C., 1970-71, Fayetteville, N.C., 1974-75; bookkeeper Babcock Center for Retarded Children, Columbia, S.C., 1971, Central Electric Power Coop., Inc., Columbia, 1972-74; sec.-bookkeeper Pee Dee Regional Transp. Authority, Florence, 1976-77; controller Florence (S.C.) Gen. Hosp., 1977—. Mem. Hosp. Fin. Mgmt. Assn., Beta Gamma Sigma. Democrat. Methodist. Home: 2901 Woodbine Ave Florence SC 29501 Office: Florence Gen Hosp 512 S Irby St Florence SC 29501

COOPER, KENNETH DEAN, computer cons. and service co. exec.; b. Pitts., Dec. 20, 1943; s. Robert Lee and Lois Mae (Shoup) C.; student U. Richmond, 1972-74, Inst. Computer Mgmt., 1963, Orange Jr. Coll., 1968; m. Ellen Elyse Shuler, Dec. 31, 1971; 1 son, Bucknell Dean. Shift supr. Mellon Nat. Bank, Pitts., 1964-65; programmer Mobay Chem. Co., Pitts., 1965-68; asso. analyst Martin-Marrietta, Orlando, Fla., 1968-69; mgr. programming Automated Bus. Services, Pitts., 1969-71; pres. D&E Consultants, Pitts., 1970-72; mgr. systems support Garfinckle's, Washington, 1972-76; mgr. tng. and edn., staff ops., tech. evaluation, logistics and adminstrn. orientation, Cutler-Williams Co. Dallas, 1976—; dir. Cims Group, Dallas. Served with USAF, 1962-68. Mem. Dallas Darts Assn., N.Am. Darts Assn., Internat. Platform Assn., Am. Legion, VFW. Contbr. articles to profl. jours. Home: 1302 River Oaks Dr Flower Mound TX 75028 Office: 2655 Villa Creek Dr Suite 205 Dallas TX 75234

COOPER, LOUIS IRWIN, pediatrician; b. Savannah, Ga., Jan. 15, 1948; s. Sol and Rachel (Radetsky) C.; B.S., U. Ga., 1969; M.D., Med. Coll. of Ga., 1973; children—Steven Benjamin, Amy Rachelle. Intern, Nat. Naval Med. Center, Bethesda, Md., 1973-74, resident in pediatrics, 1974-77; commd. ensign U.S. Navy, 1972, advanced through grades to lt. comdr., 1976; staff pediatrician Naval Regional Med. Center, Charleston, S.C., 1977—; clin. instr. pediatrics Med. U. S.C., Charleston, 1977—. Mem. youth commn. B'rith Shalom Beth Israel Congregation, Charleston, 1978. Diplomate Am. Acad. Pediatrics, Nat. Bd. Med. Examiners. Fellow Am. Acad. Pediatrics; mem. AMA, Am. Acad. Pediatrics, Charleston County Med. Soc., Phi Delta Epsilon. Jewish. Office: Dept Pediatrics Naval Regional Med Center Charleston SC 29408

COOPER, MELVIN DULEY, JR., ednl. adminstr.; b. Memphis, Aug. 12, 1940; s. Melvin Duley and Sydney Mae (Wilson) C.; A.B., Columbia U., 1962; M.Ed., Memphis State U., 1971. Tchr. English, Shelby County Schs., Memphis, 1963-65, Memphis U. Sch., 1965-69; account exec. Robert F. Sharpe & Co., Memphis, 1969-70; dir. devel. Hutchison Sch., Memphis U. Sch., Memphis, 1970-75, McCallie Sch., Chattanooga, 1975—. Bd. dirs. Memphis Opera Theater, 1974-75, Chattanooga Opera Assn., 1975—, St. George's Day Sch., Germantown, Tenn., 1973-75; pres. alumni chpt. Coll. Edn., Memphis State U., 1974-75. Mem. Nat. Assn. Ind. Schs. (devel. com. 1976-79, chmn., 1977-79), Council Advancement and Support of Edn. (ind. schs. adv. com. 1973-75), Kappa Delta Pi. Episcopalian. Home: 3702 Indian Trail Chattanooga TN 37412 Office: McCallie Sch Chattanooga TN 37404

COOPER, NORMAN LEE, lawyer; b. Birmingham, Ala., Feb. 1, 1940; s. Norman Tellous and Berta Ruth (Roe) C.; B.S., U. Ala., 1963, LL.B., 1964; m. Catherine Joy Clark, Aug. 18, 1962; children—Clark Andrew, Catherine Ruth. Admitted to Ala. bar, 1964, since practiced in Birmingham; asso. firm Cabaniss, Johnston, Gardner, Dumas & O'Neal, 1966-71, mem. firm, 1972—. Served to capt., AUS, 1964-66. Mem. Am. (council litigation sect. 1975-76, 79—, sec. 1976-78, award of achievement 1975, young lawyers sect.), Ala. State (pres. young lawyers' sect. 1974-75, award of merit 1976), Birmingham (sec.-treas. 1972) bar assns., Beta Gamma Sigma, Omicron Delta Kappa. Presbyn. Home: 2831 Southwood Rd Birmingham AL 35223 Office: Cabaniss Johnston Gardner Dumas & O'Neal First Nat-So Natural Bldg Birmingham AL 35203

COOPER, RICHARD GRANT, physician, educator; b. N.Y.C., Mar. 8, 1934; s. Sidney Preston and Helen Lucille (Kyle) C.; B.S., U. Ky., 1956, M.S., 1960; Ph.D. (NIH fellow in hematology), U. Tex., 1964; D.O., Coll. Osteo. Medicine and Surgery, 1976; m. Sylvia Jane Edmondson, Jan. 31, 1970. Teaching asst. U. Ky., 1958-59; teaching and research asst. U. Tex., 1960-63; asst. prof. physiology and agrl. chemistry U. Mo., 1963-72; asso. prof. physiology Coll. Osteo. Medicine and Surgery, Des Moines, 1972-75; now asso. prof. clin. sci. Okla. Coll. Osteo. Medicine and Surgery, Tulsa. Mem. Am., Okla. osteo. assns., Am. Heart Assn. (council on thrombosis), AAAS, N.Y., Iowa acads. sci., Sigma Xi. Home: 7424 E 53d Pl Tulsa OK 74145 Office: Okla Coll Osteopathic Medicine and Surgery PO Box 2280 Tulsa OK 74101

COOPER, ROBERT ELBERT, state supreme ct. justice; b. Chattanooga, Oct. 14, 1920; s. John Thurman and Susie Inez (Hollingsworth) C.; B.A., U. N.C., 1946; J.D., Vanderbilt U., 1949; m. Catherine Pauline Kelly, Nov. 24, 1949; children—Susan Florence Cooper Hodges, Bobbie Cooper Martin, Kelly Ann, Robert Elbert. Admitted to Tenn. bar; asso. firm Kolwyck & Clark, 1949-51, Cooper & Barger, 1951-53; asst. atty. gen. 6th Jud. Circuit Tenn., 1951-53; judge 6th Jud. Circuit Tenn., 1953-60, Tenn. Ct. of Appeals, 1960-70; presiding judge Eastern Div., Tenn. Ct. of Appeals, 1970-74; justice Tenn. Supreme Ct., Chattanooga, 1974—, chief justice, 1976-78; chmn. Tenn. Jud. Council, 1967—; mem. Tenn. Jud. Standards Commn., 1971—; chmn. Tenn. Code Commn., 1976—. Elder, Second United Presbyn. Ch., 1963—, chmn. bd. trustees, 1966-73; bd. dirs. St. Barnabas Nursing Home and Apts. for Aged, 1966-69; mem. exec. bd. Cherokee council Boy Scouts Am., 1960-64. Served with USN, 1941-46. Recipient Merit awards Alhambra Shrine Temple, Shrine Hosp. for Crippled Children, Lexington, Ky., 1966, Chattanooga Met. YMCA. Mem. Am., Tenn., Chattanooga bar assns., Conf. Chief Justices, Tenn. Jud. Conf., Am. Legion, Order of Coif, Phi Beta Kappa, Kappa Sigma, Phi Alpha Delta. Democrat. Clubs: Masons (33 deg.), K.T.; Shriners (potentate Alhambra Temple 1966); Royal Order Jesters. Home: 196 Woodcliff Circle Signal Mountain TN 37377 Office: Hamilton County Justice Bldg Chattanooga TN 37402

COOPER, ROBERT FRANKLIN, JR., banker; b. Ellisville, Miss., Oct. 19, 1913; s. Robert Franklin and Emily Lamar Moore (Gibson) C.; A.B., Washington and Lee U., 1935; J.D., U. Louisville, 1938; m. Mary Miller Wells, Sept. 16, 1943; children—Mary Emily Cooper Haygood, Robert Franklin III. Admitted to Ky. bar, 1938, U.S. Supreme Ct. bar, 1941; spl. agt. FBI, 1939-67; v.p., trust officer, 1968—. Mem. Am. (real property, probate and trust law sect. 1970—), Fed., Ky., Miss., Hinds County bar assns., Estate Planning Council of Miss., Soc. Former Spl. Agts. FBI, Mountain Retreat Assn. of Montreat (N.C.) (dir. 1952-57), Jackson (Miss.) C. of C., Kappa Sigma. Presbyterian. Clubs: North Jackson Kiwanis, Knife and Fork (Jackson). Home: 1335 Linden Pl Jackson MS 39202 Office: 1030 First Nat Bank Bldg 248 E Capitol St Jackson MS 39201

COOPER, ROBERT GILBERT, librarian; b. St. Louis, Feb. 24, 1930; s. Robert Kehr and Irma Emilie (Wagner) C.; B.S. in Edn., Union Coll., 1952; M.S. in L.S., U. So. Calif., 1966; m. Vivian Bernice Rabun, Aug. 9, 1953; children—Teresa Lynette, Stanley Wayne. Tchr., Tex. Conf. Seventh-day Adventists, Ft. Worth, 1952-62; librarian Loma Linda U., 1962-67, Findley Meml. Library, Southwestern Adventist Coll., Keene, Tex., 1967—. Mem. Tex. Library Assn. Home: 407 N College Dr Keene TX 76059 Office: Findley Meml Library Southwestern Adventist Coll Keene TX 76059

COOPER, ROBERT LEE, elec. engr.; b. Alvarado, Tex., Nov. 16, 1925; s. Charles M. and Conseula (Merideth) C.; B.S. in Elec. Engring., Tex. A. and M. U., 1948; m. Katherine Ruth Thompson, Oct. 17, 1959; children—Charles J., Joan Catherine, Stephen Ralph. Rep., Sperry Rand Corp., Gt. Neck, N.Y., 1948-61; dist. mgr. Varian Assos., Dallas and Los Angeles, 1961-64; applications engr. Bell and Howell Co., Albuquerque and Huntsville, Ala., 1964-67; specialist engr. Boeing Co., Huntsville, 1967-70; sr. reliability engr. Fed. Electric Corp., Huntsville, 1970-72; sr. engr. Sperry Rand Corp., Huntsville, 1972-78; mem. tech. staff Rockwell Internat., Huntsville, 1978—. Served with USNR, 1944-46. Recipient Apollo Achievement award NASA, 1970, Skylab Achievement award, 1974. Registered profl. engr., Ala. Mem. Nat., Ala. socs. profl. engrs. Methodist.

COOPER, TERRY JACK, corp. exec.; b. Bakersfield, Calif., Nov. 2, 1941; s. N.B. and Jane (Lay) C.; B.A., U. Tex., 1965; student U. Geneva, Switzerland, 1962-63; postgrad. U. Houston, 1965-67. Biomathematician, Baylor Med. Center, Houston, 1965-66; geophys. engr. Geophys. Services, Inc., Houston, 1966-67; analyst Goddard Space Flight Center, Greenbelt, Md., 1967-68; pres. Terry's Interstate, Inc., Tyler, Tex., 1968—; pres. Interstate Motel Supply Co., Inc., 1973—, Root-Mass Energy Inc., 1979—; v.p. Nautilus Balloon Works, Ltd.; guest lectr. on poetry and bus. for colls. and high schs. Active YMCA. Winner Houston poetry contest awards. Mem. Tex. Restaurant Assn., Audubon Soc., Tex. Archaeol. Soc., Archaeol. Inst. Am., Tex. Poetry Soc., AAAS, Tex. Solar Energy Soc., Assn. Energy Engrs., Nat. Hotel and Motel Assn., Balloon Fedn. Am., N. Tex. Fencers League, Tyler C. of C., Phi Delta Theta. Independent. Club: Willowbrook Country. Author: I Am Love and Other Poems, 1969. Editor of Some Friends, 1972—. Home: 310 Fannin St Tyler TX 75701 Office: PO Box 6395 Tyler TX 75711

COORPENDER, LINDA MARIE TIMPHONY, speech pathologist; b. New Orleans, Nov. 25, 1946; d. John and Jeanne Louise (Mahe) Timphony; B.A. (Am. Legion scholar), Northwestern State U. of La., 1968, M.A. in Spl. Edn., 1972; m. William Corryden

Coorpender, May 28, 1968; children—Steven John, Tracye Marie. Teaching asst. Northwestern State U. of La., 1968, fellow, 1972; tchr. lang. arts Port Sulphur (La.) Elem. Sch., 1969; tchr. English and French, Port Sulphur High Sch., 1970; pub. sch. speech therapist Pinellas County, Fla., 1972, Rapides Parish, La., 1973-75; speech pathologist VA Med. Center, Alexandria, La., 1975—. Cub Scout den leader Boy Scouts Am., 1977-78; mem. YWCA; active Equal Employment Opportunity Com., 1976—, Fed. Woman's Program Com., 1977—. Sigma Alpha Theta scholar, 1972-73. Mem. La. Assn. Mental Health, Am. Speech and Hearing Assn., La. Laryngectomy Assn. Roman Catholic. Home: 3206 Rigolette Rd Pineville LA 71360 Office: VA Med Center Shreveport Hwy Alexandria LA 71301

COORPENDER, WILLIAM GEORGE, med. adminstr.; b. Alexandria, La., June 4, 1943; s. George Banks and Lois Virginia (Gray) C.; B.S., La. Tech. U., 1968. Personnel asst. M.D. Anderson Hosp., Houston, 1968-70; personnel officer So. Nat. Bank, Houston, 1970-73; asst. v.p., personnel dir. Allied Bank Tex., Houston, 1973-74; dir. personnel Seton Med. Center, Austin, Tex., 1974-77; dir. personnel Schumpert Med. Center, Shreveport, La., 1977—. Mem. N.W. La. Personnel Assn., La. Soc. Hosp. Personnel Dirs. (pres. 1980), Am. Soc. Hosp. Personnel Administrn. Office: Schumpert Med Center 915 Margaret Pl Shreveport LA 71101

COOTS, KENNETH RAY, truck leasing co. exec.; b. Cullman, Ala., Oct. 17, 1944; s. Ottis Ray and Willodean (Mann) C.; student Jacksonville State Coll., 1963-65; B.A.A., Auburn U., 1969; m. Barbara June Watts, May 20, 1972; 1 dau., Sunny Rae. Supr., Engring. Weights Control Group, Hayes Internat. Corp., Birmingham, Ala., 1965-67; br. mgr. Saunders Leasing System, Cleve., Brantford, Ont., Can., Roanoke, Va., Charleston, W.Va., Stanley, Va., Kingsport, Tenn., Taylorsville, N.C., Detroit, 1976-78; dir. properties Sanders Leasing System, Birmingham, Ala., 1969—. Served with U.S. Army, 1967. Mem. Va. Car and Truck Rental and Leasing Assn. (pres. 1974-75), Bldg. Owners and Mgrs. Assn., Ala. Truck Rental and Leasing Assn., Nat. Truck Rental and Leasing Assn. Republican. Methodist. Club: Lions. Home: 2045 Chandaway Dr Pelham AL 35124 Office: 201 Office Park Dr Birmingham AL 35223

COPE, FRANK EUGENE, ins. co. exec.; b. Barberton, Ohio, May 10, 1929; s. Carl Bertrant and Marie Louise (Good) C.; student Akron U., 1947, Jacksonville U., 1957; m. Bonnie Carolyn Cannon, July 12, 1952; children—Susan Elaine, Janet Carolyn, Michael Eugene. Draftsman, Babcock & Wilcox, Barberton, 1945-48; owner Cope Cleaners, Barberton, 1948-50, 54-57; with Gulf Life Ins. Co., Jacksonville, Fla., 1957—, v.p., 1978—. Served with USN, 1950-54. Mem. Nat. Assn. Life Underwriters, Jacksonville Assn. Life Underwriters, Gen. Agts. and Mgrs. Assn., Am. Heart Assn. Baptist. Clubs: Univ., Ponte Vedra, Masons (32 deg.). Home: 4715 Verona Ave Jacksonville FL 32210 Office: 1301 Gulf Life Dr Jacksonville FL 32207

COPELAND, ALVIN CHARLES, fast food co. exec.; b. New Orleans, Feb. 2, 1944; s. William Allen and Augustine Marie (Comeaux) C.; student public schs., New Orleans; m. Patty K. White, Nov. 4, 1977; children—Alvin, Bonnie, Chris, Ali. Owner, pres. A. Copeland Enterprises, Inc. (Popeye's Famous Fried Chicken), New Orleans, 1972—; dir. Contemporary Arts Center. A.d.c., Gov. Edwin Edwards, 1975; named Marketer of Yr., Am. Mktg. Assn., 1977; hon. state senator La., citizen New Orleans. Mem. Nat. Restaurant Assn., Internat. Franchise Assn. Roman Catholic. Clubs: Mardi Gras Krewes. Home: Metairie LA Office: 1 Popeyes Plaza 1333 S Clearview Pkwy Jefferson New Orleans LA 70121

COPELAND, EMILY AMERICA, assn. exec.; b. Tifton, Ga.; d. Jerry and America (Vaughn) Copeland; A.B., Spelman Coll., 1937; B.S. in L.S. (Carnegie grantee) Atlanta U., 1942; M.S., Columbia, 1948, postgrad., 1959-60; postgrad. N.Y. U., 1949-50, U. S.C., 1969. Tchr., Tift County Indsl. High Sch., Tifton, 1937-38; librarian Finley High Sch., Chester, S.C., 1938-41; library asst. Atlanta U. Library, summers 1938-40, 42; head librarian Gammon Theol. Sem., Atlanta, 1942-44; acquisitions librarian Atlanta U., 1944-46; reference, sch. work sst. N.Y. Pub. Library, N.Y.C., 1945-46; head dept. library sci. S.C. State Coll., 1946-51; prof., chmn. dept. library service Fla. A. and M. U., Tallahassee, 1951-75; pres., founder Black Research Information Coordinating Service, Inc., 1972—. Recipient certificate of merit Spelman Coll., 1968. Mem. S.C. Library Devel. Com., 1947-51, S.C. Library Edn. Planning Com., 1948-51; mem. Fla. com. Columbia Campaign Fund, 1967-69. Mem. Am. (mem. nat. planning com. 1956-62, E.P. Dutton McRae award com. 1971, mem. right to read com. pub. library div. 1972—, minority recruitment cons. 1972), Southeastern, Fla. (pres. 1953-56) library assns., Smithsonian Instn. (asso.), Information Industry Assn., Marquis Biog. Library Soc. Author: A Handbook for the Guidance of Students in School Library Intership, 1964; A Guide to Minority Resources, 1973. Contbr. articles to profl. jours., World Book Ency., Black Librarian in Am. Home: 614 Howard Ave Tallahassee FL 32304 also 1212 Peachtree St Tifton GA 31794 Office: Petroleum Bldg 222 W Pensacola St Tallahassee FL 32304

COPELAND, EUGENE HERMAN, JR., architect, planner; b. Martinsville, Va., Apr. 7, 1934; s. Eugene Herman and Mary (Hurd) C.; B.S. in Bldg. Design, Va. Tech., 1955; m. Ann McColman, May 24, 1958; children—Allison, Sarah Lee, Letitia. Archtl. intern David L. Ragland, Danville, Va., 1956-58; asso. Albert C. Woodroof, Sr., Albert C. Woodroof, Jr., Greensboro, N.C., 1958-62; architect and planner Odell Assos., Inc., Charlotte, N.C., 1962-80, pres., dir., 1978-80; founder, prin. E.H. Copeland, Jr., architect and planner, Charlotte, 1980—. Active fund dr. United Arts Council, 1974, United Way, 1979; mem. study commn. Charlotte Uptown Devel. Authority, 1977; bd. dirs. Central Charlotte Assn., 1979, Myers Park Home Owners Assn., Myers Park Found. Served to capt. U.S. Army, 1956. Registered architect, Va., N.C., S.C., Ohio, Mich. Mem. AIA (past pres. Charlotte chpt., v.p. N.C. assn. 1980), Am. Inst. Cert. Planners, Va. Tech. Alumni Assn. (past pres., dir. Carolina chpt., Alumni Service award Carolina chpt. 1973), Charlotte C. of C. (chmn. state legis. task force 1974-75). Methodist. Clubs: Commonwealth of Va., Charlotte Athletic (dir. 1975-79, sec. 1979), Greensboro City, Charlotte Country, Myrtle Beach Tennis. Prin. works include: Hampton Va. Coliseum, Limestone Coll. Library, Camp Lejeune Marine Corps Base, others. Home: 2044 Sherwood Ave Charlotte NC 28207 Office: 120 Brevard Ct Charlotte NC 28202

COPELAND, HUNTER ARMSTRONG, real estate financing exec.; b. Birmingham, Ala., Oct. 22, 1918; s. Miles Axe and Leonora (Armstrong) C.; student U. Ala.; m. Courtney Bass, May 27, 1978; children—Susan Diane Copeland Locke, Hunter Armstrong, John McGregor, Robert Miles, Ann Armstrong. Engaged in mortgage appraisal and brokerage, 1946—; mortgage appraiser Prudential Ins. Co., Birmingham, 1946-54; mortgage broker Huntoon-Paige, N.Y.C., 1954-57; pres. Huntoon, Copeland & Hedin, N.Y.C., 1958-70; exec. dir. Hunter Copeland & Assos., N.Y.C., 1970-75, pres., Birmingham, 1977—; v.p. Colwell Co., N.Y.C., 1970-75; pres. Copeland Tresnan & Hornblower, Inc., N.Y.C., 1975-77; trustee Md. Nat. Realty Trust, Balt. Bd. dirs. United Way, New Canaan, Conn.; trustee Silver Hill Found., New Canaan, Nat. Council on Alcoholism for So. Conn. Served to maj., inf., bn. comdr. ETO, U.S. Army, 1941-45; from lt. col. to col., USAF Res., 1951-53. Decorated Silver Star medal, Bronze Star medal with 4 oak leaf clusters, Purple Heart with 1 oak leaf cluster, Korean Service medal. Mem. Mortgage Bankers Assn. Am., Mortgage Bankers Assn. N.Y. (gov.), Nat. Rifle Assn., Commerce Exec. Soc., C. of C. of Birmingham, Nat. Skeet Assn., Internat. Platform Assn., Nat. Historic Soc., Ala. Hist. Soc., Newcomen Soc., USAF Assn., Nat. Trust for Hist. Preservation, Res. Officers Assn., Chi Phi. Kiwanian. Clubs: Union League, New Canaan Field, Relay House; Birmingham, Country of Birmingham, Campfire of Am. Home: 3915 Knollwood Dr Birmingham AL 35243 Office: The Bank For Savings Suite 1138 Birmingham AL 35203 also 14 E 52d St New York NY 10022

COPELAND, IAN ADIE, talent agy. exec.; b. Damascus, Syria, Apr. 25, 1949 (parents Am. citizens); s. Miles Axe and Lorraine Elizabeth Copeland; grad. high sch.; m. Connie Walden, Aug. 26, 1978; 1 dau., Chandra. Agt., John Sherry Enterprises, London, Eng., 1971-72; partner Sherry Copeland Artists, London, 1972-75; booking agt. Paragon Agy., Macon, Ga., 1977—; writer music for rock group The Police, rock artist Klark Kent. Served with U.S. Army, 1967-71. Decorated Bronze Star. Home: Box 364 1155 Will Scarlet Way Lake Wildwood Macon GA 31210 Office: Paragon Agy PO Box 4408 560 Arlington Pl Macon GA 31208

COPELAND, JAMES EVERETT, educator; b. Plainview, Tex., June 10, 1937; s. William Ford and Golda Loraine (Stern) C.; B.A. in German Lit. magna cum laude, U. Colo., 1961; Ph.D., Cornell U., 1965. Instr., Cornell U., Ithaca, N.Y., 1964-65; asst. prof. U. Calif., Davis, 1965-66; asst. prof. Rice U., Houston, 1966-69, asso. prof. dept. German linguistics, 1969—, chmn. dept. linguistics, 1969—; vis. asst. prof. Cornell U., summer 1967; field supr. Tel/Aphek Archaeol. Excavations, Israel, summers, 1978-79. Mem. Linguistic Soc. Am., MLA, Phi Beta Kappa. Author: A Stepmatricial Generative Phonology of German, 1970; contbr. articles to profl. jours. Home: 1309 Bomar St Houston TX 77006 Office: Rice Univ 6100 S Main St Houston TX 77001

COPELAND, JAMES WILLIAM, state supreme ct. justice; b. Woodland, N.C., June 16, 1914; s. Luther C. and Nora (Benthall) C.; A.B., Guilford Coll., 1934; J.D. with honors, U. N.C., 1937; m. Nancy Hall Sawyer, Oct. 11, 1941; children—Emily, James W., Buxton S. Admitted to N.C. bar, 1936; individual practice law, Woodland and Murfreesboro, N.C.; mem. N.C. State Senate, 1951, 53, 57, 59, chmn. jud. com., 1957, chmn. appropriations com. 1969; mayor of Woodland, 1938-41, Murfreesboro, 1947-51; judge N.C. Superior Ct., 1961-75; asso. justice N.C. Supreme Ct., 1975—. Chmn. Bd. Elections, Northampton and Hertford Counties; mem. N.C. Adv. Budget Commn., 1957-61; del. Dem. Conv., 1956. Served as lt. USN, 1942-46. Mem. Am. Bar Assn., N.C. Bar Assn. Clubs: Masons, Shriners, Rotary. Home: 407 E High St Murfreesboro NC 27855 and Raleigh Towne Apts 21 521 Wade Ave Raleigh NC 27605 Office: PO Box 1841 NC Supreme Ct Raleigh NC 27602

COPELAND, JIMMY BRYANT, univ. adminstr.; b. Carroll County, Ga., Dec. 9, 1924; s. Joseph Bryant and Annie Lee (Jackson) C.; B.S.A., U. Ga., 1948; M.S., Clemson U., 1958; Ph.D., U. Wis., 1966; m. Barbara Bargeron, July 16, 1948; children—Carol Copeland Russell, Ann Copeland Vickery. Fieldman Pet Dairy Products Co., Washington, Ga., 1948-53; asst. agrl. editor Clemson U., 1953-59, head agrl. communications, 1959-65, asso. dir. Coop. Extension Service, 1965—. Served with USAAF, 1943-46; PTO. Kellogg Found. fellow, 1964; Sears Roebuck Agrl. scholar, 1947; recipient Pioneer Ace award, Am. Assn. Agrl. Coll. Editors, 1960. Mem. Blue Key, Gamma Sigma Delta. Baptist (deacon). Club: Clemson Rotary (dir. 1968-69). Home: 109 Mountain View Dr Clemson SC 29631

COPELAND, MARY JONES, nurse; b. Coweta County, Ga., Feb. 4, 1930; d. John Robert and Mattie Lou (Beckom) Jones; R.N., Lutheran Hosp., Vicksburg, Miss., 1952; B.S. in Health Adminstrn., St. Joseph's Coll., N. Windom, Maine, 1978; m. Harold William Copeland, Aug. 30, 1952; children—Mary Ellen, Sally Ann. Head nurse Newnan (Ga.) Hosp., 1951-52, Polio Clinic, Vicksburg, 1952-53; supr. Grady Meml. Hosp., Atlanta, 1953-57; mem. nursing staff South Fulton Hosp., East Point, Ga., 1963—, asst. dir. nurses, 1971, dir. nursing services, 1971—; bd. dirs. Fulton County (Ga.) chpt. Am. Cancer Soc.; lectr. in field. Tchr. Bible sch. Ch. of Christ, East Point, 1953—; bd. dirs. sec. Ga. AGAPE Adoption Agy. Mem. Am. Nursing Assn., Ga. Nurses Assn., Ga. League for Nurses, Ga. Soc. for Nursing Service Adminstrs., South Fulton Hosp. Vol. Aux. (dir.), Metro-Atlanta Drug Corp. Author: Straight Talk to Christian Women, 3d edit., 1977. Home: 2760 Luther Dr East Point GA 30344 Office: 1170 Cleveland Ave East Point GA 30344

COPELAND, MELBA MERCHANT, univ. adminstr.; b. Carthage, Miss.; d. Edward Waylotte and Libby (Coleman) Merchant; student Wayne State U., 1954; B.S., Rust Coll., 1950; M.S., Tenn. State U., 1954; postgrad. So. Ill. U., 1975, Delta State U., 1977; m. William H. Copeland, May 31, 1958; 1 son, Vincent Heard. Tchr. homemaking Walnut Grove (Miss.) public schs., Hickory (Miss.) public schs., Carthage (Miss.) public schs., 1950-56; asst. prof. homemaking Miss. Valley State U., Itta Bena, 1956-58, acting head homemaking, 1956-57, dietitian, 1959-75, operation mgr., 1975-77, asst. food service dir., 1978—; substitute tchr. Orange County Schs., Orlando, Fla., 1953; advisor and cons. in food service. Health and welfare rep. Wesley United Meth. Ch., Greenwood, Miss., 1974-79. Recipient Citation for meritorious service Miss. Valley State U. Alumni Assn., 1971. Mem. Internat. Food Service Assn., Rust Coll. Alumni Assn., Tenn. State U. Alumni Assn., Phi Delta Kappa, Zeta Phi Beta. Clubs: A.C.W. White Social, Progressive, United Meth. Women, Order Eastern Star, Heroines of Jerico. Home: 102 Magnolia Circle Itta Bena MS 38941 Office: Miss Valley State Univ PO Box 151 Itta Bena MS 38941

COPELAND, MURRAY M., physician, educator; b. McDonough, Ga., June 23, 1902; s. Edward Meadows and Mary Elizabeth (Speer) C.; A.B., Oglethorpe U., 1923, D.Sc., 1955; M.D., Johns Hopkins U., 1927; m. Jean Brown, June 20, 1931. Intern, City Hosp., Balt., 1927-28; fellow Mayo Clinic, Rochester, Minn., 1929-30, Meml. Hosp., N.Y.C., 1930-33; resident surgery Union Meml. Hosp., Balt., 1933-37; instr. surgery U. Md., 1937-44, Johns Hopkins Med. Sch. and Hosp., 1937-46; chief surgery Kennedy VA Hosp., Memphis, 1946-47; prof. oncology, dir. dept. Georgetown U. Med. Center, Washington, 1947-60; asst. dir. M.D. Anderson Hosp. and Tumor Inst., 1960-62, prof. surgery, 1963—, asso. dir., 1962-67; v.p. internat. affairs U. Cancer Found., also prof. surgery U. Tex. M.D. Anderson Hosp. and Tumor Inst., 1963—; prof. surgery U. Tex. Med. Sch., Houston, 1971—; nat. project dir. Nat. Large Bowel Cancer Project, Nat. Cancer Inst., 1971—; clin. cons., clin. center Nat. Cancer Inst., NIH, USPHS, 1953-68, chmn. cancer control com., 1956-58, mem. nat. adv. cancer council, 1958-61, 66-69; dir.-at-large Am. Cancer Soc., 1957-67, nat. pres., 1964-65, pres. D.C. div., 1951-53; mem., chmn. Am. Joint Com. for Cancer Staging and End Result Reporting, 1959-69, Distinguished Service award, 1972; adv. com. Cancer Control Program, Bur. State Services, USPHS, 1963-66. Served from maj. to col., M.C., U.S. Army, 1942-45. Decorated Legion of Merit; recipient Distinguished Service award U. Tex.-M.D. Anderson Hosp. and Tumor Inst., 1968, Distinguished Service plaque as chmn. Commn. Cancer A.C.S., 1965. Diplomate Am. Bd. Surgery. Hon. fellow Am. Coll. Radiology; mem. Am. Assn. Cancer Research, Am. Med. Soc. Vienna (hon. life), Am. Radium Soc., James Ewing Soc. (past v.p., sr. mem. Annual award 1970), N.Y. Acad. Scis., Soc. Med. Cons. to Armed Forces, So. Surgeons Club (past pres.), So. Surg. Assn., Am. Orthopaedic Assn. (hon.), Am. Acad. Orthopaedic Surgeons (hon.), Soc. Head and Neck Surgeons, Internat. Union Against Cancer (mem. council 1966-78, v.p. for N.Am. 1970-74, sec.-gen. 10th Internat. Cancer Congress 1967-70), Southeastern Surg. Congress (pres. 1969, Distinguished Service award 1971, sec. gen. Internat. Study Group for Detection and Prevention of Cancer 1976-79). Author: (with C.F. Geschickter) Tumors of Bone, 1949. Contbr. numerous articles, textbook chpts. on problems of cancer. Home: 1600 Holcombe Blvd Houston TX 77030 Office: 6723 Bertner Ave Houston TX 77030

COPENHAVER, WILFRED MONROE, educator; b. Westminster, Md., Dec. 26, 1898; s. Clayton Monroe and Mary Ellen (Myers) C.; A.B., Western Md. Coll., 1921; Ph.D., Yale U., 1925; m. Ethel Marker, Dec. 31, 1927; children—Carl M., Richard M. Instr. anatomy U. Rochester, 1925-27, asst. prof., 1927-28; asst. prof. anatomy Coll. Physicians and Surgeons, Columbia U., N.Y.C., 1928-40, asso. prof., 1940-52, prof., 1952-67, prof. emeritus, 1967—, chmn. dept., 1957-66; prof. anatomy, interim chmn. U. Miami Med Sch., 1967-69, adj. prof., 1969—. NIH grantee, Fla. Heart Assn. grantee, 1968-69. Mem. AAAS, Am. Assn. Anatomists, Am. Soc. Zoologists, Electron Microcope Soc. Am., Soc. Exptl. and Biol. Medicine, Soc. Study Growth, Harvey Soc., N.Y. Acad. Scis., Sigma Xi. Author: (with D.E. Kelly and R.L. Wood) Bailey's Textbook of Histology, 17th edit., 1978. Contbr. articles to profl. jours. Home: 5980 SW 63d Ct Miami FL 33143 Office: Dept Anatomy Med School Univ Miami PO Box 520875 Biscayne Annex Miami FL 33152

COPPARI, LAWRENCE AMERICUS, mech. engr.; b. White Plains, N.Y., Jan. 5, 1946; s. Americus Victor and Jean Ann (Fiscella) C.; B.M.E., U. Va., 1968, M. Engring., 1970; Ph.D. in Mech. Engring., Va. Poly. Inst. and State U., 1977. Tchr. math. and physics Rock Hill Acad., Charlottesville, Va., 1970-71; pvt. investigator Uffinger and Assos., Charlottesville, 1970-72; grad. research asst. Va. Poly. Inst. and State U., Blacksburg, 1974-77; mech. engr. Tenn. Eastman Co., Kingsport, 1977—. Served to lt. U.S. Army, 1972-74. Recipient Research award Va. Poly. Inst. and State U., 1978; NDEA fellow U. Va., 1969. Mem. ASME, Sci. Research Soc., Sigma Xi. Contbr. articles to profl. jours. Home: 125 Crown Colony Kingsport TN 37660 Office: Tenn Eastman Co Bldg 54D Kingsport TN 37662

COPPIN, JOHN STEPHENS, artist, muralist, portrait painter; b. Mitchell, Ont., Can., Sept. 13, 1904; s. Thomas Pascoe and Maude (Levette) C.; stu., Stratford Collegiate Inst., 1918-21, Wicker Art Sch., 1923-27, study trip, Europe, 1938; m. Sidni Lovelace, Feb. 7, 1948; 1 son, Torry John. Art dir. Mich. Motor News, 1930-60; life drawing instr., 1928; free lance artist and illustrator, 1928—; portrait painter. Recipient Scarab gold medals, 1940, 1944, 1946, 48; Detroit Inst. Arts popular prize, 1933, 1939, 1946, 1950; Carl F. Clark award, 1953. Murals in Mich. Bar Assn. Bldg., Lansing, Detroit Central High Sch., Detroit Gas Co., Adam Strohm Hall, Detroit Pub. Library; works in Mich. Hist. Mus., Mich. Bar Assn. Bldg., Detroit Inst. Arts, Nat. Historic Mus., Mich. Capitol Bldg., Lansing, Alfred P. Sloan, Jr. Mus., Flint, Mich., Frederiksborg, Denmark, others. Portraits include Edgar A. Guest, Alvan McCauley, Mrs. Alfred Glancey, George Romney, Dr. Henry Vaughan, George W. Stark, Gordon J. Van Wylen; ofcl. portraits ex-governors Wagoner, Kelly and Sigler, G. Mennen Williams; Henry Ford, Paul Paray, Alec Guinness, Wm. S. Knudsen, James M. Roche and others; numerous commissioned portraits of prominent persons; hist. paintings Mich. State U. Fellow Internat. Inst. Arts and Letters; mem. Am. Fedn. Artists, Sarasota, Longboat Key art assns. Clubs: Prismatic (hon. pres.), Scarab (past pres.), Detroit Press, Acanthus (Detroit); St. Dunstan's Guild, Cranbrook (past pres.) (Bloomfield Hills, Mich.); Sarasota Yacht; Bird Key Yacht. Selected works of John S. Coppin, 1948; contbr. articles on art and travel. Home and Studio: 3D Key Towers S 1750 Benjamin Franklin Dr Sarasota FL 33577

COPPO, RICHARD HENRY, mech. engr.; b. Healdsburg, Calif., June 6, 1936; s. Mario Dominic and Maybelle Irene (King) C.; B.S. in Chem. Engring., U. Calif. at Berkeley, 1958; M.M.E., Sacramento State Coll., 1972; m. Gloria Isola Battella, June 22, 1958; children—Michael Paul, Carol Ann. Process chem. engr. Reichhold Chems. Corps., South San Francisco, 1958-59; design engr. Aerojet Nuclear Systems Co., Sacramento, 1961-66, sr. engr., 1966-72; supervisory engr., prin. engr. Nuclear Power div. Babcock & Wilcox, Lynchburg, Va., 1972—. Served with U.S. Army, 1959-61. Registered profl. engr., Va. Mem. ASME, Am. Nuclear Soc. (treas. Va. sect. 1976). Democrat. Roman Catholic. Home: 1045 Moreview Dr Lynchburg VA 24502 Office: Nuclear Power Gen Div PO Box 1260 Lynchburg VA 24505

COPPRIDGE, ALTON JAMES, urologist; b. Roanoke, Va., Dec. 8, 1926; s. William Maurice and Ferrie Patterson (Choate) C.; B.A., U. N.C., 1949; M.D., U. Va., 1953; m. Helen Allen Burnett, June 24, 1950; children—William Allen, Virginia Choate. Intern N.C. Meml. Hosp., Chapel Hill 1953; resident U. Iowa, Iowa City, 1954-56, U. Mich., Ann Arbor, 1956-59; practice medicine, specializing in urology, The Coppridge Urologic Group, Durham, N.C., 1959—; asst. clin. prof. urology Duke, Durham, 1970—, U. N.C., Chapel Hill, 1968—. Served with AUS, 1944-46. Diplomate Am. Bd. Urology. Fellow A.C.S.; mem. Am., S.E., Carolina urol. assns., AMA, N.C., Durham-Orange County (pres. 1978) med. socs., Phi Delta Theta, Phi Chi. Democrat. Presbyterian. Clubs: Durham Pistol and Rifle, Hope Valley Country, Safari Internat., Asso. Investors Durham (pres. 1948), Kiwanis. Contbr. articles to profl. jours. Home: 3605 Rugby Rd Durham NC 27707 Office: 923 Broad St Durham NC 27705

CORBETT, BRADFORD GARY, plastics and chems. co. exec.; b. N.Y.C., Oct. 5, 1937; s. Arthur and Luetta J. (Smith) C.; B.A., Wagner Coll., N.Y.C., 1960; m. Gunhilde Grunde, Oct. 29, 1960; children—Bradford Gary, Pamela, Todd. Sales serviceman Barrett div. Allied Chem. Corp., 1960-65, dir. sales plastics and bldg. products, 1965-66; pres. Universal Pipe & Plastics, Inc., 1966-70; pres. Robintech., Inc., Ft. Worth, 1970-74, chmn. bd., chief exec. officer, 1974—; chmn. bd. Tex. Rangers Baseball Club, Inc.; dir. First Nat. Bank Ft. Worth; chmn. bd. Plastiline, Inc. Active Internat. Trade Conf. of S.W., Southwestern Expn. and Fat Stock Show, Tex. Christian U. Research Found.; trustee Wagner Coll.; mem. adv. council Big Bros. Am. Recipient Spirit of Achievement award Jr. Achievement of Tarrant County, 1976. Mem. Am. League Profl. Baseball Clubs (exec. mem.), Young Pres.'s Orgn. Clubs: Petroleum; Met. (N.Y.C.); Aardvark Soc.; Shady Oaks Country; River Crest Country. Office: PO Box 2342 Fort Worth TX 76101

CORBETT, SARA TAYLOR, educator; b. Lancaster, S.C., Feb. 17, 1930; d. Ira Edward and Drucilla Idelle (Hinson) Taylor; student Berry Coll., 1947-51; B.S., U. Tenn., 1965, M.S., 1965; postgrad. U. S.C.; m. Leon W. Corbett, Jr., Dec. 17, 1952; children—Leon Edward, Walter Jeffery Craig Taylor. Bus. edn. tchr. Mt. Pisgah High Sch., Kershaw, S.C. 1951; bus. and distributive edn. tchr. Wagener (S.C.) High Sch., 1952-69; distributive edn. tchr. Wilson Vocat. Center,

Columbia, S.C., 1969-70; instr., dept. head devel. studies Midlands Tech. Coll., Columbia, 1970—. Co-chmn. Wagons-to-Wagener, 1979-80 Henry R. Richert grantee, 1967-68. Mem. Nat. Bus. Edn. Assn., Devel. Studies Assn., Am. Vocat. Assn., S.C. Edn. Assn. (life), Alpha Delta Kappa. Methodist. Club: Wagener Garden (pres. 1961, sec. 1970, treas. 1979). Home: PO Box 115 Wagener SC 29164 Office: Airport Campus Midlands Technical College West Columbia SC 29169

CORBITT, DUVON CLOUGH, educator; b. nr. Pearson, Ga., July 4, 1901; s. Martin S. and Minnie Frazier (Faircloth) C.; student Meridian Coll., 1918-20; A.B., Asbury Coll., 1923; M.A., Emory U., 1926; Ph.D., U. N.C., 1938; m. Roberta Day, June 3, 1924; 1 son, Duvon Clough. Head dept. English Candler Coll., Havana, Cuba, 1927-29, 31-43, 45-46; chmn. history dept. Columbia (S.C.) Coll., 1943-45; prof. history Asbury Coll., Wilmore, Ky., 1946-75, chmn. social studies div., 1946-67, research prof., 1974-78, research prof. emeritus, 1978—. Vis. prof. Fla. State U., Ohio State U., 1944, U. Omaha, 1945; lectr. Nat. Def. Edn. Act Lang. Inst., Vanderbilt U., 1963. Bd. dirs. Wildwood Chapel Mission, 1961-80. Recipient Marti Centenniel medal Cuba, 1955; decorated officer Carlos J. Finlay Order Merit (Cuba); Ky. Col. Mem. Latin Am. Studies Assn., Am., East Tenn., So. hist. assns., Sociedad Cubana de la Historia de la Medecina, Caribbean Studies Assn. Republican. Author: The Chinese in Cuba, 1944; A Study of the Chinese in Cuba 1847-1947, 1971. Contbr. to Latin America: A Guide to Historical Literature; also numerous articles, book revs. to profl. lit. Research in history of Cuba and the Caribbean. Home: 205 E Morrison St Wilmore KY 40390

CORBITT, GRETCHEN JOHNSON, educator; b. Delway, N.C., Dec. 20, 1920; d. Leondias Lafayette and May Octavia (Garner) Johnson; student Mars Jr. Coll., 1938-40; B.A., Meredith Coll., 1943; postgrad Appalachian State U., 1969; m. John Calvin Corbitt, Dec. 22, 1949; children—Nathan, Alzada Portillos, Gretchen Corbitt Robinson, Rebekah Corbitt Stephens. Tchr. gen. music Stanley County, N.C., 1965-66, Marion Sch., McDowell County, N.C., 1966—; dir. Foothills Children's Theater, Marion, N.C., 1972-73; pvt. tchr. piano lessons, 1952—; dir. West Marion Boys Choir, 1975-76; columnist McDowell News, Black Mountain News. Mem. Early Am. Soc., Music Educator Nat. Conf., N.C. Educators Conf., Nat. Guild of Piano Tchrs., McDowell Arts and Crafts Assn., N.C. Symphony Soc. (v.p. McDowell chpt. 1974—). Baptist. Club: Fedn. of Bus. Women (pres. local dist. chpt. 1953-55). Author: No Woman Had Gone, 1976. Home: PO Box 303 Ridgecrest NC 28770 Office: South State St Marion NC 28752

CORBITT, ROBERTA DAY, educator; b. Blue Mound, Kans., Oct. 20, 1902; d. Everett Webster and Anna Lucile (Bundy) Day; student Asbury Coll., 1921-23, Emory U., 1924-26; A.B., U. Chgo., 1941, M.A., 1941; Ph.D., U. Ky., 1955; m. Duvon Clough Corbitt, June 3, 1924; 1 son, Duvon Clough. Prof., Candler Coll., Havana, Cuba, 1937-43, 45-46; instr. history Columbia (S.C.) Coll., 1943-45; prof. Spanish, Asbury Coll., Wilmore, Ky., 1946—, chmn. div. langs., 1955-65, 66-68; dir. Wildwood Chapel Mission in Ky. Mountains, 1959—. Named to Order of Ky. Cols., 1965; named Outstanding Lady Tchr., Asbury Coll., 1972. Mem. Am. Assn. of Tchrs. of Spanish and Portuguese, Latin Am. Studies Assn., Midwest Council for Latin Am. Studies, NEA, Ky. Edn. Assn., Carribean Studies Assn., Asbury Alumni Assn. (recipient A award 1972), Phi Sigma Iota. Republican. Methodist. Club: Asbury Anns. Contbr. articles to profl. jours. Home: 205 E Morrison St Wilmore KY 40390 Office: Asbury College Wilmore KY 40390

CORBOY, LOU ANN LANCASTER, social worker; b. Dallas, Feb. 12, 1939; d. Charles Dean and Grace (Stephens) Lancaster; B.A. in Anthropology, U. Tex., 1960, M.S.W., 1972; m. Michael Robert Corboy, Sept. 6, 1975. Adminstrv. asst. Braniff Internat. Airlines, Dallas, 1960-69; adminstrv. asst., exec. sec. F.S. Smithers & Co., Inc., N.Y.C., 1969-70; adminstr. Dallas County Mental Health and Mental Retardation Center, 1972-78; coordinator consultation and edn., coordinator Irving Mental Health Center, Dallas. Bd. dirs. Dallas Epilepsy Assn.; mem. adv. bd. Dallas Ind. Sch. Dist., Spl. Edn. Dept., 1976, Nat. Task Force on Consultation and Edn., 1976. Named Goodfellow Outstanding Student, U. Tex. Yearbook, 1960. HEW grantee, 1976-77. Mem. Nat. Assn. Social Workers (dir. Tex. chpt.), Acad. Certified Social Workers, Nat. Council Community Mental Health Centers, Alpha Delta Pi. Roman Catholic. Clubs: Las Colinas Country, Slipper, Cotillion, 500, Inc. (Dallas). Author: (with Joe Fogle) Competency Assessment Model for Consulation and Education, 1976. Co-author, exec. producer manual and video tape The Good Vibes Workshop, 1977-78. Home: 3883 Turtle Creek Dallas TX 75219

CORCORAN, VINCENT JOHN, elec. engr.; b. Chgo., Oct. 7, 1934; s. Vincent Anthony and Mae (DeNardo) C.; student Fournier Inst. Tech., 1952-55; B.S. (A.J. Schmidt Found. scholar), U. Notre Dame, 1957; M.S., U. Ill., 1958; postgrad. Ill. Inst. Tech., 1958-63; Ph.D., U. Fla., 1968; m. Anne Marie Fitzgerald, June 29, 1957; children—Kevin V., Margaret M., Kathleen M., Karen M., Brian J. Mem. staff U. Chgo. Lab. Applied Scis., 1958-62; v.p. Astromarine Products Corp., Melrose Park, Ill., 1962-63; sr. research scientist, aerospace div. Martin Marietta corp., Orlando, Fla., 1963-73; research staff mem. Inst. Def. Analyses, Arlington, Va., 1973—. Adj. prof. Rollins Coll., Winter Park, Fla., 1972-73; cons. radiation Stanford Co., 1962, Motorola, Inc., 1963, Martin Marietta Corp., 1967-68; dir. Q.E.D. Corp., 1968-73, Ecoterra, Inc., 1971—; chmn. working group D (lasers) Adv. Group on Electron Devices. Recipient Achievement award Martin Marietta Co., 1965. Mem. IEEE. Clubs: Notre Dame Alumni; Fournier Alumni (v.p. 1961-63) (Chgo.). Contbr. articles in field to profl. jours. Home: 2034 Freedom Ln Falls Church VA 22043 Office: 400 Army-Navy Dr Arlington VA 22202

CORDELL, ALFRED ROBERT, med. educator; b. Union, S.C., Oct. 16, 1924; s. Carl Eugene and Ann Louise (Elsmore) C.; B.S., U. N.C., 1944; M.D., Johns Hopkins, 1947; m. DeWitt Bynum Cromer, June 4, 1955; children—Alfred Robert, Franklin Cromer, Carl DeWitt, Mark Bynum. Intern Johns Hopkins Hosp., Balt., 1947-48; resident Yale VA Service, Newington, Conn., 1948-50, N.C. Baptist Hosp., Bowman Gray Sch. Medicine, Winston Salem, 1952-56; vis. instr. U. Buffalo Med. Sch., 1956-57; dir. surg. research Bowman Gray Med. Sch., Winston Salem, N.C., 1957-59, instr., 1957-61, asst. prof., 1961-65, asso. prof., 1965-70, prof., 1970—, chmn. sect. cardiothoracic surgery, 1979—, attending surgeon N.C. Bapt. Hosp., 1957—. Bd. dirs. N.C. Heart Assn., 1965—. Served with AUS, 1950-52. Recipient grants N.C. Heart Assn., NIH, Nat. Heart Inst. Diplomate Am. Bd. Surgery, Am. Bd. Thoracic Surgery, Nat. Bd. Med. Examiners. Mem. A.C.S., Am. Surg. Assn., Am. Assn. Thoracic Surgery, So. Surg. Assn., So. Thoracic Surg. Assn., Southeastern Surg. Congress, Am. Coll. Cardiology, Soc. Vascular Surgery, Soc. Thoracic Surgeons, Internat. Cardiovascular Soc., Internat. Surg. Soc., So. Soc. Vascular Surgery (mem. council), AMA, Am. Heart Assn. (fellow council on cardiology), N.C. Heart Assn., Pan Pacific Surg. Assn., Sigma Xi. Editor: Complications of Intrathoracic Surgery, 1979; contbr. articles to profl. jours. Home: 349 Arbor Rd Winston Salem NC 27104 Office: Bowman Gray Med Sch Winston Salem NC 27103

CORDELL, JERRY RALPH, real estate co. exec.; b. Elizabethton, Tenn., Jan. 11, 1942; s. Milburn Earl and Leta Evelyn (Eggers) C.; B.S., E. Tenn. State U., 1963; postgrad. U. Tenn., 1974—; children—Amy Beth, Aaron Brent. With Union Camp Corp., Morristown, Tenn., 1969-73; sales asso. Home Realty Co., Decatur, Ala., 1973, sales mgr., 1973-75; sales mgr. So. Oaks Realtors, Decatur, 1975-76; owner, mgr. Heritage Homes, Decatur, 1976—, Athens, Ala., 1978—; pres. Investment Properties, Inc., 1973-78; lectr. Calhoun Community Coll. Active Boys Scouts Am.; chmn. March of Dimes, Decatur, 1974-75, Morgan County, Ala., 1974-75; com. chmn. Spirit of Am. Festival, Decatur; dir. Decatur (Ala.) Our Little Miss Pageant, 1974-75, Miss Tenn. Valley Exposition Beauty Pageant, 1974-76. Served with U.S. Army, 1963-69. Decorated Air medal with 15 oak leaf clusters, Army Commendation medal; cert. residential specialist. Mem. Morgan County Bd. Realtors (pres. 1976-77, dir. 1978— Realtor of Yr. 1977), Ala. Assn. Realtors (state dir. 1976-80), Ala. Realtors Inst. (regional dir. N. Ala. Dist.), Realtors Nat. Mktg. Inst., Jaycees. Democrat. Baptist. Club: Masons. Home: 1612 Dandridge St SW Decatur AL 35601 Office: 1402 6th Ave SE Decatur AL 35601

CORGI, REMY (TELEMACHUS), financial co. exec.; b. Eng., May 1, 1928; s. Harry and Freida (Fotherington-Thomas) C.; came to U.S., 1965, naturalized, 1976; M.A. in Econs., Oxford U., 1949. Dept. mgr. Imperial Chem. Industries, Ltd. (Eng.), 1955-65; mgmt. cons., London, 1965-66; pres. South Mortgage Co., Atlanta, 1967—; lectr. macro-econs. Merde Poly. Inst., 1960-63. Bd. dirs. Second Montessori Sch. of Atlanta. Mem. League U.S. Savs. and Loan Instns. (area chmn.). Democrat. Baptist. Clubs: West Paces Ferry Racquet (Atlanta); Royal Thames Yacht (Eng.). Home: The Habersham Pharr Ct Atlanta GA 30305 Office: South Mortgage Co 3928 Ivy Rd Atlanta GA 30342

CORKILL, JAMES MERRIC, engring. cons.; b. Enid, Okla., Aug. 14, 1945; s. John Merric and Alyce Vinita (Mitchell) C.; B.S. in Environ. Design, U. Okla., 1975; student Ill. State U., 1964-65; m. Janice Gail Christy, Dec. 17, 1977; children—Shannon Merric, Christa Rhea. Commd. capt. U.S. Army, 1965, advanced through grades to maj., 1979; loss prevention cons. Factory Mut. Engring., Maryland Heights, Mo., 1975, resident cons., 1976; sec.-treas. Two Prairie Oil Co., Inc., Carlisle, Ark., 1977—. Decorated Air medal, Army Commendation medal, Bronze Star. Mem. Nat. Fedn. Ind. Businessmen (action council mem. 1978-79), Am. Mgmt. Assn., Ark. Oil Marketers Assn., So. Bldg. Code Congress Internat., Res. Officers Assn., Carlisle C. of C., VFW (post comdr.), Am. Legion. Republican. Baptist. Club: Lions. Home: PO Box 604 Carlisle AR 72024 Office: Route 2 Box 15B Carlisle AR 72024

CORKRIN, MARTHA ANNE, indsl. editor; b. Newark, June 21, 1943; d. Blaine Edward and Ellen Leah (King) Shoun; student East Tenn. State U., 1961; B.A., Augusta (Ga.) Coll., 1975; m. Clay Wayne Corkrin, May 15, 1962 (Dec. Sept. 1972); children—Tami Kaye and Toni Gaye (twins), Patrick Darrin. Writer, asst. women's editor Johnson City (Tenn.) Press-Chronicle, 1961-62; library asst. Cambrai-Fritsch Library, Darmstadt, W. Ger., 1964-65; asst. femina editor European edit. Stars & Stripes, 1965-66; sec. to chmn. polit. sci. dept. East Tenn. State U., 1966; writer, asst. news editor Morristown (Tenn.) Citizen-Tribune, 1966-67; news and features writer Augusta (Ga.) Chronicle, 1972; editor, photographer, writer, designer Graniteville Bull., Graniteville Co. (S.C.), 1976—; participant Working Women Conf., 1979. Lay reader St. Bartholomew's Episcopal Ch., North Augusta, S.C., also editor The Scroll newsletter. Named Outstanding Young Woman of Yr., Gen. Fedn. Women's Clubs, 1978. Mem. Internat. Assn. Bus. Communicators (awards dist. II 1977), Carolinas Assn. Bus. Communicators (awards 1977, 78), Augusta Assn. Bus. Communicators (pres. 1978), Greater Augusta Advt. Club (award 1977, 78, 79). Contbr. articles to various publs., also poetry. Home: 619 Kershaw Dr Belvedere SC 29841

CORLETT, WILLIAM ALBERT, aerospace engr.; b. Talala, Okla., Mar. 5, 1938; s. William Forest and Floy Opal (Gill) C.; B.S. in Mech. Engring., U. Okla., 1962; m. Patricia Anne Harrison, May 31, 1964; children—William Edward, Cynthia Anne, Mary Anne. Aerospace engr. NASA Langley Research Center, Hampton, Va., 1962—, supr., head exptl. methods sect., 1975-77; mgr. unitary plan wind tunnel facilities, 1977-79, head unitary wind tunnel sect., 1979—; cons. aerodynamic revisions Hawk missile U.S. Army Missile Command, 1969. Recipient Apollo achievement award NASA, 1969, achievement award, 1976. Mem. Am. Inst. Aeros. and Astronautics, Air Force Assn. Baptist (deacon). Contbr. articles to profl. jours. Home: 24 Laurelwood Rd Newport News VA 23602 Office: NASA Langley Research Center Hampton VA 23665

CORLEW, JOHN GORDON, lawyer, state ofcl.; b. Dyersburg, Tenn., July 13, 1943; s. Emmett Atkins and Margaret (Swann) C.; B.A., U. Miss., 1965; J.D., Vanderbilt U., 1968; m. Elizabeth Lee Scott, July 8, 1967; children—John Scott, William Heath. Admitted to Miss. bar, 1968; law clk. U.S. Dist. Judge, Miss., 1968-69; individual practice law, Pascagoula, Miss., 1969—; mem. Miss. State Senate, 1974-80. Mem. Am. Bar Assn., Fed. Bar Assn. (past Miss. v.p.), Miss. Bar Assn., Jackson County Bar Assn. (past pres.). Democrat. Methodist. Office: PO Box 1959 Pascagoula MS 39567

CORLEY, ELLEN CATHERINE, speech pathologist; b. Columbia, S.C., July 24, 1951; d. John Walter and Nell Catherine (Jones) C.; B.A., Columbia Coll., 1973; M.S.P., U. S.C., 1977. Distbr., Vivian Woodard Cosmetics, Columbia, 1973-74; speech pathologist Oconee County Schs., Walhalla, S.C., 1974-76, Sch. Dist. Greenville County, S.C., 1977-80; pvt. practice speech pathology, Greenville, 1980—; profl. clown, mime, story teller. Mem. Am. Speech, Lang. and Hearing Assn., Internat. Assn. Logopedics and Phoniatrics, S.C. Speech and Hearing Assn., Greenville County Speech and Hearing Assn. Episcopalian. Producer film: A Stranger No More, 1977. Home: 413 Cary St Greenville SC 29609

CORLEY, JOHN BRYSON, physician; b. Calgary, Alta., Can., Aug. 29, 1913; s. Robert Bryson and Anna May (Amos) C.; B.A. with honors in Psychology, U. Alta., 1936, M.D., 1942; m. Lidje Corley de Jong, May 23, 1947; children—Nolly Elisabeth, James Bryson. Intern, Univ. Hosp., Edmonton, Alta., 1942; practice medicine, Sundre, Alta.; resident Col. Belcher Hosp., Calgary, 1946-47; family physician Chinook Med. Clinic, Calgary, 1946-73; chief examiner Coll. Family Physicians Can., 1969-73; asst. prof. dept. ednl. planning and assessment Faculty Medicine, U. Calgary (Alta., Can.), 1969-73; asso. prof. dept. family practice Med. U. S.C., Charleston, after 1973, now prof., also chief div. evaluation; dir. Canadian Project for Devel. Post-grad. Tng. in Family Medicine, 1967-70. Served to maj. Canadian Army, 1942-45; ETO. Mem. Canadian Med. Assn. (chmn. sect. gen. practice 1962-64), Coll. Family Physicians Can. (hon. treas. 1969-71), Am. Soc. Clin. Hypnosis (1st v.p. 1971-72). Asso. editor Self Assessment, Jour. Continuing Edn. Home: 588 Oyster Rake Kiawah Johns Island SC 29455

CORLEY, THOMAS EDWARD, physician; b. Prentiss, Miss., Feb. 28, 1938; s. Suber Singleton and Willie Rite (Morie) C.; B.S., Millsaps Coll., 1959; M.D., U. Miss., 1963; m. Caroline Moore, Sept. 3, 1961; children—Thomas Edward, Cheryl Ann, Alice Traci. Intern, U. Miss. Med. Center, 1963-64; practice medicine specializing in urology, Pompano Beach, Fla., 1972—; mem. staff N. Broward, Cypress Community hosps., Pompano Beach, Imperial Point Med. Center, N. Ridge Gen. Hosp., Ft. Lauderdale, Fla. Served to comdr. M.C., USN, 1964-72. Diplomate Am. Bd. Urology. Mem. Broward County Med. Assn., Fla. Med. Assn., AMA, Am. Urol. Assn., Am. Fertility Soc. Home: 1580 SE 9th St Deerfield Beach FL 33441 Office: 1 W Sample Rd Pompano Beach FL 33064

CORLIN, RODNEY BRUCE, mgmt. cons.; b. Detroit, June 2, 1951; s. Sherwin Walter and Charlotte Corlin; B.S. in Elec. Engring., M.I.T., 1973; M.B.A. (Celanese fellow), Harvard U., 1977. Cons., Tech. Mgmt., Inc., Cambridge, Mass., 1973-74; sr. engring. programmer Instron Corp., Canton, Mass., 1974-75; analyst Am. Mgmt. Systems, Inc., Arlington, Va., 1977—. Mem. Assn. M.B.A. Execs. Home: 1301 S Scott St Apt 727 Arlington VA 22204 Office: 1515 Wilson Blvd Arlington VA 22209

CORMACK, DONALD EDWARD, engring. cons. co. exec.; b. Baton Rouge, Oct. 27, 1943; s. Leeman Jewell and Madge Marcille (Cole) C.; B.S. in Math., Northwestern State Coll., 1966; A.S. in Computer Sci., Tulane U., 1971; m. Mary Ellen Monk, Sept. 10, 1966; children—Deborah Lee, Nichole Marie. Production technician Union Carbide Corp., Taft, La., 1966-69, computer technician, 1969-72; systems analyst Biles & Assos., Houston, 1972-76, project mgr., 1976-77; projects mgr. Setpoint, Inc., Houston, 1977-79, dept. mgr., 1979—, sec.-treas., 1978—. Registered profl. engr., Calif. Mem. Instrument Soc. Am., Am. Inst. Chem. Engrs. Home: 22343 N Rebecca Burwell St Katy TX 77450 Office: 901 Threadneedle St Suite 150 Houston TX 77079

CORNELIUS, CYNTHIA KAY, social worker; b. Midland, Tex., Oct. 4, 1954; d. Bryant Thompson and Maggie Lee Cornelius; B.A., Eastern N.Mex. U., 1976; M.S.W., Ariz. State U., 1978. Directory assistance operator Southwestern Bell Telephone, Midland, 1971; sales clk. G.F. Wacker's, Midland, 1971-72; asst. dir. black affairs Eastern N.Mex. U., 1974-75, asst. Office of Asst. to V.P. Student Affairs, 1975-76, counselor Upward Bound program, 1976; social work Eastern N.Mex. Rehab. Service Center for Handicapped, Inc., Clovis, 1975; assembly line worker Tex. Instruments, Midland, 1977; psychiat. social worker VA Hosp., Tucson, 1977-78; caseworker Tex. Dept. Mental Health and Mental Retardation, San Angelo, 1978—. Recipient N.Mex. Black Econ. League, Black Leadership Conf. Youth Citizen award, 1975. Mem. Nat. Assn. Social Workers, Nat. Assn. Black Social Workers, Am. Assn. Mental Deficiency, Council on Social Work Edn., NAACP, Nat. Council Negro Women, Delta Sigma Theta. Baptist. Home: 102 W 19th St San Angelo TX 76901 Office: San Angelo Center Carlsbad TX 76934

CORNELL, JOHN FRANK, engring. reprographics co. exec.; b. Wilkes-Barre, Pa., July 26, 1942; s. Frank John and Ann (Potsko) C.; B.A., King's Coll., 1966; postgrad. U. Detroit, 1972; m. Carol Ann Johnson, July 16, 1966; children—John Christopher, Jeffrey Todd. Plant mgr. photo products dept. E.I. duPont de Nemours, Brevard, N.C., 1966-68, tech. sales rep., Niles, Ill., 1968-72; v.p., co-owner Engring. Reprographics Assos., Inc., Greenville, S.C., 1972—; acting dir., sec. Ind.-U.S. Internat. Packaging Corp., Easely, S.C., 1978—. Bd. dirs. Northwood Little League, 1979, Pebble Creek Country Club Homeowners Assn., 1979-80; active YMCA Indian Guides. Mem. Nat. Micrographics Assn., Internat. Reprographic/Blueprinters Assn., Southeastern Blueprinters Assn., C. of C. Republican. Methodist. Club: St. Giles Soccer. Home: 5 Ginger Ln Taylors SC 29687 Office: Route 5 Donkle Dr Greenville SC 29609

CORNELSON, GEORGE HENRY, textile co. exec.; b. Spartanburg, S.C., July 12, 1931; s. George Henry and Elizabeth (Woodward) C.; student Davidson Coll., 1949-51; B.S., N.C. State U., 1953; postgrad. Harvard U., 1953-54; m. Ann Martin Shaw, Oct. 6, 1956; children—George Henry, Martin S., Scott M., Elizabeth W. With Clinton Mills, Inc. (S.C.), 1954—, v.p., 1958, exec. v.p., 1970, pres., 1979—, also dir.; dir. Elastic Fabrics of Am., Ft. Washington, Pa., M.S. Bailey Bankers, Clinton, S.C. Mem. Greater Clinton Planning Commn., 1969. Served with USAF, 1955-57. Named Outstanding Young Alumnus, N.C. State U., 1965. Mem. Clinton C. of C. (pres. 1969, dir. 1966-68), S.C. C. of C. (dir. exec. com. 1975-78), S.C. Textile Mfrs. Assn. (pres. 1979—), Am. Textile Mfrs. Inst. Presbyterian. Club: Lions (dep. dist. gov. 1969-70). Home: Merrie Oaks Clinton SC 29325 Office: Drawer 1215 Clinton SC 29325

CORNET, BRUCE, paleopalynologist; b. Bryn Mawr, Pa., Aug. 31, 1945; s. Walter Bruce and Elizabeth Birge C.; student Fairleigh Dickinson U., 1963-66; B.A. with high honors, U. Conn., 1968-70, M.S., 1973; Ph.D., Pa. State U., 1977; m. Virginia Jean Skoll, Jan. 29, 1972 (div. 1979). Sr. geologist Gulf Research & Devel. Co., Houston, 1977—. Hon. curator paleobotany Houston Mus. Natural Sci.; bd. dirs. Dilton House Homeowners Assn., 1979-80. Mem. Am. Assn. Stratigraphic Palynologists, Bot. Soc. Am., Am. Inst. Biol. Scis., Soc. Vertebrate Paleontology, Paleontol. Soc., Houston Gem and Mineral Soc., Bromeliad Soc., Sigma Xi, Phi Kappa Phi, Phi Zeta Kappa. Republican. Home: Unit 138 7900 Westheimer Rd Houston TX 77063 Office: Gulf Research and Devel Co Houston Tech Services Center PO Box 36506 Houston TX 77036

CORNETT, KENNETH ROSS, investment exec.; b. San Antonio, Apr. 28, 1942; s. Julian Arthur and Ruby D. (Garrett) Mack; B.S., SW Tex. State U., 1965; m. Penny Jean Bickerstaff, Aug. 2, 1963; children—Kevin, Kyle, Casey. With Burroughs Wellcome & Co., Beamont, Tex., 1965-66; stockbroker Paine, Webber, Jackson & Curtis, Houston, 1970-73; partner Sandman & Cornett, Houston, 1974-76, Cornett & Assos., Houston, 1977, Cornett-Mead & Assos., Houston, 1977-78, Cornett Investment Corp., 1979—. Served as capt. Med. Service Corps, U.S. Army, 1966-70. Decorated Bronze Star. Mem. Internat. Assn. Fin. Planners, Coll. Fin. Planning. Club: Optimist (pres. Houston Downtown 1975-76). Home: 223 Green Forest Dr Spring TX 77373 Office: 11947 N Freeway Suite 610 Houston TX 77060

CORNISH, ROBERT SANFORD, educator; b. Mpls., Apr. 29, 1925; s. Harvey Clifford and Ethel Bertha (Johnson) C.; student Humboldt State Coll., 1947; A.A., U. Calif., Berkeley, 1949, B.A. in Architecture, 1951, M.C.P., 1958; postgrad. U. Pa., 1956-57. Self-employed city planner, San Francisco, 1960-62; project dir. Wilsey, Ham & Blair, San Mateo, Calif., 1962-64; prin. planner Assn. Bay Area Govts., Berkeley, 1964-69; prof. regional planning Tex. A. & M., College Station, 1969—; partner Veedercrest Vineyards, Napa County, Calif.; Fulbright sr. scholar U. Tehran, 1978, U. Stockholm, 1979. Mem. Citizens Planning Adv. Com., College Station, 1974, Community Center Site Selection Study Com., 1975-77; del. Tex. Assembly on Land Use, 1974. Served with U.S. Mcht. Marines, 1943-47. Recipient Higher Edn. ACT grant, 1974—. Mem. Am. Soc. Planning Ofcls., Am. Planning Assn. (v.p. Tex. chpt. 1973-77, Outstanding Service award 1971, 77, Outstanding Merit award 1973, Outstanding Service award 1977), Am. Inst. Cert. Planners (exec. com. Tex. chpt., chmn. planning com.). Episcopalian. Club: Houston Yacht. Contbr. articles to profl. jours. Home: 1214 Orr St College Station TX 77840

CORNWALL, E(SPIE) JUDSON, clergyman, author; b. San Jose, Calif., Aug. 15, 1924; s. Espie James and Beulah Vera C.; student So. Calif. Coll., 1941-44; m. Eleanor Louise Eaton, June 20, 1943; children—Dorothy Darlene, Eleanor Jean, Justine Iverna. Ordained to ministry Assemblies of God, 1946, Evangelical Ch. Alliance, 1976; pastor, Stirling City, Calif., 1946-47, Kennewick, Wash., 1948-54, Yakima, Wash., 1955-58, Eugene, Oreg., 1959-72; tchr. Central Wash. Sch. Bible, Selah, 1956-58; author: Let Us Praise, 1973; Let Us Draw Near, 1977; Let Us Abide, 1977; Let Us Enjoy Forgiveness, 1978; Let Us Be Holy, 1978; Heaven, 1978; Please Receive Me, 1979. Home: 2850 Dove Pond Rd Grapevine TX 76051 Office: 210 Abrams Richardson TX 75081

CORNWELL, EUGENE (GENE) HOWE, JR., publisher; b. Healdton, Okla., June 11, 1929; s. Eugene Howe and Mary Katherine (Parrett) C.; B.A. in English and Edn., Baylor U., 1950; m. Mildred Ogles, June 11, 1948; 1 dau., Katherine Jean Cornwell Brooks. Contract circulation distbr. Waco (Tex.) Tribune Herald, 1950-55; tchr. Waco public schs., 1955-56; contract circulation distbr. Beaumont (Tex.) Enterprise and Jour., 1956-58, city circulation mgr., 1958-61, circulation mgr., 1962-72, bus. mgr., 1973-75, pub., 1975—; sr. v.p. The Enterprise Co., Beaumont. Mem. exec. com. Central City Devel. Corp., Beaumont, 1978—; bd. councilors St. Elizabeth Hosp., Beaumont. Mem. Beaumont C. of C., Tex. Daily Newspaper Assn., Am. Newspaper Pubs. Assn., Tex. Assn. Bus., Tes. Research League. Presbyterian. Clubs: Rotary, Beaumont. Home: 680 Goodhue Rd Beaumont TX 77706 Office: 380 Walnut St Beaumont TX 77701

CORPORON, WILLIAM LEWIS, physician; b. Independence, Kans., Jan. 10, 1945; s. Lewis Leonard and Helen Maxine (Church) C.; B.A., Phillips U., 1967; M.D., U. Okla., 1972; m. Melinda Ann Gordy, Mar. 20, 1965; children—William Travis, Melinda Katherine, Anthony Coulter. Intern, Bapt. Med. Center, Oklahoma City, 1972-73; practice gen. medicine, Perry, Okla., 1973-75; gen. practice, med. dir. Family Medicine of Marlow (Okla.), 1975—; mem. staff Talley Walker Hosp., Marlow, Duncan (Okla.) Regional Hosp. Chmn. Marlow Med. Adv. Com., 1978—. Recipient Okla. Trauma Research Soc. Recognition award, 1977; Fellow Am. Acad. Family Practice; mem. Stephens County Med. Assn. (pres. 1977-78), AMA (Physicians Recognition award 1978), Okla. Med. Assn., Blue Key. Republican. Presbyterian (elder). Club: Lions. Home: 1401 S 9th St Marlow OK 73055 Office: 505 N 4th St Marlow OK 73055

CORPUZ AMBROSIO, ERLINDA BALANCIO, pediatrician; b. Itogon, Mt. Province, Philippines, Mar., 1943; d. Ricardo R. and Petra (Balancio) C.; came to U. S., 1965; B.A. in Medicine, M.D., 1965; m. Jan. 6, 1968; children—Cecilia, Ruth. Intern, Church Home and Hosp., Balt., 1965-66; resident in pediatrics Lincoln Hosp., Bronx, N.Y., 1966-68, chief, 1968-69, fellow in neonatology, 1969-70; practice medicine specializing in pediatrics, Spencer, W.Va., 1971—; chief staff Roane Gen. Hosp., 1975-76, sec., 1972-74; asst. instr. Albert Einstein Coll. Medicine, Yeshiva U., 1968-70; part-time pub. health clinician Dept. Health N.Y.C., 1970-71. Diplomate Am. Bd. Pediatrics. Mem. AMA, W.Va. State Med. Assn., W.Va. Med. Inst., Parkersburg Acad. Home: 502 Parkersburg Rd Spencer WV 25276 Office: 300 Hospital Dr Spencer WV 25276

CORRADA, BALTASAR, Congressman; b. Morovis, P.R., Apr. 10, 1935; s. Romulo and Ana Maria (Del Rio) C.; B.A. in Social Scis., U. P.R., 1956, J.D., 1959; m. Beatriz Betances, Dec. 24, 1959; children—Ana Isabel, Francisco Javier, Juan Carlos, Jose Baltasar. Admitted to P.R. bar, 1959; practiced in San Juan, 1959-76; chmn. Civil Rights Commn. of P.R., 1970-72; pres. editorial bd. P.R. Human Rights Rev., 1971-72; mem. 95th Congress as resident commr. from P.R. Founder, dir. P.R. Teleradial Inst. Ethics. Mem. Fed., P.R. bar assns. New Progressive. Roman Catholic. Club: Exchange. Home: 154 Tulipan St Rio Piedras PR 00927 Office: Ho of Reps Washington DC 20515

CORRADO, BENJAMIN WILLIAM, marketing cons.; b. Bklyn., July 16, 1911; s. Anthony and Genevieve (La Guardia) C.; student Sch. Commerce, N.Y. U., 1930-32; m. Virginia M. McCormick, June 23, 1939. Chief statisician, investment counsellor Standard Statistics Co.; news editor, Washington editor Am. Machinist; Cleve. editor Iron Age mag.; metals and beverage specialist Poor's Pub. Co.; asst. pub. relations dir. Am. Iron and Steel Inst., 1946-48; coordinator advt., spl. asst. to pres. Market Research Dir., Publicker Industries, Inc., 1948-50; research cons., beverage Specialist, 1950-55; v.p. charge market research Nat. Distillers Products Co., 1955-66; v.p. industry relations Nat. Distillers & Chem. Corp., 1966-72; marketing cons., broker Benjamin W. Corrado Assos., 1972—. Jr. economist, munitions br. WPB, 1943; v.p. dir. Bourbon Inst.; v.p., dir. Ky. Distillers Assn.; v.p. Md. Distillers Assn.; author nat. liquor consumption estimate by states and by types, 1950-54; per diem cons. NPA, 1951-52. Recipient indsl. marketing award of merit for best pub. research Am. Machinist, 1945. Mem. Am. Legion, Nat. Assn. Bus. Economists, Am. Marketing Assn. Asso. Cooperage Ind. Am. Club: Nat. Press (Washington). Author: Distilled Spirits Industry-Public Revenues, 1943; Newsweek Liquor Advt. Exp. Mags., 1951, 52, 53, 54; Trne's Beer Consumption Report, 1952, 53; Am. Mag. Wine Consumption Report, 1952, 53; Liquor Marketing Handbook, 1954, 55; Alcoholic Beverage Control, 1973; U.S. News Wine and Spirits Mktg. Bull., 1974-80; contbr. articles to nat. mags. Home: 401 Briny Ave Pompano Beach FL 33062

CORRELL, NOBLE OTTO, JR., surgeon; b. Robinson, Ill., July 16, 1920; s. Noble Otto and Margaret (Hull) C.; B.S., Ind. State U., 1942; M.S., U. Ill., 1950, M.D., 1950; m. Violet Butler, June 25, 1944. Intern, U.S. Naval Hosp., San Diego, surg. resident VA Hosp., Hines, Ill., 1951-54; thoracic resident and fellow Presbyn.-St. Lukes Hosp., Chgo., 1955-57; chief-of-surgery Community Meml. Gen. Hosp., LaGrange, Ill., 1962-64, Luth. Gen. Hosp., Park Ridge, Ill., 1965-67, pres. med. staff, 1970-72; asso. clin. prof. U. Ill., 1973—; dir. continuing med. edn. Cypress Community Hosp., Pompano Beach, Fla., 1975-78. Pres., Margaret H. Correll Research Found. Served from ensign to lt. USNR, 1942-46. Fellow Am. Coll. Chest Physicians; mem. Midwest Surg. Soc., Am. Council Med. Staffs (v.p. 1972-80, pres. No. Ill. chpt. 1971-73), Ill. Thoracic Surg. Soc. (founder, pres. 1970). Contbr. articles to profl. jours. Home: 2360 NE 8th Ave Pompano Beach FL 33064 Office: 501 E Osceola St Stuart FL 33494

CORSARO, WINNIE LOUISE, real estate broker; b. Livingston, Tex., June 19, 1939; d. Ulys S. and Beatrice (Stokes) McKinney; student Alvin Jr. Coll., 1957-58, Coll. of Mainland, 1970-72; m. Frank John Corsaro, June 28, 1958; children—Kimberly Denise, Kathi Dawn, Frank John. Mgr., E. I. Tarin & Co., Alta Loma, Tex., 1970-74; partner Tarin & Corsaro, Realtors, Alta Loma, 1974-75; owner Corsaro Real Estate, Alta Loma, 1975—; owner The Lemon Tree Dress Shop, Alta Loma; parnter C & O Investments, Alta Loma, 1974—. Pres., Santa Fe Indsl. Devel. Found.; chmn. Santa Fe Adv. Com.; mem. Santa Fe Charter Commn. Lic. real estate broker, Tex. Mem. Tex., Nat. assns. realtors, LaMargue-Texas City, Gulf Coast bds. realtors, Bus. Women of Am., Beta Sigma Phi (named Girl of the Year 1969). Home: 12228 11th St Santa Fe TX 77510 Office: C & O Center Santa Fe TX 77510

CORSE, JOHN DOGGETT, lawyer; b. Jacksonville, Fla., Mar. 16, 1924; s. Herbert Montgomery and Carita Ann (Doggett) C.; B.S., U.S. Naval Acad., 1946; LL.B., U. Va., 1957; m. Margaret Murchison, Aug. 4, 1951; children—Carita Doggett, Cameron Murchison, John Doggett, Margaret Murchison. Admitted to Fla. bar, 1957, Ga. bar, 1974; partner firm Ulmer, Murchison, Ashby & Ball, Attys. at Law, Jacksonville, 1957-75; subsequently partner firm Powell, Goldstein, Frazer & Murphy, Attys. at Law, Atlanta; pres. Great Am. Mgmt. Corp., Atlanta, 1972-75, chmn. bd., 1975; mng. trustee Great Am. Mortgage Investors, 1972-75; sr. v.p., dir. UniCapital Corp., Atlanta, 1972-75. Served with USN, 1943-54. Mem. Am., Fla., D.C., Va., Ga. bar assns., Jacksonville Area C. of C. (dir.). Episcopalian. Clubs: Timuquana Country, Fla. Yacht (Jacksonville); Piedmont Driving (Atlanta). Editor-in-chief Va. Law Rev., 1956-57. Home: 3250 Farmington Rd NW Atlanta GA 30339 Office: 1100 Citizens Southern National Bank Bldg 35 Broad St NW Atlanta GA 30303

CORSELLO, LILY JOANN, educator; b. Newark, Mar. 30, 1953; d. Joseph DiFalco and Antonietta (Gandolfo) C.; B.A., Fla. State U., 1974; M.Ed., Fla. Atlantic U., 1977. Media coordinator, sec. Church-by-the-Sea, Fort Lauderdale, Fla., 1968-71; student asst. Fla. State U., 1972-73; lang. arts tchr. Plantation (Fla.) High Sch., 1974—; drama and communications tchr., coordinator John Robert Powers Sch. Modeling, 1978—; mem. ops. com. Sta. WAFG, 1974-75. Mem. Nat. Council Tchrs. English, Am. Personnel and Guidance Assn., NEA, Nat. Educators Fellowship, Fla. Council Tchrs. English (lobbyist 1978), Fla. Teaching Profession and Classroom Tchrs. Assn. (rep. 1975), Lambda Iota Tau. Republican. Baptist. Club: Ft. Lauderdale Pilot (area Anchor asst. coordinator Outreach com. 1979). Home: 4521 NE 18th Ave Fort Lauderdale FL 33334 Office: 6901 NW 16th St Plantation FL 33313

CORSO, JOSEPH VICTOR, chem. engr.; b. Bklyn., Oct. 24, 1918; s. Salvatore John and Vita Anna (Pisano) C.; B.S., Poly. Inst. Bklyn., 1951, postgrad., 1951-52, 56, 57; m. Kitty Gray Duncan, Sept. 21, 1952; children—Barbara Ann, Lisa Cheryl, Cathy-Jo, Tina Sue. Jr. chemist N.Y.C. Dept. Water Supply, Bklyn., 1943-44; sr. chemist Drew Chem. Co., N.Y.C., 1944-50; asst. chief chemist Hogan Labs., N.Y.C., 1950-51; chemist N.Y.C. Transit Authority, 1951-59; asst. gen. chemist Consol. Edison Co., N.Y.C., 1959-66; asso. research engr. Dearborn chem. div. W.R. Grace, Lake Zurich, Ill., 1966-68; project chem. engr. Gilbert Assos., Reading, Pa., 1968-77; staff specialist, water and waste treatment engr. Brown & Root Inc., Houston, 1977—; cons. engr. water and waste treatment. Bd. dirs. Amityville (N.Y.) Schs., 1967-68; chmn. awards com. Reading Sci. and Engring. Fair, 1969-77. Registered profl. engr., Pa. Mem. Profl. Engrs. Soc., Nat. Assn. Corrosion Engrs., Reading Chemists Club (corr. sec. 19/0-74), Am. Chem. Soc. Roman Catholic. Patentee in field. Home: 7207 LaEntrada Dr Houston TX 77083 Office: Brown & Root Inc PO Box 3 Houston TX 77001

CORTES, ARSENIO C., mfg. engr.; b. Cuba, Sept. 26, 1949; came to U.S., 1962, naturalized, 1979; s. Arsenio P. and Estrella C. (Izaguirre) C.; B.S. in Elec. Engring. cum laude, U. Fla., 1975, M.S. in Elec. Engring., 1976; m. Denise Samuels, June 26, 1976. Technician, Gen. Electric, Gainesville, Fla., 1976, process engr., 1976-78, mgr. mfg. engring., El Paso, Tex., 1978-79, Daytona Beach, Fla., 1979—. Cons. Crisis Center, Gainesville, 1975-77. Four times named to pres.'s honor roll, U. Fla. Mem. Tau Beta Pi, Sigma Tau, Eta Kappa Nu. Home: 608 Devon St Port Orange FL 32019 Office: PO Box 2500 Daytona Beach FL 32015

CORWIN, JOYCE ELIZABETH STEDMAN, constrn. co. exec.; b. Chgo.; d. Cresswell Edward and Elizabeth Josephine (Kimbell) Stedman; student Fla. State U., U. Miami; m. William Corwin, May 1, 1965; children—Robert Edmund Newman, Jillanne Elizabeth Newman. Investment rep. A.M. Kidder & Co., N.Y.C., 1954-56; pres. Am. Properties, Inc., Miami, Fla., 1966-72; v.p. Stedman Constrn. Co., Miami, 1971—; owner Joy-Win Horses, Gray lady ARC, 1969-70; guidance worker Youth Hall, 1969-70; sponsor Para Med. Group of Coral Park High Sch., 1969-70. Hostess, Republican presdl. campaign, 1968; aide Rep. Nat. Conv., 1972. Mem. Dade County Med. Aux. (chmn. directory com. 1970), Fla. Psychiat. Soc. Aux., Vizcayans, Fla. Morgan Horse Assn. Clubs: Coral Gables Junior Women's (chmn. casework com. 1959-63), Riviera Country, Coral Gables Country, Royal Palm Tennis. Home: 3929 Granada Blvd Coral Gables FL 33134 also Windrift Farm Ocala FL 32686

CORWIN, WILLIAM, physician; b. Boston, Oct. 28, 1908; M.D., Tufts Coll., 1932; m. Frances M. Wetherell (dec.) m. 2d, Joyce S. Newman, 1965. Intern Wesson Meml. Hosp., Springfield, Mass., 1932-33; physician Met. State Hosp., Waltham, Mass., 1933-37, asst. supt., 1937-42; research fellow Harvard, 1937-46; practice medicine, specializing in psychiatry, Springfield, Mass., 1946-54, Miami, Fla., 1954—; mem. staff Jackson Meml. Hosp., Miami; instr. psychiatry Boston U., 1937-46, Tufts Coll., 1941-46; clin. asso. prof. psychiatry U. Miami, 1955-70, clin. prof., 1970—. Dir. Pan Am. Bank, Coral Gables. Past mem. State Fla. Adv. Com. on Mental Health; agy. operations com. United Fund. Bd. dirs. Family and Childrens Services Miami. Served to lt. col. M.C., USAAF, 1942-46. Diplomate Am. Bd. Psychiatry and Neurology, Am. Bd. Forensic Psychiatry. Fellow Am. Psychiat. Assn. (life), Am. Coll. Psychiatrists; mem. AMA, S.Fla. Psychiat. Soc. (councillor). Contbr. articles on physiology of schizophrenia to profl. publs. Home: 3929 Granada Blvd Coral Gables FL 33134 Office: Dupont Plaza Center Miami FL 33131

CORY, G. LEE, bank exec.; b. Evanston, Ill., Oct. 27, 1939; s. Gordon E. and Frances (Lee) C.; B.A., Davidson Coll., 1961; M.B.A., U. N.C., 1964; grad. Stonier Grad. Sch. Banking, 1973; m. Cokey Still, Nov. 10, 1961; children—Lacey, Lee, Cannon. Mgmt. asso. Wachovia Bank & Trust Co., Winston-Salem, N.C., 1964-65, asst. cashier, Raleigh, N.C., 1965-66, asst. cashier to v.p. comml. lending, Wilmington, N.C., 1966-73; with Citizens & So. Nat. Bank of S.C., Greenville, 1974—, v.p. in charge Greenville office, 1974-75, sr. v.p. in charge western region, 1975—, also dir. Bd. dirs. Greenville Symphony Assn., 1975—; mem. Redevel. Authority Bd., vice chmn. steering com. for community devel. program and v.p., bd. dirs. Greenville Housing Found., City of Greenville, 1975-79; bd. dirs., mem. exec. com. United Way of Greenville County, 1977—; v.p. YMCA Met. Greenville, 1978-79, bd. dirs., 1979—; bd. dirs. Blue Ridge council Boy Scouts Am., 1979-80. Served to 1st lt. Transp. Corps., U.S. Army, 1961-63. Mem. Am. Inst. Banking, S.C. Bankers Assn., Robert Morris Assos., Piedmont Econs. Club, Greater Greenville C. of C. (dir. 1975-79, v.p. econ. devel. 1979—). Methodist. Clubs: Poinsett (gov.), Greenville Country, Greenville Kiwanis. Office: 47 Camperdown Way Greenville SC 29602

CORY, JAY ROBERT, indsl. designer; b. Milw., Oct. 6, 1942; s. Halsey William and Anita Betrice (Zarwell) C.; B.S., Ill. Inst. Tech., 1968, M.S., 1974; m. Carol Lee Burgess, Aug. 7, 1965; children—Beth Linette, Jane Noelle. Program cons. Ill. Inst. Tech. Research Inst., Chgo., 1967-68; patent mktg. dir., product designer Pro Internat. Corp., Dayton, Ohio, 1969-70; design asso. Richard Ten Eyck Assos., Wichita, Kans., 1971-76; spl. project dir. Chgo. Pneumatic Drill Div., Sherman, Tex. and Enid, Okla., 1976-79; owner Jay R. Cory Indsl. Design, Sherman, 1979—, My Secretary, Sherman, 1979—; partner music pub. and rec. co., Sherman and Nashville. Vice pres. Faith and Life Ministries, Andover, Kans., 1974-77; Sunday sch. supt. Baptist Ch., 1972-76, music minister, 1977-79. Mem. Indsl. Designers Soc. Am. (student merit award 1968), Human Factors Soc. Office: 106 N Travis Sherman TX 75090

COSBY, RICHARD, coll. adminstr., coach; b. Jonestown, Miss., Mar. 23, 1943; s. Rhenette and Laura Cosby; B.S., Delta State U., 1968; postgrad. U. Tenn., 1970-72; m. Martha Ketton, May 27, 1977; children—Richard, Carlos. Dir., Headstart, Jonestown, 1965; tchr., athletic coach Quitmon County High Sch., Marks, Miss., 1968-70; dir. community social work Delta Health Center, Mound Bayou, Miss., 1972-73; asst. prof. sociology, coordinator community field work, athletic coach Stillman Coll., 1973—, research asst., dir. social work areas, Pakistan, 1974. Mem. Jonestown Bd. Aldermen, 1966-72; mem. planning bd. Barnes Br. YMCA, Tuscaloosa, Ala., 1974-79; me. Vol. Action Bd., Tuscaloosa, 1977-79. Fulbright-Hays scholar, 1974. Mem. Ala. Center Higher Edn., Nat. Assn. Social Workers, Nat. Coaches Assn., NEA. Baptist. Clubs: Social Work, Coach Social. Research rural twps. Home: 5729 18th Ave Tuscaloosa AL 35401 Office: PO Box 4877 Stillman Coll Tuscaloosa AL 35401

COSSAR, GEORGE PAYNE, lawyer, state legislator; b. Webb, Miss., Aug. 26, 1907; m. children—John, Bill. George Payne. Lawyer; mem. Miss. Ho. of Reps., 1944-48, 52—. Mem. exec. com. Council of State Govts. Mem. Omicron Delta Kappa, Phi Alpha Delta, Sigma Nu. Methodist. Mason (Shriner), Rotarian. Home: Box 50 Charleston MS 38921 Office: Mississippi House of Reps Jackson MS 39201

COSTA, JAMES FRANCIS, oil co. profl.; b. Westerly, R.I., Feb. 1, 1945; s. Frank Mendosa and Mary Elizabeth (Garcia) C.; B.S., U. Conn., 1972; m. Christine Olive Walsh, Aug. 21, 1965; children—Tina Marie, Kelley Ann. With Shell Oil Co., various locations, 1971—, sr. distbn. analyst, Houston, 1979—. Troop com. Girl Scouts Am.; scoutmaster Boy Scouts Am. Served with USMC, 1963-67; Vietnam. Mem. Smithsonian Assos. Democrat. Roman Catholic. Office: One Shell Plaza Rm 2781 Houston TX 77001

COSTANTINO RAYMOND VALENTINO, ins. co. exec.; b. Newark, Aug. 13, 1927; s. Carmello and Tersa (Sedoti) C.; C.L.U., Am. Coll., 1970 m. Betty Cook, May 29, 1952; children—Sharon, Valerie, Raymond Scott. With Ind. Life & Accident Ins. Co., Jacksonville, Fla., 1945—, asst. v.p., 1977-79, v.p., dir. tng. and mgmt. devel., 1979—. Mem. Ga. Assn. Life Underwriters (recipient George Connor award 1973), Jacksonville Area C. of C., Nat. Assn. Life Underwriters (trustee), Am. Soc. C.L.U.'s, Gen. Agts. and Mgrs. Conf. Nat. Assn. Life Underwriters. Democrat. Baptist. Clubs: Doughtery Civitan (past pres.), Toastmasters, Masons. Home: 4204 San Servera Dr N Jacksonville FL 32217 Office: 1 Independent Dr Jacksonville FL 32276

COSTELLO, KATHRYN ROPER, med. center adminstr.; b. Jasper, Ga., Apr. 20, 1942; d. Embra Arthur and Martha Elizabeth (Morrison) Roper; diploma Gulf Park Jr. Coll., 1959; B.A., U. Ky., 1963, M.A., 1973; m. Daniel E. Costello, Dec. 31, 1977; children—John Preston, Henry Cornelius. Mgr., Sta. WBKY-FM, 1960-61; producer U. Ky. Roundtable, Sta. WHAS, Louisville, 1960-62, fgn. student advisor U. Ky., Lexington, 1963-65, 71-73; instr. anthropology Paducah (Ky.) Jr. Coll., 1965-68; program specialist Ky. Ednl. TV Network, Lexington, 1970-71; asst. to mayor Lexington-Fayette Urban County Govt., 1973-75; dir. public info. Vanderbilt Med. Center, Nashville, 1975-73, asst. v.p. med. affairs Vanderbilt U., 1978—, asst. prof. med. adminstrn. Sch. Medicine, 1979—; cons. in field. Regional chmn. Assn. Am. Med. Colls. Group on Public Relations, 1979; bd. dirs. Lexington Center, Jr. League of Lexington, Jr. League of Nashville, McNeilly Day Home, Comprehensive Devel. Center Lexington, Experiment in Internat. Living. Recipient Mike award Sta. WBKY, 1960, others. Mem. Am. Rural Health Assn. (dir. 1977—), Public Relations Soc. Am., Women in Communications, Internat. Communications Assn., Tate Mountain Assos. Episcopalian. Clubs: Md. Farms Racquet and Country, Univ. Home: 6653 Jocelyn Hollow Rd Nashville TN 37205 Office: Vanderbilt U Med Center 1116 21st Ave S Nashville TN 37232

COSTES, NICHOLAS CONSTANTINE, govt. ofcl.; b. Athens, Greece, Sept. 20, 1926; s. Constantine Nicholas and Anna (Papadopoulou) C.; came to U.S., 1948, naturalized, 1959; diploma Sci. Sch., Athens Coll., 1945; student Athens Nat. Tech. U., 1945-48; A.B., Dartmouth, 1950, M.S. (George W. Davis scholar), 1951; M.A., Harvard, 1962, M.E., 1962; M.S., N.C. State U., 1955, Ph.D. (Ford Found. fellow), 1965; m. Polytime Andros, Nov. 22, 1958; children—Constantine Nicholas, Anna, Christina Smaragtha. Teaching fellow dept. civil engring. N.C. State U., Raleigh, 1951-53, instr., 1962-63; materials engr. N.C. State Hwy. and Public Works Commn., Raleigh, 1953-56; research civil engr. U.S. Army Cold Regions Research and Engring. Lab., Hanover, N.H., 1956-62; sr. staff scientist Space Scis. Lab., Marshall Space Flight Center, NASA, Huntsville, Ala., 1965—; team leader soil mechanics investigation sci. team Apollo II; co-investigator lunar geology expt. Apollo 12, 13, soil mechanics expt. Apollo 14-17; cons. geotech. engring., 1965—. Recipient Dartmouth Soc. Engrs. prize, 1951; cert. of appreciation NASA, 1970, Group Achievement award Lunar Roving Vehicle Team, 1971, Invention award, 1971; Astronauts' Silver Snoopy award, 1972; Norman medal ASCE, 1972, Registered profl. engr., N.C., Ill. Fellow ASCE (chmn. program com. aerospace council 1973-75, exec. com. aerospace div. 1976—, vice-chmn. 1979-80); mem. Nat. Soc. Profl. Engrs., AAAS, Soc. Am. Mil. Engrs., Am. Inst. Aeros. and Astronautics (Outstanding Aerospace Engr. award 1976, Martin Schilling award 1979), Am. Geophys. Union, Soc. Engring. Sci., Dartmouth Soc. Engrs., Soc. Harvard Engrs. and Scientists, Assn. Civil Engrs. Greece (hon.), Sigma Xi, Phi Kappa Phi, Chi Epsilon. Greek Orthodox. Contbr. articles and tech. reports to profl. jours. Home: 4216 Huntington Rd SE Huntsville AL 35802 Office: Space Scis Lab GC Marshall Space Flight Center Huntsville AL 35812

COSTON, DONALD THOMAS, well service co. exec.; b. Hattiesburg, Miss., Mar. 26, 1940; s. Robert Wheeler and Ernestine Ruth (Dickie) C.; B.A., N.Mex. Highlands U., 1972; postgrad. Colo. State U., 1973; children—Donald Thomas, Donna Michelle. Field engr. Radiation, Inc., Thailand, 1968-70; airport mgr. Bible's Flying Service, Las Vegas, 1972-74; head electronics tech. dept. Lamar (Colo.) Community Coll., 1974-76; chief instr. tng. dept. Petty-Ray Geophys. Co., Houston, 1976-78; tech. tng. specialist Schlumberger Well Services Co., Houston, 1976-78, mgr tng. and devel., 1978—. Adviser performing and visual arts Houston Ind. Sch. Dist. high schs. Served with U.S. Army, 1960-66. Mem. Am. Soc. Tng. and Devel., Soc. Tech. Communications, Internat. Indsl. TV Assn., Soc. Exploration Geophysicists. Home: 2409 Long Reach Sugar Land TX 77478 Office: PO Box 2175 Houston TX 77001

COSTON, L. P., educator; b. Kaufman, Tex., Feb. 5, 1936; B.S. in Agr., East Tex. State U., Commerce, 1957, M.S. in Biology and Edn., 1963; Ph.D., Inst. Tech. and Inst. Design, 1969; married; 1 child. Tchr. high schs. in Tex., 1957-59, 62-64; dir. ednl. media, prof. gen. biology and microbiology Henderson County Jr. Coll., Athens, Tex., 1965-70; prof. instructional tech. and instructional design, dir. Learning Resource Center, Memphis State U., 1970-73; prof. chmn. instructional media, dir. ednl. resources Tex. State Tech. Inst., Waco,

1973-75; dir. learning resources Midland (Tex.) Coll., 1975-79, Kilgore (Tex.) Coll., 1979—; pres. Tenn. Audiovisual Assn., 1973-74; cons. in field. Served with AUS, 1959-61. Mem. Am. Soc. Tng. and Devel., Assn. Edn. Communications and Tech., Tex. Assn. Ednl. Tech. (regional v.p. 1976-77), Tex. Jr. Coll. Assn., Tex. Tech. Soc., Tri Beta, Phi Delta Kappa. Author articles, curriculum materials. Address: Box 1963 Kilgore TX 75662

COTHRAN, ALEXANDER FORREST, drilling co. ofcl.; b. Oklahoma City, July 3, 1933; s. Elmer Klyce and Alberta (Rice) C.; B.S. in Commerce, Tex. Christian U., 1954; m. Virginia Nell Peeler, June 10, 1961; children—Adair, Leah. Personnel officer Rowan Drilling Co., Ft. Worth, 1957-68; devel. officer Tex. Christian U., Ft. Worth, 1968-79, asst. dir. devel., 1979-80; bus. mgr. Chico Drilling Co., Inc., Ft. Worth, 1980—; dir. 1st Nat. Bank, Bonham, Tex., 1971-77; treas. Council for Advancement and Support of Edn., Dist. IV., 1977—. Bd. dirs., mem. fin. com. Univ. Christian Ch., Fort Worth, 1965—; v.p., treas. Ft. Worth Ballet Assn., 1972-74, bd. dirs., 1972—. Served with U.S. Army, 1955-57. Recipient Corp. award Jr. Achievement, 1964. Mem. Am. Alumni Assn., Am. Coll. Pub. Relations Assn., Democrat. Mem. Disciples of Christ. Club: Colonial Country, Petroleum (Ft. Worth); Ferndale (Pittsburgh, Tex.). Home: 3641 Country Club Circle Fort Worth TX 76109 Office: Texas Christian U University Drive Fort Worth TX 76129

COTHRAN, OSCAR RICHARD, JR., vocat. and career edn. cons.; b. Seneca, S.C., Apr. 19, 1920; s. Oscar Richard and Olive Newton (Nealy) C.; B.S., Clemson U., 1950, M.Ed., 1962, advanced guidance certificate, 1970; m. Lula Moore, Apr. 25, 1943; children—Oscar Richard, III, Henry Moore, Margaret Olive, Frances Estelle. Clk., bookkeeper Dunean Mills, Greenville, S.C., 1938-41; tchr. Greenville County (S.C.) Sch. Dist., 1950-72, vocat. and career edn. cons., 1978—; counselor Woodmont High Sch., Piedmont, S.C., 1972-78, also dir. adult edn. Sec. Greenville Met. Sewer Commn., 1970-79. Served with USAAF, 1941-45. Cryovac scholar, 1973. Mem. Am., S.C. personel and guidance assns., Nat., S.C. vocat. guidance assns. Baptist. Clubs: Augusta Road Ruritan, Masons, Woodmen of World. Home: Route 4 Box 133 Piedmont SC 29673 Office: Sch Dist Greenville County 301 Camperdown Way Greenville SC 29602

COTTO-CERVERA, GREGORIO, hosp. ofcl.; b. San Juan, P.R., Mar. 20, 1920; s. Felix and Antonia (Cervera-Lopez) Cotto-Romero; B.B.A. magna cum laude, U. P.R., 1969; m. Lydia Orellana-Rivera, June 5, 1948; children—Carmen D., Gregorio, Ada de los A., Lydia II, Maria A., Lynda, Daniel, Janet. Chief auditor non-appropriated funds Korea, U.S. Army, 1955-60; comptroller Caribe Crown Cap Corp., San Juan, P.R., 1967-69; audit mgr. Hurdman and Cranstoun, San Juan, 1970-73; dir. fin. U. Sacred Heart, San Juan, P.R., 1973-76; chief fin. officer, comptroller Tchrs.' Hosp., Hato Rey, P.R., 1976—; prof. cost acctg. Coll. Sacred Heart, Santurce, P.R., until 1976. Served as sgt. U.S. Army, 1940-62. C.P.A. Mem. Hosp. Fin. Mgmt. Assn. (dir. 1977—), Am. Inst. C.P.A.'s, N.Y. Soc. C.P.A.'s, P.R. Coll. C.P.A.'s, Nat. Assn. Accountants. Roman Catholic. Author: Depreciation Practices in Puerto Rico, 1972. Home: Block 26 Lot 12 St 6 Villa Carolina PR 00630 Office: Tchrs' Hosp Gen PO Box 4708 San Juan PR 00936

COTTON, ELEANOR GREET, educator; b. El Paso, Tex., Jan. 30, 1923; student U. Tex., 1940-44; B.A., Tex. Western Coll. (now U. Tex., El Paso), 1950, M.A., 1952, postgrad., 1964-70; postgrad. U. Minn., 1964, U. Tex., Austin, 1967; Ph.D., U. N.Mex., 1973; m., 1944; 1 dau.; m. 2d, 1952 (div. 1968). Instr. dept. English, U. Tex., El Paso, 1960-71, instr. dept. linguistics, 1971-73, asst. prof., 1973-78, asso. prof., 1979—, evaluator El Paso Public Schs., 1973; lectr. in field. Bd. dirs. St. Clement's Episcopal Parish Sch., El Paso, 1967-68, El Paso Assn. Day Care Centers, 1975—. Named Outstanding Faculty Woman of Yr., U. Tex., El Paso, 1970-71. Mem. MLA, SW Council Fgn. Lang. Tchrs., Mexican-Am. Edn. Assn. (sec. 1969), Tex. Assn. Teaching English to Speakers of Other Langs. (v.p. 1974, pres. 1975), Linguistic Assn. SW. Contbr. chpts. to The Mexican-American Curriculum, 1970, articles and revs. to profl. jours. Office: U Tex El Paso TX 79968

COTTON, EUGENE CHARLES, ins. co. exec.; b. Brookhaven, Ga., Mar. 5, 1937; s. James Thomas and Alba (Kelly) C.; student Ga. State U., 1956-59; m. Lorraine Sandra Holtberg, Aug. 28, 1965; children—Charles Thomas, Courtney Anne. With Coastal States Life Ins. Co., Atlanta, 1955—, now v.p. Lay leader YMCA Indian Guides, 1976-77. Served with USAR, 1960. Baptist. Home: 2122 Strasburg Ct Dunwoody GA 30338 Office: 260 Peachtree St Atlanta GA 30302

COTTON, JOHN PIERCE, headmaster; b. Winchester, Mass., Nov. 25, 1937; s. Dana Meserve and Geraldine (Pierce) C.; A.B., Harvard U., 1960; M.A., U. Colo., Boulder, 1967; m. Deborah Eliott, Sept. 18, 1960; children—John Eliott, Sarah Pierce, Nathaniel Curtis Hasty, Ethan Sprague. Sr. master upper sch. Colo. Acad., Englewood, 1964-68; headmaster Kimball Union Acad., Meriden, N.H., 1968-74, St. Andrew's Sch., Boca Raton, Fla., 1974—. Served with USNR, 1960-62. Mem. Fla. Council Ind. Schs. (dir. 1976-78, now v.p.), Ind. Schs. No. New Eng. Assn. (pres. 1972-74), Diocese of S.E. Fla. Sch. Bd. Assn. (v.p.)., Headmasters Assn. Episcopalian. Club: Harvard (Boston). Home and Office: Saint Andrews School Saint Andrews Blvd Boca Raton FL 33434

COTTON, LAWRENCE FRANK, Realtor; b. Colon, Panama, May 16, 1937; s. Ernest Lawrence and Edith Agatha (Wikran) C.; B.S., U.S. Air Force Acad., 1959; m. Sharon deRussy Stillman, June 23, 1959; 1 son, Lawrence Robert. Commd. 2d lt. USAF, 1959, advanced through grades to maj., 1979; service in Vietnam, Japan and Okinawa; ret., 1979; Realtor, San Antonio, 1979—. Decorated D.F.C. with oak leaf cluster, Meritorious Service medal with oak leaf cluster, Air medal with 10 oak leaf clusters, Air Force Commendation medal. Mem. Order Daedalians. Republican. Mem. Union Ch. Home: 5102 Linda Colonia San Antonio TX 78233 Office: 12030 Perrin Beitel San Antonio TX 78217

COTTRELL, DAN FESMIRE, clergyman, educator; b. Humboldt, Tenn., Jan. 19, 1940; s. Clois Bradfield and Lucille (Fesmire) C.; B.A., David Lipscomb Coll., 1962, M.A., Harding Grad. Sch. Religion, 1970; M.A., Abilene Christian Coll., 1972; Ed.D. Candidate, U. Miss.; m. Linda Gale Billops, Aug. 16, 1964; children—Christopher Alan, Stephen Craig, Cynthia Leigh. Minister Gallatin Rd. Ch. of Christ, Nashville, 1966-67, West Memphis (Ark.) Ch. of Christ, 1967-71; instr. religion Freed-Hardeman Coll., Henderson, Tenn., 1971-71; minister Broadway Ch. of Christ, Paducah, Ky., 1978-80, Concord Rd. Ch. of Christ, Brentwood, Tenn., 1980—. Vis. chaplain, U.S. Congress, 1968. Pres. Cottrell Publs., 1974—, chmn. blood drive Chester County Red Cross, 1973—. Recipient Freedoms Found. award, 1968. Mem. Ch. of Christ. Author: The Cross and The Crown, 1975, Christ Our Contemporary, 1965, The Christian and Civil Government, 1971; Preaching First Principles, 1976. Club: Civitan. Home: Box 305 Brentwood TN 37027

COTTRELL, SAMUEL, IV, computer co. exec.; b. St. Louis, June 9, 1944; s. Samuel and Elise (Mardorf) C.; B.S., U. Ill., 1967; m. Mary Wooddell, Shepherd, Mar. 30, 1968; children—Brian Timothy, Samuel. Jr. engr. Potomac Electric Power Co., Washington, 1967; sr. systems analyst Advanced Computer Tech. Corp., Arlington, Va., 1969-72, sr. cons., 1972-73, gen. mgr., 1973-75, v.p., 1975—. Mem. exec. com. Arlington YMCA Youth Program. Served with U.S. Army, 1967-69. Mem. Assn. Computing Machinery. Unitarian. Home: 5913 Williamsburg Blvd Arlington VA 22207 Office: 1501 Wilson Blvd Arlington VA 22209

COTTRILL, CAROL MALOTT, pediatric cardiologist; b. Cin., May 9, 1937; d. Ralph William and Antoinette Marie (Meyer) Malott; B.S., U. Cin., M.D., 1971; m. J. Thomas Rolfes; children—John, Aaron, Elgin, Hope, Carl, Ben. Intern, Good Samaritan Hosp., Cin., 1971-72, resident in pediatrics, 1972-73; fellow in pediatric cardiology U. Ky. Coll. Medicine, Lexington, 1973-75, clin. tutor, 1974-75, instr., 1975-76, asst. prof. pediatrics, 1976—. Bd. dirs. Birthright Assn., 1978—. Diplomate Nat. Bd. Med. Examiners, Am. Bd. Pediatrics. Fellow Am. Acad. Pediatrics, Am. Coll. Cardiology; mem. Southeastern Soc. for Pediatric Cardiology, Am. Heart Assn., Ky. Heart Assn. Roman Catholic. Contbr. articles and abstracts to profl. jours. Home: 1234 Scoville Rd Lexington KY 40502 Office: Dept Pediatrics U Ky Med Center Lexington KY 40536

COTTS, GERHARD K., psychiatrist; b. Berlin, Germany, July 4, 1907; s. Otto and Else (Pinner) C.; came to U.S., 1935, naturalized, 1941; M.D., Kaiser Wilhelm U., Berlin, 1933; children—Susan Cotts Watkins, Gerald V., Virginia A. Intern, U. Berlin Med. Sch.; tchr., researcher U. Strasbourg (France) Med. Sch., 1933-35, Tulane U. Med. Sch., 1935-44; exec. dir. Deverevux Schs., Devon, Pa., 1944-45; clin. dir. Lynchburg (Va.) State Tng. Sch., regional dir. Central Va. Mental Health Clinics, 1945-51; dir. Montgomery County Mental Health Clinic, Rockville, Md., 1954-55; practice medicine specializing in psychiatry, Arlington, Va., 1947—. Unitarian. Home: 115 20 Hickory Cluster Reston VA 22090

COUCH, BUFORD JAMES, real estate exec.; b. Batesville, Ark., Aug. 17, 1916; s. Ralph and Ruby Adelle (Holmes) C.; B.S. M.E., U. Okla., 1938; grad. U.S. Army Command and Gen. Staff Coll., 1957-58, George Washington U., 1961-62; m. Gloria Jean Moxon, Mar. 28, 1941; children—David Michael, Diane Couch Fitzgerald. Commd. in U.S. Army, 1940, advanced through grades to lt. col.; ret. 1967; ordnance officer Mil. Dist. Washington, 1958-61; tech. liaison officer U.S. Army Arctic Test Bd., 1961-64; depot comdr., San Antonio, 1964-67; dir. properties Baker-Crow Co., Dallas, 1967-73; v.p. Wayne Duddlesten Inc., Houston, 1973—. Decorated Legion of Merit, Korean Silver Star; certified property mgr. Mem. Inst. Real Estate Mgmt., Houston Apt. Assn. Home: 1700 Seaspray St #1239 Houston TX 77008 Office: 50 Briar Hollow Houston TX 77027

COUCH, JAMES HOUSTON, engr.; b. Easley, S.C., June 5, 1919; s. A. Waverly and Gertrude (Foster) C.; B.S., Clemson U., 1941, M.S., 1952; grad. Inst. Materials Handling Tchrs., Northwestern U., 1969; grad. Materials Handling Inst., Purdue U., 1972; m. Sarah Crenshaw, Jan. 11, 1942; children—James F., Dorothy C. Couch Stafford. Asst. prof. indsl. engring. Clemson (S.C.) U., 1941-56, asso. prof. indsl. engring., 1956—; research engr. Lockheed Aircraft Corp., part time, Lockheed-Ga. Co., part-time 1955-69. Bd. dirs. Foundry Edn. Found., Cleve. Mem. Am. Welding Soc. (Meritorious award 1964, Adams Meml. membership award 1965), Am. Soc. Metals, Am. Foundrymen's Soc. Author: Manufacturing Processes and Materials, 1967; Engineering Manufacturing Processes, 1960. Home: 408 College Ave PO Box 826 Clemson SC 29631

COUCH, JOHN ALEXANDER, cell biologist, comparative pathologist; b. Washington, Feb. 12, 1938; s. Raymond Carl and Rubye Frances (Wates) Couch; B.S., U. Ala., 1961; M.S., Fla. State U., 1964, Ph.D., 1971; m. Susan Carolyn Barrett, July 3, 1963; children—Catherine Susan, John Alexander. Teaching asst. in biology Fla. State U., Tallahassee, 1961-64; research biologist U.S. Nat. Oceanic and Atmospheric Adminstrn. Lab., Oxford, Md., 1964-71; cell biologist, pathologist U.S. EPA Lab., Gulf Breeze, Fla., 1971—; adj. prof. in biology U. West Fla., Pensacola, 1975—; scientist, aquanaut Man-in-the-Sea, Tektite II Project, U.S. Dept. of Interior, V.I., 1970. Mem. Soc. Protozoologists, Soc. Invertebrate Pathology, Southeastern Soc. Electron Microscopists, Gulf Estuarine Research Soc., Sigma Xi. Contbr. articles to profl. jours. Home: 3565 Hopestill Rd Pensacola FL 32503 Office: US EPA Lab Gulf Breeze FL 32561

COUCH, RICHARD WESLEY, botanist; b. Pryor, Okla., Mar. 30, 1937; s. John Wesley and Ola Blanche (Stephens) C.; B.S. in Agrl. Edn., Okla. State U., Stillwater, 1959; M.S. in Agronomy and Botany, U. Tenn., Knoxville, 1961; Ph.D. in Botany and Biochemistry (NASA fellow 1963-65), Auburn (Ala.) U., 1966; m. Jane Mitchell, June 2, 1960; children—Juli Jane, Cathy Ellen. With Tenn. Extension Service, Union City, 1961-63; mem. faculty Athens (Ala.) Coll., 1965-73; prof. biology Oral Roberts U., Tulsa, 1973—; cons. in field. Mem. Nat. Assn. Biology Tchrs., Nat. Sch. Tchrs. Assn., Aquatic Plant Mgmt. Soc., Okla. Acad. Sci. (pres. 1979-80). Baptist. Author papers in field. Address: Dept Natural Scis Oral Roberts Univ Tulsa OK 74171

COUGHLIN, JOYCE DESMOND, physician; b. Buffalo, Jan. 13, 1924; s. Francis Desmond and Evelyn (Joyce) C.; A.B., Canisius Coll., 1944; M.D., U. Buffalo, 1947; m. Jean Ann Fitzhenry, June 14, 1947; children—J. Desmond Jr., Paul William, Tara Kathleen. Intern U. Buffalo at N.Y., 1948-52; resident Sisters of Charity, Buffalo, 1947-48, Buffalo Gen., USAA hosps., 1948-52; practice medicine specializing in urology, Asheville, N.C., 1954—; chief staff St. Joseph's Hosp., Asheville, 1963, Meml. Mission Hosp., Asheville, 1969; clin. asst. prof. urology Duke, N.C., 1974—; sr. cons. U.S. VA Hosp., Oteen, N.C., 1958—, Margaret Pardee Hosp., Hendersonville, N.C., 1960—. Dir. 1st. Union Nat. Bank, Asheville, 1967—; bd. dirs. United Fund, Buncombe County, 1962-72; chmn. U. N.C. Ashville Found. Inc., 1973—. Served as capt. U.S. Army, 1952-54. Fellow A.C.S.; mem. Am., So. Am. urol. assns., Carolina Urol. Soc., So. Soc. Urol. Surgeons, AMA, So. Med. Assn., N.C. State, Buncombe County med. socs. Clubs: K.C., Biltmore Forest Country (bd. govs. 1973-79). Home: 414 Vanderbilt Rd Asheville NC 28803 Office: 1 Doctors Park Asheville NC 28801

COUGHRAN, SAMUEL JAMES, JR., product devel. exec.; b. Buena Park, Calif., Sept. 24, 1926; s. Samuel James and Elizabeth R. (Black) C.; B.A., Fullerton Coll., 1948; B.S.M.E., U. Calif. at Los Angeles-Davis, 1950; m. G. Jean Adams, Jan. 5, 1946; children—Victoria Anne Coughran Cooke, Jeffrey Adams. Sales engr. Ken Sprinkler Mfg. Co., Vista, Calif., 1950; engr. tng. Towner Mfg. Co., Santa Ana, Calif., 1950-52, project engr., 1952-55, asst. chief engr., 1955-59; project engr. Rome Industries, Cedartown, Ga., 1959-62, chief devel. engr., 1962-70, dir. product devel., 1970—. Lectr. in field. Served with USAF, 1944-45. Mem. Am. Soc. Agrl. Engrs. (chmn. various coms. 1969-71), Forest Products Research Soc. (chmn. timber com.). Republican. Methodist. Author numerous publs. in field. Patentee in field. Home: 339 Woodlawn Cedartown GA 30125 Office: PO Box 48 Cedartown GA 30125

COUHIG, MARCELLE REESE, trade exec.; b. New Orleans, June 2, 1916; d. George Wilson and Marcelle Josephine (Jacquet) Reese; student Tulane U., Loyola U. of the South, Harvard U.; m. Sam A. LeBlanc, Jr., Feb. 22, 1938; children—Sam A., Marcelle LeBlanc Stephenson; m. 2d, Robert Emmet Couhig, July 15, 1948; children—Robert E., Owen Couhig Kemp, Kevin Hearsey, Mark St. John. Buyer Maison Blanche, New Orleans, 1946-48; founder Fairview, West Feliciana Parish, La., 1966; founder, pres. Asphodel Village Corp., Ltd., Jackson, La., 1968—. Mem. fin. com. La. Restoration Alliance, 1979—; mem. La. Mental Health Bd., 1965-66; chmn. steering com. Rep. candidate for Gov., 1979. Mem. Jackson Assembly, La. Travel Promotion Assn., Ladies Aux. for Nat. Pest Control. Republican. Roman Catholic. Author: Asphodel Cook Box, 1969. Address: Route 2 Jackson LA 70748

COULIANOS, CONSTANTINOS HARALAMPOS, master mariner, marine surveyor; b. Greece, July 18, 1916; s. Haralampos Themistocles and Vassiliki Constantinou (Tsigonias) C.; came to U.S., 1940, naturalized, 1955; grad. Posidon Mcht. Marine Acad., 1938, Radar Sch., N.Y.C., 1957, N.Y. Meteorology Sch., 1957, N.Y. Mcht. Marine Sch., 1957; m. Franzi Siggelkow, Mar. 23, 1944; children—Harry, Katina. Chief officer, master Mcht. Marine during World War II for Western Shipping Corp., N.Y.C.; chief officer for Orion Shipping Corp., N.Y.C., 1950-54; harbour pilot V.I. Govt., 1955-57; master various cargo-tanker ships Global-Orion Shipping Corp., N.Y.C., 1957-65; dir. Coulianos Maritime Agy., St. Thomas, V.I., 1972—. Mgr. family's personal real estate. Chmn. fund raising A.R.C., 1972-73; mem. V.I. Taxicab Commn., 1972-74, V.I. Urban Renewal Bd., 1973-76. Pres. U.S.O., 1971-73; chmn. bd. Community Chest, 1968-74. Served with inf., Greek Army, 1938-39. Recipient award P.R. League Against Cancer, 1970. Mem. St. Thomas-St. John C. of C. (dir.), U.S. Navy League (dir.), Andros Soc. N.Y., Mental Health Assn. St. Thomas, V.I. Hist. Soc., St. Thomas Pub. Info. Assn., Nat. Geog. Soc. Republican. Greek Orthodox. Rotarian. Club: V.I. Yacht (commodore 1966-68, 72-76). Author: Liquid Roads, 1961. Home: 14 Norre Gade Charlotte Amalie St Thomas VI 00801 Office: 78 Crystal Gade Charlotte Amalie St Thomas VI 00801

COULLIETTE, JAMES HORACE, ret. physicist and educator; b. Houston County, Ala., Feb. 11, 1899; s. John T. and Bertie M. (Harrison) C.; A.B., Birmingham-So. Coll., 1918, A.M., 1919; Ph.D., Columbia U., 1941; m. Edith Ray Ruff, Sept. 1973; 1 dau. by previous marriage—Margaret Joan Coulliette Thompson. Instr. in sci. Selma (Ala.) High Sch., 1919-20; instr. physics U. Ga., Athens, 1920-21, Emory U., 1921-22, Hunter Coll., N.Y.C., 1925-27; prof. physics Birmingham So. Coll., Birmingham, Ala., 1927-41; physicist Am. Cast Iron Pipe Co., Birmingham, 1941-45; physicist, dir. Indsl. Research Inst., U. Chattanooga (Tenn.), 1945-60; prof. physics U. Miami (Fla.), 1960-65, chmn. dept. physics, 1961-65. Mem. Am. Phys. Soc., AAAS, Am. Optical Soc., Sigma Xi. Democrat. Methodist. Rotarian. Address: 818 Success Ave Lakeland FL 33801

COULTER, HILDA HUCKABY, florist; b. Phenix City, Ala., June 16, 1924; d. Hiram Chester and Julia Lavada (Fuller) Huckaby; student Perry Bus. Coll., Columbus, Ga., 1956-58; m. Charles Thomas Coulter, Jan. 19, 1941; children—Hilda Ruth Coulter Bentley, Evelyn Charlotte Coulter Fulgham. With Coulter's Flowers, Phenix City, 1941—, owner, 1968—. Pres. Russell Betterment Assn. Aux., 1954-55; mem. ofcl. bd. Hillside Meth. Ch., Phenix City; mem. adv. bd. Salvation Army, Columbus, Ga., 1972—; active Ala. Hist. Assn., Russell County Hist. Assn. Mem. Ala. Assn. Florists, Columbus-Phenix City Assn. Florists (pres. 1955-56). Featured in articles McCall's mag., 1955, Reader's Digest, 1955, Birmingham (Ala.) News, 1955. Home: 3403 13th Ave PO Box 716 Phenix City AL 36867 Office: 611 14th St PO Box 716 Phenix City AL 36867

COULTER, JOHN ALFRED, data processing cons.; b. Phila.; s. John Stanley and Helen (Miller) C.; B.S., Purdue U.; m. Marilyn Marie Sawyer, Jan. 7, 1963; children—Dorothy Jayne, John Alfred. Commd. 2d lt. U.S. Army, 1942, advanced through grades to col., 1963; ret., 1966; quality control engr. Allied Chem., Hopewell, Va., 1966-67; systems analyst URS Co., Falls Church, Va., 1968-69; sr. systems analyst, dept. data processing City of Richmond, Va., 1969-74; pres., dir. Dominion Mgmt. Assos., Inc., Richmond, 1975—; pres. Diversified Builders, Inc., Richmond, 1978—. Decorated Legion of Merit; Greek Disting. Service medal. Mem. Am. Soc. Quality Control (past pres.), Ret. Officers Assn. (past pres.). Clubs: Bull and Bear (Richmond); Warwick Yacht and Country (Newport News, Va.). Home: 6300 Hackney Pl Richmond VA 23234 Office: 304 Turner Rd Suite I Richmond VA 23225

COULTER, S. LUTHER, lawyer; b. San Angelo, Tex., Mar. 21, 1913; s. Boon Loughridge and Lou Ella (Winslow) C.; B.A., Trinity U., 1936; M.A., U. Iowa, 1937; J.D., St. Mary's U. Sch. Law, 1963; m. Mildred Lorine Jones, Apr. 16, 1938; children—Mary Fae Coulter McKay, James Winslow. Mgr., Coulter's Arcade, San Angelo, Tex., 1937-42; spl. agt. F.B.I., Washington, 1942-63; admitted to Tex. State bar, 1963; asso. law firm Dibrell, Gardner & Dotson, San Antonio, Tex., 1963-67; atty., counselor for bus. affairs Trinity U., San Antonio, 1967-80. Trustee, United Presbyn. Homes. Mem. Am., San Antonio bar assns., State Bar of Tex., San Antonio Estate Planners Council (program chmn. 1973-74, v.p. 1973-74, dir. 1971-74), Soc. Former Spl. Agts. FBI, Nat. Soc. Sons Am. Revolution. Presbyn. (elder 1941—, trustee 1975-77). Clubs: San Antonio Knife and Fork (pres. 1976-77), Kiwanis (dir. 1972-73), Argyle. Home: 330 Alamo Heights Blvd San Antonio TX 78209 Office: 330 Alamo Heights Blvd San Antonio TX 78209

COUNTS, GURDON WRIGHT, JR., physician; b. Prosperity, S.C., Nov. 12, 1933; s. Gurdon Wright and Violet Marjorie (Epting) C.; B.S., Newberry Coll., 1955; M.D., Med. Coll. S.C., 1959; m. Elizabeth Mae Rickenbacker, Dec. 20, 1959; children—Gurdon Wright III, Karl F., Walter E., Philip J., Anthony J. Intern, Greenville (S.C.) Gen. Hosp., 1960, resident, 1961-62; practice medicine, specializing in family practice, Prosperity, S.C., 1961, Batesburg-Leesville, S.C., 1964—; mem. staff Lexington County Hosp. Mem. Leesville Town Council, 1973-74, 75-76, 77-78, mayor pro tem, 1976-77, acting mayor, 1977; trustee Newbury Coll., 1979—. Served with USAF, 1962-64. Named Batesburg-Leesville Young Man of Year, Jaycees, 1967. Mem. AMA, S.C., Ridge (sec.-treas. 1972-75, pres. 1976-79) med. socs., Batesburg-Leesville C. of C. (dir. 1965-69), Batesburg-Leesville Jaycees (pres. 1967-68, state dir. 1968-71, (hon. life mem.). Lutheran (mem. ch. council 1965-68, 70-73, 74-76, 79-81, vice chmn. congregation 1974-76). Home: 501 E Church St Leesville SC 29070 Office: Box 409 Batesburg SC 29006

COURAGE, MAXWELL BISHOP, clergyman; b. Pushthrough, Nfld., Can., June 9, 1912; s. William Reeves and Effie Martha (Way) C.; came to U.S., 1922, naturalized, 1931; B.A., Hobart Coll., 1935; grad. Gen. Theol. Sem., 1938, S.T.B., 1947, M.Div., 1973; m. Patricia Ann Smith, Apr. 18, 1952; children—Bruce, Mark, Cynthia. Ordained to ministry Episcopalian Ch., 1938; priest in charge Emmanuel Episcopal Ch., East Syracuse, N.Y., 1938-40; curate Calvary Ch., Summit, N.J., 1940-41, All Angels' Ch., N.Y.C., 1946-47; rector Trinity Ch., Wethersfield, Conn., 1947-50; supr. Tioga/Tompkins Mission Field, Candor, N.Y., 1966-70; conciliation counselor 7th Jud. Dist., N.Y. State Conciliation Bur., Rochester, 1971-73; pvt. practice as marriage counselor, Canandalgua, N.Y., 1973-75. Served to lt. col. AUS, 1942-46, 50-66. Mem. Am. Assn. Marriage and Family Counselors (emeritus), Ret. Officers Assn. Republican. Address: 45 Sea Harbor Dr E Ormond Beach FL 32074

COURINGTON, PAT MURPHY, JR., real estate broker; b. Birmingham, Ala., June 7, 1941; s. Pat Murphy and Tommie Dorris (Williams) C.; B.A. in Bus. Adminstrn., Birmingham-So. Coll., 1970; m. Martha Jane Paul, Sept. 5, 1965; 1 dau., Chella Anne. Vice pres., mgr. Carolina Printing Center, Columbia, S.C., 1965-70; v.p., mgr. Sand Mountain Pub. Co., Inc., Albertville, Ala., 1970-75; broker, owner Courington Real Estate, Albertville, 1972—; dir. Sand Mountain Newspapers, Inc., Carolina Printing Center, Inc., Fla. Sun Printing, Inc., Sand Mountain Pub. Co., Inc., Central Bank. Vice chmn. Albertville Housing Authority, 1976; bd. dirs. Albertville Downtown Action Assn., 1978; pres. Mountain Valley Council on Arts, 1975-76, 78-79. Served with U.S. Army, 1962-63. Paul Harris Fellow, Rotary Internat., 1978; cert. real estate broker, residential specialist, Nat. Assn. Realtors. Mem. Marshall County Bd. Realtors (dir. 1979—, v.p. 1980), Albertville C. of C. (v.p. 1979, pres. 1980), Nat. Assn. Realtors, Marshall Homebuilders Assn., Nat. Assn. Homebuilders, Realtors Nat. Mktg. Inst. Democrat. Methodist. Clubs: The Club Inc., Albertville Rotary (pres. 1976-77, dir. 1974-78), San Mountain Tennis Assn. (pres. 1977). Home: 4 Sycamore Ln Albertville AL 35950 Office: PO Box 734 107 N Carlisle St Albertville AL 35950

COURSON, JON LOUIS, JR., bottling co. exec.; b. Plant City, Fla., Feb. 23, 1930; s. Jon L. and Clemmie (Thomas) C.; student John B. Stetson U., 1947; m. Peggy Jeanne Davis, Aug. 13, 1955; children—Lyris, Elaine, Jon Louis III, Gregory. Sales mgr. Dr. Pepper Bottling Co., Opp, Ala., 1961-63; sales mgr. Pepsi-Cola Bottling Co., Dothan, Ala., 1963-67, controller, Tampa, Fla., 1967—; bd. dirs. Exchange Bank of Temple Terrace. Apptd. Hillsborough County Citizens Solid Waste Task Force, 1978. Mem. Fla. Soft Drink Assn., S.E. Pepsi-Cola Bottlers Assn. (v.p.), Fla. West Coast Bottlers Assn. (sec.), Am. Inst. Corp. Controllers, Temple Terrace C. of C. (pres., 1978-79). Clubs: Temple Terrace Golf and Country (v.p. 1978, bd. dirs. 1975-78), Palma Ceia Golf and Country, Sertoma Club of Tampa (pres. 1973-74, Disting. Club Pres.). Office: Pepsi Cola Bottling Co of Tampa PO Box 17175 Tampa FL 33682

COURTNEY, NEWTON J., hosp. ofcl.; b. St. Joseph, Mo., Apr. 22, 1943; s. Newton J. and Dorothy Rosa C.; student San Antonio Coll., 1965-69; B.B.A. in Personnel Mgmt., St. Mary's U., San Antonio, 1972; m. Maria Mercedes Romero, Sept. 25, 1965; children—Scott Jay, Monica Marie. Sr. counselor Camp Geiger Boy Scout Summer Camp, 1961; credit mgr. trainee Montgomery Ward & Co., 1969-70; unit clk., asst. dir. dept. unit mgmt. S.W. Tex. Meth. Hosp., San Antonio, 1970-73, dir. central services, 1973-1975, bus. office mgr., patient fin. services, 1975—. Active Nat. Assn. Eagle Scouts. Served with USAF, 1961-69; Vietnam. Mem. San Antonio Consumer Credit Assn., Tex. Hosp. Assn. Hosp. Accts. Baptist. Home: 14503 Slash Pine Woods San Antonio TX 78249 Office: Southwest Texas Methodist Hospital 7700 Floyd Curl Dr San Antonio TX 78229

COUTS, MARY FRANCES, nurse; b. Eatonton, Ga., May 23, 1921; d. Leon Forrest and Mary Will (Adams) Echols; R.N., Gen. Hosp. Sch. Nursing, Greenville, S.C., 1943; m. Harry Thomas Couts, May 3, 1944; children—Brenda Couts Cavanah, Jean Couts Bigger, Diane Couts Haston. Staff nurse Spartanburg (S.C.) Gen. Hosp., 1943-44, Flagler Hosp., St. Augustine, Fla., 1944-45; staff nurse, head nurse Meml. Hosp., Clarksville, Tenn., 1954-56; staff, pvt. duty nurse Rutherford Hosp., Murfreesboro, Tenn., 1956-58; pub. health nurse, Clarksville, 1966-69; staff nurse, mgr. infirmary Austin Peay State U., Clarksville, 1972-77. Mem. Am., Tenn. nurses assn., S.C. Gen. Hosp. Alumni Assn. Democrat. Baptist. Home: Route 1 Box 617 Cross Plains TN 37049

COUVE, ROBERT EDWARD, psychotherapist; b. Evanston, Ill., June 11, 1944; s. Forest Franklin and Clara Marie (Kaub) C.; B.A., Valaparaiso U., 1967; M.S.W., Our Lady of the Lake U., 1973; m. Janus Marie Cooper, Dec. 14, 1968; 1 dau., Amanda Joan. Rehab. technician Tex. rehab. Commn., San Antonio State Hosp., 1968-73; psychotherapist Adult Mental Health Clinic, Robert B. Green Hosp., San Antonio, 1973-74; psychotherapist, sch. cons., clin. field instr. U. Tex. Health Sci. Service Center, San Antonio, 1974-76; pvt. practice psychotherapist Robert E. Buxbaum & Assos., Inc., San Antonio, 1976—. Mem. Am. Assn. Marriage and Family Therapists, Nat. Assn. Social Workers, Acad. Cert. Social Workers. Lutheran. Home: 13726 Stoney Hill San Antonio TX 78231 Office: 4545 Centerview Dr Suite 140 San Antonio TX 78228

COVAN, JAMES PARKER, indsl. hygienist; b. Urbana, Ill., Aug. 23, 1940; s. Jack Phillip and Thelma Elizabeth (Parker) CoV.; student U.S. Naval Acad., 1958-59; B.S. in Chemistry, Tex. A&M U., 1962, M.E. in Indsl. Engring., 1974; m. Brenda Sample, June 14, 1964; children—Faith, Hope, Heather. Shift supr. Procter & Gamble, Dallas, 1967-70; safety analyst Phillips Chem. Co., Pasadena, Tex., 1974-76; indsl. hygiene engr. Tenneco, Inc., Houston, 1976-79, staff indsl. hygienist, 1979—. Served with U.S. Navy, 1958-59, USNR, 1962-67, 70-72; comdr. Res. Decorated Air Medal (2). Mem. Am. Chem. Soc., Am. Indsl. Hygiene Assn., Am. Soc. Safety Engr. Republican. Baptist. Home: 15319 Torry Pines Rd Houston TX 77062 Office: PO Box 2511 Houston TX 77001

COVEN, RONALD LEO, wholesale oil jobber; b. Hall County, Ga., Sept. 30, 1938; s. Russell H. and Inus (Martin) C.; B.S. in Bus. Adminstrn., U. Ga., 1961; m. Linda Rhodes McLanahan, Dec. 30, 1961; children—Ronald Leo, II, Frances Elaine, Martin Thomas. Sales-service mgr. Fla. Food Products Co., Orlando, Fla., 1963-65; retail tng. instr. Shell Oil Co., 1965-70; pres. Handy Oil Co., Forest City, N.C., 1970—; v.p. Citizens Fuels Co., Asheville, N.C., 1974—; sec. Old Dominion Bandag, Appalachia, Va., 1978—; pres. Kingsport Fuels, Inc. (Tenn.), 1972—. Served with USAR, 1962-63. Mem. Tenn. Oil Marketers Assn. (dir. E.Tenn. div. 1979-80), Forest City Fuel Dealers Assn. (pres. 1971), Jaycees. Republican. Methodist. Clubs: Ridgefields Country, Kingsport Civitan, Moose, Elks. Home: 644 Fleetwood St Kingsport TN 37660 Office: 233 New Beason Well Rd Kingsport TN 37660

COVER, NORMAN BERNARD, EDP adminstr.; b. Ephrata, Pa., Mar. 25, 1935; s. Barney Blainey and Chelta V. (Huff) C.; student Jacksonville U., 1955; m. Violet Hurmagene Winouski, Nov. 26, 1960; children—Brian Lee, Keith Alex. Tabulator operator State Farm Fire & Casualty Co., Bloomington, Ill., 1952-53, programming operator State Farm Mut. Auto Ins. Co., Jacksonville, Fla., 1954-56, shift supr., EDP, 1957-61, asst. supt. EDP, State Farm Ins. Co., Winter Haven, Fla., 1962-67, EDP supt., 1968-78, data processing mgr., 1979—. Chmn. data processing adv. com. Polk Community Coll., 1976—. Cert. data processor. Fellow Data Processing Mgmt. Assn. (internat. v.p. mem. services 1977-78, S.E. regional v.p. 1975-77, Individual Performance awards). Democrat. Club: Sertoma (chmn. Stamp Out Crime com. 1975—). Home: 1825 6th St SE Winter Haven FL 33880 Office: 3425 Lake Alfred Rd Winter Haven FL 33880

COVIN, THERON MICHAEL, mental health exec.; b. Repton, Ala., Feb. 27, 1947; s. Fisher Bert and Doris (Knight) C.; A.A., Jeff Davis Coll., 1968; B.S., Troy State U., 1969, M.S., 1971; Ed.S., U. Ala., 1973; Ed.D., U. Sarasota, 1975; postgrad. U. Utah, 1974, Auburn U., 1975-77; m. Jo Ann Bell, Dec. 24, 1977. Asst. mgr. Dining Hall, Glorieta (N.Mex.) Bapt. Assembly, 1967, mgr. dining hall, 1968; asst. to dir. activities Ala. Bapt. Children's Home, Troy, 1969, dir. remedial edn. and asst. to dir. activities, 1969-71, psychometrist, dir. remedial edn., 1971; pvt. practice marriage and family counseling, Troy, 1971—; spl. edn. cons., psychometrist Ala. public schs. and Ft. Rucker Dep. Schs., 1971—; instr. psychology Troy State U., 1971-75, Freshman counselor U. Ala., 1972; co-dir. Help-A-Crisis Center, Troy, 1973-75; child devel. asso. trainer Area 23 Headstart, Troy, 1975-78; psychology/sociology instr. Lomax Hannon Jr. Coll., Greenville, Ala., 1975-78; cons. psychometrist E. Central Mental Health Center, Troy, 1975-78; marriage and family counseling intern E. Central Mental Health, Troy and Project Uplift, Auburn, 1976-77; social worker/psychometrist Ala. Bapt. Children's Home, Troy, 1977—; speed reading instr. So. Reading Lab., Troy, 1977; spl. services coordinator Area 23 Headstart, 1977-79; local dir. Child and Family Mental Health Project, HEW, Troy, 1977—; asst. prof. Sch. Edn., adj. faculty Auburn (Ala.) U., 1978—; psychologist S.E. Ala. Youth Services Youth Facility, Ozark/Dothan, Ala., 1979—. Mem. Inter-Agy. Coalition, Community Support Project, State Dept. Mental Health, 1978—; mem. asso. steering com. Ala. Child Devel., 1977. Recipient Compatriot in Edn. award Kappa Delta Pi, 1979. Mem. Ala. Mental Health Counselors Assn., Ala. Council on Family Relations, Ala. Conf. of Social Work, Am. Mental Health Counselors Assn., Am. Personnel and Guidance Assn., Ala. Personnel and Guidance Assn., Ala. Assn. Marriage and Family Counselors, Gulf Coast Assn. Marriage and Family Counselors, Am. Assn. Marriage and Family Counselors, AAUP, Phi Delta Kappa, Kappa Delta Pi, Gamma Beta Phi, Psi Lambda, Circle K. Baptist. Contbr. articles to profl. jours.; book reviewer Am. Personnel and Guidance Jour., 1978—; editorial adv. com. Exceptional People, 1978—. Home: PO Box 166 Ariton AL 36311 Office: PO Box 429-ABCH Elm St Troy AL 36081

COVINGTON, CECIL LYONS, electronics co. exec.; b. Dallas, Nov. 21, 1911; s. William Roper and Mary Eliza (Lyons) C.; A.B. cum laude, Baylor U., 1933; LL.B., Nat. U., 1939, M.P.L., S.J.D., 1940; m. Phyllis Ruth McIntyre, Feb. 17, 1943; 1 son, Mark Roper. Adminstrv. asst. PWA Washington, 1933-40; clk. to Senator Tom Connally of Tex., 1940-41; spl. asst. on contracts OSRD, 1941-43; spl. asst. to dir. tng., facilities service VA, in charge review contracts negotiated with all schs. and colls. Ark., La., Okla., Miss., Kans., Tex., Mo., 1946-53; contract adminstr. Texas Instruments, Inc., 1953-56, controller apparatus div., 1956-58, mgr. govt. contracts adminstrn., 1958-61, mgr. govt. contracts and banking relations, 1962-63, mgr. govt. relations, 1964-66, adminstrv. asst. to chmn. bd., 1967, contracts mgr. govt. products div., 1968, mgr. govt. relations equipment group, 1969—; adj. prof. Grad. Sch. Mgmt., U. Dallas. Served as lt. USNR, 1944-46. Mem. Fin. Execs. Inst. (govt. bus. com.), Nat. Security Indsl. Assn. (procurement adv. com.), N.A.M. (nat. def. com.), Sigma Nu Phi. Presbyterian. Clubs: Chandlers Landing Yacht (Dallas); Twin Points (Hot Springs, Ark.). Home 9531 Windy Hill Rd Dallas TX 75238 Office: 13500 North Central Expressway Dallas TX 75222

COVINGTON, EARL GENE, lawyer; b. St. Louis, Nov. 10, 1939; s. Earl Lloyd and Mary J. (Johnson) C.; B.B.A., U. Tex., 1962; J.D., U. Houston, 1969; m. Pamela Marquis Smither, July 28, 1967. Acct., Arthur Young & Co., Ft. Worth, 1963-64, Ernest Leavitt, Houston, 1964-66; tax specialist Ernst & Whinney, Houston, 1967-72; admitted to Tex. bar, 1967; atty. Urban Coolidge Attys., Houston, 1973-74; pres. firm Covington & Reese, P.C., Houston, 1974—; dir. Mariner Corp., Houston. Pres., Univ. Arms Townhouses, 1969-70; pres. Bayou Woods Assn. Property Owners, 1978-79, dir., 1979—. Served with USMCR, 1962-68. Mem. Tex. Soc. C.P.A.'s, Houston Bar Assn., Tex. Bar Assn., Am. Bar Assn., Am. Inst. C.P.A.'s. Home: 9145 Kenilworth St Houston TX 77024 Office: 1700 W Loop St Suite 1460 Houston TX 77027

COVINGTON, ROBERT NEWMAN, educator; b. Evansville, Ind., Sept. 9, 1936; s. George M. and Roberta (Newman) C.; B.A., Yale U. 1958; J.D., Vanderbilt U., 1961; m. Paula Anne Hattox, July 29, 1972. Admitted to Tenn. bar, 1961; asst. prof. Vanderbilt U. Sch. Law, Nashville, 1961-64, asso. prof., 1964-69, prof., 1969—, asso. dean, 1972-75; cons. Tenn. State Law Library Commn., 1965-75; chmn. So. Law Review Conf., 1963-64; mem. Labor Law Group Trust, 1969—; vis. prof. U. Mich., 1971, U. Calif. at Davis, 1975-76; adminstrv. law officer Calif. Agrl. Labor Relations Bd., 1975. Pres. Henry County (Tenn.) Young Democrats Club, 1959. Mem. Am., Tenn. bar assns., Am. Judicature Soc., Assn. Am. Law Schs. (chairperson sect. labor relations law 1975, sect. prelegal edn. and admission to law schs. 1975), Am. Arbitration Assn., Order of Coif, Phi Beta Kappa, Phi Delta Phi. Democrat. Episcopalian. Club: University (pres. 1968-70) (Nashville). Author: Problems in Professional Responsibility: Insurance, 1966; co-editor: (with Thomas G. Roady Jr.) Essays in Procedure and Evidence, 1961; (with others) Cases and Materials on Legal Methods, 1969; (with A. Caghan) Social Legislation, 1971, 2d edit., 1974; (with J. Jones and A. Cagham) Discrimination in Employment, 1971, 3d edit., 1976; contbr. articles to legal jours. Home: 907 Estes Rd Nashville TN 37215

COWAN, CHARITY ALLENE, educator; b. Lancaster, Ky., Oct. 1, 1924; d. John Theo and Julia Mae (Stevens) Cowan; B.S., Eastern Ky. U., 1946; M.A., U. Ky., 1952, postgrad., 1959-60. Tchr., Locust St. Sch., Erlanger, Ky., 1946-58; gen. supr. Erlanger-Elsmere Bd. Edn., 1958-76, asso. supt. supervision, 1976—. Named An Outstanding Educator, Eastern Ky. U., 1975. Mem. Assn. Childhood Edn. (state sec. 1956-58, chpt. pres. 1968—), NEA (life mem., br. pres. 1967-69), Eastern State U. Alumni Assn. (life), U. Ky. Alumni Assn. (life), Ky. Edn. Assn., Assn. for Childhood Edn. Internat. (life), Ky. Assn. Ednl. Suprs., Assn. Supervision and Curriculum Devel., Ky. Assn. Supervision and Curriculum Devel., Ky. Assn. Sch. Adminstrs., AAUW (v.p. 1964-66; program chmn. 1964-66), Ky. PTA (life), Ind. Order Foresters, Kappa Delta Pi, Phi Delta Kappa, Delta Kappa Gamma (pres. Zeta chpt. 1974-76). Baptist (sec. chmn. kindergarten 1964-77). Home: 440 B Graves Ave Erlanger KY 41018 Office: 500 Graves Ave Erlanger KY 41018

COWAN, JOEL HARVEY, real estate exec.; b. Marietta, Ga., June 23, 1936; s. Charles A. and Bernice (Kemp) C.; B.S., Ga. Inst. Tech., 1958; m. R. Geraldine Matthews, Dec. 21, 1957; children—Joel H., Mark Kemp, Jennifer Matthews. Pres. Phipps Land Co., Atlanta, 1968-76; owner, pres. Cowan & Assos., FSB Fin. Corp., 1976—; chmn. bd. Fayette State Bank, Peachtree City, Ga.; dir. Interstate Gen. Corp., San Juan, P.R., Nat. Bank Ga., Atlanta, IRT Property Co., Atlanta, Leadcil, Inc., Atlanta. Chmn. Gov.'s Commn. on Planned Growth, 1973. Trustee, Rabun Gap-Nacoochee Sch., Rabun Gap, Ga.; bd. dirs. Central Atlanta Progress. Kiwanian. Home: 102 Pebble Point Peachtree City GA 30269 Office: Box 2204 Peachtree City GA 30269

COWAN, SWAFFIELD, cons. elec. engr.; b. Moss Point, Miss., Dec. 1, 1907; s. Oliver Bingham and Mary (Swaffield) C.; B.S. in Elec. Engring., U. S.C., 1929; E.E., 1931; m. Anne Bryan Lawton, July 2, 1935; children—Anne Lawton (Mrs. Wade H. Barber), William Swaffield. With N.Y.C. R.R., 1929-30; teaching fellow U. S.C., Columbia, 1930-31; with S.C. Power Rate Investigating Com., Columbia, 1931, Underwriters Labs., Inc., Chgo., 1935-46; with Factory Ins. Assn., Charlotte, N.C., 1946-72, sr. elec. engr., 1960-72; cons. elec. engr., Georgetown, S.C., 1972—. Mem. Elec. Council Underwriters Labs., Chgo., 1956-72. Bd. dirs. Joint Indsl. Council, 1967-72. Registered profl. elec. engr., Ill., N.C. Mem. Am. Inst. E.E. (chmn. textile com. 1952-54, mem. gen. industry applications com. 1952-65, safety com., 1961-65, industry div. com., 1961-65), I.E.E.E. (life, mem. industry applications soc. 1965—, chmn. group safety com. 1966-69, mem. group tech. operations dept. 1966-69, mem. textile industry com. 1966-75), Nat. Fire Protection Assn. (mem. nat. elec. code correlating com. 1966-72, chmn. machine tool elec. standards com. 1956-72, chmn. elec. equipment maintenance com. 1968-72), Internat. Assn. Elec. Insps., N.C., S.C. socs. engrs. Contbr. articles to profl. jours. Address: 29 Palmetto St Georgetown SC 29440

COWAN, TED, state legislator Okla.; b. Stillwater, Okla., May 27, 1940; s. Robert Bruce and Mildred Elizabeth (Todd) C.; B.A. in Chemistry, Kans. State Tchrs. Coll., Emporia, 1963; m. Patricia Clark Wettack, Aug. 3, 1963; children—Drew, Elizabeth, Matthew. Cons. chemist Richard J. Bigda & Assos., Tulsa, 1972—; mem. Okla. Ho. of Reps. from 79th Dist., 1974—. Republican. Presbyterian. Address: 4233 S Pittsburg St Tulsa OK 74135

COWARD, RAYMOND, lawyer, ret. army officer; b. Searcy, Ark., Feb. 10, 1909; s. Emmett T. and Mary A. (Gentry) C.; B.A., Coe Coll., 1933; J.D., U. Iowa, 1935; diploma FBI Acad., 1941; postgrad. U. Mich., 1943, U. Vienna (Austria), 1946; M.B.A., U. Ala., 1966; grad. Command and Gen. Staff Coll., 1949; m. Phyllis Lee Furr (dec.); children—Raymond Lynn, Janet Anne. Admitted to Iowa bar, 1935, U.S. Supreme Ct. bar, 1948, D.C. bar, 1956; practiced in Cedar Rapids, Iowa, 1935-41; spl. agt. FBI, 1941-43; served from 2d lt. cav. to col. Judge Adv. Gen.'s Corps, U.S. Army, 1943-63; legal officer in Eng., France, Belgium, Luxembourg, Austria, Germany, Italy, Japan, Korea and Okinawa; asst. legal attache U.S. Embassy, Havana, Cuba; 3 tours of duty in Washington; gen. counsel to Surgeon Gen. Army, 1956-58; mem. bd. rev. Dept. Army, 1958-59; ret., 1963; asso. prof. bus. law La. State U., Baton Rouge, 1963-65; vis. lectr. bus. law U. Ala., Tuscaloosa, 1965-66; lectr. bus. law U. Tex., Arlington, 1966-67; asst. prof. polit. sci. and econs. Tex. Wesleyan Coll., Ft. Worth, 1968-69; lectr. internat. law U. Tex., Arlington, 1979—. Decorated Bronze Star medal, Combat Infantryman's badge, Purple Heart; recipient (as mem. com. on edn. about Communism of Am. Bar Assn.) Freedoms Found. at Valley Forge award, 1973, 74. Mem. Am. Bar Assn. (book reviewer Jour. 1960—, Merit award 1974, mem. adv. com. on Law Day 1974-78, mem. adv. com. on law and nat. security 1977—), Pi Kappa Delta. Mason (32 deg.). Contbr. articles on law to profl. jours.; author, columnist, lectr. nat. internat. affairs; poet. Address: 1022 S Cooper Suite 202 Arlington TX 76013

COWART, CARL MINER, banker; b. Douglas, Ga., Sept. 27, 1947; s. Emmett Jackson and Dorothy Eudell (Miner) C.; B.S., U. S.C., 1969; grad. sch. Bank Adminstrn. U. Wis., Madison, 1977; m. Virginia Melina Jones, Apr. 15, 1972; children—David Andrew, Ashley Virginia. Staff auditor S.C. Nat. Bank, Columbia, 1969-70, audit supr., 1970-71, audit officer, 1971-72, audit officer EDP, 1972-77, asst. gen. auditor, 1977-79, sr. v.p., gen. auditor, 1979—. Chartered bank auditor, cert. internal auditor, S.C. Mem. Inst. Internal Auditors, Nat. Assn. Accts. Baptist. Home: 500 Mill Creek Rd Lexington SC 29072 Office: PO Box 21367 Columbia SC 29221

COWART, GRIGGSBY THOMAS, physician; b. Atlanta, Aug. 19, 1919; s. Griggsby Thomas and Gilley Pearl (Johnson) C.; A.B., Emory U., 1941, M.D., 1944; m. Anne Henderson, Mar. 4, 1944; children—Dorothy Anne, Griggsby Thomas. Intern, Emory U. Hosp., Atlanta, 1944-45, asst. resident surgery, 1945-46; resident urology Lawson VA Hosp., Chamblee, Ga., 1948-51; chief of urology Atlanta VA Hosp., 1951-54, cons., 1954—; individual practice medicine, specializing in urology, Atlanta, 1954—; clin. asst. prof. surgery Emory U. Sch. Medicine, 1964—. Dir. So. Fed. Savs. and Loan Assn., Atlanta. Served to capt. M.C., AUS, 1946-48. Diplomate Am. Bd. Urology. Fellow A.C.S.; mem. A.M.A., So. Med. Assn., Am., Southeastern, Ga. Urol. assns., Phi Beta Kappa, Sigma Nu. Contbr. articles to profl. jours. Home: 18 Blackland Rd NW Atlanta GA 30342 Office: 384 Peachtree St Atlanta GA 30308

COWGILL, BARBARA ELLEN, business exec.; b. Union City, Tenn., Oct. 29 1947; d. Charles Louis and Margaret Josephine (Hilliard) Markwell; A.A., Itawamba Jr. Coll., 1967; B.S., Miss. State U., 1969; m. Frank E. Cowgill, Jr., Dec. 27, 1969; children—Charles Michael, Catherine Michelle. Asst. security officer Honeywell Co., St. Louis, 1969, receptionist, 1969-70, sec., El Paso and Memphis, 1970-74; legal adminstr. firm Waring, Cox, Sklar, Allen, Chafetz & Watson, Memphis, 1974-80; bus. mgr. Pediatric Allergy Group, P.A., Memphis, 1980—. Mem. Assn. Legal Adminstrs. Clubs: Am. Dachshund, Memphis Kennel. Office: 848 Adams St Memphis TN 38103

COWGILL, ROBERT, oncologist; b. Rockville Center, N.Y., Jan. 27, 1944; s. Harry B. and Ann O. (Taylor) C.; B.A., U. Va., 1965, M.D., 1969; m. Diane MacNeill, Mar. 2, 1974; children—Jessica, Kimberly, Jennifer, Daniel, Julia. Intern, Emory U. Hosp., 1969; resident in surgery Ga. Baptist Hosp., Atlanta, 1972-76; fellow in surg. oncology Meml. Sloan-Kettering Cancer Center, N.Y.C., 1976-78; practice medicine specializing in surg. oncology, Atlanta, 1978—; med. dir. Hospice Atlanta, Inc. Pres., N.W. Unitarian Congregation, Atlanta, 1979; bd. dirs. Ga. div. Am. Cancer Soc. Served with U.S. Army, 1970-72. Am. Cancer Soc. fellow, 1976-78. Mem. Med. Assn. Atlanta, Med. Assn. Ga., Ga. Hospice Orgn. Democrat. Contbr. articles in field to profl. jours. Home: 980 Crest Valley Dr NW Atlanta GA 30327 Office: 960 Johnson Ferry Rd Atlanta GA 30342

COWLES, MARK, retail stores exec.; b. N.Y.C., Mar. 9, 1923; s. Louis and Tillie (Forim) Cohen; ed. high sch.; m. Arlene Hollander, May 14, 1961; children—Stefan, Daryll, Tracy, Stuart. Operator, Bond Clothiers, Rochester, N.Y., 1941-42; underwriter Woodridge Coop. Ins. Co., 1946-48; salesman Majestic Splties. Co., Cleve., 1948-66, Erwin J. Klineman Corp., N.Y.C., 1966-67; with Hecht's Tall Shops, Memphis, 1967—, pres., 1975—; pres. Hecht's Inc. and Tall Gals Inc., 1976—. Bd. dirs. Temple Israel Brotherhood. Served with U.S. Army, 1943-45; ETO. Mem. Memphis C. of C., Mchts. Assn. Little Rock. Democrat. Home: 5635 Sycamore Grove Memphis TN 38117 Office: 109 S Highland St Memphis TN 38111

COWLES, MILLY, educator; b. Ramer, Ala., May 29, 1932; d. Russell Fail and Sara (Mills) Cowles; B.S., Troy State U., 1952; M.A., U. Ala., 1958; Ph.D. (grad. fellow), 1962. Tchr. pub. schs., Montgomery, 1952-59; asst. then asso. prof. Grad. Sch. Edn., Rutgers U., 1962-66; asso. prof. U. Ga., 1966-67; prof. early childhood devel. and edn. Sch. Edn., U. S.C., Columbia, 1967-73; prof. Sch. Edn., U. Ala. at Birmingham, 1973—, asso. dean, 1974-80, dean Sch. Edn., 1980—. Cons. So. Edn. Found., Atlanta, Ga. Inst. Higher Edn. U. Ga., also numerous sch. systems throughout Northeast and South; chief cons. Williamsburg County (S.C.) Pub. Schs., 1968—. Pres. bd. dirs. 2d Reformed Ch. Nursery Sch., New Brunswick, N.J., 1963-66. Named Outstanding Pub. Educator, Capstone Coll. Edn. Soc. U. Ala., 1977. Mem. Am. Ednl. Research Assn., Soc. for Research Child Devel., A.A.A.S., Am. Assn. U. Profs., Nat. Council Tchrs. English, Internat. Reading Assn., Nat. Assn. for Edn. Young Children, N.E.A. (mem. parent involvement com. elementary, kindergarten and nursery educators dept. 1972—), Assn. for Supervision and

Curriculum Devel. (mem. council on early childhood edn. 1969-71), Am. Psychol. Assn., N.Y. Acad. Sci., Kappa Delta Pi (chpt. treas. 1964-66), Delta Kappa Gamma. Editor, contbg. author: Perspectives in the Education of Disadvantaged Children, 1967. Contbr. articles to profl. jours. Home: 4000 Rock Ridge Rd Birmingham AL 35210

COWLING, HERFORD TYNES, photographic engr., movie producer, explorer, ret. air force officer; b. Nansemond County, Va., Aug. 20, 1890; s. John Phillips and Caroline Weaver (Tynes) C.; student George Washington U., 1912-13; m. Virginia Hardin, Jan. 14, 1927. Chief photographer U.S. Reclamation Service, 1909-16; traveled extensively in U.S., Canada and Mexico, 1913-16; headed cinematographic expdn., 1917, to Formosa. Philippines, Indo-China, Siam, Malay States, Indonesia, Australia, Tasmania, China, Japan, New Zealand and South Sea Islands, producing Paramount—Burton Holmes Travel Films; produced motion pictures of Europe, 1919, including France, Belgium, Germany, Austria, Switzerland, Czechoslovakia, Italy, also Algeria, Tunisia, Tangier, Morocco, Sicily, Spain, Egypt, Palestine, Turkey, Cuba and Mexico, 1921-23; expdns. to Brit. East Africa, Uganda, Belgian Congo and The Sudan, filming big game hunting, 1922; India, Kashmir, Tibet, Burma, Sumatra, Malaysia, 1924; China war corr. Fox News Movietone Films, produced motion picture of coronation of Maharaja of Kashmir, 1926; tech. dir. teaching films dept. Eastman Kodak Co., 1927-32; ofcl. photographer Century of Progress, Chgo., 1933; supr. motion picture prodn. U.S. Nat. Parks Service, 1934; tech. dir. div. motion pictures and sound rec. U.S. Nat. Archives, Washington, 1935-37; tech. asst. to adminstr. Nat. Unemployment Census, Washington, 1937; sr. administrv. asst. Dept. Commerce, 1938-40, then chief photog. services U.S. Dept. Labor. Served with USAAF, 1941-46, USAF, 1946-50; col. USAF ret. Fellow Royal Photog. Soc. (Gt. Britain); mem. U.S. Govt. Photog. Soc. (pres. 1915-16, hon. mem.), Biol. Photographic Assn., Am. Soc. Cinematographers, Soc. Motion Pictures Engrs., S.A.R. Mason (Shriner). Clubs: Explorers (fellow) (N.Y.C., also Washington); Army-Navy Country, Army and Navy (Washington). Home: 808 S Ode St Arlington VA 22204

COX, BAXTER SYDNOR, III, mech. engr.; b. Richmond, Va., Dec. 30, 1936; s. Baxter Sydnor, Jr. and Virginia Thomas (Wright) C.; student Christopher Newport Coll., 1963-64, Catawba Valley Tech. Inst., 1969-70; m. Vivian Lucille Morton, Apr. 15, 1972; children by previous marriage—Jerry, Syd, Stuart. Machinist, engr. Newport News Shipbuilding & Drydock Co. (Va.), 1959-68; salesman Smith-Courtney Co., Richmond, 1968-72; sales engr. Miller Fluid Power Co., Bensenville, Ill., 1972—; tchr. hydraulic systems and airlogic seminars. Com. chmn. Boy Scouts Am., 1974-77. Served with Va. N.G., 1955-63. Mem. Fluid Power Soc. Baptist. Clubs: Masons, Catawba Shrine. Home: Route 5 Box 127 Hickory NC 28601

COX, BERTHA MAE HILL (MRS. WILLIS L. COX), educator, author; b. Kosse, Tex., Mar. 10, 1901; d. Marshall Victor and Ollie Evelyn (Phifer) Hill; student S.W. Tex. U., 1922, Baylor U., 1923, So. Meth U.; B.S., North Tex. State U., 1935, M.S., 1950; m. Willis L. Cox, June 8, 1924. Prin. rural sch., Harmony, Tex., 1918; acting postmaster, Kosse, Tex., 1919-21; tchr. pub. schs., Kosse, 1922-24, Dallas County, 1925-29; prin. Dallas City Schs., 1930-33, tchr., 1934-64; tchr. Dallas Ind. Sch. Dist., after 1964, now ret.; founder, now dir. emeritus Kessler Park United Meth. Ch. Day Sch., Dallas; author, dir. Kessler Park United Meth. Ch. Bicentennial Celebration, 1976. Named Tchr. of Year, Dallas Times Herald, 1950. Mem. Dallas Assn. Childhood Edn. (pres. 1938, state sec.-treas., 1940), Speech Arts Tchrs. (pres. 1954), NEA (life), Tex. Tchrs. Assn. (life), Tex. Parents and Tchrs. Assn. (hon. life), Wesleyan Service Guild (hon. life), Kappa Delta Pi, Delta Kappa Gamma. Democrat. Methodist. Author: True Tales of Texas, 1949; Susan's Happy Year, 1957; Let's Read about Texas, 1963; Our Texas, 1964; also ch. sch. materials for Meth. Ch.; editor: Tell Us about Texas, 1947; The Texans Texas to Today, 1972; editorial adviser Ideas readers series, 1973; contbr. articles to profl. jours. Home: 1130 N Winnetka St Dallas TX 75208

COX, CLARK, journalist; b. Jefferson, N.C., Feb. 21, 1943; s. Scott Joseph and Juanita Geneva (Weiss) C.; grad. high sch.; m. Brenda Sue Bowers, Oct. 30, 1971 (div.); m. 2d, Helen Jeanette Parks, June 9, 1979. Reporter, Watauga Democrat, Boone, N.C., 1963; editor, Blowing Rocket, Blowing Rock, N.C., 1964; editor Marshville (N.C.) Home, 1965; editor Henry County Jour., Bassett, Va., 1966-67; reporter Messenger and Intelligencer, Wadesboro, N.C., 1969-71; sports editor Richmond County Daily Jour., Rockingham, N.C., 1971-73, investigative reporter, 1974-77, asst. editor, 1977—; freelance journalist, 1967-69, 73-74. Active Big Bros. Am. Recipient Sport reporting award N.C. Press Assn., 1971, 72, 1st place investigative reporting award, 1974. Mem. Friends of Earth. Democrat. Club: Lions. Home: 110 Shannon Dr Rockingham NC 28379 Office: PO Box 1888 Rockingham NC 28379

COX, CLAUDE CALVIN, writer, radio-TV producer; b. Denton, Tex., Dec. 9, 1928; s. Claude Cecil and Olive May (Neff) C.; B.A. in Journalism, N. Tex. State U., 1949; M.A. in Clin. Psychology, U. Kans., 1951; m. Glorida Lee Dice, June 16, 1955; children—Gloria Cecille, Barbara Joyce. Pub. relations dir. Am. Investors Life Ins. Co., Dallas, 1952; editor Ins. Jour., Dallas, 1953; writer, producer weekly TV program Tex. in Review, Dallas, 1954-55; regional newsman CBS-TV, N.Y., Los Angeles, 1956; asst. news dir. Sta. KRLD-TV, Dallas, 1957-60; pub. relations dir. Six Flags over Tex., Ga., and Mid Am., Great S.W. Corp., 1961-67; writer-producer Baptist Hour, Powerline, Soulsearchers radio programs So. Bapt. Conv., Ft. Worth, 1968—; instr. photo-journalism U. Kans., summer 1956; cons. Tyndale House Pubs., Chgo., 1974—. Cons. Tex. Tourism Assn., 1963-67; pres. Tex. Travel Counselors Assn., 1963; bd. dirs. Tex. Indian Affairs, 1962-64; Elder, chmn. of bd. and congregation 1st Christian Ch. (Disciples of Christ), Arlington, Tex. Served to lt. comdr. AC, USNR, 1953. Recipient Ann. award Nat. Press Club, 1956, Outstanding Layman's award Religious Heritage Am., 1970. Mem. AFTRA, Screen Actors Guild, Nat. Assn. Psychol. Researchers, Pub. Opinion Survey Inst. Republican. Author: Religious Landmarks of America, 1975; Streams in the Desert, 1977; Success in Black, 1978. Home: 2115 Coral Dr Arlington TX 76010 Office: 6350 W Freeway Fort Worth TX 76150

COX, CONRAD MICHAEL, mfg. co. exec.; b. Johnson City Tenn., Sept. 4, 1944; s. W.B. and Ruth (Corpening) Cox; M.S., E. Tenn. State U., 1966, M.B.A., 1968; postgrad. U. Tenn., 1978. Staff asst. to regional mgr. and v.p. Texaco, Inc., Atlanta, 1969-74; v.p. Cameron Real Estate Co., Columbia, S.C., 1974-76; gen. mgr. Craig Oil Co., Marianna, Fla., 1976-77; account mgr. S.E., Maremont Corp., Atlanta, 1977—; speaker, lobbyist S.C. Petroleum Council, 1972-74. Mem. S.C. Petroleum Council, S.C. Real Estate Bd., Nat. Assn. Real Estate Bds., Fla. Petroleum Council. Republican. Methodist. Clubs: U.S. Lawn Tennis Assn., Atlanta Lawn Tennis Assn. Home and Office: 2315 N Forest Dr Marietta GA 30062

COX, DONALD EMERY, chem. engr.; b. Joplin, Mo., June 12, 1921; s. William Emery and Vera Leona (Hall) C.; B.S. in Chem. Engring., Okla. State U., 1943; m. B. Marie Chauncey, July 3, 1943; children—Albert Emery, Anita Emily, Raymond Emery. With chem. div. PPG Industries, Corpus Christi, Tex., 1943-78; v.p., gen. mgr. Refinery Terminal Fire Co., Corpus Christi, 1978—; cons. environ. engr., 1978—. Bd. dirs. Community Devel. Corp. of Corpus Christi, v.p., 1978—; bd. dirs. Lower Nueces River Water Supply Dist., also pres., 1972—; mem. Coastal Bend Council Govts., 1966—, chmn., 1966-68, exec. com., 1966—; mem. Corpus Christi Zoning and Planning Commn., 1959-63; environ. quality com. Council Govts., 1972—, chmn., 1972-76; adv. com. Nueces River Basin Water Planning, vice chmn., 1977-78; trustee Corpus Christi YWCA, 1970-76, pres., 1974-76. Recipient Community Service award PPG Industries, 1973, named Corporate Citizen of Year, 1976; registered profl. engr. Fellow Am. Inst. Chem. Engrs. (chmn. Coastal Bend sect. 1978, Service to Society award 1978); mem. Am. Chem. Soc., Corpus Christi C. of C., Air Pollution Control Assn. Democrat. Presbyterian. Clubs: Cactus and Succulent, S. Tex. Engrs. Patentee in field. Home: 369 W Saxet Dr Corpus Christi TX 78408 Office: PO Box 4162 Corpus Christi TX 78408

COX, EDWIN, III, chem. engr.; b. Richmond, Va., Oct. 31, 1931; s. Edwin and Virginia (DeMott) C.; B.S., Va. Mil. Inst., 1953; M.Ch.E., U. Va., 1960; m. Sally Dreyfus Carr, Oct. 30, 1965; children—Virginia Meade, Edwin Carr, James Maxwell, William Hatcher. Pres., Commonwealth Lab., Inc., Richmond, 1964—; partner Edwin Cox Assos., Richmond, Va., 1963—. Pres., Historic Richmond Found., 1971-73; chmn. Richmond Independence Bicentennial Commn., 1971-76; capt. Va. Army N.G., 1956-66; col. Res. Served with U.S. Army, 1953-56. Fellow Am. Inst. Chemists; mem. Am. Inst. Chem. Engrs., Am. Soc. Metals, Air Pollution Control Assn., Sons of Revolution in Va. (pres. 1976-78, gen. v.p. 1979—), Soc. Colonial Wars (council 1964-70, 76-79), Va., Nat. socs. profl. engrs., Fertilizer Soc. (London), Va. Acad. Sci., Inst. Metals (London), Soc. Chem. Industry (London), Chemists Club, N.Y. Engrs. Club. Episcopalian. Clubs: The Commonwealth, Country Club of Virginia, Focus Club, 2300 Club. Home: 7111 Pine Tree Rd Richmond VA 23229 Office: 2209 E Broad St Richmond VA 23223

COX, FLOYD BROOKS, JR., dentist; b. Gallipolis, Ohio, Feb. 23, 1920; s. Floyd Brooks and Mary Adele (Wallman) C.; student W.Va. U., 1938-41; D.D.S., U. Mich., 1944; postgrad. U. Ala., 1946-47; m. Marjorie Thomas Ballengee, Aug. 17, 1949; 1 dau., Mary Elizabeth. Staff dentist Manhattan Project, Oak Ridge, 1944-46; pvt. practice dentistry, Morgantown, W.Va., 1948—; mem. staff St. Vincent Pallotti Hosp., Morgantown, Monongalia Gen. Hosp., Morgantown. Bd. dirs. Monongalia chpt. ARC, 1954-62, chmn., 1961; bd. dirs. Park Hills Community Assn., 1962-63. Served with USPHS, 1946-48; capt. USAF, 1952-53. Mem. Am., W.Va., Monongalia County (pres. 1958) dental assns., Am. Endodontic Soc., S.R., U.S. Power Squadron (charter), U.S. Pony Clubs, No. W.Va. Automobile Assn. (dir.), Psi Omega. Roman Catholic. Elk. Clubs: Suncrest Garden, Cotillion. Home: 32 Bates Rd Morgantown WV 26505 Office: 344 Spruce St Morgantown WV 26505

COX, GLENDA EVONNE, legal adminstr.; b. Troup, Tex., Apr. 5, 1937; d. John Henry and Eula Mae (Kilgore) Barkley; degree in Bus. Adminstrn., Fed. Inst., 1956; m. Don D. Cox, Oct. 1, 1960; children—Janis, Larry. Office mgr., sec. Clapp & Beall, Attys., Tyler, Tex., 1956-60; sec. Sleeper, Boynton, Burleson, Williams & Johnston, Attys., Waco, Tex., 1960-62; sec. Bracewell, Reynolds & Patterson, Attys., Houston, 1962-66; office mgr., sec., Reynolds, Allen & Cook, Attys., Houston, 1966-75, legal adminstr., 1975—; mem. adv. bd. and faculty North Harris County Coll., Houston, 1979-80. Mem. Assn. Legal Adminstrs. (chpt. pres. 1979-80). Republican. Baptist. Home: 906 Twin Falls St Houston TX 77088 Office: 16th Floor 1100 Milam Bldg Houston TX 77002

COX, HEADLEY MORRIS, JR., univ. dean; b. Mt. Olive, N.C., July 25, 1916; s. Headley Morris and Frank (English) C.; A.B., Duke U., 1937, M.A., 1939; postgrad. U. Colo. Sch. Oriental Langs., 1944-45; Ph.D., U. Pa., 1958; m. Irene Todd, June 26, 1940; children—John Morris, Debora English Cox Gunnels, Thomas Headley. Educator, Clemson U., 1939—, successively instr., asst. prof., asso. prof., prof. English, head dept. English, 1950-69, dean Coll. Liberal Arts, 1969—; sr. Fulbright lectr. U. Graz (Austria), 1958-59. Served with Intelligence, USN, 1944-46. Mem. MLA, Phi Beta Kappa. Methodist. Home: 213 Riggs Dr Clemson NC 29631 Office: 801 Strode Tower Clemson U Clemson SC 29631

COX, HOLLIS UTAH, veterinarian, microbiologist; b. Holdenville, Okla., Mar. 4, 1944; s. Hollis Roy and Molinda Edline (Powell) C.; B.S., Okla. State U., 1965, D.V.M., 1967; Ph.D., La. State U., 1973; m. Debra Dawn Campbell, Dec. 4, 1976; children—Lindy Belle, Hollis Utah. Pvt. vet. med. practice, Choctaw, Okla., 1969-70; project veterinarian, spl. lectr. NIH-La. State U., Baton Rouge, 1970-73; asst. prof. microbiology Auburn (Ala.) U., 1973-75; asso. prof. vet. bacteriology La. State U., Baton Rouge, 1975—, chief clin. diagnostic sect., 1980—; cons. to pvt. vet. practices, 1975—. Campaign chmn. for vets. United Way, 1978. Served to capt. USAF, 1967-69; Vietnam. Diplomate Am. Coll. Vet. Microbiologists; cert. specialist in microbiology Am. Acad. Microbiology, Am. Soc. Clin. Pathologists. Mem. Am. Vet. Med. Assn., La. Vet. Med. Assn., Baton Rouge Area Vet. Med. Assn. (pres. 1980), Am. Assn. Vet. Med. Colls., Am. Soc. Microbiology, Am. Assn. Vet. Lab. Diagnosticians, Kenilworth Civic Assn., Sigma Xi, Phi Zeta, Phi Eta Sigma, Alpha Psi. Baptist. Clubs: La. State U. Union, Masons, Shriners, Rosicrucian Order. Contbr. articles to profl. jours. Home: 1323 Kenilworth Pkwy Baton Rouge LA 70808 Office: Dept of Veterinary Microbiology Louisiana State University Baton Rouge LA 70803

COX, IRENE DICKSON, educator; b. Grassy Creek, N.C., Oct. 12, 1917; d. John Alexander and Ruby Esther (Thompson) Dickson; B.S., Appalachian State U., 1938; Certificate in Spl. Edn., Radford Tchrs. Coll., 1973; m. George Dewey Cox, Dec. 24, 1940; children—Bill Dickey, Nathalia Sue. Tchr. English and French, Lansing (N.C.) High Sch., 1938-39; tchr. Mountain Park (N.C.) Elementary Sch., 1939-40; tchr. English, Va.-Carolina High Sch., Grassy Creek, N.C., 1940-60, Ashe Central High Sch., Jefferson, N.C., 1961-67; tchr. spl. edn. Mt. Rogers Sch., Whitetop, Va., 1971-76; girls basketball coach Va.-Carolina High Sch., 1940-57. Registrar, Grassy Creek Precinct, 1967-80; nat. def. chmn. DAR, 1970-76; v.p. UDC, 1974-76, pres., 1976-77, mem. edn. com. N.C. div., 1977-80, chmn. awards com. Ashe County chpt., 1978-80; pres. Ashe County Friends of Library, West Jefferson, N.C., 1979-80; publicity chmn. dist. 7, N.C. Extension Homemakers Assn., 1978-80, pres. Grassy Creek club, 1979-80. Recipient scholarship, Appalachian State U., 1972, Radford (Va.) State Tchrs. Coll., 1973. Home: Route 1 Box 6 Grassy Creek NC 28631

COX, JENNINGS GODDIN, educator; b. Richmond, Va., July 23, 1945; s. William Jennings and Mary Elizabeth (Goddin) C.; B.A., Randolph-Macon Coll., 1967; M.S., Va. Commonwealth U., 1969; Ph.D., U. Mo., 1974; m. Patricia Ball Harrison, Aug. 12, 1967; 1 son, Patrick Jennings. Counselor, Central State Hosp., Commonwealth of Va., Petersburg, 1969-71, U. Mo., Columbia, 1972-73; psychologist in pvt. practice, Dallas, 1975—; asso. prof. U. Tex. Health Sci. Center, Dallas, 1975—; dir. counseling services Longwood Coll., Farmville, Va., 1980—; cons. Mental Health Center, 1974-77, Tex. Rehab. Commn., 1975-79, Dallas Ind. Sch. Dist., 1976-78. Rehab. Services Adminstrn. grantee, 1967-68, 71-73; Research Soc. Am. grantee, 1976; Instl. Research grantee, 1977, 78. Mem. Am. Psychol. Assn., Nat. Rehab. Assn., Am. Personnel and Guidance Assn., Dallas Mental Health Assn., Dallas Psychol. Assn., Omicron Delta Kappa, Pi Epsilon Mu. Democrat. Episcopalian. Contbr. articles to profl. jours. Home: 7008 Lakeshore Dr Dallas TX 75214 Office: 5323 Harry Hines Blvd Dallas TX 75235

COX, JOHN THOMAS, JR., lawyer; b. Shreveport, La., Feb. 9, 1943; s. John Thomas and Gladys Virginia (Canterbury) C.; B.S., La. State U., 1965, J.D., 1968; m. Tracey Lou Tanquary, Aug. 27, 1966; children—John Thomas III, Stephen Lewis. Asso., Sanders, Miller, Downing & Kean, Baton Rouge, 1968-70; asso., Blanchard, Walker, O'Quin & Roberts, Shreveport, La., 1970-71, partner, 1971—; dir. So. Saw Co., Inc., Shreveport. Adv. bd. mem. La. Law Inst., 1969—; guest lectr. bus. law Centenary Coll. La., 1973—. Served with AUS, 1963-70. Mem. Am., La., Shreveport bar assn., La. Defense Lawyers Assn., Petroleum Club Shreveport, Shreveport C. of C. (mem. com. on indsl. devel. 1975—), Order of Coif, Phi Kappa Phi, Omicron Delta Kappa. Democrat. Presbyn. (elder 1977—). Clubs: Rotary (dir. 1979-80), Country (Shreveport, La.). Home: 555 Dunmoreland Dr Shreveport LA 71106 Office: PO Drawer 1126 Shreveport LA 71163

COX, LINDSAY WHEELER, JR., assn. exec.; b. Winston-Salem, N.C., Mar. 2, 1931; s. Lindsay Wheeler and Margaret Matthew (Noel) C.; student Appalachian State U., 1949-51; B.S. in Landscape Architecture, N.C. State U., 1959; degree in Municipal Adminstrn., U. N.C., Chapel Hill, 1964; m. Peggy Nix Lyerly, June 12, 1954; children—Betsy Lin, Stephen Lyerly, David Noel. Community planner State of N.C., 1958-61; partner Townsend & Cox, Landscape Architects & Planning Cons., Greenboro, N.C., 1961-62; chief planner Kavanaugh-Smith & Co., Greenboro, 1962-63; planning dir. Guilford County (N.C.), 1963-69; exec. dir. Piedmont Triad Council Govts., Greensboro, 1969—. Lectr. in field. Pres. Green Valley Park, N.C. Land Use Congress, 1973. Bd. dirs. Gov.'s Beautification Com., 1970-73. Served with USN, 1951-54. Mem. Gov.'s State and Local Task Force, Nat. Assn. Regional Councils (bd. dirs. 1973-75), U.S. (pres. 1973-74), N.C. (pres. 1971-72) regional council dirs. assns., Am. Planning Assn. (N.C. chpt. pres. 1968), Am. Inst. Cert. Planners, Nat. County Planning Dirs. Assn. (bd. dirs. 1968), Internat. City Mgmt. Assn. Rotarian. Club: Sertoma (Man of Year 1967). Contbr. articles to profl. jours. Home: 1304 Hobbs Rd Greensboro NC 27410 Office: 2120 Pinecroft Rd Greensboro NC 27407

COX, MARY ELIZABETH BLEVINS, career counselor; b. Memphis, Jan. 10, 1941; d. David and Mary Marie (Sharpe) Blevins; B.A., San Diego State Coll., 1970; M.A., Montclair State Coll., Upper Montclair, N.J.; J.D., U. San Diego, 1978; 1 son, Anthony Maurice. Service order writer Pacific Telephone Co., 1964-67; ednl. opportunities adv. San Diego State Coll., 1968-70; counselor Paterson (N.J.) State Coll., 1970-71; asst. dir. residence halls Montclair State Coll., 1971-73; asst. residence dean U. Calif., San Diego, 1974-76, residence counselor, 1976-78; Reginald Heber Smith fellow Neighborhood Legal Aid, Richmond, Va., 1978—. Mem. Am. Personnel and Guidance Assn. Lutheran. Home: 320 Kirkland Dr Apt D Richmond VA 25227 Office: 823 E Main St Richmond VA 23219

COX, RALPH FREDERICK, printing co. exec.; b. Boston, June 6, 1923; s. Edward J. and Hilda Catherine (Kunkel) C.; B.S., Babson Coll., 1949; m. Mary Eleanor Connelly, Feb. 4, 1950; children—Carolyn Louise, Ralph Frederick, Cynthia Ann. Sales rep. Lever Bros. Co., 1950-52, Westfield River Paper Co., 1952-57, Continetal Can Co., 1957-66; exec. v.p. Hibbert Co., 1966-72; pres. Hibbert-So., Inc., Houston, 1972—; dir. Hibbert Co., Retail Direct Corp., Hibbert-Laman, Denver, Printing Industries of Gulf Coast. Served to capt. U.S. Army, 1942-45. Decorated Bronze Star medal. Mem. Am. Mgmt. Assn., Mail Advt. Service Assn., Internat., Houston Direct Mail/Mktg. Assn. Republican. Roman Catholic. Home: 6019 Coral Ridge St Houston TX 77069 Office: 6855 Wynnwood St Houston TX 77008

COX, RAYMOND GEORGE, geophysicist, electronics mfg. co. exec.; b. Toronto, Ont., Can., Mar. 13, 1921; s. Silas and Helen Mary (Street) C.; came to U.S., 1954, naturalized, 1977; B.Sc., U. Toronto, 1944; m. Fabiola Burgos, June 23, 1954; 1 dau., Roxana Helen. Geophysicist Imperial Oil Co., Edmonton, Alta., Can., 1945-46; geophysicist Tropical Oil Co., Bogota, Colombia, 1946-48; geophysicist Carter Oil Co., Tulsa, 1948-54; geophysicist Internat. Petroleum Co., Talara, Peru, 1948-54, Caiberian, Cuba, 1955; geophys. supr. Petroleo Brasileiro S.Am., Rio de Janiero, Brazil, 1956-62; v.p. internat. ops. Geo Space Corp., Houston, 1963—. Mem. Am. Mgmt. Assn. (co-chmn. 1974, speaker), Soc. Exploration Geophysicists, European Assn. Exploration Geophysicists, Assn. Mexicano Exploration Geophysicist, Can. Geophys. Soc. Republican. Roman Catholic. Pioneered comml. bus. with U.S.S.R., Albania, Romania, People's Republic of China. Home: PO Box 1383 Boca Raton FL 33432 Office: 5803 Glenmont Dr Houston TX 77081

COX, RONALD BAKER, ednl. adminstr., mech. engr.; b. Chattanooga, Sept. 27, 1943; s. Fred T. and Mary B. Cox; B.S., U. Tenn., 1965, M.S., 1968; Ph.D., Rice U., 1970; M.B.A., Vanderbilt U., 1980; m. Nancy Charline Barger, June 12, 1965; children—Kathy, David, Sherry. Design engr. DuPont Co., Chattanooga, 1965-66; chief engr. Inds. Boiler Co., Chattanooga, 1966-68; asst. prof. mech. engring. U. Tenn., Chattanooga, 1970-72, asso. prof., dir. research, 1972-78, prof., dean Sch. Engring., 1979—; dir. vehicle research program U.S. Dept. Transp., 1974-76; mgmt. and engring. cons. to govt. and industry. Chmn. Congl. Campaign, 1976. Named an Outstanding Young Men of Am., U.S. Jaycees, 1979. Mem. ASME (pres. 1979-80), Greater Chattanooga Area C. of C., Tenn. Soc. Profl. Engrs. (dir.), Nat. Soc. Profl. Engrs., Sigma Xi, Tau Beta Pi. Club: Chattanooga Engring. (pres. 1980). Contbr. articles to profl. jours. Office: Sch Engring U Tenn Chattanooga TN 37401

COX, SANDERS BROWNLOW, JR., solid state physicist; b. Dallas, Aug. 31, 1945; s. Sanders Brownlow and Clara Sue (Haywood) Cox; B.S., So. Methodist U., 1967; M.A., U. Tex.-Arlington, 1973; m. Linda Sue Dupree, June 4, 1967; children—Meredith, Brandon. Grad. asst. physics U. Tex.-Arlington, 1971-73; program mgr., sr. process engr. Tex. Instruments Inc., Dallas, 1973—; lectr. U. Tex.-Arlington, 1975—; cons. radiation effects. Served to capt. USAF, 1967-71. Mem. Arnold Air Soc. (nat. ops. officer 1966-67), IEEE, Am. Phys. Soc., ASTM, Sigma Pi Sigma. Project officer underground nuclear tests, researcher radiation effects, semicondr. devices, quantum theory solids, energy band theory. Contbr. articles to profl. publs. Home: 2728 Aspen Ct Plano TX 75075 Office: MS976 Tex Instruments Inc Dallas TX 75222

COX, WILLIAM ANDREW, cardiovascular thoracic surgeon; b. Columbus, Ga., Aug. 3, 1925; s. Virgil Augustus and Dale Jackson C.; student Presbyn. Coll., 1942-43, Harvard U., 1944-45, Cornell U., 1945; B.S., Emory U., 1950, M.D., 1954; M.S. in Surgery, Baylor U., 1960; m. Nina Recelle Hobby, Jan. 1, 1948; children—Constance Lynn Cox Rogers, Patricia Ann Cox Brown, William Robert, Janet Elaine. Commd. 1st lt. M.C., U.S. Army, 1954, advanced through grades to col., 1969; intern Brooke Army Med. Center, San Antonio, 1954-55, resident in gen. surgery, 1956-60; resident in cardiovascular thoracic surgery Walter Reed Army Med. Center, Washington, 1960-62, staff cardiothoracic surgeon, 1962; asst. chief cardiothoracic surgery Letterman Gen. Hosp., 1962-65; chief dept. surgery and cardiothoracic surgery 121 Evacuation Hosp., Seoul, Korea, cons. cardiothoracic surgery Korean Theatre, 1965-66; asst. chief cardiothoracic surgery Brooke Army Med. Center, 1965-69, chief, 1969-73; ret., 1973; clin. prof. cardio-thoracic surgery U. Tex. Sch. Medicine, San Antonio, 1971—; practice medicine specializing in cardiovascular thoracic surgery, Corpus Christi, Tex., 1973—; cons. cardio-thoracic surgery Brooke Army Med. Center, San Antonio, 1977—; dir. disaster med. care region 3A Tex. State Dept. Health, 1973—; mem. Coastal Bend council Gov. Emergency Med. Service Commn., 1979—; chief staff Meml. Med. Center, 1980. Served to lt. USN, 1945-48. Decorated Legion of Merit; recipient A Prefix award Surgeon Gen. Army; diplomate Am. Bd. Surgery, Am. Bd. Thoracic Surgery. Fellow Am. Coll. Chest Physicians; mem. AMA, Soc. Thoracic Surgeons, Denton A. Cooley Cardiovascular Surgery Soc., Tex. Med. Assn., So. Thoracic Surgery Assn., Nueces County Med. Soc., Corpus Christi Surg. Soc., 38th Parallel Med. Soc. Republican. Presbyterian. Clubs: Yacht (past commodore presidio)(San Francisco); T-Bar-M Racquet Corpus Christi Country; Fort Sam Houston Officer's (San Antonio). Contbr. numerous articles in field to profl. jours. Home: 5214 Wooldridge Rd Corpus Christi TX 78413 Office: 2601 Hospital Blvd Corpus Christi TX 78405

COYNER, RANDOLPH STRATTON, JR., educator, accountant; b. Winston-Salem, N.C., July 28, 1944; s. Stratton and Patricia Firestone (Chatham) C.; A.B., U. Miami, 1967, M.B.A., 1968; postgrad. U. Md., 1970-74, Ga. State U., 1976; m. Diana Dawson, June 14, 1964; children—William James, Charles Christopher. Sr. accountant, cons. Peat, Marwick, Mitchell and Co., Washington, 1968-70; instr. U. Md., College Park, 1970-74; mgr. Internal Audit Ryder System, Inc., Miami, Fla., 1974-75; asst. prof., acting chmn. Fla. Atlantic U., Boca Raton, 1975—; pres. Exec. Consultants Internat., Inc. C.P.A., N.C., Md. Mem. Nat. Assn. Accountants (chpt. pres., dir., regional officer), Am. Inst. C.P.A.s, Phi Eta Sigma (pres. 1966-6), Omicron Delta Kappa (treas. 1967-68). Home: 1901 S Ocean Blvd 508 Boca Raton FL 33432

CRABTREE, JACK TURNER, lawyer; b. Mountain View, Okla., Feb. 23, 1936; s. Andrew J. and Dorrit (Turner) C.; Mus. B., Oklahoma City U., 1960, J.D., 1964; divorced; children—Elizabeth Kaye, Deborah Anne, Jacqueline Sue, Nancy Lea. Admitted to Okla. Supreme Ct. bar, 1964, U.S. Supreme Ct. bar, 1967, Dist. Ct. Western Dist. Okla. bar, 1964, U.S. Ct. Appeals 10th Circuit bar, 1965; practiced in Oklahoma City, 1964—; mem. firm Matthews, Buck, Cain, Crabtree & Lynn, 1965-67, Buck, Crabtree, Ransdell & Buford Inc., 1967-79, Jack T. Crabtree & Assos., P.C., 1979—; adj. prof. law Oklahoma City U. Sch. Law, 1972—; Dir. Quail Creek Bank N.A. Chmn. Okla. Environ. Protection Authority, 1972. Mem. Oklahoma County (Outstanding Young Lawyer, 1970, chmn. com. specialization 1975), Okla. (chmn. legal assts. com. 1975-78), Am. (com. legal assts. 1974—, council gen. practice sect. 1973-77, 79—) bar assns., Kappa Alpha, Phi Alpha Delta, Blue Key. Democrat. Presbyterian. Home: 6432 Brandywine Oklahoma City OK 73116 Office: 6242 N Western Suite 201 Oklahoma City OK 73118

CRABTREE, MATTIE JO, nurse epidemiologist, educator; b. Cherokee County, Ala., Nov. 4, 1930; d. W.W. and Oma M. Lane; B.S., Jacksonville State U., 1950, M.S., 1973, B.S. with honors in Nursing, Lurleen B. Wallace Sch. Nursing, 1976; M.A. in Mgmt., Central Mich. U., 1977; postgrad. U. Ala., 1977—; m. Burlies Crabtree, Oct. 17, 1952; children—Steven, Gregory. Tchr., Sand Rock High Sch., Leesburg, Ala., 1950-51, Valley Head (Ala.) High Sch., 1951-52; chief technologist Campbell's Clinic, Chattanooga, 1957-62, Finney's Clinic, Gadsden, Ala., 1962-68, Cherokee County Hosp., Centre, Ala., 1969-71; ednl. coordinator Bapt. Meml. Hosp., Gadsden, Ala., 1971-78, nurse epidemiologist, 1976—, dir. systems design, 1978—; dir. Gadsden State Jr. Coll., 1971-78. Mem. Nat. League of Nursing, Ala. Nursing Assn., NEA, Ala. Edn. Assn., Ala. Nursing Assn., N.E. Ala. Soc. Med. Technologists, Ala. State Soc. Med. Technologists, Am. Soc. Med. Technologists, Am. Soc. Clin. Pathologists, Assn. Practitioners of Infection Control. Baptist. Home: Route 6 PO Box 325 Fort Payne AL 35967 Office: Baptist Memorial Hospital 1007 Goodyear Ave Gadsden AL 35903

CRABTREE, ORNAL WILLIAM, truck leasing co. exec.; b. Mobile, Ala., Nov. 29, 1930; s. Nell Veronica (O'Connor) Crabtree Kruithoff; stepson Albert George Kruithoff; student Tulane U., 1951-52, U. Ala., 1948-49, Ga. State Tchrs. Coll., 1955-60; children—Schuyler Elizabeth, Michael William, Patrick William. Buyer, A & P Tea Co., Mobile, 1948-51, New Orleans, 1952-55, Atlanta, 1955-60; sales rep. Toni Co., Atlanta, 1960-61, Charlotte, N.C., 1962-63, John Crosland Co., Charlotte, 1963-65; sec.-treas. Phoenix-Atlanta Inc., Atlanta, 1965-68; sales coordinator to v.p. Saunders Leasing System, Birmingham, Ala., 1968—, also dir. Active Boy Scouts Am.; co-chmn. Birmingham unit Cancer Crusade, 1974. Served with inf. U.S. Army, 1951-52. Mem. N.Am. Gasoline Tax Conf., Car and Truck Leasing Assn., Nat. Assn. Truck Stop Operators, Am. Assn. Motor Vehicle Adminstrs., Ky. Cols. Democrat. Roman Catholic. Clubs: Elks, Sales Mktg. Execs. (dir. 1979), The Club Birmingham. Home: 2833 Montevallo Rd Birmingham AL 35223 Office: 201 Office Park Dr Birmingham AL 35223

CRABTREE, THEODORE EUGENE, accountant; b. Mobile, Ala., July 28, 1931; s. Theodore and Addie Lee (Burton) C.; student Ala. State Vocat. Trade Sch., 1955-56, U. Ala., 1956-60, Springhill Coll., 1960-62, U. South Ala., 1973-74; m. Valrie Louise Mabrey, May 29, 1951; children—Theodore Eugene, Sandra Lynn. Order clk. Mobile Paint Mfg. Co., 1955; cost accountant Brookley AFB, Mobile, 1955-66; pvt. pub. accounting practice Mobile, 1958-66; prin. Theodore E. Crabtree & Assos., Mobile, 1966—. Served with USAF, 1951-55. Registered pub. accountant, Ala.; enrolled to practice before IRS. Served to tech. sgt. Ala. Air N.G. Mem. Nat. Soc. Pub. Accountants, Ala. Assn. Pub. Accountants (dir. 1969-73, 77—, chpt. pres. 1969-71), Nat. Assn. Enrolled Agts., Ala. Soc. Enrolled Agts. (founder, incorporator), Air Force Sgts. Assn. Club: Masons (3 deg.). Home: 52 E Charmingdale Dr Mobile AL 36608 Office: 3750 Moffat Rd Mobile AL 36618

CRACKEN, L. WILLIAM, computer mfg. co. exec.; b. N.Y.C., Jan. 6, 1920; s. William and Rachel C.; B.A., Denver U., 1954; M.S., George Washington U., 1956; M.B.A., U. Tex., 1976; m. Marilyn Morris, June 5, 1955; children—Rachel Elizabeth, John Robert William. Commd. U.S. Air Force, 1942, advanced through grades to col., 1974; served in combat SW Pacific, 1942-44, Korea, 1951-52; later sr. staff officer NATO; dir. computer services Air Force Logistics Command, ret., 1974; with Datapoint Corp., San Antonio, 1976—, now dir. master prodn. planning; asso. prof. U. Md., 1959-63. Bd. dirs. San Antonio Little Theater, 1972-74. Decorated Legion of Merit, Bronze Star, others. Mem. Am. Inst. Indsl. Engrs., Soc. Mfg. Engrs., AAUP, Am. Mgmt. Assn. Republican. Episcopalian. Club: Masons. Office: Datapoint Corp 9725 Datapoint Dr San Antonio TX 78284

CRADDICK, THOMAS RUSSELL, state legislator; b. Beloit, Wis., Sept. 19, 1943; s. Russell F. and Beatrice (Kowalick) C.; B.B.A., Tex. Tech U., 1965, M.B.A., 1966; m. Nadine Nayfa, Sept. 6, 1969; children—Christi Leigh, Thomas Russell. Instr., Tex. Tech U., 1966; v.p., dir. CBC, Inc., Midland, Tex., 1965-72; v.p., dir. Gulf States Enterprises, Inc., Midland, 1965-72; pres., dir. Field Creek Pecan Farms, Inc., Midland, 1968-72, Tri-State, Inc., Midland, 1972-75; v.p. sales Well Fluids Corp., 1975-78; sales rep. Mustang Mud Inc., 1978—; mem. Tex. Ho. of Reps., Austin, 1968—. Adv. dir. Clover House in Permian Basin; bd. dirs. Midland Boys Club. Mem. Nat. Tex. Tech Ex-Students Assn. (past dir.), Tex. Tech Ex-Students Assn. (past pres. Midland chpt.), Midland Jr. C. of C. (past dir.). Lion. Home: 3108 Stanolind St Midland TX 79701 Office: 408 W Wall St Midland TX 79701

CRADDOCK, CHARLES RUSSELL, mgmt. and tax cons., numismatist, philatelist; b. Waco, Tex., Aug. 19, 1916; s. Charles Yancey and Lillian (Russell) C.; student Lamar Tech. U., 1947-48; U. Houston, 1950-51; m. Bonnie Maxine Partin, June 26, 1947 (dec.); m. Nancy Ruth Sowell, June 14, 1964; children—Kathleen Mary, John Robert, Cathy Lynn, Charles Edwin. Pres., Craddock Bus. Services, Inc., Bus. Cons., Houston, 1949—; asst. sec., treas. Global Truck & Equipment, Inc., Houston, 1972—. Pres., Aldine Mustang Booster Club, 1968-71. Served to tech. sgt. AUS, 1942-46. Mem. Sons Republic Tex., Am., Tex., Can. numismatic assns., DAV (life), Nat. Soc. Pub. Accts., Tex. Assn. Public Accts., Internat. Bank Note Soc., Numismatics Internat., Soc. Paper Money Collectors, Latin Am. Notaphilic Soc., Am. Philatelic Soc. Mason (32 deg., Shriner), Lion (Outstanding Service award 1956), K.T.; mem. Order Eastern Star. Home: 618 W Parker Blvd Houston TX 77091

CRADDOCK, RUSSELL PATTERSON, audiologist; b. LaRue County, Ky., Aug. 17, 1917; s. David Bennett and Margaret Beatrice (Patterson) C.; B.S., Hampton Inst., 1972; M.Ed., U. Va., 1973; m. Nancy Louise Penoyar, Oct. 13, 1956. Embalmer, funeral dir., Franklin, Ky., 1947-50; enlisted U.S. Army, 1950, advanced through grades to capt., 1962; served in Japan, 1960-62; with Counter-Intelligence Corps, 1950-62; ret., 1964; clin. audiologist Florence (S.C.) ENT Clinic, 1973—. Served with USAAF, 1940-45; CBI, ETO. Mem. Am. Speech Lang. and Hearing Assn., S.C. Speech and Hearing Assn., VFW, Am. Legion, Ret. Officers Assn., Res. Officers Assn., Am. Mil. Retirees. Clubs: Pee Dee Shrine, Masons, Knights Templar. Home: 2815 W Boxwood Ave Florence SC 29501 Office: 441 W Cheves St Florence SC 29501

CRAFT, WILLIAM JACOB, univ. ofcl.; b. Gaffney, S.C., Oct. 14, 1941; s. William McElveen and Ruth Ann (Hord) C.; B.S. in Applied Math., N.C. State U., 1963, B.S. in Physics, 1963; M.S. in Engring. Mechanics (NSF fellow), Clemson U., 1969, Ph.D. in Engring. Mechanics (NSF fellow), 1970; m. Elizabeth Ann Fullerton, May 29, 1965; children—Lydia Elizabeth, Sonia Ann, Michael Jacob. Tutor dept. applied math. U. Sydney (Australia), 1964-66; instr. dept. engring. mechanics Clemson (S.C.) U., 1971; sr. engr. Structures div. Martin Marietta Corp., Orlando, Fla., 1971-72; group engr., vis. prof. mech. engring. N.C. Agrl. and Tech. State U., Greensboro, 1972-74, asso. prof., 1974-77, dir. grad. engring. program, 1976—, asst. dean Sch. Engring., 1977—; engring. cons. Lawrence Livermore (Calif.) Lab., 1979. Registered profl. engr., N.C. Mem. Am. Acad. Mechanics, Am. Soc. Engring. Edn., Sigma Xi. Contbr. articles to profl. jours.; patentee in field. Home: 5505 Wild Turkey Rd Whitsett NC 27377 Office: Sch Engring NC Agrl and Tech State U 312 N Dudley St Greensboro NC 27411

CRAGO, H. CARMAN, II, packaging cons.; b. Wheeling, W.Va., Aug. 23, 1921; s. Homer C. and Ethel (Kittle) C.; A.B., W.Va. U., 1943; postgrad. U. Pitts., 1950-51; m. Sarah Kathleen Carter, Aug. 4, 1945; children—David Hughes, John Carman. Adminstrv. asst. Hazel-Atlas Glass Co., Wheeling, W.Va., 1944-49, product mgr. beverage containers, 1950-55; dist. sales mgr. Glass div. Continental Can Co., Cleve., 1955-56, Clin. 1957-60. Midwest area mgr., Chgo., 1961-64; regional mgr. Knox Glass, Inc., Palestine, Tex., 1964-69; mgr. S.W. region Glass Containers Corp., Dallas, 1969-70; nat. sales mgr. Obear-Nester Glass, 1971-74; gen. sales mgr. Windor Industries, Inc., Dallas, 1974-75; cons. Par-Pak Co. Inc., Narberth, Pa., 1975-77; pres. Crago & Co. Inc., Packaging Cons., 1977—. Served to lt. (j.g.) USNR. 1943-44. Mem. Nat. Assn. Bus. Econs., Ret. Officers Assn. Washington, Phi Delta Theta Alumni Assn. Presbyn. (elder). Mason. Club: Admirals (Dallas). Home and office: 7606 Chattington Dr Dallas TX 75248

CRAIG, LOUIS ELWOOD, chem. co. exec.; b. Clifton Hill, Mo., Dec. 10, 1921; s. Clyde Allen and Elsie (Metcalf) C.; A.B., Central Coll., 1943; Ph.D. in Organic Chemistry, U. Rochester, 1948; m. Lorene Virginia Higgins, July 17, 1943; children—James Allen, David Andrew, Margaret Louise, Barbara Jean. Chemist Am. Cyanamid Co., Stamford, Conn., 1943-46; research fellow U. Rochester, 1946-48; research chemist Gen. Aniline Film Corp., Easton, Pa., 1948-54; dir. research John Deere Chem. Co., Tulsa, 1954-59, dir. research and tech. service, 1959-61, dir. marketing services, 1961-65; mgr. market research and devel. Kerr-McGee Chem. Corp., Oklahoma City, 1965-67, Western area marketing mgr., 1967-68, v.p. mfg., 1968-70, v.p. chem. mfg. div., 1972-76, dir. mfg. services, 1976-77, v.p. info. services Kerr-McGee Corp., Oklahoma City, 1970-72, dir. info. div., 1977—. Mem. Am. Chem. Soc. (past chmn. Tulsa sect.), AAAS, Am. Mgmt. Assn. Contbr. articles to profl. jours. Patentee. Home: 4921 NW 32d St Oklahoma City OK 73122 Office: Kerr McGee Center Oklahoma City OK 73125

CRAIG, MARGARET LEWIS, educator; b. Oak Grove, La., Jan. 7, 1920; d. Leon Lee and Leonie LeMay (Cochran) Lewis; B.S. with distinction, Miss. Coll., 1958, M.S., 1959, M.Guidance and Counseling, 1960; Ed.D. (fellow), U. So. Miss., 1966; m. Paul Moore Craig, Sept. 16, 1935; children—Paul Moore, Margaret Lillian. Tchr., Jackson (Miss.) Sch. System, 1958-63; asst. prof. Miss. Coll., Clinton, 1965-67; mem. faculty Northwestern State U., Natchitoches, La., 1967-68; mem. faculty dept. edn. Valdosta (Ga.) State Coll., 1968—, prof., 1977—. Pres. Lowndes Assn. for Retarded Citizens, 1974. Mem. NEA, AAUP, Ga. Assn. Educators, Internat. Reading Assn. (Ga. council), Kappa Delta Pi, Phi Delta Kappa, Alpha Delta Kappa. Home: 806 Tanglewood Dr Valdosta GA 31601 Office: Valdosta State Coll Valdosta GA 31601

CRAIG, ROBERT E. LEE, physician; b. Toledo, Oct. 7, 1936; s. Robert L. and Virginia Mae (Trautman) C.; A.B., Harvard U., 1958, M.P.H. (NASA fellow), 1967, S.M. in Hygiene (NASA fellow), 1968; M.D., C.M., McGill U., 1962; m. Elisabeth M. Welter, June 24, 1961; 1 son, Graham Robert. Intern Royal Victoria Hosp., Montreal, Que., Can., 1962-63; resident in occupational medicine Harvard Sch. Pub. Health, 1966-68, TVA, 1968-69; gen. practice medicine, Wilmington, Vt., 1965-66, specializing in occupational medicine, Chattanooga, 1968—; asst. med. dir. TVA, 1971-74, med. dir., 1974—; clin. asst. prof. Clin. Edn. Center, U. Tenn. Coll. Medicine, Chattanooga, 1975—. Served as capt. M.C., USAF, 1963-65. Diplomate Am. Bd. Preventive Medicine. Fellow Occupational Med. Assn., Am. Acad. Occupational Medicine, Am. Coll. Preventive Medicine; mem. AMA, Tenn., Chattanooga-Hamilton County med. socs., Tenn. Occupational Med. Assn. (sec.-treas. 1971-73, pres. 1973-75), Am. Nuclear Soc. (standards com. 1970—). Home: 7112 Saratoga Ln Chattanooga TN 37421 Office: Edney Bldg Chattanooga TN 37401

CRAIG, SYDNEY POLLOCK, trust co. exec.; b. Noblesville, Ind., Jan. 28, 1921; s. Sydney Pollock and Kathryn (Couden) C.; B.S. in Sci., Purdue U., 1947; m. Elizabeth White, Nov. 18, 1941; children—Sydney Pollock, III, Michael Craig Nabong. Co-mgr. David A Noyes & Co., 1960-65; v.p. Lincoln Nat. Bank, Ft. Wayne, Ind., 1965-68; sr. v.p. Worcester Bancorp (Mass.), 1968-73; exec. v.p. S.E. 1st Nat. Bank, Miami, Fla., 1973-74; pres., S.E. Banks Trust Co., N.A., Miami, 1974—. Mem. bd. investment trustees Greater Miami Opera Assn.; trustee Arthur Vining Davis Found. Served with USAAF. Decorated Air medal. Mem. Am. Bankers Assn., Boston Security Analysts Soc., Fla. Bankers Assn. Clubs: Riviera Country, Bankers. Office: 100 So Biscayne Blvd Miami FL 33131

CRAIG, THOMAS E., accountant; b. Moulton, Ala., Sept. 25, 1915; s. R. Clyde and Lassie (Fretwell) C.; student pub. schs. of Leon County, Tallahassee Partner Pentland & Cowles, C.P.A.'s, Tampa, Fla., 1952-63. Cowles, Craig, Silverman & Wooten, C.P.A.'s, Tampa, 1963—. Served with USAAF, World War II. C.P.A., Fla. Mem. Am. Inst. C.P.A.'s, Fla. Inst. C.P.A.'s. Clubs: Propellor, University (Tampa). Home: 4350 Kennedy Apt 33 Tampa FL 33609 Office: 100 Twiggs St Tampa FL 33602

CRAIGHEAD, GORDON FULTON, JR., hotel and real estate devel. exec.; b. Pitts., Apr. 2, 1925; s. Gordon Fulton and Gladys (McKinnon) C.; student Carnegie Inst. Tech., 1943, U. Rochester, 1943-44; B.S., B.Mgmt. Engring., Rensselaer Poly. Inst., 1947; B.S. in Hotel Adminstrn., Cornell U., 1949; m. Eugenia Anne Garard, Sept. 10, 1951; children—Eugenia Anne, Barbara Evans, Cameron Garard. Steward, Madison Hotel, Atlantic City, N.J., 1949-50; asst. mgr. Hidden Valley Inn, Somerset, Pa., 1950; mgr. Langwell Hotel, Elmira, N.Y., 1951; resident mgr. The Inn, Ponte Vedra Beach, Fla., 1952; asst. mgr. Cloister Hotel, Sea Island, Ga., 1952-57; restaurant mgr. Marshall Field & Co., Chgo., 1957-60; asst. dir. Presbyn.-St. Lukes Hosp., Chgo., 1960-66; v.p. Sea Pines Co., Hilton Head Island, S.C., 1966-72; pres. Atlantis Devel. Co., Hilton Head Island, 1972—, Island Realty. Mem. Beaufort County Council, 1977—; pres. bd. dirs. Beaufort County United Way, 1974, 75; chmn. bd. trustees Episcopal Ch. Home, Charleston, S.C. Served to lt. (j.g.) USNR, 1943-46. Mem. Hilton Head Island (dir., pres. 1969, 76), Beaufort County (dir.) chambers commerce, Hilton Head Island Bd. Realtors, Cornell Soc. Hotelmen (regional v.p. 1970). Republican. Episcopalian. Clubs: Oglethorp (Savannah, Ga.); Sea Pines, Hilton Head Golf (Hilton Head Island). Home: 19 Beach Lagoon Rd Hilton Head Island SC 29928 Office: Island Realty Inc 19 Coligny Plaza Hilton Head Island SC 29928

CRAIGHEAD, MOSES NATHANIEL, civic worker; b. Penhook, Va., Apr. 28, 1928; s. Morman Garfield and Ora (Edwards) C.; student Patrick Henry Community Coll., 1974-75; m. Eleanor Virginia Redd, Nov. 20, 1948; children—Eleanor Rose, Elaine Renae. With DuPont, Martinsville, Va. 1954—. Vice pres. Samuel H. Hairston Elementary Sch., Preston, Va., 1960-61; pres. George W. Carver High Sch. P.T.A., Fieldale, Va., 1969-71; mem. bd. Patrick Henry Community Coll., 1972—. Mem. Henry County Democratic Exec. Com., Spencer, Va., 1971—. Mem. N.A.A.C.P. (pres. 1970—), Martinsville-Henry County Voters League. Mem. Christian Ch. (deacon 1955, chmn. bd. 1964—). Mason. Home: Route 1 Box 78 Spencer VA 24165 Office: 315 Fayette St Martinsville VA 24112

CRAIN, BERRY, JR., chem. engr.; b. Memphis, Aug. 11, 1941; s. Berry and Inez Rovine (Claud) C.; B.S., Miss. State U., 1963; M.S., Okla. State U., 1965, Ph.D. (NASA trainee), 1973; m. Diane Rhodes Hoke, Aug. 23, 1963; children—Gregory, James, Scott, Bradley. Staff engr. Savannah River plant E. I. du Pont de Nemours & Co., Aiken, S.C., 1970—. Served with USAR, 1968-70. Mem. Sigma Chi. Methodist. Clubs: Aiken Sertoma (pres. 1975-76, dist. gov. W. Central dist. 1976-77, 1977-78, disting. pres. 1975-76, disting. gov. 1976-78). Home: 138 Vivion Dr Aiken SC 29801 Office: Savannah River Plant Aiken SC 29801

CRAIN, JOHN WALTER, hist. soc. adminstr.; b. Amarillo, Tex., July 11, 1944; s. John Clyde and Roma (McDowell) C.; B.A., U. Tex., Austin, 1967; M.A., S.W. Tex. State U., 1970; cert. in arts adminstrn., Harvard U., 1975; m. Mary Stuart Hemingway, Aug. 18, 1973; 1 son, John Matthew. Dir., Star of the Republic Mus., 1971-76; dir. Dallas Hist. Soc., 1976—; mem. adv. bd. Tex. Hist. Records; mem. bd. commerce Dallas Nat. Bank. Mem. Hist. Preservation League (trustee, exec. com.), Tex. State Hist. Assn., Am. Assn. State and Local History, Am. Assn. Museums, East Dallas C. of C. Methodist. Office: PO Box 26038 Dallas TX 75226

CRAIN, WILLIAM HENRY, curator; b. Victoria, Tex., July 19, 1917; s. William Henry and Margaret James (McFaddin) C.; student Tex. Mil. Inst., 1933-36; B.A., U. Tex., 1940, M.A., 1943, B.F.A., 1947, M.F.A., 1949, Ph.D., 1965. Resident playwright Artillery Lane Theatre, San Augustine, Fla., 1950-51; dir. David G. Benjamin Inc., Austin, Tex., 1957-59 Austin Mfg. Corp., 1957-59; publicity asst. drama dept. U. Tex., Austin, 1959-60; humanities research asso. II, 1965-70; curator Hoblitzelle Theatre Arts Library, Austin, 1970—; dir. Waterloo Press, 1971—. Bd. dirs. Austin Civic Theatre, 1961-64, Paramount Theatre for Performing Arts, 1976—. Served with AUS, 1941-45. Recipient Cross of Mil. Service, U. D.C., 1961. Mem. Am. Theatre Assn., Sons Republic Tex., Serra Internat., Phi Eta Sigma, Phi Kappa Phi, Delta Kappa Epsilon. Roman Catholic. Clubs: Serra (treas. 1978-79), Austin Players. Writer numerous plays produced including Brains and Eggs, 1948, The Muddled Magician, 1957, Sir Marmaduke Miles, 1976, Sweet Old Thing, 1961, The Reluctant Caesar, 1977. Home: 2511 San Gabriel Austin TX 78705 Office: 7204 B Humanities Research Center PO Box 7219 Austin TX 78712

CRAMER, FORREST EUGENE, paper mfg. co. exec.; b. Franklin, Ohio, Dec. 20, 1922; s. Orville Thomas and Catherine Mae (Painter) C.; E.E., Internat. Corr. Schs., 1952; m. Dona Maxine Ferguson, Dec. 26, 1944; children—Virginia, Richard, Ronald. Staff, Western Electric Co., 1941-42, Aeronca Aircraft Co., 1942-46; electrician Longview Fiber Co., 1947-57; elec. supt. U.S. Gypsum Co., 1957-60; elec. instrument supt. Boise Cascade Corp., Wallula, Wash., 1960-67, maintenance supt., Wallula, 1967-69, maintenance supt. DeRidder, La., 1969-70, resident mgr., Bataan, Philippines, 1970-72, Newcastle, N.B., 1972-73 project engr., De Ridder, 1973-74, resident mgr. Elizabeth, La., 1974—; lectr. in field; dir. Bataan Pulp & Paper Mills. Commr. Recreation Dist. 3 Allen Parish, La., 1975—. Served with A.C., U.S. Army, 1942-45. Hon. state senator La.; ofcl. brother City of Samal, Philippines; recipient Civic Service award City of Oakdale (La.), 1980. Mem. Oakdale (La.) C. of C. (dir. 1975—), Am. Legion. Democrat. Methodist. Clubs: Allen Country (dir. 1977—, pres. 1980), Rotary (pres. Oakdale 1980), Lions, Elks. Home: PO Drawer C Elizabeth LA 70638 Office: PO Drawer 520 Elizabeth LA 70638

CRAMER, LAURA SCHWARZ, realtor; b. St. Louis, Aug. 13, 1925; d. Frederick William and Gertrude Margaret (Kipp) Schwarz; A.B., Duke U., 1947; M.A., Washington U., 1948; m. Robert R. Cramer, Oct. 29, 1949; children—Anne Randolph, Carol Parker, Laura Forster. Model, John Robert Powers Agy., N.Y.C., 1946; grad. asst. dept. psychology Washington U., St. Louis, 1947-48, instr., 1948-49; psychometrist Clayton (Mo.) pub. schs., 1961; dir. testing Columbia Sch., Rochester, N.Y., 1964-71; asst. registrar and counselor for women students St. John Fisher Coll., Rochester, N.Y., 1971-72, registrar, dean of women, 1972-76; sales exec. Sea Pines Plantation Co., Hilton Head Island, S.C., 1976—. Bd. dirs. Vol. Service Bur., St. Louis, 1960-61, Monroe County Hosp. Aux., 1974-76, St. Louis Community Music Sch., 1959-61; bd. mem. St. Louis Inst., chmn., 1960. Jesse M. Barr fellow, 1947-48. Mem. Nat. Assn. for Women Deans, Adminstrs. and Counselors, Hilton Head Island Bd. Realtors, AAUW, Jr. League Savannah, Sea Pines Two Million Dollar Club, Phi Beta Kappa, Sigma Xi. Club: Zonta (charter) (Hilton Head Island). Home: PO Box 3091 Hilton Head Island SC 29928 Office: Sea Pines Plantation Co Hilton Head Island SC 29948

CRAMER, WADE LEE, electronics co. exec.; b. Sioux Falls, S.D., Aug. 25, 1948; s. Richard Dale and Joan Patrica C.; B.S. in Elec. Engring., Tex. Tech U., 1971; m. Sarah Ann Bruffey, Jan. 15, 1972; children—Leah Denise, Kenneth Adam, Karen Elizabeth. Quality assurance engr. Tex. Instruments, Inc., Dallas, 1972-75, quality reliability supr., 1975-79, quality reliability mgr., 1979—. Mem. Am. Soc. for Quality Control. Office: Tex Instruments Inc PO Box 6015 Dallas TX 75222

CRAMER, WILLIAM MONROE, bus. exec.; b. St. Louis, Oct. 12, 1928; s. George Hallock and Pearl (Patterson) C.; B.S. in Elec. Engring., U. Tex., 1955; m. Patsy June Fleming, Nov. 22, 1977; children by previous marriage—Wayne William, Gary Lewis, Bradley. With Rockwell Internat. Co., Anaheim, Calif., 1955-70, supr. Minuteman and Navy ground support equipment, 1963-66, Minuteman flight control equipment, 1966-70; pres. Research Tech. Inc., Dallas, 1971-72; pres., chief exec. officer Seaco Computer Display, Garland, Tex., 1972-75, Century 21 Prodns., Dallas, 1977-78; pres. Lone Star Equities, Dallas, 1979—. Served with USNR, 1947-50. Mem. Am. Mgmt. Assn. Elk. Home: 3311 Chaparral St Dallas TX 75234 Office: 4248 Armstrong Dallas TX 75205

CRAMP, DONALD ARTHUR, hosp. adminstr.; b. Meaford, Ont., Can., Dec. 23, 1936; s. Reginald Graham and Sarah Agnus (Robinson) C.; B.A., U. Western Ont., 1960; M.Sc., Columbia U., 1962; m. Lynda Marie D'Acunto, Feb. 14, 1970; 1 son, Donald Arthur. With Bank of Am., San Francisco, 1962-64; with Gen. Motors Corp., Oshawa, Ont., 1964-66; asst. adminstr. South Nassau Communities Hosp., Oceanside, N.Y., 1966-70; dir. Highland View Hosp., Cleve., 1970-71; sr. v.p. Cuyahoga County Hosp. Systems, 1971-76; exec. dir. Univ. Hosp., U. Louisville, 1976—; asst. prof. Sch. Medicine, Case Western Res. U., Cleve., 1970-76; guest lectr. N.Y. Sch. Adminstrv. Medicine, Columbia, 1966-70. Bd. dirs. Nassau Heart Assn., 1967-70. Fellow Am. Pub. Health Assn., Am. Coll. Hosp. Adminstrs.; mem. Am. Hosp. Assn. (chmn. research and publ., pub. gen. sect. 1971—), Beta Theta Pi. Club: Nat. Exchange (dir. 1967-70). Contbr. to profl. publs. Home: 8809 Peterborough Dr Louisville KY 40222 Office: Univ Hosp Preston and Walnut Sts Louisville KY 40202

CRANE, FRANCES HAWKINS, artist; b. Johntown, Tex., July 8, 1928; d. Henry Cleo and Laura Elizabeth (Jenkins) Hawkins; ed. Del Mar Coll., 1948; studied under Mrs. K.K. Simpson, and Frederic Taubes; m. Gene Calvin Crane, May 10, 1946; children—Cindie Crane Rogers, Cheryl Elizabeth. Exhbns. include Highland Mall Gallery, Austin, Tex., Prichard Gallery, Houston, Heath and Brown Gallery, Houston, Salado (Tex.) Gallery, Bellas Artes Gallery, Kerrville, Tex., Jerry Smith Gallery, Alice, Tex., Corpus Christi Mus.; represented in permanent collections Corpus Christi Mus., Lyndon Baines Johnson Library. Recipient top awards local, state, nat., internat. shows. Mem. S. Tex. Traditional Art Assn. (sec.-treas. Corpus Christi chpt. 1970-76), Nat. League Am. Pen Women, Internat. Platform Assn., Hill Country Arts Found., Internat. Soc. Artists. Home: 5058 Wingfoot St Corpus Christi TX 78413 Office: 5832 Macardle Rd Corpus Christi TX 78412

CRANE, JOHN STEVEN, architect; b. Melrose Park, Ill., Mar. 6, 1945; s. Sherwood and Lorraine (Plachota) C.; B.Arch., Tex. Tech. U., 1968; M.A., Washington U., St. Louis., 1971; m. Cynthia Russell Maddox, Aug. 3, 1968; children—Jonathan Barrett, Christopher Todd, Andrew Maddox. Staff architect Golemon & Rolfe Assos., Inc., Houston, 1968-70, Lawrence D. White, Architects, Ft. Worth, 1972; project mgr. Caudill, Rowlett, Scott, Architects, Houston, 1972-75; prin. Goleman & Rolfe Assos., Inc., Houston, 1975—, also dir. Washington U. fellow, 1970. Mem. AIA. Methodist. Home: 2339 Goldsmith St Houston TX 77030 Office: 3000 S Post Oak St Suite 1200 Houston TX 77056

CRANE, MARILYN JOYCE, paleontologist; b. Grand Rapids, Mich., May 10, 1931; d. H.D. and Dorris (Northrup) Crane; B.S., Mich. State U., 1953, M.S., 1955. Geologist, Ind. Geol. Survey, Bloomington, 1955-56; paleontologist Humble Oil & Refining Co. (now Exxon), 1956—. Mem. Nat. Audubon Soc. (charter Houston, sec. 1971, v.p. adminstrv. affairs 1977—), Am. Assn. Petroleum Geologists, Soc. Econ. Mineralogists, and Paleontologists, Houston Geol. Soc., Gulf Coast Soc. Econ. Mineralogists and Paleontologists, Conservation Arts of Houston, Houston Outdoor Club (v.p. membership 1975-77), Corpus Christie Outdoor Club (sec. 1965, chmn. Christmas bd. count 1967); Ornithology Group (chmn. 1972, 73). Contbr. articles to profl. jours. Home: 12690 Briar Patch Houston TX 77077 Office: PO Box 2180 Houston TX 77001

CRANE, PAUL SHIELDS, surgeon; b. Oxford, Miss., May 2, 1919; s. John Curtis and Florence (Hedleston) C.; B.S., Davidson Coll., 1941, D.Sc., 1969; M.D., Johns Hopkins, 1944; m. Sophie Earle Montgomery, June 2, 1942; children—Virginia Crane Gleser, John Curtis, Letitia, Janet Crane Adams, James. Intern, resident surgery Union Meml. Hosp., Balt., 1944-46, 51-52; fellow surgery Johns Hopkins Hosp., Balt., 1960-62; med. missionary to Korea, Bd. World Missions, Presbyn. Ch. U.S., 1947-69, dir., chief surgeon Presbyn. Med. Center, Chonju, Korea, 1948-69; asst. chief surgery VA Hosp., Atlanta, 1969-70; asso. Miller Clinic, Nashville, 1970—; clin. prof. surgery Yonsei U., Seoul, Korea, 1964-69; asst. clin. prof. surgery Emory U., Atlanta, 1969, Vanderbilt U., 1971—. Chmn. Korean Presbyn. Mission, 1956; mem. gen. assembly mission bd. Presbyn. Ch. in U.S., 1979; dir. Program for Intestinal Parasite Eradication in Korea through Korean Assn. Vol. Agys.; chmn. Philatelic Soc. Korea; council mem. Korea br. Royal Asiatic Soc. Bd. dirs. Med. Benevolent Found., Yonsei U., Wilson Leprosy Colony, Korea. Served as 1st lt. M.C., AUS, 1946-47; to maj. Res., 1956-58, 60, 65, 68. Decorated Commendation medal, Order Cultural Merit (Korea); recipient UN World Day of Health medal Korea, 1963. Mem. A.C.S., Tenn. Acad. Medicine, Nashville Surg. Soc. Presbyn. (elder). Author: Korean Patterns, 1967; Tennessee Taproots, 1976; Tennessee's Troubled Roots, County Tails, 1979. Writer monthly column Korea Times Newspaper, Seoul, 1964. Contbr. articles to profl. jours. Home: 1203 Riverside Rd Old Hickory TN 37138 Office: 602 Gallatin Rd Nashville TN 37206

CRANE, RUTH ANN, mgmt. cons.; b. Cleve., Oct. 26, 1928; d. Orson Eugene and Elsie Caroline (Miller) Hunt; A.S., U. Tulsa, 1949; student Sch. Law, U. Tulsa, 1950, Sch. Law U. Mo., at Kansas City, 1951, U. Utah, 1956; B.A., U. Tulsa, 1971, M.A., 1972; m. Charles Belden Crane, Dec. 28, 1951; children—Cynthia Ann, Charles Bretton. Cons., City County Health Dept., 1972-73; pres. Crane Consultants, Inc., Tulsa, 1973—. Mem. Civil service Commn., City of Tulsa, 1974—, chmn., 1978—; chmn. Work Edn. Council Tulsa, 1977-78. Mem. Tulsa C. of C. (vice chmn. career edn. task force 1976), Assn. Mgmt. Cons. (trustee), Am. Soc. Tng. and Devel., Tulsa Personnel Assn., Adminstrv. Mgmt. Soc., Psi Chi, Tulsa Bus. and Profl. Womens Club. Presbyterian. Club: Toastmasters. Author: (with Marcine H. Goad) Self-Evaluation Career Guide, 1978. Office: 5043 Fulton St S Suite 7 Tulsa OK 74135

CRANE, TERRY, antique dealer; b. Muncie, Ind., Feb. 9, 1929; s. Earl Franklin and Georgia Hedden (Byers) C.; B.A. in Fine Arts, Northwestern U., 1951. Designer, Lord & Taylor, N.Y.C., 1953-55, Contemporary Interiors, Houston, Ft. Worth, 1955-63; owner, operator Terry Crane Assos., Ft. Worth, 1963—, Crandale Galleries, Ft. Worth, 1972—. Mem. Am. Soc. Interior Designers. Republican. Clubs: Ridglea Country, Ft. Worth Club. Home: 4901 Westridge St Fort Worth TX 76116 Office: 4949 Byers St Fort Worth TX 76107

CRANE, WILLIAM HARRY, educator; b. Montgomery, Ala., Mar. 21, 1925; s. Harold Curtis and Alvira (Landon) C.; student Clemson Coll., 1943, Duke, 1946-47; B.S., M.S., U. Ala., 1950; m. Joanna Breedlove, Sept. 1970; children—(by previous marriage) Dorothy Jean (Mrs. Alan Adams), Lucy Anne (Mrs. Duane Newby), Mary Elizabeth (Mrs. Clifford Hornady), Suzanne Victoria (Mrs. Cantrell Allen). Partner, Crane, Jackson & Thornton, C.P.A.'s, Montgomery, 1953-64 Crane & Crane, C.P.A.'s, Montgomery, 1964-67; pres. William H. Crane & Co., C.P.A.'s, Montgomery, 1967-79; asst. prof. acctg. Auburn U., Montgomery, 1979—. Budget dir., exec. com. United Appeal, Montgomery, 1962-64. Bd. dirs. Montgomery chpt. A.R.C. Served with inf. AUS, 1943-45. Decorated Purple Heart with 2 clusters, Bronze Star medal, Silver Star medal; named Ky. col.; C.P.A., Ala. Mem. Ala. Soc. C.P.A.'s (chmn. council 1964-65), Am. Inst. C.P.A.'s, Montgomery Assn. C.P.A.'s (pres. 1961-62), Delta Sigma Pi. Methodist. Club: Rotary (dist. gov. 1969-70, Paul Harris fellow 1979). Home: 3300 Drexel Rd Montgomery AL 36106 Office: Auburn U Montgomery AL 36117

CRANFILL, WILBURN FRANKLIN, food broker; b. Winston-Salem, N.C., June 1, 1920; s. David Calvin and Mattie Elizabeth (Chandler) C.; student Mars Hill Coll., 1941-42, Piedmont Bible Coll., 1946-47, Food Service Inst., 1971; m. Ella Louise Threatt, Oct. 21, 1948; children—David Hoyt, Donald Eugene. With Am. Home Foods, 1947-48, Pilot Brokerage Co., 1948-54, 55-58, Cates Pickle Co., 1954-55, Cranfill Merchandising Service, 1958-59; with Southgate Brokerage Co. of Raleigh, Inc., 1959—, dir., pres., treas., 1971—, merged with Mktg. Concepts, Inc., Raleigh, 1978, now chmn. bd., pres. Cons. in field personology, 1969—. Served with AUS, 1943-46; PTO. Named Optimist of Year, 1966. Mem. Raleigh Food Brokers Assn. (pres. 1961, 74), Nat. Food Brokers Assn. (regional dir. 1975-76), Asso. Brokers Am. (chmn. bd., past pres., v.p.). Baptist (chmn. bd. deacons 1964). Clubs: Optimist of Raleigh (pres. 1964-65), Optimist Internat. (N.C. dist. gov.-elect 1975-76, gov. 1976-77), Pinehurst Country. Home: 3325 Buffaloe Rd Raleigh NC 27604 Office: 500 St Mary's St Raleigh NC 27608

CRANFORD, THOMAS EDWARD, banker; b. Oberlin, La., Sept. 7, 1932; s. Thales Elton and Annie May (Robinson) C.; B.S., La. State U., 1953, M.S., 1955; m. Phyllis Kay Doggett (dec.); children—Frances (Mrs. David W. Holmes, III), Phyllis Kay. With Whitney Nat. Bank, New Orleans, 1953, La. Nat. Bank, Baton Rouge, 1954; trust officer, cashier Bunkie Bank & Trust Co. (La.), 1957-60; v.p., sr. real estate officer First Miss. Nat. Bank, Hattiesburg, 1960—; faculty La. State U., 1953-55, U. So. Miss., 1961-65. Active, South Miss. Art Assn., Muscular Dystrophy. Served to capt., inf. AUS, 1955-57. Presbyterian. Clubs: Masons, Elks, Kiwanis. Home: 3212 Brookwood Dr Hattiesburg MS 39401 Office: PO Box 1231 Hattiesburg MS 39401

CRANSTON, JOHN WELCH, historian; b. Utica, N.Y., Dec. 21, 1931; s. Earl and Mildred (Welch) C.; B.A., Pomona Coll., 1953; M.A., Columbia U., 1964; Ph.D., U. Wis., 1970. Asst. prof. history West Tex. State U., 1970-74, U. Mo., Kansas City, 1970, Rust Coll., Holly Springs, Miss., 1974—. Served with U.S. Army, 1953-55. Nat. Endowment for Humanities fellow, 1976. Mem. Am. Hist. Assn., Phi Alpha Theta. Democrat. Episcopalian. Contbr. hist. articles to profl. lit. Address: Box 241 Holly Springs MS 38635

CRANTON, ELMER MITCHELL, physician; b. Haverhill, Mass., Sept. 17, 1932; s. Watson Hallet and Laura Mae (Mitchell) C.; M.D., Harvard U., 1964; student U. Colo., 1957-59, U. Erlangen (W. Ger.), 1959-60; m. Nancy Elise Neece, May 13, 1961; children—John Allen, Anne Elizabeth, Catherine Louise, Jennifer Lynn. Rotating intern U.S. Naval Hosp., Pensacola, Fla., 1964-65, gen. surg. staff, 1965; gen. practice medicine, Encinitas, Calif., 1969-72, Arcadia, Calif., 1972-75; chief of staff USPHS Indian Hosp., Talihina, Okla., 1975-76; practice medicine specializing in family practice, preventive medicine and holistic medicine, Trout Dale, Va., 1976—; med. dir. Mt. Rogers Clinic, Trout Dale, 1977—. Mem. human resources com. Mt. Rogers Planning Dist. Commn., 1977-78; tchr., med. advisor Vol. Rescue Squads, Mt. Rogers, 1977—; pres. bd. trustees Poseidia Inst. Centers for Interdisciplinary Research, 1979—. Served with USN, 1951-58, 64-69; USPHS, 75-76. Diplomate Am. Bd. Family Practice. Fellow Am. Acad. Family Physicians, Am. Acad. Med. Preventics, Internat. Coll. Applied Nutrition; mem. Am. Holistic Med. Assn. (pres. 1980—), Smyth County Med. Soc. (pres. 1980), Internat. Found. Preventive Medicine, AMA, Med. Soc. Va., S.W. Va. Med. Soc., Va. Acad. Family Physicians, Acad. Orthomolecular Psychiatry, Internat. Acad. Preventive Medicine, Internat. Acad. Parapsychology and Medicine, Am. Geriatrics Soc., Am. Soc. Bariatric Physicians, Mensa, Alpha Epsilon Delta. Republican. Methodist (trustee 1979—). Home: Route 1 Box 5 Trout Dale VA 24378 Office: Mount Rogers Clinic Ripshin Rd PO Box 44 Trout Dale VA 24378

CRAPP, TONY EDWARD, city ofcl.; b. Miami, Fla., July 8, 1952; d. Seth and Pauline (Harris) C.; A.B. cum laude, Harvard U., 1974; M.P.A. (Woodrow Wilson fellow), Princeton U., 1976; m. Beatrice Horton, May 2, 1971; children—Tony Edward, Seth James. Econ. planner Metro Dade County, Fla., 1976-77, supr. program planning and devel., 1977, community devel. planner, 1977-78; dir. bus. devel. City of Miami Dept. Trade and Commerce Devel., 1978—; corp. mem. Miami Dade Neighborhood Housing Services, Inc. Mem. Am. Planning Assn., Internat. City Mgmt. Assn., Nat. Council Urban Econ. Devel. Democrat. Baptist. Clubs: Harvard, Princeton (Miami). Office: 100 N Biscayne Blvd Miami FL 33132

CRATER, HAROLD LESLIE, educator; b. Newark, Sept. 1, 1938; s. Harold L. and Olive V. (Morisen) C.; B.A., Wagner Coll., 1960; M.Ed., Rutgers U., 1963; Ph.D., U. Tex., 1972; m. M. Wendy Walton, Aug. 20, 1960; children—Mark, Wayne, Dorothy. Tchr. sci., Warwick, N.Y., 1960-69, Austin, Tex., 1972-74; asst. prof. physics U. Miss., University, 1974—; ednl. cons. Union Carbide Corp., 1967-69. Recipient Disting. Service award Warwick Valley Tchrs. Assn., 1965. Mem. Nat. Sci. Tchrs. Assn., Miss. Sci. Tchrs. Assn., Am. Assn. Physics Tchrs., Miss. Assn. Physicists, Miss. Acad. Scis. (chmn. youth activities com.), Assn. for Edn. of Tchrs. in Sci., Sch. Sci. and Math. Assn., Soc. for Coll. Sci. Tchrs., Phi Delta Kappa (treas. chpt.). Lutheran. Contbr. articles to publs. including Sci. Tchr., Sci. and Children, Sch. Sci. and Math., Jour. Chem. Edn. Office: Dept Physics U Miss University MS 38677

CRATER, JOHN LEE, mfg. co. exec.; b. Elkin, N.C., July 17, 1943; s. John Alfred and Anne Ruth Crater; A.B., Western Carolina U., 1965; m. Nancy Denton, June 7, 1964; children—Timothy, Laurie, Leah, Mary. Jr. indsl. engr. Sunbeam Corp., Elkin, 1965-67; employment supr. Lufkin Rule Co., Raleigh, N.C., 1967-68; indsl. relations mgr. Uniroyal Inc., Scottsville, Va., 1968-70; with Gen. Electric Co., Wilmington, N.C., 1970-77, mgr. employee and community relations, Dothan, Ala., 1977—; instr. Des Moines Area Community Coll. Chmn. adv. council Dothan Vocat. Center; bd. dirs. Ala. State Employment service Improvement Com.; bd. dirs. United Way; active Boy Scouts Am. Mem. Wiregrass Personnel Assn., Dothan C. of C., Assn. U.S. Army, Am. Mgmt. Assn. Presbyterian. Club: Kiwanis.

CRAVEN, CLYDE WESLEY, JR., nuclear engr., sci. research co. exec.; b. Gibonville, N.C., Sept. 24, 1934; s. Clyde W. and Ruby (Glosson) C.; B.S. in Nuclear Engring., U. Tenn., 1961, M.S., 1963, Ph.D. in Engring Sci., 1965; m. Wanda Parrett, June 14, 1952; children—Vicky Lynn Loveless, Cheryl Ann Graham. Mem. faculty nuclear engring. U. Tenn., 1964-65; tech. asst. to asso. dir. for reactor and engring. scis., Oak Ridge (Tenn.) Nat. Lab., 1965-70, tech. asst. to asso. dir. for biomed. scis., 1970-72, asso. dir. environ. program, 1972-74, dir. regional environ. assessment program, 1972-74, dir. regional and urban studies dept., 1974-75; dir. engring., environ. and research services staff Sci. Applications, Inc., Oak Ridge, Tenn., 1975—, v.p., 1978—; pres. Polaris Travel, 1978—. Served with USAF, 1954-57. Mem. Am. Nuclear Soc., AAAS. Contbr. numerous articles on nuclear sci. and engring. to profl. jours. Home: 110 Artesia Dr Oak Ridge TN 37830 Office: 800 Oak Ridge Turnpike Oak Ridge TN 37830

CRAVEN, DOUGLAS CHARLES, elec. engr.; b. Cookeville, Tenn., Sept. 8, 1952; s. Charles Curtis and Cora Beatrice (York) C.; B.S. in Elec. Engring. magna cum laude, Tenn. Tech. U., 1974; m. Pamela June Vick, June 15, 1974; children—Stephen Douglas, Robert Andrew. Elec. engr. TVA, Daisy, Tenn., 1974-79, asst. elec. maintenance supr. Sequoyah Nuclear Plant, 1979—. Named Putnam County True Gentleman, 1970; Eagle Scout, Boy Scouts Am., 1967. Engring. Devel. scholar, 1971; Upper Cumberland Sci. Fair scholar, 1971. Mem. IEEE, Am. Nuclear Soc., Order of the Engr., Tau Beta Pi, Eta Kappa Nu, Phi Kappa Phi, Kappa Mu Epsilon. Methodist. Home: 1013 Ambrose Ln Hixson TN 37343 Office: PO Box 2000 Daisy TN 37319

CRAVEN, HAROLD LLOYD, govt. ofcl.; b. Reynoldsville, Pa., June 24, 1924; s. Thomas Harold and Elizabeth Jane (Shindledecker) C.; student DuBois Bus. Coll., 1946, Penn Airmotive Aviation Sch., 1947, Armed Forces Info. Sch., 1949, U. Calif. Extension at San Francisco, 1949, Oklahoma City U., 1950, U. Md., 1961, Air U., 1964; Ph.B., Am. Bible Inst., 1976; D.D. (hon.), Sacerdotal Order Universal Life, 1979; m. Arthurette Lucille Forth, May 15, 1945; children—Nola (Mrs. Donald M. Lynch), Howard Randolph. Writer-editor U.S. Dept. Air Force, 1947-60; historian Allied Air Forces So. Europe, Naples, Italy, 1960-62; staff writer Airman Mag., Washington, 1962-65; writer-editor News For Farmer Coops., Washington, 1966; editor Transp. Procs., Baileys Crossroads, Va., 1966-70; editor Translog Mag., Baileys Crossroads, 1970-74; dep. pub. affairs officer U.S. Mil. Traffic Mgmt. Command, Baileys Crossroads, 1974—. Dir. grad. activities Silva Mind Control of No. Va., Annandale, 1972—; lectr. parapsychology ORB Inst., Washington, 1975. Served with USAAF, 1943-46. Mem. Am. Parapsychol. Research Assn., Inst. Noetic Scis., Assn. Research and Enlightenment, ORB Found., Psychorientology Studies Internat., Mankind Research Found., Soc. for Application of Free Energy. Editor Kwajalein Kaleidoscope, 1952; Westover Yankee Flyer, 1955; The Viking, 1956. Home: 14993 Alaska Rd Woodbridge VA 22191 Office: 5611 Columbia Pike Baileys Crossroads VA 22041

CRAVEN, JAMES MILLARD, mfg. co. exec.; b. Jackson Springs, N.C., July 17, 1930; s. James C. and Martha A. (Pusser) C.; student public schs., Ellerbe, N.C.; m. Kathleen Freeman, Sept. 5, 1950; children—Richard C., Donna Kay, Stephen M., Jennifer D. Served with U.S. Army, 1948-68, ret., 1969; pres. Carolina Galvanizing Corp., Aberdeen, N.C., 1969-78; chmn. New South Industries, Southern Pines, N.C., 1978—. Mem. Republican Exec. Com., 1976-79; county commr. Moore County, N.C., 1978—. Mem. C. of C. (dir. 1977-79), Am. Hot-Dip Galvanizing Assn. (dir. 1977—), Artechial Pre-Cast Assn., V.F.W. Republican. Methodist. Club: Masons. Home: PO Box 44 Pinebluff NC 28378 Office: 120 N Bennett St Southern Pines NC 28387

CRAVEN, ROY CURTIS, JR., educator, art gallery dir.; b. Cherokee Bluffs, Ala., July 29, 1924; s. Roy Curtis and Edna (Morris) C.; B.A., U. Tenn., Chattanooga, 1949; M.F.A., U. Fla., 1956; m. Lorna Elizabeth Andreae, Sept. 19, 1948; children—Curtis A., Hillary Y. Photographer, Chattanooga Times, 1946-47; head dept. art Stratford Coll., Danville, Va., 1950-51; instr. art U. Chattanooga, 1952-53; graphic design Purse Advt., Chattanooga, 1952-54; mem. faculty U. Fla., Gainesville, 1954—, prof. art, 1967—, dir. univ. art gallery, 1966—; past mem. bd. Southeastern Museums Conf., Fla. Arts Council; one-man exhbns. in various U.S. museums and galleries, paintings rep. public and pvt. collections. Served with USAAF, 1942-46. Sr. Fulbright research scholar, 1962-63; grantee U.S. Dept. Edn., 1968-73, Am. Philos. Soc., 1977. Fellow Royal Soc. Arts; mem. Asia Soc., Assn. Asian Studies, Am. Assn. Museums, Fla. Art Mus. Dirs. Assn., Phi Beta Kappa. Author: Ceremonial Centers of the Maya, 1974; Concise History of Indian Art, 1976. Home: 6818 NW 65th Ave Gainesville FL 32601 Office: Univ Gallery Univ Fla Gainesville FL 32611

CRAVENS, MARGARET EVELYN JOHNSON, motel exec.; b. nr. Versailles, Ky., May 11, 1919; d. Denny Johnson and Bethel (Goodpaster) Johnson Cox; student Draughn Bus. Coll., Springfield, Mo., 1943, U. Ky., 1951, Sch. Civil Def., 1959, Quality Inns, Inc. Motel Mgmt. Sch., 1969; m. Dennis Carl Cravens, Aug. 7, 1937; children—Dennis Wayne, Glenn Allen, Margaret Gayle. Office mgr. Cravens & Cravens, Inc., Lexington, Ky., 1946-50; gen. mgr. Quality Inn, N.W. Lexington, 1968—; pres., dir. Motel Developers, Inc. Chmn. Lexington-Fayette County Recreational, Tourism and Conv. Commn., 1975-77. Bd. dirs., past sec. Lexington Center, Inc. Chmn. commn. on missions, mem. bd. stewards Epworth Methodist Ch., 1961-65, sponsor, counselor World Friendship Group of Girls, 1953-57. Bd. dirs. Nathanael Methodist Mission, Ky. Historic Mansions Preservation Found. Mem. Greater Lexington C. of C. (dir. 1974-77), Am. (dir., exec. com. 1980—), Ky. (pres. 1978-79), Lexington (pres. 1975) hotel-motel assns. Home: 423 Clinton Rd Lexington KY 40502 Office: Quality Inn NW 1050 Newtown Pike Lexington KY 40505

CRAVER, THOMAS BURKE, textile co. exec.; b. Lexington, N.C., Apr. 6, 1917; s. Herman Roswell and Glenna (Dale) C.; B.S. in Commerce, U. N.C., 1938; m. Edna Buchanan, Dec. 23, 1939; children—Beverly, Thomas Burke, James. Office mgr. Burlington Industries, Greensboro, N.C., 1938-42, head hosiery prodn. planning dept., 1946-49; controller Leon-Ferenbach, Inc., N.Y.C., 1950-56; v.p. Madison Throwing Co. (N.C.), 1957-67; pres. Paducah (Ky.) Throwing Co., Inc.; pres., treas. Craver Enterprises, Inc., Paducah. Chmn., Charter Study Com., Mountain Lakes, N.J., 1965; bd. dirs. Mountain Lakes-Boonton (N.J.) Little League Baseball League, 1964-68. Served with USN, 1943-46. Mem. Asso. Industries of Ky. Republican. Home: 285 Springwell Ln Paducah KY 42001 Office: 200 Tennessee St Paducah KY 42001

CRAVEY, ETHELYN JOYCE, nursing supr.; b. Richton, Miss., Sept. 21, 1922; d. Perriman Sheppard and Josiephine (Hutto) Brewer; R.N., South Miss. Infirmary, Hattiesburg, 1943; m. John Marvin Cravey, Aug. 13, 1966; 1 dau., Janis Louise. Operating room supr. South Miss. Infirmary, Hattiesburg, 1943-45; operating room supr. Laurel (Miss.) Gen. Hosp., 1945; office nurse, asst. in surgery Med. Center, Laurel, 1945-58; supr. Central Service, Jones County Community Hosp., Laurel, 1969—. Leader, Gulf Pines council Girl Scouts U.S.A., 1963-65. Mem. Am. Soc. Central Service Personnel. Republican. United Methodist. Home: Route 1 Box 229 Ovett MS 39464 Office: PO Box 607 Laurel MS 39440

CRAWFORD, ANDY WILLIAM, veterinarian; b. Ashland, Miss., Feb. 23, 1904; s. J.A. and Ella (Elliott) C.; student U. Tex., 1923-24, Millsaps Coll., 1924-25; D.V.M., Kan. State Coll., 1930; m. Muriel Hallock, July 29, 1931; children—Jo Anne, Pat. Gen. practice vet. medicine, Rolling Fork, Miss., 1933-40, 45—; also cons. animal health and nutrition. Mem. sec. agr.'s hog cholera eradication com. Sheriff Sharkey County, Miss., 1946-51, 56-59. Served with AUS, 1940-45; col. Res. Mem. Am. Vet. Med. Assn. (v.p., 1961-62, house dels., ednl. council), Am. Bovine Practitioners Assn. (past pres.), Am. Soc. Agrl. Cons. Mason, Rotarian. Home: 400 Race St Rolling Fork MS 39159 Office: 305 Race St Rolling Fork MS 39159

CRAWFORD, BARBARA NOBLES, assn. exec.; b. Kinston, N.C., Dec. 20, 1952; d. LeRoy and Hazel Lee (Gray) Nobles; B.A., U. N.C., Greensboro, 1974; M.Ed., U. Va., 1978; m. Kermit Anthony Crawford, Apr. 28, 1974. Adminstrv. asst. Leesona Corp., Greensboro, 1974; counselor State of N.C., U. N.C., Greensboro, 1975; housing referral rep. Greensboro Housing Authority, 1976-77; grad./research asst., consultative resource center U. Va., Charlottesville, 1978; counselor community orgn. Family Services Inc., Charlottesville, 1978; project dir. Citizen Involvement project OAR/USA-NIC, Charlottesville, 1979—; cons., trainer, facilitator criminal justice, sch. adminstrn., career devel. workshops. Coordinating Council Charlottesville Human Resources Assn., 1979—; active NAACP. Escheats scholar, 1972; Gov.'s scholar, 1977; I-Dare-You-Book awardee, 1970. Mem. Am. Personnel and Guidance Assn., Assn. Non-White Concerns, NAACP, Nat. Assn. Blacks in Criminal Justice, Phi Delta Kappa. Home: 13 Copeley Hill Apt 5 Charlottesville VA 22903

CRAWFORD, CARL LEROY, physician; b. Grinnell, Ia., Oct. 26, 1928; s. William Lester and Eva Wilma (Flanigan) C.; B.S., U. N.M., 1953; M.D. (fellow), Med. Coll. Ga., 1965; m. Joe Ann Simmons, Nov. 22, 1959; 1 dau., Constance S. Tchr. sci. high sch., Ia., 1953-56; profl. service rep. Geigy Pharm., Macon, Ga., 1957-61; intern Macon (Ga.) Hosp., 1965-66; gen. practice medicine, Americus, Ga., 1966-68, Warner Robins, Ga., 1968—; mem. med. staff Americus and Sumter County Hosp., 1966-68, Houston County Hosp., Warner Robins, 1968—; med. dir. Plains (Ga.) Convalescent Home, 1966-67; coll. physician Ga. Southwestern Coll., 1967; med. dir. Hallmark Nursing Home, Warner Robins, 1968—, Peachbelt Nursing Home, 1974-75. Profl. v.p. Houston County chpt. Am. Cancer Soc., 1969-77; pres. Houston County Assn. Exceptional Children, 1971-74. Bd. dirs. ARC, chmn. Houston County Bloodmobile program, 1971-77; bd. dirs. Atlanta Regional Blood Program, 1974-76, Warner Robins chpt. Houston County United Givers Fund, Blue Shield of Ga., Columbus; chmn. adv. bd. Salvation Army, 1972-75. Served with AUS, 1946-49. Recipient Citizen of Yr. award Warner Robins Jaycees, 1971; Community Service award Warner Robins C. of C., 1973. Diplomate Am. Bd. Family Practice. Mem. AMA, Am. (fellow), Ga. acads. family physicians, Am. Heart Assn., So. Med. Assn., Med. Assn. Ga., 3d Dist. (sec.-treas. 1967-69, pres. 1974-77), Peachbelt (pres. 1977-78) med. socs., Warner Robins C. of C. (dir. 1975-77), Air Force Assn. (life), Soc. Medalists, Franklin Mint Collectors Soc., Med. Coll. Ga. Alumni Assn., Alpha Kappa Kappa. Republican. Episcopalian. Rotarian. Club: Houston Lake Country (Perry, Ga.). Home: 109 Deerwood Circle Warner Robins GA 31093 Office: 1410 Russell Pkwy Warner Robins GA 31093

CRAWFORD, DAVID EARL, univ. adminstr.; b. Birmingham, Ala., Oct. 27, 1941; s. Earl Stanley and Josephine Elizabeth C.; B.S., Montevallo U., 1962; postgrad. U. Ga., 1962-64; M.S. in Mgmt., Memphis State U., 1977; m. Nancy Little, Jan. 20, 1968; 1 dau., April Michele. Research chemist So. Research Inst., Birmingham, 1964-71; mgr. teaching labs. Coll. Medicine, U. Ala., Birmingham, 1971-74; dir. core teaching services Center for Health Scis., U. Tenn., Memphis, 1974-78, dir. ednl. support services, 1978—; lectr. in field. Mem. Assn. for Multidisciplinary Edn. in Health Scis. (v.p. 1979-80), Nat. Assn. Coll. Aux. Services. Home: 2547 Mackinnon Dr Memphis TN 38138 Office: Center for Health Scis U Tenn 8 S Dunlap St Room 7 Memphis TN 38163

CRAWFORD, FREDERICK LELAND, II, air force officer; b. Leesville, La., Dec. 7, 1945; s. Frederick Leland and Cleota Izell (Morrison) C.; B.B.A., Okla. U., 1968, M.B.A., 1978; M.L.A., Tex. Christian U., 1974; m. Kay Lang Stewart, Mar. 29, 1975; children—Matthew Frederick, Courtney Erin. Commd. 2d lt., U.S. Air Force, 1968, advanced through grades to maj., 1971; missile launch officer Grand Forks (N.D.) AFB, 1968-70; navigator trainee Mather AFB, Calif., 1970-71; navigator instr. Carswell AFB, Tex., 1971-74; asst. prof. aerospace studies Okla. U., Norman, 1975-77; nat. admissions counselor for AF ROTC, Norman, 1977—, comdt. of cadets, 1978-79; productivity and manpower analyst Hdqrs. USAF, 1979—. Referee Little League. Decorated D.F.C., 9 Air medals, Air Force Commendation medal; recipient Linzi trophy for flying excellence, 1971. Mem. Air Force Assn., Sigma Chi. Office: AF/MPMZ Pentagon Washington DC

CRAWFORD, HORACE RANDOLPH, diversified industry exec.; b. Haskell, Tex., Mar. 4, 1928; s. John Milton and Annie Maud (Williams) C.; B.Ch.E., Tex. Tech. U., 1949; M.S., U. Tex., 1954, Ph.D. (Humble Oil fellow), 1958; m. Mary Louise Holcombe, July 10, 1955; children—Michael Earl, Donald Kevin, Nancy Esther, Barbara Ann. Engine opr. Sun Oil Co., Rio Grande, Tex., 1949, plant chemist, 1950, petroleum engr., Corpus Christi, Tex., 1953, gas engr., Silver, Tex., 1954-55; instr. math., Humble Oil fellow, U. Tex. at Austin, 1956-57; research asso. Western Co., Dallas, 1957-59, research group supr., 1959-61, asst. div. mgr., 1961-63, mgr. chem. engring. dept., 1963-67, mgr. contract research and devel. dept., Richardson, Tex., 1967-68; mgr. chem. engring. Enserch Corp., Dallas, 1969-72, dir. fuels sect. corp. devel. and research, 1972-74, dir. Sanitech div., 1974-75; dir. process and new product devel. NIPAK, 1975-77; mgr. oil gas sales Enserch Exploration, Inc., 1977-78; pres. Cangro Fertilizer, 1978—; staff engr. Conoco, 1979—. Vice-chmn. fin. North Trail Dist. Boy Scouts Am., 1971, chmn. fin., 1972, chmn. dist., 1973-75, chmn. relationships, 1976—, Merit award, 1977, Silver Beaver award, 1978. Served with U.S. Army, 1950-52. Registered profl. engr. Mem. Engring. Soc. Tex. Tech. (pres. 1948-49), Am. Inst. Chem. Engrs. (chmn. Dallas 1968, dir. 1969-77, Engr. of Yr. award 1973), N.Tex. Gas Men's Assn., Am. Soc. Gas Engrs. (pres. SW chpt. 1972-73, nat. dir. 1972-74), Petroleum Engrs. Club, Nat. Solid Waste Mgmt. Assn., Internat. Platform Assn., Sigma Xi, Alpha Chi, Phi Lambda Upsilon, Kappa Mu Epsilon, Tau Beta Pi, Omega Chi Epsilon (pres. Tex. chpt. 1954). Club: Optimist (pres. Richardson 1963-64, dir. 1965-66). Contbr. articles to profl. jours. Patentee in field. Home: 20406 Laverton Katy TX 77450 Office: 5 Greenway Plaza E Suite 2630 Houston TX 77046

CRAWFORD, JAMES FRANKLIN, economist; b. Tabor, Iowa, May 16, 1920; s. Frank Mitchell and Loie Marie (Yerger) C.; A.B., Peru Coll., 1941; M.A. in Econs., U. Colo., 1952; Ph.D., U. Wis., 1957; m. Miriam Weirick, Aug. 14, 1949; children—Cathy Ann, David. Instr. econs. U. Wis., Madison, 1955-56, program dir. U.S. State Dept. Program for German Indsl. Relations Trainees, 1955-56; asst. prof. econs. Ga. State U., Atlanta, 1956-58, asso. prof., 1958-60, prof., 1960—, chmn. dept. econs., 1962—. Mem. Gov.'s Joint Study Com. on Full Employment in Ga., 1976-77; mem. community disputes settlement panel Am. Arbitration Assn., 1970—; mem. region 3 econ. stablzn. com. Office of Emergency Planning, 1970—; trustee Ga. Council on Econ. Edn., 1972—. Served to lt. (j.g.) USN, 1942-46. Mem. Indsl. Relations Research Assn. (pres. Atlanta chpt. 1978-80), Atlanta Econs. Club (pres. 1976-77), Am., So. econs. assns., Pi Gamma Mu, Kappa Delta Pi, Alpha Kappa Psi, Omicron Delta Epsilon. Editor: Readings in Modern Economics, 1977; Principles of Economics, 1956; contbr. articles and revs. to profl. jours. Office: Dept Economics Ga State U Atlanta GA 30303

CRAWFORD, JOHN MILTON, JR., assn. exec.; b. Tyler, Tex., Jan. 7, 1939; s. John Milton and Winifred (Robinson) C.; B.B.A., U. Tex., 1961; m. Carolyn Tyson DeVault, Aug. 29, 1963; 1 son, John Milton III. Field rep. U. Tex. Ex-Students Assn., 1961-62; asst. promotional dir. S.W. Republic Corp. 1965; exec. dir. Tex. Nursing Home Assn., 1965-69 (all Austin, Tex.); exec. v.p. Screen Printing Assn. Internat., Fairfax, Va., 1969—; mem. environ. conservation bd. Graphic Arts Industry; guest lectr. univs., 1966-67. Loan exec. United Fund, 1965; mem. exec. com. printing and pub. sect. Nat. Safety Council. Served with Intelligence Corps, AUS, 1962-65. Recipient SPOKE Jaycee award, 1961; Sparkplug Jaycee award, 1970, 71. Mem. Tex. Soc. Washington, Am. (certified assn. exec., awards com., pub. affairs com., bd. mem. membership dirs. council, bd. mem. conv. and expn. mgrs. council President's club), Washington socs. assn. execs., Internat. Platform Assn., Inst. Organizational Mgmt. (curriculum com., task force), Soc. Assn. Mgrs. (charter mem.), Meeting Planners Internat. (charter mem.), Postal Commerative Soc., U. Tex. Longhorn Alumni Band, Graphic Arts Assn. Execs., Nat. Assn. Exposition Mgrs., Nat. Hist. Soc., Cowboy Hall of Fame (life), U. Tex. Ex-students Assn. (life), Delta Sigma Pi (life). Baptist. Editor: Caring, 1965-69, Spotlight, 1961-62, 65-66, Highlights, 1965. Contbr. articles to newspapers, mags. in U.S., abroad. Home: 11206 Lapham Dr Oakton VA 22124 Office: 10015 Main St Fairfax VA 22031

CRAWFORD, MARIAN COX, educator; b. Jackson, Miss., Mar. 3, 1940; d. Selby Marion and Myrtle Marie (Peyton) Cox; B.S., Miss. State Coll. for Women, 1962; M.B.E., U. Miss., 1970, Ph.D., 1975; children—Robert Peyton, Stephen Selby. Instr., N.W. Ala. State Jr. Coll., 1970-72, U. Miss., 1972-74; asst. prof. bus. adminstrn. U. Ark., Little Rock, 1974-79, asso. prof., 1979—. Mem. Am. Bus. Communication Assn., Nat. Bus. Edn. Assn., Adminstrv. Mgmt. Soc., Am. Vocat. Assn., DAR, Alpha Kappa Psi, Beta Gamma Sigma, Delta Kappa Gamma, Delta Pi Epsilon. Baptist. Home: 10 New Haven Ct Little Rock AR 72207 Office: 33d and University St Little Rock AR 72204

CRAWFORD, NICKEY LEWIS, horse breeding assn. exec.; b. Franklin, N.C., Nov. 13, 1949; s. Herbert Lewis and Marie (Shope) C.; student Guilford Tech. Inst., Jamestown, N.C.; m. Dixie Pressley Crawford, Oct. 16, 1969; children—Matthew Scott, Melissa Ashley. Prodn. foreman Martin Marietta Aggregates, Jamestown, 1974; registrar Ashmore Bus. Coll., Thomasville, N.C., 1975; gen. mgr. Protection Systems, High Point, N.C., 1976; farm mgr. Richard Petty Farms, Level Cross, N.C., 1979—. with Am. Paint Horse Assn. Tng. and Breeding Center. Served with USMC, 1970-73. Mem. N.C. Paint Horse Assn. So. Baptist. Club: Masons.

CRAWFORD, OLIVER RAY, real estate, investments, service contract exec.; b. Amarillo, Tex., July 19, 1925; s. George Gordon and Bell Elizabeth (Allston) C.; student Wash. State Coll., 1943-44, S. Tex. Sch. Law, 1953-55; m. Nancy Rose Hudson, Sept. 22, 1979; children by previous marriage—Lynda Ann, Carolyn Rae, Alan Richard. Div. mgr. Phillips Petroleum Co., Midland, Tex., 1947-52; mgr. tax and tile dept. Houston Oil Co. Tex., 1952-56; asst. to gen. mgr. Southwestern Settlement and Devel. Co., Jasper, Tex., 1956-59; gen. mgr. Southwestern Timber Co., 1959-73; v.p. Eastex, Inc., 1956-73; v.p., treas. Jasper Timber Co., Newton Timber Co., Bleakwood Timber Co., San Augustine Timber Co., 1960-72; pres. Eastern Tex. Cable TV Services, Inc., 1967-71; asst. to pres. Temple Industries, 1973-74; partner firm real estate investment and counseling, Austin, Tex., 1974-75; exec. v.p. Metro Contract Services, Houston, 1975-76; v.p., sec., treas. Tex. Commodore Enterprises, Austin, 1976—; chmn., pres. Tecom Inc., Austin, 1976—, Chaparral Valley Properties, Inc., 1979—; dir. First State Bank, Jasper. Mem. Tex. Alcoholic Beverage Commn., 1965-69; pres. So. Forest Research Inst., 1963-75; adv. com. Tex. Forest Service, 1957-74; dir. Tex. forest industries com. Am. Forest Products Industries. Founder, pres. Jasper Youth Baseball Assn., 1958-74; bd. dirs. ARC, Operation Orphans, Inc., Tex. Law Enforcement Found.; mem. century council Tex. A. and M. U.; trustee Southwest Research Inst., Tex. A. and M. U. Research Found.; v.p., bd. dirs. Tex. chpts. Leukemia Soc. Am.; mem. regent's devel. council Lamar U. Served as fighter pilot USAAF, 1943-45; brevet maj. gen. U.S. Air N.G. Named Man of Month, East Tex. C. of C., 1961; recipient hon. Lone Star Farmer degree Tex. Assn. Future Farmers; Forest Mgmt. award Nat. Lumber Mfrs. Assn.; Mr. East Texas award, operating dirs. of Tyler County Dogwood Festival, 1967; Sportsman Conservationist of Yr. award Tex. Outdoor Writers Assn., 1970; Forest Conservation award Nat. Wildlife Fedn., 1966; decorated comdr.'s cross of the Order of Merit (Fed. Republic Germany). Hon. life mem. Jasper Youth Baseball, Nat. Congress PTA, Future Farmers Am.; mem. Tex. Forestry Assn. (dir., pres. 1970-71), Sportsman's Clubs Tex. (pres. 1975-76), Combat Pilots Assn., Jasper C. of C. (pres. 1964), Def. Orientation Conf. Assn., Confederate Air Force (life). Presbyterian. Home: 7507 Step Down Cove Austin TX 78731 Office: 3636 Executive Center Dr Suite 201 Austin TX 78731

CRAWFORD, PATRICIA ELIZABETH BUSH, ednl. and rehab. counselor; b. Kittery, Maine, Mar. 28, 1951; d. Ernest Robert and Elizabeth Mary (Maloney) Bush; A.B. in Sociology, St. Mary's U., Halifax, N.S., Can., 1973; M.A. in Edn., E. Carolina U., 1975, M.S. in Rehab. Counseling, 1977. Planner, tng. officer Onslow County Fund, Inc., Jacksonville, N.C., 1973-74; univ. residence adminstr., E. Carolina U., Greenville, N.C., 1975-77, counselor, 1977—; faculty advisor Gamma Sigma Sigma service sorority. Active N.C. Symphony Assn. Rehab. internship grantee, Halifax, 1977; certified ednl. counselor, N.C. Mem. Am. Personnel and Guidance Assn., Am. Coll. Personnel Assn., Am. Sch. Counselor Assn., Am. Rehab. Counseling Assn. Roman Catholic. Club: Bus. and Profl. Women's Assn. Research in rehab. of children. Home: Wilson Wood 1605-7 Kent Dr Wilson NC 27893 Office PO Box 2726 East Carolina Univ Greenville NC 27834

CRAWFORD, RUTH W., educator; b. Macon County, Ala., Mar. 15, 1927; d. Moses and Pastoria (Young) Whitlow; B.S. in Elementary Edn., Tuskegee (Ala.) Inst., 1950, M.Ed. in Elementary Edn., 1960, M.Ed. in Supervision, 1973; m. George W. Crawford; children—Doris Crawford Oloyede, Deloris, George W., Georgia Ruth Crawford Anthony. With Pike County (Ala.) Bd. Edn., Troy, 1950—, tchr. Title I reading, 1965-72, supr. instruction, 1973—. Mem. NEA, Ala., Pike County edn. assns., LWV, Ala. Reading Assn., Ala. Assn. Public Continuing Adult Edn., Epsilon Beta, Dir. Supervision Dir. Instruction, Assn. Supervision and Curriculum Devel. Club: Daus. of Elks. Certified as tchr., supr. instruction, adult edn., Ala. Home: 204 Carver Dr Troy AL 36081 Office: PO Box 456 Troy AL 36081

CRAWFORD, THOMAS HENRY, chemist, univ. adminstr.; b. Louisville, Oct. 22, 1931; s. Thomas Marion and Margaret Stella (Cummins) C.; B.S., U. Louisville, 1958, Ph.D., 1961; m. Wanda June Allison, June 19, 1954; children—Sherri Lynn Gary, Thomas Barry. Asst. prof. chemistry U. Louisville, 1961-66, asso. prof., 1966-70, prof., 1970—, chmn. dept. chemistry, 1971-72, 74, acting dean Coll. Arts and Scis., 1973, faculty asso. office of pres., 1975-77, asst. exec. v.p. for adminstrn., 1977-79, asso. v.p. acad. affairs, 1979—; vis. asst. prof. chemistry Columbia U., N.Y.C., summer 1965; vis. asso. prof. Calif. Inst. Tech., Pasadena, 1968-69. Served with USNR, 1951-53. Recipient Metroversity Instructional Devel. award, 1979. Mem. Am. Chem. Soc., AAAS. Democrat. Author: (with Gray, Hammond, and Osteryoung) Models in Chemical Science, 1971; (with Gray and Swanson) Project Acac, 1972. Home: 2502 Windsor Forest Dr Louisville KY 40272 Office: Acad Affairs Belknap Campus U Louisville Louisville KY 40208

CRAWFORD, WILLIAM DONHAM, utility co. exec.; b. Little Rock, June 22, 1923; s. Sidney Robert and Blanche (Donham) D.; B.S., U.S. Naval Acad., 1947; M.S., Calif. Inst. Tech., 1948; m. Colene King; children—Carol, Bruce, Philip. Chief, Office of Sci. and Tech., Pan Am. Union, 1949-50; mem. tech. and adminstrv. staff AEC, 1951-54; nuclear power specialist Middle South Utilities, 1955-56, asst. sec., asst. treas., 1956-59, v.p., 1963—; v.p., adminstrv. v.p. Consol. Edison Co., N.Y.C., 1963-69; pres Edison Electric Inst., N.Y.C., 1969-77 chmn. bd. Gulf State Utilities Co., Beaumont, Tex., 1978—; vice chmn. Thomas Alva Edison Found.; dir. First City Bancorp. Tex., 1st Security Bank, Beaumont; mem. adv. bd. Comml. Nat. Bank, Little Rock. Served with C.E., U.S. Army, 1951-54; with USN, 1947-49. Mem. East Tex. C. of C. (dir.), Edison Electric Inst., Nat. C. of C., Tex. Research League, Helium Breeder Assos., Am. Nuclear Energy Council, Atomic Indsl. Forum, S.W. Power Pool. Baptist. Clubs: Beaumont, Beaumont County, Baton Rouge Country; Boston (New Orleans); Met. (Washington). Office: 285 Liberty St Beaumont TX 77701

CRAWFORD, WILLIAM EDWIN, clergyman; b. Temple, Tex., Dec. 19, 1918; s. William Edwin and Mattie Margaret (Heard) C.; B.A., Baylor U., 1941; B.D., Southwestern Bapt. Theol. Sem., 1952; m. Mary Inez Gilliam, Mar. 10, 1940; children—Dan Reavis, Bob Floyd. Ordained to ministry Southern Baptist Conv., 1939; asso. pastor South Main Bapt. Ch., Houston, 1959-56; pastor West End Bapt. Ch., Houston, 1956-60, 1st Bapt. Ch., Nacogdoches, Tex., 1960-67; dir. missions Golden Triangle Assn., Nederland, Tex., 1967-70; dir. missions Waco Bapt. Assn. (Tex.), 1970-74; dir. devel. Southwestern Bapt. Theol. Sem., Fort Worth, 1974—. Served as capt. AUS, 1942-44. Trustee Houston Bapt. U., 1960-61, East. Tex. Bapt. Coll., 1961-67, Southwestern Bapt. Theol. Sem., 1966-73; mem. exec. com. Southern Bapt. Conv., 1960-66; mem. exec. bd. Bapt. Gen. Conv. Ten., 1964-67. Home: 3800 Ashford St Fort Worth TX 76133 Office: PO Box 22000 Fort Worth TX 76122

CRAWLEY, JOHN EMMETT, JR., chem. engr.; b. Alton, Va., Mar. 31, 1920; s. John Emmett and Gladys Elwyn (Martin) C.; B.S. in Chem. Engring. Va. Poly Inst. 1941, M.S., 1947; m. Ruth Williams, Dec. 27, 1946; children—Robert Arthur, William Edward, Donald Eugene. Research and devel. engr. Du Pont Co., Charleston, W.Va., 1947-50, asst. tech. supt., 1950-52, sr. process engr., Wilmington, Del., 1952-64, Orange, Tex., 1964-70, staff engr., 1970—. Mem. Orange Community Action Com., 1974-75, YMCA, 1966—. Served to maj. AUS, 1941-46. Mem. Am. Inst. Chem. Engrs., Sigma Xi. Republican. Presbyterian (elder). Lions. Home: 2109 Treemont Ln Orange TX 77630 Office: PO Box 1089 Orange TX 77630

CRAWLEY, RONALD EDWARD, air force officer; b. Winston Salem, N.C., Dec. 23, 1938; s. John Skahan and Margaret Camellia (Isenhour) C.; B.A., La. Tech. U., 1971; M.A., St. Mary's U., 1976; m. Lillie Faye McIntyre, Oct. 25, 1959; children—Camellia Anne, Ronald Edward. Commd. lt. U.S. Air Force, 1957, advanced through grades to capt. radio operator, Eng. and Turkey, 1957-61, airlift command and control technician, U.S. and Europe, 1961-70, comdr. U.S. Air Force Honor Guard, Washington, 1971-74, mil. sci. instr., officer tng. sch. Lackland AFB, Tex., 1974-75, sr. counselor, 1975-77, plans and programs officer for hdqrs., Air Force ROTC, Maxwell AFB, Montgomery, Ala., 1977-79; chief institutional research Community Coll. of Air Force, Maxwell AFB, 1979—; instr. sociology and psychology Our Lady of the Lake U., San Antonio. Certified master instr. mil sci. Air Tng. Command, USAF; recipient profl. performance award as counselor Officer Tng. Sch., 1977. Mem. Air Force Assn., Am. Personnel and Guidance Assn. Baptist. Home: 1243 High Point Rd Montgomery AL 36109

CRAYCROFT, JOSEPH MARTIN, ins. co. exec.; b. Meade County, Ky., June 7, 1936; s. Joseph Morris and Mary Jane (Mills) C.; B.A., Bellarmine Coll., 1959; postgrad. Spalding Coll., 1959-62; m. Mary Martha Powers, Apr. 23, 1966; children—Kimberly Ann, Scott Joseph. Tchr. public schs., Brandenburg, Ky., 1959-65; with Craycroft Ins. & Real Estate Agy., Louisville, 1965-71; tchr. real estate Craycroft Real Estate Sch., 1972-77; owner Craycroft Enterprises, Louisville, 1969-70; gen. agt., pres. Craycroft Ins. Assos., Inc., Louisville, 1980—; cons. in field. Mem. Nat. Assn. Life Underwriters. Democrat. Roman Catholic. Club: Church. Home: 507 Quails Run Louisville KY 40207 Office: PO Box 6512 Louisville KY 40207

CREASY, JACK OGDEN, II, hosp. mgmt. co. exec.; b. Columbia, Mo., Nov. 16, 1935; s. Jack Ogden and Ida May (McCurry) C.; B.S. in B.A., U. Mo., 1958; m. Sharon Kay Vander Ploag, Mar. 10, 1979; children by previous marriage—Ted, Jay, Julie, Cindy, Jeff. Ops. mgr. CIDA Investment Co., Columbia, Mo., 1960-67; personnel mgr. U. Mo. MED Cont., Columbia, 1967-75; personnel specialist Humana Inc., Tampa, Fla., 1975-77; employee relations mgr. Am. Medicorp, Dallas, 1977-78, dir. human resources, Birmingham, Ala., 1978-79; v.p. Hosp. Affiliates Mgmt. Corp., Tampa 1979—; dir. Am. Health Profiles, 1978-79. Mem. adv. Birmingham ARC, 1978-79. Served with U.S. Army, 1958-60. Mem. Am. Soc. Hosp. Personnel Dirs., Fla. Hosp. Assn., Am. Soc. Hosp. Edn. and Tng., Tampa C. of C. Office: 205 S Hoover Blvd Tampa FL 33609

CREEK, JOHN DENNIS, mfg. co. exec.; b. Roswell, N.Mex., Apr. 5, 1951; s. Webster Bennett and Edna Ore (Lott) C.; B.A., Tex. Tech. U., 1974, postgrad., 1974-75; m. Billie Lou Kingsbery, June 19, 1976. Field technician Tait-Andritz Co., Lubbock, Tex., 1976, sales staff, 1977-78, sales mgr., 1978, dir. mktg., 1978—, v.p., 1980—; cons. U. Wis., Madison, 1978-79. Mem. TAPPI, Am. Inst. Mining Engrs. Republican. Baptist. Clubs: Rotary, Lubbock Country. Home: 4811 Tamanaco Ct Arlington TX 76013 Office: 1010 Commonwealth Blvd S Arlington TX 76063

CREEK, MARY LOU, retail store exec.; b. Carnegie, Pa., Sept. 16, 1927; d. John David and Olive May (Coup) Marshall; student Indiana (Pa.) State Tchrs. Coll., 1945, Ad-Art Studio Sch., Pitts., 1946-49; m. Lewis Elmore Creek, Mar. 8, 1952. Artist, G.C. Murphy Co., McKeesport, Pa., 1946-59; owner Comml. Art Service, Auburndale, Fla., 1960-79; artist Scotty's, Inc., Winter Haven, Fla., 1970-73, advt. prodn. mgr., 1973—. Bd. dirs. Polk County Assn. for Retarded Citizens, 1975—, chmn. publicity com., 1975—; bd. dirs. Scotty's Employees Fed. Credit Union, 1978—. Republican. Mormon. Illustrator: The Practical Nurse, 1964; Practical Nurse Education, a Manual of Nursing Measures for Practical Nursing, 1965. Home: 123 Tempsford Rd Auburndale FL 33823 Office: PO Box 939 Winter Haven FL 33880

CREEL, NICHOLAS, chem. engr.; b. Galveston, Tex.; s. Luke and Anna (Dicklich) C.; B.S. in Chem. Engring., Tex. A&M U., 1950; m. Aug. 2, 1941 (dec.); children—Nicholas, Dennis Alan, Jeffrey L. With Signal Oil and Gas Co., 1950-65, Coastal State Petrochem. Co., 1965-66; mgr. ops. Fluor Engrs., 1966-69; project engr. SIP Corp., 1969; sales engr. Petrolite Corp., 1969-72; environ. engr. Crown Central Pet Corp., 1972-73; project engr. J.F. Pirtchard Co., 1973, HK Ferguson Co., 1973-77; sr. project engr., project mgr. Stubbs Overbeck Co., 1977— (all Houston). Served to 1st lt. AUS, 1943-45. Decorated DFC, Air medal with 3 clusters. Conservative. Home: 4600 Beechnut St #109CC Houston TX 77096 Office: 8585 Commerce Park Dr Houston TX 77036

CREMINS, WILLIAM DANIEL, lawyer; b. Boston, Feb. 21, 1939; s. Eugene Joseph and Dorothy (Forbes) C.; B.A., St. Bonaventure U., 1960; J.D., George Washington U., 1967; m. Susan P. Shenkman, June 25, 1960; children—Kathryn, Michael, Jennifer. Admitted to Va. bar, 1967; partner, prin. Mackall, Mackall & Cremins, Fairfax, 1967-74; individual practice, Fairfax, 1974—; lectr. No. Va. Community Coll., Annandale. Bd. dirs. Brookfield P.T.A., 1970-71, Brookfield Swim Club, Inc. Served to 1st lt. AUS, 1961-63. Mem. Am. Bar Assn., Va. Bar Assn., Fairfax Bar Assn. (pres. 1980), Am. Judicature Soc., Am., Va. trial lawyers assns., Am. Arbitration Assn. (panel arbitrators), Delta Theta Phi. Home: 11924 Richland Ln Herndon VA 22070 Office: 4041 University Dr Fairfax VA 22030

CRENSHAW, ALLEN, III, photographer, advt. agy. exec.; b. Dallas, Oct. 8, 1944; s. Allen and Jackie Youvonne (Mansfield) C.; student N. Tex. State U., 1964-67, Art Center, 1968-70; B.F.A., Austin Coll., 1975; children by previous marriage—Andrew, Kelly. Asso. producer Ernie Zehms Prodns., Los Angeles, 1969, Ednl. Film Prodns., Los Angeles, 1969-70; pres. Crenshaw Studio, Inc., Denison, Tex., 1970—; owner, mgr. The Great Tintype Conglomerate, Dension, 1974—; instr. photography Austin Coll., 1973-76. Pres. trustees 1st Presbyn. Ch. Served with USMCR, 1962-67. Recipient awards AP Mng. Editors, Nat. Photographers Am. Mem. Denison C. of C. (dir.), Profl. Photographers Am. Democrat. Home: 1215 S Fairbanks St Denison TX 75020 Office: 930 W Main St Denison TX 75020

CRENSHAW, TENA LULA, librarian; b. Coleman, Fla., Dec. 15, 1930; d. Herbert Joseph and Nellie Jackson (Wicker) Crenshaw; B.S., Fla. So. Coll., 1951; postgrad. U. Fla., 1952-55; M.L.S. (Univ. scholar), U. Okla., 1960. Tchr. pub. schs., Coleman, Fla., 1952-55, St. Petersburg, Fla., 1955-57, Houston, 1957-59; tech. librarian Army Rocket & Guided Missile Agy., Redstone Arsenal, Huntsville, Ala., 1960-61; acquisitions librarian Martin Marietta Corp., Orlando, Fla., 1961-64; reader services librarian John F. Kennedy Space Center, NASA, Fla., 1964-66; research info. analyst, specialist, Lockheed Missiles and Space Co., Palo Alto, Cal., 1966-68; head services to pub. A.W. Calhoun Med. Library, Emory U., Atlanta, 1969—. Mem. High Mus. Art, Spl. Libraries Assn. (treas. S. Atlantic chpt. 1970-72, chmn. membership com. 1973, v.p. 1973-74, pres. 1974-75, mem. resolutions com. 1975-77, mem. archives com. 1978—, mem. biol. scis. div. nominating com. 1974—, chmn. 1977-78), Med. Library Assn., Southeastern (mem. new directions com. 1972-74), Ga. (careers in librarianship com. 1974—, automation com. 1978—) library assns. Am. Soc. for Info. Sci., D.A.R., Alpha Delta Pi, Kappa Delta Pi. Democrat. Episcopalian. Contbr. to Spl. Libraries Assn. Newsletter. Home: 1810 NW 23d Blvd Gainesville FL 32605 Office: U Fla Edn Library 1500 Norman Hall Gainesville FL 32611

CRESIMORE, JAMES LEONARD, food broker; b. Statesville, N.C., Jan. 24, 1928; s. Fred Clayton and Cleo (Edison) C.; B.S. in Bus. Adminstrn., High Point Coll., 1949; m. Mary Josephine Conrad, June 3, 1956; children—James Conrad, Jennifer Cheryl, Joel Clayton. Gen. mgr. Home Service Stores, Inc., High Point, N.C., 1948-50; co-founder, sec. Red Dot Food Stores, Inc., 1952-56; sec. Consol. Wholesale Corp., 1952-56; owner Village Super Market, High Point, 1953-56; co-owner Bunker Hill Packing Corp., Bedford, Va., 1964—, chmn. bd., co-owner Asso. Brokers, Inc., Raleigh, N.C., 1956—; founding dir., chmn. bd. State Bank Raleigh. Chmn. Mayor's Manpower Com., Raleigh. Chmn. Wake County Republican Com., 1963—, del. nat. conv. San Francisco, 1964; 4th Congl. dist.; mem. platform com. Rep. Nat. Convention, Miami, Fla., 1968. Mem. advisory bd. Salvation Army; trustee Pheiffer Coll. Served with U.S. Army, 1950-52. Mem. Sales and Marketing Execs. Internat. (mem. bd., pres. Raleigh, now v.p.), Raleigh (past pres.), Nat. (lt. regional dir.) food brokers assns., Raleigh C. of C. (dir. 1973-74). Rotarian. Home: 3720 Williamsborough Ct Raleigh NC 27609 Office: 3309 Drake Circle Raleigh NC 27609

CRESSMAN, ARTHUR RAYMOND, JR., steel co. exec.; b. Darby, Pa., Aug. 2, 1947; s. Arthur Raymond and Lorraine E. C.; student U. Kans., 1965-67, U. Md., 1972-74, U. Chgo., 1973-74, Harrow Inst., London, 1974-75; m. Constance A. Smith, Mar. 11, 1972; children—Arthur R., Jacqueline A. Mgr. ops. Itel Corp./Computer Dimensions Inc., Dallas, 1975-77; mgr. regional sales Dallas Pipe & Supply Inc., 1977-78; pres., chief operating officer Intercontinental Pipe & Steel Inc., Dallas, 1978—. Served with U.S. Navy, 1967-75. Mem. Nat. Assn. Steel Pipe Distbrs., Kans. Independent Oil and Gas Assn., Phi Kappa Tau. Clubs: Brookhaven Country (Dallas); Dallas County Republican Men's. Office: 8340 Meadow Rd #134 Dallas TX 75231

CREVENNA SINGER, HILDA, soprano; b. Frankfort Am Main, Germany, Dec. 11, 1892; d. Theodor and Amy Gertrude (Gordon) Plieninger; student Hoch'Sches Konservatorium, Frankfort, 1906-11; student with Guerrina Fabbri, prof. Moratti, Milan, Italy; m. Werner Singer, Mar. 16, 1958; children by previous marriage—Alfredo Crevenna, Theo R. Crevenna. Leading soprano in Carmen, Der Rosenkavalier, Don Giovanni, Marriage of Figaro, La Boheme, Madame Butterfly, Berlin Opera House, 1928-33, Staedtische Oper, Frankfort Am Main, 1930-31; appeared in leading roles in maj. opera houses in Munich, Germany and Basel, Switzerland; appeared in numerous solo recitals throughout Europe; soprano soloist with BBC, London, 1929-30, also London Philharmonic Orch.; rec. artist Electrola Records, 1928-31; instr. voice N.Y. Coll. Music, N.Y.C., 1947-68, N.Y. U., N.Y.C., 1968-70. Mem. Nat. Assn. Tchrs. of Singing. Address: 3614 SE 10th Ave Cape Coral FL 33904

CREWS, D'ANNE MCADAMS (MRS. JAMES EDWARD CREWS, JR.), merc. co. exec.; b. Huntsville, Tex., Nov. 1, 1934; d. W.D. and Annette A. (Turner) McAdams; B.B.A. with high honors, So. Meth. U., 1954; M.A., Sam Houston State U., 1967; m. James Edward Crews, Jr., June 1, 1957; children—Kay Allison, Kelly Anne. Sec. to dir. Tex. Dept. Corrections, Huntsville, 1954-57; certification clerk for univ., sec. to dir. edn. dept. Sam Houston State U., Huntsville, 1961-66; partner McAdams Co., Huntsville, 1966—. Dir., sec. Walker County Tchrs. Fed. Credit Union, 1964-66. Chmn. Mayor's Commn. on Status of Women, Huntsville, 1970-72; pres. Huntsville P.T.A., 1969-70; chmn. cookie sales, Girl Scouts U.S.A., Huntsville, 1970-71; active Huntsville Enrichment Activities Program, 1969-74; co-chmn. heritage com. Bicentennial Commn. Huntsville, 1974-76; mem. bd. Huntsville Public Library, 1976-79; mem. Walker County (Tex.) Hist. Commn., 1977—; bd. dirs. Walker County unit Am. Cancer Soc., sec., treas., 1970-76. Named Girl of Year Beta Sigma Phi, 1958, 62, 65, Outstanding Young Woman of Am., 1970; recipient medal of Appreciation S.A.R., 1975. Mem. D.A.R. (chpt. librarian 1972-74, chpt. curator 1974-76), Daus. Am. Colonists (capt. John Utle chpt., regent 1973-75, state rec. sec. 1973-75, state 1st vice regent, 1975-77 state regent 1977-79), Daus. Republic of Tex. (pres. Houston chpt. 1975-77, corresponding sec. gen. 1977-79), Tex. Congress Parents and Tchrs. (hon. life), Huquenot Soc. Tex., Huguenot Soc. of Founders Manakin in Colony Va., Nat. Soc. Sons and Daus. of the Pilgrims, U.S. Daus. 1812, U. D.C., Huntsville Meml. Hosp. Aux. (pres. 1972-73, life), Sam Houston State U. (life; dir., treas. 1972-75, pres. 1975-76), So. Meth. U. alumni assns., Zeta Tau Alpha Alumnae (pres. chpt. 1977-79). Methodist. Clubs: Huntsville Band Boosters (sec. 1977-78), Huntsville Study (pres. 1972-73). Compiler, editor: Huntsville and Walker County, Texas: A Bicentennial History. Home: 253 Royal Oaks Huntsville TX 77340 Office: 1215 Sam Houston Ave Huntsville TX 77340

CREWS, HAROLD RICHARDSON, clin. chemist; b. Sylvania, Ga., Aug. 31, 1934; s. George Mills and Eva Marie (Scott) C.; student South Ga. Coll., 1958-60, Ga. Southwestern Coll., 1960-62, U. Miami, 1966-67; m. Barbara McFarlane, Feb. 27, 1970; children—Karen Hope, Mark Richardson. Chemist, U.S. Naval Hosp., San Diego, 1953-55, Med. Coll. S.C., 1963-66; research asso. cardiovascular medicine Miami Heart Inst., Miami Beach, Fla., 1966-68; asso. dir. research and devel. cardiovascular medicine Parkway Gen. Hosp., North Miami Beach, Fla., 1968-71; sr. mgr. research and devel., corp. tech. advisor and cons. Coulter Electronics, Inc., Hialeah, Fla., 1971—. Served with USNR, 1953-57; Korea. NIH grantee, 1963. Mem. Am. Chem. Soc., Am. Assn. Clin. Chemists, Can. Soc. Clin. Chemists, AAAS. Research on arteriosclerosis and atherosclerosis; patentee in field. Office: 440 W 20th St Hialeah FL 33010

CREWS, MALCOLM KNIGHT, city ofcl.; b. Arcadia, Fla., Apr. 2, 1923; s. Chester Arthur and Florence Hortenze (Meliza) C.; student S.Fla. Jr. Coll., 1968-69; m. Betty G. Lanier, Apr. 16, 1955; children—Dennis Mark, Keith Knight. Asst. operations clk. Lodwick Aviation Mil. Acad., 1941-44; asst. sec.-treas. Avon Park Citrus Growers Assn. (Fla.), 1944-51; city clk., treas., tax collector city of Avon Park, 1951-55, city clk., treas., 1967—; gen. mgr. Wells Better Homes Co., Avon Park, 1955-60; sec.-treas. Wells Motor Co., Avon Park, 1960-67; appraiser, v.p. Heartland Fed. Savs. and Loan Assn. Hardee County, Wauchula, Fla., 1960—. Mem. Chrysler Corp. Accountants Inst. (life), Fla. Assn. Realtors, Fla. Municipal Finance Officers Assn., Fla. Assn. Assessing Officers, Fla. Pollution Control Assn., Avon Park C. of C. (past pres.), Internat. Inst. Municipal Clks., Ridge League Municipalities (pres. 1975-76), Avon Park Area Bd. Realtors (past pres.). Baptist (treas., deacon, Sunday sch. tchr.). Club: Lions (past pres.). Home: 421 E State St Avon Park FL 33825 Office: City Hall Avon Park FL 33825

CREWS, POLLY ANN, art center adminstr., broadcasting co. exec.; b. Little Rock, Aug. 20, 1929; d. Curren Goldman and Pauline Brooks (Britt) Wood; student U. Central Ark., 1947-48, Draughons Bus. Coll., 1948-49; m. Bill J. Crews, Nov. 23, 1952 (div.); children—Britt, Stuart, Leslie, Laurie, Tipton, Todd. Sec., Ark. State Dept. Revenue, 1949-52; engring. sec. Gardner-Denver Co., Quincy, Ill., 1952-53; office mgr. Fort Smith (Ark.) Psychiat. Clinic, 1969-74; spl. affairs dir. Sta. KLMN-TV, Fort Smith, 1978—, hostess show People Places and Polly, 1978—; dir. Fort Smith Art Center, 1975—. Bd. dirs. Ark. State Bd. Cerebral Palsy, 1977-78; mem. adv. bd. Sparks Regional Med. Center, Fort Smith, 1977—. Mem. Fort Smith/Van Buren Advt. Club, Bus. and Profl. Women, Soroptomists. Presbyterian. Author weekly newspaper column. Office: 423 N 6th St Fort Smith AR 72901

CREWS, WILLIAM DARYL, cons. engr.; b. Chickasha, Okla., Mar. 31, 1927; s. Ralph William and Beryl (Callahan) C.; student Rice U., 1945-48; B.S., U. Colo., 1949; postgrad. U. So. Cal., 1949-50, U. Tulsa, 1953-56; m. Dortha Louise Parsons, Oct. 14, 1950; children—Darryl Lee, Gary Wayne, Peggie Lynn, Rebecca Louise. Research chemist, engr. Cities Service Research and Devel. Co., Tulsa, 1950-59; ind. cons. engr., Tulsa, 1959—; prin. Crews Prodn. Co., Ltd., Beeline Ranch Ltd., Beeline Devel. Corp.; propr. mgr. farm and ranching ops. Served with USNR, 1944-46, AUS, 1950-52. Registered profl. engr., lic. real estate broker, Okla. Mem. Soc. Petroleum Engrs., Kappa Sigma. Patentee well stimulation techniques. Home: 2625 E 67th St Tulsa OK 74136 Office: 3015 E Skelly Dr Tulsa OK 74105

CREWS, WILLIAM PRESTON, lawyer; b. Shreveport, La., June 7, 1931; s. William P. and Bertha Mae (Richey) C.; B.S., Northwestern State U., 1960; J.D., Loyola U., 1970; m. Suzanne Wimberly, July 30, 1977; children—Steven David, Kimberly Ann. Owner, mgr. Central La. Claim Service, Natchitoches, 1958-70; admitted to La. bar, 1970; mem. firm Watson, Murchison, Crews, Arthur & Corkern, Natchitoches, 1970—. Faculty Northwestern State U., Natchitoches, 1972—. Pres. local Boy Scouts Am., 1967; pres. Weaver Elementary Sch. P.T.A., 1967; mem. Natchitoches Planning and Zoning Commn., 1963-67. Served to capt. AUS, 1950-58. Decorated Bronze Star. Mem. Am., La., Natchitoches, Red River Parish bar assns., Nat. Assn. Def. Attys., La. Assn. Def. Council, Natchitoches Parish C. of C. (pres. 1968), V.F.W. Elk. Home: Route 3 Box 305B Natchitoches LA 71457 Office: 110-112 Denis St Natchitoches LA 71457

CRIBBETT, ALBERT FRANKLIN, coll. adminstr.; b. Tavares, Fla., Aug. 31, 1928; s. Robert and Thelma Anne (Blair) C.; B.S. in Agr., U. Fla., 1950, M.S. in Agr., 1966; m. Norma Teresa Fernandez, June 8, 1952; children—Larry Stephen, Glenn Robert, Lana Caroline. Herdsman, Meeks Hereford Ranch, Dalhart, Tex., 1950-51, Lorraine Farms, Macon, Ga., 1951, 53-54; asst. agrl. agt. County of Orange, Orlando, Fla., 1954-62; extension dir. County of Pasco, Dade City, Fla., 1962-65; asst. prof. extension farm mgmt. U. Fla., 1965—, asst. to provost of agr., 1965-68, dir. spl. programs Inst. Food and Agrl. Scis., 1968-76, exec. asst. agrl. affairs, 1976—. Gen. mgr. Pasco County Fair Assn., 1962-65. Served with USAF, 1951-53. Recipient U. Fla. Student Agrl. Council Service award, 1973; 4-H Service award, 1957. Mem. Alpha Zeta, Gamma Sigma Delta, Epsilon Sigma Phi. Democrat. Presbyterian. Home: 1815 NW 22d Terr Gainesville FL 32605 Office: 1008 McCarty Hall U Florida Gainesville FL 32611

CRIM, BENJAMIN EDWARD, engr.; b. Fulton, Ala., Sept. 25, 1949; s. Edward Manning and Margie Olivia (Nelson) C.; student Southeastern La. U., 1967-69; B.S., La. State U., 1971; m. Vicki Diane Prejean, June 24, 1972; children—Christopher Edward, Carly Diane, Jennifer Lynn. Asst. plant engr. Edward Hines Lumber Co., Hines, Oreg., 1972-74, plant engr., 1974-77; design engr. Temple Assos. Engring. div. Diboll, Tex., 1977-78, forest products group leader, 1978—. Registered profl. engr., Tex., Ark., La., Miss., Tenn., Oreg. Mem. Nat. Soc. Profl. Engrs., Tex. Soc. Profl. Engrs., Forest Products Research Soc., Am. Forestry Assn., Tex. Forestry Assn. Democrat. Baptist. Home: 903 Meadow Ln Lufkin TX 75901 Office: 700 N Temple Dr Diboll TX 75941

CRIM, ELOISE HINKLE, probation officer; b. Glenville, W.Va., Jan. 19, 1927; d. Willie Otis and Edna Dale (Barker) Hinkle; student W.Va. Wesleyan U., 1943-44; B.S. in Social Work, W.Va. U., 1947, certificate in social work, 1948; M.S. in Social Work, Va. Commonwealth U., 1959. Child welfare worker W.Va. Dept. Pub. Assistance, Charleston, 1947-50, asst. dist. child welfare supr., 1950-59, dist. child welfare supr., 1959-60; social worker W.Va. Rehab. Center, Institute, W.Va., 1961-62; probation officer, tng. supr., adult probation dept. 13th Jud. Circuit, Charleston, W.Va., 1962-74, asst. chief probation officer, 1974—; bd. dirs., pres. Kanwha County Probation and Parole Council. Named Social Worker of Year, Charleston br. Nat. Assn. Social Workers, 1975-76. Mem. W.Va. Assn. Crime and Delinquency (treas., dir., past pres.), Nat. Assn. Social Workers (past sec. W.Va. chpt.), Acad. Certified Social Workers, Nat. Council Crime and Delinquency, Kanawha County, State and Fed. Probation and Parole Council, Democrat. Home: 512 Nancy St Charleston WV 25311 Office: 718 Morris St Charleston WV 25311

CRINER, BEATRICE HALL, editor; b. Hamilton, Ill., Nov. 25, 1915; d. Henry Nelson and Nellie (Hyer) Hall; A.B., Monmouth Coll., 1937; postgrad. Northwestern U., 1942, Lake Forest Coll., 1942, Harvard, 1943; m. Calvin L. Criner, Dec. 18, 1953. Sec., Stowe Thread Co., Belmont, N.C., 1945-51; asso. dir. spl. study religion Am. Council Edn., Washington, 1951-53; bus. mgr. Lees McRae Coll., 1953-56; registrar, 1956-62, tchr., 1956-61; chief examiner admissions office U. N.C., Chapel Hill, 1963-66; editor N.C. Dept. Edn., Raleigh, N.C., 1966—; mng. editor Longview Jour., Raleigh, 1967-70. Mem. Am. Assn. U. Women, Longview Writers, Delta Kappa Gamma, Kappa Delta. Author with Calvin L. Criner: Jobs in Public Service, 1974; Jobs in Personal Service, 1974; also books for juveniles. Address: PO Box 26403 Raleigh NC 27611

CRINER, JAMES ELLIS, elec. engr., former naval officer; b. Ripley, Tenn., Feb. 12, 1918; s. James Alfred and Rosa Agnes (New) C.; student Lake Forest Coll., 1950-51, U. Ill., 1948-49; B.S., U.S. Naval Postgrad. Sch., 1958; m. Ruth Elizabeth Hall, Dec. 15, 1945; children—James Ellis, David Hall, George Keith, Nancy Suzanne. Enlisted as apprentice seaman USN, 1938, advanced through grades to capt., 1972; tchr. USN Warrant Officer Electronic Engrs. Sch., Washington, 1947-48; tchr. elec. sci. U.S. Naval Acad., Annapolis, Md., 1963-66; comdg. officer Naval Electronic Systems Engring. Center, Charleston, S.C., 1973-77, ret., 1977. Served with U.S. Army, 1935-38. Decorated Bronze Star medal, Navy Commendation medal. Mem. IEEE, U.S. Naval Inst., Armed Forces Communications and Electronics Assn. Clubs: Masons, Shriners. Home: 1234 N Trinity Dr Charleston SC 29407

CRISP, MARTHA LYN, ednl. adminstr.; b. Mangum, Okla., Sept. 27, 1937; d. Hardy C. and Hattie Mae (Shumate) Crisp; B.S., Southwestern State U., 1970; M. Ed., W. Tex. State U., 1972; children—Jan E., Tim E., Philip L. Tchr. Miami Ind. Sch. Dist., 1970-71, Lamb County (Tex.) Schs., 1971-73; counselor Amarillo (Tex.) Ind. Sch. Dist., 1972—, mem. faculty adv. com., 1976—; dir. spl. edn. Bailey County, Tex., 1977-79; office mgr. Your Laundry & Dry Cleaners, Pampa, Tex., 1964-68; accountant Joy Oil Tool Mfg. Co., Oklahoma City, 1960-64, Cities Service Oil Co., Bartlesville, Okla.; sch. supr. Burleson County, Tex., 1979—. Treas. chpt. NOW, 1976—; active Women's Polit. Caucus. Mem. Am., Tex. personnel and guidance assns., Am. Sch. Suprs. Assn., Tex. Assn. Supervision and Curriculum Devel., Tex. Ednl. Diagnosticians, Council Exceptional Children, Tex. State Tchrs. Assn. (life), NEA, Tex. Coll. Tchrs. Assn., Tex. History Club, Delta Psi Kappa. Democrat. Unitarian. Home: 3401 Lynette St Amarillo TX 79109 Office: Box 3067 College Station TX 74840

CRITCHLOW, DONALD EARL, ednl. psychologist; b. Baker County, Oreg., Mar. 29, 1929; s. Lloyd Joseph and Alice Mae (Tucker) C.; B.S., Eastern Oreg. State Coll., 1954; M.A., Coll. of Idaho, 1956; Ph.D., U. Iowa, 1964; postgrad. Holy Trinity Sem., Irving, Tex., 1979—; m. June Evelyn Naomi Rasmussen, Aug. 23, 1950; children—Carmel Jeannien, Kevin Don. Prin., tchr. Idaho Pub. Schs., Marsing and Meridian, 1951-52, 54-60; asst. prof., chmn. dept. edn. St. Ambrose Coll., Davenport, Iowa, 1960-64; prof. edn. Our Lady of the Lake U., San Antonio, 1966-70; prof. edn. and psychology, dir. reading-learning clinic Laredo (Tex.) State U., 1970-79; cons. testing, reading and spl. edn. to colls., univs., pub. sch. systems. Pres. Meridian (Idaho) Council PTA, 1956-60, hon. life mem. Idaho Congress PTA's. Served with USNR, 1946-48. Mem. Am., Tex. psychol. assns., Internat. (pres. Tex. state council 1976-77), Tex. reading assns., Tex. Assn. Profs. of Reading (pres. 1975-76), Council Exceptional Children, Kappa Delta Pi. Roman Catholic. Club: Elks. Author: Dos Amigos Verbal Language Scales, 1973; Reading and the Spanish Speaking Child, 1973. Contbr. articles and book reviews to profl. jours. Home: 555 Del Mar Blvd Laredo TX 78041

CRITCHLOW, SUSAN MELISSA, pub. relations exec., graphic art cons.; b. Gainesville, Fla., Dec. 24, 1950; d. James Carlton and Mildred Estelle (Pringle) Barley; B.A., U. South Fla., 1972, M.A. in Speech Communication with honors, 1973; m. Warren Hartzell Critchlow, Jr., Aug. 18, 1973. Asst. dir. pub. relations Goodwill Industries of N. Fla., Inc., 1973-74; dir. pub. relations St. Luke's Hosp., Jacksonville, Fla., 1974; dir. informational services Greater Orange Park Community Hosp., Orange Park, Fla., 1974—; pres. Susan Critchlow & Assos., SC&A Pub. Co., Inc., Orange Park, 1976—. Named N.E. Fla. Bus. Communicator of Month, 1975, 78. Mem. Fla. Hosp. Assn. Public Relations Council (bd. dirs. 1976-78, Gold award 1975, Silver award 1976), Jacksonville Hosp. Pub. Relations Council (chmn. 1975-77), Fla. Pub. Relations Assn. (Golden Image award 1975, 76, 77, 78), Pub. Relations Soc. Am. Democrat. Episcopalian. Club: Pilot of Orange Park. Home: 210 Kettering Ct Orange Park FL 32073 Office: PO Box 1316 Orange Park FL 32073

CRITES, SHERMAN EDWIN, communications co. exec.; b. Chadron, Nebr., Jan. 12, 1918; s. Frederick A. and Marion (Hart) C.; student Nebr. State Coll., 1934-37; B.S., Mass. Inst. Tech., 1941; M.S., N.Y. U., 1947; m. Florence Virginia Stiles, Dec. 22, 1940; children—Sherman Edwin, Patricia L., James F. Various engring.

positions Pan Am. World Airways, N.Y.C., 1941-47, asst. prof. A. and M. Coll. of Tex., 1947-49, asso. prof. 1949-50; product planning engr. aircraft gas turbine div. Gen. Electric Co., Lynn, Mass., 1950-52, mgr. new product planning, Evendale, Ohio, 1952-55, from mgr. product planning to mgr. mktg., small aircraft engine dept., Lynn, 1955-60; v.p., gen. mgr. transmission products dept. ITT Kellogg, Raleigh, N.C., 1960-62; pres., chief exec. officer Aero Electronics, Inc. (now Aerotron, Inc.), Raleigh, 1962-65, pres., chmn. bd., 1965-71; pres., chmn. bd. C.H. Electronics, Inc., Raleigh, 1971—, also dir. Mem. Gov.'s Tech. Utilization Adv. Bd. for State of N.C., 1967-68; active various community drives. Bd. dirs. United Fund Wake County, 1965-70. Mem. Am. Horse Show Assn. Club: Carolina Country. Home: 5250 Castlebrook Dr Raleigh NC 27604 Office: PO Box 14042 Raleigh NC 27620

CROCKER, VIRGINIA LEAMAN, state legislator; b. Clinton, S.C., Sept. 9, 1951; d. Claude Arthur and Myra Leaman (Adair) C.; B.A., Columbia (S.C.) Coll., 1973; postgrad. U. S.C. Mem. legis. staff to gov. S.C., 1973-74; public info. specialist Dept. Parks, Recreation and Tourism S.C., 1974-75; adminstrv. asst. to state senator, 1975-76; asst. dir. admissions Presbyn. Coll., Clinton, 1976—; mem. S.C. Ho. of Reps. from 15th Dist., 1977—. Bd. dirs. Area Six Lung Assn.; 1st youth vice chmn. Laurens County Democratic Party, 1973; alt. del. Dem. Nat. Conv., 1972. Mem. Clinton Bus. and Profl. Women's Club, Am. Legion Aux., Laurens Community Council, Laurens County Arts Council, Columbia Coll. Alumnae Assn., Clinton High Booster Club, Alpha Psi Omega. Episcopalian. Office: PO Box 975 Broad St Clinton SC 29325

CROCKETT, CROSCINA ODELL, med. technologist; b. New Orleans, Oct. 19, 1939; d. Crossley Pompy and Margaret (McCann) Odell; B.S. in Med. Tech., Xavier U., New Orleans, 1961; M.Sc. in Microbiology (Warner-Lambert grad. scholar 1973), Tulane U., 1976; m. Nolen John Crockett, July 21, 1962; children—Theresita, Nolen John, Monica. Successively intern, staff technologist, supr. clin. chemistry USPHS Hosp., New Orleans, 1960-68; clin. and research technologist Tulane U. Med. Sch., 1968-71; mem. faculty Xavier U., 1971—, asst. prof. med. tech., 1977—; asst. coordinator New Orleans citywide clin. chemistry lectures; mem. adv. council La. High Blood Pressure Control Program; adv. council allied health counseling program New Orleans public schs. Mem. sponsors council youth dept. Old Zion Baptist Ch., New Orleans. Mem. Am. Soc. Med. Tech., Am. Soc. Clin. Pathologists, La. Soc. Med. Tech., New Orleans Soc. Med. Technologists (pres. elect 1979), Am. Soc. Clin. Chemistry, Alpha Delta Theta. Democrat. Baptist. Author lab. manual. Home: 4901 Chantilly Dr New Orleans LA 70126 Office: Med Tech Bldg Xavier Univ Palmetto and Pine Sts New Orleans LA 70125

CROCKETT, EDWARD MERCER, state ofcl.; b. Austin, Tex., July 24, 1921; s. Cecil Leslie and Helen Gardner (Brown) C.; B.B.A., U. Tex., 1950; postgrad. Kans. State Coll., 1951; m. Ann Gertrude Wood, May 14, 1950; children by previous marriage—Edward Alexander, Patricia Joan. Template maker, prodn. clk., prodn. engr. Lockheed Aircraft Corp., Burbank, Calif., 1940-42; commd. 2d lt., U.S. Army Air Corps, 1942, advanced through grades to lt. col. U.S. Air Force, 1963; numerous positions including jet fighter pilot, aircraft comdr. in RC-121 Constellations; ret., 1965; dir. health referral program for med. rejectees Ga. Dept. Public Health, Atlanta, 1965-67, program mgr. Crippled Children's Program, 1967—; asst. prof. air sci. Kans. State Coll., 1949-53. Spl. nat. field commr. Boy Scouts Am., 1962-65. Served with USAAF, 1942-45. Decorated Air Force Commendation medal, Air medal; recipient Outstanding Service award Explorer Service Nat. Council Boy Scouts Am., 1965. Mem. Air Force Assn. (charter), Ga. Public Health Assn., Am. Acad. Health Adminstrs. Methodist. Home: 4383 Beach View Dr SE Smyrna GA 30080 Office: 47 Trinity Ave SW

CROCKETT, SHAREN ANN DEACON, home economist; b. Spargursville, Ohio, Dec. 19, 1942; d. William and Roberta (Marhoover) Deacon; B.S., Harding U., 1967; M.S., Ohio State U., 1968; m. Jimmie Wayne Crockett, Dec. 28, 1969; children—Elizabeth Ann, Julie Renee. Mem. faculty Harding U., Searcy, Ark., 1968—, asso. prof. home econs., 1980—. Sec., Rose Bud (Ark.) PTA, 1976-77, membership chmn., 1978-79. Mem. Am. Home Econs. Assn., Ark. Home Econs. Assn. (state bd. 1977-76), White County Assn. Children Under Six (pres. 1976-77, sec. 1978-79), Ark. Assn. Children Under Six (historian 1979, chmn. parenting com. 1980), Ark. Advocates for Children and Families. Mem. Ch. of Christ. Home: Route 1 Rose Bud AR 72137 Office: Box 813 Harding U Searcy AR 72143

CROCKETT, STANLEY THEODORE, electronics co. exec.; b. Port Arthur, Tex., Aug. 20, 1924; s. Jesse Emmett and Dora Elizabeth (Jackson) C.; student U. Houston, 1945-48, U. Ala., 1948-49; m. Audrey Lee Booth, June 20, 1945; children—Stanley Theodore, Audrey Lee. Regional sales mgr. Olympic Internat., N.Y.C., 1960-67, nat. sales mgr., 1970-73; nat. sales mgr. TV Mfrs. Am., Chgo., 1968-69; regional sales mgr. Capehart Corp., N.Y.C., 1974—. Served with U.S. Navy, 1942-45; PTO. Named hon. Ky. col. Episcopalian. Clubs: The Club, Downtown, St. Andrews Soc. Mid-South. Home and Office: 4133 Sharpsburg Dr Birmingham AL 35213

CROFT, CHARLES BENJAMIN, architect; b. Enid, Okla., Nov. 10, 1927; s. Glenn W. and Esther (Lewis) C.; Design and Planning, Technologico y de Estudios Superiores de Monterrey (Mexico), 1952; B.Arch., U. Tex., 1953; div.; children—David, Cathy, Janet, Charles B., Carol. Draftsman-designer John Linn Scott & Asso., Austin, Tex., 1953-54; architect, designer Fehr & Granger Architects, Austin, 1954-59; asso. partner John G. York & Asso., Harlingen, Tex., 1959-60; partner Taniguchi & Croft, Harlingen, 1960-62; asso. partner Jessen Assos., Austin, 1966-72; owner Charles B. Croft, Harlingen, 1962-66, Croft Assos., Austin, 1972—. Cons. architect Valley Regional Airport, Cameron County, 1963-65. Precinct presiding judge Cameron County Democratic Com., 1960-66, precinct chmn., 1964-66; del. Tex. Dem. Conv., 1960, 64. Bd. dirs. YMCA, Harlingen, 1960-63. Served with USMC, 1946-48; PTO. Recipient Honor award Tex. Soc. Architects, 1962, Merit award, 1962. Mem. A.I.A. (chpt. pres. elect 1966, 76. chpt. sec. 1974, v.p. 1975, pres. 1976), Tex. Soc. Architects (dir. 1978-80). Home: 7131 Woodhollow Apt 132 Austin TX 78731 Office: 3724 Jefferson Austin TX 78731

CROFT, RAYMOND CONWAY, bus. machines co. exec.; b. Darby, Pa., July 31, 1939; s. Leslie W. and Mary Virginia (Shinault) C.; student Va. Poly. Inst., 1957-59, No. Mich. U., 1960-62; m. Arsilia Isabel Vinas, Dec. 21, 1960; 1 son, Glenn Ellis. Systems marketing rep. IBM Corp., San Antonio, 1964-73; dist. sales mgr. Docutel Corp., Houston, 1973-74; div. mgr. sales tng. Xerox Corp., Dallas, 1976—. Served to capt. USAF, 1959-64. Mem. Am. Soc. Tng. and Devel., Internat. Word Processing Assn. Republican. Episcopalian. Home: 612 Durango Circle S Irving TX 75062 Office: 1341 W Mockingbird St Dallas TX 75247

CROFT, TERRENCE LEE, lawyer; b. St. Louis, Apr. 13, 1940; s. Thomas L. and Anita B. (Brown) C.; A.B., Yale U., 1962; J.D. with distinction, U. Mich., 1965; m. Merry Patton; children—Shannon Storey, Kristin Kendall, Bethann Bates. Admitted to Mo. bar, 1965, Ga. bar, 1970, Fla. bar, 1970; asso. firm Coburn, Croft, Sheperd & Herzog, St. Louis, 1965-69; asso. firm Hansell, Post, Brandon & Dorsey, Atlanta, 1969-73; litigation partner Huie, Brown & Ide, Atlanta, 1973-75, Huie, Ware, Sterne, Brown and Ide, 1976-77, Huie, Sterne, Brown & Ide, 1977, Kutak, Rock & Huie, 1978—. Mem. State Bar Ga., State Bar Fla., Am., Atlanta bar assns., Lawyer's Club of Atlanta. Home: 3 Basswood Circle Atlanta GA 30328 Office: 1200 Standard Fed Savs Bldg Atlanta GA 30303

CROMARTIE, ERNEST WILLIAM, II, lawyer; b. Richland County, S.C., June 6, 1945; s. Ernest William and Charlie Mae (Harrison) C.; B.A., Mich. State U., 1968; J.D. cum laude, George Washington U., 1971; m. Ranette White, Dec. 20, 1971; children—Ernest William, III, Antoinette Bouvier. Admitted to S.C. bar, 1971, since practiced individually in Columbia; dir. Kitani Found. Del., Richland County Democratic Conv., 1976, S.C. Dem. Conv., 1976; mem. Columbia Dem. Exec. Com., 1976—, Columbia Zoning Bd. Adjustment and Appeals, 1976-79. Mem. Am. Bar Assn., Am. Trial Lawyers Assn., S.C. Bar Assn., S.C. Trial Lawyers Assn., Richland County Bar Assn., E. Columbia Jaycees, Alpha Phi Alpha. Methodist. Clubs: Optimist, Masons, Elks. Home: 2213 Lorick Ave Columbia SC 29204 Office: 1926 Hampton St Columbia SC 29201

CROMER, JERRY HALTIWANGER, educator; b. Anderson, S.C., Apr. 4, 1935; s. Phillip and Ethel Irene (Tribble) Cromer; B.S., Wofford Coll., 1957; postgrad. Med. U. S.C., 1957-58; M.S., U. S.C., 1965; Ph.D., Vanderbilt U., 1968; m. Anne Olevia Palmer, June 9, 1962; children—Jeffrey Philip, James Edward. Instr. biology Vanderbilt U., Nashville, 1965, teaching fellow, 1966-67; asst. prof. biology Converse Coll., Spartanburg, S.C., 1968-73, asso. prof., 1973—, organizer, dir. pre-profl. med. and paramed. programs, 1971—. Served as ensign USNR, 1959-61. USPHS tng. grantee, 1963-64; faculty research grantee Converse Coll., 1968, 73. Mem. A.A.A.S., Assn. Southeastern Biologists, S.C. Acad. Scis., Sigma Xi. Presbyn. Home: 202 Shelton Dr Spartanburg SC 29302

CRONE, BONNIE WARREN, editor; b. South Africa, Oct. 22, 1934; d. John Willis and Della Ruth (West) Warren; 1 son, Nathan Earl. Editorial rep. Better Homes and Gardens, New Orleans, 1968—; contbg. writer New Orleans Mag., 1967-77, columnist Around the Belt, 1967-77, editor, 1977-78. Bd. dirs. Cultural Attractions Fund; mem. women's com. New Orleans Philharmonic Symphony Soc.; bd. dirs. France La. Festival. Mem. New Orleans Art Assn. (pres.), New Orleans Mus. Art, Nat. Fedn. Press Women, Press Club New Orleans, Women in Communications. Recipient 1st place trophy New Orleans Press Club, best feature story, 1972, best sports column, 1971. Home: 3652 River Oaks Dr New Orleans LA 70114 Office: 6666 Morrison Rd New Orleans LA 70126

CRONE, DAVID CHRISTIAN, JR., plant engr., engring. cons.; b. Allentown, Pa., Nov. 17, 1948; s. David Christian and Jeanne (Ross) C.; B.M.E., Le Tourneau Coll., 1972; postgrad. N.C. State U., 1977; m. Karen Kleppinger, June 21, 1969; children—Christina, Timothy. Mfg. engr. Stemco Mfg. Co., Garlock Inc., Longview, Tex., 1971-72, indsl. engr., 1972-74; plant engr. AP Parts Co. div. Questor Corp., Goldsboro, N.C., 1974-79; pres. Engring. Consultant, 1979—. Mem. Am. Inst. Indsl. Engrs. (sec. E. Tex. chpt. 1972-73), Soc. Mfg. Engrs., Am. Welding Soc. Baptist. Clubs: Adamsville Lions, BMW Riders, Studebaker Drivers, Nat. Rwy. Hist. Home: 113 Marie Ave Goldsboro NC 27530 Office: 113 Marie Ave Goldsboro NC 27530

CRONIN, GERARD THOMAS, community devel. cons.; b. Pitts., Dec. 23, 1947; s. John Michael and Mary Veronica (White) C.; B.A. in Philosophy, U. Tenn., Knoxville, 1969. Planner, OEO, VISTA vol., Camden, Ark., 1969-72; project mgr., chief exec. officer Ind. Community Cons., Inc., Hampton, Ark., 1972—; field asst. dept. human service U. Tenn., 1975—, dept. family and community medicine U. Ark. Med. Sci. Campus, Little Rock. Mem. Am. Soc. Tng. and Devel., Rural Housing Alliance, Nat. Assn. Bus. and Mgmt. Cons. Democrat. Roman Catholic. Author: Guide to Fundraising and Proposal Writing, 1975; Arkansas Social Service Advocacy Handbook, 1976, rev. edits., 1977, 78; The Non-Profit Board of Directors Workshop; editor: Directory of Community Development Information Sources, 1976; pub. Mt. Ida Reporter. Home and Office: PO Box 141 Hampton AR 71744

CRONISTER, JERRY R., educator; b. Amarillo, Tex., Dec. 22, 1933. B.S. in Edn., West Tex. State U., Canyon, 1956, M.Ed. in Elem. Edn. and Guidance, 1958; Ph.D. in Spanish Lang. and Pre-Columbian History, Universidad Interamericana, Saltillo, Mex., 1971. Tchr. spl. reading Booker (Tex.) Sch., 1973—; dir. Booker Neurol. Impress Reading Lab. Mem. NEA (life), Tex. State Tchrs. Assn. (life). Author handwriting system The Autokinetic Way; author various teaching aids in reading, math., history and lang. arts, specializing in aids for the learning-disabled. Office: Box 2010 Amarillo TX 79105

CRONK, ALFRED EDWARD, educator; b. Hudson, Wis., July 1, 1915; s. Walter Eli and Alma Serena (Simonson) C.; B.S., Coll. St. Thomas, 1937; M.S., U. Minn., 1946; m. Nora Viola Pepin, Sept. 7, 1940; children—Andrew, Alfred, Susan, Nancy. Math. and physics instr. Cretin High Sch., 1940-43; instr. U. Minn., 1943-46, asst. prof., 1946-53, asso. prof., 1953-56; prof., head dept. aerospace engring. Tex. A. and M. U., College Station, 1956-78, emeritus, 1978—; cons. Mpls.-Honeywell, Gen. Mills Co., 3 M Co., Fluidyne Engring. Corp., 1950-56. Fellow Tex. Acad. Scis., Am. Inst. Aeros. and Astronautics (asso.); mem. Am. Soc. Engring. Edn. (chmn. aero. div. 1951-52), Soc. Flight Test Engrs., Sigma Xi, Tau Beta Pi, Sigma Gamma Tau, Theta Tau. Club: Briarcrest Country (Bryan, Tex.). Home: 727 N Rosemary St Bryan TX 77801 Office: Tex A and M U College Station TX 77843

CROOK, DONALD HUBERT, JR., marriage and family counselor; b. Birmingham, Ala., June 18, 1946; s. Donald Hubert and Bettye Kincaid (Kosloff) C.; B.S., Troy (Ala.) State U., 1968, M.S., 1979; postgrad. U. Ala., 1979—; m. Bobbie Shaw, Feb. 14, 1976; children—Ashley Shy, Charles Louis, Donald Hubert, III. Instr. biology Bay County Sch., Panama City, Fla., 1968-69; area mgr. Sandoz Pharms Co., Montgomery, Ala., 1969-78; clin. dir. Family Counseling Center, Elba, Ala., 1978-79; mem. part-time faculty Shelton State Community Coll., Tuscaloosa, Ala., 1979—; grad. research asst. U. Ala., 1979—. Bd. dirs. Autanga County Fair Assn., 1974-78. Mem. Am. Personnel and Guidance Assn., Am. Mental Health Counselors Assn., Ala. Personnel and Guidance Assn., Ala. Mental Health Counselors Assn., Ala. Jaycees (pres. 1976; regional award 1974, Brownfield award 1975). Home: 447-A 30th Pl Tuscaloosa AL 35401 Office: 1014 N Drayton St Elba AL 36323

CROOK, HOWARD WILSON, real estate developer, appraiser; b. Monroe, N.C., Aug. 12, 1912; s. Jeff E. and Emma (Wilson) C.; A.B. in Econs., U. Tex., El Paso, 1969, M.A. in Econs., 1972; m. Nancy A. Hawthorne, Nov. 28, 1934; children—Nancy E. Crook Marcus, Howard H., James J., Belinda B. Crook Cole, Richard J. Owner, H.W. Crook Realty Co., El Paso, 1948—; pres. H.W. Crook Constrn. Co., Inc., El Paso, 1948—, H.W. Crook, Inc., El Paso, 1955—, Coronado Hills Shopping Center, Inc., El Paso, 1955—. Certificate in real estate, Calif. Mem. El Paso Bd. Realtors, Am. Soc. Appraisers (regional gov. 1969-74), Nat. Bus. Economists, Nat. Assn. Real Estate Brokers, El Paso C. of C. Democrat. Roman Catholic. Club: Horizon Country (El Paso). Contbr. article to Appraisal Jour. Home: 22 Cumberland Circle El Paso TX 79903 Office: 3824 Tompkins Ave El Paso TX 79930

CROOK, ROBERT LACEY, state senator, lawyer; b. Bolton, Miss., Apr. 22, 1929; s. Walter Barber and Louise (Lacey) C.; student U. Miss., 1952-53; LL.B., Jackson Sch. Law, 1965; m. Brigita Vija Nerings, Sept. 20, 1953; children—Robert Lacey II, Hubert William. Operator, Ruleville (Miss.) Dry Cleaners, 1953-60; Miss. dir. Civil Def., Jackson, 1960-64; admitted to Miss. bar, 1965, since practiced in Ruleville; mem. firm Robert L. Crook; mem. Miss. Senate, 1964—. Served with USMC, 1949-51. Mem. State Civil Def. Dirs. Assn. (nat. v.p. 1962-63), Am., Miss. bar assns., Am. Legion, S.C.V., Order Stars and Bars. Democrat. Home: 3615 Crane Jackson MS 39216 also 125 N Oak Ave Ruleville MS 38771 Office: 800 N Division Ave Ruleville MS 38771

CROOK, ROY MAX, pipeline co. exec.; b. Heard County, Ga., May 11, 1945; s. William L. and Annie Z. (Witcher) C.; B.A. in Chemistry, W.Ga. Coll., 1967; postgrad. U. Md., 1968-69; m. Christie Ann Jackson, Aug. 18, 1967. With Plantation Pipe Line Co., 1966-67, 69—; pipeline technologist, 1975-76, div. engr. Western Div., Baton Rouge, 1976—. Served with AUS, 1967-69. Mem. Am. Chem. Soc., Nat. Assn. Corrosion Engrs., Nat. Rifle Assn. Baptist. Home: 14112 Harwood Ave Baton Rouge LA 70816 Office: PO Box 708 Blount Rd Baton Rouge LA 70714

CROOKS, THADIS WAYNE, air force officer; b. Mount Pleasant, Tex., Aug. 1, 1940; s. A.E. and Nannie (Cox) C.; B.B.A., Tex. A&M U., 1962; m. Marion B. Kubichek, Feb. 19, 1966; 1 dau., Emily Paige. Commd. 2d lt. USAF, 1962, advanced through grades to lt. col., 1978; fighter pilot, Vietnam, 31st TAC fighter wing, 1966-67; instr. pilot Webb AFB, Tex., 1968-72; air ops. staff officer Hdqrs., Pentagon, 1972-76; comdr. 71st sudent squadron Vance AFB, Okla., 1978—. Decorated Silver Star with oak leaf cluster, D.F.C. with oak leaf cluster, Air medal with 14 oak leaf clusters, Air Force Commendation medal; Gallantry Cross with silver star (Vietnam). Mem. Air Force Assn. Republican. Methodist. Home: 2053 Lantern Ln Enid OK 73701 Office: 71st Student Squadron Vance AFB OK 73701

CROOKS, WILLIAM BATTLE, JR., communications co. exec.; b. Meridian, Miss., June 14, 1915; s. William Battle and Alma (Knighton) C.; B.S., Davidson Coll., 1938; m. Saramel Repsher, Nov. 12, 1949; children—Saramel (Mel) Repsher, Sally Repsher. Asst. mgr. Gt. So. Hotel, Meridian, 1939-41; sales mgr. Sta. WTOK, Meridian, 1946-53; v.p., sales mgr. So. TV Corp., Meridian, 1953—, also dir.; sec.-treas., dir. Brookhaven Coca-Cola Bottling Co. (Miss.), Repsher-Crooks Inc.; sec., dir. Campbellsville Coca-Cola Bottling Co. (Ky.); dir. Miss. Power Co., H-C-R Inc., Citizens Nat. Bank. Pres., Meridian Indsl. Found., 1964-65; pres. Choctaw Area council Boy Scouts Am., 1972, exec. com., 1972—; bd. visitors Davidson Coll., 1976-79. Served with USAF, 1941-46. Decorated DFC, 3 Air medals; named Jaycees Young Man of Year, 1948, 49; King of Mardi Gras, Meridian Jr. Aux., 1966; recipient Silver Beaver award Boy Scouts Am., 1976. Mem. Meridian C. of C. (pres. 1959). Baptist (deacon). Clubs: Northwood Country, Downtown, Timberlake Fishing, Univ., Optimist Internat., Jaycees (pres. Meridian 1947, 48). Office: PO Box 2988 Meridian MS 39301

CROOM, BOBBY HAROLD, convenience store exec.; b. Zebulon, N.C., June 28, 1938; s. James Bearl and Irona (Long) C.; B.S.M.E.A., N.C. State U., 1960; postgrad. Ohio State U., 1962; M.B.A. (Bus. Found. scholar), U. N.C., 1968; m. Sandra Bunn, June 11, 1960; children—David Allen, Susan Elizabeth. Researcher on propulsion systems 8' structures lab. NASA, Langley, Va., 1963-66; v.p. Northgate Shopping Center, Durham, N.C., 1968-72, Sea Pines Co., comml. real estate, Hilton Head Island, S.C., 1973-75; pres. United Gen. Stores, Hilton Head Island, 1976—, also dir.; cons. Kiawah Island Co., 1975-76. Served with USAF, 1960-63. Mem. S.C. Assn. Convenience Stores (dir., sec.), Nat. Assn. Convenience Stores, Internat. Council Shopping Centers. Baptist. Office: 51 S Forest Beach Dr Hilton Head Island SC 29928

CROOM, DAN R., sales exec.; b. Knoxville, Tenn., Apr. 18, 1951; s. James Guthrie and Waneta (Bowman) C.; student Chowan Coll., 1969-71; B.A., Wake Forest U., 1973; postgrad. Rollins Coll., 1977; m. Jill Wallace Robison, Jan. 18, 1975. Dist. mgr. for Fla. div. Douglas Battery Mfg. Co., Orlando, Fla., 1974-77; dist. mgr. Central Fla., ACF/Carter Carburetor Div., Orlando, 1977—. Scuba instr. YMCA, 1975—. Recipient ACF/Carter Carburetor Century Club award for outstanding sales performance and territorial mgmt., 1978; cert. scuba diving instr.; cert. CPR instr. Mem. Automotive Boosters (treas. 1979—). Clubs: Cracker Investment (v.p. 1979—), Toastmasters (sgt.-at-arms 1979). Home: 4708 Harwich St Orlando FL 32808 Office: PO Box 15367 Orlando FL 32858

CROOM, ESTELLE LUCKEY, life ins. co. exec.; b. Gibson, Tenn., Dec. 22, 1917; d. Fred Wilson and Corinne (Fly) Luckey; ed. high sch.; m. John Guthrie Croom, Mar. 3, 1933; children—John Harold, Wilson Buckley, Michael Luckey. Sec. Humboldt (Tenn.) 1st Baptist Ch., 1945-46; with John M. Senter & Sons, ins. and real estate, Humboldt, 1954-66; pres. Croom & Cobb Insurors, Humboldt and Bells, Tenn., 1966-59; sec. Mid-West Nat. Life Ins. Co., Nashville, 1969-71, v.p., 1971-79, exec. v.p., mem. exec. com., 1976—, also dir.; dir. Mid-West Nat. Life Co., Webster's Ency. Sales, Crusade Enterprises Inc., Am. Lab. Inst. Pres. Humboldt Band Parents Club, 1965-66. Mem. Tenn. Assn. Life Inst. Cos., Nashville Assn. Life Underwriters Nat. Ins. Assn. (conv. co-chmn. 1976). Baptist. Club: Humboldt Bus. Women's (pres. 1963-64). Home: 135 Honeysuckle Ln Humboldt TN 38343 Office: 1161 Murfreesboro Rd Nashville TN 37217

CROOM, FREDERICK HAILEY, mathematician; b. Lumberton, N.C., Aug. 6, 1941; s. Robert DeVane and Anna Rosalyn (Currie) C.; B.S. in Math. (John M. Morehead scholar), U. N.C., 1963, Ph.D. in Math. (Woodrow Wilson, NSF fellow), 1967; m. Henrietta B. Brown, Aug. 17, 1963; children—Elizabeth Bonner, Frederick Hailey. Asst. prof. math. U. Ky., Lexington, 1967-71; asst. prof. U. of South, Sewanne, Tenn., 1971-74, asso. prof., 1974—. Treas. Sewanee Civic Assn., 1973, sec., 1974, bd. dirs.; chmn. Sewanee Community Chest, 1975; pres. Sewanee PTA, 1976. NSF, Babcock Found. grantee, 1972-76. Mem Am. Math. Soc., Math. Assn. Am., AAUP, Phi Beta Kappa, Sigma Xi (chpt. pres. 1976-77), Omicron Delta Kappa, Pi Kappa Alpha. Democrat. Episcopalian. Club: U. of South Faculty (pres. 1974). Author: Basic Concepts of Algebraic Topology, 1978; contbr. articles and reviews to math. jours. Home: Tennessee Ave Sewanee TN 37375 Office: Univ of South Sewanee TN 37375

CROOM, WILLIAM HENRY, systems analyst, ret. naval officer; b. Mooringsport, La., Feb. 13, 1932; s. William Henry and Theo (Smart) C.; B.S., U.S. Naval. Acad., 1954; B.S., U.S. Naval Postgrad. Sch., 1961; M.S., U. So. Calif., 1975; m. Donna Mae Martin, Mar. 29, 1958; children—William, Pamela. Commd. ensign U.S. Navy, 1954, advanced through grades to comdr., 1975; comdg. officer VT-7, 1970; air officer U.S.S. Lexington, 1971, Naval Air Systems Command, 1972-75; staff engr. Gen. Research Corp., McLean, Va., 1975-77; sr. research analyst Presearch Inc., Arlington, Va., 1977—. Security committeeman Pinewood Lake Assn., 1972-77. Decorated Air medal, Navy Commendation medal. Mem. U.S. Naval Inst., Am. Def. Preparedness Assn. Democrat. Methodist. Clubs: Toastmasters, Assn.

Old Crows, Masons. Home: 4312 Cedarlake Ct Alexandria VA 22309 Office: 2361 S Jefferson Davis Hwy Arlington VA 22202

CROOM, WILLIAM STERLING, physician; b. Morrilton, Ark., July 3, 1925; s. Adlai Stevenson and Margaret Price (Harris) C.; student Phillips U., 1943, Harding Coll., 1943, Abilene Christian Coll., 1943-44; M.D., U. Okla., 1948; m. Karen Ausburn, June 3, 1968; children—William Sterling, Brad Franklin, Christian. Intern, U. Ind. Med. Center, Indpls., 1948-49; resident internal medicine U. Okla. Hosp., 1949-52; pvt. practice internal medicine, Oklahoma City, 1952-53, Lubbock, Tex., 1953—; mem. staff Methodist, St. Mary's hosps., (both Lubbock); courtesy staff W. Tex. Hosp., Lubbock; clinical asst. internal medicine U. Okla. Hosps., 1952-53; asso. clin. prof. medicine Tex. Technol. U., 1972—. Served to lt. USNR, 1954-56. Diplomate Am. Bd. Internal Medicine. Fellow. Am. Coll. Chest Physicians; mem. A.C.P., Tex. Acad. Internal Medicine, Am. Heart Assn., Tex. Med. Assn., Phi Chi. Republican. Mem. Ch. of Christ. Club: Lubbock Country. Home: 6219 Kenosha Dr Lubbock TX 79413 Office: 3801 19th St Lubbock TX 79410

CROSA, PETER JAMES, ins. adjuster; b. Detroit, July 10, 1951; s. James Rafael and Adela Camelia C.; A.A., Miami-Dade Community Coll., 1971; student Ins. Inst. Am., 1976-79; m. Lorraine Debra Ouida, Apr. 4, 1971; children—Robyn, Beth, Emilé. With Allstate Ins. Co., Miami, Fla., 1969-73, Crawford & Co., Sarasota, Fla., 1973-76, Continental Ins. Co., Sarasota, 1976-78; regional gen. adjuster Am. Internat. Adjustment Co., Atlanta, 1978—; chmn. Adjustech Pubs., Bradenton, Fla., 1978—; lectr. in field. Mem. South Fla. Claimsmens Assn., Sarasota-Bradenton Claims Assn., West Coast Claims Assn. Author booklets.

CROSBY, CHRISTOPHER STEVENSON, lawyer; b. Charlotte, N.C., Sept. 4, 1951; s. Vernon Perry and Ottie (White) C.; B.A., East Carolina U., 1972; J.D., Wake Forest U., 1975; m. Rosalie Gates, Nov. 10, 1978. Admitted to N.C. bar, 1975; law clk. to judge N.C. Supreme Ct., 1975-76; asso. firm McElwee, Hall & McElwee, North Wilkesboro, N.C., 1976-77; asst. atty. gen. N.C. Dept. Justice, Raleigh, 1977-79; sr. partner Christopher S. Crosby, P.A., 1979—; pres. Castlewood Corp., Kings Mountain, N.C. Mem. legal adv. bd. Dorothea Dix Hosp., Raleigh. Mem. N.C. Bar Assn., Am. Bar Assn., N.C. Acad. Trial Lawyers, Assn. Trial Lawyers Am., Fed. Bar Assn., Nat. Guard Assn., Aircraft Owner Pilots Assn., Phi Sigma Phi, Phi Alpha Theta, Phi Delta Phi, Sigma Phi Epsilon. Democrat. Presbyterian. Club: Masons. Home: 405 Edgemont Dr Kings Mountain NC 28086 Office: 107 W King St Kings Mountain NC 28086

CROSBY, GERRY WORTH, assn. exec.; b. Savannah, Ga., Mar. 17, 1929; d. John and Ida Worth; B.A., Armstrong Coll., 1950; student U. Miami, U. Ga.; children—Glenn R., Pamela J. Credit and collections mgr. Variety Children's Hosp., Miami, Fla., 1951-52; substitute tchr. Dade County (Fla.) Sch. Bd., 1964-69; reporter, asso. editor S. Dade County News Leader, 1964-70; exec. v.p. South Dade C. of C., Miami, 1970—; freelance writer, contbr. to UPI, Miamian, Fla. Bankers, 1965—. Chmn. adv. bd. Public Safety Dept. Recipient Outstanding Citizens award Perrine-Cutler Ridge Jr. C. of C., 1968; 1st and 2d place awards AP Fla., Armed Service pub. relations award, POW award, mental health award, others. Mem. Women in Communications, Mental Health Guidance Center, Am. C. of C. Execs., Pvt. Indsl. Council. Home: 8450 201st St SW Miami FL 33189

CROSBY, JOHN CAMPBELL, author; b. Milw., May 18, 1912; s. Frederick Gifford and Edna (Campbell) C.; student Yale U., 1931-33; m. Katharine J.B. Wood, Dec. 1, 1964; children—Michael, Margaret, Alexander, Victoria. Reporter, Milw. Sentinel, 1933; reporter New York Herald Tribune, 1935-41, columnist, 1946-65; columnist London Observer, 1965-75. Served to capt. AUS, 1941-46. Recipient Newspaper Guild award, George Polk award, Peabody award. Author: Out of The Blue, 1951; Love and Loathing, 1962; Sappho In Absence, 1970; Literary Obsession, 1973; Contract On President, 1973; Affair of Strangers, 1975; Nightfall, 1976; Company of Friends, 1977; Dear Judgment, 1978; Party of the Year, 1979. Home: Esmont VA 22937

CROSBY, ROBERT LEE, JR., wirebound co. exec.; b. Norfield, Miss., Jan. 25, 1931; s. Robert Lee and Nancy Elizabeth (Moak) C.; B.S., La. State U., Baton Rouge, 1953; m. Ann Marie Morel, June 13, 1953; children—Robert Lee III, Julie Ann, Jeffrey Thomas, John Michael. Gen. accountant Armstrong Tire & Rubber Co., Natchez, Miss., 1956-57; sr. auditor Basil M. Lee & Co., C.P.A.'s, Baton Rouge, 1957-60; pres., chief exec. officer, dir. Am. Box Co., Fernwood, Miss., 1960—. Served to sgt. U.S. Army, 1953-56. Mem. Wirebound Box Mfg. Assn. (dir.), Miss. Wildlife Assn., Assn., U.S. Army, Miss. Mfrs. Assn., Nat. Wooden Pallet and Container Assn., Nat. Wood Box Assn., U.S. C. of C., McComb C. of C., Magnolia (Miss.) C. of C., Pi Kappa Alpha. Republican. Roman Catholic. Club: Lions. Office: PO Box 179 Fernwood MS 39635

CROSE, ELIZABETH ANN, speech pathologist; b. Louisa, Ky., Apr. 5, 1950; d. Homer Thurman and Ardith Frances (Bellomy) Smith; B.A. with distinction, U. Ky., 1972; M.A., Marshall U., 1976; m. John Lewis Crose, June 15, 1974; 1 dau., Kelly Ann. Speech and lang. pathologist Boyd County Schs., Catlettsburg, Ky., 1972—; pvt. practice speech and lang. pathology, Ashland, Ky., 1979—; asst. buyer Little People Nook, Ashland, 1974—. Mem. health adv. com. Boyd County Headstart program, 1978-79. Cert. speech pathologist, Ky.; named Young Career Girl, Ashland Bus. and Profl. Women's Club, 1972; Marshall U. grad. assistantship, 1975-76. Mem. Am. Speech, Lang. and Hearing Assn. Presbyterian. Home: 4727 Canterbury Ct Ashland KY 41101 Office: PO Box 522 Catlettsburg KY 41129

CROSS, ELMO GARNETT, JR., lawyer, state senator; b. Richmond, Va., Feb. 19, 1942; s. Elmo Garnett and Catherine (Gillis) C.; B.S., U. Richmond, 1963; LL.B., T.C. Williams Sch. Law, 1966. Admitted to Va. bar, 1966; staff accountant A.M. Pullen & Co., Richmond, 1968-71; asso. firm Wade and Cross, Richmond, 1972-7; mem. Va. State Senate, 1976—. Mem. Hanover Democratic Com. Served with U.S. Army, 1966-68. Mem. Va. State Bar Assn., Hanover Bar Assn. Methodist. Office: 3212 Cutshaw Ave Richmond VA 23230

CROSS, JOSEPH MILTON, JR., planning cons. co. exec.; b. Suffolk, Va., Dec. 23, 1945; s. Joseph Milton and Ella (Ashburn) C.; B. City Planning, U. Va., 1969, M.Public Adminstrn., 1971; postgrad. George Washington U., 1974; children—Joseph Austin, Camille Christian. Project architect Joseph T. Norris & Assos., Charlottesville, Va., 1969-71; asst. dir. planning Baldwin & Gregg, Ltd., Norfolk, Va., 1972-76; pres. Cross & Assos., Norfolk, 1976-77; founding partner Planning Mgmt. Assos., Newport News, Va., 1977—, Cross Devel. Co., Virginia Beach, Va., 1978—. Sec., Feldman Chamber Music Soc., 1978—. Served to lt. U.S. Army, 1971-72. Mem. Am. Inst. Cert. Planners, Am. Planning Assn. (exec. com. Va. chpt. 1978—), Va. Soc. Economists, Va. Citizens Planning Assn., Va. Jr. C. of C., Norfolk Jr. C. of C. (dir. 1974—). Methodist. Home: 1000 Hanover Ave Norfolk VA 23508 Office: 700 Newmarket Bldg Suite 312 Newport News VA 23605

CROSS, LOUISE PORTLOCK, mfg. co. exec.; b. Norfolk, Va., Jan. 20, 1907; d. William Seth and Mary Louise (Fanshaw) Portlock; grad. high sch.; m. James Byron Cross, July 17, 1929; 1 dau., Blanche Louise. With J.B. Cross, Inc., Norfolk, 1952—, exec. pres., 1959-60, pres., chief exec. officer, 1960—. Mem. Phi Sigma Alpha (charter). Episcopalian. Clubs: Order Eastern Star, Altrusa Internat., Ladies Oriental Shrine N.Am. Home: 500 Pacific Ave Virginia Beach VA 23451 Office: 3797 Progress Rd Norfolk VA 23502

CROSS, MAXWELL S., auto co. exec.; b. Bludna, Poland, July 5, 1912; s. Joseph P. and Mary Lynne (Fisher) C.; came to U.S., 1921, naturalized, 1933; student econs. and finance, 1953; m. Claire Moss, Sept. 5, 1970; children—Phyllis Cynthia, Joel S., Marlene Roberta, Lawrence S., Gale Mindy. With U.S. Auto Radiator Co., Inc., N.Y.C., 1933—, pres., 1940—, chmn. bd. dirs., 1961—. Pres., 1770 N. Bay Shore Dr. Corp., Miami, Fla., 1956—, 1109 N.W. 22d St. Corp., Miami, Fla., 1956—, McRoss Realty Corp., N.Y.C., 1942—. Mem. OPA, 1942-46, N.Y.C. Patrol Corps, 1943-45, Local Sch. Bd. Dist., N.Y.C., 1952-62 (chmn. 1957-58), Bklyn. Community dist. Planning Bd., 1963, SSS, 1963—; active Lemberger Home for Aged. Recipient Mayor's Com. on Achievement award Mayor City N.Y., 1958; Bd. Edn. award Sch. Bd., N.Y.C., 1957; certificates of appreciation Pres. U.S., 1968, 70. Mem. Asso. Industries N.Y. State, Inc., Auto Radiator Assn. N.Y. State, Inc. Democrat. K.P. Home: 11120 SW 73d Ct Miami FL 33156 Office: 1109 NW 22d St Miami FL 33156

CROSS, VIRGINIA ROSE, chemist; b. Portland, Oreg., May 15, 1950; d. Remi Joseph and Rose Matilda (Schallberger) C.; B.S. with high honors, Oreg. State U., 1972; Ph.D. in Phys. Chemistry, M.I.T., 1976; m. John P. Cross, Aug. 17, 1974. Sr. research chemist Celanese Plastics Co., Greer, S.C., 1976-80, Exxon Chem. Co., Bayport, Tex., 1980—. Mem. Am. Chem. Soc., S.C. Acad. Sci., Sigma Xi. Contbr. articles to profl. jours. Home: 3419 Ledgestone Houston TX 77059 Office: PO Box 4309 Houston TX 77210

CROSS, WARD HUBERT, ins. co. exec.; b. Polo, Ill., Jan. 2, 1917; s. William and Elizabeth Jane (Cox) C.; B.S. in Agr., U. Ill., 1941; m. Dureth Anne Stoner, Jan. 2, 1942 (dec.); children—Dennis Ward, Harriett Elizabeth (Mrs. William R. Hendrickson); m. 2d, Helen Marie Taylor Brown, Apr. 16, 1966; step-children—Sharon Ann Brown (Mrs. Robert Bunting), Larry De Witt Brown. Farm adviser Agrl. Extension Edn., De Kalb County, Ill., 1946-52; ins. mgmt. Country Cos., Bloomington, Ill., 1952-67, Tex. Farm Bur. Ins. Co.'s Waco, Tex., 1967—. Lectr. loss prevention. Mem. Nat. Safety Council Farm Conf., 1960—. Bd. dirs. Southwestern Ins. Info. Service, 1974-76. Served with AUS, 1941-46; ETO. Recipient Advt. Fedn. Silver Medal award, 1974. Mem. Nat. Inst. Farm Safety (pres. 1966-67), Nat. Assn. Mutual Ins. Co.'s, Nat. Fire Protection Assn. (Surburban, Rural Fire Prevention, Promotion com. 1959—, chmn. com. elec. code agr. 1976—), Am. Soc. Agrl. Engrs. (mem. electric power and processing com., chmn. com. elec. code agr. 1976—). Methodist (trustee). Clubs: Advt. of Waco (pres. 1973-74); Toastmasters. Home: 5619 Lake Jackson Waco TX 76710 Office: 7420 Fishpond Rd Waco TX 76710

CROSS, WILLIAM ALAN, nuclear engr.; b. Barberton, Ohio, July 18, 1948; s. Dowell Douglas and Loretta Cecilia (Rarick) C.; B.S. Nuclear Engring. Sci. with honors, U. Fla., 1974; m. Patricia Lucille Love, Aug. 14, 1970; children—Leanne, Daryl. Licensing engr. Fla. Power Corp., 1974; nuclear power supply planning engr. TVA, 1974-75; plant engr. Crystal River Nuclear Plant (Fla.), 1975-77, tech. specifications engr., 1977-78, reactor engr., 1978-79, ops. engr., 1979—. Recipient Research award IEEE Nuclear Sci. and Plasma Soc., 1974. Mem. Am. Nuclear Soc. (cert. of appreciation 1974). Home: PO Box 1564 Crystal River FL 32629 Office: PO Box 1240 Crystal River FL 32629

CROSSLAND, EDWARD JOHN, seismograph co. exec.; b. Okmulgee, Okla., Jan. 17, 1927; s. Samuel Hess and Iva (Jones) C.; B.S., U. Tulsa, 1954; m. Joyce Gardner, Dec. 27, 1963; children—Joy Lorraine, Iva Lynn, Lisa Pauline. Engr., Philco Corp., Phila., 1950-51; research engr. Seismograph Service Corp., Tulsa, 1951-56, mgr. new product devel., 1957-59, engring. mgr. voting machine div., 1959-65, nat. marketing mgr. voting products, 1966-68, exec. engring. cons. P.E.D./Seiscor Div., 1969—. Mem. Okla. State Bd. Registration for Profl. Engrs., 1962-67, chmn., 1966-67. Trustee Tulsa State Fair Bd., 1956-57. Served with USAAF, 1945-49. Registered profl. engr., Okla. Mem. Nat., Okla. socs. profl. engrs. Patentee in field. Home: 7022 E 64th Pl Tulsa OK 74133 Office: 6200 E 41st St PO Box 1590 Tulsa OK 74102

CROSSON, STEPHEN THOMAS, real estate appraiser; b. Dallas, Mar. 22, 1945; s. Earl T. and Mary Frances (McCauley) C.; B.B.A., N. Tex. State U., 1968; postgrad. So. Meth. U., 1974—. Chief appraiser Oak Cliff Savs. & Loan Assn., Dallas, 1972-73; regional supr. appraisal div. First Tex. Fin. Corp., 1973-74, mgr. appraisal adminstrn., 1974-76; chief exec. officer Crosson Dannis, Inc., Dallas, 1977—. Recipient Letter of Merit, Pan Am. Appraisal Conf., 1976. Mem. Am. Inst. Real Estate Appraisers, Estate Appraisers, Soc. Real Estate Appraisers. Home: 3701 Turtle Creek Blvd Apt 6-C Dallas TX 75219 Office: 8350 N Central Expy Suite 1140 Dallas TX 75206

CROSSWELL, CAROL MCCORMICK, lawyer; b. Buffalo, Dec. 21, 1928; d. Albert L.L. and Helen (McDowell) McCormick; student Radcliffe Coll.; LL.B. cum laude, U. Buffalo, 1948; postgrad. Columbia U., 1960, (fellow) Harvard U. Sch. Internat. Law, 1961; m. William J. Crosswell (dec.); m. 2d, Gilbert Wheatland Smith, Feb. 2, 1952 (div. Feb. 1972); children—Carol, Linda. Admitted to N.Y. bar, 1948, Washington bar, 1953, Fla. bar, 1967; mem. legal staff UN, 1948-51; mem. U.S. Govt. Psychol. Strategy Bd., 1951-53; U.S. del. Inter Am. Council Jurists, Santiago, Chile, 1960; practiced in N.Y.C., 1950—, Palm Beach, Fla., 1967—; mem. firm Weidon and Crosswell, 1950-66, Winkle Sims Kenny & Crosswell, 1979—; prof. internat. bus. transactions Nova Law Sch. Mem. Fla. Marine Commn., 1968—. Bd. dirs. Jr. League, Millard Fillmore Hosp., Buffalo, Save the Children Fedn., Gebbie Found. Inst.; bd. govs. Nova U. Law Center. Mem. Soc. Women Geographers, Fellows of Harvard. Clubs: Indian Harbor Yacht (Greenwich, Conn.); Buffalo Country; N.Y. Skating, Olcott Yacht (N.Y.C.); Palm Beach Yacht, Sail Fish, Beach (Palm Beach, Fla.); Royal Can. Yacht (Toronto, Ont.). Author: Protection of International Personnel, 1956; Financing Foreign Investment, 1962; International Business Techniques, 1963; International Business Law and Knowhow, 1980. Home: 1204 N Ocean Blvd Palm Beach FL 33480 also Cherrycroft Burt NY Office: 249 Royal Palm Way Palm Beach FL 33480

CROTTS, MARCUS BOWMAN, mech. engr.; b. Winston-Salem, N.C., Aug. 6, 1931; s. Marcus James and Daphne (Bowman) C.; B.Mech.Engring., N.C. State U., 1953; postgrad. in bus. adminstrn. Wake Forest U., 1954; M.S. in Mech.Engring., U. Ill., 1956; m. Margo Jackson, May 12, 1955; children—Van, Laura. Asso. engr. Duke Power Co., Winston-Salem, 1947-49; Mech. engr. Babcock & Wilcox Co., Canton, O., 1950-51, Western-Electric Co., Winston-Salem, 1954-55; partner Crotts & Saunders Engring., Inc., Winston-Salem, 1956—; owner Crotts Enterprises, Inc., Salem Equipment Co.; dir. Electronic Data Control, Objective Industries. Trustee N.C. State U.; bd. mgrs. Nazareth Childrens Home, 1968-78; pres. alumni assn. N.C. State U.; dist. commr. Boy Scouts Am. Served to lt. USAF, 1954-56. Recipient Archimedes Engring. Achievement award Calif. Soc. Profl. Engrs., 1979; Disting. Engring. Achievement award U. Ill., 1980; registered profl. engr., N.C., S.C., Va. Mem. ASME (life past nat. v.p., mem. council), Soc. Mfg. Engrs. (past chmn. Winston-Salem chpt., Piedmont chpt., nat. dir., past regional chmn., Nat. Soc. Profl. Engrs., Numerical Control Soc., Profl. Engrs. N.C. (dir.), N.C. Soc. Engrs. (pres. 1979-80, dir.), Instn. Prodn. Engrs. (Eng.), Am. Machine Tool Distbrs. Assn. (sec., dir.), Winston-Salem C. of C., Alumni Assn. N.C. State U. (dir., past pres.), Phi Kappa Phi, Tau Beta Pi, Theta Tau, Pi Tau Sigma. Mem. United Ch. Christ (deacon, elder, trustee). Rotarian (dir., pres. Stratford club, dist. gov. 1980-81). Clubs: Forsyth Country; Engineers (past pres.) (Winston-Salem). Contbr. numerous articles on metric conversion to tech. jours. Home: 10 Gomar Lane Winston-Salem NC 27106 Office: PO Box 5058 4000 Silas Creek Pkwy Winston-Salem NC 27103

CROUCH, ANNA BELLE, educator; b. Springfield, Mo., Nov. 11, 1918; d. Joseph Earl and Iva Mae (Garoutte) Crouch; B.S., S.E. Mo. State U., 1942; M.R.E., So. Bapt. Theol. Sem., 1947; M.A., Columbia, 1967; postgrad. So. Bapt. Theol. Sem. Sch. Sacred Music, 1947-48, East Carolina U., summers 1958, 69, 70, Union Theol. Sem., summers 1962, 64, Va. State Coll., 1968, Coll. William and Mary, 1970-71, Evangel Coll., 1978. Tchr. pub. schs. Barton and Newton Counties, Mo., 1938-40; asst. chief clk. Post Pubs., Fort Crowder, Mo., 1942-45; youth dir. First Bapt. Ch., Florence, Ala., summer 1947; young people's sec. Mo. Bapt. Woman's Missionary Union, Jefferson City, 1948-54; dir. music, edn. Rosemary Bapt. Ch., Roanoke Rapids, N.C., 1955-58; asst. dean women Chowan Coll., Murfreesboro, N.C., 1958-66, prof. women's phys. edn., 1958-60, prof. hygiene, 1960-63, prof. music, 1958-62, prof. religion, 1959-63, prof. profl. devel., 1960-69, 75-77, prof. speech, 1961—. Dir. music Murfreesboro (N.C.) Bapt. Ch., 1966-71, Branchville (Va.) Bapt. Ch., 1973-74; speech correctionist Southampton (Va.) Pub. Schs., 1970. Mem. Murfreesboro Hist. Assn., 1971—; flood vol. worker, Cape Girardeau, Mo., 1937; vol. youth dir., worker among service men and women, Neosho, Mo., 1942-45; field worker with women county jail and Waverly Sanitarium, Louisville, 1945-48; mem. Roanoke Rapids (N.C.) Hosp. Guild, 1956-58; modeling dir. Roanoke-Chowan Beauty Pageants, 1960-72, spl. award, 1967; rep. Mo. Baptist Gen. Assn., Panama, 1952; mem. Hertford County Bicentennial Commn., 1974—; chmn. Hertford County Fine Arts Bicentennial Com., 1974—; mem. travel and recreation com. Coastal Plains Devel. Assn., 1976—. Named Hertford County Citizen of Week, 1979. Mem. N.C. Speech and Drama Assn., So. Speech Communication Assn., Speech Communication Assn. Am., Jr. Coll. Speech Assn., Chowan Community Concert Assn., Chowan Coll. Speakers Bur., N.C. Hist. Soc., Murfreesboro C. of C. (Chowan Coll. rep. to women's div. 1973—, dir. women's div. 1975-77, 80—, chaplain 1975—, mem. bicentennial com. 1976, Woman of Month Women's div. 1975), Internat. Platform Assn. Democrat. Baptist (youth leadership rep. Mo. Bapt. Inter-Racial Council, 1950-54, dir. Woman's Missionary Union, adult Sunday Sch. supt. asst. Sunday Sch. tchr., mem. choir 1974—). Clubs: Murfreesboro Federated Woman's (v.p. 1977-79), Chowan Coll. Women and Wives (pres. 1980). Contbr. articles to profl. jours. Home: 411 Union St Murfreesboro NC 27855 Office: Marks Hall Room 320 Chowan College Murfreesboro NC 27855

CROUCH, EARL RUSSELL, JR., ophthalmologist; b. Richmond, Va., Feb. 20, 1943; s. Earl R. and Agnes (Massey) C.; B.S. magna cum laude, U. Richmond; 1965; M.D., Med. Coll. Va., 1969; m. Edith L. Paulette, Dec. 28, 1968; children—Earl Russell III, Richard John Page. Intern, U. Hosps., Med. Coll. Va., Richmond, 1969-70; resident in ophthalmology U. Ill. Eye and Ear Infirmary, Chgo., 1972-75; fellow in pediatric ophthalmology Nat. Med. Center, Children's Hosp., Washington, 1975-76; practice medicine specializing in ophthalmology, Norfolk, Va., 1976—; instr. in ophthalmology U. Ill. Eye and Ear Infirmary, 1974-75, George Washington U., 1975-76; cons. pediatric ophthalmology USPHS Hosp., 1977, Portsmouth Naval Hosp., 1978; asst. prof. ophthalmology Eastern Va. Med. Sch., Norfolk, 1976-79, asso. prof., 1979—, asst. prof. pediatrics, 1979—, vice chmn. dept. ophthalmology, 1977—. Served with USPHS, 1970-72. Heed Ophthalmic Found. fellow, 1975-76; diplomate Am. Bd. Ophthalmology. Fellow A.C.S., Am. Acad. Ophthalmology and Otolaryngology; mem. Va. Assn. Ophthalmology and Otolaryngology, Am. Assn. Ophthalmology, Assn. for Research and Vision in Ophthalmology, Am. Assn. Pediatric Ophthalmology and Strabismus, Costenbader Pediatric Ophthalmology Soc., Tidewater Eye Soc. (sec. 1977-78), Norfolk Acad. Medicine, Va. Med. Soc., U. Ill. Alumni Assn., Phi Beta Kappa, Omicron Delta Kappa. Contbr. articles on ophthalmology to profl. jours. Home: 2109 Windward Shore Dr Virginia Beach VA 23451 Office: Bldg 20 Koger Executive Center Norfolk VA 23502

CROUCH, (NORA) JOSEPHINE, librarian; b. Hereford, Tex.; d. Joseph Evvy and Nora (Betts) Crouch; B.S., Ga. Coll., 1942; M.L.S., George Peabody Coll., 1950. Librarian, Boy's High Sch., Rome, Ga., 1942-44, Parker High Sch., Greenville, S.C., 1944-46; library supr. Bartow (Fla.) Sch. System, 1946-47; librarian high sch., Aiken, S.C., 1950-53; chief librarian Aiken County Pub. Library, 1954-58; dir. Aiken-Bamberg-Barnwell-Edgefield Regional Library, Aiken, 1958—. Appointed dir. to establish 1st S.C. Regional Demonstration Library, 1958—; library rep. 2d to 9th S.C. Gov.'s Conf. Bus., Industry, Edn. and Agr., 1960-68; mem. S.C. Gov.'s Conf. Pub. Libraries, 1965; mem. S.C. Gov.'s Conf. State-wide Traffic Safety, 1961-63; mem. spl. com. S.C. Progress, 1962. Sec. Dibble Meml. Library Bd., 1963—, S.C. Council Common Good, 1968-69, 69-70. Mem. A.L.A., Southeastern, S.C. (chmn. pub. library sect. 1956-58, mem. exec. bd. 1956-58, 64-70, mem. state exec. com. 1965-69, pres. 1966, 67; A.L.A. fed. relations coordinator 1963-65), Central Savannah River Area library assns., AAUW (state bd. 1957-58, br. bd. 1958—; state div. parliamentarian 1965-67; exec. bd. 1964-67; br. pres. 1966-67), Council for Common Good (sec. 1968-70), Aiken County Hist. Soc., Hist. Aiken Found. Club: Pilot. Contbr. to profl. publs. Home: 823 Fermata Pl SW Aiken SC 29801 Office: 224 Laurens Ave SW Aiken SC 29801

CROUCH, WILLIAM ELLSWORTH, internist, cardiologist; b. Pitts., July 31, 1943; A.B., Princeton U., 1965; M.D., Columbia U., 1960; m. Rosalie Kelsey, June 3, 1967; children—Katherine Anne, Richard William. Intern, Roosevelt Hosp., N.Y.C., 1969-70, resident in internal medicine, 1970-73, fellow div. cardiology, dept. medicine, 1973-75; practice medicine specializing in internal medicine and cardiology, Charleston, S.C., 1975—; mem. staff, chmn. combined dept. internal medicine Roper Hosp. and St. Francis Xavier Hosp., 1979—; mem. staff Baker Hosp. Diplomate Am. Bd. Internal Medicine. Mem. A.C.P., Am. Coll. Cardiology, Am. Heart Assn., Med. Soc. S.C., Charleston County Med. Assn. Episcopalian. Office: 122 Bull St Charleston SC 29401

CROW, ALONZO BIGLER, educator; b. Warren, Pa., Aug. 27, 1910; s. Charles Rohrer and Mary Donaldson (Wilson) C.; student Pa. State Forest Sch., 1928-29, U. Mont., 1929-30, U. Pitts., 1930; B.S., N.C. State Coll., 1934; M.Forestry, Yale, 1941; m. Margaret Belle Rinaman, June 22, 1935; children—Nancy (Mrs. Joseph Hamlin Barham, Jr.). Jr. forester, research forester U.S. Forest Service, Mo., Pa., Md., 1934-40; farm forester U.S. Soil Conservation Service, Md., 1941-44; regional cons. Am. Forestry Assn., Md., Del., Ill., W.Va.,

1945-46; asst. prof. Sch. Forestry and Wildlife Mgmt., La. State U., Baton Rouge, 1946-52, asso. prof., 1952-64, prof., 1964-76, prof. emeritus, 1976—. Recipient Sci. Faculty Fellowship, NSF, 1958, 60, Teaching award Gamma Sigma Delta, 1964. Mem. Soc. Am. Foresters (Disting. Service award for La. 1975), Am. Forestry Assn., Forest Farm Assn., La. Forestry Assn., Sigma Xi, Phi Kappa Phi, Gamma Sigma Delta, Alpha Zeta, Xi Sigma Pi. Home: 1957 Cherrydale Ave Baton Rouge LA 70808

CROW, JAMES SYLVESTER, banker; b. Mobile, Ala., June 23, 1915; s. James S. and Elizabeth (Jackson) C.; student U. Ala., 1946-48; grad. Rutgers Sch. Banking, 1959; m. Dorothy Charbonnet Farwell, Sept. 21, 1974; children by previous marriage—Michele Marie (Mrs. John Z. Higg, III), Denise Anne (Mrs. Walter C. Andrews, Jr.), Marcia Lynn, Deborah Jane. Clk. First Nat. Bank Mobile, 1932-41, 45-48, mgr. bond dept., 1949-50, asst. cashier, 1951, asst. v.p., 1952; sales mgr. Hendrix & Mayes Investment Bankers, Birmingham, Ala., 1952-53; asst. cashier First Nat. Bank Birmingham, 1954-55, asst. v.p., 1955-56, v.p., 1957-60, sr. v.p., 1961-66, exec. v.p., 1966-67; v.p. finance So. Ry. Co., Washington, 1967-70; exec. v.p. First Nat. Bank Mobile, 1970-71, pres., 1971-74, chmn. bd., 1974-79; pres., chmn. bd. First Bancgroup Ala., 1973-79; dir. Ala. Gt. So. R.R., La. So. R.R., Ala. Dry Dock & Shipbldg. Co., Lerio Corp. Trustee So. Research Inst.; trustee, pres. Ala. Ind. Colls. Assn., 1979—. Mem. Ala. Banker Assn. (v.p. 1966-67), Newcomen Soc. N.Am. Episcopalian. Clubs: Birmingham Country, Downtown (Birmingham); Metropolitan (Washington and N.Y.C.). Home: PO Box 68 Montrose AL 36559 Office: PO Box 1467 Mobile AL 36621

CROW, JOHN DAVID, football coach; b. Marion, La., July 8, 1935; s. Harry D. and Velma J. Crow; B.B.A., Tex. A&M U., 1958; m. Carolyn Gilliam, July 2, 1954; children—John David, Annalisa, Jeannie. Profl. football player St. Louis Cardinals, 1958-65, San Francisco 49ers, 1966-68; asst. coach U. Ala. football team, 1969-71, Cleve. Browns Profl. Football Team, 1972-73, San Diego Chargers Profl. Football Team, 1974-75; athletic dir., head football coach N.E. La. U., Monroe, 1976—; mem. Lombardi Award Selection Com. Past chmn. Ouachita (La.) Parish Arthritis Fund drive. Recipient Heisman trophy, 1957, Walter Camp trophy, 1957; unanimously named All-Am.; named Top Coll. Football Player, Sports mag., 1957, La. Collegiate Coach of Year, 1978; named to Nat. Football League All-Star Team. Mem. Am. Football Coaches Assn. Methodist. Office: 700 University Dr Monroe LA 71209

CROW, LESTER DONALD, educator, author; b. Dundee, Ohio, Mar. 31, 1897; s. William Caldwell and Mary (Olmstead) C.; A.B., Ohio U., 1923, L.H.D., (hon.), 1972; M.A., N.Y. U., 1924, Ph.D., 1927; LL.D., St. Lawrence U., 1975; Litt.D.(hon.), Mt. Union Coll., 1976; m. Alice von Bauer, June 11, 1927 (dec. Jan. 1966); m. 2d, Rosamond M. Hardy, July 9, 1969. Tchr. high schs., Ohio, 1919-22, Pelham, N.Y., 1924-26; prof. edn. Mary Washington U., Fredericksburg, Va., 1926-27; asst. prof. edn. Leigh U., Bethlehem, Pa., 1927-28; prof. edn. N.Y. U., 1929-30; dir. edn. Pelham Inst., N.Y.C., 1930-32; faculty Bklyn. Coll., 1932-67, emeritus prof. edn., 1967—. Mem. com. to evaluate secondary schs. Middle Atlantic States Colls. and Secondary Schs., 1947-49; pres. Midwood Park Property Assn., Bklyn., 1955-65; mem. U.S. govt. commn. to set up Tchr. Edn. Program, Japan, 1950-51. Recipient Certificate of Merit, Ohio U. Alumni Assn., 1970; Alumni award Mt. Union Coll., 1974. Mem. Am. Personnel and Guidance Assn. (life), N.Y. Acad. Sci. (life), Kappa Delta Pi (hon. life), Phi Delta Kappa (life). Club: N.Y. Schoolmaster's (pres. 1965-66). Author numerous books including An Introduction to Education, 1947, 3d edit., 1974; Educational Psychology, 1948, rev. edit., 1963; Introduction to Guidance, 1951, 2d edit. 1961; Child Psychology, 1953; Readings in General Psychology, 1954; Sex Education in a Growing Family, 1959; How to Study, 1963; Psychology and Human Adjustment, 1967; General Psychology, rev. edit., 1972; Human Development and Adjustment, 1973; As the Crow Flies (autobiography), 1977; Personality, 1978; Psychology of Childhood and Adolescence; Development of Self-Discipline, 1980; also articles in profl. jours. Home: 5300 Washington St Apt 301D Hollywood FL 33021

CROW, NEIL EDWARD, physician; b. Belton, Tex., July 12, 1926; s. Floyd Charles and Mary (Martin) C.; student Henderson Coll., 1943-44, Tex. Christian U., 1944-45; B.S., U. Tex., 1946; M.D., U. Ark., 1951; m. Mary Katherine Claxton, Sept. 11, 1948; children—Neil E., Katherine Lee. Intern U. Ark. Med. Center, 1951-52, splty. tng. in radiology, 1953-56, asso. clin. prof. radiology, 1960-75, prof. clin. radiology, 1975—; gen. practice medicine, Hope, Ark., 1952-53; radiologist Holt-Krock Clinic and Sparks Med. Center, Fort Smith, Ark., 1960—; chief of staff, trustee Sparks Regional Med. Center, 1975—. Cons. USPHS, USAF Surgeon Gen. Pres., Ft. Smith Sch. Bd., 1971-72. Trustee Ark. Poly. Coll., 1972—, Sparks Regional Med. Center, 1974—. Served to lt. (j.g.) USNR, 1944-47; to lt. col. USAF, 1953-60; now col. M.C. Res. Diplomate Am. Bd. Radiology. Mem. Am. Coll. Radiology, A.M.A., Ark. Med. Soc., Air Force Assn., Am. Fedn. Clin. Research, U. Ark. Sch. Medicine Alumni Assn. (pres. 1972-74), Alpha Omega Alpha, Phi Chi. Democrat. Presbyn. Contbr. articles to profl. jours. Home: 19 Berry Hill Rd Fort Smith AR 72903 Office: 1500 Dodson Ave Fort Smith AR 72901

CROW, WILLIAM CECIL, cons., former govt. ofcl.; b. Oneonta, Ala., Oct. 4, 1904; s. Mandeville McAlpin and Flora Jane (Brice) C.; A.B., Maryville Coll., 1924; A.M., U. Chgo., 1929; LL.D., Maryville College, 1969; m. Mary Lucille Johnson, July 5, 1935; 1 son, William Cecil. Asst. prof. econs., Ala. Poly. Inst., 1930-35; with U.S. Dept. Agr., 1935-72, successively with Bur. Agrl. Econs., 1935-42, War Food Adminstrn. and Prodn. and Marketing Adminstrn., 1942-53, dir. transp. and facilities research div., and liaison with state depts. of agr. Agrl. Marketing Service, 1953-63, dir. transp. and facilities research div. Agrl. Research Service, 1963-72; cons. food mktg. facilities and systems, Africa, Asia, Australia, Europe, N.Am., Central Am., S.Am. Mem. Arlington (Va.) Com. of 100; chmn. Arlington County Pub. Utilities Commn. Trustee Presbytery of Washington. Decorated Chevalier de l'Ordre du Merite Agricole (France); Order of Long Leaf Pine (N.C.); recipient Achievement award Nat. Assn. Produce Market Mgrs., also plaque for exceptional service; Superior Service award U.S. Dept. Agr.; citation Greater Phila. Movement; named Ky. Col. Hon. life mem. Nat. Assn. Refrigerated Warehouses; mem. Am. Agrl. Econs. Assn., AAAS. Presbyterian. Club: Springfield Golf and Country. Author many publs. Home and office: 1258 N Buchanan St Arlington VA 22205

CROWDER, BILLY CALHOUN, wholesale co. exec.; b. Little Rock, May 7, 1930; s. Wesley Hays and Bernice C.; student Ark. Tech. Coll., 1948-49, Little Rock Jr. Coll., 1952-54; m. Mary Lynn Puddephatt, Aug. 11, 1950; children—Glenn, Larry, Ellen. With S.E. Ark. Supply Co., 1949-51, 51-56, mgr. br., 1956-60; co-owner, gen. mgr. Central Ark. Supply Co., Little Rock, 1960—, also pres. Central Ark. Supply of Conway. Served with USAF, 1951-52. Recipient Order of Arrow, Boy Scouts Am. Episcopalian. Club: Maumelle Golf and Country. Home: 11 Brookridge Rd Little Rock AR 72205 Office: 1000 Rushing Circle Little Rock AR 72205

CROWDER, CAMELLIA HUFFMAN, congl. sec.; b. Roanoke, Va., Oct. 1, 1940; d. Walter Watson and Irene Frances (Craft) Huffman; grad. Nat. Bus. Coll., 1959; m. Steve E. Crowder, June 5, 1971; 1 son, Steven Edward. Sec. to M. Caldwell Butler, Roanoke, 1959-62; legal sec. law firm Eggleston, Butler & Glenn, 1962-72; sec. to Congressman M. Caldwell Butler, Roanoke Dist. Office, 1972—. Mem. Va. Assn. Legal Secs. (Va. Legal Sec. of Year 1969), Roanoke Valley Legal Secs. Assn. (Legal Sec. of Year 1965, pres. 1968-69). Republican. Baptist. Home: Route 2 Box 56 Fincastle VA 24090 Office: PO Box 865 Roanoke VA 24005

CROWDER, CHARLIE CLEMONS, JR., municipal ofcl.; b. Danville, Va., July 26, 1940; s. Charlie Clemons and Avis Louise (Griffith) C.; B.S., Va. Mil. Inst., 1962; M.S., George Washington U., 1978; m. Carolyn Marie Willis, June 16, 1962; children—Coni, Christin, Catherine. Commd. 2d lt., U.S. Army, 1962, advanced through grades to capt., 1965; combat engr. unit comdr., Ft. Meade, Md., 1962-64; post engr., Aschaffenburg, Germany, 1964-66; comdr. Port Constrn. Co., Ft. Belvoir, Va. and Qui Nhon, Vietnam, 1966-67; post engr., Tobyhanna (Pa.) Army Depot, 1968; ret., 1968; dir. pub. works City of Danville, 1969-72; mgr. store engring. Asso. Service Corp., Danville, Va., 1972-73; adminstrv. engr., asst. to dir. pub. utilities, City of Pensacola, Fla., 1973, water supt. dept. pub. utilities, 1973-76; chief engr. dept. pub. utilities City of Newport News (Va.), 1976—. Decorated Bronze Star (U.S.); Order of Merit 2d Class (Vietnam). Mem. Internat. City Mgmt. Assn. (affiliate mem.). Baptist. Mason. Home: 474 Harcourt Pl Newport News VA 23602 Office: Dept Pub Utilities Newport News VA 23607

CROWDER, ROBERT DOUGLAS, educator; b. Nashville, June 21, 1934; s. Noble Douglas and Eleanor Clare (Fulghum) C.; B.A., Vanderbilt U., 1956, M.A., 1960, Ph.D., 1967. Fulbright lectr. U. Lyon (France), 1958-59; instr. Vanderbilt U., 1960-64; dir. Vanderbilt U. in France, 1964-65; asso. prof. fgn. langs. N. Tex. State U., Denton, 1965—, chmn. dept. fgn. langs. and lits., 1979—. Fulbright scholar, U. Poitiers (France), 1957-58. Mem. AAUP, Am. Assn. Tchrs. French, Tex. Assn. Coll. Tchrs., Tenn. Hist. Soc., SAR, Sons Confederate Vets. Democrat. Home: 2525 Turtle Creek Blvd Dallas TX 75219 Office: Dept Fgn Langs and Lits N Tex State U Denton TX 76203

CROWE, BYRON DAN, food co. exec.; b. Atlanta, Jan. 14, 1939; s. William Dan and Mary Ruth (Harper) C.; B.A. in Econs., Harvard U., 1962; m. Ruth A. Hearn, Feb. 1, 1980; children by previous marriage—Byron Dan, Dean Christopher, Leslie Jeanne. Fgn. exchange trader Bankers Trust Co. N.Y., 1962-65; fin. cons. dir. various corps., 1965-74; pres. GRF, Inc., mgmt. cons., Atlanta, 1974-77; pres. Munch Corp., food mfr., Forest Park, Ga., 1977-79; pres. Whitehorse Properties, Inc., Barnesville, Ga., 1980—; dir. Whitehorse Parks, Inc. Lic. real estate broker, Ga. Mem. Ga. Cattlemen's Assn. Club: Associated Harvard. Home: Route 1 Barnesville GA 30204 Office: Old 41 Hwy North Barnesville GA 30204

CROWE, ROBERT DENNING, lawyer; b. Richmond, Mo., July 24, 1899; s. Thomas William and Laura Belle (Penny) C.; A.B., Central Meth. Coll., 1922; J.D., U. Mo., 1926; m. Ewing Hardy, Dec. 5, 1936; children—Jean Meredith Crowe Rustvold, Robert Denning II. Admitted to Okla. bar, 1925; individual practice law, Enid, 1926-29, Oklahoma City, 1934—; asst. atty. gen. State of Okla., 1929-34; pres. Crowe & Crowe, Inc., Oklahoma City, 1971—. Mem. Am. Bar Assn., Okla. Bar Assn., Oklahoma County Bar Assn., Newcomen Soc. N.Am., Oklahoma City C. of C., Acacia, Phi Alpha Delta. Democrat. Methodist. Home: 1702 Camden Way Oklahoma City OK 73116 Office: 666 First Nat Center W Oklahoma City OK 73102

CROWE, THOMAS ASHLEY, educator; b. Birmingham, Ala., Feb. 15, 1947; s. Alden Emerson and Mary Frances (Ashley) C.; B.A., U. Ala., 1973, M.A., 1975; Ph.D. (Bd. Suprs. scholar), La. State U., 1980; m. Sandra Kay Cross, Sept. 22, 1966; children—Mark Alden, Bradley Thomas. Speech pathologist Earl K. Long Mem. Hosp., Baton Rouge, 1976-77; asst. prof. dept. communicative disorders U. Miss., University, 1977—; lectr. in field. Served with USAF, 1967-71. Decorated Air Force Commendation medal. Recipient Outstanding Tchr. award, dept. communicative disorders U. Miss., 1978. Mem. Am. Speech-Lang.-Hearing Assn. (cert. clin. competence), Miss. Speech and Hearing Assn. Contbr. chpts. to books, articles to profl. jours. Home: 3308 S Lamar Ext Oxford MS 38655 Office: Dept Communicative Disorders U Miss University MS 38677

CROWELL, JOHN KENNETH, govt. ofcl.; b. Los Angeles, May 15, 1950; s. John Henry and Carrie E. (Williams) Bright; B.S. in Acctg., Okla. U., 1974; grad. Oliver Wolcott Tech. Sch., 1968; m. Joni M. Zardiackas, July 2, 1976; 1 son, Michael James. Toolmaker, Mitral Corp., Torrington, Conn., 1966-69; adminstr. Eastern Motors, Altus, Okla., 1971-74; auditor Def. Contract Audit Agy., Conn. and Tex., 1974-75; auditor Dept. Labor, Dallas, 1975-77; mem. staff of dir. Office Spl. Counsel, Dept. Energy, Dallas, 1977—; chmn. Am. Employee Benefits, Dallas, 1977—. Served with USAF, 1970-74. Mem. Govt. Accountants Assn., Automated Data Processing Counsel. Republican. Baptist. Club: Barton Dads (pres.). Home: 2209 Cambridge St Irving TX 75061

CROWELL, VIRGINIA SMITH, educator; b. Mount Airy, N.C., May 18, 1923; d. Thomas William and Sarah Kate (Banner) Smith; A.B. summa cum laude, Queens Coll., Charlotte, N.C., 1945; M.A., Emory U., 1963; M.Ed., U. N.C., 1972; m. John Eugene Crowell, Apr. 26, 1956. Tchr. biblical studies Selma, Elkin-Jonesville and Thomasville, N.C., 1945-55; tchr. Anne Arundel County (Md.) Schs., 1958-60; dir. religious edn. First Methodist Ch., Athens, Ga., 1962-67, Myers Park Meth. Ch., Charlotte, 1967-70; counselor, instr. psychology Coker Coll., Hartsville, S.C., 1973-76, acting dean students, 1975; instr. in psychology Surry Community Coll., 1976-77; instr. human devel. Yadkin Valley Employment and Tng. Services, summer 1977; counselor, instr. social studies and English, Surry County Extended Sch. Day Program, 1977-80. Mem. goodwill mission to Congo, Africa, 1970, Costa Rica, 1973. Mem. Am. Personnel and Guidance Assn., Am. Mental Health Counselors Assn., N.C. Mus. History Assos., Surry County (N.C.) Hist. Soc. Democrat. Home: 264 Hylton St Mount Airy NC 27030 Office: 105 Davis Arcade Mount Airy NC 27030

CROWLEY, HAROLD JAMES, real estate broker; b. Chickasha, Okla., Aug. 3, 1924; s. Harold James and Thelma Lee (Graves) C.; student Kansas City Jr. Coll., 1942-43; B.S., U. Colo., 1947; m. Mary Elizabeth Oden, July 16, 1949; children—Sharon (Mrs. William Hartwell Baughn), Elizabeth. With Gulf Oil Corp., Tulsa, Houston, 1947-63, budget and econs. staff adviser, 1959-63; with Peebles Realty Co., Houston, 1963-64; co-owner Stewart and Crowley Realtors, Houston, 1964-66; owner Jim Crowley Co., Houston, 1966—; owner, pres. Jim Crowley Comml. & Investment Properties, Inc., Houston, 1975—; pres. Crowley/Sprinkle, Inc., Houston, 1975—. Instr. real estate Houston Community Coll., 1973-77. Served with USNR, 1942-46. Mem. Nat. Assn. Realtors (cert. comml. and investment mem.), Tex. Assn. Realtors, Houston Property Exchange (chmn. mktg. com. 1975), Tex. Property Exchangers (Tex. Exchanger of Yr. 1977, pres. 1980), Soc. Exchange Counselors, Bellaire C. of C. (dir. 1973-75), Sigma Nu. Rotarian. Home: 5006 Creekbend Houston TX 77035 Office: 6235 Beechnut Houston TX 77074

CROWNOVER, KENNETH ANDREW, combustion engr.; b. Hillsboro, Tenn., July 6, 1930; s. Charles Perry and Lela (Wilder) C.; B.A., U. Ala., 1975; postgrad. in history, 1975-79; E.E., U. Tenn., 1955; m. Mildred Louise Harris, July 25, 1953; 1 son, Danny Kenneth. With Republic Steel Corp., Gadsden, Ala., 1956—, combustion engr., 1967—, energy coordinator, chmn. energy conservation com. So. dist., 1979—. Chmn. record book PTA, 1966; com. chmn. Boy Scouts Am., 1965; dir. edn. deacon Ch. of Christ, 1964-69. Served with USN, 1951-54. Mem. Ala. Hist. Assn., Gadsden Concert Assn., Republic Steel Suprs. Club. Democrat. Club: Civitan. Home: 609 S 4th St Gadsden AL 35901 Office: 174 S 26th St Gadsden AL 35904

CROXTON, THOMAS CLYBURN, JR., electronics and photog. co. exec.; b. Kershaw County, S.C., May 3, 1942; s. Thomas Clyburn and Willie Inez (Young) C.; student Clemson Coll., 1960-62; degree in Electronic Tech., Massey Tech. Inst., 1965; m. Sylvia Joan Newell, Mar. 4, 1967; children—Dawn, Tracie, Matt. Electronic maintenance technician Kinder Foto Internat., Charlotte, N.C., 1965-69, asst. plant engr., 1969-72; mgr. prodn. equipment PCA Internat., Matthews, N.C., 1972-75, dir. equipment mfg., 1975—. Recipient Employer of Yr. award N.C. Assn. for Retarded Citizens, 1977. Mem. Soc. Mfg. Engrs., Am. Mgmt. Assn., Nat. Rifle Assn. Republican. Presbyterian. Club: Woodmen of the World. Home: 9619 Alexis Dr Charlotte NC 28212 Office: 801 Crestdale Ave Matthews NC 28105

CROZER, ROBERT PAGE, food co. exec.; b. Bryn Mawr, Pa., Feb. 21, 1947; s. George Knowles and Neville Carlyle (Leary) C.; B.A., U. Va., 1969, M.B.A., 1972; m. Thornton Taliaferro Flowers, Feb. 19, 1977. Security analyst Elkins, Morris, Stroud, Phila., 1973; product mgr. Flowers Industries, Thomasville, Ga., 1974-76, dir. mktg., 1977-78, pres. Convenience Food div., 1979—, also dir. Bd. dirs. Crozer-Chester Hosp. Mem. Am. Mktg. Assn. Episcopalian. Clubs: St. Anthony Hall, Gulph Mills Golf, Merion Cricket, Lyford Cay; Univ. (N.Y.C.). Office: Flowers Industries Box 1338 Thomasville GA 31792

CROZIER, OUIDA G., counselor; b. Clermont, Fla., Oct. 21, 1947; s. Charles E. and Ouida R. (Hinson) C.; A.A., U. Fla., 1967, B.A., 1969; M.Ed., U. S.C., 1973; postgrad. Center for Whole Person, Phila., 1976-77; cert. program in carpentry Midlands Tech. Coll., 1978. Tchr., Sumter, S.C., 1969-70, 70-71; adminstrv. asst. U. S.C., 1971-72; instr. human services dept. Midlands Tech. Coll., Columbia, S.C., 1972-76, acting dept. head, 1975-76, prof. tng. program psychotherapy, 1976-77, instr. dept. social sci., 1977-78, instr. woodworking and cabinetry, 1978-79, coordinator CETA program for women in non-traditional careers, 1979—; self employed in custom woodworking, Columbia, 1978-79; individual practice counselling, 1978—; mental health counselor Morris Village Alcohol and Drug Addiction Treatment Center, Columbia. Recipient award for service Assn. Women Students, U. Fla., 1967; award Columbia Lumber Co., 1978; award Altrusa Internat., 1978; named Outstanding Student Carpentry Program, Midlands Tech. Coll., 1973. Mem. Assn. Women in Psychology, Assn. Gay Psychologists. Methodist. Club: Lambda Alliance (Columbia).

CRUES, BOBBY JIM, investment banker; b. Plainview, Tex., Oct. 7, 1935; s. John Vernon and Cora Lee (Pedigo) C.; B.B.A., Tex. Tech U., 1959; m. Georgia Marie Morse, Aug. 1, 1970; stepchildren—Kenneth Wayne Tennison, Steven Earl Tennison, Ronald Lee Tennison. Trainee, Texhoma Gins Inc., Dallas, 1959-61; broker Parker, Ford & Co., Plainview, Tex., 1961-63; with Eppler, Guerin & Turner, Inc., 1963—, asst. br. mgr. Midland, Tex., 1972—, asst. v.p., 1980—. Mem. West Tex. Golf Assn. (dir. 1971-78, pres. 1975-77), Alpha Tau Omega, Zeta Eta. Episcopalian. Clubs: Plainview Country, Lions, Elks. Home: 1601 N Midkiff Apt 101 Midland TX 79701 Office: 110 Vaughn Bldg Midland TX 79701

CRUM, JOSEPH EARL, child psychologist; b. Sewickley, Pa., Aug. 6, 1940; s. Jack Wallace and Dorthea Maxwell (Newcomer) C.; B.A., Fla. State U., 1966, Ph.D., 1973; M.A., Memphis State U., 1967; m. Linda Lee Boggess, Aug. 18, 1962 (div. Feb. 1971); children—Jeffery Scott, Jodi Sharlene. Staff psychologist Pinellas County Child Guidance Clinic, St. Petersburg, Fla., 1967-70; intern clin. child psychology State U. N.Y. Upstate Med. Center, Syracuse, 1972-73; fellow in clin. child psychology Sch. Medicine, N.C. Meml. Hosp., Chapel Hill, 1973-74; chief psychol. services Child and Family Comprehensive Mental Health Center, Clearwater, Fla., 1974-78; dir. div. child and adolescent devel., head dept. psychology All Children's Hosp., St. Petersburg, Fla., 1978—. Served with USCG, 1958-62. Fellow Am. Orthopsychiat. Assn.; mem. Am. Psychol. Assn., Soc. Research in Child Devel., Soc. Pediatric Psychology, Assn. Child Psychology and Psychiatry, Phi Kappa Phi. Contbr. author: Mother-Infant Interaction, 1975. Home: FO Box 14056 Saint Petersburg FL 33733 Office: 801 6th St S Saint Petersburg FL 33701

CRUM, LAWRENCE LEE, educator; b. Brownsville, Tex., July 25, 1933; s. John Mears and Mary Louise (Kistler) C.; B.B.A., U. Tex. at Austin, 1954, M.B.A., 1956, Ph.D., 1961. Asst. prof. finance U. Fla. at Gainesville, 1959-63; asso. prof., 1963-65; asso. prof. U. Tex. at Austin, 1965-69, prof. fin., 1969—, chmn. dept., 1969-76; econ. cons. Irving Trust Co., N.Y.C., 1961-70; cons. Am. Bankers Assn., Washington, 1969-71, Crocker Nat. Bank, San Francisco, 1973, Republic Nat. Bank, Dallas, 1976—, Tex. Bankers Assn., Austin, 1977; dir., chmn. pro tem San Antonio br. Fed. Res. Bank of Dallas, 1980—. Ford Found. fellow Fed. Res. Bank Atlanta, 1963-64; Alpha Kappa Psi scholar, 1954. Mem. Am. Finance Assn., Am. Econ. Assn., Financial Mgmt. Assn., Beta Gamma Sigma, Phi Kappa Phi, Austin Investment Club. Republican. Author: Time Deposits in Present Day Commercial Banking, 1964; Transition in the Texas Commercial Banking Industry, 1970; Competition for the Commercial Banking Industry in an Electronic Payments System, 1971; co-author: The Development of State-Chartered Banking in Texas, 1978. Home: 3920 Sierra Dr Austin TX 78731 Office: Dept Finance Univ Texas Austin TX 78712

CRUM, WELDON, auditor; b. Bisbee, Tex., Mar. 16, 1928; s. Bathurst Dewey and Zelma Flory (Barfield) C.; B.B.A., Tex. Wesleyan Coll., 1968; m. Jewel Hunn, June 21, 1947; children—Donald Weldon, Bryan Keith. Asst. credit mgr. Leonard's Dept. Store, 1946-48; unit head credit and collection Montgomery Ward & Co., 1948-49; auditor City of Ft. Worth, 1949-74; pvt. practice as internal auditor, Hurst, Tex., 1974—; auditing cons., 1946—. Hon. dep. sheriff Tarrant County, 1963—; life mem. K.T. Eye Found. Served with USMCR, 1944-46, 50-51; Korea. Mem. Inst. Internal Auditors, Nat. Assn. Govt. Accountants, Intergovtl. Employees Assn., Century Club Southwestern Christian Coll., Police Res. Officers Assn., DAV (life), VFW (life), Marine Corps Assn. Democrat. Mem. Ch. of Christ. Mason (32 deg., Shriner, K.T.). Home: 905 Royal Terrace Hurst TX 76053

CRUMBLEY, GEORGE PIERCE, JR., advt. exec.; b. Atlanta, June 15, 1923; s. George Pierce and Mary (Hicks) C.; A.B., Emory U., 1949; m. Sarah Carolyn Hardy, July 4, 1944; children—Thomas McMahan, Chery Marie. Sales mgr. WSB-TV, Atlanta, 1948-57;

southeastern mgr. Headley-Reed Radio-TV Reps., 1957-59, CBS Radio, 1959-62; pres. Crumbley, Robertson, Riley Advt., Inc., 1962—. Chmn. DeKalb County Cancer Crusade, 1965-67; chmn. spl. study com. Ga. Industries for Blind. Bd. dirs. Met. Atlanta Better Bus. Bur.; trustee Churches Home for Bus. Girls. exec. dir. Peach Bowl, Inc. Served with USAAF, 1942-46; lt. col. Res. ret. Mem. Atlanta Advt. Club (dir.), Nat. Fedn. Advt. Agys. (pres. 1975-76), Alpha Delta Sigma, Sigma Delta Chi. Methodist. Mason, Lion (life dir. Lighthouse for Blind; past dist. gov., internat. dir. 1974-76). Home: 873 Castle Falls Dr NE Atlanta GA 30329 Office: 20 Marietta St NW Atlanta GA 30303

CRUMBO, MINISA, artist; b. Tulsa, Sept. 2, 1942; d. Woodrow and Lillian (Hogue) C.; student Tex. Western U., El Paso, 1961-62, U. Colo., Boulder, 1970-71, Taos (N.Mex.) Acad. Fine Arts, 1972-74, Sch. Visual Arts, N.Y.C., 1974-75; children—Woody Carter, Chris Carter. One-woman shows: Gilcrease Inst. Am. History and Art, Tulsa, 1976, Tulsey Town Gallery, Tulsa, 1975, USSR, 1978-79, Roy Clark Ranch Party-TV Spl., 1976, Pottawatomie Agy. and Cultural Center, Shawnee, Okla., 1977, Okla. Gov.'s Spl. Showing, 1976, Adobe Gallery, Las Vegas, 1977; traveling exhbn. Indian Art Show, U. Oreg., 1977; exhibited Pushkin Mus., Moscow, 1979, Montreux (Switzerland) Jazz Festival, 1979; represented in permanent collections at Heard Mus., Phoenix, Gilcrease Inst. Am. History and Art, Philbrook Art Center, Tulsa, U. Tulsa Art Center, also pvt. collections in U.S. and Europe; guest artist instr. Taos Pueblo Day Sch. Center. Recipient Graphics award for pencil drawing Creek Woman, 29th Am. Indian Exhbn. at Philbrook Art Center. Mem. Native Am. Ch. Home: 6630 E 60th Pl Tulsa OK 74145 Office: 3225 S Norwood St Tulsa OK 74135

CRUMMER, ROGER NELSON, communications co. exec.; b. Essexville, Mich., Dec. 21, 1931; s. John Ernest and Ethel Linea (Nelson) C.; B.S., Mich. State U., 1957; m. Jacqueline Sue Meade, Oct. 7, 1960; children—Laura Ann, James Einar, Margaret Leigh. Sr. engr. Creole Petroleum Corp., Maracaibo, Venezuela, 1957-64; supervisory engr. Page Communications Engrs., Inc., Washington, 1964-67; v.p. Telcom, Inc., Vienna, Va., 1967-75; pres. Novacom, Inc., Fairfax, Va., 1975—. Communications systems cons. Republic Venezuela, Fed. Mil. Govt. Nigeria, Republic Bolivia, Hashemite Kingdom Jordan, Kingdom Saudi Arabia. Served with USN, 1949-53. Mem. IEEE. Republican. Home: 4127 Lenox Dr Fairfax VA 22032 Office: 10720 Main St Fairfax VA 22030

CRUMP, CHARLES METCALF, lawyer; b. Memphis, Oct. 9, 1913; s. Dabney Hull and Mary Hadden (Metcalf) C.; B.A., Southwestern at Memphis, 1934; LL.B., U. Va., 1937; m. Diana Temple Wallace, July 20, 1940; children—Charles Metcalf, Philip Hugh Wallace, Stephen Beard. Admitted to Tenn. bar, 1936, U.S. Supreme Ct. bar, 1946; asso. firm Metcalf, Metcalf & Apperson, Memphis, 1937-40; partner Apperson, Crump, Duzane & Maxwell, and predecessors, Memphis, 1940—; dir. Commerce Union Bank of Memphis, Ripley Industries, Inc. Mem. Tenn. Gen. Assembly, 1939-43; sec. Shelby County Democratic Exec. Com., 1939-50; pres. Chickasaw council Boy Scouts Am., 1953; pres. Sheltered Occupational Shop, Memphis, 1963; v.p. United Fund, Memphis, 1955; mem. nat. exec. council Episcopal Ch., 1964-70, v.p. ho. of deps. Gen. Conv., 1967-70. Served with USNR, 1944-46; PTO. Recipient Outstanding Citizen award Memphis Jr. C. of C., 1943; award of merit for contbn. Tenn. Bar Assn., 1964. Mem. Memphis, Shelby County (dir., treas., sec. 1971-73), Tenn., Am. bar assns., Am. Coll. Probate Counsel, Estate Planning Council Memphis. Democrat. Clubs: Rotary, (pres., 1977-78), Memphis Country, Tenn. Contbr. notes and decisions to Va. Law Rev., 1935-37. Home: 4110 Tuckahoe Ln Memphis TN 38117 Office: 2610 - 100 N Main Bldg Memphis TN 38103

CRUMP, DANNY ROSS, accountant; b. Nathcitoches, La., June 12, 1948; s. Thomas Ross and Mildred Ruth (Haskins) C.; B.S., N.E. La. U., 1970; m. Janie Louise Roberts, June 14, 1969; children—Shawn Christopher, Shane Christian. Accountant, Progressive Savs. & Loan Co., Natchitoches, 1970-71; accountant Ouachita Valley Tech., Inc., Monroe, La., 1972-75; instr. N.E. La. Vocational Sch., Winnsboro, La., 1975-78; asst. dir. Baton Rouge Vocat. Tech. Sch., 1978—; bus. adviser Mastercrafter's Corp. Alderman, Village of Baskin, 1977—; treas. Franklin Parish Firemen's Assn., Franklin Park Rescue Squad; active Baskin PTA. Named Outstanding Young Man of Franklin Parish, Winnsboro Jaycees, 1977. Mem. La. Vocational Assn. (pres. trade and indsl. div.), La. Fireman's Assn., Winnsboro Jr. C. of C. (v.p., Jaycee of Year 1977). Democrat. Home: 7753 Gov Davis Baton Rouge LA 70811 Office: 3250 N Acadian Thruway Baton Rouge LA 70805

CRUMP, EUGENE LITTLE, JR., utility co. exec.; b. Lynchburg, Va., Aug. 4, 1941; s. Eugene Little and Louise (Keeling) C.; B.S., U. Richmond, 1964; m. Mary Jane Hoxie, Sept. 3, 1966; children—Lindsay, Josh. With Va. Dept. Hwys., Richmond, 1965-66, Richmond C. of C., 1966-70; exec. dir. Team of Progress, Richmond, 1970; mgr. govtl. and community affairs Va. Electric & Power Co., Richmond, 1970—; dir. Thermo Press Corp., Richmond; cons. in field. Bd. dirs. Big Bros., Richmond, 1965-67; pres. Fan Dist. Assn., 1971; asst. to chmn. United Way, Richmond, 1974. Recipient YMCA award for service to youth. Mem. Va. C. of C., Richmond C. of C. (legis. com. 1975-79), Utility State Govt. Orgn. Presbyterian. Clubs: Commonwealth, Bull and Bear. Home: 1612 Hanover Ave Richmond VA 23220 Office: PO Box 26666 Richmond VA 23261

CRUMP, JANICE ELLIOTT, librarian; b. Albert, Okla., May 25, 1932; d. Jewell and Goldie (Brown) Elliott; B.A. in English, U. Sci. and Arts Okla., Chickasha, 1953; M.Ed. in Library Sci., S.W. Okla. U., Weatherford, 1973; m. Kenneth E. Crump; children—Ken, Kathy. Social worker Dept. Pub. Welfare, Chickasha, 1963-67; tchr. English, Apache (Okla.) Pub. Schs., Dist. #1-6, 1968-73, librarian, 1973—. Mem. Okla. Library Assn., NEA, Okla. Edn. Assn., Apache Edn. Assn. Certified in library sci., English and journalism, Okla. Home: 23 Dusky Valley Ln Chickasha OK 73018 Office: Chickasha Jr High Sch 1000 S 9th Chickasha OK 73018

CRUMP, MARJORIE VIRGINIA DODSON, univ. adminstr.; b. Smithville, Tex., Sept. 12, 1924; d. P. J. and Marjorie (Dietz) Dodson; B.A., Baylor U., 1946. M.A., 1962; m. Stephen Henry Crump, Jr., Oct. 24, 1947. Adminstrv. asst. to librarian Baylor U., Waco, Tex., 1946-60, research asst. devel. dept., 1960-61, asst. dean women, 1961-64, asst. dean students, 1964-72, asso. dean students, 1972—, chmn. univ. council, 1972-74. Women's council Waco Symphony Assn.; exec. bd. Wesley Found. at Baylor U.; bd. dirs. Bluebonnet council Girl Scouts U.S.A., 1975-77; pres. Waco br. Arthritis Found., 1979—. Named Outstanding Alumna, Baylor U., 1966. Mem. Nat. (nominating com. 1971-72, com. on concerns for students 1972-74, adv. bd. univ. sect. 1975-77, nominating com. 1979-80), Tex. (membership chmn., 1963-65, sec. 1965-66, 2d v.p. 1967, program chmn., pres. 1969-71) assns. women deans and counselors, Am. Assn. U. Women (bull. editor Waco br. 1962-64, 1st v.p. Waco 1966-67, pres. 1967-68, conv. chmn. Tex. div. 1975), Friends Waco Pub. Library, Waco C. of C. (vice chmn. youth council 1972-73, image com. 1976-78), Mortar Bd., Phi Gamma Nu, Alpha Lambda Delta, Kappa Alpha Theta. Baptist. Home: Route 10 Box 368 Waco TX 76708

CRUMP, MARY RUTH, historian; b. Fairfax, Ala., Sept. 7, 1921; d. John Patterson and Katie Louise (Crowder) Royal; student public schs., Fairfax; m. Charles Henry Crump, July 21, 1939; children—John Scott, Charles Frederick, Phoebe Clare. Sec., librarian Fairfax Sch., 1947-49; high sch. sec., Lanett, Ala., 1949-67; asst. recreation dir., Lanett, 1953-54; historian Chambers County, Ala., 1974—. Active Boy Scouts Am., 1949—, recipient Silver Beaver award, 1975; bd. dirs. Historic Chattahoochee Commn. Recipient award of merit Ala. Hist. Commn., 1975. Hon. lt. col. Ala. Militia, 1977. Mem. Nat. Hist. Soc., Ala. Hist. Soc., Chattahoochee Valley Hist. Soc., Lee County Hist. Soc., Tallapoosa County Hist. Soc., East Ala. Geneal. Soc., N.E. Ala. Geneal. Soc., Muscogee County (Ga.) Geneal. Soc., Nat. Trust for Hist. Preservation, Colonial Dames XVII Century (chpt. pres. 1979—). Methodist. Co-author: Bluffton-Lanett, Alabama, 1971; contbr. chpts. to books. Feature writer mag. Alabama Life. Home: 212 S 5th Ave Lanett AL 36863

CRUMP, RICHARD LOY, ednl. adminstr.; b. Mt. Holly, N.C., Sept. 2, 1935; s. Richard Lexington and Effatta Mae (Dagenhart) C.; B.S., Western Carolina U., 1957; M.A.T., Jacksonville U., 1970; Ed.D., Nova U., 1975; m. Betty Abernethy, Sept. 10, 1955; 1 son, Jon Richard. Tchr. math., chmn. dept. Oceanway (Fla.) Jr. High Sch., 1962-64; tchr. math. N.B. Forrest High Sch., Jacksonville, Fla., 1964-70; tchr. math., dept. chmn. Ed White High Sch., Jacksonville, 1970, curriculum coordinator, 1970-76; asst. prin. Terry Parker High Sch., 1976-78; prin. Sandalwood Jr. High Sch., 1978—; part-time instr. Jones Coll., 1970-71, Fla. Jr. Coll., 1971—. Served with USN, 1958-62. Mem. Duval County Council Tchrs. of Math. (past pres.), Nat. Assn. Sch. Adminstrs., Fla. Assn. Sch. Adminstrs., Fla. Council Tchrs. of Math., Phi Delta Kappa (past pres.). Presbyterian. Home: 2313 Dogwood Lane Orange Park FL 32073 Office: 2750 John Prom Blvd Jacksonville FL 32216

CRUMP, THOMAS RICHARD, lawyer; b. Seguin, Tex., Oct. 14, 1945; s. Tom and Helen Margaret (Smith) C.; B.S. in Geology, St. Mary's U., summa cum laude, 1969, J.D., 1971. Faculty, St. Mary's U., San Antonio, 1965-67; with Petty Geophys. Engring. Co., Tex. and Okla., 1966-73; admitted to Tex. bar, 1972, Supreme Ct. of Tex. bar, 1972, U.S. Tax Ct. bar, 1974; pvt. practice law, 1973—; officer, dir. Crump & Knobles, Inc., Seguin, Tex., 1973—, Nash Manor, Inc., Seguin, 1975—, Tri-County Operating Co., 1979—; Countywide Title Co., 1976—; C.K. Prodn. Co., 1980—; examiner real estate titles for Title Ins. Co. of Minn., Safeco Title Ins. Co., U.S. Life Title Ins. Co. of Dallas, Pioneer Nat. Title Ins. Co., Am. Title Ins. Co. of Miami, Chgo. Title Co., Tex. Title Guaranty Co., Stewart Title Co. Mem. Am. Trial Lawyers Assn., Nat. Water Slide Assn. (asso.), New Braunfels C. of C., Tex. Trial Lawyers Assn., Am. Bar Assn., Tex. Bar Assn., San Antonio Bar Assn., Guadalupe County Bar Assn., Tex. Assn. Bank Counsel, Am. Mgmt. Assn., Outdoor Amusement Bus. Assn., Tex. Assn. Realtors, Delta Theta Phi, Delta Epsilon Sigma. Patentee on seismic prospecting invention. Address: 109 W Gonzales St Seguin TX 78155

CRUMPTON, JOHN MABREY, JR., coll. pres.; b. Gainesville, Fla., Sept. 24, 1934; B.S., Auburn U., 1959, M.Ed. (NSF fellow), 1962; Ed.D., N.C. State U., 1973. Tchr. sci., public schs., West Point, Ga., 1960-61; tchr. math. Muscogee County (Ga.) Bd. Edn., 1961-63; tchr. math. Brevard County (Fla.) Bd. Public Instrn., 1963-64, math. curriculum supr., 1964-65, data processing dir., 1965-67; with IBM, Sacramento, Calif., and Raleigh, N.C., 1967-75, account mgr., 1972, edn. mktg. rep., 1973-74, productivity rep., 1974-75; pres. Durham (N.C.) Tech. Inst., 1975—. Cons., Dorothea Dix Hosp., Raleigh, 1972-73; bd. dirs. Durham Day Care Council, 1975-79, Durham Vol. Services Bur., 1975—, Wake County (N.C.) Rehab. and Cerebral Palsy Center, 1976—; bd. dirs., mem. exec. com. N.C. State U. Edn. Found., 1977—; mem. conservation task force Nat. Energy, Edn., Bus. and Labor Conf., 1978-79. Served with U.S. Army, 1954-56. Recipient awards including Regional Mgrs.'s Productivity award IBM, 1974; named Boss of Yr., Bartlett Durham chpt. Am. Bus. Women's Assn., 1976. Mem. Greater Durham C. of C. (dir. 1976-79), AAUP, Phi Delta Kappa. Author: Modern Mathematics for Parents, 1965; contbr. articles to profl. jours.; editor and contbr. Teleprocessing Newsletter, 1970-71. Office: PO Drawer 11307 Durham NC 27703

CRUNK, WILLIAM ATKINS, JR., educator; b. Troy, Ala., Sept. 29, 1948; s. William Atkins and Sue Helen (Kennedy) C.; B.A., Mansfield State Coll., 1970; M.S., Va. Commonwealth U., 1972; Ph.D., U. of S.C., 1975; 1 son, Kristopher Corey. Rehab. counselor blind Raleigh (N.C.) Lions Clinic, 1969; tchr. Horseheads (N.Y.) Sch. Dist., 1971; vocat. rehab. counselor, work evaluator City of Chesterfield, Va., 1972-73; psychiatric specialist Moncrief Army Hosp., Ft. Jackson, S.C., 1973-75; staff mem. Gen. Electric Inst. U. of S.C., 1973-75, asst. dir. undergrad. rehab. service program, 1973-75; asst. supr. staff devel. for vocat. rehab. City of Montgomery, Ala., 1975—; asst. prof. dept. counselor edn. U. Ala., 1975—, also coordinator of rehab. tng., dir. univ. student rehab. services center, coordinator practicum and clin. experiences. Mem. advisory bd. 13th Pl., Birmingham, Ala., 1975—; mem. advisory bd. Birmingham Work Release Center, 1976—; outread vol. Crisis Center, Birmingham, 1976—; chmn. family ministry Bluff Park (Ala.) Methodist Ch., 1977—. Served with U.S. Army, 1970-71. Grantee in field. Certified rehab. counselor, Ala. Mem. Am. Personnel and Guidance Assn., Nat., Ala. rehab. assns., Am. Assn. Marriage and Family Counselors, Nat. Rehab. Counseling Assn., Assn. for Counselor Edn. and Supervision, So. Assn. for Counselor Edn. and Supervision, N. Am., Ala. adlerian socs., Phi Delta Kappa. Democrat. Guest editor: Journal of Elementary Sch. Guidance and Counseling, 1975. Contbr. in field. Home: 4301 Dolly Ridge Ln Birmingham AL 35243 Office: School of Education University College University of Alabama Birmingham AL 35294

CRUSE, IRMA BELLE RUSSELL, former telephone co. exec.; b. Hackneyville, Ala., May 3, 1911; d. Charles Henry and Nellie Dunn (Ledbetter) Russell; student Birmingham-So. Coll., 1927-28; corr. student U. Chgo., U. Wis., U. Minn., intermittently 1958-68; A.B. in Journalism, U. Ala.; m. Jesse Clyde Cruse, Dec. 22, 1931; children—Allan Baird, Howard Russell. With So. Bell and successor South Central Bell, Birmingham, Ala., 1928-44, 54-76, pub. relations supr., 1965-68, rate supr., 1968-76. Free lance writer, 1956—. Mem. bd. Festival of Arts, Birmingham, 1970—; v.p. Birmingham Council Clubs, 1973-74; pres. Jefferson County Radio and TV Council, 1971-72; Past. mem. Quota Club of Birmingham, pres., 1976-77. Recipient numerous awards including Freedoms Found. award, 1967-69; Beautiful Activist, 1972; nominated Women of Year, Birmingham, 1971, 72, 75, Woman of Achievement Met. Bus. and Profl. Women's Club, 1970-71. Mem. Birmingham Bus. Communicators, Ala. Writer's Conclave (pres. 1973-74), Birmingham Council Clubs (sec. 1973-74, dir. 1979-80), Birmingham Met. Bus. and Profl. Women (pres. 1970-71), Women in Communications (pres. 1970-71), Birmingham Bus. Communicators (pres. 1968-69), Women's C. of C., Freedoms Found. of Valley Forge, Telephone Pioneers Am. (editor newsletter 1970—), Ala. State Poetry Soc. (program chmn. 1972-74, editor Muse Messenger 1977—). Baptist. Contbr. articles to various publs. Home: 136 Memory Ct Birmingham AL 35213

CRUSE, JULIUS MAJOR, JR., physician, educator; b. New Albany, Miss., Feb. 15, 1937; s. Julius Major and Effie (Davis) C.; B.A., U. Miss., 1958, B.S. with honors, 1958; D.Microbiology with honors (Fulbright fellow), U. Graz, Austria, 1960; M.D., U. Tenn., 1964, Ph.D. in Pathology (USPHS fellow), 1966. USPHS postdoctoral fellow in pathology U. Tenn., 1964-67; faculty U. Miss., University, 1967—, research prof. immunology, prof. biology, Grad. Sch., 1967-74, asst. prof. pathology, Sch. Medicine, 1973-74, prof. pathology, 1974—, asso. prof. microbiology, 1974—, dir. grad. studies program in pathology, 1974—. Lectr. pathology U. Tenn. Coll. Medicine, Memphis, 1967—; adj. prof. immunology Miss. Coll., 1977—. Recipient Coll. Am. Pathologists and Am. Soc. Clin. Pathologists award continuing edn., 1976; book collection named in his honor at U. Wis., Madison. Fellow AAAS, Royal Soc. for the Promotion of Health, Am. Acad. Microbiology, Intercontinental Biographical Assn.; mem. Am. Assn. Pathologists and Bacteriologists, Am. Soc. for Exptl. Pathology, Am. Chem. Soc., British, Canadian socs. for immunology, Am. Soc. Microbiology, Internat. Acad. Pathology, Am. Assn. Immunologists, AMA (Physician's recognition award 1969, 75), Am. Inst. Biol. Scis., Am. Soc. Clin. Pathologists, Canadian Soc. Microbiologists, N.Y. Acad. Scis., Soc. for Experimental Biology and Medicine, Societe Francaise d'Immunologie, Reticuloendothelial Soc., Transplantation Soc., Electron Microscopy Soc. Am., Internat. Platform Assn., Am. Assn. for History of Medicine, Sigma Xi, Phi Kappa Phi, Phi Eta Sigma, Alpha Epsilon Delta, Gamma Sigma Epsilon, Beta, Beta, Beta. Episcopalian. Author: Immunology Examination Review Book, 1971, rev. edit., 1975; Introduction to Immunology, 1977. Contbr. articles to profl. jours. Home: 1122 Avon Way Jackson MS 39206 Office: Dept of Pathology University of Miss Medical Center 2500 N State St Jackson MS 39216

CRUSE, ROBERT RIDGELY, chemist; b. Tucson, Aug. 20, 1920; s. Samuel Ridgely and Hellen Gurganus (Patrick) C.; B.S., Antioch Coll., 1942; postgrad. Ohio State U., 1946, U. Ariz., 1951-52, Trinity U., 1956-58; m. Pauline Julia McIntire, Mar. 1, 1947; 1 son, Harold McIntire. Research engr. Battelle Meml. Inst., Columbus, Ohio, 1942-47; real estate broker, owner-developer Los Ranchitos Subdivisions, Tucson, 1947-53; analytical chemist, hydrometallurgist U.S. Bur. Mines, Tucson, 1953-55; indsl. chemist S.W. Research Inst., San Antonio, 1955-61; research chemist Allied Chem. Corp., nitrogen div., Hopewell, Va., 1961-68; research chemist Food Crops Utilization Research Lab., U.S. Dept. Agr., Weslaco, Tex., 1968—. Instr. chemistry Trinity U., San Antonio, 1956-57. Mem. ofcl. election bd. Pima County, Ariz., 1948-55. Fellow Am. Inst. Chemists, A.A.A.S.; mem. Am. Chem. Soc. (abstractor chem. abstracts service 1963—), Lower Rio Grande Valley Hort. Soc., Chemists Club N.Y. Home: 1106 W 3d St Weslaco TX 78596 Office: Mile 3 1/4 E and E State Hwy Box 388 Weslaco TX 78596

CRUSIUS, MILTON WOOD, oil co. exec.; b. Mobile, Ala., May 9, 1922; s. Milton Wood and Georgie G. (Ranew) C.; B.S. in Geology, U. Tex., 1949; m. Lois L. Lovell, June 14, 1947; children—Timothy, John Bryan. Geophysicist, Humble Oil & Refining Co. (now Exxon Co., U.S.A.), Houston, 1949-64, data analyst, 1966-70, tech. writer earth scis., 1970—; geologist and geophysicist Argus Oil Explorations Africa Ltd., Cape Town, S. Africa, 1964-66. Served with USN, 1940-46. Mem. Soc. for Tech. Communication (chmn. Houston chpt. 1974-75), Am. Assn. Petroleum Geologists. Author: (with Dearl T. Russell) Geology of El Rancho Cima, 1963; contbr. articles on geology of S. Africa to profl. jours. Home: 7139 Galleon St Houston TX 77036 Office: 495 South Tower PO Box 2180 Houston TX 77001

CRUSOE, EDWIN EDGAR, IV, master mariner; b. Lakeland, Fla., Mar. 23, 1938; s. Edwin Edgar and Muriel Valerie (Christian) C.; B.S. in Nautical Sci., Calif. Maritime Acad., 1960. Served as lt. j.g. U.S. Navy, 1960-62; served from 3d mate to master U.S. Mcht. Marines, 1962-72; bar and harbour pilot Port of Key West, Fla., 1972—; marine surveyor, cons.; chmn. Monroe County Port Authority Adv. Com.; mem. Key West Port and Transit Authority; pres. Key West Bar Pilots. Past chmn. Monroe County Career Service Council; campaign chmn. Monroe County Democratic Party, 1976; mem. Monroe County Dem. Exec. Com., 1976-78. Mem. Masters, Mates and Pilots, Am., Fla. pilots assns., Propeller Club of Key West (past pres., commendation), Key West C. of C., Nat. Assn. Marine Surveyors. Episcopalian. Clubs: Masons; Shriners; Elks; Arcane Order, Jesters. Author: (poetry) Wanderings, 1970. Home: Route 2 Box 306 Summerland Key FL 33042 Office: PO Box 848 Key West FL 33040

CRUTCHER, DEBORAH GAYLE, speech pathologist, educator; b. Owensboro, Ky., Sept. 5, 1952; d. Robert W. and Juanita M. (Salmon) C.; B.S., Murray (Ky.) State U., 1974, M.S., 1978. Speech pathologist Carroll County public schs., Huntingdon, Tenn., 1974-75; substitute tchr. Marshall County public schs., Benton, Ky., 1976-78; speech pathologist, instr. Murray State U., 1979—; condr. workshops on communication disorders of aging. Project dir. grant on aging Fed. Adminstrn. on Aging, 1979—. Mem. Am. Speech and Hearing Assn. (cert. clin. competence), Ky. Speech and Hearing Assn., Second Voice Club Western Ky. Office: Spl Edn Dept Communication Disorders Murray State U Murray KY 42071

CRUTE, JAMES BYRON, banker; b. Farmville, Va., Mar. 23, 1943; s. James Ligon and Geraldine (Buckles) C.; B.S. in Acctg., U. Richmond, 1970; m. Beatrice Tiller, Apr. 17, 1971; children—Kenneth Byron, Jamie Danielle. Auditor, Peat, Marwick, Mitchell & Co., Richmond, Va., 1970-74; with First and Mchts. Nat. Bank, Richmond, 1974—, asst. v.p., 1975-76, v.p., 1976-78, v.p., controller, 1978—. C.P.A., Va. Mem. Am. Inst. C.P.A.'s, Va. Soc. C.P.A.'s. Home: 1417 Westshire Ln Richmond VA 23233 Office: First and Mchts Nat Bank PO Box 27025 Richmond VA 23261

CRUZ, GILBERT RALPH, historian, educator; b. San Antonio, Dec. 6, 1929; s. Gilbert and Hilaria (Rivas) C.; student Assumption Sem., 1949-55; B.A. in History, St. Mary's U., 1968, M.A., 1970; Ph.D. in Am. History, St. Louis U., 1974; postgrad. Cath. U. Am., summer, 1962; m. Martha Oppert, Nov. 24, 1970; children—Andrés Antonio, Miguel Luis. Mem. faculty St. John's Sem., San Antonio, 1967; asst. prof. Am. history Pan Am U., Edinburg, Tex., 1970-71, 73—; vis. prof. U. Tex., San Antonio, summer 1978; cons. various sch. dists. in Tex., 1971-78. Deanery moderator Cath. Youth Orgn., 1962-64; mem. staff Indian Creek Camp, Boy Scouts Am., Ingram, Tex., 1957, Nat. Philmont Ranch, Cimarron, N.Mex., 1957; bd. dirs. Community Care Center, Kerrville, Tex., 1964. Sr. Fulbright grantee, Colombia, 1979; recipient O'Connor Presidio La Bahia award Sons of Republic of Tex., 1970, 75. Mem. Tex. State Hist. Assn., Am. Studies Assn., Tex. Assn. Coll. Tchrs., So. Tex. Soc. Sci. Tchrs. (dir. 1979-80), Tex. Cath. Hist. Soc., Southwestern Council Latin Am. Studies, Tex. Assn. Chicanos in Higher Edn., Phi Alpha Theta. Democrat. Roman Catholic. Author: Our Lady Queen of the Americas: A Religious Drama on the Historical Events of Guadalupe, 1956; (with Jane Talbot and Edward Simmen) Chicano Bibliography, 1973; (with Martha O. Cruz) A Century of Service: The Catholic Church in the Lower Rio Grande Valley, 1978; contbr. articles to jours. and mags. Home: 401 Driftwood St San Antonio TX 78239 Office: Dept History Pan Am U Edinburg TX 78539

CRUZAN, CHARLES GRANT, physicist; b. Cushing, Okla., Feb. 23, 1912; s. Ulysses Grant and Mamie Amanda (Montgomery) C.; B.S., Okla. State U.. 1934, M.S., 1938; m. Leonore Scott, May 25, 1937; children—Carlyn G., Marletta (Mrs. Raymond Howard Walker), Jo Ann (Mrs. James Charles Smith), Donald C. Asst. mathematician Okla. State U., Stillwater, 1937-38; instr. math. and physics Woodward (Okla.) Jr. Coll., 1938-41; instr. Tech. Schs. USAF, Chanute Field, Ill., 1941-43; with Phillips Petroleum Co., Bartlesville, Okla., 1946-77, chief physicist Patent div., 1947-77. Pres. McKinley Sch. P.T.A., Bartlesville, 1948-49; mem. adv. com. Washington County, Bartlesville, 1973-74; asst. dist. commr. Boy Scouts Am., Bartlesville, Okla., 1967-69. Del. State Rep. Conv., 1971-72. Served to comdr. USNR, 1943-46. Mem. Am. Phys. Soc., Am. Legion (pres. 1955-56, dir. 1950-58), Pi Mu Epsilon, Kappa Delta Pi. Baptist (pres. mens brotherhood 1963-64). Mason (32 deg.), Lion (pres. 1969-70). Clubs: Hillcrest Country; Frank Phillips Mens (Bartlesville, Okla.). Home: 1950 Dewey Bartlesville OK 74003

CRYDER, JERRY LEE, psychotherapist; b. Elberton, Ga., Aug. 2, 1948; s. Royal Glenn and Maebelle (Scott) C.; B.A., U. Ga., 1970, M.S.W., 1973; m. Jean Herlong, June 7, 1970; children—Jeffrey Elliott, Jessica Elizabeth. Dir., Elbert-Madison County Mental Health Center, Elberton, 1973—; pvt. practice psychotherapy, Elberton, 1978—. Mem. Nat. Assn. Social Workers, Ga. Assn. Social Workers. Baptist. Home: Route 1 Box 149 Elberton GA 30635

CUADRANTE, MINERVA R. (MRS. JOSE YOLANDO HERNANDEZ), physician; b. Naga, Phillippines, Oct. 20, 1937; d. Arsenio F. and Mercedes (Relunia) Cuadrante; A.A., U. Santo Tomas, 1956-58, M.D., 1962; m. Jose Yolando Hernandez, Dec. 17, 1966; children—Jay Yolando, Myra Jane, Maureen Juliet. Intern St. Clare's Hosp., Schenectady, 1964-65; resident internal medicine Springfield (Mass.) Hosp., 1965-66, pediatrics Trumbull Meml. Hosp., Warren, Ohio, 1966-68, pathology Allentown (Pa.) Hosp., 1969-70; now pvt. practice, Quincy, Fla. Roman Catholic. Office: 109 N Madison Quincy FL 32351

CUATRECASAS, PEDRO MARTIN, research exec., educator; b. Madrid, Spain, Sept. 27, 1936; s. Jose and Martha C.; came to U.S., 1947, naturalized, 1955; A.B., Washington U., St. Louis, 1958, M.D., 1962; m. Carol Zies, Aug. 15, 1959; children—Paul, Lisa, Diane, Julia. Intern, resident internal medicine Osler Service, Johns Hopkins Hosp., Balt., 1962-64, asst. physician, 1972-75; clin. asso., clin. endocrinology br. NIH, Nat. Inst. Arthritis and Metabolic Diseases, Bethesda, Md., 1964-66, spl. USPHS postdoctoral fellow Lab. Chem. Biology, 1966-67, med. officer, 1967-70; professorial lectr. biochemistry George Washington U. Sch. Medicine, 1967-70; asso. prof. pharmacology and exptl. therapeutics, asso. prof. medicine, dir. div. clin. pharmacology, Burroughs Wellcome prof. clin. pharmacology Johns Hopkins Sch. Medicine, 1970-72, prof. pharmacology and exptl. therapeutics, asso. prof. medicine, 1972-75; v.p. research, devel. and med. Wellcome Research Labs., dir. Burroughs Wellcome Co., Research Triangle Park, N.C., 1975—; adj. prof. Duke, 1975—; adj. prof., mem. adv. com. Cancer Research Program, U. N.C., 1975—. Bd. dirs. Burroughs Wellcome Fund. Recipient John Jacob Abel prize in pharmacology, 1972, Laude prize Pharm. World, 1975. Mem. Am. Soc. Biol. Chemists, Am. Soc. for Pharmacology and Exptl. Therapeutics, Am. Soc. for Clin. Investigation, Am. Fedn. for Clin. Research, Spanish Biochemical Soc., Md. Acad. Scis. (Outstanding Young Scientist of Year 1970), Am. Cancer Soc., Endocrine Soc., Am. Chem. Soc., Am. Diabetes Assn. (Eli Lilly award 1975), Sigma Xi. Democrat. Editor: Receptors and Recognition Series, 1975; Jour. of Solid-Phase Biochemistry, 1975. Mem. editorial bd. Jour. Membrane Biology, 1972, Internat. Jour. Biochemistry, 1972, Molecular and Cellular Endocrinology, 1973, Biochimica Biophysica Acta, 1973. Contbr. articles to profl. jours. Home: 626 Kensington Dr Chapel Hill NC 27514 Office: 3030 Cornwallis Rd Research Triangle Park NC 27709

CUBA, BENJAMIN JAMES, lawyer; b. San Antonio, Dec. 12, 1936; s. Ben and Patricia (Machalek) C.; A.A., Temple Jr. Coll., 1957; B.B.A., U. Tex., 1959; J.D., Baylor U., 1963; m. Bernadette Theresa Haney, Sept. 4, 1964; children—Benjamin Courtney, Tristan Konrad. Admitted to Tex. bar, 1964, U.S. Supreme Ct. bar, 1978; mem. firm Benjamin J. Cuba, P.C., and predecessor firms, Temple, Tex., 1964—. Dir. Temple Savs. Assn. Mem. Bell, Lampasas and Mills Counties Bar Assn. (pres. 1973-74), Tex. Assn. Bank Counsel, Tex. Assn. Savs. and Loan Counsel, Tex. Bar Found., State Bar Tex., Tex. Assn. Def. Counsel, Temple C. of C., Phi Delta Phi. Office: PO Box 1003 Temple TX 76501

CUCCO, MICHAEL A., advt. agy. exec.; b. Berea, Ohio, June 15, 1948; s. Albert and Patricia Ann (Leslie) C.; B.S. in Polit. Sci., Golden Gate U., 1972; m. Claudia Michaud, June 20, 1979. Staff cons. Payne-Maxie, San Francisco, 1972-74; acct. exec. Abelson-Frankel, Chgo., 1974-76; v.p. mktg. The William Lacy Co., Austin, Tex., 1976-77; pres. Macom, Inc., Austin, 1977—; cons. in field. Mem. Am. Mktg. Assn. (v.p. Austin chpt. 1979). Home: 4810 Canyon Bend Circle Austin TX 78735 Office: 1800 Austin National Bank Tower Austin TX 78701

CUDAHY, WILLIAM BREWER, banker; b. Chgo., Jan. 23, 1912; s. Edward Ignatius and Leonore (Brewer) C.; B.A. magna cum laude, Harvard U., 1934; J.D., Northwestern U., 1937; m. Evelyn Wilkinson, Apr. 5, 1951; children—Joseph Michael, Victoria Fenton. Sec., dir. Callaghan & Co., Chgo., 1937-41; asst. sec. No. Trust Co., Chgo., 1945-51; v.p. Am. Nat. Bank & Trust Co., Chgo., 1951-60; dir. 1st Nat. Bank in Palm Beach (Fla.), Steego Corp., West Palm Beach; mayor Palm Beach, 1977-78. Served as lt. USCG, 1941-45; ETO, PTO. Named to Coll. Sailing Hall of Fame. Mem. Nat. Fedn. Fin. Analysts. Republican. Episcopalian. Clubs: Everglades (dir.), Bath and Tennis (dir.) (Palm Beach). Home: 742 Slope Trail Palm Beach FL 33480

CUESTAS, RAUL ANTONIO, JR., physician; b. Boquete, Panama, Apr. 13, 1946; came to U.S., 1962; s. Raul Antonio and Josefa Maria (Gomez) C.; B.A., U. Minn., 1967, Ph.D., 1972, M.D., 1972; m. Yolanda Cuestas; children—Luis, Marco. Intern, U. Minn. Hosps., Mpls., 1972-73, resident, 1973-74, fellow in neonatology, 1974-76; practice medicine specializing in neonatology, Shreveport, La., 1977—; mem. staff Willis-Knighton Hosp.; mem. staff, dir. nurseries Schumbert Med. Center, Shreveport, 1977—; asst. prof. pediatrics U. Minn., Mpls., 1976-77. Diplomate Am. Bd. Pediatrics. Fellow Am. Acad. Pediatrics. Home: 836 Sweetbriar St Shreveport LA 71105 Office: 915 Margaret Pl Shreveport LA 71101

CULBERSON, JAMES OLIN, educator; b. Shannon, Ga., Apr. 5, 1932; s. John Thompson and Willie Mae (Colston) C.; B.S., Bob Jones U., 1953; M.A., Columbia Bible Coll., 1957; M. Ed., U. S.C., 1960; Ed.D. (Counseling fellow), U. Ga., 1970; m. Janice May Jaquith, Jan. 11, 1958; children—Pamela May, John Clifford, Sarah Elizabeth, James Olin Jr. Circulation mgr. Sword Pubs., Wheaton, Ill., 1957-58, gen. mgr., 1958-59; tchr., prin. Bur. Indian Affairs, Juneau, Alaska, 1960-62; tchr. pub. high sch. Floyd County, Ga., 1963-67; counselor pub. schs. Gordon County, Ga., 1968-69; asso. prof. counseling and guidance U. So. Miss., Hattiesburg, 1970-75, prof. counseling psychology, 1976—, dir. Social and Rehab. Services program, 1972—. Cons. to Pub. Services Careers Workshop, Miss., 1971, Bur. Hearings and Appeals, HEW, Miss., 1975—, Ednl. Professions Devel. Act Vocat. Workshop, Miss., 1973. Chmn., Com. Exceptional Children, Gordon County, Ga., 1968. Mem. Region IV Rehab. Educator's Council, 1972—. Served with AUS, 1953-55. Recipient Excellence in Teaching award U. So. Miss., 1975. Mem. Am., Miss. Personnel and Guidance Assns., Am. Psychol. Assn., Nat. Rehab. Counseling Assn., Nat. Vocat. Guidance Assn., Assn. for Counselor Edn. and Supervision, Phi Delta Kappa, Kappa Delta Pi. Baptist. Contbr. articles to profl. jours. Home: 207 Beverly Ln Hattiesburg MS 39401

CULBERSON, RANDALL EDWARD, nuclear engr.; b. Coral Gables, Fla., Apr. 25, 1952; s. Reid Taylor and Betty Lou (Hands) C.; A.A., Miami Dade Jr. Coll., 1972; B.S.E.E. summa cum laude, U. Fla., 1974. Designer, Donald Weeks & Assos., Miami, Fla., 1971-72; reactor engr. Va. Electric & Power Co., Surry, 1976—. Va. High Sch. Football and Soccer ofcl.; NCAA and U.S. Soccer Fedn. referee. Served with USN, 1974-76. Mem. Nat. Soc. Profl. Engrs., IEEE, Fla. Engring. Soc., Am. Nuclear Soc., United Soccer Fedn. Ofcl. Assn., Hampton Roads Jaycees (dir.), Tutoring Soc., Eta Kappa Nu. Republican. Baptist. Contbr. articles on design of mobile nuclear generating plant to profl. jours. Home: 966-2 Marcus Dr Newport News VA 23602 Office: Surry Nuclear Power Station PO Box 315 Surry VA 23883

CULBERTSON, JOHN DENNIS, counselor; b. Greenville, S.C., Aug. 18, 1947; s. John Bolt and Ellie (Barbare) C.; B.S., U. S.C., 1969; M.S. (scholar), N.D. State U., 1978; m. Eunice Virginia Watson, June 7, 1969; children—John David, Ellen Barbare. Commd. 2d lt. U.S. Air Force, 1969, advanced through grades to capt., 1973; squadron exec. officer Minot AFB, N.D., 1975-77, ret., 1977; grad. asst. U. N.D., Grand Forks, 1978; grad. asst., intern The Counseling Center, U. S.C., Columbia, 1978-79; pvt. practice counseling, Columbia, 1979; discussion leader students, staff, faculty. Vol. group leader Parenting Skills, Columbia Area Council on Child Abuse. Mem. Am. Personnel and Guidance Assn., S.C. Personnel and Guidance Assn., Am. Sch. Counselors Assn., S.C. Sch. Counselors Assn., Assn. for Specialists in Group Work, S.C. Assn. for Measurement and Evaluation in Guidance, Assn. for Non-White Concerns in Personnel and Guidance, S.C. Assn. for Non-White Concerns in Personnel and Guidance, NEA, S.C. Edn. Assn., Am. Legion, others. Methodist. Home: 1886 Westmoreland Dr Florence SC 29501

CULBERTSON, KATHERYN CAMPBELL, lawyer, state ofcl.; b. Tom's Creek, Va., Aug. 14, 1920; d. Robert Fugate and Mary E.V. Campbell (Leonard) Culbertson; B.S., East Tenn. State U., 1940; B.S. in L.S., George Peabody Library Sch., 1942; J.D., YMCA Night Law Sch., 1968. Librarian, Bur. Ships Tech. Library, U.S. Navy Dept., Washington, 1945-49, 51-53; librarian Lincoln Elementary Sch., Kingsport, Tenn., 1949-50, 50-51; librarian Regional Library, Tenn. State Library and Archives, Johnson City, 1953-61; dir. extension services library Met. Govt. Nashville and Davidson County, 1961-71; Tenn. state librarian and archivist, 1972—; admitted to Tenn. bar, 1969; since practiced in Nashville. Mem. library com. Pres.'s Com. Employment of Handicapped, 1966—; mem. library com. Nat. Bus. and Profl. Women's Found., 1968-70; pres. Tenn. Fedn. Bus. and Profl. Women's Clubs, Inc., 1974-75. Mem. Am., Tenn. bar assns., Am., Southeastern, Tenn. library assns., D.A.R. Republican. Clubs: Zonta, Business and Professional Women's (pres. 1970-71) (Nashville). Contbr. to Ency. of Edn. Home: 800 Glen Leven Dr Nashville TN 37204 Office: 403 7th Ave N Nashville TN 37219

CULBERTSON, RICHARD DONNELL, lawyer, state govt. ofcl.; b. San Antonio, July 26, 1945; s. Harvey Rex and Loyce Linnell (du Menil) C.; B.A., Tex. Christian U., 1967; postgrad. U. Tex. Law Sch., 1967-69, U. Tex., Arlington, 1972-79. Admitted to Tex. bar, 1970; individual practice law, Fort Worth, 1970-74; atty., heading child support collection Tex. Dept. Human Resources, Fort Worth, 1974—. Candidate, Tarrant County Water Bd., 1971, 72, 74. Mem. Am. Bar Assn., Tex. Bar Assn., Fort Worth-Tarrant County Bar Assn., Assn. Trial Lawyers of Am., Fort Worth-Tarrant County Young Lawyers, Tex. Archaeol. Assn., Tex. Hist. Assn., Fort Worth Jaycees. Roman Catholic. Clubs: Central Cath. (pres. 1977-79), Third Order St. Francis, K.C. Contbr. articles to geneal. publs. Home: 6428 Arthur Dr Fort Worth TX 76134 Office: 1322 Electric Service Bldg Fort Worth TX 76102 also Tex Dept Human Resources 308 E 4th St Fort Worth TX 76102

CULBERTSON, THOMAS DALE, JR., architect; b. St. Ignatius, Mont., Sept. 5, 1938; s. Thomas Dale and Virginia (Ames) C.; B.S., Va. Poly. Inst., 1962, M.Urban Planning, 1964; married; children—Tracy, Brandy. Instr. architecture Va. Poly. Inst. and State U., Blacksburg, 1963-64; staff Ward & Hall, Springfield, Va., 1964-69; staff P. Salditt & Assos., McLean, Va., 1969-73; individual practice architecture, Spotsylvania, Va., 1973—. Bd. dirs. Spotsylvania chpt. ARC. Registered architect, D.C., Md., Va. Mem. AIA. Mormon. Office: PO Box 366 Spotsylvania VA 22553

CULBERTSON, WALTER LEROY, petroleum co. exec.; b. Dederick, Mo., July 29, 1918; s. Alfred and Ethel Ida (Belong) C.; B.S.M.E., Kans. State U., 1939; m. Wanda Marian Atkins, Sept. 30, 1940; children—Philip, Robert. With Phillips Petroleum Co., 1939—, v.p., Bartlesville, Okla., 1964-78, sr. v.p. corp. planning and budgeting, Bartlesville, 1978—. Mem. ASME, Nat. Soc. Profl. Engrs., Am. Inst. Chem. Engrs. Republican. Mem. Christian Ch. (Disciples of Christ). Club: Bartlesville Hillcrest Country.

CULBRETH, HENRY WILSON, clergyman; b. Madison County, Tex., Sept. 9, 1919; s. Henry and Mada Olivia (Whitten) C.; B.A., Assemblies of God Grad. Sch., Springfield, Mo., 1975, M.A., 1976; m. Verta Ercil Janway, Sept. 15, 1943; children—Henry Allen, Cecil Wayne, Timmie Ray, Daniel Richard. Ordained to ministry, Assemblies of God Ch., 1943; pastor chs., 1943-58; sec.-treas. Ark. Dist. Assemblies of God, 1958-69; missionary, Philippines, 1969-74; dean of men Am. Indian Bible Inst., Phoenix, 1974-75; mem. faculty Trinity Bible Inst., Ellendale, N.D., 1975-77; exec. dir. Teen Challenge of Ark., Inc., Little Rock, 1977—. Mem. Internat. Soc. Gen. Semantics. Address: 6804 W 34th St Little Rock AR 72204

CULBRETH, RAYWARD BILL, clergyman; b. Columbia, Ala., Dec. 17, 1921; s. Jesse A. and Ettie (Webb) C.; A.B., Howard Coll., 1944; B.D., So. Bapt. Theol. Sem., 1947, Th.M., 1948, Th.D., 1951; m. Ella Florine Eaton, June 3, 1943; children—Karen F., Randall E. Ordained to ministry Baptist Ch., 1942; pastor, Choccolocco, Ala., 1942-44, New Haven, Ky., 1945-47, Clermont, Ky., 1947-49, First Bapt. Ch., Miami, Fla., 1949-58, Miami Springs (Fla.) Bapt. Ch., 1958-61, Met. Bapt. Ch., Washington, 1961-66, Huffman Bapt. Ch., Birmingham, 1966-72, First Bapt. Ch., South Miami, 1972-77, Westwood Bapt. Ch., Birmingham, 1977—. Moderator Miami (Fla.) Bapt. Assn., 1957; mem. Christian life commn. So. Bapt. Conv., 1958-61, mem. Sunday Sch. Bd., 1962-66; pres. D.C. Pastor's Conf., 1966; mem. Ala. Bd. Missions, 1967-72; mem. exec. bd., chmn. evangelism com. Birmingham Bapt. Assn., 1968; chmn. Evangelism com. Miami Bapt. Assn., 1973-74. Chmn. bd. Cook Springs Home for Sr. Citizens 1968-72. Recipient Freedoms Found. Valley Forge Freedom award, 1962. Address: 2349 Forrestdale Blvd Birmingham AL 35214

CULL, JOHN G., JR., psychologist, author; b. Venice, Ill., Nov. 9, 1934; s. John G. and Geneva M. (Crippen) C.; B.S. with distinction, Tex. A. and M. U., 1959, Ed.M. in Counseling, 1960; Ph.D. in Clin. Psychology, (HEW scholar), Tex. Tech. U., 1967; m. Linda Abbott, June 29, 1957; children—David, Dana, Rebecca. Teaching asst. dept. end. and psychology Tex. A. and M. U., College Station, 1959-60; lectr. (part-time) dept. psychology, Tex. Tech. U., Lubbock, 1961-64; rehab. counselor, lectr.; Tex. Inst. for Rehab. and Research, Baylor U. Coll. of Medicine, Houston, 1962-64; staff psychologist South Plains Adult Mental Health Clinic, Lubbock, 1964-65; asst. commr. State Dept. Vocat. Rehab., Richmond, Va., 1965-66; asso. prof. dept. rehab. counseling Sch. of Community Services, Va. Commonwealth U., Richmond, 1966-72, dir. regional counselor tng. program, 1966-72, prof., 1972-77, dir. regional continuing edn. program, 1972-77, prof. dept. rehab. counseling, 1977; adj. prof. psychology and edn., U. Va., 1971-72; prof. clin. counseling, psychology and guidance dept. Our Lady of Lake U. San Antonio, 1977—; cons. in program planning and devel. to rehab. agys. and mental retardation commns. in various states, 1968—; tech. cons. to Rehab. Services Adminstrn., HEW, 1968—; pvt. practice clin. psychology, Tex., 1977—; mem. Nat. Task Force on Welfare Reform and Rehab. Planning, HEW, 1972-73; panel moderator rehab. Warsaw, Poland, 1978. Va. del. to White House Conf. on Aging, Washington, 1972; mem. Criminal Justice Council of Central Shenandoah Valley, Staunton, Va., 1972-75; chmn. Human Resources Planning Council, Central Shenandoah Valley (Va.), 1971-74; chmn. State Com. on Employment, Retirement and Income, Gov.'s Post-White House Conf. on Aging, Richmond, Va., 1972-73; mem. advisory bd. Regional Rehab. Research Inst., U. Md., 1968-70; bd. dirs. Valley Workshops, Inc., pres., 1970-73. Served with USNR, 1951-59, 64-66. Recipient Outstanding Community Achievement award Valley Workshops, Inc., 1973, Community Service award Sara Bonwell Hudgins Regional Center, 1975, Contributions to Rehab. award U. Tel-Aviv Sch. Medicine, 1977, Community Service award Peninsular Assn. for Retarded Children, 1976; named Adm. in Tex. Navy, 1976. Mem. Am. Psychol. Assn., Internat. Assn. of Applied Psychology, Internat. Assn. of Rehab. Facilities (mem. edn. and tng. com. 1971-72), Council of Rehab. Edn., Am. Personnel and Guidance Assn., Am. Correctional Assn., Nat. Rehab. Assn., Am. Assn. of Workers for the Blind (Nat. citation 1975), Nat. Assn. for Retarded Citizens, AAAS. Author sixty books on counseling, rehab. and psychology, latest being: (with R.E. Hardy) Group Counseling and Therapy Techniques in Special Settings, 1974, Hemingway: A Psychological Portrait, 1977, Social and Rehabilitation Services for the Blind, 1972, Physical Medicine and Rehabilitation Techniques in Spinal Cord Injury, 1977; contbr. numerous articles and chpts. to books in field; editor: Am. Lecture Series in Social and Rehab. Psychology, 1972—. Office: 411 SW 24th St San Antonio TX 78285

CULLEN, GEORGE EDWARD, JR., educator; b. Orange, Mass., Mar. 29, 1926; s. George Edward and Helen Rita (Congdon) C.; A.A., Boston U., 1949, B.S. in Journalism, 1951; M.S. in Journalism, W.Va. U., 1965, Ph.D., 1979; m. Hester Allen Nock, Apr. 30, 1955; children—Helen, Laura, Mary, George Edward III. Asst. prof. aerospace studies W.Va. U., Morgantown, 1961-65; mem. faculty Hampton (Va.) Inst., 1970—, asso. prof. mass media arts, 1979—. Served with USAAF, 1944-46, USAF, 1951-69. Recipient Cert. of Merit, Spl. award for outstanding service Hampton Edn. Assn., 1970; State Dept. grantee, Ghana, 1975, So. Fellowships Fund fellow, 1978-79. Mem. Assn. Edn. in Journalism, Am. Legion, Sigma Delta Chi (life), Kappa Tau Alpha. Author: Talking to a Whirlwind, 1980; editor Airlifter mag., 1956-58, Profiles in Communication mag., 1971. Home: 115 Culotta Dr Hampton VA 23666 Office: Box 6432 Hampton Inst Hampton VA 23668

CULLER, FRED BENJAMIN, JR., psychologist; b. High Point, N.C., Oct. 14, 1949; s. Fred Benjamin and Vivian Baxine (Beck) C.; A.B., High Point Coll., 1971; M.A., E. Carolina U., 1972; m. Linda Marie Fox, Mar. 9, 1977. Chmn. dept. psychology Fayetteville (N.C.) Tech. Inst., 1973—. Mem. Am., N.C. psychol. assns., NEA, N.C. Assn. Edn., N.C. Community Coll. Social Sci. Instrs. Assn. (dir. 1975—). Democrat. Baptist. Home: 1214 Ward's Ferry Rd Lynchburg VA 24502 Office: PO Box 5236 Fayetteville NC 28303

CULLINANE, JOSEPH, advt. and pub. relations exec.; b. Boston, June 26, 1927; s. Joseph P. and Marie (McGuire) C.; B.S., Suffolk U., 1950; m. Pearl Cerwonka, Mar. 2, 1958; children—Glen, Michael, Scott. Reporter Boston Record-Am., 1947-52; publicity dir. Westinghouse Broadcasting Co., Boston, 1952-58; advt./pub. relations dir. CBS Radio, Boston, 1958-67; pub. relations dir. Bendix Corp. Launch Support div., Kennedy Space Center, Fla., 1965-67, space div. Rockwell Internat., Kennedy Space Center, 1967-70; mgr. corp. pub. affairs Rockwell Internat., Pitts., 1970-74, dir. communications Rockwell-Collins, Dallas, 1974—. Cons. network news ABC-TV, Cape Kennedy AF Sta., Fla., 1965-67. Tchr. Pitts. Jr. Achievement, 1968; pub. relations aide Internat. Youth Sci. Tour, Kennedy Space Center, 1973; pub. relations dir. Nat. Alliance Businessmen, Pa., 1969-70. Served with USNR 1944-46; PTO. Mem. Aviation and Space Writers Assn., Space Pioneers Assn., Pub. Relations Soc. Am. (dir. Kennedy Space Center 1968-69), Tex. Pub. Relations Assn. (Best of Tex. trade show award 1978), Pub. Affairs Council Washington. Club: Press (Dallas). Office: Rockwell-Collins 1200 N Alma Rd Dallas TX 75207

CULLISON, WILLIAM LESTER, assn. exec.; b. Balt., Aug. 26, 1931; s. William Lester and Margaret Elizabeth (Quick) C.; B.S., U.S. Mcht. Marine Acad., 1953; LL.B., LaSalle Extension U., 1968; M.B.A., Fla. Atlantic U., 1975; m. Lorraine Stella Wirtz, Dec. 24, 1953; 1 dau., Beth Lynn. Research coordinator Am. Petroleum Inst., 1957-60, asst. dir. sci. and tech., 1960-68; tech. sec. TAPPI, Atlanta, 1968-70, dir. tech. ops. 1970—, treas., 1975—; book reviewer for Soc. Research Adminstrs. Served with USNR, 1954-55. Mem. ASME, Am. Soc. Assn. Execs. (cert. assn. exec.), Ga. Soc. Assn. Execs. (pres.). Republican. Episcopalian. Mason (Shriner). Home: 1905 Six Branches Dr Roswell GA 30076 Office: 1 Dunwoody Park Atlanta GA 30338

CULP, DELOS POE, univ. pres. emeritus, constrn. co. exec.; b. Clanton, Ala., July 26, 1911; s. Joseph Daniel and Lela (Popwell) C.; student Jacksonville State Coll., 1932-34; B.S., Auburn U., 1937, M.S., 1940; Ed.D., Columbia, 1949; m. Martha Edwardine Street, Dec. 23, 1934; children—Martha Jean, James David, John Stephen. Tchr., prin. Chilton, Butler counties, Ala., 1935-42; supt. Chilton County Schs., Ala., 1942-46; supr. pub. sch. trans., asst. dir. div. adminstrn. and finance State Dept. Edn., Montgomery, Ala., 1946-51; prof. edn. Ala. Polytech. Inst., 1951-54; pres. Livingston State Coll., 1954-63; pres. Ala. Coll., Montevallo, 1963-67; pres. E. Tenn. State U., Johnson City, 1967-77, pres. emeritus, 1977—; exec. v.p. Powell Constrn. Co., 1977—. Dir. First Peoples Bank. Mem. com. on studies Am. Assn. State Colls. and Univs., 1970—. Chmn. Nat. Commn. on Safety Edn., 1965—; mem. survey team for Philippine Sch. Bur. Survey, 1959-60; mem bd. advisers Meth. Children's Home, Selma, Ala.; mem. nat. com. on exploring Boy Scouts Am., 1971—. Mem. Ala. Edn. Commn. (exec. dir. 1957-59), Ala. Edn. Assn. (chmn. policies commn. 1965—), Ala. Acad. Sci., Am. Assn. Sch. Adminstrs., Ala. Hist. Assn., Kappa Delta Pi, Kappa Phi Kappa, Phi Delta Kappa, Phi Kappa Phi. Democrat. Methodist. Rotarian. Home: 903 Beech Dr Johnson City TN 37601

CULP, JAMES FRANKLIN, Realtor, appraiser, counselor; b. Temple, Tex., Feb. 14, 1918; s. Reuben Owen and Sadie (Hunt) C.; B.B.A., U. Tex., Austin, 1939; m. Robbie Walker, Sept. 1, 1942; children—Joan Culp Shinkle, James Franklin. Owner, Culp Real Estate, Temple, 1939—. Served with USNR, 1942-46. Mem. Tex. Assn. Realtors (v.p. 1952), Am. Inst. Real Estate Appraisers (v.p. 1971-72, gov. council 1968-70), Am. Soc. Farm Mgrs. and Real Estate Appraisers, Am. Soc. Real Estate Counselors, Temple Bd. Realtors (pres. 1949-50, 53-54), Sigma Alpha Epsilon. Methodist (steward 1950-58). Home: 1408 N 13th St Temple TX 76501 Office: 13 W Central St Temple TX 76501

CULP, MARTHA EDWARDINE STREET (MRS. DELOS POE CULP), former educator, civic worker; b. Gadsden, Ala., Nov. 4, 1915; d. Alonzo Cranford and Mattie (Miller) Street; student Jacksonville State Coll., 1932-34; B.S., Auburn U., 1940; postgrad. Columbia U., 1948; m. Delos Poe Culp, Dec. 23, 1934; children—Martha Jean Culp Flanigan, James David, John Stephen. Tchr. elementary grades, Ala. schs., 1934-42; sec. to sch. supt. Chilton County, Ala., 1942-45; tchr. pub. Kindergarten, Tappan, N.Y., 1948-49; tchr., Marbury, Ala., 1950-51, Auburn, Ala., 1952-53; coll. registrar Livingston U., 1957-63. Past bd. dirs. Easter Seal Soc. for Crippled Children and Adults; bd. dirs. East Tenn. Council for Hearing Impaired, Methodist Ch., Washington County Assn. for Handicapped, Carroll Reece Mus., United Way; past chmn. Tenn. Developmental Disabilities Adv. Council, 1975-78; charter mem. Unaka Com.; mem. admissions bd. Greene Valley Devel. Center; mem. Inter-Agy. for Handicapped. Recipient Outstanding Service award Easter Seal Soc., 1975. Mem. D.A.R. (regent 1974-77), UDC (state 2d v.p.), Nat. League Am. Pen Women, Johnson City Area C. of C. (past pres. women's div., state dir., Outstanding Mem. award 1973), Watauga Valley Art League (charter), Delta Kappa Gamma, Kappa Delta Pi. Clubs: Faculty Women's (past pres.); Monday; Music. Contbr. articles to newspapers and mags.; artist, speaker. Home: 903 Beech Dr Johnson City TN 37601

CULP, WILLIAM COMBS, radiologist; b. McAlester, Okla., Sept. 7, 1942; s. Chesley Key and Irma Lucille (Combs) C.; M.D., U. Okla., 1967; m. Theresa Anthony, July, 1966; children—Jenniffer Lynette, William Combs, Laura Susanne, Thomas Allen. Intern, U. Okla., 1967-68; resident U. Tex., 1971-74; practice medicine specializing in diagnostic radiology, Ft. Smith, Ark., 1974—; chief radiology St. Edwards Med. Center, Ft. Smith, 1978—; asst. clin. prof. U. Ark. Pres., Ft. Smith Symphony Assn., 1978-79. Served with USCG, 1968-70. Named U.S. nat. champion Catalina 22 Sailboat, 1978. Mem. Am. Coll. Radiology, Cooley Soc., So. Med. Assn., AMA, Radiol. Soc. N.Am., U.S. Yacht Racing Union. Methodist. Club: Galveston Yacht. Author: Shallow Water Sailing, 1976; contbr. articles to profl. jours. Office: 318 N Greenwood St Fort Smith AR 72907

CULPEPPER, JOHN CECIL, JR., real estate exec.; b. Cameron, Tex., Dec. 29, 1936; s. John Cecil and Mary Lake (Henderson) C.; LL.B., J.D., U. Tex., Austin, 1963; m. Mary Ann Massengale, Aug. 12, 1961; 1 son, John Cecil, III. Pres., Culpepper Realty Co., College Station, Tex., 1963—; owner, mgr. Culpepper Properties, College Station, 1963—; admitted to Tex. bar, 1963; mem. faculty U. of Shopping Center; chmn. bd. Homestead Savs. and Loan Assn., College Station; dir. First Bank and Trust Co., Bryan, Tex. Bd. dirs. U. Tex. Sch. Law, 1964-67. Licensed real estate broker, Tex. Mem. Internat. Council Shopping Centers. Club: Pope and Young (1st v.p.). Asso. editor Tex. Law Rev., 1962-63, life mem., 1975—. Home: 2701 Burton St Bryan TX 77801 Office: PO Drawer JC College Station TX 77840

CULPEPPER, MILTON IRVING, JR., lawyer; b. Meridian, Miss., June 14, 1929; s. Milton Irving and Margaret Medora (Brown) C.; student Spring Hill Coll., 1946-48, U. Houston, 1953-54, S. Tex. Law Sch., 1955; LL.B., Cumberland Sch. Law, 1969; m. Betty Jean Wimpee, June 4, 1949; children—Michael Irving, Donna Gene, Margaret Jane. Admitted to Ala. bar, 1969; facilities mgr. Cities Service Oil Co., Birmingham, Ala., 1955-69; legal counsel and asst. to chmn. dept. surgery U. Ala., Birmingham, 1969—, instr., 1971—, lobbyist to Ala. Legis., 1971; asso. legal counsel and asst. to pres. U. Ala. Health Services Found., Birmingham, 1973—, sec. 1973—, treas., 1973, mem. fin. com., 1974—, now spl. asst. to chmn., legal counsel; spl. lectr. in hosp. adminstrn. Sch. Community and Allied Health Resources, 1972-74; cons. Health Care Adminstrn., 1972-74. Area chmn. oil industry Community Chest Dr., 1962. Served with USNR, 1947-52. Recipient Meritorious Service award Sigma Delta Kappa, 1968, Book award Lawyers Coop. Admiralty, 1968. Mem. Am., Ala., Birmingham bar assns., Nat. Health Lawyers Assn., Am. Judicature Soc., Am. Mgmt. Assn., Am. Soc. Law and Medicine, Birmingham C. of C. (health services com. 1977-78), Relay House. Republican. Baptist (trustee local ch. 1969-70, chmn. fin. com. 1969-70). Club: Altadena Valley Golf and Country (bd. govs.). Home: 2504 Woodmeadow Pl Birmingham AL 35216 Office: 1901 7th Ave S Birmingham AL 35294

CULPEPPER, WALTER EDMUND, obstetrician and gynecologist; b. Shreveport, La., July 6, 1935; s. W.J. and Vadna (Burkett) C.; M.D., La. State U., 1960; m. Carolyn Owens, June 28, 1957; children—Walter Edmund, Brian Scott, Clint Alan. Intern, Confederate Meml. Med. Center, Shreveport, 1960-61; resident in obstetrics and gynecology St. Thomas Hosp., Vanderbilt U. Hosp., Nashville, 1961-64; practice medicine specializing in obstetrics and gynecology, Rosenberg, Tex., 1966—; mem. staff Polly Ryon Hosp.; health officer Fort Bend County, 1972—. Served with M.C., U.S. Army, 1964-66. Diplomate Am. Bd. Obstetrics and Gynecology. Fellow Am. Coll. Obstetricians and Gynecologists. Democrat. Methodist. Home: 500 Bayou Dr Richmond TX 77469 Office: 5180 Ave H Rosenberg TX 77471

CULVERHOUSE, HUGH FRANKLIN, lawyer, football team owner; b. Birmingham, Ala., Feb. 20, 1919; s. Harry Georg and Grace Mae (Daniel) C.; B.S., U. Ala., 1941, LL.B., 1947; m. Joy McCann, Nov. 14, 1942; children—Gay Culverhouse Chapman, Hugh Franklin. Admitted to Fla. bar, 1955, Ala. bar, 1947; asst. atty gen. State of Ala., Montgomery, 1947-49; spl. atty. asst. regional counsel Office of Chief Counsel IRS, Atlanta and Jacksonville, Fla., 1949-56; mem. firm Culverhouse, Tomlinson, Mills and Anderson, and predecessors, Jacksonville and Miami, Fla., 1956—, now sr. partner; pres., majority owner Tampa Bay Buccaneers, Nat. Football League, Tampa, Fla., 1974—; v.p., dir. Port Everglades Steel Corp.; co-owner, pres., dir. Miami Internat. Mdse. Mart, Inc.; co-owner v.p., dir. Mode, Inc., Housing Investment Corp.; dir. Host Internat., Inc., Gator Distbrs., Inc., Barnett-Winston Co., Tampa Electric Co., Major Realty Corp., Cator Trailers Corp., George Washington Corp., McMillen Corp., Barnett Banks of Fla., Inc., Peninsular Life Ins. Co.; partner, owner, developer various real estate projects, Fla., Ind., Ohio; mem. faculty U. Ala. Sch. Bus. Adminstrn. Co-founder, 1st pres. Family Consultation Service, Jacksonville; vice chmn. bd. trustees Jacksonville U.; mem. bd. visitors Coll. Commerce and Bus. Adminstrn., U. Ala.; del., U.S. Ambassador 1976 Winter Olympics, Innsbruck, Austria; active United Fund of Jacksonville. Served with USAAF, 1941-46, USAF, 1951-53. Mem. Am. Judicature Soc., Am., Ala., Fla., Dade County, Birmingham, Miami, Jacksonville (chmn. tax sect. 1957-59) bar assns. Republican. Episcopalian. Clubs: Timuquana, Fla. Yacht, River, Univ. (Jacksonville); Indian Creek County, LaGorce Country, Surf, Jockey, Palm Bay (Miami); Ponte Vedra (Ponte Vedra Beach, Fla.); Univ., Palm Ceia Golf and Country (Tampa). Contbr. articles to legal jours. Office: 655 Florida Bank Bldg Jacksonville FL 32202

CUMBIE, CALVIN ARTIMUS, univ. adminstr.; b. Athens, Tex., July 19, 1922; s. Artimus and Rubie (Richardson) C.; B.A., North Tex. State U., 1943, M.A., 1948; B.S., Tex. Christian U., 1953, M.Ed., 1951; grad. U.S. Army Command and Gen. Staff Coll., 1973, Indsl. Coll. Armed Forces, 1975. Tchr., San Marcos Mil. Acad., 1946-47; instr. Tex. Mil. Coll., 1947-49; asst. registrar Tex. Christian U., 1949-54, registrar, 1954—. Served to col. AUS, 1942. Recipient Valuable Alumnus award Tex. Christian U., 1973; Meritorious Service award Selective Service System, 1977. Mem. Mil. Order World Wars, Assn. U.S. Army, Res. Officers Assn., Ret. Officers Assn., Am. (pres. 1972-73), Tex. (pres. 1962-63), So. (pres. 1968-69, Distinguished Service award 1969) assns. collegiate registrars and admissions officers, Assn. Tex. Colls. and Univs. (pres. div. dirs. and deans supplemental programs 1960-61), North Tex. State U., Tex. Christian U. (sec. 1962-63) ex-student assns., Phi Delta Kappa, Alpha Phi Omega, Pi Omega Pi, Alpha Sigma Lambda. Baptist. Club: Rotary. Home: 3141 Cockrell Ave Fort Worth TX 76109 Office: Sadler Hall Tex Christian U Fort Worth TX 76129

CUMBIE, MICHAEL HOWARD, ins. co. exec.; b. Hope, Ark., Oct. 9, 1947; s. Howard Franklin and Pauline Ruth (Burns) C.; A.A., American River Jr. Coll., Sacramento, 1974; B.S., U. Ark., 1977; m. Aven Gene Youmans, Aug. 28, 1977; 1 son, Matthew Howard. Vice pres. data processing Mother Lode Bank, Placerville, Calif., 1969-74; ops. mgr., pilot Placerville Mcpl. Airport, 1975; computer systems analyst, Fayetteville, Ark., 1977-78; life underwriter Lincoln Nat. Life Ins. Co., Fayetteville, 1978—. Served with USMC, 1968-69. Registered rep. Nat. Assn. Securities Dealers. Mem. N.W. Ark. Assn. Life Underwriters, N.W. Ark. Estate Planning Council, Fayetteville Jaycees. Republican. Lutheran. Office: Lincoln Nat Life Ins Co PO Box 1403 Suite 401 1st Pl Fayetteville AR 72701

CUMBIE, RICHARD ORLAND, hosp. adminstr.; b. Duncan, Okla., June 8, 1934; s. Orland Wade and Lorene (Boles) C.; B.S. in Edn., E. Central Okla. State U., 1963; B.S., Okla. Bapt. U., 1969; m. Nancy Jane Bryant, Feb. 10, 1957; children—Kenneth Orland, Janice Lynn. Adminstr. Wetumka (Okla.) Gen. Hosp., 1966-70, Community Hosp., Elk City, Okla., 1970-76, Afton (Okla.) Hosp. Authority, 1976-77, E.P. Clapper Meml. Med. Center, Waynoka, Okla., 1977—; project dir. Freedom Health Center. Mem. Health Care Council, Swoda, 1973-76. Served with U.S. Army, 1957-59. Mem. Okla. Hosp. Fin. Mgmt. Assn., Okla. Hosp. Assn. Baptist. Home: PO Box 164 Waynoka OK 73860 Office: 500 S Nickerson St Waynoka OK 73860

CUMERFORD, WILLIAM RICHARD, fund raising pub. relations exec.; b. Stroudsburg, Pa., Dec. 3, 1916; s. Reginald Read and Helen (Ryall) C.; student R.I. State U., 1935; B.S., U. Maine, 1937; postgrad. in Journalism, Columbia U., 1937, Barry Coll., 1974-76; D. Humanics (hon.), Salem Coll., 1976; m. Rosemary Fisher, Nov. 21, 1939; 1 dau., Helen Diane Cumerford Dorney. Exec. in fund raising Boy Scouts Am., Ft. Dodge, Iowa, Corning, N.Y. and Denver, 1937-45; campaign dir. Marts & Lundy, N.Y.C., 1945; founder Cumerford Corp., fund raising cons., Kansas City, Mo., 1949, cons., 1949—; founder Ryall Corp., pub. relations, Kansas City, Mo., 1952, cons., 1952—; founder Cumerford Service Corp., deferred gift cons. firm, Ft. Lauderdale, Fla., 1970, cons., 1970—; v.p. Tulsa U., 1950; lectr. Barry Coll.; speaker in field. Nat. adviser fin. service, bd. dirs. So. Fla. council Boy Scouts Am.; bd. dirs. Ft. Lauderdale Jr. Achievement; trustee Missouri Valley Coll., 1975-77. Recipient Distinguished Eagle award Miami (Fla.) council Boy Scouts Am., 1975; award Leavenworth (Kans.) Jr. C. of C., 1939, Ft. Dodge Jr. C. of C., 1941. Mem. Am. Assn. Fund Raising Counsel (exec. com., dir.), Nat. Soc. Fund Raisers (organizer, dir. So. Fla. chpt.), Am. (accredited), Fla. pub. relations assns., Ft. Lauderdale C. of C., So. Fla. Better Bus. Bur., Kansas City Advt. and Sales Club, Council Advancement and Support Edn., Navy League. Republican. Roman Catholic. Clubs: Kansas City (Mo.); Rotary, Coral Ridge Yacht, Club Internat., Marina Bay; Elks (Ft. Lauderdale). Author: Planned Giving, Vol. I, 1957, Vol. II, 1960; contbr. numerous articles on fund raising to profl. jours. Home: 4010 Galt Ocean Dr Apt 1604 Fort Lauderdale FL 33308

CUMMING, DWIGHT HERBERT, public relations co. exec.; b. Ft. Worth, May 2, 1949; s. Richard Alton and Foye Rebecca (Gilley) C.; B.A., Tex. Christian U., 1974; m. Jaynie Diane Jackson, Mar. 10, 1979. Editorial positions, feature writer Ft. Worth Press, a Scripps-Howard paper, 1974-75; account man Media Reps. Inc., Dallas, 1975-76; owner, operator D.H. Cumming & Assos., Ft. Worth, 1976—; cons. in field. Active Am. Cancer Soc. Mem. Alpha Delta Sigma, Kappa Sigma. Methodist. Club: Steeplechase of Ft. Worth. Office: D H Cumming & Assos 2917 Morton St Fort Worth TX 76107

CUMMING, JOSEPH BRYAN, JR., journalist; b. Augusta, Ga., Feb. 26, 1926; s. Joseph Bryan and Virginia Neville (Burum) C.; student Jr. Coll. Augusta, 1942-43; A.B., U. of South, 1947; postgrad. Emory U.; m. Emily Wright, Oct. 2, 1948; children—Joseph Bryan, Douglas Oliver, Walter Whittier, Anne Burum. Salesman, asst. mgr. Burum Co., Augusta, 1947-55; salesman, Frank Willard Prodns., Atlanta, 1956; reporter Atlanta bur. Newsweek Mag., 1957-61, bur. chief, 1961-79; instr. mag. writing U. Ga., 1975-76; instr. creative writing Clayton Jr. Coll., 1972-73. Chmn. adv. panel Ga. Council for Arts and Humanities. Served with USN, 1944-46, with USNR, 1946-64. Mem. Inquiry Club, Sigma Delta Chi. Episcopalian. Contbr. articles to Esquire mag., 1962, 71, 77, poem to Harpers. Home and Office: 2604 Parkside Dr NE Atlanta GA 30305

CUMMINGS, CONRAD MILTON, oil co. exec.; b. Shreveport, La., July 1, 1933; s. Horald Carson and Gladys (Martin) C.; B.S. in Petroleum Engring., Tex. A. and M. U., 1955; m. Beverly Carol Arrant, Aug. 18, 1956; children—Leigh, Connie, Ross. Jr. engr. Lion Oil Co. (name now changed to Monsanto Corp.), El Dorado, Ark., 1955-56, staff engr., Houston, 1958-60, dist. engr., Pratt, Kans., 1960-64, regional engr., Houston, 1964-68, planning coordinator, 1968-70; sr. v.p. McRae Consol. Oil & Gas Inc., Houston, 1970—, also dir.; dir. McRae Oil Corp. Petrofunds, Inc., McRae Exploration, Inc., La. Gas Purchasing Corp., La. Gas Intrastate Inc. Served with AUS, 1956-58. Mem. Soc. Profl. Engrs., Independent Petroleum Assn. Am. Republican. Presbyn. (deacon 1966-69, elder 1969-71). Clubs: Houston Athletic; Champions Golf; Shreveport, Petroleum (Shreveport). Home: 10626 Glenway St Houston TX 77070 Office: 800 Dresser Tower 601 Jefferson St Houston TX 77002

CUMMINGS, JAMES BERNARD, hosp. adminstr.; b. Albany, N.Y., Sept. 25, 1944; s. Bernard J. and Eleanor (Nodine) C.; B.A. in Bus. Adminstrn., Broward Coll., 1979; m. Joyce C. Nierenberg, Jan. 6, 1973; children—Joseph Edward, Kimberly Dawn. Account clk. Foremost Dairies, Tampa, Fla., 1963-65; asst. office mgr. So. Bakeries, Tampa, 1965-66, asst. corp. purchasing agt., Atlanta, 1966-69; account clk. State of Fla., Tallahassee, 1969-71, purchasing agt., 1971-76, dist. gen. services mgr., Ft. Lauderdale, 1976-79; bus. mgr. South Fla. State Hosp., Hollywood, 1979—. Mem. Nat. Purchasing Mgmt. Assn., Fla. Purchasing Mgmt. Assn. Democrat. Roman Catholic. Office: 1000 SW 84th Ave Hollywood FL 33025

CUMMINGS, MARY VOIGT, guidance counselor; b. Eagle Grove, Iowa, Sept. 23, 1937; d. Wilson Burns and Evelyn Louise (Allen) V.; B.S., Northwestern U., 1959; M.A., U. South Fla., 1977; m. William G. Cummings, Jr., June 20, 1959; children—William G., III, Ann, Joan, Louise, Betsy. Guidance counselor Pinellas Park Sr. High Sch., Largo, Fla., 1977—; mem. Pinellas County Curriculum Com.; mem. adv. com. Eckerd Coll. Upward Bound, Belcher Elem., Oak Grove Middle and Pinellas Park schs. Pres. planning com. Morton Plant Hosp., 1977; vestrywoman Episcopal Ch. of Ascension, Clearwater, Fla., 1978. Named Clearwater Outstanding Young Woman, Jr. League of Clearwater, 1975. Mem. Am. Personnel and Guidance Assn., Fla. Personnel and Guidance Assn., Suncoast Personnel and Guidance Assn., Pinellas County Tchrs. Assn., Clearwater Jr. League (past pres.). Republican. Home: 1829 Nottingham Ln Clearwater FL 33516 Office: 6305 118th Ave N Largo FL 33543

CUMMINGS, ROXIE DEAN, sch. adminstr.; b. Kyle, Tex., Oct. 29, 1940; d. Adolph Marion and Emma Irene (Koch) Hill; student Tex. Woman's U., 1958-60; B.A., Baylor U., 1961; postgrad. U. Houston, 1967-73, M.A., 1973; postgrad. Sam Houston State U., 1975; m. George B. Cummings, Feb. 6, 1960; children—Darla Audrene, Stuart Britt. Tchr. public schs., Wichita Falls, Tex., 1961-63, Burkburnett, Tex., 1963-65; speech pathologist Aldine Ind. Sch. Dist., Houston, 1965-74, spl. edn. supr., 1974-77, asst. dir. spl. edn., 1977—; cons. in field; condr. staff devel. workshops for tchrs. Mem. John Hill Blue Ribbon Edn. com., 1978-79. Recipient Chpt. Achievement award Delta Kappa Gamma. Mem. Am. Speech and Hearing Assn. (cert. of clin. competence), Tex. Speech and Hearing Assn., Council for Exceptional Children, Houston Area Assn. Communication Disorders, Aldine Assn. for Children with Learning Disabilities, Aldine Tchrs. Assn., Tex. Council of Suprs. Speech, Hearing and Lang. Programs, Delta Kappa Gamma. Home: 2 Goodson Dr Apt 304 Houston TX 77060 Office: 14910 Aldine-Westfield Rd Houston TX 77032

CUMMINS, ANN SINCLAIR, sch. psychologist; b. Joplin, Mo., July 3, 1931; d. John Taylor and Lula Vivian (Sanders) Sinclair; A.A., Ward-Belmont Coll., 1951; student So. Meth. U., 1951-52; B.A., U. Fla., 1970, M.Ed., 1973, Edn. Specialist, 1973; m. Wade L. Cummins, 1952; children—Virginia Ann, Robert Jeffrey, Charles Scott, William Christopher. Counselor, Crisis Intervention Center, Gainesville, Fla., 1970-71; therapist Marion-Citrus Mental Health Center, Ocala, Fla., 1973; therapist Citrus Mental Health Center, Inverness, Fla., 1973; counselor Inverness Middle Sch., 1974; psychologist Citrus County Schs., Inverness, 1974—. Certified sch. psychologist, Fla. Mem. Am., Fla. personnel and guidance assns., Am., Fla. assns. measurement and evaluation in guidance, Nat., Central Fla., Fla. assns. sch. psychologists. Democrat. Episcopalian. Home and Office: 402 Lake Shore Dr W Inverness FL 32650 Office: 1507 W Main St Inverness FL 32650

CUMMINS, CLAIRE MARIE, dietitian; b. Cin., Feb. 4, 1923; d. Alfred Joseph and Charlotte Marie (Soelter) Gerhardt; B.S., Coll. of Mt. St. Joseph on the Ohio, 1945; m. Alvin Joseph Cummins, June 14, 1947; children—Sandra M. Cummins Stallings, Gregory O., Judith Ann. Intern, Case Western Reserve Coll., Lakeside Hosp., 1946; asst. adminstrv. dietitian Good Samaritian Hosp., Dayton, Ohio, 1946-47, Georgetown U. Hosp., Washington, 1947-48; therapeutic dietitian Pa. Hosp., Phila., 1948-50; vol., relief dietitian W.F. Bould Hosp., Memphis, 1965-67; consulting dietitian, Memphis, 1967-69; nutrition cons., Memphis, 1969—; guest lectr. nutrition dept. community medicine Center Health Scis., U. Tenn., 1976-77; guest lectr. breast cancer dept. health, recreation and phys. edn. Memphis State U., 1976. Mem. nutrition com. Memphis Regional Med. Program, 1970-72; chmn. nutrition symposia 3 and 4 Memphis Area Nutrition Council, 1972-73, v.p., 1973-74, pres., 1975, chmn. ways and means symposium, 1974, chmn. hospitality symposium 6, 1975; mem., sec. exec. bd. J.K. Lewis Center for Sr. Citizens, 1972—; charter mem. statewide nutrition adv. com. Tenn. Commn. on Aging, 1972-75; vol. Reach to Recovery Program, Am. Cancer Soc., Memphis, 1973—, vice chmn., 1976-77, chmn., 1977-79, coordinator Tenn. div., 1979—. Mem. Am., Tenn., Memphis Dist. (chmn. community nutrition 1970-72) dietitic assns., Soc. for Nutrition Edn., Gerontol. Soc., Mastectomy Assn. (founder Memphis area chpt. 1977). Roman Catholic. Clubs: U. Tenn. Faculty Womens Club; Womens Auxiliary to Memphis and Shelby County Med. Soc. Home: 4320 Chickasaw Cove Memphis TN 38117

CUMMINS, GEORGE CLARK, computer specialist; b. Drew, Miss., Mar. 15, 1934; s. Willis Richard and Mary Lee (Clark) C.; student Milw. Sch. Engring., 1959-61; B.S. in Math., Miss. Coll., 1972; m. Nell Conger, July 23, 1954; children—Sherri Lynne, George Clark, Tom Wilson. Computer specialist, U.S. Army, C.E., Vicksburg, Miss. dist., 1966—, asst. to chief ADP Center, alternate ADP coordinator, 1970—; tchr. Alcorn State U., 1975-77, Hinds Jr. Coll., 1977—. Served to 1st lt. U.S. Army, 1956-66. Mem. Engrs. Club Vicksburg. Methodist. Home: 201 Signal Hill Dr Vicksburg MS 39180 Office: PO Box 60 Vicksburg MS 39180

CUMPTON, BROMAN DAVID, chem. mfg. co. exec.; b. Muncie, Ind., Sept. 8, 1939; s. Anchor Lee and Dorothy G. (Hixon) C.; student Palm Beach Jr. Coll., 1957-60, Ball State U., 1960-62; m. Barbara Anne Ervin, June 30, 1967; children—Broman David II, Brian Daniel. Buyer, Farrel-Birmingham Co., Ansonia, Conn., 1962-63; project asst. Nat. Sugar Inc., N.Y.C., 1963; with acctg. dept. Sugar Cane Growers Co-op, Belle Glade, Fla., 1965-66; mgr. adminstrn. Quaker Oats Co., Belle Glade, 1966—. Active Glades Youth Baseball, 1966—; bd. dirs. Glades Assn. for Retarded Citizens, 1978—. Served with U.S. Army, 1963-65. Mem. Nat. Assn. Purchasing Mgmt., Am. Soc. Sugar Cane Technologists, Asso. Industries of Fla., Fla. C. of C., Lake Okeechobee Traffic Council, Nat. Assn. Accountants. Democrat. Presbyterian. Clubs: Kiwanis, Elks. Home: 941 SE 3d St Belle Glade FL 33430 Office: PO Box 759 Airport Rd Belle Glade FL 33430

CUNDEY, PAUL EDWARD, JR., cardiologist; b. Phila., Sept. 9, 1936; s. Paul Edward and Ann Elizabeth (Morris) C.; B.A., LaSalle Coll., 1958; M.D., Temple U., 1962; m. Katharine Zerbey, Aug. 1, 1959; children—Richard David, Paul Edward III, Heath John, Elizabeth Ann. Intern, Temple U. Med. Center, 1962-63; resident in cardiology Med. Coll. Ga., 1965-69, fellow in cardiology, 1967-69; research fellow Nat. Heart Inst., 1968-70; practice medicine specializing in cardiology, Augusta, 1970—; asso. prof. medicine sect. cardiology Med. Coll. Ga., 1976—; mem. specialized services com. E. Central Ga. Health Systems, 1977—. Served with U.S. Army, 1963-65. Diplomate Am. Bd. Internal Medicine, Am. Bd. Angiology. Fellow A.C.P., Am. Coll. Angiology, Am. Coll. Cardiology (asso.); mem. AAAS, Am. Fedn. Clin. Research, Am., Ga. (dir. 1977—, exec. com. Richmond County div. 1972—), heart assns., AMA, Am. Soc. Echocardiography, Richmond County Med. Soc. Author articles and abstracts. Home: 2710 Wellington Dr Augusta GA 30909 Office: 1003 Chafee Ave Augusta GA 30904

CUNNINGHAM, ANN ROSCOE, coll. adminstr.; b. Fort Worth, Jan. 6, 1942; d. Odell and Irene (Fite) R.; B.S., Baylor U., 1964, M.S., 1966; postgrad. U. Tex., Austin, 1966-67, U. Calif., Berkeley, 1969-70, N. Tex. State U., 1976-78; children—Tracy Colleen, Erin Delise. Instr. phys. edn., intramural dir. Baylor U., Waco, Tex., 1965-66; instr. health, phys. edn., early childhood edn. McLennan Community Coll., Waco, Tex., 1966-74; instr. phys. edn. Mountain View Coll., Dallas County Community Coll. Dist., 1975-77, div. chmn. phys. edn.-health, athletic dir. men's and women's programs, 1977—, div. chmn. phys. edn-health-aviation tech., fine arts, 1979—. Baylor faculty scholar, 1964, 65, Houston Endowment Fund scholar, 1968, Faculty devel. grantee, 1976, 78, 79. Mem. AAHPER, Amateur Fencers League Am., U.S. Volleyball Assn., Tex. Assn. Health, Phys. Edn. and Recreation, Tex. Jr. Coll. Tchrs. Assn., Tex. Assn. Intercollegiate Athletics for Women. Office: Mountain View Coll 4849 W Illinois St Dallas TX 75211

CUNNINGHAM, ATLEE MARION, JR., aero. engr.; b. Corpus Christi, Aug. 17, 1938; s. Atlee Marion and Carlos Dean (Shepherd) C.; B.S. in Mech. Engring., U. Tex., 1961, M.S. in Mech. Engring., 1963, Ph.D., 1966; m. Diana Wahl Bonelli, July 17, 1976; children by previous marriage—Christopher Atlee, Scott Patrick, Sean Michael. Research scientist Def. Research Lab., Austin, Tex., 1965; engring. specialist Gen. Dynamics Corp., Fort Worth, 1965—; vis. indsl. prof. So. Meth. U. Inst. Tech., Dallas, 1969-70; vis. asso. prof. aero. engring. U. Tex., 1978—; cons. NASA, USAF, U. Tex. Vice pres. Tex. Fine Arts Assn., Fort Worth, 1972. Served with USN, 1962-64. Welding Research Assn. fellow, 1961-62; NATO fellow, 1964-65. Fellow AIAA (asso.; tech. reviewer jours.); mem. Sigma Xi. Contbr. articles to profl. jours.; pioneer in subsonic, transonic and supersonic steady and oscillatory aerodynamics method. Home: 2212 Windsor Pl Fort Worth TX 76110

CUNNINGHAM, CLARENCE MARION, chemist, educator; b. Cooper, Tex., July 24, 1920; s. Willie Lee and Naomi Mae (Stokes) C.; B.S., Tex. A&M U., 1942; M.S., U. Calif., 1948; Ph.D., Ohio State U., 1954; m. Janet Ruth Kohl, Sept. 14, 1951; children—Elizabeth Jane, Daniel Marvin, Steven Charles, Margaret Helen. Asst. prof. Calif. Poly. State U., San Luis Obispo, 1948-49; cryogenic engr., cons. H.L. Johnston, Inc., Columbus, Ohio, 1951-53; vis. research prof. Ohio State U., Columbus, summer 1961; mem. faculty Okla. State U., Stillwater, 1954—, asso. prof. chemistry, 1959—; cons. in field. Vice pres. Stillwater United Way, 1959-60, bd. dirs., 1958-62; v.p. Stillwater YMCA, 1958-61; bd. dirs. Payne Community Action Bd., 1965-69; bd. dirs., v.p. Stillwater Neighborhood Nursery, 1968-72, 78—; sec. Payne County Dem. Central Com., 1964-67, 75-77. Served to capt. U.S. Army, 1942-46. Recipient Silver Beaver award Boy Scouts Am., 1976; Research Corp. Am. grantee, 1955-56; NASA grantee, 1966-72. Mem. AAAS, Am. Phys. Soc., Am. Chem. Soc., AAUP (chpt. pres. 1964-65, state pres. 1965-67), Okla. Acad. Sci. Democrat. Quaker. Club: Kiwanis. Author: A Student's Guide for General Chemistry, 1977. Home: 924 Lakeridge Ave Stillwater OK 74074 Office: Dept Chemistry Okla State Univ Stillwater OK 74074

CUNNINGHAM, DORYLEA, elem. counselor; b. Lindsay, Okla., Feb. 20, 1933; d. Floyd Monroe and Mary Oma (Stephens) Barefoot; student Okla. U., 1951-53, Wichita U., 1953-55; B.S., U. Sci. and Arts of Okla., 1965; M.Ed., East Central U., 1976; postgrad. Webster Coll., 1977, Okla. U., 1979; m. James Nelson Cunningham, Apr. 3, 1953; children—Karen, Sally Ann, John Alan. Tchr., Doyle Sch., Lindsay, 1967-69; tchr. Lindsay Sch., 1969-76, elem. counselor, 1976—; biofeedback ednl. cons. Sr. advisor, mem. regional bd. Girl Scouts U.S.A.; bd. dirs. PTA. Mem. NEA, Okla. Edn. Assn., Okla. Personnel and Guidance Assn. (dir., pres. Region IV), Am. Personnel and Guidance Assn., Am. Sch. Counselors Assn., Biofeedback Soc. Am., Delta Delta Delta, Delta Kappa Gamma. Methodist. Home: 305 West Creek Lindsay OK 73052 Office: 302 SW 8th Lindsay OK 73052

CUNNINGHAM, E. BRICE, lawyer; b. Buffalo, Tex., Feb. 17, 1931; s. Hattie and Tessie (Roblow) C.; B.A., Howard U., 1960, LL.B., 1960; m. Rosie Nell Portis, Mar. 6, 1964; children—Ledner Vernard, Michele Denise, Elana Brice. Admitted to Tex. bar, 1960, U.S. Ct. Appeals, 1966, U.S. Supreme Ct. bar, 1972; asso. counsel W.J. Durham, Dallas, 1960-64; mem. firm Finch, Lockridge & Cunningham, Dallas, 1964-68; individual practice, Dallas, 1968-75; sr. partner Cunningham, Greenidge & Gaines, 1977-79; pres. E. Brice Cunningham, P.C., Dallas, 1979—; hearing officer City of Dallas, 1974—; mcpl. judge City of Dallas, 1971-72. Mem. Dallas City Plan Commn., 1973-76; vice chmn. Park South br. YMCA, Dallas, 1969-71, chmn., 1970-71. Bd. dirs. Children's Aid Soc. Served with AUS, 1948-54. Recipient Black Hist. Achievement award United Meth. Ch., 1979; cert. of merit J. L. Turner Legal Assn., 1979; A. Maceo Smith Community Service award; cert. of service City of Dallas; cert. of recognition Pilgrim Rest Bapt. Ch. Mem. State Bar Tex., Dallas Bar Assn., Prince Hall. Mason. Club: Idlewild (Dallas). Home: 2210 Van Cleave Dallas TX 75216 Office: 4118 S Oakland Ave Dallas TX 75215

CUNNINGHAM, EMORY O., publisher; b. Kansas, Ala., Mar. 17, 1921; s. Emory O. and Belle (Kelly) C.; B.S. in Agrl. Sci., Auburn U., 1948; m. Jeanne Loftis, Dec. 21, 1951; children—James Emory, David Lee, Sara Jeanne, Mary Lou. Pub. Progressive Farmer and Southern Living, 1967—; pres. Progressive Farmer Co., 1968—; dir. Birmingham Trust Nat. Bank, Ala. Gas Corp. Bd. dirs. Audit Bur. Circulation, Ala. Heart Assn., Salvation Army, So. Research Inst., Callaway Gardens Found.; exec. bd. Birmingham Area council Boy Scouts Am. Bd. govs. Internat. Ins. Seminar, Inc. Named Man of Year, Birmingham Advt. Club, 1971; recipient Hall of Fame award Miss. Gulf Coast Jr. Coll., 1973, Henry Johnson Fisher award as mag. pub. of year, 1975, Free Enterprise award Nat. Farm-City Week Com., 1979; named Man of Year in Service to Rural Alabamians, 1975; recipient Communicator of Yr. award Sales and Mktg. Execs. Internat., 1977. Mem. Agrl. Pubs. Assn. (pres., dir.), Mag. Pubs. Assn. (vice chmn., treas., dir.), Newcomen Soc. N.Am. (chmn. Ala. chpt.), Ala. Acad. of Honor. Home: 2441 Vestavia Dr Birmingham AL 35216 Office: 820 Shades Creek Pkwy Birmingham AL 35209

CUNNINGHAM, GUY ALLEN, retail home furnishings co. exec.; b. Longview, Tex., May 22, 1952; s. Basil William and Opal (Randle) C.; student Kilgore Coll., 1970-72, Tex. Tech. U., 1972, N. Tex. State U., 1973. Designer, salesperson Rick Furniture Co., Dallas, 1973-74; partner Trend Furniture & Interiors, Longview, 1974-78, operating partner, 1978—; tchr. interior design Kilgore Coll., 1975-76; dir. Downtown Devel. Corp. Mem. Interior Design Soc., Illuminating Engring. Soc. (affiliate), Longview C. of C., Kappa Alpha Order. Clubs: Kiwanis, Mason. Office: 215 E Tyler St Longview TX 75601

CUNNINGHAM, JAMES JOSEPH, cons. engr.; b. Pawtucket, R.I., Mar. 17, 1927; s. Thomas Joseph and Mildred Claudia (Sunderland) C.; B.S. in Civil Engring., Ga. Inst. Tech., 1953; m. Clara Smith, Feb. 25, 1966; children—James, Gary, Bruce, Alva, Arlene. With Humble Oil & Refining Co., 1953-71, sr. staff engr., 1968-71; chief engr. Stubbs, Overbeck & Assos., Inc., Houston, 1971-73, mgr. Beaumont and La. ops., 1975—; co-owner, pres. Am. Engring. Assos., Inc., Houston, 1973-75. Bd. dirs. Water Dist. Indian Shores, Huffman, Tex., 1969, 70; pres. Indian Shore Civic Assn., 1969-70; mem. Steering Com. for Flood Control in Hardin County (Tex.), 1979—. Served with USAAF, 1945-47. Registered profl. engr., Tex., La. Mem. ASCE, Nat. Soc. Profl. Engrs., Tex. Soc. Profl. Engrs., La. Engring. Soc., Bus. and Profl. Men's Club Beaumont, Young Men's Bus. League Beaumont, Chi Epsilon. Clubs: West Beaumont Rotary, Pinewood Country. Patentee in field. Office: Suite 950 Petroleum Bldg Beaumont TX 77701

CUNNINGHAM, JOHN RANDOLPH, software specialist; b. Alexandria, La., July 17, 1954; s. John Adolphus and Zelma Audrey (Cox) C.; student La. State U., Shreveport, 1972-73, 73-74, Baton Rouge, 1973-74; B.S., La. Tech. U., 1976; m. Teresa Ellen Toms, Jan. 22, 1977. Software specialist South Central Bell, New Orleans, 1977—. Mem. Assn. for Computing Machinery, Upsilon Pi Epsilon. Baptist. Home: 285 Whisperwood Slidell LA 70458 Office: 3500 N Causeway Room 810 Metairie LA 70035

CUNNINGHAM, LILLIE SUMMERS, former ednl. adminstrn.; b. Hornbeak, Tenn., Apr. 26, 1912; married, 1 child. B.S. in Pre-Med., La. State U., Baton Rouge, 1937; postgrad. Peabody Coll., Nashville, Memphis State U. Tchr. Obion County (Tenn.) schs., Hornbeak, 1937-42, 1948-61; Librarian Lake County (Tenn.) schs., Tiptonville, 1943-45, dir. fed. projects, 1966-79; guidance counselor Obion County schs., Troy, 1963-66. Mem. program com. W. Tenn. Kidney Found. Mem. NEA, Tenn. Edn. Assn., Internat. Reading Assn., Tenn. Right to Read, Tenn. Assn. Sch. Adminstrs. Home: PO Box 145 Hornbeak TN 38232 also 3519 Kenwood Memphis TN 38122

CUNNINGHAM, MARY ELIZABETH, nursing adminstr.; b. Hornell, N.Y., Dec. 20, 1933; d. Harry G. and Helen M. (Jones) C.; diploma St. Mary's Hosp. Sch. Nursing, 1954; B.S. in Nursing, U. Rochester, 1960, M.S., 1961. Staff nurse St. Mary's Hosp., Rochester, N.Y., 1954-57, various head nursing positions, clin. instr. maternal and child health nursing, 1958; staff nurse blood mobile unit Monroe County chpt. ARC, Rochester, 1957-58; clin. instr. Highland Hosp. Sch. Nursing, Rochester, 1959-60, instr. acute nursing, 1961-62; dir. edn. St. Ann's Home, Rochester, 1962-63, Cedars of Lebanon Health Care Center, Miami, Fla., 1964-74; dir. nursing Towne House Convalescent Center, Miami, 1974-75; staff nurse Med. Personnel Pool, Miami, 1975-76, North Miami (Fla.) Gen. Hosp., 1976; nursing service adminstr. Lake Community Hosp., Leesburg, Fla., 1976—. N.Y. State Regents scholar, 1958. Mem. Am. Nurses Assn., Fla. Nurses Assn. (dir. 1972-74), Fla. Soc. Nursing Service Adminstrs., Coll. Cuban Nurses in Exile (hon. mem.). Home: 950 SW 145th St Ocala FL 32671 Office: 700 N Palmetto St Leesburg FL 32748

CUNNINGHAM, PAUL JOHNSTON, surgeon; b. Princeton, Ky., Oct. 10, 1928; s. Paul Clement and Marie (Johnston) Cunningham; B.S., U. Ky., 1950; M.D., U. Louisville, 1955; m. Billie J. Freeman, Aug. 25, 1952; children—Suzanne, Cynthia, Paul Raymond. Intern, resident in surgery U. Tex. Med. Br. Hosp., Galveston, 1955-56, 1956-62, now mem. staff, clin. asst. prof.; practice medicine specializing in surgery, Galveston, 1962—; mem. Galveston Surg. Group Assos.; mem. staff, past pres. med. staff St. Mary's Hosp., mem. staff Galveston Meml. Hosp. Mem. exec. com. 17th dist. Tex. Republican Exec. Com., 1972—; bd. regents Galveston Coll. Served as capt. M.C., USAF, 1957-59. Diplomate Am. Bd. Surgery. Mem. A.C.S., Southwestern Surg. Congress, Singleton Surg. Soc., Galveston County Med. Soc., Galveston C. of C. (past dir.). Office: 200 University Blvd Suite 907 Galveston TX 77550

CUNNINGHAM, ROGER GRADY, chiropractor; b. Dallas, Sept. 5, 1944; s. Samuel Grady and Gladys Sue (Burford) C.; A.A., North East Miss. Jr. Coll., 1964; D.Chiropractic (Am. Chiropractic Assn. scholar), Nat. Coll. Chiropractic, Lombard, Ill., 1967; m. Nancy Lee Dollar, Nov. 18, 1972; children by previous marriage—Roger Grady, David; 1 stepdau., Kristie. Chiropractor, Cunningham Chiropractic Clinic, Ripley, Miss., 1967—. Cub scoutmaster Tallahatchie dist. Boy Scouts Am., 1973-77. Mem. Miss. (dir., sec.-treas. 1972), Am. chiropractic assns., Miss. Asso. Chiropractors (bd. dirs. 1979-80), Ripley Jaycees (charter), Ripley Civitan Club (pres. 1977). Mem. Ch. of Christ. Home: Dumas Rd Ripley MS 38663 Office: 903 Main St Ripley MS 38663

CUNNINGHAM, WILLIAM JOSEPH, internat. commerce exec.; b. Valatie, N.Y., Sept. 18, 1925; s. Roy Edward and Ruth Gladys (Carney) C.; B.S. in Chemistry and Math., Siena Coll., 1949, postgrad. in phys. chemistry, 1952-53; m. Elca Galmeijer, Dec. 27, 1950; children—Kevin, Brian, Gayle, Roy III. Asst. sales mgr. W.&L.E. Gurley Co., Troy, N.Y., 1951-53; v.p., gen. mgr. Sprague Elec. Co., P.R., Mexico and Tex., 1953-71, dir. Mexican affiliate cos., 1970-72; cons., gen. mgr. constrn. Maule Industries, Miami, Fla., 1972-74; pres. Galmeijer Inc., Miami, 1974—. Bd. dirs. St. Lukes Episcopal Hosp., Ponce, P.R., 1968-70, Museo de Arte de Ponce, 1968-69. Served with U.S. Army, 1943-45. Decorated Purple Heart; recipient 4 REECO awards U.S. Sec. of State, 1968-72. Mem. Elec. Industries Assn. P.R. (pres. 1966-67), P.R. Mfrs. Assn. (v.p. 1968-70), Am. Chem. Soc., Regional Export Expansion Councils. Republican. Roman Catholic. Clubs: Curacoa (Netherlands Antilles) Yacht, Ponce Country (pres. 1965-67). Office: 8410 NW 53d Terr Suite 121 Galmeijer Inc Miami FL 33166

CURBO, DEBORAH ANN TUCKER, hosp. personnel adminstr.; b. Blackstone, Va., Nov. 14, 1953; d. Clyde Jackson and Margaret Odle (Chrane) Tucker; student U. Tenn., Knoxville, 1972-74, San Jacinto Coll., 1975-76, U. Houston, 1977—; m. Charles Bruce Curbo, Aug. 31, 1974. Asst. buyer Kelly Mfg. Co., Houston, 1976-77; dir. personnel Gulf Coast Hosp., Baytown, Tex., 1977—. Mem. Am. Soc. for Hosp. Personnel Adminstrn., Tex. Soc. for Hosp. Personnel Adminstrn., Houston Soc. for Hosp. Personnel Adminstrn., Am. Hosp. Assn., Tex. Hosp. Assn., Baytown Panhellenic Assn., Phi Mu Alumni, Beta Sigma Phi. Club: Pinehurst Garden. Home: 7311 Ironwood Ln Baytown TX 77521 Office: Gulf Coast Hosp 2800 Garth Rd Baytown TX 77521

CURLEE, LEWIS ELTON, orthopedic surgeon; b. Marshville, N.C., Dec. 30, 1928; s. Seaborn and Mary (Smith) C.; student Appalachian U., 1943-45, Duke, 1945-46; M.D., Wake Forest U., 1950. Intern, Emory U., Atlanta, 1950-51; resident in orthopedic surgery Duke U., Durham, N.C., Charlotte (N.C.) Meml. Hosp., 1951-53, Tulane U., New Orleans, 1953-54; fellow Nuffield Inst., Oxford, Eng., 1955-56; resident in orthopedic surgery N.Y. U., Bellevue Med. Center, N.Y.C., 1957; practice medicine specializing in orthopedic surgery, Concord, N.C., 1957—; chief orthopedic surgery Cabarrus Meml. Hosp.; med. dir. Cabarrus Nursing Center, Bryan Nursing Center, Concord; med. examiner Cabarrus County, N.C., 1972—; med. examiner FAA, Concord, 1974—; dir. Speed & Custom, Inc., Concord, Cheese Chateau Enterprises Ltd. Mem. Hist. Preservation Soc. of N.C., Concord, 1958—; founding patron Charlotte (N.C.) Symphony. Served with USAF, 1954-56. Diplomate Am. Bd. Orthopedic Surgery. Fellow A.C.S., Am. Geriatric Soc., Am. Fracture Assn., Internat. Coll. Surgeons, Am. Acad. Orthopedic Surgeons; mem. Am., N.C., Cabarrus County, So., World, Pan Am. med. assns., N.C., Eastern orthopedic assns., Pan Pacific Surgical Assn., Southeastern Surgical Congress, Royal Soc. Medicine (London), Am. Coll. Emergency Physicians, Am. Coll. Sports Medicine, Am. Trauma Soc. (founder), Am. Assn. Automotive Medicine, Christian Med. Soc., Flying Physicians Assn., Assn. Mil. Surgeons, Nat. Rehab. Assn., A.C.L.U., Am. Med. Soc. Vienna, Flying Drs. Africa, Orthopedic Research Found., D.A.V. Democrat. Methodist. Club: Cabarrus Country. Home: 109 Country Club Dr Concord NC 28025 Office: 103 Country Club Dr Concord NC 28025

CURNUTT, ESTHER CLARK, public relations exec.; b. Texon, Tex., June 16, 1935; d. J. Linton and Ann (Martin) Clark; student San Angelo Coll., 1953-55; B.J., U. Tex., 1957; M.A., Sul Ross State U., 1959; postgrad. U. Inc., 1963, U. Miss., 1966, U. Tex., 1968; m. Harry O. Curnutt, Feb. 1, 1966; 1 son, Clark Denton. Society editor Pecos (Tex.) Enterprise 1957-58; grad. teaching fellow Sul Ross State U., Alpine, Tex., 1958-59; tchr. English, journalism, San Antonio Ind. Sch. Dist., 1959-66; tchr./dist. public relations N.E. Ind. Sch. Dist., San Antonio, 1966-67; chmn. dept. journalism San Antonio Coll., 1967-71; owner/operator Esther Curnutt Public Relations, San Antonio, 1976—. Mem. Mayor's Commn. on Status of Women, San Antonio, 1974-76, v.p., bd. dirs. Nat. Women's Employment and Edn. Bd., 1979—; mem. Bexar County Women's Polit. Caucus, 1978-79, Leadership-San Antonio, 1978-79. Named Outstanding High Sch. Journalism Tchr., Newspaper Fund Inc., 1962; Newspaper Fund Inc. journalism fellow 1963. Mem. LWV (1st v.p. 1977-79), Women in Communications (pres. 1974-76), Internat. Bus. Communicators, Tex. Public Relations Soc., San Antonio Conservation Soc. Methodist. Clubs: Women's Polit. Ad-Hoc Com., Suburban Bankers Wives Aux. (pres. 1974-75). Address: 126 Five Oaks St San Antonio TX 78209

CURRAN, HELEN, educator; b. Chgo., Aug. 6, 1916; d. Samuel Audley and Edna (Sandiford) Curran; student Lewis Inst. Tech., 1935-37; B.S., Ill. Inst. Tech., 1946; M.E. in Guidance and Counseling, U. Ill., 1952; postgrad. Internat. Inst. Edn., 1957, U. Maine, 1962, U. London, 1963, No. Ill. U., 1964; Advanced certificate in ednl. adminstrn., U. Ill., 1966; m. William Zorn, 1937 (div.); 1 dau., April; m. 2d, J.W. Fenner, May 10, 1972. Tchr. pub. schs., Maywood, Ill., 1946-47, tchr., Fox Lake, Ill., 1947-49, guidance dir., dean girls, 1949-57; dean girls, Peoria Heights, Ill., 1957-59, dir. guidance, 1959-63, adminstrv. asst., dir. curriculum, McHenry (Ill.) Pub. Schs., 1963-66, asst. supt., 1966-71; asst. supt. instrn. Tech. Information Center, Charleston, S.C., 1972—; staff tchrs. summer sessions The Citadel; asst. prof. psychology Bapt. Coll., Charleston, 1974—. Mem. adv. bd. Advocacy for Retarded Citizens; bd. dirs. Orphans of the Storm. Mem. Ill. Assn. Sch. Adminstrs., Ill., Nat. edn. assns., Ill., Nat. assns. women deans and counselors, Nat., Ill. assns. supervision and curriculum, Internat. Transactional Analysis Assn., Am. Legion Aux., Delta Kappa Gamma. Office: Tech Information Center 64 Society St Charleston SC 29401

CURRENT, GLOSTER BRYANT, JR., food co. exec.; b. Cin., Jan. 8, 1946; s. Gloster Bryant and Leontyne Ruth (Kelly) C.; B.A. cum laude, Howard U., 1957; M.B.A., U. Pitts., 1972; m. Yvonne Davis, Dec. 28, 1974. With long lines dept. AT&T, Washington, 1967-71; brand mgr. Ivory bar soap Procter & Gamble Co., Cin., 1972-77; brand mgr. Hawaiian Punch drink mix R.J. Reynolds Foods Co., Winston-Salem, N.C., 1977-79, group brand mgr. Hawaiian Punch beverages, 1980—. Vice chmn. Cin. United Appeal drive, 1977; mem. allocations com. Winston-Salem United Appeal, 1979. Served to 1st lt. USAR, 1968-70. Mem. Am. Mgmt. Assn., Howard U. Alumni Assn., Delta Sigma Rho, Tau Kappa Alpha, Kappa Alpha Psi (past nat. officer). Baptist. Home: 3141 Parrish Rd Winston-Salem NC 27105 Office: RJR Industries Winston-Salem NC 27102

CURREY, THOMAS ARTHUR, ophthalmologist; b. Itawamba County, Miss., July 9, 1933; s. Charles Edward and Anna Laura (Williams) C.; student U. Miss., 1952-55; M.D., U. Tenn., 1958; m. Carol Ann Clabaugh, Nov. 7, 1959; children—Thomas Arthur, Russell. Intern, City of Memphis Hosp., 1958-59; practice family medicine Amory, Miss., 1959-62; resident in ophthalmology U. Tenn. Hosp., Memphis, 1962-65; practice medicine specializing in ophthalmology, Memphis; mem. staffs Meth. Hosp., Bapt. Hosp., St. Jo Hosp.; asst. clin. instr. U. Tenn., 1966-79. Fellow Am. Coll. Surgery; mem, AMA, So. Med. Assn., Am. Acad. Ophthalmology, Tenn. Acad. Ophthalmology, Memphis Soc. Ophthalmology. Baptist. Patentee direct operating ophthalmoscope. Home: 87 Wallace Rd Memphis TN 38117 Office: 1900 Kirby Pkwy Memphis TN 38138

CURREY, WILLIAM ROY, public relations exec.; b. Charleston, W.Va., Dec. 28, 1944; s. William Earl and Iva Virginia (Justice) C.; B.A., Marshall U., 1968; m. Jean Ann McCue, Mar. 21, 1947; children—Mathew, Sarah, Elizabeth. Public relations and advt. mgr. Cabell Wayne United Fund, Huntington, W.Va., 1967-68; asst. to v.p. public relations Appalachian Power Co., Charleston, 1968-74; asst. gen. mgr. Kanawha Valley Regional Transp. Authority, Charleston, 1974-75; mgr. public relations eastern U.S., FMC, South Charleston, W.Va., 1975-80, dir. public relations U.S. and internat. ops., Phila., 1980—; mem. adv. com. dept. communications W.Va. State Coll. Mem. bd. advs. U. Charleston; mem. Charleston Fireman's Civil Service Commn.; mem. publicity com. United Fund.; founding bd. dirs., Jr. Achievement of Charleston, 1973-75; mem. South Charleston Bicentennial Commn., 1976-77. Mem. Nat. Alliance Businessmen, Public Relations Soc. Am., Internat. Assn. Bus. Communications, Charleston Advt. Club (bd. dirs., award for public relations program 1978-79), W.Va. Communicators, W.Va. Press Assn. (asso.), Chlorine Inst. (chmn. public affairs com.) W.Va. Mfrs. Assn. (chmn. public relations com.), Electric League of Charleston (sec.-treas. 1970-72). Republican. Methodist. Clubs: Exchange, Edgewood Country. Developer award winning mktg. program for Charleston Area Public Bus System, 1974. Home: Route 2 Box 243-A Hurricane WV 25326 Office: PO Box 8126 South Charleston WV 25303

CURRIE, CHARLES LEONARD, coll. pres.; b. Phila., July 9, 1930; s. Charles Leonard and Elizabeth Katherine (Harper) C.; A.B., Boston Coll., 1955; M.S., 1956; Ph.L., Weston Coll., 1956; Ph.D., Catholic U. Am., 1961; S.T.B., Woodstock Coll., 1962, S.T.L., 1964; D.Sc. (hon.), Bethany Coll., 1974 Joined S.J., Roman Catholic Ch., 1950; postdoctoral researcher Nat. Bur. Standards, 1962, Can. Nat. Research Council, 1963-65, Cambridge (Eng.) U., 1965-66; asst. prof. chemistry Georgetown U., 1966-72; pres. Wheeling (W.Va.) Coll., 1972—; bd. dirs. Xavier U., St. Joseph's U. Chmn. W.Va. Bd. Miner Tng., Edn. and Cert., 1974-79; bd. dirs. Oglebay Inst., Wheeling, United Way of Upper Ohio Valley, W.Va. Humanities Found., Institute. Dept. Def. grantee, 1968-71; Am. Chem. Soc. (Petrol Research Fund) grantee, 1963-65; NSF grantee, 1969-72. Mem. Am. Chem. Soc., Chem. Soc. (London), Wash. Acad. Sci., N.Y. Acad. Sci., AAUP, Am. Assn. Univ. Adminstrs., W.Va. C. of C. (dir.), Common Cause, Assn. Jesuit Colls. and Univs. (dir.), W.Va. Assn. Pvt. Colls. (dir.), Wheeling Area C. of C. (dir.), Sigma Xi. Clubs: Rotary; Univ. (Pitts.). Contbr. articles to chem. jours., 1959-73. Office: Wheeling Coll Wheeling WV 26003

CURRIE, DONALD MORGAN, physician; b. Hamilton, Ohio, May 18, 1947; s. John M. and Doris L. (Gribble) C.; student Baylor U., 1965-67, Rice U., 1967-68; M.D., U. Tex. Southwestern Med. Sch., 1972; M.S. in Rehab. Medicine, U. Wash., 1977; m. Laurel Beth Mc Clure, Oct. 16, 1971; children—Rachel Elizabeth, Andrew Morgan. Intern, Baylor U. Med. Center, Houston, 1972-73, resident, 1972-75; resident rehab. medicine U. Wash. Sch. Medicine, 1975-77; practice medicine specializing in phys. medicine, rehab., pediatric rehab., San Antonio, 1977—; mem. staff Audie Murphy VA Hosp., 1977—, Bexar

County (Tex.) Hosp. Dist. Teaching Hosps., San Antonio, 1977—; co-med. dir. Spina Bifida Clinic, Robert B. Green Hosp., 1978-80; med. dir. Spina Bifida Evaluation Center, Santa Rosa Children's Hosp., San Antonio, 1980—; crippled children's services physician Tex. Dept. Health, 1979—; co-med. dir. San Antonio Easter Seal Treatment Center, 1977—; cons. phys. medicine and rehab. Santa Rosa Med. Center, Bapt. Meml. Hosp., Met. Gen. Hosp., St. Luke's Luth. Hosp., 1977—; asst. prof. phys. medicine and rehab. U. Tex. Health Sci. Center, San Antonio, 1977—. Mem. Mastersingers chorus San Antonio Symphony Orch., 1979—. Diplomate Am. Bd. Phys. Medicine and Rehab. Mem. Am. Acad. of Phys. Medicine and Rehab., Tex. Phys. Medicine and Rehab. Soc., Am. Congress of Rehab. Medicine, AMA, Tex. Med. Assn., Christian Med. Soc., Am. Spina Bifida Assn., Bexar County Med. Soc., Orten Soc. Contbr. articles in field to med. jours. Home: 2414 Wilderness Hill San Antonio TX 78231 Office: 7703 Floyd Curl Dr San Antonio TX 78284

CURRIE, OVERTON ANDERSON, lawyer; b. Hattiesburg, Miss., Nov. 28, 1926; s. Edward Alexander and Terry (Anderson) C.; A.S., Marion Inst., 1944; B.B.A., U. Miss., 1948, LL.B., 1949; B.D., Emory U., 1958, M.Div. 1968; LL.M., Yale U. 1958; m. Lavona Stringer, Dec. 31, 1949; children—Iva Terry, Overton Anderson, Martha Lavona, Lucy Flora, Judy Stringer. Admitted to Miss. bar, 1949, Ga. bar, 1959; practiced law, Hattiesburg, 1949-55; mem. faculty Yale U. Law Sch., 1958-59; partner firm Smith, Currie & Hancock, Atlanta, 1959—; county pros. atty., 1952-55; spl. asst. atty. gen. State of Miss., 1954-55; adj. prof. law Emory U., 1966-73, Fla. State U., 1973; lectr. on constrn. law for local trade assns. Served with U.S. Mcht. Marine Corps, USNR, 1944-46. Mem. Am. Bar Assn. (nat. chmn. sect. public contract law 1971-72, nat. chmn. com. constrn. cases sect. litigation 1978-80. ho. of dels. 1972-74), Atlanta Bar Assn. (chmn. continuing legal edn. com. 1975-76), Ga. Bar Assn. (chmn. legal econs. com. 1979-80), Am. Arbitration Assn. (nat. dir.). Club: Kiwanis (Atlanta). Home: 1055 Nawench Dr Atlanta GA 30327 Office: 2600 Peachtree Center Harris Tower Atlanta GA 30303

CURRIN, WILLIAM DODSON, tobacco co. exec.; b. Oxford, N.C., Oct. 8, 1930; s. Rux Dodson and Doris (Watkins) C.; A.B., Duke U., 1951; postgrad. in German, U. N.C., 1951, in Spanish, 1965-66; grad. exec. bus. course U. Va., 1966; m. Ann Neely Brothers, July 5, 1952; children—Rux Brothers, Neely Ann. With Liggett Group Inc., Liggett & Myers Tobacco Co., Durham, N.C., 1954—, gen. mgr. factory ops., 1972—, v.p. mfg., 1972—, also dir. Liggett & Myers Tobacco Co.; dir. Investor's Consol. Ins. Co., 1974—. Bd. dirs. exec. com. John Avery Boy's Club, Durham, 1972, N.C. Museum Life and Sci., Durham, 1973—; bd. dirs. Durham Council on Alcoholism, 1973—, chmn. bd., 1979; chmn. bd. Epworth United Meth. Ch., Durham, 1979. Served to lt., arty. U.S. Army, 1952-54. Recipient Service to Youth award YMCA, 1973; Spl. Service award Boy's Club Am., 1977; named Hon. Citizen of Tex., 1974. Mem. Am. Mgmt. Assn., Va. State C. of C., Greater Durham C. of C. (Boss of Yr. 1973), Durham Mgmt. Club (top mgmt. bd. 1973-79, Spl. Service award 1979). Republican. Club: Hope Valley Country.

CURRY, ALEXANDER FRAZIER, educator; b. Glasgow, Ky., Apr. 26, 1943; s. Green Veeton and Susie Lee (Burbridge) C.; B.S. in Math., Ky. State U., 1964; M.Ed. in Secondary Counseling, U. Louisville, 1970; m. Carla Tyree, Oct. 15, 1966; 1 dau., Stacy Carrese. Adminstrv. trainee Am. Tobacco Co., 1964-65; tchr. math. public schs., Ky., 1965-71; counselor public schs., Ky., 1971-79; tng. specialist, div. program and pupil evaluation Jefferson County schs., Louisville, 1979—; mem. Ky. Career Edn. Adv. Council. Pres. Louzion Fed. Credit Union, Zion Baptist Ch., Louisville. Mem. Am. Personnel and Guidance Assn., NEA (past del.), Ky. Personnel and Guidance Assn., Ky. Edn. Assn. (dir., mem. bd. negotiation), Jefferson County Counselor Assn. (pres. sr. high div.), Jefferson County Tchr. Assn. (dir.), Jack and Jill Am., Urban League, Ky. State Coll. Alumni Assn. Democrat. Author handbook. Home: 2209 High Pine Dr Louisville KY 40214 Office: 675 River City Mall Louisville KY 40201

CURRY, DOUGLAS ARTHUR, illustrator; b. Parkersburg, W.Va., June 6, 1944; s. Russell Doyle and Ethel Ann (Twyman) C.; grad. Famous Artist Sch., 1970; student in bus.; m. Donna Aschner, Dec. 22, 1978. With Norman Harwell & Assos., River Oaks, 1968-69; tech. illustrator, display artist, lead illustrator Vought Co., Grand Prairie, Tex., 1969—. Served with USAF, 1963-65. Mem. Air Force Assn. Republican. Baptist. Office: 9314 W Jefferson Grand Prairie TX 75050

CURRY, JOHN CHARLES, JR., mgmt. cons.; b. Hattiesburg, Miss., July 22, 1935; s. John Charles and Marguerite (Twilley) C.; B.S. in Indsl. Engring., Ga. Inst. Tech., 1958, M.S. in Indsl. Mgmt., 1972; m. Grace Lynn Ouzts, Sept. 23, 1961; children—John Charles III, Twilley Ann. Sr. mgmt. cons. Henderson, Lindsay & Michaels, Inc., Greenville, S.C., 1958-72; v.p. textile mktg. Summerour & Assos., Inc., Atlanta, 1972-75; sr. partner Roberts, Curry & Co., mgmt. cons., Greenville, 1975—. Served with USNR, 1953-61. Mem. Am. Inst. Indsl. Engrs. (auditor Greenville chpt. 1966-70), Am. Textile Mfrs. Inst., N.C. Textile Mfrs. Assn., Greenville C. of C., Ala. Textile Mfrs. Assn. Methodist. Club: Greenville Country. Office: Roberts Curry & Co 8 Williams St Greenville SC 29601

CURRY, LAURA JUNE, educator; b. Cin., Jan. 13, 1928; d. Willard Lyle and Laura Mabel (Hauck) Curry; B.S. in Edn., U. Ala., 1950; M.S. in Edn., U. Va., 1962; postgrad. U. Miami, 1966—. Tchr. English Cleburne County High Sch., Heflin, Ala., 1950-52; tchr. elementary sch. Graymont Sch., Birmingham, Ala., 1952-57, Sherwood Forest Sch., Norfolk, Va., 1957-61; tchr. reading Norfolk pub. schs., 1961-66, coordinator reading instrn. throughout system, 1968—. Instr. extension div. U. Va., 1963-66, 68—. Mem. Internat., Va. State (chmn. gen. conf. 1974, pres. 1974-75) reading assns., Va. Assn. Children with Learning Disabilities (rec. sec. 1972-73, certificate 1973), N.E.A., Edn. Assn. Norfolk, Nat. Soc. Study Edn., Va. Edn. Assn., Assn. for Supervision and Curriculum Devel., Am. Ednl. Research Assn., Alpha Lambda Delta, Alpha Delta Kappa, Sigma Delta Pi, Kappa Delta Pi. Methodist (adminstrv. bd. 1970-73, 76—, chmn. commn. edn. 1976—, tchr. 1970—). Home: 8105 Deerfield Dr Norfolk VA 23518

CURRY, MARTIN WAYNE, computer service co. exec.; b. Bridgeport, W.Va., Mar. 11, 1936; s. Melvin Wayne and Margaret A. (Steinbeck) C.; student Morris Harvey Coll., 1954-55, U. Wis., 1957-58, 63-64; m. Marjorie Ann Curry, Oct. 12, 1957; children—Pamela Jean, Paula Ann, Margaret Lorene. Vice pres. Lennox Studios, Chgo., 1965-67; dir. personnel Pa. Life Ins. Co., Madison, Wis., 1967-69; account rep. Fla. Forms, Inc., 1969-76, pres., 1976—; organizer, chmn. bd., pres. Curry Bus. Systems, Inc., Jacksonville, Fla., 1976—; pres. Computer Shack, Jacksonville, 1979—. Served with USAF, 1955-65. Republican. Clubs: Masons (Worshipful master 1976), Shriners. Home: 5443 Wynnewood Dr Jacksonville FL 32207 Office: Curry Bus Systems Inc 3336 Beach Blvd Jacksonville FL 32207

CURRY, MARY EARLE LOWRY (MRS. PEDEN GENE CURRY), poet; b. Seneca, S.C., May 13, 1917; d. Ullin Sidney and Mary Sloan (Earle) Lowry; student Furman U., 1944-45; m. Peden Gene Curry, Dec. 25, 1941; children—Eugene Lowry, Mary Earle. Mem. Aux. Rotary, Charleston, S.C., 1972-74. Mem. Internat. Platform Assn., Centro Studie Scambi Internat. Roma, United Meth. Women. Methodist. Club: Meth. Ministers Wives (pres. dist. 1973-74). Author: Looking Up, 1949; Looking Within, 1961; Hymn, 1973. Contbr. poems to lit. jours. and periodicals. Home: 410 Auld Brass Rd Walterboro SC 29488

CURRY, MICHAEL PAUL, arts adminstr.; b. London, Oct. 17, 1952; s. Thomas Noel and Ruby Anderson (Harte) C.; came to U.S., 1974; ed. U. London, 1971-74. Asst. tech. stage mgr. Newpalm Prodns., Chelmsford Civic Theatre, U.K., 1970-71; in various positions, profl. theatre, U.K., 1971; adminstr. Fine Arts Found., Lafayette, La., 1974—. Bd. dirs. Friends of La. Pub. TV, 1978—; mem. music panel La. Arts Council Adv. Bd., 1977. Mem. Assn. La. Arts and Artists (state treas. 1978-79), La. Fedn. Music Clubs (dist. dir. 1977-79), Assn. Coll., Univ. and Community Arts Adminstrs., Internat. Soc. Performing Arts Adminstrs. Mem. Ch. of Eng. Office: PO Box 53320 Lafayette LA 70505

CURRY, STEPHEN MARTINDALE, quantum electronics and applied optics cons.; b. Dallas, Sept. 4, 1944; s. Duncan Ford and Frances Janella (Martindale) C.; B.S. in Physics and Math. (H.T. Clark scholar 1963-67), So. Methodist U., 1967; M.S. in Physics (NSF fellow 1967-71), Stanford U., 1969, Ph.D., 1972. Research asso. Stanford U., 1972-73; asst. prof. physics U. Tex., Dallas, 1973-78; Sloan Found. fellow Columbia U., 1977-78; sr. research scientist Vought Corp., Dallas, 1978-79; sci. cons. Curry Assos., Dallas, 1979—. Mem. Am. Phys. Soc., Optical Soc. Am., Optical Soc. Tex. (pres. 1979-80), Phi Beta Kappa, Sigma Xi, Phi Eta Sigma. Author papers on laser spectroscopy. Home: 2114 Vega Ct Grand Prairie TX 75050

CURTIN, BERNADETTE MARY, counselor; b. Balt., Oct. 19, 1949; d. Richard Willis and Anne Margaret (Brady) Black; B.A., Ladycliff Coll., 1971; M.S., U. Dayton, 1973; m. Aug. 25, 1973. Admissions counselor Ladycliff Coll., Highland Falls, N.Y., 1971-72; asst. dir. placement U. Dayton (Ohio), 1972-73; dir. student affairs Strayer Coll., Washington, 1974-76; placement counselor No. Va. Community Coll., Alexandria, 1976—; lectr., cons. in field. Bd. dirs. Ladycliff Coll. Alumni, 1971-72. Mem. Am. Personnel and Guidance Assn., Va. Coll. Placement Assn., Alpha Chi. Home: 370 N Granada St Arlington VA 22203 Office: No Va Community Coll Beauregard St Alexandria VA 22311

CURTIS, BETTIE JEAN, educator; b. Orange, Tex., July 8, 1935; s. Shelton and Ophelia B. Broussard; B.A. in Bus. Edn., Wiley Coll., 1956; M.A. in Bus. Edn., Tex. So. U., 1963; postgrad. U. Houston, 1961-63, Lamar U., 1976; m. James I. Curtis, Aug. 26, 1963. Med. sec. Orange (Tex.) Meml. Hosp., 1956-59; tchr. bus. W. Orange-Stark High Sch., Orange, 1958—; ct. reporter Port Arthur, Tex., 1963; mem. faculty Lamar U., summer 1979. Fin. sec. Mount Olive Bapt. Ch., 1958-79; bd. dirs. United Fund, 1974—, Lamar Tchr. Center, 1976-79. Recipient Dedicated Service award Wallace High Sch.; named Selected Tchr. of Yr., West Orange-Cove Consol. Ind. Sch. Dist., 1972, 79. Mem. Tex. State Tchrs. Assn. (pres. dist. V. 1977-79, dir.), Tex. Classroom Tchrs. Assn., W. Orange-Cove Classroom Tchrs. Assn. (pres.), NEA, Tex. Bus. Edn. Assn., Nat. Bus. Edn. Assn., Delta Sigma Theta. Home: 2801 Fairway St Orange TX 77630

CURTIS, CARL THOMAS, physician; b. Rayne, La., June 3, 1932; s. Carl Dwight and Inza (Gillentine) C.; B.S., U. Southwestern La., 1955; M.D., La. State U., 1956; m. Barbara Nell Rosinski, May 2, 1976; children by previous marriage—Sharon Elizabeth, Dwight Thomas, Karon Louise. Intern, Confederate Meml. Med. Center, Shreveport, La., 1956-57; pvt. practice gen. medicine, Rayne, 1959—; staff Rayne Branch Hosp., 1959—; vis. staff Lake Charles (La.) Charity Hosp., 1973—; asso. staff Our Lady of Lourdes Hosp., Lafayette, La., 1975—; clin. asst. prof. dept. family practice La. State U. Sch. Medicine, 1976—. Served with USAF, 1957-59. Diplomate Am. Bd. Family Practice. Fellow Am. Acad. Family Physicians; mem. AMA, So., La., Acadia Parish med. assns., La. State U. Interfraternity Council (pres. 1956-57), La. State U. Undergrad. Med. Soc., Phi Kappa Phi, Phi Beta Pi. Democrat. Methodist. Home: 820 F St Rayne LA 70578 Office: 301 S Chevis St Rayne LA 70578

CURTIS, CHARLES GARNSEY, travel agent; b. Chgo., Aug. 10, 1926; s. George G. and Marie S. (Smith) C.; B.A., Beloit (Wis.) Coll., 1950; m. Betty L. David, Jan. 4, 1975; children—William W., James S. Pres. Am. & Internat. Travel Service, Inc., Memphis, 1953—. Deacon Idlewild Presbyterian Ch., Memphis, 1955-68. Served with USN, 1944-46. Mem. Inst. Certified Travel Agts. (life), Memphis Travelers Aid Soc., Am. Soc. Travel Agts. Republican. Presbyterian. Clubs: Memphis Skal, Univ., Summit, Whitehaven Rotary. Home: 2189 Kimbrough Woods Pl Germantown TN 38138 Office: 8 N 3d St Memphis TN 38103

CURTIS, CHARLES LEE, advt. exec.; b. St. Louis, Nov. 23, 1945; s. Charles Leonard and Doris Earline (Petty) C.; B.J., U. Mo., 1967, M.A., 1968; m. Gloria Jean Beiser, June 25, 1966; children—Daniel Charles, Gregory Lee. Advt. mgr. Monsanto Co., St. Louis, 1968-71; account exec. Marsteller Inc., Chgo., 1971-73; v.p. Adplan, Inc., Chgo., 1973-77; pres. Curtis Advt., Inc., Chgo., 1977-78; account supr. Trary-Locks Advt. Co., Dallas, 1978—. Dir. public relations Citizens for Mikva, Chgo., 1974, 76, 78; dir. Democratic Com. Evanston, Ill., 1976. Office: 1407 Main St Dallas TX 75202

CURTIS, CHARLIE MONROE, univ. dean; b. Gandy, La., Nov. 27, 1917; s. Leo and Emmaline (Sandel) C.; B.S., La. State U., 1940, M.S., 1952, Ph.D., 1958; m. Lillie Leola Fish, Feb. 16, 1941; children—Thomas David, JoAnn Curtis. Vocational agr. tchr. Leesville (La.) public schs., 1940-42, Anacoco (La.) public schs., 1945-49; mem. faculty La. State U., Baton Rouge, 1949-52, 62—, asso. dean Coll. of Agr., dir. Sch. of Vocat. Edn. and prof. vocat. agrl. edn., 1972—; with La. Dept. Edn., Baton Rouge, 1952-62; cons. in field. Active Pollard Estates Civic Assn., 1958—. Served with U.S. Army, 1942-45. Recipient Disting. Service Plaque, So. Agrl. Edn. Conf., 1963; Outstanding Prof. award Alpha Gamma Rho, 1978. Mem. La. Vocat. Assn., La. Vocat. Agr. Tchrs., Am. Vocat. Assn., Nat. Vocat. Agr. Tchrs. Assn., La. Edn. Assn., Gamma Sigma Delta, Phi Delta Kappa, Phi Kappa Phi, Alpha Zeta, Alpha Tau Alpha. Democrat. Methodist. Club: Kiwanis. Contbr. articles in field to profl. jours.; editor Summaries of Vocat. Agr. Research, So. Region, 1964-69; asso. editor Am. Assn. Tchr. Educators in Agr. Jour., 1966-69. Home: 1555 S Columbine St Baton Rouge LA 70808 Office: 208 Stubbs Hall La State Univ Baton Rouge LA 70803

CURTIS, EDGAR JONAH, JR., textile co. exec.; b. Charlotte, N.C., June 9, 1941; s. E.J. and Louise (Tucker) C.; B.S. in Mktg., U. S.C., 1964, M.B.A. in Mktg., 1965; m. Patricia Kathern Russell, June 8, 1964; children—Sharyn Patricia, Christina Karen. With Amoco Oil Co., Atlanta, 1965-69; v.p., gen. mgr. Stewart-Warner Corp., Atlanta, 1972-79, Southeastern regional mgr., Chgo., 1969-72; v.p., gen. mgr. H. F. Livermore, Boston, also v.p. fgn. ops., Greenville, S.C., 1979—; mem. faculty DeKalb Coll., 1979. Bd. dirs. So. Auto Show. Mem. Ga. Automotive Wholesalers (dir.). Presbyterian. Clubs: Masons, Scottish Rite. Address: 123 Sugar Creek Ln Greer SC 29651

CURTIS, JAMES ROBERT, folding carton co. exec.; b. Danbury, Conn., Jan. 29, 1938; s. Nelson George and Sarah Frances (Knepp) C.; Asso. in Bus., Nichols Coll., 1959; student U. Bridgeport, 1960-61; div.; children—Pamela Brooks, Christine Sarah, James Robert. With Curtis Packaging Co., Sandy Hook, Conn., 1960-78, pres., 1976-78; pres. Roanoke Box Inc. (Va.), 1978—; dir. Curtiscorp, Sandy Hook, Roanoke Box Inc. Mem. Internat. Mgmt. Council (chmn. top mgmt. adv. bd. 1975-78), Young Presidents Orgn., Paperboard Packaging Council. Episcopalian. Home: 3318K Circle Brook Dr Roanoke VA 24014 Office: 621 Ashlawn St Box 4086 Roanoke VA 24015

CURTIS, JAMES ROBERT, JR., radio sta. exec.; b. Longview, Tex., Aug. 18, 1945; s. James Robert and Sarah DeRue (Armstrong) C.; B.B.A., Tex. Christian U., 1967; postgrad. Am. Inst. Fgn. Trade, 1968; m. Sue Skaggs, Aug. 18, 1967; children—Jason Skaggs, Elizabeth Ann. With Radio Sta. KFRO, Longview, Tex., 1967—, v.p., 1968—; mem. staff Radio Sta KHAT, Phoenix, 1967-68; v.p., co-owner Workmans Oil; partner Mac Investments, 1974—; co-owner J&L Petroleum, 1976—. Mem. city commn. City of Longview, 1975—, mayor, 1977-78; bd. dirs. Longview Mus. Arts Center, Greater Longview United Fund. Mem. Christian Ch. Home: 2012 Sunshine Sq Longview TX 75601 Office: PO Box 792 Longview TX 75601

CURTIS, JAMES WYLIE, psychologist; b. Madison, Ind., July 3, 1913; s. Wylie Ralph and Gertrude (Allison) C.; A.B., U. Ky., 1937, M.S., 1938; postgrad. Princeton, 1942-43, Universidad de Panama, 1946-47; m. Mildred Louise Fisher, Apr. 29, 1942; children—James W.A., Carol Ann. Cons. psychologist Ill. Div. Vocational Rehab., Springfield, 1947-69; staff psychologist Meml. Hosp.; personnel cons. Capitol Bank of Springfield, Town and Country Bank, 1962-69; prof. Lincoln Land Community Coll., also chmn. behavioral sci. div., 1969-73. Cons. psychologist Sangamo Electric Co., Hosp. Order St. Francis. Served from 1st lt. to lt. col., USAAF, 1941-47. Recipient medal of Merit Am. Numismatic Assn., 1955, medal of Merit. Central States Numismatic Soc., 1950, Heath Lit. award, Am. Numismatic Assn., 1957, Lit. award, Chgo. Coin Club, 1955. Fellow Royal Numismatic Soc., A.A.A.S.; mem. Sociedad Numismatica de Mexico, Am. Numis. Assn. (gov.), Ill., Midwestern psychol. assns., Springfield Personnel Assn. (dir. 1960-72), Am. Research Center Egypt. Egypt Exploration Soc., Pi Kappa Alpha. Club: Windcrest Golf. Author: (tests) Curtis Completion Form, 1953; Curtis Classification Form, 1951; Curtis Checking Test, 1954; Curtis Interest-Aptitude Index, 1952; Curtis Interest Scale, 1959; Curtis Capacity Test, Curtis Cross Reference Test, Curtis Com- putation Test, 1965; (books) Media of Exchange in Ancient Egypt, 1951; The Tetradrachms of Roman Egypt, 1957; The Coinage of Roman Egypt, 1956; United States Pattern Coin Handbook, 1949; (monographs) Coinage of Pharaonic Egypt, 1956, Domitius Domitianus and His Coinage, 1957; Pictorial Coin Types at the Roman Mint at Alexandria, 1955; A Study of the Relationship Between Hypnotic Susceptibility and Intelligence, 1943; Administration of the Purdue Pegboard Test to Blind Individuals, 1950. Home: 634 Weatherly Dr San Antonio TX 78239

CURTIS, JOHN AVERY, mgmt. exec.; b. Bklyn., Apr. 10, 1909; s. Osborn and Edna (Onderdonk) C.; B.A., Yale, 1930; m. Helen Frances Brown, June 11, 1938 (dec.); children—Katherine Edna (Mrs. Douglas Vernon Rigler), Helen Virginia (Mrs. John Guyton Knepper), John Avery, Joanne Louise (Mrs. Jeremiah Evarts); m. 2d, Mrs. Stewart Jones Schmalbach, Aug. 21, 1971. Press agt., mgr. Charles Hopkins Prodns., Inc., N.Y.C., 1930-32; v.p., gen. mgr. First Div. Pictures, Inc., Hollywood, Calif., 1932-36; advt. mgr. Current History mag., N.Y.C., 1936-38; pres. Casman, Cook & Curtis, 1938-40; advt. mgr., asst. pub. Atlantic Monthly mag., Boston, 1940-42; v.p. Halstead Traffic Communications Corp., N.Y.C., 1941-45; mgr. mobile communications div. Farnsworth div. Internat. Tel. & Tel. Corp., Ft. Wayne, Ind., 1945-50, mgr. power equipment div., 1956; mgr. track equipment div. Pullman Standard Mfg. Co., Chgo., 1950-53, gen. mgr. sales Westinghouse Tube div., Elmira, N.Y., 1953-55; dir. marketing ACF Electronics div., Washington, 1957-62; v.p., gen. mgr. marketing div. Electronics Assos., Inc., Long Branch, N.J., 1962-68; founder, pres. Center for Excellence, Inc., 1968—. Mem. Am. Soc. Engring. Edn., Computers in Edn. (founder), Nat. Acad. Engring. (adv. com. on issues in ednl. tech. commn. on edn.). Co-editor Educational Telecommunications Delivery Systems. Presbyterian. Clubs: Yale (N.Y.C). Contbr. articles to profl. jours. Patentee in field. Home: 107 Walnut Hills Dr Williamsburg VA 23185

CURTIS, JOYCE VIRGINIA CHEWNING, artist, educator; b. Dallas, Dec. 7, 1931; d. Ellis E. and Velma M. Chewning; B.A., Abilene Christian U., 1952; postgrad. Tex. Christian U., 1954, Baylor U., 1956, Ramon Froman Sch. Art, 1967-68; m. Jimmy H. Curtis, June 5, 1955; children—Michelle, Marcia L. Tchr. art Bowie (Tex.) public schs., 1952, Ft. Worth public schs., 1953-55, Hillsboro (Tex.) public schs., 1955-60; faculty Hill Jr. Coll., Hillsboro, 1973—, head dept. art, 1975—; exhibited in one-person shows at Ft. Worth Christian Coll., 1967, Studio Gallery, Waco, Tex., 1965, The Patrician, Hillsboro, 1976; exhibited in group show at Bond's Alley Art Show, Hillsboro, 1970-79; represented in permanent collections; condr. workshops Hillsboro and Abilene (Tex.) for sch. system. Named artist of yr. Abilene Christian U., 1978. Mem. Southwestern Watercolor Soc., Nat. Council Art Adminstrs. Mem. Ch. of Christ. Author, illustrator: Historic Hillsboro, sketches of homes and bldgs., 1979. Home: Route 3 Box 189 Hillsboro TX 76645

CURTIS, MARIE ANN, educator; b. Arkansas City, Kans., July 14, 1948; d. James Melanchthon and Eleanor Lucille (Blandy) Ellinger; student Cowley County Community Jr. Coll., 1967-69; B.A., Tex. Tech. U., 1971; M.A., Adams State Coll., 1975; Ed.D., U. Ariz., 1979; m. Donald Ray Curtis, June 27, 1971; 1 dau., Staci Renee. Gen. office worker Maurer-Neurer, Inc., Arkansas City, 1966-69; counselor Colo. Sch. for Deaf and Blind, Colorado Springs, 1971-73, Tex. Rehab. Commn., Lubbock, 1973-74, Spl. Services Office, Rehab. Center, U. Ariz., Tucson, 1976-77; teaching asst. Rehab. Center, U. Ariz., Tucson, 1977-78; pvt. practice rehab. cons., Austin, Tex., 1978-79; asst. prof. Stephen F. Austin State U., Nacogdoches, Tex., 1980—. Mem. Nat. Rehab. Assn., Nat. Rehab. Counseling Assn., Am. Personnel and Guidance Assn., Am. Rehab. Counseling Assn., Am. Deafness and Rehab. Assn., Nat. Assn. of the Deaf, Conv. Am. Instrs. of the Deaf. Democrat. Baptist. Home: PO Box 6126 Stephen F Austin State U Nacogdoches TX 75962 Office: Dept Sch Services Stephen F Austin State U Nacogdoches TX 75962

CURTIS, MARY GERVASE BARNETT (MRS. BUFORD C. CURTIS), publisher, genealogist, author; b. Little Rock, June 8, 1924; d. Edgar Wheeler and Nellie (O'Neal) Barnett; grad. high sch.; m. Buford C. Curtis, Sept. 19, 1943; children—Mary Michele Curtis Hill, Buford C., Robert Thornton Higgins, Eura Melisa Curtis Dittfurth, Sidney Watson, Katherine Victoria. Editor, pub. South Fort Worthian, weekly, 1954-56, Strickland & Allied Families Query & Answer Exchange, quar., 1958—; owner Arrow Printing Co., Ft. Worth, 1953-76; founder, pres. Am. Reference Publishers, Inc., 1967-72; pres. In Print Books, Inc., 1972—; publisher, bibliographer, owner Mag. of Bibliographies, 1972—; dir. Ft. Belknap Archives, Inc., 1971—; owner Family Tree Shoppe, Ft. Worth. Chmn. ramp com. Tarrant County of Tex. Hist. Survey Com., 1959-66; judge genealogy and heraldry Okla. State Fair, 1972-74. Fellow Tex. Geneal. Soc. (charter mem., rec. sec. 1960-74, chmn. writers and editors workshop 1976); mem. Ft. Worth

Geneal. Soc. (charter mem., chmn. publicity 1959-60), Tex., Cath. (pres. Ft. Worth 1959—), Tarrant County (dir. 1962—, rec. sec. 1962-63) hist. socs., Cath. Daus. Am., S.W. Council Geneal. and Hist. Socs. (sec. 1973), S.W. Archivists (charter). Author: Early East Tennessee Tax Lists. Editor: Stirpes, Quar. Tex. Geneal. Soc., 1973-76. Home: 3812 Lafayette Fort Worth TX 76107

CURTIS, RICHARD HARVEY, constrn. co. exec.; b. Balaklava, South Australia, Apr. 23, 1931; came to U.S., 1971; s. John William and Winifred Bramhall (Fidler) C.; B. Applied Sci., U. Adelaide, 1952; m. Eleanor Robson, Apr. 3, 1956; children—Robert Harvey, Helen Louise. Chem. engr. Powergas Corp. of Australia, Melbourne, 1953; chem. engr. Powergas Corp., Stockton-on-Tees, Eng., 1953-61, head devel., 1961-64, chief engr., 1964-68, div. tech. dir., 1968-71; dir. engring. Davy McKee Corp. (formerly Davy Powergas Inc.), Lakeland, Fla., 1971-72, v.p. engring., 1972—. Mem. com. Boy Scouts Am., 1975-77, merit badge counselor, 1975—. Chartered engr., U.K.; registered profl. engr., Fla., La., N.Mex., Ariz., Ohio, Oreg., Wis., Del. Fellow Inst. Gas Engrs. U.K.; mem. ASME, Am. Inst. Chem. Engrs., Fla. Engring. Soc. (sr.), Nat. Soc. Profl. Engrs. Episcopalian. Clubs: Lone Palm Golf, Lakeland Yacht and Country, Continental Country, Deep Six Scuba Diving, Univs. Lodge (Durham, Eng.). Home: 141 Skyland Dr Lakeland FL 33803 Office: PO Drawer 5000 Lakeland FL 33803

CUSH, JOSEPH WILBUR, dentist; b. Natchitoches, La., Aug. 22, 1929; s. Samuel and Angeline Marie (Catanese) C.; student Centenary Coll., 1946-48; D.D.S., Loyola U. of So., 1953; m. Beverly Jean Burch, Aug. 21, 1954; children—Joseph Wilbur, Derrie Anne, Gregory Samuel, Bryan Stephan, Angela Marie. Intern oral surgery Charity Hosp., New Orleans, 1953-54; resident oral surgery Confederate Meml. Med. Center, Shreveport, La., 1956-58; pvt. practice oral surgery, Shreveport, 1958—; mem. staffs La. State Sch. Medicine Post Grad. Dept. Dir. United Merc. Bank. Pres. N.W. La. Cancer Soc., 1970. Bd. dirs. Doctor's Hosp., 1965-75. Served with USAF, 1954-56. Fellow Acad. Internat. Dentistry; mem. Am. Dental Soc. of Anesthesiology, Am., La., 4th Dist. (pres. 1965) dental assns., Pierre Fauchard Acad., Shreveport C. of C. (dir. 1976, 77, v.p. 1979), Delta Sigma Delta, Am. Legion. Roman Catholic. K.C., Rotarian. Clubs: Serra, Pierremont Oaks Tennis, East Ridge Country, University. Home: 307 Deborah St Shreveport LA 71106 Office: 915 Shreveport Barksdale Hwy Shreveport LA 71105

CUSTODI, GEORGE LOUIS, chem. co. exec.; b. Trani, Italy, Oct. 2, 1942; s. Angelo Luigi and Vera (Moscatelli) C.; came to U.S., 1956; naturalized, 1959; B.S. in Chem. Engring., Iowa State U., 1964; M.S. in Chem. Oceanography, Tex. A. and M. U., 1971; m. Sandra Leah Lackey, Aug. 1, 1970; children—Victoria Ann, Andrea Christine. Mgr. Lab. Services Commonwealth Lab., Inc., Richmond, Va., 1972-74; supr. E.I. DuPont de Nemours & Co., Inc., Richmond, 1974—. Instr. Naval Reserve Officers Sch., Richmond, 1972-74. Served to lt. USN, 1964-70; mem. Res. Sun Oil scholarship, 1970-71; Welch Found. fellow, 1970-71. Mem. Am. Inst. Chem. Engrs. (vice chmn. 1974-75: Tidewater chpt. chmn. 1975), Am. Inst. Chemists, U.S. Naval Inst., Naval Res. Officer Assn., Water Pollution Control Fedn., Church Hill Residents Assn., Knights of St. Patrick, Delta Tau Delta. Lutheran. Contbr. articles to profl. jours. Home: 4469 Old Fox Ct Midlothian VA 23113 Office: E I du Pont de Nemours and Co PO Box 27001 Richmond VA 23261

CUTHBERTSON, BERTHA MARIE, hosp. exec.; b. Dallas, Oct. 23; d. John N. and Marie Katherine (Walker) Prewitt; student Oklahoma City U., 1942, Okla. U., 1963, 73; m. Jordan Leon Cuthertson, Mar. 31, 1935; children—Michael T., Ronald D. With Halliburton's Dept. Store, Oklahoma City, 1932-41; civilian supply officer USAAF, 1941-44; adminstr. Mid-Del Manor Nursing Home, Midwest City, Okla., 1963-68; dir. vols. and public relations South Community Hosp., Oklahoma City, 1968—; bd. dirs. Okla. Health Scis. Fed. Credit Union; leader seminars and workshops. Active local March of Dimes, Cancer Soc. Mem. Am. Soc. Dirs. Vol. Services, Public Relations Soc. Am., Okla. Soc. Dirs. Vol. Services (exec. bd. 1974, editor newsletter 1979), Okla. Soc. Public Relations, Central Okla. Soc. Dirs. Vol. Services, Am. Bus. Women's Assn. (Woman of Yr. 1974). Democrat. Clubs: Ivy Garden (Midwest City); Order Eastern Star. Address: 3505 Shady Brook Dr Midwest City OK 73110

CUTLER, DONALD ELWYN, hosp. adminstr.; b. Cold Water, Mich., Apr. 12, 1947; s. Elwyn Edward and Rowena Belle (Hosmer) C.; B.A., Roberts Wesleyan Coll., 1969; M.S.W., U. Okla., 1975; M.B.A., Central State U., 1977; m. Linda Ruth Schwab, May 26, 1967; children—Kimberly R., Edward Elwyn. Caseworker, Monroe County (N.Y.) Dept. Social Services, 1969-72; dir. social services Deaconess Hosp. and Home, Oklahoma City, 1972-77, acctg. mgr. and social services cons. Deaconess Hosp., 1978—; dir. admitting/social services Univ. Hosp., Oklahoma City, 1977-78; mem. curriculum adv. com. U. Okla. Sch. Social Work; mem. profl. adv. bd. Okla. Home Health Care Agy.; treas., bd. dirs. Okla. Health Services Fed. Credit Union. Mem. citizens screening com. Juvenile Bur. Oklahoma County, 1975—; coach referee, dir. N.W. Oklahoma City Soccer Assn., 1979; mem. bd. adminstrn., treas. ins. and retirement bd., and chmn. moral issues and social action com. Okla. Conf. Free Methodist Ch.; mem. social action council Free Meth. Ch. N. Am. N.Y. State Regents scholar, 1965-69. Mem. Nat. Assn. Social Workers, Acad. Cert. Social Workers, Hosp. Fin. Mgmt. Assn. Home: 3917 NW 58th Terr Oklahoma City OK 73112 Office: 5501 N Portland St Oklahoma City OK 73112

CUTTER, ERRAL, steel co. exec.; b. Pitts., Dec. 7, 1943; s. Alex and Mary Rose (Burke) C.; student Norwich U., 1961-62; B.S. in Geology, Waynesburg (Pa.) Coll., 1965; m. Madeline J. Cutter, May 29, 1964; children—Gary, Lisa. Mgmt. trainee U.S. Steel Co., 1965-66; dist. mgr. Randustrial, Inc., 1966-69; gen. mgr. Structuramics, Inc., Syracuse, N.Y., 1969-71; S.E. regional mgr. Steel-Span, Inc., Bena, Va., 1971-78; dist. mgr. Inryco, Inc. div. Inland-Ryerson Steel, Bena, 1978—. Club: Richmond Engrs. Office: Rt 3715 Bena VA 23018

CUTTINO, CHARLES LYNUM, III, oral surgeon; b. Sumter, S.C., Nov. 19, 1940; s. Charles Lynum and Elizabeth (Marsh) C.; B.S., Clemson U., 1962; D.D.S., Med. Coll. Va., 1966; m. Peggy J. Jepsen, Aug. 8, 1964; children—Charles Marsh, David Scott. Intern, Wilford Hall USAF Hosp., Lackland AFB, Tex., 1966-67; intern in oral surgery Med. Coll. Va., Richmond, 1969-70, resident in oral surgery, 1970-72, asst. clin. prof. oral surgery, 1972—; practice oral surgery, Richmond, Va., 1972—; v.p. Peters, Malbon, Green & Cuttino, Assos., Ltd., Richmond, 1972—; mem. active staff St. Mary's Hosp., Richmond Meml. Hosp., Johnston-Willis Hosp., Retreat Hosp., Chippenham Hosp., Henrico Doctors' Hosp.; mem. courtesy staff Imperial Hosp., Richmond Eye Hosp., Stuart Circle Hosp. Bd. dirs. Am. Cancer Soc., Richmond, 1974-78. Served with USAF, 1966-69. Diplomate Am. Bd. Oral and Maxillofacial Surgery. Mem. ADA, Am. Soc. Oral and Maxillofacial Surgeons, Va. Soc. Oral Surgeons, Richmond Dental Soc., Atwood Wash Soc., Sigma Xi, Delta Kappa Alpha, Omicron Kappa Upsilon, Sigma Zeta, Psi Omega. Methodist. Home: 512 Welwyn Rd Richmond VA 23229 Office: 3217 Grove Ave Richmond VA 23221

CUTTS, VIRGINIA ALLEN PAIRO (MRS. HARVEY CLARK CUTTS), former advt. exec.; b. Atlanta, Jan. 12, 1903; d. Louis Prescott Pairo and Lucy Walthall Jones Pairo; A.B., Oglethorpe U., 1924; m. Harvey Clark Cutts, Apr. 12, 1962; 1 stepdau., Caroline Cutts (Mrs. Randall Edmund Jones). Sales promotion Allyn & Bacon Pub. Co., 1924-25; advt. mgr. Philbosian, home furnishings, 1925-27, J.M. High Dept Store, 1928, Loeb Advt. Agy., 1929-35, Loeb & Pairo, 1935-47; owner Pairo Advt. Agy., Atlanta, 1947-66. Mem. housing com. YWCA, 1934-35; active A.R.C., Am. Heart Assn., Jr. Achievement. Mem. Fashion Group, Inc. (sec. 1953-54), Advt. Fedn. Am., Atlanta Advt. Club (dir. 1953-58), Am. Women in Radio and TV, Atlanta Hist. Soc., Atlanta Art Assn., Atlanta Symphony Guild (policy bd. 1959-62, v.p. 1961-63), D.A.R., English-Speaking Union, Atlanta Opera Guild. Episcopalian. Club: Piedmont Driving (Atlanta). Pub.: Maum Nancy (Susan Merrick Haywood). Home: Greenville GA 30222 also 3701 Scenic Hwy Pensacola FL 32504

CYLC, RICHARD MARION, computer services co. exec.; b. Chester, Pa., Aug. 15, 1931; s. Walter F. and Angela M. (Twarog) C.; asso. degree Pa. Mil. Coll., 1958, B.S. in Bus. Adminstrn., 1961; m. Ilona M. Lajca, June 13, 1953; children—Richard Marion, Stephen, David, Valerie Ann. With Sinclair Refining Co., 1953-68, sr. indsl. engr., 1965-67, mgr. gen. systems, 1967-69; overall coordinator consolidation and relocation BP & Sohio (merger with Sinclair Refining Co. 1969), Atlanta and Cleve., 1969-70; with Nat. Data Corp., Atlanta, 1970—, v.p. processing ops., facilities mgmt. div., 1977—. Pres. parish council Holy Cross Roman Catholic Ch., 1979—. Served with USAF, 1947-51; Korea. Mem. Am. Mgmt. Assn., PMC Alumni Assn. (capt. 1976—). Republican. Club: Nottaway Swim (membership chmn., dir. 1973-76). Home: 3774 East Brook Ct NE Atlanta GA 30340 Office: Nat Data Corp 12 Corporate Sq Atlanta GA 30329

CZARNIECKI, MYRON JAMES, III, art museum dir.; b. San Francisco, May 28, 1948; s. Myron James, Jr. and Laura Maxine (Atwood) C.; A.B., Wabash (Ind.) Coll., 1971; postgrad. Sch. Art Inst. Chgo., 1971-72; m. Anne Frances Dixon, Nov. 20, 1976; 1 son, Mark James. Photographer, then audio/visual supr. Art Inst. Chgo., 1971-74; dir. edn. and state services Ringling Mus. Art, Sarasota, Fla., 1974-76; dir. Miss. Mus. Art, Jackson, 1976—; lectr. Art Inst. Chgo.; cons. Nat. Endowment Arts and Humanities; bd. dirs. Miss. Inst. Arts and Letters, 1978—. Mem. Internat. Council Museums, Am. Assn. Museums, Southeastern Museums Conf., Miss. Museums Assn. (v.p. 1978-80). Author lectr. series, exhbn. catalogs. Office: PO Box 1330 Jackson MS 39205

CZYSZCZON, JOHN ALBERT, aluminum mfg. co. exec.; b. Chester, Pa., Aug. 29, 1940; s. Albert and Monica C.; B.S. cum laude, Widener Coll., Chester, 1970; m. Joan M. Jarusinska, May 25, 1968; children—Gregory, Christopher, Jonathan. Maintenance dispatcher Gen. Motors Corp., Wilmington, Del., 1965-70, hourly employment and tng. sect., personnel dept., 1970-74; asst. plant personnel mgr. Reynolds Metals Co., Chester, 1974-77, plant personnel mgr., Bristol, Va., 1977—. Mem. Employers Adv. Com. to Va. Employment Commn., 1978—; chmn. placement improvement Bristol Coll. Bd. Advs., 1979—. Served with U.S. Army, 1962-65. Mem. Am. Soc. Personnel Adminstrn. Roman Catholic. Home: 343 Monticello Dr Bristol VA 24201 Office: Reynolds Metals Co 750 Old Abingdon Hwy Bristol VA 24201

DABBS, BRUCE RANDAL, mfg. co. exec.; b. Pine Bluff, Ark., May 10, 1954; s. Albert Glen and Betty Jo (Krisell) D.; student U. Central Ark., 1972-74; B. Indsl. Engring. summa cum laude, Ga. Inst. Tech., 1977; m. Susan L. Rongey, June 10, 1977. Farmer, Humphrey, Ark., 1972-77; mgr. nonwovens contract converting Buckeye Cellulose, Columbus, Miss., 1977-78, fng. opns. mgr., nonwovens contract converting, 1978-79, nonwovens prodn. area mgr., Memphis, 1979—. Mem. Am. Inst. Indsl. Engrs., Tau Beta Pi, Phi Kappa Phi. Mem. Ch. of Christ. Home: 3611 Allandale St Memphis TN 38111 Office: 2899 Jackson Ave Memphis TN 38108

DABBS, JOHN WILSON THOMAS, physicist; b. Nashville, Dec. 11, 1921; s. John Wilson Thomas and Ruth (Fuqua) D.; B.S., U. Tenn., 1944, Ph.D., 1955; m. Elizabeth Jane Hicks, Sept. 16, 1945; children—Carol Jane, John Richard, David Frederick. Research asst. Metall. Lab., U. Chgo., 1944-45; jr. engr. Applied Physics Lab., Johns Hopkins U., Balt., 1945; physicist Oak Ridge Nat. Lab., 1946—, sr. staff physicist, 1968—; pres. Oak Ridge Devel. Corp., 1973-78; v.p. Pic-Air, Inc., Oak Ridge, 1971-76; pres. Elographics, Inc., Oak Ridge, 1976-77, treas., 1977—. Fulbright lectr. Instituto de Fisica, San Carlos de Bariloche, Argentina, 1961; vis. scientist Centre d'Etudes Nucleaires, Saclay, France, 1967-68. Pres., Karns (Tenn.) Community Club, 1956. Served with ordnance AUS, 1945-46. Fellow Am. Phys. Soc.; mem. Oak Ridge C. of C. (chmn. local industry com. 1972), Mobile Steam Soc. (pres. 1973), Delta Tau Delta. Republican. Home: 106 Osage Rd Oak Ridge TN 37830 Office: PO Box X Oak Ridge TN 37830

DABBS, MIRIAM ADAIR (MRS. CHESTER NORWOOD DABBS), journalist, artist; b. Rialto, Calif., May 6, 1908; d. Watts McIntosh and Betty (Pearson) Adair; B.A., Miss. State Coll. for Women, 1930; m. Chester Norwood Dabbs, Dec. 24, 1933; 1 son, Willis Norwood. English instr., Jones County Jr. Coll., Ellisville, Miss., 1933-34; instr. Am. history Northwest Jr. Coll., Senatobia, Miss., 1935-36; soc. editor Clarksdale (Miss.) Daily Register, 1942-47; feature writer, corr. Clarion-Ledger, Jackson, Miss., 1964-76; corr. Jackson Daily News, 1968-76, Press-Scimitar, Memphis, 1969-74, Here's Clarksdale mag., 1973—. Exhibited one-man shows Galeries Raymond Duncan, Paris, France, 1970, 71, 74, 77, 79, Ligoa Duncan Gallery, N.Y.C., 1971, 77, Mcpl. Mus. Art, Paris, 1974, Luxembourg Palace Mus., 1978, also regional exhbns.; works represented in pvt. and museum collections; lectr. in field, 1972. Chmn., Missionary Soc. Bapt. Ch., 1952-53; mem. Clarksdale Beautification Commn., chmn., 1952-54, 56-63, sec., 1955, 68; Bicentennial historian, Clarksdale, 1974-75. Recipient Beautification Merit award, Miss. C. of C. community program at Clarksdale, 1961; Prix de Paris for painting Bridge to Sunrise, 1970, for The Rising Flood, 1974, for Where Eagles Rest, 1977, for Feeding Time, 1978; Palme d'Or, Internat. Festival Paintings, St. Germaine de Pres, Paris, 1974, 78. Mem. Nat. League Am. Pen Women (award; editor Pen Drifts, 1957), Accademia Italia delle Arti e del Lavoro (gold medallion), Ulster-Scot Hist. Soc. (Belfast, Ireland), D.A.R. Clubs: Clarksdale Woman's (past pres.), Town and Country Garden (Clarksdale, Miss.). Author: Idyls of the Delta: Coahoma, 1948; The Passing Storm; Sepaled Horns; Sonnets From India, 1962. Contbr. articles on founding families of Miss. to tech. lit. Research in genealogy. Home: 321 Maple St Clarksdale MS 38614

DABNEY, RICHARD LAWSON (DICK), writer; b. Charlottesville, Va., Oct. 26, 1933; s. Wythe Overton, Jr., and Reba Adams (Lawson) D.; Ph.D. in Am. Civilization, George Washington U., 1971; m. Dana Elisabeth Trice, Aug. 9, 1969; children—Vaden, John, Norah. Teaching fellow George Washington U., Washington, 1968-69, mem. faculty, 1969-72; author: (novels) Old Man Jim's Book of Knowledge, 1973, The Honor System, 1976, (biography) A Good Man: The Life of Sam Ervin, 1976; weekly columnist Washington Post; monthly columnist Side Streets, Washingtonian mag. Recipient fiction award Nat. Endowment for Arts, 1975. Office: Editorial Page Washington Post 1150 15th St NW Washington DC 20071

DAENECKE, ERIC, lawyer, former UN advisor; b. Bklyn., Jan. 24, 1914; s. August and Ida (Brosowski) D.; B.S., Am. U., Washington, 1944, M.A., 1947 Ph.D., 1950; J.D., U. Balt., 1954; LL.M. cum laude, U. Manila, 1964; D.C.L., U. Santo Tomas, Manila, 1966; m. G. Alma Schwenn, Apr. 5, 1936 (dec.); children—William Eric, Maryellen Daenecke Lawlor. Chief of finance GAO and Dept. Labor, Washington, 1935-56. pub. adminstrn. adviser Dept. State, 1957-70; interregional advisor UN, N.Y.C., 1970-77; tchr. Strayer Coll., Washington, 1951-56, U. Md. Far East Br., 1967-70, grad. law U. Santo Tomas, Manila 1964-66; minister Christian Ch., Washington, 1953-56. Mem. Am. Inst. C.P.A.'s, Fed., Inter-Am. bar assns., Am. Accounting Assn., Rosicrucian Order. Club: Lawyers. Author: Tales of Mullah Nasr-Ud-Din, 1960; More Tales, 1961. Home: 5640 Wood St Port Orange FL 32019

DAGGY, ROBERT EDWARD, lit. archive curator, educator; b. New Castle, Ind., July 28, 1940; s. George Edward and Anna Louise (Linn) D.; B.A., Yale U., 1962; postgrad. Columbia U., 1962-63, Ball State U., 1965-66; M.A., U. Wis., 1968, Ph.D., 1971. Asst. to archivist Yale U. Archives, 1963-65; tchr. Darlington Sch. for Boys, Rome, Ga., 1965-67; asst. prof. ednl. policy studies and history U. Wis., Madison, 1971-73; cons. Thomas Merton Legacy Trust, Louisville, 1973-74; curator, asso. dir. Thomas Merton Studies Center, Bellarmine Coll., 1974—, lectr. div. edn., 1975—; lectr. dept. ednl. founds. U. Louisville, 1974—; advisor, lectr. to various groups holding programs, seminars on Thomas Merton. Mem. Am. Public Health Assn., Am. Assn. Coll. Tchrs. Edn., Ky. Ednl. Assn., Ky. Council on Archives, Alcoholism Council Ky., Am. Contract Bridge League, Louisville Bridge Assn., Yale Assn. Ky. Clubs: Louisville East End Democratic, Yale of Ind. Contbr. articles to profl. jours.; editor: Introductions East and West: The Foreign Prefaces of Thomas Merton, 1980. Home: 425 W Ormsby Ave Apt 706 Louisville KY 40203 Office: Thomas Merton Studies Center Bellarmine Coll Newburg Rd Louisville KY 40205

DAGLEY, JOHN CARL, educator; b. Newton, Ill., Oct. 3, 1942; s. Howard M. and Mary L. D.; B.A., Culver-Stockton Coll., 1964; M.S. in Edn., Ind. U., 1965; Ph.D., U. Mo., 1972; m. Peggy Leamer, June 5, 1968; children—Ryan Matthew, Ross Mitchell. Admissions counselor Culver-Stockton Coll., Canton, Mo., 1965-66, instr. psychology, 1966-68; staff counselor, intern U. Mo., Columbia, 1969-71, asst. dir. nat. career devel. guidance, counseling, placement project, 1971-72; asst. prof. counseling and human devel. services U. Ga., Athens, 1972-79, asso. prof., 1979—; cons pubs. schs., Ga., Fla., W.Va., Ky., Ala., S.C., Mo. Served with USCGR, 1966-72. Mem. Am., Ga. personnel and guidance assns., Nat., Ga. (pres. 1975-77) vocat. guidance assns., Assn. for Counselor Edn. and Supervision, Am. Vocat. Assn., Am. Psychol. Assn. Contbr. articles to profl. jours. Home: 100 Featherwood Hollow Athens GA 30601 Office: 408 Aderhold Hall Athens GA 30602

D'AGNESE, HELEN JEAN (MRS. JOHN J. D'AGNESE), artist; b. N.Y.C., July 6, 1922; d. Leonardo and Rose (ReDavid) De Santis; student City U. N.Y., 1940-42, Oakland Art Inst., 1954-56; m. John J. D'Agnese, Oct. 29, 1942; children—John, Linda, Diane, Michele, Helen, Gina, Paul. One-man shows Maude Sullivan Gallery, El Paso, 1964, John Wanamaker Gallery, Phila., 1966, U. N.Mex., 1967, Karo Manducci Gallery, San Francisco, 1968, Tuskegee Inst. Carver Mus., 1968, Lord & Taylor Gallery, N.Y.C., 1969, Harmon Gallery, Naples, Fla., 1970, Fontainbleau, Miami, 1970, Reflections Gallery, Atlanta, 1972, Williams Gallery, Atlanta, 1973, Red Piano Gallery, Hilton Head, S.C., 1975, Terrace Gallery, Atlanta, 1975, Americana Gallery, Tex., 1977, Kraskin Gallery, Atlanta, Howard Gallery, Amelia Island, Fla., 1978, others; exhibited in group shows Musseo des Artes, Juarez, Mexico, 1968, Benedictine Art Show, N.Y.C., 1967, Southeast Contemporary Art Show, Atlanta, 1968, Atlanta U., 1969; represented in permanent collections Pres. Jimmy Carter, Atlanta, DeKalb Library, Atlanta, Mario Spada Gallery, Juarez; series of liturgical paintings exhibited at various churches, also at Mus. Contemporary Art at the Vatican, Rome, Italy. Judge art show Mt. Loretto Acad., El Paso, 1967; art demonstration and lectr. Margaret Harris Sch., Atlanta, 1970; artist-in-residence Montessori Sch., 1978-79. Recipient Gold medal Accademia Italia delle Arte, 1979. Mem. Atlanta Lawn Tennis Assn. Club: Tennis (Atlanta). Address: 1683 Knob Hill Ct NE Atlanta GA 30329

DAHLBERG, LEOLA LENORA, educator; b. Geneva, N.Y., Mar. 14, 1923; d. Arthur Chester and Lenora (Damuth) D.; B.A., Cornell U., 1945; M.Ed., Syracuse U., 1961; children—Arthur, Elizabeth Dahlberg Meade. Tchr. educable mentally retarded and elementary, Dryden, N.Y., 1955-61; tchr. educable mentally retarded Dade County (Fla.) Pub. Schs., Miami, 1961-71, tchr. specific learning disabilities, 1971—. Pres., Spotlight Community Players Theater, 1975-77. Recipient Certificate of Recognition, Assn. Spl. Class Tchrs. and Parents of the Handicapped, 1971. Mem. Fla. Textbook Council, Fla. Fedn. Council for Exceptional Children (pres. 1975-76), Internat. Platform Assn., United Tchrs. of Dade, Alpha Chi Omega, Alpha Delta Kappa (Honoris Causa award 1978), Phi Delta Kappa, Epsilon Tau Lambda. Republican. Presbyterian. Home: 11537 SW 81st Rd Miami FL 33156 Office: 8455 SW 119th St Miami FL 33156

DAHLBERG, PETER BLACK, actuary; b. San Antonio, Sept. 25, 1952; s. Hugh Black and Mary Carlton (Lutrick) D.; B.B.A., U. Tex., Austin, 1973, M.B.A., 1974; m. Elizabeth Gail McGill, May 27, 1973; 1 son, Eric Christopher. Actuarial trainee Southwestern Life Ins. Co., summer 1971, Govt Personnel Mut. Life Ins. Co., summer 1972, TCC Ins. Services, 1973-74; actuarial asst. Great Am. Res. Ins. Co., 1974, various positions, 1974-78, v.p., actuary, 1978—; v.p., actuary J.C. Penney Life Ins. Co. Recipient Outstanding Student award U. Tex. Coll. Bus., 1974. Fellow Soc. Actuaries; mem. Am. Acad. Actuaries, Actuaries Club S.W., Phi Kappa Phi, Alpha Kappa Psi. Baptist. Club: Centre Tennis. Office: 2020 Live Oak St Dallas TX 75221

DAHNE, ROBERT ALOYSIUS, real estate broker, pub. relations, advt. agy. exec., author, publisher; b. Owatonna, Minn., Aug. 19, 1921; s. Julius August and Teresa Marie (Zengerle) D.; grad. high sch.; m. Virginia Schilling Nye, May 27, 1953; children—William, James, Marie, Thomas. With Vero Beach Press Jour., 1948-50, McKee Jungle Gardens, Vero Beach, Fla., 1950-52, Fla. State Game and Fish Commn., 1952-60, Marineland of Fla., 1960-62; pres. R.A. Dahne & Assos., pub. relations, advt., 1965-75; pres. Am. Attractions, Inc., 1964-74; exec. dir. Fla. Pub. Relations Assn., Inc., 1972-77 (all Leesburg, Fla.); realtor, owner Leesburg Real Estate Service, (Fla.), 1975—. Served with USMCR, World War II. Mem. Mensa, Leesburg Bd. Realtors, Lake County C. of C. (pres. 1977). Lion, Elk. Club: Racquet (Harbor Island, Fla.). Author: Salt Water Fishing, 1952. Contbr. numerous articles, stories, newspapers and mags. Home: 1002 S 9 St Leesburg FL 32748 Office: 2100 N Citrus Blvd Leesburg FL 32748

DAILY, LOUIS, ophthalmologist; b. Houston, Apr. 23, 1919; s. Louis and Ray (Karchmer) D.; B.S., Harvard U., 1940; M.D., U. Tex. at Galveston, 1943; Ph.D., U. Minn., 1950; m. LaVerl Daily, Apr. 5, 1958; children—Evan Ray, Collin Derek. Intern, Jefferson Davis Hosp., Houston, 1943-44; resident in ophthalmology Jefferson Davis

Hosp., 1944-45, Mayo Found., Rochester, Minn., 1947-50; individual practice medicine, specializing in ophthalmology, Houston, 1950—; asso. prof. clin. ophthalmology U. Tex. at Houston, 1972—, Baylor Med. Sch., Houston, 1950—. Vice-pres. bd. dirs. Mus. Med. Sci., 1973-80, pres., 1980. Served as lt. (j.g.) USNR, 1945-46. Diplomate Am. Bd. Ophthalmology. Fellow A.C.S., Internat. Coll. Surgeons; mem. Soc. Prevention of Blindness (med. chmn. Tex. 1968-70), Contact Lens Assn. Ophthalmologists (exec. bd. 1976-78), Tex. Ophthal. Assn. (pres. 1963-64), Houston Ophthal. Soc. (pres. 1970-71), numerous other med. socs., Sigma Xi, Alpha Omega Alpha. Jewish. Clubs: Doctors, Harvard (dir. 1965-66) (Houston). Editorial bd. Jour. Pediatric Ophthalmology, 1964-68; asso. editor Eye, Ear, Nose and Throat Monthly, 1962-65, Jour. Ophthalmic Surgery, 1970; contbr. numerous articles to profl. publs., also contbr. to books. Home: 2523 Maroneal St Houston TX 77030 Office: 1517 Med Towers Houston TX 77030

DAINS, CLYDE CECIL, natural gas co. ofcl.; b. Enid, Okla., Sept. 11, 1920; s. Roscoe J. and Katie Ruth (Combs) D.; B.A., Phillips U., 1946; postgrad. U. Okla., 1946-47, Okla. State U., 1950-51; m. Leah Jean Gates, July 11, 1943; children—Robert Bruce, Kathryn Lynn Dains Fellows, Ann Kristin Dains Schneider. Reporter, Enid Events, 1938-42, 45-46; editor The Haymaker, 1941-42, Garfield County Legal News, 1945-46; corr. The Daily Oklahoman, 1947-51; asst. prof. journalism, dir. public relations Central State U., Edmond, Okla., 1947-51; personnel dir., purchasing agt. City of Enid, 1953-55; sales rep. Okla. Natural Gas Co., Tulsa, 1955-58, supr. dealer sales, 1958-62, asst. dir. advt. and promotion, 1962-63, mgr. mktg. services, 1963—. Pres., Community Chest, Enid, 1947. Served as pilot USAAF, 1942-45, 51-53; Korea. Mem. Am. Mktg. Assn. (pres. Tulsa chpt. 1969-70), Am. Advt. Assn. (pres. Tulsa chpt. 1978-79), Okla. Press Assn., So. Gas Assn., Public Utilities Communicators Assn. Presbyterian. Clubs: Tulsa Country, Petroleum, Rotary (dir. 1977) (Tulsa); Masons. Home: 9769 S Lakewood Tulsa OK 74136 Office: 624 S Boston St Tulsa OK 74102

DALE, DOROTHY HUGHES, r.r. exec.; b. Mobile, Ala., Feb. 8, 1919; d. Cyril A. and Elizabeth (Castle) Hughes; grad. Draughon's Bus. Coll., Jackson, Miss., 1936; m. Seabron S. Dale, Sept. 26, 1940 (dec. May 1962); children—Robin Dale Fuller, Thomas Douglas, Richard Stephen. Exec. sec. Overstreet & Town, Architects, Jackson, 1937-40; exec. asst., specification writer William I. Rosamond & Assos., Architects, Columbus, Miss., 1950-75; contributions solicitor Miss. U. for Women Found., Columbus, 1975; corp. asst. sec.-treas. Columbus and Greenville Ry., 1975—. Mem. Columbus Planning Commn., 1969-71. Mem. Nat. Assn. Jr. Auxs. (corr. sec., rec. sec. 1957-59), Columbus Jr. Aux. (pres. 1959-60), D.A.R. (regent 1965-68), Cherokee Garden Club (charter mem., past pres.), Antiquities Assn. (charter mem., past treas.), Hist. Columbus, Inc., Columbus Civic Arts Council (treas.), Miss Arts Assn., Lowndes County Hist. Soc. (dir.), Lowndes County Mental Health Assn. (treas.), Nat. Trust Hist. Preservation, United Cerebral Palsy (past sec.), Smithsonian Assos. Methodist. Clubs: Columbus Country, Soroptimist (charter mem., past sec.) (Columbus). Home: 1118 11th St N Columbus MS 39701 Office: PO Box 6000 Columbus MS 39701

DALE, GEORGE WILLIAM, sales cons., real estate broker; b. Coldwater, Kans., July 15, 1912; s. George William and Nellie (Haynes) Dale; B.A. in Bus., Fairmount Coll., 1936; postgrad. U. Kans., 1945-50; m. Mary Woodard, 1977; 1 son, Roger Dean. Tng. course planner N.Am. Aviation, Kansas City, Kans., 1941-44; operations mgr. Consumers Co-op. Assn., Kansas City, Mo., 1944-54; pres. Pallister Mfg. Co., Wichita, Kans., 1954-57; pres. Hollidays Blueprint & Supply, Inc., Wichita, 1957-65; realtor, cons., Eureka Springs, Ark., 1966—; counselor SCORE, SBA. Mem. Eureka Springs Real Estate Bd. (pres. 1968-70). Mem. Christian Ch. (chmn. bd. elders 1946-50). Mason (Shriner). Address: PO Box 25302 Charlotte NC 28212

DALE, JOHN IRVIN, III, chemist; b. Knoxville, Tenn., May 14, 1935; s. John Irvin, Jr., and Cecile Lurline (Chandler) D.; B.S., Carson-Newman Coll., 1956; M.A., U. N.C., 1959; Ph.D., U. Va., 1963; m. Emily Louise Fornes, Sept. 1, 1962 (dec. Apr. 1979); 1 dau., Susan Marie. Grad. teaching asst. U. N.C., 1956-58; asso. chemist Oak Ridge Nat. Labs., 1957-58; with Tenn. Eastman Co., research labs., Kingsport, Tenn., 1962-67, organic chems. div., 1967—, sr. chemist devel. and control dept., 1967-69, sr. chemist dyes dept., 1969-73, sr. chemist hydroquinone dept., 1973, sr. chemist intermediate dept., 1973-76, acting head chem. staff, intermediate dept., 1976-77, sr. chemist devel. and control dept., 1977—. Mem. Kingsport Citizens Adv. Com., 1965-67; dir. Kingsport Girls Club, 1965-68. Justice of peace Sullivan County, Tenn., 1969-72. Shell Found. fellow, 1961-62; recipient Pres.'s and Bd. Visitors prize, Soc. of Sigma Xi, U. Va., 1964. Mem. Am. Chem. Soc., Am. Inst. Chem. Engrs., Carson-Newman Coll. Alumni Assn., Nat. Assn. Timetable Collectors, Tenn. Farm Bur., Sigma Xi, Alpha Chi Sigma, Blue Key. Republican. Presbyterian. Contbr. articles to profl. jours. Patentee in field. Home: Route 16 Gray TN 37615 Office: Tennessee Eastman Co Kingsport TN 37662

DALE, SAM E., JR., ednl. adminstr.; b. Harmon, La., July 10, 1921; s. Sam E. and Willie Edith (Pann) D.; B.S. in Vocat. Agr., La. State U., Baton Rouge, 1947, M.S. in Vocat. Agr., 1954, Ph.D. in Vocat. Agr., 1972; m. Cathleen Trichel; 1 dau., Cathy Sue. With Catahoula Parish Sch. Bd., Jonesville, La., 1948—, supervising prin., 1969-72, dir. career and vocat. edn., 1973-79, supt., 1979—. Mem. adv. council La. State U.; mem. supts. council La. Bd. Elem. and Secondary Edn. Mem. La. (legis. com.), Catahoula Parish (pres.) tchrs. assns., La. Vocat. Assn., La. Agr. Tchrs. Assn., Am. Vocat. Assn., La. Supts. Assn., Gideons, Am. Legion, Phi Delta Kappa. Lion. Home: PO Box 56 Sicily Island LA 71368 Office: PO Box 308 Jonesville LA 71343

DALE, STEPHEN WAYNE, chemist; b. Greensboro, N.C., Feb. 16, 1943; s. Wayne Byron and Virginia (Learned) D.; B.S., Emory U., 1964; M.A. (grantee) Duke U., 1966, Ph.D., (grantee), 1969; postgrad. in bus. adminstrn. U. N.C., Chapel Hill, 1970-71; m. May 31, 1968 (div. 1972). Quality control engr. nuclear fuel dept., Gen. Electric Co., Wilmington, N.C., 1970-76, mgr. chem. metall. testing lab., 1976-78, mgr. chem. mfg. engring., 1978—. Served as lt. USPHS, 1968-70. Mem. N.C. Acad. Sci., AAAS, Sigma Xi, Phi Delta Theta. Episcopalian. Home: 5102 Belgrave Circle Wilmington NC 28403 Office: PO Box 780 Wilmington NC 28402

DALEHITE, WILLIAM MOORE, JR., lawyer; b. Clarksdale, Miss., Dec. 27, 1943; s. William Moore and Katherine (Ballard) D.; B.A. in English, U. Miss., 1965, J.D., 1972; m. Helen Harvey Ludlam, July 2, 1966; children—Robert Lawrence, Katherine Kimberlin. Admitted to Miss. bar, 1972; mem. firm Steen Reynolds Dalehite & Currie, Jackson, Miss., 1972—. Served to capt., inf., AUS, 1965-69. Decorated Silver Star, Bronze Star with oak leaf cluster. Mem. Jackson Young Lawyers Assn. (treas. 1974-75), Miss. State, Am. bar assns., Miss. Opera Assn. (bd. dirs. 1975-78), Omicron Delta Kappa, Pi Kappa Alpha, Delta Theta Phi. Methodist. (adminstv. bd. 1974-76). Home: 915 Briarfield Rd Jackson MS 39211 Office: PO Box 900 Jackson MS 39205

DALEY, EDWIN CHARLES, city ofcl.; b. Erie, Pa., Sept. 16, 1948; s. Lawrence Neal and Anna Ruth (Dobbins) D.; B.A., Slippery Rock State Coll., 1973; M.P.A., U. Pitts. 1975; m. Karen Roberta Knowlton, June 13, 1970; children—Heather Marie, Holly Ann. Adminstrv. asst. City of New Castle (Pa.), 1973-74; human services dir. Lawrence County (Pa.), 1974-75; asst. city mgr., community devel. dir. City of Dodge City (Kans.), 1975-78, city mgr., 1978-80; city mgr. City of Fairmont (W.Va.), 1980—. Served with USMC, 1969-72. Mem. Internat. City Mgmt. Assn., Acad. for Profl. Devel., Am. Soc. for Public Adminstrn., Am. Planning Assn. Methodist. Office: City of Fairmont Fairmont WV 26554

DALILI, HAMID, physician; b. Tabriz, Iran, Nov. 5, 1934; s. Taghi Mohammed and Khanom Balla (Bolugh) D.; came to U.S., 1964, naturalized, 1975; M.D., U. Teheran, 1961; m. Louise Maria Foret, July 25, 1974; children—Cameron T., Curtis, Carla, Dean H., Dawn M. Intern, West Suburban Hosp., Oak Park, Ill., 1964-65; resident Mt. Sinai Hosp., Chgo., 1965-67, Charity Hosp., New Orleans, Tulane U., 1967-69; physician in charge of Outpatient Clinics, Royal Inst. Social Services, Iran, 1963-64; instr. anesthesiologist dept. surgery/anesthesiology Tulane U., 1969-71, asst. prof. anesthesiology, 1971—; anesthesiologist West Jefferson Gen. Hosp., 1973—; clin. asst. prof. anesthesiology La. State U. Med. Sch., 1976—. Served with Iranian Armed Forces, 1961-63. Diplomate Am. Bd. Anesthesiology. Fellow Am. Coll. Anesthesiologists. Mem. A.M.A., La., Jefferson Parish med. socs., Am., La. State socs. anesthesiologists, Internat. Anesthesia Research Soc. Home: 10 Tennyson Pl New Orleans LA 70114 Office: 4500 11th St Marrero LA 70072

DALLMAN, GLENN ROBERT, library dir.; b. Oconomowoc, Wis., July 31, 1927; s. Henry William and Alma (Baehler) D.; B.A. magna cum laude, Northland Coll., 1950; M.Ed., U. Wis. at Milw., 1954; M.S. in L.S., Case Western Res. U., 1962; m. Charlotte Marie Frank, June 26, 1954; children—Jeffry Paul, Jaclyn Marie. Tchr. Trinity High Sch., Fort Lauderdale, Fla., 1950-51; tchr., prin. Lutheran Tchrs. Tng. Coll., Ibakachi, Nigeria, 1951-57; tchr., librarian Concordia Coll., Portland, Oreg., 1957-58; tchr. Luth. High Sch., Cleve., 1959-61; librarian Cleveland Heights (Ohio) Pub. Library, 1961-62; dir. library Indian River Community Coll., Fort Pierce, Fla., 1962-66, St. Petersburg Jr. Coll., Clearwater, Fla., 1966—. Served with USNR, 1945-46. Mem. ALA, Southeastern, Fla., St. Lucie County (dir., pres., 1965-66) library assns., Fla. Assn. Community Colls. Home: 1806 Sunrise Blvd Clearwater FL 33520 Office: 2465 Drew St Clearwater FL 33515

DALRYMPLE, DAVID EDWARD, physician; b. Elkhart, Ind., Nov. 10, 1936; s. Thurlow Edward and Irene Guinevere (Northrop) D.; A.B., DePauw U., 1958; M.S., Purdue U., 1960; postgrad. Ind. U., 1960-61; M.D., U. Chgo., 1965; m. Carol Mae Anderson, Aug. 2, 1959; children—David Northrop, Brian Anderson. Intern State U. Iowa, 1965-66, resident, 1966-68; NIH fellow Washington U. Sch. Medicine, St. Louis, 1968-69; practice medicine specializing in internal medicine and endocrinology, Atlanta, 1971—; chmn. patient care and dietary com., equipment com., exec. com., chmn. dept. medicine Northside Hosp., Atlanta. Vis. clin. instr. Med. Coll. Ga., Augusta, 1969-70. Mem. med. com. drug abuse Sandy Springs (Atlanta), Ga.; mem. North Fulton County Med. Care Program. Served with AUS, 1969-71; med. officer Specialized Treatment Center, Ft. Gordon. Recipient Resident award State U. Iowa, 1965. Diplomate Am. Bd. Internal Medicine, Am. Bd. Med. Examiners. Fellow A.C.P.; mem. Am. Fedn. for Clin. Research, Med. Assn. Atlanta (trustee No. dist., past jr. trustee), Med. Assn. Ga. (splty bd. peer rev.), Am., Ga. socs. internal medicine, AMA, Diabetes Assn. Atlanta (pres., chmn., dir.), Ga. Diabetes Assn. (dir.), Ga. Thoracic Soc., Ga. Wildlife Fedn., Sigma Xi, Alpha Tau Omega. Episcopalian. Club: Flying. Editorial bd. Atlanta Medicine. Contbr. articles to profl. jours. Home: 5515 Whitewood Ct Dunwoody GA 30338 Office: 6500 Vernon Woods Dr Atlanta GA 30328

DALTON, JESS NEWMAN, lawyer; b. Independence, Kans., Feb. 3, 1912; s. Edward Andrew and Floss Ellen (Newman) D.; A.B., Washburn U., Topeka, 1934, J.D., 1937; grad. Advanced Mgmt. Program, Harvard, 1952; H.H.D. (hon.), U. Ams., Mex., 1978; m. Elaine Virginia Courtney, Dec. 7, 1957; children—Nancy McNeese, Laurie Louise, Jess Newman, Cornelia Virginia, Molly Adrienne. Admitted to Mexican bar, 1939; since practiced in Mexico City; partner firm Basham, Ringe & Correa, Mexico City, 1937-45, Goodrich, Dalton, Little & Riquelme, 1945—; chmn. bd. Mexico City Valley Coca Cola Bottling Co., Scott Paper Co. Mex., Pan Am. Ins.; dir. Mexican subs.'s Procter & Gamble, Owens-Corning Fiberglas, Burlington Industries, Aluminum Co. Am., others; dir. Am. Standard, N.Y.C., Borden Inc., N.Y.C., Sistemas Banco de Comercio Mexico City. Past chmn. fund drive Mexico City Community Chest; past pres. Am. Soc. Past chmn. bd. dirs. Am. Brit. Cowdray Hosp., Mexico City; bd. dirs., chmn. exec. com. U. Ams., Puebla, Mexico, 1965—. Recipient Disting. Alumni award Washburn U., 1959. Mem. S.A.R., Sons Am. Colonists. Clubs: University, River (N.Y.C.). Home: 2570 Paseo de la Reforma Pvt 115 Mexico City 10 Mexico Office: 355 Paseo de la Reforma PO Box 93 Bis Mexico City 5 Mexico

DALTON, JOHN NICHOLS, gov. Va.; b. Emporia, Va., July 11, 1931; s. Ted R. and Mary (Turner) D.; A.B., William and Mary Coll., 1953; J.D., U. Va., 1957; m. Edwina Jeanette Panzer, Feb. 18, 1956; children—Katherine Scott, Ted Ernest, John Nichols, Mary Helen. Admitted to Va. bar, 1957; lt. gov. Va., 1974-77; gov. Va., 1978—. Pres., Young Republican Fedn. Va., 1960; treas. Va. Rep. Com., 1960, gen. counsel, 1961-72. Mem. Va. Ho. of Dels., 1966-72, Va. Senate, 1973. Served to 1st lt. AUS, 1954-56. Mem. Am. Legion, Sigma Alpha Epsilon. Mason (Shriner, 33 deg.), Moose, Odd Fellow. Home: 411 4th St Radford VA 24141 also Executive Mansion Richmond VA 23219

DALTON, LARRY RAYMOND, chemist, biochemist; b. Belpre, Ohio, Apr. 25, 1948; s. Leonard William and Calla Virginia (Maylee) D.; B.S., Mich. State U., 1965, M.S., 1966; A.M., Harvard U., 1971, Ph.D., 1972. Asst. prof. chemistry Vanderbilt U., Nashville, 1971-73, asso. prof., 1973-77, research prof. biochemistry, 1977—, physiology, 1979—; asso. prof. chemistry SUNY, Stony Brook, 1976—; cons. Varian Assos., Palo Alto, Calif., 1971-74, Bruker Physik, Karlsruhe, W.Ger., 1975; distinguished cons. Spring Arbor Coll., Mich., 1972—; vis. prof. chemistry U. Tex., Austin, 1977—; cons. IBM Corp., 1978. Mem. select com. on advancement of univ. Vanderbilt U., 1973-74; mem. Nashville Speakers Bur., 1972-77; judge Tenn. High Sch. Debate Tournament. Recipient research career devel. award NIH, 1976—, Camille and Henry Dreyfus Tchr.-Scholar award, 1975—; award for meritorious research Sigma Xi, 1966; Young Leader award Spring Arbor Coll., 1973, Undergrad. Teaching award Vanderbilt U., 1973; Alfred P. Sloan Found. fellow, 1974-77; NIH predoctoral fellow, 1966-70; Harvard U. fellow, 1966. Mem. Am. Chem. Soc., Am. Phys. Soc., Sigma Xi, Pi Mu Epsilon, Phi Kappa Phi, Phi Eta Sigma, Tau Sigma. Author: Saturation Transfer Spectroscopy, 1978. Contbr. articles to Jour. Chem. Physics, Chem. Physics, Proc. Nat. Acad. Sci., Chem. Physics Letters, Phys. Review, Jour. Phys. Chemistry. Co-discoverer saturation transfer spectroscopy. Home: 2140 Acklen Ave Nashville TN 37212 Office: Vanderbilt University Dept of Biochemistry Nashville TN 37232

DALY, JAMES WILLIAM, obstetrician, gynecologist; b. Chgo., Jan. 5, 1931; s. John F. and Helen L. (Hendricks) D.; B.S., U. Santa Clara, 1951; M.D., Loyola U., Chgo., 1955; m. Geraldine Jane Callaghan, June, 1953; children—Daniel F., Timothy P., Rebecca A. Intern, St. Mary's Mercy Hosp., Gary, Ind., 1955-56; chief profl. services USAF Hosp., Lockbourne AFB, Ohio, 1957-59; commd. capt. U.S. Air Force M.C., 1959, advanced through grades to maj., 1966; resident Wilford Hall USAF Hosp., San Antonio, 1959-62, chief gynecology service, 1963-68, tng. officer, 1963-68; asso. prof. obstetrics and gynecology U. Fla., 1968-77, prof., 1977—, dir. tumor div., 1968—; cons. in field. Diplomate Am. Bd. Obstetrics and Gynecology. Fellow Am. Coll. Obstetrics and Gynecology; mem. Soc. Gynecol. Oncologists, AMA, Am. Radium Soc., Fla. Med. Assn., Am. Cancer Soc. Alachua County (Fla.) Med. Soc., S. Atlantic Soc. Obstetricians and Gynecologists, Felix Rutledge Soc. Republican. Roman Catholic. Contbr. articles to med. pubs. Home: 1115 NW 52d Terr Gainesville FL 32605 Office: Dept Obstetrics-Gynecology Coll Medicine U Fla Gainesville FL 32610

DAMATO, DAVID JOSEPH, SR., design engr.; b. Chgo., Aug. 7, 1953; s. Joseph Charles and Evelyn Elaine (Darling) D.; B.E.E., Devry Inst. Tech., Chgo., 1974; m. Elizabeth Earle Foster, Aug. 14, 1976. Field service engr. Taylor Instrument Co., Birmingham, Ala., 1974-75; design engr. B. E. & K. Inc., Birmingham, 1975-79, mgr. engring. computer services, 1979—. Active Boy Scouts Am.; firefighter; paramedic. Mem. IEEE, Nat. Soc. Profl. Engrs., Instrument Soc. Am. (sr.), Am. Legion. Methodist. Contbr. article to profl. jour. Home: 3105 Blue Lake Dr Birmingham AL 35243 Office: PO Box 2332 Birmingham AL 35201

D'AMATO, NICHOLAS ANTHONY, physician, ret. naval officer; b. Tampa, Fla., Sept. 30, 1931; s. Pietro and Mary (Falsone) D'A.; B.S. in Biology, Springhill Coll., 1953; M.D., Tulane U., 1957; m. Irma Jo Plaisance, Aug. 23, 1958; children—Nicholas Anthony, James, Mark, Paul, Irma Marie. Intern, Charity Hosp., New Orleans, 1957-58; commd. lt. U.S. Navy, 1958, advanced through grades to capt., 1971; ret., 1979; resident in pathology U.S. Naval Hosp., St. Albans, N.Y., 1960-64; staff pathologist U.S. Naval Hosp., Portsmouth, Va., 1964-67, chmn. lab. dept., 1967-79; dir. labs. DePaul Hosp., Norfolk, 1979—; adj. prof. biology Norfolk State U., 1979—; prof. pathology Eastern Va. Med. Sch., Norfolk, 1974—. Decorated Navy Commendation medal. Diplomate Am. Bd. Pathology. Fellow Am. Coll. Pathologists; mem. Acad. Clin. Lab. Physicians and Scientists, Assn. Clin. Scientists, Va., Tidewater socs. pathology. Editor Naval Hosp. Med. Bull., 1968-75. Editor: Cytology Manual, 3d edit., 1976. Home: 4029 Wyndybrow Dr Portsmouth VA 23703 Office: DePaul Hosp Norfolk VA 23505

D'AMBROSIA, ROBERT DOMINICK, orthopedic surgeon; b. Ellwood City, Pa., Dec. 25, 1938; s. Alphonse and Agnes (D'Amore) D'A.; B.A., Washington and Jefferson Coll., 1960; M.D., U. Pitts., 1964; m. Barbara Ann Faycik, Oct. 17, 1964; children—Lisa Ann, Christopher John, Robert Matthew, Peter Alphonse. Intern, U. Colo., Denver, 1964-65; resident in orthopedic surgery U. Pitts., 1967-70; fellow in rheumatology St. Margarets Rehab. Hosp., Pitts., 1970; practice medicine specializing in orthopedic surgery, Sacramento and Davis, Calif., 1970-76; asst. prof. orthopedic surgery U. Calif., Davis, 1971-75, asso. prof., 1975-76; prof., head dept. orthopedics La. State U. Med. Center, New Orleans, 1976—; mem. staff Charity Hosp. La., Hotel Dieu Hosp., Childrens Hosp., Jo Ellen Smith Meml. Hosp., Mercy Hosp. Served with M.C., USAF, 1965-67. Diplomate Am. Bd. Orthopedic Surgery. Mem. Am., So. med. assns., La., Orleans Parish med. socs., Am. Rheumatism Assn., Am. Acad. Orthopedic Surgeons, A.C.S., Orthopedic Research Soc., 20th Century, La. orthopedic assns., Greater New Orleans Orthopedic Soc., New Orleans Grad. Med. Assembly, AAUP, Assn. Am. Med. Colls., Assn. Orthopedic Chairmen, Am. Orthopedic Soc. for Sports Medicine, La. chpt. Arthritis Found., Phi Beta Kappa, Alpha Omega Alpha. Author: Musculoskeletal Disorders: Regional Examination and Differential Diagnosis, 1977; mem. editorial bd. Orthopedic Survey, 1976—, Orthopaedics, 1977—, Jour. of Continuing Edn. in Orthopedics, 1977—. Home: 3624 Red Oak Ct New Orleans LA 70114 Office: 1542 Tulane Ave New Orleans LA 70112

DAME, RICHARD FRANKLIN, JR., marine ecologist; b. Charleston, S.C., Nov. 16, 1941; s. Richard F. and Lawrence May (Heisser) D.; B.S., Coll. of Charleston, 1964; M.A., U. N.C., 1967; Ph.D. (Baruch fellow), U. S.C., 1971; m. Amanda Roberts, Apr. 29, 1967; children—Caroline LaRoche, Elizabeth Stewart. Prof. marine sci. and ecology U. S.C. Coastal Carolina Coll., Conway, 1971—, also research asso. Belle W. Baruch Inst. Marine Biology and Coastal Research, U. S.C., Georgetown, 1971—, and research asso. Inst. Ecology, U. Ga., Athens, 1978. Bd. dirs. Litchfield Beaches Property Owners Assn., 1972-76; vestryman Trinity Episcopal Ch., 1979—. NSF grantee, 1972-75, 78-80; EPA grantee, 1974-75. Mem. Am. Soc. Zoologists, Am. Soc. Limnology and Oceanography, Southeastern Estuarine Research Soc., Ecol. Soc. Am., Nat. Shellfisheries Assn., Sigma Xi. Episcopalian. Author newspaper corr. course Oceans and Man, 1976, 77, 79; editor: Marsh Estuarine Systems Simulation, 1979; research on ecology of marsh-estuarine systems. Home: Route 2 Box 80 C 3 Pawleys Island SC 29585 Office: University of South Carolina Coastal Carolina College Conway SC 29526

DAMORE, MICHAEL HARRY, architect; b. Chgo., Mar. 2, 1949; s. Marion Harry and Elsie (Olson) D.; B.Arch., Okla. State U., 1973; m. Sharon Jeane Hoover, Sept. 28, 1974. Archtl. designer Skidmore, Owings & Merrill, Chgo., 1973-76, studio head, sr. designer, Houston, 1976—, participating asso., 1977-80, asso. partner, 1980—; design critic U. Houston, Rice U. Mem. Houston C. of C. AIA, Tex. Soc. Architects. Lutheran. Architect, Charles Stark Draper Lab. Bldg., Cambridge, Mass., Central Trust Center, Cin., First Fed. Savs. & Loan Assn. Bldg., Little Rock, Westchase Nat. Bank Bldg., Houston. Home: 5011 Spruce Forest St Houston TX 77091 Office: 5251 Westheimer Suite 200 Houston TX 77056

DANBURG, JEROME SAMUEL, physicist; b. Houston, Dec. 21, 1940; s. August and Rosalie (Bornstein) D.; B.S. in Physics, Mass. Inst. Tech., 1962; Diplom in Physics (Fulbright scholar), Freie Universitat Berlin, West Berlin, Germany, 1964; Ph.D. in Physics, U. Calif. at Berkeley, 1969; m. Gudrun Ella Ernestine Scholz, Sept. 8, 1965; children—Aron Ralf, Andrea Leda, Sylvia Freia, Sonja Rebecca. Asso. physicist Brookhaven Nat. Lab., Upton, N.Y., 1969-72; sr. research geophysicist Shell Devel. Co., Houston, 1973—. Mem. Am. Phys. Soc., Soc. Exploration Geophysicists, Geophys. Soc. Houston. Contbr. articles on elementary-particle physics to profl. jours. Home: 7611 Burning Hills Dr Houston TX 77071 Office: Shell Devel Co PO Box 481 Houston TX 77001

DANCER, JACK TOM, surgeon; b. Boswell, Okla., Dec. 10, 1935; s. Dudley D. and Bessie B. (Gilbreath) D.; M.S., U. Ariz., 1957; M.D., George Washington U., 1961; m. Joy S. Bell, May 23, 1957; children—Sheila Joy, Brian C., Brice D., Blake D. Intern U. Okla. Med. Center, Oklahoma City, 1961; resident U. Okla. Health Scis. Center, Oklahoma City, 1962-66; practice medicine, specializing in gen. surgery Shattuck, Okla., 1968—; gen. surgeon Newman Med. Center, Shattuck, 1968—. Bd. dirs. Gov. Okla. Com. to Combat Cancer, 1973—. Served to capt., M.C., USAF, 1966-68. Am. Cancer

Soc. grantee, 1964-65. Diplomate Am. Bd. Surgery. Mem. A.C.S., Southwestern Surg. Soc., A.M.A., Northwest Med. Assn., Northwest Med. Soc. (pres. 1973), Delta Chi. Republican. Methodist (dir.). Home: 515 E 7th St Shattuck OK 73858 Office: Newman Med Center Inc Shattuck OK 73858

DANCZ, ROGER LEE, musician; b. Ludington, Mich., May 25, 1930; s. Roy Stanley and Viola Lenore (Boston) D.; B.Mus. cum laude, Stetson U., 1952; Mus.M., Peabody Coll., 1958; m. Phyllis Ann Jones, June 2, 1952; 1 son, Steven. Dir. instrumental music Martin County Schs., Stuart, Fla., 1952-53; profl. trumpet player, 1951-65; dir. bands, U. Ga., Athens, 1955—, asso. prof., 1971—; guest condr., adjudicator South and Southwest. Served with U.S. Army, 1953-55. Recipient Music in Sports award Broadcast Music Inc., 1976. Mem. Nat. Assn. Jazz Educators (past pres. Ga. chpt.), Ga. Music Educators Assn. (past pres.), Coll. Band Dirs. Nat. Assn. (past pres. So. div.), Music Educators Nat. Conf., Gridiron Soc., Phi Beta Mu (past pres. Ga. chpt.), Phi Mu Alpha Sinfonia, Pi Kappa Lambda, Ye Mystic Krewe, Kappa Kappa Psi. Columnist Athens Banner-Herald, 1970—. Home: 680 Pinecrest Dr Athens GA 30605 Office: Dept Music U Ga Athens GA 30602

DANDRIDGE, RICHARD EUGENE, elec. engr.; b. Dallas, Dec. 24, 1936; s. Alva Eugene and Edna May (Huckabee) D.; Indsl. Elec. Engring. degree U. Tex., Arlington, 1960; m. Helen Ann Dorman, Mar. 22, 1958; children—Chris Eugene, Cindy Dawn. Engr. trainee Dallas Power & Light Co., 1955-58; estimator Fisk Electric Co., Dallas, 1961-65, purchase agt., 1965-66, project mgr., 1965-68; project engr. Ling-Oliver-O'Dwyer Electric Inc., Dallas, 1968—, office mgr., 1969—. Mem. Duncanville (Tex.) Planning Bd., 1961; mayor, Lakewood Village, Tex., 1977-78. Mem. Internat. Brotherhood Elec. Workers, C. of C. Little Elm Area (dir.). Democrat. Baptist. Club: Masons. Office: Ling-Oliver-D'Dwyer Electric Inc 727 S Central Expressway Richardson TX 75080

DANDRIDGE, WILLIAM SHELTON, orthopedic surgeon; b. Atoka, Okla., May 21, 1914; s. Theodore Oscar and Estelle (Shelton) D.; B.A., U. Okla., 1935; M.D., U. Ark., 1939; M.S., Baylor U., 1950; m. Pearl Sessions, Feb. 3, 1941; 1 dau., Diana Dawn. Intern St. Paul's Hosp., Dallas, 1939-40; surgical residence Med. Arts Hosp., Dallas, 1940; commd. 1st lt. USAF, advanced through grades to lt. col., 1950; chief reconditioning service and reconstructive surgery Ashburn Gen. Hosp., McKinney, Tex., 1945-46; neurosurg. resident Brooke Army Med. Center, San Antonio, 1946-47; orthopedic surg. resident, 1947-50; chief orthopedic service and gen. surgery Francis E. Warren AFB, Cheyenne, Wyo., Travis AFB, Susan, Cal., 1950-51; chief orthopedic service and gen. surgery Shepherd AFB, 1951-52; comdg. officer, chief orthopedic service, chief gen. surgery Craig AFB Hosp., Selma, Ala., 1952-53; practice medicine specializing in orthopedic surgery Muskogee, Okla., 1954-69, 72—; active staff Muskegon Gen. Hosp.; med. dir. Rehab. Center, Okmulgee, Okla.; orthopedic econs. McAlester (Okla.) Gen. Hosp., VA Hosp., Muskogee. Exec. mem. Eastern Okla. council Boy Scouts Am. Fellow A.C.S., Internat. Coll. Surgeons; mem. Am. Fracture Assn., Nat. Found. (adviser 1958-61), N.Y. Acad. Sci., Okla. State, Pan-Am. So., Aerospace med. assns., A.M.A., Eastern Okla. Counties med. socs., S.W. Surg. Congress, Am. Rheumatology Soc., Democrat. Methodist. Mason (32 deg., K.T. Shriner, Jester), Lion. Club: Muskogee Country. Contbr. articles to profl. jours. Home: 3504 University Blvd Muskogee OK 74401 Office: 1601 W Okmulgee St Muskogee OK 74401

DANESH, YOUSEF, polit. scientist; b. Rasht, Iran, Sept. 21, 1925; permanent resident in U.S., 1968; s. Ebrahim and Ommal Bani D.; LL.B., U. Tehran, 1957, B.A., 1958; M.A., So. Ill. U., 1962, Ph.D., 1964; m. Behjat Bakhti, Jan. 7, 1949; children—Farah, Forough, Mehrdad. Head, Iranian Office Customs Internat. Coop., 1963-65; exec. dir. Iran Mcpl. Assn., 1965-67; head Iranian Office Customs Studies and Planning, 1967-68; lectr. Tehran U., 1963-68; mem. faculty So. U., Baton Rouge, 1968—, prof. polit. sci., 1975—. Acting mayor of Arak, 1965; exec. mem. Internat. Union Local Authorities, 1965-67. Mem. Am. Polit. Sci. Assn., Assn. Muslim Scientists, Internat, Polit. Sci. Assn., Southwestern Social Sci. Assn., So. Polit. Sci. Assn., La. Polit. Sci. Assn., La. Acad. Sci., Phi Kappa Phi, Phi Delta Kappa. Muslim. Author: Principle of Local Government, 1970; co-author: Comparative Local Government, 1965; contbr. articles to profl. jours.

DANFORTH, FRANCES MUELLER (MRS. WILLIAM PAUL DANFORTH), civic worker; b. Austin, Tex., Mar. 23, 1914; d. Rudolph George and Laura Emma (Von Boeckmann) Mueller; B.J., U. Tex., 1935, B.A., 1936; M.S., Columbia, 1938; m. William Paul Danforth, Aug. 16, 1942; children—William Paul, Douglas Mueller, Donald Lee. Grader dept. journalism U. Tex., Austin, 1934; asst. dir. Interscholastic League Press Bur., U. Tex., 1936-37, asst. editor Alcalde, monthly alumni mag., 1936-37, 38-42; editor Star Points, nat. papers Delta Delta Delta Chgo., 1968-70. Pres., Austin Symphony League, 1967-68; state v.p. Tex. Women's Assn. Symphony Orchs., 1970; pres. Austin Vol. Bur., 1966-68. Bd. dirs., sec. U.S.O., 1971-72; bd. dirs. Symphony Orch. Soc.; bd. dirs., sec. Cen-Tex. chpt. A.R.C., pres. Altenheim, 1961-62. Mem. Women in Communications, Mortar Board, Delta Delta Delta. Lutheran (pres. ch. women 1972-74). Clubs: Settlement, Lawyers Wives (mem. bd., sec. 1973-74), Woman's Forum (sec. 1972-74) Austin Woman's (v.p. 1977—) (Austin). Home: 1400 West Ave Austin TX 78701

DANIEL, DAN, U.S. congressman; b. Chatham, Va., May 12, 1914; s. Reuben Earl and Georgia (Grant) D.; m. Ruby McGregor; 1 son, Jimmie Foxx. Formerly asst. to chmn. bd. Dan River Mills, Inc.; mem. Va. Ho. of Dels., 1959-68; mem. 91st-96th congresses from 5th Va. Dist. Decorated Croix du Merite (France); recipient Star of Italian Solidarity 1st class; Service to Mankind award; George Washington Honor medal. Mem. Am. Legion (past nat. comdr.), Va. State C. of C. (past pres.), Omicron Delta Kappa (hon.). Democrat. Baptist. Address: Pittwood RFD 7 Danville VA 24541

DANIEL, GARY SHELTON, ednl. adminstr.; b. New Orleans, Mar. 20, 1948; s. Guy Shelton and Lydia Doris Daniel; B.A., Northwestern La. State U., 1972; M.Ed. with honors, U. New Orleans, 1975; Ed.S. with honors, U. Fla., 1977; additional studies in Rome. High sch. bus. tchr. Jefferson Parish Sch. Bd., Gretna, La., 1973-74, middle sch. social sci. tchr., 1974; intern Career Planning and Placement Center, U. Fla., Gainesville, 1977; ednl. researcher, evaluator Dallas Ind. Sch. Dist., 1977—. Mem. Am. Personnel and Guidance Assn., Nat. Vocat. Guidance Assn., Am. Ednl. Research Assn., S.W. Ednl. Research Assn., Dallas Historic Preservation League. Republican. Author articles and reports. Home: 6946 Walling Ln Dallas TX 75231 Office: Dept Research and Evaluation Dallas Ind Sch Dist 3700 Ross Ave Dallas TX 75204

DANIEL, HENRIETTA BELL, pharmacist; b. Houston, Sept. 17, 1943; d. Henry and Bernice (Thompson) Bell; B.Ph. and Med. Tech., Tex. So. U., 1968; m. Donald F. Daniel, Jan. 19, 1979. Pharmacy mgr. Mading-Ducan Drugs, Inc., Houston, 1968-69, Target Stores, Inc., Houston, 1969-76; chief pharmacist Riverside Gen. Hosp., Houston, 1976-80; staff pharmacist VA Med. Center, Houston, 1980—; adult basic edn. instr. Houston Ind. Sch. System, 1966-68; cons. Riverside Clinic Drug Abuse Center, Medicus Corp., Houston. Cert. intravenous admixture cons. Mem. Nat. Pharm. Assn., Houston Pharm. Assn., Tex. Soc. Hosp. Pharmacists, Black Women for Social Change, NAACP, Houston Urban League, Timber Crest Civic Assn. Democrat. Methodist. Home: 3349 Prospect St Houston TX 77004 Office: 3204 Ennis St Houston TX 77004

DANIEL, HOWARD GRADY, diagnostic radiologist; b. Gainsville, Ga., Sept. 27, 1942; s. Horace Grady and Evelyn (Perry) D.; B.A., Emory U., 1964, M.D., 1968; m. Donna Ilene Thomas, June 24, 1967; children—Christine Anne, Karen Lynn. Rotating intern U.S. Naval Hosp., Newport, R.I., 1968-69; resident in diagnostic radiology health scis. center Okla. U., Oklahoma City, 1972-75, fellow in diagnostic ultrasound, chief resident in diagnostic radiology, 1975-76, asst. prof., 1976-78; diagnostic radiologist and ultrasonagrapher Oklahoma City Clinic, 1978—; establisher diagnostic ultrasound depts. VA and Presbyn. hosps., Oklahoma City, 1978. Served to lt. comdr. USNR, 1968-72. Diplomate Am. Bd. Radiology; mem. AMA, Okla. Med. Soc., Oklahoma County Med. Soc., Am. Inst. Ultrasound in Medicine, Am. Coll. Radiology. Republican. Methodist. Club: Lost Hound Hunt (Edmond, Okla.). Office: Oklahoma City Clinic 701 NE 10th St Oklahoma City OK 73104

DANIEL, RALPH WINFIELD, electronics engr., fraternal exec.; b. Greensboro, N.C., Sept. 27, 1940; s. Ray Edward and Hattie Rema (Jones) D.; B.S., N.C. State U., 1964. Mem. Mu Beta Psi, 1960—, nat. v.p., 1961-63, nat. editor, 1962-63, nat. pres., 1963-64, exec. sec., 1965—; research, design and devel. engr. Lockheed Ga. Co., Marietta, 1966—. Mem. Am. Theatre Organ Soc., Theatre Hist. Soc., Guild Carilloneurs N. Am., Atlanta Zool. Soc., Atlanta Lankmarks. Lutheran. Address: 3401 Hickory Crest Dr Marietta GA 30064

DANIEL, ROBERT WILLIAMS, JR., congressman; b. Richmond, Va., Mar. 17, 1936; s. Robert Williams and Charlotte (Bemiss) D.; B.A., U. Va., 1954-58; M.B.A., Columbia, 1961; children—Robert, Charlotte, Nell. Fin. analyst J.C. Wheat Co., Richmond, 1961-62; instr. econs. U. Richmond Sch. Bus., 1963; with CIA, Washington, 1964-68; owner, operator Brandon Plantation, Prince George County, Va., 1968—; mem. 93d-96th congresses from Va. Mem. Commonwealth of Va. Bd. Conservation and Econ. Devel., 1972; mem., sec. Prince George County Planning Commn., 1972; mem. mktg. com. Va. Farm Bur., 1971-72; trustee Atlantic Rural Expn., Sheltering Arms Hosp., Richmond; watchdog of Treasury 93d-95th Congresses. Served with AUS, 1959. Recipient Service award Ams. for Constl. Action, 1973-78; Nat. Associated Businessmen's award; Nat. Fedn. of Small Businesses award; Douglas MacArthur Meritorious Service award, 1975; Lafayette Freedom award, 1975. Mem. Phi Beta Kappa, Phi Kappa Psi. Republican. Episcopalian (vestryman 1968-72). Clubs: N.Y. Yacht; Metropolitan (Washington); Commonwealth (Richmond); Moose. Home: Brandon Plantation Spring Grove VA 23881 Office: 2236 Rayburn House Office Bldg Washington DC 20515

DANIELL, HERMAN BURCH, pharmacologist; b. Cadwell, Ga., May 25, 1929; s. Walter and Ruby Florence (Burch) D.; B.S., U. Ga., 1951, M.S., 1963; Ph.D., Med. Coll. S.C., 1966; m. Ottie Lorraine Smith, June 30, 1957; children—Kimberley, Anthony, Walter. Owner-pharmacist retail pharmacies, Savannah, Ga., 1953-62; instr. U. Ga. Sch. Pharmacy, Athens, 1962-63; NIH research fellow Med. Coll. S.C., Charleston, 1964-66, instr. pharmacology, 1966-67, asso. in pharmacology, 1967-68, asst. prof., 1968-70, asso. prof., 1970-78, prof. pharmacology, 1978—. Served to capt., Med. Service Corps, AUS, 1951-53. USPHS research grantee, 1968-77, S.C. Heart Assn. research grantee, 1966-73. Mem. Am. Soc. Pharmacology and Exptl. Therapeutics, Sigma Xi, Kappa Sigma, Rho Chi. Episcopalian. Lion. Contbr. articles to profl. jours. Home: 1549 Burningtree Rd Charleston SC 29412 Office: Dept Pharmacology Med U SC Charleston SC 29401

DANIELLS, ELEANOR GRACE, educator; b. Wacousta, Mich., Apr. 30, 1916; d. Will Carleton and Iva (Bliss) D.; Mus.B., Fla. State U., 1939; Mus.M., Northwestern U., 1944. Tchr. pub. schs. Midland, Mich., 1940-43, Decatur, Mich., 1944-45; asso. prof. music edn. Culver Stockton Coll., Canton, Mo., 1945-58; tchr. music Escuela Americanna, San Salvador, El Salvador, 1958-61, U. Tampa (Fla.), 1961-62; asso. prof. music edn. E. Tenn. State U., Johnson City, 1962—. Mem. E. Tenn. Vocal Assn., Nat., Tenn. edn. assns., Music Educators Nat. Conf., Tenn. Music Educators Assn., Viola de Gamba Soc. Am., Phi Kappa Phi, Pi Kappa Lambda, Mu Phi Epsilon, Delta Kappa Gamma, P.E.O. Sisterhood, Sigma Kappa. Presbyterian. Home: 1502 Chickees St Johnson City TN 37601 Office: East Tennessee State U Box 24480 Johnson City TN 37601

DANIELPOUR, MEHRI M., sculptor; b. Teheran, Iran; d. Ibrahim and Akhtar (Farokh-Tavana) Moatamed; came to U.S., 1944, naturalized, 1950; student Art Students League, 1953-55, Phoenix Sch. of Design, 1954-56; m. Sayid Danielpour, Nov. 9, 1954 (dec.); children—Richard, Debbie. Freelance sculptor, Palm Beach, Fla., 1965—; tchr. sculpture Lighthouse Gallery and Sch. of Art, Tequesta, Fla., 1970—; owner, dir. Gallery Worth Ave., Palm Beach, 1975—; major commns. include: portrait sculpture of His Highness, Crown Prince Reza, 1969, Her Imperial Majesty, Empress Farah of Iran (gold medal), 1969, Portrait bust of His Imperial Majesty, the Shah of Iran, 1970, Year of the Child sculpture West Palm Beach Public Library, 1979. Mem. Norton Mus. and Sch. Art, Worth Ave. Assn., Palm Beach C. of C. Home: 233 La Puerta Way Palm Beach FL 33480

DANIELS, ALLEN JERROLD, hotel/motel supply co. exec.; b. Bklyn., June 4, 1946; s. Irving D. and Selma C. Daniels; A.A., Miami Dade Jr. Coll., 1967; B.A., Fla. Atlantic U., 1969, M.B.A., 1971. Teller, Washington Fed. Savs. & Loan Assn., Miami Beach, Fla., 1966-67; sr. asst. mgr. Household Fin. Corp., Miami, 1967-68; loan officer and credit analyst Hialeah-Miami Springs (Fla.) First State Bank, 1968-70; credit mgr. Mary Carter Industries, Miami, 1970-72, Cain & Bultman Inc., Miami, 1972; regional mgr. Famco Services, Inc., Miami, 1972-73; fin. services mgr. Edward Don & Co., Miami, 1973—. Mem. Nat. Assn. Credit Mgmt. (chmn. internat. com.), So. Fla. Credit Mgmt. Assn. (pres. 1977-78). Democrat. Jewish. Home: 9231 NW 32 Pl Sunrise FL 33321 Office: 1550 N Miami Ave Miami FL 33136

DANIELS, DAVID H., accountant, banker; b. Winter Garden, Fla., Feb. 12, 1953; s. George J. D.; B.S. in Econs., U. Pa., 1974; M.B.A., U. Fla., 1975; M.S.M., Rollins Coll., 1980; grad. S.E. Banking Corp. Sch., 1976; A.B.A., Grad. Comml. Lending Sch., 1979; student Sch. of Banking, La. State U., 1980. Asst. v.p. comml. and real estate loans S.E. Nat. Bank, Orlando, Fla., 1979—, instr. profl. courses; adj. prof. Rollins Coll., Winter Park, Fla., 1979; cons. Project Bus. Jr. Achievement, 1977-79. Mem. Indsl. Devel. Commn. Mem. Robert Morris Assn. (treas.), Nat. Assn. Accountants, Assn. M.B.A. Execs., Inst. Internal Auditors, Am. Fin. Assn., Mortgage Bankers Assn., Inst. Mgmt. Acctg., Am. Bankers Assn., Am. Inst. C.P.A.'s, Fla. Inst. C.P.A.'s, Central Fla. Assn. C.P.A.'s and Bankers (sec.-treas.), Econs. Club Central Fla., Leadership Orlando, C. of C., Phi Kappa Phi. Home: PO Box 488 Windermere FL 32786 Office: 201 E Pine St Orlando FL 32801

DANIELS, DIANNE SUSAN, state ofcl.; b. Pauls Valley, Okla., Nov. 16, 1940; d. Henry Winton and Gladys Susan (Richardson) D.; student U. Ark., 1960-61; B.B.A., U. Okla., 1964. Clk. First Nat. Bank & Trust Co., Oklahoma City, 1964-65; supr. credit woman Sunray DX Oil Co., Tulsa, 1965; asst. cashier Am. Exchange Bank & Trust Co., Norman, Okla., 1966-73, asst. v.p., 1973; bank examiner state of Okla., 1973—; instr. women and fin. mgmt. Okla. Center for Continuing Edn., U. Okla., Norman, 1974. Ky. col. Mem. United Daus. Confederacy, D.A.R. (outstanding jr. mem. Black Beaver chpt. 1968, 69). Baptist. Home: 820 W Eufaula St Norman OK 73069 Office: 4100 Lincoln Blvd Oklahoma City OK 73105

DANIELS, HARRIET EARNESTINE, nurse, adminstr.; b. Shamrock, Fla., Oct. 10, 1937; d. Willie Lee and Carrie Elvira (Anderson) D.; B S., Fla. A&M U., 1960; M.Nursing, U. Fla., 1971, postgrad., 1976. Sch. nurse Fla. A&M High Sch., Tallahassee, 1960-61; head nurse U. Fla. Med. Center, Gainesville, 1963-71, supr. obstetrics-gynecology, 1971-73, asst. dir. nurses, 1973—. Bd. dirs. Upjohn Health Care Services. Fla. State Bd. Regents grantee, 1975-76. Mem. Zeta Phi Beta. Methodist. Clubs: Ebony Women's (treas. 1977-79), Order Eastern Star. Home: 1215 SE 13th St Gainesville FL 32601

DANIELS, LORRAINE ELEANOR, univ. adminstr.; b. Jacksonville, Fla. May 6, 1934; d. Albert and Jeanette (Bailey) Morrison; B.S., Bethune Cookman Coll., 1955; M.S., U. Fla., 1968, Ed.D. (Experienced Tchr. fellow), 1974; children—Yvette, Elton, Kerry. Instr. math. Jacksonville Public Schs., 1955-68, counselor, 1968-72; counselor for youth opportunity progams, tchr., counselor, coordinator adult basic edn. Fla. Jr. Coll., Jacksonville, 1969-74; dir. spl. ESAA funded programs for potential drop-outs U. North Fla., Jacksonville, 1974—; cons. Making Acad. Improvement, Duval County Schs. Active, NAACP, YWCA. NSF grantee, 1963-64. Mem. Am. Personnel and Guidance Assn., Assn. Non-White Concerns, Fla. Personnel and Guidance Assn., Delta Sigma Theta. Democrat. Home: 2811 Begonia Rd Jacksonville FL 32209 Office: U North Fla PO Box 17074 Pottsburg Sta Jacksonville FL 32216

DANIELS, MARION LUCILE LEATHERS, educator; b. Decatur, Ga., Sept. 6, 1924; B.A., Agnes Scott Coll., 1945; M.A., Emory U., 1964, Ph.D., 1969; m. Paul G. Kuntz. Tchr. Latin, Lovett Sch., Atlanta, 1963-66; asst. prof. classics Ga. State U., 1966-69, asso. prof. classics, 1969-73, prof. classics, 1973, Regents prof. classics, 1975—, acting chmn. dept. fgn. langs., 1974-75, chmn., 1975—. Named Tchr. of Yr. in Latin, State of Ga., 1965; recipient Semple award, 1965; Am. Council Learned Socs. grantee, 1970, 73, 76. Mem. Classical Modern Fgn. Lang. Assn. Ga. (v.p. 1968-69), Am. Philol. Assn., Archaeol. Inst. Am. (exec. bd. Atlanta chpt. 1960-72), Classical Assn. Mid-West and South, Renaissance Soc. Am., Classical Soc. Am. Acad. in Rome (sec.-treas. 1970-74), Classical Assn. Am. Sch. Classical Studies, Soc. Ch. History, Vergilian Soc., Am. Soc. Aesthetics, MLA, Internat. Neo-Platonic Soc., Soc. Philosophy Religion, Internat. Soc. Neo-Latin Studies, Medieval Acad. Am., Phi Beta Kappa, Phi Kappa Phi (sec. Ga. chpt. 1974), Omicron Delta Kappa. Author, translator: The Colloquim of the Seven About Secrest of the Sublime, 1975; author: The Crowned Salamander: A Study of the Metaphysics of Guillaume Postel, 1980; editor: (with Paul G. Kuntz) Harmony and the Pythagorean Tradition, 1979. Home: 1655 Ponce de Leon St Atlanta GA 30307 Office: Ga State U Univ Plaza Atlanta GA 30303*

DANIELS, ROGER DALE, chem. co. exec.; b. Ft. Gay, W.Va., May 20, 1938; s. Henry D. and Murvel (Lynch) D.; B.S., Va. Poly. Inst., 1961; postgrad. U. Mich.; m. Judith Smith, Dec. 27, 1959; children—Craig, Philip. With Dow Chem. Co., 1961—, research Inorganic Chems., Midland, Mich., 1961-74, group leader, 1970-74, Freeport, Tex., 1975-77, dir. resources, research dept., 1977—; presl. interchange exec. Pres.'s Commn. on Personnel Interchange, Washington, 1974-75. Pres., Lake Jackson Little League, 1977-78. Recipient Presdl. award, 1975. Mem. Am. Inst. Chem. Engrs., ASME, Am. Chem. Soc., Tau Beta Pi. Lutheran. Clubs: Riverside Country. Patentee in field. Home: 131 Poinciana Lake Jackson TX 77566 Office: A-2301 Bldg Dow Chem USA Freeport TX 77541

DANNA, ANTHONY CHRISTOPHER, printing co. exec.; b. Monroe, La., Dec. 19, 1945; s. Sam Christopher and Mary Frances (Moreci) D.; student La. Tech. U., 1964-65; m. Kathy Lynette Smith, Oct. 1, 1977; 1 son, Samuel Colby; children by previous marriage—Anthony Michael, Thomas Matthew. Shift supr. printing, multiple packaging div. Olinkraft Co. div. Johns Manville Corp., West Monroe, La., 1976—. Basketball coach, leadership dir. Boys Clubs Am., 1975-76. Served with USAF, 1966-70. Roman Catholic. Home: 410 Lakeshore Dr Monroe LA 71203 Office: PO Box 488 Jonesboro Rd West Monroe LA 71291

DANNER, DAVID WILLIAM, educator; b. Anderson, Ind., Oct. 12, 1940; s. Donald G. and Charlotte (Flynn) D. B.A., Coll. Wooster, 1962; student Edinburgh U., Scotland, 1960-61; B.Div., Princeton Theol. Sem., 1965; M.Ed., Temple U., 1970, Ed.D., 1974; m. Elizabeth Beck Reichardt, Aug. 27, 1966. Ordained to ministry Presbyterian Ch., 1965; asst. minister First Presbyn. Ch., Easton, Pa., 1965-66; asst. minister edn. St. John's Presbyn. Ch., Devon, Pa., 1966-68; English tchr. Valley Forge Jr. High Sch., 1968-74; teaching asso., lectr. Temple U., Phila., 1971-73; adj. prof. edn. Va. Commonwealth U. Richmond, 1975—; dir. adult edn. St. John's United Ch. of Christ, 1976—; asso. prof. Christian edn. Presbyn. Sch. Christian Edn., Richmond, 1974—. Recipient Preaching award-Mary Long Greir prize Princeton Sem., 1964; United Presbyn. Ch., Presbyn. Ch. U.S., Assn. Presbyn. Ch. Educators grantee, 1978. Mem. Assn. Profs. and Researchers in Religious Edn., Am. Psychol. Assn., Assn. Childhood Edn. (pres. Richmond br. 1978-80), Religious Edn. Assn., Assn. Presbyn. Ch. Educators. Republican. Office: 1205 Palmyra Ave Richmond VA 23227

DANNER, LORAIN DUFFIN, sec., bookkeeper; b. Ft. Smith, Ark., June 1, 1924; d. Everett Mearl and Ida (Killion) Duffin; student pub. schs., Ft. Smith; m. John Francis Danner, June 20, 1948; children—John Mearl, James Paul, Mark Richard, Rebecca Ann. Supr., Welcome Wagon Internat., Ark., 1963-70; med. sec., bookkeeper Joseph & Killough Clinic, Searcy, Ark., 1974—. Pres. White County (Ark.) Council Extension Homemakers, 1963-65; specialist in children's Sunday sch. work Ark. Bapt. Conv., 1947—. Clubs: Searcy Beethoven (pres. 1973-75), Extension Homemakers. Home: 812 Merritt St Searcy AR 72143 Office: 1300 S Main St Suite 101 Searcy AR 72143

DANOS, GARY JUDE, physician; b. New Orleans, Dec. 5, 1945; s. Lehman Joseph and Josie Teresa (Paternostro) D.; B.S., Loyola U. South, 1967; M.D., Tulane U., 1971; m. Carlos Ann Dominguez, Dec. 20, 1969; children—Suzanne Michelle, Ashley Elizabeth. Intern dept. surgery Tulane U., Charity Hosp., New Orleans, 1971-72, resident in surgery, 1972-76; pvt. practice medicine, specializing in surgery, New Orleans, 1976—; partner Surg. Clinic of East, New Orleans, 1976—; clin. asst. prof. Tulane U., 1978—; mem. staff Meth. Hosp., 1976—. Fellow A.C.S., AMA, Alton Ochsner Surg. Soc., La. Surg. Soc., La. State Med. Soc., Orleans Parish Med. Soc. Roman Catholic. Home: 3325 Vincennes Pl New Orleans LA 70125 Office: 5640 Read Blvd New Orleans LA 70127

DANOWSKI, ELIZABETH JOAN, rehab. counselor; b. Forest City, Pa., Jan. 24, 1935; d. Stephen and Mary (Tursic) Selinsky; R.N., St. Joseph's Hosp. Sch. Nursing, 1957; B.A., Marshall U., 1975, M.A., 1978; children—Michael, Stephen, Paul, Marianne. Nurse, St. Joseph's Hosp., 1954-57, VA Hosp., Syracuse, N.Y., 1957-58, Deaconess Hosp., Cleve., 1958-60, Miner's Hosp., Raton, N.Mex., 1968; nursing supr. Cabell Huntington Hosp., Huntington, W.Va., 1970-73; nursing counselor Community Mental Health Center, Huntington, 1976-77; rehab. house counselor, rehab. counselor Div. Vocat. Rehab., Huntington, 1978—. Mem. Am. Personnel and Guidance Assn., Nat. Rehab. Assn., Nat. Rehab. Counseling Assn., Kidney Found. Home: 101 W 11th Ave Huntington WV 25701 Office: 929 1/2 4th Ave Huntington WV 25701

D'ANTIGNAC, WILLIAM MICHAEL, banker; b. Augusta, Ga., Nov. 24, 1952; s. Cecil Auverne and Kathryn Virginia (Smith) D'A.; B.A., Augusta Coll., 1975, M.B.A., 1980; m. Diann Melinda Corgill, Jan. 25, 1975; 1 son, William Michael. Customer service rep. Ga. R.R. Bank, Augusta, 1973-74, asst. mgr. customer service, 1975-76, trust ops. mgr., 1977, trust ops. officer, 1978—. Active United Way, Heart Fund, Cancer Soc., Georgians for Good Govt. Mem. Am. Inst. Banking, Chi Delta Psi. Roman Catholic. Club: Gold G. Home: 3024 Angela St Martinez GA 30907

D'ANTONIO, ALBERT, JR., bus. exec.; b. N.Y.C., May 23, 1941; s. Albert and Jean D'A.; student Coll. of Ins., N.Y., 1970-72, U. Houston, 1973—; m. Linda J. Walsh, Feb. 9, 1963; children—Denise, Albert, III. Salesman, New York Life Ins. Co., 1963-64, John Hancock Ins. Co., L.I. City, N.Y., 1964-69; v.p. Sidney W. Fairchild Co., N.Y.C., Houston, 1969—. Served with USAF, 1959-63. Mem. Houston Life Underwriters, Houston N.W. C. of C. Roman Catholic. Clubs: Meml. N.W., El Dorado Country. Home: 8302 Twining Oaks St Spring TX 77379 Office: 3100 Eastside St Houston TX 77098

DANTZLER, RICHARD, realtor; b. Winter Haven, Fla., May 5, 1931; s. E. R. and Olive B. Dantzler; B.A. in Agrl. Econs., U. Fla., 1953; m. Clara Whelchel, June 19, 1954; children—Rick, Todd, Brad. With Swift & Co., Moultrie, Ga., 1953-54; realtor, Winter Haven, 1956—; dir. Exchange Bank Polk County, Haven Fed. Savs. & Loan Assn. Mayor, Winter Haven, 1962-64; trustee Winter Haven Hosp., Inc.; mem. exec. com. Winter Haven Area Devel. Council. Served to capt. AUS, 1954-56. Mem. Am. Inst. Real Estate Appraisers, Winter Haven C. of C. Club: Elks. Office: PO Box 192 Winter Haven FL 33880 also 277 Magnolia Ave SW Winter Haven FL 33880

DANVERS, ANN ADAMS, med. technologist; b. Mitchell County, Ga., Mar. 7, 1936; s. Orr and Iva V. (Jones) Adams; A.S., Ga. Southwestern Coll., 1955; B.A., Fla. Internat. U., 1977; M.B.A., Nova U., 1979; m. Richard F. Danvers, Jan. 7, 1955 (div. Mar. 1971); children—Gloria Ann Danver Rodriguez, Sandra Danvers Hagan, Richard, Michael, Stephen, Vicky. EKG technician, med. technician Winter Park (Fla.) Meml. Hosp., 1963-67; asst. chief technician Palm Springs Gen. Hosp., Hialeah, Fla., 1968-70, chief technician, 1970-71; clin. lab. mgr. Palmetto Gen. Hosp., Hialeah, 1971—. Mem. Clin. Lab. Mgmt. Assn. Home: 8540 NW 182d St Hialeah FL 33015 Office: Palmetto Gen Hosp 2001 W 68th St Hialeah FL 33010

DAPPRICH, JOHN WILLIAM, interior designer; b. Dearborn, Mich., Mar. 6, 1937; s. Elton and Ellen (Ketchum) D.; student Easter U., 1956-57; diploma Kendall Sch. Design, 1962. Interior designer Burdines Dept. Stores, Miami, Fla., 1963-64, Jordan Marsh Dept. Store, Miami, 1964-66; interior designer Waldo Perez Interiors, Coconut Grove, Fla., 1967-68; owner Dapprich Interiors, Coconut Grove, 1968-70; dir. interior design Deltona Corp., Miami, 1970—. Served with AUS, 1957-59. Mem. Am. Inst. Designers. Interior designer pent-house Joe Garagiola, Marco Island, 1970, also interior designer for Jack Paar, Key Biscayne, 1972, Henry Kissinger, Key Biscayne, 1972, Gene Sarazen, Marco Island, 1972, Ken Venturi, Marco Island, also Adm. Rickenbacker, Senator George Smathers, Ara Parseghian; TV commls. for Bob Griese of Miami Dolphins hotels include Marco Beach Hotel, Marco Island, Fla., Key Biscayne (Fla.) Hotel, Tierra Verde Hotel, St. Petersburg, Fla. Home: 3927 Douglas Rd Coconut Grove FL 33133

DARBY, NORMA JEAN, health clinic adminstr.; b. Mt. Hope, W.Va., Apr. 7, 1935; d. Clifford Rufus and Mabel Jane (Cales) Darby; Advanced Secretarial Certificate, Beckley (W.Va.) Coll., 1954, A.B.A., 1975; B.S. in Bus. Adminstrn., Concord Coll., 1979. Typist, Beckley Coll., 1953-54; sec. to asst. area med. adminstr. United Mine Workers Am. Welfare & Retirement Fund, Beckley, 1954-64; asst. adminstr. Dr. Thomas Walker Meml. Health Found., Inc., Beckley, 1964-79, So. W.Va. Health Services, Inc., 1979—. Mem. Med. Group Mgmt. Assn., Beckley C. of C., Beta Sigma Phi. Democrat. Methodist. Home: 201 Tanner Dr Beckley WV 25801 Office: PO Box 50 302 Stanaford Rd Beckley WV 25801

DARDEN, CONRAD LYNN, lawyer; b. Tyler, Tex., June 6, 1934; s. Robert Webster and Willie Oleta (Jones) D.; B.A., Baylor U., 1956; J.D., U. Tex., 1959; m. Margaret Alice Furr, June 16, 1956; children—Kimberly, Victoria, Sally. Admitted to Tex. bar, 1959; with Kouri, Banner & Darden, Wichita Falls, Tex., 1959-61; adminstrv. asst. to U.S. Congressman Graham B. Purcell, Jr., Washington, 1961-62; partner Humphrey, Gibson & Darden, Wichita Falls, 1962-69, Gibson, Darden & Hotchkiss, Wichita Falls, 1969—. Mem. Civil Def. Adv. Commn., 1960; chmn. Wichita Falls Planning Bd., 1960-65; dir. Wichita Falls Citizens Adv. Com., 1965—; chmn. bd. N. Tex. Mental Health Clinic, Inc., 1965-68; bd. dirs. Tex. Mental Health and Mental Retardation Found.; dir. Vol. Services Council State Hosp. and Spl. Schs. for Tex., 1965-66; chmn. bd. Wichita County Mental Health and Mental Retardation Center, 1969-73; mem. Tex. Mental Health and Retardation Bd., 1973-79; bd. dirs. Children's Aid Soc. West Tex., 1965-74. Del. Dem. Nat. Conv., 1972, 74; chmn. finance council Tex. Dem. Com., 1975-76. Recipient awards U. Tex. Bar Assn., 1958, U. Tex. Counsel, 1959, Wichita Falls Mental Health Assn., 1973. Mem. Am., Tex. bar assns., Delta Sigma Pi, Delta Theta Phi. Democrat. Baptist. Mason (32 deg., Shriner), Rotarian. Home: 4310 Ridgemont St Wichita Falls TX 76309 Office: City National Bank Bldg Wichita Falls TX 76301

DARDEN, JOHN WALDON, III, jewelry co. exec.; b. Conway, S.C., Dec. 15, 1945; s. John Waldon, Jr., and Hannah Ross (Smith) D.; B.S. in Bus., U. S.C., 1969; Diamond certificate Gemological Inst. Am., 1977; student Holland Sch. for Jewelers, 1976; m. Susan Ann Wright, Nov. 18, 1971; children—Stuart L., Elizabeth Ross. With Darden's Jewelers, 1969—, mgr., Lancaster, S.C., 1969-73. mgr., Conway, S.C., 1973-74, mgr., Myrtle Beach, S.C., 1974-75, pres. Darden's Jewelers of Conway, Myrtle Beach, Lancaster, and Georgetown, 1975—; cons. Nat. Profl. Jewelers Inst. Commr. housing Conway Housing Authority; bd. dirs. Conway Downtown Council. Mem. Conway C. of C., S.C. Mchts. Assn. (v.p.), S.C. Retail Jewelers Assn. (pres. 1975-76, 76-77), Retail Jewelers Am. (council of affiliated services), Am. Gem Soc. (registered jeweler), Lancaster Jaycees (bd. dirs., state dir.). Democrat. Methodist (chmn. adminstrv. bd., fin. com.). Clubs: Lancaster Toastmasters, Conway Lions (dir.). Home: 907 Lakeside Dr Conway SC 29526 Office: 331 Main St Conway SC 29526

DARE, EDWARD DAVID, med. service adminstr.; b. Evansville, Ind., Apr. 9, 1939; s. Sherman Edward and Anna Marie (Baker) D.; student Vincennes U., 1958-60; B.S., U. Evansville, 1963; m. Lawanda Joyce Steffey, June 20, 1960; children—Scott, Daniel, Steven. Teaching supr. Sch. Tech., Carle Clinic, Urbana, Ill., 1964-66; dir. nursing and personnel mgr. Marshfield (Wis.) Clinic, 1966-73; regional mgr. Hyland div. Baxter-Travenol, Costa Mesa, Calif., 1973-76; clinic adminstr. Med. Arts Clinic, Emporia, Kans., 1976-78; adminstr. Internal Medicine Group, El Paso, Tex., 1978—; exec. sec. Med. Equipment, Inc., 1976—; cons. to Emporia State U., 1976—; coroner Wood County, Wis., 1968-73. Alderman, Marshfield City Council, 1970-73. Named Outstanding Young Man, Marshfield Jaycees, 1972. Mem. Am. Soc. Clin. Pathologists, Med. Group Mgmt. Assn., Emporia C. of C., Registry of Med. Technologists, Nat. Rifle Assn., Nat. Muzzle Loading Rifle Assn. Club: Masons. Author: Guidebook to Laboratory Procedures, 1970; Sixty-Three Hours, 1977. Home: 4713 Tumbleweed Ave El Paso TX 79924 Office: 1250 Cliff St Suite 5A El Paso TX 79902

DARLING, LEROY ANTHONY, microelectronics exec.; b. Bangor, Maine, Nov. 24, 1922; s. Harold Eugene and Minnie (Haywood) D.; B.S. (Calvin Nealy scholar), U. Maine, 1947; M.S., Bklyn. Poly. Inst., 1952; m. Geraldine Violette, Sept. 29, 1943; children—Michele, Lynne. Asst. project engr., project engr., sr. chemist, sect. head, materials processes lab. Sperry Gyroscope Corp., L.I., N.Y., 2945-56; design specialist, supr. ANIP program Douglas Aircraft Corp., El Segundo, Calif., 1956-59; tech., dir., dir. research lab. Lear-Siegler, Inc., Santa Monica, Calif., 1959; dept. mgr., microelectronics center TRW Systems, 1963-68; dir. engring. ops., microelectronics div. Teledyne Systems Co., 1968-70; chief engr. microelectronics ops. Allen-Bradley Co., 1970-71; mgr. ops. engring. and microelectronic center Gen. Dynamics Corp., 1971-77; dir. microelectronics div. Martin Marietta Corp., Orlando, Fla., 1977—; tchr. evening div. Farmingdale Inst. Tech., 1954-56; cons. high polymer chemistry. Certified mfg. engr. Mem. Am. Chem. Soc., Sigma Xi. Roman Catholic. Republican. Patentee in field. Office: PO Box 5837 MP 189 Orlando FL 32805

DARNELL, CLARENCE STANLEY, mfg. co. exec.; b. Bristol, Va., Dec. 4, 1945; s. Robert Guy and Edna (Wilson) D.; student U. Tenn., 1975; m. Patricia Ford, July 9, 1965; 1 son, Stephen Michael. With Bristol Metals, Inc., Bristol, Tenn., 1964-80, mgr. engring. estimating, 1976-80; lead designer Engring. Co., Kingsport, Tenn., 1980—; pres. Rhondell Enterprises; curriculum cons. Va. High Drafting Dept., 1977—. Mem. ASME, ASTM. Home: Route 6 PO Box 312 Bristol TN 37620 Office: 2608 E Center St Kingsport TN 37664

DARNELL, RILEY CARLISLE, state legislator Tenn.; b. Clarksville, Tenn., May 13, 1940; s. Elliott Sinclair and Mary Anita (Whitefield) D.; B.S., Austin Peay State U., 1962; J.D., Vanderbilt U., 1965; m. Mary Penelope Crockarell, June 2, 1963; children—Neil Whitefield, Duncan Edward, Mary Eve, Penelope Joy. Admitted to Tenn. bar, 1965; gen. practice, 1965-66, 69—; mem. Tenn. Ho. of Reps. from 67th Dist., 1971—, treas. house caucus, 1971—, sec. house com. ways and means, chmn. joint house-senate fiscal rev. com., 1975—. Served to capt. AUS, 1966-69. Democrat. Mem. So. Legislative Conf. (vice chmn. jud. com. 1976—), Nat. Conf. State Legislators (jud. task force). Mem. Ch. of Christ (deacon 1971—). Club: St. Bethlehem Civitan. Home: 603 Waterloo Clarksville TN 37040 Office: 221 S 3d St Clarksville TN 37040

DARRACOTT, HALVOR THOMAS, ret. govt. ofcl.; b. Wichita Falls, Tex., Aug. 21, 1910; s. Charles William and Allie Mae (Moore) D.; B.S., Drury Coll., 1933; M.S. in Physics, U. Ark., 1939; m. Margaret Jane Mitchell, May 24, 1940; children—Hattiejane, William Michael, James Patrick. Reporter, editor Springfield (Mo.) Leader-Press, 1933-38; instr. math. and physics Fayetteville (Ark.) High Sch., 1939-41; commd. 2d lt. Signal Corps, U.S. Army, 1941, advanced through grades to col., 1962; bn. comdr. Hdqrs. Seventh Army, Germany, 1952-54; chief adminstrv. div. research and devel. lab., Ft. Monmouth, N.J., 1954-55, asst. dir. research, 1955-56; chief electronics br. Office Chief Signal Officer, Washington, 1956-58; dep. signal officer Hdqrs. Mil. Dist. Washington, 1958-59; chief electronics br. experimentation div. FAA-Nat. Aviation Facilities Experimentation Center, Atlantic City, 1959-62, ret., 1962; exec. engr. Adler Electronics Co., New Rochelle, N.Y., 1962-63; communication cons., Atlantic City, 1963-64; supervising gen. engr. U.S. Army Materiel Command Hdqrs., Washington, 1964, sr. supervisory phys. scientist in tech. forecasting, 1964-68; chief Ops. Analysis div. U.S. Army Advanced Materiel Concepts Agy., Alexandria, Va., 1968-71, supr. phys. sci., chief Technol. Forecasting div., 1971-74, chief Communications-Electronics div., 1974-75; chief Communications and Control Systems, Office Systems Devel., Hdqrs. U.S. Army Devel. and Readiness Command, Alexandria, 1975-79. Recipient certificate of appreciation Ft. Dix, 1962, others. Fellow Washington Acad. Sci.; mem. I.E.E.E. (sr.), Am. Phys. Soc., Am. Inst. Physics, Am. Math. Soc., Math. Assn. Am., A.A.A.S., Assn. U.S. Army, Washington Ops. Research Council, Armed Forces Communications and Electronics Assn., Am. Acad. Polit. and Social Sci., Am. Acad. Arts and Scis., Sigma Pi Sigma, Kappa Delta Pi. Mason (Shriner), Kiwanian (pres. 1969-70, lt. gov. 1979-80). Contbg. author: Technological Forecasting for Industry and Government, 1968. Contbr. articles to profl. jours. Home: 3325 Mansfield Rd Falls Church VA 22041

DARROW, GEORGE RICHARD, metals mfg. co. exec.; b. Memphis, Dec. 11, 1921; s. Henry Baldwin and Annie Warren (O'Neal) D.; student Ga. Sch. Tech., 1939-41; B.A., U. Louisville, 1957; m. Elvira Elizabeth Sauer, Sept. 8, 1956; 1 dau., Nancy Lynn Darrow Maclin. With, Reynolds Metals Co., Richmond, Va., 1941—, finishing and corrosion control sect. dir., engring. and tech. services, mill products div., 1968—. Registered profl. engr., Calif. Served with USN, 1943-46; PTO. Mem. Am. Chem. Soc., Am. Electroplaters Soc. (dir. 1978—). Republican. Lutheran. Patentee in field. Home: 205 Tamarack Rd Richmond VA 23229 Office: Reynolds Metals Co PO Box 27003 Richmond VA 23261

DARTEZ, LOUIS AVERY, typographer, rancher; b. Lafayette, La., Dec. 12, 1925; s. Joseph Avery and Marie (LeBlanc) D.; student in Journalism and Bus. Adminstrn., U. Houston, 1956-59, 62-63; m. Barbara Ann Jackson, Oct. 13, 1951. Engring. clk. Stone & Webster Engring. Corp., Houston, 1946-48; supr. non-tech. sect. Mathieson Chem. Co., Balt., 1949-52; adminstrv. asst. to v.p. dept. engring. Tellepsen Constrn. Co., Houston, 1952-59; founder, owner, operator Dart Type Co., Houston, 1959—; rancher Round Top Farm, Houston; owner Dart Aircraft Leasing & Chartering, Houston, Am. Manor Apts., Houston; partner Greenlea Land Devel., Houston; speaker on small bus. mgmt., typography and communications to sch. groups. Served with USAAF, 1943-46, USAF, 1948-49. Mem. Printing Industries Assn. Houston (pres. 1970-71, award of appreciation and recognition 1974), Nat., Houston (pres. 1974) composition assns., Printing Craftsmen Club, Houston Litho Club, Gen. Aviation Pilots Assn., Attakapas Hist. Soc. Republican. Roman Catholic. Contbr. articles on typography to tech. publs., newspapers; author copyfitting charts; contbr. editor Graphics S.W. Mag., 1968-70; geneal. research, including extensive travel, 1956—. Office: 3313 D'Amico St Houston TX 77019

DAS, BRAJA MOHAN, civil engr., educator; b. Cuttack, India, Mar. 2, 1941; s. Gour M. and Snehalata (Patnaik) D.; came to U.S., 1966, naturalized, 1973; B.Sc. with honors, Ravenshaw Coll., India, 1959; B.S. in Civil Engring., U. Coll. Engring., Burla, India, 1963; M.S. in Civil Engring., U. Iowa, 1968; Ph.D., U. Wis., 1972; m. Janice Fay Quinley, Sept. 6, 1969; 1 dau., Valerie Jean. Asst. engr. irrigation Govt. of Orissa, India, 1963-66; civil engr. Ill. Div. Hwys., 1967-69; soils engr. Walter Lum Assos., Inc., Honolulu, 1972-73; asst. prof. dept. civil engring. Tri-State U., Angola, Ind., 1973-75; asso. prof. civil engring. S.D. State U., Brookings, 1975-78; asst. prof. civil engring. U. Tex., El Paso, 1978—. Mem. ASCE, Am. Soc. for Engring. Edn., ASTM, Internat. Soc. Soil Mechanics and Found. Engring., Chi Epsilon. Democrat. Baptist. Author: Introduction to Soil Mechanics, 1980; contbr. articles on found. engring. and soil mechanics to profl. publs. Home: 440 San Blas Dr El Paso TX 79912 Office: Civil Engring Dept Univ Texas El Paso TX 79968

DAS, LACHHMAN, indsl. engr., airlines exec.; b. Hajipur, India (now West Pakistan), Sept. 21, 1935; s. Mool and Hukmi Devi (Gulati) Chand; came to U.S., 1964, naturalized, 1973; m. Lalita Khosla, Oct. 10, 1960; children—Micky Naveen, Tony Sanjiv. Project leader, indsl. engr. Matson Nav. Co., San Francisco, 1965-68; with Pan Am. World Airways, 1968—, specialist engr., project engr., supr., mgr. systems analysis, supt. ops. systems support, 1975—; staff ops. analyst United Airlines Co., San Francisco, 1974-75; owner (with wife) 2 travel agys., Houston area. Registered profl. engr., Calif. Sr. mem. Am. Inst. Indsl. Engrs. Hindu. Clubs: Lions, Toastmasters. Contbr. articles to profl. jours. Home: 16423 Clearcrest Dr Houston TX 77059 Office: Pan Am PO Box 58938 Houston TX 77058

DAS, SALIL KUMAR, biochemist; b. Rangoon, Burma, Dec. 21, 1940; s. Santi R. and Provabati Das; came to U.S., 1962, naturalized, 1966; I.Sc., Calcutta U., 1956, B. Sc., 1958, B. Sc. with honors, 1959, M. Sc., 1961; D.Sc., 1974; Sc. D., Mass. Inst. Tech., 1966; m. Anjusri Das, May 31, 1968; Research asst. Mass. Inst. Tech., Cambridge, 1962-66, research asso., 1966; research asso. dept. physics U. Ariz., Tucson, 1966-67; research asso. dept. chemistry Grad. Inst. Tech., Little Rock, Ark., 1967-68; research asso. Duke, Durham, N.C., 1968-69; asst. prof. Meharry Med. Coll., Nashville, 1969-74, asso. prof., 1974—. Recipient Univ. medal Calcutta U., 1961, Cressy Morrison award N.Y. Acad. Scis., 1967, grant NIH, 1972—, Travel grantee Am. Inst. Nutrition, 1975. Fellow, Am. Inst. Chemists; mem. Am. Inst. Nutrition, N.Y. Acad. Scis., Am. Oil Chemists Soc., Am. Chem. Soc., Inst. Food Technologists, AAAS, Biochem. Soc. (London), Am. Contract Bridge League (life master), Sigma Xi. Contbr. articles to profl. jours. Home: 937 Giant Oak Dr Nashville TN 37217 Office: Biochemistry Meharry Medical College 1005 18th Ave N Nashville TN 37208

DASILVA, ERCIO MARIO, surgeon; b. Cataguazes, Brasil, Oct. 19, 1924; s. Mario and Rosa (Pinto) daS.; came to U.S., 1951, naturalized, 1963; M.D., U. Minas Gerais (Brasil), 1949; m. Doris H. daSilva, Aug. 22, 1953; children—Robert, Suzanne. Intern, St. Mary's Hosp., Huntington, W.Va.; resident St. Josph Hosp., Lexington, Ky., Millard Fillmore Hosp., Buffalo; pvt. practice surgery, Columbia, S.C., 1961—; chief surg. service S.C. State Hosp., Columbia, 1961—; surg. cons. Midland Tng. Center, Columbia, 1963—. Diplomate Am. Bd. Colon and Rectal Surgery. Mem. Columbia Med. Soc., Am. Soc. Colon and Rectal Surgeons, Piedmont Soc. Colon and Rectal Surgeons. Home: 448 Winstain Dr Columbia SC 29210 Office: SC State Hosp Columbia SC 29202

DASPIT, KATHARINE, banker; b. Houma, La., Sept. 29, 1920; d. Robert Valentine and Margaret Lee (Butler) D.; student La. State U., Baton Rouge, 1937-39; B.A. cum laude, Southwestern La. Inst., 1942; M.B.A., Tex. A. and M. U., 1971. Tchr., Cut Off High Sch., Lafourche Parish Sch. Bd., Thibodaux, La., 1942-43; joined WAC, 1943, commd. 2nd lt., 1945, advanced to maj., 1960, ret., 1963; comdr. 25th squadron Walker AFB, Roswell, N.Mex., 1952, 24th squadron, Carswell AFB, Ft. Worth, 1953; chief WAF procurement 3504th USAF Recruiting Group, Lackland AFB, San Antonio, 1954-58; chief printing and publs. div., asst. dir. adminstrv. services Pacific Air Forces Bases Command, Hickam AFB, Hawaii, 1958-60, dir. adminstrv. services, 1960-62; chief career mgmt. and ednl. guidance div. Hdqrs. Air Force Flight Test Center, Edwards AFB, 1962-63, chief quality control br., 1963, chief data control br., 1963; tchr. Bayou Blue Elementary Sch., Lafourche Parish Sch. Bd., 1963-64, East Houma Elementary Sch., Terrebonne Parish Sch. Bd., Houma, 1967; programmer La. State Computer Center, Baton Rouge, 1968-69; personnel officer 1st. Nat. Bank Houma, 1972—. Mem. AAUW (2d. v.p. Houma-Thibodaux br. 1976—), Personnel Mgmt. Assn. S. Central La. (chpt. sec. 1976, v.p. 1977, pres. 1978), Nat. Assn. Bank Women, Res. Officers Assn., Ret. Officers Assn. Democrat. Roman Catholic. Toastmaster. Home: Route 5 Box 294 Houma LA 70360 Office: PO Box 6096 Houma LA 70361

DASTE, BARRY MICHAEL, social scientist; b. New Orleans, Feb. 19, 1943; s. Verdun Roger and Marie Louise (Roper) D.; B.A., U. New Orleans, 1966; M.S.W., La. State U., 1968; 3d yr. cert. in social work Tulane U., 1971; m. Beverly Ann Rodriguez, Mar. 2, 1968; 1 dau., Bonnie Maria. Social worker Charity Hosp., New Orleans, 1966, Orleans Sch. Bd., 1966-67, 69-70, DePaul Mental Health Center, 1968-69; asso. prof. social work La. State U., Baton Rouge, 1971—, coordinator internships, 1975—; cons. pvt. orgns., state depts. Served with USMC, 1960-65. NIMH fellow, 1965-68; Childrens Bur. fellow, 1970-71. Mem. Acad. Cert. Social Workers, La. Assn. Criminal Justice Social Workers, Council on Social Work Edn., La. Conf. Social Welfare. Contbr. ten articles to profl. jours. Home: 9137 Baronne Dr Baton Rouge LA 70809 Office: Sch Social Welfare La State U Baton Rouge LA 70803

DASTUGUE, FERNAND JOSEPH, JR., physician; b. New Orleans, Apr. 26, 1922; s. Fernand Joseph and Frances Eliza (Brownson) D.; B.S., Tulane U., 1941, M.D., 1944; m. Shirley Louise Labbe, Dec. 10, 1955; children—Patrice L., Suzanne M., Michele C. Intern Charity Hosp., New Orleans, 1944-45; asst. dept. anatomy Tulane U., 1946-47; resident internal medicine Charity Hosp., 1947-50; staff physician VA Center, Biloxi, Miss., 1950-60; staff physician Ochsner Clinic, New Orleans, 1960—, head sect. on gen. internal medicine, dept. internal medicine, 1976—; sec. staff Ochsner Found. Hosp., 1966-69; clin. asso. prof. dept. internal medicine Tulane U. Sch. Medicine, New Orleans, 1976—. Served to comdr., USNR, 1945-46, 52-54. Diplomate Am. Bd. Internal Medicine (recertified 1974). Mem. A.C.P. (life), A.M.A., So. Med. Assn., Orleans Parish Med. Soc., New Orleans Acad. Internal Medicine, Cath. Physicians Guild, Phi Beta Kappa, Omicron Delta Kappa, Alpha Omega Alpha. Democrat. Roman Catholic. Clubs: Empire, New Orleans Opera (New Orleans). Home: 35 Colony Rd Gretna LA 70053 Office: 1514 Jefferson Hwy New Orleans LA 70121

DATTILO, DONALD PHILLIP, electronic design engr.; b. Louisville, Feb. 5, 1945; s. Phillip Francis and Lucy (Thompson) D.; B.A., Bellarmine Coll., 1969; M.B.A., U. Louisville, 1972, B.S. in E.E., 1977. With Gen. Electric Co., Louisville, 1969-71; electronic design engr. Am. Industries, Louisville, 1971-72; cons. engr., system design Verback Asso., Louisville, 1972-73; pres. Dattilo Co., Louisville, 1973—. Served with USAF, 1971-72. Mem. IEEE, Indsl. Designers

Soc. Am., Ky. Hypnotic Soc., Am. Inst. Indsl. Designers, Am. Soc. Inventors. Roman Catholic. Club: Louisville Aero. Author: P. C. Artwork Techniques, 1975; Replacing Relay Bands with Circuit Boards, 1977; Monolithic Circuit Design, 1977; Functional Circuit Design, 1978; contbr. articles to profl. jours. Patentee in field. Home: 2302 Taylorsville Rd Louisville KY 40205

DAUB, OSCAR CARL, educator; b. Irvington, N.J., Sept. 12, 1941; s. Oskar Karl and Olga Adeline (Schmidt) D.; A.B., Wheaton Coll., 1963; M.A., Rutgers U., 1964; Ph.D., U. Ga., 1972. Instr. English, Gordon Coll., Wenham, Mass., 1965-68, U. Ga., Athens, 1971-72; asst. prof. Savannah (Ga.) State Coll., 1972-78 asso. prof., 1978—; Fulbright lectr. U. Iceland, 1976-77. Vestryman, St. Michael's Episcopal Ch. Mem. Conf. on Christianity and Lit., So. Atlantic Modern Lang. Assn., S.E. Renaissance Conf., Lambda Iota Tau, Phi Kappa Phi, Phi Beta Kappa. Home: 5507 Magnolia Ave Savannah GA 31406 Office: Dept English Savannah State Coll Savannah GA 31404

DAUBENSPECK, WAYNE MARTEL, clergyman; b. Selinsgrove, Pa., Nov. 25, 1904; s. Lloyd Mosheim and Della Almeda (Burns) D.; A.B., Susquehanna U., 1927; grad. Susquehanna Theol. Sem., 1930; m. Ethel Mason, July 15, 1931; children—Richard Edward, Ruth Elizabeth (Mrs. G. Keith Kistler), Henry Mason. Ordained to ministry Luth. Ch., 1930; minister ch., Oshkosh, Nebr., 1930-35; chaplain Nebr. Dist. CCC, 1936-38, U.S. Penal System (Northeastern and Ft. Leavenworth), 1938-40; Luth. service pastor Japan and Korea, 1954-63; pastor St. David's Ch., Kannapolis, N.C. 1964-70; ret., 1970. Served as chaplain AUS, 1940-54, commd. 1st. lt., 1935; col. Res. ret. Decorated Bronze Star medal. Mem. V.F.W. (chaplain N.C. dept. 1973). Mason (32 deg.). Home: 208 W 22d St Kannapolis NC 28081

DAUGHDRILL, JAMES HAROLD, JR., coll. adminstr.; b. LaGrange, Ga., Apr. 25, 1934; s. James Harold and Louise Coffee (Dozier) D.; student Davidson Coll., 1952-54; A.B., Emory U., 1956; D.D., Davidson Coll., 1974; B.D., M.Div., Columbia Theol. Sem., 1967; m. Elizabeth Anne Gay, June 26, 1954; children—James Harold, Louisa Risha, Elizabeth Gay. Ordained to ministry Presbyn. Ch. of U.S.; pres. Kingston Mills, Inc., Cartersville, Ga., 1956-64; minister St. Andrews Presbyn. Ch., Little Rock, 1967-70; sec. stewardship Presbyn. Ch. of U.S., 1970-73; pres. Southwestern Coll., Memphis, 1973—. Trustee Frank E. Seidman Award Fedn., Brooks Meml. Art Gallery, Hutchison Sch. Mem. Econ. Club Memphis, Tenn. Council Pvt. Colls (past chmn.), Assn. Presbyn. Colls (dir.), Coll. Athletic Conf. (past pres.), So. Coll. Univ. Union (past pres.), Omicron Delta Kappa. Clubs: Memphis Country, Racquet Club of Memphis. Author: Man Talk, 1972. Asso. editor Presbyterian Outlook, 1978. Home: 671 West Dr Memphis TN 38112 Office: 2000 N Parkway Memphis TN 38112

DAUGHERTY, BILLY JOE, banker; b. Timpson, Tex., Jan. 31, 1923; s. David Albert and Kate (Smith) D.; grad. Tyler Comml. Coll., 1942; postgrad. So. State Coll., 1945-47; grad. Southwestern Grad. Sch. Banking, So. Meth. U., 1969; student Nat. Credit Lending Sch., U. Okla., 1969; m. Martha Carroum, May 14, 1942; children—Stephen Michael, Tony Fares, Kathryn Love. Asst. v.p., asst. trust officer First Nat. Bank Magnolia (Ark.), 1947-52; plant acct. Republic Steel Corp., Magnolia, 1953-54; with Union Nat. Bank, Little Rock, 1954-70, v.p., cashier, 1965-70; exec. v.p., dir., sec. to bd. dirs. First State Bank & Trust Co., Conway, Ark., 1970-73, pres., dir., sec. to bd. dirs., 1973—. Dir. Ark. Banking Sch. Mem. adv. bd. Salvation Army, 1967-70; bd. dirs. Met. YMCA, Little Rock, 1966-70; chmn. Columbia chpt. ARC, Magnolia, 1952; mem. budget com. United Fund Pulaski County (Ark.), 1962-65; treas. City Beautiful Com. Little Rock, 1965-67; treas. Ark. br. Am. Assn. UN, 1965-67; pres. Heart of Ark. Travel Assn., 1971-74; pres., dir. United Fund of Faulkner County, 1972; state treas. Radio Free Europe, 1960-72; chmn. Faulkner County Heart Fund Campaign, 1971. Sec. to bd. dirs., trustee Union Nat. Found.; bd. dirs. Ark. Heart Assn., 1971-75, chmn. bd., 1975—; trustee Ark. Baptist Med. Center, sec.-treas., 1965-69; bd. dirs. Am. Heart Assn., Goodwill Industries Ark., 1975—. Served with USAAF, 1943-46. Mem. Little Rock Clearing House Assn. (v.p. 1969, pres. 1965-66, sec.-treas. 1967-68), Ark. Bankers Assn. (pres. jr. bankers sect. 1950; bank dirs. adv. com. 1971—, dir. 1979—), Conway C. of C. (pres. 1975). Baptist (supt. Sunday sch.; chmn. bldg. com. 1964-66; chmn. bd. deacons 1962-63; mem. finance com. 1960-68, chmn. stewardship com. 1968). Clubs: Top of Rock (dir. 1969—); Little Rock; Conway Country; Pleasant Valley Country; Western Hills Country (dir., sec. 1968-69). Home: 22 Riviera Dr Conway AR 72032 Office: First State Bank & Trust Co Oak and Front Sts Conway AR 72032

DAUGHERTY, DAVID HENRY, bank exec.; b. Pitts., Nov. 16, 1934; s. Carroll Roop and Miriam Rogers (Craiglow) D.; B.A., Wesleyan U., 1956; M.B.A., U. Pa., 1961; m. Mary Catherine Goins, June 18, 1960; children—David Henry, Jr., Anne Goins. Second v.p. securities The Fidelity Mut. Life Ins. Co., Phila., 1961-71; pres. Valley Forge Investment Mgmt., King of Prussia, Pa., 1971-74; v.p., dir. Funds, Inc., Houston, 1974-78; v.p., sr. trust investment officer First Nat. Bank & Trust Co., Tulsa, 1978—. Served as officer USMC, 1956-59. Mem. Fin. Analysts Okla., English Speaking Union. Republican. Episcopalian. Home: 4015 S Victor St Tulsa OK 74105

DAUGHERTY, FREDERICK ALVIN, judge; b. Oklahoma City, Aug. 18, 1914; s. Charles L. and Felicia A. (Mitchell) D.; LL.B., Cumberland U., 1934; postgrad. Oklahoma City U., 1934-35, LL.D. (hon.), 1974; postgrad. U. Okla., 1936-37; D.Hum., Okla. Christian Coll., 1976; m. Marjorie E. Green, Mar. 15, 1947 (dec. Feb. 1964); m. 2d, Betsy F. Amis, Dec. 15, 1965. Admitted to Okla. bar, 1937; practiced in Oklahoma City, 1937-40; mem. firm Ames, Ames & Daugherty, Oklahoma City, 1946-50, Ames, Daugherty, Bynum & Black, Oklahoma City, 1952-55; judge dist. ct. 7th Jud. Dist. Okla., 1955-61; U.S. dist. judge Western, Eastern, No. dists. Okla., Oklahoma City, 1961—; chief judge Western Dist. Okla., 1972—. Mem. profl. adv. com. Okla. County Assn. Mental Health, 1963-70; mem. exec. com. Oklahoma City Council on Alcholism, 1964—, Okla. Med. Research Found., 1966-69. Nat. bd. govs. A.R.C., 1963-69, 3d vice chmn., 1968-69, nat. fund vice chmn. Okla., 1956-58; trustee United Fund Greater Oklahoma City, 1961—, v.p., 1960, pres., 1961; bd. dirs. Community Council Oklahoma City and County, pres., 1967-69. Served with AUS, 1940-45; PTO; 1950-52; Korea; served to maj. gen. Okla. N.G., 1934-64. Decorated Legion of Merit with two oak leaf clusters, Bronze Star with oak leaf cluster, N.G. Assn. Distinguished Service medal; recipient Okla. Distinguished Service medal, recipient award to mankind Oklahoma City Sertoma Club, 1962, Outstanding Citizen award Oklahoma City Jr. C. of C., 1965, U. Okla. Distinguished Service citation, 1973, Distinguished Alumni citation Cumberland Law Sch., Samford U., 1974; named to Okla. Hall of Fame, 1969. Mem. Okla., Am., Fed. bar assns., Am. Bar Found., Oklahoma City C. of C. (dir. 1960-61, 66-67, 71-72, 77—), 45th Inf. Div. Assn. (pres. mus. bd. 1974—), Amvets, Am. Legion, Assn. U.S. Army (Okla. pres. 1962-65, adv. bd. dirs. 1964-70), Okla. N.G. Assn. (pres. 1947), VFW, Mil. Order World Wars (chpt. comdr. 1968-69), Sigma Alpha Epsilon, Phi Delta Phi. Episcopalian. Kiwanian (pres. Oklahoma City 1957), Mason (33 deg., Shriner, Jester). Club: Oklahoma City Men's Dinner (exec. com. 1963-65, pres. 1966-69). Home: 1800 Coventry Ln Oklahoma City OK 73120 Office: US Courthouse Oklahoma City OK 73102

DAUGHERTY, KENNETH EARL, research co. exec., educator; b. Pitts., Dec. 27, 1938; s. Thomas Hill and Laura Elizabeth (Schuda) D.; B.S. in Chemistry, Carnegie-Mellon U., 1960; Ph.D. in Analytical Chemistry (DuPont, Shell Oil, Standard Oil, NSF fellow), U. Wash., 1964; M. Bus. Econs., Claremont Grad. Sch., 1971; m. Joan Kay Ogrosky, Dec. 22, 1961; children—Brian Earl, Kirsten Kay. Chemist, Marbon Chem.-Borg Warner, Washington, W.Va., 1960; research chemist Rohm and Haas Corp., Bristol, Pa., 1964; group leader, sr. staff Amcord, Riverside, Calif., 1966-71; asso. prof. chemistry U. Pitts., 1971-73; dir. research and devel. Gen. Portland Inc., Dallas, 1973-77; dir. energy and materials sci. Inst. Applied Scis., North Tex. State U., Denton, 1977-79, prof. chemistry, 1979—; pres. KEDS Inc., KD Cons., 1977—; adj. prof. chemistry U. Pitts., 1973—, N. Tex. State U., Denton, 1974—. Cons. in field. Served to maj. AUS, 1964-66, Res., 1966—. Decorated Army Commendation medal. Fellow Am. Inst. Chemists; mem. Research Soc. Am., ASTM, Rilem, Nat. (transp. research bd.), N.Y. acads. scis., Am. Ceramic Soc., Am. Chem. Soc. (chpt. pres. 1960), Applied Spectroscopy Soc., Sigma Xi, Pi Kappa Alpha, Omicron Delta Epsilon, Phi Lambda Upsilon, Alpha Chi Sigma. Republican. Methodist. Clubs: Masons, Shriners, Rotary. Author numerous publs. in field. Patentee in field. Home: 317 Lakeland Dr Lewisville TX 75067 Office: Dept Chemistry North Tex State U Denton TX 76203

DAUGHERTY, LARRY GENE, gen. contractor; b. Fall Brook, Calif., Dec. 17, 1937; s. Francis Edward and Dorothy Donna (LongmiLe) D.; student pub. schs.; m. Patricia Gail a4tFick, Nov. 19, 1971; 1 son, Shane Anthony. Salesman, N4tionwide Builders Co., Des Moines, 1962-64, Universal Builders Co., Little Rock, 1964-69; sales mgr. Smith Bros. Const0n. Co., N. Little Rock, 1969-73; owner, operator Daugherty Constrn. Co., Blytheville, Ark., 1973—, Blytheville Home Improvement Center, 1973—; bd. dirs. Ark. Home Improvement Council. Mem. Nat. Home Improvement Council, Nat. Remodelers Assn., Ark. Amateur Trap Shooters Assn. (dir.). Club: Blytheville Noon Lions. Home: PO Box 1221 Blytheville AR 72315 Office: 101 W Main St Blytheville AR 72315

DAUGHTRIDGE, VERNON FLETCHER, JR., lawyer; b. Rocky Mount, N.C., Aug. 11, 1926; s. Vernon Fletcher and Blanche Hester (Riley) D.; B.S. in Commerce, U. N.C., 1950; J.D., 1952; children—Susan H. Daughtridge Stephenson, Vernon Fletcher III, Blanche Lynne Daughtridge Duncan, Gladys Lee Daughtridge Leyshon. Admitted to N.C. bar, 1952, U.S. Supreme Ct., 1973; pvt. practice law, Wilson, N.C., 1952—. Served with U.S. Navy, 1944-46. Mem. N.C., Wilson County (pres. 1956-58), 7th Jud. Dist. (pres. 1959-60) bar assns., N.C. State Bar, N.C. Soc. of Cin., SCV, SAR. Democrat. Episcopalian. Clubs: Masons, Shriners, Elks. Home: 1004 Treemont Rd Wilson NC 27893 Office: PO Box 885 Suite 515 First National Bank Bldg Wilson NC 27893

D'AURIA, RICHARD EDWARD, Spanish linguist, educator; b. Bklyn.; s. Enrico and Josephine (De Angelis) D'A.; B.S., N.Y. U., 1962; M.A., U. P.R., 1968, Ph.D., 1974; m. Carmen Acevedo Garcia, Oct. 11, 1962; children—Riccardo Enrico, Bianca Maria. Asso. prof. Spanish lang. and lit. U. P.R., Rio Piedras, 1969—, asst. prof. Profl. Sch. of Translating, 1971—. Huntington Found. grantee to study in Spain, 1961-62; recipient cert. of merit for disting. service to community, Cambridge, Eng., 1978. Fellow Internat. Biog. Assn.; mem. South Atlantic, Am. modern lang. assns., Am. Assn. Tchrs. Spanish and Portuguese, Puerto Rican Assn. U. Profs., Spanish Heritage Assn., Internat. Platform Assn., Nat. Geog. Soc., Latin Am. Assn. Linguistics and Philology, Christian Family Movement, Sigma Delta Pi. Author: El tema hispanico en la obra de Ramiro de Maeztu, 1968; El problema de Espana en la literatura del siglo XVIII, 1974; El universo poético de Estaban Manuel Villegas, 1979; La problemática de traducir Jabberwocky, 1980. Home: Calle 24 B1Q 42-8 Sta Rosa Bayamon PR 00619 Office: Dept Hispanic Studies POB BB U PR Rio Piedras PR 00931

DAUSER, FREDDIE WARDEN, social worker; b. Tuscaloosa, Ala., Apr. 26, 1936; s. Eugene Frederick and Lois Virginia (Warden) D.; B.S., Memphis State U., 1958; M.S. in Social Work, U. Tenn., 1972; now postgrad. U. Ala.; m. Renate Veikins, May 31, 1959; children—Alfred Lawrence, John Eugene. Salesman, U.S. Plywood Corp., 1959-61; store mgr. Sam Shainberg Corp., 1961-63; chief child support Memphis and Shelby County Juvenile Ct., 1964-70; community services supr. Tenn. Dept. Human Services, Nashville, 1972-76; chief social work Bryce Hosp., Tuscaloosa, 1976—; lectr., field instr. Sch. Social Work, U. Tenn., 1972-76, U. Ala., 1976—; cons. youth aid div. Tuscaloosa County Sheriff's Office, 1978—. Vol. hunter safety instr., Tenn., 1973-76, Ala., 1976—. Lic. cert. social worker, Ala.; NIMH maternal and child welfare grantee, 1970-72, 79-80. Mem. Am. Acad. Cert. Social Workers, Nat. Assn. Social Workers, Nat. Rifle Assn. (life). Presbyterian. Home: 1439 50th Ave E Tuscaloosa AL 35404 Office: Bryce Hospital Tuscaloosa AL 35401

DAUSSMAN, GROVER FREDERICK, cons. engr.; b. Newburgh, Ind., May 6, 1919; s. Grover Cleveland and Madeline (Springer) D.; student U. Cin., 1936-38; Carnegie Inst. Tech., 1944-45, George Washington U., 1948-56; B.S. in Elec. Engring., U. Ala., 1963, postgrad., 1963-64, 77; postgrad. Indsl. Coll. Armed Forces, 1955, 63; Ph.D. (hon.), Hamilton State U., 1973; m. Elli Margrite Kilian, Dec. 27, 1941; children—Cynthia Louise (Mrs. Kenneth E. Quinn), Judith Ann, Margaret Elizabeth (Mrs. Robert T. Davidson). Coop. engr. Sunbeam Elec. Mfg. Co., Evansville, Ind., 1936-38; engr. draftsman Phila. Navy Yard, 1941-42; resident engr. supr. shipbldg. USN, Neville Island, Pa., 1942-45; engr. Pearl Harbor Navy Yard, 1945-48; with Bur. Ships, USN, Washington, 1948-56; with Guidance and Control Tech. Liaison, Army Ballistic Missile Agy., Huntsville, Ala., 1956-58, chief program coordination Guidance and Control Lab., 1958-60; chief program coordination Astrionics Lab., Marshall Space Flight Center, Huntsville, 1960-62, staff asst. for advanced research and tech. Astrionics Lab., 1962-70; engring. cons., 1970—; project dir. fallout shelter surveys Mil. Dept. Tenn., 1971-73; head drafting dept. Alverson-Draughon Coll., Huntsville, Ala., 1974-77; instr. Ala. Christian Coll., 1977-79; engring. draftsman Reisz Engring. Co., Huntsville, 1979—; chief engr. Sheraton Motor Inn, Huntsville, 1979; sr. engr. Sperry Support Services, 1980—. Recipient cert. Hon. Service, USN, 1945; Performance Award certificate U.S. Army, 1960; NASA Apollo Achievement award, 1969. Registered profl. engr., Ala., Va., D.C. Mem. U. Ala. Alumni Assn., Ala. (Engr. of Yr. award 1968, chpt. pres. 1966-67, state dir. 1962-65, 68-71), Nat. socs. profl. engrs., I.E.E.E. (sr. mem., sect. chmn. N.Ala. sect. 1961-62, engring. mgmt. chpt. chmn. 1964-65, mem. adminstrv. com. engring. mgmt. soc. 1966—, sec. soc. 1969—, Engr. of Yr. award 1969, research com. 1965-67, dir. S.E. region, mem. inst. bd. dirs. 1972-73), A.A.A.S., Am. Def. Preparedness Assn. (post dir. Tenn. Valley), Am. Inst. Aeros. and Astronautics, Am. Soc. Naval Engrs., Missile, Space and Range Pioneers, U.S. Naval Inst., Assn. U.S. Army, Internat. Platform Assn., Huntsville Assn. Tech. Socs. (sec. 1969-71, v.p., dir.), Marshall Space Flight Center Retirement Assn. (pres. 1974—). Democrat. Mem. United Ch. of Christ (sec. ch. council 1965-66, vice moderator Ala-Tenn. Assn. 1965-68, bd. dirs. S.E. conv. 1965-66). Home: 1910 Colice Rd SE Huntsville AL 35801 also Apt 3114 125 S Reynolds St Alexandria VA 22304 Office: Suite 700 1755 S Jefferson Davis Hwy Arlington VA 22202

D'AVANTE, SHIRLEY JEANETTE, pharmacist; b. Tex., July 15, 1945; B.S. in Pharmacy, Tex. So. U., 1969; B.S. in Nursing, Tex. Woman's U., 1979; postgrad. El Centro Coll., 1976—; children—Brian, Desmond. Pharmacist, St. Luke & Tex. Children's Hosp., Houston, 1970-73, Meml. S.E. Hosp., Houston, 1973-75, M.D. Anderson Hosp., Houston, 1975; coordinator pharmacy services Dallas County Mental Health-Mental Retardation Dist. 5, Dallas, 1975—. Sec., Dallas Urban League, 1976-77, award, 1976. Mem. Nat. Council Negro Women (membership chmn. 1976—), Am. Soc. Hosp. Pharmacists, Am., Dallas County pharm. assns., Tex. Pharmacists Assn., Delta Sigma Theta, Lambda Kappa Sigma. Mem. African Methodist Episcopal Ch.

DAVENPORT, FOUNTAIN ST. CLAIR, electronic engr.; b. Harmony, N.C., Jan. 16, 1914; s. Dennis F. and Margaret E. (Winfield) D.; B.S., U. Miami, 1950; postgrad. U. Miami, U. Balt., Johns Hopkins, U. Fla., Rollins Coll., Brevard Engring. Coll., 1952-64; M.S., Fla. Inst. Tech., 1970; m. Jane Helena Hermann, June 11, 1948 (dec. Sept. 1973); 1 dau., Sylvia Jane; m. 2d, Joyce Allen Huff, Mar. 16, 1974. Engr., Bendix Aviation Corp., Towson, Md., 1951-53; project engr. Vitro Labs., Eglin AFB, Fla., 1953-55; engr. A, RCA Missile Test Project, Patrick AFB, Fla., 1955-60; supr. radar engring., guided missiles range div. Pan Am. World Airways, Inc., Patrick AFB, Fla., 1960-65, sr. systems engr. Aerospace Services Div., 1965-77; individual practice cons. engring., 1977—. Cons. N.R.C., Churchill Research Range, Man., Can., 1966-67; faculty Fla. Inst. Tech., 1958-60, 62-63, mem. edn. com., 1964. Mem. staff Brevard Assn. for Advancement of Blind. Served with USN, 1934-37; with USNR, 1942-45. Life mem. Friends Melbourne Library; patron Indian River Players. Mem. IEEE, Am. Ordnance Assn. (life), Missile and Space Pioneers (life), Soc. Wireless Pioneers (life). Mason (32 deg.). Home: 2110 Shannon Ave Indialantic FL 32903

DAVENPORT, GEORGE KEEFE, computer co. exec.; b. N.Y.C., Dec. 30, 1937; s. Fred Morris and Dorothy Frances (Keefe) D.; B.A., Lehigh U., 1959; B.S. in Indsl. Mgmt., C.W. Post Coll., 1962; cert. orgn. devel. W. Ga. Coll., 1978; m. Phyllis Joan Dallin, Oct. 12, 1963; children—Dierdre Kirsten, Christopher Prescott. Indsl. engr., Grumman Aircraft Co., Bethpage, N.Y., 1955-62; sales rep. IBM, Jacksonville, Fla., 1962-67; prin. engr. Reliability Engring. Bendix Co., Cape Kennedy, Fla., 1967-70; area mgr. Xerox Data Systems, Jacksonville, 1970-76; br. mktg. mgr. energy Sperry Univac Co., Bellaire, Tex., 1976—; asso. prof. indsl. mgmt. U. Fla., Brevard Coll., 1967-72; mem. quality control and reliability adv. com. Brevard Jr. Coll., Cape Kennedy, 1967-72; mem. fund raising com. 5th Congl. Dist. Fla., 1970. Recipient New Technology Utilization award NASA, 1969. Mem. Am. Mgmt. Assn., Instrument Soc. Am., Data Processing Mgmt. Assn., Am. Inst. Indsl. Engrs., Soc. Am. Mil. Engrs. Methodist. Clubs: Atascocita (Humble, Tex.); Univ. (Houston). Author: Statistical Calibration, 1967; Reliability Objectives, 1970; Introduction to Data Processing, 1971, others; contbr. articles to profl. jours. Home: 19627 Sweet Forest Ln Humble TX 77338 Office: 4393 Viewridge Ave San Diego CA 92123

DAVENPORT, WILLIAM HAROLD, mathematician; b. Jackson, Tenn., Dec. 21, 1935; s. John Heron and Mary (Troutt) D.; B.S. in Engring. Physics, U. Tenn., 1962; M.S. in Math., Tex. A. and M. U., 1966; Ph.D. in Math., U. Ala., 1971; m. Mary Janice Johnson, Mar. 18, 1960; children—Mark Edson, Amber Yvette; m. 2d, Sandra Elaine Holloway, July 30, 1973; children—William Harold, David Carleton. Aerospace technologist NASA Manned Spacecraft Center, Houston, 1962-64; research mathematician Brown Engring. Co., Huntsville, Ala., 1966-67; teaching fellow, instr. math. U. Ala., University, 1967-71; mathematician U.S. Army Missile Command, Huntsville, 1971-72; asst. prof. math. U. Petroleum and Minerals, Dhahran, Saudi Arabia, 1972-77; asst. prof. math. Columbus (Ga.) Coll., 1977—. Served with USN, 1954-58. Mem. Am. Math. Soc., Sigma Pi Sigma, Phi Kappa Phi, Pi Mu Epsilon. Home: 3748 Meadowcliff Dr Columbus GA 31907 Office: Dept Math Columbus Coll Columbus GA 31907

DAVID, AMIEL, petroleum engr.; b. Haifa, Israel, June 7, 1939; s. Bezalel and Ziona (Kovalsky) D.; came to U.S., 1959, naturalized, 1970; B.S. in Petroleum Engring., U. Tulsa, 1964; M.S. in Chem. Engring., U. Pa., 1966; M.B.A., U. Pitts., 1976; Ph.D. in Petroleum Engring., Stanford U., 1968; m. Zmira Charash, Dec. 28, 1965; children—Hod, Sharon. With Gulf Research and Devel. Co., 1968-78, sr. research engr., Fa., 1974-77, staff engr., Houston, 1977-78; div. staff engr. Superior Oil Co., Houston, 1978—. Chmn. Israelis in Pitts., 1972. Served with Israeli Air Force, 1957-59. Mem. Soc. Petroleum Engrs. (pres. Pitts. sect. 1976-77), Sigma Xi, Pi Epsilon Tau, Omicron Delta Kappa, Sigma Gamma Epsilon. Jewish. Author research papers in field. Home: 5707 Spanish Oak Houston TX 77066 Office: 2202 Timberloch Pl Suite 100 The Woodlands TX 77380

DAVID, JAMES RICHARD, life ins. agt.; b. Poteau, Okla., Apr. 22, 1950; s. Ray Orville and Dorothy Jane (Bailey) D.; B.S. in Bus., Okla. State U., 1973; m. Cynthia Jane Moran, June 1, 1979; children—Candice Michelle, Regan Moran. Spl. agt. Northwestern Mut. Life Ins. Co., Muskogee, Okla., 1973-77, dist. agt., 1977—; pres. James R. David and Assos., Inc., Muskogee, 1977—; instr. Life Underwriter Tng. Council, 1976-77. C.L.U. Mem. Nat. Assn. Life Underwriters, Okla. Assn. Life Underwriters (v.p.), Muskogee Assn. Life Underwriters, Am. Soc. C.L.U.'s, Million Dollar Round Table, Northwestern Mut. Life Dist. Agts. Assn., Muskogee Tax and Estate Planning Council (pres.), Muskogee C. of C. Democrat. Methodist. Clubs: Muskogee Country, Elks, Noon Lions (Muskogee). Home: PO Drawer AE Muskogee OK 74401 Office: 219 N 3d St Muskogee OK 74401

DAVID, YADIN BEZALEL, med. engr., educator; b. Haifa, Israel, Nov. 25, 1946; s. Bezalel and Ziona (Kovalsky) D.; came to U.S., 1972, naturalized, 1978; Asso. Engr., Israel Inst. Tech., 1972; B.S.E.E., W.Va. U., 1974, M.S., 1975; m. Rebecca Lask, Jan. 23, 1968; children—Tal, Daniel. Head technician Armamant Authority Devel., Israel, 1969-72; instr. elec. engring. W.Va. U., Morgantown, 1974-75, asst. prof. anesthesia, med. center, since 1979—, dir. biomed. engring., 1976—; design engr. Rockwell Internat. Co., Cedar Rapids, Iowa, 1975-76; pres. Tal/Dan Health Care Cons. Engr., Morgantown, 1978—; lectr. in field. Served with Israeli Air Force, 1965-68. Kirkland scholar, 1973-74. Mem. IEEE, Nat. Fire Protection Assn., Assn. for Advancement of Med. Instrumentation, Eta Kappa Nu. Jewish. Club: B'nai B'rith. Home: 1312 Perry Ave Morgantown WV 26505

DAVIDGE, BILLY LLOYD, govt. ofcl.; b. Collins, Miss., July 14, 1927; s. Thomas Hiram and Lela Nancy (McAlpine) D.; student pub. schs., Hammond, La.; m. Nell LaFleur, Sept. 24, 1949; children—Billy Lloyd, Deborah Nancy Davidge Piediscalzo, Kurt LaRay. With E.V. McCollum & Co., oil exploration, Tulsa, 1947-60, chief surveyor, to 1960; with Office Pub. Works, Baton Rouge, 1961—, asst. to office engr., 1970-77, chief internal services, 1977—. Served with USNR, 1945-46; PTO. Home PO Box 448 Natalbany LA 70451 Office: PO Box 44155 Baton Rouge LA 70804

DAVIDOFF, ROBERT, photographer; b. Bklyn., June 5, 1926; s. David and Jessie (Levine) D.; grad. Sch. Modern Photography, 1950; m. Sara Litwen, Mar. 2, 1947; children—Kenneth Edward, Michael Lee, Daryl Reid. Free lance photographer, Lakewood, N.J., 1947-49; photographer Lorstan Thomas Studios, N.Y.C., 1950-55; owner, mgr. Bob Davidoff Studios, Palm Beach, Fla., 1960—; ofcl. photographer Breakers Hotel, Palm Beach, 1968—. Served with USN, 1944-46. Decorated Silver Star. Photographs have appeared in local, nat. and internat. newspapers and mags. Office: Breakers Hotel Palm Beach FL 33480

DAVIDS, ROBERT NORMAN, uranium exploration geologist; b. Elizabeth, N.J., Apr. 27, 1938; s. William Scheible and Anna Elizabeth (Backhaus) D.; A.B. in Geology, U. Va., 1960; M.S., Rutgers U., 1963, Ph.D., 1966; m. Carol Ann Landauer, Apr. 20, 1957; 1 son, Robert Norman. With Exxon Co. USA, 1966—, uranium geologist, Denver, 1971-72, Albuquerque, 1972-78, supervisory geologist Tex. area exploration, Corpus Christi, 1978—. Active local Little League Baseball, Jr. Achievement. NSF grad. fellow, 1964-65. Mem. Geol. Soc. Am., AIME, Soc. Econ. Paleontologists and Mineralogists (treas. Gulf Coast sect. 1971), Am. Assn. Petroleum Geologists, Explorers Club, Sigma Xi, Beta Theta Pi. Author papers. Home: 6126 San Ramon Dr Corpus Christi TX 78413 Office: Wilson Tower Bldg Corpus Christi TX 78401

DAVIDSON, ANNE DEVINE, speech pathologist; b. Tulsa, Nov. 20, 1945; d. Matthew Joseph and Louise M. (DeLay) Devine; B.S., U. Tulsa, 1968, M.A., 1970; m. Kenneth Lawrence Davidson, Dec. 17, 1966; children—Rebecca, Deborah. Speech-lang. pathologist Pryor (Okla.) public schs., 1967, Okmulgee (Okla.) Rehab. Center, 1969, Children's Med. Center, Tulsa, 1970, Columbus AFB, Columbus, Miss., 1971-72, Coop. Sch. for Handicapped Children, Vienna, Va., 1973, Rehab., Inc., Alexandria, Va., 1974-76, Devel. Center, Tulsa, 1977; instr., clin. supr. Okla. State U., Stillwater, 1977—; owner, operator Open Circle Natural Foods, Stillwater. HEW fellow, 1968. Mem. Am. Speech-Lang. and Hearing Assn., Okla. Speech and Hearing Assn. Unitarian. Office: Hanner Hall Okla State U Stillwater OK 74074

DAVIDSON, BEN NIXON, speech pathologist; b. Abilene, Tex., Oct. 26, 1934; s. Buell Benjamin and Sabra Chleo (Nixon) D.; B.S.Ed., Abilene Christian U., 1964; M.A., Calif. State U., Long Beach, 1969; m. Grace Elizabeth Lindly, Oct. 11, 1978; children—David, Rusty, Dusty, Lea Ann, Windy. Speech therapist, public schs., Port Lavaca, Tex., 1964-65, Abilene, Tex., 1965, Breckenridge, Tex., 1965-67; dir. spl. edn. Region IX Edn. Service Center, Wichita Falls, Tex., 1968-71; program coordinator N.Tex. Rehab. Center, Wichita Falls, 1971-72; speech therapist public schs. Sweetwater, Tex., 1972-74; project Throutwo dir. W.Tex. Rehab. Center, Abilene, 1974—. Served with USMC, 1952-56, USAF, 1957-61. Mem. Am. Speech and Hearing Assn., Tex. Speech and Hearing Assn., Council Exceptional Children, Teaching Tex. Tots Consortium. Mem. Ch. of Christ. Home: Route 3 Box M-175 Merkel TX 79536 Office: 4601 Hartford St Abilene TX 79605

DAVIDSON, MRS. CHARLES (KATE S. DAVIDSON), educator; b. Emporia, Va., May 13, 1910; d. John William and Ida Florence (Hill) Saunders; student Chowan Coll., 1926-27; A.A., Louisburg Coll., 1927-28; summer student Forest Coll., 1928, 29. Longwood Coll., 1932; m. Charles Reuber Davidson, July 1, 1933; 1 dau., Katharine Saunders (Mrs. John Byers Horner). Tchr. Emporia High Sch., 1930-33, 1946-50, substitute tchr., 1950—. Gen. chmn., dir. Greenville Tb Assn.; 2d v.p. Southside area council Girl Scouts U.S.A.; dir. Southside Area Planning Bd., A.R.C.; sec. Emporia Band Boosters Club; mem. state nursing scholarship com. Tb and Respiratory Disease Assn.; pres. Greenville Meml. Hosp. Aux.; rep. dir. Va. Tb Assn., also dist. rep.; pres. Southside Region Lung Assn.; v.p. Southside Lung Assn., Petersburg Dist. Lung Assn.; mem.-at-large bd. dirs. Va. Lung Assn.; bd. dirs. Commonwealth council Girl Scouts U.S.A., Richmond council Girl Scouts U.S.A.; bd. dirs. Va. Lung Assn.; pres. Southside Region Lung Assn.; mem. Petersburg Dist. Corp. Bd. Missions; mem. Ann. Va. Conf., United Methodist Ch., mem. ch. and soc. bd.; coordinator Christian social involvement United Meth. Women of Petersburg Dist.; rec. sec. pub. affairs Ch. Hosp. Aux.; hon. mem. Greensville Meml. Hosp. Aux., 1979—; 1st v.p. Hermitage Guild Petersburg Dist. Mem. PTA (asst. dist. dir. Southside area, dir. Emporia, Va.), U.D.C. (pres local chpt.; registar), Va. Hist. Soc., Butts Tavern Assn. (dir., trustee), Woman's Soc. Christian Service (promotion sec. corr.; edn. ch. pres., Dora Armstrong zone leader, pres., mem. bd. Petersburg dist.), United Meth. Women (pres. Petersburg dist., chmn. community improvement projects), Va. Fedn. Woman's Clubs (chmn. leadership devel.). Methodist (supt. CradleRoll, mem. bd. edn., mem. ch. adminstrv. bd., dir.). Clubs: Emporia Ladies Golf Assn. (pres.), Riparian Federated Woman's (pres. Garden Club, v.p.; credentials chmn. Southside dist.), Woman's (past pres., parliamentarian, edn. chmn., mental health chmn.), Emporia Federated Garden, Wednesday. Home: 506 Ingleside Ave Emporia VA 23847

DAVIDSON, CHARLES NELSON, physicist; b. Kankakee, Ill., Oct. 19, 1937; s. Arthur Nelson and Maxine Elizabeth (Garrett) D.; B.S., The Citadel, Charleston, S.C., 1959; Ph.D. (NSF fellow), Fla. State U., 1962; m. Juanita Louise Davey, Aug. 1, 1959; children—Charles Nelson, Kevin Arthur, Timothy Michael. Nuclear effects officer U.S. Army Combat Devels. Command CBR Agy., Ft. McClellan, Ala., 1962-66, physicist Combat Devels. Command Inst. Nuclear Studies, Ft. Bliss, Tex., 1966-68, sci. adviser to comdr. U.S. Army Nuclear Agy., Ft. Bliss, 1968-77; sci. adviser to comdr. U.S. Army Nuclear and Chem. Agency, Ft. Belvoir, Va., 1977—; asso. prof. dept. chemistry Jacksonville (Ala.) State Coll., 1965-66. Vice pres. Yucca council Boy Scouts Am., El Paso, Tex., 1976-77, tng. chmn., 1968-70, asst. scoutmaster, 1974-77, cubmaster, 1969-72, 73-76, dist. chmn., 1970-72, cubmaster Keystone Area council, 1972-73, Nat. Capital Area council, 1978—; coach Little League Baseball, 1969, 73. Bd. dirs. Southwestern Sun Carnival Assn., 1972-77, El Paso Girls Clubs, 1977. Served as capt. U.S. Army, 1962-64. Decorated Army Commendation medal. NSF postdoctoral fellow, 1962. Mem. Am. Chem. Soc., Am. Nuclear Soc. Roman Catholic. Rotarian (treas. 1974-75, v.p. 1975-76, pres. 1976-77). Contbr. articles to profl. jours. Home: 10838 Greene Dr Lorton VA 22079 Office: US Army Nuclear and Chem Agy Fort Belvoir VA 22060

DAVIDSON, GORDON BYRON, lawyer; b. Louisville, June 24, 1926; s. Paul Byron and Elizabeth (Franz) D.; A.B., Centre Coll., 1949; J.D., U. Louisville, 1951; LL.M., Yale, 1952; m. Geraldine B. Geiger, Dec. 21, 1948; children—Sally Burgess, Stuart Gordon. Asst. Army staff judge advocate of First Army, Govs. Island, N.Y., 1952-54; law clk. Mr. Justice Stanley Reed, Supreme Ct. of U.S., Washington, 1954; partner Wyatt. Grafton and Sloss, 1955—; lectr. U. Louisville Law Sch., 1958—. Dir. Courier-Jour. & Louisville Times Co., WHAS, Inc., Standard Gravure Co., Armor Elevator Co. Inc., Hermitage Farm, Inc. Pres. Louisville Central Area, Inc., 1971-73; chmn. River City Mall Com., 1973-74, Ky. Cultural Complex Com., 1977-78; chmn. Louisville Devel. Com.; mem. Ky. Derby Festival Com.; mem. Louisville Commn. Fgn. Relations. Bd. dirs., chmn. Norton-Children's Hosps., Inc., Louisville Fund for Arts; trustee St. Francis High Sch., Centre Coll., Internat. Center of U. Louisville. Served as cadet midshipman U.S. Mcht. Marine Acad., 1944-45; 1st lt. AUS, 1952-54; Korea. Recipient Louisville Citizen of Yr. award, 1973-74; Mayor's Fleur de Lis award, 1974. Fellow Am. Bar Found.; mem. Am. Law Inst., Am., Ky., Louisville, Fed. bar assns., Louisville Area C. of C. (v.p., dir.), Phi Delta Theta, Omicron Delta Kappa, Phi Kappa Phi. Democrat. Presbyn. Clubs: Harmony Landing Country; Jefferson (bd. govs.), Louisville Country (bd. govs.); Tavern; Lawyer's; Pendennis; Delray Beach. Home: 435 Lightfoot Rd Louisville KY 40207 Office: 28th Floor Citizens Plaza Louisville KY 40202

DAVIDSON, JAMES JOSEPH, III, lawyer; b. Lafayette, La., July 27, 1940; s. James Joseph and Virginia Lee (Dunham) D.; B.A., U. Southwestern La., 1963; J.D., Tulane U., 1964; m. Kay Cecile Holloway, Aug. 7, 1962; children—Kimberly Kay, James Joseph IV, Lynda Leigh, Virginia Holland. Admitted to La. bar, 1964; mem. firm Davidson, Meaux, Sonnier & Roy, Lafayette, 1964—. Bd. dirs. Jr. Achievement Greater Lafayette, 1968-71, sec., 1969-71; mem. exec. bd. Evangeline Area council Boy Scouts Am., 1969—; bd. dirs. U. Southwestern La. Found., 1979—, Wesley Found., Meth. Student Center, 1970-71, Acadiana Mental Health Center, 1971-72. Fellow Am. Bar Found.; mem. Am. Judicature Soc., Am. Bd. Trial Advocates, Nat. Assn. R.R. Trial Counsel, La. Assn. Def. Counsel (dir. 1975-77), Acadiana Defense Council (treas. 1970), Am., La. (mem. house of delegates 1970—), Lafayette Parish bar assns., Southwestern La. Alumni Assn. (dir. 1970-71), Phi Alpha Delta, Kappa Sigma. Methodist (mem. bd. stewards 1970—). Rotarian (dir. 1966, treas. 1967). Club: Oakbourne Country (dir. 1974-77). Home: 539 Girard Park Dr Lafayette LA 70501 Office: PO Drawer 2908 Lafayette LA 70502

DAVIDSON, JOELINE DILLARD, med. technologist; b. Bessemer, Ala., Oct. 4, 1942; d. Joel and Laura (Smith) Dillard; B.S. in Chemistry, U. Ala., 1963, B.Mus. in Voice, 1967; M.T., Birmingham Bapt. Hosp., 1964; M.B.A. candidate Ga. State U.; m. John Pratt Davidson, Aug. 27, 1966. Staff technologist Highland Bapt. Hosp., Birmingham, Ala., 1964; chemistry technologist Druid City Hosp., Tuscaloosa, Ala., 1967-69; staff technologist McGuire VA Hosp., Richmond, Va., 1969; blood bank supr. Druid City Hosp., 1969-73; lab. mgr. W. Ga. Med. Center, LaGrange, 1974—. Mem. Ala. State Assn. Blood Banks (dir. 1971-73), Am. Soc. Med. Tech., Ga. Soc. Med. Tech. (chmn. adminstrv. sect. of sci. assembly), Chattahoochee Valley Clin. Lab. Mgmt. Assn. (charter chmn. 1978). Methodist. Home: PO Box 1786 LaGrange GA 30241 Office: 1514 Vernon Rd LaGrange GA 30240

DAVIDSON, KENNETH LEE, ednl. adminstr.; b. Klamath Falls, Oreg., Apr. 4, 1943; s. Harry and Floy (Maxwell) D.; B.A. in Social Studies, Northeastern Okla. State U., Tahlequah, 1966, M.A. in Adminstrn., 1969; postgrad. in Early Childhood Devel., Tex. So. U., Houston, 1973; m. Brenda; 1 son, Tony. Chmn. social studies Stilwell (Okla.) High Sch., 1966-68; dir. Cookson Hill Head Start, Tahlequah, 1971-76; supt. Watts (Okla.) Schs., 1976—. Chmn. Adair County Am. Red Cross, 1967-73. Mem. Nat. (past treas.), Okla. State (past pres.) head start dirs. assns., Warner, Okla. advisory com. on Early Childhood Devel. Home: Box 374 Stilwell OK 74960 Office: Box 10 Watts OK 74964

DAVIDSON, PHILIP HAROLD, banker; b. East Grand Rapids, Mich., Aug. 20, 1944; s. Harold Elton and Jeanne Elizabeth (Ulrich) D.; B.A., U. Mich., 1966; M.B.A., Western Mich. U., 1967; Ph.D., U. Ill., 1971; m. Kay Marie Heikkinen, Nov. 25, 1966; 1 son, Matthew Philip. Economist, research dept. Fed. Reserve Bank, Richmond, Va., 1970-73; economist Bank of Va. Co., Richmond, 1974, v.p., 1975—; mem. adj. faculty U. Richmond, 1971-74, Va. Commonwealth U., 1977-78. Bd. dirs. Housing Opportunities Made Equal, Richmond, 1975—, pres., 1977. Mem. Richmond First Club (dir. 1974-77), Am. Econ. Assn., Nat. Assn. Bus. Economists, Am. Bankers Assn. Club: Downtown (Richmond). Author: Banking Tomorrow, Managing Markets Through Planning, 1978; contbr. articles in field to profl. jours. Home: 3811 Seminary Ave Richmond VA 23227 Office: PO Box 25970 Richmond VA 23260

DAVIDSON, WILLIAM HAROLD, mgmt. cons.; b. Dayton, Ohio, Sept. 22, 1928; s. Oscar Roy and Anna Mary (Fisher) D.; student Miami U., Ohio, 1946-48; B.B.A., U. Dayton, 1954; M.B.A., Ind. U., 1955; m. Patricia Lucille Kernan, Apr. 23, 1949; children—Jill, Patricia, William Harold, Maribeth, Sally. Dir. mgmt. devel. Chrysler Corp., Detroit, 1955-63; v.p. Booz, Allen & Hamilton, Chgo., 1963-67; pres. Davidson-Kernan Corp., Ft. Worth, 1967—, also dir.; dir. Visa Travel, Inc.; tchr. U. Detroit, 1958-62. Pres. Warren (Mich.) Bd. Edn., 1961-62. Served with USNR, 1948-52. Republican. Roman Catholic. Clubs: Rivercrest Country, Ft. Worth. Home: 6009 Merrymount St Fort Worth TX 76107 Office: 5501 W Rosedale St Fort Worth TX 76107

DAVIES, GARTH HODSON, mktg. communications cons.; b. Oldham, Eng., May 26, 1936; s. Christopher Hodson and Phyllis (Dunkerly) D.; student N.W. Lincolnshire Tech. Coll. (Eng.), 1952-54. Journalist series of newspapers Gainsborough and Lincolnshire, Eng., 1954-57; group advt. dir. newspaper industry, Scunthorpe, Eng., 1957-64; mktg. dir. pub. co. and liquor conglomerate, Nassau, Bahamas, 1964-67; v.p., mng. dir. Interpublic Group of Cos., N.Y.C., also affiliate offices in Nassau, Freeport, Miami, Fla., London, Eng., 1967-70; pres., chmn. bd. Trans-Atlantic Mktg. Partners Group, Nassau, 1971—, offices Miami, Haiti, Cayman Islands, Can., U.K.; pres., chmn. Cayman Islands News Bur. Group, Cayman Islands and Miami; pres. IMPS Corp., Miami. Registered fgn. agt. for Cayman Islands govt., U.S. Dept. Justice. Mem. Public Relations Soc. Am., Inst. Public Relations (U.K.), Savs. Insts. Mktg. Soc. Am., Inst. Mktg. (U.K.), Advt. Fedn. Greater Miami, West India Com. (London). Anglican. Clubs: Mutiny, Alley, Rotary Internat. (Grand Cayman). Home: 2649 S Bayshore Dr Suite 1605 Miami FL 33133 also West Wind Bldg Box 1111 Grand Cayman British West Indies Office: Box 330106 Coconut Grove Miami FL 33133 also Box 1111 Grand Cayman British West Indies

DAVIES, ROSALIE MAY, media specialist; b. Chgo., Apr. 6, 1938; d. Charles B. and May G. Johnson; B.A. in English, No. Ill. U., 1960; M.A. in English, U. Ill., 1961; M.A. in Library Sci., U. South Fla., 1976; divorced; children—Jessica E., Heather D., Perry O. Instr., Am. Girls Coll., Izmir, Turkey, 1961-64, New Haven Coll. (now U. New Haven), West Haven, Conn., 1966-67; soprano soloist Temple Beth Shalom, Montreal, Que., Can., 1967-69, United Ch. of Can., Montreal West, 1969-70; dir. music 1st Unitarian Ch., New Orleans, 1970-72; media specialist Nina Harris Exceptional Student Center, Pinellas Park, Fla., 1976—; dir. music Unitarian-Universalist Ch., Clearwater, Fla., 1977-80; supr. computer cataloging U.S. Fla., Tampa, 1976; one-woman recitals of music, drama, poetry, multi-media prodns. H.W. Wilson scholar, 1976; cert. English tchr., librarian elem., secondary, jr. coll. level, Fla. Mem. Pinellas County Assn. Librarians and Media Specialists. Democrat. Unitarian-Universalist. Home: 75 Suncrest Dr Safety Harbor FL 33572 Office: 6000 70th Ave N Pinellas Park FL 33535

DAVILA, CARMEN AMALIA, advt. agy. exec.; b. Santurce, P.R., Feb. 3, 1948; d. Gervacio and Aida Josefina (Iragavidez) D.; B.A., Coll. Sacred Heart, 1971, A.S., 1978; student U. P.R., 1971. Med. technologist Gubern's Hosp., Fajardo, P.R., 1971; med. technologist Laboratorio Clinico Landron, Santurce, 1971-73; med. technologist ARC Blood Bank, Rio Peidras, P.R., 1974-77; copywriter Lopito, Ileana & Howie, Santurce, 1978; chief copy writer retail dept. JWT MFP Advt., Santurce, 1978, copywriter consumer div., 1979—. Mem. free-lance advt. staff Popular Democratic Com., 1979. Mem. Am. Soc. Clin. Pathologists, P.R. Coll. Med. Technologists. Popular Democrat. Roman Catholic. Home: 1354 Magdalena Ave Condado PR 00907 Office: Edificio MFP 60 Calle C Caparra Heights San Juan PR 00922

DAVIS, ALBERT WADDELL, III, food mfg. co. exec.; b. Columbus, Ga., Aug. 27, 1940; s. Albert Waddell and Virginia (Roberts) D.; B.B.A., U. Ga., 1962; m. Judith Pope, Oct. 27, 1962; children—Bradley Pope, Averett Waddell. Mgr. REA Express Office, Jackson, Tenn., 1962-63, terminal mgr., Jackson, Miss., 1964; life underwriter Mut. of N.Y. Life Ins. Co., Columbus, 1964-65; with Tom's Foods subs. Gen. Mills, Columbus, 1965—, nat. sales mgr., 1978—. Sales adv. to nat. champion co. Jr. Achievement, Columbus, 1967. Dir., chmn. fin. com. Jackson (Tenn.) Jaycees, 1962-63. Mem. Alpha Kappa Psi. Methodist. Club: Columbus Country. Office: 900 8th St Columbus GA 31902

DAVIS, AUGUSTUS HUGHES, JR., urban planning cons.; b. Morehead City, N.C., Nov. 21, 1935; s. Augustus Hughes and Mildred (Lesesne) D.; B.S., N.C. Central U., 1965, J.D., 1967; m. Valerie Jean Euell. With claims dept. Allstate Ins. Co., Bronx, N.Y.C., 1967; asst. to pres. Borough of Bronx (N.Y.), 1968; dep. dir. South Bronx Model Cities, 1968-70; dir. Bridgeport (Conn.) Model Cities, 1970; dir. Multi-Racial, Inc., mgmt. and urban planning cons., New Orleans, 1970—, v.p., 1972—. Served with USAF, 1954-58. Recipient Service award Bronx Congress on Racial Equality, 1968. Mem. N.A.A.C.P. (life), N.C. Central U. Alumni Assn., 369th Vets. Assn., Kappa Alpha Psi. Office: 2610 Esplanade Ave New Orleans LA 70119

DAVIS, BEN REEVES, newspaper editor; b. Huntington, Ark., Apr. 1, 1927; s. Lester Belton and Jessie (Reeves) D.; B.A. in Journalism, U. Ala., 1949; m. Margaret Lee Rogers, Nov. 26, 1950 (div.); 1 son, Ben Reeves; m. 2d, Helen Duke Ellis, Oct. 22, 1977. Reporter, Selma (Ala.) Times-Jour., 1949-50; mng. editor Jasper (Ala.) Mountain Eagle, 1950-52; sports writer, copy editor Birmingham (Ala.) News, 1952-56; mng. editor Tuscaloosa (Ala.) News, 1956-64; mng. editor Montgomery Advertiser and Ala. Jour., 1964-78. Served with USNR, 1945-46. Mem. A.P. Mng. Editors Assn., Ala. A.P. Assn. (pres. 1964-65, 76-77), Sigma Delta Chi, Pi Kappa Phi. Methodist. Home: 3156 Malone Dr Montgomery AL 36106

DAVIS, BERTHA GERMIZE, artist; b. Vilno, Lithuania, July 15, 1918; d. Abraham and Dvora Germaize; student Stewart Van Orden, Pan Am. Coll., 1960-61, Fred Samuelson and James Pinto, Art Inst. of San Miguel Allende, Mex., 1965, Harold Phenix, 1972-73, Ed Whitney, 1973-74, Bud Shackelford, 1976, Zoltan Szabo, 1977, Morris Shubin, 1977; children—Sylvia Davis Caplan, Doryn. Owner, operator art gallery, Houston, Tex., 1969-72; asst. mgr. Art Internat., Houston, 1972-75; asst. mgr. Kirt Niven Gallery, Dallas, 1977-78; major one-woman shows include: Pan Am. Coll., 1960, Jewish Community Center, Houston, McAllen State Bank, 1974, U. Tex. Health Sci. Center, Dallas, 1979, also La Cuidadela, Monterey, Mexico, also Houston Pub. Library; group shows include: Watercolor Soc. Houston, S.W. Watercolor Soc., Am. Painters in Paris, Cooperstown Art Exhibit, Issac Delgado Mus. Art, New Orleans, Corpus Christi Art Found., Salmagundi Club, N.Y.C., 1979, Gallery-TWO, Dallas, Laguna Gloria Mus., Austin, Tex., 1979; showings in Marsha London Gallery, N.Y.C., Nat. Design Center, N.Y.C., Fontainbleau Gallery of N.Y., Deportivo Israelita de Mexico, Laguna Gloria Mus.; awards judge Temple Emanuel Art Show, Dallas, 1979. Mem. Tex. Fine Art Assn., S.W. Watercolor Soc., Richardson Civic Art Assn., Artist Sculptors Contemporary Assn., Art League of Houston, Houston Art Assn., Catharine Lorillard Wolf Art. Prin. illustrator: Open Dallas, 1976. Works pub. in various publs. including La Revue Moderne des Arts de la Vie, 1965, 68, 69, Repertorium Artis Guide Europeen des Beaux Arts, 1966-67, Artists U.S.A., 1973-76. Home: 715 Gaylewood Dr Richardson TX 75080

DAVIS, BURL EDWARD, educator; b. Edenwold, Tenn., Sept. 8, 1930; s. John T. and Lydia Frances (Richards) D.; B.A., David Lipscomb Coll., 1953; M.S., Clemson U., 1962; Ph.D., Mich. State U., 1968; m. Frances Dawn Bartlett, Feb. 22, 1952; children—Kathy Aleta, Mary Kay, Phyllis Deanna, Michael Edward. Ordained to ministry Ch. of Christ, 1946; minister various locations, 1953-58; asso. editor, dept. agrl. communications Clemson (S.C.) U., 1958-65; research asst. dept. communications Mich. State U., East Lansing, 1964-68; prof. communication Abilene Christian U., Abilene, Tex., 1969—, dir. mass communication program, 1975—, dir. Center for Religious Communications Research, 1977—; pres. World Christian Broadcasting Corp., Abilene, Tex., 1977-80; cons. to numerous orgns. Advisor for campaigns various local, state polit. candidates, 1972-74; research dir. Citizens for Better Community, Abilene, 1976. Recipient Trustees' award as outstanding tchr. Abilene Christian U., 1973, spl. recognition award Abilene Assn. for Mental Health, 1972. Mem. Internat. Communication Assn., Assn. for Edn. in Journalism, Am. Speech Communication Assn., World Christian Communication Assn., So. Speech Assn. Mem. Ch. of Christ. Research and publs. in field. Home: 2002 Cedar Crest Rd Abilene TX 79601 Office: Box 8034 Abilene Christian U Abilene TX 79601

DAVIS, CALVIN REESE, mortician; b. Toccoa, Ga., Sept. 17, 1942; s. Frank Young and Laura (Stovall) D.; A.A. in Acctg., Gordon Mil. Coll., Barnesville, Ga., 1962; B.S. in Biology, Georgetown U., 1965; M.S. in Mortuary Sci., Gupton-Jones Coll., Atlanta, 1977; m. Patricia Williams Davis, June 16, 1967; children—Karen Elizabeth, Frank Young. Vice pres., gen.mgr. Acree-Davis Funeral Home, Toccoa, 1970—. Bd. dirs. Am. Cancer Soc., Toccoa, 1979; mem. Toccoa-Stephens County Parks and Recreation Dept. Bd., 1979; mem. adminstrv. bd. First United Methodist Ch., Toccoa; mem. Toccoa-Stephens County Devel. Bd. Served with U.S. Army, 1966-70. Decorated Purple Heart, Bronze Star. Mem. Nat. Selected Morticians, Nat. Funeral Dirs. Assn., Ga. Funeral Dirs. Assn. (chmn. 1979-80), Am. Mgmt. Assn., Jaycees, Am. Legion, VFW. Democrat. Clubs: Kiwanis, Toccoa Golf, Masons. Home: 110 E Franklin St Toccoa GA 30577 Office: 350 S Pond St Toccoa GA 30577

DAVIS, CARL LEWIS, psychiatrist; b. Pulaski, Tenn., Dec. 26, 1930; s. Jack Bernard and Bertha (Turest) D.; B.A., Vanderbilt U., 1951; M.D., U. Tenn., 1954; m. Ruth Weingart, June 21, 1953; children—Jay Alan, Bruce Norman, Patricia Lynn. Intern, Baylor U. Hosp., Dallas, 1954-55; resident in psychiatry Charity Hosp., New Orleans, 1957-60; practice medicine specializing in psychiatry and psychoanalysis, New Orleans, 1960—; mem. staff Touro Infirmary, Coliseum House, Charity Hosp.; clin. asso. prof. psychiatry La. State U. Med. Center; tng. and supervising analyst New Orleans Psychoanalytic Inst. Served with USPHS, 1955-57. Fellow Am. Psychiat. Assn.; mem. AMA, Internat. Psychoanalytical Assn., Am. Psychoanalytic Assn., New Orleans Psychoanalytic Soc. (sec.-treas. 1976-77, pres. 1979-81), La. Psychiat. Assn. (chmn. com. standards of practice and peer review). Home: 5566 Jacquelyn Ct New Orleans LA 70124 Office: 3412 Prytania St New Orleans LA 70115

DAVIS, CAROL IRENE, speech pathologist; b. Lincoln, Nebr., Feb. 28, 1945; d. Ralph Doman and Genevieve Opal (Davidson) McCall; B.S. in Edn., U. Nebr., 1967, M.A. in Speech Pathology, 1968; Ph.D. in Speech Pathology, U. Fla., 1971; M.R.E., New Orleans Bapt. Theol. Sem., 1974; m. Wallace Terry Davis, June 2, 1974; 1 son, Joshua Mark. Speech pathologist public schs., Falls City, Nebr., 1968-69; cons. W. Ala. Mental Health Center, Demetropolis, 1973-74; teaching fellow dept. counseling psychology New Orleans Bapt. Sem., 1973-74; alcoholism counselor Skid Row Men's Mission, New Orleans, 1972-74; lang. pathologist, curriculum devel. for profoundly retarded children Parents and Retarded Children Sch., New Orleans, 1974-77; speech pathologist Mobile County Public Schs., Ala., 1978; pvt. practice speech-lang. pathology and devel. disabilities, owner-dir. Speech and Hearing Center, Mobile, Ala., 1977—; cons. So. Region Health Systems HEW, Mid-South Home Health Agency for Home-bound Geriatrics; spl. cons. in lang. devel. S. Ala. Head Start Programs. Dir. Falls City (Nebr.) Community Theatre, 1968-69; vol. tchr. Women's Prison, Fla., 1969-71; vol. social worker for women New Orleans Central Lock-up, 1973; vol. Service to Poverty Programs, Mobile, 1979; tchr. theology Oakdale Bapt. Ch., 1979. VA fellow, 1969-72; Fla. Bapt. Conv. scholar, 1973-74; So. Bapt. Conv. Home Mission Bd. fellow in alcoholism studies, 1973-74; La. Devel. Disabilities grantee, 1974-76; recipient cert. of appreciation Gator Exchange Club, Gainesville, Fla., 1970, cert. of award for vol. service Project Head Start, Mobile, 1979. Mem. Am. Speech and Hearing Assn., Ala. Speech and Hearing Assn., Mobile Speech and Hearing Assn., Sigma Alpha Eta. Club: Kappa Delta (v.p. alumnae, Lincoln, Nebr., 1967, pres. 1968). Contbr. papers to profl. confs. and publs. in field. Home: 3110 Riviere Du Chien Loup E Mobile AL 36609 Office: Speech and Hearing Center Suite 3 Quadrangle Professional Offices 3263 Demetropolis Rd Mobile AL 36609

DAVIS, CAROLYN SUE ROSE, nurse; b. Quincy, Mass., Aug. 2, 1950; d. Robert Taylor and Mildred Frances (Barrow) Rose; B.S. in Nursing, U. S.C., 1975, M.Nursing, 1977; m. John L. Davis, Nov. 16, 1968 (div. Nov. 1974). Staff nurse, nursing supr. Beaufort (S.C.) Meml. Hosp., 1971-77; charge nurse Lexington County Hosp., West Columbia, S.C., 1977; head nurse labor, delivery and nursery, relief nursing supr. Beaufort Meml. Hosp., from 1977, now asst. dir. nursing. Nat. adv. bd. Am. Security Council; mem. Republican Nat. Com., 1976-78. Registered nurse. Mem. Am. Nurses Assn. S.C. Perinatal Assn., Low Country Nurses Assn., Greater U. S.C. Alumni Assn. Home: 3016 Hickory St Burton SC 29902 Office: Beaufort Meml Hosp Ribault Rd Beaufort SC 29902

DAVIS, CHARLES BRINKLEY, criminalogist; b. Moultrie, Ga., Mar. 9, 1946; s. Charlie Rufus and Lillie Bea (Brinkley) D.; A.A., Manatee Jr. Coll., 1969; B.S., Fla. State U., 1970; m. JoAnn Francis Kastrop, May 27, 1963; children—Charlie Marvin, Kenneth Wade. Dep., investigator Sheriff's Dept., Sarasota, Fla., 1962-70; spl. agt. Fla. Dept. Law Enforcement, Tallahassee, 1970-78; bur. chief Fla. Dept. Criminal Law Enforcement, Tallahassee, 1972-75, tng. specialist, 1975-78; security adminstr. Tex. Instruments, Dallas, 1978, mgr. corporate investigations, 1979—; cons. in field. Deacon, Baptist Ch., Tallahassee, 1972-78, chmn. ch. trustees, 1973-76. Served with USAF, 1958-62. Palmer Bank grantee, 1969-70. Mem. Am. Soc. Indsl. Security, Internat. Assn. Identification, Nat. Policy Officers Assn. Democrat. Home: 6009 Fawnvalley Dr Rowlett TX 75088 Office: PO Box 225474 M/S 262 Dallas TX 75265

DAVIS, CHARLES ELTON, librarian; b. Manhattan, Kans., Sept. 28, 1927; s. Charles Etherington and Ethel Manie (Ward) D.; B.A., Union Coll., Lincoln, Nebr., 1951; M.A., Kans. State U., 1961; M.S. in L.S., U. So. Calif., 1967; m. Frances B. Anderson, July 8, 1951; children—Charles Eric, Charman Eliece. Dean men, tchr. Highland Acad., Portland, Tenn., 1951-55, Campion Acad., Loveland, Colo., 1955-56; tchr., librarian Mt. Pisgah Acad., Candler, N.C., 1956-61; tchr., registrar, Librarian Bass Meml. Acad., Lumberton, Miss., 1961-63; tchr., librarian San Pasqual Acad., Escondido, Calif., 1963-66; asst. librarian, head public services Loma Linda (Calif.) U., 1966-68; dir. libraries, archivist, prof. library sci. So. Missionary Coll., Collegedale, Tenn., 1968—. Served with U.S. Army, 1946-47. Mem. ALA, Southeastern Library Assn., Tenn. Library Assn., Chattanooga Area Library Assn., Soc. Am. Archivists, Tenn. Archivists, Am. Assn. State and Local History. Seventh-day Adventist. Home: PO Box 629 Collegedale TN 37315 Office: McKee Library Southern Missonary Coll Collegedale TN 37315

DAVIS, CHARLES G., savs. and loan exec.; b. Augusta, Ga., Feb. 2, 1947; s. George H. and Ruth (Rozar) D.; B.B.A., U. Ga., 1969; m. Dianna Andrews, Dec. 28, 1967; children—Jeffrey C., Brian G. In-charge acct. Peat, Marwick, Mitchell & Co., Atlanta, 1969-72; sr. acct. DuBose & Co., Waycross, Ga., 1972-73; adminstrv. mgr. Am. Broadcasting ABC Record & Tape Sales Corp., Atlanta, 1973-76; v.p. fin. Macon Fed. Savs. & Loan (Ga.), 1976—; tchr. courses Am. Inst. C.P.A.'s, Savs. and Loan Inst. Fin. Edn. Served with Ga. N.G., 1971-77. C.P.A., Ga. Mem. Ga. Soc. C.P.A.'s, Am. Inst. C.P.A.'s, Fin. Mgrs. Soc. for Savs. and Loans, Nat. Assn. Accts., Phi Kappa Phi, Beta Alpha Psi. Club: Macon Exchange. Home: 150 Castlegate Rd Macon GA 31210 Office: 201 2d St Macon GA 31201

DAVIS, CLAUDE-LEONARD, lawyer; b. Augusta, Ga., Feb. 16, 1944; s. James Isaac and Mary Emma (Crawford) D.; A.B.J., U. Ga., 1966, J.D., 1974; m. Margaret Earle Crowley, Dec. 30, 1965; 1 dau., Margaret Michelle. Radio broadcaster, Washington, Ga., 1958-61; real estate salesman, Athens, Ga., 1962-65; bus. cons., Palm Beach, Fla., 1970-71; admitted to Ga. bar, 1974; atty., asst. to dir. of extension U.S. Dept. Agr./U. Ga. Coop. Extension Service, Athens, 1974—; cons. Congl. Office of Tech. Assessment; univ. lectr. agrl. law. Mem. council of advisers U. Ga.; sec. Ga. State Coordination and Adminstrn. Com., 1979-80. Served to capt. U.S. Army Res., 1966-70. Decorated Army Commendation medal; recipient Thomas Whitehead award Chi Psi Ednl. Trust, 1975; Outstanding Alumnus award Chi Psi, 1973; Profl. Achievement award Epsilon Sigma Phi, 1974. Mem. Am. Bar Assn., State Bar Ga., Bar Western Jud. Circuit, U.S. Assn. County Agrl. Agrs., Ga. Assn. County Agrl. Agrs., U.S. Assn. Extension 4-H Agts., Ga. Assn. Extension 4-H Agts., Alpha Alpha Delta of Chi Psi. Club: Owls. Contbr. articles to various jours. and mags. Office: Conner Hall Suite 203 U Ga Athens GA 30602

DAVIS, DANELLA BETH, editor; b. Loraine, Tex., Aug. 1, 1939; d. Oscar Britton Porter and Ella Elvera (Sweatt) Porter Freeman; grad. Abilene (Tex.) Beauty Coll., 1958; m. Bob D'Wayne Davis, Nov. 14, 1973; children—Malia Beth, Margo Lynette. Hairdresser, exec. sec., Colorado City, San Antonio, Stanton, Tex., 1959-70; women's editor, asst. to pub. Fort Stockton Pioneer, 1970-73; asst. to editorial page editor, mem. women's dept. Amarillo Globe News, 1974; with pub. relations dept. Pioneer Corp., Amarillo, 1974-75, editor employee mag., 1975—; judge beauty pageants including Miss Tex. Nat. Teen-Ager, 1975. Recipient Addy award of merit Amarillo Advt. Club, 1976. Mem. Internat. Assn. Bus. Communicators (chpt. pres. 1978), Tex. Press Women (recipient awards, winner state press sweepstakes 1978; dist. pres.), Amarillo C. of C., Beta Sigma Phi. Republican. Presbyterian. Clubs: Desk and Derrick, Toastmistress. Home: 2809 W 28th St #131 Amarillo TX 79109 Office: 301 Taylor St Amarillo TX 79163

DAVIS, DAVID BOOTEN, counselor; b. Huntington, W.Va., Feb. 8, 1917; s. Maurice Booten and Myrtle Bell (Dean) D.; B.A., Marshall U., 1939; M.Ed., Ohio U., 1947; postgrad. UCLA, Los Angeles State U. Tchr., Chesapeake Union Exempted Village Sch. Dist., 1944-45; supervising prin. Washington Twp. Schs. and The Plains Local Schs., 1945-50; tchr., supervising critic Plains Sch.; extension tchr. Ohio U., 1945-50; prin. Harrisonburg (Va.) Tng. Sch. for Madison Coll., 1950-51; asst. prof. Madison Coll., 1950-51; tchr., counselor Montebello (Calif.) Schs., 1951-65; prin. Chesapeake (Ohio) High Sch., 1965-66; coordinator spl. programs, guidance dir. Chesapeake Union Exempted Village Sch. Dist., 1966—. Leader, Boy Scouts Am. Recipient fellowship grant for counselors edn.; cert. high sch. and elem. supr., high sch. and elem. prin., supt., high sch. and elem. counselor. Mem. Am. Assn. Sch. Adminstrs., Am. Personnel and Guidance Assn., Ohio Schs. Counselors Assn., Nat. Vocat. Guidance Assn., Chesapeake Edn. Assn., Chesapeake Counselors Assn. Club: Masons. Home: 2942 Chase St Huntington WV 25704 Office: PO Box 458 Chesapeake OH 45619

DAVIS, DAVID KEITHLEY, petroleum co. exec.; b. Sayre, Okla., July 19, 1926; s. Orville Keithley and Ruth (Johnson) Wilson; student Oklahoma City U., 1943-44, 46-47; student Cameron State Coll., 1955; m. Wanda Jean Martin, July 20, 1944; children—David Michael, Derek Hamilton, D'Et Suzanne. Chief geophysicist Frankfort Oil Co., Dallas, 1958-62; exec. v.p. Longhorn Prodn. Co., Dallas, 1962-64; exec. v.p. Exploration Surveys Inc., Dallas, 1964-71; pres. Computer Systems Corp., Dallas, 1967-71; partner Natural Gas Finders Inc., Dallas, 1971-78; owner D.K. Davis: Geosci., Austin, 1972—; mng. dir. Energy Research Assos., Dallas, 1975-77; sr. v.p. Tex. Ind. Producers and Royalty Owners Assn., 1978—. Served with USAAF, 1944-45. Mem. Soc. Exploration Geophysicists, Dallas Geol. Soc., Dallas Geophys. Soc., Houston Geophys. Soc., Dallas Petroleum Club, Petroleum Engrs. Club, Internat. Oceanographic Found., Mensa. Republican. Baptist. Clubs: Onion Creek Country, Masons (32 degree, Shriner). Home: 4613 Pinehurst Dr S Austin TX 78747 Office: 1770 Austin Nat Bank Tower Austin TX 78701

DAVIS, DONALD GORDON, JR., librarian, educator; b. San Marcos, Tex., Aug. 15, 1939; s. Donald Gordon and Ethel Dorothy (Henning) D.; B.A., UCLA, 1961; M.A., U. Calif., Berkeley, 1963, M.L.S., 1964; Ph.D., U. Ill., 1972; m. Avis Jane Higdon, Dec. 6, 1969; children—Lucinda Ellen, Samuel Higdon, Caroline Louise. Adminstrv. asst. Biola Coll. Library, La Mirada, Calif., 1961-62; sr. library asst. U. Calif., Berkeley, 1961-64; sr. reference librarian Fresno State Coll. Library, 1964-68, head dept. spl. collections, 1966-68; asst. prof. library sci. U. Tex., Austin, 1971-77, asso. prof., 1977—; bd. dirs., v.p. Logos Bookstore, Austin, Pres. PTA Robert E. Lee Sch., Austin, 1979-80; mem. adv. bd. America: History and Life, 1979—. Newberry Library fellow, 1974. Mem. Am. Hist. Assn., ALA (chmn. library history round table 1978-79), Am. Printing History Assn., Assn. Am. Library Schs., Assn. Bibliography History, Christian Librarians Fellowship, Conf. Faith and History, Hymn Soc. Am., Orgn. Am. Historians, Tex. Assn. Coll. Tchrs., Tex. Library Assn., Heritage Soc. Austin. Presbyterian. Author: The Association of American Library Schools, 1915-1968, 1974; Reference Books in the Social Sciences and Humanities, 1977; American Library History: A Bibliography, 1978, others. Editor Jour. Library History, 1976—. Home: 3900 Ave C Austin TX 78751 Office: Grad Sch Library Sci Univ of Tex Austin Box 7576 University Station Austin TX 78712

DAVIS, DORIS LYNN MATTHEWS, journalist; b. Roanoke, Va., Nov. 14, 1945; d. H. Paul and Nina (McLelland) Matthews; student Taylor U., 1963-65; B.S. in Journalism, U. Md., 1967; m. Lamar Waldo Davis, Dec. 21, 1968; 1 son, Jason Edward. Information asst. Balt. Internat. Airport, 1967-69; ednl. communicatons asst. Washington Sanitarium and Hosp., Washington, 1969; publs. asst. U. Md., Balt., 1970-71; asso. dir. univ. relations U. Md., Baltimore County, 1972; dir. publs. Hollins (Va.) Coll., 1973-76, pub. relations cons., 1976-77; freelance writer, editor, photographer, 1977—. Vol. worker home for juvenile delinquent girls, Balt., 1968; vol. worker Balt. City Jail, 1967-69; program designer Balt. Symphony, 1972. Recipient Golden Rule award Md. Girl Scouts, 1968; Writing award Newsweek, 1973; award N.Y. Art Dirs. Club, 1975; writing and editing awards Va. Pres Assn.; awards Nat. Fedn. Press Women; several awards Am. Alumni Council, Am. Coll. Pub. Relations Assn., Council for Advancement and Support of Higher Edn. Mem. Roanoke Valley Lawyers' Wives Assn. (v.p.). Republican. Home: Sinking Creek New Castle VA 24127

DAVIS, DOUGLAS JAMES, accountant; b. Bronxville, N.Y., Feb. 1, 1952; s. James Foster and Irene F. Davis; B.S., U. Fla., 1974, M.B.A., 1977. Research asst. Bur. Econ. and Bus. Research, Gainesville, Fla., 1975-77; sr. accountant Touche Ross & Co., Jacksonville, Fla., 1977—. C.P.A., Fla. Mem. Grad. Bus. Assn. (pres. 1977), Am. Inst. C.P.A.'s, Fla. Inst. C.P.A.'s, Assn. M.B.A. Execs., U. Fla. Alumni Assn. Clubs: Z Connection Sports Car, Southside Bus. Men's. Contbr. articles to profl. jours. Office: Suite 2801 Independent Sq Jacksonville FL 32202

DAVIS, DOUGLAS RAYMOND, ry. exec.; b. Meridian, Miss., Sept. 9, 1942; s. Raymond Pollack and Annie Lucille (Lowe) D.; B.S. in Civil Engring., Miss. State U., 1965; m. Virginia Lynn Salter, Jan. 22, 1966; children—Dara Lane, Douglas Lance, Raymond Selby. With So. Ry., Somerset, Ky., summers 1963, 64; with Frisco Ry, 1965-71, process engr., Springfield, Mo., 1970-71; with Atlanta & St. Andrews Bay Ry., 1971—, chief engr., 1973-79, gen. supt., Panama City, Fla., 1979—. Mem. Am. Ry. Engring. Assn., Am. Ry. Bridge and Bldg. Assn., Am. Assn. R.R. Supts. Democrat. Baptist. Office: Atlanta & St Andrews Bay Ry PO Box 669 Panama City FL 32401

DAVIS, DREXEL REED, state ofcl.; b. Shelbyville, Ky., July 18, 1921; s. E. Forest and Myrtle Francis (Stacy) D.; student Georgetown Coll., 1940-42; m. Sarah Lillis, Oct. 15, 1947; children—Drexel R., Ann Lillis. Dep. clk. Ky.'s Ct. of Appeals, 1948-52, 56-63, clk., 1964-67; adminstrv. asst. Ky. Sec. of State, Frankfort, 1952-56; dist. mgr. Investors Heritage Life Ins. Co., Frankfort, 1969-72; treas. State of Ky., Frankfort, 1972-75, 79—, sec. of state, 1975-79. Served with Signal Corps, U.S. Army, 1942-45. Mem. Southeastern Nat. Treasurers Assn. (chmn.), Am. Legion, VFW. Democrat. Clubs: Lions (dist. govt.), Masons, Shriners. Office: Treasury Dept New Capitol Annex Frankfort KY 40601*

DAVIS, EDWARD LEE, mfg. co. ofcl.; b. Martinsville, Va., Nov. 27, 1943; s. Carl Evans and Nellie Louise (Connevey) D.; B.S. in Indsl. Engring., Va. Poly. Inst., 1965; m. Margaret Jean Rebuck, Mar. 13, 1965; children—Jeffrey Scott, Stephen Mark. Jr. methods engr. Babcock & Wilcox Co., Barberton, Ohio, 1965-66, methods engr., 1966-68, foreman nuclear internals shop, 1968-69, sr. method engr., 1969-70; mfg. engr. Ingersoll Rand Co., Mocksville, N.C., 1970-72, supr. mfg. engring., 1972-78, mgr. mfg. planning, 1979—. Treas., Rollingreen Civic Assn., 1975-76, pres., 1976-77. Mem. Soc. Mfg. Engrs. (cert.), Alpha Pi Mu. Republican. Methodist. Club: Masons. Home: 4507 Woodsman Way Winston-Salem NC 27103 Office: PO Box 868 Mocksville NC 27028

DAVIS, ELEANOR STEWART, ins. claims adjusting co. exec.; b. Carrollton, Ga., Sept. 28, 1939; d. Paul Wilson and Bernice Irene (Lovvorn) Roberts; student public schs., Carrollton; m. George Travis Davis, May 20, 1977; children—Mary Cynthia Stewart, Deborah Davis Hargrove, Gregory Scott Stewart, Michelle, Lisa. With Retail Credit Co., Atlanta, 1958-60; with Crawford and Co., Atlanta, 1964—, asst. corp. sec., 1977—, dir. employee benefits, 1977—, plan and claim adminstr., 1978—. Mem. Internat. Found. Employee Benefit Plans, Am. Hosp. Assn., Ga. Claims Assn., Atlanta Claims Assn. Democrat. Methodist. Home: 2535 Cardinal Lake Circle Duluth GA 30135 Office: 5620 Glenridge Dr Atlanta GA 30328

DAVIS, ELISE MILLER (MRS. LEO M. DAVIS), author; b. Corsicana, Tex., Oct. 12, 1915; d. Moses Myre and Rachelle (Daniels) Miller; student U. Tex., 1930-31; m. Jay Albert Davis, June 27, 1937 (dec. June 1973); 1 dau., Rayna Miller (Mrs. Michael Edwin Loeb); m. 2d, Leo M. Davis, Aug. 23, 1974. Freelance writer, 1945—; buyer and dir. Jay Davis, Inc., Amarillo, Tex., 1956-73. Mem. Am. Soc. Journalists and Authors. Author: The Answer Is God, 1955. Contbr. articles to periodicals including Reader's Digest, Woman's Day, Nation's Business, others. Home: 3906 Old Mill Rd Waco TX 76710

DAVIS, ELIZABETH MARDRE, educator, civic worker; b. Lumpkin, Ga.; d. Wilson Little and Sarah (Bivins) Mardre; student U. Calif. at Berkeley 1927; B.S., Auburn U., 1929; m. Hartwell Davis, Feb. 24, 1933; children—Hartwell, Letitia Dowdell. Tchr. English, Clift High Sch., Opelika, Ala., 1929-33, Lanier High Sch., Montgomery, Ala., 1934-36, 39, Robert E. Lee High Sch., Montgomery, 1952-68, Jefferson Davis High Sch., Montgomery, 1968-69. Mem. Ala. Citizens Adv. Ednl. Council, Ala. Com. for Better Schs., Inc.; pres. Montgomery Know-Your-Schs. Com., 1951-52. Trustee Carnegie Library Assn. Mem. Montgomery County Republican Exec. Com., 1956-66, 71-73; vice chmn. Rep. State Exec. Com., 1961-62; mem. Congl. Dist. and State Republican exec. coms., 1960-66; pres. Montgomery County Rep. Women, 1970-72. Mem. United Church Women (pres. Montgomery 1951-53, pres. Ala. 1955-57, mem. adminstrv. and exec. coms. gen. dept. 1957-58), D.A.R., Daus. Am. Colonists, Colonial Dames 17th Century, Magna Charta Dames, LWV (exec. bd. Montgomery 1952-54), Auburn U. Alumni Assn. (v.p. 1946-48), Kappa Delta, Phi Kappa Phi, Kappa Delta Pi. Methodist. (exec. com., sec. promotion Ala.-W. Fla. Woman's soc. 1952-58, mem. Ala.-W. Fla. Conf. Bd. Missions 1960-62). Clubs: 20th Century Literary (pres. 1944-45, 72-73), Hypatia Lit. (pres. 1944-45), Panjandrum Lit. (pres. 1948-49, 74-75). Home: 2216 Allendale Pl Montgomery AL 36111

DAVIS, ERNST MICHAEL, educator; b. Victoria, Tex., Oct. 12, 1933; s. Robert and Helen (Lamprecht) D.; B.A., N. Tex. State U., 1956, M.A., 1962 Ph.D., U. Okla., 1966; m. Claudia Dixon, July 21, 1973; 1 dau., Dana Annette. Research asso. U. Tex. at Austin, 1966-68, asst. prof., 1968-70; asst. prof. U. Tex. at Houston, 1970-73, asso. prof., 1973—; cons. environ. engring., water pollution abatement, waste treatment, ecological effects of discharges. Served with Chem. Corps, AUS, 1956-58. Recipient Disting. Alumni citation North Tex. State U., 1979; diplomate Am. Acad. Environ. Engrs.; USPHS scholar, 1964-66. Registered profl. engr., Tex. Mem. Water Pollution Control Fedn., Am. Water Works Assn., Internat. Assn. Water Pollution Research, Assn. Environmental Engring. Profs., Tex. Soc. Profl. Engrs. Beta Beta Beta, Kappa Sigma. Contbr. articles to profl. jours. Home: 5410 Darnell St Houston TX 77096 Office: U Tex Sch Pub Health PO Box 20186 Houston TX 77025

DAVIS, EVELYN BABB, educator; b. Chelesea, Mass., May 11, 1923; d. George E. Babb and Marie A. LaPorte; student Chandler Secretarial Sch., 1942; B.S. in Bus. Adminstrn., Boston U., 1947; M.S. in Bus. Edn., U. Fla.; m. Ellis A. Davis, Aug. 10, 1957; 1 dau., Tracey L. Sec., Boston YMCA, 1942-43; exec. sec. Brigham's, Inc., Cambridge, Mass., 1947-49; tchr. S. Broward High Sch., Hollywood, Fla., 1951-52; instr. bus. U. Fla., Gainesville, 1952-57, Pensacola (Fla.) Jr. Coll., 1960-68. Recipient Fla's Outstanding Bus. Educators award, 1976. Mem. Fla., Escambia (pres., dir.), Am. vocat. assns., Fla. (dir.), Escambia, Nat., So. bus. edn. assns., Fla. Bus. Tchrs. Educators Council (past pres.), Delta Pi Epsilon (past pres., nat. historian), Alpha Omicron Pi (hon mem.), Kappa Delta Pi, Pi Lambda Theta (past pres.). Republican. Presbyterian. Contbr. articles to profl. jours. Home: 1700 E Scott St Pensacola FL 32503 Office: Coll Edn Univ W Fla Pensacola FL 32504

DAVIS, GARNETT STANT, accountant; b. Mt. Vernon, Tex., Oct. 24, 1916; s. James Stant and Ivey (Hightower) D.; student E. Tex. State Tchrs. Coll., 1938-39; B.B.A., Tex. Tech. Coll., 1942; M.S., Tex. A. and M. U., 1943; LL.B., So. Meth. U., 1947; m. Emogene Campbell, Oct. 3, 1943; children—Patricia Jean, Cynthia Ann, Mary Helen. Grad. asst. Tex. A. and M. Coll., 1942-43; instr. Tex. Tech. Coll., 1943-44; mem. staff Haskins & Sells, Dallas, 1944-46; asst. prof. Tex. Christian U. 1946-48; admitted to Tex. bar, 1948; asso. prof. Tex. Coll. Arts and Industries, 1948-51; partner Hart, Veale, Davis & Co., 1951-53, Veale, Davis & Kendall, 1953-55; pvt. accounting practice, 1955-65; partner Davis & Olson, Kingsville, Tex., 1965—. Named Kingsville Lion of the year, 1966. C.P.A., Tex. Baptist (deacon). Club: Lions (Kingsville). Home: 720 Santa Clara St Kingsville TX 78363 Office: 701 E King Kingsville TX 78363

DAVIS, GERALD WAYNE, electronics co. exec.; b. Birmingham, Ala., Apr. 20, 1939; s. Earl Otis and Dorothy M. D.; student Brunswick Coll., 1965; 1 son, Gerald Dwayne. With Powerll Electronics Co., Huntsville, Ala., 1967-70, Gulf Electronics Co., Huntsville, 1970-71; mem. outside sales staff Hall-Mark Electronics Co., Huntsville, 1971-75, outside sales mgr., 1975-76, mgr. distbn. center, Austin, Tex., 1976—. Served with USN, 1961-65. Clubs: Masons, Shriners Home: 12401 Blue Water St Austin TX 78758 Office: Hall-Mark Electronics Co 10109 Mckalla St Suite F Austin TX 78758

DAVIS, GORDON WILLIAM, educator; b. Galva, Ill., Oct. 7, 1910; s. William George and Beatrice (Gordon) D.; A.B., Knox Coll., 1934; M.S., Washington U., 1938. Asst. plant physiology Washington U., 1935-39; head sci. dept. Leadwood (Mo.) High Sch., 1937-39; tch. sales dir. Printograph Co., Kansas City, Mo., 1939-41; instr. sci., English, math. Morgan Park Mil. Acad., Chgo., 1941; head sci. dept. Elkader (Ia.) Jr. Coll., 1941-42; asst. prof., sci. supr. Winthrop Coll., Rock Hill, S.C., 1957-58; prof. biology and chem., chmn. sci. dept., Frederick Coll., Portsmouth, Va., 1958-59; asst. prof. chem. and math. Ferris State Coll., Big Rapids, Mich., 1959-63; asso. prof. phys. scis. Miami-Dade Jr. Coll., Miami, 1963—. Commd. capt. AUS, 1942, advanced through grades to lt. col., Res., 1953; chem. br. advisory S.C. Mil. Dist., also chem. U.S. Army Res. adviser for chem. units, Charleston, S.C., 1953-57. Mem. Mo. Acad. Sci., Res. Officers Assn., Armed Forces Chem. Soc., Nat. Honor Soc., Nat. Sci. Tchrs. Assn. (life), AAUP (pres., founder Miami-Dade Jr. Coll. chpt. 1966—), Am. Chem. Soc., Dade County Classroom Tchrs. Assn., Am. Assn. Physics Tchrs., Am. Ordnance Assn. (life), NEA, Fla. Edn. Assn., Assn. for Higher Edn., Internat. Platform Assn., Fla. Acad. Sci., Sigma Xi, Phi Sigma. Club: Chemist. Home: 10545 NW 28th Ave Miami FL 33147

DAVIS, GUY CLAUDE, JR., anesthesiologist; b. Gainesville, Fla., July 16, 1943; s. Guy Claude and Mary Frances (Elrod) D.; A.B., Emory U., 1965, M.S., 1969, M.D., 1972, Ph.D., 1972; m. Sally Ann Bridges, July 16, 1966; 1 dau., Mary Kay. Intern, Grady Meml. Hosp., Atlanta, 1972-73; resident Emory U. Affiliated Hosps., Atlanta, 1973-75; asst. prof. anesthesiology Duke U. Med. Center, Durham, N.C., 1975-76; anesthesiologist, med. dir. bioengring. Crawford W. Long Meml. Hosp., Atlanta, 1976—; practice medicine specializing in anesthesiology, Atlanta, 1976—; mem. staff Crawford W. Long Meml. Hosp., Jesse Parker Williams Meml. Hosp.; clin. asst. prof. anesthesiology Emory U. Mem. Am. Soc. Anesthesiologists, Internat. Anesthesia Research Soc., AMA, Biometric Soc., Am. Statis. Assn. Baptist. Home: 1671 Council Bluff Dr Atlanta GA 30345 Office: 35 Linden Ave Atlanta GA 30308

DAVIS, H. DON, chem. engr.; b. Abilene, Tex., May 20, 1947; s. Howard B. and Loyce Avanell (Shelton) D.; student Odessa Coll., 1965-67; B.S. in Chem. Engring. with honors, Tex. Tech. U., 1970; postgrad. in Chem. Engring. U. Houston, 1970—; m. Norma Louise Zachry, June 10, 1967; children—Jon Don, Louise Rose. Chem. engr. Shell Chem. Co. Deer Park, Tex., 1970-72, Shell Oil Exploration Co., Houston, 1972-74, Shell Oil Prodn. Co., Houston, 1974; v.p. engring., partner Petromas Inc., Houston, 1974—. Registered profl. engr., Tex. Mem. Tex. Soc. Profl. Engrs., Am. Inst. Chem. Engrs. (treas. chpt.), San Jacinto Kennel Club, Italian Greyhound Club Am. (treas., author bimonthly column Italian Greyhound mag. 1974—), Italian Greyhound Club Greater Houston pres., editor newsletter 1975—), Tex. Assn. Phi Theta Kappa Chpts. (pres. 1966-67), Phi Theta Kappa (pres. chpt. 1966-67), Tau Beta Pi (pres. chpt. 1969-70). Mem. Ch. of Christ. Home: 1811 Winding Creek St Pearland TX 77581 Office: 8235 Lockheed St Houston TX 77061

DAVIS, HAROLD EDWARD, JR., psychiat. social worker; b. St. Petersburg, Fla., Oct. 22, 1932; s. Harold Edward and Pauline Rebecca D.; B.S. in Bus. Adminstrn., U. Tampa, 1958; M.S.W., Fla. State U., 1970; postgrad. U. South Fla., Tampa, 1975; m. Alice Carolyn York, Dec. 25, 1952; children—Debra Adair, Alisanne Elisabeth, Timothy Edward. Supr., Fla. Parole Commn., 1960-62; social worker, supr. Fla. Public Welfare Dept., Tampa, 1962-70; social worker Hillsborough County Schs., Tampa, 1970—; instr. U. Tampa MacDill AFB Campus, 1974—; caseworker Pinellas Epilepsy Found., St. Petersburg, 1978—. Served with USMC, 1950-52. Lic. marriage and family counselor, Fla. Mem. Fla. Vis. Tchrs./Sch. Social Workers Assn., Nat. Assn. Social Workers, Phi Delta Kappa. Author: Alcoholics and Problem Drinkers, 1976. Home: 3908 Moran Rd Tampa FL 33618 Office: 411 E Henderson St Tampa FL 33602

DAVIS, HARTWELL, lawyer; b. Auburn, Ala., Dec. 18, 1906; s. Christopher Hartwell and Elizabeth Myrick (Dowdell) D.; student U. Fla., 1923-24; B.S., Auburn U., 1928; Woodrow Wilson Meml. scholar U. Va. Law Sch., 1929-30; LL.B., Emory U., 1931, LL.D., 1970; m. Elizabeth Mardre, Feb. 24, 1933; children—Hartwell, Letitia Dowdell (Mrs. R. Wilkins Hamill, III). Clk. Bradenton Bank & Trust Co. (Fla.), 1924-25; admitted to Ga., Ala., Fla. bars, 1931, since practiced at Opelika and Montgomery, Ala.; asst. U.S. atty. Middle Dist. Ala., 1932-51, U.S. atty., 1953-62; atty. City of Montgomery, 1951-53; spl. asst. atty. gen. Ala., 1964-71. Del., S.E. jurisdictional confs. Meth. Ch., 1948, 52, 56; mem. Meth. Gen. Bd. Evangelism, 1952-56; sec.-treas. Meth. Ala. Conf. Bd. Lay Activities, 1945-60. Pres. Montgomery YMCA, 1938-40, bd. dirs., 1935-57; chmn. Ct. Honor, Tuckabatchie area Boy Scouts Am., 1951-52, chmn. merit badge com., 1953; bd. dirs. Ala. Meth. Children's Home, 1953-76, 1st v.p., 1973-74; trustee George Wheeler Meml. Scholarship Fund, 1941-71. Mem. Fed., Am., Ala., Montgomery bar assns., C. of C., Am. Judicature Soc., Am., Ala. trial lawyers assns., Sigma Nu, Phi Alpha Delta, Theta Alpha Phi. Republican. Kiwanian (pres. 1938). Clubs: Capital City, Tuesday Evening Social, Montgomery Fresh Air Domino. Home: 2216 Allendale Pl Montgomery AL 36111 Office: 1st Alabama Bank Bldg Montgomery AL 36104

DAVIS, JACK (WILLIAM), JR., hosp. personnel adminstr.; b. Watonga, Okla., Dec. 21, 1945; s. Jack W. and Orpha L. (Mayhall) D.; B.S. in Psychology, Central State U., Edmond, Okla., 1972, B.B.A. in Mgmt., 1972, M.B.A. in Mgmt., 1974; m. Lynda S. Carpenter, Sept. 5, 1975. Field rep. Retail Credit Co., Oklahoma City, 1972-74; adminstr. Watonga Mcpl. Hosp., 1974-75; dir. personnel South Community Hosp., Oklahoma City, 1976—. Precinct treas. Oklahoma County (Okla.) Republican Party, 1979. Served with U.S. Army, 1966-68; Vietnam. Mem. Am. Hosp. Personnel Assn., Am. Soc. Personnel Adminstrn. (accredited personnel mgr.), Okla. Hosp. Personnel Assn., Oklahoma City Personnel Assn. (co-chmn. 1978-79). Methodist. Home: Route 1 Box 197-L Oklahoma City OK 73111 Office: 1001 SW 44th St Oklahoma City OK 73109

DAVIS, JACK CARLSON, tng. sch. exec.; b. Kansas City, Mo., Dec. 30, 1925; s. William G. and Lila (Carlson) D.; B.F.A., Kansas City Art Inst., 1953; asso. in bus. Kansas City Jr. Coll., 1957; student Acadamie Julian, Paris, France, 1948; m. Phyllis Ileana Lakin, Nov. 21, 1947; children—Brett Carlson, Normandy Marie, Glen Barry, Kathryn Lorraine, Edgar Bearn. Asst. advt. mgr. Davis Paint Co., Kansas City, Mo., 1952-55; advt. mgr. Keystone Trailer Co., Kansas City, 1955-57, Central Tech. Inst., Kansas City, 1957-63; exec. v.p. Atlantic Sch., Kansas City, 1963-71, pres., 1971-73; v.p. Nat. Systems Corp., Newport Beach, Calif., 1969-73; founder, exec. v.p. Westervelt Travel Inst. Ltd., London, Ont., Can., 1973-76; founder, pres. Westport Tng. Corp., Inc., Kansas City, Mo., 1976-78; asst. dir. Southeastern Acad., Kissimmee, Fla., 1979—. Served with USNR, 1943-46. Home: 229 Loraine Dr Altamonte Springs FL 32701

DAVIS, JAMES EARL, sci. adminstr.; b. Russellville, Ohio, Dec. 27, 1934; s. James Clyde and Mabel Anna (Hook) D.; B.S. in Mech. Engring. and Indsl. Engring., Ohio U., 1962; postgrad. in Optics, UCLA, 1960-64, U. Rochester, 1967; M.S. in Fin., U. Houston, 1978; m. Mona Constance Leonard, Nov. 16, 1961; one son, James Jeffrey. Engr. FMA Inc., microfilm recorders, El Segundo, Calif., 1960-62; sr. engr. Houston Fearless Co., photo enhancement and projectors, Los Angeles, 1962-65; tech. staff Hughes Aircraft Co., Culver City, Calif., 1965-68; supr. Apollo camera calibration lab. Johnson Space Center, Lockheed Electronics Co., Houston, 1968-71, data processing lab., 1971-73, mgr. remote sensing data analysis research, 1973—. Registered profl. engr., Tex. Mem. Nat. Mgmt. Assn., Optical Soc. Am., Soc. Photo-Optical Instrumentation Engrs., Soc. Photog. Scientists and Engrs., Beta Theta Pi. Contbr. articles to profl. publs. Home: 15710 Diana Ln Houston TX 77062 Office: 1830 NASA Rd 1 Houston TX 77058

DAVIS, JAMES ELSWORTH, food chain exec.; b. Henderson, Ark., July 31, 1907; s. William M. and Ethel (Chase) D.; student U. Idaho, 1925-27; m. Florence Novinger, Jan. 27, 1932; children—Dorothy Jean Davis Smith, Andrew Dano. Pres., Economy Wholesale Grocery Co., 1939-42, v.p., dir., 1925—; exec. v.p., dir. Winn & Lovett Grocery Co., 1946-50, chmn. bd., 1950-55; chmn. bd., dir. Winn-Dixie Stores, Inc., 1955—; v.p. Economy Wholesale Distbrs., Inc.; chmn. bd., dir. Am. Heritage Life Ins. Co.; pres., dir. D.D.I. Inc., Danov Corp., Estuary Corp.; chmn. trustees Am. Century Mortgage Investors, dir. Barnett Nat. Bank of Jacksonville. Vice pres. Winn-Dixie Stores Found.; pres. Elsworth Davis Family Found. Bd. dirs. Bolles Sch., St. Luke's Hosp. Assn.; trustee Bethune-Cookman Coll., Daytona Beach, Fla. Served from capt. to lt. col. AUS, 1943-45; officer charge Q.M.C. Market Center, N.Y.C., 1944-45; perishable foods, ETO, MTO, NATOUSA. Decorated Legion of Merit. Mem. Nat. Assn. Food Chains, Alpha Kappa Psi, Sigma Chi. Mem. Christian Ch. Home: 3960 Ortega Blvd Jacksonville FL 32210 Office: 5050 Edgewood Ct Jacksonville FL 32203*

DAVIS, JAMES MINOR, JR., utility co. exec., mech. engr.; b. Raeford, N.C., May 9, 1936; s. James Minor and Betsy S. (Sessoms) D.; B.S.M.E., N.C. State U., 1958; m. Patsy Ann McLean, July 19, 1958; children—Martha Jeanette, James Owen, Julie Ann. Test engr. Pratt & Whitney Aircraft Co., East Hartford, Conn., 1961-65; with Carolina Power & Light Co., Raleigh, N.C., 1965—, mgr. rates and regulation dept., 1976-79, v.p. fuel and materials mgmt. group, 1979—. Pres. Episcopal Laymen, Diocese N.C., 1971-73; vestryman St. Michael's Episcopal Ch., Raleigh, 1974-76. Served with USAF, 1958-61. Registered profl. engr., N.C. Mem. N.C. Soc. Engrs., Profl. Engrs. N.C., Nat. Soc. Profl. Engrs. Republican. Office: PO Box 1551 Raleigh NC 27602

DAVIS, JESSE DUNBAR, lawyer; b. Burden, Kans., June 19, 1908; s. Jesse Bowman and Hazel (Dunbar) D.; student U. Okla., 1926-28; LL.B., U. Tulsa, 1944; m. Frances Lou Vinson, June 19, 1929; children—Sydney (Mrs. Donald George Dove), Brett Vinson. Asst. mgr. Long-Bell Lumber Co., Muskogee, Okla., 1928-32, gen. mgr., Tulsa, 1933-48, div. mgr., Kansas City, Mo., 1949-57; admitted to Okla. bar, 1944, U.S. Supreme Ct. bar, 1950, Mo. bar, 1959, Fed. bar, 1963; v.p., dir. Tamko Asphalt Products, Inc., Joplin, Mo., 1958-59; gen. counsel Southwestern Lumberman's Assn., Kansas City, Mo., 1960-65, corporate sec., 1962-65; gen. practice law, Kansas City, Mo., Tulsa, 1960—; mgmt. cons., Tulsa, 1965—; realtor, Tulsa, Columnist, Retail Lumberman Mag., 1962-65; cons. industry Sch. Forestry, U. Mo., 1962-65; tchr. bus. law U. Mo., 1946-65; tchr. real estate law U. Tulsa, 1969-76; v.p., dir., asso. editor Retail Lumberman Pub. Co., Kansas City, 1962-65. Served to lt. USNR, 1944-46. Recipient Civic award Tulsa YMCA, 1946-47. Mem. Am. Judicature Soc., Lawyers Assn. Kansas City, Tulsa Bd. Realtors (dir. 1970-72, treas. 1971, corporate sec. 1972), Tulsa C. of C. (Civic award 1939), Res. Officers Assn. U.S. (life), Claremore C. of C. (dir. 1972-74, v.p. 1973-74), Am., Fed., Tulsa County, Rogers County, Kansas City bar assns., S.A.R., Am. Legion (life mem. Okla.), U.S. Navy League, Mid-Am. Lumbermens Assn., Nat. Lumber and Bldg. Material Dealers Assn. (dir. 1962-64), Tulsa County Hist. Soc. (life), Phi Delta Theta, Phi Beta Gamma. Republican. Presbyn. Clubs: University (charter mem.), Kiwanis (pres. Tulsa 1941, sec.-treas. Tex.-Okla. dist. 1942, charter mem. Claremore, Okla.). Home: 3231 S Utica Ave Tulsa OK 74105 Office: 3233 S Utica Ave Tulsa OK 74105

DAVIS, JESSE EDWIN, JR., wood products exec.; b. Atlanta, Feb. 4, 1910; s. Jesse Edwin and Eufa (Swilling) D.; B.S., Ga. Sch. Tech., 1933; LL.B., Woodrow Wilson Coll., 1937; m. Sarah Etta Fitzpatrick, Apr. 7, 1938; children—Carolyn W. (Mrs. Edward W. Riser), Sarah K. (Mrs. M. Rick Taylor), Jesse Edwin III, Marion H. Admitted to Ga. bar, 1937; sales rep. Atlantic Steel Co., 1937-43, Tidewater Supply Co., 1943-49; v.p., treas. Thackston-Davis Supply, 1949-59; with Marwin Co., 1959—, pres., treas., 1959— (all Columbia). Chmn. religious work com. Columbia YMCA, 1956—, also bd. dirs. Trustee, United Community Services. Mem. Columbia Com. of 100, Sigma Chi, Alpha Kappa Psi, Pi Delta Epsilon. Baptist (deacon). Mason (Shriner), Lion. Home: 4829 Carter Hill Rd Columbia SC 29206 Office: PO Box 9126 Atlas Rd Columbia SC 29209

DAVIS, JIMMIE GLEN, aluminum co. exec.; b. El Dorado, Ark., Feb. 1, 1938; s. Hudie Dale and Orlene (Smith) D.; B.S.E., So. Ark. U., 1962; m. Carolyn Brewer, Feb. 1, 1958; children—Jimmie, Jeffery, Joel. Draftsman, So. Extrusions, Inc., Magnolia, Ark., 1958-62, customer service mgr., 1962-65, field salesman, Kansas City, Mo., 1965-68, plant mgr., Ardmore, Okla., 1968-71, sales mgr., Magnolia, 1971-77; fabrication plant mgr. Howmet Aluminum Corp., Magnolia, 1977-79, mfg. mgr., 1979—. Mem. Magnolia Jr. C. of C. (bd. dirs. 1971-72). Democrat. Baptist. Home: Route 2 PO Box 369 Magnolia AR 71753 Office: 1617 N Washington St Magnolia AR 71753

DAVIS, JOE EBB, grocery store exec., elec. co. exec.; b. Axtel, Tex., Feb. 11, 1936; s. George W. and Willie Irene (Frazier) D.; student public schs., Abilene, Tex.; m. Billie Jane Tidwell, Feb. 22, 1958; children—David Clark, Joe Bob, Bo Shannon. Pres., Abilene Pump & Electric, Inc., 1964—; pres., founder Skinny's, Inc., Abilene, 1974—. Served with U.S. Army, 1958-60. Mem. Nat. Elec. Contractors, Tex. Oil Jobbers, Gen. Contractors Assn., Nat. Elec. Contractors Assn., Petroleum Equipment Inst. Republican. Office: Abilene Pump & Electric Inc 5189 Texas Ave Abilene TX 79605

DAVIS, JOE WALTER, ret. ch. ofcl.; b. Hobart, Okla., Aug. 11, 1913; s. Lee and Willie (Stewart) D.; B.S., Southwestern U., 1935; B.C.S., Benjamin Franklin U., Washington, 1942; m. Ethel Lois Wiemers, Apr. 24, 1937; children—Edith Marie (Mrs. Alan W. Loveland), Eugene Stewart, George Edward, Mary Ellen (Mrs. Phillip H. Arnold), Elizabeth Ann (Mrs. Michael S. Hime). Identification officer FBI, Washington, 1937-42, spl. agt., 1942-44; auditor Southwestern U., 1944-54; treas., bus. mgr. television, radio and film United Meth. Communications, 1954-76, asst. gen. treas. Council Finance and Adminstrn., 1973. Past mem. bd. mgrs., bus. finance com. of broadcasting and film commn. Nat. Council Chs. Sch., bd. sec., Georgetown, Tex., 1951-54. Home: 210 Emery Dr Nashville TN 37214

DAVIS, JOHN EDWARD, JR., educator; b. Welch, W.Va., Nov. 18, 1922; s. John Edward and Bessie Irene (Cline) D.; student Randolph-Macon Coll., 1939-41; B.A., U. Va., 1947, M.A., 1949, Ph.D., 1955; m. Katherine Vivian Smith, Aug. 27, 1949; 1 son, John Edward III. Instr. biology Washington and Lee U., 1949-51, 54-56; asst. prof. biology Wake Forest U., 1956-62, asso. prof., 1962-67, prof., 1967-68; chmn. dept. biology Madison Coll., Harrisonburg, Va., 1968-71, acting provost, 1971-72, provost div. arts and scis., 1972-73, prof. biology, 1973—; vis. prof. biology Washington and Lee U., 1977; cons. N.C. State Dept. Edn.; mem. study commn. allied health scis. State Council Higher Edn. Va. Ednl. coordinator Madison Coll. United Fund, 1973. Mem. adv. com. Rockingham Meml. Hosp. Sch. Nursing. Served with M.C., AUS, 1942-46. Phipps and Bird research fellow, 1948; research asso. N.C. Heart Assn., 1962; Am. Cancer Soc. research fellow, 1963. Mem. A.A.A.S., Assn. Southeastern Biologists, Va. Acad. Sci., N.Y. Acad. Scis., Sigma Xi, Kappa Alpha. Republican. Methodist. Elk. Clubs: Spotswood Country, Harrisonburg Kiwanis. Contbr. articles profl. jours. Research in biology, effects of radiation on coronary blood vessels, avian embryology. Home: Forest Hills Harrisonburg VA 22801

DAVIS, JOY LYNN, investment co. exec.; b. N.Y.C., Feb. 4, 1945; d. Irving and Irene Gloria Davis; student public schs., North Miami, Fla. Clk.-typist, sec. Texaco Inc., Long Island City, N.Y., 1962-66; asst. cashier Shearson Hayden Stone, Inc., N.Y.C., 1966-67, sec. asst., 1967-72; 2d v.p. investments Shearson Loeb Rhoades Inc., Ft. Lauderdale, Fla., 1972—. Pres. bd. dirs. Manors of Inverrary Condominium XI Assn., Inc., 1979—. Mem. Greater Miami/Fort Lauderdale Stock Brokers Soc., Fort Lauderdale Bond Club (bd. dirs.). Home: 4174 Inverrary Dr Lauderhill FL 33319 Office: 3099 E Commercial Blvd Fort Lauderdale FL 33308

DAVIS, JOYCE LORAYNE, ednl. counselor; b. Port Arthur, Tex., Aug. 5, 1930; d. Thomas I. and Annie (Hoffpauir) D.; A.A., Lon Morris Jr. Coll., 1950; B.A. in Math., U. Tex., Austin, 1952, M.Ed. in Ednl. Psychology, 1955; postgrad. U. Tex., Dallas, 1976; m. Charles Fredric Stahl, Aug. 28, 1954 (div. Nov. 1977); children—Charles Gregory Stahl, Lisa Kathryn Stahl. Registrar, Allan Jr. High, Austin, 1952; shipping clk. Gulf Oil Co., Port Arthur, Tex., 1952; tchr. math. Woodrow Wilson Jr. High Sch., Port Arthur, 1952-53; coop. tchr. core curriculum public schs., Kyle and Buda, Tex., 1953-54; tchr. math. McCallum High Sch., Austin, 1954-56, public schs., Manitou Springs, Colo., 1956-57, Austin High Sch., 1957-58; counselor Pearce Jr. High Sch., Austin, 1958-60; counselor Lanier Jr. High Sch. and tchr. math. Lanier High Sch., Austin, 1962-63; tchr. math. Lanier High Sch., 1965; counselor Austin Ind. Sch. Dist., 1965—, O. Henry Jr. High, 1965-71, 72—, Murchison Jr. High Sch., 1971-72. Proofreader legis. Tex. Senate Spl. Session, summer 1978. Lic. psychologist, various tchr. certs., Mem. NEA (life), Tex. State Tchrs. Assn., Austin Assn. Tchrs., Tex. Personnel and Guidance Assn. (legis. chmn. 1973-76, Spl. Legis. award 1974, Spl. award for ednl. research 1976), Central Tex. Personnel and Guidance Assn., Tex. Psychol. Assn., Alpha Delta Kappa. Democrat. Methodist. Office: O Henry Jr High Sch 2610 W 10th St Austin TX 78703

DAVIS, JOYCE LOUISE, educator; b. Miami, Fla., July 17, 1941; d. Arthur Henry and Willie Mae (Wilson) Sheppard; B.A., Miami Dade-Fla. Atlantic Coll., 1968; M.E., U. Miami, 1978; m. Robert Scott Davis, Dec. 16, 1967. Tchr. public schs., Miami, 1968, media specialist, 1970-72, exceptional child tchr., 1972-73, activities dir., 1972—, counselor, 1977-78; tchr. Snapper Creek Elem. Sch., Miami, 1970—; cons. in field. Sec., City Council, Miami, 1974-75. Mem. Am. Fedn. Tchrs., United Tchrs. of Dade, Am. Personnel and Guidance Assn., Beta Sigma Phi (pres. 1976-77). Presbyterian. Address: 8215 SW 63 Pl Miami FL 33143

DAVIS, JULIAN CARLYLE, psychologist, ins. agt.; b. Quincy, Fla., Feb. 8, 1921; s. Julius C. and Bonnie Jean (Marquardt) D.; m. Betty Lou Morris, Mar. 14, 1953; children—Zachary, Shannon, Richard, Marianne. Intern, N.H. State Hosp. and Mental Hygiene Clinic, Concord, 1944-45; psychologist Fla. State Hosp., Chattahoochee, 1946-48, dir. psychology, 1948-79; with Benson Ins. Assos., Naples, Fla., 1979—; vis. lectr. Fla. State U., 1975, Fla. Law Enforcement Acad., 1966; cons. Fla. Children's Commn., 1962, Dade County Chiefs of Police, 1954, Fla. Legislative Investigating Com., 1964. Chmn., Gadsden Cancer Crusade, 1967, Chattahoochee March of Dimes, 1970. Mem. Gadsden County Sch. Bd., 1961-68. Bd. dirs. State Cancer Crusade Com., 1968-70, Gadsden chpt. ARC, 1960-66, R.F. Munroe Sch., Quincy, Fla., 1969-70. Nat. Inst. Mental Health Hosp. Improvement grantee. Mem. Am., Southeastern, Fla. psychol. assns., Fla. Sch. Bd. Assn. (dir. 1967, v.p. 1968), Kappa Alpha. Episcopalian (mem. Mission bd. 1955—). Club: Gadsden Country. Author: (with Foreyt) Mental Examiners Source Book, 1975; Rorschach Location Charts, 1949. Contbr. articles to profl. jours. Home: 324 Palm Dr Apt 2 Naples FL 33942 Office: 1315 Fifth Ave S Naples FL 33942

DAVIS, KAREN ELAINE, ins. co. mgr.; b. Galveston, Tex., Feb. 17, 1942; d. John Duke and Anne (Olsen) Winchester; B.S., U. Tex., 1964; postgrad. U. Houston, 1964-65; m. Benjamin Lee Davis, July 30, 1965; children—Bradford Winchester, Benjamin Duke. Tchr., Texas City (Tex.) Ind. Sch. Dist., 1965-66, Galveston Ind. Sch. Dist., 1967-68; sr. computer analyst Am. Nat. Ins. Co., Galveston, 1974-75, computer div. sect. mgr., 1976—; guest lectr. data processing Tex. A. and M. Maritime Acad., 1976—. Area chmn. March of Dimes, Galveston, 1972; mem. Goals for Galveston Com., 1975, Friends of Rosenberg Library; bd. dirs. Am. Cancer Soc., Galveston, 1976-77, Galveston Arts Center; mem. Galveston County Jr. League, Inc. Mem. AAUW, Data Processing Mgmt. Assn. (dir.), DAR, Galveston Hist. Found., Galveston County Panhellenic Assn., Alpha Delta Pi. Republican. Methodist. Home: 56 Le Brun Ct Galveston TX 77551 Office: 1 Moody Plaza 19 Market St Galveston TX 77550

DAVIS, KEITH EUGENE, psychologist, educator; b. Clifton, N.C., May 15, 1936; s. Ted Eugene and Mary Flossie (Roland) D.; B.A., Duke U., 1958, Ph.D., 1963; m. Dorothy Ann Reeves, Feb. 23, 1968; 1 dau., Kristin; children by previous marriage—Rachel, Rebecca, Jessica. Instr. psychology Princeton (N.J.) U., 1961-62; asst. prof. psychology U. Colo., Boulder, 1962-67, asso. prof., 1967-70, dir. grad. program in social-personality psychology, 1967-70; prof., chmn. dept. psychology Livingston Coll., Rutgers U., New Brunswick, N.J., 1970-73; provost of univ. U. S.C., Columbia, 1974-78, prof. psychology, 1973—; mem. population research study sect. Nat. Inst. Child Health and Human Devel., 1973-76; mem. psychol. scis. subcom., mental health research edn. rev. com. NIMH. Participant Greater Columbia Forum, 1973-74, bd. dirs., 1974-76, pres. past participants, 1974-75; state plan adv. com. S.C. Dept. Mental Health, 1976-78, chmn., 1976-78; bd. dirs. Columbia Area Mental Health, 1976—, chmn. fin. com., 1977-79, chmn. search com. for dir., 1978. Woodrow Wilson Nat. fellow, 1958-59; So. Fellowships Fund fellow, 1958-61, many others. Mem. Am. Psychol. Assn., Am. Sociol. Assn., Nat. Council on Family Relations, Soc. for Descriptive Psychology (1st pres. 1979-81), Phi Beta Kappa, Omicron Delta Kappa. Democrat. Presbyterian. Author: Advances in Experimental Social Psychology, vol. 2, 1965; editor Advances in Descriptive Psychology, 1980; contbr. articles in field to profl. jours. Home: 1808 Catawba St Columbia SC 29205 Office: Dept Psychology Univ of SC Columbia SC 29208

DAVIS, LAWRENCE MICHAEL, accountant; b. Phila., Nov. 30, 1948; s. Paul and Marjorie (Goldburgh) D.; B.S., U.S. Mil. Acad., 1971; B.S. in Bus. Adminstrn., Auburn U., 1978, M.B.A., 1978; m. Lorraine Condon, July 11, 1971. Audit asst. Arthur Andersen & Co., Atlanta, 1978—. Served to capt. U.S. Army, 1971-76. Mem. Ga. Soc. C.P.A.'s (asso.), West Point Soc. Atlanta, Assn. Grads. U.S. Mil. Acad., Auburn U. Alumni Assn., Alumni Assn. Central High Sch. Phila., Beta Alpha Psi. Home: 3054C Clairmont Rd Atlanta GA 30329 Office: 25 Park Pl Atlanta GA 30303

DAVIS, LAWRENCE WILLIAM, personnel adminstr.; b. Concord, N.C., Feb. 1, 1938; s. Lawrence William and Betty Beatrice (Hord) D.; B.S., Appalachian State U., 1964; postgrad. N.C. State U., 1964-65; m. Kaye Elizabeth Joye, Nov. 24, 1966; children—Christopher K., William C. Tchr. history, coach high sch. Bessemer City, N.C., 1964; veterans employment rep. Employment Security Commn. N.C., Gastonia, 1965-66; personnel dir. Yarn div. Am. & Efird Mills Inc., Mt. Holly, N.C., 1966-73, Washington Group, Inc., Winston-Salem, N.C., 1973-77; personnel mgr. truck assembly plant Freightliner Corp., Charlotte, N.C., 1977—. Past pres. Blue Ridge Safety Council. Served with USAF, 1955-59, Army N.G., 1959—. Mem. Am. Soc. Personnel Adminstrs., Gaston County Personnel Assn., Am. Legion. Democrat. Baptist. Home: Belwood Dr Belmont NC 28012 Office: Freightliner Corp Mt Holly NC 27120

DAVIS, LEONARD RICHEY, architect; b. Charleston, Ill., Sept. 4, 1943; s. Donald Eckerd and Dorothy Dale (Richey) D.; B.A., Auburn (Ala.) U., 1968; grad. Summer Planning Inst., Ga. Inst. Tech., 1973; m. Annette Elizabeth Trucks, Dec. 28, 1966; children—Austin, Carrie. With various archtl. firms, Orlando, Fla., 1968-71; v.p. Environ. Design Group, Orlando, 1971-72; v.p. charge design King Helie Planning Group, Orlando, 1972-74; propr. Dick Davis, architect, Orlando, 1974-76; partner Leibin-Davis Partnership, Orlando, 1976—. Chmn. downtown improvement com. College Park Mchts. Assn., 1979; mem. Orlando Bd. Zoning Adjustment. mem. bldg. com. Winter Park (Fla.) First United Methodist Ch. Mem. AIA, Fla. Planning and Zoning Assn. (state dir., 1st v.p. Central Fla. chpt. 1974—). Republican. Home: 1522 Charlotte Ln Orlando FL 32804 Office: 2626 Edgewater Dr Orlando FL 32804

DAVIS, LEVI HAMILTON, city ofcl.; b. Akron, Ohio, Nov. 16, 1945; s. Levi Franklin and Pearl (Blair) D.; B.S. in Edn., Tex. Christian U., 1971; M.A. in Urban Affairs (N. Central Tex. Council Govt. fellow 1972), U. Tex., Arlington, 1973; m. Nellie Louise Ellis, Sept. 1970. Adminstrv. intern N. Central Tex. Council Govts., 1973; with City of Dallas, 1975—, dir. Office Human Devel., 1977-79, asst. to city mgr., 1979—. Bd. dirs. Child Care Assn. Dallas, Dallas UN Assn., Dallas Vol. Action Agy., Dallas Council Alcoholism. Served with USAF, 1967-70. Mem. Internat. City Mgmt. Assn. (bd. advs. acad.), Urban Mgmt. Assts. N. Tex. (pres. 1974), Com. 100, Am. Soc. Public Adminstrn., Tex. City Mgmt. Assn. Methodist. Club: Uptown Exchange. Author: A Giant in History: The History of the Dallas/Fort Worth Regional Airport Controversy, 1977. Address: City Hall Room 105 Dallas TX 75201

DAVIS, LOUIS, JR., retail chain exec.; b. Ft. Benning, Ga., July 13, 1949; s. Louis and Fannie R. Davis; student Ala. A&M U., 1967-68, Columbus Coll., 1970-72. With Ledger-Enquirer newspaper, Columbus, Ga., 1974-76, account exec., 1976; advt. mgr. Montgomery Ward & Co., Columbus, 1977—. Mem. Alpha Phi Alpha. Democrat. Office: Montgomery Ward & Co 3091 Manchester Expressway Columbus GA 31904

DAVIS, LOURIE BELL, ins. co. exec.; b. Las Vegas, N.Mex., Apr. 8, 1930; d. Currie Oscar and Irene Rodgers Bell; B.S. in Edn., W. Tex. State U., 1959; m. Robert Eugene Davis, Aug. 21, 1950; children—Judith Anne, Robert Patrick. Project leader Nat. Bank of Tulsa, 1968-71, Blue Cross/Blue Shield of Okla., Tulsa, 1971-75, 77—, project coordinator Corp. Data Base, 1977, mgr. systems support, 1977-78, mgr. planning and control, 1979—; instr. computer sci. Tulsa Jr. Coll., 1975-76. Cert. data processing Inst. Cert. Computer Profls. Mem. Assn. Systems Mgmt. (chpt. award 1978, Internat. Merit award 1980; instr.), Am. Mgmt. Assn., Tulsa Area Systems Edn. Assn., Faculties of Okla. Colls. and Univs. Soc., NEA, Okla. Edn. Assn., Sigma Chi. Republican. Presbyterian. Clubs: Mensa Internat., Intertel. Home: 2403 W Oklahoma St Tulsa OK 74127 Office: 1215 S Boulder St Tulsa OK 74102

DAVIS, MARJORIE, embryologist, educator; b. Elkhart, Kans., Mar. 13, 1935; d. Harry and Lena Smith; B.S., Panhandle State Coll., 1959; M.A., Kans. U., 1962, Ph.D., 1970; 1 son, Roger. Instr. biology Mankato (Minn.) State U., 1962-67; instr. Kans. State U., Manhattan, 1966-69, asst. prof., 1972-75; asst. prof. Mo. Western Coll., St. Joseph, 1970-72; asst. prof. med. biology Okla. Coll. Osteo. Medicine and Surgery, Tulsa, 1975—. Mem. AAAS, Am. Assn. Anatomists, Soc. for Study Reproduction, Soc. Am. Zoologists, AAUP, AAUW, Sigma Xi. Methodist. Home: 3816 E 105th St Tulsa OK 74136 Office: Oklahoma College Osteopathic Medicine and Surgery 1111 W 17th St Tulsa OK 74104

DAVIS, MARJORIE FRY, arts patron; b. Natchez, Miss.; d. Louis and Regina G. Fry; student Newcomb Coll., 1936-40; m. Walter Davis, June 15, 1939; children—Patricia, Walter III. Exhibits pvt. collection art to benefit small communities. Mem. Mayor's Com. of Cultural Resources. Bd. dirs. Womens Com., New Orleans Symphony, New Orleans Womens Opera Guild, Davis Family Fund; bd. dirs. New Orleans Speech and Hearing Clinic, also v.p., trustee New Orleans Mus. of Art, La. Arts and Sci. Center, La. State Mus.; bd. dirs. Council of Arts for Children, La. Arts Council. Clubs: Plimsoll, International House. Home: 1819 Octavia St New Orleans LA 70115 Office: PO Box 6099 New Orleans LA 70174

DAVIS, MARTHA H., librarian; b. Macon, N.C., Feb. 14, 1920; d. Raymond A. and Bessie M. (Satterwhite) Harris; A.B., Greensboro Coll.; B.S. in L.S., U. N.C.; m. William Edward Davis, II, Apr. 17, 1942; children—Harriet, Betsy Davis Cresenzo, William Edward, Allen Hunter. Asst. librarian Olivia Raney Library, Raleigh, N.C.; librarian Portsmouth (Va.) Public Library, Mary Bayley Pratt Children's Library, Chapel Hill, N.C., Hugh Morson High Sch., Raleigh, Ruffin (N.C.) High Sch., Reidsville (N.C.) Jr. High Sch.; instr. children's lit. Meredith Coll.; now dir. Rockingham County (N.C.) Public Library System. Bd. dirs. Rockingham County Fund, Inc.; chmn. Reidsville Library Commn., 1958-59, Piedmont Triad Library Council; bd. dirs. Girl Scouts U.S.A., 1959-60. Mem. ALA, Southeastern Library Assn., N.C. Library Assn. (sec. public library sect.), Gen. Alumni Assn. Greensboro Coll. (pres. 1959-61). Democrat. Methodist. Clubs: Tuesday Afternoon Reading, Little Gardens Garden (pres.), Penrose Park Country. Office: 527 Boone Rd Eden NC 27288

DAVIS, MARTINA CAMPBELL, public relations exec.; b. Bowling Green, Ky., Aug. 30, 1932; d. Martin Joseph and Mollye Dean (Raymer) Campbell; student David Lipscomb Coll., 1950-52; B.S., U. Ky., 1954; M.A., Morehead State U., 1975; m. Paul Ford Davis, June 24, 1956; children—Laura Ellen, Mariana, Joseph Stark. Home economist Ky. Utilities, Elizabethtown, 1954-55; head dept. home econs. Freed Hardeman Jr. Coll., Henderson, Tenn., 1955-56; city planning aide City of Morehead (Ky.), 1975-77; coordinator of communications and devel. St. Claire Med. Center, Morehead, 1977—. Bd. dirs. Wilderness Rd. council Girl Scouts U.S.A., 1969-74, 1st v.p., 1971-74; pres. Rowan County LWV, 1972; sec. citizens com. Morehead Girls Center, 1973; sec. Morehead Park and Recreation Commn., 1976, Morehead-Rowan County Joint Planning Commn., 1976—; chmn. Morehead All Ky. City Program, 1976; chmn. Rowan County Land Use Workshop, 1976, Gateway ADD Transp. Com., 1976-79; bd. dirs. Cave Run Devel. Assn., 1977—; mem. Morehead Recreation, Tourism and Conv. Commn., 1978—. Recipient Cert. of Appreciation, Ky. Dept. Child Welfare, 1973; Citation of Appreciation, Am. Legion, 1975; Honor award in recognition of service Conservation Dist. Bd. Suprs., 1977; Award of Excellence in Hosp. Public Relations, Ky. Hosp. Assn., 1978. Mem. Ky. Soc. Hosp. Public Relations, Am. Soc. for Hosp. Public Relations, Nat. Pub. Assn., Kappa Delta (province pres. 1973). Mem. Ch. of Christ. Clubs: Bus. and Profl. Women, Morehead State Univ. Woman's. Home: Route 5 Morehead KY 40351 Office: 222 Medical Circle Morehead KY 40351

DAVIS, MATT MCKINNEY, III, rancher; b. San Antonio, June 11, 1932; s. Matt McKinney, Jr. and Edna Mayne (Lewis) D.; B.S., Tex. A. and I. U., 1957; postgrad. Tex. A. and M. U., 1956, U. Tex., 1956-57; m. Jimmie Lee Henson, Dec. 21, 1963; children—Rebecca Mae, Dixie Lee, Clay Matthew. Salesman, Anderson Machinery Co., Corpus Christi, Tex., 1958-59; rancher, Atascosa County, Tex., 1959—. Mem. Charlotte Vol. Fire Dept., 1970—; bd. dirs. Econ. Opportunities Devel. Corp. Atascosa, Karnes and Wilson counties, 1969—, Community Council S. Central Tex., Inc., 1973—. Served with USMC, 1950-52. Decorated Purple Heart with 2 gold stars. Mem. Am. Nat., Atascosa County (charter) cattleman's assns., Tex. and Southwestern Cattle Raisers Assn., Performance Registry Internat. (life), Ind. Cattlemans Assn., Atascosa County Farm Bur. (dir. 1965—), DAV (life), Am. Legion, Nat. (life), Tex. rifle assns., VFW (life). Clubs: Rotary (sec.; pres. Charlotte 1975-76); Odd Fellows. Home: PO Box 100 Charlotte TX 78011

DAVIS, MATTIE MAE, ednl. adminstr.; b. Columbia, S.C., Apr. 8, 1942; d. Prophet and Eugenia D.; A.B. cum laude, Allen U., 1963; M.A. with honors, N.Y. U., 1969; Ph.D. in Counselor Edn., U. S.C., 1978. Tchr. social studies St. Helena High Sch., Beaufort, S.C., 1963-66, Wilson High Sch., Florence, S.C., 1966-71; prof., dir. counseling Allen U., Columbia, 1971-77; adj. prof. U. S.C., Columbia, 1975-77, cons. Certified tchr. chemistry, history, counseling, secondary sch. prin., S.C. Mem. Am. Personnel and Guidance Assn., Am. Sch. Counselor Assn., Assn. Measurement and Evaluation, Am. Coll. Personnel Assn., Assn. Humanistic Edn. and Devel., Counselor Edn. Doctoral Student Assn. Methodist. Home: PO Box 3731 Columbia SC 29230

DAVIS, MENDEL JACKSON, congressman; b. North Charleston, S.C., Oct. 23, 1942; s. Felix Charles and Elizabeth (Jackson) D.; B.S., Coll. Charleston, 1966; J.D., U. S.C., 1970; m. Suzanna Henley, Nov. 25, 1965; 2 children. Admitted to S.C. bar, 1970; mem. staff Rep. L. Mendel Rivers, 1970-71; mem. 92d-96th Congresses from S.C. Named One of Outstanding Young Men of Am., 1972. Mem. S.C. State, Am. bar assns., Air Force Assn., Navy League. Democrat. Methodist. Mason, Elk. Office: 2161 Rayburn Bldg Washington DC 20515

DAVIS, MICHAEL ANDREW, ins. co. exec.; b. Fort Worth, Mar. 13, 1948; s. Jack Taylor and Ann Mae Davis; B.B.A. in Acctg. N. Tex. State U., 1970; m. Bridget Morey, June 7, 1969; 1 son, Keith Merrill. Mgr., Hardees Food Systems, Denton, Tex., 1963-73; agt. State Farm Ins., Grapevine, Tex., 1973—. Mem. Sch. Bd. Grapevine, 1977—; chmn. Grapevine Tax Equalization Com., 1976-77; mem. Grapevine Planning and Zoning Com., 1974-77; vice chmn. Grapevine Adv. Com. on Community Edn., 1975-77. Mem. Grapevine C. of C. (dir. 1976—, pres. 1980-81), Presidents Club. Baptist. Club: Kiwanis. Home: 3312 Marsh Ln Grapevine TX 76051 Office: 1003 Main St Grapevine TX 76051

DAVIS, MICHAEL LEE, physician; b. Houston, Dec. 23, 1947; s. John L. and Vera M. (Ford) D.; B.A. cum laude, Houston Bapt. Coll., 1971; M.D. with high honors, U. Tex. Med. Br., 1974; m. Alma Leila Crumm, Jan. 2, 1970; children—Matthew, Barbara, David. Ordained to ministry Bapt. Ch., 1965; asso. pastor First Bapt. Ch., Humble, Tex., 1969-71; youth and music minister First Bapt. Ch., Alvin, Tex., 1971-72; interim music dir. First Bapt. Ch., Sweeny, Tex., 1978; intern John Sealy Hosp., Galveston, Tex. 1974-75, resident, 1975-77; practice medicine, specializing in family practice, Sweeny, 1977—; chief of staff Sweeny Community Hosp., 1977—; mem. cons. bd. Home Health Home Care Assn., Brazoria County, Tex., 1978—; mem. staff Davis Med. Clinic, Sweeny. Recipient Cert. of Appreciation, Sweeny Community Hosp. Bd., 1978; diplomate Am. Bd. Family Practice. Mem. AMA, Aircraft Owners and Pilots Assn., Alpha Omega Alpha. Democrat. Home: 1401 Hilltop Dr Sweeny TX 77480 Office: 411 Main St Sweeny TX 77480

DAVIS, MILTON VICTOR, surgeon; b. Shreveport, La., Nov. 11, 1920; s. Ephem Henry and Rose (Pinsker) D.; student U. Tex., Austin, 1938-41; M.D., Southwestern Med. Coll., 1944; m. Vera Nell Erwin, July 29, 1944; children—Rachael Vicki, Margery Davis Miller, Barbara Davis Sibley, Diann Davis Hogan. Intern Parkland Hosp., Dallas, 1947; resident VA Hosp., Dallas, 1947-50, Baylor and Parkland hosps., Dallas, 1950-52; practice medicine specializing in thoracic and cardiovascular surgery, 1952—; attending staff Drs. Hosp.; sr. attending Parkland Meml. Hosp.; hon. staff Children's Hosp.; pres. Swiss Ave Med. Bldg., Inc., 1965-70; chmn. med. care adv. com. Tex. Dept. Human Resources, 1974-78; mem. Legis.'s Med. Profl. Liability Study Commn., 1975-77. Mem. Dallas County Sch. Bd., 1968-80, v.p., 1977-80. Served with U.S. Army, USAF, 1945-47. Diplomate Am. Bd. Surgery, Am. Bd. Thoracic Surgery. Fellow ACS, Am. Coll. Chest Physicians; mem. Am. (mem. residency review com. thoracic surgery 1972-78), Tex. (speaker ho. dels. 1978—, alt. del. to AMA) med. assns., Dallas County Med. Soc., Southwestern Surg. Congress, Am. Assn. Thoracic Surgery, So. Thoracic Surg. Assn. (pres. 1968), Soc. Thoracic Surgeons. Reform Jewish. Clubs: Lakewood Country, Dallas. Contbr. articles in field to med. jours. Home: #4 Nonesuch Rd Dallas TX 75214 Office: Northlake Doctors Bldg 10405 E Northwest Hwy Suite 208 Dallas TX 75238

DAVIS, MONTE VINCENT, scientist; b. Cove, Oreg., Apr. 29, 1923; s. Ruben Francis and Pomona Virginia (Stackland) D.; B.A., Linfield Coll., 1949; M.A., Oreg. State U., 1951, Ph.D., 1956; m. Nancy Elaine Adler, May 5, 1973; children—Sheri Lou, Teri Lynn. Sr. scientist Gen. Elec. Co., Richland, Wash., 1951-57; group leader, project engr. Atomics Internat., Canoga Park, Calif., 1957-61; prof. U. Ariz., Tucson, 1961-73; dir. Neely Nuclear Research Center, prof. nuclear engring. Ga. Inst. Tech., Atlanta, 1973—; pres. MND, Inc. Served with USAF, 1943-46. Recipient numerous grants from industry and govt. Fellow Am. Nuclear Soc.; mem. Am. Physics Soc., Internat. Solar Energy Soc., Soc. Nuclear Medicine, Sigma Xi. Club: Druid Hills Golf. Contbr. articles profl. jours. Home: 1207 Reeder Circle NE Atlanta GA 30306 Office: 900 Atlantic Dr Atlanta GA 30332

DAVIS, MONTIE GRANT, physicist, educator; b. Nashville, Aug. 15, 1936; s. Harold Odell and Mildred May (King) D.; B.A., Vanderbilt U., 1958; M.S., U. Tenn., 1966, Ph.D., 1968; m. Janice Elaine Sandlin, May 26, 1962; children—Montie Grant, Monica Leigh. Radiol. physicist Tenn. Dept. Pub. Health, Nashville, 1960-63; research project dir. ARO Inc., Tullahoma, Tenn., 1963-66, 67-69, cons., 1970—; pvt. cons., Nashville, 1969-71; coordinator phys. scis. U. Tenn., Nashville, 1971-75, asst. vice chancellor, 1975-77, asso. dean arts and scis., 1977-79; prof. physics U. Tenn., Tullahoma, 1979—. Scoutmaster, troop com. mem., asst. scoutmaster Middle Tenn. council Boy Scouts Am. Bd. dirs. YMCA, Hendersonville, 1969-70. Mem. Am. Phys. Soc., Tenn. Acad. Sci., Sigma Xi. Methodist. Club: Indian Lake Swim and Tennis. Contbr. articles to profl. jours. Research on nitric oxide molecule. Home: 107 Hillcrest Dr Hendersonville TN 37075 Office: Univ Tenn Space Inst Tullahoma TN 37388

DAVIS, NEIL OWEN, newspaper exec., educator; b. Hartford, Ala., Aug. 15, 1914; s. Charles Francis and Katherine Anderson (West) D.; B.S., Auburn U., 1935; m. Henrietta Worsley, Nov. 5, 1938; children—Katherine Davis Savage, Henrietta Lee Davis Blackman, Neil Owen. Reporter, Dothan (Ala.) Jour., 1935; editor N. Ga. Jour., Rossville, 1936; editor Auburn (Ala.) Bull., 1937-75, editor, pub., 1937-75, editor emeritus, 1975—; prof. journalism Auburn U., 1976—; pres. Bull. Pub. Co., Inc., 1939-75; sec. Auburn Broadcasting Co., Inc., 1947-75. Bd. dirs. United Fund, 1958, 70-74; sec. Lee County Democratic Com., 1952-68, mem. Ala. Dem. Exec. Com. 3d Dist., 1948-56; mem. bd. Christian edn. Presbyterian Ch. in U.S., 1959-68, mem. ad interim com. to write New Confession of Faith, 1968-75, ruling elder 1st Presbyn. Ch., Auburn, Ala., moderator John Knox Presbytery, 1979; trustee Agnes Scott Coll., Decatur, Ga.; participant U.S. Presdl. Adv. Commn. on Rural Poverty, 1966-67; mem. So. Regional Council, 1968—; participant So. Regional Edn. Bd. coms., 1958-64; chmn com. to study Auburn Pub. Schs., 1976; mem. Ala. Ethics Commn.; mem. adv. council humanities Auburn U. Served from 2d lt. to maj. USAAF, 1942-45. Recipient Pub. Service award Jaycees, 1941; numerous editorial awards Ala. Press Assn., 1938-75; Herrick Editorial award Nat. Editorial Assn., 1954, 59, 62; Nieman Found. fellow Harvard U., 1941-42. Mem. Auburn C. of C. (dir. 1955-56, 1967-68), Ala. Press Assn. (pres. 1947), Sigma Delta Chi, Omicron Delta Kappa, Lambda Chi Alpha. Author: (with others) Newsmen's Holiday, 1942; contbr. article to Nation Mag., 1947. Home: 241 Cary Dr Auburn AL 36830 Office: 8094 Haley Center Auburn U Auburn AL 36830

DAVIS, NORMAN EMANUEL, maintenance contract co. exec.; b. Waycross, Ga., Apr. 6, 1941; s. Verdell and Joanna Davis; B.S., Tuskegee Inst., 1966, postgrad. 1966-67; postgrad. U. Ga., 1976-77; m. Minnie Ole James Nov. 25, 1961; children—Norman Emanuel, Anthony Keith, Corey Verda. Planner for City of Tuskegee (Ala.), 1969-78; pres. Dial-A-Maid, Inc., 1972—. City program planner Child Day Care Program, 1972-78; pres. bd., planner Macon County Adult Activity Center Program, 1974-76; program planner Sr. Citizens Program, 1969-70; mem. Macon County Medicare and Medicaid Adv. Bd., 1969-76, Macon County Mental Health Bd., Macon County Retardation and Rehab. Exec. Bd., 1970-77. Served with USN, 1961-63. Recipient Jaycees Scotsman award, 1974; Outstanding Achievement award Pro-Plan Internat., 1973. Mem. Am. Soc. Planning Ofcls., Internat. Guild for Resource Devel., Macon County Monumental and Hist. Soc., Am. Legion, Tuskegee Jaycees, Omega Psi Phi. Democrat. Baptist. Clubs: Elks, Electrolex, Shriners, Masons (32 deg.). Home: PO Box 286 Tuskegee Institute AL 36088

DAVIS, OLGA STEPHANIE SAMPLES, playwright, educator; b. San Antonio, Mar. 13, 1949; d. Eugene and Browning McKinney Samples; B.A. in Fine Arts-Theatre, U. Tex., Austin, 1973; M.A. in Higher Edn., U. Tex., San Antonio, 1976; m. Clinton Davis, Mar. 13, 1974; Instr., St. Mary's U., San Antonio, 1973-74, 78; co-dir. student activities St. Philip's Coll., San Antonio, 1979, instr. dept. speech and drama, theatre dir., 1973—. Bd. dirs. San Antonio Little Theatre, 1978—, San Antonio chpt. Big Bros. and Sisters of Am., 1977—; mem. Fine Arts Commn., San Antonio, 1977-79; mem. Arts Council San Antonio. Nat. Endowment for Humanities grantee, 1976. Mem. Dramatists Guild N.Y.C., Speech Arts Assn. San Antonio, Nat. Black Theatre Alliance, S.W. Craft Center, Delta Sigma Theta. Methodist. Office: Dept Speech and Drama St Philip's Coll 2111 Nevada St San Antonio TX 78203

DAVIS, OLIVIA ANNE CARR (MRS. TOM LUCIAN DAVIS), author; b. Leeds, Eng., Dec. 4, 1922; d. Henry Marvell and Olive Frances Kate (Rumble) Carr; ed. Camden Sch. for Girls, London, Eng., pvt. tutors; m. Tom Lucian Davis, Oct. 13, 1943; children—Sebastian, Miranda, Penelope. Came to U.S., 1951, naturalized, 1956. Sec., Mil. Intelligence, War Office, London and Oxford, Eng., 1941-44. Recipient Emily Clark Balch award Va. Quar. Rev., 1969. Mem. Authors Guild, Audubon Soc., Smithsonian Assos., Nat. Trust for Historic Preservation. Author: The Last of the Greeks, 1968; The Steps of the Sun, 1972; The Scent of Apples, 1973. Contbr. short stories to lit. quars. and anthologies U.S. and abroad. Home: 6828 Floyd Ave Springfield VA 22150 Office: care Curtis Brown Ltd 575 Madison Ave New York City NY 10022

DAVIS, PALMER MCKIEVER, JR., seismograph co. exec.; b. Conway, S.C., July 12, 1936; s. Palmer McKiever and Adell (Foxworth) D.; student U. Clemson, 1954-56; m. Shelby Jean Shelley, July 23, 1955; children—Palmer, Elizabeth, Steve, Melissa, Christopher, Donna Jean. With Horry Telephone Co-op, Conway, S.C., 1956-65, plant mgr., 1965-66; carrier engr. Superior Cable Corp., Hickory, N.C., 1966-68, sr. field engr. Superior Continental Corp., Hickory, 1968-69, supr. customer service Continental Telephone Electronics Corp., Euless, Tex., 1970, transmission engr. Continental Trading Corp., Miami, Fla., 1970-71, sales engr., 1971-74, gen. sales mgr., 1974; mgr. ind. telephone industry sales, seiscor div. Seismograph Service Corp., Tulsa, 1975-76, nat. sales mgr. telephone products, 1976-79, asst. v.p. sales, 1979—. Mem. Ind. Telephone Pioneer Assn., Aircraft Owners and Pilots Assn. Democrat. Methodist. Home: 7311 E 58th St Tulsa OK 74145 Office: Seismograph Service Corp PO Box 1590 Tulsa OK 74102

DAVIS, PATRICK REESE, mfg. co. exec.; b. Anson, Tex., Nov. 19, 1935; s. James and Mattie (Roach) D.; B.S. in Mktg., Abilene Christian U., 1957, B.S. in Gen. Bus., 1957; m. Norma Jean Kidwell, Dec. 3, 1956; children—Debra Jean, Michael Reese, Cary Camille. Bus. mgr. Jim Ned Ind. Sch. Dist., Tuscola, Tex., 1958-61; pres. Ruane Homes, Inc., Abilene, 1961-65; dir. contracts/sales Teledyne Corp., Lewisburg, Tenn., 1967-75; pres. Omega Prodn., Inc., machine shop and electronic assembly, Cedar Park, Tex., 1975—; dir. 1st Nat. Bank Cedar Park. Mem. Cedar Park City Council, 1976-77. Mem. Ch. of Christ (deacon 1960-79). Home: 300 Cardinal Ln Cedar Park TX 78613 Office: 381 Hwy 1431 Cedar Park TX 78613

DAVIS, PAUL BEAMON, JR., ins. co. exec.; b. Portsmouth, Va., Oct. 27, 1948; s. Paul Beamon and Ruth (Burbage) D.; B.S. in Indsl. Mgmt., Fin. and Econs., U. Richmond, 1971. Rep., Equitable Life Assurance Soc. U.S., 1971—; mgr. life dept. SIR-CO Ins. Agy., Richmond, Va., 1977-79; owner, pres. Davis and Assos., Richmond, 1980—. Mem. Tuckahoe Vol. Rescue Squad, Inc., 1974—, bd. dirs., 1978—, chmn. ins. com., 1976—. Served with arty. U.S. Army, 1972-73. Registered health underwriter; equity qualified agt.; cert. emergency med. technician; cert. CPR. Mem. Richmond Assn. Life Underwriters, Va. Assn. Life Underwriters, Nat. Assn. Life Underwriters, Richmond Assn. Health Underwriters (pres. 1980—), Va. Assn. Health Underwriters, Nat. Assn. Health Underwriters, Richmond Beekeepers Assn. (pres. 1980), Southampton Greys Musket Team, North-South Skirmish Assn. Episcopalian. Home: 6415 Kensington Ave Richmond VA 23226 Office: 6415 Kensington Ave Richmond VA 23226

DAVIS, PRESTON CALDWELL, internist; b. Beckley, W.Va., Sept. 17, 1915; s. Robert Keith and Sue Irene (Caldwell) D.; A.B., B.S., W.Va. U., 1949; M.D., Med. Coll. Va., 1951; children—Elizabeth Ann, Rebecca, Susan Caldwell. Intern, Charleston (W.Va.) Gen. Hosp., 1952; resident in internal medicine Charleston Gen. and Beckley Meml. hosps., 1959-62; pvt. practice specializing in internal medicine, Beckley, 1962—; physician Raleigh and Fayette County Health Depts.; commr. health Beckley Police Dept.; cons. W.Va. Lung Assn.; organizer dir. med. residency tng. program Beckley Appalachian Hosp., 1968-72. Diplomate Am. Bd. Internal Medicine. Fellow A.C.P.; mem. AMA, W.Va., Raleigh County (past pres.) med. socs., W.Va. Thoracic Soc. (past pres.), Am. Soc. Internal Medicine. Episcopalian. Club: Elks. Home: 501 Maxwell Hill Rd Beckley WV 25801 Office: PO Box 50 Beckley WV 25801

DAVIS, RICHARD MCKEATING, chem. co. exec.; b. Dallas, Nov. 9, 1944; s. Raymond Ashley and Iva Lee (Selby) D.; student Pan Am. U., 1969-72; d. Laura Meredith, Aug. 19, 1966; 1 son, Cody Duane. Individual practice acctg., McAllen, Tex., 1969-75; asst. to pres. Tide Products, Inc., Edinburg, Tex., 1975—, plan adminstr. employee profit sharing trust. Bd. dirs., exec. com., adminstrv. com. chmn. ARC, Hidalgo County, 1979—. Mem. Nat. Soc. Public Accts., Valley Accts. Assn. (1st pres. 1973-75). Methodist. Clubs: Rotary (chmn. found. com. 1979-80), Pan Am Flying (dir. 1979—). Home: 118 Hibiscus St McAllen TX 78501 Office: 800 N Closner St Edinburg TX 78501

DAVIS, RICHARD RICHARDSON, univ. adminstr.; b. Kennedy, Ala., Dec. 7, 1923; s. Oron V. and Ethel M. (Richardson) D.; B.S., Auburn U., 1947; M.S., Purdue U., 1949, Ph.D., 1950; m. Ruth A. Booras, Dec. 18, 1945; children—Richard R., J. David, Thomas L. Asst. prof. to prof., asso. chmn. dept. agronomy Ohio Agrl. Research and Devel. Center, also Ohio State U., 1950-78, asst. dir. Center, 1969-78; asst. to v.p. div. agr., forestry and vet. medicine Miss. State U., 1978—. Served with USNR, 1943-46. Cert. agronomist Am. Registry of Cert. Profls. in Agronomy, Crops and Soils. Fellow Am. Soc. Agronomy (pres. 1969-73), AAAS; mem. Crop Sci. Soc. Am. (pres. 1974), Internat. Turfgrass Soc. (pres. 1969-73), Sigma Xi, Phi Kappa Phi, Alpha Zeta, Gamma Sigma Delta. Baptist. Tech. editor in crops Agronomy Jour., 1965-67; contbr. articles to jours., bulls., books and mags. Office: PO Box 5386 Mississippi State MS 39762

DAVIS, ROBERT CARTER, JR., physician; b. Chgo., Sept. 21, 1939; s. Robert Carter and Hilda Blount (Brown) D.; M.D., Emory U., 1964; m. Hulda Eileen Markillie, Mar. 14, 1964; children—Edward Campbell, Kathleen Morgan, Robert Carter. Intern and resident The N.Y. Hosp., Cornell U., 1964-68; attending gastroenterologist Crawford W. Long Meml. Hosp. of Emory U., Atlanta, 1972—; clin. asst. prof. medicine and digestive diseases Emory U. Sch. Medicine, Altanta, 1973—. Served with M.C., U.S. Army, 1968-71. Fellow Am. Coll. Gastroenterology; mem. A.C.P., Am., Ga. (pres.) socs. gastrointestinal endoscopy, Med. Assn. Atlanta (trustee 1972-77), Emory Med. Alumni Assn. (pres.), Alpha Omega Alpha. Republican. Roman Catholic. Clubs: Capital City, German, Clin. Soc. Contbr. articles to med. jours. Home: 3218 Nancy Creek Rd Atlanta GA 30327 Office: 25 Prescott St NE Atlanta GA 30308

DAVIS, ROBERT NORMAN, hosp. adminstr.; b. Plainfield, N.J., July 30, 1938; s. Norman DuBois and Geraldine Elizabeth (Sliker) D.; B.S. civil engring., Pa. State U., 1960; M.S. in Mgmt., Rensselaer Poly. Inst., 1970; m. Barbara Ann House, Aug. 26, 1961; children—Keith Robert, Kathryn Beth, Karl Thomas. Dir. plant ops. Am. Hosp. Assn., Chgo., 1964-68; dir. mgmt. engring. Hosp. Assn. of N.Y., Albany, 1968-72; asso. exec. dir. United Hosp., Portchester, N.Y., 1973-75; regional mgr. Arthur Young & Co., N.Y.C., 1975, Medicus Systems Corp., Nashville, 1976-79; pres. Resource Devel. Assos., Hendersonville, Tenn., 1979—; asso. adminstr. Vanderbilt Univ. Hosp., Nashville, 1979—. Bd. dirs., treas. Middle Tenn. Youth Soccer Inc., 1979—. Served with M.S.C., USAF, 1960-63. Mem. Hosp. Mgmt. Systems Soc. (dir. 1972-75), Am. Coll. Hosp. Adminstrs. Baptist. Contbr. articles to profl. jours. Home: 243 Hidden Lake Rd Hendersonville TN 37075 Office: Vanderbilt U Hosp Adminstrn AA 1214 Nashville TN 37232

DAVIS, ROBERT RICHARD, clergyman; b. Cleve., Dec. 1, 1933; s. George Milton and Edith Manilla (Randall) D.; A.B., Taylor U., Upland, Ind., 1958; B.D., United Theol. Sem., Dayton, Ohio, 1961, M.Div., 1977; m. Betty E. Godsey, Sept. 7, 1958; children—Deborah Annette, Rebekah Louise. Ordained to ministry Presbyterian Ch., 1964; pastor Williamsburg Meth. Ch., 1959-61, Alto Meth. Ch., Kokomo, Ind., 1961-64; asso. pastor 1st Presbyn. Ch., Miami, Fla., 1964-66; pastor Hazelwood (N.C.) Presbyn. Ch., 1966-71; adminstrv. v.p. Westminster Christian Sch., Miami, 1971-73; sr. pastor Old Cutler Presbyn. Ch., Miami, 1973—; moderator Asheville (N.C.) Presbytery, 1970. Recipient Nat. Freedom Found. award, 1969, 74, 75, 77. Mem. Platform Speakers Am., Nat. Freedom Found. Republican. Author: Portraits From the Pages, 1977. Contbr. articles to mags. Office: 14401 Old Cutler Rd Miami FL 33158

DAVIS, RONALD KENNETH, gen., vascular surgeon; b. Waynesboro, Va., Sept. 7, 1935; s. Bruce B. and Essie (Newman) D.; student W.Va. U., 1956-57, Va. Poly. Inst., 1957-58, U. Richmond, 1959-63; M.D., Med. Coll. Va., 1963; m. Eleanor S. Davis, 1978; children—Rahn Timothy, Matthew Kent, John Robert, Jonathan Paul. Intern, Med. Coll. Va., Richmond, 1963-64, resident, 1964-69, asst. clin. prof. surgery, 1970—; practice medicine specializing in gen. and vascular surgery, Richmond, 1970—; asst. chief dept. surgery St. Mary's Hosp., 1974-77, chief, 1978-80. Served with AUS, 1966-68. Diplomate Am. Bd. Surgery. Fellow A.C.S., Internat. Coll. Surgeons; mem. Alpha Omega Alpha, Sigma Zeta, Alpha Sigma Chi. Contbr. articles to profl. jours. Home: 3020 Mount Hill Dr Midlothian VA 23113 Office: 5855 Bremo Rd Richmond VA 23226

DAVIS, RONALD LEWIS, mech. engr.; b. Jackson, Tenn., Dec. 18, 1940; s. Bruce and Elizabeth Lucille (Marshall) D.; B.S., Lambuth Coll., 1962; B.S.M.E., Naval Postgrad. Sch., Monterey, Calif., 1967; M.S., U. Tenn., Knoxville, 1974; m. Carolyn June Ward, Apr. 15, 1962; children—Malea Ward, Marianna Lynn. Furnace engr. Owens Corning Fiberglas Corp., Jackson, 1971-73; dir. engring. and safety Jackson-Madison County Gen. Hosp., 1973—; lectr., cons. in field. Served to lt. comdr. U.S. Navy, 1962-71. Decorated Naval Commendation medal. Registered profl. engr., Tenn. Mem. Nat. Soc. Profl. Engrs., U. Tenn. Nat. Alumni Assn. (pres. Madison County chpt. 1978—), ASME, Am. Chem. Soc., Am. Soc. Hosp. Engring., Nat. Fire Prevention Assn. Methodist. Clubs: Lions, Masons. Home: 46 Rutherford Ave Jackson TN 38301 Office: Jackson-Madison County Gen Hosp 708 W Forest Ave Jackson TN 38301

DAVIS, SUSAN SCOTT, civic worker; b. Kearney, Nebr.; d. Thomas Jefferson and Mary Estelle (Grant) Scott; A.B., U. Nebr., 1918, Nebr. State Tchrs. Coll., 1919; M.A., Columbia U., 1935; m. Gaylord Davis, July 4, 1925; 1 dau., Susanne Davis Newberry. Dir. tng. sch., dept. kindergarten Nebr. State Tchrs. Coll., 1914-16; mem. casts plays in N.Y. theatres, 1921-23. Mem. Council Juvenile Planning Group, Asheville and Buncombe County, N.C., 1956-59; sec. exec. com. Buncombe County Com. White House Conf. Children and Youth, 1960; dir. Children's Welfare League, Asheville, N.C., 1949, 52, 60, pres., 1955-57; bd. dirs. Family and Children's Service Agy., Asheville, N.C., 1948-55, Asheville Community Concerts Assn., 1973—; mem. Family and Children's Services Buncombe County Planning Council, 1967—. Bd. dirs. United Social Services, 1955-60, Candelight Concerts, Inc., 1960-63; Civic Arts, Inc., 1960-68, Asheville Community Concerts Assn., 1972—; bd. dirs. Asheville Day Nursery, 1960-62, 68—, v.p., 1963-64, pres., 1964-66. Mem. Buncombe County Republican Women's Club, 1963—; mem. Women's Nat. Rep. Club, N.Y.C., 1963—, mem. nat. council, 1963—, mem. membership com., 1969—; mem. exec. com. permanent conf. Buncombe County Planning Council, 1965-70. Mem. English-Speaking Union, Ikebana Internat., Pi Beta Phi. Republican. Christian Scientist. Clubs: Biltmore Forest Country, The Duetters (founder 1947). Home: T-4 Crowfields Dr Asheville NC 28803

DAVIS, T. ALBERT, psychiatrist; b. Madison, Fla., July 26, 1940; s. James Bishop and Florida (Langford) D.; B.S. in Chemistry with honors, U. Fla., 1962; M.D., Emory U., 1967; m. Carolyn Garnie Thomas, Feb. 5, 1978; 1 dau. by previous marriage, Brooke. Intern, St. Vincent's Hosp., N.Y.C., 1967-68; resident in psychiatry Emory U., Atlanta, 1968-71; practice medicine specializing in psychiatry, Valdosta, Ga., 1978—; dir. alcohol treatment program Peachtree-Parkwood Hosp., Atlanta, 1973-76; dir. psychiat. services, asso. chmn. dept. Ga. Bapt. Hosp., Atlanta, 1976—; asso. clin. prof. Emory U. Sch. Medicine, 1973—; mem. psychiat. panel Med. Care Found.; med. dir. Center for Personal and Family Growth, S. Ga. Health Assos., Valdosta; owner Georgian Collectors, Antiques, Ltd. Served to maj. USAF, 1971-73. Communicable Disease Center research grantee to Limbe, Haiti, 1965-66. Mem. AMA, So. Med. Assn., Ga. Psychiat. Assn., Ga. Mental Health Assn. (chmn. personnel com.). Democrat. Episcopalian. Home: 300 Georgia Ave Valdosta GA 31601 Office: 1706 Patterson St Valdosta GA 31601

DAVIS, TERRY HUNTER, JR., lawyer; b. Charlottesville, Va., Mar. 19, 1931; s. Terry Hunter and Mattie (Parsons) D.; B.A., Va. Mil. Inst., 1953; LL.B., U. Va., 1958; m. Mary Jane Davis, Sept. 3, 1960; 1 son, Terry Hunter III. Admitted to Va. bar, 1958; atty. law firm Thacher, Proffitt, Prizer, Crawley & Wood, N.Y.C., 1958-60; law clk. to Hon. Walter E. Hoffman, Chief U.S. Dist. Judge, Norfolk, Va., 1960-61; partner law firm Taylor, Gustin, Harris, Fears & Davis, Norfolk, Va., 1961—. Republican candidate for Va. House of Dels., 1967, 1969. Served with AUS, 1953-55. Named to State Electoral Bd. City Norfolk, 1970-73, chmn., 1972. Mem. Norfolk-Portsmouth, Va. State, Am. bar assns., Am. Judicature Soc., S.A.R., Norfolk C. of C. Clubs: Norfolk Yacht, Virginia, Kiwanis. Contbg. author to: The Virginia Lawyer's Basic Practice Handbook, 2d edn., 1964. Home: 7451 North Shore Rd Norfolk VA 23505 Office: 5735 Poplar Hall Dr Bldg Norfolk VA 23502

DAVIS, TERRY LYNN, respiratory therapist; b. Atlanta, Dec. 6, 1952; s. James Earl and Betty June (Futral) D.; B.S., Ga. State U., 1975; m. Denise Rene Conley, Aug. 5, 1977. Supr. evening shift respiratory therapy dept. Cobb Gen. Hosp., Austell, Ga., 1975-76, asst. dir., 1976-77, dir. respiratory therapy dept., 1977—. Bd. advs. Ga. Lung Assn., 1979—. Recipient Ga. Lung Assn. award for presentation of a community program for people with chronic obstructive pulmonary disease, 1978; registered respiratory therapist, 1976. Mem. Met. Atlanta Respiratory Therapy Mgrs. Assn. (pres. 1977), Am. Assn. Respiratory Therapy, Ga. Soc. Respiratory Therapy (dir. 1980). Contbr. animal lab. data recorded on cassette tape, 1975.

DAVIS, THOMAS PARKS, univ. adminstr.; b. Mobile, Oct. 30, 1942; s. John Carlin and Eileen (Parks) D.; B.S.C., Spring Hill Coll., Mobile, Ala., 1964; M.A., U. Ala., 1970. Successively tchr., counselor, dir. activities, vice prin. McGill Inst., Mobile, 1964-73; dir. public relations McGill-Toolen High Sch., Mobile, 1973-78; dir. S.W. Ala. Regional Office, U. Ala., Mobile, 1978—; cons. in field, 1972—. Chmn. Mobile United Fund for Mobile Diocese Catholic Dept. Edn., 1969-72, 74-75; bd. dirs. Mobile/Malaga Sociedad, 1976—, U. Ala. Alumni Assn., 1974—. Mem. Nat. Assn. Coll. Admissions Counselors, Nat. Assn. Secondary Sch. Prins., Am. Personnel and Guidance Assn., Am. Sch. Counselor Assn., Ala. Personnel and Guidance Assn. (dist. sec. 1978—), Ala. Assn. Collegiate Registrars, Ala. High Sch. Athletic Assn., Phi Delta Kappa. Democrat. Clubs: Met., Internat. Trade. Home: 1963 Calmes St Mobile AL 36606 Office: 3729 Cottage Hill Rd Mobile AL 36609

DAVIS, VERONICE H., program analyst; b. Preston, Ga., May 3, 1949; d. Ross Dean and Mae Thelma (Dew) Hawkins; B.S., Ft. Valley (Ga.) State Coll., 1971; postgrad. Jacksonville (Ala.) State U. Mgmt. analyst Anniston (Ala.) Army Depot, 1971-73, program analyst, 1974—; mgmt. analyst Aviation Systems Command, St. Louis, 1973-74; mem. Incentive Awards Com., 1977, Telecommunications Rev. Bd., 1977; upward mobility counselor, 1977; combined fed. campaign coordinator, 1977-78. Recipient Letter of Appreciation (3), Anniston Army Depot, 1976-79, Quality Increase award, 1976, Outstanding Performance appraisal, 1976. Mem. Am. Def. Preparedness Assn. Baptist. Address: Route 7 Box 458-J Oxford AL 36203

DAVIS, WALTER PERRY, landman; b. Oklahoma City, Aug. 19, 1932; s. Walter Randolph and Palma Ione (Baulch) C.; B.S. in Agr., Tex. A & M U., 1955; m. Edna Mae Hunt, June 24, 1955; children—Dracinda, Thomas Jefferson, Walter, Joseph. Farm planner Soil Conservation Service, Denten and Merkel, Tex., 1955-57; feed dealer, elevator mgr. Kimble Milling Co., Merkel, 1957-61; plant operator helper El Paso Natural Gas Products Co., Odessa, Tex., 1961-63; elevator mgr., Dalhat, Tex., 1963-65; loan officer Fed. Land Bank, Plainview, Clint and New Boston, Tex., 1963-72; ind. petroleum landsman and lease purchasing, New Boston, 1972—. Mem. Am. Assn. Petroleum Landmen, E. Tex. Assn. of Landmen. Democrat. Southern Baptist. Clubs: Mason, Scottish Rite. Home: PO Box 336 New Boston TX 75570

DAVIS, WENDELL, mktg. cons.; b. Detroit, June 18, 1933; s. Christian Doerr and Alberta Luella (Scramlin) D.; student U. Fla., 1952, St. Petersburg (Fla.) Jr. Coll., 1978, Lake Sumter (Fla.) Community Coll., 1979; m. Josephine Elizabeth Campbell, Aug. 24, 1960; children—James Wendell, Debra Allee, Anita Jo Yount, Douglas Jerry Yount, Jo Elizabeth. Operating exec. Terminal Van Lines, St. Petersburg, 1952-59; mgr. Acme Moving & Storage, Key West, Fla., 1960-61, Key West Moving & Storage, 1961-62; gen. mgr. Thomas Moving & Storage, Sanford, Fla., 1962-64; owner Triangle Moving and Storage, Eustis, Fla., 1963-78; v.p. mktg. Terminal Van Lines, St. Petersburg, 1977-78; owner Raintree Books, Eustis, 1963—; individual practice as mktg. cons., 1979—. Precinct committeeman Lake County (Fla.) Republican Exec. Com., 1980—; del. Fla. Dem. Conv., 1976-77; trustee Eustis City Library, 1976—. Recipient Public Service cert. Harry-Anna Crippled Childrens Hosp., 1975; Golden Wings Advt. award St. Petersburg, 1979. Mem. Sales and Mktg. Execs. Club, Fla. Movers and Warehousemans Assn., Nat. Inst. Cert. Moving Cons., Movers and Warehousemens Assn. Am., Am. Booksellers Assn., Fla. Direct Mail Mktg. Assn., Early Ford V8 Club Am. Club: Elks. Editor: Florida Early V8 Times, 1972-73; Terminal Van Lines Times, 1978-79. Home: 517 Orange Ave Eustis FL 32726 Office: 432 N Eustis St Eustis FL 32726

DAVIS, WINBORN ELTON, med. facilities cons.; b. Heflin, La., Aug. 26, 1917; s. John Henry and Joanna (McKinney) D.; student La. Poly. Inst., 1935-37; B.A., La. State U., 1940; M.S.W., Tulane U., 1948; m. Edith Claire Causey, Aug. 5, 1940; 1 son, David Michael. Family service supr. U.S. Dept. Agr., Thibodaux, La., 1941-42; social worker VA, Shreveport, La., 1946-47; chief div. mental health La. Dept. of Hosps., Baton Rouge, 1949-51, dir. tng. and research, 1958-61, asst. dir., 1962-63, dir., 1964; asso. prof. mental health Southeastern La. Coll., Hammond, 1952-55; dir. La. Evaluation Center for Exceptional Children, New Orleans, 1956-57; adminstr. Student Health Service, asso. prof. mgmt. La. State U., 1965-70, adminstr. dept. psychiatry Sch. Medicine, 1970-71, asst. dean for adminstrn. Sch. Medicine, 1971-73; lectr. dept. psychiatry Tulane U., 1950-79, adj. asso. prof. Sch. Pub. Health, 1970-79. Mgmt. cons. health facilities, 1957—; exec. sec. La. State Bd. Examiners for Nursing Home Adminstrs., 1979—; spl. cons. U.S. Surgeon Gen., 1964-68; mem. La. Bd. Examiners Cert. Social Workers, 1974-78. Mem. adv. council La. Commn. on Aging, 1963-66; mem. adv. com. Baton Rouge Family Ct., 1957-61; sec. Gov.'s Com. on Mentally Retarded, 1959-60; sec. State Adv. Com. on Edn. Handicapped, 1950-55. Chmn. adv. council Protestant Childrens Home, 1964-65; dir. Baton Rouge Guidance Center, 1952-54. Trustee La. State Employees Retirement System, 1962-66, chmn., 1964-66; bd. dirs. La. Dept. Hosps. Credit Union, 1961-64. Served to lt. (j.g.) USNR, 1942-45. Mem. Nat. Assn. Social Workers (charter mem., mem. cabinet div. of profl. standards), La. Conf. on Social Welfare (pres. 1961-63), La. Psychiat. Assn., La. Health Care Assn., La. Hosp. Assn. Democrat. Baptist. Author: (with James A. Knight) Manual for Comprehensive Mental Health Clinics, 1964. Contbr. articles to profl. jours. Home: 5057 Whitehaven St Baton Rouge LA 70808

DAVISON, FREDERICK CORBET, univ. pres.; b. Atlanta, Sept. 23, 1929; s. Frederick Collins and Gladys (Carsley) D.; D.V.M., U. Ga., 1952; Ph.D., Iowa State U., 1963; L.H.D. (hon.), Presbyn. Coll., 1977; LL.D. (hon.), Mercer U., 1978; m. Dianne Castle, Sept. 3, 1952; children—Frederick Corbet, William C., Anne. Pvt. practice vet. medicine, Marietta, Ga., 1952-58; research asso. Iowa State U., Ames, 1958-59, asst. prof., 1960-63, asso. inst. for atomic research, 1960; asst. dir. sci. activities Am. Vet. Med. Assn., Chgo., 1963-64; dean sch. vet. medicine U. Ga., Athens, 1964-66; vice chancellor Univ. System Ga., Atlanta, 1966-67; pres. U. Ga. at Athens, 1967—; dir. Fed. Savs. & Loan Assn. Mem. rural devel. com., pres., 5th region Boy Scouts Am.; mem. Council of Synod of Ga. Trustee Presbyn. Coll., Clinton, S.C. Recipient Disting. Achievement award Iowa State U., 1978. Mem. Am. (council on biol. and therapeutic agts.), Ga. vet. med. assns., Inst. Lab. Animal Research of Nat. Acad. Scis., Nat. Com. on Pharmacy and Vet. Medicine, Sigma Xi, Phi Kappa Phi, Sigma Alpha Epsilon, Omega Tau Sigma, Alpha Zeta, Phi Zeta, Gamma Sigma Delta. Contbr. articles to profl. jours. Home: Office: U Ga Athens GA 30601

DAVISSON, NELSON MARC, dentist, army officer; b. Winchester, Ind., Sept. 16, 1938; s. Ray Marcus and Garnet Rebecca (Addington) D.; A.B., DePauw U., 1960; D.D.S., Ind. U., 1964; m. Patricia Ann Crossen, Aug. 24, 1963; children—George William Tennis, Lani Catherine. Commd. capt. U.S. Army, 1964, advanced through grades to col., 1980; practice dentistry, Ft. Gordon, Ga., 1964-68, Viet-Nam, 1968-69, Fort Sam Houston, Tex., 1969-70; asst. chief crown and bridge service Walter Reed Hosp., Washington, 1971-72; chief crown and bridge service dental detachment, Ft. Leavenworth, Kans., 1972-77, 87th Med. Detachment, APO N.Y., 1977—. Decorated Bronze Star, Army Commendation medal. Diplomate Am. Bd. Prosthodontics. Fellow Am. Coll. Prosthodontists; mem. ADA, VFW, Psi Omega. Mem. Ch. of Jesus Christ of Latter-day Saints (elder 1971—). Home: 1020 De Leon Dr 303 Dunedin FL 33528 Office: 87th Med Detachment (DS) APO NY 09105

DAWES, CHARLES EDWARD, mfg. co. exec.; b. Peoria, Okla., Feb. 7, 1923; s. Charles Gates and Lottie (Nonkesis) D.; A.A., Joplin (Mo.) Jr. Coll., 1950; B.S., U. Ark., 1953; m. Lorraine Mercer, Apr. 16, 1948; children—Charla Rene, Kevin Lawrence. Mgr. mfg. Vickers, Inc., Joplin, 1953-57; sales engr. Sebastian Diesel Co., Joplin, 1957-59; gen. mgr. Duplex Mfg. Co., Ft. Smith, Ark., 1959-77; v.p. Flanders Industries, Inc., 1977—. Chief, Ottawa Indians of Okla.; sr. counselor Inter-tribal Songchiefs Okla. Bd. dirs. Ark.-Okla. Regional Edn. and Promotion Assn.; trustee St. Edward Mercy Med. Center; bd. dirs., pres. Abilities Unlimited, Inc.; bd. dirs., mem. exec. com. Ft. Smith United Fund; mem. adv. bd. Seneca Indian Sch. Served with USAAF, 1943-46. Mem. Am. Soc. Tool and Mech. Engrs., Ft. Smith C. of C. (dir.), Personnel Assn. N.W. Ark., Western Ark. Purchasing Assn., Mfg. Execs. Assn. (pres. Ft. Smith), Nat. Congress Am. Indians, Okla. Inter-Tribal Council. Republican. Presbyterian. Mason. Home: 2010 Wolfe Ln Fort Smith AR 72901 Office: 1901 Wheeler Fort Smith AR 72901

DAWKINS, MATHER EMORY, cons. sanitary engr.; b. Andalusia, Ala., Dec. 11, 1921; s. Frank C. and Minnie P. (Chesser) D.; B.C.E., U. Fla., 1947, M.S., 1950; m. Elizabeth Burkett, Apr. 21, 1944; children—Carolyn Dawkins Stemland, Richard Emory. Asst. campus engr., plant supr. U. Fla., Gainesville, 1947-50; sanitary engr. USAF Hdqrs., SAC, Omaha, 1951-52, Hdqrs., Tech. Tng. Air Force, Gulfport, Miss., 1952; sanitary engr. Fla. State Bd. Health, Jacksonville, 1953-55, Reynolds, Smith and Hills Co., Jacksonville, 1955-62; pres., chief engr. Dawkins & Assos., Inc., Orlando, Fla., 1962—; cons. engr., Orlando, 1965—. Mem. bd. visitors Coll. Engring., U. Central Fla., 1977—; bd. dirs. U. Central Fla. Found., Inc., 1978—. Served from 2d lt. to capt. U.S. Army, 1943-46; ETO. Decorated Bronze Star, Silver Star, Purple Heart; recipient Environ. Protection award U. Central Fla., 1975; diplomate Am. Acad. Environ. Engrs. Mem. ASCE, Am. Public Works Assn., Am. Water Works Assn., Water Pollution Control Fedn. (Arthur Sidney Bedell award 1960), Fla. Pollution Control Assn., Fla. Water and Pollution Control Operators Assn. (hon.), Fla. Engring. Soc. (Named Engr. of the Year 1979), Profl. Engrs. in Pvt. Practice, Fla. Inst. Cons. Engrs., Nat. Soc. Profl. Engrs., Inst. for Solid Wastes, Inst. for Mcpl. Engrs., Fla. Audubon Soc., Orlando Area C. of C., Indsl. Devel. Council of Mid-Fla., Tau Beta Pi. Methodist. Clubs: Citrus (Orlando); Gator Boosters. Author: Florida Sewerage Guide, 1954; editorial bd. Overflow Mag., 1965—. Home: 3513 Marwood Dr Orlando FL 32806 Office: PO Drawer 14024 Orlando FL 32857

DAWSON, EARL BLISS, educator; b. Perry, Fla., Feb. 1, 1930; s. Bliss and Linnie (Callaham) D.; B.A., U. Kans., 1955; student Bowman Gray Sch. Medicine, 1955-57; M.A., U. Mo., 1960; Ph.D., Tex. A. & M. U., 1964; m. Winnie Ruth Isbell, Apr. 10, 1951; children—Barbara Gail, Patricia Ann, Robert Earl, Diana Lynn. Research instr. dept. obstetrics and gynecology U. Tex. Med. br., Galveston, 1963-67, research asst. prof., 1967-70, research asso. prof., 1970—; cons. Interdeptl. com. on Nutrition for Nat. Defense, 1965-68; cons. Nat. Nutrition Survey, 1968-69. Served with USNR, 1951-52. Nutrition Research fellow, 1960-61; NSF scholar, 1961-62; Nat. Insts. Health Research fellow, 1962-63. Mem. Am. Chem. Soc., Tex., N.Y. acad. scis., AAAS, Am. Inst. Physicists, Am. Inst. Nutrition, Am. Soc. Clin. Nutrition, Soc. Environmental Geochemistry and Health, Sigma Xi, Phi Rho Sigma. Baptist. Mason. Club: Mic-O-Say (Kansas City, Mo.). Contbr. numerous articles to profl. jours. Home: 15 Chimney Corners LaMarque TX 77568 Office: Dept Obstetrics and Gynecology U Tex Med Br Galveston TX 77550

DAWSON, GARY LYNN, mktg. co. exec.; b. Washington, Dec. 22, 1948; s. Harry Samuel and Gladys (Avey) D.; student Abilene Christian U., 1966-68, Southwestern State Coll., 1969-70; B.L.S., U. Okla., 1979; m. Carol Ann Heidegger, Oct. 13, 1967; children—Kimberlie Yvonne, Christopher Erin. Photographer, Altus (Okla.) Times Democrat, 1969-72; with GC Services Corp., Houston, 1972—, asst. v.p. market devel., 1975-78, nat. mktg. mgr. tng., 1978—. Bd. dirs. Birnhamwood Homeowners Assn. Served with USAF, 1968-72. Recipient photog. awards Dept. Def., USAF, Okla. Press Assn. Mem. Hosp. Fin. Mgmt. Soc. Republican. Mem. Ch. of Christ. Home: 30 N Deerfoot Circle The Woodlands TX 77380 Office: 6330 Gulfton St Houston TX 77081

DAWSON, JAMES IRA, coll. dean; b. Goshen, Ala., Jan. 14, 1925; s. Jesse Lee and Charlotte (Vann) D.; B.S., Ala. A&M U., 1953; M.Ed., Tuskegee Inst., 1963; Ph.D., Pa. State U., 1969; A.S. in Mortuary Sci., Jefferson State Coll., 1972; m. Gloria C. Peterson, July 24, 1942; 1 dau., Delarise Dawson Hamilton. Vet. coordinator Butler County Bd. Edn., Greenville, Ala., 1949-51; tchr. sci. public schs., Grenshaw County, Ala., 1953-55; tchr. vocat. agr. Elba (Ala.) City Schs., 1955-67; chmn. agr-bus. edn. Ala. A&M U., Normal, 1969—, asso. dean for extension, 1972—, prof. stats. and research, 1969—. Pres. bd. dirs. Huntsville Madison County Community Action Agy.; treas. NAACP, Huntsville; mem. Huntsville Human Rights Council; proposal reader Huntsville Manpower Council; bd. dirs. So. Rural Devel. Council, Ala. Black Caucus on Aging. Served with USAAF, 1943-46. Mem. Ala. Edn. Assn., NEA, Nat. Community Devel. Soc., Ala. Funeral Dirs. Assn., Nat. Funeral Dirs. Assn., Ala. Embalmers Assn., Nat. Embalmers Assn., Ala. Land-Grant Council, Phi Beta Sigma. Democrat. Methodist. Club: Masons. Author: Business Leadership in Agricultural Industry, 1968; Making Vocational Agriculture Relevant for the Disadvantaged, 1971; Helping Lay Leaders Improve Their Community, 1972. Home: 836 Tannahill Dr Huntsville AL 35802 Office: PO Box 53 Normal AL 35762

DAWSON, PAUL DOW, ednl. adminstr.; b. Cin., June 1, 1943; s. Glenn and Cleo R. D.; B.S., U. Cin., 1965; M.Ed., Miami U., 1968; Ed.D., U. Cin., 1976; m. Joy Elaine Goertemiller, Aug. 21, 1965; children—Benjamin Dow, Tiffany Dawn, Andrew Glenn. Tchr., Princeton City Schs., Cin., 1965-70; grad. teaching asst. U. Cin., 1970-71; asst. headmaster/prin. Seven Hills Schs., Cin., 1971-76; headmaster Sumner Acad., Nashville, 1976—. Pres., Cancer Soc. Sumner County, 1977-78, ednl. dir., 1978-80. Benedict Bot. Sci. grantee and honor fellow U. Cin., 1963-64. Mem. Nat. Assn. Elem. Sch. Prins., Am. Assn. Biology Tchrs., Nat. Assn. Ind. Schs., Am. Assn. Internat. Edn., Nat. Assn. Secondary Sch. Prins., Assn. Individually Guided Edn., Nat. Sci. Tchrs. Assn., Ohio Forestry Assn., Phi Delta Kappa, Kappa Delta Pi. Presbyterian. Contbr. articles to profl. jours. Home: 591 Indian Lake Rd Hendersonville TN 37075 Office: PO Box 944 Nichols Ln Gallatin TN 37066

DAWSON, RAYMOND LESLIE, pulp and paper co. exec.; b. St. Louis, Apr. 2, 1942; s. Escal Durward and Hazel Marie (Cooper) D.; A.A., Neosho County Community Coll., 1962; B.S. in Chemistry, U. Tulsa, 1965; postgrad. Inst. Paper Chemistry, 1965-66; M.S. in Chemistry, N.E. La. U., 1969; m. Janet Lee O'Connor, Dec. 27, 1964; children—Brian Edward, Wendy Kay, Matt Douglas. Research chemist Olinkraft Inc., West Monroe, La., 1966-69, sr. research chemist, 1969-73, mgr. pulp and paper devel., 1973—. Bd. dirs. Little Theatre Monroe, 1977; asst. pack master Cub Scouts, Ouachita council Boy Scouts Am., 1974-76, council camporee chmn., 1976, 77. Mem. TAPPI (dir. SW sect. 1972—, chmn. 1976), Am. Chem. Soc. (chmn. Ouachita Valley sect. 1974). Democrat. Methodist. Contbr. articles to profl. jours. in field; patentee improved couch roll. Home: 2804 Lamy Circle Monroe LA 71201 Office: PO Box 488 West Monroe LA 71291

DAWSON, ROBERT EDWARD, ophthalmologist; b. Rocky Mountain, N.C., Feb. 23, 1918; s. William and Daisy (Wright) D.; B.S., Clark Coll., 1939; M.D., Meharry Med. Coll., 1943; m. Julia Belle Davis, Mar. 10, 1950; children—Dianne Elizabeth, Janice Elaine, Robert Edward, Melanie Loraine. Intern Homer G. Phillips Hosp., St. Louis, 1943-44, resident, 1944-46; preceptor Duke Hosp., 1946-50, clin. instr. ophthalmology, 1968-70; practice medicine, specializing in ophthalmology, Durham, N.C., 1943-55, 57—; mem. attending staff ophthalmology Lincoln Hosp., Durham, 1946-55; cons. ophthalmology N.C. Central U. Health Service, Durham, 1950-64; chief ophthalmology and otolaryngology Lincoln Hosp., Durham, 1959-76; mem. attending staff ophthalmology Watts Hosp., Durham, 1966-76; mem. attending staff ophthalmology Durham County Gen. Hosp., v.p. med. staff, 1976-78; med. dir. Lincoln Hosp., Durham, 1968-70; lectr. ophthalmology Lincoln Hosp. Sch. Nursing, 1948-56; clin. asso. Duke U., 1969-75, clin. asst. prof. ophthalmology, 1975-80; mem. N.C. Adv. Com. on Med. Assistance, 1972-74; mem. adv. bd. N.C. State Commn. for Blind, 1965-75; mem. Gov.'s Adv. Com. Med. Assistance; regional surg. dir. Eye Bank Assn. Am., Inc., 1968-79. Mem. Durham Council Human Relations, 1967-69; mem. Pres. Com. on Employment of Handicapped, 1971-79. Bd. dirs. Durham County Tb Assn., 1950-54, Better Health Found., 1960-66, Durham Community House, 1966-68, Lincoln Community Health Center, Nat. Soc. Prevention Blindness, Am. Cancer Soc., Durham United Fund, Durham County Mental Health Center, 1976-79, Found. for Better Health of Durham County Gen. Hosp., 1975-79; trustee Durham Acad., 1969-72, Meharry Med. Coll., 1971—, N.C. Central U.; mem. bd. mgmt. Meharry Med. Coll. Alumni Assn.; chmn. bd. dirs. Lincoln Pvt. Diagnostic Clinic; bd. visitors Clark Coll., Atlanta. Served as maj. M.C., USAF, 1955-57. Diplomate Am. Bd. Ophthalmology, Pan Am. Med. Assn. Fellow A.C.S., Acad. Ophthalmology and Otolaryngology; mem. Am. Assn. Ophthalmology, Soc. Eye Surgeons, A.M.A., Nat. Med. Assn. (trustee 1971—, pres. 1979-80), Old North State Med. Soc. (pres. 1966-67), Durham Acad. Medicine (pres. 1967-68), N.A.A.C.P., Durham Bus. and Profl. Chain, C. of C., Meharry Nat. Alumni Assn. (past pres.), Alpha Omega Alpha, Alpha Phi Alpha (past pres.), Sigma Pi Phi (pres.), Chi Delta Mu. Democrat. Mem. A.M.E. Ch. (stewards bd. 1968-75). Mason (32 deg., Shriner). Club: Toastmasters (pres. 1969-70). Home: 817 Lawson St Durham NC 27701 Office: 512 Simmons St Durham NC 27701

DAWSON, ROYCE EDMUND, surgeon; b. Owensboro, Ky., Aug. 26, 1925; s. John M. and Nellie E. (Easton) D.; B.S., Western Ky. U., 1948; M.D., Vanderbilt U., 1952; m. Lucy Henderson Buford, July 10, 1954; children—John L., Lucy Henderson, Mary Gillespie. Intern, Vanderbilt Univ. Hosp., Nashville, 1952-53, resident, 1953-58; practice medicine specializing in surgery, Owensboro, 1958—; mem. staffs Owensboro-Daviess County Hosp., Our Lady of Mercy Hosp.; mem. Ky. State Bd. Licensure, 1972—; dir. Owensboro Fed. Savs. & Loan Assn., Green River Rural Electric. Bd. dirs. Green River Comprehensive Health Planning Council, 1969—, Tri-State Health Planning Council, 1971—; mem. Green River Health Planning Com., 1969-78, Tri-State Health Planning Com., 1971-78. Served with AUS, 1942-46. Diplomate Am. Bd. Surgery, Am. Bd. Thoracic Surgery. Mem. A.C.S., So. Thoracic Surg. Assn., Daviess County Med. Soc. (mem. bd. censors 1970-73, pres. 1979-80), Ky. Surg. Soc., H. William Scott Jr. Soc., A.M.A., Southeastern Surg. Assn. Presbyterian (mem. bd. deacons 1970-73). Contbr. articles to profl. jours. Home: 1607 Fawn Dr Owensboro KY 42301 Office: 2707 Breckenridge St Owensboro KY 42301

DAWSON, SAMUEL COOPER, JR., motel co. exec.; b. Alexandria, Va., Sept. 21, 1909; s. Samuel Cooper and Edna French (Horner) D.; grad. Episcopal High Sch., Alexandria, 1928; B.A. in Commerce, U. Va., 1932; m. Frances Margaret Boatwright, Mar. 24, 1945; children—Samuel Cooper III, Marion Boatwright. Tchr. sci. St. Christopher's Sch., Richmond, Va., 1932-36; underwriter Md. Casualty Co., Balt., 1936-39; mgr. Penn-Daw Motor Hotel, Alexandria, 1939-73; pres. Penn-Daw Hotels Corp., Alexandria, 1960-73, Penn-Daw Shopping Center, Alexandria, 1958-72; owner, operator Camp Alleghany for Girls, Lewisburg, W.Va.; bus. mgr. Episcopal High Sch. Past pres. Va. Travel Council. Served with USNR, 1942-46; capt. Res.; group comdr. 47 res. units Washington area. Recipient Hall of Fame award Hospitality magazine, 1961; Distinguished Service award Am. Motor Hotel Assn., 1964. Mem. Am. Automobile Assn. (past chmn. No. Va. adv. bd.), Va. Hotel Assn. (past pres.), Va. Motel Assn. (past pres.), Alexandria Jr. C. of C. (past pres.; Outstanding Young Man award 1942), Washington (past pres.), Nat. (dir.) restaurant assns., Am. Motor Hotel Assn. (past pres., chmn. legislative affairs com.), Washington Civil War Round Table, S.A.R. (past pres. George Washington chpt.). Episcopalian. Club: Army Navy Country (Arlington, Va.). Home: 206 N Quaker Lane Alexandria VA 22304 Office: PO Box 56 Alexandria VA 22313

DAWSON, THOMAS JOHNSON, metall. engr.; b. Bells, Tex., Jan. 10, 1914; s. Vol Montgomery and Julia (Smith) D.; student So. Meth. U., 1931-34, Miss. State Coll., 1942-45, N.C. State Coll., 1955, U. Mich., 1956, U. Miss., 1956-59; B.S., U. So. Miss., 1959; m. Audie Hawkins, Dec. 21, 1939; children—Julia Marie (Mrs. A. D. Bishop), Aron Vol, Ruby Kay (Mrs. Jessie Lawrence Meyers), Nancy Jo (Mrs. James Richard Hock), Sue Ellen (Mrs. Richard Douglas Jennings). Quality control supt. Ingalls Shipbldg. Corp., Pascagoula, Miss., 1942-61, chief metallurgist, 1950-61, tchr. tng. program, 1955; supervising engr. hull unit Naval Ships Engring. Center, Washington, 1961-74; cons. metall. engr. U.S. Naval Facilities Engring. Comd., Alexandria, Va., 1974—. Tchr. program engring. sci. and mgmt. war tng. Miss. State Coll., 1944, 45; lectr. U. Miss., 1959, U. Wis.-Madison, 1962, U. R.I., 1975, U.S. Naval Acad., 1976-77, Naval Post Grad. Sch., 1977; moderator hull constrn. Submarine Circularity and Repair Conf., Norfolk, Va., 1971; mem. Gov. Miss. Adv. Com. on Atomic Energy, 1956-61, Com. on Spl. Report to White House Conf. on Edn., 1958-60; adviser Dept. Transp. Tng. Bridge Engrs.; cons. in field. Bd. dirs., chmn. organizing United Cerebral Palsy of Jackson County (Miss.), 1955-61, chmn. com. program services, 1958—, v.p. state assn., 1956-61, regional mem. nat. program services com., 1958-59; treas. Jackson County League for Better Govt., 1959. Recipient Silver certificate Am. Soc. for Metals-ASTM, 1969. Registered profl. engr., Miss., Calif.; certified marine gas chemist. Mem. ASME (com. devel. sect. on pressure vessels for humane occupancy), Am. Soc. Metals (hon. life), Am. Welding Soc. (A.G. Bissel award 1972, Dist. Meritorious award 1973, chmn. com. preparation sect. 54 Welding Handbook 1956-60, vice chmn. com. on underwater welding), Soc. Nondestructive Testing, Marine Gas Chemists Assn., Great Books Found. (moderator 1955-58). Methodist. Elk. Contbr. articles to profl. publs. Patentee in field. Home: 6632 Moly Dr Falls Church VA 22046 Office: 200 Stovall St Alexandria VA 22332

DAY, A. DEWITT, landscape architect; b. Alco, La., July 15, 1936; s. Onnie Laska and Armittie Lavancie (Starks) D.; B.S. in Landscape Architecture, La. State U., 1958-63; m. Nancy Jane Miller, June 21, 1958; children—Byrom Dewitt, Christopher Daniel. With U.S. Corps of Engrs., Mobile, Ala., 1963-65, U.S. Forest Service, Jackson, Miss., 1965-67; pvt. practice landscape architecture A. Dewitt Day & Asso., Jackson, 1967—; guest lectr. La. State U., Baton Rouge, 1964-67, Miss. State U., 1967—; lectr. in field; notary pub., Jackson, 1976—. Served with USAF, 1955-58. Mem. Am. Arbitration Assn., Am. Soc. Landscape Architects (chpt. pres. 1977), AIA, Landscape Architects Registration Bd. (pres. 1976-77), Bass Angler Soc. Am., Ducks Unltd., Miss. Art Assn. Baptist. Contbr. articles to profl jours. Home: 3515 Runnymede Rd Jackson MS 39211 Office: 5466 Office Park Dr Jackson MS 39206

DAY, HOWARD MALCOLM, clergyman, counselor, educator; b. Mulberry, Fla., Dec. 14, 1914; s. James Samuel and Olive Beatrice (Wilhelm) D.; A.B., John B. Stetson U., 1936; M.Div., So. Bapt. Theol. Sem., 1940; M.Ed., U. Fla., 1962; m. Elizabeth Marie Ransom, June 5, 1939; 1 son, James Frederick. Ordained to ministry So. Bapt. Ch., 1936; commd. lt. (j.g.) U.S. Navy, 1940, advanced through grades to comdr., 1945, served dist. chaplain 15th Naval Dist., wing chaplain First Marine Air Wing, base chaplain Camp Pendleton, div. chaplain 2d Marine Div., ret., 1961; instr. St. John's River Community Coll., Palatka, Fla., 1962—, pres. faculty senate, 1977-79; instr., counselor, pastor Paran Bapt. Ch., Grandin, Fla., 1964—. Pres., Civic Round Table, 1973-74; bd. dirs. Teen Town, 1968-70; pres. Putnam Community Concert Assn., 1965-66, bd. dirs., 1966-74; pres. Putnam County Ambassador's Club, 1963. Mem. Fla. Assn. Community Colls. (pres. St. John's River Community Coll. chpt.), Ret. Officers Assn., Am. Assn. Ret. Persons, Pi Kappa Phi, Theta Alpha Phi. Republican. Club: Rotary (v.p., pres. Palatka, 1971-73). Home: 120 Crestwood Ave Palatka FL 32077 Office: St John's Ave Palatka FL 32077

DAY, MARY WINIFRED GARVEY (MRS. GEORGE EARL DAY), Realtor; b. Chgo., May 5, 1932; d. William and Mary Patricia (Kennedy) Garvey; student U. Tex., 1971, Richland Coll., 1972-73; m. George Earl Day, Jan. 15, 1955; children—Patricia Ann, Shawn Michael, Kathleen Mary. Asso. editor Bell Telephone Labs., White Sands Missile Range, N.M., 1961-67; city editor Richardson (Tex.) Daily News, 1968; dir. pub. relations Drs. Hosp. Found., Dallas, 1969-72; owner Mary Day/Media Design, Richardson, 1972-75; realtor Henry S. Miller Co., Dallas, 1975—. Recipient Key to City Corpus Christi (Tex.), 1971. Mem. Nat. Fedn. Press Women (dir. 1970-71), Women in Communications (dir. 1973-74), Am., Tex. socs. hosp. pub. relations dirs., Profl. Photographers Am., Tex. Press Women (dir. 1966-73), Tex. Pub. Relations Assn., Dallas Hosp. Council (pub. relations com. 1969-72), Nat., Tex. assns. realtors, Dallas Bd. Realtors, Women's Council Realtors. Roman Catholic (bd. dirs. ch. 1974—). Clubs: Canyon Creek Country (Richardson); Press (Dallas). Home: 1614 Baltimore St Richardson TX 75081 Office: 215 White Rock St N Dallas TX 75238

DAY, NERINE CAROLYN PARLIAMENT, fin. co. exec.; b. Watertown, S.D., Sept. 12, 1942; d. Clinton H. and Helen (Bender) Parliament; student S.D. State U., 1960-62; m. C. Michael Day, Nov. 26, 1977; 1 son, Ronald Allan. Sec., Fed. Civil Service, VA Hosp. and Social Security Adminstrn., Alexandria, La., 1963-66; legal sec. firm Gist, Methvin and Trimble, Alexandria, 1969-72; investment broker A.G. Edwards & Sons, Alexandria, 1972-78, br. mgr., 1978—; adj. investments instr. La. Coll., Pineville, 1976-80. Mem. Alexandria Women's Commn., 1978-80; pres. adv. bd. Alexandria Regional Mental Health Center, 1979-80; mem. adv. bd. YWCA, Alexandria, 1977—; pres. Cantral La. Mental Health Assn., 1975-77. Named Outstanding Young Woman in La., La. Jaycees, 1976. Mem. Nat. Assn. Female Execs., Alexandria-Pineville C. of C. (dir. 1979-80, treas. 1980), Bus. and Profl. Women (v.p. 1975-76). Republican. Episcopalian. Home: 348 Windermere Blvd Alexandria LA 71301 Office: PO Box 7328 Alexandria LA 71306

DAY, RAE GORE, hosp. adminstr.; b. Riga, Latvia, Oct. 4, 1921; d. Solomon Boris and Maria (Gos) Gore; came to U.S., 1933, naturalized, 1939; R.N., Kings County Hosp., 1942; postgrad. Johns Hopkins U., 1951-53; B.S. in Nursing, U. Washington, 1963; postgrad. The Citadel, 1969; M.A., U. Iowa, 1971; postgrad. U. Tenn., Nashville, 1979. Staff nurse to asst. chief VA Dept. Medicine, various locations, 1947-67; dir. div. clin. nursing Med. Univ. Hosp., Charleston, S.C., 1967-69; dir. nursing Mental Health Inst., Mt. Pleasant, Iowa, 1969-72; dir. dept. nursing Iowa Meth. Med. Center, Des Moines, 1972-74; asst. adminstr. Parkview Hosp., dir. Parthenon Pavilion, Nashville, 1974—; cons., surveyor extended care facilities dept. social service State of Iowa, 1971-73. Served with Nurse Corps, U.S. Army, 1943-46. Mem. Am. Soc. Nursing Service Adminstrs. of Am. Hosp. Assn., Nashville Mental Health Assn., Middle Tenn. Health Service Adminstrn. (ad hoc com. for mental health planning). Club: Am. Legion. Office: 2401 Murphy Ave Nashville TN 37203

DAY, RICHARD EUGENE, mining co. exec.; b. Mound City, Kans., Jan. 6, 1933; s. Lambert P. and Geneva (Johnson) D.; student Kans. U., 1951-52, postgrad., 1955-56; B.S., Kans. State U., 1955; J.D., Washburn U., 1965; m. Ruth Wells, Aug. 29, 1954; children—Diane, Linda. Indsl. waste chemist, Wichita, Kans., 1956-59; ops. supr. water pollution control dept. City of Wichita, Kans., 1959-63; admitted to Kans. bar, 1965, N.Mex. bar, 1966; house counsel, asst. sec. United Nuclear Corp., Santa Fe and Albuquerque, 1965-74; gen. counsel Pa. Glass Sand Corp. subs. ITT, Berkeley Springs, W.Va., 1974—, v.p., 1975—. Pres., Santa Fe Kearney PTA, 1966-67; pres. Santa Fe PTA Council, 1967-68; mem. Santa Fe Mayor's Council on Youth Affairs, 1968-69; bd. dirs. Mo. Mining Industry Council, 1974—. Mem. W.Va. Mfrs. Assn. (dir., exec. com.), Pa. Sand and Gravel Assn., Kans. Bar Assn., N.Mex. Bar Assn., Am. Bar Assn., Phi Alpha Delta, Acacia. Clubs: Woodmont Rod & Gun, Elk. Home: Route 4 Box 468 Berkeley Springs WV 25411 Office: PO Box 187 Berkeley Springs WV 25411

DAY, RICHARD ROBERT, rehab. counselor; b. Opelika, Ala., Jan. 2, 1944; s. Robert William and Bernice Ethyl (Hocutt) D.; B.S. in Econs., Auburn (Ala.) U., 1965, M.S. in Psychology, 1972; Ph.D. in Counselor Edn. (grad. asst. 1972-74), U. Va., 1974; m. Priscilla Ann Grist, Jan. 14, 1967; children—Lisa, Leslie, Lori. Mktg. analyst Shell Oil Co., 1966-70; dir. spl. projects Mountain Empire Community Coll., Big Stone Gap, Va., 1975-76; asst. prof. counseling and guidance Troy (Ala.) State U. 1976-78; asst. prof. human devel. counseling George Peabody Coll., Nashville, 1976-78; dir. research and staff devel. Ark. Enterprises for Blind, Little Rock, 1978—; pvt. counselor, cons. in field. Mem. Am. Personnel and Guidance Assn., Ark. Psychol. Assn., Assn. Workers for the Blind, Ark. Personnel and Guidance Assn., Phi Delta Kappa. Baptist. Club: Lions. Home: 50 Kingspark Rd Little Rock AR 72207 Office: 2811 Fair Park Blvd Little Rock AR 72214

DAY, ROBERT CLARK, JR., food service co. exec.; b. Montgomery, Ala., Dec. 29, 1948; s. Robert Clark and Jane Maysey (Matthews) D.; B.A., U. South, Sewanee, Tenn., 1971; postgrad. Oxford (Eng.) U., summer 1972; m. Elizabeth Slaton Thompson, June 2, 1973; children—Kathryn Slaton, Elizabeth Matthews, Robert Clark. Tchr. English, McGill-Toolen High Sch., Mobile, 1971-72; reporter Mobile Press Reporter, 1972-73; public info. dir. Spring Hill Coll., Mobile, 1973-75; public relations asst. Morrison Inc., Mobile, 1975—. Bd. dirs. S.W. Ala. chpt. Am. Lung Assn.; Bikeathon planning com. Mobile chpt. Am. Diabetes Assn.; trustee Wilmer Hall; mem. vestry, jr. warden, asst. youth dir. Christ Episcopal Ch., Mobile. Clubs: Mobile Press, Athelstan, Mystic Soc. (Mobile). Author weekly humor column Azalea City News, Mobile, 1979—. Home: 327 McDonald Ave Mobile AL 36604 Office: 4721 Morrison Dr Mobile AL 36625

DAY, WILLIAM RAY, aerospace mfg. co. exec.; b. Cumberland Gap, Tenn., May 30, 1940; s. Otis and Ruby Day; B.S., U. Tenn., 1963; m. Loretta K. Porter Dec. 31, 1965; 1 dau., Lisa Kay. Systems analyst Kraft Foods, Chgo., 1963-66, Univ. Computing Co., Dallas, 1969-73; sr. systems analyst Lykes Pasco Co., Dade City, Fla., 1973-74; data processing mgr. Vought Corp., Dallas, 1974—. Served to 1st lt. U.S. Army, 1966-68. Decorated Army Commendation medal. Baptist. Home: 2309 Chapel Hill Ln Arlington TX 76014 Office: Vought Corp PO Box 6114 Dallas TX 75222

DAYTON, BENJAMIN BONNEY, physicist, educator; b. Rochester, N.Y., Feb. 25, 1914; s. Howard Hay and Helen (Thrall) D.; B.S., Mass. Inst. Tech., 1937; M.S., U. Rochester, 1948; postgrad. Western Carolina U., 1973, 74, U. N.C. at Asheville, 1976; m. Irene Catherine Glossenger, Oct. 16, 1943; children—David B., Glenn C. Research supr. Distillation Products Industries, Rochester, 1940-53; dir. research, tech. dir. Consol. Vacuum Corp., Rochester, 1953-68; tech. dir. vacuum div. Bendix Corp., Rochester, 1968-69, chief scientist, sci. instruments and equipment div., 1969-71; cons., 1971-72; tchr. sci. Henderson County Pub. Schs., N.C., 1973-79; cons. H.J. Ross Assos., Miami, 1974-78; staff lectr. George Washington U., 1966, 68; mem. advisory panel Nat. Bur. Standards, 1965-71; chmn. advisory com. vacuum tech. Am. Nat. Standards Inst., 1964-71. Trustee Roberts Wesleyan Coll., N. Chili, N.Y., 1951-61. Mem. Am. Phys. Soc., Am. Sci. Affiliation, Am. Vacuum Soc. (pres., 1961, hon. life; dir., 1954-57, 59-62), Vacuum Soc. Japan (hon. life), N.C. Assn. Educators. U.S. editor Vacuum, 1959-72; edit. bd. Rev. Sci. Instruments, 1953-55. Editor: Glossary of Terms Used in Vacuum Technology, 1958. Contbr. articles to profl. jours. Home: 209 S Hillandale Dr East Flat Rock NC 28726

DEACON, SARAH MARIE, nurse; b. Galveston, Tex., Oct. 1, 1940; d. Michael Joseph and Grace Lucille (Oliver) Barrett; A.A.S., Galveston Coll., 1968; student U. Houston, 1979—; m. Edward T. Deacon; children—Thomas Walter, Todd Wayne, Stephen Edward. Office nurse, Galveston, Tex., 1962-71; staff nurse, supr. Alvin (Tex.) Community Hosp., 1972-74, asst. dir. nursing service, 1974-77, dir. nursing service, 1977-78; intensive care nurse USPHS Hosp., Nassau Bay, Tex., 1978—; mem. vocat. tech. adv. com. Alvin Community Coll. Mem. med. adv. bd. Brazoria County March of Dimes; instr. CPR, Brazoria County Heart Assn. Mem. Tex. Hosp. Nurses Assn., Tex. Nurses Assn. Roman Catholic. Home: 2316 Kingsway Dr League City TX 77573 Office: USPHS Hosp 2050 Space Park Dr Nassau Bay TX 77058

DEAKINS, DANIEL RULE, bldg. services exec.; b. Athens, Tenn., Jan. 23, 1950; s. Dan B and Delois Sue (Rule) D.; student Tenn. Tech. U., 1968-72; 1 dau., Lesli Suzanne. Chief exec. officer Collegiate Services, Inc., Tallahassee, 1972-77, Nashville, 1978—; exec. dir. So. Scholarship Found., Tallahassee, 1977; cons. bldg. mgmt. Active Capital City Tiger Bay Club; bd. dirs. March of Dimes. Mem. Bldg. Owners and Mgrs. Assn., Entrepreneurs Internat., Lowery-Nickerson Real Estate Investment Group, Better Bus. Bur. Methodist. Home: Route 2 Lewisburg Pike Franklin TN 37064 Office: One Plus Executive Center Nashville TN 37219

DEAKYNE, DEAN JAY, II, utility co. exec.; b. Upland, Pa., July 11, 1926; s. George Fallows and Edyth Bennett Deakyne; B.A., U. Pa., 1954; m. M. Jane Desmond, Dec. 26, 1945; children—Dean Jay II, Andrew Desmond. Mem. petroleum chem. research staff Sun Oil Co., Norwood, Pa., 1945-54; field sales engr. Celanese Corp., N.Y.C., 1954-60; indsl. sales mgr. Simoniz Co., Chgo., 1960-63; resident mgr., sales mgr. Alphaloy Corp., Chgo., 1964-72; pres. Utilities Service and Operating Corp., New Smyrna, Fla., 1972—. Served with USNR, 1944-46. Mem. Fla. Pollution Control Operators Assn., Nat. Water Improvements Assn. Episcopalian. Club: Smyrna Yacht, Masons. Home: 1 Esther Ct New Smyrna Beach FL 32069 Office: 202 Julia St New Smyrna Beach FL 32069

DEAL, FREDERICK GORDON SCOTT, dentist; b. San Antonio, Tex., Jan. 6, 1940; s. Harry Edward and Grace Margaret (Webster) D.; B.A., U. Calif. at Berkeley, 1963; D.D.S., U. Calif. at San Francisco, 1973 m. Angela Boynton, June 4, 1965;

children—Frederick Gordon Scott, Markham Nathan, Jamie Alston. Intern, USPHS, Galveston, Tex., 1973-74; pvt. practice dentistry, Clearwater, Fla., 1974—. Elder, Ch. of Jesus Christ of Latter Day Saints, 1976—. Served with USAF, 1963-68. Licensed dentist, Fla., Calif. Mem. Upper Pinellas, West Coast dental socs., Fla. Dental Assn., ADA, Brigham Young Acad. Dentistry, Zeta Psi.

DEALEY, JOSEPH MACDONALD, newspaper exec.; b. Dallas, July 18, 1919; s. Edward Musgrove and Clara (MacDonald) D.; A.B., U. Tex., 1941; m. Doris Carolyn Russell, Jan. 18, 1947; children—Joseph MacDonald, Russell Edward, Pamela Carolyn, Frances Patricia. Reporter, Dallas Morning News, 1942-50, asst. sec., 1950-55, dir., 1952—, sec., 1955-60, pres., 1960-80; chmn. bd., chief exec. officer A.N. Belo Corp., 1980—. Pres., county chpt. ARC, 1961-63; vice chmn., mem. bd. govs. Am. Nat. Red Cross; mem. exec. com. Community Council Greater Dallas, 1960—, pres., 1965-66; bd. dirs. Dallas Citizens Council, 1960—, pres., 1964-65; bd. dirs. Childrens' Med. Center, 1950—, pres., 1964-67; bd. dirs. Dallas Council Social Agys., 1958—; trustee Dallas Theater Center, Dallas Bar Found., Southwestern Med. Found.; bd. dirs. Dallas County United Way, 1961—, mem. exec. com., 1962—, v.p., 1963-65, pres., 1967, campaign chmn., 1966-67; bd. dirs. United Community Funds and Councils Am.; bd. dirs. State Fair Tex.; mem. U. Tex. Devel. Bd. and Chancellor's Council, chmn., 1967-68. Served to lt. USAAF, 1942-46. Mem. Dallas C. of C. (dir.), Am. (dir.), So. (dir., pres. 1969) newspaper pubs. assns., Tex. Daily Newspaper Assn. (mem. exec. com., pres. 1969), Press Club Dallas, Sigma Delta Chi, Phi Delta Theta. Clubs: Dallas Country, Koon Kreek, Las Colinas Country. Home: 4332 Arcady St Dallas TX 75205 Office: Dallas Morning News AH Belo Corp Communications Center Dallas TX 75222

DEAN, ANNE GWYNNE FREY, nurse; b. Piketon, Ohio, Sept. 9, 1942; d. Robert Fredrick and Anne Wynn (Crace) Frey; student Colo. Coll., 1960-61, Ohio U., 1970-72; A.D.N., San Antonio Coll., 1974; student U. Tex. Health Sci. Center, 1978—; m. Michael Fox Dean, Dec. 16, 1961 (div. June 1979); children—Heather Elizabeth, Michael Bruce, Lara Anne. Nurse intern in critical care nursing Bexar County Hosp., San Antonio, Tex., 1974, staff nurse surg. intensive care, 1974-75, charge nurse recovery room, 1975-77, operating room supr., 1978-79; dir. Outpatient Surgery Center, S.W. Tex. Meth. Hosp., San Antonio, 1979—. Art cons. dept. plastic surgery U. Tex. Health Sci. Center; Sunday Sch. tchr., 1970-72; chairperson Nursing Students of Tex. Conv., 1974; mem. admissions and standards com. San Antonio Coll., 1974. Winner 1st place painting and sculpture award, Pike County Fair, 1971. Mem. Tex. Assn. Post Anesthetic Nurses, Assn. Operating Room Nurses, Nat. League of Nursing, Jacques Costeau Soc., Nat. Space Inst., Nat. Geog. Soc., Smithson Soc. Episcopalian. Clubs: Nat. Order of Foresters. Home: 2102 Orange Blossom St San Antonio TX 78247 Office: 7700 Medical Dr San Antonio TX 78229

DEAN, BELPHRY JUNE, ednl. adminstr.; b. Hendrix, Okla., Dec. 31, 1946; s. Andrew Jackson and Marzee (Kemp) D.; B.S., Central State U., 1970; postgrad. U. Okla., 1978—; m. Sharon Ann McCullough, June 14, 1969; 1 son, Erron. Mgr., Coco Fed. Credit Union, Oklahoma City, 1970-72; asst. v.p. Med. Center State Bank, Oklahoma City, 1973-75; field rep. Gen. Electric Credit Corp., Oklahoma City, 1975-77; purchasing agt. Oklahoma City Schs., 1977—. Chmn. fin. com., bd. dirs. Merry Mahoney Health Center, Inc., 1973-75. Mem. Urban League of Oklahoma City, Nat. Assn. Purchasing Mgmt., Am. Bankers Assn., Am. Mgmt. Assn., Purchasing Mgmt. Assn. Oklahoma City, Alpha Phi Omega, Omega Psi Phi. Democrat. Baptist. Club: Kiwanis (pres. 1978-79). Home: 32 NE 64 St Oklahoma City OK 73105 Office: 900 N Kelin St Oklahoma City OK 73106

DEAN, BOB WESLEY, mech. engr.; b. Birmingham, Ala., Aug. 6, 1924; s. Robert Leon and Gertrude (Griffith) D.; B.Mech. Engring., Auburn U., 1945; M.S. in Engring., U. Ala., 1948; m. Martha Stone Grace, July 15, 1944; children—Robert Allbritton, Elizabeth Cary, Thomas Wesley, DeForest DeSha, David Bryant. Various positions, 1948-52; mfrs. rep. F. J. Evans Engring. Co., Atlanta, 1952-57; design engr. Robert & Co., Atlanta, 1957-62; with Mallory & Evans, Inc., Scottdale, Ga., 1962—, v.p., project engr., 1965—; asso. Mech. Engring., Inc., Scottdale, Ga., 1965-70. Mem. State Ga. Bd. Examiners Warm Air Heating Contractors, 1970—. Registered profl. engr., Ind., Pa., Calif., Miss., Ala., Ga., Fla., Tenn., S.C., N.C., Nebr., N.Y., Va., Ky., Del., Minn., Ark. Mem. Am. Soc. Heating, Refrigeration and Air Conditioning Engrs. (chpt. pres. 1963-64). Patentee in field. Home: 760 Old Ivy Rd NE Atlanta GA 30342 Office: 646 Kentucky St Scottdale GA 30079

DEAN, BRENDA JOYCE, chem. technician; b. Greenville, S.C., July 8, 1951; d. Walter Woodrow and Mary Jane (Rollins) Dean; student Furman U., 1969-70; A.S. in Chem. Technology, Greenville (S.C.) Tech. Coll., 1972-74. Chem. technician, carcinogen project, indsl. hygiene group, Los Alamos (N.Mex.) Sci. Lab., 1974-77. Mem. Am. Chem. Soc. (technician affiliate). Methodist. Contbr. articles to chem. jours. Home: 396 P Greentree Apts Taylors SC 29687

DEAN, CAROLYN SUE, advt. agy. exec.; b. Oklahoma City, May 15, 1949; d. John Davison And Mary Eugenia (Lindly) Cross; B.S. in Journalism, Okla. State U., 1971. Audio visual dir. Asso. Advt. Agy., Wichita, Kans., 1972-75; broadcast prodn. mgr. Lane & Leslie Advt. Co., Hutchinson, Kans., 1975-76; advt. coordinator Advt. Concepts, Wichita, 1976-77; sales prodn. supr. Sta. WKY Radio, Oklahoma City, 1977-78; advt. dir. Sweet 'n Legal USA, Oklahoma City, 1978-79; mgr. Tupper Advt. Inc., Oklahoma City, 1979—; free lance writer and fashion model. Mem. public relations bd. Girls Scouts U.S.A., 1978—. Recipient Best TV Writer of the Year Addy award, 1973-74. Mem. Nat. Press Woemn, Wichita Advt. Club. Republican. Home: 11614 Surrey Hills Blvd Yukon OK 73099 Office: 6051 N Brookline St Suite 124B Oklahoma City OK 73112

DEAN, DAVID ALLEN, lawyer, govt. counsel; b. Chattanooga, Jan. 14, 1948; s. William Berry and Elizabeth (Connor) D.; B.B.A., So. Meth. U., 1969; J.D., U. Tex., 1973; m. Kathleen Humphreys, June 26, 1971; 1 dau., Hillary Diane. Admitted to Tex. bar, 1973; asst. dir. Tex. Office Comprehensive Health Planning, Austin, 1973; adminstrv. asst. to Gov. Tex., Austin, 1974, legal counsel to Gov. Briscoe, 1975-78. Mgr. campaign, legal counsel Briscoe Campaign Com., 1974-78; gen. counsel to Gov. Clemento, 1979—. Trustee, Dean Meml. Learning Center, Dallas; bd. dirs. Girlstown U.S.A., Whiteface, Tex.; mem. fin. com. 1st United Methodist Ch.; co-chmn. Highland Lakes chpt. Ducks Unltd.; mem. Bergstrom-Austin Community Council, Laguna Gloria Art Found. Mem. State Bar Tex., Dallas, Travis County (Tex.) bar assns., U. Tex. Ex-Students Assn. (life), Am. Quarter Horse Assn., Sigma Alpha Epsilon. Democrat. Clubs: Headliners, Bachelors, Idlewild, Terpsichorean, Dervish, Calyx. Home: 3902 Greenmountain Ln Austin TX 78759 Office: Gov's Office Capitol Bldg Austin TX 78711

DEAN, DAVID PARKS, oil co. exec.; b. Detroit, Tex., July 23, 1898; s. William Alexander and Minnie (Lee) D.; student Austin Coll., 1915-16, U. Tulsa, 1916-17; B.A., Okla. U., 1920; m. Ruby Macy Boren, Mar. 12, 1953. Geologist, Waite Phillips Co., later Barnsdall Oil Co., 1921-30; partner Dean Bros., 1931-48; pres. Great Expectations Corp., Fort Worth, 1948—, Uncertain Oil Corp., 1976—. Trustee Reformed Theol. Sem., Jackson, Miss., 1968-77. Served as pvt. U.S. Army, World War I, to capt. AUS, World War II. Recipient 50 yr. award Am. Assn. Petroleum Geologists, 1969, Austin Coll., Sherman, Tex., 1966. Presbyterian. Author: Smackover Rose, 1967, adaptation for play, 1971; (poetry) My Little Dog's Tail, 1972. Home: 2125 Park Pl Ave Fort Worth TX 76110 Office: Oil and Gas Bldg Fort Worth TX 76102

DEAN, DENIS ALLEN, lawyer; b. Detroit, Jan. 29, 1942; s. Allen C. and Mildred Ella (Stevens) D.; B.A., U. Miami, 1963, J.D., 1966; m. Sherrilynn Jean Huerkamp, Mar. 16, 1973; children—Denis Allen, Daron Andrew. Admitted to Fla. bar, 1966—; research asst. State Atty.'s Office of Dade County, 1964-66; asst. state atty. 11th Jud. Circuit Fla., 1966-70; asso. Eugene P. Spellman, Miami, Fla., 1970-79, Dean & Hartman, P.A., 1980—. Mem. Fla. Bar Grievance Com., 1972-75; instr. criminal law and procedure Miami Dade Jr. Coll., 1969-71; mem. bd. arbitration N.Y. Stock Exchange, 1973—. Mem. Am., Fed., Dade County bar assns., Assn. Trial Lawyers of Am., Acad. Fla. Trial Lawyers, Nat. Assn. Criminal Def. Attys. (dir.). Home: 12680 Hickory Rd North Miami FL 33181 Office: New World Tower Penthouse 100 N Biscayne Blvd Miami FL 33132

DEAN, HARRY BROOKS, psychoanalyst; b. Macon, Ga., Aug. 8, 1919; s. Samuel Alexander and Lula Lee (Lowe) D.; A.B., Mercer U., 1941; M.D., U. Ga., 1944; student Phila. Psychoanalytic Inst., 1952-57; m. Mary Lucy Hattrich, June 14, 1942; children—David L., Christopher C., Carol K. Intern, Macon Hosp., 1944-45, resident in internal medicine, 1945-46; pvt. practice gen. medicine, Unadilla, Ga., 1947-50; clin. dir. Norristown (Pa.) State Hosps., 1955-57; instr. psychiatry Jefferson Med. Coll., Phila., 1955-57; asso. prof. psychiatry U. Miami (Fla.) Sch. Medicine, 1957-58, clin. asso. prof., 1958-79; pvt. practice medicine specializing in psychoanalysis, Coral Gables, Fla., 1958-79. Served to capt. M.C., U.S. Army, 1946-48. Diplomate Am. Bd. Psychiatry and Neurology. Mem. Dade County, Fla. med. assns., S. Fla. Psychiat. Soc., Am. Psychiat. Assn., Fla. Psychoanalytic Soc. (pres. 1972-74), Am., Internat. psychoanalytic assns., Alpha Omega Alpha. Home: 2001 Lee Dr Valrico FL 33594

DEAN, JAMES DUDLEY, power engr.; b. Lake Charles, La., Nov. 29, 1946; s. Elmo Clyde and Helen Jennie (Bordelon) D.; B.E.E., La. State U., 1973; m. Kathleen Ann Warneke, June 16, 1967; children—Michelle Elizabeth, James Michael. Design engr. E.I. duPont Co., Martinsville, Va., 1973, energy conservation coordinator, 1974, power engr., 1974, power services supr., 1975-77; power area supr. atomic energy div. SPR, Aiken, S.C., 1977—. Gen. chmn. Martinsville and Henry County 4th of July Celebration, 1977; exec. dir. Martinsville Sr. Citizen's Winterization Program, 1976-78. Served with USAF, 1966-70. Named Outstanding Young Man of Year, Martinsville, 1977. Mem. IEEE, Nat. Soc. Profl. Engrs., S.C. Soc. Profl. Engrs. (sec.-treas. chpt. 1978-79, chpt. pres. 1979-80), Am. Legion, Jaycees (past pres. Martinsville chpt., awards 1976, 77), Eta Kappa Nu. Republican. Lutheran. Home: 13 Deerwood Dr Aiken SC 29801

DEAN, LLOYD, clergyman, educator; b. East Chicago, Ind., Aug. 17, 1930; s. Bert T. and Minty (Creech) D.; B.S., Morehead U., 1958, M.A., 1959; m. Arvetta Dorcas Plank, Oct. 2, 1954. Ordained to ministry United Pentecostal Ch. Internat., 1962; pastor Morehead United Pentecostal Ch., 1959—; tchr., counselor Felicity (Ohio) Franklin High Sch., 1959-63; counselor Carter County Sch. System, Grayson, Ky., 1963-70, Rowan County High Sch., Morehead, Ky., 1970—; Ky. Sunday sch. dir. United Pentecostal Ch., Internat., 1957-69, sec.-treas. Ky., 1969-73; dir. Dean & Creech Reunions Am.; owner Dean's Greenhouse, 1972-78. Served in USAF, 1953-57. Recipient Am. Farmer degree Ky. Future Farmers Am., 1951. Mem. Ky., Rowan County edn. assns., Nat. PTA of United Pentecostal Ch., Rowan County Personnel and Guidance Assn. (pres. 1970-71, 76-77), Rowan County Hist. Soc. (pres. 1977-80), Rowan County Farm Bur. (dir.). Republican. Editor Ky. dist. news United Pentecostal Ch., 1957-69. Home: Route 6 Box 498 Morehead KY 40351 Office: Rowan County High Sch Morehead KY 40351

DEAN, LYDIA MARGARET CARTER (MRS. HALSEY ALBERT DEAN), food and nutrition cons., author; b. Bedford, Va., July 11, 1919; d. Christopher C. and Hettie (Gross) Carter; grad. Averett Coll.; B.S., Madison Coll., 1941; M.S., Va. Poly. Inst. and State U., 1951; postgrad. U. Va., Mich. State U.; m. Halsey Albert Dean, Dec. 24, 1941; children—Halsey Albert, John Carter, Lydia Margarae. Dietetic Intern, therapeutic dietitian St. Vincent de Paul Hosp., Norfolk, Va., 1942; physicist U.S. Naval Operating Base, Norfolk, 1943-45; clin. dietitian, asso. prof. Va. Poly. Inst. and State U., 1946-51, asso. prof. nutrition, 1951-53; community nutritionist Roanoke, Va., 1953-60; dir. nutritions and dietetics dept. Southwestern Va. Med. Center, Roanoke, 1960-67; food and nutrition cons. Nat. Hdqrs. ARC, Washington, 1967-73, vol., 1973—; nutrition scientist, cons. Dept. Army, Washington, 1973—, also Dept. Agr., ARC. Cons. Am. Dietetic Assn., 1969—, dir. Communications, 1974-75; mem. task force White House Conf. Food and Nutrition, 1969—; chmn. fed. com. Interagy. Com. on Nutrition Edn., 1970-71; now tech. rep. to AID; chmn. Crusade for Nutrition Edn., Washington, 1970—; asso. prof., dir. coordinated undergrad. degree programs U. Hawaii, 1974-75; participant, cons. Nat. Nutrition Policy Conf., 1974; speaker Food Technologists Ann. Meeting. Fellow Am. Pub. Health Assn.; mem. Am. Dietetic Assn., Bus. and Profl. Women's Clubs (cons. 1970—), Am. Home Econs. Assn. (rep. and treas. Joint Congl. Com.), AAUW, Food Service Execs. Assn., Internat. Platform Assn. Author: (with Virginia McMasters) Community Emergency Feeding, 1972; Help! My Child Won't Eat Right, 1973; The Complete Gourmet Nutrition Cookbook, 1978; How to Eat Well and Right, 1978; contbr. articles to profl. jours. Home: 7816 Birnam Wood Dr McLean VA 22101

DEAN, ROBERT GAYLE, JR., musician, producer, composer; b. Marion, N.C., Nov. 22, 1939; s. Robert Gayle and Helen Louis D.; student Mannhiem (Germany) Music Conservatory, 1958-59, Massey Bus. Coll., Atlanta, 1963. Salesman music store, Atlanta, 1960-65; mgr. music store, Coral Gables, Fla., 1965-66; pvt. music tchr., Atlanta, 1966-67; studio musician, Atlanta, 1970, Nashville, 1973—; studio musician, producer, song writer, arranger, pub., owner, pres. Myownah Music, Inc., Owlofus Music, Inc., Soul Country & Blues, Inc., Dean's List Publishing, Nashville. Served with U.S. Army, 1957-59. Recipient 6 ASCAP awards, 1975. Mem. Nashville Fedn. Musicians, Nashville Songwriters Assn., ASCAP/BMI, Country Music Assn., Nat. Rifle Assn., Nat. Acad. Recording Arts and Scis. Republican. Baptist. Club: Half Fast Walking (New Orleans). Composer: I Want To Hold You In My Dreams Tonight, 1975; Ode To Olivia, 1975; It's Not Funny Anymore, 1975. Home: 270 Tampa Dr Nashville TN 37211 Office: PO Box 110546 Nashville TN 37211

DEAN, SARAH KATHERINE, educator; b. Orlinda, Tenn., May 31, 1926; d. Ray H. and Nelle E. (Babb) D.; A.B., Georgetown Coll., 1948; M.R.E., So. Bapt. Theol. Sem., 1954; M.A., Peabody Coll., 1958; Ed.D., Nova U., 1980—. Dir. youth activities First Bapt. Ch., Winchester, Ky., 1948-51, Pensacola, Fla., 1951-52, Danville, Ky., 1954-55; dean women, asst. prof. sociology and anthropology Belmont Coll., Nashville, 1955-68; v.p., dean students Eckerd Coll., St. Petersburg, Fla., 1968-78, dir. women's studies, asst. prof. sociology, 1978—; cons. in field. Jones Found. grantee, 1957-58; NSF grantee, 1965; recipient Outstanding Alumni award Georgetown Coll., 1974; Outstanding Educator of Yr., 1972. Mem. AAUW, Nat. Assn. Women Deans, Adminstrs., So. Sociol. Soc., Fla. Personnel and Guidance Assn. Nat. Assn. Student Personnel, Nat. Women's Studies Assn., Tenn. Deans Assn. (pres. 1966-67), Delta Omicron, NOW. Baptist. Contbr. articles to profl. jours.

DEAN, WILLIAM ROOSEVELT, coll. pres., clergyman; b. Clarksburg, W.Va., Oct. 16, 1933; s. Raymond O. and Dessie May (Cox) D.; B.A., Bob Jones U., 1958, M.A., 1963; B.D., 1965; postgrad Marshall U., 1959; m. Nancy Thornton Dean, Aug. 27, 1957; children—Lori Ann, Andrew William. Prin. elem. sch., W.Va., 1957-59; ordained to ministry Methodist Ch., 1967; pastor chs., N.Y., 1959-62; dean of men So. Meth. Coll., Orangeburg, S.C., 1965-74, prof. Greek and philosophy, 1965-74, coll. pres., 1974—; chmn. com. schs. and colls. So. Meth. Ch., 1978—; pastor Charleston Heights So. Meth. Ch., 1968-70, Hebron So. Meth. Ch., 1970-74. Served with USCG, 1953. Mem. Am. Assn. Higher Edn., Gen. Conf. Bd. Christian Edn. So. Meth. Ch. Home: 350 Pinehill Rd Orangeburg SC 29115 Office: 760 Broughton St Orangeburg SC 29115

DEANE, FREDERICK, JR., banker; b. Boston, Aug. 5, 1926; s. Frederick and Julia (Coolidge) D.; M.B.A. with distinction, Harvard U., 1951; m. Dorothy Legge, Dec. 21, 1948; children—Dorothy Porcher, Eleanor Dodds, Frederick III. With Bank of Va. and Bank of Va. Co. (formerly Va. Commonwealth Bankshares), 1953—, now chmn. bd., chief exec. officer of both; dir. Chessie System, Inc., C.&O. R.R., B&O R.R. Bd. dirs. Va. Mus. Found., Endowment Assn. of Coll. William and Mary, Va. Found. Ind. Colls., Federated Arts Council Richmond, Va. Inst. Pastoral Care, Va. Diocesan Center. Served to 1st lt. U.S. Army, 1944-47, 51-53. Mem. Richmond Soc. Fin. Analysts (pres. 1963-64), Nat. Fedn. Fin. Analysts Socs., Am. Bankers Assn., Assn. Bank Holding Cos. (chmn. 1979-80), Assn. Res. City Bankers, Fin. Analysts Fedn., C. of C. U.S. (econ. policy com. 1965-69), Young Pres.'s Orgn. (exec. com., chpt. pres. 1971-72). Republican. Episcopalian (vestryman, lay reader, mem. fin. com.). Clubs: Farmington Country (Charlottesville); Harvard of Virginia (pres. 1969-70, v.p. 1960, pres. Bus. Sch. sect. 1960); Brook, Harvard (N.Y.C.); Commonwealth, Country of Va. (Richmond); Met. (Washington); Hasty Pudding Inst. of 1770; Mid-Ocean (Bermuda). Home: 110 W Hillcrest Ave Richmond VA 23226 Office: 1011 W Broad St Rd PO Box 25970 Richmond VA 23260

DEAR, WAYNE ENGLEHARDT, cardiologist; b. Austin, Tex., Mar. 29, 1934; s. Raymond H. and Irene (Wittmann) D.; B.A., U. Tex., 1955; M.D. with honors, Bayler Coll. Medicine, 1962, M.S. in Physiology; m. Cynthia Boyd, June 24, 1978; children by previous marriage—James Wittmann, Margaret Marie, William Jessen. Intern, Hosp. of U. Pa., Phila., 1962-63, resident dept. medicine, 1963-65; Bur. Vocat. Rehab. Tng. of HEW grantee, fellow as med. cons. George Morris Piersel Rehab. Center, U. Pa., Phila., 1963-64, neurol. cons., 1964-65; USPHS cardiovascular tng. grantee Robinette Found., U. Pa., Phila., 1965-66, Southeastern Pa. Heart Assn.-Robinette Found. grantee, 1965-66; USPHS, Nat. Heart Inst. fellow dept. medicine Baylor Coll. Medicine, Houston, 1966-67; practice medicine specializing in cardiology, Houston, 1967—; asst. clin. instr. medicine U. Pa., Phila., 1963-66; clin. instr. medicine Baylor Coll. Medicine, Houston, 1967-70, asst. clin. prof. medicine, 1970—; staff St. Luke's Episcopal Hosp., Houston, 1967—, Tex. Children's Hosp., Houston, 1967—; courtesy staff Meth. Hosp., Houston, 1967—, Hermann Hosp., Houston, 1967—; staff physician Ben Taub Gen. Hosp., Houston, 1967—; cons. in cardiology Montgomery County Hosp., Conroe, Tex., 1972—. Served with USN, 1955-57, USNR, 1957-63. Diplomate Am. Bd. Internal Medicine. Fellow A.C.P., Am. Coll. Cardiology, Houston Soc. Internal Medicine, Council Clin. Cardiology; mem. Osler Soc., Phila. Physiol. Soc., Harris County Med. Soc., Tex. Med. Assn., Tex. Soc. Internal Medicine, Am. Heart Assn., Houston Heart Assn. (dir. 1968-74, v.p. exec. bd. 1972-74, v.p. exec. com. 1979, pres.-elect 1980), Houston Acad. Medicine, Baylor Med. Alumni Assn., Tex. Med. Found., Sierra Club, Alpha Omega Alpha, Delta Tau Delta, Scabbard and Blade, Phi Beta Pi. Clubs: Houston Cardiology, Drs. of Houston, Univ., Brazos River. Contbr. articles to profl. jours. Home: 306 Longwoods Ln Houston TX 77024 Office: 6560 Fannin St Suite 1520 Houston TX 77030

DEARING, JAMES WALLACE, savs. and loan assn. exec.; b. N.Y.C., Dec. 13, 1943; s. James A. and Elsie M. Dearing; B.S., Fla. State U., 1966; m. Gail Pittman, Apr. 23, 1966; children—Michael, Jennifer. With First Fed. Savs. and Loan, Fort Lauderdale, Fla., 1971—, mgr. mortgage loans, 1976-77, dir. mortgage loan div., 1977—. Served with USAF, 1966-71. Decorated Air medal. Mem. Inst. Fin. Edn., South Fla. Mortgage Officers Soc. Roman Catholic. Office: 301 E Las Olas Blvd Fort Lauderdale FL 33302

DEARING, NOVA LEE, ednl. cons.; b. Avalon, Tex., Jan. 21, 1904; d. Orrin Cardwell and Della Eulala (Tapp) Harvey; Tchr.'s Cert., Trinity U., Waxahachie, Tex., 1926; m. Olin Clyde Dearing, Oct. 8, 1922 (dec., 1942); children—Olin Clyde, Catherine Dearing Day. Pvt. practice as speech tchr., Waxahachie, 1926-28; elem. tchr. Brous Pvt. Sch., Ft. Worth, 1938-40; co-founder, tchr., unit dir., parent-relations coordinator, dir. admissions, spl. asst. to pres. Brown Schs. for Exceptional Children, Austin, Tex., 1940-77, cons., 1977—. Vol. worker nursing homes and handicapped children. Mem. Am. Assn. on Mental Deficiency (life; regional sec. 1958-73, treas. 1958-73), Council for Exceptional Children (nat. bd. dirs. 1960-63, co-founder local chpt., local and state officer), Mental Health Assn. (local and state officer), Nat. Conf. Social Workers, State Tchrs. Assn., Austin Community Services. Baptist. Clubs: Order Eastern Star (worthy matron, 1961-62, grand officer), D.A.R., Zonta (dist. treas. 1972-74, internat. nominating com. 1972-74, monitor internat. conv., Germany, 1976). Home: 5411 Montview St Austin TX 78756

DE ARMAS, FREDERICK ALFRED, educator; b. Havana, Cuba, Feb. 9, 1945; s. Alfredo and Ana Maria (Galdos) de Armas; came to U.S., 1959; naturalized, 1969; B.A. magna cum laude, Stetson U., 1965; Ph.D. (Carnegie fellow), U. N.C., 1968. Asst. prof. Spanish, La. State U., Baton Rouge, 1968-73, asso. prof., 1973-78, prof., 1978—; chmn. fgn. langs., 1979—; vis. asso. prof. U. Mo., Columbia, summer 1977. Nat. Endowment for Humanities stipend, summer 1979. Mem. Modern Lang. Assn., Comparative Lit. Assn., Renaissance Soc. Am., Asociacion Internacional de Hispanistas, Am. Assn. Tchrs. Spanish and Portuguese, Am. Assn. Tchrs. French, Asociacion de Filologia y Linguistica de la America Latina. Author: The Four Interpolated Stories in the "Roman Comique," 1971; Paul Scarron, 1972; The Invisible Mistress, 1976. Editor: El Sastre del Campillo (Luis de Belmonte Bermudez), 1975. Contbr. articles to profl. jours. Home: 8345 Perkins Rd Baton Rouge LA 70810 Office: Dept Fgn Langs Louisiana State U Baton Rouge LA 70803

DE ASES, ELIDA FABELA, state social services adminstr.; b. Alice, Tex., May 5, 1918; d. Horacio Jaime and Marta Mata (Ochoa) Fabela; A.A., Del Mar Coll., 1965; student A&I U., intermittently, 1953-62, Beeville Coll., intermittently, 1970-74; m. Jan. 1, 1937; children—Edna Elodia Ramirez Soto, Lauro Ramirez; m. 2d, Juvencio G. De Ases, June 28, 1945; children—Aida Ester De Ases Reed, David Roy. Sec., War Food Adminstrn., Sinton, Tex., 1945-50;

stenographer Tex. Dept. Public Welfare, Sinton, 1950-65; field worker Tex. Dept. Human Resouces, Sinton, 1965-76, supr. Aid to Families with Dependent Children, Sinton, 1976—, also supr. Food Stamp Program. Past pres. Ladies Aux. of GI Forum, Sinton. Mem. Tex. Public Welfare Assn., Tex. Public Employees Assn. Democrat. Roman Catholic. Club: Sinton Bus. and Profl. Woman's. Office: Tex Dept Human Resources Sodville Rd Sinton TX 78387

DEATON, FAE ADAMS, mental health worker; b. Phila., Feb. 19, 1932; d. Charles Sizemore and Dorothea Lucia (Adams) Deaton; Mus.B., Salem Coll., 1953; postgrad. U. Alaska, 1968-69, Alaska Methodist U., 1969, Wright State U., 1971-73; M.S. in Edn., Old Dominion U., 1975, Norfolk State U., 1978—; children—Dorothea Fae Stein, Caroline Louise Stein, Eric Charles Stein. Tchr. music, Mifflin, Ohio, 1953-54; supr. high sch. USN Dependents Sch., Argentia, Nfld., 1956-57; tchr. USAF Dependents Sch., Croughton, Eng., 1960-63, Upper Heyford, Eng., 1963-64; mag. editor Scott AFB, Ill., 1966-67; mem. staff Hist. and Fine Arts Mus., Anchorage, 1968-70; music and arts reviewer Anchorage Evening Times, 1968-70; publicity chmn., mem. publicity staff Alaska Council on Arts, 1969-70; counselor Youth Services Bur., Dayton, Ohio, 1973; engring. research aide Wright Patterson AFB, Dayton, 1973; writer Dayton Daily News, 1973; counselor, patient advocate Norfolk (Va.) Free Clinic, 1975-76; adminstrv. asst. Old Dominion U., Norfolk, 1975-76; tchr., counselor Blessed Sacrament Sch., Norfolk, 1976-77; mem. mental health team, young adolescent unit, milieu therapy Portsmouth (Va.) Pschiat. Center, 1977-79, children's unit, 1979—. Mem. Tidewater Profl. Assn. on Child Abuse, 1978—, Tidewater Rape Info. Services, Norfolk, 1978—; adminstr./author Sexual Abuse Helpline of Tidewater 1979—; mem. VBDSS Sexual Abuse Testament Team, 1979—; mem. ad hoc com. Coalition on Sexual Abuse, 1980—; mem. admissions/release bd. Norfolk Lakehouse Girls Detention Home, 1978-79; chmn. task force spl. children Children's Art Center, Norfolk, 1979—; bd. dirs. Norfolk Little Theater, 1977-78; historian Alaska Arts Club; mem. Elmendorf AFB Sch. Bd., 1967-68. Mem. Am., Va., Hampton Roads personnel and guidance assns., Am. Orthopsychiat. Assn., Nat., Va. assns. specialists in group work, Nat., Va. mental health counselors assns., Nat. Sch. Counselors Assn., Nat. League Am. Pen Women, Elem. Sch. Counselors Assn., Va. Elementary Sch. Counselors Assn., Va. Council Social Welfare (dir. Tidewater area 1978—, membership chmn. 1979-80), Tidewater Expressive Art Therapies Assn., Tidewater Mental Health Assn., Va. Opera Assn. Guild, Chrysler Mus. Assn., Alaska Press Club. Home: 1176 Pickett Rd Norfolk VA 23502 Office: 301 Fort Ln Portsmouth VA 23704

DEAUX, JAMES DEWITT, III, record industry exec.; b. Heidelberg, Germany, Feb. 8, 1948 (parents Am. citizens); s. James DeWitt and Hildegarde Augustine Johanna (Straub) D.; div.; 1 dau., Julie Diane. Salesman, Sears Roebuck & Co., Atlanta, 1967-68; computer operator Trust Co., Bank, Atlanta, 1969-71, Coll. William and Mary, Williamsburg, Va., 1974; salesman Warner-Elektra-Atlantic Corp., Atlanta, 1974—. Office: WEA Corp 250 Villanova Dr Atlanta GA 30336

DEAVER, HENRY CLAYTON, JR., master mariner; b. Tarboro, N.C., July 27, 1925; s. Henry Clayton and Daisy Belle (Briley) D.; student U.S. Mcht. Marine Acad., 1946; m. Anna Virginia Thomas, Oct. 15, 1955. Third mate Am. Pacific S/S Co., 1946; 2d mate Blidberg-Rothchild S/S Co., 1947-50; 3d mate Amoco Shipping Co. (became div. Standard Oil of Ind. 1957), 1950-51, 2d mate, 1951-53, chief officer, 1953-57, master mariner S/S Amoco Conn., S/S Amoco Del., S/S Amoco La., S/S Amoco Va., 1957—. Served with USMC, 1943-46; ATO, MTO, PTO. Mem. Council Am. Master Mariners, Marine Sq. Club. Baptist. Clubs: Masons, Shriners. Home: 4316 Knob Rd Richmond VA 23235

DEAVER, PETE EUGENE, civil engr.; b. Ft. Worth, Mar. 8, 1936; s. Elmer Jack and Mattie Alline (Kelley) Deaver; student Cramwell Inst., 1957; B.S., U. Tex. Arlington, 1968; m. Birdie Jo Foster, Apr. 30, 1954; children—Pete Eugene, Stephen Lewis, Mickey Jo, Robert. Aircraft engr. Gen. Dynamics Corp., Ft. Worth, 1957-61; project engr. ejection seat studies Kirk Engring. Co., Bethpage, N.Y., 1961-64; sr. engr. Ling Tempco Vought Aeros., Dallas, 1964-65; stress engr. Boeing Aircraft Co., Seattle, 1965-66; sr. aero. engr. Gen. Dynamics Corp., Albuquerque, 1966-74; owner, operator Deaver Engring. Co., cons. constrn. and industry, Henrietta, Tex., 1974—. Served with USNR, 1952-54. Registered profl. engr., N.Mex., Tex. Mem. Tex. Water Pollution Control Assn., NW Tex. Water Utilities Assn., Am. Helicopter Soc., Soc. Exploration Geophysicists, Tex., Nat. socs. profl. engrs. Baptist. Mason (32 deg.). Author: Basic Stress Analysis for Engineers and Draftsmen, 1967. Address: PO Box 442 Henrietta TX 76365

DEAVERS, DANIEL RONALD, physiologist; b. Normal, Ill., Oct. 23, 1943; s. Ronald B.E. and Evelyn I. Deavers; B.S., San Diego State U., 1967, M.S., 1969; Ph.D., Cornell U., 1976; m. Marilyn Irene Humphrey, June 11, 1966. Postdoctoral fellow, cardiovascular trainee USPHS, Dalton Research Center, U. Mo., Columbia, 1976-78, instr. physiology Med. Sch., 1978; instr. physiology and biophysics Sch. Medicine, U. Louisville, 1979—. Mem. Am. Physiol. Soc., Am. Soc. Zoologists, Internat. Hibernation Soc., AAAS, Ky. Acad. Sci. Author papers in field. Home: 212 Parliament Sq Louisville KY 40206 Office: Dept Physiology and Biophysics Univ Louisville Med Sch Louisville KY 40232

DEBAKEY, LOIS, educator; b. Lake Charles, La.; d. S. M. and Raheeja (Zorba) DeB.; B.A., Tulane U., 1949, M.A., 1959, Ph.D., 1963. Asst. prof. English, Tulane U., asst. prof. sci. communication Med. Sch., 1963-65, asso. prof. sci. communication, 1965-66, prof. sci. communication, 1966-68, lectr., 1968—; prof. sci. communications Baylor Coll. Medicine, Houston, 1968—; mem. biomed. library rev. com. Nat. Library Medicine, Bethesda, Md., 1973-77. Recipient Bausch & Lomb award; Disting. Service award Am. Med. Writers Assn., 1970. Mem. Assn. Tchrs. of Tech. Writing, Council Basic Edn. (commn. on writing), Inst. Soc., Ethics and the Life Scis., Nat. Assn. Sci. Writers, Internat. Soc. Gen. Semantics, Council Biology Editors (dir. 1973-77, chmn. com. on editorial policy 1971—), So. Assn. Colls. and Schs. (exec. council Commn. on Colls.), AAAS, Conf. Coll. Composition and Communication, Nat. Council Tchrs. English (com. on sci. writing), Soc. Health and Human Values, Soc. Tech. Communication, Am. Soc. Info. Sci., NIH Alumni Assn., Phi Beta Kappa. Sr. author: The Scientific Journal: Editorial Policies and Practices, 1976; editorial bd. Health Communications, and Informatics; Cardiovascular Research Center Bull., 1971—, Forum on Medicine, Tulane Studies in English, 1966-68; contbr. articles to profl. jours. Office: Baylor Coll Medicine 1200 Moursund St Houston TX 77030

DE BAKEY, MICHAEL E(LLIS), surgeon; b. Lake Charles, La., Sept. 7, 1908; s. Shaker Morris and Raheeja (Zerba) DeB.; B.S., Tulane U., 1930, M.D., 1932, M.S., 1935, LL.D., 1965; Dr. honoris causa, U. Lyon (France), 1961, U. Brussels (Belgium), 1962, U. Ghent (Belgium), 1964, U. Athens (Greece), 1964, U. Turin (Italy), 1965, U. Belgrade (Yugoslavia), 1967; Lafayette Coll., 1965, U. Cin., 1969, McNeese U., 1972; D.Sc., D'Youville Coll., 1967, U. Mich., 1967, Fla. State U., 1968, MacMurray Coll., 1971, Hahnemann Med. Coll. and Hosp., 1973; Hon. Faculty of Medicine U. Chile, Santiago, 1964; Dr. Med. Scis. (hon.), Aristotelean U. of Thessaloniki (Greece), 1971; D.Sc. honoris causa, Assumption Coll., 1971, L.I. U., 1971, Ft. Lauderdale U., 1970, Loyola U. of South, 1965, St. John's U., Jamaica, N.Y., 1970; Hon. Dr., Ljubljana U., 1971; M.D. honoris causa, U. Louvain; LL.D. (hon.), Southwestern U., Georgetown, Tex., 1968; H.H.D., Centenary Coll., Shreveport, 1979; m. Diana Cooper, Oct. 15, 1936; children—Michael Maurice, Ernest Ochsner, Barry Edward, Denis Alton. Intern Charity Hosp., New Orleans, 1932-33, asst. in surgery, 1933-35; asst. in surgery U. Strasbourg (France), 1935-36; asst. surgery U. Heidelberg (Germany), 1936; instr. surgery Tulane U., 1937-40, asst. prof., 1940-46, asso. prof., 1946-48; prof. surgery, chmn. dept. Baylor U., Houston, 1948—, v.p. med. affairs, 1968—, chief exec. officer Baylor Coll. Medicine, 1968-69, pres., 1969-78, chancellor, 1978—, Disting. Service prof., 1968—; surgeon in chief Ben Taub Gen. Hosp., Houston, 1963—; practice medicine Ochsner Clinic, New Orleans, 1946-48; sr. attending surgeon, dir. Cardiovascular Research Center, Methodist Hosp., Houston, 1967-75; dir. Nat. Heart and Blood Vessel Research and Demonstration Center, Baylor Coll. Medicine, 1975—; mem. nat. adv. council St. Jude Children's Research Hosp., Memphis, 1978; hon. faculty medicine U. Chile, Santiago, 1964; bd. dirs., cons. Am. Med. Bldgs., 1978; cons. staff, mem. exec. com. St. Luke's Episcopal Hosp., Houston; cons. surgery M.D. Anderson Hosp. and Tumor Inst., Tex. Children's Hosp., Houston; clin. prof. surgery U. Tex. Dental Br., Houston, 1971-72; distinguished prof. surgery Tex. A. and M. U., 1972—; cons. Tex. Inst. Rehab. and Research, Brooke Gen. Hosp., Ft. Sam Houston; area cons. thoracic surgery to VA, 1946—; mem. adv. bd. Pa. Regional Tissue and Transplant Bank, 1979; mem. med. adv. com. sec. of def., 1948-50; chmn. com. on surgery NRC, 1953, mem. exec. com., 1953; mem. adv. council Inst. Advanced Research in Asian Sci. and Medicine, 1978; mem. task force Commn. for Reorgn. Exec. Br. Govt.; mem. Nat. Adv. Health Council, 1961-65, Nat. Adv. Council Region Med. Programs, 1965—, Civilian Health and Med. Adv. Council Office Asst. Sec. Def.; mem. med. adv. bd. Am. Hosp. of Paris, 1971—; mem. com. NRC-Nat. Acad. Scis., 1978—; cons. cardiovascular surgery to surgeon gen. U.S. Air Force; mem. adv. council Nat. Heart Inst.; chmn. Albert Lasker Clin. Med. Research Jury awards, 1973, Citizens for Treatment High Blood Pressure, 1974, numerous other adv. positions. Bd. visitors Tulane U., 1970—; founders bd. Transylvania U., 1979; trustee S.W. Research Inst., 1972—; mem. Com. of 1000 for Better Health Regulations, Washington, 1978. Served as col., Office of Surgeon Gen., AUS, 1942-46, surg. cons. to surgeon gen., 1946—. Decorated Legion of Merit, knight comdr. Order of Merit Italian Republic, Grand Cross Order Leopold (Belgium), Presdl. Medal of Freedom; recipient Rudolph Matas award, 1954; Hektoen Gold medal AMA; Internat. Soc. Surgery Distinguished Service award, 1958, 59; Distinguished Service award AMA, 1959; Albert Lasker award for clin. research, 1963; St. Vincent prize med. scis. U. Turin, 1965; Orden del Libertador Gen. San Martin, Argentina, 1965; Hunterian medal St. George's Hosp. Med. Sch., London, Eng., 1966; Centennial medal Albert Einstein Med. Center, 1966; Eleanor Roosevelt Humanities award, 1969; P.A. Gertzin medal Internat. Med. Sci. Orgn. of Surgeons, Moscow, 1971, medallion Tex. Med. Center, 1972, Spl. Recognition award Merck Sharp & Dohme, 1971, Distinguished Citizens award Rotary Club, 1972, USSR Acad. Sci. 50th Anniversary Jubilee medal, 1973, Ann. award honoring distinguished mems. of soc. U. Detroit, 1978; Edwin and Lee Ducat Humanitarian award Bd. Dirs. of Diabetes Juvenile Found., Washington, 1978, numerous others; named Dr. of Year Med. World News, 1965, Med. Man of Year, 1966; hon. fellow Inst. Medicine of Chgo., 1965. Diplomate Am. Bd. Surgery, Am. Bd. Thoracic Surgery, Nat. Bd. Med. Examiners. Fellow A.C.S. (ann. award extraordinary performance 1973), Am. Coll. Cardiology (hon.), Royal Coll. Surgeons (Eng.) (hon.); mem. Internat Cardiovascular Soc. (pres. N.Am. chpt. 1964), Southwestern Surg. Congress (pres. 1952), Soc. Vascular Surgery (pres. 1953), M.E. DeBakey Internat. Cardiovascular Soc., AMA, Tex. Med. Assn. Council on med. edn. and hosps. 1971—), Am., So., Western surg. assns., Am. Assn. Thoracic Surgery (pres. 1959), Soc. Clin. Surgery, Soc. U. Surgeons, Internat. Soc. Surgery, Soc. Exptl. Biology and Medicine, Sociedad Nacional de Cirugia, Am. Acad. Achievement (gov.), AAAS, Am. Assn. Cancer Research, Am. Soc. Contemporary Medicine and Surgery (pres. 1971—; achievement award 1973), Am. Trauma Soc. (founding), N.Y. Acad. Scis., World Med. Assn., Philos. Soc. Tex., Mexican Acad. Surgery, Cuban Med. Assn. in Exile (hon.), Udruzenje Kirurga Jugoslavia (hon.), Acad. Medicine of Turin (fgn. hon. asso.), Phila. Acad. Cardiology (hon.), Royal Acad. Medicine (Belgium) (hon.), Am. Geriatric Soc., Am. Heart Assn. (founding mem. council cerebrovascular disease, mem. council on thrombosis), C. of C., Sigma Xi, Alpha Omega Alpha. Democrat. Episcopalian. Clubs: Rotary (hon. Houston); Cosmos, University (Washington); Press (Houston). Author: (with Robert Kilduffe) Blood Transfusion, 1942; (with Gilbert W. Beebe) Battle Casualties, 1952; (with Alton Ochsner) Textbook of Minor Surgery, 1955; (with T. Whayne) Cold Injury, Ground Type, 1958; (with Antonio M. Gotto, Jr.) The Living Heart, 1977; A Surgeon's Diary of a Visit to China, 1974. Editor surg. vols. AUS Medical History of World War II; Year Book of General Surgery, 1958—. Editorial bd. surg. jours.; mem. editorial adv. bd. Biomed. Materials and Artificial Organs, 1971—. Home: 5323 Cherokee St Houston TX 77005 Office: 1200 Moursund Ave Houston TX 77030

DE BARDELEBEN, WILLIAM DEE, JR., utility co. exec.; b. Montgomery, Ala., Sept. 24, 1945; s. Willie Dee and Elsie Mae (Woodall) DeB.; B.S. in Bus. Adminstrn., Auburn U., 1967; M.B.A., Ga. State U., 1970; m. Mary Ethel English, Nov. 22, 1975; children—Jennifer Lea, Alsie Jane. With Ga. Power Co., Atlanta, 1967—, student acct., 1967-69, jr. acct., 1969-70, adminstrv. asst., 1973, fin. analyst, 1973-75, supr. fin. services, 1975-76, mgr. fin. adminstrn. and analysis, 1976-78, asst. comptroller corp. acctg., 1978—. Vestryman, treas. St. Margaret's Episcopal Ch., Woodbridge, Va., 1971-73; vestryman Holy Trinity Episc. Ch., Decatur, Ga., 1978—. Served to capt. C.E. U.S. Army, 1970-73. Mem. Edison Electric Inst. (acctg. prins. com.), Nat. Soc. Rate of Return Analysts, Nat. Acctg. Assn., Southeastern Electric Exchange, Inst. Property Taxation, Phi Gamma Delta. Office: 270 Peachtree St NW Atlanta GA 30303

DE BAUN, CHARLES WITTER, physician; b. Monsey, N.Y., Dec. 4, 1907; s. John Nelson and Myrtle Dell (Witter) De.; B.S., N.Y. U. at Washington Square, 1932, M.D., N.Y. U. Coll. Medicine, 1940; m. Thordis Alice Johansen July 26, 1941; children—Charles John, Jane Thordis DeBaun Andrews, Susan Lynne DeBaun Conrad. Lab. technician neuropathology N.Y. State Dept. Mental Hygiene, Thiells, 1932-36; intern Norwegian Hosp., Bklyn., 1940-41; commd. 1st lt. U.S. Army, 1942, advanced through grades to col. USAF, 1961; asst. med. dir. BC-BS, Chgo., 1962-70, asst. v.p., 1962-70; practice medicine, Laredo, Tex., 1970—. Diplomate Am. Bd. Preventive Medicine. Fellow Am. Coll. Preventive Medicine; mem. Air Force Assn. (past pres. Ill.), Tex., Am. med. assns., Aerospace Med. Assn., Pub. Health Assn., Alpha Omega Alpha. Home: 2019 O'Kane St Laredo TX 78040

DE BLASI, IGNATIUS ANGELO, health care exec.; b. Bklyn., Sept. 10, 1946; s. Joseph and Mary (Peleno) DeB.; B.A., SUNY, 1967; m. Suzanne Sallenger, Apr. 27, 1975; children—Michael, Kathleen, James, Jon. Salesman, Sears, Roebuck & Co., L.I., N.Y., 1964-68; with Edwards & Hanley, Garden City, L.I., 1968-72; asst. to pres. E. Gate Med., L.I., 1972-73; pres. Relsco, Inc., Louisville, 1973—. Bd. dirs. Lyndon Recreation Assn., Louisville, 1977-78. Mem. Mktg. Specialists (dir. 1978-79), Bus. Mgrs. Assn., Am. Sex Edn. Assn., Am. Pub. Health Assn., Nat. Abortion Fedn. (dir. 1977—), Nat. Abortion Rights Action Com. Democrat. Roman Catholic. Club: Standard Country. Home: 1103 Stone Spring Way Louisville KY 40222 Office: 200 S 7th St Louisville KY 40202

DE BOER, LLOYD MARTIN, educator; b. LaCrosse, Wis., Nov. 20, 1923; s. Martin J. and Alice (Mulder) DeB.; student Wis. State Tchrs. Coll. at LaCrosse, 1941-43, Brown U., 1943-44; B.S., U. Ill., 1947, Ph.D., 1957; M.B.A., Harvard U., 1950; m. Virginia A. Rano, Aug. 28, 1948; dau., Patricia A. Research asst. Mass. Inst. Tech., 1947-48; teaching asst., instr., asst. prof., asso. prof. mktg. U. Ill., 1950-66; prof. bus. adminstrn. Parsons Coll., 1966-67; asso. prof. advt. U. Ill., 1967-68, prof. mktg. Kent State U., 1968-75, dir. D. Bus. Adminstrn. program 1972-74, dir. Bur. Mgmt. Devel., 1974-75; prof. bus. adminstrn. George Mason U., Fairfax, Va., 1975—, chmn. dept., 1975-77, dean Sch. Bus. Adminstrn., 1977—. Cons. 3M, Gen. Telephone and Electronics, Pillsbury Co., others. Served with USAAF, 1943-46. Mem. Am. Mktg. Assn., AAUP, Am. Inst. Decision Scis., Alpha Kappa Psi, Phi Kappa Phi, Beta Gamma Sigma. Home: 4100 Sideburn Rd Fairfax VA 22030 Office: Sch Bus Adminstrn George Mason U 4400 University Dr Fairfax VA 22030

DE BOISBLANC, JACQUES FELIX, transmission parts co. exec.; b. New Orleans, Dec. 24, 1944; s. Felix Joseph and Hellen (Weigand) de B.; B.S. in Mech. Engring., La. State U., 1967; M.B.A., Tulane U., 1972. Engr., Boeing Corp., New Orleans, 1967-68; salesman Gulf Plastics, New Orleans, 1969-70, Latter & Blum, New Orleans, 1973-74; chief exec. officer, pres. The Clinic, New Orleans, 1975—. Mem. Automatic Transmission Rebuilders Assn. (treas.). Roman Catholic. Clubs: Sea Scamps (sec.), Hank Stram's. Home: 7824 Breakwater Dr New Orleans LA 70124 Office: 2067 Poydras St New Orleans LA 701 2

DEBUSK, EDITH M., lawyer; b. Waco, Tex., April 12, 1912; d. Otto Clifton and Margaret (Hatcher) Mann; LL.B., Dallas Sch. Law, 1941; certificate So. Methodist U. Sch. Law, 1941; m. Manuel C. DeBusk, June 13, 1941. Atty., Regional Atty.'s Office, O.P.A., Dallas, 1942; asso. atty. Office of Karl F. Steinmann, Balt., 1945-46, mem. firm DeBusk & DeBusk, Dallas, 1946—. Vice pres. Killeen Savs. & Loan Assn., The Teeling Mortgage Co., Inc.; officer, dir. DeBusk Corp., Tex. Mortgage Liquidation Corp.; officer East Town Osteo. Hosp. Corp. Former mem. Tex. Gov.'s Com. on Aging; dir. Dallas Citizens Commn. on Action for Aging, Inc., del. to White House Conf. Children and Youth 1960, Conf. on Aging, 1961; former dir. Dallas United Cerebral Palsy Assn., Tex. Soc. Aging, Dallas County Community Action Com., Inc., Crossroads Community Center; former mem. div. aging Council of Social Agys., Citizen's Traffic Commn.; former sec. and legal adviser Tex. Fedn. Bus. and Profl. Women's Clubs. Bd visitors Freedoms Found. at Valley Forge, 1964-66; trustee DeBusk Found. Named Woman of Month, Dallas Mag., 1948; Woman of Week, Balt., 1945; recipient George Washington honor medal Freedoms Found. Fellow Tex. Bar Found.; mem. State Bar Tex. (bar jour. com. 1975-76), Am. (chmn. subcom. state and local taxation, sect. real property, probate and trusts 1978—), Dallas bar assns., Women's Council of Dallas County, Bus. and Profl. Women's Club Dallas (past pres.), Kappa Beta Pi (past dean Alpha Psi chpt. and province IV). Presbyn. Club: Altrusa (past pres. Dallas; pres. internat. 1963-65). Home: 7365 Elmridge Dr Dallas TX 75240 Office: First Nat Bank Bldg Dallas TX 75202

DE CAMP, IRENE FRANCES, fin. and estate planner; b. Maynard, Iowa, Oct. 2, 192; d. Floyd L. and Effie Jane (Martin) Parker; student Rollins Coll., Winter Park, Fla., Fla. Atlantic U., Am. Coll.; C.L.U., 1978; m. Gayle Schilling de Camp, July 18, 1949 (dec. Dec. 1976). Part-time tchr. Orange County pub. schs., Orlando, Fla., 1952-65; various secretarial positions, 1962-71; dir., sec.-treas. Toga Films, Inc., Ft. Lauderdale, Fla., 1965—; pres. de Camp Realty, Inc., de Camp Enterprises, Inc., Ft. Lauderdale, 1978—; fin. and estate planner Home Life Ins. Co. N.Y., Ft. Lauderdale, 1972—; dir. Royal Group, Inc.; asst. sec.-treas. A. Massengill Devel. Co., Inc.; cons. to bus. Trustee, mem. planned gifts com. Boca Raton (Fla.) Community Hosp., 1976—. Mem. Nat. Assn. Life Underwriters, Nat. Secretaries Assn., Internat. Assn. Fin. Planners (chpt. sec. 1979-80), Million Dollar Round Table, Nat. Assn. Securities Dealers, Broward County Assn. Life Underwriters, Am. Soc. C.L.U., Fla. Soc. Cert. Profl. Secs., Nat. Assn. Female Execs., Am. Mgmt. Assn., AAUW, Henderson Mental Health Center Aux. (sec. 1979-80), Republican. Baptist. Clubs: Whale and Porpoise, Kentucky (pres. 1979), Tower, Americana, Order Eastern Star, Soroptimists. Home: 4325 NE Country Club Dr 22 Ave Fort Lauderdale FL 33308 Office: 5554 N Federal Hwy 4th Floor Fort Lauderdale FL 33308

DE CASTONGRENE, RUSSELL OTHOMAR, JR., systems engr.; b. Indpls., June 16, 1931; s. Russell O. and Cecelia J. (Dessert) de C.; student Jackson Jr. Coll., 1948-49, Vincennes U., 1949-50; B.S. in Aero. Engring., Purdue U., 1953; postgrad. U. Fla., 1967-69; M.C.E., Tex. A. and M. U., 1975, D.Eng., 1976; m. Patricia Mary Murphy, Feb. 7, 1959; children—Russell Othomar, Michelle Marie, Martin James, Richard Hugo, Peter William. Engr., McDonnell Aircraft Co., St. Louis, 1953; with E.W. Bliss Co., Phila. and Yokosuka, Japan, 1956-58, RCA, Camden, N.J., 1958-60; cons. M. & T Co., Phila., 1960-62; engr. Gen. Electric Co., King Of Prussia, Pa., 1962-63, Daytona Beach, Fla., 1963-69, San Antonio, 1969-71; research and teaching asst. Tex A. and M. U., 1972-75; systems engr. Shell Oil Co., Houston, 1975—. Served to lt. (j.g.) USNR, 1953-56. Registered profl. engr., Fla., Tex.; certified fallout shelter analyst. Mem. Am. Inst. Aeros. and Astronautics, Am. Aviation Hist. Soc., Am. Soc. Naval Engrs., ASCE, Naval Inst., Naval Res. Assn. Home: 27126 Kane Ln Conroe TX 77302 Office: Shell Oil Co PO Box 2099 Houston TX 77001

DE CELL, HERMAN BRISTER, lawyer, former state senator Miss.; b. Yazoo City, Miss., Sept. 26, 1924; s. John Eldridge and Lucile (Brister) De C.; B.B.A. with distinction, U. Miss., 1948; LL.B., Harvard, 1950; m. Harriet Causey, Aug. 11, 1951; children—Alice, Brister, Causey. Admitted to Miss. bar, 1950; mem. firm Henry, Barbour & DeCell, Yazoo City, 1950—; instr. U. Miss. extension, 1951-56; mem. Miss. Senate, 1959-80. Chmn., Yazoo Community Action, Inc., 1965—; del. Democratic Nat. Conv., 1964, state conv., 1960, 64, 68, 72. Trustee, Yazoo Library Assn. Served with U.S. Army, 1943-46; PTO. Methodist. Home: 14 Woodlawn St Yazoo City MS 39194 Office: PO Box 960 Yazoo City MS 39194

DECHERT, DANIEL STRATTON, computer services co. exec.; b. Winchester, Va., Mar 31, 1934; s. Robert Beck and Mary Kathryn (Quick) D.; A.B. in Econs., Coll. William and Mary, 1956; m. Mary Ellen Macdonald, Mar. 2, 1957; children—Elizabeth Macdonald, D. Stratton. Project dir. Newport News Shipbldg. & Dry Dock Co. (Va.), 1959-66; mgr. Ernst & Ernst, Winston-Salem, N.C., 1966-72; pres. Hosp. Data Center of Va., Inc., Norfolk, 1972—, also dir.; pres. Va. Micrographics, 1975—, Hosp. Collection Service Va., 1976—. Mem. adv. com. Electronic Computer Programming Inst. Tidewater (Va.). Served with Signal Corps, U.S. Army, 1957-59. Mem. Data

Processing Mgmt. Assn. (pres. 1977, dir.), Shared Hosp. Systems Assn. (vice-chmn. 1979), Nat. Microfilm Assn., Va. Hosp. Assn., Nat. Hosp. Collectors Assn. (vice-chmn. 1979), Soc. Cert. Data Processors, Soc. Computer Medicine, Inst. Certification Computer Profls. (certified in data processing), Adminstrv. Mgmt. Soc. (cert. adminstrn. mgr.), Nat. Acad. Adminstrv. Mgrs. Republican. Episcopalian. Clubs: Hampton Rds. Cotillion, Virginia Beach (Va.) Racquet, Harbor. Author: (with others) Management Accounting for the Furniture Manufacturer, 1971. Home: 1601 Barnard's Cove Rd Virginia Beach VA 23455 Office: 962 Norfolk Sq Norfolk VA 23502

DE CINTRON, EMMA VARGAS, ednl. counselor; b. Yauco, P.R., Aug. 8, 1926; d. Jose Bocheciampi and Maria Teresa Rivera de Vargas; B.A. in Sociology summa cum laude, Inter Am. U., San German, P.R., 1973, M.A. in Counseling and Guidance summa cum laude, 1974; postgrad. in psychology Centro Caribeño Estudios Postgraduados; m. Jorge N. Cintron, Feb. 14, 1948; children—Lisi C. Yazquez, Ileana C. Vazquez. Weekly columnist newspaper El Mundo, San Juan, P.R., 1979—; advisor for dormitories Inter Am. U., San German, P.R., 1978-79, part time prof. dept. edn., 1976-77, cons. orientation center, 1974-76; bus. mgr. U. P.R. Law Rev., Rio Piedras, 1963-71. Mem. Humanist Assn., Am. Personnel and Guidance Assn., Puerto Rican Guidance Assn., Phi Delta Kappa (editor Phi-De-Ka). Methodist. Clubs: Lions (Domadora), Grandmothers, San German. Contbr. articles to newspapers including El Mundo, Impacto, Colinas, Puerto Rico Evangelico. Home and Office: Box 3263 Inter American University Campus San German PR 00753

DECKARD, CHARLES, financial exec.; b. nr. Bloomington, Ind., June 1, 1927; s. James Andrew and Nora (Sipes) D.; B.S., Ind. U., 1951; m. Emily Jane Dwyer, Dec. 25, 1948; children—Norita Charlene, Charles Kevin, Mark Alison. Instr. Ind. U., 1951-52; with Bendix Corp., South Bend, Ind., 1951-61, asst. to mgr. internal audit staff, 1956-61; controller Sheffield Corp., Dayton, Ohio, 1961-66; div. controller Automation and Measurement div. Bendix Corp., Dayton, 1966-69, Automotive Electronics div., Balt., 1969-70, Newport News, Va., 1971-75, controller Electronics and Engine Control Systems group, 1975—. Served with AUS, 1945-46. Methodist. Club: Four Seasons Towne (founding trustee, treas.) (Dayton). Home: 1 Digges Dr Newport News VA 23602 Office: 615 Bland Blvd Newport News VA 23602

DECKER, ALFRED STANLEY, mech. engr.; b. Springfield, Ill., Feb. 18, 1930; s. Daniel Webster and Helen Grace (Vogel) D.; B.S. in M.E., State U. Iowa, 1959; m. Patricia Ann Buck, Nov. 20, 1963; children—Denise M., Deborah G., Nancy E. With Owens Illinois Inc., Toledo, 1959-69, Anchor Hocking Corp., Lancaster, Ohio, 1969-70; mgr. machine devel. Univis div. Itek Corp., Fort Lauderdale, 1970-73; staff mech. engr. Motorola Inc., Fort Lauderdale, 1973—. Served with U.S. Army, 1950-52: Korea. Mem. ASME, Nat. Soc. Profl. Engrs., Pi Tau Sigma, Tau Beta Pi. Baptist. Patentee in field. Home: 660 Glenwood Ln Plantation FL 33317 Office: 8000 Sunrise Blvd W Fort Lauderdale FL 33313

DECKER, HAROLD LEE, gallery exec.; b. Norfolk, Va., June 22, 1945; s. Sam and Rose (Kayer) D.; B.A. in Polit. Sci. cum laude, Old Dominion U., 1967; m. Barbara Berson, Nov. 25, 1967; 1 son, Bradley Harris. Vice pres. Old Dominion Brokerage Co., Norfolk, 1965—; pres. Harold Decker Galleries, Norfolk, 1970—; tchr. art Norfolk Pub. Schs., 1977-78. Pres., Tidewater Regional Ballet, 1977-78; bd. dirs. Tidewater Arts Council, 1975-77, Temple Israel, 1977—, Met. Arts Congress, 1978-80, Chrysler Mus. Library Com., Norfolk 200; mem. City of Norfolk Commn. of Arts and Humanities, 1978-80; chmn. Tidewater Ballet Assn., 1979-80; bd. dirs. Nat. Assn. Regional Ballet, 1979—, Va. Stage Co., 1979—; mem. Internat. Azalea Festival Com., 1978, 79, 80; mem. Chrysler Mus., Va. Mus., Met. Mus. Art, Jewish Community Center Tidewater. Served with U.S. Navy, 1967-70. Mem. Tidewater, Virginia Beach, Chesapeake Bay artists assns., Profl. Picture Framers Assn. (pres. Tidewater chpt. 1966-67), Am. Crafts Council, Va. Crafts Council, Ceramic Designers Assn., Tidewater Craftsman's Guild, Am. Art Dealers Assn., Nat. Audubon Soc., Norfolk C. of C. Jewish. Clubs: B'nai B'rith, Kiwanis, Tidewater Yacht and Country, Cape Henry Bird. Home: 1601 Longdale Dr Norfolk VA 23518 Office: PO Box 14248 Norfolk VA 23518

DECKER, JOSEPHINE I., clinic adminstr.; b. Barling, Ark., May 24, 1933; d. Ralph and Ada A. (Claborn) Snider; student public schs., Muldrow, Okla.; m. William Arlen Decker, Feb. 4, 1952; 1 son, Peter A. With Southwestern Bell Telephone Co., Fort Smith, Ark., 1951-52; with Holt Krock Clinic, Fort Smith, 1952—, bus. mgr., 1970—. Bd. dirs. Sparks Credit Union, Adv. Council Northside and Southside high schs., Fort Smith, Fort Smith Credit Bur. Mem. Credit Women Internat., Soc. Cert. Consumer Credit Execs. Home: 508 SE Sam Houston Muldrow OK 74948 Office: Holt Krock Clinic 1500 Dodson Ave Fort Smith AR 72901

DEDO, RICHARD GREGG, orthopedic surgeon, educator; b. Detroit, Jan. 11, 1935; s. Homer H. and Dorothy (Gregg) D.; B.A., U. Kans., 1957; M.D., Northwestern U., 1964; m. Barbara Lynn Isely, Feb. 4, 1967; children—Katherine Anne, William Scott, Rebecca Lynn. Intern Chgo. Wesley Hosp., 1964-65; resident Northwestern U., Chgo., 1965-69; instr. orthopaedic surgery The Children's Mem. Hosp., Chgo., 1969-70; asst. prof. dept. orthopaedic surgery Jacksonville (Fla.) Hosps. Ednl. Program, 1970—. Served as navigator, USAF, 1957-60. Fellow Am. Acad. Orthopaedic Surgeons. Episcopalian. Home: 8629 La Losa Dr W Jacksonville FL 32217 Office: 321 Marshall Taylor Bldg Jacksonville FL 32207

DEDRICK, JOHN HENRY, metals co. exec.; b. Milw., July 10, 1913; s. John Henry and Mathilde Ernestine (Phlamer) D.; B.S. in Chem. Engring., U. Wis., 1935; postgrad. metallurgy Pa. State U., 1936-37; D.Sc., Mass. Inst. Tech., 1948; m. Irene McWhorter, Apr. 1959. With Reynolds Metals Co., 1950—, dir. basic research, 1966-70, exec. asst. to exec. v.p. research and devel., 1970-72, gen. dir. metall. research div., Richmond, Va., 1972—. Fellow Am. Inst. Chemists; mem. Am. Soc. Metals, AIME, Brit. Inst. Metals, Va. Acad. Sci., Sigma Xi, Alpha Chi Sigma. Clubs: Sertoma (Richmond), Mass. Inst. Tech. of Va. (v.p.). Contbr. chpts. to books, numerous articles to profl. jours. Patentee field phys. metallurgy. Home: 7618 Cornwall Rd Richmond VA 23229 Office: 4th and Canal Sts Richmond VA 23218

DEE, NORBERT, civil engr., environ. planning adminstr.; b. Milw., Feb. 22, 1942; s. Norbert Victor and Mavis (Kastrova) Domagalski; B.S., Marquette U., 1965; M.S., Johns Hopkins U., 1966, Ph.D. (fellow), 1970; m. Nena Phyllis Keen, Aug. 19, 1967; children—Jenna Lin, Jeffrey Kim. Environ. planner Battelle Lab., Columbus, Ohio, 1970-75; asst. dept. mgr. Battelle, Resources Mgmt. Dept., Columbus, 1975-77; mgr. environ. programs Battelle So. Corp., Atlanta, 1977—. Mem. ASCE, Sigma Xi. Contbr. numerous articles on environ. planning and evaluation to profl. publs. Home: 1744 Eastgate Dr Stone Mountain GA 30087 Office: 101 Marietta St Atlanta GA 30303

DEER, ELVA MAE, librarian; b. Pitts., Sept. 4, 1926; d. Lewis Hutchinson and Martha (Caughey) D.; B.A., Bethany (W.Va.) Coll., 1948; M.S., U. Ark., 1952; M.A. in L.S., U. Denver, 1971; Fulbright summer scholar U. Poona (India), 1962. Tchr., Pulaski County (Ark.) Spl. Sch. Dist., 1949-59; tchr. Indpls. Public Schs., 1959-65; with Peace Corps, Ethiopia, 1965-67, Indpls., 1967-71; asst. prof. edn. West Tex. State U., Canyon, 1971—; mem. Ind. State-Wide Curriculum Com. Library Sci. AAUW scholar, 1978, 79; East-West grantee, 1964. Mem. NEA, Tex. Tchrs. Assn., Randal County Tchrs. Assn., Tex. Assn. Coll. Tchrs., ALA, Tex. Library Assn. Democrat. Home: 411 Thompson Ln Canyon TX 79015 Office: W Tex State U Box 208 Canyon TX 79015

DEERE, RUNYAN ELTON, educator; b. Rolla, Ark., May 13, 1919; s. Elijah Bithon and Frances Lee (Overton) D.; B.S., U. Ark., 1942, M.S., 1963; Ph.D. (Kellogg Found. fellow, Gen. Motors Corp. fellow), U. Wis., 1966; m. George Etta Barnette, July 7, 1943; children—Linda Frances, Robert Thomas. County extension agt. Coop. Extension Service, U. Ark., 1946-53, state subject matter specialist, 1953-56, dist. field supr., 1956-72, state program leader health edn., 1972—; adj. prof. Coll. Edn., U. Ark., 1975—, adj. prof. public health edn. Coll. Medicine, 1979. Served with U.S. Army, 1942-46. Mem. Soc. Public Health Edn., Am. Rural Health Assn., Adult Edn. Assn. U.S., Rural Sociol. Soc., Ark. Public Health Assn., Omicron Delta Kappa, Alpha Zeta, Gamma Sigma Delta, Epsilon Sigma Phi. Baptist. Club: Rotary (Little Rock). Home: 7419 Gable Dr Little Rock AR 72205 Office: 1201 McAlmont St PO Box 391 Little Rock AR 72203

DEERING, RONALD FRANKLIN, librarian; b. Paxton, Ill., Oct. 6, 1929; s. Minor Franklin and Grace Gilmore (Perkins) D.; B.A. summa cum laude, Georgetown Coll., 1951; B.D., So. Bapt. Theol. Sem., 1955, Th.D., 1961; M.S. in Library Sci., Columbia, 1967; m. Edith Ann Proctor, June 12, 1966; children—Mark David, Daniel Timothy. Ordained to ministry Bapt. Ch., 1950; instr. religion Georgetown (Ky.) Coll., 1951; pastor Blue River Bapt. Ch., Salem, Ind., 1955-58; instr. Greek, So. Bapt. Theol. Sem., Louisville, 1958-61, research librarian, 1962-67, asso. librarian, 1967-71, librarian, 1971—. Recipient Lilly Fund grant, 1967. Mem. Am. Assn. U. Profs., Am. Acad. Religion, Soc. Bibl. Lit., Phi Alpha Theta, Sigma Tau Delta, Beta Phi Mu. Home: 3111 Dunleith Ct Louisville KY 40222

DEES, ANTHONY ROANE, assn. exec.; b. Pikeville, N.C., Sept. 19, 1937; s. Claude Edward and Lois Winifred (Jackson) D.; B.A., U. N.C., 1959, M.S. in L.S., 1964; m. Leslie Gray McNeill, Sept. 27, 1975. Catalogue librarian Washington and Lee U., Lexington, Va., 1962-67; catalogue librarian, then curator manuscripts U. Ga., Athens, 1967-77, mem. faculty, 1967-77; dir. Ga. Hist. Soc., Savannah, 1977—; mem. faculty Armstrong State Coll., Savannah, 1979—. Mem. Soc. Am. Archivists, Soc. Ga. Archivists, Southeastern Library Assn., Ga. Library Assn. Democrat. Roman Catholic. Club: Rotary. Author articles, weekly newspaper column. Home: 112 W Taylor St Savannah GA 31401 Office: 501 Whitaker St Savannah GA 31401

DEES, JAMES WILLYN, psychologist; b. Atlanta, July 15, 1936; s. James O'Reagan and Bertha Louise (Jones) D.; B.A., Emory U., 1958; Ph.D., U. Tenn., 1962; m. Joyce Ann Wood, May 26, 1963; children—Kathryn Joyce, Beverly JoAnne, Amy Elizabeth. Sr. engring. psychologist McDonnell Aircraft Corp., St. Louis, 1962-65; asst. prof. U. Akron, 1965-67; sr. scientist Human Resources Research Orgn., Dothan, Ala., 1967-75; prof. Wallace Community Coll., U. Ala. and Troy State U., 1975-76; ops. research systems analyst U.S. Army Aviation Bd., Ft. Rucker, Ala., 1976—. Lectr., Washington U., 1964-65; cons. Goodyear Aerospace Corp., 1965-67, Center for Urban Studies, Akron, 1966-67. Mem. Am., Southeastern psychol. assns., Human Factors Soc., Soc. Aviation Psychologists, Mil. Testing Assn., Sigma Xi, Sigma Nu. Presbyterian. Contbr. articles to profl. jours. Inventor of motion picture mirror stereoscope. Home: 900 Richmond Rd Dothan AL 36301 Office: US Army Aviation Bd Fort Rucker AL 36360

DEES, LAFON CARABO, mfrs. rep.; b. Bennettsville, S.C., Aug. 13, 1937; s. Willie Ray and Allie Lee (Carabo) D.; A.B., Wofford Coll., Spartanburg, S.C., 1959; m. Elizabeth Winston Clark, June 15, 1963; 1 dau., Kimberly Ann. Mktg. rep. Armstrong Cork Co., Buffalo, also Syracuse, N.Y. and Houston, 1962-68; sales mgr. Stewart Co., Dallas, 1968-72, gen. sales mgr., 1972; mfrs. rep. Lane Co., Atlanta, 1972—. Pres., North Harbor Club, Inc., 1976—; 1st v.p. Underwood Hills Sch. PTA, 1977-78. Served to 1st lt. U.S. Army, 1959-62. Mem. Internat., Ga. home furnishings reps. assns., Ga. Home Furnishings Assn. Methodist. Home and Office: 425 N Harbor Dr NW Atlanta GA 30328

DEES, SALLY BICE, research microbiologist; b. Montgomery, Ala., July 5, 1933; d. Stoughton Nathaniel and Sibyl Carolyn (Simpson) Bice; B.A., Huntingdon Coll., 1955; M.S., Ga. State U., 1970; children—Deborah Diane Samuels, Laura Carolyn Wood, Marza Katherine Stewart. Microbiologist, Ala. State Health Dept., Montgomery, 1955-57, Ga. State Health Dept., Atlanta, 1957-61; research microbiologist Center for Disease Control, Atlanta, 1961—; lectr. in field. Trainer, scheduler Contact Teleministries, 24-Hour Crisis Line, 1977-78. Cert. specialist in public health and med. lab. microbiology. Mem. Am. Soc. Microbiology, Sigma Xi. Author articles on fatty acid composition of various bacteria and how this technique can be applied to taxonomy and identification of these organisms. Office: Center for Disease Control Bldg 5 Room 112 1600 Clifton Rd Atlanta GA 30333

DEESE, JOHN THOMAS, drug chain exec.; b. Pensacola, Fla., Feb. 7, 1948; s. William Ira and Elizabeth (Trippe) D.; student N.C. State U., 1966-68; m. Mary Lana Bolen, June 22, 1968; children—Mary Patricia, Julie Trippe. Layout artist Sears Roebuck & Co., Raleigh, N.C., 1968-71, asst. advt. mgr., 1971-73, advt. and sales promotion mgr., 1973-74, cons., zone advt. layout artist, Greensboro, N.C., 1974-76; advt. dir. Kerr Drug Stores, Inc., Raleigh, 1976—. Umpire, coach Little League, commr. umpires, 1977-79; tutor elem. sch., 1978-79; chmn. publicity PTA, 1978-79. Recipient Proctor & Gamble creative award, 1979; Golden Triangle creative award, 1978; Merchandising certificate Sears, 1969, Div. Mgmt. certificate, 1969. Mem. Triangle Ad Club, Audit Bur. Circulations. Office: Kerr Drug Stores Inc PO Box 30249 Raleigh NC 27622

DE FAZIO, RICHARD ANTHONY, mgmt. cons.; b. North Tonawanda, N.Y., June 14, 1946; s. Dominic R. and Teresa B. (Bucciarelli) DeF.; A.B., Niagara U., 1966; B.S., SUNY, Buffalo, 1975, M.B.A., 1976; m. Karen Long, July 1, 1972. Cost analyst N.Y. State Power Authority, Lewiston, 1967-74; v.p. ops. Ops. Analysis Co., Buffalo, 1974-76; exec. v.p. Ops. Mgmt. Group, Inc., Atlanta, 1976—. Served with USAF, 1966-69. Mem. AIME. Home: 903 Angeline Ct Lilburn GA 30247 Office: 330 Buckeye Rd Atlanta GA 30341

DE FOOR, IRA THOMAS, educator; b. Hahn, Tex., Mar. 17, 1919; s. Tant Thomas and Maggie Elizabeth (Lewandowski) DeF.; B.S., N. Tex. State U., 1948, M.S., 1949; m. Vada Mae Kunkel, May 8, 1948; children—Ronald Thomas, Lanny Paul, Kelley Jane. Supr. men's activity program N. Tex. State U., Denton, 1953-69, asst. dir. health, phys. edn. and athletics, 1961-69, asst. dir. health, phys. edn. and recreation, 1969-73, facilities-equipment coordinator, 1969-73, asst. prof. div. health edn., 1973—. Served with U.S. Army, 1943-46; PTO. Mem. AAHPER, Tex. Assn. Health, Phys. Edn. and Recreation, Tex. Dental Assn., Phi Delta Kappa. Democrat. Roman Catholic. Home: 1407 Kendolph Dr Denton TX 76201 Office: Men's Bldg Room 109A N Tex State U Denton TX 76203

DE FOREST, AGNES BATTELLE BONELL (MRS. LIONEL THEODORE DE FOREST), club woman; b. Manitou, Colo., 1908; d. Benjamin Walter and Agnes (Bailey) Bonell; student U. Hawaii, St. Mary's Coll., Dallas, Manaolu Coll., Hawaii, Sam Houston State U., Tex.; m. Lionel Theodore De Forest, 1929; children—Alice Battelle (Mrs. Emil Henry Klatt, Jr.), Amber DeForest Sharp. Pres. United Ch. Women, Beaumont, Tex.; regent George Washington chpt. D.A.R., Galveston, Tex., 1963-65, state chmn. D.A.R. Mag., 1964-67, Good Citizens, 1967-69; v.p. Episcopal Churchwomen Diocese Tex., 1966-68; regional chmn. Nat. Cathedral; instr. yoga exercises. Mem. D.A.R. (S.C. chaplain), Descs. of Signers Declaration of Independence (pres.-gen. 1972-75, editor Spirit of 76 newsletter), Mayflower Descs., Pilgrim John Howland Soc., Women Descs. Ancient and Honorable Arty. Co., Colonial Dames XVII Century (chpt. pres.). Republican. Episcopalian. Address: Star Route 5 Box 121A Beaufort SC 29902

DEFOREST, JOHN WILLIAM, psychologist; b. Sewanee, Tenn., Dec. 5, 1946; s. John Theophilus and Anne Louise (Gammon) DeF.; B.S., Southwestern U., 1969; M.A., U. Houston, 1972; m. Nancy Penelope VanKleef, Aug. 30, 1969; children—Rachel Marie. Staff psychologist Tex. Research Inst. Mental Scis., Houston, 1972-74; program dir. Gulf Coast Regional Mental Health/Mental Retardation Center, Galveston, Tex., 1974-77, asso. service dir., 1977-78, service dir., 1978—; instr. Houston Community Coll., 1973-75. Bd. mem. Bayor Chantilly Civic Club, 1978—. Southwestern U. beneficiary scholar, 1965-69; Tex. Research Inst. Mental Scis. fellow, 1971-72. Mem. Am. Assn. Mental Deficiency, Am. Psychol. Assn., Nat. Rehab. Assn., Tex. Psychol. Assn. Democrat. Episcopalian. Home: 4912 Live Oak St Dickinson TX 77539 Office: 507 Tremont St Galveston TX 77553

DE FOREST, LIONEL THEODORE, clergyman; b. Boston, Aug. 20, 1905; s. John T. and Lavinia (Monish) DeF.; B.A., St. John's Coll., Greeley, Colo., 1927; B.D., Episcopal Theol. Sch., Cambridge, Mass., 1929, M.Div., 1973; LL.B., E. Tex. Coll. Law, Beaumont, 1944; B.S., Sam Houston State U., Huntsville, Tex., 1965; m. Agnes Battelle Bonell, Sept. 30, 1929; children—Amber (Mrs. James C. Sharp, Jr.), Alice Battelle (Mrs. Emil H. Klatt, Jr.), Steve Scott (Mrs. David J. Rossi, dec.). Ordained priest Episcopal Ch., 1929; priest-in-charge St. Andrew's Ch., La Junta, Colo., 1929-31; asst. rector Christ Ch., Houston, 1931-34; rector Good Shepherd Ch., Houston, 1934-38, St. George's Ch., Port Arthur, Tex., 1938-40, St. Cyprian's Ch., Lufkin, Tex., 1940-41; admitted to Tex. bar, 1944; asst. city atty., Beaumont, Tex., 1944-47; exec. dir. Boys Haven, Beaumont, 1947-48; rector Grace Episcopal Ch., Galveston, Tex., 1948-65, St. John's Ch., Marlin, Tex., 1945-49; chaplain, tchr., asst. headmaster Beaufort (S.C.) Acad., 1969-73; priest-in-charge Ch. of the Heavenly Rest, Estill, S.C., 1972-76, Sheldon Chapel, McPhersonville, S.C., 1976—; civilian Episc. chaplain USMC Tng. Depot, Parris Island, S.C., 1971—; mem. exec. com. Episcopal Diocese Tex., 1932-35, sec., 1935-41, mem. standing com., 1966-69, pres. standing com., 1969; pres. Port Arthur Ministerial Assn., 1939, Galveston Ministerial Assn., 1950, Marlin Ministerial Assn., 1966. Bd. dirs. Port Arthur chpt. ARC, 1938-40, Galveston chpt., 1948; pres. adv. bd. Salvation Army, Beaufort, 1977—. Republican. Elk, Mason (Shriner), Rotarian (pres. Beaufort 1970-71). Editor Tex. Churchman, 1932-35. Address: Star Route 5 Box 121A Beaufort SC 29902

DE FRANK, VINCENT, condr.; b. L.I. City, N.Y., June 18, 1915; s. Nicholas and Della (Proudford) DeF.; student Juilliard Sch. Music, 1934-36, Ind. U., 1950-52; D.Mus. (hon.), Southwestern U., Memphis, 1974; m. Jean Marie Martin, Aug. 26, 1960; children—Vincent Nicholas, Philip Martin. Cellist Detroit Symphony Orch., 1939-40, St. Louis Symphony, 1947-50; condr. Memphis Symphony Orch., 1952—, also Memphis Little Symphony, Memphis Youth Symphony; music supr. Memphis-Hebrew Acad., 1969—; mem. adv. panel Tenn. Arts Commn., 1970—; guest condr. Memphis Civic Ballet, Memphis Opera Theatre, Tenn. All-State Orch., Sewanee Summer Music Center, Jackson (Miss.) Symphony, Nashville Symphony and Little Symphony, Quincy (Ill.) Symphony. Served with AUS, 1940-45. Mem. Memphis Music Inc., Am. Symphony Orch. League, Violin Cello Soc., Conductors' Guild, Nat. Soc. Lit. and Arts, Nat. Rifleman Assn. Club: Petroleum (Memphis). Office: 3100 Walnut Grove Rd Suite 402 Memphis TN 38111

DEFROSCIA, GERARD, auditor; b. Coatesville, Pa., Nov. 3, 1946; s. William J. and Fern Velda DeF.; B.S. in Bus. Adminstrn., Drexel U., 1969. Cost analyst Lukens Steel Co., Coatesville, 1969-71; staff acct. McGraw-Hill Book Co., Hightstown, N.J., 1971-73; sr. auditor Audit Bur. of Circulations, Chgo., 1973—.

DE GAISH, MELADE S., vocat. adminstr.; b. Sweetwater, Tex., Dec. 24, 1933; s. Shaheen Shaff and Lurece (Samara) DeG.; B.S., Tex. Tech. U., Lubbock, 1957; M.S., Tex. A. and I. U., 1971; m. Mary Darlene Ganam, July 4, 1960; children—Mark Steven, Miriam Ann, Darlene Ann, Brett John, Debra Ann. Tchr. and coach, then elementary adminstr. Robston (Tex.) Ind. Sch. Dist., 1959-69; vocat. tchr. Gregory (Tex.)-Portland Ind. Sch. Dist., 1969-75, vocat. adminstr., 1975—; v.p. Invesco 74, Corpus Christi, Tex., 1978—; cons. in field. Served with AUS, 1957-59. Recipient Outstanding Service award Robstown Ind. Sch. Dist., 1968-69. Mem. NEA, Tex. Tchrs. Assn., Am. Vocat. Assn., Tex. Vocat. Tech. Assn., Tex. Assn. Dirs. and Suprs. Occupational Edn. and Tech. (state dir.), Nat. Council Local Adminstrs. Democrat. Roman Catholic. Club: Lions (pres. Portland 1970-71; named Lion of Year 1975). Home: Box 664 Portland TX 78374 Office: Box 338 Gregory TX 78359

DEGEROLAMI, STANLEY CARL, social worker; b. San Antonio, Jan. 9, 1950; s. Quinto and Helen Gertrude (Barger) DeG.; B.S.W., Our Lady of Lake Coll., San Antonio, 1975, M.S.W., 1976; children—Giovanni Battista, Carla Leal. Sports editor Alamo Messenger, San Antonio, 1969-70; attendant, counselor, rehab. therapist technician Austin (Tex.) State Hosp., 1970-73; rehab. therapist technician San Antonio State Hosp., 1973-74; adminstrv. asst. St. Joseph's Ch., San Antonio, 1974-75; adminstr., exec. dir. Salvation Army Home for Girls, San Antonio, 1976-79; child placement worker Tex. Dept. Human Resources, San Antonio, 1979-80; med./psychiat. caseworker, chief social services Giddings (Tex.) State Home and Sch., 1980—; field instr. social work Antioch Coll., San Antonio, 1978-79, Incarnate Word Coll., San Antonio, 1978-79, Our Lady of Lake U., 1976-79. Lic. child care adminstr. Mem. Nat. Assn. Social Workers. Democart. Roman Catholic. Home: 211 Golden Crown San Antonio TX 78223 Office: PO Box 600 Giddings TX 78942

DE GEROME, JAMES HENRY, III, internist, gastroenterologist; b. Newark, May 11, 1940; s. James Henry and Helen Paterno (Ciluzzi) DeG.; B.S., Georgetown U., 1962; M.S., N.Y.U., 1963; M.D., N.J. Coll. Medicine, 1968; m. Cornelia Ann Byron, Aug. 5, 1965; children—James Henry IV, Alison, Julie Ann. Intern, N.J. Coll. Medicine, 1968-69, resident internal medicine, 1969-70; fellow gastroenterology Wilford Hall USAF Med. Center, San Antonio, 1971-73; dir. internal medicine and gastroenterology Scott AFB, Ill.,

1973-74; pvt. practice specializing in gastroenterology and internal medicine, Delray Beach, Fla., 1974—. Served with M.C., USAF, 1970-74. Decorated Air Force Commendation Medal; diplomate Am. Bd. Internal Medicine. Fellow A.C.P.; mem. AMA, Am. Soc. Gastrointestinal Endoscopy, Palm Beach County Med. Soc., Fla. Med. Assn., Am. Gastroenterol. Assn., Georgetown U. Alumni Assn. Roman Catholic. Club: Quail Ridge Racquet. Office: 250 Dixie Blvd Suite 201 Delray Beach FL 33444

DE GRAFFENRIED, WILLIAM RYAN, state senator; b. Tuscaloosa, Ala., Apr. 2, 1950; s. William Ryan and Margaret Nell (Maxwell) deG.; B.S., U. Ala., 1975; LL.B., Cumberland Sch. Law, 1975; m. Georgia Ann Bailey, June 5, 1971; children—William Ryan, III, Frances Margaret. Clk., Office Ala. Atty. Gen.-Office U.S. Atty. Gen., 1975; admitted to Ala. bar, 1975; dist. atty. Tuscaloosa County, 1975-76; partner firm Hubbard, Waldrop, Tanner & deGraffenried, Tuscaloosa, 1976—; mem. Ala. Senate from 16th Dist., 1978—, vice chmn. judiciary com.; dir. Tuscaloosa Hotel Co., Inc. Mem. Am. Bar Assn., Ala. Bar Assn., Ala. Trial Lawyers Assn., Tuscaloosa County Bar Assn., Tuscaloosa County Trial Lawyers Assn., Cattlemen's Assn., Tuscaloosa Jaycees. Democrat. Presbyterian. Club: Tuscaloosa Exchange. Home: 48 Academy Dr Tuscaloosa AL 35406 Office: 808 Lurleen Blvd N Tuscaloosa AL 35401

DEGRAZIA, JOSEPH ANTHONY, physician; b. Rochester, N.Y., Sept. 22, 1934; s. Joseph Anthony and Bessie D.; B.A., Harvard Coll., 1956; M.D., Tufts U., 1960; m. Anne G. Batchelor, July 30, 1957; children—Henry, Anthony, William. Intern, U. Chgo., 1960-61; fellow in endocrinology and radioisotopes, U. Wash., Seattle, 1961-63; resident in medicine U. Calif., San Francisco, 1963-66, NIH spl. fellow in clin. pathology, 1966-68; asst. prof. radiol. div. nuclear medicine Stanford (Calif.) U. Med. Sch., 1968-74; practice medicine specializing in nuclear medicine, Santa Cruz, Calif., 1974-76; dir. nuclear medicine Community Hosp., Santa Cruz, 1976; dir. med. edn. Spartanburg (S.C.) Gen. Hosp., 1976—; asst. dean, asso. prof. radiologic (nuclear) medicine Med. U. S.C., Charleston, 1976—; pres. CSI Corp., 1978—. Recipient grants HEW, 1967-75, Appalachian Regional Council, 1978—. Mem. Soc. Nuclear Medicine, Spartanburg County Med. Assn., S.C. Med. Assn., AMA, Assn. Hosp. Med. Edn., Am. Assn. Physicists in Medicine, Nuclear Medicine Soc. Contbr. articles to profl. jours. Home: PO Box 4457 Spartanburg SC 29303 Office: 101 E Wood St Spartanburg SC 29303

DE GROOT, SYBIL GRAMLICH, psychologist, educator; b. Evanston, Ill., Feb. 28, 1928; d. Charles Christian and Mary Edith (Thompson) Gramlich; A.A., Stephens Coll., 1946; B.A. in Psychology, Ohio State U., 1947, M.A. in Exptl. Psychology, 1950, Ph.D. in Engring. Psychology, 1968; m. Robert Carstens de Groot, July 3, 1950 (div. 1963); children—Robert Jason, Jon Christian, Annika. Rockette, Radio City Music Hall, N.Y.C., 1948; research asst. Inst. for Co-op Research, Johns Hopkins U., Balt., 1950-51; psychophysicist of vision U.S. Naval Med. Research Lab., Groton, Conn., 1951-52; propr., dir. Sch. of Dance, Old Greenwich, Conn., 1952-58; counselor to teenagers Old Greenwich-Riverside Community Center, 1952-53; staff. psychologist Dunlap and Assos., Darien, Conn., 1958-62; research asso. Bur. Ednl. Research and Service, Coll. Edn., Ohio State U., Columbus, 1962-66, research asso. Div. of Info. and Computer Scis., Coll. Engring., 1967-68; asst. prof. dept. psychology Mont. State U., Bozeman, 1968-72; asso. prof. dept. psychology, research dir. Sch. of Hotel, Food, and Travel, Fla. Internat. U., Miami, 1972-74, asso. prof. div. indsl. engring. tech., 1974—, dir. Grad. Teaching Assts. Tng. Program, 1970-72, spl. asst. to the dean on affirmative Action, 1975—; sci. cons. to Fla. Home Econs. Assn., 1973— pub. opinion survey cons. to State of Mont., Office of Water Resources, 1971-72. Cub Scout Den mother, Old Greenwich, 1960-61. NSF fellow, 1967-68; Air Force Office of Sci. Research grantee, 1977, USAF research fellow, 1976, NASA design fellow, 1975. Mem. Human Factors Soc., Am. Psychol. Assn., Am. Soc. Engring. Educators, Soc. Women Engrs. (scholarship chairperson Fla. sect. 1978-80), AAUW, LWV, Soc. Engring. Psychologists, Internat. Ergonomics Assn., Bus. and Profl. Women, Rockette Alumnae Assn., Kappa Kappa Gamma. Republican. Congregationalist. Contbr. articles on human factors psychology to profl. jours. Home: 12765 SW 54th St Miami FL 33175 Office: Fla Internat U Tamiami Trail Miami FL 33199

DE HART, ROBERT CHARLES, research co. exec.; b. Laramie, Wyo., Aug. 16, 1917; s. Charles Edward and Harriet Irene (Tapling) DeH.; B.S., U. Wyo., 1938; M.S., Ill. Inst. Tech., 1940, Ph.D., 1953; m. Ethel M. Thompson, Sept. 20, 1941 (dec. Apr. 1970); children—Michael R., Dayle Ann; m. 2d, Marion W. McDonald, Aug. 21, 1970. Design engr. Standard Oil Co., Wood River, Ill., 1940-46; asso. prof. Mont. State U., Bozeman, 1946-53; analyst Armed Forces Spl. Weapons Project, Washington, 1953-58; mgr. structural mechanics S.W. Research Inst., San Antonio, 1958-59, dir. structural research, 1959-72, v.p., 1972—. Lectr., George Washington U., Washington, 1955-58. Mem. ASCE, ASME, N.Y. Acad. Scis., Sigma Xi, Phi Kappa Phi, Tau Beta Pi, Sigma Tau. Home: 403 LaJara St San Antonio TX 78209 Office: 8500 Culebra Rd San Antonio TX 78284

DE HART, SHEPPARD ALLEN, ednl. adminstr.; b. nr. Stuart, Va., Sept. 3, 1926; s. Samuel A. and Losia (Weaver) De H.; student Cleve. Bible Coll., 1945-47; grad. Mpls. Sch. Art, 1951; student U. Heidelberg (Germany), 1952; B.A., High Point Coll., 1955; M.A., U. Va., 1957; postgrad. Duke U., 1960-61, Fla. State U., 1961; m. Flora Ballowe, Sept. 3, 1956. Free-lance artist advt. and decorating Park Place, Danville, Va., 1948-49; adminstrv. asst. Va. Mil. Dist., 1948-50; columnist Danville Comml. Appeal, 1949-50; ordained to ministry Am. Christian Ch., 1950; pastor Meth. Chs., Martinsville, Va., 1950-51, Rochelle, Va., 1965-67; dir. counseling services Louisburg (N.C.) Coll., 1957-71, lectr. exptl. psychology, 1968—, dir. public affairs, 1973—. Chmn., Franklin County Indsl. Devel. Com., 1963-76; founder Franklin County (N.C.) Arts Council, 1979. Served with U.S. Army, 1951-53. Recipient Internat. Creativity award, 1972; Disting. Citizen award, 1979, Merit award Washington Garden Club, 1979. Mem. Am. Psychol. Assn., N.C. Psychol. Assn., Assn. Coll. and Univ. Arts Adminstrs., Nat. Entertainment for Coll. Activities Assn. (co-founder 1960), So. Hist. Soc., Am. Personnel and Guidance Assn., Coll. News Assn., NEA (Leadership award 1973), AAUP, Am. Hiking Soc., Am. Adventurers Assn., Appalachian Mountains Club, Appalachian Trail Conf., Sierra Club. Democrat. Contbr. articles to various mags. and newspapers. Home: Route 1 Greencroft Louisburg NC 27549 Office: Louisburg Coll Louisburg NC 27549

DE HAVEN, JOHN MICHAEL, broadcasting co. exec.; b. Allentown, Pa., Aug. 17, 1926; s. John Francis and Emma Irene DeH.; B.S. in Bus. Adminstrn., U. Pitts., 1950; m. Gail Ann Horner, June 7, 1952; children—Michelle Jude, Jeffery Kevin. Account exec. Sta. WWSW, 1950-62; pres., gen. mgr. Pa. State Reps., 1962-66; nat. sales mgr. Susquehanna Broadcasting Co., N.Y.C., 1966-74; v.p. gen. mgr. Sta. WLTA, Atlanta, 1974—. Served with U.S. Navy, 1944-46. Sec. Dunwoody (Ga.) Sr. Baseball Assn. Mem. Atlanta Broadcast Exec. Club. Club: Lions. Office: 1459 Peachtree Rd NE Atlanta GA 30309

DE HAVEN, MARIE, nurse; b. Sawyer, Okla., July 30, 1938; d. George K. and Mattie Mae (Beach) Johnson; grad. Mercy Hosp. Sch. Nursing, Oklahoma City, 1962; m. Forest Richard DeHaven, Aug. 14, 1958; children—James Kenneth, Rosanna Marie. Operating room nurse supr. Hayden H. Donahue Mental Health Inst., Norman, Okla., 1962—.; preceptor South Oklahoma City Jr. Coll., 1977-78. Mem. Okla. Nurses Assn., Am. Nurses Assn., Assn. Operating Room Nurses, Central Service Assn., Paint Horse Show (sec. 1976-78), Norman Round-Up Club (sec.-treas. 1975). Baptist. Home: Route 4 Box 88CC Norman OK 73071 Office: Box 151 Norman OK 73070

DEIBERT, LAVERNE MALINDA, accountant; b. Clifton, Tex., Sept. 21, 1927; d. Henry William and Anna Augusta (Walsleben) Hampe; Asso. in Bus. Adminstrn., Central Tex. Jr. Coll., 1972; children—Clayton, Michael, Sue, Claire, Yvette, Donna, Fred, William. Owner, operator Lavern's Bake Shop, Clifton, 1961-67; salesman Tupperware, Killeen, Tex., 1969-72; chief fin. officer, asst. personnel dir. City of Harker Heights, Tex., 1973—. Mem. Am. Bus. Womens Assn., Mcpl. Fin. Officers Assn., Parents Without Partners. Lutheran. Home: 3913 Westcliff Rd Killeen TX 76541 Office: City of Harker Heights 120 Harley Dr Harker Heights TX 76541

DEIDESHEIMER, HAROLD JACOB, advt. exec.; b. N.Y.C., Feb. 1, 1917; s. Charles Phillip and Adeline (Erdenbrecher) D.; student pub. schs.; m. Mary Ann Moroni, Jan. 26, 1958; 1 dau., Annamaria E. Dir. printing Hazard Advt. Co., N.Y.C., 1948-53; salesman, printing cons. Reiman Conway Assos., N.Y.C., 1953-55; prodn. mgr., dir. printing and purchasing Harris & Whitebrook & Co., Miami Beach, Fla., 1955-57; prodn. mgr. C.J. LaRoche & Co., N.Y.C., 1957-58; asso. mgr. advt. prodn. controls Gen. Food Corp., White Plains, N.Y., 1959-64; adminstrv. mgr., account exec. firm Bishopric Green Fielden Advt., Miami, Fla., 1966-71; pres. Financial Plaza Advt. Co., Ft. Lauderdale, Fla., 1971—. Recipient Cronite awards Art Dirs. Club N.Y., 1952. Miami, 1956, Detroit, 1958; Advt. Achievement award Instns. Mag., 1977. Address: 2100 NW 12th Ave Fort Lauderdale FL 33311

DEILER, FREDERICK GEORGE, environ. biologist; b. New Orleans, June 19, 1921; s. Theodore G. and Myrtle C. (Bolt) D.; B.S., Tulane U., 1943, M.S., 1960; m. Peggy Anne Smith, Nov. 27, 1947; children—Barbara A., David F., Michael K. Research asst. Biloxi (Miss.) Lab., 1949-52; biologist Freeport Sulphur Co., New Orleans, 1952-62, sr. biologist Freeport Research & Devel., 1962-71, adminstr. biol. and environ. services, 1971-79, mgr. environ. public relations, 1979—. Bd. dirs. New Orleans Area/Bayou-River Health Systems Agy., 1977—; co-chmn. legis. com. La. Sch. Bd. Assn., 1974-75, pres. sch. bd., 1971—; chmn. Plaquemines dist. Boy Scouts Am., 1957-59; mem. La. Atty. Gen.'s Sci. Adv. Com., 1974—; bd. dirs. Ecology Center La., 1973—, La. Nature Center, Inc., 1973—. Recipient Regional Merit award Nat. Assn. Environ. Edn., 1975; Arthur Sidney Bedell award for extraordinary personal service in water pollution control, 1975; Spl. Service award La. Water Pollution Control Assn., 1976; Water or Air Conservationist of Year, La. and Nat. wildlife fedns. and Sears Roebuck & Co., 1977; awards Boy Scouts Am.; named Boss of Yr., La Bas chpt. Am. Bus. Women's Assn., 1979. Mem. La. Acad. Scis., La. Mosquito Control Assn., La. Water Pollution Control Assn., Water Pollution Control Fedn., Nat., La. air pollution control assns., Gulf State Council Wildlife, Fisheries and Mosquito Control, Mid-Continent Oil and Gas Assn. (air and water conservation com.), La. Wildlife Biologists Assn., La. Environ. Profls. Assn., Urban Pest Control Assn., Sigma Xi. Contbr. articles to profl. jours. Roman Catholic. Home: 210 Ollie Dr Belle Chasse LA 70037 Office: 821 Gravier St New Orleans LA 70161

DEINZER, HARVEY THEODORE, educator; b. Monroe, Mich., Dec. 24, 1908; s. Edwin Frederick and Emily Marie (Meissner) D.; A.B., U. Mich., 1932, M.B.A., 1933, Ph.D., 1947; J.D., U. Fla., 1955; m. Margaret Emily Reed, June 18, 1934; 1 son, Robert Reed. Accountant, Ernst & Ernst, Detroit, 1933-37; with F. E. Ross & Co., Ann Arbor, Mich., 1937-38; staff cons. Pub. Adminstrn. Service, Chgo., 1938-39; fiscal analyst, bus. economist U.S. Govt., Washington, 1942-43; prof. accounting Shrivenham Am. U., 1945; asso. prof. accounting U. Fla., Gainesville, 1947-49, prof., 1949-73, prof. emeritus, 1973—, interim prof. law, 1960. Served to 1st lt. AUS, 1943-46. Mem. Am. Econ. Assn., Order of the Coif, Beta Gamma Sigma, Phi Delta Phi. Author: Development of Accounting Thought, 1965; contbr. articles to profl. jours. Home: 928 NW 21st Terr Gainesville FL 32603

DEITENBECK, WILLIAM HESSION, clin. engr.; b. New Orleans, Apr. 25, 1945; s. Hugo and Elaine (Hession) D.; B.S. in Indsl. Tech., U. Southwestern La., 1973, B.S. in E.E., 1979; m. Lauralee Brisbin, Dec. 10, 1966; children—Erich, Alexander, Max. Head clin. engring. dept. Lafayette (La.) Gen. Hosp., 1970—; instr. U. Southwestern La. Served with U.S. Navy, 1963-69. Cert. biomed. equipment technologist, cert. clin. engr. Mem. IEEE, Am. Soc. Hosp. Engrs., Assn. Advancement of Med. Instrumentation, Nat. Fire Protection Assn., Mid-La. Health Systems Agy., Inc., La. Hosp. Assn., Eta Kappa Nu, Sigma Tau Epsilon, Nat. Eagle Scout Assn. Republican. Roman Catholic. Home: 305 Cleveland St Lafayette LA 70501 Office: 1214 Coolidge St Lafayette LA 70505

DEITZ, ROBERT LEE, JR., health care exec.; b. Charleston, W.Va., Mar. 15, 1945; s. Robert Lee and Eva Mae (Boggess) D.; B.S. in B.A. cum laude, W.Va. State Coll., 1972. Prodn. coordinator FMC Corp., Charleston, 1965-68; logistics and transp. coordinator Union Carbide Corp., South Charleston, W.Va., 1968-72; dir. purchasing Charleston Area Med. Center, 1973—. Mem. Tri-State Hosp. Purchasing Mgmt. Assn. (pres. 1978-79), Nat. Assn. Hosp. Purchasing/Material Mgmt., Am. Soc. for Hosp. Purchasing/Material Mgmt., Southeastern Hosp. Assn. Home: 6548 Roosevelt Ave SE Charleston WV 25304 Office: 3000 MacCorkel Ave SE Charleston WV 25304

DEIVANAYAGAM, SUBRAMANIAM, indsl. engr.; b. Tirunelveli, India, Nov. 15, 1941; s. Deivanayagam and Gomathy Subramaniam; came to U.S., 1969; B.Engring., Annamalai U., 1963, 66; Ph.D., Tex. Tech U., 1973; m. Ratna Sambasivam, Jan. 17, 1971; children—Vikram, Harsha. Indsl. engr. Enfield India Ltd., Madras, 1963-64; lectr. Thiagarajar Coll. Engring., Madurai, India, 1966-69; research asst. Tex. Tech U., Lubbock, 1969-72, research asso., 1973-75, asst. prof., 1975-76; asso. prof. indsl. engring. U. Tex., Arlington, 1976—; cons. Gen. Dynamics, Ft. Worth. Registered profl. engr., Tex. Mem. Am. Inst. Indsl. Engrs., Human Factors Soc., Aerospace Med. Assn., Sigma Xi, Tau Beta Pi, Alpha Pu Mu. Contbr. articles to profl. jours. Home: 4715 Oak Valley Arlington TX 76016 Office: Dept Indsl Engring U Tex Arlington TX 76019

DE JARNETTE, JAMES EDWARD, psychoanalyst, psychotherapist; b. Atlanta, Mar. 22, 1948; s. Charles Nathan and Sarah Holmes (Phillips) deJ.; B.A., Shorter Coll., 1970; M.A., W.Ga. Coll., 1971; Ph.D., Sussex Coll., 1975. Exec. dir. Middle Ga. Counseling Center, Macon, 1972—; exec. dir. Power Ferry Psychotherapy Clinic, 1976—; exec. dir. deJarnette and Assos., Beverly Hills, Calif., 1979—; chmn. bd. dirs. Leonidas Ltd., Inc.; bd. dirs. Alpha-Omega Enterprises, Inc.; chmn. bd. trustees Center for Meditative Living, Inc. Bd. dirs. Ga. Mental Health Assn., 1975, Macon/Bibb County Mental Health Assn., 1975. Fellow Am. Orthopsychiat. Assn., Am. Acad. Behavioral Sci.; mem. Am. Mental Health Counselors Assn., Nat. Psychiat. Assn., Internat. Soc. Adlerian Psychology, Pi Gamma Mu. Republican. Episcopalian. Contbr. articles to profl. jours. Office: Suite 590 Macon Federal Tower Macon GA 31201

DE LA BURDE, ROGER ZYGMUNT, corporate dir., investor, scientist; b. Katowice, Poland, Sept. 22, 1931; s. Rudolph Z. and Helena (Swiatek) delaB.; came to U.S., 1957, naturalized, 1965; M.S., Krakow (Poland) U., 1952, Ph.D., 1959; Ph.D. in Engring., Tech. Hochscule Aachen (Germany), 1961; M.Eng. in Indsl. Mgmt., Krakow Poly. Inst., 1956; m. Brigitte E. Stoltenberg, June 7, 1958; children—Clette-Alison, Corina Margot. Mgr. internat. div. Krakow Mfg. Co., 1952-56; sculptoral asst. with Fritz Wotruba; scientist Roswell Park Meml. Inst., Buffalo, 1957-59; project leader Armour & Co., Chgo., 1959-61; sr. scientist Philip Morris Corp., Richmond, Va., 1961-68; dir. Fed. Inst. Indsl. Research, Lagos, Nigeria, 1968-69; dir. Consol. Indsls. Inc., Richmond, Va., 1964-77; sec. treas., Powhatan, Va., 1968—; dir. Quester Investments, 1978—; adviser to UN Indsl. Devel. Orgn., 1968—. Sculptor and collector African and modern art, 1955—; collections exhibited at: Va. Mus. Art, Richmond, 1970, Lagos, Nigeria, 1969, Windsor, Powhatan, Va., 1974, Mala Galeria, Prague, Czechoslovakia, 1976, Pryzmat Galeria and Art Galeria, Krakow, Poland, 1977, Studio Galeria, Warsaw, Poland, 1978; dir. of ethnographic expdns. in Africa, 1969, 1973, 75. Named Art Collector of the Year, Va. Mus., 1972; recipient Patent medal award Philip Morris Corp., 1971, 76, 78, Polish Nat. Tech. award, 1952, U.S. Hide Assn. award, 1961. Fellow AAAS, Am. Inst. Chemists; mem. Am. Chem. Soc., Sci. Research Soc. of Am. (hon. mem.). Clubs: Island (Nigeria); Briarwood; 2300 (Richmond); Artists (Poland). Contbr. articles on chemistry, investments and African arts to profl. publs.; patentee new processes and products. Home: Route 2 Box 168 Powhatan VA 23139 Office: Philip Morris Research Center Box 26583 Richmond VA 23261

DE LA GARZA, E(KIKA), congressman; b. Mercedes, Tex., Sept. 22, 1927; s. Dario and Elisa (Villarreal) de la G.; student Pan Am. Coll., Edinburg, Tex., 1947-48; LL.B., St. Mary's U., San Antonio, 1951; m. Lucille Alamia, May 29, 1953; children—Jorge Luis, Michael Alberto, Angela Dolores. Admitted to Tex. bar, 1951; mem. Tex. Ho. of Reps. from Hidalgo County, 1953-64; mem. 89th-96th Congresses 15th Dist. Tex. Served with USNR, World War II, with AUS, Korea. Democrat. Office: 1434 Longworth House Office Bldg Washington DC 20515

DELAHOUSSAYE, CURTIS MARTIN, plaster contracting co. exec.; b. Lafayette, La., Dec. 28, 1925; s. John Wesley and Marie Therese (Martin) D.; grad. high sch.; m. Merry Clem Cosper, Sept. 23, 1971; children—Cynthia, Curtis, Albert, Daniel, Gregory, Don, Richard, Dominique, Andre. Pres., chief estimator J.W. Delahoussaye & Sons, Inc., Lafayette, La., 1948—; pres. C.M.D., Inc., Lafayette, 1966-74. Chmn., Lafayette Airport Commn., 1967. Served with AUS, 1944-46. Decorated Bronze Star, Purple Heart. Mem. La. Thoroughbred Breeders Assn. (dir.), Internat. Assn. Wall and Ceiling Contractors, Asso. Gen. Contractors, Am. Subcontractors Assn., Confederate Air Force, VFW. Democrat. Roman Catholic. Home: Route 1 Box 59C1F Broussard LA 70518 Office: 427 N Sterling Ave Lafayette LA 70501

DELAHUNT, JOHN CLARK, hosp. adminstr.; b. N.Y.C., July 23, 1918; s. Joseph William and Mary Tanner D.; B.S. in Pharmacy, Union U., 1941; m. Orpha May Small, July 5, 1943; children—Joseph, Helen, Deborah, John Clark; m. Elizabeth Park, Aug. 18, 1968; 1 son, Robert. Commd. 2d lt. U.S. Army, 1942, advanced through grades to col., 1971; mem. staff Air Force Insp. Gen.'s office, 1962-66; comdr. 801st Air Evacuation Squadron, Vietnam, 1967-68; adminstr. USAF Hosp., Tokyo, 1966-58; ret., 1971; asst. prof. U. Tex. Med. Sch., Dallas, 1971-77; staff pharmacist, asst. adminstr. Caruth Meml. Hosp., Dallas, 1978—; chmn. Pharmacy Theft Prevention Com., Dallas County, 1977-80. Active Big Bros. Assn. Decorated Legion of Merit (2), Air medal (3), Bronze Star (2). Mem. Am. Pharm. Assn., Am. Ret. Officers Assn., Tex. Soc. Cons. Pharmacists, Tex. Pharm. Assn., Dallas County Pharm. Assn. (dir. 1977-78), Dallas Ret. Officers Assn. (v.p. 1976-77). Roman Catholic. Club: Brookhaven Country (Dallas). Home: 3544 Ainsworth St Dallas TX 75229 Office: 7850 Brookhollow Dr Dallas TX 75235

DE LAITSCH, DALE M., educator; b. Colfax, Wis., Dec. 18, 1922; B.S., U. Chgo., 1944; B.A., St. Olaf Coll., 1946; Ph.D. in Chemistry, U. Minn., 1950; m. Marion Karlsbroten, July 30, 1945; children—David Martin, Paul George. Asst. prof. chemistry U. Southwestern La., Lafayette, 1950-52, asso. prof., 1952-63, prof., 1963—. Served to 1st lt. USAAF, 1943-46. Mem. Am. Chem. Soc. Address: Dept Chemistry U Southwestern La Lafayette LA 70501

DE LAITSCH, MARION KARLSBROTEN, educator; b. Spring Grove, Minn., Mar. 25, 1921; d. Martin E. and Marie (Otterness) Karlsbroten; B.A., St. Olaf Coll., 1942; M.A., U. Minn., 1950; m. Dale M. DeLaitsch, July 30, 1945; children—David M., Paul. Instr. English, Bethel Coll., St. Paul, 1948-50; asst. prof. English, U. Southwestern La., Lafayette, 1952—. Organist 1st Lutheran Ch., Lafayette, 1963—, mem. ch. council, 1964-69. Mem. AAUW (sec. La. div. 1964-66, pres. Lafayette br. 1954-58, recipient fellowship unit named in honor 1969), S. Central Modern Lang. Assn., Delta Delta Delta. Democrat. Lutheran. Home: 116 Girard Woods Dr Lafayette LA 70503 Office: PO Box 1210 Univ Southwestern La Lafayette LA 70501

DELANEY, PAUL EDWARD, radio exec.; b. Concord, Mass., Feb. 23, 1944; s. Ansel Rice Smart and Virginia Lillian (Leisch) Smart; student N.E. Broadcasting Sch., 1962-63; m. Sandra Jo Wainscott, Dec. 22, 1978; children—Patrick, Ryan; 1 stepdau., Shannon. News dir. Sta. WKKO, Cocoa, Fla., 1968-69; announcer, music dir. Sta. WBEC, Pittsfield, Mass., 1969-73; v.p., gen. sales mgr. Sta. WQSR, Sarasota Radio Co., St. Petersburg, Fla., 1973-79; account exec. WFLA-AM-FM, St. Petersburg, 1979—. Mem. St. Petersburg Advt. Fedn., St. Petersburg C. of C., Tampa Sales and Mktg. Execs. Democrat. Baptist. Home: 6201 103d Ave N Pinellas Park FL 33702 Office: WFLA-AM-FM 3530 1st Ave N Saint Petersburg FL 33713

DE LANEY, THOMAS CALDWELL, JR., museum exec.; b. Danville, Va., Jan 1, 1918; s. Thomas C. and Ethel (Loving) D.; B.S., Spring Hill Coll., 1941; M.A., U. Ala., 1952; m. Lois Jean Fitzsimmons, July 20, 1960. Dean U. Mil. Sch., Mobile, Ala., 1941-56; founder, supt. Julius T. Wright Sch. for Girls, Mobile, 1956-65; mus. dir. City of Mobile, 1965—. Mem. bd. Providence Sch. Nursing, 1956-59. U.S. Civil War Centennial Commn., 1958-65; rep. Mobile County Ala. First Capital Commn., 1961-65. Historian Mobile 250th Anniversary Celebration, 1961, Mobile Civil War Centennial Comm., 1961-65, Mobile Sesquicentennial Comm., 1969. Bd. dirs. Mobile Civic Music Assn., Mobile Symphony, Historic Mobile Preservation Soc. Recipient Ala. Penwomen award, 1962. Mem. Ala. Hist. Assn. (pres. 1962-63), Mobile Art Assn. Rotarian. Author: Deep South, 1942; Remember Mobile, 1948, 69; The Story of Mobile, 1953, 61; Madame Octavia Walton LeVent, 1961; Mary McNeil Fenollosa, 1963; The Phoenix Volunteer Fire Company of Mobile 1838-1888, 1967; The First Hundred Years, 1968; Craighead's Mobile, 1968;

Confederate Mobile, 1971; Raphael Semms-Rear Admiral, Confederate States Navy, Brigadier General, Confederate States Army. Home: 8 S Ann St Mobile AL 36604 Office: 355 Government St Mobile AL 36602

DELANEY, WILLIAM JOSEPH, mfg. co. exec.; b. Oak Park, Ill., Oct. 10, 1945; s. William Joseph and Stephanie Constance (Swartz) D.; B.S. in Material Sci., Purdue U., 1967; student engring. Gen. Electric Co., 1967-70; M.S., U. Calif., Berkeley, 1970. Mgr. European nuclear fuel sales, mgr. nuclear tech. licensing Gen. Electric Co., San Jose, Calif., 1970-77, mgr. internat. sales and bus. devel., Hickory, N.C., 1977-79, mgr. mfg. tech. ops., 1980—. Purdue Alumni scholar, 1963-67; Gen. Electric grantee, 1969-70; registered profl. engr., Calif. Mem. C. of C. Presidents Club, Sigma Chi. Republican. Club: Lake Hickory Country. Home: 2070 2d St Dr NW Hickory NC 28601 Office: PO Box 2188 Hickory NC 28601

DE LANGE, DANIEL H., data processing co. exec.; b. Gaylord, Mich., July 1, 1936; s. Walter and Harriet (Koning) DeL.; A.B., Calvin Coll., Grand Rapids, Mich., 1961; M.S., Mich. State U., E. Lansing, 1963; m. Joyce Schregardus, Aug. 19, 1955; children—Daniel Mark, Kristina Joy, Gregory Scott, Phillip Ray. High sch. tchr., prin. Westminster Sch., Miami, Fla., 1963-67; with mktg. dept. IBM Corp., Miami, 1967-68; exec. asst. to gov. of Fla., 1968-69; pres. Computer Time Sharing, Inc., Miami, 1969—; dir. CT Systems, Inc.; cons. in field. Grantee NSF, AEC. Mem. Nat. Micrographics Assn., Data Processing Mgmt. Assn. Presbyterian. Author, designer in field. Address: 13220 SW 208th St Miami FL 33177

DE LANY, WILLIAM HURD, JR., engring. and constrn. co. exec.; b. Lexington, Ky., Apr. 5, 1918; s. William Hurd and Evelyn Alice (Gray) DeL.; A.B., Columbia U., 1940, B.S. in Chem. Engring., 1941; m. Margaret Byrd Mauney, Aug. 23, 1942; children—William Hurd, David Stephen, Janet Lynne. Chem. engr. E. I. Dupont, Co., Wilmington, Del., 1941-46; process and project engr. Blaw Knox Constrn. Co., Chem. Plants div., Pitts., 1946-52; project engr. Catelvtic Constrn. Co., Phila., 1952-54; lead design dept. Wm. K. Hood & Assos., York, Pa., 1954-55; supr. engr. Chem. Constrn. Co., N.Y.C., 1955-63; chief engr. Nitram Chemicals Co., Tampa, Fla., 1963-67; project mgr. Davy Powergas, Inc., Lakeland, Fla., 1967—. Mem. Am. Inst. Chem. Engrs., Nat. Soc. Profl. Engrs., Fla. Engring. Soc. Republican. Home: PO Box 5131 Lakeland FL 33803 Office: Drawer 5000 Davy McKee Corp Lakeland FL 33803

DE LA PARTE, LOUIS ANTHONY, lawyer; b. Tampa, Fla., July 27, 1929; s. Louis and Dulce (Santa Cruz) de la P.; B.A., Emory U.; LL.B., U. Fla.; m. Helen C. White, Nov. 23, 1957; children—Louis David, Martha Ann. Admitted to Fla. bar; practice law, Tampa; spl. asst. atty. gen. State of Fla., 1953; asst. county solicitor, Hillsborough County, Fla., 1957-60; asst. state atty. 13th Jud. Circuit, 1960-61; mem. Fla. Senate, 1966—, senate pres. pro tempore, 1973-74, pres., 1974—. Mem. Fla. Ho. of Reps., 1962-66; del. Democratic nat. conv., 1964; mem. Gov.'s Commn. Capital Punishment, 1972, public employees rights com. Supreme Ct., 1973-74, Joint Legis. Uniform Probate Code Com. and Joint Legis. Criminal Code Com., 1973-74. Trustee, U. Tampa. Served to capt. USAF, 1953-56. Recipient Allen Morris award, 1967, 71, 73; Outstanding State Legislator award Fla. Young Dems., 1972; named Most Valuable Senator St. Petersburg (Fla.) Times, 1969, 70, 71, 74, Legislator of Year Fla. Assn. Retarded Children, 1969-74, Legislator of Year Fla. Vol. Health Assns., 1970, Legislator of Year, Pros. Attys. Assn., 1972. Mem. Am., Fla. bar assns., Am., Fla. trial lawyers assns., Greater Tampa C. of C. (past bd. govs.), Fla. Blue Key, Phi Delta Phi, Eta Sigma Phi, Sigma Alpha Epsilon. Roman Catholic. Home: 8003 N Rome St Tampa FL 33604 Office: 403 N Morgan St Tampa FL 33602

DE LA PENA, CORDELL AMANDO, pathologist; b. Honolulu, Apr. 30, 1934; s. Eusebio de Guzman Awanan and Virginia Uyeno de Costa; M.D., U. Santo Tomas, Manila, 1958; m. Linda Laron Lapuz, Apr. 1, 1957; children—Leslie, Nina, Cordell Amado. Intern, St. John's Hosp., Lowell, Mass., 1960-61; resident New Britain (Conn.) Gen. Hosp., 1963-67; pathologist St. Mary's Hosp., Clarksburg, W.Va., 1967, Union Protestant Hosp., Clarksburg, 1967; pathologist United Hosp., Inc., Clarksburg, 1967-78, pres. med. staff, 1974-75, bd. dirs., 1974-75, chief pathologist, dir. lab. and blood bank, 1978—; cons. VA, St. Joseph's, Stonewall Jackson Meml. hosps.; pres. Harrison County Cancer Soc., 1974-76. Diplomate Am. Bd. Pathology. Fellow Coll. Am. Pathologists, Am. Soc. Clin. Pathologists; mem. Internat. Acad. Pathology, Am., W.Va. med. assns., W.Va. Pathol. Soc. (treas. 1975-77, pres.-elect 1977-80), Harrison County Med. Soc. (treas. 1977-78, pres.-elect 1979-80), Nat. Skeet Shooting Assn., W.Va. Bird Dog Club (pres. 1972). Club: Masons. Contbr. med. jours. Home: 209 Candlelight Dr Clarksburg WV 26301 Office: United Hosp Clarksburg WV 26301

DELAPENA-LAPUZ, ERLINDA LARON, physician, pathologist; b. Manila, P.I., Nov. 26, 1933; d. Eriberto Mallari and Teodora Quiero (Laron) Lapuz; M.D., U. Santo Tomas, 1957; m. Cordell DeLaPena, Apr. 1, 1957; children—Leslie, Nina, Cordell. Intern, St. John's Hosp., Lowell, Mass., 1959-60; attending physician Tewksbury (Mass.) Hosp., 1960-63; resident in pathology Mercy Hosp., Pitts., 1967-71; instr. pathology U. Pitts. Med. Sch., 1967-71; chief lab. service VA Hosp., Clarksburg, W.Va., 1971—; courtesy staff United Hosp. Center; asst. prof. Coll. Nursing, Salem (W.Va.) Coll., 1978; asst. prof. Alderson Broddus Coll., Philippi, W.Va. Diplomate Am. Bd. Pathology. Mem. Am. Soc. Clin. Pathology, AMA, W.Va. Med. Assn., W.Va., Assn. Pathologists. Roman Catholic. Club: Clarksburg Country. Contbr. articles med. jours. Home: 209 Candlelight Dr Clarksburg WV 26301 Office: Veterans Administration Hospital Clarksburg WV 26301

DE LA SIERRA, ANGELL O., coll. adminstr.; b. Santurce, P.R., Feb. 28, 1932; s. Juan and Barbara de la S.; B.S., U. P.R., 1954; M.S., Coll. City N.Y., 1958; Ph.D., St. John's U., 1963; m. Judith Sheffer-Lavalle, Dec. 31, 1960; children—Angell II, John Arthur, Daniel Gerard, Barbara Grace, Denise Roxanne. Research analyst Smithsonian Instn., Washington, 1963-64; research chemist Defense Atomic Support Agy., Washington, 1964-65; NIH fellow Georgetown U., Washington, 1965-67; vis. prof. Faculty of Medicine, U. P.R., 1967-68, dir. Faculty of Natural Scis., 1968—. Lectr. on univ. and community interactions at various academic and civic orgns. Served with USAF, 1963-70. Mem. Am. Phys. Soc., Am. Chem. Soc., N.Y. Acad. Scis., Biophys. Soc., Sigma Xi. Author: Neoplastic Cell Transformation, 1963; contbr. articles to profl. jours. Home: 1-7 Faculty Residence U PR Cayey PR 00633

DE LCO, WILHELMINA RUTH, state legislator Tex.; b. Chgo., July 16, 1929; d. William Patrick and Juanita Marie (Heath) Fitzgerald; B.A., Fisk U., Nashville, 1950; m. Exalton A. Delco, Jr., Aug. 23, 1952; children—Deborah Diane, Exalton A., III, Loretta Elmire, Cheryl Pauline. Trustee Austin Ind. Sch. Dist., 1968-74; mem. Tex. Ho. of Reps. from 37D Dist., 1975—, chmn. com. on higher edn. Del. Tex. Democratic Conv., 1972-74, vice chmn., 1974-76; mem. So. Regional Edn. Bd. Recipient numerous awards for civic and community work. Catholic. 1805 Astor Pl Austin TX 78721

DE LEON, DORA LUCILA, ednl. cons.; b. Odem, Tex., July 10, 1934; d. Leo Cosme and Maria Guadalupe (Carrales) DeLeon; B.A., Pan Am. U., 1958, M.A., 1974. Tchr. elementary sch. McAllen (Tex.) Ind. Sch. Dist., 1958-72; counselor coll. assistance migrant program St. Edwards U., Austin, Tex., 1972; counselor jr. high sch., Mercedes, Tex., 1974-75; cons. Region One Edn. Service Center, Edinburg, Tex., 1976—. Chmn. Hidalgo County March of Dimes, 1965, 68, 69, 70. Mem. Rio Grande (pres.), Am., Tex. personnel and guidance assns., NEA (life), Tex. Tchrs. Assn. (life), AAUW. Democrat. Roman Catholic. Home: 700 Jackson Ave Apt 194 McAllen TX 78501 Office: 1900 Schunior St W Edinburg TX 78539

DELEON, EDWIN LAZARO, oral surgeon; b. Aguadilla, P.R., Jan. 20, 1937; s. Candido E. and BeLen (Sein) DeL.; B.A., Fla. State U., 1961; D.M.D., U. Louisville, 1965; m. Helen Amelia Sheppard, Sept. 9, 1960; children—Melinda Amelia, Jon Deni. Intern, Hillsborough County Dental Research Clinic, 1965-66; oral surgery resident U. Tenn. Meml. Research Center and Hosp., 1966-69; pvt. practice oral surgery, Madison, Tenn., 1969—. Served with USAF, 1954-58. Fellow Royal Soc. Health, Internat. Assn. Oral Surgeons; mem. Am. Soc. Oral and Maxillofacial Surgeons; Southeastern Soc. Oral Surgeons, ADA, Nashville Dental Assn., Psi Omega. Episcopalian. Contbr. numerous articles to dental jours. Office: 500 Lentz Dr Madison TN 37115

DELERAY, JANE WITHROW, speech pathologist; b. Kansas City, Mo., July 10, 1953; d. John Blake, Jr. and Gladys Ellen (Petersen) Withrow; B.S. in Edn., Baylor U., Waco, Tex., 1975, M.S. in Speech Pathology and Audiology, 1976. Speech pathologist Mesquite (Tex.) Ind. Sch. Dist., 1977—; vice chmn. com. spl. edn. Admission Rev. Dismissal. Sec.-treas. Geode Prodns., Inc., ednl. video tapes, 1978. Mem. Am. Speech and Hearing Assn., Tex. Speech and Hearing Assn., Dallas Assn. Speech Pathologists and Audiologists, Zeta Phi Eta. Home: 2844 Capella Circle Garland TX 75043 Office: 1607 Sierra St Mesquite TX 75149

DELERAY, JOHN EARLY, exptl. psychologist; b. San Gabriel, Calif., Sept. 30, 1946; s. Wilfred Louis and Ruth Tomlinson (Pinckney) D.; B.A., Whittier Coll., 1968; M.S., Baylor U., 1971, Ph.D., 1973. Teaching asst. in psychology Baylor U., Dallas, 1971-73; exptl. psychologist in pvt. practice, Dallas, 1973—; cons. in field to bus., industry, social service orgns., 1971—; invited lectr. in rehab. and social tech., 1973—. Mem. Dallas Assn. Behaviorists (pres. 1975-76), Am., Dallas psychol. assns., Nat. Rehab. Assn., Alpha Sigma Phi. Spl. research in operant conditioning, videotape, 1971-73, human behavior, 1971—. Home: 4700 Dorset Rd Dallas TX 75229 Office: 11422 Harry Hines Blvd Dallas TX 75229

DELGADILLO-MOYA, CLAUDIO, botanist; b. Tezoyuca, Mex., Feb. 18, 1945; s. Rafael Delgadillo-Zaldivar and Gracia Moya-Gonzalez; B.S., U. Nat. Autonoma Mexico, Mexico City, 1967; M.S., U. Tenn. at Knoxville, 1969; Ph.D., Duke, Durham, N.C., 1973; m. Teresa Chavez-Benitez, Sept. 7, 1974; children—Claudia, Ivan. Grad. asst. U. Tenn. at Knoxville, 1967-69; lab. instr. Duke U., 1970-72; asst. prof. U. Nat. Autonoma de Mexico, 1973-78, researcher, 1973-78; prof. botany U. Autonoma Metropolitana, Mexico City, 1978—; vis. scientist Instituto de Investigaciones sobre Recursos Bioticos, Julapa, Mexico, 1979-80. Sigma Xi grantee, 1968; Orgn. for Tropical Studies grantee, 1969. Mem. Sociedad Botanica de Mexico, Am. Bryological and Lichenological Soc., Calif. Bot. Soc., Internat. Assn. Plant Taxonomy, Sigma Xi. Contbr. articles to profl. jours. Home: Cartago 80 Lomas Estrella Mexico City Mexico Office: Departamento de Botanica Apartado Postal 70-233 Mexico 25 DF Mexico

DELGADO-GARCÍA, RAMIRO, physician, educator; b. Bogotá, Colombia, Dec. 7, 1928; came to U.S., 1971; s. Ramiro and Susana de Delgado) D.-G.; B.A., N.S. del Rosario Coll., Bogotá, 1944; M.D., U. Nacional Colombia, Bogotá, 1950; A.E. (French Govt. fellow), U. Paris, 1958; R.F. (Ford Found. Population Council fellow), Worcester Found. Exptl. Biology, 1962; m. Michele Durand, Nov. 8, 1956; children—France, Paul. Intern, Nat. U. San Juan de Dios Hosp., Bogotá, 1949-50; dir. Community Health Center, Galán, Colombia, 1951-52, Puente Nacional, Colombia, 1953-54; asst. prof. Sch. Medicine, U. Nacional, Bogotá, 1958-59; prof. Sch. Medicine, U. del Valle, Cali, Colombia, 1959-64, dir. Population Research Center, 1964-71; prof. internat. health and population Tulane U. Sch. Public Health and Tropical Medicine, New Orleans, 1971—, head population sect. dept. applied health scis., 1971—; cons. internat. health WHO, AID, NASA, UN, Am. Public Health Assn., others, 1972—. Rockefeller Found. grantee, 1965-71, 79—; AID grantee, 1972-79. Mem. Am. Public Health Assn., Population Assn. Am., Internat. Union for Sci. Study Population, Latin Am. Assn. Human Reprodn., Nat. Geog. Soc., Smithsonian Instn. Assos., Lake Hillsdale Property Owners Assn. Colombian Liberal Party. Roman Catholic. Club: Population. Author: El Dilema de la Población en la América Latina, 1968; O Dilema Populacional na America Latina, 1968; contbr. numerous articles to profl. jours. Home: 81 Dove St New Orleans LA 70124 Office: 150 S Liberty St New Orleans LA 70112

DELGADO-PASAPERA, GERMAN ALBERTO, educator; b. Anasco, P.R., Apr. 14, 1928; s. Luis Mario Delgado-Lugo and Maria Pasapera-Tio; B.A., Poly. Inst. P.R., 1952; M.A., La. State U., 1964; postgrad. U. Madrid, 1975-76; m. Maria del Pilar Acevedo-Defillo, Mar. 11, 1967. Tchr. secondary public schs., Mayaguez, 1953-54; research asst. Coll. Agr. and Mechanic Arts, U. P.R., Mayaguez, 1954-55, asst. registrar, 1955-59, acting registrar, 1959-60, dir. admissions, 1960-63, instr. history, 1962-63, 67-70, asst. prof., 1970-73, asso. prof., 1973—; asst. dir. admissions Inter Am. U. P.R., San German, 1965-66, dir. fin. aid, 1966-67; lectr. geography, extension div. U. P.R., Rio Piedras, 1966, instr. humanities, 1967-69. Recipient plaque of merit, dept. social sci. U. P.R., Mayaguez, 1974; diploma Anasco Cultural Centre, 1974; plaque Festival Bellas Artes, Anasco, 1976; diploma of honor Festival Carnaval Mayaguez, 1976. Mem. Am. Acad. Polit. and Social Sci., Acad. Polit. Sci., Internat. Studies Assn., Caribbean Historians, Am. Assn. Tchr. Spanish and Portuguese, AAUP, Nat. Hist. Soc., Nat. Trust for Hist. Preservation, Sociedad Puertrriquena de Escritores, Asociacion Puertorriquena de Profesores Universitarios (dir. U. P.R., Mayaguez, 1973-75), World Acad., Internat. Platform Assn., Sociedad de las Letras Puertorriquenas. Author: Desde el Fondo del Pecho (poems), 1964; (with F. Lluch-Mora and R. Torres-Delgado) Puerto Rico en la Geografia Universal de Malte-Brun, 1979; asso. editor Atenea Jour. of Sch. of Arts and Scis., U. P.R., Mayaguez, 1969-75; contbr. articles, short stories and poems to profl. publs. Home: 9 (altos) Nereidas Mayaguez PR 00708 Office: G 334 C U PR Mayaguez Campus Mayaguez PR 00708

DE LLANO, RODRIGO RUBÉN, import co. exec.; b. Laredo, Tex., Oct. 12, 1927; s. Matias and Dolores (Villareal) D.; B.S. in Indsl. Engring., Cornell U., 1949; postgrad. Madrid U., 1949-50; Sorbonne U., Paris, 1952-53; m. Marilyn Y. Rolnick, Sept. 25, 1958; children—Shira Y, Rodrigo R., Dolores D. Mng. partner Tex. Hat Co., Laredo, 1954-62; pres., chmn. DeLlano's Mex. Products Co., Laredo, 1963—; chmn. Doreli S.A., Nuevo Laredo, Mex., 1968-70, Mex-Moc, S.A., Nuevo Laredo, Mex., 1969-70. Republican. Office: PO Box 506 Laredo TX 78040

DELLIAN, KURT ADOLPH, color and textile chemist; b. Huglfing, W. Ger., June 19, 1920; came to U.S., 1965, naturalized, 1972; s. Otto and Centa (Reich) D.; Ph.D. Dr. rer. nat., Tech. U. Munich, 1950; m. Anna Almuth Sentpaul, Feb. 4, 1949. Supr., Perutz-Agfa, Munich, W. Ger., 1950-53; chemist Aktiengesellschaft Hoechst, Frankfurt am Main, W. Ger., 1953-58, tech. mgr. Hoechst do Brazil, 1958-65, supr. Am. Hoechst, W.Warwick, R.I., 1965-68; tech. mgr., research asso. Ciba-Geigy, Greensboro, N.C., 1968—; adj. prof., mem. grad. faculty dept. textile chemistry N.C. State U., Raleigh. Mem. Am. Assn. Textile Chemists and Colorists, Am. Chem. Soc., Nat. Geog. Soc., Greensboro Art Assn. Roman Catholic. Contbr. articles to profl. publs.; patentee dye application and auxiliaries; lic. artist painter and pvt. tchr. Home: 1201 Wakefield Rd Greensboro NC 27410 Office: Ciba-Geigy Corp Swing Rd Greensboro NC 27409

DELLINGER, RICHARD PHILLIP, physician; b. Andrews, S.C., Mar. 8, 1947; s. David Fred and Ada (Nettles) D.; B.S., Clemson U., 1968, M.S., 1970; M.D., Med. U. S.C., 1975; m. Jennie Duraine McRae, Dec. 2, 1967; children—Barton, Michael. Commd. capt. M.C., U.S. Air Force, 1970, advanced through grades to lt. col., 1980; intern Wilford Hall USAF Med. Center, San Antonio, 1975-76; resident in internal medicine, 1976-78, fellow in pulmonary medicine, 1978-80. Decorated Bronze Star. NSF fellow, 1968-70; Duke Found. scholar, London, 1974. Mem. AMA (mem. med. service council), Tex. Med. Assn., A.C.P. (asso.), Am. Coll. Chest Physicians (asso.), Bexar County Med. Soc., Air Force Soc. Physicians, Alpha Omega Alpha. Home: 6222 Rue Sophie San Antonio TX 78238 Office: Dept Pulmonary Medicine Wilford Hall USAF Medical Center San Antonio TX 78236

DELLINGER, SUSAN ELAIN, mgmt. cons.; b. Elwood, Ind., Dec. 30, 1942; d. Norwood Everett and Mary Evelyn (Roush) Allen; B.S., Ind. U., 1965; M.A., U. Fla., 1970; Ph.D., U. Colo., 1973; m. Robert D. Dellinger, Aug. 21, 1964; 1 son, Jade Roush. High sch. tchr. English and drama Broad Ripple High Sch., Indpls., 1965, Leto High Sch., Tampa, Fla., 1965-67, Chofu High Sch., Tokyo, 1968, Fessenden High Sch., Ocala, Fla., 1969; instr. U. Colo., Boulder, 1971-73; prof. U. Oreg., Eugene, 1973-74; adj. prof. U. South Fla., Tampa, 1975; mgmt. devel. trainer Gen. Telephone Co. Fla., Tampa, 1975—; mgmt. cons. IBM, GTE, USN, City of Tampa, LWV, Nat. Secs. Assn. Bd. dirs. Mental Health Assn. Hillsboro County, Drug Abuse Coordinating Council, YMCA, Gulf Ridge council Boy Scouts Am., Tampa Downtown Devel. Council; v.p. Women's Survival Center. Recipient Women Helping Women award Joint Women's Service Clubs, 1977. Mem. Am. Mgmt. Assn., Speech Communication Assn., Athena Soc. Profl. Women (v.p.). Democrat. Presbyterian. Author: (with B. Deane) Communicating Effectively, 1980. Home: 794 High St Land O'Lakes FL 33539 Office: PO Box 110 Mail Code 1077 Tampa FL 33601

DELOACH, HERMAN HOLMES, electronic mfg. co. exec.; b. Monroe, La., Apr. 19, 1932; s. Albertus Lee and Helen (Gray) DeL.; student N.E. La. State U., 1955; B.S., La. Poly. Inst., 1958; M.S., N.C. State U., 1962; m. Jane Loraine McClendon, Dec. 23, 1951; children—Tammy, Guy. Mem. tech. staff, microwave electronics design engr. Bell Telephone Labs., Greensboro, N.C., 1958-73; pres., owner Deltronics Inc., Jamestown, N.C., 1970—, Z-Five, Inc., Jamestown, N.C., 1979—. Served with USN, 1951-55. Registered profl. engr., La. Mem. Jamestown Bus. Alliance, IEEE, Tau Beta Pi. Democrat. Home: 5119 W Wendover St Greensboro NC 27410 Office: Deltronics Inc PO Box 1119 101 Depot St Jamestown NC 27282

DE LONG, EDGAR EMILE, computer systems analyst; b. New Orleans, Aug. 15, 1928; s. Ormond Marx and Delta M. (Simeneaux) De L.; B.A., St. Leo (Fla.) Coll., 1979; m. Ruth Clare Bell, Sept. 12, 1953; children—Janelle Lynne, Thomas Edward, Gerianne Lee. Served as enlisted man, U.S. Navy, 1944-58; commd. ensign, U.S. Navy, 1958, advanced through grades to lt. comdr., 1966; project officer, long range missiles and space systems, operational test and evaluation, Norfolk, Va., 1962-65; dir. surface missile systems schs., Dam Neck, Va., 1966-69, ret., 1969; customer service mgr. Ednl. Computer Corp. subs. EDP Tech., Strafford, Pa., 1969-74; asso. mgr. advanced systems System Devel. Corp., Integrated Systems, Inc., Virginia Beach, Va., 1974-78; dep. mgr. Virginia Beach ops. Sperry Univac Corp., 1979—; cons. in field; sec.-treas. London Bridge Fabric Barn Inc., Virginia Beach, 1976-79. Mem. various civic commns. City of Virginia Beach, 1961—; pres. numerous civic leagues City of Virginia Beach, 1964-77; bd. dirs. Council of Civic Orgns., Virginia Beach, 1974-77; pres. Eastern Va. Thorobred Assn., youth baseball, 1978-79. Recipient George Washington honor medal, Freedoms Found., Valley Forge, Pa., 1967, 68. Episcopalian. Club: Masons. Contbr. articles to mil. mags.; researcher effects of nuclear radiation on C-band radars. Home: 1500 Hidden Cove Virginia Beach VA 23454 Office: Sperry Univac Corp Suite 500 Pembroke 4 Virginia Beach VA 23462

DE LONG, JAMES FRANCIS, physician; b. Dayton, Ohio, Sept. 3, 1946; s. Pearl Francis and Betty Catherine (Esterline) DeL.; B.S., U. Dayton, 1968; M.D., U. Cin., 1972; m. Linda Faye Brown, Dec. 20, 1969; children—Cori Michelle, James Francis. Intern, U. Tex., Galveston, 1972-73; resident U. Okla., Oklahoma City, 1973-75, fellow nuclear medicine, 1975-76; practice medicine specializing in nuclear medicine, Fairfield, Ala.; mem. staffs Lloyd Noland Hosp.; asst. clin. prof. radiology U. Ala., Birmingham, 1976—. Diplomate Am. Bd. Internal Medicine, Am. Bd. Nuclear Medicine. Fellow A.C.P.; mem. Am. Coll. Nuclear Physicians, Soc. Nuclear Medicine (pres. Ala. chpt. 1979—), AMA, Jefferson County Med. Soc., Birmingham Acad. Medicine. Republican. Baptist. Club: Optimist (sec. 1978—). Contbr. articles to profl. jours. Home: 1159 Riverchase Pkwy W Birmingham AL 35244 Office: Lloyd Noland Hospital 701 Ridgeway Rd Fairfield AL 35064

DEL RE, ROBERT, cons. civil engr.; b. N.Y.C., June 3, 1930; s. Nicholas and Virginia (Higginbotham) Del Re; B.S., Marietta Coll., 1952, B.S. in Petroleum Engring., 1973; m. Joyce Maley, Aug. 20, 1971. Engr., Greeley and Hansen, Chgo., 1957-71, asso., 1971, resident engr. in field office, Knoxville, Tenn., 1963-64, resident engr. in overseas office at City of Panama, Republic of Panama, 1964-69, resident rep., br. office, Tampa, Fla., 1971—. Patron, Tampa Bay Art Center, Friends of Morning Star Sch., Tampa Preservation; bd. dirs. Sand Castle Assn. Served with CEC, USNR, 1952-55. Registered profl. engr., Calif.; diplomate Am. Acad. Environ. Engrs. Fellow ASCE; mem. Fla. Engring. Soc., Nat. Soc. of Profl. Engrs., Soc. Am. Mil. Engrs., Fla. Pollution Control Assn., Am. Arbitration Assn., Earthquake Engring. Research Inst., Inter-Am. Assn. San. Engring., Am. Soc. Quality Control, Am. Water Works Assn., Tampa Hist. Soc., Pi Epsilon Tau, Alpha Tau Omega. Clubs: Carrollwood Village Golf and Tennis; University (Chgo.). Home: 10-130 White Trout Ln Tampa FL 33618 Office: Greeley and Hansen 1211 N Westshore Blvd Tampa FL 33607

DEL RIO-ESTRADA, CARLOS, microbiologist; b. Mexico City, Feb. 28, 1923; s. Aurelio del Rio and Josefina Estrada; Chemist-Microbiologist, Inst. Politecnico Nacional, Mex., 1948; M.Sc. (Buenos Aires Conv. fellow), Cornell U., 1950, Ph.D. (NIH fellow), 1953; m. Marta Elena Guerra, Sept. 23, 1964;

children—Marta Sylvia, Carlos Renato, Alexandra Rosa, Eduardo Andres. Dir. control Syntex Labs., Mex., 1953-56; mem. faculty U. Nacional Autonoma de Mex., 1957—, prof. microbiology, 1965—, head dept., 1968-74, acad. sec. coordination of scis., 1974-77; vis. researcher Duke U., 1964-66; specialist OAS, Washington, 1968-69; head sci. dept. Inst. Italo Latino Americano, Rome, 1972-74; head spl. project Center Econ. and Social Studies 3d World, Mexico City, 1978-79, adv. to dir. gen., 1979-80; dir. gen. CATMEX, S.A., Mexico City, 1980—; vis. prof. Inst. Politecnico Nacional Grad. Sch., 1953, 56, U. Autonoma Metropolitana Xochimilco, 1977; invited lectr. U. Libre de Bruxelles (Belgium), 1979; organizer, participant internat. confs.; pres. organizing com. X Internat. Congress Clin. Chemistry, Mex., 1978; pres. Leeuwenhoek Symposium, Mex., 1976; gen. coordinator XXIX Pugwash Conf., Mex., 1979. Mem. Am. Acad. Microbiology, Acad. de la Investigacion Cientifica, Asn. Mex. Microbiologia (founder 1949, pres. 1953-54, 55-56), Soc. Quimica de Mex. (founder 1956), Soc. Mex. de Bioquimica (founder 1957). Club: Cornell Mex. (pres. 1976-78). Home: 575 Las Flores Mexico 20 DF Mexico Office: 752 Ejercito Nacional Ave Mexico 5 DF Mexico

DEL-ROSARIO, ERNESTO, ins. co. exec.; b. Yauco, P.R., Nov. 17, 1911; s. Ulises and Josefa E. (Olivieri) Del-R.; student Yauco Comml. Coll., 1928-29; m. Josefina Masini, July 24, 1936; children—Elliette A. (Mrs. Jose H. Pico), Juan E. Asst. postmaster U.S. Post Office, Yauco, P.R., 1929-37; income tax inspector P.R. Treasury Dept., San Juan, P.R., 1937-41; pub. accountant, tax practice, San Juan, P.R., 1941-42; comptroller Coop. Azucarera Los Canos, Arecibo, P.R., 1942-62; br. mgr. Nationwide Ins. Cos., Hato Rey, P.R., 1962-77, resident v.p. for P.R., 1975-77, cons., 1977-78; pres. P.R. Ins. Guaranty Assn., 1975-78, exec. dir., also of Life, Disability and Health Ins. Guaranty Assn., 1978—. Hon. mem. Civic Crusade for Traffic Safety, 1975-76. Mem. P.R. Coll. C.P.A.'s, Nat. Soc. Pub. Accountants, Nat. Soc. Coop. Accountants. Roman Catholic. Clubs: Elks, Casino De Puerto Rico, Bankers Club of Puerto Rico. Home: M-207 Villa Caparra Guaynabo PR 00657 Office: PO Box 272 Hato Rey PR 00919

DEL VALLE, IGNACIO GONZALEZ, lawyer; b. Havana, Cuba, Apr. 7, 1944; s. Ambrosio Gonzalez and Silvia (Fonts) del V.; came to U.S., 1960, naturalized, 1966; B.S. in Chem. Engring., La. State U., 1965, M.S., 1970; postgrad. in mathematics U. Fla., 1965-66; J.D., U. Miami, 1973; m. Olga Maria Rodriguez Pajon, June 5, 1965; children—Jorge Ignacio, Beatriz. Mem. devel. center staff Chemstrand div. Monsanto Co., Pensacola, Fla., 1965-66; research engr. Esso Research Labs., Baton Rouge, 1966-69; cons. engr., project mgr. Nat. Planning & Constrn. Corp., Coral Gables, Fla., 1969-72; admitted to Fla. bar, 1974; clk. firm Salley, Barns & Pajon, Miami, Fla., 1972-73, asso. firm, 1973-75, partner, 1975-80; partner firm Salley, Barns, Payon, Guttman & del Valle, Miami, 1980—; dir., officer Miami Imperial Lands, Inc., 1975—, Totalbank, Miami, 1976—, Lime Groves, Inc., 1977. Mem. Am. Inst. Chem. Engrs., Am., Fla., Dade County bar assns., Lawyers Title Guaranty Fund, Tau Beta Pi, Phi Lambda Upsilon. Republican. Roman Catholic. Patentee process for preparation of low sulfur fuel oil. Home: 7955 SW 108th St Miami FL 33156 Office: Suite 700 100 Biscayne Blvd Miami FL 33132

DEL VALLE, JOSE ANTONIO, utility co. exec.; b. San Juan, P.R., May 1, 1935; s. Dionisio and Alejandrina (Vazquez) DelV.; B.B.A., U. P.R., 1957; M.B.A., Inter Am. U., 1969; m. Blanca Colon, Nov. 14, 1959; children—Niurka, Sandra, Viviana. Auditor, Office of Controller of P.R., 1957; with P.R. Water Resources Authority, San Juan, 1957—, controller, 1974-75, dir. adminstrn., 1974-78, dir. customers service, 1978—. Mem. P.R. Inst. Internal Auditors (v.p. 1966), Nat. Assn. Accountants. Roman Catholic. Clubs: Lions (past pres.). Office: PR Water Authority San Juan PR 00936

DELZER, DONALD JOHN, radiologist; b. Napoleon, N.D., Oct. 31, 1940; s. Jacob and Edna (Naaz) D.; B.A., UCLA, 1965; M.D., U. N.Mex., 1972. Intern, U. Okla., Oklahoma City, 1972-73, resident in radiology, 1973-75, resident in nuclear medicine, 1975-76; practice medicine specializing in radiology and nuclear medicine, Chickasha, Okla., 1976—; guest faculty U. Okla. Health Scis. Served with USMC, 1965-66. Diplomate Am. Bd. Radiology. Mem. AMA, Okla. Med. Assn., Grady County Med. Assn., Am. Coll. Radiology (cert.), Am. Soc. Nuclear Physicians, Am. Inst. Ultrasound in Medicine, Armed Forces Inst. Pathology. Republican. Lutheran. Club: Elks. Office: PO Box 1333 Chickasha OK 73018

DEMARTINI, WILLIAM DILLON, psychologist; b. White Plains, N.Y., June 15, 1948; s. Walter and Dawn Elizebeth (Dillon) DeM.; A.A., Miami-Dade Jr. Coll., 1968; B.A., Jacksonville U., 1970; M.S., Nova U., 1973; Ed.S., U. Louisville, 1975; Ed.D., Ind. U., 1979. Suicide prevention worker Jacksonville, Fla., 1970-71; dir. guidance Nova U., Ft. Lauderdale, Fla., 1971-72; instr. Div. Continuing Edn., Ind. U., Bloomington, 1975-77; pvt. practice psychology, Ft. Lauderdale, 1978—; dir. counseling and student services Coll. for Human Services, Fla. campus. Delta Theta Tau ednl. grantee, 1976-78; lic. psychologist, marriage counselor, Fla. Mem. Am. Ednl. Research Assn., Am. Personnel and Guidance Assn., Am. Psychol. Assn., World Future Soc., Nat. Vocat. Assn. (com. on gifted), Assn. to Advance Ethical Hypnosis. Roman Catholic. Contbr. articles to books, profl. jours. Address: 500 NE Victoria Terr Fort Lauderdale FL 33301

DE MELLO, WALMOR CARLOS, educator; b. Florianopolis, Brazil, Sept. 11, 1931; s. John Carlos and Alba (Baptiste) DeM.; B.S., Colegio Catarinese, 1949; M.D., U. Brazil, 1955, D.M., 1964; m. Celina Storino, Sept. 15, 1956; children—Alexandre, Andriana, Claudia, Patricia. Prof. dept. pharmacology Sch. Medicine, U. P.R., Rio Piedras, 1970-71, prof., dir. dept. pharmacology, 1972—. Cons. Am. Heart Assn., 1973. Nat. Heart and Lung Inst. grantee, 1966—, P.R. Heart Assn. grantee, 1968-71. Mem. Sociedade Brasilera de Biologia, Am. Physiol. Soc., Biophys. Soc., N.Y. Acad. Scis. Author: The Specialized Tissues of the Heart, 1961; Electrical Phenomena in the Heart, 1973; Intercellular Communication, 1977. Home: 0-12 C St Extension Alto Apolo-Guaynabo PR Office: Dept Pharmacology Med Scis Campus PO Box 5067 San Juan PR 00936

DEMETRIOUS, MARY, state ofcl.; b. Florence, S.C., Feb. 27, 1950; d. Chris Nicholas and Katina Demetra (Pappas) D.; B.A., Randolph-Macon Woman's Coll., 1972. Intern, Sen. Ernest Hollings, Washington, 1971; state field coordinator McGovern for Pres., S.C., 1972; field coordinator Jenrette for Congress, Florence, S.C., 1974; regional dir. S.C. Human Affairs Commn., Florence, 1975-76; project coordinator S.C. Reorgn. Commn., Columbia, 1976—; cons. State Bd. Tech. and Comprehensive Edn. Mem. exec. com. S.C. Council for Human Rights, 1975; alt. del. Democratic Nat. Conv., 1972; mem. steering com. New Dem. Coalition, 1973-74; vice chmn. Dem. Party of S.C., 1976-78; mem. Nat. Dem. Com., 1976-78; del. Dem. Nat. Conv., 1980; chmn. Darlington County Dem. Party; mem. S.C. adv. com. ERA. Mem. Am. Soc. Pub. Adminstrn., Assn. State Dem. Chmn., AAUW, Alston Wilkes Soc. Greek Orthodox. Home: 112 Wells St Darlington SC 29532 Office: PO Box 22 Darlington SC 29532

DE MINO, STEVEN LOUIS, ins. co. exec.; b. N.Y.C., Aug. 19, 1935; s. Evelyn Rachel (Morra) DeM.; A.A.S. in Indsl. Mgmt., B.S. in Bus. Adminstrn., Adelphi U., m. Feb. 1, 1958; children—Steven Louis, Robert John, Adam Christopher. Indsl. mgr. Manuel San Juan Co., San Juan, P.R., 1969-70; mgr. mfg. Motorola Co., Vega Baja, P.R., 1970-71; prodn. mgr. Travelers Corp., Orlando, Fla., 1975—. Served with U.S. Army, 1954-56. Recipient citation Jr. Achievement of P.R. Mem. Nat. Rifle Assn. (life), Profl. Businessmen's Assn. Central Fla. Republican. Roman Catholic. Home: 801 North St Rolling Hills Golfview Longwood FL 32750

DEMOPULOS, CHRIS, engring. co. exec.; b. Texarkana, Tex., Oct. 30, 1924; s. Frank C. and Helen G. (Murzicos) D.; B.S. in Engring., Tex. A. and M. U., 1947; m. Sophia S. Soteropulos, Nov. 12, 1950; children—Anastasia Elaine, Paul Chris. Cons. engr. E.M. Freeman Assos., Shreveport, La., 1947-52; pres. Demopulos & Ferguson, Inc., Shreveport, 1953—. Bd. dirs. Met. YMCA Shreveport, 1966-79. Served with USAAF 1943-45. Decorated Air medal with cluster. Registered profl. engr. La., Tex., Ark., Okla., Pa.; mem. Bd. Registration Profl. Engrs. and Land Surveyors State of La., 1977—. Fellow ASCE (pres. Shreveport chpt. 1960-61); mem. Am. Cons. Engrs. Council (dir. 1974-75), Nat. Soc. Profl. Engrs., La. Engring. Soc. (dir. 1962-64), Tex. Soc. Profl. Engring., Soc. Am. Mil. Engrs. (pres. Shreveport post 1969-70), Am. Concrete Inst., Am. Legion, Shreveport Art Guild, C. of C. Mem. Greek Orthodox Ch. Clubs: Tex. A. and M. Alumni, Houston Engrs., Shreveport, Rotary, Shreveport Country. Home: 331 Janie Ln Shreveport LA 71106 Office: 600 Petroleum Tower Shreveport LA 71101

DE MOSS, JERRY VAUGHN, exec. search and mgmt. cons. exec.; b. Los Angeles, Feb. 14, 1934; s. Lloyd Barrow and Ora May (Condon) DeM.; B.S. in Bus. Adminstrn., UCLA, 1956; m. Janet Ruth Brant, July 2, 1965; children—Suzanne Ruth, David Vaughn, Anne Marie. Dist. mgr. Caribbean Area Moore Bus. Forms de P.R., San Juan, 1960-66; franchisee Kelly Services, Inc., San Juan, 1966-71; founder, pres. CAREERS Inc., San Juan, 1971—, J.V. DeMoss & Asso., cons. firm representing Plant Location Internat., Brussels, 1976—. Bd. dirs. Better Bus. Bur. P.R., 1971—; bd. dirs., exec. com. United Fund P.R., San Juan, 1974—; bd. dirs. Traveller's Aide P.R., San Juan, 1972-74. Served to comdr. USN, 1956—. Recipient cert. of merit United Fund P.R., 1976. Mem. Naval Res. Assn. (founder, pres. San Juan chpt. 1967), P.R. Mfrs. Assn., Res. Officers Assn. Clubs: Rotary (pres. 1977-78), Bankers of P.R. Palmas del Mar, Beach. Office: Suite 1919 Banco Popular Center Hato Rey PR 00918

DEMPSEY, ALFRED LEE, audio visual specialist; b. Nowata, Okla., July 10, 1951; s. John Alfred and Catheline Louise (Marler) D.; degree in electronic tech. United Electronics Inst., 1972; A.Child Devel., Stephen F. Austin U., 1975; m. Judy Kaye Jeffery, Mar. 11, 1972; 1 son, Jonathan Lee. Technician, Ashdown Radio and TV, Ashdown, Ark., 1964-69; owner Whatever Tape Shop, Ashdown, 1969; electronic technician Hamby's TV Service, Little Rock, 1970-72; chief electronic technician Tex. Community Antenna, Nacogdoches, Tex., 1972-75; audio-visual supr. Stephen F. Austin U., Nacogdoches, 1975-77; audio visual dir. Garland (Tex.) Ind. Sch. Dist., 1977—; audiovisual, photography, video and multi-image cons. Recipient God and Country award, Boy Scouts Am., 1965. Mem. Nat. Audio-Visual Assn., Assn. Audio-Visual Technicians, Assn. for Ednl. Communications and Tech., Assn. for Multi-Image (chpt. officer). Republican. Club: Christian Service Brigade. Home: 1914 Meridian Way Garland TX 75040 Office: 221 S 9th St Garland TX 75040

DEMPSEY, BRUCE HARVEY, museum dir.; b. Camden, N.J., July 4, 1941; s. Lawrence Aloysius and Esther Audrey (Harvey) D.; B.A., Fla. State U., 1964, M.F.A., 1966; m. Gabriele Katharina Heerling, July 12, 1970; 1 son, Lawrence Maximilian. Faculty, Fla. State U., Tallahassee, 1966-75, gallery dir., 1969-75, instr. Fla. State U. Study Center, Florence, Italy, 1967-68; dir. Jacksonville (Fla.) Art Mus., 1975—. Mem. fine arts adv. bd. State of Fla. Fine Arts Council, 1974-76, grant rev. panel, 1979; mem. adv. bd. Jacksonville Arts Assembly; visual arts adviser Fla. Div. Cultural Affairs, 1973-76; mem. Duval County Arts Assembly, 1975—; mem. art purchase panel Fla. Ho. of Reps., 1979. Bd. dirs. Tallahassee Arts Council, 1973-75; mem. Fla. Bicentennial Com., 1974-76. U.S.-Chinese Relations travel-in-aid grantee, 1975. Mem. Fla. Art Mus. Dirs. Assn. (treas. 1977), Am. Assn. Museums, Internat. Council Museums. Home: 2415 Mandarin River Ln Mandarin FL 32223

DEMPSEY, FREDERICK GERARD, JR., med. service co. exec.; b. Ft. Bliss, Tex., June 17, 1949; s. Frederick Gerard and Rosalie Laura D.; student U. Notre Dame, 1967-68; B.B.A., U. Ky., 1971; M.B.A., Ga. State U., 1977; m. Diann Page Vicars, Aug. 28, 1971; children—James Paul, David Michael. Gen. mgr. Med. Soc. Services, Inc., also asst. exec. dir. Med. Assn. Atlanta, 1977—; mem. adv. com. on med. assts. Atlanta Jr. Coll., 1978—. Served to capt. U.S. Army, 1971-78. Decorated Commendation medal. Mem. Am. Assn. Med. Soc. Execs., Ga. Soc. Assn. Execs., U. Ky. Alumni Assn., Ga. State U. Alumni Assn., Beta Gamma Sigma. Roman Catholic. Office: Medical Society Services Inc 875 W Peachtree St NE Atlanta GA 30309

DEMUNBRUN, DONNE O'DONNELL, physician; b. St. Paul, Aug. 26, 1926; d. Francis Joseph and Julia Theresa (Hoffmann) O'Donnell; B.S., U. Ky., 1948, M.S., 1949; M.D., U. Louisville, 1954; m. Truman Weldon DeMunbrun, Mar. 17, 1948; children—Michael Jerome, Steven Murphy, Julie Frances, Suzanne. Intern, St. Anthony's Hosp., Louisville, 1955-56; gen. practice of medicine, Shively, Ky., 1956—; mem. staff Aububon Hosp., Sts. Mary and Elizabeth Hosp., S.W. Jefferson Community Hosp. Diplomate Am. Bd. Family Practice. Mem. Am. Acad. Family Physicians, Ky. Med. Assn., Jefferson County Med. Assn. (v.p. 1975-76). Republican. Home: 3004 Beals Branch Dr Louisville KY 40206 Office: 4731 Rockford Plaza Shively KY 40216

DE NAPLES, MARK ANTHONY, physician; b. Atlantic City, Mar. 22, 1936; s. Anthony and Hedwiga Honora (Hanska) DeN.; B.A., U. Pa., 1958; M.D., Jefferson Med. Coll., 1962. Intern, Lankenau Hosp., Phila., 1963; resident in neurosurgery U. Va., Charlottesville, 1966-70; group practice neurosurgery, Norfolk, Va., 1970-71; asst. prof. neurol. surgery Med. Coll. Ga., Augusta, 1971-74; group practice neurosurgery, Corpus Christi, Tex., 1974—; mem. staff Meml. Med. Center, Spohn Hosp., Corpus Christi. Served with USN, 1964-66. Diplomate Am. Bd. Neurol. Surgery. Fellow A.C.S.; mem. Am. Assn. Neurol. Surgeons, AMA, Tex. Med. Assn., So. Neurosurg. Soc. Club: Corpus Christi Country. Home: 5229 St Andrews Dr Corpus Christi TX 78413 Office: 2418 Morgan Ave Corpus Christi TX 78405

DENDINGER, JAMES ELMER, physiologist; b. Long Beach, Calif., Nov. 13, 1943; s. Elmer Clare and Marylee Pearl (Black) D.; B.S., Calif. State U., Long Beach, 1969, M.A., 1971; Ph.D., U. Mass., 1975; m. Dolores Marie Madden, June 13, 1975. Asst. prof. biology James U., Harrisonburg, Va., 1975—. Served with U.S. Army, 1965-67. Grantee, So. Regional Edn. Bd., 1977-78, James Madison U., 1977-78, 79-80. Mem. AAAS, Va. Acad. Sci., Am. Soc. Zoologists, Sigma Xi, Beta Beta Beta. Contbr. articles to profl. jours. Home: Rt 1 Box 149K Weyers Cave VA 24486 Office: Dept Biology James Madison U Harrisonburg VA 22807

DENG, JUENCHIN, seafood technologist, educator; b. Taiwan, Apr. 19, 1945; came to U.S., 1969, naturalized, 1979; s. Chii-Shen and Cheng-Mei D.; B.S., Taiwan Nat. Coll. Marine Sci., 1968; M.S., U. Ga., 1971, Ph.D., 1974; m. Chii-Shya Deng, Aug. 14, 1971; children—Justin, Austin. Research asst. U. Ga., 1969-74; asst. prof. dept. food sci. and human nutrition U. Fla., Gainesville, 1974-79, asso. prof., 1979—. Dept. Energy grantee, 1978-80; Dept. Commerce grantee, 1978-79. Mem. Inst. Food Technologists, Tropical and Subtropical Fisheries Technologists, Atlantic Fisheries Technologists, N.Y. Acad. Scis., Sigma Xi, Gamma Sigma Delta. Office: Dept Food Sci and Human Nutrition U Fla Gainesville FL 32611

DENISON, HENRY CLARK, elec. engr.; b. Norman, Okla., Sept. 17, 1900; s. Jesse Irvin and Ada Irene (Naylor) D.; B.S., U. Okla., 1924; m. Mary Ella McBride, Apr. 23, 1927; children—Gilbert Walter, Harvey Clark. Student engr. Dallas Power & Light Co., 1924-25; test engr. Gen. Electric Co., Schenectady, 1925-26; statis. engr. Kansas City (Mo.) Power & Light Co., 1926-29; with Okla. Gas & Electric Co, Oklahoma City, 1929-65; elec. design engr. Benham-Blair & Affiliates, Oklahoma City, 1965-67; elec. study and design engr. C.H. Guernsey & Co., Oklahoma City, 1967-69; elec. cons., Oklahoma City, 1972—. Precinct chmn. Republican party, 1964. Registered profl. engr., Okla. Mem. Nat. (life), Okla. (life; municipal affairs com. 1972) socs. profl. engrs., I.E.E.E. (life), Sigma Tau, Eta Kappa Nu. Club: Engring. (Oklahoma City). Contbr. articles in field to profl. jours. Home: 2816 NW 25th St Oklahoma City OK 73107

DENISTON, PATRICIA SWAN, coll. adminstr.; b. N.Y.C., Sept. 29, 1935; d. Anthony E. and Dorothy L. (Kemmer) Swan; B.S., U. Tampa, 1963; M.A., U. South Fla., 1968; Ed.D., U. Fla., 1975; m. Dale R. Deniston, Jan. 29, 1977; children—Robert Paul Miller, Ruth Ansley Deniston. Classroom tchr., media specialist Hillsborough County (Fla.) Bd. Pub. Instrn., 1963-66, 68-69; librarian Tampa (Fla.) Cath. High Sch. 1959-70; prof., media specialist Polk Community Coll., Winter Haven, Fla., 1971-72, dir. learning resources, 1972—; del. Fla. Gov.'s Conf. on Libraries and Info. Services, 1978; cons. in field. U. Fla. fellow, 1969-70. Mem. ALA, Assn. for Ednl. Communications and Tech., Fla. Library Assn., Fla. Assn. for Media in Edn. (pres. elect 1979), Pi Lambda Theta, Kappa Delta Pi, Phi Kappa Phi. Asso. editor Fame newsletter, 1973-74. Home: 4 Eagles Nest Winter Haven FL 33880 Office: 999 Ave H NE Winter Haven FL 33880

DENIUS, FRANKLIN WOFFORD, lawyer; b. Athens, Tex., Jan. 4, 1925; s. S. F. and Frances (Cain) D.; B.B.A., LL.B., U. Tex., 1949; m. Charmaine Hooper, Nov. 19, 1949; children—Frank Wofford, Charmaine. Admitted to Tex. bar, 1949, practiced in Austin, 1949—; partner firm Clark Thomas Harris Denius & Winters, 1949-75; gen. counsel Delhi-Taylor Oil Corp., 1962-64, Delhi Pipeline Corp., 1950-64; founder, sec., dir. Telecom Corp., Tex. Capital Corp.; dir. Delhi Internat. Oil Corp., Capital Nat. Bank Austin, So. Union Co., Supron Energy Corp., Red Ball Motor Freight, Inc.; chmn. legal com. R.R. Commn. Adv. Council on Pipeline Safety; atty. Tex. High Sch. Coaches Assn.; mem. legal com. Nat. Assn. Electric Utilities, 1965-72. Chmn. Austin United Fund Spl. Schs. div., 1960, Pacesetters div., 1961, Schs. div., 1964, gen. chmn., 1968, pres., 1972, chmn. bd., 1973; bd. dirs. Tex. Research League; chmn. steering com. Sch. Bond Campaign, 1964; mem. Wofford Cain Found.; sec., bd. dirs. Tex. Longhorn Edn. Found.; gen. counsel Better Bus. Bur. Austin; pres. Young Men's Bus. League Austin; pres., exec. council Austin Ex-Students Assn. U. Tex.; chmn. United Way Austin, 1973; trustee Austin Ind. Sch. Dist., 1970-73, Schreiner Coll. Served AUS, 1943-45; ETO. Decorated Silver Star medal with two oak leaf clusters, Purple Heart; recipient Outstanding Young Man of Austin award Jr. C. of C., 1959. Mem. State Bar Tex., Am., Tex., Travis County (past dir.) bar assns., Austin C. of C., Athens C. of C., Tex. Philos. Soc. Presbyterian (deacon, elder, trustee). Clubs: Longhorn (past pres.), West Austin Optimist (past dir.), Headliners (pres., v.p., sec., trustee, mem. exec. com.), Masons. Home: 3703 Meadowbank Dr Austin TX 78703 Office: PO Box 2177 Austin TX 78768

DENMAN, ANDREW JACKSON, optometrist; b. Atlanta, Aug. 8, 1915; s. Julius L. and Minnie Irene (Murphy) D.; D.Optometry, So. Coll. of Optometry, 1949, Dr. Ocular Sci., 1963; m. Ruth H. Schillinger, Sept. 28, 1940; children—Andrew Jackson, Steven W., Sylvia L. Pvt. practice optometry Athens, Ga., 1949—. Trustee So. Coll. of Optometry, 1960-68. Served with AUS, 1943-45. Recipient Man of Year award Ga. Optometric Assn., 1957. Mem. Am., Ga. (pres. 1957) optometric assns., Am. Acad. Optometry, S.E. Ednl. Congress Optometry (pres. 1956), Omega Delta. Presbyn. (elder 1956). Kiwanian (pres. 1956, lt. gov. 7th div. 1958). Home: 230 Beechwood Dr Athens GA 30601 Office: 489 N Milledge Ave Athens GA 30601

DENMAN, BEN P., ins. co. exec.; b. Brownwood, Tex.; student Howard Payne Coll.; B.B.A. with high honors, U. Tex. at Austin, 1942; m. Nell Denman; children—W. Edwin, Marajen. Formerly sec.-treas. wholesale grocery firm, Brownwood; with Southwestern Life Ins. Co., Dallas, 1951—, successively salesman, regional mgr., v.p., agy. dir., exec. v.p., 1969-73, chief operating officer, 1972-73, pres., 1973—; v.p., dir. Southwestern Life Corp.; chmn. exec. com. Southwestern Gen. Life Ins. Co. Served with USNR, World War II. C.L.U. Mem. Am. Coll. Life Underwriters (mem. devel. bd.). Presbyn. (elder). Club: Bent Tree Country. Address: PO Box 2699 Dallas TX 75221*

DENNETT, EDWARD MOORE, mfg. co. exec.; b. Central Falls, R.I., Mar. 10, 1935; s. Edward Moore and Gertrude May (Pelote) D.; B.S., Worcester Poly. Inst., 1957; m. Katherine L. Kapesis, June 15, 1957; 1 son, Mark E. Sales engr. Sangamo Electric Co., Birmingham, Ala., 1960-62, dist. mgr., 1963-68, sales mgr. automotive and indsl. div., Springfield, Ill., 1969, asst. regional mgr., Atlanta, 1970-71, mgr. mktg. and sales Oliver div., Atlanta, 1972-75, regional mgr. Sangamo-Weston, Inc., Atlanta, 1976, nat. sales mgr., 1977, v.p. nat. sales, 1977, v.p., dir. mktg., 1977—. Served to 1st lt. AUS, 1958-60. Registered profl. engr., Fla., Miss. Mem. IEEE, Alpha Tau Omega. Republican. Roman Catholic. Clubs: K.C., Civitan. Contbr. articles to profl. jours. Office: PO Box 48400 Atlanta GA 30362

DENNEY, WOODROW WILSON, JR., poultry co. exec.; b. Griffin, Ga., June 30, 1940; s. Woodrow Wilson and Ruth Brooks (Austin) D.; student N. Ga. Coll., 1958-61; B.B.A., U. Ga., 1961-63; m. Nancy Irene Chasteen, Apr. 12, 1968; children—Courtney Leigh, Austin Kirk. Ins. salesman N.Y. Life Ins. Co., 1964; acct. Gold Kist Inc., Canton, Ga., 1964-66, sales mgr., Durham, N.C., 1966-73, mgr. poultry and meat internat. sales div., Atlanta, 1973-75, div. sales mgr., Athens, Ga., 1975—. Served with USAF, 1963. Mem. Nat. Broiler Council, Ga. Poultry Processors (dir.). Democrat. Baptist. Club: Rotary (West Athens, Ga.). Home: 170 Sweet Gum Dr Athens GA 30605 Office: Gold Kist Inc 355 Oneta St Athens GA 30603

DENNIS, CARLICE WENDYL, steel co. exec.; b. Kingston, Okla., Sept. 30, 1939; s. Carlice Garland and Mary Lois (Haynie) D.; B.B.A., Central State U., 1970; m. Rozanne Swick, Dec. 30, 1970; children—Marc Anthony, Khristin Wyn. With W & W Steel Co., Oklahoma City, 1961-71, gen. mgr., Norman, Okla., 1971-73, v.p., gen. mgr., 1973—. Served with U.S. Army, 1957-60. Mem. Norman C. of C. Republican. Methodist. Home: 9516 Regal Ln Oklahoma City OK 73132 Office: 2932 W Tecumseh Rd Norman OK 73069

DENNIS, EARL WILSON, JR., army officer; b. Ft. Collins, Colo., Nov. 30, 1942; s. Earl Wilson and Betty Elaine (Sperr) D.; B.S., U. So. Colo., 1968; grad. U.S. Army Command and Gen. Staff Coll., 1978; m. Karen Elaine Smith, Dec. 27, 1973. Commd. 2d lt., U.S. Army, 1968, advanced through grades to maj., 1979; aero scout platoon comdr., Ft. Riley, Kans., 1972-73; cavalry troop comdr., Ft. Knox, Ky., 1974-75, command instr. pilot, 1975-76, mgr. data processing center, 1977-79, aviation detachment exec. officer, Japan, 1979—. Decorated Bronze Star, Army Commendation medal, Air medal with 7 oak leaf clusters, Meritorious service medal; certified flight instr. FAA; licensed multiple-lines ins. agt., Colo. Mem. Army Aviation Assn. Am. (life), N.G. Assn. U.S. (life), So. Colo. State Coll. Alumni Assn. (life), Assn. U.S. Army. Republican. Presbyterian. Clubs: Ft. Riley Flying (pres. 1972-73), So. Colo. State Coll. Vets. (pres. 1967-68). Home: PO Box 202 Palo Pinto TX 76072 Office: US Army Aviation Detachment Japan APO San Francisco CA 96343

DENNIS, FRANK ALLEN, educator; b. Athens, Tenn., June 15, 1943; s. Dow Neil and Bonnie Mae (Nipper) D.; B.A., Tenn. Wesleyan Coll., 1965; M.A., Miss. State U., 1966, Ph.D., 1970; m. Linda Joyce Minge, July 17, 1965; 1 dau., Farrah Lauri. Sports editor Athens (Tenn.) Press, 1961-62, Daily Post-Athenian, 1962-64; minister Sweetwater (Tenn.) Ch. of Christ, 1964-65; instr. history Delta State U., Cleveland, Miss., 1968-70, asst. prof. history, 1970-73, asso. prof., 1973-77, prof., 1977—. Mem. So. Hist. Assn., Miss. Hist. Soc. (dir. 1972-75), AAUP. Democrat. Lion. Editor: Kemper County Rebel: The Civil War Diary of Robert Masten Holmes, C.S.A., 1973. News and notices editor Jour. Miss. History, 1971-74, bibliog. editor, 1974—; editor: Southern Miscellany: Essays in Honor of Glover Moore, 1981. Home: 105 Colonial Dr Cleveland MS 38732 Office: Delta State U Cleveland MS 38732

DENNIS, HENRY ARNOLD, newspaper editor; b. Concord, N.C., Dec. 7, 1891; s. Amanuel Haywood and Ida May (Utley) D.; A.B., Duke U. (formerly Trinity Coll.), 1913; m. Essie Thomas Daniel, Dec. 25, 1919; children—William Baker, Doris Tharrington, Ruth. Editor, Greenville (N.C.) Reflector, 1913; reporter Raleigh (N.C.) News & Observer, 1913-14; news editor Rocky Mount (N.C.) Telegram, 1914; editor Henderson (N.C.) Daily Dispatch, 1915—, pres., 1922—; pres. N.C. R.R. Co., 1945-46; N.C. editor Tobacco Internat., 1915—; dir. Henderson Home Savs. & Loan Assn., 1935—. Mem. N.C. Dem. Exec. Com., 1936-40; mem. Henderson Sch. Bd., 1936-42, Vance County Sch. Bd., 1942-48; tchr. men's Bible class City Road Meth. Ch.; trustee Maria Parham Hosp., Henderson. Named Boss of Yr., Henderson Jaycees, 1974, Man of Yr., Henderson-Vance County C. of C., 1975; recipient plaque Henderson Mchts. Assn., 1974. Mem. N.C. Asso. Press Club (past pres.), Am. Soc. Newspaper Editors, N.C. Assn. Evening Dailies (past pres.), N.C. Press Assn. (pres. 1957-58), Eastern N.C. Press Assn. (pres. 1957-58), Henderson C. of C. (past pres.). Clubs: Odd Fellows, K.P.; Duke U. Half Century (pres. 1968). Contbr. articles to various newspapers. Home: 309 Burwell Ave Henderson NC 27536 Office: PO Box 93 Henderson NC 27536

DENNIS, RICHARD GARRETT, pharmacist; b. Wichita Falls, Tex., June 11, 1951; s. Charles Loyd and Doris LaVelle (Garrett) D.; B.S. in Pharmacy, Southwestern State Coll. (now Southwestern Okla. State U.), 1974; m. Terry Lynn Richardson, Aug. 18, 1972; 1 son, Levi Garrett. Intern, Starr Pharmacy, Moore, Okla., 1974, Graves Drug Co., Arkansas City, Kans., 1974, Pierce Pharmacy, Muskogee, Okla., 1975; staff pharmacist Drs. Hosp., Tulsa, 1975-77, dir. pharmacy, 1977—, founding mem. nutritional support team; mem. faculty Southwestern Okla. State U. Mem. Am. Soc. Parenteral and Enteral Nutrition, Okla. Soc. Hosp. Pharmacists. Home: 8804 N 120th E Ave Owasso OK 74055 Office: 2323 S Harvard St Tulsa OK 74114

DENNIS, RUTLEDGE MELVIN, educator; b. Charleston, S.C., Aug. 16, 1939; s. David and Ora Jane (Porcher) D.; B.A., S.C. State Coll., 1965; M.A., Wash. State U., 1969, Ph.D., 1975; m. Sarah Helen Bankhead, Aug. 16, 1967; children—Tchaka Lateef, Imaro Aki, Kimya Nuru, Zuri Sanyika. Asso. prof. sociology Va. Commonwealth U., Richmond, 1971—, coordinator Afro-Am. studies, 1971-78. Commr., Richmond Redevel. and Housing Authority, 1976—, Housing Opportunities Made Equal, 1976—; co-coordinator Southeastern Regional African Seminar, 1973-76; mem. Eastern Va. Internat. Consortium, 1972-77. Served with U.S. Army, 1960-63. Ford Found. grantee, 1970—; Nat. Endowment Humanities grantee, 1978; NIMH grantee, 1980-82; recipient Outstanding Citizens award Boys' Club Richmond, 1976. Mem. African Heritage Assn., AAAS, Assn. Study Afro-Am. Life and Culture, Am., So., Va. (exec. com. 1974-75) sociol. assns., NAACP. Editor: (with others) The Afro Americans: Social Science Perspectives; editorial bd. Pan-African Studies Jour., 1976. Home: 3015 Sunset Ave Richmond VA 23221 Office: 820 W Franklin St Richmond VA 23284

DENNIS, WILLIAM BURL, hosp. ofcl.; b. Franklinton, N.C., Sept. 26, 1949; s. Charlie Robert and Pattie Jane (King) D.; diploma Croft's Bus. Coll., 1970; m. Linda Mae Rose, May 3, 1975; 1 son, Christopher Scott. Asst. to chief central processing Duke U. Hosp., Durham, N.C., 1972-74, asst. chief, 1974-76, asso. chief, 1976-77, chief sterile processing and sterilization, 1977-79, asst. dir. pharmacy and sterile processing, 1979—; instr. Durham Tech. Inst., 1978—. Served with USNR, 1970-72. Mem. N.C. Assn. Hosp. Central Service Personnel (pres. 1976-78), Am. Soc. Hosp. Central Service Personnel (pres. 1980). Baptist. Home: Route 1 Box 379-O Bahama NC 27503 Office: Box 3078 Duke U Hosp Durham NC 27710

DENNISON, JERRY LEE, retail office supply co. exec.; b. Leitchfield, Ky., May 22, 1947; s. Ronald M. and Alice Marie D.; diploma Spencerian Bus. Coll., 1969; A.S., Western Ky. U., 1975; m. Patricia Jeanette Davis, Sept. 19, 1965; children—Sonya, Staci, Jarred. Mgr. EDP, Ky. So. Coll., Louisville, 1965-67; supr. EDP, Western Ky. U., Bowling Green, 1967-68; asst. mgr. Bank Data Center, Bowling Green, 1968-70; instr. EDP, Spencerian Coll., Louisville, 1971-72, Somerset (Ky.) Vocat.-Tech. Sch., 1972-77; mgr. EDP, Crane Co., Ferguson, Ky., 1977-79; owner, mgr. Dennison Office Supply Co., Russell Springs, Ky., 1979—; vol. faculty Somerset Community Coll., 1972-77. Pres. Russell Springs Elem. Sch. PTA, 1973-74, v.p., 1974-75. Mem. Data Processing Mgmt. Assn. Russell County C. of C. Mem. Ch. of Christ. Home: Route 1 Box 104-A Russell Springs KY 42642 Office: Dennison Office Supply Key Village Center Russell Springs KY 42642

DENNISTON, GARRETT LEE, audiologist; b. Montgomery County, Ky., June 12, 1950; s. Winfred Elwood and Manetta Mae (Hatfield) D.; B.A., Milligan Coll., 1972; M.A., E. Tenn. State U., 1975; m. Donna Sue Loving, Aug. 25, 1973; 1 son, Garrett Allan. Audiologist, Asheville (N.C.) Ear, Nose & Throat Assos., 1975—; pres., chief stockholder Hear-Care, Inc.; noise cons. Active Buncombe County (N.C.) Assn. for Retarded Citizens; bd. dirs. Tanglewood Theatre. Lic. audiologist, N.C. Mem. Am. Speech and Hearing Assn. (cert. clin. competence), Audiol. Resource Assn. (sec.-treas. 1976—), Am. Tinnitus Assn. (cert. therapist), Soc. Med. Audiology, Am. Auditory Soc., N.C. Speech, Hearing and Lang. Assn., Phi Kappa Phi, Kappa Delta Pi. Home: 65 W Kensington Rd Asheville NC 28804 Office: Asheville Ear Nose & Throat Assos 131 McDowell St Asheville NC 28801

DENSON, JACK MC VAY, petroleum co. exec.; b. San Antonio, Apr. 16, 1927; s. John LaClede and Mary Lou (Stinson) D.; student U. Tex., 1944, Southwestern U., 1944-45; B.S. in Naval Sci. and Tactics, U. Tex., 1947, B.S. in Petroleum Engring., 1948; m. Betty Joyce Gray, Aug. 4, 1964. Petroleum engr. Tex. Co., Buckeye, N.Mex., Midland, Tex., Snyder, Tex., Sundown, Tex., Lamesa, Tex., 1948-59, Cosden Petroleum Corp., Big Spring, Tex., 1959-63; petroleum engr. Am. Petrofina Co. Tex., Big Spring, 1963-64, dist. engr., 1964-66, asst. dist. mgr., 1966-71, asst. dist. mgr., Tyler, Tex., 1971-73, dist. mgr., 1973-78, mgr. outside ops., Dallas, 1978—. Asst. dir. Big-Spring-Howard County Dept. Civil Def., 1963-70. Served with USNR, 1944-46, 51-53. Registered profl. engr., La., Tex. Mem. Am. Petroleum Inst. (dir. E. Tex. chpt. 1973—), Soc. Petroleum Engrs. (chmn. E. Tex. chpt. 1979), Tyler Petroleum Club. Home: 1718 S College Tyler TX 75701 Office: Box 2159 Dallas TX 75221

DENSON, ROBERT NEAL, hosp. adminstr.; b. San Antonio, Sept. 23, 1942; s. J. C. and Birdie May (Leaverton) D.; B.S., S.W.Tex. State U., 1972; M.S. H.C.A., Trinity U., 1973; m. Mary Ellen Thurman, Dec. 22, 1967; children—Marissa Deanna, Krista Leah. Adminstrv. resident, asst. to dir. hosps. Ind. U. Hosps., Indpls., 1973-75; adminstrv. dir. radiology Parkview Meml. Hosp., Ft. Wayne, Ind., 1975-76; asst. adminstr. support services Riveredge Hosp., Forest Park, Ill., 1977; adminstr. Coon Meml. Hosp., Dalhart, Tex., 1977-78, Littlefield (Tex.) Med. Center, 1978—. Mem. adult living com. County Extension Agy., Littlefield, 1978; bd. dirs. Littlefield chpt. ARC, 1978. Mem. Tex. Hosp. Assn., Am. Hosp. Assn., Dalhart C. of C. (chmn. med. service com. 1977). Baptist. Clubs: Masons, Rotary. Home: 1223 W 13th St Littlefield TX 79339 Office: Littlefield Med Center 1500 S Sunset St Littlefield TX 79339

DENT, DANNY VAL, lawyer; b. Atlanta, Jan. 3, 1946; s. Vincent Val and Martha Virginia (Prather) D.; B.A., Tex. Christian U., 1968; J.D., Tex. Tech. U., 1971; postgrad Judge Adv. Gen. Sch. U. Va., 1971; m. Dee Ann Huff, Aug. 3, 1968; children—Dawn Alison, David Victor. Admitted to Tex. bar, 1971; adult probation officer Tarrant County, Tex., Ft. Worth, 1971; partner firm Eastland, Crow & Dent, Hillsboro, Tex., 1974—; county atty. Hill County, 1979—. Pres., Hill County Tex. Cancer Soc., 1976-77, crusade chmn., 1976; crusade chmn. Hill County United Way, 1977—. Served with U.S. Army, 1971-75. Recipient Hill County Cancer Soc. Distinguished Service award. Mem. Am, Hill County (sec. 1976-77, pres. 1979) bar assns., State Bar Tex., Tex. Trial Laweyrs Assn., Tex. Criminal Def. Lawyers Assn., Ky. Colonels Assn. Democrat. Presbyterian. Club: Optimist (pres. Hillsboro). Home: 339 Carr St Hillsboro TX 76645 Office: PO Box 840 Hillsboro TX 76645

DENT, HARDY LEE, JR., profl. assn. exec.; b. Hale Center, Tex., Dec. 3, 1920; s. Hardy Lee and Clara (Allen) D.; student C. of C. Inst., 1957, U. Colo., 1958-59; m. Juanita Carmickle, Apr. 17, 1946; 1 child, Hardy Lee. Mgr. Ponca Wholesale Co., Austin, 1947-50; owner Dent Service Sta., Hale Center, 1951-56; gen. mgr. Hale Center C. of C., 1956—. Exec. dir. Fed. Housing Authority, Hale Center, 1966—. Guest instr. Tex. Firemen and Fire Marshalls Sch., Tex. A&M U., 1972—. Chief Hale Center Vol. Fire Dept., 1953—; sec. Community Fund Bd., Hale Center, 1968—; coordinator Disaster and Clean-up orgn. tornado disaster, 1965. Bd. dirs. Salvation Army, Hale Center, Community Action Center; mem. Hale Center Indsl. Found., 1971—. Served with AUS, 1941-46, 50-51. Recipient Service to Youth award Am. Legion, 1962, Service to Youth award 4-H Club, 1965, Lion of Year award, 1964-65, Citizen of Year award Hale Center C. of C., 1976. Mem. C. of C. Execs. Assn. West Tex. (dir. 1976, Mgr. of Year 1978), Tex. C. of C. Mgrs. Assn., Interstate Assn. Chamber Execs., Panhandle Assn. Chamber Execs., South Plains Assn. Chamber Execs., Panhandle Fireman's Assn. (pres. 1967, sec.-treas. 1969-74, 77—), Internat. Assn. Fire Chiefs. Lion (sec.-treas. 1970-75, zone chmn. 1974-75). Baptist. Home: 407 Main St Hale Center TX 79041 Office: City Hall Main St Hale Center TX 79041

DENT, JOHN ROBERT, phys. scientist; b. Rainelle, W.Va., Oct. 26, 1932; s. George Livingston and Reba Ammi (Reid) D.; B.S., Va. Poly. Inst., 1957, postgrad., 1969; postgrad. Rensselaer Poly. Inst., 1967; m. Bonnie Heather Plahte, Aug. 15, 1953; 1 son, John Robert II. Sr. engr. Melpar, Falls Church, Va., 1957-63; project engr. Tri-State Electronics, Falls Church, 1963-64; with Harry Diamond Labs., Washington, 1964—, chief research and devel. br., 1973—. Instr. Va. Poly. Inst., Blacksburg, 1956; cons. to Gen. Abram's sci. adviser, Republic of Vietnam, 1969. Judge regional sci. fair judge Fairfax and West Prince William Counties (Va.), 1965—; dir. regional contest Acad. Model Aeronautics, Washington, 1971-73. Served with AUS, 1953-55. Recipient Hinman award for annual outstanding tech. leader Harry Diamond Labs., 1971; Research and Devel. Tech. Achievement award Dep. Sec. Army, 1972, 75. Mem. IEEE, Sci. Research Soc. Am., Sigma Xi. Patentee in field. Home: 9932 Clearfield Ave Vienna VA 22180 Office: Harry Diamond Labs 2800 Powder Mill Rd Adelphi MD 20783

DENT, WOODWARD GUIDRY, casing mfg. co. ofcl.; b. Orangeburg, S.C., July 9, 1952; s. William Prickett and Mary Ethel (Guidry) D.; grad. U. S.C., 1974; m. Jeanette Carroll, Aug. 22, 1972; children—Michelle Elizabeth, Edie Carroll. Dist. mgr. Progressive Farmer Ins. Co., Orangeburg, 1973-75; owner The Back Door night club, St. Matthews, S.C., 1975-77; owner/mgr. quality assurance dept. Teepak Co., Columbia, S.C., 1977—. Served with U.S. Army, 1971. Mem. Order of Arrow. Republican. Roman Catholic. Home: PO Box 71 Saint Matthews SC 29135 Office: Teepak PO Box 11925 Columbia SC 29211

DENTON, THOMAS, chem. co. exec.; b. Fall River, Mass., Dec. 12, 1916; s. Harry and Ellen (Taylor) D.; student public schs., Fall River, Mass.; student in journalism Brown U., indsl. engring. U. Tenn.; children—Margaret, Leslie, Mark, Laurel. With Fall River Herald News, 1932-39, U.S. Dept. Navy, 1939-46, Wesinghouse Corp., 1946-50; with Union Carbide Co., Oak Ridge, 1953-69, indsl. engr., 1955-61, writing analyst, 1961-69; mgr. comml. ops. Chem. Separations Corp., Oak Ridge, 1969—; cons. Zagar Co., Cleve., Acraloc Co., Oak Ridge. Clubs: Elks, Oak Ridge Country. Contbr. articles to tech. jours. Home: 102 Keystone Ln Oak Ridge TN 37830 Office: Tech Park Oak Ridge TN 37830

DENTON, THOMAS STEWART, investments co. exec.; b. Louisville, Oct. 12, 1945; s. Stewart Benjamin and Jane Alma (Wiggers) D.; student U. Miss., 1964-68; B.S., Murray State U., 1969, postgrad., 1974-77; m. Janet Lee Scott, Dec. 11, 1976. Asst. parts mgr. Don Corlett Volkswagen, Louisville, 1962; v.p., sec.-treas. Scoden Inc., Murray, Ky., 1979—. Mem. Public Service Research Council. Served with USAF, 1969-73. Recipient cert. of appreciation Murray State U. Super Racer Club, 1978. Mem. Murray State U. Alumni Assn., Americans Against the Union Control of Govt., Am. Hunting Union, Am. Numismatic Assn. (life). Club: Mason (Valley Sta., Ky.). Home: 812 N 20th St Murray KY 42071 Office: 100A N 6th St Murray KY 42071

DENTON, WAYNE LAVERT, JR., biochemist, ednl. adminstr.; b. Greenwood, Miss., Nov. 15, 1943; s. Wayne Lavert and Edna (Naaman) D.; B.S. in Chemistry, Delta State Coll., 1965; Ph.D. in Biochemistry, Okla. State U., 1970; m. Rosemary Correro, July 6, 1962; children—D'Wayne, Stephanie. Lab. technician Okla. State U., 1965-66, research asst. dept. biochemistry, 1966-70; asst. prof. chemistry U. Southwestern La., Lafayette, 1970-72, dir. research and sponsored programs for univ., 1973—, acting dir. U. Southwestern La. Conf. Center, 1978-79, cons., past dir. Crawfish Research Center. Loan exec. United Giver's Fund of Lafayette, 1973-74; univ. chmn. United Givers Fund Drive, 1978-79, div. chmn., 1979-80; chmn. univ. liaison for La. Gulf Coast Oil Expn., 1979; asst. dist. commr. Evangeline council Boy Scouts Am., 1975-78; bd. govs. La. Arthritis Found., 1975-77. Mem. Nat. Council Univ. Research Adminstrs., Sigma Xi (pres. U. Southwestern La. chpt. 1975). Roman Catholic. Clubs: Rotary (dir. Lafayette chpt. 1978-79, treas. 1979-80, mem. internat. group study exchange to Australia 1975), K.C. Home: 134 Oakleaf Dr Lafayette LA 70503 Office: USL Box 42331 Lafayette LA 70504

DENT O'NEILL, BEVERLY, writer, pub. relations and mktg. cons.; d. DeWitt Talmadge and Lois Geraldine (Givens) Dent; student U. Houston, 1958-61, So. Meth. U., 1963-65; m. Richard H. O'Neill, June 21, 1971. Columnist, Bellaire (Tex.) Texan, 1954-60; feature writer Houston Chronicle, 1956-62; pub. speaker, mistress of ceremonies fashion shows, convs., 1956-61, 72—; actress, singer, comedienne summer stock cos., Cripple Creek and Denver, Colo., 1959-61, little theaters, Dallas, 1964-67, radio and TV, 1963—; copywriter, media dir. A.E. Hardy & Heinke Advt. Co., Dallas, 1963-66; copywriter Glenn Advt. Co., Dallas, 1967; copy chief, media dir. McCrary-Powell Advt. Co., Dallas, 1967-70; feature writer Houston Post, 1970—; pvt. practice cons. advt., pub. relations, mktg., Houston, 1970—; freelance writer newspapers and mags., 1978—; corr. Suburbia Reporters, Beacon & Post; Nat. Assn. Broadcasters, Hollywood Assn. Broadcasters radio and TV spot judge, 1969, 70. Youth dir., Harris County Multiple Sclerosis Found., cons., 1959, 60. Recipient awards for advt., poetry, short stories, feature writing, editorials, oil painting, piano. Mem. Theta Sigma Phi. Home: 5555 Little Lake Bellaire TX 77401

DEODATI, JOSEPH BENJAMIN, aero. engr.; b. San Antonio, Dec. 17, 1916; s. Michael N. and Lydia (Rotondi) D.; B.S., Tex. A. and M. U., 1939 M.S., Calif. Inst. Tech., 1946, Aero. Engr., 1947; m. Mildred Perkins, Mar. 2, 1944; children—Debora Breger, Joseph Benjamin. Commd. ensign USN, 1941, advanced through grades to comdr., 1953; naval aviator, World War II; aero. engr., Pacific and Atlantic fleets, U.S.; ret., 1961; dir. research, engring. systems engring. div. Pnuemo Dynamics Corp., Bethesda, Md., 1961-63; aero. engr. advanced programs Gen. Dynamics Corp., Ft. Worth, 1963—. Decorated Air medal with two gold stars. Mem. Nat. Mgmt. Assn., Navy League U.S. (dir.), Air Force Assn., Am. Security Council, Calif. Inst. Tech. Alumni Assn., Sigma Xi. Club: De Cordova Bend Country. Home: 2512 Ridgmar Blvd #1 Fort Worth TX 76116 Office: PO Box 748 Fort Worth TX 76101

DE PASQUALE, NICHOLAS DOMINIC, aerospace exec.; b. Balt., June 5, 1927; s. George C. and Carmella M. (Tuminella) DeP.; B.E., Johns Hopkins U., 1951; M.S. (Sloan fellow), Mass. Inst. Tech., 1971; m. Mary Carol Cooper, Apr. 21, 1951; children—Michael N., Deborah. With Martin Marietta Corp., 1951—, asst. project engr., Orlando, Fla., 1958-61, program mgr., 1961-67, program dir., 1967-73, dir. tactical weapons systems program, 1973-75, v.p. tactical weapons systems, 1975-76, v.p. guided projectiles, 1976-77, v.p., dep. gen. mgr. prodn. ops., 1977—. Served with USNR, 1945-46. Mem. IEEE, Am. Ordnance Assn., Am. Inst. Aeros. and Astronautics, Armed Forces Communications and Electronics Assn., Assn. U.S. Army. Home: 1881 Shiloh Ln Winter Park FL 32789 Office: PO Box 5837 MP-292 Orlando FL 32855

DEPEL, JAMES ANTHONY, educator; b. Oklahoma City, July 4, 1936; s. William Emil and Ruby Valentine (Osterlow) D.; B.A. in Edn., Central State Coll., Edmond, Okla., 1962. Tchr. public schs., New Orleans, 1962-63; tchr., coach public schs., Bowie, Ariz., 1963-64; tchr. public schs. Mangum, Okla., 1964-65, Hefner Jr. High Sch., Oklahoma City, 1965-73; tchr., coach Western Oaks Jr. High Sch., Putnam City Sch. Dist., Bethany, Okla., 1974—. Served with USMCR, 1955-72. Mem. Okla. Ednl. Assn., NEA. Author: The Baseball Handbook for Coaches and Players, 1976. Home: 5912 NW 41st St Apt 215 Oklahoma City OK 73122 Office: 7200 NW 23d St Bethany OK 73008

DE PÍNERO, EUROPA GONZÁLEZ GARRIGA (MRS. JOSE A. DE PINERO), educator; b. Aguadilla, P.R., Feb. 1, 1918; d. Juan C. Gonzalez Giocoechea and Maria Garriga Chacon; B.A. in Edn., U. P.R., 1938, profl. diploma, 1954; M.A. in Edn., N.Y. U., 1956, Ed.D., 1965; J.D., Inter-Am. U. P.R., 1978; m. Jose A. de Pinero, Dec. 22, 1939; children—Jose Juan, Luis Roberto, Europa Maria de Pínero del Valle, Imgard L. Tchr. elementary, jr. and high schs., prin. P.R. Dept. Pub. Instrn., 1938-58, asst. supt., supt. schs., 1960-65; instr. edn., supr. students U. P.R., 1958-60; prof., chmn. dept. edn. Inter Am. U. P.R., Hato Rey, 1966-70, dean acad. affairs, 1970-73, prof. grad. studies Sch. Edn., 1974—. Mem. cons. com. for devel. vocational and tech. edn. P.R. Dept. Edn.; cons. P.R. Dept. Sch. Prins., 1968—; mem. sch. bd., pres. acad. com. Caribbean Consol. Schs. P.R., 1967-69. Recipient awards for outstanding ednl. work. Mem. Am. Assn. Colls. Tchr. Edn. (Distinguished Achievement award 1969), Assn. for Supervision and Curriculum Devel., Assn. for Childhood Edn. Internat., Am. Assn. for Higher Edn., Nat. Inst. for Advanced Study in Teaching Disadvantaged, Nat. Assn. for Edn. Young Children, Nat. Home Study Council, Am. Acad. Polit. and Social Sci., N.E.A. (life), Tchrs. Assn. P.R., Am. Assn. U. Profs., N.Y. U. Alumni Assn. P.R. (past pres.). Author: Tendencias Ideas Pedagogicas: Su Aplicacion en Puerto Rico, 1971; Accountability and Change in Education, 1972; Schools in Transition, 1973; El Director de las Escuelas Publicas de Puerto Rico: Sus Problemas, Intereses y Necesidados, 1973; Del Quehacer Educativo Puertorriqueno, 1974; Evaluación del Maestro, Sistema de Mérito: Relación con el Derecho Administrativo, 1978; contbr. articles to ednl. jours. Home: 372 R Lamar St Hato Rey PR 00918

DE PINGRE, MAJOR, office supply co. exec.; b. Leesville, La., May 31, 1928; s. Adrien Edward and Madeline Ethel (Kirby) DeP.; B.A., La. State U., 1952; m. Patricia Lee Catron, Mar. 27, 1953; children—Benny Louis, Margaret Ann. Owner, Webster Printing Co., Inc., Minden, La., 1959—; pres. Major Office Supply, Meadowpark Nursing Center, Inc., Shreveport; owner Meadowview Nursing Homes, Minden, 1963-72. Pres. Webster Parish Tb Assn., 1958-59; treas. New March of Dimes, 1959-60, publicity chmn., 1956-60; pres. Am. Field Service, Webster Parish chpt., 1960-61; publicity chmn. Charlie Hennigan Day, 1964; mem. N. La. Health Systems Agy., Inc.; pres. Minden Little Theatre, 1964-66; chmn. comml. div. Webster United Fund, 1964; chmn. camping and activities com. Yatasi council Boy Scouts Am., 1960-61, dist. commr., 1960-61, 66; pres. chpt. ARC, 1965-66; publicity chmn. Webster's Centennial, 1971; v.p. Com. to Get Mus., 1974; mem. Cultural Affairs Com., 1973; vice chmn. Webster Parish Democratic Exec. Com., 1960-74; del. La. Dem. Conv., 1980; bd. dirs. Webster Parish Cancer Bd., Easter Seal Soc.;

chmn. bldg. dedication com. 1st Baptist Ch., 1978. Served with USN, 1946-48. Recipient Outstanding Jaycee Local Pres. State La., Jr. C. of C., 1959-60, Distinguished Service award Jr. C. of C., 1969. Mem. Am. Legion (publicity chmn. 1958-59, comdr. Wiley-Pevy post 1976-77), Dorcheat Hist. Assn. (pres. 1977), Minden C. of C. (dir. 1961-62, chmn. ann. banquet 1976, 78, chmn. free enterprise com. 1979-80), Minden Jr. C. of C. (pres. 1959-60), Webster Parish La. State U. Alumni Assn. (pres. 1962-63). Club: Tennis and Aquatic (Minden) Author: History of the First Baptist Church, 1844-1969. Home: 1001 E Chrislo Dr Minden LA 71055 Office: 116 Pearl St Minden LA 71055

DERHAM, JOHN PICKENS, JR., banker; b. Green Sea, S.C., Apr. 27, 1896; s. John Pickens and Loula Jackson (McGougan) D.; B.S., Clemson U., 1917; m. Sarah Louella Ivy, Apr. 19, 1968; 1 dau. by previous marriage—Mary L. (Mrs. J.P. Roberts); stepchildren—Anne A. (Mrs. Gilbert Coleman), Bert L. Angle. With Seaboard R.R., 1920-66, beginning as devel. agt., successively contracting freight agt., comml. agt., dist. freight agt., asst. freight traffic mgr., all Jacksonville, Fla., freight traffic mgr., asst. v.p., both Norfolk, Va., 1920-54, v.p., Richmond, Va., 1954-66; sr. v.p., dir. Barnett Bank of Winter Haven (Fla.), 1966—. Served to 1st lt., inf., U.S. Army, 1917-19. Mem. Nat. Freight Traffic Assn. (life), Nat. Def. Transp. Assn. (life), Jacksonville Traffic Club (life, past pres.), Fla. Traffic Assn., Future Farmers Am. (hon.), Future Farmers Fla. (hon.), Newcomen Soc. N.Am. Clubs: Masons, Shriners; Grenelefe Golf and Racquet; Lake Region Yacht and Country (Winter Haven). Home: 700 Mirror Terr Winter Haven FL 33880 Office: 11 5th St Winter Haven FL 33880

DERIAN, PAUL SAHAK, physician; b. L.I., N.Y., July 25, 1922; s. Sahak B. and Renee (Tabore) D.; student N.Y. U., 1940-41; B.A., U. Va., 1946, M.D., 1947; children—Michael, T. Craig, Renee Brooke. Intern St. Vincent's Hosp., N.Y.C., 1951-52; resident orthopedic surgery U. Va., Charlottesville, 1952-53; sr. resident, 1956-57; resident Alfred I. Dupont Inst., Wilmington, Del., 1954-55, Children's Hosp., Cerebral Palsy, Reisterstown, Md., 1955, Rehab. Center, Fisherville, Va., 1955; practice medicine specializing in orthopedic surgery, Pineville, W.Va., 1953-54, Marion, O., 1959; instr. orthopedic surgery Ohio State U., 1958-60, also chief orthopedic surgery F.C. Smith Clinic; asso. prof., chief orthopedic surgery U. Miss. Med. Center, Jackson, 1960-66, prof., chief orthopedic surgery, 1966-77, also adj. prof. law; individual practice, Marion, Va., 1977—; vis. lectr. Sch. Law, Oxford; cons. Jackson VA Hosp., 1960—, Keesler AFB, Biloxi, Miss.; adj. prof. U. Miss. Sch. Law, Oxford, dir. Medicolegal program Univ. Med. Center. Served with USNR, 1942-45. Fellow Nat. Pollo Found., 1956-57. Diplomate Am. Bd. Orthopedic Surgery, also examiner; fellow Am. Acad. Orthopedic Surg., A.C.S.; mem. AMA, Miss. State, So., Va., Ohio, W.Va. med. assns., Soc. Nuclear Medicine, Am. Med. Colls., AAUP, Miss. Assn. Medicine (bd. advisers), Southeastern Surg. Congress, Tri-County, Central, Hinds County med. socs., Am. Assn. Surgery of Trauma, Miss. Orthopedic Soc. (pres. 1968-69), Research Soc. Am., Nat. Rehab. Soc., Am. Arthritic and Rheumatology Soc., Société Internationale de Chirurgie Orthopedique et de Traumatologie, Am. Civil Liberties Union, Sigma Xi, Raven Soc. (U. Va.). Author: Outline Orthopedic Surgery, 1968; An Introduction to Medicine and the Law; Legal Aspects of Nursing, 1974; Adult Orthopedic Problems, Roads Textbook Surgery, 1977. Contbr. articles to profl. jours. Home: Radio Hill Rd Marion VA 24354

DERN, ALVIN, securities dealer; b. Bayonne, N.J., Mar. 5, 1931; s. Leon and Frances Rose (Silverman) D.; B.B.A., Rutgers U., 1952; postgrad. N.Y.U., 1955-58; m. Phyllis Ann Popper, Dec. 27, 1958; children—Mark Richard, Karen Beth. Gen. partner J. B. Hanauer & Co., Newark, N.J., 1960-68; pres. Dern & Co., Inc., Miami, Fla., 1968-78, Hamilton/Cooke & Co. of Fla., Inc., Miami, 1978—; dir. Dern's Selected Funds, Inc., East Orange, N.J. Served with USNR, 1952-54. Mem. Municipal Forum N.Y. Mason. Club: Kings Bay Yacht and Country. Office: 444 Brickell Ave Miami FL 33131

DE ROBERTIS, EDNA ESTELLA (MRS. FRED DE ROBERTIS), civic worker; b. Birmingham, Ala., Nov. 25, 1901; d. Edward and Dorothy (Cagle) Crealey; student U. Tenn., 1920-22, Chgo. Musical Coll., 1929; m. Fred De Robertis, Feb. 25, 1923; children—Giulia De Robertis Neubert, Rosa Maria De Robertis Faulkner. Organizer, pres. Knox Clean Air League, 1968—; pres. City Assn. Women's Clubs, 1962-64, bd. dirs., 1951—, rec. sec., 1958-60, chmn. fine arts, 1974-78; clean air chmn. Clean Environment Council, 1969-75; charter and hon. life mem., bd. dirs. James White Fort Assn., 1964—; hon. life mem. PTA, pres., 1951-52; bd. dirs. Knox County unit Arthritis Found., 1965-75; mem. nat. cancer research team cancer prevention study Am. Cancer Soc.; chmn. clean air community action program Ossoli Circle, 1968-72, mem. music com., 1976-77; mem. citizen's adv. com. Knoxville-Knox County Met. Planning Commn., 1976-77; mem. citizen adv. council Knoxville Transit Authority, 1978-79. Recipient spl. achievement award Knox County Bd. Commrs., 1976. Mem. Tenn. Fedn. Women's Clubs (state dir. 1964-76, dir. Dist. II 1949-75, chaplain Dist. II 1972-74, chmn. fine arts dept. and pub. speaking 1964-66, music 1966-68, leadership devel. 1972-74), W.C.T.U. Baptist. Clubs: Knoxville Woman's (pres. 1949-50, dir. 1936—, chmn. music 1974-76, historian 1978-79), Ladi-Kiwan, ADi Pi Mothers (corr. sec. 1957-58), Eastern Star. Home: 1302 Luttrell St Knoxville TN 37917

DE ROJAS, ARTURO, advt. exec.; b. Matanzas, Cuba, Apr. 5, 1948; s. Agustin Jose and E. Laura (de la Portilla) de R.; came to U.S., 1961, naturalized, 1972; B.F.A., Tex. Christian U., 1969; 1 son, Cristian Dale. Copy dir. Group Three Advt. Corp., Ft. Lauderdale, Fla., 1974-76; v.p., creative dir. Group Two Advt., Inc., Ft. Lauderdale, 1976-78; freelance writer/producer, Ft. Lauderdale, 1978—. Recipient awards Am. Advt. Fedn. Mem. Advt. Club Ft. Lauderdale, Sigma Phi Epsilon, Alpha Delta Sigma (past chpt. pres.).

DERR, PAUL JACOB, retail store exec.; b. Akron, Ohio, Feb. 15, 1929; s. Dwight Luther and Hazel Mae (Boise) D.; student Ohio No. U., 1947-48; m. Erma Susany, June 11, 1950; children—Mark Luther, Brian Louis, Paula Mae. With M. O'Niel's Co., Akron, 1948-56, asst. buyer, 1954-56; buyer home fashions Trask's Dept. Store, Erie, Pa., 1956-59; owner DeGar Interiors, Punta Gorda, Fla., 1959-62; asst. v.p. 1st Fed. Savs. and Loan, Punta Gorda, 1962-64; with Sears Roebuck & Co., 1964—, store mgr., 1974-76, group mdse. mgr., Birmingham, Ala., 1976—. Mem. exec. council Boy Scouts Am., Florence, S.C., 1975-76; pres. United Way, Florence, 1976; mem. Human Resources Adv. Council, 1977-79. Served with USMC, 1950-52. Republican. Episcopalian. Home: 3429 Portsmouth Dr Birmingham AL 35226 Office: 1531 2d Ave N Birmingham AL 35203

DERRICK, BUTLER CARSON, JR., congressman; b. Sept. 30, 1936; s. Butler Carson and Mary English (Scott) D.; student U. S.C., 1954-58; LL.B., U. Ga., 1965; D.Hum. (hon.), Lander Coll.; m. Suzanne Mims; children—Lydia Gile, Butler Carson, III. Admitted to S.C. bar, 1965; partner law firm Derrick & Byrd, Edgefield; mem. S.C. Ho. of Reps., 1969-74; mem. 94th to 96th Congresses from 3d Dist. S.C. Sr. warden Trinity Episcopal Ch. Recipient certificate of award S.C. Law Enforcement Officers Assn.; named S.C. Conservationist of Yr., Nat. Wildlife Fedn., 1977. Mem. Am., S.C. bar assns., S.C. J. C. of C. (Outstanding Young Man of Year 1971-72, pres.), Edgefield County Fish and Game Assn. (pres.). Clubs: Masons, Lions. Office: 133 Cannon House Office Bldg Washington DC 20515

DERRICK, HOMER, banker, ins. exec.; b. Lexington, Va., Dec. 10, 1906; grad. U. S.C., Am. Inst. of Banking; m. Mabel Ellison Beckham, 1924; children—Homer, Jeanne Derrick Morris, Betsy Derrick Calvo. Vice pres. S.C. Nat. Bank, Columbia and Greenville, 1926-50; pres. Carolina Nat. Bank, Easley and Pendleton, S.C., 1951-54; founding pres. Gt. Eastern Life Ins. Co., Greenville, 1950-55, Atlantic & Gulf States Ins. Co., Easley, Eastern Fire & Casualty Ins. Co., Greenville; bd. dirs. Freedom Life Ins. Co., Greenville, 1950-57; chmn. bd. dirs., pres. First Nat. Bank, Lexington, Va., 1955-73; chmn. bd. dirs. First Eastern Securities Corp., First Eastern Fin. Corp., pres., bd. dirs. Fin. Internat. Corp., Washington, 1965-67; bds. dirs. Lexington Cadillac-Pontiac Inc., Appalachian Fruit Growers Coop. Assn., Raphine, Va.; partner The Sherwood Co., Lexington. Democrat. Episcopalian. Clubs: Lexington Golf, Country, English-Speaking Union. Home: Windswept Lexington VA 24550 Office: Drawer 1111 Lexington VA 24450

DERRICK, WILLIAM SHELDON, physician; b. Millville, Pa., Mar. 5, 1916; s. Bruce Berger and Margaret (Mosteller) D.; B.A., George Washington U., 1940, M.D., 1942; m. Alice Marie Cowing, May 30, 1942; children—Lynn Sheldon, Bruce William. Intern Allegheny Gen. Hosp., 1942-43; fellow surgery Cleve. Clinic Found., 1943; resident anesthesiology Walter Reed Gen., Mt. Alto Vets., Gallinger Municipal, and George Washington U. hosps., 1945-48; asso. anesthesiology Harvard Med. Sch., 1948-54, also head sect. anesthesiology Peter Bent Brigham Hosp., Boston, 1948-54; cons. anesthesia VA Hosp., Rutland Heights, Mass., Murphy Army Hosp., Waltham, Mass., and VA Hosp., West Roxbury, Mass., 1950-54; head dept. anesthesiology U. Tex. System Cancer Center, M.D. Anderson Hosp., Houston, 1954-77; cons. anesthesia St. Joseph's Hosp., Houston, 1955-77; prof. anesthesiology U. Tex., 1954—; mem. med. staff Center Pavilion Hosp., 1967-77; vis. mem. grad. faculty Tex. A & M U., 1968-71; prof. anesthesiology U. Tex. Med. Sch., 1968—. Recipient Alumni Achievement award George Washington U., 1957; scholarship Mass. Inst. Tech., 1960; award for service as trustee Am. Registry Inhalation Therapists, 1972. Served to maj. M.C., U.S. Army, 1943-46. Diplomate Am. Bd. Anesthesiology. Mem. Am. Coll. Anesthesiologists, Tex. Gulf Coast Anesthesia Soc. (pres. 1959-60), So. Soc. Anesthesiologists (pres. 1965-66), So. Med. Assn. (chmn. sect. anesthesiology 1967), Doctors Club Houston (pres., gov. 1969), Tex. Med. Found. (charter). Presbyterian. Clubs: Aesculapian (Harvard); Bayou Rifles, Greater Houston Gun, Harvard, Houston Racquet, Houston Tennis Patrons, Knife and Fork, Les Amis du Vin (pres. 1971), Univ., Univ. Tex. Faculty (pres, 1969-71) (Houston); Congl. Country, George Washington U. (Washington). Developed techniques of subarachnoid alcohol block for control of pain, 1956; co-developer mech. respiratory assistor, 1949. Home: 2808 University Blvd Houston TX 77005

DESAI, CHANDRAKANT S., educator; b. Nadisar, Gujarat, India, Nov. 24, 1936; came to U.S., 1964, naturalized, 1973; m. Sankalchand P. and Kamala M. (Kothari) D.; B.E., U. Bombay, 1959; M.S. (fellow), Rice U., 1966; Ph.D. (fellow), U. Tex., Austin, 1968; m. Patricia L. Porter, Apr. 28, 1969; children—Maya C., Sanjay C. Engr., various govt. and pvt. agencies, India, 1959-64; research civil engr. U.S. Army C.E. Waterways Expt. Sta., Vicksburg, Miss., 1968-74; prof. dept. civil engring. Va. Poly. Inst. and State U., Blacksburg, 1974—; cons. to pvt. and govt. agencies. Chmn., Internat. Com. on Numerical Methods in Geomechanics, 1976—. Recipient Meritorious Civilian Service award U.S. C.E., 1972; Alexander von Humboldt-U.S. Sr. Scientist award German Govt., 1976; NSF grantee, 1976; Dept. Transp. grantee, 1977; registered profl. engr., Missp. Mem. ASCE, Inst. of Structural Engrs. (London), Internat. Soc. Rock Mechanics, Internat. Soc. Soil Mechanics and Found. Engrs. Co-author: Introduction to Finite Element Method, 1972; author: Elementary Finite Element Method, 1979; co-editor: Numerical Methods in Geotechnical Engineering, 1977; gen. editor Internat. Jour. for Numerical and Analytical Methods in Geomecanics, 1977—; editor procs. various confs. and symposia; contbr. articles to profl. jours. Home: 2307 San Marcos St Blacksburg VA 24060 Office: Dept Civil Engring Va Poly Inst and State Univ Blacksburg VA 24061

DESAI, HARSHKUMAR CHIMANLAL, civil engr.; b. Hansot, Gujarat, India, Nov. 21, 1929; s. Chimanlal Pranvallabhdas and Savita Chimanlal (Vakil) D.; came to U.S., 1964, naturalized, 1974; B.Engring. in Civil Engring., Baroda U., 1954; M.S. in Civil Engring., Columbia, 1966, postgrad., 1966-67; postgrad. Vanderbilt U., 1968-70; m. Prafulla Rameshchandra Hansoty, May 21, 1957; children—Sujata, Amit. Asst. marine surveyor Bombay Govt., 1954-57; asst. civil engr. Kandla (India) Port, 1957-62, Gujarat Refinery, New Delhi, 1962; civil engr. Gujarat Fertilizers Co., Baroda, 1963-64; structural engr. ports Parsons, Brickerhoff, Quade & Douglas, N.Y.C., 1965-66; structural designer Frederic R. Harris, N.Y.C., 1966-67; structural designer bldgs. James Ruderman, N.Y.C., 1967, Weiskopf & Pickworth, N.Y.C., 1967-68; structural designer bridges Barge, Wagoner & Sumner, Nashville, 1968-69; structural designer marine works Van Houten Assos., N.Y.C., 1970-72; sr. structural engr. marine works Frederic R. Harris, Gt. Neck, N.Y., 1972-73; project engr. marine terminals Brown & Root, Houston, 1974—. Registered profl. engr., N.Y., Tex., Calif. Fellow ASCE; mem. Am. Inst. Steel Constrn., Am. Concrete Inst. Hindu. Contbr. articles to profl. jours. Home: 7806 DelGlen Ln Houston TX 77072 Office: Marine Terminals Dept Brown & Root PO Box 3 Houston TX 77001

DE SALME, WILLA HITCHCOCK, guidance counselor, educator; b. Cisco, Tex., May 30, 1931; d. Thomas Henry and Orphia (Culberson) Hitchcock; B.S. in Edn., Mc Murray Coll., 1953; M.Ed., Tex. Woman's U., 1965; children—Charles DeSalme, Randy Joe DeSalme. Tchr., Atascosa (Tex.) Pub. Schs., 1953-55; Beeville (Tex.) Pub. Schs., 1955-56; Randolph AFB (Tex.) Pub. Schs., 1957-62, Fallbrook (Calif.) Pub. Schs., 1962-79; coach girls' basketball and track Breckenridge (Tex.) Schs., 1979—. Mem. Tex., Breckenridge tchrs. assns., NEA, Am. Fedn. Tchrs., Tex. High Sch. Coaches Assn. Democrat. Baptist. Home: 1705 W Walker St Breckenridge TX 76024 Office: 500 W Lindsey St Breckenridge TX 76024

DE SANDERS, WILLIAM DWAYNE, automobile exec.; b. Logan, Utah, Aug. 17, 1920; s. Neil James and Nina (Gallacher) De S.; student U. Mo., 1942; m. Alice Madaline Jones, Oct. 31, 1942; children—Alice, Sue, William. Sales mgr. Lone Star Cadillac Co., Dallas, 1945-53, pres., chmn. bd., 1956—; pres. Village Cadillac Co., Dallas, 1953-56; pres. El Dorado Realty & Investment Co., Dallas, 1965—, Lone Star Acceptance Co., Dallas, 1956—; dir. Am. Bank & Trust Co., Dallas, 1960—, Republic Savs. & Loan Assn., Dallas, 1957—; v.p., dir. Addison Airport, Inc., Dallas, 1956-78. Chmn. bd. dirs. Tex. div. Am. Cancer Soc., 1966-67, Dallas chpt., 1963-64; Served to maj. USAAF, World War II. Decorated D.F.C., Purple Heart. Mem. Dallas C. of C., Dallas New Car Dealer Assn., Nat. Cadillac Dealer Council (chmn. 1966), Sigma Chi. Home: 4237 Westway Pl Dallas TX 75205 Office: 2301 Ross Ave Dallas TX 75201

DE SANTIAGO, ELVIRA TORO, acct., educator; b. Cabo Rojo, P.R., Dec. 5, 1925; d. Sebastian Toro Lugo and Aurora Sanchez; B.B.A. cum laude, Catholic U. P.R., 1967, M.B.A., 1971; m. Julio Santiago Garcia, Aug. 16, 1947; children—Juan, Elvira, Julio. Acct., Villariny & Santiago Assos., Ponce, P.R., 1958-67; instr. acctg. Cath. U. P.R., Ponce, 1968-73, chmn. dept. acctg.-econs., 1973-76, asst. prof., 1974-78, asso. prof., 1978—; mem. adv. bd. P.R. Higher Edn.; cons. in acctg. and fin. Mem. AAUP, Cath. Bus. Edn. Assn., Phi Delta Kappa. Roman Catholic. Researcher C.P.A. practice in P.R. Home: A-95 Extension Mariani Ponce PR 00731 Office: PO Box 671 Ponce PR 00731

DE SAUSSURE, RICHARD LAURENS, JR., surgeon; b. Macon, Ga., Dec. 29, 1917; s. Richard Laurens and Margaret (Hamilton) DeS.; A.B., U. Va., 1939, M.D., 1942; m. Phyllis Helen Falk, June 12, 1948; children—Alexis, Richard Laurens III, Denise. Intern, U. Va. Hosp., Charlottesville, 1942-43, resident neurosurgery, 1946-47; vol. fellow neurosurgery Cin. Gen. Hosp., 1947-48; asst. chief neurosurgery Kennedy VA Hosp., Memphis, 1949-50, chief neurosurgery, 1950; practice medicine specializing in neurosurgery, Memphis, 1950—; clin. prof. neurosurgery U. Tenn. Coll. Medicine; chief staff Bapt. Meml. Hosp., Memphis, pres., 1966; mem. courtesy staff Meth., St. Joseph, William F. Bowld, John Gaston hosps. (all Memphis); pres. Mid-South Found. Med. Care, 1975; chmn. Semmes-Murphey Clinic, 1973. Served from 1st lt. to maj. with M.C., AUS, 1943-46; ETO. Decorated Bronze Star medal; recipient Superior Leadership award Memphis area C. of C., 1966. Diplomate Am. Bd. Neurol. Surgery (mem. bd. 1966-72, sec. 1970-73). Mem. Tenn. Med. Assn. (speaker ho. of dels. 1969-71), Am. Assn. Neurol. Surgery (v.p. 1956), Congress Neurol. Surgeons (past pres.), A.C.S. (chmn. adv. council neurol. surgery 1964-69), Am. Acad. Neurol. Surgeons (v.p.), Memphis and Shelby County Med. Soc. (v.p.), Am. Assn. Neurol. Surgeons (pres. 1975-76). Home: 4290 Heatherwood Ln Memphis TN 38117 Office: 201 Med Plaza North 920 Madison Ave Memphis TN 38103

DES CHAMPS, JOHN LEFEBER, mech. engr.; b. Muskogee, Okla., Apr. 23, 1913; s. John William and Mary B. (Cordray) D.; B.S., Okla. State U., 1936; m. Ludie B. Sullivan, July 18, 1933; children—Michael, Mary Lee (Mrs. Guy L. Butler). Chief engr. Allied Steel Products Corp., Tulsa, 1939-47; Star Mfg. Co., Oklahoma City, 1947-59; self-employed cons. structural engr., Oklahoma City, 1959-69; chief engr. Harter Concrete Products Corp., Oklahoma City, 1969—. Instr. structural steel design U. Tulsa, Engring. Def. Program, 1941-43. Scoutmaster, Boy Scouts Am., Oklahoma City, 1956-57, merit badge counciler, 1956—; little league baseball coach, Oklahoma City, 1953-54. Paul Harris fellow Rotary Found., 1976; registered profl. engr., Okla., Tex., Ind., Tenn. Baptist (deacon 1954—). Rotarian (charter pres. 1949-50). Home: 3716 NW 25th St Oklahoma City OK 73107 Office: Harter Concrete Products 1628 W Main Oklahoma City OK 73103

DESCHLER, LEWIS, II, lawyer; b. Washington, Aug. 17, 1931; s. Lewis and Virginia (Cole) D.; student Duke, 1949-50, George Washington U., 1956-57; B.S., Washington and Lee U., 1953, J.D., 1955. Admitted to Md. bar, 1955, D.C. bar, 1956, Fla. bar, 1957; practiced in Boca Raton, Fla., 1960-63; partner firm Deschler Reed & Critchfield, Boca Raton, 1963—; chmn. bd. Boca Raton Fed. Savs. & Loan Assn., 1966—; adv. dir. Lawyers' Title Services Inc. Served to lt. USNR, 1955-59. Mem. Am. Bar Assn., Fla. Bar Assn., Md., D.C. bars, Boca Raton C. of C. Episcopalian. Club: Exchange (pres. 1961). Home: 2000 N Ocean Blvd Apt 205 Boca Raton FL 33432 Office: 555 S Federal Hwy Boca Raton FL 33432

DE SERRES, FREDERICK JOSEPH, geneticist; b. Dobbs Ferry, N.Y., Sept. 24, 1929; s. Frederick J. and Helen Marie (Henshaw) de S.; B.S. in Biology, Tufts U., 1951; M.S. in Botany, 1953, Ph.D. (fellow) in Botany, Yale U., 1955; m. Christine Marie Covone, Sept. 18, 1954; children—Mark, John Paul, David, Jonathan, Lianne. Sr. staff biologist Oak Ridge Nat. Lab., 1957-72; experimenters rep. NASA Biosatellite Program, 1964-68; coordinator environ. mutagenesis program Oak Ridge Nat. Lab., 1969-72; lectr. U. Tenn., 1971-73; adj. prof. dept. pathology U. N.C., Chapel Hill, 1973—; chief environ. mutagenesis br. Nat. Inst. Environ. Health Scis., Research Triangle Park, N.C., 1972-76, asso. dir. for genetics, 1976—; cons. EPA, 1971, 76-79, Nat. Inst. Drug Abuse, 1976, genetics study sect. NIH, 1967, NASA Bioscis. Expt. Survey, 1968; U.S. coordinator Biol. and Genetic Consequences Project, U.S.-USSR Environ. Protection Agreement, 1972—; chmn. panel on mutagenesis and carcinogenesis U.S.-Japan Coop. Med. Sci. Program, 1972—; chmn. subcom. environ. mutagenesis HEW com. to coordinater toxicology and related programs, 1972—; mem. com. on assessment of nitrate accumulation in environment Div. Biology and Agr., NRC 1970-72; chmn. various workshops on environ. pollutants and mutagenesis, 1961-79. Recipient NIH Dir.'s award, 1976. Mem. Genetic Soc. Am., Internat. Assn. Environ. Mutagen Soc., Radiation Research Soc., Am. Soc. Cancer Research, Environ. Mutagen Soc. (pres. 1973-76, editor newsletter 1969-72, ann. award 1979), Internat. Commn. Protection Against Environ. Mutagens and Carcinogens (vice-chmn. 1976—). Contbr. numerous articles on mutations and carcinogenetic chems. to sci. jours.; editorial bd. Radiation Botany, 1965-74, Jour. Toxicology and Environ. Health, 1975—; editor Jour. Environ. and Exptl. Botany, 1975-77, Mutation Research, 1973—; asso. editor: Chemical Mutagens, vols. 5 and 6. Home: 632 Rock Creek Rd Chapel Hill NC 27514 Office: Nat Inst Environ Health Scis Research Triangle Park NC 27709

DE SHA, RALPH HUNTER, food co. exec.; b. Newport, Ky., Oct. 20, 1921; s. Alonzo Hamilton and Myrtle Jennie (Cox) DeS.; student U. Iowa, 1940-41; B.A., Beloit Coll., 1949; m. Lillian Elmenthaler, Apr. 8, 1957; children—Ralph Hunter, Craig Richardson. With Oscar Mayer & Co., Madison, Wis., 1950-63; v.p. Gwaltney Inc., Smithfield, Va., 1965-68, The Kroger Co., Cin., 1968-76; pres. Protein Foods Corp., Ltd., Gainesville, Ga., 1976—. Served with U.S. Army, 1943-46. Mem. Gainesville C. of C., Inst. Food Technologists, Sudan-Am. Bus. Council, U.S. C. of C., Am. Legion. Republican. Presbyterian. Home: 548 Tommy Aaron Dr Gainesville GA 30501 Office: 794 Main St Gainesville GA 30501

DE SHAZO, GARY FORREST, lawyer; b. Bolivar, Tenn., Feb. 5, 1945; s. Warren and Verna Mayfield (Scott) DeS.; B.A., Tex. Christian U., 1967, M.A., 1970; J.D., U. Tex., 1973; m. Carolyn Youngblood, July 11, 1969; children—Scott Forrest, Darcie Caroline. Contract adminstr. Gen. Dynamics AeroSpace, Ft. Worth, 1968-71; admitted to Tex. bar, 1973; legis. asst. Tex. Ho. of Reps. 1973; exec. dir., gen. counsel Tex. Criminal Def. Lawyers Assn., Austin, 1973-76; pvt. practice law, Austin, 1976—; instr. econs. Tex. Christian U., 1970; exec. sec. Lawyers Polit. Action Com.; dir. Criminal Def. Lawyers Project, Austin, 1974-76. Mem. State Bar Tex., Travis County Bar Assn., Sigma Alpha Epsilon (chpt. pres. 1966). Baptist. Mng. editor Voice for the Def., 1973-76. Home: 3705 Hillbrook Dr Austin TX 78731 Office: 508 First Fed Plaza Austin TX 78701

DESIDERIO, DOMINIC MORSE, JR., educator; b. McKees Rocks, Pa., Jan. 11, 1941; s. Dominic Morse and Jewell Aline (Hull) D.; B.A., U. Pitts., 1961; S.M., Mass. Inst. Tech., 1964, Ph.D., 1965; m. Julia Marie Thomas, Oct. 9, 1965; children—Annette Marie, Dominic Michael. Research asst. Mass. Inst. Tech., Cambridge, 1962-65; research chemist Am. Cyanamid Co., Stamford, Conn., 1966-67; asst. prof chemistry Baylor Med. Sch., Houston, 1967-71, asso. prof., 1971-77; prof. neurology (chemistry), dir. Stout Neurosci. Mass. Spectrometry Lab., U. Tenn. Center for Health Scis., Memphis, 1977—; Cons. Recipient fellowships Internat. Assn. for Exchange of Students, 1962, Intra-sci. Research Found., 1971-75. Mem. Am. Chem. Soc. (awards com. 1972-75), Am. Inst. Chemists, AAAS, Am. Soc. Mass Spectrometry, AAUP (sec. 1972-73), N.Y. Acad. Sci., Sigma Xi. Office: U Tenn Center Health Scis 800 Madison Ave Memphis TN 38163

DE SOMBRE, ROBERT MAGNUS, publisher; b. Washington, Oct. 7, 1915; s. John William and Helena (Magnus) de S.; student pub. schs.; m. Patricia Ann Sullivan, Apr. 17, 1948; children—Diane, Patricia Ann, Joanne. With Kiplinger Washington Letters, 1942-50; with Gulf Pub. Co., Houston, 1950—, v.p., dir., 1956-68, sr. v.p., dir., 1968—; dir. Gulf Printing Co., Internat. Tng. Co. Mem. Am. Petroleum Inst., Houston C. of C., Direct Mail Advt. Assn. (past gov.), Am. Bus. Press (past dir.), Assn. 2d Class Mail Publs. (dir.). Club: Houston. Home: 4410 Ingersoll St Houston TX 77027 Office: 3301 Allen Pkwy Houston TX 77019

DE SORBO, DONALD GARY, nurse, hosp. adminstr.; b. Amsterdam, N.Y., Apr. 4, 1951; s. Louis and Philomena (Russo) DeS.; A. Applied Sci., Fulton-Montgomery Community Coll., 1973; B.S. in Nursing, Alfred U., 1974; m. Carol Martuscello, June 5, 1971; children—Tara, Todd. Dir. nursing Cuba (N.Y.) Hosp., 1976; asst. dir. legis. program N.Y. State Nurses Assn., Albany, 1977; dir. nursing Leesburg (Fla.) Hosp., 1977-78, Seminole Meml. Hosp., Sanford, Fla., 1978—; mem. health adv. com. Seminole Community Coll. Mem. Am. Nurses Assn., Fla. Nurses Assn., Nat. League Nursing, Am. Soc. Nursing Service Adminstrs., Jaycees. Home: 717 Galloway Ct Winter Springs FL 32707

DE SOUSA, PAULO JOSE NOBREGA MOITA TEIXEIRA, elec. engr.; b. Nova Lisboa, Angola, Jan. 25, 1947; s. Francisco Teixeira and Liberdade Lusitana (Moita) deS.; came to U.S., 1971; Licenciatura, U. Luanda, Angola, 1970; M.S., U. Mo., 1972, Ph.D., 1976; m. Susan Gloria Allison, June 1, 1974; children—Vasco Phillip, Alexandra Allison, Andrew Nicholas. Undergrad. asst. U. Luanda, 1968-69; engr.-in-tng. Companhia Portuguesa de Electricidade, Lisbon, Portugal, 1970; instr. Luanda, 1971-75; research asst. elec. engring. U. Mo., Columbia, 1973-74; engr./scientist Rockwell Internat. Co., Dallas, 1976—; lectr. in field. City of Luanda scholar, 1964-70; U. Luanda Overseas fellow, 1971-75; Rotary Internat. grad. fellow, 1971-72. Mem. IEEE, Nat. Mgmt. Assn., Richardson Jaycees, Tau Beta Pi, Eta Kappa Nu. Club: Internat. House. Home: 1908 Wyndemere Ln Garland TX 75042 Office: 1200 N Alma Rd M/S 420-180 Richardson TX 75081

DESPALJ, PAVLE, music dir. and condr.; b. Blato, Yugoslavia, June 18, 1934; came to U.S., 1967, naturalized, 1974; s. Sime and Katica (Kalogjera) D.; grad. Zagreb (Yugoslavia) Music Acad., 1960; m. Majda Radic, Feb. 8, 1964; children—Nadja, Simon. Music dir. Zagreb Symphony, 1962-67, Fla. Symphony, Orlando, 1970—; prin. condr. Zagreb Philharmonic, 1978—; guest condr. Zagreb Opera, various symphonies; founder Zadar Music Festival, 1960, Belgrade Chamber Orch., 1966. Recipient Zagreb City award, 1965, award in recognition of outstanding achievement in arts Council Arts and Scis. for Central Fla., 1977. Composer mus. works, including: Variations for Orchestra, 1957; Violin Concerto, 1959; Alto Saxophone Concerto, 1963. Office: 320 N Magnolia Orlando FL 32802

DES PORTES, CALVIN JOHNSTON, JR., elec. and biomed. engr.; b. Columbus, Ga., Nov. 1, 1928; s. Calvin and Margaret (Garrard) Des P.; B.S.E.E., Jakson State U., Nashville, 1953, Ph.D. in Elec. Engring., 1974; D.Sc., Sussex (Eng.) Coll. Tech., 1975; m. Alice Elizabeth Chamison, Aug. 20, 1955. Pres., Elec. Circuits Unltd., Columbus, 1976—. Served in USN, 1948-52. Mem. IEEE, Nat. Soc. Profl. Engrs., Ga. Soc. Profl. Engrs., N.C. Soc. Engrs., Soc. Am. Mil. Engrs., Illuminating Engring. Soc. N. Am. Presbyterian.

DESSLER, GARY, educator, author, cons.; b. N.Y.C., June 8, 1942; s. Alexander and Laura Dessler; B.S., N.Y. U., 1966; M.S., Rensselaer Poly Inst., 1967; Ph.D., CUNY, 1972; m. Claudia Offman, Mar. 19, 1970; 1 son, Derek. Asst. prof., asst. dean Fla. Internat. U., Miami, 1971-74, asso. prof., asso. dean, 1974-78, prof. Sch. Bus. and Organizational Scis., 1978—. Mem. Acad. Mgmt. Author: Organization and Management: A Contingency Approach, 1976, 2d edit., 1978; Management Fundamentals, 2d edit., 1979; Personnel Management: Modern Concepts and Techniques, 1978; Organization Theory: Integrating Structure and Behavior, 1979; Human Behavior: Improving Performance at Work, 1980; contbr. articles to profl. jours. Home: 11551 SW 106th Terr Miami FL 33176 Office: Sch Bus Fla Internat U Tamiami Trail Miami FL 33199

DE STEIGUER, JOSEPH EDWARD, economist, govt. ofcl.; b. Port Arthur, Tex., Nov. 22, 1945; s. Joseph Emanuel and Ione (Hudson) De S.; B.B.A., Lamar U., 1968; M. Forestry, Stephen F. Austin State U., 1974; Ph.D., Tex. A&M U., 1979. Field rep. A.C. Nielsen Co., Chgo., 1968-69; mgr. market research AMF Tuboscope Inc., Houston, 1969-71; research asst. forestry Stephen F. Austin State U., Nacogdoches, Tex., 1972-73; specialist remote sensing U.S. Geol. Survey, U.S. Dept. Interior, Bay St. Louis, Miss., 1974-75; research asso. forest econs. Texas A&M U., College Station, 1975-79; economist U.S. Forest Service, U.S. Dept. Agr., Princeton, W.Va., 1979—. Mem. Soc. Am. Foresters, Am. Forestry Assn., Tex. Forestry Assn., Forest Products Research Soc., Am. Soc. Photogrammetry, Sigma Xi, Xi Sigma Pi. Contbr. articles to sci. publs. Home: 4333 Asbury St Port Arthur TX 77640 Office: US Forest Service US Dept Agr Box 152 Princeton WV 24740

DETHLOFF, HENRY CLAY, historian; b. New Orleans, Aug. 10, 1934; s. Carl Curt and Camelia (Jordan) D.; B.A., U. Tex., Austin, 1956; M.A., Northwestern State U. (La.), 1960; Ph.D., U. Mo., 1964; m. Myrtle Anne Elliott, Aug. 27, 1961; children—Clay, Carl. Mem. faculty dept. history U. Southwestern La., Lafayette, 1962-69, asso. prof., 1967-69; asso. prof. history Tex. A&M U., College Station, 1969-75, prof., 1975—; dir. Southwestern Archives and Manuscripts Collection, U. Southwestern La., 1964-68. Served with USNR, 1956-58. Mem. La. Hist. Assn. (dir. 1968-71), Econ. Hist. Assn., So. Hist. Assn., Agrl. History Assn., Tex. Hist. Assn., Phi Beta Phi, Phi Alpha Theta, Sigma Chi. Democrat. Methodist. Author books in field including: Americans and Free Enterprise, 1979. Office: Dept History Tex A&M Univ College Station TX 77843

DETJEN, EDWARD YEAMANS, veterinarian; b. Tulsa, Mar. 13, 1921; s. Otto E. and Hazel G. (Yeamans) D.; student Okla. A. and M. Coll., 1940; D.V.M., Tex. A. and M. Coll., 1943; m. Jeanne Akin, June 3, 1944; children—Stephen Richard, Gary Akin, David John. Veterinarian, City Vet. Hosp., Tulsa, 1943-45; pvt. vet. practice, Pawnee, Okla., 1945-46, Guthrie, Okla., 1946—; beef cattle breeder, citrus grower. Mem. Am., Okla. (pres. 1962) vet. med. assns., Guthrie C. of C., Tex. Citrus Exchange, Rio Tex., Edinburg citrus assns., Sigma Chi. Republican. Roman Catholic. Address: Route 3 Guthrie OK 73044

DE TONNANCOUR, PAUL ROGER GODEFROY, library adminstr.; b. Fall River, Mass., May 22, 1926; s. R. Godefroy and Emilie (St. Germain) de T.; A.B. cum laude, Providence Coll., 1952; M.S., Simmons Coll., 1953; m. Mary E. Fenno, Apr. 9, 1955; children—Paul Godefroy, Camille Marie. Asst. librarian Enoch Pratt Library, Balt., 1953-54; chief librarian, tech. analyst Armco Steel Corp., Balt., 1954-56; mgr. info. services Gen. Dynamics, Ft. Worth div., 1957-69, mgr. info. programs, 1969—; cons. Modern Lang. Assn. Am.; cons. on sci. information personnel U.S. Office Edn. John Cotton Dana lectr., 1966. Singer Ft. Worth Opera Assn., Chorus. Active United Fund; mem. exec. com. Big Bros. Tarrant County. Trustee Cosmopolitan Internat., 1961-63. Served with USNR, 1943-46. Named Boss of Year, Am. Bus. Women's Assn., 1965. Mem. ALA, Fort Worth Art Assn., Spl. Libraries Assn., (adv. council, chmn. aerospace div.), Am. Soc. Info. Sci., Delta Epsilon Sigma. Episcopalian, (vestryman). Mason. Club: Fort Worth Boat. Author: The Exploitation of Technical Information, 1966. Co-author: Science Information Personnel, 1963. Contbr. articles to profl. jours. Home: 6332 Genoa Rd Fort Worth TX 76116 Office: PO Box 748 Fort Worth TX 76101

DETTBARN, WOLF-DIETRICH, pharmacologist; b. Berlin, Ger., Jan. 30, 1928; s. Erwin Bruno and Maria Magdalena (Conrady) D.; came to U.S., 1958; naturalized, 1968; M.D., U. Göttingen, 1953; m. Christine Anneliese Keune, Sept. 15, 1960; children—Donata-Andrea, Henning-Christian. Intern, Univ. Clinic, Göttingen, 1953-54; research asso. biol. dept. Ciba Co., Basel, 1954-55; research asso. Physiol. Inst., U. Saarland, Homburg, Saar, 1955-58; research asso. neurology Columbia U., N.Y.C., 1958-61, asst. prof., 1961-67, asso. prof., 1967-68; prof. pharmacology Vanderbilt U., Nashville, 1968—; mem. corp. Marine Biol. Lab, Woods Hole, Mass. Grantee NIH, 1958. Mem. Am. Physiol. Soc., Am. Soc. for Pharmacology and Exptl. Therapeutics, Am. Soc. Neurochem., Soc. Gen. Physiologists, Soc. for Neurosci., Soc. for Toxinology, Harvey Soc., AAAS. Contbr. articles to profl. jours. Home: 4422 Wayland Dr Nashville TN 37215 Office: Vanderbilt U Dept Pharmacology Nashville TN 37232

DETTWILLER, GEORGE FREDERICK, beer wholesaler; b. Memphis, Oct. 8, 1932; s. Edgar Ellis and Elsie Mai (Stroud) D.; A.B. in Philosophy, Vanderbilt U., 1954; m. Martha Ann Dietz, June 8, 1972; children—Kimberly, Sarah, George, Helene, Ann Kathryn. Pres., owner Cardett Distbg., Nashville, 1956—; pres., owner DET Distbg. Co., Nashville, 1973—. Exec. com. Muscular Dystrophy Assn., Nashville, 1978-79. Recipient Miller Masters award Miller Brewing Co., 1976, 77, 78. Mem. UN Assn. (dir. 1981, chmn. UN Day Nashville/Davidson County 1979), Tenn. Malt Beverage Assn. (dir.). Episcopalian. Clubs: City, Cumberland, Richland Country. Home: 151 Valley Forge Dr Nashville TN 37205 Office: 613 11th Ave N Nashville TN 37203

DETWILER, SAMUEL B(ERTOLET), JR., scientist; b. Wabasha, Minn., Sept. 21, 1909; s. Samuel Bertolet and Kate E. (Price) D.; B.S. in Chemistry, George Washington U., 1934; A.M. in Chemistry, U. Ill., 1941; 1 dau. by previous marriage, Margaret Mary; m. 2d, Kathryn N. Prater, Apr. 1972. Engr. comml. standardization fire prevention engring. Nat. Bur. Standards, Washington, 1927-37; chemist Regional Soybean Lab., U.S. Dept. Agr., Urbana, Ill., 1937-41; asst. to chief Bur. Agrl. and Indsl. Chemistry, Washington, 1941-49, tech. program specialist, 1949-53, asst. to dep. adminstr. Agrl. Research Service, 1953-72; research asso. Fedn. Am. Socs. for Exptl. Biology, Bethesda, Md., 1972-76. Recipient Service award D.C. Inst. Chemists, 1963; Service award Chem. Soc. Washington, 1966; Service award Washington Acad. Scis., 1974. Mem. Am. Chem. Soc., Am. Oil Chemists Soc., Am. Inst. Chemists, AAAS. Club: Cosmos (Washington). Died May 21, 1978. Home: 2300 Pimmit Dr Idylwood Towers 801-W Falls Church VA 22043

DEUSER, LARRY MARTIN, elec. engr.; b. Indpls., June 2, 1940; s. Emil Martin and Anna Elizabeth (Troutman) D.; B.S.E.E., Purdue U., 1962, M.S.E.E., 1964; Ph.D., U. Tex., 1975; m. Carole Louise Reinken, Mar. 4, 1960; children—Tamra Kay, Sheryl Lynn, Karen Marie. Instr. engring. Purdue U., West Lafayette, Ind., 1962-64; mem. tech. staff Hughes Aircraft Co., Culver City, Calif., 1964-67; research engr. asst. Dept. Elec. Engring., U. Tex., Austin, 1967-68, research engr. asso. Applied Research Labs., 1968-77; engr./scientist applied scis. group, Tracor, Inc., Austin, 1977—. Commr., City of Austin Electric Utility Commn., 1978—; v.p. Austin Neighborhoods Council, 1978—; treas. Austin Alliance for Smooth Transition, 1977—; pres., bd. dirs. United Action for the Elderly, 1972-77. Purdue U. scholar, 1962. Mem. IEEE, Acoustical Soc. Am., Sigma Xi. Baptist. Club: Kiwanis. Contbr. articles in field to profl. jours. Home: 11800 Mustang Chase Austin TX 78759 Office: 6500 Tracor Ln Austin TX 78721

DEUTERMAN, JOHN LYNDON, mfg. co. exec.; b. Elgin, Ill., Aug. 21, 1940; s. Joel LeRoy and Margaret Livingston (Johnston) D.; B.A. in Psychology, Northwestern U., 1962; M.S. in Counseling Psychology, George Williams Coll., 1973; m. Diane Vivienne LeLoup, June 30, 1962; children—Joel Andre, Daniel Lyndon, Bradford John, William Fredrick. Project dir. Marplan, Chgo., 1962-67, Container Corp. Am., Carol Stream, Ill., 1967-72; pres. Deuterman Research Services, Chgo., 1972-74; mgr. mktg. research Texize Chem. Co., Greenville, S.C., 1974-78; dir. mktg. research Kayser Roth Corp., Greensboro, N.C., 1978—; lectr. Ill. Inst. Tech., Northwestern U., Atlanta U. Active Greenville Crisis Intervention, 1974-78; Jr. Achievement counselor, 1969; regional rep. Boy Scouts Am., Lombard, Ill., 1971-73; research dir. local and regional polit. candidates, 1968, 70, 76; crisis tng. counselor. Mem. Am. Mktg. Assn. (speaker nat. conf. 1968, seminars 1976, 78), Soc. Consumer Affairs Profls., Chi Phi, Alpha Phi Omega. Contbg. editor: Qualitative Research in Marketing, 1976; contbr. articles to publs. Home: 106 Fairidge Ct Jamestown NC 27282 Office: 2303 W Meadowview St Greensboro NC 27407 also PO Box 77057 Greensboro NC 27407

DEUTSCH, PAUL MICHAEL, psychologist; b. N.Y.C., May 23, 1949; s. Samuel P. and Elaine (Simpson) D.; B.A., Rollins Coll., 1971; M.Rehab. Counseling, U. Fla., 1972, postgrad., 1975—; m. Nancy N. Wayman, May 22, 1971; 1 dau., Laura Leigh. Counselor, Fla. Dept. Health and Rehab. Services, Orlando, 1972-73; counselor Rehab. Resources, Orlando, 1973-76; pvt. practice rehab. counseling and guidance Rehab. Counseling Cons., Orlando, 1976—; dir. Center for Rehab., Orlando, 1977—. Founder Central Fla. chpt. Nat. Paraplegic Found.; bd. dirs. Fleury Found., Easter Seals Soc. Orlando. Rehab. Services Adminstrn. fellow, 1971-72. Mem. Am. Congress Rehab. Medicine, Nat., Am., Fla. rehab. counselors assns., Assn. Measurement and Evaluation Guidance, Am. Personnel and Guidance Assn., Eta Rho Pi, Pi Lambda Theta. Republican. Jewish. Office: 60 Columbia St W Orlando FL 32806

DEUTSCH, STUART JAY, indsl. and systems engr.; b. Manhattan, N.Y., Mar. 11, 1943; s. Meyer and Pauline D.; B.S., Mich. State U., 1965; Ph.D., U. Wis., 1970; m. Carol A. Powers, Jan. 20, 1968; children—Geoffrey, Jason. Project engr. Shulton Inc., Clifton, N.J., 1965-66; spl. process engr. Avco, Lycoming and Stratford, Conn., 1966-68; asst. prof. ops. research Poly. Inst. Bklyn., 1970-72; asso. prof. indsl. and systems engring. Ga. Inst. Tech., Atlanta, 1972-78, prof., 1978—; cons. in field. Ford Found. grantee, 1969-70, Nat. Inst. Law Enforcement and Criminal Justice, 1974—. Mem. Ops. Research Soc. Am., Am. Statis. Assn., Atlanta Lawn Tennis Assn. Contbr. articles to tech. publs. Editorial bd. Evaluation Quar., 1976—. Home: 4604 Waterford Ct Dunwoody GA 30338

DEVALL, CHARLES KLINGMAN, newspaper exec.; b. Mount Vernon, Tex., Nov. 7, 1908; s. Charles Robert and Leila (Milam) D.; student John Tarleton State Coll., 1925-26; B.J., U. Tex., 1931; m. Lyde Gwynne Williford, July 15, 1939. Owner-pub. Kilgore (Tex.) Herald, 1935-40, Kilgore Daily News Herald, 1940-79, pub. emeritus, 1997—; cons. Donrey Media Group; dir. Kilgore Ceramics Corp., Kilgore Nat. Bank, Kilgore Indsl. Found., Inc. Pres., Tex. Good Rds. Assn., 1956-58. Mem. Tex. Democratic party Exec. Com., 1934-38, presdl. elector, 1940; trustee Tex. So. U., 1947-51; chancellor's council U. Tex. at Austin. Served to lt. comdr. USNR, 1942-45. Recipient George Washington awards Freedoms Found. Valley Forge, Pa., 1956, 63; Appreciation award East Tex. Freedom Forum, 1968. Mem. Tex. Daily Newspaper Assn. (named Tex. Newspaper Leader of Yr. 1979), So. Newspaper Assn., Tex. (past pres., N.E. Tex. (past pres., award 1964) press assn., Kilgore C. of C. (past pres., Man of Yr. 1969), Sigma Delta Chi, Kappa Tau Alpha (hon.). Presbyn. (elder). Lion (past pres. Kilgore). Clubs: Laird Country (Kilgore); Cherokee (Longview, Tex.); Headliners (Austin). Home: 820 Crimwood Ln Kilgore TX 75662 Office: 304 Allied Citizens Bank Bldg PO Box 1939 Kilgore TX 75662

D'EVEGNEE, CHARLES PAUL, state ofcl.; b. Liege, Belgium, Aug. 4, 1939; came to U.S., 1959, naturalized, 1963; s. Charles Clement and Fernande Francoise (Godet) d'E.; B.A., Brigham Young U., 1966; M.A., U. Conn., 1969, J.D., 1974; m. Marie Therese Barnich, Apr. 17, 1962; children—Chantal, Charlie. Group pension underwriter Conn. Gen. Life Ins. Co., Hartford, 1969-72; legal cons. Frank B. Hall & Co., N.Y.C., 1974-76; mem. firm Meidinger & Assos., Richmond, Va., 1976-78; dir. benefits devel. Commonwealth of Va., Richmond, 1978—; pres. Industries Internat. Corp., Richmond, 1979—. Served with U.S. Army, 1960-63. Mem. Internat. Found. Employee Benefit Plans, Am. Mgmt. Assn., Richmond C. of C. Club: Kiwanis. Author: (with Guyenot) European Antitrust Law, 1976. Home: 10307 Pebblebrook Place Richmond VA 23233 Office: Commonwealth of Virginia 302 Finance Bldg Capitol Sq Richmond VA 23219

DE VELASCO, JOAQUIN FERNANDEZ, educator; b. Havana, Cuba, May 20, 1920; came to U.S., 1961, naturalized, 1967; s. Joaquin F. and Maria Josefa (Olivera) DeV.; B.A., Inst. de la Habana, 1938; J.D., U. Havana, 1942; M.A., Middlebury Coll., 1972. Admitted to Cuban bar, 1942; individual practice law, Havana, 1942-52; chief lawyer Bur. Info. Tribunal de Cuentas de Cuba, Havana, 1952-61; asso. prof. Spanish, Wofford Coll., Spartanburg, S.C., 1963—. Recipient diploma of honor Havana Bar Assn., 1947. Mem. South Atlantic MLA, Am. Assn. Tchrs. of Spanish and Portuguese, Sigma Delta Pi. Roman Catholic. Author: La Novela Picaresca, 1955; La Comedia Rural de Benavente, 1957. Office: Wofford Coll N Church St Spartanburg SC 29301

DEVER, ELNEITA LENORE, psychologist; b. Washington, Dec. 7, 1943; d. James B. and Lois A. (Biggs) Hightower; B.S., Prairie View A&M U., 1966, Ed.M., 1968; Ed.D., North Tex. State U., 1975; m. Wayman Todd Dever, May 31, 1967; children—Schreese, Angela. Research asst. Prairie View A&M U., 1965-66, instr. psychology, 1966; staff nurse ICU, Baylor Hosp., Dallas, 1966-67; counseling psychologist Counseling and Testing Center, North Tex. State U., Denton, 1972—, asst. dir. program devel., 1977—; cons. to Dallas (Tex.) Ind. Sch. Dist., 1971—. Vice pres. Community Ethnic Relations Bd., Denton, 1977-78. Recipient Outstanding Student Service award North Tex. State U., 1977. Mem. Am. Nurses Assn., Am. Personnel and Guidance Assn., Phi Delta Kappa. Democrat. Mem. A.M.E. Ch. Home: 1914 Emerson Ln Denton TX 76201 Office: PO Box N T Sta Denton TX 76203

DEVILLE, LINDA GAIL, hosp. fin. adminstr.; b. Opelousas, La., Dec. 31, 1953; d. John Earl and Earline S. Fontenot; student La. State U., 1971-74; B.S. in Bus. Adminstrn., U. Southwestern La., 1976; m. Stefan L. Deville, Aug. 4, 1973; 1 dau., Dana. Medicare-Medicaid clk. Ville Platte (La.) Gen. Hosp., 1975, bus. office mgr., 1976-77, acting fin. mgr., 1977-78, fin. mgr., 1978—; fin. adviser. Mem. La. Hosp. Fin. Mgmt. Assn. (chmn. credit and collection com. 1980). Office: Ville Platte Gen Hosp 800 E Main St Ville Platte LA 70586

DE VINE, BILLIE MACK, agrl. co. exec.; b. Gadsden, Ala., Feb. 23, 1945; s. Charles Durwood and Ida Nell (Blanton) De V.; B.S. in Acctg., Jacksonville State U., 1968; postgrad. in fin. U. S. Fla., 1970-71; postgrad. Sch. Bus. Adminstrn., Harvard U., 1978; m. Shirley Jean Pitspatrick, Mar. 16, 1966; children—Charles Durwood, Cynthia Denise. Vice pres., dir. Bay-Con Industries, Inc., Tampa, Fla., 1971-74; sec.-treas. Automatic Merchandising Inc., Tampa, 1974-75; chief fin. officer Gt. So. Equipment Co., Inc., Tampa, 1975-76; v.p., chief operating officer Am. Agronomics Corp., Tampa, 1976-77, pres., Arcadia, Fla., 1977—, also dir.; dir. Am. Orange Corp., Coastline Corp., Funshine Corp. Served with U.S. Army, 1966-68. Mem. Am. Acctg. Assn., Nat. Acctg. Assn., Am. Mgmt. Assn. Internat. Platform Assn., Aircraft Owners and Pilots Assn. Pres.'s Assn. Democrat. Clubs: Elks, Rotary. Home: PO Box 1665 Brandon FL 33511 Office: 4600 W Cypress St Tampa FL 33511

DEVIS, DONALD ALBERT, social worker; b. Massillon, Ohio, May 11, 1912; s. Henry and Viola Phillips D.; B.A., Bethany Coll., 1934; M.S.W., Ind. U., 1948; m. Martha Snyder, Mar. 13, 1942; children—David, Bronwyn. Instr., Ind. U., 1948-50; commd. 2d lt. U.S. Army, 1950, advanced through grades to col., 1966; chief social worker Walter Reed Army Hosp., 1952-55, Letterman Army Hosp., San Francisco, 1959-62; ret., 1966; asst. prof. dept. psychiatry Med. Sch. Emory U., Atlanta, 1966—. Mem. Gov.'s Adv. Council on Mental Health, 1976—; mem. adv. council ARC, San Francisco, 1960-62. Served with AUS, 1942-46. Named Social Worker of Yr., No. Ga. chpt. Nat. Assn. Social Workers, 1974, Mental Health Worker of Yr., Atlanta Mental Health Assn., 1979. Mem. Nat. Assn. Social Workers, Ga. Conf. Social Work, Nat. Conf. Social Welfare, Acad. Cert. Social Workers, Kappa Alpha. Democrat. Unitarian. Club: Community Friendship. Author: Social Work with Families, 1980. Home: 241 W Parkwood Rd Decatur GA 30030 Office: 80 Butler St Atlanta GA 30303

DEVORE, MARGARET BOWEN (MRS. ROBERT N. DEVORE), physician; b. Troy, S.C., Dec. 29, 1930; d. William R. and Ruth (McAlister) Bowen; B.A. magna cum laude, Winthrop Coll., 1951; M.D., Med. Coll. S.C., 1955; m. Robert N. DeVore, Aug. 31, 1952; children—Robert Douglas, Thomas Lee and John Anthony (twins), Margaret Ann and William George (twins). Intern Med. Coll. S.C., 1955-56; gen. practice Oceana, W.Va., 1957-59, Jackson, S.C., 1959-62; resident anesthesiology, 1962-64; instr. anesthesiology dept. Med. Coll. of Ga., Augusta, 1964-65, asst. prof. anesthesiology, 1966-70, asso. prof., 1970-73, prof., 1973—, asso. dean sch. medicine students. Diplomate Am. Bd. Anesthesiology. Mem. AMA, Ga., Richmond County med. socs., Am. Soc. Anesthesiologists, Am. Assn. Med. Colls. (womens liaison officer), Alpha Omega Alpha. Baptist. Home: 405 5th St Jackson SC 29831 Office: Med Coll Ga Augusta GA 30902

DE VORE, PAUL WARREN, educator; b. Parkersburg, W.Va., July 18, 1926; s. Harry and Eleanor Sarah (Dunn) DeV.; B.S., Ohio U., 1950; M.A., Kent State U., 1954; Ed.D., Pa. State U., 1961; postdoctoral fellow U. Md., 1965-66; m. Eleanor Condron, Apr. 7, 1952; children—Michelle Ann, Phillip Charles. Instr. public schs., Chagrin Falls, Ohio, 1950-53; asst. prof. Grove City Coll., 1953-56; asst. prof. SUNY, Oswego, 1956-60, dir. div. indsl. arts and tech. SUNY, 1960-67; prof. tech. edn. W.Va. U., Morgantown, 1967-75, prof., chmn. tech. edn., 1975—; cons. NSF, U.S. Office Edn. Chmn. campaign United Fund, Oswego, 1962-63. Served with USN, 1944-46. Named Outstanding Tchr. W.Va. U., 1970-71. Mem. Am. Council Indsl. Arts Tchr. Edn., Am. Soc. Engring. Edn., Soc. History of Tech., AAAS, World Future Soc., Epsilon Pi Tau. (Disting. Service award 1976). Author: Technology: An Intellectual Discipline, 1964; Education in a Technological Society, 1971; Technology and the New Liberal Arts, 1976. Home: 668 Colonial Dr Morgantown WV 26505 Office: Allen Hall Dept Technology W Va U Morgantown WV 26506

DE VRIES, DAVID LEE, research adminstr.; b. Holland, Mich., Aug. 11, 1943; s. Martin and Catherine DeV.; B.A., Calvin Coll., 1965; M.A., U. Ill., 1967, Ph.D., 1970; m. Martha C. Christian, Aug. 21, 1965; children—Todd, Mark, Matthew. Research asso. U. Ill., Urbana, 1969-70; research scientist, asst. prof. Johns Hopkins U., Balt., 1970-75; research scientist Center Creative Leadership, Greensboro, N.C., 1975-76, dir. research, 1976—. Mem. Am. Psychol. Assn., Am. Ednl. Research Assn., Acad. Mgmt. Author: (with others) Team Games Tournament, 1980; mem. editorial bd. Research in Higher Edn., 1974—. Home: 1612 Red Forest St Greensboro NC 27410 Office: PO Box P-1 Greensboro NC 27402

DEVRIES, ELLA SCALES, educator; b. Wedowee, Ala., Apr. 16, 1943; d. Less and Mary Scales; B.S., Ala. State U., 1965; M.A., U. Nebr., 1970, Ph.D., 1976; m. James DeVries, July 23, 1975. Tchr. secondary English, Selma, Ala., 1965-69; research asst. U. Nebr., 1969-70; tchr., Selma, 1970-71; instr. U. Nebr., 1971-75; asst. prof. English, coordinator ednl. opportunities program in rhetoric U. Ill., Urbana, 1975-77; asst. prof. English, coordinator writing lab. Clark Coll., Atlanta, 1977—. Active NAACP. Named Outstanding Tchr. of Year, U. Nebr., 1974. Mem. Modern Lang. Assn., Nat. Council Tchrs. of English. Democrat. Methodist. Home: 1425 Adams Dr SW Atlanta GA 30311 Office: Clark College Atlanta GA 30314

DE VRIES, GEORGE HENRY, scientist, educator; b. Paterson, N.J., Dec. 22, 1942; s. Henry and Jeanette (Greydanus) De V.; B.S., Wheaton Coll., 1964; postgrad. U. Ill., 1964-69; m. Helen McKean, Aug. 21, 1965; children—Jori Elizabeth, James Thomson. Postdoctoral fellow Albert Einstein Coll. Medicine, Bronx, N.Y., 1969-72; asst. prof. biochemistry Med. Coll. Va., Richmond, 1972-76, asso. prof. biochemistry, 1976—; cons. neurobiol. program NSF, 1976—. NIH grantee, 1973—; Roche Found. fellow, 1975-76; NSF grantee, 1978—; Nat. Multiple Sclerosis Soc. grantee, 1977—. Mem. Am. Soc. Neurochemistry, AAAS, Am. Soc. Biol. Chemists, Internat. Soc. for Neurochemistry, Am. Chem. Soc., Soc. for Neurosci. Presbyterian. Contbr. articles to profl. jours. Home: 2329 Tuscora Rd Richmond VA 23235 Office: Dept Biochemistry Med Coll Va MCU Sta Box 614 Richmond VA 23298

DEW, JESS EDWARD, chem. engr.; b. Okemah, Okla., July 18, 1920; s. Jess Edward and Colleen (Norman) D.; student Okla. Mil. Acad., 1939-41; B.S. in Chem. Engring., U. Okla., 1943; M.S., Mass. Inst. Tech., 1948; m. Mary Ann Burns, Jan. 3, 1944; children—Anne, Stephen Dodson, David Burns. Asst. chem. engr. Exxon, Baytown, Tex., 1943-47; chem. engr. Standard Oil Ind., Tulsa, 1948-52; v.p. John Deere Chem. Co., Pryor, Okla., 1952-63; gen. supt. John Deere Planter Works, Moline, Ill., 1963-65; v.p. Arkia Chem. Corp., Helena, Ark., 1965-69; project mgr. Chem. Constrn. Co., N.Y.C. hdqrs., 1969-74, posts include Eng., Argentina, Arabia, Algeria; cons. engr., 1974-78; constrn. mgr. W.R. Holway & Assos., Tulsa, 1978—; pres., dir. Pryor Indsl. Conservation Co., 1961-63. Mem. Pryor Municipal Utility Bd., 1955-60, Pryor City Council, 1962-63; Rivers and Harbor Commn., Helena, 1966-70; adv. com. Sacred Heart Acad., 1967-69. Registered profl. engr., Okla. Mem. Am. Inst. Chem. Engrs., ASME, Sigma Xi, Beta Theta Pi, Alpha Chi Sigma, Tau Beta Pi. Republican. Roman Catholic. Clubs: Tulsa, Okmulgee Country, Elks, Rotary. Contbr. articles to profl. jours. Patentee in field. Home: 120 S Prairie St Okmulgee OK 74447 Office: 4111 S Darlington St Tulsa OK 74135

DEW, JOHN KENNETH, radio sta. exec.; b. Detroit, Nov. 5, 1939; s. Albert Nelson and Irene (Morris) D.; student U. Mich. (Nat. Merit scholar), 1958-60; B.A., Wayne State U., 1963, postgrad., 1963-66; m. Marsha; children—Mary Elizabeth, Kimberly Ann and Julie Lynn (twins). Producer, dir. pub. relations WXYZ radio and TV, Detroit, 1958-66; dir. advt., sales Orange Blossom Diamond Rings div. Traub Co., Detroit, 1966-68, San Francisco, 1968-70; account exec. Sta. KABL, San Francisco, 1970-71; gen. mgr. Sta. WWWW, Detroit, 1971-73; v.p. Belo Broadcasting Corp.; v.p., gen. mgr. Stas. WFAA-AM and KZEW-FM, Dallas, 1973-76; v.p., gen. sales mgr. Radio Sta. KENR, Houston, 1976—; cons. broadcast mgmt. Tchr., St. Leo High Sch., Detroit, 1963, Howard Sch. Broadcasting, Detroit, 1972-73; columnist Observer newspaper, Detroit, 1963-66. Mem. Avon Players, Rochester, Mich., 1971-73; mem. adv. bd. Abe Lincoln Awards Com.; mem. com. Pin Oaks Charity Horse Show, Houston; mem. Ft. Bend County Fair Advt. Com., Houston Livestock Show and Rodeo Com. Mem. Assn. Broadcast Execs. Tex. Clubs: Variety, Adcraft (Detroit); Pecan Plantation Country (Richmond, Tex.); Newk's Racquet; Meadowcreek Racquet (treas. 1980-81), Quail Valley Country (Houston). Home: 2826 Meadowcreek Dr Houston TX 77459 Office: KENR 2 Greenway Plaza E Houston TX 77046

DEWAR, MILDRED (JO) ELLER (MRS. DONALD NORMAN DEWAR), librarian; b. Wilkesboro, N.C., Nov. 9, 1925; d. Charles Franklin and Golda (Velt) Eller; student Brevard Coll., 1942-44; diploma Jr. Coll., 1944; A.B., Berea Coll., 1946; B.S. in L.S., U. N.C., 1948; postgrad. Barry Coll., U. Fla., U. Miami; m. Donald Norman Dewar, Mar. 6, 1954; 1 dau., Heather. Tchr., librarian Mountain View High Sch., Hays, N.C., 1946-47; chief librarian Tenn. Wesleyan Coll., Athens, 1948-50; dept. head U. Tex. Library, Austin, 1951; librarian U.S. Army Spl. Services, Ft. Jackson, S.C., 1951-52; chief post library system, Ft. Stewart, Ga., 1952-54; librarian Olsen Jr. High Sch., Dania, Fla., 1955-56; librarian Lauderdale Manors Sch., Ft. Lauderdale, Fla., 1956-63; head readers services Miami-Dade Jr. Coll. Library, Miami, Fla., 1963-70; library dir. Miami-Dade Community Coll., South, 1970—; mem. library task force S.E. Fla. Consortium; mem. learning resources standing com. Fla. Council Instructional Affairs; vis. instr. library edn. U. Ga., summer 1967. Co-exec. dir. Nat. Library Week Fla., 1966. Mem. AAUW (past br. v.p.), Am., Fla. library assns., Fla. Assn. Sch. Librarians (past pres.), Delta Kappa Gamma. Author articles in field. Home: 3520 Crystal View Ct Coconut Grove FL 33133 Office: 11011 SW 104 St Miami FL 33156

DEWAR, TIMOTHY SMITH, psychologist; b. Eastman, Ga., Aug. 26, 1942; d. Rosser Malone and Nelle Malone (Edwards) Smith; B.A., U. Ga., 1963, M.S., 1965, Ph.D., 1970; m. Robert Alexander Dewar, Feb. 14, 1975. Asst. prof. psychology Troy (Ala.) State U., 1969-70; adj. asst. prof. psychology W. Ga. Coll., Carrollton, 1970-71; rehab. coordinator Work Oriented Rehab. Center, Daytona Beach, Fla., 1974; therapist Human Resources Center, Daytona Beach, 1974-75, dir. Deland (Fla.) office, 1975-78; pvt. practice psychology, South Daytona, Fla., 1978—. Chmn. Citizens for Planned Growth and Devel., 1972; pres. Coronado Beach Civic Assn., 1973-74; mem. Volusia County Environ. Council; pres. West Volusia Social Services Planning Council. Mem. Am. Psychol. Assn., Fla. Psychol. Assn., Fla. Health and Social Services Assn., Volusia County Profl. Psychologists Assn. (chmn.), New Smyrna Audubon Soc. (v.p. 1972-73), Fraternal Order of Police Aux. Presbyterian. Office: 2763 S Ridgewood South Daytona FL 32019

DEWBERRY, INEZ S., educator; b. Delta, Ala., Aug. 28, 1915; d. Oscar Lee and Bessie (Gibson) Stephens; B.S. in Edn., Jax State U., 1956; M.S. in Spl. Edn., Auburn (Ala.) U., 1965; m. James Laurence Dewberry. Tchr. spl. edn. Randolph County (Ala.) schs., Wedowee, 1935—. Mem. NEA, Ala., Randolph County edn. assns. Home: Rt 1 Box 100 Lineville AL 36266 Office: Box 295 Wedowee AL 36278

DE WITT, ROBERT JOTHAN, geologist; b. Paterson, N.J., Jan. 13, 1928; s. Donald Ashtenau and Mary Winifred (Swezey) De W.; B.A., Rutgers U., 1957, M.S., 1958; m. Doris Marie Hulings, Oct. 9, 1965; children—Donald James, Mary Catherine. Micropaleontologist, Shell Oil Co., Houston, 1958-61; research geologist Exxon Prodn. Research Co., Houston, 1961—. Served with U.S. Army, 1948-54. Mem. Geol. Soc. Am., Assn. Petroleum Geologists, Sigma Xi. Contbr. sci. articles to profl. jours. Home: 411 Ashford Forest Dr Houston TX 77079 Office: PO Box 2189 Houston TX 77001

DE WREE, EUGENE ERNEST, valve mfg. co. exec.; b. Fairbanks, Alaska, June 26, 1930; s. Henry Joseph and Bertha Agnes DeWree; grad. Cogswell Engring. Coll., 1955, Stanford Grad. Sch. Bus., 1978; m. Shirley May Russo, Apr. 16, 1955; children—Angela Kathryn, Mary Rebecca, Thomas Albert, Babette Gabrielle, Jane Elizabeth. Project engr. Heat & Control Co., San Francisco, 1955-59; chief applications engr., then market mgr. Wesix Electric Heater Co., San Francisco, 1959-65; account mgr. Fisher Controls, San Francisco, 1965-76; market and sales mgr. TRW Mission, Houston, 1976—; dir. Creative Capers, San Francisco and Houston. Mem. Belmont (Calif.) Personnel Bd., 1965; com. chmn. Boy Scouts Am., 1970. Served to capt., arty. U.S. Army, 1951-53; Korea. Named Outstanding Jaycee of Yr., 1966. Mem. Am. Mgmt. Assn., Am. Nuclear Soc., Valve Mfg. Assn., Water Pollution Control Fedn. Republican. Roman Catholic. Clubs: Pine Fores Country, Plaza; Engrs. (San Francisco). Home: 16203 Champions Dr Spring TX 77373 Office: PO Box 40402 Houston TX 77040 also 8760 Clay Rd Houston TX 77080

DE WYS, JANE NEGUS, geologist; b. Portland, Oreg., Apr. 24, 1924; d. Howard Curtiss and Cleo (Brockhausen) Negus; B.A. with honors in Geology, Miami U., Oxford, Ohio, 1946; postgrad. U. Wis., 1946-48, U. Wyo., 1947, Ohio State U., 1951-53, U. Calif., Los Angeles, 1964-66, Tex. Tech. U. Law Sch., 1969-71; Ph.D. in Geology, W.Va. U., 1979—; m. Egbert Christiaan deWys, Apr. 7, 1949 (div. 1971); children—Wendela, Tanya, Mark, Matthew. Curator, Geology Mus., U. Wis., Madison, 1946-48; geologist Shell Oil Co., Midland, Tex., 1948-49; instr. geology Case Western Res. U., Cleve., 1949; geologist Mene Grande Corp., Caracas, Venezuela, 1951-53; research asso. Ohio State Research Found. Ohio State U., Columbus, 1953-58; instr. geology adult edn. Van Nuys (Calif.) High Sch., 1958-60; design engr. Sierra Engring., Sierra Madre, Calif., 1960-63; sr. scientist Calif. Inst. Tech. Jet Propulsion Lab., Pasadena, 1963-66; mgr. First Grand Teton Ltd., Jackson, Wyo., 1972-74; gen. mgr. Jackson Hole Cable TV, Jackson, 1974-76, cons. on open univ., 1976—; research geologist, asst. dir. Environ. Studies Lab. U. Utah Research Inst., Salt Lake City, 1976-77; research asso. Devonian Shales Program geology dept. W.Va. U., Morgantown, 1977—; lectr. in field; mem. NASA review panel for extraterrestrial resource utilization program U.S. Bur. Mines, 1967-68. Active YWCA, Denver, 1960-70; advisor to sch. bd., Lubbock, Tex., 1970-71. Served with U.S. Cadet Nurse Corps, 1943-44. Recipient NASA citation for Magnet Experiment on Surveyor Spacecraft, 1968; NSF award, 1968. Mem. Am. Assn. Petroleum Geologists, Geol. Soc. Am., Am. Geophys. Union, Utah Geol. Assn., Nat. Air Pollution Control Assn., Nat. Honor Soc., AAUW, CAP, Sigma Xi, Sigma Gamma Epsilon, Phi Sigma, Delta Zeta, Phi Kappa Phi. Baptist. Contbr. articles to profl. jours. Home: 917 Revere St Morgantown WV 26506 Office: Geology Dept WVa U Morgantown WV 26505

DEXTER, MICHAEL ADAM, devel. co. exec.; b. Houston, Tex., Mar. 17, 1942; s. John Fay and Kathleen Elizabeth (Rider) D.; B.A. in History and Econs., Tex. A & M U., 1964; m. Helen Marie Hagaman, June 23, 1966; children—Adam Todd, Matthew John, Erin Elizabeth. Area sales mgr. Xerox Corp., Houston, 1965-74; project mktg. mgr. Gerald D. Hines Interests, Houston, 1974-76; dir. mktg. Century Devel. Corp., Houston, 1976-78; v.p., br. mgr. Cushman & Wakefield of Tex. Inc., Houston, 1978—. Real Estate Broker, Tex. Mem. Houston Bd. Realtors, Assn. Former Students Tex. A & M U. Roman Catholic. Club: Brae Burn Country, Onion Creek Country, A & M Century. Home: 4111 Drummond St Houston TX 77025 Office: Houston TX

DEY, MURIEL FOSTER, jewelry designer; b. Willimansett, Mass., June 16, 1909; d. Harry Schuyler and Florence (Grady) Foster; A.B., Ohio Wesleyan U., 1930; M.A., Ohio State U., 1931; student Craft Students League of N.Y., 1947-50; m. Andrew B. Dey, Sept. 8, 1936. Asso. prof. art Hillsdale (Mich.) Coll., 1931-34; asst. editor The Art Digest, N.Y.C., 1934-36; jewelrymaker, De Land, Fla., 1951—; exhibited in group shows Fla. Craftsmen's Ann. State Craft Shows, 1951-68, U.S. Dept. State Am. Jewelry World Tour, 1953-55, Mus. of Contemporary Crafts, N.Y.C., 1957, Dallas Mus. Fine Arts, 1958, Walker Art Center Design Quar. #33, Mpls., 1955, Am. Fedn. Art Travelling exhibition, 1958-59, The Egg and the Eye, Los Angeles, 1967, Stetson U., De Land, 1958, 68, Jacksonville (Fla.) U., 1972; represented in permanent collections Smithsonian Instn., Washington; juror Halifax Art Festival, Daytona Beach-Ormond Beach, Fla., 1977, Ringling Mus. 6th Ann. Crafts Festival, Sarasota, Fla., 1977; bd. dirs. De Land Mus., 1976—. Mem. Fla. Craftsmen (pres. 1958), Am. Craftsmen's Council (Fla. rep. 1959-62). Address: 431 N Sans Souci De Land FL 32720

DE YOUNG, JOHN, aero. engring. scientist; b. Detroit, Apr. 20, 1919; s. Fred and Mary (Kaspareth) DeY.; B.S. with honors, Wash. State U., 1943; postgrad. U. Chgo., 1947-48, Stanford U., 1955-56; Ph.D., U. Tex., Arlington, 1975; m. Ann Wythe Sinclair, May 20, 1974; children—Leslie V., John W., Forrest, V. Mitzi, Talia, Anemarie. Research scientist NASA Ames Research Center, 1944-56; prof. Instituto Tecnologica de Aeronautica, Brazil, 1956-62; sr. aerodynamicist Grumman Corp., Bethpage, N.Y., 1962-68; sr. engring. scientist specialist Vought and Kentron, Hampton, Va., 1968—; cons. in field. Served with USMC, 1935-39, USN, 1944-46. Asso. fellow AIAA; mem. Sigma Xi, Tau Beta Pi, Sigma Gamma Tau. Democrat. Episcopalian. Contbr. articles to profl. jours.; sponsor John DeYoung aerospace scholarship U. Tex., Arlington. Home: 157 Columbia Ave Hampton VA 23669 Office: Kentron Internat Inc 3221 N Armistead Ave Hampton VA 23666

DHILLON, HARPAL SINGH, mgmt. cons.; b. Punja Sahib, Pakistan, Dec. 7, 1939; came to U.S., 1968, naturalized, 1976; s. Harnand Singh and Mohinder Kaur (Randhawa) D.; B.S., Punjab U., 1958, B.S. in Engring. with honors, 1962; M.S., Okla. State U., 1969; Ph.D., U. Mass. 1973; m. Sarjit Kaur, Jan. 10, 1971; children—Pepe, Mona. Lectr., Thapar Coll. Engring., Punjab, India, 1962-64; group engr. Brooke Bond Tea Co., Assam, India, 1964-68; group leader Mitre Corp., McLean, Va., 1973-79; pres. Engring. and Econs. Research, Inc., Falls Church, Va., 1979—; adj. prof. U. Md., Am. U. Mem. Ops. Research Soc. Am., Inst. for Mgmt., Phi Kappa Phi. Contbr. articles to profl. jours. Home: 132 N Ithaca Ct Sterling VA 22170 Office: Engring and Econs Research Inc 7700 Leesburg Pike Falls Church VA 22043

DIAL, EDWARD LAMAR, beverage mfg. co. exec.; b. Oxford, Ga., Nov. 10, 1909; s. Barney Edward and Lottye Lamar (Morgan) D.; student U. Oglethorpe, Atlanta, 1929-30; m. Nov. 23, 1930; children—Nancy Michael, Bernie Lamar, Benjamin Edward. Founder, pres. Jus-Made Inc., Dallas, 1945—, also dir.; v.p. Fla. Julep Corp., Dallas, 1972—, also dir.; prodn. mgr., dir. Crazy Chake Corp., Dallas, 1972-74. Elder, Scofield Meml. Ch., Dallas, 1975—; bd. dirs. Christian Indian Mission, Dallas. Served with USNR, 1944; ETO. Recipient Nat. Championship award Jet Spray Corp., Waltham, Mass., 1977. Club: Christian Men's Breakfast (Dallas). Owner trade mark registrations. Home: 2971 Sunbeck Circle Dallas TX 75234 Office: Jus-Made Inc 250 Comstock St Dallas TX 75208

DIAMOND, HARVEY JEROME, machinery mfg. co. exec.; b. Charlotte, N.C., Dec 7, 1928; s. Harry B. and Jeanette R. (Davis) D.; B.B.A., U. N.C., 1952; m. Betty L. Ball, May 22, 1953; children—Michael A., Leah Beth, David A., Abby. Sales mgr. Dixie Neon Supply House, Charlotte, N.C., 1951-61; pres., sr. exec. officer Plasti-Vac, Inc., Charlotte, 1961—; pres., chmn. bd. Diamond Supply, Inc., Charlotte, 1971—; del. White House Conf. Small Bus., 1979, 80; mem. regional dist. export council Dept. Commerce, 1980—. Instr. Practical Politics in Action, Charlotte C. of C., 1966, 67, 68, 78; bd. dirs. OIC, Charlotte; mem. adv. bd. Phieffer Coll., Misenheimer, N.C., 1979—; vice chmn. Mecklenburg Democratic Com., 1970-72, chmn., 1974-75, treas., 1972-74, del. Dem. Nat. Conv., 1972. Served with U.S. Army, 1952-54. Recipient awards March of Dimes, 1966, U.S. Dept. Commerce 1967. Mem. Soc. Plastic Engrs. (award 1970), Nat. Eelctric Sign Assn., Small Bus. Assn. S.E. (dir. 1979). Jewish. Clubs: Charlotte Athletic, Masons, Shriners, Cotswold Optimist. Author: (manual) Introduction to Vacuum Forming, 1976; patentee in field of plastic thermoforming machinery. Home: 6929 Folger Dr Charlotte NC 28211 Office: PO Box 5543 Charlotte NC 28225

DIAMOND, HINDI ALTMAN, mag. editor; b. N.Y.C., Sept. 11; d. Saul and Esther (Kijewski) Altman; student C.Z. (Panama) Jr. Coll., 1947-49, U. Miami (Fla.), 1966-69; children—Linda, Stephen, Mark. Reporter, photographer Panama Am., daily English newspaper, 1951-58; Panama corr. for McGraw-Hill Co. and Vision mag., 1951-61; founder, editor Industria Turistica mag. Diamond Pub. Co., South Miami, Fla., 1957—; pub., editor Panama/This Month, 1958-65; free-lance writer for Miami Herald, Miami News, also other newspapers, 1966—; chmn. Date With the Press, talk show, Sta. WKAT, Miami Beach. Fla. Bd. dirs. Am. Jewish Com., 1966—, editor Newsletter, 1969—. Mem. Am. Soc. Mag. Photographers (chmn. Fla. chpt. 1960—), Women in Communication, Coral Gables C. of C. (dir., chmn. public relations). Author: Your Name in the News, 1974. Home: 7250 SW 126th St Miami FL 33156 Office: Industria Turistica PO Box 52 South Miami FL 33143

DIANA, MATTHEW VICTOR, bus. exec.; b. Cin., Nov. 17, 1934; s. Joseph and Mary C. (Andrews) D.; B.B.A., U. Cin., 1957; children—Joseph Edwin, Holly Lynn. With Keebler Co., 1960-69, new product devel. mgr., Atlanta, to 1969; v.p. indsl. div. Raley Bros., Inc., Atlanta, 1970-76; pres. Oxford Foods Co., Inc., San Antonio, 1976-77; v.p. mktg. Stanley Smith Security, Inc., San Antonio, 1977—. Mem. adv. council Hamilton County (Ohio) Juvenile Ct., 1960-62. Mem. Am. Mktg. Assn. (treas. 1979-80), Am. Soc. Indsl. Security, Nat. Fedn. Ind. Bus., San Antonio C. of C. (research and planning council), Sigma Chi, Sigma Sigma. Clubs: Conroy Square Racquet, Highpoint Tennis. Home: 12221 Blanco 1502 San Antonio TX 78216 Office: 3355 Cherry Ridge San Antonio TX 78230

DIANA, MICHELE NICHOLAS, counselor; b. Union City, N.J., May 31, 1927; s. Santo and Angela (Scilla) D.; B.S. in Psychology, Fordham U., 1951; M.S. in Guidance, Creighton U., 1967; m. Gloria Vivian Sirico, June 17, 1950; children—Michael Peter, Patricia Ann, Stephen Neal. Enlisted U.S. Navy, 1944; served 1944-46; commd. 2d lt. U.S. Army, 1951, advanced through grades to lt. col., 1966; ret., 1972; supr. adjustive services Sarah Bonwell Hudgins Regional Center for Retarded Citizens, Hampton, Va., 1972-74; vocat. rehab. evaluator and unit supr. Va. Dept. Rehab. Services, Newport News, 1974-79; pvt. practice counseling, Newport News, 1979—; parent effectiveness trainer Christopher Newport Coll., social service agencies; vocat. cons. to attys. and ins. cos. Pres., Peninsula Orgn. Exceptional Children, 1974-76; chmn. adv. bd. Riverside Hosp. Community Mental Health Center, 1976-77; chmn. Newport News Spl. Edn. Adv. Council, 1976-77, mem., 1975—. Decorated Meritorious Service medal; lic. profl. counselor, Va. Mem. Va. Vocat. Evaluation and Work Adjustment Assn. (pres.), Am. Personnel and Guidance Assn., Nat. Rehab. Assn., Nat. Assn. Retarded Citizens, Va. Personnel and Guidance Assn. Home and Office: 14 E Governor Dr Newport News VA 23602

DIASIO, CLARA FLORA (MRS. JOSEPH S. DIASIO), ret. physician; b. N.Y.C.; d. Angell and Victoria (Alba-Rosa) Benedict; Ph.G., Columbia, 1923; B.S., N.Y. U., 1925; M.D., N.Y. Med. Coll., 1929; m. Dr. Joseph S. Diasio, Oct. 22, 1933; children—Matthew Roger, Robert Bart Intern St. Cecilia Hosp., Bklyn., 1929-30; resident pediatrics N.Y. Foundling Hosp., N.Y.C., 1930-31, asst. vis. pediatrician, 1931-36; asst. vis. pediatrician Columbus, N.Y. Postgrad. hosps., 1931-36; asst. allergist St. Lukes Hosp., 1931-36; vis. physician N.Y.C. Dept. Health Baby Clinics, 1931-36; examining physician Western Electric Co., 1943-44; physician Genesee Meml. Hosp., Batavia, N.Y., 1956-74; sch. physician Oakfield Ala. Central Sch., Oakfield, N.Y., 1957-74; practice medicine, Oakfield; hon. physician St. Jerome Hosp., Batavia, 1974—, Culpeper (Va.) Meml. Hosp.; vol. physician Culpeper Meml. Hosp. Nursing Home, 1977—; physician Spotsylvania County (Va.) Schs. Mem. emeritus AMA, N.Y. State, Genesee County (pres. woman's aux. 1951; chmn. disaster med. care com. 1958-74; chmn. CD com. 1960-74) med. socs., Va. chpt. Am. Acad. Pediatrics; mem. Med. Soc. Va., Culpeper County Med. Soc., Genesee County Cancer Soc. (chmn. ednl. com. 1952-54), Omicron Phi Epsilon. Club: Oakfield Study (pres. 1958). Contbr. articles in field to med. publs. Home: 305 Chestnut Dr POB 213 Culpeper VA 22701

DIAZ, MARIA IGNACIA ZAMORA, nurse; b. Falfurries, Tex., Apr. 17, 1947; d. Abel and Glemencia (Garza) Zamora; B.S. in Nursing, Tex. Woman's U., Denton, 1971, M.S., 1977; m. Sam C. Diaz, Nov. 29, 1969; 1 son, Jason. Staff/charge nurse St. Luke's Hosp., Houston, 1970-71; instr. nursing Alvin (Tex.) Jr. Coll. Nursing Sch., 1971-73; part-time house supr. Homestead Hosp., Houston, 1971-73; instr. nursing Pan Am. U., Edinburg, Tex., 1973-77, U. Tex. Sch. Nursing, Galveston, 1977-78; dir. nurses Rio Grande State Center Mental Health-Mental Retardation, Harlington, Tex., 1978-79; faculty nursing dept. Pan Am. U., Edinburg, Tex., 1979—; mem. adv. nursing bd. Southmost Coll., Brownsville, Tex. Mem. Tex. Nursing

Assn., League United Latin Am. Citizens (charter mem., pres. council 655, 1973-75). Roman Catholic. Home: PO Box 2 Edinburg TX 78539 Office: Pan Am U Edinburg TX 78539

DIAZ, NILS JUAN, nuclear engr., educator; b. Moron, Cuba, Apr. 7, 1938; came to U.S., 1961, naturalized, 1968; s. Rafael G. and Dalia R. (Rojas) D.; B.S. in Mech. Engring. with high honors, U. Villanova, Cuba, 1960; M.S. in Nuclear Engring., U. Fla., 1964, Ph.D., 1969; m. Zenaida G. Gonzalez, Oct. 9, 1960; children—Nils, Ariadne, Allene. Sr. engr. and head of planning Ministry of Industry, Cuba, 1959-61; research asso. nuclear engring. scis. dept. U. Fla., Gainesville, 1966-69, asst. prof. nuclear engring., 1969-74, asso. prof., 1974-79, prof., 1979—, dir. nuclear facilities, 1978—; cons. to Babcock & Wilcox Co., Fla. Power & Light Co., Fla. Power Corp., Govt. Venezuela, ExXon Nuclear Co., and others; pres., prin. engr. Fla. Nuclear Associates, Inc., 1976—. Recipient Boynton award, 1974. Mem. Am. Nuclear Soc. (vice chmn. Fla. sect. 1977-80), Am. Soc. Engring. Edn., Am. Public Health Assn., Am. Acad. Polit. and Social Sci., Fla. Acad. Scis., AAAS, Sigma Xi. Roman Catholic. Contbr. articles on nuclear engring. and nuclear engring. edn. to profl. jours.; inventor in field. Office: 202NSC Dept of Nuclear Engring Scis Univ Fla Gainesville FL 32611

DIAZ-COLLER, CARLOS, physician; b. Villahermosa, Tabasco, Mex., Sept. 2, 1916; s. Jose Diaz-Coller and Maria Gonzalez; M.D., Army Med. Sch., Mex., 1945; M.P.H., Harvard U., 1948; m. Ana Maria de la Garza, Dec. 17, 1945; children—Carlos, Jose Alberto, Mario, Juan Antonio and Anna Maria Elisa (twins). Del. from Mex., WHO, 1956, 57, 58; exec. bd. alt. WHO, 1956-57, v.p. exec. bd., 1958-59; del. from Mexico to directing council Pan-Am. San. Orgn., 1956-57, exec. com., 1957-58, pres. exec. com., 1958-59; del. from Mex., XV Pan Am. San. Conf., 1958; dir. div. exptl. studies in pub. health Ministry Pub. Health and Welfare, Mex., 1957, 58; former chief dept. profl. edn., chief editorial services Pan Am. Health Orgn. of WHO; now chief nat. program for accident prevention, undersecretariat of health Ministry Health and Welfare, Mex. Pub. health supr. Mexican Army, 1948-56; dir. Sch. Pub. Health, Mexico, 1953. Mem. Mexican Pub. Health Soc. (pres. 1957-58), Am. Pub. Health Assn., Nat. Geog. Soc. Editor: Jour. Mexican Pub. Health Soc., 1955-58. Home: California 180 Mexico 21 DF Mexico Office: P Miranda 177 5to piso Mexico 19 DF Mexico

DIAZ-LÓPEZ, MANUEL, mech. engr.; b. Ciales, P.R., Aug. 13, 1936; s. Manuel Diaz Resto and Lucila L. López; B.S. in Mech. Engring., Coll. Agr. and Mech. Arts, Mayaquez, P.R., 1959; m. Carmen Ileana Toro, Jan. 28, 1961; children—Karin Gisela, Kira Rebeca. Line supr. P.R. Water Resources Authority, San Juan, 1959-61, line supr. E, 1961-65, estimator, tech. studies supt., 1965-70, work programming gen. supt., 1970-74, constrn. and improvement gen. supt., 1974-76, gen. supt. warehouse operations, 1976—. Mem. IEEE, Coll. Engrs. and Surveyors P.R., Elec. Engrs. Soc. P.R. Roman Catholic. Home: S-5-15 Catarata St Rio Piedras PR 00926 Office: Gen PO Box 4267 San Juan PR 00926

DIAZ-NORIEGA, JOSÉ MIGUEL, electronics component co. exec.; b. Mexico City, May 1, 1929; s. José and Emilia deDiaz (Noriega) Diaz de la Fuente; B.A., Universidad de Oviedo (Spain), 1948; B.S., Stanford U., 1951, M.S., 1952; m. María del Carmen Sotres, Aug. 22, 1953; children— María José, José Miguel, María del Carmen, Francisco Javier, Juan Ignacio, Teresa de Jesús, Ignacio. Gen. Elec. fgn. student scholar, 1952-53, electronics and elec. small appliance mgr. Gen. Electric de México, S.A., 1954-56; mgr. engring. Sylvamex Electrónica, S.A., 1956-58; mfrs. rep., 1958-62; pres., gen. mgr. Electrey, S.A., Monterrey, Mex., 1962—. Asst. prof. Instituto Tecnológico y de Estudios Superiores de Monterrey. Dir. Christian Family Movement, 1964-69. Mem. IEEE (sr.), Soc. Automotive Engrs. Roman Catholic. Club: Casino del Valle Athletic (Monterrey). Patentee in field; designer test and mfg. machines for fuses and breakers. Home: 425 Río Colorado Colonia del Valle NL México Office: Apartado 1393 Monterrey NL México

DIAZ-RIVERA, LUIS RAFAEL, educator; b. Santa Isabel, P.R., Nov. 8, 1940; s. Rafael and Matilde Diaz; A.S., U. P.R., 1962, B.A., 1964, prof. diploma, 1968, M.A., 1970; Ph.D., Lehigh U., 1976; m. Betty Vega, June 1, 1968. Tchr., counselor, prin., supr. public schs., Santa Isabel, 1964-70; prof. edn. Cath. U. P.R., 1970-77, Inter Am. U., Ponce, P.R., 1978-79; World U., Ponce, P.R., 1979—; dean acad. affairs U. Ponce, 1977-78; cons. to pvt. schs., 1970—; mem. bd. Colegio ERGOS. Vol. counselor to community youth; adv. CREA (rehab. centers for drug addicts). Mem. Am. Personnel and Guidance Assn., Tchrs. Assn. P.R., Rehab. Counselors Assn. P.R., Phi Delta Kappa (pres. 1974, Disting. Kappan award 1976). Author articles in field. Home: A-10 San Miguel Santa Isabel PR 00757 Office: World U Ponce PR 00731

DI BARROS, EDUARD, educator; b. N.Y.C., July 22, 1929; s. John and Ethel (Murry) Di B.; B.A. in Sociology, Norfolk, (Va.) State Coll., 1961; M.Ed., U. Va., 1970; children—Kelly Marie, Eduard. Probation officer Juvenile and Domestic Relations Ct., Norfolk, 1962-63; guidance counselor Mary M. Bethune High Sch., Halifax, Va., 1963-68, Dunbar and E.C. Glass high schs., Lynchburg, Va., 1968-70; admissions counselor St. Paul's Coll., Lawrenceville, Va., 1970-71; guidance counselor, resource tchr. John Adams Middle Sch., 1971-77; guidance counselor, resource tchr. Hammond Secondary Sch., Alexandria, Va., 1971-77, learner effectiveness in-sch. tchr., 1977—; guidance counselor George Mason Elem. Sch., 1979—; home sch. counselor Hammond Jr. High Sch., 1979—, George Washington Jr. High Sch., 1979—, T.C. Williams High Sch., 1979—. Treas., Alexandria Polit. Action Com. for Educators, 1975—; bd. dirs. Alexandria United Way, 1972—; Nat. Capital area rep. Big Bros., 1971-72. Served with USN, 1948-52. Mem. Am. Personnel and Guidance Assn., NEA, Va., Alexandria edn. assns., NAACP (v.p. Alexandria 1971—), Urban League, Hopkins House Assn. Democrat. Roman Catholic. Club: K.C. Home: 438 N Armistead St #101 Alexandria VA 22312 Office: 4646 Seminary Rd Alexandria VA 22304

DIBRELL, GEORGE EDWARD, city mgr.; b. Dallas, Sept. 22 1928; s. Waymen Eugene and Maude (Helton) D.; B.B.A., So. Meth U., Dallas, 1951; LL.B., U. Tex. at Austin, 1957; M.P.A., U. So. Calif. 1976; m. Georgene Valas, May 30, 1953; 1 dau., Deborah Jeanne Admitted to Tex. bar, 1956; pvt. practice law, Austin, 1956-57; asst city atty., Port Arthur, Tex., 1958-62, city mgr., 1962—; adj. prof Lamar U. Bd. dirs. Port Arthur Coll. Found., Port Arthur council Camp Fire Girls; bd. councilors St. Mary's Hosp. Recipient Good Citizenship award S.A.R., 1975; named Outstanding Community Leader, Tex. chpt. Bus. and Profl. Women's Club. Mem. State Bar Tex., Jefferson County, Am. Port Arthur bar assns., C. of C., Internat. Tex. (pres. region 6, dir. 1973, v.p. 1977, pres. 1979, Merit award 1974, Innovation award 1978) city mgmt. assns., Tex. Municipal League (dir. 1976-78), Municipal Fin. Officers Assn., Phi Alpha Delta Sigma Nu. Mason, Rotarian. Home: 3919 Platt Port Arthur TX 77640 Office: City Hall 444 4th St Port Arthur TX 77640

DICHARRY, ROY MAURICE, petroleum engr.; b. Convent, La. Dec. 30, 1932; s. Benjamin Joseph and Felicie Marie (Donaldson) D. B.S. in Petroleum Engring., La. State U., 1956; m. Patricia Ruth Naquin, June 9, 1956; children—Roy Maurice, Kevin, Cheryl, Debra, Daryl, Tricia. Drilling and prodn. engr. Chevron Oil Co. div. Standard Oil Co. of Tex., Snyder, 1956-61, staff reservoir engr., Houston, 1961-65, div. reservoir engring., 1965-66, sr. reservoir engr., 1966-69, Sacroc unit engr., western div., Snyder, 1969-70, div. reservoir engr., Midland, 1970-71, div. petroleum engr., supr. petroleum engrs., 1971-75, sr. engring. asso. Chevron Oil Field Research, La Habra, Calif., 1975-76, project leader Chevron Services Co.-Aramco Reservoir Mgmt. Project, Houston, 1976-78, mgr., 1979—; lectr. co. seminars. Mem. Am. Gas Assn. (res. com.), Am. Petroleum Inst., Soc. Petroleum Engrs. (asso.), Pi Epsilon Tau. Roman Catholic. K.C. Contbr. articles to profl. jours. Home: 1026 Drava Ln Houston TX 77090 Office: 36487 Houston TX 77036

DICKENS, CHARLES ALLEN, petroleum co. exec.; b. Mount Gilead, N.C., Nov. 26, 1932; s. Alonzo Newton and Elizabeth Ann (Haywood) D.; B.S., N.C. State U., 1954; m. Helen Theresia Baudendistel, Jan. 4, 1958; children—Karen Ann, Constance Lynn, Pamela Jean, Kimberly Susan. Asst. chem. engr., chem. engr., sr. chem. engr., project chem. engr. Texaco, Inc., Beacon, N.Y., Port Arthur, Tex., 1954-63, sr. engr., London, 1963-65, project engr., Brussels, 1965-67, mgr. additive sales, Brussels, 1967-69, asst. sales mgr., additive div., Chgo., 1969-72, Houston, 1972—. Served with USAF, 1955-57. Fellow British Inst. Petroleum; mem. Am. Inst. Chem. Engrs., Am. Soc. Lubrication Engrs., Am. Mgmt. Assn., Soc. Automotive Engrs., Engrs. Council of Houston, Scabbard & Blade, Sigma Xi, Tau Beta Pi. Republican. Clubs: Texaco Country, Westador Residents.

DICKENSON, FREDERICK JOSEPH, JR., author; b. Chgo., Jan. 18, 1909; s. Frederick Joseph and Mary Jane (Dempsey) D.; student U. Ill., Urbana, 1928; m. B. Margaret Erickson, June 4, 1937; children—Margaret Ann, Virginia (Mrs. John Walker), Elizabeth (Mrs. John Rudolf). Reporter, asso. editor Chgo. Daily News, 1929-31, Wis. News, Milw., 1932-34, Newark Star-Eagle, 1935-38, King Features Syndicate, Inc., N.Y.C., 1938—; author illustrated newspaper adventure strip Rip Kirby, 1952—. Clubs: Mt. Kisco (N.Y.) Country, Nat. Press. Author: Kill 'Em With Kindness, 1950; How to Iron a Telephone Book, 1959. Contbr. fiction stories, essays and articles to leading periodicals. Home: 6035 E Peppertree Way Sarasota FL 33581 Office: King Features 235 E 45th St New York City NY 10017

DICKENSON, PRISCILLA PYE, speech pathologist; b. N.Y.C., Apr. 13, 1948; d. Huburt E. and Mildred K. (Petersen) Pye; student Grinnell (Iowa) Coll., 1968-69; B.A. summa cum laude, U. Houston, 1975, M.A., 1976. Speech pathologist VA Hosp., Houston, 1975-76, Methodist Hosp., Houston, 1976-77; dir. speech pathology services Shoal Creek Hosp., Austin, Tex., 1978—; supr. U. Tex. Speech and Hearing Clinic; cons. Austin Speech, Lang. and Hearing Center. Acad. scholar U. Houston, 1973-76; Houston VA Hosp. trainee. Mem. Am. Speech and Hearing Assn., Tex. Speech and Hearing Assn. Contbr. articles to profl. jours. Office: Shoal Creek Hosp 3501 Mills Ave Austin TX 78731

DICKERSON, JOHN GASTON, fin. exec.; b. San Antonio, Aug. 27, 1946; s. Ralph Lee and Isabelle (Gaston) D.; B.A., U. Tex., Austin, 1975, M.B.A., 1980. Gen. mgr. Austin (Tex.) Community Project, 1972-74, pres., 1974-76; gen. mgr. Wheatsville Food Co-op., Austin, 1976-77, pres., chmn. bd., 1978—; cons. in field. Recipient Sord award for acad. excellence Grad. Sch. Bus., U. Tex., Austin, 1979. Mem. Amnesty Internat., Co-op. League U.S.A. (dir. 1978—), Consumer Co-op. Mgrs. Assn. (dir. 1979—), Co-op. Resource Center (dir. 1978—), Consumer Co-op. Alliance. Democrat. Office: 2901 Lamar St Austin TX 78705

DICKERSON, LARRY RICHARD, counselor, educator; b. Parsons, Kans., Oct. 18, 1943; s. Lester Clyde and Belva Alice (Taylor) D.; student U. of Central Ark., 1961-62; B.A., U. Ark., 1965; M.A. (fellow), U. Iowa, 1967, Ph.D., 1971; m. Marita Ann Moore, June 28, 1969; children—Valerie Ann, Larry Richard, Daniel Lucas. Work adjustment counselor Curative Workshop, Milw., 1967-68; rehab. counselor N.Y. Commn. for the Blind, Bronx, 1968-69; work evaluator and supr. Goodwill Industries Inc., Iowa City, summer, 1970; counselor Counseling Center, Coe Coll., Cedar Rapids, Iowa, 1970-71; practicum supr. and instr. U. Iowa, Iowa City, 1969-71; sr. research scientist, asst. prof. Ark. Rehab. and g. Center, U. Ark., Fayetteville, 1971-73, asso. prof., program dir. Center for Continuing Edn. in Rehab., 1974-76; asso. prof., coordinator rehab. of the blind grad. program U. Ark., Little Rock, 1977-79, prof., chmn. rehab. and spl. edn., 1979—; asso. prof. U. Wis., Menomonie, 1973-74; mem. Nat. Adv. Council on Vocat. Rehab., 1972-73; mem. client service adv. bd. Ark. Enterprises for the Blind, 1974-76; cons. to various rehab. orgns., 1971—; pvt. practice psychol. counseling, 1972—. Mem. Am. Rehab. Counseling Assn. (mem. research awards com. 1973-74), Nat. Rehab. Counseling Assn., Am. Assn. Workers for Blind (pres. region VI 1978-80), Am. Personnel and Guidance Assn., Nat. Soc. for Prevention of Blindness (v.p. state chpt. 1979—), Vocat. Evaluation and Work Adjustment Assn., Nat. Rehab. Assn. Mem. Christian Ch. Club: Lions. Contbr. articles on counseling and rehab. to profl. jours.; editorial bd. Jour. Visual Impairment and Blindness, 1979—. Home: 909 N Mississippi Ave Little Rock AR 72207 Office: 33d St and University Ave Little Rock AR 72204

DICKERSON, THOMAS HOWARD, landscape architect; b. Knox County, Tex., Feb. 7, 1944; s. Doris and Ernestine Ruby (Howard) D.; B.S., Tex. Tech. U., 1966; m. Cheryl Kaye Matthews; children—Thomas Eric, Dinita Leigh. Asst. supt. parks Dallas Park and Recreation Dept., 1966-70; sales mgr. Lambert Landscape Co., Dallas, 1970-72; gen. mgr. Green Valley Nurseries, Inc., Dallas, 1973-75; pres. Enviro-Industries, San Antonio and Dallas, 1974—; landscape designer, cons. Baylor U. Med. Center, 1969-79; instr., mem. horticulture adv. bd. Dallas County Jr. Coll.; cons. in field. Recipient Beautification award 1972, Landscape Design award, 1976. Registered landscape architect, Tex. Mem. Tex. Turfgrass Assn. (dir.), Tex. Indsl. Weed Control Assn. (dir.), Tex. Nurseryman's Assn. Mem. Ch. of Christ (tchr.). Contbr. articles to profl. jours. Home: 10309 Vinemont Dallas TX 75218 Office: 1700 East Gate Dr Dallas TX 75041

DICKEY, JOHN COKE, obstetrician and gynecologist; b. Abilene, Tex., June 26, 1934; s. Claude H. and Opal A. (Isom) D.; B.A., McMurry Coll., 1955; M.D., U. Tex., Dallas, 1959; m. Joanne Robinson, June 10, 1955; (div. May 1976); children—Jeffrey C., Denise Anne, David Coke, Jason Charles; m. 2d, Delores Marie Wilson, July 6, 1976. Instr. biology McMurry Coll., 1955; rotating intern Parkland Meml. Hosp., Dallas, 1960-61, resident in obstetrics and gynecology, 1962-65; pvt. practice specializing in obstetrics and gynecology, Denison, Tex., 1965—; chief of staff Denison Meml. Hosp., 1975-76, chief obstetrics and gynecology service, 1968-70; mem. Grayson County Bd. Health, 1969-72; bd. dirs. Texoma Region Blood Bank, 1976—. Mem. Denison City Council, 1973-75. Served with M.C., USAF, 1960-62. Diplomate Am. Bd. Obstetrics and Gynecology. Fellow Am. Coll. Obstetrics and Gynecology, Central Assn. Obstetrics and Gynecology; mem. Tex. Soc. Obstetricians and Gynecologists, Am. Assn. Laproscopists, AMA, Tex. Med. Assn, Alpha Chi, Theta Kappa Psi. Presbyterian. Clubs: Texoma Racquet, Rod and Gun, Denison Country. Home: 231 N Eddy St Denison TX 75020 Office: 100 Memorial Dr Denison TX 75020

DICKEY, LEE DOWLING, aerospace co. engring. exec.; b. Lubbock, Tex., Jan. 2, 1928; s. Emory Dowling and Lucy Golden (Hooten) D.; student E. Tex. State U., 1944-45; B.S., Tex. Technol. U., 1951; m. Lena Mae Payne, Apr. 12, 1949; children—Jerry Lee, Richard Allan, Sharon Kay. Jr. engr. J.B. Payne & Assos., Enid, Okla., 1951; with Vought Systems div. LTV Aerospace Corp., Dallas, 1951—, supr. elec. electronic design, 1963-71, acting chief systems design, 1971-72, supr. armament, crew systems and elec./electronic design, 1972-74, chief systems design, 1974-76, chief configuration control and design support, 1976-78, mgr. design support, 1978—; instr. aerospace design So. Meth. U., 1969, Naval Air Sta., Dallas, 1970. Coach, Little League Baseball, 1961-63; post com. mem. exploring div. Boy Scouts Am., 1975-76. Bd. dirs. Arlington Christian Youth Center. Served with USAAF, 1946. Mem. IEEE, Aerospace and Electronics Systems Soc. (pres. 1975-76, dir.). Mem. Ch. of Christ (deacon). Contbr. to Power Semiconductor Applications, vol. II, 1972. Research on application of solid state switching to aircraft elec. systems. Amateur radio operator. Home: 1615 White Way Dr Arlington TX 76013 Office: PO Box 225907 Dallas TX 75265

DICKEY, RAYMOND ADELLE, hosp. ofcl.; b. Halls Summit, Kan., Dec. 3, 1921; s. William Raymond and Elsie Venita (Mitchell) D.; student Fla. So. Coll., 1962-65, Central Mo. State Coll., 1968; B.S. in Accounting summa cum laude, Jones Coll., Orlando, Fla., 1972; M.B.A., N.Y. Inst. Tech., Orlando, 1976; m. Helen Jean Killian, Oct. 16, 1943; children—Eugene Raymond, Mary Helen (Mrs. James Theodore Franke), Thomas Mark. Served with U.S. Army Air Force, 1942-46, 48-68, ret., 1968; dean Jones Coll., 1972-75; fiscal officer Holiday Hosp., Orlando, 1975—. Cons. data processing, 1972—. Decorated Commendation medal with oak leaf cluster; named hon. citizen State of Nev., 1949. Mem. Inst. Internal Auditors, U.S. Chess Fedn., Phi Theta Pi. Democrat. Methodist. Mason (Shriner). Home: 1633 Hollis Dr Orlando FL 32807 Office: Holiday Hospital Orlando FL 32807

DICKIE, LAURANCE PORTER, architect; b. Birmingham, Ala., Apr. 9, 1950; s. Henry Tirril and Maureen Elizabeth (Reynolds) D.; B.Arch. with honors, U. Tenn., Knoxville, 1975. A founder, dir. Nicaraug n Assistance Group at Knoxville and Managua, Nicarauga, 1973-75, cons., 1975-79; partner Tensiletecture, Knoxville, 1975-79; contract adminstr., corp. sec. J. H. Deatherage Co. Inc., archtl., engring. co., Knoxville, 1975-77; contract adminstr. Dearthick and Henley Architects, Chattanooga, 1977-79; head constrn. contract adminstrn. Rañon McIntosh Bernardo & Ramirez, Architects & Planners, Inc., Tampa, Fla., 1979—. Diving instr. YMCA. Mem. Constrn. Specification Inst. (pres. Chattanooga chpt.), AIA (Reynolds Design award 1975), Tenn. Soc. Architects (chmn. exhbts. com.). Roman Catholic. Research, devel. lightweight tensile roof membrains. Home: 4003 S Westshore Blvd Tampa FL 33611 Office: 515 Bay St Tampa FL 33606

DICKINSON, EDMUND JOHN, transp. cons.; b. Spokane, Wash., Mar. 31, 1920; s. Floyd Sylvester and Clara Anna (Thien) D.; B.S. in Civil Engring., Gonzaga U., 1942; m. Mary LeRoux, June 30, 1973; children—William, Robert, John, James, Frederick. Structural engr., Corps Engrs., Spokane, 1942-43; airport engr. CAA, Boise, Idaho and Salem, Oreg., 1946-53; airport mgr., engr. City of Pendleton, Oreg., 1953-55; transp. cons. James C. Buckley Inc., N.Y.C., 1955-69, pres., Washington, 1969-76; pres. Edmund J. Dickinson & Assos., transp. cons., Arlington, Va., 1977-78; v.p. J.R. Crenshaw & Assos., Inc., transp. cons., Falls Church, Va., 1978—. Served to lt. USNR, 1943-46. Registered profl. engr., airport exec. Mem. Alpha Sigma Nu. Address: 3800 N Fairfax Dr Apt 914 Arlington VA 22203

DICKINSON, WILLIAM LOUIS, congressman; b. Opelika, Ala., June 5, 1925; s. Henry K. and Bernice (Lowe) D.; LL.B., U. Ala., 1950; m. Barbara Edwards, Mar. 10, 1977; children by previous marriage—Chris, Mike, Tara, Bill. Admitted to Ala. bar, 1950, practiced in Opelika, 1950-63; judge Opelika City Ct., 1951-53; judge Ct. Common Pleas, 1953-59; judge Juvenile Ct. Lee County, 1953-59; judge 5th Jud. Ct. Ala., 1959-63; asst. v.p. So. Ry. System, Montgomery, Ala., 1963-64; mem. 89th-96th congresses from 2d Ala. Dist.; mem. com. on house armed services, joint com. on printing, com. on house adminstrn. Chmn. Opelika Bd. Edn., 1960-61; mem. Gov.'s Indsl. Com. of 100, 1963-64; dir. Lee County Civil Def., 1961-62. Past pres. Ala. Mental Health Assn. Chmn. Ala. Republican Congl. Del.; pres., bd. dirs. Lee County Mental Health Clinic; bd. dirs. Lee County Rehab. Center. Served with USNR, World War II. Named Man of Year, Opelika Jr. C. of C., 1961, One of Four Outstanding Young Men in Ala., 1961. Mem. Ala. Bar Assn., U. Ala. Alumni Assn., Sigma Alpha Epsilon. Clubs: Masons, Kiwanis, Elks. Office: Rayburn House Office Bldg Washington DC 20515

DICKSON, CONSTANTINE JOHN, broadcaster; b. Benicia, Calif., May 21, 1913; s. John Diamond and Katie Connie (Skathetis) D.; student Ark. State U., 1931; engring. grad., Ark. State Trade Sch. Engring., 1941; m. Georgia Marie Allen, Apr. 29, 1935; 1 son, Robert Lee. Operator carbon plant Alcoa Corp., Jones Mills, Ark., 1942-44; sales mgr. KWFC Radio, Hot Springs, Ark., 1945-50; mgr. MWFC Radio, Hot Springs, 1951-54; owner, mgr. KBLO Radio, Hot Springs, 1955-61; mgr. KFOY-TV, Hot Springs, 1962-64; sales mgr. KBHS Radio, Hot Springs, Ark., 1965-68, owner, mgr. KGUS Stereo FM Radio, 1969—. Bd. dirs. Hot Springs Boy Club, 1950-54, Garland County Red Cross, 1952-56. Mem. Ark. Broadcasters (dir. 1952-58), Am. Broadcast Assn. (sec.-treas. 1958-62), Ark. Navy League (sec.-treas. 1956-60), Hot Springs C. of C. Greek Orthodox (pres. Ch. Council 1966-70, deacon 1971-75). Democrat. Clubs: Elks, Moose, Lions (past pres.), K.P. Club: Belvedere Country. Home: 34 Circle Dr Hot Springs AR 71901 Office: 208 1/2 Broadway Hot Springs AR 71901

DICKSON, JAMES GILMER, civil engr.; b. Freeport, Tex., May 2, 1922; s. John Lafayette and Lillian Elliott (Dingle) D.; B.S. in Civil Engring., U. Tex., 1943; m. Ora Wehring, Sept. 1, 1941; children—James Gilmer, Linda S. Resident engr. Tex. Hwy. Dept., San Antonio, 1946-48; pres. Dunbar & Dickson, Lake Jackson, Tex., 1948-50, 53-64, 75—; pres., vice chmn. Limbaugh Engrs. Inc., Albuquerque, 1970-74; dir. First Freeport Nat. Bank, 1955-78; chmn. bd. First Freeport Corp., 1978—. Vice pres. Block 78 Co., Freeport, 1954—; partner Dickson-Dingle Realty Co., Freeport, 1954—. Served with C.E., AUS, 1944-46, 50-53. Registered profl. engr., Tex., La. Fellow ASCE (chmn. exec. com. Tech. Council on Aerospace 1973-74), Tex., N.Mex., Nat. socs. profl. engrs., Houston Engring. Sci. Soc., Brazosport C. of C. (pres. 1958). Clubs: Riverside Country, Kiwanis. Home: 54 Caraway Common Lake Jackson TX 77566 Office: PO Box 540 Lake Jackson TX 77566

DICKSON, ROY SHELTON, JR., petroleum co. exec.; b. Lewiston, Ida., Aug. 29, 1933; s. Roy S. and Ethel (Means) D.; B.S., U. Tulsa, 1958; m. Cassandra G. Bennett; children—Laura Ann, Julia Kay, Roy Shelton III. Sci. computer programmer research and devel. Phillips Petroleum Co., Bartlesville, Okla., 1957, systems analyst computing dept., 1958-61, supt. computing systems computing dept., 1961-62, supr. tech. programming systems, 1962-65, dir. computing systems and evaluations, 1965-67, asst. mgr. operations div., 1967-69, mgr. ops. div., 1969-74, mgr. computing, 1974-75, mgr. info. services, 1975—. Vice pres. SHARE, Internat., 1964-65, pres., 1965-66. Chmn. Bartlesville chpt. ARC. Served with USMCR, 1952. Mem. Assn. Computing Machinery. Author: (with others) Data Processing in 1980-85, 1976. Home: Route 3 Box 289 Bartlesville OK 74003 Office: Info Services Div Phillips Petroleum Co Bartlesville OK 74003

DICKSON, SANDLER HARVEY, environ. engr.; b. West Palm Beach, Fla., Oct. 16, 1935; s. Maurice and Sophie Esther (Shuman) D.; B.C.E., U. Fla., 1958; M.P.H. (USPHS scholar), U. Minn., 1964; m. Barbara Brenda Levy, June 16, 1963; children—Helene, Carolyn, Brian. Environ. engr. USPHS, various locations, 1958-70; environ. engr. Fla. Div. Health, Jacksonville, 1970-72, Dept. Environ. Regulation, Tallahassee, 1972—, J. P. Action Realty, Inc., 1979—. Mem. Tallahassee Sesquicentennial Com., 1973-74; mem. steering com., action auction WFSU TV pub. TV, 1974-75; ofcl. host Gov.'s Inauguration, 1975. Mem. exec. bd. Leon County Bicentennial, 1975-76; bd. dirs. Springtime Tallahassee, 1975-78; Krewe chief Spanish Krewe, 1979. Mem. Fla. Engring. Soc. (bicentennial chmn., corr. sec. Big Bend chpt. 1976-77, sec.-treas. 1977-78, v.p. 1978-79), Nat. Soc. Profl. Engrs., Water Pollution Control Fedn., Pi Lambda Phi. Democrat. Jewish (v.p. Temple Israel Brotherhood, dir. Temple Israel 1979—). Home: 729 Kenilworth Rd Tallahassee FL 32312 Office: 2600 Blairstone Rd Tallahassee FL 32301

DICKSON-PORTER, CLAUDIA BLAIR, librarian; b. Memphis, Oct. 22, 1925; d. Walton Avery and Annie Laurie (Tate) Tucker; B.S., U. Nebr., Omaha, 1964; M.L.S., N. Tex. State U., Denton, 1971, Ph.D., 1979; m. Benjamin A. Dickson, June 5, 1945 (div.); children—Susan Dickson Morrison, Andrea Dickson Darby, Donna Dickson Stephens, Reid W., Bryan A.; m. 2d, William G. Porter, Feb. 8, 1978. Tchrs. schs. in Nebr. and Hawaii, 1964-71; librarian Nat. Assn. Retarded Citizens, Arlington, Tex., from 1971; dir. Regional Office TAS VI, Research and Tng Center in Mental Retardation Tex. Tech. U.; dir. planning Tex. Planning Council for Devel. Disabilities, Tex. Dept. Mental Health/Mental Retardation, 1979-80; program specialist Office of Devel. Disabilities, Office of Human Devel., Fed. Region VI, Dallas, 1980—; tchr. community services courses El Centro Jr. Coll., Dallas. Mem. Spl. Libraries Assn., Southwestern, Tex. library assns., Am. Assn. Mental Deficiency, Council Exceptional Children, Metroplex Council Health Sci. Librarians, Soc. S.W. Archivists, Local History Soc., Phi Delta Kappa. Author, compiler in field. Home: 1618 Oakwood St Arlington TX 76012 Office: 1200 Main Tower Dallas TX 75201

DI DEA, ARTHUR ANTHONY, dentist; b. N.Y.C., Jan. 4, 1925; s. Charles and Rebecca (Schmeltzer) DiD.; B.S. with honors, City U. N.Y., 1945; postgrad. Washington U., St. Louis, 1945-47; D.D.S., U. Ill., 1952; m. Viola Mae Rodenmayer, Feb. 8, 1947; children—Barbara (Mrs. David Haines Phillips), Mark Brian, Linda Katherine, Gregory Scott, Karen Lee. Tchr. gen., qualitative and quantitative chemistry Harris Tchrs. Coll., St. Louis, 1947; research bacterial chemist St. Louis Health Dept. Endemic Typhus Fever Study, 1948; asst. prof. oral histology, pathology and operative dentistry U. Ill., 1952-53; practice dentistry, Orlando, Fla., 1955—; dental staff Winter Park (Fla.) Hosp., also Fla. Hosp., Orlando, 1956-62. Chief Hawkeye tribe Indian Guides of YMCA, Orlando, 1963-64, nation chief, 1965; pres. PTA, 1970; active Little League, Cub Scouts Am. Bd. dirs. Civic Theater, 1963-66. Served as 1st lt. AUS, 1953-55. Mem. Fla. (ins. chmn. 1965), Orange County (program chmn. 1970) dental socs., Kappa Alpha, Phi Beta Pi, Omicron Kappa Upsilon, Psi Omega. Episcopalian (mem. vestry 1970-74, jr. warden 1971-73). Clubs: Masons, Shriners, Order Eastern Star, Exec. (pres. 1966-68), Sertoma (chmn. bd. 1963, 65, pres. 1964), Univ. (Winter Park). Contbr. articles to profl. jours. Home: 1921 N Forest Ave Orlando FL 32803

DIDION, JAMES JERRETT, real estate co. exec.; b. Sacramento, Dec. 20, 1939; s. Frank R. and Eduene J. D.; A.B. in Polit. Sci., U. Calif., Berkeley, 1961; m. Gloria K. Geisler, Aug. 25, 1962; children—Kelley Suzanne, Steven James, Lori Anne. With Coldwell Banker Co., 1962—, resident mgr. Sacramento office, 1969-71, v.p., 1969-71, sr. v.p., regional mgr., Houston, 1971—; dir. Med. Center Bank. Served with USAF, 1957-58. Mem. Internat. Council Shopping Centers, Urban Land Inst., Houston Bd. Realtors, Nat. Bd. Realtors, Houston C. of C. Clubs: Lakeside Country (Houston); Sutter (Sacramento). Office: 2500 W Loop S Houston TX 77027

DIEDERICH, J(OHN) WILLIAM, newspaper exec.; b. Ladysmith, Wis., Aug. 30, 1929; s. Joseph Charles and Alice Florence (Yost) D.; Ph.B., Marquette U., 1951; M.B.A. with high distinction (Baker scholar), Harvard U., 1955; m. Mary Theresa Klein, Nov. 25, 1950; children—Mary Theresa Diederich Evans, Robert Douglas, Charles Stuart, Michael Mark, Patricia Anne, Donna Maureen (dec.), Denise Brendan, Carol Lynn, Barbara Gail, Brian Donald, Tracy Maureen, Theodora Bernadette, Tamara Alice, Lorraine Angela. With Landmark Communications, Inc, Norfolk, Va., 1955—, exec. v.p. fin., 1973-78, exec. v.p. community newspapers, 1978—, chmn. bd., 1977—, also dir.; chmn. bd., dir. Community Dailies, Inc., 1978—; bd. dirs. Landmark Charitable Found.; instr. Boston U., 1954, Old Dominion U., 1955-59. Served to lt. col USMC. Mem. Inst. Newspaper Controllers and Fin. Officers, Nat. Assn. Accountants, Am. Numismatic Assn., Nat. Geneal. Soc., Wis. Geneal. Soc., Pa. Geneal. Soc., Sigma Delta Chi. Roman Catholic. Clubs: Harbor (Norfolk); SAR. Office: 150 W Brambleton Ave Norfolk VA 23501

DIEDRICH, RICHARD JOSEPH, architect; b. South Bend, Ind., May 8, 1936; s. Arthur Joseph and Lucille D.; Diploma in Architecture, École Des Beaux Arts Americaines, Fountainbleau, France, 1960; B.Arch., U. Ill., 1961, M.Arch., 1962; m. Francyne Dawn Leontios, June 10, 1961; children—Dawn Marie, Lisa Lee, Andrea Lynn. Archtl. designer Richardson Severns Scheeler & Assos., Champaign, Ill., 1961-62; design critic U. Ill. Sch. Architecture, 1961-62; archtl. designer Swensson & Kott, Nashville, 1963-64; architect, v.p. Miller Waltz Diedrich, Architects, Milw., 1965-77; pres. MWD Architects, Atlanta, 1978—. Mem. Whitefish Bay Bd. Appeals, 1968-71; v.p. N. Decatur Youth Assn., 1975-76. Mem. AIA (past pres. Milw. chpt.), Wis. Architect (past pres.). Clubs: Atlanta City, Druid Hills Country. Archtl. works include: Avondale Sta., Atlanta Rapid Transit, Student Center, U. Ga. Home: 1316 N Decatur Rd Atlanta GA 30306 Office: 235 Peachtree St NE Suite 1101 Atlanta GA 30303

DIEHL, LOUIS CALVIN, air force officer; b. Huntington, W.Va., Sept. 15, 1942; s. Louis Adler and Emmy Lou D.; B.S. in Bus. Mgmt., W.Va. Inst. Tech., 1965; M.B.A., U. N.D., 1976; m. Karen Evans, Oct. 26, 1968; 1 son, Roderick Evan. Commd. 2d lt. USAF, 1966, advanced through grades to maj., 1979; procurement and contracting officer, 1966—; flight comdr. 321st Strategic Missile Wing, 1974-77; dep. chief quality assurance, Wichita, Kans., 1977-79; officer-in-charge Dept. Def. Joint Services assignment, contract adminstrn. services residency, Ft. Worth, 1979—. Decorated Air Force Commendation medal, Air Force Meritorious Service medal. Mem. Soc. Advancement Mgmt., Nat. Contract Mgmt. Assn., Sigma Iota Epsilon.

DIEHR, DAVID B., YMCA exec.; b. Toledo, June 4, 1939; s. Harlan E. and Lillis R. (Consaul) D.; A.B. in Sociology, Coll. William and Mary, Williamsburg, Va., 1961; postgrad. George Williams Coll., Chgo., 1961-63; m. Kathryn D. Welsh, Apr. 2, 1966; 1 son, Erik William. Phys. dir. YMCA of Xenia (Ohio) and Greene County, 1964-68, YMCA, Joliet, Ill., 1968-74; exec. dir. Northwest family br. San Antonio YMCA, 1974-77; gen. dir. YMCA Waco (Tex.), 1977—; YMCA aquatic field agt., S.W. Ohio, 1966-68, Chgo. area, 1972-74, S. Tex., 1974-75, S.W. region commr., 1975—, mem. Nat. YMCA operating councils on aquatics and competitive swimming and diving. Mem. YMCA Phys. Edn. Soc. (pres. region I, 1972-74, chmn. Chgo. area 1971-73; named Phys. Edn. Dir. of Year region I, 1974), Assn. Profl. YMCA Dirs., AAHPER, Am. Swimming Coaches Assn., U.S. Power Squadron, Fellowship Christian Athletes, League Am. Wheelmen, Omicron Delta Kappa. Republican. Presbyterian (ruling elder 1975-77). Club: Rotary (Waco). Home: 606 Brint Ln Robinson TX 76706 Office: 1115 Columbus Ave Waco TX 76701

DIENER, MARY ELEANOR MCMATH, author, co. exec.; b. Washington, July 20, 1929; d. Mercer Bailey and Margaret Therese (Chase) McMath; student Internat. Coll. Japan, 1948; B.A., Manhattanville Coll., 1951; M. Human Service Adminstrn., Antioch U., 1978; m. William Harrison Diener, Sept. 3, 1951; children—Eric, Paul, Lawrence, Valerie. Econ. researcher, analyst Gen. Motors of Brazil, Sao Paulo, 1951-53; asst. dir. fed. funding analysis Cultural Union of Brazil-U.S.A., Sao Paulo, 1955-57; feature writer Bazilian Business, U.S. C. of C.-Brazil, 1958-61; feature writer, Sao Paulo advt. rep. Times of Brazil, 1958-61; dir. food and med./dental project Social Services of Vila Alpina, 1961-65; dir. data processing, computer programming and med. asst. program Career Tng. Inst., 1965-67; editor, display advt. mgr. The Citizen, weekly newspaper, Sarasota, Fla., 1966-68, account rep., creative writer Center for Marketing and Research, Sarasota, 1969-71; pres. Diener & Assos., Inc., communications cons., mgmt., ednl. planning and devel., mktg., Research Triangle Park, N.C., 1971—. Mem. metric speakers bur. Bur. Standards, U.S. Dept. Commerce; del. White House Conf. Small Bus., also chmn. N.C. del.; mem. N.C. Small Bus. Adv. Council, 1980—. Recipient 4th Dist. Addy award for best black and white newspaper campaign in advt., 1972. Fellow Internat. Poetry Soc., Internat. Acad. Poets; mem. Women in Communications, U.S. Metric Assn. (mid Southeastern regional dir.), Am. Mgmt. Assn., Am. Assn. Pub. Opinion Research, So. Assn. Pub. Opinion Research, Nat. League Am. Pen Women (pres. 1972-74), Am. Advt. Fedn. (past dir.), Nat. Assn. Women Bus. Owners (nat. dir., state pres.), U.S. C. of C. Republican. Roman Catholic. Co-author: Economic Survey of Brazil, 1953; author: When The Sun Goes Down (poetry), 1969; Just Living (poetry), 1979. Office: PO Box 12052 50 Park Dr Research Triangle Park NC 27709

DIENHART, CHARLOTTE MARIE, educator; b. Sioux Falls, S.D., Aug. 14, 1923; d. Arthur Peter and Mae (Donahue) Dienhart; B.S., Coll. St. Catherine, 1945; M.S., State U. Iowa, 1947; postgrad. U. Minn., 1956-58, Emory U. Sch. Medicine, 1962-64; Ph.D., Mich. State U., 1960. Research asst. U. Minn., 1947-48, grad. teaching asst. physiology, 1957-58; instr. dept. biology Coll. St. Catherine, 1948-57; grad. teaching asst. anatomy Mich. State U., 1958-60; mem. faculty Emory U., Atlanta, 1960—, asst. prof. anatomy, 1966—, asso. prof. allied health, 1975—. Served to lt. comdr. Med. Service Corps, USNR. Mem. AAAS, N.Y. Acad. Scis., So. Soc. Anatomists, Ga. Acad. Sci., Sigma Xi, Sigma Delta Epsilon, Omicron Nu. Beta Beta Beta. Author: Basic Human Anatomy and Physiology, 1967, 3d edit., 1979. Home: 1943 N Decatur Rd NE Atlanta GA 30307

DIERCKS, FREDERICK OTTO, govt. ofcl.; b. Rainy River, Ont., Can., Sept. 8, 1912; s. Otto Herman and Lucy (Plunkett) D.; B.S., U.S. Mil. Acad., 1937; M.S.C.E., M.I.T., 1939; M.S. in Photogrammetry, Syracuse U., 1950; m. Kathryn Frances Transue, Sept. 1, 1937; children—Frederick William, Lucy Helena. Commd. 2d lt. U.S. Army, 1937, advanced through grades to col., 1952; comdg. officer U.S. Army Map Service, Washington, 1957-61; dir. U.S. Army Coastal Engring. Research Center, Washington, 1964-67; ret., 1967; asso. dir. U.S. Coast and Geodetic Survey (now Nat. Ocean Survey), Rockville, Md., 1967-74; U.S. mem. commn. cartography Pan. Am. Inst. Geography and History, OAS, 1961-67, alt. U.S. mem. directing council, 1970-74, exec. sec. U.S. nat. sect., 1974—. Decorated Legion of Merit (U.S.); Grand Cross of Order of King George II (Greece); Most Exalted Order of White Elephant (Thailand). Registered profl. engr., D.C. Fellow ASCE; mem. Am. Soc. Photogrammetry (pres. 1970-71), Sigma Xi. Republican. Presbyterian. Clubs: Masons, Army-Navy, Cosmos (Washington). Home: 9313 Christopher St Fairfax VA 22031 Office: 6001 Executive Blvd Rockville MD 20852

DIES, DOUGLAS HILTON, assn. exec.; b. St. Paul, Sept. 9, 1913; s. Edward Jerome and Ma ceta (Cole) D.; A.B., Harvard, 1934; postgrad. Oxford U., 1934-35; m. Mary Frances Doreen Harding, Nov. 25, 1939; children—Harding Mogridge, Andrea Frances. Editorial staff Grand Forks (N.D.) Herald, summer 1933, Mpls. Star, summer 1934, London Sunday Chronicle, summer 1935; staff London bur. U.P., 1935-38, Knoxville (Tenn.) Jour., 1938-40; pub. relations dept. Westinghouse Electric Co., 1940-41; staff A.P., Cleve., 1941-42; pub. relations, staff U.S. Bd. Econ. Warfare, Washington, 1942-43; pub. relations, Washington, 1946—; editor Washington Correspondence, weekly newsletter on oilseeds and fats industry, 1947—; asso. world trading corps, 1947—; asst. to pres. Nat. Inst. Oilseed Products, 1947—; Washington rep. Pillsbury Co., 1956-64, East Asiatic Co., 1956—, Woodward & Dickerson, Inc., 1958—; asst. sec., bur. raw materials Am. Vegetable Oils and Fats Industries, 1961-62, sec., 1962—; exec. sec. Am. Council Ind. Labs., 1963—; guest lectr. fgn. trade Georgetown U., 1966—; mem. agrl. tech. adv. com. on oilseeds and products for multilateral trade negotiations, 1975. Mem. Republican City Com., Alexandria, 1953-61. Served from ensign to lt. comdr., USNR, 1943-46. Mem. S.R. (gov. D.C. 1956-62), Mil. Order World Wars, Sigma Alpha Epsilon. Episcopalian (vestryman). Clubs: Harvard (N.Y.C., Washington); University, Oxford-Cambridge (Washington). Editor: Chemurgie Digest, 1950-53. Home: 505 Robinson Ct Alexandria VA 22302 Office: 1725 K St NW Washington DC 20006

DIES, FEDERICO, scientist, educator; b. Paris, Mar. 17, 1936; s. Haroldo and Pilar (Angulo) D.; M.D., Universidad Autónoma de México, 1959; Ph.D., U. Rochester, 1966; m. Rosa María Cobos, Aug. 11, 1962; children—Juan Antonio, Gonzalo. Asst. chmn. dept. clin. physiology Instituto Nacional de la Nutrición México, 1965-70; med. dir. Eli Lilly Co., Mex., 1970-72; chmn., prof. physiology and pharmacology dept. Sch. Medicine, Universidad Autónoma de San Luis Potosí (Mex.), 1973—. Nat. Acad. Medicine (Mex.). Fellow A.C.P.; mem. Academia de Investigación Científica, Sociedad Mexicana de Ciencias Fisiológicas (pres. 1973-75), Sociedad Mexicana de Nutrición y Endocrinología (Alfonso Rivera award 1967, pres. 1973-74), Internat., Am. socs. nephrology, N.Y. Acad. Scis., Am. Physiol. Soc., Academia Nacional de Medicina (Dr. Eduardo Liceaga award 1972), Asociación Latinoamericana de Ciencias Fisiológicas (sec.). Contbr. articles to profl. jours. Home: 1030 Fray Diego de la Magdalena San Luis Potosí SLP Mexico Office: 2405 Venustiano Carranza San Luis Potosí SLP Mexico

DIETSCHE, HEINZ BRENT JURGEN, clin. psychologist; b. Mannheim, Germany, Aug. 2, 1919; s. Erwin Karl and Erna (Gobelbecker) D.; came to U.S., 1924, naturalized, 1924; B.A., Stanford U., 1942, M.A., 1949; postgrad. U. Denver, 1943-44, U. So. Calif., 1946, U. Tenn., 1952; hon. doctorate, Am. U., 1974; m. Anna Jewell Price, June 25, 1956; children—Michael, Marcelle, Elizabeth. Intern, Inst. for Juvenile Research, Chgo., 1951-52, Calif. State U. at San Jose, 1940-41, 47, U. Calif. at Los Angeles, 1946; clin. and asst. chief psychologist Eastern State Psychiat. Hosp., Knoxville, Tenn., 1952-64; pvt. practice clin. psychology, Knoxville, 1953-54; instr. U. Tenn. Meml. Hosp., Knoxville, 1962-63; psychol. asst. Eastern State Hosp., Vinita, Okla., 1964, asst. chief psychologist, 1964-65, dir. psychol. services, 1965-75; pvt. practice clin. psychology, Vinita, 1966—; cons. Head Start, Vinita Sch. System, Taft State Hosp., Home of Hope. Served with AUS, 1942-45. Mem. Am., Southwestern, Okla. psychol. assns., AAAS, Okla. Ednl. Psychol. Assn., Menninger Found., So. Marriage Counseling Assn., Nat. Rehab. Assn., Nat. Rehab. Counseling Assn., Am. Group Psychotherapy Assn., Am. Ednl. Research Assn., Vinita C. of C., Am. Legion. Contbr. articles to profl., trade jours. Home: House #9 4th St PO Box 69 Eastern State Hosp Vinita OK 74301 Office: Adminstrn Bldg Eastern State Hosp Vinita OK 74301

DIETZE, CHARLES EDGAR, clergyman; b. Savannah, Ga., Jan. 21, 1919; s. Ernest and Mary (Fetzer) D.; A.B., Transylvania Coll., 1940; B.D., Lexington Theol. Sem., 1944; D.D., Atlantic Christian Coll., 1965; m. Mary Nettie Peavyhouse, Dec. 28, 1940; children—Mary Katherine Dietze Ballance, Charles William. Ordained to ministry Christian Ch. (Disciples of Christ), 1943; pastor, Ky., 1940-55; v.p. Lexington Theol. Sem. (Ky.), 1955-65; regional minister Christian Ch. in N.C., Wilson, 1965—. Vice pres., bd. higher edn. Christian Ch., 1966-68, pres. ccnf. regional ministers, 1976-77; fraternal visitor chs. in Kenya, S.Africa, Zaire, Liberia, 1976. Trustee Atlantic Christian Coll., Wilson. Recipient Distinguished Service award Henderson (Ky.) Jr. C. of C., 1951. Spl. Centennial citation Lexington Theol. Sem., 1965; named outstanding young man Ky., Jr. C. of C., 1951. Mem. N.C. Council Chs. (pres. 1972-73). Author: God's Trustees, 1976. Editor: N.C. Christian, 1965—. Contbr. articles to profl. jours. Home: 805 Trinity Dr Wilson NC 27893 Office: Box 521 Wilson NC 27893

DIGGS, MELVIN M., lawyer; b. Trenton, Tex., Apr. 11, 1914; s. Harvey Washington and Juanita (Moore) D.; A.B., Tex. Christian U., 1936; LL.B., Georgetown U., 1941; m. Virginia Haley, May 3, 1948; children—Susan, Nancy, Ann. Admitted to Tex. bar; lawyer U.S. Govt., Ft. Worth, 1945—; 1st asst. U.S. atty. No. Dist. Tex., Ft. Worth, 1958-65, U.S. atty., 1965-68, 1st asst. U.S. atty., 1958-73; speedy trial act cons. to U.S. cts. No. Dist. Tex., Ft. Worth, 1975—. Served with AUS, 1941-45. Mem. State Bar. Tex., Fed., Tarrant County bar assns., Mil. Intelligence Assn., Texas Christian U. Ex-Lettermen's Assn. (past pres.). Club: Colonial Country (golf com.) (Ft. Worth). Home: 4316 Briar Haven Rd Fort Worth TX 76109

DIGGS, STEVEN FRANKLIN, advt. agy. exec., radio/TV prodn. co. exec.; b. Oak Ridge, July 3, 1952; s. Herbert Boyd and Verna (Calvert) D.; B.A. in Speech, David Lipscomb Coll., 1974; m. Bonita Louise Crosby, Aug. 8, 1976. Salesman, sales mgr. Dave Floyd & Assos., Nashville, 1974-76; in house advt. and public relations dir. Lloyd White Co., Erie, Pa., 1976-77; owner, pres. The Franklin Group, Inc., Nashville, 1977—. Recipient Southwestern Pub. Co. Club 100 award, 1970. Republican. Mem. Ch. of Christ. Published and recorded musical composition Flight 408. Home: 4608 Xavier Dr Antioch TN 37013 Office: 22 Music Sq W Nashville TN 37203

DILL, ANNE HOLDEN, educator; b. Poplarville, Miss., Mar. 7, 1920; d. James Houston and Florence Elizabeth (Henley) Holden; B.A., U. Ala., 1954, M.A., 1955; Ed.S., 1970; postgrad. U. Miss., 1975-78; m. Elmer Dill, Jan. 25, 1941; children—Winston E., Jane Ann, Caroll Elizabeth Dill Norman. Civilian worker Navy Dept., Washington, World War II; instr. Western world lit. U. Ga. Extension Div., Dublin, 1965-66; instr. English, Gadsden (Ala.) State Jr. Coll., 1966—. Hon. lt. col. staff of Gov. George C. Wallace, 1972. Fellow Internat. Platform Assn.; mem. Am. Assn. Women in Community and Jr. Colls., Ala. Assn. Coll. English Tchrs., S. Central Modern Lang. Assn., Nat. Council Tchrs. of English (judge writing programs 1975-79), Southeastern Conf. English in 2 Yr. Coll., Ala. Council Tchrs. of English, Conf. Coll. Composition and Communication, NEA, Ala. Edn. Assn., Ala. Jr. Coll. Assn., AAUW, DAR. Democrat. Baptist. Research on female characters and roles of women in So. lit. Home: 850 Walnut St Gadsden AL 35901 Office: Gadsden State Jr Coll English Dept George Wallace Dr Gadsden AL 35903

DILL, ROBERT EARL, rubber co. exec.; b. Port Arthur, Tex., Oct. 3, 1923; s. Luther Taylor and Anna Naomi (Parker) D.; B.S. in Agrl. Econ., Tex. A. and M. U., 1950; m. Nellie McBride, July 18, 1953; children—Claire E., Celia A. With Gulf Oil Corp., Port Arthur, 1941-42; lab. technician Neches Butane Products Co., Port Neches, Tex., 1951-57; lab. supr. Firestone Synthetic Rubber & Latex Co., Orange, Tex., 1957-69, personnel rep., 1969—. Bd. dirs. Jr. Achievement, Beaumont, Tex., 1975—, v.p. programs, 1978-79. Served with USAAF 1943-45. Mem. S.W. Placement Assn., Am. Soc. for Personnel Adminstrn., Sabine-Neches Personnel Assn. Baptist. Club: Masons. Address: PO Box 1269 Orange TX 77640

DILLAHUNT, PAUL HUSTON, II, cardiologist; b. Columbus, Ohio, July 31, 1948; s. Paul Huston and Jain (Huston) D.; B.S., Ohio State U., 1970; M.D., 1973; m. Barbara Jean Burkey, July 15, 1972; 1 dau., Christina Jane. Intern, Los Angeles County, U. So. Calif. Med. Center, 1973-74; resident in internal medicine Jacksonville (Fla.) Hosps. Edn. Program, Div. U. Fla. Coll. Medicine, 1974-76; cardiology fellowship Jacksonville Health Edn. Program, 1976-78; practice medicine specializing in cardiology, Jacksonville, 1978—; clin. instr. internal medicine in cardiology U. Fla., Jacksonville, 1978—; mem. staff Baptist Med. Center, Jacksonville. Diplomate Am. Bd. Internal Medicine. Asso. fellow Am. Coll. Cardiology; mem. AMA, A.C.P., Phi Beta Kappa. Office: 820 Prudential Dr Suite 606 Jacksonville FL 32207

DILLAHUNTY, WILBUR HARRIS, U.S. atty.; b. Memphis, June 30, 1928; s. Joseph Silas and Octavia (Jones) D.; J.D., U. Ark., 1954; m. Emma Cox, Nov. 25, 1948; 1 dau., Sharon Kaye. Admitted to Ark. bar; practiced, West Memphis, Ark., 1954-58; U.S. atty. Eastern Ark., Little Rock, 1968-79; exec. asst. to adminstr. SBA, 1979—; West Memphis city atty., 1958-68. Served with AUS, 1945-48. Named Young Man of Year, Crittenden County, Ark., 1961. Mem. Crittenden County Bar Assn. (past pres.), Omicron Delta Kappa, Delta Theta Phi. Club: Meadowbrook Country (West Memphis). Home: 9710 Catskill Rd Little Rock AR 72207

DILLARD, EARLE STERLING, ins. exec.; b. Man, W.Va., Apr. 24, 1925; s. Andrew Sterling and Margaret Grace (Keiffer) D.; student Marshall U., 1953-54; m. Naomi Ruth Ferrell, Aug. 31, 1947; children—Dan Earle, Cherilyn Ruth, David Ferrell, Kevin Andrew, Kerry Paul, Julie Beth. Supr. agts. Security Ins. Co., Huntington, W.Va., 1948-54; pres. Dollar Stores Corp., Huntington, 1971-79, Harlo Corp., Huntington, 1971—; pres., treas. Bloss & Dillard, Inc., Huntington, 1954—; pres. Ins. Mgrs., Inc., Columbus, Ohio, 1977—, Agts. Ins. Markets, Inc., Richmond, Va., 1979—; dir. Huntington Fed. Savs. Loan Assn. Chmn., Huntington Mayor's Adv. Com., 1967-69; pres. Huntington YMCA, 1969-71; v.p. Marshall U. Big Green Scholarship Found., 1980—. Served with USCG, 1943-46; ETO. W.Va. Ins. Agts. Co. Man of Yr., 1977; YMCA Layman of the Yr., 1964. Mem. W.Va. Ins. Assn. (pres. 1969), Am. Assn. Mng. Gen. Agts. (pres. 1974-75), W.Va. Surplus Lines Assn. (pres. 1979—), Am. Legion, V.F.W., C. of C. Baptist. Clubs: Guyan Country, Masons, Lions (pres. 1964-65). Home: 1934 S Englewood Rd Huntington WV 25701 Office: 517 9th St Huntington WV 25701

DILLARD, JAMES HARDY, II, state legislator Va.; b. Charlottesville, Va., Nov. 21, 1933; s. George Budd and Carra Winder (Garrett) D.; B.A., Coll. William and Mary, Williamsburg, Va., 1955; M.A., Am. U., 1970; m. Joyce Woods Butt, 1955; children—Virginia, Elizabeth, Anne, Christy. Tchr., Fairfax County Va., 1959-66, 69—; regional dir. sch. services div. Am. Fgn. Policy Assn., Atlanta, 1966-69; mem. Va. Ho. of Dels. from 19th Dist., 1971—. Mem. Fairfax County Vacat. Edn. Adv. Commn., Springfield (Va.) Youth Activities Com.; chmn. state relations Save Mason Neck Com.; mem. bd. Planned Parenthood Va.; alt. del, Republican Nat. Conv., 1976. Served with USN, 1955-57. Named Outstanding Young Tchr., Lee High Sch., 1965; Outstanding Young Man, Springfield Jaycees, 1966. Mem. Nat., Va., Fairfax County (dir.) edn, assns., Nat., Va. councils social studies, Internat. Lightning Assn., Phi Delta Kappa. Episcopalian. Clubs: Potomac River Jazz, Nat. Yacht. Address: 4709 Briar Patch Ln Fairfax VA 22032

DILLARD, NORMA JEAN, practical nurse; b. Spartanburg, S.C., Mar. 22, 1938; d. John Marshall and Lena (Boyter) Burnett; R.T., Spartanburg Gen. Hosp., 1959; L.P.N., R.D. Anderson Vocational Sch. Practical Nursing, 1972; m. Howard E. Dillard, May 24, 1966 (dec. 1971); children—Cheryl Jean, Homer Howard. X-ray dept. Spartanburg Gen. Hosp., 1957-62; with x-ray clinic, Spartanburg, 1962-64, Startex Bleachery, S.C., 1964-66; emergency room licensed practical nurse Spartanburg Gen. Hosp., 1972-74, Mountview Nursing Home, Spartanburg, 1975-76, Lakeview Nursing Home, Spartanburg, 1976, Camp Haven Nursing Home, Inman, S.C., 1976—. Mem. Greer Community Concert Choir, 1978, 79. Mem. Am. Registry Radiologic Technologists (registered), Nat. Fedn. L.P.N.'s, State Bd. Nursing of S.C. Baptist. Home: Route 1 Box 38 Duncan SC 29334 Office: Blackstock Rd Inman SC 29349

DILLARD, ROBERT GARING (GARY), JR., oil co. exec.; b. Clarendon, Tex., June 18, 1931; s. Robert Garing and Hazel Lynn (Bourland) D.; B.S. in Chemistry, U. Calif. at Los Angeles, 1956; m. Marilyn Ann Broderick, Dec. 28, 1954; children—Mary Catherine, Lynne Anne, Robert Gregary, Carolyn Jean, Jamie Ann, Laurie Diane. Joined Shell Chem. Co., 1956, asst. dept. mgr. ops., Houston, 1963, asst. dept. mgr. market devel. unit Martinez plant, 1964, ops. mgr. Martinez, plant, 1965, plant supt. Shell Point plant, 1966, Houston plant, 1968, plant mgr. Geismar plant, 1969-71, mgr. staff adminstrn., Houston, 1971-74; mgr. Deer Park mfg. complex Shell Oil Co., 1974-76, gen. mgr., Houston, 1976—. Bd. dirs. Bishop Estates Civic Bd., 1965; trustee Nottingham Forest Civic Assn., 1969; chmn. archtl. control com. Wilchester Civic Assn., 1976-77. Served with USN, 1950-53. Mem. Am. Chem. Soc., Tex. Chem. Council (exec. com., chmn. air conservation com.), Tex. Assn. of Bus., Tex. Mid-Continent Oil and Gas, Greater Houston Area Bus. Roundtable (chmn. policy com.), Houston C. of C. (mfrs. com.). Roman Catholic. Clubs: Lakeside Country, Houston Yacht.

DILLARD, RODNEY JEFFERSON, real estate broker; b. Short Hills, N.J., Jan. 1, 1939; s. Albert Jefferson and Anne E. (Willingham) D.; student Morristown Sch. (N.J.), 1953-55, Salisbury Sch. (Conn.), 1955-57; B.A., Rollins Coll., 1961; m. Anne Palfrey Lanston, June 10, 1961; children—Courtney Lanston, Carter Jefferson. With A.M. Kidder Co., N.Y.C., 1961-62; with Previews Inc., N.Y.C., 1962-63, Palm Beach, Fla., 1963-79, regional v.p. 1967-70, v.p., 1970-79; pres., chmn. bd. Illus. Properties, Inc., Palm Beach, 1976—; v.p., dir. Sotheby Park Bernet Internat. Realty Corp., 1979—. Mem. Internat. Real Estate Fedn. Clubs: Palm Beach Yacht, Bath and Tennis (Palm Beach); Travelers (Paris); Windermere Island (Eleuthera, Bahamas). Home: 315 Tangier Ave Palm Beach FL 33480 Office: 155 Worth Ave Palm Beach FL 33480

DILLAWAY, ROBERT BEACHAM, tech. utilization and mktg. cons.; b. Washington, Nov. 10, 1924; s. Robert Gardiner and Ida Louise (Clark) D.; B.S. in Mech. Engring. and Math., U. Mich., 1945; M.S. in Physics, U. Ill., 1951, Ph.D., 1953; postgrad. UCLA, 1953-58; m. Beverly Ann Hercer, Nov. 14, 1971; children—Ronald C., Blair B., R. Keith, Brian P. Maschler, Lauren D. Maschler, Ted A. Maschler. Research and devel. staff mem. Carrier Corp., Syracuse, N.Y., 1945-46, Engring. Research Assos., Washington, 1946-48; prof. mech. engring., U. Ill., 1948-53; aerospace engr.-mgr. N. Am. Aviation Co. div. Rockwell Internat., Los Angeles, 1953-68; asst. to sec. navy for systems analysis, 1968-69; dir. labs., research and devel. programs U.S. Army Materiel Command, Washington, 1969-75; sr. v.p. Cons. Diesel Electric Co., Greenwich, Conn., 1975-76; cons. U.S. Ho. of Reps. Sci. and Tech. Com., Washington, 1976-77; cons. to U.S. and fgn. corps. and govts., 1977—; pres. Global Def. Products Inc., 1977-79. Active PTA, Woodland Hills, Calif., 1956-60; bd. dirs. Los Angeles West Valley YMCA, 1959; pres. alumni bd. U. Ill., 1974-75. Recipient Disting. Alumni award U. Ill., 1975. Fellow ASME, AIAA, Am. Helicopter Soc., Am. Arbitration Assn. (arbitrator), Nat. Aero. Assn. (dir. 1962-72), Am. Def. Preparedness Assn., Assn. U.S. Army, Sigma Xi, Phi Sigma Kappa, Pi Mu Epsilon. Clubs: Cosmos, Army Navy. Author: Fluid Mechanics, 1965; contbr. articles to profl. jours.; patentee in field. Home: 1306 Ballantrae Ct McLean VA 22101 Office: 1901 N Ft Myer Dr Arlington VA 22209

DILLEY, JERRY DALE, diversified industry exec.; b. Dallas, Nov. 24, 1931; s. Loniel Elmer and Mary Magdeline (Graves) D.; student Crozier Tech. Sch., Dallas, 1948-49, Dallas Art Inst., 1946-50; m. Carol Parker, Apr. 5, 1974; children—Marilyn Smith, Paul E., Lori Browning, Wesley C., Trey O., Cassandra K. Shopman, Welding Lab., Dallas, 1948-50, designer, 1950-51, chief engr., 1951-53; v.p., chief engr. Metal Structures Corp., Grapevine, Tex., 1954-58, v.p., gen. mgr., 1958-62; v.p., gen. mgr., dir. Rollform Corp., Dallas, 1961-63; pres., dir. Dilley Corp., 1961-65; exec. v.p., dir. Omega Industries, Inc., Grapevine, 1965—. Recipient award for painting Dallas Mus. Fine Arts, 1941. Mem. Nat. Coil Coaters Assn., Am. Mgmt. Assn., Order Foresters. Home: 1115 Hughes Rd Grapevine TX 76051 Office: 404 Dallas Rd Grapevine TX 76051

DILLIN, JAKE THOMAS, JR., hosp. adminstr.; b. Jonesboro, Ark., Aug. 19, 1945; s. Jake Thomas and Beatrice B. (Ervin) D.; student La. State U., 1964-67; B.S., U. South Fla.; m. Dec. 26, 1965; 1 dau., Traci. Clin. chemist lab. Tampa (Fla.) Gen. Hosp., 1966-71; dir. dept. paramed. tng. Bus. U. of Tampa, 1968-73; toxicologist, lab. mgr. v.p. bd. Doctors Lab. Services, Inc., Tampa, 1972-74; pres. Central Fla. Biols., Orlando and Tampa, 1974-76; lab. adminstrv. dir. Holiday div. Orlando Regional Med. Center, Inc., 1976-79, adminstrv. dir. pharmacies, 1979—; owner Tom Dillin Photography Studio, 1969-72; one-man shows: Tampa Photo, Holiday Hosp. Mem. Orlando Choral Soc. Messiah Chorus, 1977—, Bach Festival Choir, 1979—, U.S. Gymnastics Fedn., 1976—; Pres. bd. dirs. YMCA Lakemont gymnastic group. Licensed, certified med. lab. supr., Fla. Mem. Am. Assn. Clin. Chemists (Recognition award 1978), Am. Soc. Law and Medicine, Am. Soc. Quality Control, Soc. Biomed. Equipment Technicians (charter), Internat. Soc. Blood Transfusion (Paris), Clin. Lab. Mgmt. Assn., Assn. Drug Detection Labs., Med. Electronics and Data Soc. (charter), Tampa Jr. C. of C. (Miss Tampa Pageant chmn. 1972), Jaguar Club Fla. (founder, pres.), E Jag N.Am. (area coordinator). Home: 7529 Compass Dr Orlando FL 32807 Office: Orlando Regional Med Center Orlando FL 32806

DILLMAN, GEORGE FRANKLIN, fin. and mgmt. cons.; b. Coronado, Calif., Sept. 5, 1934; s. Wilbur Mitchell and Meadie (Ables) D.; student Abilene Christian Coll., 1952; B.S., B.B. A., U. Tex., 1958; m. Virginia Gayle Yeary, Sept. 1, 1961; children—Leesa Gayle, Mitchell Lynn, Virginia Louise, Laura Lynn. Asso., Bus. Research Corp. Tex., Austin, 1957-61; dir. econ. research Pacific Western Properties, Inc., Los Angeles, 1961; dir. corporate relations, econ. research Diversa, Inc., Dallas, 1961-62, corp. sec., 1962-65, v.p., corp. sec., dir., 1965-67; chmn. bd., pres. Bonanza Internat. (Bonanza Steak House), 1965-67; chmn. Dillman & Assos. (formerly Dillman-Berry & Assos.), Dallas, 1968—; chmn. exec. com., dir. Richardson Savs. & Loan Assn., 1965-76; chmn. Security Savs. Assn., 1974-75; chmn. exec. com. Dallas Internat. Bank, 1974-76. Mem. univ. bd. Pepperdine U., Los Angeles. Mem. bd., past pres. Dallas Assembly; chmn. Tex. Tourist Devel. Agy., Pub. Health Services Bd. of Dallas County. Served with USNR, 1952-60. Democrat. Mem. Ch. of Christ. Contbr. articles to profl. and ch. jours. Home: 13361 Peyton Dr Dallas TX 75214 Office: 4600 Olin Dallas TX 75240

DILLON, CLARENCE EDWARD, clergyman; b. South Charleston, W.Va., Jan. 30, 1933; s. James Wesley, Sr., and Hurtle Gladys (King) D.; student W.Va. State Coll., 1955-64, Morris Harvey Coll., 1963-64; m. Shirley Ann Hill, Apr. 3, 1953; children—Karen Lynn (Mrs. Johnnie Hayes Milstead), Sharon Kay (Mrs. Anthony Eugene Pompelia), Angela Carol (Mrs. Mark Barnett), Judith Ann. Lab. asst. chemist Union Carbide Chems. Co., 1951-64; ordained to ministry Ch. of God-Anderson, Ind., 1965; pastor 1st Ch. of God, Point Pleasant, W.Va., 1964-67, Rock Creek Ch. of God, Bessemer, Ala., 1967-72, Parkview Ch. of God, Meridian, Miss., 1972-75, First Ch. of God, Princeton, W.Va., 1975—. Chmn. Ala. Ministers Fellowship Ch. of God, 1970-71; active numerous regional ch. bds. and coms., chmn. Miss. credentials com., 1974-75, camp meeting program com.; chmn. W.Va. State Ministerial Assn.; sec. W.Va. Gen. Assembly; trustee Warner So. Coll., Lake Wales, Fla. Served with AUS, 1953-55; ETO. Mason. Home: 1815 Honaker Ave Princeton WV 24740 Office: 301 Mahood Ave Princeton WV 24740

DILLON, JAMES LEE, pub. and communications co. exec.; b. Martinsville, Va., Dec. 17, 1928; s. Alton Milton and Betty Ruth (Thomas) D.; B.S., Va. Commonwealth U., 1952; postgrad Harvard U.; children—Christopher S., Mark T. Planning and service mgr. Norfolk (Va.) Newspapers, Inc., 1955-61; dir. sales devel. Richmond Newspapers, Inc., 1961-65, asst. to advt. dir., 1965, asst. advt. dir., 1966-68, advt. dir., 1969-72, bus. mgr., 1972-73, v.p., gen. mgr., 1973-77; v.p. Media Gen., Inc., Richmond, 1977—. Chmn. bd. Richmond Montessori Sch., 1968; v.p. R.E. Lee council Boy Scouts Am., 1977-79; bd. dirs. Better Bus. Bur., Richmond, 1970-73. Served with USMC, 1953-55. Mem. Am. Newspaper Pubs. Assn., So. Newspaper Assn., Internat. Newspaper Advt. Execs., Va. Press Assn., Advt. Club Richmond, Greater Richmond C. of C., Sales and Mktg. Execs. Club. Clubs: Commonwealth, Bull and Bear. Office: 333 E Grace St Richmond VA 23219

DILLON, ROGER HOWARD, ednl. adminstr.; b. Oak Park, Ill., Oct. 19, 1936; s. Phil Stiver and Esther Alleen (Hopkins) D.; B.S., Purdue U., 1963; Ph.D., Mich. State U., 1973; m. Georgiana Williams Hutter, Oct. 1, 1960; children—Sheri Lyn, Lee Ann. Coordinator supervision programs Purdue U., W. Lafayette, Ind., 1963-64; tchr. secondary schs., Bath, Mich., 1964-65; conf. cons. Mich. State U., East Lansing, 1965-67; dir. edn. and tng. St. Lawrence Hosp., Lansing, Mich., 1971-72; dir. ops. S.E. Tenn. Area Health Edn. Center, Chattanooga, 1973-76; dir. research, devel. and ednl. resources U. Tenn. Coll. Medicine, Chattanooga, 1976—, instr. Higher Mgmt. Inst., 1974-76. Bd. dirs. Tenn. Valley Lions Kidney Found., 1974-79, v.p., 1978-79. Served with USN, 1956-59. Mem. Am. Ednl. Research Assn., Am. Assn. Higher Edn., Am. Acad. Polit. and Social Scis., Assn. Ednl. Communications and Tech., Am. Mgmt. Assn., Health Edn. Media Assn., Health Scis. Communication Assn., Iota Lambda Sigma, Phi Delta Kappa. Clubs: Lions (v.p. 1976-77), Bal Harbor Yacht; Masons. Instrumental in devel. of preventive and rehab. programs for southeast Tenn., northwest Ga. and northeast Ala. regional areas. Home: 4924 Lake Haven Dr Chattanooga TN 37416 Office: College of Medicine Univ of Tenn Suite 400 921 E 3d St Chattanooga TN 37403

DI LORETO, DANIEL VICTOR, JR., broadcasting co. exec.; b. Ravenna, Ohio, Sept. 21, 1944; s. Daniel Victor and Rose M. (Ferrara) DiL.; B.S. in Advt. and Mktg., U. Fla.; m. Elaine Breton, Nov. 10, 1965; children—Victor, Denise. Account exec. Miami Herald, 1966-69; sales mgr. Storz Broadcasting Co., Miami, 1969-71; gen. sales mgr. Cox Broadcasting Co., Miami, 1971-75; v.p., gen. mgr. Storer Broadcasting Co., Miami, 1975—; vol. instr. dept. communications U. Miami. Active United Way, Miami, Muscular Dystrophy, Miami. Mem. South Fla. Broadcasters Assn., Miami Ad Fedn (dir.), Nat. Assn. Broadcasters, Fla. Assn. Broadcasters, Alpha Delta Sigma. Roman Catholic. Office: 710 Brickell Ave Miami FL 33131

DILS, ROBERT JAMES, educator; b. Dayton, Ohio, Oct. 2, 1919; d. Lawrence Elsworth and Maudie Marguerette (Koogler) D.; B.S., Eastern Ky. U., 1939-43; M.A., Marshall U., 1960; postgrad. Ohio State U., 1962-64; m. Juanita B. Graber, Aug. 9, 1947; children—Susan (Mrs. Leroy Mayne), Robert James II, Norma, Jo. Tchr. Ashland (Ky.) High Sch., 1948-51, Jr. Coll., Ashland, 1951-57; chmn. sci. dept. Paul G. Blazer High Sch., Ashland, 1958-62; asso. prof. sci. Marshall U., Huntington, W.Va., 1964—. Mem. exec. com. Tri-State council Boy Scouts Am., 1970—; radiol. def. officer Cabel County Civil Def., 1968—. Served with USAAF, 1943-45. Decorated Air medal. NSF grantee. Mem. AAAS, Phi Delta Kappa, Kappa Delta Pi. Republican. Baptist (deacon 1964—). Home: 2514 Elm St Ashland KY 41101 Office: 3d Ave and 16th Huntington WV 25701

DILWORTH, BILLY D., newspaperman; b. Martin, Ga., Oct. 4; 1934; s. B.Q. and Pearl (Davis) D.; student journalism U. Ga. Ga. editor Anderson (S.C.) Ind., 1953-63; state editor Atlanta Times, 1964-65; state editor Athens (Ga.) Daily News, 1967-72, roving editor, columnist, 1975—; state editor Anderson Independent, 1972-75; host programs radio sta. WLET, Toccoa, Ga., 1960—, sta. WSPA-TV, Spartanburg, S.C., 1968—. Mem. Ga. Scholarship Commn., 1971—. Recipient A.P. award reporting and news photo, 1963; nominee Disk Jockey of Yr., Country Music Assn., 1974-75, 75-76, 77-78, 78-79. First newsman to announce Presdl. candidacy of Jimmy Carter. Address: Box 117 Carnesville GA 30521

DILWORTH, EDWIN EARLE, obstetrician; b. Jasper, Ala., June 28, 1914; s. Tranny and Bertie (Caldwell) D.; A.B., U. Ala., 1936; M.D., Tulane U., 1940; m. Neida May Humphrey, June 17, 1939; children—John Edwin, Robert Earle, Nancy. Intern, Shreveport Charity Hosp., 1940-41, resident, 1941-44; pvt. practice medicine specializing in obstetrics and gynecology, Shreveport, 1959-60; chief of service dept. obstetrics and gynecology Schumpert Meml. Med. Center, Shreveport, 1951, pres. staff, 1954; chief of service dept. obstetrics and gynecology Confederate Meml. Med. Center, Shreveport, 1954-76, pres. staff, 1959; clin. prof. obstetrics and gynecology La. State U. Sch. Medicine, Shreveport, 1967—. Head med. div. United Way, 1972. Served to capt. M.C., AUS, 1944-46; ETO. Diplomate Am. Bd. Obstetrics and Gynecology (also recert.). Fellow Am. Coll. Obstetrics and Gynecology (founding), A.C.S.; mem. Central, So., Southeastern assns. obstetrics and gynecology. Club: Shreveport Skeet. Contbr. articles to profl. jours. Home: 660 Thora St Shreveport LA 71106 Office: 865 Margaret Pl Shreveport LA 71101

DIMICH, DENISE, occupational therapist; b. South Bend, Ind., Jan. 18, 1952; d. George and Grace (Milovich) D.; student Ind. U., 1970-72; B.S., Med. Coll. Ga., 1974. Staff occupational therapist in psychiatry Meml. Hosp., Sarasota, Fla., 1974-76, sr. therapist in psychiatry, 1976-79, service coordinator dept. occupational therapy, 1979—; occupational therapy intern supr. in psychiatry, 1974-78, center coordinator clin. edn. Occupational Therapy Dept., 1979—; sec. ednl. council, med. coll. Ga., 1979-81. Mem. Am. Occupational Therapy Assn. Club: Palm Aire Tennis. Home: 3325 Bee Ridge Rd Sarasota FL 33579 Office: 1901 Arlington St Sarasota FL 33580

DIMINO, MICHAEL J., endocrinologist; b. Norristown, Pa., Mar. 12, 1942; s. Joseph and Theresa D.; B.S., Villanova U., 1964; Ph.D., Rutgers U., 1971; m. Anne V. Tiblis, Sept. 11, 1965; children—Michael J., Stephen P., Anne M. Asst. research biochemist U. Mich. Med. Sch., Ann Arbor, 1971-73; research asso. Sinai Hosp., Detroit, 1973-78; asst. prof. Wayne State U. Sch. Medicine, Detroit, 1976-78; asso. prof. biochemistry Eastern Va. Med. Sch., Norfolk, 1979—. NIH fellow, 1968-71, 72-73; NSF grantee, 1978—. Mem. Am. Physiol. Soc., Endocrine Soc., Soc. for Exptl. Biology and Medicine, Soc. for Study of Reprodn., Sigma Xi. Roman Catholic. Contbr. articles on endocrinology to profl. jours. Home: 2205 Hidden Creek Ct Virginia Beach VA 23454 Office: Eastern Va Med Sch PO Box 1980 Norfolk VA 23501

DIMITROFF, EDWARD, chemist; b. Nancy, France, Feb. 27, 1927; s. Stantcho Stantcheff and Marguerite Louise (Virrion) D.; student U. Medicine, Nancy, 1946-48; B.S., U. Denver, 1956; M.S., St. Marys U., San Antonio, 1965; m. Dorothy Mae Queen, Nov. 24, 1951; children—John, Monique. Came to U.S., 1950, naturalized, 1955. Aero. research chemist Naval Ordnance Test Sta., China Lake, Calif., 1956-59; mgr., dir. energy tech. ops. S.W. Research Inst., San Antonio, 1959—. Fellow Am. Inst. Chemists; mem. Am. Chem. Soc., ASTM, Soc. Automotive Engrs. Contbr. articles to profl. jours. Home: 4838 Rollingfield Dr San Antonio TX 78228 Office: 6220 Culebra Rd San Antonio TX 78284

DIMLER, MICHAEL, pediatric surgeon, educator; b. S.I., N.Y., Apr. 21, 1943; s. William Alexander and Anna (Fadok) D.; B.S., Fordham U., 1964; M.D., Georgetown U., 1968; m. Ellen Patricia Zagrella, July 16, 1966; children—Jennifer Lynn, Justin Patrick. Intern surgery Georgetown U. Hosp., Washington, 1968-69, gen. surgery resident, 1969-74; fellow pediatric surgery Cin. Children's Hosp., 1974-76; asst. prof. surgery, chief div. pediatric surgery E. Tenn. State U. Coll. Medicine, Johnson City, 1976—. Served to lt. col. M.C., U.S. Army, 1976-79. Diplomate Am. Bd. Surgery. Mem. Assn. Acad. Surgery, Tenn. Med. Assn., Tenn. Pediatric Assn., Washington/Carter/Unicoi Med. Soc. Roman Catholic. Contbr. articles to profl. jours. Home: 413 Lamont St Johnson City TN 37601 Office: PO Box 19 750A E Tenn State Univ Coll Medicine Johnson City TN 37601

DINCULEANU, NICOLAE, mathematician, educator; b. Padea, Romania, Feb. 26, 1925; came to U.S., 1976, naturalized, 1980; s. Nicolae and Frusina (Lusca) Dobrescu; Engr., Poly. Inst. Bucarest, 1950; licencié in Math., U. Bucarest, 1951, Ph.D., 1957; m. Elena Constantinescu, Feb. 9, 1959. Prof. math. U. Bucarest, Romania, 1950-78; vis. research prof. U. Fla., Gainesville, 1971-76, prof. dept. math., 1976—; dep. dir. Math. Inst. of Romanian Acad., 1965-75; vis. prof. Queen's U., Kingston, Ont., Can., 1966-67; disting. Mellon vis. prof. U. Pitts., 1970-71. Recipient prize of Romanian Acad., 1964; NSF grantee, 1972-74. Mem. Am. Math. Soc. Christian Orthodox. Author 4 univ. textbooks, monographs; contbr. articles to profl. publs. Home: 610 NW 22nd St Gainesville FL 32603 Office: Walker Hall Math Department University of Florida Gainesville FL 32611

DINGER, DONALD BRACKETT, govt. ofcl.; b. Providence, Nov. 30, 1935; s. Fred Bert and Marguerete Elsie (King) D.; B.S., U. R.I., 1958; M.S., George Washington U., 1964, A.P.S., 1978; m. Grace Ann Monroe, Aug. 13, 1960; 1 dau., Lynn Ann. Elec. power sources research engr. Engr. Research and Devel. Labs., U.S. Army, Fort Belvoir, Va., 1958-61, nuclear electromagnetic pulse effects project leader, 1961-65, dir. Army Nuclear Electromagnetic Pulse Effects Lab., 1965-71, asso. tech. dir. for research and devel., 1971-78, tech. dir., 1978—. Founder, Mt. Vernon (Va.) Civic Assn., 1963. Recipient Commanders award for sci. achievement U.S. Army, 1965; Civilian Meritorious Service award Dept. Army, 1979. Fellow Wash. Acad. Sci.; mem. IEEE, Am. Def. Preparedness Assn., Sigma Xi, Omega Rho. Presbyterian (deacon 1971-73, elder 1975-77). Clubs: Belle Haven Country, Mansion House, Mansion House Yacht. Contbr. articles to profl. jours. Home: 9008 Volunteer Dr Alexandria VA 22309 Office: Commander US Army Mobility Equipment Research and Development Command Attn DRDME-ZT Fort Belvoir VA 22060

DINGFEIDER, STEVEN PETER, psychologist, mental health service adminstr.; b. Mpls., May 9, 1944; s. Sigbert and Elizabeth (Neu) D.; B.A., U. Minn., 1966; M.A., Ind. State U., 1968, Ph.D., 1971; m. Claire Elaine and Shechter, Dec. 19, 1965;

children—Jennifer Ann, Scott Allen, Heidi Lynn. Psychologist, Moore-Porter Evaluation Clinic, Terre Haute, Ind., 1968; sch. psychologist Vigo County (Ind.) Sch. Corp., Terre Haute, 1969-70; clin. psychologist Katherine Hamilton Mental Health Center, Terre Haute, 1970-72, program dir., 1972-74; chem. dependency coordinator No. Pines Unified Services Center, Cumberland, Wis., 1973—. Chmn. Vigo County Coordinating Council on Alcohol and Drug Abuse, 1972-74; adj. prof. psychology Ind. State U., Terre Haute, 1972; mem. drug abuse com. Ind. State Dept., 1972-74; cons. psychologist Gibault Sch. for Boys, Terre Haute, 1974; area dir. Sandhills Mental Health Center, Pinehurst, N.C., 1977—. Mem. Gov.'s Advisory Council on Alcohol and Drug Abuse, State of Ind., 1974. Recipient Becker award Ind. State U., 1968. Mem. Am., Ind. (chmn. div. sch. psychology 1973-74) psychol. assns., Ind. Assn. of Counselors on Alcohol and Drug Abuse (v.p. 1973-74), Wis. Assn. Community Human Services Program, Wis. Assn. Chem. Abuse Coordinators (chmn. 1976), Area Dirs. Assn. for N.C. (sec.-treas. 1979—), Lambda Psi Sigma, Phi Delta Kappa. Address: Box 554 Seven Lakes West End NC 27376

DINGLEDINE, RAYMOND CARLYLE, JR., historian; b. Petersburg, Va., Jan. 15, 1919; s. Raymond Carlyle and Agness Browne (Stribling) D.; B.A., U. Va., 1940, M.A., 1941, Ph.D., 1947; m. Emily Elizabeth Reel, Aug. 17, 1943; children—Anne S., Raymond Carlyle, III, Emily Merritt, Elizabeth R. Asst. prof. history Ala. Poly. Inst., 1947-48; asst. prof. James Madison U. (formerly Madison Coll.), Harrisonburg, Va., 1948-51, asso. prof., 1951-60, prof., 1960—, head dept. history, 1965—. Mem. Harrisonburg City Council, 1970, 72—, Harrisonburg Recreation Commn., 1972—; exec. bd. Valley Program for Aging Services, Fisherville, Va., 1974—; mem. Harrisonburg-Rockingham Independence Bicentennial Commn., 1974—; elder Presby. Ch., Harrisonburg, 1949—, trustee, 1969—. Served to 1st. lt. Signal Corps and AC, U.S. Army, 1942-46. Mem. Am., So. hist. assns., Orgn. Am. Historians, Va. Social Sci. Assn. (pres. 1967-68), Va. Hist. Soc., Phi Beta Kappa, Omicron Delta Kappa, Phi Alpha Theta. Club: Kiwanis (pres. Harrisonburg chpt. 1970-71). Author: (with Lena Barksdale and Marion Nesbitt) Virginia's History, 1956, rev. edit., 1964; Madison College: The First Fifty Years, 1908-1958, 1959; contbr.: America, The Middle Period: Essays in Honor of Bernard Mayo, 1973; contbr. articles to encys. Home: 320 West View St Harrisonburg VA 22807 Office: Dept History James Madison U Harrisonburg VA 22801

DINNING, JAMES SMITH, nutritionist, educator; b. Franklin, Ky., Sept. 28, 1922; s. James Starks and Fanny Blanch (Smith) D.; B.S., U. Ky., 1946; Ph.D., Okla. State U., 1948; D.Sc.(hon.), Mahidol U., Bangkok, Thailand, 1975; m. Sally Sue Hensley, Oct. 28, 1944; children—Kay Sue, James M., Robin J., Randal. Starks prof. biochemistry Sch. Medicine, U. Ark., Little Rock, 1948-60; asso. dir. Rockefeller Found., N.Y.C., 1960-75; prof. nutrition, U. Fla., Gainesville, 1975—. Recipient Lederle Med. Faculty award, 1958, Mead Johnson award, 1964; grantee fed. agys. Mem. Am. Inst. Nutrition, Am. Soc. Biol. Chemists, Soc. Exptl. Biology and Medicine, Sigma Xi. Democrat. Editor: Jour. Nutrition, 1979—. Contbr. articles on nutrition to research publs. Home: 2554 SW 14th Dr Gainesville FL 32608

DIODENE, ALONZO NELSON, JR., physician; b. New Orleans, July 10, 1941; s. Alonzo and Gladys Marie (Knoll) D.; B.S., La. State U., 1963, M.D., 1967; m. Jeanelle Jude Bourgeois, June 15, 1963; children—Paula Jeanelle. Intern, Charity Hosp. La., New Orleans, 1967-68; resident in surgery Ochsner Found. Hosp., New Orleans, 1968-69; resident in orthopedic surgery Walter Reed Gen. Hosp., Washington, 1969-72; fellow in hand surgery, 1976-77; commd. capt. U.S. Army, 1969, advanced through grades to lt. col., 1976; asst. chief orthopedic services, chief hand surgery services Dwight David Eisenhower Army Med. Center, Fort Gordon, Ga., 1977-80; ret., 1980; practice medicine specializing in orthopedic surgery, New Orleans, 1980—. Diplomate Am. Bd. Orthopedic Surgery. Fellow Am. Acad. Orthopedic Surgeons, Soc. Mil. Orthopedic Surgeons. Roman Catholic. Democrat. Office: 1538 Louisiana Ave New Orleans LA 70115

DI PIETRO, ROBERT JOSEPH, linguist, educator; b. Endicott, N.Y., July 18, 1932; s. Americo and Mary DiP.; B.A., SUNY, Binghamton, 1954; M.A., Harvard U., 1955; Ph.D., Cornell U., 1960; m. Vincenzina Angela Giallo, Sept. 5, 1953; children—Angela Maria, Mark Andrew. Instr., English, Boston Sch. Modern Lang., 1955-56; instr., grad. fellow Cornell U., Ithaca, N.Y., 1957-60; jr. lectr. linguistics U. Rome, 1960; asst. prof. linguistics Georgetown U., Washington, 1961-64, asso. prof., 1964-69, prof., 1969-78, Andrew Mellon disting. lectr. linguistics, 1975-77, head div. Italian, 1966-68; prof., chmn. dept. langs. U. Del., 1978—; sr. lectr. linguistics U. Madrid, 1963-64; mem. adv. bd. Polish-Am. Contrastive Study Project, 1974—. Decorated cavaliere ufficiale (Italy); Fulbright grantee, 1960, 63. Mem. Am. Assn. Tchrs. Italian (chpt. pres. 1968-69), Linguistic Soc. Am., AAAS, Am. Anthrop. Assn., Linguistics Assn. Can. and U.S. (exec. bd. 1974—), Washington Linguistics Club (pres. 1967-68), Nat. Italian Am. Found. (dir. 1979—). Author: (with F.B. Agard) Sounds of English and Italian (Vol. I), 1965, Grammatical Structures of English and Italian (Vol. II), 1965, rev. edit., 1969, Language Structures in Contrast, 1971, rev. edit., 1978; Language as Human Creation, 1976; Semiotics of Musical Theatre, 1979; contbr. articles in field to profl. jours.; book rev. editor Modern Lang. Jour., 1972-77; founder, editor Interfaces newsletter, 1974—; mem. editorial bd. Italian-Americana, the N.A.B.E. Jour., 1979—.

DIPLACIDO, FRANCIS PAUL, JR., dentist; b. Phila., Dec. 25, 1934; s. Francis Paul and Elizabeth Marie (deMaria) DiP.; B.S. in Biology, St. Josephs Coll., 1956; D.D.S., U. Pa. Sch. Dentistry, 1962; postgrad. U. Pa. Grad. Sch. Medicine, 1965; m. Noreen M. Bamford, June 14, 1969; children—Francis Paul, III, Damon Samuel, Denise Elizabeth. Resident oral surgery U. Pa., 1965-68; pvt. practice oral surgery, Fort Myers, Fla., 1968—. Sec., S.W. Fla. Flyers; treas., dir. Flordeco, Inc. Pres., Lee County Health Adv. Council; bd. dirs. Lee County YMCA, S. Central Fla. Health Systems Council. Served with AUS, 1962-65. Diplomate Am. Bd. Oral Surgery. Mem. Am., Fla. dental assns., Southwest Fla. Dental Soc. (pres. 1974), Am. Soc. Oral Surgeons, Internat. Assn. Oral Surgeons, Internat. Soc. Maxillofacial Surgeons, Am. Dental Soc. Anesthesiology, Southeastern Soc. Oral Surgeons, Fla. Soc. Oral and Maxillofacial Surgeons. Republican. Roman Catholic. Clubs: Cypress Lake Country, Royal Palm Yacht (Ft. Myers). Home: 6696 Overlook Dr Fort Myers FL 33901 Office: 3900 S Broadway Fort Myers FL 33901

DIPPY, THEODORE ALBERT, physician; b. Phila., June 25, 1925; s. Robert Henry and Clara Jean (Dorzenbach) D.; B.S., Emory U., 1950, M.D., 1953; m. Elizabeth Cannon, Dec. 29, 1962; children—Theodore A., Reece Culloden, Philip Alan, Lee Kimball, Mark Christopher. Intern, Piedmont Hosp., Atlanta, 1953-54; resident Ga. Bapt. Hosp., 1954-56; pvt. practice medicine specializing in pediatrics Winter Park, Fla., 1956—; head pediatric dept. Fla. Hosp., Orlando, 1956-66, staff, 1966—; mem. staff Winter Park Meml. Hosp., Mercy Hosp., Orlando; med. dir. United Cerebral Palsy, Orlando, Fla., 1958—. Mem. Orange County Sch. Bd., 1978—. Served with USAAF, 1943-45. Mem. Am. Acad. Pediatrics, Am. Acad. Cerebral Palsy and Devel. Disabilities, Orange County Med. Soc., Fla. Med. Assn., Internat. Platform Assn. Home: 921 N Lake Sybelia Dr Maitland FL 32751 Office: 220 Edinburgh Dr Winter Park FL 32789

DIRKS, KENNETH RAY, pathologist, army officer, clin. adminstr.; b. Newton, Kans., Feb. 11, 1925; s. Jacob Kenneth and Ruth Viola (Penner) D.; M.D., Washington U., St. Louis, 1947; m. Betty Jean Worsham, June 9, 1946; children—Susan Jan, Jeffery Mark, Deborah Anne, Timothy David, Melissa Jane. Rotating intern St. Louis City Hosp., 1948, asst. resident in gen. surgery, 1948-49; resident in pathology VA Hosp., Jefferson Barracks, Mo., 1951-53, resident in pathology, asst. chief lab. service, Indpls., 1953-54; resident in pathology Letterman Army Hosp., San Francisco, 1956-57; fellow in tropical medicine and parasitology, La. State U., Central Am., 1958; asst. in pathology Washington U. Sch. Medicine, St. Louis, 1952-53; asst. chief, lab. service, VA Hosp., Jefferson Barracks, Mo., 1953; instr. pathology U. Ind. Med. Center, Indpls., 1953-54; commd. capt. M.C. U.S. Army, 1954, advanced through grades to maj. gen., 1976; dir. research, Med. Research and Devel. Command, Washington, 1968-69, dep. comdr., 1969-71, comdr., 1973-76; dep. comdr. Med. Research Inst. Infectious Diseases, Ft. Detrick, Frederick, Md., 1972-73, comdr., 1973; comdr. Fitzsimons Army Med. Center, Denver, 1976-77; supt. Acad. Health Scis., Fort Sam Houston, 1977—. Decorated Legion of Merit with one oak leaf cluster, Army Commendation medal with one oak leaf cluster; diplomate Am. Bd. Pathology. Fellow Coll. Am. Pathologists, Internat. Acad. Pathology. Contbr. articles to med. jours. Office: Acad Health Scis US Army Fort Sam Houston TX 78234

DI SANTO, GRACE JOHANNE DEMARCO (MRS. FRANK MICHAEL DI SANTO), poet, civic worker; b. Derby, Conn., July 12, 1924; d. Richard and Fannie (DeMarco) De Marco; student N.Y. U. Sch. Journalism, 1941-43; A.B. in English, Belmont Abbey Coll., 1974; m. Frank Michael Di Santo, Aug. 30, 1946; children—Frank Richard, Bernadette Mary, Roxanne Judith. Newswriter, Australian Asso. Press, N.Y.C., 1942-43; staff reporter Ansonia Sentinel, Derby, 1943-45; feature writer, drama critic Bridgeport Herald, New Haven, 1945-46; editor monthly bull. Pa. State Coll. Optometry, Phila., 1947-48; free-lance writer, 1949-54; founder, pres. Broad Investors Ltd., Morganton, N.C., 1966-67. Pres. Burke County chpt. N.C. Symphony Soc., 1968-70; mem. exec. bd. Community Concerts Assn., 1962-73; Burke County chmn. nat. humanities series Woodrow Wilson Fellowship Found., 1971-73. Bd. dirs. Burke county chpt. March of Dimes, 1966-72; trustee N.C. Symphony Soc., 1965-73; trustee, bd. dirs. North State Acad., Hickory, N.C., 1973—. Mem. Am. Acad. Poets, Poetry Council N.C., N.C. Poetry Soc., Delta Epsilon Sigma. Republican. Roman Catholic. Clubs: Grandfather Golf and Country (Linville, N.C.); Mimosa Hills Golf. Author: (poems) The Eye Is Single. Address: 218 Riverside Dr Morganton NC 28655 also Grandfather Golf and Country Club Linville NC 28646

DISCH, JAMES GEORGE, educator; b. Houston, Nov. 21, 1947; s. Dorothy Ethel (Seaman) D.; B.S. cum laude, U. Houston, 1969, M.Ed., 1970; P.E.D., Ind. U., 1973; m. Cathryn Freeman, Dec. 18, 1976. Instr., asst. intramural dir. U. Houston, 1970-71; research asst. Ind. U., 1971-73; adj. asst. prof. edn. statistics U. Houston, 1973-78; asst. prof. dept. health and phys. edn. Rice U., Houston, 1973-79, asso. prof., 1979—; statis cons. master's and doctoral theses U. Houston, 1975—, Health and Tennis Corp. Am., 1974—, Dallas Cowboys, 1977—; statis. adv. U.S. Olympic Com. on Track and Field, 1978—. Recipient Honorable Mention Service award U.S. Volleyball Assn., 1975, Brown Coll. Teaching Excellence award Rice U., 1975-76; NDEA Title IV fellow Ind. U., 1971-73. Mem. AAHPER and Dance (sec. nat. measurement and evaluation council 1979-80), Am. Ednl. Research Assn., Tex. Assn. Health, Phys. Edn. and Recreation, Phi Eta Sigma, Omicron Delta Kappa, Phi Delta Kappa, Phi Epsilon Kappa. Contbr. articles in field to profl. jours. Home: 6511 Wanda Ln Houston TX 77074 Office: Dept Health and Phys Edn Houston TX 77001

DISEND, DAVID SAUL, ednl. adminstr.; b. Lakewood, N.J., Nov. 26, 1952; s. William and Binnie Bella (Kursh) D.; B.A., New Coll., Fla., 1975; M.A.T., Duke U., 1977; postgrad. Coll. William and Mary, 1977. Tutor, Pomfret (Conn.) Sch., 1973; instr. New Coll., Sarasota, Fla., 1974-75; acad. dean Christchurch (Va.) Sch., 1976—, instr. English dept., 1976, head dept. English, 1976; test center dir. Ednl. Testing Service, Christchurch, Va., 1977—. Mem. Internat. Soc. Gen. Semantics, Assn. Supervision and Curriculum Devel., Council Basic Edn., Va. Assn. Tchrs. English, Nat. Council Tchrs. of English, Potomac and Chesapeake Assn. Coll. Admissions Counselors, Assos. for Research on Pvt. Edn. Jewish. Contbr. poems to lit. publs. and articles on edn. to profl. publs.; cons. editor The Clearinghouse, 1979—. Address: Christchurch School Christchurch VA 23031

DISHER, DAVID ALAN, data processing co. exec.; b. Chgo., Apr. 15, 1944; s. Hugh George and Beatrice Rose (Selmanovitz) D.; S.B.E.E. (Levy Engring. scholar), Mass. Inst. Tech., 1965, S.M.E.E. (Inst. fellow), 1966; m. Vivian Doak, Apr. 15, 1979; children by former marriage—Carol Ann, Karl Theodore. Mathematician Shell Devel. Co., Houston, 1966-68; sr. engr. Tex. Instruments Co., Houston, 1968; research geophysicist Geocom Inc., New Orleans, 1969-70; owner, dir. research Disher Cons. Service, Houston, 1970-73; chmn. bd. dirs., pres. Seismic Programming Corp., Houston, 1973—; chmn. bd. dirs. Seismic Programming Internat. Corp., Houston. Mem. Soc. Exploration Geophysicists, IEEE, European Assn. Exploration Geophysicists, Mensa. Inventor in field. Home and Office: 1006 Redfish Hitchcock TX 77563

DISSLY, DONALD DYER, research co. exec.; b. Lewistown, Mont., Jan. 7, 1922; s. William Gustav and Ella Maude (Dyer) D.; B.A., Reed Coll., 1941; B.S. in Bus. and Engring. Adminstrn., Mass. Inst. Tech., 1943; m. Elizabeth Tator, June 4, 1942; children—Cheryl Patricia, Kathryn Louise. Prodn. research engr. Douglas Aircraft Co., Santa Monica, Calif., 1943-44; in charge engring. and research Boss Mfg. Co., Kewanee, Ill., 1946-50; civilian chief mfg. div. U.S. Army Q.M.C. Depot, Jeffersonville, Ind., 1950-54; in charge research and devel. Louisville Courier Jour. and Times Co., Louisville, 1954-64; dir. Research Inst. Am. Newspaper Pubs. Assn., Easton, Pa., 1964-66; pres. Dissly Systems Corp., Easton, 1966-74; pres. Dissly Research Corp., Easton, 1970-76, chmn. bd., Louisville, 1976—, also dir. Trustee, Easton Hosp. Bd., 1969-73. Served with USAAF, 1944-46; PTO. Mem. Nat. Micrograinic Assn. Club: Jefferson (Louisville). Home: 3600 Falls Bluff Ct Louisville KY 40222 Office: 620 S 5th St Louisville KY 40202

DISSTON, HARRY, author, bus. exec., horseman; b. Red Bank, N.J., Nov. 23, 1899; s. Eugene John Kauffmann and Frances Matilda Disston; A.B., Amherst Coll., 1921; m. Valerie Ivy Duval, Mar. 26, 1930 (dec. 1951); children—Robin John Duval, Geoffrey Whitmore; m. 2d, Catherine Sitler John, Aug. 26, 1960. With N.Y. Telephone Co., 1921-32, with AT&T, N.Y.C., 1932-60, exec. tng. student, dist. traffic supt., sales engr., dist. mgr., adv. staff engr., adv. staff exec. ind. co. relations, 1951-60; coordinator devel. activities, placement dir. Grad. Sch. Bus. Adminstrn., U. Va.; v.p. Equine Motion Analysis, Ltd., 1979—; dir. horse and cattle leasing AMVEST Leasing Corp., Charlottesville, Va. Aide-de-camp to gov. Va.; chmn. Louisa County Electoral Bd.; mem. Va. Bd. Mil. Affairs; chmn. finance com. Republican party Va.; chmn. Louisa County Rep. Com. Vice pres., dir. Park Ave. Assn Mem. exec. com. Episcopal Diocese of Va., also pres. council, region 15; trustee Grant Monument Assn., Va. Outdoors Found.; bd. dirs. Atlantic Rural Expn., Lee-Jackson Found.; chmn., bd. dirs. Charlottesville-Albemarle Clean Community Commn., 1978—. Served from maj. to col., cav. and gen. staff corps, 1941-46; PTO; comdg. officer 107th Regtl. Combat Team, N.Y.N.G., 1947-57; brig. gen. ret. Awarded Legion of Merit, Bronze Star with oak leaf cluster; comdr. Order of Boliver; Philippine Liberation Medal; Medal of Merit with Swords, Free Poland. Mem. Am. Horse Shows Assn. (judge, steward, tech. del.), Vets. 7th Regt., N.Y. Soc. Mil. and Naval Officers World Wars (past pres.), Vet. Corps Arty., Mil. Order Fgn. Wars, Mil. Order World Wars, Am. Legion, Res. Officers Assn. (chpt. pres.), St. Georges Soc., St. Andrews Soc., Va. Thoroughbred Assn., U.S. Pony Clubs (gov.), Phi Beta Kappa, Phi Kappa Psi. Clubs: Torch (pres. Charlottesville-Albermarle); Union; Amherst; Church of New York; Farmington Country, Greencroft, Jack Jouett Bridle Trails (pres.) (Charlottesville, Va.); The Pilgrims; Keswick Hunt, Keswick of Va. Author: Equestionnaire, 1947; Riding Rhymes, 1951; Know About Horses, 1961; Young Horseman's Handbooks, 1962; Elementary Dressage, 1971; Beginning Polo, 1973; several mag. articles on mil., equine and bus. subjects; contbr. to Ency. Brit. Home: Hidden Hill Farm Keswick VA 22947 Office: 1 Boar's Head Pl Charlottesville VA 22901

DITCHEY, ROBERT LOUIS, airline exec.; b. Pottsville, Pa., Jan. 9, 1941; s. Francis Joseph and Ruth Virginia (Leymeister) D.; B.S., U.S. Naval Acad., 1962; M.S. in Aero. Engring., Naval Postgrad. Sch., 1969; Aero. Engr., Calif. Inst. Tech., 1973; m. Barbara A. Boretsky, Oct. 13, 1962; children—Robert L., Carol R., Adrienne B. Commd. ensign U.S. Navy, 1962, advanced through grades to lt. comdr., 1976; served with Patrol Squadron 10, N. Atlantic, Iceland, Norway, 1964-67; ordnance officer U.S.S. Enterprise, 1969-71; with Patrol Squadron 50, Alaska, Japan, Guam, 1973-76; comdg. officer Naval Facility, San Nicolas Island, Calif., 1971-73; dir. maintenance adminstrn. and contracts Nat. Airlines, Inc., Miami, Fla., 1976—. Sec. of Navy scholar, 1971. Mem. Calif. Inst. Tech. Alumni Assn., Sigma Xi. Home: 7191 Bamboo Ct Miami Lakes FL 33014 Office: PO Box 592055 Airport Mail Facility Miami FL 33159

DITTRICH, GAINES STANDLEY, cons.; b. Decatur, Tex., Apr. 22, 1943; s. Wilbur Orville and Marilu (Plaxco) D.; B.A., Tex. Christian U., 1965, M.A., 1968; m. Sandy Ann Jones, Dec. 22, 1973; children—Shea Corbin, Shanna Dichelle, Shawn Dittrich. Credit analyst 1st Nat. Bank of Ft. Worth, 1961-67; economist Tex. Elec. Service Co., Ft. Worth, 1967-68; asst. v.p. 1st City Nat. Bank, Houston, 1968-72; v.p. Pepsi Co. Transp., Tulsa, 1972; asst. v.p. 1st City Bancorp., Houston, 1972-74; v.p. BancOkla. Corp., Tulsa, 1974-76; sr. v.p Bank of Okla., 1976-79; partner Smith/Biffle/Dittrich, Tulsa, 1979—; adv. dir. Merc. Bank & Trust Co., Tulsa, 1974—, City Bank & Trust Co., Tulsa, 1974-75, Southwest Tulsa Bank, 1976—. Mem. Growth Strategy Task Force City of Tulsa; mem. adminstrv. bd. Christ United Methodist Ch., 1974—, chmn., 1977-78. Mem. Nat. Assn. Bus. Economists, Planning Execs. Inst., Am. Econs. Assn., Am. Mktg. Assn. Republican. Home: 4738 S Boston Pl Tulsa OK 74105 Office: 408 Philtower Tulsa OK 74103

DIX, IRENE HISTORIA, counselor; b. Birmingham, Ala., Dec. 5, 1945; d. Tommie Lee and Ella B (Striggers) D.; B.A., U. Ala., Birmingham, 1973, M.A., 1978; m. Posey Lewis Jr., Dec. 8, 1973 (div.). Counselor trainee Ala. Youth Services, Roebuck, 1977—; tchr. Ala. Dept. Mental Health, Birmingham, 1977; trainee assertiveness continuous edn. workshops. Cert. tchr., Ala. Mem. Am. Personnel and Guidance Assn., Ala. Edn. Assn. Democrat. Baptist. Home: 212 23d St SW Birmingham AL 35211

DIXON, EVA CRAWFORD JOHNSON, librarian; b. Evinston, Fla., Aug. 28, 1909; d. William Alpheus and Willie (Crawford) Johnson; A.B. in Edn. with honors, U. Fla., 1937, M.A., 1948; postgrad. Fla. State U., 1950, Appalachian State Tchrs. Coll., 1955; m. Thomas Gordon Dixon, Dec. 14, 1935 (div. 1944). Tchr. English, librarian Jefferson High Sch., Monticello, Fla., 1945-47; audio-visual dir. Jefferson County Schs., 1948-50; tchr. English, librarian Maigs (Ga.) High Sch., 1954-55; librarian Chipola Jr. Coll., Marianna, Fla., 1955-57, dir. library services, 1958-80, emeritus, 1980—, chmn. student aid and scholarship com., 1961-65. Elder, 1st Presbyterian Ch. Marianna, 1976—, chmn. witness/evangelism com., 1978-80, parliamentarian Fla. Presbytery, 1979—. Mem. Jefferson County Edn. Assn. (pres. 1948-50), Fla. Edn. Assn. Honor Socs. (chmn. 1950-51), Bus. and Profl. Women's Club (pres. 1958-59, 62-63), Fla. Fedn. Bus. Profl. and Women's Clubs (dist. dir. 1962-63), Women of 1st Presbyn. Ch. (pres. 1962-63), Nat. Assn. Parliamentarians, Kappa Delta Pi. Contbr. articles to profl. jours. Home: 506 Kelson Ave Marianna FL 32446

DIXON, HAL BERNARD, restaurant exec.; b. Wake Forest, N.C., Mar. 6, 1928; s. Dudley Burgwin and Cynthia Lou (Crowder) D.; grad. Wake Forest Coll., 1951; student N.C. State Coll., 1951, U. Chattanooga, 1962-63; m. Starr Faye Stone, Sept. 29, 1951; children—Hal Bernard, Valerie Starr, Candace Starr, Vanessa Starr. Successively credit and sales mgr., sales mgr., gen. sales mgr., dir. mktg. Ch. of God Pub. House, Cleveland, Tenn., 1955-74; pres. M.I.T., Inc., Wilson, N.C., Dixon Enterprises, Cleveland; partner Foursquare, nursing home, Whiteville, N.C., Dixon & Dixon Enterprises, Wilson; v.p., dir. Dixon Food Service, Inc., Wilson; dir., sec. 1st Citizens Bank of Cleveland. Mem. and former chmn. Bradley County Bd. Edn. Pres. North Cleveland Towers. Bd. dirs. United Tenn. League, Nashville, 1973—; mem. pres.'s council Lee Coll. Served with AUS, 1946-47. Mem. Christian Booksellers Assn. (dir. Colorado Springs 1960-69, sec. 1967-69). Rotarian. Club: Cleveland Optimist (pres. 1966-67). Home: 3545 Edgewood Circle NW Cleveland TN 37311 Office: 907 Ward Blvd Wilson NC 27893

DIXON, JAMES RAY, herpetologist; b. Houston, Aug. 1, 1928; s. Carl C. and Ione Z. (McCann) D.; B.A., Howard Payne Coll., 1950, M.S., 1957; Ph.D., Tex. A&M U., 1961; m. Mary Ellen Finley, Feb. 28, 1953; children—Maya, James, Tana, Dawn, Toby. Asst. prof. Tex. A&M U., College Station, 1956-61, asso. prof., 1967-71, prof., 1971—, chief curator Tex. Coop. Wildlife Collections, 1967—; asst. prof. N.Mex. State U., Las Cruces, 1961-65; curator herpetology Los Angeles County Mus. Natural History, 1965-67; adj. asso. prof. U. So. Calif., 1965-67. Served with USMC, 1950-53; Korea. Recipient grants NSF, 1964, Am. Philos. Soc., 1969, Organized Research Funds, Peru, 1968, Venezuela Acad. Sci., 1974-76, Sigma Xi, 1960, 62, 65. Mem. Soc. Study Amphibians and Reptiles (pres. 1974), Tex. Acad. Sci. (pres. 1973-74), S.W. Assn. Naturalists (pres. 1970), Am. Soc. Ichthyologists and Herpetologists (gov. 1966-68), Herpetologists League (gov. 1968-71), Biol. Soc. Wash., Chihuahuan Desert Inst. (bd. scientists), So. Calif. Acad. Sci., Sigma Xi. Baptist. Contbr. articles to profl. jours. Home: 705 Inwood St Bryan TX 77801 Office: Dept Wildlife Fisheries Scis Tex A&M U College Station TX 77843

DIXON, JOSEPH MOORE, ophthalmologist; b. Roanoke, Va., Sept. 22, 1910; s. Paul and Anna (Kinsey) D.; student Va. Poly. Inst., 1929-31; M.D., Med. Coll. Va., 1935; postgrad. Washington U., St. Louis, 1946-47; m. Virginia Matthews, June 27, 1941;

children—John, Joseph, Mary. Fellow in ophthalic pathology Armed Forces Inst. Pathology, 1948-49; resident Cin. Gen. Hosp., 1949-51; pvt. practice medicine specializing in ophthalmology, Birmingham, Ala., 1952—; pvt. practice gen. medicine, Roanoke, Va., 1937-40; clin. prof. ophthalmology U. Ala. Med. Center. Mem. rev. com. USPHS, HEW, 1963-65. Served to lt. col. AUS, 1940-45; CBI. Mem. AMA (chmn. sect. on ophthalmology 1974-76), Am. Assn. Ophthalmology (pres. 1964-70), Contact Lens Assn. Ophthalmologists (pres. 1968-69), Ala. Acad. Ophthalmology (pres. 1965-66), Am. Acad. Ophthalmology and Otolaryngology. Baptist (deacon). Club: Explorers. Contbr. articles to profl. jours. Home: 3529 Brookwood Rd Birmingham AL 35223 Office: 516 Med Towers Birmingham AL 35205

DIXON, RICHARD ERWIN, physician; b. Nashville, Sept. 15, 1942; s. Erwin and Lucile (Grimsley) D.; A.B., Princeton U., 1964; M.D., Vanderbilt U., 1969; m. Sarah Lee Dawson, Aug. 26, 1967; children—Rebecca Reilly, Ashley Elizabeth. Intern, U. Wash., Seattle, 1969-70, resident in medicine, 1970-71; med. dir. USPHS, 1971; med. epidemiologist Center for Disease Control, Atlanta, 1971-73, chief hosp. infections br., 1973-74, sr. med. resident Mass. Gen. Hosp., Boston, 1974-75, fellow in infectious diseases, 1975-76, chief hosp. infections br. Center for Disease Control, Atlanta, 1976—; asst. clin. prof. Emory U. Med. Sch., Atlanta, 1976—. Diplomate Am. Bd. Internal Medicine. Fellow A.C.P., mem. Am. Soc. Microbiology, Infectious Disease Soc. Am. Editor: Isolation Techniques for Use in Hospitals, 1975; contbr. numerous articles to profl. jours. Office: Center for Disease Control Atlanta GA 30333

DIXON, RICHARD FRANKLIN, advt. co. exec.; b. Cedar Rapids, Iowa, Mar. 28, 1946; s. Everett Dee and Maxine (Burke) D.; M.B.A., U. Iowa, 1969; m. Margaret Ganaway Cornick, June 23, 1973; children—Mark Shepherd. Exec. trainee Jordan Marsh, Fla., 1969-70; acct. supr. Chenault Assos., N.Y.C., 1970-72; mgr. advt. and mktg. Cunard Lines Ltd., N.Y.C., 1973-75; pres., account supr. The Dixon Group, Norfolk, Va., 1978—. Bd. dirs. Va. Orch. Group, 1978—. Mem. Advt. Club Tidewater (dir. 1978—), Internat. Assn. Bus. Communicators, Va. Soc. Hosp. Public Relations. Home: 7317 Ruthven Rd Norfolk VA 23505 Office: 409 Duke St Norfolk VA 23510

DIXON, WALLACE CLARK, JR., biologist; b. Winston-Salem, N.C., Dec. 18, 1922; s. Wallace Clark and Lillian E. (Figg) D.; A.B., Eastern Nazarene Coll., 1946; A.M., Boston U., 1947, Ph.D., 1956; m. Alice Marie George, May 30, 1946; children—Rebecca, David. Instr. in biology Boston U., 1946-47, asst. prof. biology, 1956-59, asso. prof., 1959-65, prof., 1965-68; asst. prof. biology Eastern Nazarene Coll., 1947-54; chmn. dept. natural sci. Eastern Ky. U., 1968—, asso. dean Coll. Natural and Math. Scis., 1979—; pres. Ky. Conf. Life Scis., 1973. USPHS grantee in cytology, 1955-61. Mem. Assn. Gen. and Liberal Studies, Am. Assn. Higher Edn., AAAS. Democrat. Unitarian. Clubs: Kiwanis (pres. 1975), Internat. Torch (pres. 1976) (Richmond, Ky.). Contbr. articles on adrenocortical cytology in mice, rats, to profl. jours., 1956-63. Home: Route 2 Lakewood Estates Richmond KY 40475 Office: Meml Sci 224 Eastern Ky U Richmond KY 40475

DOAN, PATRICIA NAN, librarian; b. Fayetteville, Ark., Oct. 27, 1930; d. William Rader and Olga (White) Rogers; B.A., U. Ark., 1951; m. John Cannon Doan, Apr. 2, 1950; children—William Curtis, Sarah Cannon, Mary Virginia. Librarian, Okmulgee (Okla.) Pub. Library, 1967—. Treas. Okmulgee Art Guild, 1969-71; sec. Okmulgee County Devel. Council, 1971—, Creek Nation Council House Bd., 1975—. Mem. Okmulgee Meml. Hosp. Found. Mem. Am., Okla. (sec. pub. library div. 1970) library assns., Okmulgee County Genealogical Soc. (v.p. 1970), Sigma Alpha Iota, Zeta Tau Alpha. Democrat. Episcopalian. Author: Index of the 1907 Census of Okmulgee, Oklahoma, 1971. Home: 540 N Morton St Okmulgee OK 74447 Office: 218 S Okmulgee St Okmulgee OK 74447

DOANE, HAROLD EVERETT, record co. exec.; b. N.Y.C., Oct. 17, 1904; s. Thomas J. and Mary S. (Blaisdell) D.; student Edison Sch. Arts, 1919-23, Columbia, 1924; m. Mary G. Gardner, Dec. 20, 1936 (div. 1941) ; m. 2d, Faith S. Tracy, Oct. 17, 1943 (div. 1966); children—Priscilla Clare (Mrs. Ramiro Tello-Saldano), Richard Henry Tracy; m. 3d Vivian Dillon Dunn, May 3, 1966. Asst. cameraman D.W. Griffith Orienta Point Studios, Mamaroneck, N.Y., 1921-22; radio announcer sta. WGBU, Fulford, Fla., 1925-26, WBNY, N.Y.C., 1926-27, WMCA, 1927 WKBQ, 1927-28; owner radio sta. WCOH, Mt. Vernon, N.Y., 1928-29; research engr., N.Y.C., 1929-35; dir. Gramercy Pictures Corp., N.Y.C., 1935-37; producer Spotlight Prodns., Inc., 1940-41; tech. operations dir. War Finance Com., N.Y. State div. U.S. Treasury Dept., N.Y.C., 1941-44; gen. mgr. Art Records, Miami, Fla., 1945-59, pres., 1959—. Mem. Nat. Acad. Rec. Arts and Scis., N.Y. Advt. Club. Republican. Home: 5800 Marlin Dr Plantation Isles FL 33317 Office: 991 SW 40th Ave Plantation FL 33317

DOBBINS, LOY HENDERSON, counselor; b. Arcadia, La., Feb. 4, 1920; s. W.M. and Vera R. (Carter) D.; B.S., La. State U., 1947, M.S., 1949, Ph.D., 1968; m. Joyce Maxine Baker, Dec. 25, 1945; children—Ruth Anne Dobbins Bennett, Denise Joyce. Instr. Livingston (La.) Parish Sch. Bd., 1947-49; agrl. tchr., Claiborne Parish Sch. Bd., Homer, La., 1949-65; research asso. La. State U., Baton Rouge, 1965-68, instr., 1968-70; tchr. high sch., East Baton Rouge, 1970; asso. prof. vocational guidance Southern U., Baton Rouge, 1970-77, prof., 1977—. Mem. Claiborne Parish Democratic Com., 1965-66. Served with 77th inf. div. AUS, 1942-45. Decorated Purple Heart, Bronze Star. Hon. state farmer, 1965; U.S. Office Edn. grantee, 1965-67. Mem. NEA, La. Tchrs. Assn., La., Am. ednl. research assns., Nat. Vocational Guidance Assn., Am. Personnel and Guidance Assn., Am. Vocational Assn., Nat. Vocational Agrl. Tchrs. Assn., Am. Counselor Edn. and Supervision, Am. Assn. Measurement in Edn. and Guidance, Alpha Zeta Phi Kappa Phi, Phi Delta Kappa, Alpha Tau Alpha, Gamma Rho. Methodist. Clubs: Mason, Shriners. Home: 3045 Potomac Dr Baton Rouge LA 70808 Office: Coll Education Southern Univ Baton Rouge LA 70813

DOBBS, GEORGE ALBERT, retail corp. exec.; b. Atlanta, Oct. 16, 1943; s. Albert F. and Ruby Lee (Haynes) D.; B.A., Cornell U., 1966, M.B.A., 1972; m. Wanda Faye Keahey, Apr. 27, 1976; step-children—Sherry Lynne, Kenneth Lee, Rodney Eugene, Pamela Denise. Retail store mgr. Alterman Foods, Atlanta, 1960-72; ind. mng. cons. George A. Dobbs & Assos., Decatur, Ga., 1972-78; retail mgr. K-Mart Corp., Decatur, 1978—; notary public, 1976—. Named Small Bus. Mgr. of Year, Dekalb Businessman's Assn., 1974. Mem. Ga. Small Bus. Mgrs. Assn. (Recognition cert. for contbns. 1976), Dekalb Businessmen's Assn., Dekalb Sheriff's Posse, Ga. Sheriff's Assn. Republican. Baptist. Clubs: Capital City, Masons, Shriners. Office: K-Mart Corp 2901 Clairmont Rd NE Atlanta GA 30033

DOBES, WILLIAM LAMAR, JR., dermatologist; b. Atlanta, Apr. 16, 1943; s. William Lamar and Sara (Wilson) D.; B.A., Emory U., 1965, M.D., 1969; m. Martha Husmann, June 16, 1966; children—Margaret Alison, William Shane. Intern Grady Meml. Hosp., Atlanta, 1969-70; fellow dermatology Mayo Clinic, 1970-71; fellow U. Miami, 1971-73; clin. instr. Emory U. Sch. Medicine, Atlanta, 1973-77, asst. prof. dermatology, 1977—, dir. immunofluorescense lab.; mem. staff Crawford Long, West Paces Ferry, Grady Meml., Ga. Bapt. hosps. (all Atlanta); chmn. profl. edn. unit Atlanta unit Am. Cancer Soc., also bd. dirs.; mem. Ga. med. bd. Lupus Found. Diplomate Am. Bd. Dermatology. Mem. Soc. Investigative Dermatology, Am. Acad. Dermatology, So., Ga., Pan Am. med. assns., A.M.A., A.C.P., Am. Soc. Dermatologic Surgery, Atlanta Dermatol. Assn. (pres.), N.Am. Clin. Dermatologic Soc., Soc. Tropical Dermatology, Atlanta Clin. Soc., Emory U. Med. Alumni Assn. (pres. 1980), Phi Delta Theta (past pres.), Phi Chi (past pres.). Club: Cherokee Town & Country (Atlanta). Contbr. articles to profl. jours. and texts. Home: 2898 Rivermead Dr Atlanta GA 30327 Office: 478 Peachtree St Atlanta GA 30308 also Dept Dermatology Emory U School Medicine Atlanta GA 30308

DOBROVOLSKY, NICHOLAS WASIL, counseling psychologist; b. Beaver Meadows, Pa., Feb. 19, 1935; s. Nicholas and Theresa (Goida) D.; B.S. summa cum laude, Troy State U., 1973, M.S., 1974; Ph.D., Tex. A&M U., 1977; m. Edna Arlean Smith, June 1, 1957; children—Michael J., Pamela A., Janice L., Thomas E., David A., Laura J. Commd. airman U.S. Air Force, 1954, advanced through grades to maj., 1966; aviation cadet, Houston, 1955; navigator/bombadier, Salina, Kans., 1956-58; instr. navigator, Wichita, Kans., 1958-61; student pilot, Enid, Okla., 1962; pilot, Waco, Tex., 1962-66; combat pilot, Vietnam, 1966-67; flying safety officer, Oklahoma City, 1967-70; maintenance officer/squadron comdr. Maxwell AFB, Montgomery, Ala., 1970-74; ret., 1974; counseling psychologist personal counseling service Tex. A&M U., 1974—. Decorated D.F.C., Meritorious Service award, Air medal with 5 oak leaf clusters, Air Force Commendation medal; lic. psychologist, Tex. Mem. Am. Assn. Family and Marriage Therapy, Am. Personnel and Guidance Assn., Am. Soc. Clin. Hypnosis, Nat. Register Health Service Providers, Tex. Psychol. Assn., Brazos Valley Psychol. Assn. (pres.), Phi Delta Kappa. Roman Catholic. Office: Personal Counseling Service 017 YMCA Bldg Tex A&M U College Station TX 77843

DOBSON, DONALD ALFRED, elec. engr.; b. Evanston, Ill., Feb. 19, 1928; s. Alfred Topping and Agnes Lucille (Park) D.; B.S. in Elec. Engring., Northwestern U., 1950, Ph.D., 1955; M.S.E.E., M.I.T., 1951. Research asso. Northwestern U., Evanston, 1951-54; engr. Indsl. Research Products, Franklin Park, Ill., 1952; sr. engr. Sperry Gyroscope Co., Great Neck, N.Y., 1954-59; sr. tech. specialist N. Am. Aviation, Columbus, Ohio, 1959-63; research staff mem. Inst. Def. Analyses, Arlington, Va., 1963—; instr. physics Adelphi Coll., Garden City, N.Y., 1956. Mem. IEEE, Sigma Xi, Tau Beta Pi, Eta Kappa Nu, Pi Mu Epsilon. Home: 6800 Fleetwood Rd Apt 420 McLean VA 22101 Office: 400 Army-Navy Dr Arlington VA 22202

DOBSON, GERARD RAMSDEN, educator; b. Lynbrook, N.Y., May 4, 1933; s. Edward Ramsden and Harriet (Bowman) D.; B.S., Fla. So. Coll., 1955; Ph.D., Fla. State U., 1964; m. Kay Ann Tauscher, June 16, 1962; children—Charles, Thomas, Edward. Asst. prof. chemistry U. Ga., 1963-67; asso. prof. chemistry U. S.D., 1967-69; asso. prof. chemistry North Tex. State U., 1969-72, prof. chemistry, 1972—. Mem. Clarke County (Ga.) Republican Exec. Com., 1964-67, Denton County (Tex.) Rep. Exec. Com., 1974-80. NSF grant, 1969-72; Petroleum Research Fund grant, 1963-72; Robert A. Welch Found. grant, 1971—. Mem. Am. Chem. Soc., Royal Soc. Chemistry, Soc. Sigma Xi, Beta Beta Beta, Pi Kappa Phi, Alpha Chi Sigma (dist. counselor 1974-76, grand master of ceremonies 1976—), Phi Lambda Upsilon. Club: Masons. Editor: The Hexagon of Alpha Chi Sigma. Contbr. numerous articles to sci. jours. Home: Box 273 Justin TX 76247 Office: Dept Chemistry North Tex State U Denton TX 76203

DOBYNS, ROY ARMSTEAD, coll. dean; b. Bristol, Va., Jan. 31, 1931; s. Roy Armstead and Francis (Williams) D.; A.B., Carson-Newman Coll., 1953; M.A., Vanderbilt U., 1954; Ph.D., George Peabody Coll., 1963; m. Kathryn Louise Williams, June 19, 1955; children—Roy, John, Joe. Asst. prof. math. La. Coll., 1956-58; prof. math. McNeese State U., 1958-68; chmn. dept. math Georgetown Coll., 1968-73; prof., chmn. div. sci. and math Clayton Jr. Coll., 1973-75; acad. dean Carson-Newman Coll., Jefferson City, Tenn., 1975—. Served with AUS, 1954-56. Recipient Ford grant, 1961-62; NSF fellowship, 1963. Mem. Math. Assn. Am. (chmn. Ky. sect. 1971-73), Nat. Council Tchrs. Math. Baptist (deacon 1964—). Author: Programmed Guide to Trigonometry, 1968; Programmed Guide to Algebra, 1969; Programmed Guide to Algebra & Trigonometry, 1970; Programmed Guide to Elementary Functions, 1971; Programmed Guide to Calculus, 1979. Home: Route 4 Box 446A Talbott TN 37877

DOCKERY, EDWARD BURRELL, JR., wholesale exec.; b. Tuscaloosa, Ala., Apr. 22, 1945; s. Edward Burrell and Grace Evelyn (Hughes) D.; B.S. in C.E., U. Ala., 1968; m. Vickie Janelle Marshall, Sept. 2, 1967; children—Edward Burrell, Tyler Martin. Field jr. engr. Schlumberger Well Services, Lake Charles, La., 1963-68, field engr., Houma, La., 1968-69; with Electric Motor & Supply Co., Tuscaloosa, Ala., 1969—, pres., 1979—. Sec., Greater Tuscaloosa area Youth for Christ, 1977, chmn., 1978-79. Mem. Elec. Apparatus Service Assn., Nat. Assn. Elec. Distbrs. Baptist. Club: City Salesmen's. Home: 10 Hickory Forest Tuscaloosa AL 35401 Office: 1601 15th St Tuscaloosa AL 35401

DOCKERY, THOMAS HARLOWE, accountant; b. Asheville, N.C., Apr. 9, 1930; s. Grover William and Grace Wagner (Garnflo) D.; B.S., U. S.C., 1955; postgrad. Jacksonville U., Fla. Jr. Coll.; m. Laverna Rebecca Robinson, May 19, 1951; children—Dorothy K. (Mrs. Douglas K. Wilder), V. Joanne Dockery Wheeler, Jill C., Robin K. Accounting supr. U.S. Fidelity & Guaranty Co., Columbia, S.C., 1955-60, Jacksonville, Fla., 1960-63; acct. Duval Motor Co., Jacksonville, 1960-63; pres. Acctg. & Bus. Service Inc., 1962-77; self-employed acct., Jacksonville, 1963-72, Keystone Heights, Fla., 1972-77; comptroller Smoky Mountain Enterprises, Inc., Buck Stoves, Inc., Asheville, N.C., 1977-79; pvt. practice acctg., Asheville, 1979—; owner Aaron Printing Industries, Allegro Pub. Co.; tchr. taxation Fla. Jr. Coll., Jacksonville, 1972, N.C. State U. Extension. Pres., P.T.A., Sherwood Elementary Sch., 1962. Served with USMCR, 1948-52. Mem. Fla. Accts. Assn. (pres. N.E. chpt. 1971), Jacksonville C. of C. (chmn. com. better bus. div. 1970-72), Clay County C. of C. (dir., treas. 1973), Asheville C. of C., N.C. Soc. Accts. (sec.-treas., tax seminar speaker), Nat. Soc. Pub. Accountants. Clubs: Toastmasters (v.p. 1961), Mars Hill Coll. Volleyball. Home: Route 6 Box 715 Fairview NC 28730 Office: 830 Fairview Rd Asheville NC 28803

DOCTOR, VASANT MANILAL, educator; b. Surat, India, Mar. 19, 1926; s. Manilal Ramlal and Kusum (Bhambhani) D.; M.S., U. Wis., 1951; Ph.D., Tex. A & M U., 1953; m. Pushpa Broker, Nov. 17, 1953; children—Shreenath, Uday, Ravi. Came to U.S., 1949, naturalized, 1973. Asst. prof. biochemistry U. Tex. M.D. Anderson Hosp., Houston, 1953-59, asso. prof. dental br., 1959-62; chief biochemist H.A. Ltd., Pimpri, India, 1962-65; asso. prof. biochemistry U. Houston, 1965-67; prof. biochemistry Prairie View (Tex.) A. & M. U., 1967—. Cons. U. Houston Biochemistry and Biophysics dept., Houston Research Inst. Committeeman Sam Houston Area council Boy Scouts Am., 1957-62. NIH grantee 1961-62; Am. Cancer Soc. grantee, Welch Found. grantee, 1968, Research Career Devel. award NIH, 1959-64. Mem. Am. Soc. Biol. Chemists, Soc. Exptl. Biology and Medicine, AAAS, Sigma Xi. Contbg. author: Nucleic Acids, 1965. Contbr. numerous articles to sci. jours. Home: 2115 10th St Hempstead TX 77445 Office: Chemistry Dept Prairie View A & M U Prairie View TX 77445

DODD, CAROLE ALMA, systems analyst; b. Los Angeles, May 31, 1942; d. Charles Worley and Betty Elizabeth (Sawaya) Dodd; student Los Angeles City Coll., 1960-61; A.A., Los Angeles Metro. Coll., 1966. Tabulation operator Carnation Milk Co., Los Angeles, 1962-63, 1401 computer operator, 1964; programmer Union Oil Co., Los Angeles, 1966-67; sr. programmer analyst TransAmerica Ins., Los Angeles, 1967-70; tech. cons. Omnis Corp., Dallas, 1970-71; programmer/analyst DPAINC, Dallas, 1971, First Nat. Bank, Dallas, 1972-75; systems analyst/project leader Affiliate Computers, Dallas, 1975—. Mem. Nat. Geog. Soc., Franklin Mint Soc. Democrat. Roman Catholic. Office: 1712 Commerce St Dallas TX 75222

DODD, JAMES LEE, mfg. co. exec.; b. Birmingham, Ala., Aug. 17, 1947; s. Lester Lee and Effie Louvee (Nicholas) D.; B.S., Calif. State U., Fresno, 1974; M.B.A., U. S. Ala., 1977; m. Glenda Anne Goode, July 14, 1967; 1 dau., Jennifer Cambria. Indsl. engr. Ingalls Shipbldg. Co., Pascagoula, Miss., 1974-75; budget analyst Teledyne Continental Motors, Mobile, Ala., 1975-76, pricing supr., 1976-77; mgr. pricing and planning Fleetguard div. Cummins Engine Co., Cookeville, Tenn., 1977-78, mgr. acctg., 1978—. Served with USN, 1968-72. Mem. Nat. Assn. Accountants, Nat. Mgmt. Assn. Home: 1281 E 7th St Cookeville TN 38501 Office: Route 8 Cookeville TN 38501

DODD, LAWRENCE ROE, lawyer; b. Alexandria, La., Oct. 17, 1944; s. Sylvester Abner and Annie Ruth (Chandler) D.; B.A., La. State U., 1966, J.D., 1972; m. Nancy Meagher, Apr. 11, 1979; children—Bruce Wayne, Laurence Scott, Chandler Layne. Research asso. La. State U. Inst. of Continuing Legal Edn., Baton Rouge, 1971-72; admitted to La. bar, 1973; mem. firm Kizer & Kizer, Baton Rouge, 1973-76, Dodd, Achée and Burt, Baton Rouge, 1976—; dir. JTL Electronics, Inc., Baton Rouge, 1973-75, F.C. Schaffer & Assos., Inc., Baton Rouge, 1974-75. Instr. law and banking Am. Inst. Banking, Baton Rouge, 1975-76. Mem. Theta Xi. Lion. Clubs: Southwood Racquet; City (Baton Rouge); Walden. Editor: Recent Developments in the Law of Maritime Torts, 1972. Home: 1241 Thoreau Dr Baton Rouge LA 70808 Office: 4744 Jamestown Ave Baton Rouge LA 70808

DODD, WILLIAM RAY, JR., elec. engr.; b. Mobile, Ala., Mar. 16, 1945; s. William R. and Mary E. (Evans) D.; B.S. in Elec. Engring., Auburn U., 1967; m. Juanita Marie Bailey, June 12, 1967; children—Robert, John. Engr. elec. design Chrysler Corp., Huntsville, Ala., 1968-69; instrumentation engr. Deering Milliken Co., LaGrange, Ga., 1972-73; elec. design engr. Lummus Co., Columbus, Ga., 1973-74; cons. elec. engring. Patchen Migledorff & Assos., Atlanta, 1974-76; chief facilities engr. Amoco Fabrics Co., Inc., Hazlehurst, Ga., 1976-79; dir. engring. Amoco Container Co., Norcross, Ga., 1979—. Served to capt. USAF, 1969-72. Registered profl. engr., Ga. Mem. IEEE, ASHRAE, Am. Soc. Mil. Engrs., Nat., Ga. socs. profl. engrs., Illuminating Engrs. Soc. Home: 100 Conner Ave Hazlehurst GA 31539 Office: Amoco Container Co 1858 Meca Way Norcross GA 30093

DODDS, JOSEPH J., surgeon; b. Farrell, Pa., Feb. 9, 1929; s. Joseph Burns and Julia (Scott) D.; B.S., Univ. Pitts., 1951, M.D., 1955; m. Vina Mae Elder, June 19, 1954; children—Lynn Eider, Sandra Allison. Intern, Shadyside Hosp., Pitts., 1955-56; resident Mayo Clinic, Rochester, Minn., 1958-62; practice medicine specializing in surgery, Chattanooga, 1962—; clin. prof. U. Ky.; pres. Patterns, Inc.; dir. S.E. Tenn. Area Health Edn. Center, Inc., Profl. Systems Inc., Chattanooga. Mem. Tenn. Manpower Commn.; v.p. United Health Mgmt. Orgns., Inc. Bd. dirs. Ga.-Tech. Regional Health Commn., chmn., 1976-77; bd. dirs. Tenn. Edn. and Med. Services, Inc.; dir. med. ops., bd. dirs. Waldens Ridge Emergency Services, Inc.; mem. Tenn. State Health Coordinating Council. Served with USAF, 1956-58. Diplomate Am. Bd. Surgery. Fellow A.C.S., Southeastern Surg. Congress, Am. Soc. Abdominal Surgeons, Royal Soc. Health, Pan. Pacific Surg. Assn., Pan. Am. Med. Assn.; mem. AMA, So. Med. Assn., Fedn. Am. Hosps. (pres. 1971-72, dir.), Tenn., Chattanooga and Hamilton County med. socs., Royal Coll. Medicine. Republican. Presbyterian (deacon). Clubs: Capital, Lions. Home: 1105 E Brow Rd Signal Mountain TN 37377 Office: 628 Morrisons Springs Rd Chattanooga TN 37415

DODGE, EVA FRANCETTE, physician; b. New Hampton, N.H., July 24, 1896; d. George Francis and Winnie Josephine (Worthem) D.; A.B., Ohio Wesleyan U., 1919, H.H.D., 1969; postgrad. Johns Hopkins U., 1920-23; M.D., U. Md., 1925; postgrad. U. Vienna, 1930-31. Intern, U. Hosp., Balt., 1925-26, resident obstetrics, 1926-27; acting prof. obstetrics Womans Christian Med. Coll., Shanghai, China, 1928-29; obstetric cons. Ala. Dept. Health, Montgomery, 1937-42; practice medicine, Winston-Salem, N.C., 1932-37; asso. med. dir. Planned Parenthood Fedn. Am., N.Y.C., 1943-45; asst. prof. obstetrics and gynecology U. Ark. Sch. Medicine, Little Rock, 1945-46, asso. prof., 1947-60, prof., 1960-64, prof. emerita, 1964—; dir. maternal and infant care project Detroit, 1964-66; dir. East Ark. Family Planning Project, Ark. Health Dept., Little Rock, 1969-72, dir. Ark. Family Planning Program, 1972-78, vol. in sex edn., 1978—; obstetric cons. Children's Bur., 1940-41; speaker on family planning and adolescent problems. Bd. dirs. New Hampton Sch., 1962—. Named Woman of Year, Little Rock Democrat, 1951; recipient Alumni award, gold key U. Md. Sch. Medicine, 1967; Tom T. Ross award Ark. Pub. Health Assn., 1976; Ross award, 1977; plaque and citation Ark. Family Planning Council, 1979. Fellow A.C.S., Am. Coll. Obstetrics and Gynecology; mem. Am. Med. Women's Assn. (v.p. 1938, Blackwell achievement award 1977), Pan Am. Med. Women's Assn. (pres. 1964-66), Pan Am. Assn., AMA, Central Assn. Obstetrics and Gynecology, Am. Assn. Sterility, Internat. Platform Assn., Delta Kappa Gamma. Clubs: Travelers Century, Altrusa (pres. Winston-Salem 1933) (Little Rock). Contbr. articles to med. jours. Home: Quapaw Tower Little Rock AR 72202

DODGE, GEORGE BURTON, artist; b. Meriden, Conn., Mar. 31, 1945; s. Daniel Clark and Helen Agnes (Lichtenberger) D.; Fine Arts diploma, Ringling Sch. Art, 1973, B.F.A., 1974; M.S., Troy State U., 1978; m. Margaret Ann Toevs, Feb. 10, 1968; children—Alexander John-Christian, Christina Mary-Elizabeth, Anastasia Dana-Katherine, George Burton. Art dir. CBS Radio & TV, Montgomery, Ala., 1974-76; prof. visual arts, dir. art communications Troy (Ala.) State U., 1976-78; now area dir. Low Income Housing Devel. Corp. Ala. and public relations dir. Pike County Crime Prevention Task Force; one-man shows include: Sarasota (Fla.) Bank & Trust, 1970, Ringling Sch. Art, Sarasota, 1972, Auburn (Ala.) U., 1974, Troy (Ala.) U., 1976, Jasmine Hills Folk Festival, Wetumpka, Ala., 1978; group shows include: U. Hartford (Conn.), Wadsworth Athenaeum, 1963, Ringling Sch. Art, 1969-72, Manatel Jr. Coll., Bradenton, Fla., 1973; represented in permanent collections: Jasmine Hills of Wetumpka. Mem. Phi Theta Kappa, Gamma Beta Phi. Mormon. Home and office: 120 Montgomery St Troy AL 36081

DODGE, NANCY ROBINS (N.R.), data processing exec.; b. N.Y.C., July 20, 1950; d. Robert and Muriel (Daughtry) Hughes; student Hartwick Coll., 1967-68, Oneonta State Coll., 1968-69; honor grad. Computer Learning Center, 1974. Adminstrv. sec. Nat. Bank of Washington, 1970-72; free-lance public relations cons., 1972-73; br. sec. Nat. Savs. & Trust, Washington, 1973-74; programmer/analyst Datatel, Inc., Alexandria, Va., 1974-77; pvt. data processing cons., 1978-79; sr. programmer/analyst Basics Info. Systems, Inc., Alexandria, 1979—; instr. Computer Learning Center, Springfield, Mass., 1978-79. Mem. Am. Bus. Women's Assn. (treas. 1978), Assn. Computer Programmers and Analysts, Nat. Symphony Assn., Smithsonian Assn. Club: Order Eastern Star. Contbr. articles to profl. jours. Home: 7951 Woodpecker Way Alexandria VA 22306 Office: 3700 Mount Vernon Ave Alexandria VA 22305

DODSON, CALAWAY H., botanist; b. Selma, Calif., Dec. 17, 1928; s. Homer C. and Leona W. (Jones) D.; A.B., Fresno State Coll., 1954; M.A., Claremont Coll., 1956, Ph.D., 1959; m. Piedad Marmol Cevallos, Jan. 15, 1960; children—Debra A., David C., Thomas A. Dir., Instituto Botanico, Universidad de Guayaquil (Ecuador), 1959-60; taxonomist and curator of living plants Mo. Bot. Garden, St. Louis, 1960-64; course coordinator Orgn. for Tropical Studies, San Jose, Costa Rica, 1966; prof., curator herbarium U. Miami (Fla.), 1964-74; dir. Marie Selby Bot. Gardens, Sarasota, Fla., 1973—; pres. Rio Palenque Sci. Center, Inc., Ecuador, 1976—. Enlisted in U.S. Army, 1946, ret. 1961. Mo. Bot. Garden research fellow, 1956-58-59; Dunmar Found. research fellow, 1957-58; NSF grantee, 1961-79. Mem. Am. Soc. Plant Taxonomists, Soc. Study of Evolution, Assn. Tropical Biology, AAAS, Am. Inst. Biol. Scis., Am. Orchid Soc., Internat. Assn. Plant Taxonomy, Sigma Xi. Republican. Club: Kiwanis. Contbr. articles to profl. jours.; author: Agentes de Polinización y Su Influencia Sobre la Evolución en la Familia Orquidacea, 1964; The Orchid Flower, Its Pollination and Evolution, 1966; Biology of the Orchids, 1967; Flora of the Rio Palenque Science Center, Los Rios Province, Ecuador, 1978. Home: 3210 Old Oak Dr Sarasota FL 33579 Office: 800 S Palm Ave Sarasota FL 33577

DODSON, CHARLES LEON, JR., chemist, educator; b. Knoxville, Tenn., Mar. 15, 1935; s. Charles Leon and Margaret Glen (Berry) D.; B.S., Emory and Henry Coll., 1957; M.S., U. Tenn., 1962, Ph.D., 1963; m. Vernell Laura Woodard, Sept. 6, 1958; children—Alyssa, Bronwyn. Postdoctoral fellow U. Birmingham (Eng.), 1963-64, Nat. Research Council, Ottawa, Ont., Can., 1964-66; mem. faculty U. Ala., Huntsville, 1966—, asso. prof. chemistry, 1969—; vis. prof. Oxford (Eng.) U., 1972-73. Mem. Am. Chem. Soc., Am. Phys. Soc., Blue Key, Sigma Xi, Sigma Pi Sigma. Contbr. articles to profl. jours. Home: 1403 Appalachee Dr Huntsville AL 35801 Office: PO Box 1247 Huntsville AL 35807

DODSON, CHESTER LEE, geologist, educator; b. Eastland, Tenn., Dec. 18, 1921; s. Earnest and Ida (Wallace) D.; B.S., W.Va. U., 1950, M.S., 1953; m. Lena Laurene Sapp, June 14, 1947; children—Jennifer, Cynthia. Geologist, Mineral Deposits br. U.S. Geol. Survey, Washington, 1952-54, Grand Junction, Colo., 1954-57, project chief Water br., Decatur, Ala., 1957-61, Murphy, N.C., 1961-63; dir. Water Research Inst., asst. prof. geology W.Va. U., Morgantown, 1963—. Served with AC, U.S. Army, 1942-46. Fellow Geol. Soc. Am.; mem. Am. Geophys. Union, Nat. Water Well Assn., Am. Water Resources Assn., W.Va. Acad. Sci., Soil Conservation Soc. Am., AAAS, Morgantown Area C. of C. (chmn. environ. improvement com. 1972-74). Club: Rotary. Researcher ground-water hydrology. Home: 438 Civitan St Morgantown WV 26505

DODSON, EUGENE BENEDICT, TV exec.; b. Woodward, Okla., Nov. 25, 1912; s. William Benedict and Minnie (Richard) D.; B.A., U. Okla., 1933; m. Grace Beaulieu, Apr. 4, 1941; children—Jean Ann (Mrs. Jean D. Hibbs), George. Reporter, Okla. News, Oklahoma City, 1933-34, Daily Oklahoman, Oklahoma City, 1934-42; reporter, deskman Asso. Press, Washington, 1945-47; news editor Daily Transcript, Norman, Okla., 1947-49; promotion mgr. WKY Television System, Oklahoma City, 1949-51, adminstrv. asst. 1951-54, dir. radio operations, 1954-55, asst. mgr., 1955-56, acting mgr., 1956-57; mgr. WSFA-TV, Montgomery, Ala., 1957-58, WTVT, Tampa, Fla., 1958-77; exec. v.p. WKY-TV Television System, Inc. (name now Gaylord Broadcasting Co.), 1970-75, pres., 1975-77, vice chmn. bd., 1977-79; ret., 1980. Past mem. CBS-TV affiliates adv. bd. for Dist. No. 3. Campaign chmn. Tampa United Fund, 1965, pres., 1968-69; pres. Tampa Horse Show Assn., 1966-75, chmn. bd., 1975-78; pres. Tampa Citizens Safety Council, 1965, Tampa Philharmonic Assn., 1962-66; fellow U. Tampa. Served with AUS, 1942-45. Decorated Legion of Merit (U.S.); Order of Vasco Nunez de Balboa (Republic of Panama); recipient Silver Medallion of Brotherhood award Fla. Region NCCJ, 1974; Silver medal Tampa Advt. Fedn., 1974; Abe Lincoln Merit award So. Bapt. Radio and TV Commn., 1977; named Citizen of Yr., Civitan Club, Tampa, 1967. Mem. Nat. (TV bd. dirs. 1974-79), Fla. (dir., past pres.) assns. broadcasters, Broadcast Pioneers, Greater Tampa C. of C. (pres. 1969-70), Sigma Delta Chi. Episcopalian. Rotarian (pres. Tampa club 1966-67). Clubs: University, Tampa Yacht and Country, Palma Ceia Golf and Country. Home: 10703 Carrollwood Dr Tampa FL 33618

DODSON, JAMES CLIFTON, mech. engr.; b. Shreveport, La., Nov. 1, 1946; s. Butler and Lois (Wilson) D.; B.S., La. Tech. U., 1969, M.S., 1970; m. Melaney Moore; 1 son, James Clifton. Field engr. trainee Halliburton Services, Laurel, Miss., 1970-71, field engr., 1971-72, engr. pump research sect. Mech. Research and Devel. Dept., Duncan, Okla., 1972—. Unit commr. Boy Scouts Am., Duncan, Okla., 1973-74, explorer adviser, 1974-75, Eagle scout. Recipient Young Engr. of Year award South Central chpt. Okla. Soc. Profl. Engrs., 1976. Am. Machine Foundry fellow, 1969-70. Registered profl. engr., Okla. Mem. Am. Inst. Mining, Metall. and Petroleum Engrs., Okla. Soc. Profl. Engrs. (chpt. sec.), Nat. Rifle Assn., Nat. Soc. Profl. Engrs., Pi Kappa Alpha, Pi Tau Sigma. Club: Elks. Patentee in field. Office: PO Drawer 1431 Duncan OK 73533

DODSON, RONALD FRANKLIN, cell biologist, exptl. pathologist; b. Paris, Tex., Feb. 14, 1942; s. Benjamin Franklin and Vera (Eubank) D.; A.A., Paris Jr. Coll., 1962; B.A., East Tex. State Coll., 1964, M.A., 1965; Ph.D., Tex. A. & M. U., 1969; m. Sandra Jim Roberson, Nov. 13, 1965; children—Diana Lynn, Debra Kay. Teaching asst. East Tex. State U., 1964-65; grad. coll. fellowship in electron microscopy Tex. A. and M. U., 1965-69; research asso. dept. anatomy U. Tex. Med. Sch., 1969-70; instr. depts. neurology and pathology Baylor Coll. Medicine, 1970, asst. prof. neurology and pathology, 1971-77, adj. asst. prof., 1977—; chief dept. cell biology and environ. scis. U. Tex. Health Center, Tyler, 1977—; ultrastructural research in cerebrovascular disease and respiratory diseases. Mem. Am. Heart Assn. (fellowship in stroke council 1971—), British Brain Research Assn., Tex., N.Y. acad. scis., A.A.A.S., Am. Men and Women of Sci., Am. Chem. Soc., Am. Inst. Biol. Sci., Southwest Sci. Forum, Tex. Soc. Electron Microscopy, Electron Microscopy Soc. Am., Soc. Neurosci., Am. Thoracic Soc. Home: 2918 Bain Pl Tyler TX 75701 Office: U Tex Health Center PO Box 2003 Tyler TX 75710

DOENGES, RUDOLPH CONRAD, educator; b. Tonkawa, Okla., Dec. 7, 1930; s. Rudolph Soland and Helen (Lower) D.; A.B. magna cum laude, Harvard, 1952, M.B.A., 1954; D.Bus. Adminstrn., U. Colo., 1965; m. Ellen Ione Gummere, Oct. 5, 1963; children—Rudolph Conrad, John Soland, William Gummere. Gen. mgr. Doenges-Long Motors Inc., Colorado Springs, Colo., 1958-61; asst. prof. U. Tex. Grad. Sch. Bus., Austin, 1964-67, asso. prof., 1967-74, prof., 1974—, asso. dean, 1972-76, chmn. finance dept., 1976—. Served to lt. (j.g.) Supply Corps, USNR, 1954-58. Harvard Nat. scholar, 1948-54; Ford Found. Dissertation fellow, 1963-64. Mem. Am. Econ. Assn., Am., Southwestern (pres.) finance assns., Financial Mgmt. Assn., Southwestern Fedn. Adminstrv. Disciplines (pres. 1976-77), Phi Beta Kappa, Beta Gamma Sigma, Phi Kappa Phi, Delta Sigma Pi. Republican. Methodist. Rotarian. Author: (with others) Case Problems in Financial Management, 1968; (with G.A. Jentz) Consumer Credit in Texas, 1969. Editor: (with H.A. Wolf) Readings in Money and Banking, 1968; asso. editor finance Social Sci. Quar., 1966-74. Contbr. articles to profl. jours. Home: 3500 Hillbrook Circle Austin TX 78731

DOERGE, JIMMIE FRANCES, educator; b. Stephens, Ark., Jan. 2, 1931; d. Jack and Dessie Tillie (Crumpler) Parker; B.S., Northwestern State U., 1951; M.Ed., La. State U., 1974; postgrad. La. Tech. U., 1975-78; m. George Leonard Doerge, Dec. 19, 1954. Typewriting tchr. Northwestern State U., Natchitoches, La., 1951-56; bus. tchr. Sarepta High Sch., 1951-56; bus. tchr. and counselor Ayers Bus. Sch., Shreveport, La., 1952-57; classroom tchr. lang. arts-social studies Caddo Parish Sch. Bd., Shreveport, 1956-67; secondary sch. bus. tchr. Northwood High Sch., Shreveport, 1967—, head dept. bus., 1967—. Mem. Nat. Bus. Edn. Assn., NEA, La. Bus. Edn. Assn., So. Bus. Edn. Assn., La. Edn. Assn., Caddo Tchr. Assn., Delta Kappa Gamma, Kappa Kappa Iota. Democrat. Baptist. Clubs: Ladies Aux. Brotherhood Locomotive Engrs., North Highlands Woman's (game night chmn. 1976-79). Office: Northwood High Sch 754 Wesley Shreveport LA 71107

DOGGETT, LLOYD ALTON, II, state senator; b. Austin, Tex., Oct. 6, 1946; s. Lloyd and Alyce Doggett; B.B.A., U. Tex., Austin, 1967, J.D., 1970; m. Elizabeth Belk, Jan. 1968; children—Lisa, Catherine. Admitted to Tex. bar, 1971; mem. firm Doggett & Jacks, Austin, 1975—; mem. Tex. Senate from 14th Dist., 1973—. Named one of Ten Best Tex. Legislators, Tex. Monthly, 1979; One of Five Outstanding Young Texans, Tex. Jaycees, 1977. Mem. Tex. Trial Lawyers Assn., Tex. Young Lawyers Assn., Austin Young Lawyers Assn. (named Outstanding Young Lawyer in Austin 1978). Democrat. Methodist. Home: 1906 Sharon Ln Austin TX 78703 Office: 332 State Capitol Austin TX 78711

DOHERTY, THOMAS ROSS, dentist, oral implantologist; b. Pine Bluff, Ark., Aug. 13, 1938; s. Neumie Ray and Pocahontas (Guthrie) D.; student U. Ark. at Monticello, 1956-59; D.M.D., Washington U., 1964; m. Ruth Esther Willoughby, Dec. 31, 1963; children—Christopher Michael, Johnathan Maxwell. Asso. of Drs., Pine Bluff, Dumas, Ark., 1966-67; pvt. practice dentistry, Pine Bluff, 1967—; mem. dental staff Jefferson, Davis hosps., sec. dental staff, 1968. Chmn., Nat. Children's Dental Health Week, 1968-69; dental dir. Office Econ. Opportunity, 1967-69. Mem. Pine Bluff Municipal Airport Commn. Served to capt. Dental Corps, AUS, 1964-66; maj. Res. Diplomate Am. Bd. Oral Implantology. Fellow Acad. Gen. Dentistry; mem. Am. Dental Assn., Ark., Jefferson County (pres. 1974), Armed Forces dental socs., Acad. Gen. Dentistry, Am. Acad. Implant Dentistry, Exptl. Aircraft Assn., Aircraft Owners and Pilots Assn., C. of C., Flying Dentists, Quiet Birdmen, Exptl. Aircraft Assn., Xi Psi Phi. Mason (Shriner). Club: Little Rock Hangar. Home: 904 Wisconsin St Pine Bluff AR 71601 Office: 1700 Doctors Dr Pine Bluff AR 71603

DOI, YUTAKA, physicist; b. Osaka, Japan, Nov. 26, 1936; s. Hiroshi and Hiroko (Tsuyama) D.; came to U.S., 1967, naturalized, 1978; B.A., Keio U., 1960; B.S., Osaka U., 1967; M.S., San Francisco State U., 1970; m. Michiko Ishikawa, Nov. 26, 1972; children—Masao, Mary. Officer bank Mitsui Bank, 1960-62; guest research Lawrence Berkeley (Calif.) Radiation Lab., 1969-71; engr. Hewlett-Packard Co., Tokyo, 1972-74; health physicist radiologist U. Miami (Fla.), 1977-79; elec. engr. Communication div. Motorola, Ft. Lauderdale, Fla., 1979—. Recipient Honor prize Japanese Assn. Pvt. Instns., 1952; grad. fellow San Francisco State U., 1968-69. Registered profl. engr., Fla. Mem. IEEE. Buddhist. Inventor in field. Home: Apt F207 4007 N University Dr Sunrise FL 33321 Office: 8000 W Sunrise Blvd Fort Lauderdale FL 33322

DOIG, MARION TILTON, III, biochemist, educator; b. Charleston, S.C., Sept. 29, 1943; s. Marion Tilton, Jr., and Dulcie Marshall (Mahn) D.; B.S. (Alumni scholar, 1961-65), Coll. of Charleston, 1966; M.S., U. South Fla., 1971, Ph.D., 1973; m. Patricia Ann Bloder, June 6, 1966; children—Chadwick Marshall, Bryan Tilton. Analytical chemist Fed. Water Pollution Control Assn., HEW, Athens, Ga., 1965-68; asso. prof. chemistry dept. Coll. of Charleston (S.C.), 1974—; vis. asst. prof. chemistry dept. U. South Fla., Tampa, 1973-74; adj. prof. biochemistry dept. Med. U. S.C. Recipient Sigma Xi research award, 1972. Mem. Am. Chem. Soc., AAAS, S.C. Acad. Sci. Methodist. Home: 2100 Bishop Dr Charleston SC 29407 Office: Chemistry Department College of Charleston Charleston SC 29401

DOKE, MARSHALL J., JR., lawyer; b. Wichita Falls, Tex., June 9, 1934; s. Marshall J. and Mary Jane (Johnson) D.; B.A. magna cum laude, Hardin-Simmons U., 1956; LL.B. magna cum laude, So. Meth. U., 1959; m. Betty Orsini, June 2, 1956; children—Gregory J., Michael J., Laetitia Marie. Admitted to Tex. bar, 1959; asso. firm Thompson, Knight, Wright & Simmons, Dallas, 1959, 62-65; founding partner Rain Harrell Emery Young & Doke, 1965—. Lectr. govt. contract law So. Meth. U., 1965—. Mem. bd. visitors Law Sch. So. Meth. U., Dallas, 1966-69, mem. legal com. bd. trustees, 1976—; mem. bd. young assos. Hardin-Simmons U., Abilene, Tex., 1964-69; bd. dirs. Hope Cottage-Children's Bur., Dallas, 1964-72, pres., 1969-70; bd. dirs. Dallas Theater Center, 1976—, sr. v.p., 1979—; gen. counsel Republican party Tex., 1976-77. Served with JAGC, U.S. Army, 1959-62. Mem. Internat. Trade Assn. Dallas (chmn. and pres. 1979-80), Am. (chmn. sect. pub. contract law 1969-70, mem. ho. of dels. 1970-72, 74—), Fed., Dallas bar assns., State Bar Tex., Dallas C. of C. (chmn. consular corps subcom. 1972-79, chmn. internat. com. 1979—), So. Meth. U. Law Sch. Alumni Assn. (pres. 1977-78). Methodist (chmn. com. edn. 1967-68). Editor Am. Bar Assn. Ann. Developments in Govt. Contract Law, 1975—. Home: 6910 Dartbrook Dallas TX 75240 Office: Republic Bank Tower Dallas TX 75201

DOLAN, JOHN BERNARD, real estate broker; b. Phila., July 10, 1916; s. Joseph David and Anna Elizabeth (Feeley) D.; B.S., Drexel U., 1940; M.S., Temple U., 1945; Ph.D., Carnegie Inst., 1949; m. Dorothy M. Breakey, Dec. 26, 1939; children—John B., Dorothy, Fred J., Barbara Ann. Pres. Boiler Service, Inc., Phila., 1948-60; v.p. Bateman & Co., Realtors, Boca Raton, Fla., 1962-72; pres. John B. Dolan & Co., Inc., Boca Raton, Fla., 1972—; adv. bd. Univ. Nat. Bank, Boca Raton, 1970—. Pres. Multiple Listing Service, 1971-72. Mem. sch. adv. bd. Broward County, Fla., 1964-65. Served with U.S. Merchant Marines, 1943-44. Named Realtor of the Year, 1970, 75. Mem. Fla. Assn. Realtors (v.p. 1974—), Boca Raton Bd. Realtors (pres. 1970—), Am. Soc. M.E., Engring. Club Phila., Nat. Assn. Realtors, Aircraft Owners and Pilots Assn. Roman Catholic. Club: Boca West Golf. Contbr. articles to profl. jours. Home: Star Route Box 118 Bryson City NC 28713 Office: 1299 S Ocean Blvd Boca Raton FL 33432

DOLAN, JOHN TERRY, polit. assn. exec.; b. Norwalk, Conn., Dec. 20, 1950; s. Joseph William and Margaret (Kelly) D.; B.A. in Govt., Georgetown U., 1972, postgrad., 1979. Cons. politics, 1972-75; exec. dir. Nat. Conservative Polit. Action Com., Arlington, Va., 1975-78, chmn., 1978—; admitted to D.C. bar; chmn. Nat. Conservative Research and Edn. Found., Washington Legal Found.; bd. dirs. Conservative Nat. Com., Conservatives Against Liberal Legislation; treas. Ams. for Nuclear Energy. Mem. Am. Assn. Polit. Cons., D.C. Bar, Am. Bar Assn. Roman Catholic. Office: 1500 Wilson Blvd #513 Arlington VA 22204

DOLE, RICHARD FAIRFAX, JR., lawyer, educator; b. Lowell, Mass., July 12, 1936; s. Richard Fairfax and Grace Priscilla (Haynes) D.; A.B. magna cum laude, Bates Coll., Lewiston, Maine, 1958; LL.B. with distinction, Cornell U., 1961, LL.M., 1963; S.J.D., U. Mich., 1966; m. Linda Ann Ingols, Nov. 12, 1961; children—Richard Fairfax, Robert Paul, Mary Grace. Admitted to Maine bar, 1961, N.Y. bar, 1962, Iowa bar, 1966, Tex. bar, 1979; with U. Iowa, 1964-78, prof., 1969-78; E.W. Young prof. law U. Houston, 1978—; Iowa commr. Uniform State Laws, 1969-79. Mem. Am. Law Inst., Am. Bar Assn., Tex. Bar Assn., Order of Coif, Phi Beta Kappa, Delta Sigma Rho, Phi Kappa Phi. Unitarian. Home: 9144 Kenilworth Dr Houston TX 77024 Office: U Houston Coll of Law 4800 Calhoun St Houston TX 77004

DOLENZ, BERNARD JOSEPH, neuropsychiatrist; b. W. Bend, Wis., July 10, 1933; s. Joseph and Martha (Kircher) D.; B.S., U. Okla., 1953, M.D., 1957; m. Billie Reyna, Oct. 11, 1959; children—Bruce, Brenda, Brigid, Erian, Beverly. Intern, Boston City Hosp., 1957, Harris Hosp., Ft. Worth, 1958; resident in neurology and psychiatry U. Tex. Med. Branch, Galveston, 1958-60, U. Tex. Southwestern Med. Sch., Dallas, 1960-61; founder Ft. Worth Neuropsychiat. Hosp., 1962-71, dir., 1971—; practice medicine specializing in neuropsychiatry, Ft. Worth, 1962—; mem. bd. dirs. for Neuro-Psychiat. and Health Services, Inc., Newport Beach, Calif., 1971; clin. instr. Tulane Med. Sch. Named Hon. citizen, Dallas, 1973. Mem. Am., N. Tex. psychiat. assns., Titus Harris Soc., Tarrant County Med. Soc., Tex. Med. Assn., Ft. Worth Internist Club, Mensa; hon. mem. SETAF (European) Med. Soc. Clubs: Rotary. Author: Nothing Will Stop Me, Not Even Death, 1974; Bariloche Connection, 1976. Contbr. articles to profl. med. jours. Home: 1410 Mistletoe Rd Fort Worth TX 76110 Office: 1 Summit Ave Fort Worth TX 76102

DOLEZAL, CHARLES HENRY, educator; b. La Grange, Tex., June 28, 1939; s. Henry Lambert and Doris Emma (Jurasek) D.; B.S., U. Tex., 1961, M.Ed. (Pub. Law fellow), 1965, Ph.D., 1968; m. Carroll Elizabeth Faust, Oct. 2, 1968; children—Carl Travis, Christi Elizabeth. Speech therapist Del Valle (Tex.) Pub. Sch., 1961-63; tchr. Austin (Tex.) pub. schs., 1963-64; exec. dir. Austin (Tex.) Cerebral Palsy Center, 1966-68; psychologist, dir. admissions Marbridge Found., Austin, Tex., 1964-66; program coordinator Austin (Tex.) State Sch., 1968-70; faculty S.W. Tex. State U., San Marcos, 1970-71; supt. Rio Grande State Center for Mental Health and Mental Retardation, Harlingen, Tex., 1971-72; supt. Corpus Christi (Tex.) State Sch., 1972-74; faculty Tex. A. and I. U., Corpus Christi, 1974-77, chmn. dept. spl. edn. S.W Tex. State U., San Marcos, 1977—; asso. prof. in charge of spl. edn. program. Cons. Marbridge Found., 1970-71; adviser Del Mar Jr. Coll. Mental Health Program, 1973-77. Easter Seal Soc. fellow, 1962. Mem. Am. Psychol. Assn., Am. Assn. Mental Deficiency, Council on Exceptional Children, Kappa Delta Pi, Phi Delta Kappa, Sigma Alpha Eta, Psi Chi. Democrat. Episcopalian. Mason, Rotarian. Author: Manual for Teachers of Minimally Brain-injured Children, 1968. Home: Route 1 Siesta Verde 21A San Marcos TX 78666

DOLEZAL, HENRY, ret. judge; b. Perry, Okla., Jan. 11, 1905; s. James H. and Ella (Kesl) D.; A.B., U. Okla., 1926, LL.B., 1933; student U. Chgo., 1930-31. Admitted to Okla. bar, 1933, pvt. practice, Perry, 1933-35, 37-38, 46-48; asso. dist. judge, Noble County, Okla., 1969-75; county atty. Noble County, 1935-37, county judge 1938-41; city atty., Perry, 1937-38. County adviser to registrants under Selective Service Law, 1940-41, 46-72; mayor City of Perry, 1947-49, 51-57; mem. Okla. Ho. Reps., 1957-64. Chmn. finance com. Noble County Rep. Central Com., 1948-52, chmn. central com. 1954-58. Served to maj. AUS, 1941-46. Mem. Am., Okla., Noble County (pres. 1953-55) bar assns., Am. Judicature Soc., Internat. Platform Assn., VFW (comdr. post 1948-49), Am. Legion (chaplain Okla. dept. 1960). 40 and 8, Phi Delta Phi, Presbyn. (elder, clk. session 1966-69). Mason (32 deg., K.T.), Rotarian (pres. Perry 1946-47), Odd Fellow, Knight of Pythias; mem. Order of Eastern Star, White Shrine of Jerusalem. Home: 1102 Delaware St Perry OK 73077 Office: County Courthouse Perry OK 73077

DOMBALIS, CONSTANTINE NICHOLAS, clergyman; b. Norfolk, Va., July 30, 1925; s. Nicholas John and Helen Florence (Matinos) D.; B.A., Greek Orthodox Theol. Sem., 1947, B.Th., 1949; postgrad. (Gregory Taylor scholar), Harvard, 1949-50; S.T.B., Gen. Episcopal Theol. Sem., 1951; postgrad. Columbia, 1952; m. Mary Chris Fourgis, June 6, 1954; children—Nicholas, Christopher. Ordained to ministry Greek Orthodox Ch., 1954; pastor Sts. Constantine and Helen Greek Orthodox Ch., Richmond, Va., 1954—; lectr. dept. humanities Va. Union U., Richmond; dir. Dominion Nat. Bank. Mem. Nat. Presbyters Bd. of Greek Archdiocese; vicar Greek Archdiocese of Va.; rep. Nat. Council Chs., 1970—; pres. Va. Council of Chs., 1975-76; v.p. Mediterranean Inst., U. Richmond, 1970-71; founder, Pre-Naturalization Classes (cited by Freedom Found.), 1958; mem. Richmond Human Relations Commn., 1970-72; pres. UN Assn. Central Va., 1972—, Boys Club, 1971; mem. Va. Gov.'s Electricity Cost Commn., 1975, Va. Bd. Vocat. Rehab., 1974—; Bd. dirs. James Branch Cabell Library, Va. Commonwealth U., Near East Found., 1978-80; bd. govs. United Givers Fund, 1966-69; trustee Hellenic Coll., 1980—. Recipient citation award D.A.R., 1968. Mem. Richmond Area Ministers Assn. (pres. 1964). Club: James River Catfish. Contbr. articles to profl. jours., mags. and newspapers, sermons to numerous books. Home: 304 Sandalwood Dr Richmond VA 23229 Office: 30 Malvern Ave Richmond VA 23221

DOMBRO, ROY SANDOR, biochemist; b. Bklyn., Oct. 21, 1933; s. Max and Esther (Shapiro) D.; B.S., Bklyn. Coll., 1954; M.S., U. Wis., 1956, Ph.D. in Biochemistry, 1958; m. Marcia Ann Winters, Sept. 10, 1967; children—Rayna Lisette, Meryl Elana. Research asso. Rockefeller U., N.Y.C., 1958-64, Inst. for Muscle Disease, N.Y.C., 1964-65; asst. prof. biochemistry and surgery Albert Einstein Coll. Medicine, Bronx, 1965-70; research asst. prof. surgery U. Miami (Fla.), 1970—; chemist VA Hosp., Miami, 1970—; instr. chemistry Miami Dade Community Coll., Miami, part-time, 1974-75. Mem. Am. Chem. Soc., Phi Beta Kappa, Sigma Xi. Jewish. Contbr. articles to chem. and med. jours. Home: 9841 SW 123d St Miami FL 33176 Office: 1201 NW 16th St Miami FL 33125

DOMBROWSKI, MADGE COHEA (MRS. CASEY WILLIAM DOMBROWSKI), photographer; b. Westville, Okla., Sept. 6, 1918; d. William E. and Ina Clyde (Greer) Cohea; B.S., Okla. Coll. for

Women, 1939; grad. N.Y. Inst. Photography, 1945, Edwards Sch. of Color, 1940; m. Casey William Dombrowski, July 3, 1943; children—Carol Jo (Mrs. Don Kitchen), Linda Norene (Mrs. Frank Edgell), Peggy Sharon (Mrs. Tom Porter), John Casey, Alan Wayne. Co-partner Cohea Studio, Frederick, Okla., 1938-80; news corr., writer Okla. Pub. Co., Oklahoma City, 1958-70, Lawton (Okla.) Morning Press, 1959-80, Wichita Falls (Tex.) Morning Press, 1958-80; news writer Sta. KTAT, Frederick, Okla., 1960-80. Lectr. on photography to various civic and womens clubs. Publicity chmn. Frederick Community Theater, 1970-72, Heart Fund, 1974-75; past mem. Frederick Ann. Fine Arts Festival; mem. Frederick Bicentennial Com., 1975. Bd. dirs. Campfire Girls, 1960-72. Recipient Plaque as Frederick's most useful citizen Lions Club, 1967, awards Okla. Press Assn. Writers' Contest, 1976-77. Mem. Frederick C. of C., Okla. Coll. for Women Alumni Assn. (dir. 1967-68), Friends of Library, Okla. Press Assn. for Women, Nat. Fedn. Press Women, Tillman County Hist. Soc. (charter), Beta Sigma Phi (census com. 1980, Woman of Yr. 4 chpts. 1980). Mem. Christian Ch. (tchr. Sunday sch. 28 years, supt. 1976-78). Club: Black Kat Bus. Women's (pres. 1943, 60-70) (Frederick). Home: 1401 Melissa St Frederick OK 73542 Office: 112 W Grand Ave Frederick OK 73542

DOMEYER, NANCY, psychotherapist, marriage and family counselor; b. Mt. Vernon, N.Y., Oct. 28, 1941; d. George and Helen Marie (Foley) Fasenfeld; A.B. cum laude, Fla. So. Coll., 1963; postgrad. Fla. State U., 1963-64; M.S.W., Tulane U., 1965; m. A. William Domeyer, June 26, 1965; 1 son, Todd William. Psychiat. social worker Touro Infirmary, New Orleans, 1965-67; coordinator out-patients, psychiat. social worker St. Louis State Hosp., 1967-69; mem. faculty Washington U. Sch. Social Work, 1968-69; supr., marriage and family counselor Family Counseling Center, Boca Raton, Fla., 1970-74; pvt. practice psychol. counseling, Delray Beach, Fla., 1974—. Mem. Nat. Assn. Social Workers, Acad. Certified Social Workers, Am., Fla. assns. marriage and family therapists, Am. Assn. Sex Educators, Counselors and Therapists, Fla. Clin. Social Workers, AAUW. Home: 24 Eleuthera Dr Ocean Ridge FL 33435 Office: 798 NE 2d Ave Delray Beach FL 33444

DOMINGUEZ, DANIEL, accountant; b. Buenos Aires, Argentina, Oct. 20, 1945; s. Vicente and Josefa (Santangelo) D.; came to U.S., 1964, naturalized, 1970; B.A., U. Houston, 1968, M.S., 1970; m. C. Naomi Liendo, Dec. 15, 1966; children—Andrea, Daniel, Mark, Bryan. Staff accountant Seidman & Seidman, C.P.A.'s, Houston, 1968, sr. accountant 1970-71, mgr. taxes, 1971-72, mgr. in charge profl. devel., scheduling, 1972-73, prin., 1974—, partner in charge of tax dept., 1977—. Chmn., mem. allocations com. United Ways of Houston, and Harris County (Tex.) Gen. Services Com.; bd. dirs. Tex. Youth Camps. Recipient Standard Oil of Tex. scholarship, 1967-68, Heine fellowship, 1968-69. C.P.A., Tex. Mem. Tex. Soc. C.P.A.'s, Am. Inst. C.P.A.'s. Mem. Spanish Bible Chapel (trustee, elder 1971—). Home: 8215 Twin Hills Houston TX 77071 Office: 700 Dresser Tower Houston TX 77002

DOMINGUEZ, JAMES FRANCIS, dentist; b. New Orleans, June 13, 1920; s. James Louis and Frances Beatrice (Buchert) D.; B.S., Tulane, 1943; D.D.S., Loyola U., New Orleans, 1945; m. Estelle Viola Haase, Jan. 24, 1945; 1 dau., Carlos Ann (Mrs. Gary Jude Danos). Individual practice dentistry, New Orleans, 1945—. Dir. Assn. Upper State St. Inc., 1966—. Served with USNR, 1943-45, 52-54, comdr. (ret.). Mem. C. Victor Vignes Hon. Dental Fraternity, ADA, La., New Orleans dental assns., Xi Psi Phi. Roman Catholic. Home: 2323 State St New Orleans LA 70118 Office: 2233 Jefferson Hwy New Orleans LA 70121

DOMINGUEZ, SYLVIA MAIDA, educator; b. Mercedes, Tex.; d. Jesus J. and Adela (de la Garza) Vasquez; certificate St. Louis Inst. Mus., student U. Mexico, B.A., Our Lady of the Lake Coll., San Antonio, 1957, M.Ed., 1958; M.A., U. Ariz., 1968; Ph.D., U. Ariz., 1971; m. John F. Dominguez, Aug. 15, 1959; 1 son, John J. Instr. Spanish and English, Our Lady of the Lake Coll., 1956-59; tchr. So. Palm Garden Sch., Mercedes, 1959-60; instr. Pan Am. U., Edinburg, Tex., instr., after 1960, asso. prof., 1976-78, prof., 1978—; lectr., cons. McAllen (Tex.) Bilingual Inst., 1970—; leader bilingual edn. workshops Weslaco, Tex., 1971-75, McAllen, 1971-73, Brownsville, Tex., 1971, Edgewood Ind. Sch. Dist., San Antonio, 1974—; mem. advisory bd. McAllen Bilingual Edn., 1970-72. Active Democratic Women of Hidalgo County, Tex., 1961—. Mem. Alliance Pan Am. Round Tables Western Hemisphere (sec. 1964-66), Am. Assn. Tchrs. Spanish and Portuguese, Southwestern Council Latin Am. Studies, Tex. Assn. Coll. Tchrs., Inter-Am. Soc., Southwestern Social Sci. Assn., South Central Modern Lang. Assn., Southwestern Sociol. Assn., League Women Voters, AAUW, Alpha Psi Omega, Alpha Chi, Sigma Delta Pi, Sigma Tau Delta, Kappa Delta Pi, Kappa Gamma Pi. Roman Catholic. Author: Lest We Forget, A Poem, The Chekov Theatre, The Christmas Twins, 1953-56; La Comadre Maria, 1973, Christmas on the Rio Grande, 1973; Samuel la Carretilla, 1974; La Comadre Maria Instruction-Production System, 1976; Curanderismo: a Dramatic Portrayal. Home: 621 S 10th St Edinburg TX 78539 Office: Dept Fgn Langs Pan American U Edinburg TX 78539

DOMINIAK, GERALDINE FLORENCE, accountant; b. Detroit, Sept. 28, 1934; d. Benjamin Vincent and Geraldine Esther (Davey) D.; B.S., U. Detroit, 1954, M.B.A., 1956; Ph.D., Mich. State U., 1966. Audit supr. Coopers & Lybrand, 1958-63; asst. prof. U. Detroit, 1965-68; asso. prof. Mich. State U., 1968-69; prof. acctg. Tex. Christian U., Ft. Worth, 1969—, chmn. dept., 1974—; Arthur Young prof. acctg. Fla. A&M U., 1977. Ford Found. fellow, 1964-65; C.P.A., Mich. Mem. Am. Inst. C.P.A.'s, Am. Acctg. Assn., Assn. Govt. Accts., Nat. Assn. Accts., Am. Womans Soc. C.P.A.'s, Tex. Soc. C.P.A.'s, AAUP. Roman Catholic. Author: (with J. Edwards and T. Hedges) Interim Financial Reporting, 1972; (with J. Louderback) Managerial Accounting, 1975. Home: 4401 Cardiff St Fort Worth TX 76133 Office: Sch Bus Tex Christian U Fort Worth TX 76129

DOMINICK, WAYNE DENNIS, computer scientist, educator; b. Chgo., Oct. 19, 1946; s. Edwin Frank and Helen (Kmiec) D.; B.S., Ill. Inst. Tech., 1968; M.S., Northwestern U., 1974, Ph.D., 1975; m. Joan Theresa Knox, Jan. 3, 1971; children—Brian Keith, Wendy Dion. Royal E. Cabell fellow Northwestern U., Evanston, Ill., 1974-75; computer sci. cons., Evanston and Lafayette, La., 1971—; asso. prof. computer sci. U. Southwestern La., Lafayette, 1975—; v.p. Info. Mgmt., Inc., Lafayette, 1978—, Optimum Info. Systems, Inc., Columbus, Ohio, 1979—. Served with U.S. Army, 1969-71. Mem. Am. Soc. Info. Sci. (chmn. spl. interest group/numeric data bases br. 1977—), Assn. Computing Machinery. Contbr. articles to profl. jours. Home: 225 Lippi Blvd Lafayette LA 70508 Office: PO Box 4 4330 U Southwestern La Lafayette LA 70504

DOMINY, MATTHEW, Army officer; b. Bayshore, N.Y., Nov. 30, 1946; s. Charles Reeve and Sheila (Paige) D.; B.S., Bucknell U., 1969; M. Engring., U. Fla., 1977. Commd. 2d. lt., C.E., U.S. Army, 1969, advanced through grades to capt., 1974, service Vietnam with 169, 92d Engr. bns., 1971, co. comdr. Co. C, 54th Engr. Bn., Wildflecken, W. Ger., 1972-73, engr. staff officer hdqrs. 130th Engr. Brigade, Hanau, W. Ger., 1973-74, bn. ops. officer hdqrs. 317th Engr. Bn., Eschborn, W. Ger., 1974-76, assignment officer engr. lts., hdqrs. Dept. Army, Mil. Personnel Center, Alexandria, Va., 1977-78, distbn. mgmt. officer, 1978—. Decorated Meritorious Service medal, Bronze Star; registered profl. engr., Fla. Mem. ASCE, Internat. Star Class Racing Assn., Fla. Engring. Soc., Assn. U.S. Army, Tau Beta Pi, Lambda Chi Alpha. Mem. Order of DeMolay (life). Home: 14481 Brentwood Ct Woodbridge VA 22193 Office: 200 Stovall St Alexandria VA 22332

DOMIT, MOUSSA MAJED, mus. adminstr.; b. Mazarat-raffah, Lebanon, May 24, 1932; s. Majed M. and Jamileh (Khoury) D.; came to U.S., 1953, naturalized, 1967; B.A., Ohio State U., 1961, postgrad., 1961-62; M.S., So. Conn. State Coll., 1967; postgrad. Yale U., 1964-66. Instr. in art history Columbus Coll. Art and Design, 1962-64; curator intra-univ. loan collection, registrar collections Yale U. Art Gallery, 1966-68; asso. dir. Corcoran Gallery Art, Washington, 1968-70, lectr. in art appreciation Corcoran Sch. Art, 1968-70; curator Nat. Gallery of Art, Washington, 1970-72; lectr. in art history Hood Coll., 1971-72; asso. dir. N.C. Mus. Art, Raleigh, 1972-74, dir., 1974—. Bd. advisors U. Ga. Mus. Art, Athens, 1976—; sec. N.C. Art Com., 1974—. Mem. Assn. Art Mus. Dirs., Am. Assn. Museums, Nat. Soc. Lit. and the Arts, N.C. Art Soc. (dir.). Author: George Lee: Recent Color Photography, 1969; American Impressionist Painting, 1973; Saliba Douaihy: A Retrospective Exhibition, 1978. Office: NC Museum Art 107 E Morgan St Raleigh NC 27611*

DOMURAT, RICHARD FRANCIS, design and bldg. cons.; b. New Britain, Conn., July 11, 1940; s. Frank Boleslav and Josephine Hedwig (Laskowsi) D.; student Washington U., St. Louis, U. Hartford (Conn.); m. Bette-Jane Christine Zenga, Nov. 30, 1963; children—Kimberly Ann, Kristine Elise. With Bank Bldg. Corp., St. Louis, 1958-73, constrn. supt., 1962-67, constrn. project mgr., 1967-69, mgr. constrn., mem. mgmt. group, 1969-73; self-employed cons., 1973-74; mgr. constrn., mem. exec. com. Finacial Bldg. Consultants, Atlanta, 1974-75; S.E. div. mgr. Bank Consultants of Am., Denver, 1975-76; pres., chief exec. officer, chmn. bd. Design/ Build Concepts, Atlanta, 1976—; cons. Mem. Holy Spirit Cath. Ch. Bd. Edn., Atlanta. Served with AUS, 1962-63. Certified in constrn., Fla.; licensed gen. contractor, Tenn., Fla., Va. Mem. Nat. Assn. Rev. Appraisers (sr.). Author: Manual of Design and Construction for Banks, 1974. Instrumental in architecture and bldg. of over 300 finanical facilities, 1957—. Home: Atlanta GA 30327 Office: Design/Build Concepts 5600 Roswell Rd Prado N 390 Atlanta GA 30342

DONAHUE, HAYDEN HACKNEY, psychiatrist; b. El Reno, Okla., Dec. 4, 1912; s. Henry Hilton and Mamie (Hackney) D.; student U. S.D., 1930-31; student U. Kans., 1932-34, B.S., 1939, M.D., 1941; m. Helen Patricia Toothaker, Feb. 22, 1947; children—Erin Kathleen, Kerry Shannon, Patricia Marie. Intern, U. Ga. Medicine Hosp., 1941-42, USAAF Sch. Aviation Medicine, 1943; chief hosp. operations VA, Washington, 1946; asst. mgr., acting mgr. VA Hosp., North Little Rock, Ark., 1946-49; dir. edn. and research Ark. State Hosp., 1949-51; asst. med. dir. Tex. Bd. Hosps. and Spl. Schs., 1951-53; dir. mental health Okla., 1953-59; asst. supt., dir. projects Ark. State Hosp., 1959-61; supt. Central State Griffin Meml. Hosp., Norman, Okla., 1961-79; chief cons. psychiatry Okla. State Penitentiary, 1963—; cons. psychiatry USAF Hosp., Tinker Field, 1964—, Okla. Crime Bur., 1964—; asst. dir. Okla. Dept. Mental Health, 1966-70, dir., 1970-78; asso. prof. psychiatry Ark. Sch. Med., 1949-51, 60-61; lectr. legal medicine U. Tex. Sch. Law, 1952-53; cons. asst. prof. neurology and psychiatry U. Okla. Sch. Medicine, 1954-58, asso. prof. psychiatry, 1969-79; clin. prof. psychiatry behavioral scis., 1967—; dir. Okla. Inst. Mental Health Edn. and Tng., 1979—; instr. psychology Okla. State U., 1958-59; mem. faculty Southwestern Homicide Inst., U. Okla.-U. Tex., 1953—. Mem. Okla. Med. Research Commn., 1963-78, Gov. Okla. Adv. Mental Health Planning Com., 1963-68, Gov. Okla. Com. Alcoholism, 1962-70, Okla. Mental Health Planning Com., 1963-68, Adv. Com. to Mental Health Authority, 1963-70, Okla. and Ark. Gov.'s Commn. White House Conf. Aging, 1959-61, 69; mem., chmn. Okla. State Health Planning Commn., 1974—; nat. adv. council White House Conf. on Aging, 1959-61, chmn. sect. mental health and aging, 1960-61, vice chmn. Okla. com. White House Conf. Children and Youth, 1959, 69—; adviser to Okla. com. Pres.'s Com. on Employment Handicapped, 1957-59, 61—; rep. 2d Latin Am. Seminar Mental Health, WHO, Buenos Aires, 1963; council mental health tng. and research So. Regional Edn. Bd., 1954-59; sec. sect. psychopharmacology U.S.-Mexican Psychiat. Conf., 1963; mem. exec. com. Okla. Crime Commn., 1969-74; chmn. Crime Commn. Com. on Juvenile Delinquency, 1969-74, mem., 1974-79; chmn. Okla. Council on Juvenile Delinquency Planning, 1969—; chmn. Okla. Mental Health Authority, 1970-78; mem. Okla. Alcohol Authority, 1970-78, Okla. Drug Treatment and Rehab. Authority, 1970-78, Com. Reorgn. Exec. Govt. Okla., 1971-74, Health Planning Council, 1965-69; med. adv. bd. United Cerebral Palsy Assn. Okla., 1969-79; chmn. spl. study group Am. Psychiat. Assn.-Am. Bar Assn.; mem. faculty and adv. com. Children's Hosp., Oklahoma City, 1975—; adviser subcom. on nat. health ins. Com. Ways and Means, U.S. Ho. of Reps., 1975—. Bd. dirs., v.p. Okla. Alcoholism Council; bd. dirs. Sr. Citizens Okla.; bd. dirs., treas. Pan Am. Tng. Exchange in Psychiatry, 1961-65; bd. dirs. Wesley Found., U. Okla., 1962—, chmn., 1963-68; bd. dirs. Assn. Med. Supts. Mental Hosps., pres., 1975; mem. council Am. Assn. Psychiat. Adminstrs. Served with M.C., USAAF, 1942-46. Recipient Outstanding Service awards Okla. Mental Health Assn., 1962, Okla. Psychol. Assn., 1962; Leadership and Teaching award Psychiat. Tech. Assn., Ark.; Donahue Appreciation Day proclaimed in Okla., 1959; A.H. Robins community service award Okla. State Med. Assn., 1979; commendation outstanding leadership and service Okla. Conf. Juvenile Delinquency, 1978; Hayden H. Donahue Mental Health Inst. named in his honor by joint resolution House and Senate Okla., 1977. Fellow Am. Psychiat. Assn. (pres. Okla. dist. br. 1963, del. Okla. 1969—, chmn. budget com., treas. 1968-72, chmn. ad hoc com. legis. network), Am. Assn. Mental Deficiency, Am. Geriatrics Soc., AAAS, Am. Coll. Psychiatrists (a founder, regent 1965—, treas. 1966-72, pres. 1975-76, Bowis award 1975, Outstanding Service commendation 1976); mem. Mid-Continent, Okla. (pres. 1962-66) psychiat. assns., Am. Med. Correctional Assn., Nat. Acad. Religion and Mental Health, Nat., Okla. (pres. 1969) rehab. assns., Am., Okla. (chmn. council pub. health 1962-, ho. of dels. 1964-76) med. assns., Nat. Assn. Mental Health (nat. profl. adv. council 1959-68), Nat. Assn. Mental Hosp. Program Dirs. (organizing com. 1958-59), Brookings Inst. Mental Health and Govt., Am. Bar Assn. (commr. commn. mentally disabled 1973—, mem. exec. com. 1973—). Methodist (steward). Rotarian. Contbr. articles to med. and profl. jours. Home: 1109 Westbrooke Terr Norman OK 73069 Office: Box 151 Norman OK 73070

DONALD, DERBONNE RAY, mech. engr.; b. Many, La., Mar. 14, 1949; s. Harvey James and Cathrine Jane (Mitchell) D.; B.S. in Mech. Engring., La. State U., 1972. Engr., Newport News (Va.) Shipbuilding Co., 1972—. Mem. ASME. Office: 3010 Shelly St Baton Rouge LA 70805

DONALDSON, BILLY JOE, computer programmer/analyst; b. Ft. Benning, Ga., July 5, 1949; s. Joe T. and Edna L. (Brawner) D.; student Columbus (Ga.) Coll., 1980—. Asst. to dir. Datamatics Inc., Columbus, Ga., 1973-74; computor supr. Columbus (Ga.) Coll., 1974—; data processing sect. Columbus Med. Center, 1979—; owner, pres. Software Designs Co., Fortson, Ga., 1979—, free-lance computer programmer/analyst 1979—. Served with U.S. Army, 1971-73 Mem. Am. Soc. Personnel Adminstrn., Columbus (Ga.) Jaycees, Delta Sigma Pi. Republican. Baptist. Home: Route 1 Box 53 Fortson GA 31808 Office: PO Box 8151 Columbus GA 31908

DONALDSON, ELVIS SMITH, JR., physician; b. Bowling Green, Ky., Apr. 19, 1945; s. Elvis Smith and Ruth Payne (McElroy) D.; B.S., Tulane U., 1967; M.D., U. Ky., 1971; m. Marcia L. Boyd, May 24, 1969; 1 son, Smith. Intern, Med. U. S.C., Charleston, 1971-72; resident in ob-gyn So. Ill. U., 1972-75, U. Ky., 1975-77; asst. prof. ob-gyn U. Ky., Lexington, also dir. residency program. Am. Cancer Soc. fellow, 1976-77, 79—. Fellow Am. Coll. Obstetricians and Gynecologists; mem. AMA, Ill. Med. Soc., Ky. Ob-Gyn Soc., Ky. Med. Assn., Fayette County Med. Soc., John W. Greene, Jr. Gynecol. Soc. Contbr. articles to profl. jours. Office: U Ky Med Center Dept Ob-Gyn 800 Rose St Lexington KY 40536

DONALDSON, LORAINE, economist; d. Lonnie Milton and Lois Lorene (Young) D.; B.S.B.A. with high honors, U. Fla., 1960, M.A. (Univ. fellow 1960, J. H. Miller scholar 1960), 1961; D.B.A. (Univ. fellow), Ind. U., 1965. Research asst. Internat. Devel. and Research Center Ind. U., 1963-64; asst. prof. econs. Ga. State U., 1964-66, asso. prof., 1955-70, prof., 1970—; bd. dirs. Atlanta Assn. Internat. Edn., 1976-79. Bd. dirs. Pine Hills Civic Assn., Atlanta, 1973—. Recipient Achievement award Beta Gamma Sigma, 1960. Mem. Am. Econ. Assn., Soc. Internat. Devel. Author: Development Planning in Ireland, 1966; contbr. articles to profl. jours. Office: Ga State U Univ Plaza Atlanta GA 30303

DONATELLI, FELIX FRANCIS, pharmacist; b. Newport, Ky., Aug. 29, 1929; s. Mario and Angela Sophie (Ferrara) D.; B.S.P., U. Fla., 1951; m. Barbara Ann Donatelli; children—Nick, Felicia, Steve. Pharmacist, mgr. Liggett-Rexall Stores, 1951-58; founder Donatelli's Pharmacies, Lakeland, Fla., 1959; pres. Donnaco, Inc., D & F Goaves; dir. Holiday Nursing Homes, Inc. Mem. utilization rev. com. Presbyn. Extended Care Facility, 1954; dir. Pharmashield, 1967-70. Head basketball coach St. Joseph Falcons, 1970-74. Founder Gator Youth Athletic Assn., gen. mgr., 1967-75; dir. Polk County Heart Assn., 1968-70; chmn. Citizens Adv. Com. City of Lakeland, Lakeland Planning and Zoning Bd., 1969; mem. Gov.'s Medicaid Com., 1967; mem. Host Task Force, Lakeland, 1975; mem. pharmacist adv. panel Drug Topics, 1974; bd. dirs. Orlando Diocese Bd. Edn. Named vol. of year Fla. Heart Assn., 1969, outstanding young man Lakeland Jr. C. of C., 1965, Fla. pharmacist of the year, 1964, 65. Served with USNR, 1951. Mem. Fla. (pres. 1965), Polk County (pres. 1960) pharm. assns., Nat. Assn. Retail Druggists, U. Fla. Coll. Pharm. Alumni Assn. (pres. 1966), Lakeland C. of C. (dir. 1975—, host task force, chmn.). Rotarian (dir.). Clubs: Lakeland Yacht and Country; Woodlake Tennis. Home: 2256 Collins Ln Lakeland FL 33803 Office: 821 Oleander St Lakeland FL 33801

DONATO, ANTONIO TUASON, physician; b. Manila, Philippines, Mar. 29, 1939; s. Ramon Donato and Amparo Gatdula Tuason; A.A., U. Sto. Tomas Manila, 1957, M.D., 1962; m. Marilyn Javier Ranada, May 23, 1964; children—Mary Anne, Bernadette L., Pauline T., Jude A., Grace C., James A. Intern Perth Amboy (N.J.) Gen. Hosp., 1963; resident surgery Hosp. St. Raphael, New Haven, 1964-68; cardiothoracic resident Henry Ford Hosp., Detroit, 1968-69, Boston U. Med. Center, 1969-71; resident pathology Western Mass. Hosp., Westfield, 1971-72; practice medicine specializing in thoracic, cardiovascular and gen. surgery VA Hosp., Salem, Va., 1972-75, Roanoke, Va., 1975—; clin. asso. in thoracic surgery Boston U., 1970-71; asst. prof. surgery U. Va. Sch. Med., Charlottesville, 1972-77, asst. clin. prof. surgery, 1977—; vis. surgeon U. Va. Hosp., 1972—; thoracic and vascular surgery cons. Salem VA Hosp., 1975—; dir. acad. programs and surg. residencies, attending staff Community Hosp. Roanoke Valley, Roanoke, 1975—, also Roanoke Meml. Hosp. Diplomate Am. Bd. Surgery, Am. Bd. Thoracic Surgery. Fellow A.C.S., Internat. Coll. Surgeons, Am. Coll. Chest Physicians, Southeastern Surg. Congress; mem. AMA (Physicians Recognition award 1969, 72, 75), Med. Soc. Va., Roanoke Acad. Medicine, Va. Surg. Soc., So. Thoracic Surg. Assn., Assn. VA Surgeons, Soc. Philippine Surgeons in Am., Assn. Philippine Practicing Physicians Am., Am. Acad. Med. Dirs. (charter mem.), Roanoke Thoracic and Cardiovascular Surg. Soc., Philippine Yale New Haven Assn. (pres. 1966-67), Philippine Med. Assos. New Eng. (pres. 1970-71), Philippine-Am. Assn. S.W. Va. (pres. 1974-75). Roman Catholic. Clubs: Lions, Knights of Rizal. Contbr. articles to sci. and med. jours. Home: 3707 Alton Rd Roanoke VA 24014 Office: 1215 3rd St Roanoke VA 24016

DONAUBAUER, ELTON HENRY, univ. administr; b. Marion, Tex., Nov. 9, 1921; s. Edwin O. and Melanie (Schultze) D.; B.A., Sul Ross State Coll., 1949, M.A., 1950; M.Ed., George Peabody Coll. for Tchrs., 1951; m. Dorothy Mauryne Lindley, Oct. 17, 1947; children—Melanie, Allyn, Craig. Asst. mgr. J. C. Penney Co., New Braunfeis, Tex., 1939-42, 1946; prof. edn., polit. sci. S.W. Tex. Jr. Coll., Uvaide, 1949-50; dir. pub. relations Community Chest, Nashville, 1951-54, Allegheny County, Pitts., 1954-55; regional dir., dir. info. services Pa. United Fund, 1955-57; instr. Watkins Inst. High Sch., Nashville, 1952-54; mem. pub. relations adv. com. United Community Funds and Councils of Am., Inc., 1955-57, mem. United Fund adv. com., 1957-60; exec. dir. United Fund of Shenango Valley Area, Sharon, Pa., 1957-60; exec. dir. Community Chest, United Fund, Health and Welfare Council, Pulaski County, Little Rock, 1960-64; dir. devel. and planning George Peabody Coll. for Tchrs., also lectr. Sociology and Social scis. Watkins Inst., Nashville, 1964-68; dir. devel. U. Ark., Fayetteville, 1968-75, exec. dir. for devel., 1975—; pres. S.W. Regional Conf. United Community Funds and Councils Am., 1963—; part-time instr. social scis. Little Rock U. Chmn. United Fund Campaign, 1970; div. chmn. Washington Regional Hosp. Devel. Campaign; co-chmn. Ridgehouse campaign, Fayetteville; chmn. Washington County United Way; pres. United Community Services of N.W. Ark., 1974—; mem. adv. bd. Washington County Juvenile Ct.; pres. Fayetteville Council Civic Clubs, 1976-77; mem. Ridge House Renovation Com., chmn. Community Appearance Task Force; vice chmn. Fayetteville Planning Commn.; mem. com. on taxation and ednl. fundraising Council for Advancement and Support of Edn., 1977—; bd. dirs. Westark Boy Scout Council; bd. dirs., pres. United Fund Fayetteville, United Community Services, Fayetteville; mem. adv. bd. Salvation Army, 1980—; mem., adv. house corp. Phi Gamma Delta, 1980—; vol. cons. Ft. Smith Arts Center, 1980—, Ft. Smith Little Theatre, 1980—, ARC, Ft. Smith, 1980—. Served with USAAF, 1945-46. Recipient Service to Mankind award Sertoma Club, 1976; Bus. Person of Yr. award Phi Beta Lambda, 1977. Mem. Pub. Relations Soc. Am., Am. Judicature Soc., Ark., Springdale, Fayetteville chambers commerce, Am. Mgmt. Assn., Nat. (dir.), S.W. socs. fund raisers, Internat. Platform Assn., Washington County Hist. Soc., Phi Delta Kappa, Kappa Delta Pi. Methodist (bd. pres. Meth. men). Rotarian (pres. Fayetteville 1975-76, dir.). Home: 320 Oakwood Fayetteville AR 72701

DONCHIAN, RICHARD DAVOUD, econ. analyst; b. Hartford, Conn., Sept. 21, 1905; s. Samuel B. and Armenouhi A. (Davoud) D.; A.B., Yale U., 1928; C.F.A., U. Va., 1964; m. Alma C. Gibbs, Feb. 9, 1957. With Hemphill Noyes & Co., N.Y.C., 1933-35; Samuel

Donchian Rug Co., Hartford, 1935-38; pres. Fin. Supervision, Inc., 1938-42; econ. analyst Shearson-Hammill & Co., N.Y.C., 1946-48; investment advisor, 1948-60; pres., dir. Futures Inc., 1948-60; dir. commodity research, account exec. Hayden, Stone & Co. (now Shearson Loeb Rhoades Inc.), N.Y.C., 1960-69, v.p., 1970-76, sr. v.p. investments, 1976—; advisor Commodity Trend Timing Fund, 1979—; dir. Donchian Mgmt. Inc., Ft. Lauderdale, Fla., Fin. Supervision Inc., Greenwich, Conn.; mem. N.Y. Cotton Exchange, Commodity Exchange, Inc., Amex Commodities Exchange. Statis. control officer, USAAF, 1942-45. Mem. N.Y. Soc. Security Analysts, Am. Statis. Assn., Inst. Chartered Fin. Analysts, Fin. Forum. Republican. Presbyterian (elder). Clubs: N.Y. Commodity, Yale, Down Town Assn. (N.Y.C.); Yale (Ft. Lauderdale, Fla.); Univ. (Hartford); Scarsdale Golf; Appalachian Mountain. Author articles and monographs. Home: 133 Pompano Beach Blvd Pompano Beach FL 33062 also Country Club Apts Hartsdale NY 10530 also Bomoseen VT 05732 Office: 3099 E Commercial Blvd Fort Lauderdale FL 33308 also 2 Greenwich Plaza Greenwich CT 06830

DONEGAN, DENNIS PATRICK, bldg. supply co. exec.; b. Dickson, Tenn., Aug. 30, 1945; s. Verlie Lee and Edna Iomagene D.; B.S. in Mktg., Austin Peay State U., 1969; M.B.A., U. Tenn., 1971; m. Cathie Lee DeWoody, Aug. 13, 1967; children—Diana, Kelly, Rachel. Loan officer Nashville City Bank & Trust Co., 1969-76; credit mgr. Peterbilt Motors Co., Madison, Tenn., 1976-78; credit and cash mgr. Franklin Builders Supply Co., Inc., Nashville, 1978—. Served with U.S. Army, 1965-67. Mem. Nat. Assn. Credit Mgmt., Nashville Assn. Credit Mgmt. Methodist. Home: 124 Grandview Circle Old Hickory TN 37138 Office: 612 10th Ave N Nashville TN 37203

DONESKY, GARRY LEROY, hosp. adminstr.; b. Vernon, B.C., Can., Aug. 15, 1947; s. Conn J. and Doris D.; came to U.S., 1973; B.A. in Bus. Adminstrn., Andrews U., Berien Springs, Mich., 1971; m. Barbara Joyce Howson, May 5, 1968; 1 dau., Tamara Rochelle. Asst. dir. personnel N. York Branson Hosp., Willowdale, Ont., Can., 1971-73; dir. personnel, asst. adminstr. Hialeah (Fla.) Hosp., 1973-77; pres. Watkins Meml. Hosp., Ellijay, Ga., 1977—; dir. SAHHS, Inc. Trustee, Smyrna (Ga.) Hosp.; mem. bd. Gilmer Arts Council. Mem. Ellijay C. of C. (dir. 1978—), Am. Acad. Med. Adminstrs., Aircraft Owners and Pilots Assn. Republican. Adventist. Clubs: Lions Internat., Ellijay Running. Home: PO Box 845 Ellijay GA 30540 Office: PO Box 346 Ellijay GA 30540

DONKIN, ROBERT GORDON, mgmt. cons.; b. Cleve., Apr. 16, 1923; s. Robert Forster and Louise (Hess) D.; B.S.M.E., Case Inst. Tech., 1944; postgrad. U.S. Naval Acad., 1944; m. Marilyn Ann Mitzel, Dec. 23, 1944; children—Marilyn Ann Donkin Walters, Elizabeth Louise Donkin Ayers, Diana Jeanne Donkin Grigg. Design engr. Towmotor Corp., 1946-47; chief engr. Webster Products Corp., 1947-48; chief mech. designer Swartwout Co., 1949-50, asst. gen. supt., 1951-54, mgr. steam specialties mfg., 1955-56; gen. supt. Rockwell Mfg. Co., Chgo., 1957-58, works mgr., 1959-62, gen. mgr., Tulsa, 1962-63; mng. asso., gen. mgmt. cons. div. mgmt. services Arthur Young & Co., Tulsa, 1964-66, prin., 1967-68, dir., partner, 1969-73; pres. Indsl. Relations Services, Inc., Tulsa, 1973—; exec. v.p. Selindex, Inc., 1976—. Served to ensign USNR, 1942-46. Mem. Am. Prodn. and Inventory Control Soc. (pres. Tulsa chpt. 1975-76), Phi Delta Theta. Republican. Methodist. Club: Mason. Patentee centrifuge. Home: 5408 E 38th St Tulsa OK 74135 Office: 2300 E 14th St Suite 302 Tulsa OK 74104

DONLEY, JOAN PETRELLA, internist; b. Wheeling, W.Va., Aug. 9, 1948; d. August and Jeannette E. (Lupinetti) Petrella; B.S., W.Va. U., 1970, M.D., 1974; m. Gregory J. Donley, June 6, 1970; children—Gregory Ryan, Sarah Elizabeth. Intern, Baylor U. Med. Center, Dallas, 1974-75; resident in internal medicine Meth. Hosp., Dallas, 1975-78; practice medicine, specializing in internal medicine, Dallas, 1978—; staff physician Med. City Hosp., Dallas, 1979—, Richard (Tex.) Med. Center, 1979—. Diplomate Am. Bd. Internal Medicine. Mem. A.C.P., Dallas Acad. Internal Medicine, Am. Med. Women's Assn. Roman Catholic. Office: 7777 Forest Ln Dallas TX 75230

DONNELL, HAROLD DOUGLAS, SR., landscape architect; b. Mobeetie, Tex., Dec. 29, 1925; s. Arlander C. and Ada (Douglas) D.; student Kans. State Tchrs. Coll., 1944; B.S. in Agr., Tex. Tech. U., 1956, postgrad. 1955-56; m. Virginia Hartman, Dec. 15, 1945 (div.); children—Harold D., Dennis Lee, Sandra Donnell Kimbro, Peggy Sue, Jill Ruth; m. 2d. Patricia Voelker Taylor, March 1978. Owner floral shop and nursery, Champaign, Ill., 1949-50; product supr. Procter & Gamble Def. Corp., Amarillo, Tex., 1950-55; landscape architect, horticulturist City of Dallas, 1956-57; office mgr. Brown & Root Engring., Houston, 1957-59; individual practice landscape architecture, 1959-71; pres. Peaches of Tex., Inc., Fruit Builders, Inc.; cons. for numerous orchards, Tex., Calif., Mex. Active P.T.A., Boy Scouts Am., Little League. Served with USAF, 1943-46. Mem. Tex. Soc. Landscape Architects. Mem. Christian Ch. Club: Masons (32 deg., Shriner). Home: 3235 La Quinta Missouri City TX 77459

DONNELLAN, THOMAS ANDREW, archbishop; b. N.Y.C., Jan. 24, 1914; s. Andrew and Margaret (Egan) D.; A.B., St. Joseph's Sem., 1939; J.C.D., Catholic U. Am., 1942. Ordained priest Roman Catholic Ch., 1939; chancellor Archdiocese of N.Y., 1958-62; synodal judge Marriage Tribunal, 1950-58; rector St. Joseph's Sem., 1962-64; bishop of Ogdenburg, N.Y., 1964-68, archbishop of Atlanta, 1968—. Mem. canon law com. and com. for liaison with maj. superiors of religious men. Trustee Catholic U. Decorated knight grand cross Knights Holy Sepulchre. Mem. Nat. Conf. Catholic Bishops (adminstrv. bd.), Sacred Congregation Religious and Secular Insts. Address: 756 W Peachtree St NW Atlanta GA 30308*

DONNELLY, LLOYD WILLIAM, JR., corp. exec.; b. Tillamook, Oreg., Mar. 15, 1927; s. Lloyd W. and Margaret Mary (Mulveny) D.; B.S.M.E., Tex. A. and M. U., 1950; m. Marjorie Bowen Donnelly, Aug. 27, 1949; children—Kathleen, Peter, Nancy, Mark. Engr., Monsanto, Tex. City, Tex., 1951-58, engring. mgr., Springfield, Mass., 1958-61, mfg. supt., Cin., 1961-65; dir. engring. Geigy Chem. Co., Mobile, Ala., 1965-68; v.p., mgr. So. Tech. Services, Mobile, 1968-71; v.p. chem. div. Daniel Internat. Corp., Greenville, S.C., 1971—, group v.p. engring., 1973—. Served with USNR, 1944-46. Registered profl. engr., Tex., La., Miss., Mass. Mem. S.C. Soc. Profl. Engrs., Nat. Soc. Profl. Engrs., Am. Inst. Chem. Engrs., ASME. Home: 10 Westchester Rd Greenville SC 29615 Office: Daniel Bldg Greenville SC 29602

DONOHUE, HELEN SHAY, speech pathologist, audiologist; b. Ansonia, Conn., Jan. 26; d. Thomas Francis and Margaret (Buckley) Shay; B.S., So. Conn. State Coll., 1948; M.A., Columbia U., 1958; profl. diploma U. Bridgeport, 1961; m. Thomas C. Donahue, Dec. 7, 1943. Speech and hearing therapist New Haven Public Schs., 1958-68; pvt. practice speech pathology, audiology, Boca Raton, Fla., 1969—; cons. in field. Bd. dirs. Riviera Civic Assn., 1975. Mem. Am. Speech and Hearing Assn. (cert. clin. competence), AAAS, AAUW, Pi Lambda Theta. Home: 260 NE Spanish Trail Boca Raton FL 33432

DONOVAN, TIMOTHY PAUL, historian; b. Terre Haute, Ind., Dec. 25, 1927; s. Harry Thomas and Gretchen Alma (Stakeman) D.; B.A., U. Okla., 1949, M.A., 1950, Ph.D., 1960; m. Eugenia Matella Trapp, June 1, 1950; children—Kevin, Rebecca, David, Richard. Instr., Okla. Mil. Acad., 1950-52, chmn. humanities div., 1952-57; teaching asst. U. Okla., 1957-60; asst. prof. history Tex. Tech U., 1960-63, asso. prof., 1963-68, prof., 1968-69; prof. U. Ark., Fayetteville, 1969-76, chmn. dept. history, 1976—. Recipient Distinguished Teaching award Standard Oil, 1968. Mem. Am., Ark., So. hist. assns., Orgn. Am. Historians, Popular Culture Assn., Phi Alpha Theta. Democrat. Roman Catholic. Author: Henry Adams and Brooks Adams, 1961; Historical Thought in America: Postwar Patterns, 1973. Home: 1503 Cedar St Fayetteville AR 72701 Office: Dept History U Ark Fayetteville AR 72701

DOODY, LOUIS CLARENCE, JR., accountant; b. New Orleans, Feb. 5, 1940; s. Louis Clarence and Elsie Clair (Connors) D.; B.C.S., Tulane U., 1963; m. Mary Evelyn Barba, Nov. 13, 1965; children—Dana Lori, Mary Lyn, Kathleen Louise. Accountant, Louis C. Doody, C.P.A., 1963-68, partner Doody and Doody, C.P.A.'s, 1969—. C.P.A., La., Tex., Miss. Mem. Am. Inst. C.P.A.'s, La. Soc. C.P.A.'s. Home: 231 Atherton Dr Metairie LA 70005 Office: 1160 Commerce Bldg 821 Gravier St New Orleans LA 70112

DOOLEY, ELMO SHARBER, physiologist; b. Davidson, Tenn., Feb. 23, 1924; s. Brooks L. and Katherine F. D.; B.S., Tenn. Poly. Inst., 1953; M.S., U. Tenn., 1955, Ph.D., 1957; m. Betty Jenkins, Oct. 2, 1945; children—Joseph B., Walter S., Bryan N. Clin. microbiologist Cumberland Med. Center, 1957-58; environ. physiologist U.S. Army Med. Research Lab., 1958-62; aerospace physiologist USAF Aerospace Med. Research Lab., 1962-64; prof. physiology Tenn. Tech. U., Cookeville, 1964—; cons. NASA, USAF Systems Command. Served with USAF, 1942-45, 50-51. Fellow Royal Soc. Health; mem. Aerospace Med. Assn., Am. Soc. Microbiology, Am. Fedn. Clin. Research, Tenn. Acad. Sci., Am. Acad. Microbiology. Co-author book; contbr. articles to profl. jours. Office: Biology Dept Tenn Tech Univ Cookeville TN 38501

DOOLEY, J. RONALD, coll. career specialist, writer; b. Walker County, Ga., Mar. 26, 1947; s. Earl C. and Drucilla A. (Dodd) D.; student U. Ga., 1966; B.B.A., West Ga. Coll., 1970, M.Ed. in Counseling, 1976; m. Patricia Coleman, June 21, 1975. Jr. high sch. tchr., 1970-74; poet in residence Lane Coll., 1975-76, Union U., 1975-76, Lambuth Coll., 1975-76, Jackson Community Coll., 1975-76; counselor Midlands Coll., 1977-78, career specialist, 1979—; books include: Shades of Yesterday, 1974; Old Hickory Review, 1975; editor: Poetry Anthology for the Tennessee Arts Commission, 1975. Mem. S.C. Tech. Edn. Assn., Ga. Assn. Educators, Am. Personnel and Guidance Assn., Assn. Humanistic Edn. and Devel. Home: 504 S Beltline St Columbia SC 29205

DOOLITTLE, KATHERINE HUTTON-PIERCE, acct.; b. Greensboro, N.C., Oct. 9, 1948; d. Charles Coble and Annie Lee (Thompson) Hutton; B.A. in Math. (Roxie Armfield King Scholar), U. N.C., 1970; M.A. in acctg., U. Fla., 1979; m. Jack Douglas Doolittle, July 14, 1979. Mktg. coordinator First State Bank, Toms River, N.J., 1972-73; group adminstr. Equitable Life Assurance Soc., Gainesville, Fla., 1973-75; chief acct. Environ. Sci. and Engring., Gainesville, 1975-76, controller, 1976—; tax and systems cons. C.P.A., Fla. Mem. Nat. Assn. Accts., Am. Soc. Women C.P.A.'s, Profl. Services Mgmt. Assn., Am. Inst. C.P.A.'s (asst. sec.-treas. 1980), Fla. Inst. C.P.A.'s, Beta Alpha Psi. Republican. Methodist. Office: Environ Sci and Engring PO Box 13454 Gainesville FL 32604

DORAN, MICHAEL DESMOND, psychologist, educator; b. Manchester, Eng., Jan. 20, 1923; came to U.S., 1948, naturalized, 1952; s. John Joseph and Elizabeth Doran; A.B., Fla. State U., 1955, M.A., 1956, Ph.D., 1965; m. Merle Beatrice Souter, Aug. 20, 1956. Asst. prof. psychology U. Tampa (Fla), 1956-61, 63-65; asst. prof. psychology East Tenn. State U., Johnson City, 1965-67, asso. prof., 1967-70; asso. prof. psychology The Citadel, Charleston, S.C., 1970-78, prof., 1978—. Served with USAF, 1948-52. Citadel Devel. Found. research grantee, 1974, 77. Mem. Am. Psychol. Assn., Southeastern Psychol. Assn., Charleston Area Psychol. Assn., Phi Beta Kappa, Sigma Xi, Phi Kappa Phi. Contbr. articles to profl. jours. Patentee in book constrn. Home: 106 Old Point Rd Charleston SC 29412 Office: Dept Psychology The Citadel Charleston SC 29409

DORCY, DARYL BIRNIE, state ofcl.; b. Santa Ana, Calif., Jan. 1, 1945; s. Lawrence Holmes and Doris Mae (Scranton) D.; B.A. in Polit. Sci., U. Calif., Berkeley, 1967; postgrad. San Francisco State Coll., 1967-68. Budget examiner Tex. Legis. Budget Bd., Austin, 1968-73, project coordinator for zero-base budgeting, 1973-74, sr. examiner pub. health, 1973-76; mgmt. audit dir. Tex. Dept. Mental Health and Mental Retardation, Austin, 1976—. Mem. Am. Mgmt. Assn., Am. Acad. Polit. and Social Sci., Austin Soc. Public Adminstrn., Navy League U.S. Democrat. Clubs: Phi Delta Theta Alumni. Club: Kiwanis. Home: 6506 East Hill Dr Austin TX 78731 Office: Tex Dept Mental Health and Mental Retardation Box 12668 Austin TX 78711

DOREMUS, OGDEN, lawyer; b. Atlanta, Apr. 23, 1921; s. C. Estes and Mary (McAdory) D.; B.A., Emory U., 1946, J.D., 1949; m. Carolyn Wooten Greene, Aug. 30, 1947; children—Celia Jane, Frank O., Dale Marie. Admitted to Ga. bar, 1947; asst. solicitor gen., Atlanta, 1947-49; partner firm Smith Field Doremus & Ringel, Atlanta, 1949-60, Falligant Doremus & Karsman, Savannah, Ga., 1960-72, Ogden Doremus, P.C., Metter, Ga., 1972—; prof. Woodrow Wilson Sch. Law, Atlanta, 1948-50. Mem. Atlanta City Council, 1950-53; mem. Savannah Govtl. Reorgn. Commn., 1960-61. Trustee Ga. Conservancy. Served with USAAC, 1942-46; ETO. Named Young Man of Year, Atlanta, 1951. Mem. Am. Bar Assn., State Bar Ga., Savannah Bar Assn., Sierra Club. Clubs: Savannah Golf; Chatham, Chatham Tennis; Willow Lake Country (Metter). Home: Route 2 Box 188A Metter GA 30439 Office: 52 N Broad St Metter GA 30439

DORFMAN, MYRON HERBERT, petroleum co. owner; b. Shreveport, La., July 3, 1927; s. Samuel Yandell and Rose (Gold) D.; B.S., U. Tex., 1950, M.S., 1972, Ph.D., 1975; children—Shelley Fonda Dorfman Roberts, Cynthia Renee. Geologist, engr. Sklar Oil Co., Shreveport, 1950-56, mgr. prodn. and devel., 1957-59, partner, 1958-59; owner Dorfman Oil Properties, Shreveport, 1950-71, Austin, Tex., 1971—; asst. prof. petroleum engring. U. Tex., Austin, 1974-76, asso. prof., 1976-78, prof., chmn. dept., 1978—, dir. Center for Energy Studies, 1974—, Disting. lectr. Soc. Petroleum Engrs., 1978-79. Pres., Shreveport Community Council, 1966; mem. bd. La. Gov.'s Com. for Employment Handicapped, 1966-68; bd. dirs. La. Youth Opportunity Center, Shreveport, 1966-71, A.R.C., Caddo Parish, La., 1964-71; pres. La. Mental Health Center, Shreveport, 1967; chmn. geothermal resources com. Interstate Oil Compact Commn. Served with USNR, 1945-46; PTO; ATO. Recipient medal State of Israel, 1963. Registered profl. engr., Tex. Fellow Geol. Soc. Am.; mem. Am. Geophys. Union, Nat. Acad. Scis., Am. Assn. Petroleum Geologists, Soc. Profl. Well Log Analysts, Am. Inst. Mining, Metall. and Petroleum Engrs., Shreveport Geol. Soc., Petroleum Club Shreveport, Shreveport Jewish Fedn. (pres. 1967), Pi Epsilon Tau, Tau Beta Pi, Phi Kappa Phi. Club: Shreveport Skeet (pres. 1964). Contbr. articles to profl. jours. Home: 770 E Bee Cave Rd Austin TX 78746 Office: Dept Petroleum Engring U Tex Austin TX 78712

DORION, WALLACE JOHN, JR., advt. exec.; b. New Orleans, Nov. 9, 1930; s. Wallace John and Henrietta Patricia (Kenney) D.; A.B., La. State U., 1953; m. Jacqueline Stanley, Mar. 28, 1960; children—Brandon John, Christopher William. Owner, exec. Dorion Advt. and Public Relations, New Orleans, 1977—; instr. Loyola U., 1969-70. Area bd. dirs. Heart Fund, 1970-71; bd. dirs. New Orleans Ad Club, 1970-73 Served to 1st lt. USAF, 1954-55. Recipient various art dirs. awards. Asso. mem. Public Relations Soc. Am., La. Assn. Broadcasters. Clubs: Chaine des Rotisseurs, Les Amis du Vin. Home: 338 Homestead Ave Metairie LA 70005 Office: 111 Iberville St New Orleans LA 70130

DORN, RICHARD ALDEN, banker; b. Chgo., June 13, 1938; s. Otto A. and Mildred G. (Hasenbank) D.; B.A., Monmouth Coll., 1961; student Valparaiso U., 1957-58; m. Judith Mack, Jan. 14, 1967; children—Julia, Richard. Mem. investment research staff St. Louis Union Trust Co., 1963-65, portfolio mgr., 1966-69; investment officer Nat. Blvd. Bank, Chgo., 1969-71; v.p., trust investment officer El Paso Nat. Bank, 1971—. Treas., mem. exec. com., mem. met. bd. YMCA. Served with U.S. Army, 1961-63. Mem. Fin. Analysts Fedn., Chgo. Fin. Analysts Soc., El Paso Estate Planners Council, El Paso Hist. Soc. Lutheran. Club: Kiwanis (v.p.). Home: 804 Royal Oak St El Paso TX 79932 Office: PO Drawer 140 El Paso TX 79980

DORN, RICHARD DONALD, oil and gas lease broker; b. Tulsa, Oct. 8, 1923; s. Kenneth C. and Laura Mae (Crooks) D.; B.S., U. Tulsa, 1950; m. Ann Adelle Miller, Sept. 11, 1950; children—Patricia Ann, Tracy. Dist. landman Cities Service Oil Co., Oklahoma City, 1950-65; ind. oil and gas operator and producer, 1965-68; ind. oil and gas lease broker, Oklahoma City, 1968—; cattle rancher; pres. Creo Oil Co., Inc. Served with USAAF, World War II. Mem. Am., Oklahoma City assns. petroleum landmen, Sigma Chi. Republican. Presbyn. Mason (K.T.). Home: 7208 Shoreline Dr Oklahoma City OK 73132 Office: Cravens Bldgs Oklahoma City OK 73102

DORNBUSH, KIRK TERRY, financial cons.; b. Atlanta, Oct. 31, 1933; s. Kirk and Claire Louise (Saperstein) D.; B.A., Vanderbilt U., 1955; m. Marilyn Jane Pierce, June 23, 1956; children—Laura M., Kirk Terry, Claire L. Partner, Courts & Co., Atlanta, 1955-69; propr. The Dornbush Co., Atlanta, 1969—; chmn. bd. Thermo Materials Corp.; dir. Southeastern Bonded Warehouses, 1st Women's Bank, N.Y. Venture Fund, Inc. Mem. Atlanta exec. finance com. Jimmy Carter presdl. campaign. Served to capt., USAR, 1955-63. Mem. Atlanta Soc. Fin. Analysts. Episcopalian. Clubs: Commerce, Capital City, Cherokee Town and Country, Amelia Island Plantation. Home: 3061 W Pine Valley Rd Atlanta GA 30305 Office: 2 Peachtree St Atlanta GA 30303

DORNENBURG, PETER RAYMOND, orthopaedic surgeon; b. Pitts., Apr. 13, 1943; s. Delbert Donald and Theodora Catherine (Kearns) D.; B.A., St. Vincent Coll., 1965; M.D., U. Pitts., 1969; m. Suzanne Digby Perrine, Aug. 30, 1969. Intern, Vanderbilt U. Hosp., Nashville, 1969-70, resident in gen. surgery, 1970-71, resident in orthopaedic surgery, 1971-74; practice medicine specializing in orthopaedic surgery, Little Rock, 1976—; clin. instr. dept. orthopaedic surgery U. Ark. for Med. Scis., Little Rock, 1976—; cons. Spina Bifide Clinic, Ark. Children's Hosp., 1976—. Served to lt. comdr., M.C., USNR, 1974-76. Diplomate Nat. Bd. Med. Examiners, Am. Bd. Orthopaedic Surgery. Fellow Am. Acad. Orthopaedic Surgeons, A.C.S. (chmn Ark. com. on trauma 1979—); mem. Ark. Orthopaedic Soc. (sec.-treas. 1977-78, pres. 1978-79), Ark. Med. Soc., Pulaski County Med. Soc., Mid-Central States Orthopaedic Soc. Club: Ark. Hand. Home Route 1 Box 15 Roland AR 72135 Office: Suite 210 1 St Vincent Circle Little Rock AR 72205

DOROUGH, VIRGINIA ANN, computer programmer; b. Birmingham, Ala., Dec. 26, 1930; d. Joseph Southern and Gladyce Mildred (Wilson) Dorough; B.S., U. Ala., 1952, postgrad., 1964-65; postgrad. Ga. State Coll., 1964; certificates Am. Inst. Banking, 1967, 69, 71, 75; grad. Sch. Banking South, 1973. Tchr. sci. Munford (Ala.) High Sch., 1952, Cahaba Heights Jr. High Sch., Birmingham, 1952-53; loan clk. First Nat. Bank of Birmingham, 1953-55; reservations agt. Eastern Airlines, Birmingham and Atlanta, 1955-64; programmer 1st Ala. Bank of Birmingham, 1965-67, systems analyst, 1967-75, asst. cashier, 1969-76, mgr. system support, 1975-76; mgr. systems First Ala. Bancshares, Inc. Birmingham, 1977-78, sr. programmer analyst Central Computer Services, Inc., Birmingham, 1978-79; systems programmer AKRA-DATA Inc., Birmingham, 1979—. Mem. planning com. U. Ala. Ann. Data Processing Conf., 1968-72. Recipient Bausch & Lomb Hon. Sci. award, 1948. Mem. Data Processing Mgmt. Assn., Am. Soc. Women Accountants (pres. 1972-73), Mountain Brook Bus. and Profl. Women's Club (v.p. 1972-73, pres. 1974-75), AAUW, Assn. for Computing Machinery (treas. So. Region conf. 1976), Freedom Found. at Valley Forge, Beta Sigma Phi (chpt. pres. 1976-77). Methodist. Soroptimist (pres. 1975-76); mem. Order Eastern Star (worthy matron 1957-58). Home: 2140 Shadybrook Lane Birmingham AL 35226 Office: AKRA-DATA Inc 2320 7th Ave S Birmingham AL 35233

DORR, JOHN ROBERT, owner petroleum land mgmt. co.; b. Pecos, Tex., Aug. 25, 1938; s. John Joseph and Dorothy Rosalie (Ulrich) D.; B.B.A., U. Okla., 1961; m. Gerta Sue Prendergast, Apr. 2, 1960; children—John Joseph, Dede Sue Helen, John Robert, Jan Elizabeth. With Amarada Petroleum, Tulsa, 1961-62; cotton farmer, rancher, Pecos, 1962-70; ind. oil and gas lease broker and oil producer Petroleum Land Mgmt. Co., Pecos, 1970—; dir. First State Bank, Matador, Tex. Pres., Reeves County Sch. Trustees, 1968-74; adv. bd. Permian Basin Grad. Center, Midland, Tex., 1975—. Served with USAF, 1961-62. Mem. Pecos C. of C. (bd. dirs. 1972-75), W. Tex. C. of C., Am. Petroleum Inst., Permian Basin Landman's Assn., Am. Assn. Petroleum Landmen, Permian Basin Petroleum Assn. (pres. 1974), Ind. Petroleum Assn. Am. (dir. 1975). Home: 8 Winding Way Pecos TX 79772 Office: 212 Security State Bank Bldg Pecos TX 79772

DORRIS, HENRY CLAY, physician, air force officer; b. Morton, Miss., July 8, 1911; s. John Henry and Helen (Evans) D.; B.S. cum laude, Millsaps Coll., 1934; M.D., Tulane U., 1938; m. Elizabeth Snelson Aycock, Nov. 23, 1940; children—Anne Elizabeth Dorris Buchness, John Clay, Katherine Dorris Fisackerly. Intern, Charity Hosp., New Orleans, 1938-39; resident Emory U.-Grady Meml. Hosp., Atlanta, 1939-40; practice medicine specializing in internal medicine, Winona, Miss., 1940-41, 45-48, Denver, 1948-50, USAF, 1948—; physician Fitzsimmons Gen. Hosp., 1948-50; commd. capt., M.C., U.S. Air Force, 1940, advanced through grades to brig. gen., 1967; comdr. U.S. Air Force Med. Center, Nagoya, Japan, 1953-55; surgeon Air Force, Mobile (Ala.) Air Materiel Area, 1955-61; vice comdr. Wilford Hall U.S. Air Force Med. Center, San Antonio, 1961-64; dir. profl. services Surgeon Gen. U.S. Air Force, Washington, 1964-68; surgeon Hdqrs. Command Andrews AFB, 1968-69; comdr. U.S. Air Force Med. Center, Keesler AFB, Miss., 1969-72; chief flight surgeon U.A. Air Force, 1965-71; med. mem. Congressional Mission to Poland, 1966. Deacon, First Presbyn. Ch., Biloxi, 1975. Decorated Legion of Merit, D.S.M. Diplomate Am. Bd.

Internal Medicine. Fellow A.C.P. (gov. 1967), Am. Coll. Chest Physicians; mem. Aerospace Med. Assn., Am. Heart Assn., Council on Clin. Cardiology, AMA, Soc. Air Force Physicians (pres. 1964-67). Club: Rotary. Chmn. editorial bd. U.S. Air Force Med. Service Digest, 1964-67. Home and office: 207 South Shore Dr Biloxi MS 39532

DORRIS, PEGGY RAE, educator; b. Holly Bluff, Miss., Feb. 27, 1933; d. Hugh B. and Alta E. (Stampley) D.; B.S. with distinction, Miss. Coll., 1956; M.S., U. Miss., 1963, Ph.D., 1967. High sch. sci. tchr. Benton, Miss., 1956-57, Wilmot, Ark., 1957-61, Pontotoc, Miss., 1961-62; teaching asst. U. Miss., 1962-66, NSF fellow, 1965-66; prof. biology, chmn. Henderson State U., Arkadelphia, Ark., 1972—. Mem. Arkadelphia Water and Sewer Commn. NSF grantee, 1960-62. Mem. AAAS, Am. Arachnologists, Ark. Acad. Scis., Miss. Acad. Scis., Kans. Entomol. Soc., Journalists of Am. Microscopical Soc., Arachnologists of S.W., Audubon Soc., Phi Kappa Phi, Beta Beta Beta, Delta Kappa Gamma (v.p., sec.). Baptist. Contbr. articles to profl. publs. Home: 125 Evonshire St Arkadelphia AR 71923 Office: Box H-642 Arkadelphia AR 71923

DORSCH, LOUIS MILTON, ret. research dir.; b. Washington, Nov. 25, 1908; s. Louis Michael and Marie (Pflieger) D.; student Wood's Comml. Sch., 1922-23; m. Viva Mae Patzack, May 2, 1952. Research specialist Newspaper Info. Service, Washington, 1923-42; librarian Scripps-Howard Newspaper Alliance, Washington, 1942-45; asst. dir. dept. research Army Times Pub. Co., Washington, 1945-50, dir. dept., 1950-72, ret., 1972. Mem. Assn. Oldest Inhabitants D.C., Canadian County Hist. Soc. (life). Lutheran. Elk. Contbd. daily syndicated column, 1925-72; compiler numerous publs. Home: 2607 S Ridgecrest Dr El Reno OK 73036

DORSETT, CORA MATHENY, librarian; b. Camden, Ark., July 15, 1921; d. Walter Stanton and Cora (Smith) Matheny; B.S. in Edn. summa cum laude, Centenary Coll. La., 1963; M.L.S., U. Miss., 1965, Ph.D., 1972; postdoctoral study U. Okla., 1974. Tchr. pub. schs., Shreveport, La., 1963-64; dir. Pine Bluff and Jefferson County Pub. Library, Pine Bluff, Ark., 1965—. Alpha Chi fellow, 1962-63; recipient Social Sci. award Chi Omega, 1963. Mem. Am., Ark., Southwestern library assns., Jefferson County Hist. Assn., Kappa Delta Pi. Episcopalian. Home: 1305 W 35th Ave Pine Bluff AR 71603 Office: 200 E 8th Ave Pine Bluff AR 71601

DORSETT, FRANCES ELLEN, psychotherapist; b. Shreveport, Jan. 7, 1938; d. Omar Lamar and Pauline (Hinds) Head; B.A., Baylor U., Waco, Tex., 1959; M.Ed. (Houston Personnel and Guidance Assn. scholar 1977), U. Houston, 1978. Tchr., Houston Ind. Sch. Dist., 1959-76; clin. psychologist's counselor, researcher, text illustrator, Houston, 1964-79; psychotherapist Houston Internat. Hosp., 1979—; leader workshops. Mem. NEA, Am. Personnel and Guidance Assn., Holistic Health Assn., Tex. Tchrs. Assn., Tex. Personnel and Guidance Assn., Houston Tchrs. Assn. Home: 7168 S Dairy Ashford St Houston TX 77072 Office: 6441 Main St Houston TX 77030

DORSETT, HERBERT FRANKLIN, hosp. adminstr.; b. Branford, Fla., Oct. 21, 1933; s. Alford Owen and Georgia Willard (Howell) D.; B.A. in Music, Stetson U., 1955; postgrad. U. Md., Europe, 1957; M.H.A., Baylor U., 1965; m. Nettie A. Sharrock, Nov. 12, 1955; children—Jerry, Carol, Jon Andrew, Johanna. Commd. 2d lt. U.S. Army, 1955, advanced through grades; dir. personnel and adminstrn. 44th Med. Brig., Saigon, Vietnam, 1966-67; adminstr. dept. medicine Walter Reed Gen. Hosp., Washington, 1967-68; ret., 1968; dept. head, program dir. ITT Sheraton Corp., Boston, 1968-72; dept. head Multivest Internat., Inc., Indpls., 1972-73, pres., 1973-74; pres., part owner Aegis Corp., Indpls., 1974-75; chief exec. officer Fawcett Meml. Hosp., Port Charlotte, Fla., 1975—. Bd. dirs. Charlotte County (Fla.) YMCA, 1978-79. Decorated Bronze Star, Army Commendation medal. Mem. Am. Hosp. Assn., Fla. League Hosps. (pres. 1980—), Omicron Delta Kappa, Pi Kappa Phi. Republican. Presbyterian. Clubs: Charlotte Harbor Yacht, Rotary (pres. club 1978-79) (Port Charlotte). Office: 101 NW Olean Blvd Port Charlotte FL 33952

DORSETT, LAWRENCE PRESTON, mech. engr.; b. York, Pa., June 29, 1938; s. George Chesley and Helen Lawrence (Walker) D.; B.S. in Engring. Physics, Lehigh U., 1958; M.S. in Engring. Mechanics, U. Kans., 1970; m. Ann Monica Ziomek, Aug. 22, 1964; 1 dau., Helen Elaine. Enlisted in U.S. Navy, 1958, advanced through grades to lt.; missile officer U.S.S. Dewey, 1970-73; nuclear ship supt. Charleston (S.C.) Naval Shipyard, 1973-76; project engr. anti-ship missile def. systems Naval Surface Weapons Center, 1976-78; ret., 1978; now sr. naval architect, prin. engr. Stanwick Corp., Charleston. Mem. U.S. Naval Inst., Sigma Xi, Tau Beta Pi, Sigma Tau, Sigma Pi Sigma. Research on steel joist-concrete slab constrn.; patentee gen. purpose launching system. Home: Route 3 Box 308 John's Island SC 29455 Office: PO Box 7445 Charleston SC 29405

DORSETT, WALTER E., JR., newspaper editor; b. Waynesboro, Pa., Apr. 3, 1947; s. Walter E. and Florence Prescott (Beckner) D.; B.A., Wake Forest U., 1969, also postgrad. Copy editor Winston-Salem (N.C.) Journal, 1968-70, 73-76, editorial writer, 1970-71, bus. editor, 1971-73, Sunday news editor, 1976-79, asst. news editor, 1979-80; dep. chief of copy desk Lexington (Ky.) Herald, 1980—. Mem. rank-order register U.S. Dept. State Fgn. Service, 1974-76. Mem. Phi Delta Phi. Democrat. Roman Catholic. Home: 1435 Forbes Rd Apt 18 Lexington KY 40505 Office: 239 W Short St Lexington KY 40507

DORSEY, BENJAMIN WILLIAM, constrn. co. exec.; b. New London, Conn., May 14, 1936; s. Thomas Francis and Helen Mary (Collins) D.; B.A., Bowdoin Coll., 1959; M.B.A., U. Maine, 1968; m. Karin Sylvia Swanson, June 26, 1965 (div.); children—Matthew William, Julie Ingrid, Alison Karin. Tchr., Kents Hill (Maine) Sch., 1963-66; research asst. Dept. Commerce and Industry, State of Maine, Augusta, 1968, dir. research, 1969, dir. operational services, 1970-71, dep. commr., 1972-73; mgr. facility siting Daniel Constrn. Co., Greenville, S.C., 1974—. Served with USN, 1959-63. Republican. Roman Catholic. Office: Daniel Constrn Co Daniel Bldg Greenville SC 29602

DORSEY, DANIEL ROBERDEAU, JR., computer co. exec.; b. Corpus Christi, Nov. 19, 1944; s. Daniel Roberdeau and Florence Agatha (Yeskawich) D.; student Va. Poly. Inst., 1963-67; B.S. in Physics, Old Dominion Coll., 1969, M.S. in Physics, 1971; postgrad. (USPHS fellow), U. Chgo., 1972. Programmer, Computer Scis. Corp., Hampton, Va., 1972-73, 74-75; programmer, physicist U.S. Naval Air. Devel. Center, Warminster, Pa., 1973-74; programmer, physicist, sr. computer systems analyst Control Data Corp., Rockville, Md., 1975—. Mem. Am. Phys. Soc., Assn. Computing Machinery, Inc., Met. Opera Guild, Inc., Am. Radio Relay League. Club: Ski of Washington. Contbr. articles to profl. jours. Home: 1060 Cambridge Crescent Norfolk VA 23508 Office: 1151 Seven Locks Rd Rockville MD 20854

DORSEY, HAROLD WINSTON, clergyman; b. Shelbyville, Ky., Dec. 31, 1916; s. Earl Vanhorn and Angie Marie (Hancock) D.; A.B., Ky. Wesleyan Coll., 1938, D.D., 1959; B.D., Emory U., 1941; m. Irene Cochran, Aug. 31, 1941; 1 son, Edwin Cochran (dec.). Ordained to ministry Meth. Ch., 1940; minister various congregations, 1942—, Pikeville (Ky.) United Ch., 1960-63; dist. supt. Danville dist. United Meth. Ch., 1963-69; minister Epworth United Ch., Lexington, Ky., 1969-75, First United Meth. Ch., Ashland, Ky., 1975-79, supt., Lexington, 1979—. Del. Southeastern Jurisdictional Conf., 1968, 72, 76; alternate del. Gen. Conf. United Meth. Ch., 1968, 72, 76, 80; mem. Southeastern Jurisdictional Council, 1968-76; chmn. various bds. and agencies Ky. ann. conf. United Meth. Ch.; chmn. Ky. Conf. Bd. Pensions, 1976—, co-chmn. Pension Funding Crusade, 1977. Trustee Ky. Wesleyan Coll., Good Samaritan Hosp.; bd. govs. Lexington-Shrine Hosp. Ky. col.; named to Floyd County Hall of Fame, 1959. Clubs: Masons, Shriners, Kiwanis. Home: 215 Caralpa Rd Lexington KY 40502 Office: Room 206 1018 New Circle Rd NE Lexington KY 40505

DORSEY, JASPER NEWTON, journalist, educator; b. Marietta, Ga., Jan. 19, 1913; s. John Tucker and Annie (Coryell) D.; A.B., U. Ga., 1936, postgrad. Lumpkin Law Sch., 1935-36; m. Callender Hull Weltner, Oct. 16, 1937; children—Sally Dorsey Danner, John Tucker (dec.). With So. Bell Tel. & Tel. Co., Inc., 1937-61, 68-78, v.p., chief exec. Ga. ops., Atlanta, 1968-78; mgr. govt. relations AT&T, Washington, 1962-68; dir. Fulton Nat. Corp., Fulton Nat. Bank, Atlanta; columnist Atlanta Jour.-Constn.; contbg. editor Sky mag.; adj. prof. mgmt. U. Ga.; charter mem. adv. bd. Coll. Bus. Adminstrn., U. Ga. Mem. adv. bd. Salvation Army, Atlanta; sight-saving chmn. Ga. Soc. Prevention Blindness, 1975-76; sec., mem. World Congress Center Authority; former state dir. Ga. Friendship Force, Atlanta Boys Club, Kidney Found. Ga.; past hon. bd. dirs. Ga. Engring. Found., Ga. Econ. Council; former chmn., mem. exec. com. U. Ga. Found., Atlanta; trustee Ga. Student Ednl. Fund, Athens, Ga. 4-H Found., Ga. Found. Ind. Colls.; charter mem. adv. bd. U. Ga. Henry Grady Sch. Journalism, pres., 1972-74; former mem. exec. com. bd. visitors Emory U., Atlanta; charter mem. pres.'s adv. bd. Med. Coll. Ga.; chmn. Richard B. Russell Found., Atlanta; former chmn. bd. govs. Atlanta Community Service Awards; adv. council Ga. Agrirama Authority; past bd. dirs. YMCA, Ga. Easter Seal Soc., NCCJ, Ga. Conservancy; past state fund chmn. ARC. Served to lt. col., inf., U.S. Army, 1941-46. Recipient Blue Key award U. Ga., 1967; Outstanding Contbn. to U. Ga. award Student Body, 1969; Alumni Merit award U. Ga., 1970; Georgian of Year award Ga. Assn. Broadcasters, 1971; Distinguished Georgian award Pub. Relations Soc. Am., 1974; named Citizen of Year for Cobb County, Ga., Marietta Daily Jour., C. of C., 1974; Alumnus of Year award Henry Grady Sch. Journalism, U. Ga., 1976; Community Service award Women's C. of C. Atlanta, 1977; William Booth award Salvation Army, 1977; Atlanta Salesman of Yr. award Atlanta Sales & Mktg. Execs. Atlanta, Inc., 1977; Pres.'s award Kidney Found. Ga., 1977; Pres.'s award Cobb County C. of C., 1977; Hon. Lifetime Mem. award Atlanta Jaycees, 1977; Free Enterprise award Ga. Found. Ind. Colls., 1978; Big Heart award Ga. Assn. Retarded Citizens, 1979; Citizen of Year, N. Ga. Civitan Clubs and Buckhead Rotary Club, 1979; J. W. Fanning award Leadership Ga., 1980. Mem. Ga. (past pres., chmn. bd., now hon. chmn. bd., life dir.), Atlanta (former dir.), chambers commerce, Soc. Colonial Wars, Newcomen Soc. N. Am., U. Ga. Alumni Assn. (nat. pres. 1967-69, chmn. bd. 1969-73), Blue Key, Sphinx, Gridiron, Greek Horsemen, Omicron Delta Kappa, Sigma Delta Chi, Sigma Iota Epsilon, Phi Delta Theta, Beta Gamma Sigma, Phi Kappa Phi, Delta Sigma Rho, Tau Kappa Alpha. Presbyterian (elder, past trustee, deacon, Sunday sch. supt.). Clubs: Rotary, Capital City, Commerce, Peachtree Golf, Piedmont Driving (Atlanta); President's (U. Ga.). Office: So Bell Telephone & Telegraph Co PO Box 3231 Atlanta GA 30302

DORTA, PAULINO, JR., med. technologist, educator; b. Hatillo, P.R., Feb. 2, 1949; s. Paulino and Juana (Perez) D.; B.S., U. P.R., 1971, grad. cert. in Med. Tech., 1972, M.S. cum laude, 1978. Instr., Arecibo (P.R.) Regional Coll., U. P.R., 1972, lab. asst. biology dept., 1975-77, asst. prof., 1979—, chmn. dept. biology, 1980—; med. technologist Dr. Susoni's Hosp. Lab., Arecibo, 1973-74. Jury mem. N. and W. Sci. Fair, Inter Am. U. P.R., 1973-74; govt. bd. Regional Colls. State League, 1973-74, faculty rep., 1979—; govt. bd. Med. Tech. Coll. P.R., 1974-75. NIH grantee, 1975-77. Mem. P.R. Soc. Microbiology, Am. Soc. Microbiology. Roman Catholic. Home: Buzon L55 Arecibo PR 00612 Office: PO Box 1806 Arecibo PR 00612

DORTA-DUQUE, JORGE ENRIQUE, architect, gen. contractor-developer; b. Havana, Cuba, Apr. 6, 1932; came to U.S., 1961, naturalized, 1976; s. Manuel Antonio and Carmen (Ortiz) D.; B.S., Havana U., 1959, D.Sc., 1960; m. Maria L. Mecalling, Nov. 8, 1958; children—Maria L., Jorge J., Carmen. Chief designer E. Abraben Assos., Miami, Fla., 1961-64; architect G.M. Fein Assos., Miami, 1964-69; pres. J. Dorta-Duque Constrn. Co., Miami, 1969-79; pres. J. Dorta-Duque Assos., Miami, 1969-77; sr. v.p., gen. mgr. Southeast Enterprises, Miami, 1977—; pres. Buigas & Assos., Architects, 1977—. Fellow Soc. Am. Registered Architects; mem. AIA, Assn. Cuban Architects, Fla. Planning and Zoning Assn., Soc. Civil Engrs., S. Fla. Gen. Contractors Assn., Internat. Assn. Housing Sci. Democrat. Roman Catholic. Clubs: K.C., Miramar Yacht. Home: 5645 SW 87th St Miami FL 33143 Office: 500 NW 165th St Miami FL 33169

DOSCHER, JÜRGEN HENRY, JR., lawyer; b. Houston, Jan. 5, 1921; s. J. Henry and Maynette (Shearn) D.; B.A., Amherst Coll., 1942; M.A., Hardin-Simmons U., 1973; J.D., U. Tex., 1948. Law clk. Supreme Ct. Tex., 1949-50; admitted to Tex. bar, 1948; partner, Wagstaff, Alvis, Pope, Doscher & Charlton, 1950-66; practiced in Abilene, Tex., 1966—; adj. prof. law McMurry Coll., Abilene, 1969—. Mem. Dodge-Jones Found., 1973—. Bd. dirs. Abilene Fine Arts Mus., 1971-72, W. Tex. Rehab. Center, Abilene. Served to capt. USNR, 1942-46. Mem. Am., Abilene (pres. 1971-72) bar assns., State Bar Tex., Sons Rep. Tex., Phi Gamma Delta, Phi Delta Phi. Club: Country (Abilene). Home: 2301 Sayles Blvd Abilene TX 79605 Office: Citizens Nat Bank Bldg Abilene TX 79601

DOSKOCIL, ANNIE MARY, librarian; b. Cyclone, Tex., July 11, 1930; d. Joseph and Matilda (Manak) Doskocil; B.A., U. St. Thomas, 1960; M.L.S., U. Tex., 1966. Tchr. parochial schs., Houston, 1952-64; librarian Our Lady of Perpetual Help Jr. Coll., Bellaire, Tex., 1965-66; librarian Marian High Sch., Bellaire, 1966-68, 68-71, dir. learning resource center, 1971-77; librarian Incarnate Word Acad., Houston, 1968-71; librarian Marian Christian High Sch., Houston, 1978—. Mem. Cath. Library Assn., Tex. Library Assn. Home: 10800 Fondren Houston TX 77096 Office: 11101 S Gessner Houston TX 77071

DOSS, ARDEN GLEN, JR., lawyer; b. Miami, Fla., July 1, 1942; s. Arden Glen and Margaret (McGuire) D.; B.A., Harvard, 1964; LL.B., Yale, 1967; m. Diane Kay Butcher, June 5, 1966; children—Arden Glen, Amber Diane. Admitted to Fla. bar, 1968; since practiced in Miami; partner, Sage Gray Doss Lynch & Castro, 1979—; dir. S.E. SBIC, Inc. Bd. dirs. Fla. Philharm. Mem. Am., Fla., Dade County bar assns. Clubs: Bath, Miami, Bankers, Coral Oaks Tennis, Sunset Tennis, La Gorce Golf and Country. Home: 2680 Natoma St Miami FL 33133 Office: Suite 2350 One Biscayne Tower Miami FL 33131

DOSS, DIANA JOHNSON, counselor; b. McMinnville, Tenn., June 24, 1948; d. W.L. and Leah Maie (Ellis) Johnson; B.S.Ed., Tenn. Tech. U., 1970, M.A. Ed., 1971; m. John R. Doss III, Jan. 13, 1979. Counselor, testing Nashville State Tech. Inst., 1971-79, head counseling and testing, 1979—. Mem. Tenn. Coll. Personnel Assn., Tenn. Personnel Guidance Assn., Middle Tenn. Personnel and Guidance Assn., Am. Personnel and Guidance Assn., Tenn. Vocat. Assn., Tenn. Tech. Edn. Council, Am. Vocat. Assn., Phi Kappa Phi, Kappa Delta Pi. Baptist. Office: 120 White Bridge Rd Nashville TN 37209

DOSS, JANE BUSKILL, educator; b. Houston, Sept. 27, 1932; d. Norman Griffin and Merle (Bassett) Buskill; B.S., Winthrop Coll., 1954; postgrad. U. Ky., 1954-55, 64-65; M.S., Jacksonville State U., 1968; m. James White Doss, Aug. 22, 1954; children—Jamie Lee, Jerry Dean, Jeffrey Van. Health, phys. edn., recreation tchr. Cassidy Elem. and Morton Jr. High Schs., Lexington, Ky., 1955-56, Thornwood Prep. Sch. for Girls, Rome, Ga., 1958-61; teaching fellow, instr. health, phys. edn., recreation U. Ky., Lexington, 1954-55, Shorter Coll., Rome, Ga., 1961-66; asst. prof. Berry Coll., Mt. Berry, Ga., 1966—; cons., work shop dir. phys. edn., recreation, camping. Bd. dirs. Presbytery Camp. Mem. AAHPER and Dance, Ga. Assn. Health, Phys. Edn. and Recreation (dist. chmn. 1966-67, 69-70, state v.p. recreation 1975-76, dance chmn. 1977-79, pres.-elect 1980-81), So. Dist. Assn. Health, Phys. Edn., Recreation and Dance, (sec. coll. div. 1977-80), Nat. Recreation Assn., Ga. Recreation Assn., So. Dist. Assn. Phys. Edn. for Coll. Women, Delta Kappa Gamma. Presbyterian. Home: 207 Dodd St Rome GA 30161 Office: Berry Coll Box 847 Mount Berry GA 30149

DOSTER, JAMES FLETCHER, educator; b. Tuscaloosa, Ala., Dec. 8, 1912; s. James Jarvis and Mabel (Cowart) D.; A.B., U. Ala., 1932; M.A., U. Chgo., 1936, Ph.D., 1948; postgrad. Harvard (research fellow), 1953-54; m. Nina Hall, Dec. 22, 1936; children—James Hall, Nina Katherine (Mrs. Michael S. Stoddard). Instr. U. Ala., 1936-39, 40-44, asst. prof., 1948-55, asso. prof., 1955-62, prof. history, 1962—, Distinguished Sr. fellow Center for Study So. History and Culture, 1977—; instr. Samford U., Birmingham, 1944-45; asso. Danforth Found., 1950-53; vis. prof. U. Houston (Tex.), 1956, U. Western Ont. (Can.), 1965. Cons. Creek Nation, 1957-65, 68-73; lectr. U. Chattanooga, 1961, 63. Vice pres. Tuscaloosa Sesqui-Centennial Com., 1963-64. Mem. S.A.R. (chpt. pres. 1965-66), Ala. Acad. Sci. (v.p. 1961-62), Ala. (exec. com. 1959-70), So. (exec. com. 1958-61) hist. assns., Tuscaloosa Hist. Soc. (trustee 1960-73, pres. 1960-62), Forest Hist. Soc., Phi Beta Kappa, Delta Chi, Phi Delta Kappa, Kappa Delta Pi. Democrat. Methodist. Researcher in history of Am. railroads. Author: Alabama's First Railroad Commission, 1881-1885, 1949; Railroads in Alabama Politics, 1875-1914, 1957; The Creek Indians and Their Florida Lands, 1974. Contbr. articles on railroad history to profl. jours. Home: 10 Guilds Woods Tuscaloosa AL 35401 Office: PO Box 1955 U Ala University AL 35486

DOTSON, BILLY JUNIOR, physicist; b. Liberal, Kans., Sept. 11, 1920; s. William Clarence and Bertie Isabelle (Gorman) D.; B.A., Southwestern Coll., 1942; M.A., Amherst Coll., 1943; m. Rowena V. Knisely, Dec. 4, 1943; children—Brian Mark, Marsha Gale, Darlene Joy. Instr. physics and math. Amherst Coll., 1943-44; research physicist Mobil Research and Devel. Corp., Dallas, 1944—. Chmn. zoning bd. adjustments, Grand Prairie, Tex., 1962. Mem. Am. Inst. Mining, Metall. and Petroleum Engrs., Soc. Petroleum Engrs. (tech. symbols reviewer), Sigma Xi. Republican. Methodist. Contbr. articles to profl. jours. Patentee in field. Home: 611 Turner Blvd Grand Prairie TX 75050 Office: 3600 Duncanville Rd Dallas TX 75236

DOTSON, ROBERT LEE, psychologist; b. Caretta, W.Va., Mar. 9, 1924; s. Jasper Madison and Lucy Eunice (Gardner) D.; B.A., W.Va. Wesleyan Coll., 1949; B.S. in Edn., Concord Coll., 1952; M.A., Marshall U., 1956; D.Sc., London Inst. Applied Research, 1973; m. Virginia Ruth Burke, Nov. 4, 1950. Tchr., Big Creek High Sch., War, W.Va., 1952-55, 56-58, Edinburg (Ind.) Pub. Schs., 1955-56; psychologist W.Va. Rehab. Center, Institute, 1958-67, 68—; chief clin. psychologist Mammoth Cave Comprehensive Care Center, Glasgow, Ky., 1967-68. Served with U.S. Army, 1943-45. Mem. Am. (asso.), W.Va. (treas. 1969-72) psychol. assns., Nat. Register Health Service Providers in Psychology, Nat. Rehab. Assn., Assn. Advancement of Psychology. Presbyterian. Home: PO Box 451 Eleanor WV 25070 Office: Institute WV 25112

DOTSON, RONALD LYNNEWOOD, chemist; b. Grafton, W.Va., Jan. 13, 1935; s. Russell G. and Helen M. (Putnam) D.; A.A., Potomac State Coll., 1959; B.S. in Chemistry, Marshall U., 1962; Ph.D. with honors in Chemistry, La. State U., 1970; m. Barbara Burdett, May 31, 1959; children—Kimberly Lynn, Gregory Stewart. Grad. teaching asst. Purdue U., W. Lafayette, Ind., 1962-63; chemist, plant process research and devel. Dow Chem. Co., Plaquemine, La., 1963-66; grad. teaching asst. La. State U., Baton Rouge, 1966-70; sr. research chemist Diamond Shamrock Corp., Painesville, O., 1970-74; research asso., sr. research asso., scientist Olin Chems. Group, Charleston, Tenn., 1974—. Served with USN, 1952-56. Mem. Am. Chem. Soc., Electrochem. Soc., Sigma Phi Omega, Phi Lambda Upsilon. Republican. Methodist. Mason. Contbr. articles to profl. jours. Patentee in field. Home: 4044 Tomahawk Circle Cleveland TN 37311 Office: PO Box 248 Lower River Rd Charleston TN 37310

DOTT, ANDREW BERWICK, obstetrician-gynecologist; b. N.Y.C., Sept. 16, 1942; s. Andrew B. and Louise (Barten) D.; student U. Pa., 1960-61; A.B., Haverford Coll., 1964; M.D. (Internat. fellow), Columbia U., 1968; M.P.H. (Maternal and Child Health fellow), Tulane U., 1974; m. Caroline Jean Pilcher, Oct. 28, 1977; children—Andrew, Mary, Amy. Clin. clk. St. Mary Hosp. Med. Sch., London, summer 1967; intern dept. surgery U. Wash. Hosp., Seattle, 1968-69, resident in orthopaedics, 1971-72; officer, research asso. Injury Control Research Lab., USPHS, Providence, 1969-71; clinic instr. dept. physiology Brown U., Providence, 1969-71; clin. dir. Desire/Fla. Neighborhood Health Center, New Orleans, 1972; med. dir. New Orleans Model Cities Health Program, 1973; research asso. La. Family Planning Program, New Orleans, 1974; resident in gen. preventive medicine Tulane U. Hosp., New Orleans, 1972-74, resident physician dept. ob-gyn Charity Hosp., 1974-77, clin. instr. dept., 1978—; practice medicine specializing in ob-gyn, 1978. Mem. joint com. of users Interagy. Data Sharing Project, New Orleans City Health Dept., 1972-74; mem. project rev. com. New Orleans Area Health Planning Council, 1973-76; mem. gov.'s adv. com. State of La. Med. Policy Adv. Bd., 1974—. Diplomate Nat. Bd. Med. Examiners, Am. Bd. Preventive Medicine. Jr. fellow Am. Coll. Ob-Gyn; mem. La. Med. Assn., Am. Coll. Preventive Medicine. Contbr. articles to profl. jours. Home: 479 Lowerline St New Orleans LA 70118 Office: 1328 Aline St New Orleans LA 70115

DOTTS, PHILIP CRAIG, banker; b. Norristown, Pa., Mar. 10, 1950; s. George Stong and Elsie (Rowe) D.; B.S., Davidson Coll., 1972; postgrad. in econs. U. Minn., 1972-73; m. Kathleen Lynette Wells, Aug. 26, 1972. Vice pres. Plasti-Vac Inc., Diamond Supply, Inc., Charlotte, N.C., 1972-74; asst. v.p. Northwestern Bank, Charlotte, 1974-77; v.p., mgr. comml. loan dept. Central Bank Ala., N.A., Huntsville, 1977—; del. White House Task Force on Small Bus. Del., Democratic Nat. Conv., 1972; co-dir. Carolinas Region Dem. Nat. Telethon, 1973-74; dir. Huntsville dist. Boy Scouts Am.; mem. budget rev. com. Huntsville City Schs. Served with AUS, 1974. NSF grantee, 1968-69. Mem. Charlotte C. of C. Ala. Bankers Assn., Ala. Young Bankers, Nat. Assn. Accts., Huntsville C. of C., Robert Morris Assos.

Democrat. Episcopalian. Home: 1602 Sun Valley Pl Huntsville AL 35801 Office: 127 West Side Sq Huntsville AL 35804

DOTY, GLEN ANDERSON, cons. engr.; b. Pharr, Tex., Feb. 1, 1924; s. Lee Anderson and Cora Alice (Fitch) D.; B.S. in Civil Engring., U. Tex., Austin, 1948; M.S. in San. Engring., 1949; m. Montrue Irvin, July 28, 1945; children—Jimmy Anderson, Sue Ann Doty. Dir. research Tex. State Dept. Health, 1949-51; city mgr. City of Alice, Tex., 1951-54, City of Breckenridge, Tex., 1954-57; dir. environ. health services Dallas Health Dept., 1957-59; regional engr., asst. regional mgr. Wallace & Tirenan div. Pennwatt Corp., Dallas, 1959-75; dir. client devel. Black & Veatch, Dallas, 1975—. Mem. Farmer's Branch (Tex.) City Council, 1968-74; mem. flood control com. Dallas County, 1970-74. Served with USMC, 1942-45. Decorated Bronze Star, Purple Heart. Mem. Am. Waterworks Assn., Tex. Water Conservation Assn., Fedn. Pollution Control Fedn., ASCE, Tex. Soc. Profl. Engrs. Republican. Methodist. Home: 3055 Eric Ln Dallas TX 75234 Office: 5728 LB Johnson Freeway Dallas TX 75240

DOTY, JIMMY ANDERSON, san. engr.; b. Weslaco, Tex., July 6, 1950; s. Glen Anderson and Montrue (Irvin) D.; B.S. in Civil Engring., U. Tex., 1972; M.S. in San Engring., U. Ill., 1974. Engring. aide Tex. Dept. Health, Austin, 1973; asst. div. mgr. Dallas Water Utilities, 1974-78; field engr. Can-Tex. Industries, Mineral Wells, 1978-80; sales engr. Gifford-Hill-Am., Dallas, 1980—. Served with U.S. Army, 1973. U.S. EPA trainee, U. Ill., 1973-74. Registered profl. engr., Tex. Mem. Water Pollution Control Fedn., Am. Water Works Assn., Tex. Soc. Profl. Engrs., Tex. Water Utilities Assn., Res. Officers Assn. Republican. Home: 7791 Royal Ln Dallas TX 75230 Office: Box 47127 Dallas TX 75247

DOUGAN, MICHAEL BRUCE, historian; b. Burbank, Calif., Feb. 26, 1944; s. Will Leigh and Helen Frances (North) D.; A.B. cum laude, S.W. Mo. State Coll., 1966; A.M., Emory U., 1967, Ph.D., 1970; m. Carol Helen Warner, Mar. 30, 1970. Asso. prof. history Ark. State U., 1970—. NDEA fellow, 1966-69; Nat. Endowment Humanities fellow, 1975; Newberry Library fellow, 1979. Mem. Ark. Hist. Assn. (4th v.p.), Craighead County Hist. Soc. (pres.), So. Hist. Assn., Am. Assn. Legal History, State Hist. Soc. Mo., Soc. S.W. Archivists, Civil War Roundtable of Ark. Unitarian. Author: Confederate Arkansas, 1976. Office: Box 1739 State University AR 72467

DOUGHERTY, BILLY BUELL, petroleum engr.; b. Guymon, Okla., Jan. 31, 1950; s. Carl Vernon and Anna Jo (Hagelberg) D.; B.S., Okla. State U., 1972; m. Deborah Ann King, June 6, 1970; children—Colby Bryce, Brandon Scott. Roustabout, Exxon Co. U.S.A., Grand Isle, La., 1972-73, engring. technician, New Orleans, 1973-75; drilling engr. Continental Oil Co., Houston, 1975-76; drilling engr. Cleary Petroleum Corp., Oklahoma City, 1976-77; owner, mgr. petroleum cons. firm, Oklahoma City, 1977—. Mem. Soc. Petroleum Engrs. (v.p. tech. club 1971-72). Home and Office: 1621 Oak Creek Edmond OK 73034

DOUGHERTY, CARY MCCONNELL, JR., hosp. adminstr.; b. New Orleans, July 17, 1946; s. Cary McConnell and Jean Percy (Highfill) D.; B.S., La. State U., 1965-69; M.P.H., Tulane U., 1973-75; m. Patricia Elaine Skyring, Aug. 24, 1968; children—Jeannette Cary, Elizabeth Stewart, Cary McConnell. Med. record adminstr. USPHS, 1970-73; asst. in fin. Alton Ochsner Med. Found., New Orleans, 1975-76; asst. adminstr. and dir. fin. Eye and Ear Inst. La., New Orleans, 1976-77, v.p. for fin., 1977-78, v.p. and adminstr., 1978—; trustee So. Eye Bank; instr. in fin. acctg., preceptor Tulane U. Served with USPHS, 1970-73. Mem. Am. Coll. Hosp. Adminstrs., Hosp. Fin. Mgmt. Assn., Am. Med. Record Assn., La. Young Adminstrs. Forum. Episcopalian. Club: Lions (New Orleans). Home: 2400 Jefferson Ave New Orleans LA 70115 Office: 145 Elk Pl New Orleans LA 70112

DOUGHERTY, FRANCIS KELLY, ins. co. exec.; b. Lubbock, Tex., May 15, 1953; s. Francis Kelly and Mary Anne (Odell) D.; B.A. in Math., U. Dallas, 1975, B.A. in Physics, 1975; m. Bonnie Lee Burch, June 14, 1975; 1 dau., Anne Katherine. Actuarial trainee Ranger Nat. Life Ins., Houston, 1976-77; mgr. time sharing services Phila. Life Ins. Co., Houston, 1977—. U. Dallas scholar, 1971-75; Rice U. fellow, 1975-76. Fellow Life Mgmt. Inst. Republican. Roman Catholic. Home: 10500 Valley Forge #168 Houston TX 77042 Office: PO Box 2465 Houston TX 77001

DOUGHERTY, FRANCIS STEARNS, marine products distbg. co. exec.; b. Mpls., Nov. 9, 1921; s. William Park and Marian (Stearns) D.; student Dartmouth Coll., 1941; B.S., U.S. Naval Acad., 1945; m. Julia Vincent Ravenel, Nov. 1, 1946; children—Renee, Frances, Park. Account exec. A.E. Chew Export Co., N.Y.C., 1948-51; founder, pres., owner Dougherty Marine Products Co., Charleston, S.C., 1954—. Pres., Charleston Opera Co., 1972-74, bd. dirs., 1977—; active Charleston Symphony Guild, 1978—. Served to lt. USN, 1945-46, 52-53. Mem. Nat. Marine Distbrs. Assn. (pres. 1976-77). Republican. Episcopalian. Clubs: Carolina Yacht, Charleston Country, Rotary. Home: 50 Legare St Charleston SC 29401 Office: Dougherty Marine Products Co 2040 Savage St Charleston SC 29407

DOUGHERTY, J(OHN) CHRYS(OSTOM), lawyer; b. Beeville, Tex., May 3, 1915; s. John Chrysostom and Mary V. (Henderson) D.; B.A., U. Tex., 1937; LL.B., Harvard U., 1940; diploma Inter-Am. Acad. Internat. and Comparative Law, Havana, Cuba, 1948; m. Mary Ireland Graves, Apr. 18, 1942 (dec. July 1977); children—Mary Ireland, John Chrysostom IV; m. 2d, Bea Ann Smith, June 16, 1978. Admitted to Tex. bar, 1940; atty. Hewit & Dougherty, 1940-41; partner firm Graves & Dougherty, 1946-50, Graves, Dougherty & Greenhill, Austin, Tex., 1950-57, Graves, Dougherty & Gee, 1957-60, Graves, Dougherty, Gee & Hearon, 1961-66, Graves, Dougherty, Gee, Hearon, Moody & Garwood, 1966-73, Graves, Dougherty, Hearon, Moody & Garwood, 1973—; spl. asst. atty. gen., 1949-50. Dir. Austin Nat. Bank. Hon. French consul for Tex., Austin, 1971—. Mem. Tex. Submerged Lands Adv. Com., 1963-72, Tex. Bus. and Commerce Code Adv. Com., 1964-66, Gov.'s Com. Marine Resources, 1970, Colo. River Basin Water Quality Mgmt. Study Com., 1972-73, Legis. Property Tax Com., 1973-75. Bd. dirs. Advanced Religious Study Found., 1955—, Greenville Clark Fund; trustee Nat. Pollution Control Found., 1966—, St. Stephen's Episcopal Sch., 1966—, U. Tex. Law Sch. Found., 1971—. Served as capt. C.I.C., U.S. Army, 1941-44, Judge Adv. Gen. Corps. 1944-46, maj., 1953—. Fellow Tex. Bar Found., Am. Bar Found.; mem. Am. Arbitration Assn. (mem. nat. panel arbitrators 1958—, S.W. adv. council 1965—), Internat. (patron), Am., Travis County (pres. 1976-77) bar assns., State Bar Tex. (chmn. sect. taxation 1965-66, pres. 1979-80), Internat., Am. fgn. law assns., Internat. Acad. Estate and Trust Law, Am. Law Inst., Am. Soc. Internat. Law (exec. council 1959-62), Inter-Am. Bar Assn., World Assn. Lawyers, Cum Laude Soc. (hon.), Phi Beta Kappa, Phi Eta Sigma, Beta Theta Pi (dir. Tex. Beta Students Aid Fund). Presbyterian. Editorial bd. editors: Appellate Procedure in Tex., 1964, 2d edit., 1976. Contbr. Bowe, Estate Planning and Taxation; Texas Lawyers Practice Guide, 1967, 71; How to Live and Die with Texas Probate, 1968; Texas Estate Administration, 1975. Home: 6 Green Lanes Austin TX 78703 Office: Austin Nat Bank Tower PO Box 98 Austin TX 78767

DOUGHERTY, JACK FRANCIS, petroleum co. exec.; b. Durango, Colo., July 4, 1916; s. Frank and Barbara (Nelson) D.; B.Sc., Calif. Inst. Tech., 1938, M.Sc., 1939; m. Ruth Anne Castagnetti, Aug. 30, 1958; children—Christine, William, Mari-Sue, Patrick, Lisa, Erin. Geologist, FPC, Washington, 1939-41, Phillips Petroleum Co., Amarillo, Tex., 1941-46; v.p. DeGolyer & MacNaughton, Cons. Engrs., Dallas, 1946-51; v.p. Empire Trust Co., N.Y.C., 1951-54; gen. partner Lambert Oil Exploration, Ltd., N.Y.C., 1954-57; independent cons., N.Y.C., 1957-60; founder/pres. Oil & Gas Futures, Inc., N.Y.C., 1960-63; chmn., chief exec. officer Oil & Gas Futures, Inc. of Tex., Houston, 1963-76; dir., v.p. Norwegian Oil Corp., 1974-76; dir., mem. exec. com. Post Oak Bank, Houston, 1968—; founder, pres. JFD, Inc., Houston, 1976—; gen. partner Susitna Explorers, Ltd., Houston, 1977—. Registered profl. engr., Tex. Mem. Am. Soc. Petroleum Geologists, Soc. Petroleum Engrs. Club: Petroleum (Houston). Home: 10 S Briar Hollow Ln #91 Houston TX 77027 Office: 2200 S Post Oak Rd Houston TX 77056

DOUGHERTY, NATHAN SAM, JR., research engr.; b. Murray, Ky., Aug. 15, 1939; s. Nathan Sam and Naomi Elizabeth (Coile) D.; B.S., U. Tenn., Knoxville, 1962; M.S., U. Tenn., Tullahoma, 1970; m. Carol Marie Roggli, Nov. 6, 1976; children—Helen Lynn, James Edward; stepchildren—Edward Carmack, Tiffany Ann. Coop. scholarship Sverdrup/ARO Inc., operating contractor USAF Arnold Engring. Devel. Center, Tenn., 1958-62, engr. test/installations, propulsive system test facilities, 1962-67, data analyst for ground and flight tests, 1967-71, research project engr. advanced test techniques research, ground and flight, 1971-79, program mgr. for wood conversion industries at co. hdqrs., Tullahoma, 1979—. Active Tullahoma Ch. Bantam Basketball League, 1974-79; bd. dirs. Tullahoma Am. Little League, 1976; pres., commr. Pop Warner Jr. Football League of Coffee County, Tenn., 1976-77. Lic. profl. engr., Tenn., Ky. Mem. AIAA (spl. award for tech. achievement Tenn. sect. 1971), Tenn. Soc. Profl. Engrs. (young engr. of yr. Tullahoma 1967), Sigma Xi. Presbyterian. Contbr. articles to tech. publs. Patentee aerodynamic noise suppression device. Home: 209 Kaywood Ave Tullahoma TN 37388 Office: ARO Inc Sverdrup Corp 101 W Lincoln St Tullahoma TN 37388

DOUGHERTY, WILLIAM H., JR., banker; b. Liberty Borough, Pa., 1930; grad. U. Pitts., 1952. Pres., dir. NCNB Corp., N.C. Nat. Bank, Charlotte, NCNB Properties Inc.; dir. NCNB Mortgage Corp., TranSouth Fin. Corp., Coca-Cola Bottling Co. Consol.; trustee Tri-South Mortgage Investors, Atlanta. Trustee Johnson C. Smith U., Carmel Acad., Charlotte, Pfeiffer Coll., Misenheimer, N.C.; bd. dirs. Mercy Hosp., Inc.; trustee Fin. Acctg. Found. Mem. Assn. Bank Holding Cos. (dir.), Assn. Res. City Bankers, Fin. Execs. Inst., Am. Inst. C.P.A.'s. Clubs: Charlotte Athletic (dir.), Carmel Country (dir.) (Charlotte). Home: 3801 River Ridge Rd Charlotte NC 28211 Office: One NCNB Plaza Charlotte NC 28255

DOUGLAS, BARTON THRASHER, lawyer; b. Gainesville, Fla., Mar. 23, 1908; s. James Byers and Rebecca (Hicklin) D.; J.D., U. Fla., 1932; m. Monica Karlene Darling, May 30, 1958; children—Barton A. J. Zachariah Hicklin II, Alexander Scott II, Monica Karlene. Admitted to Fla. bar, 1932, Tex. bar, 1935, U.S. Supreme Ct. bar, U.S. 5th Circuit Ct. Appeals; practiced in Gainesville, 1932—. Served to lt. comdr. USNR, 1942-45, judge advocate U.S. Naval Forces Western Australia. Mem. Am., Fla. State, Tex. State, Fed. bar assns., Academia Internationali Lex Et Scientia, Eighth Jud. Bar Assn. (past pres.), Delta Chi. Democrat. Presbyterian (elder). Clubs: Elks, K.P., Masons. Home: 612 NE 4th Ave Gainesville FL 32602 Office: 103 N Main St Gainesville FL 32601

DOUGLAS, BEN HAROLD, physiologist; b. Sontag, Miss., Feb. 20, 1935; s. Benona H. and Mary Nell (Rich) D.; B.S., Miss. Coll., 1956; Ph.D., U. Miss., 1964; m. Jo Ann Rugland, Aug. 16, 1953; children—Pamela, Benny. Instr. medicine U. Miss. Med. Center, Jackson, 1964-65, asst. prof., 1965-68, asso. prof., 1968-78, prof. anatomy, 1978—; vis. investigator Med. Research Council blood pressure unit Western Infirmary, Glasgow, Scotland, 1973-74; mem. med. adv. bd. Am. Heart Assn. Council on High Blood Pressure Research. Mem. Am. Physiol. Soc., Soc. Gynecol. Investigation, Am. Assn. Anatomists, Am. Heart Assn. (established investigator), Miss. Heart Assn. (dir., Silver Disting. Achievement award), Miss. Acad. Sci. (dir.), Central Soc. Clin. Research. Author 2 books; mem. editorial bd. Jour. Clin. and Exptl. Hypertension, 1979—; contbr. to publs. in field. Home: 425 N Canton Club Circle Jackson MS 39211 Office: Dept Antomy U Miss Med Center Jackson MS 39216

DOUGLAS, CRAIG HAMILTON, pediatric ophthalmologist; b. Louisville, June 15, 1947; s. James Bruce and Marjorie Elaine (Hamilton) D.; B.A., Vanderbilt U., 1969; M.D., U. Louisville, 1973; m. Pamela Ann Grubbs, June 7, 1969; children—Kevin Hamilton, Kristin Ann, Keith Cooper. Intern, U. Louisville, 1973-74; resident in ophthalmology Wills Eye Hosp., Phila., 1974-77, chief resident, 1976-77; pediatric ophthalmology fellow Wills Eye Hosp., 1977-78; practice medicine specializing in pediatric ophthalmology, Louisville, 1978—; clin. instr. dept. ophthalmology, U. Louisville, 1978—; staff Children's, Suburban, Baptist East hosps.; cons. in presch. screening Soc. Prevention of Blindness, Louisville 1978—; ophthalmic cons. Louisville Headstart programs, 1978—. Diplomate Am. Bd. Ophthalmology. Mem. AMA, Kentucky Med. Assn., Ky. Ophthalmology Soc., Jefferson County Ophthalmology Soc., Am. Acad. Ophthalmology, Am. Assn. for Pediatric Ophthalmology and Strabismus. Presbyterian. Contbr. articles to profl. jour. Home: 609 Maryhill Ln Louisville KY 40207 Office: 4E Suburban Med Plaza 4001 Dutchmans Ln Louisville KY 40207

DOUGLAS, DEANNA MAE, artist; b. Belleville, Ill., July 20, 1949; d. Allison A. and Mary Elouise (Nangle) Douglas; B.F.A., U. So. Miss., 1971; M.F.A., U. Miss., 1973. Asst. prof. art Miss. State U., Mississippi State, 1973—; nat. juried exhbns. include: LaGrange (Ga.) Nat. Print and Drawing Exhbn. (purchase award), 1974, New Photographics Exhbn., Ellenburg, Wash., 1974, Amarillo (Tex.) Artist Studio Exhbn. (purchase award), 1974, Am. Contemporary Arts and Crafts Slide Competition, Palm Beach, Fla., 1974, Nat. Cape Coral (Fla.) Exhbn., 1975, 76, Shreveport (La.) Parks and Recreation Nat. Exhbn., 1975, Auburn (Ala.) Nat. Drawing and Print Exhbn., 1976, N.Mex. Internat. Exhbn., Clovis, 1976, Kutztown (Pa.) Nat. Drawing and Sculptors Exhbn., 1977. Mem. Southeastern Coll. Art Conf., Southeastern Graphics Council, Phi Kappa Phi. Home: 326 Critz St Starkville MS 39759 Office: Dept Art Box 5182 Miss State U Mississippi State MS 39762

DOUGLAS, DOROTHY LORENE, oil co. exec.; b. Dallas, Mar. 29, 1944; d. Joseph D. and Clara Belle (Lucas) Johnson; student So. Meth. U., 1965-66; m. Apr. 9, 1971; children—Renee, Michael, Stacey. With Rep. Vanguard Ins. Co., Dallas, 1962-65; sec. to chmn. bd. and pres., lease records and div. orders mgr. May Petroleum Inc., Dallas, 1965-75, adminstrv. v.p., corp. sec., 1975—; pres. John Edward May, Inc., Dallas, 1978-79; sec., dir. Bravo Prodn. Co., Dallas, 1976—, J.E. May, Inc., Dallas, 1976—, Valor Oil Co., Dallas, 1979—; sec., v.p. May Personal Investments, Inc., Dallas, 1977—. Mem. Am. Soc. Corp. Secs. Republican. Baptist. Office: 4925 Greenville Ave Suite 1000 Dallas TX 75206

DOUGLAS, ELLEN HOPSON, educator; b. Bainbridge, Ga., Mar. 8, 1928; d. Sidney D. and Franzena (Robinson) Hopson; B.S., Ft. Valley State Coll., 1947; M.A., Columbia U., 1968; m. Jimmie Clarence Douglas, May 25, 1950. Tchr., Emery High Sch., Dalton, Ga., 1947-48, Dickerson Tng. Sch., Vidalia, Ga., 1948-56, T.J. Elder High Sch., Sandersville, Ga., 1956-59, Aaron Elem. Sch., Millen, Ga., 1959-67, Burgess Landrum High Sch., Millen, 1967-69, Wrens (Ga.) Elem. Sch., 1969-70; faculty dept. music edn. Paine Coll., Augusta, Ga., 1970—, asst. prof. music edn., coordinator of music, 1977—, faculty rep. to trustee bd., 1977—. Mem. Ga. Music Edn., Music Educators Nat. Conf., Black Women Academician. Democrat. Baptist. Club: Order of Eastern Star. Contbr. music sect. A Humanistic Approach to Interdisciplinary Art Studies, 1973. Home: PO Box 566 Millen GA 30442 Office: 1235 15th St Augusta GA 30901

DOUGLAS, NEHEMIAH ELIAS, educator; b. Jamaica, W. Indies, May 21, 1924; s. Isaac and Sarah Jane (Clark) D.; came to U.S., 1954, naturalized, 1973; student Zion Coll., 1954-55; Th.B., Am. Bapt. Theol. Sem., 1958; A B., Fisk U., 1961; M.Div., Vanderbilt U., 1971, D.Ministry, 1974; m. Glenda Dean McDaniel, Aug. 27, 1958; children—Fitzroy E., Herman Seabrook, Nehemiah Elias Jr., Robbie Sarah. Dir. Bapt. Ednl. Center, Charleston, S.C., 1961-64, Cooperative Bapt. Work, Nashville, 1964-66; editor youth lit. Nat. Bapt. Pub. Bd., Nashville, 1966-77; asst. prof. theology and social sci. Am. Bapt. Coll. of Am. Bapt. Theol. Sem., Nashville, 1972—. Ordained to ministry, Baptist Ch., 1956; asso. minister Ebenezer Missionary Bapt. Ch., Nashville, 1956-77, pastor, 1977—; dean ednl. dept. Tenn. Missionary Bapt. State Conv., 1973—. Mem. Am. Acad. Religion, N.A.A.C.P., Nashville Ministers Conf., Interdenominational Ministers' Fellowship, Nashville Bapt. Dist. Assn. (dean ednl. dept. 1968-76, pres. 1976—). Home: 1400 N 6th St Nashville TN 37207 Office: 2624 Morena St Nashville TN 37208

DOUGLAS, WAYMON JOE, drywall co. exec.; b. Lexington, Tenn., Feb. 24, 1933; s. John Wilburn and Lydia Ann (Tyler) D.; m. Virginia Lee Todd, Aug. 20, 1955; children—Deborah, Ledonna, David, Darrell. Finisher, Laminated Drywall Systems, Memphis, Tenn., 1947-55; supr. So. Drywall Co., Louisville, 1955-57; mgr. Silliman Drywall Co., Lexington, Ky., 1957-64; owner, operator Douglas Drywall Co., Lexington, 1964—; v.p. Quali-Con, Inc., Lexington, 1970-74; dir. Douglas Machine Co., Lexington. Mem. Nat. Home Builders Assn., Lexington Home Builders Assn. (dir.), Jessimine County Home Builders Assn. (dir.). Republican. Mem. Ch. of Christ. Patentee in field. Home: 2905 Nakomi Dr Lexington KY 40503 Office: 151 Payne St Lexington KY 40508

DOUGLASS, BETTY RUTH, steel weldments mfg. co. exec.; b. Vanceburg, Ky., Feb. 28, 1928; d. Carl D. and Myrtle W. (Setters) McCally; student U. Ky., 1946-47, Brevard Community Coll., 1963-67; B.A. in Bus. Econs., Rollins Coll., 1972; m. Howard A. Douglass, Sept. 15, 1956; children—Eric Douglass, Christopher. Computer control specialist Computer Applications, Kennedy Space Center, Fla., 1965-66 sect. leader ITT Federal Electric Corp., Kennedy Space Center, 1966-74; analyst, buyer Teledyne Brown Engring., Decatur, Ala. 1975-80; buyer Matthews Machine Co., Inc., Decatur, 1980—. Alternate, Brevard County Republican Exec. Com., 1974. Recipient Quality award ITT, 1974; Manned Spaceflight Awareness award NASA and ITT, 1968. Mem. Fed. Electric Mgmt. Assn. (v.p. 1974-75), N. Ala. Purchasing Assn. Republican. Mem. Christian Ch. Office: PO Box 2004 101 Lenwood Rd SW Decatur AL 35601

DOUGLASS, CURTIS LINDSEY, elec. co. engr.; b. Gilmer, Tex., Dec. 20, 1929; s. Robert George and Christell (Lindsey) D.; B.S., So. Meth. U., 1952; m. Owenda Lee Hardy, Oct. 27, 1956; children—Caren Lynn, Cathy Ann. Elec. design engr. Tex. Power & Light Co., Dallas and Waco, Tex., 1948-57, Phillips Petroleum Co., McGregor, Tex., 1957; engring. mgr. Fed. Pacific Elec. Co., Dallas, 1958—. Lectr. ground fault applications for equipment protection. Registered profl. engr., Tex. Mem. I.E.E.E., Constrn. Specifications Inst., Delta Chi. Methodist. Author articles in field. Home: 1417 Boca Chica Dr Dallas TX 75232 Office: 901 Regal Row Dallas TX 75247

DOUGLASS, ROBERT JOSEPH, forest products cons.; b. Moline, Ill., Sept. 8, 1913; s. Ralph Allison and Fannie Josephine (Moore) D.; student Augustana Coll., 1933-34; B.S., U. Miss., 1937; m. Hattie Jane Holmes, Feb. 2, 1947; children—Jane Douglass Rhodes, Robert Joseph, Jr. Area mgr. Weyerhaeuser Corp., Tacoma, 1954-61; v.p. mktg. Gen. Plywood Corp., Louisville, 1961-63; pres., chmn. bd. Gamble Bros., Inc., Louisville, 1963-73; forest products cons.; dir. Martin Sweets Co., Reliance Universal, Inc., Plastic Parts, Inc., H.J. Scheirich Co., Gusdorf, Inc., St. Louis. Mem. Ky. Forestry Council. Trustee Boy Scouts Am. Served to lt. comdr. USNR, 1941-46. Mem. Nat. Forest Products Assn. (dir.), Internat. Woodworking Machinery and Furniture Supply Fair (dir.), Sigma Chi. Clubs: Rotary, Flight, Louisville Country, Pendennis (Louisville); Stuart (Fla.) Yacht and Country, Mid-River Country; Atlantis (Fla.) Golf; Mariner Sands Golf. Home: Hutchinson House 205N 1555 NE Ocean Blvd Stuart FL 33494

DOUMIT, CARL JAMES, chemist; b. New Iberia, La., Jan. 11, 1945; s. Clement Bourgeois, Jr. and Agnes (John) Doumit; B.S., U. Southwestern La., 1967; M.S., Tulane U., 1970, M.A., 1971, Ph.D., 1973; m. Karen Ann Reed, Dec. 27, 1969; 1 son, Kevin John. Instr., coordinator gen. chemistry labs. Tulane U., 1967-72; prof. chemistry Miss. U. for Women, 1973-79; postdoctoral research fellow U. Ala., 1979—. Chmn., Rhodes Scholarship Com., 1978-79; gdv. Mortar Board, 1975-78. Mem. Am. Chem. Soc., Miss. Acad. Scis., Sigma Xi. Republican. Roman Catholic. Home: 905 6th Ave S Apt 3 Columbus MS 39701 Office: Miss U for Women PO Box W-40 Columbus MS 39701

DOUTHIT, J. DOUGLAS, oil co. exec., chem. engr.; b. Beeville, Tex., Oct. 1, 1933; s. Jesse Dunlap and Fay Doris (Patty) D.; B.S., Tex. A&M U., 1954; m. Jeanene Charles, Feb. 17, 1962. Jr. gas engr. Texaco Inc., Erath, La., 1954-55; gas engr. Texaco Inc., Houston, 1956-60, Midland, Tex., 1960-67, project engr., New Orleans, 1967-68, supr., 1968-70, supt. gas ops., 1970-71, asst. div. supt. (gas) offshore div., 1971-73 div. supt. (gas) offshore div., 1973—. Sunday sch. tchr. So. Bapt. Ch., 1979—; tutor adult literacy classes, 1978—. Served with C.E., U.S. Army, 1956. Registered profl. engr., Tex. Mem. Gas Processors Assn. (dir. chpt. 1972-74). Republican. Club: Toastmasters (adminstrv. v.p. 1975-76, sgt. of arms 1971-72). Office: 1501 Canal St New Orleans LA 70160

DOUTHITT, CAMERON BENNETT, mortgage co. exec.; b. Flynn, Tex., Dec. 17, 1942; s. Briston D. and Ona Vermelle (Petty) D.; B.S. (engring. scholar), U. Houston, 1964, Ed.D. (fellow), 1971; M.S., Sam Houston State U., 1966; children—Tiffany Ann, Ronald Joseph. Instr. math Alvin (Tex.) Community Coll., 1966-68, dir. math lab., 1971, dir. research and devel., 1975-76, dir. free studies, 1972-75, dean research planning and devel., 1976-79, v.p., 1976-79; area mgr. Suburban Coastal Mortgage Co., Clear Lake City, Tex., 1979—. Mem. Houston-Galveston Area Manpower Adv. Bd. Mem. Nat. Council Resource Devel. (pres.), Alvin C. of C., Math Assn. Am., AAUP, Tex. Jr. Coll. Tchrs. Assn., Am. Audio Tutorial Congress, Assn. Instl.

Research. Author: (with Joe McMillan) Trigonometry, 1978; contbr. articles to profl. jours. Home: 2920 Country Club Dr Pearland TX 77581 Office: 1350 Nasa Rd 1 Houston TX 77058

DOUTY, HELEN IRENE, clothing specialist; b. Loganton, Pa., Apr. 6, 1916; d. George T. and Mayme E. (Kahl) D.; B.S., Cornell U., 1942, M.S., 1948; Ph.D., Fla. State U., 1962. Tchr. public high sch., N.Y. State, 1942-48; instr., asst. prof. home econs. U. Hawaii, 1948-58; asso. prof. clothing, somatology Auburn U., 1962—. Mem. Am. Home Econs. Assn., Assn. Coll. Profs. Textiles and Clothing, AAUP, Soc. Med. Anthropology, Am. Public Health Assn., Sigma Xi, Omicron Nu, Delta Kappa Gamma. Unitarian. Research in somatology, clothing and behavior; contbr. articles to profl. jours. Home: 323 Payne St Auburn AL 36830 Office: Sch of Home Econs Auburn U Auburn AL 36830

DOW, CHARLES DAVID, telecommunications co. exec.; b. Marion, Va., Nov. 2, 1939; s. Charles Harris and Marian Elizabeth (Fernsler) D.; B.S.E.E., Ind. Inst. Tech., 1965; postgrad. ops. research Fla. Inst. Tech., 1965-66; hon. degree, Tsinghua U., Peking, 1980; m. Dian Darby, Mar. 24, 1961; children—Scott David, Ted Andrew, Kurt Daniel. Engr. spl. circuits Gen. Telephone Co., Ft. Wayne, Ind., 1961-65; mgr. data retransmission br. ITT-Federal, Cape Canaveral, Fla., 1965-66; sr. engr., program mgr. Westinghouse Co., Balt. and Dallas, 1967-69; tech. dir. Systems Tech. div., Varo Inc., Garland, Tex., 1970-72; dir. mktg., bus. devel. Reliance Electric Telecommunications Corp., Bedford, Tex., 1973—; lectr. in field. Pres., Plano (Tex.) Sports Authority, 1973-74, v.p., 1974-75; active Tex. Amateur Baseball Congress, 1976-80; adv. bus. planning 1st. Baptist Acad., Dallas, 1978-79. Served with USAF, 1958. Recipient Award for Excellence EDN magazine, 1969. Mem. Am. Mktg. Assn., Inst. Mgmt. Scis., Ops. Research Soc. Am., Ind. Telephone Pioneer Assn., AAUP. Home: 400 High Brook Dr Richardson TX 75080 Office: Reliance Electric Telecommunications Corp 2100 Reliance Pkwy Bedford TX PO Box 919 76021

DOW, NORMAN GAIL, tool co. exec.; b. Corpus Christe, Tex., Sept. 29, 1936; s. William Percy and Effie Adyce (Lord) D.; B.B.A., U. Calif., Domingues Hills, 1972; postgrad. Pepperdine U.; m. Norma Dee Banks, Sept. 3, 1965; children—Teresa Yarmer, Jim Yarmer, Melinda Dow, Billy Dow. Gen. mgr. Moore Prodn. Equipment Co., Odessa, Tex., 1960-63; West coast mgr. Gray Tool Co., Los Angeles, 1963-67, western regional mgr., 1967-75, div. mgr., 1975—. Served with USAF, 1956-59. Mem. Instrument Soc. Am., Am. Nuclear Soc., Gulf Coast Gas Measurement Soc. Baptist. Clubs: Univ., Elks. Home: 11706 S Kirkwood St Stafford TX 77477 Office: PO Box 2291 Houston TX 77001

DOW, ROBERT FREDERICK, physician; b. N.J., May 11, 1908; s. John Francis and Johanna (O'Dea) D.; B.S., Georgetown U., 1930, M.D., 1934; m. Dorothy Marie Davis, July 23, 1938; children—Robert Frederick, John D. Intern, St. Josephs Hosp., Paterson, N.J., 1934-35, resident, 1935-36; preceptorship in phys. medicine Northwestern U., 1939; practice medicine specializing in phys. medicine and rehab., Paterson, N.J., 1939-42, Bethesda, Md., and Washington, 1946-53, Montclair, N.J., 1953-74; ret., 1974; head dept. phys. medicine Georgetown U., until 1953; cons. VA, 1947-74, Army Med. Center, 1946-53; founding pres. Handi-crafters, Inc.; cons. Univ. Med. Center. Vice chmn. advisory com. Lee Country (Fla.) Bd. Commrs. on Multi-Purpose Sr. Citizen's Centers, 1977; pres. Cape Coral, Fla. chpt. Am. Assn. Ret. Persons, Inc., 1977; founding mem. Cape Coral United Council Sr. Citizens, 1977—. Served to maj. M.C. U.S. Army, 1942-46. Diplomate Am. Bd. Phys. Medicine and Rehab. Mem. N.J. Soc. Phys. Medicine, Med. Soc. N.J., AMA, Internat. Congress Rehab. Medicine, Am. Congress Phys. Medicine, Am. Acad. Phys. Medicine, Delta Chi, Alpha Kappa Kappa. Author: Treatment of Military Casualties, 1943. Home: 3352 SE 19th Ave Cape Coral FL 33904

DOW, THOMAS WENDELL, psychiatrist; b. Boston, Oct. 7, 1939; s. Wendell Adams and Elise Rose (Mullaney) D.; B.S., Boston Coll., 1961; M.D., U. Vt., 1965; postgrad. McGill U., 1968-71; m. Anne Campbell Shea, June 11, 1960; children—David Wendell, Abra Elise. Intern, Lakeland (Fla.) Gen. and Polk County (Fla.) hosps., 1965-66; resident psychiatry Douglas Hosp., Verdun, Que., 1968-69, Jewish Gen. Hosp., Montreal, 1969-71; practice medicine specializing in psychiatry Orlando, Fla., 1971—; mem. staffs Orlando Regional Med. Center, Fla. Hosp., Lucerne Gen. Hosp.; psychiat. cons. Orlando Regional Med. Center Community Mental Health Center, 1972—, Cath. Social Services, 1973-77, Hillcrest Halfway House, 1971-73, Orange County Sch. System, 1977—; clin. asst. prof. U. South Fla. Coll. Medicine, 1978—. Mem. citizens advocacy com. Emotionally Disturbed Children of Central Fla., Orlando. Trustee, chmn. planning and evaluation com. Mental Health Bd. Central Fla., 1974—; bd. dirs., chmn. profl. adv. com. Thee Door of Orange County Drug Abuse Program, 1971-74; bd. dirs. Orange County Mental Health Assn. Served to capt. M.C., USAF, 1966-68. Diplomate Am. Bd. Psychiatry and Neurology. Mem. Am., Can. psychiatric assns., Am. Group Psychotherapy Assn., Am., Fla. med. assns., Orange County Med. Soc., Fla. Psychiat. Soc. (br. pres. 1975—), Am. Acad. Child Psychiatry. Democrat. Unitarian. Club: Bay Hill Country. Home: 6083 Tarawood Dr Orlando FL 32811 Office: 85 W Miller St Orlando FL 32806

DOWBEN, ROBERT MORRIS, physician; b. Phila., Apr. 6, 1927; s. Morris and Zena (Brown) D.; A.B., Haverford Coll., 1946; M.S., U. Chgo., 1947, M.D., 1949; m. Carla Lurie, June 20, 1950; children—Peter Arnold, Jonathan Stuart, Susan Laurie. Intern, U. Chgo. Clinics, 1949-50; research fellow U. Oslo, Norway, 1950-51; fellow Johns Hopkins Hosp., Balt., 1951-52; resident medicine U. Pa. Hosp., Phila., 1952-53; dir. radioisotope unit VA Hosp., Phila., 1953-55; asst. prof. medicine Northwestern U., Chgo., 1957-62; asso. prof. biology Mass. Inst. Tech., Cambridge, 1962-68; lectr. medicine Harvard U., 1962-68; prof. med. sci. Brown U., Providence, 1968-72; prof. biophysics, physiology and neurology U. Tex. Health Sci. Center, Dallas, 1972—; cons. neurologist Childrens Hosp., Scottish Rite Hosp., Presbyn. Hosp., Baylor Hosp., 1972—. Bd. dirs. Greenhill Sch., 1974—. Served to capt. USAF, 1955-57. Lalor fellow 1960. Recipient Distinguished Service award Assn. Neuromuscular Diseases, 1964. Mem. Am. Physiol. Soc., Am. Soc. Biol. Chemists, Am. Chem. Soc., Soc. Exptl. Biology and Medicine, Biophys. Soc., Soc. for Clin. Investigation, Biochem. Soc. (London), Faraday Soc. (London), Sigma Xi, Phi Beta Kappa. Mem. Soc. of Friends. Author: Biological Membranes, 1969; General Physiology, 1971; Cell Biology, 1972. Contbr. articles to profl. jours. Home: 7150 Eudora Dr Dallas TX 75230 Office: 5323 Harry Hines Blvd Dallas TX 75235

DOWD, CLARK WAYNE, state senator; b. Texarkana, Ark., Nov. 1, 1941; s. Tillman Harold and Blanche (Pope) D.; B.B.A., So. State Coll., Magnolia, Ark., 1964; LL.B., U. Ark., Fayatteville, 1966; m. Carolyn Margaret Walker, Apr. 17, 1965; children—Chad Everett, Joseph Walker. Admitted to Ark. bar, 1966, since practiced in Texarkana; partner firm Tackett, Moore, Dowd & Harrelson, 1971—; dep. pros. atty. Miller County, 1968-69; city atty., Texarkana, 1972; mem. Ark. Senate from 12th Dist., 1979—. Mem. Am. Bar Assn., Ark. Bar Assn., Tex. Bar Assn., Ark. Trial Lawyers Assn., Tex. Trial Lawyers Assn., S.W. Ark. Bar Assn., Miller County Bar Assn., Bowie County (Tex.) bar Assn., Texarkana Bar Assn. (past pres.). Democrat. Methodist. Home: 20 Broadmoor St Texarkana AR 75502 Office: 421 Hickory St Texarkana AR 75502

DOWDLE, NASH JAMES, oil co. exec.; b. Chgo., Dec. 4, 1923; s. John Joseph and Myrtle (FitzMaurice) D.; student Grinnell Coll., 1942-43, U. Notre Dame, 1943-44, Mt. St. Mary's Coll., Md., 1945-46; m. Joyce Corinne Bechtold; children—Nash James, Kathleen Mary, Timothy Joseph, Mary Virginia, Kelly Frances, Jane Murphy. Founder, Tex. Am. Oil Co., Midland, 1956, pres., chief exec. officer, 1956-69; chmn. Western Oil Shale Corp., Midland, 1965-69, Tex. Am. Sulfur Co., Midland, 1965-69; chmn. bd., pres., chief exec. officer Dowdle Oil Corp., Midland, 1969—; pres., chmn. Shamrock Oil Corp., 1979—; pres. Can. Shamrock Oil Ltd., West Vancouver, B.C., 1979—; chmn. bd., chief exec. officer Internat. Petroleum Reserves, N.V., Netherlands Antilles and Eng., 1977—. Trustee St. Mary's Coll., Notre Dame, Ind., 1968-72; co-founder City of Midland Swim Team, 1965. Served to lt. as pilot USAAF, 1942-46. Mem. Am. Petroleum Inst., Permian Basin Petroleum Assn., Tex. Mid-Continent Oil and Gas Assn. Roman Catholic. Clubs: Midland Country, Petroleum (Midland, Dallas), Racquet. Home: 2006 Sinclair St Midland TX 79701 Office: 300 W Wall St Suite 1315 Midland TX 79701 also 4718 Woodvalley Pl West Vancouver BC Canada

DOWDY, RONALD RAYMOND, air force officer; b. Columbus, Ga., Sept. 5, 1944; s. Lester Henry and Dorothy Louvoise (White) LeVine; B.S., U. Md., 1968; M.S., Troy State U., 1974, Ed.S., 1976; m. Susan Carol, Sept. 5, 1968; children—Veronica, Richard. Commd. 2d lt. U.S. Air Force, 1968, advanced through grades to maj., 1979; aircraft comdr., Vietnam, 1969-70; instr. pilot Moody AFB, Ga., 1970-73; sect. comdr. Squadron Officer Sch., Maxwell AFB, Ala., 1973-76; aircraft comdr. Charleston AFB, S.C., 1976—; cons., tchr. in field. Decorated D.F.C., Bronze Star with V device, Air medal with 4 oak leaf clusters, Air Force Commendation medal with 2 oak leaf clusters (U.S.); Cross of Gallantry (Vietnam). Mem. Am. Personnel and Guidance Assn., Order Daedalians. Home: 102 Botany Bay Blvd Charleston SC 29405 Office: 20th MAS Charleston AFB SC 29404

DOWIAK, DANIEL JOSEPH, environ. engr.; b. Passaic, N.J., Jan. 5, 1950; s. Benjamin J. and Helen (Serafin) D.; Electronic technician, R.E.T.S., Nutley, N.J., 1969-71; B.S., N.J. Inst. Tech., 1978; m. Susan Ann McManus, June 17, 1972; 1 dau., Jennifer. Installation technician Western Electric, Union, N.J., 1970-75; environ. engr. Am. Cyanamid, Wayne, N.J., 1975-78; environ. cons. Trinity Cons., Dallas, 1978-79; environ. engr. Tex. Oil & Gas Corp., Dallas, 1979—. Mem. Am. Inst. Chem. Engrs., Water Pollution Control Fedn., Air Pollution Control Assn. Russian Orthodox. Office: Fidelity Union Tower Dallas TX 75201

DOWLER, JAMES ROSS, advt. exec.; b. Royal, Ill., Apr. 19, 1925; s. Emery Ross and Ethel (Burroughs) D.; B.S., U. Ill., 1949, M.S., 1950; m. Helen Jean Ernst, Feb. 19, 1950; 1 son, Ross Matthew. News reporter Champaign (Ill.) News-Gazette, 1948-49; pub., owner Adams County Republican, Brighton, Colo., 1950-51; advt. supr., mgr. Shell Chem. Co. div. Shell Oil Co., N.Y.C., 1954-70, Atlanta, 1970-75, San Ramon, Calif., 1976-77, Houston, 1977—. Served with USAAF, 1943-45, USAF, 1951-53. Decorated Bronze Star. Mem. Sigma Delta Chi. Republican. Methodist. Author: Partner's Choice, 1958; Fiddlefoot Fugitive, 1970; Laredo Lawman, 1970; Copperhead Colonel, 1972. Inventor parlor games Dai Jobi, 1955, Moon Tag, 1957. Home: 3303 Riverlawn Dr Kingwood TX 77339 Office: One Shell Plaza Houston TX 77001

DOWLING, JACQUES MACCUISTON, sculptor, painter, juror, writer; b. Texarkana, Tex., Oct. 19, 1906; d. Charles Edward and Viola John (Estes) MacCuiston; tchrs. certificate Coll. Marshall, 1923; art student Loyola U., Frolich's Sch. Fine Art, Los Angeles, NAD, Art Students League, N.Y.C.; Ph.D., Colo. State Christian U. One-woman shows: Fedn. Dallas Artist, 1950, Rush Gallery, 1958, Sartor's Gallery, Sheraton-Dallas, Dallas Auditorium, 1960; exhibited in group shows: Dallas Mus. Fine Arts, Mus. N.Mex., Fedn. Dallas Artists, Sartor's Galleries, Ney Art Mus., Oak Cliff Soc. Fine Arts, Sheraton-Park, Washington, Phillips Mill Fall Exhbn., New Hope, Pa., 1967-74, others; selected sculpture, 1st S.W. ann. show Mus. N.Mex., 1957; represented in permanent collections: corps., pvt. homes; former columnist En Passant for newspaper chain. Recipient 1st in sculpture, 2 best in show, 1st in oil painting Fedn. Dallas Artist, 1950, 51, 52, 53, 54, 55, 56; Sweepstakes award for sculpture 1st S.W. Ann. Arts and Crafts Show, 1954; 3 journalism awards, 1963; hon. certificate award Dallas Fed. Bus. Assn., 1964; Gold medal Internat. Acad. Lit., Arts and Sci., Tommaso Campanello, Rome, 1972; 1st in profl. sculpture 4th dist. N.J. Fedn. Women's Club, 1972-74, 1st in profl. sculpture state exhbn., 1972-74; 3d in sculpture Yardley Art Assn. Spring Show, 1972, 2d, 1973, Acad. of Italy with gold medal Accademia Italia, Parma, 1979, many others. Fellow Internat. Inst. Arts and Letters (life); mem. Nat. Soc. Arts and Letters, St. Catherine's Bus. and Profl. Guild (past pres.), Cousteau Soc. (founding), Sr. Citizens Delaware Valley (past pres.), Am. Contract Bridge League, U.S. Chess Fedn., Woodmere Art Gallery (life), Internat. Acad. Lit., Arts and Sci. (life golden album mem.), C. of C. South Hunterdon (hon.). Republican. Episcopalian. Clubs: Order Eastern Star (grand officer 1959-68), Solebury Farmers (past pres.), Kalmia (past pres.); Middle Bucks Chess (charter). Former pub., editor-in-fact Anchor News. Home: 335 NW Midway Blvd Port Charlotte FL 33952

DOWLING, JERRY CLAIR, geol. engr.; b. Rapid City, S.D., Nov. 2, 1928; s. Clarence Burdette and Hanna Marie (Bartlett) D.; B.S. in Geol. Engring., S.D. Sch. Mines and Tech., 1951; m. Helen Marie Krallman, Aug. 25, 1962; children—Julie Marie, William Gregory. With Hercules Powder Co. 1951-61, Fenix & Scisson, Inc., Ky., Ill. and Nev., 1962-64, Peter Kiewet Sons Co., Mo., Va., Nev. and Alaska, 1964-71; chief engr. Cowin & Co., Birmingham, 1971—. Served with AUS, 1956-58. Registered profl. engr., Ala., Pa.; cert. mine foreman, Ala., W.Va., Ky., Tenn., Pa. Mem. Am. Inst. Mining, Metall. and Petroleum Engrs., Nat. Soc. Profl. Engrs. Republican. Roman Catholic. Home: 4169 Churchill Dr Birmingham AL 35213 Office: 1 18th St SW Birmingham AL 35211

DOWNEY, JAMES CECIL, educator, musicologist; b. Grand Bay, Ala., Feb. 13, 1931; s. James Fred and Thelma Mattie (Hamilton) D.; B.A., Wm. Carey Coll., 1958; M.Mus., U. So. Miss., 1963; Ph.D., Tulane U., 1968; m. Phyllis Carolyn Barber, Jan. 25, 1952; children—James Vance, Joy Lyndell, Jennifer Ann, Robert Joel. Prof. music lit. William Carey Coll., Hattiesburg, Miss., 1966—; tchr./musician So. Bapt. Chs., Mobile, Ala., 1954-60. Music critic Hattiesburg Am., 1966—; reviewer Jour. Soc. Ethnomusicology, Yearbook of Inter-Am. Inst. Mus. Research, Register of Miss. Folklore Soc. Project dir. Forrest County (Miss.) Library Bd., 1975—. Served with AUS, 1954-56. Recipient Younger Humanist fellowship Nat. Endowment for the Humanities, 1970-71; Jaap Kunst prize Soc. Ethnomusicology, 1964. Mem. Am. Musicol. Soc. (sec.-treas. Gulf States chpt. 1968-69), Miss. Folklore Soc. (pres. 1974-75), Phi Tau Chi, Omicron Delta Kappa, Phi Mu Alpha, Pi Gamma Mu. Contbr. Grove's Dictionary of Music and Musicians. Home: Route 3 Box 245 Sumrall MS 39482 Office: Box 198 Wm Carey Coll Hattiesburg MS 39401

DOWNEY, WILLIAM GERALD, JR., lawyer, ret. banker, ret. army officer; b. Bklyn., June 20, 1914; s. William Gerald and Mary Veronica (Ryder) D.; B.S.S., Coll. City N.Y., 1937; M.A., Catholic U., 1938; J.D., Georgetown U., 1951; certificate internat. law, U. Mich., 1937, Latin Am. area tng., 1946; student U. Iceland, 1941-42; grad. Command and Gen. Staff College, 1962; diploma Anglo-Irish Lit., Trinity Coll., Dublin, 1976; m. Ellen Wagle, Apr. 17, 1942 (dec.); 1 son, William G. III (dec.); m. 2d, Laufey Arnadottir, June 5, 1947; children—Richard, Elizabeth, Mary, Catherine, William Gerald IV, Karen. Commd. 2d lt. inf. res., 1936, advanced through the grades to col. Judge Adv. Gen.'s Corps, 1964, ret., 1969; chief internat. law br., 1946-50, Group Judge Adv., Formosa, 1952-54; sr. partner Downey & Lennhoff, Springfield, Va.; practice law, Va. and Washington; founder, past chmn. bd. No. Va. Bank; pres. Springfield Corp.; fellow internat. law Cath. U., 1936-37; fellow internat. law, Georgetown U., 1937-40, instr. govt., 1937-40; prof. internat. law Soochow U. Law Sch., 1952-54. Mem. Fairfax County Democratic Com.; del. Va. Dem. Conv., 1960, 64, 68; candidate Va. State Senate, 1963. Mem. Springfield C. of C. (pres. 1961-62, dir.), Washington, Va. bar assns. Clubs: Kiwanis (pres. Springfield 1961-62, 78-79; lt. gov. 10th div. Capital dist. 1974-75, dist. chmn. internat. relations 1976-77, ofcl. rep., dist. chmn. Va. 1977-78, chmn. past lt. govs. com.); Army-Navy, Army-Navy Country; Morgan Horse. Author articles on mil. and internat. law. Contbr. to Ency. Brit. Home: Crest View 1005 Crest Ln McLean VA 22101 Office: Springfield Plaza Profl Bldg PO Box 6 Springfield VA 22150

DOWNEY-PRINCE, ELEANOR PAULINE LONG, med. researcher; b. Birmingham, Ala., Nov. 27, 1942; d. Roger Winston and Ruby Pauline (King) Long; A.B., Birmingham So. Coll., 1964; postgrad. U. Ala., 1965-67, 68—; m. Stanford H. Downey, Jr., July 4, 1964 (div.); children—Stanford Harmon III, Jonathan Michael; m. 2d, Daniel Scott Prince, May 27, 1977. Lab. asst. Seale Harris Clinic, 1959-60; cancer research technologist Meml. Inst. Pathology, Birmingham, Ala., 1960-64, anthropology and clin. pathology research asso., 1963—, now coordinator research activities; statis. cons. Gravlee Labs, 1972-73; bd. dirs. Info. and Document Mgmt. Inc., 1974—; cons. Ga. Hosp. Assn., 1972. Med. sec. to dr., 1960-62; high sch. tchr., Trussville, Ala., 1963-64. Mem. A.A.A.S. (award 1960), Internat. Cancer Congress, Internat. Acad. Pathology, Ala. Acad. Sci., Am. Assn. Phys. Anthropologists, Am. Statis. Assn., Caucus for Women in Statistics, Nat. Orgn. Women, Nat. Audubon Soc., Nat. Wildlife Assn., Ala. Tng. Network, Alpha Chi Omega (adv. bd. 1964—), Kappa Delta Epsilon. Unitarian (Sunday sch. tchr., pianist, mid-south coordinator camp and conf. center). Co-author book. Contbr. numerous articles to profl. jours. Home: 373 Laredo Dr Birmingham AL 35226 Office: 1025 S 18th St PO Box 3453-A Birmingham AL 35205

DOWNING, VINCENT FRANCIS, writer, editor; b. Utica, N.Y., Oct. 19, 1911; s. Maurice F. and Alice (Claesgens) D.; B.S., Rensselaer Poly. Inst., 1935; postgrad. U. Rochester Med. Sch., 1936-37, 1939-40, Grad. Sch., 1946-47; m. Hildegarde F. Luhde, Apr. 15, 1944; children—Diane Margot, Richard Ernest. Chemist, Skenandoa Rayon Corp., Utica, 1935-36; research fellow U. Rochester, 1937-39; head sanitation sect. U.S. Army Engrs., Boston, 1945-46; physicist Am. Brake Shoe Co., Mahwah, N.J., 1947-50; chemist Lederle Labs., Pearl River, N.Y., 1950-57, patent, med. writer, 1957-63, medicolegal editor, 1963-69, med. editor, 1969-77. Scoutmaster, Rockland County council Boy Scouts Am., 1954-56, neighborhood commr., 1952-53, dist. chmn., 1951-52; chmn. Village Spring Valley (N.Y.) Housing Authority, 1967-75; jobs coordinator Westchester-Rockland-Putnam met. Nat. Alliance Businessmen, 1970-72; publicity dir. for Abbeville County, S.C. Gov.'s Beautification and Community Improvement Program, 1978—; pres. Spring Valley Library Assn., 1957-62; treas. Ramapo chpt. ARC, 1952-56, chmn., 1956-57, dir. Rockland County chpt., 1957-60. Trustee Finkelstein Meml. Library, Spring Valley, 1962-77; chmn. membership com. Abbeville County Mus. Assn., 1978—. Served with AUS, 1940-45. Mem. Am. Chem. Soc., AAAS, N.Y. Acad. Sci., Am. Med. Writers Assn. (editor Newsletter 1972-75), Drug Info. Assn., Sigma Xi. Clubs: Rotary, Lions. Contbr. articles to sci. jours.; columnist Press & Banner, Abbeville Medium, 1978—. Home: 501 Greenville St PO Box 834 Abbeville SC 29620

DOWNS, BRANDI ELIZABETH, artist; b. McComb, Miss., Aug. 11, 1932; d. Jack Denson and Martha Ethel (Bornman) Hammack; B.F.A., Miss. State Coll. Women, 1955; m. William K. Douglas, Dec. 23, 1956; children—Martha Anne, William K., Christine Rachel. Artist, WLBT-TV, Jackson, Miss., 1955, Gorden Marks Advt., Jackson, 1955-57, Dallas Times Herald, 1957-58, Whaley Studio, Dallas, 1958; art dir. Jiffy Printing, Dallas, 1958-59; tchr. art Dallas Pub. Schs., 1959-62; art cons. Ovutron Corp., Las Vegas; one-man shows Municipal Art Gallery, Jackson, 1955, French Quarter Gallery, New Orleans, 1967-71, Sheraton Gallery, San Juan, P.R., 1968, La Concia Gallery, San Juan, 1972, Our Lady of Holy Cross, 1971, San Geronimo Gallery, San Juan, 1973, French Quarter Design, New Orleans, 1974-75, Symmetry Gallery, New Orleans, 1976-77; exhibited in group shows Norfolk (Va.) Mus., 1953, Nat. Kappa Pi Exhbn., 1954. Recipient 1st prize Colonial Dames Art award, Columbus Miss., 1954; 1st prize Allison Wells, 1955; silver medal Tommaso Campanella Soc., Rome, 1970, Gold medal, 1972. Mem. Am. Artist Profl. League, Soc. N. Am. Artists, Nat. Health Fedn. Home: PO Box 128 Ruby SC 29741 Office: 828 A Bourbon St New Orleans LA 70116

DOWNS, JAMES TICKELL, III, physician; b. Dallas, Tex., Oct. 2, 1917; s. James Tickell and Florence Elizabeth (Erich) D.; B.A., U. Tex., 1938, M.D., 1941; m. Helen Mar Looney, Nov. 22, 1939; children—Helen Elizabeth, Judith Ann, Mary Frances, Susan Rebecca. Intern, Detroit Receiving Hosp., 1941-42; resident John Sealy Hosp., Galveston, Tex., 1945-48; pvt. practice medicine specializing in obstetrics and gynecology, Dallas, 1948-51; partner Drs. Alexander, Downs & Brunken, Dallas, 1951—; clin. prof. obstetrics and gynecology Southwestern Med. Sch., 1956—; mem. staff Baylor U. Med. Center, Presbyn. Hosp., Parkland Meml. Hosp. (all Dallas). Chmn. health panel Community Council of Dallas, 1972. Served with M.C., AUS, 1942-46. Decorated Bronze Star. Mem. Am., Tex. (ho. dels. 1960-80) med. assns., Dallas County Med. Soc. (pres. 1974), Dallas-Ft. Worth Obstetrics and Gynecology Soc. (pres. 1962), Tex. Assn. Obstetrics and Gynecology (pres. 1969), Am. Coll. Obstetrics and Gynecology (chmn. Tex. sect. 1965-68), Willard R. Cooke Obstetrics and Gynecology Soc., Phi Rho Sigma, Sigma Chi. Episcopalian. Contbr. articles to med. jours. Home: 4011 University St Dallas TX 75205 Office: 3600 Gaston St Dallas TX 75246

DOWNS, JON FRANKLIN, educator; b. Bartow, Fla., Sept. 15, 1938; s. Clarence Curtis and Frankie (Morgan) D.; student Ga. State Coll., 1956-58; B.F.A., U. Ga., 1960, M.F.A., 1969. Dir. The Beastly Purple Forest (marionettes) U. Ga., 1968, Dracula: A Horrible Musical, DeKalb Coll., 1971, Streetcar Named Desire, DeKalb, 1974, others; actor Wedding in Japan, N.Y.C., 1960, Dark at the Top of the Stairs, N.Y.C. and tour, 1961, Night Must Fall, DeKalb Coll., 1970, others; designer Sweeney Todd, DeKalb Coll., 1970, Romulus, 1971, Grass Harp, 1972, others; author, dir. Gold, tour, summer 1974-75, The Vigil, tour, summer 1975, 76; drama dir. DeKalb Coll., Clarkston, Ga., 1969—. Writer, dir. play Tokalitta, on tour of Ga., summers 1973,

74, 76. Ga. Dept. Planning and Budget arts sect. grantee, 1973, 74. State and Nat. Bicentennial Commn. grantee, 1975. Mem. Southeastern (state rep. 1971-73), Ga. (exec. bd. 1970-73 79-80) theatre confs. Author: The Illusionist, 1979. Home: 1124 Forrest Blvd Decatur GA 30030 Office: DeKalb Coll 555 N Indian Creek Dr Clarkson GA 30021

DOYLE, BEVERLY SUE, nursing adminstr.; b. Greencastle, Ind., Sept. 26, 1940; d. Frederick William and Doris Imogene (VanBuskirk) Caspar; grad. St. Joseph Infirmary Sch. Nursing, 1962; m. Gerald Carey Doyle, Feb. 23, 1963; children—Shawn, Kevin, Jennifer. Staff nurse pediatrics St. Joseph Infirmary, Louisville, 1962, Jewish Hosp., Louisville, 1962-63, St. Catherine's Hosp., Kenosha, Wis., 1963-64; asst. instr. urology, neurology and orthopedics St. Joseph Hosp., Ft. Wayne, Ind., 1964-65; staff nurse acute area float Parkview Meml. Hosp., Ft. Wayne, 1965-67; office nurse, Louisville, 1967-69; staff nurse emergency dept. St. Joseph Infirmary, Louisville, 1967-69, staff nurse emergency dept. Hillcrest Med. Center, Tulsa, 1969-70, supr., 1970-73; tng. supr. med. coordinator Central Ambulance Service, Tulsa, 1973-77; tng. dir. Emergency Med. Tng. Services, Tulsa, 1979—; in-service coordinator emergency dept. St. John's Hosp., Tulsa, 1977-79; ednl. and outreach coordinator emergency med. services St. Francis Hosp., Tulsa, 1979—; sch. nurse Marquette Sch., Tulsa, 1973; faculty participant various workshops, 1969—. Mem. Emergency Dept. Nurses Assn. (state rep. 1971-74, regional rep. 1974-76), Okla. State Emergency Med. Service Council (vice chmn. 1974), Am. Trauma Soc. (dir. Okla. div. 1974-77), Am. Heart Assn. Office: 6161 S Yale St Tulsa OK 74177

DOYLE, CHARLES THOMAS, banking exec.; b. Mangum, Okla., Aug. 3, 1934; s. Roy L. and Mattie B. (Carter) D.; A.A., Kemper Mil. Acad., 1954; B.B.A., U. Okla., 1956; M.B.A., U. Houston, 1961; m. Mary Ellen Hipp, Aug. 25, 1956; children—Matthew, David, Denise, Patrick, Christopher. Mgr. indsl. relations Union Carbide Corp., 1956-69; mgmt. cons., Houston and Galveston, Tex., 1969-72; pres., dir. 1st State Bank, Hitchcock, Tex., 1972—; chmn. bd. U.S. Mgmt. Corp., Houston, 1972—; pres., dir. Bank of West, Galveston, 1974—; dir. Buffalo Savs. & Loan Assn., Copperstone Constructors, Inc. City commr., Texas City, Tex., 1964—; chmn. legislative com. Houston-Galveston Area Council, 1971-72; vice chmn. Houston-Galveston Regional Transp. Coordinating Com., 1971-72. Bd. dirs., charter mem. Galveston County Community Action Council; bd. dirs., vice chmn. Bay Area Heart Assn., 1972-73; pres. Coll. of Mainland Found. Served with Armed Forces, 1956-58. Mem. Galveston County Mayors and Councilmen Assn. (pres. 1968-69), Texas City Jaycees (life), Am. Acad. Polit. and Social Sci., Indsl. Relations Research Assn., Am. Mgmt. Assn., Am. Acad. Mgmt., Texas City Mcpl. League, Am. Arbitration Assn., U. Houston, U. Okla. alumni assns., Phi Gamma Delta, Beta Gamma Sigma, Omicron Chi Epsilon, Sigma Iota Epsilon. Club: Houston. Contbr. articles to profl. jours. Home: 1526 19th Ave N Texas City TX 77590 Office: 8128 Hwy 6 Hitchcock TX 77563

DOYLE, ELIZABETH DORR, nursing supr.; b. Augusta, Ga., Mar. 7, 1938; d. Paul Ferris and Dessie (McConnell) Dorr; R.N., St. Joseph's Infirmary, 1958; B.S. in Nursing, Med. Coll. Ga., 1978, grad. student, 1978—; m. Francis Ivins Doyle, Oct. 7, 1961; children—Angela Elizabeth, Margaret McConnell. Staff nurse Talmadge Hosp. of Med. Coll. Ga., Augusta, 1958-66, head nurse operating room, 1966-72, supr. operating room, 1972—, supr. postanesthesia recovery, 1972—; nurse cons. Davis & Geck div. Am. Cyanamid Co. Mem. Am. Nurses Assn., Assn. Operating Room Nurses. Roman Catholic. Home: 744 Fairfield Augusta GA 30909 Office: 1120 15th St Augusta GA 30912

DOYLE, ELIZABETH LEWIS, advt. exec.; b. San Francisco; d. Alvin Edward and Doris (Joyce) Lewis; B.A., Mich. State U., M.S. in Med. Journalism; m. Walter Arnett Doyle. Book editor Apothecary mag., Boston; columnist Am. Druggist mag., N.Y.C.; editor-in-chief, writer Beacon mag., Boston; med. columnist Boston Today mag.; pres. Doyle Advt., Lexington, Ky.; asst. prof. English composition North Shore Community Coll., Beverly, Mass.; cons., lectr. in field. Mem. women's guild Lexington Philharm. Orch. Mem. Am. Advt. Fedn. (numerous awards), Lexington C. of C., Theta Sigma Phi, Kappa Delta Pi. Republican. Clubs: Lexington Advt.; Women's City (Boston). Author: Momma Miser Finds Electronic Solutions to the Problems of Everyday Life, 1979, Momma Miser Finds Algebraic Solutions to the Problems of Everyday Life, 1979, How to Find the Best Job for You, 1979; The Old Lady and the Banker, 1980. Home: 1628 Nicholasville Rd Lexington KY 40503 Office: 1628 Nicholasville Rd Lexington KY 40503

DOYLE, JAMES MICHAEL, chem. co. exec.; b. Milw., Dec. 31, 1948; s. Donald Joseph and Dorothy Jane (Noeth) D.; B.B.A., U. Southwestern La., 1971; m. Charlotte Ann Ardoin, May 19, 1973; children—Angela Marie, Craig Michael. Sales rep. Mass. Mut. Life Ins. Co., 1972-73; sales rep., then sales mgr. Coastal Chem. Co., Abbeville, La., 1973-76, v.p. mktg. and sales, 1976—. Mem. Natural Gas Processors Assn., Nat. Assn. Chem. Distbrs. Republican. Roman Catholic. Home: 2323 Camella St Abbeville LA 70510 Office: PO Drawer C Abbeville LA 70510

DOYLE, JOHN ROBERT, JR., author; b. Dinwiddie County, Va., Jan. 22, 1910; s. John Robert and Marian Stickley (Binford) D.; B.A., Randolph-Macon Coll., 1932; M.A., U. Va., 1937, Bread Loaf Sch. English, 1941; postgrad. U. N.C., 1944-45; m. Clarice Alise Slate, June 13, 1942; 1 dau., Gwendolen Binford (Mrs. Lawrence Colwyn Hurst). Head dept. English, Dinwiddie (Va.) High Sch., 1932-40; instr. English, Clemson U., 1940-41; asst. prof. English, The Citadel, 1941-44, asst. prof., 1946-57, assn. prof., 1957-63, prof., 1963-75, prof. emeritus, 1975—, dir. Fine Arts Series, 1965-75. lectr. in physics U. N.C., 1944-45; lectr. lit. Stephens Coll., 1945-46; vis. prof. Am. lit. Univs. Cape Town and Witwatersrand, 1958; author books including: The Poetry of Robert Frost, 1962; William Plomer, 1969; Francis Carey Slater, 1971; Thomas Pringle, 1972; Arthur Shearly Cripps, 1975; William Charles Scully, 1978; founding editor of The Citadel Monograph Series; contbr. articles and essays to periodicals. Pres. Charleston Civic Ballet, 1963-65; chmn. fine arts events S.C. Tri-Centennial, 1970. Recipient Smith-Mundt grant to S. Africa, 1958; Daniel Disting. Teaching award, 1968; Algernon Sidney Sullivan award, The Citadel, 1971. Mem. Poetry Soc. S.C. (past pres., dir. writing group 1947-75, award of merit 1971), Modern Lang. Assn. Am. (chmn. conf. So. lit. 1965, world lit. written in English 1967), Am. Studies Assn. (past dir.), Coll. English Assn., Phi Beta Kappa. Home and office: Rives Ave McKenney VA 23872

DOYLE, ROBERT ALAN, psychiatrist; b. Chgo., June 12, 1935; s. Robert Morrison and Carmen Clara (Dorweiler) D.; B.S., Mich. State U., 1957; postgrad. Yale U., 1957-61; M.D., Duke U., 1963; m. Anne de Peyster Cary Tilton, May 10, 1969; children—Henry von Hoff Stoever, Brude Dickenson S., Anne de Peyster Cary. Intern, Lenox Hill Hosp., N.Y.C., 1963-64; resident in psychiatry Duke U. Med. Sch., Durham, N.C., 1964-69; practice psychiatry, Fort Lauderdale, Fla., 1969—; mem. staff Broward Gen. Med. Center, Beach Hosp., Holy Cross Hosp.; cons. Priory Hosp., London, 1975—. Served to capt., M.C., USAF, 1966-68. Mem. AMA, Am., Fla., Broward County psychiat. assns., Fla., Broward County med. assns., Duke U. Sch. Medicine Alumni Assn., Am. Philatelic Soc., Fort Lauderdale Museum, Ft. Lauderdale Opera Guild (dir.), Ft. Lauderdale Symphony Soc., Royal Philatelic Soc. (London), Royal Hort. Soc., Nat. Geneal. Soc., Md. Geneal. Soc. Episcopalian. Club: Yale (dir.). Home: 987 Hillsboro Mile Hillsboro Beach FL 33062 Office: 1109 Las Olas Blvd E Fort Lauderdale FL 33301

DOYLE, WALTER ARNETT, dentist; b. Los Angeles, Aug. 9, 1933; s. Walter James and Ruth Estelle (Journey) D.; D.D.S., Emory U., 1959; M.S. in Pedodontics, Ind. U., 1961; cert. in Orthodontics, Boston U., 1976; m. Elizabeth Lewis, July 18, 1977; children—Shannon, Elizabeth, Sarah, Walter Arnett. Practice dentistry specializing in pedodontics and orthodontics, Lexington, Ky., 1962—; instr. pedodontics Ind. U., Indpls., 1961-62; instr. (part-time) pedodontics U. Ky., 1964-65, guest lectr. pedodontics dept. community dentistry, 1972-74, asst. field prof. dept. community dentistry, 1972-74; vis. asso. prof. pedodontics Northwestern U., Chgo., 1972-74; vis. clin. prof. pedodontics Boston U. Sch. Grad. Dentistry, 1975—; pres. Renaissance Lab., Lexington, 1970—; v.p. Doyle Advt., Lexington, 1978—; dental cons. to Medcom, Inc., 1974—; cons. and contbr. to Health Info. Systems, Inc., 1972-74. Bd. dirs. Ky. Dental Service Corp., 1964-69; trustee Hunter Found., 1972-74. Recipient Thomas Hinman award, 1971, 77; S.S. White Centennial Teaching fellow, 1959; diplomate Am. Bd. Pedodontics (examining mem. 1968-75). Fellow Am. Acad. Pedodontics, Am. Coll. Dentists, Internat. Coll. Dentists, Royal Soc. Health; mem. Am. Soc. of Dentistry for Children (pres. 1976-77, sec. treas. 1973-74), Am. Soc. Preventive Dentistry (pres. Ky. unit 1972-73), Lexington Council for the Arts, Smithsonian Instn. Clubs: Sierra, Keeneland, Rotary. Contbr. articles on pedodontics to profl. publs. Home and Office: 1628 Nicholasville Rd Lexington KY 40503

DOYON, GÉRARD MAURICE, art historian; b. Manchester, N.H., Apr. 6, 1923; s. Arthur Eugène and Yvonne Mina (Gagne) D.; B.F.A., Manchester Inst., 1945; A.B., St. Anselm's Coll., 1951; postgrad. Ecole des Beaux-Arts, Paris, 1952, Ecole du Musée du Louvre, 1952; M.A., Boston U., 1954, Ph.D., 1964; m. Marie Thérèse Françoise Favreau, Sept. 1, 1945; children—Suzette Doyon Bernard, Denise Doyon Jared, Léon. Prof. art, chmn. dept. St. Anselm's Coll., 1952-60; prof. humanities Miami-Dade Community Coll., 1961-63; prof. art, chmn. dept. Fla. Atlantic U., 1963-68; prof. art history, chmn. dept. Washington and Lee U., Lexington, Va., 1968—. Served with U.S. Army, 1943-45. Decorated Bronze star; Croix de Guerre. Fulbright fellow, 1951-52; Danforth scholar, 1963-64. Mem. Va. Mus. Assn., Southeastern Coll. Art Assn., Alliance Francaise. Roman Catholic. Contbr. articles to profl. jours. Home: 911 Shenandoah Rd Lexington VA 24450 Office: Art Dept Washington and Lee U Lexington VA 24450

DOZIER, CARROLL T., bishop; b. Richmond, Va., Aug. 18, 1911; s. Curtis M. and Rose A. (Conaty) D.; A.B., Holy Cross Coll., 1932, LL.D., 1973; postgrad. N. Am. Coll., Gregorian U., Rome. Ordained priest Roman Catholic Ch., 1937, consecrated bishop, 1971; curate St. Vincent's Ch., Newport News, Va., 1937-41, St. Joseph's Ch., Petersburg, Va., 1941-45; dir. Soc. Propagation of Faith, 1945-54; pastor Christ the King Ch., Norfolk, Va., 1954-71; 1st bishop of Memphis, 1970—; mem. lay apostolate com., from 1972; named papal chamberlan, 1954, domestic prelate, 1962, Recipient Bill of Rights award ACLU, 1972; Cath. Human Relations award, Memphis, 1973. Address: 1325 Jefferson Ave Memphis TN 38104*

DOZIER, WILLIAM ALBERT, elec. engr.; b. Winfield, Ga., Mar. 11, 1932; s. Thomas Albert and Josie Large (Hall) D.; B.E.E., Ga. Inst. Tech., 1956; m. Martha Virginia Morris, May 24, 1958; children—William Albert, Steven Daniel. With Ga. Power Co., Columbus, 1955—, dist. engr., 1969-71, div. planning engr., 1971—. Named Engr. of Year, Ga. Power Engring. Assn., 1974, Columbus chpt. Ga. Archtl. and Engring. Soc., 1974. Registered profl. engr., Ga. Mem. I.E.E.E., Ga. Soc. Profl. Engrs. Methodist. Contbr. articles to Electrical World mag. Originator 3 stake method of locating faults on underground cables using radar; inventor dead cable certifier; patentee in field. Home: 5921 Leonard's Ct Columbus GA 31904 Office: PO Box 1220 Columbus GA 31902

DRAEGER, KENNETH EARL, chem. engr.; b. Seguin, Tex., Apr. 28, 1920; s. Arthur Andrew and Cora Lydia (Schaper) D.; B.S., U. Tex., 1941, M.S., 1942; m. Ethel Agnes Bellanger, Apr. 11, 1945; children—Jean Draeger Ramey, Marilyn Draeger Traynham. Chem. engr. Tex. Co., Port Arthur, 1942-47; chem. engr., engring. asso. Humble Oil Co., Baton Rouge, 1947-63; engring. asso. Esso Research & Devel. Co., Linden, N.J., 1963-65; sr. engring. asso. Exxon Co., Baton Rouge, 1965—. Mem. Am. Inst. Chem. Engring. Methodist. Patentee in field. Office: PO Box 2226 Baton Rouge LA 70821

DRAGSTEDT, CARL ALBERT, JR., ret. army officer, educator; b. Chgo., Apr. 21, 1921; s. Carl Albert and Ethel Elizabeth (Johnson) D.; B.A., U. Chgo., 1949; B.S. magna cum laude, U. Md., 1962; M.A.T., Rollins Coll., 1966; postgrad. (NDEA grantee) Fla. State U., 1967, Winthrop Coll., 1968; m. Louise Graham, May 14, 1947; children—Marsha Louise (Mrs. Ronald E. Ferguson), Carl Albert III, Laurel Maureen (Mrs. Lance C. Kimrey), Graham Lester, Leslie Carol (Mrs. John Hansen), Dana Selene, Carla Jane. Commd. 2d lt. U.S. Army, 1943, advanced through grades to maj., 1964; Japanese lang. officer, Osaka and Kyoto, Japan, 1946-48, 50-54; counter-intelligence officer, Japan, Germany, U.S., 1946-64; instr. Army Lang. Sch., Monterey, Cal., 1949-50; ret., 1964; tchr.-coach Oak Ridge High Sch., Orlando, Fla., 1964—. Sportswriter Orlando Sentinel Star, 1964—; tchr. Orange County (Fla.) Adult Edn. Program, Orlando, 1968—; instr. Valencia Community Coll., Orlando, 1974-75; adj. prof. Fla. So. Coll., Orlando, 1978—. Coach McCoy AFB (Fla.) Swim Team, 1971; coach Little League, Orlando, 1964-65; financial adviser Boy Scouts Am., Ludwigsburg, Germany, 1959-60. Named Outstanding Tchr. Nat. Honor Soc., 1970, 74, 76, 77, 79. Mem. Fla. Edn. Assn., Nat. Counter Intelligence Assn., Nat. Mil. Intelligence Assn., Nat. Interscholastic Swim Coaches Assn., Security and Intelligence Fund, Am. Security Council, Assn. Ret. Intelligence Officers, Fla. Athletic Coaches Assn., Delta Upsilon. Republican, Methodist (adminstrv. bd. 1972—). Coach All Am., Hon. Mention high sch. swimmers. Home: 1438 Gibson Dr Orlando FL 32809 Office: 6000 Winegard St Orlando FL 32809

DRAKE, ALBERT ESTERN, educator; b. Stamping Ground, Ky., June 12, 1927; s. John and Dullia D.; B.S., U. Ky., 1950, M.S., 1951; Ph.D., U. Ill., 1958; postdoctoral (NSF grantee) N.C. State U., 1959, 63, U. Fla., 1960; m. Katherine Ashby, June 22, 1952; children—Alan Sanford, Paul Steven, Jane, Philip David. Research asst. to research asso. U. Ill., 1953-59; from asso. prof. to prof. Auburn U., 1959-63; dir. computer center W.Va. U., 1963-66; prof. statistics U. Ala., 1966—. Cons. industry. Served with USMCR, 1945-46; PTO. Ford Found. grantee, 1975-76. Mem. Am. Statis. Assn. (pres. Ala. chpt. 1971-72), Am. Inst. Decision Scis. (nat. sec. 1973-74, nat. council 1969-72, 75-77), Biometrics Soc., Am. Agrl. Econs. Assn., Mu Sigma Rho, Chi Alpha Phi, Gamma Sigma Delta, Pi Mu Epsilon, Beta Gamma Sigma, Alpha Iota Delta. Club: Black Bear Booster (pres. 1976). Contbr. articles to profl. jours. Editorial bd. Jour. Decision Scis., 1969-71. Home: 280 Woodland Hills Tuscaloosa AL 35405 Office: U Ala Tuscaloosa AL 35486

DRAKE, GEORGE SHELDON, copier equipment co. exec.; b. Detroit, Nov. 25 1941; B.S., Lawrence Inst. Tech., 1970; M.B.A., Mich. State U., 1972; m. Mary J. Smith, Jan. 13, 1962; children—Christine, Stephanie, George S., II. Research technicican Ford Motor Co., Dearborn, Mich., 1963-65; tech. rep. Xerox Corp., Detroit, 1965-67, field service mgr., 1967-70, sales rep., 1970-72, br. service mgr., Fort Wayne (Ind.) br., 1972-74, sales mgr., Mich. br., Detroit, 1974-76; v.p. internat. service mgr. Apeco Corp., Evanston, Ill., 1976-77, v.p. ops., 1977-78; pres. Am. Photocopy Equipment Co., Atlanta, Ga., 1978—. Served with USCG, 1959-63. Mem. Atlanta C. of C., Gwinnet C. of C., Dekalb C. of C., Better Bus. Bur., Nat. Office Machine Dealers Assn. Home: 4629 Buckline Circle Atlanta GA 30338 Office: 5952 Peachtree Industrial Blvd Norcross GA 30071

DRAKE, JUNE DUNN, real estate broker, writer; b. Chgo., July 16, 1930; d. Gustave and Ann (Klein) Tilley; student U. Mo., 1948, Northwestern U., 1949; grad. Realtor Inst., Orlando, Fla., 1973; m. Ben Robert Drake, July 11, 1953 (div. 1970); children—Mitchell Alexander, Barbara Ann, Christopher Addison. Program mgr. Sta. WBKB-TV, Chgo., 1951-52; copy chief Sta. WTVJ-TV, Miami, Fla., 1952-53; owner, mgr. Creative Copy Unltd., Inc., Miami, 1966—; producer, writer films and TV shows, including Number One at the Fair (Film Writers Guild prize), 1965, numerous films for Fla. Devel. Commn., 1963-69; lectr. Greater Miami Real Estate Exchangors, 1977-79. Bd. dirs. Miami Shores Presbyn. Ch., 1960-66. Mem. Farm and Land Inst. (dist. v.p. 1980—), Realtors Nat. Mktg. Inst. (cert. comml. investment mem.), Nat. Assn. Realtors, Fla. Assn. Realtors (Realtor Asso. of Yr. 1976), Miami Bd. Realtors (Realtor Asso. of Yr. 1974), Women's Council Realtors (Woman of Yr. Miami chpt. 1973, pres. South Dade chpt. 1973, dist. v.p. 1974-75, treas. Fla. chpt. 1979, v.p. 1980), Fla. Real Estate Exchangors (dist. v.p. 1977-80), Acad. Creative Real Estate, Internat. Fedn. Realtors, Broward Real Estate Exchangors, Internat. Platform Assn., Keyes Million Dollar Sales Club, Cultural Arts Guild, Phi Mu. Clubs: Zonta Internat., Miami Shores Country, Menage, Viscayans; Jockey (Miami). Author: Radio and Television Copy Writing, 1954; editor humor column Fla. Realtor mag., 1976-79. Home: 432 NW 111th Terr Miami Shores FL 33168 Office: Keyes Co 100 N Biscayne Blvd Miami FL 33132

DRAKE, ROBERT ELDON, ophthalmologist; b. Baconton, Ga., Jan. 29, 1924; s. Edward Plummer and Carolyn Lucille (Redding) D.; student Centenary Coll., 1941-42. La. State U., 1942-43, Tulane U., 1943-44; M.D., La. State U., 1948; m. Bettye Bedell Boss, Dec. 31, 1947 (div.); children—Robert Eldon, Suzanne Elene, Kenneth Boss; m. 2d., Jo Ann Williams, July 1, 1962; 1 son, Jesse Joseph. Intern, Touro Infirmary, New Orleans, 1948-49; resident in ophthalmology Smith Eye Clinic 1965-67, Mobile (Ala.) Gen. Hosp., 1967-68, Scheie Eye Clinic, Phila., 1974; individual practice medicine, specializing in ophthalmology Winter Pk. (Orange County), Fla., 1953-64, Orlando (Orange Co.) Fla., 1968—. Pres., Winter Park (Fla.) Little League, 1958-64, Orlando (Fla.) Broncos Football team, 1972-74. Served with USNR, 1942-45, to capt., USAF, 1951-53. Mem. AMA, So. Med. Assn., Fla. Med. Assn., Orange County Med. Soc., Am. Acad. Ophthalmology. Democrat. Methodist. Author: Descendants of Exum Drake, Vol. III, 1977, Vol. IV, 1978. Home: 842 N Laurel Ave Orlando FL 32803 Office: 1226 E Colonial Dr Orlando FL 32803 also 303 E Magnolia Ave Eustis FL 32726

DRAKE, RONALD BLAINE, resort sales and marketing exec.; b. Pitts., Apr. 19, 1946; s. Russell Blaine and Betty Jane (Fulton) D.; student U. Kans., 1964-66, 68-70, Memphis State U., 1966-67; m. Brenda Eloise Moore, Feb. 20, 1971. Mgmt. trainee Holiday Inn, Lawrence, Kans., 1970, asst. innkeeper, Salem, Oreg., 1971, innkeeper, St. Augustine, Fla., 1971-72, food and beverage mgr., Fort Myers, Fla., 1972, asst. innkeeper, Fort Myers Beach, Fla., 1972-73, innkeeper, 1973; food and beverage mgr. Lehigh Corp., Lehigh Acres, Fla., 1973-76, resort dir., 1976-79, dir. resort sales and mktg., 1979—; cons. Edison Community Coll., 1975-76; vocat.-tech. cons., Lee County, Fla., 1976-77. Mem. Econ. Devel. Com., Lee County, Fla.; mem. Greater Fort Myers Royal Ambassadors. Served with USMC, 1967. Mem. Nat. Tour Brokers Assn., Fla. Soc. Assn. Execs., S.W. Travel Industry Assn., S.W. Fla. Chef's Assn., Lee County Hotel/Motel Assn. (pres.), Lee County Restaurant Assn., Met. Fort Myers C. of C., Sigma Alpha Epsilon. Republican. Methodist. Club: Rotary (pres. 1978-79) (Lehigh Acres). Home: 309 8th Ave Lehigh Acres FL 33936 Office: 225 E Joel Blvd Lehigh Acres FL 33936

DRAKE, VAUGHN PARIS, JR., telephone co. exec.; b. Winchester, Ky., Nov. 6, 1918; s. Vaughn Paris and Margaret Turney (Willis) D.; student U. Ky., 1936-41; m. Lina Louise Wilson, May 5, 1946; 1 son, Samuel Willis. With Gen. Telephone Co. Ky., Lexington, 1945—, asst. engr., 1945-50, field engr., 1950-54, dist. engr., 1954-56, div. engr., 1956-57, depreciation engr., 1957-62, gen. valuation and cost engr., 1962—. Mem. profl. adv. bd. Zoning Commn., Lexington and Fayette County (Ky.), 1955-57. Served with AUS, 1941-45. Registered profl. engr., Ky. Mem. Nat., Ky. (chmn. engrs. in industry sect. 1967-68, Outstanding Engr. in Industry award 1979) socs. profl. engrs., IEEE (sr.), Ky. Hist. Soc. Author: (manual) Conduit Engineering for Telephone Engineers, 1958. Home: 633 Portland Dr Lexington KY 40503 Office: 9th Floor First Security Plaza Lexington KY 40592

DRAPER, ROBERT BRUCE, architect; b. Gainesboro, Tenn., July 28, 1927; s. Herbert Ridley and Hallie (Reeves) D.; student U. Chgo., 1947-48, Frank Lloyd Wright Found., 1948-50; m. Jane Helen Caplinger, Dec. 11, 1953; children—Cynthia, Christopher Louis, Elizabeth. Draftsman, designer Chgo. firms William F. Deknatel, and Barancik & Conte, 1951-52; draftsman, designer Marr & Holman, Nashville, 1952-53 gen. practice architecture, Nashville, 1953—. Served with USNR, 1945-46. Mem. Soc. Am. Registered Architects. Episcopalian. Mason (32 deg.). Club: Harbor Island Yacht (past commodore). Home: 613 Estes Rd Nashville TN 37215 Office: 200 4th Ave N Nashville TN 37219

DRAPER, WILLIAM LEONARD, physician; b. Atlanta, Jan. 18, 1925; s. William Loyt and Belva (Ducote) D.; student Birmingham-So. U., 1942-43, Emory U., 1943-44; M.D., Baylor U., 1948; m. Beverly Blue Steele, Aug. 21, 1947; children—Diane, Kerry, Laura, Steven. Intern, Jefferson Hillman Hosp., Birmingham, Ala., 1948-49; resident Baylor U. Coll. Medicine Affiliated Hosps., Houston, 1951-54; practice medicine specializing in otolaryngology, Houston, 1954—; clin. asso. prof. otolaryngology Baylor Coll. Medicine and U. Tex. Med. Sch., Houston. Served as lt. (j.g.) USNR, 1942-45, 49-51. Mem. Harris County Med. Soc., Tex. Med. Assn., AMA, Tex. (past pres.), Houston (past pres.), otolaryngol. assns., Tex. Soc. Otolaryngology, Am. Soc. Ophthalmol. and Otolaryngol. Allergy (past pres.), Am. Rhinol. Soc. Presbyterian. Home: 2131 Brentwood St Houston TX 77019 Office: 1400 Hermann Profl Bldg Houston TX 77030

DRASEN, RICHARD FRANK, mfg. co. exec.; b. Chgo., Jan. 16, 1930; s. Frank Bernard and Margaret Louise (Lindsteadt) D.; student Mich. State U., 1943-49, Northwestern U., 1954-55, U. Calif. at Los Angeles, 1956-58, 1960-61, Calif. State U. at Northridge, 1961-63. Teacher, dir. The Academy, Los Angeles, 1959-61; mgr. communications United Parcel Service, Los Angeles also N.Y.C., 1961-68; mgr. pub. relations and communications Signal Oil & Gas Co., Los Angeles also Houston, 1968-74; mgr. pub. affairs Burmah Oil,

Inc., N.Y., 1974-75, Burmah Oil & Gas Co., Houston, 1975-77; mgr. pub. relations—energy R.J. Reynolds Industries, Inc., Winston-Salem, N.C., 1977-78; v.p. corp. affairs Howell Corp., Houston, 1978-80; mgr. public relations MAPCO, Inc., Tulsa, 1980—. Pres. Tara Homeowners Assn., 1960. Served with AUS, 1951-53. Mem. Internat. Assn. Bus. Communicators, Nat. Investor Relations Inst. Clubs: Univ., Houston, Warwick. Office: 1801 S Baltimore Ave Tulsa OK 74119

DRAWDY, VANCE BRABHAM, lawyer; b. Orangeburg, S.C., Jan. 29, 1928; s. Lonnie Wesley and Agnes Jane (Wilson) D.; B.A. cum laude, Furman U., 1952; J.D. (Root Tilden scholar), U. S.C., 1955; m. Mary Earle, Aug. 4, 1962; children—Vance Earle. Admitted to S.C. bar, 1955; asso. Rainey, Fant & Horton, Greenville, S.C., 1955-62, partner, 1963-70; pres. Horton, Drawdy, Marchbanks, Chapman & Brown, Greenville, 1970—; sec., dir. Patewood Corp., Greenville; dir. Pleasantburg Warehouse Co., Greenville. Gen. counsel S.C. Republican party, 1972-74; mem. S.C. Election Law Study Com., 1975—; mem. Tax Bd. of Review, 1976—; chmn. Hist. Preservation Commn.; bd. dirs. County Hist. Soc. Served as 1st lt. Signal Corps, AUS, 1947-49. Mem. Am. Bar Assn., Am. Judicature Soc., S.C.V. (comdr.). Clubs: Elks, Poinsett, Exchange (pres. 1974-75) (Greenville). Home: Route 6 Box 623 Piedmont SC 29673 Office: 307 Pettigru St Greenville SC 29603

DRERUP, JOHN WILLIAM, shoe co. exec.; b. Brookfield, Mo., May 22, 1922; s. Alphonse Lawrence and Mary (Killion) D.; B.S., Murray State U., 1947; postgrad. U. S.D., 1943, Washington U. Law Sch., 1946-47; m. Margaret Burrus, Oct. 9, 1948; children—Patricia, John William. Salesman, Bay Bee Shoe Co., Inc., Dresden, Tenn., 1949-51, sales mgr., v.p., 1951-62, pres., 1962-78, chmn. bd., 1978—; pres. First Realty Co., 1969—; partner Venture Investment Co.; dir. Farmers Exchange Bank, Benton Co. Broadcasting, DCM Co. Mem. U. Tenn. Devel. Council, U.S. Jaycees (past nat. dir.). Served with Signal Corps, U.S. Army, 1943-46. Named Young Man of Year, Jr. C. of C., 1956, Civitan award for outstanding work in community, 1978. Mem. Shoe Travlers Assn., Am. Legion. Roman Catholic. Club: Rotary, Moose. Home: 1015 Woodlawn St Union City TN 38261 Office: 140 Hillcrest St Dresden TN 38225

DRESDEN, GARY ANDREW, obstetrician, gynecologist; b. N.Y.C.; s. Arnold and Ruth Geraldine (Fisher) D.; B.S., McGill U., 1963; degree in medicine and surgery U. Bologna, 1968; m. Trudy Jean Ownes; children—Scott Charles, Bryan Lory, Dara Rayne. Intern, St. Barnabus Med. Center, Livingston, N.J., 1969-70; resident Baypoint Med. Center, St. Petersburg, Fla., 1970-73; practice medicine specializing in ob-gyn, St. Petersburg, 1973—; mem. staffs Bayfront Med. Center, St. Petersburg Gen. Hosp., Rutland Hosp.; pres., chmn. bd. All Women's Health Center, Inc., 1975—, Lakeland Women's Health Center, 1975—, Ft. Meyer's Women's Health Center, 1975—; pres. Dresden & Tickton M.D.'s, P.A., St. Petersburg, 1976—; asst. clin. prof. dept. ob-gyn, U. South Fla. Founder, 1st pres. Thom Howard Acad. Parents Assn. Fellow Am. Coll. Obstetricians and Gynecologists; mem. So. Med. Assn., Fla. Med. Assn., Pinellas County Med. Assn. Club: Feather Sound Country. Home: 2755 Bullard Dr Saint Petersburg FL 33520 Office: 6499 38th Ave N Saint Petersburg FL 33710

DRESSLER, ROBERT, elec. engr.; b. N.Y.C., May 5, 1925; B.S. in Elec. Engring., Columbia, 1946, M.S. in Elec. Engring., 1948; postgrad. Bklyn. Poly. Inst., 1948, 57, Northeastern U., 1962-67. Vice pres. research and devel. Paramount Pictures, N.Y.C., 1946-51; v.p. Chromatic TV Labs, Ins., N.Y.C., 1951-57; exec. v.p. Autometric Corp., N.Y.C., 1957-61; dir. advanced systems research and engring. Raytheon Corp., 1961-68; pres., chief exec. officer Riker-Maxson Corp., 1968-73; exec. v.p. Crown Industries, Tampa, Fla., 1973-75, pres., 1975—. Served with USNR, 1943-46. Recipient Nat. TV Systems Com. Award for color TV standards. Mem. I.R.E. (sr.), Am. Inst. E.E., Am. Soc. Photogrammetry, N.Y. Acad. Sci., Am. Phys. Soc., Am. Optical Soc., Am. Mgmt. Assn., Air Force Assn., Am. Rocket Soc. (sr.), Am. Geophys. Union, Soc. Motion Picture and TV Engrs. Patentee electric analogue circuit and method, others in field. Home: 2611 Bayshore Blvd Tampa FL 33609 Office: 3825 Henderson Blvd Tampa FL 33609

DRESZER, ANDREW EDWARD, public relations exec.; b. Washington, Mar. 9, 1951; s. Richard Joseph and Anna Kamila (Monseu) D.; student U. Md., 1969-71; B.S. in Forestry, N.C. State U., 1973; m. Cynthia Jean Baron, Mar. 4, 1972; children—Andrea Jean, Eric Joseph. With Belair Exxon, Bowie, Md., 1970; with Jacobs Transfer, Inc., Washington, 1970-71; summer forestry technician Westvaco Corp., Rupert, W.Va., 1973; asst. night mgr. Kerr Drugs, of Cameron Village, Raleigh, N.C., 1971-73; inventory forester Union Camp Corp., Savannah, Ga., 1974; supr. coop. forest mgmt. Westvaco Corp., Bleached Bd. Div., Appomattox, Va., 1974-78, public relations mgr., Covington, Va., 1978—. Indsl. chmn. Greater Alleghany United Fund dr., 1979-80, v.p., 1980—; pres. Sacred Heart Cath. Ch. Council, 1978—; co-chmn. sustaining membership enrollement Stonewall Jackson dist. Boy Scouts Am., 1979—; mem. Covington Downtown Devel. Com., 1979—; mem. Va. 5th Planning Dist. Pvt. Industry Council, 1979—; bd. dirs. Salvation Army, 1978—. Recipient Young Forester Leadership award Am. Foresters Soc., 1979; So. Forest Inst. Pres.'s award, 1978; cert. of appreciation Am. Forest Inst., 1977-78; co-recipient Nat. Arbor Day Found. award, 1977; cert. of merit, Va. Public Relations Soc., 1978. Mem. Va. Forestry Assn., Forest Industries Council, Forest Products Assn., So. Forest Inst. (del. 1977-78), Forest Farmers Assn., Soil Conservation Soc. Am., Va. Agribus. Council, Soc. Am. Foresters, Conservation Council Va. (del. 1976—), Internat. Assn. Bus. Communicators, Xi Sigma Pi, Gamma Sigma Delta. Roman Catholic. Home: 242 Detroit St Covington VA 24426 Office: Westvaco Corp Covington VA 24426

DREW, HORACE RAINSFORD, JR., lawyer; b. Jacksonville, Fla., Jan. 1, 1918; s. Horace Rainsford and Margaret Louise (Phillips) D.; B.S. in Bus. Adminstrn., U. Fla., 1940, LL.B., 1941, J.D., 1967; m. Rae Berger, Oct. 28, 1944; children—Shelley Louise, Robert Fairbanks, Horace Rainsford III. Admitted to Fla. bar, 1941; estate tax examiner Office Internal Revenue Agt. in Charge, Jacksonville, 1946-50; practice law, Jacksonville, 1951—; partner Buck, Drew, Ross & Short. Bd. dirs. Childrens Home Soc. Fla., Family Consultation Service, Duval County unit Am. Cancer Soc., 1962-71; founder, trustee Episcopal High Sch., Jacksonville; trustee Frank Lubbock Miller, Jr. Ednl. Found.; founding mem. So. Acad. Letters, Arts and Scis. Served to maj. F.A., AUS, 1941-45; ETO; lt. col. Res. (ret.). Mem. Am., Fla. (chmn. estate and gift tax com. 1956-58, chmn. tax sect. 1959-60), Jacksonville (chmn. spl. liaison tax com. Southeastern region 1962-63, chmn. com. on taxation 1955-56, 64-65) bar assns., Am. Judicature Soc., Jacksonville C. of C., Am. Security Council (nat. adv. bd.), Fairbanks Family in Am. (life), Internat. Order Blue Gavel, Phi Delta Phi, Sigma Alpha Epsilon. Episcopalian. Clubs: River; San Jose Country, San Jose Yacht (commodore 1978); Officers U.S. Naval Air Sta. (Jacksonville). Home: 861 Waterman Rd N Jacksonville FL 32207 Office: Fla Title Bldg Jacksonville FL 32202

DREWRY, GARTH RICHARD, radiologist; b. Kingsville, Tex., Aug. 28, 1928; s. Raymond George and Ingeborg Marie (Lokensgard) D.; B.S. with highest honors, Yale U., 1948; M.D. cum laude, Harvard U., 1952; m. Anne Carolyn Seashore, Dec. 30, 1960; children—Raymond George, David Harold, Elizabeth Anne, Douglas Garth. Intern in medicine Mass. Gen. Hosp., Boston, 1952-53; fellow in radiology U. Minn. Hosps., Mpls., 1953-56; staff radiologist Merritt Hosp., also Children's Hosp. of East Bay, Oakland, Calif., 1958-59; practice medicine specializing in radiology, Tampa, Fla., 1959—; radiologist Tampa Gen. Hosp.; clin. asst. prof. radiology Coll. Medicine, U. South Fla. Vice pres. Unitarian Ch. of Tampa, 1967; mem. Hillsborough County Pub. Edn. Study Commn., 1967, Hillsborough County Bd. Pub. Instruction, 1968; trustee Hillsborough Community Coll., 1969-71, Tampa Prep. Sch., 1978—; mem. Yale Alumni Bd., 1972; bd. dirs. Hillsborough Assn. for Gifted Edn., 1972; chmn. Citizens Adv. Com. to Pub. Schs., 1975-76. Served with USAF, 1956-58. Diplomate Am. Bd. Radiology, Am. Bd. Nuclear Medicine. Fellow Am. Coll. Radiology; mem. Radiol. Soc. N.Am., AMA, Fla., Hillsborough County med. assns., Fla., Fla. West Coast (pres. 1968-69) radiol. socs., Soc. Nuclear Medicine, Colegio Interamericano de Radiologia, Am. Cancer Soc. (dir. Hillsborough chpt. 1972—, v.p. 1974-75), Phi Beta Kappa, Sigma Xi, Alpha Omega Alpha. Clubs: Harvard (pres. 1968); Yale (pres. Bay Area club 1966). Home: 901 S Oregon Ave Tampa FL 33606 Office: 1 Davis Blvd Tampa FL 33606

DREWRY, JOSEPH SAMUEL, JR., chem. plant designer; b. Boykins, Va., Feb. 16, 1921; s. Joseph Samuel and Lucy (Moore) D.; B.S., Va. Mil. Inst., 1942; postgrad. U. Richmond, 1952; m. Virginia Daniel Pearson, June 12, 1948; children—Christopher Morris, Martha Kay. Asst. chief engr. Va.-Carolina Chem. Co., Richmond, 1946-62; chief engr. Armour Agrl. Chem. Co., 1962-67; v.p., dir. Kiernan-Gregory Corp., Atlanta, 1967—. Active Boy Scouts Am.; pres. Hammond Sch. PTA, 1969-71, N. Fulton County PTA, 1979-80. Decorated Bronze Star Medal, Purple Heart, Legion of Merit. Registered profl. engr., Ga. Mem. Nat. Fertilizer Assn. (dir.), Va. Mil. Inst. Alumni Assn. (pres. Atlanta chpt. 1966-68). Methodist (ofcl. bd. 1979-80). Clubs: Masons, Shriners. Home: 6640 Williamson Dr NE Atlanta GA 30328 Office: 173 W Wieuca Rd NE Atlanta GA 30342

DREWRY, WILLIAM ALTON, educator; b. Dyess, Ark., Oct. 23, 1936; s. C. Clarence and Cathleen (Ford) D.; Asso. Sci., Ark. Tech., 1956; B.S., U. Ark., 1959, M.S., 1961; Ph.D., Stanford, 1968; m. Bette Ann Cooper, Sept. 5, 1959; children—William Boyd, Bette Cathleen, Leslie Ann. Instr., U. Ark., Fayetteville, 1960-62, asst. prof., 1965-68; research asst. Stanford U., Palo Alto, Calif., 1962-65; asso. prof. dept. civil engring. U. Tenn., Knoxville, 1968-73, prof., 1973-76; prof., chmn. dept. civil engring. Old Dominion U., Norfolk, Va., 1976—. Cons. numerous industries and govt. agys. Registered profl. engr., Ark., Tenn., Va. Mem. Assn. Environ. Engring. Profs., ASCE, Am. Soc. Engring. Edn., Water Pollution Control Fedn., Am. Water Works Assn., Nat. Soc. Profl. Engrs., Sigma Xi, Tau Beta Pi, Chi Epsilon. Contbr. articles to profl. jours. Office: Dept Civil Engring Old Dominion U Norfolk VA 23508

DREWYER, ROLAND PAUL, civil engr., photographer; b. Waco, Tex., Feb. 17, 1935; s. Cecil Arnold and Sarah Edna (Arnold) D.; student Baylor U., 1953-54, 57-59; B.S. in C.E., U. Tex., 1961; m. Madelyn Elizabeth Coppin, Aug. 22, 1958; children—Roland, Patricia. Div. engr., City Waco, 1961-64; bridge design engr. Tex. Hwy. Dept., Waco, 1964-66; mgr. civil structural design group Dow Chem. Co., Houston, 1966-70; chief civil structural engr. J.F. Pritchard & Co., Houston, 1970-73; project mgr. Lummus Co., Houston, 1973—. Served with C.E., AUS, 1954-57. Registered profl. engr., Tex., Ark., La. Baptist (deacon). Home: 13307 Butterfly Ln Houston TX 77079 Office: 3000 S Post Oak Rd Houston TX 77056

DREY, ALAN, marketing services co. exec.; b. N.Y.C., Aug. 3, 1924; s. Adolf and Ruth (Fribourg) D.; student Carleton Coll., 1942-44; m. Hollis M. Kistler, June 20, 1946; children—Alan Bruce, Robert Edwin, Hollis Ann; m. 2d, Nancy J. Bruns, Feb. 19, 1972. Account exec. Lawrence H. Selz Orgn., Chgo., 1946-49; advt. dir. Hudson-Ross, Inc., 1951-52; v.p. Walter Drey, Inc., 1953-60; pres. Alan Drey Co., Inc., Chgo., 1960—; pub. Casper (Wyo.) Morning Star, 1949-52; v.p. Star Pub. Co., 1949-55; chmn. bd. Market Devel. Corp., St. Louis, 1964—, also dir.; chmn. bd. Drey/Bach Corp., N.Y.C., 1979—, also dir. Served to capt., USAAF, 1943-46. Decorated Air medal with 2 oak leaf clusters, Purple Heart, D.F.C. Mem. Direct Mail Mktg. Assn. Chgo. (past pres., dir.). Clubs: Tavern, Carlton (Chgo.); Key Biscayne (Fla.) Yacht. Home: 10 Island Drive Key Biscayne FL 33149 Office: 104 Crandon Blvd Miami FL 33149

DRINKWATER, GARY WADE, indsl. tech.; b. Franklin, La., Aug. 19, 1944; s. Minor Earl and Jessie May (Shoemaker) D.; B.S. in indsl. tech., La. State U., Baton Rouge, 1973; m. Karen Louise Bourgoyne, Jan. 21, 1967; children—Amanda Kaye, Allison Leigh. Fabrication production engr. J. Ray McDermott, Morgan City, La., 1974, offshore estimator, 1974-75, offshore field engr., 1975, planning engr. offshore div., 1976, installation coordinator world's deepest offshore platform Shell Cognac, 1976-78, chief engr. offshore div. Gulf of Mexico ops., 1978-80, div. mgr. offshore Gulf of Mexico ops., 1980—. Served with U.S. Army, 1968-72. Decorated Bronze Star medals, D.F.C., Air medal (19). Mem. Am. Welding Soc. Republican. Methodist. Club: Mason. Home: 1152 W Camelia St Thibodaux LA 70301 Office: PO Box 188 Morgan City LA 70380

DRINNON, JAMES EARL, JR., univ. adminstr.; b. Morristown, Tenn., Feb. 8, 1939; s. James Earl and Margaret (Boyd) D.; B.S., U. Tenn., 1966, J.D., 1962, Ed.D., 1971; m. Gail Drinnon, Mar. 19, 1960; children—Jim, Margie, Will. Admitted to Tenn. bar; spl. agt. FBI, Mo., Calif., N.Y., 1962-65; practiced law, Morristown, 1965; asst. gen. counsel U. Tenn, Knoxville, 1965-71, exec. asst. to pres., 1972-73, v.p. adminstrn., 1973-74; exec. asst. to chancellor U. Tex. Med. Units, Memphis, 1971-72; chancellor U. Tenn., Chattanooga, 1973—; bd. dirs. Tenn. Student Assistance Agy., Tenn. Com. for Humanities. Bd. dirs. ARC, Chattanooga; mem. exec. bd. Central YMCA, Chattanooga. Mem. Nat. Assn. Coll. and Univ. Attys., Tenn. Bar Assn., Am. Assn. Higher Edn., Am. Assn. State Colls. and Univs., Am. Council Edn., Greater Chattanooga C. of C. (dir.). Episcopalian. Clubs: Rotary, Masons, Shriners. Office: U Tenn Chattanooga TN 37401

DRISKELL, BERTRAN NORMAN, agronomist, cons.; b. Wilmer, Ala., Feb. 26, 1915; s. Dewitt Chapman and Iva Veronica (Pierce) D.; grad. Perkinston Jr. Coll., 1941; B.S. with honors, Miss. State U., 1942, M.S., 1946; Ph.D., Pa. State U., 1950; m. Bessie Lu York, Dec. 23, 1942; children—Boyce Norman, Julian Dale, Helen Anette. Asso. prof. La. State U., Baton Rouge, 1949-59; soil specialist U. Ky., Lexington, 1959-62; prof. chemistry and bacteriology U. Ala., Mobile, 1962-64; agronomist, cons. McMillan-Harrison Fertilizer Co., Grand Bay, Ala., 1964—; owner, mgr. Denham Lab. Vice pres. Mobile Extension Council, 1967-79; chmn. Town of Wilmer Planning Commn., 1976-80. Served with U.S. Army, 1942-46; ETO. Recipient Leadership award Mobile County, 1967; internat. minerals cert. Mem. Ala. Soil Fertility Soc. (pres. 1973-74), Soil Sci. Soc. Am., Southeastern Turf Grass Assn., Forestry Assn. Am., Creation Research Soc., Catlemen's Assn., Farm Bur., Sigma Xi, Phi Theta Kappa, Gamma Sigma Delta. Democrat. Baptist. Club: Tanner Williams Civics. Contbr. articles to profl. and religious publs. Home: Route 1 Box 15 Wilmer AL 36587 Office: PO Box 726 Grand Bay AL 36541

DRISKELL, CARL ROWLAND, elec. engr.; b. Forsyth, Ga., June 5, 1939; s. Cecil Searcy and Mary Susan (Bullard) D.; B.E.E., Ga. Inst. Tech., 1962, M.S., 1964; m. Nancy Lee Mastin, Aug. 20, 1966; children—Robert Scott, John Mark. Systems engr. Western Electric Co., Atlanta, 1962-63; asst. research engr. Ga. Tech. Engring. Expt. Sta., Atlanta, 1964-68, lectr. dept. elec. engring., 1967-68; electronics engr. Naval Tng. Equipment Center, Orlando, Fla., 1968-74; electronics engr. Army Tng. Device Agy., Orlando, 1974-76; electronics engr. Project Mgr. for Tng. Devices, Orlando, 1976-77; phys. scientist Dep. Chief of Staff for Research and Devel., Washington, 1977-78; lead project officer, product mgr. Armor Tng. Devices, Orlando, 1979, chief configuration and data mgmt., project mgr. for tng. devices, 1980—. Mem. IEEE, Sci. Research Soc. Am., Eta Kappa Nu, Tau Beta Pi. Home: 105 N Spring Trail Maitland FL 32751 Office: US Army Project Mgr for Tng Devices Code SC Orlando FL 32813

DRISKELL, ELOISE WHITEHURST, psychologist; b. Wauchula, Fla., Mar. 19, 1919; d. Wilbur Walton and Lemmie (Carlton) Whitehurst; B.A., Fla. So. Coll., 1939; M.A., Western Carolina U., 1968; children—Jeff Lott, Jess Driskell. Dir. pupil personnel services, sch. psychologist, dir. exceptional children Hardee County Schs., Wauchula, Fla., 1972—. Adviser to registrants Selective Service Bd., 1968—; mem. steering com. Fla. Learning Resource Systems. Delta Kappa Gamma fellow, 1967. Mem. Am., Fla. personnel and guidance assns., Am., Fla. sch. counselors assns., Am. Assn. Mental Deficiency, Nat., Fla. assns. sch. psychologists, Fla. Adminstrs. of Pupil Personnel Services, Fla. Assn. Sch. Adminstrs., Fla. Assn. Suprs. of Instrn., Council Adminstrs. of Spl. Edn., Council of Exceptional Children, Bus. and Profl. Womens Club, Delta Kappa Gamma. Democrat. Home: PO Box 517 Wauchula FL 33873

DROSSOS, ANGELO, investment co. exec.; b. San Antonio, Oct. 31, 1928; s. John Angelo and Demetra (Rigopoulos) D.; student U. Tex., 1946-47; student St. Mary's U., San Antonio, 1950, postgrad. in law, 1956-57; m. Lillie Fotenopulos, Dec. 4, 1960; children—Debra, John. With Shearson, Hammill & Co. (merged with Shearson Hayden, Stone, Inc. 1974, now Dean Witter & Co., Inc.), San Antonio, 1963—; pres. San Antonio Spurs. Bd. dirs. YMCA; pres. bd. dirs. St. Sophia Greek Orthodox Ch., San Antonio. Served with U.S. Army, 1950-52. Mem. Nat. Basketball Assn. (dir.). Office: care San Antonio Spurs Hemisfair Arena PO Box 530 San Antonio TX 78292*

DRUCKER, DAVID H., obstetrician and gynecologist; b. Bklyn., Aug. 8, 1939; s. Sterling S. and Clara (Haber) D.; A.B., Cornell U., 1961; M.D., SUNY, Bklyn., 1965; m. Eve Marie Lehrman, Aug. 23, 1964; children—Heather and Scott (twins), Brian. Intern, L.I. Jewish Hosp., New Hyde Park, N.Y., 1965-66; resident in obstetrics and gynecology Meadowbrook Hosp., East Meadow, N.Y., 1966-70; chief obstetrics and gynecology USAF Hosp., Robins AFB, Ga., 1970-72; pvt. practice specializing in obstetrics and gynecology L.I., 1972-75, Chattanooga, 1975—; chief obstet. and gynecol. service East Ridge Community Hosp. Bd. dirs. Chattanooga Jewish Day Sch., 1977—. Served to maj. M.C., USAF, 1970-72. Diplomate Am. Bd. Obstetrics and Gynecology (also recert.). Fellow Am. Coll. Obstetrics and Gynecology, Am. Fertility Soc.; mem. Am. Assn. Gynecol. Laparoscopists. Republican. Jewish. Club: Walden (Chattanooga). Home: 1508 Independence Ln Chattanooga TN 37421 Office: 4547 Brainerd Rd Chattanooga TN 37411

DRUCKER, GERALD DAVID, editor, publisher; b. N.Y.C., Mar. 23, 1923; s. Max and Ray (Clara) D.; B.A., U. N.C., 1943; postgrad. Columbia U., 1954, N.Y. Inst. Finance, 1957; m. Bettina Brown, July 11, 1964; children—Linda Fairbanks, Susan Wood. Sales mgr. ZIV United Artists, 1955-60; account exec. Katz Agy., N.Y.C., 1960-73; pres. Gerald Drucker Assos., N.Y.C., 1973-77; pres. Greystone Publishers Inc., pub. Sandlapper Mag., Columbia, S.C., 1978—. Served to lt. USNR, 1943-46. Mem. Sales Marketing Club, Communicating Arts Soc., Columbia Media Club, Columbia Advt. Club. Club: Westchester Country. Home: 1825 St Julian Pl Columbia SC 29204 Office: 3830 Forest Dr Columbia SC 29204

DRUCKER, MEYER, educator; b. Denmark, S.C., Aug. 10, 1937; s. Morris and Ida Belle (Andronosky) D.; B.S., U. S.C., 1959, J.D., 1966; M.A., Am. U., 1961; m. Barbara Loewe, June 12, 1966; children—Deborah, Kenneth. With Sears, Roebuck & Co., Columbia, S.C., 1955-58; supervisory accountant U.S. GAO, Washington, 1959-63; lectr. in acctg. U. S.C., 1963-66, prof. acctg. and bus. law, 1975—; sr. internal auditor Burlington Industries, Greensboro, N.C., 1966-67; controller Maxon Shirt Co., Greenville, S.C., 1967-68; head dept. acctg. Midlands Tech. Coll., Columbia, 1968-70; asso. prof. acctg. U. N.C., Charlotte, 1970-75; cons. in tax and bus. related work. Del., county and state Democratic Party convs., 1976, 78; head tax clinic for indigent taxpayers, 1971-79. Served with U.S. Army, 1956-58. Mem. Am. Inst. C.P.A.'s, Am. Bar Assn., Am. Acctg. Assn., Inst. Internal Auditors, S.C. Bar Assn., N.C. Inst. C.P.A.'s, Adminstrv. Mgmt. Soc., Nat. Assn. Accountants. Democrat. Jewish. Contbr. articles to profl. jours. Home: 231 Heathwood Dr Spartanburg SC 29302 Office: U SC Spartanburg SC 29303

DRUDE, RICHARD BERNARD, JR., gastroenterologist; b. New Orleans, Aug. 9, 1950; s. Richard Bernard and Adeltte Elaine (Melkie) D.; B.S., La. State U., 1972, M.D., 1975; Intern, Earl K. Long Meml. Hosp., Baton Rouge, 1975-76, resident in internal medicine, 1975-78, chief resident, 1978; gastroenterology fellow Alton Ochsner Med. Found., New Orleans, 1978-80; faculty La. State U. Med. Sch., New Orleans, 1976-78, Tulane U. Med. Sch., New Orleans, 1979-80; joined USAFR, 1973; gastroenterologist Eglin AFB, Ft. Walton, Fla., 1980—; lectr. in field. Diplomate Am. Bd. Internal Medicine. Mem. ACP. Roman Catholic. Club: Tennis. Contbr. articles to profl. jours. Office: 1516 Jefferson Hwy Jefferson LA 70121

DRUM, MARKEL KENT, speech pathologist; b. Chanute, Kans., Dec. 13, 1948; s. Kenneth Martin and Virginia Arlene (Williams) D.; B.A. in Audiology and Speech Pathology, Kans. U., 1970; M.S. in Speech and Hearing Scis., Washington U., St. Louis, 1972; m. Jennifer Kay Enke, Nov. 14, 1970; children—Christopher Markel, Calista Joy. Tchr. hearing impaired Tucker-Maxon Oral Sch., Portland, Oreg., 1972-74; ednl. specialist Tenn. Dept. Edn., Jackson, 1974-75; deaf edn. specialist Middle Tenn. State U., Murfreesboro, 1975-76; staff audiologist VA Med. Center, Murfreesboro, 1976—; extension instr. U. Tenn., Knoxville, 1975; cons. Nashville Met. Sch. System, 1977. Bd. dirs. Murfreesboro Community Theatre, 1976, 78, 79. Recipient Suggestion award VA, 1977. Mem. Am. Speech and Hearing Assn., A.G. Bell Assn. Deaf, Am. Orgn. Edn. Hearing Impaired, Tenn. Speech and Hearing Assn. Home: 2326 Halls Hill Pike Murfreesboro TN 37130 Office: Audiology and Speech Pathology Service VA Medical Center Murfreesboro TN 37130

DRUMM, MORRIS DON, govt. ofcl.; b. Royse City, Tex., Dec. 2, 1943; s. John Morris and Jimmie Nell (Burks) D.; B.A., East Tex. State U., Commerce, 1966, M.A., 1967, postgrad., 1970—; m. Cynthia Ann Howard, Dec. 17, 1966; children—Stephanie Ann, Lee Ann. Claims examiner VA, Waco, Tex., 1967-73, legal rating specialist,

1973—; area 2 rep. VA Adminstr.'s com. on youth, 1974-75. Part-time instr. polit. sci. McLennan Community Coll., Waco, Tex., 1970—. Patron, bd. dirs. Waco Civic Theater. Mem. Am., Southwestern polit. sci. assns., Dallas Summer Mus. Guild, Pi Sigma Alpha, Alpha Phi Omega (sec. chpt. 1964-65), Phi Delta Kappa. Democrat. Methodist (v.p. Mary and Joseph class 1974-75, vice chmn. adminstrv. bd., treas. Agape class 1977—). Contbr. Polit. Sci. Utilization Directory, 1975. Home: 5412 Lake Lindenwood Waco TX 76710 Office: 1400 N Valley Mills Dr Waco TX 76710

DRUMMOND, GARY DAVID, data systems exec.; b. Toronto, Ont., Can., May 4, 1944; s. David Bogie and Margaret Lillian (Thompson) D.; student Kent State U., 1963-64, Cerritos Coll., 1965-66; m. Dorothy Elaine Bush, Mar. 4, 1967 (div.); children—Jeffrey David, Jay Charles; m. 2d, Bridgett A. Brennan, Aug. 4, 1979. Salesman, Sears Roebuck and Co., Los Angeles, 1965-67, Addressograph Multigraph Corp., San Francisco, 1967-71, San Bernardino, Calif., 1971-72, Las Vegas, Nev., 1972-73; founder, pres., chief exec. officer Spl. Service Systems, Inc., Tulsa, 1973—. Served with USMCR, 1975. Mem. Data Processing Mgmt. Assn., Nat. Assn. Accountants, Okla. Bankers Assn., Independent Bankers Assn. Okla., Okla. Hosp. Assn., Pres.'s Assn. Republican. Mem. Ch. of Nazarene. Office: 10514 E Pine St Tulsa OK 74116

DRUMMOND, KENNETH HERBERT, sci. project exec.; b. Riverside, Calif., Jan. 19, 1922; s. Finlay Mackay and Eva Mary (Holland) D.; student Bates Coll., 1941-43; B.S., U. Ariz., 1949; postgrad. Tex. A. and M. U., 1950-57; m. Marion Emily Deane, May 14, 1955; children—Laurie, Finlay, Carter. Asso. in oceanography Tex. A. and M. U., College Station, 1950-57; asst. dir. Smithsonian Astrophys. Obs., Cambridge, Mass., 1957-60; asst. to chancellor U. Calif. at San Diego, 1960-62; Washington rep. Tex. Instruments, 1960-67; exec. sec. panel industry and investment Commn. on Marine Sci., Exec. Office Pres., Washington, 1967-68; dir. program devel. Teledyne, Inc., Washington, 1969-72; asst. to pres. Ensco, Inc., Springfield, Va., 1972-76; program dir. Marine Resources Centers, State of N.C., 1976-77; asst. to dean, dir. spl. projects Center for Wetlands Resources La. State U., Baton Rouge, 1977—. Served with USNR, 1943-46; PTO. Fellow AAAS, Tex. Acad. Sci., Explorers Club; mem. Nat. Space Club, Marine Tech. Soc., Nat. Ocean Industries Assn. (dir. 1972-76), Circumnavigators Club. Mason (32 deg.). Author: (with Eloise Engle) Sky Rangers, 1965. Editor: (with C.A. Whitten) Contemporary Geodesy, 1959. Home: Windy Bend Box 217 Greenwell Springs LA 70739 Office: Center Wetland Resources La State U Baton Rouge LA 70803

DRUMMONDS, DAVID LESLIE, mech. engr.; b. Birmingham, Ala., Apr. 26, 1948; s. Robert Monroe and Leslie Alice (Fulton) D.; B.S., U. Ala., 1970, M.S. (NDEA fellow), 1973. Asst. engr. Northrop Services, Inc., Huntsville, Ala., 1971-72; instr. engring. Jefferson State Jr. Coll., Birmingham, 1973-75; sr. engr. So. Co. Services, Inc., Birmingham, 1972—. Registered profl. engr., Ala., Ga., Fla., Miss. Mem. Nat. Soc. Profl. Engrs., Pi Mu Epsilon, Pi Eta Sigma, Pi Tau Sigma, Tau Beta Pi. Methodist. Home: 2200 Brookdale Ln Birmingham AL 35216 Office: PO Box 2625 Birmingham AL 35202

DRURY, JOHN TERRY, chem. mktg. dir.; b. Atlanta, Mar. 11, 1947; s. Carroll R. and Runell S. D.; B.B.A., U. Ga., 1969; m. Patricia House, Nov. 3, 1973. Ins. broker, 1969-73; sales rep. Premier Fastener, Chamblee, Ga., 1973; v.p. mktg. and sales Tesco Chems., Marietta, Ga., 1973-77; dir. mktg. Great Lakes Chem. Corp., Aquabrom div., West Lafayette, Ind., 1977—, also dir. mktg. Aquabrom div., Marietta, Ga., 1978—. Bd. dirs. Council on Aging, Family Counseling Service, Athens, Ga., 1970. Mem. Nat. Swimming Pool Inst., Internat. Spa and Tub Inst. Home: 4800 River Farm Rd Marietta GA 30067 Office: 1850 Airport Industrial Park Dr Marietta GA 30062

DRURY, LEONARD LEROY, oil co. exec.; b. Gillespie, Ill., Nov. 5, 1928; s. Roy August and Regina Loretta (Finnegan) D.; B.S., St. Louis U., 1950; M.B.A., U. Houston, 1957; m. Myra Lee Klunk, June 30, 1951; children—Denise Ann, Marilyn Jo. With Shell Oil Co., 1953—; mgr. systems programming, N.Y.C., 1966-68, mgr. data processing, Menlo Park, Calif., 1968, mgr. accounting, 1968-69, mgr. bus. systems div., N.Y.C. and Houston, 1969-71, mgr. planning, Houston, 1971-73, mgr. planning and tech., Houston, 1973-75; asst. treas. financing, Houston, 1975-77; gen. mgr. info. and computer services, Houston, 1977—. Active United Way, Salvation Army, Houston. Served in C.E., U.S. Army, 1951-53. Mem. Fin. Execs. Inst., Data Processing Mgmt. Assn., Am. Petroleum Inst., Sigma Iota Epsilon. Roman Catholic. Clubs: University, Lakeside Country (Houston); Rotary. Home: 12414 Old Oaks Dr Houston TX 77024 Office: PO Box 2463 Houston TX 77001

DRURY, LLOYD LEONARD, mfg. co. exec.; b. New Orleans, Oct. 12, 1925; s. John Joseph and Evelyn (Nebel) D.; student U.S. Mcht. Marine Acad., 1946; B.S., La. State U., 1949; M.B.A., Loyola U., 1961; Ph.D., Rochdale Coll., 1972; D.D., Ch. Universal Brotherhood, 1975; Ph.D., Pacific So. U., 1976; m. Betty Bray Byrne, July 10, 1946; children—Lloyd Leonard, David Bray, Susan Joan, Denise Ann. Marine engr. Grace Lines, Inc., N.Y.C., 1945-46; field engr. Calif. Co., New Orleans, 1949; various tech. and mgmt. positions Gen. Electric Co., 1949-59, corp. exec., New Orleans, 1959—; mgmt. cons.; lectr. La. State U., Tulane U.; cons. psychologist. Div. leader United Fund, New Orleans, 1960; leader Jr. Achievement, New Orleans, 1969-71; mem. Alumni council La. State U.; v.p. First Evang. Ch., 1972. Served with USN. Named hon. La. State Senator; recipient Gen. Electric managerial achievement awards. Registered profl. engr. Mem. Nat. Soc. Profl. Engrs., Soc. Naval Architects and Marine Engrs., Am. Soc. Indsl. Security, La. Engring. Soc. Clubs: Metairie Country, Beau Chene Golf and Raquet. Home: 4465 Bancroft Dr New Orleans LA 70122

DRURY, THOMAS JOSEPH, bishop; b. County Sligo, Ireland, Jan. 4, 1908; s. Michael and Margaret (Lannon) D.; student St. Benedict's Coll., Atchison, Kan., 1926-29; A.B., Kenrick Sem., 1931-35. Ordained priest Roman Catholic Ch., 1935; asst. and pastor Sacred Heart Cathedral, Amarillo, Tex., 1935-45; pastor St. Elizabeth's Ch., Christ the King Ch., Lubbock, Tex., 1956-61; bishop Diocese of San Angelo, 1961-65; consecrated, 1962; bishop Diocese of Corpus Christi, 1965—. Sec. Matrimonial Ct., 1935, promotor of justice, 1938—, defender of the bond, 1939—; diocesan dir. Confraternity of Christian Doctrine, 1936, Soc. Propagation of the Faith, 1936—, Cath. Action, Holy Name Soc.; mem. bd. Diocesan Adminstrn., 1938—. Chmn. Amarillo council Boy Scouts Am.; v.p. Amarillo Cath. Welfare Bur. Served to maj. Chaplains Corps, USAAF, 1945-47, USAF, 1949-55. Editor, bus. mgr. Texas Panhandle Register, 1936-38. Home: 4109 Ocean Dr Corpus Christi TX 78411 Office: 620 Lipan St Corpus Christi TX 78401

DRY, OWEN LEE, steel fabrication co. exec.; b. Galveston, Tex., Jan. 13, 1942; s. Lee Owen and Ellen Erna (Rodefeld) D.; B.S. in Math., U. Houston, 1976; m. Gail Lynn Wallace, Apr. 2, 1965; children—Owen Lee, James Michael, Jill Deann. With Wyatt Industries, Inc., Houston, 1963-78, mgr. systems and procedures, 1972-78, mgr. value analysis, 1976-78, mgr. prodn. Steel Tank Constrn. Co. subs., 1978—. Mem. Soc. Am. Value Engrs. Republican. Baptist. Home: 21222 Park Wick Ln Katy TX 77450 Office: PO Box 3052 Houston TX 77001

DRYDEN, DAVID CHARLES, journalist, public relations counselor; b. Tulsa, Apr. 29, 1947; s. Charles B. and Lona Kathryn (Ratterree) D.; student U. Okla.; m. Carolyn Sue Samara; 1 son, Paul David. Asst. bus. editor Tulsa Daily World, 1967; local govt. affairs reporter The Daily Oklahoman, 1968-77; v.p. E.H. Public Relations, Inc., 1977-78; editor The Downtowner, 1977-78; asso. editor Best Years, 1977-78, fin. columnist, 1977—; owner, mgr. Diversified Income Services, 1977—; mgr. public relations Okla. div. Am. Automobile Assn., 1978—; editor Okla. Traveler, 1978—. Bd. dirs. Hist. Preservation, Inc., 1972, Kidney Found. Okla., 1980—; sec.-treas. Okla. Hwy. Users Fedn., 1980. Mem. Acad. Polit. Sci., Public Relations Soc. Am., Sigma Delta Chi. Republican. Baptist. Clubs: Oklahoma City Gridiron, Oklahoma City Press. Home: 221 NW 20th St Oklahoma City OK 73103 Office: PO Box 60425 Oklahoma City OK 73146

DRYDEN, WILLIAM, farmer; b. Auburn, Ala., Mar. 20, 1905; s. Charles A. and Mabel Claire D.; B.S., Auburn U., 1926, M.A., 1933; postgrad. Columbia, 1927-28, Carnegie Mellon U., 1928-30; postgrad. Beca de la U., U. Nacional de Colombia, 1947; m. Evelyn McKillip. Exec. sec. Sch. Chemistry, Auburn (Ala.) U., 1930-45, asst. dean Grad. Sch., dir. research found., 1945-49; faculty univ. relations div. Oak Ridge (Tenn.) Asso. Univs., 1949-53; owner William Dryden Poultry Farm, Fort Myers, Fla., 1953-64; owner Dryden Swine Farms, Wabash, Ind., 1960—. Commr. Lee County Mosquito Control Dist., Ft. Myers, 1958—, sec.-treas., 1960—. Bd. dirs. Lehigh Acres Gen. Hosp., Fort Myers, 1965-71; chmn. bd. dirs. St. Luke's Parochial Sch., Fort Myers, 1958-62; bd. dirs. Canterbury Sch., Fort Myers, 1970—. Mem. Fla. Anti-Mosquito Assn. (pres. 1975-76, hon. life), Sigma Phi Epsilon. Democrat. Episcopalian (del. nat. conv. 1970). Elk, Rotarian (pres. 1958-60). Club: Royal Palm Yacht. Address: Route 14 PO Box 362 Fort Myers FL 33905

DUANE, CAMILLE (MRS. FRANK DUANE ROSENGREN), research cons.; b. San Antonio, Sept. 28, 1926; d. Emmett Thomas and Camille Georgette (Lodovic) Sweeney; B.A., Incarnate Word Coll., 1948; M.S., Our Lady of the Lake Coll., 1951; m. Frank Duane Rosengren, Jan. 13, 1951; 1 dau., Emily Duane Ferry. Script reader for various N.Y. prodn. firms, 1954-58; reference librarian, cataloger Met. Mus. Art, N.Y.C., 1959-61; circulation and reference librarian San Antonio Coll., 1964-67; registrar, librarian Inst. Texan Cultures, San Antonio, 1967-70; freelance research cons. on history and fine arts, San Antonio, 1970—; v.p. Rosengren's Books, Inc., San Antonio, 1970—. Mem. Citizens for a Better Environment, San Antonio, 1971-74; mem. San Antonio Symphony Soc., 1964-72; mem. women's com. Bexar County Democratic Women, 1963—; bd. dirs. San Antonio Conservation Soc., 1964-68, v.p. pub. relations, 1966-68. Mem. Am. Booksellers Assn., Ind. Bookseller Assn. (v.p.), ALA, AAUP, ACLU. Home and Office: 801 Garraty Rd San Antonio TX 78209

DUANE, FRANK, author; b. Chgo., Aug. 8, 1926; s. Frank and Florence (Kedney) Rosengren; B.A., U. Chgo., 1951; fellow Yale, 1955-56; m. Emily Camille Sweeney, Jan. 13, 1951; 1 dau., Emily Duane Ferry. Pres. Rosengrens Books, San Antonio, program cons. sta. KENS-TV, San Antonio, 1963-70; staff writer Omnibus, 1956-57; workshop coordinator Elinor Morgenthau New Dramatists Workshop, N.Y.C., 1954-55; producer On The Spot, KENS-TV, 1961-71; editor El Abrazo, 1967—; chief spl. features HemisFair, 1968; exec. producer KLRN-TV, San Antonio-Austin, 1968—; exec. dir. Presentation Assos. Bd. dirs. Music Theatre, Inc.; chmn. adv. bd. Coll.-Community Creative Arts Center, Our Lady of Lake Coll.; dir. concept devel. Telesis, 1972—. Served with USAAF, 1944-46. Mem. Dramatists Guild, Writers Guild of Am., Acad. TV Arts and Scis., Nat. Assn. Ednl. Broadcasters, San Antonio Theatre Council, U. Chgo. Alumni Assn. Writer various plays, motion picture, TV shows including: Jimmy and the River, 1958; Guitar, 1959; Prophets of Light, 1966; Pilgrims to the West, 1971; After Cortez, 1973; Anywhere From Orpheus, 1975; To Harness the Rain, 1979. Home: 801 Garraty Rd San Antonio TX 78209

DUBACH, HAROLD WILLIAM, oceanographer, sci. cons.; b. St. Joseph, Mo., Nov. 25, 1920; s. Henry William and Susan (Cornelius) D.; A.B., Baker U., 1942; postgrad. U. Chgo., 1942-43, Johns Hopkins, 1949-51; m. Roberta Pauline Rose, Sept. 26, 1946; children—Linda Joy, Deborah Ann, Nancy Lee, David Wesley. Research meteorologist Thunderstorm Project, U.S. Weather Bur., Chgo., 1946-48; research oceanographer U.S. Naval Hydrographic Office, Washington, 1948-60; oceanographer, dep. dir. Nat. Oceanographic Data Center, Washington, 1960-69; oceanographer, asst. dir. Center for Marine Devel., Coastal Plains Regional Commn., 1969-73; head marine industries dept. Beaufort (S.C.) Tech. Inst., 1973-75; cons. oceanography Savannah River Lab., E.I. DuPont de Nemours Co., Inc., ERDA, Aiken, S.C., 1975-76; coordinator Ocean Outfall Project, N.C. Office Marine Affairs, Raleigh, 1976-77; dir. N.C. Marine Resources Center, Ft. Fisher, N.C., 1977-78; dist. mgr. Star-News, Wilmington, Del., 1978—. Panel examiner in meteorology U.S. Civil Service Commn., 1957-60, in oceanography, 1954-63; mem. Fed. Adv. Com. Water Pollution, 1966-69; chmn. U.S. delegation Working Group on Marine Data Systems, Internat. Council Exploration of Seas, 1968. Pres. Bellemead (Md.) Citizens Assn., 1955-56; lay del. Balt. Conf. Meth. Ch., 1956-71, N.C. Conf. Meth. Ch., 1979—. Bd. dirs. Youth Services Inc., Landover Hills, Md., 1956-57. Served to capt. USAAF, 1942-46. Recipient CIA-U.S. Navy Commendation, 1959; Superior Accomplishment award U.S. Navy, 1962, commendation award for invention, 1967, Distinguished Alumni award Baker U., 1970. Mem. Am. Meteorol. Soc., Internat. Oceanographic Found., Marine Tech. Soc., Fla. Oceanographic Soc., Oceanographical Soc. Japan, Australian Marine Scis. Assn., Cousteau Soc., Smithsonian Assos. Methodist (trustee 1956-57; ofcl. bd. 1956-71, adminstrv. bd. 1975—, mem. social concerns com. 1967; steward). Author books, tech. reports, book reviews and papers profl. jours. Mem. editorial bd. Geoscience Documentation (London, Eng.). Patentee in field. Home: 4609 Dean Dr Wilmington NC 28405 Office: Star-News Newspapers PO Box 840 Wilmington NC 28402

DU BARD, (NETTIE) ETOILE, educator; b. Grenada, Miss., May 1, 1921; d. William Vassar and Zollie Luther (Young) DuBard; B.S., Mary Hardin-Baylor Coll., 1942; M.A., George Peabody Coll., 1950; postgrad. (scholar), Central Inst. for Deaf, Washington U., St. Louis 1960-62; Ph.D., U. So. Miss., 1967. Tchr., Robstown, Tex., 1942-43, Port Arthur, Tex., 1946-49, Jackson, Miss., 1950-53, Apopka, Fla., 1953-54, Natchez, Miss., 1954-55; speech pathologist, Natchez, 1955-60; dir. Sch. for Children with Lang. Disorders, U. So. Miss., Hattiesburg, 1962—, Disting. prof., 1976—. Served with USNR, 1943-45. Mem. Am., Miss. speech and hearing assns., Bell Assn. for Deaf, Council fdr Exceptional Children, Assn. for Children with Learning Disabilities, Miss. Assn. for Epilepsy, Pi Tau Chi, Omicron Delta Kappa. Roman Catholic. Author: Teaching Aphasics and Other Language Deficient Children, 1974, 76. Home: 3806 Pearl St Hattiesburg MS 39401 Office: Box 8137 Southern Station Hattiesburg MS 39401

DUBAY, ROLAND CHARLES, ednl. adminstr.; b. Unterreichenbach, Germany, Mar. 7, 1949; s. Charles John and Alice Gisela (Burke) D (parents Am. citizens); B.A., U. S.C., 1971, M.A., 1980. State project developer Title I Programs, Higher Edn. Act of 1965, Columbia, S.C., 1979—. Polit. campaign mgr., Richland County Young Rep. Club, 1977, sec., 1977-78, chmn., 1978, newsletter editor, 1978-79; committeeman, Lykesland Precinct and exec. com. mem. Richland County Rep. Party, 1978-79, del. to state conv., 1978, chmn., editor newsletter, 1979, chmn. speakers com., 1979. Active Easter Seal Soc. S.C., 1979—. Served with USN, 1971-76; to lt., USNR, 1976—. Recipient S.C. State Legis. internship, 1978. Mem. Columbia Jr. C. of C., Columbia Navy League, Naval Res. Assn., U. S.C. Alumni Assn., Columbia Soc. for Prevention of Cruelty to Animals, V.F.W. (adj. post 641, 1979-80, Newsletter editor, 1979-80, chmn. post 641, polit. action com., 1979-80), U. S.C. Soc. of Public Adminstrn. (program chmn. 1978), S.C. Assn. Higher Continuing Edn. Presbyterian. Clubs: Columbia First Tues., Jonathan Maxcy. Home: 2244 Newell Rd Columbia SC 29209

DUBERG, JOHN EDWARD, research scientist; b. N.Y.C., Nov. 30, 1917; s. Charles Augustus and Mary (Blake) D.; B.S., Manhattan Coll., 1938; M.S., Va. Polytech. Inst., 1940; Ph.D., U. Ill., 1948; m. Mary Louise Andrews, June 11, 1943; children—Mary Jane, John Andrews. Field engr. Cauldwell Wingate Builders, N.Y.C., 1938-39; research fellow Va. Polytech. Inst., 1939-40; research asst. U. Ill., 1940-43; aero. research scientist Langley Labs., NACA, Langley Field, Va., 1943-46; research engr. Standard Oil Co. (Ind.), Chgo., 1946-48; chief structures research Langley Lab. NACA, 1951-56; mgr. aero. mechanics Aeronutronics, Glendale, Cal., 1956-57; prof. structures U. Ill., 1957-59; asst. to chief theoretical mechanics div. Langley Research Center, NASA, Langley AFB, Va., 1959-61, tech. asst. to asso. dir., 1961-64, asst. dir., 1964-68, asso. dir., 1968—; instr. U. Va. Extension, 1944-45; adj. prof. George Washington U.; dir. Joint Inst. Advancement of Flight Scis., 1971. Dir. Newport News Savs. & Loan Assn. Mem. NACA adv. com. on materials, 1950, adv. com. on structures, 1951-55, NASA, 60-63; mem. materials adv. bd. Nat. Acad. Scis., 1950; mem. subcom. profl., sci. and tech. manpower Nat. Manpower Adv. Com., Dept. Labor, 1971; participant Fed. Exec. Inst., Charlottesville, Va., 1971. Trustee Peninsula United Fund, 1963—, campaign chmn., 1965-66; sci. adv. bd. Va. Asso. Research Center; pres. Greater Tidewater Fed. Exec. Assn., 1975-76; bd. dirs. Peninsula Jr. Nature Mus.; mem. Pres.'s Adv. Council Christopher Newport Coll., 1973-75, vice chmn. council, 1976. Fellow AIAA (asso.), N.Y. Acad. Scis., Va. Acad. Scis., AAAS, Va. Soc. Profl. Engrs., Engrs. Club Va. Peninsula (pres. 1955), Sigma Xi, Gamma Alpha, Phi Kappa Phi, Sigma Tau, Tau Beta Pi. Episcopalian (mem. vestry). Rotarian (pres. 1967-68). Club: James River Country. Contbr. numerous articles to profl. jours. Home: 4 Museum Dr Newport News VA 23601 Office: Langley Research Center Hampton VA 23665

DUBI, MICHAEL, cons. mental health and retardation; b. N.Y.C., Oct. 20, 1943; s. Bernard and Belle (Wilsker) D.; B.A., L.I. U., 1967, M.S., 1974; m. Jeanne Thomas, Oct. 23, 1969. Cons., Woodburn Center, Annandale, Va., 1978—; psychologist Letchworth Village Devel. Center, N.Y.C., 1977-78; program coordinator Westchester Devel. Center (N.Y.), 1976-77; mental health retardation cons., N.Y., N.J., Va., 1977—; dir. Commonwealth Affirmative Industries, Inc.; mem. vol. faculty Malcolm King Coll., N.Y.C., 1977-78. Mem. Internat. Soc. Profl. Hypnosis (regional v.p. 1977-78), Am. Personnel and Guidance Assn., Am. Rehab. Counselors Assn. Contbr. articles to profl. jours. Home: 3205 Lothian Rd Fairfax VA 22031

DUBITSKY, KAREN ANN, community relations exec.; b. N.Y.C., Apr. 27, 1947; d. Louis and Helen Rose (Weiss) Hersh; B.A. with honors in Religion and Philosophy, Am. U., 1969; M.A., U. Miami, 1972; student U. Va., 1965-67; m. Ira Lee Dubitsky, June 1, 1972; children—Juli Lynn, Lori Jeann. Instr. religious lit. Miami-Dade Coll., Fla., 1971; lectr. in religion, coordinator residential acad. planning U. Miami (Fla.), 1972-74, acad. adv., 1974; mgr. public and community relations Burger King Corp., Miami, 1976—. Internat. v.p. B'nai B'rith Youth Orgn., 1964-65; mem. Fla. exec. bd. Anti-Defamation League, 1980; del. Worldwide Conv. Internat. Relations, U. Va., 1966; founder Coupons for the Elderly, 1973; youth council dir. Temple Beth Am., 1971-72. Recipient Excellence in Citizenship and Scholarship award B'nai B'rith, 1965; Gov.'s award for Arts, Fla., 1980; NDEA fellow, 1970-72. Mem. Public Relations Soc. Am., Am. Philos. Soc., Fla. Philos. Soc., Am. Acad. Religion. Home: 13800 SW 78 Court Miami FL 33158 Office: 7360 N Kendell Dr Miami FL 33156

DU BOIS, EUGENE ELI, educator; b. Rochester, N.Y., Mar. 2, 1937; s. Eugene E.R. and Ursula R. (Johnson) DuB.; A.B., Hillsdale (Mich.) Coll., 1960; M.S., Boston U., 1962; Ed.D. (Kellogg fellow), Wayne State U., 1966. Asst. to v.p. Jr. Coll. Dist. St. Louis, 1963; adminstrv. asst. to pres. Monroe Community Coll., Rochester, 1963-67; mem. faculty Boston U., 1967-73, asso. prof. edn., 1970-73, coordinator spl. services 1972-73; exec. sec. spl. interest groups Am. Assn. Community and Jr. Colls., Washington, 1973-75; Nat. Edn. prof. Nova U., Ft. Lauderdale, Fla., 1975—, dir. Inst. for Staff Devel., 1977—; cons. in field. Trustee Garland Jr. Coll., Boston, 1971-76; bd. dirs. Montgomery Neighborhood Center, Rochester, 1965-66. Kellogg fellow, 1962-64; recipient Alumni Achievement award Hillsdale Coll., 1973. Mem. Adult Assn. U.S., Am. Assn. Higher Edn., Am. Assn. Community and Jr. Colls., Assn. Profs. Higher Edn., Commn. Profs. Adult Edn., Tau Mu Epsilon, Phi Delta Kappa, Phi Sigma Epsilon. Baptist. Club: Boston U. Contbr. articles to profl. jours. Home: 455 S Pine Island Rd Fort Lauderdale FL 33324

DUBOSE, CARUS KISNER HICKS, microscopist; b. Fairmont, W.Va., May 9, 1929; s. Carus Searight and Laura Louise (Kisner) Hicks; student U. Tenn., 1948-51; m. Mary Estelle Fulmer, Aug. 25, 1957; children—C. Michael, William H., James F. Lab. supr. metall. engring. Oak Ridge Nat. Lab., 1955—; founder, chmn. Internat. Metallographic Exhibit, 1968—. Bd. dirs. Oak Ridge Arts Council, 1964-68; pres. Oak Ridge Arts Festival, 1968-69; asst. scoutmaster Boy Scouts Am., 1971—. Served with USAF, 1951-55. Mem. Internat. Metallog. Soc. (founding bd. mem. 1967-75), Am. Soc. Metals, Electron Microscopy Soc. Am. Mem. United Ch. (dir. ch.). Co-editor of Microstructures Jour., 1970-72; asso. editor of Metallog. Rev. Jour., 1972-74; editor: Internat. Metallographic Exhibit Jour.; contbr. articles profl. jours., photomicrographs to periodicals and encys. Developer specimen preparation techniques for electron and optical microscopy, 1962-72. Home: 101 Pelham Rd Oak Ridge TN 37830 Office: Oak Ridge National Laboratory Oak Ridge TN 37830

DU BOSE, CHARLES WILSON, lawyer; b. Sumter, S.C., Mar. 2, 1949; s. Frank Elsivan and Fannie Louise (Wilson) DuB.; A.B. magna cum laude, Harvard U., 1971; J.D., U. Va., 1974. Admitted to Ga. bar, 1974, U.S. Supreme Ct., 1979; asso. firm Kutak, Rock & Huie, and predecessor firms, Atlanta, 1974-79, partner, 1979—. Bd. deacons Peachtree Presbyterian Ch., Atlanta. Mem. Am. Bar Assn., Am. Judicature Soc., State Bar Ga., Atlanta Bar Assn., Lawyers Club Atlanta. Editorial bd. Va. Law Rev., 1972-74. Home: 1217 Cumberland Rd NE Atlanta GA 30306 Office: 1200 Standard Fed Savings Bldg Atlanta GA 30303

DU BOSE, DOROTHY GAMBLE (MRS. WILLIAM SNELTON DU BOSE), civic worker; b. St. Louis, Dec. 23, 1925; d. Andrew Suter and Dorothy (Gollier) Gamble; student Swarthmore Coll., 1942, 43, Tex. Christian U., 1964, 67; m. William Snelton Du Bose, Jan. 14, 1944; children—Dorothy, Frances, Julie, William Snelton, Suter Gamble. Vice pres. W.S. Du Bose, Inc., Ft. Worth, 1956—. Bd. mem. Family Service Assn. Tarrant County (Tex.), 1964-66; v.p. Fort Worth (Tex.) Art Center Guild, 1963; mem. Charitable Solicitations Commn., Fort Worth, 1965—; asso. mem. Mayor's Com. on Status of Women, 1971; pres. Tex. Council on Crime and Delinquency, 1977—. Bd. dirs. North Tex. chpt. Arthritis Found., Tarrant County YWCA. Mem. Soc. for Study Democratic Instns., Am. Civil Liberties Union (bd. mem. pres. Greater Ft. Worth chpt. 1971), Nat. Orgn. Women (pres. Ft. Worth chpt. 1970-72, legislative coordinator Tex.). Democrat. Episcopalian. Research and publs. on women in prison and their children. Home: 2928 Owenwood St Fort Worth TX 76109 Office: Suite 234 2630 West Freeway Fort Worth TX 76109

DUBOSE, JACK MARK, food co. exec.; b. Gonzales, Tex., Jan. 21, 1930; s. Warren Lee and Merle (Houston) D.; B.A., Baylor U., Waco, Tex., 1951; m. Dyna Lynn Vordenbaum, Oct. 17, 1959; children—Tara, Mark, Sean. Partner, Continental Produce Co., Gonzales, 1954—; owner Jack Dubose Farms; pres. Rainbo Acre Farms, Inc.; pres. Dubose Foods Inc.; mem. Tex. Egg Mktg. Bd., 1958—; vice chmn., dir. Am. Egg Bd. Served to 1st lt. USAF, 9151-53; Korea. Mem. Tex. Egg Council (dir., past pres.), Tex. Poultry Fedn. (past pres.), Nat. Egg Co. (dir., past pres.), Southeastern Poultry and Egg Assn. (dir., pres. 1977). Methodist. Clubs: Rotary (past pres.), Elks (Gonzales). Home: 1503 Gardien St Gonzales TX 78629 Office: Box 16 Gonzales TX 78629

DUBOSE, ROBERT N(EWSOM), clergyman; b. Hartsville, S.C., Sept. 4, 1914; s. John Boyd and Belle (Newsome) DuB.; A.B., Wofford Coll., 1936; B.D., M.Div., Duke, 1942; D.D., Salem Coll., 1946; m. Marie King, Sept. 10, 1937; children—Mary Virginia (Mrs. Jean Derrick), Barbara Anne (Mrs. J.M. Terry). Ordained to ministry Meth. Ch., 1939; pastor, Jamestown, 1937-39, Lake View, 1939-40; asso. pastor Asbury Ch., Durham, N.C., 1940-41; dir. religious activities Duke U., 1945-48; exec. sec. Commn. Christian Higher Edn., Assn. Am. Colls., 1948-51; pastor First Meth. Ch., Whitmire, S.C., 1951-54, Shandon Meth. Ch., Columbia, S.C., 1954-60; dist. supt. Spartanburg Dist., S.C. Conf., 1960-65; pastor Buncombe St. Meth. Ch., Greenville, S.C., 1965-71; pastor 1st United Meth. Ch., Myrtle Beach, S.C., 1971-77, pastor emeritus, 1977—; lectr., writer, 1977—; dir. Grand Strand Parish. Mem. bd. edn. S.C. Conf., Meth. Ch., 1968-72. Pres. Myrtle Beach Camp Ground Ministry Commn. Past pres., dir. Columbia chpt. ARC, S.C. fund chmn., 1963-65; pres. S.C. Crippled Children's Soc.; chmn. Caroling Program, 1969-70; mem. S.C. Tricentennial Com., 1969-70, Mayor's Adv. Com., 1969-70; adv. bd. Mental Health Clinic; dir. Jr. League Speech and Hearing Clinic. Vice chmn. bd. trustees Wofford Coll; chmn. bd. trustees Spartanburg Jr. Coll., 1967-68, exec. com., 1969-72. Vice Chmn. bd. dirs. U.S.C. Wesley Found.; trustee Meth. Home Aging; chmn. S.C. Meth. Credit Union; mem. Pres.'s Selection Com. Columbia Coll., 1977. Served as chaplain AUS, 1943-45; PTO. Recipient Alumni Assn. award Wofford Coll., 1961; citation Myrtle Beach C. of C., 1977. Mem. S.C. Conf. Meth. Ch. (chmn. conf. com. Christian vocation, chmn. credit com., chmn. interboard com. S.C.), Lambda Chi Alpha. Rotarian. Author articles on Christian edn. Editor: College and Church (ofcl. publ. Assn. Am. Colls.), 1948-51. Home: Litchfield Country Club Pawleys Island SC 29585

DU BROFF, RICHARD EDWARD, elec. engr.; b. Chgo., June 14, 1948; s. Warren Cannon and Suzanne (Stern) DuB.; B.S., Rensselaer Poly. Inst., Troy, N.Y., 1970; M.S. (grad. research asst. 1970-76), U. Ill., 1972, Ph.D., 1976; m. Janet Ellen Rice, Sept. 10, 1978. Research asso. U. Ill., 1976-78; elec. engr. research and devel. Phillips Petroleum Co., Bartlesville, Okla., 1978—; cons. hydrologist to city engr. Bartlesville, 1978—. Vol., Vol. Action Center Champaign County (Ill.), 1977. Registered profl. engr., Ill., Okla. Mem. IEEE, Am. Geophys. Union, Sigma Xi, Tau Beta Pi, Eta Kappa Nu, Phi Kappa Phi. Republican. Jewish. Author papers in field. Home: Route 2 Box 142D Bartlesville OK 74003

DUCHESNEAU, DONALD ANTONIO, retailing dairy co. exec.; b. Providence, Apr. 10, 1935; s. Antonio Joseph and Elizabeth Caldwell (Taylor) D.; B.S., Stetson U., 1956; M.B.A., Mich. State U., 1956; m. Dorothy Anne Ferruzzi, Aug. 20, 1955; children—Donald A., Darrell A., Dorothy A. Store mgr. supermarket Winn Dixie Stores Inc., Jacksonville, Fla., 1952-64, grocery buyer and merchandiser, 1961-63; mgr. sales planning Gen. Foods Corp., White Plains, N.Y., 1963-66, regional sales mgr., 1966-68; v.p. sales and ops. Farm Stores Inc., Miami, 1968-73; exec. v.p., dir. 1974-79; exec. v.p. Pacemaster Inc., Miami, also Farm Stores Inc., Miami, 1976-79; v.p. Hill Bros. Credit Union, Miami, 1974—, also dir.; instr. mktg. Youngstown (Ohio) U., 1965-66. Recipient award Nat. Assn. Food Chains, 1956. Mem. Am. Mktg. Assn., Nat. Assn. Convenience Stores. Republican. Roman Catholic. Club: Jockey. Author: An Introduction to Food Chain Mergers, 1956. Home: 7975 SW 69th Terr Miami FL 33143 Office: Farm Stores Inc 5800 NW 74th Ave Miami FL 33166

DUCK, JOHN ROBERT, JR., nuclear ins. cons.; b. Yeadon, Pa., Mar. 10, 1943; s. John Robert Duck and Blanche Gertrude (Himmelsbach) Nail; B.S., U.S. Naval Acad., 1965; M.B.A., Harvard U., 1973; m. Mary Clare Peebles, Oct. 8, 1977. Real estate investment analyst State Mut. Life Assurance Co., Worcester, Mass., 1973-74; nuclear cons. Marsh & McLennan, Inc., N.Y.C., 1974-77, asst. v.p., mgr. Marsh & McLennan Nuclear Cons., So. Region, nuclear cons., Dallas, 1977—. Served with USN, 1965-71; to lt. comdr., USNR. Mem. ASME, Am. Nuclear Soc., Naval Reserve Assn., U.S. Naval Acad. Alumni Assn., U.S. Naval Inst., Assn. of MBA Execs., Am. Mgmt. Assn., Atomic Indsl. Forum, Harvard U. Alumni Assn. Club: Strategy and Tactics. Office: 400 N Akard St Dallas TX 75201

DUCKETT, ROSS, state legislator Okla.; b. Stuttgart, Ark., Oct. 23, 1924; s. Thomas Ross and Mabel Ann (Henderson) D.; B.S., Okla. State U., 1947, M.S., 1951; LL.D., Oklahoma City Southwestern Coll., 1976; m. Charline Miller, May 25, 1946; children—Charlotte Ann, Thomas Ross, III. Tchr., prin., supt. pub. schs., Okla., 1947-63; pres. Gt. Plains Life Ins. Co., 1964—; interim pres. Oklahoma City Southwestern Coll., 1975; mayor City of Mustang, 1965-69; mem. Okla. Ho. of Reps. from 98th Dist., 1973—; sec.-treas. Assn. Central Okla. Govts Named Outstanding Christian Legislator, Okla. Assn. Christian Schs., 1978, 80. Mem. Nat. Assn. Legislators, Oklahoma City, Mustang, S. Oklahoma City chambers commerce. Democrat. Baptist. Author articles. Address: 1886 W Lake Park Dr Mustang OK 73064

DUDIK, ROLLIE M., hosp. adminstr.; b. Hartford, Conn., Sept. 29, 1935; s. Martin and Iola Maxine (Hamilton) D.; M.B.A., U. Calif., Santa Ana, 1977. Gen. mgr. Freedman Artcraft Engring., Charlevoix, Mich., 1970-73; exec. v.p. Harrison Community Hosp., Cadiz, Ohio, 1973-77; dir. institutional rev. Dade Monroe PSRO, Miami, Fla., 1977-78; exec. dir. Fla. Keys Meml. Hosp., Key West, 1978—. Served with U.S. Army, 1956-62. Mem. Am. Inst. Indsl. Engrs., Am. Acad. Med. Adminstrs., Hosp. Fin. Mgmt. Assn., Hosp. Mgmt. Systems Soc., Am. Soc. Law and Medicine, Nat. Assn. Flight Instrs., Nat. Assn. Accts., Nat. Counterintelligence Corps Assn. Clubs: Rotary, Kiwanis. Home: 207 SC Key West by the Sea S Roosevelt Blvd Key West FL 33040 Office: 600 Junior Coll Rd Key West FL 33040

DUDLEY, BROOKE FITZHUGH, found. exec.; b. East Orange, N.J., Oct. 22, 1942; s. Benjamin William and Jean (Peeples) D.; A.B. in Econs., Colgate U., 1966; m. Susan Sanford, Sept. 20, 1969; 1 dau., Catherine Sanford. Sales mgr. De La Rue Instruments, Phila., 1968-71; comml. banker Bankers Trust Co., N.Y.C., 1966-68, Provident Nat. Bank, Phila., 1972-74; dir. admissions/financial aid St. Stephen's Episcopal Sch., Austin, Tex., 1974-78; exec. dir. U. Tex. Law Sch. Found., Austin, 1978—; mem. com. U. Tex. Devel. Bd., 1978—. Trustee, chmn. devel. com. Austin Evaluation Center; trustee Austin Repertory Theater; founding mem. bd. Day Sch., Austin; mem. Symphony Square Com.; usher St. David's Episcopal Ch.; Republican campaign mgr., N.Y.C., 1966-68. Served with U.S. Army, 1962-64. Mem. Council Advancement and Support Edn., Tex. Soc. Assn. Execs., Austin Non-Profit Execs. Assn. Episcopalian. Office: U Tex Law Sch Found 2500 Red River Rd Austin TX 78705

DUDLEY, CLARENCE RAYMOND, JR., lawyer, C.P.A.; b. Birmingham, Ala., May 13, 1921; s. Clarence Raymond and Mayme Agnes (Rencher) D.; B.S., Birmingham So. Coll., 1949; LL.B., Jones Law Sch., 1956; m. Sarah Frances Stewart, Mar. 23, 1946; children—Stewart Ray, Richard Ernest. Admitted to Ala. bar, 1957; staff U.S. Treasury Dept., Birmingham, 1949-52; partner F.W. Nichols & Co., Birmingham, 1952-55; sr. partner Dudley, Hopton-Jones, Sims & Freeman, Birmingham, 1955—; chmn. bd. Pollution Control-Walther Inc., Birmingham, 1972—; pres. N. Ala. Industries, Birmingham, 1976—; developer Jackson Mall-Holiday Inns, St. Petersburg, Clearwater and Clearwater Beach, Fla., 1962—, Slidell, La., 1967—; dir., organizer City Nat. Bank Birmingham, 1967—; dir. Southland Bancorp, C.E. Walther Inc., Affiliated Accounting Firms Internat. Served with inf., U.S. Army, 1943-46. Mem. Ala. Bar Assn., Ala. Soc. C.P.A.'s, Am. Inst. C.P.A.'s, Newcomen Soc. Am. Methodist. Clubs: Vestavia Country, Relay House, Athelstan, Masons, Shriners. Home: 2848 Vestavia Forest Dr Birmingham AL 35216 Office: 2101 Magnolia Ave S Birmingham AL 35205

DUDLEY, JOHN RICHARD, architect; b. Ft. Smith, Ark., Sept. 8, 1931; s. John Gant and Melba (Bibb) D.; B.Arch., Tex. A&M U., 1954; m. Elizabeth Ann Brown, Sept. 11, 1953; children—Mary Lou, John Grant. Architect, Wirtz, Calhoun, Tungate & Jackson, Houston, 1954-60; architect Bush & Dudley, Waco, 1960-76; pres. Dudley & Assos., Inc., Architects, Waco, 1976—; mem. McLennan County Hist. Survey Com. Bd. dirs. Hist. Waco Found., 1973—, pres., 1977-78; bd. dirs. Art Center, 1975-78, Better Bus. Bur., 1975-78. Served to 1st lt. arty., AUS, 1956-57. Mem. Tex. Soc. Architects (past dir.), AIA, Soc. Archtl. Historians. Baptist. Home: 2612 Woodmont Circle Waco TX 76710 Office: 406 Citizens Tower Waco TX 76703

DUDRICK, STANLEY JOHN, surgeon, educator; b. Nanticoke, Pa., Apr. 9, 1935; s. Stanley Francis and Stephania Mary (Jachimczak) D.; B.S., Franklin and Marshall Coll., 1957; M.D., U. Pa., 1961; m. Theresa M. Keen, June 14, 1958; children—Susan Marie, Paul Stanley, Carolyn Mary, Stanley Jonathan, Holly Anne, Anne Theresa. Intern, Hosp. of U. Pa., Phila., 1961-62, resident, fellow Harrison dept. surg. research, 1962-67, mem. sci. staff, Harrison dept. surg. research, 1967-72, asso. surgeon, 1967-72; practice medicine, specializing in surgery, Phila., 1967-72, Houston, 1972—; chief surgery Phila. VA Hosp., 1967-72; asst. physician Phila. Gen. Hosp., 1967-72; instr. surgery U. Pa. Sch. Medicine, 1966-67, asso. in surgery, 1967-68, asst. prof., 1968-69, asso. prof., 1969-72, prof., 1972; chief surg. services Hermann Hosp., 1972—; prof., chmn. dept. surgery U. Tex. Med. Sch. at Houston, 1972—; cons. in surgery M.D. Anderson Hosp. and Tumor Inst., 1973—; sr. cons. in surgery and medicine Tex. Inst. for Rehab. and Research, 1974—. Mem. Anatomical Bd. State of Tex., 1973—; Am. Bd. Surgery examiner, 1974-78, dir., 1978—; Chmn. sci. adv. com. Tex. Med. Center Library, 1974; mem. food and nutrition bd. NRC-Nat. Acad. Scis., 1973—; mem. sci. adv. com. Nat. Found. for Ileitis and Colitis; DaCosta orator Philadelphia County Med. Soc.; mem. merit rev. bd. on nutrition VA. Bd. dirs. Found. for Children, Houston, Harris County unit Am. Cancer Soc. Decorated knight Order St. John of Jerusalem Knights Hopitaller; recipient VA citation for significant contbn. to med. care, 1970; Mead Johnson award for research in hosp. pharmacy, 1972; Seale Harris medal So. Med. Assn., 1973; AMA-Brookdale award in medicine, 1975, Great Texan award Nat. Found. Ileitis and Colitis, 1975, Modern Medicine award, 1977; Schaufus Tech. Achievement award Parenteral Drug Assn., 1978, also others. Fellow A.C.S. (vice chmn. pre and post-operative com. 1975 dir. South Tex. chpt. 1977—), Philippine Coll. Surgeons (hon.); mem. AMA (Goldberger award in clin. nutrition 1970), Am. Surg. Assn., Soc. Univ. Surgeons (exec. council 1974-78), Assn. for Acad. Surgery (founders group), Internat. Soc. for Parenteral Nutrition (pres. 1978), Houston Gastroent. Soc., Tex. Surg. Soc., Tex. Med. Assn. (com. nutrition and food resources), Harris County med. Soc., Am. Radium Soc., Am. Soc. Parenteral and Enteral Nutrition (pres. 1977), Am. Gastroenterol. Assn., James Ewing Soc., Ravdin-Rhoads Surg. Assn., Soc. Surg. Chmn., So. Surg. Assn., Southwestern Surg. Congress, Surg. Biology Club II, Western Surg. Soc., Halsted Soc., Allen O. Whipple Surg. Soc. Am. Inst. Nutrition, Soc. Clin. Surgery, Soc. for Surgery of Alimentary Tract, Am. Assn. for Surgery of Trauma, Am. Soc. Clin. Nutrition, Alaska Med. Assn., AAAS, Am. Assn. for Lab. Animal Sci., AAUP, Am. Burn Assn., Am. Coll. Emergency Physicians, Am. Coll. Nutrition, Am. Fedn. for Clin. Research, Am. Soc. Clin. Investigation, Assn. Am. Med. Colls., Collegium Internationale Chirurgiae Digestivae, Fedn. Am. Socs. for Exptl. Biology, Houston Acad. Medicine, Houston Ostomy Assn., Houston Surg. Soc., John Morgan Soc., Minn. Surg. Soc. Nutrition Today Soc., Pan Am. Med. Assn., Pan-Pacific Surg. Assn., Societe Internationale de Chirurgie, S.E. Surg. Congress, So. Gut Club, So. Med. Assn., So. Soc. Clin. Surgery, Tex. Med. Found., Univ. Assn. for Emergency Med. Services, Phi Beta Kappa, Sigma Xi, Alpha Omega Alpha. Editor: Manual of Surgical Nutrition, 1975, Manual of Preoperative and Postoperative Care, 1979; asso. editor Nutrition in Medicine, 1975—; editorial cons. Jour. of Trauma, 1972—; editorial bd. Annals of Surgery, 1975—, Infusionstherapie und Klinische Ernahrung, 1974—, Nutrition and Cancer, 1977—, Practical Gastroenterology, 1977—, Corr. Soc. Surgeons, 1978—, Infusion, 1978—, Jour. Parenteral and Enteral Nutrition, 1977—; contbr. chpts. to books, articles to profl. jours.; inventor new technique of intravenous feeding (intravenous hyperalimentation). Home: 527 Saddlewood St Houston TX 77024 Office: U Tex Med Sch 6431 Fannin Houston TX 77030

DUFAU, CLEMENT JOHN, real estate broker; b. New Orleans, June 27, 1911; s. John T. and Louise (Sarradet) D.; student Holy Cross Coll., 1928, Tulane U., 1929-31; m. Hazel O. Pierre, Oct. 6, 1936; 1 dau., Jean Ann. Pres., prin. owner Dufau Petroleum Co., 1955-63; oil jobber New Orleans area, Phillips 66; owner, mgr. Clem Dufau, Realtor, New Orleans, 1963—; dir. Nat. Bank of Commerce, Jefferson Parish; dir. Am. Savs. & Loan Assn. Mem. finance com. Fitzmorris for Gov. Campaign, 1979. Served with AUS, 1942-43. Named Man of Year, Holy Cross Coll., 1977. Mem. East Bank C. of C. (past chmn. 1955-59, past dir.), Nat. Assn. Realtors, Nat. Mktg. Inst., Real Estate Bd. New Orleans, Real Estate Bd. La., K.C. Democrat. Roman Catholic. Home: 771 Robert E Lee Blvd New Orleans LA 70124 Office: 806 Perdido St New Orleans LA 70112

DUFF, SYLVIA LINDAUER, tobacco co. ofcl.; b. Louisville, Oct. 1, 1950; d. Sylvester John and Clara Marie (Gruber) Lindauer; grad. Sullivan Bus. Coll., 1969; student U. Louisville, 1975-77; m. Thomas Martin Duff, Mar. 20, 1970; children—Lisa Renee, Stephanie Lynn. Stenographer, Brown & Williamson Tobacco Co., Louisville, 1969, sec., 1969-70, sr. sec., 1970-72, exec. sec., 1972-76, salary analyst, 1976-78, compensation adminstr., 1978—. Mem. Am. Compensation Assn., Louisville Personnel Assn. (membership com.). Democrat. Roman Catholic. Home: 2308 Youngland Ave Louisville KY 40216 Office: 1600 W Hill St Louisville KY 40232

DUFF, WILLIAM GRIERSON, elec. engr.; b. Alexandria, Va., Dec. 16, 1936; s. Johnnie Douglas and Annetta Osceola (Rind) D.; B.E.E., George Washington U., 1959, postgrad., 1959-72; M.S., Syracuse U., 1969; D.Sc. in Elec. Engring., Clayton U., 1977; m. Joan Lilla King, June 27, 1964; children—Warren David, Valerie Lynn, Dawn Elizabeth. Mgr. advanced systems tech. dept. Atlantic Research Corp., Alexandria, 1959—; asst. prof. Capitol Inst. Tech., Kensington, Md., 1972—; instr. Inst. for Electromagnetic Compatibility, Don White Cons., Inc., Germantown, Md. Counselor, Meth. Sr. High Youth Group, 1965-73. Recipient D.A.R. Good Citizenship award, 1955; Math. award George Washington High Sch., Alexandria, 1955. Mem. IEEE (chmn. Washington chpt. EMC Group, asso. editor EMC Group Newsletter 1970—), Am. Inst. E.E. (Best Paper award 1961), George Washington U. Engring. Alumni Assn. (pres. 1963-64), Sigma Tau, Theta Tau. Clubs: Springfield Golf and Country; Occoquan (Va.) Water Ski (pres. 1976). Author: EMI Handbook, vol. 5, EMI Prediction and Analysis Techniques, 1972; Mobile Communications, 1976. Contbr. articles to profl. jours. Home: 10507 Clipper Dr Fairfax Station VA 22039 Office: 5390 Cherokee Ave Alexandria VA 22314

DUFFELL, GORDON MICHAEL, physician; b. Macon, Ga., Nov. 23, 1935; s. Gordon L. and Helen (Clark) D.; B.A., Emory U., 1957, M.D., 1961; m. Carol Jackson, Dec. 28, 1958; children—Lisa, Carol Anne, Michael, Susan, Sarah. Intern, Emory U. Affiliated Hosps., Atlanta, 1961-62, resident, 1962-63, 65-69; asst. prof. medicine, specializing in pulmonary diseases, Emory U., 1969-74, asso. prof., 1974—, dir. div. pulmonary diseases, 1976—. Served to capt. USAF, 1963-65. Diplomate Am. Bd. Internal Medicine, Am. Bd. Pulmonary Diseases. Fellow A.C.P., Am. Coll. Chest Physicians; mem. AMA, Ga., med. assns., Am. Fedn. Clin. Research, Am., Ga. (pres. 1975-77) thoracic socs. Methodist. Home: 2751 Breckenridge Ct Atlanta GA 30345 Office: 1365 Clifton Rd NE Atlanta GA 30322

DUFFEY, DONALD CREAGH, educator; b. Winchester, Va., Feb. 9, 1931; s. Hugh Sisson and Vera (Lynch) D.; B.S., Va. Poly. Inst., 1953; M.A., Rice U., 1955; Ph.D., Ga. Inst. Tech., 1959; m. Elizabeth Mallard, Aug. 25, 1965. Asst. prof. dept. chemistry Miss. State U., State College, 1960-62, asso. prof., 1962-67, prof., 1967—; fellow Pa. State U., 1959-60, U. Pa., 1964-65; vis. prof. U. Cin., 1967-68, Max-Planck-Institut, Gottingen, 1968, U. Utah, 1979, U. Va., 1980. Fellow Am. Inst. Chemists; mem. Am. Chem. Soc., Sigma Xi, Phi Kappa Phi. Contbr. articles to profl. jours. Home: PO Box 35 State College MS 39762

DUFFIELD, CHARLES ALLEN, printing co. exec.; b. Kingsport, Tenn., Aug. 10, 1942; s. James Clyde and Nita B. (Norris) D.; B.S., E. Tenn. State U., 1972; m. Sallie Louise Gillenwater, Aug. 24, 1963; children—Sherry, Vicki, Robin. Owner electronic repair center, 1959-64; technician Kingsport Broadcasting Co., 1959-64; with Kingsport Press, 1964—, sales project specialist, 1976-77, div. supt., 1977—. Pres., Colonial Heights Service Club, Kingsport, 1976; Jr. Achievement counselor, 1973, 74; treas. Colonial Heights Girls Athletic Commn., 1979-80; chmn. Miller Perry Sch. PTA Booster Club, 1978, 79; coach Colonial Heights Girls Volleyball Team, 1979. Recipient Pres.s award Colonial Heights Service Club, 1976. Republican. Baptist. Club: Eagles. Address: 811 Sir Echo Dr Kingsport TN 37662

DUGAN, KENNETH LAVOYD, athletic dir.; b. Huntsville, Ala., Apr. 14, 1935; s. W.F. and Dolly T. Dugan; B.S., David Lipscomb Coll., Nashville, 1957; M.A., Middle Tenn. State U., 1961; postgrad. Peabody Coll., 1964-65; m. Diane Frazier; children—Christi, Mike, Kurt. Baseball coach, asso. prof. phys. edn. David Lipscomb Coll., 1960—, athletic dir., 1968—; baseball coach World Games, St. Petersburg, Fla., 1974, Pan-Am. Games, Mexico City, 1975, Belgium Baseball Fedn., Antwerp, 1975, 79. Served with AUS, 1957-59. Named Dist. 24 Coach of Year, Area 5 Coach of Year, Nashville Banner Man of Year. Mem. Nat. Intercollegiate Athletic Dirs. Assn., Am. Assn. Coll. Baseball Coaches. Mem. Ch. of Christ. Author: How to Organize and Coach Winning Baseball, 1971, (revision) Teaching Individual and Team Sports, 1972; also articles. Office: David Lipscomb Coll Nashville TN 37203

DUGAN, MILDRED CLAIRE, pediatrician; b. Ft. Worth, Sept. 21, 1929; d. Hugh and Lena Florine (Schneider) Dugan; B.A., Tex. Christian U., 1951; M.D., Southwestern Med. Sch., 1955. Intern Harris Hosp., Ft. Worth, 1955-56; mem. staff Carswell Air Force Hosp., 1956-59, 62-73; resident in pediatrics Washington U. Med. Sch., St. Louis, and St. Louis Children's Hosp., 1959-61; fellow in adolescent medicine Harvard Med. Sch., Boston, 1961-62; practice medicine specializing in pediatrics, Ft. Worth, 1962-73; instr. in pediatrics Washington U. Sch. of Medicine, St. Louis, 1959-61; cons. to Spl. Edn. Bd. of Ft. Worth pub. schs., 1968-70; med. adviser Cystic Fibrosis N. Regional Dist., 1971-75; pediatric cons. to City Pub. Health and County Pub. Well Baby Clinics for State of Tex., 1970-74. Bd. dirs. N. Tex. chpt. Nat. Cystic Fibrosis Research Found., 1973-75. Diplomate Am. Bd. Pediatrics. Fellow Royal Soc. Health (Eng.), Am. Acad. Pediatrics, Pan-Am. Med. Assn.; mem. Am., Tex. pub. health assns., Tex. Med. Found., Cystic Fibrosis Found., Dallas So. Clin. Soc. (asso.), AMA, So., Tex. med. assns., Am., Internat. women's med. assns., Tex. Assn. Children Learning Disability, Am. Assn. Physician-Surgeons, Nat. Audubon Soc., Tex. Christian U. Women's Alumni Assn., Internat. Platform Assn., Alpha Chi, Alpha Epsilon Iota. Baptist. Contbr. articles to med. jours. Home: 7158 Tamarack Rd Fort Worth TX 76116

DUGAN, RICHARD FRANKLIN, fish and wildlife biologist; b. Sugar Grove, Ill., July 27, 1916; s. Ralph Emory and Nettie Frances (Bunnel) D.; student Aurora (Ill.) Coll., 1934-35; B.S. in Agr., U. Ill., 1938; B.S. in Forestry/M.F. in Wildlife Mgmt., U. Mich., 1941; postgrad. in outdoor recreation Tex. A and M U., 1967-68; m. Lucile Helen Shoger, June 19, 1941; children—Richard, Mary, Phyllis, Carol. Timber surveyor U.S. Forest Service, Ore., 1940; agrl. aide Soil Conservation Service, U.S. Dept. Agr., Mich., 1941, biologist/woodland conservationist, N.J., 1958-59, biologist/recreation specialist, Va., 1960-77; asst. prof. forestry and wildlife mgmt. W.Va. U., 1942-57. Mem. Wildlife Soc., Soil Conservation Soc. Am. (life), Am. Fisheries Soc., Nat. Recreation and Parks Assn., Am. Forestry Assn., Nat. Audubon Soc., Smithsonian Instn., Nat. Assn. Conservation Dists., Izaak Walton League (life), Nat. Wildlife Fedn. (life), Nat. Rifle Assn. (life), Alpha Zeta, Xi Sigma Pi. Baptist (past deacon). Lion. Contbr. articles profl. jours. Home: 4306 Chickahominy Ave Richmond VA 23222

DUGGAN, ARTHUR ALEXANDER, farm coop. exec.; b. Austin, Tex., June 6, 1941; s. Arthur Pope and Mary Josephine (Turner) D.; B.B.A., U. Tex., Austin, 1963, M.B.A., 1965; m. Regina Margaret Rausch, May 19, 1973; children—Brian Keith, Darla Lynn, Cynthia Dawn. Sales trainee Lincoln-Mercury div. Ford Motor Co., St. Louis, 1965-66; acct. exec. Eastman Dillon Union Securities, Dallas, 1966-71; sales rep. Premier Indsl., Inc., Amarillo, Tex., 1971-73; office mgr. Panhandle Ins. Agy., Amarillo, 1973-74; asst. gen. mgr. Perryton Equity Exchange (Tex.), 1974-79; gen. mgr. Sooner Coop., Inc., Okeene, Okla., 1979—. Mem. Nat. Soc. Accts. for Coops., Am. Contract Bridge League (life master), Delta Sigma Pi, Sigma Iota Epsilon, Alpha Tau Omega. Republican. Methodist. Home: 502 N 2d St Okeene OK 73763 Office: 301 E Oklahoma St Okeene OK 73763

DUGGAN, MINOR, physician, editor; b. Cork, Ireland, Apr. 9, 1924; s. Cornelius and Eugenia (Sposchum) D.; M.B., B.Ch., B.A.O., Univ. Coll., Cork, Nat. U. Ireland 1952; m. Doloria Arlene Zelasko, July 10, 1959. Came to U.S., 1958, naturalized, 1963. Asst. editor Merck Manual, Merck Sharp and Dohme, 1961-64; dir. med. services White Labs., Inc., div. Schering Corp., Kenilworth, N.J., 1967-70; dir. med. illustration and publs. dept. Miami (Fla.) Heart Inst., 1970—. Mem. Assn. Med. Dirs., Am. Med. Writers Assn., Am. Assn. for History Medicine, Drug Information Assn., Brit. Med. Assn., A.M.A. Home: 251 Winston Blvd Apt 1820 Miami Beach FL 33160 Office: Miami Heart Inst 4701 N Meridian Ave Miami Beach FL 33140

DUKE, BUFORD WOODROW, JR., architect; b. Dallas, June 17, 1938; s. Buford W. and Mildred (Becker) D.; Asso. in Architecture, Arlington State Coll. (Tex.), 1958; student Inst. Technilogico De Monterrey, Mexico, 1960; B.Arch., U. Tex., 1962; m. Ruth Adele Stout, Aug. 24, 1958; children—Belinda Gayle, Tanya Adele. Architect-in-tng. with C. Marley Green, Houston, 1962-64; project designer The Perkins & Will Partnership, Washington, 1964-68; sr. corp. v.p. and prin. for design Benham-Blair & Affiliates, Inc., Oklahoma City, 1977—; pres. Gwathmey-Duke, Inc., Falls Church, Va., 1968-74; pres., dir. Benham-Blair-Winesett-Duke, Inc., 1974-77; mem. adv. bd. Family Savs. & Loan Corp. Va., 1974-77. Major archtl. works include: U. Md. Modular Housing, 1972; Distributive Edn. Clubs of Am. Hdqrs. Facilities, Reston, Va., 1974; Energy Efficient Office Bldg., Sacramento (Calif. State Competition winner; Owens Corning Energy award), 1978; Conoco Research Labs., Ponca City, Okla., 1977; Halliburton Research Labs., Duncan, Okla., 1978; Los Alamos Lab. Support Complex, 1979; Energy Scis. Research Labs., Oak Ridge, 1980. Recipient Am. Wood Council Design for Better Living award, 1974. Mem. AIA, Guild Religious Architecture, Am. Underground Space Assn., Soc. Am. Mil. Engrs. Democrat. Methodist. Club: Greens Golf and Country. Office: 1200 Northwest 63rd St Oklahoma City OK 73156

DUKE, CHARLES RICHARD, educator; b. W. Stewartstown, N.H., July 6, 1940; s. George T. and Evelyn M. (Murray) D.; B.E., Plymouth (N.H.) State Coll., 1962; M.A., Middlebury (Vt.) Coll., 1968; Ph.D., Duke U., 1973; m. Jonquelyn Simpson, May 20, 1973. Chmn. English dept. Sunapee (N.H.) High Sch., 1962-68; mem. faculty Plymouth State Coll., 1968-78; prof. English Murray (Ky.) State U., 1978—; dir. Western Ky. Writing Project; cons. sch. systems, dir. Project Write. Mem. Nat. Council Tchrs. English, New Eng., N.H. assns. tchrs. English, AAUP, Popular Culture Assn., Am. Film Inst., Ky. Council Tchrs. English. Author: Creative Dramatics and English Teaching, 1973; Teaching Fundamental English Today, 1976; Teaching Literature Today, 1979; also articles. Office: English Dept Murray State U Murray KY 42071

DUKE, DANIEL GIST, ophthalmologist; b. Shreveport, La., Jan. 21, 1947; s. Chalmers Bledsoe and Mozelle (Gist) D.; B.A., U. Tex., Austin, 1969, M.D., San Antonio, 1973; m. May 30, 1969; children—Lisa, Daniel. Intern, Bexar County Hosp., San Antonio, 1973-74; resident Mayo Clinic, Rochester, Minn., 1977; practice medicine specializing in ophthalmology, San Antonio, 1977—; clin. instr. dept. surgery U. Tex., 1977—. Tex. Legis. Merit scholar, 1971-72. Diplomate Am. Bd. Ophthalmology. Mem. Am. Acad. Ophthalmology, Bexar County Med. Soc., Tex. Med. Assn. Democrat. Office: 8601 Village Dr #212 San Antonio TX 78217

DUKE, DONALD EDWARD, acct.; b. Manchester, Tenn., May 5, 1930; s. John W. and Leona Deshon (Dodd) D.; B.S., U. Tenn., 1955; M.S., Columbia U., N.Y.C., 1958; Ph.D., U. Ga., 1974; m. Katherine Billingsley, Aug. 10, 1958; 1 son, Donald Edward. With Arthur Andersen & Co., N.Y.C., 1955-58, Peat, Marwick Mitchell & Co., C.P.A., Dallas, 1958-62; controller Indsl. Life Ins. Co., Dallas, 1962-65; controller Boise Cascade Internat. Inc., Boise, 1965-68; asst. prof. Tenn. Tech. U., Cookeville, 1969-71; asst. prof. U. Ga., Athens, 1971-72; prof. U. Tenn., Nashville, 1972-79; prof. acctg. Tenn. State U., Nashville, 1979—; pres., dir. Don Duke Investments, Inc., 1973—. Served with AUS, 1951-53. C.P.A., Tenn., Tex. Mem. Am. Acctg. Assn., Tenn. Soc. C.P.A.'s, Am. Inst. C.P.A.'s, Republican. Baptist. Home: 269 Forest Lawn Dr Brentwood TN 37027 Office: Dept Acctg Tenn State U Nashville TN 37203

DUKE, ELEANOR LYON, microbiologist; b. Marfa, Tex., Apr. 12, 1918; d. William Luther and Eleanor Ida (McCamant) Lyon; B.A., Tex. Coll. Mines and Metallurgy, 1939; M.A., U. Tex., Austin, Tex., 1945, Ph.D., 1967; m. Jack Newton Duke, Dec. 2, 1939. Instr. to prof. dept. biol. scis. Tex. Western Coll., 1940-53; asst. prof. dept. biol. scis. U. Tex., El Paso, 1953-60, asso. prof., 1960-76, prof., 1976—; research vol. William Beaumont Army Med. Center. Named Outstanding Ex, Alumni Soc. U. Tex. at El Paso, 1974. Mem. Am. Micros. Soc. (exec. com. 1976-79), Tex. Assn. Coll. Tchrs. (state pres. 1970), AAAS, Soc. Protozoologists, Electron Micros. Soc. Am., Ecol. Soc. Am., N.Y. Acad. Scis., Tex. Acad. Sci., Biol. Photog. Soc., AAUP, Am. Phycol. Soc., Am. Soc. Limnology and Oceanography, DAR. Clubs: Eastern Star, Daughters of Nile. Contbr. to Biology of Diatoms, 1977. Research on diatoms and cannabis. Home: 2819 Aurora St El Paso TX 79930 Office: Dept Biol Scis Univ Tex El Paso TX 79968

DUKE, JAMES HENRY, JR., water resources engr.; b. San Antonio, Aug. 18, 1942; s. James Henry and Evelyn Augusta (McLennan) D.; B.S. civil engring., U. Tex., 1966, M.S. civil engring., 1967; Ph.D., Colo. State U., 1971; m. Virginia Earl Carter, Aug. 27, 1966; children—James Henry III, John Earl. Vis. asst. prof. civil engring. U. Tex., Austin, 1971-72; asso., sr., prin. engr. Water Resource Engrs., Inc., Austin, 1972-76; prin. cons. engr. James H. Duke, Jr., Austin, 1976—. Treas., Summitt Sch. P.T.A., Austin, 1979-80. Registered profl. engr., Tex. Mem. ASCE, Am. Water Resources Assn., Am. Geophys. Union, Chi Epsilon. Contbr. articles in field to profl. jours. Home: 5303 Pony Chase Austin TX 78759

DUKE, RUSSELL WARREN, chemist; b. Dallas, Mar. 14, 1946; s. Henry Greene and Margaret May (Boatner) D.; Ph.D. in Biophys. Chemistry, U. Louisville, 1974; m. Pamela Fern Moses, Aug. 19, 1966; children—Geoffrey Russell, Gregory Michael. Trainee, NSF, 1969-73; instr. chemistry Jefferson Community Coll., Louisville, 1972-74; postdoctoral fellow Universite Paris-Sud, Laboratoire de Physique des Solides, Orsay, France, 1974-75, Instituttet for Kemiindustri, Danmarks Tekniske Hojskole, Lyngby, Denmark, 1975-76, Inst. Materials Sci., U. Conn., Storrs, 1976; dir. clin. lab. Doctors Health Facilities, Dallas, 1976—. Recipient Statens Teknisk Videnskabelige Forskningsrad (Denmark), 1975; George C. Marshall fellow, 1974-75. Mem. Am. Chem. Soc., Am. Phys. Soc., Biophys. Soc., Am. Soc. Clin. Pathologists, Am. Assn. Clin. Chemists, Sigma Xi, Kappa Alpha Order, Phi Lambda Upsilon. Office: Clin Lab Doctors Hosp 9440 Poppy Dr Dallas TX 75218

DUKESHIRE, CLARENCE CORTLAND, textile mfg. co. exec.; b. Cambridge, Mass., May 11, 1928; s. Clarence Cortland and Ella Phoebe D.; B.A., Bentley Coll., Waltham, Mass.; m. Dolores Vedovelli, Nov. 4, 1950; children—Sharon, Carolyn, Kathleen. Salesman, United Elastic Corp. div. J.P. Stevens, Greensboro, N.C., 1950-68; pres. Piedmont Braid Co., Burlington, N.C., 1968-73; exec. v.p. Olympic Narrow Fabrics, Inc., Graham, N.C., 1973—. Served with 82nd Airborne, 1946-48. Republican. Roman Catholic. Club: Greensboro Country. Home: 5003 Laurinda Dr Greensboro NC 27410 Office: 501 Maple St Ext Graham NC 27253

DUKLER, ABRAHAM EMANUEL, chem. engr., univ. ofcl.; b. Newark, Jan. 5, 1925; s. Louis and Netty (Charles) D.; B.S., Yale U., 1945; M.S., U. Del., 1950, Ph.D., 1951; m. Nancy Brace, Aug. 15, 1975; children—Martin Alan, Ellen Leah, Malcolm Stephen. Process engr. Rohm & Haas Co., Phila., 1945-48; research engr. Shell Oil Co., Houston, 1950-52; asst. prof. dept. chem. engring. U. Houston, 1952-56, asso. prof., 1956-61, prof., 1961—, dean engring., 1976—; exec. dir. State of Tex. Energy Council, 1973-75; cons. to Shell Devel. Co., 1971, U.S. Nuclear Regulatory Commn., 1976—, Brookhaven Nat. Lab., 1977. NSF fellow, 1967. Fellow Am. Inst. Chem. Engrs. (Research award 1970); mem. Am. Chem. Soc., ASME, AAAS, Nat. Acad. Engring., Am. Soc. Engring Edn. (Edn. Research lectureship award 1976), AAUP, Sigma Xi, Tau Beta Pi. Contbr. numerous articles on chem. engring. to profl. jours.

DULL, CARL AREY, JR., ins. co. exec.; b. Winston-Salem, N.C., Jan. 5, 1918; s. Carl Arey and Nora Mae (Alspaugh) D.; B.S. cum laude in Bus. Adminstrn., Wake Forest U., 1939; m. Mary Chitwood Cooper, June 15, 1946; children—Sybil Jane Dull Edwards, Keith R.; 1 dau. by previous marriage, Donna Dull Hurt. Realtor, ins. agt., Winston-Salem, 1939-41; with Integon Corp., Winston-Salem, 1946—, sec., v.p., asst. treas., 1960-79, v.p., asst. treas., 1979, pres., chief exec. officer, 1979—, chmn. subs. Commr., Winston-Salem Housing Authority; trustee Salem Acad. and Coll., 1969-77; trustee Denmark Loan Fund, Wake Forest U., 1965—. Served to lt. comdr. USNR, 1941-46. Mem. N.C. Fin. Analyst Soc., N.C. Council on Econ. Edn. (trustee 1976—), Winston-Salem C. of C. (dir. 1976-78). Conservative Democrat. Mem. Moravian Ch. Clubs: Forsyth Country, Rotary. Office: Integon Corp 420 N Spruce St Winston-Salem NC 27102

DULL, JULIA HILTON, mfg. co. ofcl.; b. Monroe, N.C., Mar. 6, 1950; d. Willie Wriston and Ruth Lorraine (Walters) Hilton; B.A., U. N.C., 1973, M.Ed., 1976; m. Calvin Ray Dull, Oct. 1, 1977; 1 dau. by previous marriage, Rebecca Lynn Dayvault; 1 son, Jeremy Calvin. Tng. asst. Belk Stores Services, Inc., Charlotte, N.C., 1969-71; tchr. Cabarrus County Schs., Concord, N.C., 1973-75; mgr. mgmt. devel. PCA Internat., Inc., Matthews, N.C., 1975—; columnist That's Life, The SE News, 1976-78; mgmt. cons., 1978—; part-time tchr., lectr., 1978—. Prin.'s cert., N.C.; tchr.'s cert., N.C. Mem. Am. Soc. Tng. and Devel., Am. Inst. Indsl. Engrs., Metrolina Citizens Band Club, Beta Sigma Phi. Democrat. Methodist. Home: 3508 Old Monroe Rd Matthews NC 28105 Office: 801 Crestdale Ave Matthews NC 28105

DULMAGE, HOWARD TAYLOR, microbiologist, govt. ofcl.; b. Bridgeport, Conn., July 13, 1923; s. Harlan and Margaret Park (Taylor) D.; grad. Phillips Acad., 1940; B.S., U. Ill., 1947; Ph.D., Rutgers U., 1951; m. Eileen Mary Alders, May 30, 1953; children—Howard Taylor, Mary-Margaret Eileen. Sr. research microbiologist Abbott Labs., North Chicago, Ill., 1950-62; dir. research Nutrilite Products, Inc., Lakeview, Cal., 1962-67; research microbiologist, location/research leader Agrl. Research Service, U.S. Dept. Agr., Brownsville, Tex., 1967—. Served with AUS, 1943-46. Recipient Merit certificate for outstanding research U.S. Dept. Agr., 1970, Disting. Service medal, 1978. Fellow Am. Inst. Chemists; mem. Soc. Invertebrate Pathologists, Am. Soc. Microbiology, Entomol. Soc. Am., Am. Chem. Soc. Mason, Kiwanian. Prodn. and standardization of microbial insect control agts. Home: 8 Edgewater Pl Brownsville TX 78520 Office: US Dept Agr PO Box 1033 Brownsville TX 78520

DUMMER, DYEANN REDDIG, pub.; b. Cin., Nov. 5, 1939; d. Henry Shur and Thelma (Dye) Reddig; student Northwestern U., 1957-59, Ohio State U., 1959-60; m. Richard Henry Dummer, May 15, 1971; children by previous marriage—Kenneth, Sharon, Cathleen; 1 son, Geoffrey. Prin. data control supr. Link. div., Singer Corp., Sunnyvale, Calif., 1968-70; office mgr. S. Fla. distbn. center, Wechsler Coffee Co., Boca Raton, Fla., 1970-72; asso. realtor, Park Place Assos., Winter Pk., Fla., 1975-76. Bd. dirs. Girl Scouts U.S.A., Citrus council, Winter Pk., 1978—, recipient service certificate of appreciation, 1977. Mem. Fla. Mag. Assn. (pub. chmn. 1978-79), Altamonte C. of C., Fla. Mfd. Housing Assn., Orlando Area Advt. Fedn., Fla. Press Assn. Asst. pub. Mobile Home News, Altamonte Springs, Fla., 1976-77, pub., 1977—. Home: 410 Santa Maria Way Longwood FL 32750 Office: 409 Lake Howell Rd Maitland FL 32751

DUMONT, RICHARD ALLEN, personal services co. exec.; b. Malone, N.Y., Jan. 24, 1939; s. Lillian (Dame) D.; B.A., Syracuse U., 1960; m. Michele Tuyes, Jan. 24, 1979. Med. rep. Lederle Labs. div. Am. Cyanamid Co., Pearl River, N.Y., 1965-69; asst. to v.p. Bestline Products Inc., Elk Grove, Ill., 1973-76; mng. dir. U.K., London, Eng., 1972-73, dir. self improvement, 1976-78; pres. RAM Enterprises self improvement, Atlanta, 1978—; cons. Golden Products South Africa, Nu-You, Inc. Bd. dirs. Peppertree Lake Homeowners Assn., Atlanta. Served with USNR, 1960-65. Mem. Delta Upsilon. Democrat. Methodist. Home: 47 Basswood Circle Atlanta GA 30328 Office: 2245 Perimeter Park Suite 7 Atlanta GA 30341

DUNAWAY, ALTON A., steel products co. exec.; b. Columbia, Miss., Apr. 27, 1912; s. Clinton E. and Mae (Roberts) D.; B.A., La. Tech. U.; grad. advanced mgmt. program Harvard Bus. Sch.; m. Margaret E. Lawton, July 3, 1940 (dec.); 1 dau., Patricia Carol. Sales rep. Continental Supply Co., Shreveport, La., 1936-40, mem. treasury dept., Dallas, 1940-42; chief dep. U.S. shipping commr. U.S. Coast Guard, Jacksonville, Fla., 1942-45; div. credit mgr. Continental Supply Co., Ft. Worth, 1946-49, Tulsa, 1949-50; asst. sec., credit mgr. Ideco div. Dresser Industries, Dallas, 1950-51; asst. sec., asst. treas., asst. credit mgr. Continental Supply Co., Dallas, 1952-57; asst. sec., asst. treas., asst. credit mgr. Continental Supply Co. Ltd., 1952-57; asst. sec. Youngstown Sheet & Tube Co., Dallas, 1958-61; v.p. Continental Emsco Co. div., Dallas, 1958-61; exec. v.p., gen. mgr. sales Superior Iron Works & Supply Co., Inc., Shreveport, 1962—, Pelican Supply Co., Shreveport, 1964—; sales mgr. Salem Chem. Co., Shreveport, 1964—; dir. Superior Iron Works & Supply Co. Inc. Regional chmn. Harvard Bus. Sch. Fund, 1965-66; mem. Bus. Industry Polit. Action Com. Mem. Harvard Bus. Sch. AMP Assn. (pres. 1959), U.S. C. of C., So. Gas Assn. (mem. adv. council 1963—), Petroleum Equipment Suppliers Assn. (chmn. suppliers com. 1969—), Mid-Continent Oil and Gas Assn., Ind. Petroleum Assn. Am., Am. Petroleum Inst., Internat. Assn. Oil Well Drilling Contractors (asso.). Republican. Baptist. Club: East Ridge Country; Dallas Petroleum, Shreveport Petroleum. Home: 8312 Suffolk Dr Shreveport LA 71106 Office: 1842 Barton Dr Box 7002 Shreveport LA 71107

DUNAWAY, DONNA ELIZABETH KASTLE, computer scientist, co. exec.; b. Ft. Worth, Mar. 16, 1935; d. Joseph A. and Susie (Garrett) Kastle; B.A., Tex. Christian U., 1956; M.S., So. Meth. U., 1969, Ph.D., 1972; children—Diane Elizabeth, Thomas Kastle. Owner, pres. Ditrec Corp., Dallas, 1971—; computer sci. researcher Tex. Instruments, Inc., 1973-79; mgr. software devel. Advanced Bus. Communications, Inc., 1979—. Mem. Math. Assn. Am., Assn. Computing Machinery, Kappa Kappa Gamma. Presbyn. Home: 3706 Dartmouth St Dallas TX 75205

DUNBAR, BONNIE JEANNE, ceramics engr., aerospace technologist; b. Sunnyside, Wash., Mar. 3, 1949; d. Robert C. and Ethel F. (Parker) D.; B.S. in Ceramic Engring. with honors, U. Wash., 1971, M.S., 1975; Ph.D. in Bioengring., U. Houston, 1980. Engr., Boeing Aerospace, 1972-73; grad. research asst. U. Wash., Seattle, 1973-75; vis. research asso. Harwell Labs., Oxford, Eng., 1976; sr. research engr. space div. Rockwell Internat., Downey, Calif., 1976-78; sr. systems engr. NASA Johnson Space Center, Houston, Tex., 1978—. Recipient Engr. of Yr. award, 1978. Mem. Am. Ceramic Soc., Nat. Inst. Ceramic Engrs. (chmn. nat. ethics com.), Soc. of Women Engrs., AIAA, Royal Air Force Sport Parachuting Assn., Kappa Delta. Contbr. articles on ceramic engring. to profl. publs. Home: 702 Whitecap Dr Seabrook TX 77586 Office: NASA JSC CH6 Johnson Space Center Houston TX 77058

DUNBAR, JAMES CURTIS, physician; b. Mountain Home, Ark., Nov. 21, 1921; s. Felton F. and Eilleen (Love) D.; M.D., U. Ark., 1946. Intern Luth Hosp., Cleve., 1946-47; practice medicine, Mountain Home, 1949—. Served from lt. (j.g.) to lt. comdr. M.C., USNR, 1943-49; PTO. Fellow Am. Coll. Angiology, Am. Geriatrics Soc.; mem. N.Y. Acad. Scis., A.M.A., Ark., Baxter County med. socs., U. Ark. Alumni Assn. Mem. Christian Ch. Home: 806 E 9th St Mountain Home AR 72653 Office: 617 S Baker St Mountain Home AR 72653

DUNBAR, JAMES WILLIAM, audiologist; b. Kansas City, Mo., Nov. 3, 1953; s. Chester Earle and Dorothy May (Alexander) D.; B.A., U. No. Colo., 1975, M.A., 1976. Audiologist, B. Philip Cotton and Stephen J. Toner, physicians, Panama City, Fla., 1977—. Cert. audiologist, Fla. Mem. Am. Speech and Hearing Assn. (cert. clin. competence), Fla. Speech and Hearing Assn., Am. Auditory Soc., Am. Tinnitus Assn. Democrat. Home: 2100 W Beach Dr Apt E203 Panama City FL 32401 Office: 634 E Business 98 Panama City FL 32401

DUNCAN, DONN ROBERT, psychologist; b. Frostproof, Fla., Nov. 18, 1922; s. Robert William Angel and Vera Mabel (Moyer) D.; B.S., U. Fla., 1946, M.A. 1950, M.R.C., 1960, Ed.D., 1962; m. Donna Hiers, June 7, 1963; children—Donn Robert, II, Phillip J., James R. Diplomatic courier U.S. Dept. State, Washington, 1952-53; state auditor Fla. Auditing Dept., Tallahassee, 1953-54; bus. mgr. Fla. Alcoholic Rehab. Program, Avon Park, 1954-59; psychologist Mental Health Center of Polk County, Inc., Lakeland, Fla., 1962-78; pvt. practice psychology and group psychotherapist Lakeland (Fla.) Manor Hosp., 1962-73; pres. Donn R. Duncan & Sons, Inc.; pres., gen. mgr. Duncan Groves, Inc., Lakeland, 1956—; partner J & D Partnership, Lakeland, 1973—; sec.-treas. Pack Groves, Inc. Served to 1st lt. AUS, 1943-46, India; 50-52, Japan. Mem. Am. Psychol. Assn., Acad. Psychologists in Marriage Counseling, Am. Assn. Marriage and Family Counselors, Diplomatic Courier Assn., Am. Legion, Beta Alpha Psi, Alpha Phi Omega. Club: Masons. Home: 5510 Old Scott Lake Rd Lakeland FL 33803

DUNCAN, HARRY ERNEST, educator; b. Hartford, W.Va., Nov. 20, 1936; s. William Robert and Margaretta (Harris) D.; B.S., W.Va. U., 1959, M.S., 1961, Ph.D., 1966; m. Carmela Rose Mangano, June 14, 1958; children—Deborah Ann, Pamela Sue, Harry Ernest. Asst. prof. plant pathology N.C. State U., Raleigh, 1965-70, asso. prof., specialist-in-charge, Plant Pathology Extension, 1970-77, prof., specialist-in-charge plant pathology extension, 1977—. Mem. Pesticide Assn. N.C. (bd. dirs. from 1972), Corn Growers Assn. N.C. (bd. dirs. from 1977), Am. Phytopathol. Soc., Sigma Xi, Epsilon Sigma Phi, Gamma Sigma Delta. Roman Catholic. Home: 201 Chatterson Dr Raleigh NC 27609 Office: PO Box 5397 NC State Univ Raleigh NC 27650

DUNCAN, JAMES LOUGHLIN, bishop; b. Greensboro, N.C., Sept. 11, 1913; s. Robert and Mary (Loughlin) D.; B.A., Emory U., 1935, M.A., 1936; B.D., U. of South, 1939, D.D., 1962; m. Evelyn Burgess, July 25, 1942 (dec. Jan. 1967); children—Mary Anna (Mrs. Edward B. Waters), John Robert, James Loughlin; m. 2d, Mrs. Elaine B. Gaither, Oct. 7, 1957. Ordained to ministry Episcopal Ch., 1938; asst. rector in Atlanta, 1939-40; rector in Rome, Ga., 1940-45, Winter Park, Fla., 1945-50, St. Petersburg, Fla., 1950-61; suffragan bishop Episcopal Diocese So. Fla., 1961-69; bishop S.E. Fla., 1969-79; ret., 1980. Exchangee, U.S.-S. African Program, 1961. Chmn. Dade County Community Relations Bd., 1965. Mem. Kappa Alpha (knight comdr. 1957-58).

DUNCAN, JOHN EBLEN, religious assn. exec.; b. Chattanooga, Aug. 1, 1925; s. Ronald Clarence and Nellie Mae (Gray) D.; student Wis. State U., 1943-44, Tenn. Temple Coll., 1951-53; A.B., Samford U., 1955, M.S., 1968; postgrad. Carver Sch. Missions, 1962, So. Baptist Sem., 1963; m. Elnor Kathleen Gardenshire, June 29, 1946; 1 son, John Charles. Ordained to ministry, 1951; pastor Hickory Valley Bapt. Mission, Chattanooga, 1953-54; asst. pastor Roebuck Plaza Bapt. Ch., Birmingham, Ala., 1954-55; pastor Mt. Pleasant Bapt. Ch., Pell City, Ala., 1956-59; dir. missions St. Clair Bapt. Assn., Ashville, Ala., 1959-62, Shelby Bapt. Assn., Columbiana, Ala., 1962—. Adv. bd. mem. Shelby County Youth Aid Bur.; bd. mem. Shelby County R.S.V.P. Served with USAAF, 1943-46. Certified trainer adult edn. techniques. Mem. Am., Ala. personnel and guidance assns., So. Bapt., Ala. (pres. 1976-77) confs. dirs. of associational missions, Assn. for Specialists in Group Work. Democrat. Clubs: Civitan Internat. Contbr. articles to religious publs. Home: 101 Myrtle St Columbiana AL 35051 Office: PO Box 888 Columbiana AL 35051

DUNCAN, JOHN JAMES, congressman; b. Scott County, Tenn., Mar. 24, 1919; married, four children. Asst. atty. gen., 1947-56; dir. law, Knoxville, Tenn., 1956-59, mayor, 1959-64; mem. 89th-96th congresses from 2d dist. Tenn. Served with U.S. Army, 1942-45. Mem. Am., Tenn., Knoxville bar assns., Am. Legion (comdr. Tenn. 1954), V.F.W. Presbyn. Republican. Office: 2458 Rayburn House Office Bldg Washington DC 20515*

DUNCAN, MARVIN EARL, educator; b. Greenville, N.C., Nov. 23, 1939; s. Leroy and Mary Duncan; B.S., N.C. Central U., 1962, M.A., 1963; Ph.D., Mich. State U., 1972; div.; children—Carolyn Ann, Crystal Lynn, Francine. Dir., Learning Resources Center, N.C. Central U., 1963-72, dir., prof. edn., 1972—; cons. planning. Title V-D fellow, 1970-72. Mem. Assn. Edn. Communication Tech., N.C. Assn. Educators, Phi Delta Kappa. Democrat. Baptist. Home: 521 Nelson St Durham NC 27707 Office: NC Central U Durham NC 27707

DUNCAN, PAUL, printmaker, communications cons., educator; b. Columbia, S.C., July 10, 1909; s. William Whiteford and Myrtle Frances (Gibson) D.; B.A., U. Ala., 1934; postgrad. Corcoran Sch. Art, 1967-75, Georgetown U., 1973-74; m. Gwendolyn Margaret Drolet, Feb. 6, 1937; children—Paula D. Hereford, Denis D. Hasty, Jean Laurens. With Montgomery (Ala.) Advertiser, 1926-30, Anniston (Ala.) Star, 1934, Knoxville News-Sentinel, 1935-36, AP, Montgomery and Birmingham, Ala., 1937-42; with Office of Govt. Reports, Nat. War Labor Bd., Office Economic Stabilization of Exec. Office Pres., Washington, 1942-46; adminstrv. asst. U.S. Senator Lister Hill, Washington, 1946-51; dir. information and reports Tech. Coop. Adminstrn. Dept. State, Washington, 1951-53; information cons. Pres.'s Com. on Scientists and Engrs., Washington, 1956-58; owner, cons. on mass communications and pub. affairs co., Washington, 1953-77. Prints exhibited in Corcoran Gallery Art, 1969-71. Bd. dirs. Performing Arts Assn., Foley, Ala. Decorated Comdr. Most Noble Order Crown, King of Thailand, 1960. Recipient First prize printmaking, Corcoran Sch. Art, 1971. Mem. Phi Gamma Delta. Democrat. Presbyterian. Author: Motivate, Teach, Train, 1952 (handbook). Editor: The Scientific Revolution: Challenge and Promise, 1959. Home and Studio: Magnolia Springs AL 36555

DUNCAN, POPE ALEXANDER, coll. pres.; b. Glasgow, Ky., Sept. 8, 1920; s. Pope Alexander and Mabel (Roberts) D.; B.S., U. Ga., 1940, M.S., 1941; Th.M., So. Bapt. Theol. Sem., 1944, Th.D., 1947; postgrad. U. Zurich (Switzerland), 1960-61; m. Margaret Flexer, June 30, 1943; children—Mary Margaret Duncan Jones, Annie Laurie Duncan Kelly, Katherine Maxwell. Instr. physics U. Ga., 1940-41; fellow So. Bapt. Theol. Sem., 1944-45; dir. religious activities Mercer U., 1945-46, Roberts prof. church history, 1948-49; prof. religion Stetson U., 1946-48, 49-53; prof. ch. history Southeastern Bapt. Theol. Sem., 1953-63; dean Brunswick Coll., 1964; pres. S. Ga. Coll., Douglas, 1964-68; v.p. Ga. So. Coll., Statesboro, 1968-71, pres., 1971-77; pres. Stetson U., Deland, Fla., 1977—; chmn. council pres.'s So. Consortium for Internat. Edn., 1974-75; mem. coll. commn. So. Assn. Colls. and Schs., 1978—; bd. dirs. Nat. Assn. Ind. Colls. and Univs., 1980—. Pres. Wake Forest Civic Club, 1959-60, Ga. Assn. Colls., 1968-69; pres. Coastal Empire Council Boy Scouts Am., 1973-74. Mem. Am. Hist. Assn., Am. Soc. Ch. History, Douglas-Coffee County C. of C. (dir. 1966-68), Statesboro-Bulloch County C. of C. (dir. 1971-77), Deland C. of C. (dir. 1977— v.p. 1980), Fla. Council of 100, Phi Beta Kappa, Omicron Delta Kappa, Phi Kappa Phi, Phi Delta Kappa, Kappa Delta Pi, Pi Mu Epsilon, Phi Eta Sigma, Sigma Phi Sigma. Democrat. Baptist. Rotarian (dir. 1965-66, 1970-72, pres. 1967-68). Author: Our Baptist Story, 1958; The Pilgrimage of Christianity, 1965 Hanserd Knollys, 1965. Home: 418 N Woodland Blvd Deland FL 32720

DUNCAN, SYLVIA ANNA, advt. and pub. relations exec.; b. Galveston, Tex., Feb. 28, 1944; d. Clifford G. and Marcella Octavia Paisley; student U. Houston, 1967, So. Methodist U., 1969, N.Y. U., 1976; 1 dau., Monique. Personnel asst. Tex. Eastern Transmission Co., Houston, 1965-69; editor Nat. Bank Commerce, Dallas, 1969-72; pub. relations exec. Lone Star Gas Co., Dallas, 1972-73; freelance writer, 1973-76; news media coordinator Transco Companies, Inc., Houston, 1976-77; pres., owner S. Duncan Inc., Houston, 1977—. Mem. spl. gifts com., gen. fund com. Mus. Fine Arts, Houston; coordinator drug abuse communication programs Mental Health and Retardation Centers, Dallas. Mem. Internat. Assn. Bus. Communicators (Merit award 1970, Overall Outstanding Achievement award 1978), Women in Bus. Communications, Houston Advt. Fedn. Episcopalian. Club: Houston Press. Home: 10220 Memorial St Apt 51 Houston TX 77024 Office: 3303 Louisiana St Suite 145 Houston TX 77006

DUNCAN, WILLIAM ADAM, JR., clergyman, guidance counselor; b. Newton Center, Mass., Apr. 27, 1918; s. William A. and Milner Florence (Sammons) D.; A.B., Mercer U., 1947; diploma in Urban Planning, Ga Tech. U.; B.D., Southwestern Baptist Theol. Seminary, 1951, M.Div., 1951, Ph.D., 1978; m. Edna Pearl Shaw, Apr. 11, 1946; children—Adam Chandler, Malcomb Sammons, Robert Bruce. Ordained to ministry So. Baptist Conv., 1946; pastor First Baptist Ch., Hahira, Ga., 1951-52, Sereven, Ga., 1952-54; dir. missions Daniell Bapt. Assn. of Ga., 1954-57, Ogeechee Bapt. Assn. Ga., 1957-58; dir. assn. programs Piedmont Bapt. Assn., Greensboro, N.C., 1958-77; pvt. practice guidance counseling, East Point, Ga., 1977—; pres. Anglo-Mexican Counseling Service. Served with U.S. Army, 1942-46; with USAFR, 1968-79. Mem. Nat. Rifle Assn., N.C. States Sheriffs Assn., Am. Assn. Adminstrs., Atlanta Bapt. Ministers Conf., CAP, Air Force Chaplains Assn., Am. Radio Relay League, Ga. Sport Shooters, Gun Owners Am., Bass Assn. Am. Contbr. articles to ch. publs. Home and Office: 2239 Headland Dr East Point GA 30344

DUNFEE, WILMA ROSE, ednl. counselor; b. Willow Lake, S.D., May 26, 1934; d. Wesley Fred and Elsena Johanna (Meester) Busse; B.S. in Edn., No. State Tchrs. Coll., Aberdeen, S.D., 1960; M.Ed., U. Nev., Las Vegas, 1969; m. J. Roger Dunfee, June 2, 1963; 1 dau., Heidi Lou. Tchr., Rosedale Sch. Dist., Willow Lake, 1952-54, Roosevelt Sch., Watertown, S.D., 1954-56, Franklin Sch., Great Falls, Mont., 1956-58, Hyde Park Jr. High Sch., Las Vegas, 1958-59; tchr. English and social studies Jim Bridger Jr. High Sch., Las Vegas, 1959-66; reading specialist Von Tobel Jr. High Sch., Las Vegas, 1966-67, counselor, 1967-69; counselor K.O. Knudtsen Jr. High Sch., Las Vegas, 1969; tchr. English, U. Nev., Las Vegas, 1969-70; counselor Valley High Sch., Las Vegas, 1970-78; counselor R.E. Lee High Sch., Tyler, Tex., 1978—. Bible study tchr., 1973-77; Brownie 1 leader Girl Scouts U.S.A., 1972-74; bd. dirs. Vacation Bible Sch., 1978. Mem. Am. Personnel and Guidance Assn., Civic Music Assn., Piney Woods Counselors Assn. Republican. Club: FBI Wives of Tyler. Office: 411 E Loop 323 Tyler TX 75701

DUNFORD, BIRTIES RAY, indsl. engr.; b. Detroit, Dec. 29, 1933; s. Warner Gordon and Helen Louise (Guard) D.; A.A., St. Petersburg Jr. Coll., 1960; B.S. in Indsl. Engring., U. Fla., 1963; m. Billie Jean Hodson, Nov. 3, 1954; children—Belinda Dennise, William Gordon. Asst. mgr. St. Petersburg Beach, Fla., 1959-60; tech. asst. Western Electric Co., Winston-Salem, N.C., 1961-62; systems mgr. Reynolds Metals Co., Va., also Ky., 1963-68; supr. GTE Data Services Corp., Tampa, Fla., 1968-79, adminstr., 1979—; exec. dir. Interservice, Tampa, 1970—. Committeeman, Gulf Ridge council Boy Scouts Am., 1968-74, commr., 1964-67. Served with USCGR, 1954-58. Mem. Am. Inst. Indsl. Engrs. (dir. 1972-73, treas. 1973-74, sec. 1974-75, pres. 1976-77), SHARE (project mgr. 1973-75), Tesdata Users Group (v.p. 1978-79). Democrat. Clubs: Tampa Trident, Fishing of Am. Home: 8312 W Hiawatha St Tampa FL 33615 Office: PO Box 2602 Tampa FL 33601

DUNHAM, CLARENCE TYRONE, JR., sch. dist. adminstr.; b. Houston, June 7, 1935; s. Clarence and Annie Mae D.; student Wiley Coll., 1953-55; m. Lois M. Lacey, May 11, 1966; children—Anthony, Cythia, Craig, Janice. Operation supr. Houston Ind. Sch. Dist., 1964-71, supt. vehicle maintenance, 1971-78, warehouse mgr., food service, 1978—; chmn. Area 10 Improvement Cooperation Bd., 1975-76. Mem. Tex. Tchrs. Assn., Houston Supr. Assn. (pres. 1976-78). Baptist. Home: 4811 Kashmere St Houston TX 77026 Office: Houston Ind Sch Dist 2000 Lyons Ave Houston TX 77020

DUNLAP, CLARKE, ednl. adminstr.; b. Rolla, Mo., Jan. 8, 1929; s. D. Edward F. and Etta D (Kofahl) D.; A.A. cum laude, Los Angeles City Coll., 1973; B.A. in Econs., U. Wash., 1954; M.A., Am. U. Sch. Fgn. Service, 1960; postgrad. U. Tex. Law Sch., 1954-55, George Washington U. Law Sch., 1955-56; m. Diana Tamara Jacykewycz, Apr. 21, 1968 (div. 1971). Intelligence officer CIA, 1956-61, U.S. Dept. State, 1961; free-lance writer, 1962-67; instr. geography Woodbury U., Los Angeles, 1967-70; instr. polit. sci. Los Angeles Trade Tech. Jr. Coll., 1968-73; instr. polit. sci. West Coast U., Los Angeles, 1967—; instr. phys. geography, Am. history and Am. govt. Columbia Coll., Los Angeles, 1976—; research coordinator univ. affairs U. So. Calif., Los Angeles, 1978—. Served with USN, 1946-48, 51-52; Korea. George Burley scholar in sci., 1973. Mem. Assn. Am. Geographers, Am., Nat. geog. socs., Va., Mo., Ky. hist. socs., Viking Soc. for No. Research, S.R., SAR, SCV, Gen. Soc. War of 1812, English Speaking Union, St. Andrews Soc. of Los Angeles, Mensa, Sigma Tau Gamma. Home: 2553 Larkin Rd 25 Lexington KY 40503

DUNLAP, E. T., educator; b. Cravens, Okla., Dec. 19, 1914; s. C.C. and Ida (McWhirter) D.; B.S., Southeastern Okla. State U., 1940; M.S., Okla. State U., 1942, Ed.D., 1956; LL.D. (hon.), Oklahoma City U., 1962, John Brown U., 1968, Oral Roberts U., Pepperdine U., 1979; m. Opal O. Jones, June 3, 1934; 1 son, E.T. Tchr., prin. Latimer County (Okla.) schs., 1936-38, supt. schs., 1938-42; high sch. insp. Okla. Dept. Edn., 1942-45; supt. schs., Red Oak, Okla., 1945-51; pres. Eastern Okla. State Coll., 1952-61; chancellor Okla. System Higher Edn., 1961—; chmn. bd. Fed. Student Loan Mktg. Assn. Mem. Okla. Ho. of Reps. from Latimer Co., 1947-51, chmn. edn. com., 1947-51. Recipient Silver Beaver award Boy Scouts Am., 1960, commendation resolution Okla. Legislature, 1976; inducted into Okla. State U. Alumni Hall of Fame, 1977. Mem. NEA, Am. Assn. Sch. Adminstrs., Am. Assn. Higher Edn., Nat. Soc. Study Edn., Okla. Edn. Assn., Okla. Assn. Sch. Adminstrs., Okla. Polit. Sci. Assn., Okla. Hist. Soc., Oklahoma C. of C., Phi Delta Kappa, Pi Kappa Alpha. Democrat. Methodist. Clubs: Lions, Oklahoma City Men's Dinner, Shriners. Author papers, reports in field. Home: 5304 Stonewall Dr Oklahoma City OK 73111 Office: 500 Education Bldg State Capitol Complex Oklahoma City OK 73105

DUNLAP, JOE EVERETT, dentist; b. Delaware, Ohio, May 11, 1930; s. Arthur Calvin and Mary Irene (Jones) D.; student Ohio Wesleyan U., 1949-50, 54; D.D.S., Ohio State U., 1959; m. Mary Susan King, June 17, 1959; children—Marlene, Todd, David, Sherrie, Dru. With Fla. Instl. Dental Service, Gainesville, Ft. Myers, 1959-60; individual practice dentistry, Clearwater, Fla., 1961—; sr. mem. dental group Dunlap, Vance, Deal, Szeto & Assos.; partner Susie Q's—The Lamp and Accessory Gallery. Served to 2d lt. Med. Service Corps, AUS, 1950-53. Mem. Am., Fla., West Coast Dist. dental assns. Author: Surviving in Dentistry: The Sources of Stress; The Beginning Dental Practice; The First Year. Mem. editorial bd. Dental Econs. mag.; contbr. articles to dental jours., articles and photographs to regional publs. Home: 1816 Lombardy Dr Clearwater FL 33515 Office: 1455 Sunset Point Rd Clearwater FL 33515

DUNLAP, MARTHA WILLIAMS, printing co. exec.; b. Smiths Grove, Ky. Smiths Grove, Ky., Sept. 26, 1949; d. Woodrow and Lucy Pearl (Majors) Williams; grad. pub. schs.; m. Roger Lewis Dunlap, June 29, 1978; 1 son, Larry Ray Williams. With Castner Knott, Nashville, 1967; with Shrimp Boats, Inc., Nashville, 1967-68; word processing supr. Baird Ward Printing Co., Nashville, 1968—. Home: Route 2 Rocky Fork Rd Smyrna TN 37167 Office: PO Box 539 Powell Ave Nashville TN 37202

DUNLAP, NAOMI GIBSON, psychologist; b. Meridian, Tex., Oct. 10, 1911; d. John Wheat and Callie Jane (Taylor) Gibson; B.A., Baylor U., 1949; M.A., U. Tex. at Austin, 1950, Ph.D., 1961; m. Artie Reynolds Dunlap, Nov. 24, 1932 (dec.); 1 dau., Norma Dell (Mrs. Jack Thomas Harris). Clin. psychologist VA Center, Temple, Tex., until 1975; part-time pvt. practice clin. psychology, Austin, Tex., 1976—. Mem. Am. Psychol. Assn., Southwestern Psychol. Assn., Tex. Psychol. Assn. Home: 3204 W Ave T Temple TX 76501

DUNLOP, BRENTON DELANEY, word processing co. exec.; b. Alexandria, Va., Aug. 22, 1949; s. George Lee and Mary Ellen (Drayton) D.; B.S. in B.A., Va. State U., 1971; m. Shirley Blagmon, Dec. 15, 1969; 1 dau., Tara Tyge. Prodn. control specialist Ford Motor Co., Metuchen, N.J., 1971-72; advanced mktg. rep. IBM Corp., Washington, 1972-75; regional mktg. mgr. Addressograph/Multigraph Corp., Washington, 1976-78; dist. mgr. Micom Data Systems, Inc., Washington, 1978—; founder land speculation bus. Mem. Am. Mgmt. Assn. Christian Ch. Club: K.P. Office: 1815 N Fort Myer Dr Arlington VA 22209

DUNN, BYRON G., engring. cons.; b. Ft. Worth, Feb. 4, 1928; s. William O. and Maude (Parker) D.; student Wayland Coll., 1948, Tex. Tech. U., 1948-50; m. Jo Ann Alexander, Aug. 31, 1950; children—Margaret Ann, W. Byron, Mary Kathleen. With Firestone Tire & Rubber Co., 1950-55; owner Byron Dunn & Assos., Muskogee, Okla., 1956-61; pres. Continental Mfg. & Engring. Co., Muskogee, 1961-66; exec. v.p. Sonics Internat Inc., Dallas, 1967-70; pres. Pyrotech, Inc., Dallas, 1970—, Byron Dunn Engring. Co., 1979—; chmn. bd. Delta Fine Wire Co., 1979—. Mem. adv. bd. Am. Security Council; mem. Rep. Nat. Com., 1978—. Served in USNR, 1946-48. Mem. Nat. Fire Protection Assn. Patentee. Home: 6831 Orchid Ln Dallas TX 75230

DUNN, CHARLES ALLEN, crops specialist; b. Elkhart, Kans., Oct. 20, 1941; s. Willis Allen and Verna Louise (Williams) D.; B.S., Okla. State U., 1964, M.S., 1969; Ph.D., N.C. State U., 1973; m. Sharon Kay Harper, June 17, 1962; children—David Allen, Christopher Audie. Insp., plant pest control div. U.S. Dept. Agr., Agrl. Research Service, Sikeston, Mo., 1964-67; agronomist Tex. A. and M. U., Yoakum, 1973-76; extension crops specialist Okla. State U., Stillwater, 1976—; co-dir. Agronomic Cons. Okla. Recipient Grad. Excellence award Okla. State U. Grad. Coll., 1968. Mem. Crop Sci. Soc. Am., Soil Sci. Soc. Am., Am. Soc. Agronomy, Am. Soybean Assn., Am. Peanut Research and Edn. Assn., So. Weed Sci. Soc., Okla. Soybean Assn., Sigma Xi. Democrat. Lutheran. Clubs: U.S. Dept. Agr. (Stillwater, Okla.), Sons of Hermann. Office: 376 Agr Hall Okla State U Stillwater OK 74074

DUNN, HARLEY EUGENE, mfg. co. exec.; b. DeQueen, Ark., Mar. 30, 1942; s. John L. and Maggie J. (Ross) D.; ed. public schs., Littlefield, Tex.; m. Donna Jean Mead, May 5, 1973. Mktg. cons. Dallas, 1968-74; pres. Design South, Asheville, N.C., 1974-77; exec. v.p., mktg. dir. Buck Stove, Asheville, 1977—; pres. Rocky Mountain Buck Stove, Boulder, Colo., 1978—; dir. Smoky Mountain Enterprises, Delta Buck Stove, Brunk and Dunn, Inc. Served with USAF, 1963-67. Mem. Nat. Assn. Home Builders, Wood Energy Inst., Fireplace Inst. Mem. Christian Ch.

DUNN, HARRISON A., constrn. co. exec.; b. Tellico Plains, Tenn., Sept. 22, 1920; s. Charles Edmund and Ella (Ware) D.; ed. pub. schs.; m. Tennie Arlene Cochran, Jan. 10, 1943; children—Harrison David, Pamela (Mrs. David Brockwell Kidd). Employed with various constrn. firms, 1940—; with Brock & Blevins Co., Ins., Rossville, Ga., 1950—, mgr. power constrn., 1958—, v.p., 1969—, dir., 1969—. Mem. Big Bros. Assn. Baptist. Mason (Shriner). Home: 7109 Saratoga Ln Chattanooga TN 37421 Office: 200 W Gordon Ave Rossville GA 40741

DUNN, HENRY HAMPTON, editor; b. Floral City, Fla., Dec. 14, 1916; s. William Harvey and Nannie L. (Hemrick) D.; student Mercer U., Macon, Ga., U. Tampa (Fla.); m. Charlotte Rawls, Aug. 16, 1941; children—Janice Kay, Henry Hampton, Dennis Harvey. Mem. staff Tampa (Fla.) Times, 1936-58, city editor, 1946-51, mng. editor, 1951-58; polit. analyst and newscaster WCKT-TV, Miami, 1958-59; pub. relations dir. Peninsula Motor Club, 1959—, also v.p.; editor Fla. Explorer. Adv. council Gordon Keller Sch. Nursing, 1955-72, chmn. 1956-59, adv. bd. Salvation Army, 1953—, chmn., 1955-56; dir., past pres. United Cerebral Palsy of Tampa, state pres.; dir., treas. Tampa A.R.C.; selections com. Girl Scouts; dir., v.p. Vis. Nurses Assn. Greater Tampa 1956, pres., 1973-74, also life mem.; mem. Nat. AAA Traffic and Safety Com., Nat. AAA Pub. Relations Com., Nat. AAA Hwy. Com.; mem. West Central Fla. Com. Mil. Assistance to Safety and Traffic; chmn. Citizen's Adv. com. Tampa Urban Area Transp. Study. Charter trustee Bd.; trustee Pensacola Preservation Bd.; charter trustee Historic Tallahassee Preservation Bd.; trustee Historic Tampa/Hillsborough County Preservation Bd.; pres. DWI Counterattack Tampa-Hillsborough County; mem. Carrollwood Civic Assn.; dir. Girl's Club of Tampa, Hillsborough County unit Am. Cancer Soc.; adv. com. Hillsborough Community Coll.; bd. dirs. Hillsborough Community Mental Health Center, Inc., Rough Riders Inc.; v.p. Friends of Library, Tampa/Hillsborough County Public Library. Served to maj. USAF, World War II; MTO. Decorated Bronze Star, 5 Battle Stars. Recipient award for best news story A.P., 1946; Award of Merit, Fla. Hist. Soc.; Torch award Citrus County C. of C., 1969; Jefferson Davis medal United Daus. Confederacy; Outstanding Service award Dick Pope chpt. Fla. Pub. Relations Assn., 1973; Fla. History award Peace River Valley Hist. Soc., 1974; Cooper-Taylor award Jaycees, 1974; Distinguished Pub. Service award U. Tampa, 1975, Achievement medal, 1978; Outstanding Alumnus award U. Tampa, 1976; Fla. Patriot, Fla. Bicentennial Commn., 1976. Mem. Am. Legion, Tampa C. of C. (tourist com., mem. hwy. com.), Fla. Hist. Soc., Hist. Assn. So. Fla., U. Tampa Alumni Assn. (past pres.), Asso. Press Assn. Fla. (pres. 1955-56), Internat. Platform Assn., Tampa Hist. Soc. (pres. 1973-74, D.B. McKay award 1978), Old Timers Assn. Hillsborough County (pres. 1975-76, dir.), Sigma Delta Chi (pres. Fla. West Coast chpt. 1954-55). Baptist. Mason, Rotarian (pub. relations chmn., bd. dirs., pres. Tampa, dist. gov., dist. rep. to R.I. legis. council 1977, 80, Paul Harris fellow); mem. Order Eastern Star. Author: Re-Discover Florida; WDAE, Florida's Pioneer Radio Station; Yesterday's Tampa; Yesterday's St. Petersburg; Yesterday's Clearwater; Yesterday's Tallahassee; Florida Sketches; Accent Florida; Yesterday's Lakeland; Back Home-The History of Citrus Country, Fla. Hist. writer Fla. Trend mag., Tampa Tribune, Tampa Times; writer syndicated hist. column. Home: 10610 Carrollwood Dr Tampa FL 33618 Office: 1515 N Westshore Blvd Tampa FL 33607

DUNN, JAMES LYNWOOD, univ. adminstr.; b. Shacklefords, Va., Aug. 13, 1939; s. Aubrey Mason and Mary Bernice (Carlton) D.; B.S., Richmond Profl. Inst., 1962; M.S., Va. Commonwealth U., 1972; m. Mary Catherine Sellers, June 17, 1961; children—Maurice Aubrey, Michael Llewellyn. Instr. mgmt. and acctg. Smithdeal-Massey Bus. Coll., Richmond, Va., 1962-64; asst. dir. devel. Va. Commonwealth U. (formerly Richmond Profl. Inst.), Richmond, 1964—, dir. alumni activities, 1970—. Treas., Robious Elem. Sch. PTA, 1974-75; chmn. steering com. Greenfield Elem. Sch. PTA, 1975, pres., 1975-76; dist. v.p. Chesterfield County (Va.) Council PTA's, 1977-79. Mem. So. Coll. Placement Assn. (chmn. adv. com. 1970), Va. Coll. Placement Assn. (pres. 1967-68, Merit award 1970), Council for Advancement and Support of Edn., Am. Alumni Council, Am. Coll. Public Relations Assn., Adminstrv. Mgmt. Soc., Va. Alumni/Devel. Adminstrs. Presbyterian. Clubs: Rotunda, Kiwanis. Home: 11031 Sydelle Dr Richmond VA 23235 Office: Va Commonwealth U 828 W Franklin St Richmond VA 23284

DUNN, JOHN LELAND, high fidelity store exec.; b. Wewoka, Okla., May 15, 1948; s. Walter James and Wenona (Latimer) D.; student Lubbock Christian Coll., 1966-67, Sayre Jr. Coll., 1967-68, Okla. Christian Coll., 1968; m. Lucy Perez, Apr. 5, 1975; children—Jennifer Rebecca, Victoria Elizabeth. Mgmt. trainee Radio Shack/Tandy Corp., Oklahoma City, 1969-70, mgr. stores, Memphis, 1970-71, New Orleans, 1971-72, Houma, La., 1972, Ft. Lauderdale, Fla., 1972-73, North Palm Beach, Fla., 1973, San Antonio, 1974-75, Norman, Okla., 1975—. Mem. Norman Jaycees, Mchts. Assn. Southland Mall Houma. Republican. Mem. Ch. of Christ. Office: Radio Shack div Tandy Corp 602 E Johnson St Norman OK 73071

DUNN, MARIE CLOAR, tax accountant; b. Love County, Okla., Feb. 2, 1921; d. George Calvin and Lallie Myrtle (Sweat) Cloar; student Ardmore (Okla.) Bus. Coll., 1939, Southeastern State Coll., 1968, E. Central State Coll., 1975; m. Oklahoma Lee Dunn, June 16, 1940 (dec.); children—Dan A., Debora Irene. Legal sec. E.W. Schenk, atty., Ardmore; self-employed tax accountant, Fox, Okla.; dir. region 3, Okla. Rural Water Assn., 1973—; tchr. simplified rural water dist. bookkeeping system; notary pub. Mem. Nat. Soc. Pub. Accountants, Nat. Assn. Tax Consultors, Okla. Farm Bur. Democrat. Baptist. Clubs: Ohoyohoma Indian Women's, Philharmonic Music (Ardmore). Address: Fox OK 73435

DUNN, REGINALD MURL, phys. therapist; b. Mexico, Mo., Jan. 11, 1952; s. Glenn Edward and Mavis Murline (Kellogg) D.; B.S. in Phys. Therapy, Loma Linda U., 1975; m. Desamparados Lizandra Montalvá, Sept. 5, 1976; 1 child, Amado Reimundo. Head dept. phys. therapy Med. Center Hosp., Punta Gorda, Fla., 1976, co-dir. phys. therapy, 1976-77; co-dir. phys. therapy DeSoto Meml. Hosp., Arcadia, Fla., 1977-78; co-dir. phys. therapy Punta Gorda (Fla.) Care Center, 1976-78, dir. phys. therapy, 1978—. Mem. Am. Phys. Therapy Assn. Adventist. Home: 742 NW Lakeview Blvd Port Charlotte FL 33952 Office: Life Care Center Punta Gorda 733 E Olympia Ave Punta Gorda FL 33950

DUNN, ROBERT GEORGE, III, lawyer; b. Richmond, Va., Sept. 17, 1940; s. Robert George and Rosalie Holiday (Tyler) D.; B.B.A., McMurry Coll., 1966; J.D., St. Mary's U., 1971; m. Elizabeth Sabra Hartsfield, Dec. 21, 1971; 1 son, Robert George. Admitted to Tex., Ga. bars, 1972; asst. dist. atty. Collin County (Tex.), 1972-74; individual practice law, Donalsonville, Ga., 1974—. Served with U.S. Army, 1968-69. Mem. Tex., Ga., Am., Pataula Circuit bar assns., Donalsonville Jaycees (pres. 1976-77, Spoke award 1977), Am. Legion. Episcopalian. Clubs: Lions (Donalsonville); Descs. Signers Declaration Independence. Home: 1719 Williams Dr Donalsonville GA 31745 Office: PO Box 1024 218 W Second St Donalsonville GA 31745

DUNN, RONALD HOLLAND, engring. and mgmt. exec.; b. Balt., Sept. 15, 1937; s. Delmas Joseph and Edna Grace (Holland) D.; student U. S.C., 1956-58; B.S. in Engring., Johns Hopkins U., 1969; m. Verona Lucille Lambert, Aug. 17, 1958; children—Ronald H., Jr. (dec.), David R., Brian W. Field engr. Balt. & Ohio R.R., Balt., 1958-66; chief engr. yards, shops, trackwork DeLeuw, Cather & Co., D.C., 1966-73; mgr. engring. support Parsons

Brinckerhoff-Tudor-Bechtel, Atlanta, 1973-76; dir. railroad engring. Morrison-Knudsen Co., Inc., Boise, Idaho, 1976-78; v.p. Parsons Brinckerhoff CENTEC, Inc., McLean, Va., 1978—. Mem. adv. com. track engrs. U.S. Dept. Transp. Chmn., Cub Scout Pack, 1972-73, committeeman, 1973-75. Mem. Am. Mgmt. Assn., Am. Ry. Engring. Assn., ASCE, Am. Pub. Transit Assn., Soc. Am. Mil. Engrs., Roadmasters and Maintenance of Way Assn. of Am., Am. Ry. Bridge and Bldg. Assn., Ry. Tie Assn., Inst. of Rapid Transit, Phi Kappa Sigma. Methodist. Author tech. publs., profl. articles. Guest of Japan Ry. Civil Engring. Assn. observing, inspecting railroad and rail rapid transit facilities in Japan, 1972. Office: Suite 220 8301 Greensboro Dr McLean VA 22102

DUNN, TERRENCE HERBERT, voluntary agencies ednl. adminstr.; b. Painesville, Ohio, Jan. 20, 1947; s. Herbert H. and Hilma M. (Heikkila) D.; B.A., Salem Coll., 1968; M.A., Bowling Green State U., 1976; m. Beverly Rae Sugaski, Feb. 9, 1973; 1 son, Terrence Ian. With Firelands Area Council Boy Scouts Am., Sandusky, Ohio, 1969-73; admissions/fin. aid counselor Firelands Campus, Bowling Green State U., Huron, Ohio, 1973-75; resident adminstr. Am. Humanics, Inc., High Point (N.C.) Coll., 1976—; personnel cons. Nat. council Boy Scouts Am., 1976-79. Mem. program com. High Point YWCA, 1979—; camping and activities chmn. Boy Scouts Am., High Point, 1979, nat. chmn. Search Lab. Program, Nat. Explorers Pres.'s Congress, 1978-79, commodore Sea Exploring, 1976-79; mem. Tarheel Triad council Girl Scouts U.S.A., 1976-79. Recipient Big Bronze Horn award Boy Scouts Am., 1976; Sebago award Camp Fire Girls, 1974. Mem. Am. Personnel and Guidance Assn., Am. Coll. Personnel Assn., Assn. Profl. Dirs. YMCA. Episcopalian. Club: Rotary. Home: 2615 Ernest St High Point NC 27263 Office: 933 Montlieu Ave High Point NC 27262

DUNSTAN, EDGAR MULLINS, med. cons.; b. Rio de Janeiro, Brazil, Mar. 7, 1902 (parents Am. citizens); s. Albert Lafayette and Sarah (Silvey) D.; B.S., U. Ga., 1923; M.A., Mercer U., 1924; M.D., Emory U., 1928; m. Florene Anita Johnson, Aug. 26, 1926; 1 dau., Dorothy Dunstan Brown. Intern, Ga. Bapt. Hosp., Atlanta, 1928-29; resident Elkins (W.Va.) City Hosp., 1929-31; chief resident Baylor U. Hosp., Dallas, 1930-31; practice medicine specializing in internal medicine, Atlanta, 1946-70; cons. VA Hosp., Atlanta, 1970—; instr. internal medicine med. sch. Emory U., Atlanta, 1946-76. Active Civil Def., Atlanta. Served with M.C., AUS, 1941-46. Recipient Aven Citizenship Cup, Fulton County Med. Soc., 1955. Diplomate Am. Bd. Internal Medicine. Fellow A.C.P.; mem. A.M.A., Am. Heart Assn. Democrat. Baptist (deacon). Contbr. articles to prof. jours. Home: 710 Pinetree Dr Decatur GA 30030 Office: VA Hosp 1670 Clairmont Rd Decatur GA 30033

DUNTON, JAMES GERALD, assn. exec.; b. Circleville, Ohio, Nov. 10, 1899; s. Oscar Howard and Florence (Nightengale) D.; A.B., Harvard, 1923, M.Ed., 1928; m. Dorothy Winfough, Oct. 10, 1944. Free lance author, 1925-34; Fed. Projects dir., Ohio, 1935-37; spl. rep. Fed. N.W. Terr. Sesquicentennial Commn., 1938; editor Ohio Democracy, 1939-40; Ohio field rep. Office Govt. Reports, Exec. Office of Pres., 1940-41; dir. spl. activities Office Sec. Def., 1950-61; exec. dir. Va. Health Care Assn., 1965-75; Washington rep. Am. Chess Found., 1962—; adv. council Oliver Wendell Holmes Assn., 1966—. Mem. vets. com. Presdl. Inaugurations, 1965, 69, 77; pres. Nat. Capital U.S.O., Washington, 1966-67; mem. Nat. Council of U.S.O., 1966—; Va. State Adv. Com. Adult Services, 1972; distinguished sponsor 100th Anniversary 1st Battle of Bull Run, 1961. Served with Ambulance Corps, A.E.F., U.S. Army, 1918-19, to maj. AUS, World War II, Korea. Recipient certificate of appreciation Nat. Press Club, 1955, Commendation award Pres.'s Com. on Employment of Handicapped, 1963; decorated Army Commendation medal; hon. fellow Truman Library Inst. Mem. U.S. Army Hon. Ret. Res., SAR, Am. Legion (Nat. Comdr.'s award 1975), Vets. World War I, V.F.W., Res. Officers Assn., U.S. Army Ambulance Service Assn., Mil. Order World Wars, Ohio Soc. Washington, Soc. of Va. Presbyterian (elder). Clubs: Harvard (Washington), Nat. Assn. Execs. Author: Wild Asses, 1925; Murders in Lovers Lane, 1927; Maid and a Million Men, 1928; Counterfeit Wife, 1930; Honey's Money, 1933; Queen's Harem, 1933; (anthology) C'est La Guerre, 1927. Contbr. articles to mags., newspapers. Address: 2820 Bisvey Dr Falls Church VA 22042

DUPLAA, ETHEL CLAIRE, nurse; b. New Orleans, Nov. 8, 1934; d. August Rudolph and Ethel Elizabeth (Dorhauer) D.; R.N., Tulane U., 1953. Emergency room nurse Touro Infirmary, 1955, head nurse emergency room, 1960, nursing office supr., 1960; mem. staff nurse Charity Hosp. New Orleans, 1956, head nurse, 1957-60; industrial nurse clinic, New Orleans, 1962-65; head clinic, New Orleans, 1965-73; plant nurse Equitable Shipyards Inc., New Orleans, 1973-75, dir. med. services, 1975—, head 1st aid depts., 1975—; instr. vision conservation Am. Assn. Occupational Health Nurses, 1978. Mem. New Orleans, La. indsl. nurse assns., Am. Assn. Occupational Health Nurses, Greater New Orleans Assn. Occupational Health Nurses (treas.). Democrat. Roman Catholic. Home: 6035 Colbert St New Orleans LA 70124 Office: Equitable Shipyards Inc PO Box 8001 New Orleans LA 70182

DUPLANTIER, ADRIAN GUY, judge; b. New Orleans, Mar. 5, 1929; s. Robert and Amelie (Rivet) D.; J.D. cum laude, Loyola U., New Orleans, 1949; m. Sally Thomas, July 15, 1951; children—Adrian G., David L., Thomas, Jeanne M., Louise M., John C. Practice law, New Orleans, from 1950; judge Civil Dist. Ct., Parish of Orleans, 1974-78; judge U.S. Dist. Ct., Eastern Dist. of La., New Orleans, 1978—; lectr. Loyola U., 1960-80; mem. La. Senate, 1960-74; 1st asst. dist. atty., New Orleans, 1954-56. Del., Democratic Nat. Conv., 1964; chmn. adv. com. Jesuit High Sch.; Served with USNR. Mem. New Orleans Bar Assn., Am. Bar Assn., La. Bar Assn., Loyola U. Law Sch. Alumni Assn. (past pres.), Alpha Sigma Nu. Editor-in-chief Loyola Law Rev., 1948-49. Office: 500 Camp St New Orleans LA 70130

DUPREE, EMMETT LEE, JR., surgeon; b. Jasper, Fla., Feb. 27, 1939; s. Emmett Lee and Jimmie (Byrd) D.; A.B., Emory U., 1961, M.D., 1965. Intern Emory U. Hosp., also Grady Meml. Hosp., Atlanta, 1965-66; resident in gen. surgery Mayo Grad. Sch. Medicine, Rochester, Minn., 1966, 69-72; practice medicine specializing in gen. surgery, Jacksonville, Fla., 1972—; mem. staff St. Vincent's Med. Center, Riverside, University, St. Luke's, Bapt. Meml. hosps. Bd. dirs. DuVal County unit Am. Cancer Soc. Served with M.C., USNR, 1967-69. Diplomate Am. Bd. Surgery. Mem. Am., Fla. med. assns., Duval County Med. Soc., Priestly Surg. Soc., Mayo Alumni Assn. Contbr. articles to med. jours. Home: 4436 McGirts Blvd Jacksonville FL 32210 Office: 1820 Barrs St Jacksonville FL 32204

DUPREE, THOMAS RANDALL, advt. writer; b. Norfolk, Va., Nov. 27, 1949; s. Harry Randall Dupree and Betty Jean (Luper) Bearss; B.A. in Polit. Sci. and Theatre, Millsaps Coll., 1971; M.A. in Journalism, U. Ga., 1974; m. Mary Elizabeth Narrow, Sept. 18, 1971 (div. 1974). Mem. Sunday staff Clarion-Ledger/Jackson (Miss.) Daily News, 1965-71; newsman UPI, 1969-71; info. specialist Coll. Agr. Expt. Stas., U. Ga., Athens, 1971-75; copy chief, broadcast prodn. mgr. Gordon Marks & Co., Jackson, 1975-79; asso. creative dir. Advt. & Mktg., Jackson, 1979—; freelance scriptwriter Miss. Authority Ednl. TV, 1977—; freelance rock writer, 1971-77; contbr. to Rolling Stone, Playboy, Oui, Creem, Billboard, Record World, Fusion, Changes, Circus; books include: The Rolling Stone Record Review, 1974; actor New Stage Theatre. Named Copywriter of Year, Greater Jackson Advt. Club, 1977. Mem. Am. Film Inst., Mensa, Intertel, Lambda Chi Alpha. Methodist. Home: PO Box 16113 McWillie Station Jackson MS 39206 Office: PO Box 873 Jackson MS 39205

DUQUE, HOMER ADOLPH, city ofcl.; b. Belcher, La., Mar. 27, 1918; s. Adolph and Ann (Bullard) D.; student La. Poly., 1939-40; B.A., Centenary Coll., La., 1947; m. Melba Juanita Sisemore, Feb. 15, 1940; 1 dau., Melba Kathryn. Dist. mgr. Shreveport Times, 1946-50; mgr. B.H. Rainwater Ins. Agy., Ruston, La., 1950-55; exec. dir. Ruston Housing Authority, 1956—. Sec., v.p., pres. Housing Council La., 1967—. Served with USNR, 1943-45; PTO. Mem. Nat. Assn. Housing and Redevel. Ofcls., Am. Legion, V.F.W. Democrat. Baptist. Home: 1805 Huey Dr Ruston LA 71270 Office: 615 N Farmerville St Ruston LA 71270

DURAN, MIGUEL HERRERA, tech. tng. supr.; b. Ysleta, Tex., Sept. 30, 1934; s. Matilde and Feliciana (Herrera) D.; student N.Mex. State U., 1954, Capitol Engring. Inst., 1971, Upper Iowa U., 1978; m. Emma G. Luna, Aug. 3, 1955; children—Edsel Lee, Wyatt Ross, Mary Lynn, Michael. Electronics field engr. RCA Service Co., Cherry Hill, N.J., 1959-67; telemetry systems engr. Lockheed Electronics Co., Houston, 1967-72; tech. tng. supr. E-Systems, Inc., Garland, Tex., 1972—; instr. tech. insts. and B.S. in electronic tech. programs. Served with USAF, 1955-59. Cert. mfg. engring. technologist. Mem. IEEE, Am. Soc. Mfg. Engrs. (sr.). Democrat. Roman Catholic. Home: 1202 Carroll Dr Garland TX 75041 Office: E-Systems Inc Space Systems Dept 4-50350-W PO Box 226118 Dallas TX 75266

DUREMDES, GENEROSO DIVINAGRACIA, surgeon; b. Davao, Philippines, Nov. 13, 1937; s. Godofredo D. and Soledad D. (Divinagracia) D.; M.D., Far Eastern U., 1960; m. Janelle F. Bermejo, May 18, 1961; 1 son, Gene B. Intern, St. Elizabeth Hosp., Elizabeth, N.J., 1962-63; resident in surgery Bronx Municipal Hosp. Center, Albert Einstein Coll. Medicine, 1963-67; chief resident, asst. instr. gen. surgery Albert Einstein Coll. Medicine, Yeshiva U., Bronx, N.Y., 1967-68; chief resident, instr. pediatric surgery Wyler Children's Hosp., U. Chgo., 1968-69; staff surgeon Princeton (W.Va.) Community Hosp., 1969—; pres. Princeton Surg. Group, Inc., 1976—. Diplomate Am. Bd. Surgery. Fellow A.C.S., Southeastern Surg. Congress; mem. AMA, So., W.Va. med. assns., Soc. Philippines Surgeons in Am. Baptist. Clubs: Gideon Internat. Contbr. articles to med. jours. Home: PO Box 1719 Princeton WV 24740 Office: Med Arts Clinic PO Box 1374 Princeton WV 24740

DURHAM, DONALD LEE, oceanographer; b. McKinney, Ky., May 1, 1942; s. Russell E. and Nina J. (Denham) D.; A.B. cum laude, Centre Coll., 1964; M.A., Tex. A&M U., 1967, Ph.D., 1972; m. Nancy Elizabeth Graves, July 29, 1967; children—Kimberly Elizabeth, Russell Graves. Research engr. E.I. Dupont de Nemoire Research Lab., Richmond, Va., 1964; research asst. Tex. A&M U., College Sta., 1965-69, research asso., 1969-72; research oceanographer U.S. Army Engr. Waterways Expt. Sta., Vicksburg, Miss., 1972-78; oceanographer Naval Ocean Research & Devel. Activity, Nat. Space Tech. Labs., Station, Miss., 1978—; environ. and engring. cons. Corning Glass Works, De Gaw Engring. Co., Tex. Instruments, Inc., A.H. Glenn & Assos. and other firms, 1965—. Mem. troop com. Andrew Jackson council Boy Scouts Am., 1976-78; mem. bldg. com. chmn. YMCA, Vicksburg, 1973-78. Recipient Service awards Dept. of Army, 1974, 75, U.S. Pres.'s Letter of Commendation, Dept. Army, 1976, Spl. Achievement Commendation, Dept. Navy, 1979. Mem. Am. Soc. Oceanography, Marine Tech. Soc., Am. Soc. of Limnology and Oceanography, Am. Geophys. Union, ASCE (reviewer 1975-79), Miss. Acad. Scis., Phi Beta Chi (pres. 1963-64), Sigma Xi. Methodist (adminstrv. bd.). Clubs: Kiwanis (Disting. Service award 1978, dir. 1973-78), Lions. Contbr. articles on oceanography and environ. engring. to sci. jours. Home: 489 Lakeshore Dr HW Carriere MS 39426 Office: NORDA Code 115 NSTL Station MS 39529

DURHAM, FLOYD WESLEY, JR., economist, educator; b. Yuma, Ariz., Feb. 9, 1930; s. Floyd Wesley and Inez (Irvin) D.; B.A., N. Tex. State U., 1951, M.A., 1952; Ph.D., U. Okla., 1963; m. Patricia Keehan, May 24, 1973; children—Mark Kipling, Ronald Chappell. Claimsman, Liberty Mutual Ins. Co., Boston and Ft. Worth, 1955-58; mem. faculty dept. econs. Tex. Christian U., Ft. Worth, 1960—, prof., 1971—. Cons. econs., 1964—. Pres., Suicide Prevention Tarrant County, 1968-69. Bd. dirs. Ft. Worth Literacy Council, 1963-70. Served with AUS, 1953-55. Danforth Found. grantee, 1969-70. Mem. Am., So. econ. assns., Southwestern, Western social sci. assns., A.A.U.P., Beta Gamma Sigma, Omicron Delta Epsilon, Lambda Chi Alpha. Author: A Pilot Methodological Study to Determine Dibilitating Conditions, 1967; The Trinity River Paradox: Flood and Famine, 1976. Contbr. articles to profl. jours. Home: 4701 Boulder Run Fort Worth TX 76109

DURIG, JAMES ROBERT, chemist, coll. dean; b. Washington, Pa., Apr. 30, 1935; s. Roberta Wilda (Mounts) D.; B.A., Washington and Jefferson Coll., 1958, D.Sc. (hon.), 1979; Ph.D. in Phys. Chemistry, M.I.T., 1962; m. Katherine Marlene Sprowls, Sept. 1, 1955; children—Douglas Tybor, Bryan Robert, Stacey Ann. Asst. prof. chemistry U. S.C., 1962-65, asso. prof., 1965-68, prof., 1968-70, Ednl. Found. prof. chemistry, 1970-73, prof., 1973—, dean Coll. Sci. and Math., 1973—. Served with Chem. Corps, U.S. Army, 1963-64. Recipient Russell award U. S.C., 1968; Alexander von Humboldt Sr. Scientist award Govt. of W. Ger., 1976. Mem. Am. Chem. Soc. (S.E.-Piedmont sect. Charles A. Stone award 1975, Memphis sect. So. Chemist award 1976), Am. Phys. Soc., Soc. Applied Spectroscopy, Coblentz Soc. (award for outstanding research in molecular spectroscopy 1970, governing bd. 1972-76, pres. 1974-76), Internat. Union Pure and Applied Chemists (chmn. sub-commn. on infrared and Raman spectroscopy 1975—, mem. commn. on molecular spectra and structure 1978—), Blue Key Soc., Phi Beta Kappa (pres. Alpha chpt. S.C. 1970), Sigma Xi, Phi Lambda Upsilon. Presbyterian. Research, numerous publs. in field; editor: Vibrational Spectra and Structure, 8 vols., 1972-77; editor Jour. Raman Spectroscopy, 1979—; mem. editorial bd. Jour. Molecular Structure, 1972—. Office: Coll Sci and Math U SC Columbia SC 29208

DURKEE, DALE CROWELL, pub. utility co. exec.; b. Elyria, Ohio, June 9, 1938; s. Orin Eugene and Harriett Amelia (Crowell) D.; B.B.A., Baldwin-Wallace Coll., 1960; M.B.A., Case-Western Res. U., 1964; m. Carol Sue Casey, Aug. 11, 1962; 1 son, Tyler Aaron. Sr. job analyst Fed. Res. Bank of Cleve., 1960-63; mgr. exec. and staff devel. Central Nat. Bank of Cleve., 1963-67; mgr. recruitment and tng. Stouffer Foods Corp., Cleve., 1968; asst. dir. personnel May Dept. Stores Co., 1968-72; mgr. orgn. devel. and tng. Fla. Power and Light Co., Miami, 1972—; asso. Wyvern Research Assos., San Francisco, 1980—. Chmn. Westside solicitations Boy Scouts Am., Cleve., 1970-72; mem. gen. adv. bd. Miami-Dade Community Coll., 1977—; mem. adv. bd. S.E. Electric Exchange Public Utility Mgmt. Program, 1979-80; mem. adv. bd. for adult learning Fla. Internat. U., 1977-78. Served with USCGR, 1956-66. Recipient Danforth award for leadership, 1956. Mem. Human Resource Planning Soc. (profl. devel. com.), Am. Soc. Tng. and Devel. (dir. Miami chpt. 1977—), Am. Soc. Personnel Adminstrn., Cleve. Jr. C. of C. (dir. 1971-72, Outstanding Dir. award, Keyman award), Case-Western Res. U. Grad Sch. Bus. Alumni (dir. 1970-72). Republican. Lutheran. Home: 8430 SW 142d Ave Miami FL 33183 Office: 9250 W Flagler St Miami FL 33152

DURLACH, MARCUS RUSSELL, mech. engring. cons., artist; b. Bklyn., Jan. 27, 1911; s. Marcus Russell and Nellie Kinard (Schureman) D.; M.E., Stevens Inst. Tech., 1933; M.Sc., Cornell U., 1946; m. Jeannette Vivian Lorber, June 29, 1941; children—Marcus Russell, Richard Stevens. Tchr. Bklyn. Tech. High Sch., 1934-41; test engr., supr. U.S. Navy, Charleston, S.C., 1941-45; asso. prof. engring. U. S.C., Columbia, 1945-52; cons. engr., sr. partner Durlach, O'Neal & Jenkins, Columbia, 1946—. Mem. S.C. Bd. Engring. Examiners. Exhibited in one-man shows at Columbia Coll., Ft. Jackson Gallery, Columbia Mus. Art; exhibited in group shows at Columbia Gallery, Columbia Mus. Art represented in permanent collections. Chmn. curriculum com. Midlands Tech. Inst., Columbia, 1969-78. Recipient various art awards. Registered profl. engr., N.C., S.C., Ga., Nev., Wis. Fellow Am. Soc. M.E. (profl. practice com. 1972—), Am. Soc. Heating Ventilation Air Conditioning Engrs.; mem. Artists Guild Columbia (pres. 1973-74), S.C. Guild of Artists, Nat. (dir. 1966-69), S.C. (pres. 1964), Columbia (pres. 1957) socs. profl. engrs., S.C. Watercolor Soc. (pres.), So. Watercolor Soc. (pres. 1979—), S.A.R. Rotarian (pres. club 1963-64). Home: 6025 Lakeshore Dr Columbia SC 29206 Office: 2119 Santee Ave Columbia SC 29205

DURNEY, JOHN HENRY, mayor; b. Mt. Kisco, N.Y., Aug. 10, 1917; s. William H. and Elizabeth T. (Hoffman) D.; student Columbia U., 1937-38; grad. N Am. Flight Sch., 1943; m. Ann Carol Oberdorf, June 17, 1972; children—Beatrice E. Durney Reis, Katherine S.; stepchildren—Timothy, Edmund. With Suburban Propane Co., Whippany, N.J., 1940—, regional mgr., 1961—; dir. Community Bank of West Pasco, Port Richey, Fla., 1970—; police commr. City of Port Richey, 1967-75, mcpl. judge, 1967-75, mayor, 1967-75, 78—; mem. Ind. Fire Co., Mt. Kisco, 1941—. Mem. Citizens Com. for Improved Law Enforcement, State of Fla., 1967-70; mem. engring. and constrn. com. Fire Prevention Conf., State of Fla., 1967-69; mem. New Port Richey Transp. Com., 1976-77; founder Group of Concerned Citizens and Parents to Bring Sch. Bus Safety to Pasco, 1973; bd. dirs. Pinellas-Pasco Dist. Mental Health Bd., 1978—; mem. Gov.'s Pasco County Adv. Com., State of Fla., 1970-74; alt. mem. L.P. Gas Adv. Com., State Treasurers Office, State of Fla., 1967—. Served to capt. USAF. Recipient Outstanding Citizen award Greater New Port Richey Jaycees, 1965; Service to Mankind award West Pasco Sertoma Club, 1973; Disting. Service citation Am. Cancer Soc., 1969, Cert. of Appreciation, City of Port Richey, 1975. Mem. Greater New Port Richey C. of C. (dir. 1975-77), Mcpl. Judges Assn., Ga. LP Gas Assn., Air Force Assn. Clubs: Moose, Eagles, Elks, Lions (pres. 1964—). Office: PO Box 309 Port Richey FL 33568

DURNIAK, JAMES DENNIS, aero. engr.; b. Sewickley, Pa., Oct. 24, 1946; s. Peter Richard and Nell Francis (Routh) D.; B.S., LeTourneau Coll., 1968; M.S., Air Force Inst. Tech., 1977; m. Sharon Marie Moore, Aug. 23, 1969. Heavy equipment engr. R.G. Le Tourneau Inc., Longview, Tex., 1967-68; commd. 2d lt. USAF, 1969, advanced through grades to capt., 1972; navigator Grand Forks AFB, 1974-75; project engr., turbofan engine, Wright Patterson AFB, Ohio, 1977—, F-107 liaison with USN, Washington, 1978—. Decorated DFC, Air medal with 4 oak leaf clusters. Mem. Am. Inst. Aeros. and Astronautics, Air Force Assn. Roman Catholic. Home: 205 Yoakum Pkwy Apt 720 Alexandria VA 22304 Office: JCMPO-PM 3 Washington DC 20360

DUSEK, EDWIN RALPH, research lab. exec.; b. San Angelo, Tex., Dec. 30, 1924; s. John J. and Lucille (Schuch) D.; B.A., U. Mo., 1947; M.A., State U. Iowa, 1949, Ph.D., 1951; m. Mary Helen Armstrong, Aug. 15, 1952; children—David Armstrong, Jonathan Thomas. Asst. prof. psychology U. Ark., 1951-53; research psychologist Quartermaster Research and Devel. Lab., Natick, Mass., 1953-56; chief psychology lab. Army Research Inst. Environ. Medicine, 1960-71, dir. individual tng. and performance lab., 1971-72; dir. individual testing and performance lab. Army Research Inst. for Behavioral and Social Scis., Alexandria, Va., 1973—. Bd. dirs. Needham (Mass.) YMCA, 1969-71. Served with USAAF, 1943-46. Fellow Human Factors Soc., Am. Psychol. Assn.; mem. Research Soc. Am. (past br. pres.), Sigma Xi. Author reports, articles. Home: 6309 Mori St McLean VA 22101 Office: 5001 Eisenhower Alexandria VA 22233

DUST, GERALD EDWARD, restaurant chain exec.; b. Joplin, Mo., Sept. 7, 1954; s. Orville Gerald and Enid Marjorie (Pribble) D.; student Mo. So. State Coll., 1974-77; m. Ruby Jo Dake, Mar. 27, 1976; children—Travis Edward, Tisha Lynett. Technician, ABC Ambulance, Joplin, 1970-72; mgr. Derby Oil Co., Joplin, 1973-76; office mgr. State Farm Ins. Co., Joplin, 1976-77; dist. mgr. Taco Hut, Inc., Joplin, 1977-78, asst. franchise dir., Tulsa, 1978-80, franchise dir., 1980—. Served with USMC, 1972-74. Mem. Nat. Inst. Food Industry, Mo. Restaurant Assn., Jaycees. Mormon. Home: 5947 E 26th St Tulsa OK 74114 Office: Taco Hut Inc 3621 S 73d E Ave Tulsa OK 74145

DUTTON, BOB WAYNE, accountant; b. Borger, Tex., Mar. 12, 1947; s. Bob and Mary Frances (Ball) D.; B.B.A., Tex. Technol. U., 1969; m. Lettie Ann Ingram, Jan. 28, 1968; children—Robin Elizabeth, Lara Ann. Auditor, Fed. Res. Bank of Dallas, 1972-73; staff accountant Elms, Faris & Co., C.P.A.'s, Midland, Tex., 1974-76, partner, 1977—; dir. Diversified Warehousing, Inc. Served with Security Agy., U.S. Army, 1969-72. Decorated Bronze Star; recipient 1st pl. project award in environment Tex. Jaycees, 1975-76, named Outstanding Young Man Am., 1976. Mem. Am. Inst. C.P.A.'s, Tex. Soc. C.P.A.'s, Am. Inst. Banking, Midland C. of C., Odessa Jaycees (sec.-treas. 1975-76, dir. 1976-77). Methodist. Club: Midland Rotary. Home: 1901 Hughes St Midland TX 79701 Office: PO Box 2519 Midland TX 79702

DUVAL, CLAUDE BERWICK, lawyer, state senator; b. Houma, La., Oct. 24, 1914; s. Stanwood and Mamie (Richardson) D.; student La. State U., 1931-32; LL.B., Tulane U., 1937; m. Betty Bowman, Apr. 6, 1938; 1 dau., Dorothy. Admitted to La. bar, 1937; practiced in Houma, 1937—; mem. law firm Duval, Arceneaux, Lewis & Funderburk; chmn. bd. First Nat. Bank Houma; dir. Pelican Lake Oyster & Packing Co., Ltd., Duval-Whitney-Stevenson, Inc. Mem. La. Senate, 1967—. Mem. com. ARC, 1947-48; chmn. 3d Congl. dist. Area Cancer Drive, 1949-50; mem. devel. council Tulane U., 1958; trustee Pub. Affairs Research Council; bd. dirs. Council for Better La.; state chmn. Radio Free Europe, 1968. Campaign mgr. deLesseps S. Morrison, Democratic candidate for gov. La., 1959; candidate for lt. gov. La., 1963. Served from 2d lt. to capt. USMCR, 1941-46; PTO. Decorated Bronze Star, Purple Heart, Letter of Commendation, Presdl. Unit Citation recipient award as Outstanding Young Man of Year, Houma Jr. C. of C., 1947. Mem. Am., La. (ho. of dels. 1957-60, mem. law reform com.) bar assns., Am. Legion (La. comdr. 1950; mem. nat. exec. com. 1952-54), La. State (pres. 1961-62), Houma (pres. 1959) chambers commerce, Young Men's Bus. Clubs La. (state pres. 1948). Democrat. Episcopalian. Mason (Shriner), Elk, Rotarian (pres. 1958), Houma Exchange (pres. 1940). Home: 18 Country Club Dr Houma LA 70360 Office: 504 Belanger St Houma LA 70360

DUVAL, CLIVE LIVINGSTON, II, state senator Va.; b. N.Y.C., June 20, 1912; s. Clive Livingston and Augusta Harper (Lynde) DuV.; grad. magna cum laude Groton Sch. 1931; B.A. summa cum laude, Yale, 1935, LL.B., 1938; m. Susan Holdrege Bontecou, June 21, 1940; children—Susan D. (Mrs. Robert Phipps), Clive Livingston, David R., Daniel H. Admitted to N.Y. bar, 1939, D.C. bar, 1957, Va. bar, 1970; practiced in N.Y.C., 1938-42, Poughkeepsie, N.Y., 1946-51; spl. asst. to undersec. Dept. Army, Washington, 1951-52; asst. gen. counsel Dept. Def., Washington, 1953-55; gen. counsel USIA, Washington, 1955-59; asso. law firms Milbank, Tweed, Hadley and McCloy, Washington, 1959-71, Bean, Kinney, Korman & Hylton, Arlington, Va., 1971—. Mem. Va. Ho. of Dels., 1966-72, Va. Senate, 1972—, chmn. Senate Democratic Caucus, 1980—. Mem. Va. Citizens Consumer Council, 1968—, Democratic State Central Com. Va., 1968-76. Served to lt. comdr. USNR, 1942-46. Named Outstanding State Legislator in U.S. for achievements in conservation legislation Nat. Wildlife Fedn., 1969. Mem. Va., D.C., Arlington bar assns., Arlington, Fairfax chambers commerce, Nat. Trust for Historic Preservation, Izaac Walton League, Sierra Club, Va. Wildlife Fedn., Am. Legion, VFW (judge adv. 1968—), Nat. Press Club. Democrat. Presbyn. Clubs: Yale, Metropolitan (Washington). Home: 1214 Buchanan St McLean VA 22101 Office: PO Box 749 Arlington VA 22216

DU VAL, MILES P., JR., ret. naval officer; b. Portsmouth, Va., Apr. 19, 1896; s. Miles P. and Minnie Lee (Chalkley) DuV.; B.S., U.S. Naval Acad., 1918, student U.S. Naval War Coll., 1925-26; U.S. Naval Post Grad. Sch., 1930-31; M.F.S., Fgn. Service Sch., Georgetown U., 1937. Commd. ensign USN, 1918, and advanced through grades to capt., 1945; served as comdg. officer, U.S.S. Dupont, 1933-35, participated in naval demonstration off Cuban ports, 1933-34; sec. Shore Sta. Devel. Bd., Navy Dept., Washington, 1936-38; comdg. officer U.S.S. Antares, 1939-40; capt. of port, Balboa, C.Z., in charge marine operations of Pacific subdiv. of Panama Canal, 1941-44; planned and coordinated enlargement of Balboa Harbor, 1942-43; developed high level terminal lake plan for operational improvement of Panama Canal, 1943; comdg. officer U.S.S. Dade, 1944-46, participated in Okinawa campaign, 1945; designated as Navy Dept. liaison officer and coordinator for modernization studies of Panama Canal by Sec. of Navy, 1946; ret. active service, 1949. Vice pres., gen. cons. John F. Stevens Hall of Fame com., 1969—. Bd. dirs. Gorgas Meml. Inst. Tropical and Preventive Medicine. Decorated Legion of Merit (Army), 1945, World War I Victory medal with Atlantic and Grand Fleet clasps, 1918, Am. Defense with Fleet and Base clasps, 1939-41, Am. campaign, 1941-44, Aslatic-Pacific campaign with bronze star, 1945. Recipient Roger Brooke Taney award Md. div. Sons Confederate Vets.; medal of honor Nat. Soc. D.A.R.; Gold medallion Am. Revolution Bicentennial Commn. Fellow A.A.A.S.; mem. Va. Hist. Soc., Naval Hist. Found., Soc. of Va. in Washington (past v.p.), Permanent Internat. Assn. Nav. Congresses (life), U.S. Naval Inst., U.S. Strategic Inst., Soc. Am. Mil. Engrs., Panama Hist. Soc. (corr. mem.), Panama Canal Soc. of Washington (pres.), Panama Canal Natural History Soc. (past v.p.), Baronial Order Magna Charta, Mil. Order Crusades, Jamestowne Soc., Phi Alpha Theta (hon.). Clubs: Explorers; Cosmos, Army and Navy (Washington); Yacht (N.Y.C.). Author: Series on Panama Canal: Cadiz to Cathay, 4th edit., 1975; And the Mountains Will Move, 2d edit., 1969; Let the Waters Rise, 1980; Matthew Fontaine Maury: Benefactor of Man Kind, 1964; Sam Houston: The Washington of the Vast Southwest, 1966; George Rogers Clark: Conqueror of the Old Northwest, 1970; John Frank Stevens: Civil Engineer, Explorer, Diplomat and Statesman, 1976; also papers on interoceanic canal history and problems. Home: 5120 King William Rd Richmond VA 23225

DU VAL, ROBERT GLINN, accountant; b. West View, Va., Nov. 9, 1912; s. William Vernon and Mary Blanche (Glinn) DuV.; B.S., U. Richmond, 1950; M.B.A., U. Chgo., 1951. Pvt. practice bookkeeping and accounting, Richmond, Va., 1931-40; asst. prof. accounting U. Southwestern La., Lafayette, 1952-63, asso. prof., 1963-78; asso. prof. acctg. Fla. Internat. U., 1978-79; field auditor Horwath & Horwath, Chgo., summers 1952-57. Served with AUS, 1941-47. Decorated Bronze Star; C.P.A., Va., La. Mem. Phi Beta Kappa Assn. of S.W. La. (pres. 1972-73), La. Soc. C.P.A.'s (sec.-treas. chpt. 1962-64), AAUP, La. Assn. Higher Edn., Am. Accounting Assn., Delta Sigma Pi, Phi Beta Kappa. Baptist. Address: Box 4811 Shreveport LA 71104

DUVALL, ARLINE MARIE, educator; b. Sherwood Forest, Md., Nov. 2, 1927; d. Grover Cleveland and Beulah Vivian (Skipper) D.; B.S.P.H.N., U. N.C., 1956; M.P.H., U. MIch., 1959; Ed.D., Columbia U., 1972. Phys. sci. aide USN Engring. Exptl. Lab., Annapolis, Md., 1944; nurse Annapolis Emergency Hosp., 1948; public health nurse Anne Arundel County (Md.) Health Dept., 1948-55, public health nursing supr., 1955-58; instr. U. Ala. Sch. Nursing, University, 1959-62; asst. prof. nursing Vanderbilt U. Sch. Nursing, Nashville, 1962-68; asso. prof. nursing Clemson (S.C.) U. Coll. Nursing, 1971-75, dir. baccalaurate program in nursing, 1973-76, prof. nursing, 1975—. USPHS trainee, 1954-55, 69-70, Bixler scholar, 1968-69. Mem. Nat. League Nursing (accreditation visitor 1975—), Am. Nurses Assn., Am. Public Health Assn., AAUP, S.C. Public Health Assn., Sigma Theta Tau, Delta Kappa Gamma, DAR, Nat. Soc. Descendents Mareen Duvall. Democrat. Episcopalian. Home: 219 Grove Dr Clemson SC 29631 Office: Clemson U Coll Nursing Clemson SC 29631

DVORETZKY, ISAAC, petroleum co. exec.; b. Houston, Jan. 24, 1928; s. Max and Anna (Greenfield) D.; B.A., Rice U., 1948, M.A., 1950, Ph.D. in Chemistry, 1952; m. Zelda Benowitz, June 29, 1958; children—Rachel Leah, Aaron Benjamin, Rebecca Esther. With Shell Oil Co., various locations, 1952—, mgr. unconventional raw materials dept., Emeryville, Calif., 1969-72, mgr. profl. recruitment, univ. relations Shell Devel. Co. div., Houston, 1972—. Exchange scientist Royal Dutch/Shell Lab., Amsterdam, 1958-59; mem. council Gordon Research Confs., 1972—. Bd. dirs. San Francisco Bay Area Sci. Fair, 1971-72; mem. grad. council Rice U., 1977-79; mem. Houston Commn. for Jewish Edn., 1976-78; v.p. Houston Kashruth Assn., 1979—. Mem. Am. Chem. Soc., Phi Beta Kappa Alumni Assn. Greater Houston (dir. 1976-78), Phi Beta Kappa, Sigma Xi, Phi Lambda Upsilon. Jewish (synagogue officer, trustee). Contbr. articles to profl. jours. Patentee hydrocarbon chemistry and catalysis. Home: 9714 Kit St Houston TX 77096 Office: PO Box 1380 Houston TX 77001

DWIGGINS, CLAUDIUS WILLIAM, JR., chemist; b. Amity, Ark., May 11, 1933; s. Claudius William and Lillian (Scott) D.; B.S., U. Ark., 1954, M.S., 1956, Ph.D. (Am. Oil Co. fellow, Coulter-Jones scholar), 1958. With U.S. Dept. of Energy, Bartlesville (Okla.) Tech. Center, 1958—, chemist, 1958-60, project leader surface physics project, 1960-65, project leader petroleum composition research project, 1965—. Mem. Am. Chem. Soc., N.Y. Acad. Scis., A.A.A.S., Am. Crystallographic Assn., Am. Inst. Physics, Sigma Xi (sec. 1966-67), Alpha Chi Sigma, Delta Sigma Phi (treas. 1952). Contbr. articles to profl. jours. Home: 1211 S Keeler St Bartlesville OK 74003 Office: US Dept Energy Bartlesville OK 74003

DWYER, MICHAEL THOMAS, accountant; b. Somerville, N.J., July 21, 1945; s. Paul Richard and Elizabeth Claire (McBrairty) D.; B.B.A., Angelo State U., 1972; m. Sara K. Peyton, Aug. 15, 1970; children—Erin Elizabeth. With Arthur Andersen & Co., Houston, 1972—, audit mgr., 1976—. Sec., treas. Southmeadow Property Owners Assn., Houston. Served with USAF, 1966-70. Mem. Tex. Soc. C.P.A.'s, Am. Inst. C.P.A.'s. Office: 425 Soledad Suite 600 San Antonio TX 78205

DYCHE, JAMES DOAK, ranch exec.; b. El Paso, Tex., Dec. 4, 1951; s. M.F. Dees; ed. Tex. A&M. Mgr., Pecos County Airport, Ft. Stockton, Tex., 1971-72, Dyche Ranch, Ft. Stockton, 1973—; owner Western Enterprises; ind. oil field welder; riding instr., since 1972—; trainer show horses; judge Quarter horse shows. Pres., Pecos County Sheriffs Posse, 1979—. Mem. Profl. Rodeo Cowboys Assn., Am. Quarter Horse Assn., Tex. Quarter Horse Assn., Tex. Polled Hereford Assn., Am. Police Res. Address: PO Box 329 Fort Stockton TX 79735

DYE, BRAD, lt. gov. Miss.; b. Charleston, Miss., Dec. 20, 1933; s. Bradford Johnson and Maylise (Dogan) D.; B.A. in Bus. Adminstrn., U. Miss., 1957, postgrad. Sch. Law, 1959; m. Donna Bess Bailey; children—Hamp, Ford, Rick. Admitted to Miss. bar, 1959; practiced in Grenada, Miss., 1959-61; mem. Miss. Ho. of Reps., 1959-63, Miss. Senate, from 1963; mem. U.S. Senate Judiciary Com., 1961-64, Miss. Workmen's Compensation Commn., 1965-67; dir. Miss. Agrl. and Indsl. Bd., 1968-71; treas. State of Miss., Jackson, 1972-76, lt. gov., 1980—; pres. Jackson Savs. and Loan Assn., 1976-79. Mem. adminstrv. bd. Galloway United Meth. Ch.; chmn. Grenada County Cancer Drive, 1959, Miss. Heart Assn., Central Miss. chpt. ARC; bd. dirs. United Way, fund chmn., 1968; former coach minor league baseball and football Northside YMCA, now basketball coach; bd. dirs. Andrew Jackson council Boy Scouts Am. Mem. U. Miss. Bus. Alumni Assn. (charter pres.), Phi Alpha Delta, Pi Kappa Alpha. Office: Office of Lt Gov State Capitol Bldg Jackson MS 39205

DYE, FRANKLIN HADDOX, state ofcl.; b. Honolulu, Aug. 6, 1927; s. Harry A. and Lyau D. (Dung) D.; student U. Toledo, 1948-49; B.S., Boston U., 1952, Ed.M., 1955; Ph.D., Ohio State U., 1968; m. Dora Elaine Kelly, Aug. 6, 1960; 1 dau., Nani Elaine Kelly. Instr., Colby Jr. Coll., New London, N.H., 1952-57; speed typing specialist, edn. cons. Royal Typewriter Co., N.Y.C., 1957-61, 62-64; chmn. dept. bus. Mass. Bay Community Coll., Boston, 1961-62; instr. Eastern Ill. U., 1964-65; research asso. Nat. Center for Research in Vocat. Edn., Columbus, Ohio, 1965-67; vocat. tchr. Ferris State Coll., Big Rapids, Mich., 1967-68; prof. No. Ill. U., DeKalb, 1968-71, Chgo. State U., 1971-74, N.E. La. U., Monroe, 1974-77; div. dir. G.B. Cooley Hosp. for Retarded Citizens, W. Monroe, La., 1977-79; state supr. vocat. edn. for the handicapped La. Dept. Edn., Baton Rouge, 1979—; nat. lectr. vocat. office edn., 1964—, vocat. spl. needs edn., 1968—; cons. Chgo. Title and Trust Co., 1971-73, Field Enterprises Edn. Corp., Chgo., 1973-74, Ouachita Parish Personnel System, Monroe, 1978-79. Served with U.S. Army, 1945-47. Recipient citation Office Edn. Assn., 1974. Mem. Am. Vocat. Assn., La. Vocat. Assn., Nat. Bus. Edn. Assn., Council for Exceptional Children, Nat. Assn. Vocat. Edn. Spl. Needs Personnel, Ouachita Assn. for Retarded Citizens, Pi Omega Pi, Delta Pi Epsilon. Presbyterian. Clubs: Rotary, Shriners, Masons, High 12 Internat. Author: (with others) Typewriting Speed/Control Builders, 1972; contbr. articles to profl. publs. Office: La Dept of Education PO Box 44064 Baton Rouge LA 70804

DYER, CAROLYN ELIZABETH, nurse, hosp. ofcl.; b. Lucedale, Miss., July 11, 1945; d. Horace Edward and Dorothy Lavelle (Gibson) D.; lic. practical nurse Richmond P. Hobson Tech. Inst., 1969; Asso. Nursing, George Corley Wallace Community Coll., 1974. Technician-scrub Bryan W. Whitfield Meml. Hosp., Demopolis, Ala., 1964-69, practical nurse, 1969-74, registered nurse, 1974—, supr. operating room dept., 1979—. Mem. Am. Nurses Assn., Ala. Nurses Assn., U. Ala. Alumni Assn., Am. Horse Protection Assn., Marengo County Nursing Soc. Baptist. Home: PO Box 269 Demopolis AL 36732 Office: PO Box 890 Demopolis AL 36732

DYER, DEWEY ALFRED, naval officer, former corp. exec.; b. North Andover, Mass., June 23, 1925; s. Edward D. and Rose (Desjardins) D.; Yale, 1944, Suffolk U., 1951, 1952; m. Jean Boyington, Mar. 19, 1946; children—Dwight, Jackqueline, Dianne, Daniel, David. Operator flying sch. and charter service, Lawrence, Mass., 1947-50, constrn. co., North Andover, 1950-52; sr. field engr. Kemper, Boston, 1952-57; dir. community and employee relations Raytheon, Lexington, 1957-60; mng. dir. indsl. systems div. Blickman, Weehawken, N.J., 1960-62; asst. v.p. operations Canteen Corp., Chgo., 1963-65, dir. concessions div., v.p., 1965—; chmn. bd. Sportscene Pub. Corp., N.Y.C., 1962-67; v.p. ITT Food Services, 1968-70; sr. v.p. Great No. Corp., 1970-71; chmn. bd., pres., chief exec. Applied Mgmt. Sci. Corp., 1970-78; recalled to active duty at capt. U.S. Navy, 1979; now spl. asst. to chief naval edn. and tng., Pensacola, Fla.; dir. Green Mt. Communications and Publs.; founder chmn. Les Savants Internaux, Ltd. Mem. faculty Merrimack Coll., 1960-62. Mem. Lawrence Citizens Com. for Indsl. Devel., 1956-58. Bd. dirs., pres. Essex County Bd. Trade, 1956-63. Trustee St. Jude Found., St. John's Mil. Acad., Delafield, Wis., Outdoors Unltd. Served with USNR, 1943-47. Mem. Mass. Soc. Profl. Engrs., Silver Wings. Roman Catholic. Author several books on mgmt., aviation; writer syndicated column in mgmt. field. Home: 4320 Roxborough Pl Coventry Estates Pensacola FL 32504 Office: CNET HQ Code 019 Bldg 624 USNAS Pensacola FL 32508

DYER, DOLORES, psychologist; b. Ft. Worth; d. William Leon and Frances Louise (Cargill) D.; B.A. with highest honors, N. Tex. State U., 1963; grad. (scholar) So. Meth. U. Grad. Sch., 1964-65; Ph.D. (fellow), Southwestern Med. Sch., U. Tex., Dallas, 1973; 1 son, Michael Dexter Allen. Adminstr., Child and Adolescent Community Mental Health Center, Dallas, 1969-70; asst. to dir. Dallas County Mental Health and Mental Retardation Center, 1970-73, project dir. Dallas County Comprehensive Child Care Program, 1973; dir. Dallas Commn. on Children and Youth, 1974; pvt. practice psychology, Dallas, 1975—; tchr. Adult Sch. Continuing Edn., So. Meth. U.; trainer Suicide Prevention Center of Dallas; trainer group tng. program Dallas Group Psychotherapy Soc. Mem. children and youth adv. com. Dallas Office of Human Devel.; bd. dirs. Dallas County Mental Health Assn. Mem. Am., Tex., Dallas psychol. assns. Democrat. Episcopalian. Clubs: The 500 Inc. Home: 4031 Inwood Rd Dallas TX 75209 Office: 2505 Wycliff Dallas TX 75219

DYER, IRWIN ALLEN, univ. dean; b. Dahlonega, Ga., Feb. 8, 1921; s. Marion Lon and Carrie Caldonia (Moose) D.; B.S.A., U. Ga., 1946, M.S.A., 1947; Ph.D., U. Ill., Champaign-Urbana, 1950; m. Allene Liddell Hodgson, Nov. 26, 1943; children—Barbara Louise Dyer Currie, Irwin Allen, Patricia Anne Dyer Reil. Research asst. U. Ga., 1946-47, U. Ill., 1947-50; asst. prof. U. Ga., Athens, 1950-51, asso. prof., 1951-52; adv. Ministry Agr., El Salvador, C.Am., 1952-54; asso. prof. Wash. State U., Pullman, 1955-61, prof., 1961-78, chmn. nutrition program, 1968-70, asso. dean Grad. Sch., 1970-75, chief party to U. Jordan, Amman, head dept. animal prodn. and protection, 1975-77, prof. animal scis., asso. dean Grad. Sch., 1977-78; dean Coll. Agr., Tex. A&I U., Kingsville, 1978—, prof. nutrition, Title XII officer, 1978—. Served to lt. comdr. USNR, 1943-46. Recipient award of Appreciation, Wash. Beef Commn., 1973, plaque Wash. Cattle Feeders, 1973. Mem. AAAS, Am. Inst. Nutrition, Am. Inst. Biol. Scis., Am. Registry Cert. Animal Scientists, Am. Soc. Animal Sci. (Disting. Service award Western sect. 1975), Council Agrl. Sci. and Tech., Sigma Xi, Alpha Tau Alpha, Aghon, Chi Gamma Iota. Republican. Presbyterian. Club: Kiwanis (Disting. Service award 1977). Author: Sheep Production in Arid and Semi-arid Areas, 1979; editor: (with C. C. O'Mary) The Feedlot, 1972, 2d edit., 1977; Commercial Beef Cattle Production, 1973, 2d edit., 1978; Animal Growth and Nutrition, 1969; contbr. articles in field to profl. jours. Home: W 1217 W Santa Gertrudis Ave Kingsville TX 78363 Office: Tex A&I U Kingsville TX 78363

DYER, ROBERT GLENN, mfg. co. exec.; b. North Baltimore, Ohio, Oct. 18, 1940; s. Emery Glenn and Ethel Otoey (Farris) D.; B.S. in Speech, Defiance (Ohio) Coll., 1963; B.A. in Acctg., Baldwin-Wallace Coll., Berea, Ohio, 1975; M.B.A., U. Dallas, 1977; m. Regina C. Dominick, Aug. 28, 1961; children—Charles E., Sheryl A., Laura A., Robert A., Timothy E. Cost acct. Chrysler Corp., Twinsburg, Ohio, 1963-74; adminstrv. mgr. S & K Excavating Co., Stow, Ohio, 1974-75; corporate records retention supr. Frito-Lay, Inc., Dallas, 1976-77; acct. analysis cons. Robert Half & Assos., Dallas, 1977; div. controller Kolmar Labs. Inc., Denton, Tex., 1977-78; corporate controller Fred F. Hunter Corp., Galveston, Tex., 1978—. Mem. Nat. Assn. Accts., Inst. Mgmt. Accts., Am. Soc. Personnel Adminstrn. (treas. 1977-78), Am. Mgmt. Assn., Planning Execs. Inst., Delta Mu Delta. Home: 5507 Yacht Club Dr Dickinson TX 77539 Office: 2228 Broadway St Galveston TX 77550

DYKERS, JOHN REGINALD, JR., physician; b. Jacksonville, Fla., Sept. 25, 1935; s. John Reginald and Vance Estelle (Peacock) D.; B.S., Davidson Coll., 1956; M.D., U. N.C., 1960; m. Dorothy Esther Dover, June 25, 1960 (div.); children—Dorothy Anne, John Reginald; m. 2d, Jackie Lynn Sigmon, June 29, 1977 (div.); 1 son, Thomas Andrew. Intern, USN, Pensacola, Fla., 1962-64; practice family medicine, Siler City, N.C., 1964—; chief med. staff Chatham Hosp.; asst. prof. U. N.C. Med. Sch., Chapel Hill, 1974—; mem. Internat. Congress on Trichomoniasis, Czechoslovakia, 1977; pres. New Hope Farm, Inc., 1966—, brown Fuquay Enterprise Inc., 1974—, Dugan Parker Med. Center, Inc., 1970—. Chmn. Chatham County Planning Council for Devel. Disabled. Fellow Am. Coll. Family Physicians; mem. Am. Acad. Family Practice, Chatham County Med. Soc. (pres. 1968), Med. Soc. N.C. Club: Rotary. Contbr. articles to profl. jours. Home: Route 3 Box 565 Siler City NC 27344 Office: PO Box 565 Siler City NC 27344

DYKES, JAMES EDGAR, educator; b. Wetumpka, Ala., Aug. 11, 1919; s. Reuben Owen and Sunie (Cannon) D.; student Washington U., St. Louis, 1939-41; B.A., Auburn U., 1946-47; M.B.A., Tex. Tech U., 1953; m. Mary Jane Roth, Nov. 28, 1942; children—Stephen Van, Michael James. Advt. mgr. Nolin Mfg. Co., Montgomery, Ala., 1947-49; copywriter Craig & Webster, advt. agy., Lubbock, Tex., 1952-53; instr. Fla. State U., Tallahassee, 1948-50; asst. prof. Tex. Tech U., Lubbock, 1950-53; prof., head advt. sequence William Allen White Sch. Journalism, U. Kans., Lawrence, 1953-73; prof. Sch. Bus. and Commerce, Troy (Ala.) State U., 1973—; free-lance creative and exec. work in advt. Served with USMCR, 1943-45. Newspaper Advt. Execs. Assn. fellow, 1962; Am. Assn. Advt. Agys. fellow, 1965. Mem. Am. Acad. Advt. (pres. 1965), Assn. Edn. in Journalism (chmn. advt. div. 1968), Assn. Indsl. Advertisers. Methodist. Club: Kiwanis. Author: (with others) Principles of Advertising, 1963. Home: 116 Pine St Troy AL 36081

DYKES, WILLIS GERALD, agrl. equipment devel. co. exec.; b. Vicksburg, Miss., July 7, 1941; s. Willis Eugene and Annie (Bishop) D.; B.M.E., Miss. State U., 1965; m. Tina Vivian Hazzlerigg, Nov. 7, 1965; children—Brian Gerald, Adam Christopher. Mech. engr., C.E., U.S. Army, 1965-74; pvt. practice cons. mech. design engring., Vicksburg, 1974-76; pres. Lasco, Inc., Vicksburg, 1976—. Registered profl. engr., Miss. Mem. Am. Soc. Agrl. Engrs. Methodist. Patentee in elec. methods of plant control. Home: 802 Santa Rosa Dr Vicksburg MS 39180 Office: PO Box 187 Vicksburg MS 39180

EACHUS, ALVIN REED, constrn. engr.; b. Nyssa, Oreg., Feb. 7, 1937; s. Louis and Edith Elaine (Burns) E.; student Los Angeles City Coll., 1957-60; m. Gail Margret Airoldi, Apr. 7, 1979; children—Lyle, Shari, Tammy, Alvin. Staff various small archtl. cos. Los Angeles, 1960-63; draftsman, job capt. Daniel, Mann, Johnson & Mendenhall, Architects and Engrs., Los Angeles, 1963-66; facilities engr. McDonnell Douglas Co., Los Angeles, 1967-70; freelance contractor, Lewisville, Tex., 1970-72; draftsman, job capt. Wheeler & Stefoniak, Architects, Dallas, 1972-74; draftsman, designer J.L. Williams Contractors, Dallas, 1974-75; field constrn. engr. Collins Radio Group, Rockwell Internat. Co., Richardson, Tex., 1975—. Res. dep. Dallas County Sheriff's Dept., 1976—. Served with USMC, 1954-57. Jewish. Club: Elks. Office: Collins Radio Group Rockwell Internat Co 1200 N Alma Rd Richardson TX 75081

EADES, ERBERT BROWN, advt. exec.; b. Fayette County, Ky., Oct. 1, 1920; s. Thomas Stamper and Mattie Virginia (Dearing) E.; student U. Ky., 1944; m. Maude Rose Hendrickson, Jan. 23, 1976; children by previous marriage—Ellen Marie Fore, Linda Brown Bradley, Diane Gail Stephens. With Herald Leader Co., Lexington, Ky., 1947-59; mgr. H & L Advt. Agy., Lexington, 1959-63; advt. dir. The Blood-Horse, Lexington, 1963—; pres. Am. Horse Publs., 1978-79. Dir. auto. safety campaign 4-H Clubs, Ky., 1966, 67, 68; div. leader United Funds, Lexington, 1962-64; div. leader Central Bapt. Hosp., Lexington, 1966-68; supt. Sun. sch. Broadway Christian Ch., Lexington, 1950-75. Served to lt. col., U.S. Army, 1942-47; ETO. Decorated Bronze Star medal, Purple Heart. Mem. Mag. Pub. Assn., Am. Horse Pubs., Ky. Breeders Assn., Res. Officers Assn. Democrat. Christian Ch. Clubs: Rotary, Lexington Country, Lafayette, Lexington Advt., Thoroughbred of Am. Home: 1988 Favell Ct Lexington KY 40503 Office: 1736 Alexandria Dr Lexington KY 40504

EADIE, JOHN MICHAEL, brokerage firm exec.; b. N.Y.C., Oct. 29, 1934; s. George Crawford and Marjorie Alice (Whitehorne) E.; B.S., U. Pa., 1957; children—Katrina, Alita, Larry. Edn. filmstrip producer, to 1968; account exec. Merrill, Lynch, Fenner, Pierce & Smith, Fort Lauderdale, Fla., 1968—; mem. Fort Lauderdale Employees Pension Adv. Bd., 1967-77. Mem. adv. bd. Sister City Program, 1968—; mem. Fort Lauderdale Opera Guild, 1962-77. Mem. U. Pa. Alumni Assn. (v.p. 1966-77). Presbyterian. Clubs: Fort Lauderdale Bond, Lauderdale Yacht. Home: 333 Sunset Dr Fort Lauderdale FL 33301 Office: Merrill Lynch Pierce Fenner Smith 1 Financial Plaza Fort Lauderdale FL 33394

EADS, JAMES ROBERT, social worker; b. Harlan, Ky., July 22, 1937; s. Edgar Thomas and Hattie Nora (Goff) E.; B.A., U. Ky., 1965; M.S.S.W. (Martha Davis scholar), U. Louisville, 1969; m. Sherry Lynn Pope, Apr. 18, 1969; children—Judi Lynn Wood (stepdau.), Dawn Michelle. Program coordinator Fayette County Children's Bur., Lexington, Ky., 1969-70; commd. capt. U.S. Army, 1970, advanced through grades to maj., 1979; with Army Mental Hygiene Services, U.S.A., Germany, 1970-79; chief social work service Darnall Army Hosp., Ft. Hood, Tex., 1979—. Mem. Bell County Child Welfare Bd., Belton, Tex., 1977—. Served with AUS, 1958-61. Mem.

Nat. Assn. Social Workers, Acad. Cert. Social Workers, Am. Assn. for Marriage and Family Therapy, Nat. Register Clin. Social Workers. Home: 4117 Antelope Trail Temple TX 76501 Office: Social Work Service Darnall Army Hosp ITEDDAC Fort Hood TX 76544

EADS, PAUL THOMAS, electronic instruments co. mktg. exec.; b. Houston, Dec. 31, 1938; s. Jack and Eula (Locke) E.; B.S., U. Houston, 1962; m. Winnie Mae Munger, July 8, 1960; children—Todd Alan, Troy Haven. Lab technician Computers Inc., Houston, 1961-64; sales rep. Camco, Maracaibo, Venezuela, 1964-65, engring. research, Houston, 1965-67, sales applications engr., 1967-70, mgr. mfg. rep., 1972-73, elec. products mgr., 1973-75, mktg. mgr., 1975-77; pres. Apensco, Inc., mfrs. reps., Houston, 1975—; staff sales cons. Camco, Inc., Houston, 1977-79, staff gas lift tech., 1979—; tchr. U. Tex. Indsl. Tng. Bur., 1969-75; tchr. gas lift tech. and application engring. pvt. seminars, Houston, New Orleans, Lafayette, Alaska, Peru, Egypt, Brunei, Jakarta. Mem. Gulf Coast Gas Measurement Soc., Am. Inst. Metall. Engrs. (Soc. Petroleum Engrs. Home: 6210 Wynnwood St Houston TX 77008 Office: 7100 Ardmore St Houston TX 77021 also PO Box 7732 Houston TX 77007

EAGAN, DAVID LEE, retail exec.; b. St. Louis, Jan. 10, 1946; s. Noel Harper and Jenna (Lee) E.; B.S., Middle Tenn. State U., 1968; m. Janice Kay Thurston, Jan. 6, 1968; 1 son, David Lee II. With Cain Sloan Co., Nashville, 1968—, buyer, 1971-76, div. mdse. mgr., 1976—, mem. corp. steering com., 1978-79. Served with Air N.G., 1966-72. Mem. Nashville C. of C. Republican. Mem. Ch. of Christ. Club: Masons. Home: 2116 Hartland Dr Franklin TN 37064 Office: 501 Church St Nashville TN 37219

EAGER, JAMES DOUGLAS, ins. co. exec.; b. Newton, N.J., Mar. 19, 1953; s. John William and Eleanor Louise (Weaver) E.; B.B.A., So. Meth. U., 1975; postgrad. Baylor U. Clerical asst. Eppler Guerin & Turner, Dallas, 1975; mdse. control staff Horchow Collection, Dallas, 1975; mktg. rep. Crum Forster Co., Little Rock, 1976—. Bd. dirs. Woodway Boys Club, 1977—. Mem. Assn. M.B.A. Execs., Inc. Republican. Presbyterian. Club: Fidelis Lodge. Home: 1912 Greenmountain Dr Apt 160-I Little Rock AR 72212 Office: PO Box 7670 Little Rock AR 72217

EAGLSTEIN, WILLIAM HOWARD, physician; b. Kansas City, Mo., Mar. 27, 1940; s. Max A. and Mildred Eaglstein; M.D., U. Mo., 1965; m. Janet Strickland, Aug. 23, 1979. Intern, Kings County Hosp., Bklyn., N.Y., 1965-66; resident in dermatology U. Miami (Fla.) Sch. of Medicine, 1966-69; practice medicine specializing in dermatology Miami, Fla., 1971—; asst. prof. dept. dermatology U. Miami Sch. Medicine, 1971-75, asso. prof., 1975—; vis. prof. Nagoya (Japan) City Coll. Sch. of Medicine, 1976; dir. internat. clin. studies Bur. of Indian Affairs, Chinle, Ariz., 1973-74; Inst. de Formacion Agropecuria, Tucupita, Venezuela, S. Am., 1974; mem. staff Jackson Meml. Hosp., Miami. Served with USN, 1969-71. Diplomate Am. Bd. Dermatology. Mem. Am. Acad. Dermatology and Syphilology, Fla. Soc. Dermatology, Soc. of Investigative Dermatology, Soc. of Mil. Dermatologists, AMA, Am. Fedn. Clin. Research, Sigma Xi. Author: (with D.M. Pariser) Office Techniques for Diagnosing Skin Diseases, 1978; contbr. numerous articles on dermatology to med. jours. Home: 574 NE 96th St Miami Shores FL 33138 Office: Univ Miami School of Medicine PO Box 520875 Miami FL 33152

EAKIN, FRANK EDWIN, JR., educator; b. Roanoke, Va., Sept. 4, 1936; s. Frank Edwin and Vera Constance (Taylor) E.; B.A., U. Richmond, 1958; B.D., So. Bapt. Theol. Sem., 1961; Ph.D., Duke U., 1964; m. Frances Joan Crockett, June 28, 1958. Instr., Duke U., 1963-64; vis. asst. prof. religion Wake Forest U., Winston-Salem, N.C., 1964-65; instr. Duke U., Durham, N.C., 1965-66; asst. prof. U. Richmond (Va.), 1966-69, asso. prof., 1969-75, prof. religion, 1975—, chmn. dept., 1978—. Am. Council Edn. fellow, 1975-76; Gurney Harriss Kearns fellow Duke U., 1962-63. Mem. Soc. Bibl. Lit., Phi Beta Kappa, Omicron Delta Kappa. Episcopalian. Author: The Religion and Culture of Israel, 2d edit., 1977; Religion in Western Culture: Selected Issues, 1977; contbr. articles to profl. jours. Home: 7013 Bandy Rd Richmond VA 23229 Office: Dept Religion U Richmond Richmond VA 23173

EARL, POLLY ANNE, historian, editor, preservation cons.; b. N.Y.C., Aug. 24, 1943; d. Oscar A. and Anne C. Jose; B.A., Sweet Briar Coll., 1965; M.A. (Hagley fellow), U. Del., 1968, also postgrad.; m. John Andrew Scafidi, Aug. 12, 1966 (div.); m. 2d, N. Clarkson Earl IV, July 1, 1972 (div.); 1 son, Andrew Tobin. Grad. asst. community design planning commn. U. Del., Newark, 1969-70, instr., 1973; asst., editor publs. Winterthur (Del.) Mus., 1970-73, asso. editor, 1973-74; co-chmn. Winterthur Conf., 1974; instr. Coll. of Lake County, Greyslake, Ill., 1976—; adj. asst. prof. Fla. Atlantic U., Boca Raton, 1979-80; cons. N.Y. State Hist. Mus.; grant reviewer Nat. Endowment for Humanities div. public programs; co-editor Technological Innovation and the Decorative Arts, 1974. Nat. Endowment for Humanities fellow, 1968-69; Eleutherian Mills Hist. Library grant-in-aid, 1970; cert. on quantitative methods for historians, Newberry Library, Chgo., 1976. Mem. Am. Hist. Assn., Orgn. Am. Historians, Soc. for History of Tech. and Culture, Nat. Trust for Hist. Preservation, Fla. Hist. Soc., Fla. Trust for Hist. Preservation, LWV (2d v.p. West Palm Beach 1979-80). Clubs: Tennis (Palm Beach); Soc. of 4-Arts. Contbr. sects. to books and biog. dictionaries; contbr. articles to profl. jours. Home: 209 Sea Spray Ave Palm Beach FL 33480 Office: History Dept Florida Atlantic U Boca Raton FL 33431

EARL, WALTER RUPERT, counselor, psychometrist: b. Newport News, Va., June 21, 1932; s. Henry Samuel and Lola Clayton (Brown) E.; B.A., Randolph Macon Coll., 1955; M.Div., Union Theol. Sem. in Va., 1960; M.S. in Edn., Old Dominion U., 1970; children—James Samuel, Stephen Walter, David Andrew. Ordained to ministry United Methodist Church, 1955; clergyman various locations, Va. Conf., 1954-66; dir. Westley Found., Old Dominion U., Norfolk, Va., 1966-68, counselor, 1968—, coordinator of testing, 1970—, chmn. dept. acad. counseling and testing, 1975—, coordinator workshops on standardized tests, div. continuing studies; pvt. practice Walter R. Earl and Assos., Counseling and Testing, Norfolk, 1978—. Pres. Civic League, 1969, 71; pres. various PTA's, 1969, 73, 74. Lic. counselor, Va. Mem. Am. Personnel and Guidance Assn., Va. Personnel and Guidance Assn., Am. Coll. Personnel Assn., Va. Coll. Personnel Assn. (pres., 1978-79, chmn. acad. counseling, 1975—), Hampton Roads Personnel and Guidance Assn., Assn. for Measurement in Evaluation and Guidance, Va. Ednl. Research Assn., Omicron Delta Kappa. Unitarian. Author workbook How to Get Ready for College Boards, 1978; contbr. papers in field to profl. confs., publs. Office: Academic Counseling and Testing Old Dominion University Hampton Blvd Norfolk VA 23508

EARLE, JOSEPH ELIAS, constrn. co. exec.; b. Anderson, S.C., Dec. 7, 1946; s. Samuel Hammond and Belle Acker (Boggs) E.; B.S., Erskine Coll., 1969; m. Idali Elizabeth Rodriguez, Jan. 11, 1976; children—Beth, Kevin, Tiffany. Internal auditor Dan River Inc., Greenville, S.C., 1969-70; fin. analyst Daniel Internat. Corp., Greenville, 1970-74, controller Caribbean div., San Juan, P.R., 1974-76, subs. controller, Greenville, 1977-78; controller Daniel Constrn. Co., Greenville, 1978—. Chmn. budget and rev. bd. United Way; bd. dirs. Urban League. Served with Army N.G., 1969-74. Club: Kiwanis. Home: 102 Silvercreek Ct Greer SC 29651 Office: Daniel Bldg Greenville SC 29602

EARLES, EDGAR LEE, broadcasting co. exec.; b. Gretna, Va., Feb. 22, 1935; s. G.L. and Docie Bye (Bolling) E.; student Roakake Bible Coll., Elizabeth City, N.C.; m. Yvonne Marie Motley, Aug. 30, 1955; children—Tammy Lee, Timothy Douglas, Trecia M. Served with USAF, 1956-76; service in Morocco, Libya, Vietnam; ret., 1976; sales mgr. Blue Motor Co., Defuniak Springs, Fla., 1975-76, Sta. WGTX, Defuniak Springs, 1976-77; v.p. Euchee Valley Broadcasting, Defuniak, Fla., 1977-78, pres., 1978—. Pres. Walton Middle Sch. Band Parents, 1968-69, Walton Sr. High Band Parents, 1971-73, Walton County Assn. Retarded Citizens, 1979; bd. dirs. Walton County Heart Fund, 1979. Named Young Man of Year, DeFuniak Jaycees, 1971; recipient Outstanding Citizen award DeFuniak Springs Jaycees, 1978. Mem. Nat. Assn. Broadcasters, Religious Broadcasters Assn., Fla. Assn. Broadcasters. Democrat. Mem. Ch. of Christ. Club: Kiwanis. Address: Euchee Valley Broadcasting PO Box 627 DeFuniak FL 32433

EARLY, CHARLES THOMAS, chem. co. exec.; b. Knoxville, Tenn., Mar. 3, 1933; s. Charles Thomas and Mary Nan E.; B.S. in Mech. Engring., U. Tenn., 1957; m. Eleanor Ann Brogden; children—Sherry Marlene, Marian Renee, Anita Gail. With Eastman Kodak-Tenn. Eastman Co., Kingsport, 1957—, now mgr. plant maintenance. Officer Community Club; trustee United Methodist Ch.; mem. exec. bd. Sequoyah council Boy Scouts Am., chmn. Warriors Path dist. Registered profl. engr., Tenn. Mem. ASME, Nat. Soc. Profl. Engrs., U. Tenn. Alumni Assn. Republican. Club: Kiwanis. Office: Tenn Eastman Co PO Box 511 Bldg 75 Kingsport TN 37660

EARLY, JOHN LEVERING, lawyer; b. Staunton, Va., Dec. 19, 1896; s. Charles E. and Ida (Clark) E.; A.B., Washington and Lee U.; LL.B., U. Va., 1923; m. Maebelle C. Brooks, June 2, 1924; 1 son, Charles Edward. Admitted to Va. bar, 1923, W.Va. bar, 1924, Fla. bar, 1924; practice law, Welch, W.Va., 1923-24, Sarasota, Fla., 1924—; cattleman, breeder thoroughbred Shorthorns. Mem. Sarasota-Bradenton (Fla.) Airport Authority, 1951-53. Mem. Ho. Reps., 1933-39; municipal judge, 1944-46; mayor City Sarasota, 1951-53. Served as pvt., inf., 1918-19. Recipient Pres.'s award Asbury Coll., 1980; Ky. col. Mem. Sarasota County Bar Assn. (pres.), Am. Legion, D.A.V., Helping Hands (pres.), Rodeheavers Boy's Ranch Assn., Founders Club, Fla. Sheriffs Boys Ranch, Order of Coif. Methodist. Mason, Odd Fellow. Home: 1841 Oak St Sarasota FL 33577 Office: 920 1st Fed Bldg Sarasota FL 33577

EARP, LINDA, singer, actress, dancer; b. Salisbury, N.C., Apr. 18, 1948; d. Clyde Webster and Grace Lee (Parks) Earp; B.A. with honors in dramatic art, U. N.C., 1970; m. Benjamin Berman, Nov. 17, 1972. Appeared with Harmony and Grits Show, Cerromar Beach Hotel, P. R., 1973-77, Regency Hyatt, Atlanta, 1973, Shangri La Hotel, Singapore, 1978, Carlton Hotel, S. Africa, 1978-79, Dusit Thani Hotel, Bangkok, 1978, Fountainbleau and Konover Hotel, Miami, 1975-76, Oakdale Theatre, Wallingford, Conn., 1976, Union Plaza Hotel, Las Vegas, 1976, Pinehurst Hotel, N.C., 1978, many others; TV appearances on own spls., Bangkok, 1978, P.R., 1976, also To Tell the Truth, 1971, Jerry Lewis Muscular Dystrophy Telethon, Las Vegas, 1976, N.Y.C., 1974, Kid's Corner Children's Show, 1972-77, Moliere's Doctor in Spite of Himself, 1970, Cruise Lines, 1976-79; Broadway appearances include Christmas Carol, 1970, Touch, 1971; Cabaret, off-Broadway, 1971; also Summer Stock, little theatre appearances; performer at White House for First Family, 1976. Recipient Teenager of the Year award C. of C., 1966; Rotary Service award, 1966; United Daus. of Confederacy Essay award, 1961; William Morris Agy. Found. scholar, 1969; named Miss Broadway, 1971, Order of Valkyries, 1971. Mem. Actors Equity Assn. Baptist. Recordings: Peace Song, 1972; To See the World, 1972, others. Address: 1724 Boatswain Pl Stuart FL 33494

EARVIN, LARRY LEE, research orgn. exec.; b. Chattanooga, Feb. 23, 1949; s. William Lee and Clara Mae (Ware) E.; B.A., Clark Coll., 1971; M.S., Ga. State U., 1973; postgrad Emory U., 1974—; m. Valerie Belinda Johnson, Dec. 8, 1974; 1 son, William Jarrett. Planning intern DeKalb County, Ga., 1972-73, asst. dir. Atlanta Housing Study Policy Center, Clark Coll., 1973-75, asst. dir. So. Center for Studies in Pub. Policy, 1975—; adj. prof. Atlanta U. HUD fellow, 1972; Nat. Endowment for the Humanities fellow, 1976; United Negro Coll. Fund Faculty fellow, 1976-77; Faculty fellow Transp. Systems Center, Cambridge, Mass., 1978-79. Mem. Am. Inst. Planners, Am. Soc. Planning Ofcls., Nat. Assn. Planners, Conf. Minority Pub. Adminstrs., Phi Beta Lambda, Alpha Phi Alpha. Democrat. Methodist. Author: Housing in Atlanta: Toward Neighborhood Investment by Residents, 1975; A Neighborhood Approach to Urban Planning, 1976. Home: 154 Peyton Rd SW Atlanta GA 30311 Office: 240 Chestnut St SW Atlanta GA 30314

EASLEY, MARY KATHREN WILLIAMS, juvenile counselor; b. McAlester, Okla., Dec. 12, 1952; d. Claude Harold Williams and Hazel Marie Burris (White) W.; asso., Eastern Okla. State Coll., 1973; B.A., Okla. State U., 1975, M.S., 1979; m. Gregory M. Easley, May 9, 1955; 1 stepson, Dennis J. Easley. With Layden & Layden Attys., McAlester, Okla., 1975-76; juvenile counselor State of Okla., Ct. Related and Community Services, Wilburton, Okla., 1976-77, McAlester, 1977-79, Perry, Okla., 1979—; cons. in field. Dept. Insts., Social and Rehabilitative Services scholar, 1978-79. Mem. AAUW, Am. Personnel and Guidance Assn. Democrat. Baptist. Contbr. articles in field to profl. jours. Home: 1302 E 6th Stillwater OK 74074 Office: PO Box 327 Perry OK 73077

EASON, CHARLES HUBERT, indsl. supplies co. exec.; b. Birmingham, Ala., Aug. 17, 1930; s. Marvin J. and Ethel R. E.; B.S., U. Ala., 1957; m. Martha L. Matson, Sept. 20, 1957; children—Martha Ann, Charles Clifton. Project engr. Am. Cast Iron Pipe Co., Birmingham, 1957-68; mgr. foundry sales Perry Supply Co., Birmingham, 1968-70, v.p., 1970-72, pres., 1972—; pres. Eason Inc., casting brokerage co., Birmingham, 1979—. Mem. higher edn. scholarship campaign, Birmingham So. Coll., 1977; active Jr. Achievement, 1965—; chmn. sustaining membership, Warrior Dist., Boy Scouts Am., 1974-78. Served with U.S. Army, 1951-53. Decorated Bronze Star. Mem. Am. Foundrymen's Soc. (chmn. 1972, chmn. nat. conv. 1979), Nat. Mgmt. Assn. (vice-chmn. Ala. council 1967—), Foundry Ednl. Found., Asso. Industries Ala., U.S. Indsl. Council. Democrat. Methodist. Clubs: The Club, Downtown, Inverness Country, Civitan. Researcher metall. engring. and foundry ops., lectr. foundry confs. Home: 464 Crumly Chapel Rd Birmingham AL 35214 Office: Perry Supply Co 831 1st Ave N Birmingham AL 35201

EAST, CHARLES ELMO, JR., advt. exec.; b. Baton Rouge, La., Dec. 5, 1949; s. Charles Elmo and Sarah (Simmons) E.; B.A. in Journalism, La. State U., 1971. Successively state desk copy editor, gen. assignment reporter, edn. writer Times-Picayune, New Orleans, 1971-73; co-founder, editor Gris-Gris, Baton Rouge, 1973; successively advt. and pub. relations copywriter Weill/Strother, Inc., Baton Rouge, 1973-74, exec. v.p., 1974-79; partner Weill/Strother/East, Inc. 1979—. Recipient Journalism awards La. State U., 1969, 70, 71. Hodding Carter award, 1971, Mpls. Star award, 1970. Democrat. Presbyterian. Club: City (Baton Rouge). Office: Weill/Strother/East Inc PO Box 645 Baton Rouge LA 70821

EAST, CHARLES ROBERT, life ins. co. exec.; b. Tulsa, Apr. 13, 1936; s. Robert Wendell and Geraldine Rachel (Stewart) E.; student U. Okla., 1954-55; B.A., U. Tulsa, 1959, M.A., 1962; m. Carmelita J. McDaniel, Aug. 24, 1958; children—Dawn Michelle, Heather Danielle. Placement specialist No. Natural Gas Co., Omaha, 1962-63, unit personnel adminstr., 1963-64, personnel dir., 1965; spl. agent Nat. Life Ins. Co. of Vt., Omaha, 1965-68; sales dir. New Eng. Mut. Life, Houston, Tex., 1968-79; asst. gen. agt. Mass. Mut. Life, Houston, 1979—. Bd. dirs. Unity Ch. of Christianity, Houston, 1974-75, Cypress United Meth Ch., 1977-79; Served with U.S. Army, 1962. Recipient various life ins. mgmt., sales, quality and service awards. Mem. Houston Assn. Life Underwriters, Houston Assn. Chartered Life Underwriters (dir.), Am. Soc. of Chartered Life Underwriters, Houston Estate and Fin. Forum, Million Dollar Round Table, Psi Chi., Sigma Chi Alumni Assn. Republican. Methodist. Clubs: Sons of the Am. Revolution. Home: 18111 Mountfield Dr Houston TX 77084 Office: 1610 Bank of SW Bldg Houston TX 77002

EAST, DOROTHY GAIL, sch. counselor; b. Atlanta, Oct. 16, 1940; d. Robert Leon and Verna Dorothy (Bryce) Gordon; A.B., Emory U., 1962; M.Ed., Ga. State U., 1972; m. Donald Paul East, July 15, 1962. Tchr. English, then tchr. remedial reading Forest Park (Ga.) Jr. High Sch., 1962-69; tchr. English, Morrow (Ga.) Jr. High Sch., 1969-70, guidance counselor, 1970—, chmn. English dept., 1966-70. Mem. Am., Ga. sch. counselors assns., Am. Personnel and Guidance Assn., PTA. Episcopalian. Home: Route 4 Box 91 Foster Rd McDonough GA 30253 Office: Morrow Jr High Sch Maddox Rd Morrow GA 30260

EASTERLING, CHARLES ARMO, lawyer; b. Hamilton, Tex., July 22, 1920; s. William Hamby and Jenny Arilla (Jackson) E.; B.B.A., Baylor U., 1950; LL.B., 1951, J.D., 1969; m. Irene Alice Kelm, Apr. 25, 1943; children—Charles David, Danny Karl, Jan Irene Easterling Taylor. Admitted to Tex. bar, 1950; sr. asst. city atty. City of Houston, 1952-64; partner firm Easterling & Easterling, Houston, 1964—; city atty. City of Pasadena (Tex.), 1969—; instr. South Tex. Coll. Law, 1954-69. Served to lt. col. USAAF, 1943-46. Mem. State Bar Tex., Houston-Harris County Bar Assn., Res. Officers Assn., Phi Alpha Delta. Democrat. Methodist. Clubs: Kiwanis (pres. club 1958) Masons, Shriners (potentate 1971, vice chmn. bd. trustees Shriners Hosps. for Crippled Children-Galveston, (Tex., unit 1978—). Home: 5103 Sleepy Creek St Houston TX 77017 Office: 1121 Walker Ave Suite 1100 Houston TX 77002

EASTMAN, JAMES NEWELL, JR., historian; b. Callaway, Nebr., Nov. 12, 1936; s. James Newell and Helen Ida (Siel) E.; A.B., Doane Coll., Crete, Nebr., 1958; M.A., U. Nebr., 1960; postgrad. U. Okla., Auburn U., Air Command and Staff Coll., Air War Coll., U. Mich.; m. Hertha Ann Hardwick, Feb. 14, 1956; children—James Newell, III, Mary E., Paul E., Patrick G., Charles W. Civilian historian with USAF, 1960—; dep. historian USAF Europe, Wiesbaden, W. Ger., 1970-72; dep. dir. Albert F. Simpson Hist. Research Center, USAF, chief research bd. Montgomery Maxwell AFB, Ala., 1972—; dir. USAF historians course; instr. Auburn U., Montgomery. Active Boy Scouts Am., 1965—, asst. dist. commnr., 1970-72; active local youth baseball and basketball. Fellow Inter-Univ. Consortium Social and Polit. Research, 1977; recipient various Boy Scout awards. Mem. Am. Hist. Assn., Phi Alpha Theta. Democrat. Club: Elks. Editor: Aces and Aerial Victories, the USAF in Southeast Asia, 1977; contbr. numerous articles to profl. jours. Home: 4433 N Gaskell Circle Montgomery AL 36106 Office: Albert F Simpson Hist Research Center Maxwell AFB AL 36112

EASTMAN, JAMES ROBERT, city ofcl.; b. Saginaw, Mich., Feb. 19, 1928; s. Lawrence C. and Blanche E. Hitchcock; student UCLA, 1945, Los Angeles City Coll., 1946, U. Tenn., 1977-78; m. Loretta I. Grissom, May 1, 1950; children—Lisa Devon, Charles Kent, James Chris, Robert Bruce. News dir. Tex. and Tenn. radio stas., 1951-67; v.p. Advt. Assos., Nashville, 1967-73; dir. mktg. Nashville Met. Transit Authority, Nashville, 1973—; faculty applied transit mktg. U. So. Calif., 1978. Pres. PTA of elem. sch., 1971, jr. high sch., 1973, high sch., 1975, life mem., 1971—; press sec. various polit. campaigns, 1966—. Served with USN, 1946, 52-53. Recipient award Nashville Jaycees, 1958; AP News award, 1965. Mem. Am. Mktg. Assn. (pres. Nashville chpt. 1979-80), Am. Public Transit Assn. (mktg. steering com. 1973—), Tennesseans for Better Transp. (transit com. 1978—), Nashville Advt. Fedn. Democrat. Baptist. Clubs: Glencliff Aquatic 1978-79), Nashville Swim (v.p. 1979—). Editor, pub. Franchise Newsletter, 1970-72. Home: 209 Wallace Rd Nashville TN 37211 Office: Nashville Met Transit Authority 60 Peabody St Nashville TN 37210

EASTMAN, JOHN ALLEN, ins. co. exec.; b. Detroit, July 22, 1940; s. Jesse Earl and Gertrude Ethel Monica (Thomas) E.; B.S., U. Tex., 1972, postgrad. 1972-73; m. Rose Marie Cangiamilla, Apr. 16, 1977; children by previous marriage—Deborah Lynn, Felicia Maria, John Erik; 1 stepdau., Belynda Noel Cleveland. With Electronic Designs, Inc., Dallas, 1964-65; engring. technician Howell Instruments, Inc., Ft. Worth, Tex., 1965-72, sr. engring. technician, 1966-72; spl. agt. Prudential Ins. Co. of Am., Ft. Worth, 1974-75, devel. mgr., 1975—. Served with USAF, 1960-64. Named Prudential Regional leader, 1974, 75, 77, 78, 79; Prudential Pres.'s Citation as Outstanding Unit, 1978, 79. Mem. Nat. Assn. Life Underwriters, Gen. Agts. and Mgrs. Assn., Mensa. Roman Catholic. Home: 5907 Walden Trail Arlington TX 76016 Office: 1200 Summit Ave Suite 500 Fort Worth TX 76102

EATON, WILLIAM E., utility co. exec.; b. Russellville, Ark., Mar. 21, 1945; s. Thomas Loren and Mary Jane (West) E.; student Little Rock U., 1963-65; B.A. in Sociology, Ark. Poly. Coll., 1968; m. Sharon Lynn Hall, Dec. 18 1966; children—Julie Diane, Traci Jean, Myra Kay. Engrs. asst. Western Ark. Telephone Co., Russellville, Ark., 1965-68; with Continental Telephone Co., 1968—, bus. office mgr., Booneville, Ark., 1975-77, supr. customer service center, Gentry, Ark., 1977—. Alderman, City of Gentry, 1977-78. Served with U.S. Army, 1968-71; capt. Ark. N.G. Decorated Bronze Star, Army Commendation medal. Mem. Gentry C. of C. (sec. 1976-77, sec.-treas. 1977-78). Methodist. Clubs: Masons, Lions (sec. 1976-78, dir. 1978-79, 1st v.p. 1979-80). Home: 350 Otis St Gentry AR 72734 Office: Continental Telephone Co Corner Main and Nelson Sts Gentry AR 72734

EAVENSON, LESTER WRIGHT, radiologist; b. Kaifeng, Honan, China, Dec. 3, 1922; s. Ira Dennis and Nancy (Miller) E. (parents Am. citizens); B.S., Delta State U., 1943; M.D., U. Tenn., 1947; m. Carolyn Webb, June 18, 1945; children—Carol, Denise, Lester Wright, Nancy. Intern, John Gaston Hosp., Memphis, 1947-48; gen. practice medicine, Natchez, Miss., 1948-53; fellow, mem. staff Ochsner Found. Hosp., New Orleans, 1953-59; with So. Bapt. Hosp., New Orleans, 1959—, dir. dept. radiology, nuclear medicine and ultrasound, 1972—; asso. prof. radiology Med. Sch., Tulane U., New Orleans. Chmn. med. advisory com. La. Bd. Nuclear Energy. Served to capt. M.C., USAF, 1950-52. Diplomate Am. Bd. Radiology, Am. Bd. Nuclear Medicine. Mem. AMA, Am. Coll. Radiology, Am. Coll.

Nuclear Medicine, Am. Roentgen Ray Soc., Radiol. Soc. N.Am., Soc. Nuclear Medicine, La. Med. Soc., Radiol. Soc. La. (past pres.), Alpha Omega Alpha, Phi Chi. Democrat. Baptist. Club: Rotary (New Orleans). Home: 5412 Yale St Metairie LA 70003 Office: 2700 Napoleon Ave New Orleans LA 70115

EBAUGH, ELIZABETH BROWN (MRS. FRANK WRIGHT EBAUGH), civic worker; b. Jacksonville, Tex.; d. John Lemuel and Jewel (Newton) Brown; B.A., U. Colo., 1925; M.A., Tchrs. Coll., Columbia, 1927; m. Frank Wright Ebaugh, Feb. 22, 1930; 1 dau., Betty Jane (Mrs. Gordon B. McFarland, Jr.). Kindergarten tchr., Port Arthur, Tex., 1927-30. Mem. bd. Jacksonville (Tex.) Pub. Library, 1944-76, pres., 1944-46, curator, organizer Vanishing Texana Mus., 1965—. Mem. Cherokee County Hist. Survey Com., 1964—, Jacksonville Bicentennial Bd. Recipient Appreciation plaques Jacksonville Library, 1969, 79. Mem. D.A.R. (charter; registar 1965—), Chi Omega. Presbyterian (historian 1965-66). Home: 428 S Patton St Jacksonville TX 75766

EBAUGH, FRANK WRIGHT, cons. indsl. engr., investments exec.; b. New Orleans, July 31, 1901; s. John Lynn and Mary (Wright) E.; B. in Chem. Engring., Tulane U., 1923; m. Elizabeth Brown, Feb. 22, 1930; 1 dau., Betty Jane (Mrs. Gordon B. McFarland, Jr.). Engr., asso. mgmt. Texas Co., 1923-34; partner retail firm, Jacksonville, Tex., 1934-54; mgr., partner Ebaugh & Brown Investments, Jacksonville, 1955-62; prin. Frank W. Ebaugh, Profl. Engr., dir., mem. fin. com. Palestine Savs. & Loan Assn. Pres. Upper Neches River Municipal Water Authority; dir. Tex. Indsl. Devel. Council; vice chmn. Tex. Mapping Adv. Com.; sec. Tex. Coordinating Water Com.; pres. Neches River Devel. Assn.; Mem. panel chmn. Cherokee County (Texas) War Price and Ration Board, 3 years. Mem. regional com. of Girl Scouts Am.; mem. Cherokee County Hist. Survey Com., Jacksonville Bicentennial Bd.; bd. dirs. Neches River Conservation Dist.; mem. bd. Jacksonville Pub. Library. Named Man of Month, East Tex. C. of C., 1953; named Man of Year, Lions Club, 1953; honored as Distinguished Visitor Tex. Senate; Appreciation Plaque erected in Jacksonville Library, 1969. Mem. Nat. Soc. Profl. Engrs., Tex. Soc. Profl. Engrs. (chmn. water com., life mem.), E. Texas C. of C., Jacksonville C. of C. (past pres., dir., chmn. water resources com.), Am. Chem. Soc. (life mem.), AAAS, Tex. Acad. Sci., Tex. Water Conservation Assn. Presbyn. (elder, trustee). Clubs: Headliners (Austin); Rotary, Country of Jacksonville (past pres.). Patentee Ebaugh Mixer. Home: 428 S Patton St Jacksonville TX 75766 Office: Box 1031 Jacksonville TX 75766

EBBS, JOHN DALE, educator; b. Carbondale, Ill., Sept. 26, 1925; s. Charles and Dora (Fox) E.; A.B., U. N.C., Chapel Hill, 1948, M.A., 1949, Ph.D., 1958; m. Dorothy Ruth Churchwell, Mar. 14, 1953; children—Laura Ebbs Benjamin, Charles Curtis. Tchr. English, Clinton (N.C.) High Sch., 1949-50; instr. English Tex. A. and M. U., 1950-54; grad. instr. English, U. N.C. at Chapel Hill, 1955-58; asso. prof. English, High Point (N.C.) Coll., 1958-59; asst. prof. Tex. A. and M. U., College Station, 1959-60; asso. prof. East Carolina U., Greenville, N.C., 1960-63, prof. English, 1963—, dir. Pockets of Excellence project, 1973—; supr. English for State of N.C., 1966-67; vis. prof. English, U. Nebr., Lincoln, 1967-68. Served with USAAF, 1943-45. Decorated D.F.C., Air medal with five oak leaf clusters; named Outstanding Tchr. at East Carolina U., 1978; Z. Smith Reynolds Found. grantee to Eng., summer 1973. Mem. Modern Lang. Assn. Am., Mediaeval Acad. Am., Nat. Council Tchrs. English, NEA, N.C. Assn. Educators, Phi Delta Kappa. Democrat. Methodist. Club: Exchange Greenville. Author: The Principle of Poetic Justice Illustrated in Restoration Tragedy, 1973; Manual of Style for Research Writing, 1976; editor: Early Methodism in Greenville, North Carolina, 1979; A History of the Jarvis Meml. United Methodist Church, 1979. Contbr. articles, revs. to state, nat. jours. Home: 1202 Drexel Ln Greenville NC 27834 Office: E 5th St Greenville NC 27834

EBEL, JOHN ANDREW, instl. pharmacist; b. N.Y.C., Nov. 26, 1927; s. John A. and Lucy Maria (Newton) E.; A.A., U. Coll., U. Fla., 1960; B.S. in Pharmacy, with honors, U. Fla., 1962, postgrad. 1963-66; m. Betty Jane Melissa Moore, Sept. 5, 1953; children—James Andrew, Jean Elizabeth. Intern pharmacist Attwood & Rogers, Inc., Jacksonville, Fla., 1962, community pharmacist, 1962-63; staff pharmacist Shands Teaching Hosp. and Clinics, U. Fla., Gainesville, 1963-64, pharmacist supr. and preceptor, 1964-65, asso. dir. pharm. services, 1965-66; dir. pharm. services Tallahassee (Fla.) Meml. Regional Med. Center, 1966—; clin. instr. hosp. pharmacy Fla. A&M U., Tallahassee, 1968—; instr. pharmacology dept. nursing edn. Tallahassee Community Coll., 1977—; cons. hosp. pharmacy Fed. Correctional Instn., Bur. Prisons, Tallahassee, 1967—, Eaton Labs. div. Norwich Pharmacal Co., 1969—, Gadsden Meml. Hosp., Quincy, Fla., 1977; mem. drug formulary adv. com. State of Fla. Dept. of Health and Rehabilitative Services, 1975—; mem. continuing edn. com. Fla. Bd. Pharmacy, 1970-76. Coach, Baseball Atom and Cub program, Tallahassee, 1969-73; mem. pack com. Suwanee Valley council Boy Scouts Am., 1971-72. Recipient Merck Pharm. Chemistry award 1962, Johnson & Johnson Pharm. Adminstrn. award, 1962; J. Hillis Miller Meml. scholar, 1961. Mem. Am. Soc. Hosp. Pharmacists (Fla. del. 1968-72, dir. 1972-75), Fla. Soc. Hosp. Pharmacists (dir. 1967—, pres. 1969-70), Fla. Pharmacy Assn. Jour. (chmn. public relations com. 1973-74, dir. 1978—), Southeastern Soc. Hosp. Pharmacists (sec. treas. pro-tem 1972), Leon County Pharmacy Assn., Am. Pharm. Assn. (mem. Ho. Dels. 1972), Phi Eta Sigma, Rho Chi, Phi Kappa Phi. Democrat. Club: Kiwanis. Contbr. articles in field to profl. jours.; editorial bd. Therapeutics, 1976—. Home: 2103 Woodstock Ln Tallahassee FL 32303 Office: care Pharmacy Tallahassee Meml Regional Medical Center 1300 Miccosukee Rd Tallahassee FL 32303

EBERHARDT, DUANE ORRIN, economist, educator; b. Sauk City, Wis., Dec. 10, 1934; s. Edgar William and Luella Anna (Geiger) E.; B.S. in Physics, San Diego State Coll., 1956; M.A. in Econs., U. So. Calif., 1968, Ph.D. in Econs., 1970; m. Melva Lee Gibson, June 22, 1960; children—Anne, Lynn, John, Catherine, Richard, Allyson, Kent, Mauree. Engr., Convair div. Gen. Dynamics, San Diego, 1956-62; engr. and fin. research specialist Lockheed Aircraft Corp., Burbank, Calif., 1962-69; asst. prof. bus. adminstrn. No. Ariz. U., Flagstaff, 1969-73; head dept. bus. adminstrn., prof. econs. Angelo State U., San Angelo, Tex., 1973—. Scoutmaster, Boy Scouts Am., 1973—. Served to capt., nav., USAF, 1956-59. Piper prof., 1979. Mormon. Author: Economic Analysis of Supersonic Transport Markets, 1968; An Econometric Overhead Model for an Aerospace Firm, 1970; Financial Management, 1975. Home: 2817 Vista Del Arroyo San Angelo TX 76901 Office: Angelo State U San Angelo TX 76901

EBERLE, WILLIAM FRANCIS, stockbroker; b. Beallsville, Ohio, Aug. 22, 1915; s. George and Katie Beall (Hunnel) E.; B.C.S., Benjamin Franklin U., 1933-36; m. Gertrude Eloise Johnson, Sept. 3, 1937; children—John Donald and Judith Lee (twins). Mem. faculty Fenn Coll. (now Cleve. State U.), 1963-64; purchasing agt. Thomas Machine, Glenshaw, Pa., 1939-41; asst. purchasing agt. Chambersburg Engring. Co. (Pa.), 1941-42; sr. buyer Kaiser Frazer Corp., Warren, Ohio and Ypsilanti, Mich., 1942-46; with Diamond Shamrock Corp., 1946—, mgr. purchasing adminstrn., Cleve., until 1970, project purchasing mgr., La Porte, Tex., 1970-78; account exec. All Am. Mgmt. Corp., Nassau Bay, Tex., 1978—. Mem. adminstrv. bd. trustees Seabrook (Tex.) Methodist Ch. Mem. Nat. Assn. Purchasing Mgmt. (certified purchasing mgr.), Purchasing Mgmt. Assn. Houston. Clubs: Clear Lake Country, Shriners, Masons. Home and office: 2007 Back Bay Ct Nassau Bay TX 77058

EBERSOLE, ALVA VERNON, educator; b. Liberal, Kans., June 27, 1919; s. Alva Vernon and Eleanor Lucia (Cash) E.; B.A., Mexico City Coll., 1949; M.A., 1951; Ph.D., U. Kans., 1957; m. Carmen Iranzo, Sept. 24, 1949. Asst. instr. Spanish, U. Kans., Lawrence, 1952-57; instr. Spanish, U. Ill., Champaign, 1957-59; asst. prof. Spanish, U. Mass., Amherst, 1959-61, asso. prof., 1961-62; prof., head dept. Spanish, Adelphi U., Garden City, N.Y., 1962-68; prof. Spanish, U. N.C., Chapel Hill, 1968—. Served with USMC, 1937-41, USNR, 1944-45. Mem. AAUP, Modern Lang. Assn., Am. Assn. Tchrs. Spanish and Portuguese (pres. N.C. chpt. 1973-74), Sigma Delta Pi, Pi Delta Phi. Author: G. de Castro, El Narciso en su opinion, 1969; Seleccion de comedias del Siglo de Oro, 1973; J.R. de Alarcón, El Texedor de Segovia, 1974; Jose de Cañizares, dramaturgo olvidado, 1975; J.R. de Alarcón, La verdad sospechosa, 1976; Lope de Vega, Las ferias de Madrid, 1977; Perspectives de la Comedia, 1978; Pedro Ciruelo, Reprobación de las supersticiones y hechicertas, 1978. Editor: Hispanofila, 1957—. Estudios de Hispanofila, 1962—. Office: Dept Romance Langs U NC Chapel Hill NC 27514

EBERSOLE, WILLIAM GLENN, publisher; b. Arcadia, Fla., Sept. 30, 1924; s. Glenn Robert and Dora Pelot Ebersole; B.A. in Journalism, U. Fla., 1949, M.A., 1957; m. Wanda Edleweiss Cowart, Aug. 6, 1950; children—Glenda Raye, William James. Student apprentice Arcadian, Arcadia, Fla., 1939-42; linotype operator Gainesville (Fla.) Sun, 1948-49, advt. mgr., 1950-51, advt. dir., 1951-64, v.p., 1964—, gen. mgr., 1966-71, publisher, 1971—; exec. v.p. N.Y. Times Affiliated Newspaper Group, 1975—. Bd. dirs. Boys Club, Gainesville, Univ. United Methodist Ch., Gainesville, United Way, Gainesville; pres. J.J. Finley PTA, Gainesville, 1965-66, 73-74. Served with USAAF, 1943-46. Decorated D.F.C., Air medal with 3 oak leaf clusters. Mem. Am. Newspaper Pub. Assn., So. Newspaper Pub. Assn., Fla. Newspaper Advt. Execs., Internat. Newspaper Advt. Execs., Nat. Newspaper Assn., Fla. Press Assn. Club: Gainesville Golf and Country. Home: 1424 NW 14th Ave Gainesville FL 32605 Office: 101 SE 2d Pl Gainesville FL 32602

ECABERT, PETER L., lawyer; b. Ohio, Sept. 10, 1948; s. Claude M. and Mary E.; B.S. in Bus. Adminstrn., Georgetown U., 1970; J.D., Ohio No. U., 1974; LL.M., Boston U., 1977; m. Constance L. Critten, Apr. 24, 1971; children—Christina, Angela. Tax specialist Deloitte Haskins & Sells Co., Lexington, Ky., 1974-79; admitted to Ohio bar, 1974, Ky. bar, 1979; asso. mem. firm Harbison, Kessinger, Lisle & Bush, Lexington, 1979—. C.P.A., Ky. Mem. Am. Bar Assn., Ky. Bar Assn., Ohio Bar Assn., Am. Soc. C.P.A.'s, Ky. Soc. C.P.A.'s, Bluegrass Estate Planning Council. Republican. Roman Catholic. Home: 3513 Boston Rd Lexington KY 40503 Office: 101 E Vine St Lexington KY 40507

ECHENIQUE, JORGE, urologist; b. Havana, Cuba, Oct. 20, 1925; s. Enrique F. and Elena Lutgarda (Gonzalez) E.; came to U.S., 1961, naturalized, 1966; M.D., U. Havana, 1950; m. Nuria Rovira, Jan. 7, 1956; children—Jorge Enrique, Nuria Elena. Intern, Mt. Sinai Hosp., Miami Beach, Fla., 1961-62; resident Jackson Meml. Hosp., Miami, 1962-66; practice medicine specializing in urology, Havana, 1951-61, Miami, 1967—; chief div. urology Mercy Hosp., Miami, 1978—; clin. asst. prof. dept. urology U. Miami. Diplomate Am. Bd. Urology. Fellow A.C.S.; mem. AMA, Dade County Med. Assn., Fla., Greater Miami, So. urol. assns., Am. Urol. Assn., Southeastern Sect. of Am. Urol. Assn., Am. Assn. Clin. Urologists, Royal Soc. Medicine, Am. Fertility Soc. Greater Miami Urol. Soc. Roman Catholic. Clubs: Country Coral Gables, Big Five, Inc. Office: 2931 Coral Way Miami FL 33145

ECHOLS, BARBARA ELLEN, med. center adminstr.; b. Atlanta, Ga., Sept. 29, 1934; d. Harold Thomas and Ellen Ertice (Lyon) Echols; M.B.A., Wake Forest U., 1978; m. William G. Anlyan, July 5, 1973; children by previous marriage—Barbra Ellen Bucci, Laura Marie Bucci. Technician EEG lab. Johns Hopkins Hosp., Balt., 1952-54, chief EEG lab., 1954-66; asst. sch. hygiene and pub. health Johns Hopkins U., 1967-69; asst. to pres. Assn. Am. Med. Colls., Washington, 1969-71; dir. office grants and contracts Duke U. Med. Center, Durham, N.C., 1971-77, coordinator spl. and regulatory programs, 1977—. Mem. Assn. MBA Execs., Internat. Union for Health Edn., Inst. of Soc., Ethics & Life Scis. Author: The Commonsense Guide to Good Eating, 1978; contbr. articles in field to profl. jours. and chpts. to books. Home: 1516 Pinecrest Rd Durham NC 27705 Office: Duke Univ Medical Center Durham NC 27710

ECK, EDGAR CLARENCE, SR., elec. co. exec.; b. Richmond, Va., Jan. 8, 1913; s. Edgar Paul and Mary Elizabeth (Pohlig) E.; student schs., Richmond; m. Mary Anne Chase, May 7, 1938; children—Mary Chase, Edgar Clarence, Virginia K., Francis T., Patricia A. Br. mgr. Westinghouse Electric Supply Corp., Richmond, Va., 1950-55; with Southeastern Electric Supply Corp., Richmond, 1956—, now chmn. bd.; chmn. bd. EBB Investment Corp., Richmond. Mem. Va., Richmond chambers commerce. Roman Catholic. Clubs: West End Cath. Men's, Hermitage Country, K.C. (4 deg.). Home: 7708 Stuart Hall Rd Richmond VA 23229 Office: 8-S Harvie St Richmond VA 23220

ECK, RONALD WARREN, civil engr., educator; b. Allentown, Pa., May 11, 1949; s. Warren Edgar and Viola Minnie (Ruth) E.; B.S. in Civil Engring., Clemson U., 1971, Ph.D., 1975. Research asst. dept. civil engring. Clemson U., Clemson, S.C., 1972-73, teaching asst., 1974—; asst. prof. dept. civil engring. W.Va. U., 1975—; project dir. workshop on heating and cooling bldgs. with coal, W.Va. Bd. Regents, 1979—; prin. investigator W.Va. Dept. of Hwys., 1977—. NDEA fellow, 1971-74; registered profl. engr., W.Va. Mem. ASCE (pres. W.Va. sect. 1979-80), Am. Soc. Engring. Edn. (campus activity coordinator for W.Va. U. chpt. 1977-80), Nat. Soc. Profl. Engrs., Inst. of Transp. Engrs., Am. Road and Transp. Builder's Assn., Am. Soc. Photogrammetry. Contbr. articles on transp. systems and engring. to profl. jours. Home: 487 Lawnview Dr Morgantown WV 26505 Office: WVa Univ Morgantown WV 26506

ECK, WALTER WILLIAM, pharmacist, hosp. adminstr.; b. Ironton, Mo., May 27, 1943, s. John Joseph and Irene (Kovachick) E.; student Alexian Bros. Sch. Radiologic Tech., 1963, Gradwhol Sch. Lab. Tech., 1964; B.S. in Pharmacy, U. Houston, 1973; postgrad. Sam Houston State U.; m. Sherry Lee Britton, May 1, 1965; children—Michael Troy, Heather Leigh. With Western Bapt. Hosp., Paducah, Ky., 1964-65, St. Joseph Hosp., Houston, 1971-72; dir. pharmacy, asst. adminstr. materials mgmt. Madison County Hosp., Madisonville, Tex., 1965—; with Eckerd Drug, Houston, 1971-73; lectr. nursing sch. and orgns., local orgns. Mgr. Little League, 1973—, bd. dirs., v.p. Minor League, 1976-78, v.p. Major League, 1979—; active Brazos Valley Drug Abuse Com., 1977-79, chmn., 1979. John W. Dargavel Found. scholar, 1971. Mem. Am. Soc. Med. Technologists, Am. Registry Radiologic Technologists, Am. Soc. Hosp. Pharmacists, Am. Pharm. Assn., Tex. Pharmacy Assn., Brazos Valley Pharmacy Assn. Roman Catholic. Home: Shady Creek Rd Madisonville TX 77864 Office: 100 W Cross St Madisonville TX 77864

ECKENBERGER, JOHN EDWARD, II, social worker; b. Frederick, Okla., Oct. 13, 1942; s. John Edward and Doris Ellen (Jones) E.; B.A., Southwestern Okla. State U., Weatherford, 1964; M.S.W., U. Okla., 1970; m. Cora Louise Haynes, Oct. 4, 1964; children—John William, Symphony Louise. County adminstr. Okla. Welfare Dept., Medford, 1967-69; social worker Okla. Dept. Corrections, Lawton, 1969-75; pvt. practice marriage and family counseling, Lawton, 1972-75; dir. social work services United Meth. Boys Ranch, Gore, Okla., 1975—. Mem. Internat. Transactional Analysis Assn., Acad. Cert. Social Workers, Okla. Bd. Registered Social Workers, Okla. Assn. Children's Homes and Agys. Democrat. Methodist. Home and office: Route 1 Box 258 Gore OK 74435

ECKENFELDER, WILLIAM WESLEY, JR., environ. and water resources engr.; b. N.Y.C., Nov. 15, 1926; B.C.E., Manhattan Coll., 1946; M.S., Pa. State U., 1948; M.C.E., N.Y. U., 1954; m. Kathy Hurley; children—Larry, Janice, Jennifer. Instr., Manhattan Coll., 1951, asst. research prof., 1953-57, asso. prof., 1957-65; prof. civil engring. U. Tex., Austin, 1965-69; Distinguished prof. environ. and water resources engring. Vanderbilt U., 1970—; cons. UN, State of Israel, industry, municipalities, cons. engrs. Recipient Indsl. Wastes medal Fedn. Sewage and Indsl. Waste Assn., 1957, Kenneth Allen award N.Y. State Sewage and Indsl. Waste Assn., 1957; N.C. State Coll. research fellow, 1947; Pa. State Coll. research fellow, 1948. Fellow Instn. Pub. Health Engrs., Am. Inst. Chemists; mem. Internat. Assn. Water Pollution Research (hon.), Water Pollution Control Fedn., Am. Chem. Soc., ASCE, Am. Soc. Engring. Edn., Am. Inst. Chem. Engrs., Instn. Pub. Health Engrs., Instn. Sewage Purification, N.Y. Acad. Sci., TAPPI, Sigma Xi, Chi Epsilon. Author: Water Quality Engineering, 1970; (with D.L. Ford) Water Pollution Control, 1970; (with Carl E. Adams, Jr.) Process Design Techniques For Industrial Waste Treatment, 1974; contbr. numerous articles on water pollution control to profl. jours. Office: Vanderbilt U Dept Environ and Water Resources Engring Program Nashville TN 37235

ECKERLIN, HERBERT MARTIN, mech. engr., educator; b. N.Y.C., Oct. 23, 1935; m. Herbert A. and Anna M. (Gruber) E.; B.S. in Mech. Engring., Va. Poly. Inst., 1958; M.S., N.C. State U., 1968, Ph.D., 1972; m. Juliana E. Vanderberg, Aug. 2, 1958; children—Herbert C., Mariana E., Lawrence M., Margaret E. Test engr. Norfolk Naval Shipyard, Portsmouth, Va., 1958-59; efficiency engr. Va. Electric & Power Co., 1959-60; thermodynamic engr. Combustion Engring., Windsor, Conn., 1960-65; sr. research engr. Corning Glass Works, Raleigh, N.C., 1965-68; asso. prof. mech. engring. N.C. State U., Raleigh, 1968—; pres. Energy Conserve Ltd., 1977-79; cons. solar and energy conservation, 1974-79; guest lectr. seminars on energy to local civic orgns., 1975-79. Mem. ch. council Holy Trinity Luth. Ch., 1975-78; mem. NW Raleigh Community Adv. Com., 1975-79. Recipient Outstanding Extension award N.C. State U., 1978; NASA Summer Faculty fellow, 1974; registered profl. engr., N.C. Mem. ASME, Phi Kappa Phi, Sigma Xi. Lutheran. Club: Toastmasters Internat. Contbr. articles on energy conservation and engring. to profl. jours.; patentee in field. Home: 4313 Azalea Dr Raleigh NC 27612 Office: Mechanical and Aerospace Engring PO Box 5246 NC State Univ Raleigh NC 27650

ECKERT, VERA LILLIAN, poet; b. Wichita Falls, Tex., Nov. 17, 1911; d. Everett Beal and Mary Elinor (Luck) Stonecipher; m. Henry Patrick Eckert, July 4, 1937; children—Gloria June Eckert Reed, Janet Rose Eckert Kemp, Henry Dale. Author: The Legacy of Santa Fe and other Poems of the Southwest, 1972; poet laureate Tex. Fedn. Women's Clubs, 1975-76; poet laureate alt. of Tex., 1976-77. Recipient Clark Ashton Smith-Lilith Lorraine Meml. award, 1970, Poetry Soc. Tex. ann. awards, 1970—, State Poet Laureate contest citation Tex. Ho. of Reps., 1975. Mem. Tex. Fedn. Women's Clubs (dist. officer 1976-78, poet laureate 1979-80), Poetry Soc. Tex. (counselor 1970—), DAR, Woman's Forum of San Angelo (Tex.). Home: 2723 L S U Ave San Angelo TX 76901

ECKHARDT, ROBERT CHRISTIAN, congressman; b. Austin, Tex., July 16, 1913; s. Joseph Carl Augustus and Norma (Wurzbach) E.; B.A., U. Tex., 1935, LL.B., 1939. S.W. regional dir. Office Coordinator Inter-Am. Affairs, Austin, 1944-46; admitted to Tex. bar, 1939, practice law Austin, 1939-42, 46-48, Dallas, 1948-50, Houston, 1950-67; mem. Tex. Ho. of Reps., Austin, 1958-67; mem. 90th-96th Congresses from 8th Tex. Dist., mem. interstate and fgn. commerce com., chmn. consumer protection and fin. subcom., 1977-78, chmn. subcom. on oversight and investigations, 1979—; chmn. Democratic Study Group, 1975-76. Served with USAAF, 1942-44. Mem. State Bar Tex. Democrat. Author: (with Charles L. Black, Jr.) Tides of Power, 1976. Office: 1741 Longworth House Office Bldg Washington DC 20515 also 8632 Fed Bldg 515 Rusk Houston TX 77002

ECKOLS, HOWARD LOYD, banker; b. Luling, Tex., Mar. 23, 1930; s. Lewis Vernard and Gladys (Colwell) E.; student Tex. Tech., 1947-48; B.B.A., S.W. Tex. State U., 1954; m. Martha Lynn Wilson, Jan. 24, 1954; children—Timothy, Linda. State auditor State of Tex., Austin, 1954-55; mgr. data processing Shell Oil Co., Houston, 1956-62, Tex. Commerce Bank, 1962-69; mgr. data processing Houston Nat. Bank, 1969-73, corr. banking dept., 1973—, asst. v.p., 1965-75, v.p., 1975—. Bd. dirs. S.W. Tex. State U. Ex-Students Assn. Served with USN, 1948-49. Mem. Data Processing Mgmt. Assn. (dir. Houston chpt. 1965—). Home: 7219 Bayou Forest Dr Houston TX 77088 Office: Box 2518 Houston TX 77001

ECKSTEIN, ROBERT EPHRAIM, ins. agt.; b. N.Y.C., Dec. 22, 1928; s. Frederick and Edith (Anrig) E.; B.A., La. State U., 1946-50; J.D., Loyola U., New Orleans, 1974; m. Ernestine Lehman, June 3, 1951; children—Linda Lee, Michael Lehman. Life ins. agt. Equitable Life Assurance Soc. U.S., New Orleans, 1951—. Pres. New Orleans chpt. Cystic Fibrosis Found., 1957-58. Served with USNR, 1947-53. Recipient Nat. Quality award Nat. Assn. Life Underwriters, 1952; named to Equitable's Hall of Fame, 1969, named to Million Dollar Round Table, 1957. Mem. New Orleans Estate Planning Council (pres. 1971-72), New Orleans Life Underwriters Assn. (v.p. 1956-57, chmn. ethics com. 1970-74, New Orleans Life Ins. Man of Yr. 1973), Zeta Beta Tau. Republican. Jewish. Author articles in field. Mem. Loyola Law Rev. Home: 530 Lowerline St New Orleans LA 70118 Office: 600 Commerce Bldg New Orleans LA 70112

EDDIN, M(ARY) EDNA, economist; b. Daisy, Tenn., Nov. 8, 1941; d. Tip and Floretta Wright; B.A., Berea Coll., 1965; M.A., Am. U., 1969; Ph.D., U. S.C., 1976; m. M. Shehab Eddin, Oct. 1, 1964. Research asst. Am. Council Edn., Washington, 1963-66; economist Dept. Commerce, Washington, 1966-67; instr. econs. Gardner-Webb Coll., Columbia, S.C., 1969-73, planning and devel. cons., 1973-75; asso. prof. econs. Brescia Coll., 1976-78; sr. economist HUD, Louisville, 1978—. Mem. AAUP, Am. Econ. Assn., So. Econ. Assn., Am. Polit. Sci. Assn., ACLU, Pi Sigma Alpha, Omicron Delta Epsilon, Phi Delta Kappa. Author: Attitude Toward Business in Relations to Economic Knowledge, 1976; contbr. articles to profl. jours. Office: HUD Louisville Area Office Louisville KY 40201

EDDIN, M. SHEHAB, educator, adminstr.; b. Cairo, Egypt, July 20, 1932; s. Mohammed Hassan Shehab and Asala (Eltabeiy) E.; B.A., U. Cairo, 1958; M.A., Am. U., Washington, 1963, Ph.D., 1966, postdoctoral research, 1967; postdoctoral research U.N.C., Chapel Hill, 1972-73, Grad. Sch. Dept. Agr., Washington, 1967-68; m. Mary Edna Wright, Oct. 1, 1964; 1 dau., Ahlam. Came to U.S., 1960, naturalized, 1970. Mgr. tannery, Cairo, 1946-50; tchr. English and Arabic, Syria, U.A.R., 1950-60; supr. distbn. World Confn. Orgns. of Teaching Professions, Washington, 1962-65; asst. prof. polit. sci. and econs. Western Carolina U., Cullowhee, N.C., 1967-69; prof. Gardner-Webb Coll., Boiling Springs, N.C., 1969-75; project adminstr. Dept. Parks, Recreation and Tourism, State of S.C., Columbia, 1973-74; owner, dir. pvt. evening sch. adult edn., Cairo, 1952-55; adminstrv. asst., asst. dir. Mus. Rokn-Helwan, Cairo, 1955-58; mem. Egyptian Ednl. Mission to Syria, 1958-60, also instr. English civilization and Arabic, Shaabiya Inst., Syria; planning and devel. cons., Columbia, S.C., Owensboro, Ky., 1974-78; planner Green River Area Devel. dist., Owensboro, 1977-78; regional economist U.S. C.E., Louisville, 1978—. Mem. Am. Polit. Sci. Assn., Am. Soc. Internat. Law, Am. Acad. Polit. and Social Scis., Internat., So. polit. sci. assns., Middle East Inst., Am. Econ. Assn., Am. Planning Assn., Am. Civil Liberties Union, Delta Mu Delta, Pi Sigma Alpha. Author: Pan-Arabism and the Islamic Tradition: Ideology and Political Consensus, 1967. Contbr. articles to jours. Rotarian. Home: PO Box 1886 Louisville KY 40201 Office: Corps Engrs Louisville KY 40201

EDDY, DOUGLAS MANN, architect; b. Saginaw, Mich., Apr. 23, 1942; s. Clarence Nathan and Loretta Marguerite (McKeith) E.; B.Arch., U. Ariz., 1970; m. Carole E. Scott, June 26, 1965; children—Heather, Shannon. Vice-pres. for health facility design William Wilde and Assos., Tucson, 1970-74; sr. planner Med. Planning Assos., Malibu, Calif., 1974-75; dir. cons. services Herman Miller, Zeeland, Mich., 1975-78, regional planning mgr., Atlanta, 1978-79; founder, Tekton Devel. Corp., 1980—. Served with USAF, 1962-66. Mem. Am. Inst. Architects, Am. Hosp. Assn., Am. Assn. Hosp. Planners. Home: 2075 Six Branches Dr Roswell GA 30076 Office: 3565 Piedmont Rd Atlanta GA 30305

EDDY, GEORGE GAGE, JR., ret. army officer, educator, author, cons.; b. Washington, Sept. 26, 1921; s. George Gage and Josephine Murray (Tracy) E.; A.B., U. Mich., 1945; M.B.A., Babson Coll., 1958; Ph.D., U. Tex., 1974; m. Joele Germaine Moene, July 6, 1946; children—Christopher, Robin. Enlisted in U.S. Army, 1942, advanced through grades to col., 1966; insp. gen. Def. Supply Agy., 1962-64; bn. comdr. 4th Armored Div., Germany, 1965-66; comdr. munitions depot complex, Germany, 1966-68; gen. staff officer for logistics Dept. Army, Washington, 1968-69; ret., 1969; tchr. bus. policy U. Tex., Austin, 1973—; bus. case researcher and writer, 1972—; mgmt. cons., Austin, 1974—; feature writer West Lake Picayune, 1976—; pres. Southwestern Mgmt. Services, Ltd. Mem. city council City of West Lake Hills (Tex.), 1972-73, 74—, mayor pro tem, 1977—; mem. West Lake Hills Planning and Zoning Commn., 1972. Decorated Legion of Merit with oak leaf cluster, Joint Service Commendation medal, Purple Heart. Mem. Acad. Mgmt., Case Research Assn., Mil. Order World Wars, Am. Def. Preparedness Assn., Assn. U.S. Army, U.S. Armor Assn., Beta Gamma Sigma, Sigma Iota Epsilon. Contbr. articles to profl. jours. Home: 809 Terrace Mountain Dr Austin TX 78746 Office: Dept Mgmt U Tex Austin TX 78712

EDEL, JOHN JACOB, geophys. co. exec.; b. Phila., Sept. 16, 1939; s. Leonard Jacob and Dorothy Williams E.; E.E., Bucknell U., 1962; m. Janice Elizabeth Savoy, Jan. 14, 1967; children—Gretchen Elizabeth, Pamela Clare, Samuel Orion. With Western Geophys. Co., 1966—, asst. resident mgr., Cairo, Egypt, 1972-74, resident mgr., Karachi, Pakistan, 1974-76, supr. various fgn. ops., 1976-78, supr. gulf coast marine crews, Houston, 1978—. Served with USAF, 1962-66. Mem. European Assn. Exploration Geophyscists. Republican. Episcopalian. Office: 10001 Richmond St Houston TX 77042

EDEN, MARK ALLAN, ins. agy. exec.; b. Bklyn., Feb. 28, 1946; s. John Jerome and Lorraine (Tannenbaum) E.; B.S. in Acctg., Fla. State U., 1968; M.B.A. in Fin., Ga. State U., 1971; m. Margie Cohen, July 15, 1970; children—Jason Mitchell, Brent Michael. Margin analyst Reynolds & Co., Atlanta, 1969; counselor Moye Fin. Assos., Inc., Atlanta, 1971-74; partner Lagana & Eden, Atlanta, 1974—; mem. advanced underwriting adv. bd. Indpls. Life Ins. Co., 1978—. Chmn. young execs. div. Atlanta Jewish Welfare Fedn., 1979-80. Served with Ga. Army N.G., 1968-74. Named Agt. of Year, Indpls. Life, 1976; Outstanding Young Man of Am., U.S. Jaycees, 1976. Mem. Chartered Life Underwriters, Nat. Assn. Life Underwriters, Nat. Assn. Securities Dealers, Am. Soc. Chartered Life Underwriters, Atlanta Estate Planning Council, Million Dollar Round Table, Fla. State U. Alumni Assn., Fla. State U. Boosters Assn., Lambda Chi Alpha. Jewish. Club: Standard. Home: 1397 Epping Forest Dr Atlanta GA 30319 Office: 1465 Northside Dr 28 Atlanta GA 30318

EDGAR, THOMAS FLYNN, chem. engr., educator; b. Bartlesville, Okla., Apr. 17, 1945; s. Maurice Russell and Natalie May (Flynn) E.; B.S. in Chem. Engring., U. of Kans., 1967; Ph.D. in Chem. Engring., Princeton U., 1971; m. Donna Jean Proffitt, July 15, 1967; children—Rebecca, Jeffrey. Process engr., Continental Oil Co., Balt., 1968-69; asst. prof. chem. engring. U. Tex. at Austin, 1971-76, asso. prof., 1976—, dir. In Situ Lignite Gasification Project; cons. Newton Steele Co., Teknekron, Inc., Mobil Oil Corp., Elgin-Butler Brick, Co., Nat. Bur. Standards, U.N. Devel. Program; v.p. CACHE Corp., Cambridge, Mass., 1980—; dir. Am. Automotive Control Council, 1978-80. Registered profl. engr., Tex.; recipient outstanding counselor award Am. Inst. of Chem. Engring., 1974, good prof. award, U. Tex. at Austin, Am. Inst. Chem. Engring. student chpt., 1974; named outstanding young mem. S. Tex. section of Am. Inst. Chem. Engring., 1976. Mem. Am. Inst. Chem. Engring., Soc. of Petroleum Engrs., Tau Beta Pi, Phi Lambda Upsilon, Omicron Delta Kappa, Am. Inst. Chem. Engrs. (exec. com. S. Tex. Sect. 1977). Methodist. Author numerous articles, book chpts., papers and reports; editor profl. jour., 1977—. Home: 5409 Highland Crest Austin TX 78731 Office: Dept Chem Engring U Tex Austin TX 78712

EDGE, DONALD (RICHARD), architect; b. Detroit, Jan. 25, 1927; s. Ernest R. and Grace (Beymer) E.; B.Arch., U. Mich., 1951; m. Alice Nan Divine, June 2, 1956; children—Barbara Carol, Karl Richard, Nancy Lynn. Draftsman for various archtl. firms, Detroit, 1951-52; asso. with William Manly King, architect, West Palm Beach, Fla., 1954-58; partner Plockleman, Powell and Edge, Palm Beach, Fla., 1958-60; prin. Donald R. Edge, architect, Palm Beach, 1960-64; mem. archtl. staff Maass, Edge and Willson, West Palm Beach, 1964-66, Powell, Edge and Willson, Palm Beach, 1966-67, Powell-Edge archtl. firm, West Palm Beach area, 1967-77; pres. The Edge Firm Inc., West Palm Beach, 1977—. Major works include: Palm Beach County Courthouse, 1970, Fla. Hosp., Orlando, 1954-80, Fla. Hosp. Satellite, Altamonte Springs, Rush Found. Hosp., Meridian, Miss., 1969-78, Orthopedic Clinic, Winter Park, Fla., 1973. Bd. dirs. Crippled Children's Soc., 1966-79. Served with USN, 1945-46. Recipient Appreciation award Fla. Hosp., Orlando, 1979; Appreciation award Crippled Children's Soc., 1977. Mem. AIA (mem. com. on architecture for health 1970-80, rep. to Nat. Fire Protection Assn. 1978-80), Fla. State Bd. Architecture (pres. 1960), Fla. Assn. Architects, Am. Hosp. Assn., Am. Assn. for Hosp. Planning, Nat. Fire Protection Assn., Fla. Hosp. Assn. Republican. Office: 444 Bunker Rd West Palm Beach FL 33405

EDGE, JAMES WESLEY, oil co. exec.; b. Rattan, Okla., Mar. 1, 1934; s. John Diamond and Dollie Mae Edge; B.S. in Petroleum Engring., U. Okla., 1956; m. Geraldine Sue Bryant, Apr. 17, 1954; children—James Michael, Teri Lynn. Petroleum engr. Tenneco, Wichita Falls and Oklahoma City, 1956-64; cons. engring., Oklahoma City, 1964-65; with Ashland Exploration, Inc., Houston, 1965—, v.p. planning and econs., 1977—. Registered profl. engr., Tex. Mem. Soc. Petroleum Engrs., Am. Petroleum Inst., Ind. Petroleum Assn. Am., Planning Execs. Inst., N. Am. Soc. Corp. Planning. Republican. Baptist. Home: 10703 Valley Forge Houston TX 77042 Office: PO Box 1503 Houston TX 77001

EDGE, ROBERT LANEER, communications cons.; b. Los Angeles, Sept. 8, 1925; s. Dan and Mary Gertrude (Baker) E.; B.S., Omaha U., 1962; M.S. in Elec. Engring., Stanford U., 1965; grad. Advanced Mgmt. Program, Harvard U., 1968; m. Mary Catherine Boyce, Mar. 14, 1945; children—Rebecca Lynn, Jeffrey Glenn, Claudia Mary. Enlisted in USAAF, 1943, commd. 2d lt., 1945, advanced through grades to maj. gen. USAF, 1974; service in Japan and Germany; dep. dir., then dir. Command Control and Communications, Hdqrs. USAF, Washington, 1971-75, asst. chief staff communications and computer resources, 1975-77; ret., 1977; ind. cons. in communications and computers, Springfield, Va., 1977—. Decorated D.S.M., Meritorious Service medal, Joint Services Commendation medal. Mem. Armed Forces Communications-Electronics Assn., Air Force Assn., Order Daedalians. Author articles in field. Address: 8408 Willow Forge Rd Springfield VA 22152

EDGECOMB, CLARK RAYMOND, JR., mktg. cons.; b. Kansas City, Mo., Aug. 28, 1918; s. Clark Raymond and Eddie Robertson E.; indsl. engring. certificate Calif. Inst. Tech., 1942; m. Virginia Baynton Starky, Sept. 3, 1938; children—Clark Raymond III, Karen Lee, John Robb. Mgr. sales devel. U.S. Schlumberger Well Services, Houston, 1943-69; mgr. tech. services Royal Resources and Imperial Am. Oil Co., Houston, 1969-71; exec. dir. Energy Research and Edn. Found., Houston, 1971-73; pres. Record Service Center, Houston, 1973-78; owner, pres. Edgecomb & Assos., mktg. cons., Houston; dir. Los Diez Land Corp., Knowledge Box, advt. agy. Pres., chmn. bd. Houston Internat. Trade and Travel Fair, 1964-65. Mem. Am. Assn. Petroleum Geologists, Am. Inst. Mining, Metall. and Petroleum Engrs. Republican. Episcopalian. Clubs: Houston Petroleum; Sugar Creek (Tex.) Country. Home: 4 Charleston St S Sugar Land TX 77478 Office: Edgecomb & Assos 3110 Eastside Suite 11 Houston TX 77098

EDGERTON, A. FREEMAN, lawyer; b. Coushatta, La., Oct. 22, 1919; s. Clarence Eugene and Daisy Bell (Gardner) E.; B.A., La. State U., 1940, J.D., 1976; m. Kerttu Sofia Maria von Ammondt Friman, Feb. 26, 1946. Ins. sales E.T. Edgerton Agy., Asheville, N.C., 1940-42; owner, operator ins. agy., Charlotte, N.C., 1948-73; admitted to La. bar, 1977, N.C. bar, 1977; legal research asst. to judge La. Ct. Appeal, Baton Rouge, 1977-78; asso. firm Watson, Blanche, Wilson & Posner, Baton Rouge, 1978—; dir. State Nat. Capital Corp., State Nat. Life Ins. Co., Delta Nat. Life Ins. Co. Pres., Charlotte br. English-Speaking Union, 1962-72; chmn. dept. fin. Diocesan Council, Episcopal Diocese N.C., 1957-66; bd. dirs. Greater Carolinas chpt. ARC, 1962-70. Served with U.S. Army, 1942-46. C.L.U. Mem. N.C., La., Am., Baton Rouge bar assns., Phi Alpha Delta, Phi Kappa Phi, Omicron Delta Kappa, Kappa Alpha. Democrat. Clubs: Charlotte City; City (Baton Rouge); Blowing Rock (N.C.) Country. Home: 7982 Brandon Dr Baton Rouge LA 70809 Office: 505 North Blvd PO Box 2995 Baton Rouge LA 70821

EDGERTON, RICHARD, restaurant/hotel owner; b. Haverford, Pa., May 2, 1911; s. Charles and Ida Bonner E.; m. Marie Lytle Page, Oct. 24, 1936; children—Leila, Margaret, Carol. Pres./owner Lakeside Inn Properties, Inc., Mt. Dora, Fla., 1935—; co-owner 19 Burger King restaurants, Pa., 1966—; gen. mgr., pres. Buck Hill Falls (Pa.) Co., 1961-65; pres., chief exec. officer Eustis Sand Co., Mt. Dora, Fla.; founding dir. Fla. Service Corp., Tampa; dir. First Nat. Bank, Mt. Dora. Mem. Gov.'s Little Cabinet, 1955-61. Trustee Berry Coll.; bd. dirs. Mt. Dora Community Trust Fund. Served to lt. USNR, 1944-46; ETO. Mem. Am. (dir.), Fla. (past pres.), NH. (past pres.) hotel and motel assns., Newcomen Soc., Welcome Soc., Pa. Soc. Clubs: Miami; Mt. Dora Yacht, Mt. Dora Golf. Home: 3d and McDonald Sts Mt Dora FL 32757 Office: 234 W 3d Ave Mt Dora FL 32757

EDGINGTON, WALTER ROY, electronics co. exec.; b. Guthrie Center, Iowa, Apr. 26, 1925; s. Thomas William and Helen Violet (Schrader) E.; B.S., M.S., Georgetown U., 1954; m. Florence Mary Kowaleski, Nov. 9, 1949; children—Eric Michael, Bruce Edward. Various civilian positions U.S. Army, 1949-66, intelligence specialist, 1954-62, ops. analyst, 1962-66, program mgr. Communications Projects, 1966-69; mgr. Monmouth Engring. Center GTE Sylvania Inc., New Shrewsbury, N.J., 1969-71, mgr. office Springfield, Va., 1967-71, v.p. govt. relations, Arlington, Va., 1972—. Served with U.S. Army, 1946-49. Mem. Armed Forces Communications and Electronics Assn. (dir. 1977—), Am. Def. Preparedness Assn., Assn. U.S. Army, Electronic Industries Assn. (chmn. export/import com. 1976—), Navy League U.S., Nat. Security Indsl. Assn. (dir. 1977—), Air Force Assn. Clubs: International, Capitol Hill, Aviation. Home: 4843 Dodson Dr Annandale VA 22003 Office: 1800 N Kent St Arlington VA 22209

EDISEN, CLAYTON BYRON, psychiatrist; b. Chgo., Apr. 5, 1927; s. Byron Parker and Elsie Eleonore (Mielke) E.; Ph.B., U. Chgo., 1949, M.D., 1953; postgrad. Tulane U., 1954-57; m. Barbara Schreier, Dec. 1, 1968; children—Niki Paul Bradley, Brenda Pumphrey, Laura Ingrid, Glenn Knute, Lynn Kirsten. Research asso. Ill. Dept. Pub. Welfare, Manteno State Hosp., 1953; rotating intern U. Chgo. Clinics, 1953-54; asst. vis. physician Charity Hosp. La., New Orleans, 1954-56, resident psychiatry, 1956-57; med. dir., psychiatrist Lincoln Parish Guidance Center, Ruston, La., 1955-56, Monroe (La.) Area Guidance Center, 1957-58; practice medicine specializing in psychiatry, New Orleans, 1957—; prof. exptl. communications designs dept. tchr. edn. Tulane U., New Orleans, 1973—. staff cons. Childrens Bur., New Orleans, 1958-60; mem. staff DePaul Hosp., 1957—, Touro Infirmary, 1958-72, Coliseum House, 1974—; USPHS fellow in psychiatry Tulane U. Sch. Medicine, 1954-57, instr. psychiatry, 1956-57, faculty Sch. Social Work, 1958-60; lectr. Ann. Life Inst., Jewish Fedn. New Orleans, 1961. Chmn., U. Chgo. Alumni Found. Bd., New Orleans, 1962-63. Served with U.S. Army, 1945-47. Hon. state senator La. Senate, 1976. Diplomate Am. Bd. Neurology and Psychiatry, Pan Am. Med. Assn. Fellow Am. Geriatric Soc., Sci. Council Internat. Coll. Angiology; mem. Am. (Physicians Recognition award 1969), So. med. assns., La., Orleans Parish, Second Dist. med. socs., Am. Group Psychotherapy Assn., La. Group Psychotherapy Soc. and Inst., Am. (panelist), La., Canadian (corr. 1966), World psychiat. assns., New Orleans Psychiat. Forum, New Orleans Area Psychiat. Soc., Royal Soc. Health (London), Assn. Am. Physicians and Surgeons, Am. Heart Assn., N.Y. Acad. Scis., Am. Soc. Videology, Internat. Platform Assn., Greater New Orleans Area C. of C., Sigma Xi. Contbr. articles to med. jours. Home: 515 Broadway New Orleans LA 70118 Office: Suite 305 1636 Toledano St New Orleans LA 70115

EDLIN, JOHN CHARLES, physician, educator; b. Wilmington, Del., June 16, 1943; s. Frank Edward and Eleanor Laura (Frederick) E.; B.S. in Psychology, Duke U., 1965; M.D., U. Tenn., 1968; m. Mailand Lorenda Stevens, Aug. 23, 1969; children—Mark Steven, Scott Charles, Matthew Shawn. Intern and resident in pediatrics Med. Center, Duke U., Durham, N.C., 1969-71; fellow in growth and devel. U. London (Eng.), 1971; fellow in adolescent medicine Children's Hosp., Harvard U., Boston, 1972-73; asst. prof., dir. adolescent medicine dept. pediatrics, Southwestern Med. Sch., U. Tex., Dallas, 1973-77, asst. prof. depts. pediatrics and internal medicine, dir. adolescent medicine program, 1977—; med. dir. Dallas County Juvenile Detention Center, 1977—; mem. adv. bd. Dallas County Juvenile Dept., 1977—; cons. Timberlawn Hosp., Baylor Coll. Dentistry, Western State Coll. Colo. Mem. Soc. for Adolescent Medicine (exec. council), Am. Acad. Pediatrics, Tex. Acad. Pediatrics, Am. Soc. for Adolescent Psychiatry, N.Tex. Soc. for Adolescent Psychiatry. Mem. United Church of Christ. Home: 4821 Twinpost Dr Dallas TX 75234 Office: Southwestern Med Sch U Texas Dept Pediatrics 5323 Harry Hines Blvd Dallas TX 75235

EDMISTEN, RUFUS LIGH, state ofcl.; b. Watauga County, N.C., July 12, 1941; B.A. with honors, U. N.C.; LL.B. with honors, George Washington U.; married; 1 dau. Admitted to N.C. bar, 1967, D.C. bar; formerly chief aide to U.S. Senator Sam J. Ervin; dep. chief counsel U.S. Senate Select Com. on Presdl. Campaign Activities (Watergate Com.); chief counsel, staff dir. U.S. Senate Judiciary Subcom. on Separation of Powers; counsel U.S. Senate Judiciary Subcom. on Constl. Rights; atty. gen. State of N.C., Raleigh, 1974—. Bd. advisers Lees-McRae Coll. Served with U.S. Army, 1966-67. Recipient Wildlife Conservation award Watauga County, N.C., 1962; Good Govt. award State of N.C., 1969. Mem. N.C., D.C., Am., Fed. bar assns., Nat. Assn. Attys. Gen. Democrat. Club: Masons. Office: Dept Justice Justice Bldg Corner Fayetteville and Morgan Sts Raleigh NC 27611*

EDMISTON-VANDERVOORT, PAMELA ANN, designer; b. Mobile, Ala., Feb. 9, 1949; d. James Dean and Jewel Rebecca E.; student Brevard Jr. Coll., 1967-68; m. H. A. H. Vandervoort, May 7, 1977. Trainer, mgr., owner Trilogy Farms, Miami, 1974-78; v.p. Into of Fla., Inc., Miami, 1974—; owner Trilogy Pet Farms II, Princeton, Fla., 1979—. Mem. Am. Horse Show Assn., So. Fla. Horse Show Assn. Methodist. Home and Office: 24700 SW 152d Ave Princeton FL 33032

EDMONDS, DONALD RAY, systems engr.; b. Jersey City, Mar. 16, 1937; s. Clarence Raymond and Marilyn (Hrinyak) E.; B.S., B.A., Rutgers U., 1960; M.S., Ohio State U., 1966, Ph.D., 1973; m. Clydene Ann Jones, Dec. 19, 1965; children—Catherine Joy, Douglas Jones. Research asso./asst. Ohio State U., Columbus, 1963-66; sr. operations research analyst N. Am. Rockwell Corp., Columbus, O., 1966-68; research asso. Ohio State U., Columbus, 1968-69; lectr. U. So. Calif., Los Angeles, 1969-70; asst. prof. U. Utah, Salt Lake City, 1971-74; sr. research analyst Presearch, Inc., Arlington, Va., 1974-76; asst. prof. U. So. Calif., Los Angeles, 1976-77; sr. staff scientist George Washington U., Washington, 1977-78; dept. staff Mitre Corp., McLean, Va., 1979—; cons. Summit Research Corp., Gaithersburg, Md., 1977—; asso. professorial lectr. George Washington U., dept. operationsresearch, Sch. Gen. Studies, 1977—. Served with USAF, 1960-63. Mem. Ops. Research Soc. Am., Mil. Ops. Research Soc., IEEE, Am. Inst. Indsl. Engrs., AAAS, Washington Ops. Research/Mgmt. Sci Council, Beta Theta Pi. Republican. Unitarian. Home: 5004 Regina Dr Annandale VA 22003 Office: 1820 Dolley Madison Blvd McLean VA 22102

EDMONDS, HENRY DAVID, counselor; b. Anderson, S.C., Oct. 14, 1938; s. Henry N. and Helen K. (Johnson) E.; A.A., Anderson Coll., 1959; B.A. in Psychology, Furman U., 1961, M.A., 1970; m. Mary Judith Hance, Dec. 18, 1960; children—Steven, Lisa. Social worker S.C. Dept. Social Services, Anderson, 1964; counselor S.C. Employment Security Commn., Anderson, 1965—; instr. Tri County Tech. Coll., Limestone Coll.; chmn. bd. Anderson-Oconee Head Start Child Devel.; mem. adv. com. Tri County Tech. Coll. Mem. Am., S.C. (asso.) psychol. assns., Anderson Assn. Service Agys. (past pres.), Anderson-Oconee Mental Health Assn. Baptist. Home: 1404 Forest Ln Anderson SC 29621

EDMONDS, VERNON H., educator; b. Clinton, Okla., Dec. 18, 1927; s. Clarence Lee and Mary Jane (Hurd) E.; A.A., Okla. State U., 1952, B.A., 1954; M.S., Purdue U., 1955; Ph.D., U. Mo., 1960; m. Gloria Graves King, Aug. 26, 1955; 1 son, Kevin. Instr. psychology and sociology Cottey Coll., Nevada, Mo., 1956-58; asst. prof. sociology U. South Fla., Tampa, 1960-63, Fla. State U., Tallahassee, 1963-67; prof. sociology Coll. William and Mary, Williamsburg, Va., 1967—. Pres. ACLU of Fla., 1966-67; chmn. ACLU Tallahassee, 1964-67; mem. nat. bd. dirs. ACLU, 1965-67. Served with USAAF, 1946-49. NSF grantee, 1970-72. Mem. Am. Sociol. Assn., Nat. Council Family Relations, So. Sociol. Soc. Asso. editor Jour. Marriage and Family; prin. author: Social Behavior, 1967. Home: 2 Travis Ln Williamsburg VA 23185 Office: College of William and Mary Williamsburg VA 23185

EDMONDSON, DAVID VIRGIL, banker; b. Chattanooga, Nov. 5, 1928; s. Clarence W. and Grace B. (Williams) E.; B.B.A., U. Chattanooga, 1950; postgrad. Sch. Banking of South, La. State U., 1978; m. Lucile Joyce Mansfield, Apr. 23, 1955; children—Annis Edmondson Trevartren, Margaret, David. Mgmt. trainee So. Wood Preserving Co., 1950-52; pres. Edmondson Coll., 1952-74; asst. head retail div. Am. Nat. Bank, Chattanooga, 1974-80, sr. v.p., 1980—. Bd. dirs. Better Bus. Bur. of Chattanooga, 1956—, Diabetes Assn., Chattanooga, 1975—, Jr. Achievement, Chattanooga, 1978—, Conv. and Visitors Bur., Chattanooga, 1976—; mem. Tenn. Bd. Vocat. Edn., 1961—. Mem. Am. Inst. Banking, Consumer Bankers' Assn. Methodist. Clubs: Signal Mountain (Tenn.) Golf and Country, Kiwanis (pres. chpt. 1971-72, lt.-gov. dist. 1978-79). Office: Am Nat Bank 8th and Market Sts Chattanooga TN 37402

EDMONDSON, JEANNETTE BARTLESON, state govt. ofcl.; b. Muskogee, Okla.; d. A. Chapman and Georgia S. Bartleson; student Hollins Coll., Roanoke, Va., 1942; B.A., U. Okla., 1946; m. J. Howard Edmondson, May 15, 1946; children—James Howard, Jeanne Edmondson Watkins, Patricia Edmondson Zimmer. Sec. of state of Okla., 1979—. Chmn. Okla. chpt. Am. Heart Assn., 1979-81. Mem. Kappa Alpha Theta, Phi Epsilon Omega. Democrat. Methodist. Address: 101 State Capitol Oklahoma City OK 73105

EDMONDSON, RUBY JOHNSON, educator; b. Jefferson, S.C., July 3, 1942; d. Carl M. and Annie Bell (Campbell) Johnson; B.S., Atlantic Christian Coll., 1966; M.A., Appalachian State U., 1969; Ed.D., Nova U., 1976; postgrad. U. N.C. Charlotte and Greensboro, Western Carolina U. U. S.C.; m. Alton Edmondson, Sept. 1, 1972. Tchr., Buford Elementary Sch., Lancaster, S.C., 1966-68, Rowan Tech. Inst., Salisbury, N.C., 1969-74; counselor Concord (N.C.) City Sch. System, 1974-79; psychologist Charlotte-Mecklenburg Sch. System, 1979—. Mem. Mayor's Commn. on Status of Women,

1970-75; rep. United Fund, 1973-74. Certified elementary tchr., N.C., S.C., counselor N.C., psychologist, N.C. Mem. Am., N.C. personnel and guidance assns., NEA, N.C. Assn. Educators, Assn. Classroom Tchrs., Bus. and Profl. Women's Club. Presbyterian. Home: 2632-C Park Rd Charlotte NC 28029 Office: 1501 Euclid Ave Charlotte NC 28209

EDMUNDS, EDWARD WAYNE, mktg. exec.; b. New Brunswick, N.J., June 29, 1945; s. Edward Edmund and Shirley Barbara E.; student U.S. Naval Acad., 1963-64; A.B. in Phys. Geology, Colgate U., 1967; postgrad. Fla. State U., 1967; m. Diane Margaret Kasten, July 1, 1970; children—Shawn Michael, Jarret Christian. Sales engr. Huntington (W.Va.) Alloy Products div. Internat. Nickel Co., 1967-69; account exec. Southeastern Personnel Co., Atlanta, 1969-70; sales engr. Tube Sales, Inc., div. Superior Tube Co., Atlanta, 1970-71; sales metallurgist Rolled Alloys, Inc., Detroit, 1971-76; mgr. market research and devel., mgr. conversion and direct sales, mgr. advt. Teledyne Allvac, Monroe, N.C., 1976—. Mem. U.S. Senatorial Club of Nat. Republican Senatorial Com. Served with USNR, 1964-69. Mem. Nat. Assn. Corrosion Engrs., Am. Welding Soc., ASTM, AIME, Metall. Soc., Soc. Petroleum Engrs., Am. Soc. Metals, Marine Tech. Soc., Am. Tube Assn., TAPPI, Am. Mgmt. Assn., Tech. Adv. Com. Metal Properties Council, Delta Upsilon, Colgate Alumni Assn. Episcopalian. Club: Carmel Country. Home: 1714 Lost Tree Ln Charlotte NC 28211 Office: 2020 Ashcraft Ave Monroe NC 28110

EDMUNDS, FRANCES RAVENEL, found. exec.; b. Charleston, S.C., Dec. 11, 1916; d. Augustine T. and Harriott (Buist) Smythe; B.S., Coll. Charleston, 1937, LL.D. (hon.), 1977; m. S. Henry Edmunds, 1943 (dec.); children—Harriott Edmunds Lumpkin, Eliza Edmunds Cleveland, Langdon. Headed staff Historic Charleston Found., since 1947; trustee Spoleto Festival Two Worlds, Historic House Assn. Am., Thomas Jefferson Meml. Assn.; chmn. Drayton Hall council Nat. Trust; mem. president's adv. council historic preservation, Dept. Interior. Recipient Louise Dupont Crownshield award, Nat. Trust; conservation service award, Dept. Interior. Mem. Nat. Trust, Am. Assn. State and Local History, Soc. Archtl. Historians. Presbyterian. Lectr., contbr. articles in field. Home: 10 Bedon's Alley Charleston SC 29401 Office: 51 Meeting St Charleston SC 29401

EDMUNDS, JAMES SMITH, III, writer, photographer; b. New Iberia, La., Sept. 25, 1951; s. James Smith and Eva Louise (Fry) E.; B.A. in Philosophy with distinction, U. Southwestern La., 1973; m. Susan Violet Hester, Jan. 1, 1973. Grad. asst. U. Southwestern La., 1973-75; dir. dept. art Mt. Carmel Acad., New Iberia, 1975-77; freelance writer and photographer contbg. to Newsweek, New Orleans Times-Picayune, Renaissance, Francaise, Louisianne, Daily Iberian, Figaro, Dallas Times-Herald; contbg. editor Gris-Gris, Baton Rouge. Mem. Nat. Press Photographers Assn. Office: PO Box 2185 New Iberia LA 70560

EDMUNDS, JAMES TELFORD, lawyer; b. Amsterdam, N.Y., Sept. 12, 1931; s. Allen Telford and Margaret Rhea (Sleight) E.; student U. Richmond, 1949-51, Columbia Coll., 1951-52, Columbia Law Sch., 1952-53; LL.B., U. Richmond, 1955; children—Jeanne Louise, Thomas Arthur, Mark Allen, Andrew Griffing; m. 2d, Harriett Kaminsky Bishop, July 17, 1977. Admitted to Va. bar, 1955, U.S. Supreme Ct. bar; practiced in Kenbridge, 1955—; town atty., Kenbridge, 1966—; mem. Va. Senate from 17th Dist., 1972-80, mem. adv. com. on professions and occupations, 1973. Sec.-treas., dir. Kenbridge Industries, Inc.; mem. adv. bd. Fidelity Nat. Bank; guest lectr. Southside Community Coll. Sec., Lunenburg County Planning Commn., 1960-70; Mem. Va. Democratic Central Com., mem. Dem. Nat. Platform Com., 1976; chmn. joint subcom. Alcohol and Drug Abuse, Va. Gen. Assembly, 1975-77; vice chmn. Senate Dem. Caucus, 1976-80. Bd. dirs. Va. Mental Health Found.; mem. Va. State Crime Commn., 1976-80, Va. Adv. Legis. Council, 1978-80, Nat. Conf. State Legislatures, 1979-80. Named Jaycee Outstanding Young Man of Year, 1966. Mem. Va., 10th Circuit bar assns., McNeill Law Soc., Delta Theta Phi, Phi Gamma Delta. Methodist. Lion. Club: Bull and Bear (Richmond). Home: 110 N Pine St Kenbridge VA 23944 Office: 115 5th St Kenbridge VA 23944

EDNEY, FRED RIPPY, aluminum co. exec.; b. Hendersonville, N.C., Sept. 9, 1917; s. Fred Earchel and Nannie Minerva Edney; A.B., U. N.C., 1941, LL.B., J.D., 1943; m. Charlotte Poland, Mar. 28, 1958. Admitted to N.C. bar, 1943, Va. bar, 1943; atty. Reynolds Metals Co., Louisville, 1943-61, asst. gen. counsel, 1961-71, gen. atty., 1971-72, exec. asst., 1972, v.p. corp. adminstrn. and personnel, Richmond, Va., 1972—; dir. Alumina Transport Corp., Broad St. Road Corp., Bushnell Plaza Devel. Corp., El Campo Aluminum Co., Latas de Aluminium Reynolds, Inc., Lomer Devel. Corp., Mill Pond Devel. Corp., New Eastwick Corp., Ocean Trailer Transport Corp., Presdl. Devel. Corp., Presdl. Manor Corp., Presdl. Plaza Corp., numerous Reynolds subsidiaries, Reyship Can. Ltd., Reywest Devel. Corp., Sirco Systems, Inc., So. Gravure Services, Inc., Tilo Co. Inc., Weybosset Hill Devel. Corp.; pres., dir. Reynolds Metals Co. Found.; v.p. personnel and labor relations, dir. Caribbean Steamship Co. S.A., Reynolds Haitian Mines, Inc., Reynolds Jamaica Mines Ltd. Mem. Henrico County (Va.) Republican Com., 1979—; mem. adv. com. U. Richmond Sch. Bus., 1979—. Mem. Am. Bar Assn., Va. Bar Assn., Ky. Bar Assn., N.C. Bar Assn., Richmond Bar Assn., Am. Soc. Personnel Adminstrn., Nat. Lawyers Club, Order of Coif, Phi Delta Phi. Republican. Presbyterian. Clubs: Internat. (Washington); Marco Polo (N.Y.C.). Editor-in-chief N.C. Law Rev., 1941-43. Home: 101 Woodhall Dr Richmond VA 23229 Office: 6601 W Broad St Box 27003 Richmond VA 23261

EDWARDS, BENJAMIN FRANKLIN, JR., biophys. scientist; b. Lufkin, Tex.. Sept. 24, 1923; s. Benjamin Franklin and Celcie (Pena) E.; B.S., S.F. Austin State U., 1950; M.S., Tex. A. and M. U., 1960; Ph.D., U. Houston, 1973; m. Hazel Leroy Stanford, Dec. 19, 1964; children—Mary Carol, John Christopher. Sr. structures engr. Vought Aircraft Co., Dallas, 1957-58; instr. sci. and math. U. Dallas, 1958-60; asst. prof. physics S.F. Austin State U., Nacogdoches, Tex., 1960-63, N.E. La. State U., Monroe, 1963-64; chief biophysics sect. Physiometrics Research Lab., VA Hosp., Houston, 1966-67; prin. scientist Lockheed Electronics Co., Houston, 1967-80; sr. research scientist Technology Inc., Houston, 1980—; cons. scientist, deptl. staff U. Houston Clear Lake Campus. Served with USAAF, 1942-46, with M.S.C., USAF, 1950-53; PTO. NSF summer research fellow U. Rochester, 1960; recipient performance commendations Lockheed Electronics Co., Apollo Achievement award NASA, 1969. Mem. Tex. Acad. Sci., Tex. Archaeol. Soc., Nat. Mgmt. Assn., Am. Assn. Physics Tchrs. Clubs: Houston Yacht, San Leon Sailing. Developed model for electron probe analysis of thin biol. materials. Home: 1438 Saxony Ln Houston TX 77058

EDWARDS, BRENDA DIANE, speech pathologist; b. Sabine Parish, La., Aug. 1, 1951; d. Ernest G. and Bessie M. (Armstrong) McComie; B.A., Northwestern State U., Natchitoches, La., 1974, M.A., 1975; m. E.L. Edwards, III, Dec. 19, 1976; 1 dau., Stacey Diane. Speech pathologist Caddo Parish Public Schs., Shreveport, La., 1975-76; speech and hearing cons. Spl. Edn. Evaluation Center, Shreveport, 1976-78, evaluation coordinator, 1979—; cons. Nat. Assn. Spl. Edn. Registered speech pathologist, La. Mem. Am. Speech and Hearing Assn. Democrat. Baptist. Club: La. State U. Med. Center Wives (pres. 1978-79). Home: 5856 S Lakeshore D-4 Shreveport LA 71119 Office: Spl Edn Evaluation Center 4150 Linwood Ave Shreveport LA 71108

EDWARDS, BRIAN ALFRED, naval officer; b. Rockaway Beach, N.Y., July 18, 1943; s. Alfred William and Evelyn May (Edger) E.; B.A., Valparaiso U., 1967; B.S., M.S., U.S. Naval Postgrad. Sch., Monterey, Calif., 1972; diploma U.S. Naval Destroyer Sch., 1973; studied engring. Duty Officer Sch., 1978; m. Mary Marcella Hill, 1976. Commd. ensign USN, 1967, advanced through grades to lt. comdr., 1977; main propulsion asst. U.S.S. Estes, 1968; advanced tech. tng. U.S. Naval Postgrad. Sch., 1969-73; temp. duty Destroyer Devel. Group, Newport, R.I., 1973; engr. officer U.S.S. Trippe, 1973-75, Tomich Propulsion Engring. Tng. Facility, Great Lakes, Ill., 1976, U.S.S. Sellers, 1976-77; temp. duty Naval Shipyard, Charleston, S.C., 1977; staff supt. Shipbldg., Pascagoula, Miss., 1977-80; assigned to Ship Repair Depot, Guantanamo Bay, Cuba. Decorated Cross of Gallantry with palm (Republic Vietnam). Mem. Am. Soc. Naval Engrs., Marine Tech. Soc., Oceanic Soc., U.S. Naval Inst., Internat. Oceanic Fedn., Alpha Phi Omega. Lutheran. Contbr. poem to Orpheus Rebound, 1966. Office: SRD US Naval Station Guantanamo Bay FPO NY

EDWARDS, DEL MOUNT, bus. exec.; b. Tyler, Tex., Apr. 12, 1953; s. Welby Clell and Davida (Mount) E.; A.A. cum laude, Tyler Jr. Coll., 1974; B.B.A., Baylor U., 1976. Corp. coordinator Dillard Dept. Stores, Inc., Fort Worth, Tex., 1976-77; v.p. W. C. Supply, Inc., Tyler, 1977—; pres., owner Walker Auto Spring, Inc., Shreveport, La., 1978—; v.p. W. C. Square, Inc., 1976—. Mem. Council Fleet Specialists, Tyler Area C. of C., Smith County Hist. Soc., SCV (treas. camp 124). Baptist. Clubs: Tyler Petroleum, Willow Brook Country (Tyler). Home: Mountwood Ranch Route 2 Box 213 Tyler TX 75704 Office: WC Square Front at Bonner Sts Tyler TX 75710

EDWARDS, DENNIS CHARLES, co. exec.; b. Kansas City, Mo., Mar. 17, 1951; s. Charles Isome and Catherine Anne (Kabardis) E.; B.S. in Mech. Engring., U. Mo., Rolla, 1973, M.S., 1974; m. Roberta Sue Farley, Mar. 23, 1968; children—Dennis Charles, Derek Jason. Project engr. research and devel. Fiber Industries Inc., Charlotte, N.C., 1974-79; area supr. Cigarette Tow Maintenance and Services, 1979—. Mem. Soc. Automotive Engrs., ASME, Sigma Xi. Greek Orthodox. Office: Celanese Fibers Co PO Box 1000 Narrows VA 24124

EDWARDS, EDWIN WASHINGTON, gov. La.; b. Marksville, La., Aug. 7, 1927; s. Clarence W. and Agnes (Brouillette) E.; J.D., La. State U., 1949; m. Elaine Schwartzenburg, Apr. 5, 1949; children—Anna Laure, Victoria Elaine, Stephen Randolph, David Edwin. Admitted to La. bar, 1949; gen. practice in Crowley, La 1949-66; sr. founding partner firm Edwards, Edwards & Broadhurst, 1954—; mem. Crowley City Council, 1954-62, La. Senate from 35th dist., 1964-65; mem. 89-92d congresses 7th dist. La.; gov. La., 1972—. Chmn., Interstate Oil Compact Commn., 1974-77, Ozark Regional Commn., 1974—. Served with USNR, World War II. Mem. So. Gov.'s Conf. (energy com.), Nat. Gov.'s Conf. (rural and urban devel. com., nat. resources and environ. mgmt. com., task force on fgn. trade and tourism), Internat. Rice Festival, Crowley C. of C., Crowley Indsl. Found., Am. Legion. Democrat. Catholic. Club: Lions. Home: Governor's Mansion Baton Rouge LA 70804 Office: PO Box 44004 Capitol Station Baton Rouge LA 70804

EDWARDS, ELLA CHANDLER, librarian; b. Pueblo, Colo., July 17, 1934; d. Robert Gray and Nell (Orman) Chandler; B.A., Northwestern State Coll., Natchitoches, La., 1968; M.S., La. State U., Baton Rouge, 1973; m. Clarence Jeptha Edwards, Jan. 23, 1953; children—Clarence Jeptha, Marguerite Herries, Mathilde Hollingsworth. Cataloging asst. Magale Library, Centenary Coll. La., Shreveport, 1969-72, acquisitions librarian, 1972-74, cataloger, head tech. processes, 1974-75, asst. dir., 1975—, acting dir., 1975-76; So. Colls. and Univs. Assn. exchange librarian to Joint Univ. Libraries, Nashville, 1972. Mem. AAUP, La. Library Assn., Nat. Soc. Colonial Dames Am. (registrar, mem. Shreveport com.), La. Trails Council, Shreveport Jr. League, DAR, Ozark Soc., Shreveport Preservation Soc., Kappa Delta Pi. Republican. Episcopalian. Home: 928 Monrovia St Shreveport LA 71106 Office: Magale Library Centenary Coll La Shreveport LA 71104

EDWARDS, HORACE RAY, civil engr., land surveyor, county ofcl.; b. Wedowee, Ala., Apr. 2, 1933; s. William McKinley and Hattie Elizabeth (Wright) E.; student Auburn U., 1951-53, Internat. Corr. Schs., 1958-59; m. Ann Eloise Mitchell, Nov. 12, 1960; children—George William, James Ray. With Ala. Hwy. Dept., 1953-75, project engr., 1961-71, dist. engr., 1971-75; county engr. Randolph County, Ala., 1975-79; dir. Self Ins. Co. for Ala. Counties, 1977—; Calhoun County engr., 1979, Chilton County, 1979—. Mem. Randolph County High Sch. PTA, 1975-79; deacon Eron Bapt. Ch., 1973-75; chmn. deacons 1st Bapt. Ch., Wedowee, Ala., 1975-79; bd. dirs. Randolph Indsl. Devel. Assn., 1977-79; vol. fireman, Wedowee, 1975-79; city councilman, Wedowee, 1978-79. Served with USN, 1955-57. Registered profl. engr., land surveyor, Ala. Mem. Assn. County Engrs. Ala. (sec.-treas. 1978-79, v.p. 1979-80), Am. Congress Surveying and Mapping, Ala. Soc. Profl. Land Surveyors. Clubs: Kiwanis (sec.-treas. 1975-79), Masons, Gideons Internat. Home: 105 Pine Cone Circle Clanton AL 35045

EDWARDS, HUGH RANDALL, coll. pres., civil engr.; b. Orange County, Va., Nov. 9, 1941; s. Hugh Chester and Arlene (Roberts) E.; B.S. in Civil Engring., Va. Poly. Inst., 1964, M.S. in San. Engring., 1965, Ph.D. in Civil Engring., 1970; m. Anna Wallace, June 25, 1965; children—Suzan, Todd, Tom. Instr. dept. engring. Va. Poly. Inst., Wytheville br., also asst. football coach; asst. prof. engring. and math. Wytheville Community Coll., chmn. engring tech. and bus. scis. div., coordinator applied sci. programs; ednl. cons. to Bluefield State Coll.; engring. cons. to Harwell Constrn. Co., 1969-72, Appalachian Power Co., State Water Control Bd., Fairfax County, Va.; dean of instrn. Germanna Community Coll., Fredericksburg, Va., 1969-72; provost of Parham Rd. campus J. Sargeant Reynolds Community Coll., 1972-76; pres. New River Community Coll., Dublin, Va., 1976—; mgmt. consl. to various community colls. in Va.; mem. adv. bd. Nat. Bank & Trust Co., Germanna br., Va., 1970-72; mem. instructional programs adv. com. State Council Higher Edn. for Va.; chmn. research com. Adv. Council of Presidents to the Chancellor of Va. Community Coll. System, 1978-79. Athletic dir. Blue Star Youth Football Program, Mechanicsville, Va., 1973-74; ednl. chmn. United Way Campaign, Pulaski County, Va., 1977; mem. Pulaski County Planning Commn.; v.p. Robin Ridge Civic Assn., 1973-74; bd. govs. Va. Operators Tng. Center, 1975—; mem. vestry Christ Episcopal Ch., Pulaski, Va.; bd. dirs. Saint Albans Found., Dalton Theater; trustee Pre-sch. Kindergarten Day Sch., St. Episcopal Ch., Wytheville, Va. Mem. Am. Assn. Higher Edn., Pulaski County C. of C. (past pres., dir.), Water Pollution Control Fedn., Sigma Xi, Phi Kappa Phi, Tau Beta Pi, Chi Epsilon, Omicron Delta Kappa. Club: Rotary (pres. 1979—). Home: 4 Staff Village Dublin VA 24084 Office: New River Community College Drawer 1127 Dublin VA 24084

EDWARDS, ISHMELL HENDREX, coll. dean; b. New Albany, Miss., July 29, 1949; s. Jonathan and Nannie Lou (Foster) E.; grad. Rust Coll., Holly Springs, Midd., 1971; m. Josephine Stennis, Jan. 9, 1970; children—Marcus LaZerick, Kevin Ishmell. Asst. dir. phys. plant Rust Coll., 1971-74, dir. athletics and student activities, then tennis and softball coach, 1974-79, asso. dean student affairs, 1979—; mem. publicity com. Holly Springs Tennis Assn., 1979. Troup leader local Boy Scouts Am., 1976-78; adv. Holly Springs YMCA, 1974-79. Recipient Outstanding Service award Rust Coll. Mem. NCAA (dir. nat. youth sports program), U.S. Lawn Tennis Assn., Nat. Intramural Recreational Sports Assn., Nat. Intercollegiate Athletic Dirs. Assn., Nat. Intercollegiate Coaches Assn., Nat. Assn. Athletic Dirs., NAACP, Omega Psi Phi. Democrat. Methodist. Home: Route 4 Box D-5 Holly Springs MS 38635 Office: Box 702 Rust Ave Holly Springs MS 38635

EDWARDS, JACK, congressman; b. Birmingham, Ala., Sept. 20, 1928; s. William Jackson and Sue (Fuhrman) E.; B.S. in Commerce and Bus. Adminstrn., U. Ala., 1952; LL.B., U. Ala., 1954; m. Jolane Vander Sys, Jan. 30, 1954; children—Susan Lane, Richard Arnold. Admitted to Ala. bar, 1954; pvt. practice, Mobile, 1954-58; gen. atty. G., M. & O. R.R., 1958-64; legal adviser Emergency Port Operations Mobile, 1961-64; mem. 89th-96th Congresses, 1st Dist. Ala. Mem. House Republican Leadership; vice chmn. House Rep. Conf.; ranking Rep. subcom. on def. appropriations. Chmn. America's Jr. Miss Pageant, 1960; pres. Ala. Deep Sea Fishing Rodeo, 1956-57; div. chmn. Mobile United Fund, 1960; mem. transp. adv. com. Mobile City Planning Commn., 1960-64. Served with USMC, 1946-48, 50-51. Named one of outstanding young men U.S. Jr. C. of C., 1964. Mem. Am., Ala., Mobile (sec. 1956) bar assns., Mobile Jr. Bar Assn. (pres. 1957), Mobile Jr. C. of C. (pres. 1961-62), Kappa Alpha (pres. 1951-53), Omicron Delta Kappa. Presbyn. Office: House Office Bldg Washington DC 20515

EDWARDS, JAMES EDWIN, lawyer; b. Clarkesville, Ga., July 29, 1914; s. Gus Calloway and Mary Clara (McKinney) E.; student U. Tex., 1931-33; B.A., George Washington U., 1935, J.D. cum laude, 1946; m. Frances Lillian Stanley, Nov. 22, 1948; children—Robin Anne, James Christopher, Clare (Mrs. Ronald C. Wilkson). Admitted to Fla. bar, 1938, practiced, Cocoa, Fla., 1938-42; divisional asst. Dept. of State, 1945-50; practice law, Ft. Lauderdale, 1951—; asst. city atty., Ft. Lauderdale, 1961, 63-65; city commr., Coral Springs, Fla., 1970-76, mayor, 1972-73; pres., dir. Ocean Beach Improvement Co. Chmn., Ft. Lauderdale for Eisenhower, 1952; Republican county parliamentarian, 1954-59; pres. Rep. Attys. Club Broward County, 1960-64. Served to lt. USCGR, 1942-45; lt. col. USAF Res. ret. Mem. Fla., Broward County bar assns., Fla. Sportsmen's Assn. (pres. 1967-68), Fla. Conservative Union (chpt. pres. 1976), Delta Sigma Rho, Pi Gamma Mu, Phi Delta Phi, Phi Sigma Kappa. Clubs: Rotary, Broken Woods Golf and Racquet, S.E. Fla. Dressage and Combined Tng. Author: Myths About Gems, 1978. Home: 10 Covered Bridge Dr Coral Springs FL 33065 Office: Suite 510 Bank of Coral Springs Bldg 3300 University Dr Coral Springs FL 33065

EDWARDS, JAMES HARRELL, state senator N.C.; b. Pitt County, N.C., Nov. 25, 1926; s. James Josiah and Ella Stokes (Edwards) E.; student Atlantic Christian Coll., Wilson, N.C., 1944-45, 47-48, E. Carolina U., Greenville, N.C., 1948-49, U. Miami (Fla.), 1961; m. Trelby Bumgarner Edwards, June 30, 1967; children by previous marriage—James L., Charles Thomas, Ella Ann Edwards Compton, John Harrell. Accountant, Raynor & Harris Tobacco Warehouse, Greenville, 1948-53; adjuster N.C. Farm Bur., Raleigh, 1953-59. Southeastern Adjustment Co., Inc., Hickory, N.C., 1959—, pres., 1975—; pres. Carolinian, Inc.; mem. N.C. Ins. Study Commn., 1971-72; Democratic precinct chmn., Raleigh, 1953-56; mem. N.C. Ho. of Reps. from 34th Dist., from 1975; now mem. N.C. Senate. Served with USNR, 1944-47. Recipient Honor award Am. Fedn. Police, 1975. Mem. N.C. Adjusters Assn., Nat. Assn. Ind. Ins. Adjusters, Internat. Assn. Loss Adjusters, Internat. Assn. Aaron Investigators, Nat. Assn. Fire Investigators, N.C. Assn. Licensed Detectives, Pvt. Protective Services Assn. Charlotte, VFW, Am. Legion, Hickory Mchts. Assn., Order Long Leaf Pine. Lutheran. Clubs: Shrine, Elks, Moose. Home: Route 3 Box 118 Granite Falls NC 28630 Office: 420 7th Ave SW Hickory NC 28610

EDWARDS, JAMES MELVIN, wholesale co. exec.; b. N.Y.C., Feb. 25, 1942; s. Jackson A. and Natalie E.; B.S. in Bus. Adminstrn., Boston U., 1963; m. Carole Ann Goldberg, June 6, 1964; children—Jon Stuart, Meredith Joy. Mgr., dist. mgr., asst. treas., treas. Associated Ind. Theatres, N.Y.C., 1963-65; with Tujax Electric Supply Co., 1965-73, v.p., 1970-73, br. mgr., 1965-73; v.p., br. mgr. Consol. Electric Supply Co., Hollywood, Fla., 1973-76, v.p. hdqrs., Miami, 1976—. Bd. dirs. Temple Solel, Hollywood, 1976-80; sustaining mem. Republican Nat. Com., 1976-80; life mem. Rep. Party, 1979—. Mem. Illuminating Engring. Soc. N.Am., Young Execs. of Today div. Nat. Assn. Elect. Distbrs. Club: Lions (1st v.p. 1977-78). Home: 4322 Lincoln St Hollywood FL 33021 Office: 3800 NW 31st Ave Miami FL 33142

EDWARDS, JAMES WESLEY, JR., auditor; b. Wakefield, Va., Aug. 16, 1951; s. James Wesleya and Ina Ellie (Bryant) E.; A.A. in Bus., Richard Bland Coll., 1970-72; B.S. in Bus. and Acctg. Va. Commonwealth U., 1973. Cost acct. E.R. Carpenter Co., Richmond, Va., 1973-74; auditor A, field services Dept. Taxation, Commonwealth of Va., Richmond, 1974-76, auditor A, corp. income tax tech unit, 1976-77, auditor B, miscellaneous tax sect., 1977—. Mem. ch. adminstrv. and council on ministries Wakefield United Methodist Ch., 1970-73, tchr. Sunday sch., 1967-73, ch. youth dir., 1970-73; part time local pastor Claremont United Meth. Ch., 1973—. Club: Masons (Wakefield). Home: Wilson Ave Wakefield VA 23888

EDWARDS, JOHN DIXON, JR., engring. co. exec.; b. Wake County, N.C., Jan. 28, 1933; s. John Dixon and Magnolia (Woody) E.; B.S., N.C. State U., 1956, M.S., 1958; m. Ida Gerlene Hinnant, Sept. 10, 1954; children—Mark D., Alan Bradford. Designer, N.C. State Hwy. Commn., Raleigh, 1956-58; transp. planner City of Cin., 1958-62; with Traffic Planning Asso., Inc., Atlanta, 1962-77, pres., 1965-77; v.p. Richard P. Browne Assos., 1977—. Lectr. Ga. Inst. Tech., 1965—. Mem. Atlanta Urban Design Com., 1978—. Mem. Am. Inst. Planners (chpt. sec. 1962), Inst. Traffic Engrs. (pres. Ga. 1962-63, mem. tech. council 1968-70, internat. dir. 1972-76, dir. cons. council, Herman J. Hoose Disting. Service award 1973), Transp. Research Bd., Atlanta C. of C. (task force on transp.), Met. Atlanta Transp. Improvements Council (dir., exec. com. 1974—). Contbg. author: Urban Design Manual, 1965; Revised Traffic Engineering Handbook, 1973-74, 1973. Home: 3912 Sheldon Dr NE Atlanta GA 30342 Office: 1175 Peachtree St Atlanta GA 30361

EDWARDS, (FLOYD) KENNETH, journalist, educator; b. Salina, Kans., Sept. 29, 1917; s. Floyd Altamus and Grace Frances (Miller) E.; A.B., Fort Hays State U., 1940; M.S., 1970; m. Virginia Marie Lewark, Sept. 10, 1970; children—Elaine Patricia, Diana, Kenneth, John Michael, Melody, Daniel J. Ins. sales exec., Denver, 1947-50; reporter Sterling (Colo.) Daily Jour., 1950, editor, 1950-52; editor Waverly (Iowa) Newspapers, 1953-55; editor, pub. Edina (Minn.) Courier Newspapers, 1955-56; v.p., editor Mpls. Suburban Newspapers, Hopkins, Minn., 1956-65; editor, gen. mgr. Valley of the

Sun Newspapers, Tempe, Ariz., 1968; instr. Mankato (Minn.) State U., 1970-72, asst. prof., 1972-73; asso. prof. U. Ala., 1973—; cons. on newspaper mgmt. Pres. Calhoun-Harriet Home Owners Assn., Mpls., 1958-60; bd. dirs. Hennepin County Assn. for Mental Health, 1959-60, S.W. Activities Council, 1960-61, S.W. High Sch. PTA, Mpls., 1960-61. Served with USN, World War II. Grantee Ford Found., 1976, U. Ala., 1977. Recipient awards for community service and editorial writing. Mem. Inst. Newspaper Controllers and Fin. Officers (mem. tech. advisory bd. 1977-78), Assn. for Edn. in Journalism, Soc. Profl. Journalists, Nat. Conf. of Editorial Writers. Contbr. articles to profl. jours. Author newspaper profit planning and management manual. Home: 9 Camellia Park Tuscaloosa AL 35401 Office: Dept of Journalism University of Alabama 1482 University AL 35486

EDWARDS, LEE, savs. and loan exec.; b. N.Y.C., Apr. 23, 1923; s. Walter and Anna Veronica E.; A.B., U. Mass., 1950; m. Frances Myrtle White, Nov. 10, 1970. Gen. mgr. Sta. WZRO, Jacksonville Beach, Fla., 1951-57; pub. Beach News, Jacksonville Beach, 1958-62; dir. pub. relations Volkswagen Am., Jacksonville, Fla., 1963-69; v.p. 1st Fed. Savs. and Loan Assn., Jacksonville, 1971—; mem. adv. council Fla. Jr. Coll. Served with USMC, 1942-46. Decorated Purple Heart; recipient award Fla. Press Assn., 1961, Am. Advt. Fedn., 1966, 75, 76, Major Media citation of Excellence, 1973-74. Mem. Savs. Instns. Marketing Soc. Am., Fla. Savs. and Loan League, Fla. Pub. Relations Assn. Home: 4336 Venetia Blvd Jacksonville FL 32210 Office: First Fed Savs and Loan Assn 300 W Adams St Jacksonville FL 32202

EDWARDS, MARVIN H. MICKEY, Congressman; b. Cleve., July 12, 1937; s. Edward A. and Rosalie (Miller) E.; B.A. in Journalism, Okla. U., 1958; J.D., Oklahoma City U., 1969; m. Carolyn Sue Lindley, Feb. 14, 1974. Editor, Muskogee (Okla.) Daily Phoenix, 1958-59; reporter, editor Oklahoma City Times, 1959-63; dir. pub. relations Beals Advt. Agy., Oklahoma City, 1964-68; editor Pvt. Practice mag., 1968-73; spl. legis. cons. Republican Steering Com., Washington, 1973-74; tchr. law and journalism, Oklahoma City, 1975-76; mem. 95th-96th Congresses from 5th Okla. Dist. Bd. dirs. Am. Conservative Union. Recipient Freedoms Found. medal, 3 times; named Outstanding Young Man of Am., 1973. Mem. Sigma Delta Chi, Phi Delta Phi. Episcopalian. Clubs: Mason (32 deg.); Kiwanian. Author: Hazardous to Your Health, 1972. Office: 1223 Longworth House Office Bldg Washington DC 20515*

EDWARDS, PATTI SUE, nurse; b. Sasakwa, Okla., Nov. 11, 1941; d. Wiley S. and Elleen G. (Greer) Jones; R.N., St. Anthony Sch. Nursing, Oklahoma City, 1966; postgrad. E. Central U., Ada, Okla., 1979; children—Andrea, Steven, Chandra, Mark. Nursing supr. Wewoka (Okla.) Meml. Hosp., 1966-73, Seminole (Okla.) Mcpl. Hosp., 1973-75, asst. dir. nursing, 1975-77, dir. nursing, 1977-79, asst. dir. nursing, 1979—. Mem. Am. Nurses Assn., Okla. Assn. Nursing Adminstrs., St. Anthony's Alumni Assn. Roman Catholic. Home: 318 W Third St Wewoka OK 74884

EDWARDS, PAUL DAVID, assn. exec.; b. Akron, Ohio, Oct. 5, 1946; s. John Paul and Loraine Virginia (Rhodes) E.; B.S., U. Fla., 1974; m. Felicia Angela Monell, June 24, 1972; children—Cory Alan, Brian Craig. Mgr. public relations Kissimmee Osceola County C. of C., 1974-75, exec. v.p., 1975-78; dir. tourism Kissimmee St. Cloud Conv. and Visitors Bur., Kissimmee, Fla., 1978—. Bd. dirs. United Way, 1978—, ARC, 1975—, Ret. Sr. Vol. Program, 1975—. Served with USMC, 1968-70; Vietnam. Mem. Kissimmee St. Cloud Jaycees (pres. 1977-78), Am. C. of C. Execs., Fla. Public Relations Assn., Hotel Sales and Mktg. Assn., VFW, Am. Legion. Republican. Lutheran. Club: Rotary. Home: 1055 Partin Dr Kissimmee FL 32741 Office: 310 Dyer Blvd Kissimmee FL 32741

EDWARDS, RANDALL ALLAN, health ins. co. exec.; b. Rome, Ga., Jan. 8, 1944; s. Ernest W. and Lois Harbin (Little John) E.; B.S. in Bus. Adminstrn., Berry Coll., 1966; m. Wanda Faye Fowler, June 6, 1966; 1 dau., Deitra Fay. Clk., The Kroger Co., Rome, 1960-66; auditor GAO, Atlanta, 1966-69; acct. Blue Cross and Blue Shield of Ga., Columbus, 1969-70, mgr., 1971-72, dir., 1973-76, corp. auditor, sr. corp. internal auditor, 1977—, chmn. dist. V and VI fin. groups, 1976, chmn. internal audit group, 1978. Chmn. fin. com. Metro Columbus Urban League, 1979-80. Served with U.S. Army, 1966-68. Mem. Nat. Assn. Accts. (pres. Chattahoochee Valley chpt. 1976, Outstanding Bd. Mem. 1972, 79), Def. Preparedness Assn., Berry Coll. Alumni Assn. Republican. Methodist. Club: 100 (Columbus). Home: 3641 Ginger Dr Columbus GA 31904 Office: 2357 Warm Springs Rd Columbus GA 31906

EDWARDS, RAOUL DURANT, writer, cons.; b. N.Y.C., Nov. 3, 1928; s. Louis Durant and Gloss Edwards; student N.Y. U., 1957-58, U. Chgo., 1970-72; m. Jean Guthrie, Nov. 22, 1958; children—Guthrie Hamilton, Jonathan Valentine. Asst. mng. editor Am. Banker, N.Y.C., 1953-62, Washington bur. chief, 1962-63; asst. to bd. FDIC, Washington, 1963-66; dir. public relations Bank Adminstrn. Inst., Park Ridge, Ill., 1966-70; prin. R.D. Edwards & Assos., Park Ridge, 1971-73, Falls Church, Va., 1973—; asso. editor U.S. Banker mag., 1977—; guest lectr. Va. Commonwealth U., Richmond, 1977—. Del., Va. Rep. State Conv., 1978. Mem. N.Y. Fin. Writers Assn., Am. Soc. Bus. Press Editors. Republican. Baptist. Club: Exchequer. Gen. editor ATM Program Success. Contbr. articles to newspapers, mags., jours. Home and office: 5927 Merritt Pl Falls Church VA 22041

EDWARDS, RAYMOND LEWIS, social worker; b. Dayton, Ohio, Sept. 18, 1931; s. Raymond Lewis and Irene (Basham) E.; B.A., Fla. So. Coll.; M.S.W., Fla. State U., Ph.D., 1966; m. Mona Lou Gearheart, Jan. 15, 1955; children—Glenn Alan, Alisa Lynne. Social worker Dept. Public Welfare, State of Fla., Leon County (Fla.) Mental Health Clinic; counselor Family Service Agy., Ft. Lauderdale, Fla., Marriage and Family Counseling Clinic Fla. State U.; marriage and family counselor Juvenile Welfare Bd. of Pinellas County, Fla., St. Petersburg, 1967-72, dir., 1972—. Served with USAF, 1951-56. Mem. Nat. Assn. Social Workers, Nat. Council on Family Relations, Am. Orthopsychiat. Assn., Fla. Assn. Health and Social Services. Club: Masons. Contbr. articles to profl. jours. Office: 4140 49th St N Saint Petersburg FL 33709

EDWARDS, RICHARD WAYNE, psychologist; b. Nashville, May 23, 1933; s. Arthur Brannon and Ethel Pauline (Lamar) E.; B.A., Vanderbilt U., 1956; M.A., George Peabody Coll., 1959; L.H.D. (hon.), London Inst. Social Scis., 1973; postgrad. U. Chgo., 1964-66. Instr., asst. dir. spl. ednl. services Evansville (Ind.) Coll., 1959-62; asst. supt. Ill. Visually Handicapped Inst., Chgo., 1962-66; exec. dir. Community Services for Blind, Inc., Atlanta, 1966-73; clin. dir. Coastal Area Community Mental Health Center, Brunswick, Ga., 1973—; adj. prof. psychology DeKalb Coll., 1966-73, Brunswick Jr. Coll., 1973-74. Mem. adv. bd. WABE-FM, pub. radio, Atlanta, 1971-73; lay reader, vestryman St. Mark's Episcopal Ch., Brunswick; trustee St. Mark's Towers, Brunswick; mem. adv. bd. campaign publicity United Way, Brunswick. Served in Signal Corps, U.S. Army, 1956-57. Recipient Beaver award for community achievement Sta. WSB, Atlanta, 1971. NSF fellow, 1961. Mem. Am., Ga. (dir. 1961-62, Achievement award 1962) assns. workers for blind, Am. Personnel and Guidance Assn., Am. Psychol. Assn., Theta Chi, Psi Chi. Clubs: Woodmen of World, Northside Kiwanis. Contbr. articles on psychology and psychology of visually handicapped to profl. mags. and jours. Home: 4030 Riverside Dr Brunswick GA 31520 Office: 1609 Newcastle St Brunswick GA 31520

EDWARDS, ROBERT C., ch. assn. adminstr.; b. Jefferson City, Mo., Aug. 2, 1932; s. Robert C. and Marjorie (Woods) E.; B.J., U. Mo., Columbia, 1959; postgrad. Loyola U., New Orleans, 1973; m. Norma A. Roth, Sept. 2, 1953; children—Debra, Kirk, Cheri, Mitch, Kelley, Eric, Jill, Chris. News dir., radio stations, Moberly, Mo., 1958-59, Freeport, Tex., 1959-60, Portsmouth, Va., 1960, Janesville, Wis., 1960-63, Holland, Mich., 1963-64, Jour. and Courier, Lafayette, Ind., 1964-70; sr. editor AAA, Washington, 1970-72; dir. communications and councils Cath. Diocese Richmond (Va.), 1972—, mem. pastoral council, 1975—, mem. nat. steering com., 1977—. Served with USAF, 1952-56. Mem. Richmond Public Relations Assn., Religious Public Relations Council, World Assn. Christian Communicators, Nat. Pastoral Planners Conf., Diocesan Parish and Pastoral Council Personnel Conf. Roman Catholic. Office: 811 Cathedral Pl Richmond VA 23220

EDWARDS, SCOTT SAMUEL, JR., lawyer; b. Atlanta, Apr. 16, 1915; s. Scott Samuel and Maggie (Harris) E., Sr.; LL.B., Woodrow Wilson Coll., 1941; m. Jeanette Victoria Smith, Nov. 14, 1945; 1 son, David Scott. Admitted to Ga. bar, 1941, practiced in Marietta, Ga., 1946—; asst. county atty., Cobb County, 1948-53; atty. City of Marietta, 1948-60, Kennestone Hosp., Marietta, 1948-73. Served with Signal Corps, AUS, 1941-45; PTO. Mem. Am., Ga., Cobb County (pres. 1955-56) bar assns., Am. Legion. Presbyn. Club: Civitan (pres. 1952-53). Home: 330 S Woodland Dr Marietta GA 30064 Office: 216 Washington Ave Marietta GA 30060

EDWARDS, WILLIAM BRUNDIGE, III, chemist; b. Phila., Oct. 10, 1942; s. William Brundige and Elizabeth (Burr) E.; B.A., Lehigh U., 1964; Ph.D., U. Pa., 1969. Research asst. Wyeth Labs., Inc., Radnor, Pa., 1964-65; postdoctoral fellow Synvar Research Inst., Palo Alto, Calif., 1969-70; research organic chemist Philip Morris, Inc., Richmond, Va., 1970—. Allied Chem. Co. fellow, 1967-68; Busch fellow, 1968-69; DuPont fellow, summers 1966-68. Mem. Am. Chem. Soc., AAAS, Chem. Soc. London, Sigma Xi. Contbr. articles to profl. jours. Home: 207 Kirkland Dr Richmond VA 23227 Office: Philip Morris Research Center Box 26583 Richmond VA 23261

EDWARDS, WILLIAM HAWKINS, physician; b. Nashville, Mar. 16, 1927; s. Leonard Wright and Mary Alene (Hawkins) E.; B.A., Vanderbilt U., 1949, M.D., 1953; m. Frances N. McGaughy, Dec. 27, 1952; children—William Hawkins, Mary Frances, Norton M., Sarah Elizabeth. Intern, Vanderbilt Hosp., 1953-54, resident in surgery, 1954-55, 56-59; resident in surgery U. Calif. at Los Angeles Hosp., 1955-56; fellow in cardiovascular surgery Baylor Meth. Hosp., Houston, 1959-60; practice medicine specializing in surgery, Nashville, 1960—; mem. staff St. Thomas, Vanderbilt hosps. Mem. med. adv. bd. Medcom, Inc.; trustee State Volunteer Mut. Ins. Co., Served with USN, 1944-45. Fellow ACS; mem. Tenn. Med. Assn. (speaker ho. of dels.), AMA, So. Thoracic Surg. Assn., Am. Coll. Chest Physicians, Internat. Cardiovascular Soc., So. Surg. Assn., So. Med. Assn., Soc. Vascular Surgery, So. Assn. Vascular Surgery. Editor: Vascular Surgery, 1975. Contbr. articles to profl. jours. Home: 50 Concord Park Nashville TN 37205 Office: 4230 Harding Rd Suite 205 Nashville TN 37205

EDWARDS, WILLIAM MYRON, chem. engr.; b. San Diego, Aug. 28, 1932; s. William Tell and Goldie May (Self) E.; B.S., UCLA, 1954; M.S. in Chem. Engring., U. Houston, 1971, Ph.D., 1973; m. Marian Edwards; children—David, John, Karen, Thomas. With Shell Chem. Co., Long Beach, Calif., New Orleans, N.Y.C., Houston, 1954-69; teaching asst. U. Houston, 1969-73, Pullman Kellogg, Houston, 1973-79; staff research engr. Shell Devel. Co., Houston, 1979—. Mem. Am. Inst. Chem. Engrs. (Outstanding Publ. award S. Tex. sect. 1975), Phi Beta Kappa, Sigma Xi. Office: Shell Devel Co Westhollow Research Center PO Box 1380 Houston TX 77001

EDWARDS, WILLIAM RAYMOND, dentist; b. Richmond Hill, N.Y., Apr. 10, 1914; s. Vivian and Mabel Lucy (Keay) E.; student U. Fla., 1932-33, U. Miami, 1933-34; D.D.S., Washington U., St. Louis, 1938; m. Shirley Bonawit, Nov. 14, 1959; children—Bonnie Keay, Barbara Sisson. Individual practice dentistry, Fort Lauderdale, Fla., 1938-41, 45—. Served with AUS, 1941-45. Fellow Fla. State Dental Soc.; mem. Am. Dental Assn. (life), Fla. Acad. Dental Practice Adminstrn., East Coast Dist. (pres. 1955-56), Atlantic Coast dist., Pi Kappa Alpha, Xi Psi Phi, Omicron Kappa Upsilon. Home: 3080 NE 47th Ct Fort Lauderdale FL 33308 Office: 3015 Bayview Dr Fort Lauderdale FL 33306

EDWARDS, WILLIAM RYON, textile mfg. co. exec.; b. Spartanburg, S.C., May 31, 1940; s. Oscar Manning and Helen (Bearden) E.; student Clemson U., 1958-60, Wofford Coll., 1960-62; m. Martha Anne Canaday, June 7, 1963; children—Jenny Lea, William Ryon, Kenneth Bruce. Mgmt. trainee Reeves Bros., Inc., Spartanburg, 1964, asst. mgr. inventory control, 1964-69, mgr. inventory control, 1969—. Pres. Travelers Protective Assn., 1971; del. S.C. Democratic Conv., 1976. Mem. Adminstrv. Mgmt. Soc. (pres. 1977-78, asst. dir. area 4 S.C. 1978-80). Baptist. Home: 201 Wadsworth Blvd Spartanburg SC 29301 Office: Reeves Bros Inc PO Box 5788 Spartanburg SC 29304

EDWIN, JAMES MATTHEWS, agrl. engr.; b. Humboldt, Tenn., Nov. 15, 1919; s. John Edgar and Clara Dell (James) M.; B.S. Agrl. Engring., U. Tenn., 1942; M.Agrl. Engring., N.C. State U., 1956; m. Mary Louise Milligan, June 8, 1946; children—John, David, Howard, Mary. Instr., U. Tenn., Knoxville, from 1946, asst. prof. agrl. engring., to 1956; asso. prof. agrl. engring. U. Ark., Fayetteville, 1956—. Served with USAAF, 1942-45. Mem. Am. Soc. Agrl. Engrs. (chmn. Tenn. and Ark. sects.), Am. Soc. Engring. Edn., Gamma Sigma Delta, Alpha Epsilon. Democrat. Baptist. Inventor water shielded flame cultivation cotton and soybean production machine. Home: 311 Adams St Fayetteville AR 72701 Office: Agrl Engring Dept U Ark Fayetteville AR 72701

EFFINGER, GEORGE ALEC, writer; b. Cleve., Jan. 10, 1947; s. George Paul and Ruth Carolyn (Uray) E.; student Yale U., 1965-66, 69-70, N.Y. U., 1968-69; m. Beverly Anon Kandrac, Mar. 14, 1977. Free-lance writer, 1970—; novels include What Entropy Means to Me, 1972, Relatives, 1973, Those Gentle Voices, 1976, Felicia, 1976, Death in Florence, 1978, Heroics, 1979; short story collections include Mixed Feelings, 1974, Irrational Numbers, 1976, Dirty Tricks, 1978; tchr. sci. fiction Tulane U., New Orleans, 1974. Mem. Sci. Fiction Writers Am., Authors Guild. Address: Box 15183 New Orleans LA 70175

EFIRD, KILLIAN DANIEL, corrosion engr.; b. Birmingham, Ala., Oct. 25, 1944; s. K.P. and Mary Frances (Daniel) E.; B.S. in Chem. Engring., N.C. State U., 1967; M.S. in Materials Engring., U. Fla., 1970; m. Judith Jean Huffman, Sept. 4, 1965; children—Jennifer Jean, Mary Katherine. Materials engr. Dow Chem. Co., Plaquemine, La., 1967-69; sr. project engr. Internat. Nickel Co., Inc., Wrightsville Beach, N.C., 1971-77; sr. corrosion engr. Occidental Petroleum (Caledonia), Ltd., Aberdeen, Scotland, 1977—; lectr. in field. Pres. Wrightsville Beach PTA, 1972-74; youth advisor St. Paul's Luth. Ch., Baton Rouge, 1967-69, Univ. Luth. Ch., Gainesville, Fla., 1969-71, St. Matthews Ch., Wilmington, N.C., 1971-77. Mem. Nat. Assn. Corrosion Engrs. (Young Authors award 1975, symposium chmn. 1978), ASTM (chmn. subcom. 1975-77), Electrochem. Soc., Am. Soc. Metals. Democrat. Contbr. articles to tech. jours. Home: 3800 Carmel Acres Charlotte NC 28211 Office: Engineering Dept Occidental Petroleum (Caledonia) Ltd 127 Causewayend Aberdeen AB2 3TP Scotland

EFTHEMES, GEORGE H., archtl. engr.; b. Wheeling, W.Va., Oct. 8, 1911; s. Harry and Ann (Baxter) Efthemeopulas; student W.Va. U., 1930-31, 32-33, Nat. U., Washington, 1934; student Fairmont State Tchrs. Coll., 1936; m. Sarah Selepak, Jan. 1, 1933; children—Dorothy Jean, George H. Project engr. Fed. Emergency Relief Adminstrn., Wheeling, 1934; field engr. Works Progress Adminstrn., 1935; gen. contractor Efthemes Constrn. Co., 1945-58; city planner City of Benwood (W.Va.), 1959-60, City of North Mechem (W.Va.), 1959; cons. City of Grafton (W.Va.), 1960—; planning cons., lectr., 1962—; cons. for shopping malls, devel., schs., housing in S.E.; 1964-68; civil engr., head planning Naval Dist., Washington, 1968-69; civil engr., head planning Dept. Def., 1969-73; lectr., cons., developer mfg. facilities, Ohio, Pa., Fla., 1974—. Exec. dir. Citizens Com., Inc., Wheeling; 1st pres. Warwood Civic Assn., Hellenic Athletic Assn. Recipient numerous awards, trophies and plagues. Mem. Gen. Contractors Assn. (charter), Govt. Constrn. Engrs. Soc. (charter), Nat. Assn. Govt. Engrs. (sec.-treas.), Concrete Reinforcing Inst., Specifications Writers Assn., Am. Soc. Planning, Ofcls., Soc. for Coll. Accreditation, Am. Concrete Inst., Internat. Platform Assn. Greek Orthodox. Home: 2230 Chapline St Wheeling WV 26003

EGAN, MARK STEPHEN, geophysicist; b. Cleve., Mar. 29, 1953; s. Robert Francis and Ruth (Volzer) E.; B.S. in Physics and Math., Duquesne U., 1975; M.S. in Acoustics, U. Houston, 1978; m. Paulette Kathryn Dockal, May 29, 1976. Geophysicist, Geophys. Service, Inc., Houston, 1975—. Mem. Soc. Exploration Geophysicists (asso.), AAU. Democrat. Roman Catholic. Home: 2518 Long Reach Dr Sugarland TX 77478 Office: Geophys Service Inc PO Box 2803 Houston TX 77001

EGGEN, RODMAN ALAN, energy cons.; b. Louisville, Feb. 1, 1948; s. Freeman Mathias and Mary Lowe (Tichenor) E.; B.S. in Metall. Engring. (Univ. scholar), Vanderbilt U., 1970, postgrad. in Metall. Engring., 1970-71; research fellow, M.B.A., Tulane U., 1974; m. Alexandra Perrien, Dec. 26, 1975. Research engr. U.S. Steel Corp., Chgo., 1969-71; terr. mgr. Exxon Co. U.S.A., Houston, 1974-76; pres. Hansbrough Energy Systems Co., New Orleans, 1976—; dir. Ascension Processing Co. Served with AUS, 1971-72. Recipient cert. of appreciation Mayor of New Orleans, 1974. Mem. Am. Soc. Metals, Am. Mktg. Assn., Cousteau Soc. Club: Sierra. Research on field-ion microscopy. Office: PO Drawer 1776 Covington LA 70433

EGGERS, PAUL WALTER, lawyer; b. Seymour, Ind., Apr. 20, 1919; s. Ernest H. and Ottie (Carre) E.; B.A., Valparaiso U., 1941; LL.B., U. Tex., 1948; m. Virginia McMillin Streeter, Feb. 23, 1974; 1 son, Steven Paul. Admitted to Tex. bar, 1948; practiced in Wichita Falls, 1948-69; mem. firm Eggers, Sherrill & Pace, 1952-69; gen. counsel U.S. Treasury Dept., Washington, 1969-70; practice, Dallas, 1971—. Pres., Wichita Falls Symphony, 1960-62. Chmn., Wichita County Republican Party, 1966-67; chmn. Rep. State Task Force on Revenue and Fiscal Policy, 1967; Rep. candidate for gov. of Tex., 1968, 70. Commr. Pres. Assay Commn., 1972—. Trustee Episcopal Ch. Bldg. Fund, Dallas Symphony Orch., St. Mark's Sch. of Tex., 1974—; bd. dirs. Student Loan Marketing Assn., 1973-78; adv. council St. Paul Hosp., 1974—; dir. Dallas County ARC, 1974—, Dallas Civic Opera Assn., 1978—. Served to maj. AUS, 1941-46. Mem. State Bar Tex., Am. Bar Assn., Am. Judicature Soc. Episcopalian (chancellor diocese Dallas 1979—). Home: 3131 Maple St Apt 1D Dallas TX 75201 Office: 1407 Main St Dallas TX 75202

EHART, ROSALIE BOSWELL, educator; b. Indpls.; d. John Bruce and Edith K. (Harvey) Boswell; student Barry Coll., 1963-64; B.A., U. Miami, 1965, postgrad., 1969—; M.S. (NSF fellow), Colby Coll., 1969; postgrad. Fla. Atlantic U., 1975—; m. William McMein Ehart (div. Aug. 1957); children—Jan Bruce, Penelope Margaret, William McMein; m. 2d, Clive Dorrn, Dec. 20, 1979. Columnist, Diario las Americas, 1954-55; pres., chmn. bd. Collins Pharmacal Co., 1955-59; tchr. biology Mays Sr. High Sch., Goulds, Fla., 1966-70, Portobello Secondary Sch., Edinburgh, Scotland, 1971-72, Miami Edison Sr. High Sch., 1970-71 72—. Mem. Women's Congress on Housing, 1956, 57; dir. Am. Homes Com. for Miami Jr. Woman's Club, 1952, dir. social activities, 1953-54, NSF fellow, summers 1966-69; Fulbright fellow, 1971-72. Mem. AAUW, Theosophical Soc., English-Speaking Union, Daus. of Brit. Empire, Mensa, Brit. Floridian Club. Roman Catholic. Home: 1224 Tangier St Coral Gables FL 33134 also 26 Southland Rise Langford Biggleswade Bedfordshire SG18 9PP England

EHLE, ALBERT LAWRENCE, neurologist; b. Seattle, July 16, 1940; s. Albert Risbell and Josephine (Matzger) E.; B.S., Wash. State U., 1962; M.S., U. Wash., 1967, M.D., 1967; m. Virginia Louise Forman, June 5, 1967; children—Gregory Lawrence, Keri Louise. Intern, Cornell Med. Sch.-N.Y. Hosp., N.Y.C., 1967-68; resident in neurology U. Calif., San Francisco, 1971-73; asst. prof. neurology U. Ariz., Tucson, 1973-76; asst. prof. neurology U. Tex. Southwestern Med. Sch., Dallas, 1976-79, asso. prof., 1979—. Served to maj. M.C., U.S. Army, 1968-71. Diplomate Am. Bd. Psychiatry and Neurology, Am. Bd. Qualification in Electroencephalography. Mem. Am. Acad. Neurology, Am. EEG Soc., Soc. for Neurosci. Contbr. articles to profl. jours.; contbg. author books. Office: Dept Neurology Southwestern Med Sch U Tex 5323 Harry Hines Blvd Dallas TX 75235

EHLERS, HERBERT EDMUND, homebuilding co. exec.; b. Orange, N.J., June 28, 1939; s. Herbert E. and Marion Elizabeth (Danner) E.; B.A. with honors and distinction (Texaco fellow), Lehigh U., 1962, M.S. (Mgmt. Sci. fellow), 1964; children—Scott David, Ashley Susan. Vice pres. Parker Hunter Inc., Pitts. and Largo, Fla., 1968-75, C.S. McKee and Co. Inc., Largo, 1975-76, Colin Hochstin Co., Largo, 1976, U.S. Home Corp., Clearwater, Fla., 1977—; adj. prof. Fla. Inst. Tech. Grad. Sch. Bus.; pres. Real Estate Analysts Group, N.Y.C., 1974-75. Club: Countryside Country (Clearwater). Home: 2649 Winding Wood Dr Clearwater FL 33519 Office: PO Box 5000 Clearwater FL 33518

EHLMAN, WILLIAM GEORGE, mktg. exec.; b. Milw., Apr. 11, 1938; s. Neal Leroy and Verona Catherine (Reinbold) E.; B.S. in Bus. Adminstrn., Marquette U., 1960; M.B.A., Am. U., 1969; m. Carolyn Jean Sollenberger, Aug. 14, 1971. Vice pres. Career Consultants, Washington, 1966-68; nat. account rep., Sperry Univac, 1968-72; v.p. Eastern ops. Holosonics, Inc., Springfield, Va., 1972—; sec., treas. dir., Va. Mortgage Co., Annandale, 1975-78; dir. mktg. Hunter Assos. Lab., Inc., 1978—; corp. dir., founder, Va. Mortgage Co., Joe Theismann's Restaurant Inc.; nat. speaker Am. Soc. Quality Control. Active Congl. and State Legis. campaigns; mem. Red Fox,

Corrotoman civic assns. Served with C.E., U.S. Army. 1961-63. Registered fin. advisor. Mem. Am. Soc. Nondestructive Testing (nat. speaker), Soc. Mfg. Engrs. (nat. speaker), Armed Forces Communications and Electronics Assn., Assn. for Advancement Med. Instrumentation, Mortgage Bankers Assn. Club: Potomac River Yacht (commodore). Contbr. tech. papers in field of holography to confs. and publs. Home: 5033 Linette Ln Annandale VA 22003 Office: 9001 Braddock Rd Springfield VA 22151

EHMANN, WILLIAM DONALD, chemist; b. Madison, Wis., Feb. 7, 1931; s. William F. and Victoria V. (Koperski) E.; B.S., U. Wis., 1952, M.S., 1954; Ph.D., Carnegie Inst. Tech., 1957; m. Nancy M. Gallagher, July 16, 1955; children—William James, John Michael, James Thomas, Kathleen Elizabeth. NSF postdoctoral asso. Argonne (Ill.) Nat. Lab., 1957-58; asst. prof. chemistry U. Ky., 1958-63, asso. prof., 1963-66, prof., 1966—, chmn. dept. chemistry, 1972-76, Disting. prof. Coll. Arts and Scis., 1968-69, univ. research prof., 1977-78. Recipient Alumni Research award U. Ky. Alumni Assn., 1964; Fulbright research scholar, 1964-65. Mem. Am. Chem. Soc., Ky. Acad. Sci., Fulbright Alumni Assn., Meteorical Soc., Internat. Assn. Geochemistry and Cosmochemistry, Soc. Environ. Geochemistry and Health, Phi Eta Sigma, Phi Lambda Upsilon, Phi Kappa Theta. Roman Catholic. Contbr. articles on radiochemistry, geochemistry and chemistry of the moon to profl. jours.; among first scientists to study returned lunar samples from Apollo and Russian moon missions. Home: 769 Zandale Dr Lexington KY 40502 Office: Dept Chemistry U Ky Lexington KY 40506

EHRENTHAL, FRANK F., architect, planner, educator; b. Budapest, Hungary, Jan. 22, 1910; s. Alexander S. and Eugenie (Deutch) E.; came to U.S., 1939, naturalized, 1944; student U. Padua, Italy, 1928-29, Brunn Inst. Tech., Czechoslovakia, 1929-32; D.Arch., U. Firenze, Italy, 1935; L.H.D. (hon.), Starr King Sch. for Ministry, Berkeley, 1966; m. Julie Ann Deutch, 1941; children—Robert (adopted), Ann, Sylvia. Asso. various archtl. firms, Czechoslovakia, Italy, U.S., 1931—; pvt. practice architecture, San Francisco, 1946-63; vis. lectr. various colls. and univs., 1948-63; prof. architecture and urban design Pa. State U., 1963-66, Okla. State U., 1966-68; prof., chmn. urban design program Center for Urban and Regional Studies, Coll. Architecture, Va. Poly. Inst. and State U., Blacksburg, 1968-69, prof., chmn. urban and regional planning and urban design programs Environ. and Urban Systems div. Coll. Architecture and Urban Studies, 1969-70, prof. urban and regional studies, chmn. urban design program, 1970-80, prof. emeritus, 1980—. Recipient Grand prize Archtl. Forum, NAMP Competition, 1952, honorable mention Franklin Delano Roosevelt Meml. Competition, Washington, 1960, Spl. honorable mention Centro Direzionale Fontivegge Bellocchio Internat. Competition, Perugia, Italy, 1971, hon. mention Rainbow Center Plaza Competition, Niagara Falls, 1972. Past chmn. com. on extension, San Francisco Council Chs.; past mem. Mayor's San Francisco Forward Com. Task Force. Mem. Fedn. Am. Scientists, A.I.A., Am. Inst. Planners, Internat. Fedn. Housing and Planning, Assn. Collegiate Schs. Architecture, Assn. Collegiate Schs. Planning, Am. Assn. U. Profs., A.C.L.U., UN Assn. of U.S.A., Va. Citizens Planning Assn. (past dir.), Lambda Alpha, Tau Sigma Delta. Mason. Pub. writing A.I.A. Jour., work various profl. publs. Home: 2413 Southgate Sq Reston VA 22091

EHRHARDT, FRANZ, oil co. exec.; b. Erfurt, Germany, Feb. 24, 1936; s. Liemar and Ada-Rita (Veit) E.; came to U.S., 1975; student Trade and Commerce Sch., Germany, 1956-58; P.M.D., Harvard Bus. Sch., 1973. Mem. mktg. dept. Aral AG, Bochum, Germany, 1958-64; region mgr. Marathon Oil Co., Frankfurt, Germany, 1964-68; mgr. retail mktg., co. dir. Conoco, Hamburg, Germany, 1968-72; gen. mgr. mktg. Conoco Europe, London, 1972-75; coordinator worldwide retail mktg. Conoco Inc., Houston, 1976—. Office: Conoco Inc 5 Greenway Plaza E Houston TX 77046

EHRIG, NILA JUNE POE, educator; b. Denton, Tex., Nov. 1, 1948; d. Clifton F. and Martha Ludene (Brown) Poe; B.S. in Homemaking Edn., SW Tex. State U., 1970; M.S. in Edn., Prairie View A&M U., 1979; m. Al Wayne Ehrig, June 10, 1967; children—Bart, Sheryll. Tchr. homemaking Horace O'Bryant Jr. High Sch., Key West, Fla., 1970-71; homebound tchr. spl. edn. Gonzales (Tex.) High Sch., 1972-73, homemaking tchr., 1973-74; homemaking tchr. Academy High Sch., Temple, Tex., 1974—. Mem. Am. Personnel and Guidance Assn., NEA, Am. Vocat. Assn., Vocat. Homemaking Tchrs. Assn. Tex., Tex. Tchrs. Assn., Tex. Personnel and Guidance Assn., Gonzales Young Homemakers of Tex. (hon.). Methodist. Home: PO Box 355 Little River TX 76554 Office: Route 2 Temple TX 76501

EHRLICH, GERALDINE ELIZABETH, mgmt. cons.; b. Phila., Nov. 28, 1939; d. Joseph Vincent and Agnes Barbara (Campbell) McKenna; B.S. in Instl. Mgmt., Drexel Inst. Tech., Phila., 1958; m. S. Paul Ehrlich, Jr., June 20, 1959; children—Susan Patricia, Paula Jeanne, Jill Marie. Intern, USPHS, 1959; supervisory dietitian ARA Service Co., Phila. and San Francisco, 1959-65; dietary mgmt. cons. HEW, 1967-68; nutrition cons. hypertension research team U. Calif., Micronesia, 1970; regional sales dir. Marriott Corp., 1976-78; dir. sales and profl. services coll. and health care div. Macke Co., Cheverly, Md., 1978, gen. mgr. health care div., 1978-80, v.p. ops., 1980—; mem. Health Systems Agy. No. Va., 1976-77; chmn. health care adv. bd. Fairfax County (Va.), 1973-77. Vice chmn. Fairfax County Community Action Agy., 1973-77; treas. Fairfax County Democratic Com., 1969-73; trustee Fairfax Hosp., 1973-77. Mem. Am. Dietetic Assn., Assn. Mil. Surgeons, LWV, Fairfax County Nutrition Com. Club: Internat. Women's. Home: 6512 Lakeview Dr Falls Church VA 22041 Office: 1 Macke Circle Cheverly MD 20781

EHRLICH, STEPHEN JEFFREY, mech. engr.; b. Bklyn., Jan. 4, 1943; s. Edwin Kenneth and Fae (Reiss) E.; B.S. in Mech. Engring. cum laude, Newark Coll. Engring., 1970; m. Harriet Rose Meyers, Jan. 30, 1965; children—Mark Lee, Richard Scott. Sr. tech. aide Bell Telephone Labs., Whippany, N.J., 1965-70; sr. devel. engr. Black & Decker Mfg. Co., Towson, Md., 1970-73; sr. engr. BioQuest Corp., Cockeysville, Md., 1973-76; engring. group leader Motorola Corp., Fort Lauderdale, Fla., 1976—. Chmn. troop Boy Scouts Am., 1977-79. Mem. Soc. Mfg. Engrs., Soc. Plastic Engrs., Tau Beta Pi, Tau Alpha Pi, Pi Tau Sigma. Patentee in field. Home: 4331 NW 93d Way Sunrise FL 33321 Office: 8000 W Sunrise Blvd Fort Lauderdale FL 33322

EICH, WILBUR FOSTER, III, physician; b. Tuskegee, Ala., June 26, 1938; s. Wilbur Foster and Lula Olivia (Dudley) E.; B.A., Huntingdon Coll., 1960; M.D., Tulane, 1964; m. Eugenia Glass Graves, May 31, 1963; children—Paul Foster, Mark Samuel, Donna Eugenia. Intern, Lloyd Noland Hosp., Fairfield, Ala., 1964-65; resident in pediatrics U.S. Naval Hosp., Portsmouth, Va., 1967-69; pediatrician Infants' and Children's Clinic, Florence, Ala., 1971—; pres.-elect med. staff Eliza Coffee Meml. Hosp., 1979; clin. asst. prof. U. Ala., Birmingham, 1976—. Vol., Project Hope, Brazil, 1973; trustee Huntingdon Coll., Montgomery, Ala., 1977—. Served with USN, 1965-71. Diplomate Am. Bd. Pediatrics. Fellow Am. Acad. Pediatrics, Am. Acad. Cerebral Palsy and Devel. Medicine; mem. AMA, So. Med. Assn., Med. Assn. Ala., Lauderdale County Med. Soc., Christian Med. Soc. Episcopalian. (lay reader). Home: 201 Flurnoy Ave Florence AL 35630 Office: 412 Cedar St S Florence AL 35630

EIDSON, JOHN OLIN, educator; b. Johnston, S.C., Dec. 10, 1908; s. Olin Marvin and Margaret (Rushton) E.; A.B., Wofford Coll., 1929, Litt.D. (hon.), 1954; M.A., Vanderbilt U., 1930; Ph.D., Duke U., 1941; m. Perrin Cudd, Aug. 7, 1952. Faculty U. Ga., Athens, 1936-68, beginning as instr. English, successively dean Coordinate Coll., dir. U. Center in Ga., dean Coll. Arts and Scis., 1957-68; pres. Ga. So. Coll., Statesboro, 1968-71; vice chancellor U. System of Ga., 1971-76; Fulbright prof. U. Bonn (Germany), 1977-78; vis. prof. Am. lit. U. Freiberg (Germany), 1956. Mem. senate Nat. Assn. State Univs. and Land-Grant Colls., 1963-66. Mem. Atlanta Municipal Edn. Adv. Com., 1971—. Exec. bd. Atlanta area council Boy Scouts Am., 1973—, exec. bd. Inst. Internat. Edn., 1976—. Served from lt. to maj., inf., AUS, 1942-46; lt. col. Res. Recipient M.G. Michael award for research, 1950. Mem. Am. Studies Assn. (v.p. southeastern 1964-66, pres. 1966-68), Am. Assn. State Colls. and Univs. (mem. grad. com.), Conf. Acad. Deans So. States (pres. 1967-68), Nat. Council Colls. Arts and Scis. (exec. bd. 1965-68), English Assn., Tennyson Soc., MLA, S. Atlantic MLA, Newcomen Soc. N.Am., Sphinx, Phi Beta Kappa (pres. U. Ga. chpt. 1957-58, chmn. S. Atlantic dist. 1958-61, pres. Coastal Ga.-Carolina 1970-71), Pi Kappa Delta, Phi Kappa Phi, Delta Phi Alpha (nat. sec. 1929-34, mem. nat. council 1969—), Tau Kappa Alpha, Kappa Delta Pi, Phi Delta Kappa, Kappa Phi Kappa. Methodist. Rotarian. Author: Tennyson in America, 1943; Charles Stearns Wheeler: Friend of Emerson, 1951; (with W. W. Davidson) Reading for Pleasure, 1948. Editor: Georgia Rev., 1950-57, mem. editorial bd., 1957-74. Contbr. articles and revs. to scholastic jours. Home: 362 Valley Green Dr NE Atlanta GA 30342

EINSPRUCH, NORMAN GERALD, univ. ofcl., elec. engr.; b. N.Y.C., June 27, 1932; s. Adolph and Mala (Goldblatt) E.; B.A. in Physics, Rice U., Tex., 1953; M.S. in Physics, U. Colo., 1955; Ph.D. in Applied Math., Brown U., 1959; m. Edith Melnick, Dec. 20, 1953; children—Eric, Andrew, Franklin. Mem. tech. staff Central Research Labs., Tex. Instruments, Inc., Dallas, 1959-62, mgr. electron transport physics br., 1962-68, dir. advanced tech. lab., 1968-69, dir. technology, chem. materials div., 1969-72, dir. Central Research Labs., 1972-75, asst. v.p., 1975-77; prof. dept. elec. engring. Sch. Engring. and Architecture, U. Miami, Coral Gables, Fla., 1977—, dean Sch. Engring. and Architecture, 1977—. Fellow Am. Phys. Soc., Acoustical Soc. Am., IEEE; mem. Am. Inst. Indsl. Engrs., Am. Soc. Engring. Edn., AAAS, Sigma Xi, Phi Kappa Phi, Eta Kappa Nu, Tau Beta Pi. Contbr. numerous articles on solid state physics, electronics, acoustics to profl. jours. Home: 1415 Trillo Ave Coral Gables FL 33146 Office: PO Box 248294 Coral Gables FL 33124

EISELE, GARNETT THOMAS, judge; b. Hot Springs, Ark., Nov. 3, 1923; s. Garnett Martin and Mary (Martin) E.; student U. Fla., 1940-42, Ind. U., 1942-43; A.B., Washington U., 1947; LL.B., Harvard, 1950, LL.M., 1951; m. Kathryn Fraygang, June 24, 1950; children—Wendell A., Garnett Martin, Kathryn M., Jean E. Admitted to Ark. bar, practiced in Hot Springs, 1951-52, Little Rock, 1953-69; asso. firm Wootten, Land and Matthews, 1951-52, Owens, McHaney, Lofton & McHaney, 1956-60; asst. U.S. atty., Little Rock, 1953-55; individual practice, 1961-69; U.S. dist. judge, Little Rock, 1970—. Legal adviser to gov. Ark., 1966-69. Del. Ark. 7th Constl. Conv., 1969-70. Trustee U. Ark., 1969-70. Served with AUS, 1943-46, ETO. Mem. Am., Ark., Pulaski County bar assns., Am. Law Inst., Am. Judicature Soc. Office: US Post Office and Courthouse Little Rock AR 72203*

EISEN, SUSAN HARRIET, speech and lang. pathologist; b. Ossining, N.Y., Apr. 8, 1950; d. Eugene Leo and Barbara (Schnapp) E.; B.S., U. Fla., 1972, M.Ed., 1974; postgrad. Boston U., summers 1970, Northwestern U., summer 1979. Speech pathologist Alachua County Schs., Gainesville, Fla., 1975—, Champus Medicaid and Medicare, Gainesville, 1977—, Therapy, Inc., Gainesville, 1977—; adminstr., owner D.B.A. Ednl. Therapy Service, Gainesville, 1977—; cons. Children's Med. Services, Gainesville, 1977—. Mem. Democratic Nat. Com., 1977-79; mem. Nat. Resource Def. Council. Notary public. Mem. Am. Speech and Hearing Assn., Council for Exceptional Children, Found. for Exceptional Children. Jewish. Club: B'nai B'rith Women. Address: PO Box 12215 Gainesville FL 32604

EISENBERG, DIANE KAY, utility co. exec.; b. Fulton, N.Y., Aug. 27, 1949; d. Harry Leonard and Harriet (Ferst) Alpert; B.S. in Communications cum laude, U. Fla., 1972; m. Herman I. Eisenberg, Dec. 22, 1968. Mgr., Ott, Hertner, Ott & Assos., mgmt. cons., Miami, Fla., 1972-73; personnel adminstr. Fla. Power & Light Co., Miami, 1973-75, sr. devel. and tng. specialist, 1975—; cons. in communications, public speaking, mgmt. devel. Recipient Creative Publs. award Phi Beta Phi, 1972, outstanding young woman of Am. award, 1979. Mem. AAUW, Am. Soc. Tng. and Devel., Public Relations Soc. Am. (past pres.). Home: 15305 SW 78th Ct Miami FL 33157 Office: 9250 W Flagler St Miami FL 33174

EISENBERG, HARRY VICTOR, plastic surgeon; b. N.Y.C., May 8, 1945; s. Joseph and Faye (Simon) E.; B.A., Boston U., 1968, M.D., 1968; m. Lya Etta Chamikles, June 21, 1969; children—Davina Hera, Erica Beth. Intern, Maimonides Hosp., Bklyn., 1968-69, resident in gen. surgery, 1969-73; emergency physician Orange Meml. Hosp., Orlando, Fla., 1973-75; resident in plastic surgery Orange Meml. Hosp., Orlando, 1975-77; pvt. practice plastic surgery, Maitland, Fla., 1977—; mem. staff Fla. Hosp., Lucerne Hosp., Winter Park (Fla.) Meml. Hosp. Diplomate Am. Bd. Surgery, Am. Bd. Plastic Surgery. Mem. AMA (Physicians Recognition award 1971, 74, 77), A.C.S., Am. Coll. Emergency Physicians, Am. Soc. Plastic and Reconstructive Surgeons, Fla. Med. Assn., Fla. Soc. Plastic and Reconstructive Surgeons, S.E. Soc. Plastic and Reconstructive Surgeons, Orange County Med. Soc. Jewish. Home: 255 Spring Lake Hills Dr Maitland FL 32751 Office: 451 N Maitland Ave Maitland FL 32751

EISENBERG, HOWARD MICHAEL, neurosurgeon; b. N.Y.C., May 4, 1939; s. Monroe L. and Regina (Fish) E.; B.A., Syracuse U., 1960; M.D., SUNY, N.Y.C., 1964; children—Nancy M., John A. Resident fellow in surgery Cornell Med. Sch., N.Y. Hosp., N.Y.C., 1964-66; resident fellow in neurosurgery Harvard U., Boston, 1966-70, instr. surgery, 1972-75; asso. prof. neurosurgery U. Tex., Galveston, 1975—; head, pediatric neurosurgery U. Tex. Hosps., Galveston, 1975-80, chief div. neurosurgery, 1980—. Served to lt. comdr. USN, 1970-72. Fellow A.C.S.; mem. Nat. Assn. Advancement Sci., Internat. Soc. Pediatric Neurosurgery, Am. Assn. Neurol. Surgeons, Congress Neurosurgeons, Soc. Neurosci., Sierra Club. Clubs: Galveston Yacht, U.S. Yacht Racing Union. Contbr. articles to profl. jours.; editor: (with R. L. Suddith) The Cerebral Microvasculature, Investigation of the Blood-Brain Barrier, 1980. Office: Div Neurosurgery U Tex Med Br Galveston TX 77550

EISENFELD, LEONARD IRWIN, pediatrician, neonatologist; b. Pitts., June 16, 1946; s. Harry and Bessie G. (Ruben) E.; B.A., Washington and Jefferson Coll., 1967; M.D., Yale U., 1971; m. Vicki Ilene Port, June 29, 1969; children—Matthew Mitchell, Amy Michele. Pediatric intern U. Pitts. Children's Hosp., 1971-72, pediatric resident, 1972-74; fellow perinatal medicine U. Ala., Birmingham, 1976-78; practice medicine specializing in pediatrics Redstone Arsenal, Ala., 1974-76, Birmingham, 1976-77, Huntsville, Ala., 1977-79, New Orleans, 1979—; mem. staff, chief sect. neonatology Ochsner Found. Hosp., East Jefferson Gen. Hosp., New Orleans; instr. pediatrics U. Ala., Huntsville, 1975-78, asst. prof. pediatrics, 1978-79; clin. asst. prof. pediatrics Tulane U., 1979—. Served to maj. M.C., U.S. Army, 1974-76. Diplomate Am. Bd. Pediatrics, Nat. Bd. Med. Examiners. Fellow Am. Acad. Pediatrics; mem. Ala. Acad. Pediatrics, So. Perinatal Assn., So. Soc. Pediatric Research, La. Med. Assn., Madison County Med. Soc. Contbr. articles to profl. jours.

EISMA, JOSE ALBARRACIN, physician; b. Jolo, Sulu, Philippines, Oct. 18, 1939; came to U.S., 1964, naturalized, 1973; s. Marcelo L. and Rosa A. (Albarracin) E.; A.A., Silliman U., Philippines, 1958; M.D., U. Santo Tomas (Manila), 1963; m. Lenora Womack, Sept. 14, 1977; 1 son, Joseph Alan. Rotating intern Wilson Meml. Hosp., Johnson City, N.Y., 1964-65, med. resident, 1965-67; med. resident Kingsbrook Jewish Med. Center, Bklyn., 1967-68; gen. internist Reynolds Army Hosp., Ft. Sill, Okla., 1971-73; resident in pulmonary disease Brooke Army Med. Center, Ft. Sam Houston, Tex., 1973-74; chief med. staff, chief of medicine, med. dir. respiratory therapy dept., chmn. infection control com. West (Tex.) Community Hosp., 1978—. Served to lt. col. M.C., Army N.G., 1975-80. Diplomate Am. Bd. Family Practice. Fellow Am. Acad. Family Physicians, Am. Coll. Angiology (asso.); mem. A.C.P., Am. Soc. Internal Medicine, Am. Thoracic Soc., Am. Heart Assn., Am. Med. Writers Assn. Clubs: Res. Officers Assn., Tex. N.G. Assn., Assn. U.S. Army, Assn. Mil. Surgeons of U.S. Contbr. article to profl. publ. in field. Home: 1406 N Reagan St West TX 76691 Office: 300 N Reagan St West TX 76691

EISMAN, DIANE BATSHAW, physician; b. Chgo., Apr. 26, 1937; d. Robert and Anne (Holtzer) Batshaw; S.B., U. Chgo., 1957; M.D., U. Ky., 1969; m. Eugene Herbert Eisman, Aug. 18, 1958; 1 dau., Clara Jessica. Intern, U. Ky., 1969; physician Dade County Dept. Pub. Health, Miami, Fla., 1970-71, Student Health Services, U. S.C., Columbia, 1971-72; acting dir. disease control Dade County Dept. Pub. Health, Miami, 1972-73; practice family medicine with Eugene Eisman, Miami, 1974—; mem. staff Pkwy. Gen. Hosp., North Miami Gen. Hosp. Recipient Physicians Recognition award AMA, 1973-76, 76-78; diplomate Am. Bd. Family Practice. Fellow Am. Acad. Family Physicians; mem. Dade County Med. Assn., Royal Soc. Medicine (affiliate), Am. Physicians Fellowship, Fla. Med. Assn., Heart Assn. Greater Miami, Am. Med. Womens Assn., Am. Jogging Assn., Sierra Club, Internat. Oceanographic Found. Jewish. Home: 8551 NE Bayshore Dr Miami FL 33138 Office: 12860 Biscayne Blvd North Miami FL 33181

EISMAN, EUGENE HERBERT, physician; b. N.Y.C., Mar. 29, 1936; s. Frank and Mae (Shapiro) E.; S.B., U. Chgo., 1958; M.S., U. Miss., 1961; M.D., U. Ky., 1966; m. Diane Barbara Batshaw, Aug. 22, 1936; 1 dau., Clara Jessica. Intern, Univ. Hosp., Lexington, Ky., 1966-67, resident in medicine, 1967-70; practice medicine specializing in internal medicine, North Miami, Fla., 1971—; chief dept. internal medicine North Miami Gen. Hosp. Served with U.S. Army, 1970-72. Mem. Am. Coll. Cardiology, Am. Heart Assn., Dade County Med. Assn., Fla. Med. Divers Assn., Active Divers Assn. Office: 12860 Biscayne Blvd Suite 108 North Miami FL 33181

EITELBACH, WARREN CHESTER, steamship exec.; b. N.Y.C., May 3, 1918; s. Maximmian Frederick and Lillian Burgess (Reid) E.; student U. Houston, 1950, San Jacinto Coll., 1972; m. Olive Marie Leonard, June 20, 1948; children—Leonard, Frederick, Gerrit, Elaine, Eric, Laurie. Stevedore supr. Lykes Bros. Steamship Co., Houston, 1949-56, West Gulf stevedoring mgr., 1956-71, ops. mgr. West Gulf, 1971-73, asst. v.p. West Gulf ops., 1973-79, v.p. West Gulf ops., 1979—; pres., dir. Southside Services, Inc.; pres. Terminal Services Houston, Inc.; dir. Jay's Crane Rental, Inc. Served with U.S. Maritime Service, 1934-49. Mem. West Gulf Maritime Assn., Nat. Cargo Bur., Nat. Assn. Stevedores (dir.), Nat. Rifleman's Assn. Quaker. Club: Masons. Home: Box 737 Friendswood TX 77546 Office: 6821 Ave V Houston TX 77011

EKBERG, DONALD ROY, fishery adminstr.; b. Hinsdale, Ill., Dec. 23, 1928; s. Roy H. and Evelyn B. (Newman) E.; B.S., U. Ill., 1950, Ph.D., 1957; M.S., U. Chgo., 1952; m. Anneliese G. Nattermann, May 27, 1961; children—Kenneth, Dale. Physiologist, Gen. Electric Co., Phila., 1958-65; mgr. bioscis. Gen. Electric Co., King of Prussia, Pa., 1965-71, mgr. applied sci., Bay St. Louis, Miss., 1971-76; chief environ. and tech. services div. NOAA, Nat. Marine Fisheries Service, St. Petersburg, Fla.; adj. prof. Drexel Inst., 1969-71. Served to lt., USAF, 1952-54; to col. Res., 1952—. USPHS fellow U. Kiel (Germany), 1959-60. Mem. Soc. Gen. Physiologists, Am. Soc. Zoologists, Am. Physiol. Soc., Sigma Xi. Unitarian. Contbr. articles to profl. jours. Home: 1376 Ambassador Dr Clearwater FL 33516 Office: 9450 Koger Blvd Saint Petersburg FL 33702

EKERY, FRED NICHOLAS, physician; b. El Paso, Jan. 13, 1939; s. Leon John and Albina (Simon) E.; B.A. in Biol. Sci., U. Tex., 1959; M.D., 1963; m. Dorothy Maria DiNardo, June 5, 1965; children—Deborah, Rachel, Laura. Intern Parkland Meml. Hosp., Dallas, 1963-64, resident 1965-66, R.B. Hite fellow in hematology, oncology, 1966-67; resident in internal medicine III and IV med. divs. Bellevue Hosp., N.Y.C., 1964-65; practice medicine specializing in internal medicine and med. oncology, El Paso, 1969-77; cons. in hematology U.S. Army, Japan, 1967-69, R.E. Thomasen Gen. Hosp., El Paso, 1969-75; asso. prof. medicine Tex. Tech U., El Paso, 1975-80; bd. advisers El Paso Cancer Treatment Center, 1974-77. Served with U.S. Army, 1967-69. Recipient Sardonyx award U. Tex. at El Paso, 1959; diplomate Am. Bd. Internal Medicine, Am. Bd. Oncology. Mem. El Paso County Med. Soc., Tex., Am., med. assns., Alpha Omega Alpha. Greek Orthodox. Home: 4256 Park Hill Dr El Paso TX 79902 Office: 2800 N Stanton St El Paso TX 79902

EKWALL, MERTON LEON, psychiatrist, neurologist; b. Fairfield, Nebr., Feb. 26, 1922; s. John Wesley and Ruth Elvira (Berguist) E.; student Nebr. Wesleyan U., 1940-43; M.D., U. Nebr., 1946; m. Bonnie Marie Sutton, Aug. 30, 1946; children—Pamela, John Stephen, Debra Marie, William Wallace. Intern, Santa Barbara (Calif.) Cottage Hosp., 1946; resident in psychiatry Norfolk (Nebr.) State Hosp., 1948-50; resident in neurology Wis. Gen. Hosp., Madison, 1950; practice medicine specializing in psychiatry and neurology, Jacksonville, Fla., 1953-65, Tallahassee, Fla., 1965—. Served with USNR, 1940-45, 51-53. Mem. AMA, Am., So., Fla. (past pres.) psychiatric socs., Am. (pres. 1977—), So. EEG socs. Republican. Methodist. Clubs: Rotary, Mason. Home: 3380 W Lakeshore Dr Tallahassee FL 32312 Office: 1326 N Magnolia Dr Tallahassee FL 32303

ELAD, EMANUEL, analytical instrumentation exec.; b. Kutno, Poland, May 7, 1935; s. Yishaiau and Esther Altman; came to U.S., 1965, naturalized, 1975; B.S., Technion U., Israel, 1960, M.S., 1964; Ph.D. in Elec. Engring. (fellow 1966-67), U. Calif., Berkeley, 1968; M.B.A., U. Tenn., Knoxville, 1977; m. Hanna Wakman, May 26, 1959; children—Orly, Doronne, Joel. Research engr. Atomic Energy Commn. Israel, Haifa, 1960-65, LBL, Berkeley, 1965-68; tech. dir. Nuclear Diodes Co., Prairie View, Ill., 1968-69; with ORTEC, Inc., Oak Ridge, 1969—, gen. mgr. materials analysis div., 1975—, v.p., 1977—. Served with Israeli Air Force, 1953-56. Mem. IEEE, Sigma Xi, Eta Kappa Nu, Phi Kappa Phi. Jewish. Club: Oak Ridge Tennis.

Author research papers. Home: 102 Canterbury Rd Oak Ridge TN 37830 Office: 100 Midland Rd Oak Ridge TN 37830

ELAM, ANDREW GREGORY, II, ins. co. exec.; b. Winchester, Va., Feb. 6, 1932; s. Andrew Gregory and Francis Clayton (Gold) E.; A.B., Presbyn. Coll., 1955; m. Rebecca Rhea Cole, Oct. 26, 1958; children—Andrew Gregory III, Philip Cole, Dawna Francis. Adminstrv. asst. Citizen's and So. Nat. Bank, Columbia, S.C., 1955-56; nat. exec. dir. Pi Kappa Phi, Sumter, S.C., 1956-59; pres. Carolina Potato Co., Inc., West Columbia, S.C., 1959-61; mem. pub. relations staff Kendavis Industries Internat., Inc., Fort Worth, 1961-63; dir. sales promotion Pioneer Am. Ins. Co., Fort Worth, 1963-64, dir. pub. relations and sales promotion, 1964-66, asst. v.p., 1966-68, v.p., mem. exec. com., 1968-71, dir., 1970-71; v.p. pub. relations and sales promotion Gt. Am. Res. Ins. Co., Dallas, 1972—J.C. Penney Life Ins. Co., Dallas, 1978—. Mem. pub. relations adv. council Am. Council Life Ins., Washington, 1971—; mem. pub. relations com. Tex. Life Conv., 1970—. Mem. pub. info. adv. com. Am. Cancer Soc., Tex. div., 1969—, chmn., 1972-77, exec. com., bd. dirs., 1972-77; vice-chmn. pub. relations com. Tarrant County United Fund, 1967; campaign leader Community Pride Campaign Performing Arts, 1969. Bd. dirs. Fort Worth Community Theatre, 1971-72; bd. dirs., treas., vice-chmn. Tarrant County unit Am. Cancer Soc., 1963-71, bd. dirs. Dallas County unit, 1972—; bd. dirs. Baylor U. Med. Center Found., 1979—; adv. bd. Charles A. Sammons Cancer Center. Mem. Life Ins. Advertisers Assn. (dir. communications workshop 1970-71, exec. com. 1973—, chmn. So. Round Table 1972), Pub. Relations Soc. Am., Tex. Pub. Relations Assn. (dir. 1966), Indsl. Editors Fort Worth (pres. 1968), Meeting Planners Internat. (nat. conv. program chmn. 1979), Fort Worth C. of C. (chmn. publ. com. 1970), Dallas Advt. League. Presbyterian (deacon 1966-68; ruling elder 1969-71). Home: 7730 Chattington St Dallas TX 75248 Office: 2020 Live Oak Dallas TX 75221

ELAM, JAMES DONALD, univ. adminstr.; b. Birmingham, Ala., Apr. 8, 1933; s. James Walter and Betty Viola (Bates) E.; B.S., U. Tenn., 1955; M.Div., Luth. Theol. Sem., 1959; D.Min., Lexington Theol. Sem., 1972; m. Audrey Grace Wagner, June 5, 1956; children—James Michael, Donald Mark, Kevin Douglas. Ordained to ministry, Lutheran Ch., 1959; pastor Holy Trinity Luth. Ch., Anderson, S.C., 1959-62, Faith Luth. Ch., Lexington, Ky., 1962-67; field underwriter Mutual Life Ins. Co. of N.Y., Lexington, 1967-69; asso. dir. Ketchum, Inc., Pitts., Pa., 1969-70; dir. annual fund Transylvania Coll., Lexington, 1970-71; asso. v.p. for univ. relations and devel. U. Ga., Athens, 1973—. Bd. trustees Luth. Sch. Theology, Chgo., 1971-72, Wittenberg U., 1970-72. Recipient Pres.'s award, Jr. C. of C., 1960; U.S. Steel Alumni Incentive award, 1976. Mem. Council for Advancement and Support of Edn., Am. Assn. Univ. Adminstrs., C. of C., Am. Assn. Assn. Mgrs., Gridiron Secret Soc., Delta Tau Delta. Democrat. Presbyterian. Club: Athens Country. Contbr. articles in field to profl. jours. Home: 320 Cedar Creek Athens GA 30605 Office: Univ Ga Alumni House Athens GA 30602

ELAM, MARY GLENDINNING, interior designer; b. Huntsville, Ala., Sept. 28, 1927; d. James S. and Anne (Holden) Glendinning; B.S. in Interior Design, U. N.C., 1971; m. Harper Johnston (Jack) Elam, III, Aug. 30, 1947; children—George Martin, John Claibourne, Erin Patricia. Apprentice in interior design Guilford Galleries, Greensboro, N.C., 1969-70; free lance interior designer, 1970-73; pres. Mary Elam Design Inc., Greensboro, 1973—. Commr., City of Greensboro Zoning Commn. Mem. Am. Soc. of Interior Designers (profl. mem.; dir. Carolinas chpt. 1977—), N.C. Preservation Soc. Presbyterian. Home: 110 S Park Dr Greensboro NC 27401 Office: 2110 N Elm St Greensboro NC 27408

ELAM, PATRICIA LEE, free-lance writer; b. Ashland, Ky., Apr. 28, 1950; d. James Harve and Mildred Elizabeth (Hayes) E.; B.A. in Journalism, U. Ky., 1972; M.A. in Communications, Morehead State U., 1975; M.A. in Cinema, N.Y. U., 1981. Regional reporter, columnist, film and theater critic Ashland (Ky.) Daily Independent, 1973; grad. asst. tchr. div. communications Morehead State U., 1974-75; exec. dir. Lexington (Ky.) Rape Crisis Center, Inc., 1975-77; wife abuse specialist, researcher Louisville-Jefferson County (Ky.) Criminal Justice Commn., Louisville, 1978; radio personality Sta. WCMI, Ashland, 1979; del. Rape and Its Victims Conf., Nat. Inst. Law Enforcement and Criminal Justice. Mem. exec. com. Lexington Task Force on Battered Women; chairperson task force Ky. Women's Agenda Coalition. Mem. Nat. Bus. and Profl. Women's Club, Nat. Woman's Party, Nat. Women's Polit. Caucus, Ky. Women's Polit. Caucus, ACLU, Ky. Civil Liberties Union, N. Central Women's Studies Assn., Ky. Pro ERA Alliance, Sigma Delta Chi, Women in Communications. Home: 2511 Woodland Ashland KY 41101 Office: 53 Washington Sq New York NY

ELBLING, PAUL URBAIN, restaurant services exec.; b. Orbey, France, Aug. 22, 1940; came to U.S., 1967, naturalized, 1977; s. E. Rene and Fernande E. (Dissler) E.; cert. d'Aptitude Profl., Brevet de Maitrise, France, 1963; m. Marie Antionette, Apr. 30, 1966. Chef, Das Golden Kreitz, Baden-Baden, Germany, 1962-63, Rotisserie Zur Kloke, Baden-Baden, 1963-66; chef Restaurant Chez Francois, Washington, 1967-68; exec. chef for Pres. of U.S., 1969; chef for spl. dinners at Nat. Hotel, Washington, 1969-70; propr., exec. chef LaPetite France Restaurant, Richmond, Va., 1970—. Served to sgt. French Army, 1959-62. Recipient Humanitarian award Little Sisters of the Poor, 1978; Universal Dining award, 1979; Disting. Achievement award No. Seaboard region of Hadassah, 1979; Cert. of Commendation, Supreme K.C., 1979; Disting. Achievement award Am. Heart Assn., 1978; Humanitarian award Gov. of Va., 1978; Gold Medal award, Paris, France, 1965. Mem. Am. Acad. Chefs (award 1978), Am. Culinary Fedn. Ednl. Inst. (trustee 1978-79), Va. Chefs Assn. (founder 1976, pres. 1976-79), Va. Restaurant Assn. (dir. 1979-80), Internat. Wine Soc. (chevalier 1978—), Am. Culinary Fedn. (eastern regional dir. 1977-79), Cordons Bleus, Wintergreen Assn. Roman Catholic. Club: Hermitage Country. Editor, pub.: Chef Paul's La Petite France, 1978; author: Inexpensive Beef Cuts Made Special, 1973. Home: 10114 Deepwood Circle Richmond VA 23233 Office: 2912 Maywill St Richmond VA 23230

ELDER, HARVEY LYNN, mathematician; b. Mayfield, Ky., Apr. 23, 1934; s. Harvey Arthur and Fannie Dodds (Scholes) E.; B.A., Murray State U., 1955; M.A. in Edn., 1957; A.M., U. Ill., 1961, Ph.D., 1968. Mem. faculty dept. math. Murray (Ky.) State U., 1957—, prof., 1977—. Mem. Nat. Council Tchrs. Math., Kenlake Council Tchrs. Math. (pres.), Math. Assn. Am., Euclidean Math. Club, Phi Delta Kappa. Mem. Ch. of Christ. Home: 75 Shady Oaks Murray KY 42071 Office: Dept Math Murray State Univ Murray KY 42071

ELDRIDGE, FRANCIS LEE, constrn. co. exec.; b. Martinsville, Ind., Oct. 19, 1938; s. Albert Charles and Doris Ladine (Hubbard) E.; B.S. in Bus. Adminstrn., Hamilton State U., 1962. Pres., chmn. bd. F.L. Eldridge & Co., Inc., Bradenton, Fla., 1978—; owner Eldridge Properties Fla.; v.p. First Saratoga Mortgage Co.; mem. Ind. Group of Manatee and Saratoga Counties. Served to sgt. U.S. Army, 1957-60. Certified gen. contractor; registered real estate broker. Mem. Nat., Fla. assn. realtors, Am. Inst. Constructors, Nat. Assn. Home Builders, Gulf Coast Builders Exchange. Democrat. Clubs: Masons, Shriners, Anna Maria Island Privateers. Office: 1713 Manatee Ave W Bradenton FL 33505

ELDRIDGE, PETER JOHN, fishery biologist; b. New Bedford, Mass., Feb. 6, 1937; s. Carlton C. and C. Frances Eldridge; B.S., U. Mass., 1959; M.A., Coll. William and Mary, 1962; Ph.D., U. Wash., 1975; m. Joan F. Tyler, Dec. 20, 1968; children—Kelly, Christine Elizabeth. Asst. marine scientist Va. Inst. Marine Scis., 1965-67; asst., then asso. marine scientist S.C. Dept. Wildlife and Marine Research, 1972-78; biol. statistician Charleston (S.C.) lab. Nat. Marine and Fisheries Service, NOAA, 1978—; mem. stats. and sci. com. S. Atlantic Fishery Mgmt. Council. Served to capt. U.S. Army, 1962-65. Mem. Am. Inst. Fishery Research Biologists (dist. dir. Carolina), Am. Fisheries Soc., Nat. Shell Fish Assn., Common Cause, Sigma Xi. Roman Catholic. Author articles, reports in field. Home: 761 Stiles Dr Charleston SC 29412 Office: PO Box 12607 Charleston SC 29412

ELEBASH, HUNLEY AGEE, bishop; b. Pensacola, Fla., July 27, 1923; s. Eugene Perrin and Ann (Agee) E.; B.S., U. of South, 1944, B.D., 1950, D.D., 1969; m. Maurine Ashton, Nov. 2, 1946; children—David Hunley, Brett Randolph. Ordained to ministry Episcopal Ch., 1950; rector in Jacksonville, Fla., 1950-57, Wilmington, N.C., 1957-65; exec. sec. Diocese East Carolina, 1965-68, bishop coadjutor, 1968-73, bishop, 1973—. Sec. Diocese Fla., 1953-57; del. Gen. Conv. Episcopal Ch., 1961, 64, 67; pres. Fourth Province of Episcopal Ch., 1975-79. Served to 1st lt. USMCR, 1943-46. Fellow Coll. Preachers, Washington, 1958. Home: 1905 Live Oak Pkwy Wilmington NC 28403 Office: 305 S 3d St Wilmington NC 28401

ELEQUIN, CLETO, JR., physician; b. Antique, Philippines, Oct. 18, 1933; s. Cleto and Enriqueta (Tengonciang) E.; M.D., Far Eastern U. (Philippines), 1957; m. Nancy Johnson, May 14, 1958; children—Tracy, Thomas Kyle, Stuart Scott. Rotating intern Good Samaritan Hosp., Lexington, Ky., 1957-58; gen. practice resident Central Bapt. Hosp., Lexington, 1958-59; psychiat. resident State Hosp., Danville, Pa., 1959-60, 61-62; psychiat. resident with child psychiatry State Hosp., New Castle, Del., 1962-63; staff physician Eastern State Hosp., Lexington, 1960-61, dir. Fayette County Project, dir. intensive treatment service, 1964-67, supt., 1969-71; dep. commr. Dept. Mental Health, State Ky., 1967-69; practice medicine, specializing in family practice, Pecos, Tex., 1971-72, Austin, Tex., 1974—; asst. dep. commr. Tex. Dept. Mental Health and Mental Retardation, Austin, 1973-74, dep. commr. mental health, 1974; attending psychiatrist U. Ky. Med. Center, 1964-71, Good Samaritan Hosp., 1969-71, Central Bapt. Hosp., 1966-71; cons. psychiatrist U. Ky. Student Health Service, 1965-71, Peace Corps, 1966-68, Bur. Rehab., State Ky., 1965-71, Blue Grass Community Care Center, 1967-71, Covington (Ky.) Community Care Center, 1969-71, Hazard Community Care Center, 1969-71, Danville (Ky.) Community Care Center, 1969-71, Maysville (Ky.) Community Care Center, 1969-71; clin. instr., asst. clin. prof. dept. psychiatry U. Ky. Med. Center, 1964-69, asso. clin. prof., 1969-71. Mem. Profl. Adv. Council Community Mental Health-Retardation Center, Lexington, 1967-71; mem. Lexington Hosp. Council, 1969-71. Mem. AMA, Am. Psychiat. Assn., Tex. Med. Assn., Travis County Med. Soc., Austin Psychiat. Soc., Assn. Med. Supts. Mental Hosps., Am. Acad. Family Physicians. Home: 7109 Montana Norte Austin TX 78731 Office: 942 Peyton Gin Rd Austin TX 78758

ELEUTERIUS, CHARLES KEMUEL, phys. oceanographer; b. Biloxi, Miss., Nov. 28, 1940; s. Lionel Adam and Martha Elizabeth (Tiblier) E.; B.S., U. So. Miss., 1965, M.S., 1969; postgrad. Tex. A. & M., 1971; m. Mary Earle Beemon, July 3, 1964; 1 dau., Mary Beth. Head, computer center Gulf Coast Research Lab., Ocean Springs, Miss., 1965-72, head phys. oceanography sec., 1972—; tech. rep. State of Miss. on superport siting; tech. advisor Gulf Regional Planning Commn., reviewer environ. affairs; instr. mathematics, statistics, computer sci.; mem. Miss. Mineral Resources Inst. Served with U.S. Army, 1962; with Army N.G., 1961-67. Mem. Assn. for Computing Machinery, Miss. Acad. Scis., Am. Fisheries Soc., Gulf Estuarine Research Soc., Littoral Soc. Methodist. Contbr. articles to profl. jours. Home: 2504 Ridgewood Rd Ocean Springs MS 39564 Office: Shearwater Dr Ocean Springs MS 39564

ELEY, MICHAEL HENRY, biochemist; b. LaGrange, Ga., Mar. 2, 1943; s. Sherman Elmer and Netsie Lee (Wyatt) E.; A.B. in Biology, West Ga. Coll., 1965; M.S. in Biochemistry, U. Ga., 1968, Ph.D. in Biochemistry, 1970; m. Betty Jane McClain, Mar. 14, 1964; children—Alexandra Cheree, Aaron Timothy. Lab. teaching asst. biology West Ga. Coll., 1963-65; lab. technician biochemistry U. Ga., 1965-66, NSF grad. trainee biochemistry, 1966-70, research asso. biochemistry, 1970-71; USPHS fellow Clayton Found. Biochem. Inst., U. Tex., Austin, 1971-74; asst. prof. biology, adj. asst. prof. chemistry U. Ala., Huntsville, 1974—; cons., researcher. Mem. adminstrv. bd. Lakewood United Methodist Ch., 1977-79; mem. St. Joseph Sch. Bd., 1975-79, pres., 1976-79; mem. Holy Family Sch. Bd., 1979. NSF grantee, 1975-79; So. Regional Edn. Bd./Alfred P. Sloan Found. grantee, 1978. Mem. Am. Chem. Soc., Am. Soc. Microbiology, AAAS, AAUP, NEA, Sigma Xi, Beta Beta Beta. Contbr. articles research jours, lectr. in field. Home: 3317 Clifford Rd Huntsville AL 35810 Office: Dept Biology Univ Ala Huntsville AL 35807

ELFSTROM, DOROTHY LILLIAN BETTENCOURT (MRS. WALTER WILLIAM ELFSTROM), author; b. Galveston, Tex.; d. Henry Joseph and Margaret (Rowan) Bettencourt; grad. Draughon's Bus. Coll.; m. Walter William Elfstrom (dec.); children—Dorothy Elfstrom Bailey, Bill, Henry. Weekly columnist Galveston Island Mirror; daily columnist Texas City Daily Sun; poet laureate Galveston County; poet laureate State of Tex. Recipient 1st pl. awards Nat. Fedn. Press Women, 1963, Tex. Press Women, 1963. Author: Challenge of the Seasons, 1963; Fireside Fancies, 1960; Voyager on the Sea of Life, 1971; Seeker, 1974. Writer various songs including But I Just Can't Say Goodbye; You're Way Behind the Beat, Lovely Galveston; What Are you Trying to Find; At Taps Time I Have a Date With You; Not for Keeps; You Have Shaken Up My World; I Know You've Got to Go; Now You Won't Let Me Be; No Plastic Heart for Me; I Have Captured an Old-Fashioned Christmas; I Fell in Love with You in Old San Antonio; That Good Old-Fashioned 14 Karat Band. Contbr. to numerous mags., newspapers. Home: 3815 Ave S Galveston TX 77550

ELIAS, SAMY E. G., educator; b. Cairo, Egypt, June 28, 1930; came to U.S., 1956, naturalized, 1964; s. Elias Girgis and Tahia N. (Kassabgy) E.; B.S., Cairo U., 1955; M.S., Tex. A. and M. U., 1958; Ph.D., Okla. State U., 1960; m. Janice Lee Craig, Aug. 21, 1960; children—Mona Lee, Tresa Jean, Cecilia Ruth. Grad. asst. Tex. A. and M. U., College Station, 1957-58; grad. asst. Okla. State U., Stillwater, 1958-60; asst. prof. indsl. engring. Kans. State U., Manhattan, 1960-61; exec. asst. to chmn. bd. Orgn. of Mil. Factories, Egypt, 1961-62; asso. prof. indsl. engring., Kans. State U., 1962-65; asso. prof. indsl. engring. W.Va. U., Morgantown, 1965-67, prof., 1967-69, chmn. dept. indsl. engring., 1969-76, spl. asst. to univ. pres. for personal rapid transit, 1970-77, Claude Worthington Benedum prof. transp., 1976—; cons. Kansas City Transit, N.Y. Transit Authority, N.Y. Transit Authority Police Dept., Omaha Transit Co., Cin. Transit Co., W.C. Gilman & Co., Inc., Brown Engring., others. Mem. Region VI Planning and Devel. Council, Morgantown, 1972—. Recipient Americanism medal D.A.R., 1977. Mem. Am. Inst. Indsl. Engrs. (Transp. and Distbn. award 1979), Soc. Am. Value Engring., Am. Soc. Engring. Edn. (vice chmn. indsl. engring. div. 1972-73), Soc. for Computer Simulation. Episcopalian. Home: 322 Baldwin St Morgantown WV 26505 Office: 151 Engring Bldg WVa U Morgantown WV 26506

ELING, THOMAS EDWARD, pharmacologist; b. Cin., Oct. 26, 1941; s. Joseph Edward and Gertrude Mary Eling; B.S., U. Cin., 1963, M.S., 1964; Ph.D. (NIH fellow), U. Ala., 1968; m. Mary Blecken, Nov. 29, 1969. Postdoctoral fellow U. Iowa, Iowa City, 1968-70; asst. prof. pharmacy U. Cin., 1971; pharmacologist Nat. Insts. Environ. Health Scis., Research Triangle Park, N.C., 1971—. Mem. AAAS, Am. Soc. Pharmacology and Exptl. Therapeutics. Contbr. articles to profl. jours. Office: PO Box 12233 Research Triangle Park NC 27709

ELKAN, GERALD HUGH, microbiologist; b. Berlin, Aug. 3, 1929; came to U.S., 1935; s. George Herman and Eva Joan (Karger) E.; A.B., Brigham Young U., Provo, Utah, 1950; M.S., Pa. State U., 1966; Ph.D., Va. Poly. Inst and State U., 1958. Mem. faculty N.C. State U., Raleigh, 1958—; prof. microbiology, 1967—, asst. dean research, 1977-79; cons. Army Research Office. Pres. Wake County Young Democratic Clubs, 1968; exec. com. N.C. Dem. Party, 1970-74. Served with AUS, 1951-53; lt. col. Res. Fulbright research fellow, Uppsala, Sweden, 1963-64; research grantee NSF, 1959-78, AID, 1976-81. Fellow Am. Acad. Microbiology; mem. AAAS, N.C. Acad. Scis. (exec. dir. 1975), N.C. Bacteriology Soc. (pres. 1970), Soc. Microbiology, AAUP, Soc. Gen. Microbiology, Netherlands Soc. Microbiology, World Acad. Arts and Scis., Sigma Xi (nat. dir. 1983, nat. lectr. 1974-78), Phi Sigma, Gamma Sigma Delta, Phi Kappa Phi. Contbr. articles prof. jours. Home: 606 Stacy St Raleigh NC 27607 Office: Dept Microbiology NC State Univ Raleigh NC 27650

ELKINS, JAMES ANDERSON, JR., banker; b. Galveston, Tex., Mar. 24, 1919; s. James Anderson and Isabel (Mitchell) E.; grad. Hill Sch., 1937; B.A., Princeton, 1941; m. Margaret Wiess, Nov. 24, 1945; children—Elise, James Anderson III, Leslie K. With First City Nat. Bank, Houston, 1941—, v.p., 1946-50, pres., 1950-60, chmn. bd., 1960—, also dir.; dir. Eastern Airlines, Cameron Iron Works, Am. Gen. Ins. Co., Houston, Freeport Minerals, Inc., N.Y.C. Trustee U. Houston, Baylor Coll. Medicine, Princeton. Episcopalian. Home: 101 Farish Circle Houston TX 77024 Office: First City Nat Bank Houston TX 77001

ELKINS, JAMES ANDREW, JR., lawyer; b. Little Rock, Jan. 24, 1940; s. James Andrew and Doris (O'Neal) E.; A.B., U. of South, 1962; J.D., U. Ga. 1965; m. Martha Lee Allen, Nov. 11, 1963; children—James Andrew, Allen Lee, Martha Lee. Admitted to Ga. bar, 1965; asso. firm Roberts and Thornton, Columbus, Ga., 1965-69, Roberts, Elkins & Kilpatrick, Columbus, 1969-71, Martin, Jones & Layfield, Columbus, 1971-72; individual practice law, Columbus, 1972-73; partner firm Elkins & Flournoy, Columbus, 1973—. Bd. dirs. Pioneer Little League Columbus, Inc., 1977-79, sec., 1978-79; mem. Com. on Drug Abuse Control, 1971-75. Mem. Am. Trial Lawyers Assn., Ga. Trial Lawyers Assn., Ga. Assn. Criminal Def. Lawyers, State Bar Ga., Chattahooche Bar Assn. Republican. Episcopalian. Club: Columbus Lawyers. Home: 6130 Canterbury Dr Columbus GA 31904 Office: PO Box 1724 Columbus GA 31902

ELKINS, JEAN GODMAN, pharmacist, hosp. ofcl.; b. Scott County, Ky., Jan. 29, 1934; d. Granville Allen and Arva Mae (Dixon) Godman; B.S., U. Ky., 1956; m. Rainey Miller Elkins, Dec. 10, 1976. Pharmacist, Western Bapt. Hosp., Paducah, Ky., 1956-66, Med. Arts Pharmacy, Paducah, 1966-68, Bapt. Med. Center-Princeton, Birmingham, Ala., 1968-69; chief pharmacist Lourdes Hosp., Paducah, 1970—; ectr. in field. Bd. dirs. Jackson Purchase Area Health Edns. Systems. Mem. Ky. Pharm. Assn., Am. Soc. Hosp. Pharmacists, 1st Dist. Pharm. Assn., SE Soc. Hosp. Pharmacists, Ky. Soc. Hosp. Pharmacists. Bus. and Profl. Women's Club (pres. Paducah 1974-76, dir. Dist. 1977-78, woman of yr. 1978, pres. Murray, Ky., 1978-79). Democrat. Baptist. Club: Order of Eastern Star. Home: Route 8 Box 98 Clark ine Rd Paducah KY 42001 Office: Lourdes Hosp 1530 Lone Oak Rd Paducah KY 42001

ELKINS, LARRY OWEN, research and devel. engr.; b. Old Hickory, Tenn., Sept. 28, 1937; s. Ezra Byford and Mazell Helen (Brown) E.; B.S., Vanderbilt U. 1959, M.S., 1962, Ph.D., 1966; m. Patricia Ann Jones, Feb. 18, 1961; children—Larry DeWayne, Patrick Owen. Engrs. aide Tenn. Products and Chem. Corp., Chattanooga, Tenn., 1957; chem. engr. in charge of prodn. Ashland Oil Refining Co., Canton, Ohio, 1959, E. I. Du Pont Cellophane Plant, Old Hickory, Tenn., 1960-61, Dacron Plant, 1962, chem. engr. in charge of research and devel. Research & Devel. Lab., 1965-67; with Air Force Systems Command, Air Force Armament Lab., Eglin AFB, Fla., chem. engr., 1967-72, chief of high explosives processing lab./chem. engr., 1972-77, dir. programs and support, research and devel. labs., 1977-79, tech. dir. high explosives research and devel. lab., 1979—. Mem. Am. Inst. Chem. Engrs., Am. Chem. Soc., Am. Def. Preparedness Assn., Sigma Xi, Kappa Mu Epsilon, Beta Club. Democrat. Ch. Christ. Home: 1 Wimbledon Way Shalimar FL 32579 Office: Air Force Armament Lab Eglin AFB FL 32542

ELKINS, SAMUEL MICHAEL, ins. agt.; b. Hazelhurst, Ga., June 26, 1946; s. Isadore and Etta Ruth (Friedberg) E.; B.A., U. Ga., 1968; m. Toni M. Elkins, June 9, 1968; children—Stephanie Elise, Eric Marcus. Agt., Pilot Life Ins. Co., Columbia, S.C., 1974—, rep., field adv. com., S.C. and Western N.C., 1979-80. Served with U.S. Army, 1969-70. Recipient Man of Yr. award Gen. Agts. and Mgrs. Assn., 1973, 74, 76-78; Agt. of Yr. award Pilot Life Ins. Co., Columbia, 1970-78. Mem. S.C. Life Leaders, Columbia Life Underwriters Assn. (dir. 1972-74), Million Dollar Round Table (fin. coordinator Columbia 1977-78). Jewish. Home: 4136 Sandwood Dr Columbia SC 29206 Office: Pilot Life Ins Co 2132 Devine St Columbia SC 29205

ELKINS, SUZANNE, speech pathologist; b. Los Angeles, Mar. 26, 1942; d. G.D. and Mary Alice (Pereira) Hindman; B.A., U. Tex., Austin, 1964; M.Ed., S.W. Tex. State U., San Marcos, 1979; m. Byron W. Elkins, July 16, 1965; children—Mary Kristin, Sharon Louise. Speech therapist Port Neches (Tex.) Ind. Sch. System, 1964-65; dir. speech therapy Easter Seal Soc., Crippled Children's Center, McAllen, Tex., 1966-67; tchr. hard of hearing Laguna Salada Union Sch. Dist., Pacifica, Calif., 1967-70; speech therapist M&S Tower, San Antonio, 1979—, Bapt. Hosp. System. Mem. Am. Speech Lang. Hearing Assn., Tex. Speech Lang. Hearing Assn.

ELLEFSON, GEORGE EDWIN, JR., elec. engr.; b. Fort Smith, Ark., June 19, 1929; s. George Edwin and Cecil (Soard) E.; B.S. in E.E., U. Ark., 1954; student U. N.Mex., 1954-55; m. Dorothy Claire Stannus, Aug. 28 1952; children—Dorothy Lynn, Jane Ann. Staff engr., Sandia Corp., Albuquerque, 1954-55; engr. Reynolds Metals Co., Jones Mills, Ark., 1955-56; elec. mgr. Erhart, Eichenbaum, Rauch, Blass architects, Little Rock, 1956-60; engr. Leo L. Landauer & Assos., Inc., Little Rock, 1960-61; prin. G.E. Ellefson & Assos., Inc., Little Rock, 1961-70; gen. partner Ecology Dynamics Assos., Ltd., Little Rock 1970-73; area tech. mgr. Am. Standards Testing Bur., Inc., Little Rock, 1973—. Served with USN, 1947-50. Named

Engr. of Distinction, Engrs. Joint Council, 1974. Mem. IEEE (sr), Assn. Energy Engrs. (charter), Am. Cons. Engrs. Council (recipient engring. excellence award 1968), Am. Mgmt. Assn., N.Y. Acad. Scis. Presbyterian (elder). Home: 1421 N University Apt S 336 Little Rock AR 72207 Office: 1200 Summit Av Little Rock AR 72202

ELLENBURG, LAURA DIANE, coll. adminstr.; b. Greeneville, Tenn., Dec. 15, 1954; d. Ernest Edward and Barbara Mae (Hartman) Ellenburg; B.A., U. Tenn., 1975, M.S., 1976. Resident counselor U. Tenn., Knoxville, 1973-75; tchr. Greene County (Tenn.) schs., 1976-77; coordinator of career office Tusculum Coll., Greeneville, Tenn., 1977-79, asst. dean students, 1979—; career cons.; equal opportunity coordinator. Mem. NOW (treas. 1977-78), Nat. Soc. of Lit. and the Arts, Am. Personnel and Guidance Assn., Coll. Placement Council, So. Coll. Personnel and Placement Assn., Tenn. Coll. Personnel and Placement Assn., Tenn. Personnel and Guidance Assn. Democrat. Author: (with others) Creative Social Studies, 1976. Home: Route 1 PO Box 362F Midway TN 37809 Office: Tusculum Coll Greneville TN 37743

ELLENSON, EUGENE PETER, univ. adminstr.; b. Chippewa Falls, Wis., Mar. 24, 1921; s. Eugene Argard and Catherin (Flinn) E.; A.B. in Journalism, U. Ga., 1943; M.Ed., U. Miami, 1947; m. Jeanne Marie Center, Jan. 24, 1951; children—Donna Susan, Eugene Mark. Coach, Miami (Fla.) Sr. High Sch., 1947-49; asst. coach U. Miami, 1950-59; asst. coach U. Fla., Gainesville, 1960-69, asst. athletics dir., 1970-73, dir. Gator Boosters, 1974—, asst. prof. phys. edn., 1971-74. Capt., United Way, 1970-80. Served with AUS, 1939-46, 51-52. Decorated Silver Star, Bronze Star, Purple Heart; Russian medal of valor. Mem. Am. Football Coaches Assn., Nat. Assn. Athletic Dirs., Nat. Football Found. and Hall of Fame, Sigma Alpha Epsilon, Blue Key, Omicron Delta Kappa, Sigma Delta Chi. Democrat. Roman Catholic. Clubs: Gainesville Golf and Country. Author: ABC's of Offensive Line Play, 1961; Coaching Line Backers and the Defensive Perimeter, 1972. Home: 3525 8th Ave NW Gainesville FL 32605 Office: PO Box 13796 Gainesville FL 32604

ELLERBE, JAMES HARGETTE, state ofcl.; b. Rockingham, N.C., Oct. 4, 1933; s. Hiram Hicks and Jimmie (Hargette) E.; B.S., E. Carolina Coll., 1956; M.Ed., N.C. State U., Raleigh, 1970; m. Helen Elizabeth Austin, July 15, 1956; children—Vickie Beth, James Austin. Tchr., Hopewell (Va.) schs., 1956-57; supr. Nationwide Ins. Co., Raleigh, 1957-63; dir. manpower devel. N.C. Dept. Community Coll., Raleigh, 1963-70, div. dir., 1970—; cons. in field. Chmn. Johnston County Bd. Edn., 1979, Johnston County Library Bd., 1964-72; mem. Clayton Planning Bd., Clayton Library Bd. Served with USAR, 1957. Mem. Am. Vocat. Assn., Nat. Sch. Bds. Assn., N.C. Vocat. Assn., N.C. Sch. Bds. Assn., Nat. Council Staff Program and Orgn. Devel., Phi Lambda Kappa, Iota Sigma Lambda. Democrat. Baptist. Clubs: Clayton Rotary, Masons. Home: 415 Canady St Clayton NC 27520 Office: Education Bldg Raleigh NC 27611

ELLIOT, JEANN NIELSEN, mktg. exec.; b. Chgo., Dec. 30, 1924; d. William August and Grace Estella (Ottow) Ninneman; student Layton Art Sch., Milw., 1944; grad. Ind. U., 1950, Butler U., 1952; m. George Elliot, Apr. 18, 1964; 1 son, Robert James Becker. Advt. mgr. Regency Electronics, Indpls., 1949-54, also asst. distbr. sales mgr., office mgr.; partner Cody Advt., Chgo., 1956-60; account exec. Burton Browne Advt., Chgo., 1954-56; advt. mgr. ITT Distbr. Products, Lodi, N.J., 1960-62; sales promotion mgr. Triad Transformer div. Litton Industries, Inc., Venice, Calif., Huntington, Ind., 1962-65; advt. mgr. Fairchild DuMont Labs., Clifton, xxN.3, 1965-69; editor, writer advt. Monroe Calculator Div. Litton Industries, Inc., Morris Plains, N.J., 1975; mktg. services adminstr. ITT Decca Marine, Inc., Palm Coast, Fla., 1978—. Pres., Syracuse Operetta Co.; sec. Young Republicans; active Red Cross Motor Corps, Syracuse Chorale, Palm Coast Chorus, Palm Coast Civic Assn. Recipient First Place award sculpture Palm Coast Art Show, 1978. Mem. Los Angeles Advt. Women, LWV (dir.). Republican. Home: 55 Federal Ln Palm Coast FL 32037 Office: Box G US 1 and St Joe Rd Palm Coast FL 32037

ELLIOT, LARION JOSEPH, sch. adminstr.; b. New Orleans, Sept. 7, 1919; s. Francis B. and Enols Marie (Hanemann) E.; B.S. in Math., Spring Hill Coll., 1943; S.T.L., St. Louis U., 1950. Joined S.J., 1938, ordained priest Roman Catholic Ch., 1949; dir. Jesuit sem. bur. S.J., 1965-74; pro tem dir. Jesuit missions S.J., 1970-71; sec. Jesuit High Sch., New Orleans, 1951-57; sec. Jesuit High Sch., Tampa, Fla., 1957-59, pres. 1959-65, 76—; dir. alumni and devel., 1974-76. Bd. dirs. Tampa chpt. ARC; bd. dirs. Internat. Ednl. Devel., Inc. Mem. Tampa C. of C. Home and Office: Jesuit High Sch 4701 N Himes Ave Tampa FL 33614

ELLIOT, SIMON, lawyer; b. Wilno, Poland, Feb. 4, 1912; s. Eliakimowicz and Nelkin E.; came to U.S., 1936, naturalized, 1943; LL.B., N.Y. U., 1945, J.D., 1969; m. Dec. 31, 1949; children—Mark, Helen. Admitted to N.Y. bar, 1947; founding partner Maquinaria Minera SA, Motolinia, Mexico, 1947—, Kenaf Mexicano SA, Mesones, Mexico; pres. Industrias Sorel SA, Mexico, 1966—; exec. v.p. Fibras Vitricas Mex SA, Monserrat, Mexico, 1968—. Vice pres. Pre Bar Assn., 1941—; founder, legal counsel New Americans for the Democratic Party, 1945—. Home: Sierra Gorda 39 Mexico 10 DF Mexico

ELLIOTT, CLARENCE WILLARD, accountant; b. Hampton, Ark., Oct. 9, 1936; s. Clarence Willard and Madge (Lyon) E.; B.S., Ark. A. and M. Coll., 1958; M.B.A., U. Ark., 1960, Ph.D., 1964; m. Sherry Carolyn Kennedy, Sept. 3, 1960; children—Clarence Willard III, Erin Gaye. Cost accountant Duracraft Boats, Inc., Monticello, Ark., 1957-58; instr. U. Ark., Fayetteville, 1959-62; asst. prof. accounting St. Josephs Coll., Rensselaer, Ind., 1962-64; asso. prof. accounting La. State U., Baton Rouge, 1964-74, prof., 1974-79, also dir. placement Coll. Bus. Adminstrn.; partner Gondron, Walker, Ourso, Efferson & Elliott, C.P.A.'s, Baton Rouge, also Nederland, Tex., 1979—. Auditor, R.J. Flynn, C.P.A., Rensselaer, 1962-64; cons. internat. div. Ethyl Corp., Baton Rouge, summer 1966; cons. Harbor Banana Distbrs., Inc., Long Beach, Cal., Aluminum Products Co., New Orleans, Basil M. Lee & Co., C.P.A.'s, Baton Rouge; cons. edn. and tng. Arthur Young & Co., 1968-69; mem. faculty Inst. Ins. Marketing. Recipient service award La. LP-Gas Assn., 1968. C.P.A., La. Mem. Am. Inst. C.P.A.'s, La. Soc. C.P.A.'s (chpt. pres.), Alpha Chi, Beta Alpha Psi, Beta Gamma Sigma. Contbr. numerous articles to profl. jours. Home: 3848 N Bluebonnet Rd Baton Rouge LA 70809

ELLIOTT, DAVID ROSS, diversified industries exec.; b. Pontiac, Mich., June 22, 1943; s. Leonard Emerson and Dorothy Priscilla (Tuson) E.; B.A., Mich. State U., 1965; m. Kathleen Ruth Kleinert, Oct. 2, 1965; children—Melissa Marie, Craig Andrew. With The Continental Group, Inc., 1969—, asst. indsl. relations mgr., Augusta, Ga., 1969-70, div. mgmt. devel. supr., div. supr. employee relations, N.Y.C., 1970-72, indsl. relations mgr., Augusta, Ga., 1972-77, dir. personnel planning and mgmt. devel., 1977-78; v.p. human resources Kinark Corp., Tulsa, 1978—; guest lectr. Augusta Coll., TAPPI, Internat. Mgmt. Club. Chmn. edn. div. United Way, 1973. Served with AUS, 1966-69. Decorated Purple Heart medal, Bronze Star medal. Mem. Am. Soc. Personnel Adminstrs., Ga. Bus. and Industry Assn., Augusta C. of C., Am. Soc. Tng. and Devel., Personnel Assn. Augusta (dir.). Republican. United Methodist. Clubs: West Lake Country, Indian Springs Country. Home: 6531 E 86th Pl Tulsa OK 74133

ELLIOTT, ETHEL WARREN, ednl. adminstr.; b. Enterprise, Ala., Jan. 30, 1931; d. Joe and Dora (Stanley) Warren; B.S., Ala. State U., 1951, M.Ed., 1960, Ed.S., 1977; children—Michael, Gail. Tchr., Covington County (Ala.) public schs., 1951-53, Santa Rosa County (Fla.) public schs., 1955-73; acting prin. T.R. Jackson Elem. Sch., Milton, Fla., 1973-74; attendance supr. Santa Rosa County Sch. Bd., Milton, 1974-76, dir. fed. programs, 1976—, title IX coordinator, 1976—. Parliamentarian, Democratic Womens Club Santa Rosa County, 1978; mem. adv. com. Kiddie Kampus PTA; mem. Fla. Panhandle Health Systems Agy.; mem. adv. com. Santa Rosa 4H Clubs. NSF fellow, 1965. Mem. Santa Rosa Prins. and Suprs. Assn. (pres.), Fla. Assn. Sch. Adminstrs., Am. Assn. Sch. Adminstrs. Club: Order Eastern Star. Home: PO Box 403 Milton FL 32570 Office: PO Box 271 Milton FL 32570

ELLIOTT, GLORIA HADANICH, mental health center exec.; b. Washington, Pa., Mar. 7, 1947; d. George and Victoria M. (Guzik) Hadanich; student Mt. Aloysius Jr. Coll.; B.S. in Edn. with high honors, California (Pa.) State Coll., 1969; M.S. in Counselling with highest honors, Shippensburg State Coll., 1975. Govt. career trainee Bur. Classification and Pay, Pa. Office Adminstrn., Harrisburg, 1970-71; youth devel. counselor Youth Devel. Centers, Pa. Dept. Pub. Welfare, Waynesburg, Loysville, 1971-73; caseworker, group home supr. Bradford County Mental Health-Mental Retardation, Sayre, Pa., 1974; exec. dir. Counselling Services Center of Southeastern Erie County, Inc., Corry, Pa., 1975-78; dir. partial hospitalization and group homes Mental Health Services Roanoke Valley, Roanoke, Va., 1978—; adj. prof. U. Va., Roanoke, 1979—; cons. Cuyahoga County Mental Health-Mental Retardation, 1977-78; cons. mgmt., adminstrn., human relations tng., women's issues, 1978—; a founder Telinform and Community Care Council, 1975-77. Bd. dirs., sec. Erie County Citizens Coalition for Human Recources, 1978-; bd. dirs. Anchor House, 1975-77, Child Care Coordinating Council; mem. youth adv. com. YWCA, 1969, active Tri-Hi Y; coordinator March of Dimes, 1972; mem. Mental Health-Mental Retardation Task Force on Erie County Case Mgmt. and BSU Functions. Certified in rural mental health adminstrn., U. Wis.; certified in rehab. counselling, in filial therapy, goal planning, guided group interaction. Mem. Am. Personnel and Guidance Assn., Nat. Rehab. Counselors Assn., Assn. for Specialists in Group Work, Am. Mental Health Counselors Assn., Rural Mental Health Assn., Va. Personnel and Guidance Assn., Va. Assn. Specialists in Group Work, Va. Mental Health Counselors Assn. (state sec.), Council Exceptional Children, Va. Mental Health Providers Assn., Profl. and Managerial Women's Network, Roanoke Fine Arts Council, YMCA. Contbr. articles to profl. publs.

ELLIOTT, J(AMES) ROBERT, chief dist. judge; b. Gainesville, Ga., Jan. 1, 1910; s. Thomas M. and Mamie Lucille (Glenn) E.; Ph.B., Emory U., 1930, LL.B., 1934; m. Brownie C. Buck, Aug. 3, 1949; children—Susan G., James Robert. Admitted to Ga. bar, 1934, engaged in corporate and trial practice; U.S. dist. judge Middle Dist. Ga., from 1962, now chief judge. Mem. Ga. Ho. of Reps., 1937-49; mem. Democratic Nat. Com., 1948-56. Served as lt. (s.g.) USNR, World War II; PTO. Mem. Ga. Jr. C. of C. (pres. 1941-42), Ga. Bar Assn., Lambda Chi Alpha, Phi Delta Phi. Kiwanian. Office: PO Box 2017 Columbus GA 31902*

ELLIOTT, JAMES WILLIAM, clergyman, bus. exec.; b. Larrence County, Ala., Sept. 28, 1942; s. Charles and Gertrude E.; student Tuskegee Inst., Ky. State U., Simmons U., Louisville; m. Mar. 8, 1969; children—James William, Joy, Paris; stepchildren—Herman Crosson, Gerri Mosley. Mgr. city sales Am. Bible Soc., N.Y.C.; engr. So. Ry. System, Louisville; ordained to ministry Baptist Ch.; pastor New Jerusalem Bapt. Ch., Louisville; owner, mgr. Warehouse Paint Center, Louisville; dir. Amber Internat., Louisville. Served with U.S. Army. Mem. Nat. Fedn. Ind. Businessmen, Gen. Splty. Assn., Nat. Bus. League, Ky. Minority Bus. Assn. (founder, dir.), NAACP, Urban League, SCLC, Louisville Econ. Devel. Corp. Clubs: Masons, Lions. Home: 2005 Garland Ave Louisville KY 40210 Office: 1411 Olive St Louisville KY 40210

ELLIOTT, JANE HARRISON, printing co. exec.; b. Tampa, Fla., Feb. 6, 1927; d. John Norton and Mary Lou (Bachman) H.; student U. Ala., 1945-47; m. M. Leo Elliott Jr., June 15, 1948 (dec. Apr. 1979); children—M. Leo III, Barbara Lynn, Sheila Tracy; m. 2d, Uldric Thompson, III, Jan. 5, 1980. With Free Press Pub Co., Inc., Tampa, 1966—, v.p., editor newspaper, 1967—. Mem. Tampa Hist. Soc. (dir.), Jr. League Tampa (dir.), Alpha Delta Pi. Episcopalian. Clubs: Ponte Vedra, Tampa Yacht and Country, Golf View Garden, Chiselers. Home: 4513 Culbreath Ave Tampa FL 33609 Office: Free Press Pub Co Inc 401 E Platt St Tampa FL 33602

ELLIOTT, JOHN FRANKLIN, clergyman; b. Neosho, Mo., June 11, 1915; s. William Marion and Charlotte Jeanette (Crump) E.; student Maryville Coll., 1933-35; A.B., Austin Coll., 1937; postgrad. Louisville Presbyn. Sem., 1937-38, U. Tenn., 1938, Dallas Theol. Sem., 1939-40; B.D., Columbia Theol. Sem., 1942, M.Div., 1971; D.Litt. (hon.), Internat. Acad., 1954; m. Winifred Margaret Key, July 6, 1939; children—Paul Timothy, Stephen Marion, Andrew Daniel. Ordained to ministry Presbyn. Ch., 1942; founder Emory Presbyn. Ch., Atlanta, 1941, Wildwood Presbyn. Ch., Salem, Va., 1950; pastor Wylam Presbyn. Ch., Birmingham, Ala., 1942-47, Salem Presbyn. Ch., 1947-51, Calvary Presbyn. Ch. Ind., Fort Worth, 1952—; founder, pastor Grace Presbyn. Ch. Ind., Roanoke, Va., 1951-52; headmaster Colony Christian Sch., Ft. Worth, 1968—. Bd. dirs., pres. Salem (Va.) Nursing Assn., 1949; charter mem. Fellowship Independent Evang. Chs., 1950—, pres., 1967, nat. sec., 1971; founder, dir. Ft. Worth Home Bible Classes, 1954—; dir. Spanish Publs., Inc., 1969—; bd. dirs. Ind. Bd. for Presbyn. Home Missions, 1956-74; dist. committeeman Longhorn council Boy Scouts Am., Ft. Worth, 1960-66; bd. dirs. Union Gospel Mission, Ft. Worth, 1965-70, pres., 1968; mem. U.S. Coast Guard Aux., Ft. Worth, 1967—; pilot, chaplain, col. CAP, Ft. Worth, 1970—, chmn. nat. chaplain com., 1979—; ministerial adviser bd. dirs. Reformed Theol. Sem., Jackson, Miss., 1973—; chaplain Tex. Constl. Conv., 1974; bd. dirs. Scripture Memory Fellowship Internat., 1979—. Bd. dirs. Graham Bible Coll., 1966-74. Fellow Philos. Soc. Great Britain (Victoria Inst.), Royal Geog. Soc., Huguenot Soc. of London. Clubs: Ft. Worth, Ridglea Country, Ft. Worth Boat, Rotary. Home: 3980 Edgehill Rd Fort Worth TX 76116 Office: 4800 El Campo Ave Fort Worth TX 76107

ELLIOTT, KENNETH CHARLES, trucking co. exec.; b. Burkburnet, Tex., May 31, 1924; s. Wilbur Allen and Zebie (Gray) E.; B.B.A., U. Tex., Austin, 1945; m. Marcene Simmons, Dec. 2, 1944; children—Linda D., Kenneth Clayton. Vice-pres. Comml. Oil Transp., Fort Worth, 1957-68; exec. v.p. Bray Lines, Inc., Cushing, Okla., 1968-73; owner, pres. D & H Trucking, Tulsa, 1973-76; chmn. bd., pres. Redwing Carriers, Inc., Tampa, Fla., 1976—. Mem. Nat. Tank Truck Carriers Inc., Ala. Trucking Assn., Fla. Trucking Assn., Tampa C. of C. Republican. Baptist. Clubs: Elks, Masons. Home: 4218 Fairway Run Tampa FL 33624 Office: PO Box 426 Tampa FL 33601

ELLIOTT, LARRY DARNELL, corp. rep.; b. Springfield, Tenn., Oct. 4, 1953; s. A.B. and Ozellia (Woodard) E.; B.S. cum laude, Austin Peay State U., 1976; postgrad. (fellow) Howard U. Law Sch., 1976-79. Dist. exec. Middle Tenn. council Boy Scouts Am., Nashville, 1976-77; rep. Gen. Motors Acceptance Corp., Clarksville, Tenn., 1978—; instr. Austin Peay State U., 1978. Active coms. Boy Scouts Am., Tenn. Dem. Party. Mem. Phi Alpha Theta (polit. sci. award 1976), Alpha Phi Omega. Contbr. feature article to Nashville mag. Home: S-151 Glendale Gardens Clarksville TN 37040 Office: General Motors Acceptance Corp 1156 Pettus Clarksville TN 37040

ELLIOTT, NANCY GUEST, educator; b. Cherokee County, S.C., June 20, 1946; d. Lester Carlisle and Ellen Estelle (Loftis) Guest; B.S., Limestone Coll., 1968; M.Ed., Clemson U., 1975; m. Nicholas Scott Elliott, July 19, 1969 (div.); children—Nanci Jill, Nicholas Scott. Tchr. home econs. Landrum (S.C.) High Sch., 1968-69; tchr. Belton (S.C.) Middle Sch., 1969-73; instr. reading and study skills Anderson (S.C.) Coll., 1975—. Mem. Internat. Reading Assn., Western Coll. Reading Tchrs. Assn. Methodist. Home: C 7 Concord Apts Anderson SC 29621 Office: Anderson Coll Anderson SC 29621

ELLIOTT, PAUL CHARLES, oil co. exec.; b. Terre Haute, Ind., Sept. 23, 1933; s. Ross Edward and Maybelle (Reichert) E.; B.S. in Chem. Engring., Rose Poly. Inst., 1955; postgrad. Purdue U., 1955, Wharton Sch. Bus., U. Pa., 1958-59, Grad. Sch. Bus., Harvard U., 1971; m. Sally Nancy Sibley, Dec. 17, 1960; children—Elizabeth, Paul, Robert, Jennifer. With Socony Mobil Oil Co., Paulsboro, N.J., 1955-60, Comml. Solvents Corp., Terre Haute, 1960-62; with Marathon Oil Co., Findlay, Ohio, 1962-74, mgr. refinery exports, 1972-74; founder, pres., chief exec. officer Tampimex Petroleum Corp., Houston, 1974-78; pres., chief exec. officer Concord Petroleum Corp., Houston, 1978—; instr. chemistry Findlay Coll. Evening Sch., 1965-67. Precinct committeeman Republican Com. Terre Haute, 1960-62, ward chmn., 1961-62; deacon 1st Presbyterian Ch., Findlay, 1967-69. Served with USN, 1956-57. Recipient Purdue U. Nat. Scholar award, 1951, Hemingway medal Am. Legion, 1952. Mem. Am. Petroleum Inst., Am. Chem. Soc., Am. Inst. Chem. Engrs., World Trade Club Houston, Petroleum Club Houston. Clubs: Houston, Houston Racquet, Pine Forest Country, Harvard, Houston Athletic, Rotary. Home: 10810 Oak Creek St Houston TX 77024 Office: 1776 Yorktown St Houston TX 77056

ELLIOTT, ROBERT BURL, orthopaedic surgeon; b. Kirksville, Mo., Dec. 30, 1919; s. Burl Dennis and Beatrice (Corbin) E.; A.B., U. Iowa, 1941, M.D., 1943; M.S., U. Minn., 1951; m. Georgia Anne Lindley, Aug. 24, 1950; children—Robert Burl, Stephen Corbin, Gregory Taylor. Intern, Md. Gen. Hosp., Balt., 1944; Cole fellowship in orthopaedic surgery U. Minn., Mayo Clinic, 1944-47; practice orthopaedic surgery, Houston, 1948—; instr. orthopaedic surgery Lillie Jolly Sch. Nursing, Meml. Hosp.; chmn. orthopaedic sect., former chief surgery, dir. acad. orthopaedics Meml. Bapt. Hosp.; instr. clin. faculty Baylor U. Med. Sch.; asso. prof. U. Tex. Med. Sch. Diplomate Am. Bd. Orthopaedic Surgery, Am. Acad. Orthopaedic Surgery. Fellow A.C.S., Internat. Coll. Surgeons (pres. Tex. 1970-71, mem. U.S. bd. regents 1976-80); mem. Am. Fracture Assn. (pres. 1969-71; bd. govs.), Tex. Orthopaedic Soc., So., Pan-Am. med. assns., Houston Surg. Soc., ASTM (F-4 award merit 1977, exec. bd. 1968—, chmn. osteosynthesis sect. 1968—, chmn. orthopedics subcom. 1974—), Royal Soc. Medicine, Am. Nat. Standards Inst. (med. devices tech. adv. bd. 1973—), Internat. Standards Orgn. (tech. com. surg. implants, U.S. tech. adv. group), Western Orthopaedic Assn., Pan Am. Assn. Orthopaedics and Traumatology (founding), Houston Orthopaedic Club, Am. Orthopaedic Foot Soc. (chmn. ednl. com.), Sam Houston Trail Assn. (bd. dirs. pres. 1971-73), Sociedad Latino-Americana de Ortopedia y Traumatologia, Spectators Orthopaedic Club, Sigma Alpha Epsilon, Phi Rho Sigma. Clubs: Masons, K.T., Shriners, Elks. Editorial bd. Health Devices, 1974—. Home: 10902 Wickwild Dr Houston TX 77024 Office: Memorial Hospital Profl Bldg Suite 414 7777 Southwest Freeway Houston TX 77074

ELLIOTT, ROBERT LEE, JR., utility exec.; b. Baird, Tex., Apr. 14, 1937; s. Robert Lee and Rama A. (Dickey) E.; B.B.A., Tex. Tech. U., 1960; m. Rita L. Dye, July 24, 1964; 1 son, Robert Lee. With Pruitt Supply Co., Amarillo, Tex., 1960-65, Graybar Electric Co., Amarillo, 1966-70, Harris & Patterson Cons. Engrs., Amarillo, 1971-75; mgr. Rita Blanca Electric Co-op Inc., Dalhart, Tex., 1975—. Active Rural Friends/ACRE, Washington, 1975—. Mem. West Tex. C. of C., Dallam-Hartley Counties C. of C., Am. Mgmt. Assn. Baptist. Clubs: Lions XIT Rangers. Office: Hwy 87 N Dalhart TX 79022

ELLIOTT, ROBERT PERRY, JR., indsl. engr.; b. Winchester, Va., Jan. 21, 1942; s. Robert Perry and Dorothy Elizabeth (Thomas) E.; student Gen. Motors Inst., 1972, 79; m. Carolyn Patricia Rockwell, May 17, 1962; children—Kimberlee Ann, Robert P. Engr. Abex Corp., 1964-68; indsl. engr. supr. parts div. Gen. Motors Corp., Martinsburg, W.Va., 1968—. Bd. dirs. Lake Holiday Estates. Served with USNR, 1960-64. Home: Box 120 Cross Junction VA 22625 Office: 1000 Warm Springs Ave Martinsburg WV 25401

ELLIOTT, SHIRLEY RAE, med. technologist; b. Binghamton, N.Y., Oct. 21, 1922; d. John Rook and Carrie Marie (Keeney) Reynolds; student Duke U., 1940-42, U. Tex., 1942-43; m. Floyd S. Elliott, Nov. 13, 1943; children—Linda Rae, Teresa Marie, Rita Kay, Susan Irene, John Roger, Katherine Claire, Floyd S. With VA Hosp., Nashville, 1956—, supervisory med. technologist, 1972—; instr. med. technology Vanderbilt U.-VA, 1972—. Mem. Am. Soc. Clin. Pathologists, Am. Soc. Med. Tech., Royal Soc. Health, Internat. Soc. Lab. Tech., Tenn. Soc. Clin. Microbiology. Methodist. Home: 1007 Bentley Circle Gallatin TN 37066 Office: 1310 24th Ave SW Nashville TN 37203

ELLIOTT, WALTER MAC, banker; b. Laurel, Miss., Sept. 19, 1947; s. William Harold and Mary Alice Elliott; B.B.A., U. Miss., 1969; student Grad. Sch. Banking of South, La. State U., 1979; m. Barbara Jean Ellard, Dec. 20, 1969. Asst. cashier, mktg. officer First Nat. Bank of Laurel, 1972-73; from asst. v.p. to v.p. Bankers Trust Savs. & Loan Assn., Laurel, 1974-75; successively asst. v.p., v.p., sr. v.p., exec. v.p., sr. credit officer Nat. Bank of Commerce of Miss., Starkville, 1975—; guest lectr. Miss. State U. Mem. exec. council, fin. chmn. Boy Scouts Am.; bd. dirs. Starkville C. of C., Miss. Econ. Council, East Miss. Council. Served to 1st lt. U.S. Army, 1969-72; Vietnam. Decorated Army Commendation medal. Mem. Am. Bankers Assn., Miss. Bankers Assn., Ducks Unltd. (zone chmn.), Am. Legion, Presbyterian. Club: Starkville Country (pres., sec.). Home: Route 4 Old West Point Rd Starkville MS 39759 Office: 1 NBC Plaza Starkville MS 39759

ELLIOTT, WILLIAM WAYNE, mfg. co. exec.; b. Russell, Kans., Dec. 16, 1943; s. Patrick Joseph and Helen Rose (Heronema) E.; B.A., St. Thomas U., 1964; m. Wilma Jean Ohl, June 3, 1967; 1 dau., Michelle Paige. Mem. advt. sales staff Wichita Eagle-Beacon, Wichita, Kans., 1966-68; stock broker Stiefel Nicolaus Corp., Wichita, 1968-70; mfrs. rep. Schnadig Corp., Omaha, Des Moines, 1970-74; pres. Bumper Inc., Richardson, Tex., 1974—. Served with USAF, 1964-66. Mem. Southwest Roadrunners Assn., Southwest Furnishings Assn., Furnishings Mfrs. Assn., Nat. Home Furnishings

Mfrs. Assn. Clubs: Dallas Golf Assn. (dist. dir.), K.C. Home and Office: 444 Birch Ln Richardson TX 75081

ELLIOTT, WILLIE LAWRENCE, educator; b. Cin., July 18, 1948; s. Harry Thomas and Mary O'Neal E.; B.A., Ky. State U., 1971; M.S.W., U. Ky., 1973; children—Wymanette Lois, Willye. Caseworker, Dept. Public Welfare, Frankfort, Ky., 1971-73; child welfare worker Dept. Child Welfare, Lexington, Ky., 1973-74; therapist Pee Wee Valley Prison, Louisville, 1974; asst. prof., field coordinator, dept. sociology Ky. State U., Frankfort, 1974—; asst. dir. pre-retirement project, cons. U. Louisville. Mem. Assn. Black Social Workers, Nat. Assn. Social Workers, Ky. Assn. Social Work Educators, Council Social Work Educators, Kappa Alpha Psi. Democrat. Mem. Churches of Christ. Club: Frankfort Tennis. Home: Combs Hall Frankfort KY 40601 Office: Hathaway Hall Dept Sociology Frankfort KY 40601

ELLIS, BRYAN KEITH, owner advt. agy.; b. Houston, Aug. 26, 1949; s. Arthur Smith and Margie Aletha (Main) E.; B.S. in Photography and Journalism, Sam Houston State U., 1972; m. Debra Jean McMillian, Apr. 28, 1974. Free-lance photographer-journalist, Austin, Tex., 1972-73; mem. mktg. and sales staff Huntsville Honda, 1974-75; photojournalist Huntsville (Tex.) Item, 1975; owner, operator Advent Advt. & Communication, Huntsville, 1976—. Office: Advent Advt & Communication 1320 17th St Huntsville TX 77340

ELLIS, DAVID EIFION, geologist; b. Johnstown, Pa., Oct. 23, 1947; s. John E. and Charlotte Ruth (Rowland) E.; B.S. with honors, Allegheny Coll., 1969; M.Phil., Yale U., 1973, Ph.D., 1977. Research asso. dept. geophys. sci. U. Chgo., 1977-78; research scientist Conoco, Inc., Ponca City, Okla., 1978-79, research group supr., 1979—. Served with U.S. Army, 1969-71. Recipient award for outstanding research Sigma Xi, 1969; William E. Ford prize Yale U., 1976; William E. Ford fellow, 1972, 73, 74. Mem. Geol. Soc. Am., Geochem. Soc., Mineral. Soc Am., Am. Geophys. Union, Sigma Xi. Contbr. articles to profl. jours. Home: 301 W Hartford St Apt 410 Ponca City OK 74601 Office: 1000 S Pine St Ponca City OK 74601

ELLIS, ELMO ISRAEL, broadcasting exec.; b. Birmingham, Ala., Nov. 11, 1918; s. Samuel B. and Bertha F. (Seletz) Israel; A.B., U. Ala., 1940; M.A., Emory U., 1948; postgrad. Am. Mgmt. Assn., 1959, Emory U., 1965; m. Ruth M. Ballinger, Dec. 26, 1944; children—Janet Faye, William Bryan. Dir. publicity, prodn. mgr. Sta. WSB, Atlanta, 1940-42, dir. scripts and prodn., 1947—, prodn. mgr., 1948-52, mgr. programming WSB Radio (AM-FM), 1952-63, v.p., gen. mgr., 1963—; v.p. Cox Broadcasting Corp., 1969—; dir. Citizens and So. Nat. Bank, East Point, Ga.; writer-producer network radio programs NBC, ABC, CBS and Mut. Broadcasting System, 1942-46; mem. Mut. Affiliates Adv. Council; writer-producer We The People radio program, Great Jury Trials, FBI in Peace and War, CBS Sch. of the Air, Continental Celebrity Club, 1946; mem. faculty Ga. State U., Emory U. Bd. dirs. Ga. Safety Council, v.p., 1968-69; hon. chmn. Ga. PTA, 1975-76; mem. Ga. Industry Adv. Com.; chmn. No. Ga. Operational Area Emergency Communications Com.; pub. relations advisor Ga. Heart Assn.; mem. Gov.'s Com. on Employment Handicapped, Gov.'s Commn. on Ga. White House Conf. on Handicapped Individuals; adv. panel Ga. Nutrition Council; adv. bd. Consumer Credit Services Greater Atlanta; adv. com. Atlanta League Women Voters; bd. advisors Atlanta chpt. UN Assn.; mem. Atlanta area council Boy Scouts Am., Friends of Library Emory U.; vice chmn. S.E. regional adv. bd. Anti-Defamation League, B'nai B'rith; mem. hon. com. Interracial Council for Bus. Opportunity, Atlanta; adv. council Sch. Bus. Adminstrn., Ga. State U.; bd. dirs. Atlanta Landmarks, Internat. Radio and TV Found., Ga. Arthritis Found., Jr. Achievement Greater Atlanta, Arthritis Found., Fulton-Dakalb-Clayton chpt. Nat. Found.-March of Dimes, Atlanta Mental Health Assn.; bd. dirs., chmn. exec. com. Radio Advt. Bur.; exec. com. Atlanta chpt. Am. Jewish Com.; trustee, charter mem. pres.'s council Oglethorpe U.; asst. to dir. Dem. Nat. Conv., 1952, 56, 60, 64. Served to capt. USAAF, 1942-46. Recipient Silver medal award Atlanta Advt. Club, 1965; Peabody award, 1966; Alfred P. Sloan award, 1966; Citizen of Year award Ga. Assn. Broadcasters, 1965; Sch. Bell award Ga. Edn. Assn., 1967, 74, 75; Distinguished Alumnus award U. Ala., 1971; Abraham Lincoln award So. Baptist Radio-TV Commn., 1972, 77; Silver Beaver award Boy Scouts Am., 1972; Pioneer Broadcaster Ga. award Di Gamma Kappa, 1972; Gavin Radio Program Conf. Distinguished Broadcaster award, 1972; award Freedoms Found., 1970, 72, 73, George Washington Honor medal, 1972; News Editorial award Nat. Found. Hwy. Safety, 1974; Atlanta Braves Sportsman award, 1974; Abe Goldstein award Anti-Defamation League, 1975; Gold Boot award March of Dimes, 1975; George Erwin award Ga. Assn. Realtors, 1975; 1st pl. Best Editorial award AP, 1977; 1st pl. Gen. Editorial Excellence award UPI, 1977; numerous others; named Gavin Mgr. of Year, 1971. Mem. Radio Advt. Bur. (chmn.), Ga. AP Broadcasters (chpt. pres.), Nat. Assn. FM Broadcasters (dir.-at-large, past chmn. bd.), Ga. Assn. Broadcasters (dir., past pres. Jack Williams Cancer Research award 1974), Emory U., U. Ala. alumni assns., Ga. C. of C. (bus. image task force), Nat. Congress Parents and Tchrs. (hon. life), Ga. Sch. Food Service Assn. (hon. life), Sigma Delta Chi. Clubs: B'nai B'rith (exec. com. Gate City lodge), Standard, Commerce. Author: (with others) Radio Station Management, 1948, 60; Opportunities in Broadcasting, 1977; Happiness is Worth the Effort, 1970; Sleepy Hollow Poems. Home: 6345 Aberdeen Dr NE Atlanta GA 30328 Office: 1601 W Peachtree St NE Atlanta GA 30309

ELLIS, GARY MELTON, estate adminstr.; b. Houston, Oct. 20, 1943; s. Robert Lee and Alma Gladys (Hoskins) E.; B.A., New Sch. Social Research, 1968; M.B.A., U. Houston, 1977; m. Kaye Marlene Berkey, Mar. 12, 1977. Pvt. practice translater, expediter, Paris, 1968-70; pvt. practice estate mgr., Houston, 1971—; cons. finance/marketing. Del. Tex. Democratic Senatorial Dist. Conv., 1975. Krueger fellow, 1962; licensed salesman real estate Tex. Mem. Houston Jr. C. of C. (dir. 1977—), Houston Bd. Realtors, Tex. Assn. Realtors, Nat. Assn. Real Estate Bds., Assn. M.B.A. Execs., Futurist Soc., English Speaking Union. Lutheran. Clubs: Finance, Houston S.W. Civic. Home: 1052 Monarch Oaks St Houston TX 77055 Office: 8243 Hartford St Houston TX 77017

ELLIS, JAMES CALVIN, III, accountant; b. Meridian, Miss., Sept. 17, 1947; s. James Calvin and Mary Elizabeth (Moore) E.; B.A., Miss. State U., 1970, M.A., 1971, B.S., 1973; m. Georgia Ann Howell, June 6, 1970; children—Amy Elizabeth, Adam Howell, Robert Elliott. Staff accountant McDaniel & Co., C.P.A.'s, Dothan, Ala., 1973-76; partner McDaniel & Co., C.P.A.'s, Dothan, 1976—. Served with inf. U.S. Army, 1972. C.P.A., Ala. Mem. Am. Inst. C.P.A.'s, Ala. Soc. C.P.A.'s. Methodist. Club: Houston County Kiwanis (sec.-treas. 1977-78). Home: 1130 Appian Way Circle Dothan AL 36303 Office: PO Box 6356 Dothan AL 36302

ELLIS, KENNETH GARY, edn. specialist; b. Klamath Falls, Oreg., Feb. 23, 1945; s. Maynard Charles and Leona Josephine (Keifer) E.; B.S. in Psychology, So. Oreg. State Coll., 1973; M.A. in Human Resource Mgmt., Pepperdine U., 1976; m. Lesley Helen Kearns, June 10, 1967; children—Kevin, Yvonne. Vocat. rehab. specialist VA, White City, Oreg., 1972-73; edn. specialist CONAVCRUITDIST, Seattle and Butte, Mont., 1973-75, San Diego, Calif., 1975-77; edn. specialist COMNAVCRUITAREA SEVEN, Dallas, 1977—. Served with USN, 1967-71; Vietnam. Mem. Am. Vocat. Assn., Tex. Vocat. Tech. Assn., Am. Soc. Tng. and Devel., Nat. Assn. Industry Edn. Coop., Tex. Vocat. Guidance Assn., Am. Personnel and Guidance Assn., Tex. Personnel and Guidance Assn., Tex. Career Guidance Assn., Nat. Vocat. Guidance Assn., Am. Sch. Counselors Assn., Mil. Educators and Counselors Assn. Republican. Baptist. Research on Vietnam vets. and self-disclosure, Mont. high sch. students and the ASVAB. Home: 1100 Shady Pine Ct Bedford TX 76021 Office: Suite 501 1499 Regal Row Dallas TX 75247

ELLIS, LARRY JOSEPH, coal mining co. exec.; b. Welch, W.Va., Apr. 8, 1950; s. Joe Bill and Kathleen (Martin) E.; B.S., U. Ky., 1972; m. Patricia Lynn Womack, Mar. 15, 1971; children—Brian Chadwick and Paul Stephen (twins). Tchr., Tazwell County (Va.) Bd. Edn., 1972-75; supr. indsl. relations Consolidation Coal Co., Itmann, W.Va., 1975-76; dir. labor relations Hawley Coal Mining Corp., Keystone, W.Va., 1976—. Mem. Am. Mgmt. Assn., So. W.Va. Personnel Assn. Baptist. Club: Elks. Home: Route 3 Box 123 Bluefield VA 24605 Office: Drawer J Keystone WV 24852

ELLIS, MILDRED TERESA, speech-lang. pathologist; b. Jackson, Miss., Sept. 13, 1948; d. Wilbert Marvin and Mildred Christine (Burns) E.; B.A., U. Miss., 1972, M.Communicative Disorders, 1975. Speech-lang. pathologist Desoto County Schs., Southaven, Miss., 1971-73, LeFlore County Schs., Greenwood, Miss., 1973-74, Humphrey County Schs., Belzoni, Miss., 1975-76, Tate County Schs., Senatobia, Miss., 1976-77; staff Project RUN-Early Edn. program N. Miss. Retardation Center, Oxford, 1977—, speech-lang. pathologist, 1978—; univ. affiliated faculty U. Miss., also adj. instr. communicative disorders, 1978—. Licensed speech-lang. pathologist Miss. Mem. Am. Speech-Lang.-Hearing Assn. (cert. clin. competence), Council for Exceptional Children, Am. Assn. for Edn. of Severely/Profoundly Handicapped, Am. Assn. on Mental Deficiency, Miss. Speech and Hearing Assn., Nat. Assn. Retarded Citizens, Miss. Assn. Retarded Citizens, Zeta Tau Alpha (dir. house corp. 1978—, pres. alumnae chpt. 1979—). Home: College Hill Duplexes Apt 4 Oxford MS 38655 Office: N Miss Retardation Center PO Box 967 Oxford MS 38655

ELLIS, MORRIS RAY, educator; b. Amherst, Tex., July 28, 1944; s. Norman and Thelma (Golleher) E.; B.A. in Accounting, Harding Coll., 1967; M.A. in Theatre and Pub. Address, Stephen F. Austin State U., 1972; m. Melinda Leigh Heath, May 17, 1971; 1 dau., Heather Rae. Jr. auditor Ark. State Div. Legis. Audit, 1967-69; instr. speech Harding Coll., Searcy, Ark., from 1971, now asst. prof. speech, tech. dir. theatre. Mem. S.W. Theatre Assn. Mem. Ch. of Christ. Home: Box 211 Route 1 Judsonia AR 72081 Office: Box 666 Sta A Searcy AR 72143

ELLIS, QUINCY AMBROSE, III, coll. adminstr.; b. Belton, Tex., Sept. 3, 1941; s. Quincy Ambrose, Jr. and Becky (Everett) E.; B.B.A., N. Tex. State U., Denton, 1963; M.Ed., Springfield (Mass.) Coll., 1976; m. Nell Marie Gerth, June 30, 1973; children—Mark Quincy, Paul Bradley, Chad Ramsey. Personnel supr. VARO Inc., Garland, Tex., 1966-69; personnel mgr. Baifield Industries, Carrollton, Tex., 1970; v.p. ops. and personnel Dallas Met. YMCA, 1970-76; dir. personnel Dallas County Community Coll. Dist., 1976—; part-time instr. El Centro Coll., Dallas; speaker, cons. in field. Chmn. program com. and personnel com. Arlington (Tex.) YMCA, 1975-77. Served with USNR, 1963-65. Mem. Am. Soc. Personnel Adminstrn., Coll. and Univ. Personnel Assn., Dallas Personnel Assn. (past v.p.), Sigma Phi Epsilon. Baptist. Author manuals, tng. programs. Home: 1707 Kingsborough Arlington TX 76015 Office: 1707 Kingsborough Arlington TX 76015

ELLIS, ROBERT FRANKLIN, computer specialist; b. Richmond, Va., July 20, 1938; s. Lawrence William and Blanche (Seymour) E.; student Capital U. Ohio, 1965-66, George Washington U., 1972-73, Chapman Coll., 1974-76; m. Betty Lou Roberts, July 5, 1956; children—Robin Lynne, Jerilyn Suzanne. Computer programmer Def. Gen. Supply Center, Richmond, 1956-64; computer programmer Data Systems Automation Office, Columbus, Ohio, 1964-66; computer systems analyst Def. Supply Agy. Adminstrv. Support Center, Alexandria, Va., 1966-67; programmer analyst Systems Engring. Corp., Richmond, 1967-68; computer specialist Def. Gen. Supply Center, Richmond, 1968-69; computer specialist U.S. Army Computer Systems Command, Fort Belvoir, Va., 1969-71, Dept. Justice, Washington, 1971-72; supervisory computer specialist U.S. Army Computer Systems Command, Fort Belvoir, 1972-74, computer specialist, support group, Fort Lee, Va., 1974—. Named Boss of Year, Am. Bus. Womens Assn., 1972. Mem. Ch. of Christ. Home: 424 Nottingham Dr Colonial Heights VA 23834 Office: USACSC Support Group Fort Lee VA 23801

ELLIS, THOMAS BLAIR, accountant; b. Bedford, Va., Nov. 9, 1954; s. Thomas Ray and Jean Lamberth (Bauer) Ellis; B.S.B.A. in Acctg., Appalachian State U., 1977; m. Wendy Badgett, June 9, 1979. Housing dir. Center for Continuing Edn., Boone, N.C., later bus. mgr.; with Jefferson Standard Ins. Co., Boone, 1980—. Mem. Grandfather Mountain Area Motel Assn. (pres. 1978-79), Boone C. of C., Boone Jr. C. of C. (internal dir., 1978, publicity dir. 1979, named Rookie of Yr. 1978). Republican. Presbyterian. Home: 114 Oak St Apt 7 Boone NC 28607 Office: 901 E King St Boone NC 28607

ELLIS, THOMAS FORDTRAN, III, transp. co. exec.; b. Galveston, Tex., Feb. 19, 1950; s. Thomas Gordtran and Betty Lu (Dalehite) E.; B.B.A. in Fin. and Acctg., U. Tex., Austin, 1972; m. Sally Anne Ballard, June 3, 1972; children—Carrie Elizabeth, Daniel Fordtran. Partner, Ellis Interest, Houston, 1970-77, v.p., dir., 1974-78; stockbroker Underwood, Neuhaus & Co., Houston, 1972-74; pres. Ellis Transp. Co., Houston, 1978—, Ellis Interests, Inc., Houston, 1978—; dir. Trinity Valley Barge Line, Inc. Bd. dirs. Nat. River Acad., Helena, Ark. Mem. Am. Waterways Operators, Republican. Roman Catholic. Home: 11606 Cherryknoll St Houston TX 77077 Office: 7700 San Felipe St Suite 250 Houston TX 77063

ELLIS, WILLIAM TINSLEY, lawyer; b. Ft. Lauderdale, Fla., May 26, 1933; s. Thomas and Marcella (Tinsley) E.; B.A., Emory U., 1955; J.D., N.Y. U., 1958, LL.M., 1969; m. Judith L. Williams, July 21, 1957; children—William, Marcella, John, Ralph. Admitted to Fla. bar, 1958; mem. firm Ellis Spencer Butler & Kisslan, Hollywood, Fla., 1958—; adj. prof. law Nova U., Ft. Lauderdale, 1975. Founding chmn. Hollywood YMCA, 1962. Trustee Nova U. Vice-pres., S.Fla. Ednl. Center, Inc., 1964. Mem. Greater Hollywood Bar Assn. (past pres.), Alpha Tau Omega, Phi Delta Phi. Methodist. Club: Fort Lauderdale Yacht. Home: 917 N South Lake Dr Hollywood FL 33022 Office: PO Box 6 Hollywood FL 33022

ELLISON, CARY MACK, mech. engr.; b. Houston, Aug. 27, 1948; s. Raymond Hermalee and Opal (Dell) E.; B.S. in Mech. Engring., La. State U., 1971, postgrad. (Univ. fellow), summer 1972; M.S. in Mech. Engring., U. Houston, 1975; m. Cynthia Ann Ellison, Jan. 29, 1972; 1 son, Evan Mack. Design engr. Mission Mfg. Co., Houston, 1971-72; design engr. Vetco Offshore, Houston, 1972-74, mgr. completion equipment, 1976—; project engr., stress analyst Hydril Co., Houston, 1974-76. Registered profl. engr., Tex. Mem. Nat. Soc. Profl. Engrs., Tex. Soc. Profl. Engrs., ASME, Pi Tau Sigma, Tau Beta Pi. Patentee multi-positional lock for ram type blow out preventors. Home: 10322 Pine Pass Houston TX 77070 Office: Vetco Offshore 3726 Dacoma St Houston TX 77092

ELLISON, DARRELL F., employment agy. exec.; b. Olwien, Iowa, Jan. 19, 1941; s. Ode O. and Ruth F. E.; B.A. in Bus. Adminstrn., U. Nebr., 1965. Dir. ops U.S., Personnel Pool Am., Ft. Lauderdale, Fla., 1965-70; owner, pres. Help Unltd., Inc., Atlanta, 1970—. Served with USAF, 1958-62. Decorated Legion of Merit. Mem. Young Pres. Assn., Pinellas Industry Council. Republican. Lutheran. Home: 1900 Piedmont Rd Marietta GA 30062 Office: 711 W Peachtree St NE Atlanta GA 30308

ELLISON, LUTHER FREDERICK, oil co. exec.; b. Monroe, La., Jan. 2, 1925; s. Luther and Gertrude (Hudson) E.; student Emory U., 1943-44; B.S. in Petroleum Engring., Tex. A. and M. U., 1949, B.S. in Geol. Engring., 1950; m. Frances Z. Williams, July 17, 1948; children—Constance Elizabeth, Carolyn Williams. Jr. petroleum engr. Sun Prodn. Co., Kilgore and McAllen, Tex., 1950-52, area petroleum engr., Garcia Field, Tex., 1952-54, Delhi (La.) unit engr., 1954-60, asst. region supt., Dallas, 1960-62, dist. drilling engr., Corpus Christi, 1962-63, dist. engr., McAllen, 1963-65, supr. engring., Dallas, 1965-66, div. chief petroleum engr., 1966-70, region mgr. engring., 1970-76, region mgr., 1976-78, dir. devel., 1978—; pres., dir., mem. exec. com. Nabors-Sun Drilling Co.; dir., mem. exec. com. East Tex. Salt & Water Disposal Co. speaker in field. Vice pres. PTA of Northwood Jr. High Sch., Dallas, 1967-68, pres., 1968-69. Served with USNR, 1943-46. Registered profl. engr., Tex., La. Mem. Tex.-Mid-Continent Oil and Gas Assn. (Outstanding Achievement award 1964, chmn. area 1964-65, mgr. north region, operating com.), Am. Petroleum Inst., Soc. Petroleum Engrs., Dallas Engrs. Club, Petroleum Engrs. Club, Dallas Petroleum Club, Parents League, Sigma Alpha Epsilon (pres. 1944-45). Presbyterian (elder). Clubs: Northwood (Dallas), Lions. Home: 7442 Overdale St Dallas TX 75240 Office: 12850 Hillcrest Rd Dallas TX 75230

ELLISON, THORLEIF, engr.; b. Lyngdal, Norway, May 13, 1902; s. Andreas Emanuel and Gemalie (Svensen) E.; C.E., Christiania Coll. Tech., 1924; postgrad. George Washington U., U. Va.; m. Reidun Ingeborg Skonhoft, Jan. 1, 1932; children—Earl Otto, Thorleif Glenn, Sonja Karen. Came to U.S., 1928, naturalized, 1933. Supervising engr. GSA, Washington, 1948-57; supervising airport and airways service engr. FAA, 1957-61 chief airways engring. AID, Iran, West Pakistan, Turkey, 1961-67; cons. engr., Washington, Va., 1942—; supervising structural engr. for reconstrn. of The White House, 1949-52; mission dir. Bethlehem, Israel, Holy Land Christian Mission, Kansas City, 1968-71; instr. engring George Washington U., 1974-77. Active Christian Bus. Men's Com., Washington, Boy Scouts Am. Registered profl. engr. Mem. Nat. Soc. Profl. Engrs. (dir.), Sons of Norway (pres. Washington chpt.), Norwegian Soc. (treas.). Presbyterian (ruling elder). Home: Svennevik Rosfjord 4580 Lyngdal Norway also 6324 Telegraph Rd Alexandria VA 22310

ELLISTON, LURA DUFF, designer, poet; b. Ft. Worth, July 20, 1933; d. Fred Addison and Lura Duff (Elliston) M.; student Duke, 1951-52, U. Tex., 1952-54; m. George Edward Nowotny, Jr., Aug. 14, 1954 (div. Aug. 14, 1973); children—Edward Duff, George Edward III, Addison Dance. Owner, Interiors Ltd., Ft. Smith, Ark., Mulberry Bush Center, Ft. Smith; pres. 3729 Corp. Bd. dirs. Sebastian County Mental Health Assn., 1963-69, Ark. Assn. Mental Health 1966-72; gov. Western Ark. Counciling and Guidance Center, 1969-74; dir. Spark's Hosp. Guild, 1964—), pres., 1973-74; dir. Community Concert Assn., 1963—; pres. Ft. Smith Affiliation of the Arts, 1968; co-chmn. arts festivals, 1964, 65, 70; leadership cons. Nat. Assn. Retarded Children, 1968-69; mem. Retardation Com. State Health Planning, 1968-69; mem. Sebastian County Youth Services Commn., 1973-74; mem. Comprehensive Health Planning Council, 1969-74; del. Nat. Symposium on Alternatives to Incarceration of Youth, 1974. Republican committeewoman 3d Congl. Dist., 1962-64, 68-70; charter mem. County Rep. Women, 1961—, vice chmn., 1976—; co-chmn. Rep. United Campaign, 1962; sec. Rep. State Conv., 1968; justice of peace, 1973-74. Trustee Old Fort Museum, 1968-74, 75—, pres., 1971-72; trustee St. John's Sch. for Children with Learning Disabilities, 1971-74; mem. adv. bd. St. Edward's Mercy Hosp., 1967-69; bd. govs. Sebastian County Juvenile Detention Center, 1974; chmn. Ft. Smith Art Center Antique Show, 1978 Recipient first place award, Ark. Arts Festival, 1968; named one of outstanding young women of Am., 1966, One of 100 Ark. Women of Achievement, Ark. Presswomen, 1979 hon. girl Ft. Smith Girl's Club, 1978. Mem. Jr. League Ft. Smith, La. Assn. Ind. Royalty Owners, D.A.R., Delta Delta Delta. Episcopalian (pres. ch. women 1961-62). Clubs: Hardscrabble Country, Town (Ft. Smith). Author: New Look Trio, 1970. Founder, designer Ft. Smith Children's Museumobile, 1965; author vol. art enrichment program Ft. Smith Pub. Schs., 1969; design concept mini parks City of Ft. Smith, 1972. Home: 4106 S 25th St Fort Smith AR 72903

ELLISTON, WILLIAM JACKSON, JR., structural engr.; b. Nashville, July 23, 1934; s. William Jackson and Dorothy Lea (Leake) E., Sr.; B. Engring. cum laude, Vanderbilt U., 1957; m. Mary De Heckman; children—William J., III, Elizabeth Harding Elliston Culp, Jeffrey Benson Ligon. Cons. engr., prin. asso. Ross H. Bryan & Assos., Nashville, 1957-65; asst. gen. mgr., chief engr. Span-Deck, Inc., Franklin, Tenn., 1965-57; partner Bass-Elliston & Assos., Architects and Engrs., Nashville, 1967-70; prin. Wm. Elliston & Assos., Cons. Engrs., Nashville, 1970—. Bd. dirs. Samaritans, Inc., Nashville, 1970—; class chmn. Living Endowment Fund, Vanderbilt U., Nashville, 1971-77; tchr. Sunday sch. St. Henry's Catholic Ch., Nashville, 1971-77; mem. major gifts com. Vanderbilt U., 1979. Lic. profl. engr., Tenn. Mem. Nat. Soc. Profl. Engrs., Cons. Engrs. Council, Pre-stressed Concrete Inst., ASCE. Contbr. articles to profl. jours. Office: 3200 West End Ave Suite 405 Nashville TN 37203

ELLSWORTH, LUCIUS FULLER, univ. ofcl., historian; b. Wooster, Ohio, July 6, 1941; s. Clayton Sumner and Frances Lindemuth (Fuller) E.; B.A. with high honors, Coll. of Wooster, 1963; M.A. (Andelot fellow) U. Del., 1966, Ph.D. (Rovensky fellow), 1971; m. Linda Diane Vollmar, July 3, 1969. Acting coordinator of Hagley Grad. program U. Del., 1968-69, adj. instr. history, 1968-69; vis. honors prof. Villanova (Pa.) U., 1968; asst. prof. history U. West Fla., Pensacola, 1969-74, asso. prof., 1974-78, prof., 1978—, provost of Alpha Coll., 1975-79, dean Coll. of Arts and Scis., 1979—; grant proposal reviewer Nat. Endowment for the Humanities, 1975, 76, 77; cons. to div. history Sec. of State, State of Fla., 1977, N.Y. State Dept. Edn., 1969, Pensacola Jr. Coll., 1970, Chipla Jr. Coll., 1973; mem. Task Force on Research and Service, State U. System, Fla., 1975-76. Chmn. Escambia County (Fla.) Bicentennial Festival Com., 1972-75. Am. Council on Edn. fellow, 1975-76; Nat. Trust for Hist. Preservation grantee, 1975, Fla. Endowment for Humanities Project grantee, 1978—. Mem. Orgn. of Am. Historians, Am. Hist. Assn., Econ. History Assn., Agrl. History Soc. (Edwards award 1969), Soc. for History of Technology, Am. Assn. for Higher Edn., Fla. Hist. Soc. (dir. 1979—, mem. Arthur Thompson Meml. award com. 1974, 78), Phi Alpha Theta. Democrat. Presbyterian. Author: (with Brooke Hindle) Technology in Early America, 1966; The American Leather Industry, 1969; The Americanization of the Gulf Coast, 1803-1850, 1972; Traditionalism and Change: The New York Tanning Industry in the Nineteenth Century, 1975. Home: 9330 Scenic Hwy Pensacola FL 32504 Office: Univ of West Florida Pensacola FL 32504

ELLSWORTH, THOMAS JAMES, mayor; b. Hot Springs, Ark., Aug. 3, 1926; s. Ernest and Leah Blumenstiel; B.S., U. Ark., 1949; m. Julia Gilliam, Nov. 20, 1948; children—Thomas James, John C. Owner, Hot Springs Surg. Supply, 1953-79; alderman Hot Springs City Council, 1962-70, mayor City of Hot Springs, 1971—. Served with USN, 1944-46. Mem. Ark. Mcpl. League Exec. Com., Hot Springs C. of C. (past dir.), U.S. Conf. Mayors, Internat. City Mgmt. Assn., Nat. League Cities, Am. Soc. Public Adminstrn. Episcopalian. Clubs: Lions (past pres.), Elks. Home: 11 Glen St Hot Springs AR 71901 Office: 123 Convention Blvd Hot Springs AR 71901

ELLWOOD, B(UD) M. BASIL, JR., mgmt. cons.; b. N.Y.C., Aug. 27, 1927; s. Basil M. and Irene (Cooney) E.; student pub. schs., Hempstead, N.Y.; m. Lee Marie Rush, Sept. 1, 1951; 1 dau., Ava Marie. Mng. prin. Lifson, Wilson, Ferguson & Winick, Houston and Dallas, 1959-64; v.p. ops. Fleming & Sons, Dallas, 1964-70; exec. v.p. Wessendorff Nelms, Houston, 1970-76; mng. prin. Ellwood & Assos., Houston, 1976—. Served with USN, 1944-47. Mem. Soc. Mfg. Engrs. Club: Plaza. Home: 1646 S Gessner Houston TX 77063 Office: 3811 Richmond St Suite 111 Houston TX 77027

ELLZEY, CARLOS FRANK, JR., univ. adminstr.; b. Galveston, Tex., Jan. 7, 1941; s. Carlos Frank and Orine Maude (Heimerle) E.; B.S., Fla. State U., 1975, M.S., 1979; m. Mary Elizabeth Allen, June 9, 1972; children—Julie-Ann, Richard Allen, Heather Elizabeth. Mgr. sales and service Hobart Equipment Co., Tallahassee, Fla., 1965; cons. Met. Ins. Co., Tallahassee, 1965-66; electronic technician Lanier Bus. Machines, Tallahassee, 1966-67; pres. Profl. Data Systems, Inc., Tallahassee, 1967-69; dir. data processing Fla. Edn. Assn., Tallahassee, 1969-73; mgmt. analyst Fla. State U., Tallahassee, 1973-75; computer systems coordinator Fla. Bd. Regents, Tallahassee, 1975-78; dir. univ. computing Fla. A&M U., Tallahassee, 1978—; mgmt. and systems cons. Mem. adv. council Sch. Dist., Tallahassee, 1978-79. Served with USAF, 1961-64. Mem. Coll. and Univ. Systems Exchange, Assn. Instl. Researchers, Fla. Assn. Instl. Researchers, Fla. Assn. Ednl. Data Processing, Coll. and Univ. Machine Records. Democrat. Mem. United Ch. Home: 2961 Foxcroft Dr Tallahassee FL 32308 Office: Box 189 Fla A&M U Tallahassee FL 32307

ELMAGHRABY, SALAH ELDIN, ops. researcher, indsl. engr., educator; b. Fayoum, Egypt, Oct. 21, 1927; came to U.S., 1954, naturalized, 1970; s. Abdel Fattah and Leila (Orabi) E.; B.S., Cairo U., 1948; M.Sc., Ohio State U., 1955; Ph.D., Cornell U., 1958; m. Amina Ishac, July 9, 1964; children—Leila, Wedad J., Karima N. Asso. prof. ops. research, Yale U., New Haven, 1962-67; vis. asso. prof. ops. research Cornell U., Ithaca, N.Y., 1967; prof. ops. research and indsl. engring. N.C. State U., Raleigh, 1967—, asso. head indsl. engring. and grad. adminstr., 1971-75; cons. in field. Mem. Am. Inst. Indsl. Engrs. (Disting. Research award 1970), Sigma Xi, Alpha Pi Mu, Phi Kappa Phi, Tau Beta Pi. Author: Some Network Models in Management Science, 1970; Activity Networks, 1977. Editor: (with J.J. Moder) Handbook of Operations Research, Vols. 1 and 2, 1978; dept. editor Indsl. Engring. Trans., 1976—; adv. bd. Ency. Computer Sci. & Tech. Home: 124 Perquimans Dr Raleigh NC 27609 Office: PO Box 5511 NC State U Raleigh NC 27650

ELMES, DAVID GORDON, psychologist; b. Newton, Mass., Feb. 15, 1942; s. Leslie and Ruth (Adams) E.; B.A., U. Va., 1964; M.A., 1966, Ph.D., 1967; m. Anne Louise Lawrence, June 7, 1963; children—Matthew David, Jennifer Anne. Mgmt. trainee C & P of Va., 1963; asst. prof. Washington and Lee U., Lexington, Va., 1967-71, asso. prof., 1971-74, prof., 1975—; research asso. Human Performance Center, U. Mich., 1973-74. Bd. dirs. Rockbridge Mental Health Clinic, 1968-73; ofcl., coach Little League Baseball and Basketball, 1969-77. Mem. Va. Acad. Sci., Psychonomic Soc. Author: Readings in Experimental Psychology, 1978; contbr. articles to profl. jours. Home: 3 Westside Ct Lexington VA 24450 Office: Washington and Lee U Lexington VA 24450

EL-MESSIDI, KATHY GROEHN, communications exec.; b. Detroit, Jan. 23, 1946; d. Thomas Emil and Helen Margaret (Schreck) Groehn; B.A., U. Mich., 1967; M.A., So. Oreg. Coll., 1971; Ph.D., U. Okla., 1976; m. Adel El-Sayed Ali El-Messidi, Sept. 14, 1974. Reporter, Grosse Pointe (Mich.) News, 1966, Christian Sci. Monitor, Boston, 1967-69; publicity writer Harry & David & Jackson and Perkins Cos., Oreg., 1970-71; radio writer Sta. WNAD, Norman, Okla., 1973; instr. history U. Okla., 1972-75; public relations writer, Houston, 1976-78; communications mgr. Bovay Engrs., Inc., Houston, 1978-80; communications cons. CRS Group, Inc., Houston, 1980—, Turner, Collie & Braden, Inc., Houston; asso. Rice U., Houston. Mem. Internat. Assn. Bus. Communicators, Women in Communications, Am. Hist. Assn., Am. Pen Women, Phi Alpha Theta. Christian Scientist. Club: Galveston Country. Author: Grosse Pointe, Michigan: Race Against Race (Am. Pen Women 1st pl. award for informational books), 1972; The Bargain: The Story Behind the 30-year Honeymoon of GM and the UAW, 1980. Home: 14502 Magic River Dr Cypress TX 77429 Office: CRS Group 1100 Milam St Suite 500 Houston TX 77001

ELMORE, JACK STANLEY, Realtor; b. Savannah, Ga., Aug. 31, 1922; s. William Lawrence and Lillian Pauline (Weldon) E.; grad. Miami Police Acad., 1946, Bolan Acad., 1948; m. Suzanne Prager, Dec. 17, 1954; 1 son, Thomas Louis. With Miami Police Dept., 1946-75, capt., 1968-75; pres. Elmore Realty Co., Coral Gables, Fla., 1975—. Served with USN, 1938-45. Mem. Navy League U.S. (pres. Miami council 1976-77), Southwest Real Estate Brokers Assn. (pres. 1963), Nat. Assn. Real Estate Bds., Miami Bd. Realtors. Democrat. Congregationalist. Clubs: Elks, Masons, Shriners. Home: 1145 Mariana Ave Coral Gables FL 33134 Office: 5111 SW 8th St Miami FL 33134

ELMORE, JOHN HOWARD, clin. audiologist; b. Denver, Sept. 29, 1944; s. Howard Willis and Bambi (Balzano) E.; B.A. in Speech Pathology, Adams State Coll., 1968; M.A. in Audiology (VA fellow), No. Ill. U., 1971. Commd. 2d lt. Med. Service Corps, U.S. Army, 1971, advanced through grades to capt., 1976; chief audiology dept. Ft. Jackson Hosp., Columbia, S.C., 1971-74, U.S. Army Hosp., Landstuhl, W. Ger., 1974-75, U.S. Army Hosp., Nurnburg, W. Ger., 1975-76; ret., 1976; pvt. practice clin. audiology, Beloit, Wis., 1976-78; capt. Biomed. Sci. Corps, U.S. Air Force, 1979; dir. audiol. services Tinker AFB, Oklahoma City, 1979—. Mem. Am. Speech and Hearing Assn. (cert. clin. competence), Joint Mil. Audiology Soc. (v.p.), Am. Racquet Ball Assn. Roman Catholic. Editor Mil. Audiology jour., 1975-76. Address: Tinker AFB PO Box 45607 Oklahoma City OK 73145

ELMORE, SAMUEL ELTINGE, pediatrician; b. Chgo., July 16, 1914; s. Samuel Eltinge and Jane McCrady (Bacot) E.; A.B., U. N.C., 1936; M.D., Harvard U., 1940; m. May Carroll Miles, Dec. 19, 1941; children—Samuel Eltinge III, Miles, Harriette W., Nancy B. Intern, Charity Hosp., New Orleans, 1940-41, resident in pediatrics, 1941-42; fellow in pediatrics Tulane U. Med. Sch., New Orleans, 1947-48; pvt. practice pediatrics, Spartanburg, S.C., 1948—; mem. staff Spartanburg Gen. Hosp., 1948—, chief of staff, 1959-60; chief Rheumatic Fever Clinic, Spartanburg, 1958—; mem. staffs Mary Black Hosp., Doctors Meml. Hosp. Served with USN, 1942-47. Decorated Silver Star medal. Diplomate Am. Bd. Pediatrics. Mem. Am. Acad. Pediatrics, AMA, S.C. Med. Assn., Spartanburg County Med. Soc. (pres. 1965-66). Republican. Episcopalian. Home: 1075 Partridge Rd Spartanburg SC 29302 Office: 147 Oakwood Ave Spartanburg SC 29302

ELMORE, THOMAS STEPHEN, indsl. engr.; b. Gastonia, N.C., Apr. 19, 1952; s. Robert Porter and Catherine (Moore) E.; B.S. in Engring. Ops., N.C. State U., 1974, M.S. in Indsl. Engring., 1976; M.B.A., East Carolina U., 1979; m. Helen Zoe Pantazis, May 26, 1979. Research asst. Human Ecology Inst., Raleigh, N.C., 1974-75; teaching and research asst. N.C. State U., 1975-76; sr. mgmt. engr. Carolinas Hosp. and Health Services, Raleigh, 1976—; dir. mgmt. engring. Lenoir Meml. Hosp., Kinston, N.C., 1977-79, Durham County Gen. Hosp., Durham, 1979—, Pitt County Meml. Hosp., Greenville, N.C., 1979—. Tchr., Grey Stone Bapt. Ch., Durham, 1979—. Named Outstanding Sr. in Engring. Ops., N.C. State U., 1974. Mem. Am. Inst. Indsl. Engrs., Hosp. Mgmt. Systems Soc. (research com.), Fellowship Christian Athletes. Democrat. Office: PO Box 12546 Raleigh NC 27605

ELOVITZ, MARK HARVEY, lawyer; b. Pitts., May 20, 1938; B.A. cum laude, N.Y. U., 1960, Ph.D. (Honors scholar), 1973; M.H.L., Jewish Theol. Sem. Am., 1962; J.D. cum laude, Cumberland Sch. Law, 1977; m.; 3 children. Rabbi, 1964; asso. rabbi Temple Beth-El, Cedarhurst, N.Y., 1967-69; rabbi Temple Beth-El, Birmingham, Ala., 1970-77; law clk. U.S. Atty.'s Office, No. Dist. Ala., summer 1976; admitted to Ala. bar, 1977; mem. firm Denaburg, Schoel, Meyerson & Ogle, Birmingham, 1977-79; individual practice law, Birmingham, 1979—; cons., panelist Pub. Programs div. Program Devel. Bd., Nat. Endowment for Humanities; past vice chmn. Ala. Com. for Humanities and Pub. Policy; cons. Outreach Program, Birmingham Crisis Center; lectr. Nat. Jewish Welfare Bd. Lecture Bur. Past pres. Birmingham Area Legal Services Corp., Inc.; bd. dirs. Birmingham Jewish Community Center, Positive Maturity, Inc. Served to capt. USAF, 1964-67. Decorated Commendation medal. Mem. Inst. Religion and Mental Health, Rabbinical Assembly Am., New York Bd. Rabbis, Am., Ala., Birmingham bar assns., Am. Trial Lawyers Assn., Ala. Assn. Trial Lawyers, Phi Beta Kappa. Author: A Century of Jewish Life in Dixie: The Birmingham Experience, 1974; (with John Kirklin and John Durant) The Right to Die: Medical Ethics, Law and Human Values, 1976. Contbr. legal and religious articles to profl. jours. Address: Suite 407 Woodward Bldg Birmingham AL 35203 also 3728 Dover Dr Mountain Brook AL 35223

ELSAS, LOUIS JACOB, II, geneticist; b. Atlanta, Feb. 10, 1937; s. Herbert Rothschild and Edith (Levy) E.; B.A., Harvard U., 1958; M.D., U. Va., Charlottesville, 1962; m. Nancy Elder Terrell, July 15, 1961; children—Nancy Louise, Margaret Edith, Louis Jacob. Intern, Yale U. Hosp., 1963-65; resident New Haven Hosp., 1965-68; asst. prof. Yale U., 1968-70; dir. div. med. genetics Emory U. Sch. Medicine, Atlanta, 1970—, asso. prof. pediatrics, 1972-78, prof., 1978—. Chmn. bd. dirs. The Patch, Inc., 1975—; mem. health adv. com. Nat. Found. March of Dimes, 1977—. Recipient Mosby Scholarship award, 1962; John Horsley Meml. award for biomed. sci. research, 1972; research career devel. award Nat. Inst. Child Health and Devel., 1973-78; diplomate Am. Bd. Internal Medicine. Mem. Am. Fedn. for Clin. Research, AAAS, Am. Soc. for Human Genetics, Atlanta Genetics Soc. (chmn., treas. 1972—), Soc. Pediatric Research, Endocrine Soc., Am. Soc. Clin. Investigation, Am. Soc. for Biol. Chemists, Soc. for Inherited Metabolic Disorders (pres. 1977-79), Sigma Xi (pres. Emory chpt. 1977-78). Contbr. articles, chpts. to med. jours., texts. Home: 858 Oakdale Rd Atlanta GA 30307 Office: PO Drawer AM Emory U Atlanta GA 30322

ELSASSER, GEORGE FREDERICK, JR., physician; b. Portsmouth, Va., Feb. 15, 1925; s. George Frederick and Bertha Mae (Rountree) E.; student William and Mary Coll. (now Old Dominion U.), 1942-43, Hampden-Sydney Coll., 1943-44; M.D., Med. Coll. Va., 1948; m. Madaline Avila O'Kane, Dec. 13, 1949; children—Demaris Ann Elsasser Wheeler, Carolyn Avila, George Frederick, Richard Rainey, Maryann Moss. Intern, U.S. Naval Hosp., Portmouth, Va., 1948-49; resident in pathology Naval Med. Center, Bethesda, Md., 1949-50; resident in internal medicine Duke U. Hosp., Durham, N.C., 1954-56; pvt. practice internal medicine, Norfolk, Va., 1956—; attending physician DePaul Hosp., Norfolk Gen. Hosp.; dir. muscle disease Clinic, Med. Center Hosp.; asso. prof. medicine Eastern Va. Med. Sch., 1975—. Served with USNR, 1943-48, U.S. Navy, 1948-54. Diplomate Am. Bd. Internal Medicine. Mem. A.C.P., Am. Soc. Internal Medicine, Am. Heart Assn. Council on Clin. Cardiology, Muscular Dystrophy Assn. Am., Norfolk Acad. Medicine, Med. Soc. Va., AMA, N.Y. Acad. Scis., Med. Coll. Va., Duke U., Old Dominion U. alumni assns., Phi Chi. Methodist. Club: Norfolk Yacht and Country. Home: 5220 Studeley Ave Norfolk VA 23508 Office: 530 Wainwright Bldg 229 W Bute St Norfolk VA 23510

ELSEY, KATHERINE JONES, ret. educator; b. Sheridan, Wyo., Apr. 30, 1914; d. Archie Israel and Edith Lorraine (Neff) Jones; student Kans. City Jr. Coll., 1932-33; B.S.M., U. Mo., 1937; M.Ed., U. Houston, 1954; m. Dan Giard Elsey, Dec. 24, 1939; children—Dan Jr., Katherine Anne. Tchr., Lowell Sch., Aurora, Mo., 1937-40; supr. elementary music Corpus Christi (Tex.) Ind. Sch. Dist., 1947-55; spl. music tchr. Boulder Valley (Colo.) Ind. Sch. Dist., 1955-65; instr. music U. Colo. Boulder, summers 1956-64; asst. prof. music Lamar U., Beaumont, Tex., 1965-79; cons. in field. Mem. Music Educators Nat. Conf., Tex. Music Educators Assn., Tex. Assn. Coll. Tchrs., Delta Kappa Gamma Soc. Internat. (chpt. Outstanding and Dedicated Service award 1976-77), Sigma Alpha Iota (patroness). Contbr. articles to profl. jours. Research in field. Home: 835 Howell St Beaumont TX 77706

ELSTER, ROBERT ERIC, hosp. adminstr., naval officer; b. Oakland, Calif., July 31, 1948; s. Robert Edward and Leanor Eileen (Dalton) E.; A.B. in History, Georgetown U., 1969; M.H.A., George Washington U., 1972; m. Eleanor Dyer Ansel, July 7, 1973. Adminstrv. resident Welborn Bapt. Hosp., Evansville, Ind., 1971-72; commd. ensign U.S. Navy, 1970, advanced through grades to lt. comdr., 1979; adminstv. positions Nat. Naval Med. Center, Bethesda, Md., 1972-74; head med. facilities projects office, Pensacola, Fla., 1974-77; med. constrn. officer Naval Hosp., Orlando, Fla., 1977—. Mem. Am. Hosp. Assn., Am. Coll. Hosp. Adminstrs., Assn. Western Hosps., U.S. Naval Sailing Assn. Republican. Office: Naval Regional Medical Center Orlando FL 32813

ELSTON, ROBERT CHARLES, printing co. exec.; b. N.Y.C., Feb. 2, 1931; s. Bert and Mary (Mulhern) E.; A.B., Providence Coll., 1952; m. Juanita D. Lee, Aug. 7, 1965; children—Stephen J., Mary Elizabeth, Maura Jean, Susan Margaret. Asst. to dir. research Geigy Chem. Corp., Ardsley, N.Y., 1952-55; quality control supr. Dexter Press, West Nyack, N.Y., 1955-57; v.p., gen. mgr. World Color, Inc., Ormond Beach, Fla., 1957-65, pres., 1965—. Chmn., Cancer Drive Daytona Beach, 1964; chmn. Citizens for Ormond Beach, 1966; mem. Ormond Beach Planning Bd., 1971; chmn. Scoop Jackson Com., 1972, Volusia County Planning Bd., 1974. Mem. Graphic Arts Tech. Found., Nat. Assn. Photo Lithographers, Southeastern Photo Platemakers Assn., Printing Industries Fla. Democrat. Home: 623 John Anderson Dr Ormond Beach FL 32074 Office: World Color Inc PO Box 1327 Ormond Beach FL 32074

ELY, ALLEN JUDSON, JR., mfg. co. exec.; b. Elizabeth, N.J., Jan. 13, 1925; s. Allen Judson and Elizabeth (Fehl) E.; B.S. in Mech. Engring., Lehigh U., 1947; m. Patricia M. Phelps, May 1, 1948 (div. 1978); children—Elizabeth Ely Morris, Margaret Ely Hixson, Allen Judson, Scott David; m. 2d, Cecilia A. Bilowich, June 10, 1978. Engr., Standard Oil Co. N.J., Linden, 1947; engr. Taylor Forge Inc., Chgo., 1947-70, prodn. control mgr., 1954-56, mgr. engring., 1956-62, v.p. engring., 1962-64, v.p. mfg., 1964-66; pres. Tinnie Merc. Co., Roswell, N.Mex., 1970-79, chmn. bd., 1979—; chmn., pres., dir. Globe Universal Scis., Inc., El Paso, 1970; pres., dir. Ben Miller, Inc., El Paso, 1970, Hyer Boot Co.; pres. Cotter Corp., Golden, Colo., 1971-74; dir. Sunbell Corp., Albuquerque, Realities, Inc., Denver. Served with U.S. Mcht. Marine, 1944-46. Clubs: El Paso Country, El Paso. Home: 606 Coeur d'Alene Circle El Paso TX 79922 Office: PO Box 9637 El Paso TX 79986

ELY, WINSTON THEODORE, clothing mfg. co. exec.; b. Detroit, Sept. 2, 1918; s. Roy Sanford and Leigh (Ryan) E.; ed. in Toronto, Ont., Can.; m. Barbara Grace Spalding, Apr. 27, 1940; children—Edward Winston, Judith Leigh, Bartlett Spalding. Mng. dir. Sunshine Uniform Supply Co., Ltd., Toronto, 1940-46; pres. Ely Corp., Detroit, 1950-67, Detroit Overall Mfg. Co., 1960-67, Winston Uniform Co., Double Springs, Ala., 1963—; chmn. bd. Garment Corp. Am., Miami, Fla., 1967—, Cadillac Mfg. Co., Mayaguez, P.R., 1968—, Cadillac Shirt Corp., Mayaquez, 1968—. Spl. hon. cons. Puerto Rican Econ. Devel. Adminstrn., 1963—. Mem. Founders Soc., Detroit Inst. Arts. Republican. Methodist. Home: 9048 SW 62d Terr Miami FL 33173 Office: Garment Corp Am 9156 SW 87th Ave Miami FL 33176 also Cadillac Industries Box 435 Mayaguez PR 00708

EMBERTON, WALLACE AARON, automotive mfg. co. exec.; b. Louisville, Oct. 27, 1933; s. Huey Denzmore and Lola Mae (Smith) E.; student Western Ky. U., 1966, Ariz. State Coll., 1974, Stanford U., 1975, Air U., U. N.C., 1978; m. Mary D. Reagan, July 6, 1953; children—Jacqueline, Joyce, Janet. Served as enlisted man U.S. Air Force, 1952-56; commd. 2d lt. U.S. Air Force, 1962, advanced through grades; ret., 1962; with Sorensen Mfg. Co., a Gulf & Western Co., Glasgow, Ky., 1962—, procurement mgr., 1974—. Decorated Bronze Star with oak leaf cluster. Mem. Nat. Assn. Purchasing Mgmt. Mem. Churches of Christ. Home: 105 Lyon St Glasgow KY 42141 Office: Sorensen Mfg Co 1115 Cleveland St Glasgow KY 42141

EMBRY, CARLOS BROGDON, JR., newspaper exec.; b. Louisville, July 29, 1941; s. Carlos Brogdon and Zora (Romans) E.; B.S., Western Ky. U., 1963; B.D., Adler U., 1970; M.A., Edison Coll., 1972; postgrad. Duke U., 1969, Blackstone Sch. Law., 1968; m. Wanda Lou Ralph, Aug. 26, 1962; children—Laura Ann, Barbara Ann, Carlos Brogdon III. Editor, Ohio County Messenger, Beaver Dam, Ky., 1963-73; judge Ohio County Court, Hartford, Ky., 1974-77; v.p. Embry Newspapers, Inc., Beaver Dam, 1978—; program coordinator Ohio County Fiscal Court, Beaver Dam, 1978—; co-owner Embry's Valley Shopping Center, 1974—. Treas., Republican party, 1977—; mayor City of Beaver Dam, 1970-73. Mem. Ky. Weekly Newspaper Assn. (pres. 1970-71), Beaver Dam Retail Merchants Assn., Ohio County C. of C. Baptist. Clubs: Mason, K.T., Lion, Moose. Home: Old Hartford Rd Box 202 Beaver Dam KY 42320 Office: Embry Newspapers Inc 220 N Main St Beaver Dam KY 42320

EMDEN, KAREN ANNE, educator, lawyer; b. Piermont, N.Y., Mar. 8, 1947; d. John Anthony and Helen Roxanne (Rafter) Gallucci; B.A., Coll. William and Mary, 1973, J.D., 1976, postgrad., 1979; m. Willard F. Emden, Jr., Jan. 28, 1966; 1 dau., Patricia. Admitted to Va. bar, 1976; atty.-at-law, Williamsburg, Va., 1976—; asst. prof. Sch. Bus. Adminstrn., Coll. William and Mary, 1976—. Mem. Am., Mid-Atlantic Regional (sec.-treas. 1978-79, v.p. 1979-80) bus. law assns., Am., Va. State, Va. Women's bar assns., Am., Va. trial lawyers' assns. Democrat. Roman Catholic. Home: 45 Mile Course Williamsburg VA 23185 Office: Sch Bus Adminstrn Coll William and Mary Williamsburg VA 23185

EMENS, STEVEN COUNTISS, lawyer; b. Sheffield, Ala., Feb. 20, 1950; s. Arthur Greenhill and Martha Elizabeth (Countiss) E.; B.S., U. No. Ala., 1972; M.B.A., U. Ala., 1976, J.D., 1976. Admitted to Ala. bar, 1976; staff atty. Lauderdale Legal Services, Florence, Ala., 1976-77; mng. atty. Dallas County Legal Services, Selma, Ala., 1977-78; asst. dir. clin. program U. Ala. Sch. Law, Tuscaloosa, 1978—; state coordinator emergency legal services in natural disasters; cons. in field. Mem. Am., Ala. bar assns., Assn. Trial Lawyers Am., Nat. Legal Aid and Defenders Assn., Phi Alpha Delta. Methodist. Club: Lions, Kiwanis. Home: 404-B 8th Ave NE Tuscaloosa AL 35401 Office: 912 4th Ave Tuscaloosa AL 35401

EMERSON, ANN PARKER, dietitian, educator; b. Twin Lakes, Fla., Dec. 3, 1925; d. Charles Dendy and Gladys Agnes (Chalker) Parker; B.S., Fla. State U., 1947; M.S., U. Fla., 1968; m. Donald McGeachy Emerson, Sept. 22, 1950; children—Mary Ann, Donald, Charles Parker, William John. Research dietitian Coll. Medicine U. Fla., Gainesville, 1962-68, dir. dietetic edn., 1968-74, dir. dietetic internship program, 1968-75, dir. program clin. and community dietetics, 1974—; mem. Commn. Dietetic Registration, 1974-77. VA Allied Health Manpower grantee, 1974-81; HEW Allied Health Manpower grantee, 1975-78, 78—. Mem. Am., Fla. dietetic assns., Altrusa Internat. (pres. Gainesville chpt. 1977-78). Democrat. Roman Catholic. Club: Jr. League. Office: Box J184 JHMHC Gainesville FL 32610

EMERSON, DAVID EDWIN, chemist; b. Checotah, Okla., May 15, 1932; s. David Ervin and Della Elizabeth (Fennell) E.; B.S. in Chemistry, Southeastern State U., Durant, Okla., 1955; postgrad. W. Tex. State U., 1966-68; m. Ermyne Faith Snodgrass, Aug. 21, 1953; children—Joe David, Sally Gayle, Terry William. Civilian instr. U.S. Air Force, Amarillo, Tex., 1955-57; chemist Helium Research Center, U.S. Bur. Mines, Amarillo, 1957-59, supervisory chemist, 1959-62, chief br. lab services, 1962-71, chief unit of tech. services, 1971-75, chief sect. tech. services, 1975-78, chief sect. of research and analytical services, helium ops., 1978—. Mem. chem. tech. adv. com. Amarillo Coll.; elder First Christian Ch., Amarillo. Served with U.S. Army, 1956-62. Mem. Am. Chem. Soc. Contbr. articles to profl. jours.; patentee in field. Home: Route 5 Box 891 Amarillo TX 79118 Office: Box H4372 Amarillo TX 79101

EMERSON, ELMA JOSEPHINE HENDERS, dietitian; b. Dancy, Ala., May 13, 1920; d. Fred Whitacre and Celia Martha Smith Henders; B.S., Ala. Coll. for Women, 1942; postgrad. UCLA, 1945-46; m. Charles Leon Emerson, Dec. 3, 1947. Civilian dietitian Prisoner of War Camp, Aliceville, Ala., 1944-45; dietetic intern Good Samaritan Hosp., Portland, Oreg., 1946-47; dietitian St. Francis Hosp., San Francisco, 1947-49; dietitian VA Hosp., Oakland, Calif., 1949, chief dietetics, Spokane, Wash., 1963-67, Amarillo, Tex., 1967-69, Roseburg, Oreg., 1969-71, Vancouver, Wash., 1971-77; chief dietitian VA Med. Center, Dublin, Ga., 1977—. Chmn. bond drive, Roseburg, 1969, 70, Oakland, 1959; chmn. Combined Fed.

Campaign, Vancouver, 1974. Recipient public service award VA, 1968. Mem. Am. Dietetic Assn., Am. Soc. for Hosp. Food Service Adminstrs., Ga. Dietetic Assn., U. Montevallo Alumni Assn., DAR, Smithsonian Assos., Nat. Archives Assos., U.S. Capitol Hist. Soc. Republican. Episcopalian. Clubs: Marines (San Francisco); Cherry River Navy (Richwood, W.Va.).

EMERSON, GERALDINE MARIELLEN, med. scientist, gerontologist, educator; b. Greensboro, N.C., Dec. 30, 1925; d. William Silas and Buna Launa (Thornton) Blakely; grad. Jacksonville, (Fla.) Jr. Coll., 1946; B.A. in Chemistry and Psychology, U. Miami (Fla.), 1949; postgrad. Northwestern U., 1951-52; Ph.D., U. Ala., 1960; m. Jack Drew Emerson, Nov. 26, 1946 (dec. Sept. 1971); 1 son, William Kenneth. Research asst. U. Ala. Med. Center, Birmingham, 1953-59, teaching asst., 1955-60, instr. physiology and biochemistry, 1960-61, instr. biochemistry, 1961-64, asst. prof., 1964-77, asso. prof., 1977—, mem. admissions com. Sch. Dentistry, 1972-74, mem. Univ. Council, 1973-75, affirmative action com., 1976-78; asso. Max Planck Institut für Hirnforschung, Frankfurt am Main, W. Ger., 1977-78; dir. Am. Investors Ins. Co. Adv. council Jefferson County RSVP, 1973—, chmn., 1975-77. Fellow AAAS, Am. Inst. Chemists (chmn. elect Ala. chpt. 1974, chmn. 1975, councillor 1976-78), Psi Chi; mem. Ala. Acad. Sci. (vice-chmn., v.p. 1966-68, chmn. local arrangements com. 1974, editorial bd. Jour. 1976-78, 2d v.p. 1978, pres. elect 1979, pres. 1980), Am. Physiol. Soc., Soc. for Cryobiology, Ala. Soc. Med. History (sec.-treas. 1958-59), N.Y. Acad. Sci., Ala. Hist. Assn., Fla. Citrus Growers, Sigma Xi (treas. U. Ala. chpt. 1964-66, pres.-elect 1975, pres. 1976). Editor: Aging. Contbr. articles on endocrinology, gerontology and neurophysiology to sci. jours. Home: 2800 Vestavia Forest Pl Birmingham AL 35216 Office: Room 217 Volker Hall Box 316 Univ Station U Ala in Birmingham Birmingham AL 35294

EMERSON, HORACE MANN, III, former r.r. exec.; b. Wilmington, N.C., Jan. 22, 1914; s. Horace Mann and Laura Placida (Clark) E.; student pub. and pvt. schs., Sumter, Columbia, S.C.; m. Susan LeRoy Carr, June 1, 1943; children—Susan C. (Mrs. Nicholas H. Bancks), Laura C. Clk., A.C.L. R.R., Wilmington, N.C., 1934-47, gen. agt., Jacksonville, Fla., 1947-51, asst. gen. freight agt., Wilmington, N.C., 1952-57, asst. treas., 1957-58, treas., Wilmington and Jacksonville, 1958-61, asst. v.p. traffic, 1961-67; sr. asst. v.p. traffic Seaboard Coast Line R.R. Co., Jacksonville, 1967-68, v.p. freight traffic, 1968-73; sr. v.p. traffic S.C.L. Industries, 1973-76, ret.; sr. v.p., dir. S.C.L. R.R., Louisville & Nashville R.R.; chief traffic officer Ga. R.R., A.&W.P. R.R., W. Ry. of A., C.C.&O. R.R., 1973-76, ret., 1976; dir. Central R.R. Co. S.C., Columbia, Newberry & Laurens R.R., Seacoast Transp. Co., S.C. Pacific Ry. Co. Served to capt. U.S. Army, 1943-46, 51-52. Mem. Assn. ICC Practitioners, Nat. Freight Traffic Assn., Fla. Traffic Assn., N.Y. Traffic Club, Jacksonville Area C. of C. Democrat. Episcopalian (mem. vestry 1970-73). Clubs: Timuquana Country, River, University, Meninak, Ponte Vedra (Jacksonville, Fla.). Home: 2970 St Johns Ave Jacksonville FL 32205

EMERSON, K(ARY) C(ADMUS), sci. cons.; b. Sasakwa, Okla., Mar. 13, 1918; s. Earle Evans and Diva Elisabeth (Wilkins) E.; B.S., Okla. State U., 1939, M.S., 1940, Ph.D., 1949; m. Mary Rebecca Williams, Aug. 13, 1939; children—William K., James B., Robert E. Commd. officer U.S. Army, 1940, advanced through grades to col.; ret. from active duty, 1966; asst. prof. Okla. State U., 1946-49, adj. prof., 1971—; staff Armistice Commn., Korea, 1958-59; tech. liaison Office Chief R & D, Army Dept., Washington, 1959-60; asst. for research Office Sec. Army, Washington, 1961-79, acting dep. asst. sec. army, 1973-75, acting asst. sec. army, 1975-79, dep. for sci. and tech., 1976; mem. Army Sci. Bd., 1978—. Research asso. Smithsonian Instn., 1960-79; collaborator U.S. Dept. Agr., 1959—; instr. Far East br. U. Md., 1959; mem. Def. Com. on Research, 1967—, U.S. Panel Systematics and Taxonomy, 1968—, NATO Panel I Long-term Studies, 1970—. Decorated Legion of Merit, Bronze Star, Purple Heart; recipient Exceptional Civilian Service award Army; Outstanding Civilian Service award Dept. Def. Fellow Entomol. Soc. Am., Washington Acad. Sci., Explorers Club; mem. Biol. Soc. Washington (exec. bd. 1969—), Soc. Tropical Medicine and Hygiene, Soc. Systematic Zoology, Wildlife Disease Assn., Entomol. Soc. Washington, A.A.A.S., Sigma Xi, Alpha Zeta, Phi Sigma. Club: Cosmos (Washington). Author or co-author numerous books; mem. editorial bd. 2 sci. jours.; contbr. articles to profl. jours. Home: 560 Boulder Dr Sanibel FL 33957

EMERSON, O.D., accountant; b. Hillsboro, Tex., June 25, 1909; s. Ollie D. and Sudie (Johnson) E.; B.B.A., Baylor U., 1932; spl. courses LaSalle U., N.Y. U.; m. Myrtle Mae Hennigan, Feb. 17, 1933; 1 son Philip Edward. Disbursing officer Tex. Relief Commn., 1933-36; agt. U.S. Bur. Internal Revenue, 1936-45; pub. accounting O.D. Emerson, Jr., C.P.A., Hattiesburg and McComb, Miss., 1945-61, Emerson & Emerson, C.P.A.'s, Hattiesburg, Columbia and McComb, Miss., 1961—; sec., treas. Pearl River Land Co.; dir. S. Miss. Oil Corp. Meridian Vendors, Inc. Former lectr. accounting U. So. Miss. Trustee St. Bernard Hosp. Mem. Am. Inst. Accountants, Tex., Miss. socs. C.P.A.'s. Methodist. Clubs: Metropolitan, Masons. Home: Route 3 Box 124 Sumrail MS 39482 Office: 610 W Pine St Hattiesburg MS 39401

EMERSON, ROBERT BISCAL, chemist, physicist; b. Nashville, Mar. 17, 1909; s. Winiford Frank and Roberta (Griffith) E.; M.S., La. State U., 1950; grad. Army Command and Gen. Staff Coll., 1948; D.D.; m. Opal Lynelle Duke, Nov. 3, 1934; children—Robert B., Jin. Commd. 2d lt. U.S. Army, 1935, advanced through grades to col., 1952; mem. Spearhead Planning Staff, 1944, top secret control officer, 1944-46, G-4 Base sect., ETO, 1944-46, dir. command and gen. staff dept. U.S. Army Res. Sch., 1951-57, instr. or dir. for command and gen. staff subjects, Ft. Sill, Okla., 1953-57, Ft. Sam Houston, Tex., 1957, comdg. officer 4225 Logistical Command (C), 1957-62; ret., 1962; asst. to forensic chemist State of Fla., Tampa, 1926; control chemist Victor Chem. Works, Nashville, 1927; chief chemist Fla. Match Co., St. Petersburg, 1928-29; owner Emerson Testing Labs., St. Petersburg, 1930-38; forensic chemist State of Fla., St. Petersburg, 1930-36; asso. chemist Gable Clin. Labs., St. Petersburg, 1930-38, Hurst Labs., St. Petersburg, 1936-38; owner Emerson Testing Labs., Baton Rouge, 1948—; now researcher parapsychology and biophysics. physics instr. La. State U., 1948-53; sr. research chemist, staff research asso. Chem. Aluminas, Kaiser Chems., Baton Rouge, 1953-74. Decorated Legion of Merit, Bronze Star medal. Mem. Am. Phys. Soc., Am. Chem. Soc., Nat. Geog. Soc., Fla. Soc. Med. Technicians, TAPPI, AAAS, Inst. Fundamental Studies Assn., Internat. Platform Assn., Center Integrative Edn., So. Rubber Group, Catalysis Soc., Mil. Order of World Wars, Am. Theosophical Soc., Inst. Psychorientology, Inst. Noetic Scis., Am. Bicentennial Research Inst., Nat. Ret. Tchrs. Assn., Am. Parapsychology Research Found., Acad. Parapsychology and Medicine, La., Am. socs. psychical research, Fla., Toronto socs. for psychical research, Human Dimensions Inst., Lindisfarne Assn., Humanity Found., Spiritual Frontiers Fellowship, Inst. for Humanistic and Transpersonal Edn., Holistic Health Assn., Army Transport Soc., Nat. Assn. Uniformed Services, Nat. Investigations Com. Aerial Phenomena, Internat. Imagery Assn., Monroe Inst. Applied Scis., New Horizons Research Found., Rosicrucians, Phi Eta Sigma, Phi Lambda Upsilon, Phi Kappa Phi, Sigma Pi Sigma. Patentee in field. Home: 1560 Stephens Ave Baton Rouge LA 70808 Office: 1560 Stephens Ave Baton Rouge LA 70808

EMERSON, ROBERT WINCHESTER, radio sta. exec.; b. Jackson, Tenn., Aug. 24, 1922; s. Robert Wesley and Mary Margaret (Withers) E.; B.A., U. of South, 1943; postgrad. Northwestern U., 1946; m. Blanche Stuart Somervill, Oct. 29, 1960; children—Maude Caroline, Robert Winchester. Copy chief Radio Sta. WTJS, Jackson, Tenn., 1946, sales mgr. WTJS AM-FM, 1970, v.p. WTJS and WKIR-FM, 1973—, dir., 1975—. Founder, Jackson Recreation Center, 1953, bd. dirs., 1953-71, chmn. bd., 1963-65; founder Episcopal Day Sch., Jackson, 1970, bd. dirs., 1970—. Served with AUS, 1942-46; Tenn. N.G., 1953-66, U.S. Army Res., 1966-71. Named Jackson's First Veteran of Year, VFW, 1965. Mem. Nat., Tenn. assns. broadcasters, VFW, Am. Legion, Res. Officers Assn. U.S., Alpha Tau Omega. Episcopalian. Clubs: Rotary, Jackson Golf and Country, Isle Dauphine Country. Home: 15 Oakmont Pl Jackson TN 38301 Office: 122 Radio Rd Jackson TN 38301

EMERSON, WALTER CARUTH, artist, educator; b. Dallas, Jan. 24, 1912; s. Walter Caruth and Ruby Dale (Chisholm) E.; B.A., So. Methodist U., 1941; student Southwestern Sch. Theatre, 1934-35; student of John Knott, 1932-33, Olin Travis, 1926-27; m. Mary Elizabeth Hicks, July 15, 1961; children—Mary Jane, William Ross. Art dir. Pollock Paper Corp., Dallas, 1937-52; creator, instr. courses in art and art history So. Meth. U., Dallas, 1940-63; producer Pencil Personalities, Sta. WFAA-TV, Dallas, 1958; art dir. Food and Drug div. Hunt Oil Co., Dallas, 1963-69; instr. art and art history Christian Coll. S.W., Dallas, 1969-70, Dallas Community Coll. Dist., 1972-74; founder, dir. Art Acad. Dallas, 1974—; lectr. throughout U.S. on art and art history, 1977—; editorial cartoonist Dallas Morning News, 1941, N.Y. Mirror, 1956-58; represented in permanent collection Tex. State Mus. Founder Americans Unified, 1979. Served with USN, 1941-45. Recipient best in class award Cherokee Nat. Mus., 1976. Mem. Better Bus. Bur. Dallas, New Eng. Historic Geneal. Soc. Republican. Club: Dallas Knife and Fork (past pres.), Park Cities Rotary (past pres.), Dallas County Council Rotary Pres.'s (past pres.). Author: The Truth about Santa Anna, 1973; author, illustrator Art Alive, internat. syndicated feature column, 1979—. Home: 3637 Haynie Ave Dallas TX 75205 Office: 3400 University Blvd Dallas TX 75205

EMERT, GEORGE HENRY, chemist; b. Sevier County, Tenn., Dec. 15, 1938; s. Victor K. and Hazel E.; B.A., U. Colo., 1962; M.S.; Colo. State U., 1970; Ph.D., Va. Poly. Inst. and State U., 1973; m. Billie Bush, June 10, 1967; 4 daus. Research technician U. Colo. Med. Sch., 1961-63; researcher Stanford U. Marine Research Sta., 1966; microbiologist Colo. Dept. Public Health Labs., 1967-69; research fellow Va. Poly. Inst. and State U., Blacksburg, 1970-73, NDEA fellow, 1971-72; research asso. dept. chemistry U. Colo., 1973-74; sr. applications biochemist Gulf Oil Corp., Merriam, Kans., 1974-75, supr. biochem. tech., 1975-77, dir. biochem. tech., 1977-79; adj. asst. prof. microbiology U. Kans., 1977-79; dir. biomass research center U. Ark., Fayetteville, 1979—. Served with Spl. Forces, U.S. Army, 1963-66. Mem. Am. Chem. Soc., Soc. Complex Carbohydrates, Am. Inst. Chem. Engrs., Soc. Indsl. Microbiology, Audubon Soc., Sigma Xi, Phi Lambda Upsilon. Home: 2451 Elaine St Fayetteville AR 72701 Office: 415 Adminstrn Bldg U Ark Fayetteville AR 72701

EMERY, EDGAR MILTON, chemist; b. River Rouge, Mich., Mar. 7, 1928; s. Edgar Joseph and Isabel (Picard) E.; B.S., U. Mich., 1951; M.S., Seton Hall U., 1963; children—Donna Jean, Richard Charles. Paint chemist Hock Paint and Chem. Co., Phoenixville, Pa., 1951-52; analytical chemist Allied Chem. Co., Frankfort, Pa., 1952-53, mass spectrometrist, Glenolden, Pa., 1953-56; research chemist, then sr. research chemist Colgate—Palmolive Co., Jersey City and Piscataway, N.J., 1956-77; sr. analytical chemist Pullman Kellogg Co., Houston, 1977—. Mem. Am. Chem. Soc., Am. Soc. for Mass Spectrometry (dir. 1974-76), Am. Oil Chemists Soc., Applied Spectroscopy Soc., Quantum Chemistry Program Exchange, ASTM (chmn. mass spectrometry com. 1974-76), AAAS. Contbr. articles to profl. jours. Home: 6623 Vialinda Dr Houston TX 77083 Office: 16200 Park Row Houston TX 77084

EMERY, LEON, pastor, religious assn. exec.; b. Tigerville, S.C., Aug. 20, 1919; s. John Perry and Minnie Delia (Lindsey) E.; A.A., North Greenville Jr. Coll., 1951-54; B.A., Miss. Coll., 1956; student New Orleans Bapt. Theol. Sem., 1959; m. Jessie Mae Plumley, Apr. 11, 1941; children—Sharon Emery Hardin, Ronald Leon. Ordained to ministry Baptist Ch., 1950; supt. missions Washington Bapt. Assn., Greenville, Miss., 1962-63; asso. sec., coop. missions dept. Miss. Bapt. Conv. Bd., Jackson, 1963-74, ch. adminstrn. cons., 1974-76, dir. ch. adminstrn., pastoral ministries dept., 1977—. Served with inf. U.S. Army, 1942-45. Decorated Bronze Star. Mem. Miss. Assn. Children Under Six, So. Assn. Children Under Six, So. Bapt. Research Fellowship, Miss. Bapt. Religious Edn. Assn. Club: Crosswind Flying. Home: 1060 Fairway St Jackson MS 39212 Office: Miss Bapt Conv 515 Mississippi St PO Box 530 Jackson MS 39205

EMERY, RICHARD RAY, educator; b. Poplar Bluff, Mo., July 20, 1933; s. Clyde Ray and Ethel Irene (Wagster) E.; Mus.B., B. Mus. Edn., Bethany Coll., 1960; M. Mus. Edn., Wichita State U., 1965; postgrad U. Mo., Kansas City, 1969-71, Luther Rice Sem., Jacksonville, Fla.; m. Marilyn Kay Janssen, Aug. 26, 1956; children—Jeffrey, Kristin, Kerry. Tchr., Marysville (Kans.) High Sch., 1960-62, Greensburg (Kans.) High Sch., 1962-64; instr. Union U., Jackson, Tenn., 1965-69; asst. prof. music U. Ark., Little Rock, 1970-74; asso. prof. John Brown U., Siloam Springs, Ark., 1974—, chmn. dept. music, 1974-80; cons. on ch. music. Bd. dirs. Pulaski Acad., Little Rock, 1973-74, United Fund, 1972-74. Served with USCG, 1951-54. Mem. Internat. Music Honor Soc., Am. Choral Dirs. Assn. (life), Nat. Assn. Schs. Music, So. Bapt. Ch. Music Conf., Nat. Assn. Tchrs. Singing, Am. Choral Found., Hymn Soc. Am., Nat. Ch. Music Fellowship, Ark. Choral Dirs. Assn., Music Educators Nat. Conf., Phi Mu Alpha (life). Home: Lake Forest Heights Rt 2 Siloma Springs AR 72761 Office: John Brown U Box 2053 Siloam Springs AR 72761

EMILY, JAMES LEE, plastic engr.; b. Henderson, Ky., Apr. 12, 1913; s. Robert L. and Birdie Jane (Jenkins) E.; student U. Ky., 1931-32; m. Geneva Hargis, Oct. 7, 1939 (div. 1964); children—Michael, Robert, James, Raymond; m. 2d, Martha Elizabeth Peele, May 23, 1965. Operator, mfg. foreman Tri State Plastics, Henderson, 1947-52; mfg. foreman, maintenance supr. Kusan Inc., Nashville, 1952-57; dept. head, engr. Gen. Time, Athens, Ga., 1957-69; plastic molding engr. Square D Co., Asheville, N.C., 1971—. Served with U.S. Army, 1935-36. Mem. Soc. Plastics Engrs. Democrat. Home: 21 Maplewood Rd Asheville NC 28804 Office: Square D Co Asheville NC 28802

EMMETT, JOHN ROY, otologist; b. West Palm Beach, Fla., Mar. 29, 1943; s. Roy C. and Katrine D. Emmett; B.S. in Applied Biology, Ga. Inst. Tech., 1965; M.S. in Physiology and Biochemistry, Baylor U., 1968; M.D., George Washington U., 1970; 1 dau., Kathleen Brooks. Intern in surgery, then asst. resident in gen. surgery Duke U. Med. Center, 1970-72; sr. asst. resident, then resident in otolaryngology U. N.C. Hosp., Chapel Hill, 1972-76; practice medicine specializing in otolaryngology, Memphis, 1976—; mem. staff Memphis Eye and Ear Hosp., 1976—, pres., chief staff, 1978—; mem. staff VA Hosp., Memphis, 1977—, Shea Clinic, Memphis, 1976—; instr. U. N.C. Med. Sch., 1976—; clin. asst. prof. U. Tenn. Med. Sch., 1976—. Teaching fellow Baylor U., 1965-66; Anson A. Biglow scholar, 1967, Health Profession scholar, 1967; recipient Alexander A. Horwitz Surgery award George Washington U. Med. Sch., 1970, Hoffman-LaRoche award, 1970; diplomate Am. Bd. Otolaryngology. Mem. Am. Audiology Soc., Assn. Am. Physicians and Surgeons, Am. Acad. Ophthalmology and Otolaryngology, Am. Council Otolaryngology, Nat. Hearing Assn., Memphis Soc. Otolaryngology, Tenn. Acad. Otolaryngology, William Beaumont Research Soc., Politzer Soc., Sentac. Author numerous papers in field. Home: 768 Eventide Dr Germantown TN 38138 Office: 1080 Madison Ave Memphis TN 38104

EMMETT, ROY RAY, advt. co. exec., publisher; b. Phila., May 7, 1943; s. Frederic H. and Janet (Hagerich) E.; B. Design, U. Fla., 1965; m. Patricia Ann Miller, Apr. 15, 1978; 1 son, Jason Allen. Art dir. Ross Hancock Advt. Agy., Miami, 1969-70; owner/designer Roy Emmett Design Studio, Inc., Miami, 1971-74; v.p./designer Beeper Ads Inc., Miami, 1974-77, owner, pres., 1977—; pub. Telecourier mag., Miami Shores, Fla., 1978—; advt., mktg. cons. to radio common carrier industry. Served with Signal Corps, U.S. Army, 1966-68. Mem. Telocator Network Am. of Assn. Radio Common Carrier Cos. (asso.), Can. Radio Common Carrier Assn. (asso.), Radio Common Carrier Mfrs. and Exhibitors Assn. (chmn. 1978—). Republican. Presbyterian. Home: 1260 NE 132d St N Miami FL 33161 Office: Beeper Ads Inc 9822 NE 2d Ave Miami Shores FL 33138

EMMETT, WALTER CHARLES, bus. brokerage firm exec.; b. Lawrence, Mass., July 6, 1925; s. Walter Thornton and Agnes Owens E.; student Dartmouth Coll., 1942-43, 46-47; m. Laurel Stinnett Emmett, Nov. 21, 1975; children—Jeffrey, Nancy, Scott; stepchildren—Wayne, Victoria Dammier. Owner, pres. Emmett Bus. Brokers, Inc., Amarillo, Tex., 1978—; owner Your Graphics Are Showing, Amarillo, 1977-79; salesman Ada Realtors, Amarillo, 1976-78; salesman Stevenson Motor, 1969-74, Russell Buick, 1974-76. Bd. dirs. Maverick Boys Club. Served with A.C., USN, 1943-46. Mem. Nat. Assn. Realtors, Nat. Panel Consumer Arbitrators, Inst. Cert. Bus. Counselors, Center Entrepreneurial Mgmt., Tex. Assn. Realtors, Amarillo Bd. Realtors. Episcopalian. Clubs: Downtown Kiwanis (bd. dirs. 1979-80). Home: 2611 Henning St Amarillo TX 79106 Office: 1616 S Kentucky St B-101 Amarillo TX 79102

EMORY, SAMUEL THOMAS, geographer, educator; b. Durham, N.C., June 22, 1933; s. Samuel Thomas and Mary (Dortch) E.; A.B., U. N.C., 1954, M.A., 1959; Ph.D., U. Md., 1964; m. Sylvia Greer Callaway, July 12, 1958; children—Samuel Thomas III, Greer Callaway. Instr. geography Mary Washington Coll., Fredericksburg, Va., 1959-60, asst. prof., 1960-65, asso. prof., 1965-68, chmn. dept. geography, 1960-79, prof., 1968—; adj. faculty Va. Commonwealth U., Richmond, 1960—, U. Richmond, 1965—, Command and Staff Coll., U.S. Marine Corps, Quantico, Va., 1975—. Chmn., City of Fredericksburg Planning Commn., 1960-75; presdl. elector, 1968; chmn. Fredericksburg Republican party City Com., 1965-77, chmn. 28th Senatorial Dist. Com., 1978—; chmn. Fredericksburg Downtown Design Com., 1978—; bd. dirs. Planning Dist. 16, 1978. Mem. Assn. Am. Geographers (treas. div. 1978—), Am. Geog. Soc., Va. Geog. Soc. Sigma Xi. Republican. Episcopalian. Clubs: Fredericksburg Country; Skytop (Pa.). Editor Va. Geographer, 1965-75. Home: 608 Hawke St Fredericksburg VA 22401

EMSWILER, JOSEPH MICHAEL, constrn. co. ofcl.; b. Balt., May 4, 1947; s. Maurice Eugene and Marie Elizabeth (Semon) E.; B.S. in Acctg., Villanova U., 1969; M.B.A., La. State U., 1979; m. Mindy Ester Valenzuela, June 30, 1970; children—William Joseph, Mindy Lynne, David James, Michael Justin. Acct. George Hyman Constrn. Co., Inc., Bethesda, Md., 1971-73; treas., controller Demory Bros., Inc., Rockville, Md., 1973-75; controller Crest, Inc., Beaumont, Tex., 1975-77; treasury mgr. Nichols Constrn. Corp., Baton Rouge, 1977—; pres. Acctg. Corp. Am. Served with inf., AUS, 1969-71; Vietnam. Decorated Air medal. Mem. Am. Mgmt. Assn., Assn. M.B.A.'s. Roman Catholic. Home: PO Box 261 Baton Rouge LA 70821 Office: PO Box 2750 Baton Rouge LA 70821

ENDICOTT, JAMES NESBIT, otolaryngologist; b. Princeton, Ind., Feb. 10, 1941; s. James N. and Marie (C.) E.; A.B., Wabash Coll., 1963; M.D., Ind. U., 1967. Intern, Tampa (Fla.) Gen. Hosp., 1967-68, resident in gen. surgery, 1968-69; resident in otolaryngology U. South Fla. Coll. Medicine, Tampa, 1969-72; practice medicine specializing in otolaryngology, Tampa, 1975—; asst. prof. otolaryngology Hahnemann Med. Sch. Hosp., Phila., 1973-75; asso. prof. surgery, chief head and neck service, and div. otolaryngology U. South Fla. Coll. Medicine, Tampa, 1975—; instr. Hillsborough Community Coll.; mem. staff Tampa Gen. Hosp.; mem. otolaryngology staff Naval Hosp., Phila., 1972-75. Served to lt. comdr. USN, 1972-75. Diplomate Am. Bd. Otolaryngology. Fellow A.C.S., Am. Acad. Ophthalmology and Otolaryngology; mem. AMA, Am. Council Otolaryngology, Am. Acad. Facial Reconstructive Surgery, Soc. Univ. Otolaryngologists, Hilsborough County Med. Assn. (mem. welfare com. 1977), Fla. Soc. Otolaryngology. Office: 13000 N 30th St Tampa FL 33612

ENDO, AKIRA, condr.; b. Shido, Japan; s. Hikotaro and Reiko (Tezuka) E.; came to U.S., 1954, naturalized, 1964; B.Music, U. So. Calif., 1962, M.Music, 1964; m. Susan Jane Ward, Sept. 7, 1962; children—Stephanie Tamiko, Gregory Tadashi, Julie Kimiko. Music dir. Long Beach (Calif.) Symphony, 1966-68; music dir., prin. condr. Am. Ballet Theatre, 1969-78; resident condr. Houston Symphony, 1974-75; music dir. Austin (Tex.) Symphony, 1975—; condr. for Nat. Edn. Network for Dance in Am. series; recs. for Crystal Records. Winner Dimitri Mitropoulos Internat. Competition for Condrs., 1968, 69. Home: 8853 Mountain Ridge Circle Austin TX 78759 Office: 1101 Red River Austin TX 78701

ENDRESS, WILLIAM JOSEPH, mobile home park exec.; b. Evansville, Ind., May 5, 1942; s. William Joseph and Margaret (Clevelin) E.; student U. So. Miss., 1961-63; A.A., U. Evansville, 1968, B.F.A., 1970; m. Janie Rose, Feb. 2, 1963; children—William Joseph III, Jill Rose. Artist, Whirlpool Corp., Evansville, 1963-66; comml. artist Keller Crescent, Evansville, 1968, Creative Press, Inc., also account exec., 1969-73; pres., owner Lazy Days Mobile Village, Inc., also owner Sun-Up-South Corp., Ft. Myers, Fla., 1973—; mem. Fla.-Lee County Constrn. and Lic. Bd., 1976-78; bd. dirs. Ft. Myers Mobile Home Adv. Bd., 1975—. Recipient Disting. Salesman award So. Ind. Sales and Mktg. Execs., 1973. Mem. S.W. Fla. Mobile Home Assn. (pres. 1976-78), Fla. Mobile Home Assn. (dir. 1976-78), Lee County C. of C., U. Evansville Alumni Assn., Better Bus. Bur., Alpha Tau Omega. Roman Catholic. Clubs: Ft. Myers Rod and Gun, N. Ft. Myers Rotary (dir. 1977-30). Home: 1267 Osceola Dr Fort Myers FL 33901 Office: 2524 N Tamiami Trail North Fort Myers FL 33903

ENFIELD, KURT FERDINAND, bus. machine co. exec.; b. Frankfurt, Germany, July 23, 1921; s. Henry and Alice (Bluethental) E.; came to U.S., 1939, naturalized, 1944; grad. Buxton Coll. Eng., 1937; m. Dorothy Was, Sept. 9, 1977; children from previous marriage—Gwen, Jill, Richard. Partner, Enfield's Camera Shop, Miami Beach, Fla., 1939-53; pres. Enfield's Bus. Products Co., Miami, 1955—. Treas. Temple Israel, Miami. Served with AUS, 1944-46.

Decorated Bronze Star. Mem. Miami Beach C. of C., Bus. Products Council Assn. (pres. 1972-73), Nat. Microfilm Assn., Internat. Word Processing Assn. Democrat. Jewish. Clubs: Bayshore Service, Tiger Bay Polit., Standard, Jockey, B'nai B'rith. Home: 3301 5th Ave NW Apt 1010 Miami FL 33137 Office: 4000 NW 30th Ave Miami FL 33142

ENGE, ERIC FRANK, chem. mfg. co. exec.; b. Drexel Hill, Pa., Apr. 4, 1949; s. Frank and Phyllis (Black) E.; B.A., Muhlenberg Coll., 1971; M.B.A., Lehigh U., 1972; m. Cheryl Dee Dunlop, July 24, 1971; children—Scott Daniel, Brett Alan. Fin. analyst Rohm and Haas Co., Phila., 1972-73, plant controller, Rohm and Haas Calif. Inc., Hayward, 1973-76, mgr. fin. and acctg. Rohm and Haas Tenn. Inc., Knoxville, 1976—. Advisor, Knoxville Jr. Achievement, 1976-78; loaned exec. United Way Knoxville, 1978-79; pres. Gulfwood Recreation Assn., 1978-79. Mem. Nat. Assn. Accountants, Gulfwood Mixed Bowling League (v.p. 1977-79). Office: Rohm and Haas Tenn Inc 730 Dale Ave Knoxville TN 37921

ENGEL, WALBURGA VON RAFFLER (MRS. A. FERDINAND ENGEL), linguist; b. Munich, Germany, Sept. 25, 1920; d. Friedrich J. and Gertrud (Kiefer) von Raffler; D.Litt., U. Turin (Italy), 1947; M.S., Columbia, 1951; Ph.D., Ind. U., 1953; came to U.S., 1949, naturalized, 1955; m. A. Ferdinand Engel, June 2, 1957; children—Lea Maxine, Eric Robert von Raffler. Faculty, Bennett Coll., Greensboro, N.C., 1953-55, Morris Harvey Coll., Charleston, W.Va., 1955-57, City Coll. of City U. N.Y., Adelphi U., 1957-58, N.Y. U., 1957-59, U. Florence (Italy), 1959-60, Istituto Post Universitario Organizzazione Aziendale, Italy, 1960-61, Bologna Center of Johns Hopkins U., 1964; faculty Vanderbilt U., Nashville, 1965—, asso. prof. linguistics, 1966-77, prof., 1977—, chmn. com. on linguistics Nashville Univ. Center, 1974-79; vis. prof. U. Ottawa, 1971-72, Inst. for Lang. Scis., Tokyo, 1976; grant evaluator NSF and Can. Council. Free lance journalist, 1949-58. Mem. AAUP, AAAS, Internat. Linguists Assn. (chmn. nominating com.), Linguistic Soc. Am. (anniversary film com.), Internat. Assn. Applied Linguistics (research com. on discourse analysis), Internat. Sociol. Assn. (research com. on sociolinguistics), Societas Linguistica Europea, Inst. Nonverbal Communication Research, Internat. Assn. Study of Child Lang. (v.p. 1975-78). Author: Il Prelinguaggio Infantile, 1964; Language Intervention Programs, 1975; (color film) Children's Acquistion of Kinesis. Editor: Child Language, 1975—; co-editor: Baby Talk and Infant Speech, 1976, Views of Language, 1975, Aspects of Non-verbal Communication, 1977, 80; Language Acquisition and Developmental Kinesis, 1978; guest editor Word, Internat. Jour. Sociology of Lang.; adv. bd. Jour. Child Lang. Contbr. articles to profl. publs. Home: 372 Elmington Ave Nashville TN 37205

ENGELHART, ISABEL KINCHELOE, writer, ednl. cons.; b. Chgo., Oct. 10, 1904; d. William Wing and Sarah Anne (MacLean) Kincheloe; Ph.B., U. Chgo., 1925, A.M., 1936, postgrad., 1941-53; m. Max Dissette Engelhart, Apr. 21, 1956. Tchr. English, Chgo. Pub. Schs., 1928-41, 48-53, cons. bur. curriculum, 1941-49, prin. James Madison and Bryn Mawr elementary schs., 1956-62, South Shore High Sch., 1962-66; tchr. English, Chgo. Tchrs. Coll., 1953-56; lectr. U. Chgo., 1949, 51, U. Wis., Madison, 1950, 52, Northwestern U., Evanston, Ill., 1951-52; cons. in field. Ford Found. fellow, 1953. Mem. N.C. Lit. and Hist. Soc., Chgo. Prins. Assn., Nat. Council Tchrs. English, Campus Club Duke U., Delta Kappa Gamma. Methodist. Author: (with Harry Paul) English—Books I-IV, 1948, Junior English, 1951; (with Harold Anderson) Advanced Reading Skill Builders, 1956; (with Eva Pumphrey) Adventures for You, 1962, Adventures Ahead, 1962, 68; (with Lester Cook) Adventures in Values, 1969; Reading Tests, 1969. Home: 2419 Perkins Rd Durham NC 27706

ENGERRAND, DORIS DIESKOW, educator; b. Chgo., Aug. 7, 1925; d. William Jacob and Alma Wilhelmina (Cords) D.; B.S. in Bus. Adminstrn., N. Ga. Coll., 1958, B.S. in Elementary Edn., 1959; M. Bus. Edn., Ga. State U., 1966, Ph.D., 1970; m. Gabriel H. Engerrand, Oct. 26, 1946; children—Steven, Kenneth, Jeannine. Tchr., dept. chmn. Lumpkin County High Sch., Dahlonega, Ga., 1960-63, 65-68; tchr., Gainesville, Ga., 1965; asst. prof. Troy (Ala.) State U., 1969-71; asst. prof. bus. Ga. Coll., Milledgeville, 1971-74, asso. prof., 1974-78, prof., 1978—, chairperson dept. bus. edn. and office adminstrn., 1978—. Named Outstanding Tchr. Lumpkin County Pub. Schs., 1963, 66, Outstanding Educator bus. faculty Ga. Coll., 1975. Mem. Am. Bus. Communication Assn. (nat. dir., v.p. SE region), Internat. Communication Assn., Soc. Tech. Communication, NEA, Ga. Assn. Educators, Acad. Mgmt., So. Mgmt. Assn., Nat., Ga. (v.p.) bus. edn. assns., Am., Ga. vocat. assns., Nat. Secs. Assn., Ninety-nines Internat. (chmn. N. Ga. chpt. 1975-76, named Pilot of Year N. Ga. chpt. 1973). Methodist. Contbr. articles on bus. edn. to profl. publs. Home: 1674 Pine Valley Rd Milledgeville GA 31061 Office: Ga Coll Milledgeville GA 31061

ENGLAND, ARTHUR JAY, JR., state chief justice; b. Dayton, Ohio, Dec. 23, 1932; s. Arthur Jay and Elsbeth (Weiskopf) E.; B.S., U. Pa., 1955, LL.B. magna cum laude, 1961; LL.M. in Taxation, U. Miami (Fla.), 1971; m. Morley Tenenbom, June 24, 1959; children—Andrea, Pamela, Ellen, Karen. Admitted to N.Y. bar, 1961, Fla. bar, 1961; asso. firm Dewey, Ballantine, Bushby, Palmer & Wood, N.Y.C., 1961-64; partner firm Culverhouse, Tomlinson, Taylor & DeCarion, Miami, 1964-69, Scott McCarthy Steel Hector & Davis, Miami, 1969-70, Paul & Thomson, Miami, 1973-74; spl. tax counsel Fla. Ho. Reps., 1971-72; consumer adv., spl. counsel to gov. Fla., 1972-73; justice Supreme Ct. Fla., 1975—, chief justice, 1978—; dep. chmn. Conf. Chief Justices; chmn. council state ct. reps. to Nat. Center for State Cts. Served with AUS, 1955-57. Mem. Am. Law Inst., Conf. Chief Justices (dep. chmn. 1979-80), Order of Coif, Beta Gamma Sigma. Jewish. Author reports, articles in field. Home: 1002 Kenilworth Rd Tallahassee FL 32312 Office: Supreme Ct Fla Tallahassee FL 32304

ENGLAND, CAROL JOYCE, speech pathologist, educator; b. Houston, Sept. 7, 1948; d. Vernie Lee and Barbara Joyce Farris; B.A., Sam Houston State U., 1973; M.A., U. Houston, 1976; m. William Olin England, Feb. 14, 1974. Speech pathologist Dyer Vocat. Sch., pvt. instn. for retarded citizens, Leona, Tex., summer 1973, Aldine Sch. Dist., Houston, 1973-74, Lakeview Elem. Sch., Ft. Bend Ind. Sch. Dist., Stafford, Tex., 1974-77; resource and speech pathologist severely handicapped children M.R. Wood Campus, Ft. Bend Dist., 1977-79; remedial reading instr. Willowridge High Sch., 1979—; clinic supr. Sam Houston State U., 1979. Dir. children's Sunday sch. dept. Calvary Baptist Ch., Rosenberg, Tex., alt. ch. pianist. Cert. early childhood handicapped, severely profoundly handicapped, mental retardation, learning disabilities, profl. speech therapy Tex. Mem. Am. Speech and Hearing Assn. (cert. clin. competency), Council for Exceptional Children, Tex. State Tchrs. Assn., Tex. Speech and Hearing Assn., Houston Area Assn. for Communication Disorders (continuing edn. com.), Assn. for Retarded Citizens, Psi Chi. Republican. Baptist. Home: 2219 N Belmont St Richmond TX 77469 Office: 500 Dulles Ave Stafford TX 77477

ENGLAND, LONDON THURMAN, radio sales exec.; b. Winters, Tex., May 12, 1919; s. George Floy and Molly Maud (Moore) E.; grad. Tyler Comml. Coll., 1938; m. Mary Anna Seibel, Sept. 25, 1940; children—London Thurman, Judy. Engr., announcer KIUN Radio, Pecos, Tex., 1938-38, KLUF Radio, Galveston, Tex., 1938-41, KTRH Radio, Houston, 1941-52, Graybar Elec. Co., 1952-56; dist. mgr. radio and FM sales, broadcast products div. Harris Corp., Houston, 1956—. Served with USNR, 1944-46; PTO. Mem. IEEE, Soc. Broadcast Engrs., Tex., La. assns. broadcasters. Club: Long Meadows Country (Houston). Home: 5210 Kinglet St Houston TX 77035 Office: 7000 Regency Sq Houston TX 77036

ENGLAND, LYNNE LIPTON, speech pathologist; b. Youngstown, Ohio, Apr. 11, 1949; d. Sanford Yale and Sally Lipton; B.A. cum laude, U. Mich., 1970; M.A., Temple U., 1972; postgrad., Tulane U., 1978—; m. Richard E. England, Mar. 5, 1977. Sr. speech therapist Rockland Children's Hosp., Orangeburg, N.Y., 1972-74; clin. audiologist Rehab. Inst. Chgo., 1974-76; childhood aphasia therapist Jefferson Parish Sch. System, Gretna, La., 1977-78; pvt. practice speech pathology, New Orleans, 1973—. Mem. Am. Speech and Hearing Assn., Am. Congress Physical Medicine and Rehab., Tulane U. Student Bar Assn., Tulane Law Women's Assn., Phi Delta Phi. Jewish. Home: 7927 Birch St New Orleans LA 70118

ENGLAND, MARTHA JEAN GOULD, educator; b. Fayetteville, Ark., May 13, 1938; d. Walter Earl and Jimmie Opal (Bryant) Gould; B.S. in Edn., U. Ark., 1960; M.Ed., Tex. Woman's U., 1979; m. John Rogers England, Apr. 12, 1963; children—Mary Rebecca, Anderson Allen. Tchr. pub. schs., Dallas, 1960-65, Carrollton, Tex., 1975-77; tchr. Woodlake Elementary Sch., Carrollton, Tex., 1977—. Mem. Am. Personnel and Guidance Assn., Internat. Reading Assn., NEA, Tex. State Tchrs. Assn., Peter's Colony Hist. Soc., A.W. Perry Homestead Mus. Soc., Phi Delta Kappa. Democrat. Home: 3132 Chestnut Rd Carrollton TX 75007

ENGLE, LARRY ALBERT, engring. co. exec.; b. Kansas City, Mo., Aug. 21, 1942; s. William Albert and Helen LaVerne (Weyenth) E.; student Kansas City Jr. Coll., 1960-61, U. Mo., 1961-64. With Western Electric, Kansas City, Mo., 1960-63; with Electro-Motive Div. Gen. Motors, Los Angeles, 1966-68; with Triangle Engring. Co., Houston, 1971—, corp. purchasing dir., 1979—. Mem. Nat. Assn. Purchasing Mgmt., Am. Mgmt. Assn. Office: 12300 Amelia Dr Houston TX 77045

ENGLISH, ARTHUR WILLIAM, anatomist, physiologist, educator; b. Port Hueneme, Calif., Oct. 20, 1945; s. Thomas E. and Mary Louise (Murphy) E.; B.S., U. Oreg., 1967; B.S. in Pharmacy, U. Ill., Chgo., 1970, Ph.D. in Anatomy, 1974; m. Sue Hutchinson, Mar. 23, 1970; children—Kelly Eileen, Colin Matthew. Teaching asst. Coll. Pharmacy, U. Ill., Chgo., 1968-69, dept. anatomy, 1970-74; research asst. dept. pathology Abraham Lincoln Coll. Medicine, 1969-71; instr. dept. anatomy Emory U., Atlanta, 1974, 76, asst. prof. anatomy and research asso. regional rehab. research and tng. center, 1976—; mem. com. for evolutionary biology and systematics Field Mus. Natural History, 1971-74. Grantee Nat. Inst. Arthritis Metabolism and Digestive Diseases, 1978—, Nat. Inst. Neurol. Communicative Disorders and Stroke, 1979—. Mem. Am. Assn. Anatomists, Am. Soc. Zoologists, Am. Soc. Mammalogists, AAAS, Sigma Xi, Rho Chi. Contbr. articles to profl. jours. Home: 2119 Desmond Dr Decatur GA 30033 Office: Dept Anatomy Emory U Atlanta GA 30322

ENGLISH, DAVID RICHARD, tng. specialist; b. Lansing, Mich., Sept. 30, 1950; s. George E. and Carolyn E. E.; B.A. with honors, U. Fla., 1972, M.Ed. in ednl. adminstrn., 1980. With Sunland Tng. Center Health and Rehab. Services, Orlando, Fla., 1975-76, Gainesville, Fla., 1976—, in-service coordinator, 1975-77, tng. specialist, 1977—; cons. mgmt./human relations tng. Mem. Am. Assn. Mental Deficiency, Am. Soc. Tng. and Devel., Council Exceptional Children, Assn. for Severely Handicapped, Delta Sigma Phi. Home: 2480 Forest Way Gainesville FL 32605 Office: PO Box 1150 Gainesville FL 32602

ENGLISH, EDWARD JOSEPH, security systems co. exec.; b. Bklyn., Aug. 23, 1947; s. Bernard Augustine and Mary Elizabeth (Lloyd) E.; B.B.A. in Acctg., St. Francis Coll., N.Y.C., 1968; M.B.A. in Acctg., Pace U., 1978; m. Linda Vasquez, Nov. 3, 1973. Sr. auditor Peat Marwick Mitchell & Co., N.Y.C., 1968-71; supr. internal audit Paine Webber Jackson & Curtiss Inc., N.Y.C., 1971-74; asst. comptroller N.Y. div. Inleasing Corp., Providence and N.Y.C., 1975; regional comptroller Am. Dist. Telegraph Corp., Alexandria, Va., 1975—; tax cons. Roman Catholic. Club: K.C. Home: 8130 Carrick Ln Springfield VA 22151 Office: Am Dist Telegraph Corp PO Box 4144 Alexandria VA 22303

ENGLISH, GLENN LEE, JR., congressman; b. Cordell, Okla., Nov. 30, 1940; s. Glenn and Marcella (Rainbolt) C.; B.A. in Gen. Bus., Accounting and Econs., Southwestern State Coll., 1964; m. Jan Pangle, 1970. Petroleum landman, Cordell, 1973-74; mem. 94th-96th congresses from Okla. 6th Dist., 1974—. Staff worker Calif. State Assembly, 1967-68, U.S. Ho. of Reps., 1965; exec. dir. Okla. Democratic Com., 1969-73; mem. Dem. Research Orgn. Mem. Congl. Rural Caucus. Home: Cordell OK Office: US Ho of Reps Washington DC 20515

ENGLISH, MARIE R., painter; b. Jefferson County, Ga., Oct. 28, 1910; d. John Frank and Mattie Bell (Black) Raley; B.S. in Natural Scis., Ga. State Coll. for Women, 1931; m. Robert Lamar English, July 13, 1932; children—William Franklin, Robert Lamar, Samuel Donald, Jack Raley. Tchr. Avera (Ga.) High Sch., 1931-33; tchr. Edgehill Jr. High Sch., Gibson, Ga., 1938-40, prin., 1950-52; prin. Grange Jr. High Sch., 1942-48; tchr. Gibson (Ga.) High Sch., 1948-49, Louisville (Ga.) Acad. Jr. High Sch., 1953-65; ret., 1965; painter oils, watercolors, pastels, acrylics, 1965—; founder Marie's Paintings, Louisville. Active campaign for Bill English elected Ga. State Senator, 21st Dist., 1976; tchr. adult Sunday Sch. class, organist Louisville Methodist Ch.; spl. mem. United Meth. Women. Mem. NEA, Ga. Ednl. Assn., Gertrude Art Assn., U.S. Artists Am., DAV, Boy's Ranch Sheriffs Assn., Ga. Vets. Assn. Club: Garden. Home and office: Route 1 Box 234 Louisville GA 30434

ENGLUND, GAGE BUSH, dancer, educator; b. Birmingham, Ala., Sept. 7, 1931; d. Morris Williams and Margaret Wallace (Gagé) Bush; student Sweet Briar Coll., (Ford Found. scholar) Sch. Am. Ballet, 1960; m. Richard Bernard Englund, Dec. 1, 1959; children—Alixandra, Rachel Rutherford. Founder Birmingham Civic Ballet, 1952; mem. Robert Joffrey Ballet, N.Y.C., 1957-60, soloist, 1959-60; mem. Am. Ballet Theatre, N.Y.C., 1960-63, Huntington Dance Ensemble, L.I., N.Y., 1968-69; soloist Dance Repertory Co., 1969-72; tchr. ballet, asso. chmn. Friends of Am. Ballet Theatre, N.Y.C., 1972—; mem. scholarship com. Am. Ballet Theatre Sch., N.Y.C., 1974—; dir. Ala. By-products Corp., 1971-77. Bd. dirs. Children's Hosp. Clinic, Birmingham, 1955-57, Ala. State Ballet, 1967—, Birmingham Civic Ballet, 1952-67, Spoleto Festival of Two Worlds, 1980—; trustee Ballet Theatre Found., 1974—, v.p. bd. trustees, 1980—. Recipient Silver Bowl award Birmingham Festival of Arts, 1955; named Queen of Birmingham Festival of Arts, 1957. Mem. Am. Guild Mus. Artists, Colonial Dames Ala., Jr. League N.Y.C. Episcopalian. Club: Lakewood Country. Home: PO Box 469 Point Clear AL 36564 Office: 322 W 78th St New York NY 10024

ENGMAN, ROBERT PAUL, chemist; b. Yankton, S.D., Jan. 7, 1951; s. Burdette Laverne and Ruth (Pollman) E.; B.A., U. Tex., Austin, 1973; m. Martha Sue Hale, May 28, 1977; 1 son, Christopher Robert. With Dow Badische Corp., Freeport, Tex., 1973—, prodn. chemist Caprolactan I, 1974-75, prodn. chemist Hydroxylamine II, 1975—. Mem. Phi Beta Kappa, Phi Kappa Phi, Psi Lambda Upsilon. Republican. Methodist. Home: 948 Mulberry St Brazoria TX 77422 Office: Dow Badische Corp 602 Copper Rd Freeport TX 77541

ENNIS, JOHN MATTHEWS, dermatologist; b. Huntsville, Ala., Aug. 19, 1936; s. Lawrence and Lucy Matthews (Mastin) E.; student Ga. Inst. Tech., 1954-56, Vanderbilt U., 1956-57; M.D., Med. Coll. Ala., 1961; m. Lorraine Gaston, June 9, 1961; children—Shelby Lorraine, Todd Mastin, Patrick Gaston, Lucy Matthews. Intern, Walter Reed Gen. Hosp., Washington, 1961-62; resident in dermatology U. Ala. Med. Center, Birmingham, 1966-67, 68-69, Lloyd Noland Hosp., Fairfield, Ala., 1967-68; practice medicine specializing in dermatology, Huntsville, Ala., 1969—; mem. staff Huntsville Hosp., 1969—, chief div. medicine, 1975; mem. staff Med. Center Hosp., Crestwood Hosp.; pres. John M. Ennis, M.D., P.A., Huntsville, 1971—; pres. Profls. Data Processing Assn., Inc., Huntsville, 1975-76. Trustee, Huntsville Symphony Orch. Assn.; exec. com. Tenn. Valley council Boy Scouts Am., 1980—. Served with USAF, 1960-66. Fellow Am. Acad. Dermatology; mem. Southeastern Dermatol. Assn., Ala. Dermatol. Soc. (pres. 1975-76), So., Madison County (trustee) med. assns., Alpha Omega Alpha. Home: 1507 Toney Dr SE Huntsville AL 35802 Office: 410 Sivley Rd SW Huntsville AL 35801

ENOCH, JAY MARTIN, visual scientist, educator; b. N.Y.C., Apr. 20, 1929; s. Jerome Dee and Stella Sarah (Nathan) E.; B.S. in Optics and Optometry, Columbia U., 1950; postgrad. Inst. Optics U. Rochester, 1953; Ph.D. in Physiol. Optics, Ohio State U., 1956; m. Rebekah Ann Feiss, June 24, 1951; children—Harold Owen, Barbara Diane, Ann Allison. Asst. prof. of physiol. optics Ohio State U., Columbus, 1956-58, asso. supr. of Mapping and Charing Research Lab., 1957-58; fellow Nat. Phys. Lab., Teddington, Eng., 1959-60; research instr. dept. ophthalmology Washington U. Sch. Medicine, St. Louis, 1958-59, research asst. prof., 1959-64, research asso. prof., 1965-70, research prof., 1970-74; fellow Barnes Hosp., St. Louis, 1960-64, cons. ophthalmology, 1964-74; research prof. dept. psychology Washington U., St. Louis, 1970-74; grad. research prof. ophthalmology and psychology U. Fla. Coll. Medicine, Gainesville, 1974—, dir. Center for Sensory Studies, 1976—, grad. research prof. physics, 1979—. Mem. nat. adv. eye council, Nat. Eye Inst., NIH, 1975-77; exec. com., com. on vision NAS-NRC, 1971-74; mem. U.S. Nat. Com. of Internat. Commn. for Optics, NRC, 1976—; mem. nat. sci. adv. bd. Retinitis Pigmentosa Found., 1977—; U.S. rep. Internat. Perimetric Soc., 1974—; trustee Illuminating Engrs. Research Inst., 1978—. Served to 2d lt. U.S. Army, 1951-52. Recipient Career Devel. award NIH, 1963-73. Fellow AAAS, Am. Acad. Optometry (Glenn A. Fry award 1972, Charles F. Prentice medal award 1974), Optical Soc. Am. (chmn. vision tech. 1974-76), Am. Acad. Ophthalmology Otolaryngology (asso.); mem. Assn. for Research in Vision and Ophthalmology (pres., chmn. bd. trustees 1972-73, Francis I. Proctor medal 1977), Internat. Strabismological Assn. Internat. Soc. for Clin. Electroretinography, Biophys. Soc., Psychonomic Soc., Am. Soc. for Photobiology, AAUP, Am. Psychol. Assn., Contact Lens Soc. of U.K., Sigma Xi. Contbr. numerous articles on visual sci., receptor optics, perimetry, contact lenses and infant vision to sci. jours.; contbr. chpts. in field to med. books; editorial bd. Vision Research, 1974—, Internat. Ophthalmology, 1977—; asso. editor Sight-Saving Rev., 1974—, Sensory Processes, 1974—. Home: 3845 NW 34th Pl Gainesville FL 32601 Office: Dept Ophthalmology PO Box J284 JHMHC Univ Florida Coll Medicine Gainesville FL 32610

ENOS, RICHARD EDWARD, social work educator; b. Honolulu, May 29, 1937; s. Manuel and Marie (Furtado) E.; B.A., Colo. Coll., 1960; M.S.W., U. Denver, 1966; D.S.W., U. Utah, 1976; m. Susan Ellen Cannon, Apr. 29, 1961; children—Craig Edward, Gary William, Marnie Elaine. Caseworker, Lane County Public Welfare Commn., Eugene, Oreg., 1962-64; social worker Solano County Mental Health Service, Fairfield, Calif., 1965; dir. educo therapy program and Larimer Children's Center, Poudre Sch. Dist., Ft. Collins, Colo., 1966-68; asst. prof. sociology and social welfare Colo. State U., Ft. Collins, 1968-73; asst. prof., dir. social work program N. Tex. State U., Denton, 1975—; social work cons. social agencies; bd. dirs. Denton Area Crisis Center, 1976—. Served with AUS, 1960-62. NIMH trainee, 1964-66; cert. Acad. Cert. Social Workers. Mem. Nat. Assn. Social Workers (clin. registry), Council Social Work Edn., Tex. Assn. Undergrad. Social Work Educators, Tex. Evaluation Network, Larimer County Mental Health Assn. (v.p. 1970-72), Alpha Delta Mu (Southwestern region v.p.), Sigma Chi. Roman Catholic. Contbr. articles to profl. jours. Home: 2610 Royal Acres Denton TX 76201 Office: Dept Sociology and Anthropology North Texas State U Denton TX 76203

ENRIGHT, JOHN RICHARD, physician; b. Sicily Island, La., Oct. 24, 1936; s. Clarence Edward and Julia Irma (Stutson) E.; student La. Tech. U., 1954-57; M.D., La. State U., 1961; m. Monette Ann Moreau, June 10, 1959; children—Ellen Marie, Sharon Anne, Mary Colleen. Intern, Confederate Meml. Med. Center, Shreveport, La., 1961-62, resident in urology, 1968-72; pvt. practice medicine, Winnfield, La., 1964-68; pvt. practice medicine, specializing in urology, Lake Charles, La., 1972—; instr. La. State U. Med. Sch., 1971—. Served with USNR, 1962-64. Mem. Calcasieu Parish Med. Soc. (pres. 1979), La. State Med. Soc., AMA, A.C.S. Republican. Methodist. Office: 234 S Ryan St Lake Charles LA 70601

ENRIQUEZ, CRISTINO CATUD, radiologist, internist-cardiologist; b. Batangas, Philippines, Dec. 5, 1941; s. Elpidio Macaraeg Enriquez and Cristeta Catud; M.D., U. East, Manila, 1964; m. Erlinda Buenaventura, Oct. 21, 1972; children—Louis, J. David. Intern, St. Mary's Hosp., Waterbury, Conn., 1965-66; resident Hosp. St. Raphael, New Haven, 1966-68, Carney Hosp., Boston, 1968-69; fellow in cardiology Baylor U., 1969; fellow in pulmonary diseases Yale U., 1971; resident in radiology U. Miami, 1974-77; practice medicine specializing in internal medicine and radiology, Plantation, Fla., 1977—; pres., chmn. bd. S. Atlantic CFM, Inc.; pres. Celin Investment Enterprises, Celin Car Brokers, Inc. Recipient cert. appreciation Philippine Med. Assn. New Eng., 1969. Diplomate Am. Bd. Radiology. Mem. AMA, Broward County Med. Assn., Am. Coll. Cardiology, Fla. Radiol. Soc., Interam. Coll. Radiology, Assn. Philippine Practicing Physicians in Am. Roman Catholic. Office: 1417 S University Dr Plantation FL 33324

ENSENAT, LOUIS ALBERT, physician; b. Merida, Mexico, Oct. 24, 1916; s. Frank and Guadalupe F. (Ensenat) E.; B.S., Tulane U., 1938, M.D., 1941; M.Sc. in Medicine, U. Pa., 1953; m. Ruth Ogden, July 9, 1943; children—Gloria Louise, Tinita Ruth, Louis Albert, Rita Joan, Barbara Jean, Michael Monroe. Intern, Charity Hosp., New Orleans, 1941-42; resident surgery Charity Hosp., Monroe, La., 1942, Lakeshore Hosp., New Orleans, VA hosp., New Orleans, Batavia, N.Y.; fellow in surg. pathology Tulane U. Sch. Med.; preceptorship in surgery Biloxi (Miss.) VA Hosp.; staff surg. VA Hosp., Montgomery, 1946-52; pvt. practice surgery, Pasadena, Tex., 1952-63, New Orleans, 1963—; adminstr. Mercy Hosp. Pasadena, 1954-63, chief surgery, 1954-63. Founder, dir. Gulf Coast Home Bulders, Inc. Trustee Big State Factors Corp. Served from lt. (j.g.) to lt. comdr. USN, 1942-46. Decorated Purple Heart. Diplomate Am. Bd. Surgery, Am. Bd. Abdominal Surgery. Fellow French Soc. Phlebology, Am. Coll. Angiology (v.p.); mem. Hawthorne Surg. Soc., Am. Soc. Abdominal Surgeons, N.Y. Acad. Scis., Am. Med. Writers' Assn. Author articles in field. Home and Office: 7630 Jeannette Pl New Orleans LA 70118

ENSIGN, MARK RUSSELL, acct.; b. Cin., Jan. 26, 1948; s. Grayson Harter and Grayce Marie (Steele) E.; student Moberly Jr. Coll., 1965-66; student Amarillo Coll., 1966-67, Tex. A. and M. U., 1967-68; B.S., W. Tex. State U., 1969; dip. Internat. Accts. Soc., 1974; m. Joy Dell Fewell, Aug. 20, 1971. Phys. scientist Helium Ops. U.S. Govt., Amarillo, Tex., 1968-71, 73; acct. H.V. Robertson & Co., Amarillo, 1973-78; pvt. C.P.A., Amarillo, 1978—; cons. in field. Dir., sec.-treas. Rhema Christian Sch. System, Amarillo, 1977-79; elder, asso. pastor Maranatha Fellowship, 1978-79. Served with USN, 1971-72. C.P.A., Tex.; recipient Award of Appreciation, Maranatha Fellowship, 1977. Mem. Am. Inst. C.P.A.'s, Tex. Soc. C.P.A.'s. Christian Ch. Club: Rotary. Home: 1911 Karen St Amarillo TX 79106 Office: 1709 Avondale St Amarillo TX 79106

ENSLEN, GEORGE CLINTON, real estate co. exec.; b. Cleve., Mar. 1, 1925; s. George C. and Genevieve A. (Pryber) E.; B.A., Denison U., 1949; m. Helga E. Kreis, Jan. 11, 1974; children—Lisa Gray, William Bradley. Exec. v.p., dir. Asso. Surveys Co., Wayne, N.J., 1954-73; pres., chmn. bd. Mgmt. Asso. Fla., Inc., Miami, 1974—, dir., 1974—. Served with USAAF, 1943-45. Mem. Evaluator Inst., Nat. Assn. Review Appraisers, Am. Soc. Appraisers, Soc. Real Estate Appraisers (asso.), Sigma Alpha Epsilon. Republican. Episcopalian. Clubs: Palm Bay, Racquet, Ocean Reef (Miami). Home: 1196 N E 87th St Miami FL 33138 Office: 275 Forest Ave Paramus NJ 07652 also 9999 NE 2d Ave Suite 118 Miami FL 33138

ENSOR, ERIC FRANK, mfg. co. exec.; b. Passaic, N.J., Oct. 7, 1952; s. Frank John and Eileen Mildred (Williams) E.; B.A., Duke U., 1974, postgrad. Law Sch., 1974-75, M.B.A., 1977; m. Pamela Love Smith, May 25, 1974; 1 son, Michael. Plant mgr. Birnn Candy Co., Highland Park, N.J., 1977-78; sr. product planner Motorola Inc., Fort Lauderdale, Fla., 1978—. Home: 3529 NW 73 Way Coral Springs FL 33065 Office: 8000 W Sunrise Blvd Fort Lauderdale FL 33065

ENSSLIN, ROBERT FRANK, JR., advt. agency exec.; b. Jacksonville, Fla., Feb. 22, 1928; s. Robert Frank and Pauline (Harper) E.; A.B. in Art, U. N.C., 1950; grad. U.S. Army Command and Gen. Staff Coll., 1969, U.S. Army War Coll., 1978; m. Fae Finter, Sept. 29, 1951; children—Robert Frank, Clyde F., Paul H., John B. Advt. exec. Sears Roebuck & Co., Tampa, Fla., 1950-61; v.p. Louis Benito Advt., Tampa, 1961-67; pres. Ensslin Advt. Agy., Tampa, 1967-78, chmn. bd. dirs., 1978—. Trustee, U. Tampa, Shimberg Found.; chmn. Downtown Council; exec. com. Mchts. Assn. Greater Tampa; v.p. United Way of Greater Tampa; mem. Armory Bd. State of Fla. Served with U.S. Army, 1950-53; served to brigade comdr. Army N.G., 1956—. Recipient Silver medal Am. Advt. Fedn., 1971, Jaycee Disting. Service award, 1963, SME Top Mgmt. award, 1979. Mem. Am. Assn. Advt. Agys. (chmn. S.E. council), Tampa Advt. Fedn. (trustee, ad profl. of year 1961), Assn. U.S. Army (dir. Suncoast chpt.), Am. Acad. Advt., Fla. N.G. Officers Assn. Democrat. Methodist. Clubs: Tampa Yacht and Country, Davis I. Yacht, Univ. of Tampa; Army and Navy (Washington). Home: 132 Chesapeake St Tampa FL 33606 Office: 102 W Whiting St Tampa FL 33602

ENTMAN, STEPHEN SAUL, physician; b. N.Y.C., June 19, 1943; s. Sidney and Rose Anne (Newman) E.; B.A. cum laude, Harvard Coll., 1964; M.D., Duke U., 1968; m. Catherine Alice Sivils, Apr. 15, 1973; children—Elizabeth Ann, Margaret Perry. Intern, Childrens Hosp., Boston, 1968-69; resident Hosp. U. Pa., 1969-73; pvt. practice medicine, specializing in obstetrics and gynecology, Columbia, S.C., 1975-77; asst. prof. obstetrics and gynecology U. S.C. Sch. Medicine, Columbia, 1977-80, Vanderbilt U. Sch. Medicine, Nashville, 1980—. Served with M.C., AUS, 1973-75. Diplomate Nat. Bd. Med. Examiners, Am. Bd. Obstetrics and Gynecology. Mem. Am. Coll. Obstetricians and Gynecologists, Am. Fertility Soc., Assn. Profs. Gynecology and Obstetrics, Am. Soc. Psychosomatic Obstetrics and Gynecology. Jewish. Office: Dept Obstetrics and Gynecology Vanderbilt U Hospital Nashville TN 37232

EPPERLY, JOHN DAVID, lawyer; b. Floyd, Va., Oct. 14, 1920; s. Isaac Lafayette and Linda (Weddle) E.; B.S.C., U. Va., 1941, LL.B., 1947, J.D., 1970; m. Judy Martin, Oct. 4, 1968; children—Carolyn M., John David, Jr., Elizabeth R., Anne Marie. Admitted to Va. bar, 1947; since practiced in Martinsville; mem. firm Broaddus, Epperly, Broaddus & Warren, 1947—; mem. rules, appointees selection coms. Supreme Ct. Va. dir. Lester Group Inc., Am. Standard Homes Corp. Instr. comml. law U. Va., 1960-64. Mem. Am., Va. (v.p. 1970-71), Martinsville-Henry County (pres. 1970-71) bar assns., Raven Soc., Internat. Soc. Barristers, Am., Va. trial lawyers assns., Am. Coll. Trial Lawyers, Order of Coif, Omicron Delta Kappa. Elk, K.P. Home: 211 Thomas Heights PO Box 1342 Martinsville VA 24112 Office: 106 E Main St Martinsville VA 24112

EPPERSON, DAVID ROSS, architect, planner; b. Miami, May 27, 1939; s. Thiel Otis and Helen Amanda (Ross) E.; B.Arch., U. Fla., 1965; M.S., Fla. State U., 1972, Ph.D., 1978; m. Merrie-Jayne Tallamy, Apr. 9, 1965; 1 son, David Ross. Project architect Kemp, Bunch and Jackson, Architects, Jacksonville, Fla., 1965-69; sch. cons. architect State of Fla., Tallahassee, 1969-73; project mgr. Eoghan N. Kelley and Assos., Architects, Sanford, Fla., and Atlanta, 1973-75; dir. archtl. and engring. facilities research Fla. Dept. Edn., Tallahassee, 1975—; cons. in field. Fla. Bd. Regents grantee, 1979; registered profl. architect, Fla., Ga., Tex.; cert. Nat. Council Archtl. Registration Bds. Mem. AIA, Council of Ednl. Facilities Planners, Fla. Sch. Planners Assn., Train Collectors Assn., Fla. State U. Alumni Assn., U. Fla. Alumni Assn., Theta Chi, Kappa Delta Pi, Phi Delta Kappa. Episcopalian. Author: (with others) The Exceptional Child in the Open Middle School, 1972; Design Criteria for Florida Public Schools, 1978; Construction Guidelines for Educational Facilities, 1980. Home: 4072 Roscrea Dr Tallahassee FL 32308 Office: Fla Dept Edn Knott Bldg Tallahassee FL 32301

EPPS, JAMES HAWS, III, lawyer; b. Johnson City, Tenn., Sept. 15, 1936; s. James H. and Anne (Sessoms) E.; grad. Episcopal High Sch., Alexandria, Va., 1955; B.A., U. N.C., 1959; J.D., Vanderbilt U., 1962; m. Jane Mahoney, Oct. 9, 1976; children by previous marriage—James Haws IV, Sara Stuart. Admitted to Tenn. bar, 1962, U.S. Supreme Ct., 1967, other fed. cts.; now partner Powell & Epps, Johnson City, Tenn. City atty. Johnson City, 1967—; past dir. ET & WNC Transp. Co., E. Tenn. & Western N.C. R.R., Tennolina Corp., Appalachian Air Lines, Inc., Appalachian Flying Service, Inc. Mem. Tenn. Law Revision Commn., 1970-71. Mem. budget com. United Fund, Johnson City, 1964-68, former mem. bd. dirs.; former legal adviser and mem. Appalachian council Girl Scouts Am.; mem. adv. bd. Salvation Army; mem. Civil Def. Adv. Bd. Mem. county exec. com. Democratic party. Past bd. dirs. Tenn. Mental Health Assn., Washington County Mental Health Assn. Mem. Fed. (asso.), Am. (mem. transp. com. adminstrv. law sect.), Tenn. (mem. continuing legal edn. com. 1971-74), Washington County (past pres.) bar assns., Am. Judicature Soc., Am., Tenn. trial lawyers assns., Tenn. Municipal Attys. Assn., Assn. ICC Practitioners (former mem. com. profl. ethics and grievances), Motor Carrier Lawyers' Assn. (bd. govs. Transp. Law Jour.), Am. Counsel Assn., Nat. Assn. R.R. Trial Counsel, Lawyers Com. for Civil Rights Under Law, Tenn. Municipal Attys. Assn., Supreme Ct. Hist. Soc., Nat. Inst. Municipal Law Officers, C. of C. (govtl. affairs com.), Tennesseans for Better Transp., Tenn. Taxpayers Assn., Internat. Platform Assn., Nat. Legal Aid Defender Assn., Tenn. Correctional Assn., Tenn. Lung Assn., Nat. Rifle Assn., Tipton Haynes Hist. Assn. (dir.), Phi Delta Phi, Phi Delta Theta. Episcopalian (vestryman, 1965-68, 70-71, clk. 1968, 70, 71, layreader). Clubs: Elks (legal counsel 1963-67), North Johnson City Business (dir., pres. 1966-67), Hurstleigh, Johnson City Country; Nat. Lawyers, Unaka Rod and Gun, Highland Stable. Home: 705 Judith Dr Johnson City TN 37601 Office: 115 E Unaka Ave Johnson City TN 37601

EPPS, JAMES VERNON, ins. co. exec.; b. Kingstree, S.C., Aug. 12, 1928; s. John Vernon and Opal (McKnight) E.; student U. S.C., 1946-50; m. Dorothy Jean Rast, Dec. 26, 1951; children—John Vernon II, James Steven, Leah Elizabeth. Farmer, cattleman, realtor, Lake City, S.C., 1956—. Pres. Epps-McLendon Co., Inc., Lake City, 1960—; dir. Lake City State Bank. Mem. econ. opportunity commn. Lake City United Fund, 1966-69, chmn., 1963; pres. Lake City P.T.A., 1957-58; mem. Florence County Planning Council, 1964-70; mem. Lake City Zoning Commn., 1972-73. Trustee Presbyn. Home of S.C., 1974—, now chmn. bd. Mem. Lake City Bd. Realtors (pres.), S.C. Ind. Ins. Agts., Carolina Assn. Profl. Ins. Agts. (pres.), Lake City C. of C. (pres. 1961), Phi Kappa Sigma (pres. 1950). Presbyterian (deacon, elder). Clubs: Lions (pres. 1956-57, dep. dist. gov.), Lake City Band Booster (pres.), Pee Dee Coin (pres.). Home: 119 2d Ave Lake City SC 29560 Office: 249 W Main St PO Box 1348 Lake City SC 29560

EPPS, ROBERT FLEETWOOD, III, coll. adminstr.; b. Kingstree, S.C., Dec. 3, 1940; s. Robert Fleetwood and Mildred Leonora (Moye) E.; B.S. in Mech. Engring., Duke U., 1963; M.S. in Mech. Engring., Clemson U., 1968; postgrad. in occupational edn. N.C. State U., 1970-73; m. Mary Elizabeth Elliott, June 25, 1966; children—Elliott Fleetwood, William Lawrence. Mech. engr. U.S. Marine Corps Air Sta., Cherry Point, N.C., 1963-66; asso. engr. IBM, Research Triangle Park, N.C., 1969-70; dean of instrn. Aiken (S.C.) Tech. Coll., 1973—. Chmn., Aiken County Heart Assn., 1975-76, pres.-elect. 1976-77, pres., 1977-78, mem. state heart fund com., 1977—. Mem. ASME, Am. Soc. Engring. Edn., Am. Vocat. Assn., S.C. Vocat. Assn., S.C. Tech. Edn. Assn. (pres.-elect 1978-79, pres. 1979-80), Council Occupational Edn., S.C. State Employees Assn. (dir. 1976-78), Epsilon Pi Tau. Episcopalian. Club: Kiwanis (pres. Aiken chpt. 1978-79). Home: 106 Kemberly Dr NW Aiken SC 29801 Office: Aiken Tech Coll Drawer 696 Aiken SC 29801

EPSTEIN, BARRY MICHAEL, computer communications co. exec.; b. Indpls., Dec. 16, 1939; s. Alex and Sylvia (Weissman) E.; B.S.E.E. with honors, Purdue U., 1961, M.S.E.E., 1963; m. Patricia Lee Burnstein, Aug. 26, 1962; children—Robert, Bradley. Mem. tech. staff Bell Telephone Labs., Whippany, N.J., 1963-68; mgr. equipment devel. Univ. Computer Co., Dallas, 1968-71; asst. v.p. telephone industry Action Communication Systems, Dallas, 1971—; cons. computer systems. Bd. dirs. Temple Shalom, Dallas, 1974-79; prs. Northwood Hills Sch. Parents Group, Dallas, 1976. Eastman fellow, 1961-62; Purdue Alumni scholar, 1959-61; Square D scholar, 1958-59. Mem. IEEE. Patentee electronics, communications, med. electronics. Home: 7523 Cliffbrook St Dallas TX 75240 Office: 4401 Beltwood Pkwy S Dallas TX 75234

ERBELE, LEO ALBERT, physician; b. Mandan, N.D., Jan. 8, 1927; s. Albert Frederick and Anna (Goldmann) E.; student Creighton U., 1944-45; B.A., U. N.D., 1949, B.S., 1950; M.D., Bowman Gray Sch. Medicine, 1952; m. Josephine Phelps Matthews, Apr. 26, 1973; children by previous marriage—John, Olivia, Peter, Mary. Intern City Hosp., Winston-Salem, N.C., 1952-53; gen. practice medicine, Clover, S.C., 1953-54, Marion, N.C., 1954-55; residency tng. Bowman Gray Sch. Medicine, Winston-Salem, 1955-59; asso. pathologist Macon (Ga.) Hosp., 1959-61, dir. labs., 1961-65; now engaged in pvt. practice. Served as sgt. USAAF, 1945-47. Diplomate in anatomic pathology and clin. pathology Am. Bd. Pathology, Am. Bd. Nuclear Medicine. Fellow Am. Soc. Clin. Pathologists, Coll. Am. Pathologists; mem. So. Med. Assn. Home: 3379 Osborne Pl Macon GA 31204 Office: 1021 Daisy Park Macon GA 31208

ERDEY, RODNEY NICHOLAS, ins. agent, real estate broker, bldg. contractor; b. Livingston, La., Nov. 6, 1949; s. Nicholas Louis and Ethel Helen (Beregi) E.; M.S., La. State U., 1971; m. Linda Susan Kracmer, July 3, 1969; 1 dau., Tisha Nicole. With Erdey Ins. Agy., Inc., Livingston, 1971—, v.p., sec., treas., 1973—; owner Erdey Real Estate, Livingston, 1970-78. Treas., Livingston United Methodist Ch. Lic. bldg. contractor. Mem. Livingston Bd. Realtors (dir. 1978-79, sec. 1979-80), Livingston Area Jaycees (v.p. 1976-77, sec., treas. 1975-76, dir. 1977-79), La. Assn. Independent Ins. Agts. Democrat. Home: PO Box 425 Livingston LA 70754 Office: 132 S Magnolia St Livingston LA 70754

ERDMAN, DAVID WILLIAMS, lawyer; b. Camp LeJeune, N.C., July 4, 1949; s. Lawrence Huntington and Anna Marian (Williams) E.; B.S. in Engring., Duke, 1971; J.D., Georgetown U., 1975. Cons., Occupational Safety and Health Adminstrn., N.C. Dept. Labor, Raleigh, 1973; investigator campaign finances Watergate Com., U.S. Senate, Washington, 1973; internship coordinator N.C. Inst. Govt., Raleigh, 1974; admitted to N.C. bar, 1975; atty. N.C. Dept. Pub. Edn., Raleigh, 1975-76; mem. campaign staff N.C. Gov. Jim Hunt, Raleigh, 1976; atty. firm Wardlow, Knox, Knox, Robinson & Freeman, Charlotte, N.C., 1977—; mem. Mecklenburg County Commn. Status of Women, 1977-78; mem. N.C. Employment Security Commn., 1978—. Del. Democratic Nat. Conv., Miami, Fla., 1972; mem. Presdl. campaign staff Senator Henry M. Jackson, 1976; 3d vice chmn. Mecklenburg County Dem. Com., 1977-78; treas. Mecklenburg County Young Dems., 1977-78; dir. fundraising N.C. Young Dems., 1977-78. Angier B. Duke scholar 1967-71. Mem. Am. (nat. pres. div. law students 1974-75, inventor Juriscan Nat. Computerized Job Bank 1974), Mecklenburg County (governing bd. young lawyers sect. 1977-80) bar assns. Methodist. Office: 1490 City Nat Center 200 S Tryon St Charlotte NC 28202

ERFE, JOSE ASPERIN, psychiatrist; b. Philippines, Dec. 1, 1937; s. Pedro D. and Mauricia O. (Asperin) E.; came to U.S., 1969; M.D., U. Philippines, 1962; m. Purita F. Erfe, Mar. 1, 1964; children—Ma. Elizabeth, Jose. Intern, U. Philippines-Philippine Gen. Hosp. Med. Center, 1961-62, resident in psychiatry, 1962-65; asst. med. dir. Procter & Gamble-Philippines, 1965-67, med. dir., 1967-69; staff physician Eastern State Hosp., Williamsburg, Va., 1969-71, resident psychiatry, 1971-74, clin. dir., 1977—; asst. dir., clin. Western State Hosp., Staunton, Va., 1974-75; dir. Central State Hosp., Petersburg, Va., 1975-77; clin. asst. prof. psychiatry Med. Coll. Va., Richmond, 1976—. Diplomate Am. Bd. Psychiatry and Neurology. Mem. Am. Psychiat. Assn., Neuropsychiat. Soc. Va., Inc., Va. Soc. Adolescent Psychiatry. Home: 105 Sabre Dr Williamsburg VA 23185 Office: Eastern State Hosp Williamsburg VA 23185

ERFFT, KENNETH REYNDERS, ednl. cons.; b. Chgo., Nov. 14, 1908; s. Victor Athen and Ethel (Reynders) E.; A.B., No. Mich. U., 1932; M.A., U. Richmond, 1936, D.S.C., 1967; Litt.D., Maclean Coll., 1947; LL.D., No. Mich. U., 1961; m. Nancy Fontaine Creath, June 8, 1940. Instr. Ironwood (Mich.) High Sch., 1932-34; clk. bd. edn. Petersburg (Va.) pub. schs., 1936-42; bus. mgr. Furman U., Greenville, S.C., 1946-54; comptroller Pa. State U., 1954-57; v.p., treas. Rutgers State U., 1957-62, Thomas Jefferson U., 1962-64; pres. Kenneth R. Erfft Assos., Inc., ednl. cons., Phila. 1964-66; v.p. Duquesne U., Pitts., 1966-72; exec. dir. Nationwide Conf. Edn. Centers, Inc., Atlanta, 1972-74; pres. Univ. Center in Va., Richmond, 1974-78. Chmn. bd. dirs. Afuture Fund, Carlisle-Asher Enterprises, Pennell Corp., Phila. Mem. adminstrv. com. for Calif. and Western Conf. Cost and Statis. Study, 1955-57. Served from lt. (j.g.) to comdr. USNR, 1942-46. Decorated knight Sacred Order Constantinian of St. George; recipient Disting. Alumnus award No. Mich. U., 1979. Mem. Eastern Assn. Coll. and U. Bus. Officers (pres.), AAUP, Middle States Assn., Delta Sigma Phi, Phi Epsilon, Tau Kappa Alpha, Omicron Delta Kappa, Theta Omicron Rho. Club: Internat. Torch. Co-author: Administrators in Higher Education, 1962. Editorial com. College and University Business Administration, rev. edits. Home: 1004 Hathaway Tower 2956 Hathaway Rd Richmond VA 23225 Office: Suite 210 4905 Radford Ave Richmond VA 23230

ERICKSON, DAVID THEODORE, petroleum engr.; b. Delta, Colo., June 1, 1951; s. Carl John and Mary Blanche (Wortham) E.; B.S., Colo. Sch. Mines, 1973. Asso. engr. Continental Oil Co., Hobbs, N.Mex., 1974, engr., 1975; social coordinator AIME, Hobbs, 1975-76; prodn. engr. Continental Oil Co., Oklahoma City, 1977-78, supervising reservoir engr., Lake Charles, La., 1978—. Registered profl. engr., N.Mex. Mem. Soc. Petroleum Engrs., Am. Inst. Mining, Metall. and Petroleum Engrs. Republican. Home: 413 Glover St Lake Charles LA 70605 Office: 901 Lakeshore Dr Lake Charles LA 70601

ERICKSON, JOHN ALBIN, architect; b. Tacoma, Apr. 17, 1946; s. Carl Albin and Frances Elizabeth (Stitt) E.; student U. Tex., Arlington, 1964-65, U. Tex., Austin, 1966-72; m. Susan Margaret Hurley, Sept. 27, 1969; children—Derek, Jason, Jeremy. Draftsman, Fehr & Granger, Architects and Planners, Austin, Tex., 1967-69; designer/draftsman Roger Erickson, Architect, Engr., Austin, 1969-70; designer Walter Carrington Bldg., Austin, 1970-72; asso. in charge of design Environ. Design Group, Austin, 1972-74; design and prodn. coordinator Architects Partnership, Dallas, 1974-75; dir. design Killebrew/Rucker/Asso., Inc., Wichita Falls, Tex., 1975—; design cons. Image Advt. 1979-80, All Saints Episcopal Ch., 1979-80. Recipient First Place awards in residential single family design, Tex. Inst. Bldg. Design, 1972; registered architect, Tex. Mem. AIA, Tex. Soc. Architects. Episcopalian. Archtl. works include The Bluffs at Lakeway, 1972, Patient Services Bldg., Wichita Falls State Hosp., 1978. Home: 5306 Pyrenees St Wichita Falls TX 76310 Office: 600 Petroleum Bldg Wichita Falls TX 76301

ERICKSON, RONALD EUGENE, metal co. exec.; b. Savannah, Ga., Feb. 2, 1942; s. Theodore W. and Margaret A. (Wilson) E.; B.A., U. Ga., 1966; M.B.A., Columbia U., 1968; m. Virginia White Murray, Oct. 13, 1975; children—Lucy, Chrisy. Investment banker Kohlmeyer & Co., New Orleans, 1968-73; asst. to the pres. Delta Metals, Inc., Savannah, Ga., 1974-77, v.p., gen. mgr., 1977-79, pres., chief exec. officer, 1979—, also dir. Mem. Savannah Sheet Metal Contractors Assn. Episcopalian. Clubs: Oglethorpe, Savannah Golf. Home: 418 E Liberty St Savannah GA 31402 Office: Delta Metals Inc 218 E Lathrop Ave Savannah GA 31401

ERICSON, RUTH ANN, psychiatrist; b. Assaria, Kans., May 15; d. William Albert and Anna Mathilda (Almquist) Ericson; student So. Meth. U., 1945-47; B.S., Bethany Coll.; M.D., U. Tex., 1951. Intern, Calif. Hosp., Los Angeles, 1951-52; resident in psychiatry, U. Tex. Med. Br., Galveston, 1952-55; psychiatrist Child Guidance Clinic, Dallas, 1955-63; clin. instr. Southwestern Med. Sch., Dallas, 1955; practice medicine specializing in psychiatry, Dallas, 1955—; cons. Dallas Intertribal Council Clinic, 1974—, Dallas Ind. Sch. Dist., U.S. Army, Welfare Dept., Tribal Concerns, alcoholism, Adv. Bd. Intertribal Council. Mem. Am. Med. Women's Assn. (corr. sec. 1980—), Paleopath. Soc. So., Tex., Dallas med. assns., Am. Psychiat. Assn., Am. Geriatric Soc., Dallas Area Women Psychiatrists, Alumni Assn. U. Tex. (Med. Br.), Navy League (life), Air Force Assn., Tex., Dallas (pres. 1972-73) archaeol. socs., Alpha Omega Alpha, Delta Psi Omega, Alpha Psi Omega, Pi Gamma Mu, Lambda Sigma, Alpha Epsilon Iota. Lutheran. Home: 4007 Shady Hill Dr Dallas TX 75229 Office: 2339 Inwood Rd #22 Dallas TX 75235

ERMER, CHARLES MARTIN, steel co. exec.; b. Balt., July 25, 1941; s. Charles Martin and Elsa (Flatt) E.; B.E.S., Johns Hopkins U., 1962, Ph.D., 1972; M.B.A., Ga. State U., 1979; m. Phyllis Mary Hughes, June 25, 1977. Elec. foreman Bethlehem Steel Corp., 1962-68; mem. tech. staff Bell Telephone Labs., 1972-75, Analytic Scis. Corp., 1975-77, mgr. indsl. engring. Atlantic Steel Co., Atlanta, 1977—. Mem. IEEE, Am. Inst. Indsl. Engrs., Beta Gamma Sigma. Home: 489 Pinetree Dr Atlanta GA 30305 Office: Atlantic Steel Co PO Box 1714 Atlanta GA 30301

ERNEST, ALBERT DEVERY, JR., banker; b. Mobile, Ala., June 7, 1930; s. Albert Devery and Dorothy (Griffith) E.; B.A. in Econs., U. Va., 1954; grad. Advanced Mgmt. Program, Harvard U., 1974; m. Donna Barnett Sims, Nov. 20, 1954; children—Albert Devery, Lise Sims. Mgmt. trainee St. Regis Paper Co., N.Y.C., 1954, asst. to v.p. Timberlands div., 1958-61; founder, pres. Albert Ernest Enterprises, Investment and mgmt. consultants Jacksonville, Fla., 1961-76, Allied Timber Co., Inc., Jacksonville, 1965-73; exec. v.p. Barnett Bank of Jacksonville, 1976-77, pres., 1977—, chief exec. officer, 1979—; dir. Barnett Mortgage Co., St. Regis Paper Co. Trustee Jacksonville U., 1975—; bd. dirs. Arts Assembly of Jacksonville, 1978—, North Fla. council Boy Scouts Am., 1978— Chanel 7, Public Broadcasting Co., 1978—, Cummer Gallery Art, 1979—, Jacksonville Community Council, Inc., 1978—, Jacksonville Symphony Assn., 1979—; chmn. Central Jacksonville, Inc., 1979—; pres. Leadership Jacksonville, 1977-78, dir., 1978—; trustee Southside Country Day Sch., 1971-78, pres., 1974-76; mem. exec. com. United Way of Jacksonville, 1978—, co-chmn. Keel Club, 1979—. Mem. Am., Fla. bankers assns., Jacksonville Area C of C. (gov., com. of 100 1976—), Fla. Forestry Assn. (dir. 1961—, pres. 1973-74), Forest Farmers Assn. (dir. 1960, pres. 1970-72), Ga. Forestry Assn. (dir. 1970-74). Democrat. Episcopalian. Clubs: River (charter, dir. 1978—), Harvard (N.Y.C.), Fla. Yacht, Ponte Vedra, Timuquana Country, Farmington Country, Deerwood; Meninak (dir. 1978—) (Jacksonville). Home: 8070 Lakecrest Dr Jacksonville FL 32216 Office: 100 Laura St Jacksonville FL 32231

ERNOUF, ANITA BONILLA, educator; b. Santurce, P.R., Feb. 22, 1920; d. John and Dolores (Asencio) Bonilla; B.A., Hunter Coll., 1944; M.A., Columbia U., 1946, Ph.D., 1970; m. Edward Ernouf, Feb. 8, 1946; children—Edward, Roderic. French, Spanish and Portuguese examiner U.S. Postal Service, N.Y.C., 1942-44; research asst., librarian Hispanic Inst. Columbia U., 1945-47; asst. prof. Spanish,

Hollins Coll., Va., 1947-60; prof. Longwood Coll., Farmville, Va., 1960—, chmn. dept. fgn. langs., 1972-79. Mem. NEA, Va. Edn. Assn., AAUW (past pres.), AAUP, Am. Assn. Tchrs. Spanish and Portuguese, Tchrs. French, Am. Council on Teaching Fgn. Langs., Va. Fgn. Lang. Assn. (pres. 1972-73, pres. elect 1978). Home: 312 Randolph St Farmville VA 23901 Office: Longwood College Farmville VA 23901

ERNST, EDWARD ALBERT, anesthesiologist; b. Cin., Jan. 16, 1926; s. Emerson T. and Elizabeth A. (Nordman) E.; student Ohio State U., 1946-48; M.D., Temple U., 1952; m. Dorothy Webster, Dec. 26, 1947; children—Pamela, Timothy, Valery, Beverly. Gen. practice medicine, Lodi, Ohio, 1953-65; resident in anesthesiology, NIH postdoctoral research fellow U. Fla., 1968-69; asst. prof. anesthesiology Case Western Res. U. Sch. Medicine Univ. Hosps., Cleve., 1969-75; asso. prof., 1975-78; dir. dept. anesthesiology Cleve. Met. Gen. Hosp., 1975-78; prof., chmn. dept. anesthesiology U. Ala., Birmingham, 1978—. Served with USAF, 1943-46. Diplomate Am. Bd. Anesthesiology, Nat. Bd. Med. Examiners. Mem. Am. Coll. Anesthesiology (examiner), Am. Soc. Anesthesiologists (regional dir. nat. preceptorship program 1974-77), Ala. Med. Assn., AMA, Internat. Soc. Oxygen Transport to Tissue, Ala. Soc. Anesthesiologists, Jefferson County Med. Assn. Reviewer, Am. Jour. Physiology, 1971—; author: The Quantitative Practice of Anesthesia, 1980; also articles. Office: 619 S 19th St Birmingham AL 35293

ERRANTE, FRANK GERARD, musician; b. N.Y.C., Jan. 11, 1941; s. Frank Joseph and Chrystine (Musacchio) E.; B.A., Queens Coll., 1963; Mus.M., U. Wis., 1964; A.Mus.D., U. Mich., 1970; diplome d'Honneur, Academie Internationale, Nice, France, 1974. Tchr. orchestral music N.Y.C. Public Schs., 1964-67; instr. clarinet Eastern Mich. U., 1968-69; artist-in-residence New South Wales State Conservatorium of Music, Sydney, Australia, 1979; mem. faculty Norfolk (Va.) State U., 1970—, asso. prof. music, 1973-75, prof., 1975—; prin. clarinetist Norfolk Symphony Orch., 1971-74, Va. Opera Assn., 1974-78; solo recitals Carnegie Hall, N.Y.C., 1978, Wigmore Hall, London, 1979; rec. artist CRI. Named Tchr. of Year, Norfolk State U., 1972-73; recipient 2d prize Internat. Gaudeamus Competition, 1976. Mem. Internat. Clarinet Soc., Nat. Assn. Coll. Wind and Percussion Instrs., Coll. Music Soc., Music Educators Nat. Conf., Am. Soc. Univ. Composers, Nat. Assn. Composers, AAUP. Author: A Selective Clarinet Bibliography, 1973; contbr. articles to profl. jours. Home: 4116 Gosnold Ave Norfolk VA 23508 Office: Dept Music Norfolk State U Norfolk VA 23504

ERVIN, ALLEN DELANO, constrn. co. exec.; b. Greenbank, W.Va., Aug. 17, 1942; s. Allen Dale and Ethel Viola E.; B.A. in Bus. Adminstrn., Bridgewater Coll., 1970; M.B.A., Mt. St. Mary's Coll., Emmitsburg, Md., 1979; m. Kathryn Roberta Marvel, Aug. 14, 1965; children—Allen David, Daniel Robert, Kathryn Elizabeth. Vice-pres., Lantz Constrn. Co., Broadway, Va., 1972-76; corp. controller Perry Engring. Co., Inc., Winchester, Va., 1977-78, exec. v.p., 1979—, also dir. Served with USN, 1966-68. Mem. Am. Mgmt. Assn. Presbyterian. Home: 1808 Wayland Dr Winchester VA 22601 Office: PO Box 439 Winchester VA 22601

ERVIN, ROBERT MARVIN, lawyer; b. Marion County, Fla., Jan. 19, 1917; s. Richard William and Carrie Marvin (Phillips) E.; B.S. in Bus. Adminstrn., U. Fla., 1941, LL.B., 1947, J.D., 1965; m. Frances Cushing, Dec. 25, 1941; children—Anne Cushing Ervin Rowe, Robert Marvin. Admitted to Fla. bar, 1947, since practiced in Tallahassee; exec. partner firm Ervin, Varn, Jacobs, Odom & Kitchen, 1964—; mem. Fla. Constnl. Revision Commn., 1966-68; chmn. bd. visitors Fla. State U. Coll. Law, 1974-76, founder Ervin Scholarship Fund. Served with USMCR, World War II. Recipient Disting. Service award Stetson U., 1966, Armed Forces League, 1966. Fellow Am. Coll. Trial Lawyers, Internat. Acad. Trial Lawyers, Am. Bar Found., Fla. Bar Founds.; mem. Am. Law Inst., Am. Judicature Soc., Am. Bar Assn. (ho. dels. 1966—, bd. govs. 1979—), Tallahassee Bar Assn. (past pres.), Fla. State Bar (pres. 1965-66, gov. 1959-66; Disting. Service award 1966), Phi Alpha Delta. Baptist. Home: 1434 Crestview Ave Tallahassee FL 32303 Office: PO Box 1170 Tallahassee FL 32302

ERWIN, HERBERT CLARK, diesel engine distbg. co. exec.; b. Detroit, Oct. 6, 1931; s. Adolphus Oren and Emma Rubena (Clark) E.; B.A., Hillsdale (Mich.) Coll.; m. Shirley June Whitton, Feb. 8, 1957; children—Laura Lynn, Gale Elizabeth, David Clark. Instr., spl. service rep. Detroit Diesel Engine div. Gen. Motors Corp., 1956-57; sales engr. L.B. Smith Inc., Syracuse, N.Y., 1958; service mgr. O'Donnell-Quigley Co. Inc., Syracuse, 1959-68, parts and service mgr., 1968-69, mktg. mgr., 1969-76; gen. mgr. ops. Gen. Engine and Equipment Co., Tampa, Fla., 1976—; cons. Internat. Inst. Trade Schs. Served with USAF, 1951-54. Mem. Soc. Automotive Engrs. Republican. Clubs: Propeller, Sertoma, Tampa Bay Buccaneer Booster. Home: 1013 Saxon St Brandon FL 33511 Office: 8311 Sabal Industrial Blvd Tampa FL 33601

ERWIN, JEAN HOCKING, educator; b. Ottawa, Ont., Can., Dec. 15, 1920; d. William James and Margaret Pearl (Logan) Hocking; came to U.S., 1959; student Riverdale Coll., 1934-38; B.A. with honors, U. Toronto, 1942; M.S., Iowa State U., 1960, Ph.D., 1969; m. Kenneth Wesley Erwin, Aug. 25, 1951. Collegiate tchr., Ottawa, London, Toronto, Ont., Can., 1943-66; instr. home econs. Iowa State U., Ames, summer 1968; asso. prof. Wash. State U., Pullman, 1969-71; prof. U. Tenn., Martin, 1971—. Sec., past pres. adv. bd. Easter Seal Center; active United Methodist Women. Gen. Foods fellow, 1967-69. Mem. AAUP, AAUW, Internat. Fedn. Home Econs., Nat., Tenn., So. assns. edn. young children, Am., Can., Tenn., Toronto home econs. assns., Iowa State U. Alumnae Assn., Nat., Southeastern councils family relations, Soc. Research in Child Devel., U. Toronto Alumnae, Merrill Palmer Alumnae, Consumers Assn. Can., Tenn. Edn. Assn., U. Tenn. Century Club, Phi Kappa Phi, Omicron Nu, Psi Chi. Club: Order Eastern Star. Author: Families, 1967. Home: 162 Glenwood Dr Glenwood Estates Martin TN 38237 Office: 305F Gooch U Tenn Martin TN 38238

ERWIN, WILLIAM MACK, psychologist; b. Gould, Okla., Jan. 4, 1940; s. Edwin Mack and Loraine (Duckworth) E.; B.A., Tex. Tech. U., 1963, Ph.D., 1971; m. Janis Richardson, Sept. 8, 1962; children—Crystal, Amy. Psychologist, Tex. Christian U., 1969-71; asst. prof. West Tex. State U., 1971-75; practice psychology, Amarillo, Tex., 1975-79, Lubbock, Tex., 1979—; tchr. and cons. for local agys.; bd. dirs. Rape Crisis Center, Amarillo, Opportunity House, Amarillo, Juliette Fowler Homes, Dallas. Mem. Potter-Randall County Psychol. Soc., Southwestern Psychol. Assn., Tex. Psychol. Assn., Am. Psychol. Assn. Mem. Christian Ch. (Disciples of Christ). Club: Rotary. Home: 8105 Salem Ave Lubbock TX 79424 Office: 4316 23 St Lubbock TX 79410

ERXLEBEN, ALBERT ERNEST, educator, state ofcl.; b. Savannah, Ga., June 21, 1921; s. Albert August and Lila Mae (Alcorn) E.; student U. Fla., 1939-41; postgrad. Fla. State U., 1977—; m. Frances Virginia Lee, Feb. 2, 1951; children—Bonnie Mae Erxleben Bussard, Albert Ernest II, William Lee. Various editorial positions newspapers Fla., Ga., N.C., 1942-54; night city editor Fla. Times-Union, Jacksonville, 1954-64, edn. editor, 1964-66; coordinator public info. Fla. Dept. Edn., Tallahassee, 1966—; cons., lectr. in field. Served with AC, U.S. Army, 1940. Mem. Sunshine State Sch. Public Relations Assn. (co-founder), Jacksonville News Club (co-founder, sec.-treas. 1956-66). Democrat. Methodist. Home: 310 Inglewood Dr Tallahassee FL 32301 Office: Fla Dept Edn LL-24 Capitol Tallahassee FL 32301

ESCH, LEROY TED, EDP exec.; b. Paducah, Ky., July 21, 1943; s. Chester Leroy and Estella May (Bridgeman) Brooking; student U. Tenn. at Knoxville, 1961-70; m. Billie Jean Davis, Aug. 30, 1963; children—Russell Ted, Robert Davis. Programming analyst Comml. Data Processing, Knoxville, 1964-68; systems analyst Millers Dept. Store, Knoxville, 1968-69; systems analyst Knoxville Computer Center, 1969—, treas., gen. mgr., 1971—, v.p., 1978, exec. v.p., chief operating officer, 1979—, also dir.; instr. data processing. Certified data processor. Mem. Seymour Vol. Fire Dept. Mem. Data Processing Mgmt. Assn. (treas. 1973-75, v.p. 1975-76, pres. Knoxville chpt. 1977-78). Democrat. Baptist. Clubs: Optimists (athletic coach), Kiwanis. Home: Route 5 Seymour TN 37865 Office: PO Box 457 Knoxville TN 37901

ESCOTT, LLOYD HARRISON, retail exec.; b. Cushing, Okla., Sept. 10, 1948; s. Lloyd Elmer and Mildred Belle (Smith) E.; student Okla. State U., 1966-69; m. K'Lynne Michelle Jarvis, June 6, 1976. With Escott's Red Bud, Cushing, Okla., 1962; stock clk. Reasor's Red Bud, Tahlequah, Okla., 1968-69; dairy mgr. Escott's Discount Foods, Cushing, 1969-72; asst. mgr. Reasor's Discount Foods, Tahlequah, 1972-73, store mgr., 1973-74, pres. Escott's Inc. d.b.a. Escott's Discount Foods, 1975—. Bd. dirs. Cushing Agri-Civic Center Trust, 1977. Mem. Cushing C. of C. (v.p. 1979), Okla. Retail Grocers Assn., Nat. Assn. Retail Grocers. Republican. Baptist. Clubs: Cushing Jaycees, Rotary Internat. Office: 310 E Broadway Cushing OK 74023

ESKENAZI, JACOB VICTOR, lawyer; b. Miami, Fla., Sept. 10, 1932; s. Victor A. and Marie E.; student U. Miami, 1950-51; B.A., Tulane U., 1955; LL.B., U. Fla., 1960; m. Elaine Nadene Ofsanko, June 29, 1963; children—Victor Joseph, Stacy Marie. Admitted to Fla. bar; spl. agt. FBI, Phila., 1961-64; asst. State Atty.'s Office, Miami, 1964-66; asst. U.S. atty, Miami, 1966-71; fed. pub. defender, Miami, 1971-75; U.S. magistrate, Miami, 1975-77; U.S. atty. for so. dist. of Fla., Miami, 1977—; supervising atty. clin. law program U. Miami, Nova U. Served with USNR, 1955-58. Mem. Am. Bar Assn., Fed. Bar Assn., Fla. Bar, Naval Res. Assn., Audubon Soc., Nat. Wildlife Fedn. Democrat. Unitarian. Club: Masons. Office: 300 Ainsley Bldg Miami FL 33132

ESKRIDGE, JOHN IRA, bank holding co. exec.; b. Waxahachie, Tex., Jan. 28, 1940; s. William L. and Dora Lorene (Griffin) E.; B.S., Rice U., 1963; m. Loretta Marie Verret, June 2, 1970; children—Laurie Ann, John Ira. Audit supr. Ernst & Ernst, Houston, 1963-68; sr. v.p., controller Mac-Gregor Park Nat. Bank, Houston, 1968-70; audit mgr. Peat Marwick Mitchell & Co., Jacksonville, Fla., 1970-74; sr. v.p., controller Republic of Tex. Corp., Dallas, 1974—. Mem. Am. Inst. C.P.A.'s, Tex. Soc. C.P.A.'s, Bank Adminstrn. Inst., Rice Athletic Alumni Assn. Republican. Baptist. Club: Dallas Exchange (pres.). Home: 705 Rocky Canyon Arlington TX 76012 Office: PO Box 222105 Ervay and Pacific Dallas TX 75222

ESLER, ANTHONY JAMES, novelist, historian; b. New London, Conn., Feb. 20, 1934; s. James Arthur and Helen (Kreamer) E.; B.A., U. Ariz., 1956; M.A., Duke U., 1958, Ph.D., 1961; postgrad. (research fellow) U. London, 1961-62; m. Carol Eaton Clemeau, June 17, 1961; children—Kenneth Campbell, David Douglas. Asst. prof. history Coll. William and Mary, Williamsburg, Va., 1962-67, asso. prof., 1967-72, prof., 1972—; vis. prof. history Northwestern U., Evanston, Ill., 1968-69. Fulbright fellow, 1961-62, Am. Council Learned Socs. fellow, 1969-70, William and Mary research fellow, 1975-76. Mem. Am. Hist. Assn., Authors Guild. Author: The Aspiring Mind of the Elizabethan Younger Generation, 1966; Bombs, Beards and Barricades: 150 Years of Youth in Revolt, 1971; Generational Studies: A Basic Bibliography, 1980; (hist. fiction): Castlemayne, 1974; Hellbane, 1975; Lord Libertine, 1976; Forbidden City, 1977; Pirate, 1978; Babylon, 1980; Bastion, 1980; editor: The Youth Revolution: Conflict of Generations in Modern History, 1974. Home: 1523 Jamestown Rd Williamsburg VA 23185

ESLINGER, TROY RHUDY, coll. adminstr.; b. Ringgold, Ga., Aug. 7, 1919; s. Eulus Newell and Rebecca Lucinda (Rhudy) E.; A.B., Centre Coll. Ky., 1948; M.Div., Louisville Presbyn. Sem., 1951; H.H.D. (hon.), Centre Coll., 1966; H.H.D. Morehead State U., 1976; m. Margaret E. Howard, Jan. 30, 1942; children—Margaret Lucinda Eslinger Noe, Rodric Hunter, Michael, James, Robert, Stephan. Ordained to ministry Presbyterian Ch., 1951; pastor chs., Millersburg, Ky., Pineville, Ky., Lexington, Ky., 1951-61; pres. Lees Coll., Jackson, Ky., 1961—. Mem. Regional Health Planning Council; chmn. ARC, Breathitt County. Served with AUS, 1942-45; chaplain maj., Ky. Army N.G., 1960-73, ret. Mem. Nat. Council Ind. Jr. Colls. (dir.), Am. Council Edn. Democrat. Club: Kiwanis (past pres.). Home: 708 Washington St Jackson KY 41339 Office: 601 Jefferson Jackson KY 41339

ESOGBUE, AUGUSTINE ONWUYALIM, indsl. engr., educator; b. Kaduna, Nigeria, Dec. 25, 1940; s. Nwanze Esogbue and Helen Nwakauso; came to U.S., 1961; B.S. in Elec. Engring., U. Calif., Los Angeles, 1964; M.S. in Indsl. Engring., Columbia U., 1965; Ph.D. in Systgms Engring. and Ops. Research, U. So. Calif., Los Angeles, 1968. Research asso. Schs. of Engring. and Medicine, U. So. Calif., Los Angeles, 1965-68; devel. engr. Water Resources Center, Sch. Engring. and Applied Sci., U. Calif., Los Angeles, 1966-67; asst. prof. dept. ops. research Case Western Res. U., Cleve., 1968-72; asso. prof. Sch. Indsl. and Systems Engring., Ga. Inst. Tech., Atlanta, 1972-77, prof., 1977—; adj. prof. community medicine Morehouse Sch. Medicine, Atlanta; asso. faculty U. Seminar on Water Resources and Pollution, Columbia U., N.Y.C., 1970—; v.p. Atlantic Systems, Inc., Atlanta, 1972—; mem. water resources adv. group Atlanta Regional Commn., 1977—; book and tech. paper reviewer for various sci. jours., 1968—. Fellow AAAS; mem. Am. Inst. Indsl. Engrs., IEEE, Inst. of Mgmt. Scis., Nat. Acad. Scis., Ops. Research Soc. Am., NRC (mem. sci. panel 19/3), Sigma Xi. Contbr. numerous articles on ops. research and systems engring. to profl. publs.; asso. editor Health Ops. Research Newsletter, 1976, Jour. of Math. Analysis and Applications, 1977, Jour. Computer Sci., 1979; advisory editor Internat. Journal of Fuzzy Sets and Systems, 1977—. Home: 1510 Loch Lomond Trail SW Atlanta GA 30331 Office: School of Industrial and Systems Engring Ga Inst Tech Atlanta GA 30332

ESPARZA, THOMAS, SR., univ. sports dir.; b. Edinburg, Tex., May 21, 1921; s. Greg and T.R. (Tirsa) E.; student Allen Mil. Acad., 1943; B.S., Tex. A. & I. U., 1948, M.S., 1951, Ph.D., 1977; m. Esther La Madrid, June 1, 1949; children—Tommy Jr., Steven, Teylene. Coach Edinburg (Tex.) Consol. Ind. Sch. Dist., 1948-68, adminstrv. asst., 1963-65, instructional media cons., 1963-65, athletic events mgr., 1957-68, health, phys. edn. cons., 1950-68; dir. intramurals dept. phys. edn., Pan Am. U., Edinburg, 1968—, univ. chmn. steering com. Nat. Phys. Edn. and Sports Week; mem. steering com. Met. Bank, 1973—. Cons. edn. City Park bd., 1968—; coordinator dist. I, Spl. Olympics, 1976-78; workshop cons. health and phys. edn. to various schs., 1968—; pres. Edinburg Tchrs. Credit Union, 1958-65, Pan Am. U. Credit Union, 1970. Bd. dirs. Am. Cancer Soc., 1948-73, v.p. Edinburg unit, 1976, edn. dir. Edinburg unit, 1977—. Served with USNR, 1946-48. Mem. Tex. High Sch. Coaches Assn., Tex. Assn. Health Phys. Edn., Recreation, NEA, AAHPER, Tex. State Tchrs. Assn., N.I.A., Edinburg C. of C., Hidalgo County Hist. Soc. (bd.), Am. Legion (comdr. post 1970-75, 15th dist. baseball chmn. 1975—, 3d div. baseball chmn. 1975—, state baseball chmn. 1980—, mem. state Americanism, constn. and by-laws, credentials coms. 1976—), D.A.V. (life). Author numerous publs. in field. Home: 811 S 16th Ave Edinburg TX 78539

ESPIN, ROBERTO RAFAEL, JR., fin. co. exec.; b. Havanna, Cuba, Oct. 8, 1945; came to U.S., 1960, naturalized, 1975; s. Roberto R. and Mercedez E.; B.S., U. Fla., 1969; m. Luisa Rojo, July 25, 1969; children—Roberto A., Jose I., Juan C. With Leo Burnett Advt. Agency, San Juan, P.R., 1969-72; v.p. Roesco Realty, San Juan, 1972-75; pres. Appco Fin. Corp., Coral Gables, Fla., 1975—. Mem. Fla. Premium Fin. Assn. (dir. 1976—). Republican. Roman Catholic. Club: Ocean Reef (Largo, Fla.). Office: Appco Finance Corp 811 Ponce De Leon Coral Gables FL 33134

ESPINOLA, AURELIO A., forensic pathologist; b. Isabela, Philippines, June 25, 1940; s. Victorino Levitania Espinola and Esperanza Parungao Aurelio; came to U.S., 1969, naturalized, 1972; M.D., Manila Central U., Philippines, 1963; m. Rosa V. Molle; children—Rommel, Leilani. Intern pathology Detroit Meml. Hosp., 1971-72; resident pathology Wayne State U., Detroit, 1972-76; fellow forensic pathology Wayne County Med. Examiner's Office, Detroit, 1976-77; pathologist, physician Tex. Dept. Correction, Huntsville, 1977-78; asst. med. examiner Harris County Med. Examiners Office, Houston, 1978—. Mem. Coll. Am. Pathologists, Am. Soc. Clin. Pathologists, Tex. Med. Assn., Harris County Med. Soc., Houston Soc. Clin. Pathologists. Roman Catholic. Home: 9503 Hexham Ct Spring TX 77373 Office: 1502 Taub Loop Houston TX 77030

ESTEB, ADLAI ALBERT, ret. clergyman, author; b. La Grande, Oreg., Nov. 17, 1901; s. Lemuel Albert and Addretta (Koger) E.; B.Th., Walla Walla Coll., 1931; M.A., Calif. Coll., Peiping, China, 1953; Ph.D., U. So. Calif., 1944; m. Florence Edna Airey, Feb. 5, 1923; children—Adeline, Lucille. Ordained to ministry Seventh-day Adventist Ch., 1923; missionary to China, 1923-37; pastor Seventh-day Adventist Ch., Long Beach, Calif., 1938-40; sec. home missionary dept. So. Calif. Conf. Seventh-day Adventist Ch., 1940-46, Pacific Union Conf. Seventh-day Adventist Ch., Glendale, Calif., 1946-50; editor Go, Jour. for Adventist Laymen, gen. conf. Seventh-day Adventist Ch., Washington, 1950-70; vis. prof., lectr. Christian ethics Andrews U., Berrien Springs, Mich., 1955-75, ret. Cited as poet laureate of denomination by pres. World Conf., 1966; named Alumnus of Yr., Walla Walla Coll., 1979. Mem. China Soc. of So. Calif. (pres. 1946-50), Oriental Fellowship (pres. 1963), Phi Beta Kappa, Phi Kai Phi, Phi Kappa Phi. Author: Driftwood, 1947; Firewood, 1952; Sandalwood, 1955; Morning Manna, 1962; Rosewood, 1964; Scrapwood, 1967; (poetry) Redwood, 1970; Kindle Kindness, 1971; The Meaning of Christmas, 1972; When Suffering Comes, 1974; Straight Ahead, 1974. Home: Route 1 Box 345 Warsaw VA 22572

ESTES, DELL MCGLOTHREN, occupational therapist; b. Pace, Fla., Dec. 26, 1940; d. Ernest E. and Lanie (Ellis) McGlothren; B.S., U. Fla., 1962; postgrad. in edn. U. S.C., 1965; teaching certificate in Spl. Edn., U. So. Ala., 1966; now postgrad. in edn. and allied health scis. U. Ala., Birmingham; m. John E. Estes, June 27, 1958; children—Brenda, Alisa, John E. Therapist, S.C. Soc. Crippled Children and Adults, Georgetown, 1963-65; tchr. Winyah High Sch., Georgetown, 1963-64, Summerville (S.C.) Elementary Sch., 1964-65; spl. edn. tchr. Monroeville (Ala.) Elementary Sch., 1966-67; staff therapist to supr. rehab. dept. Monroe County Hosp., Monroeville, from 1967—; cons. Monroeville and Evergreen Nursing Homes, 1974-76; therapist, Jackson, Ala., 1975-76; cons. nursing home activities Monroe County Health Dept. Vol. ARC; leader Girl Scouts U.S.A., 1966-70; mem. adv. council Ret. Seniors Vol. Program; pres. United Methodist Women, Monroeville; pres. Monroe chpt. ARC. Mem. Am., Ala. occupational therapy assns. Club: Vanity Fair Golf and Tennis. Home: 801 Old Forest Rd Birmingham AL 35243 also PO Box 447 Monroeville AL 36460 Office: Regional Tech Inst U Ala Birmingham AL 35205

ESTES, GERALD WALTER, newspaper exec.; b. Memphis, Apr. 21, 1928; s. Edward Leon and Grace Virginia (Knight) E.; student Memphis State U., 1949-50; m. Mary Charlene Owen, Nov. 7, 1953 (div. July 1975); children—Patricia (Mrs. Roy Brian Tischler), Charles Edward, Susan Lynn, Jacqueline Ann; m. 2d, Bernice O'Mery, Mar. 20, 1976. Research asst. Washington Star News, 1954-56, asst. prodn. mgr., 1956-68; prodn. mgr. Richmond (Va.) Newspapers, S.E. Media, Inc., 1968-69, gen. mgr., 1969-73, v.p., 1969—; v.p. Media Gen., Inc., 1974-77, sr. v.p., 1977—. Served with USAF, 1946-49. Mem. Richmond C. of C., Central Richmond Assn., So. Newspaper Pubs. Assn., So. Printing Prodn. Inst. Republican. Methodist. Clubs: Bull and Bear, Salisbury Country, Research in newspaper automation and computerized newspaper prodn. facility. Home: 6505 River Rd Richmond VA 23229 Office: 333 E Grace Richmond VA 23219

ESTES, MOREAU PINCKNEY, IV, lawyer, business exec.; b. Nashville, Oct. 10, 1917; s. Moreau Pinckney and Lillian (Cole) E.; student Vanderbilt U., 1935-37; LL.B., Cumberland U. Law Sch., 1938; m. Bertha Lewis, Jan. 14, 1941; children—Moreau Pinckney V, Robert Lewis, Victoria Susanne. Admitted to Tenn. bar, 1938; practiced in Nashville, 1938-41; bldg. contractor, Nashville, 1940-42; asst. employees service dir. Vultee Aircraft, Nashville, 1942; bldg. contractor, Nashville, 1946-53; dir. Davidson County Farm Bur., Nashville, 1950-56; v.p. Davidson Farmers Co-Op, 1955-56; gen. mgr. Harpeth Valley Utilities Dist. of Davidson and Williamson Counties, Tenn., 1963-67; pres. Hillsboro-Harpeth Corp; v.p. Rivermont Farms, Inc., property adminstr. State of Tenn., 1964-67, atty. property div., 1962-64; asst. commr. Tenn. Dept. Conservation, 1975. Del. Democratic State Conv., 1951; sec. Williamson County Dem. Primary Commn., 1967-69. Served as 1st lt. Signal Corps, AUS, 1942-46. Mem. Nashville Home Bldrs. Assn. (pres. 1951, dir. 1952), Tenn. Horsemens Assn., (dir. 1964), Tenn. Hist. Assn., Nashville Tennis Assn. (municipal singles and doubles champion 1939, 40, dir. 1969-72), Tenn., Nashville bar assns., Am. Judicature Soc., Internat. Platform Assn., Davidson County Farm Bur., Nat. Audubon Soc., Smithsonian Assos., Nat. Hist. Soc., Vanderbilt Alumni Assn., Am. Legion, Delta Kappa Epsilon. Democrat. Methodist (steward 1940-50). Clubs: Inglewood Sch. Men's (pres. 1946, 48), Percy Priest Sch. Men's (pres., 1963), Wildwood Swimming and Tennis (founder, 1st chmn. bd.). Home: Wildwood Dr Route 8 Brentwood TN 37027 Office: 19th Floor Life and Casualty Tower Nashville TN 37219

ESTES, NOLAN, univ. prof.; b. Rio Hondo, Tex., June 22, 1930; s. Clarence M. and Eva (Boyd) E.; B.S., U. Corpus Christi, 1950; M.Ed., U. Tex., 1954; postgrad. Baylor U., 1956; D.Ed., Harvard, 1958; m. Mildred Johnson, Aug. 9, 1951; children—Dennis, Blake, Kevin, Brian. Tchr. math. and sci., athletic dir. Bruni (Tex.) High Sch., 1950-51; adminstrv. intern Bur. Lab. Schs., U. Tex., Austin, 1953-54; elementary tchr. Waco (Tex.) Ind. Sch. Dist., 1954-55, prin. Lake

Waco Sch., 1955-59; ednl. tv instr. Tex. Dept. Edn. and Baylor U., Waco, 1956-57; staff mem. Center for Field Studies, Harvard Grad. Sch. Edn., 1957-58; asst. supt. instrn. Chattanooga Pub. Schs., 1959-62; vis. lectr. edn. U. Chattanooga, 1960-62; vis. lectr. edn. U. Ariz., summer 1962; supt. schs. Sch. Dist. Riverview Gardens, St. Louis County, Mo., 1962-66; Washington intern in edn. as spl. asst. to asso. commr. edn. Bur. Elementary and Secondary Edn., 1965-66, dir. div. Plans and Supplementary Centers, 1966, dep. asso. commr., 1966-67, asso. commr. edn., 1967-68; supt. schs., Dallas Ind. Sch. Dist., 1968-70; prof. ednl. adminstrn. U. Tex. Mem. ops. adv. com. Nat. Com. on Assessing Progress of Edn.; mem. adv. and policy com. ERIC Clearing House on Tchr. Ednl.; pres. Council Gt. Cities Schs., 1977. Vice chmn. Greater Chattanooga United Fund, 1962; pres. St. Louis County Sch. Dist. AV Corp. Bd., 1964. Bd. dirs. Circle Ten council Boy Scouts Am., Chattanooga Symphony Orch.; mem. adv. bd. trustees Carson-Newman Coll., Jefferson City, Tenn.; trustee, mem. exec. com. St. Louis Ednl. Television Commn.; trustee U. Corpus Christi. Served with AUS, 1951-53. Decorated Bronze Star. Recipient Outstanding Officer of Year award Chattanooga Jr. C. of C., 1961-62, Sch. of Year award Nation's Sch. Competition as supt. schs., 1965, Distinguished Alumnus awards U. Corpus Christi, 1966, Dallas Bapt. Coll., 1969. S.D. Shankland Meml. scholar, 1968. Mem. NEA (life), PTA (nat. treas.), Assn. for Supervision and Curriculum Devel., Tex. Assn. Sch. Adminstrs. (v.p. 1977), Tex. Tchrs. Assn., Tex. Elementary Sch. Prins. Assn. (past dist. pres.), Tenn. Assn. for Supervision and Curriculum Devel. (past pres.), Sigma Epsilon, Phi Delta Kappa. Home: 8 Lake Trail Austin TX 78746 Office: EdB310 Univ Tex Austin TX 78712

ESTES, SIDNEY HARRISON, ednl. adminstr.; b. Atlanta, Jan. 18, 1932; s. William Harrison and Fannie Mae (Webster) E.; B.A., Lincoln U., 1953; M.A., Atlanta U., 1959; Ed.D., Ind. U., 1967; m. Barbara Ann Brown, Apr. 10, 1971; children—Sidmel, Edward, Cheryl, Christopher. Assembly worker Lockheed Aircraft Corp., Marietta, Ga., 1955-56; case worker Fulton County Dept. Public Welfare, Atlanta, 1956-57; tchr. Slater Elem. Sch., Atlanta, 1957-63; prin. Ralph Robinson Elem. Sch., Atlanta, 1963-68; asso. dir. Edn. Improvement Project, Atlanta, 1968-69, exec. dir., 1969-71; dir. doctoral program in ednl. adminstrn. Atlanta U., 1971-73; asst. supt. for instrnl. planning and devel. Atlanta Public Schs., 1973—. Chmn., Atlanta Clean City Commn.; mem. exec. bd. Atlanta Area council Boy Scouts Am. Served with Mil. Intelligence, U.S. Army, 1953-55. Recipient Silver Beaver award Boy Scouts Am., 1974. Mem. Am. Assn. Sch. Adminstrs., Nat. Soc. for Study of Edn., Assn. Supervision and Curriculum Devel., Phi Delta Kappa, Alpha Phi Alpha. Home: 1244 Shore Dr Atlanta GA 30311 Office: Atlanta Public Schs 2930 Forrest Hill Dr SW Atlanta GA 30315

ESTES, TIMOTHY BRUCE, mktg.-sales co. exec.; b. Atlanta, Sept. 3, 1949; s. Bruce Edward and Charlotte Marie (Jones) E.; A.A., Gordon Mil. Coll., 1969; 1 yr. Bible degree Fla. Bible Coll., 1970; B.B.A., U. Ga., 1972; m. Margaret Ann Winchester, Apr. 7, 1973; children—Timothy Paul, Jonathan Mark, Stephen Michael. Mgr. trainee J.C. Penney Co., Decatur, Ga., 1973; account exec. Ivan Allen Co., Marietta, Ga., 1973—; mktg. cons. Estes & Assos. Internat., Powder Springs, Ga. Served with U.S. Army, 1970. Football scholar, 1968-70. Mem. Yagar Dreambuilders Assn., Am. Mktg. Assn. (v.p. 1971-72), Pi Kappa Alpha (v.p. 1971-72). Club: Free Enterprize.

ESTILL, CHARLES REUEL, found. exec.; b. Chgo., Dec. 17, 1914; s. Reuel Cape and Hazel Genevieve (Kast) E.; A.B., Colgate U., 1939; m. Dorothy Eleanor Murphy, Sept. 21, 1940; children—Patric Genevieve, Michael Reuel. Sales, mgmt. positions R.H. Macy, N.Y.C., 1939-41; account exec. Young & Rubicam, Inc., N.Y.C., 1941-47; v.p., dir. Reuel Estill & Co., N.Y.C., 1947-54; dir. devel. Clarkson Coll. Tech., Potsdam, N.Y., 1954-58; v.p. Johns Hopkins Instns., Balt., 1958-67, U. Miami, Coral Gables, Fla., 1967-73; pres. Charles Estill & Co., Miami, 1973-76, Sarasota Meml. Hosp. Found., 1976—. Chmn. bd. Hospice of Sarasota, Inc., 1979. Served with USNR, 1942-45. Decorated Bronze Star. Mem. Nat. Assn. Devel. Officers (career recognition award 1970, nationally outstanding devel. officer of decade 1974), Am. Coll. Public Relations Assos. Republican. Clubs: Univ. Sarasota, Miami, Fox Fire Country, Forest Lakes Country. Home: 8625 Midnight Pass Rd Apt 208B Sarasota FL 33581 Office: Sarasota Meml Hosp Fund 1865 Hawthorne St Sarasota FL 33579

ESTRADA, GEORGE HENRY, food service co. adminstr.; b. San Antonio, Feb. 10, 1940; s. Emilio and Susie (Martinez) E.; student E. Carolina U., 1969-71; m. Barbara J. Estrada, Apr. 8, 1977; stepchildren—Michael, Chris. Served as enlisted man U.S. Marine Corps, 1957-77; with ARA Food Services Co., 1977—, food prodn. mgr. Fla. State U., Tallahassee, 1977-78, asst. dir. food services U. N.C. at Greensboro, 1978-79, dir. food services Michel Tire Corp., Dothan, Ala., 1979—. Mem. Am. Numis. Assn., Non-Commd. Officers Assn. Home: 2108 Honeysuckle Rd Fox Run Apts Apt 246 Dothan AL 36301 Office: Michelin Tire Corp Industrial Rd Dothan AL 36301

ESTRADA, HAYDEN FRANCIS, corp. exec.; b. Hot Springs, Ark., Mar. 4, 1935; s. Leon Pius and Maude Elizabeth (Fields) E.; B.S. in Math. and Chemistry, Memphis State U., 1960; Ph.D. in Commerce (hon.), London Inst., 1973; m. Emma Cardona y King, Apr. 4, 1959; children—Hayden Francis IV, Robert Leon, John Alan. Quality control engr. for procurement mil. supplies U.S. Govt., 1960-61; engr. Apollo Capsule, Westinghouse Aerospace Div., 1961-63, with Ampex Corp., 1963-69; pres. Profl. Reps., also Info. Processing Supplies, Atlanta, 1970—; pres. Am. Info. Processing Supplies; dir. Word Processing Supplies Inc.; dir. and officer Atlantic Info. Supplies. Served with U.S. Army, 1957. Recipient commendation White House, 1968; numerous sales awards. Mem. Am. Soc. Quality Control, Am. Mgmt. Assn., AAAS, Pres.'s Assn., Nat. Office Products Assn., Nat. Office Machine Dealers Assn., Electronics Reps. Assn., Internat. Word Processing Assn. Roman Catholic. Clubs: Elks, K.C., Kiwanis. Office: 230 Marray Dr Atlanta GA 30341 also 2101 SIH 35 Suite 300 Austin TX 78741

ETCHISON, ANNIE LAURIE, librarian, artist; b. Cana, N.C., Dec. 5, 1908; d. John W. and Nana (Cain) Etchison; A.B., Western Res. U., 1939, B.L.S., 1940. Librarian, Cleve. Pub. Library, 1941-42; chief librarian Langley AFB, Va., 1942-44; supervisory librarian U.S. Army, Hawaii, 1945; chief librarian Armed Forces Western Pacific, Phillipines, Okinawa 1945-46; command librarian 2d Dist. U.S. Army, Europe, 1947-49, U.S. Air Force, Alaska, 1950-52; librarian recruitment Dept. Army, Washington, 1952-54; staff librarian U.S. Army, Korea, 1954-55; librarian Dept. Navy, Washington, 1956; chief librarian Ft. Bragg, N.C., 1957-63; staff librarian Hdqrs. 3d U.S. Army, Atlanta, 1963-72; library dir. U.S. Army Europe, 1972-78; cons. automation of libraries and library design. Awarded U.S. Army Meritorious Service medal, Armed Forces Achievement citation, 1978. Pioneer in library service for armed forces; designed 1st automated library system in U.S. Army. Home: RFD 5 Box 58 Mocksville NC 27028

ETHEREDGE, ROBERT FOSTER, lawyer, state legislator; b. Birmingham, Ala., July 14, 1920; s. Joel H. and Nell (Cain) E.; A.B., U. Ala., 1946, LL.B., 1949; m. Joanna Carson, Aug. 28, 1948; children—Robert Foster, Carson, Nancy. Admitted to Ala. bar, 1949; since practiced in Birmingham; mem. firm Spain, Gillon, Riley, Tate, & Etheredge and predecessor firms, 1949—. Mem. Ala. Ho. of Reps., 1963—. Mem. adv. com. Family Ct.; pres. Ala. Soc. Crippled Children and Adults, 1971-73; chmn. profl. div. United Appeal. Bd. dirs. Jefferson County Socs. for Crippled Children and Adults, North Central Ala. Rehab. Facility. Served to 1st lt. AUS, 1943-46. Mem. Am. (mem. state legislative com.), Birmingham bar assns., Ala. State Bar, Am. Legion, V.F.W., Relay House, Ala. Law Inst., Farrah Law Soc., Ala. Def. Lawyers Assn., Internat. Assn. Ins. Counsel, Am. Judicature Soc., Omicron Delta Kappa, Pi Kapps Alpha. Democrat. Methodist. Elk, Eagle, Rotarian. Club: Country of Birmingham. Home: 3748 Locksley Dr Birmingham AL 35223 Office: John A Hand Bldg Birmingham AL 35203

ETHERIDGE, FRANK ROBINSON, indsl. distributor co. exec.; b. Atlanta, July 4, 1927; s. Girard G. and Frances (Robinson) E.; B.S. in B.A., Temple U., 1951; m. Edna Ruth Scott, Feb. 21, 1954; 1 dau., Lynne Renee Etheridge Kelley. Mgr., P.F. Kane, Inc., Phila., 1948-51; partner Miller Bearings, Lakeland, Fla., 1951-56; pres. Miller Bearings of Ocala (Fla.) Inc., 1956-58, Miller Bearings of Tampa (Fla.), Inc., 1961-62, Acme Conveyor Co., Inc., Sanford, Fla., 1970-75, FRE Enterprises, Inc., Orlando, Fla., 1971-76, Orange Plating Inc., Orlando, 1972—; pres. Gondas Corp. Internat., Miami, Fla., 1974-76; pres. Miller Bearings of Orlando, 1957-70, chmn. bd., 1970—. Bd. dirs. Loch Haven Art Center, Orlando, 1953-55, John Young Mus. and Planetarium, Orlando, 1953-55, Fla. Symphony Soc., Orlando, 1953-55, Lakeland (Fla.) Jr. C. of C., 1953-55. Served with USN, 1945-46; PTO. Mem. Purchasing Mgmt. Assn. Central Fla., Purchasing Mgmt. Assn. Fla., Bearing Specialists Assn., Power Transmission Distbrs. Assn., So. Indsl. Distbrs. Assn., Nat. Assn. Wholesale Distbrs. Baptist. Clubs: Country of Orlando, Citrus, Masons (Shriner). Author, illustrator: Bearing Basics, 1963; Caring for Bearings, 1963; Bearing Failures, 1963. Home: Orlando FL 32804 Office: 17 S Westmoreland St Orlando FL 32802

ETIENNE, JOSEPH EDGAR, audiologist; b. Cannelton, Ind., Dec. 2, 1954; s. Edgar F. and Helen K. E.; A.B., Ind. U., 1976, M.A., 1977; m. Darlina McBride, Nov. 24, 1976. Audiologist Middle Ga. Cooperative Ednl. Service Agy., Ft. Valley, 1977-78; tchr. hearing impaired, audiologist Dooly County (Ga.) Bd. Edn., Vienna, 1978-79; clin. audiologist Bristol (Va.) Regional Speech and Hearing Center, 1979—; cons. in field. Mem. Am. Speech Lang. and Hearing Assn., Ga. Assn. Educators, NEA, Va. Speech and Hearing Assn. Roman Catholic. Home: 1613 Fairmount Ave Bristol VA 24201 Office: Memorial Hall Bristol VA 24201

ETTER, RICHARD LEE, physician; b. Waco, Tex., Nov. 17, 1912; s. Hall and Nogya (McBride) E.; B.S., The Citadel, 1935; B.A., U. Houston, 1936; M.A., Baylor U., 1937; M.D., George Washington U., 1943; m. Nancy L. Schnack, Nov. 16, 1977; 1 dau., Patricia Lee Etter Womack. Intern, Hermann Hosp., Houston, 1943, resident, 1945-47; with Houston Allergy Clinic, 1947—, sr. partner, 1949—; asso. prof. medicine U. Tex. Med. Sch., Houston, 1970—; clin. asst. prof. medicine Baylor Coll. Medicine, Houston, 1965—; chief emeritus allergy dept. Hermann Hosp., U. Tex., 1978—. Served to maj., M.C., U.S. Army, 1943-47. Decorated Bronze Star medal. Mem. Am. Coll. Allergists, Am. Acad. Allergy, Am. Assn. Clin. Immunology and Allergy, Tex. Med. Assn., S.W. Allergy Forum, So. Med. Assn., Houston Allergy Soc. Republican. Episcopalian. Clubs: Masons, Shriners. Home: 2705 Essex Terrace Houston TX 77027 Office: 444 Hermann Profl Bldg 6410 Fannin St Houston TX 77030

ETTIEN, JAMES THOMAS, surgeon; b. Chattanooga, Mar. 23, 1941; s. Todd and Rose Jane (Verhey) E.; B.A. in English, U. of South, Tenn., 1963; M.D., Med. Coll. Ga., 1971; student Ga. State U., 1966-67; m. Janey Cureton, Sept. 14, 1963; 1 son, James Keith. Intern in surgery Vanderbilt Hosp., Nashville, 1971-72; resident in ophthalmology Med. Coll. Ga., 1972, resident in orthopaedic surgery, 1973-74, resident in surgery, 1974-76; practice medicine specializing in surgery, Gastonia, N.C., 1976-78, Largo, Fla., 1979—; attending surgeon VA Hosp., Forest Hills div., Augusta, Ga., 1978—, mem. med. records com., 1978-79; surg. cons. Eisenhower Med. Center, Fort Gordon, Ga., 1978—; asst. prof. dept. surgery Med. Coll. Ga., Augusta, 1978—; gen. and vascular surgeon Diagnostic Clinic, 1979—; mem. staff Gastonia Surg. Assos., 1976-78; mem. Med. Research Found. Ga., 1978-79. Served with USAF, 1963-66. Diplomate Am. Bd. Surgery. Fellow Internat. Coll. Surgeons; mem. Med. Assn. Ga., Southeastern Surg. Congress, Assn. Acad. Surgery, A.C.S. (candidate), William H. Moretz Surg. Soc., So. Med. Assn., AMA, Richmond County Med. Soc., Pancreas Club, Alpha Omega Alpha. Republican. Episcopalian. Contbr. articles on surgery to med. jours. and chpts. to books on surgery. Home: 2345 Kings Pointe Dr Largo FL 33540 Office: 1551 W Bay Dr Largo FL 33540

EUBANK, BRENDA SUE, ins. adjusting co. ofcl.; b. Daviess County, Ky., Oct. 8, 1948; d. Dan and Juanita (Tanner) Eubank; student Western Ky. U., 1966, Ky. Wesleyan Coll., 1970-73, U. Louisville, 1973-76. Exec. sec. to exec. v.p. Ky. Wesleyan Coll., Owensboro, 1971-73; exec. sec. to pres. U. Louisville, 1973-76; adminstrv. asst. ops. Crawford & Co., Atlanta, 1977—. Mem. Internat. Word Processing Assn., Adminstrv. Mgmt. Soc. Democrat. Methodist. Office: 5620 Glenridge Dr NE PO Box 5047 Atlanta GA 30302

EUBANKS, MICHAEL RAY, lawyer; b. Lumberton, Miss., Sept. 21, 1940; s. Michael Joseph and Nell Elizabeth (Bass) E.; student Phillips Acad., 1954-58; B.B.A., Tulane U., 1962, J.D., 1965; m. Sue Ellen Griffin, Aug. 10, 1968; children—Michelle, Christy Leigh, Mark Webster. Admitted to La. bar, 1965, Miss. bar, 1966; individual practice law, Lumberton, Miss., 1966-71; partner firm Eubanks Temple & Hudson, Purvis, Miss., 1971—, sr. partner, 1971—; atty. Lamar County Bd. Suprs., 1972-79, City of Lumberton, 1970—; served as judge City of Lumberton, 1968-70. Exec. dir. Lumberton C. of C., 1973-77. Mem. gov.'s staff State of Miss., 1971-79. Recipient Regional Improvement award Tulane Alumni Fund, 1976; Miss. alumni rep. Philips Acad., 1973—. Mem. Am., Miss., La., S. Central Miss., Lamar County bar assns., Am., Miss. trial lawyers assns. Democrat. Methodist. Clubs: T, Tulane U. Home: 702 W Main Ave Lumberton MS 39455 Office: Courthouse Sq Purvis MS 39475

EUBANKS, WALTER EDWARD, educator; b. Memphis, Jan. 1, 1925; s. William B. and Erma Lee (Balch) E.; student Howard Coll., 1947-49, Amarillo Coll., 1975, Wayland Bapt. Coll., 1975-78; m. Dora Lee Wheeler, Dec. 10, 1948; children—Larry Edward, Pamela Ann Eubanks Davis. Mem. Big Spring (Tex.) Police Dept., 1953-63; chief police City of Sweetwater, Tex., 1963-69; criminal justice coordinator West Central Council Govt., Abilene, Tex., 1969-70; chmn. public safety edn. Amarillo (Tex.) Coll., 1970—, asst. vocational prof. 1975—. Served with AUS, 1942-45. Mem. Tex. Jr. Coll. Tchrs. Assn., Tex. Police Assn., Assn. Law Enforcement Educators, Tex. Sheriffs Assn., NRA. Clubs: Masons, Shriners. Home: 6700 Falcon St Amarillo TX 79109 Office: 22d and Washington Sts Amarillo TX 79178

EULER, ARTHUR RAY, pediatric gastroenterologist; b. Hammond, Ind., Oct. 20, 1942; s. John Stanley and June Alice Biestek; B.S., Purdue U., 1965; M.D., Ind. U., 1969; m. Becky Suzanne Brashares, Feb. 2, 1967; children—Elizabeth Suzanne, Katherine Anne. Intern, Riley Hosp., Indpls., 1969-70, resident in pediatrics, 1970; resident Harborn Gen. Hosp., 1973-74; asst. prof. pediatrics UCLA Sch. Medicine, 1976-77; chief div. pediatric gastroenterology U. Ark. Med. Scis. Campus, Little Rock, 1977—. Served with USNR, 1970-73. Cystic Fibrosis fellow, 1973-75. Mem. Am. Gastroenterology Assn., Am. Fedn. Clin. Research, Am. Acad. Pediatrics, Central Ark. Pediatric Soc., Am. Soc. Parenteral and Enteral Nutrition, Western Gastroent. Assn., N. Am. Soc. Pediatric Gastro-enterology, So. Calif. Soc. Gastro-intestinal Endoscopy, So. Calif. Soc. Gastroenterology, Midwest Gut Club, So. Soc. Pediatric Research, AAAS. Home: 3208 Breckenridge Dr Little Rock AR 72207 Office: 804 Wolfe St Little Rock AR 72201

EULISS, RAY COOPER, automobile dealer; b. Burlington, N.C., Dec. 18, 1932; s. Cyrus Manning and Myrtle (Cooper) E.; A.B. summa cum laude, Elon Coll., 1953; M.B.A., U. N.C., 1955; m. Alice Dunn Carlyle, Aug. 28, 1954; 1 son, Cyrus Manning. Bus. mgr., treas. Alamance Motors, Inc., Burlington, 1955-63, exec. v.p. 1963-72, pres., 1972—; dir. Wachovia Bank & Trust Co., Burlington, N.C. Campaign dir., pres. United Way, Burlington, 1962, 63; pres.'s bd. advisors Elon Coll., 1974—; trustee Meml. Hosp. Alamance County, 1960—. Recipient Distinguished Service award Jr. C. of C., 1962; named Alamance County Young Man of Year, 1963; Distinguished Service award United Fund, 1963; Pres.'s award United Way, 1966. Mem. Chevrolet Dealer Council, Nat. Automobile Dealers Assn., N.C. Automobile Dealers Assn. (dir. 1960-61), Burlington Mchts. Assn. (dir. 1958-61), U. N.C. Alumni Assn. (life), Burlington-Alamance C. of C. Democrat. Methodist. Clubs: Alamance Country, Greensboro City, Kiwanis, Masons. Home: May's Lake PO Box 917 Burlington NC 27215 Office: PO Drawer 2228 The Alamance Rd Burlington NC 27215

EUTON, MICHAEL FRED, landscape architect; b. Houston, Aug. 10, 1938; s. William Robert and Lillie Bertha (Wischer) E.; student U. Tex. at Austin, 1956-59, Massey Bus. Coll., Houston, 1972. Sales mgr. Civic Reading Club, Houston and San Antonio, 1960-62; designer Davis Landscape Service, Houston, 1962-66; landscape architect Mike Euton Landscape Service, Barker, Tex., 1966—; lectr. in field. Exec. com. Democratic Party Harris County, Tex., 1966-68; del. Harris County Conv., 1960—, Tex. State Conv., 1960, 64, 68, 72, 74; precinct election judge, 1976; mem. U.S. Senator William A. Blakley's Harris County Campaign Staff, 1961; active campaign Dolph Briscoe for Gov., 1968, 72, 74. Mem. Tex. Soc. Landscape Architects, Tex. Farm Bur., Barker Heritage and Preservation Soc. (charter mem., sec. 1976, pres. 1977—, chmn. bd. 1979—), U. Tex. Ex-students Assn., C. of C. Club: One-Hundred (Houston). Address: 3506 Barker-Cypress St Barker TX 77413

EVANS, ALFONSO JACKSON, educator; b. Orangeburg, S.C., Oct. 11, 1933; s. John Gary and Florence Virginia (Frederick) E.; B.S. in Biology and Phys. Edn. (Scholar), S.C. State Coll., 1957, M.S. in Guidance, Supervision and Adminstrn., 1965; Ed.D. in Ednl. Adminstrn., U. S.C., 1977; m. Angie Evelyn Holmes, June 8, 1957; children—Letitia Alene Alfonso Jackson, Curtis Malcolm, Ericka Jillene. Tchr. biology, att. football coach W. Gresham Meggett High Sch., Charleston, S.C., 1959-62, prin., head football coach, 1962-69; asst. dir. guidance and testing Charleston County Pub. Schs., 1969-70; edn. extension agt. S.C. Dept. Edn., Charleston, 1970-72, chief supr. edn. products center, 1972—; resource cons. for ednl. info. dissemination. Mem. local events com. for Charleston County Tri-Centennial for Charleston County Schs., 1970; mem. cast Porgy and Bess, Charleston County Tri-Centennial Prodn., 1970; chmn. Palmetto Dist. Boy Scouts Scouts Am., 1970-72. Served with U.S. Army, 1957-59. Recipient Silver Beaver award Boy Scouts Am., 1973. Mem. Assn. for Supervision and Curriculum Devel., (asso.), Phi Delta Kappa (Mu Alpha chpt.), Omega Psi Phi. Frat. Baptist. Club: Masons. Home: 31 Race St Charleston SC 29403

EVANS, BEATRICE SINGLETON, ednl. counselor; b. Florence, S.C., May 29, 1931; d. Nathaniel Earl and Bertha Beatrice (Singletary) S.; B.S., S.C. State Coll., 1955; M.S., 1970; m. Robert Shaw Evans, Dec. 28, 1955; children—Robert Shaw, Fredrick Marshall, James Malcolm. Tchr. Hazel Elementary Sch., Hampton, S.C., 1955-58; mem. guidance dept. S.C. State Coll., Orangeburg, 1960-73; student coordinator vocat. edn. Orangeburg City schs., 1973-76; guidance counselor Claflin Coll., Orangeburg, 1976—. Bd. dirs. United Way, Orangeburg, S.C., 1977—; mem. advisory com. Mt. Pisgah Baptist Ch., Orangeberg, S.C., 1977, advisory council, Columbia, S.C. for Orangeberg, Bamberg, and Calhoun counties; Mental Health Assn.; Nat. Council of Negro Women, Robt. Shaw Wilkinson assembly #220, Palmetto-Los Country Health Systems Agency. Recipient United Way Vol. award, 1977; Jack & Jill of Am. Service certificate, 1977; Noteworthy Americans plaque, 1976. Mem. Am., S.C. personnel and guidance assns., Am. Measurement and Evaluation in Guidance, Nat. Assn. Non-White Concerns, Am. Coll. Personnel Assn., C. of C. (sub. com.). Democrat. Clubs: Delta Sigma Theta, Nat. Assn. of Univ. Women, Orangeberg chpt. Links, Eastern Star #258, VFW Ladies Aux. Post-8166. Home: 1736 Walker Ave Orangeburg SC 29115 Office: PO Box 1534 State College Orangeburg SC 29115

EVANS, BERNICE JONES, home economist, educator; b. Eagle Lake, Tex., Sept. 10, 1942; d. Burnett and Sophia Beaulah (Einkauf) Jones; student SW Tex. State U., 1960-62; B.S., U. Mary Hardin Baylor, 1964; M. Ed., Prairie View A&M U., 1979; m. W.C. Evans, Aug. 18, 1962; children—Edward Joe, John Rylan. Tchr. homemaking Rogers (Tex.) High Sch., 1964-66, Acad. High Sch., Little River Acad., Tex., 1966—. Mem. Tex. State Tchrs. Assn. (life), Vocat. Homemaking Tchrs. Assn. Tex., Am. Home Econs. Assn., Am. Personnel and Guidance Assn., Am. Vocat. Assn., Tex. Personnel and Guidance Assn. Baptist. Address: Box 458 Little River TX 76554

EVANS, BILLY LEE, Congressman; b. Tifton, Ga., Nov. 10, 1941; A.B., U. Ga., 1963, LL.B., 1964; m. April Durrough, 1971; children—Christopher, William Corry, Paul Jason, Autumn Lee. Admitted to Ga. bar, 1965; individual practice law, Macon, Ga., 1965-76; mem. Ga. Ho. of Reps., 1969-76; mem. 95th and 96th Congresses from 8th Ga. Dist., mem. Pub. Works and Transp. com., House Judiciary com., Small Bus. com., Select Com. on Drug Abuse. Mem. Macon, Ga. bar assns., Ga. Farm Bur. Democrat. Clubs: Elk, Moose, Eagles, Masons, Shriners. Office: 113 Cannon House Office Bldg Washington DC 20515

EVANS, BRUCE DAVISH, educator; b. Rochester, N.Y., Oct. 31, 1935; s. Harry M. and Margaret E.; B.S., Kent State U., 1956; M.B.A., U. Mich., 1958; postgrad. N. Tex. State U., 1967-70; m. Viva S. Andrus, June 22, 1957; children—Lori Ellyn, Bryce C. Asst. to pres. Hamilton Reins. Pools Co., Atlanta, 1962-64; v.p. Transport Ins. Group, Dallas, 1964-67; lectr. N. Tex. State U., Denton, 1967-70; asso. prof. Grad. Sch. Mgmt., U. Dallas, 1969—; exec. dir. Risk Mgmt. Inst., Irving, Tex., 1972—; cons. on gen. and risk mgmt. matters to numerous corps.; expert witness on reins. issues in fed. cts. Mem. Planning and Zoning Commn. Renner, 1969-77; area liaison City of

Dallas Communications, 1977-79. C.P.C.U. Mem. Risk and Ins. Mgmt. Soc. Contbr. articles to profl. jours.; author: (with Margaret Evans) Research Paper Guide, 1979. Home: 7032 Creek Bend St Dallas TX 75252 Office: Sch Mgmt U Dallas Irving TX 75061

EVANS, CALVIN AUGUSTUS, banker; b. Columbus, Ga., Dec. 10, 1945; s. Calvin Wilkes and Catherine S. (Sentell) E.; B.A., U. Ga., 1968, M.B.A., 1970; m. Sherry Hinson, Aug. 1, 1970; 1 son, Calvin Augustus. Asst. cashier Trust Co. of Columbus, 1971, asst. v.p., 1972-74, v.p., 1974-79, sr. v.p., 1979—; instr. mktg. Troy State U., 1979. Mem. budget com. United Way, Columbus, 1976; bd. dirs. ARC, 1971, Jr. Achievement, Columbus, 1974—, Boys Club, Columbus, 1976—. Mem. Assn. U.S. Army, Omicron Delta Epsilon. Club: Kiwanis. Home: 1618 Elmwood Dr Columbus GA 31908 Office: PO Box 8808 Columbus GA 31908

EVANS, CHARLES WESLEY, state legislator; b. Jacksonville, Fla., Feb. 19, 1939; s. Robert Lee and Leona Evelyn Evans; B.A. in History, Arlington (Tex.) State Coll., 1965; J.D., So. Meth. U., 1967; m. Patricia Anne, June 8, 1963; children—Lisa Ann, James Wesley. Mem. Tex. Ho. of Reps., 1973—, vice chmn. local govt. com., 1974, vice chmn. adminstrn. com., 1974-76, chmn. govtl. orgn. com., 1978—, chmn. jud. affairs com., 1976—; mem. Hurst City Council, 1970-72. practice law, Hurst, Tex. Served with USN, 1957-61. Named Man of Month, Hurst (Tex.) Jaycees, 1972; recipient Disting. Service award State Bar Tex., 1973. Mem. N.E. Tarrant County Bar Assn., Hurst-Euless-Bedford C. of C., Phi Kappa Theta. Democrat. Baptist. Home: 809 Bedford Ct W Hurst TX 76053 Office: 729 Bedford Euless Rd Hurst TX 76053

EVANS, DARDANELLA LISTER, nurse, writer, engring. co. exec.; b. Vernon, Tex., Jan. 26, 1921; d. Jack and Jenna Ferol (Bradley) Lister; grad. U. Okla. Sch. Nursing, 1943; grad. Nat. Landscape Inst., 1959; m. Kent E. Evans, May 21, 1946; children—Karen Louise Evans Ulehla, Sharon Jean Evans Wilson. With Okla. Pub. Co. and Sta. WKY, 1939-40; nurse U. Hosp. and Crippled Childrens' Hosp., Oklahoma City, 1940-43; vol. nurse Sch. Immunization Community Program, Dallas, 1958-69; key market editor for N.Y. publs. including Radio & TV Weekly, 1964-71, U.S. Tobacco Jour., 1964-71; v.p. Atlas Engring. Services, Inc., Atlanta, 1976—; free lance writer health and safety, 1939—. PTA room rep. Lakewood, Long and Woodrow Wilson high schs., Dallas, 1953-69; girl scout leader Lakewood Sch. council Girl Scouts U.S., 1956-63; Sunday sch. tchr. Skillman Ave. Ch. of Christ, 1962-65. Served with U.S. Army Nurse Corps, 1943-46. Mem. Women in Communications, Am. Heart Assn., Nutrition Today Soc., Nat. Writers Club, Associated Bus. Writers Am., Smithsonian Nat. Assn., Am. Trauma Soc., DeKalb North Art Alliance, Silver Lake Civic Assn., Nat. Safety Council. Republican. Mem. Ch. of Christ. Club: Atlanta Athletic. Author: Nest Not in My Hair!, 1978; contbr. poetry to various lit. publs. Home: 1273 Ragley Hall Rd Atlanta GA 30319 Office: 3808 Green Industrial Way Chamblee GA 30341 also PO Box 81292 Atlanta GA 30366

EVANS, DAVID ARTHUR, computer scientist, oceanographer; b. Gloucester, U.K., Aug. 5, 1939; s. Arthur and Estelle Vida (Phillips) E.; came to U.S., 1965; B.A., St. John's Coll., Cambridge (Eng.) U., 1960; Ph.D., Balliol Coll., Oxford (U.K.) U., 1964; m. Christine Ann Rees, July 28, 1962; children—Rosemary Helen, Hugh David. Research asst. nuclear physics lab. Oxford U., 1963-65; research asso. particle physics U. Calif., Riverside, 1965-67; asst. prof. physics SUNY at Buffalo, 1967-74; marine scientist Deepsea Ventures, Gloucester Point, Va., 1976-79; sr. marine scientist, also dir. computer center Va. Inst. Marine Sci., Gloucester Point, 1979—; asso. prof. marine sci. Coll. William and Mary, Williamsburg, Va., 1979—. Mem. Sigma Xi. Anglican. Editor: Nuclear Research Emulsions, Vol. II, 1973. Home: Box 428 Gloucester Point VA 23062 Office: Va Inst Marine Sci Gloucester Point VA 23062

EVANS, DE ETTE BRITT, ednl. diagnostician; b. Taylor, Ark., May 30, 1938; d. Denman and Lomer Britt; B.S. in Elementary Edn. with honors, N. Tex. State U., Denton, 1965; M.Ed. in Spl. Edn., Stephen F. Austin State U., Nacogdoches, Tex., 1973; div.; children—Aurelia, Cara. Tchr., Eskimo children for Bur. Indian Affairs, Emmonak, Alaska, 1965-68; tchr. educable retarded, Center, Tex., 1971-73; ednl. diagnostician, Marshall, Tex., 1973-74, Panola County Coop., Carthage, Tex., 1974—; condr. workshops. Mem. NEA, Am. Personnel and Guidance Assn., (chmn. Assessment Techniques 1977 conv.), E. Tex. assn. ednl. diagnosticians (pres. 1977-78), Tex. Tchrs. Assn. (chmn. lang and/or learning disability sect. 1976), Council Exceptional Children (workshops), Measurement and Evaluation in Guidance (nat. membership chmn.), Tex. Assn. Measurement and Evaluation in Guidance (pres. 1980—), E. Tex. Sch. Women's Council, Phi Delta Kappa, Alpha Delta Kappa. Methodist. Author: Screening for Exceptionalities, 1978; Evans Visual Motor Scale, 1980; also papers. Address: 300 Meadowlake Dr Longview TX 75604

EVANS, DWIGHT LAMAR, process engr.; b. Jasper, Ala., Oct. 27, 1951; s. William B. and Vera (Morrow) E.; B.A., U. North Ala., 1974; m. Elizabeth Ann Mason, Dec. 19, 1971; children—Kristopher, Lori. Chemist, 3M Co., Decatur, Ala., 1974-78, process engr., 1978—. Mem. Ch. of Christ. Home: 1608 Marion St Decatur AL 35601 Office: PO Box 2206 Decatur AL 35602

EVANS, EDDIE JOSEPH, JR., personnel exec.; b. Houma, La., Aug. 26, 1949; s. Eddie Joseph and Rose Mary Labat E.; B.S. in Econs. and Finance, Nicholls State U., 1971; m. Loretta Ann Hidalgo, Dec. 16, 1976; children—Cade Aaron, Jeff Robert. Mail clk. U.S. Post Office, 1971-73; personnel and accounts receivable clk. T. Baker Smith Engrs., Houma, 1973-75; office mgr Baton Black div. Hudson Engring. Corp. subs. J. Ray McDermott, Morgan City La., 1975-78; corp. personnel mgr. J. Ray McDermott, New Orleans, 1978-79; group personnel dir. McDermott Shipyard, Morgan City, 1979—. Mem. Am. Mgmt. Assn., Personnel Mgrs. Am., Bus. Adminstrn. Alumni Assn. Nicholls State U. (treas. 1979-80), Delta Sigma Pi. Democrat. Roman Catholic. Home: 113 Malibou Blvd Houma LA 70360 Office: PO Box 188 Morgan City LA 70380

EVANS, EDWARD ERNEST, land planner, landscape architect; b. Oak Ridge, June 16, 1945; s. Ernest Coleston and Marie Odile (Ricci) E.; B.L.A., N.C. State U., 1969; M.L.A., Harvard U., 1974; m. Mary Virginia Hughey, Dec. 21, 1968; 1 dau., Collyn Luneau. Land planner, landscape architect, resource analyst Oceanic Properties, Honolulu, 1969; with T. Bradshaw & Assos., Lauderdale-by-the-Sea, Fla., 1973; resource analyst EDAW, Inc., Mpls., 1973; landscape architect Miller, Wihry, Lee, Louisville, 1974, Walton, Madden, Cooper, A.I.A., Riverdale, Md., 1975; v.p., bus. mgr., land planner, partner Jordan/Evans Assos., P.A., Charlotte, N.C., 1976—; pres. Charter Oaks Farms, Inc.; landscape contractor, gen. contractor; curriculum adv. Catawba Valley Tech. Inst., 1979. Served to capt. C.E., USAR, 1969-72. Decorated Army Commendation medal for design and constrn.; registered landscape architect, Mass., Ky. Md., N.C., S.C., Tex.; registered landscape contractor, N.C.; Harvard U. regional field service grantee, 1973. Mem. Urban Land Inst., Am. Soc. Landscape Architects, Am. Planning Assn., Am. Landscape Contractors Assn., N.C. Landscape Contractors Assn. Lutheran. Clubs: Charlotte Kiwanis; Harvard of Charlotte. Office: PO Box 31312 Charlotte NC 28231

EVANS, EDWIN CURTIS, physician; b. Milledgeville, Ga., June 30, 1917; s. Watt Collier and Bertha Hall (Chambers) E.; B.S., U. Ga., 1936; M.D., Johns Hopkins U., 1940; m. Marjorie Claire Wood, Nov. 19, 1945; children—Nancy Claire, Edwin Courson, Marjorie Ann, Jane and Jill (twins), Carol. Intern, Hartford (Conn.) Hosp., 1940-42; chief resident in internal medicine Balt. City Hosp., 1946-47; fellow in pathology Hosp. of U. Pa., Phila., 1947-48; practice medicine specializing in internal medicine, Atlanta, 1948—; mem. staff Ga. Bapt. Hosp., chief staff, 1973-79; mem. staff Grady Meml. Hosp.; clin. asso. prof. medicine Emory U.; pres. bd. Atlanta Blue Shield, 1969. Served with M.C., AUS, 1942-46. Diplomate Am. Bd. Internal Medicine. Fellow A.C.P. (gov. for Ga. 1972-76), Am. Coll. Chest Physicians; mem. AMA, Am. (pres. 1972-73), Ga. (pres. 1963) socs. internal medicine, So. Med. Assn. (chmn. council 1978-79), Med. Assn. Atlanta (pres. 1973-74), Diabetes Assn. Atlanta (pres. 1958), Ga. Diabetes Assn. (pres. 1965-66), Med. Assn. Ga., Am. Heart Assn., Inst. of Medicine, Nat. Acad. Scis., Phi Chi. Methodist. Club: Cherokee Town and Country. Home: 500 Westover Dr NW Atlanta GA 30305 Office: 340 Boulevard NE Atlanta GA 30312

EVANS, HAZEL ATKINSON, polit. ofcl.; b. Atlanta, Aug. 16, 1931; d. Alex P. and Hazel (Thomas) Robert; student Marjorie Webster Jr. Coll., Washington, 1951; m. W. Reed Talley, Sept. 11, 1951; children—W. Reed Talley, Alex R.; m. 2d, Robert Winfield Evans, Nov. 30, 1968. Mem. State Democratic Com. Manatee, Pinellas County, 1962—; mem. Dem. Nat. Com., 1968—, mem. exec. com., 1973-80; mem. State Central Com. Dem. Exec. Com., Fla., 1966—; sec. Young Dem. Clubs Fla., 1962-63, v.p., 1963-64; del. Dem. Nat. Conv., 1964, 68, 72, 76, mem.-at-large exec. com., 1976; del. Nat. Dem. Mid-Term Conf., Kansas City, 1974, Memphis, 1978; mem. arrangements com. Dem. Nat. Conv., 1976, 1980; chmn. 6th Congl. dist. Dem. com., 1976—; del. Fla. Dem. Conv., 1975, 77, 79. Mem. Gov.'s Adv. Com. Pinellas County; Commr. Pinellas County Housing Authority, 1972—, vice chmn., 1975. Bd. dirs. Fla. Heart Assn., Fla. Mental Health Assn., Ringling Mus. Art, United Fund Manatee, Pinellas County. Recipient Meritorious award Am. Heart Assn., 1960, 64, 66, President's award Young Democrats Fla., 1963, 64. Mem. Beta Sigma Phi. Home: 1146 41st Av NE St Petersburg FL 33703

EVANS, JAMES DANSBY, lawyer; b. Butler, Ala., Sept. 30, 1948; s. Albert Henry and Josephine (Dansby) E.; B.A., Davidson Coll., 1970; J.D., U. Ala., 1973; m. Mildred Brett Morris, May 27, 1972; children—Evelyn Beaty, Rachael Purcell. Admitted to Ala. bar, 1974; law clk. Tuscaloosa Title Co. Inc., Tuscaloosa, 1972-73, Supreme Ct. of Ala., Montgomery, 1973-74; mem. firm William L. Utsey, Butler, 1974-77; mcpl. judge, 2 cities, 1975-76; dist. atty. 1st Jud. Circuit of Ala., Choctaw, Clarke and Washington counties, 1977—; mem. adv. com. on proposed law enforcement sch. Patrick Henry State Jr. Coll., Monroeville, Ala. Co-chmn. Bicentennial Commn. of Choctaw County, 1975-76; incorporator, bd. dirs. Ballet and Theatre Arts Performing Cos., Inc., Gilbertown, Ala.; mem. bd. advisors Ala. Hist. Commn.; lay leader First United Methodist Ch., Butler, 1978, 79, 80. Recipient award of merit Ala. Hist. Commn., 1978. Mem. Am. Bar Assn., Ala. Bar Assn., Choctaw County Bar Assn., 1st Jud. Circuit Bar Assn., Am. Law Enforcement Officers Assn., Ala. Dist. Attys. Assn., Nat. Dist. Attys. Assn., Fraternal Order of Police, Ala. Sheriffs Assn. (hon.), Farrah Law Soc., Ala. Hist. Assn., Davidson Coll. Alumni, U. Ala. Nat. Alumni Assn., Choctaw County Hist. Soc. (charter pres. 1978-80), Clarke and Washington County Hist. Socs. Historic Meridian Found., Phi Alpha Delta, Pi Kappa Phi. Democrat. Clubs: Lions (1st v.p.), Choctaw Country (Butler); Downtown (Meridian, Miss.). Home: 1105 Jeff St Butler AL 36904 Office: Choctaw County Courthouse Butler AL 36904

EVANS, JAMES HARVEY, mfg. co. exec.; b. Charleston, S.C., Aug. 8, 1946; s. Raymond Travis and Stella Mae (Bell) E.; B.S. in Indsl. Mgmt., Clemson U., 1968; M.B.A., The Citadel, 1977; m. Carolyn Gale Broad, Aug. 11, 1967; 1 son, James Travis. Planner, scheduler Avco Lycoming Co., Charleston, 1969-71; materials specialist Simplicity Mfg. Co., Lexington, S.C., 1971-72; prodn. supr. Exxon Chem. Co., Summerville, S.C., 1972-73; asst. to material control mgr. Teledyne Co., Walterboro, S.C., 1973-74; prodn. planning supr. Robert Bosch Corp., Charleston, 1974—. Mem. Am. Prodn. and Inventory Control Soc. Baptist. Home: 724 Creekside Dr Charleston SC 29412 Office: PO Box 10347 Charleston Heights SC 29405

EVANS, JAMES MIGNON, architect; b. Memphis, May 9, 1938; s. Mignon Kemper and Louise Elizabeth (Fulcher) E.; B.A., Rice U., 1960; M.F.A. (Lowell M. Palmer fellow), Princeton U., 1962; m. Gayle Jean Dupont, Aug. 25, 1965; children—Matthew Moseby, Benjamin Dupont, Bolin Briscoe. Designer, Perkins & Will Partnership, Washington, 1965-66; designer Doxiadis Assos., Inc., Washington, 1967-68; designer Gassner Nathan & Partners, Memphis, 1969—, v.p., 1977—. Trustee Grace-St. Luke's Episc. Sch. Served with AUS, 1963-65. Mem. AIA (pres. Memphis chpt.; Gulf States honor award 1978), Tenn. Soc. Architects (dir.). Episcopalian. Clubs: Univ. Memphis, Wolf River Soc. Architect: Phys. Edn./Convocation Center, U. Tenn., Martin, 1975, Miles Coll. Library, 1977, Fort Pillow State Historic Area Interpretive Center, 1978. Home: 1604 Vinton Ave Memphis TN 38104 Office: 265 Court Ave Memphis TN 38103

EVANS, JAMES PRICE, III, hotel ofcl.; b. Robinson, Ill., Oct. 12, 1946; s. Kent B. and Wilburta (Beasley) E.; B.S. in Bus., Eastern Ill. U., 1968; postgrad. Northeastern U., 1976; m. Sherryl Ann Evans, Dec. 27, 1975; 1 dau., Stacy Allyn. Meeting mgr., prodn. mgr. DNB Mgmt., 1971-72; conv. mgr. Ambassador Hotel, dir. sales Northshore Sheraton Inn Hotel, Chgo., 1973-74; sales mgr. Sheraton Corp., Chgo., 1972-73; dir. sales Sheraton Royal, Kansas City, Mo., 1974-75; dir. sales and mktg. Hyatt Hotels Corp. H.R. Cambridge, 1975-77, Hyatt Regency New Orleans, 1977—; regional sales rep. 5 other Hyatt Regency Hotels. Served with U.S. N.G., 1968-74. Named Dir. of Sales of Quarter, Sheraton Corp., 1973, 74, Dir. of Sales of Year, Hyatt Hotels Corp., 1976. Mem. Hotel Sales Mgmt. Assn., Nat. Assn. Exhibit Mgrs. Methodist. Home: 300 Woodmead St Gretna LA 70053 Office: 500 Polydras Plaza New Orleans LA 70140

EVANS, JANET JUNE (COLEMAN), broadcasting exec.; b. Fishtrap, Ky., June 3, 1935; d. Ireland and Flossie Jane (Williamson) Coleman; student Bowling Green Bus. U., 1953-54, Marshall U., Williamson, 1966-67, 70, So. W.Va. Community Coll., 1972-74. Sec., Appalachian Power Co., Williamson, W.Va., 1954-55; officers personnel clk. U.S. Army, Ft. Sill, Okla., 1957-58; sec. U.S. Probation Office, Detroit, 1961-62; sec./clk. market news Dept. Agr. Tobacco Div., Lexington, Ky., 1963-64; sec. propane div. Ashland Oil & Refinery (Ky.), 1964-65; sec./bookkeeper Superior Motor Co., Williamson, 1965-66; with Harvit Broadcasting Corp., owner Sta.-WBTH-AM and Sta.-WXCC-FM, Williamson, 1966—, adminstrv. asst., 1968-77, asst. to pres., 1977-79, v.p., gen. mgr., 1979—. Public relations person City of Williamson, 1978-79. Mem. W.Va. Broadcasters Assn., Am. Women in Radio and TV, Nat. Secs. Assn. (pres. Tug Valley chpt. 1968-69, treas. 1977-79), Ky. Fedn. Women's Clubs (community improvement chmn. 7th dist. 1978-80). Democrat. Clubs: D.A.R., Women of Moose, Order Eastern Star, Belfy Area Woman's (pres. 1977-78), White Shrine of Jerusalem (worthy scribe 1975-76). Home: PO Box 1335 Williamson WV 25661 Office: PO Box 261 5 1/2 E Second Ave Williamson WV 25661

EVANS, JOEL KENT, hort. mfg. co. exec.; b. Oak Hill, W.Va., Feb. 20, 1943; s. L. E. and Mary Pauline E.; B.S., W.Va. Inst. Tech., 1966; postgrad. W.Va. U., 1969—; m. Cora A. Halstead, July 17, 1965; children—Jessica, Christinia. Retail merchandiser Kroger Co., Cin., 1960-70; mgr. sales planning Gillette Co., Boston, 1970-75; gen. sales mgr. United Brands Floriculture, Miami, 1976—; cons. in field. Mem. Fla. Assn. Realtors, Fla. Foliage Assn. (corp. sec. 1978—), Fla. Nurserymen and Growers Assn. Club: Elks. Home: 16842 SW 79th Pl Miami FL 33157 Office: United Brands Floriculture 17455 SW 157th Ave Miami FL 33157

EVANS, JOHN DERBY, telecommunications co. exec.; b. Detroit, June 3, 1944; s. Edward Steptoe and Florence (Allington) E.; A.B., U. Mich., 1966; m. Susan Blair Allan, Apr. 7, 1973; 1 son, John Derby. Pres., Evans Communications Systems, Inc., Charlottesville, Va., 1970-72; v.p., gen. mgr. Capitol Cablevision Corp., Charleston, W.Va., 1972-76; regional mgr. Am. TV & Communications Corp., Denver, 1974-76; telecommunications cons. to asst. sec. for planning and devel. Dept. HEW, Washington, 1976—; exec. v.p., chief ops. officer Arlington (Va.) Tele Communications Corp., 1976—. Served to lt. USN, 1966-70. Mem. Nat. Cable TV Assn. (pres.'s award 1979), Va. Cable TV Assn. (dir. 1979—), Soc. Motion Picture TV Engrs. Republican. Episcopalian. Clubs: Farmington Country, Boars Head Sports (Charlottesville, Va.), Old Dominion Boat (Alexandria, Va.). Home: 1023 Delf Dr McLean VA 22101 Office: Arlington Tele Communications Corp 2707 Wilson Blvd Arlington VA 22201

EVANS, JOYCE STEWART, ednl. adminstr.; b. Dallas, Apr. 4, 1933; d. John Benton and Phyllis Joyce (Burnton) Howell; B.S., Tex. Women's U., 1964, M.A., 1965; Ph.D., U. Tex., 1971; m. Joe Mack Evans, July 3, 1970; children—Christi, Mark, Phyllis, Patricia, Pamela. Tchr., Odessa (Tex.) Ind. Sch. Dist., 1958-63; intern in speech pathology Dallas Speech and Hearing Center, spring, 1964; speech therapist Mesquite (Tex.) Ind. Sch. Dist., 1965-66; spl. edn. tchr. Midland (Tex.) Ind. Sch. Dist., 1966-67; research asst. dept. spl. edn. U. Tex. at Austin, fall 1968, spring 1969, research asso., summer 1968, 69; early childhood specialist, early childhood program S.W. Ednl. Devel. Lab., Austin, 1970-71, resource specialist, 1971-72, program coordinator II, 1972-74, acting dir., 1974-75, dir. spl. projects div., 1975—; vis. prof. U. Tex., 1979—. Bd. dirs. Found. Exceptional Children, 1978—; bd. govs. Council Exceptional Children, 1977—; program chmn. Research Theatre, 1978-79; mem. nat. com. on early childhood edn., 1971-72, Nat. Com. Div. Early Childhood Edn. and Learning Disabilities, 1973—. Am. Businessman's scholar, 1963-64; Midland Assn. for Deaf scholar, 1967; Midland Ind. Sch. Dist. Bldg. scholar, 1966; U.S. Office Edn. fellow, 1963-65; Tex. Woman's U. fellow, 1964; U. Tex. fellow, 1967-69. Mem. Nat. Soc. Study of Edn., Assn. Children With Learning Disabilities, Nat. Assn. for Edn. Young Children, Am. Ednl. Research Assn., Nat. Assn. Public Continuing and Adult Edn., S.W. Ednl. Research Assn. Author: Change: The Pre-Teen and Early Teen Years, 1977; School/Home Observation and Referral System, 1978; Storybooks for Toddlers (series of 3), 1979; also articles. Home: 5807 Trailridge Circle Austin TX 78731 Office: 211 E 7 St Austin TX 78701

EVANS, LOU ANN, bus. exec.; b. Daughtery, Tex., Aug. 30, 1938; d. Melvin Willard and Odessa May Turner; m. Donald Evans, Dec. 1, 1956; children—Vicki Sheryl, Michael Don, Kristi Lynn. Purchasing sec. Shaw & Estes, Garland, Tex., 1956-61; purchasing sec. Tex. Instruments, Inc., Dallas, 1962-70, asst. buyer, 1970-72, corp. adminstr. supply buyer, 1972—. Mem. Purchasing Mgmt. Assn. Office: 13500 N Central Expressway Dallas TX 75265

EVANS, LYLE KENNETH, JR., pedodontist; b. Gainesville, Tex., June 1, 1935; s. Lyle K. and Margaret (Kelly) E.; student U. Tex., 1954-57; D.D.S., Baylor U., 1962; certificate in pedodontics, U. Rochester, 1966; 1 son, Jonathan Carter. Resident in pedodontics, The Eastman Dental Center, Rochester, N.Y., 1964-66; pvt. practice dentistry and pedodontics, San Antonio, Tex., 1966—; pedodontic mem. of search com. for head of dept. pedodontics U. Tex. Health Sci. Center, 1974; pecan grower, San Antonio, 1974—. Served to capt. U.S. Army, 1962-64. Recipient Clinic award Tex. Dental Assn., 1969; Certificate of Achievement, U.S. 5th Army Hdqrs., Certificate of Appreciation, San Antonio Dist. Dental Soc., 1970; licensed dentist, Tex. Mem. Am., Tex. dental assns., San Antonio Dist. Dental Soc., Tex. Pedodontic Assn., Southwestern Soc. Pedodontists, Am. Acad. Pedodontics, Am. Soc. Preventive Dentistry, Am. Soc. Dentistry for Children, Tex. Pecan Growers Assn., Internat. Acad. Preventive Medicine. Delta Sigma Delta, Kappa Alpha. Home: 11429 Mission Trace San Antonio TX 78230 Office: 7254 Blanco Rd San Antonio TX 78216

EVANS, MACK NELSON, textiles co. exec.; b. Spencer, Va., Apr. 18, 1940; s. Hubert M. and Pearlie (Joyce) E.; diploma in acctg. Danville Tech. Inst., 1963; A.A.S., Patrick Henry Community Coll., 1975; B.S. in Mgmt., Averett Coll., 1979; m. Margaret W. Weaver, Feb. 14, 1964; children—Nelson, Brock, Craig. Prodn. coordinator Bassett-Walker, Martinsville, Va., 1964-66, cost engr., 1968-69; indsl. engr. Sale Knitting Co., Martinsville, 1969-75, shift supr., 1975—; pres. WEB's, Inc., Martinsville. Served with USMC, 1966-68. Mem. Am. Inst. Indsl. Engrs., Am. Soc. Quality Control. Baptist. Patentee in field. Home: 1006 Maplewood Ct Martinsville VA 24112 Office: 306 Broad St Box 5191 Martinsville VA 24112

EVANS, MARILYN BAILEY, state legislator; b. Deland, Fla., Nov. 19, 1928; d. Cecil Cabanis and Augusta Davis (Mann) Bailey; B.A., Duke U., 1950; children—Hugh M., Daniel, Cecile, Mary Louise. Substitute tchr. schs. in Fla., 1970-75; real estate salesperson Evans-Butler Realty, Melbourne, Fla., 1973—; mem. Fla. Ho. of Reps. from 46th Dist., 1976—, chmn. Brevard County legis. del., 1979—; also chmn. Republican Caucus, mem. ad hoc com. on aging, 1978, now mem. edn., health and rehab. services, and natural resources coms.; sec. Pinewell Corp. Sec. legis. affairs Fla. conf. United Methodist Women; bd. dirs. Big Bros. and Big Sisters Fla.; mem. adv. council Continuing Edn. Women, Eau Gallie High Sch.; mem. Fla. State Republican Com. Recipient Woman of Year award Melbourne C. of C., 1976; Goof Govt. award Melbourne Jaycees, 1977-78; Outstanding Polit. Contbns. award Fla. Council Community Mental Health, 1978; Very Important Person award Human Rights Adv. Com. for the Mentally Retarded, 1978; Rep. of Yr. award Fla. Assn. Retarded Citizens, 1979; Outstanding Legis. Service award Fla. Assn. Community Colls., 1979, others. Mem. AAUW (chpt. legis. chmn.), Nat. Rep. Legislators Assn., Am. Legis. Exchange Council, LWV, Melbourne Area C. of C., Melbourne Area Bd. Realtors, United Meth. Women (life), Panhellenic P.E.O., Delta Delta Delta Alumae Assn. Home: 321 Lynn Ave Melbourne FL 32935 Office: 1495 N Harbor City Blvd Melbourne FL 32935

EVANS, MARY ANN, county exec.; b. Smyth County, Marion, Va., Feb. 22, 1942; d. Joseph Emory and Ruth Hazel (Burnop) Cress; grad. in bus. Marion Jr. Coll., 1962; m. Robert C. Evans, Dec. 29, 1970; children—Michael David, Steven Walter, Deanna Jill. Sec., Dr. Pepper Bottling Co., Marion, Va., 1962-71; exec. sec. Smyth County Bd. Suprs., Marion, 1971—, asst. county adminstr., 1977—. Mem. Nat. Assn. Counties, Va. Assn. County Adminstrs. Mem. First Ch. of God. Home: PO Box 126 Atkins VA 24311 Office: PO Box 188 Marion VA 24354

225 WHO'S WHO IN THE SOUTH AND SOUTHWEST

EVANS, MICHAEL LEE, newspaper exec.; b. Pasco, Wash., Nov. 11, 1950; s. George William and Clara Cecilia E.; A.A. in Bus., Angelina Jr. Coll., 1971; B.B.A., Stephen F. Austin State U., 1974; m. Patricia Kaye Zinkula, May 22, 1972. Warehouse checker Brookshire Bros. Warehouse, Lufkin, Tex., 1969-74; ad salesman Lufkin (Tex.) News, 1974—, asst. advt. mgr., 1976-78, advt. mgr., 1978—. Mem. Hudson Vol. Fire Dept., 1975—, historian, 1978—; advt. adviser Angelina County Bike-A-Thon Against Cancer Com., 1979. Mem. Internat. Newspaper Advt. Execs., Tex. Daily Newspaper Assn., Tex. Newspaper Advt. Mgrs. Assn., Nat. Rifle Assn. Democrat. Roman Catholic. Clubs: Crown Colony Country, Angelina Rifle and Pistol. Home: Route 8 Box 840 Lufkin TX 75901 Office: PO Box 1089 Ellis and Herndon Lufkin TX 75901

EVANS, PAT TERRELL, state govt. exec.; b. New Orleans, June 5, 1931; d. Paul Wallace and Catherine (Rappold) T.; B.A., Southeastern La. U., 1953; m. Harry L. Evans, Aug. 5, 1950; children—Debra, Matthew, Erin. Tchr., public schs., Baton Rouge, 1953-55; TV personality Sta.-WBRZ, Baton Rouge, 1956-58, documentary film producer, 1960-72; dir. La. Bur. for Women, Baton Rouge, 1973—. Founder, La. Women's Polit. Caucus, Baton Rouge Rape Crisis Center; mem. Baton Rouge Commn. on Women; bd. dirs. YWCA, Baton Rouge. Recipient Service award Welfare Rights Orgn. Mem. Baton Rouge Mental Health Assn., Women in Communications, Narcotics Anonymous (cert.). Democrat. Roman Catholic. Research on women offenders in La., rape in La., women in blue collar work in La. Office: 530 Lakeland Baton Rouge LA 70801

EVANS, PHILLIP RANDOLPH, oil co. exec.; b. Houston, Feb. 2, 1939; s. Reginald Desmond and Mabel Claire (Brown) E.; B.S. in C.E., Tex. A. and M. U., 1961, M.B.A., 1962; m. Doris Ingram, June 28, 1958; children—Kimberly Jan, Kay Lynn. Engr., data mktg. mgr. S.W. Bell Telephone, Houston, 1962-68; with Control Data Corp., 1968-69; corp. communications mgr. Occidental Petroleum Corp., 1969-74; mgr. telecommunications and radio/electronics Ashland Oil, Inc., Ashland, Ky., 1974—; telecom curriculum advisor Tex. A. and M. U., College Sta., 1972-79, Ohio U., Athens, 1978-79. Founding pres. Ashland Tri-State Recreational Assn., 1978-79; area chmn. Citizens Advocacy Com., 1975; chmn. Boy Scouts Am. family fund dr., 1977; div. chmn. United Way, 1976-77; pres., dir. Candlelight Plaza Civic Club, 1970-71; advisor, Jr. Achievement, 1963-65. Mosher Steel scholar, 1959-61. Mem. Am. Petroleum Inst., Internat. Communications Assn. (dir. 1977-79), Energy Telecom Elec. Assn. (dir. 1976-78). Republican. Baptist. Clubs: Rotary (dir. 1978-79), Atra Tennis, Atra Skiing. Home: 4605 Royale Ct Ashland KY 41101 Office: PO Box 391 Ashland KY 41101

EVANS, RITA POETTER, social worker; b. Atlanta, May 15, 1949; d. Louis Jerome and Mable (Reece) Poetter; B.S. in Psychology, U. Ga., 1971, M.S.W., 1975; m. James Henry Evans, July 17, 1971; children—Kristen Renee, Carrie Elizabeth. Vol. coordinator, services supr. Douglas County (Ga.) Dept. Family & Children Service, Douglasville, Ga., 1971-74; field placement North DeKalb Family & Youth Clinic, Doraville, Ga., 1974-75, also counselor Mental Health Inst.; dir. social services Anneewakee Treatment Center, Douglasville, 1975—; cons. in field. Placement chmn. Service League of Douglas County, Inc., 1975, pres., 1976-77, mem. adv. bd., 1977-78. Lic. marriage and family counselor, Ga.; named Douglas County Outstanding Young Woman of the Year, 1978, 1 of 5 Outstanding Young Women in Ga., 1980. Mem. Nat. Assn. Social Workers, Acad. Cert. Social Workers, Am. Assn. Marriage and Family Therapists (clin. mem.), Soc. Hosp. Social Work Dirs., Nat. Assn. Christian Social Workers, Am. Orthopsychiat. Assn. Baptist. Office: 4771 Anneewakee Rd Douglasville GA 30135

EVANS, ROBERT ARTHUR, neuroradiologist; b. San Francisco, Apr. 6, 1928; s. Arthur Thomas and Hazel (Bronson) E.; A.B. with great distinction, Stanford U., 1947, A.M., 1948; M.D., Columbia U., 1952. Intern, Columbia-Presbyn. Med. Center, N.Y.C., 1952-53, asst. resident in medicine, 1953-54, asst. resident in radiology, 1954-59; trainee Nat. Cancer Inst., 1957-59; instr. radiology Columbia U., N.Y.C., 1959; research fellow Nat. Heart Inst., 1959-60; instr. radiology Stanford U., 1960-61, instr. pediatrics, 1960-61; Nat. Inst. Neurol. Disease and Blindness spl. fellow in neuroradiology Neurol. Inst. N.Y., Columbia-Presbyn. Med. Center, N.Y.C., 1962-64; asso. prof. radiology Baylor Coll. Medicine, Houston, 1964—; mem. staff Meth. Hosp., Ben Taub Gen. Hosp., Tex. Children's Hosp., VA Hosp., all in Houston. Served in USNR, 1956-57. Recipient Zabriskie prize Columbia U., 1951. James Picker Found. grantee, 1961-63. Mem. AMA, Am. Soc. Neuroradiology, Am. Coll. Radiology, Am. Acad. Neurology, Am. Assn. Neurol. Surgeons, Rocky Mountain Neurosurg. Soc., Tex. Med. Assn., Harris County Med. Soc., Houston Neurol. Soc., Phi Beta Kappa, Alpha Omega Alpha, Phi Chi. Office: Methodist Hosp Houston TX 77030

EVANS, ROSEMARY KING (MRS. HOWELL DEXTER EVANS), librarian; b. Forsyth, Ga., Nov. 16, 1924; d. Wiley Gwin and Mary (Goggans) King; B.S., Tift Coll., 1957; librarian's certificate Woman's Coll. of Ga., 1963; M. Library Edn., U. Ga., 1972, postgrad. in library edn., 1975; m. Howell Dexter Evans, June 29, 1945; children—Joseph Williams, Curtis McKenney. Tchr. elementary sch., Forsyth, Ga., 1946-48, 54-62; librarian Mary Persons High Sch., Forsyth, 1962-73; catalog librarian Tift Coll., Forsyth, 1973-74; head librarian Stratford Acad., Macon, Ga., 1974-77; head librarian, asst. prof. Gordon Jr. Coll., Barnesville, Ga., 1977—. Spiritual edn. chmn. PTA, 1960-61. Named Star Tchr., 1966. Mem. Nat., Ga., Monroe County (sec. 1959-60, v.p. 1961-62, pres. 1962-63) edn. assns., Ga. (dist. pres. 1965), Southeastern library assns., Delta Kappa Gamma. Methodist (chmn. local edn. bd. 1964-65, chmn. commn. on Christian vocation 1965—, exec. com., tchr. adult Bible class). Clubs: Jaycettes, Woman's (1st v.p. 1955-56, chmn. edn. dept. 1959-60, chmn. pub affairs dept. 1961-62) (Forsyth). Office: Gordon Junior Coll Barnesville GA 30204

EVANS, RUTHANA WILSON, educator; b. Roxie, Miss.; d. James and Luberta (Wade) Wilson; B.S., Tougaloo Coll., 1955; postgrad. (NDEA grantee) U. Ill., 1965, (NDEA grantee) N.C. Coll., 1967; M.S., Delta State Coll., 1971; m. Lit Parker Evans, Jr., Mar. 22, 1957; children—Cedric Glenn, Valerie Denise. Elem. tchr., Shaw, Miss., 1955-57; tchr., curriculum chmn. Nailor Elementary Sch., Cleveland, Miss., 1957-60, tchr., librarian H.M. Nailor Sch., 1960-62, librarian, 1963-64; library supr. Bolivar County Dist. 4 elementary schs., Cleveland, 1965-67; curriculum resources tchr. ednl. TV Jackson, Miss., 1968-70; librarian Parks and Pearman elem. schs., Cleveland, 1968-70; cons. Greenville (Miss.) Elem. Sch., 1970; edn. dir. Miss. Head Start activities, Cleveland, 1970—. Librarian, Presch. Story Hour, 1964-66, Little Rascals kindergarten, 1966-68; organizer elementary sch. library program Bolivar County, 1969; job trainer Neighborhood Youth Corps, Cleveland, 1969; trainer man power program Step, Cleveland, 1970—; cons. Indianola (Miss.) presch. activities, 1971; organizer inventory, classification system Head Start, 1970. Sec., Negro's Citizens Com. Cleveland, 1957-61, P.T.A., Shaw, Miss., 1955; active Boy Scouts Am.; librarian Bapt. Tng. Union, Cleveland, 1972—. Mem. Miss. Personnel and Guidance Assn., Miss., Bolivar County tchrs. assns., NEA, NAACP, Nat. Black Child Devel. Assn., ALA, Miss. Library Assn., Negro Voters League. Democrat. Clubs: East Side High Sch. Band Booster (treas. Cleveland 1972), Athena Social (treas. 1971), Women's (sec. Cleveland 1970). Contbr. articles to profl. jours. Home: 816 Cross St Cleveland MS 38732 Office: 321 S Sharpe St Cleveland MS 38732

EVANS, THELMA BERNICE, educator; b. Seguin, Tex., Mar. 6; d. Simon and Pearl (Littlejohn) Miller; A.A., St. Philip's Jr. Coll., 1957; B.S. Huston-Tillotson Coll., 1960; M.Ed., Prarie View Coll., 1967; cert. counselor Trinity U., 1970; m. Robert Lee Evans, Jan. 4, 1942. Instr., Hicks Beauty Sch., San Antonio, 1955-57; tchr. Sch. for Deaf and Blind, Austin, Tex., 1959-66; tchr. Brackenridge High Sch., San Antonio, 1966-74, Wheatley High Sch., San Antonio, 1974—. Mem. Alamo Ceramic Assn., Good Neighbors Guild, Daffodils Civic and Social Assn., AAUW, Cts. of Calanthe, Nat. Council Negro Women, Princess of Omar, Mother's Service Orgn., St. Philip's Coll. Alumni Assn., Huston-Tilston Coll. Alumni Assn., Prarie View Coll. Alumni Assn., Phi Delta Kappa, Epsilon Pi Tau, Iota Phi Lambda. Baptist. Home: 613 Virginia Blvd San Antonio TX 78203 Office: 400 Temple St San Antonio TX 78210

EVANS, THOMAS IRVIN, pharmacist; b. Haleyville, Ala., Sept. 24, 1947; s. Pet and Jewel Mae (Irvin) E.; B.S.Ph., U. Miss., 1970; emergency med. technician II, U. Ala., Huntsville, 1977. Pharmacist T.K.E. Drug Co., 1970-72; relief pharmacist, cons. primary health care, Tupelo, Miss., 1972-73; mgr. Med. Arts Pharmacy, Hamilton, Ala., 1974; instr. emergency med. tech. N.W. Ala. State Tech. Coll., Hamilton, 1977—; partner, designer Ethel's Florist and Antiques, Hamilton, 1978—; dir. pharmacy Lister Hill Hosp., Hamilton, Ala., 1974—; mem. adj. faculty Sch. Pharmacy, Samford U., 1977-79; cons. pharmacist Marion County Nursing Home, 1974—; v.p. Dist. Pharmacy Meeting, 1973, pres., 1974; pres. Convention Music Co., 1977—. Mem. Am. Pharm. Assn., Southeastern Hosp. Soc. Pharmacists, Ala. State Pharm. Assn., Hamilton High Sch. Alumni Assn. (pres. 1975). Democrat. Methodist. Club: Fraternal Order Police. Home: Route 6 Box 102 Hamilton AL 35570 Office: 1315 Military St Hamilton AL 35570

EVANS, TRUMAN MEREDITH, aerospace engr.; b. Joshua, Tex., Jan. 24, 1928; s. John Thomas and Lillian (Chaney) E.; B.S.A.E., Tex. A&M U., 1953; M.S.E.A., So. Meth. U., 1971; m. Kathryn (Kay) Marie Campbell, June 16, 1950; children—Taylor Meredith, Terri Leigh. Apprentice, Santa Fe R.R., 1944-50; design engr. aerodynamics Vought Corp., Dallas, 1953-56, test engr. gas dynamics labs., 1956-59, engring. specialist engring. labs., 1959-70, sr. engr., 1970-72, project engr. test ops., 1972—; instr. aerospace engring. U. Tex., Arlington, 1978—. Active Boy Scouts Am., 1960-72. Served with USN, 1946-47. Registered profl. engr., Tex. Fellow AIAA (asso.); mem. Inst. Environ. Scis. (sr.), Nat. Rifle Assn., Air Force Assn., Arlington Sportsman's Club. Republican. Mem. Ch. of Christ. Clubs: Optimists (pres. Arlington, 1964-65, lt. gov. Zone H, N. Tex. Dist. 1968-69, gov. 1971-72, internat. v.p., dir. 1975-76), Masons. Home: 124 Mill Creek Dr Arlington TX 76010 Office: Vought Corp PO Box 225907 Dallas TX 75265

EVANS, VAN AUBREY, research and devel. exec.; b. Valley Park, Miss., May 22, 1940; s. James William and Cleo Evelyn (Hale) E.; B.S., Miss. Coll., 1968, M.B.A., 1970; m. Linda M. Murrah, June 30, 1972. Mgr. acctg. Westinghouse Electric Corp., Vicksburg, Miss., 1963-71; auditor Miss. Power and Light Co., 1971-72; mgr. new ventures Miss. Research and Devel. Center, Jackson, 1972—; v.p., dir. Venture Mgmt., Inc., 1978-80, chmn. bd., pres., 1980—. Bd. dirs. N. Jackson Enrichment Found., 1979—, Tech. Commercialization Center, 1978—; tchr. entrepeneur devel. workshop. Recipient Public Service award SBA, 1977. Mem. Miss. Indsl. Devel. Council. Democrat. Baptist. Club: Shriners. Home: 105 McRee St Clinton MS 39056 Office: PO Box 2470 Jackson MS 39205

EVANS, WILLIAM BRYCE, educator; b. Ft. Worth, Apr. 25, 1929; s. Selby Herman and Lula Merle (Woodham) E.; A.A., Clarke Coll., 1949; B.S., Miss. Coll., 1951, postgrad. New Orleans Bapt. Sem.; M.A., U. So. Miss., 1953; postgrad. doctoral program La. State U., 1954-70; Ph.D., Walden U., 1979; m. Joan Davis Evans, Sept. 25, 1950; children—Dinah, Donnie, Dana. Instr. speech U. So. Miss. Hattiesburg, 1953-54; chmn. dept. speech Clarke Coll., Newton, Miss., 1954-67; instr. speech pathology, U.S. Ala., Mobile, 1967—, dir. speech & hearing clinic, 1967-74, chmn. Tchr. Edn. com., 1975-76, apptd. grad. faculty, 1976—; cons. in field. Mem. Miss. state bd. dirs. Am. Cancer Soc.; County chmn. March of Dimes, 1960. Licensed speech pathology, Ala., Miss. Mem. Nat., Miss., edn. assns., Am., Miss. speech assns., Am., Ala. (certificate clin. competance 1968) speech and hearing assns. Baptist. Clubs: Lions, Kiwanis, Masons. Author: Visible Phonics and Articulation, 1973, Improving Your Speech, 1976. Editor: Ala. Jour. of Speech and Hearing, 1970-73. Home: Route 2 PO Box 440 Lucedale MS 39452 Office: Dept Speech Pathology Audiology Univ of S Alabama Mobile AL 36688

EVANS, WILLIAM BUELL, mathematician; b. Monticello, Miss., June 5, 1918; s. Walter Price and Lillian G. (Hancock) E.; B.S. with highest honors in Math. and Chemistry, U. So. Miss., 1939; M.S. in Math. and Physics, La. State U., 1941; M.S. in Meteorology, Mass. Inst. Tech., 1944; Ph.D. in Math., U. Ill., 1950; m. Margaret Polk Peters, Oct. 12, 1945; children—Patricia Irene, Margaret Faye, David Buell. Instr. in math. A. and M. Coll. Tex., College Station, 1941-42; asst. prof. math. U. Ill., Urbana, 1948-50; asso. prof. math. Ga. Inst. Tech., Atlanta, 1950-60; vis. asso. prof. engring. math. U. Calif., Los Angeles, 1960-64; prof. math. Emory U., Atlanta, 1965—, prof. biometry, 1965—, acting chmn. dept. biometry, 1969-71, dir. Computing Center, 1965—. Served with USAAF, 1942-46, 51-53. Mem. Math. Assn. Am., Biometry Soc., Am. Math. Soc., Soc. Indsl. and Applied Math., Assn. Computing Machinery, Sigma Xi, Phi Kappa Phi. Baptist. Contbr. articles on applied math. and meteorology to sci. publs. Home: 2901 Rockingliam Dr Atlanta GA 30327 Office: Uppergate House Emory U Atlanta GA 30322

EVANS, WILLIAM LEE, cytologist; b. Calvert, Tex., Aug. 28, 1924; s. James Herman and Lilly Australia (O'Neal) E.; B.A. with honors, U. Tex., Austin, 1949, M.A., 1950, Ph.D., 1955; m. Lillian Mary Madden, July 30, 1948; children—Kathy, David, Susan. Mem. faculty U. Ark., Fayetteville, 1955—, asso. prof. zoology, 1962-68, prof., 1968—. Served with AUS, 1942-46, USAF, 1950-51. Decorated Air medal with oak leaf cluster. NIH grantee, 1959-61, U. Ark. Found. grantee, 1979. Mem. Ark. Acad. Sci. (treas.), Am. Genetic Assn., AAAS, Am. Philatelic Soc., Sigma Xi, Phi Beta Kappa, Phi Eta Sigma. Contbr. articles to profl. jours. Home: 111 Nolan Ave Fayetteville AR 72701

EVELSIZER, RONALD LEE, educator; b. Bloomington, Ill., Sept. 3, 1932; s. Paul Vernon and Edna Rachel (Ellis) E.; B.S., Ill. State U., 1955, M.S., 1964; Ed.D., U. Ala., 1968; m. Patricia Anne Johnson, June 13, 1954; children—Lee Anne, Julie, Tracy, Richard. Tchr. deaf Quincy (Ill.) Pub. Schs., 1955-59, 60-61, tchr. mentally retarded, 1959-60; prin. Speech and Hearing Center, Birmingham, Ala., 1961-63; program chmn. edn. deaf U. Ala., University, 1963—, dir. undergrad. study in communicative disorders, 1971—, project dir. deaf-blind-retarded, 1974—; field reader and cons. U.S. Office Edn., 1969-72. Adv. bd. SE Regional Center for Deaf/Blind. U.S. Office Edn. grantee, 1967-71; Ala. Dept. Mental Health grantee, 1975-80. Mem. A.G. Bell Assn. for Deaf, Am. Orgn. for Edn. of Hearing Impaired, Am. Instructors Deaf, Associated Coll. Educators of Hearing Impaired, Am. Mus. Nat. History, Smithsonian Instn. Methodist. Clubs: Masons, Shriners, Lions. Contbr. articles to profl. jours. Home: 12-G Northwood Lake Northport AL 35476 Office: PO Box 1903 University AL 35486

EVERETT, DON LEE, automobile dealer, clergyman; b. Houston, Dec. 7, 1924; s. Freeman and Minnie Kate E.; M.Th., Union Theol. Sem., Houston, 1966; m Feb. 19, 1973; 1 son by previous marriage, Michael Dwyane. Ins. salesman Golden State Mut. Ins. Co., Los Angeles, 1957-62; salesman Jim Sanders Ford, Houston, 1967-69, Frizzell Pontiac, Houston, 1969—; owner, operator Everett Auto Broker Service, Houston, 1966—; ordained to ministry Baptist Ch., 1967; asst. pastor Bethel Bapt. Ch., Houston, 1967-73, Met. Christian Methodist Episcopal Ch., Houston, 1973—, Washington Chapel, Sweeney, Tex., 1974-75. Served with USN, 1942-45. Mem. Religious Businessmens Fellowship, Profl. Business Men's Club, NAACP, Urban League Houston. Democrat. Home: 5502 South Acres Houston TX 77048 Office: 5001 Grigg Rd Houston TX 77021

EVERETT, HARLEY WILLIAMSON, communication corp. exec.; b. Waltham, Mass., Oct. 1, 1948; s. Harley Davidson and Lily Elizabeth (Fox) E.; Asso. Sci., Central Va. Community Coll., 1976; B.S., U. Tampa, 1978. Mgr., Martek Inc., Lynchburg, Va., 1972-74; asst. acct. corp. fin. Gen. Telephone & Electric Data Services, Tampa, Fla., 1977-78; comptroller Precision Communication Services, Inc., Tampa, 1978—; ind. cons., 1977—. Served with AUS, 1968-72. Mem. Ch. of Christ. Home: 4615 Tennyson Ave Tampa FL 33609 Office: Precision Communication Services Inc 2609 DeLeon St Tampa FL 33609

EVERETT, JAMES MURPHY, ednl. adminstr.; b. Hickman, Ky., Mar. 29, 1945; s. Raymond Douglas and Margaret Estelle (Rogers) E.; B.S. in Vocat. Agr., Murray State U., 1967, M.S. in Horticulture, 1968, postgrad., 1969-79; m. Louetta Wheeler, Dec. 16, 1967; 1 dau., Cindy Carol. Clerical asst. to head dept. agr. Murray (Ky.) State U., 1963-68; area extension specialist in horticulture and youth U. Ky. Co-op Extension Service, 1968-69; tchr. vocat. agr. Fulton County (Ky.) Bd. Edn., 1969-72; coordinator and chief adminstr. Fulton County Area Vocat. Edn. Center, Hickman, 1972—. Bicentennial adv. to bd. Internat. Banana Festival, 1974, parade participant, 1973-78; pres. Fulton County Bicentennial Inc., 1973-77; mem. county voter registration com. Fulton County Young Democrats, 1975-79; state del. White House Conf. on Informational Services and Libraries, Washington, 1979; music dir. First Bapt. Ch., Clinton, Ky., 1967-76, Hickman, 1976—; mem. Fulton County Band Program, 1957-63; bd. dirs. Jackson Purchase Regional Mus., 1974—, Fulton County Conservation Dist., 1973—, vice chmn., 1976; mem. Gov.'s Indsl Devel. Adv. Team, 1976; del. Gov.'s Local Govt. Issues Conf., 1976. Recipient Outstanding Achievement award Fulton County Bicentennial, 1974, Leadership award Fulton County Edn. Assn., 1973, Cert. of Merit Goodyear Tire & Rubber Co., 1974. Mem. Ky. Assn. Sch. Adminstrs., W. Ky. Assn. Sch. Adminstrs., Fulton County-Hickman C. of C. (pres. 1976, 79, Citizen of Year 1976), Vocat. Indsl. Clubs Am. (Appreciation award 1974, regional adv. 1975-76), Nat. Council Local Adminstrs., Ky. Council Local Adminstrs., Ky. Assn. Conservation Dists. (state com. on youth 1975-78), Nat. Vocat. Assn., Ky. Vocat. Assn. Clubs: Optimist (program chmn. 1979-80), Rotary. Home: Route 4 Cottonwood Dr Hickman KY 42050 Office: PO Box 199 Hickman KY 42050

EVERETT, KARL MENOHER, JR., gerontology health care cons., educator; b. Latrobe, Pa., Aug. 13, 1935; s. Karl Menoher and Nell Irene (McCullough) E.; R.N. with honors, div. nursing, Coll. Medicine, N.Y. U., 1958; grad. U.S. Fgn. Service Inst., Washington, 1970-71; B.A. cum laude, U. Md., 1974; postgrad. U. Okla., Norman, 1978—; m. June Kay Lenz, Dec. 10, 1960; children—Dianna Lynn, Christopher Douglas. Instr. clin. urology Coll. Medicine, div. nursing N.Y. U., N.Y.C., 1958-59; mem. staffs N.Y. U.-Bellevue Med. Center, N.Y.C., 1955-59, N.Y. U. Postgrad. Hosp., N.Y.C., 1958-59; commd. 2d. lt. U.S. Army, 1959, advanced through grades to maj., 1967; served Brooke Army Med. Center, San Antonio, 1959, Walter Reed Army Med. Center, Washington, 1959-60, Vets. Hosp. Center, Norman, 1977—; intelligence officer Dept. Def., apptd. mem. ad hoc com. Nat. Security Council, 1968-69; pvt. negotiator UN Command, Korea, with People's Republic of China and Dem. People's Republic N. Korea, 1971-75; dir. Directorate of Security F.A. Center and Ft. Sill, Okla., 1975-77, ret., 1979; pres., chmn. bd. dirs. Okla. World Consultants, Inc., Norman, 1977-78; sr. asso. Karl M. Everett & Assos., Norman, 1979—; cons. N.E. Asian bus. affairs Am. U., Washington, 1975—; lectr. comparative internat. jud. systems overseas br. Los Angeles City Coll., 1975; mem. vis. faculty John F. Kennedy Center, Fayetteville, N.C., 1977—; bd. dirs. SEC LTD, Rockville, Md., 1974-77. Mem. Cleveland County Christmas Store, Norman, 1977—; county chmn. membership com. Cleveland County Democratic Party Leadership Club, Norman, 1979. Decorated Bronze Star, Joint Services Commendation medal; recipient Ogden D. Mills scholarship award, 1958, various U.S. mil. awards, ministerial level awards Govt. Republic of Korea. Mem. Am. Geriatrics Soc., Gerontol. Soc., Am. Nurses Assn., Res. Officers Assn. U.S., Tulsa C. of C. (com. on govt., 1977-78). Clubs: Masons (Mystic Circle, Lawrence, Ind.), Scottish Rite, Shrine (Everett, Wash.), Shrine Club of Korea (life). Researcher hemodialysis and cardiac catheterization, 1955-58; contbr. articles on socio-polit.-econ. problems Cambodia and S.E. Asia to publs. Home: 1305 Spruce Dr Norman OK 73069

EVERETT, PETER CASE, bus. and indsl. cons.; b. Jackson, Miss., Oct. 16, 1940; s. Robert Brayton and Katherine (Lohse) E.; B.B.A., U. Miss., 1964; M.B.A., Miss. Coll., 1978; m. Dorothy Marion Bray, Aug. 28, 1965; children—Dorothy Elizabeth, Robert Arthur, Peter Benjamin, James Case. Product mgr. ITT Telecom, Milen, Tenn., 1965-69; asst. gen. mgr. Bruce Paneling & Molding, Covington, Tenn., 1969-72; mgr. field services br. Miss. Research & Devel. Center, Jackson, 1972—; partner PTP Co., Jackson, 1973-75; pres. Everett, Walters, Pickering & Assos., Jackson, 1978—; mgmt. instr. Miss. Coll., 1979—. Mem. mission council and vestry, treas. and sr. warden Episcopal Ch., 1968-72. Served with USMC, 1968. Mem. Covington Tipton County C. of C. (chmn. mfg. council 1970-71, mem. indsl. com. 1970-72). Clubs: Lions (sec., dir. 1968-69), ITT Mgmt. (sec. 1976-77). Home: 5029 Sunnyvale Dr Jackson MS 39211 Office: PO Drawer 2470 Jackson MS 39205

EVERETT, WOODROW WILSON, JR., elec. engr.; b. Newton, Miss., Oct. 11, 1937; s. Woodrow Wilson and Katherine Elizabeth (Thrash) E.; B.E.E., George Washington U., 1959; M.S., Cornell U., 1965, Ph.D., 1968; m. Cherry Donna Sarff, Aug. 23, 1958; children—Woodrow, Cherry Leanne. Project engr. Scott Paper Co., Mobile, Ala., 1959; project engr. Atlantic Research Corp., Ithaca, N.Y., 1962-64; dir. postdoctoral program Rome Air Devel. Center, 1964-75; chmn. bd. N.E. Consortium for Engring. Edn., Bridgeport, N.Y., 1975-; chmn. Southeastern Center for Elec. Engring. Edn.; dir. Device Assos. Corp. of N.Y., Masonwood Inc., Data Functions Inc., Groton Community Devel. Corp. Pres. Groton (N.Y.) Youth Center, 1965-68; dir. CD, Town of Groton, 1967-71; pres. Groton Village Bd. Appeals, 1966-71; chmn. Groton Planning Bd., 1968-69. Served with USAF, 1959-62. Fellow IEEE. Democrat. Author 4 books in field.

Office: FTU-SORC 7300 Lake Ellenor Dr Orlando FL 32809 also Cherwood-Oneida Lake Walnut Rd Bridgeport NY 13030

EVERHART, CLYDE HUGH, internist; b. Lexington, N.C., Jan. 31, 1948; s. Clyde Casper and Virgie Lee (Beck) E.; B.S., N.C. State U., 1969; postgrad. U. Ga., 1969-70; M.D., Bowman Gray Sch. Medicine, 1974. Intern, Med. Coll. Va., Richmond, 1974-75; resident in medicine N.C. Bapt. Hosp., Winston-Salem, 1975-77; N.C. Lung Assn. fellow in pulmonary diseases Bowman Gray Sch. Medicine, Winston-Salem, 1977-78, instr. internal medicine, div. pulmonary disease, 1979—; practice medicine specializing in internal medicine and chest disease, Morehead City, N.C., 1978-79; mem. staff N.C. Baptist Hosp. Mem. A.C.P., Am. Thoracic Soc., N.C. Lung Assn. Home: PO Box 10638 Winston-Salem NC 27108 Office: Dept Medicine Div Pulmonary Disease Bowman Gray Sch Medicine Winston-Salem NC 27103

EVERHEART, JOHN CHARLES, indsl. engr.; b. Leonard, Tex., Nov. 3, 1934; s. David Robert and Dorothy Elizibeth (Simpson) E.; student Sherman (Tex.) public schs.; m. Margaret Louise Williams, June 10, 1956; 1 son, Michael David. Indsl. engr. Quaker Oats Co., 1956-58; procurement specialist, indsl. engr. E Systems, Inc., Greenville, Tex., 1958-79, supr. property mgmt. control, plant engring. facilities, 1979—. Former pres. Hunt County React; former pres. men's Bible class North Baptist Ch., Greenville, now deacon. Mem. Soc. Mfg. Engrs. (hon.). Democrat. Club: Hunt County CB. Office: PO Box 1056 Greenville TX 75401

EVERMAN, HENRY ESLI, JR., educator; b. Lexington, Ky., May 8, 1941; s. Henry Esli and Margaret Jane (Ball) E.; B.A. (6th Dist. PTA scholar), U. Ky., 1963; M.A., La. State U., 1965, Ph.D., 1970; m. Linda Suzanne Heath, Jan. 2, 1971. Instr. La. State U., Alexandria, 1965-67, teaching asst., Baton Rouge, 1967-70; faculty soci sci. Eastern Ky. U., Richmond, 1970—, asso. prof. social sci. dept., 1974—; instr. extension work England AFB, Alexandria, La., 1965-67; speaker, lectr. religious, hist., ednl. meetings. Mem. Ky. Hist. Soc. Democrat. Mem. Christian Ch. (Disciples of Christ). Author: The History of Bourbon County, 1785-1865, 1977; contbr. articles to ency. and jour. of history. Home: Redwood Dr Richmond KY 40475 Office: Eastern Kentucky University Box 997 Richmond KY 40475

EVERTON, EARLE LEA, utility co. exec.; b. Norfolk, Va., Oct. 14, 1932; s. Harry Lea and Thelma Virginia (Parsons) E.; B.S. in Elec. Engring., Va. Poly. Inst. and State U., 1959; m. Grace Iannuzzi, July 6, 1957. Elec. engr. Harrisonburg (Va.) Electric Commn., 1958-60, asst. supt., 1960-62; elec. engr. City of Lakeland (Fla.) Dept. Water and Electric Utilities, 1962-72, asst. supt. transmission and distbn., 1972-77, supt. transmission and distbn., 1977—. Served with USN, 1951-53. Registered profl. engr., Fla. Mem. Am. Public Power Assn., Nat. Soc. Profl. Engrs., Fla. Soc. Profl. Engrs. Club: Elks. Home: 1629 Sims Pl Lakeland FL 33803 Office: City of Lakeland Dept Water and Electric Utilities PO Box 368 Lakeland FL 33802

EVERY, RAYMOND CALVIN, social worker; b. Anderson, S.C., July 5, 1927; s. Karl O'Bryant and Victoria (Taylor) E.; B.A. magna cum laude, Furman U., 1951; postgrad. U. Utah, 1954-55; M.S.W., U. Wash., Seattle, 1957; children—Brant, Monique, Paul. With VA Med. Centers, Tacoma, Wash., Phoenix, Los Angeles, and Lyons, N.J., 1957-69; asst. chief VA Med. Center, New Orleans, 1969—; spl. lectr. Tulane U., La. State U. Sch. Social Work, 1969—. Served with U.S. Army, 1946-47. Mem. Nat. Assn. Social Workers, Acad. Cert. Social Workers, Am. Assn. Sex Counselors, Educators, Therapists (cert.). Editor-in-chief Nat. Assn. Social Workers La. State chpt. Newsletter, 1977—. Office: 1601 Perdido St New Orleans LA 70146

EVETT, RUSSELL DOUGHERTY, physician; b. Norfolk, Va., Feb. 1, 1932; s. Edward Hall and Elizabeth (Dougherty) E.; B.S., Randolph-Macon Coll., 1953; M.D., Med. Coll. Va., 1957; M.S. in Medicine, Mayo Clinic and U. Minn., 1963; m. Mary Gail Kirby, Aug. 18, 1956; children—Stephen, Anne, Gail, John. Intern, DePaul Hosp., Norfolk, 1957-58; fellow in internal medicine Mayo Clinic, Rochester, Minn., 1960-63; pvt. practice internal medicine, Norfolk, 1964—; pres. med. staff Leigh Meml. Hosp., Norfolk, 1970-72; chmn. dept. internal medicine Norfolk Gen. Hosp., 1972-74; asso. prof. medicine Eastern Va. Med. Sch., 1974—; mem. staff Med. Center Hosps., Chesapeake Gen. Hosp., DePaul Hosp. Served with USNR, 1958-60. Diplomate Am. Bd. Internal Medicine. Mem. Va. Gastroenterol. Soc. (pres. 1975-77), Norfolk Acad. Medicine (pres. 1976-77), Med. Soc. Va., AMA, So. Med. Assn., A.C.P., Phi Beta Kappa, Omicron Delta Kappa, Alpha Omega Alpha. Methodist. Clubs: Norfolk Yacht and Country, Harbor. Home: 6147 Studeley Ave Norfolk VA 23508 Office: 530 Wainwright Bldg Norfolk VA 23510

EVINS, STARLING CLAUDE, urologist; b. Danville, Ky., Aug. 6, 1944; s. Charles Parker and Billie (Early) E.; B.S., Davidson Coll., 1966; M.D., U. Ky., 1970; m. Mary Richard Shearer, June 22, 1968; children—Holly Elizabeth, Stephen Parker. Intern, Med. U. S.C., 1970-71, resident in gen. surgery, 1971-72, resident in urology, 1974-77, asst. prof. urology, 1977-78; urologist Franklin (Tenn.) Urol. Assos., 1978—, v.p., 1978—; mem. staff Williamson County Hosp., vice chief of staff, 1980. Served with M.C., USAF, 1972-74. Dana scholar, 1963-66; Burlington scholar, 1965-66; Moseby scholar, 1969-70; recipient Physicians Recognition award AMA, 1973, 76; diplomate Am. Bd. Urology. Mem. AMA, Am. Urol. Assn., So. Med. Assn., Soc. Univ. Urologists, Williamson County Med. Soc., Alpha Omega Alpha. Presbyterian. Contbr. articles to med. jours. Home: 215 4th Ave S Franklin TN 37064 Office: 1325 Carter's Creek Pike Franklin TN 37064

EWART, JUDITH CHANEY, computer systems analyst; b. Richmond, Va., June 1, 1949; d. Raleigh Calloway and Mary Claire (Hardy) Chaney; B.S., Coll. William and Mary, 1971, M.B.A., 1977; m. George Daniel Ewart, Oct. 30, 1971. Computer programmer Christopher Newport Coll., Newport News, Va., 1971-72; computer programmer Coll. William and Mary, Williamsburg, Va., 1972-75, prodn. control supr., 1975-76, sr. systems analyst, 1976—. Mem. adj. faculty Thomas Nelson Community Coll., Hampton, Va., 1972-74, 77—, Christopher Newport Coll., 1978—. Mem. Internat., Va. (pres. 1977-78) assns. ednl. data systems, Beta Gamma Sigma. Democrat. Baptist. Home: 27 Marina Dr Newport News VA 23602 Office: Computer Center College William and Mary Williamsburg VA 23185

EWAYS, MUNIR SALEM, retail co. exec.; b. Ramallah, Palestine, May 20, 1937; s. Salem Musa and Nima Miriam (Essis) E.; came to U.S., 1937, naturalized, 1964; certificate of accounting Reading (Pa.) Bus. Inst., 1957; certificate of proficiency U. Pa., 1963; m. Ann Marie Parker, Aug. 10, 1957; children—Kathleen Marie, Karen Ann, Kay Elizabeth, Kristina Lynne. Auditor Dana Corp., Toledo, 1964-65, asst. plant controller, Parish div., Detroit, 1965-66, plant controller, 1966-67; dir. systems and data processing Am. Brakeblok div. ABEX Corp., Winchester, Va., 1967-68; pres., treas. Salem M. Eways, Inc., Charlottesville, Va., 1968—; cons. in field. Chmn. Multiple Sclerosis Fund Drive, Charlottesville, 1970-71; bd. dirs. Charlottesville YMCA, 1977—; fund raising chmn. 1st Bapt. Ch. Charlottesville, 1974-75, deacon, 1970-77; trustee 1st Monte Vista Land Trust, 1977—. Mem. Oriental Rug Retailers Am. (dir., past pres., now sec.), Retail Floor Covering Inst. (dir.), Charlottesville-Albemarle C. of C. (v.p.), World Trade Assn. (co-founder Blue Ridge chpt.), Textile Mus., Nat. Home Furnishings Assn., Nat. Assn. Accountants. Republican. Baptist (chmn. body of deacons 1978-79). Club: Fairview. Home: 314 Eastbrook Dr Charlottesville VA 22901 Office: 1417 N Emmet St Charlottesville VA 22901

EWEN, JOEL JOACHIM, telephone equipment mfr.; b. Bklyn., Nov. 6, 1934; s. Frederic and Dorothea (Werker) E.; student Mass. Inst. Tech., 1952-54, Bklyn. Poly. Inst., 1955-56, N.Y. U., 1958-59; Hon. Prof. Degree, U. Cauca, Colombia, 1967; m. Petra Barrera, Apr. 1, 1956; children—George, Alexander, Michael. Testman, A.T. & T., N.Y.C., 1954-55; telephone engr. Western Elec. Co., N.Y.C., 1956-59, Telefonbau und Normalzeit, Frankfurt and N.Y.C., 1959-62; sr. telephone engr. Adler Electronics, New Rochelle, N.Y., 1962-65; dept. chmn., prof. U. Cauca, Popayan, Colombia, 1966-67; mgr. telephone switching Telcom, Inc., 1967-69; with I.T. & T., N.Y.C., 1969-71; pres. Tele-Path Industries, Inc., Roanoke, Va., 1972—. Mem. IEEE, Armed Forces Communications and Electronics Assos., Ind. Telephone Pioneers Assn., U.S. Ind. Telephone Assn. Contbr. articles to trade jours. Patentee in field. Home: Rancho Mexico Lithia VA 24110 Office: 1711 Granby St NE Roanoke VA 24012

EWERZ, NANCY MAUREEN, sch. counselor; b. Tyler, Tex., Feb. 18, 1926; d. John Aaron and Pearl (Wiltshire) Neill; B.S. in Edn., Tex. Tech. U., Lubbock, 1963, M.Ed., 1971; m. Robert Ray Ewerz, Mar. 17, 1945; children—Robert Stephen, John William, Michael Ray, David Neill. Tchr., Lubbock Ind. Sch. Dist., 1963-68; tchr., then spl. edn. counselor and ednl. programmer Irving (Tex.) Ind. Sch. Dist., 1968-74, counselor, 1974—. Chpt. pres. Lubbock PTA, 1955-56, 59-60. Mem. Am., Tex., N. Central Tex. personnel and guidance assns., Tex. Sch. Counselor Assn., Am. Sch. Counselor Assn., Tex. PTA (hon. life mem.). Mem. Christian Ch. (Disciples of Christ). Home: 4117 Dorris Rd Irving TX 75062 Office: 901 O'Connor Rd Irving TX 75061

EWING, JOHN KIRBY, realtor, ind. oil operator, investor; b. Mercedes, Tex., Apr. 23, 1923; s. Emile Kelty and Edna Lillian (Olson) E.; student U.S. Naval Acad., 1941-42; B.A., U. Tex., 1946; m. Virginia Wilson, Oct. 2, 1970; children—Steven Calder, Charlotte Kelty, Robin Virginia, Holly Cross. Staff asst. to gov. of Tex., 1943-46; asst. purchasing agt. Estate of John H. Shary, Mission, Tex., 1946-47; mortgage banker David C. Bintliff & Co., Inc., Houston, 1947-52; self-employed bldg. contractor and residential subdiv. developer, Houston, 1952-54; mortgage loan mgr. Ringer Properties, Inc., Houston, 1954-57; partner Curtis & Ewing, realtors, Houston, 1957—; sales cons. Wilson Mfg. Co., Inc., oilwell drilling and servicing equipment, Wichita Falls, Tex., 1970-74, dir., 1973-77, v.p., 1974-75, pres., 1975-76; pres. Wichita Clutch Co., 1975-76; pres., dir. Mt. Royal Mining & Exploration Co., 1973—, Old Ontario Mining Co., 1973-77. Active local Boy Scouts Am., 1935-63, chmn. Buffalo Dist. Friends of Scouting, 1962-78, Western div. show chmn., 1977; active fund raising United Way, 1950-51, 55. Election judge Harris County, 1958-64; sec. credentials com. Tex. Democratic Com., 1952, mem. Harris County exec. com., 1958-65, del. convs., 1952-64. Bd. dirs. Mental Health Assn. Houston, 1969-74, pres., 1970-73; bd. dirs. Tex. Assn. Mental Health, 1970—. Recipient Distinguished Service award Nat. Assn. Mental Health, 1973. Mem. Houston Bd. Realtors, Nat. Assn. Real Estate Bds., Am. Foundrymen's Soc., Tex. Assn. Realtors, U.S. Naval Acad. Alumni Assn. (past pres., dir. Houston chpt.), Nat. Rifle Assn. (life), Bayou Rifles, Silver Spur, Kappa Alpha, Pi Sigma Alpha. Methodist (ofcl. bd. 1966-68, 69-71, 72-74, 78—. Clubs: Masons, Kiwanis (dir. Houston 1967-69). Home: 1508 Kirby Dr Houston TX 77019 Office: 616 Southwest Tower 707 McKinney Ave Houston TX 77002

EWING, SIDNEY ALTON, veterinarian; b. Emory University, Ga., Dec. 1, 1934; s. Aubrey Coleman and Grace Eliza (Prickett) E.; B.S.A., D.V.M., U. Ga., 1958; M.S., U. Wis., 1960; Ph.D., Okla. State U., 1964; m. Margaret Jane Steffens, Aug. 16, 1963; children—Holly Annette, Ann Krull, Leah Grace. Instr., U. Wis., 1960; mem. faculty Okla. State U., Stillwater, 1960-65, 68-72, prof., head dept. vet. parasitology, microbiology and public health, 1968-72, 79—; asso. prof. Kans. State U., 1965-67; prof., head dept. Miss. State U., 1967-68; dean Coll. Vet. Medicine, U. Minn., St. Paul, 1973-78; mem. adv. bd. Morris Animal Found., Denver, 1967-69, cons., 1969—; mem. animal health com. NRC, 1971—. Recipient Outstanding Tchr. of Year award Okla. State U. Coll. Vet. Medicine, 1970. Mem. N.Y. Acad. Scis., AVMA, Minn. Vet. Med. Assn., Okla. Vet. Med. Assn., Am. Assn. Vet. Parasitologists, World Assn. Advancement Vet. Parasitology, Am. Soc. Parasitologists, Conf. Research Workers in Animal Diseases, Sigma Xi, Phi Kappa Phi, Phi Zeta, Alpha Zeta, Alpha Psi (past nat. pres.), Gamma Sigma Delta, Aghon, Omicron Delta Kappa. Office: Dept Vet Parasitology Microbiology and Public Health Okla State U Stillwater OK 74078

EXUM, JAMES ARTHUR, JR., social worker; b. Tyler, Tex., July 29, 1944; s. James Arthur and Eula Mildred (Kent) E.; B.A., Baylor U., 1968; M.R.E., Southwestern Baptist Sem., 1971; M.S. in S.W., U. Tex., Arlington, 1973; m. Sally Arnold, June 15, 1968; 1 son, James Arthur. Dir. 24 hour service Family Service Assn., Ft. Worth, 1971-73, counselor, psychotherapist, 1973-76; dir. Rural Mental Health Center Terrell State Hosp., Waxahachie, Tex., 1976—; pvt. practice psychotherapy, Waxahachie, 1976—. Bd. dirs. United Way Waxahachie, YMCA Waxahachie, Ellis County (Tex.) Heart Assn. Mem. Nat. Assn. Social Workers, Assn. Rural Mental Health, League Am. Wheelmen. Club: Rotary. Home: 103 Chieftain St Waxahachie TX 75165 Office: 114 S Rogers St Waxahachie TX 75165

EXUM, LENA, educator; b. Yazoo City, Miss., Nov. 30, 1927; d. Richard Ledbetter and Lena (Dixon) E.; B.A., Miss. State Coll. for Women, 1949; M.A., U. N.Mex., 1958. Tchr. pub. schs., Yazoo City, 1949-53, Albuquerque, 1956-57; instr. English, Tyler (Tex.) Jr. Coll., 1958. Mem. Kappa Mu Epsilon, Eta Sigma Phi, Delta Kappa Gamma. Baptist. Home: 3900 Old Bullard Rd Tyler TX 75701 Office: English Dept Tyler Jr Coll Tyler TX 75701

EZELL, OLIVER EUGENE, health scientist, educator; b. Lafayette, Ga., Sept. 1, 1948; s. Alfred Oliver and Hilda Sue (Griffin) E.; B.S., Asbury Coll., 1970; M.S., Purdue U., 1973; Ed.D., U. Tenn., 1975; m. Cynthia Jo Snyder, Oct. 17, 1970. Classroom tchr. Western Schs., Kokomo, Ind., 1970-71, Webb Sch. of Knoxville (Tenn.), 1973-74; grad. teaching asst. health edn. Purdue U., West Lafayette, Ind., 1971-73; grad. teaching asst. U. Tenn., Knoxville, 1973-74, asso. prof., 1974—; cons. in field. Mem. AAHPER (del. nat. assembly 1978—), Am. Sch. Health Assn., Tenn. Assn. Health, Phys. Edn. and Recreation (pres. 1980—), Tenn. Acad. Health Educators, Internat. Racquetball Assn., Chattanooga Track Club, Brainerd Golf Club, Phi Delta Kappa (pres., research coordinator Chattanooga chpt. 1978—). Researcher aging, death, child abuse, dental health, nonsmoker's rights, human sexuality. Editorial bd. Tenn. Jour. Health, Phys. Edn. and Recreation. Home: 4215 Melinda Dr Chattanooga TN 37416 Office: Health Phys Edn and Recreation Dept MacLellan Gymnasium Chattanooga TN 37402

FABBI, BRENT PETER, chemist; b. Reno, Mar. 1, 1938; s. Baptiste Peter and Frances Rita (Barnes) F.; B.S., U. Nev., Reno, 1963, M.S., 1965; m. Delia Yolanda Juillerat, Apr. 23, 1962; children—Lisa Frances, Edmund Baptiste, Teresa Ruth. Sr. research asso. Nev. Bur. Mines, Reno, 1963-67; project chief, X-ray spectroscopy, br. analytical labs. U.S. Geol. Survey, Menlo Park, Calif., 1967-76, chief br. analytical labs., Reston, Va., 1976—. Served with U.S. Army, 1960-66. Recipient Spl. Achievement award U.S. Geol. Survey, 1975. Mem. Am. Chem. Soc., Soc. Applied Spectroscopy, Geol. Soc. Washington, Assn. Nationale de Recherche Technique, Centre De Recherches Petrographiques et Geochimiques France (asso. group mem.), Sigma Xi, Sigma Nu. Democrat. Roman Catholic. Home: 9810 Meadow Knoll Ct Vienna VA 22180 Office: US Geol Survey Nat Center Reston VA 22092

FABRE, FRED RUFFIN, automobile repairman; b. Baton Rouge, Sept. 22, 1939; s. Joseph Ruffin and Bessie S. (Solomon) F.; student La. State U. Engaged in automobile repair, 1961—; owner Carriage House Garage, Baton Rouge, 1978—; cons. Rolls-Royce restorations, 1971—. Bd. dirs., trainer, coordinator drug end., counsellor Genesis House, crisis center, Baton Rouge, 1970-71. Recipient various service awards. Mem. Antique Automobile Club Am. (officer; award for article 1978), Rolls-Royce Owners Club, Rolls-Royce Enthusiats Club, Bentley Drivers Club, BMW Owners Assn., Vintage BMW Owners Club, Capital Area Health Planning Council. Contbg. tech. editor R-R Owners Club. Home: 4063 Mohican St Baton Rouge LA 70805 Office: 8450-A Madrid St Baton Rouge LA 70814

FABRE, LOUIS FERNAND, psychiatrist; b. Akron, Ohio, Sept. 13, 1941; s. Louis Fernand and (Tait) F.; B.S., Akron U., 1962; Ph.D., Case-Western Res. U., 1966; M.D., Baylor U., 1969; m. Betty M. Nichols, Feb. 14, 1975; children by previous marriage—Amy Marie, Holly Susanne. With Tex. Research Inst. Mental Scis., Houston, 1960-73, chief alcoholism research, 1972-73; intern Meth. Hosp., Houston, 1969-70; resident in psychiatry Baylor Hosp., 1970-73; practice medicine specializing in psychiatry, Houston, 1973—. NIH travel fellow. Mem. Internat. Soc. Endocrinology, Endocrine Soc., Am. Fedn. Clin. Research, AMA, Am. Physiol. Soc., Am. Psychiat. Assn., Phi Sigma Alpha. Home: 1714 South St Houston TX 77098 Office: 5503 Crawford St Houston TX 77098

FABRY, PAUL ANDREW, internat. assn. exec.; b. Budapest, Hungary, June 19, 1919; s. Andrew and Ilona (Gombos) F.; B.A., Godollo Jr. Coll., 1937; Ph.D., U. Budapest, 1942, J.D., 1943; m. Louise Hitchcock Fair, May 15, 1958 (div. 1968); children—Lydia Louise, Alexa Fair; m. 2d, Angela Andrews Rutledge, May 8, 1971 (div. 1979). Came to U.S., 1949, naturalized. War corr. Central European Press Service, Warsaw, Poland, Berlin Germany, Vienna, Austria, Zurich, Switzerland, Budapest, 1943-44; sec. Fgn. Office, Budapest, 1945; head Prime Minister's Cabinet, Budapest, 1945-46; charge d'affaires of Hungary, Ankara, Turkey 1946-47; fgn. corr. Istanbul, Turkey, 1948-49; sect. chief Radio Free Europe, N.Y.C., 1950-53; free lance writer, lectr., N.Y.C., 1954; pub. relations adviser E.I. du Pont de Nemours & Co., Wilmington, Del., 1955-62; mng. dir. Internat. House, New Orleans 1962—. Rep. Internat. Red Cross, Vienna-Budapest, 1945-46; adv. bd. Istanbul U., 1948-49, Internat. Econ. Cooperation Com., N.Y.C.; v.p. Cultural Services, Inc., N.Y.C., 1953-54; moderator Fact and Opinion, WYES-TV, 1965-74. Active United Fund, Wilmington, 1955-60. Trustee, mem. exec. com. New Orleans Ednl. TV Found., 1970-75. Served as capt. Royal Hungarian Artillery, 1943. Mem. Pub. Relations Soc. Am., World Trade Centers Assn. (v.p., treas. 1969—). Fgn. Press Assn., New Orleans Bd. Trade, C. of C. Home: 1127 Bourbon St New Orleans LA 70116 Office: 607 Gravier St New Orleans LA 70130

FACE, EDWARD JOSEPH, banker; b. N.Y.C., Apr. 7, 1927; s. John C.G. and Edna Mae (O'Malley) F.; B.S. in Bus. Adminstrn., U. S.C., 1953; postgrad. Am. Inst. Banking, 1966, Grad. Sch. Banking, U. Wis., 1969, Air Command and Staff Coll., 1971, Indsl. Coll. Armed Forces, 1974; m. Theresa Dean Eurey, June 13; children—Edward Joseph, John G., James M., Cheryl J. Vice pres. Comml. Banking div. Bank of Va., Richmond, 1960—. Past pres. Pinedale Farms Civic Assn. Served with USN, 1944-48, to lt. col. USAFR, 1952-80. Mem. Sales and Mktg. Execs. Richmond (Salesman award 1971), Am. Mgmt. Assn. (lectr.), Va. Nat. Guard Assn., Nat. Guard Assn. U.S., Air Force Assn., Am. Soc. Mil. Comptrollers, Am. Inst. Banking, Lambda Chi Alpha, Alpha Kappa Psi. Presbyterian. Clubs: Masons (Scottish Rite, 32 deg.), Shriners, Optimist (past pres.). Home: 9522 Ridgefield Rd Richmond VA 23229 Office: 8th and Main St Richmond VA 23260

FACKELMAN, ROBERT HENRY, newspaper exec.; b. Ponca, Nebr., Oct. 19, 1907; s. Herman Carl and Jeanette (Pomeroy) F.; student Midland Coll., 1923-25; B.J., U. Mo., 1927; postgrad. Harvard U., 1941-42; m. Anna Laura Torbert, June 6, 1928; 1 dau., Ann Karen (Mrs. Frank Nixon). Editor, pub. Baxter Springs (Kans.) Citizen, 1927-28, Raymondville (Tex.) Chronicle, 1929-40, Morristown (Tenn.) Sun, 1950-52; editor, gen. mgr. Winter Haven (Fla.) News-Chief, 1943-50; pub. Cleveland (Tenn.) Banner, 1952-54; v.p. So. Newspapers, Inc., 1954-58; pres. Newspaper Service Co., Inc., 1953—; pres. Gulf Coast Newspapers, Inc., 1958—; pres. Ruston (La.) Pubs., Inc., Tarpon Springs (Fla.) Leader, Inc. Served in USAAF, 1941-42. Mem. Am., So. (dir. 1970-74) newspaper pubs. assns. Author: Publishers Primer; (novel) Hijackers Aboard. Address: 408 S Bonita Ave Panama City FL 32401

FAGAN, MAURICE JAMES, JR., dentist; b. Coventry, R.I., Dec. 4, 1921; s. Maurice James and Ellen Louisa (Albro) F.; B.S., Providence Coll., 1943; student Balt. Coll. Dental Surgery, 1944-47; D.D.S., U. Md., 1947; m. Ruth Pearl Mcdonald, June 28, 1947; children—Maurice James III, Malford, Mark, Mitchell, Laurie Anne, Margo Jean. Practice dentistry, Wakefield, R.I., 1947, Atlanta, 1956—; asso. in geriatrics, cons. Malford Thewlis Geriatric Clinic, 1947-56, Dental Masters, Inc.; founder dental health program South Kingston (R.I.) Sch. Dept. 1948, dir., 1948-50; instr. USAF Med. Service, Atlanta, 1959-64; pres. Dental Practice Plan Inc. Founder, 1960, since pres., chmn. bd. dirs., trustee Maurice J. Fagan Meml. Dental Hosp., Dentistry for Aged and Handicapped, Atlanta; cons. Gale Clinic, Narragansett, R.I., 1957—; lectr. and tchr.; sec. Internat. Research Com. for Oral Implantology. Served from pvt. to lt. col. USAF, 1942-72. Decorated knight of Malta with title of Sir by Queen Juliana of Netherlands, 1975; officier Ordre de la Ville de Paris; recipient Silver Medal of Honor, Paris, 1973, Gold Medal of Honor, Republic of France, 1973. Fellow Am. Acad. Gen. Dentistry, Internat. Coll. Oral Implantologists (a founder 1972), Royal Soc. Health, Acad. Implants and Transplants; mem. Royal Soc. Medicine (asso.), So. Acad. Oral Implantology (founder; pres. 1969-70), Am. Prosthodontic Soc., Am. Acad. Implant Dentistry, Am., Ga. dental assns., No. Dist. Dental Soc., Am. Geriatric Soc., Am. Soc. Geriatric Dentistry, Assn. Advance Ethical Hypnosis, Res. Officers Assn., Am. Soc. Clin. Hypnosis, Acad. Gen. Dentistry, Associazone Nazionale Implantoprotesi Orale, Psi Omega. Author: Dental Practice Planning; How to Succeed in Dentistry; New Concepts in Implant Dentistry; Treatment of Severe Alveolar Atrophy, Vol. I.; The Interplant Techniques Manual; asst. editor Jour. Oral Implantology. Inventor dental implants. Contbr. articles to profl. jours. Home: 5360 Peachtree-Dunwoody Rd NE Atlanta GA 30342 Office: 960 Johnson Ferry Rd NE Atlanta GA 30342

FAGAN, TIMOTHY CHARLES, clin. pharmacologist; b. Phoenix, Mar. 22, 1947; s. George Philip and Barbara Caroline (Griswold) F.; A.B. in Psychology (Nat. Merit scholar), Stanford U., 1969; M.D., UCLA, 1973; m. Susan Virginia Eastman, June 19, 1970; children—Ian Timothy, Elissa Susanne. Intern, Wadsworth VA Hosp., Los Angeles, 1973-74, resident in internal medicine, 1974-76; fellow in clin. pharmacology Med. U. S.C., Charleston, 1976-78, asst. prof. medicine and pharmacology, 1978—; clin. asso. physician Nat. Inst. Gen. Med. Scis., 1979—. Mem. A.C.P., Am. Soc. Clin. Pharmacology and Therapeutics, Am. Soc. Internal Medicine. Contbr. articles to profl. jours. Office: 171 Ashley Ave Charleston SC 29403

FAGERBURG, DAVID RICHARD, chemist; b. Rockford, Ill., Aug. 5, 1942; s. Richard Burton and Marjorie Charlotte (Hagaman) F.; B.S., Calif. State U., Long Beach, 1967; Ph.D. in Chemistry, U. Wash., 1970; m. Nila Maureen Wilson, Mar. 6, 1965; children—Eric, Carla, Brian, Paul, Kurt, Luann. Quality assurance analyst McDonnell-Douglas Aircraft, Long Beach, Calif., 1965-67; research chemist Tenn. Eastman Co., Kingsport, Tenn., 1970-73, sr. research chemist, 1973-79, research asso., 1979—. NDEA fellow, 1967-70. Mem. Am. Chem. Soc. Republican. Mormon. Patentee in field. Home: 3812 Cimmaron Dr Kingsport TN 37664 Office: PO Box 511 Kingsport TN 37662

FAGG, CHARLES FREDERICK, hosp. adminstr.; b. McKinney, Tex., Apr. 16, 1939; s. Clyde Lee and Arlyn Beatrice (Myrick) F.; B.A. in Zoology, U. Tex., 1965; postgrad. North Tex. State U., 1967; M.S. in Health Care Adminstrn., Trinity U., San Antonio, 1973; m. Kay Carlton Solomon, Nov. 28, 1964; children—Lisa Arlyn, Charles Frederick II and Stephen Lee (twins). Instr. biology L.O. Bell High Sch., Bedford, Tex., 1964-67; med. service rep. Parke-Davis & Co., Dallas, 1967-71; asso. dir. Harris Hosp-Meth., Ft. Worth, 1973—; exec. dir. Harris Meth. Found. Active United Way, Leadership Ft. Worth, YMCA. NSF grantee, 1966. Mem. Am. Coll. Hosp. Adminstrs., Am. Hosp. Assn., Tex. Hosp. Assn., U. Tex. Alumni Assn., Sigma Iota Epsilon. Methodist. Clubs: Longhorn, Rotary. Home: 9 Crosslands St Fort Worth TX 76132 Office: 1300 W Cannon St Fort Worth TX 76104

FAGGETT, HARRY LEE, educator; b. Greensboro, N.C., Jan. 10, 1921; s. Walter Lee and Lucy Ann (Clymer) F.; B.S., Hampton Inst., 1941; A.M., Boston U., 1945, Ph.D., 1947; m. Cardis Donahue, June 10, 1969; children—Heather Lee, Barry Allan. Tchr., N.C. schs., 1941-44; mem. faculty N.C. Coll., Durham, 1945-46, Morgan State Coll., 1948-53, Fla. A. and M. U., 1953-57, Central State Coll., Ohio, 1957-59, So. U., La., 1959-60, 61-69, Queensborough Coll., L.I., N.Y., 1960-61, Prairie View U., Tex., 1969-73, Jackson (Miss.) State U., 1973-74; prof. English, S.C. State Coll., Orangeburg, 1974—. Mem. Modern Lang. Assn., Nat. Council Tchrs. of English, AAUP, Coll. Lang. Assn., Phi Beta Sigma. Episcopalian. Club: Masons. Author: Minorities in Shakespeare, 1972; author fiction, essays, poetry. Home: 1160 Hickory Dr Orangeburg SC 29115

FAGLIE, KAY MARIE RUNDQUIST, nurse; b. Jamestown, N.Y., Feb. 4, 1948; d. Gust William and Betty Mae (Parsons) Rundquist; student Ga. State Coll., Atlanta, 1966-67; diploma St. Joseph's Infirmary Sch. Nursing, Atlanta, 1969; m. Jerry Columbus Faglie, June 26, 1969; 1 son, Shawn Christopher. Staff nurse St. John's McNamara Hosp., Rapid City, S.C., 1969-72, Dekalb Gen. Hosp., Decatur, Ga., 1972-73; staff nurse emergency dept., asst. to dir. nursing service, nurse coordinator utilization rev., supr. emergency dept. Candler Gen. Hosp., Savannah, Ga., 1973-78; community health nurse I, women, infants, and children program Berkeley County Health Dept., Moncks Corner, S.C., 1979; office nurse Berkeley Family Practice, Moncks Corner, 1979—. Cert. instr. in basic life support Am. Heart Assn.; registered nurse, S.D., Ga., S.C. Mem. Nat. Emergency Dept. Nurses Assn., Am. Heart Assn., Ga. Heart Assn. Lutheran. Home: Route 5 Box 278-A Edward Dr Moncks Corner SC 29461 Office: Berkeley Family Practice New US Hwy 52 PO Box 787 Moncks Corner SC 29461

FAHERTY, MICHAEL EDWARD, bus. cons.; b. Pierce, W.Va., Mar. 25, 1935; s. Michael Richard and Mary Kathern (Sheetz) F.; B.B.A. cum laude, Fairmont State Coll., 1960; m. Patti A. Daugherty, Oct. 19, 1957; children—Kathleen Ann, Patrick Weldon, Maureen Ellen. Mgmt. trainee U.S. Steel, Pitts., 1960-62; corp. staff analyst Celanese Corp., N.Y.C., 1962-65, plant controller, Cumberland, Md., 1965-67; v.p., controller N.C. N.B. Bank, 1967-68, v.p., treas., dir. planning NCNB Corp. and N.C. Nat. Bank, Charlotte, 1968-69; treas., v.p. planning, dir. major contracts negotiations Recognition Equipment Group, Dallas, 1969-77; sr. v.p. finance, dir. Datapoint Corp., San Antonio, 1971-77; pres. MI Co., Inc., 1977—. Served with USMCR, 1953-57. Home: 3035 Quakertown Rd San Antonio TX 78230 Office: 8400 Data Point Dr San Antonio TX 78230

FAHEY, DARRYL RICHARD, chemist; b. Grand Forks, N.D., July 13, 1942; s. Richard M. and Gladys (Durnell) W.; B.S., U. N.D., 1964, Ph.D., 1969; m. Karin M. Rekdal, June 11, 1966; 1 son, Ryan. Sr. research chemist Phillips Petroleum Co., Bartlesville, Okla., 1968—. Mem. Am. Chem. Soc., Organic Reactions Catalysis Soc., Sigma Xi. Republican. Episcopalian. Contbr. numerous articles to sci. jours. Patentee in field. Home: 6301 King Dr Bartlesville OK 74003 Office: 88-F Phillips Research Center Bartlesville OK 74004

FAHEY, JOHN AUGUSTINE, educator; b. Medford, Mass., Apr. 23, 1923; s. John Augustine Fahey and Delia Agnes (Nee) F.; student Brown U., 1946-48; B.S., U. Md., 1960; M.Ed., Coll. William and Mary, 1966; m. Barbara Ann Haag, June 23, 1945; children—Kathleen Fahey Piper, John, Barbara. Commd. aviation cadet, U.S. Navy, 1942, advanced through grades to comdr., 1959; officer in charge ground sch. U.S. Naval Airship Tng. Program, 1952-53; dir. U.S. Navy Lang. Sch., 1957-60; liaison officer to comdr. in chief Soviet Forces, Germany, 1960-62; exec. officer USS Thuban, 1962-63, ret., 1963; master Norfolk Acad., 1964-66; instr. dept. fgn. langs. Old Dominion U., Norfolk, Va., 1966-68, asst. prof., 1969-73, asso. prof., 1974—, chmn. dept., 1976-79. Mem. Democratic Exec. Com., Virginia Beach, 1968-72; del. Va. Dem. Conv., 1968. Recipient Distinguished Faculty award, Old Dominion U., 1974. Mem. Am. Assn. Tchrs. Slavic and East European Langs. (past pres. Va. chpt.), Fgn. Lang. Assn. Va. (pres. 1976), Modern Lang. Assn., Am. Council Tchrs. Fgn. Langs., U.S. Naval Inst., Nat. Slavic Honor Soc. Club: Rotary. Author: Cartoon View of Russia, 1968. Contbr. articles to profl. jours. Home: 901 Pillow Dr Virginia Beach VA 23454 Office: Dept Fgn Langs Old Dominion U Norfolk VA 23508

FAHRINGER, CATHERINE HEWSON, savs. and loan exec.; b. Phila., Aug. 1, 1922; d. George F. and Catherine G. (Magee) Hewson; diploma Inst. Fin. Edn., 1965; 1 son by previous marriage, Francis George Beckett; m. Edward F. Fahringer, July 8, 1961. Public relations clk. Dade Savs. and Loan Assn., Miami, Fla., 1958-59, asst. sec., pub. relations, 1959-61, asst. v.p., 1961-67, v.p., 1967-74, sr. v.p., 1974-75, sr. v.p., sec., 1975-79, sr. v.p., head savs., personnel and mktg. div., 1979—. Mem. Public Health Trust Dade County, Fla., 1974—, sec., 1976-79, chmn., 1979—; mem. exec. com. and council Dade County CETA Consortium, 1973—; co-chmn. United Way Panel C., Miami, 1977—, mem. priorities and allocations com., 1978—, trustee, 1980—; mem. woman's adv. bd. Fla. Internat. U., 1978; trustee, v.p. Fla. Internat. U. Found., 1979; bd. dirs. John Elliott Blood Center, 1979; trustee Dade County Vocat. Edn. Found., 1978—, Downtown Miami Mchts. Assn., 1979-80. Named Woman of Yr., Dade County Bus. Profl. Women's Club, 1974; Woman of Yr. in Fin., Zonta Internat., 1975; recipient Trailblazer award, Women's Council of 100, 1977. Mem. Inst. Fin. Edn., (past pres. Greater Miami chpt.; nat. dir.), Savs. Loan Marketing Soc. (past pres.), Am. Soc. Personnel Mgrs., Fla. Savs. Loan League, Am. Soc. Personnel Adminstrs., Internat., Nat., Fla., Dade County bus. profl. women assns. Democrat. Congregationalist. Clubs: Coral Gables Country, Bankers. Contbr. speeches and articles to profl. jours. Office: Dade Savs 101 E Flagler St Miami FL 33131

FAIN, BOBBY COOK, mfg. engr.; b. Lexington, Ky., July 16, 1938; s. Curtis Cook and Edna Elizabeth (Teater) F.; student U. Ky., 1972; m. Linda Sue Whalen, Nov. 14, 1968; 1 son, Robert Curtis. Indsl. engr. Kawneer Co., Cynthiana, Ky., 1967-70; standards engr. Oster Corp., McMinnville, Tenn., 1972-74; mfg. engr. Koehring Atomaster, Bowling Green, Ky., 1976—. Served with USAR, 1957. Mem. Soc. Mfg. Engrs. Home: Route 4 Box 324A Bowling Green KY 42101 Office: 2701 Industrial Dr Bowling Green KY 42101

FAIN, GEORGE RAMEY, JR., newspaper pub.; b. Hendersonville, N.C., July 20, 1944; s. George Ramey and Mary (Ratchford) F.; A.B., Davidson Coll., 1966; m. Marilyn Botts, Aug. 14, 1966; 1 son, Christopher. Advt. sales rep. Hendersonville Times-News, 1968-72, advt. dir., 1972-74, v.p., pub., gen. mgr., 1974—. Bd. dirs. Henderson County Sheltered Workshop, YMCA; mem. Hendersonville Chorus. Served with AUS, 1966-68. Mem. N.C. Press Assn. (dir.), Greater Hendersonville C. of C. (dir.). Presbyterian. Clubs: Hendersonville Lions, Hendersonville Country. Home: 1215 Chanteloupe Dr Hendersonville NC 28739 Office: PO Box 490 Hendersonville NC 28739

FAIN, JIM, publisher; b. Norman Park, Ga., Sept. 12, 1920; s. James Edward and Mary (McCalman) F.; B.A., Emory U., 1941; m. Jill Carpenter, June 30, 1967; 1 son, Mike. Mng. editor Columbus (Ga.) Ledger, 1946-47; news editor Atlanta Jour., 1947-53; editor Dayton Daily News, 1953-76; editor Miami News, 1974-76; pub. Austin (Tex.) American-Statesman, 1976—. Served to maj. USAAF; to brig. gen. Res. Office: 308 Guadalupe St PO Box 670 Austin TX 78767

FAIRBAIRN, GRADY LYNN, corp. ofcl.; b. Kosse, Tex., Jan. 17, 1938; s. Andrew Grady and Ida Ruth (Mitchell) F.; B.B.A., U. Tex., Austin, 1961; M.B.A., Pepperdine U., 1977; m. Mary Alma Bond, Sept. 16, 1961; children—Sherri Lynn, James Alison, Mary Elizabeth. Sales rep. Phillips Petroleum Co., Dallas and Shreveport, La., 1963-67; buyer Collins Radio Co. Div. Rockwell Internat., Richardson, Tex., 1967-68, personnel mgr., 1968-70, mktg. adminstr., 1970-72, subcontract mgr., 1972-74, contract mgr., 1974-75, program planning and control analyst, 1975-77, program planning and control mgr., 1975—. County del. Rep. party, 1976; tax com. Goals for Plano, Tex., 1978-79. Served with U.S. Army, 1961-63. Mem. Nat. Mgmt. Assn., Mgmt. by Objectives Inst., Greater Dallas Res. Officers Assn. Methodist. Clubs: Richardson Jaycees (life), Plano Future Farmers Am. Alumni Assn., Delta Sigma Pi Alumni Assn. Club: Masons. Home: 1020 Kirnwood Dr Plano TX 75075 Office: 1200 N Alma Dr Richardson TX 75081

FAIRBANKS, HAROLD VINCENT, metall. engr., educator; b. Des Plaines, Ill., Dec. 7, 1915; s. Oscar William and Muriel (Hulet) F.; B.S. in Chem. Engring., Mich. State U., 1937, M.S. in Phys. Chemistry, 1939; postgrad. Mass. Inst. Tech., 1939-40; m. Marilyn Elizabeth Markussen, July 20, 1951; children—Elizabeth Muriel, William Martin. Instr. in chem. engring. U. Louisville (Ky.), 1940-42; asst. prof. dept. chem. engring. Rose Poly. Inst., 1942-46; asst. prof. dept. chem. engring. W.Va. U., Morgantown, 1946-49, asso. prof. metall. engring., 1949-55, metall. engr. Engring. Expt. Sta., 1949—, prof. metall. engring., 1955—, asso. chmn. dept. chem. engring., 1973—; adviser for mining and metall. engring. dept. Taiwan Provincial Cheng Kung U., Republic of Free China, 1957-59; cons. to various mfg. firms, govt. agys. and utility cos., 1939—. Tau Beta Pi scholar, 1933-34; registered profl. engr., Ind., W.Va. Fellow AAAS; mem. Am. Inst. Metall. Engrs., Am. Inst. Chem. Engrs., ASTM, Nat. Soc. Profl. Engrs. (pres. Morgantown chpt. 1962-64), IEEE, Internat. Metallographic Soc., Instrument Soc. Am., Profl. Engrs. in Edn. (W.Va. state chmn. 1966-69), Nat. Assn. Corrosion Engrs., Am. Ordnance Assn., Am. Powder Metallurgy Inst., W.Va. Acad. Sci. (chmn. engring. sci. sect. 1969), Acoustical Soc. Am., W.Va. Soc. Profl. Engring., Am. Soc. Metals, Chinese Inst. Engrs., Sigma Xi, Tau Beta Pi, Phi Mu Alpha, Phi Kappa Phi. Contbr. numerous articles on corrosion and metall. engring. to profl. jours. Home: 909 Riverview Dr Morgantown WV 26505 Office: Dept of Chemical Engineering West Virginia Univ Morgantown WV 26506

FAIRBANKS, MARILYN MARKUSSEN, educator; b. Minden, Nebr., Apr. 7, 1925; d. John Martin and Elizabeth (Aabel) Markussen; B.A., U. Nebr., 1947, M.A., 1948; Ed.D., W.Va. U., 1972; m. Harold V. Fairbanks, July 20, 1951; children—Elizabeth Fairbanks, William Fairbanks. Tchr., U. Nebr. High Sch., Lincoln, 1946-47, mem. research team field studies in child devel. dept. ednl. psychology, 1947-49; instr. psychology W.Va. U., Morgantown, 1949-51, instr. coll. edn., 1952-57, instr. reading, human resources and edn., 1968-73, asst. prof., 1973-77, asso. prof., 1977—; asso. prof. fgn. lang. and lit. dept. Cheng Kung U., Tainan, Taiwan, 1957-59. Named Outstanding Tchr. in Coll. of Human Resources and Edn., W.Va. U., 1976-77. Mem. Internat., Nat. Coll. reading assns. Presbyterian. Contbr. articles to scholastic jours. Home: 909 Riverview Dr Morgantown WV 26505 Office: WVa U Morgantown WV 26506

FAIRBURN, JOHN ALDEN, investment banker; b. N.Y.C., June 2, 1940; s. A.J.B. and Reba Peo F.; B.S., Bowling Green State U., 1964. Exec. dir. Lorain County Regional Airport Authority, Lorain, Ohio, 1960-62; chief exec. officer Fairburn Marine Aviation, Bucyrus, Ohio, 1962-70; chief exec. officer John Fairburn & Co., Mortgage Bankers, Melbourne Beach, Fla., 1970—, J.A. Fairburn securities, Melbourne Beach, 1974—. Fin. commr. City of Melbourne Beach, 1971-73. Mem. Nat. Assn. Security Dealers, Securities Investors Protection Corp. Republican. Episcopalian. Club: Elks (past treas.). Home: 1203 Atlantic Ave Melbourne Beach FL 32951 Office: 902 Oak St Melbourne Beach FL 32951

FAIRCHILD, DAVID ARTHUR, material handling engring. co. exec.; b. Midvale, Idaho, Oct. 26, 1939; s. Arthur Allen and Lois Mildred (Clark) F.; B.S. in Sci. Edn., Magic Valley Christian Coll., 1961; postgrad. (Univ. fellow) Abilene Christian U., 1961; postgrad. in Chemistry, Wadley Research Inst. Baylor U., 1962-67; m. Lloyd Ann Rawdon, Mar. 6, 1959; children—David Arthur, II, Jeffry Scott, Glenda Lawaine, Angela Christine. Vice pres. mktg. Medimation, Inc., Ft. Worth, 1969-73; v.p. contract adminstrn. Thomas Systems, Inc., Ft. Worth, 1974—; bd. dirs. Coll. Am., Petersburg, Tenn.; pres. Godley (Tex.) Ind. Sch. Dist. Sch. Bd., 1975-80. Republican. Mem. Chs. of Christ. Club: Lions. Home: PO Box 218 Godley TX 76044 Office: PO Box 18629 Fort Worth TX 76118

FAIRCHILD, JOSEPH VIRGIL, JR., accountant, educator; b. New Orleans, Nov. 25, 1933; s. Joseph Virgil and Georgiana Malone (Bourgeois) F.; B.S., La. State U., 1956, M.B.A., 1963, Ph.D., 1975; m. Judith Anne Champagne, Aug. 12, 1961; children—Georgiana, Joseph, Benjamin. Geologist, United Core, Inc., Houston, 1956-57; asso. accountant Humble Oil & Refining Co., New Orleans, 1963-64; sr. accountant L. A. Champagne & Co., C.P.A.'s, Baton Rouge, 1964-67, partner, 1967-68; owner J.V. Fairchild, C.P.A., Thibodaux, La., 1969—; asst. prof. accounting Nicholls State U., Thibodaux, La., 1969-75, asso. prof., 1975-76, prof. accounting, 1976—. Served with USAF, 1957-60, USAFR, 1960—. Named Outstanding Tchr., Nicholls State U. Yearbook, 1972. C.P.A., La. Mem. Am. Inst. C.P.A.'s, Soc. La. C.P.A.'s, Nat. Accounting Assn., Geol. and Mining Soc. of Am. Univs., Southwestern Soc. Sci. Assn., Res. Officers Assn., Beta Alpha Psi, Delta Sigma Pi, Delta Mu Delta. Clubs: Lions, K.C. Home: 412 Plater Dr Thibodaux LA 70301 Office: Nicholls State Univ Thibodaux LA 70301

FAIRES, DUNN THOMAS, educator; b. Commerce, Tex., Mar. 14, 1949; s. Tom Flow and Willie Louise (Dunn) F.; B.S., E. Tex. State U., 1971, M.S., 1972, Ed.D., 1977. Asst. instr. dept. industry and tech. E. Tex. State U., Commerce, 1971-72, 75-76, adj. instr., 1976-77; tchr. Plano (Tex.) Ind. Sch. Dist., 1972-75, Richardson (Tex.) Ind. Sch. Dist., 1977-78; tchr. Adult Edn. Dept. Parks and Recreation, City of Plano, 1972-74; asst. prof. dept. indsl. edn. and tech. Northeastern Okla. State U., Tahlequah, 1978—. Chmn. bd. Hunt, Rains, Delta Tri-County chpt. ARC, 1976-77; mem. Commerce Emergency Corps, 1970-72, 75-78, sec. treas., 1976, chief, 1977; pres. Ch. of Christ, E. Tex. State U. Bible Chair, 1969-70. Recipient Outstanding Presdl. Leadership award Sigma Tau Epsilon, 1970. Mem. Am., Tex., Okla. indsl. arts assns., Am. Vocat. Assn., Faculties of Okla. Coll. and Univ. System, Tex. Vocat. Tech. Assn., Am. Council Indsl. Arts Tchr. Edn. (sec.-treas. Okla. chpt. 1979-80), Nat. Assn. Indsl. and Tech. Tchr. Educators, Phi Delta Kappa, Epsilon Pi Tau, Kappa Delta Pi, Sigma Tau Epsilon, Iota Lambda Sigma (pres. chpt. 1980, chmn. nat. adv. council 1977-78). Home: 1005 N Callie Ave Tahlequah OK 74464 Office: Indsl Edn and Tech Northeastern Okla State U Tahlequah OK 74464

FAIRFIELD, AL, real estate devel. co. exec.; b. Blytheville, Ark., Aug. 26, 1934; s. A.B. and Ethel B. (Denton) F.; B.B.A. in Bus. Mgmt., So. Methodist U., 1958; m. Barbara Ann Hoffman, Feb. 11, 1978; children—Stephan Brown, Cynthia Lynn. Apprentice to various architecture, homebldg. and lumber businesses, 1958; ind. custom homebuilder, Houston, 1959-61; owner, operator Al Fairfield Builder, Inc., Houston, 1961-66; chmn., pres. Fairfield Co., Houston, 1967—; pres., chief exec. officer 8 corps.; gen. mng. partner 8 partnerships and joint venture. Bd. dirs. Musicfest, Houston. Served with U.S. Army, 1954-56; ETO. Recipient Housing Mktg. award Housing Guidance Council, 1964. Mem. Urban Land Inst., Nat. Assn. Homebuilders, Houston C. of C., Houston Better Bus. Bur. Republican. Presbyterian. Clubs: Houston Ski (dir., past pres.), Houston Racquet, Rotary. Innovator and designer of communities, homes, townhomes, office bldgs.; author manual on new town devel. Home: 5001 Woodway #1802 Houston TX 77056 Office: 9575 Katy Freeway Suite 300 Houston TX 77024

FAIRLEIGH, MARGARET HILLS, lawyer; b. Atlanta, Apr. 11, 1912; d. Albert Lyman and Georgia (Burns) Hills; LL.B. Woodrow Wilson Coll. Law, 1939 m. George DuRelle Fairleigh, June 29, 1951; stepchildren—Kathryn (Mrs. Roger W. Allen Jr.), Henrietta (Mrs. Charles M. Sparacino). Admitted to Ga. bar, 1940; asso. Poole, Pearce & Hall, Atlanta, 1942-51, partner (name later changed to Poole, Pearce & Cooper), 1951-71; individual practice law, Decatur, Ga., 1971—. Dir. Fed. Defender Program, Inc., 1974—. Mem. Atlanta Estate Planning Council, Gov.'s Commn. on Status of Women, 1968-70. Mem. Atlanta Legal Aid Soc. (pres. 1966), Am., Ga., Atlanta, Decatur-DeKalb bar assns., Am. Judicature Soc., DeKalb C. of C. (dir. 1976). Presbyn. Home: 486 Princeton Way NE Atlanta GA 30307 Office: 1 W Court Sq Decatur GA 30030

FAIRMAN, JARRETT SYLVESTER, retail co. exec.; b. Anderson, Ind., Feb. 22, 1939; s. Charles Lawton and Ruth (Rich) F.; B.S., Purdue U., 1961; m. Delores Rae Anderson, Nov. 13, 1960; children—Adele Suzanne, Jarrett Scott, Angela Christine. Exec. trainee, div. mgr. Sears, Marion, Ind., 1963-67, merchandise mgr., asst. store mgr., Bloomington, Ind., 1967-69, asst. retail sales mgr. sporting goods, Chgo., 1969-71, territorial mdse. mgr. sporting goods, toys and bus. equipment, Dallas, 1971-78; regional v.p. retail ops. White's Home and Auto Stores, 1978—. Served with U.S. Army, 1961-63. Republican. Lutheran. Home: 1608 Centenary St Richardson TX 75081 Office: 3910 Callfield Rd Wichita Falls TX 76328

FAIRWEATHER, CHARLES WALTER, III, lawyer; b. Lovington, N.M., June 5, 1936; s. Charles and Effie (Merony) F.; A.B., U. Calif. at Los Angeles, 1960; J.D., So. Meth. U., 1963; m. Ruth Marie Collins, Apr. 11, 1970; children—Rebecca Lynn, Gregory Scott, Jon Christopher. Admitted to Tex. bar, 1963; asst. county atty. Potter County, Tex., 1964-67; partner firm Fairweather & Hale, Amarillo, Tex., 1967—. Trustee, Wilson Pub. Trust, Temple, Tex. Mem. Nat. Assn. Def. Lawyers in Criminal Cases, Tex. Criminal Def. Lawyers Assn., Phi Beta Kappa, Phi Delta Phi. Episcopalian. Clubs: Amarillo Country, Amarillo, Amarillo Yacht. Home: 4603 Olsen Blvd Amarillo TX 79109 Office: 310 W 6th Amarillo TX 79101

FAIRWEATHER, GLADSTONE HENRY, health center exec.; b. Jamaica, W.I., Nov. 30, 1935; s. Arnold Darrell and Miriam Loretta Fairweather; B.A., William Jewell Coll., 1960; M.S., So. Ill. U., 1962; M.H.A., U. S.C., 1970; 1 child. Asso. dir. tng. and devel. N.Y.C. Health and Hosp. Corp., 1970-72; exec. dir. Greensborough Neighborhood Health Center, Westchester County (N.Y.) Health Dept., 1972-75; dir. ambulatory services Meharry Med. Coll., Nashville, 1974-78; exec. dir. Matthew Walker Health Center, Nashville, 1979—; instr. health care adminstrn. Belmont Coll., 1978-78. Elder Lord's Chapel, Nashville. Mem. Nat. Assn. Health Execs. (pres. Nashville chpt. 1975-79), Am. Coll. Hosp. Adminstrs., Nat. Assn. Community Health Centers, Am. Hosp. Assn., Tenn. Hosp. Assn., Nat. Assn. Health Services Execs., Am. Public Health Assn. Home: 1701 Primrose St Nashville TN 37212 Office: 1501 Herman St Nashville TN 37208

FAISON, FRANK ALLEN, county mgr.; b. Richmond, Va., Nov. 14, 1929; s. Patrick L. and May (Trusheim) F.; B.S., Va. Poly. Inst., 1951, M.S., 1952; postgrad. U. Chgo., 1959-60; grad. Army Command and Gen. Staff Coll., 1976; m. Marilyn Roth, Sept. 13, 1958; children—E. Lawrence, David L., Elizabeth L., Patricia L. Adminstrv. asst. City LaGrange Park (Ill.), 1956-59, city mgr., 1961-67; dir. pub. works City of St. Charles (Ill.), 1959-61; city mgr., Danville, Va., 1967-71, Pensacola, Fla., 1971-78; county mgr. Henrico County (Va.), 1978—. Lectr. Va. Commonwealth U., Pensacola Jr. Coll., U. W. Fla. Mem. Met. Econ. Devel. Council Richmond. Served with C.E., U.S. Army, 1952-56, now col. Res. Decorated Bronze Star medal. Mem. Internat. City Mgmt. Assn. (mem. Acad. for Profl. Devel.; bd. dirs. 1974-76), Fla. City and County Mgrs. Assn., Nat. Assn. County Ofcls., Mil. Order World Wars, Res. Officers Assn. (life), Omicron Delta Kappa,

Chi Epsilon. Clubs: Pensacola Exec., Richmond Exec. Home: 2006 Fon du lac Rd Richmond VA 23229

FALCON, JOSE EDGAR, advt. agy. exec.; b. Mayaguez, P.R., June 4, 1934; s. Isidoro Falcon and Luz Maria Tebar; B.B.A., Boston Coll., 1956; m. Elba M. Blanes, Feb. 26, 1965; children—Vilma Milagros, Edgardo Francisco. Mgr., Muebleria Falcon Inc., San Juan, P.R., 1956-58, gen. mgr., 1960-68; account exec. Communications Art Co., San Juan, 1968-71; dir. public info. and advt. ITT All Am. Cables & Radio Co., San Juan, 1971; gen. mgr. Sta. WQBS, La Gran Cadena, San Juan, 1971-74; v.p. Promo Inc., Rio Piedras, P.R., 1974-77, pres., 1978—. Served with U.S. Army, 1958-60. Mem. Sales and Mktg. Execs. Assn., Nu Sigma Beta. Roman Catholic. Club: Riomar Golf. Home: 0-34 California St Mallorca Guaynabo PR 00657 Office: Promo Inc La Electronica Inc Bldg Suite 310 Rio Piedras PR 00927

FALKENBURY, STEPHEN DOUGLAS, JR., engring. and construction mgmt. co. exec.; b. Staten Island, N.Y., Apr. 9, 1928; s. Stephen Douglas and Lillian Rosalee (Schultz) F.; B.S. in Civil Engring., The Citadel, 1949; postgrad. U.S. Army Engring. Sch., 1956-57, Def. Lang. Inst., 1962; m. Jean Carole Gainer, Jan. 16, 1960; children—Stephen Douglas III, John William, Pamela Carole, Paul Howard. Commd. 2d lt. U.S. Army, 1949; advanced through grades to lt. col., 1965; chief constrn., mgmt. br., Ft. Belvoir, 1957-60; dep. dist. engr., Balt., 1965-67; constr. bn. comdr., Korea, 1967-68; asst. div. engr., Huntsville, Ala., 1968-70; ret., 1970; v.p. devel. Medicenters of Am., Memphis, 1970-74; pvt. practice engring. and construction mgmt. consulting, Memphis, Charlotte, N.C. and Honduras, 1974—; pres. Falkenbury & Assos., Charlotte, N.C., 1974—; pres., adminstr. Five Oaks Nursing Center, Concord, N.C. Mem. advisory bd. Boy Scouts Am., Memphis, 1971-73; delegate N.C. Republican Conv., 1976. Decorated Bronze Star, Purple Heart, Dept. Def. Meritorious Service medal; registered profl. engr., Md.; certified gen. contractor Fla., Ariz., S.C., N.C., Va. Mem. Nat. Soc. Profl. Engrs., Am. Inst. Mgmt., Am. Mgmt. Assn., Am. Health Care Facilities Assn. Episcopalian (vestryman). Clubs: Mason Shriner. Home: 2019 Cassamia Pl Charlotte NC 28211 Office: 413 Winecoff School Rd Concord NC 28025

FALKNER, PAMELA POLLARD, realtor, accountant; b. Helena, Ark., Sept. 29, 1949; d. Robert Edward and Doris Marie (Carlton) Pollard; B.S. U. Tenn., Knoxville, 1970; M.S., Memphis State U., 1977; m. Terrell Manning Falkner, Dec. 19, 1970. Broker, Falkner Realty, Hughes, Ark., 1973—; dir. tax services Agro Systems Corp., Memphis, 1977-79; gen. partner Hickman, Falkner & Assos., Memphis, 1979—. Mem. Am. Inst. C.P.A.'s, Ark. Soc. C.P.A.'s, Beta Gamma Sigma, Beta Alpha Psi, Phi Kappa Phi. Methodist. Club: Town and Country Garden (pres. 1976). Home: 201 Tournament St West Memphis AR 72301 Office: 5384 Poplar St Suite 411 Memphis TN 38117

FALLON, JAMES THOMAS, hosp. adminstr.; b. Cin., Oct. 15, 1949; s. James Robert and Virginia Mary (Schmutte) F.; B.A., U. Cin., 1971; M.H.A., Xavier U., 1974; m. Sandra Lee Dudek, Sept. 14, 1974. Nurse's aid Vets. Hosp., Cin., 1970-72; adminstrv. resident St. Joseph Riverside Hosp., Warren, Ohio, 1973-74; health planner Mahoning Valley Health Planning Assn., Youngstown, Ohio, 1974-76; adminstr. Marcum and Wallace Meml. Hosp., Irvine, Ky., 1976—; mem. Estill Health Care, Inc., 1978—; chmn. Estill County Blood Donor Program, 1977—. Served with U.S. Army, 1971-72. Mem. Alumni Assn. Xavier U. Hosp. and Health Adminstrn. Program. Roman Catholic. Club: Irvine-Ravenna Kiwanis (pres. 1979-80). Home: 710 Elm St Ravenna KY 40472 Office: 201 Richmond Ave Irvine KY 40336

FALLS, ROY EMERSON, clergyman; b. Roxton, Tex., June 27, 1920; s. William Bruce and Sarah Ann (Gregory) F.; Th.M., Bible Bapt. Sem., 1952; B.S. in Edn., N. Tex. State U., 1963; m. Eula V. Alexander, Oct. 24, 1947; children—Linia Gail Falls Francis, Ronald Keith. Printer, Fort Worth Star-Telegram, 1940-78; public sch. tchr., Euless Tex., 1974-77; real estate broker, Ft. Worth, 1978-79; ordained to ministry Baptist Ch., 1962; pastor Faith Bapt. Ch., Euless, 1970—. Active precinct level Republican party, 1970-78. Mem. Internat. Typog. Union, Nat. Assn. Realtors, World Bapt. Fellowship of Pastors. Served with AUS, 1941-45. Author: Biography of Life of J. Frank Norris, 1975. Home: 3708 Denton Hwy Fort Worth TX 76117 Office: Faith Bapt Ch 304 Pipeline Rd Euless TX 76039

FALUDI, JEFFREY ERIC, ophthalmologist; b. Phila., Sept. 17, 1943; s. Heinz K. and Shirley F.; B.S., La. State U., 1965, M.D., 1970; m. Jo Ann Townsend, Nov. 4, 1966; children—Jeffrey Eric, Jason Christopher. Intern, Confederate Meml. Med. Center, Shreveport, La., 1970-71; resident Greater Balt. Med. Center, 1973-76; pvt. practice medicine, specializing in ophthalmology, Shreveport, 1976—; clin. instr. La. State U. Sch. Medicine, 1976—; mem. staff P & S Hosp., Schumpert Hosp., Doctors Hosp., VA Hosp., Highland Hosp. Bd. dirs. Shreveport Assn. of Blind. Served to capt., M.C., AUS, 1974-76. Diplomate Am. Bd. Ophthalmology. Fellow Am. Acad. Ophthalmology; mem. La. Med. Soc., Shreveport Med. Soc. Methodist. Office: 1513 Line Ave Suite 210 Shreveport LA 71101

FAMULARY, JOSEPH LAWRENCE, social scientist; b. Long Branch, N.J., Aug. 12, 1943; s. Joseph Carmen and Nancy Lowe (Ivins) F.; B.A., Monmouth Coll., N.J., 1968; M.A., U. Md., 1976; m. Carol Suddreth, Oct. 15, 1973; 1 dau., Sherry Lynn. Tchr. lang. arts Hammarskjold Jr. High Sch., East Brunswick, N.J., 1968; tchr. social studies, gifted and talented West Caldwell High Sch., Lenoir, N.C., 1977—. Monmouth scholar, 1966; Monmouth County Freeholders scholar, 1964-66; NJ. Contractors scholar, 1965; Lenoir Caldwell County C. of C. scholar, 1978. Mem. Am. Hist. Assn., Nat. Geog. Soc., N.C. Assn. Educators, NEA, Phi Alpha Theta. Home: 336 Hilltop St Hudson NC 28638

FANCHER, EVELYN PITTS, librarian; b. Marion, Ala.; d. D.C. and Nell Lenora Pitts; B.S., Ala. State U., 1946; M.S.L.S., Atlanta U., 1961; Ed.S., George Peabody Coll., 1969, Ph.D., 1974; m. Charles B. Fancher, Dec. 20, 1947; children—Charles B., Mark Pitts, Adrienne Lenore. Tchr. biology, chemistry public schs., Marion, Ala., 1946-56; library tech. asst. A&M U., Huntsville, 1956; dir. media center Council High Sch., Huntsville, Ala., 1959-62; circulation, reference librarian, instr. Tenn. State U., Nashville, 1962-74, dir. univ. library, 1975—. Mem. ALA, Southeastern Library Assn., Tenn. Library Assn., Mid State Library Assn., Nashville Library Club, AAUW, Phi Delta Kappa. Congregationalist. Home: 3948 Drakes Branch Rd Nashville TN 37218 Office: Brown-Daniel Library Tenn State Univ Nashville TN 37203

FANDRICH, ROBERT THOMAS, JR., environ. engring. exec.; b. Milw., Mar. 10, 1939; s. Robert Thomas and Erika (Gilomen) F.; B.S., U. Wis., Madison, 1961; M.S., Purdue U., 1964; m. Judith Ellin Fieschko, Oct. 28, 1961; children—Robert Thomas III, Laura Judith, Christopher Grant. Designer Torrington Bearing Co. (Conn.), 1961-63; project engr. A. C. Electronics Co., Milw., 1964-67; mgr. dept. environ. engring. Harris Electronic Systems div., Melbourne, Fla., 1967—; lectr. in field. Instr. Marquette U., 1965, Milw. Sch. Engring., 1966. Mem. Inst. Environ. Scis. (panel on cost effectiveness in dynamic testing 1974), Mensa, Internat. Meditation Soc. Unitarian. Contbr. articles to profl. jours. Home: 549 US A1A Satellite Beach FL 32937 Office: PO Box 37 Melbourne FL 32901

FANG, CHENG SHEN, educator; b. Taipei, Taiwan, Mar. 29, 1936; s. Ho Chin and Lai Mai F.; came to U.S., 1962, naturalized, 1976; Ph.D. in Chem. Engring., U. Houston, 1968; m. Fei-Ying Cheng, Oct. 5, 1972. Shift supr. Ammonia Plant Taiwan Fertilizer Inc., 1960-62; asst. prof. chem. engring. U. Southwestern La., Lafayette, 1969-74, asso. prof., 1975—; cons. in field. NSF grantee, 1970-72 75; Dept. Conservation State of La. grantee, 1975-76. Mem. Am. Inst. Chem. Engrs. Contbr. articles in field to profl. jours. Home: 215 N Philo Lafayette LA 70506 Office: PO Box 4-4130 Lafayette LA 70504

FANG, CHING SENG, civil engr., marine scientist, educator; b. Chung-Ching, China, Nov. 23, 1938; came to U.S., 1962, naturalized, 1972; s. Tien and Funchuen I. Fang; B.S., Nat. Taiwan U., 1961; M.S., N.C. State U., 1964, Ph.D., 1969; m. Carol Sang, June 18, 1966; children—Edward, James. Research asst. dept. agrl. engring. N.C. State U., 1962-64, teaching asst., 1964-65, research asst. dept. civil engring., 1965-67, research asso. and teaching asst. dept. engring. mechanics and civil engring., 1967-68; research engr. Camp, Dresser & McKee Co., Boston, 1968-69; asst. prof. and marine scientist Va. Inst. Marine Sci., U. Va., Gloucester Point, 1969-70, head dept. phys. oceanography and hydraulics, 1970—; asso. prof. dept. marine sci. Coll. of William and Mary, Williamsburg, Va., 1974-78, prof., 1979—; gen. mgr. Coastal Environ. Associates, Inc., Gloucester Point, 1971—; environ. engring. cons. to UN, 1976. Mem. ASCE, Am. Geophys. Union. Contbr. numerous articles on hydrodynamics, environ. engring. and marine sci. to profl. jours. Home: 325 Yorkville Rd Grafton VA 23692 Office: Virginia Inst of Marine Science Gloucester Point VA 23062

FANJUL, ALFONSO GERONIMO, land co. exec., sugar producer; b. Havana, Cuba, Sept. 30, 1909; s. Higinio and Maria (Estrada) F.; came to U.S., 1959; B.A., Cath. U. Am., 1931; m. Lillian Gomez Mena, Sept. 9, 1936; children—Alfonso Jose, Lillian Fanjul Azqueta, Jose, Alexander, Andres. Vice pres. Cuban Trading Co., Havana, 1934-59, Nueva Compania Azucarera Gomez Mena, Havana, 1937-59, Manati Sugar Co., Havana, 1947-59, Francisco Sugar Co., Havana, 1945-59, Czarnikow-Rionda Co., N.Y.C., 1940-69; chmn. bd. Osceola Farms Co., Palm Beach, Fla., 1960—, New Hope Sugar Co., Palm Beach, 1961—, Flo-Sun Land Corp., Palm Beach, 1969—; dir. Fla. Sugar Cane League, 1965—. Trustee Biscayne Coll., Miami, Fla., 1963—, Palm Beach Day Sch., 1968—. Mem. Fla. Sugar Marketing and Terminal Assn. (dir. 1977—). Roman Catholic. Clubs: Everglades, Seminole Golf, Bath and Tennis, Meadow. Home: 109 Wells Rd Palm Beach FL 33480 Office: 316 Royal Poinciana Plaza Palm Beach FL 33480

FANNIN, LARRY DONNELL, educator; b. LaGrange, Ga., Nov. 23, 1951; s. Sallie Fannin; D.Pharmacy, Mercer U., 1975. With Reed's Discount Drugs, Atlanta, 1971-74; instr. to students in profl. practice rotation Ga. Bapt. Hosp., Atlanta, 1974-75; dir. pharmacy services S.W. Community Hosp., Atlanta, 1975-77; dir. Drug Info. Edn. Center, asst. prof. clin. pharmacy and co-dir. supervised internship program Fla. A. and M. U., Tallahassee, 1977-78, dir. undergrad. clin. programs, and asst. prof. clin. pharmacy, co-dir. supervised internship program, 1978—. Registered pharmacist, Ga. Mem. Am. Pharm. Assn., Nat. Pharm. Assn., Am. Soc. Hosp. Pharmacists, Am. Assn. of Colls. of Pharmacy, Kappa Psi. Democrat. Methodist. Club: Y's Men Internat. Orgn. Home: 1346 Terrace St Tallahassee FL 32303 Office: Fla A and M Univ Tallahassee FL 32307

FANNIN, TROY EDWARD, optometrist, educator; b. Sandy Hook, Ky., Jan. 19, 1925; s. Floyd Mitchell and Elizabeth (Hayes) F.; B.S., U.S. Mcht. Marine Acad., 1945; B.S., Dr. Optometry, Ohio State U., 1952; m. Cecile Mae Owen, Nov. 24, 1949; 1 dau., Heather Fay. Marine engr. Isthmian S.S. Co., 1945-46, Coastwise S.S. Co., 1946-47; instr. U. Houston Coll. Optometry, 1954-56, asst. prof., 1965-68, asso. prof., 1968-73, prof., 1973—, chmn. dept. clin. scis., 1974-79, optics tract coordinator, 1979—; vis. asso. prof. U. Calif. at Berkeley, summer 1969; pvt. practice optometry, Houston, 1956-65. Served to lt. USNR. Diplomate Nat. Bd. Optometry. Mem. Am. Acad. Optometry (past chmn. sect. meetings), Am., Tex., Harris County optometric assns., Am. Assn. U. Profs., Tex. Assn. Coll. Tchrs., Editorial Council Am. Acad. Optometry, Assn. Optometric Educators, Beta Sigma Kappa. Unitarian. Home: 13334 Bretagne Dr Houston TX 77015

FANNING, JOHN WOOD, assn. exec.; b. Grand Rapids, Mich., Jan. 17, 1932; s. Francis Burke and Audrey (Young) F. B.S., U. Ill., 1953; m. Hannah Call, Dec. 20, 1958; children—Audrey, David, Mary. With Boy Scouts Am., 1955—, dist. exec., Des Plaines, Ill., 1955-60, Kermit and Odessa, Tex., 1960-67, Lawton, Okla., 1967-69, field dir., Tulsa, 1969-73, scout exec., Pikeville, Ky., 1973-79, scout exec., Lake Charles, La., 1979—. Recipient Vigil honor, Order of the Arrow Boy Scouts Am. Mem. Sigma Pi. Republican. Mormon. Club: Rotary. Home: 2917 Creole St Lake Charles LA 70601 Office: 304 S Ryan St Lake Charles LA 70601

FANNING, ROBERT ALLEN, lawyer; b. Dallas, Nov. 3, 1931; s. Charles Allen and Beryl Julia (Buckner) F.; B.B.A., Baylor U., 1953; J.D., So. Meth. U., 1960; m. Carolyn Parker Hedges, Aug. 6, 1960; children—Barry H., Marc H. Admitted to Tex. bar, 1959; since practiced in Dallas; mem. firm Fanning Harper, Wilson, Martinson & Fanning, P.C., Dallas, Profl. Corp., 1960—. Mem. bd. visitors So. Meth. U. Sch. Law, 1969-72; mem. adv. council Southwestern Bapt. Theol. Sem., 1966-68; mem. devel. council Baylor U., 1965-73. Trustee Annuity Bd. So. Bapt. Conv., 1971-79, past vice chmn.; Nat. Bd. Fellowship Christian Athletes; past chmn. bd. trustees San Marcos Baptist Acad. Served to 1st lt. USAF, 1954-56. Recipient Distinguished Service medal, San Marcos Acad., 1970. Mem. Am. Judicature Soc., Am., Tex. State, Dallas bar assns., S.W. Legal Found., Tex. Assn. Defense Counsel, Delta Theta Phi. Clubs: Dallas, City, Insurance (Dallas), Masons, Shriners. Home: 3605 Crescent Dr Dallas TX 75205 Office: 4040 First Nat Bank Bldg Dallas TX 75202

FANSHIER, CHESTER, metal products mfg. exec.; b. Wilson County, Kans., Mar. 2, 1897; s. Thomas J. and Nora Bell (Maxwell) F.; m. Ina Muriel Goens, Apr. 12, 1918; 1 dau., Norma Elaine (Mrs. Robert B. Rice). Gen. mgr. Bart Products Co., 1932-39; pres. gen. mgr. Metal Goods Mfg. Co., 1939—. Commr. Tulsa Presbytery to 156th Gen. Assembly, Presbyn. Ch. U.S.A., 1944; pres Sunday Eve. Fedn. (chs.), 1937-38. Recipient Wisdom award Honor, 1970; Gutenberg Bible award. Registered profl. engr. Okla. Mem. Am. Soc. M.E. (life mem.), Am. Soc. Testing Materials, Am. Def. Preparedness Assn. (life), Nat. Rifle Assn. Am. (life), Nat., Okla. (charter) socs. profl. engrs., Okla. Rifle Assn., Profl. Photographers Am., SAR. Presbyn. (elder). Clubs: Rotary (pres. 1956-57), Engineers of Bartlesville (charter mem.; past dir.). Home: 1328 Cherokee Ave Bartlesville OK 74003 Office: 309 W Hensley Blvd Bartlesville OK 74003

FANT, ALBERT REESE, architect; b. Anderson, S.C., Feb. 5, 1928; s. Charles William and Susan Dorothy (Bell) F.; B.Arch., Clemson U., 1949; m. Sara M. Haynie, June 21, 1957; children—Al, Todd, David. With Charles W. Fant, architect, Anderson, S.C., 1949-56; partner Fant & Fant, Anderson, 1956—. Chmn., Anderson City Planning and Zoning Commn., 1956-68. Trustee Anderson Coll., Anderson YMCA. Served to lt. U.S. Army, 1951-53. Mem. A.I.A. Baptist. Kiwanian. Home: 114 Carter Oak Dr Anderson SC 29621 Office: 109 1/2 Sharpe St Anderson SC 29621

FANT, SADIE PATTON, speech pathologist; b. Guntown, Miss., Jan. 26, 1933; d. Samuel Hoyle and Mary Francis (Parker) Patton; B.S., Miss. State Coll. Women, 1956, M.S., 1968; postgrad. Miss. U. Women, 1976; m. Arnold Lee Fant, Aug. 9, 1953; children—Frances Yvonne Yarbrough, Richard Lee. Tchr., Aliceville (Ala.) High Sch., 1956-57, New Hope High Sch., Columbus, Miss., 1957-58; tchr. W. Lowndes Elementary Sch., Columbus, Miss., 1959-61, Knee-Hi Kindergarten, Columbus, 1962-64; speech pathologist Columbus Public Schs., 1968—; spl. edn. examiner Miss. U. Women regional screening team, 1968—. Sec., Lowndes County Emergency Radio Net, 1977—; pres. Stokes Beard PTA, 1962-66, Columbus PTA City Council, 1967-71; sec. bd. dirs. Foster Group Home, Inc., Columbus, 1975-77; mem. Lowndes County Dem. Com., 1975—. Certified speech pathology, Am. Speech and Hearing Assn.; Miss. State Coll. for Women fellow, 1966-68. Mem. Am. Law Enforcement Officers Assn. (sec. 1976—), Miss. Speech Hearing Assn., Nat., Miss. (pres.-elect 1980-81), Lowndes County assns. retarded citizens. Democrat. Baptist. Clubs: Columbus Positive Mental Attitude, Tombigbee Citizens Band Radio, Nat. C.B. Possee. Contbr. articles to profl. jours. Home: 1122 Waterworks Rd Columbus MS 39701 Office: 723 22d St S Columbus MS 39701

FARALLI, THOMAS STEVEN, city ofcl.; b. Beloit, Wis., May 19, 1946; s. Leonard Joseph and Suzanne Elizabeth Faralli; B.S. in Recreation and Parks Adminstrn., U. Wis., LaCrosse, 1972; M.Ed. in Therapeutic Recreation, U. South Ala., 1979. Recreation supr. City of Monroe (Wis.), 1972-73; dir. parks, recreations and forestry City of Watertown (Wis.), 1974-75; dist. supr. recreation City of Mobile, 1975—; mem. therapeutic recreation adv. bd. U. South Ala., mem. adj. faculty, 1979—. Pres., Mobile Gulf Coast chpt. Muscular Dystrophy Assn., 1978—. Recipient Freedoms Found. award, 1977. Mem. Nat. Recreation and Park Assn., Am. Recreation and Park Soc., Ala. Recreation and Parks Soc. (dist. pres. 1977-78, dir. 1978-79), Wis. Parks and Recreation Assn., Sigma Lambda Sigma. Home: 6451 Old Shell Rd Apt 807 Mobile AL 36608 Office: 2301 Airport Blvd Mobile AL 36606

FARBER, GEORGE ALLAN, dermatologist; b. Miami, Fla., Jan. 4, 1934; s. Charles R. and Clara M. (Milman) F.; B.S., La. State U., 1955, M.D., 1959; m. Nancy Graves, Dec. 26, 1955; children—George Allan, Michael G., Jeffrey N., Guy C., Scott O. Intern So. Bapt. Hosp., New Orleans, 1959-60; resident Charity Hosp. of New Orleans, 1963-66; pvt. practice dermatology, 1966—; commd. 2d lt. M.C., U.S. Air Force, 1955, advanced through grades to lt. col., 1965; chief aviation medicine and mil. pub. health Luke AFB, Phoenix, 1960-63; flight surgeon, chief dermatology and syphilology Cam Ranh Bay, Viet Nam, 12th U.S. Air Force Hosp., 1966-67; chief dermatology service and cons. to Surgeon Gen. for S.E. region U.S. Air Force Med. Referral Center, Keesler AFB, Miss., 1967-70, ret., 1970; mem. staff Charity Hosp. New Orleans, Sara Mayo Hosp., East Jefferson Hosp., So. Bapt. Hosp.; asst. prof. medicine Tulane U. Sch. of Medicine, New Orleans, 1970-75, asso. prof., 1976—, clin. asso. prof. dermatology, 1975—; chmn. bd., pres. Zenith Polyfactoring Corp., 1963—; mng. partner Elk Place Med. Plaza, New Orleans, 1972—; partner Farlee Co., New Orleans, 1972—; dir. Fairground Corp. Decorated Air medal with 3 oak leaf clusters, Bronze Star; diplomate Am. Bd. Dermatology. Mem. Am. Acad. Dermatology, Am. Soc. Dermatologic Surgery (pres. 1978-79), Am. Assn. Physicians and Surgeons, Assn. Mil. Dermatologists (life), So. Med. Assn., Am. Assn. Cosmetic Surgeons, Internat. Soc. Cosmetic Surgery, Air Force Soc. Internists and Allied Specialists, La. Dermatol. Soc., AMA, La. State, Orleans Parish med. socs., South Central Dermatol. Assn., Hotel and Apt. Owners Assn., Civil Service Employees Assn., Bldg. Owner and Mgrs. Assn., Alpha Tau Omega, Phi Chi. Democrat. Methodist. Clubs: Chateau Golf and Country, Westbank Petroleum. Contbr. articles to med. jours. Home: #5 Chateau Petrus Ct Kenner LA 70062 Office: 144 Elk Pl Suite 1604 New Orleans LA 70112

FARIA, EDWARD CYRINO, health care adminstr.; b. Peabody, Mass., Aug. 12, 1924; s. Celestino and Laura (Lucio) F.; student U. S.C., 1948-50, 1956-60, U.S. Armed Forces Inst., 1957-58, So. Ill. U., 1961-65; certificate USAF Sch. Aviation Medicine Air U., 1955; m. Gloria Jewel Harrison, Jan. 15, 1944; children—Gloria Dawn, Evelyn Celeste, Elizabeth Vermel. Served as enlisted man USAAF, 1942-46, USAF, 1950-67, advanced through grades to chief master sgt. USAF, 1960; med. adminstrv. specialist USAAF, 1942-46; chief storekeeper VA Regional Office, S.C., 1946-50; med. adminstrv. supt. Lawson AFB Hosp., Ga., 12th Air Force Surgeons' Office, Wiesbaden, Germany, Spangdahlem Air Base, Toul-Rostere Air Base, France, 1950-67; adjutant Spandahlem Air Base, 1951-54; exec. officer Mil. Air Transport Service, Scott AFB, Ill., 1961-62, chief adminstrv. services, 1965-66; asst. adminstr. Myrtle Beach (S.C.) AFB Hosp., 1966-67; sr. instr. med. adminstr. USAF Med. Service, USAF Med. Sch., Gunter AFB, Ala., 1954-60; ret., 1967; loan guarantee analyst VA Regional Office, Columbia, S.C., 1967; personnel statistician U.S. Army Hosp., Ft. Jackson Hosp., S.C., 1967-68; adminstr. Columbia (S.C.) Area Mental Health Center, 1968—; cons. in community mental health; instr. health care adminstrn., psychiat. residency Hall Psychiat. Inst., Columbia. Chmn. deacons Seventh Day Adventist Ch., Montgomery, Ala., 1957-58, supt. Sabbath Sch., Columbia, 1966-67, asst. supt. Sabbath Sch., Orangeburg, S.C., 1975-76, ednl. sec., 1975-76. Fellow Am. Acad. Med. Adminstrs.; mem. Adminstrv. Mgmt. Soc., Assn. Mental Health Adminstrs., Soc. Personnel Adminstrn., USAF Assn., S.C., Am. hosp. assns., Am. Cancer Soc., Heart and Lung Assn., Southeastern Statisticians, Smithsonian Inst. Assos. Clubs: Armed Forces, Am. Legion, DAV, VFW, Elks (hon.), Optimists (v.p. internat. 1971-72). Author: Medical Services Financial Management, 1959; Base Level Medical Checklist for Self Inspection, 1954, 3d rev. edit., 1956. Home: Route 2 Box 127A3 Saint Matthews SC 29135 Office: 1618 Sunset Dr Columbia SC 29203

FARINACCI, CHARLES JOSEPH, physician, former educator; b. Cleve., Jan. 12, 1906; s. Vincent and Clementina Maria (Doria) F.; B.A., Case Western Reserve U., 1927; M.D., U. Md., 1930; m. Eva Elizabeth Erlach, Sept. 11, 1947; children—Nicholas Armin, E. Doria, George Clement. Intern, Cleve. City Hosp., 1930-31, resident, 1931-32; resident Akron (O.) People's Hosp., 1932-33; commd. 1st lt. U.S. Army, 1935; advanced through grades to col., 1944; asst. prof. pathology Colo. U. Sch. Medicine, 1950-53; asso. prof. pathology Baylor U. Sch. Medicine, 1954-57; prof. pathology U. Tex. Health Sci. Center, 1972-77, ret., 1977; pathology cons. Anderson Cancer Hosp., Houston, 1954-57; pathologist Nix Hosp., San Antonio, 1961-72, USAF Wilford Hall Med. Center, San Antonio, 1962—. Decorated Bronze Star; Mil. Order Brit. Empire. Decorated knight Order of St. Agatha, Republic of San Marino, 1944. Mem. Coll. Am. Pathologists, Am. Soc. Clin. Pathologists, Internat. Acad. Pathology, A.M.A. Contbr. articles profl. jours. Home: 121 Five Oaks Dr San Antonio TX 78209 Office: 7703 Floyd Curl Dr San Antonio TX 78284

FARISH, STEPHEN THOMAS, JR., singer, condr.; b. Columbia, Va., May 5, 1936; s. Stephan Thomas and Jessie Virginia (Jones) F.; B.S., East Carolina U., 1958; Mus.M., U. Ill., 1959, D. Mus. Arts, 1962; m. Anna Withers Montgomery, May 31, 1958; children—Stephen David, Virginia Kaye. Dir. choirs First Meth. Ch., Urbana, Ill., 1960-62; minister of music St. Andrew Presbyn. Ch., Denton, Tex., 1964-72, Universal Christian Ch., Ft. Worth, 1972-76; mus. dir., producer Denton County Music Assn., Inc., 1967—; asst. prof. music North Tex. State U., 1962-67, asso. prof., 1967-72, prof., 1972—; lectr. in field. Pres. Greater Denton Arts Council, 1975-77. Mem. Nat. Assn. Tchrs. Singing (Texoma regional gov. 1978—), Nat. Choral Dirs. Assn., Assn. Choral Dirs., Phi Mu Alpha Sinfonia, Pi Kappa Lambda, Phi Kappa Phi, Kappa Delta Pi. Methodist. Home: 1900 Emerson St Denton TX 76201 Office: Sch of Music North Tex State U Denton TX 76203

FARLER, PATRICK NEWMAN, chewing gum co. exec.; b. Nashville, Oct. 13, 1951; s. Newman B. and Blanche Lynn F.; B.S. in B.A., Belmont Coll., 1974; m. Sara Jane Bishop, Jan. 24, 1975; children—Ashley Newman. Clk., Hyde Park Food Stores, Nashville, 1966-68, Kroger Co., Nashville, 1968-75; salesman Food Mktg. Services, Inc., Nashville, 1974-76; ter. mgr. Topps Chewing Gum, Inc., Nashville, 1976—. Mem. Nashville Bapt. Bowling Assn. (pres. 1978—, dir. 1978—), Antioch Jr. C. of C. (external v.p. 1975-76). Baptist. Home: 294 Ocala Dr Nashville TN 37211

FARLEY, CLARA MOONEAN, bookstore propr.; b. Guntersville, Ala., June 30, 1936; d. Geddis Grafton and Mary Mae (Martin) Mulligan; student U. North Ala., 1954-56; Asso. Sci., Pensacola Jr. Coll., 1978; B.S., SUNY, Albany, 1979; postgrad. U. West Fla., 1979—; m. Owen Eli Farley, Jr., Dec. 27, 1956; children—Owen E. III, Deborah Vernice, Rebecca Mae. Office sec. Gilbert Sch., Florence, Ala., 1954-56; tchr. Escambia Christian Sch., Pensacola, Fla., 1966-77; owner-mgr. Moonean's Antiques, Pensacola, 1967-68; owner, mgr. Farley's Old & Rare Books, Pensacola, 1975—. Gray lady ARC, Iwakuni, Japan, 1958-60. Cert. tchr., Fla.; notary public; lic. appraiser. Mem. So. Assn. Children Under Six, Fla. Assn. Children Under Six, Pensacola Assn. Children Under Six, Pensacola Friends of Public Library, Pensacola Historic Preservation Soc., Antiquarian Bookman. Democrat. Mem. Ch. of Christ. Home: 2031 Morningside Dr Pensacola FL 32503 Office: 310 N Perry St Pensacola FL 32503

FARLEY, DANIEL WAYNE, social worker; b. Princeton, W.Va., Feb. 9, 1944; s. Clyde L. and Ina Helen (Tabor) F.; B.S. in Bus. Adminstrn., Concord Coll., Athens, W.Va., 1967; M.S.W., W.Va. U., 1971; m. Bettye Sue Conner, Aug. 21, 1966; children—Kathy Jo, Julia Anne. Successively social worker, supr., adminstr. W.Va. Dept. Welfare, Princeton, 1967-73; dir. social service div. health and welfare ministries W.Va. conf. United Methodist Ch., 1973-78, exec. dir. health and welfare agys., 1978-79; exec. v.p., chief adminstrv. officer Glenwood Park United Meth. Home, 1979—; adj. instr. S.W. Va. Community Coll., Concord Coll., Coll. Grad. Studies, Charleston, W.Va.; lay speaker, diaconal minister United Meth. Ch. Mem. Acad. Cert. Social Workers, Am. Coll. Nursing Home Adminstrs., W. Va. U. Alumni Assn., Concord Coll. Alumni Assn., Nat. Assn. Social Workers (chpt. pres.), W.Va. Welfare Conf., Nat. Assn. Health and Welfare Ministries, W.Va. Wildlife Fedn., Nat. Rifle Assn. Democrat. Clubs: Elks, Civitan (pres. Princeton 1973-74, dist. gov. 1978-79, Honor Keys 1979). Author papers in field. Home: 507 Walnut St Princeton WV 27440 Office: Route 1 Box 464 Princeton WV 24740

FARLEY, GAIL CONLEY, librarian; b. Mead, Okla., July 9, 1936; s. William Conley and Marguerite Gaines (Austin) F.; B.S. in History, Sul Ross State U., Alpine, Tex., 1957; M.S. in L.S., East Tex. State U., Commerce, 1970. Served with U.S. Army, 1957-60; tchr. San Felipe Ind. Sch. Dist., Del Rio, Tex., 1963-64; tchr. Natalia (Tex.) Ind. Sch. Dist., 1964-65; librarian Medina Valley Ind. Sch. Dist., Castroville, Tex., 1965-77, La Pryor (Tex.) Ind. Sch. Dist., 1977-78, McCamey (Tex.) Ind. Sch. Dist., 1978—. Reporter Medina County Sheriff's Res., 1973-75, pres., 1975-77. Mem. Tex. Library Assn., Tex. Assn. Sch. Librarians, Tex. Profl. Educators, Nat. Rifle Assn., Tex. Rifle Assn. (life). Home: PO Box 965 McCamey TX 79752 Office: PO Drawer 1069 McCamey TX 79752

FARMER, BLAINE JACKSON, JR., agri-bus. exec.; b. Knoxville, Tenn., Feb. 4, 1928; s. Blaine Jackson and Retha (Fortner) F.; B.S., U. Tenn., 1949; postgrad. U. N.C., Chapel Hill, 1966; m. Anne Dean, June 5, 1948; children—Dean, Reid, Charles. Vice pres. Agrico Chem. Co. div. Continental Oil Co., Memphis, 1948-72; group v.p. marketing Agrico Chem. Co. div. Williams Cos., Tulsa, 1972; v.p., gen. mgr. Agri Products div. ConAgra, Inc., Knoxville, 1972—; dir. Dean-Planters Warehouses, Inc., Park Nat. Bank, Knoxville. Bd. dirs. Tennessee Valley Agrl. and Indsl. Fair; elder Presbyn. Ch. U.S.A. Served with USAF, 1951-53. Mem. Greater Knoxville C. of C. (dir.), Tenn. Feed Mfrs. Assn. (past pres., dir.), Sigma Chi. Clubs: Cherokee Country, Rotary. Home: Route 23 Topside Rd Half Mile West Knoxville TN 37920 Office: PO Box 671 Knoxville TN 37901

FARMER, CHERYL LEE, humanist, educator; b. Ft. Wayne, Ind., Oct. 15, 1948; d. Joseph J. and Mae Marie (Shriver) Gambee; B.A., Ariz. State U., 1971; M.A. with honors, Ball State U., 1975; Specialist in Ednl. Counseling, with honors, George Peabody Coll. for Tchrs., 1977; m. Vernon Dwayne Farmer, Dec. 19, 1970; stepchildren—Tony, Kim, Shari. Tchr. English, Motley High Sch., Columbus, Miss., 1971; substitute tchr. Las Vegas Sch. Systems, 1972; tchr. English, Quarrendon Secondary Sch., Aylesbury, Buckinghamshire, Eng., 1972-73; vol. community counselor RAF Upper Heyford (Eng.) Hosp., also pvt. vol. counselor RAF, Bicester, Eng., 1974-77; tchr. English, Bray (Okla.) High Sch., 1977—; vol. community, pvt. counselor. Mem. Okla. Edn. Assn., NEA, Am. Personnel and Guidance Assn., Am. Sch. Counselors Assn., Nat. Honor Soc. Club: Officers (Ft. Sill, Okla.). Home: 560 Redwood Dr Duncan OK 73533 Office: Box 711 Bray High Sch Bray OK

FARMER, J(ESSIE) JOSEPHINE ANDREWS, educator; b. Beckly, W.Va., Nov. 18, 1909; d. John Milton and Sarah Adella (Ewart) Andrews; B.S., W.Va., U., 1933; M.Ed., U. Va., 1953; postgrad. U. Fla., 1965; m. Walter Ashby Farmer, Oct. 6, 1977. Tchr. math. Crichton (W.Va.) High Sch., 1935-42; tchr., head math. dept., St. Lucie County High Sch., Fort Pierce, Fla., 1942-52; tchr., head math. dept. Dan McCarty High Sch., Fort Pierce, 1952-70. Mem. accredition com. So. Assn. Secondary Schs., 1951-58. Recipient St. Lucie County star teacher award, 1968; winner ribbons oil paintings W.Va. State Fair, 1974, 75, 76. Mem. St. Lucie County Classroom Tchrs. Assn. (pres. 1948-50), AAUW (2d v.p. 1966), Ft. Pierce PTA (treas. 1945-51), Nat. Council Tchrs. Math., NEA, Nat. Ret. Tchr. Assn., Smithsonian Assos., Nat. Trust Hist. Preservation, DAR, English Speaking Union, St. Andrews Soc. Fla., Am. Antiques and Craft Soc., Delta Kappa Gamma (pres. 1962-64). Author: (tchrs. manual) Mathematics Essentials, 1953; Up-dating Mathematics, 1956. Home: 4109 El Prado Blvd Tampa FL 33609

FARMER, JAMES D., accountant; b. Cin., June 3, 1947; s. Rutherford D. and Thelma (Cook) F.; B.B.A., Eastern Ky. U., 1969; M.S. in Accounting (Ernst & Ernst fellow), Ohio State U., 1970; m. Diane Albert, Sept. 10, 1965; children—Stephanie Dyan, Rebecca Danae. Instr. Wright State U., 1970-71; accountant Price Waterhouse & Co., C.P.A.'s, Tampa, Fla., 1971-77. Recipient Yeager, Ford & Warren award for outstanding accounting student Eastern Ky. U., 1968. C.P.A., Fla. Mem. Am. Accounting Assn., Am. Inst. C.P.A.'s, Fla. Soc. C.P.A.'s, Tampa C. of C., Omicron Alpha Kappa. Republican. Mem. Reformed Ch. (deacon 1973-75, 77-79). Home: 3609 Hudson Ln Tampa FL 33618 Office: 2800 First Fla Tower Tampa FL 33602

FARMER, JOSEPH CLARENCE, JR., surgeon, educator; b. Fayetteville, N.C., Oct. 14, 1937; s. Joseph Clarence and Bettie (Eatman) F.; M.D., Duke, 1962; m. Margery Jean Newton, Aug. 19, 1957; children—Joseph Clarence III (dec.), Thomas Hackney Richardson. Intern Duke Med. Center, 1962-63, intern, resident in surgery, 1964-65, fellow in thoracic surgery, 1965, resident otolaryngology, 1967-70; mem. faculty Duke U., 1970—, asso. prof. otolaryngology, 1975—, mem. CORE faculty F.G. Hall Lab. Environ. Biomed. Research, 1970—; attending physician Durham VA Hosp., 1979—; clin. asso. Nat. Cancer Inst., 1965-67; cons. Durham County Gen., Mcpherson hosps., Durham. Bd. dirs. Center for Hearing Impaired Children, Durham; formerly v.p. bd. trustees Durham Acad. Served with USPHS, 1965-67. C.V. Mosely scholar, 1962. Diplomate Am. Bd. Otolaryngology. Fellow Am. Acad. Ophthalmology and Otolaryngology, A.C.S., Laryngological, Rhinological, Otological Soc.; mem. Undersea Med. Soc., Assn. U. Otolaryngologists, Sigma Xi, Alpha Omega Alpha. Episcopalian (past vestry). Club: Triangle Traders (pres.). Contbr. articles to profl. jours., chpts. to books. Home: 3020 Harriman Ave Durham NC 27705

FARMER, MARY JO SAMS, electronics co. mgr.; b. Birmingham, Ala., Jan. 21, 1932; s. Sidney Ernest and Iva Lee (Payne) Sams; cert. human relations Clayton Jr. Coll., Morrow, Ga., 1975; grad. Motorola Mgmt. Inst.; m. Walter E. Farmer, Sept. 18, 1950. Various secretarial positions, 1953-68; mgr. Kare Products Co., Atlanta, 1968-71; order process mgr. Motorola Communications and Electronics, Inc., Decatur, Ga., 1971—. Methodist. Home: 2152 Hwy 138 Jonesboro GA 30236 Office: PO Box 1920 Decatur GA 30031

FARMER, ROBERT EDWARD, JR., research forester; b. Rehoboth Beach, Del., Dec. 3, 1930; s. Robert Edward and Katherine Hyde (Watson) F.; B.S., U. Mich., 1953, M.F., 1958, Ph.D., 1961; m. Rima J. Nickell, May 14, 1960; children—Brian, Alan. Plant geneticist, U.S. Forest Service, So. Hardwoods Lab., Stoneville, Miss., 1961-67; plant physiologist TVA, Norris, Tenn., 1967—; adj. prof. ecology U. Tenn., Knoxville, 1977—. Vice-pres. Tenn. Citizens for Wilderness Planning, 1976. Served to 1st lt., 1953-55. Rackham grad. fellow, 1961. Fellow AAAS; mem. Tenn. Native Plant Soc. (pres. 1978), Soc. Am. Foresters, Ecol. Soc. Am. Unitarian. Contbr. articles to sci. publs. Home: 99 Reservoir Rd Norris TN 37828 Office: TVA Forestry Norris TN 37828

FARMER, ROBERT MICHAEL, data processing co. exec.; b. Los Angeles, Jan. 20, 1943; s. Robert Preston and Helen Margaret (Shultz) F.; B.S. in Fin., UCLA, 1965; postgrad. Calif. State U., Northridge, 1965-66; m. Georgene Lamoine Thoe, Aug. 28, 1965; children—Robert Lincoln, Jennifer Lee. Fin. analyst Union Oil Co. of Calif., Los Angeles, 1966-72; treas. Electronic Data Systems Corp., Dallas, 1972—; past pres. EDS Employees Fed. Credit Union. Served to 1st lt. U.S. Army, 1967-69. Decorated Army Commendation medal. Office: Electronic Data Systems Corp 7171 Forest Ln Dallas TX 75230

FARMER, THOMAS SHELBY, chem. co. exec.; b. New Orleans, Sept. 2, 1931; s. John Walter and Elizabeth Shelby (Buck) F.; B.S. in Chem. Engring., Tulane U., 1952; M.S.E. in Chem. Engring., Princeton U., 1953; m. Ann Wood, Sept. 27, 1955; children—Jeanne, John, Thomas. Various tech. managerial positions Standard Oil of N.J. affiliates, 1953-57; mgr. planning Esso Chem., Inc., N.Y.C., 1967-68; v.p. EssoChem Europe, Brussels, 1968-71; pres. Borg-Warner Chems., Chgo., 1971-77; pres. Internat. group Hooker Chem. Co., Houston, 1978—; dir. Winnebago Industries; pres. Chem. Industries Council Midwest, 1976-78. Mem. pres.'s council Tulane U. Served to cpl. U.S. Army, 1953-55. Recipient Harold Levy Alumni award Tulane U., 1962; registered profl. engr., Tex. Mem. Am. Chem. Soc., Am. Inst. Chem. Engrs., AAAA, Sigma Alpha Epsilon, Alpha Chi Sigma. Republican. Presbyterian. Clubs: Chicago Yacht, Houstonian, Carleton. Office: 1980 S Post Oak Rd Houston TX 77056

FARNELL, MICHAEL JOSEPH, ednl. adminstr.; b. Birmingham, Ala., June 2, 1942; s. Joseph and Normalea (Jernigan) F.; B.A., U. Tex., Arlington, 1965; M.Div., Gen. Theol. Sem., 1970; M.Ed., N. Tex. State U., 1973; m. Poupette Bekhor, June 2, 1969. Peace Corps vol., Iran. 1965-67; youth dir. YMCA, Dallas, 1970-71; research asst. counseling and testing center N. Tex. State U., Denton, 1971-72; human devel. instr. Richland Jr. Coll., Dallas, 1972-73; counselor Houston Community Coll. System, 1973-74, coordinator of testing, 1974—; cons. in field to various corps. and agencies. Mem. Am. Personnel and Guidance Assn., Am. Rehab. Counseling Assn., Assn. Measurement and Evaluation in Guidance, Assn. Specialists in Group Work, Tex. Jr. Coll. Tchrs. Assn., Jr. Coll. Student Personnel Assn. Tex., SE Tex. Area Coll. Health Assn. (charter), Gerontol. Soc. Democrat. Episcopalian. Author various publs. in field. Home: 7334 Mar Vista Dr Houston TX 77083 Office: 320 Jackson Hill Houston TX 77007

FARR, RUSSELL HAYNES, investment cons.; b. Blytheville, Ark., Feb. 20, 1923; s. Russell Carter and Mabel Anna (Haynes) F.; B.S. in Bus. Adminstrn., U. E.Fla., 1950; B.A., Shaw U., 1975, Edison Coll., 1976; Ph.D. in Humanities (hon.), Calif. Western U., 1975; m. Mary Sue Piercy, July 22, 1944; 1 son, Gary Russell. Partner, then owner R.C. Farr & Sons Oil Co., Blytheville, 1946-78; partner, then owner Delta Propane Co., Blytheville, 1955-78; ind. investment cons., Blytheville, 1978—; dir. Blytheville Fed. Savs. & Loan Assn. Past pres. Chickasawba chpt. ARC, Blytheville Bowling Assn.; pres. Blytheville United Way, 1980-81. Served with AUS, 1942-46, 51-52. Decorated Bronze Star, Purple Heart. Mem. Ind. Cons. Am. (gov. 1979—), Blytheville C. of C. (past pres.), Am. Soc. Quality Control, Nat. Assn. Accountants, Nat. Mgmt. Assn., U. Ark. Alumni Assn., 11th Armored Div. Assn., Air Force Assn., VFW (life), Am. Legion, Sigma Alpha Epsilon. Baptist. Clubs: Nat. Sojourners (past pres. Blytheville), Blytheville Country (past pres.), Masons. Home: 1805 Eastgate St Blytheville AR 72315 Office: 398 S 3d St Blytheville AR 72315

FARR, WILLIAM HOWARD, ops. research analyst, statistician; b. Youngstown, Ohio, Feb. 3, 1946; s. Howard Samuel and Jean Louise (Foltz) F.; B.A., Wittenberg U., 1968; M.S. (NSF trainee), Fla. State U., 1970, Ph.D. (NSF trainee 1970-71, Univ. fellow 1971-72), 1973; m. Patricia A. Hudak, Aug. 28, 1971. Asst. prof. math. scis. Johns Hopkins U., 1973-76; ops. research analyst, combat integration div. Naval Surface Weapons Center, Dahlgren, Va., 1976-77, ops. research analyst quality assurance br. FBM Geoballistics div., 1977—. Unit commr. Balt. Area council Boy Scouts Am., 1974-76, Nat. Capital Area council, 1976-77, asst. dist. commr. Fredericksburg, Nat. Capital Area council, 1978—; mem. ch. council, trustee Redeemer Lutheran Ch., Fredericksburg, Va., 1978—. Served with USAF, 1973. Recipient Woodbadge award Nat. Capital Area council Boy Scouts Am., 1978. Mem. Am. Statis. Soc., Sigma Xi, Phi Kappa Phi. Clubs: Rappahannock Twirlers Sq. Dance, Potomac Promenaders Sq. Dance. Contbr. articles to profl. jours. Home: Route 11 Box 1634 Fredericksburg VA 22401 Office: K-56 Naval Surface Weapons Center Dahlgren VA 22448

FARRALD, ROBERT RALPH, pub.; b. Purdon, Tex., Mar. 6, 1940; s. Hubert James and Dixie (Rogers) F.; B.A., Creighton U., 1963; M.S., U. Nebr., 1966; postgrad. Creighton U., 1963-65, U. Guam, 1966-68, U. S.C., 1969—; m. Carol Joan Fisch, June 5, 1965; children—Michele, David, Christopher, Jamie. Tchr. remedial reading Marion High Sch., Omaha, 1962-63; tchr. Madonna Sch. for Exceptional Children, Omaha, 1963-65; clinician in child study clinic U. Nebr., Omaha, 1965-66; testing-guidance cons. Sch. psychologist and reading cons. Guam Dept. Edn., Agana, 1966-68; contract counselor VA, Guam, 1966-68; counseling psychologist Guam Dept. Vocat. Rehab. and Rehab. Sheltered Workshop, 1966-68; cons. Head Start and presch. programs Guam and for Trust Ter. of U.S., 1966-68; asst. prof. U. Guam, 1966-68; grad. fellow U. S.C., Columbia, 1968-69; dir. psychol. services center and spl. edn. div. Region One Ednl. Service Center, Edinburg, Tex., 1969-71; instr. U. Tex., Austin, 1969-71, Pan Am. U., 1969-71; vis. prof. State Coll. Ark., 1969-71; vis. prof. Continuing Edn. Center, Sioux Falls, S.D., 1971-73; developer, cons. Title III project, Sioux Falls, 1970-71; dir. Title III Project, 1971-73; cons. to various schs. in field; pvt. cons., Elsa, Tex., 1973-78; pres., chief editor Adapt Press, Sioux Falls, 1973—; mem. adv. com. Title VI Projects, Guam, 1967-68; mem. adv. bd. for Vocat. Rehab., Rio Grande Valley, 1969-70, Cameron County-Head Start programs, 1969-70. Recipient Pacesetters award U.S. Office Edn., 1973; U. Nebr. fellow, 1965-66, U. S.C. fellow, 1968-69. Mem. Internat. Assn. for Children With Learning Disabilities, Council for Exceptional Children, Internat. Reading Assn., Assn. Children with Learning Disabilities, Tex. Assn. Children with Learning Disabilities, Tex. Council for Exceptional Children, Tex. Internat. Reading Assn. Roman Catholic. Home: PO Box 1478 Elsa TX 78543 Office: 1209 W Bailey St Sioux Falls SD 57104

FARRAR, BEVERLY JAYNE CLARK, ednl. psychologist; b. Albuquerque, Nov. 6, 1928; d. Jack Murphy and Jane (Thomas) Clark; B.A., So. Meth. U., 1949, M.A., 1967; M.Ed., E.Tex. State U., 1971, postgrad., 1971-75; m. R.L. Farrar, July 1, 1949; 1 dau., Dorothy Jane. Tchr. high sch. English, social studies, Allen, Tex., 1949; part-time instr. speech and English Sam Houston State U., Huntsville, Tex., 1949-51; tchr. English and speech jr. high sch. Houston Ind. Sch. Dist., 1951-52, high sch., 1953-55; tchr. spl. edn. Dallas Ind. Sch. Dist., 1952-53, tchr., counselor elem. schs., 1969-71; tchr. secondary English and speech Harlingen (Tex.) Ind. Sch. Dist., 1957-63; speech therapist Longview (Tex.) Ind. Sch. Dist., 1963-69; asso. psychologist elem. schs. Richardson (Tex.) Ind. Sch. Dist., 1971—; participant in-service workshops for tchrs. Leader, Camp Fire Girls, Longview, 1964-68; active Lake Highlands Youth Commn., 1974-79; mem. Lake Highlands United Meth. Commn. on Missions, 1978, adminstrv. bd., 1979. Cert. classroom tchr., speech/lang. therapist, ednl. counselor, ednl. diagnostician, psychol. asso. Mem. NEA, Tex. Edn. Assn., Richardson Edn. Assn., Tex. State Tchrs. Assn., Am. Speech, Hearing, Lang. Assn. (cert. in speech pathology), Tex. Speech, Hearing, Lang. Assn., Dallas Psychol. Assn., Tex. Psychol. Assn., AAUW (rec. sec., Harlingen 1962, v.p., Longview 1968-69, study group chmn. Dallas 1978-79), Delta Kappa Gamma (chpt. achievement award 1973, chpt. pres. 1974-76, chmn. Dallas County council 1977-79). Democrat. Methodist. Club: Altrusa Internat. (program coordinator, Richardson). Home: 10220 Mapleridge Dallas TX 75238 Office: REEU Spring Valley Annex 13530 Spring Grove Dallas TX 75240

FARRELL, CHARLES PATRICK, data processor; b. Bronx, N.Y., Sept. 16, 1946; s. Edward Raymond and Frances Florence (Maier) F.; B.A. in Econs. magna cum laude, Fordham U., 1976. Systems analyst Fed. Res. Bank N.Y., 1969-75; project leader fin. and credit systems W.T. Grant Co., 1975-76; systems analyst Blue Cross of N.Y., 1976-77; programmer, analyst 1st Nat. Bank in Ft. Myers (Fla.), 1977-78; sr. programmer Va. Nat. Bank, Norfolk, 1978—. Served with AUS, 1967-69. Roman Catholic. Home: 231 Spanish Trace Dr Altamonte Springs FL 32701 Office: Research and Devel Div 711 E Altamonte Dr Altamonte Springs FL 32701

FARRELL, EDMUND JAMES, assn. exec., educator, author; b. Butte, Mont., May 17, 1927; s. Bartholomew J. and Lavinia H. (Collins) F.; A.B., Stanford J., 1950; M.A., 1951; Ph.D., U. Calif. at Berkeley, 1969; m. Jo Ann Hayes, Dec. 19, 1964; children—David, Kevin, Sean. Chmn. English dept. James Lick High Sch., San Jose, Calif., 1954-59; supr. secondary English, U. Calif. at Berkeley, 1959-70; field rep. Nat. Council Tchrs. English, 1970-71, asst. exec. sec., 1971-73, asso. exec. dir., 1973-78; adj. prof. English U. Ill., Urbana, 1973-78; prof. English edn. U. Tex., Austin, 1978—; speaker at local, state and nat. confs. of English tchrs., 1954—; cons. to NDEA Insts., 1965-68; reader compositions for advanced placement program, Rider Coll. Princeton, N.J., 1969, 72-77; participant revision of lit. objectives Nat. Assessment of Ednl. Progress, Denver, 1972-73, 78; chmn. English discipline com. Coll. Entrance Exam. Bd., 1974-79. Served with USNR, 1945-46. Mem. Nat. Council Tchrs. of English, Tex. Joint Council Tchrs. English, Calif. Assn. Tchrs. of English (pres. 1962-63), Phi Delta Kappa. Unitarian. Author: Exploring Life Through Literature, 1964, Counterpoint in Literature, 1967, Projection in Literature, 1967, Outlooks in Literature, 1973; Fantasy: Forms of Things Unknown, 1974; Science Fact/Fiction, 1974; Comment, 1975; Myth, Mind, and Moment, 1976; I/You, We/They, 1976; Traits and Topics, 1976; Up Stage/Down Stage, 1976; To Be, 1976; Conflict in Reality, 1976; Arrangement in Literature, 1979; Purpose in Literature, 1979. Home: 6500 Sumac St Austin TX 78731 Office: Dept Curriculum and Instruction U Texas Austin TX 78712

FARRENS, GERALD ELMER, utility forestry contractors exec.; b. Stanton, Nebr., Feb. 7, 1923; s. Elmer and Alma Opal (Cantrell) F.; B.A. in Econs., Rollins Coll., Winter Park, Fla., 1948; m. Irma Jean Cartwright, May 27, 1949; children—Gloria Jean, Richard Bruce, Katherine Elaine. With Farrens Tree Surgeons, Inc., 1941—, v.p., gen. mgr., 1967—. Trustee I.S.A. Research Trust, Am. Nat. Standards Inst. Served with U.S. Army A.C., 1943-45. Mem. Nat. (pres. 1977-78), Utility arborist assns., Internat. Soc. Arboriculture, Am. Forestry Assn., Fla. Inst. Park Personnel, Am. Soc. Consulting Arborists, Arlington Area C. of C., Nat. Rifle Assn., Aircraft Owners and Pilots Assn., Sigma Nu (life). Presbyterian. Clubs: Gateway Rifle and Pistol of Jacksonville, Fla. Aero. Inc., Univ. Club. Jacksonville. Home: 2025 River Rd Jacksonville FL 32207

FARRI, ELIAS PETER, physician; b. Providence, Jan. 26, 1930; s. Antonio and Julia (Monacelli) F.; B.Sc. in Pharmacy, Temple U., 1957; D.O., Phila. Coll. Osteopathic Medicine, 1961; m. Margaret Gutenberger, June 19, 1965; children—Michael, Melinda. Pvt. practice gen. medicine, Phila., 1962-71, Ft. Myers, Fla., 1971—; mem. staff Ft. Myers Community Hosp. Served with USNR, 1948-50; with U.S. Army, 1951-53. Mem. Fla. Osteopathic Med. Assn., Pa. Osteo. Med. Assn., Rho Chi. Home: 3571 Heritage Ln Heritage Farms Fort Myers FL 33908 Office: 1178 Cypress Lake Dr Fort Myers FL 33907

FARRIER, SYDNEY STRANGE, social worker; b. Dallas, Sept. 11, 1946; d. Robert Lee and Marion Inez (Barrett) Strange; B.S. in Sociology, Trinity U., 1968; postgrad. U. Tex., Austin, 1969; M.S.S.W., U. Tex., Arlington, 1970; postgrad. N. Tex. State U., Denton; m. Robert Clem Farrier, Aug. 6, 1971; children—Sara Sydney, Joseph Robert. Triage social worker Presbyterian Psychiat. Out-Patient Clinic, 1970-72; instr. psychiatry U. Tex. Med. Sch., Dallas, 1972-75; dir. social work Richardson (Tex.) Med. Center, 1977—. Mem. Nat. Assn. Social Workers, Assn. Cert. Social Workers, Tex. Hosp. Assn., Dirs. Hosp. Social Work. Home: 6900 Wildgrove St Dallas TX 75214 Office: 401 W Campbell St Richardson TX 75080

FARRINGER, JOHN LEE, JR., surgeon; b. Bowling Green, Ky., Sept. 4, 1920; s. John Lee and Zora (Lawson) F.; B.A., Vanderbilt U., 1942; M.D., U. Tenn., 1945, M.S., 1950; m. Mary Margaret Smith, Mar. 8, 1947; children—John Lee, III, Janice Ann, Mary Jill. Intern, Harris Meml. Meth. Hosp., Ft. Worth, 1946; resident John Gaston and U. Tenn. Hosp., Memphis, 1949-54; practice surgery, Nashville, 1954—; asst. clin. prof. surgery Vanderbilt U. Sch. Medicine, 1956—; chief surgery Baptist Hosp., Nashville, 1966-69, pres. staff, 1971, vice chief staff, 1973-75, chief of staff, 1976-78. Coordinator, Battle Nashville Centennial Commemoration, 1964—; chmn. Met. Hist. Commn., Nashville, 1966-73; exec. bd. Middle Tenn. council Boy Scouts Am., 1961—; pres. Davidson County Found. for Med. Care, 1973-75; mem. Statewide Health Coordinating Council, 1977—. Bd. dirs. Davidson County unit Am. Cancer Soc., Davidson County Council Retarded Children, Police Assistance League, Profl. Systems Nashville, Tenn., Middle Tenn. Health Systems Agy.; trustee Parkview Hosp., 1970-73. Served with AUS, 1943-45. Diplomate Am. Bd. Surgery. Fellow A.C.S., Southeastern Surg. Congress, So. Surg. Assn., Am. Geriatric Soc.; mem. Nashville Acad. Medicine (dir. 1970-73), Davidson County Med. Soc. (dir. 1970-73), So. Med. Assn., Nashville Surg. Soc. (pres. 1973), Harwell Wilson Surg. Soc. (pres. 1977-78), Co. Mil. Historians, Nashville Area C. of C., Alpha Kappa Kappa. Clubs: Richland Country, Nashville City, University (Nashville). Contbr. articles to surg. jours. Home: 2325 Golf Club Lane Nashville TN 37215 Office: 1919 Hayes St Nashville TN 37203

FARRIOR, JOSEPH BROWN, physician; b. Tuscaloosa, Ala., Dec. 22, 1911; s. J. Brown and Evelyn (Searcy) F.; B.S., U. Fla., 1932; M.D., Tulane U., 1936; M.S., U. Mich., 1942; m. Beverly Hall, Nov. 16, 1945; children—Jay, Annie. Resident in otolaryngology Roosevelt Hosp., N.Y.C., 1937-38, Univ. Hosp., Ann Arbor, Mich., 1938-42; instr. U. Mich., 1939-42; instr., asst. prof. Tulane U., 1945-48; otologist Oschner Clinic, 1945-48; practice medicine specializing in ear surgery, Tampa, Fla., 1948—; chief otolaryngology, clin. prof. U. of S. Fla. Coll. of Medicine, 1972-76, prof. emeritus, 1977—; chief otolaryngology Tampa Gen. Hosp., 1948-68; chief otolaryngology St. Joseph's Hosp., 1969-76. Served to lt. col. M.C., U.S. Army, 1942-46. Decorated 4 Bronze Stars; recipient Billings Gold medal AMA, 1959, 69; Gold medal in otolaryngology Am. Acad. Ophthalmology and Otolaryngology, 1973, Wherry Meml. lectr., 1976; recipient 18 sci. exhibit awards; diplomate Am. Bd. Otolaryngology. Fellow Am. Acad. Ophthalmology and Otolaryngology, ACS; mem. Am. Otol. Soc., Otosclerosis Study Group, The Triological Soc., AMA (Physicians Recognition award). Presbyterian. Clubs: Rotary, Tampa Yacht and Country, Palma Ceia Golf and Country. Author 4 atlases Tympanoplasty in 3-D, 1968-73; contbr. articles on otolaryngology to med. jours. Home: 1909 Oakmont Ave Tampa FL 33609 Office: 509 Bay St Tampa FL 33606

FARRIS, ANDREW HENRY, sales tng. cons.; b. Rochester, Minn., Nov. 19, 1943; s. Henry George and Margaret Mary (Gasparbridge) F.; B.A. in Journalism, So. Ill. U., 1971. Sales rep. Atlanta Jour. and Constn., 1971; account exec. Atlanta Mag., 1972-73; sales rep. Media Networks, Inc., Atlanta, 1973-75, Mid-Atlantic regional sales mgr., 1975-76, Southeastern regional sales mgr., 1976-77, sales devel. mgr., 1977-79; pres. Andrew H. Farris, Inc., Atlanta, 1979—; tchr. DeKalb Community Coll. Served to 1st lt., AUS, 1966-69. Decorated Purple Heart, Air Medal, Bronze Star, Silver Star. Named No. 1 salesman Media Networks, Inc., 1974; recipient cert. of appreciation DeKalb Community Coll., 1978. Mem. Mag. Advt. Reps. of South (pres. 1976-77), Nat. Assn. Sales Tng. Execs. Roman Catholic. Home and Office: 422 Jefferson Circle Atlanta GA 30328

FARRIS, CHARLES EDWARD, educator; b. Sallisaw, Okla., Nov. 3, 1922; s. John Oliver and Mary Flavia (Griffith) F.; A.B., Northeastern State U., Tahlequah, Okla., 1947; M.S.W., St. Louis U., 1951; m. Lorene Sanders, Mar. 7, 1947. Supt. Bellefontaine Farms, St. Louis, 1951-53; exec. dir. Girls Home, St. Louis, 1953-59; social worker Family Service, Miami, 1959-60; social worker, supr. Fla. Dept. Pub. Welfare, Miami, 1960-61, Dept. Health, Edn., Welfare, Atlanta, 1961-64; exec. dir. Family & Children's Service, Shreveport, La., 1964-67; asso. prof. social work Barry Coll., Miami, 1967—. Del., Council on Social Work Edn., N.Y.C., 1973-77. Served with Air Corps, U.S. Army, 1943-46. Democrat. Presbyterian. Editorial bd. Abstracts for Social Workers, 1974-75. Contbr. articles on Am. Indian to profl. jours. Home: 900 NE 89th St Miami FL 33138 Office: 11300 NE 2nd Ave Miami FL 33161

FARRIS, DAVID EARL, mfg. co. exec.; b. Forest, Miss., June 23, 1953; s. Alton B. and Irene (King) F.; B.S., Miss. State U., 1975, masters degree, 1976; m. Susan Anne Foster, June 11, 1977. Prodn. mgr. Morton Mfg. Co., Inc. (Miss.), 1976-78, v.p., 1978—. Mem. ofcl. bd., mem. pastor-parish com. Morton United Methodist Ch. Mem. Nat. Wooden Pallet and Container Assn., Miss. Mfrs. Assn., Morton C. of C. (dir.), Miss. State U. Alumni Assn. (pres. 1978-79). Club: Lions (Morton). Home and Office: Drawer K Morton MS 39117

FARRIS, FRANK MITCHELL, JR., lawyer; b. Nashville, Sept. 29, 1915; s. Frank Mitchell and Mary Frances (Lellyett) F.; B.A., Vanderbilt U., 1937; student N.Y. Law Sch., 1939; m. Genevieve Baird, June 7, 1941; 1 dau., Genevieve Baird. Admitted to Tenn. bar, U.S. Supreme Ct. bar; mem. firm Clayton & Farris, 1939-40, 40-41; conciliation commr., def. counsel 12th Naval Dist., Treasure Island, Cal., 1944; partner firm Farris, Evans & Evans, Nashville, 1946-71, Farris, Warfield & Kanaday, and predecessors, 1975—. Dir., gen. counsel Cherokee Ins. Co., Nashville, 1947—; dir., counsel 3d Nat. Bank, Nashville; dir. Cherokee Equity Corp. Chmn. commrs. Watkins Inst., Nashville, 1953-76. Trustee, gen. counsel, exec. com. George Peabody Coll., 1969-79; mem. bd. trust Vanderbilt U. Served to lt. USNR, World War II. Mem. Am. Bar Assn., Bar Assn. Tenn., Beta Theta Pi, Phi Delta Phi. Presbyn. Clubs: University, Belle Meade Country, City (Nashville). Home: 940 Overton Lea Rd Nashville TN 37220 Office: 3d Nat Bank Bldg Nashville TN 37219

FARRIS, GENEVIEVE BAIRD (MRS. FRANK MITCHELL FARRIS, JR.), civic worker; b. New Orleans; d. Thomas Barton and Cecilia K. (Kearny) Baird; grad. Arlington Hall Jr. Coll., 1936; B.A., Agnes Scott Coll., 1938; m. Frank Mitchell Farris, Jr., June 7, 1941; 1 dau., Genevieve Baird. Press and publs. U.S. Postal Censorship, New Orleans, 1942-44. Area chmn. Heart Fund, Nashville, 1965, United Givers Fund, 1968, 72, 73. Bd. dirs. Nashville Childrens Theatre, 1948—, exec. bd., pres., 1969-72; bd. dirs. Nashville Travelers Aid Soc., 1956—, pres., 1963-64; bd. dirs. Nat. Travelers Aid Soc., 1964-72; dir. Davidson County Hort. Soc., 1968-72, v.p., 1965-67, 71-73, 73-74, pres., 1975—; sec. bd. Day Care Home Retarded Children, 1970-72, pres., 1973-74; chmn. women's div. fund raising campaign Peabody Coll., 1977-78. Mem. Davidson County Lawyers Aux. (pres. 1961), Jr. League. Presbyn. Clubs: Bellemeade Country, Centennial, Md. Farm Racquet. Home: 940 Overton Lea Rd Nashville TN 37220

FARRIS, JEFFERSON DAVIS, univ. adminstr.; b. Springdale, Ark., Sept. 30, 1927; s. Jeff D. and Loretta J. (Grunder) F.; B.S. in Engring., U. Central Ark., 1949; M.A., Peabody Coll., 1950; M.P.H. (USPHS fellow), U. Mich., 1957; Ed.D., U. Ark., 1963; m. Patricia Ann Camp, July 31, 1948; children—Rebecca, Elizabeth, Jefferson Davis, III. Tchr. pub. high sch., Pine Bluff, Ark., 1950-57; dir. pub. health edn. Ark. State Dept. Health, Little Rock, 1957-61; prof. health edn. U. Central Ark., 1961—, chmn. dept. health and phys. edn., 1961-68, dean, 1968-75, univ. pres., 1975—; civilian aide to Sec. of Army, 1979—; mem. adv. com. Nat. Endowment Humanities; mem. Ark. Gov's. Council on Youth Fitness. Bd. dirs. Conway (Ark.) Meml. Hosp., 1971—. Served with USN, 1946-48. Named Layman of Yr., Ark. Assn. Dentistry for Children, 1970. Mem. Ark. Assn. Acad. Deans (pres. 1968-75). Methodist. Club: Rotary (pres. local club). Editor: A Guide for School Health Education, 1956; Handbook for Elementary Physical Education, 1964. Home: 140 Donaghey St Conway AR 72032 Office: Office of Pres U Central Ark Conway AR 72032

FARRIS, MARY ANN, health care services adminstr.; b. Clarksville, Ark., May 2, 1936; d. Rheual Wesley and Lillian Estes (Eichenberger) Mickel; B.S., Coll. of Ozarks, 1959; diploma in nursing Ark. Bapt. Hosp. Sch. of Nursing, 1968; student DePaul U., Chgo., 1954-55, Tex. State Coll. for Women, 1955-56; m. Robert Edmond Farris, Jr., Dec. 29, 1957; children—Robert Wesley, Martha Susan. Charge nurse Clarksville (Ark.) Hosp., 1968-70; dir. nursing Mickel Nursing Home, Clarksville, 1970-76, asst. adminstr., 1972—; adminstr. Mickel's Infant Infirmary, Clarksville, 1973—. Den leader West Ark. Area council Cub Scouts Am., 1968-70, den leader coach, 1970-72. Recipient Human Services award, 1977; Fulbright scholar to Denmark, 1958; qualified mental retardation practitioner. Mem. Ark. League for Nursing, Nat. League for Nursing, Ark. Nursing Home Assn. (Service award 1976), Am. Assn. on Mental Deficiency, D.A.R., UDC. Methodist. Club: Order Eastern Star. Home: PO Box 549 Clarksville AR 72830 Office: PO Box 250 Clarksville AR 72830

FARRIS, ROBERT EARL, oil co. exec., retail trade co. exec.; b. Etowah, Tenn., Mar. 7, 1928; s. Garvin B. and Edna E. (Phillips) F.; student pub. schs., Nashville; m. Dorothy Ann Wright Oct. 2, 1948; children—Julia Ann, Robert E. Sales rep. for Indsl. Tractor and Equipment Co., Nashville, 1947-49; territorial rep. of sch. supplies and equipment Nashville Products Co., 1950-52; asst. sales promotion mgr. The Toni Co., Nashville and Chgo., 1958-60, field rep., 1952-55, products test area supr., 1956-58; pres. Swimco, Inc., Nashville, 1960—; partner Durango Oil Co., Nashville, 1967—; propr. Mgmt. Services Co., Nashville, 1961—; pub. Swimmers mag. mem. Better Bus. Bur., Nashville, 1969—; dir. Nashville Electric Service, 1976—. Troop scout master Cumberland council Boy Scouts Am., 1950-52; mem. water safety com. ARC, 1968-70, chmn., 1969-70, mem. exec. com., 1974—, chpt. chmn.; mem. Davidson County Republican Steering Com., 1964-66; liason officer for Tenn. del. to Republican Nat. Conv., 1968; Republican nominee for Tenn. State Ho. of Reps., 1972; supt. of Sunday schs., United Meth. Ch., Nashville, 1956-58; Sunday sch. tchr. Forest Hills United Meth. Ch., 1968-78, trustee, 1968—, chmn. Council of Ministries, 1970-72, bldg. com. chmn., 1969-75; pres. Jamaican-Am. Meth. Men's Fellowship, 1968-70; bd. dirs. Kidney Found. of Tenn., 1971-73; trustee Riverside Hosp. Served with USMC, 1946-51. Recipient Certificate of Merit, Assn. of Nat. Advertisers, 1959. Mem. Sales and Mktg. Execs., Nashville C. of C. Club: Kiwanis (pres. 1975-76, pres.'s award 1976). Home: 5039 Hillsboro Rd PO Box 15906 Nashville TN 37215 Office: 1400 8th Ave Nashville TN

FARRIS, SAMUEL HARDY, JR., bank exec.; b. Memphis, Jan. 18, 1933; s. Samuel Hardy and Floy Volentine (Barrow) F.; student U. Miss., 1950-52; B.S., Miss. State U., 1957, M.B.A., 1959; grad. La. State U. Sch. Banking, 1976; m. Martha Faye Nicholas, Apr. 16, 1954; children—Samuel Hardy, III, Martha Catherine. Agt., Prudential Ins. Co. Am., 1963-73; trust officer United So. Bank (formerly Bank of Clarksdale), Clarksdale, Miss., 1973—, also loan officer, system coordinator, sr. v.p. Served to 1st lt. U.S. Army, 1954-57. Mem. Am. Coll. Life Underwriters Baptist. Club: Rotary (Clarksdale). Office: PO Box 1059 Clarksdale MS 38614

FARRISS, MICHAEL ATLEE, acct.; b. Richmond, Va., Sept. 11, 1952; s. Emmett R. and Margaret Farriss Cairns; B.S. with high honors, Va. Commonwealth U., 1974, M.B.A., 1978; m. Cynthia G. Tignor, June 3, 1973; 1 son, Christopher Ryan. Officer, IRS, Richmond, 1974-78; plant acct. Philip Morris, U.S.A., Richmond, 1978-79, lead plant acct., 1979-80, sr. ops. analyst, 1980, supr. leaf systems devel., 1980—. Barbara Elaine Major Meml. scholar, 1972-74. Mem. Nat. Assn. Accts. (dir. communications Richmond-Jackson chpt. 1980—), Inst. Mgmt. Acctg. (cert. mgmt. acct.), Assn. M.B.A. Execs., Tau Kappa Epsilon. Home: 6910 Manning Rd Chesterfield VA 23832 Office: Philip Morris USA PO Box 26603 Richmond VA 23261

FARROW, MICHAEL GEORGE, JR., toxicologist; b. Altoona, Pa., Aug. 17, 1939; s. Michael George and Katharine Dolores Farrow; B.S., Juniata Coll., 1961; M.S., W.Va. U., 1964; Ph.D., 1970. Postdoctoral student W.Va. U., 1970-73; research pharmacologist Wyeth Labs., Phila., 1973-78; toxicologist JRB Assos., Inc., McLean, Va., 1978—; dir. JRB Labs., McLean, 1980—; lectr. Cabrini Coll., 1976. NIH fellow, 1962-67; Nat. Cancer Inst. grantee, 1967-73. Mem. Environ. Mutagen Soc., European Teratology Soc., Am. Genetic Assn., Mid-Atlantic Reprodn. and Teratology Assn., Genetic Toxicology Assn., Am. Coll. Toxicology, Teratology Soc. Home: 2940 Waterford Ct N Vienna VA 22180 Office: 8400 Westpark Dr McLean VA 22102

FARVER, ALVIN D., dentist; b. Topeka, Ind., Oct. 25, 1893; s. Moses A. and Mary Elizabeth (Hostetler) F.; D.D.S., Ind. U., 1914; m. Marie Ellen Troyer, June 20, 1918; children—Frances Charlene (Mrs. Jack E. Farley), Gloria Jean (Mrs. Richard L. Payton), Patricia Ann (Mrs. Jerry R. Lusk). Practice gen. dentistry, Middlebury, Ind., 1914-27, restorative dentistry, Miami Beach, Fla., 1940—; presented clinics to numerous dental groups, 1945—; instr. gold inlays, crown and bridge group Dade County Dental Research Clinic, 1948—; cons. in restorative dentistry Miami VA, 1954-58. Served to 1st lt. Dental Corps, U.S. Army, 1917-19; AEF. Fellow Am., Internat. colls. dentists; mem. Am. Dental Assn. (1st v.p. 1962-63), Ind., Fla. (pres. 1959-60), East Coast Dist. (pres. 1942-43), Miami (pres. 1940—), Miami Beach, Chgo. dental socs., Dade County Dental Research Clinic (pres. 1952-53), Am. Acad. Restorative Dentistry, Am. Legion, 40 and 8, Xi Psi Phi. Conglist. Mason (Shriner, K.T.). Home: 4291 Nautilus Dr Miami Beach FL 33140 Office: 333 Arthur Godfrey Rd Miami Beach FL 33140

FARWELL, HAROLD FREDERICK, JR., educator; b. Oak Park, Ill., Apr. 9, 1934; s. Harold Frederick and Dorothy Delma (Cobb) F.; B.A., U. Chgo., 1960, M.A., 1961; Ph.D., U. Wis., 1970; m. W. Joyce George, Feb. 10, 1961; children—Douglas George, Beth Elene, Amy Kathleen, Ellen Claudia. Instr. English Drake U., Des Moines, Iowa, 1960-61; teaching asst. U. Wis., 1961-66; asst. prof. English U. Cin., 1966-70; asso. prof. English Western Carolina U., Cullowhee, N.C., 1970-79; vis. prof. English, Baylor U., 1979-80. Served with USNR, 1958-60. Mem. Modern Lang. Assn., Am. Studies Assn., Melville Soc., Am. Fedn. Tchrs. (pres. local chpt.), Phi Gamma Delta. Editor, Arts Jour., 1978—. Home: 2633 Lake Oaks Waco TX 76710

FASCELL, DANTE B., congressman; b. Bridgehampton, L.I., N.Y., Mar. 9, 1917; s. Charles A. and Mary (Gullotti) F.; J.D., U. Miami, 1938; m. Jeanne-Marie Pelot, Sept. 19, 1941; children—Sandra J., Toni F., Dante J. Admitted to Fla. bar, 1938, practiced in Miami, 1938-41, 46—; legal attache state legis. del. Dade County, 1947-50; mem. Fla. Ho. of Reps., 1950-54; mem. 84th-96th Congresses from 15th Dist. Fla. Served as officer U.S. Army, 1942-46. Named one of ten outstanding legislators Fla. Legislature, 1951, 53; one of five outstanding men in Fla., Fla. Jr. C. of C., 1951. Mem. Miami Jr. C. of C. (pres. 1947-48), Am., Dade County, Fed., D.C. bar assns., Fla. Bar, Am. Legion, Mil. Order World Wars, Kappa Sigma. Democrat. Clubs: Lions, Italian-American (pres. 1947-48), Dade County Young Democratic (pres. 1947-48) (Miami, Fla.). Home: 6300 SW 99th Terr Miami FL 33156 Office: House Office Bldg Washington DC 20515

FASHBAUGH, HOWARD DILTS, JR., lawyer; b. Monroe, Mich., Jan. 31, 1922; s. Howard Dilta and Ninetta Esther (Greening) F.; B.S.E. in Chem. Engring., U. Mich., 1947, M.S.E., 1948, M.B.A. with high distinction, 1960; J.D. cum laude, Wake Forest U., 1972; m. Joyce Dallas MacCurdy, Dec. 25, 1946; children—James Howard, Linda Carol, Patricia Lee. Mgr. engring. and mfg. Dow Corning Corp., Midland, Mich., 1952-70; admitted to Va. bar, 1973, Mich. bar, 1975; asso. firm Williams, Worrell, Kelly & Greer, Norfolk, Va., 1972-76, partner firm, 1976-77; corp. counsel Va. Chems., Inc., Portsmouth, 1977—. Chmn. adv. bd. Salvation Army, Midland, 1967-69, Portsmouth, 1975—. Served to lt. USNR, 1943-46, 50-52. Decorated Bronze Star. Mem. Am. Bar Assn., Va. Bar Assn., Portsmouth Bar Assn., Norfolk-Portsmouth Bar Assn., Beta Gamma Sigma. Presbyterian. Clubs: Kiwanis (past pres.). Home: 2504 Sterling Point Dr Portsmouth VA 23703 Office: 3340 W Norfolk Rd Portsmouth VA 23703

FASKEN, DAVID R(OBERT), oil producer; b. Toronto, Ont., Can., Apr. 22, 1915; s. Robert Winstanley and Mae (Farland) F.; student San Rafael Mil. Acad. Jr. Coll., 1932-34, U. San Francisco, 1935. Livestock breeder, Tex., Cal., 1939—; pres. Midland Farms Co., Tex., 1943-44, Palafox Exploration Co., Midland and Laredo, Tex.; ind. oil producer, 1953—. Republican. Episcopalian. Club: Olympic (San Francisco). Home: Circle Dr Ross CA 94957 Office: First Nat Bank Bldg Midland TX 79701

FASO, PAUL LEO, photographer; b. Buffalo, Mar. 15, 1945; s. Carl Peter and Rosella Barbara (Privetera) F.; B.A., State U. N.Y. at Buffalo, 1970. Advt., sales dir. Williams Contracting Co., Atlanta, 1971-72; pres. Exploratory Concepts, multi-media prodn. co., producer slide shows, Atlanta, 1972—; free lance photographer, Atlanta, 1972—. Served with 82d Airborne div. U.S. Army, 1963-66. Researched impact of photographs on mentally retarded. Home: Atlanta GA

FAUBION, JERRY TOLBERT, fiber and chem. co. exec., mgmt. cons.; b. Pidcoke, Tex., June 9, 1917; s. Roy Arthur and Lilly (Pendleton) F.; B.S. in Engring. Adminstrn., Tex. A. and M. U., 1940; m. Rena Louise Derouen, July 20, 1940; 1 son, Roy Michael. Mech. and chem. engr. Dow Chem. Co., Freeport, Tex., 1942-43, supt. prodn. control, 1943-55, mgr. prodn. coordination, 1955-57, mgr. planning and distbn., 1957-63, mgr. organic chems., Midland, Mich., 1963-64, mgr. packaging dept., 1964-65; pres. Dow Badische Co., Williamsburg, Va., 1966-75, also dir.; pres., dir. Faubion Enterprises, Inc., Williamsburg, Va., 1976—; dir., mem. audit and exec. coms. United Va. Bank of Williamsburg; dir., mem. exec. and compensation coms. Va. Chems. Inc.; dir., mem. audit and compensation com. Chesapeake Corp. of Va.; dir., chmn. audit com. United Va. Bankshares, Inc., Richmond; chmn. bd., dir. The Tintometer Co., Williamsburg; dir. RV Chems. Ltd., London; chmn. bd., dir. Virchem SA/NV, Brussels; dir. HCB Chemicals Corp., Portsmouth, Va.; lectr. Coll. William and Mary, 1978. Mem. city council City of Freeport (Tex.), 1950-51; mem. Brazosport (Tex.) Ind. Sch. Bd., 1952-57, pres., 1955-57. Trustee Community Hosp., Freeport, Tex., 1960-61; bd. dirs. Williamsburg (Va.) Community Hosp., 1970—. Registered profl. engr., Tex. Presbyn. (elder). Home: Box BT Williamsburg VA 23185 Office: Faubion Enterprises Williamsburg VA 23185

FAUCHEUX, ROBERT RONALD, JR., lawyer; b. New Orleans, Nov. 28, 1950; s. Robert Ronald and Beulah Marie (Roussel) F.; B.S., La. State U., 1972; J.D., Loyola U., New Orleans, 1975; m. Diana Marie Laiche, Mar. 9, 1969; children—Robert Ronald III, Julienne Chantelle. Admitted to La. bar, 1975; asso. partner firm Becnel & Faucheux, Reserve, La., 1975—; legal counsel St. John The Baptist Parish Sch. Bd. and Police Jury, Vol. Indigent Defenders Bd. 29th Jud. Dist. Ct.; dir. Faucheux Chevrolet, Inc. Served with U.S. Army Res., 1972—. Mem. Am. Bar Assn., La. Bar Assn., 29th Jud. Dist. Bar Assn., Assn. Trial Lawyers Am., La. Trial Lawyers Assn., Nat. Assn. Criminal Def. Lawyers. Democrat. Roman Catholic. Home: 45 Country Club Dr LaPlace LA 70068 Office: Becnel & Faucheux 109 W 7th St Reserve LA 70084

FAUGHN, LARRY OVELL, ins. agt.; b. Crider, Ky., Feb. 23, 1943; s. Oburn Ovell and Lattie Loraine (Holt) F.; student Western Ky. U., 1961-63; m. Sandra Kaye Davis, May 16, 1964; children—Melanie Lee, Melisa Lynn. With Lincoln Income Life Ins. Co., Princeton, Ky., 1964-69; ind. agt. State Farm Ins. Cos., Princeton, 1969—. Bd. dirs. Pennyrile Allied Community Services, 1976; chmn. Caldwell County unit Am. Cancer Soc., 1976. Recipient career achievement awards State Farm Ins. Cos., 1970-79; W.W. Billip's Spirit of Success award, 1977; named an Outstanding Am. in South, 1975. Democrat. Baptist. Club: Elks (Princeton). Home: Route 1 Box 312A Princeton KY 42445 Office: State Farm Ins Cos 108 E Court Sq Princeton KY 42445

FAUGHT, JOHN CHARLES, telephone co. exec.; b. Eden, Tex., Apr. 29, 1942; s. Damon William and Flora Lucille (Wheeler) F.; A.A., San Angelo Jr. Coll., 1964; B.B.A., Angelo State Coll., 1967, M.B.A., 1976; m. Robbie Ann Gilliam, Aug. 26, 1967; children—Robin Angela, John Charles. With Gen. Telephone Co. of S.W., 1967—, revenue acctg. mgr., 1974-77, cost. acctg. mgr., 1977-78, info. systems dir., 1978—. Mem. fin. com. 1st Baptist Ch. Mem. Nat. Assn. Accts., Am. Mgmt. Assn. Home: 2706 Jann Dr San Angelo TX 76901 Office: 2701 S Johnson San Angelo TX 76901

FAUGHT, TIM DON, pub. relations exec.; b. Navo, Tex., July 24, 1934; s. Leon Allison and Anna Belle (Dooley) F.; B.A., N. Tex. State U., 1955, M.Ed., 1965; children from previous marriage—Brian Keith, Kent Stephen, Melinda Leigh. Advt. copywriter A. Harris & Co., Dallas, 1955-56, asst. buyer fabrics, 1956; tchr. Sunset High Sch., Dallas, 1959-63; publs. editor Southern Union Gas Co., Dallas, 1963-67; supr. sales promotion Tex. Power & Light Co., Dallas, 1968-70; dir. pub. relations Harris Hosp., Ft. Worth, 1970-79; public relations cons., Houston, 1979—. Trustee, Tex. Boys Choir Ft. Worth,

1974—, bd. dirs., 1976—. Served with AUS, 1956-58. Mem. Internat. Assn. Bus. Communicators (pres. 1969, chmn. bd. 1970, recipient Editor of Year award Dallas, 1969, Eddy award, Dallas, 1968), Pub. Relations Soc. Am., Tex. Soc. Hosp. Pub. Relations. Republican. Presbyterian. Home: 8100 Cambridge Dr 6 Houston TX 77054

FAULCON, NETTIE DEMORY, aerospace technologist; b. Halifax County, N.C., Dec. 7, 1947; d. Wilford and Susie Mae (Hunter) Demory; B.S., Norfolk (Va.) State Coll., 1970; M.S., George Washington U., 1978; m. Kenneth Carl Faulcon, Aug. 22, 1970; 1 son, Kenneth Carl. Student trainee engring. Langley Research Center, NASA, Hampton, Va., 1967-70, electronic engr., 1970—. Mem. Nat. Tech. Assn., NAACP, Delta Sigma Theta. Democrat. Baptist. Author papers in field. Home: 908 Sanderlin Ln Virginia Beach VA 23462 Office: Mail Stop 238 Hampton VA 23665

FAULCONER, ROBERT JAMIESON, pathologist; b. Sedlescombe, Sussex, Eng., July 11, 1923; s. Robert Hoffman and Gladys Alice (Jamieson) F.; came to U.S., 1925, naturalized, 1932; B.S., Coll. William and Mary, 1943; M.D., Johns Hopkins, 1947; m. Virginia Myrl Davis, Aug. 11, 1945; children—Anne, Elizabeth, Mary Waite, John. Intern. Johns Hopkins, 1948-48, fellow, 1948-49; resident, Presbyn.-U. Pa. Med. Center, Phila., 1949-52; pathologist, DePaul Hosp., Norfolk, Va., 1954—; pathologist, dir. labs., 1965-79; clin. prof. pathology Med. Coll. Va., 1972-79; prof. pathology Eastern Va. Med. Sch., 1974—, chmn., 1978—; cons. pathologist U.S. Naval Hosp., Portsmouth, Va., 1958—, U.S. VA, Hampton, Va., 1956—. Bd. visitors Coll. William and Mary; nat. bd. dirs., mem. exec. com. Am. Cancer Soc. Served with USNR, 1943-46, M.C., U.S. Army, 1952-54. Recipient J. Shelton Horsley award of merit Va. div. Am. Cancer Soc., 1966. Mem. Am. Soc. Clin. Pathologists, Coll. Am. Pathologists, Am. Assn. Anatomists, AMA, Am. Soc. Clin. Oncology. Episcopalian. Clubs: Commonwealth (Richmond, Va.): Yacht and Country (Norfolk, Va.). Home: 1507 Buckingham Ave Norfolk VA 23508 Office: Eastern Va Med Sch 700 W Olney Rd Norfolk VA 23507

FAULK, DAVID REYNOLDS, savs. and loan exec.; b. Monroe, La., Jan. 18, 1907; s. William Crowther and Sarah Celia (Milling) F.; m. Alma Laura Reveley, Apr. 28, 1927; children—Oscie Ozella, Jo Anne Cecelia, Laura Elizabeth. Founder Faulk Creamery, 1931; owner Dutch Girl Dairy Stores, 1951—, Faulk Investments, 1946—, Faulk Constrn. Co., 1967—. Dir., underwriter SW Tex. Meth. Hosp.; dir., underwriter Hemis-Fair, San Antonio, 1968, ambassador to W. Europe, 1963. Clubs: St. Anthony, K Dinner, Sportsman. Republican. Methodist. Home: 121 Shavano Dr San Antonio TX 78231 Office: 1908 W Olmos Dr San Antonio TX 78201

FAULKNER, JAMES HERMAN, publisher; b. Lamar County, Ala., Mar. 1, 1916; s. Henry L. and Ebbie (Johnson) F.; B.J., U. Mo., 1936; m. Evelyn Irwin, Apr. 15, 1937; children—James Herman, Henry Wade. Co-owner, co-pub. The Baldwin Times, Bay Minette, Ala., 1936-74, pub. emeritus, editorial writer, 1974—; co-owner, co-pub. The Onlooker, Foley, Ala., 1969-74, Fairhope (Ala.) Courier, 1970-74; co-owner South Alabamian, Jackson, 1974-78; pres. Faulkner Radio, Inc.; owner radio stas. WLBB, WBTR, Carrollton, Ga., WBCA and WWSM, Bay Minette, WGAA, Cedartown, Ga., WAOA and WFRI, Opelika, Ala.; sr. v.p. David Volkert & Assos., architects and engrs., Mobile, Ala., New Orleans, Washington, Miami, Fla.; founder, pres. Loyal Am. Life Ins. Co., Mobile, 1955-57; chmn. bd. Alpine Industries, Inc., Bay Minette, 1975-79; pres., dir. Gulf Area Ins. Agy., Inc., Bay Minette, 1964-74. Mayor, Bay Minette, 1940-43; mem. Ala. Dem. Com.; del. Dem. Nat. Conv., 1948, 52; Ala. state senator, 1951-55; candidate gov. Ala.; fin. chmn. Ala. Dem. campaign, 1976; chmn. Baldwin County Hosp. Bd., 1964-74, Bay Minette Housing Authority, Bay Minette Municipal Airport Com., 1968—, Pub. Edn., Bldg. Com. of Bay Minette, 1967—, Indsl. Devel. Bd. Bay Minette, 1968—; chmn. adv. bd. James H. Faulkner State Coll., 1971—; mem. Ala. Commn. on Higher Edn., 1978—. Bd. dirs Ala. Safety Council, 1967—, Ala. Crippled Children's Soc.; bd. dirs. Ala. div. Am. Cancer Soc., chmn., 1960-61; state chmn. Cancer Fund Drive: chmn. bd. dirs. Ala. Christian Coll., Montgomery, 1966—. Served with USAAF, World War II. Named Man of Year, Bay Minette, 1965; named Journalist of Year (weekly newspaper), U.S. Steel Corp., 1966. Mem. Ala. Press Assn. (pres. 1939), Ala. (dir. 1947—), Newcomen Soc., Bay Minette (pres.) chambers commerce, Am. Legion, 40 and 8, Sigma Delta Chi. Rotarian. Home: 705 E 5th St Bay Minette AL 36507 Office: 102 W 2d St Bay Minette AL 36507

FAURI, DAVID P., ednl. adminstr.; b. Lansing, Mich., July 22, 1940; s. Fedele F. and Iris (Peterson) F.; A.B., U. Mich., 1962; M.P.A., U. Mich., 1964; Ph.D., Syracuse U., 1972; m. Judith M. DeLeau, Mar. 16, 1968. Adminstrv. asst. City of Ann Arbor (Mich.), 1964; research asso. and Peace Corps vol. Inst. Adminstrn., U. Ife, Ibadan, Nigeria, 1964-66; mgmt. analyst, social services specialist State of Wash., Olympia, 1966-68; research asso. Syracuse (N.Y.) U. Sch. Social Work, 1969-71; dir. Office of Aging, City of Syracuse, 1971-72; asst. prof. Coll. Social Professions, U. Ky., Lexington, 1972-73; dir., asso. prof. U. Tenn. Sch. Social Work, Nashville, 1976—; social services tng. cons. NASA fellow, Syracuse U., 1970-72. Mem. Nat. Assn. Social Workers (br. pres. 1979—), Gerontol. Soc., Council on Social Work Edn., Am. Soc. for Pub. Adminstrn. (mem. Mid Tenn. council 1978—). Author articles on public adminstrn. and social work. Home: 6767 Pennywell Dr Nashville TN 37205 Office: Univ of Tenn Sch Social Work PO Box 90440 Nashville TN 37209

FAUST, ELMER FORD, banker; b. Shawnee, Okla., Oct. 14, 1925; s. Arthur E. and Helen Caroline (Ford) F.; student Trinity U., 1946-47; B.A., McNeese State Coll., 1961; m. Betty Ann Evans, Dec. 19, 1946; children—Jerry Lee, Mark Thomas, Candy Susan. Commd. 2d lt. U.S. Army, 1949, advanced through grades to col., 1970, ret., 1972; asst. v.p. pub. relations Nat. Bank Ft. Sam Houston, San Antonio, 1972, v.p. mktg. 1972-75, sr. v.p. mktg. and customer relations, 1975—; dir. Universal City Bank (N.A.). Served with USNR, 1943-46. Decorated Legion of Merit, Bronze Star; Cross of Armed Forces 3d class (Venezuela); recipient Air Force Assn. nat. medal of merit, 1975; Nat. Air Force Exceptional Service award, 1976, Presdl. citation, 1977. Mem. Am. Inst. Banking, Tex. Pub. Relations Assn., Bank Mktg. Assn., Air Force Assn. (life mem., pres. Tex. 1976, nat. v.p. SW region 1977, nat. dir. 1979—, Assn. U.S. Army (pres. Alamo chpt. 1976, regional v.p. 1978, regional pres. 1980), San Antonio C. of C. (armed forces com. 1972—). Methodist. Home: 5834 Winding Ridge Dr San Antonio TX 78239 Office: 1422 E Grayson St San Antonio TX 78239

FAUST, JOSEF, geologist; b. Meggen, Germany, Feb. 6, 1902; s. Heinrich and Maria (Hunoldt) F.; Diplom-Engr., Technische Hochschule-Berlin-Charlottenburg, 1927, D.Eng., 1928; m. Irmgard Kamkowski, Apr. 29, 1934; children—Margrete Irma (Mrs. Curtis G. Hookway, Jr.), Mary Jo (Mrs. Harold E. Johnson). Came to U.S., 1929, naturalized, 1942. Mining engr. Wenzeslaus Grube Moeltke, Neder Silesia, Germany, 1928-29; ingenieur Carnegie Steel Co., Pitts., 1929; geologist Hall & Briscoe, Oklahoma City, 1929-34; cons. geologist, engr., Oklahoma City, 1934—. Registered profl. engr., Okla. Mem. Am. Assn. Petroleum Geologists, Am. Assn. Profl. Engrs., Am. Assn. Petroleum Landmen, Okla. Geol. Soc., Okla. Landmen's Assn., Soc. Profl. Engrs. Oklahoma City. Rotarian. Home: 2717 Pembroke Terrace Oklahoma City OK 73116 Office: Suite 504 May-Ex Bldg 3022 NW Expressway Oklahoma City OK 73112

FAUST, PEGGY SAXON, coll. adminstr.; b. Bamberg County, S.C., May 16, 1945; d. George and Lillian (Staley) Saxon; A.A., Voorhees Jr. Coll., 1965; B.S., Voorhees Coll., 1968; M.Ed., U. S.C., 1977; m. Wilber A. Faust, July 26, 1969; 1 dau., Philice Nicole. Fin. aid asst. Benedict Coll., Columbia, S.C., 1971-78; dir. career planning and placement Voorhees Coll., Denmark, S.C., 1978—. Leader, Girl Scouts U.S.A., Denmark, 1975—. Recipient award for outstanding achievement as fin. aid asst. Benedict Coll., 1978. Mem. Am. Personnel and Guidance Assn., S.C. Personnel and Guidance Assn., NAACP, So. Coll. Placement Assn., AAUW. Democrat. Baptist. Home: Route 2 PO Box 205A9 Denmark SC 29042 Office: Voorhees Coll Voorhees Rd Denmark SC 29042

FAVARO, MARY KAYE ASPERHEIM (MRS. BIAGINO PHILIP FAVARO), pediatrician; b. Edgerton, Wis., Sept. 30, 1934; d. Harold Wilbur and Genevieve Catherine (Hyland) Asperheim; B.S., U. Wis., 1956; M.S., St. Louis Coll. Pharmacy, 1965; M.D., U. Wis., 1969; m. Biagino Philip Favaro, May 31, 1969; children—Justin Peter, Gina Sue. Instr. pharmacology St. Louis U. and St. Mary's Hosp. Sch. Practical Nurses, 1959-64; staff pharmacist U. Hosps., Madison, Wis., 1964-65; intern Albany (N.Y.) Med. Center, 1969-70, resident, 1970-71; resident in pediatrics U. S.C., Charleston, 1971-72, asst. prof. pediatrics, 1973—; pvt. practice pediatrics, 1974—. Mem. A.M.A., Am. Med. Women's Assn. Roman Catholic. Author: Pharmacology for Practical Nurses, 1963; The Pharmacologic Basis of Patient Care, 1968. Home: 1866 Capri Dr Charleston SC 29407 Office: 5060 Dorchester Rd North Charleston SC 29405

FAVELL, WILLIAM DAVID, motor express co. exec.; b. Shelby, N.C., Oct. 22, 1928; s. William B. and Mary J. (Mauney) F.; student Brevard Coll., 1947-48, Miami Art Sch., 1948-49, Coll. Advanced Traffic, 1961-62; m. Jessie P. Clark, June 25, 1950; children—William David, Mary Jane. Billing clk. Carolina Freight Carriers, Cherryville, N.C., 1949-50, rate clk., 1950-51, terminal mgr., Tampa, Fla., 1951-52; terminal mgr. Mercury Motor Express, Tampa, 1952-55, mgr. rating and billing, Columbia, S.C. and Jacksonville, Fla., 1955-65, dir. traffic, Tampa, 1965-68, dir. traffic and sales, 1968-70, v.p. traffic and sales, 1970-74, pres., chief operating officer, dir., 1974—. Served with USN, 1945-47. Mem. Tampa C. of C. (mem. transp. com. 1975-79), Fla. Trucking Assn. (dir. 1975-79), Am. Trucking Assn. (trustee found. 1979—), Common Carrier Conf. (dir. 1977-79), Nat. Def. Transp. Assn. Democrat. Baptist. Clubs: Commerce, Exchange. Office: 2511 N Grady Ave Tampa FL 33623

FAVRO, KERRY DEWAR, mfg. co. exec.; b. Pitts., May 10, 1936; s. Marius Ovidio and Iola May (Dewar) F.; B.S. in M.E. (scholar), Carnegie Inst. Tech., 1957; M.S. in M.E. (fellow), Stanford U., 1958; m. Sandra Rose Trudeau, July 17, 1967; children—Kristin Reeves, Cindy Lee, Jill Susanne. Mech. engr. Northop Corp., Hawthorne, Calif., 1958-60; mem. tech. staff Aerospace Corp., El Segundo, Calif., 1964-76; asst. v.p. Sci. Applications, Inc., Arlington, Va., 1976—. Mem. Air Force Assn., AIAA. Home: 11220 South Shore Rd Reston VA 22090 Office: 2361 Jefferson Davis Hwy Arlington VA 22202

FAWCETT, LESLIE CLARENCE, JR., accountant; b. Ft. Davis, Tex., May 12, 1920; s. Leslie Clarence and Estelle Virginia (Bloys) F.; student San Antonio Jr. Coll., 1938-41, St. Mary's U., 1947-48; B.B.A., U. Tex., 1949, M.B.A., 1951. Jr. accountant Fred E. Pflughaupt & Co., C.P.A.'s, San Antonio, 1951-52, sr. accountant, 1953-59, partner, 1960—. Served with Signal Corps, U.S. Army, 1942-45. C.P.A., Tex. Mem. Am. Inst. C.P.A.'s, Tex. Soc. C.P.A.'s. Presbyn. Home: 428 Hammond Ave San Antonio TX 78210 Office: 1222 Alamo Nat Bldg San Antonio TX 78205

FAWLEY, OKEY BROWN, JR., mental health center adminstr.; b. Morgantown, W.Va., June 8, 1938; s. Okey Brown and Ruth Louise (Watson) F.; B.S. in Acctg., W.Va. U., 1960, M.S.W., 1965; m. Pamela Marian Shelton, July 16, 1971; children—Joshua, Zachary. Mem. corp. mgmt. staff Bell Telephone of Pa., Dover, Del., and Norristown, Pa., 1960-64; social worker Veterans Psychiat. Hosp., Salem, Va., 1965-68; therapist Family Services, Roanoke, Va., 1966-67; exec. dir. 4-County Regional Community Mental Health Center, Morgantown, W.Va., 1968—; asst. prof. dept. psychiatry W.Va. U., 1968—, asst. prof. Sch. Nursing, 1969—; cons. NIMH. Coach Little League, Morgantown; organizer Need Council, Morgantown, W.Va. Assn. Mental Health Programs. Served with U.S. Army, 1960. Mem. Nat. Assn. Social Workers, Am. Quarter Horse Assn., Phi Delta Theta. Democrat. Methodist. Club: Rotary. Home and Office: 301 Scott Ave Morgantown WV 26505

FAY, THOMAS E., fin. cons.; b. Kansas City, Mo., Dec. 11, 1934; s. Earl J. and Harriett E. F.; B.B.A., St. Mary's U., 1956; m. June 27, 1964; 1 child. Salesman, Monroe Calculator, 1957-60, br. mgr., 1960-74; real estate tax counselor S.S. Aurelia and W/Dorsey Realtor, Corpus Christi, Tex., 1974—. Served to 2d lt. U.S. Army, 1956-57. Mem. Acad. Real Estate, Interx. Address: PO Box 8828 Corpus Christi TX 78412

FEAGANS, ROBERT GEARY, mech. engr.; b. Ashland, Ky., July 5, 1924; s. Guy and Hazel Edna (McIntyre) F.; B.S., U. Ky., 1948; m. Anna Louise McCalvin, Sept. 14, 1924; children—Deborah Louise, Pamella Gaye. Self-employed as mech. contractor, Ironton, Ohio and Frankfort, Ky., 1948-63; mech. engr. Rust Engring. Co., Calhoun, Tenn., 1965-68; chief mech. engr. Patchen, Mingledorff & Asso., cons. engrs., Augusta, Ga., 1969—. Pecan grower, Aiken County, S.C., 1971—. Served with U.S. Mcht. Marine, 1944-45. Registered profl. engr., Tenn., Ga. Mem. Am. Soc. Heating, Refrigerating and Air-Conditioning Engrs., Ga. Soc. Profl. Engrs. (pres. 1976-77). Home: Route 1 Box 494 Aiken SC 29801 Office: Suite 1400 Ga RR Bank Bldg Augusta GA 30902

FEAGANS, ROBERT RYAN, mktg. exec.; b. Lynchburg, Va., Jan. 11, 1918; s. Charles Burton and Minnie (Carter) F.; B.S. in Agronomy with honors, Va. Poly. Inst., 1938; m. Willie Helen Cruise, Jan. 17, 1942; children—Helen Turman Smith, Jane Carter Proctor, Robert Ryan. With So. States Coop., Inc., Roanoke, Va., 1945—, regional mgr., 1960—; farmer; v.p. Holiday Lake 4-H Ednl. Center, Inc., Appomattox, Va., 1976-77, 77-78. Vestryman, St. Paul's Episcopal Ch., Lynchburg, 1956-58; chmn. Central Va. Planning Dist. Commn. Served to capt., inf. U.S. Army, World War II; PTO. Mem. Va. Council Farmer Coops (dir.), Va., Amherst County (pres., dir.) chambers commerce, Sales and Mktg. Execs. Roanoke Valley (pres. 1975-76), Va. Agribus. Council, Retail Mchts. Assn., SAR (sec.-treas. Lynchburg chpt.), Pi Sigma Epsilon, Omicron Delta Kappa, Phi Kappa Phi, Alpha Zeta. Club: Winton Country (Amherst). Office: PO Box 12206 Roanoke VA 24023

FEATHERS, CHERYL WRIGHT, educator; b. Louisville, Apr. 23, 1952; d. Arthur William and Verna Mae (Bandy) Wright; B.A. with high honors, U. Louisville, 1974, M.Ed. with highest honors, 1977; m. Charles Leo Feathers, Jr., Jan. 25, 1975. Clothing inspector Levy Bros., Louisville, 1970-74; tchr. Jefferson County (Ky.) Bd. Edn., Louisville, 1974—. Mem. NEA, Ky. Edn. Assn., Jefferson County Tchrs. Assn., Woodcock Soc., Nat. Ret. Tchrs. Assn. (asso.), Cwens, Phi Kappa Phi. Republican. Baptist. Home: 9912 Old Third St Rd Louisville KY 40272

FEATHERSTON, CHARLES HENRY, III, Realtor; b. Wichita Falls, Tex., Jan. 6, 1925; s. Solon Richmond and Lillie Beall (Reeves) F.; B.B.A., U. Tex., Austin, 1947; m. Florence Emily Harding, Oct. 26, 1947; children—Solon Richmond III, Randall Mason, David Harding, Molly Kay. Salesman, Crestview Meml. Park, Wichita Falls, 1947-49; sales dir. Crestview Meml. Park and Mausoleum, Wichita Falls, 1949-51; realtor, developer, homebuilder, Wichita Falls, 1954-66; evangelist Billy Graham Evangelistic Film Ministry, East Tex. region, 1966-72; prin. Charles Featherston Assos., Realtors, Tyler, Tex., 1972—; v.p., dir. Village Mortgage Co., Wichita Falls; co-founder, charter chmn. Multiple Listing Service of Wichita Falls Bd. Realtors; tchr. real estate courses Midwestern U. Smith County chmn. Citizens to Elect Pres. Ford, 1976; del. Republican State Conv., 1976. Served to lt. (jg.), USNR, 1943-46, to lt. (s.g.), 1951-53; PTO. Mem. Nat. Assn. Real Estate Bds., Tex. Assn. Real Estate Bds., Tyler Bd. Realtors. Home: 3200 Silverwood St Tyler TX 75701 Office: 3923 S Broadway Tyler TX 75701

FECHTEL, VINCENT JOHN, JR., state senator; b. Leesburg, Fla., Aug. 10, 1936; s. Vincent John and Annie Jo (Hayman) F.; B.S. in Bus. Adminstrn., U. Fla., 1959; children—John, Katherine. Mem. Fla. Ho. of Reps., 1972-78, Fla. Senate, 1978—. Mem. Lake Conservation Council. Served in USNR. Mem. Lake Hist. Soc., Jacksonville Beach Hist. Soc., Leesburg C. of C., Mt. Dora C. of C., Eustis C. of C., Lake County C. of C., Lake County Bd. Realtors, Alpha Tau Omega. Republican. Roman Catholic. Clubs: Leesburg Quarterback, Elk, Kiwanian. Address: PO Box 1675 Leesburg FL 32748 also 315 W Main St Tavares FL 32778

FEDDERN, OTTO GERDT, fund-raising co. ofcl.; b. Louisville, May 25, 1941; s. Fred W. and Martha W. (Wuest) F.; Mus.B., U. Louisville, 1964, B.M.Ed., 1965, Mus.M., 1968; postgrad. N.Y. U., Vanderbilt U.; m. Linda Sue Owen, June 5, 1964. Music tchr., dir. bands Doss High Sch., Louisville, 1967-74, also organist, choir master 1st Lutheran Ch., Louisville, 1962-69 and organist, choir dir. St. Mark's United Ch. of Christ, New Albany, Ind., 1970-74; area mgr. HENCO, Inc., Selmer, Tenn., 1974—. Mem. Phi Kappa Phi. Republican. Home and Office: 9000 Seaton Springs Pkwy Louisville KY 40222

FEDERMAN, STEVEN ROBERT, physicist; b. N.Y.C., Nov. 19, 1949; s. Joseph Meyer and Adele Louise (Strome) F.; B.S., Poly. Inst. Bklyn., 1971, M.S., N.Y. U., 1976, Ph.D., 1979. Sr. research technician Hosp. for Spl. Surgery, N.Y.C., 1972-75; teaching fellow N.Y. U., N.Y.C., 1975-78, research asst., 1978-79, postdoctoral fellow, 1979; postdoctoral fellow U. Tex., Austin, 1979—. Mem. Am. Phys. Soc., Am. Astron. Soc. Home: 2306 Wickersham #1503 Austin TX 78741 Office: Astronomy Dept Univ Tex Austin TX 78712

FEENEY, THOMAS MICHAEL, rental car co. exec.; b. N.Y.C., Feb. 24, 1952; s. Richard Aloysius and Dolores Rita (Cox) F.; student La Salle Coll., 1970-74; m. Debra Francis Mazzuca, Aug. 20, 1977; 1 dau., Tara Marie. With Hertz Corp., 1974—, sr. auditor, 1974-76, controller rent-a-car div. ops. South Fla., 1976-77, mgr. Miami Airport, 1977—. Roman Catholic. Home: 11546 NW 41st St Coral Springs FL 33056 Office: PO Box 59-2196 Miami FL 33159

FEHNER, EUGENE CHARLES, cons. engr.; b. Detroit, Sept. 1, 1924; s. Eugene Phillip and Ida Marie (Gagnier) F.; B.S. in Elec. Engring., U. Ill., 1944; M.S. in Physics, Rollins Coll., 1969; m. Brunhilde G. Wyandt, Sept. 25, 1970; children—Suzanne Fehner Townes, Valerie Fehner Michael, Karen Wyandt Kenny, Bruce Wyandt, Laura Lee Fehner Meister, Lawrence Charles, Wayne Wyandt. Design engr. Ford Motor Co., Dearborn, Mich., 1947-51; design, sales engr. Gen. Electric Co., Schenectady, 1951-60, systems engring. mgr. Daytona Beach, Fla., 1966-72; systems engring. mgr. Martin Co., Orlando, Fla., 1960-66; principal firm Fehner, St. John and Assos., Inc., Orlando, 1972—; instr. U. Detroit, 1947-50, Gen. Electric Co., Schenectady, 1954-55; co-author airport master plans, engr. for design of civil and elec. constrn. at 15 Fla. and Ga. airports; Chmn. indsl. div. United Fund Daytona Beach, Fla., 1971. Served to lt. (j.g.) USN, 1943-46. Registered profl. engr., Fla., Ga., N.Y. Mem. IEEE, Fla. Engring. Soc., Fla. Inst. Cons. Engrs. Patentee in field. Author: Range Safety, Sprint Missile Systems, 1964; contbr. articles to profl. jours. Home: 460 Beloit Ave Winter Park FL 32702 Office: Terminal Bldg Herndon Airport Orlando FL 32808

FEIN, JOHN MORTON, ednl adminstr.; b. Chgo., Dec. 23, 1922; s. Louis Julius and Lola (Dubin) F.; B.A., M.A., Harvard U., 1944, Ph.D., 1950; m. Lucille Blumenthal, Sept. 11, 1946; children—David, Judith, Joanna, Laura. Teaching fellow, tutor Harvard U., Cambridge, Mass., 1944-49, instr. Spanish Am. Lit., 1949-50; mem. faculty Duke U., Durham, N.C., 1950—, prof. Romance langs., 1963—, chmn. dept., 1964-73, 79—, vice provost undergrad. edn., 1974-79, dean Trinity Coll., 1974-79; vis. prof. U. Chile, U. Catolica (Chile), 1957-58, Ind. U., 1964, Stanford U., summer 1965, U. Wyo., summer 1967, Dartmouth Coll., summer 1971. Mem. Modern Lang. Assn., Am. Assn. Tchrs. Spanish and Portuguese (exec. com.). Author: Modernismo in Chilean Literature: The Second Period, 1965. Home: 2726 Montgomery St Durham NC 27705 Office: Duke Univ Durham NC 27706

FEIN, LOUIS IRA, speech pathologist; b. N.Y.C., Apr. 9, 1941; s. Saul N. and Sally F.; B.A., L.I. U., 1966; M.S., Bklyn. Coll., 1969; m. Carla Ginsburg, Apr. 25, 1965; children—Marc, Tracy. Sr. staff therapist Bklyn. Coll. Speech and Hearing Clinic, 1966-69; dir. speech pathology Miami Dade Community Coll., 1970-74; dir. South Miami Speech Clinic, 1970—; supr. speech clinic, instr. Grad. Sch. U. Miami, 1974-75, adj. asst. prof. dept. otolaryngology Med. Sch. U. Miami, 1975—; exec. dir. United Testing Service, Inc., 1976—. Cert. speech pathologist N.Y., Fla. Mem. Am. Speech Hearing Assn., Fla. Speech and Hearing Assn., Fla. Cleft Palate Assn., Nat. Stutterers Found. Developed FAST Fein Articulation Screening Test. Office: 12390 SW 82d Ave Miami FL 33156

FEINBERG, STEPHEN LOUIS, holding co. exec.; b. Chgo., Oct. 10, 1944; s. Milton David and Jean (Brody) F.; B.B.A., U. Tex., 1967; m. Sally Hutchings, June 22, 1957; children—William L, David C. Account exec. Dominick & Dominick Inc., Houston, 1967-70; pres. Dorsar Industries Inc., El Paso, 1972—, also dir.; dir. Border Steel Rolling Mills Inc., Springer Bldg. Materials Inc., First State Bank, Circle K Corp., El Paso. Bd. dirs. St. John's Coll., United Way El Paso, El Paso Cancer Treatment Center. Home: 5028 Country Club Pl El Paso TX 79922 Office: PO Box 9858 El Paso TX 79989

FEINN, BARBARA ANN, economist; b. Waterbury, Conn., Feb. 16, 1925; d. David Harris and Dora (Brandvein) Feinn; A.B. magna cum laude, Smith Coll., 1946; M.A. (Univ. scholar), Yale U., 1947, Ph.D. (Univ. fellow), 1952; certificate Oxford (Eng.) U., 1949. Research economist 1st Nat. City Bank, N.Y.C., 1953-54; asso. economist Office Messrs. Rockefeller, N.Y.C., 1954-61; asst. to dir. N.Y. State Office for Regional Devel., N.Y.C., 1961-62; cons. economist Nelson A. Rockefeller, N.Y.C., 1963-64; pvt. cons., 1965-68; sr. council economist N.Y. State Council Econ. Advisers, N.Y.C., 1969-72; chief economist Office S.C. Gov. Columbia, 1972—, mem. bd. econ.

advisors, 1976—; adj. prof. bus. adminstrn. U. S.C., Columbia, 1972-74. Ofcl. participant White House Conf. on Balanced Nat. Growth and Econ. Devel., 1978; del. meetings on nat. balanced growth Nat. Govs. Assn., Leesburg, Va., 1977. Dir. Smith Coll. Alumnae Fund Program, N.Y.C., 1965-66, mem. spl. gifts com., 1971. Mem. Am., West. econ. assns., N.Y. Assn. Bus. Econ., Nat. Assn. Bus. Econ., Soc. Govt. Economists, Downtown Economists Luncheon Group, Atlanta Economic Club, Phi Beta Kappa. Clubs: Yale (N.Y.C.); Wildewood (Columbia, S.C.); Sea Pines (Hilton Head Island, S.C.). Contbr. articles to profl. jours. Home: 1212 Quail Run Columbia SC 29206 Office: Gov's Office Columbia SC 29201

FEINSMITH, LESLIE SEWALD, physician; b. Bklyn., Mar. 12, 1940; s. Benjamin and Betty (Kramer) F.; B.A. cum laude, Bklyn. Coll., 1961; M.D. with highest honors, N.Y. Med. Coll., 1965; m. Arlene Kessler, Aug. 11, 1963; children—Jeffrey, Jason. Intern, Montefiore Hosp., Bronx, N.Y., 1965-66; resident N.Y. Med. Coll., 1968-70, chief med. resident, 1969; fellow in nephrology U. Pa., Phila., 1971-73; pvt. practice internal medicine, Atlanta, 1973—; instr. medicine Med. Coll. Ga., Augusta, 1970-71, U. Pa., 1971-73; mem. staff. Clayton Gen. Hosp., South Fulton Hosp.; med. dir. So. States Dialysis Center, College Park, Ga., 1974-76, Clayton Dialysis Center, Jonesboro, Ga., 1979—; partner, cons. Dekalb Gwinnette Nephrology Referral Center, Decatur, Ga., 1977—; clin. asst. prof. medicine Emory U., Altanta, 1975—; pres. Atlanta Med. Specialists, 1973—. Served to maj. U.S. Army, 1969-71. Diplomate Am. Bd. Internal Medicine. Mem. Med. Assn. Ga., AMA, Clayton Fayette Med. Soc., Alpha Omega Alpha. Jewish. Author: (with Jack J. Kleid) Textbook Study Guide of Internal Medicine, vol. 11-A, vol. 11-B, 1968—; Insect Stings and Bites, Handbook of Medical Emergencies, 1970. Office: 150 Medical Way Suite A Riverdale GA 30274

FEINSTEIN, RICHARD JAY, dermatologist; b. Bklyn., Nov. 15, 1942; s. Abraham Louis and Sarah (Neuer) F.; B.A., cum laude, Bklyn. Coll., 1964; M.D., SUNY, Syracuse, 1968; m. Daria Ann Keller, May 18, 1968; children—Rachel, Lisa. Straight med. intern Georgetown Med. div. D.C. Gen. Hosp., Washington, 1968-69; resident in dermatology U. Miami (Fla.), 1971-74, asst. clin. prof., 1978—; chief dermatology, Mercy Hosp. of Miami, 1978—; apptd. by Gov. Robert Graham to Fla. Bd. Med. Examiners, 1979—; cons. in field. Served as sr. surg. USPHS, 1969-71. Diplomate Am. Bd. Dermatology. Fellow Am. Acad. Dermatology; mem. Fla. Soc. Dermatology, Miami Dermatol. Soc. (pres. 1979-80), AMA, Fla. Med. Assn., Dade County Med. Assn. Jewish. Club: Rotary (dir. Coconut Grove, Fla., 1977—). Home: 10395 SW 60th Pl Miami FL 33156 Office: Mercy Profl Bldg Suite 902 3661 S Miami Ave Miami FL 33133

FEIT, HOWARD, neurologist, educator; b. Bklyn., June 22, 1943; s. Charles and Beatrice (Zimmerman) F.; B.A., Columbia U., 1964; Ph.D., Albert Einstein Coll. Medicine, Bronx, N.Y., 1971, M.D., 1972; m. Cheryl Ann Orenstein, July 31, 1966; children—Kerry Danielle, Aaron Lee. Intern, U. Colo. Med. Center, Denver, 1972, resident in neurology, 1972-75; asst. prof. neurology Southwestern Med. Sch., Dallas, 1975—. Recipient S. Weir Mitchell award for neurol. research, 1975; grantee NIH, Muscular Dystrophy Assn. Mem. Am. Neurol. Assn., Am. Acad. Neurology, Am. Soc. for Cell Biology, Am. Soc. for Neurosci. Office: Dept Neurology Southwestern Med Sch Dallas TX 75235

FELAND, JOHN J., farm coop. exec.; b. Danville, Ky., Nov. 24, 1923; s. Armstead Milner and Elizabeth (Jackson) F.; student U. Ky., 1941-43; m. Joan Stoughton Ridlehouse, Nov. 20, 1947. With So. States Coop., Inc., Richmond, Va., 1945—, chief exec. officer, 1973—; vice chmn. Tex. City Refining, Inc., C.F. Industries, Inc.; dir. Agri-Petco Internat., First and Mchts. Nat. Bank. Mem. adv. bd. Richmond Salvation Army. Mem. Nat. Council Farmer Coops. (dir.). Clubs: Commonwealth, Downtown, Country of Va., Masons. Office: 6606 W Broad St Richmond VA 23230

FELBER, NEIL WAYNE, utility exec.; b. Enid, Okla., Apr. 10, 1952; s. Hugh Nickolas and Rosetta Mae (Patocka) F.; B.S., Okla. State U., 1973, M.S., 1974. Auditor, Arthur Andersen & Co., Tulsa, 1974-79; spl. asst. to controller Pub. Service Co. of Okla., Tulsa, 1979—. C.P.A., Okla. Mem. Am. Inst. C.P.A.'s, Okla. Soc. C.P.A.'s, Nat. Assn. Accts. Republican. Roman Catholic. Home: 1222 S 110 E Ave Tulsa OK 74128 Office: PO Box 201 Tulsa OK 74102

FELDMAN, EDMUND BURKE, artist; b. Bayonne, N.J., May 6, 1924; s. Lucian Theodore and Bertha (Seldin) F.; diploma Newark Sch. Fine and Indsl. Arts, 1941; B.F.A. (Roswell Hill prize painting 1948), Syracuse (N.Y.) U., 1949; M.A. in History of Art, UCLA, 1951; Ed.D. in Fine Arts, Columbia U., 1953; m. Lailah G. Link, Mar. 15, 1953; children—Eva Jeanne, Jessica Marion. Curator painting and sculpture Newark Mus., 1953; asso. prof. art Livingston (Ala.) State U., 1953-56, Carnegie Inst. Tech., 1956-60; head art div. SUNY Coll., New Paltz, 1960-66; vis. prof. Ohio State U., 1966; prof. art U. Ga., Athens, 1966—, Alumni Found. disting. prof., 1973—; vis. prof. aesthetic edn. U. Calif., Berkeley, 1974; bd. govs. Pitts. Plan for Art, 1964-66; adv. Ga. Council Arts, 1973-74; cons. Nat. Instructional TV Center, Bloomington, Ind., 1969-71; mem. Coll. Entrance Exam. Bd., 1969-70, Edn. Testing Service Bd., 1969-70. Served with USAAF, 1942-46. Mem. Nat. Art Edn. Assn. (pres.-elect 1979-81), Coll. Art Assn., U.S. Soc. Edn. Through Art, Nat. Art Edn. Assn. (pres. elect 1979-81), Am. Assn. Higher Edn., Kappa Pi, Phi Kappa Phi, Tau Sigma Delta. Author: Art as Image and Idea, 1967; Becoming Human Through Art, 1970; Varieties of Visual Experience, 1971; editor: Art in American Higher Institutions, 1970; chmn. editorial bd. Ga. Rev., 1977-79; mem. editorial bds. profl. jours., cons. editor art publishers. Home: 140 Chinquapin Pl Athens GA 30605 Office: Art Dept Univ Ga Athens GA 30602

FELDSTEIN, CHARLES ROBERT, educator; b. Jacksonville, N.C., Dec. 16, 1947; B.A. in English and Philosophy, E. Carolina U., 1969; M.A. in English Edn., U. Ga., 1973; cert. rational behavior therapy U. Ky. Coll. Medicine, 1974; cert. supervisory mgmt. Purdue U.-Sacred Heart Coll., 1975; postgrad. in English Edn., Pa. State U., 1977—; married. Tchr., English, Jacksonville (N.C.) Jr. High Sch., 1969-70, N. Brunswick High Sch. (formerly Leland High Sch.), Leland, N.C., 1970-72; instr. English and communications Fla. Jr. Coll., Jacksonville, 1973-75; instr. Sacred Heart Coll., Belmont, N.C., 1975-76, asst. prof. English, 1976-77; teaching asst., summer lectr. dept. English, Pa. State U., State College, 1977—. Coordinator, E. Carolina U. campus dr. Easter Seals and March of Dimes, 1968-69. Black belt in Karate. Mem. Nat. Soc. Published Poets, N.C. Soc. Poets, Phi Delta Kappa, Phi Sigma Tau (corr. sec. 1967-68, pres. 1968-69), Alpha Epsilon Pi (corr. The Lion 1966-69, corr. sec. 1967-68, pres. 1968-69, Scholarship trophy 1969). Contbr. articles, poems to profl. publs.; asst. editor: The Encyclopedia of Educational Research, 5th edit., 1980; editor Bittersweet Lit. Mag., 1976-77.

FELIX, OTIS LEANDER, govt. ofcl.; b. Christiansted, St. Croix, V.I., Nov. 7, 1915; s. James and Sarah (Barnwell) F.; ed. N.Y. Police Acad., 1951, Cin. Police Acad., 1955, Boston Sch. Criminology, 1962, FBI Nat. Acad., 1964; Ph.D. in Pub. Adminstrn., 1968; m. Edna Steele, Aug. 9, 1940; children—Priscilla (Mrs. Adrian Plunkett), Rita, Ramon, Otis. Mem. V.I. Police Dept., 1941-75, chief detectives, 1949-55, chief police, 1955-62, commr. pub. safety, 1962-69, spl. asst. to commr. pub. safety Govt. V.I., 1972-75, mem. V.I. Senate, 1975—. Mem. V.I. Law Enforcement Planning Commn. Vice-pres. Internat. Assn. Identification, V.I. Assn. Criminology. Dir. P.A.L. Served in World War II, 1945-47. Mem. A.C.S., FBI Nat. Acad. Assos. Odd Fellow. Democrat. Home: No 12 Contant St Thomas VI 00801

FELKER, PAUL HENRY, JR., bus. and sales adminstr.; b. St. Louis, July 24, 1918; s. Paul Henry and Mable Gertrude (Beal) F.; student Muskegon (Mich.) Community Coll., 1939; m. Violet Irene Gephart, Aug. 2, 1966; children by previous marriage—Kathryn Margaret, Paula June. Draftsman, E.H. Sheldon, Muskegon, Mich., 1940-41; resident insp. in charge U.S. Corps Engrs., South Bend, Ind., 1941-43; engr., tech. authority to U.S. Air Force, U.S. Rubber Co., Mishawaka, Ind., 1943-47; dist. sales engr. Dodge Mfg. Co., Mishawaka, 1948-49; prin. Ottawa Sales Engring. Co., Holland, Mich., 1949-63; mgr. Mendelsohn Elec. Supply Co., South Haven, Mich., 1963-65; project mgr., instr. sales schs. Barber-Greene Co., Aurora, Ill., 1965-69; pres. Pavidor Bldg. Corp., Englewood, Fla., 1969-76, now dir.; missionary Christian Missionary Fellowship, Indpls., Econ. Devel., Brazil, 1976-77. Mem. adv. com. div. on aging Tampa Bay (Fla.) Regional Planning Council, 1971-74; bd. dirs. Big Bros. Venice Area, Inc., 1970-75, v.p., 1972-74, pres., 1975; bd. dirs. Fish of Englewood, 1971-76, pres., 1972-75. Mem. Asolo Theatre Festival Assn., Ill. Wild Life Fedn., Airline Passengers Assn., Am. Mgmt. Assn., Nat. Geog. Soc. Congregationalist. Clubs: Kiwanis, Masons (Englewood), Shriners, Elks. Office: PO Box 1136 Englewood FL 33535

FELLOWS, STEVEN ARNOLD, audiologist; b. Decatur, Ga., Mar. 4, 1943; s. George Rudin and Dorothy (May) F.; B.A., Auburn U., 1965, M.A., 1966; m. Joan Elaine Bearden, Dec. 30, 1977; children—Scott Alan, Christopher John. Research asst. audiology Colo. State U., Ft. Collins, 1966; instr./audiologist U. Southwestern La., 1967-70; dir. NW Ga. Speech and Hearing Center, Rome, 1970-71; dir. Gordon D. Hoople Hearing and Speech Center of Rome, Inc., Ga., 1971—, also audiologist; cons. in field; dir. Alemetco Inc. Chmn. Ga. Bd. Examiners for Speech Pathology and Audiology, 1974-75; active NW Ga. Council, Boy Scouts Am., 1976—; bd. dirs. Floyd Tng. Center for Mentally Retarded, 1977-78. Lic. audiologist Ga.; registered Tinnitus clinician. Mem. Am. Speech and Hearing Assn. (cert. clin. competence), Centurion Club Deafness Research Found., So. Audiological Soc., Ga. Speech and Hearing Assn., Ga. Council of Speech and Hearing Execs., Nat. Assn. Hearing and Speech Action. Club: Optimist (v.p. chpt. 1974-75). Office: 15 John Maddox Dr Rome GA 30161

FELT, WILLIAM NORCROSS, ret. educator; b. Northboro, Mass., Sept. 24, 1904; s. George Herbert and Ella Winchester (Norcross) F.; B.A., Clark U., 1926; M.A., Middlebury Coll., 1931, D.M.L., 1951; postgrad. U. Bordeaux (France), U. Grenoble (France), U. Paris (France), U. Madrid (Spain), Harvard, Ohio State; m. Elizabeth Fay Pease, Aug. 29, 1931; 1 dau., Marcia (Mrs. John C. Abernethy). Tchr. French and history Acton (Mass.) High Sch., 1926-27; from instr. to asst. prof. Denison U., Granville, O., 1927-47; from asst. prof. to asso. prof. U. N.C., Greensboro, 1947-72; asso. dir. French NDEA Inst., U. Alaska, 1965. Franco-American Exchange scholar, Bordeaux, 1929-30; named Chevalier dans l'Ordre des Palmes academiques. Mem. Modern Lang. Assn., Am. Assn. U. Profs. (mem. nat. council, 1945-48), Am. Assn. Tchrs. French (mem. nat. council 1960-65, v.p., 1967-69, mng. trustee 1969—), South Atlantic Modern Lang. Assn., Am. Assn. Tchrs. Spanish and Portuguese. Contbr. articles to profl. jours. Home: 1003 Westridge Rd Greensboro NC 27410

FELTON, WARREN LOCKER, II, thoracic surgeon; b. Bartlesville, Okla., Oct. 25, 1925; s. Warren Locker and Elizabeth (Keller) F.; student U. Okla., 1943, U. Tex., 1943-45; B.S., Washington U., St. Louis, 1949, M.D., 1949; m. Judith Ann Mead, July 25, 1969; children—Warren Locker III, Susan Elizabeth, Richard John Conrad, Alecia Ann, Christina Jane. Intern, New Haven (Conn.) Hosp., 1949-50; resident in surgery Yale-New Haven Med. Center, 1950-56, instr., 1955-56; chief gen. surg. service Valley Force (Pa.) Army Hosp., 1956-58; practice medicine specializing in thoracic and vascular surgery, Oklahoma City, 1958—; clin. prof. surgery U. Okla., 1972—; chmn. dept. surgery Baptist Med. Center Okla. Bd. dirs. Travelers Aid Soc., Oklahoma City, 1961-64. Served with USNR, 1943-45, USAR, 1956-58. Mem. AMA, Am. Thoracic Soc., Am. Assn. Thoracic Surgery, Soc. Thoracic Surgeons, A.C.S., Southwestern Surg. Congress, Sigma Xi, Alpha Omega Alpha. Episcopalian. Clubs: Oklahoma City Golf and Country, U. Okla. Faculty Assn. Contbr. articles to profl. jours. Home: 1612 Dorchester Dr Oklahoma City OK 73120 Office: 5700 NW Grand Blvd Oklahoma City OK 73112

FELTS, CORNELIUS BUFORD, JR., grain elevator co. exec.; b. Kansas City, Mo., Mar. 31, 1928; s. Cornelius Buford and Hazel (Vandivier) F.; B.A., U. Mo., 1950; m. Jeannine Troupe, June 7, 1948; children—William Thomas, Mary Michelle, Richard Neal. Pub. accountant Arthur Young & Co., Kansas City, 1950-57; treas., dir. Simpson, Laybourne, Miller & Stark-Colo. Grain Co., Salina, Kans., 1957-59; treas. Grain Mchts., Inc., Topeka, 1959-63; pres. Garvey Elevators, Inc., Ft. Worth, 1963—, also dir.; dir. Jim Garvey Ranches, JaGee Corp., Rafter-J Ranch, Inc.; corp. officer Jim Garvey Ranches, Inc., Rafter-J Ranch, Inc., JaGee Corp. Mem. Chgo. Kansas City bds. trade; dir. treas. Ft. Worth Grain Exchange; dir. Nat. Grain and Feed Assn. Treas. Garvey Tex. Found. Served with USN, 1945-47. Mem. Am. Inst. C.P.A.'s, Fin. Execs. Inst., Ft. Worth C. of C., Newcomen Soc. N.Am. Episcopalian. Clubs: Ridglea Country (Fort Worth), Century II, Masons, Rotary. Home: Route 2 Box 255 Azle TX 76020 Office: PO Box 1688 Fort Worth TX 76101

FENDLEY, CHARLES ROBERT, yarn co. exec.; b. Pickens County, Ga., Mar. 9, 1946; s. Robert W. and Ruby Lee (Childers) F.; student public schs., Pickens; m. Linda Sue Mull, Aug. 26, 1966; 1 son, Michael Shane. Supr. 2d shift H.D. Lee Co., 1965-67; salesman Moore Furniture Co., Jasper, Ga., 1967-72; dye supr. Glen Head Inc., Jasper, 1972-74, gen. mgr., 1974-79; v.p. Jasper Yarn Processing, 1979—; dir. Amicadola Electric Membership Corp., 1972—. Served with U.S. Army, 1966-68; Vietnam. Decorated Bronze Star. Mem. Am. Assn. Textile Colorists and Chemists, Aircraft Owners and Pilots Assn. Home: Box W35A Route 1 Jasper GA 30143 Office: Jasper Yarn Processing Inc 1 Carl Sanders Ave Jasper GA 30143

FENDT, LOUIS MARION, JR., constrn. cons.; b. Waycross, Ga., Mar. 11, 1920; s. Louis Marion and Margaret Elizabeth (Owens) F.; B.M.E., N.C. State Coll., 1942; m. Daisy Nell Worth, Mar. 16, 1963. Mech. engr. U.S. Army C.E., Jacksonville, Fla., 1951-64, U.S. Army Office of Chief of Engrs., Washington, 1964-73; constrn. cons., Jacksonville, Fla., 1973—; engr., environ. specialist Fla. Dept. Environ. Regulation, 1974—, now mgr. Punta Gorda br. office and lab. South Fla. dist. Served with USAAF, 1942-46. Registered profl. engr., Vt. Mem. Pi Tau Sigma. Democrat. Methodist. Elk. Home: 1109 Appian Dr Punta Gorda FL 33950

FENDT, PAUL FREDERICK, educator; b. Callicoon, N.Y., July 4, 1933; s. Frederick and Edna (Muir) F.; B.A., Taylor U., 1957; M.Div., Duke U., 1962; M.Ed., U. N.C., 1970, Ph.D., 1976; postgrad. N.C. State U., summer 1978; m. Sept. 21, 1974; children—Frederick Paul, Mary Kathryn, Karl Hamilton, Krista Marie. Tchr. math. and sci. N.Y. State System, Central Valley, 1957-58; ordained to ministry Methodist Ch., 1962; pastor N.C. Conf., United Meth. Ch., Walstonburg and Durham, 1958-62; employment counselor Employment Security Commn. N.C., Fayetteville, 1963-64; asst. personnel dir. Duke U., Durham, 1964-67, tng. dir. employee tng. and devel., 1967-69; asso. head corr. instrn. Extension Div., U. N.C., Chapel Hill, 1969-71, asst. dir. extension for corr. instrn., 1971-75, asst. dir. extension for ind. study, 1975-77, asso. dir. extension for credit and cert. programs, 1977—, clin. asst. prof. edn. Sch. Edn., 1976—, cons. group processes Sch. Nursing, 1969-72, OEO funded project Sch. Pub. Health, 1970-71; cons. Joint Com. on Coll. Transfer Students, Spl. Subcom. on Nontraditional Edn., U. N.C., N.C. State Bd. Edn. and N.C. Assn. Ind. Colls. and Univs., 1978; lectr. in field; conf. participant Motivation and Research Process in Doctoral Candidates, 14th Annual Adult Edn. Research Conf., U. Montreal, 1973; v.p. N.C. Assn. for Emotionally Troubled, 1975—; pres. N.C. Assn. Emotionally Disturbed Children, 1973; dir. Statewide Ind. Study Program for N.C., 1975-77; chmn. Triangle Higher Edn. Consortium, 1976-78; project dir. Outreach to Inmates, N.C., 1972-79, Econo-Coll. for Inmates, 1973-79. Title I grantee, 1973-76; N.C. Com. for Continuing Edn. in the Humanities grantee, 1973-77; Z. Smith Reynolds grantee, 1972-79, Mary Reynolds Babcock grantee, 1972-79, Hillsdale Fund grantee, 1973-76. Mem. N.C. Adult Edn. Assn. (dir. 1974-79, pres. 1978), Nat. Univ. Extension Assn., Adult Edn. Assn. U.S.A. (del. 1977, 78), Durham C. of C., Am. Soc. for Personnel Adminstrn. (dir. 1968-69), Am. Soc. Tng. and Devel., Durham Personnel Assn. (pres. 1966), World Future Soc. Club: Univ. N.C. Faculty. Contbr. articles to profl. jours. Home: Route 1 Box 165A Hillsborough NC 27278 Office: 218 Abernethy Hall 002A Univ of NC Chapel Hill NC 27514

FENN, JIMMY O'NEIL, med. physicist; b. Brunswick, Ga., Nov. 18, 1937; s. Raymond Hume and Mae Elizabeth (Maxwell) F.; B.S., Lincoln Meml. U., 1963; M.S., Emory U., 1967; Ph.D., Ga. Inst. Tech., 1977; children—Daniel S., Nancy Anne, Margaret Elizabeth. Asso. dept. radiology Emory U., Atlanta, 1966-68, asst. prof. radiation therapy, 1973-74, asst. clin. prof. radiation therapy, 1975—; asst. prof., dir. div. basic radiation scis., dept. radiology Med. U. S.C., Charleston, 1968-73, 74—. Recipient Jones Scis. award Lincoln Meml. U., 1963. Mem. Am. Assn. Physicists in Medicine (past pres. Southeastern chpt.), Am. Soc. Therapeutic Radiology, Am. Pub. Health Assn., Sigma Pi Sigma. Presbyterian. Contbr. articles to profl. jours. Home: 924 Cliffwood Dr Mt Pleasant SC 29464 Office: 171 Ashley Ave Charleston SC 29403

FENNELL, MARGARET EVELYN, dietitian; b. Paterson, N.J., Mar. 17, 1936; d. John Carter and Hallie Elizabeth (Wilson) Packard; B.S., Maryville (Tenn.) Coll., 1957; m. Duncan Thomas Fennell, June 4, 1976; children by previous marriage—Lori Lynn Donaldson, Susan Beth Donaldson, Margaret Ann Donaldson. Cafeteria mgr. Duke U., 1958; clin. dietitian Ga. Bapt. Hosp., Atlanta, 1961-63, adminstrv. dietitian, 1965-79; dietitian Ga. Mental Health Inst., Atlanta, 1964; dir. dietetics Ga. Bapt. Med. Center, Atlanta, 1979—. Mem. Am. Dietetic Assn., Ga. Dietetic Assn., Am. Soc. Hosp. Food Service Adminstrs. Methodist. Home: Route 7 Box 58 Griffin GA 30223 Office: 300 Boulevard Dr Atlanta GA 30312

FENSTERMACHER, DAVID LEE, hosp. adminstr.; b. Vicksburg, Miss., Jan. 29, 1944; s. Richard Henry and Kathleen Sarah F.; B.A., U. Miss., 1966, M.B.A., 1971; M.H.A., Ga. State U., 1973; m. Alexandra Elizabeth Ross, June 18, 1966; children—David, Kathleen, Thomas. Adminstrv. asst. Univ. Hosp., Augusta, Ga., 1973-74, asst. adminstr., 1975-78, asso. adminstr., 1978—. Mem. exec. bd. Ga.-Carolina council Boy Scouts Am. Served with M.S.C., AUS, 1966-69. Decorated Air Medal, Purple Heart. Mem. Am. Coll. Hosp. Adminstrs., Am. Hosp. Assn., Ga. Hosp. Assn. Episcopalian. Home: 3108 Sussex Rd Augusta GA 30909 Office: 1350 Walton Way Augusta GA 30902

FENTON, J. JOSEPH, constrn. and real estate co. exec.; b. Duluth, Minn., Jan. 16, 1940; s. Charles and Dorothy (Doolittle) F.; B.A., Cornell U., 1961; m. Diane Elizabeth Bear, July 10, 1966; children—Rham David, Lila Amma, Jonathan Krishna. Asst. gen. mgr. Roger Sherman Rigging Co., Bloomfield, Conn., 1965-68; pres. Aquarian Age Real Estate, Virginia Beach, Va., 1971—; pres. Aquarian Age Yoga Center, 1970—, Aquarian Age Center, 1971—, Sunrise Constrn. Co., 1978—. Served to lt. USNR, 1962-65. Mem. Nat., Va., Chesapeake bds. realtors, Tidewater Assn. Homebuilders, Internat. Fedn. Real Estate Brokers, Nat. Inst. Real Estate Brokers. Club: Harbor (Norfolk, Va.). Home: 625 Timberland Trail Virginia Beach VA 23452 Office: PO Box 1566 Chesapeake VA 23320

FENTRESS, MALCOLM O'NEIL, printing co. exec.; b. Short Creek, Ky., Dec. 21, 1932; s. Elmer and Anna Katherine (Robinson) F.; grad. Leitchfield Ind. Sch. Dist.; m. Marian Sarver Smith, Oct. 11, 1953; children—Kathy, Kimberly, Kelly. Office mgr. Ernest Walker Press, Louisville, 1956-68, v.p., 1968—. Served with USAF, 1952-55. Mem. Printing Industry Assn. South, Jefferson County Farm Bur. Mem. Ch. of Christ (deacon 1973—). Clubs: Rotary (Louisville), Hon. Order Ky. Cols., U.S. CB Radio Assn. Home: 1045 Runell Rd Louisville KY 40214 Office: 841 S 6th St Louisville KY 40203

FEREBEE, JOHN SPENCER, JR., mgmt. cons.; b. Washington, Mar. 8, 1947; s. John Spencer and Louise (Barnes) F.; B.S.I.E., Lehigh U., 1969; M.B.A., Duke U., 1972; m. Nancy Stein, Oct. 11, 1969; 1 son, John Spencer III. Indsl. engr. RCA Corp., Palm Beach Gardens, Fla., 1969-70; sr. cons./mgr. Price Waterhouse & Co., Washington, 1972-77; asst. adminstr. Social and Rehab. Service, HEW, Washington, 1976-77; sr. mgr. Price Waterhouse & Co., Washington, 1978—. Mem. Greater Washington Bd. Trade, 1974—. Mem. Am. Inst. Indsl. Engrs., Am. Mgmt. Assn., Am. Prodn. and Inventory Control Soc., Hosp. Fin. Mgmt. Assn., Duke U. Grad. Sch. Bus. Adminstrn. Alumni Assn., 1972—. Club: Congressional Country (Bethesda, Md.). Home: 125 Eagles Mere Great Falls VA 22066 Office: 1801 K St NW Washington DC 20006

FERGUS-O'BRIEN, ADELE LOUISA, air force officer; b. Downey, Calif., Apr. 9, 1954; d. James Edward and Norma Adele Fergus; B.S., U. So. Calif., 1976; M.A., Webster Coll., 1978; m. George J. O'Brien, Aug. 4, 1979. Commd. 2d lt. U.S. Air Force, 1976, advanced through grades to capt., 1980; materiel control officer for dep. comdr. for maintenance complex Pope AFB, N.C., 1977—. Mem. Air Force Assn., Alpha Epsilon Phi. Republican. Presbyterian. Office: 317 TAG/MAMM Pope AFB NC 28308

FERGUSON, ALVIN LEE, office equipment co. exec.; b. Greenville, S.C., Sept. 4, 1923; s. Ross Alvin and Mary Lou (Lee) F.; B.S., U. N.C., 1950; m. Dorothy Christine Bailey, Aug. 14, 1953; children—Janine Lee, Mary Kathleen, Alvin Lee, Bari Christine, Ross Damon. Sales rep. Nat. Cash Register, Greenville, S.C., 1950, Orlando, Fla., 1951-53, Daytona Beach, Fla., 1954-63, acctg. machine sales mgr., Asheville, N.C., 1964-68, St. Petersburg, Fla., 1969, fin. mgr., Fort Lauderdale, Fla., 1970, ter. mgr., Augusta, Ga., 1971; pres. Ferguson Office Supply, Inc., Augusta, Ga., 1971—; v.p. Ocala Office Products, Inc., 1979—. Served with USAAF, 1943-45. Mem. Ga. Office Products Assn. (dir. 1979-80). Democrat. Presbyterian. Club: Augusta Country. Home: 813 Dogwood Ln Augusta GA 30909

Office: Ferguson Office Supply Inc 3125 Washington Rd Augusta GA 30907

FERGUSON, GEORGE ROBERT, lawyer; b. Learned, Miss., Aug. 13, 1933; s. George R. and Eugenia (Williams) F.; B.S., Miss. State U., 1955; LL.B., Jackson Sch. Law, 1965; m. Martha Gillespie, July 5, 1959; children—Martha Elizabeth, George Robert, Cade Drew. Admitted to Miss. bar, 1965; sales rep. Procter & Gamble Co., 1958-60; dir. advt., pub. relations Standard Life Ins. Co., 1960-64; v.p. advt., pub. relations L. E. Davis & Assos., 1964-65; pvt. practice law, Raymond, Miss., 1965—; mem. Miss. Ho. of Reps., 1968—, chmn. public utilities com.; owner, pub. Miss. Valley Stockman-Farmer mag., 1965-67. Mem. Miss. Classification Commn., 1970-73; chmn. Hinds County Christmas Seal campaign, 1971, 80. Bd. dirs. Hinds County Lung Assn., Jackson, Miss., 1969—. Served with AUS, 1956-58. Named Among Outstanding Young Men of Am., Nat. Jr. C. of C., 1969. Mem. Am., Miss., Hinds County bar assns. Presbyterian (elder 1963—). Lion (pres. 1969-70, zone chmn. 1970-71), Mason (Shriner). Home: PO Drawer 89 237 Oak St Raymond MS 39154 Office: 114 Main St Raymond MS 39154

FERGUSON, HAROLD LAVERNE, JR., lawyer; b. Cleveland, Miss., Dec. 3, 1938; s. Harold Laverne and Allene Thompson (Burford) F.; B.P.A., U. Miss., 1960; J.D., Samford U., Birmingham, Ala., 1973; m. Jamie Frances Fleming, Nov. 20, 1965; children—Harold Laverne, III, Samuel Christopher, Julie Allene. With Social Security Adminstrn., 1960-68, asst. dist. mgr., Greenville, Miss., 1967-68; engaged in retail grocery bus., Senatobia, Miss., 1968-70; admitted to Ala. bar, 1973, since practiced in Birmingham; partner firm Spain, Gillon, Riley, Tate & Etheredge, 1973-79; mem. firm Dominick, Fletcher, Yeilding, Acker, Wood & Lloyd, P.A., 1979—. Mem. Am., Ala., Birmingham bar assns. Republican. Baptist. Home: 440 Hillwood Dr Birmingham AL 35209 Office: 1700 John A Hand Bldg Birmingham AL 35203

FERGUSON, JAMES RUFUS, mech. engr., diversified co. exec.; b. Charlotte, N.C., May 17, 1943; s. Raymond S. and Sue Ramsey (Johnston) F.; B.S. in Mech. Engring., N.C. State U., 1966; M.B.A., U. N.C., 1968; m. Brenda Ann Clanton, Aug. 5, 1967; children—James Ross. Pres., chmn. bd. Ferguson Gear Co., Gastonia, N.C., 1968-70; pres. Basinere Metals, Fry Canyon, Utah, 1969-72; gen. mgr. Apparatus div. Superior Continental Corp., Keller, Tex., 1969-75; v.p., dir. FRK Industries, Shelby, N.C., 1970-73; pres. Liledoun Enterprises, Taylorsville, N.C., 1968—; pres. Liledoun Leasing, Taylorsville, 1978—; pres., chmn., dir. Systems Equipment Products Co., Hickory, N.C., 1975—; cons. Missouri Research Labs., St. Charles, Mo., 1979—. Vice pres. Alexander County (N.C.) Rescue Squad, 1968-72; mem. 6th N.C. Inf., Re-activated Civil War Regiment, 1961-70. Mem. ASME, Nat. Assn. Accountants, Aircraft Owners and Pilots Assn., Southwest Exec. Club, Petroleum Club. Presbyterian. Club: Colonial Country. Home: Route 6 PO Box 60 Taylorsville NC 28681

FERGUSON, JEFFREY WILLIAM, packaging co. exec.; b. Butler, Pa., Mar. 26, 1948; s. Harold William and Jean Beverly (Blake) F.; B.A., Lafayette Coll., 1970; M.A., U. Akron, 1973; M.B.A., U. Pa., 1977; m. Janet Arthur, Aug. 19, 1972; children—Andrew, Matthew, David. Asst. dir. admissions U. Akron (Ohio), 1971-74; dir. student services Wharton Sch., U. Pa., Phila., 1975-77; project analyst, corporate planning staff Owens-Ill., Inc., Toledo, 1977-78, adminstrv. mgr., Atlanta Plastics Plant, 1978—. Vice pres. Carlisle Civic Assn., Stone Mountain, Ga., 1979-80. Served to 1st lt. USAR, 1970-78. Mem. Am. Mgmt. Assn., Class rep. Wharton Grad. Alumni Assn. Republican. Presbyterian. Office: 3490 Hamilton Blvd SW Atlanta GA 30354

FERGUSON, JERE CLAUDE, mfg. co. exec.; b. San Francisco, June 27, 1947; s. Andrew Claude and Barbara Jeanne (McNeal) F.; B.A., R.I. Coll., 1970; M.B.A., U. Dayton, 1976; m. Nancy Beth Duckworth, June 20, 1970; children—Jere Claude, Tobi William, Elizabeth Anne. With Nat. Can Corp., Ft. Worth, 1972-73, sales office mgr., 1973—. Deacon, Tate Springs Bapt. Ch., 1978, Sunday sch. dir., 1979. Served to lt. comdr. USN, 1970-72. Mem. Naval Res. Assn. Republican. Baptist. Club: Lions. Home: 2117 Valleydale Dr Arlington TX 76013 Office: 8800 S Freeway Fort Worth TX 76104

FERGUSON, ROBERT BENJAMIN, engring. cons.; b. New Orleans, Mar. 1, 1936; s. Jackson Benjamin and Mary Louise (Cox) F.; B.S., U. Tex., 1960; postgrad. Calif. Inst. Tech., 1968; m. Carolyn Maurine Ramsey, June 6, 1959; children—Pamela Maurine, Roy Benjamin. Drilling and prodn. engr. Phillips Petroleum Co., Alvin, Tex., 1960-64; sr. prodn. engr. Signal Oil & Gas Co., Huntington Beach, Calif., 1964-66, mgr. Huntington Beach office, 1966-68, corporate mgr. computing dept., Los Angeles, 1968-70; engring. cons., Ft. Worth, 1971, Calgary, Can., 1972, P.R., 1974-75, Jakarta, Indonesia, 1976, Houston, 1976; computer systems cons. Mobil Oil Co., 1976-80; pres. PIRT Inc., 1979—. Registered profl. engr., Tex. Mem. Am. Petroleum Inst., Am. Inst. Mining, Metall. and Petroleum Engrs., Nat. Assn. Corrosion Engrs., Soc. Petroleum Engrs., Tex. Soc. Profl. Engrs. Club: Exchange (social chmn. 1967, chmn. Boy of Yr. award com. Huntington Beach, Calif.) Patentee in field. Home: 14618 Kellywood St Houston TX 77079

FERGUSON, TERRY LYNN, real estate broker; b. Waynesville, N.C., Mar. 15, 1946; s. William M. and Catherine (Muse) F.; student pub. schs., Waynesville, N.C.; student Realtors Inst., Chapel Hill, N.C.: grad. Real Estate Edn., Inc., 1974; m. Sharon Snyder, 1966; children—Brian Eric, India Lynne, William Aaron. With Deland (Fla.) Dodge, 1966-69; partner Plaza Mobile Homes, Waynesville, 1969-74; salesman Services Galore Real Estate, Waynesville, 1974-75, Century 21 Blue Ridge Realty, Waynesville, 1975; owner Blue Ridge Cottages, Waynesville, 1975-76. Lic. real estate broker, N.C., 1974; recipient Diamond award, Chrysler Corp., 1968; Century 21 AIM award, 1979. Mem. Nat. Assn. Realtors, Waynesville Jr. C. of C. (v.p. 1975), Haywood County C. of C. Home: 603 Brunswick Dr Waynesville NC 28786 Office: 306 Walnut St Waynesville NC 28786

FERGUSON, THOMAS CAMPBELL, lawyer; b. Roswell, N.M., Sept. 3, 1906; s. William Marion and Martha Ann (Harvey) F.; grad. high sch.; m. Vera Elizabeth Foster, Apr. 20, 1930. Owner-editor Liberty Hill Index, 1921-23, Blanco Courier, 1923-24; pub. Burnet (Tex.) Bull., 1924-26; floor foreman, advt. mgr. Superior (Ariz.) Sun, 1926-27; dep. dist. clk. Burnet County, 1927-28; admitted to Tex. bar, 1929, U.S. Supreme Ct., 5th Circuit Ct. of Appeals, U.S. Dist. Ct.; practiced in Burnet, 1929—; city atty., Burnet, 1932-36, Marble Falls, Tex., 1930-42, 63-66; spl. counsel County of Burnet, 1932-38; atty. Home Owners Loan Corp.; atty. City of Johnson City, 1963-68. County judge Burnet County, 1945-47; dist. judge 33d Jud. Dist. Tex., 1947-60, ret.; now state jud. officer; chmn. State Bd. Ins., 1961-62. Mem. Burnet County Sch. Bd., 1934-41; chmn. Def. Bond sales Burnet County, 1941-42; county officer U.S.O., 1940-42; county chmn. ARC, 1946-47; adult scouter Boy Scout program, 1940-80. Chmn. Burnet County Democratic Com., 1928-30; mem. Tex. Ho. of Reps., 1931-32; mem. State Dem. Exec. Com. from 10th Dist., 1933-34; mayor, Burnet, 1939-43. Bd. dirs. Lower Colorado River Authority, 1935-37, 45, 65-71; chmn. adv. bd. to registrants SSS for Burnet County, 1939-47. Served with AUS, 1942-45. Mem. State Bar Tex., Hill Country Bar Assn., Burnet County Bar Assn., Tex. Bar Found., Nat. Hist. Assn., Tex. State Hist. Soc., Tex. Hist. Found., Supreme Ct. Hist. Soc., Burnet County Hist. Commn., Sons of Republic of Tex., Sons of Confederacy, Am. Legion, 40 and 8, various geneal. and hist. assns. and family fellowships. Mem. Christian Ch. Club: Masons. Home: 208 E Post Oak St Burnet TX 78611 Office: PO Box 38 Burnet TX 78611

FERGUSON, THOMAS MORGAN, avian physiologist; b. Burnet, Tex., Nov. 8, 1915; s. Thomas Anthony and Ruth Pauline (Morgan) F.; B.A. in Chemistry, Southwestern U., Georgetown, Tex., 1936; M.S. in Biology, Tex. A&M U., 1946, Ph.D. in Zoology, 1954; m. Grace Evelyn Barnett, Aug. 28, 1938; children—Thomas M., John F., Letitia R., Leonard P. Tchr., prin. A&M Consol. High Sch., College Station, Tex., 1936-41; high sch. biology tchr., Corpus Christi, Tex., 1941-42; civilian instr. AAFTTC, Chanute Field, Ill. and Lincoln, Nebr., 1942-43; instr., then asst. prof. biology Tex. A&M U., 1946-52, asso. prof. poultry sci., 1955-65, prof., 1965—; biochemist Interdeptl. Com. on Nutrition for Nat. Def. nutrition survey team, Libya, 1957, Ethiopia, 1958, Uruguay, 1962. Active Little League, 1951-61, Boy Scouts, 1954-65; mem. adminstrv. bd. A&M United Methodist Ch., 1978-79. Served in USNR, 1943-46. USPHS postdoctoral research fellow Nat. Cancer Inst., 1953-55. Mem. Poultry Sci. Assn., Am. Inst. Nutrition, Soc. Exptl. Biology and Medicine, AAAS, Fedn. Am. Socs. Exptl. Biology, Sigma Xi, Phi Kappa Phi, Gamma Sigma Delta. Contbr. articles to sci. jours. Home: 4217 Nagle St Bryan TX 77801 Office: Tex A&M U College Station TX 77843

FERLAND, ROSS EDWARD, mech. engr., educator; b. St. Albans, Vt., July 13, 1937; s. Clement R. and Ramona G. (Ginett) F.; B.S. in Mech. Engring., Ariz. State U., 1967, M.S., 1968; Ph.D. in Mech. Engring., U. Houston, 1972; student Officer's Tng. Sch., Tex., 1966. Served as enlisted man USAF, 1955-66: commd. 2d lt. USAF, 1966, advanced through grades to capt., 1969; aerospace engr. Manned Spacecraft Center, NASA, Houston, 1968-71; value engring. group leader Hill AFB, Utah, 1972-74, nuclear hardness engr., ret., 1976; dir. aviation Weber State Coll., Ogden, Utah, 1972-77, mem. faculty, 1972-79, asso. prof. Sch. Tech., 1976-79; propr., mgr. Greenfield Leasing Services (Utah), 1978-79; dean Sch. Engring. Tech., U. Ark., Little Rock, 1979—. Recipient NASA Achievement award, 1969; registered profl. engr., Tex. Mem. Nat. Soc. Profl. Engrs., Am. Astronautical Soc., AAAS, Am. Soc. Engring. Edn., Aircraft Owners and Pilots Assn., Exptl. Aircraft Assn. Ogden C. of C., Sigma Xi. Home: Route 2 No 103 North Little Rock AR 72118 Office: 33d and University Ave Little Rock AR 72204

FERLITA, ERNEST CHARLES, educator; b. Tampa, Fla., Dec. 1, 1927; s. Giuseppe Rosario and Vincenta Rose (Ficarrotta) F.; B.S., Spring Hill Coll., 1950; S.T.L., St. Louis U., 1964; D.F.A., Yale, 1969. Joined Soc. Jesus; ordained Roman Catholic priest, 1962; asso. prof. drama and religious studies Loyola U., New Orleans, 1969—, chmn. dept. drama and speech, 1970—, chmn. bd. dirs., 1972-75. Dir. Jesuit Inst. Arts, 1973-75. Served with AUS, 1945-46. Author: The Theatre of Pilgrimage, 1971; (play) Black Medea, 1977; The Way of the River, 1977; co-author: Film Odyssey, 1976; The Parables of Lina Wertmüller, 1977. Home: 1575 Calhoun St New Orleans LA 70118

FERM, CARL AXEL, elec. engring. co. exec.; b. Kansas City, Mo., July 12, 1928; s. Axel Wallace and Jessie Elizabeth (Lowell) F.; student U. Kans.; grad. Harvard Advanced Mgmt. Program, 1975; m. Barbara Marie Reagan, June 24, 1950; children—Brita Ferm Schwenk, Cynthia Ferm Murrell, David A., Kersten Ferm Carney. Various positions elec. contractors Kansas City, 1947-60; elec. estimator, elec. engr., v.p., dir., mgr. SE div. Cloverland Contracting Co., Crystal Falls, Mich., 1960-65; elec. engr., mgr. instrument dept., constrn. mgr., v.p. process plant sales, v.p., mgr. SW div. Blount Bros. Corp., Montgomery, Ala., 1965—; pres. Blount Engring. div. Blount Internat., Ltd. Served with AC, USN, 1945-46.

FERMAN, RAY, JR., designer; b. Northwebster, Ind., July 8, 1925; s. Ray Levi and Ruth Emily (Pontious) F.; student Miss. State Coll., 1943, Okla. State U. Tech. Inst., 1976; m. Anita Faye Brewer, June 3, 1946; children—Roger B., Richard L., Ray D., Renita F. Commd. 2d lt. USAAF, 1945, advanced through grades to maj. USAF, 1963; served with Berlin Airlift, 1946-49; assigned March AFB, Calif., 1950, Korea, 1951-52, Langley AFB, Va., 1953-55, Chaumont, France, 1956-59, Lowry AFB, Denver, 1960-63; ret.; electro-mech. designer Collins Radio Co., Dallas, 1966-72; program and site mgr. div. Rockwell Internat. Collins Internat. Service Co., Oklahoma City, 1973-78; designer Rockwell Internat., Dallas, 1979—. Decorated D.F.C., Air medal with oak leaf cluster. Mem. Am. Inst. Aeros., Astronautics, Soc. Mfg. Engrs. (sr. mem.), Ret. Officers Assn. Home: 411 W Middleton St Sherman TX 75090 Office: Rockwell Internat 1110 Commerce Richardson TX 75081

FERNANDEZ, ERIC, physician; b. Havana, Cuba, Sept. 19, 1944; s. A.C. and Dolores (Navarro) F.; B.S., U. Md., 1965; M.D., U. Salamanca (Spain), 1972; m. Cheryl Ann Burr, Sept. 5, 1970; children—Katrina Lorenne, Candice Ann, Lorene Carin. Vice pres. med. staff Palm Spring Gen. Hosp., Hialeah, Fla., 1978—; clin. asst. prof. U. Miami Med. Sch., 1978—. Mem. Nat. Republican Congl. Com., 1978—. Mem. A.C.P., Am. Soc. Internal Medicine, Fla. Med. Assn., Dade County Med. Assn., Am. Security Council Edn. Found., Nat. Jogging Assn., N. Am. Vegetarian Soc., Ague. Mem. editorial research bd. Postgrad. Med. Jour. Office: 1550 W 84th St Suite 27 Hialeah FL 33014

FERNANDEZ, EVERETT ANTHONY, textile co. exec.; b. Paia, Hawaii, May 5, 1936; s. Abel Perreria and Florence (Costa) F.; student parochial schs., Wailuku, Hawaii, 1942-54; m. Margarete Weber, Sept. 28, 1958; children—Glenn, Everett, Florence, Wayne. Enlisted man U.S. Army, 1954-74; with Transco Textile's Industries, Augusta, Ga., 1974—, asst. supt. printing dept., 1979—; instr. U.S. Army Signal Sch., Ft. Monmouth, N.J., 1966-68. Decorated Army Commendation medal with 2 oak leaf clusters, Bronze Star. Mem. Internat. Mgmt. Council. Roman Catholic. Home: 3106 Scenic Dr Augusta GA 30909 Office: PO Drawer 10026 Augusta GA 30903

FERNANDEZ, JAMES EVERETT, food co. exec.; b. Tampa, Fla., Feb. 19, 1937; s. James Alphonso and Frances Marie F.; B.S., U. Tampa, 1972; m. Sylvia Diana Giglio, Aug. 31, 1957; children—Diana, Shirley, Karen, Jimmy, David, Damon. Mgr., Shoe Fair, 1959-61; br. mgr. Breakstone Sugar Creek Foods, Tampa, 1961-75; pres. Miracle Food Service Distbrs., Tampa, 1975-76; exec. v.p. Betty Ann Foods, Clearwater, Fla., 1976—. Served with USMC, 1956-59. Democrat. Roman Catholic. Home: 8319 Millwood Dr Tampa FL 33615 Office: 1770 Calumet St Clearwater FL 33518

FERNANDEZ, RICARDO JOSE, architect; b. Holguin, Cuba, Mar. 25, 1948; s. Recaredo and Etelvina (Benitez) F.; came to U.S., 1961, naturalized, 1972; B. Arch. with high honors, U. Fla., 1972; m. Mirtha M. Latour, Aug. 22, 1970; children—Ricardo Jose, Alejandro J. Archtl. intern firm Ferendino, Grafton, Spillis, Candela, Coral Gables, Fla., 1971; hotel project architect Gulf & Western Co., Dominican Republic, also asso. planner Costa Sur Resort, 1972-75; pvt. archtl. practice, Fla., Dominican Republic, Venezuela and P.R., 1975—. Mem. president's council U. Fla., 1976-77, company sponsor archtl. scholarship, 1975—. Recipient award AIA-AIA Found., 1972. Mem. AIA, Constrn. Specification Inst., Nat. Fire Protection Assn., ASTM, Am. C. of C. Santo Domingo, Greater Miami C. of C., Latin Am. Jaycees (dir.). Roman Catholic. Introduced uniform system constrn. to Dominican Republic. Author articles. Home: 1008 SW 45th Ave Coral Gables FL 33134 Office: 61 Merrick Way Coral Gables FL 33134 also 2 Jose Contreras #28 PO Box 1999 Santo Domingo Dominican Republic

FERNANDEZ, ROBERT FRANK, county ofcl.; b. Tampa, Fla., June 9, 1949; s. Frank and Rose Marie (Valenti) F.; B.S. in Bus. Adminstrn., U. Fla., 197_; postgrad. U. South Fla., 1974-75; m. Candice Marie Decker, Oct. 30, 1976. Counselor, Hillsborough County, Fla., 1971, program developer, community devel. dir., 1974-77; manpower planner City of Tampa, Fla., 1972-74; grant services chief Manatee County, Fla., Bradenton, 1977-78, asst. county adminstr., 1978—; exec. bd. Fla. Community Devel. Assn., 1976-79. Mem. Internat. City Mgmt. Assn., Fla. City and County Mgmt. Assn., State Assn. County Commrs., Nat. Assn. Counties (council intergovtl. coordinator). Democrat. Roman Catholic. Home: 5304 18th Ave W Bradenton FL 33505 Office: PO Box 1000 Bradenton FL 33506

FERNANDEZ-CAROL, ADOLFO ALBERTO, gastroenterologist; b. Havana, Feb. 8, 1932; came to U.S., 1957, naturalized, 1968; s. Adolfo A. and Carmen Dolores (Carol) Fernandez; M.D., U. Havana, 1957; m. Cristina C. Garcia, Jan. 20, 1962; children—Alvaro O., Cristina, Cecilia, Paul. Intern, resident in internal medicine Cook County Hosp., Chgo., 1957-62; fellow in gastroenterology U. Pa., Phila., 1959-60; clin. instr. medicine U. Ill., Chgo., 1962-71; practice medicine specializing in gastroenterology, Miami, Fla., 1971—; chief of medicine Am. Hosp., Miami, 1975-77; sr. attending staff Mercy Hosp., Am. Hosp. Diplomate Am. Bd. Internal Medicine. Fellow Am. Coll. Gastroenterologists; mem. A.C.P., Dade County Med. Assn., Bockus Internat. Assn. Gastroenterology, Am. Soc. Gastrointestinal Endoscopy. Roman Catholic. Club: Big Five (Miami). Home: 301 Island Dr Key Biscayne FL 33149 Office: 3661 S Miami Ave Miami FL 33133

FERNHOFF, PAUL MARTIN, physician; b. Jersey City, N.J., Jan. 16, 1946; s. Stanley Herbert and Roslyn (Sussman) F.; A.B., Rutgers U., 1967; M.D., Jefferson Med. Sch., 1971; m. Deborah Finkelstein, Mar. 23, 1969; 1 dau., Shana Miriam. Intern, Children's Hosp. of Phila., U. Pa., 1971-72, resident, 1972-74; pediatrician Center for Disease Control, USPHS, Atlanta, 1974-76; asst. prof. pediatrics Emory U. Div. Med. Genetics, Dept. Pediatrics, 1976—; pediatric cons. dept. disability ins. HEW. USPHS fellow, 1978. Fellow Am. Acad. Pediatrics; mem. Am. Soc. Human Genetics, AAAS, Soc. Inborn Errors of Metabolism, Atlanta Genetics Soc., Phi Beta Kappa, Alpha Omega Alpha, Sigma Xi. Home: 1591 Knob Hill Dr Atlanta GA 30329 Office: Drawer AM Emory U Sch Medicine Atlanta GA 30322

FERRARI, HERBERT ALFRED, anesthesiologist; b. Buenos Aires, Dec. 3, 1930; s. Alfredo Luis and Leontina (Azzati) F.; came to U.S., 1964, naturalized, 1969; B.S. Coll. Nacional Mariano Moreno, 1948; M.D., U. Buenos Aires, 1957; m. Noemi Maria Owen, Dec. 5, 1956; children—Gloria Noemi, Vivian Mabel, Victor Steven. Intern Hosp. Nacional Neuropsiquiatrico, Buenos Aires, 1954-55; resident in anesthesiology Hosp. Rawson, Buenos Aires, 1955-56, Duke Hosp., 1964-66; anesthesiologist Hosp. J.A. Fernandez, Buenos Aires, 1956-57; chief dept. anesthesiology Inst. Angel H. Roffo, U. Buenos Aires Hosp., 1957-64; asst. prof., then asso. anesthesiology Duke Med. Center, 1966-69; cons. Watts Hosp., Durham, N.C., 1967-69; clin. asso. prof. surgery (anesthesiology), then clin. prof. anesthesiology N.J. Coll. Medicine and Dentistry, Newark, 1969-72; dir. dept. anesthesiology Jersey City Med. Center, 1969-72; cons. Berthold S. Pollack Hosp. Chest Diseases, Jersey City, 1969-72; clin. prof. anesthesiology Med. Sch., U. N.C., Chapel Hill, 1972—; chmn. dept. anesthesiology Charlotte (N.C.) Meml. Hosp., 1972—. Bd. dirs. Hudson County Heart Assn., 1970; med. adv. com. Tb Respiratory Disease Assn. Central N.J., 1970; ruling elder Covenant Presbyterian Ch. Diplomate Am. Bd. Anesthesiology. Mem. Assn. Medica Argentina, Assn. Argentina de Anestesiologia, AMA, N.C. Soc. Anesthesiologists (pres. 1976-77), Internat. Anesthesia Research Soc., Am., So. med. assns., AAUP, AAAS, N.C. Med. Soc. (chmn. anesthesia sect. 1977-78), Assn. Anesthetists Gt. Britain and Ireland. Contbr. articles to med. jours. Home: 3121 Sharon Rd Charlotte NC 28211 Office: Charlotte Meml Hosp Charlotte NC 28234

FERRARO, MICHAEL ANTHONY, recreation cons.; b. Niagara Falls, N.Y., Aug. 31, 1955; s. Charles John and Elvera Eva (Denitto) F.; B.S., Fla. State U., 1977. Mgmt. trainee Ramada Inn, Niagara Falls, 1973, Sonesta Hotels, Key Biscayne, Fla. and Amsterdam, Holland, 1975-77; cons. Harris, Kerr, Forster & Co., Atlanta, 1977—; guest lectr. dept. hotel, restaurant and travel adminstrn. Ga. State U., 1977—. E.M. Statler Found. scholar, 1973-77, Am. Hotel Found. merit scholar, 1976-77; Nat. Inst. for Food Service Industry Golden Plate award, 1977. Mem. Nat. Restaurant Assn., Ga. Hospitality and Travel Assn., Soc. Hosts Alumni Assn., Common Cause, Gold Key Soc. Home: Apt 210 125 Copeland Rd Atlanta GA 30342 Office: Harris Kerr Forster & Co 5775-B Glenridge Dr NE Atlanta GA 30328

FERREE, WILLIAM ISAAC, JR., organic research chemist; b. Salem, Ind., Nov. 7, 1942; s. William Isaac and Martha Eloise (Lloyd) F.; B.A., U. South Fla., 1964; Ph.D., Purdue U., 1971. Postdoctoral research fellow Trinity U., San Antonio, 1971-73, U. Fla., Gainesville, 1973-74; analytical organic chemist Tex. Instruments Inc., Dallas, 1974-75; research chemist Liquid Paper br. Gillette Corp., Dallas, 1975-79; research mgr., 1979—. Mem. Am. Chem. Soc. Republican. Contbr. articles to profl. jours. Home: 8769 Southwestern Blvd 2147 Dallas TX 75206 Office: 9130 Markville Dr PO Box 225909 Dallas TX 75265

FERRELL, NORMA ANN, nurse; b. Cleve., Jan. 17, 1938; d. Fred Ira and Thelma Susan (Samson) Ely; L.P.N., Florence (S.C.) Vocat. Sch., 1969; R.N., Florence Darlington Tech. Coll., 1977; m. John Henry Ferrell, June 2, 1955; children—John H., William Eugene, Barbara Ronalyn, Brenda Lee. Licensed practical nurse coronary care unit McLeod Meml. Hosp., 1969-76; licensed practical nurse Bruce Hosp., Florence, 1976-77, charge nurse CCU, 1978—; charge nurse Coleman Aimar Hosp., Darlington, S.C., 1977. Mem. Am., S.C., Pee Dee nurses assns., Critical Care Nurses Assn., Continuing Edn. in S.C. Democrat. Baptist. Home: PO Box 1132 Florence SC 29503

FERRERO, JAMES JOHN, psychiatrist; b. San Antonio, Sept. 15, 1927; s. Martin P. and Lavada (Herring) F.; B.S. in Chemistry, U. Tex. at Austin, 1949; M. D., U. Tex. at Galveston, 1953; m. Betty Jean Gideon, Sept. 4, 1949; children—David, Lane, Ellen, Martha. Intern, Bapt. Meml. Hosp., San Antonio, 1953-54; resident Austin State Hosp., 1966-69; gen. practice medicine, San Antonio, 1954-66; dir. clin. programs Tex. Dept. Mental Health Mental Retardation, 1969-70; med. dir. Austin-Travis County Mental Health Mental Retardation Center, 1970-72; community psychiatrist Amarillo (Tex.) Hosp., 1972-74; psychiatrist Tex. Research Inst. Mental Scis., Houston, 1975—; pvt. practice psychiatry, Houston, 1976—; clin. asst. prof. psychiatry Baylor Coll. Medicine. Bd. dirs. Spring Shadows,

1975—; pres. PTA North Brook High Sch., 1977-78; elder Memorial Dr. Presbyterian Ch., Houston, 1976—. Served with USN, 1945-47. Mem. Tex. Med. Assn., AMA, Harris County Med. Soc., Tex., Am. psychiat. socs., Harris County Pschiat. Soc., Central Neuropsychiat. Assn. Republican. Home: 9810 Emnora St Houston TX 77080 Office: 8945 Long Point 107 Houston TX 77055

FERRIER, RICHARD BROOKS, artist, educator; b. Ft. Worth, Mar. 29, 1944; s. Samuel Foster and Opal (Brooks) F.; B.Arch., Tex. Tech. U., 1968; M.A. in Art, U. Dallas, 1972; 1 son by previous marriage, Sean Brooks. Illustrator for Lubbock (Tex.) Planning Dept., 1962-63; designer McMurty and Craig, architects, Lubbock, 1963-65; cons. in design and communication to various archtl. and engring. firms in U.S., Canada, and Great Britain, 1966—; designer Ralph Kelman & Assos., Dallas, 1969-70; illustrator constrn. documents George and George, architects, Dallas 1968-69; cons. in architecture and graphic design, Dallas, 1968—; asso. prof. architecture U. Tex., Arlington, 1968—, co-dir. Student Film Festival, 1974; guest lectr. on film in archtl. edn. U. Tex., Austin, 1977; major works include: Seagraves (Tex.) High Sch., 1967, First Bapt. Ch. Chapel, Crosbyton, Tex., 1964, Lost Creek Houses, Ft. Worth, 1979, also numerous residential bldgs.; one-man shows of paintings and drawings include: Gallery A, Taos, N.Mex., 1968, 77, Hall's Gallery, Lubbock, 1968, 69, 72, 73, 76; group shows include: Tex. Tech. Art Mus., 1968, W. Tex. Art Assn., 1972, Ft. Worth Art Mus., 1972, Dallas Mus. Fine Art, 1972, 73, U. Dallas Art Gallery, 1972, Nat. Coll. Art Show, 1972, Nat. Slide Collection-Am. Contemporary Artist, 1974-75; represented in permanent collections: Tex. Tech. U., U. Dallas, Arlington (Tex.) Pub. Library. Recipient Grumbacher award for Contbn. to the Arts, 1971, Film Instruction award Info. Film Producers Am., 1973; 10 awards for archtl. drawings Dallas AIA, 1980. Mem. AAUP, Cousteau Soc., ACLU. Producer ednl. films including Back to the Place (Va. Film award, Christchurch Internat. Film Festival award); composer of song Touch Me Back, 1976. Home: 1628 Connally Terr Arlington TX 76010 Office: U Tex Sch Architecture Arlington TX 76019

FERRIS, JOHN ACKEL, oil properties broker; b. Austin, Tex., Sept. 14, 1900; s. S.A. and Sophia (Shipley) F.; grad. Kemper Mil. Sch., 1920; m. Frances White, June 5, 1927; children—John Ackel, Frances Jeanne Ferris McCutchon. Partner S. Ferris Sons, Austin, 1924-36, John A. Ferris Men's Wear, Corpus Christi, Tex., 1937-52; oil and gas lease broker, Corpus Christi, 1953—; pres. Oil Properties, Houston, 1966—. Mem. Gulf Coast council Boy Scouts Am., 1941-66, pres., 1962-63, recipient Silver Beaver; bd. dirs. Nueces County chpt. ARC Mem. draft bd. Corpus Christi; mem. City Council Corpus Christi, 1946-49. Mem. Houston, Am. assns. petroleum landmen, Am. Security Council (adv. bd.; founder-mem. Center for Internat. Security Studies), Corpus Christi C. of C. (dir.). Republican. Roman Catholic. Clubs: Rotary (pres. 1945-46), Elks. Home and office: 2929 Buffalo Speedway Apt 512 Houston TX 77098

FERRIS, NORMAN BERNARD, historian; b. Richmond, Va., Nov. 29, 1931; s. Paul Whyte and Elizabeth (Gilette) F.; A.A., Lamar Coll., 1951; B.A., George Washington U., 1953; LL.B., Blackstone Sch. Law, 1956; M.A., Emory U., 1959, Ph.D., 1962; m. Kathleen Anne Richard, Feb. 21, 1961; children—Allison, Cheryl, Adrienne, Kennedy, Julie. Instr. history Emory U., Atlanta, 1959-60; asst. prof. U. Southwestern La., Lafayette, 1960-61; mem. faculty dept. history Middle Tenn. State U., Murfreesboro, 1962—, prof., 1969—. Mem. Tenn. Com. for the Humanities, 1979—; sec. Rutherford County Democratic Party, 1972-78. Served with USNR, 1953-56. Nat. Endowment for Humanities fellow, 1979-80. Mem. AAUP (pres. Tenn. Conf., 1978—), Am. Hist. Assn., Orgn. Am. Historians, So. Hist. Assn. Nat. Hist. Soc., Soc. Historians of Am. Fgn. Relations, ACLU. Unitarian. Author: The Trent Affair, 1977; Desperate Diplomacy, 1976. Home: Route 8 Box 178 Compton Rd Murfreesboro TN 37130 Office: Dept History Middle Tenn State Univ Murfreesboro TN 37132

FERRON, JOHN JOSEPH, trade assn. exec.; b. Massillon, Ohio, July 16, 1946; s. John Joseph and Eileen Mary (Foley) F.; B.S. in Internat. Affairs, USAF Acad., 1968; J.D., George Washington U., 1977; m. Lynn K. Hall, Dec. 19, 1970; children—Brady, Kevin. Commd. 2d lt. USAF, 1968, advanced through grades to capt., 1973; pilot in Vietnam; resigned, 1973; with Nat. Automobile Dealers Assn., McLean, Va., 1973—, asst. dir. research and dealership ops. div., 1974-78, exec. dir. research and dealership ops. group, 1978—; admitted to Va., D.C. bars. Trustee Northwood U., Midland, Mich.; pres. cluster bd. dirs. Reston (Va.) Homeowners Assn., 1978-79. Decorated D.F.C., Air medal with 7 oak leaf clusters. Mem. Am. Bar Assn., Nat. Economists Club, Am. Mgmt. Assn., Am. Mktg. Assn., Assn. Grads. USAF Acad., Va. Bar Assn. Club: Washington Golf and Country. Home: 1916 Abbottsford Dr Vienna VA 22180 Office: 8400 Westpark Dr McLean VA 22102

FERSTL, KENNETH LEON, educator; b. Richland Center, Wis., May 31, 1940; s. Joseph Henry and Vera Teresa (Grauvogel) F.; B.Mus., certificate in library sci. N. Tex. State U., 1963; M.S. in L.S., U. Wis., 1966; Ph.D., Ind. U., 1977; m. Sondra Rody Mueller, Aug. 10, 1968. Student asst. Dept. Library Sci., N. Tex. State U., Denton, 1961-62, cataloging asst., 1962-63, asst. cataloger, 1963-64, instr. Sch. Library and Info. Sci., 1969-72, lectr., 1975-78, asst. prof., 1978—; student asst. U. Wis., Madison, 1964-65, teaching asst., 1965-66, participating instr., Dept. Library Sci., Univ. Extension, 1966, acting instr. Library Sch., summer 1966, instr., 1966-67, instr. AIM program, 1967-68; head tech. services div., asst. dir. Oshkosh (Wis.) Public Library, 1967-69; asso. instr. Grad. Library Sch., Ind. U., Bloomington, 1973-74, coordinator, cons. Workshop on Library Services for Ind. Sr. Citizens, spring 1975; lectr. in field; cons. in field. Mem. pub. com. Continuing Library Edn. Network and Exchange, 1978—; mem. com. on library services to blind, elderly and handicapped Ind. Area 10 Library Services Authority, 1974-75; grant proposal reviewer div. public programs Nat. Endowment for the Humanities, 1978—. Spl. Libraries Assn. grad. scholar, 1964-65; U. Wis. teaching assistantship, spring, 1965, summer, 1965, fall, 1965, spring, 1966; Wis. Div. Library Services scholar, 1968; Ind. U. fellow, 1973-74, 74-75. Mem. Adult Edn. Assn. U.S.A., ALA (com. library services to shut-ins health and rehab. library services div. 1976-79, chairperson com. on library services to aging population reference and adult services div. 1977-78, 78-79) Fox River Valley Library Assn. (pres.-elect 1968-69), Tex. Library Assn. (sec.-treas. 1970-71), Wis. Library Assn., AAUP, Assn. Am. Library Schs., Cath. Library Assn., Freedom to Read Found., Internat. Music Library Assn., Music Library Assn., Southwestern Library Assn., Tex. Assn. Coll. Tchrs., Ind. U. Alumni Assn., N. Tex. State U. Alumni Assn., U. Wis. Alumni Assn., William Morris Soc. Nat. Book League, Beta Phi Mu, Pi Kappa Lambda, Alpha Lambda Sigma. Democrat. Roman Catholic. Contbr. articles in field to profl. jours. Home: 1505 Victoria Dr Denton TX 76201 Office: PO Box 13256 N Tex Sta Denton TX 76203

FERTL, WALTER HANS, well logging co. exec.; b. Vienna, Mar. 16, 1940; came to U.S., 1965, naturalized, 1973; s. Johann and Anna (Schiegl) F.; diploma in engring. Mining U. of Leoben, Austria, 1958; M.S., U. Tex., Austin, 1966, Ph.D., 1968; m. Irma Szabo, May 11, 1965; children—Dagmar, Tania. Asst. mgr. Austrian Oil Co., 1963-65; prodn. researcher Continental Oil Co., Ponca City, Okla., 1968-75; dir. interpretation and field devel. Dresser Atlas, Houston, 1976—; seminar leader; guest lectr. USSR, Venezuela, Austria, Turkey. Mem. Am. Assn. Petroleum Geologists, Soc. Exploration Geologists, Soc. Petroleum Engrs., Soc. Profl. Well Logging Analysts (pres. 1978-79, best paper award 1977), Can. Well Logging Soc. Author: Abnormal Formation Pressures, 1976; contbr. articles tech. jours., chpts. in books; tech. editor The Log Analyst, 1975-77. Home: 1627 Scenic Ridge St Houston TX 77043 Office: Dresser Atlas PO Box 1407 Houston TX 77001

FETNER, EDWARD HAWTHORNE, JR., structural engring. designer; b. Columbia, S.C., July 13, 1921; s. Edward Hawthorne and Mary Rosa (Benson) F.; student Aero Industries Tech. Inst., Glendale, Calif., 1941, Ryan Aero. Inst., San Diego, 1945, LaSalle Extension U., Chgo., 1950, Internat. Corr. Schs.; m. Nadine Beatrice Chapman, Dec. 12, 1943; children—Carolyn Rosa, Edward Hawthorne. Aircraft mechanic Hawthorne Sch. Aero., Orangeburg, S.C., 1941-42; sr. aircraft instr. Palmetto Sch. Aero., Columbia, S.C., 1942-45; asst. supt. maintenance Dixie Aviation Co., Columbia, 1945-48; sr. map draftsman S.C. State Hwy. Dept., Columbia, 1948-56; dir. structural plans prodn. Wilbur Smith & Assos., Columbia, 1956—; lectr. and cons. in field; cartographer; nautical navigator. Mem. U.S. Power Squadrons (past dist. comdr.). Republican. Methodist. Club: Palmetto of Columbia. Originator, owner Fishunt maps. Home: Route 4 Box 448 Chapin SC 29036 Office: Bankers Trust Tower Columbia SC 29201

FETNER, ROBERT HENRY, radiation biologist; b. Savannah, Ga., Feb. 22, 1922; s. William Westcott and Lucille Fedora (Goodrich) F.; B.S., U. Miami, 1950, M.S., 1952; Ph.D., Emory U., 1955; m. Mary Carolyn Guiney, July 8, 1972; 1 dau., Amber Goodrich. Mem. faculty Ga. Inst. Tech., Atlanta, 1955—, prof., 1963—, dir. Sch. Biology, 1964-70. Served with U.S. Army, 1942-45. Decorated Combat Infantryman's badge. Mem. Ga. Acad. Sci. (editor Bull. 1960-64), Sigma Xi, Phi Kappa Phi. Presbyterian. Contbr. articles to profl. jours. Patentee computer digitizer. Home: 2219 Walker Dr Lawrenceville GA 30245 Office: Ga Inst Tech Atlanta GA 30332

FEUER, STANLEY JEFFREY, clin. social worker; b. Norfolk, Va., May 29, 1948; s. Jules and Frieda Fern (Lachs) F. B.A., Fairleigh Dickinson U., 1970; M.S.W., Va. Commonwealth U., 1975. ViSTA vol., 1970-71; hotline coordinator Outreach Clinic, Virginia Beach, Va., 1972-73; social worker mental hygiene clinic McGuire VA Hosp., Richmond, Va., 1975—; instr. to clin. instr. psychiatry Med. Coll. Va., Va. Commonwealth U. Cert. Acad. Cert. Social Workers. Mem. Nat. Assn. Social Workers. Jewish. Club: B'nai B'rith (local rec. sec.). Home: 1033 Circlewood Dr Richmond VA 23224 Office: 1201 Broad Rock Rd Richmond VA 23249

FEUERBACHER, ALVIN LEROY, stock broker; b. Dallas, 1929; s. Harry Alvin and Lela I. (Heslep) F.; student Dallas Coll., So. Meth. U., Am. Inst. Banking; m. Josephine Altizer, Jan. 31, 1948; children—Alan, Thomas, Mitchell, Dwayne, Paul. Asst. cashier Rauscher Pierce & Co., 1951-54; cashier, asst. treas. Eppler, Guerin & Turner, Inc., stock brokers, 1954-58, account exec., 1958-64, registered prin. San Antonio br., 1964—; profl. travel photographer, speaker. Team leader Am. Cancer Soc. Fund Drive; past comdr. Red Carpet Com., San Antonio; bd. dirs. Harmony Services, Inc., Kenosha, Wis.; lay leader, tchr. Methodist Ch. Mem. San Antonio Soc. Security Analysts, Soc. for Preservation and Encouragement of Barbershop Quartet Singing in Am. (internat. dir., past pres. Southwestern dist., dean chpt. officers schs.). Contbr. articles to fraternal publ. Home: 110 Wildrose Ave San Antonio TX 78209 Office: 214 NE Loop 410 San Antonio TX 78284

FEY, MARILYN BARRETT, tax service co. exec.; b. Council Bluffs, Iowa, Apr. 6, 1937; d. Frank Joseph and Dorothy Marie (Jensen) Barrett; A.A., Va. Intermont Coll., 1957; B.A. in Health, Phys. Edn. and Recreation, State U. Iowa, 1961; children—David, Michael, Mary Beth, Tina Marie. Asst. supt. parks and recreation, Olympia, Wash., 1961-63; co-owner Crown Service Office Machines, Ft. Lauderdale, Fla., 1963-73; dist. mgr. H & R Block, Inc., Hialeah, Fla., 1974—. Treas., Redeemer Lutheran Ch., Ft. Lauderdale, 1969-72; pres. Ladies of the Ch., Abiding Savior Luth., Ft. Lauderdale, 1967-69. Mem. Zeta Tau Alpha. Republican. Office: 140 Hialeah Dr Hialeah FL 33010

FEZ-BARRINGTEN, BARIE, architect; b. N.Y.C., Dec. 28, 1937; s. Henry and Anne Fez-Barringten; B.F.A., (scholar), Pratt Inst., 1962; M.Arch. (scholar), Yale U., 1968; m. Christina, Mar., 1966. Exec. v.p. S.R.G. Corp., P.R., 1968-69; pvt. practice constrn. and mgmt. cons., N.Y.C., 1969-73; ops. exec. Peoples Protective Corp., Tenn., Ark., Brit. Honduras, 1973-74; mgr. spl. projects Gulf Oil Real Estate Devel. Co., Houston, 1974—; project architect Edward D. Stone, 1965-68; spl. advisor, cons. to sec. edn. P.R., 1968-70; investigator pollution elimination systems mayor's office N.Y.C., 1970, Ruhrgebeit, W. Ger., 1970; mem. info. sharing com. NASA; guest lectr. in field. Registered architect Iowa, Tex. Mem. AIA (treas. Jackson, Tenn.), Nat. Assn. Corp. Real Estate Execs., Nat. Council Archtl. Registration, Tex. Assn. Realtors, Am. Mgmt. Assn., Internat. Platform Assn., Assn. Gen. Contractors, Constrn. Mgmt. Inst., Nat. Homebuilders Assn., Landmark Preservation Soc., Costeau Soc. Clubs: Yale Club of Houston, Reston Country. Developer TV assisted ednl. facilities for illiterates P.R., 1968-70; author workbook manual: Project Management System, 1978; dir. devel. house designs and supporting structures especially steep slopes Tenn., 1973-74; contbr. articles to profl. publs. Home: 1408 Holleman College Station TX 77840

FICKER, VICTOR BENJAMIN, coll. pres.; b. Brookfield, Ill., Aug. 11, 1937; s. Victor and Helen (Wefler) F.; B.A., U. Fla., 1962, M.Ed., 1963, Ed.D., 1967; m. T. Merle Skinner, Aug. 3, 1962; children—Ellen, Celene, John. Chmn. div. social sci. Polk Community Coll., Winter Haven, Fla., 1967-71; dean of instrn. Paul D. Camp Community Coll., Franklin, Va., 1971-73, dean coll., 1973-78; pres. Mountain Empire Community Coll., Big Stone Gap, Va., 1978—; adj. asso. prof. Old Dominion U., Norfolk, Va., 1972—. Pres. local chpt. Am. Cancer Soc. Served with USMC, 1957-59. Mem. Community Coll. Social Sci. Assn. (dir.), Wise County C. of C. (pres.), Phi Kappa Phi, Alpha Kappa Delta, Kappa Delta Pi. Lion. (dir.). Author: Social Science and Urban Crisis, 1971, 2d edit., 1978 Deprivation in America, 1971; Man's Search for Himself, 1972; Values in Conflict, 1972; Revolution in Religion, 1973; Effective Supervision, 1975. Home: 1758 Holton Ave Big Stone Gap VA 24219 Office: PO Drawer 700 Big Stone Gap VA 24219

FICKLEN, CARTER BRAXTON, health physicist; b. Newport News, Va., July 30, 1942; s. Carter Braxton and Zella Anne (Maney) F.; student Old Dominion U., 1960-63; B.S., Coll. William & Mary, 1976, postgrad. 1976—; m. Carol Lynn Lipscomb, Jan. 11, 1964; children—Margaret Anne, Frances Braxton, Carter Braxton. Health physics technician Newport News Shipbldg., 1963-68, radiol. lab. asst., 1968-73, sr. lab. analyst, 1973-77; chief radiation safety officer NASA-Langley Research Center, Hampton, Va., 1977—; adj. lectr. occupational safety and health Thomas Nelson Coll. Vice pres. youth basketball YMCA, 1973-76, 78—; precinct chmn. Hampton City Democratic Com., 1975—. Mem. Am. Indsl. Hygiene Assn., Health Physics Soc., Laser Inst. Am., Engrs. Club Va. Peninsula, Alpha Tau Omega. Episcopalian. Clubs: Hilton Tennis (dir. 1970—, pres. 1971-73, 76) (Newport News). Home: 624 Redheart Dr Hampton VA 23666 Office: Occupational Medical Center NASA Langley Research Center Hampton VA 23665

FICKLING, JUDITH ANN, health care adminstr.; b. Lewiston, Maine, May 22, 1950; d. Howard Daniel and Sylvia Margaret (Anderson) Whiting; A.B., Coll. of Charleston (S.C.), 1972; M.S.W., U. S.C., Columbia, 1976; m. Elliott Reed Fickling, III, Aug. 24, 1974. Asso. exec. dir. S.C. Med. Care Found., Columbia, 1976—; condr. faculty health edn. workshops; cons. in field. Bd. dirs. Women's Symphony Assn., 1976-77, 80-81. Registered social worker, S.C. Mem. Am. Mgmt. Assn., Nat. Assn. Social Workers (dir. S.C. chpt. 1977-78). Presbyterian. Clubs: Spring Valley Country, Summit. Home: 1429 Berkeley St Columbia SC 29205 Office: SC Med Care Found 3325 Medical Park Rd Columbia SC 29203

FICKLING, WILLIAM ARTHUR, JR., health care co. exec.; b. Macon, Ga., July 23, 1932; s. William Arthur and Claudia Darden (Foster) F.; B.S. cum laude, Auburn U., 1954; m. Neva Jane Langley, Dec. 30, 1954; children—William Arthur III, Jane Dru, Julia Claudia, Roy Hampton. Exec. v.p. Fickling & Walker, Inc., Macon, 1954-74; pres., chmn. bd., chief exec. officer Charter Med. Corp., 1969—; dep. chmn., dir. Fed. Res. Bank Atlanta; dir. Ga. Power Co., S. Ga. Ry. Co., Riverside Ford, Bob Wilson Ford. Mem. Macon Bd. Realtors. Trustee, Wesleyan Coll., Macon. Mem. Young Pres.'s Orgn., Kappa Alpha, Delta Sigma Phi, Phi Kappa Phi. Methodist. Home: 4918 Wesleyan Woods Dr Macon GA 31210 Office: 577 Mulberry St Macon GA 31201

FIDLER, DONALD HENRY, lawyer; b. Aurora, Ill., Jan. 19, 1928; s. Nicholas P. and Susan A. (Leick) F.; B.S. in Mech. Engring., U. Notre Dame, 1949; J.D. with distinction, George Washington U., 1956; m. Patricia Booth, Apr. 18, children—Donald H., Pattie Anne. Engr., Creamery Package Co., Ft. Atkinson, Wis., 1949-50, Fairbanks-Morse Co., Beloit, Wis., 1950-53; patent examiner U.S. Patent Office, Washington, 1953-56; admitted to Va. bar, 1956, Tex. bar, 1957; atty. Varo Mfg. Co., Garland, Tex., 1956-57, Schlumberger, Ltd., Houston, 1957-70; pvt. practice in Houston, 1970—; dir. Sivco, Inc., Splty. Bindery Services, Inc. Councilman, Bunker Hill Village, Tex., 1973-78, mayor, 1979; bd. dirs. MTA, 1978-79. Served with USAF, 1950-53. Mem. Am. (ho. dels. 1971—), Va., Houston bar assns., State Bar Tex., Am. Patent Law Assn. (pres. Houston, mem. nat. council). Catholic. K.C. (past grand knight). Club: Houston Racquet. Home: 87 Williamsburg St Houston TX 77024 Office: River Oaks Bank and Trust Tower Houston TX 77019

FIDLER, WALTHER BALDERSON, lawyer; b. Sharps, Va., Apr. 18, 1923; s. Peyton Joseph and Gladys Ellen (Balderson) F.; B.A., Randolph-Macon Coll., 1944; J.D., U. Richmond, 1949; m. Martha Elizabeth Spencer, June 10, 1950; children—Kathleen McCray, Frances O., Jane E., James Robert II. Admitted to Va. bar, 1949; mem. firm Ryland, Fidler & Davis, Warsaw, Va., 1950—; counsel, dir. pub. affairs Va. Mfrs. Assn., Warsaw, 1974—. Gen. counsel Standard Products Co., Inc., 1963—, also dir.; dir. Washington & Lee Savs. & Loan Assn. Chmn., No. Neck Regional Planning Commn., Warsaw, 1966-68; mem. Va. Ho. of Dels., 1960-74. Chmn. State Bd. Corrections, 1974-76. Served as lt. (j.g.) USNR, 1943-46. Decorated Navy Commendation ribbon. Recipient Outstanding Citizen award Richmond County, Va., 1968. Mem. Farm Bur., Phi Delta Theta, Delta Theta Phi, Omicron Delta Kappa, Pi Delta Epsilon. Presbyterian (elder 1958—). Club: Ruritan (Warsaw). Home: Sharps VA 22548 Office: 26 W Richmond Rd Warsaw VA 22572

FIELD, ELIZABETH ASHLOCK (MRS. HENRY LAMAR FIELD), community vol., former govt. ofcl.; b. Little Rock, Nov. 27, 1915; d. Jesse Vernon and Felecia Irene (Bruner) Ashlock; grad. Little Rock Jr. Coll., 1934; student Washington U., St. Louis, 1934-35, U. Ark., 1962-63; m. Henry Lamar Field, Sept. 8, 1938 (dec.); children—Elizabeth (Mrs. John Randolph Wassell, Jr.). Dir. historic house mus. Angelo Marre House, 1965-71; dir. Ark. Commemorative Commn., Little Rock, 1972-74; dir. Ark. First State Capitol, Ark. Confederate Capitol; trustee Dade Heritage Trust, 1975-76; mem. Dade County Community Devel. Bd., 1977-78. Mem. Nat. Trust for Historic Preservation, Met. Mus. and Art Center, Hist. Assn. So. Fla., Am. Clan Gregor Soc., Quapaw Quarter Assn. (pres. 1972-74), Vizcayans, Fla. Trust for Hist. Preservation, Am. Biog. Inst. Research Assn., Phi Theta Kappa. Episcopalian. Home: 150 SE 25th Rd Apt 10A Miami FL 33129

FIELD, HENRY, anthropologist; b. Chgo., Dec. 15, 1902; ed. in Eng.; student Eton Coll., 1916-21, New Coll., Oxford, 1921-26; B.A., Oxford U., 1925, Diploma in Anthropology, 1926, M.A., 1929, D.Sc., 1937; research U. Heidelberg, 1926; research Peabody Mus., Harvard U., 1936-37; m. Julia Rand Allen, Feb. 6, 1953; 1 dau., Juliana Lathrop Field; 1 dau. by previous marriage, Mariana Hoppin. Anthropologist Field Mus. Natural History, 1926-41, asst. curator of phys. anthropology, 1926-36, curator, 1937-41; adviser Pres. F.D. Roosevelt, Pres. Harry S. Truman, Washington, 1941-45. Mem. archaeol. expdn. in Europe, Africa and Southwestern Asia; leader Marshall Field Archaeol. Expdns. to Europe, North Arabian Desert, Iraq, and others; mem. Harvard expdns. to S.W. Asia, USSR, Mongolia. Research fellow phys. anthropology Harvard 1950-69, hon. asso. in phys. anthropology, 1969—; adj. prof. U. Miami, 1966—; Forbes Hawkes lectr. U. Miami, Lowell Inst., Boston, 1952. Hon. mem. Glasgow Archaeol. Soc.; corr. mem. several fgn. scientific socs. Mem. U.S. and fgn. profl. and scientific socs. and assns., anthropol., archaeol., and other spl. orgns. Fellow AAAS, Royal Geog. Soc., Royal Central Asian Soc., Royal Asiatic Soc., Royal Anthrop. Inst. of Gt. Brit. and Ireland, Zool. Soc., Prehistoric Soc., and others; mem. Acad. Arts and Scis. Ams. (pres. 1964-68). U.S. del. to internat. congresses and sci. confs. Mem. U.S. mission to Moscow and Leningrad for 220th anniversary of Acad. Scis. USSR, 1945, Internat. Anthrop. Congress, Moscow, 1964, Internat. Geog. Congress, Eng., 1964. Club: Explorers (pres. Fla. chpt. 1973-79) (N.Y.). Author books on S.W. Asia including: Useful Plants and drugs of Iran and Iraq (with David Hooper), 1937; The Anthropology of Iraq, 1939, 40, 48, 51, 52; Contbns. to the Anthropology of the Caucasus, 1953; The Track of Man, 1953; Los Indios de Tepoztlan, Morelos, Mexico, 1954; Ancient and Modern Man in S.W. Asia, I, 1956, II, 1961; Bibliographies on S.W. Asia I-VII, 1953-61; Anthropological Reconnaissance in West Pakistan, 1959; North Arabian Desert Archaeological Survey, 1925-50, 1960; "M" Project for F.D.R., Studies on Migration and Settlement, 1962; Physical Anthropology of India, 1970; Arabian Desert Tales, 1977; Mongolia Diary and Mongolia Today, 1978; Trail Blazers, 1980. Editor: Peabody Mus. Russian Translation Series, 1959-72. Home: 3551 Main Highway Coconut Grove Miami FL 33133 Office: Peabody Museum Cambridge MA 02138

FIELD, JULIA ALLEN, environmental planner, writer; b. Boston, Jan. 5, 1937; d. Howard Locke and Julia (Wright) Allen; A.B. cum laude, Harvard, 1960; postgrad. Pius XII Art Inst., Florence, Italy, 1961, Harvard Grad. Sch. Design, 1964-65. Founder, v.p. Black Grove Inc., Fla., 1970—; pres. Amazonia 2000, Colombia, S.Am., 1979—; prepared environ. poster exhbn. Writing on the Wall for internat. conf. Cities in Context, U. Notre Dame, 1968; mem. Symposium Tropical Biology, Leticia, Colombia, 1969; cons. to

Forestry Dept., Simla, Himachal Pradesh, N. India, 1969; mem. Presdl. Adv. Group of Year 2000, Republic of Colombia, 1972-74, also Man and Biosphere Com., UNESCO, Colombia, 1974—; del. from Amazonia 2000 to Nat. Seminar on Ecology and Urbanization, Bogotá, Colombia, 1973. Mem. City of Miami Bicentennial Commn., 1974; pres. Acad. Arts and Scis. of the Ams., Miami, 1979—; coordinator Community of Man Task Force Horizons '76 Project, Miami; dir. La Manigua Center for Amazon Research, Colombia, 1976—; coordinator Amazonia 2000 Task Force, Colombia, 1977—; designer Amazon Pavilion, Feria Internacional, Bogotá, Colombia, 1978; Nat. U. Colombia del. to 2d Latin Am. Bot. Congress, Brasilia, 1978. Author: Essays on American Culture, 1961; (film) Man Against Nature, 1966. Editor: Game and Wild Life Preserves in the USSR, 1965; Amazonia 2000, 1978. Home: 3551 Main Hwy Coconut Grove FL 33133

FIELDEN, GEORGIA FREEMAN (MRS. C. FRANKLIN FIELDEN, JR.), interior designer, residential and comml. cons.; b. Alexandria, La., Aug. 3, 1919; d. John D. and Landis (Barton) Freeman; student fine arts Ward-Belmont, 1932-37, Blue Mountain Coll., 1937-38; B.S., George Peabody Coll., 1941; postgrad. N.Y. Sch. Interior Design, 1953; m. Clarence Franklin Fielden, Jr., July 16, 1942; children—Clarence Franklin III, Landis Michaux. Head dept. arts and crafts Camp Bon Air, Sparta, Tenn., 1939-42; asst. instr. fine arts demonstration sch. Peabody Coll., 1940-41; instr. fine arts Jackson (Miss.) Pub. Schs., 1941-42; lectr., interior designer, Colorado Springs, Colo., 1942-67; design cons., Denver, 1968—. Local pres. PTA, 1954-56. Mem. AAUW, Am. Inst. Interior Designers (Rocky Mountain publicity dir. 1957-58, sec. 1959-60, nat. com. pub. relations 1959-61), Am. Soc. Interior Designers, Constrn. Specifications Inst., Nat. Home Fashions League, D.A.R., Illuminating Engring. Soc. (asso.), Internat. Platform Assn., English Speaking Union, Huguenot Soc. of Founders Manakin in Colony Va., Huguenot Soc. London, Smithsonian Assos., Nat. Trust Historic Preservation, Assn. Preservation of Va. Antiquities, Nat. Geneal. Inst., Nat. Soc. Lit. and the Arts. Presbyterian. Clubs: Rotaryann (local v.p. 1959-60), Soroptomist; Inner Wheel (Washington). Contbr. articles to profl. jours. Home: 6800 Fleetwood Rd McLean VA 22101 Office: 260 Denver Club Bldg 518 17th St Denver CO 80202

FIELDING, VERL, farm and constrn. machinery co. exec.; b. Tampa, Fla., Nov. 16, 1919; s. Edward Lee and Maude Ethel (Miller) F.; B.S. in Bus. Adminstrn., U. Fla., 1946; m. Evelyn Mari Russell, Oct. 10, 1943; children—Edward Verl, James Russell, Charles Mark, Robert David, Janne Marie. Cost accountant Graveley Industries, Orlando, Fla., 1946-47; chief accountant Natural Gas & Appliance Co., Orlando, 1947-50; salesman Russell's Farm Supply, Palmetto, Fla., 1950-53, pres., mgr., 1953—; gen. mgr. Russell Machinery Co., Tampa, 1967—. Mem. Bd. Zoning Appeals, Manatee County (Fla.), 1968, mem. Pollution Control Bd., 1968; mem. Palmetto Fire Control Commn., Manatee County, Fla., 1976—; bd. dirs., pres. Palmetto br. Manatee County Boys Clubs; bd. dirs., treas. Fla. Coll.; bd. dirs. Future Farmers Am. Found. Hillsborough County. Served to capt. USAAF, 1941-45. Mem. Farm Equipment Dealers Assn. (dir.), Palmetto (dir.), Manatee County (dir.) chambers commerce. Democrat. Mem. Ch. Christ (elder). Club: Rotary (dir., pres. 1960-61). Home: 1816 17th St W Palmetto FL 33561 Office: PO Box 157 Palmetto FL 33561

FIELDS, ANITA MAY, nurse; b. Amarillo, Tex., Oct. 29, 1940; d. Dera and Mammie Maureen (Craig) Bates; diploma Sch. Nursing Jefferson Davis Hosp., 1962; B.S. in Nursing, Tex. Christian U., 1966; M.S. in Nursing, Northwestern State U., La., 1974; postgrad. (HEW fellow) Tex. Womans U., 1979; m. William Sidney, Feb. 3, 1968 (dec.); 1 son, William Kyle. Operating room staff nurse M.D. Anderson Hosp., 1962-63, charge nurse operating room Ben Taub Gen. Hosp., 1963-64; instr. St. Joseph Sch. Nursing, Fort Worth, 1966-69, Confederate Meml. Med. Center Sch. Nursing, 1971-72; asst. prof., coordinator nursing continuing edn. Northwestern State U., Natchitoches, La., 1972—; co-dir. planning grant La. Council Humanities. Chmn. nursing and health services ARC, Caddo chpt., 1973-77; bd. dirs. Am. Cancer Soc., 1973-77. Named Disting. Alumni Northwestern State U. Coll. Nursing, 1977; recipient Ann Magnussen award ARC, 1977. Mem. Am. Nurses Assn., La. Nurses Assn. (pres. 1979-81), Shreveport Dist. Nurses Assn. (pres. 1971—), Sigma Theta Tau. Democrat. Baptist. Club: Order Eastern Star. Home: Route 1 Box 266A2 Heflin LA 71039 Office: 1800 Warrington Pl Shreveport LA 71101

FIELDS, DONALD LEE, advt., public relations and mktg. co. exec.; b. Houston, Aug. 29, 1951; s. William and Gretta (Randle) F.; A.A., Pan Am. U., 1970; B.S. in Journalism, N.C. A&T State U., 1972. Dir. student publs. Tex. So. U., Houston, 1973-74; sr. account exec. Multi-Media Assos., Inc., Houston, 1974-76; dir. advt., public relations IV Fathoms Enterprises, Inc., Houston, 1976-77; pres. Omni Design Group Internat. Inc., Houston, 1978—. Mem. civilian action com. Met. Transit Authority, Houston, 1979. Recipient New Bus. Devel. award Nat. Assn. Market Developers, 1978. Mem. Nat. Assn. Market Developers, Public Relations Soc. Am. (chpt. sec. 1978-79), Houston Advt. Fedn. Club: Bus. and Profl. Men's (Houston). Home: 16314 Quailpark Dr Missouri City TX 77459 Office: 404 W Polk St Suite 2 Houston TX 77019

FIELDS, HARRIS JESSE, advt. exec.; b. Anguilla, Miss., Sept. 27, 1922; s. Thomas Walter and Rebekah (Blanks) F.; student Davidson Coll., 1939-41; m. Julia Warren, Sept. 15, 1977; children by previous marriage—Harris Jesse, Mary Fields Walling, Laura Fields Wolf. Copy editor Knoxville News-Sentinel, 1951-56; account exec. Lavidge, Davis & Newman, Knoxville, 1960-63; dir. mktg. Grey Hosiery Mills, Bristol, Va., 1963-68; owner, chief exec. officer Jay Fields & Assos. Advt., Bristol, 19—; lectr. communications to colls. and univs. Served with USAAF, 1942-45. Decorated Air Medal with oak leaf clusters. Mem. Am. Advt. Fedn. (gov. 7th Dist., dir.). Republican. Episcopalian. Home: 737 Sutherlin St Bristol VA 24201 Office: 601 Volunteer Pkwy Bristol TN 37620

FIELDS, JOHN W., oil dealer; b. Lucy, Tenn., Jan. 13, 1940; s. Robert L. and Cleadora Barber (Pearson) F.; B.S. in Edn., CCNY, 1963; M.B.A., Memphis State U., 1976; m. Evanett Watson, Apr. 22, 1971 (div.); children—Mickiel, John P., Jeffry. Shipping clk. Markite Corp., N.Y.C., 1961-63; store mgr. John's Barbain Stores, N.Y.C., 1963-65; bus driver N.Y.C. Transit Authority, 1965-70; maintenance coordinator Exxon Co. U.S.A., Memphis, 1971-72, clerical asst., 1972-76; sales rep., 1976-79, franchised dealer, Nashville, 1979—. Served with U.S. Army, 1958-61. Club: Masons (fin. sec. N.Y.C. 1962-67). Home: 1805 Martin St Nashville TN 37203

FIELDS, JOHN WILLIAM, veterinarian; b. Del Rio, Tex., Nov. 10, 1942; s. Herbert Wardlaw and Lois (Lewis) F.; B.S. in Chemistry, Tex. Tech. U., 1966; B.S., Tex. A. and M. U., 1968; D.V.M., Tex. A. and M. U., 1970; m. Jeryl Dugger, Aug. 12, 1966; children—Amy Elizabeth, Rebecca Catherine. Intern, U. Minn. Vet. Hosp., 1970-71; staff Pattison Animal Clinic, Cloquet, Minn., 1971-72; owner Sonora (Tex.) Animal Hosp., 1972—; pres. Sonora Communications Inc.; operator J-F Ranch Co.; v.p. Ranger Communications Inc.; del. Internat. Bovine Conf., Guadalajara, Mexico, 1977; speaker Tex.-La. Vet. Med. Assn. Conv., 1977. Dir. Airport Planning Commn. Joe Burger Municipal Airport. Named to Am. Cattle Breeders Hall of Fame. Mem. Tex. (dir., ethics and grievance com. 1976-79), Minn., Am. vet. med. assns., Am. Assn. Bovine Practitioners, Flying Veterinarians Assn., Ind. Cattleman's Assn. Tex., Tex. Acad. Vet. Practice (constn. and by-laws com. 1978-80, vice-chmn. membership and credentials com. 1980-81, v.p. 1980-81), Sigma Nu. Lion (dir.). Home: PO Box 412 Sonora TX 76950 Office: PO Box 441 Sonora TX 76950

FIELDS, MARTHA RENEE, counselor, educator; b. Little Rock, Apr. 11, 1944; d. Cleo Edison and Geneva Mae (McConnell) Wilson; B.S., Stephen F. Austin State U., 1966, M.Ed., 1970; M.A., U. Houston, 1978, postgrad. in adminstrv. edn., 1979—; children—Christopher Leon, Ronald Kevin. Home econs. tchr. Berkeley High Sch., St. Louis, 1966-68; counselor Picayune (Miss.) Jr. High Sch., 1971-72; counselor, instr. psychology and sociology Alvin (Tex.) Community Coll., 1972—; dir. Opportunity Outlook for Women, 1973-77. Consortium rep. Brazoria County Welfare Planning Council, 1973-74; clothing instr. Beauregard Activity Center for the Retarded, DeRitter, La., 1970-71; mem. Sunmeadow Community Improvement Assn., Friendswood, Tex. Gen. Electric Summer Guidance fellow, 1971. Mem. Tex. Jr. Coll. Tchrs. Assn. (chmn. counseling student personnel sect. 1979, sec. 1980), Jr. Coll. Student Personnel Assn. Tex. (newsletter editor 1977-79, sec. bd. dirs. 1979-83, program com. 1980), Alvin Community Coll. Tchrs. Assn., Stephen F. Austin Counselors Alumni Assn., Am. Personnel and Guidance Assn., Tex. Personnel and Guidance Assn., Brazoria County Counselors Assn. Methodist. Home: 530 W Castle Harbour Friendswood TX 77546 Office: Dept Counseling/Student Services Alvin Community Coll Alvin TX 77511

FIELDS, ROBERT I., ins. agt.; b. Mt. Vernon, N.Y., Jan. 26, 1934; s. Taft I. and Valaria Alva (Brown) F.; B.A., Va. Union U., 1961; postgrad. U. Del., 1961, Universite de Besancon, France, 1963; m. Carole V. Hundley, Aug. 23, 1959; children—Robert W., Monique L., Nicole L. Tchr., French, Richmond (Va.) Public Schs., 1961-65; pharm. rep. Lederle Labs., Washington, 1965-67; agt. N.Y. Life Ins. Co., Arlington, Va., 1967-74, 77—, asst. mgr., 1974-77. Treas., trustee Friends of Women Prisoners, Inc., Alexandria, Va.; charter mem. Prince William County (Va.) Park Authority. Served with U.S. Army, 1953-55. Mem. Va. Union U. Alumni Assn. (past nat. pres.), Nat. Assn. Life Underwriters, Va. Assn. Life Underwriters, No. Va. Assn. Life Underwriters (pres. 1979-80), Omega Psi Phi, Psi Nu. Democrat. Baptist. Clubs: Jack and Jill Inc. of No. Va. Home: 14513 El Rio Ct Dale City VA 22193 Office: 1500 Wilson Blvd Arlington VA 22209

FIFE, JOSEPH RAY, broadcasting exec.; b. Marion, Ind., Mar. 23, 1919; s. Joseph Ray and Maude Estelle (Day) F.; A.B., U. Kans., 1944; postgrad. Ind. U., 1946, Mich. State U., 1954; m. Melba Louise Grove, Apr. 23, 1944 (div. Oct. 1952); children—Patricia, Diane, Sarah, Marjorie; m. 2d, Johnnie Harper. Vice pres. radio sta. KYOK, Houston, New Orleans, Memphis, 1959-68; editor, pub. Tri-State Comet, Evansville, Ind., 1964-68; gen. mgr. radio sta. WGRT, Chgo., 1968-71; v.p., gen. mgr. radio sta., WIGO, Atlanta, 1971—; pres. Broadcast Sales Motivation, Atlanta, 1971—. Mem. Gov.'s Com. on Crime, 1973; mem. Mayor's Adv. Com., Houston, 1960-61. Bd. dirs. Atlanta Black Charities, 1972—; hon. life mem. Met. Atlanta Summit Leadership Congress. Served with U.S. Army, 1938-42. Named Houston Man of Yr., Houston Citizens C. of C., 1961; recipient editorial award A.P., 1971, Sch. Bell award Ga. Assn. Educators, 1975, Pacemaker award Associated Press, 1975. Mem. Nat., Ga. (Broadcaster-Citizen of Year 1974) assns. broadcasters. Mason (32 deg., Shriner). Home: 1259 Druid Knoll Dr Atlanta GA 30319 Office: 659 Peachtree St NE Atlanta GA 30383

FIGERT, PETER ANTHONY, real estate broker, former coll. adminstr.; b. Fort Wayne, Ind., June 11, 1930; s. Russell L. and Marie A. (Miller) F.; B.S., Ball State U., 1952, M.A., 1957; postgrad. U. Colo., 1960-72, Eastman Sch. Music, 1965, U. Tex., 1973-74; m. Ruth Elaine Hunt, Aug. 7, 1958; children—Mark, Michael, Anne, Amy, Alex. Tchr. pub. schs. Geneva, Wheatfield, Ind., 1952-59; dir. music Howe (Ind.) Mil. Sch., 1959-66; bandmaster Manchester Coll., North Manchester, Ind., 1966-68; lectr. Fox Bassoon Co., South Whitley, Ind., 1966-68; dir. instrumental music Odessa (Tex.) Coll., 1968-78; real estate broker, Odessa, 1978—. Pres., Odessa Civic Concert Assn., 1974-75. Bd. dirs. Presdl. Mus., Friends of the Library. Served with 38th inf. div. band, U.S. Army, 1948-55. Named Outstanding Alumnus Ball State U. Sch. Music, 1977. Mem. Coll. Band Dirs. Nat. Assn., Tex. Jr. Coll. Tchrs. Assn., Tex. Bandmasters Assn., Nat. Assn. Coll. Wind and Percussion Instrs., Am. Recorder Soc., Am. Musicol. Soc., Odessa Bd. Realtors, Phi Delta Kappa (pres. 1977), Phi Mu Alpha. Composer: Requiem for a Clown, 1970; For He That is Mighty, 1974. Contbr. articles to profl. jours. Home: 112 Monticello Dr Odessa TX 79763 Office: 518 E 8th St Odessa TX 79761

FIGG, ROBERT MCCORMICK, JR., lawyer; b. Radford, Va., Oct. 22, 1901; s. Robert McCormick and Helen Josephine (Cecil) F.; grad. Porter Mil. Acad., Charleston, S.C., A.B., Coll. of Charleston, 1920, Litt.D., 1970; student law Columbia, 1920-22; LL.D., U. S.C., 1959; m. Sallie Alexander Tobias, May 10, 1927; children—Robert McCormick III, Emily (Mrs. Richard A. Dalla Mura), Jefferson Tobias. Admitted S.C. bar, 1922, practiced in Charleston, 1922-61; circuit solicitor 9th Jud. Circuit of S.C., 1935-47, spl. circuit judge, 1957, 75, 76; dean Law Sch., U.S.C., 1959-70; sr. counsel firm Robinson, McFadden, Moore & Pope, Columbia, 1970—. Mem. S.C. Ho. of Reps., 1933-35; mem. S.C. Reorgn. Commn., 1948—, chmn., 1951-55, 71-75; gen. counsel S.C. State Ports Authority, 1942-72. Pres., Coll. Charleston Found., 1970-74, hon. life chmn., 1975—. Fellow Am. Coll. Trial Lawyers; mem. Am. (ho. dels. 1970-72, mem. fair trial-free press com. 1965-69, mem. spl. com. study legal edn. 1974-77), Inter-Am., Charleston County (pres. 1953) bar assns., Am. Law Inst., Am. Judicature Soc., Inst. Jud. Adminstrn., S.C. State Bar (pres. 1970-71, ho. of dels. 1975—), Blue Key, Phi Beta Kappa, Phi Delta Phi. Mason (grand master S.C. 1972-74). Co-author: Civil Trial Manual, 1974. Home: 1522 Deans Lane Columbia SC 29205

FIGUEROA-OTERO, IVAN, surgeon; b. San Juan, P.R., Oct. 27, 1944; s. Cruz and Berta (Otero-Hernandez) Figueroa-Castro; B.A. magna cum laude, U. P.R., 1966, M.D., 1970; m. Maria M. Colon, June 29, 1968; children—Beatriz, Maria Teresa, Berta Maria, Ivan. Intern, Univ. Dist. Hosp., Rio Piedras Med. Center, San Juan, 1970-75; cancer fellow Univ. Hosp., P.R. Med. Center, San Juan, 1972-73; chief resident surgery Univ. Dist. Hosp., 1974-75; fellow dept. pediatric surgery Variety Children's Hosp., Miami, 1975-76; fellow in pediatric surgery San Juan City Hosp., 1976-77, attending in pediatric surgery, 1977—; prof. zoology U. P.R., 1967, prof. physiology, 1968, 69, prof. surgery Sch. Medicine, 1972—. Recipient Gold Medal award Southeastern Surg. Congress, 1975, First Prize Publ., Clin. Conv. P.R. chpt. A.M.A., 1974. Mem. P.R. Sch. Medicine Alumni Assn., Tri Beta, Phi Eta Mu. Home: Clavel 1787 Mansiones Rio Piedras PR 00927 Office: 251 Chile St Hato Rey PR 00917

FIKE, JOHN WILLIAM, govt. exec.; b. Autaugaville, Ala., Jan. 4, 1922; s. Walter and Willie Fuller (Junkin) F.; B.S. in Elec. Engring., U. Ala., 1949; postgrad. U. Tenn., Chattanooga, 1950-51, U. Ala., Huntsville, 1958-60; M.S. in Mgmt., Fla. State U., 1972; m. Sara Katherine McKee, Dec. 24, 1943; children—Susan Katherine Fike Gaines, Mary Ellen Fike Forehand, John William. Field test engr. TVA, 1949-56; project engr. Anti-Missile Programs U.S. Army, Redstone Arsenal, Ala., 1956-61; asst. to future projects Marshall Space Flight Center, Ala., 1961-63; design and asst. dir. Kennedy Space Center, Fla., 1963-68, chief quality surveillance office, directorate of tech. support, 1968—; vis. lectr. U. Iowa, Iowa State U., 1970. Sr. and jr. warden Gloria Dei Episcopal Ch., 1965-68; vestryman, sec., jr. warden St. Mark's Episcopal Ch., 1978-79; v.p., bd. dirs. Kennedy Space Center Credit Union, pres. Employees Recreational Soc., 1972-74. Served with USNR, 1941-45. Mem. AIAA (publicity chmn., membership chmn.), Nat. Soc. Profl. Engrs., Am. Soc. Quality Control, Am. Rocket Soc. (sec.). Democrat. Clubs: Masons, Shrine, Elks. Editor: TVA Engineers News, 1952-55; author: Antennas, 1947; Launch Window, 1970. Home: 114 High Vies Dr Cocoa FL 32922 Office: Mail Code TO-QAL Kennedy Space Center FL 32899

FIKE, MARGARET SUE, educator; b. Charleston, S.C., Nov. 14; d. Frank Edward and Lillian Sue (Patterson) F.; A.B. in Religion and Elem. Edn., Coker Coll., Hartsville, S.C., 1968; postgrad. The Citadel, U. No. Colo., U. N.Mex. Elem. sch. tchr. Bur. Indian Affairs, Dzilth-na-o-dith-hle Sch., Navajo Reservation, N.Mex., 1969-77; tchr. Cherokee (N.C.) Elem. Sch., 1977—. Sunday sch. tchr. Navajo Mission, 1970-73; leader Boy Scouts, 1970-73, Girl Scouts, 1974; coordinator Children Inc., 1970-77, career edn. com., 1977-78. Cert. tchr., N.C., N.Mex. Mem. Nat. Fedn. Fed. Employees, Iota (pres. 1978). Democrat. Methodist. Home: Dawn-Dale Apts 10 Sylva NC 28779 Office: Cherokee Elementary Sch Cherokee NC 28719

FILAR, GEORGE REEVE, sociologist; b. Warsaw, Ind., Mar. 21, 1933; s. George Leon and Beatrice Florence (Reeve) F.; A.B. in Sociology, Valparaiso U. 1960; postgrad. Northeastern U., 1968-69; m. Joan Ruth Hicks, June 10 1957; children—Kenneth Allen, Karen Michal, David George, Donald Craig. With Cook County Welfare Dept., Chgo., 1960-61; with Dept. Pub. Welfare, Live Oak, Fla., 1961-62; rehab. counselor Div. Vocat. Rehab., Tallahassee, 1962, Tampa, Fla., 1962-65, Pasco and Hernando Counties, Fla., 1965-70, dist. dir. Bartow Dist., 1970-72, program supr. Bur. Rehab. Services, 1972-76, program supr. in charge client services and policy devel. sect., Tallahassee, 1976—. Active Boy Scouts Am., 1965-71, 77-80, troop com. chmn., 1970-71; coach Peewee Basketball and Little League Baseball, Dade City, Fla., 1966-68; chmn. Polk County Community Services Council, 1971; county council chmn. PTA, Pasco County, 1967; mem. task force com. on mental retardation Pasco County, 1967-70; mem. convocational council Episcopal Ch., Tallahassee, 1975-77, chmn., 1976, mem. diocesan exec. com., 1977, diocesean planning com., 1978, diocesean div. social ministries, 1979—, many others. Served with U.S. Army, 1952-55. Rehab. Services Adminstrn. grantee, 1968-69. Mem. Nat. Rehab. Assn. (life), Nat. Rehab. Adminstrn. Assn., Nat. Rehab. Counseling Assn., Fla. Assn. for Health and Social Services, Rho Chi Sigma. Democrat. Home: 2824 Morningside Dr Tallahassee FL 32301 Office: 1309 Winewood Blvd Tallahassee FL 32301

FILARDI, GERALD ANTHONY, urologist; b. N.Y.C., July 5, 1941; s. Ciro and Rachel Helen (Scaperrotto) F.; B.S., Iona Coll., 1962; M.D., SUNY, Bklyn., 1966; children—Gregory Christopher, KiminAnne, Daniel Robert Intern, Letterman Gen. Hosp., San Francisco, 1966-67; resident in urology Emory U., Atlanta, 1969-73; urologist Decatur (Ga.) Urol. Clinic, 1976—; mem. staff DeKalb Gen. Hosp., Decatur, Egleston Children's Hosp., Atlanta, Decatur Hosp. Served with M.C., AUS, 1966-69; Vietnam. Mem. test com. Nat. Bd. Med. Examiners, 1977—. Diplomate Am. Bd. Urology. Fellow A.C.S.; mem. So. Med. Assn., Am. Urologic Assn., Am. Fertility Soc., Atlanta Clin. Soc., Ga. Surg. Soc. Office: 755 Columbia Dr Decatur GA 30030

FILES, JOHN THOMAS, chem. mfg. co. exec.; b. Austin, Tex., Aug. 13, 1918; s. Sidney J. and Janie E. (Coffin) F.; B.S.Ch.E., U. Tex., Austin, 1941, M.S.Ch.E., 1942; m. Barbara Dow, Nov. 30, 1975; children—Lois Files Willis, Shirley Files Kowitz, Frances. Asst. chief engr. Dow Chem. Co., Freeport, Tex., 1942-45; chief exec. officer, chmn. bd. Merichem Co., Houston, 1945—. Mem. Tex. Air Control Bd., 1967; trustee S.W. Research Inst., Goodwill Industries, Engring. Found., U. Tex. Named Disting. Grad., Coll. Engring., U. Tex., 1968. Fellow Am. Inst. Chem. Engrs.; mem. Tex. Soc. Profl. Engrs., Am. Petroleum Inst., Chem. Mfrs. Assn., Tex. Mfrs. Assn., Nat. Petroleum Mfrs. Assn., Soc. Chem. Industry, Houston C. of C. (steering com. 1978-79), Tau Beta Pi. Christian Scientist. Clubs: Rotary, Lakeside Country, Athletic of Houston, Petroleum, Houston, Houston Met. Racquet. Office: PO Box 61529 Houston TX 77208

FILICHIA, JAMES JOSEPH, respiratory therapist; b. Oak Park, Ill., July 26, 1943; s. Joseph L. and Marian Y. Filichia; student Cook County Grad. Sch. Medicine, 1964; m. Danielle Gouvert, July 17, 1973; children—Adam, Lisa, James J., Angela. Staff therapist, U. Ill. Research Hosp., Chgo., 1965-67; dir. respiratory therapy U. Hosp. of Jacksonville (Fla.), 1967-73, St. Vincents Med. Center, Jacksonville, 1973—; instr. Fla. Jr. Coll.; mem. bd. advisers Fla. Lung Assn., Jacksonville; chmn. respiratory therapy adv. com. Fla. Jr. Coll. Mem. Am., Fla. thoracic socs., Am. Assn. Physician Assts., Am. Assn. Respiratory Therapy, Fla. Soc. Respiratory Therapy (dir.), Nat. Soc. Cardiopulmonary Tech. Democrat. Roman Catholic. Club: North Fla. Cruise. Inventor in field Home: 2904 Cesery Blvd Jacksonville FL 32211 Office: St Vincents Med Center Barrs and St Johns Aves Jacksonville FL 32204

FILICKY, JOSEPH GEORGE, chem. engr.; b. United, Pa., Mar. 18, 1915; s. Stephen and Julia (Cintel) F.; B.Chem. Engring., N.C. State U., 1940; m. Margaret Elizabeth Walsh, Mar. 10, 1941; children—Sandra Lee, Necia Jo-Ann. Shift supr. prodn. Hercules Inc., Belvidere, N.J. and Radford, Va., 1940-45; chem. engr. tech. service Westvaco Corp., Tyrone, Pa., 1945-63, mgr. quality control, Covington, Va., 1963-65, asst. supr., then supt. prodn., Covington, 1965—; lectr., author in field. Med. asst. CCC, 1934-36. Mem. Nat. Roster Sci. and Specialized Personnel. Mem. AAAS, Theta Tau, Phi Eta Sigma, Sigma Pi Alpha. Roman Catholic. Patentee in field. Home: Forest Hills Clifton Forge VA 24422 Office: Westvaco Corp Covington VA 24426

FILLYAW, HAROLD, educator; b. Wilmington, N.C., June 25, 1942; s. William and Mable J (Everett) F.; B.A., Fayetteville State U., 1965; A.M. (NDEA teaching fellow), U. Mich., Ann Arbor, 1971, Ph.D. (Spl. Rackham fellow 1969), 1975. Elem. sch. tchr., Pontiac, Mich., 1965-67; individual researcher U. London, 1968-69; research asst. U. Mich., 1969-70; vis. lectr. Eastern Mich. U., Ypsilanti, 1970-71; prin. Mack Sch., Ann Arbor, 1971-72, Bader Sch., Ann Arbor, 1974-75; dir. reading staff devel. public schs., Ann Arbor, 1972-74; dir. reading and learning skills center Prairie View (Tex.) A&M U., 1975-76, dir. Freshman studies English, 1976—; cons. in field. Mem. Am. Psychol. Assn., Internat. Cross-Cultural Psychol. Assn., Internat. Reading Assn., Am. Psychotherapy Assn., Nat. Council Tchrs. English, Mich. Reading Assn., Tex. Psychol. Assn., U. Mich. Alumni Assn. (life), NAACP, Hearthstone Civic Assn., Alpha Phi Alpha. Club: Hearthstone Country. Home: 15014 Elmont Dr Houston TX 77095 Office: PO Box 2684 Prairie View A&M Univ Prairie View TX 77445

FILSTRUP, SCOTT HOGENSON, metals service co. exec.; b. Evanston, Ill., Apr. 4, 1942; s. Alvin William, Jr., and Elaine H. (Hogenson) F.; B.S.C.E., Northwestern U., 1965; M.B.A., Northwestern U., 1967; m. Margaret McGinnis, Dec. 21, 1967; children—Laura Leigh, Scott Douglas. Comml. devel. supr. Monsanto Co., St. Louis, 1973-74; dir. industry planning Agrico Chem. Co., The Williams Co., Tulsa, 1974-76; mgr. planning Edgcomb Metals Co. div. Williams Co., Tulsa, 1977-78, mgr. bus. and market devel., 1978—; nat. speaker mkgt., planning, chem. and metals industries. Mem. adv. council mktg. Tulsa U.; bd. dirs. Jr. Achievement of Tulsa, 1979-81, exec., adv. and econs. awards; adv. bd. Tulsa Econ. Devel. Commn., 1978-80; bd. dirs. Community Services of Tulsa, Met. Tulsa Transit Authority; trustee Kirk of the Hills Presbyterian Ch. Recipient Alumni award Northwestern U., 1980. Mem. Am. Mktg. Assn. (pres. Tulsa chpt. 1979—), Tulsa Econs. Club (pres. 1977-79). Republican. Clubs: Rotary, Univ., Northwestern U. Alumni of Okla. (pres. 1976-79). Contbr. articles to Am. Mktg. Jour., Econs., Tulsa, others. Home: 7412 E 67th Pl Tulsa OK 74133 Office: PO Box 770 Tulsa OK 74101

FILZ, DAVID BRUCE, naval officer; b. Lawrence, Mass., Feb. 6, 1950; s. John Frederick and Elizabeth Mae (Worrells) F.; B.S., U.S. Naval Acad., 1974; postgrad. Old Dominion U., 1979—; m. Margaret Jane Mellings, June 5, 1974; children—Lindsay Hope and Julia Lauren (twins). Commd. ensign USN, 1974, advanced through grades to lt., 1978; communications officer U.S.S. Tuscaloosa, 1974-76, damage control asst. U.S.S. Nashville, 1976-78, asst. to officer in charge PERA, Norfolk Naval Shipyard, Portsmouth, Va., 1978—. Mem. Naval Acad. Alumni Assn., Naval Inst. Home: 3837 S Plaza Trail Virginia Beach VA 23452 Office: PERA (ASC) Code 1800 Norfolk Naval Shipyard Portsmouth VA 23709

FINCH, CHARLES CLIFTON, gov. Miss.; b. Pope, Miss., Apr. 4, 1927; B.A., U. Miss., LL.B., 1958; m. Zelma; 4 children. Admitted to Miss. bar, 1958; mem. Miss. Ho. of Reps., 1960-64; dist. atty. 17th Circuit Ct. Dist. of Miss., 1964-72; gov. State of Miss., 1976—. Served with U.S. Army, World War II. Mem. Am., Miss. bar assns., VFW. Democrat. Baptist. Clubs: Masons, Oddfellows, Moose, Civitan, Am. Legion. Former asso. editor Am. Trial Lawyers Jour. Office: Office of Gov Capitol Bldg Jackson MS 39205

FINCH, DAVID FERGUS, ind. oil and gas cons.; b. Marietta, Ohio, May 5, 1931; s. George Fergus and Ruth Edna (Twiggs) F.; B.S. in Petroleum Engring., Marietta Coll., 1958; postgrad. Pa. State U., 1959-60; m. Shirley Hollandsworth, May 4, 1964; 1 son, Matthew Fergus. Gas prodn. and storage engr. United Fuel Gas Co. (now Columbia Gas Transmission Co.), Charleston, W.Va., 1958-63; petroleum engr. Pennzoil Co., Parkersburg, W.Va., 1963-70; oil and gas cons., 1970—; research asst. in petroleum engring. Pa. State U., 1959-60. Served with USAF, 1950-54. Mem. Soc. Petroleum Engrs. Republican. Methodist. Clubs: Elks, Am. Legion. Office: RD 2 Box 532 Parkersburg WV 26101

FINCH, GAYLORD KIRKWOOD, research lab. exec.; b. Owosso, Mich., Nov. 16, 1923; B.S., U. Mich., 1944, M.S. in Chemistry, 1948, Ph.D. in Organic Chemistry, 1954; m. Barbara Schultz, Mar. 10, 1945; children—Gaylord Kirkwood, Pamela Sue (Mrs. Roy F. Dornsife), Christopher Robin, Robert Mitchell. Sr. chemist, acid div., Tenn. Eastman Co., Kingsport, Tenn., 1950-60, chief chemist, 1960-64, supt. acid devel. and control dept., 1964-66, asst. supt. acid div., 1966-70, asst. supt. polymers div., 1970-71, asst. supt. organic chems. div., 1971-72, dir. chems. European region Internat. Photog. div. Eastman Kodak Co., London, Eng., 1972-74, asst. gen. mgr., 1974-75, staff asst. gen. mgmt. and staff Tenn. Eastman Co., Kingsport, 1975-76, asst. dir. research labs., 1976—. Active United Fund. Served with USNR, 1944-46. Mem. Am. Chem. Soc. (chmn. local sect.), Am. Inst. Chem. Engrs., Am. Legion, Sigma Xi, Tau Beta Pi, Phi Lambda Upsilon. Republican. Presbyn. Kiwanian (local pres.), Elk, Moose. Contbr. articles to profl. jours. Patentee in field. Home: 1412 Lakeside Dr Kingsport TN 37664 Office: Tenn Eastman Co Research Labs Kingsport TN 37662

FINCH, HUGH EDSEL, real estate and ins. exec.; b. Spartanburg, S.C., June 21, 1928; s. Robert Lewis and Rosalee (Wyatt) F.; A.B., Wofford Coll., 1952; m. Sharon K. Smith, 1971; children—Michael Alan, Hugh Edsel, Alice Michelle; children by previous marriage—Deborah Elaine, Susan Denise. Newspaper reporter Spartanburg (S.C.) Herald Jour., 1952-54; tchr. Pacolet (S.C.) High Sch., 1955-56; operator, owner Hugh E. Finch Agy., ins. and real estate, Spartanburg, 1958. Mem. S.C. Ho. of Reps., 1956-66, 69-72. County chmn. March of Dimes, 1968. Mem. Nat., S.C., Spartanburg County ins. assns. Methodist. Clubs: Masons, Shriners, Lions, Ruritan (past pres.). Home: 1517 Rutherford Rd Landrum SC 29356 Office: 1265 Asheville Hwy Spartanburg SC 29303

FINCH, JOE MILTON, retail co. exec.; b. Hubbard, Tex., July 30, 1948; s. W.E. and Jimmie Sue (Lambert) F.; student McLennan Community Coll., 1970-72. With First Nat. Bank, Waco, Tex., 1969-73; mgr. Jack Eckerd Drug, Palestine, Tex., 1974-78, Temple, Tex., 1978, Waco, 1978, area supr., Dallas, 1978, area supr., eastern Okla., 1979—; cons. personnel and mgmt. Mem. Jr. C. of C. Mem. Ch. of Christ. Home: 4710 E 47th S Apt 106 Tulsa OK 74145 Office: 1103 E 41st Tulsa OK 74145

FINCH, T(HOMAS) VERNON, gynecologist; b. Hammond, La., Sept. 2, 1915; s. Thomas James and Virginia Elizabeth (Martin) F.; B.S., Tulane U., 1937; M.D., 1940; m. Glenna French, Mar. 8, 1957; children—Jan, Linda, Dale, Allison. Intern, Phila. Gen. Hosp., 1940-42, resident in obstetrics and gynecology, 1947-50; practice medicine specializing in gynecology, Sarasota, Fla., 1950—; mem. staff Sarasota Meml. Hosp., Drs. Hosp.; clin. instr. U. Pa., 1947-50. First v.p. Fla. div. Am. Cancer Soc., 1960. Served to lt. comdr. M.C., USN, 1942-47. Diplomate Am. Bd. Obstetrics and Gynecology. Fellow Am. Coll. Obstetricians and Gynecologists; mem. Am. Fertility Soc., Fla. (past pres.), Miami obstet. and gynecol. socs., So. Atlantic Assn. Obstetricians and Gynecologists. Republican. Club: Field. Office: 1801 Arlington St Sarasota FL 33579

FINCH, WILLIAM CALHOUN, indsl. engr.; b. Crossett, Ark., Aug. 6, 1926; s. William Edward and Emily Magnolia (Calhoun) F.; B.S., U. Ark., 1951; student Hendrix Coll., 1944, Miss. State U., 1967; m. Mildred Linda Boxx, Sept. 29, 1951; 1 son, William Calhoun. Field party chief for exploration Nat. Geophys. Co., Inc., Dallas, 1950-51; design and sales engr. Ernest Engring., Inc., New Orleans, 1951-52; indsl. engr. Gaylord Container Corp., Bogalusa, La., 1952-55; project engr. W.Va. Pulp & Paper Co., Charleston, 1955-61; product mgr. Alton Box Board Co., Alton, Ill., 1961-65; div. mgr. Mohasco Industries, New Albany, Miss., 1965-67; chief indsl. engr. Ingalls Shipbldg. Corp., Pascagoula, Miss., 1967-72; chief indsl. engr. Gen. Tire & Rubber Co., Columbus, Miss., 1972-74, div. mgr. indsl. engr., 1974-76; constrn. engr. Miss. Power & Light Co., near Port Gibson, 1976—; instr. Nat. Foreman's Inst., Pascagoula, Miss., 1967-72. Deacon, 1st Baptist Ch., Charleston, S.C., 1956—. Served with USN, World War II; PTO. Certified profl. engr. Mem. Am. Inst. Indsl. Engrs. (sr.; pres. Mobile chpt. 1968-70), Internat. Materials Mgmt. Soc., Ingalls Shipbldg. Mgmt. Assn., Sigma Chi (past treas.), Alpha Phi Omega (v.p. 1948-49). Democrat. Baptist. Clubs: Masons (32 deg.), Hickory Hills Country, Crown and Tiara. Author: Foremanship, 1966; Practical Planning and Scheduling for Foremen, 1972; contbr. articles on indsl. prodn. and tech. to profl. publs.; editor: Capital Investment and Engineering Economy, 1961. Home: 1 Champion Circle Route 2 PO Box 3H Water Valley MS 38965 also 1002 College St Port Gibson MS 39150 Office: Grand Gulf Nuclear Station PO Box 756 Port Gibson MS 39150

FINCHER, JOHN ALBERT, biologist, ednl. cons.; b. Union County, S.C., Sept. 8, 1911; s. Robert Charles and Addie Delilah (Murphy) F.; B.S. in Edn. magna cum laude, U. S.C., 1933, M.S., 1935; Ph.D., U. N.C., 1939; spl. student U. Minn., 1952; m. Ruby Catherine Broom, Aug. 19, 1939; children—Judith Ellen, Janice Manette, John Albert. Prin., Pineview Elem. Sch., West Columbia, S.C., 1933-34; instr. U. S.C., 1934-35; grad. asst. U. N.C., 1935-39; instr. Cumberland Coll., 1939-40; asst. prof. biology Millsaps Coll., 1940-42, asso. prof., 1942-46; prof., head dept. biology Samford U., 1946-57, asst. to pres., 1954-57, acad. dean, 1957-68, Disting. prof. biology, 1978—; pres. Carson-Newman Coll., 1968-77, pres. emeritus, 1977—; ednl. cons. Bapt. Med. Centers Sch. Nurse Anesthesia, 1978—; mem. Ala. Spl. Legis. Com. Higher Edn, 1958; pres. Mid-Appalachia Coll. Council, Inc., 1969-72. Bd. dirs. Gorgas Scholarship Found., Ala., 1947-68, Birmingham (Ala.) Sunday Sch. Council, 1956-65, Family Counseling Assn. Ala., 1956-63; bd. dirs. East End. Meml. Hosp., 1956-68, pres., 1965-68; mem. edn. commn. So. Bapt. Conv., 1958-66, chmn., 1962-66; bd. dirs. Douglas-Cherokee Econ. Authority of Tenn., 1969-77; mem. steering com. Nat. Colloquium on Christian Edn., 1975-76. Fellow AAAS; mem. Ala. Acad. Sci. (pres. 1952-53), Assn. Southeastern Biologists, Assn. Higher Edn., Am. Soc. Zoologists, Tenn. Council Pvt. Colls. (pres. 1972-74), Ala. Assn. Coll. Adminstrs. (pres. 1959-60), Phi Beta Kappa, Sigma Xi, Omicron Delta Kappa, Kappa Delta Pi, Phi Kappa Phi, Alpha Epsilon Delta, Phi Sigma Tau, Pi Kappa Alpha. Democrat. Club: Rotary. author Pres. page Today mag. Carson-Newman Coll., 1968-77; contbr. articles to profl. jours. Office: Samford U 800 Lakeshore Dr Birmingham AL 35229

FINDLEY, BENJAMIN FLAVIOUS, JR., educator; b. Richland, Wash., Jan. 1, 1947; s. Benjamin Flavious and Georgia Lee (Utterback) F.; B.S. in Bus. Adminstrn., W.Va. U., 1968, M.S. in Indsl. Relations, 1969; Ed.D. in Business Teaching, U. No. Colo., 1975; m. Karen Ann Bettencourt, May 13, 1972; children—Karolyn Annette, Susan Elizabeth. Instr. mgmt. W.Va. U., 1969-70; regional personnel supr. Pfizer Pharm. Co., N.Y.C., 1972-73; dir. bus. programs Parkersburg (W.Va.) Community Coll., 1973; instr. bus U. No. Colo., 1973-75; asst. prof. bus. Emporia State U., 1975-76; asso. prob. bus. adminstrn. and mgmt. Southeastern Okla. State U., 1976-79, dir. Mgmt. and Supervision Devel. Inst., 1979; pres. Findley Mgmt. Cons., Inc., Durant, Okla., 1978—; asso. prof. bus. adminstrn. Southwestern U., 1979—. First v.p. bd. dirs. Wesley Found., Durant, 1976-79; head usher 1st United Methodist Ch., Durant, 1976-78. Served to capt. USAF, 1970-72. Recipient Nat. Def. Transportation Assn. Academic award, 1969. Mem. Acad. Mgmt., Soc. Advancement of Mgmt., Mountain-Plains Mgmt. Assn., Orgn. Devel. Network, Delta Pi Epsilon, Kappa Delta Pi, Sigma Theta Epsilon. Democrat. Club: Kiwanis (past pres.). Author: A Practical Guide To Job Application, Interviewing, and Resume Preparation, 1979. Home: 402 San Gabriel Blvd Georgetown TX 78626 Office: Department of Business Administration Southwestern University Georgetown TX 78626

FINDLEY, DAVID FRANCIS, mathematician; b. Washington, Dec. 27, 1940; s. Ai Judson and Ida (Mercer) F.; B.S., U. Cin., 1962, M.A. in Math., 1963; Dr.Phil.Nat. in Applied Math., U. Frankfurt (W. Ger.), 1967; m. Mary Virginia Baker, Mar. 3, 1966. Asst., U. Frankfurt, 1966-68; asst. prof. math. U. Cin., 1968-75; asso. prof. math. scis. U. Tulsa, 1975—; cons. geophys. signal processing. Mem. Am. Math. Assn., Math. Assn. Am., German Math. Soc., Cambridge (Eng.) Philos. Soc., London Math. Soc., Circle Math. Palermo (Italy), Am. Statis. Assn., Inst. Math. Stats., IEEE, Soc. Exploration Geophysics. Editor: Applied Time Series Analysis, 1978; contbr. articles profl. jours. Home: 1234 E 29th St Tulsa OK 74114 Office: Univ Tulsa Tulsa OK 74104

FINDLEY, JAMES MARVIN, data processing exec.; b. Ontonagon, Mich., May 12, 1929; s. James W. and Margaret F.; student No. Mich. U., 1951; m. Betty Lou Smith, Aug. 18, 1951; children—James W., Carol A., Susan K., Nancy L., David A., Findley. Office mgr. Comml. Credit Corp., Marquette, Mich. and Cedar Rapids, Iowa, 1951-60; opns. mgr. Southwestern Investment Co., Odessa, Tex., 1960-61; v.p., sec. Nat. Data Communications, Inc., Dallas, 1961—. Methodist. Mem. Theta Omicron Rho. Home: 10506 Chesterton Dr Dallas TX 75238 Office: 5440 Harvest Hill Rd Dallas TX 75230

FINDLEY, WILLIAM EARLE, former mayor; b. Pickens County, S.C., Aug. 20, 1911; s. William Elbert and Essie (Earle) F.; ed. high sch.; m. Mary Louise Penland, Oct. 6, 1940; children—William Earle, Mary Ann. Mem. Pickens City Council, 1953-55, mayor, 1955-77; dir. Pickens Savs. & Loan Assn., Bankers Trust Co., Pickens, Laurel Hill Nursing Center. Vice chmn. Pickens County Planning and Devel. Commn., 1956—. Mem. Pickens County Mcpl. Assn. (pres. 1957, 64, 69). Methodist. Clubs: Masons, Shriners. Named Citizen of Year, Pickens, 1960. Home: 206 Hampton Ave Pickens SC 29671 Office: Town Hall Pickens SC 29671

FINE, J(AMES) ALLEN, ins. co. exec.; b. Albemarle, N.C., May 2, 1934; s. Samuel Lee and Ocie (Loflin) F.; student Pfeiffer Coll., 1957-58; B.S., U. N.C., 1961, M.B.A., 1965; m. Marie Nan Morris, Sept. 1, 1957; children—James A(llen), William Morris. Sr. accountant Haskins & Sells, C.P.A.'s Charlotte, N.C., 1961-62, Watson, Penry, & Morgan, Asheboro, N.C., 1962-64; instr. U. N.C., Chapel Hill, 1964-65; asst. prof. Pfeiffer Coll., Misenheimer, N.C., 1965-66; treas., v.p. adminstrn. Nat. Lab. for Higher Edn. (formerly Regional Edn. Lab. Carolinas and Va.), Durham, N.C., 1966-72; organizer, chmn. bd., pres., treas., dir. Investors Title Ins. Co., Inc., Chapel Hill, 1972—; chmn. bd., pres., treas. Investors Title Ins. Co. S.C., Columbia, 1973—; developer Carolina Forest, 1970—, Springhill Forest, 1977—, Stoneycreek, 1978—. Lectr. acctg. U. N.C., Chapel Hill, 1967-70. Area officer ann. alumni giving U. N.C. Chapel Hill, 1968-69, 71-74, 76—. Served with USN, 1953-57. Recipient Haskins & Sells Found. award for excellence in accounting, 1961; N.C. Assn. CPA's award for most outstanding accounting student U. N.C., 1961. Mem. Am. Inst. C.P.A.'s, N.C. Assn. C.P.A.'s, Am. Accounting Assn., CEDAR Bus. Mgrs. (chmn. nat. exec. com. 1971), Phi Beta Kappa, Beta Gamma Sigma (treas. 1961). Home: 112 Carolina Forest Chapel Hill NC 27514 Office: Investors Title Bldg Chapel Hill NC 27514

FINE, STANLEY SIDNEY, cons.; b. N.Y.C., Sept. 26, 1927; s. Morris and Sophie (Brajer) F.; student N.Y. U., 1944; B.S., U.S. Naval Acad., 1949; postgrad. Coll. William and Mary, 1955, U. Va., 1956; M.B.A., Am. U., 1959; D.B.A., Harvard U., 1971; m. Eleanore Baker, July 22, 1955 (dec.); children—Laurin A., Stephen S. Commd. ensign USN, 1949, advanced through grades to rear adm., 1972; assigned U.S.S. Manchester, 1949-51, U.S.S. Bradford, 1951-52; comdg. officer U.S.S. Hawk, 1954-56; assigned Polaris program, 1956-59; exec. officer U.S.S. Johnston, 1959-61; comdg. officer U.S.S. Lowe, 1961-63, U.S.S. Ingraham, 1965-67; comptroller Naval Ship Systems Commn., 1972-73; dir. fiscal mgmt. div. Office Chief Naval Ops., 1973-78; dir. Budget and Reports, 1975-78; pres., dir. Am. Productivity Systems, Inc., Washington; v.p. dir. United Internat. Research, Hauppage, N.Y.; sec., dir. 1st United of Miss., Jackson; dir. Redhead Corp., Shreve, Ohio. Active No. Va. Hotline. Decorated D.S.M., Legion of Merit (2). Recipient Mgmt. award Am. Soc. Mil. Comptrollers, 1971. Mem. Am. Assn. Budget and Program Analysis (dir.). Jewish. Clubs: Harvard Bus. Sch., B'nai B'rith. Contbr. articles to profl. jours.

FINEGAN, THOMAS ALDRICH, economist; b. Long Beach, Calif., Sept. 1, 1929; s. Edward Patrick and Hazel Irene (Aldrich) E.; B.A. summa cum laude, Claremont Men's Coll., 1951; M.A. in Econs. (Harry A. Millis fellow 1951-52, Univ. fellow 1952-53), U. Chgo., 1953, Ph.D. in Econs. (Ford Found. fellow), 1960. Asst. prof. econs. Princeton U., 1960-64, research asso. indsl. relations sect., 1962-64, vis. research economist, 1967, vis. sr. research economist, spring 1971; asst. prof. Vanderbilt U., 1964-65, asso. prof., 1965-70, prof., 1970—; vis. research asso. Princeton U. Woodrow Wilson Sch., spring, 1966; cons. Nat. Commn. on Employment and Unemployment Statistics, 1977-78. Served with Supply Corps USNR, 1954-57. Recipient Lawrence R. Klein award Monthly Labor Rev., 1972, Ellen Gregg Ingalls award Vanderbilt U., 1975; Dept. Labor grantee, 1967; NSF grantee, 1971-73. Mem. Am. (advisory com. on studies of labor market for economists 1974—), So. (bd. editors So. Econ. Jour. 1968-70, exec. bd. 1972-74, v.p. 1978) econ. assns., Indsl. Relations Research Assn., AAUP. Contbr. articles to profl. publs.; manuscript referee for profl. jours. Home: 1043 Davidson Rd Nashville TN 37205 Office: Box 1526 Sta B Nashville TN 37235

FINEGOLD, IRA, allergist; b. N.Y.C., June 29, 1938; s. Milton and Tillie (Silverberg) F.; B.A., Bklyn. Coll., 1959; M.S. in Pathology, U. Chgo., M.D. with honors (Salk scholar), 1963; m. Barbara Reich, June 15, 1963; children—Jonathan, Amy Beth, Andrew. Intern Bronx Municipal Hosp., Bklyn., 1963-64, asst. resident, 1964-65; sr. resident Montefiore Hosp., N.Y.C., 1967-68; resident in Montefiore Hosp., N.Y.C., 1967-68; resident in Allergy Roosevelt Hosp., N.Y.C., 1968-69 (Mead-Johnson scholar); practice medicine specializing in allergy, Hollywood, Fla., 1969—; clin. instr. medicine U. Miami at Hollywood, 1969-74, asst. clin. prof., 1974—. Served with USPHS, 1965-67. Recipient Sheard-Sanford award, Am. Soc. Clin. Pathologists, 1963. Diplomate Nat. Bd. Med. Examiners, Am. Bd. Internal Medicine, Am. Bd. Allergy, Immunology. Fellow A.C.P., Am. Acad., Am. Coll. allergy; mem. A.M.A., Fla., B.C. med. assns., Fla. Allergy Soc., Am., B.C. socs. internal medicine, Phi Beta Kappa, Sigma Xi. Author numerous publs. in field. Office: 3411 Johnson St Hollywood FL 33021

FINK, CHARLES AUGUSTIN, behavioral systems scientist; b. McAllen, Tex., Jan. 1, 1929; s. Charles Adolph and Mary Nellie (Bonneau) F.; A.A., Pan-Am. U., 1948; B.S., Marquette U., 1950; postgrad. No. Va. Community Coll., 1973, George Mason U., 1974; M.A., Cath. U. Am., 1979; m. Ann Heslen, June 1, 1955; children—Patricia A., Marianne E., Richard G., Gerard A. Journalist, UP and Ft. Worth Star-Telegram, 1950-52; commd. 2d lt. U.S. Army, 1952, advanced through grades to lt. col., 1966, various positions telecommunications, 1952-56, teaching, 1956-58, exec. project mgmt., 1958-62, def. analysis and research, 1962-65, fgn. mil. relations, 1965-67, def. telecommunications exec., 1967-69, chief planning, budget and program control office Def. Satellite Communications Program, Def. Communications Agy., 1969-72, ret. 1972; pvt. practice cons. managerial behavior Falls Church, Va., 1972-77; pres. Charles A. Fink, behavioral systems sci. orgn., Falls Church, 1978—; leader family group dynamics, 1958-67. Adv. bd. Holy Redeemer Roman Cath. Ch., Bangkok, Thailand, St. Philip's Ch., Falls Church, Va., 1971-73. Decorated Army Commendation medals, Joint Services Commendation medal. Mem. Soc. Gen. Systems Research, Am. Soc. Cybernetics, Am. Personnel and Guidance Assn., Assn. for Counselor Edn. and Supervision, Armed Forces Communications and Electronics Assn., Assn. U.S. Army. Club: K.C. Developer hierarchial theory of human behavior, 1967—, uses in behavioral, social and biol. sci. and their applications, 1972—, behavioral causal modeling research methodology, 1974—. Home: 3305 Brandy Ct Falls Church VA 22042 Office: PO Box 2051 Falls Church VA 22042

FINK, JACK EDWARD, industrialist; b. New Britain, Conn., May 29, 1914; s. Benson and Libby (Panish) F.; student pub. schs.; m. Ruth Marks, Feb. 9, 1935; children—Benson Stanley, Melinda Ann. Pres., Internat. Co., 1961—; v.p. Jonathan Logan Fin. Corp., N.Y.C.; dir. Ranger Mfg. Co. Active United Fund; trustee Marks Found., Libby P. Fink Found. Served with AUS, 1943-45. Decorated Purple Heart with cluster, Bronze Star, Silver Star (U.S.); Croix De Guerre (France). Mem. Sales Agts. Augusta (pres.). Democrat. Mason (32 deg., Shriner). Club: Westlake Country (dir.). Home: 3035 Park Ave Augusta GA 30904 Office: 2801 Wilco Ave Augusta GA 30904

FINK, JOHN WILLIAM, educator; b. Cin., July 29, 1939; s. Robert Edward and Hildegard (Wolf) F.; student Dartmouth Coll., 1957-58; B.A., U. N.Mex., 1962, M.A., 1965; M.A., Ball State U., 1972, Ed.D., 1973; m. Carolyn Parnall, June 19, 1975; children—Jason, Anne, Robert, Lara. Tchr., Cuba (N.Mex.) High Sch., 1961-62, Rio Grande High Sch., Albuquerque, 1962-65; asst. prof. U. Guam, 1965-69; instr. Ball State U., Muncie, Ind., 1969-73; asst. prof. R.I. Coll., Providence, 1973-74; Nat. Humanities Inst. fellow U. Chgo., 1975-76; asso. prof. S. Ga. Coll., Douglas, 1974—. Mem. NEA, MLA, Nat. Council Tchrs. English, Ga. Assn. Educators, Democrat. Author: (with I. Bruce Kirkham) Index to American Gift Books and Annuals, 1975. Home: 909 N Chester St Douglas GA 31533 Office: S Ga Coll Douglas GA 31533

FINK, WILLIAM JAMES, surgeon; b. Washington, June 24, 1917; s. Gail and Elizabeth (Thomas) F.; A.B., DePauw U., 1939; M.D., George Washington U., 1944; m. Frances Kay Kerlin, Mar. 5, 1945; children—William, Robert, Barbara, Barry, Bruce. Document examiner FBI, 1939-41; intern George Washington U. Hosp., 1944-45, resident in anesthesiology, 1948; surg. resident Sibley Hosp., Washington, 1945-46, VA Hosp., Coral Gables, Fla., 1948-51; surgeon VA Hosp., Fayetteville, Ark., 1951-53, chief of surgery, 1953—; clin. prof. surgery U. Ark., 1967—. Preceptor Am. Bd. Surgery, 1953-68. Served to capt. M.C., U.S. Army, 1946-48. Diplomate Am. Bd. Surgery. Mem. A.C.S., Western Surg. Assn., Southwestern Surg. Congress, Nat. Bd. Med. Examiners, Nat. Assn. VA Physicians, Assn. VA Surgeons, Sigma Nu, Phi Chi. Republican. Methodist. Club: Exchange (past pres. Fayetteville chpt.). Contbr. articles to profl. jours. Home: 1412 Elmwood Dr Fayetteville AR 72701 Office: VA Hosp Fayetteville AR 72701

FINKLEA, ROBERT WEIR, III, pub. relations exec.; b. Dallas, Mar. 30, 1944; s. Robert Weir and Jeanne Elizabeth (Leaming) F.; B.A. in Polit. Sci., N. Tex. State U., 1972. Circulation mgr. Tex. Mesquiter, Mesquite, 1959-60; sr. reporter Dallas Morning News, 1964-75; regional corr., N.Y. Times, 1968-75; asso. editor D, The Mag. of Dallas, 1975; regional corr. Bus. Week mag., Dallas, 1975-76; pres. The Consulting Group, Dallas, 1976-80; asst. mgr. public relations Diamond Shamrock Corp., Dallas, 1980—. Served with USAF, 1966, Tex. Air N.G., 1967-79. Bd. dirs. Boys Club East Dallas;

trustee Dallas-Ft. Worth chpt. Leukemia Soc. Am. Recipient Tex. Faithful Service medal. Mem. Sigma Delta Chi. Democrat. Clubs: Kiwanis (pres. 1976-77)(Dallas); Press (dir., v.p. 1977-78, certificate of excellence 1970)(Dallas). Office: Diamond Shamrock Corp Diamond Shamrock World Hdqrs Dallas TX 75201

FINLEY, ELSIE M., counselor; b. Huntsville, Tex.; d. L.T. and Bennie Ann (Ross) Jefferson; B.S. in Bus. Edn., Tex. State U. at Houston, 1952, M.Ed. in Elem. Edn., 1957; 1 son, Michael Tyrone. Tchr. classroom Houston (Tex.) Ind. Sch. Dist., 1953-63, reading, 1963-67, hosp. homebound, 1967-72, diagnostic, 1972-74, now counselor and ednl. diagnostician. Mem. Y.W.C.A., St. Anne's PTA., Riverside Little League. Den Mother Boy Scouts Am., 1973—. Mem. NEA,. Houston Classroom Assn., Am. Childhood Edn. Internat. Cert. in adminstrn., supervision, elementary, secondary, speech therapy, spl. edn. Home: 3202 Ozark St Houston TX 77021

FINLEY, GEORGE ALVIN, III, hardware distbn. co. exec.; b. Aurora, Ill., Apr. 25, 1938; s. George Alvin, II, and Sally Ann (Lord) F.; B.B.A., So. Meth. U., 1962; postgrad. Coll. Grad. Program, Ford Motor Co., 1963; m. Sue Sellors, June 20, 1962; children—Valerie, George Alvin IV. Rep. for Europe, Finco Internat., 1959-61; trainee Ford Motor Co., Dearborn, Mich., 1962-63; v.p. mktg. Internat. Motor Cars, Oakland, Calif., 1963-64, Sequoia Lincoln lease mgr., 1965; regional mgr. Behlen Mfg. Co., Dallas, 1965-67; former pres., now chmn. bd. C.C. Hardware Inc., Corpus Christi, Tex., 1967—; pres. Taurgo Industries, Inc.; guest instr. Sch. Bus., So. Meth. U.; mem. exec. com. Pro Hardware Inc., Stamford, Conn.; dir. USSI, NBC, Inc., Rite-On-Tops, Inc., BCM Marine and Indsl. Supply, AIRCO, Schmidt's Inc., Charter Savs. and Loan. Apptd. bd. mem. Nueces River Authority, 1976-82, v.p. bd.; pres. Coastal Bend Halfway Houses for Alcoholics. Recipient award for devel. full service half way houses for alcoholics, Tex., 1976-77. Mem. Nat., Tex. (past v.p.) wholesale hardware assns., Nat. Retail Hardware Assn., So. Hardware Assn., Phi Delta Theta. Democrat. Unitarian. Club: Rotary Internat. Asst. in design, engring., production, mktg. Apollo Automobile, 1963-64. Home: 3360 Ocean Dr Corpus Christi TX 78411 Office: PO Box 9153 210 McBride Ln Corpus Christi TX 78408

FINLEY, SARA CREWS, med. geneticist; b. Lineville, Ala., Feb. 26, 1930; B.S. in Biology, U. Ala., 1951, M.D., 1955; m. Wayne H. Finley; children—Randall Wayne, Sara Jane. Intern Lloyd Noland Hosp., Fairfield, Ala., 1955-56; NIH fellow in pediatrics U. Ala. Med. Sch., Birmingham, 1956-60; NIH trainee in med. genetics Inst. Med. Genetics, U. Uppsala (Sweden), 1961-62; mem. faculty U. Ala. Med. Sch., 1960—, co-dir. lab. med. genetics, 1966—, asst. prof. physiology and biophysics, 1968—, asso. prof. pub. health and epidemiology, 1975—, prof. pediatrics, 1975—; mem. staff Univ., Children's hosps.; cons. staff Lloyd Noland Hosp.; mem. ad hoc. com. genetic counseling Children's Bur., HEW, 1966; mem. Ala. Council Vol. Family Planning, 1974-75; adv. com. Internat. Conf. Human Engring. and Future of Man, 1974-75; mem. White House Conf. Health, 1965; mem. research manpower rev. com. Nat. Cancer Inst., 1977-80. Mem. Am. Soc. Human Genetics, Am. Fedn. Clin. Research, Soc. Exptl. Biology and Medicine, N.Y. Acad. Scis., So. Soc. Pediatric Research, Med. Assn. Ala., Ala. Assn. Retarded Children (Ann. Med. award 1969), Ala. Acad. Sci., Jefferson County Med. Soc., Jefferson County Pediatric Soc., Jefferson County Aid Retarded Children, Phi Beta Kappa, Sigma Xi, Alpha Epsilon Delta, Omicron Delta Kappa. Author papers on clin. cytogenetics, human congenital malformations, human growth and devel. Home: 2725 Cherokee Rd Birmingham AL 35216 Office: University Station Birmingham AL 35294

FINLEY, SIDNEY WILLIAM, II, chemist; b. Richmond, Va., Feb. 13, 1935; s. S.Clifton and Gladys Ethel (Hozier) F.; B.S., U. Richmond, 1956; m. Jean Ellen Bond, June 17, 1958; children—Sidney W. III, John C. Asso. chemist Texaco Expt. Inc., Richmond Research Labs., 1960-64, chemist, 1964-68, sr. chemist, 1968-71, project chemist, Convent, La., 1971-75, sr. project chemist, 1975-77, chief chemist, 1977—. Mem. Am. Chem. Soc., Sigma Phi Epsilon. Phi Beta Kappa, Gamma Sigma Epsilon, Sigma Pi Sigma. Baptist. Contbr. research paper in field to profl. jour. Home: 1735 Marilyn Dr Baton Rouge LA 70815 Office: PO Box 37 Convent LA 70723

FINLON, HAROLD GARLAND, civil engr.; b. Washington, Sept. 1, 1945; s. Harold Francis and Mildred (Garland) F.; B.S., Drexel Inst. Tech. 1968; M.S., Rensselaer Poly. Inst., 1974; m. Kay L. Newman, June 22, 1969; children—Michael H., Kristen E. Indsl. engr. Electric Boat div. Gen. Dynamics Co., Groton, Conn., 1968-74; scheduling engr. Power Systems Project div. Westinghouse Corp., Pitts., 1974-76; cons. Constrn. Systems Assos., Atlanta, 1976-77; sr. cost/schedule specialist Duke Power Co., Charlotte, N.C., 1978—. Mem. Guide Internat., Project Mgmt. Inst. Republican. Co-author: Information Management for Nuclear Power Stations, 1978. Home: 8621 Mulberry Grove Rd Charlotte NC 28212 Office: Duke Power Co 422 S Church St Charlotte NC 28242

FINN, RALPH IRWIN, educator; b. Boston, May 16, 1926; s. Samuel Leonard and Betty (Yoffe) F.; B.Mus., New Eng. Conservatory Music, 1951; M.A., Appalachian State U., 1958; postgrad. George Peabody Tchrs. Coll., 1967-69. Music tchr., Lake City (S.C.) Pub. Schs., 1951-56; band dir., dir. music, Darlington, S.C., 1956-62; asst. prof. music Pembroke (N.C.) State U., 1962-67; asst. prof. music Miss. U. for Women, Columbus, 1969—. Dir. Columbus Community Theatre, 1972-78; solo clarinet Starkville (Miss.) Community Orch., 1970-75. Pres., chmn. bd. Golden Triangle Ednl. Media Corp., Columbus, 1974-75. Served with USNR, 1944-46. Miss. U. for Women grantee, 1973. Mem. Music Educators Nat. Conf., Coll. Band Dirs. Nat. Assn., Nat. Assn. Coll. Wind and Percussion Instrs., Nat. Flute Assn., Internat. Clarinet Soc., Phi Delta Kappa. Jewish. Home: 322 2d St S Columbus MS 39701

FINN, RONALD DENNET, radiochemist; b. Weymouth, Mass., Aug. 15, 1944; s. Robert Fyfe and Doris Clark F.; B.S. in Chemistry, Worcester Polytechnic Inst., 1966; Ph.D., Va. Polytechnic Inst. and State U., 1971; postgrad Fla. Internat. U., 1978; m. Billie Elaine Wilkerson, Dec. 7, 1969. Research asso. depts. chemistry and med. Brookhaven Nat. Lab., Upton, N.Y., 1970-72; asso. chemist dept. physics, 1972-74; radiochemist Cyclotron Facility Mt. Sinai Med. Center, Miami Beach, Fla., 1974-75, tech. dir. radiochemistry/radiopharmacy div. nuclear medicine, 1975-80, dir. Cyclotron Facility, 1980—; adj. asst. prof. U. Miami, 1975—. Served with U.S. Army, 1970, served to capt. USAR, 1966-74. NASA fellow, 1966-69; Am. Cancer Soc. grantee, 1976-77, NIH grantee, 1979—. Mem. Am. Chem. Soc. (sec. treas. Miami subsection 1978-79), N.Y. Acad. Scis., Sigma Xi, Phi Sigma Kappa. Democrat. Contbr. articles in field to prof. jours. Home: 1210 W 60th St Miami Beach FL 33140 Office: 4300 Alton Rd Miami Beach FL 33140

FINNERTY, JOHN JOSEPH, mfg. co. exec.; b. Geneva, N.Y., Nov. 25, 1939; s. Joseph John and Dorothy K. (Marshall) F.; B.S., Rochester Inst. Tech., 1970; postgrad. Pepperdine U., 1973, Harvard U., 1977, U. Va., 1978; m. Mary F. Gringeri, June 3, 1960; children—Deborah, Michelle, Mary Ellen, Colleen. Gen. supervision mfg. engring. Stromberg Carlson Co., Rochester, N.Y., 1972-73, mgr. printed circuits, 1973-75, plant mgr., Camden, Ark., 1975-76, plant mgr., Charlottesville, Va., 1976-78, gen. mgr. telephone systems center, 1978—. Vice pres., bd. dirs. YMCA, 1978—; bd. dirs. United Way, 1976—; bd. dirs., v.p., treas. Work Shop V, 1977—. Served with USN, 1958-62. Mem. Nat. Mgmt. Assn., Soc. for Advancement Mgmt., Va. Mfrs. Assn. Home: 2540 Williston Dr Charlottesville VA 22901 Office: Stromberg Carlson PO Box 7266 Charlottesville VA 22906

FINNEY, MARY CREWS, civic worker; b. Wauchula, Fla., Oct. 18, 1922; d. Joseph and Flossie (Bailey) Crews; student Fla. State U., Tallahassee, 1942-43; m. William Bert Finney, Apr. 28, 1941; children—Sandra Gayle Finney Bowie, Mary Jan Finney Garner, William Bert II, Robert Bailey Clifton. Supr., U.S. Dept. Commerce, 1967-68; hostess Pickens County, Welcome Wagon Internat., 1954-56; interviewer S.C. Employment Security Commn., 1959-60; saleswoman, buyer Kelley Jewelry and Gift Shop, 1958-68; supr. info, referral, outreach and transp. Pickens County Council on Aging, Inc., 1974-78; mayor, Liberty, S.C., 1970-73; mem. Tri-County Tech. Com. Law Enforcement; mem. exec. bd. Pickens County Assn. Retarded Children; treas. exec. bd. Alston Wilkes Soc. Pickens County; bd. mem. Friends of Library in Sarlin Community; personnel com. Pickens County Library Bd.; mem. Area Aging on the Aging Com.; historian, archivist, exec. bd. Clemson Area Youth Theatre for Pickens County; mem. adv. com. S.C. Region I Council Govt. Public Safety; chmn. bd. Better Skills, Inc. Recipient Presdl. award Jr. C. of C., 1971; named Career Woman of Yr., Pickens County, 1972. Mem. Easley Bus. and Profl. Women's Club (historian), Am. Legion Aux. (mem. exec. bd.). Clubs: Women's Golf Assn. (pres.). Home: 15 Blue Ridge Dr Liberty SC 29657

FINNEY, WHITHAM DICKINSON, property ins. co. exec.; b. Vera, Kans., Sept. 17, 1898; s. John Edgar and Olive (Dickinson) F.; B.S., Okla. State U., Stillwater, 1923; M.S., Iowa State U., Ames, 1924; s. Gladys Irma Wray, Mar. 30, 1926; 1 son, Whitham Wray. County extension agt. Woods County (Okla.), 1924-25; engaged in automobile sales and service, Ft. Cobb, Okla., 1925-33; cashier, then pres. Washita Valley Bank, Ft. Cobb, 1939-66, now dir.; owner, mgr. Washita Valley Ins. Agy., Ft. Cobb, 1966—; engaged in ranching, 1935—; pres. Okla. Bankers Assn., 1950-51. Chmn. Black Beaver council Boy Scouts Am., 1961-64; pres. Okla. Heart Assn., 1964-65; mem. bd. Okla. Health Planning Agy., 1969-72; adv. bd. Okla. State Fair, 1963—; mem., chmn. bd. regents Okla. State U. and A&M Colls., 1965-73. Served with U.S. Army, 1918. Recipient Silver Beaver award Boy Scouts Am., 1959; Outstanding Animal Sci. award Okla. State U., 1950, Henry G. Bennett award, 1976, Alumni Hall of Fame award, 1974; Okla. Soil Conservation award, 1950; Okla. Higher Edn. Alumni award, 1973; named Hon. State Future Farmer Am., 1940; named to Okla. Hall of Fame, 1968. Mem. Okla. Hist. Soc. (pres. 1978-79), Ind. Ins. Assn., U.S. C. of C., Am. Assn. State and Local History, Nat. Assn. Historic Preservation. Republican. Methodist. Clubs: Rotary (past dist. gov.), Masons. Author genealogy and local history monographs. Home: 301 7th St Fort Cobb OK 73038 Office: 324 Main St Fort Cobb OK 73038

FIRESTONE, BRUCE MICHAEL, educator; b. N.Y.C., June 20, 1946; s. Frederick and Bobbie (Witzling) F.; B.A. with honors in English, Colgate U., 1968; M.A., U. N.C., Chapel Hill, 1970; Ph.D., U. N.C., 1975. Instr., U. N.C., 1974-75; asst. prof. English, Clemson U., 1975—; fiction reviewer Library Jour., 1975; film reviewer Raleigh Times, 1974-75. Mem. MLA, Univ. Film Assn., Soc. Cinema Studies, Popular Culture Assn., AAUP. Democrat. Jewish. Fiction editor Carolina Quar., 1973-74, editor, 1974-75; editor S.C. Rev., 1976—; editor An Introduction to Film Criticism; contbr. articles on lit. and film to jours. Film: A Thrill You Hadn't Ever Saw, 1979. Home: 39-B Daniel Dr Clemson SC 29631 Office: Dept English Clemson U Clemson SC 29631

FIRM, RUTH MARY, educator; b. N.J., July 7, 1912; d. Samuel and Grace H. (Hemingway) F.; B.S., M.A., Ph.D., Columbia U.; m. L. Allen Hangen, 1937 (div.). Rep., Office Brit. Petroleum, Washington; ARC hosp. recreation worker S.Pacific, World War II; instr. history of art Wilson Coll., Chambersburg, Pa., Mt. Holyoke Coll., S. Hadley, Mass.; mem. faculty Sweet Briar (Va.) Coll., 1960—, prof. history of art, 1969-78, emeritus, 1978—. Grantee Ford Found., 1964, N.Y. Inst. Fine Arts, summer 1965, HEW, India, summer 1970, Nat. Endowment Humanities, summer 1975; Fulbright travel grantee, Taiwan, summer 1966. Mem. Coll. Art Assn., Archaeol. Inst. Am., Assn. Asian Studies. Address: Box 86 Sweet Briar VA 24595

FIROR, DAVID LEONHARD, conservation assn. exec.; b. Athens, Ga., Nov. 4, 1923; s. John William and Mary Valentine (Moss) F.; B.S.A.E., U. Ga., 1943; postgrad. U. Ill., 1947-48; m. Margaret Louise Chick, Nov. 6, 1947 (dec.); 1 dau., Mary Catherine; m. 2d, Edna Bridges Bartlett, Oct. 16, 1976; stepchildren—Lynda Clair, Susan Maria, Charles Walton. Asst. mgr. Walton Electric Membership Corp., Monroe, Ga., 1946-47; asst. in agrl. engring. U. Ill., Champaign, 1947-48; owner, operator Briarpatch Farm, Winterville, Ga., 1948-63; comptroller Better Maid Dairy Products Inc., Athens, 1963-69, asst. mgr., 1969-70; br. mgr. Coble Dairy Products, Athens, 1970-71; so. rep. Nat. Assn. Conservation Dists., Athens, 1971—; dir. Cotton States Life & Health Ins. Co.; Mut. Ins. Co. Supr., Oconee River Soil and Water Conservation Dist., 1962-71; mem. Bd. Clarke County Commrs., 1963-70, chmn. 1964, 67, 70; mem. Democratic Exec. Com., Clarke County 1974-76. Served to 1st lt., inf. U.S. Army, 1943-46; lt. col. Res. ret. Mem. Ga. Assn. Conservation Dists. (pres. 1971), Ga. Soc. Assn. Execs., Soil Conservation Soc., Nat. Water Supply Improvement Assn. (charter), Res. Officers Assn. (life), Hon. Order Ky. Cols. Democrat. Home: 5555 Old Lexington Rd Route 3 Athens GA 30605 Office: PO Box 606 Athens GA 30603

FIRRITO, SALVATORE GIOVANNI, fin. co. exec.; b. Ragusa, Italy, Sept. 20, 1936; came to U.S., 1956, naturalized, 1973; s. Emanuele and Salvatrice (Occhipinti) F.; B.S. in Physics, U. Tulsa, 1960; M.S., Okla. State U., 1960-62; postgrad. U. de Besancon (France), summer 1966; M.A. in Internat. Bus., Thunderbird Grad. Sch. Internat. Mgmt., 1970. Tchr. physics Catholic U. P.R., Ponce, 1962-64; part-time prof. physics Coll. Petroleum Engring., Universidad Del Zulia, Maracaibo, Venezuela, 1966; geophysicist Corp. Venezolana Del Petroleo, Venezuela, 1964-67; cons. in fin. and mktg., Caracas, 1967-69; gen. mgr. Tuca Internat., Inc., Coral Gables, Fla., 1970-73; area mgr. Lone Star Life Ins. Co., Fla., 1974-76; dist. mgr. ITT Life Ins. Corp., Miami, Fla., 1976-78; asso. broker Diversified Capital Corp. of Am., Miami, 1976—. Recipient Honor awards ITT, 1977, 78, 79; Creole Petroleum scholar, 1956-60; NSF fellow, 1964. Mem. Nat. Assn. Life Underwriters, Million Dollar Round Table. Roman Catholic. Home: 3543 Estepona Ave Miami FL 33176 Office: Diversified Capital Corp of Am 8792 SW 12th St Miami FL 33178

FISCHER, DARLENE BOURG, educator; b. Raceland, La., Sept. 20, 1953; s. Richard Joseph and Nina Belle (Chabert) Bourg; B.A., Nicholls State U., 1974, M.Ed., 1978; m. Myron James Fischer, July 27, 1974. Tchr. social studies grades 4-6, Holy Rosary Elementary Sch., Larose, La., 1974—. Mem. Nat. Catholic Guidance Conf., Am. Personnel and Guidance Assn., Phi Kappa Phi, Kappa Delta Pi. Democrat. Roman Catholic. Home: PO Box 333 Larose LA 70373 Office: PO Box 40 Larose LA 70373

FISCHER, KERWIN ARMAND, orthopedic surgeon; b. Louisville, Nov. 1, 1901; s. William Arthur and Lillian Alora (Hamilton) F.; B.S., U. Louisville, 1926, M.D. 1926; postgrad. Presbyn. U., N.Y.C., 1938, N.Y. U., 1956-57; m. Ernestine Lucille Day, May 25, 1933; children—Kerwin Armand II, Sandy Day. Intern, St. Josephs Hosp., Lexington, Ky., 1926-27; resident Louisville Gen. Hosp., 1927-30, Hosp. for Ruptured and Crippled, N.Y.C., 1938-40; mem. faculty U. Louisville, 1927—, prof. orthopedic surgery, 1947—, chmn. orthopedic surgery, 1947; pvt. practice orthopedic surgery, Louisville, 1940—; mem. staff U. Louisville Hosps., Norton-Children's Hosp. Kosair Crippled Children's Hosp.; pres., dir. Orthopedic Assos., Louisville; pres. Fischer & Leatherman, P.S.C., Louisville. Served to lt. col. U.S. Army, 1942-45. Decorated Legion of Merit; recipient Distinguished Alumnus award U. Louisville Alumni and U. Louisville Med. Alumni, 1967. Mem. Am. Orthopedic Assn., Clin. Orthopedic Soc., Am. Acad. Orthopedic Surgeons, Orthopedic Guild, A.C.S., AMA, Ky. Surg. Soc., Ky., Louisville orthopedic socs., So. Med. Assn., Royal Soc. Eng. (affiliate), Alpha Omega Alpha, Delta Sigma, Phi Chi. Republican. Episcopalian. Clubs: Louisville Country, Rotary, Pendennis (Louisville). Contbr. articles to med. jours. Home: 145 Westwind Rd Louisville KY 40207 Office: 601 S Floyd St Children's Hosp Found Bldg Suite 200 Louisville KY 40202

FISCHER, KURT RONALD, mfg. co. exec.; b. Syracuse, N.Y., Dec. 23, 1954; s. Henry Johnand Helen Ann (Viel) F.; B.A., Elmira Coll., 1976; m. Sarah Elizabeth Keyser, Sept. 9, 1978. With Corning Glass Works, various locations, 1976—, recruiting specialist, Corning, N.Y., 1978-79, supr. personnel, Danville, Ky., 1979—. Bd. dirs. Jr. Achievement, 1979-80. Mem. Central Ky. Personnel Assn., Am. Soc. Personnel Adminstrs. Presbyterian. Club: Rotary. Home: 625 Longview Rd Danville KY 40422 Office: Corning Glass Works Vaksdahl Ave Danville KY 40422

FISCHER, LEE ALAN, physician; b. Chgo., Mar. 9, 1946; s. Bernard I. and Jacqueline L. (Mincer) F.; B.S., U. Ill., 1968, M.D., 1972; m. Candy Tina Kantor, Sept. 11, 1971; children—Adam Michael, Rachel Beth. Intern, then resident family practice Good Samaritan Hosp., Phoenix, 1972-74; practice family medicine, West Palm Beach, Fla., 1974—; mem. staff Drs. Hosp., Lake Worth, mem. exec. com., 1979-80, sec.-treas., 1980—. Recipient Granville Bennett award U. Ill., 1972. Diplomate Am. Bd. Family Practice. Fellow Am. Acad. Family Physicians; mem. Fla. Acad. Family Physicians (dir., chmn. public relations com.), Palm Beach County Acad. Family Physicians (pres. 1976—), Am., Fla. (del.), Palm Beach County (chmn. com. on continuing med. edn., editor Palm Beach Med. Publ.), med. assns., Omicron Delta Kappa. Jewish. Office: 1825 Forest Hill Blvd West Palm Beach FL 33406

FISCHER, MILLIE JACQUELINE CRAWFORD, hosp. pub. relations adminstr.; b. Savannah, Ga.; d. William S. and Willie Cleo Crawford; B.A., Ga. State Coll. for Women; m. John William Fischer, Jr., June 19, 1954; 1 son, Stephen Kenneth. Secretarial positions Strachan Shipping Co., U.S. Lines Co., Liberty Nat. Bank, Citizens and So. Nat. Bank; employment interviewer Ga. Dept. Labor; exec. dir. pub. relations Oglethorpe Mall Mchts. Assn.,Savannah; dir. community relations Candler Gen. Hosp., Savannah, Ga., 1973—. Bd. dirs. Arthritis Found., Savannah; past bd. dirs. Savannah Symphony Soc. Mem. Am. Soc. Hosp. Pub. Relations, Nat. Assn. Hosp. Devel., Pub. Relations Soc. of Ga. Hosp. Assn. (dir., 1st place certificate in field of pub. relations), Savannah Area C. of C., Am. Rose Soc., Savannah Rose Soc. (past pres.). Clubs: Advt. (pres. 1978-79, Silver medal award 1978, Addy award 1979). Methodist. Home: 2014 Colonial St Savannah GA 30406 Office: PO Box 9787 Savannah GA 31412

FISCHER, PATRICK CARL, computer scientist, educator; b. St. Louis, Dec. 3, 1935; s. Carl Hahn and Kathleen (Kirkpatrick) F.; B.S., U. Mich., 1957, M.B.A., 1958; Ph.D., M.I.T., 1962; m. Linda Loomis, Dec. 22, 1956 (div. Jan. 1967); 1 son, Carl; m. 2d, Charlotte Forese, Apr. 2, 1967; 1 dau., Carolyn. Asst. prof. applied math. Harvard U., Cambridge, Mass., 1962-65; asso. prof. computer sci. Cornell U., Ithaca, N.Y., 1965-68; prof. computer sci. U. Waterloo (Ont., Can.), 1968-74, chmn. dept. applied analysis and computer sci., 1972-74; prof. dept. computer sci. Pa. State U., 1974-79, head dept., 1974-78; prof., chmn. computer sci. dept. Vanderbilt U., Nashville, 1980—; cons. actuary, 1962-75; vis. asso. prof. U. B.C., 1967-68. Woodrow Wilson fellow, 1958-59; NSF grad. fellow, 1959-62, research grantee, 1964-68, 79—; grantee Nat. Research Council Can., 1968-75. Fellow Soc. Actuaries; mem. Assn. Computing Machinery (founder, chmn. spl. interest group 1968-73, editor-in-chief spl. publs.), IEEE, IEEE Computer Soc., Am. Math. Soc., Phi Beta Kappa, Sigma Xi, Phi Kappa Phi, Beta Gamma Sigma. Republican. Editor: Theory of Computation series, 1974—; asso. editor Jour. Computer and System Scis., 1968-74, editor, 1974—; editor SIAM Jour. Computing, 1974—; editorial adv. bd. Jour. Computer Langs., 1974—; contbr. to profl. jours. Office: Box 6026 Sta B Vanderbilt U Nashville TN 37235

FISCHER, WILLIAM O. (BILL), accountant; b. Houston, Nov. 19, 1943; s. William O. and Martha F.; B.S. in Edn., Concordia Coll., Seward, Nebr., 1965; student Kent State U., Case Western Res. U., W. Tex. State U.; m. Trina Baker, July 31, 1965; children—Kiersten, Eric. Tchr., Lutheran High East, Cleve., 1965-71; farmer, Dalhart, Tex., 1971-72; owner, mgr. Dumas Truck Dispatch Co., Dumas, Tex., 1972-73; office mgr. Empire Constrn. Co., Stratford, Tex., 1973—. Lutheran. Home: 724 Bennett St Dumas TX 79029 Office: 119 S Spruce St Stratford TX 79084

FISH, CLARA MAE, nurse; b. Atlanta, Aug. 31, 1916; d. Clarence Curtis and Ida Elizabeth (Scroggins) Martin; student public schs., Crowell, Tex.; m. Henry Fish. Nov. 12, 1939; children—Robert L., Gordon B., Martha E. Nurse, Mental Health Mental Retardation State Hosp., Vernon, Tex., 1974-80, psychiat. nurse Infirmary, 1974—. Mem. Nat. Soc. Published Poets, Am. Mgmt. Assn. Mem. Ch. of Christ. Author numerous poems and songs. Home: 821 N Main St Crowell TX 79227 Office: Tex State Mental Health Center North 821 N Main St Vernon TX 79227

FISH, JAMES FRANKLIN, nuclear environ. systems co. exec.; b. Worcester, Mass., Feb. 5, 1920; s. Charles Robinson and Bessie Irene (McLaughlin) F.; B.S. in Mech. Engring., Brown U., 1942; m. Julia Joan Frances Gibbs, Dec. 21, 1946; children—Joan Elizabeth (Mrs. George Hunt Rounsavall), James McLaughlin. Field engr. Pratt & Whitney Aircraft Co., London, Eng., 1942-47; asst. mgr. Fram Corp., Washington, 1947-53; with Am. Air Filter Co. Inc., Louisville, 1953—, mgr. nuclear environ. systems, 1965—; lectr. on air cleaning; mem. Atomic Indsl. Forum, 1970, Govt.-Industry Conf. on Nuclear Air Cleaning, 1965—. Pres. Hills and Dales Civic Assn., 1970-72; chmn. pack com. Cub Scouts Am. Named hon. Ky. col. Mem. ASME (chmn. com. nuclear air and gas treatment), Am. Nuclear Soc., Inst. Environ. Sci. Republican. Episcopalian. Club: Filson. Contbr. articles on air cleaning to profl. jours. Patentee in field. Home: 3415 Mt Rainier Dr Louisville KY 40222 Office: 215 Central Ave Louisville KY 40277

FISH, MARY MARTHA, economist; b. Albert Lea, Minn., July 17, 1930; B.B.A., U. Minn., 1953; M.B.A., Tex. Tech. Coll., 1957; Ph.D., U. Okla., 1963. Statis. asst. Iowa Bd. Control, 1951-53; analyst Calif. Dept. Public Health, 1953-54; statistician Tokyo Med. Lab., U.S. Army, 1954-55; instr. Odessa (Tex.) Coll., 1957-58; asst. prof., then asso. prof. econs. W. Tex. State U., 1961-66; prof. econs. U. Ala., 1966—; Fulbright lectr. U. Liberia, 1974-75; cons. Govt. Gambia, 1977-78. Mem. Am. Econs. Assn., So. Econs. Assn., Midsouth Acad. Economists. Co-author: Convicts, Codes and Contraband, 1974; contbr. articles to profl. jours. Home: 9 R Northwood Lake Northport AL 35476 Office: Box J Coll Commerce and Bus Adminstrn Univ Ala University AL 35486

FISH, ROBERT JAY, dental surgeon; b. Zanesville, Ohio, June 4, 1947; s. Sidney and Sara Mae (Rogovin) F.; B.S., Ohio State U., 1969, D.D.S., 1973. Practice gen. dentistry and dental reconstruction, Ft. Lauderdale, Fla., 1973—; pres. Fish & Lipson, Ft. Lauderdale; chmn. bd. Flying Fish Inc., RJF Assos.; dir. Dental Health Services Inc., 1975-78; asso. prof. microbiology Broward Community Coll., 1974. Mem. AAAS, Am. Soc. Clin. Hypnosis, Aircraft Owners and Pilots Assn., Am. Soc. Anesthesiologists, Alpha Omega. Author: Cosmetic and Reconstructive Dentistry, 1975. Home: 10237 NW 2d St Coral Springs FL 33065

FISHBURN, GAYE GIPSON, counselor; b. Miami, Fla., Jan. 14, 1950; d. Hubert Russel and Loray Alice (Heath) Gipson; B.A., Fla. Internat. U., 1975; M.A., U. W.Fla., 1977; m. Robert C. Fishburn, June 16, 1979. Group facilitator Fla. Internat. U., 1974; clin. resident Montanari Clin./Residential Sch., Hialeah, Fla., 1974-75; child care worker Variety Children's Hosp., Miami, 1976; facilitator, tchr. career and life planning U. W. Fla., 1977; counselor Alcohol Counseling Center, Pensacola, Fla., 1977—; cons., speaker in field. Recipient Vol. Merit award YWCA, 1978, cert. appreciation Fla. Office Volunteerism, 1978. Mem. Am. Mental Health Counselors Assn., Am. Personnel and Guidance Assn., Am. Coll. Personnel Assn., Fla. Internat. U. Alumni Assn., U. W.Fla. Alumni Assn. Club: Toastmasters.

FISHER, ADA MARKITA, physician, author; b. Durham, N.C., Oct. 21, 1947; d. Miles M. and Ada V. (Foster) F.; B.A., U. N.C., Greensboro, 1970; M.D., U. Wis., Madison, 1975. Intern Highland Hosp.-U. Rochester (N.Y.), 1975-76, resident family medicine, 1976-78, asso. chief resident, 1977-78; practice medicine specializing in family practice Greenevers, N.C., 1978-80; ancillary emergency room physician Highland Hosp., Rochester, Nicholas H. Noyes Meml. Hosp., Danville, N.Y., Lakeside Meml. Hosp., 1972-78; counselor and tchr. health sci. Madison Sr. High Sch., Rochester, 1977; clin. instr. dept. family medicine U. N.C., Chapel Hill, 1979—; chief med. officer Plain View Health Center, Greenevers, 1978-80; cons. minority med. edn., 1970—; mem. staff Duplin Gen. Hosp., Kenansville, N.C., 1978-80; basketball team physician Madison Sr. High Sch., 1977. Diplomate Am. Bd. Family Practice (is this Mem. Nat. Med. Assn., Old North State Med. Soc., State Med. Soc. of N.C., AMA, Duplin County Med. Soc. Jewish. Author several guides for black med. students; also poetry. Office: Plain View Health Center Route 2 Greenevers Rose Hill NC 28458

FISHER, BETHANY JEANNE, ednl. adminstr.; b. Detroit, June 27, 1945; d. Harry C. and Elizabeth McLean (Dulmage) Fisher; B.A., Mich. State U., 1967, Ph.D., 1976: M.A., Syracuse U., 1969. Head resident dean women's staff Syracuse U., 1969-67; asst. dir. student fin. aids office SUNY, 1969-70; coordinator student activities, asst. dir. Meml. Union, U. N.H., Durham, 1970-73; grad. teaching asst. Mich. State U., 1973-75; asst. dean office for student devel., dir. admissions, Johns Hopkins Sch. Health Services, 1975-78, asst. prof., 1975-78; v.p. student life Tex. Woman's U., Denton, 1978-80; v.p. student affairs U. Ala., Huntsville, 1980—; mem. U. N.H. Commn. on Status Women, 1971-73; coordinator ACU-I Core Cons. Programming Workshop for New Eng., U. N.H., 1973; mem. affirmative action com. Johns Hopkins U., 1975. Mem. Nat. Assn. Women Deans, Adminstrs. and Counselors, Regional Assn. Women Deans, Adminstrs. and Counselors (state v.p. 1977), Am. Assn. Coll. Registrars and Officers of Admissions, Am. Assn. Higher Edn., AAUW, Am. Coll. Personnel Assn., Am. Personnel and Guidance Assn. Mem. editorial bd. Jour. Coll. Student Personnel, 1976—; co-editor The MSU Orient, Vol. 9, Number 2, 1974. Contbr. articles to profl. jours. Office: Student Affairs U Ala Huntsville AL 35801

FISHER, DONALD WAYNE, assn. exec.; b. Pitts., Mar. 2, 1946; s. David Henry William and Jean Kerr (Crum) F.; A.A., Hinds Jr. Coll., 1966; B.S., Millsaps Coll., 1968; M.S., U. Miss. Med. Center, 1970, Ph.D., 1973; m. Lea Elizabeth Greenwood, Aug. 23, 1969; children—Kimberly Elizabeth, Jeffrey Wayne. Instr. dept. chemistry, dept. biology Hinds Jr. Coll., Raymond, Miss., 1968-74, chmn. physician asst. dept. 1972-74; instr. U. Miss. Sch. Medicine, Jackson, 1972-74; co-dir., exec. office physician assts. program U. Miss. Sch. Medicine and Hinds Jr. Coll., 1972-74; exec. dir. Am. Acad. Physicians Assts., Arlington, Va., 1973—, Assn. of Physician Asst. Programs, Arlington, 1977—; pres. Am. Acad. Physician Assts. Ednl. and Research Found.; mem. Nat. Commn. on Allied Health Edn.; mem. recertification com. Nat. Commn. on Ceritification of Physician's Assts.; mem. adv. com. for tng., devel. and utilization of physician extenders System Scis., Inc. Mem. Am. Soc. Allied Health Professions, Am. Soc. Assn. Execs., Washington Soc. Assn. Execs. Presbyterian.

FISHER, EDWARD LYNN, indsl. engr.; b. McKeesport, Pa., Oct. 21, 1952; s. George Earl and Wilma Ruth (Sypolt) F.; B.S. in Indsl. Engring., W.Va. U., 1975, M.S. in Indsl. Engring., 1978; postgrad., 1978—; m. Jackline Bendel, Aug. 23, 1975. Indsl. engr. parcel post damage reduction program U.S. Postal Service, Pitts., 1974; indsl. engr. U.S. Forest Service, Morgantown, W.Va., 1976-77; research indsl. engr., 1978—; mem. indsl. engring. adv. com. W.Va. U., 1976—. Registered profl. engr., W.Va. Mem. Am. Inst. Indsl. Engring. (pres. Monongahela chpt. 1979), U.S. Jaycees, Am. Soc. Agrl. Engrs., Sigma Xi (sec. W.Va. chpt. 1979), Tau Beta Pi, Alpha Pi Mu. Democrat. Contbr. articles to profl. jours. Home: 1338 Airport Blvd Morgantown WV 26505 Office: 180 Canfield St Morgantown WV 26505

FISHER, ELIZABETH CAVITT BOUSHALL, designer, image cons.; b. Dallas, Mar. 11, 1941; d. Francis McGee and Ruth Cavitt (Taliaferro) Boushall; student Southwestern U., 1959-61; B.A., La. State U., 1963; m. Michael Stewart Kilpatrick Fisher, Sept. 14, 1963; children—Ann Cavitt, Carolyn Stewart. Journalist, Houston Post, 1957-59, Baton Rouge State Times, 1961-63; profl. model, Houston, 1958-62; public relations dir., student program advisor Tex. A. and M. U., Meml. Student Center, College Station, 1965-67; editor Tex. Aggie mag., College Station, 1966-67; founder, faculty English, Christian Sch., Greenville, Miss., 1969-72; faculty Washington Sch., Greenville, 1972-75, St. Martin's Protestant Episcopal Sch., New Orleans, 1975; fashion cons. Doncastor Co., New Orleans, 1975-79, asst. dir. mgr., 1977-79; founder, exec. dir. Internat. Design Counsel, Inc., Metairie, La., 1977—; advt. cons. Sellers Chem. Corp., 1977-78. Mem. women's vol. com. New Orleans Mus. Art, 1976—; active Jefferson Parish Rep. Womens Orgn., Metairie, 1975—; del. Gov.'s Conf. on Women, Baton Rouge, 1976, Gov.'s Conf. on Priorities for the Future, New Orleans, 1979; pres. Conf. on Small Bus., New Orleans and Atlanta, 1979. Mem. LWV (fin. adv. bd. 1979—), AAUW, Women in Communications, Am. Mgmt. Assn., Internat. Communications Assn., Pi Delta Epsilon, Alpha Delta Pi, Theta Sigma Phi. Republican. Presbyterian. Club: The Pendinnis. Contbr. articles to profl. jours. Home: 312 Marguerite Rd Metairie LA 70003 Office: PO Box 162 Metairie LA 70004

FISHER, FRANCENIA ELEANORE, plant pathologist; b. Green Cove Springs, Fla., Sept. 23, 1924; d. Roy Dexter and Daisy (Sparkman) Fisher; B.S., Fla. State U., 1945; postgrad. U. Chgo., 1945; M.S., Mich. State U., 1946. Plant pathologist Citrus Expt. Sta., U. Fla., Lake Alfred, 1946—; researcher, cons., 1946—; cons. U. Calif., Berkeley, 1972-73; pvt. practitioner, tech. advisor, 1979—. Mem. AAAS, Soc. Econ. Botany, Am. Phytopath. Soc., Internat. Soc. Plant Pathology, Fla. Hort. Soc., Smithsonian Assos., Internat. Congress Plant Protection, Internat. Orgn. Citrus Virologists, Internat. Soc. Citriculture, Seminarium Botanicum (hon.), Ancient Order Ranales (hon.), Sigma Xi. Democrat. Episcopalian. Club: Lake Region Yacht and Country (charter mem.). Editor, pub.: World Directory of Plant Pathologists. Contbr. articles on citrus diseases caused by fungi, chem. control, biol. control, fungus diseases of insects and mites attacking citrus to profl. jours. and trade mags. Home: 1507 W Lake Cannon Dr PO Box 242 Winter Haven FL 33880 Office: U Fla Agricultural Research and Education Center PO Box 229 Lake Alfred FL 33850

FISHER, HOOVER PAGE, educator, musician; b. Sands Springs, Okla., Dec. 10, 1928; s. Roy Tenny and Letitia May (Gripe) F.; B.Mus.Edn., Okla. State U., 1950, M.S., 1954; D.M.E., U. Okla., 1969; m. Loretta Kathleen Colbert, Aug. 18, 1950; children—Roy Edmond, Steven Page, Mark Allen. Choral dir. Borger (Tex.) High Sch., 1950-51, Bartlesville (Okla.) High Sch., 1951-53, Guymon (Okla.) High Sch., 1953-61, Durant (Okla.) High Sch., 1961-65; dir. choral activities Okla. State U., 1965—. Active Boy Scouts. Mem. Am. Choral Dirs. Assn. (pres. Okla. 1970-71), Okla. Music Educators Assn. (pres. 1971-73), Music Educators Nat. Conf. (pres. S.W. div. 1975-77). Editor: Okla. Sch. Music News, 1973—. Home: 1309 Cedar Dr Stillwater OK 74074 Office: Okla State U Stillwater OK 74074

FISHER, JAMES RAYMOND, JR., social and indsl. psychologist; b. Clinton, Iowa, Apr. 29, 1937; s. James Raymond and Dorothy Cecilia (Ekland) F.; B.A., U. Iowa, 1956, B.S., 1956, M.S. in Biochemistry, 1958; M.A. in Social Psychology, U. South Fla., 1976; Ph.D., Walden U., 1978; m. Patricia Ann Zimmerman, Feb. 11, 1956 (div. Mar. 1979); children—Robert Joseph, Laura Ann, Jeanne Marie, Michael John. Chem. sales engr. Nalco Chem. Co., Chgo., 1958-63, corp. exec. Internat. div., 1964-68; freelance writer, Fla., 1969-70; researcher U. South Fla., Tampa, 1972-73; sr. cons., project mgr. for mgmt. studies Raleigh (N.C.) Police and Fairfax County (Va.) Police, 1974-75; pres., mng. dir. Psyche-ology, Inc., Tampa, 1976—; pvt. practice psychology, Tampa, 1978—; mgmt. and orgn. devel. specialist Honeywell Avionics, 1980; adj. prof. social and criminal psychology Nova U., la. Inst. Tech., Golden Gate U., U. South Fla., others.; police psychologist Pinellas Country (Fla.) Police, 1969—, Pasco-Hernando Country (Fla.) Police Acad., 1969—; cons. in field. Served with USN, 1956-58. Recipient various awards. Mem. Am. Psychol. Assn., Am. Chem. Soc., Phi Beta Kappa, Phi Eta Sigma, Omicron Delta Kappa, Phi Kappa Phi. Author: Sales Training and Technical Development, 1968; Confident Selling, 1971; The Self-Centered Self, 1974; Search for the Real Parents of My Soul, 1975; A Social Psychological Study of the Police Organization: The Anatomy of a Riot, 1978; The Police Paradox: Sick Cops or Sick System, 1980. Home: 2904 Janice Way Tampa FL 33609

FISHER, JAMES WILEY, educator; b. Holdenville, Okla., Aug. 20, 1941; s. Quentin Harley and Irene Estele (Hill) F.; B.S., Sul Ross State U., 1964; postgrad., The U. Tex., St. Mary's U., Trinity U., 1969-73, U. Tex., San Antonio, 1975-80; Ph.D. (hon.), Columbia, 1971. Tchr. Harry Rogers Jr. High, San Antonio, 1968-69, Kirby Jr. High Sch., San Antonio, 1969-72; tchr. biology Jack Yates High Sch., Houston, 1973-74; biology, agrl. S. San Antonio (Tex.) High Sch., 1974-79; adminstr. Lydke Ind. Sch. Dist., 1980—. Chmn. U. Fund Drive, 1970-72, Future Tchrs. Sponsors Div., 1970-75. Mem. com. Profl. Rights, Responsibilities, 1970-71, dist. XX T.E.P.S., 1970-72. Mem. Tex. Congress, Kirby (life, citation, 1973) P.T.A., Young Sci. Am., 1970-75. Active San Antonio council Boy Scouts of Am., 1969—. Delegate various tchrs. convs. Mem. Good Gov't League, 1968—, Students Democrats, Tex. (pres. 1964-65); com. presdl. Phys. Fitness, 1973-75, legis. Bexar County Educators, 1970-72, gov.'s Drive Safety, 1972-75. Recipient awards, citations for work in field. Mem. Student Edn. Assn., Future Tchrs. Am. (life, dist. adv., 1973-74), Tex. Sci. Tchrs. Assn., Ark., Judson, Houston, Tex., classroom tchrs. assns., Nat. Edn. Assn. (life), Alpha Sigma Kappa (life), Alpha Delta Chi, Alpha Delta Kappa. Babt. Lions. Home: 215 Blakeley Dr San Antonio TX 78209

FISHER, JOE JEFFERSON, U.S. dist. judge; b. Bland Lake, Tex.; student Stephen F. Austin Coll., 1929; LL.B., U. Tex., 1936. Admitted to Tex. bar, 1936; county atty. San Augustine County 1936-39; dist. atty. 1st Jud. Dist. Tex., 1939-46; practice law, Jasper, Tex., 1946-57; dist. judge 1st Jud. Dist. Tex., 1957-59; U.S. dist. judge for Eastern Dist. Tex., 1959-67, chief judge, 1967—. Trustee, Trinity United Meth. Ch., Beaumont, Schlesingers Geriatric Center; dist. gov., bd. dirs. Lions Internat., mem. exec. bd., mem. Tex. Lions Hall of Fame; pres. Tex. Gulf. Hist. Soc.; mem. advisory bd. Southwestern U. St. Elizabeth Hosp. Mem. Am. (chmn. jud. sect. 1957), 1st Jud. (pres. 1956), Tex. bar assns., Am. Judicature Soc., Ex-Students Assn. U. Tex. and Stephen F. Austin State U. (Hall of Fame), E. Tex., Jasper and Beaumont chambers commerce, Sons Republic of Tex., Delta Kappa Epsilon. Recipient Silver Beaver award Boy Scouts Am., 1954. Home: 130 C Caldwood St Beaumont TX 77707 Office: PO Box 88 Beaumont TX 77704

FISHER, JOHN FREMONT, physician; b. Dayton, Ohio, May 13, 1943; s. Robert Stewart and Audrey Kathryn (Johnson) F.; A.B., U. Notre Dame, 1965; M.D., Med. Coll. Va., 1969; m. Peggy Jean Ballance, July 10, 1976; children—Audrey Elizabeth and Brigid Ballance (twins), John Brendan. Intern in pediatrics U. Cin., 1969-70, resident in internal medicine, 1970-71; resident in internal medicine Med. Coll. Va., Richmond, 1974-75, fellow in infectious disease, 1975-77; practice medicine specializing in internal medicine, Augusta, 1977—; mem. staffs VA Hosp., Univ. Hosp., Eugene Talmadge Meml. Hosp.; asst. prof. medicine Med. Coll. Ga., Augusta, 1977—; Recipient Excellence in Teaching award Med. Coll. Ga., 1978, 79, Robb Davis Meml. Teaching award, 1979, Faculty of Yr. award, 1979; diplomate Am. Bd. Internal Medicine. Served with M.C., USN, 1972-74. Mem. A.C.P., Soc. for Preservation and Encouragement of Barber Shop Quartet Singing in Am. Roman Catholic. Contbr. articles to med. jours. Home: 751 Lancaster Rd Augusta GA 30909 Office: Med Coll Ga Augusta GA 30901

FISHER, JOHN MILLER, JR., constrn. engr.; b. Roanoke Rapids, N.C., July 19, 1926; s. John Miller and Cassie (Sadler) F.; B.C.E., N.C. State Coll., 1951; m. Betty J. Harper, June 23, 1969; children—Victor H., John Miller III, Betty Melissa. Engr. aide Alaska Rd. Commn., Anchorage dist., 1951-52; with Ebasco Services, Inc., N.Y.C., 1952-54, 56-78, field and office engr., Mt. Gilead, N.C., 1959-61, office engr., Farmington, N.M., 1961-64, office engr., purchasing agt., constrn. engr., Elderton, Pa., 1964-67, resident engr., constrn. supt., project supt., New Florence, Pa., 1967-72, constrn. supt., project supt., Hutchinson Island, Fla., 1972-75, project supt., Millstone 1 Radwaste, 1975-76, project supt. regional office, Atlanta, 1976-78; constrn. mgr. Gilbert Assos. Inc., Reading, Pa., 1978-79, mgr. projects, 1979—; resident constrn. services mgr. Neka and Tabriz Thermal Power Projects in Iran, 1978-79. Fallout Shelter analyst U.S. Dept. Def., 1966—. Guest lectr. Argonne Center for Ednl. Affairs, 1976, 77. Registered profl. engr., Vt., N.C., N.M., Pa., Fla. Served with USNR, 1944-46; PTO. Mem. Am. Soc. Civil Engrs., AAAS, Mensa, Internat. Platform Assn., Nat. Constructors Assn. (sec. tri-state com. 1969, vice chmn. 1970, co-chmn. 1971), Am. Arbitration Assn. (panel arbitrators). Home: Route 4 Box 171 Candler NC 28718 Office: PO Box 1498 Reading PA 19603

FISHER, JOHN MORRIS, assn. ofcl., educator; b. Fairhaven, O., Apr. 20, 1922; s. Marion Hays and Bessie (Morris) F.; A.B., Miami U., Oxford, O., 1947; postgrad. Bklyn. Law Sch., 1950-51, Northwestern U., 1954-55; LL.D., Masson Coll., 1972; m. Thelma Ison, Feb. 2, 1947; children—Steven Roger, Linda Lucille. With Belden Mfg. Co., Richmond, Ind., 1941; spl. agt. FBI, 1947-53; exec. trainee Sears Roebuck & Co., Chgo., 1953, exec. staff asst. to v.p. personnel and employee relations, 1953-57, chmn. security com., 1957-61; operating dir. Am. Security Council, 1956-57, pres., chief exec. officer, 1957—; pres. Am. Research Found., 1961—; pres. Communications Corp. Am., 1972—; organizer, pres. Fidelifax, Inc., 1956-57; chmn. merc. div. Nat. Safety Council, 1959-60, 1st vice chmn. trades and services sect., 1961-63. Chmn. Chgo. Retail Safety Conf., 1959-60; spl. adviser Ill. Supt. Pub. Instrn., 1963-64; cons. to Gov. Fla.; cons. to chmn. com. cold war edn. Nat. Gov.'s Conf., 1962-65, Ill. Civil Def. Adv. Council, 1965-68; pres. Am. Council World Freedom, 1971-72; mem. exec. com. Nat. Captive Nations Com., 1968—. Bd. visitors Freedoms Found., 1964-65; bd. dirs. Am. Fgn. Policy Inst., 1975—, James Monroe Library, 1977—. Served to 1st lt. USAAF, 1943-45. Decorated Air medal with clusters; recipient 10th Anniversary medal and scroll Assembly Captive European Nations, Order Lafayette Freedom award, 1973. Mem. Am. Soc. Indsl. Security (dir. 1959-62), Phi Kappa Tau. Republican. Presbyn. Mason. Clubs: Army Navy, Nat. Democratic, Capitol Hill (Washington). Home: Pleasant Hill Boston VA 22713 Office: Am Security Council Edn Found Library Boston VA 22713

FISHER, JOSEPH LYMAN, congressman; b. Pawtucket, R.I., Jan. 11, 1914; s. Howard Colburn and Caroline (Nash) F.; B.S., Bowdoin Coll., 1935, D.Sc. (hon.), 1965; postgrad. London Sch. Econs., 1935-36; M.A., Harvard U., 1938, Ph.D. in Econs. (teaching fellow 1946-47), 1947; M.A. in Edn., George Washington U., 1951; LL.D. (hon.), Allegheny Coll., 1966; L.H.D. (hon.), Starr King Sch. Ministry, 1971; m. Margaret Saunders Winslow, June 21, 1942; children—H. Benjamin, Caroline, Robert W., William B., Elizabeth, James H., Barbara W. Instr. econs. Allegheny Coll., 1938-40; planning technician Nat. Resources Planning Bd., 1939-43; economist Dept. State, 1943; economist, exec. officer Council Econ. Advisers, Washington, 1947-53; asso. dir. Resources for the Future, Inc., Washington, 1953-59, pres., 1959-74; mem. 94th-96th congresses from Va. 10th Dist.; trustee Analytic Services, Inc., 1968-74; vis. prof. U. Colo., 1957, U. Calif., 1971, 76; staff dir. Cabinet Com. Energy Supplies and Policies, 1955; cons. to govt. agys. Mem. Arlington County Bd., 1964-74, chmn., 1965, 71. Trustee Unitarian Universalist Assn., 1961-65, moderator, chmn. bd. trustees, 1965-77; trustee Tchrs. Ins. and Annuity Assn., 1966-74, United Planning Orgn., 1966-71; bd. dirs. Met. Washington Council of Govts., 1966-74, pres. 1969, chmn., 1970; bd. dirs. Washington Met. Area Transit Authority, 1972-74, chmn., 1972; bd. overseers Bowdoin Coll.; advisory council Electric Power Research Inst., 1973-79. Served with inf. U.S. Army, 1943-46. Mem. Am. Forestry Assn. (dir.), Am. Econ. Assn., Am. Soc. Pub. Adminstrn., AAAS, Regional Sci. Assn., Phi Beta Kappa, Phi Delta Kappa. Clubs: Century (N.Y.C.); Cosmos (Washington). Author: (with others) Resources in America's Future; World Prospects for Natural Resources. Contbr. chpts. in books, articles to profl. jours. Home: 2608 N 24th St Arlington VA 22207 Office: 223 Cannon Office Bldg Washington DC 20075

FISHER, KING, marine contracting co. exec.; b. Port Lavaca, Tex., Jan. 14, 1916; s. Charles Everett and Kittie (Moss) F.; student pub. schs., Port Lavaca; m. Jewel Tanner, Aug. 13, 1937; children—Ann Fisher Boyd, Linda Fisher LaQuay. Pres. King Fisher Marine Service, Inc., Port Lavaca, 1941—; treas. Fisher Channel & Dock Co., Port Lavaca, 1954—; dir. First Nat. Bank of Flour Bluff, Corpus Christi, First Nat. Bank of Port Lavaca (Tex.). Bd. dirs. Indsl. Found. of South. Mem. Tex. Mid-Coast Water Devel. Assn., Port Lavaca C. of C. Home: Hillcrest Chocolate Bay Port Lavaca TX 77979 Office: PO Box 108 Port Lavaca TX 77979

FISHER, LESLIE ROBERT, state ofcl. Okla.; b. Madill, Okla., Jan. 17, 1922; s. Alfred Fidela and Emma Theodosia (Gullege) F.; B.S., Southeastern State Col., Okla., 1951; Ed.M., U. Okla. at Norman, 1954, Ed.D., 1963; m. Ernestine Jewell Gilstrap, Oct. 11, 1941; children—Linda (Mrs. Larry Garrison), Susan (Mrs. Wayne Boyd), David. Coach, tchr., Springs, Okla., 1948-51; high sch. prin., Lone Grove, Okla., 1951-54; supt. schs., Mountain Home, Ringling, Okla., 1954-57, Elmore City, 1957-61, Moore, Okla., 1961-70; state supt. pub. instrn. Okla., Oklahoma City, 1970—. Vice-chmn., Okla. Commn. on Ednl. Adminstrn., pres. E. Central dist., tri-county; mem. adv. bd. Okla. State Bd. Vocat. Edn.; dir. Mid-Continent Regional Ednl. Lab.; mem. planning com. S.W. Regional Drive-in Conf., chmn. 1967; mem. Okla. State Bd. Edn., State Bd. Vocat. and Tech. Edn., Sch. Land Commn., State Accrediting Agy., State Edn. TV Authority, Air Edn. Commn.; chmn. vis. com. U. Okla. Coll. Edn. Bd. regents Colls. Served with USNR, 1942-45. Selected Outstanding Citizen of Moore, C. of C., 1961-62, Moore Jr. C. of C., 1963-68; recipient certificate Spl. Merit, Okla. Assn. Sch. Adminstrs., 1966. Mem. Am. (Okla. leader), Okla. (past pres.) assns. sch. adminstrs., NEA (life), Okla. Edn. Assn. (del. assembly, dir. credit union), Nat. Acad. Sch. Execs., Moore C. of C., Phi Delta Kappa. Club: Lions. Office: State Capitol Oklahoma City 73105*

FISHER, LEWIS ROBERT, govt. aerospace engr.; b. Paterson, N.J., May 18, 1921; s. Jacob and Rebecca (Collins) F.; B.S. in Aerospace Engring., N.Y. U., 1947; M.S. in Aerospace Engring., U. Va., Charlottesville, 1954; m. Lily Mary Brynda, Sept. 26, 1968; children—Debra, Anthony, Carolynn. Aerospace research engr. NASA Langley Research Center, Hampton, Va., 1947-59; aerospace technologist NASA Space Task Group, Houston, 1959-62; dep. mgr. engring. office Space Shuttle Orbiter Project NASA Johnson Space Center, Houston, 1962—. Served with USAAF, 1943-46. Recipient certificate of commendation NASA, 1969; registered comml. instrument pilot. Asso. fellow Am. Inst. Aeros. and Astronautics; mem. Aircraft Owners and Pilots Assn., Nat. Pilots Assn. Contbr. tech. articles in field to profl. jours. Home: 344 St Cloud Dr Friendswood TX 77546 Office: NASA Johnson Space Center Houston TX 77058

FISHER, MARK HOWARD, accountant; b. St. Petersburg, Va., May 18, 1952; s. Howard G. and Dorothy A. F.; B.B.A. in Acctg., U. Tex., 1974, M.P.A., 1975. Teaching asst. U. Tex., Austin, 1973-75; acct. tax dept. Arthur Young & Co., Houston, 1976-79, tax mgr.,

1979—; fin. v.p. Merit Drilling Co., 1979—; tax cons. Mem. Am. Inst. C.P.A.'s, Tex. Soc. Public Accts., Ind. Assn. Drilling Contractors (acctg. com.), Phi Delta Theta Alumni. Republican. Episcopalian. Clubs: Met. Racquet, Houston. Contbr. short story to College mag., 1970. Home: 102 Litchfield St Houston TX 77024 Office: 2500 Pennzoil St Houston TX 77002

FISHER, MARY BELLE, state agy. adminstr.; b. Gary, Ind., Aug. 12, 1944; d. Ernest Norman and Mildred Mary (Holland) F.; B.S. in Bus. Adminstrn., Ky. State U., 1978. Stenographer, Bur. Rehab. Services, Dept. Edn., State of Ky., Frankfort, 1963-70, prin. stenographer div. reclamation Dept. Natural Resources, 1970-73, adminstrv. sec. Office of Planning and Research, Dept. Natural Resources and Environ. Protection, 1973-77, adminstrv. asst. div. hazardous materials and waste mgmt., 1978—; adminstrv. and tech. asst. Hittman Assos., Inc., Lexington, 1977-78. Democrat. Club: Order Eastern Star. Home: 307 Ridgewood Ln Frankfort KY 40601 Office: 1121 Louisville Rd Frankfort KY 40601

FISHER, MILTON NATHAN, mfg. co. exec.; b. Newark, Nov. 25, 1921; s. Davis and Maria (Rapaport) F.; B.S. in Bus. Adminstrn., U. Fla., 1946; m. Berna Braunstein, June 9, 1946; 1 son, Jerome Peter. Pres., dir. Panelfab Internat. Corp., Miami, Fla., 1951—; pres., dir. Decor Internacional de Cuba, 1958-59; pres., dir. Dicoa Corp., 1958—, Cocoa Export Corp.; pres., dir. Panelfab Pacific, Inc., 1965—, Panelfab P.R., Inc., 1967—; dir. Panelfab Europe, Ltd. Chmn. Fla. Dist. Export Council, U.S. Dept. Commerce; mem., dir. Fla. Council Internat. Devel. Former pres., dir. Bd. Internat. Trade; former pres., bd. dirs. Internat. Center of Fla.; mem. bd. exec. advisors Coll. Bus. Adminstrn., U. Miami; chmn. bd. dirs. Dade County chpt. A.R.C. Served to maj. USAFR, 1942-45. Decorated D.F.C., Air medal with 3 oak leaf clusters. Mem. SE U.S./Japan Assn. (past chmn. Fla. del.), Tau Epsilon Phi, Beta Alpha Psi, Beta Gamma Sigma. Mason. Club: Banker's (Miami, Fla.). Home: 535 Reinante Ave Coral Gables FL 33156 Office: 1600 N W Le Jeune Rd Miami FL 33126

FISHER, RAY, photographer; b. Cleve., June 24, 1924; s. Andrew W. and Bertha (Friedman) F.; A.B., U. Miami, 1953; m. Suzanne Dubois, Aug. 9, 1953; children—Andrew Eugene, Richard Dubois, Julie Louise. Successively staff photographer, chief photographer, picture editor Miami (Fla.) Herald, 1953-69; pres. Ray Fisher Inc., Miami, 1969—; founder U. Miami Photography Center, 1953; lectr. in field; coordinator, chmn. Wilson Hicks Internat. Conf. on Visual Communication, 1957-74. Served as combat photographer U.S. Army, World War II. Decorated Purple Heart; recipient ann. awards Nat. Press Photographers Assn., 1960, 67, Picture of Year 2d place award, 1968, Wilson Hicks award, 1974. Mem. Am. Soc. Mag. Photographers (officer Fla. chpt. 1980), Internat. Center Photography, Photog. Adminstrs. Inc., Met. Mus. Art., Friends of Theatre Collection, Nat., Miami (past pres.) press photographers assns., Met. Opera Guild, Greater Miami Opera Assn., Iron Arrow, Sigma Delta Chi, Omicron Delta Kappa. Clubs: Vizcayans; Century (Univ. Miami). Home and Office: 10700 SW 72d Ct Miami FL 33156

FISHER, ROBERT EARL, electro-mech. products co. exec.; b. Lawrence County, Ind., Mar. 17, 1932; s. William Jesse and Hazel Clara (Poole) F.; B.A., Hanover (Ind.) Coll., 1953; postgrad. Ind. U., 1960-61, N.Y. U., 1978; m. Beverly M. Stone, June 22, 1956; children—Deborah, Theresa, Patrick, Kimberly, Elizabeth. Mgmt. trainee, salesman, coordinator Arvin Industries, Columbus, Ind., 1953-58; mfg. supt. Radio Corp. Am., Bloomington, Ind., 1958-65, Memphis, 1965-67; plant supt. Gen. Telephone & Electronics, Batavia, N.Y., 1967-72; mgr. mfg., plant mgr. Stackpole Components Co., Farmville, Va., 1972—; guest lectr. Southside Va. Community Coll. Served with USAF, 1953-55. Mem. Am. Mfrs. Assn., Farmville C. of C. (indsl. devel. com.). Roman Catholic. Club: Moose. Home: Route 4 Box 140 Farmville VA 23901 Office: PO Box M Farmville VA 23901

FISHER, ROLLAND ROY, mgmt. systems cons.; b. Southard, Okla., June 17, 1935; s. Roy B. and Lorene Josephine (Schnell) F.; B.S., Okla. State U., 1958, M.S., 1964; Ph.D., U. Ill., 1972; m. Earlene Yvonne Windham, Aug. 25, 1957; 1 son, Mark Adam. Commd. 2d lt. U.S. Air Force, 1958, advanced through grades to col., 1979; fuels supply officer, N.J., Korea, Calif., 1958-62; various assignments as engr. and systems analyst, 1962-69; systems analyst for computer system, logistics engr., analyst Orgn. of Joint Chiefs of Staff, Washington, 1972-78; mem. mil. faculty Nat. Def. U., Indsl. Coll. Armed Forces, Nat. War Coll., Ft. L.J. McNair, Washington, 1978-79, ret., 1979; sr. asso. Systems Research and Applications Corp., Arlington, Va., 1979—. Decorated Joint Service Commendation medal, Def. Meritorious Service medal with oak leaf cluster, Meritorious Service medal, Air Force Commendation medal with oak leaf cluster. Home: 8513 Canterbury Dr Annandale VA 22003 Office: Systems Research and Applications Corp 2425 Wilson Blvd Suite 245 Arlington VA 22201

FISHER, SEYMOUR, psychologist; b. N.Y.C., Nov. 4, 1925; s. George and Fannie (Hesselson) F.; B.A., N.Y. U., 1948; Ph Ph.D., U. N.C., 1952; postgrad. Washington Sch. of Psychiatry, 1954-55; m. Carmen Eldridge, June 20, 1959; children—Mark, Andrew. Psychol. trainee State Hosp., Raleigh, N.C., 1950; clin. psychologist trainee VA Hosp., Roanoke, Va., 1950; intern (part-time) Psychol. Clinic, U. N.C., Chapel Hill, 1950-51; trainee VA Hosp., Roanoke, Va., 1952; supervising clin. psychologist Walter Reed Army Inst. of Research, Washington, 1952-58; research psychologist Psychopharmacology Service Center, NIMH, Bethesda, Md., 1958-60, chief spl. studies unit, 1960-63; cons. NIMH, Chevy Chase, Md., 1964-66, Office of Naval Research, Washington, 1964-66, Mass. Dept. Mental Health, 1969—, FDA, 1973-77; pres. Boston Mental Health Found., Inc., 1970-72; prof. psychiatry Boston U. Sch. of Medicine, 1963-78, research prof. psychology Sch. of Grad. Dentistry, 1969-78, research prof. psychopharmacology Grad. Sch., 1965-78; prof., asso. chmn. psychiatry U. Tex. Med. Br., Galveston, 1978—. Fellow Am. Coll. Neuropsychopharmacology (asst. sec. 1973-77, chmn. constn. and rules com. 1977—), Am. Psychol. Assn., Collegium Internat. Neuro-Psychopharmacologicum; mem. AAAS, Am. Psychopathol. Assn. (mem. exec. council 1970-72), Sigma Xi, Psi Chi, Beta Lambda Sigma. Editorial bd. Psychopharmacology Service Center Bull., 1959-63; asso. editor Psychol. Record, 1960-66. Office: Dept Psychiatry and Behavioral Scis Univ Tex Med Br Galveston TX 77550

FISHER, SHIRLEY JACQUELINE, speech pathologist; b. Ft. Worth, Feb. 2, 1942; d. Jack Warren and Sarah Shirley (Smith) Woolsey; B.A., Tex. Christian U., 1965, M.S., 1976; 1 son, William Christopher Hesley. Speech pathologist Austin (Tex.) Ind. Sch. Dist., 1966-68; asst. head tchr., speech pathologist Hilltop Develop. Center, Richmond, Calif., 1972-73; program design/tng. personnel Ft. Worth State Sch., 1976-77; owner/dir. Hardwick Learning Center, Ft. Worth, 1978—. Mem. allocations com. United Way, Ft. Worth, 1976—; chmn. river parade Mayfest, Ft. Worth, 1979; mem. benefit com. Am. Cancer Soc., 1978. Tex. Christian U. scholar, 1974-76. Mem. Am. Speech and Hearing Assn., Kappa Alpha Theta. Presbyterian. Office: 1622 Rogers Rd Fort Worth TX 76107

FISHER, THOMAS JOHN, lawyer; b. Milw., Apr. 30, 1949; s. Joseph Vernon and Agnes (Gear) F.; B.A. with distinction, U. Wis., 1971, J.D., 1974; m. Margaret Jane Neu, June 6, 1974. Admitted to Wis. bar, 1974, Tex. bar, 1974; supervising atty. Tex. Rural Legal Aid, Inc., Kingsville, 1974-75; practiced law, Alice, Tex., 1975-76, Corpus Christi, Tex., 1977—; 1st asst. to county atty. Jim Wells County, Alice, 1977-78; asst. county atty. Nueces County, Corpus Christi, 1978—. Election insp. Sec. of State Tex., 1978; mem. campaign staff John Hill for Gov., Jim Wells County, Tex., 1978. Mem. Tex. Dist. and County Attys. Assn., State Bar Tex., State Bar Wis. Democrat. Home: 305 Texas St Corpus Christi TX 78404 Office: Nueces County Courthouse Corpus Christi TX 78401

FISHMAN, BARRY STUART, lawyer; b. Chgo., June 14, 1943; s. Jacob M. and Anita (Epstein) F.; B.A., U. Wis., 1965; J.D., DePaul U., 1968; m. Meredith Porte, Mar. 27, 1976. Admitted to Ill. bar, 1968, Fla., Calif. bars, 1969; partner firm Fishman & Fishman, Chgo., 1968-72; counsel real estate fin. dept. Baird & Warner, Inc., Chgo., 1972-75; counsel firm Cohen & Angel, North Miami, Fla., 1976; gen. counsel Biscayne Fed. Savs. & Loan Assn., Miami, Fla., 1977—; mem. firm Pallot, Poppell, Goodman & Slotnick, Miami, 1977—; dir. investment div. Cushman and Wakefield of Fla., 1978—. Mem. big gifts com. Greater Miami Jewish Fedn., 1977—; dir. Neighborhood Housing Services, Dade County, Fla., 1977—. Mem. Fla., Calif., Ill., Chgo., Dade County bar assns., Nat. Assn. Realtors, Real Estate Securities and Syndication Inst., Mortgage Bankers Assn. Jewish. Clubs: Aventura Country, Covennant. Home: 3625 N Country Club Dr North Miami Beach FL 33180 Office: 1790 Biscayne Blvd Miami FL 33132

FISHMAN, MARVIN ALLEN, physician; b. Chgo., Feb. 16, 1937; s. Joseph and Mary (Schneider) F.; B.S., U. Ill., 1959, M.D., 1961; m. Gloria B. Greenberg, Dec. 26, 1959; children—Bradley Stephen, Patricia Ann. Intern, Michael Reese Hosp., Chgo., 1961-62, resident in pediatrics, 1962-64; fellow in neurology Mass. Gen. Hosp., Boston, 1966-67; fellow in pediatric neurology St. Louis Children's Hosp., 1967-70; prof. pediatrics, neurology and preventive medicine Washington U. Sch. Medicine, St. Louis, 1970-79; prof. pediatrics and neurology Baylor Coll. Medicine, Houston, 1979—; dir. birth defects center St. Louis Children's Hosp., 1970-79; dir. Irene Walter Johnson Inst. Rehab. Washington U. Sch. Medicine, 1973-79; dir. sect. child neurology Baylor Coll. Medicine, 1979—. Served with U.S. Army, 1964-66. NIH fellow, 1966-70; recipient numerous grants Nat. Found. March of Dimes, Grant Found., Ga. Warm Springs Found. Mem. Am. Acad. Neurology, Am. Acad. Pediatrics, Am. Neurol. Assn., Am. Pediatric Soc., Am. Soc. Neurochemistry, Child Neurology Soc., Soc. Neuroscience, Soc. Pediatric Research, Alpha Omega Alpha. Contbr. chpts. to books; contbr. articles to med. jours. Home: 130 Plantation Houston TX 77024 Office: Dept Pediatrics 1200 Moursund Ave Houston TX 77030

FISHWICK, JOHN PALMER, railroad exec.; b. Roanoke, Va., Sept. 29, 1916; s. William and Nellie (Cross) F.; A.B., Roanoke Coll., Salem, Va., 1937, D.H.L. (hon.), 1971; LL.B., Harvard U., 1940; m. Blair Wiley, Jan. 4, 1941; children—Ellen Fishwick Martin, Anne Fishwick Posvar, John Palmer. Admitted to Va. bar, 1939; asso. firm Cravath, Swaine & Moore, N.Y.C., 1940-42; with Norfolk & Western Ry., Roanoke, 1945—, sr. v.p., 1963-70, pres., chief exec. officer, 1970—, also dir.; chmn. bd., chief exec. officer Erie Lackawanna Ry. Co., 1968-70; pres. Dereco, Inc., 1968—, Del. and Hudson Ry. Co., 1968-70; dir. Allied Chem. Corp., Shenandoah Life Ins. Co., Roanoke; chmn. r.r. industry div. Payroll Savs. campaigns, 1978, 79; bus. adv. com. Transp. Center, Northwestern U.; chmn. Va. coal research and devel. adv. com. Va. Poly. Inst. and State U. Pres., United Fund Roanoke Valley, 1960; past bd. dirs. Roanoke Fine Arts Center; trustee Va. Mus. Fine Arts, 1974-79, Va. Theol. Sem., 1974—, Roanoke Coll., 1964-72; mem. Com. for Revitalization Downtown Roanoke; past chancellor Episcopal Diocese Southwestern Va. Served with USNR, 1942-45. Mem. Assn. Am. Railroads (dir.). Democrat. Clubs: Roanoke Country, Shenandoah (Roanoke); Commonwealth (Richmond); City Tavern, Metropolitan (Washington); Duquesne (Pitts.); Union (Cleve.); Sky (N.Y.C.); Rolling Rock, Laurel Valley (Ligonier, Pa.); Hillsboro (Pompano Beach, Fla.). Home: 19 N Jefferson St Roanoke VA 24026 Office: 8 N Jefferson St Roanoke VA 24042

FITCH, HOWARD MERCER, lawyer, labor arbitrator; b. Jeffersonville, Ind., Dec. 23, 1909; s. J. Howard and Kate Orvis (Girdler) F.; B.M.E., U. Ky., 1930, M.S., 1936, M.E., 1939; J.D. magna cum laude, U. Louisville, 1942; m. Jane Rogers McCaw, Dec. 25, 1930; children—Catherine Mercer (Mrs. Charles E. Druitt), Jane Rogers (Mrs. Fitch Butterworth). Engr., Western Electric Co., Kearny, N.J., 1930-32; joined Am. Air Filter Co., Inc., as sales engr., 1936, successively prodn. mgr., mgr. legal and patent dept., asst. to exec. v.p., became mgr. Herman Nelson div., 1953, dir. ops., 1958-63, v.p., 1954-72. admitted to Ky. bar, 1942, Ill. bar, 1954, to practice before U.S. Patent Office, 1943; practiced Louisville, 1942—; partner Hunt & Fitch, 1945-58. Mem. nat. com. Atlantic Union Com., mem. Louisville Labor-Mgmt. Council. Bd. dirs. Louisville Urban League; Louisville Better Bus. Bur., Consumers Adv. Council. Registered profl. engr., Ky. Mem. ASME, ASHRAE, Am. Arbitration Assn. (panel arbitrators), Nat. Acad. Arbitrators, Am., Ky., Louisville bar assns., Hon. Order Ky. Cols., Louisville C. of C., Asso. Industries Quad Cities (past pres.), Am. Soc. Personnel Adminstrn., Louisville Personnel Assn. Episcopalian (vestryman). Rotarian. Clubs: Filson, Pendennis, Arts. Patentee in field. Home and Office: 1704 Spruce Ln Louisville KY 40207

FITCH, JOHNNY EDWARD, painting, decorating and spl. coatings contracting co. exec.; b. Durham, N.C., Sept. 7, 1934; s. Jasper Frank and Bertha Frances (Glenn) F.; grad. Durham Tech. Inst., 1956; m. Betty Irene Funderburk, Mar. 29, 1952; children—Johnny Edward, Teresa, Debbie, Kelly. Supt., J. M. Thompson Co., Raleigh, N.C., 1955-58; estimator Crain and Denbo, Inc., Durham, 1959-62; v.p. D. C. May Co., Inc., Durham, 1963—. Bd. dirs. Lions Club Industries for the Blind, Durham, 1974—; asst. treas. Ed Gwin Found. Mem. Painting and Decorating Contractors Am. (sec. 1967-74, pres. 1974-76, Durham chpt.), Constrn. Specifications Inst. Democrat. Baptist. Lion (dir. 1975-76, 79—). Home: 138 Fleming Dr Durham NC 27712 Office: 215 Morris St Durham NC 27702

FITCH, WILLIAM PILCHER, III, urologist; b. Lubbock, Tex., May 6, 1943; s. William Pilcher and Lula Elizabeth (Watkins) F.; B.A., U. Tex., 1964; M.D., Tulane U., 1967; m. Elizabeth King, Nov. 20, 1971; children—Lara Tressa, Erin Leigh. Intern, Bexar County Hosp., Dist., 1968-69, resident in surgery, 1969-70, resident in urology, 1972-76; practice medicine, specializing in urology, San Antonio, 1976—; clin. instr. U. Tex. Health Sci. Center, San Antonio, 1976—. Bd. dirs. Am. Cancer Soc. Bexar County, 1979—; trustee Alamo Hts. Ind. Sch. Dist., 1980—. Served with USAF, 1970-72. Decorated Bronze Star, Air medal; diplomate Am. Bd. Urology. Mem. Bexar County Me. Soc., Tex. Med. Assn., AMA, Am. Urologic Assn., U. Tex. Ex Students Assn. (exec. council 1976-77, pres. 1976-77). Republican. Episcopalian. Contbr. articles to profl. jours. Home: 131 E Mandalay San Antonio TX 78212 Office: 8042 Wurzbach Suite 380 San Antonio TX 78229

FITE, JAMES BATEMAN, III, mgmt. cons.; b. Roosevelt, Utah, June 16, 1945; s. James Bateman and Boneta (LeBeau) F.; B.A., Central State U., 1974, M.B.A., 1975; postgrad. Okla. State U., 1975-77; m. Carolyn Louise Barton, Aug. 25, 1973. Sales rep. S. Coast Life Ins. Co., Oklahoma City, 1967-68; state sales mgr. Horace Mann Ins. Co., Oklahoma City, 1968-71; pres. J.B. Fite, Inc. and J. Bateman Fite Agy., Oklahoma City, 1971-72; mgmt. cons. Fite-Davis, Cons. Firm, Oklahoma City, 1971—; faculty mktg. and mgmt. Okla. State U., 1976; bus. faculty Central State U., 1978—, Okla. Christian Coll., 1978—, Okla. State Tech. Inst., 1978—; coordinator mgmt. assistance program SBA, 1975—; Oklahoma City met. area trainer Nat. Alliance Businessmen, 1976—. Mem. Am. Mktg. Assn., Am. Mgmt. Assn., Assn. M.B.A. Execs., Internat. Platform Assn. Mem. Ch. of Christ. Home: 2701 Drakestone Ave Oklahoma City OK 73120 Office: 1425 W Britton Rd Oklahoma City OK 73114

FITE, JAMES ROBERT, JR., gen. contractor; b. Decatur, Ala., Dec. 30, 1950; s. James Robert and Beverly (Hodges) F.; B.S., Auburn (Ala.) U., 1973; m. Sharon Leigh Sellers, June 21, 1975. Asst. supt. Burns, Kirkley, Williams Co., Auburn, 1973-74; salesman Gobble-Fite Lumber Co., Decatur, 1974-75; propr. Fite Constrn. Co., Decatur, 1975—, Hendrix-Fite, Inc., Decatur, 1976—. Mem. Decatur Home Builders Assn., Decatur C. of C., Auburn Alumni Assn. Mem. Ch. of Christ. Club: Decatur Country. Home: 1304 Elizabeth St SE Decatur AL 35601 Office: PO Box 1808 Decatur AL 35602

FITERRE, IGNACIO EMILIO, indsl. engr.; b. Havana, Cuba, Oct. 22, 1945; s. Ignacio and Clara Teresa (Bunbury) F.; came to U.S., 1960, naturalized, 1976; B.S. in Indsl. Engring., U. Fla., 1969; M.B.A., U. Navarra, IESE, Spain, 1972; m. Maria de los Angeles R. Escobar, June 15, 1974; 1 son, Armando Eduardo. Researcher, Med. Coll. Ga., 1969-70; mktg. analyst Editorial Salvat, Barcelona, Spain, 1971-72; indsl. engr. Eastern Airlines, Miami, Fla., 1972-74, regional indsl. engr. for Caribbean, 1974-76, sr. indsl. engr. Central div., Oak Brook, Ill., 1976-78, Western div., St. Ann., Mo., 1978-79, project indsl. engr., Miami, Fla., 1979—. Mem. Am. Inst. Indsl. Engrs. (sr.). Home: PO Box 660542 Miami FL 33166 Office: Eastern Airlines Miami Internat Airport Bldg 16 Miami FL 33148

FITTON, GARVIN, lawyer b. Harrison, Ark., Oct. 5, 1918; s. David Edwards and Lulu Vance (Garvin) F.; LL.B., U. Ark., 1941, J.D., 1969; m. Martha Ann Hamilton, Sept. 22, 1941; children—John, Thomas, Ann. Admitted to Ark. bar, 1941; practice in Little Rock, 1945-52; partner Fitton & Adams, Harrison, Ark., 1952-62, Fitton & Meadows, Harrison, 1962-75; dir. Harrison Security Bank, 1952-73, Commonwealth Theatres, Inc., Harrison, 1952-76. Pres. Harrison Sch. Bd., 1959, 64, sec., 1957, 67-69; mem. Ark. Bd. Law Examiners, 1971-73. Served to maj. U.S. Army, 1941-45, col. Res. ret. Mem. Am., Ark., Boone County bar assns. Democrat. Methodist (past trustee). Clubs: Masons, Shriners, Rotary. Home: 921 W Nicholson St Harrison AR 72601 Office: 224 W Stephenson St Harrison AR 72601

FITTS, E. GRANT, corp. exec.; b. Montevallo, Ala., 1916; LL.B., U. Cin., 1940; LL.M., Harvard U., 1946. Admitted to Ala. bar, Tex. bar; asso. firm White, Bradley, Arant, All & Rose, 1946-51; partner firm Deramus, Fitts & Johnston, 1952-61; v.p., gen. counsel Am. Life Ins. Co., 1961-62; pres. Greatam. Corp., 1962-68; now chmn. bd., pres. Gulf Life Holding Ins. Co. Gulf Life Ins. Co., Jacksonville, Fla.; chmn. exec. officer Gulf United Corp.; also chmn., dir. various cos. Mem. Am. Bar Assn., State Bar Tex., Am. Judicature Soc. Office: Gulf Life Ins Co Gulf Life Center 1301 Gulf Life Dr Jacksonville FL 32207*

FITTS, JAMES WALTER, educator; b. Ft. Riley, Kans., July 17, 1913; s. Josiah Burt and Eva Rose (Freeman) F.; B.S., Nebr. State Tchrs. Coll., 1935; M.S., U. Nebr., 1937; Ph.D., Iowa State U., 1952; m. Mary M. Kocher, June 4, 1935; children—Jerry Burt, Dorothy Louise (Mrs. J.H. Johnson) Donald James. Asst. prof. soil sci. U. Nebr., 1937-48; asst. prof. soil sci. Iowa State U., 1948-52; prof. soil sci. N.C. State U., Raleigh, 1952—, head soil dept., 1956-65, dir. internat. soil fertilizer evaluation project, 1964-75; pres., Agrl. Environmental Systems, Inc., 1973—. Recipient Research award Soil Sci. Soc. N.C., 1966, Service award Chadron State Coll., 1977. Fellow Am. Soc. Agronomy, Soil Sci. Soc. Am.; mem. Soil Sci. Soc. Am. (pres. 1960), Internat. Soil Sci. Soc. (div. vice-chmn. 1960-64), Sigma Xi, Gamma Sigma Delta. Contbr. articles to profl. jours. Home: 550 N Leavitt Ave Orange City FL 32763

FITTS, KENNETH LYON, educator; b. St. Louis, Sept. 27, 1945; s. Matthew Lyon and Catherine Janet (Waugh) F.; A.B., Drury Coll., 1967; M.A., U. Ark., 1969; Ph.D., So. Ill. U., 1978; m. Ronna Dee Wightman, Aug. 27, 1967; 1 son, Kenneth Christopher. Instr. theatre Western Coll. for Women, Oxford, Ohio, 1969-70; asso. prof., chmn. drama dept. Thomas More Coll., Ft. Mitchell, Ky., 1970—, founder arts mgmt. dept., 1979; sponsor The Villa Players, Ft. Mitchell, 1969-77; lighting cons. Center Civic Opera, Covington, Ky., 1976—; cons. theatre renovation project No. Ky. Theatre Guild, 1971. Charter organizer No. Ky. exptl. edn. program Little Red Schoolhouse, 1974; active Boy Scouts Am. Mem. Am. Theatre Assn., Univ. and Coll. Theatre Assn., Ky. Theatre Assn., No. Ky. Arts Council, So. Speech Communication Assn., Nat. Collegiate Players, Kappa Alpha. Baptist. Home: 49 Lynda Ct Burlington KY 41005 Office: Thomas More Coll Box 85 Fort Mitchell KY 41017

FITZGERALD, ALBERT JOSEPH, computer co. exec.; b. Owensboro, Ky., Aug. 24, 1949; s. Thomas Wilbert and Sophia Beatrice (Miller) F.; B.A., U. Ala., 1971; M.S., Ala. A. and M. U., 1978; postgrad. Southeastern Inst. Tech., 1978—; 1 son, Patrick Joseph. Mem. tech. staff Computer Scis. Corp., Huntsville, Ala., 1968-71; sr. analyst Northrop Corp., Huntsville, 1971-74; site mgr. Potomac Research Corp., Huntsville, 1974-76; center mgr., data processing cons. Raytheon Corp., Huntsville, 1976—. Mem. IEEE, Data Processing Mgmt. Assn., Assn. for Computing Machinery, Assn. for Systems Mgmt., Huntsville Jr. C. of C. (dir. 1973-74), U. Ala. Alumni (pres. 1979—). Democrat. Baptist. Home: 1206 Kingsway Dr Huntsville AL 35802

FITZGERALD, JOSEPH MICHAEL, JR., lawyer; b. Norfolk, Va., Oct. 9, 1943; s. Joseph Michael and Grace Elizabeth (Finegan) F.; B.S., Mt. St. Mary's Coll., 1965; J.D., Cath. U. Am., 1970; LL.M., U. Miami, 1973; m. Lynne Marie Leslie, May 3, 1974. Investigator, Retail Credit Co., Miami, Fla., 1965-66; intelligence analyst Def. Intelligence Agy., Washington, 1966-70; admitted to Fla. bar; mem. firm McDermott, Will & Emery, and predecessor, Miami, 1970—; dir. Alexander Hamilton Nat. Bank, 1979—; lectr. environ. law at various symposiums and univs.; advisor to Office Environ. Affairs, Fla. Dept. State, 1971; spl. counsel Broward County Environ. Quality Control Bd., 1973—; spl. prosecutor for environ. crimes Broward County, 1975-76. Trustee, Fla. Ind. Coll. and Univs. Found., 1977—; trustee Inst. on Man and the Oceans, 1973—, chmn., 1976-77; trustee Boystown of Fla., 1978—, Kiwanis Youth Found., 1980—. Recipient award of merit Dade County Bar Assn., 1975, 76. Mem. Am., Fla., Dade County bar assns., Am. Judicature Soc., Cath. Lawyers Guild (pres. 1976-79), Serra Internat. (trustee 1979—). Democrat. Roman Catholic. Clubs: Fla. Jaycees (dir. 1971-72), Kiwanis, Miami, Surf, Bath. Home: 12300 SW 63th Ave Miami FL 33156 Office: 700 Brickell Ave Miami FL 33131

FITZGERALD, MICHAEL GARRETT, acct., author; b. El Dorado, Ark., Dec. 14, 1950; s. Johnny Fotch and Tommye Mae (Murphy) F.; B.B.A., So. State Coll., Magnolia, Ark., 1972. Acct., Southwestern Electric Power Co., Shreveport, La., 1972—; works include: Universal Pictures—A Panoramic History in Words Pictures and Filmographies, 1977; American Movies—The Forties, vol. I, 1940-44, 1980, vol. II, 1945-49, 1981. Democrat. Baptist. Home: 1310 Harold Ellen St El Dorado AR 71730 Office: 428 Travis St Shreveport LA 71104

FITZ GERALD, NORMAN DUNHAM, oil and gas co. exec.; b. Boston, June 7, 1911; s. Percival and Ethelyn (Dunham) FitzG.; S.B., Mass. Inst. Tech., 1931, S.M., 1932, ScD., 1933; m. Agnes Brown Mac Calden, Dec. 2, 1933; children—Norman Scott, Carl Hanson, Gerald Texas. Petroleum economist Standard & Poors, N.Y.C., 1933, Petroleum Adminstrv. Bd., Washington, 1934-35, U.S. Bur. Mines, Washington, 1936, dept. petroleum Chase Manhattan Bank, N.Y.C., 1936-42; dir. div. oil and gas Gt. Lakes Carbon Corp., N.Y.C., 1943-45; pres. Norman Oil Co., Abilene, Tex., 1945—. Mem. Am. Assn. Petroleum Geologists, Soc. Exploration Geophysicists, Am. Inst. Mining Metall. and Petroleum Engrs., West Central Tex. Oil and Gas Assn. (pres. 1972-73), Tex. Ind. Producers and Royalty Owners Assn. (exec. com. 1975-77), Ind. Petroleum Assn. Am. (area v.p. 1972-74, exec. com. 1974-76). Contbr. articles on petroleum econs. to profl. and trade jours. Office: PO Box 5046 Abilene TX 79605

FITZGERALD, RUSSELL GUY, coll. dean; b. Westernport, Md., Apr. 4, 1931; s. Russell Guy and Blanche Mary Fitzgerald; B.S. in Edn., Frostburg State Coll., 1955; M.A., W.Va. U., 1963, Ed.D., 1969; postgrad. Northwestern U., 1963, U. N.H., 1965; m. Elizabeth Joann Sager, Aug. 6, 1955; children—Bradley Alan, Gwen Allison. Tchr., Hagerstown (Md.) Bd. Edn., 1956-58, Garrett County Bd. Edn., Oakland, Md., 1959-60, Allegany County Bd. Edn., Cumberland, Md., 1960-68; asst. prof. edn. Concord Coll., Athens, W.Va., 1970-71; asso. prof. edn. Fairmont (W.Va.) State Coll., 1971-75; prof. edn., chmn. div. edn., dir. tchr. edn. Liberty Bapt. Coll., Lynchburg, Va., 1976-78, acad. dean, 1978—. Past pres. W.Va. Assn. Tchr. Educators. HEW grantee. Mem. Assn. Tchr. Educators, Am. Assn. Higher Edn., Am. Conf. Acad. Deans, Eastern Assn. Deans, Va. Assn. Tchr. Edn., Am. Assn. Sch. Adminstrs., Am. Ednl. Research Assn., Assn. for Supervision and Curriculum Devel., Concerned Leaders in Ednl. Adminstrn. and Research, Phi Delta Kappa. Baptist. Home: 100 Ramblewood Rd Forest VA 24551 Office: Liberty Baptist Coll Lynchburg VA 24506

FITZ GERALD-BUSH, FRANK SHEPARD, historian, poet; b. Hialeah, Fla., Oct. 11, 1925; s. Frank Shepard and Lady Irene (Coburg-FitzGerald) Bush; A.B., U. Miami (Fla.), 1953, M.A., 1964. Instr. Ransom Sch., Coconut Grove, Fla., 1957-58, St. Johns Country Day Sch., Orange Park, Fla., 1959-61; instr. in history Homestead AFB Extension, Fla. State U., 1961-64; reference librarian, curator Floridiana, John F. Kennedy Meml. Library, Hialeah, 1966-71; historian City of Opa-locka (Fla.), 1975—; dir. South Fla. Archaeol. Museum, 1975; instr. Vivian Laramore Rader Poetry Group, 1973—; author: (poetry) Native Treasure, 1943, Sonnets In Search of Sequence, 1968, Remembered Spring, 1974; (history) A Dream of Araby: Glenn H. Curtiss and the Founding of Opa-locka, 1976; contbr. numerous articles, revs. and poems to profl. jours. in Gt. Britain, France, U.S., 1942—; trustee Friends of Opa-locka Library, 1976—; mem. bd. advisers South Fla. Poetry Inst., 1975. Served with RCAF, 1943-44, Am. Field Service, 1944-45, USAF, 1951-55. Recipient Recognition award Laramore Rader Poetry Group, 1975, 76. Mem. Fla. Hist. Soc., Hist. Assn. So. Fla., Dade Heritage Trust, Irish Georgian Soc., County Kildare Archaeol. Soc. (life), Fla. Anthropol. Soc., RAF Assn. (life), Opa-locka C. of C. (asso.), S.R., SAR, Magna Charta Barons, English-Speaking Union, Viscayans, DAV (life). Author: Young Alfred: The Forgotten Prince, 1979. Home: 3030 NW 171st St Opa-locka FL 33056

FITZGIBBONS, PATRICIA MARY, ednl. specialist, univ. ofcl.; b. Pitts., July 24, 1950; d. Maurice John and Anita Elizabeth (Kelleher) F.; B.S. cum laude, Belmont Coll., 1972; M.A., George Peabody Coll. Tchrs., 1973, postgrad., 1977—. Tchr., cons. spl. edn. learning disability Delaware County Intermediate Unit, Media, Pa., 1973-75; learning disabilities tchr. Williamson County Schs., Franklin, Tenn., 1975-77; clin. instr. Project SERVE, Peabody Coll., Nashville, Tenn., 1977-78; ednl. specialist, asso. in pediatrics Vanderbilt U. Sch. Medicine, Nashville, 1978—. Bd. dirs. Williamson County Assn. Retarded Citizens, Franklin, 1977-79. Mem. Council Exceptional Children, Assn. Children Learning Disabilities, Am. Assn. Mental Deficiencies. Home: 2116 Hobbs Rd Apt N-4 Nashville TN 37215 Office: CDEC Med Center S Vanderbilt U Nashville TN 37232

FITZPATRICK, HUGH, physician; b. Richmond, Va., Dec. 6, 1921; s. Hugh and Ruby Amoretta (Gilliam) F.; B.S., Hampton Sydney Coll., 1943; M.D., Med. Coll. Va., 1950; m. Rachel Anne Lewis, Dec. 21, 1948; children—Hugh E., Stuart L., Julia L., Anne L. Intern, U.S. Naval Hosp., Phila., 1950-51; practice medicine, Asheboro, N.C., 1951-70; emergency room physician High Point (N.C.) Meml. Hosp., 1970—, chief emergency dept. staff, 1973—; health dir. Randolph County, N.C., part-time, 1970—; pres. Triad Emergency Assos.; med. adv. Rampon Products, 1976—; mem. staff High Point Meml. Hosp.; mem. courtesy staff Randolph Hosp., Asheboro; county coroner, 1954-58; dir. Jung Products Inc., Cin. Pres. bd. Randolph County Tb. and Health Assn., 1956-58; mem. Asheboro City Sch. Bd., 1962-68; Bd. dirs. Randolph Center for Exceptional Children, United Fund; mem. Asheboro-Randolph County Vocat. Adv. Council, 1975—. Served to lt. (j.g.) USNR, 1943-46, 50-51. Mem. N.C., Randolph County (pres. 1957) med. socs., Am. Acad. Gen. Practice, Am. Coll. Emergency Physicians (dir. N.C. chpt. 1974—), Theta Chi, Alpha Kappa Kappa. Presbyn. (ruling elder 1957). Democrat. Kiwanian (bd. dirs. 1956-58). Home: 117 S Main St Asheboro NC 27203

FITZPATRICK, JOE WARREN, educator; b. Waco, Tex., Mar. 18, 1925; s. Frank M. and Winnie (Warren) F.; B.S., Baylor U., 1948; M.A., U. Tex., 1950; m. Donna P. Davis, Nov. 3, 1951; children—Wynn Davis, Scott Warren. Research physicist Monsanto Chem. Co., Texas City, Tex., 1950-54; faculty Trinity U., San Antonio, 1956-66, prof. math., 1960-66; prof. math U. Tex., El Paso, 1966—. Active Yucca council Boy Scouts Am., troop com. chmn., 1973. Mem. Math. Assn. Am., Nat. Council Tchrs. Math., AAAS, Tex. Acad. Sci., Assn. for Supervision and Curriculum Devel., Sigma Pi Sigma. Home: 5813 Viewmont St El Paso TX 79912

FITZPATRICK, JOHN J., clergyman; b. Trenton, Ont., Can., Oct. 12, 1918; ed. Propaganda Fide Coll. (Italy), Our Lady of Angels Sem. (U.S.) Ordained priest Roman Catholic ch., 1942; named titular bishop of Cenae and aux. of Miami (Fla.), 1968, consecrated, 1968; named bishop of Brownsville, 1971, installed, 1971. Address: PO Box 2279 Brownsville TX 78520

FITZPATRICK, WALTER SMARTT, JR., hosp. adminstr.; b. Cookeville, Tenn., Mar. 4, 1937; s. Walter Smartt and Katherine Bernice (Harley) F.; B.S., Middle Tenn. State U., 1960; M.A.S., U. Ala., 1974; m. Peggy Jean Butts, May 29, 1957; children—Walter Smartt, Dennis Lee. Computer programmer Arnold Research Orgn., Tullahoma, Tenn., 1959-65; systems analyst Systems Engring. Labs., Ft. Lauderdale, Fla., 1965-66; data processing mgr. LTV Electro Systems, Inc., Greenville, Tex., 1966-69; v.p. Integrated Systems Tech., Dallas, 1969-70; dir. mktg. Computer Scis. Corp., Huntsville, Ala., 1970-75; chief exec. officer Cookeville (Tenn.) Gen. Hosp., 1975—. Mem. Tenn. Hosp. Assn. Mem. Church of Christ. Club: Rotary Internat. Home: 449 S Maple St Cookeville TN 38501 Office: 142 W 5th St Cookeville TN 38501

FITZWATER, JOHN WALKER, editor, publisher; b. Lexington, Ky., Dec. 16, 1939; s. Claude Burns and Martha D. (Carter) F.; student U. Ky., 1958-62; 1 son, John Walker. Mng. editor Somerset (Ky.) Jour., 1962; advt. mgr. Commonwealth Jour., Somerset, 1962-68; dir. adminstrn. U.S. Jaycees, Tulsa, 1968-70; v.p. Holland Co., Louisville, 1970-71; pub. Pittsburg (Calif.) Post-Dispatch, 1972-75; pub. San Marcos (Tex.) Daily Record, 1975-76 exec. editor, asso. pub. Daily Progress, Charlottesville, Va., 1976-79; pres., pub. Culpeper (Va.) Star-Exponent, 1979—. Mem. So. Newspaper Pubs. Assn., Va. Press Assn. Presbyterian. Club: Rotary. Home: 2723 Gatewood Circle Charlottesville VA 22901 Office: Star-Exponent 122 W Spencer St Culpeper VA 22701

FIX, IVOR, radiotherapist; b. Bloemfontein, S. Africa, June 30, 1924; came to U.S., 1960, naturalized, 1965; s. Sam and Hannah (Feldman) F.; M.B.B.Ch., U. Witwatersrand (S. Africa), 1952; diploma med. radiation therapy Royal Coll. Physicians and Royal Coll. Surgeons (London), 1956; m. Karin Katzenellenbogen, June 30, 1949; children—Gail, Alan, Brett. Intern surg. dept. Coronation Hosp., Johannesburg, S. Africa, 1952-53, intern med. dept., 1953; resident in gen. surgery Johannesburg Gen. Hosp., 1953-54; sr. house officer Christie Hosp. and Holt Radium Inst., Manchester, Eng., also asst. in med. council research betatron unit for clin. devel. of betatron and linear accelerator, 1954-56, clin. asst., 1958-59; rotating intern Mt. Sinai Hosp., N.Y.C., 1960-61, asst. attending radiotherapist, 1961-63, asso. attending radiotherapist, 1963-65; sr. radiotherapist Addington Hosp., Durban, S. Africa and cons. radiotherapist King Edward VIII Hosp., Durban, 1956-59; chief oncology and cancer co-ordinator Greenpoint Hosp., Bklyn., 1962-64; chief radiotherapy and oncology City Hosp., Elmhurst, N.Y., 1964-65; chmn. dept. radiotherapy Mt. Sinai Med. Center, Miami Beach, Fla., 1965—; cons. radiotherapist Collier County Health Dept., Immokalee, Fla., 1968—, St. Francis Hosp., Miami Beach, 1968—, Miami Heart Inst., Miami Beach, 1968—, Variety Children's Hosp., Miami, 1969—, Bahamian Govt., Princess Margaret Hosp., Nassau, 1973—. Served with S. African and Brit. Royal Navy, 1942-46. Diplomate Am. Bd. Radiology. Fellow Am. Coll. Radiology; mem. AMA, Fla. Med. Assn., Dade County Med. Assn., N.Y. Med. Soc., N.Y. County Med. Soc., Am. Therapeutic Radiologists, Am. Radium Soc., Radiol. Soc. N. Am., Fla. Radiol. Soc., Radiol. Soc. Greater Miami, Fla. Soc. Clin. Oncologists. Jewish. Home: 321 E DiLido Dr Miami Beach FL 33139 Office: 4300 Alton Rd Miami Beach FL 33140

FIX, RONALD EDWARD, civil engr.; b. Dallas, Dec. 27, 1941; s. Robert Eugene and Ida Fay (McGuire) F.; B.S. in Civil Engring., Tex. A. and M. U., 1963; postgrad. U. Tex., 1963-65. Engring. asst. Tex. Water Rights Commn., 1963-65; process engr. EIMCO Corp., Dallas, 1965-68; owner Ronald E. Fix & Assos., Tyler, Tex., 1969—. Registered profl. engr., Tex. Mem. Am., Tex. (chmn. publs. and registration com.) socs. profl. engrs., Am. Water Works Assn., Tex. Water Pollution Control Fedn., Am. Soc. C.E. (dir. Tex. sect., state chmn. C & I sect., past pres. E.Tex. chpt.), Assn. Former Students Tex. A. and M. U., Tyler Jr. C. of C. Mem. Christian Ch. Clubs: South Tyler Rotary; Smith County A. and M.; Aggie; Diamond Century. Home: Box 1015 Tyler TX 75701 Office: 103 E McDermott Allen TX 75002

FIZETTE, NORMAN BRADSTREET, pathologist; b. Buffalo, July 7, 1938; s. Robert D. and Davia (Bradstreet) F.; B.S., Stetson U., 1960; M.S., Vanderbilt U., 1964; M.D., Med. Coll. Va., 1971; m. M. Nannette Hagan, July 7, 1964; 1 son, Benjamin. Pharmacologist, FDA, Washington, 1965-67, A.H. Robins Co., Richmond, Va., 1968-69; intern in medicine Washington Hosp. Center, 1971-72; resident in clin. pathology George Washington U. Med. Center, Washington, 1972-75; clin. chemist, co dir. Radioassay Center, City of Memphis Hosp., 1975—; asst. prof. pathology U. Tenn., Memphis, 1975—. Diplomate Am. Bd. Pathology. Fellow Coll. Am. Pathologists (insp.), Soc. Advanced Med. Systems; mem. Acad. Clin. Lab. Physicians and Scientists, Assn. Clin. Scientists, AMA, Memphis Pathology Soc. (pres. 1979-80). Contbr. articles to profl. jours. Office: Inst Pathology U Tenn 858 Madison Ave Memphis TN 38163

FJELSTED, PAUL MICHAEL, data processing cons.; b. Claire W. and Iva (Peterson) F.; student Ohio State U., 1965, 66, 67, Franklin U., 1966, 67; m. Susan Beth Mackey, Apr. 1, 1967; children—Todd Michael, Amy Beth. With Neoterics, Inc., Raleigh, N.C., 1969—, Raleigh br. mgr., 1976-79, Southeast regional mgr., 1979—. Lutheran. Clubs: Wildwood Country, Joe Hines Hunt. Home: 3809 Hampstead Ct Raleigh NC 27612 Office: 3716 National Dr Raleigh NC 27612

FLACK, BRUCE CLAYTON, historian; b. Fremont, Ohio, Apr. 2, 1938; s. T. Preston and Alelia K. F.; B.A., Otterbein Coll., 1960; M.A., Ohio State U., 1961, Ph.D., 1969; m. Carol Mraz, June 10, 1961; children—Jenna, Brian. Prof. history Glenville State Coll., 1969—, chmn. div. social scis., also coordinator instl. TV; mem. W.Va. Higher Edn. Instl. TV Com., 1976—; Nat. Endowment for Humanities fellow U. Minn., 1974. Chmn., Gilmer County (W.Va.) Red Cross Blood Program, 1975-79; mem. W.Va. Archives and History Commn., 1977-78; Bd. dirs. W.Va. chpt. ACLU, 1979—. Mem. Am. Hist. Assn, Orgn. Am. Historians, So. Hist. Assn., W.Va. Hist. Assn. Club: Rotary (pres. club 1978) Glenville). Home: 907 Mineral Rd Glenville WV 26351 Office: Glenville State Coll Glenville WV 26351

FLACK, CHARLES ZORAH, JR., ins. and real estate co. exec., civic worker; b. Rutherford County, N.C., July 11, 1936; s. Charles Z. and Blanche (Thornton) F.; B.S., U. N.C., 1958; m. Jane Crowell Sawyer, Aug. 9, 1958; children—Charles Zorah III, Blair Thornton, Thomas Cooper. Mgr., Charles Z. Flack Agy., Inc., Forest City, N.C., 1958—; chmn. Planning and Zoning Commn., Forest City, N.C., 1968—; pres. Rutherford County Bd. Realtors, 1979. Pres., United Appeal of Rutherford County (N.C.), 1976, mem. exec. com., 1974—, campaign chmn., 1974, v.p., 1975; treas. Rutherford County Cystic Fibrosis chpt., 1973-75; chmn. Rutherford County chpt. ARC, 1967-68; pres., dir. Rutherford Vocat. Workshop, 1965-67; county chmn. John F. Kennedy Meml. Drive, 1964; treas. Troop 125, Boy Scouts Am., 1973—; chmn. Clinchfield Dam Subcom. in N.C., del. to Nat. Rivers and Harbours Congress, 1972; pres. Rutherford County Young Democratic Club, 1963-64; Dem. precinct committeeman and officer, Forest City, 1971-79, treas. Rutherford County Dem. Exec. Com., 1977—, del. to Nat. Dem. Conv., 1976; bd. dirs. Isothermal Health Council, 1973-74; bd. dirs., mem. exec. com. Western N.C. Tomorrow; bd. govs. U. N.C., 1977—. Recipient Disting. Service award City of Forest City, 1964; cert. residential specialist. Mem. Assn. Profl. Ins. Agts., U.S. Jaycees, Forest City Jaycees (pres. 1963-64, hon. life, Disting. Service award 1964, senator), SAR, Kappa Alpha Order (exec. council). Methodist. Clubs: Rutherford Country (pres. 1971—), Kiwanis (dir. 1974-77, pres. 1979). Home: 122 Forest Hills Dr Forest City NC 28043 Office: PO Drawer 470 Forest City NC 28043

FLAKE, HENRY FRITH, ins. exec.; b. Bunkie, La., Feb. 8, 1928; s. Edwin Lisle and Minerva (Frith) F.; student Sewanee (Tenn.) Mil. Acad., 1943-46; children—Robert Edwin, Mary Elizabeth. Cashier, Bunkie Bank & Trust Co., 1953-56; asst. mgr. Gen. Ins. Agy., Inc., Bunkie, 1956-60, pres., 1960—; part owner Drill One Cons. Inc., Bunkie and Tripoli, Libya; dir. Avoyelles Trust & Savs. Bank, Avoyelles Savs. & Loan Assn., Fidelity Credit Co. Inc. Past chmn. Avoyelles Parish ARC, Avoyelles Parish SSS; alderman, Bunkie, 1958-62. Served with USMC, 1946-48. Mem. Bunkie C. of C. Democrat. Episcopalian. Clubs: Masons, Shriners, Lions (past pres. Bunkie, dep. dist. zone chmn.), Avoyelles Country (a founder, dir., past pres.). Home: Box 368 Hwy 29 Bunkie LA 71322 Office: 111-113 W Magnolia St Bunkie LA 71322

FLAKE, JANICE LOUISE, mathematician, educator; b. Lerna, Ill., Nov. 24, 1940; d. Joseph Berlen and Carrie Eloise (Clark) Flake; B.S., Eastern Ill. U., 1961; M.A., U. Ill., 1962, Ph.D., 1973. Math. tchr., York Community High Sch., Elmhurst, Ill., 1962-69; asst. prof. math. Eastern Ill. U., Charleston, 1969-74; asst. prof. math. edn., Fla. State U., Tallahassee, 1974-77, asso. prof., 1977—; dir. Math That Makes Sense Project; cons. Recipient Edson H. Taylor award, 1961, NSF grantee, 1963, 64, 67, 68-69. Mem. Nat., Ill. (treas., 1970-72), Fla. (bd. dirs.), councils of tchrs. of math., Assn. Women in Math., Spl. Interest Group in Math. in AERA. Contbr. articles to publs. in field, papers to nat. conf. Office: 219 Education Mathematics Education Florida State Univ Tallahassee FL 32306

FLAKE, MURIEL HOWELL, psychologist; b. Kirbyville, Tex., June 6, 1925; d. H. Lee and Mittie (Sheffield) Howell; B.A., U. Houston, 1967, M.Ed., 1970; Ph.D. in Counseling Psychology, Tex. A&M U., 1975; m. Henry John Flake, Jr., Oct. 3, 1946; children—Tamara Lee, Henry John, III. Tchr. Am. history Waltrip High Sch., Houston, 1967-70, counselor, 1970-73; counselor Jersey Village High Sch., Houston, 1973-76; vis. prof. career edn. Tex. A & M U., College Station, 1976; asso. prof. psychology Houston Baptist U., 1976—, dir. counseling center, 1976—; adj. prof. U. Houston, 1977—; mem. guidance com. Coll. Entrance Exam. Bd., N.Y.C., 1971-74. Bd. dirs. Community Welfare Planning Assn., Houston, 1971-75; cons. to Presbyterian Ch. Guidance Program, Houston, 1977—. Cert. counselor, psychologist, tchr., Tex.; named Outstanding Faculty Woman of Year, Houston Bapt. U., 1977; Outstanding Counselor of Yr., Houston Personnel and Guidance Assn., 1979. Mem. Am. Psychol. Assn., Am. Personnel and Guidance Assn., Nat. Vocat. Guidance Assn. (also state and local affiliations). Presbyterian. Contbr. articles in field. Home: 2810 Georgetown St Houston TX 77005 Office: 7502 Fondren Rd Houston TX 77074

FLAKES, THOMAS JEFFERSON, JR., sch. counselor; b. LaFayette, Ala., May 9, 1947; s. Thomas Jefferson and Madie Lee (Morris) F.; B.S., Tuskegee Inst., 1969, M.Ed., 1972. Tchr. social studies Chambers (Ala.) County Bd. Edn., 1969-72; counselor Baldwin (Ga.) County Bd. Edn., 1972—; tchr. Sr. Outlook; tchr. history Baldwin High Sch., Milledgeville, Ga., 1978—. Recipient Merit award United Army Recruiting Sta., 1977. Mem. Nat., Ga. edn. assns., Baldwin Assn. Educators, Am. Personnel and Guidance Assn., Am., Ga. sch. counselor assns., Assn. Non-White Concerns in Counseling, Kappa Delta Pi, Kappa Alpha Psi. Methodist. Home: PO Box 193 LaFayette AL 36862 Office: Counseling Office Baldwin High Sch Milledgeville GA 31061

FLAM, RONALD BARRY, physician; b. Pitts., Aug. 4, 1938; s. Isadore and Sara Bertha (Levin) F.; B.S., U. Miami, 1960; M.D., U. Fla., 1964; m. Marilyn Sue Jablo, May 16, 1966; children—Jeffrey, Nikki Ruth. Intern, Jackson Meml. Hosp., Miami, Fla., 1964-65, resident in medicine, 1967-69, chief med. resident, 1969-70, practice internal medicine and cardiology, South Miami, Fla., 1970—; attending physician South Miami Hosp., 1973—, chief dept. medicine, 1980—; attending physician Larkin Gen. Hosp., 1972—; asso. physician Bapt. Hosp. Miami, 1973; v.p. med. staff South Miami Hosp., 1976, chief of staff, 1977—; clin. instr. internal medicine Sch. Medicine, U. Miami, 1971—. Served as lt. M.C., USNR, 1965-67. Diplomate Am. Bd. Internal Medicine. Fellow Am. Coll. Chest Physicians. Home: 9480 SW 91 St Miami FL 33176 Office: 6601 SW 80 St Miami FL 33143

FLAMM, JOHN CHARLES, computer services co. exec.; b. Dayton, Ohio, May 16, 1945; s. Ernest Carl and Mary Beatrice (Weber) F.; B.S. in Bus. Adminstrn., Xavier U., 1969; A.S., Dayton Jr. Coll., 1964; m. Sharon Sue Meyers, May 29, 1965; children—Jeffrey, Jennifer, Jason. Computer operator Reynolds & Reynolds Co., Dayton, 1964-65; computer programmer NCR Corp., Dayton, 1965-69, systems analyst, 1970, Atlanta, systems analyst, project mgr., Dayton, 1971-73; regional v.p. fin. systems Anacomp Inc., Sarasota, Fla., 1973—. Mem. NCR Fin. Users Group, CAP. Home: 1036 Chevy Chase Dr Sarasota FL 33580 Office: 1390 Main St Sarasota FL 33577

FLANAGAN, EDWARD MICHAEL, JR., army officer; b. Saugerties, N.Y., July 13, 1921; s. Edward Michael and Marie (Sinnott) F.; B.S., U.S. Mil. Acad., 1943; grad. U.S. Army Command and Gen. Staff Coll., Ft. Leavenworth, Kan., 1946, Armed Forces Staff Coll., Norfolk, Va., 1955, U.S. Army War Coll., Carlisle Barracks, Pa., 1959; M.A., Boston U., 1960; m. Marguerite Farrell, Dec. 26, 1945; children—Edward Michael III, Maureen Ann, Terrence Girard, Patricia Marie and Kathleen Mary (twins). Commd. 2d lt. U.S. Army, 1943, advanced through grades to lt. gen., 1972; comdg. gen. U.S. Army John F. Kennedy Center for Mil. Assistance and comdt. U.S. Army Inst. or Mil. Assistance, Ft. Bragg, N.C., 1968-71; comdr. gen. 1st Inf. Div., Ft. Riley, Kan., 1971-73; comptroller of Army, 1973; dep. comdg. gen. 8th U.S. Army, Korea, 1974-75; comdg. gen. 6th U.S. Army, San Francisco, 1975-78, ret., 1978. Decorated D.S.M., Legion of Merit with oak leaf cluster, Bronze Star, Air medal with oak leaf cluster, Army Commendation medal; Vietnam Nat. Order of Merit (knight class), Vietnam Army Distinguished Service Order 1st class, Vietnam Gallantry Cross with gold star, Vietnam Medal of Honor. Roman Catholic. Author: The Angels, A History of the 11th Airborne Division, 1948. Contbr. articles to profl. jours. Home: 2 Oystercatcher Rd Beaufort SC 29902

FLANDERS, DUDLEY DEAN, lawyer; b. New Orleans, Sept. 11, 1934; s. Elmer Dean and Frances Eleanor (Purser) F.; student Washington and Lee U., 1952-53; LL.B., Tulane, 1957; m. Mary Southgate Brewster, Aug. 28, 1959; children—Dana Mason, Elizabeth Boland, Robert Purser. Admitted to La. bar, 1957, since practiced in New Orleans; asso. firm Lemle & Kelleher, 1957-59, Elmer D. Flanders, 1959-63; partner Flanders & Flanders, 1963—. Bd. dirs. La. Assn. Mental Health, 1973—, pres., 1975-77; bd. dirs. Inst. for Human Understanding, 1971-77; chancellor Greater New Orleans Fedn. Chs., 1970-74; chmn. bd. trustees Presbytery of S. La., 1972-74; pres. trustees Evergreen Found., Evergreen Presbyn. Vocat. Sch.; trustee Mental Health Advocacy Service in La. Recipient Mental Health Bell award, 1979; Vol. Activist award, 1979. Mem. Am., La. (mem. ho. dels. 1964—, chmn. standing com. on jud. candidates 1973-78), New Orleans bar assns., New Orleans Notaries Assn. (sec. 1970-77, pres. 1977), Am. Judicature Soc. (dir. 1973-75). Presbyn. (elder 1967—). Clubs: Masons, Rotary, Pickwick, New

Orleans Lawn Tennis. Home: 2934 Palmer Ave New Orleans LA 70118 Office: 600 Loyola Ave New Orleans LA 70113

FLANDERS, HENRY JACKSON, JR., educator; b. Malvern, Ark., Oct. 2, 1921; s. Henry Jackson and Mae (Hargis) F.; B.A., Baylor U., 1943; B.D., So. Bapt. Theol. Sem., 1948, Ph.D., 1950; postgrad. U. Tenn., 1943, Union Theol. Sem., 1963, Hebrew Union Coll., 1948; m. Tommie Lou Pardew, Apr. 19, 1944; children—Janet, Jack III. Ordained to ministry Bapt. Ch., 1940; prof., chmn. dept. religion, chaplain Furman U., 1950-62; pastor First Bapt. Ch., Waco, Tex., 1962-69; prof. religion Baylor U., Waco, 1969—. Chaplain, Tex. Rangers Commn. Trustee Baylor U., Hillcrest Bapt. Hosp.; chmn. bd. Golden Gate Bapt. Theol. Sem.; mem. exec. bd. Bapt. Gen. Conv. Tex.; pres. bd. dirs. Econ. Opportunity Advancement Corp.; bd. dirs. Heart of Tex. Red Cross. Served with USAAF, 1943-45. Decorated Air medal with clusters. Mem. Baylor Alumni Assn. (pres.), Waco Bapt. Ministerial Assn. (pres.), Assn. Bapt. Profs. Religion (pres.), Soc. Bibl. Lit., Soc. for Religion and Ethics, Council on Religion and Law, AAUP (chpt. pres. 1971—), Am. Acad. Religion. Clubs: Masons, Rotary; Western S.C. Torch (Greenville, S.C.). Author: People of the Covenant, 1963; Introduction to the Bible, 1973. Home: 3820 Chateau St Waco TX 76710

FLANNAGAN, WILLIAM HAMILTON, hosp. adminstr.; b. Trevillians, Va., Sept. 14, 1920; B.S., Hampden-Sydney Coll., 1940, LL.D., 1976; m. Kathryn Middleton; children—William, John, Patricia Flannagan Sarver. Dir. hosp. services VA Hosp., Richmond, Va., 1946-49; hosp. adminstr. Hill-Burton Program Va. Dept. Health, Richmond, 1949-51; adminstr. Franklin Meml. Hosp., Rocky Mt., Va., 1951-54; pres. Roanoke (Va.) Meml. Hosps., 1954—; past mem. Va. Mental Health Study Commn.; past bd. dirs. Gov's. Adv. Com. for Planning for Regional Med. Programs in Va., Inc., Hosp. Service Assn. (Blue Cross), Roanoke Valley Regional Planning Council Health Services; past trustee Franklin Meml. Hosp., Burrell Meml. Hosp.; mem. exec. com. Southeastern Hosp. Conf. Served to 1st lt. Med. Adminstrv. Corps, U.S. Army, 1943-46. Named one of Ten Most Prominent Men in Roanoke Area, 1977. Fellow Am. Coll. Hosp. Adminstrs. (past regent), Royal Soc. Health; mem. Hosp. Fin. Mgmt. Assn., Am. (del. 1965-67), Va. (pres. 1963, dir., chmn. council on profl. relations), Carolinas-Va. (pres. 1963), Roanoke (sec.-treas. 1954-77, trustee 1971—, pres. 1977) hosp. assns., Roanoke Hosp. Council (pres.), Omicron Delta Kappa, Kappa Alpha. Presbyterian. Home: 2532 S Jefferson St Roanoke VA 24014 Office: Roanoke Meml Hosps Belleview and Jefferson Sts Roanoke VA 24033

FLANZER, JERRY PHILIP, social worker, educator; b. Chgo., June 25, 1943; s. Morris and Marcella (Shapiro) F.; B.A., Roosevelt U., Chgo., 1965; M.S.W., Case Western Res. U., 1967; D.S.W., U. So. Calif., 1973; m. Sally Esther Manesberg, Feb. 4, 1968; children—Matthew Lee, Douglas Max. Program chief subzone IV, Read Zone Mental Health Center, Ill. Dept. Mental Health, Chgo., 1967-70; asst. prof. Sch. Social Welfare, U. Wis., Milw., 1972-77; asso. prof. Grad. Sch. Social Work, U. Ark., Little Rock, 1977—, dir. Mid-Am. Inst. on Violence in Families, 1978—; pvt. clin. and research cons., 1974—. Bd. dirs. Little Rock Jewish Fedn., 1977—, Milw. Jewish Fedn., 1975-77. NIMH teaching fellow, 1971-72; C. Hias fellow, 1966-67; lic. clin. social worker, Calif.; registered social worker, Ill., Ark., Wis. Fellow Am. Orthopsychiat. Assn.; mem. Nat. Assn. Social Workers, Acad. Cert. Social Workers, Research Soc. Alcoholism. Contbr. articles to profl. jours. Home: 10807 Crestdale Little Rock AR 72212 Office: U Ark Grad Sch Social Work Little Rock AR 72204

FLATLAND, RAGNAR FORLI, dentist, educator; b. Porsgrunn, Norway, Apr. 4, 1938; came to U.S., 1958; s. Eugen J. and Anny (Forli) F.; D.M.D. with honors, U. Ala., 1963, M.S., 1971; cand. odont. U. Oslo, Norway, 1963; m. Irmgard Korner, Feb. 26, 1965; children—Bente, Steinar. Tchr. elem. schs., Norway, 1957-58; practice dentistry, Skien, Norway, 1963-64, 66-67; dental officer Norwegian Army, 1964-65, Norwegian Public Health Service, 1965-66; instr. Sch. Dentistry, U. Ala., Birmingham, 1967-71, asso. prof. dentistry, 1972-78, asst. prof. physiology and biophysics, 1973—, prof. dentistry, 1978—, chmn. dept. operative dentistry, 1975—, asso. prof. Grad. Sch., 1975-78; amanuensis U. Oslo (Norway) Sch. Dentistry, 1971-72. NIH research fellow, 1961-63; C.V. Mosby scholar, 1963. Mem. ADA, Ala. Dental Assn., Birmingham Dist. Dental Soc., Am. Assn. Dental Schs., U. Ala. Dental Alumni Assn., Sigma Xi, Delta Sigma Delta, Omicron Kappa Upsilon. Author various teaching manuals; contbr. articles on physiology to sci. jours. Lutheran. Office: Box 82 SDB Univ Sta Birmingham AL 35294

FLEET, ALBERT ZALMAN, accountant; b. Jacksonville, Fla., June 7, 1937; s. Louis Edmund and Florence Rhoda (Cohen) F.; student U. Fla., 1955-58; A.A., Jones Coll., 1960. Bookkeeper, Aichel Steel & Supply Co., Jacksonville, Fla., 1961-63; from accounting clk. to accountant/adminstrv. asst. to pres. Universal Marion Corp., Jacksonville, 1964—. Served with Q.M.C., U.S. Army Res., 1960-66. Mem. Nat. Assn. Accountants, Nat. Soc. Pub. Accountants. Democrat. Jewish. Contbr. articles profl. jours.

FLEGLE, LARRY VERNON, broadcasting exec.; b. Tampa, Fla., Aug. 9, 1948; s. Vernon Fredrick and Hazel Maxine (Keene) F.; A.A., B.A. in Speech and Broadcasting, U. South Fla.; M.A., Pepperdine U., 1977; postgrad. Nova U.; m. Tonice Maire Bell, Sept. 6, 1969; 1 dau., Krista Leann. Employment cons. Bus. Men's Clearning House, 1973-74; electronic technician VA Hosp., Tampa, 1974-75; tax auditor IRS, 1975-77; v.p. Sta. WBTG-FM, Sheffield, Ala., 1977—; pvt. practice acctg. and fin. planning, instr. Ala. Christian Coll. Mem. Sheffield (Ala.) Planning Bd.; mem. NW Ala. adv. com. Ala. Film Commn. Served with USN, 1968-72. Mem. Internat. Assn. Fin. Planners, Inst. Cert. Fin. Planners (affiliate), Am. Planning Assn., Nat. Assn. Religious Broadcasters, Colbert County C. of C. Democrat. Southern Baptist. Clubs: Kiwanis (sec. Sheffield 1979—), Antique Wireless, Internat. Radio of Am. Office: 2400 Avalon Ave Muscle Shoals AL 35660

FLEISCHER, ALLEN BARRY, beverage co. exec.; b. N.Y.C., June 5, 1946; s. Charles and Miriam F.; B.B.A., Hofstra U., 1969; m. Michele Y. Cook, Aug. 31, 1968; children—Loren Nicole, Scott Jason. Staff acct. Laventhal, Krekstein, Horwath & Horwath, N.Y.C., 1969-71; treas. Cook's Hotel & Restaurant Supply Corp., N.Y.C., 1971-73; controller Senter & Corgan, Bronx, N.Y., 1973-74; plant controller Howard Johnson's, Queens Village, N.Y., 1974-76; fin. coordinator, group controller, v.p., gen. mgr. Miami (Fla.) Pepsi Cola plant Gen. Cinema Corp., 1976—. Served with Army N.G., 1968-74. Home: 10631 SW 126th Ave Miami FL 33186 Office: 7777 NW 41st St Miami FL 33152

FLEISCHER, ARTHUR CARROLL, radiologist; b. Miami, Fla., May 15, 1952; s. Eugene and Lucille F.; B.S. in Biology magna cum laude, Emory U., 1973; M.D., Med. Coll. Ga., 1976; m. Leona Lynn, May 25, 1975; 1 son, Braden Matthew. Dir. diagnostic ultrasound, dept. radiology Med. Coll. Ga., 1973-76; intern, resident Vanderbilt U. Sch. Medicine, 1976-80, coordinator ultrasound teaching programs, Medicine, 1977—, acting dir. sect. diagnostic ultrasound, 1979—; tng. Armed Forces Inst. Pathology-Walter Reed Hosp., Washington, 1978. Bd. dirs. Couples Club, Temple, Nashville; judge horse shows. Recipient awards for sci. exhibits; Pres.'s award Am. Roentgen Ray Soc., 1977, cert. merit 1979. Mem. AMA, Radiol. Soc. N. Am., Am. Coll. Radiology, Nat. Biology Hon. Soc., Am. Inst. Ultrasound in Medicine (chmn. local chpt. 1974-76, chmn. S.E. region 1976—, award 1977), Sigma Xi. Democrat. Author: Introduction To Diagnostic Sonography, 1979; also book chpts.; contbr. articles to profl. publs. Home: 469 Saddel Dr Nashville TN 37221 Office: Dept Radiology Vanderbilt Sch Medicine Nashville TN 37232

FLEISCHMAN, SOL JOSEPH, ret. television broadcasting exec.; b. Hawkinsville, Ga., Sept. 12, 1910; s. Joseph Simon and Alma (Rockman) F.; hon. degree, U. Tampa (Fla.), 1954; m. Helen Elsberry; children—Sol Joseph, Martin Paul. Profl. musician Am. Fedn. Musicians, Tampa, 1926-32; announcer, control operator WDAE Radio, Tampa, Fla., 1928, chief announcer, 1950-57; sports dir., outdoor editor Tampa (Fla.) Daily Times, 1946-57; asst. to gen. mgr. L.S. Mitchell, 1956-57; sports, dir., pub. relations dir. WTVT Television, Tampa, 1957-75, ret.; now commentator sports, fishing report Chanel 13 WTVT-TV. Mem. Fla. Gov.'s Conservation Com., 1969-72; mem. Tampa Mayor's Bd. Pub. Recreation, Pub. Relations and Conv. Centers, 1968—. Trustee Land's For You, Inc. Served with USCG, 1942-46. Named Tampa's Outstanding Citizen, Tampa Sports Club, 1969-70; recipient Distinguished Service award U. Tampa, 1975, Merit award Fla. Boxing Assn.; Fightin' Gator award U. Fla., 1975; others. Mem. Outdoor Writers Am., Fla. Outdoor Writers Assn., Fla. League Outdoor Writers, Fla. Lunkers Assn., Fla. Sportscasters Assn. (mem. bd. 1970-73), Internat. Fishing Hall of Fame, Greater Tampa C. of C., Manatee C. of C., Sigma Delta Chi. Mason (Shriner), Rotarian. Clubs: Palma Ceia Golf and Country, Sword and Shield, Tampa University Quarterback, Touchdown (Tampa); Santa Rosa Golf; Palma Sola Golf (Bradenton); Highlands Country (N.C.); Bradenton Country. Home: 798 Northshore Dr PO Box 938 Anna Maria FL 33501

FLEISHER, HARVEY OSCAR, structural engr.; b. Ruston, La., Sept. 25, 1946; s. Oscar and Mary (Fomby) F.; B.S. in Indsl. Engring., Tex. A & M U., 1970, M.S., 1972; m. Vicky Sue Donaldson, Sept. 7, 1968; 1 dau., Laura Dianne. Research engr. The Offshore Co., Houston, 1972-77, project mgr., 1977—. Capt., U.S. Army Res., 1970—. Registered profl. engr., Tex. Mem. Soc. Petroleum Engrs. of Am. Inst. M.E., Tex. Soc. Profl. Engrs., Tex. Farm Bur. Contbr. articles profl. jours. Home: Rt 2 Box 225 Wharton TX 77488 Office: Offshore Co PO Box 2765 Houston TX 77001

FLEMENBAUM, ABRAHAM, psychiatrist; b. Cali, Colombia, Sept. 17, 1942; s. Moises and Ana (Safirstein) F.; came to U.S., 1966, naturalized, 1973; M.D., U. Del Valle Cali, 1964; m. Lily Gorenstein, Apr. 3, 1965; children—Arieh Mordecai Yechiel, Joel Nathan Zvi, Jehudit Shulamit Tamar. Intern, U. Hosp., Cali, 1964-65, Mt. Sinai Hosp., Chgo., 1966-67; resident in psychiatry U. Minn., 1967-70, chief resident, 1970-71, research fellow, instr. psychiatry, 1970-73; asst. prof., research psychiatrist Tex. Tech U. Med. Sch., Lubbock, 1973-74, asso. prof., research psychiatrist, 1974-78; prof. psychiatry La. State U. Med. Sch., Shreveport, 1978-79; asso. prof. psychiatry U. Miami (Fla.) Med. Sch., 1979—. cons. in field. Recipient William C. Menninger award, 1970. Diplomate Am. Bd. Psychiatry. Mem. Am. Psychiat. Assn. (pres. W. Tex. chpt. 1977—), Soc. Biol. Psychiatry, AAAS. Democrat. Jewish. Club: B'nai B'rith. Contbr. articles to sci. publs. Office: U Miami Med Sch Dept Psychiatry Miami FL 33101

FLEMIG, ERNEST ROBERT, aero. engr.; b. Jamaica, N.Y., Apr. 26, 1937; s. Ernest August and Isabelle Elinor (Smith) F.; B.S. in Aero. Engring., Mass. Inst. Tech., 1958; m. Claudia Ann Stevens, June 14, 1958; children—Steven B., David G., Cristy Ann. Staff engr. Mass Inst. Tech., Boston, 1956-58; with Thiokol Corp., various locations, 1961—, task team mgr., project dir., Huntsville, Ala., 1966—. Mem. Parish Council, 1974—. Served to lt. USAF, 1958-61. Recipient Outstanding Achievement award Martin Marietta Corp., 1974. Mem. Am. Inst. Aeros. and Astronautics. Roman Catholic. K.C. Clubs: Exchange (outstanding dist. dir. Ala. clubs 1976, dist./state pres. 1977-78, Outstanding Ala. Exchangeite award 1979). Contbr. to profl. jours. Patentee in boron combustion. Home: Route 1 Box 223 Guntersville AL 35976 Office: Thiokol Corp Huntsville AL 35807

FLEMING, BENTON SCOTT, savs. and loan exec.; b. Houston, Apr. 12, 1922; s. Earl Hampton and Lorena Oklahoma (Stapler) F.; student Tex. U., 1940-43, U. Houston, 1952-53; LL.B., South Tex. Sch. Law, 1951; m. Narcille Busch, Dec. 1, 1951; children—Scott, Joan, Guy, Diane. Admitted to Tex. bar, 1951; mortgage loan atty. Gen. Mortgage Corp., Houston, 1951-55; pres. Tex. Investment Corp., La Porte, 1955—; chmn. bd., pres. First State Bank, Point, Tex., 1961-68; pres. United Bus. Capital, Inc., La Porte, 1963—; pres. Bayshore Savs. Assn., La Porte, 1967—, chmn. bd., 1967—; dir. Bayshore Nat. Bank, La Porte; adv. dir. Tex. Nat. Bank of Baytown; pres. Harris County League Insured Savs. Assns., 1976. Aderman City of Shoreacres, 1973—. Served to lt. (j.g.) USNR, 1943-46. Mem. Tex. State Bar Assn., La Porte C. of C. (1st v.p. 1972-74, dir. 1972-74), Alpha Tau Omega. Episcopalian. Clubs: Houston Yacht, Rotary. Home: 616 Baywood St La Porte TX 77571 Office: 1102 S Broadway La Porte TX 77571

FLEMING, GEORGE BERNARD, indsl. sales co. exec.; b. Spokane, Wash., Jan. 17, 1911; s. Charles Agustus and Cora Agnes (Thompson) F.; B.S. in Mining Engring., U. Calif.; m. Josephine Tilden, May 25, 1933; 1 dau., Patricia Georgine. Warehouseman clk. Standard Oil Co. of Calif., S. San Francisco, 1933-35; engr. Hydril Co., Lomita Park, Calif., Odessa, Tex., Houston, Lafayette, La., 1935-41; sales rep. Rheem Mfg. Co., New Orleans, 1941-73, regional sales mgr., 1973; owner, operator Fleming Indsl. Sales Co., New Orleans, 1973—. Mem. Service Corps Ret. Execs., Theta Tau, Alpha Kappa Lambda. Clubs: Rotary, New Orleans Country, Bienville; Masons (Lafayette). Home and Office: 5528 Loyola Ave New Orleans LA 70115

FLEMING, LAWRENCE DURWOOD, univ. pres.; b. Sulphur Springs, Tex., Aug. 9, 1914; s. John Payne and Alice Lucile (Rash) F.; B.A., So. Meth. U., 1937, Th.M. 1940; D.D., McMurry Coll., 1957; m. Lurlyn January, Mar. 19, 1940; children—Jon Hugh, Pamela (Mrs. J. Kenneth Shamblin, Jr.), Martha Ann (Mrs. Stephen Curtis). Ordained to ministry Methodist Ch., 1940; pastor, Caddo-Mills-Salem, Tex., 1940-42, Dallas, 1942-44, Eastland, Tex., 1944-45; founding pastor St. Luke's United Meth. Ch., Houston, 1945-61, pres. Southwestern U., 1961—. Past pres. Tex. Council Ch.-Related Colls.; mem. World Meth. Council, also del. confs., 1961, 66, 71, 76, gen. and jurisdictional confs., 1960, 64, 66, 71; bd. dirs. univ. senate United Meth. Ch.; exec. com. Tex. Ind. Coll. Fund, Nat. Assn. Schs. and Colls. of United Meth. Ch., Ind. Colls. and Univs. of Tex.; mem. Tex. Conf. Bd. Ministry, Tex. Planning Commn. Recipient Distinguished Alumnus award So. Meth. U., 1965. Mem. Tex. Meth. Coll. Assn. (past chmn.), Am. Assn. Ind. Coll. and Univ. Presidents, Assn. Colls. and Univs. for Internat.-Intercultural Studies (past pres.), Big State Conf. Council of Presidents (past chmn.), Assn. Tex. Colls. and Univs. (pres. 1976-78), Philos. Soc. Tex. (pres. 1979—). Mason, Rotarian. Home: One Taylor Rd Georgetown TX 78626

FLEMING, LUTHER UNDERWOOD, safety cons.; b. Russellville, Ala., May 25, 1916; s. Guy and Bessie Lillian F.; B.S., Auburn U., 1957; M.A., N.Y. U., 1967; m. Marion Lea Dugan, Dec. 8, 1945; children—Frieda Lea (Mrs. John G. Stikes), Linda Sue. Safety engr. Naval Air Sta., Pensacola, Fla., 1957-60; safety engr. U.S. Army C.E., Little Rock, Washington, Canaveral, Fla. and Cin., 1961-71; safety engr. U.S. Army Safeguard Systems Command, Huntsville, Ala., 1971-73; safety engr. U.S. Army Proving Ground, Dugway, Utah, 1973-74; safety cons. d.b.a. Safety Cons. Services, Huntsville, Ala., 1975—. Served with AUS, 1938-39. Mem. Am. Soc. Safety Engrs. Democrat. Baptist. (dir. adult Sunday sch. dept. 1977—). Mason (master). Address: 1113 Brookmeade St NW Huntsville AL 35805

FLEMING, MYRTLE MADELINE, ret. educator; b. Hillman, Mich., Feb. 10, 1913; d. Thomas James and Lottie Mae (Bennett) Crank; B.S., East Tenn. U., 1949; M.S., U. Tenn., 1954; Ph.D., U. Ga., 1966; m. Charles Willus Fleming, May 16, 1932; 1 son, Charles James. Tchr., Myrtle (Mo.) High Sch., 1949-50; chmn. sci. dept. Lee Coll., Cleveland, Tenn., 1951-54, 74-76, asst. prof., 1968, asso. prof., 1969-71, prof., 1971-78, chmn. sci. dept. Emmanuel Coll., Franklin Springs, Ga., 1954-58 NSF summer grantee U. Utah, 1955, Claremont Coll., 1956, Murray State Coll., 1957, Pratt Inst., 1958, U. Ga., 1959-61. Mem. Tenn. Edn. Assn., Soc. Protozoologists, Am. Soc. Parasitologists, Southeastern Soc. Parasitologists, Am. Inst. Biol. Sci., AAUP, Tenn. Acad. Sci. Mem. Ch. of God. Contbr. articles to profl. jours. Home: Route 3 Box 32 Royston GA 30662

FLEMING, PARTEE AUGUSTUS, furniture co. exec.; b. Memphis, Nov. 4, 1916; s. Partee Augustus and Frances Green F.; A.B. cum laude, Vanderbilt U., 1939; grad. war course U.S. Coast Guard Acad., 1942; m. Marie Anita Tiblier, June 24, 1943; children—Geraldine Frances, James Partee, Anita Marie. Reporter, Nashville Tennessean, 1938-41; editor Inglewood (Calif.) Citizen, 1941-42; founder, owner, pres., chmn. bd. Fleming Fine Furniture, Memphis, 1947—. Democratic candidate for mayor of Memphis, 1959. Served to lt. (j.g.) USCGR, 1942-47. Recipient Man of Yr. award Memphis Gavel Club, 1974. Mem. Tenn. Home Furnishings Assn., Memphis Home Furnishings Assn. (pres. 1976-77, dir. 1970—), Irish Soc. Memphis (pres. 1970-71, 79-80), VFW (comdr. Memphis and Shelby County 1973-74, Jim Poole award 1974), Ret. Officers Assn., Am. Legion (vice comdr. Memphis 1970-71, chaplain 1971-75), Alpha Tau Omega (Thomas Arkle Clark award 1939). Episcopalian. Club: Moose. Author: God's Book of Remembrance, 1965; God and The Devil, 1965; Is God's Bible the Greatest Murder Mystery Ever Written?, 1980. Home: 6763 Wild Berry Ln Memphis TN 38138 Office: 2753 S Mendenhall St Memphis TN 38118 also PO Box 17216 Memphis TN 38117

FLEMING, SAMUEL HALE SIBLEY, diversified mfg. co. exec.; b. Augusta, Ga., July 15, 1934; s. William Cornelius and Sarah (Sibley) Fleming; B.S., Ga. Inst. Tech., 1958; m. Nancy Lovelace West, Nov. 29, 1958; children—Samuel Sibley, Katherine Shields, William Cornelius II, Jennifer West. Trainee photo products dept. E.I. du Pont de Nemours & Co., Parlin, N.J., 1958, 61, tech. rep. printing, indsl. products, Chgo., 1961-63, shift supr. Parlin plant, 1963-64, day supr. finishing area, 1964-65, asst. product mgr., Wilmington, Del., 1965-66, field sales mgr., Wynnewood, Pa., 1966-67, Clifton, N.J., 1967-68, dist. mgr., 1968-70, Atlanta, 1970—; dir. Linton Coal Co., Birmingham, Ala. Served to lt. (j.g.), USNR, 1958-61. Mem. Southeastern Photoplatemakers Assn., Atlanta Litho and Craftsman's Club, Sigma Alpha Epsilon, Scabbard and Blade, Annak, Omicron Delta Kappa. Presbyterian. Toastmaster. Home: 6330 Mt Brook Way NW Atlanta GA 30328 Office: 3070 NE Expressway PO Box 80368 Atlanta GA 30366

FLEMING, SIDNEY HOWELL, physician, educator; b. Lubbock, Tex., May 22, 1938; d. McKinley and Wilna Adrian (Simer) Howell; B.A., Agnes Scott Coll., 1959; M.D., Emory U., 1964; m. Julian Denver Fleming, Jr., June 28, 1960; 1 dau., Julie Adrianne. Intern Emory/VA Hosp., Atlanta, 1964-65, resident in psychiatry, 1965-68, coordinator residency tng., 1968-75; asst. prof. Emory U., 1968-75, asso. prof., 1975—, dir. residency tng., 1976-79; vis. staff Grady Hosp., Atlanta. Active Met. Atlanta Mental Health Assn., Ga. Assn. Mental Health. Diplomate Am. Bd. Psychiatry and Neurology. Mem. Am. Assn. Acad. Psychiatrists, AMA, Am. (task force curriculum on psychology of women and men 1977-79, editorial bd. above curriculum 1979—), Ga. psychiatric assns., Assn. Acad. Psychiatry, DeKalb County Med. Soc., Med. Assn. Ga. Met. Mental Health Assn., Wyo., Oreg. hist. socs. Republican. Club: Druid Hills Golf. Contbr. articles to med. jours. Home: 2238 Hill Park Ct Decatur GA 30033 Office: 1256 Briarcliff Rd Atlanta GA 30306

FLEMING, THEODORE CARL, pharm. co. exec.; b. Mishawaka, Ind., Apr. 28, 1924; s. Patrick L. and Theresa T. (Frerich) F.; B.S. in Sci., Trinity U., 1949; M.A. in Microbiology, U. Tex., Austin, 1951; M.B.A., U. Dallas, 1973; grad. advanced mgmt. program Harvard U., 1975; m. Margaret Jean Hutchinson, July 28, 1949; children—Teresa P., Kathleen Gail. Quality control dir. Armour Pharms., Ft. Worth, 1951-55; devel. dir. Alcon Labs., Ft. Worth, 1955-65, v.p. quality assurance, 1969—; pres. North Tex. Drugs Inc. Served with U.S. Army, 1943-46; ETO. Decorated Purple Heart, Bronze Star. Mem. Am. Pharm. Assn., Am. Soc. Quality Control. Democrat. Roman Catholic. Clubs: Glen Garden Country, Toastmasters (v.p. chpt.). Contbr. articles to profl. publs. Office: PO Box 1959 Fort Worth TX 76101

FLEMING, WILLIAM FRED, life ins. co. exec.; b. Dallas, Jan. 23, 1951; s. William Wilbur and Mary Dell (Ridley) F.; B.B.A. in Mgmt.-Mktg. (Ling-Tempco-Vought coop. ednl. scholar 1969), U. Tex., Arlington, 1974; m. Katherine M. Ruisinger, Apr. 22, 1978. Dir. field services Southland Life Ins. Co., Dallas, 1974-77; dir. field ops. Phila. Life Ins. Co., Houston, 1977-80, regional mgr., Dallas-Ft. Worth, 1980—. Bd. dirs. Bering Dr. Homeowners Assn. Mem. arbitration bd. Houston Better Bus. Bur.; project bus. cons. Jr. Achievement; vol. Easter Seal drives. Mem. Nat. Assn. Life Underwriters, Dallas Assn. Life Underwriters, Dallas Estate Planning Council, U. Tex. Arlington Alumni Assn. (dir. 1975—, pres. 1980), Phi Gamma Delta (past pres.). Republican. Methodist. Club: Masons (32 deg.). Office: 10300 N Central Suite 215 Bldg IV Dallas TX 75231

FLEMMING, JOHN FRANKLIN, social work cons.; b. South Norfolk, Va., Sept. 16, 1942; s. Nicholas Trafton and Elizabeth Medell (Weeks) F.; A.B., Elon Coll., 1964; M.S.W., U. N.C., 1969; m. Dell Scott Manning, July 11, 1964; children—John Trafton, Christopher Lynn, Lucia Brent. Staff social worker Person County Dept. Social Services, Roxboro, N.C. 1964-68; acting dir. social services O'Berry Center for the Mentally Retarded, Goldsboro, N.C., 1969; chief clin. social worker Onslow County Mental Health Center, Jacksonville, N.C., 1970-75; state social work cons. for maternal and child health N.C. Div. of Health Services, Raleigh, 1975—. Mem. Nat. Assn. Perinatal Soc. Workers (bd. dirs.), Acad. Cert. Social Workers, Nat. Assn. Social Workers (dist. sec.), N.C. Public Health Assn. Democrat. Presbyterian. Home: 405 Nelson Dr Jacksonville NC 28540 Office: PO Box 2091 Raleigh NC 27602

FLESHMAN, ROBERT EDWARD, educator; b. Lafayette, La., Feb. 18, 1930; s. George Stokes and Mildred Marcia (Herndon) F.; student La. Coll., 1947-49; B.A., William Jewell Coll., 1950; postgrad. La. State U., 1951, 1955, 1959; profl. student Ecole du Mime Etienne Decroux, N.Y.C., 1957-59, Moreno Inst., 1961-63. Tchr. drama Hinds Jr. Coll., Raymond, Miss., 1955-56, Jr. Dramatic Workshop, N.Y.C., 1957-58; social worker Indsl. Home for Blind, Bklyn., 1961-63; co-founder, dir. Shakespeare for Students, Ednl. Theatre, N.Y.C., 1961-63; social worker N.Y.C. Welfare Programs, Day Care Centers, 1963-68; prof. theatre Loyola U., New Orleans, 1968—, dir. Drama Therapy & Mime Conservatory, 1975—; instr. mime courses Tulane U., New Orleans, 1973, Ballet Hysell, New Orleans, 1974, psychodrama classes La. State U., Allied Health Services, 1976-77; coordinator Multi-Arts Therapy Program, New Orleans Consortium, 1974-78. Served with USAF, 1951-55. Recipient acad. grant Mime in France, Loyola U., New Orleans, 1973; HEW grantee, 1977—. Mem. Nat. Assn. Drama Therapy (founding mem., steering com.), Nat. Edn. Com. for Creative Therapies (steering com.). Author: (with Diane Carney) Scarecrow Press, 1978; (with Jerry Fryrear) Nelson Hall, 1978; contbr. numerous articles and revs. to profl. jours.; dir. Taming of the Shrew for record album, 1966. Home: 1000 Joliet St New Orleans LA 70118 Office: Dept Drama/Speech Loyola U PO Box 155 New Orleans LA 70118

FLETCHER, CLIFF, profl. hockey exec.; b. 1935; m. Donna Owens; 2 children. With Montreal Canadian Orgn., 1956-66, mgr. Verdun Jr. B team, later mgr. Jr. Canadiens; chief scout St. Louis Blues, 1966-69, asst. gen. mgr., 1969-72; gen. mgr. Atlanta Flames, Nat. Hockey League, 1972—, also v.p. Office: Atlanta Flames The Omni 100 Techwood Dr NE Atlanta GA 30303*

FLETCHER, DONNIE CARLTON, engring. and applied sci. cons.; b. Jacksonville, Fla., July 4, 1943; s. Aubrey and Claudia Grey (Andrews) F.; B.Sc. (Inst. scholar), M.I.T., 1965; Ph.D. (Inst. fellow), Calif. Inst. Tech., 1974; m. Alison Louise Watkins, Sept. 2, 1968; 1 dau., Laura. Mem. sr. sci. staff Research and Devel. Assos., Marina del Rey, Calif., 1973-76; cons. Johns Hopkins U. Applied Physics Lab., Laurel, Md., 1976-79; pres., sr. cons. Fletcher Assos., Delray Beach, Fla., 1979—. Recipient citation for service to Cape Kennedy, USAF, 1967. Mem. AAAS, Am. Inst. Physics, Caltech Alumni Soc., Sigma Xi. Author numerous classified research reports. Home: 3324 Blvd Chatelaine Delray Beach FL 33444

FLETCHER, EDITH HARRIGILL, educator; b. Hamburg, Miss., Mar. 14, 1919; d. Clarence Fulton and Alice Lee (French) Harrigill; B.S., U. So. Miss., 1941, M.A., 1960, postgrad., 1961-72; m. William W. Fletcher, Jr., July 25, 1942; children—Nancy Alice, William Wesley III. Tchr., Carson, Miss., 1941-43, Hamburg, 1943-45, Sumrall, Miss., 1949-67; spl. tchr. learning disabilities F.B. Woodley Sch., Hattiesburg, Miss., 1967—. Mem. NEA, Miss. Tchrs. Assn., Hattiesburg Classroom Tchrs. Assn. (named Outstanding Tchr. of Woodley Sch., 1976), Assn. Children with Learning Disabilities. Methodist. Address: 812 W 5th St Hattiesburg MS 39401

FLETCHER, JAMES NORRICE, retail exec.; b. Tipton County, Tenn., June 18, 1928; s. Harold Clarence and Ivie Myrtle (Turnage) F.; student Lambuth Coll., 1946-48; m. Georgia LaVerne Lamb, May 27, 1951; children—Cheryl Christine, Victoria Jane (twins), Julia Ellen, Amy Elizabeth. Trainee, Sears Roebuck & Co., Paducah, Ky., 1948-54, mdse. mgr., Fayetteville, N.C., 1954-59, zone mdse. mgr., 1959-65, mgr., Orlando, Fla., 1965-66, mgr., Roanoke, Va., 1965-69, mgr. Pembroke Mall, Virginia Beach, Va., 1969—; dir. United Va. Bank. Chmn. bd. trustees Bayside Hosp.; chmn. pastoral parish com. Haygood United Methodist Ch.; crusade chmn. Am. Cancer Soc., 1973; chmn. friends drive Va. Wesleyan Coll., 1974; chmn. Norfolk Met. br. Nat. Alliance Bus., 1971. Served with AUS, 1950-51. Recipient Boss of Yr. award Virginia Beach Jaycees, 1972, Virginia Beach br. Nat. Secs. Assn., 1971. Mem. Va. C. of C. (dir., pres. 1975). Republican. Club: Masons. Office: 4588 Virginia Beach Blvd Virginia Beach VA 23462

FLETCHER, MINOS L., III, metal finishing exec.; b. Nashville, Mar. 21, 1923; s. Minos L. and Emma B. (Shwab) F.; A.B., Harvard, 1945; m. Maryland M. Myford, Dec. 3, 1966; children—Minos IV, Sara Jane, Barry. Treas., So. Finishers Inc., 1954-58; v.p. Delta Plate Inc., Nashville, 1958-60, Master Plate Inc., Nashville, 1958-65; pres. Metal Plate, Inc., Nashville, 1965—. Mem. Nat. Assn. Metal Finishers (dir. 1979—), Nashville C. of C. Republican. Clubs: Fly, Harvard of Nashville, Nashville Exchange, Belle Meade Country. Served to capt. USAAF, 1944-51. Home: 1131 Crater Hill Dr Nashville TN 37215 Office: 7121 Cockrill Bend Rd Nashville TN 37209

FLETCHER, RILEY EUGENE, lawyer; b. Eddy, Tex., Nov. 29, 1912; s. Riley Jordan and Lelih (Gill) F.; B.A., Baylor U., 1950, J.D., 1950; m. Hattie Inez Blackwell, June 11, 1954. Admitted to Tex. bar, 1950; asst. county atty. Navarro County, Tex., 1951-52, county atty., 1952-54; pvt. practice law, Corsicana, Tex., 1955-56; asst. atty. gen. Tex., 1956-62, chief law enforcement div., atty. gen.'s dept., 1958-61; chief taxation div., atty. gen.'s dept., 1961-62; asst. gen. counsel Tex. Mcpl. League, 1962-63, gen. counsel, 1963-78, spl. counsel, 1978—. Lt. col. AUS ret. Mem. Am., Travis County bar assns., State Bar Tex., Am. Judicature Soc., Res. Officers Assn. (chpt. pres. 1979-80), Assn. U.S. Army (chpt. pres. 1965-66), Am. Legion, Judge Advs. Assn., Austin World Affairs Council, Mil. Order World Wars. Baptist. Mason. K.P. Home: 7201 Creekside Dr Austin TX 78752 Office: 1020 Southwest Tower TX 78701

FLETER, WALTER HENRY, bus. services co. exec.; b. Milw., Aug. 10, 1920; s. Gustav and Emma (Stenske) F.; B.S., Marquette U., 1947; postgrad. U. Chgo., 1948-49; children by former marriage—William, Marcia, Kurt, James. Office mgr. Inland Steel Co., Chgo., 1947-53; asst. to div. mgr. Milprint Co., Milw., 1953-54; underwriter bus. ins. Phoenix Mut. Life Ins. Co., Milw., 1954-58; mgmt. cons. A.L. Osmundson & Assos., Milw., 1957-59; sales rep. Curtis 1000 Inc., Smyrna, Ga., 1959-62, office mgr., 1962-65, sales mgr., 1965-71, mgr. sales promotion, 1971-74; mgr. mktg. Speedi-Print Co., subs., 1974-76, nat. research and devel. mgr. Curtis, 1976—; lectr. in field. Served to 1st. lt., U.S. Army, 1941-46. Mem. Sales/Mktg. Execs., Word Processing Assn., Alpha Kappa Psi (pres. Gamma Delta chpt. 1947-49). Lutheran. Home: 557 Little Rd SE Marietta GA 30067 Office: Curtis 1000 Inc 1000 Curtis Dr SE Smyrna GA 30080

FLEURY, GEORGE JENKINS, JR., surgeon; b. Leonardtown, Md., Feb. 24, 1916; s. George Jenkins and Alice Gibbons (Fenwick) F.; A.B. cum laude, Georgetown U., 1937, M.D. cum laude, 1941; m. Mary Gioninger, May 5, 1951; children—Mimi, George, Catherine, Anne, John, William, Peter, Alice. Intern, Georgetown U. Hosp., Washington, 1941-42, resident in surgery, 1946-49; resident in surgery Lahay Clinic, Boston, 1949-50, U. Pa. Hosp., Phila., 1949; practice medicine specializing in gen. surgery, Washington, 1950-54, Newport Beach, Calif., 1954-57, McLean, Va., 1957—; asso. clin. prof. surgery Georgetown U., 1957—. Served to capt. M.C., USAAF, 1942-46. Mem. A.C.S., Am. Bd. Surgery, AMA. Home: 1005 Abbey Way McLean VA 22101 Office: 1515 Chain Bridge Rd McLean VA 22101

FLINK, STEPHEN HARRY, ins. co. exec.; b. Bronx, N.Y., Apr. 20, 1941; s. Harry E. and Ruth Marion (Nelson) F.; B.S., U. Mich., 1964; M.B.A., Fairleigh Dickinson U., 1966; m. Anne Marie Gallo, 1964; children—Heather, Erik, Kristen. Field engr. Atwell, Vogel & Sterling, Inc., N.Y. and Ariz., 1963-64, ops. mgr., Newark, 1966-67, nat. engring. mgr., N.Y.C., 1967-68; dir. sales and mktg. Equifax Inc., Atlanta, 1970-73, asst. v.p. sales, 1973-75, v.p. mktg., 1975—; guest lectr. on bus. communications and sales mgmt. Mem. Mayor's Commn. Operations Safe City N.Y.C., 1969; mem. ins. com. Chatham Twp., 1968. Served with USN, 1959-63. Certified safety profl.; recipient letter of achievement Lloyd's of London, 1976. Mem. Sales Mktg. Execs., Am. Mgmt. Assn., Engring. Soc. of Detroit, Am. Soc. Safety Engrs., Am. Defense Preparedness Assn. (v.p., dir.), Nat. Geog. Soc., Soc. Fire Protection Engrs., U.S. Naval Inst. Republican. Inventor engring. template. Home: 5415 Seaton Dr Dunwoody GA 30338

FLINN, THOMAS HANCE, banker; b. Hutto, Tex., Jan. 30, 1922; s. Thomas Hance and Margaret (Bowden) F.; grad. certificate Stonier Grad. Sch. Banking, 1961; B.B.A., U. Tex., 1949; m. Georgeann Atwood, May 26, 1948; children—Mary Kathleen, Michael Hance, Mark Thomas. Securities salesman various firms, San Antonio, 1949-54; v.p., M.E. Allison & Co., San Antonio, 1955-56; asst. v.p., Groos Nat. Bank, San Antonio, 1956-59; pvt. practice investment counsel, San Antonio, 1959-60; investment counsel Scudder, Stevens & Clark, investment counsel, Dallas, 1960-63; v.p. investments United Va. Bankshares Inc., Richmond, 1964-73, sr. v.p., corporate treas., 1973—; lectr. in field; dir. United Va. Mortgage Corp. Vice-chmn. Chesterfield County (Va.) Republican party, 1966. Served with USAAF, 1942-46. Mem. Delta Sigma Pi. Republican. Presbyterian. Clubs: Bull and Bear, Meadowbrook Country, Masons (32 deg.), Shriners. Home: 3000 Kenmore Rd Richmond VA 23225 Office: 900 E Main St Richmond VA 23219

FLINT, CHARLES RAY, educator; b. Bristow, Okla., June 8, 1931; s. Robert Lee and Janie Leona F.; Liberal Arts degree Kilgore Jr. Coll., 1951; B.B.A., E. Tex. State U., 1955; m. Peggy Loretta Shepherd, Oct. 10, 1954; children—Nancy, Julia, Amy. Sr. sales rep. Texaco, Inc., Houston, 1955-72; asst. comptroller San Jacinto Coll., Pasadena, Tex., 1972-75; instr. mgmt. devel., 1975—, dept. chmn., 1977—, coordinator, 1975—. Served with U.S. Army, 1953-55. Cert. Tex. Edn. Agy. Mem. Tex. Jr. Coll. Tchrs. Assn., Tex. Jr. Coll. Mgmt. Educators Assn., Jr. Collegiate Distbr. Edn. Clubs Am., Mu Theta Alpha. Democrat. Baptist. Home: 809 Luella St Deer Park TX 77536 Office: 8060 Spencer Hwy Pasadena TX 77505

FLINT, CORT RAY, clergyman, author, cons.; b. Leedey, Okla., Mar. 17, 1915; s. Corties Ray and Kathryn (Logan) F.; B.A., Southwestern Okla. State U., 1935; postgrad. U. Okla., summers 1937, 39; Th.M., So. Bapt. Theol. Sem., 1943, Ph.D., 1952; m. Wilma Ilene Moore, Nov. 24, 1920; children—Sue Ann, Cort Ray. Tchr. pub. schs., Okla., 1935-40; ordained to ministry, Bapt. Ch., 1940; pastor, New Haven, Ky., 1941-43, Pleasant Grove Ch., Hodgenville, Ky., 1941-42, 46-47; asst. pastor Southside Bapt. Ch., Birmingham, Ala., 1947-48; pastor First Ch., Olney, Tex., 1948-50, Lynn Acres Ch., Louisville, 1951-53; adminstrv. asst. So. Bapt. Theol. Sem., Louisville, 1952-55; pastor First Ch., Anderson, S.C., 1955-66; interim pres. Anderson Coll., 1957—; pastor Bennertown Bapt. Ch., 1967-69, Meadows of Dan Bapt. Ch., Va., 1970-79; dir., pres. Anderson Sch. Theology for Laymen. Various offices Bapt. convs., Tex., Ky., 1948-53; chmn. stewardship com. S.C. Bapt. Conv., 1957-58, gen. bd., 1957—; finance com. Saluda Bapt. Assn. S.C., 1955-58. Active YMCA, Anderson County Tb Assn.; exec. bd. Blue Ridge council Boy Scouts Am. Vice chmn. bd. trustees So. Bapt. Theol. Sec., Louisville; trustee Furman U. Served as lt., chaplain, USNR, 1943-46; PTO. Mem. Anderson Ministerial Assn. (pres. 1956-57), Internat. Platform Speakers Orgn., Youth Rehab. Orgn. Mason, Odd Fellow. Clubs: Rotary, Kiwanis. Author: Grief's Slow Wisdom; To Thine Own Self Be True; Better Men or Bitter Men; Grief Is Love; The Best Is Yet To Be; The Purpose of Love. Editor: The Quotable Dr. Crane; The Quotable Billy Graham. Home: The Recluse Route 2 Box 174 Hillsville VA 24343

FLINT, JAMES HENRY, JR., accountant; b. Gatewood, W.Va., Dec. 17, 1947; s. James Henry and Delcie Virginia (Bradberry) F.; B.S., W.Va. Inst. Tech., 1974; m. Thresea Ann Dilley, July 16, 1971; children—Debra Lynn, Stacey Leigh. Cost accountant Cannelton (W.Va.) Industries, Inc., 1974, supr. cost acctg., 1974-78, planning accountant, 1978—. Served with U.S. Army, 1967-69. Decorated Silver Star, Bronze Star, Air medal. Mem. Kanawha Valley Mining Inst., Am. Legion. Baptist. Home: Route 1 Box 220 Fayetteville WV 25840 Office: Cannelton Industries Inc Cannelton WV 25036

FLIPPEN, LLEWELLYN TUCKER, dentist; b. Richmond, Va., July 8, 1933; s. James Howard and Evelyn (Tucker) F.; B.A., U. Richmond, 1954; D.D.S., Va. Commonwealth U., 1958. Rotating dental intern Wilford Hall Hosp., San Antonio, 1958-59; pvt. practice dentistry, Richmond, 1961—; asst. clin. prof. restorative dept. Sch. Dentistry, Va. Commonwealth U., 1961-80; dir. Westhampton Savs. & Loan Assn., 1973-75. Mem. alumni interfraternity council U. Richmond, 1966-69. Served to capt. USAF, 1958-61. Fellow Am. Coll. Dentistry, Internat. Coll. Dentistry; mem. Met. Acad. Dentistry (treas. 1969), Richmond Dental Soc. (dir. 1967-69, sec. 1971-73, ho. of dels. 1973-75, pres. 1978-79), Va. Dental Assn. (budget and fin. affairs com. 1972-79), Va. Assn. Professions, Am. Profl. Practice Assn., S.A.R. (chpt. pres. 1966, bd. mgrs. 1964-69), Southeastern Acad. Prosthodontics, Omicron Kappa Upsilon, Kappa Alpha, Delta Sigma Delta, Alpha Sigma Chi, Sigma Zeta. Presbyterian (chmn. bd. deacons 1971-72, elder 1972-75). Club: Bull and Bear. Home: 37 Snughaven Richmond VA 23228 Office: 4100 Brook Rd Richmond VA 23227

FLIPPEN, MENVILLE B., III, sociologist; b. San Angelo, Tex., Dec. 11, 1946; s. Menville B. and Dorothy Marie (Shealer) F.; B.S., Stephen F. Austin State U., 1969; M.A., Tex. A. and M. U., 1972; m. Cynthia Allen, Aug. 31, 1968; children—Matthew Allen, Micah Henry. Research asst. Tex. A. and M. U., College Station, 1969-72; exec. dir., sociologist Family Life Counseling Services, Still Creek Christian Farm, College Station, 1972—; cons. mental health and social services. Spl. witness Com. on Child Abuse Tex. Ho. of Reps. Mem. Am. Personnel and Guidance Assn., Christian Assn. for Psychol. Studies, Nat. Assn. Christians in Social Work. Methodist. Author booklets, seminar handbooks. Office: PO Box 48 501 University College Station TX 77840

FLIPPO, RONNIE GENE, congressman; b. Florence, Ala., Aug. 15, 1937; s. Claude and Esther (McAfee) F.; B.S., Florence State U., 1965; M.A., U. Ala., 1966; m. Faye Cooper, Nov 27, 1958; children—Ronnie Gene, Linda Gail, Brenda Faye, Lea Ella, Kelly Reid, Ryan Cooper. Accountant, Flippo & Robbins, C.P.A.'s, Florence, Ala., 1972-76; mem. Ala. Senate, 1975-76; mem. 95th-96th Congresses from 5th Ala. Dist. Chmn. March of Dimes, 1969. Mem. Am. Inst. C.P.A.'s, Ala. C.P.A.'s Soc., Nat. Assn. Accountants. Democrat. Mem. Ch. of Christ. Club: Elks. Office: 439 Cannon House Office Bldg Washington DC 20515

FLOOD, JOAN MOORE, librarian; b. Hampton, Va., Oct. 10, 1941; d. Harold W. and Estalena (Fancher) M.; B.Mus., N. Tex. State U., 1963, postgrad., 1977; postgrad. So. Meth. U., 1967-68, Tex. Women's U., 1978-79; 1 dau. by former marriage, Angie. Clk., Criminal Dist. Ct. Number 2, Dallas County, Tex., 1972-75; reins. librarian Scor Reins. Co., Dallas, 1975-80, Freytag, Marshall, Beneke, LaForce, Rubinstein & Stutzman, 1980—. Mem. Spl. Libraries Assn., Am. Assn. Law Librarians, Tex. Libraries Assn., S.W. Libraries Assn., Dallas County Library Assn., Dallas Assn. Legal Assts., Dallas Assn. Law Librarians, other orgns. Republican. Episcopalian. Home: 3829 Marquette St Dallas TX 75225 Office: 3131 Turtle Creek Blvd Dallas TX 75219

FLOOD, ROY DEVONNE, physician; b. Cofield, N.C., Apr. 27, 1940; s. Denver Roy and Martha Rosetta (Daniels) F.; B.S., N.C. A&T State U., 1961; M.D., Howard U., 1965; m. Julia Yvonne Campbell, Aug. 26, 1961; children—Roy, Geoffrey, Stacey. Intern, USPHS Hosp., S.I., N.Y., 1965-66, staff outpatient clinics, 1966-68; individual practice medicine, specializing in family practice, Murfreesboro, N.C., 1968—; pres. Murfreesboro Med. Assos. P.A., 1972—. Mem. N.C. Commn. on Sickle Cell Anemia, 1974-76; mem. N.C. Textbook Commn., 1977—. Served with USPHS, 1965-68. Diplomate Am. Bd. Family Practice. Fellow Am. Acad. Family Practice; mem. Hartford County Med. Soc., Northeastern N.C. Med. Soc., N.C. Med. Soc., Old North State Med. Soc., AMA, Nat. Med. Soc., Am. Acad. Family Physicians. Baptist. Home: Box 7 Spring Branch Rd Murfreesboro NC 27855 Office: Murfreesboro Med Assos PA 307 Beechwood Blvd Murfreesboro NC 27855

FLORA, ELEANOR MAXINE, club woman, former librarian; b. Earlham, Iowa, Mar. 3, 1915; d. Charles P. and Ethel Irene (Bricker) Benson; B.A., Simpson Coll., 1937; postgrad. Drake U., 1938, 62, U. Iowa, 1964-66, U. No. Iowa, 1971; m. Wilbur John Flora, Feb. 14, 1942; children—Julie Ann (Mrs. Robert Tudor Hill III), Suzanne Marie (Mrs. Samuel Richard Rubin), Edward. Tchr. English and speech Lincoln Lee High Sch., Albert City, Iowa, 1937-38, Baxter (Iowa) High Sch., 1938-41, Dallas Center (Iowa) High Sch., 1941-42; tchr., English, librarian Kellogg Jr. High Sch., Newton, Iowa, 1962-65; librarian Anson Jr. High Sch., Marshalltown, Iowa, 1965-73. Leader 4H, 1959-60; pres. Band Mothers, 1960-61, v.p., 1959-60; active D.A.R., P.E.O., Panhellenic. Mem. Iowa Edn. Assn. (mem. library services com. 1968-70), Marshalltown Edn. Assn. (secondary sch. library chmn. 1970-72), Iowa Sch. Librarians (dist. vice chmn. 1970-72), Pi Beta Phi (pres. alumnae club St. Petersburg, Fla.). Alpha Psi Omega, Sigma Tau Delta. Methodist. Home: 3975 100th Pl North Pinellas Park FL 33565

FLORANCE, STANLEY HUNTER, accountant; b. Baytown, Tex., Dec. 10, 1939; s. Robert Glenn and Eleanor Colliday (Jones) F.; B.B.A., U. Houston, 1962, grad. student, 1966-68; m. Myra Joyce Watson, Apr. 16, 1966; children—Janice, Joyce. Nat. bank examiner Comptroller of Currency, Treasury Dept., Dallas, 1962-64; comptroller Citizens Nat. Bank & Trust Co., Baytown, 1964-65; cashier U.S. Nat. Bank, Galveston, Tex., 1966-67; pub. accountant Arthur Andersen & Co., C.P.A.'s, Houston, 1967-72; asst. controller 1st City Bancorp. of Tex., Inc., Houston, 1972-74; controller, treas. Federated Capital Corp., bank holding co., Houston, 1974-77; sec., treas. Main & Polk Corp., Houston, 1975-77; treas., dir. Oil Base Inc., Houston, 1977-78, v.p., treas., chief fin. officer, 1978—; sec., treas., dir. La. Mud Co., Houma, 1977-79; treas., dir. Hevy Minerals, Inc., Houston, 1979—. C.P.A., Tex. Mem. Fin. Execs. Inst., Am. Inst. C.P.A.'s, Tex. Soc. Pub. Accountants, Am. Accounting Assn., Nat. Assn. Accountants, Am. Econs. and Fin. Assn. (pres. Houston 1961-62), Phi Kappa Theta (treas. Houston 1961-62, nat. gov. 1963-64). Republican (del. state conv. 1964). Home: 7923 Oakington Dr Houston TX 77071 Office: 3625 SW Freeway Houston TX 77027

FLORES, ARNOLD, labor union adminstr.; b. Rio Grande City, Tex., Oct. 31, 1936; s. Alejandro H. and Marianne S.; student St. Phillips Coll., 1961-62, San Antonio Coll., 1963-65, Jacinto Trevino Coll., 1969-70; m. Gloria Santoy, Sept. 3, 1960; children—Arnold Rocky, Manuel S. Various positions with Civil Service, 1962-68; aircraft parts classifier Service Employees Internat. Union, San Antonio, 1968-70, organizer, 1968-77, state dir., 1970-77; spl. asst. to Commr. of Immigration and Naturalization Service, Washington, 1977—. Mem. exec. bd. Nat. Council of LaRaza, 1972-77; vice-chmn. S.W. Voter Registration Edn. Project, 1972-77; mem. exec. bd. Labor Council for Latin-Am. Advancement, 1973-77, Mex. Am. Unity Council, 1972-77; Latin-Am. chmn. San Antonio Labor Council, 1973-77; founder, vice-chmn. Yaneguana Radio Corp., 1974-77. Served with USAF, 1954-58. Recipient citation Tex. Legislature, 1974; recipient numerous civic plaques, scrolls and citations; Indsl. Found. tng. grantee, 1972. Mem. Nat. AFL-CIO, Labor Council Latin-Am. Advancement. Democrat. Pentecostal. Home: 210 Holy Cross St San Antonio TX 78228 Office: 425 I St NW Washington DC 20536

FLORES, FRANCISCO JAVIER, educator; b. Lajas, P.R., Nov. 24, 1927; s. Eduardo F. and Monserrate (Jusino) F.; B.A., Inter-Am. U., 1961; M.A., U. Ala., 1965, Ph.D., 1972. Prof. bus. adminstrn. Inter-Am. U., San Germain, P.R., 1961-72, chmn. dept. econ. bus., 1972-73, 76-78, dean acad. affairs, 1978—, univ. senator, 1972-75; cons. Peat, Marwick, Mitchell & Co., 1968, Banco Economias de P.R., 1969-72; adv. Com. on Devel. Strategy for Govt. of P.R., 1974-75. Mem. Am. Acctg. Assn., Fin. Mgmt. Assn., Nat. Assn. Acctg. Home: PO Box 883 San German PR 00753 Office: Inter Am Univ San German PR 00753

FLORES, MANUEL C., JR., editor; b. Laredo, Tex., July 29, 1948; s. Manuel and Maria Luisa (Chapa) F.; B.S. in Edn., Tex. A&I U., 1970; postgrad., 1978-80; postgrad. N. Tex. State U., 197—72; m. Rosa Lydia Acevedo, Dec. 19, 1970; children—Mario, Marcos. Sports editor Irving (Tex.) Daily News, 1970-72; sports writer, columnist Corpus Christi Caller-Times, 1972-73; public relations asst. Central Power and Light Co., Corpus Christi, 1973, editor co. mag., 1972—. Served to capt. inf. U.S. Army, 1970. Mem. Internat. Assn. Bus. Communicators, Res. Officers Assn., N.G. Assn. Tex., N.G. Assn. U.S.,Leadership Corpus Christi. Democrat. Roman Catholic. Club: Corpus Christi Press. Home: 5837 Llano St Corpus Christi TX 78407 Office: Box 2121 Central Power and Light Co Corpus Christi TX 78403

FLORES, MARTIN, JR., ednl. adminstr.; b. Corpus Christi, Tex., July 30, 1936; s. Martin and Concepcion (Cano) F.; B.A., Tex. A. and I. U., 1971; M.S.W., Boston Coll., 1975; m. Adelina Torres, Apr. 12, 1959; children—Carmela, Angela, Edith, Martin Antonio. ednl. dir., caseworker Dept. Human Resources, Houston, 1963-71, appeals analyst, 1971-73, ednl. dir., 1975—; asst. prof. Tex. So. U., part-time, Houston, 1976—; Active United Fund Agy., Houston, 1977-78. Served with U.S. Army, 1959-61. Presdl. grantee Boston Coll., 1973-75. Mem. Nat. Assn. Social Workers, Council Social Work Edn., Tex. Public Employees Assn. Roman Catholic. Club: Ch. Address: 6053 Bellfort St Houston TX 77033

FLOREZ, LEOPOLDO, architect, planner; b. Pinar del Rio, Cuba, Oct. 15, 1945; s. Emilio and Juliana de la Caridad (Alvarez) F.; came to U.S., 1962, naturalized, 1971; B.Arch., U. Fla., Gainesville, 1970;

M.S. in Urban and Regional Planning, Fla. State U., Tallahassee, 1972. Archtl. designer, supr. constrn. Cook, Reiff & Assos., architects/engrs., Miami, Fla., 1969-70; planner intern Met. Dade County Dept. Housing and Urban Devel., Miami, 1970-72; asso. planner dept. adminstrn., div. state planning Fla. Bur. Land and Water Mgmt., Tallahasee, 1972-75; asst. dir. community devel. and housing Met. Dade County Office Community and Econ. Devel., 1975—. Mem. Spanish consumer adv. com. Dade County; mem. United Way Hispanic Am. Planning Council, Dade County. Recipient award Lehigh Design Competition, 1969; Miami Cuban Lyceum award, 1975, 76. Asso. mem. Am. Planning Assn. Democrat. Roman Catholic. Home: 511 SW 21st Rd Miami FL 33129 Office: 90 SW 8th St Suite 309 Miami FL 33130

FLOURNOY, DAYL JEAN, microbiologist; b. San Antonio, Dec. 17, 1944; s. Dayl J. and Bonnie B. (Earnest) F.; B.S., S.W. Tex. State U., 1965; A.S., San Antonio Coll., 1966; M.A., Incarnate Word Coll., 1968; Ph.D., U. Houston, 1973; m. Mary Virginia Patrick, June 2, 1967; children—David, Michael, Michelle. Med. technologist Santa Rosa Med. Center, San Antonio, 1966-69; teaching fellow anatomy, physiology and microbiology U. Houston, 1969-72; med. technologist St. Luke's Episcopal Hosp., Houston, 1972-73, microbiologist, 1974-75; dir. clin. microbiology and serology VA Med. Center, Oklahoma City, 1975—; adj. asst. prof. pathology and microbiology Okla. U. Health Scis. Center, Oklahoma City, 1975—, asso. mem. grad. faculty dept. microbiology, 1978—, dir. continuing edn. seminars for med. technologists, 1976-77. Head soccer coach Tri-City Athletic Assn. Recipient VA Med. Center Suggestion award, 1977; Indian Health Service scholar, 1969. Mem. Soc. for Exptl. Biology and Medicine, Am. Soc. for Microbiology. Contbr. articles on microbiology to sci. publs. Office: VA Med Center 921 NE 13th St Oklahoma City OK 73104

FLOWERS, ELLIOTT GALETIN, lawyer, petroleum cons.; b. Houston, Mar. 10, 1913; s. Louis Irwin and Hazel (Lawshae) F.; B.A., Rice U., 1934; LL.B., Tex. U., 1937; m. Elizabeth Sinclair, Jan. 22, 1957; children—Leigh (Mrs. L.F. Bonner, Jr.), Elliott Galetin, Lynn Zarr, Lucy (Mrs. A.J. Foyt, Jr.). Admitted to Tex. bar, 1937; practiced Houston, 1939-41, 47—; gen. counsel McCarthy Oil & Gas Corp., Houston, 1947-52; asso. counsel Allied Chem. Corp., Houston, 1952-71, asst. gen. counsel, 1971-78; exec. asst. to pres. Union Tex. Petroleum, Houston, 1952-78; petroleum cons., 1978—. Served to lt. comdr. USNR, 1942-47. Mem. Am., Tex. bar assns., Fed. Power Bar Assn., Ind. Petroleum Assn. (v.p. 1963-66, dir. 1966—), Mid-Continent Oil and Gas Assn. (mem. exec. mgmt., legis., legal coms. 1964—finance com. 1964-68, dir. 1970—), So. Gas Assn. (adv. council 1962-63), Houston Bar Assn. (finance and budget com. 1963-64). Author: Municipal Officials in Texas, 1939. Contbr. articles on municipal law to profl. jours. Home: 3330 Del Monte Houston TX 77019 Office: 1200 S Post Oak Rd Houston TX 77056

FLOWERS, VIRGINIA ANNE, univ. adminstr.; b. Dothan, Ala., d. Kyrie Neal and Annie Laurie (Stewart) Flowers; B.A., Fla. State U., 1949; M.Ed., Auburn U., 1958; Ed.D., Duke, 1963. Elementary tchr. Minnie T. Heard Sch., Dothan, Ala., 1949-52; secondary tchr. Dalton (Ga.) High Sch., 1952-55, personnel dir., asst. prin., 1955-61; instr. U.S. history U. Ga. Extension, Dalton, 1960-61; part-time instr. Duke, Durham, N.C., 1961-62, vis. prof., summers 1966, 67, 69, 70, asst. provost, asso. dean Trinity Coll. Arts and Scis. Duke, 1972—, acting vice provost, acting dean, 1973-74, chmn. dept. edn., asst. provost ednl. program devel., Duke, 1974—; asso. prof. edn. Columbia (S.C.) Coll., 1962-66, prof. edn., 1966-68; head dept. edn., 1966-68, asso. dean, 1969-71, dean, 1971-72; prof. elementary edn. Va. Commonwealth U., Richmond, Va., 1968-69, asso. dean Columbia Coll., 1969-71, dean, 1971-72. Mem. NEA, Nat. Orgn. Legal Problems in Edn., Am. Ednl. Research Assn., Nat. Soc. for Study Edn., AAUP, So. Assn. Colls. and Schs. (commn. on colls. and schs.), Am. Assn. Higher Edn., Kappa Delta Epsilon, Kappa Delta Pi, Delta Kappa Gamma, Alpha Kappa Gamma. Research and publs. in field. Home: Box 3272 Durham NC 27705

FLOWERS, WALTER, lawyer, former congressman; b. Greenville, Ala., Apr. 12, 1933; s. Walter W. and Ruth (Swaim) F.; A.B., U. Ala., 1955, LL.B., 1957; Rotary Found. fellow, U. London, 1957-58; m. Margaret V. Pringle, Aug. 21, 1958; children—Vivian Victoria, Walter Winkler III, Victor Woodley. Admitted to Ala. bar, 1957, Miss. bar, 1960; sr. partner firm Flowers and Shelby, Tuscaloosa, Ala., 1961-68; mem. 91st-95th Congresses, 7th Dist. Ala.; partner firm Collier, Shannon, Rill, Edwards & Scott, Washington, 1979—; disting. vis. prof. polit. sci. U. Ala. Past mem. Black Warrior council Boy Scouts Am., Tuscaloosa YMCA; former mem., chmn. Tuscaloosa Civil Service Bd.; past pres. Tuscaloosa County Mental Health Assn.; past bd. dirs. Tuscaloosa County chpt. ARC, Tuscaloosa Tb Assn. Served to 1st lt. AUS, 1958-59. Mem. Am., Miss., Ala., Tuscaloosa County bar assns., U. Ala. Alumni Assn. (past pres. Tuscaloosa County), Phi Beta Kappa, Omicron Delta Kappa, Jasons Soc., Phi Delta Phi, Sigma Alpha Epsilon. Democrat. Episcopalian. Club: Rotary. Office: 1055 Thomas Jefferson St NW Suite 308 Washington DC 20007

FLOYD, DAN WILSON, II, pharm. co. exec.; b. Booneville, Miss., Nov. 26, 1945; s. Dan Wilson and Toy (Witt) F.; B.A., U. Miss., 1968; student Cert. Med. Reps. Inst., 1975; m. Ann Clarice Kitchens, Sept. 4, 1966; children—Dan Wilson III, Whitney Ann. Profl. service rep. Syntex Labs., Memphis, 1968-72, dist. sales mgr., 1972-76, field devel. mgr., Palo Alto, Calif., 1976-77, mgr. sales adminstrn., 1977, Southeastern regional sales mgr., Tucker, Ga., 1977—. Served with NG, 1963-72. Named Nat. Rep. of Year, Syntex Labs., 1971; recipient Eagle Scout award Boy Scouts Am., 1958, God and Country award, 1957. Mem. South Atlantic Drug Club. Methodist. Address: Syntex Labs PO Box 147 Tucker GA 30084

FLOYD, ELDRA MOORE, JR., lawyer; b. Fairmont, N.C., July 19, 1920; s. Eldra Moore and Sarah Augusta (Blake) F.; B.A., Wake Forest U., 1950; J.D., U. S.C., 1948; m. Eugenia Chandler, Oct. 31, 1942; children—Michael H., Cindy M., Eldra Moore III, Eugenia, Ruth H. Admitted to S.C. bar, 1948, since practiced in Hartsville, S.C. Commr., Darlington County, 1961-64; mem. Darlington County Bd. Edn., 1968-79; mem. Darlington County Democratic Exec. Com., 1962—. Served as lt. comdr. USNR, 1940-45; PTO. Mem. Internat., Am., S.C. (mem. exec. com. 1973-75, mem. ho. of dels. 1975-77), Darlington County (pres. 1973) bar assns., Am. Judicature Soc., Assn. Ins. Attys. Episcopalian. Mason (Shriner), Lion. Home: 411 Kenwood Dr Hartsville SC 29550 Office: 125 W Home Ave PO Box 909 Hartsville SC 29550

FLOYD, JAMES THOMAS, plastic mfg. co. exec.; b. Laurens, S.C., Nov. 16, 1935; s. Willie James and Clara R. F.; B.S., Allen U., 1957; M.S., Tuskegee Inst., 1965; postgrad. U. Minn., 1966, Furman U., 1967, Morgan State Coll., 1968, Clemson U., 1974. Biology and gen. sci. tchr. Sanders High Sch., 1957-58, head football and athletic dir., biology tchr., 1960-64; chmn. sci. dept., tchr. chemistry and physics Beck High Sch., 1965-69; process engr. Union Carbide Corp., Simpsonville, S.C., 1969-72; process engr. Cryovac div. W. R. Grace & Co., Simpsonville, 1972-73, process engring. group leader, 1974-75, quality assurance and environ. affairs mgr., 1976—; adv. Sch. System, 1975-78. Mem. Greenville County Crime Commn.; bd. dirs. Greenville Housing Found. Served with U.S. Army, 1958-60. Recipient Ednl. Service award Inter-Community Fine Arts of N.C., 1974, Social Service award Allen U., 1977, J. N. Armstrong Disting. Service award Southeastern region Phi Beta Sigma, 1978, also Outstanding Community Service award 1979; NSF grantee, 1963, 64-65, 66, 68. Mem. Am. Chem. Soc., Am. Mgmt. Assn., Phi Beta Sigma Frat. (Man of Year 1974). Office: Cryovac Div PO Box 338 Simpsonville SC 29381

FLOYD, JOHN ALEX, JR., horticulturist; b. Selma, Ala., Feb. 21, 1948; s. John Alex and Louise (Johnson) F.; B.S. in Ornamental Horticulture, Auburn U., 1970; M.S. in Horticulture, Clemson U., 1972, Ph.D. in Plant Physiology-Horticulture, 1975. Agrl. sci. asst. Clemson (S.C.) U., 1973-75; head agrl. tech. program Jefferson State Jr. Coll., Birmingham, Ala., 1975-77; sr. horticulturist So. Living mag. Birmingham, 1977—, coordinator So. Country Living sect. Progressive Farmer mag., 1978—; mem. agrl. adv. com. Jefferson State Jr. Coll., Birmingham; bd. dirs. Birmingham Bot. Gardens. Recipient C.A.U.S.E. award NSF, 1977. Mem. Am. Horticulture Soc., Am. Soc. for Hort. Sci., Ala. Nurseryment Assn., Garden Writers Am., Gamma Sigma Delta, Pi Alpha Xi. Presbyterian. Co-author: Southern Living Gardening—Trees and Shrubs. Home: 8604 4th Ave S Birmingham AL 35206 Office: So Living Mag 820 Shades Creek Pkwy Birmingham AL 35201

FLOYD, JOHN B., JR., surgeon; b. Louisville, Sept. 18, 1917; s. John B. and Barbara Lois (Lanahan) F.; A.B., U. Ky., 1938; M.D., U. Louisville, 1941; M.S., Tulane U., 1949; children—Lynne Egge, John B., III, Lucy Floyd Rosson, Lanahan Max, William C.L. m. 2d, Margaret Feeback; 1 stepson, Michael Feeback. Intern, St. Elizabeth Hosp., Covington, Ky.; jr. asst. resident in medicine City Hosp., Louisville, 1942-43; resident in surgery Lexington (Ky.) Clinic and Ochsner Found., 1943-49; individual practice medicine specializing in surgery Lexington, Ky., 1949—. Served as maj. with USAF, 1955. Recipient Distinguished Service award, Ky. div. Am. Cancer Soc., 1950, Distinguished Service award, Am. Cancer Soc., 1967; pres. sr. class U. of Louisville Sch. Medicine, 1940-41; diplomate Am. Bd. Surgery. Fellow A.C.S.; mem. Southeastern Surg. Congress, Lexington Surg. Soc., Ky. Surg. Soc., Fayette County Med. Soc., AMA, Ky. Med. Assn., Ky. Hist. Soc., So. Med. Assn. Democrat. Episcopalian. Clubs: Kiwanis, Filson. Contbr. articles to profl. jours. Home: 1890 Parkers Mill Rd Lexington KY 40504 Office: 119 E Maxwell St Lexington KY 40508

FLOYD, MARY EMMA STEADMAN, counselor; b. Blythville, Ark.; d. John Ralph and Hazel (Adcock) Steadman; B.A. cum laude, Lambuth Coll., Jackson, Tenn., 1950; M.Ed., Memphis State U., 1970; m. Bryant Floyd, June 29, 1952; children—Mark Hazen, Melissa. Tchr., Dell (Ark.) Sch., 1950-51, Memphis City Schs., 1951-56; counselor Jackson (Tenn.) City Schs., 1969—. Bd. dirs. United Way, Jackson, 1978—, Jackson Arts Council, 1979—. Mem. Am. Personnel and Guidance Assn., Tenn. Personnel and Guidance Assn., Am. Sch. Counselors Assn., Tenn. Sch. Counselors Assn. (pres. 1979-80), NEA, Tenn. Edn. Assn., Jackson Edn. Assn. Methodist. Home: 29 Laurie Circle Jackson TN 38301 Office: 1341 Parkway Blvd Jackson TN 38301

FLOYD, RICHARD E., JR., ins. co. exec.; b. Texarkana, Tex., Aug. 10, 1943; s. Richard E. and Mable A. (Reeves) F.; student Texarkana Coll., 1963; B.S., Stephen F. Austin U., 1966; m. Jeannette Aquino, Dec. 20, 1968; children—John Rodney, Jimena Ruth. Coach football, Rayne, La., 1967, Queen City, Tex., 1968-69, Vivian, La., 1969-70, Karnack, Tex., 1971; ins. agt. Southwestern Life Ins. Co., Texarkana, Tex., 1971-78; dist. agt. Northwestern Mut. Life Ins., Texarkana, 1978—. Mem. Nat. Write Your Congressman, 1979—. Mem. Texarkana Life Underwriters Assn. (pres. 1979-80), Texarkana C. of C., Nat. Assn. Life Underwriters, Delta Sigma Phi. Episcopalian. Clubs: Masons (32 deg.), Million Dollar Round Table, Southwestern Life's Pres.'s Honor, Northwestern Mutuals Leaders. Home: Myrtle Springs Rd Texarkana TX 75501 Office: 515 State Line Plaza Texarkana TX 75501

FLOYD, ROBERT CECIL, import co. exec.; b. Houston, Feb. 24, 1931; s. Cecil McLauren and Olive Blanche (Wise) F.; grad. Old Vic, London, 1951; B.A., Tex. Christian U., 1954. Founder, pres., owner Fitz & Floyds Inc. fine china imports, Dallas, 1960—. Served with U.S. Army, 1954-57. Recipient Importer of Year award World Trade Center and Dallas C. of C., 1976. Office: 1371 Round Table Dr Dallas TX 75247 also 1020/2040 Dallas Trade Mart Dallas TX 75207

FLOYD, RUSSELL FREEMAN, counselor; b. Phila., May 6, 1951; s. Dave and Laura Mae (Roberts) F.; B.A., LeMoyne-Owen Coll., 1972; M.Ed., Antioch U., 1976; postgrad. E. Tex. State U., 1978—; m. Sharon Boyd, May 20, 1978. Tchr., Phila. Bd. Edn., 1972-76; tchr., coach Germantown Steven Acad., Phila., 1974-75; dir. admissions Jarvis Christian Coll., Hawkins, Tex., 1976-78; counselor U. Tex., Arlington, 1978—. Bd. dirs. East Falls Human Relations Com., 1972-73. Mem. Am. Personnel and Guidance Assn., Tex. Personnel and Guidance Assn., Nat. Council on Family Relationships, Am. Assn. Marriage and Family Counselors, Soc. for Spl. and Ethnic Studies. Democrat. Home: 900 Londonderry Ln Denton TX 76201 Office: U Tex at Arlington Davis Hall Arlington TX 76019

FLUELLEN, ALEXANDER HAMILTON, educator; b. Macon, Ga., Feb. 8, 1947; s. Alexander and Mamie Louise (Stanley) F.; B.S. (Ga. Bd. Regents scholar 1964-68), Ft. Valley State Coll., 1968; M.A. (So. fellow 1968-69), Northwestern U., 1969; Ph.D. (NDEA fellow 1971-75), Ind. U., 1975; m. Brenda Johnson, June 27, 1971; 1 dau., Alexis Belle. Asst. prof. math. Hampton (Va.) Inst., 1969-71; asso. instr. Ind. U., Bloomington, 1971-75; asso. prof. math. Clark Coll., Atlanta, 1975—. Mem. adv. bd. Nat. Creatadrama Soc., 1975—; mem. steering com., vis. scholars program Talladega Coll., 1977—. Mem. Nat. Council Tchrs. Math., Nat. Assn. Mathematicians, Soc. Indsl. and Applied Mathematicians, Math. Assn. Am., Inst. Atmospheric Studies and Remote Sensing (asso.). Methodist. Home and office: Box 320 Clark College Atlanta GA 30314

FLUME, VIOLET PAULINE BRUCE SIGOLOFF, artist; b. Huntington, W.Va.; d. Rufus Otho and Rachel (Witt) Bruce; student Huntington Coll., Trinity U., 1964-65; studied with portrait artist David Philip Wilson, 1963-64; m. Samuel Sigoloff, Oct. 20, 1945 (dec.); children—Bruce Myron, Nelson Witt; m. 2d, Lawrence J. Flume, Feb. 1, 1979. Owner, Wonderland Gallery, 1966—, Sigoloff Fine Art Gallery, San Antonio, 1972—; one-woman shows: St. Mary's U., 1966, Southwestern Fine Arts Inst., U. Tex., 1967, HemisFair, 1968, Trinity U., 1968; group shows include: River Art, 1964-68, San Antonio Art League, 1964-70; represented in pvt. collections. Chmn. edn. for family living PTA, 1962, v.p., 1964-65; art judge Hallmark Contest, 1969. Recipient 1st Pl. award in miniatures Composers, Authors and Artists Am. Nat. Exhibit, N.Y.C., 1965; named San Antonio's Outstanding Woman in Art, San Antonio Express and San Antonio Evening News, 1967. Mem. Tex. Fine Art Assn., San Antonio Art League, San Antonio River Art Group. Clubs: Acacia (pres. 1961, 64), Zonta (San Antonio). Home: 8410 Tiffany Dr San Antonio TX 78230 Office: Sigoloff Gallery 7700 Broadway San Antonio TX 78209 also Sigoloff Gallery St Anthony Hotel San Antonio TX 78205

FLY, EMERSON HAROLD, univ. adminstr.; b. Milan, Tenn., Feb. 5, 1935; s. Emerson N. and Laura Frances (Johnson) F.; student U. Tenn., Martin, 1952-54; B.S., U. Tenn., Knoxville, 1961; m. Catherine Key Wright, June 4, 1956; children—William Randolph, Brian Emerson, Laura Catherine, Karen Wright. Jr. acct. Price Waterhouse, 1960-61; asst. auditor U. Tenn., Knoxville, 1961-66, auditor, 1966-73, vice chancellor, 1973-75, asso. v.p. bus. and fin., 1975, v.p. bus. and fin., 1975—; instr. acctg. Univ. Evening Sch. Pres., Knoxville Jr. Achievement, 1979-80. Served with USNR, 1954-59. Named Govt. Employee of Year, E. Tenn. Assn. Govt. Accts., 1978-79. Mem. Inst. Internal Auditors (past pres. E. Tenn. chpt.), Tenn. Soc. C.P.A.'s, Beta Alpha Psi. Mem. Christian Ch. Club: Fox Den Country. Contbr. articles on auditing and cost control to periodicals. Home: 12289 N Fox Den Dr Knoxville TN 37920 Office: 709 Andy Holt Tower University of Tennessee Knoxville TN 37916

FLYNN, DAVID SHELDON, physicist; b. Orlando, Fla., June 2, 1942; s. Aubrey Sheldon and Juanita Opal (Tillis) F.; B.S., U. Fla., 1970; Ph.D., Duke U., 1976; m. Marilee Joanne Dunlap, Nov. 14, 1964; children—Lohra, Shauna, David, Tanya, Daniel, Marilee. Research asso. dept. physics and astronomy U. Ky., Lexington, 1976-79, vis. asst. prof., 1979-80, asst. prof., 1980—. Served with USAF, 1963-66. Mem. Am. Phys. Soc., Ky. Acad. Sci., Sigma Xi. Mormon. Office: Dept Physics and Astronomy U Ky Lexington KY 40506

FLYNN, LESLIE THOMAS, electronics engr.; b. Bklyn., May 31, 1935; s. Frank Thomas and Winifred May (McKenna) F.; B.S. (scholar), Lafayette Coll., 1955; B.A., U. Richmond, 1961; M.S., Poly. Inst. Bklyn., 1967; postgrad. Grumman Data Systems Inst., 1971; m. Shirley Marie Satterfield, Aug. 22, 1959; children—Kevin T., Colin M., Darren M. Computer system engr., mgr. telemetry configuration lunar module (Apollo Program), Grumman Aerospace Corp., Bethpage, N.Y., 1964-67, ground system mgr. OAO program Goddard Space Flight Center, Greenbelt, Md., 1967-73; ground system mgr. communications tech. satellite program SED Systems Ltd., Communications Research Center, Ottawa, Ont., Can., 1973-77; asst. mgr. system integration Systems div. Harris Corp., Melbourne, Fla., 1977—. Mem. Greenbelt (Md.) City Council, 1968; chmn. fund raising com., Holy Trinity Episcopal Ch., Bowie, Md., 1972; coach children's baseball and soccer, Bowie, 1971-73; mem. N. Gower (Ont.), Planning Bd., 1975-77; soccer coach Satellite Beach (Fla.) Little League Assn., 1977-79. Served to lt. U.S. Army, 1961-64. Decorated Army Commendation medal; Ford Found. scholar, 1951; recipient NASA Commendations, 1968, 71. Mem. Am. Mgmt. Assn., AIAA, Phi Gamma Delta. Democrat. Episcopalian. Contbr. articles in field to profl. jours. Home: 415 Maria Dr Satellite Beach FL 32937 Office: PO Box 37 Melbourne FL 32901

FLYNN, PAUL BARTHOLOMEW, newspaper co. exec.; b. Quincy, Mass., Sept. 17, 1935; s. Bartholomew Joseph and Katherine Marie (Coleman) F.; A.B., Stonehill Coll., 1957; m. Aline Therese Nicholson, Feb. 11, 1961; children—Bonnie Marie, Laureen P., Elizabeth A., Bernadette J. Sports writer The Patriot Ledger, Quincy, Mass., 1955-63, community relations dir., 1963-65; dir. public relations Mass. Tchrs. Assn., Boston, 1965-66; asst. dir. public service Democrat & Chronicle and The Times-Union, Rochester, N.Y., 1966-71, dir. public service and research, 1971-72; dir. advt. Huntington (W.Va.) Herald-Dispatch and Advertiser, 1972-74; dir. advt. Binghamton (N.Y.) Press & Sun-Bulletin, 1974-76; v.p. Gannett Newspaper Advt. Sales, N.Y.C., 1976—; dir. mktg. service Gannett Co., Rochester, N.Y., 1976-77; gen. mgr. The Journal-News, Nyack, N.Y., 1977; pres., pub. Ft. Myers (Fla.) News-Press, 1977—; dir. First Nat. Bank of Ft. Myers. Pres. Lend-A Hand Fund of SW Fla.; mem. exec. com. SW council Boy Scouts Am., Ft. Meyers; dir. Lee County (Fla.) United Way, 1978—. Served with U.S. Army, 1957-58. Recipient Disting. Service award B'nai B'rith, Cape Coral, Fla., 1979. Mem. Fla. C. of C. (dir. 1978—), Am. Newspaper Pubs. Assn., So. Newspaper Pubs. Assn., Fla. Press Assn., Met. Ft. Myers C. of C., Cape Coral C. of C., Stonehill Coll. Alumni Assn. Roman Catholic. Clubs: Royal Palm Yacht, Rangoon, Burnt Store Golf and Racquet. Editor: (with Vince Spezzano) Promoting The Total Newspaper, 1977. Office: PO Box 10 Fort Myers FL 33902

FLYNT, JOHN JAMES, JR., lawyer, former congressman; b. Griffin, Ga., Nov. 8, 1914; s. John James and Susan Winn (Banks) F.; student Ga. Mil. Acad.; A.B., U. Ga., 1936; postgrad. Emory U., 1937-38; J.D., George Washington U., 1940; grad. Command and Gen. Staff Sch., Air Corps Advanced Flying Sch., Brooks Field, Tex.; m. Patricia Irby Bradley; children—Susan Banks, John James III, Crisp Bradley. Admitted to Ga. bar, 1938; asst. U.S. atty. No. Dist. Ga., 1939-41, 45-46; mem. Ga. Ho. of Reps., 1947-48; solicitor gen. Griffin Jud. Circuit, 1949-54; mem. 83d-95th congresses from 6th Ga. Dist.; partner firm Smalley, Cogburn & Flynt, Griffin. Bd. visitors U.S. Air Force Acad., Colo.; trustee LaGrange (Ga.) Coll. Served with AUS, 1936-37, 41-45, col. Res. Decorated Bronze Star medal. Mem. Ga. (pres.), Am. (com. jud. selection, tenure, compensation) bar assns., Am. Legion, V.F.W., Phi Delta Phi, Sigma Alpha Epsilon. Democrat. Methodist (chmn. bd. stewards). Mason (Shriner). Home: Griffin GA 30224 Office: 115 N 6th St Griffin GA 30224

FOCHT, JOHN CHARLES, real estate and fin. corp. exec.; b. Lebanon, Pa., Oct. 13, 1945; s. William W. and Ethel L. F.; student Columbia Union Coll. 1968, Stetson U. Coll. Law, 1970-73; m. Lynn Templeton, Sept. 15, 1979. Pres. South Fla. Title and Guaranty Co., W. Palm Beach, 1975—, Fla. Mgmt. Enterprises, Inc., W. Palm Beach, 1974—, Mut. Funding Corp., W. Palm Beach, 1978—; real estate cons. Active Forum Club of the Palm Beaches, Better Bus. Bur. Palm Beach County. Served with USN, 1965. Lic. mortgage broker, life and health ins. agt. Mem. Title Ins. Assn. Palm Beach County, Mortgage Bankers Assn., Asso. Builders and Contractors (Gold Coast chpt.). Democrat. Club: Kiwanis (pres. Sunrise club, West Palm Beach, 1977-78). Home: 20 Country Club Rd West Palm Beach FL 33406 Office: 2831 Exchange Ct West Palm Beach FL 33409

FOCKE, JOHN HERMAN, III, physician; b. Mexia, Tex., Dec. 27, 1946; s. John Herman, Jr., and Lola Margret F.; B.S. in Chemistry, Tex. A&M U., 1969, M.S. in Biochemistry, 1971; M.D., U. Tex., Houston, 1975; m. Margaret Connell, Sept. 8, 1973; children—John Barnett, Scott Wallace. Rotating intern John Peter Smith Hosp., Ft. Worth, 1975-76, resident in family practice, 1975-78; practice medicine specializing in family practice, Mexia, Tex., 1978—; med. staff Mexia Meml. Hosp., chmn. infection control com., med. dir. respiratory therapy dept.; med. technologist, grantee Buie Hosp., Hillsboro, Tex., 1972; assembler, insp. Varo Inc., Mexia, 1970. Mem. bd. health council Mexia Ind. Sch. Dist.; bd. dirs. Bistone Vocat. Nursing Sch.; active First Presbyn. Ch. Diplomate Am. Bd. Family Practice. Fellow Am. Acad. Family Physicians; mem. AMA, Tex. Med. Assn., Am. Chem. Soc., Am. Med. Technologists, A.C.P., Flying Physicians Assn., Mexia C. of C. (dir. 1978—). Clubs: Rotary (chmn. trade and profl. relations com.), Mexia Country, Freestone Country. Home: 1003 Clark St Mexia TX 76667 Office: 515 S Canton St Mexia TX 76667

FOCKLER, JOHN KEEDY, found. exec.; b. Hagerstown, Md., Jan. 6, 1926; s. Samuel Mitchell and Mary Stitt (Keedy) F.; B.S. in Mgmt. Engring., Carnegie Mellon U., 1949; postgrad. U. Pitts., 1949-50, U.

Oslo, 1950, U. Del., 1955-56; M.B.A., Case Western Res. U., 1961; m. Barbara Ann Rossland, Apr. 24, 1954; children—John Keedy, Robert Mitchell, Anne Chandlee, Ellen Rossland. Asst. indsl. prodn. editor Bus. Week mag., N.Y.C., 1952-53, research editor, 1953-54, asst. bur. mgr., Pitts., 1956-57, bur. mgr., Cleve., 1957-62; v.p. Cleve. Devel. Found., 1963-68, exec. v.p., 1968-69; regional dir. Nat. Corp. Housing Partnerships, Washington, 1969-70; prin. John K. Fockler & Assos., housing cons., Cleve., 1970-74; exec. dir. Memphis-Plough Community Found., 1974—; tchr. bus. Ohio State U., 1963-64; tchr. econs. Cuyahoga Community Coll., 1964-67, Cleve. State U., 1967-69; tchr. bus. communications Baldwin-Wallace Coll., 1972-74. Treas., Mid-South Med. Center Council, 1976-78; v.p. Germantown (Tenn.) Arts Assn., 1976-78; pres. Memphis Conf. United Methodist Found., 1975—; mem. city council, Bay Village, Ohio, 1960-61, 64; mem. budget, accounting and fin. adv. com. City of Germantown, 1976-78; chmn. council on ministries Germantown United Meth. Ch., 1976-78; bd. dirs. Mid-South Regional Blood Center, 1978—, Lausanne Sch., 1978—. Served with U.S. Army, 1954-56. Republican. Clubs: Economic (Memphis); Summit, Delta. Home: 7101 Corsica Dr Germantown TN 38138 Office: Suite 1521 1st Tenn Bank Bldg Memphis TN 38103

FODOR, GEORGE EMERIC, chemist; b. Makó, Hungary, Feb. 13, 1932; came to U.S., 1956, naturalized, 1962; s. Imre and Ilona (Messinger) F.; dipl. chemist U. Scis., Szeged, Hungary, 1955; Ph.D. (Univ. fellow 1960-62, Robert A. Welch Found. fellow 1962-65), Rice U., 1965; m. Marjory Ann Byrne, Feb. 13, 1965; children—Cara Anne, John Emeric. With Hungarian Oil and Natural Gas Research Inst., Veszprem, Hungary, 1956, Pontiac Refining Corp., Corpus Christi, Tex., 1957-60; asst. Rice U., 1960-62; with photo products dept. E. I. duPont de Nemours & Co., Inc., Parlin, N.J., 1965-66; sr. research chemist S.W. Research Inst. San Antonio, 1966-78, sr. research scientist, 1978—. Mem. Am. Chem. Soc., Sigma Xi. Office: PO Drawer 28510 San Antonio TX 78284

FOERCH, JOSEPH HENRY, JR., social scientist; b. Milford, Conn., Nov. 6, 1916; s. Joseph Henry and Mary Jane (Hubbell) F.; grad. Refrigeration and Air Conditioning Inst., Chgo., 1939; student Texarkana Jr. Coll., 1947-49, U. Md., 1952-56, Consol. U. N.C., 1957-60, B.A., N.C. State U., Raleigh, 1967, M.Ed., 1974; postgrad. Nova U., 1978; m. Althea Elizabeth Hoadley, Aug. 31, 1941; 1 dau., Bonnie Elizabeth Foerch Timperley. Enlisted in U.S. Army, 1942, advanced through grades to lt. col., 1957; ret., 1961; chmn. dept. electronics Fayetteville (N.C.) Tech. Inst., 1961-73, chmn. dept. social sci., 1979—. Decorated Legion Merit (U.S.); Legion Merit (Korea). Mem. Am. Vocat. Assn., N.C. Vocat. Assn., NEA, N.C. Assn. Edn., Am. Assn. Sex Educators, Counselors and Therapists, N.C. Sociol. Assn., Am. Assn. Ret. Persons, Ret. Officers Assn., Res. Officers Assn., N.C. Assn Ret. Mil., Smithsonian Assos., N.C. State U. Alumni Assn. Democrat. Club: Shriners. Office: Dept Social Sci Fayetteville Tech Inst Fayetteville NC 28303

FOERSTER, DAVID WILLIAM, surgeon; b. Oklahoma City, Oct. 6, 1933; s. Hervey Adolph and Hazel Ann (Lower) F.; B.A., Yale U., 1954; M.D., U. Okla., 1958; m. Barbara Jane Davis, Dec. 26, 1968; 1 dau., Lara Jane; children by previous marriage—Scott Hervey, Steven Price, Stanton William. Intern, Univ. Hosp., Oklahoma City, 1958-59, resident in surgery 1959-62; resident in plastic surgery Barnes Hosp., St. Louis, 1963-64, St. Joseph Hosp., Houston, 1964-65; practice medicine specializing in plastic and cosmetic surgery, Oklahoma City, 1965—. Served with M.C., USAR, 1961-66. Diplomate Am. Bd. Plastic Surgery. Fellow A.C.S.; mem. Am. Soc. Plastic and Reconstructive Surgeons, Am. Soc. Aesthetic Plastic Surgery, Internat. Soc. Aesthetic Plastic Surgeons, Internat. Soc. Clin. Plastic Surgeons, AMA, Okla. Med. Assn., Oklahoma County Med. Soc. Patentee Surgitek surg. mammary support; contbr. articles to profl. jours.; research on gender dysphoria surgery. Home: 1600 Coventry Park Oklahoma City OK 73120 Office: 3131 NW Expy Oklahoma City OK 73112

FOGELMAN, AVRON B., real estate developer; b. Memphis, Mar. 1, 1940; s. Morris and Mollye Fogelman; B.A., Tulane U., 1962; m. Wendy Fogelman, Dec. 24, 1961; children—Hal, Richard, Mark. Pres., Fogelman Properties, Memphis, 1965—; dir. Guardsmark, Inc.; pres. Fogelman-Thomas Broadcasting Co.; chmn. bd. Wendy's of New Orleans. Mem., chmn. Memphis Planning Commn.; v.p. Memphis Jewish Community Center, 1974; pres. Memphis Profl. Basketball, Inc., 1973—, Memphis State Rebounders; owner Memphis Chicks Baseball Team; majority owner Memphis Rogues Soccer Club; bd. dirs. Future Memphis 1980, NCCJ; mem. Gov.'s Exec. Residence Preservation Found.; Recipient Disting. Service award Memphis State U., 1974; named to Best Ten of a Decade roster Memphis Comml. Appeal. Entrepreneurial fellow Memphis State U., 1980. Mem. Memphis Apt. Assn. (pres.), Home Builders Assn., Memphis C. of C. (bd. dirs.). Home: 5491 Shady Grove Memphis TN 38117 Office: 1000 Brookfield Rd Memphis TN 38138

FOGELMAN, MORRIS JOSEPH, physician; b. Chgo., Feb. 27, 1923; s. Joseph and Tillie (Schwartz) F.; B.A., U. Ill., 1941, M.D., 1944, M.S., 1948; children—Evan, Joe, Margo. Intern Wayne County Gen. Hosp., Eloise, Mich., 1944-45; resident Parkland Hosp., Dallas, 1948-51; research fellow dept. clin. sci. U. Ill. Coll. Medicine, Chgo., 1947-48, asst. physiology, 1947-48; asst. in physiology and pharmacology Southwestern Med. Sch., Dallas, 1948-50, fellow in surgery, 1948-52, instr. surgery, 1952-53, asst. prof. surgery, asst. prof. surgery, 1952-53, asso. prof. surgery, 1953, prof. surgery, 1954-57, clin. prof. surgery, 1957—; practice medicine specializing in surgery, Dallas, 1952—; sr. attending surgeon Parkland Meml. Hosp., Dallas, 1953; cons. physician in surgery VA Hosp., Dallas, 1954; attending surgeon Baylor Hosp., 1957, Parkland Meml. Hosp., 1952, Presbyn. Hosp., Dallas; pres. med. staff Presbyn. Hosp., Dallas, 1973, Morris J. Fogelman, MD & Assos., Dallas, 1972—; dir. surgery Baylor Med. Center, 1972—. Served to capt. M.C., AUS, 1945-47. Diplomate Am. Bd. Surgery. Fellow Am. Assn. for Surgery of Trauma; mem. Am. Assn. for History of Medicine, A.C.S., AAAS, AMA, Dallas County Med. Soc., Dallas Soc. Gen. Surgeons, Dallas So. Clin. Soc., N.Y. Acad. Sci., Tex. Med. Assn., Tex. Traumatic Surg. Soc., Sigma Xi. Author: Fluid Balance. Contbr. articles to various publs. Home: 6921 Norway Pl Dallas TX 75231 Office: 8210 Walnut Hill Ln Suite 513 Dallas TX 75231

FOGLEMAN, JOHN ALBERT, chief justice Ark. Supreme Ct.; b. Memphis, Nov. 5, 1911; s. John Franklin and Julia (McAdams) F.; student U. Ark., 1927-31; LL.B., U. Memphis (now Memphis State U.), 1934; m. Annis Adell Appleby, Oct. 24, 1933; children—John Albert, Annis Adell (Mrs. Henry M. Rector), Mary Barton (Mrs. Charles L. Williams Jr.). Admitted to Ark. bar, 1934; dep. circuit clk., Crittenden County, Ark., 1933-34; individual practice law, 1934-44; partner firm Hale & Fogleman, Marion and West Memphis, Ark., 1944-66; dep. pros. atty. Crittenden County, 1946-57; asso. justice Ark. Supreme Ct., 1967-80, chief justice, 1980—. Chmn., Ark. Jud. Commn., 1963-65; mem. Ark. Constl. Revision Study Com., 1967, Ark. Criminal Code Revision Com., 1971-75. Active Ark. and Crittenden County Democratic Central Com., until 1945. Served to 1st lt. AUS, 1944-45. Fellow Am. Coll. Trial Lawyers; mem. Ark. (past pres.), N.E. Ark., Crittenden County bar assns. Mason, Rotarian. Home: Cherry St Marion AR 72364 Office: Justice Bldg-State Capitol Little Rock AR 72201

FOISY, RICHARD EDWARD, auditor; b. Framingham, Mass., Nov. 2, 1953; s. Robert William and Rosalie Ann F.; B.B.A., U. Ga., 1974; m. Phyllis Ann Butler, Dec. 9, 1973. Acct., Texaco, Atlanta, 1975-77; auditor State of Ga., Atlanta, 1977-78, Insp. Gen. Office, Dept. Treasury, Atlanta, 1978—. Mem. Beta Alpha Psi (scholarship award), Phi Eta Sigma (award). Home: 1021 Grayson Hwy Lawrenceville GA 30245 Office: 221 Courtland Civic Bldg 4th Floor Atlanta GA 30331

FOLEY, CHARLES PATRICK, historian; b. Woodland, Calif., Apr. 5, 1933; s. Leo Vincent and Clarice F.; B.A., Calif. State U., Chico, 1959; M.A., U. Santa Clara, 1969; postgrad. U. N.Mex. 1972—; m. Linda Anne Sandoval, June 19, 1965; children—Elizabeth Maureen, Sean Patrick. Lectr. history Coll. Notre Dame, Belmont, Calif., 1965-67; instr. history Chaminade U., Honolulu, 1968-69; lectr. U. San Francisco, 1970; asst. prof. history, a dir. humanities Coll. of Santa Fe, 1971-75; asso. prof. history, chmn. social sci. dept. Tarrant County Jr. Coll., Ft. Worth, 1975—; cons. Inst. of Latin Am. Studies project U. Tex.; history cons. for ministerial program Cath. Diocese of Ft. Worth. Served with USN, 1951-55. Shell grantee, 1974. Mem. Am. Hist. Assn., Am. Cath. Hist. Assn., S.W. Social Scis. Assn., Tex. Cath. Hist. Assn., Tex. Assn. Chicanos in Higher Edn., Western Social Sci. Assn., Phi Theta Kappa, Phi Alpha Theta. Democrat. Roman Catholic. Home: 1113 Idlewood Ave Azle TX 76020 Office: Tarrant County Jr Coll NW Campus 4801 Marine Creek Pkwy Fort Worth TX 76106

FOLEY, LESTER WILLIAM, cons.; b. Mpls., Aug. 15, 1903; s. J. S. and Marie (Scanlon) F.; student Ga. Inst. Tech., 1920; A.B., U. Notre Dame, 1924; m. Edith Klug, Apr. 20, 1926; children—Jerry S., Patricia Foley Stedeford. Pres., Foley Lumber Industries, Jacksonville, Fla., 1950-76, dir.; v.p. Morales & Shumer, Jacksonville; interim ambassador to Costa Rica and Dominican Republic. Adv. bd. U. Notre Dame, St. Vincents Hosp.; adv. council Dept. Navy. Recipient award Sec. Navy; named hon. Ky. col., adm. Ga. Navy. Mem. Soc. Am. Mil. Engrs., Am. Forestry Assn., Am. Security Council, Nat. Football Found., Jacksonville C. of C., Navy League U.S., Tenn. Squires; hon. mem. N.C. Navy, Tenn. Navy, Panama Navy, Order Lafayette. Roman Catholic. Clubs: Fla. Yacht, Seminole, Timuquana, Ponte Vedra, River, Univ. (dir.). Home: 3625 Richmond St Jacksonville FL 32205 Office: 7825 Bay Meadows Way Jacksonville FL 32216

FOLEY, MARY ALICE DODD (MRS. LAWSON EDGAR FOLEY), piano tchr., civic worker; b. Roanoke, Va., Dec. 24, 1912; d. Cubert Bosworth and Fannie (Hale) Dodd; student St. Louis Inst. Music, 1932, 37, U. Va., 1939-53, Hollins Coll., 1953-55, U. Richmond, 1960-62, U. N.C., summers 1965-67; m. Lawson Edgar Foley, Apr. 12, 1933. Tchr. piano, 1933—. Mem. Roanoke (parliamentarian 1969-71, 75-79), Va. (state parliamentarian 1969-71, 1st v.p., 1968-70, chmn. bd. certification 1971-77, historian 1977-79), Nat. (chmn. certification So. div. 1977-80) music tchrs. assns. Nat. Guild Piano Tchrs., Hall of Fame, Music Tchrs. Nat. Assn., Inc. (del. People-to-People travel program), Daus. of Confederacy (pres. 1966-68), Magna Charta Dames, Soc. Descendants Knights of Most Noble Order Garter, Nat., Va. (councilor 1971-74) socs. daus. colonial wars, Huguenot Soc. Va. (rec. sec. 1971-73), Roanoke Hist. Soc., Colonial Dames XVII Century (chpt. pres. 1971-73, chmn. heraldry and coats of arms 1973-75, chmn. nat. def. 1977-79), Blue Ridge Forum (v.p. 1961-62), D.A.R. (chpt. regent 1968-71, dir. Dist. VII Va. 1971-74, chmn. friends of mus. 1974-77), Soc. Daus. Colonial Wars, Huguenot Soc. Va. (rec. sec. 1971-73, Councilor 1973-75), Wythe County, New River (charter mem. drama com.) hist. socs., Nat. Geneal. Soc., SW Va. Geneal. Soc., Alpha Pi Mu (past pres.). Methodist. Home: 6576 Laban Rd Roanoke VA 24019

FOLEY, THOMAS CARL, elec. engr.; b. Chgo., Sept. 26, 1948; s. Newman Clarence and Barbara Idelle (Thompson) F.; student Wis. State U., 1966, 69, Northland Coll., Asheland, Wis., 1968; B.S. in E.E., U. Nebr., 1972; postgrad. Fla. State U., 1975-76, U. N.C., Charlotte, 1977—; m. Pamela Louise Lewis, June 17, 1972; 1 son, Bradley L. Computer operator supr. U. Nebr. Computing Facility, 1969-73; elec. engr. Central Telephone and Utilities Corp., Lincoln, Nebr., 1973-74, Tallahassee, Fla., 1974-76, Hickory, N.C., 1976-78, mgr. ops. planning, 1978—; tchr. Catawba Valley Tech. Inst. Served with USAF, 1971-72. Mem. IEEE, Am. Mgmt. Assn., Nat. Rifle Assn. Republican. Presbyterian. Home: Route 9 Box 66 Hickory NC 28601 Office: Box 2308 Hickory NC 28601

FOLEY, THOMAS FRANCIS, pub. co. exec.; b. Towanda, Pa., Aug. 26, 1940; s. Eugene T. and Mary (Murray) F.; B.S., Bloomsburg State Coll., 1962; grad. mgmt. program U. Ga., 1975; m. Jeanne Barry, June 23, 1962; children—Linda, Thomas, Maureen, Terry. Bus. tchr. Tupper Lake (N.Y.) High Sch., 1962-65; mktg. rep. Gregg div. McGraw-Hill Book Co., Hightstown, N.J., 1965-71, dist. mgr., Dallas, 1971-73, regional mgr., Norcross, Ga., 1973-79, nat. sales mgr., N.Y.C., 1979-80, dir. mktg., 1980—. Democratic committeeman, Tupper Lake, 1963-65. Mem. Nat. Bus. Edn. Assn., So. Bus. Edn. Assn., Soc. Advancement Mgmt. Roman Catholic. Home: 3802 Fox Hills Dr Marietta GA 30067 Office: Gregg Div McGraw-Hill Book Co Box 1221 Ave of the Americas New York NY 10020

FOLK, AGNES BAGNAL, dietitian; b. Sumter County, S.C., Sept. 20, 1938; d. Robert Lee and Nina Louise (Thames) Bagnal; B.S., Winthrop Coll., 1960; m. Tommy M. Folk, Jr., July 3, 1960; children—Tommy M. III, Sallie Brown, Robert Walton. In-service intern Columbia Hosp. and Charlotte Meml. Hosp., 1960-64; caseworker-aide to families with dependent children Clarendon County Welfare Dept., Manning, S.C., 1967-69; clin. dietitian McLeod Meml. Hosp., Florence, S.C., 1969-70; dir. dietetics McLeod Regional Med. Center, Florence, 1970—; cons. Kelley Nursing Home, Kingstree, S.C., Bethea Bapt. Home, Darlington, S.C., Darlington (S.C.) Hosp., Palmetto Gen. Hosp., Marion, S.C.; instr. Florence-Darlington Tech. Sch. Mem. Am. Dietetic Assn.. Am. Hosp. Assn., Am. Soc. Food Service Adminstrs., S.C. Dietetic Assn., S.C. Diabetes Assn., Pee Dee Dist. Dietetic Assn., Florence-Darlington Diabetes Assn., Pee Dee Dist. Food Service Suprs. Assn. (adv.). Lutheran. Office: 555 W Cheves St Florence SC 29501

FOLK, EARL DONALD, biostatician; b. Corpus Christi, Tex., Mar. 16, 1939; s. Joe Washington and Louise Helen (Bartos) F. B.S., Okla. State Coll., 1961; M.S., Kan. State U., 1962, U. Wis., 1964; Ph.D., U. Okla., 1970; m. Patti Ann Hansen, Sept. 3, 1960 (dec. Aug. 1969); children—Ann Louise, Nancy Lynne. Research asst. dept. neurology U. Wis., Madison, 1962-66; chief biostatis. staff Civil Aeromed. Inst., FAA, Dept. Transp., Oklahoma City, 1968—. NIH tng. grantee, 1966-67. Mem. AAAS, Am. Statis. Assn., Biometric Soc., Statisticians in Okla. (sec. 1973-77), Pi Mu Epsilon. Home: 2825 NW 117 Oklahoma City OK 73120 Office: PO Box 25082 Oklahoma City OK 73125

FOLK, SHARON LYNN, printing co. exec.; b. Bellefontaine, Ohio, June 13, 1945; d. Emerson Dewey and Berdena Isabelle (Brown) F.; A.B., Belmont Abbey Coll., 1968. Exec. v.p. Nat. Bus. Forms Inc., Greeneville, Tenn., 1968-73, pres., chairperson of bd., 1973—; pres., chairperson of bd. Nat. Forms Co. Inc., Gastonia, N.C., 1973-79. Active YMCA Community Orch.; bd. dirs. Greeneville YMCA, 1977-80, United Way, 1980; mem. presdl. steering com. U.S. Senator Howard Baker, 1979-80. Mem. Internat. Bus. Forms Industry (chairperson indsl. relations com. 1978-80). Nat. Bus. Forms Assn., Tuesday Night Bus. Women's Bowling League, Greeneville Women's Bowling Assn. Home: 1131 Hixon Ave Greeneville TN 37743 Office: Nat Bus Forms Co Inc 100 Pennsylvania Ave Greeneville TN 37743

FOLKS, SOLOMON JOHN, power corp. exec.; b. Levy County, Fla., Feb. 2, 1920; s. Solomon Jonathan and Effie E. (Blitch) F.; A.A., U. Fla., 1942, B.S.A., 1943, M.S.A., 1950; m. Laurda Downing; children—Christine E., John C., Connie D., James J. With Fla. Power Corp., High Springs, 1953—, in consumer services, 1978—; supt. U. Fla. Agrl. Expt. Swine Farm; founding dir. Flas. Agribus. Inst.; mem. exec. com. Fla. Agrl. Hall Fame Com.; chairperson selection com. of new mems. Fla. Agrl. Hall Fame; bd. dirs. Chase Pub. Co., Lexington, 1978; mem. Fla. Adv. Com. to Sun Belt Agrl. Exposition, Moultrie, Ga., 1979-80; mem. state adv. com. Flas. Agribus. and Natural Resources Edn. Program, 1980—; bd. dirs. Nat Fox Hunters Assn., 1980. Recipient 1st Nat. Award Nat. Electric Energy Assn., 1972. Mem. Nat. Vocat. Agr. Tchrs. Assn. (hon.), Fla. Foxhunters Assn. (dir.), Fla. Forestry Assn., Fla. Horse Council, Fla. Horseman's Assn. (pres.), Fla. Duroc Swine Breeders Assn. (1st sec.), Fla. Internat. Agrl. Trade Council (dir.). Clubs: Masons (32 deg.), Shriners, Club: Gainesville Exchange. Author booklet. Home: RFD 2 Box 329 Newberry FL 32669

FOLSOM, ROBERT S., mayor Dallas; b. Dallas, Feb. 15, 1927; B.A., So. Methodist U., 1950. Mayor, City of Dallas, 1976—. Office: City Hall Dallas TX 75201

FONT, JUAN HIGINIO, physician; b. Barranquitas, P.R., Oct. 16, 1895; s. Ubaldino and Julia (Jimenez) F.; M.D., Medico-Chirurgical Coll. Phila., 1916; M.Sc., U. Pa., 1936; m. Celeste Casalduc, Apr. 30, 1921; children—Jaime Higinio, Jose Eduardo. Intern Presbyn. Hosp., San Juan, P.R., 1916-17; resident, Army Med. Sch., Washington and U.S. Gen. Hosp., 1918-20; gen. practice medicine, Cayey, P.R., 1922-32; chief ear, nose and throat clinic Presbyn. Hosp., San Juan, P.R., 1933-60, chief otolaryngology and bronchoesophagology, 1936-60, mem. staff emeritus, 1960—; cons. otolaryngologist San Juan Municipal Hosp., Auxilio Mutuo Hosp., Tchrs. Hosp., 1960—; state surgeon P.R. Nat. Guard, 1945-46. Mem. honor com. 6th Internat. Congress Otolaryngology, 1957. Bd. dirs. Chevalier Jackson Found. Served to capt., M.C., AUS, 1918-22. Recipient award Med. Alumni, Medico-Chirurgical Coll. Phila., 1963. Diplomate Am. Bd. Otolaryngology. Fellow Am. Acad. Ophthalmology and Otolaryngology, Coll. Chest Physicians (emeritus), Am. Laryngological, Rhinological and Otol. Soc., Internat. Coll. Surgeons, A.C.S.; mem. AMA (mem. ho. of dels. 1931), P.R. Med. Assn. (pres. 1936), P.R. Bd. Med. Examiners, Pan Am. Assn. Otorhinolaryngology and Bronchoesophagology, Internat. Bronchoesophagological Soc., Otolaryngological Club P.R. (pres. 1960), Am. Bronchoesophagological Assn., Sociedad Nacional Venezolana de Otorrinolaringologia, Mil. Order World Wars (comdr. P.R. chpt. 1946-47), Am. Legion (mem. exec. nat. com. 1940). Elk. Clubs: Bankers, Casino de P.R., Cornell-Penn. Contbr. articles to profl. jours. Home: 262 Robles St Santurce PR 00907 Office: PO Box 5213 Med Arts Bldg Pta de Tierra Sta PR 00906

FONTAINE, DENIS LOUIS, lawyer; b. Rumford, Maine, June 19, 1940; s. Herman and Marie F.; B.S., Fla. So. Coll., 1962; J.D., Stetson U., 1965; 1 son, Gregory Louis. Admitted to Fla. bar, 1965; asso. firm Troiano & Roberts, Lakeland, Fla., 1965-72, partner, 1966-72; individual practice law, Lakeland, 1972—; atty. Imperial Bank of Lakeland, 1966-72; town atty. Town of Polk City (Fla.), 1966-74; prosecutor City of Lakeland, 1971-72; mcpl. judge City of Lakeland, 1972-74; city atty. City of Mulberry (Fla.), 1972—; pres. Discount Auto Parts, Inc., 1979—. Vice pres. YMCA, 1974-78, bd. dirs., 1978—. Served to capt. U.S. Army, 1965-68; Vietnam. Decorated Army Commendation medal, Bronze Star; recipient Pres.'s award of leadership U.S. Jr. C. of C., 1969, Pres.'s award of achievement, 1969; named Boss of Yr., Am. Bus. Women's Assn., 1975, Polk County Legal Secs., 1976. Mem. Am. Bar Assn., Fla. Bar, Polk County Bar Assn., Polk County Trial Lawyers Assn., Lakeland Bar Assn., Tenth Jud. Circuit Bar Assn., Polk County Builders Assn., Jr. C. of C. (named Outstanding Young Man of Yr. 1972). Democrat. Roman Catholic. Clubs: Kiwanis, Lakeland Yacht, Imperial Polk Sailing. Contbr. articles to sailing publs. Home: 1418 Edgewater Beach Dr Lakeland FL 33801 Office: 2033 E Edgewood Dr PO Drawer 1900 Lakeland FL 33802

FONTENEAUX, JOSEPH EUGENE, athletic dir.; b. Houston, Sept. 8, 1949; s. Albert Gene and Patsy Ruth Fonteneaux; B.S. in Health and Phys. Edn., So. U., Baton Rouge, 1971, M.Ed., 1974; m. Joyce Marie Johnson, Aug. 23, 1969; children—Joseph Eugene, Terence Keith. Baseball coach, instr. phys. edn. LeMoyne-Owen Coll., Memphis, 1971-78; athletic dir., baseball coach, women's basketball coach, instr. health Paul Quinn Coll., Waco, Tex., 1978—. Mem. Am. Assn. Baseball Coaches, Nat. Assn. Intercollegiate Athletics, Nat. Assn. Intercollegiate Athletics Athletic Dirs. Assn., Waco Jaycees. Roman Catholic. Home: 1401 College St Apt 1409C Waco TX 76708 Office: 1020 Elm St Waco TX 76704

FONTENOT, MARTIN MAYANCE, JR., environ. engr., chemist; b. Mamou, La., May 30, 1944; s. Mayance and Hazel (Gradney) F.; B.S. in Chemistry, So. U., Baton Rouge, 1966, M.S. in Chemistry, 1974; postgrad. Joliet (Ill.) Jr. Coll., 1968-69; M.Eng., La. State U., 1978; m. Christel Yvonne Wilson, Aug. 20, 1966; children—Martin Mayance, Brodi Lin, Arloe Phillip. Instr. chemistry So. U., 1966; chemist supr. Uniroyal, Inc., Joliet, Ill., 1966-69; process chemist Monsanto Co., Texas City, Tex., 1969-71; chemist Southwestern Labs., Houston, 1971; sr. analytical/environ. chemist, staff environ. engr. CIBA-GEIGY Corp., St. Gabriel, La., 1971—. Advisor Jr. Achievement, 1970-71. Mem. Am. Chem. Soc., Indsl. Mgmt. Council of Baton Rouge, Instrument Soc. Am., Am. Indsl. Hygiene Assn., Baton Rouge Analytical Instrument Discussion Group, La. Air Pollution Assn., La. Water Pollution Assn. Roman Catholic. Patentee in field. Home: 9024 Staring Ct Baton Rouge LA 70810 Office: PO Box 11 Saint Gabriel LA 70776

FOOSE, DON HOLT, oil co. exec.; b. Beckley, W.Va., Nov. 1, 1942; s. Don Edward and Helen Blanch (Holt) F.; B.A., Marshall U., Huntington, W.Va., 1968, postgrad., 1968-70; m. Peggy Ann Wamock, June 3, 1967; 1 son, Don Edward II. Lab. technician FBI, 1961-62; asst. dir. alumni affairs Marshall U., 1967-69; asst. cost engr. C & O Ry., Huntington, 1969-70, asst. track supr., 1970, track supr., 1970-71, asst. div. engr., 1971-73, asst. dir. labor relations, 1973-74; asst. land agt. Quaker State Oil Refining Corp., Parkersburg, W.Va., 1974-75, dist. land mgr., 1975—. Active softball league. Named Ky. col. Mem. Ohio, W.Va., W.Va. Ind. oil and gas assns., Am. Assn. Petroleum Landmen (pres. Benedum chpt. 1977-79), Parkersburg Jaycees (chmn. pub. relations 1976—). Republican. Clubs: Kiwanis, Elks, Masons (32 deg.), Shriners. Home: 104 Beechwood Pl Parkersburg WV 26101 Office: PO Box 1327 Parkersburg WV 26101

FOOTE, AVON EDWARD, communications scientist; b. Burnsville, Miss., Sept. 24, 1937; s. Avon Rubel and Lila Frances (Broughton) F.; B.S., Florence State U., 1963; M.S., U. So. Miss., 1968; Ph.D., Ohio State U., 1970; m. Dorothy Veronica Gargis, Mar. 15, 1960; children—Anthony E., Kevin A., Michele. Announcer, Sta. WJOI, Florence, Ala., 1958-60; prodn. mgr. WOWL-TV, Florence, 1960-64; advt. coordinator Plough Inc., Memphis, 1964-66; faculty adviser Sta. WMSU, U. So. Miss., Hattiesburg, 1966-67; producer-dir. telecommunications Ohio State U., Columbus, 1967-69; asso. prof. broadcasting U. Miss., Oxford, 1971-72; project dir. Ohio Valley TV System, Columbus, 1972-74; mem. faculty, coordinator grad. studies Sch. Journalism and Mass Communication U. Ga., Athens, 1974—. Awards judge Ohio State awards, 1968-73; chmn. screening com. Peabody Radio-TV Awards, 1976-79; pres. Clarke Boosters, 1977-78. NDEA fellow, 1967, Nat. Acad. TV Arts and Scis. Meml. fellow, 1970. Mem. Nat. Assn. Ednl. Broadcasters, Broadcast Edn. Assn., Nat. Acad. TV Arts and Scis. Republican. Methodist. Clubs: Ushers, Rehearsal. Editor: The Challenges of Educational Communications, 1970; CBS and Congress: "The Selling of the Pentagon" Papers. 1972. Author: (with Koenig and others) Broadcasting and Bargaining, 1970; Chotankers, 1979. Editor Ednl. Broadcasting rev., 1969-73. Researcher pub. broadcasting, TV mgmt., attitudes. Contbr. articles to scholarly publs. Home: 217 Cavalier Rd Athens GA 30606 Office: Journalism Bldg Room 223 Athens GA 30602

FOOTE, KENNETH HARVEY, accountant; b. Boulder, Colo., July 29, 1922; s. Joe Clark and Alma Siegried (Wetterburg) F.; B.S., U. Colo., 1944; M.B.A., Ohio State U., 1949; postgrad. Stanford U., 1950-53; m. Caroline Barnwell Stevens, Dec. 23, 1947; children—John Stevens, Elizabeth Barnwell, Barbara Harvey. Instr., U. Colo., Boulder, 1946-48; grad. asst. Ohio State U., Columbus, 1948-49; asst. prof. U. San Francisco, 1952-54; staff accountant Peat, Marwick, Mitchell & Co., Denver, 1954-56, San Francisco, 1949-52; asst. prof. Citadel, Charleston, S.C., 1956-59; treas. William M. Bird & Co., Charleston, 1959-63; owner Charleston Profl. Bus. Service, 1964-66; asst. prof. Coll. Charleston, 1973-76; adj. prof. biometry Med. U. S.C., Charleston, 1974-77; prof. accounting, Bapt. Coll. Charleston, 1966-73, 76—, coordinator continuing edn., 1976-79; area dir. Person-Wolinsky C.P.A. Review, 1975—; dir. Southeastern C.P.A. Affiliates, 1979—. Chmn., Operation Native Son, 1967-68; trustee Edn. Found., S.C. Assn. C.P.A.'s, 1976-78. Served with USN, 1943-46. C.P.A., Calif., 1952, S.C., 1969. Mem. Mcpl. Fin. Officers Assn., Nat. Assn. Accountants (nat. dir. 1973-75), Am. Inst. C.P.A.'s, Calif., Colo. socs. C.P.A.'s, Estate Planning Council, S.C. Assn C.P.A.'s (dir. 1979—), Am. Soc. Tng. and Devel., Delta Sigma Pi, Beta Alpha Psi, Beta Gamma Sigma, Phi Beta Kappa. Episcopalian. Contbr. articles to profl. jours. Home: 28 Council St Charleston SC 29401 Office: PO Box 30214 Charleston SC 29407

FOOTO, THOMAS ANDREW, engr., cons. coal industry; b. Switchback, W.Va., Mar. 7, 1921; s. Andrew Thomas and Anna Ludmila (Palco) F.; student civil and mech. engring., W.Va. U., Stevens Inst. Tech., U. S.C.; m. Angelene Battlo, Sept. 5, 1960; children—Andrew Thomas, Marianna. Engring. asst. Pocahontas Fuel Co., Inc. (Va.), 1939-42; constrn. engr. Bowling Constrn. Co., Bluefield, Va., 1947-50; chief engr. Crozier Coal & Land Co., Elkhorn, W.Va., 1950-64; engr. assigned to asst. to pres. Consol. Coal Co., Pocahontas, 1964-65; asst. constrn. engr. W.Va. Dept. Hwys., 1965-68; chief mining engr. Consol. Coal Co., 1968-71; chief engr. Ranger div. Pittston Co., Beckley, W.Va., 1971-73; v.p. engring. Hawley Coal Mining Co., Keystone, W.Va., 1973-77; pres. Tafco, Inc., Oak Hill, W.Va., 1977—. Served with USNR, 1942-46. Registered profl. engr., W.Va. Mem. Nat. Soc. Profl. Engrs., Soc. Mining Engrs., Am. Inst. Mining, W.Va. Soc. Profl. Engrs. Democrat. Roman Catholic. Home: 102 Rollingwood Dr Beckley WV 25801 Office: 912 E Main St Oak Hill WV 25901

FOPPIANI, GREGORY RONALD, health care adminstr.; b. Bklyn., Aug. 21, 1948; s. Joseph Robert and Anna Maria F.; B.S. in Bus. Adminstrn., Ricker Coll., 1971; m. Natalie Marie Coffey, June 3, 1972; 1 son, Christopher. Adminstr., Reading (Mass.) Nursing Home, div. First Allied Corp., 1971, Town Manor Nursing Home, Lawrence, Mass., 1972; exec. adminstr. Fla. operation First Allied Corp., Orlando, 1973-75, adminstr., asst. v.p., 1975, adminstr., v.p. Fla. div., 1976—; dir. Orlando Meml. Convalescent Center, Inc., Titusville Nursing and Convalescent Center, Inc. Mem. Am. Coll. Nursing Home Adminstrs., Am. Soc. Notaries, Am. Health Care Assn., Fla. Health Care Assn. Club: Rotary. Home: 916 Puma Trail Maitland FL 32751 Office: 1730 Lucerne Terr Orlando FL 32806

FORBES, BYRON HENRY, engine parts mfg. co. exec.; b. Denver, Oct. 12, 1948; s. Byron Henry and Beaulah Lee (Bambery) F.; B.S.M.E., Tex. A&M U., 1973; postgrad. 1980—; m. Cynthia Lea Partridge, Jan. 19, 1974. Sales engr. Trane Co., Mobile, Ala., 1973-75; cost reduction engr. Fleetguard, Inc. div. Cummins Engine Co., Cookeville, Tenn., 1976, cost reduction specialist, 1977-78, group leader cost reduction, change control engring., 1978—. Coach, Women's Indsl. League Basketball, 1977, Youth League Baseball, 1977, Youth League Basketball, 1977-79, Youth League Football, 1976, 79. Mem. Soc. Value Engrs. Clubs: Optimists, Demolay. Home: Route 5 Cookeville TN 38501 Office: Route 8 Cookeville TN 38501

FORBES, HUBERT HENRY, petroleum co. ofcl.; b. Kendallville, Ind., Dec. 13, 1921; s. Leonard and Wanda (Fischer) F.; B.S. in Chem. Engring., Purdue U., 1943; m. Mary Kathryn Prevo, June 27, 1948; children—James Warren, Kathryn Lee. Research operator Hooker Electrochem. Co., Niagara Falls, N.Y., 1943-46; project engr. Velsicol Chem. Co., Marshall, Ill., 1948-55; process engr., mgr. tech. services Marathon Oil Co., Robinson, Ill., also London, Madrid, San Francisco, 1955-72, mgr. tech. service, mgr. engring. Texas City, 1972—. Mem. adminstrv. bd. Cub Scouts, Marshall, 1960-61. Sponsor, Teen Age Republicans, Robinson, 1969-72. Former bd. dirs. Lincoln Trail Jr. Coll. Found., Robinson, Robinson Youth Center; bd. dirs. Ed White Meml. Youth Center, Seabrook, Tex. Registered profl. engr., Ill., Tex. Mem. Am. Inst. Chem. Engrs. (chmn. arrangements ann. tech. meeting 1976, registration vice chmn. 83d nat. meeting 1977), Nat. Petroleum Refiners Assn., Am. Petroleum Inst., Tex. Mid-Continent Oil and Gas Assn. (tech. subcom. air and refinery effluents 1972-76), Tex. Chem. Council (air conservation, water conservation com. 1972-76), Texas City-LaMarque C. of C. (air and water subcom. environ. concerns com. 1974—), Acacia. Methodist (adminstrv. bd. 1974—, co.-chmn. Greeters Club 1975-77, pres. Meth. Men, 1979). Clubs: Rotary (pres. Marshall 1954-55), Elks. Home: 443 Bayou View Seabrook TX 77586 Office: Box 1191 Texas City TX 77590

FORBES, WILSON ALEXANDER, JR., chem. plant supr.; b. Gastonia, N.C., Aug. 17, 1939; s. Wilson Alexander and Alice Elvira (Rankin) F.; A.A., Gardner-Webb Coll., Boiling Springs, N.C., 1960; student N.C. State U., Raleigh, 1960-61, 1963; m. Loretta Lee Spirlin, Oct. 25, 1963; children—Susan Elizabeth, Sandra Elaine, Sharon Elisa. Tchr. elem. and jr. high sch. Gaston County (N.C.) Schs., 1964-67; analytical chemist W.G. Lord Plant, Burlington Industries, Cramerton, N.C., 1967-68; quality control mgr. BASF Corp., Charlotte, N.C., 1968-73, ops. supr., 1973—. Chmn., Charlotte Central Safety Com., 1977-79. Democrat. Presbyterian. Club: Optimist of Union Rd., Inc. (past v.p., sec.). Home: 904 E Forbes Rd Gastonia NC 28052 Office: BASF Wyandotte Corp 4330 Chesapeake Dr Charlotte NC 28266

FORCELL, CORA LOU BURNS, librarian; b. New Orleans, Dec. 14, 1947; d. James Richmond and Helen (Dixon) Burns; B.A., La. State U., 1970, M.L.S., 1971; m. Royal Forcell, July 27, 1974; children—Rhodasha Helensia, Royal Jamez. Library asst. Northwestern State U., Natchitoches, La., 1971-72; asst. librarian Nicholls State U., Thibodaux, La., 1972-76, asst. prof., humanities and scis. div. librarian, 1976—. Mem. ALA, La. Library Assn., Alpha Beta Alpha. Baptist. Office: PO Box 2073 Nicholls State Univ Thibodaux LA 70301

FORD, ARCHIE W., state ofcl.; b. Wooster, Ark., Jan. 25, 1906; s. Thomas N. and Minnie (Clements) F.; B.E., Ark. State Tchrs. Coll., 1928; M.S., U. Ark., 1948; LL.D., Ouachita Bapt. Coll., Arkadelphia, Ark., 1962; m. Ruby Lee Watson, Dec. 24, 1927; children—Justin Turner (dec.), Harold Watson (dec.), Joe Thomas. Formerly tchr. and ednl. adviser Civilian Conservation Corps; staff Ark. State Dept. Edn. 1941—, commr. edn., 1953—. Mem. NEA, Ark. Edn. Assn., Council Chief State Sch. Officers (pres. 1962-63), Phi Delta Kappa, Kappa Delta Pi. Democrat. Baptist. Mason. Contbd. nat. profl. mags. Office: Education Bldg Little Rock AR 72201*

FORD, BARBARA RICE DALE, advt. exec.; b. N.Y.C., May 21, 1929; d. James Lowry and Sarah Rice Geer (Gayle) Dale; B.A., Hollins Coll., Roanoke, Va., 1951; m. H. Aubrey Ford, Jr., Mar. 15, 1952 (div.); children—H. Aubrey III, Barbara Gray, James Lowry. Copy trainee, jr. copywriter, sr. copywriter Henderson Advt., Greenville, S.C., 1960-63; sr. copywriter, copy chief Cargill, Wilson & Acree, Charlotte, N.C., 1963-66, Copy chief, asso. creative dir., v.p., Atlanta, 1972-78; v.p. creative The Martin Agy., Richmond, Va., 1979—; sr. copywriter Leber, Katz, Paccione, N.Y.C., 1967-68; copy chief Martin & Woltz Advt., Richmond, 1966-72. Bd. dirs. Richmond Ballet, 1968-73, 79—. Recipient medals and awards in advt. competition. Mem. Richmond Soc. Communicating Arts (v.p. 1972-73). Episcopalian. Club: Country of Va. Author: Maymont, 1972; Big Hand for a Ballerina, 1966; Scenic Virginia, 1979. Contbr. to Art Direction Mag., Madison Ave. Mag., Jack and Jill Mag., Jr. League Mag. Home: 314 Lexington Rd Richmond VA 23226 Office: The Martin Agency 500 Allen Ave Richmond VA 23220

FORD, EDWARD SINCLAIR, JR., veterinarian; b. Montgomery, Ala., Jan. 1, 1930; s. Edward Sinclair and Sarah Francis (Giddens) F.; D.V.M., Auburn U., 1958; m. Dorothy Munson, July 21, 1967; children—Debra Gaye, Edward Sinclair III, Lawrence H., Kimbal D. With Del-Tor Veterinary Clinic, Lexington, Ky., 1958-59; sr. partner Harrison Veterinary Clinic, Cynthiana, Ky., 1959—; dir. Day Star Corp., Lexington. Chmn. Harrison County Bd. Edn., 1972-77; mem. Ky. Senate from 30th dist., 1978—. Served with USNR, 1948-52. Mem. Am., Ky., Buffalo Trace vet. med. assns., Cynthiana-Harrison County C. of C. (dir. 1969-77, v.p., pres. elect 1975, pres. 1976), Am. Legion, VFW. Democrat. Methodist. Elk, Rotarian (dir.). Club: Cynthiana Country. Home: 315 E Pike St Cynthiana KY 41031 Office: PO Box 143 Cynthiana KY 41031

FORD, GORDON BUELL, accountant; b. Greenville, Ky., Sept. 27, 1913; s. Otha and Mattye (Newman) F.; B.S., Western Ky. U., 1934; m. Glenda L. Cox, Oct. 10, 1974; children—Gordon Buell, Gayle Ford Greene, Greg. Partner Coopers & Lybrand, C.P.A.'s, Louisville, from 1934, now ret., pres. Southeastern Investment Trust, Inc.; dir. Broadway Chevrolet, Inc., Broadway Investments, Inc., Am. Car Rental, Inc., Sam Snead Enterprises, Inc., Paul Semanin Co. Inc., 845, Inc. Former mem. bd. dirs. Louisville Central Area, Inc.; trustee Gorjim Found., Louisville, 1960—. C.P.A., Ky., Tenn., Ind. Mem. Am. Inst. C.P.A. (mem. council 1965-71; v.p. 1972-73), Ky. Soc. C.P.A.'s (pres. 1948-49). Clubs: Country, Harmony Landing Country Pendennis (Louisville); Delray Dunes Country (Delray Beach, Fla.), Rotary. Author: (with L.C.J. Yeager) History of the Professional Practice of Accounting in Kentucky 1875-1965, 1967. Home: 5915 Brittany Valley Rd Louisville KY 40222 also 107 MacFarlane Dr Delray Beach FL 33444 Office: 3500 First Nat Tower Louisville KY 40202

FORD, GORDON BUELL, JR., educator, author, fin. mgmt. specialist; b. Louisville, Sept. 22, 1937; s. Gordon Buell and Rubye (Allen) F.; A.B., Princeton U., 1959; M.A., Harvard U., 1962, Ph.D., 1965; postgrad. U. Oslo (Norway), 1963-64, U. Sofia (Bulgaria), 1963, U. Uppsala, 1963-64, U. Stockholm, 1963-64, U. Madrid, 1963. Asst. prof. Indo-European and Baltic linguistics Northwestern U., 1965-72; prof. English, linguistics and teaching English as fgn. lang. U. No. Iowa, Cedar Falls, 1972-76; prof. linguistics Southeastern Research and Devel. Corp., Louisville, N.Y.C., Chgo., Delray Beach, Fla., Cedar Falls, 1972—; fin. mgmt. specialist Humana, Inc., The Hosp. Co., Louisville, 1978—; vis. asst. prof. medieval Latin, U. Chgo., 1966-67, lectr. linguistics U. Chgo. Extension, 1966-67, 70-72; asst. prof. anthropology Northwestern U. evening divs., 1971-72. Mem. Linguistic Soc. Am., Internat. Linguistic Assn., Modern Lang. Assn. Am., Am. Philol. Assn., Am. Assn. Tchrs. Slavic and East European Langs., Mediaeval Acad. Am., Societas Linguistica Europaea, Assn. for Advancement Baltic Studies, Inst. Lithuanian Studies, S.A.R., Phi Beta Kappa. Baptist. Clubs: Harvard (Chgo.); Louisville Country; Princeton (N.Y.C.). Author: The Ruodlieb: The First Medieval Epic of Chivalry from Eleventh-Century Germany, 1965; The Ruodlieb: Linguistic Introduction, Latin Text, and Glossary, 1966; The Ruodlieb: Facsimile Edition, 1967; Old Lithuanian Texts of the Sixteenth and Seventeenth Centuries with a Glossary, 1969; The Old Lithuanian Catechism of Baltramiejus Vilentas (1579): A Phonological, Morphological, and Syntactical Investigation, 1969; Isidore of Seville's History of the Goths, Vandals, and Suevi, 1970; The Letters of St. Isidore of Seville, 1970; The Old Lithuanian Catechism of Martynas Mazvydas (1547), 1971; Isidore of Seville: On Grammar, 1982; Readings in Comparative Linguistic Methodology, 1985; others. Translator: A Concise Elementary Grammar of the Sanskrit Language with Exercises, Reading Selections, and a Glossary (Jan Gonda), 1966; The Comparative Method in Historical Linguistics (Antoine Meillet), 1967; A Sanskrit Grammar (Manfred Mayrhofer), 1972; Introduction to the Comparative Study of the Indo-European Languages (A. Meillet), 1985. Home: PO Box 7847 St Matthew's Sta Louisville KY 40207

FORD, HAROLD EUGENE, congressman; b. Memphis, May 20, 1945; s. Newton Jackson and Vera (Davis) F.; B.S., Tenn. State U., also M.S.; m. Dorothy Jean Bowles, 1949; children—Harold Eugene, Newton Jake, Sir Isaac. Mem. Tenn. Ho. of Reps., 1971-74, majority whip, to 1974; mem. 94th-96th congresses from 8th Tenn. dist., mem. ways and means com., select com. on aging. Del. Democratic Nat. Conv., 1972; chmn. Black Tenn. Polit. Conv. Trustee Rust Coll.; mem. nat. adv. bd. St. Jude Children's Research Hosp.; bd. dirs. Mid-South Fair, Met. YMCA. Hon. fellow Harvard U.; named Outstanding Young Man of Year, Memphis Jaycees, 1976, Tenn. Jaycees, 1976. Mem. C. of C., Nat. Funeral Dirs. and Morticians Assn., Pi Omega Pi, Alpha Phi Alpha. Baptist. Home: 3631 Shady Hollow Ln Memphis TN 38116 Office: US House of Representatives Washington DC 20515

FORD, HENRY EDSEL, state ofcl., health cons.; b. Warren, Ohio, May 23, 1922; s. Robert Marion and Alice Bell (Ledford) F.; grad. Fla. Central Coll., 1959; Asso. Sci., Hillsborough Community Coll., 1976; m. Anna Katherine Campbell, July 30, 1950. Chem. helper E.I. DuPont de Nemours & Co., Charlestown, Ind., 1952-53, chief operator, 1953-57; various temporary positions with local bus. firms, Tampa, Fla., 1957-61; chem. operator Airco Indsl. Gases, Tampa, 1961-68; indsl. safety and health cons. Dept. Labor and Employment Security, Bur. of Workmen's Compensation, State of Fla., Tampa, 1969—. Served with USCG, 1940-45. Mem. Nat. Safety Mgmt. Soc. (state v.p. ops. 1979-80), Vets of Safety. Republican. Club: Elks. Outdoor editor Tampa Daily News, 1970. Home: 1405 E Powhattan Ave Tampa FL 33604 Office: 1313 N Tampa St Room 913 Tampa FL 33602

FORD, JOE THOMAS, state senator Ark.; b. Conway, Ark., June 24, 1937; s. Arch W. and Ruby (Watson) F.; B.S. in Bus. Adminstrn., U. Ark., 1959; m. Jo Ellen Wilbourn, Aug. 9, 1959; children—Alison, Scott. With Allied Telephone Co., Little Rock, 1959—, v.p., 1963-77, pres., 1977—, also dir.; dir. Security Savs. & Loan Assn., Conway, Ark., Comml. Nat. Bank, Little Rock; mem. Ark. Senate from 4th Dist., 1967—. Served with AUS, 1960. Mem. Ark. Telephone Assn., Fifty for the Future. Democrat. Baptist. Address: PO Box 2177 Little Rock AR 72203

FORD, JOHN SUFFERN, psychiatrist; b. Waterville, Maine, July 7, 1939; s. Elsford Q. Ford and Florence Helen Weeks; B.A., Tex. A. and M. U., 1961; M.D., U. Tex., 1965; m. Mary Ann Campbell, July 27, 1963 (div. 1979); children—Cynthia Ann, John Christopher, Curtis Alexander; m. 2d, Elizabeth Lee, 1980. Intern, John Sealy Hosp., Galveston, 1965-66, resident, 1966, 69-72; practice medicine, specializing in psychiatry, Clear Lake Psychiat. Assos., Nassau Bay, Tex., 1972—; mem. staff Clear Lake, Houston Internat. hosps. Bd. dirs. Bay Area Com. on Drug Abuse, Houston, 1975-77; bd. dirs., v.p. Bay Area Hosp. Authority, Nassau Bay, Tex., 1975. Served with AUS, 1966-69. Decorated Army Commendation medal; recipient Physician Recognition award AMA, 1977; diplomate Am. Bd. Psychiatry and Neurology. Mem. Tex. Med. Assn., Am. Psychiat. Assn., Am. Soc. for Adolescent Psychiatry, Phi Rho Sigma. Home: 18240 Nassau Bay Dr Houston TX 77058 Office: 1120 NASA Rd 1 Suite 444 Nassau Bay TX 77058 also 8303 Southwest Freeway Suite 841 Houston TX 77036

FORD, JON CHARLES, journalist; b. Cushing, Tex., Nov. 27, 1920; s. John Charles and Monterie (Swearingen) F.; B.J., U. Tex., 1942; m. Marian Benson Colley, June 17, 1942 (div. 1979); children—Jon Michael, Mary Jane, Charles Colley, Ann Shelley. Reporter Honolulu Advertiser, Hawaii, 1945; mng. editor Odessa Am., Tex., 1946-48; reporter San Antonio Express and News, 1948-49, successively mng. editor, 1949-51, asso. editor, 1952-54, state capital bur. chief, 1955-60, 63-73; chief state capital bur. Harte-Hanks Newspapers, 1970-73; polit. editor Newspapers Inc., 1974-79; press sec. to Gov. Clements of Tex., 1979—. Adminstrv. asst. Gov. Price Daniel of Tex., 1960-62. Tex. delegation reporter Republican and Democratic nat. convs. NBC News, 1968. Served with AUS, 1942-45; PTO. Recipient citations for distinguished writing Headliners Club, Austin, Tex., 1957, 75. Mem. Sigma Delta Chi. Co-author: Campaign Money, Reform and Reality in the States, 1976. Home: Posada del Rey 505 W 7th St Austin TX 78711 Office: Office of Governor State Capitol Austin TX 78711

FORD, MARY LOUISE, dietitian; b. Chgo., June 9, 1912; d. John H. and Frances (Jungen) F.; B.S., Clarke Coll., 1929-33; postgrad. in advanced nutrition Mundelein Coll., 1945. Intern, Michael Reese Hosp., Chgo., 1933-34; dietary dir. Manhattan Project Hosp., Oak Ridge, 1946; dir. dietetics George Washington U. Hosp., Washington, 1947-52, D.C. Gen. Hosp., 1952-53, Garfield Meml. Hosp., Washington, 1953-58; cons. dietitian Ann Arundel Hosp., Annapolis, Md., 1958-60; cons. dietetian to hosps., nursing homes, Winter Park, Fla., 1979—. Republican judge elections Fairfax County (Va.), 1952, 58; sustaining mem. Rep. Nat. Com., 1979. Served with Women's Med. Specialist Corps, U.S. Army, 1943-49. Mem. Am. Dietetic Assn. (registered dietitian), Fla. Dietetic Assn., Am. Soc. Hosp. Food Service Adminstrs. (pres. East Central Fla. 1979-80), Am. Hosp. Assn., U.S. Senatorial Club (nat. com.). Clubs: Central Fla. Kennel, VFW Aux. Home: 125 Gum St Longwood FL 32750 Office: 111 Lakemont St Winter Park FL 32792

FORD, NANCY PACE, hosp. exec.; b. Augusta, Ga., Nov. 4, 1949; d. Johnson Hagood, Jr. and Phyllis Nancy (Zeuch) Pace; B.S., Fla. State U., Tallahassee, 1972; m. Bruce MacLeod Ford, Feb. 16, 1974; 1 son, Matthew Judson. Various secretarial positions, 1969-71; dir. social services St. Luke's Hosp., Jacksonville, 1973—; adv. com. ABC Home Health Agy., 1979—; vol. to elderly Fla. nursing homes Fla. Dept. Health and Rehab. Services, 1977—. Mem. Nat. Soc. Hosp. Social Work Dirs. (treas. Fla. chpt. 1979), Hosp. Social Services Assn. (pres. 1976-77), Fla. Assn. Health and Social Services (sec. Duval chpt. 1977-79), DAR. Democrat. Episcopalian. Home: 2032 Samontee Rd Jacksonville FL 32211 Office: 1900 Boulevard Jacksonville FL 32206

FORD, RICHARD EDWIN, vol. orgn. exec.; b. Wabash, Ind., Feb. 27, 1939; s. Wilbur Edwin and Florence Gertrude (Jeup) F.; B.S., Ind. U., 1961. Sales rep. Ford Meter Box Co., Inc., Arlington, Va., 1961-70, dir., 1979—; fed. agy. liaison officer EPA, Washington, 1971-76: v.p. Bauman Bible Telecasts, Arlington, Va., 1976-77, also trustee. Bd. dirs. D.C. Met. Police Boys Club, 1970—, v.p., 1977-78, pres., 1979—; pres. Washington Sanitation Conf., 1975; bd. dirs. Washington Ballet, Md. Dance Theatre; bd. dirs. Eisenhower Meml. Scholarship Found., 1976—, v.p., 1977, pres., 1978-80; chmn. men's com. Nat. Debutante Cotillion, 1976-78. Mem. Am. Water Works Assn., Newport Hist. Soc. (life), Nat. Wildlife Assn. (life), Smithsonian Assos., Friends of the Corcoran, Wolf Trap Assn., Hist. Annapolis, Friends of Kennedy Center, Met. Opera Nat. Council, Soc. of Friends of Music of Ind. U. (life), Wash. Performing Arts Soc., U. Md. Charter Council, Culver Mil. Acad. Alumni Assn. (life), Nat. Steeplechase and Hunt Assn. (life), Ind. Soc. of Chgo., Hoosier Salon, Indpls. Mus. Art, Indpls. Opera Co. Republican. Methodist. Clubs: University, Capitol Hill (life). Pisces, Desiree, Polo (Washington); Columbia (Indpls.); Maxinkuckee Yacht (Culver, Ind.); Wabash (Ind.) Country; Elks. Home and Office: 2000 S Eads St Apt 1125 Arlington VA 22202

FORD, RUTH HARTING, ednl. adminstr.; b. Cleve., Nov. 12, 1934; d. Louis B. and Elvira E. (Brown) Harting; A.B., Stetson U., 1956; M.A., U. Fla., 1962; m. Robert Harold Ford, July 5, 1959; 1 son, Louis Harting. Tchr. English and history Lee Jr. High Sch., Orlando, Fla., 1956; tchr. Evans High Sch., Orlando, 1958-61, dean girls, 1962-64, dir. guidance, 1964-68; dir. guidance Winter Park (Fla.) High Sch., 1968—; adj. prof. edn. St. Leo Coll., 1979, Orlando Jr. Coll., 1959-69, Rollins Coll., 1969; cons. in guidance Fla. Dept. Edn., 1962-77, N.J. Dept. Edn., 1965-66, Ala. Dept. Edn., 1965-66; cons. to Coll. Bd., 1963—, U.S. Office of Edn., 1969-73. Chmn., Sch.-Coll. Relations com. for State of Fla., 1970—; adv. bd. Girl Scouts U.S.A., 1958; mem. Fla. Human Rights Commn., 1979, Gov.'s Biracial com., 1975; trustee Central Fla. Muscular Dystrophy Assn., 1965-68; mem. Orange County PTA Council, 1976. Named Tchr. of Yr., Orange County, 1957; Bicentennial Counselor in Fla., 1976; citation, Rotary Club

1973, Coll. Bd., 1974, U.S. Office Edn., 1973. Mem. LWV, AAUW, Coll. Bd. Council on Access Services, Fla. Personnel and Guidance Assn. (pres. 1968-69, newsletter editor 1973-78), Am. Personnel and Guidance Assn., Nat. Vocat. Guidance Assn., Fla. Sch. Counselors Assn. (v.p. 1967-68), Fla. Assn. Measurement in Guidance, Fla. Edn. Assn., NEA, Classroom Tchrs. Assn., Fla. Career Devel. Assn. (pres. 1970-71), Orange County Guidance Assn. (pres. 1963-64), Delta Kappa Gamma. Republican. Clubs: Order Eastern Star, White Shrine, Shrine Circus Mothers. Editor: Fla. Guidelines, 1973-78; editor: Handbook for Counselors, 1967; contbr. Fla. Handbook for Counselors, 1971; author: Counselor and the Computer, 1969; Changing Role of the Secondary Counselor, 1968; The Myth of Scholarship Availability, 1978; mem. editorial bd. Am. Sch. Counselors Jour., 1967-70; author: Is the SAT Coachable, 1979. Home: 2480 Deloraine Trail Maitland FL 32752 Office: 2100 Summerfield Rd Winter Park FL 32792

FORD, THOMAS JEFFERS, indsl. developer; b. Charleston, S.C., Sept. 9, 1930; s. Rufus and Mildred (Jeffers) F.; A.B., Wofford Coll., 1952; postgrad. U. N.C., 1956-58, 59-61, U. Okla., 1965-67; m. Barbara Jean Jackson, Dec. 28, 1954; children—Thomas Jeffers, Edward Rufus. Asst. mgr. Albany (Ga.) C. of C., 1956; mgr. Rock Hill (S.C.) C. of C., 1957-58; dir. trade devel. Greenville (S.C.) C. of C., 1959-60, dir. bus. and indsl. relations, 1961; exec. dir. Marlboro County Devel. Bd., Bennettsville, S.C., 1962-65, Lakeland (Fla.) Indsl. Bd., 1966-67; dir. Chesterfield-Marlboro Tech. Edn. Center, Cheraw, S.C., 1968-72; dir. area devel. dept. 6th Congl. Dist. S.C., Florence, 1973-74; dir. bus. devel. Eskridge & Long Constrn. Corp., Sanford, N.C., 1975; chief exec. officer Greater Orangeburg (S.C.) C. of C.; chief exec. officer Orangeburg County Devel. Commn., 1976-79, exec. dir., 1979—. Served with USN, 1952-53. Certified indsl. developer. Fellow Am. Indsl. Devel. Council (past mem. internat. certified indsl. devel. bd.; regent ednl. programs); mem. S.C. Indsl. Developers Assn. (past pres.), So. Indsl. Devel. Council (past dir.), Blue Key, Sigma Alpha Epsilon. Methodist. Rotarian (past club pres.). Home: 2978 Lakeside Dr NE Orangeburg SC 29115 Office: PO Box 1303 Orangeburg SC 29115

FORD, WENDELL HAMPTON, U.S. senator; b. Owensboro, Ky., Sept. 8, 1924; s. Ernest M. and Irene (Schenk) F.; student U. Ky., 1942-43; grad. Md. Sch. Ins., 1947; m. Jean Neel, Sept. 18, 1943; children—Shirley Jean Ford Dexter, Steven. Partner Gen. Ins. Agy., Owensboro, 1959-67; chief asst. to Gov. Ky., 1959-61; mem. Ky. Senate, 1965-67; lt. gov. Ky., 1967-71, gov., 1971-74; mem. U.S. senate, mem. coms. on commerce, sci. and transp., energy and natural resources; rules and adminstrn. chmn. Democratic Senatorial Campaign Com. Served with U.S. Army, 1944-46; Ky. N.G., 1949-62. Mem. Ky. Jr. C. of C. (state pres. 1954-55, nat. pres. 1956-57), Jr. C. of C. Internat. (v.p. N. Am. 1958-59), U.S. C. of C. (bd. dirs.). Democrat. Baptist. Club: Elks. Home: Sumner MD 20016 Office: US Senate Washington DC 20510

FORD, WILLIAM GERALD FRANCIS, chemist; b. Honolulu, Dec. 27, 1946; s. Harold Francis and Evelyn Norma (Kwiatkowski) F.; B.A., Oklahoma City U., 1969; Ph.D., Tex. A. and M. U., 1975; m. Laura Gardner, July 28, 1973; 1 son, William Patrick. Sr. chemist Halliburton Services, Duncan, Okla., 1975-79, devel. chemist, 1979—, Robert A. Welch fellow, 1971-75. Mem. parish council Assumption Cath. Ch. Mem. Soc. Petroleum Engrs. (chmn.), Am. Chem. Soc. (chmn.), Am. Petroleum Inst. (chmn.), Duncan Jaycees (dir., chaplain), Sigma Xi, Phi Lambda Upsilon, Kappa Sigma. Democrat. Roman Catholic. Clubs: K.C. (grand Knight 1976-79), Circle K. Home: 2 28th St S Duncan OK 73533 Office: PO Drawer 1431 Duncan OK 73533

FORDE, PERCY SAMUEL, horticulturist; b. Columbus, Ga., June 9, 1940; s. Jimmy G. and Hattie T. F.; B.S. in Agronomy, Tenn. A&I U., 1963, postgrad. in horticulture, 1963; m. Doris E. Shannon, Aug. 15, 1963; children—Percy, Keith. Lab. technician Armour Agrl. Chem. Co., Columbus, 1964-66; asst. dir. OEO, Columbus, 1966; pres. Forde & Sons Nursery-Landscaping, Columbus, 1979—. Pres., Kingview Betterment Assn., 1973-76. Mem. Nat. Fedn. Ind. Bus., Columbus C. of C., Better Bus. Bur., Ga. Minority Hwy. Contractors Assn. (pres. 1977-79). Baptist. Home: 425 N Oakley Dr Columbus GA 31907 Office: PO Box 6324 Columbus GA 31907

FORDYCE, HOMER EDMUND, civil engr.; b. Ridgeway, Mo., Aug. 1, 1916; s. Orey Francis and Mabel Edna (Baxter) F.; B.C.E., U. Wyo., 1941; m. Mary Louise Gilbert, Mar. 25, 1948; 1 son, Jerry Edmund; 1 stepdau., Mary Lee Sooter Phillips. Cons. in gen. design Marley Co., Mission, Kans., 1945-78. Mem. Mo. Republican Com., Clay County. Served with USAF, 1942-45. Mem. ASCE, Am. Concrete Inst. (v.p. Kans. chpt. 1977-78, pres. Kans. chpt. 1978). Patentee in cooling tower designs. Home: 146 El Cielo Circle Harlingen TX 78550

FORDYCE, MICHEL WARDER, psychologist; b. Boston, Dec. 14, 1944; s. Joseph Warder and Grace (Summerville) F.; AB., Emory U., 1967; postgrad San Fernando Valley State Coll., 1968; M.A., U.S. Internat. U., 1969, Ph.D., 1971. Instr. psychology Grossmont Coll., ElCajon, Calif., 1970-71; asst. prof. sociology Calif. Western U., San Diego, 1970; prof. psychology Edison Community Coll., Fort Myers, Fla., 1971—; pvt. counseling practice, Fort Myers, 1977—. Mem. Am. Personnel and Guidance Assn. Office: 1178 Cypress Lake Dr Fort Myers FL 33907

FOREMAN, EDWARD RAWSON, lawyer; b. Atlanta, May 15, 1939; s. Robert Langdon and Mary Rawson (Shedden) F.; grad. Taft Sch., Watertown, Conn., 1958; B.A., Washington and Lee U., Lexington, Va., 1962; J.D., Emory U., 1965; m. Margaret Reeves, Oct. 19, 1968; children—Margaret Trot, Mary Rawson. Admitted to Ga. bar, 1965, since practiced in Atlanta; partner firm Jones, Bird & Howell, 1971—; instr. Emory U., 1973; lectr. Ga. Inst. Real Estate, 1973, State Bar Ga. Continuing Legal Edn., 1977. Dir. Shedman Corp., 1965—. Coordinator Sat. lawyer program Atlanta Legal Aid Soc., 1970-72, adv. bd., 1972-74, bd. dirs., 1974—, pres., 1980—; mem. member's guild bd. High Mus. Art, 1972—, chmn. young men's roundtable, 1972-73, v.p. membership, member's guild, 1974-75, chmn. audience devel. Art in the Park Bicentennial project, 1975-76, mem. mus. bd. sponsors, 1976—; bd. dirs., v.p. Ansley Park Civic Assn., 1973-77; bd. sponsors Alliance Theatre, 1973-76; bd. dirs. Christian Council Met. Atlanta, 1972-74, Paideia Sch., Atlanta, 1974-76; trustee McAliley Endowment Trust, 1971—; sr. warden St. Luke's Episcopal Ch., 1975. Mem. Am., Ga., Atlanta bar assns., Lawyers Club Atlanta (sec. 1979-80), Phi Delta Phi. Clubs: Piedmont Driving, Nine O'Clocks (Atlanta); Highlands (N.C.) Country. Home: 211 The Prado NE Atlanta GA 30309 Office: Haas-Howell Bldg 75 Poplar St NE Atlanta GA 30303

FOREMAN, KENNETH JOSEPH, JR., clergyman, educator; b. Princeton, N.J., Dec. 28, 1921; s. Kenneth Joseph and Susan Allison (Lewis) F.; grad. Mt. Hermon Sch., 1938; B.S., Haverford Coll., 1942; B.D., Union Theol. Sem., Richmond, Va., 1945; Th.M. with distinction, Louisville Presbyn. Theol. Sem., 1953; Ph.D., Princeton Theol. Sem., 1977; m. Mary Frances Ogden, June 7, 1945; children—Frances Ogden Foreman Haga, Carol, Samuel Lewis, Joseph Lapsley. Ordained to ministry Presbyn. Ch. U.S., 1945; home missionary pastor Presbyn. Ch. U.S., Ashe County, N.C., 1945-48; fgn. mission evangelist, tchr. U.P. Ch. U.S.A., China, 1948-53, Korea, 1954-65, Ch. of Christ in China, 1949-52, Presbyn. Ch. in Korea, 1954-64, Korea Mission of Australian Presbyn. Ch., 1963-64; exec. dir. Hist. Found. Presbyn. and Ref. Chs., Montreat, N.C., 1969-79; prof. ch. history Reformed Theol. Sem., Jackson, Miss., 1979—. Clk., Bd. of Adjustment Town of Montreat, 1971-77. Bd. dirs. Tien Nan Middle Sch., Kunming, Yunnan, Ch. of Christ in China Yunnan Mission com. Kienshui Hosp., Pusan (Korea) Presbyn. Theol. Sem.; moderator Presbytery of Concord, Presbyn. Ch. U.S., 1972; trustee William Stuart Owen Collection of Art of Michael Gordon Owen, Jr., 1965—. Mem. Aircraft Owners and Pilots Assn., Am. Acad. Polit. and Social Sci., Am. Assn. for State and Local History, Am. Radio Relay League, Am. Soc. Ch. History, Hist. Soc. N.C., Scottish Ch. Hist. Soc., Soc. for Hist. Archaeology, Soc. Am. Archivists, Western N.C. Hist. Assn., Western N.C. Library Assn., Phi Beta Kappa. Author: Leaves From Behind the Bamboo Curtain, 1953; Speak Yunnanese, 1952; Continuing Problems of American Presbyterian Board and Agency Administration in the Nineteenth and Twentieth Centuries, 1976. Editor: Yearbook of Prayer of Christian Work in Korea, 1958; co-editor: Davidson Leader, 1935-37, Montreat Weekly News, 1940; editor, contbr. Study Papers Korea 1953, 1953; asso. editor Ashe Presbyn., 1945-48; editor Hist. Found. News, 1969-78; mem. editorial bd. Jour. Presbyn. History, 1969-79. Home: Box 2110-W Clinton MS 39056 Office: RTS-W 5422 Clinton Blvd Jackson MS 39209

FOREST, WAYNE GERARD, ins. broker; b. New Orleans, Dec. 20, 1948; s. Louis Edmond and Thelma Odile (Chenevert) F.; B.A. in Mktg., Southeastern La. U., 1972; m. Linda Rose Dupuy, Jan. 25, 1969; children—Wayne Gerard, Matthew Gerard. Comml. property and inland marine underwriting mgr. Fireman's Fund Ins. Co., New Orleans, 1972-74; br. mgr., asst. v.p. Swett & Crawford Group, New Orleans, 1975-77; exec. v.p. B & F Spl Risks, Inc., New Orleans, 1977—. Coach, Little League Football and Baseball, 1972—. Served with U.S. Army, 1969-71. Decorated Bronze Star. Mem. Nat. Assn. Profl. Surplus Line Offices, La. Surplus Line Assn. (dir.), New Orleans Ins. Exchange, Southeastern La. U. Alumni Assn., Tau Kappa Epsilon. Democrat. Roman Catholic. Home: 8880 Rosecrest Ln River Ridge LA 70123 Office: Suite 4620 1 Shell Sq New Orleans LA 70139

FORESTER, JEAN MARTHA BROUILLETTE, educator, librarian; b. Port Barre, La., Sept. 7, 1934; d. Joseph Walter and Thelma (Brown) Brouillette; B.S., La. State U., 1955; M.A. (Carnegie fellow 1955-56), George Peabody Coll. Tchrs., 1956; m. James Lawrence Forester, June 2, 1957; children—Jean Martha, James Lawrence. Librarian Howell Elementary Sch., Springhill, La., 1956-58; asst. post librarian Fort Chaffee, Ark., 1958; command librarian Orleans Area Command, U.S. Army, Orleans, France, 1958-59; acquisitions librarian Northwestern State U., Natchitoches, La., 1960; serials librarian La. State U., New Orleans, 1960-66; mem. faculty La. State U., Eunice, 1966—, asst. librarian, asst. prof., 1972—. Active Eunice Assn. Retarded Children. Mem. La. Library Assn. (sect. sec. 1971-72), UDC, Delta Kappa Gamma (chpt. parliamentarian 1972-74), Alpha Beta Alpha, Phi Gamma Mu, Phi Mu. Democrat. Baptist. Mem. Order Eastern Star. Home: 1351 Gregg Ave Eunice LA 70535

FORET, MICKEY PHILLIP, air transp. co. exec.; b. McComb, Miss., Oct. 23, 1945; s. Fadias Phillip and Christine (Brown) F.; B.S., La. State U., 1971, M.B.A., 1971; student Southeastern La. U., 1963-65; m. Mary Ann Tramonte, Aug. 12, 1966; 1 dau., Keri Lynn. Dist. rep. Nat. Convenience Stores, Inc., Houston, 1972-73; controller Am. Lakes & Land, Houston, 1973-74; mgr. accounts receivable Tex. Internat. Airlines, Houston, 1974-76, dir. cash mgmt., 1975—, asst. treas., 1978—; pres. Rubicon Indemnity Ltd., Hamilton, Bermuda, 1978—. Pres., Clear Woods Improvement Dist., 1975-78. Served in USAF, 1966-69. Mem. Am. Mgmt. Assn., Nat. Investor Relations Inst., Risk and Ins. Mgmt. Soc., Houston Council Retirement Plans, Phi Kappa Phi, Beta Gamma Sigma. Republican. Baptist. Home: 5330 Royal Pkwy Friendswood TX 77546 Office: PO Box 12788 Houston TX 77527

FORGAY, ROBERT ALAN, acct., city ofcl.; b. Atlanta, Feb. 16, 1951; s. Robert Coy and Lela Voncille (Shook) F.; B.B.A., magna cum laude, U. Ga., 1973; m. Rebecca S. Fletcher, May 19, 1973; children—Robert Alan, Ryan Adam. Acct., A.M. Pullen & Co., Atlanta, 1973-76; controller Am. Mut. Acceptance Co. Decatur, Ga., 1976-77; dir. fin. and adminstrn. City of Hapeville (Ga.), 1977—. Treas., Hapeville Employees' Credit Union, 1979—, also bd. dirs. C.P.A., Ga. Mem. Hapeville C. of C. (dir. 1979—), Am. Inst. C.P.A.'s, Ga. Soc. C.P.A.'s, Ga. CD Assn., Internat. Inst. Mcpl. Clks., Mcpl. Fin. Officers Assn., Ga. Mcpl. Mgrs. Assn. Democrat. Baptist. Club: Exchange. Home: 1857 Canberra Dr Stone Mountain GA 30083 Office: City of Hapeville 3468 N Fulton Ave Hapeville GA 30354

FORGUE, STANLEY VINCENT, physicist; b. Cleve., Oct. 6, 1916; s. Jack N. and Mary E. (Smith) F.; B.S. in Physics, Ohio State U., 1939, B.E.E., 1940, M.S. in Physics, 1940, postgrad., 1940-42; m. Dorothy Jeanne Huber, Feb. 14, 1942; children—Mary Jeanne Forgue Metz, Stanley T., Wesley V. Grad. asst. physics Ohio State U., 1939-40; asst. research engr. Ohio Engring. Expt. Sta., 1940-41; research fellow Ohio State Research Found., 1941-42; research engr., sr. mem. tech. staff, project engr., research group head RCA Labs., Princeton, N.J., 1942-72; engring. cons., tech. writer, 1972-75; asso. prof. physics Central Fla. Coll., Ocala, 1975—. Mem. several civic bds. in N.J., 1950-70. Recipient Distinguished Alumnus award Ohio State U., 1970; 5 research awards RCA; registered profl. engr., Ohio. Fellow IEEE; mem. N.Y. Acad. Scis., AAUP, Am. Inst. Physics, AAAS, Sigma Xi, Tau Beta Pi, Sigma Pi Sigma, Eta Kappa Nu, Pi Mu Epsilon. Contbr. tech. articles to profl. jours.; patentee in electronics; developer TV vidicom. Home: 3430 SW College Rd Box D-3 Ocala FL 32671 Office: PO Box 1388 Ocala FL 32670

FORGY, BYRON KEITH, surgeon; b. Louisville, Nov. 14, 1946; s. Byron Louis and Ora Jean (Hall) F.; B.A., Duke U., 1968; M.D., U. Miami, 1972; m. Margaret Dianne Seymour, June 16, 1968; children—Kelli, Kristi. Intern and surg. resident Emory U. Affiliated Hosps., Atlanta, 1972-77; mem. dept. surgery Seminole Meml. Hosp., Sanford, Fla., 1977-78, Grace Hosp., Morganton, N.C., 1978—. Diplomate Am. Bd. Surgery. Mem. N.C. Med. Soc., Morganton C. of C., Alpha Omega Alpha. Baptist. Home: 108 Woodstream Dr Valdese NC 28690 Office: 425 S King St Morganton NC 28655

FORMAN, HOWELL NORTHCUTT, JR., mgmt. cons.; b. Longview, Tex., Oct. 27, 1925; s. Howell Northcutt and Etha (Reagin) F., Sr.; B.S.M.R., Tex. A&M U., 1948; student U. of Tex., 1950-51; M.S. in Engring., Southern Methodist U., 1958; m. Ethel Caline Hantske, Aug. 27, 1949; children—Ethel Reagin, Howell, III, Stephen Hantske. Engr., E.I. DuPont de Nemours & Co., Waynesboro, Va., 1948-50; quality control mgr. Powers Mfg. Co., Longview, Tex., 1953; material control coordinator Gen. foreman, Ford Motor Co., Dallas, 1953-58; asst. prof. indsl. engring. So. Meth. U., Dallas, 1958-60, guest lctr., 1961-62, 68-72, asso. prof., 1963-68; chief indsl. engring. Haggar Co., Dallas, 1961-63; dir. indsl. engring. Baylor U. Med. Center, Dallas, 1969-72; pres. H.N. Forman Jr. & Asso., Inc., Dallas, 1958—. Chmn. bd. dirs. Dallas Area Assn. Christian Chs., 1974-75; chmn. SW Area AIIE Student Chpt., 1965-66. Served with USN, 1944-46, 1951-52. Registered profl. engr., Tex. Mem. Tex. Soc. Profl. Engrs., Nat. Soc. Profl. Engrs., Am. Soc. Agrl. Engrs., Soc. Automotive Engrs., ASHRAE. Contbr. several articles, manuals in field. Address: 3913 Caruth St Dallas TX 75225

FORMAN, LEON RONALD, city ofcl.; b. New Orleans, July 7, 1947; s. Benjamin and Nathalie (Regenboeen) F.; B.S. in Bus. Adminstrn., La. State U., 1969; grad. Zoo Mgmt. Sch., N.C. State U., 1975; m. Shelley Kancher, Aug. 11, 1973; 1 son, Daniel Nathan. Adminstrv. analyst City of New Orleans, 1972-73; dep. dir. Audubon Park Commn., City of New Orleans, 1973-77, dir., 1977—; bd. regents N.C. Zoo Mgmt. Sch. Served with U.S. Army, 1970-71. Mem. Am. Assn. Zool. Parks and Aquariums, Nat. Recreation and Parks Assn., La. Trails Assn. Jewish. Home: 852 Topaz New Orleans LA 70124 Office: PO Box 4327 New Orleans LA 70178

FORMAN, MILES AUSTIN, mktg. and mgmt. co. exec.; b. Fort Lauderdale, Fla., Mar. 7, 1947; s. Hamilton Collins and Doris Marie (Davis) F.; student Vanderbilt U., 1965-68, U. Fla., 1968-70; m. Kathryn Louise O'Donnell, Feb. 15, 1974; 1 son, Miles Austin. Pres., Am. Mktg. & Mgmt. Inc., Fort Lauderdale, 1970—, also dir.; dir. Westlawn Meml. Gardens, Inc., Fort Lauderdale, Forest Lawn Meml. Gardens of Broward County, Inc., Lauderdale Meml. Gardens, Inc.; Barnett Banks of Broward County. Bd. dirs. Stephen Foster Meml. Bd., Better Business Bur.; trustee Behavioral Scis., Nova U.; mem. budget and admissions coms. United Way. Served with AUS, 1970-76. Mem. Downtown Bus. Council, C. of C., S.A.R., Sigma Chi. Democrat. Clubs: Hundred of Broward County, Lauderdale Yacht, Marina Bay, Rolling Hills Country, Coral Ridge Yacht. Home: 1804 SE 9th St Fort Lauderdale FL 33316 Office: PO Box 640 Fort Lauderdale FL 33302

FORMBY, ELLEN SUE, speech pathologist; b. Dallas, Sept. 4, 1954; d. Ralph Leland and Doris Virginia (Webb) Fagala; B.A., Stephen F. Austin State U., 1974; student U. San Francisco, Guadalajara, Mex., summer 1972; M.A., N. Tex. State U., 1978; m. James Kenney Formby, Jan. 7, 1978. Speech pathologist Duncanville (Tex.) Ind. Sch. Dist., 1975—. Mem. Am. Speech-Hearing Assn., Dallas Assn. Speech Pathology and Audiology. Home: 9840 Sophora Circle Dallas TX 75249 Office: Duncanville Ind Sch Dist 302 E Freeman St Duncanville TX 75116

FORNEY, BILL EARL, cons. mech. and structural engr.; b. Beggs, Okla., June 23, 1921; s. Lysle Merriam and Leona May (Sigler) F.; B.M.E., Okla. U., 1948, B.C.E., 1952; postgrad. Okla. State U., 1949-51, NE Okla. State U., 1940-41, Tulsa U., 1943-44, U. Mo., 1945; m. Virginia Sue Tate, Apr. 29, 1967; children—Mike, Linda, Patricia, Richard. Design engr. Frick-Reid Co., Tulsa, 1943-44, Austin Co., Houston, 1941-42; engr. Mid Continent Petroleum, Tulsa, 1946; utilities engr. U. Okla., Norman, 1946-48; design engr. Coston & Frankfurt Cons.'s, Oklahoma City, 1948-49; div. mgr. Nat. Tank Co., Tulsa, 1949-70; owner, operator BEF Engring. Co., Tulsa, 1959—; dir., pres. So. Supply & Valve Co., Inc., Tulsa, 1966-74; mgr. engring. Maloney-Crawford Tank Co., Tulsa, 1970; lectr. in field. Bd. dirs. All Souls Unitarian Ch., Tulsa, 1976—; pres. bd. dirs. Unity Ch., Tulsa, 1952. Served with USAAF, World War II. Recipient Gold Letzeiser medal Okla. U., 1948. Mem. Engrs. Soc. Tulsa (pres. 1978-79), ASME (chmn. mid-continent sect. 1954—), ASCE, Am. Inst. Steel Constrn., Nat., Okla. cons. engrs. councils, Tau Beta Pi, Sigma Tau, Pi Tau Sigma, Rho Theta Sigma. Club: Southwood Country (dir.). Contbr. articles to profl. publs. Patentee in field. Address: 6011 E 57th St Tulsa OK 74135

FORNOS, PEDRO GENARO, internist; b. Havana, Cuba, Sept. 19, 1922; s. Pedro J. and Maria Angeles (Palencia) F.; came to U.S., 1965, naturalized, 1971; M.D., U. Havana, 1946; m. Caridad Lopez, Dec. 21, 1950; children—Pedro, Emma Maria. Intern, Univ. Hosp., Havana, 1947-49; resident Austin (Tex.) State Hosp., 1968-69, Meth. Hosp., Dallas, 1969-71; dir. pulmonary function dept. Univ. Hosp., Havana, 1961-65; dir. respiratory therapy dept., Bapt. Meml. Hosp. System, San Antonio, 1973—; pvt. practice internal medicine, San Antonio, 1971—. Diplomate Am. Bd. Internal Medicine. Fellow Am. Coll. Chest Physicians; mem. AMA, Tex., Bexar County med. assns., San Antonio Club Internal Medicine. Roman Catholic. Home: 3038 Oneida St San Antonio TX 78230 Office: 201 Med Sq Med Bldg 311 Camden St San Antonio TX 78215

FORRESTER, GARY DREW, social worker; b. Pitts., Sept. 5, 1952; s. Lamon Thomas and Dotty L. Forrester; B.S. in Social Work, W.Va. U., 1974. Drug abuse coordinator Greenbrier Valley Mental Health Clinic, Inc., Lewisburg, W.Va., 1974-78; mem. faculty W.Va. Ann. Sch. on Alcoholism and Drug Abuse, 1977, 79; drug services coordinator and chariperson in-service tng. Seneca Mental Health-Mental Retardation Council, Inc., Richwood, W.Va., 1979—. Umpire, Lewisburg (W.Va.) Little League, 1978—; mem. Youth Services Com. of the Greenbrier County Community Services Council, Inc., 1974—, Greenbrier Valley Domestic Violence Com., 1978—, Greenbrier River Hike, Bike and Ski Trail, 1979—; bd. dirs. Greenbrier Valley Council on Alcoholism and Drug Abuse, 1974-79. Recipient Cert. of Appreciation, Greenbrier County Community Services Council, 1978. Mem. Nat. Assn. of Social Workers (W.Va. rep. to profl. symposium 1975), W.Va. Orgn. of Parent Trainers (founding mem.), W.Va. Assn. on Crime and Delinquency (founding mem.), W.Va. Highlands Conservancy, Friends of the Earth, Nat. Orgn. for Reform of Marijuana Laws, Common Cause, Assn. for Rural Mental Health (mem. program com. 1978—), Solar Lobby, Environ. Action. Democrat. Unitarian. Club: Kiwanis (dir. 1979—). Home: Route 2 Box 476 Ronceverte WV 24970

FORSEE, JOE BROWN, librarian, state ofcl.; b. Fulton, Ky., Oct. 25, 1949; s. Earl Drummond and Reba Jean (Brown) F.; B.A., Murray State U., 1971; M.S. in Library Sci., U. Ky., 1972; m. Dencia Jane Nanney, Jan. 30, 1971; children—Amy Jo, David Matthew. Asso. regional librarian Ky. Dept. Library and Archives, 1973, dir. interlibrary cooperation, 1973-76; cons. Miss. Library Commn., 1976, asst. dir. adminstrn., 1976-78, dir., 1978—. Mem. Miss. Library Assn., Southeastern Library Assn., ALA. Mem. Ch. of Christ. Home: 222 Jeffries Dr Pearl MS 39208 Office: PO Box 3260 Jackson MS 39207

FORSHAY, DONALD SCOTT, book mfg. co. exec.; b. Blount County, Tenn., Oct. 8, 1946; s. Wayne W. and Burnice D. Forshay; B.S. in Mktg., East Tenn. State U., 1968; postgrad. Darden Bus. Bus., U. Va., 1978-79; postgrad. exec. devel. program. U. Tenn., 1980—; m. Judith F. Myers, Mar. 17, 1967; children—Donald Scott, John Benjamin. Mgmt. trainee Arcata Book Group, Kingsport, 1968-69, sales rep., 1970-72, dist. sales mgr., 1972-74, mgr. market planning and devel., 1974-76, mgr. book group mktg. services, 1977-79, v.p. book group mktg. services, 1979—. Mem. adminstrv. bd. Mt. View United Meth. Ch. Served with USMC, 1969. Mem. Kingsport C. of C. (co. rep.). Republican. Clubs: Eagles, Optimist (soccer and basketball coaching staff). Home: Route 3 Emory Church Rd Kingsport TN 37664 Office: 1201 N Eastman Rd Kingsport TN 37662

FORSMAN, J(AMES) PARKER, environ. and indsl. hygiene cons.; b. St. Louis, June 30, 1921; s. Guy C. and Mabel (Banks) F.; A.B., Princeton U., 1943; Ph.D. in Chemistry, Washington U., St. Louis, 1952; m. Patricia Anne Bartlett, Dec. 22, 1946; children—Sally B.,

Kathryn D. Chemist, Firestone Tire & Rubber Co., 1943-44, Tretolite Corp., 1947-48; chemist Exxon Research & Engring. Co., Tulsa, Linden, N.J., Baytown, Tex., 1952-61, research asso., 1961-71; pres. Aer-Aqua Labs., Inc., analytical and cons. labs. Houston, 1971—. Served with USNR, 1944-46. AEC grantee, 1949-52. Accredited indsl. hygienist Am. Indsl. Hygiene Assn. Mem. Am. Chem. Soc., Water Pollution Control Fedn., Water and Wastewater Analysts Assn., Am. Acad. Indsl. Hygiene, Am. Indsl. Hygiene Assn., Sigma Xi. Episcopalian. Office: 211 E Shaw St Pasadena TX 77506

FORSTER, WILLIAM HULL, army officer; b. Shelby, Miss., June 24, 1939; s. William Oskar Herman and Amy (Hull) F.; student Miss. State U., 1956-58; B.S., U. Ala., 1960; Ph.D. in Nuclear Chemistry, U. Calif., 1965; grad. U.S. Navy Test Pilot Sch., 1972, Armed Forces Staff Coll., 1976, Air War Coll., 1979; m. Belle Fair Brown, Dec. 27, 1968; children—William Hull, Robert Brown. Commd. 2d lt. U.S. Army Res., 1960, called to active duty, 1965, advanced through grades to lt. col., 1975; comdr. Hawk Guided Missile Battery, Vietnam, 1965-66; comdr. TUSLOG Detachment, Turkey, 1967-68; ops. analyst Inst. Nuclear Studies, 1968-71; comdr. 173d Assault Helicopter Co., Vietnam, 1971-72; research pilot, test program planner Space Shuttle Orbiter NASA, Houston, 1973-75; comdr. 10th Combat Aviation Bn., Ft. Lewis, Wash., 1976-78; dep. dir. Army Space Program Office, 1979—. Scoutmaster Boy Scouts Am., 1967-69. Decorated D.F.C., Bronze Star (2), Meritorious Service medal (2), Air medals (16), Army Commendation medal. AEC research asso., 1961-64. Mem. Am. Phys. Soc., AAAS. Presbyterian. Office: Army Space Program Office 5001 Eisenhower Ave Alexandria VA 22233

FORSYTHE, JACK NORMAN, psychologist; b. Iron City, Tenn., Aug. i, 1931; s. Algie N. and Gladys M. (Hensley) F.; B.S., Middle Tenn. State U., 1961, M.A., 1966; Ed.S., U. Fla., 1969. Ph.D., 1971; m. Margaret Newman, Dec. 19, 1952; children—Debra, Cynthia, Jack Norman. Sch. counselor Lawrence County High Sch., Lawrenceburg, Tenn., 1960-68; sch. psychologist, Gainesville, Fla., 1969-70; dir. counseling, staff psychologist, head psychology dept. Columbia (Tenn.) State Coll., 1970—. Pvt. practice counseling and cons. psychology, 1971—. Served with USAF, 1953-57. Mem. Am., Southeastern, Tenn., Middle Tenn. (treas., membership chmn., pres.) psychol. assns., Phi Delta Kappa, Phi Beta Phi, Kappa Delta Pi. Mason, Lion. Contbr. articles to profl. jours. Home: PO Box 7 Iron City TN 38463 Office: Columbia State Coll Columbia TN 38401

FORT, ARTHUR TOMLINSON, III, physician, educator; b. Lumpkin, Ga., Sept. 24, 1931; s. Thomas Morton and Gladys (Davis) F.; student N. Ga. Coll., 1948-50; B.B.A., U. Ga., 1952; student Memphis State U., 1957-58; M.D., U. Tenn., 1962; m. Jane Wilmer McClelland, June 15, 1957; children—Abby Lucinda, Arthur Tomlinson Jr., Juliana Melody, Ernest Arlington II. Intern, Bapt. Meml. Hosp., Memphis, 1962-63; resident obstetrics and gynecology U. Tenn., 1963-66, asst. prof., 1966-70; prof., head dept. gynecology and obstetrics La. State U. Med. Sch., Shreveport, 1971-73; prof. maternal and child health and family planning Tulane U. Med. Center, 1973-74, dir. family health program Sch. Pub. Health and Tropical Medicine, 1973-74; pvt. practice obstetrics and gynecology, Memphis, 1966-70, family practice and emergency medicine, Vacherie, La., 1975-78, attending in family practice and indsl. medicine Sara Mayo Hosp., New Orleans, 1978—; prof. Ob-gyn and family medicine La. State U. Med. Sch., Shreveport, 1979—; mem. med. com., bd. dirs. La. Family Planning Program, Caddo Parish, 1971—; mem. nat. adv. council Nat. Center Family Planning Program Devel., 1972-74; pres. Family Health Found., 1972-74. Served with USAF, 1952-57. Recipient Student Golden Apple award A.M.A., 1969. Diplomate Am. Bd. Obstetrics and Gynecology, Am. Bd. Family Practice. Fellow Am. Coll. Obstetrics and Gynecology; mem. Am. Fertility Soc., Am., So. med. assns., S.-Central Obstet. and Gynecol. Soc. Republican. Presbyn. Home 1707 Valmont St New Orleans LA 70115 Office: 1541 Kings Hwy Shreveport LA 71130

FORT, CLAIRE CAUDILL, legal adminstr.; b. Birmingham, Ala., Aug. 19, 1943; d. Joe Sanford and Elizabeth Hendon (Martin) Caudill; student Brevard Jr. Coll., 1962-63, Fla. State U., 1964-66; m. L. Heyward Fort, Nov. 21, 1967; 1 dau., Michelle. Mgmt. security div. Pan Am. World Airways, Cocoa Beach, Fla., 1961-64; adminstrv. asst. Ednl. TV Commn., State of Fla., Tallahassee, 1964-66; employment counselor Snelling & Snelling, Sumter, S.C., 1966-68; sec. to various lawyers, Columbia, S.C., 1968-75; office mgr. McNair Glenn Konduros Corley Singletary Porter & Dibble, P.A., Columbia, 1975—; mem. spl. adv. com. office adminstrn. program Coll. Bus., U. S.C., 1975—, adv. com. Coll. Gen. Studies, 1977—. Active Dem. politics; Sunday Sch. supt. St. Alban's Episc. Ch., Lexington, S.C., 1978—, mem. mission bd., 1978—, clk. mission bd., 1978—, Sunday Sch. tchr., 1976-79, mem. central deanery, Christian edn. steering com., 1980—; treas. Columbia Swimming League, 1978—. Mem. Assn. Legal Adminstrs. Office: 18th Floor Bankers Trust Tower Columbia SC 29201

FORT, GEORGE EDWARD, petroleum engring. cons.; b. Rolla, Mo., July 28, 1916; s. Rowe and Maude (Eddleman) F.; B.S., Mo. Sch. Mines, 1940; hon. profl. petroleum engring. degree U. Mo. at Rolla, 1967; m. Mary Anne Reeves, July 5, 1947 (dec. 1970); children—Georgiann, William R., George Edward II; m. 2d, Maxine I. Selliman, Nov. 30, 1973. With Pan Am. Petroleum Corp., 1940-58, successively engr. trainee S. Tex., S. La., engr. Houston, petroleum engr. S. La., field engr. Western Kan., dist. engr. Shreveport, La., 1947-50, sr. engr., Oklahoma City, 1951-58; petroleum cons. Oklahoma City 1959; partner Fort and Miller, petroleum cons. firm, 1960—. Served from pvt. to 1st lt. USAAF, 1942-45. Decorated Air medal with cluster, Purple Heart. Registered profl. engr., Okla. Mem. Engring. Club Oklahoma City, Oklahoma City Geol. Soc., Am. Petroleum Inst., Am. Inst. Mining, Metall. and Petroleum Engrs., Okla. Ind. Petroleum Assn. (past dir.), Soc. Ind. Profl. Earth Scientists (past chpt. pres.), Lambda Chi Alpha. Republican. Methodist. Club: Petroleum (past dir.). Home: 3939 NW 34th St Oklahoma City OK 73112 Office: First Nat Bank Bldg Oklahoma City OK 73102

FORTUNE, HILDA ORR, sociologist; b. Birmingham, Ala., Aug. 31, 1913; d. Henry and Nettie (Russell) Orr; B.A., Morgan State Coll., 1938; M.A., N.Y. U., 1958, Ed.D. summa cum laude, 1963; m. Roland Fortune, Sept. 1944 (dec.); 1 dau., Lois Jayne. With Balt. Urban League, 1938-41; asst. exec. dir. Nat. Council Negro Women, 1942-43; counselor personnel dept. Wright Aero. Corp., 1943-45; dir. employment dept. YWCA, Harlem, 1947-52; with Westchester Urban League, 1952-55; dir. community services dept. Urban League Greater N.Y., 1955-63; counselor psychol. services Bklyn. Coll., 1963-68, also instr. sociology; prof., coordinator sociology, chmn. social work and Afro-Am. studies programs York Coll., City U. N.Y., 1968-79; ret., 1979; cons., writer. Bd. dirs. Urban League Greater N.Y.; founder, chmn. Community Resources Com. Jamaica, 1970-74. Recipient Woman of Year award York Coll., 1975. Mem. Am. Sociol. Assn., Nat. Assn. Social Workers, AAUP, Am. Personnel and Guidance Assn. (emeritus), NEA, Nat. Council Negro Women, Delta Sigma Theta, Kappa Delta Pi, Pi Lambda Theta. Home: 4221 NW 27th St Lauderhill FL 33313

FOSBERG, IRVING ARTHUR, psychologist; b. N.Y.C., Jan. 22, 1916; s. Albert and Julia (Greenfield) F.; B.S., N.Y. U., 1937, Ph.D., 1940; M.A., Columbia, 1938; m. Betty Pearlman, Feb. 11, 1945; children—Ben, Orin, Barry. Cons. psychologist, N.Y.C., 1940-41; asst. prof. psychology Farragut Coll., Farragut, Ida., 1946-47; dir. Bur. Psychol. Service, Tulane U., New Orleans, asst. prof. psychology, 1947-48; chief psychologist VA Hosp., New Orleans, 1952-57; pres. Psychol. Service Center New Orleans, Inc., 1955—; asso. prof. Loyola U. Sch. Bus. Adminstrn., New Orleans, 1960-67, prof., 1967-78, prof. emeritus, 1978—. Vocat. cons. U.S. Dept. HEW. Served with USNR, 1941-68; now comdr. ret. Diplomate Am. Bd. Forensic Psychology. Fellow Am. Psychol. Assn., A.A.A.S., Rorschach Inst.; mem. So. Soc. Philos. Psychology, Orleans Soc. Applied Psychologists (past pres.), La. Psychol. Assn. (past pres.). Contbr. articles to profl. jours. Home: 6020 Freret St New Orleans LA 70118 Office: 8116 Hampson St New Orleans LA 70118

FOSDICK, FRANKLIN LAWRENCE, aircraft exec.; b. Ansonia, Conn., Sept. 12, 1919; s. Horace George and Maude Percy (Buck) F.; student New Haven Coll., 1946-48; B.B.A. with highest honors, So. Meth. U., 1962; M.B.A., Pepperdine U., 1978; m. Bette H. Burns, Sept. 19, 1940; 1 son, Franklin Lawrence, Jr. With Vought Corp., 1946—, mgr. material services, purchasing and operations control, Mich. div., Warren, 1963-70, chief traffic, transp. and shipping, Vought Systems div., Dallas, 1970-74, mgr. material control Vought Corp., 1974—. Chmn. liability and claims task force, mem. exec. com. traffic service div. Aerospace Industries Assn. Am., 1970-74. Pres., prin. owner Bali Hi Apts., Dallas, 1958—; dir., sec. LTV Missiles & Space Credit Union, Warren, 1964-70. Mem. freight adv. bd. Am. Airlines, N.Y.C., 1970-74. Served to 1st lt. U.S. Army, 1944-46. Mem. Purchasing Mgmt. Assn. Detroit (dir. 1969), Nat. Assn. Purchasing Mgmt. (dist. vice chmn. pub. relations 1970), Dallas Apt. Assn., Nat. Property Mgmt. Assn. (certified property mgr. 1978). Methodist (chmn. adminstrv. bd. 1973-75). Clubs: Masons (32 deg.), Shriners, Oak Cliff Country (Dallas); Village Players (Birmingham, Mich.). Home: 1639 Whitedove St Dallas TX 75224 Office: Vought Corp PO Box 226114 Dallas TX 75266

FOSS, GEORGE BRIDGES, JR., lawyer; b. Birmingham, Ala., Sept. 21, 1924; s. George Bridges and Mary Gladys (Gardien) F.; A.B., Birmingham-So. Coll., 1950; J.D., Duke U., 1951; m. Jean Elizabeth Morgan, July 14, 1956; children—Daphne Elizabeth, Anne Kanaar, Brian Gardien, Holly Thompson. Admitted to Ala. bar, 1951, Fla. bar, 1958, U.S. Supreme Ct. bar, 1955; asst. city atty., Birmingham, 1951-55, planning dir., 1955-57; partner firm Beasley & Foss, Birmingham, 1957; sr. planner, atty. City of St. Petersburg (Fla.), 1958-59; mem. firm Fowler, White, Burnett, Hurley, Banick & Knight, P.A. (and predecessor firms), Miami, Fla., 1959—. Served with U.S. Army, 1943-45. Mem. Am. Planning Assn., Am., Dade County bar assns., Fla. Planning and Zoning Assn. (pres. So. Fla. chpt. 1978), Sigma Alpha Epsilon, Omicron Delta Kappa, Phi Delta Phi. Democrat. Episcopalian. Home: 8267 SW 128th St 111 Miami FL 33156 Office: 25 W Flagler St Suite 501 Miami FL 33130

FOSSLER, DOUGLAS EARL, biophysicist; b. Miami, Fla., July 22, 1943; s. Emil Lawrence and Bonnie Lea (Klein) F.; student U. Tex., Austin, 1961-63; B.S., U. Tex., Arlington, 1972; M.A., U. Tex., Dallas, 1975; m. Rebecca Elizabeth Priour, Nov. 2, 1975; children—Douglas Earl II, Thomas Franklin. Blues guitarist, Austin, 1963-69; mgr., dir. Fossler Enterprises, Mountain Home, Tex., 1976—. Adv., Hill Country Youth Ranch, Ingram, Tex.; sgt. at arms Young Republicans, Austin, 1961. Served with Army NG, 1963. Recipient grant Nat. Assn. Retarded Citizens, 1973-75. Mem. Fedn. Am. Scientists, N.Y. Acad. Scis., AAAS, Am. Psychol. Assn., Am. Physiol. Soc., Nat. Small Bus. Assn., Sigma Nu. Contbr. articles to profl. jours. Address: FO Ranch Mountain Home TX 78058

FOSTER, ALFRED EWTON, security services exec.; b. Mobile, Ala., Oct. 3, 1928; s. Ernest Marsden and Gladys Christine (Ewton) F.; B.A., U. Ala., 1951; m. Jerry Lorece Gravely, Jan. 1, 1970; Program dir. Am. Salesmasters, Ft. Worth, 1968-70; owner, operator Dunamis Assos., mgmt. cons., Ft. Worth, 1970—; pres., chmn. bd., dir. Eagle Security Services, Ft. Worth, 1977—; chmn. bd., dir. Foster Assos., Ft. Worth, 1979—; coll. lectr. Served with USN, 1946-48. Mem. Nat. Assn. Chiefs of Police, Security Assn. Tex., Nat. Speakers Assn., Tex. Lodge of Chiefs Police. Republican. Clubs: Elks, Masons. Office: One Summit Ave Suite 805 Fort Worth TX 76102

FOSTER, BRIAN DAVID, environ. engr.; b. Bellville, Tex., Nov. 29, 1952; s. Arrell Frank and Juanita Louise (Brian) F.; B.S. in Indsl. Engring., U. Ark., 1975. Prodn. control engr. Honeywell Corp., Oklahoma City, 1972-73; methods and standards engr. Firestone Tire & Rubber Co., Russellville, Ark., 1974-75; safety and environ. engr. Gulf Oil Corp., New Orleans, 1975—; certifier crane operators; coordinator fire tng. sch.; chmn. ops. subcom. Clean Gulf Assos. coop. for spill cleanups, 1980—. Mem. Tau Beta Pi, Alpha Pi Mu, Theta Tau. Methodist. Club: Crescent City Rugby. Home: 3021 Rue Parc Fontaine Apt 114 New Orleans LA 70114 Office: 212 Loyola St New Orleans LA 70161

FOSTER, CARY DON, constrn. co. exec.; b. Thomas, Okla., Aug. 14, 1951; s. John D. and Alma R. (Graybill) F.; B.S. in Agrl. Econs., Okla. State U., 1973. Sales rep. Southwestern Pub. Co., Nashville, 1969-71; pres. Foster Constrn. Co., Inc., Clinton, Okla., 1973—. Chmn., Custer County Democratic party, 1976—; chmn. Custer County Econ. Devel. Council, 1978-79; mem. High Plains Water Adv. Task Force, 1978—. Mem. Western Okla. Home Builders Assn. Club: Clinton Rotary. Office: Route 1 Box 133 Clinton OK 73601

FOSTER, CHARLES ALLAN, chem. co. exec.; b. Portsmouth, Va., Dec. 20, 1951; s. Charles Albert and Florence (Jackson) F.; B.S. in Commerce with distinction, U. Va., 1975. Plant acct. Va. Chem., Inc., Portsmouth, 1975-77, fin. analyst, 1977-78, product mgr. splty. chems., 1978—. Pres., Va. Chems. Employees Fed. Credit Union, 1976—; bd. dirs. Big Bros.-Big Sisters of Tidewater, 1977-78. Mem. Nat. Assn. Corrosion Engrs., Am. Water Works Assn., Nat. Assn. Bedding Mfrs., Nat. Cotton Batting Inst., Beta Gamma Sigma. Episcopalian. Contbr. articles to profl. jours. Home: 1405 Claremont Ave Norfolk VA 23507 Office: 3340 W Norfolk Rd Portsmouth VA 23703

FOSTER, CHARLES RICHARD, educator; b. McKeesport, Pa., Oct. 5, 1901; s. Charles Richard and Ella May (Weible) F.; A.B., U. Pitts., 1923; M.Ed., Harvard U., 1929, Ed.D., 1937; m. Helen Forney George, Sept. 15, 1928; children—Helen Katharine Foster Eveland, Jessie May Foster Kirkland, Eleanor Ann Foster Elwood. Asst., then asso. prof. edn. Rutgers U., New Brunswick, N.J., 1930-40; dean Sch. Edn., U. Miami (Fla.), 1940-47; mem. faculty U. Fla., 1947—, dir. grad. studies in edn., 1947-66, prof. edn., 1947-66, prof. emeritus, 1966—, asst. dean, 1949-63. Recipient George Wharton Pepper prize U. Pitts. Mem. Am. Personnel and Guidance Assn., Nat. Vocat. Guidance Assn., Phi Delta Kappa (internat. pres. 1960-61, acting exec. sec. 1964), Sigma Delta Chi, Delta Sigma Rho, Theta Chi. Democrat. Episcopalian. Clubs: Kiwanis; Harvard (Miami, Fla.); Athenaeum (U. Fla.). Author: Editorial Treatment of Education in the American Press, 1937, reprinted, 1971; Psychology for Life Today, 1951, 3d rev. edit., 1971; Guidance for Today's Schools, 1957; (with others) The Teacher: Key to Better Guidance, 1979. Home: 504 NE 9th Ave Gainesville FL 32501

FOSTER, MARY SUE, affirmative employment cons. co. exec.; b. Rolla, Mo., Feb. 24, 1944; d. Samuel Franklin and Dolly (Callahan) F.; B.S., Southeast Mo. State U., 1966; M.Ed., N. Tex. State U., 1972; children—Kimberley Anne Loehr, Eric Michael Loehr. Speech therapist public schs. Ohio, Minn., Tex., 1966-74; developer employment info. service Women's Center of Dallas, 1974; co-founder Foster & Wood Assos., Dallas, 1976, owner, operator, 1976—. Bd. dirs. Girls Clubs of Dallas, Women's Center Dallas. Mem. Am. Soc. Tng. and Devel., Exec. Women Dallas, AAUW. Home: 13510 Red Fern St Dallas TX 75240 Office: PO Box 5337 Richardson TX 75080

FOSTER, WALTON ARTHUR, broadcasting exec.; b. San Angelo, Tex., Aug. 26, 1927; s. Arthur Rambo and Katie Pearl (Walton) F.; A.A., San Angelo Coll., 1948; m. Arla Vee Bishop, Feb. 17, 1950; 1 son, Walton Arthur II. Comml. mgr. sta., then gen. mgr. Sta. KTXL, San Angelo, 1948-54; comml. mgr., then gen. mgr. Sta. KTXL-TV, 1952-54; mem. staff Sta. KGKO, Dallas, 1954; mem. staff, weekend news dir. Sta. KTRK-TV, Houston, 1955; mem. staff Sta. KLIF, Dallas, 1956; founder, KIXY and KIXY-FM, pres. Solar Broadcasting Co. Inc., 1954—; founder, pres. Sta. KVRN and KVRN-FM, Sonora Broadcasting Co. Inc., 1975—; 1st violin San Angelo Symphony Orch., 1947. Founder KIXY-Dr. Raymond Cavness scholarship Fund for speech and drama Angelo State U., 1975; a founder W. Tex. Boys Ranch, Tankersley, Tex.; Democratic campaign chmn. Tom Green County Senatorial campaign, 1964. Mem. S.A.R., San Angelo Advt. (v.p. 1952-53), Assn. Broadcasting Execs. Tex., Phi Theta Kappa (chpt. pres. 1945). Clubs: Optimist (charter mem., dir. 1948, v.p. 1949-50), 20-30 (charter mem., pres. 1950-51), Press (co-organizer 1974) (San Angelo). Home: 2612 Oxford Ave San Angelo TX 76901 Office: KVRN and KVRN-FM Hwy 277 S PO Box 1216 Sonora TX 76950

FOSTER, WILLI KEAPELS, marriage and family therapist; b. Delft, Netherlands, Feb. 6, 1946; came to U.S., 1957, naturalized, 1967; d. John L. and Jetty (Hobijn) Krapels; B.A., Wake Forest U., 1968; M.Ed., N.C. State U., 1972; m. William Thomas Foster III, May 26, 1978. Head residence counselor, dept. residence life N.C. State U., Raleigh, 1969-72, area coordinator, dept. residence life, 1972-73; dir. new careers program N.C. Dept. Correction, 1973-74; dir. diagnostic center N.C. Correctional Center for Women, Raleigh, 1974-76; clin./dep. dir. Drug Action of Wake County, Raleigh, 1976—; chmn. Found. for Alcohol and Drug Studies. Cert. trainer Nat. Inst. Drug Abuse. Mem. Assn. for Drug Abuse Prevention, Wake County Mental Health Assn., Group Behavior Soc. Home: 121 Hillcrest Rd Raleigh NC 27605 Office: PO Box 12021 Raleigh NC 27605

FOSTER, WILLIAM SOUTHMAYD, former urban cons.; b. Sandpoint, Idaho, May 7, 1910; s. Walter Linder and Lucy (Southmayd) F.; B.S. in Civil Engring., Iowa State U., 1933; postgrad. city planning Mass. Inst. Tech., 1956; m. Grace Bertha Cristy, Dec. 31, 1932; children—Chester Cristy, Ross Water. Insp., engr. Iowa Hwy. Commn., 1934-39; cons. Stanley Engring. Co., 1939-42; engring. editor Am. City Mag., N.Y.C., 1942-56, editor in chief 1956-64, editor, dir., asso. publisher, 1964-65; ret., 1965; dir. Buttenheim Pub. Corp., N.Y.C. and Pittsfield, Mass., 1957-76. Mem. exec. advisory council Col. Bus. and Pub. Adminstrn. Fla. Atlantic U., Boca Raton, 1976—. Diplomate Am. Acad. Environ. Engring. Mem. Internat. City Mgmt Assn. (hon.), Inst. Mcpl. Engring. (hon.), Am. Public Works Assn. (life), Am. Water Works Assn. (life), ASCE (life). Republican. Christian Scientist. Author: Handbook of Municipal Adminstraton and Engineering, 1978. Home: 4305 D Island Circle Fort Myers FL 33907

FOUNTAIN, L. H., congressman; b. Leggett, N.C., Apr. 23, 1913; s. Lawrence H. and Sallie (Barnes) F.; A.B., U. N.C. (Wiley P. Mangrim Oratorical medal), 1934, J.D. (Mary D. Wright Debate medal 1935), 1936; m. Christine Dail, May 14, 1942; 1 dau., Nancy Dail. Admitted to N.C. bar, 1936; reading clk. N.C. Senate, 1936-41; mem. 83d-96th congresses from 2d Dist. N.C., mem. com. on fgn. affairs, com. on govt. ops.; chmn. inter-govtl. relations and human resources sub-com.; del. to UN, 1967. Mem. N C. State Senate from 4th Senatorial Dist., 1947-52; pres. Edgecombe Young Dem. Club, 1940; eastern organizer, past chmn. 2d dist. exec. com. Young Dem. Clubs N.C.; mem. Adv. Commn. on Intergovtl. Relations, 1959—. Enlisted AUS as pvt., 1942, disch. as maj. J.A.G.O., D.R.C., 1946. Elected Tarboro's Man of Year, 1948. Recipient Distinguished Pub. Service award N.C. Citizens' Assn., 1971, U. N.C. Sch. Medicine, 1973; Distinguished Congl. Service award Nat. League Cities, 1976. Mem. N.C., Edgecombe County bar assns., N.C. Farm Bur., N.C. Grange, Am. Legion. Democrat. Presbyterian (elder). Clubs: Elks, Kiwanis (past pres., lt. gov. 6th N.C. div.). Home: 1102 Panola St Tarboro NC 27886 also 4000 Cathedral Ave Washington DC 20016 Office: House Office Bldg Washington DC 20515 also Edgecombe County Bldg Tarboro NC 27886

FOUNTAIN, LEWIS SPENCER, physicist; b. McCrory, Ark., Oct. 18, 1917; s. Spencer Edward and Blanche Mae (Lewis) F.; student Ark. State Coll., 1935-36, San Antonio Coll., 1950-51; B.S., Trinity U., 1958, M.S., 1962; m. Dorothy Mae McCall, June 26, 1946; children—Nancy, Robert, Margaret, Rebecca. Mem. staff Lockheed Aircraft Corp., 1940-44; electronic technician S. H. Lynch & Co., San Antonio, 1947-48, 49-56, Slick Airways, Inc., San Antonio, 1948-49, S.W. Radio and Sound Equipment, San Antonio, 1949; research scientist S.W. Research Inst., San Antonio, 1956-64, sr. research scientist, 1964—, acting mgr. earth sci. applications sect. electronic systems div., 1971-75, project mgr. dept. geoscis., 1976—. Served with USN, 1944-46. Recipient recognition for geosci. work in Demilitarized Zone, U.S. Army and Govt. of Republic of Korea, 1977-79. Mem. Acoustical Soc. Am., IEEE, Soc. Non-destructive Testing, Sigma Xi. Methodist. Club: Masons. Contbr. articles to profl. jours.; research in geosci. Home: 127 Postwood San Antonio TX 78228 Office: 6220 Culebra Rd San Antonio TX 78274

FOUNTAIN, NELLIE LEE, sci. bookstore mgr.; b. Austin, Tex., Nov. 17, 1921; d. James Etheridge and Vera Mae (Whitaker) Stark; student pub. schs., Tex.; m. Jesse R. Fountain, Aug. 30, 1940; 1 dau., Barbara Fountain Miller. Mgr., Major's Sci. Books, Inc., Dallas, 1957—; advisor med. and sci. books to U. Tex. Health Sci. Center, Tex. Woman's U., Baylor U., various allied health schs. in S.W.; cons. to libraries, physicians, others. Mem. Christian Ch. Home: 9209 Heatherdale Dr Dallas TX 75243 Office: 2137 Butler St Dallas TX 75235

FOURCARD, INEZ GAREY, found. exec., artist; b. Bklyn., Sept. 26, 1930; d. George W. and Frances E. (MacDonald) Garey; student Pratt Inst., 1946-48; B.F.A., McNeese State U., 1963; m. Waldren Arthur Fourcard, Aug. 7, 1948; children—Chrystal Frances, Sharon Lynn, Waldren Arthur, Andrea Renee, David Marquard, Anita Lynn. Exhibited in numerous one man shows throughout U.S., also in Eng., France and Spain; mem. gifted and talented sect. of Spl. Edn. State of La., 1971-73; mem. adv. council Child Centered/Parent Tutored Kindergarden Program, 1974—; mem. La. Task Force for Community Edn., 1974-75; v.p. La. Assn. for Sickle Cell Anemia, 1974—; mem.

Calcasieu Parish Bicentennial Com., 1974—; exec. dir. Southwestern Sickle Cell Anemia Found., Lake Charles, La., 1973—. Democrat. Baptist. Important works include The Widow in pvt. collection Berlrand Russell Peace Found., London. Home: 1414 St John St Lake Charles LA 70601 Office: PO Box 3254 118 Enterprise Blvd Lake Charles LA 70601

FOUSHEE, ROGER BABSON, pub. rep.; b. Haw River, N.C., July 29, 1938; s. Joseph Baxter and Elsie Bellwood (Jenkins) F.; A.B., U. N.C., 1960, postgrad., 1960-64; m. Mary Joyce Farthing, Oct. 11, 1976. Serials asst. Wilson Library, U. N.C., 1960-62; research asst. Gov.'s Commn. Edn. Beyond High Sch., 1962; research asso., inst. of govt. U. N.C., 1963; pubs. rep. George Scheer Assos., Chapel Hill, N.C., 1964-77; So. dist. mgr. Follett Pub. Co., 1978—, S.E. regional sales mgr., 1980—. Mem. Central Bus. Dist. Com. of Chapel Hill, 1973; mem. Orange County Am. Revolution Bicentennial Commn. Chmn. Orange County Dem. Com., 1968-72; mem. N.C. Dem. Exec. Com., 1970-76; pres. Research Triangle Internat. Visitors Center, Inc., 1979—. Named one of 10 outstanding young Dems. in N.C., 1969, 72; recipient one of 3 Distinguished Dem. awards Orange County (N.C.), 1976. Mem. Chapel Hill Hist. Soc. (pres. 1969-74), So. Book Travellers Assn. (treas. 1979—), Assn. for Preservation Eno River (charter, dir. 1978—), L.Q.C. Lamar Soc., Phi Eta Sigma, Phi Alpha Theta. Clubs: Rotary, Order of Golden Fleece. Home: 1510 Southwood Dr Durham NC 27707 Office: Box 1145 Franklin St Sta Chapel Hill NC 27514

FOUTS, GEORGE MURRY, ednl. adminstr.; b. Mulberry, Fla., May 2, 1927; s. Manly H. and Irvie (Sweat) F.; B.S., Fla. So. Coll., Lakeland, 1949; M.S., Fla. State U., Tallahassee, 1954; m. Gloria Garcia; children—Beverly Dawne, George Murry. Staff Polk County Bd. Edn., Bartow, Fla., 1949—, prin. jr. high, then supervising prin., 1968-69, area supt. West area schs., 1969-70, dir. sch. facilities, 1970, now facilities bus. mgr. Chmn., Lakeland (Fla.) Housing Bd. Mem. Council Edn. Facilities Planners, Fla. Sch. Planners Assn. Clubs: Lions (past pres.), Shriners, Kiwanis. Home: 108 W Belvedere St Lakeland FL 33803 Office: PO Box 391 Bartow FL 33830

FOUTS, THOMAS STEPHEN, real estate broker; b. Jacksonville, Fla., Mar. 17, 1928; s. Merrill Louis and Blanche LaMont (Jones) F.; student U. Fla., 1947-51; m. Jacquelyn Laura Sweeting, Feb. 8, 1969; children—John, Sarah. Pres., owner Royal Tire Service, Inc., Tallahassee, 1955-59; asst. to sec. State of Fla., Tallahassee, 1959-60; agt. Prudential Ins. Co., Islamorada, Fla., 1960-70; pres. Tom Fouts Advt., Inc., Islamorada, 1964-72; asso. real estate salesman Eddie Sweeting, Broker, Islamorada, 1972-74; owner Thomas S. Fouts Realtor, Islamorada, 1974—. Mosquito commr. Monroe County, Fla., 1964-68; mem. sch. bd. Monroe County, 1977—. Real estate broker, Fla. Mem. Fla. Jr. C. of C. (state sec. 1959). Club: Masons (32 deg.). Home: Marker 81 US 1 Islamorada FL 33036 Office: PO Box 9 Islamorada FL 33036

FOWLER, BRUCE ANDREW, toxicologist; b. Seattle, Dec. 28, 1945; s. Andrew and Dolores Yvonne F.; B.S. in Fisheries, U. Wash., 1968; Ph.D. in Pathology, U. Oreg., 1972; m. Mary Glenn Oler, June 9, 1968; children—Glenn Andrew, Randall Bruce. Staff fellow, environ. toxicology br. Nat. Inst. Environ. Health Scis., Research Triangle Park, N.C., 1972-74, sr. staff fellow, lab. of environ. toxicology, 1974-77, research biologist, lab. of environ. toxicology, 1977-79, head renal and intracellular function and toxicology, lab. of organ function and toxicology, 1979—; adj. asso. prof. pathology U. N.C.; temporary adv. WHO; mem. work group Internat. Agy. for Research Against Cancer. Mem. Am. Fisheries Soc., AAAS, Am. Soc. Cell Biology, Am. Assn. Pathologists, Soc. of Toxicology, Sigma Xi, N.Y. Acad. Sci. Office: Nat Inst Environ Health Scis PO Box 12233 Research Triangle Park NC 27709

FOWLER, BRUCE WAYNE, physicist; b. Gadsden, Ala., Dec. 10, 1948; s. James Kenneth and Helen Christine (Towers) F.; B.S. in Chemistry (Gorgas fellow), U. Ala., Tuscaloosa, 1970; M.S., U. Ill., Urbana, 1972; doctoral Ph.D., U. Ala., Huntsville, 1978. Systems analyst Teledyne Brown Engring. Co., Huntsville, Ala., 1972-74; physicist Advanced Systems Concepts Office, U.S. Army Missile Research and Devel. Command, Huntsville, 1974—, chief theoretical physicist smoke ad hoc group, 1975. Certified profl. chemist. Mem. Am. Phys. Soc., Am. Chem. Soc., Ala. Acad. Sci., Sigma Xi, Sigma Pi Sigma, Pi Mu Epsilon, Alpha Chi Sigma. Contbr. articles in field to profl., indsl., govtl. publs. Home: 202-3 Utica Pl Huntsville AL 35806

FOWLER, CHRISTINE MILDRED WEEKS, real estate broker; b. Jay, Fla., Nov. 5, 1944; d. James Virgle and Gladys Mildred (Joyner) Weeks; Asso. Sci. in Bus. Adminstrn., Okaloosa Walton Jr. Coll., 1975; children—Tina, Christopher, Amy. Co-owner various businesses, 1963-74; with McDonnell Douglas Corp., Eglin AFB, Fla., 1974-79; owner, operator, pres. ACTV Realty, Inc., Ft. Walton Beach, Fla., 1979—. Past chmn. Okaloosa County chpt. Am. Heart Assn. Mem. Nat. Assn. Realtors, Fla. Assn. Realtors, Ft. Walton Beach Bd. Realtors. Baptist. Home: 234 S Bayshore Dr Valparaiso FL 32580 Office: ACTV Realty Inc 1212 E Miracle Strip Pkwy Fort Walton Beach FL 32548

FOWLER, DAVID PAUL, mech. engr.; b. Fort Worth, Nov. 28, 1924; s. Clyde John and Irene Flotia (Locklear) F.; B.M.E.,, Tex. A. and M. U., 1948; m. Mary Emma Welsh, Sept. 30, 1950; children—Sharon Ruth, Judy Renee, John Welsh, Nancy Jean, Mary Ann. Sr. engr. Am. Mfg. Co. Tex., Fort Worth, 1948-56; sales engr. Mid-Continent Supply Co., Inc., Fort Worth, 1956-60; liaison engr. Am. Machine & Foundry Co., Greenwich, Conn., 1961; mgr. sales and engring. Alamo Machine & Engring Works, Fort Worth, 1961-63; sr. research engr. Frito-Lay, Inc., Irving, Tex., 1963—. Active as Republican election clk., Dallas County, Tex. Served with USN, 1945-46. Mem. Instrument Soc. Am. (asso., nat. del. 1966, pres. N. Tex. sect. 1969), Am. Inst. Discussion (dir. Dallas chpt.), Mensa. Lutheran. Patentee in field. Home: 1726 E Union Bower Rd Irving TX 75061 Office: 900 N Loop 12 Irving TX 75061

FOWLER, DELBERT MARCOM, civil engr., energy planner, cons.; b. Ladonia, Tex., Sept. 14, 1924; s. Robert Delbert and Floy Ethel (Marcom) F.; B.S., U.S. Mil. Acad., 1945; M.S. in Civil Engring., Tex. A. and M. U., 1954; M.S. in Internat. Affairs, George Washington U., 1965; grad. Indsl. Coll. Armed Forces, 1965; m. Betty Alouise Reichey, Dec. 11, 1948; children—Kathryn Lewis (Mrs. David Irwin), John D. Marcom, Francine Floy. Commd. 2d lt. C.E., U.S. Army, 1945, advanced through grades to col., 1966; assigned Austria, 1945-48, Korea, 1950-52, West Germany, 1958-61, policy and planning positions, Washington, 1961-67, 70-72, Vietnam, 1968-69, ret., 1972; project mgr. Urban Systems Devel. Corp., Arlington, Va., 1973; regional adminstr. Fed. Energy Adminstrn., Dallas, 1973-77; sr. asso. Planergy Inc., Austin, 1978-79; pres. Fowler/Blum Energy Consultants, Inc., Dallas, 1979—. Mem. energy task force Goals for Dallas, 1976-77; mem. Austin Energy Conservation Commn., 1979. Decorated Legion of Merit, Bronze Star, Air medal. Fed. Exec. fellow Brookings Instn., 1971-72. Registered profl. engr., Tex. Mem. Nat., Tex., Dallas socs. profl. engrs., Am. Soc. Mil. Engrs., Soc. Energy Engrs., ASHRAE, Illuminating Engring. Soc., Internat. Platform Assn. Presbyterian. Author articles, papers. Home: 5708 Willow Ln Dallas TX 75230 Office: 1015 Elm St at Griffin Dallas TX 75202

FOWLER, EUGENE FRANKLIN, JR., physicist; b. Denton, Tex., Dec. 21, 1934; s. Eugene Franklin and Carrie Faye (Sample) F.; B.S. in Physics, N. Tex. State U., 1961, M.S. in Physics, 1963; m. Anita Kay Curry, June 8, 1963; children—Liesl, Julie. Mem. tech. staff Tex. Instruments, Inc., Dallas, 1962-72, project mgr., 1972-74, program mgr., 1974—; cons. in field. Served with USN, 1954-58. Licensed amateur radio operator. Mem. Am. Phys. Soc., IEEE, Naval Res. Assn., Kappa Mu Epsilon. Methodist. Home: 721 Northill Dr Richardson TX 75080 Office: PO Box 225474 Dallas TX 75265

FOWLER, HARDY BOOTH, engring. cons.; b. Waxahachie, Tex., Oct. 17, 1920; s. Homer Jasper and Zeta (Booth) Fowler; student Rice U., 1938-40; B.S. in Engring., U.S. Naval Acad., 1943; postgrad. N.Y. U., 1947-48; m. Frances Elizabeth Woolf, July 31, 1943; children—Elizabeth, Cynthia, Cristine, Hardy. With Alcoa Steamship Co., N.Y.C., 1946-48, Aluminum Co. of Am., Point Comfort, Tex., 1949, W. Horace Williams Co., New Orleans, 1950-56, H.B. Flowler & Co., Inc., Harvey, La., 1956-72; engring. cons., New Orleans, 1972—. Mem. La. Engring. Soc., Engrs. Joint Council. Democrat. Episcopalian. Clubs: La., Boston, New Orleans Country. Address: 5935 Coliseum St New Orleans LA 70115

FOWLER, JACK ROGERS, univ. ofcl.; b. Harrisville, W.Va., May 21, 1939; s. Glenn A. and Virginia R. Fowler; A.A., Allan Handcock Jr. Coll., 1962; B.S.B.A., W.Va. U., 1965, M. Indsl. Relations, 1975; m. Betty Cozad, Apr. 25, 1964; 1 dau., Joyce Lynn. Systems analyst Consol. Gas Supply Corp., Clarksburg, W.Va., 1965-67; systems analyst-programmer, extension specialist mgmt. info. W.Va. U., Morgantown, 1967-69, program leader mgmt. services, 1969—. Served with USAF, 1958-62. Mem. Nat. Assn. Collegiate Vets. (nat. pres. 1968-69), Data Processing Mgmt. Assn., W.Va. Planning Assn., W.Va. U. Alumni Assn., Am. Legion, Theta Chi Alumni. Methodist. Club: Masons. Office: West Virginia University Center for Extension and Continuing Edn 806 Knapp Hall Morgantown WV 26505

FOWLER, JAMES ALEXANDER, lawyer; b. Chgo., May 14, 1944; s. James Albert and Helen Harriet (Renard) F.; A.B., U. Ill., 1966; J.D., U. Fla., 1969; postgrad. in bus. adminstrn. U. Central Fla., 1973-76; m. Barbara J. Shirek, Jan. 24, 1970; Admitted to Fla. bar, 1970, Ill. bar, 1970; asst. city atty. City of Orlando, Fla., 1972-75; mng. partner Fowler Williams & Airth, P.A., Orlando, Fla., 1976—; city atty. City of Edgewood (Fla.), 1977—, City of Altamonte Springs (Fla.), 1979—; speaker U. Fla. Law Sch. Vice pres. East Central Fla. Regional Planning Council, 1976-77, mem., 1974—; gen. chmn. Bob Carr Mcpl. Auditorium Com., 1978; mem. Nat. Trust for Historic Preservation, 1969—. Served to capt. intelligence U.S. Army, 1970-72. Mem. Fla. Bar, Ill. Bar, Chgo. Bar Assn., Orange County Bar Assn. (mem. exec. council), Am. Bar Assn., Pi Kappa Phi, Phi Delta Phi. Republican. Roman Catholic. Kiwanian. Home: 502 Palmer St Orlando FL 32802 Office: 28 E Central PO Box 1215 Orlando FL 32802

FOWLER, PHILIP DEILY, III, mfg. co. exec.; b. Abington, Pa., June 24, 1947; s. Philip Deily and Elizabeth (Gordon) F.; B.S. in Mktg. and Mgmt., Susquehanna U., 1969; m. Teresa Carol Swain, Sept. 8, 1973. Gen. mgr. Blue Water Marina Inc., Ocean City, N.J., 1969-72; sales mgr. AMF Hatteras Yachts, New Bern, N.C., 1972-77, dir. sales, 1978—; guest lectr. mktg. and sales Craven Community Coll., New Bern, 1975—. Republican. Presbyterian. Club: Tryon Lions. Office: 2100 Kivett Dr High Point NC 27260

FOWLER, STEWART HAMPTON, agrl. scientist, research adminstr.; b. St. Paul, July 20, 1922; s. Talbert Bass and Doris Ernestine (Blitch) F.; B.S.A. with honors, U. Fla., 1947; M.S., Auburn U., 1950; Ph.D., Tex. A&M U., 1954; m. Rachel Ann Summerford, Mar. 18, 1950; children—Stewart Hampton, James, Amy Margaret. Livestock buyer Lykes Bros., Tampa, Fla., 1947; instr. in animal sci. Auburn U., 1948-51; instr. Tex. A&M U., 1951-54; asst. prof. animal husbandry U. Md., 1954-55; asso. prof. animal sci. Wash. State U., 1955-58; prof. animal sci. La. State U., 1958-69; prof., head dept. animal sci. Miss. State U., 1969-72; resident dir. research Tex. A&M Agrl. Research and Extension Center, Uvalde, 1972—. Tribal chief Longhouse office and nation chief La. YMCA Indian Guide Program, Baton Rouge, 1962-66. Served to lt. comdr. USN, 1942-46. Recipient Outstanding Teaching award La. State U. chpt. Gamma Sigma Delta, 1962. Fellow AAAS; mem. Am. Soc. Animal Sci. (Disting. Tchr. award 1970), Soc. Range Mgmt., Am. Forage and Grassland Council, Devon Cattle Assn. (exec. sec.), Am. Breed Assn. (sr. dir. and breed adv.), Sigma Xi, Alpha Zeta, Phi Kappa Phi. Methodist. Author: The Marketing of Livestock and Meat, 1957, rev. edit., 1961; Beef Production in the South, 1969, rev. edit., 1979; contbr. numerous articles to tech. and popular agrl. jours. Home: PO Drawer 628 Uvalde TX 78801 Office: PO Drawer 1051 Uvalde TX 78801

FOWLER, WATSON RODNEY, psychologist, educator; b. Lock Haven, Pa., Jan. 30, 1938; s. Watson Francis and Margaret Elizabeth (Douglass) F.; B.S., Lock Haven State U., 1965; M.A. (fellow), Calif. State U. at San Diego, 1968; Ed.D. (fellow), Ball State U., 1974; children—Travis Lindley-Park, Margaret Alyse, Shannon Marie. Exec. dir. Correctional Psychological Assoc., Inc., Muncie, Ind., 1973-76; police psychologist Del. County Police, Muncie, 1973-76; asst. prof. psychology Ball State U., Germany, Eng., Greece, Spain, 1974-76; asso. prof. counselor edn. U. Tenn., Chattanooga, 1976—; cons. Tenn. Hwy. Patrol Tactical Team, Chattanooga Police SWAT Team, Cleveland (Tenn.) SWAT Team, others, also Ind. State Police, Muncie Police, Red Bank Police Tactical Services Unit, Cambridge Home, Ind. Women's Prison, Weathers Med. Corp., Parkridge Hosp., Hamilton County Police, Chattanooga; exec. dir. Green River Crime Council, Ky., 1969-71. Served with U.S. Army, 1957-59. Named to outstanding journalist chair Lock Haven State Coll., 1963, 64; named Ky. col. Fellow Am. Acad. Crisis Interveners; mem. Am. Assn. Sex Educators, Counselors, Therapists, Am. Personnel and Guidance Assn., Assn. Counselor Educators and Supervisors, Am. Assn. Correctional Psychologists, Assn. for Specialists in Group Work, Ind. Assn. Profl. Police Officers, Tenn. Psychological Assn., Tenn. Assn. Personnel and Guidance Workers, Lookout Mt. Personnel and Guidance Assn. Clubs: Black Dragon Fighting Soc., Imua Kwan Tao Kai Karate Soc. Sho-dan (1st Black Belt) Kodakan Judo, 1966, Kwan-Tao Kai Karate, 1968, Hapkido, 1968. Home: 3428 Betty Ln Chattanooga TN 37412 Office: U of Tenn Chattanooga TN 37401

FOWLER, WILLIAM FREDERICK, coll. adminstr.; b. Turnersville, Tex., Apr. 23, 1923; s. Oscar Leonard and Letha Leona (Touchstone) F.; B.A., Baylor U., 1950, M.A., 1951; M.S., E. Tex. State U., 1977; m. Sheryl Stalcup, Mar. 11, 1974. Tech. writer Gen. Dynamics, 1951-53; ordained minister Baptist Ch., 1949; pastor ch. Ft. Worth, 1953-59, Granbury, Tex., 1959-63, Brownwood, Tex., 1963-73; asso. prof. media Tarrant County Jr. Coll., Ft. Worth, 1975-77; dir. media services Cedar Valley Coll., Lancaster, Tex., 1977-78; dir. coop. edn. Mountain View Coll., Dallas, 1978—. Served with USAAF, 1942-46. Mem. Assn. for Edn. and Communication Tech., Tex. Assn. for Ednl. Tech., Tex. Jr. Coll. Tchrs. Assn., Tex. Coop. Edn. Assn. Baptist. Home: 3005 Scott Mill Carrollton TX 75006 Office: 4849 W Illinois Ave Dallas TX 75211

FOWLER, WILLIAM WYCHE, JR., congressman; b. Atlanta, Oct. 6, 1940; s. William Wyche and Emelyn (Barbre) F.; B.A., Davidson Coll., 1962; J.D., Emory U., 1969; 1 dau., Katherine Wyche. Chief asst. to Congressman Charles Weltner, 1965; admitted to Ga. bar, 1970; asso. firm Smith Cohen Ringel Kohler & Martin, Atlanta. mem. Atlanta Bd. Aldermen, 1969-73; pres. Atlanta City Council, 1974-77; mem. 95th-96th Congresses from 5th Dist. Ga. Served with U.S. Army. Recipient Myrtle Wreath award, 1972; named Outstanding Young Man, Atlanta Jr. C. of C., 1972, Ga. Jr. C. of C., 1973. Mem. State Bar Ga. Democrat. Home: 894 Dean Dr NW Atlanta GA 30318 Office: 1504 Longworth House Office Bldg Washington DC 20515

FOWLKES, DOUGLAS LINCOLN (BUDDY), city ofcl. Atlanta; b. Cin., Jan. 18, 1928; s. Claude Leo and Faith (Robinett) F.; B.S. in Indsl. Mgmt., Ga. Inst. Tech., 1952. Alderman, City of Atlanta, 1962-73, councilman, 1974—. Asst. prof. Ga. Inst. Tech., 1966—. Mem. Atlanta Stadium Authority, 1966-74; mem. Ga. Gov.'s Council Phys. Fitness; bd. dirs. Northside Youth Orgn.; trustee Cyclorma Restoration, Inc. Mem. Ga. Tech. Athletic Hall of Fame. Democrat. Episcopalian. Home: 100 Biscayne Dr NW Atlanta GA 30309 Office: 190 3d St Atlanta GA 30332

FOWLKES, WINFORD (W.C.) CALVIN, bank exec.; b. Madison, N.C., Nov. 1, 1948; s. Calvin Lee and Doris (Hylton) F.; A.A., Middle Ga. Coll., 1972; B.S. Va. Commonwealth U., 1974; postgrad. Sch. Mortgage Banking and Real Estate, Northwestern U., 1978. Mortgage Loan rep. Piedmont Trust Bank, Martinsville, Va., 1974-76, mortgage loan supr., 1976-77, asst. mortgage loan officer, 1977-79, mortgage mktg. officer, 1979—; v.p. Lincoln Savs. & Loan Assn., Richmond, Va., 1979; lectr. Martinsville-Henry County Bd. Realtors, Va. Commonwealth U. Served with USAF, 1968-72. Mem. Va. Mortgage Bankers Assn., Martinsville-Henry County Bd. Realtors (asso.), Martinsville-Henry County Homebuilders Assn. (asso., exec. v.p. 1980), Soc. Real Estate Appraisers, Nat. Assn. Rev. Appraisers, U.S. Jaycees, Martinsville Jaycees (dir.), Rho Epsilon, Kappa Sigma. Home: 1404 Spruce St Martinsville VA 24112 Office: Piedmont Trust Bank Ellsworth St Martinsville VA 24112

FOX, DEL FRANKLIN, vocat. counselor; b. Hartford, Conn., Oct. 11, 1923; d. Marcus Irving and Lee (Olshan) Franklin; B.A., N.Y. U., 1944; M.A., U. South Fla., 1968; m. Mark Edward Fox, Jan. 14, 1951; children—Andrew Eric, Steven Alan. Copywriter, Sta. WSRR, Stamford, Conn., 1945-48; pub. relations staff Sidney Ascher and Assos., N.Y.C., 1949-51; feature writer Fla. Times Union, Jacksonville, 1952-59, Sarasota (Fla.) Mag., 1960-68; adult guidance counselor Sarasota County Vocat.-Tech. Center, 1968—; broadcaster Sta. WSPB, 1969—. Mem. Sarasota-Manatee Bi-County Commn. on Status of Women, 1975—, Fla. Gov.'s Commn. Status of Women, 1978-82; dir. Women's Center of Sarasota, Inc., 1979. Mem. Am. Personnel and Guidance Assn., Am. Vocat. Assn., Nat. League Am. Pen Women, Delta Kappa Gamma. Club: Univ. (Sarasota). Home: 4634 Higel Ave Sarasota FL 33581 Office: 4748 Beneva Rd Sarasota FL 33581

FOX, DONALD FRED, retail grocery owner; b. Wellington, Tex., June 11, 1945; s. Donald Frank and Melba Jean (Crowley) F.; student public schs., Oklahoma City; m. Audria Louise Shackleford, July 27, 1961; children—Stephen Gregory, Kelly Renee, Charla Kay. Stocker, Big Giant Super Market, Oklahoma City, 1961-63, Pic Pac Market, Memphis, 1963-65, Humpty Dumpty Supermarkets, 1965-67; collection asst. Century Finance, 1967-68; asst. dist. mgr. Daily Oklahoman, Oklahoma City, 1968; bookkeeper Big Giant-Big Green Supermarkets, Oklahoma City, 1968-71; mgr. Elmore Food Center, Elmore City, Okla., 1971-74, owner, 1974—; owner, mgr. Elmore Lumber Trade Center, Elmore City, 1977—. Chmn. Elmore City Park Bd., 1977—; local committeeman Boy Scouts Am., 1974—, dist. chmn., 1977—, mem. exec. bd. Arbuckle council, 1977—. Mem. Nat. Retail Grocers Assn., Food Mktg. Inst., Nat. Rifle Assn., Nat. Right to Work Com., Okla. Retail Grocers Assn., Okla. Lumberman's Assn., Okla. Jr. C. of C. (dist. dir. 1978), Elmore City Jr. C. of C. (pres. 1978, dir. 1979). Independent Republican. Baptist. Home and Office: PO Box 396 Elmore City OK 73035

FOX, EDWARD MICHAEL, mag. advt. sales exec.; b. Dallas, Feb. 2, 1924; s. Francis Marion and Almirah Boyce (Quinn) F.; B.A., Drake U., 1948; B.B.A., U. Tex., 1950; m. Alyce Jane Carlson, Aug. 5, 1945; children—Edward Quinn, Emily Thatcher. Asst. mgr. engring. personnel Convair Div. Gen. Dynamics Corp., Ft. Worth, 1950-52; asst. sales mgr. retail display equipment C.E. Erickson Co., Des Moines, 1953; with Meredith Corp., Dallas, 1953—, sales mgr., Chgo., 1961-75, SW mgr. advt. sales Better Homes & Gardens, 1975—; pres. Agate Club, Chgo., 1973; chmn. MPA Mktg. Com., Chgo., 1972-73. Served to comdr. USNR, 1942-45. Mem. Western Advt. Golfing Assn. (Chgo.), Navy League (Dallas), Naval Res. Assn., Retired Officers Assn., Tex. Ex-Student Assn. Republican. Episcopalian. Clubs: Tavern (Chgo.), Exmoor Country (Highland Park, Ill.), Prestonwood Country (Dallas), Lancers (Dallas), Masons. Office: 13101 Preston Rd Suite 210 Dallas TX 75240

FOX, ELLIOT MILTON, cons.; b. Deer Lodge, Mont., Aug. 30, 1920; s. Charles Adin and Beulah (Churchill) F.; A.B., Washington U., St. Louis, 1942; M.A., Columbia, 1954, Ph.D., 1970; m. Byrdann Sachs, Mar. 8, 1943; children—John, Catherine, James, Jeffrey. Investigator, Personnel Survey Bur., N.Y.C., 1950-53; lectr. govt. City Coll. N.Y., 1953-56; tng. coordinator, mgmt. and supervisory devel. Union Carbide Corp., Linde div., 1956-69; asso. dir. industry mgmt. services Am. Gas Assn., Arlington, Va., 1969-79; ind. cons., 1979—. Chmn. Stevenson-Kefauver com., Astoria, N.Y., 1956; Democratic candidate for town supr., Cortlandt, N.Y., 1963; pres. Wessynton Homes Assn., 1978. Mem. Internat. Transactional Analysis Assn., Assn. Humanistic Psychology, Am. Soc. Tng. and Devel., World Future Soc. Methodist (ofcl. bd. 1966-68). Co-editor: Dynamic Administration—The Collected Works of Mary Parker Follett, 1973. Home: 3404 Wessynton Way Alexandria VA 22309

FOX, HEWITT BATES, petroleum geologist; b. Chattanooga, Oct. 24, 1922; s. Frederick Hewitt and Lorena Grace (Bates) F.; student Tulane U., 1940-41, U. Pitts., 1943-44; B.A., U. Tex., 1947, B.S., 1948, M.A., 1948; m. Margaret Alleen Standifer, May 7, 1949; children—Frederick Hewitt, Douglas Standifer. Job analyst Atlantic Richfield Co., Dallas, 1948-51, sr. geologist, La. and Tex., 1951-56; owner, pres. Hewitt B. Fox, Inc., Corpus Christi, Tex., 1956—, Zorro Oilfield Service Corp., Corpus Christi, 1956—. Ruling elder, Grace Presbyterian Ch. Served with U.S. Army, 1943-46. Mem. Am. Assn. Petroleum Geologists, S. Tex., Corpus Christi geol. socs., SAR (past pres. Corpus Christi chpt.), Order of Arrow, Sigma Gamma Epsilon, Delta Tau Delta. Clubs: Petroleum, Carousel, Town, Corpus Christi Country. Home: 233 Cape May St Corpus Christi TX 78412 Office: Suite 900 Guaranty Bank Plaza Corpus Christi TX 78475

FOX, JOHN BRUCE, city ofcl.; b. Cleve., Oct. 25, 1941; s. John B. and Ruth Thelma (Frederick) F.; B.A., San Fernando State Coll., 1971; M.P.A. (EPA scholar), W.Va. U., 1975; m. Martha Lilia Mondragon, Mar. 20, 1975; 1 son, John Bruce. With Douglas Aircraft Corp., Santa Monica, Calif., 1965-70; sanitarian Wood County-Parkersburg Health Dept., W.Va., 1972-74; mgr. Princeton (W.Va.) Sanitary Bd., 1975-80; supt. San. Bd., Weirton, W.Va.,

1980—. Pres., United Fund of Princeton-Athens, W.Va., 1979—, asst. co-chmn. campaign dr., 1977-78, chmn. campaign dr., 1978-79, pres. of fund, 1979-80. Served with USAF, 1959-63. Mem. Princeton Jr. C. of C. (dir. 1977), Am. Legion, Nat. Water Pollution Control Fedn., Waste Water Operators Assn. Methodist. Contbr. articles to profl. jours. Home: 140 Lynnwood Manor Weirton WV 26062 Office: PO Box 707 Princeton WV 24740

FOX, JOSEPH CHARLES, JR., lobbyist co. exec.; b. Newark, Aug. 7, 1922; s. Joseph Charles and Delia Briget (Cafferty) F.; B.S., U.S. Mcht. Marine Acad., 1944; B.S., Temple U., 1960; m. Elinore Marie James, Dec. 17, 1944; 1 son, Douglas Allan. Commd. lt. (j.g.) U.S. Coast Guard, 1950, advanced through grades to capt., 1969; stationed Chgo., Wilmington, N.C. and Charleston, S.C.; comdr. sea cutters McCullough, Ingram, Bramble, and Woodbine, ret., 1975; exec. dir. Wilmington Indsl. Devel. Inc. (N.C.), 1975—, Am. Maritime Officers Service, Washington, 1978—. chmn. bd. commrs. nav. and pilotage, Wilmington. Bd. govs. Nat. Maritime Council. Mem. Democrat. Roman Catholic. Clubs: Cape Fear, Cape Fear Country, U.S. Propeller, Washington Army-Navy, Capital Yacht. Home: 1921 S Churchill Dr Wilmington NC 28403 Office: Am Maritime Officers Service 456 N St SW Washington DC 20024

FOX, MARK, accountant; b. N.Y.C., Apr. 28, 1923; s. Abraham and Rose (Rosenbaum) F.; B.B.A., Coll. City N.Y., 1943; m. Del Franklin, Jan. 14, 1951; children—Andrew Eric, Steven Alan. Sr. accountant Samuel Fischman & Co., C.P.A.'s, 1948-51; mgr., supr. J.K. Lasser & Co., C.P.A.'s, 1951-59; gen. practice pub. accounting, tax cons., mgmt. cons., Sarasota, Fla., 1959—. Served with AUS, 1943-46. Mem. Am., Fla. insts. C.P.A.'s, N.Y. State Soc. C.P.A.'s. Mason (32 deg. Shriner), Elk. Club: University. Home: 4634 Higel Ave Sarasota FL 33581 Office: Suite 909 Sarasota Bank Bldg 1605 Main St Sarasota FL 33577

FOX, MILTON ERNEST, state legislator Tex.; b. Tulsa, July 28, 1926; s. Stanley S. and Florence K. (Stephens) F.; B.S., U. Tex., 1946; m. Ruth Huffmaster, Aug. 1, 1947; children—Bryan, Marty, Helen, Susan, Clayton. With Carter Oil Co., 1946-59, Tenneco, 1959-70, Ryder-Scott Co., 1970-72; mem. Tex. Ho. of Reps. from 93d Dist., 1972—, vice chmn. energy resources com., 1975—. Mem. Lafayette (La.) Parish Sch. Bd., 1964-67. Registered profl. engr., Tex. Mem. Soc. Petroleum Engrs. Republican. Presbyterian. Home: 13510 Pinerock St Houston TX 77079 Office: Box 2910 Austin TX 78769

FOX, NELSON MOFFETT, JR., surgeon; b. Richmond, Va., June 30, 1930; s. Nelson Moffett and Matilda Ann (Drummond) F.; B.S., Hampden-Sydney Coll., 1951; M.D., Med. Coll. Va., 1955; M.S., U. Minn., 1967; m. Roxie Ann Cook, July 30, 1955; children—Judy Gray, Nelson Moffett, Ellen Anne, Mary Katheryn. Intern, Stuart Circle Hosp., Richmond, Va., 1955-56; fellow Mayo Grad. Sch., Rochester, Minn., 1959-63; pvt. practice surgery, Martinsville, Va., 1963—; cons. R.J. Reynolds Patrick Co. Hosp., 1963-76. Served with M.C., USAF, 1956-58. Diplomate Am. Bd. Surgery. Fellow A.C.S.; mem. Va. Surg. Soc., Med. Soc. Va., AMA, Priestley Soc., Continental Surg. Club, So. Med. Assn., Tau Kappa Alpha, Omicron Delta Kappa. Mem. Christian Ch. (Disciples of Christ). Home: 1227 Sam Lions Trail Martinsville VA 24112 Office: Medical Center Suite 206 Hospital Dr Martinsville VA 24112

FOX, OTIS OTTO, JR., geologist, oil co. exec.; b. Indianola, Okla., Feb. 9, 1934; s. Otis Otto and Foy Morton (Ross) F.; B.S. in Geology, U. Okla., 1956; postgrad. (Fulbright scholar), U. Freiburg, W. Ger., 1956-57; m. Nancy Murl Duncan, June 6, 1959; children—Otto, Duncan, Melanie. Petroleum geologist Exxon USA, Ft. Smith, Ark., 1960-62, Oklahoma City, 1962-63, Amarillo, Tex., 1963-64; geologist Esso Libya, Benghazi and Tripoli, Libya, 1964-69, geologic ops. mgr. Esso Exploration, Singapore, 1969-76, hdqrs. geol. advisor for Europe and Africa, Houston, 1976—. Served with USN, 1957-60. Mem. Am. Assn. Petroleum Geologists, Soc. Profl. Well Log Analysts, Southeast Asia Petroleum Exploration Soc. Presbyterian. Home: 14919 Carolcrest St Houston TX 77079 Office: 12727 Kimberly St Houston TX 77024

FOX, PAUL JOHN, chiropractic physician; b. Miami, Fla., Aug. 22, 1945; s. Paul John and Bertie Lee (Seiger) F.; student U. Tampa, 1964; D.Chiropractic, Palmer Coll. Chiropractic, 1968; m. Patricia Ann Tudor, Dec. 23, 1966; children—Paul Jason, Debra Ann, John Matthew, Tricia Ann, Jared Keith. Pres. Paul J. Fox chiropractic practice, Miami, 1970—; pres., chmn. bd. Pain Correction Clinic, Inc., 1972—; owner Backachers Farm, Gainesville, Fla. Vice pres. Children's Chiropractic Clinic of Dade County; mem. Parker Chiropractic Research Found. Recipient Ambassador award Palmer Coll. Chiropractic. Mem. Am., Fla. chiropractic assns., Dade County Chiropractic Soc., South Dade C. of C. Republican. Kiwanian (charter mem. Kendall Club). Home: 5400 NW 143d St Gainesville FL 32601 Office: 720 NW 23d Ave Gainesville FL 32601

FOX, RAYMOND GRAHAM, ednl. technologist; b. Portland, Oreg., May 31, 1923; s. George Raymond and Georgia Dorothy (Beckman) F.; B.S., Rensselaer Poly. Inst., 1943; m. Harriet Carolyn Minchin, Apr. 17, 1948; children—Susan, Christine, Ellen, Laura, John. Salesman IBM Corp., N.Y.C., 1946-48, br. mgr., 1949-56, systems mgr., 1957-65, edn. systems devel. mgr., 1965-76; cons. tech. and industry relations Va. Council for Deaf, Warrenton, Va., 1976-78, mem., 1978—; dir., chmn. tech. devel. com. Learning Tech. Inst., Warrenton, 1975—, dir. tech. programs, 1978—. Mem., Sec. of Navy Adv. Bd. on Edn. and Tng., 1972-77; cons. for tech. Va. Legis. Adv. Com. on Handicapped, 1970; mem. Nat. Def. Exec. Reserve, 1970—. Served with USNR, 1943-46. Mem. Soc. Applied Learning Tech. (pres. 1972—), Nat. Security Indsl. Assn. (chmn. tng. group 1974-76). Episcopalian. Clubs: Army & Navy (Washington); Fauquier, Fauquier Springs Country (Warrenton); Columbia Country (Chevy Chase, Md.). Patentee interactive audio visual instruction device; fixed format instruction delivery system. Home: Reynwood PO Box 376 Warrenton VA 22186 Office: 50 Culpeper St Warrenton VA 22186

FOX, ROBERT ANTHONY, counseling center exec.; b. Mobile, Ala., Oct. 1, 1928; s. William Dorrel and Mattie Miles F.; B.S. in Psychology, U. So. Miss., 1953; M.S.W., Tulane U., 1955; m. Barbara Wiseman, Dec. 3, 1949; 1 dau., Judith Kay Fox Kent. Probation officer U.S. Dist. Ct., Middle dist., Ala., 1956-58; resident dir. Methodist Children's Home, Selma, Ala., 1958-63; exec. dir. Family Counseling Center Mobile, Inc., 1963—. Dist. eye health chmn. Ala. Sight, Inc.; supt. Protestant Children's Home, Mobile, 1967-75; exec. dir. Florence Crittenton Home, Mobile, 1975-76. Served with U.S. Army, 1948-50. Mem. Am. Assn. Marriage and Family Therapists, Nat. Assn. Social Workers, Acad. Cert. Social Workers, Assn. U.S. Army, Res. Officers Assn. U.S. Methodist. Club: Lions. Home: 268 Summit Dr Mobile AL 36609 Office: 6 S Florida St Mobile AL 36606

FOX, THEODORE BERT, educator, city ofcl.; b. Jacksonville, Ala., Oct. 25, 1912; s. Cass and Jennie Magnolia (Taylor) F.; student Selma U., 1929-30, Gen. Motors Inst., 1935-36; certificate Ala. State U., 1954, Allen Electric Co. Sch., 1950, Ala. A. and M. U., 1956; m. Agnes Marshall Watley, Apr. 7, 1933; children—Sydney (Mrs. Eugene Reid, Jr.), June (Mrs. J. Mason Davis), Barbara (Mrs. Franklin Todd), Sandra (Mrs. Thomas Sudduth). Supr., Anniston (Ala.) Army Ordnance Depot, 1940-46; vocational instr. Anniston City Bd. Edn., 1946-80, tchr. Anniston Area Vocational Tech. Sch.; asso. pastor 1st Bapt. Ch.; mem. City Council Jacksonville, 1968—, mayor pro-tem, 1977—; bd. dirs. Ala. Democratic Com., 1970—. Pres. Jacksonville Civic League; bd. dirs. Jacksonville Child Care Center; mem. exec. bd. Choccolocco council Boy Scouts Am.; bd. dirs. Cottaquilla council Girl Scouts U.S. Recipient Silver Beaver award Boy Scouts Am., 1962; Outstanding Citizen award Delta Sigma Theta, 1975; Disting. Service award Ala. Vocat. Assn., Ala. NAACP. Mem. NEA, Anniston Edn. Assn. (pres.), NAACP. Baptist. (pres. Sunday sch., Bapt. tng. Union Congress). Home: 157 Spring St Jacksonville AL 36265 Office: City Hall Jacksonville AL 36265

FOXWORTH, CHARLES LEONARD, educator; b. Silsbee, Tex., Aug. 4, 1932; s. Steve Richardson and Mamie (Hopkins) F.; B.A., E. Tex. Baptist Coll., 1952; M.A., U. of Houston, 1959; Ph.D., La. State U., 1970; m. Lois Mae Hudson, May 31, 1950; children—Judy Clare Foxworth Ray, Charles David. Asst. mgr. Home Office Pay Dept., Am. Nat. Ins., Co., Galveston, Tex., 1953-60; staff data processing Tex. Eastern Transmission Corp., Shreveport, La., 1960-61; instr. history-psychology Roswell (N.Mex.) Sr. High Sch., 1961-64; chmn. Humanities Dept., Eastern N. Mex. U., Roswell, 1964-70; asso. prof., chmn. Secondary Edn., La. Tech. U., Ruston, 1971—, advisory bd. Center for Economic Edn., 1976—, dir. Social Studies Resource Center, 1973—; cons. Southern Assn. Colleges and Schs., La. State Dept. Edn. Recipient Tchr. of Yr. award, Eastern N. Mex. U., 1965, 1969, outstanding educator award, La. Tech. U., 1973-74. Mem. La. Tchrs. Assn., Assn. of Higher Edn., Nat., La., Lincoln Parish councils for social studies, AAUP, La. Philosophy of Edn. Soc., Phi Delta Kappa, Phi Alpha Theta. Democrat. Mem. Emmanuel Baptist Ch. Clubs: Breakfast Sertoma, Lion. Co-author: Louisiana's Story of Public Edn., 1972; Basic Concepts in Secondary Education, 1979; contbr. articles to profl. jours. Home: 2203 Greenbriar St Ruston LA 71270 Office: Coll of Edn La Tech U Ruston LA 71270

FRACE, CHARLES LEWIS, artist; b. Jim Thorpe, Pa., Feb. 18, 1926; s. Charles and Eleanor (Bunn) F.; grad. Phila. Coll. Art, 1952; m. Elke Roettger, Nov. 7, 1964; children—Jeffrey, Roger. One man shows include: Wedel (W. Ger.) Gallery, 1977, Cumberland Mus. and Sci. Center, Nashville, 1978; exhibited in group shows: Mzuri Safari Found. Conf., San Francisco, 1976, Woodson Art Mus., Wausau, Wis., 1977, Phila. Wildfowl Exhbn., 1979. Mem. Nat. Wildlife Fedn., Nat. Audubon Soc., Nat. Humane Soc., Nat. Platform Assn., Soc. Animal Artists, World Wildlife Fund, Mzuri Sarari Found., Game Conservation Internat., Holy Land Conservation Fund. Presbyterian. Club: Maryland Farms Racquet and Country. Illustrator books for Am. Heritage, McGraw Hill, Reader's Digest, Doubleday; recipient Christopher award for illustrations for The Wolf, 1973.

FRACKER, ROBERT GRANGER, librarian; b. Spout Spring, Va., Sept. 29, 1928; s. Dudley Granger and Ruby Walker (Page) F.; student Va. Poly. Inst. and State U., 1946-49, Ronaoke Coll., 1948; B.S., E. Tenn. State U., 1954; M.A., Appalachian State U., 1957; postgrad U. Ill., 1957-59, Duke U., 1962-65, U. N.C., Chapel Hill, 1977, N.C. Central U., 1978; m. Sandra Elizabeth Snyder, June 5, 1965; 1 dau., Mary Susan. Coach, tchr. English, social studies Beaver Creek High Sch., West Jefferson, N.C., 1954-56; counselor Univ. Council on Tchr. Edn., U. Ill., Urbana, 1957-59; mem. faculty Meredith Coll., Raleigh, N.C., 1962—, reference librarian, media coordinator Carlyle Campbell Library, 1977—. Campus chmn. United Way of Wake County, 1976. Served with U.S. Army, 1951-53. Mem. N.C. Assn. Tchr. Educators (pres. 1975-76), Internat. Phenomenological Soc., Assn. Tchr. Edn., Philosophy of Edn. Soc., Am. Soc. Mil. Insignia Collectors, Kami Kaze, Kappa Komma Kappa, Kappa Delta Pi, Phi Delta Kappa, Order Silver Sunset. Democrat. Presbyterian. Home: 307 Oak Ridge Rd Cary NC 27511 Office: Carlyle Campbell Library Meredith Coll Raleigh NC 27611

FRALICK, LAWRENCE ELDON, elec. engr.; b. Marion, Ky., Aug. 31, 1930; s. Walter Kilman and Etta Belle (Lamb) F.; Elec. Engr., U. Ala., 1963; m. Ida Belle Hamilton, Dec. 16, 1952; 1 dau., Carolyn Renee. Engring. technician U.S. Army Missile Command Metrology and Calibration Center, Redstone Arsenal, Ala., 1953-58, supervisory engring. technician, 1958-63, supervisory gen. engr., 1963-68, chief elec. engring., 1968—. Ala. communications route mgr., Madison County radio officer Ala. CD Served in Signal Corps, U.S. Army, 1951-53; Korea. Recipient pub. service certificates Am. Radio Relay League. Mem. AAAS, Assn. U.S. Army, Quarter Century Wireless Assn. (sec.-treas. Tenn. Valley chpt.), Instrument Soc. Am., Am. Radio Relay League. Methodist. Clubs: Huntsville Amateur Radio, Masons. Home: 802 Noland Blvd N Madison AL 35758 Office: US Army Metrology and Calibration Center Redstone Arsenal AL 35809

FRALIN, JANE LEE, counselor; b. Roanoke, Va., July 24, 1947; d. Riley Thomas and Pearl Evelyn (Meador) F.; B.S., Radford Coll., 1968; M.A. in Liberal Studies, Hollins Coll., 1972. Tchr., Cave Spring Elementary Sch., Roanoke, Va., 1968-71; tchr. Hardy Rd. Elementary Sch., Vinton, Va, 1972-75, counselor, 1975—. Tchr. Sunday sch., chmn. bd. Christian edn., pres. ch. circle, chmn. fin. bd., ch. bd., dir. children's dept. Ch. of the Brethren. Mem. Ronaoke Area, Va., Am. personnel and guidance assns., Va., Dist. guidance counselors assns., Am., Va. sch. counselors assns., NEA, Va., Roanoke County edn. assns., Nat., Va. PTA's, Beta Sigma Phi. Home: RFD 7 Box 76 Ran Lynn Dr SW Roanoke VA 24018 Office: 1200 Hardy Rd Vinton VA 24179

FRAME, CHRISTOPHER KRESS, oil jobbing co. exec., Realtor; b. Savannah, Ga., Mar. 16, 1944; s. Charles Wesley and Rosalind Kress (Haley) F.; student Armstrong State Coll.; B.A., U. Dallas, 1968; m. Rosemary Gastring, May 25, 1968; children—Christopher Kress, Catherine Alexandra Bennett. Realtor, Frame Co., Ridgeland, S.C., other locations S.C. and Ga., 1972—; pres. Yellow Cab Co. Inc., Savannah, 1975-79; pres. Wes Frame Inc., Ridgeland, 1968—. Sec., Jasper County Bd. Realtors, 1978. Mem. Jasper County C. of C. (pres. 1973-74), Ridgeland Bus. Assn. (treas. 1971-72), S.C. Oil Jobbers Assn., Airline Owners and Pilots Assn. Roman Catholic. Clubs: Masons, Civitan of Savannah, Oglethorpe of Savannah. Office: Wes Frame Inc PO Box 819 Ridgeland SC 29936

FRAMIL, ARMANDO RAMON, community counselor; b. Havana, Cuba, Aug. 12, 1948; s. Armando and Maria Araceli (Fernandez) F.; came to U.S., 1960, naturalized, 1976; B.A., Fla. Atlantic U., 1972; M.Ed., U. Miami, (Fla.), 1977; m. Maria Del Carmen Rodriguez, May 12, 1977. Youth counselor I, then II, Office Youth Services, Fla. State Dept. Health and Rehab. Services, 1973-77; youth caseworker III, Miami Police Dept., 1977-79, police social programs specialist, 1979—; cons. in field, 1974—; bd. dirs. Dade County Youth Adv. Bd., 1979; mem. Dade County Latin Substance Abuse Task Force, 1976, Drug Abuse Trust Fund, 1977-78. Mem. Spanish Am. League Against Discrimination, Juvenile Officers Assn. (dir. 1975-79), Nat. Assn. Social Workers, Am. Personnel and Guidance Assn., Public Offender Counselor Assn. Home: 45 SW 28th Rd Miami FL 33129 Office: 400 NW 2d Ave Miami FL 33128

FRANCIS, DONALD LEE, hosp. adminstr.; b. Eau Claire, Wis., Aug. 10, 1933; s. Daniel Herbert and Thelma Gertrude (Begley) F.; B.A., Coll. St. Thomas, 1955; M.H.A., Ga. State U., 1969; m. Joanne Virginia Ryder, May 25, 1957; children—Casey Patrick, Kelly Jane, Christopher Joseph, Constance Joanne, Kevin Donald. Mgr. prodn. and inventory control Honeywell Inc., St. Petersburg, Fla., 1959-65; indsl. engr. Lockheed-Ga., Marietta, 1965-68; adminstrv. resident Grady Meml. Hosp., Atlanta, 1968-69; asst. adminstr. N.E. Ga. Med. Center, Gainesville, 1969-72; exec. dir. Cole Hosp., Champaign, Ill., 1972-74; adminstr. Caldwell (Idaho) Meml. Hosp., 1974-79, sec. bd. trustees, 1975-79; adminstr. Pasadena (Tex.) Bayshore Hosp., 1979—. Mem. ednl. adv. com. Vallivue High Sch., Caldwell, 1976-; pres. St. Mary's Parish Council. Served to capt. USAF, 1956-59. Certified health facilities reviewer, Idaho. Mem. Am. Coll. Hosp. Adminstrs., Idaho Hosp. Assn. (pres. elect 1977-78), Fedn. Am. Hosps., Am. Mgmt. Assn., Assn. Univ. Programs in Health Adminstrn., Caldwell C. of C., Beta Gamma Sigma. Roman Catholic. Clubs: Rotary (Caldwell). Home: 16002 Clearcrest Dr Houston TX 77059 Office: Pasadena Bayshore Hosp 4000 Spencer Way Pasadena TX 77504

FRANCIS, JANET BOTTS, educator; b. Roanoke, Va., Oct. 18, 1906; d. James Berrey and Janet (Hilleary) Botts; B.A., Converse Coll., 1928; M.Ed., U. Va., 1959; postgrad. U. N.C., 1963—; m. Hansford Payne Francis, Dec. 26, 1933; children—Janet Hilleary (Mrs. Robert Hinton Crittenden), Ann Tilghman (Mrs. William Fredrick Bobzien III), Hansford. Tchr., Roanoke (Va.) Pub. Schs., 1928-33; propr. Knitting & Gift Shop, Roanoke, 1929-35; reporter, soc. editor Roanoke Times, 1942-44; tchr., counselor Lee Jr. High Sch., Roanoke, 1952-61; coordinator of guidance Jefferson Sr. High Sch., Roanoke, 1961-62; guidance dir., counselor Eastern High Sch., Mebane, N.C., 1962-66; counselor Durham (N.C.) High Sch., 1966-72; cons. area health edn. program U. N.C. Sch. Medicine, Chapel Hill, 1972-76. Pres., Jr. League of Roanoke, 1942-43; dir. Family Service Assn, Roanoke, 1942, Children's Home Soc., 1942-43; mem. Roanoke Assembly, 1928—. Recipient Freedoms Found. Tchrs. Medals; Gen. Electric fellow in guidance, 1966. Mem. NEA, N.C., Durham City assns. educators, Am., N.C. (rep. Triangle chpt.) personnel and guidance assns., Mental Health Assn., Nat., N.C. (pres.) vocat. guidance assns., Am. Sch. Counselor Assn., Assn. Coll. Admissions Counselors, Am., N.C. assns. women deans and counselors, AAUW, Kappa Delta Pi (life), Delta Kappa Gamma. Democrat. Episcopalian. Research to establish counselor scale for the Strong Vocational Interest blank 1968 women's form. Home: 505 Dogwood Dr Chapel Hill NC 27514

FRANCIS, KENNON THOMPSON, physiologist, biochemist; b. Camp Lejeune, N.C., July 8, 1945; s. James Ballard and Dorothy Elisabeth (Thompson) F.; B.S., Auburn U., 1967, M.S., 1969, Ph.D., 1972; m. Sheryl East Francis, Dec. 29, 1966; children—Connie Jill, Wendy Kay. Asst. prof. Troy State U., Montgomery, Ala., 1973-74; asso. prof. physiology phys. therapy div. Sch. Community and Allied Health U. Ala., Birmingham, 1974—; mem. nat. adv. com. Ph.D. program phys. therapy U. Calif., 1977. Served with AUS, 1970-72. Recipient grants U. Ala., 1975, 76, 77, 80, Linn Henley Charitable Trust, 1977, Med. Rehab. Research and Tng., 1977, 78, 79. Mem. Am. Physiol. Soc., Am. Coll. Sports Medicine, Am. Soc. Phys. and Exptl. Therapeutics, Sixma Xi, Alpha Eta, Gamma Sigma Delta, Pi Kappa Phi. Baptist. Contbr. articles to profl. jours. Home: 3851 Orleans Rd Mountain Brook AL 35243 Office: Sch Community and Allied Health U Ala Birmingham AL 35294

FRANCIS, RICARDO HUGH, lawyer; b. San Juan, P.R., July 4, 1935; s. Hugh Richard and Mercedes (Lajara) F.; B.A., Harvard U., 1955, LL.M., 1962; LL.B., U. P.R., 1958; m. Vanessa Vassallo, June 27, 1958; children—Valerie, Hildren. Admitted to P.R. bar; partner firm Francis & Doval, Hato Rey, P.R.; prof. taxation, corp. law and bus. planning U. P.R. Law Sch., 1962—; speaker seminars on taxation and bus. planning; mem., v.p. Revista del Colegio de Abogados de P.R., 1962-64. Mem. Am. Bar Assn. (com. on corps., banking and bus. law), Am. Assn. Trial Lawyers, NAM, Nu Sigma Beta. Clubs: Harvard of P.R. (treas.); San Juan Yacht; Met. Shooting. Home: PH-C Las Carmelitas Condominium San Jorge St Santurce PR 00912 Office: 1900 Popular Center Bldg Hato Rey PR 00918

FRANCIS, RUPERT ASHTON, physician; b. Kingston, Jamaica, Dec. 21, 1940; came to U.S., 1974; s. Cecil Leopold and Loretta Kelsada (Dume) F.; B.S., U. Man. (Can.), 1965; M.B., B.S., U. West Indies, 1973; m. Beverley Anne Thorsteinson, Sept. 18, 1965; 1 son, Paul Ashton. Teaching asst. biochemistry U. Man., Winnipeg, 1965-66; research asst. in microbiology Winnipeg Gen. Hosp., 1966-67; technician (part-time) Govt. Microbiology Lab., Kingston, Jamaica, 1967-73; intern Princess Margaret Hosp., Nassau, Bahamas, 1973-74; resident in family practice Meharry Med. Coll., Nashville, 1974-76; practice medicine specializing in family practice, Nashville, 1977—; asst. prof. div. family medicine Meharry Med. Coll., 1977—, dir. clin. services div. family medicine, 1979—; asso. med. dir. Middle Tenn. Artificial Kidney Center, Nashville, 1979—; med. dir. Dede Wallace Drug Treatment and Rehab. Center, Nashville, 1979—, cons. Dede Wallace Mental Health Center, 1976-79. Diplomate Am. Bd. Family Practice. Fellow Am. Acad. Family Physicians; mem. Nashville Acad. Medicine, R.F. Boyd Med. Soc., Tenn. Med. Assn., Nashville C. of C., NAACP. Home: 130 Morningview Ct Nashville TN 37118 Office: 1110 Buchanan St Nashville TN 37208

FRANCIS, WILBUR MORRIS, engring. co. exec.; b. Springfield, Ill., Mar. 14, 1916; s. George Bratton and Edna Louise (Morris) F.; student, Mo. Sch. of Mines, 1934-35, U. Ill., 1936-37; 1 dau., Peggy Ann. Design and constrn. engr. E.I. DuPont de Nemours & Co., Inc., Wilmington, Del., 1939-44; pres. and plant mgr. Made Rite Filter Co., Litchfield, Ill., 1945-51; partner firm Holmer L. Chastain & Assos., Decatur, Ill., 1951-60; partner Chastain-Francis & Assos., Springfield, 1960-63; engr. City of Speedway, Ind., 1963-65; pres. firm W.M. Francis & Assos., Inc., Mobile, Ala., 1965—, dir. Registered profl. engr., 9 states. Fellow ASCE, Nat. Soc. Profl. Engrs.; mem. ASME. Presbyterian. Clubs: Masons, Shriners. Home: 1816 Murray St Mobile AL 36606

FRANK, DONALD ALBERT, physician; b. Ponca City, Okla., Oct. 22, 1930; s. Edward Thomas and Violet (Benson) F.; M.D., U. Tenn., 1959; m. Martha Ann Smith, Oct. 22, 1957; children—Donald Albert, Brian Carl, Marcus Edward, Kathryn Ann. Intern, Hillcrest Med. Center, Tulsa, 1959-60; gen. practice medicine, Gruver, Tex., 1960-61, Dalhart, Tex., 1961-77; mem. staff Coon Meml. Hosp., 1961-78, chief of staff, 1976-77; resident in psychiatry, asst. instr. Baylor U., Houston, 1972; asst. clin. prof. Texas Tech U., 1975-79; mem. staff St. Anthony's Hosp., High Plains Bapt. Hosp., N.W. Tex. Hosp., Amarillo; flight surgeon FAA, physician Burlington No. R.R.; sch. physician Amarillo public schs. Past warden Episcopal Ch. Served in USAF, 1953-54. Fellow Am. Acad. Family Practice (diplomate); mem. AMA (Physicians Recognition award 1976), Tex. Med. Assn., Amarillo Art Alliance. Republican. Clubs: Masons, Shriners; Dalhart Country; Amarillo. Home: 3512 Edgewood Amarillo TX 79109 Office: 3 Medical Dr Amarillo TX 79106

FRANK, ELLEN SNOW, public broadcaster; b. Brockton, Mass., Oct. 1, 1934; d. George H. and Mary Wilson (Sproul) Snow; B.M.E. cum laude, Fla. State U., 1956, M.Mus., 1957; m. Sam H. Frank, June 3, 1955; 1 dau., Marian Elizabeth. Tchr. music Hawthorne (Fla.) High Sch., 1958-60; singer appearing with Jacksonville Symphony, Opera Co. of Jacksonville, 1967-78; program producer Sta. WJCT-FM,

Jacksonville, 1972-78; interviewer Sta. WJCT-TV, 1974-78. Mem. Nat. Pub. Radio Program Adv. Com., 1977-78; pres. Dels. council Arts Assembly of Jacksonville, 1977—; mem. Civic Music Assn. Bd., 1976-78; pres. Fine Arts Forum, 1969-71; mem. Jacksonville Community Council, 1977-78; bd. dirs. Rapides Symphony, 1979—, Central La. Art Assn., 1979—, Friends of La. Public Broadcasting, 1979—, Assn. La. Arts and Artists, 1979—; mem. community relations com. Rapides Gen. Hosp., 1979—. Nat. Endowment for Humanities grantee, 1977. Mem. Nat. Assn. Ednl. Broadcasters, Central La. Press Assn., Sigma Delta Chi. Democrat. Episcopalian. Home: Route 2 Box 27 Alexandria LA 71301

FRANK, HAROLD GENE, chemist; b. Luling, Tex., Jan. 2, 1941; s. William Oscar and Verlie Marie (Winnett) F.; B.S., S.W. Tex. State U., 1965; children—Sherri Dena, Gene Harlee. Tchr., Van Vleck (Tex.) Ind. Sch., also coach; research chemist Dow Chem. Co., Freeport, Tex., 1966-75; supr. product devel. St. Regis Paper Co., Dallas, 1975-79; tech. service engr. Cities Service Co., 1979—. Mem. Soc. Plastic Engrs. Methodist. Contbr. article to profl. Home: Route 12 Box 302 Lake Charles LA 70605 Office: 3409 W Prien Lake Rd Lake Charles LA 70605

FRANK, HARVEY, lawyer, educator; b. N.Y.C., Aug. 24, 1930; s. Leon and Hannah (Lehr) F.; B.A., N.Y. U., 1951; J.D., Harvard, 1954; LL.M., N.Y. U., 1961; m. Judith Ellen Lewis, Nov. 29, 1959; 1 son, David Lewis. Admitted to N.Y. State bar, 1954, Va. bar, 1977; practiced in N.Y.C., 1954—; atty. SEC, N.Y.C., 1957-60; asso. Wofsey, Certilman & Haft, 1960-62; partner Hays, Feuer, Porter & Spanier (name changed from Hays, Algase, Feuer, Porter & Spanier, 1968), 1963-69; partner Schwartz, Burns, Lesser & Jacoby (name changed to Burns, Jackson, Miller, Summit & Jacoby), 1970-74; prof. Marshall-Wythe Sch. Law Coll. William and Mary, Williamsburg, Va., 1974—. Served with Judge Advocates Gen. Corps, U.S. Army, 1954-56; Germany. Mem. Am. Bar Assn., Zeta Beta Tau. Jewish religion. Club: Harvard (N.Y.C.). Home: 107 Archer's Hope Dr Williamsburg VA 23185

FRANK, LORAINE SERWIN, lawyer; b. Passaic, N.J.; d. John and Katherine Serwin; B.S., Okla. State U., 1951, M.S., 1952; J.D., Okla. U., 1973; m. Reginald Hull Frank, May 31, 1952; children—Liane Renee, Lisa Roanne. Mem. home econs. faculty U. Tulsa, 1952-53, Perkins (Okla.) High Sch., 1956-58, Arkansas City (Kans.) Jr. Coll., 1960-63; field rep. U.S. Census Bur., Cowley County, Kans., 1960; condr. various surveys, 1964-65; salesman Carousel Realty, Del City, Okla., 1968-69; admitted to Okla. bar, 1974; atty. Public Defender's Office, Mcpl. Ct., Oklahoma City, 1974-75; cons. atty. child support enforcement unit Okla. Dept. Instns., Social and Rehab. Services, Oklahoma City, 1975-77; sec.-mem. Okla. Bd. Property and Casualty Rates, Oklahoma City, 1977—; sec.-mem. bd. mgrs. Okla. Ins. Fund. Mem. Okla. Bar Assn., Cleveland County Bar Assn. Presbyterian. Club: Bus. and Profl. Women's. Home: 2514 Boxwood Dr Norman OK 73069 Office: 401 Will Rogers Bldg State Capitol Oklahoma City OK 73105

FRANK, MILDRED BYE, bookkeeper, bus. exec.; b. Miami, Fla., Aug. 15, 1928; d. David A. and Eunice M. (Roberts) Bye; student Fla. State U., Mars Hill Jr. Coll.; m. William E. Frank, Feb. 22, 1948; children—David E., William E., Lois Kimberlee. Owner, bookkeeper Naples Millwork and Fixture Co. (Fla.), 1955—, also sec.-treas. Bd. dirs. Grace Luth. Ch. Republican. Home: 2284 Crayton Rd Naples FL 33940 Office: 959 1st Ave S Naples FL 33940

FRANK, PATRICIA ANNE, state senator; b. Cleve., Nov. 12, 1929; d. Paul Conrad and Mildred Patricia (Roane) Collier; B.S. in Fin. and Taxation, U. Fla., Gainesville, 1951; postgrad. Georgetown U. Law Sch., 1951-52; m. Richard H. Frank, Dec. 21, 1951; children—Stacy, Hillary, Courtney. Bus. economist anti-trust div. Dept. Justice, Washington, 1951-53; mem. staff U.S. Congressman John R. Foley, 1959-60; mem. Hillsborough County (Fla.) Sch. Bd., 1972-76, chmn., 1975-76; past mem. Hillsborough County Tax Bd., Tampa Election Bd.; mem. Fla. Ho. of Reps. from 67th Dist., 1976-78; past mem. adv. council dist. VI, Fla. Health and Rehab. Services; mem. Fla. Senate from 23d Dist., 1978—; mem. Fla. Phosphate Land Reclamation Study Commn., So. Regional Edn. Bd. Bd. dirs. Tampa YMCA, Tampa Bay Com. Fgn. Relations, Fla. Assn. Gifted Children; v.p. St. Andrews Episcopal Churchwomen. Recipient numerous service and community service awards. Mem. LWV (chpt. dir.), Hillsborough County Bar Aux. (dir.), Hillsborough County Council PTA's (1st v.p.). Home: 574 W Davis Blvd Tampa FL 33606 Office: 304 Plant Ave Tampa FL 33606

FRANK, RICHARD, urologist; b. N.Y.C., Apr. 16, 1943; s. Bernard and Anna F.; B.A. summa cum laude, Columbia U., 1963, M.D., 1967; m. Roberta Lynn Frank, Aug. 29, 1965; children—Brian Harris, Carrie Ilene. Intern, Mt. Sinai Hosp., N.Y.C., 1967-68, resident in surgery, 1968-69, resident in urology, 1971-74; instr. urology Mt. Sinai Sch. Medicine, N.Y.C., 1973-74; attending urologist Univ. Community Hosp., Tamarac, Fla., 1974—, Fla. Med. Center, Lauderdale Lakes, 1974—. Served to maj. M.C., U.S. Army, 1969-71. Diplomate Am. Bd. Urology. Fellow A.C.S.; mem. Am. Urol. Assn., Fla. Urol. Soc., AMA, Fla. Med. Assn., Phi Beta Kappa. Office: 7401 N University Dr Tamarac FL 33321

FRANK, SAM HAGER, univ. chancellor; b. King City, Mo., July 23, 1932; s. Edward Lloyd and Louise (Hager) F.; B.A., Fla. State U., 1953; M.A., Fla. State U., 1957; Ph.D., U. Fla., 1961; m. Ellen Wilson Snow, June 3, 1955; 1 dau., Marian Elizabeth. Prof. history Tift Coll., Forsyth, Ga., 1961-65, also chmn. div. social scis., 1961-65; asso. prof. history Augusta (Ga.) Coll., 1966-67; asso. prof. history Jacksonville (Fla.) U., 1967-72, prof. history, 1972-78, dean Coll. Arts and Scis., 1972-78; chancellor La. State U., Alexandria, 1979—; cons. Research Studies Inst., USAF U., Maxwell AFB, Ala., 1957-58; Fulbright prof. Osmania U., India, 1965-66; participant Conf. Acad. Deans of So. States, 1973. Served with U.S. Army, 1954-56; Korea. Mem. Am., So. hist. assns., Orgn. Am. Historians, AAUP (exec. com. Ga. sect. 1962-65), Alexandria C. of C. (bd. dirs.), Phi Mu Alpha Sinfonia, Phi Kappa Phi, Phi Alpha Theta, Pi Sigma Alpha, Phi Delta Kappa. Clubs: Rotary, Torch, Mensheviki. Author: (with M. Maurer) Air Force Combat Units of World War II, 1960; American Air Service Observation in World War I, 1961; contbr. articles on aviation, the mil. and Asia to profl. jours. Home: Route 2 Box 27 Alexandria LA 71301 Office: Chancellor La State U Alexandria LA 71301

FRANKEL, ANDREW JOEL, nuclear engr.; b. N.Y.C., Oct. 7, 1945; s. Lazar Hirsch and Estelle Rose (Fuchs) F.; B.S. in Chem. Engring., N.J. Inst. Tech., 1968; M.Engring., N.Y. U., 1970; m. Marilyn Judith Marcus, Dec. 24, 1967; children—Jennifer Lauren, Jonathan Matthew. With Combustion Engring. Inc., Windsor, Conn., 1970-77; lead engr., 1976-77; coordinator nonproliferation assessments tech. support office Oak Ridge Nat. Lab., 1977-78; mgr. data analysis Fuel-Trac div. Nuclear Assurance Corp., Atlanta, 1978—; participant Internat. Nuclear Fuel Cycle Evaluation; cons. in field. Mem. Am. Nuclear Soc., AAAS, Am. Mgmt. Assn., Tau Beta Pi, Omega Chi Epsilon. Contbr. articles to profl. jours. Home: 2595 Kings Pistol Ct Grayson GA 30221 Office: 24 Executive Park W Atlanta GA 30329

FRANKEL, LOUISE RILEY, dietitian; b. Miami, Okla., Dec. 7, 1918; d. John Markham and Ida (Prophet) Riley; B.S., Okla. State U., 1940; Dietetic Internship Cert., Harper Hosp., Detroit, 1942; student Cornell U., 1963-64; m. Joseph Frankel, May 28, 1945; children—Joseph, John Richard, Elizabeth Ann, Margaret Ruth, James Oscar. Chief dietitian Hillcrest Hosp., Tulsa, 1948-50; chief dietitian St. Edwards Hosp., Ft. Smith, Ark., 1950-51; dietitian VA, Wadsworth, Kans., 1951-58, Perry Point, Md., 1958-59, Bath, N.Y., 1959-65; chief dietetic service VA Med. Center, Waco, Tex., 1965—. Course dir. Dietetic Asst. Course, Tex. State Tech. Inst., Waco. Served with AUS, 1942-45. Registered Dietitian. Mem. Am. Dietetic Assn., Tex. Dietetic Assn., Central Tex. Dietetic Assn., Am. Soc. Hosp. Food Service Adminstrs., Am. Home Econs. Assn., Tex. Soc. Hosp. Food Service Dirs. Republican. Roman Catholic. Club: Altrusa Internat. Home: 516 Richland Dr Waco TX 76710 Office: VA Med Center Memorial Dr Waco TX 76703

FRANKLIN, ALFRED ALTON, JR., microbiologist, photographer; b. Atlanta, Dec. 15, 1947; s. Alfred Alton and Martha Jeanette (Linch) F.; B.S., U. Ga., 1970; M.A. in Microbiology, U. S.Fla., 1973; 1 son, Alfred Alton III. Research asst. chemistry dept., U. S.Fla., Tampa, 1971-72, teaching asst. biology dept., 1972; cons. microbiologist, Variety Frozen Foods, Tampa, Fla., 1971-72; research asso., Microlife Technics, Sarasota, Fla., 1972—; owner Franklin Foto, 1979—, Fla. Down Under, Inc., 1980—. Unit commr. Sunnyland council Boy Scouts Am.; bd. dirs. Fla. Bicycle Moto-Cross Assn., 1978. Mem. Am. Soc. Microbiology (award com. SE Br.), Soc. Gen. Microbiology, Soc. Applied Bacteriology, Am. Soc. Agronomy, Crop Sci. Soc. Am., Soil Sci. Soc. Am., Internat. Soc. Soil Sci., U.S. Fla. Alumni Assn. (pres. Sarasota-Manatee br. 1977-79, Nat. dir. 1977-79), Soil and Crop Soc. Fla., Photog. Soc. Am., Asso. Photographers Internat., Profl. Assn. Diving Instrs., Sigma Xi, Phi Sigma (nat. research award, 1974). Democrat. Presbyterian. Clubs: Kiwanis (dir. Gulf Coast club, 1973—, Kiwanian of Yr. 1978), SAR. Contbr. sci. papers to publs. Patentee in field. Home: 4658 Ardale St Sarasota FL 33582 Office: Box 3917 Sarasota FL 33578

FRANKLIN, ALTON DAVID, educator, musician; b. River Junction, Fla., Apr. 28, 1940; s. Benjamin Morgan and Roxie Lucille (Conrad) F.; B.A., Fla. State U., 1962, M.A. 1963, Ph.D. 1968; m. Elda Elizabeth Estep, June 4, 1960; 1 child—Elizabeth Anne. Asst. prof. music N. Ga. Coll., Dahlonega, 1964-66; asst. prof. Winthrop Coll., Rock Hill, S.C., 1966-68, asso. prof. 1968-73, prof. 1973—, coordinator grad. studies in music 1976—; mem. various musical performing groups, including Art Mooney Orch., 1957. Bd. dirs. Dahlonega Jaycees, 1964. Recipient summer study grant Winthrop Coll., 1976. Mem. Music Educators Nat. Conf., S.C. Music Educators Assn., Nat. Assn. Jazz Educators, Internat. Soc. for Jazz Research, Am. Fedn. Musicians. Contbr. articles in field to profl. jours. Home: 3019 Wimbledon Ln Rock Hill SC 29730 Office: Winthrop Coll Oakland Ave Rock Hill SC 29733

FRANKLIN, DONALD LEE, recreational vehicle mfg. co. exec.; b. Topeka, Kans., May 15, 1950; s. Art R. and Ruth M. (Perkins) F.; student in bus. adminstrn. Bethany Nazarene Coll., 1969-71; m. Lynda D. Fore, Aug. 1, 1970; 1 dau., Jennifer D. Sales rep. Odom's Jewelry, Oklahoma City, 1970-71; mem. staff Foretravel, Inc., Nacogdoches, Tex., 1971-74, v.p. mktg., 1975—. Mem. Recreation Vehicle Assn. Home: 1219 NW Stallings St Nacogdoches TX 75961 Office: 1221 N Stallings St Nacogdoches TX 75961

FRANKLIN, HERBERT, educator; b. Mason County, Ky., May 1, 1935; s. Arthur and Margaret (Tabor) F.; B.S., Ky. State U., 1960; M.A., U. Louisville, 1967; Ed.D., Ind. U., 1974; m. Dorothy Ann Bowman, Mar. 31, 1962; children—Marcus Byron, Lori Teaneale. Tchr. elem. levels Louisville (Ky.) public schs., 1962-65, counselor elem. grades, 1965-67, asst. prin., 1968-72; counselor Bur. Ednl. Placement, Ind. U., Bloomington, Ind., 1972-73; prin. Monroe County (Ind.) Community Sch. Corp., Bloomington, 1973-74; asst. prof. ednl. adminstrn. U. Fla., Gainesville, 1974-79, co-dir. Tng. Inst., 1979—; dir. Greater Franklin County Tchr. Center, Frankfort, Ky., 1979—; cons. to various sch. bds., 1972—. Served with U.S. Army, 1960-62. Named Outstanding Tchr., Dawn Byck Elem. Sch., 1963. Mem. Nat. Assn. Secondary Sch. Prins., Fla. Assn. Sch. Adminstrs., NEA, Fla. Assn. Secondary Sch. Prins., NAACP, Res. Officers Assn. of U.S., Phi Delta Kappa. Republican. Baptist. Contbr. articles on ednl. fin. to profl. publs. Address: 916 E Main St Frankfort KY 40601

FRANKLIN, JAMES LEE, data processing exec.; b. Fairfax, Ala., Apr. 13, 1921; s. James Tyler and Maggie Lee (Welsh) F.; Certificate in Data Processing and Acctg., Balt. Inst., 1965; m. Joyce Janelle Myers, Feb. 2, 1951; 1 dau., Dana Lee. Commd. sgt. U.S. Air Force, 1947, advanced through grades to chief master sgt., 1959, ret., 1965; mgr. computer ops. Auburn (Ala.) U. Computer Center, 1966-75, asst. dir., 1975-79, asst. dir. Div. Univ. Computing and Data Processing, 1979—. Served with U.S. Army, 1940-45. Decorated Air Force Commendation medal. Mem. Am. Legion. Clubs: Still Waters Golf, Methodist Men. Home: 3 Still Waters Dr Dadeville AL 36853 Office: Univ Computing and Data Processing Auburn Univ Auburn AL 36830

FRANKLIN, LAYMAN GREEN, contract research co. exec.; b. Carroll County, Va., Aug. 16, 1939; s. Artie Lee and Edith Ruth (Reynolds) F.; B.S. in Bus. Adminstrn. and Acctg., James Madison U., 1968; tchr.'s cert. N.C. Central U., 1974; postgrad. in Ednl. Adminstrn., Duke U., 1978; m. Zaida Faye Lynch, Sept. 5, 1974; children—Artie Lee, Robert Daniel, Layman Green. Tchr., Shenandoah County, Va., 1960-63; auditor GAO, Washington, 1968-70; contract coordinator Duke U., Durham, N.C., 1970-72; subcontract negotiator, office mgr. Battelle Columbus Labs., Durham, 1972—. Named Scoutmaster of Year Boy Scouts Am., Orange County, N.C., 1977, Scouter of Year, 1979. Mem. N.C. Assn. for Educators, IEEE, Am. Soc. Metals, Nat. Contracts Mgmt. Assn. Home: 622 Starmont Dr Durham NC 27705 Office: Battelle Columbus Labs 200 Park Dr Research Triangle Park NC 27709

FRANKLIN, MORRIS EMORY, JR., physician; b. Fort Worth, Aug. 10, 1942; s. Morris Emory and Dorothy (Downes) F.; B.A., N. Tex. State U., 1963; M.D., U. Tex. Southwestern Med. Sch., 1967; m. Linda Beth Plant, June 30, 1970; 1 son, Morris Emory. Intern, Robert G. Green Hosp., San Antonio, 1967-68; resident Bexar County Hosp., San Antonio, 1968-72; practice medicine, specializing in surgery, 1972—; asso. prof. surgery U. Tex. Med. Sch., 1974—; chief surgery Baptist Hosp., San Antonio, 1976; mem. staff Meth. Hosp., Bexar County Hosp., St. Francis Hosp., Colorado Springs, Colo. Served with AUS, 1972-74. Decorated Bronze Star medal. Mem. AMA, Am. Coll. Surgery. Club: Lions. Home: 5903 Northgap St San Antonio TX 78239 Office: 4242 E Southcross #4 San Antonio TX 78222

FRANKLIN, ROBERT DRURY, oil co. exec.; b. Mead, Okla., June 6, 1935; s. Sam W., Jr. and Frankie M. (Gooding) F.; B.S. in Petroleum Engring., U. Okla., 1957; LL.B., So. Methodist U., 1964; m. Barbara Jean Bellis, May 29, 1958; children—Philip, Elizabeth. Petroleum engr. Mobil Oil Co., Healdton, Okla., 1957-59; prodn. mgr. Bayview Oil Co., Dallas, 1959-64; sec.-treas. Siboney Corp., Dallas, 1964-70; pres. Northland Oils Ltd., Dallas, 1970—, Costa Resources, Inc., Dallas, 1973—; admitted to Tex. bar, 1964. Served with AUS, 1959. Mem. Dallas Bar Assn., State Bar Tex., Soc. Petroleum Engrs., Am. Inst. Mining Engrs., Ind. Petroleum Assn. Am., Kappa Sigma. Presbyterian. Club: Cipango (Dallas). Home: 6 Turtle Creek Bend Dallas TX 75204 Office: 3303 Lee Pkwy Dallas TX 75219

FRANKLIN, SIDNEY, computer co. exec.; b. London, Apr. 21, 1942; came to U.S., 1959, naturalized, 1966; s. John Herbert and Joan Sarah (Barber) F.; m. Charlotte Ann Summers, Feb. 15, 1964; children—Mary Ann, John Christopher. Ops. supr. Nat. Life Ins. Co., 1963-65, Aladdin Industries, Nashville, 1965-67; sci. systems analyst Lockheed Aircraft Corp., Houston, Atlanta, 1967-70; systems analyst State of Tenn., Nashville, 1970-72, Commerce Union Bank, Nashville, 1972-74; asst. mgr. data processing Tenn. Wholesale Drug Co., Nashville, 1974; dist. systems mgr. Mohawk Data Sci. Corp., Nashville, 1974—. Named Systems Analyst of Yr. for So. Region, 1978. Mem. Sports Car Club Am. (sec., treas., regional exec. 1964-67), Assn. Computing Machinery. Home: 1105 Greenleaf Ct Franklin TN 37064 Office: 1100 Kermit Dr Suite 23 Nashville TN 37217

FRANKLIN, WILLIAM, govt. ofcl.; b. Cin., Mar. 27, 1934; s. William A. and Louise E.F.; B.S., Okla. City U., 1971; M.B.A., Central State U., 1974; m. Diana Ross, Mar. 17, 1969; children—Bonita L., Christina M., William E., Dana G. Police officer Oklahoma City Police Dept., 1963-64; inventory mgmt. specialist USAF, Tinker AFB, Oklahoma City, 1964-71; dir. econ. devel. Urban League, Inc., Oklahoma City, 1971-73; personnel staffing specialist FAA Aero. Center, Oklahoma City, 1973—; dir. Pan-Okla. Communications, Inc., Franklin, Smith & Assos. Cons., Inc.; asst. prof. mktg. Southwestern Coll. Bd. dirs. Black Liberated Arts Center; trustee Quayle United Methodist Ch., 1979—. Served with USAF, 1953-62. Mem. Nat. Business League, NAACP, Okla. City Personnel Assn., Alpha Phi Alpha. Republican. Clubs: Mason, Optimist.

FRANKLIN, WILLIAM HAYNE, III, controller; b. Newberry, S.C., Oct. 2, 1946; s. William Hayne and Sara Cornelia (Byrd) F.; student Clemson U., 1964-65; B.S. in Accounting, Newberry Coll., 1965-68; m. Carolyn LaNelle Smith, June 18, 1967; children—Brian Downs, Kevin Ashton. Staff accountant, 1970-72; asst. controller Shakespeare Co., Columbia, S.C., 1972-74, div. controller Electronics & Fiberglass Div., 1974—. Dir. United Way, Newberry County, 1974-76. Served with Army N.G., 1969-75. C.P.A. Mem. N.C., S.C. assns. C.P.A.'s, Am. Inst. C.P.A.'s. Lutheran. Clubs: Newberry Shrine, Newberry Country, Newberry Coll. India (dir. 1979—), Masons, Shriners. Home: 2120 Pinehurst Dr Newberry SC 29108 Office: RFD 3 Newberry SC 29108

FRANKLIN-TAYLOR, ETHEL VIOLA, educator; b. Rome, Ga., Feb. 21, 1931; d. John Emory and Josephine (Rogers) Franklin; A.B. in English, Spelman Coll., 1951; M.A., Atlanta U., 1953, postgrad., 1955; postgrad. Cornell U., 1957-60, N.Y. U., 1961-63; Ph.D. in English, Ind. U., 1974. Tchr. English, Rome (Ga.) City Sch. System, 1952-65, coordinator English program, 1960-65; asst. prof. English Knoxville (Tenn.) Coll., 1965; asst. prof. English, Hampton (Va.) Inst., 1966-70, coordinator program for underachievers, 1967-70; asso. instr. Ind. U., Bloomington, 1972-74; asso. instr. N.C. A. & T. State U., Greensboro, 1974—, asst. dean Sch. Arts and Scis., 1978—; panelist, cons. Nat. Endowment for Humanities, Washington, 1976-77; reader Ednl. Testing Service, Princeton, N.J., 1977, 78; cons. various sch. systems N.C., Ga. 1975-77, Ark., 1978-79. Recipient Tchr. of Yr. award Rome City Schs., 1964. Mem. Nat. Council Tchrs. English, Conf. on Coll. Composition and Communication, S. Atlantic Modern Lang. Assn. Methodist. Contbr. research paper, cons. grant in field. Home: 27-H Covey Ln Greensboro NC 27406 Office: PO Box 164-74 Greensboro NC 27406

FRANKS, ALLEN P., lawyer, business exec.; b. Cleve., Nov. 12, 1936; s. Stanley Arthur and Helen Dorothy F.; student U. Miami, 1955-56; B.A., Case Western Res. U., 1959, B.Laws, 1963, J.D., 1968; m. Cary Bajko, Feb. 2, 1963; children—Mathew, Sara. Legal aide, Atty. Gen. State of Ohio, Cleve., 1959-60; research asst. Western Res. U. Med. Sch., Cleve., 1961-63; patent atty. B.F. Goodrich, Akron, Ohio, 1963-65; pigment lab. mgr. PPG Industries, Barberton, Ohio, 1965-66; tech. dir., lab. mgr. Reichhold Chems., Inc., Akron, Ohio, 1966-77; gen. counsel Broward County Bd. County Commrs., 1979; pres. Inst. Astral Studies, Inc., 1974—. Chmn. bd. dirs. Persephone Found., 1973-79. Fellow Am. Inst. Chemists; mem. Am. Chem. Soc., Soc. Internat. Law, N.Y. Acad. Scis., Assn. Research in Cosmecology (dir.), AAAS, Phi Delta Phi. Home: 1950 NE 31st St Pompano Beach FL 33064

FRANKS, CHARLES KOONCE, civil engr.; b. Knoxville, Tenn., Aug. 7, 1943; s. Don Gold and Myrtis Etelka (Koonce) F.; B.S., U. Tenn., 1976; m. Mary Sue Wilson, Nov. 22, 1963; children—Jamie Beth, Holly. Chief estimator Am. Duralite Corp., Loudon, Tenn., 1965-69; project mgr. Van Driel Proprietry Ltd., Melbourne, Australia, 1971-72; v.p., dir. Brownlee Kesterson, Inc., Knoxville, 1969-71, 72-77; pres., dir. Franks & Nichols, Inc., Knoxville, 1977—; tchr. civil engring. U. Tenn., 1977—. Bd. dirs. United Cerebral Palsy, 1975-78. Mem. Asso. Gen. Contractors Am. (dir.), Asso. Builders and Contractors E. Tenn., S.R. Presbyterian. Clubs: U. Tenn. Faculty, Executives, Sertoma (dir. 1969-80, Centurion award 1977, Tribune award 1978) (Knoxville). Home: 462 Hillvale Turn W Knoxville TN 37919 Office: PO Box 452 Knoxville TN 37901

FRANKS, ROBERT ERNEST, JR., cable TV exec.; b. East Orange, N.J., Oct. 8, 1944; s. Robert E. and Ada A. (Sharp) F.; A.A., Miami Dade Jr. Coll., 1969; B.A., U. Fla., 1971; m. Katherine Randolph, Aug. 26, 1967; 1 dau., Jamie Kay. Rep., Moore Bus. Forms, Gainesville, Fla., 1971-73; tax examiner Fla. Dept. Revenue, Gainesville, 1973-76; office mgr. to bus, mgr. Univ. City TV Cable Co., Gainesville, 1976-78, ops. mgr., 1979—. Coach, Gainesville Recreation Dept., 1971-74; chmn. Big Bro.-Big Sister Steering Com., Gainesville, 1972-73; treas. Vol. Action Center, Gainesville, 1976-77, v.p., 1977-78, chmn., 1978-79, bd. dirs., 1980—; participant Leadership Gainesville, 1977; mem. mid-mgmt. adv. bd. Santa Fe Community Coll., 1977, chmn., 1978-79; active United Way, 1978-80, Gold award, 1978. Mem. Gainesville Area C. of C. (chmn. econ. edn. com. 1979-80), Fla. Cable TV Assn. (lobbyist), Data Processing Mgrs. Assn., Friends of Five. Presbyterian. Clubs: Exchange (dir. 1979-80), U. Fla. Tip off (v.p. 1979-80), Elks (exalted ruler 1980-81). Home: Route 1 Box 40 T5 Gainesville FL 32601 Office: Univ City TV Cable Co 1115 NW 4th St Gainesville FL 32601

FRANTZIS, THEODOSIOS GEORGE, dentist; b. Tampa, Fla., Oct. 13, 1941; s. George Theodosios and Zula Costas (Pappas) F.; student U. Fla., 1959-60, Fla. State U., 1960-62; D.D.S., Emory U., 1966; M.S. in Dentistry, Mayo Grad. Sch. Medicine, 1971; m. Carol Elaine Timm, Dec. 12, 1971; children—Franklyn Timothy, Hariklia Maria. Mayo Found. fellow Mayo Clinic, Rochester, Minn., 1968-71; pvt. practice periodontology, Clearwater, Fla., 1971-78; asst. prof. periodontology Sch. Dentistry, Med. Coll. Va., Richmond, 1978—; lectr. in field. Served to capt., Dental Corps, U.S. Army, 1966-68. Lic. dentist, Fla., Ga., Minn., Va.; diplomate Am. Bd. Periodontology. Mem. ADA, Va. Dental Assn. (ho. of dels. 1979-80), Richmond Dental Soc. (public info. and dental health com. 1979-80), Internat. Assn. for Dental Research, Am. Assn. Dental Schs., Am. Acad.

Periodontology, Alpha Epsilon Delta. Contbr. articles to profl. jours. Home: 8156 Indian Springs Rd Richmond VA 23234 Office: Box 566 MCV Sta Richmond VA 23298

FRANTZREB, ARTHUR CARL, mgmt. cons.; b. Indpls., Feb. 5, 1920; s. Walter J. and Edith M. (Hart) F.; student Purdue U., 1938-40; B.S., Butler U., 1948; H.L.D., Mt. Senario Coll., 1974; m. Jane A. Fear, June 27, 1943; children—Richard Brent, James Alan. With Marts & Lundy, Inc., N.Y.C., 1948-52; dir. devel. Rutgers U., 1954-58; exec. v.p. G.A. Brakeley, Inc., N.Y.C., 1958-61; pres. A.C. Frantzreb & Co., N.Y.C., 1961-65; pres. Frantzreb, Pray and Assos., Inc., N.Y.C., 1964-75; pres. Frantzreb, Pray, Ferner and Thompson, Inc., Arlington, Va., 1975-76, chmn. bd., 1976-77; pres. Arthur C. Frantzreb, Inc., 1978—; editor Counseletter, contbg. columnist Fund Raising Mgmt. mag. Bd. chmn., trustee Mt. Senario Coll., 1972-78. Served to lt., AUS, 1942-46. Recipient Hanson H. Anderson Outstanding Service award, 1976. Christian Scientist. Clubs: University (N.Y.C.), Masons. Home: 6233 Kellogg Dr McLean VA 22101

FRANZ, JERRY LOUIS, cardiac surgeon; b. Decatur, Ind., Aug. 5, 1943; s. Lyle D. and Helen J. (Martin) F.; B.S. in Chemistry, Ohio No. U., 1965; M.S. in Bacteriology, U. Fla., 1967; M.D., U. Ky., 1971; m. Jennie Rose Heim, June 20, 1970. Intern surgery U. Ky. Hosps., Lexington, 1971-72; jr. asst. resident surgery Bexar County Hosp., San Antonio, 1972-73, resident surgery, 1973-76, adminstrv. resident surgery, 1975-76, resident cardiothoracic surgery, 1976-78. Diplomate Am. Bd. Surgery, Am. Bd. Thoracic Surgery. Mem. Am. Coll. Chest Physicians, Bexar County Med. Soc., AMA, Tex. Med. Assn., Assn. for Acad. Surgery, Cooley Cardiovascular Soc. Contbr. articles to profl. jours. Home: 106 Painted Post Ln San Antonio TX 78231 Office: 350 Methodist Plaza San Antonio TX 78229

FRANZ, LEO JOHN, mfg. co. exec.; b. Cin., Jan. 28, 1943; s. Ernest J. and Marie Elizabeth (Hartman) F.; A.S. in Indsl. Mgmt., U. Cin., 1964, B.B.A. in Econs., 1967; M.B.A. in Mktg., Xavier U., 1970; m. Patricia L. Gross, June 22, 1968; children—Leo John, Jennifer Marie. Regional mgr. Diamond Nat. Corp., Middleton, Ohio, 1966-70; mktg. mgr. merchandising dept. Mead Packaging, Atlanta, 1971-77; mktg. mgr. Masterack div. Leggett & Platt, Inc., Atlanta, 1977—. Vice pres. Lost Springs Civic Assn., Lilburn, Ga., 1975-76, pres., 1976-77. Recipient Achievement award, Coco-Cola Co., 1979. Mem. Nat. Soft Drink Assn., Point of Purchase Advt. Inst. Republican. Roman Catholic. Inventor display products. Home: 3792 Hollow Tree Ln Lilburn GA 30247 Office: 905 Memorial Dr SE Atlanta GA 30348

FRANZETTI, RONNIE ALLEN, computer programmer; b. Austin, Tex., Oct. 2, 1946; s. Arthur Angelo and Charlotte Louise (Sheplor) F.; B.B.A., U. Tex., Austin, 1975; m. Diana Gene Rothberger, Aug. 1, 1970; children—Adam Douglas, Leslie Kay. Tax examiner IRS, Austin, 1969-70; computer operator Tex. State Comptroller Public Accts., Austin, 1970-75, computer programmer, analyst, 1975—. Election judge local voting precinct, 1972—. Served with USNR, 1967-68; Vietnam. Home: 26 Lazy Oaks Dr Austin TX 78745 Office: 111 E 17th St Austin TX 78774

FRANZHEIM, SUSAN BETH, fin. corps. exec.; b. N.Y., Oct. 26, 1940; d. M. and Anne Kaplan; student UCLA, 1962-72; m. Kenneth Franzheim, II, Mar. 30, 1974; children—Richie, Tracy. Office mgr. Interhealth, Los Angeles, 1973; pres., cons. Franzheim Investment Co., Houston, 1974—; mgr. Franzheim Synergy Trust, Houston, 1974—; co-mgr. Xalapa Farm Tng. Center, Paris, Ky., 1976—. Chmn. bd. rehab. program Cenikor Found., Houston, 1977-80; internat. bd. dirs. Amigos de las Americas, para-med. program, Houston, 1976-77, Service award, 1977; bd. advisers population program Baylor Sch. Medicine, 1976-79; mem. Los Angeles County Dist. Atty.'s Adv. Council, 1969-73. Mem. Holistic Health Assn. (bd. dirs.). Clubs: Bayou, Houston Country; Lafayette (Lexington, Ky.); Green Boundary (Aiken, S.C.); Pisces (Washington); Doubles (N.Y.C.). Address: 2370 Transco Tower Houston TX 77056

FRASER, GEORGE B(ROADRUP), lawyer; b. Washington, May 9, 1914; s. George B. and Florence M. (Hillyard) F.; A.B., Dartmouth Coll., 1936; J.D., Harvard U., 1939; LL.M., George Washington U., 1941; m. Phebe Elizabeth Bandy, Dec. 20, 1965. Admitted to D.C. bar, 1939; individual practice law, Washington, 1939-41; atty. VA, Boise, Idaho, 1946; prof. law U. Idaho, Moscow, 1946-49; prof. U. Okla., Norman, 1949—, now David Ross Boyd prof.; vis. prof. law U. Ill., 1959, U. Mich., 1964, Hastings Coll. Law, 1966-67, 70, George Washington U., 1948, 58, Calif. Western Law Sch., 1969, Oxford (Eng.) U., 1976; cons. Okla. Legislature, 1967-68. Served with USNR, 1941-45. Mem. Okla. Bar Assn., Am. Bar Assn., D.C. Bar Assn. Contbr. articles to profl. jours., chpts. in Oklahoma Practice Book, 1965. Home: 1206 Greenbriar Ct Norman OK 73069 Office: Law Center 300 Timberdell Rd Norman OK 73019

FRASIER, MARGRET EVANGELINE SMITH, educator; b. Livingston, Tenn., Jan. 3, 1919; s. Barton Obediah and Margret Victoria (Dillon) Smith; student Milligan Coll., 1936-38; B.S., U. Tenn., Knoxville, 1940, M.S., 1963; m. Gleeson Perry Frasier, June 6, 1943; children—Delores Jo Frasier Turnbull, Eric. Tchr., Nash County, N.C., 1940-42, White County, Tenn., 1942-43, Murfreesboro (Tenn.) Central, 1945-46, Rickman (Tenn.) High Sch., 1948-50, Livingston Acad., 1950-62; asst. prof. home econs. Tenn. Tech. U., Cookeville, 1962—; owner Clothes Corner. Mem. NEA, Tenn. Edn. Assn., Middle Tenn. Tchrs. Assn., Am. Home Econs. Assn., Am. Coll. Profs. Textile and Clothing Assn., AAUP, Am. Legion Aux. (pres. 1963-70), Kappa Omicron Phi. Democrat. Christian. Home: Route 1 Box 12 Livingston TN 38570 Office: Tenn Tech U Dept Home Econs Cookeville TN 38501

FRATES, MRS. CLIFFORD LEROY, civic worker; b. Moweaqua, Ill., Jan. 15, 1908; d. William James and Gertrude (Gunderson) Rodman; student Pine Manor Jr. Coll., 1924; B.A., U. Okla., 1929; m. Clifford L. Frates, Nov. 15, 1935; children—Rodman A., Kent F. Mem. bd. ARC, Oklahoma City; dir. Community Fund Bd.; trustee Jane Brooks Sch. Deaf, Okla. Art Center, Okla. Coll. for Women; chmn. adv. bd. Mercy Hosp., now also trustee; bd. dirs. Okla. State Library League for Blind, dir. Jr. Leagues of Am.; mem. bd. Okla. Heritage Assn., Allied Arts of Oklahoma City, Oklahoma City Symphony, YWCA, Blood Inst.; mem. Children's Rehab. and Edn. Bd.; drive chmn. Central Vol. Bur.; chmn. women's div. United Fund; chmn. Art Center drive; chmn. Oklahoma City Savs. Bond Com.; chmn. Episcopal Women's Conf. Okla.; chmn. Re-act campaign for Oklahoma City Vol. Action Center, 1971. Named to Okla. Hall of Fame, 1969; recipient award NCCJ; Women in Communications award, 1979. Mem. Oklahoma City Art Assn., Phi Beta Kappa (pres. Oklahoma City alumnae 1964-66, alumna award 1978), Kappa Alpha Theta, Mortar Bd. Republican. Episcopalian (div. chmn. for Christian social relations; mem. Episcopal Bishop and Council, mem. vestry ch.). Home: 2607 Warwick Dr Oklahoma City OK 73116

FRAZE, DENNY TURNER, educator; b. Weatherford, Tex., May 28, 1940; s. Oran Lester and Laverne (Morrison) F.; student Weatherford Jr. Coll., 1958-59; B.F.A., U. Tex., Austin, 1962; postgrad. Tex. Christian U., summer 1963; M.F.A., U. Colo., 1964; postgrad. N. Tex. State U., summer 1965; m. Gwen Wright Woodson, May 26, 1978; children by previous marriage—David, Michael, Wendy Weir; stepchildren—Jennifer Reese, Byron Reese. Instr. art Amarillo (Tex.) Coll., 1965-68, acting chmn., 1967-68, asso. prof., 1968-70, chmn. dept. art, 1968—, prof. art, 1970—; one man shows: E. Tex. State U., 1977, Central Mo. State Coll., 1969, Western N.M. U., 1966, Ga. So. Coll., 1971, St. Mary's Coll., Md., 1973; group shows include: XIV Mid-Am. Annual at Rockhill-Nelson Gallery, Nat. Black and White Print Exhbn., Manhattan, Kan., New Photographics 1976, others; represented in permanent collections U. Colo. Recipient Amarillo Globe Times accolade, 1970. Mem. Tex. Assn. Schs. Art (pres. 1970-72, dir. 1970-74), Coll. Art Assn. Am., Nat. Art Edn. Assn., Amarillo Fine Arts Assn., Tex. Fine Arts Assn., Tex. Jr. Coll. Tchrs. Assn., Tex. Council on the Arts in Edn. Home: 2219 S Hayden St Amarillo TX 79105 Office: PO Box 447 Amarillo TX 79178

FRAZE, RICHARD OSBORNE, utilities exec.; b. St. Petersburg, Fla., Feb. 6, 1940; s. Ora Franklin, Jr. and Marie Valentina (Sorenson) F.; A.S.A., St. Petersburg Jr. Coll., 1962; B.S.M.E., U. S.Fla., 1968, M.S.M.E., 1970; m. Nancy I. Wallis, Aug. 7, 1965; children—Richard Edward, Nancy Marie. Engr. Fla. Power Corp., 1970-73, mech. project engr., 1973-75, chief mech. engr., 1975-77, asst. mgr. engring., 1977—. Mem. Bd. Adjustment, Pinellas Park, 1972—, Citizens Planning and Adv. Bd., 1975—. Served with U.S. Army, 1962-69. Registered profl. engr., Fla. Mem. Fla. Engring. Soc., ASME, Pinellas Model A Restorers. Home: 8065 52d Ln Pinellas Park FL 33565 Office: PO Box 14042 St Petersburg FL 33733

FRAZER, EMMETT BAXTER, surgeon; b. Auburn, Ala., Jan. 18, 1893; s. Tucker Henderson and Annie Dora (Holifield) F.; B.S., U. Ala., 1913, M.D., 1918; B.S., M.S. in Surgery, U. Minn., 1923; m. Mary Jane De Pauw Knight, Aug. 29, 1933; children—Jane DePauw, Mell Alice, Carolyn Emmett. Asst. biology U. Ala., 1913-14, instr. anatomy, 1919; intern Union Protestant Infirmary, Balt., 1918; fellow in surgery Mayo Clinic, Rochester, Minn., 1919-23; practice medicine specializing in surgery, Mobile, Ala., 1923—; pres. Mobile Infirmary, 1938-42; former chief surgery U.S. Marine Hosp., Providence Hosp. Served to comdr. M.C., USNR, World War II; PTO. Diplomate Am. Bd. Surgery (founders group), Am. Bd. Urology. Mem. A.C.S. (pres. Ala. chpt. 1961, gov. 1965-71), Am. Urol. Assn., Soc. Int. de Chirurgie, So. Soc. Clin. Surgeons (pres. 1948), So. Surg. Assn., Ala. Acad. Gen. Practice (hon.), Newcomen Soc. N.Am., Med. Soc. Mobile (pres. 1941), Mobile C. of C. Baptist. Clubs: Kiwanis, Masons (life mem.). Home: 2166 Old Shell Rd Mobile AL 36607 Office: 109 N Conception St Mobile AL 36602

FRAZER, JAMES WILLIAM, educator; b. Chgo., Feb. 20, 1928; s. Ralph Oliver and Myra Mabel (Lackland) F.; B.A., Syracuse U., 1950; Ph.D., State U. N.Y., 1964; m. Marjorie Louise Sumner, Sept. 17, 1947. Instr. zoology dept. Syracuse (N.Y.) U., 1951-52, research fellow AEC, Syracuse U., 1952-54; research project officer Nuclear Propulsion, U.S. NADC, Johnsville, Pa., 1957-59; biophysicist Biophysics and Radiation Sci. Div., USAF Sch. Aerospace Medicine, Brooks AFB, Tex., 1964-76; specialist in dental roentgenology/adj. asso. prof. pharmacology U. Tex. Health Sci. Center, San Antonio, 1976—; cons. in field; ad hoc mem. NIH study sects., 1973. Served with USN, 1946, USNR, 1955-59. NIH fellow, 1959-65. Fellow Am. Inst. Chemists; mem. AAAS, N.Y. Acad. Sci., IEEE, Union Radio Sci., Am. Nat. Standards Inst., Bioelectromagnetics Soc., Sigma Xi. Contbr. articles in field to profl. jours.; editorial reader IEEE MTT, IEEE publs.; ad hoc reviewer NSF, Exec. Office of Pres. Home: 346 Killarney Dr San Antonio TX 78223 Office: 7703 Floyd Curl Dr San Antonio TX 78284

FRAZER, MARSHALL EVERETT, physicist; b. Alva, Okla., Jan. 19, 1944; s. Everett Alfred and Genivie Erma (Irons) F.; B.S., Northwestern State Coll., 1964; Ph.D. (Morton Share fellow, 1964), U. Tex., 1974; m. Donna Mae Kirmse, Jan. 4, 1964; 1 dau., Dana Renee. Instr. physics Northwestern State Coll., Alva, 1964; research asso., applied research labs. U. Tex., Austin, 1964—; dir. Mardon, Inc. Mem. IEEE, Acoustical Soc. Am., Sigma Xi. Home: 3010 Honeytree Ln Austin TX 78746 Office: U Tex 10000 FM 1325 Austin TX 78758

FRAZIER, CAROLYN MAE CASEY, nurse; b. Huntsville, Tex., July 26, 1946; d. Carl and Addie Mae (Shipper) Casey; A.A., San Jacinto Coll. Sch. Nursing, 1971; B.S. in Nursing, Tex. Woman's U., 1977; m. William Sumpter Frazier, Aug. 5, 1966; children—Casey Rene, Kelley Shea. Nurse intensive care Rockglen Hosp., Houston, 1973-74; supr. emergency room Gulf Coast Hosp., Baytown, Tex., 1974-75, nursing supr., 1975-77; supr. critical care N.E. Med. Plaza, Humble, Tex., 1977—; instr. San Jacinto Coll. Vocat. Nursing Program, 1976-77; instr. Am. Heart Assn., 1973-78. Mem. Am. Assn. Critical Care Nurses, Emergency Dept. Nursing Assn., Am., Tex. Dist. 9 nursing assns. Democrat. Mem. Ch. of Christ. Home: 27127 Glencreek St Huffman TX 77336 Office: 10202 East Freeway Suite 210 Houston TX 77029

FRAZIER, LOY WILLIAM, JR., physiologist; b. Fort Smith, Ark., Aug. 14, 1938; s. Loy William and Allie Louise (Allen) F.; B.S., U. Tex., Arlington, 1968; Ph.D., U. Tex., 1972; m. Mary Jane White, Aug. 26, 1961; children—Loy William, Jennifer Jane. Med. technologist Grand Prairie (Tex.) Med. Lab., 1960-68; prof. physiology Baylor Coll. Dentistry, Baylor U., Dallas, 1972—, adj. prof. Sch. Nursing, 1974—. Served with USAF, 1957-60, 61-62. U. Tex. fellow, 1968-72; grantee NIH, 1975—. Mem. Am. Physiol. Soc., Soc. Exptl. Biology and Medicine, Sigma Xi. Republican. Methodist. Club: Lions (v.p.). Contbr. articles to profl. jours. Home: 1413 Austrian Rd Grand Prairie TX 75050 Office: 3302 Gaston Ave Dallas TX 75246

FRAZIER, PATRICIA KAGAN, educator; b. Alexandria Bay, N.Y., Mar. 10, 1949; d. Martin and Frances (Shelton) Kagan; student U. N.M., 1969-70; B.Mus., La. State U., 1971; M.Mus., Tex. Tech. U., 1973; m. Larry Richard Frazier, Nov. 26, 1971. Instr. Music Dept., Tenn. Tech. U., Cookeville, 1973-75; violinist Nashville Symphony Orch., 1974-75; violist, asst. prin. and violinist Knoxville Symphony, 1974-75; artist-in-residence, performer Ga. Arts Council, 1976; prin. viola Albany (Ga.) Symphony, 1975-76; violist Jackson (Miss.) Symphony, 1977-78; violinist Opryland U.S.A., Nashville, 1979—; asst. prof., artist, Miss. Valley State U., Itta Bena, 1976-79; adjudicator East Tenn. String Edn. Solo and Ensemble Festivals, 1974-75; string adjudicator West Tenn. All-State Orch. auditions, 1978-79, West Tenn. Solo and Ensemble Festival, Memphis, 1979. Nat. Endowment for Arts and Ga. Arts Council grantee, 1976. Mem. Am. Fedn. Musicians, Sigma Alpha Iota. Republican. Presbyterian. Club: Bulldog of Am. Home: PO Box 758 University MS 38677

FRAZIER, ROBERT JAMES, trade exec.; b. Martinsville, Va., Oct. 3, 1934; s. James Russell and Elizabeth (Barker) F.; B.S. in B.A., Va. Poly. Inst. and State U., 1960; children—Susan L., Deborah G., Robert James, Michael J. Mgmt. trainee Ruben H. Donnelly Corp., Washington and Balt., 1960-63; customer service mgr. Am. of Martinsville, 1963-64, Western sales service mgr., 1964-67, Atlantic dist. mgr., 1967-75, contract mgr., 1975-77, v.p., 1977—. Sec., Jaycees, 1964, internal v.p., 1965, external v.p., 1966, pres., 1967. Served with U.S. Army, 1953-56. Mem. Am. Mgmt. Assn., Alpha Kappa Chi. Office: Hairston St Martinsville VA 24112

FRAZIER, WILLIAM (JAMES), urologist; b. Gary, Ind., Aug. 20, 1942; A.B. in Biology, Fisk U., 1964; M.D., Ind. U., 1968; m. Veronica Frazier; 4 children. Intern, Baylor U. Med. Center, Dallas, 1968-69, resident in gen. surgery, 1969-70; resident in urology Barnes Hosp., St. Louis, 1972-75; practice medicine specializing in urology, Dallas, 1975—; mem. staff Baylor U. Med. Center, St. Paul Hosp., Dallas, Presbyn. Hosp., Dallas, Parkland Hosp., Dallas; cons. urologist to hosps; clin. instr. Southwestern U. Med. Sch. Chmn. public edn. dist. 23 Am. Cancer Soc., Dallas, 1978-79; bd. dirs. Am. Cancer Soc., Dallas, Operation Lift, Dallas, Spl. Care Sch., Dallas. Served to maj. USAF, 1970-72; Vietnam. Decorated Bronze Star; recipient Trailblazer award South Dallas Bus. and Profl. Women's Club, 1978; diplomate Am. Bd. Urology. Fellow A.C.S.; mem. AMA, Dallas County Med. Soc. (chmn. mediations com. 1980), Tex. Med. Assn., Nat. Med. Assn., Am. Coll. Emergency Physicians, C.V. Roman Med. Soc. (pres.). Office: Baylor Med Plaza Suite 806 3600 Gaston Ave Dallas TX 75246 also 5459 La Sierra Dr Dallas TX 75231

FRAZIER, WILLIAM EDWARD, JR., fin. co. exec.; b. Anson, Maine, Sept. 6, 1922; s. William E. and Edith M. (Gordon) F.; student Colby Coll., 1938-42; m. Mildred B. Dzwonkoski, Mar. 6, 1946; children—Janet Edith, Matthew Griffin. Vice pres. sales L.P.G. Equipment Co., Orlando, Fla., 1946-61; v.p. City Gas Co. Fla., Hialeah, 1961-64; v.p. Tropic Air Distributors Co., Melbourne, Fla., 1964-67; asso. v.p. A.G. Edwards & Sons, Orlando, Fla., 1968—. Served to capt., USAAF, 1940-45. Decorated D.F.C. Mem. Democrat. Presbyterian. Clubs: Elks, Masons. Home: 1305 Belmont Dr Orlando FL 32806 Office: 201 E Pine St Orlando FL 32802

FRECHTEL, GLADYS, med. assn. exec.; b. N.Y.C., Apr. 21, 1925; s. Samuel and Freda Messer; R.N., Beth Israel Hosp., 1946; B.S., Columbia U., 1952; M.S., Barry Coll., 1966; m. Saul Frechtel, Jan. 28, 1951; children—Mona Lee, Jonathan Lee. Adj. instr. U. Miami, Fla., 1963-67; dir. nursing S. Fla. State Hosp., Hollywood, 1962-67; dir. nursing, edn. Parkway Gen. Hosp., Miami, 1967-69, asst. adminstr., 1969-74; patient care coordinator Am. Med. Internat., Atlanta, 1974-77, coordinator edn., 1977—. Mem. Nat. League for Nursing, Nat. Soc. Performance Instruction, Am. Acad. Med. Adminstrs., Am. Nurses Assn., Am. Soc. for Health Manpower Edn. and Tng., Am. Soc. Tng. and Devel., Assn. for Edn., Communication and Tech., Health Edn. Media Assn., Am. Mgmt. Assn. Club: Altrusa. Office: American Medical International 6400 Powers Ferry Rd Atlanta GA 30339

FREDE, RALPH EDWARD, coll. adminstr.; b. Floydada, Tex., Sept. 28, 1921; s. Elmer Fred and Marjorie (King) F.; B.J., U. Tex., 1943, M.A., 1947; m. Martha Camilla Chambers, Dec. 25, 1946; children—Phyllis Frede Patrick, Bethann Frede Walmus, Ellen Frede Lynn, Sarah Jane. Mgr. pub. relations and edn. Austin (Tex.) C. of C., 1947-48; dir. student employment bur. U. Tex., Austin, 1948-50; state rep. Nat. Found. Infantile Paralysis, Austin, Tex. and Jefferson City, Mo., 1950-56; dir. devel., exec. dir. U. Houston Found., 1956-70; lectr. pub. relations U. Houston, 1956-70; dir. devel. and pub. relations, v.p. pub. affairs Baylor Coll. Medicine, Houston, 1970—. Pres. bd. dirs. Protestant Charities Houston, 1966-67; bd. dirs. Houston United Fund, 1968. Served to lt. USNR, 1943-46. Recipient Silver Beaver award Boy Scouts Am., 1950. Mem. Pub. Relations Soc. Am. (past dir.; Silver Anvil award 1965, Gold Anvil award 1972), Am. Coll. Pub. Relations Assn. (dist. chmn. 1969; Exceptional Achievement award 1965), Found. Pub. Relations Research and Edn. (pres. 1975-77), Sigma Delta Chi. Episcopalian. Clubs: Friars (U. Tex.); Rotary (pres. Houston 1977-78). Home: 849 Hickorywood Ln Houston TX 77024 Office: 1200 Moursund Ave Houston TX 77030

FREDERICK, BEEBE RAY, JR., ins. agt.; b. Ft. Deposit, Ala., Oct. 12, 1938; s. Beebe R. and Emma Lou (Golson) F.; B.S. in Bus. Adminstrn., Auburn U., 1960. Investigator, U.S. Dept. Labor, 1961-62; sales rep. Liberty Mut. Ins. Co., 1962-64, Universal Underwriters, 1964-65; real estate salesman Auerbach-Jordan Co., Montgomery, Ala., 1966-67, ins. mgr., 1967-72; with Frederick Agy., Montgomery, Ala., 1972—, pres., 1976—; v.p. Contractors Appliance & Lighting, Inc.; partner H&F Cattle Co., B&C Land Co. Mem. Montgomery County Republican Com., 1970—; bd. dirs. Young Rep. Nat. Fedn., 1971-73, del., 1971; chmn. Montgomery Young Republicans, 1971-72; alternate del. Rep. Nat. Conv., 1972, del., 1976; mem. Montgomery Riverboat Commn., 1971-74; trustee Brantwood Childrens Home, 1973-77. Served as 2d lt. U.S. Army, 1960-61. Mem. Ala. Ind. Ins. Agts. (dir. 1976-80), Ind. Ins. Agts. Montgomery (past pres.), Sales Marketing Execs. Montgomery (treas. 1976-77). Methodist. Home: 3144 Old Dobbins Rd Montgomery AL 36116 Office: 624 S Perry St Montgomery AL 36104

FREDERICK, MARGIE GARRETT, acctg. co. exec.; b. Orlando, Fla., Oct. 3, 1926; d. Walter Terry and Lillian Dale (Johnston) Garrett; student Miami Dade Jr. Coll., 1964; m. Auburn Collins Frederick, Nov. 28, 1945; children—Ronald Stephen, Karen Elaine, Beverly Carol. With payroll dept. Miami Air Depot, 1944-45; asst. bookkeeper Baldwin Ins. Agy., Miami, 1946-47; clk. Police Dept. and City of Hialeah, Fla., 1955-56; pres., acct. Margie Frederick Income Tax and Acctg. Service, Inc., Hialeah, 1959—, also dir.; dir. Aircheck, Inc. Mem. Internat. Assn. Accredited Tax Cons., Fla. Notary Pub. Assn., Nat. Genealogy Soc., Atlantic Christian Assos., Am. Bus. Womens Assn., Hialeah-Miami Springs C. of C. Mem. Ch. of Christ. Club: Pilot Internat. Home: 675 E 33rd St Hialeah FL 33013 Office: 4250 E 4th Ave Hialeah FL 33013

FREDERIKSEN, RAND TERRELL, cardiologist; b. Lubbock, Tex., Nov. 21, 1941; s. R.T. and Ruthe Simpson (Stanford) F.; student Tex. Technol. Coll., 1963; M.D., Washington U., St. Louis, 1967; m. Dixie Ward, Aug. 3, 1963; children—Ruth, David. Intern in internal medicine Ind. U. Med. Sch., Indpls., 1967-68; resident in medicine Parkland Meml. Hosp., Dallas, 1968-70; fellow in cardiology Washington U., St. Louis, 1970-71, Royal Postgrad. Med. Sch., London, 1973-74; practice medicine specializing in cardiology, Nashville, 1974—; mem. staff St. Thomas Hosp.; clin. instr. medicine Vanderbilt U., Nashville; clin. asst. prof. medicine Meharry Med. Sch., Nashville. Served to maj. MC, U.S. Army, 1971-73. Diplomate Am. Bd. Internal Medicine. Fellow Am. Coll. Cardiology. Home: 207 Lynwood Blvd Nashville TN 37205 Office: 4230 Harding Rd Nashville TN 37205

FREDETTE, VICTOR NORBERT, JR., data mgmt. exec.; b. New Bedford, Mass., Feb. 29, 1940; s. Victor N. and Roseline (De Mello) F.; student Southeastern Mass. U., 1958-60, U. No. Colo., 1972-73; m. Maureen Mabel Lewin, May 2, 1964; children—Victor Norbert III, Michelle Lee. Finishing specification writer Acushnet Co., New Bedford, Mass., 1962-65; documentation specialist Portsmouth Naval Ship Yard, N.H., 1965-71; configuration mgmt. specialist Naval Weapons Lab., Dahlgren, Va., 1971-73; data mgr. Tri-Service Cartridge Actuated Devices, Dept. Def., 1973—; data mgmt. cons. Naval Ordnance Sta., Indian Head, MD, 1973—. Mem. King George (Va.) Cub Scout Com., 1975; mem. N.H. Hwy. Safety Com., 1970-71; chmn. Elem. Sch. Home Sch. Orgn., King George County, Va., 1978-79; vice chmn. King George County Bicentennial Com., 1973-76, chmn., 1976; vice chmn. King George County Fall Festival Com., 1975, chmn., 1976; mem. King George County Hwy. Safety Com., 1979—; vice chmn. King George County Med. Services Com.,

1979—. Served with U.S. Army, 1961-62. Mem. Packaging Inst., Am. Def. Preparedness Assn., Va. Jaycees (presdl. award 1973, state chmn. 1975-76, life mem.), King George (Va.) Jaycees (award of merit 1973, pres. 1972-73). Roman Catholic. Home: RFD 2 Box 522L King George VA 22485 Office: CAD Engr Code 51211 Naval Ordnance Sta Indian Head MD 20640

FREDRIKSON, RICHARD JAMES, data processing co. exec.; b. Pontiac, Mich., Sept. 13, 1952; s. Joseph and Margaret Anna (Krug) F.; student Oakland U., 1972; B.B.A., Western Mich U., 1974; M.B.A., Fla. State U., 1975; m. Barbara Ann Lai-Sun, Dec. 22, 1977. Asst. dir. Mediation and Conciliation Service, Fla. Dept. Commerce, Tallahassee, 1974-75; office systems account mgr. IBM, Tallahassee, 1976—. Mem. Fla. Gov.'s Bd. of Arbitrators for Labor Disputes, 1975—; mem. Republican Nat. Com., 1979—. Recipient Gov. Reubin O.D. Askew Arbitrator award, 1975; F.C. Wiser award Trans World Airlines, 1971; named Mktg. Man of Yr., IBM, 1978; Fla. Dept. Commerce grantee, 1974-75. Mem. Am. Mktg. Assn. (officer), Western Econ. Assn., Assn. M.B.A. Execs. Republican. Roman Catholic. Club: Ambassador. Home: 1205 Valley Rd Albany GA 31707 Office: IBM 660 Apalachee Pkwy Tallahassee FL 32301

FREEDLE, S. DEAN, coll. adminstr.; b. Hartsville, Tenn., Jan. 5, 1932; s. Edgar Dean and Ruth Ellen (Harper) F.; B.S., Middle Tenn. State U., 1958, M.A., 1960; Ed.D., U. Tenn., 1972; m. Jenny Anderson, June 17, 1967; 1 dau., Elizabeth Ellen. Tchr., McMinnville (Tenn.) High Sch., 1958-62, Tullahoma (Tenn.) Sr. High Sch., 1962-63; prin. Central High Sch., Woodbury, Tenn., 1963-66; asst. prof. edn. Middle Tenn. State U., 1967-73, asso. prof., 1973-74; dean Sch. Edn. Miss. U. for Women, 1974—. Served with USAF, 1950-53. Mem. NEA, Miss. Assn. Edn., Assn. Supervision and Curriculum Devel., Miss. Assn. Higher Edn., Miss. Assn. Sch. Adminstrs., Phi Delta Kappa. Baptist. Research in attitude change through micro-teaching. Home: 1303 College St Columbus MS 39701 Office: Miss U for Women W-Box 280 Columbus MS 39701

FREEDMAN, ARNOLD MICHAEL, historian; b. N.Y.C., June 21, 1918; s. William Solomon and Ida (Mandel) F.; B.A., Fla. State U., 1963; M.A., U. Fla., 1964, Ph.D., 1978; m. Frederica Morris, Dec. 29, 1956 (dec. Dec. 1975). Sales mgr. Peterkin Co., N.Y.C., 1936-41; enlisted in U.S. Army, 1941, commd. 2d lt., 1943, advanced through grades to lt. col., 1962; service in Far East, Panama, C. Am., S. Am., ret., 1962; mem. faculty Palm Beach (Fla.) Jr. Coll., 1964—, prof. history, 1964—; adv. nat. def. Am. Security Council. Decorated Combat Inf. badge (2) with silver star, Bronze Star with V (5), Army Commendation medal (4), Purple Heart (3), also presdl. citations U.S., Philippines, Korea. Mem. Am. Hist. Assn., Ret. Officers Assn., Mil. Order World Wars. Democrat. Club: Masons (32 deg.). Home: 7978 Edgewater Dr West Palm Beach FL 33406 Office: 4200 S Congress Ave Lake Worth FL 33460

FREEDMAN, RICHARD SCOTT, mut. fund exec.; b. Brookline, Mass., May 12, 1942; s. David and Celia A. (Druckman) F.; B.S. in Bus. Adminstrn., U. Ariz., 1964; postgrad. in accounting U. Miami (Fla.), 1967; m. Linda D. Liner, July 1968; 1 son, Ross S. Financial analyst Ford Motor Co., Los Angeles, 1965-67; stockbroker Bache & Co., Miami, 1967-72; exec. v.p. Am. Birthright Trust Mgmt., Inc., Palm Beach, Fla., 1972—, also asst. sec. Am. Birthright Trust; pres. U.S. Fiduciary Trust Co., 1978—. Tax cons., investment adviser. Mem. Soc. Fin. Planning, Sigma Alpha Mu (chpt. treas.). Clubs: Kiwanis (organizer, charter mem. Kendall); Blue Hills Golf and Country (Canton, Mass.); Villa Del Rey Golf (Delray Beach, Fla.). Contbr. photographs and articles to nat. publs. Home: 724 Jacana Way North Palm Beach FL 33408 Office: 247 Royal Palm Way Palm Beach FL 33480

FREEHLING, PAUL ALBERT, retail exec.; b. Montgomery, Ala., Apr. 6, 1944; s. Arthur J. and Grace (McArdle) F.; B.S. in Mus.Ed., U. Ala., 1966; student Ind. U., 1964, Auburn U., 1967—, Troy State U., 1963; m. Norma Lee Hobbie, Aug. 30, 1964; children—Jessica, Jennifer. Mgr., Custom Coin Supplies, Montgomery; program dir. Boys Clubs Tuscaloosa County (Ala.), 1967-68, camp dir., 1968; mgr. sheet music dept. Art's Music Shop, Montgomery, 1969-73, gen. mgr., 1973-76, pres., 1976—; dir. Consumer Credit Corp., 1980—. Active Tukabatachee council Boy Scouts Am., 1955—. Recipient Montgomery Advt. Club award, 1975, 79; Nat. Brand Names Retailer of Year, 1972. Mem. Nat. Assn. Music Merchants, Am. Fedn. Musicians, Nat. Assn. Sch. Music Dealers, PK Music Study Club, Montgomery C. of C. (edn. com. 1978—), Montgomery Fedn. Musicians. Home: 1217 Wentworth Dr Montgomery AL 36106 Office: 149 Lee St Montgomery AL 36104

FREELAND, SUSAN MARIE, speech pathologist; b. Cedar Rapids, Iowa, Apr. 25, 1943; d. Walter Francis and Ruth Margaret (Mills) Hogan; B.A., Marquette U., 1966; M.A., U. Iowa, 1970; m. James Keith Freeland, Dec. 28, 1968; 1 son, John Edward. Speech clinician Bd. Edn., Chgo., 1967; head resident U. Iowa, 1968-70; speech pathologist Easter Seal Soc., Orlando, Fla., 1972-73; pvt. practice speech pathology, Orlando, Fla., 1974—; cons. various hosps. Active, Jr. League, Sr. Day Care Center; bd. dirs. John Young Museum Guild, Arts Guild, Audubon Soc. Recipient Sr. Acad. award Sch. of Speech, Marquette U., 1965. Mem. Am. (certificate of clin. competence), Fla. speech and hearing assns., Fla. Cleft Palate Assn. Democrat. Roman Catholic. Home: 1010 Lake Adair Orlando FL 32804 Office: 801 N Magnolia St Orlando FL 32802

FREEMAN, ALGEANIA WARREN, speech pathologist; b. Dunn, N.C., Jan. 24, 1949; d. Robert and Ada Jackson; B.S., Fayetteville State U., 1970; M.S. (grad. fellow 1970, internship award 1971), So. Ill. U., 1972; Ph.D., Ohio State U., 1977; m. Ernest Freeman, Aug. 19, 1972. Speech pathologist Americana Nursing Center, Decatur, Ill., 1972-73; instr. Norfolk (Va.) State Coll., 1973-75, asst. prof. speech pathology, 1978—; clin. supr. Ohio State U., 1975-76; chairperson speech communication dept. N.C. A. and T. State U., Greensboro, 1977-78; cons. Del. State Coll., 1978. Communication dir. City Councilman's Campaign, 1978. Recipient Outstanding Pan-Hellenic award, 1972, Teaching Asso. award Ohio State U., 1975, Outstanding Ednl. award, 1977. Mem. Am. Speech, Lang. and Hearing Assn. (cert. clin. competence), Va. Speech and Hearing Assn., Zeta Phi Beta. Clubs: Chums, Inc.; Blazer Civic (v.p. 1979). Home: 7371 Kirby Crescent Norfolk VA 23505 Office: PO Box 2384 Norfolk State U Norfolk VA 23504

FREEMAN, BEE JAY, educator; b. Scranton, S.C., July 22, 1924; d. Dollon and Creacie (McClamb) Jones; A.B., Shaw U., 1946; M.A., Atlanta U., 1970; m. Raymond Louis Freeman, Nov. 15, 1962; 1 dau., Rachael Durrell. Tchr., Dillard High Sch., Goldsboro, N.C., 1963-65; Fulbright prof. Tokyo U. of Edn., 1958-59; City Schs., 1965-69, 71-72; instr. Memphis Reading Center, 1972-73; instructional content specialist WKNO-TV, Memphis, 1973-74; script writer high sch. English series Project CABLECOM, Memphis, 1974-77; asso. prof. English, Shelby State Community Coll., 1977—. Vol. reader closed circuit radio broadcast to blind and physically handicapped WLYX. Mem. Assn. Supervision and Curriculum Devel., Nat. Assn. Ednl. Broadcasters, Coll. English Assn., Poetry Soc. Tenn., Nat. Writers Club. Democrat. Mem. Ch. Christ. Contbr. poetry to mags. Home: 811 E McLemore Ave Memphis TN 38106 Office: PO Box 4568 Memphis TN 38104

FREEMAN, BERNICE, ret. educator; b. LaGrange, Ga., Aug. 8, 1909; d. Thomas Norman and Everette (Jenkins) Freeman; A.B., Tift Coll., 1930; M.A. in English, U. N.C., 1932; Ed.D. in English, Columbia, 1952. Tchr. math. pub. schs., Dublin, Ga., 1930-31; tchr. social studies pub. schs., La Grange, Ga., 1932-42; tchr. social studies and English, Peabody Demonstration Sch., Ga. State Coll. Women, 1942-48, prin., tchr. 1948-51; dir. curriculum Troup County Schs., La Grange, 1951-67; asso. prof. edn. West Ga. Coll., Carrollton, Ga.; 1967-69, prof. edn., 1969-74, coordinator secondary edn. 1969-73, chmn. dept. secondary edn., 1973-74, ret., 1974. Del. Washington Conf. Academically Talented, 1958, White House Conf. Children and Youth, 1960; chmn. English curriculum guide com., Ga. Pub. Schs., 1960-64, mem. steering com., English curriculum guide com., 1965-68; pres. Ga. Dept. Instructional Supervision, 1961-62, co-dir. English Study in Ga., 1951-52. Bd. dirs. Troup-Harris-Cowetta Regional Library. Mem. League Women Voters (pres. Carrollton br. 1970-72), AAUW (pres. Ga. div. 1957-59), Ga. Council Tchrs. English (pres. 1947-48), Ga. Writers Assn., Ga. Acad. Social Scis., Nat. Council Tchrs. English, World Edn. Fellowship (dir. U.S. sect.), DAR (chpt. regent), Pi Lambda Theta, Kappa Delta Pi, Pi Gamma Mu, Delta Kappa Gamma. Preparation ednl. materials (with Lydia A. Thomas) The Reader's Digest, NEA (exec. com. dept. rural edn. 1965-69), Reading Skill Builder, Grade 5, Part 3, 1960. Home: 305 Park Ave LaGrange GA 30240

FREEMAN, DONALD WILFORD, real estate developer; b. Brooksville, Fla., Sept. 25, 1929; s. Fred Maxwell and Dovie (Keef) F.; B.S., U. Ala., 1953, LL.B., 1953; LL.M., N.Y. U., 1957; m. Ruby Jane Lewis, Feb. 25, 1956; children—Clifton Lewis, Susan Anne. Accountant Ernst & Ernst, Atlanta, 1953-55; admitted to Ala. bar, 1953; tax atty. Office Chief Counsel, U.S. Treasury Dept., N.Y.C., 1955-57, West Point Mfg. Co. (Ga.), 1957-58; asst. treas. Ryder System, Inc., Miami, Fla., 1958-61; v.p., dir., Henderson's Portion Pak, Inc., 1961-63; pres. Biscayne Capital Corp., 1963-66; asso. Lazard Freres & Co., N.Y.C., 1967-69; pres. James A. Ryder Corp., Miami, 1969-78, Fla. Mobile Home Communities, Inc., Vero Beach, Fla., 1978—. Served with AUS, 1946-48; PTO. C.P.A., Ga. Mem. Fla. Inst. C.P.A.'s, Phi Kappa Sigma, Beta Gamma Sigma. Episcopalian. Home: 13026 Nevada St Coral Gables FL 33156 Office: 7300 State Rd 60 Vero Beach FL 32960

FREEMAN, FRANK RAY, counselor; b. French Lick, Ind., Sept. 16, 1936; s. William Stanford and Amanda Victoria (Fentress) F.; student Ball State U., 1954-55; A.B., Bellarmine Coll., 1958; postgrad. Georgetown U., 1958-60; M.Ed., Spalding Coll., 1967; postgrad. Cath. U., 1977-79. Head social studies Providence High Sch., Clarksville, Ind., 1960-64; tchr. DeSales High Sch., Louisville, 1964-66; prin. Carr Twp. Elementary Schs., Clark County, Ind., 1966-67; instr. U. Va., Falls Church, 1967-70; counselor, asso. prof. psychology No. Va. Community Coll., 1970—; pvt. practice clin. psychology, Springfield, Va., 1977—. Lic. profl. counselor. Mem. Am. Personnel and Guidance Assn., No. Va. Personnel and Guidance Assn., Va. Edn. Assn., NEA, AAUP, ACLU, Assn. Measurement and Evaluation in Guidance. Democrat. Home: 6905 Edgebrook Dr Springfield VA 22150 Office: 8333 Little River Turnpike Annandale VA 22003

FREEMAN, GEORGE CLEMON, JR., lawyer; b. Birmingham, Ala., Jan. 3, 1929; s. George Clemon and Annie Laura (Gill) F.; B.A. magna cum laude, Vanderbilt U., 1950; LL.B., Yale U., 1956; m. Anne Colston Hobson, Dec. 6, 1958; children—Anne Colston, George Clemon III, Joseph Reid Anderson. Admitted to Ala. bar, 1956, Va. bar, 1958, D.C. bar, 1974; law clk. to Justice Black, U.S. Supreme Ct., 1956; asso. firm Hunton & Williams, Richmond, Va., 1957-62, partner, 1962—. Cons. Va. Outdoor Recreation Study Commn. Va. Gen. Assembly, 1964-65, gov's. spl. com. on water resources, 1966. Mem. Richmond Democratic Com., 1964—, chmn., 1969-72. Bd. dirs. Richmond Symphony, 1958-64, sec., 1960-64; chmn. Va. chpt. Nature Conservancy, 1962-64. Served to lt. (j.g.) USNR, 1951-54. Mem. Am. (chmn. standing com. on facilities Law Library of Congress 1967-73, mem. council sect. corp. banking and bus. law 1975-79, chmn. trade assn. com. 1969-75, chmn. ad hoc com. fed. criminal code 1979—), Va., D.C., Richmond bar assns., Am. Law Inst., Phi Beta Kappa, Phi Delta Phi, Omicron Delta Kappa. Episcopalian. Clubs: Country of Va.; Knickerbocker (N.Y.C.); Met. (Washington). Contbr. articles to profl. jours. Home: 10 Paxton Rd Richmond VA 23226 Office: PO Box 1535 Richmond VA 23212 also 919 Pennsylvania Ave Washington DC 20006

FREEMAN, IDA RUTH, artist; b. Cleve., Apr. 19, 1908; d. Aaron and Bertha Marshall; B.A., Cleve. Inst. Art, 1929; 1 dau., Ronna Freeman Brodsley. Art counselor Camp Anisfield, Huron, Ohio, 1926, 27, 28, 29; substitute art tchr. Cleve. Public Schs., Karamu House, 1929; art tchr. Akron Ohio Public Schs., 1930-41; self-employed as art tchr., Hollywood, Fla., 1979—. Mem. Cleve. Inst. Art Alumni Assn., Hollywood Art Guild, Sumi-e Soc. Am. Democrat. Office: 1909 Harrison St Room 201 Hollywood FL 33020

FREEMAN, JAMES DREW, SR., comml. and indsl. lighting mfg. co. exec.; b. Jonesboro, Ga., July 13, 1924; s. Jesse Bryan and Nell Cornelia (Woolf) F.; ed. high sch.; student Internat. Accountants Soc.; m. Zella B. Wise, Apr. 19, 1947; children—J. Drew, Josie D., Nell W. Jr. acct., George H. Dombhart, C.P.A., Charlotte, 1946-47; office mgr. Minute Grills of Charlotte, 1947-51; works acct. H.K. Porter Co. Inc., Charlotte, 1951-72; controller Benjamin div. Thomas Industries Inc., Sparta, Tenn., 1972—. Served with USN, 1942-45. Mem. Nat. Assn. Accts. Republican. Mem. Disciples of Christ. Club: Masons. Office: Benjamin div Thomas Industries Inc PO Box 180 Sparta TN 38583

FREEMAN, JERE EVANS, agribusiness exec.; b. Martin, Tenn., Oct. 13, 1936; s. T.C. Donald and Ludie Blanche (Brooks) F.; B.S., U. Tenn., Martin, 1958; M.S., U. Ill., 1961, Ph.D., 1962; M.B.A., U. Chgo., 1975; m. Barbara Jean Magnuson, Dec. 29, 1962; children—Gregory E., Kristina L., Curtis M., J. Brent. Research scientist CPC Internat. Inc., Argo, Ill., 1962-68, research sect. leader, 1968-76, dir. bus. environ. research, Englewood Cliffs, N.J., 1976-77, corp. dir. indsl. research and devel., 1977-78, mgr. tech. and capital planning N. Am. div., 1978-79; v.p. corp. devel. Gold Kist Inc., Atlanta, 1979—; co. rep. Agrl. Research Inst., Indsl. Research Inst. Judge state expn. Ill. Jr. Acad. Scis., 1962-75; active Am. Cancer Soc. Mem. Planning Execs. Inst., Am. Soc. Agronomy, Am. Assn. Cereal Chemists, Inst. Food Technologists, Sigma Xi, Gamma Sigma Delta. Contbr. articles to profl. publs.; patentee in field. Office: PO Box 2210 Atlanta GA 30301

FREEMAN, JERRE MINOR, ophthalmologist; b. Memphis; M.S., Auburn U., 1955; M.D., U. Tenn., 1963; m. Anne Dodd, June 7, 1956; children—James, John, Ashley. Intern, Bapt. Meml. Hosp., Memphis, 1964; resident in ophthalmology U. Tenn., 1965-67; dir. tng. in ophthalmology U. Tenn. Med. Center, 1968-73; practice medicine specializing in ophthalmology and cataract surgery, Memphis, 1968—; asso. clin. prof. U. Tenn. Med. Sch., 1973—. Chmn. com. devel. inexpensive intraoccular lens for implant, in 3d world countries. Served as pilot USN, 1956-59. NIH fellow, 1964; Heed fellow Harvard U. Med. Sch., 1968. Mem. AMA, Memphis Med. Assn. Presbyterian. Club: University (Memphis). Author articles, chpts. on cataracts. Home: 1509 Peabody Ave Memphis TN 38104 Office: 188 S Bellevue St Suite 405 Memphis TN 38104

FREEMAN, JOSEPH FRANCIS, III, polit. scientist; b. Evansville, Ind., Nov. 16, 1939; s. Joseph Francis and Caroline (Snow) F.; A.B., Ind. U., 1961; M.A., U. Va., 1963, Ph.D., 1969; m. Marjorie M. Morgan, Dec. 18, 1966; children—Joseph Francis, Willard. Instr., Wofford Coll., 1964-66, Emory U., 1967-69; asso. prof. polit. sci. Lynchburg Coll., 1970-77, prof., 1977—, chmn. dept. polit. sci., 1973—; participant Nat. Endowment for Humanities Spl. Summer Inst., Vanderbilt U., 1979. Mem. exec. bd. Episcopal Diocese of S.W. Va., 1974-77; candidate for Va. Ho. of Dels., 1975; mayor City of Lynchburg, 1976-78, mem. city council, 1978—; mem. Central Va. Planning Dist. Commn., 1978-80, Gov.'s Adv. Commn. Local Govt., 1980—. Earhart research fellow, 1974. Mem. Am. Polit. Sci. Assn., So. Polit. Sci. Assn. Republican. Club: Kiwanis. Author: Common Experience, 1976. Office: Polit Sci Dept Lynchburg Coll Lynchburg VA 24501

FREEMAN, JOYCE FAYE, biologist; b. Hillsboro, Tex., Nov. 22, 1934; d. George R. and Lura Lee Freeman; B.A., U. Tex., Austin, 1957; M.S., Tex. Woman's U., 1964, Ph.D., 1970. Tchr. biology Corpus Christi (Tex.) public schs., 1963, cons. secondary scis., 1973; asst. prof. Wharton (Tex.) Jr. Coll., 1968; asso. prof. biology and sci. edn. Corpus Christi State U., 1974—. NSF fellow, 1963-64. Mem. Am. Hort. Soc., Royal Hort. Soc., Tex. Acad. Sci., Tex. Assn. Radiation Biologists, Nat. Sci. Tchrs. Assn., Tex. Colls. Tchrs. Assn., Sigma Xi, Phi Theta Kappa, Beta Beta Beta, Iota Sigma Pi, Phi Delta Kappa, Pi Lambda Theta, Delta Kappa Gamma. Democrat. Mem. Ch. of Christ. Author papers in field. Office: 6300 Ocean Dr Corpus Christi TX 78412

FREEMAN, LARRY JOE, hosp. adminstr.; b. Jacksonville, Fla., Dec. 18, 1948; s. Eugene Clark and Nila Edna (Smith) F.; B.S., Fla. State U., 1970; lic. practical nurse certification Fitzsimmons Gen. Hosp., Denver, 1971; M.P.H., U. Tenn., 1975; m. Christina C. Fisher, Mar. 25, 1971; children—Joshua Joseph, Anthony Nicholas. Mgmt. trainee J.C. Penney & Co., Tallahassee, Fla., 1970-72; cons. Div. Health, Jacksonville, 1972-76; adminstr. Jacksonville Children's Hosp., Bapt. Med. Center, 1976—. Trustee Jacksonville Children's Hosp., 1976—; bd. dirs. N.E. Fla. Cancer Program, 1977—, YMCA, 1978—, N.E. Fla. chpt. March of Dimes, 1979—. Served with U.S. Army, 1971-72. Recipient Gift of Life award Emergency Med. Service Council. Mem. Am. Coll. Hosp. Adminstrs., Am. Hosp. Assn., Fla. Hosp. Assn., N.E. Fla. Hosp. Council, Jacksonville Hosp. Council. Democrat. Baptist. Club: Rotary. Home: 13259 Huguenot St Jacksonville FL 32225 Office: Jacksonville Children's Hosp Bapt Med Center 800 Prudential Dr Jacksonville FL 32207

FREEMAN, NOLEN W., police chief; b. Harrodsburg, Ky., June 12, 1931; s. William A. and Eula Virginia (Wilson) F.; B.S., Eastern Ky. U., 1970, M.A. in Criminal Justice, 1971; m. Daisy Tewney, Feb. 17, 1951; children—Nolen W., Will, Tony, Joey, Eric. Mem. Ky. State Police, 1953-58, Lexington (Ky.) Police Dept., 1958-72; police chief Gainesville (Fla.) Police Dept., 1972-76, Lexington-Fayette Urban County Div. Police, 1976—; instr., panel mem. Traffic Inst., Northwestern U.; cons. in field. Served with USMCR, 1949-53. Recipient Freedom Found. award, 1970. Mem. Internat. Assn. Chiefs Police, Ky. Assn. Chief Police (v.p. 1979), Ky. Peace Officers Assn. Address: 1409 Forbes Rd Lexington KY 40505

FREEMAN, RICHARD R., oil co. exec.; b. Buffalo, Mo., July 8, 1942; s. Clarence Bertram and Beulah Freeman; student S.W. Bapt. Coll., 1963; m. Nell Dees, Sept. 19, 1964; children—Suzanne Michelle, Chase Anthony. Supr. treasury dept. Phillips Petroleum Co., Kansas City, Mo., 1964-69; corp. cash coordinator, treasury Conoco Inc., Ponca City, Okla., 1969-76, coordinator stockholder services and stock transfer, 1976—. Mem. Ponca City Park and Recreation Bd., 1976-78; mem. adv. bd. Bd. Edn., 1974-75; Republican precinct chmn., 1977; active PTA, YMCA. Mem. S.W. Stock Transfer Assn., Am. Mgmt. Assn. Baptist. Club: Masons. Home: 2708 Kingston St Ponca City OK 74601 Office: 1000 S Pine St Ponca City OK 74601

FREEMAN, ROBERT ALFRED, ecologist, state ofcl. b. Phila., Nov. 14, 1946; s. Alfred Charles and Marion Arlene (Weber) F.; B.S., Drexel U., 1969; M.S., Colo. State U., 1970, Ph.D., 1975. Analyst, U.S. AEC, N.Y.C., 1965-66; phys. chemist Franklin Inst. Research Labs., Phila., 1967-69; field coordinator Inst. Water Research, Mich. State U., East Lansing, 1970-72; research asso. dept. biology U. Ky., Lexington, 1976-78; ecologist Ky. Div. Water Quality, Frankfort, 1979—; lectr. in field. Bd. dirs. Lexington Food Coop., 1977-78. Colo. Div. Wildlife grantee, 1972-75; EPA Symposium travel grantee, 1977. Mem. Am. Chem. Soc., Am. Fisheries Soc., ASTM, Aquatic Tech. Group, Nat. Wildlife Fedn. Universalist. Contbr. articles in field to profl. jours. Home: Star Route Box 105A Clearfield KY 40313 Office: Div Water Quality Century Plaza Frankfort KY 40601

FREEMAN, ROBERT MATTHEW, III, mech. engr.; b. Asheville, N.C., Feb. 25, 1941; s. Robert M., Jr., and Anna Lou (Rhinehardt) F.; B.S.M.E. magna cum laude, U. Pitts., 1974, M.B.A. in Fin. (Grad. Sch. Bus. fellow), 1975; m. Victoria Mary Linkovich, Nov. 19, 1966; 1 dau., Jennifer Anne. Primary cons. nuclear safety and quality assurance Swindell-Dressler Co., also lectr. nuclear systems and quality assurance Beaver County Community Coll., 1974-75; sr. project engr. Exxon Co., 1975-76, sr. econ. and planning analyst, 1977, air quality specialist Marine Dept., Houston, 1978—. Bd. dirs. Timberlake Improvement Dist., pres., 1976-77, v.p., 1978-79; area rep. Council Cypress Creek Water Dists., 1977-78. Served with U.S. Navy, 1964-73. Mem. Assn. M.B.A. Execs., Assn. Water Bd. Dirs., Air Pollution Control Assn., Am. Petroleum Inst., Western Oil and Gas Assn., Am. Inst. Mcht. Shipping, Aircraft Owners and Pilots Assn. Republican. Methodist. Authority on marine air quality control econs. and tech. Home: 13103 Lazdins Circle Cypress TX 77429

FREEMAN, SIMON DAVID, govt. ofcl., civil engr., lawyer; b. Chattanooga, Jan. 14, 1926; s. Morris and Lena Freeman; B.S. in Civil Engring., Ga. Inst. Tech., 1948; LL.B., U. Tenn., 1956; children—Anita R., Stanley A., Roger L. Engr., TVA, Knoxville, Tenn., 1948-54, atty., 1956-61, dir., 1977-78, chmn. bd., 1978—; admitted to Tenn. bar, 1957, D.C. bar, 1965, U.S. Supreme Ct. bar, 1964; asst. to chmn. FPC, Washington, 1961-65; head energy policy staff Office Sci. and Tech., Exec. Office of Pres., 1967-71; dir. energy policy project Ford Found., Washington, 1971-74; spl. energy and resources cons. U.S. Senate Commerce Com., Washington, 1974-76; mem. White House Energy Staff, 1976-77; bd. dirs. Electric Power Research Inst., U.S. Nat. Com. of World Energy Conf. Served with U.S. Mcht. Marine, 1943-44. Registered profl. engr., Tenn. Mem. Am. Bar Assn., Fed. Bar Assn., Order of Coif. Democrat. Jewish. Author: Energy: The New Era, 1974; dir. final report of Ford Found. Energy Policy Project, pub. as A Time To Choose, 1974. Home: 1431 Cherokee Trail # 122 Knoxville TN 37920 Office: 400 Commerce Ave (E12A7) Knoxville TN 37902

FREEMAN, STEPHEN WALLACE, psychologist; b. Bronx, N.Y., Aug. 8, 1941; s. Henry and Rosylind Freeman; B.Ed., U. Miami, 1963; M.A. in Counseling and Psychology, Appalachian State U., 1965; Ed.D. in Cons. Psychology, U. Tenn., 1970; m. Amy Lydia Thornton, Dec. 19, 1965; children—Amy Alecia, Kristine Dawn. Instr. psychology Sweet Briar Coll., 1966-68; supervising clin. psychologist Birth Defects Center, Knoxville, Tenn., 1970-72; cons. psychologist Community Mental Health Center, Pensacola, Fla., 1974-76, U.S. Navy, Corry Sta., Pensacola, 1978; chief psychologist Greene Valley Devel. Center, Greeneville, Tenn., 1978—; bd. dirs. Escambia County Assn. Retarded Citizens, 1975-78, N.W. Fla. Assn. Children with Learning Disabilities, 1975-78, United Cerebral Palsy of N.W. Fla., 1975-78, Epilepsy Soc. N.W. Fla., 1975-77; mem. profl. adv. bd. Fla. Assn. Children with Learning Disabilities, 1975-78. Recipient Humanitarian award United Cerebral Palsy Assn. N.W. Fla., 1976; Brotherhood award Fla. Assn. Retarded Citizens, 1977; named Outstanding Educator, Fla. Assn. for Children with Learning Disabilities, 1978. Mem. Am. Psychol. Assn., Am. Assn. Mental Deficiency, Council for Exceptional Children, Epilepsy Found. Am., Nat. Assn. Children with Learning Disabilities, Nat. Assn. Retarded Citizens. Democrat. Unitarian. Author: Does Your Child Have A Learning Disability, 1974; The Epileptic in Home School and Society, 1979; contbr. articles to profl. jours. Home: 1505 Brentwood Dr Greeneville TN 37743 Office: Greene Valley Devel Center and Hosp Greenville TN 37743

FREEMAN, THOMAS RUMPH, surgeon; b. Marshallville, Ga., Dec. 29, 1918; s. Horace T. and Annita (Rumph) F.; A.B., Emory U., 1939, M.D., 1943; m. Carol Glisson, Aug. 29, 1973; children—Lane, Thomas R., Robert H., Angela D., Lauren Annita. Intern, U.S. Naval Hosp., Portsmouth, Va., 1944; resident Emory U. Hosp., Atlanta, 1946-50; pvt. practice medicine, specializing in surgery, Savannah, Ga., 1950—; pres. med. staff Candler Hosp., Savannah, 1962-63, chmn. dept. surgery, 1978-80; mem. staff St. Joseph's Hosp., Savannah, 1950-80; mem. Meml. Med. Center, Savannah, 1955-80; mem. Surg. Assos. of Savannah, 1970—. Bd. dirs. Better Bus. Bur., Savannah, 1958-60. Served to lt. M.C., USNR, 1943-46. Diplomate Am. Bd. Surgery. Fellow A.C.S.; mem. AMA, Med. Assn. Ga., Ga. Med. Soc. (pres. 1975), Savannah Surg. Soc. (pres. 1955), Savannah C. of C. (dir. 1965-66), Hist. Savannah. Methodist. Clubs: Savannah Golf (pres. 1958-59), Oglethorpe. Engaged in pioneer surg. treatment of strokes in the South, 1958—. Home: 7519 LaRoche Ave Savannah GA 31406 Office: 200 E 31st St Savannah GA 31402

FREER, LESLIE ALBERT, gunsmith; b. Newark, N.J., Dec. 25, 1905; s. Thomas Washington and Selina Lydia (Kaelin) F.; student pub. schs., Newark, N.J.; m. Ann Elizabeth Blank, Sept. 5, 1931; 1 son, Richard Paul. Owner, Les Freer Gun Shop, Gillette, N.J., 1931-42; co-owner Freer & Kent Gun Shop, Dallas, 1946-52; with Simmons Gun Specialties, Kansas City, Mo., 1952-57; owner Les Freer Gun Shop, Houston, 1957—. Served with USN, 1942-45; ATO; PTO. Mem. Am. Def. Preparedness Assn., Nat. Rifle Assn., Tex. Rifle Assn., Bayou Rifles, Inc. Inventor in field. Home: 1714 Hollow Hook Dr Houston TX 77080 Office: 8928 Spring Branch Dr Houston TX 77080

FREESE, HOWARD LEE, engring. co. exec.; b. Charleston, W. Va., Dec. 9, 1941; s. Floyd Herschel and Laura Alice (O'Dell) F.; B.S., Columbia, 1965; M.B.A., Syracuse U., 1972; div.; children by previous marriage—Laura Katharine, Daniel Friedrich, Matthew Stephen. Jr. process engr. Union Carbide Corp., South Charleston, W.Va., 1962-63; process engr. Corning Glass Works Corp., Blacksburg, Va., 1965-67, application engr., Corning, N.Y., 1967-72; mgr. mktg. Luwa Corp., Charlotte, N.C., 1972-73, mgr. engring., 1973-75, v.p., sec., 1975—. Dist. chmn. Boy Scouts Am. Registered profl. engr., N.C. Mem. Am. Chem. Soc., Am. Inst. Chem. Engrs. (chmn. Central Carolinas sect. 1974-75), Am. Mgmt. Assn., Chem. Mktg. Research Assn., Charlotte C. of C. (mem. mktg. task force 1974), Beta Gamma Sigma, Beta Theta Pi, Theta Tau. Presbyterian. Clubs: Masons, Shriners, Owls. Contbr. articles to profl. jours. Home: 2729 Hampton Ave Charlotte NC 28207 Office: Luwa Corp PO Box 16348 Charlotte NC 28216

FREESE, SIMON WILKE, civil engr.; b. Blossom, Tex., Dec. 4, 1900; s. Wilke Harm and Novella (Hancock) F.; student So. Meth. U., 1917-19; B.S., Mass. Inst. Tech., 1921; postgrad. Trinity Coll., Cambridge U., 1923-24; m. Eunice Elizabeth Brooks, June 30, 1927; children—Eunice (Mrs. Robb H. Rutledge), John Wilke, Lee Brooks. Partner, Hawley & Freese, cons. civil engrs., Ft. Worth, 1927-28, Hawley, Freese & Nichols, cons. civil engrs., Ft. Worth, 1928-38; partner Freese & Nichols, Inc., Ft. Worth, 1938-76, chmn. bd., 1977—. Mem. Ft. Worth Bd. Edn., 1931-41. Served from maj. to lt. col., AUS, 1943-46. Mem. ASCE, Am. Water Works Assn., Nat. Soc. Profl. Engrs., Sigma Alpha Epsilon, Chi Epsilon. Mason. Club: Fort Worth. Home: 3318 Avondale St Fort Worth TX 76109 Office: 811 Lamar St Fort Worth TX 76102

FREIBURGER, E. ALLEN, mgmt. cons.; b. Chgo., Sept. 21, 1920; s. Emil Herman and Eleanor (Beringer) F.; student Northwestern U., 1939, 45, Lake Forest Coll., 1940, 41; m. Dolores Ruth Brant, June 15, 1946; children—Gary Allen, Gail Ann. Flight radio engr./cryptographer Intercontinental div. TWA, 1942-43; semi sr. engr. John M. Thorne, Inc., Washington, 1943-45; sales engr. Indsl. Condenser Corp., Chgo., 1946-48; regional sales mgr. Midwest region, govt. and indsl. div., dist. rep. radio and TV div. Philco Corp., Phila., 1948-53; regional mgr. Admiral Corp., Chgo., 1953-56; mdse. mgr. RCA Victor Div., Camden, N.J., 1956-57; gen. mgr. Concertapes, Inc., Wilmette, Ill., 1957-59; mgr. central-south region, communications systems div. ITT, Chgo., 1959-60; govt. relations mgr., videograph div. A.B. Dick Co., Chgo., 1960-63; Washington rep., mgr. NASA programs, mgr. aerospace programs, mgr. advanced tech. UNIVAC Def. Systems div. Sperry Rand Corp., St. Paul, 1963-67; dir. program devel. CEIR subs. Control Data Corp., Mpls., 1967; mgr. NASA programs, mgr. civil agys., space and def. div., mgr. NASA programs, advance systems mktg., sr. mktg. cons. Control Data Corp., Mpls., 1967-72; mktg. cons., dir. govt. mktg., dir. mktg., analytical services div. Tesdata Systems Corp., McLean, Va., 1972-73; owner Sr. Mktg. Engrs., fed. govt. bus. devel. cons., Falls Church, Va., 1973-76; dir. mktg., process systems div. LOGICON, Inc., Fairfax, Va., 1976; pres. INTERACTION, Inc., Arlington, Va., 1977—. Served with USNR, 1941-42. Mem. IEEE, Am. Inst. Aeros. and Astronautics, Sigma Pi Sigma (sustaining). Home: 3718 Tollgate Terr Falls Church VA 22041

FREIDKIN, GEORGE JACOB, cons.; b. Dallas, July 22, 1946; s. Marvin Joel and Deborah (Miller) F.; B.A., U. Ala., 1974, M.B.A., 1977. Programmer, analyst Univ. Computing Co., Dallas, 1967-69; mgr. competitive analysis Com Share, Inc., Ann Arbor, Mich., 1969-70; sr. staff cons. Cord Cons. Co., Dallas and Tuscaloosa, Ala., 1972—; instr. indsl. mgmt. U. Ala., Tuscaloosa, 1977—. Served with U.S. Army, 1970-71. Mem. Assn. Computing Machinery, Theta Xi. Home: 602 Williamsburg E 3301 Loop Rd Tuscaloosa AL 35404 Office: PO Drawer BB University AL 35486

FRENCH, CARL WESTON, JR., oil co. exec.; b. Kilgore, Tex., Oct. 19, 1937; s. Carl Weston and Louise Regina French; B.B.A., U. Houston; 1 son, Douglas Wayne. With Texaco Inc., Houston, 1953—, asst. mgr. corp. services, 1973-77, bldg. mgr., 1977—; loan officer Texaco Credit Union, 1973-77. Served with USAF, 1955-59. Mem. Houston C. of C. Republican. Club: Texaco Country (dir. 1973-76). Office: PO Box 52332 Houston TX 77052

FRENCH, CHARLES O., ofcl. Nashville and Davidson County (Tenn.); b. Charleston, S.C., Feb. 14, 1942; s. Charles E. and Martha F. (Powell) F.; B.S., Tenn. Tech. U., 1967, M.A., 1969. Dist. mgr. Rogers Galleries div. Nasco, Inc., Nashville, 1965—; dir. Nashville Thermal Transfer Corp., Collegiate Co. pub. Collegiate Guidepost. Councilman, Met. Govt. Nashville and Davidson County, 1971—, chmn. pub. works com. and historic preservation com., now pres.; mem. spl. com. on constrn. Criminal Justice Center. Cons. Taft Inst. Govt., U. Tenn., 1972-73; pres. Contemporary Designs Corp., 1976—. Mem. Mayor Nashville Council Youth Opportunity; del. Nat. League of Cities cities and revenue sharing conf., 1973; asst. chmn. Muscular Dystrophy Telethon, Nashville, 1974; bd. dirs. Hist. Nashville; nat. fund-raising chmn. Tenn. Tech. U. Served with USN, 1960-62. Mem. Nashville Area C. of C., Nashville Better Bus. Bur., Sales and Mktg. Execs. Nashville. Home: 550 Foothill Dr Nashville TN 37217 Office: 205 Metro Courthouse Nashville TN 37201

FRENCH, ELIZABETH IRENE, biologist, educator, violinist; b. Knoxville, Tenn., Sept. 20, 1938; d. Junius Butler and Irene Rankin (Johnston) F.; B.Music, U. Tenn., 1959, M.S., 1962; Ph.D., U. Miss., 1973. Tchr. music, violinist symphony orch., Kingsport, Tenn., 1962-64; tchr. music, first violinist Birmingham (Ala.) Symphony Orch., 1964-66; first violinist Knoxville Symphony Orch., 1966-68, Memphis Symphony Orch., 1970-73; NASA trainee in biology U. Miss., 1969-70; asst. prof. biology and violin Mobile (Ala.) Coll., 1973—; performing violinist Ala. Artists Series, 1978-80; faculty adv. Mobile Coll. chpt. Alpha Chi honor soc., 1977—. Pres., Clara Schumann Music Club, 1977-79. Mem. AAAS, Assn. Southeastern Biologists, Nat. Audubon Soc., Wilderness Soc., Ala. Ornithol. Soc., Am. Fedn. Musicians, Ala. Fedn. Music Clubs (state chmn. chamber music). Republican. Episcopalian. Club: Mobile Bird. Research on DDT and rat reprodn., artificial female hormones and parasites. Home: 903 James St Saraland AL 36571 Office: PO Box 13220 Mobile AL 36613

FRENCH, JIM, paper co. exec.; b. Walnut Ridge, Ark., Dec. 14, 1944; s. James Leon and Opal Mardell (Sherrell) F.; B.S. in M.E., La. State U., 1970, postgrad. 1970; postgrad. Ga. Inst. Tech., 1978, So. Meth. U., 1979; m. Charlotte Ann Smith, July 29, 1967; children—Stacey, Brian, Christopher. Calculator, Louis J. Daigre Assn., Cons. Engrs., Alexandria, La., 1967; field crewman Pan Am. Engrs., Baton Rouge, 1967-68; designer Perrault & Perrault, Inc., Baton Rouge, 1968-69; project engr. Pineville (La.) Kraft Corp., 1970-72; project engr. Calkraft Paper Co., Elizabeth, La., 1972-73; engring. supt. Mill Engring. Dept., Boise So. Co., DeRidder, La., 1973—; cons. on house plans and home improvements. Judge local and regional sci. fairs; chmn. reorgn. com. PTO, 1975, mem., 1974—. Served with USAF, 1962-66. Recipient Outstanding Tchr. award, DeRidder Jr. C. of C., 1973-75. Mem. TAPPI, Am. Forestry Assn., La. Engring. Soc. Democrat. Roman Catholic. Club: Beauregard Country. Home: 38 Birch Dr DeRidder LA 70634 Office: PO Box 1000 DeRidder LA 70634

FREUND, EMMA FRANCES, med. technologist; b. Washington; d. Walter R. and Mabel W. (Loveland) Ervin; B.S., Wilson Tchrs. Coll., Washington, 1944; M.S. in Biology, Catholic U., Washington, 1953; cert. in mgmt. devel. Va. Commonwealth U., 1975; student SUNY, New Paltz, 1977, J. Sargeant Reynolds Community Coll., 1978; m. Frederic Reinert Freund, Mar. 4, 1953; children—Frances, Daphne, Fern, Frederic. Tchr. math. and sci. D.C. Sch. System, 1944-45; technician in parasitology lab., zool. div., U.S. Dept. Agr., Beltsville, Md., 1945-48; histologic technician dept. pathology Georgetown U. Med. Sch., Washington, 1948-49; clin. lab. technician Kent and Queen Anne's County Gen. Hosp., Chestertown, Md., 1949-51; histotechnologist surg. pathology dept. Med. Coll. Va. Hosp., Richmond, 1951—, supr. histology lab., 1970—. Asst. cub scout den leader Robert E. Lee council Boy Scouts Am., 1967-68, den leader, 1968-70. Mem. Am. Soc. Med. Technology (rep. to sci. assembly histology sect. 1977-78), Va. Soc. Med. Technology, Richmond Soc. Med. Technologists, Va. Soc. Histology Technicians (dir. 1979—), N.Y. Acad. Scis., Am. Soc. Clin. Pathologists (cert. histology technician), Nat. Geog. Soc., Va. Govtl. Employees Assn., AAAS, Nat. Soc. for Histotech., Smithsonian Instn., Sigma Xi, Phi Beta Rho, Kappa Delta Pi, Phi Lambda Theta. Home: 1315 Asbury Rd Richmond VA 23229 Office: Surgical Pathology Dept Medical College of Virginia Hosp 12th and Broad Sts Richmond VA 23298

FREY, GERARD LOUIS, clergyman; b. New Orleans, May 10, 1914; s. Andrew and Marie Therese (DeRose) F.; D.D., St. Joseph's Sem. at St. Benedict's, La., 1933; postgrad. Notre Dame Sem., New Orleans. Ordained priest Roman Catholic Ch., 1938, consecrated bishop, 1967; asst. pastor, Taft, La., 1938-46, St. Leo The Great Ch., 1946-47; asst. dir. Confraternity Christian Doctrine, Archdiocese New Orleans, 1946, dir., 1946-47; pastor St. Frances Cabrini Ch., New Orleans, 1952-63, St. Frances DeSales Ch., Houma, La., 1962-67; bishop Diocese of Savannah, Ga., 1967-72, Diocese of Lafayette, La., 1972—; clergy rep. 2d Vatican Council, 1964; dir. Diocesan Friendship Corps, New Orleans, 1966; Episcopal moderator Theresians Am., from 1968. Recipient Bishop Tracy Vocation award St. Joseph's Sem. Alumni Assn., 1959. Address: 421 Lippi Blvd PO Drawer 3387 Lafayette LA 70501*

FREY, HENRY RICHARD, oceanographer; b. N.Y.C., July 16, 1932; s. Henry George and Florence Stella (Tweed) F.; B.S. in Physics, Queens Coll., City U. N.Y., 1960; M.S. in Oceanography, N.Y. U., 1966, Ph.D. in Oceanography, 1971; m. Shaney Frey, June 4, 1960; children—Kathleen, Henry Christopher, Lawrence Keith. Group leader in underwater tech. Uniroyal Research Center, Wayne, N.J., 1960-66; program mgr., ocean sci. and engring. Uniroyal Inc., Wayne, 1966-67; sr. research scientist N.Y. U., N.Y.C., 1967-73; asso. prof. oceanography Poly. Inst. N.Y., N.Y.C., 1973-76; dir. phys. oceanography Alpine Geophys. Assos., Norwood, N.J., 1976-77; chmn. N.Y.C. Mayor's Oceanographic Adv. Com., 1971-74; tech. adviser Nat. Ocean Survey, NOAA, Rockville, Md., 1977—. Served with USMC, 1952-55. Recipient Spl. tribute Internat. Underwater Film Festival, 1965, N.Y. Underwater Film Expn., 1965; Founders Day award N.Y. U., 1971; Outstanding Performance award Dept. Commerce, 1978, 79. Mem. Am. Geophys. Union, Marine Tech. Soc. (sect. chmn. 1976), Sigma Xi. Author: 130 Feet Down, 1961; Diver Below, 1967; Camera Below, 1968; Underwater Photography, 1972; editor: Resources of the Worlds Oceans, 1973; contbr. articles to jours. and mags. Home: 8103 Lewinsville Rd McLean VA 22102 Office: NOAA Nat Ocean Survey 6001 Executive Blvd Rockville MD 20852

FREY, LINDA ANN, mfg. co. adminstr.; b. Bronx, N.Y., July 30, 1954; d. Raymond Edward and Regina Katherine (Neiminski) F.; B.A., Fairfield U., 1976; M.Ed., U. N.C., Greensboro, 1978. Counselor residence life U. N.C., Greensboro, 1977; adminstrv. asst. youth leadership program Greensboro Human Relations Commn., 1977; tng. specialist Western Electric Co., Greensboro, 1978—. Mem. Am. Personnel and Guidance Assn., Nat. Vocat. Guidance Assn., Profl. Assn. Diving Instrs., Cousteau Soc. Roman Catholic. Club: Sportime Racquet. Home: 2116 Pebble Dr Greensboro NC 27410 Office: Western Electric Co PO Box 25000 Greensboro NC 27420

FRI, DAVID LEROY, mining co. specialist; b. Chillicothe, Ohio, Jan. 26, 1943; s. Elvey Clifton and Margaret Esther (Shoemaker) F.; B.B.A., Ohio U., 1965; m. Cynthia Jane Godwin, Mar. 1, 1969; children—David LeRoy, Michael Brian, Heather Nicole. With Ortho Pharm. Corp., Erie, Pa., 1969-71, Tremco Mfg. Co., Erie, Pa., 1971-73; with Victalic Co. of Am., Charleston, W.Va., 1973-79, mining specialist, 1976-79; with Colt Industries, Garlock Inc., Knoxville, Tenn., 1979—. Served with U.S. Army, 1965-69. Decorated Bronze Star Medal. Mem. So. W.Va. Coal Preparation and Engring. Soc., Am. Legion, VFW, DAV, Am. Security Council (nat. adv. bd.), Nat. Rifle Assn., Am. Def. Preparedness Assn., Ky. Mining Inst., Soc. Mining Engrs., Am. Inst. Mining, Metall. and Petroleum Engrs., Charleston Jr. C. of C. (dir. 1975). Democrat. Methodist. Address: 9503 Boliver Circle Knoxville TN 37922

FRIBERG, EMIL EDWARDS, mech. engr.; b. Wichita Falls, Tex., Apr. 11, 1935; s. John Walter and Anne (Edwards) F.; B.S. in Mech. Engring., U. Tex., 1958; m. Jo Ann Rutta, Jan. 26, 1957; children—Emil Edwards, Vicki Lynn, Joe Alan. Engr., Tex. Electric Service Co., Wichita Falls, 1958-64, engring. cons., Ft. Worth, 1964-69; cons. engr. Love, Friberg & Assos. Inc., Ft. Worth, 1969—. Pres. Cons. Engrs. Council Tex., 1979-80; chmn. Com. Automated Procedures for Engring. Cons., 1974. Served to 2d lt. C.E., AUS, 1959. Registered profl. engr., Tex., Okla., La., Miss. Mem. U. Tex. Ex-Students Assn. (life), Am. Inst. Mech. Engrs., ASME, Nat., Tex. (pres. Ft. Worth chpt. 1972-73) socs. profl. engrs., Am. Soc. Heating, Refrigerating and Air-Conditioning Engrs. (pres. Ft. Worth chpt. 1973-74, dir., chmn. Region VIII 1975-78, dir.-at-large 1979—), Delta Upsilon (pres. Tex. Found. 1969, life). Baptist. Clubs: Rotary, Ft. Worth. Contbr. articles to profl. jours. Research in field. Home: 3406 Woodford Dr Arlington TX 76013 Office: 1414 Oil & Gas Bldg Fort Worth TX 76102

FRIBOURGH, JAMES HENRY, univ. adminstr.; b. Sioux City, Iowa, June 10, 1926; s. Johann Gunder and Edith Katherine (James) F.; B.A., U. Iowa, 1949, M.S., 1949, Ph.D., 1957; m. Cairdenia Minge, Jan. 29, 1955; children—Cynthia, Rebecca, Abbie. Instr., Little Rock Jr. Coll., 1949-56; asso. prof. biology Little Rock U., 1957-59, prof., 1959-69, chmn. dept., 1959-69; vice chancellor for acad. affairs U. Ark., Little Rock, 1969-78, exec. vice chancellor, 1978—; research biologist Dept. Interior, 1959-69, Charles Pfizer and Co., Inc., 1968-69; cons. VA Hosp. Fellow AAAS; mem. Am. Fisheries Soc. (cert. fisheries scientist), Electron Microscopy Soc. Am., AAUP, Sigma Xi, Phi Kappa Phi. Episcopalian. Co-author spl. sci. report Fisheries Bur. of Sport Fisheries and Wildlife; research, publs. in field; editor: A Course of Study for Biology, 1959. Office: 33d and Univ Ave Little Rock AR 72204

FRICK, ELMER FRANKLIN, JR., electric and gas co. exec.; b. Columbia, S.C., Nov. 5, 1925; s. Elmer Franklin and Blana (Fulmer) F.; B.S., U. S.C., 1947, M.Accountancy, 1969; m. Mary Elizabeth Paschal, June 14, 1952; children—Elizabeth, Kenneth. Accountant Esso Standard Oil Co., Columbia, S.C., Charlotte, N.C., 1948-58; supr. S.C. Electric & Gas Co., Columbia, 1958-67, internal auditor, 1967—. Active United Fund. Served with AUS, 1944-45. Cert. internal auditor. Mem Inst. Internal Auditors (bd. govs. 1969-75, treas. 1972, v.p. 1975, pres. 1976, dist. v.p. 1977-78, chmn. internat. admissions com. 1978, chmn. internat. membership com. 1979), Greater Columbia, West Columbia-Cayce (dir. 1975, v.p. 1976-77, pres. 1979) chambers commerce, Beta Gamma Sigma, Beta Alpha Psi. Lutheran. Home: 1108 Evergreen West Columbia SC 29169 Office: PO Box 764 Columbia SC 29218

FRICK, JOHN DAVID, geologist; b. Conroy, Iowa, Apr. 24, 1924; s. David Randolph and Rose M. (Olson) F.; B.A., UCLA, 1948, postgrad. 1948-50; student Stanford U., 1943-44; m. Edith Elliott, Oct. 19, 1963; children—John David, Douglas R., Leila K. Area exploration geologist Humble Oil & Refining Co., Los Angeles, 1950-63; with Calif. Humble, Corpus Christi, Tex., 1963-68, Exxon, Houston, 1968-74; with Houston Oil Internat., 1974—, v.p., 1978—. Served with U.S. Army 1943-46; ETO. Mem. Am. Assn. Petroleum Geologists, Geol. Soc. Am., Am. Geophys. Union, Houston Geol. Soc., Geophys. Soc. Houston. Republican. Presbyterian. Clubs: Univ., Riverbend Country. Contbr. articles to profl. jours. Home: 7515 Olympia St Houston TX 77063 Office: 1212 Main St Houston TX 77002

FRICK, KENNETH DARE, ednl. adminstr.; b. Fort Worth, May 16, 1924; married, 6 children. B.S. in Edn., Tex. Christian U., Fort Worth, 1953, M.Ed. in Ednl. Adminstrn., 1966; postgrad in Adminstrv. Leadership, North Tex. State U., Denton, 1975—. Internat. cons. engr., North Africa, Libya, 1956-63; tchr. Hurst (Tex.) Euless Bedford Ind. Sch. Dist., 1963-66, adminstrv. officer, 1966—. Mem. NEA (life), Tex. State Tchrs. Assn., Phi Delta Kappa Internat. (Life). Certified as tchr., prin., supt., adminstr., Tex. Home: 1604 Oak Creek Dr Hurst TX 76053 Office: 1849 Central Dr Bedford TX 76021

FRIDAY, WILLIAM CLYDE, univ. pres.; b. Raphine, Va., July 13, 1920; s. David L. and Mary E. (Rowan) F.; student Wake Forest Coll., 1937; B.S., N.C. State Coll., 1941; LL.B., U. N.C., 1948; LL.D., Belmont Abbey Coll., Wake Forest Coll., 1957, Duke, Princeton, 1958, Elon Coll., 1959, Davidson Coll., 1961, U. Ky., 1970, Mercer U., 1977; D.C.L., U. of South, 1976; m. Ida Howell, May 13, 1942; children—Frances H., Mary H., Ida Elizabeth. Admitted to N.C. bar, 1948; asst. dean students U. N.C., 1948-51, asst. to pres., 1951-55, sec. of univ., 1955-56, acting pres., 1956, pres., 1956—. Mem. Nat. Com. for Bicentennial Era; past chmn. Am. Council on Edn.; chmn. Pres.'s Task Force on Edn., 1966-67; vice chmn. So. Regional Edn. Bd., 1967-69, mem. exec. com., 1969—; mem. nat. council Boy Scouts Am. Trustee Carnegie Found. for Advancement Teaching; bd. visitors Davidson Coll.; mem. Carnegie Commn. on Higher Edn.; trustee Urban Inst., 1968-73, Am. Bd. Med. Spltys., 1975—, Howard U., 1975—, Citizen Involvement Network. Served as lt. USNR, World War II. Mem. Assn. Am. Univs. (pres. 1971). Democrat. Baptist. Home: 402 E Franklin St Chapel Hill NC 27514

FRIEDBERG, HAROLD DAVID, cardiologist; b. Johannesburg, S. Africa, June 7, 1927; s. Samuel and Violet (Grodzen) F.; M.D., U. Witwatersrand, Johannesburg, 1949; postgrad. U. London (Eng.), 1949-51, U. Manchester (Eng.), 1956-58; m. Patricia Ann Barnett, June 27, 1954; children—Mandy Violetta, Adrienne Valinda, Richard Charles, Adam Seth. Came to U.S., 1964. Intern, Baragwanath Hosp., Johannesburg, 1949-50; resident Royal Coll. Physicians Affiliated Hosps., London, 1950-54, Christie Hosp., Manchester, Eng., 1956-58; cons. cardiologist Salisbury, Rhodesia, 1959-63; fellow medicine Johns Hopkins Med. Sch., Balt., 1964-65; mem. staff Milwaukee County Gen. hosp.; mem. staff Milw. VA Hosp., chief cardiology, 1966-73, cons., 1973—; cons. cardiology St. Luke's Hosp., 1968—, dir. coronary care unit and pacemaker clinic, 1972-79; cons. cardiology Mt. Sinai Hosp., 1967—, Milw. Children's Hosp., 1972— (all Milw.); asso. clin. prof. medicine Med. Coll. Wis.; prof. medicine U. South Fla., Tampa, 1979—; sci. adviser to Cardiac Pacemakers, Inc., St. Paul, St. Jude Med. Inc., St. Paul. Fellow A.C.P., Am. Coll.

Chest Physicians, Am. Coll. Cardiology, Am. Heart Assn. Council Clin. Cardiology, Royal Coll. Physicians (London); mem. Wis. Heart Assn. (dir. 1970-78, pres. 1973), N.Am. Soc. Pacing and Electrophysiology (founding mem.), AAAS, Laennec Soc. Asso. editor Jour. Electrocardiology. Contbr. articles to profl. jours., chpts. to med. books. Home: 701 Lands End Longboat Key FL 33548 Office: PO Box 522 Longboat Key FL 33548

FRIEDEL, ROBERT OLIVER, physician; b. Flushing, N.Y., Aug. 4, 1936; s. August W. and Denise G. (D'Aoust) F.; B.S., Duke U., 1958, M.D., 1964; m. Susanne Weber, June 30, 1961; children—Christine, Scott, Karin, Linda. Intern, Duke U. Med. Center, Durham, N.C., 1964-65, resident psychiatry, 1967-70; practice medicine specializing in psychiatry, Durham, 1970-74, Seattle, 1974-77, Richmond, Va., 1977—; asst. prof. psychiatry and pharmacology dept. psychiatry Duke U. Med. Center, Durham, 1970-73, asso. prof. psychiatry, 1973-74, asst. prof. pharmacology, 1973-74; asso. prof. psychiatry and pharmacology U. Wash. Sch. Medicine, Seattle, 1974-77, dir. div. psychopharmacology, 1974-77, vice chmn. and dir. clin. services dept. psychiatry and behavioral scis., 1975-77; prof., chmn. dept. psychiatry Med. Coll. Va., Va. Commonwealth U., Richmond, 1977—, mem. staff hosp. Served to lt. comdr. USPHS, 1965-67. Recipient Research Scientist Devel. award NIMH, 1970-75. Diplomate Am. Bd. Psychiatry and Neurology. Fellow Am. Psychiat. Assn.; mem. Am. Psychopath. Assn., Soc. Biol. Psychiatry, Am. Soc. Pharmacology and Exptl. Therapeutics, Am. Coll. Neuropsychopharmacology, Am. Fedn. Clin. Research, Am. Soc. Neurochemistry, AAAS, Med. Soc. Va., Alpha Omega Alpha. Author: (with F.R. Hine, E. Pfeiffer, G. Maddox and P. Hein) Behavioral Science: A Selective View, 1972; contbr. articles on psychopharmacology to profl. jours. Home: 13722 Hickory Nut Point Midlothian VA 23113 Office: Dept Psychiatry Med Coll Va PO Box 710 1200 E Broad St Richmond VA 23298

FRIEDENBERG, KAREN ROSEN, educator; b. Savannah, Ga., May 3, 1949; d. Emanuel Fredrick and Thelma Zena (Reed) Rosen; student U. Ga., 1967-69, U. N.C., summer 1969, Harvard U., summer 1970; B.S., Emerson Coll., 1971, postgrad., 1971-72; cert. Katherine Gibbs Sch., 1972; m. Harry Friedenberg, Sept. 8, 1974. Women's editor weekly talk show WERS Radio, 1971; asst. registrar Emerson Coll., Boston, 1971-72; part-time tchr. Barbizon Sch., Boston, 1974: asst. to v.p., dir. advt. and public relations Jordan Marsh Co., Boston, 1973-74; broadcast coordinator, sr. staff copywriter Rich's, Atlanta, 1974-76; advt. and public relations dir. Northlake Mall Shopping Center, Atlanta, 1976-77, Lenox Sq. Shopping Center, Atlanta, 1977; advt. and prodn. cons. to small businesses; instr. Art Inst. Atlanta, Emory U., Atlanta, 1977-78; instr. advt. and public relations Bauder Coll. Fashion, Atlanta, 1979—. Bd. dirs. Feminist Action Alliance, 1975-76; v.p. public relations Nat. Council Jewish Women, 1977-78; mass media com., television coordinator DeKalb unit Am. Cancer Soc., 1977-78; press coordinator Lady Tara Golf Classic, 1975, COPE, 1978; active Atlanta High Mus. Art, 1979—, Young Careers Guild, 1979—. Named An Outstanding Young Woman of Am., 1976. Mem. Women in Communications, Ga. C. of C. (judge Stay and See Ga. Week 1978). Jewish. Clubs: Atlanta Ad 2 (publicity dir. 1975, v.p. public relations 1976), Atlanta Advt. (dir., publicity dir. 1977-78), Atlanta Press. Home: 60 Angus Trail Atlanta GA 30328

FRIEDMAN, ALAN WARREN, educator; b. Bklyn., June 8, 1939; s. Leon and Anne (Markowitz) F.; B.A., Queens Coll., 1961; A.M., N.Y. U., 1962; Ph.D., U. Rochester, 1966; children—Eric Lawrence, Scot Bradley, Lorraine Eve. Teaching asst. U. Rochester, 1963-64; mem. faculty U. Tex., Austin, 1964—, prof. English, 1976—, dir. plan II, 1972-76; Fulbright prof. Am. lit. U. Lancaster (Eng.), 1977-78. Founder, chmn. Neighborhood Assn., Austin, 1973; chmn. Austin Democratic Precinct Conv., 1972; del. state and county Dem. convs., 1972, 73; bd. dirs. Hillel Found., U. Tex. Fellow Nat. Endowment Humanities, 1970-71; grantee U. Tex., 1970-71, 77-78, 81. Mem. MLA, AAUP (chpt. pres. 1979-80), ACLU, Common Cause, Tex. Assn. Coll. Tchrs., Omicron Delta Kappa. Jewish. Author: Lawrence Durrell and The Alexandria Quartet: Art for Love's Sake, 1970; Multivalence: The Moral Quality of Form in the Modern Novel, 1978; editor: Forms of Modern British Fiction, 1975. Office: English Dept Univ Tex Austin TX 78712

FRIEDMAN, ALLEN SAUL, bus. exec.; b. Salisbury, Md., Apr. 26, 1952; s. Harry and Toby (Gorowsky) F.; B.S., Phila. Coll. Textiles and Sci., 1974; m. Karen Anapol, June 9, 1974. Merchandising rep. fibers div. Allied Chem. Corp., N.Y.C., 1974-76; regional mgr. Viking Carpets, Inc., N.Y.C., Miami, Fla., 1976-79; asst. mgr. Cooper Distbrs., Inc., Miami, 1979—. Home: 492 NW 165th St Rd Miami FL 33169 Office: 10 W 33d St New York NY 10001

FRIEDMAN, JULIAN RICHARD, lawyer; b. Savannah, Ga., Oct. 9, 1936; s. W. Leon and Evelyn Sarah (Bodziner) F.; B.A., Emory U., 1956; J.D. cum laude U. Ga. Sch. Law, 1959; LL.M. in Taxation, N.Y. U. Law Sch., 1964; m. Em Olivia Bevis, Dec. 27, 1974; children—Esther Bess, Sheldon Arthur. Admitted to Ga. bar, 1958; asso. W. Leon Friedman, Savannah, 1959, 61-63, Cheatham, Bergen & Sparkman, Savannah, 1960; asso. Adams, Adams, Brennan & Gardner, Savannah, 1965—, partner, 1968—; instr. taxation Armstrong State Coll., 1966-71; lectr. Continuing Legal Edn. programs State Bar Ga. Nat. Honor scholar, U. Chgo., 1956-57; teaching fellow, N.Y. U., 1963-64; recipient outstanding grad. award, Phi Delta Phi, 1959, Henry Shinn Meml. award, 1959. Mem. Savannah Estate Planning Council (pres. 1972-73), Am., Ga., Savannah bar assns., Fed. Bar Assn. (pres. Savannah chpt. 1971-72), Phi Beta Kappa, Phi Kappa Phi, Omicron Delta Kappa, Pi Sigma Alpha, Phi Delta Phi. Jewish. Mem. B'nai B'rith. Contbr. articles profl. jours. Home: Star Route 1 Box 25W Bluffton SC 29910 Office: 15 Drayton St Savannah GA 31402

FRIEDMAN, LYNN JOSEPH, rehab. counselor; b. New Orleans, Jan. 12, 1949; d. Leonard Cerf and Paula Rose (Levy) Joseph; B.S. in Edn., La. State U., 1970; M.Ed., U. Tex., 1971; m. Herbert Sol Friedman, June 25, 1972; children—Rebecca, Naomi. Tchr., Orleans Parish Sch. Bd., New Orleans, 1971-73; ednl. dir. Gates of Prayer Religious Sch., New Orleans, part-time 1971-75; vocat. rehab. counselor La. State Div. Vocat. Rehab., Metairie, 1973-76, sr. counselor, 1976-79, master counselor, 1979—. Active Marriage Encounter, New Orleans, 1978-79. Named Counselor of the Year, La. Rehab. Counseling Assn., 1979; recipient certs., Nat. Assn. Retarded Citizens, 1974, Goodwill Industries, 1976, Magnolia Sch., 1976; cert. rehab. counselor. Mem. Nat. Assn. Rehab. Counselors, La. Assn. Rehab. Counselors, Am. Rehab. Counselors Assn. Democrat. Jewish. Home: 4721 Loveland St Metairie LA 70002 Office: 433 Metairie Rd Suite 206 Metairie LA 70005

FRIEDMAN, MORTON HENRY, anatomist, educator; b. Uniontown, Pa., Apr. 16, 1938; s. Benjamin and Jennie (Bremler) F.; B.A., Washington and Jefferson Coll., 1960; M.A., Hofstra U., 1964; Ph.D., U. Tenn., 1969; children—Laurence Erik, Scott Justin-Marl. USPHS trainee U. Tenn. Med. Units, Memphis, 1964-69; instr. dept. anatomy Sch. Medicine, W.Va. U., Morgantown, 1969-70, asst. prof., 1970-73, asso. prof., 1973—, vice chmn. Com. on Admissions, 1976-78, chmn., 1979—. Bd. dirs. LWV, Morgantown, 1979. U.S. Dept. Energy grantee, 1977—, also numerous others. Mem. Am. Assn. Anatomists, So. Soc. Anatomists, Am. Soc. Cell Biology, Electron Microscopy Soc. Am., AAAS, N.Y. Acad. Sci., W.Va. Health Systems Agy., W.Va. Lung Assn., NAACP. Democrat. Jewish. Club: B'nai B'rith. Home: 909 Brierwood St Morgantown WV 26505 Office: Dept of Anatomy Sch of Medicine WVa Univ Med Center Morgantown WV 26506

FRIEDMAN, RICHARD NATHAN, lawyer; b. Phila., June 13, 1941; s. Martin Harry and Caroline (Fruchtman) F.; B.A., U. Miami, 1962, J.D., 1965; LL.M. in Taxation, Georgetown U., 1967; m. Catherine Helen Gulotta, Nov. 7, 1970; 1 dau., Melissa Danielle. Admitted to Fla. bar, 1965; staff atty. SEC, Washington, 1965-66; asso. firm Feldman & Warner, Washington, 1966-67; individual practice law, Miami, Fla., 1968—; adj. prof. U. Miami, 1972-76; arbitrator N.Y. Stock Exchange, 1973—. Founder, pres. Am. Stockholders Assn., Inc., 1971-74, Stop Transit-Over People, Inc., 1975—; mem. endowment com. U. Miami, 1970—; mem. Soc. Univ. Founders, U. Miami, 1980. Recipient cert. of merit Dade County Bar Assn., 1972-73; cert. of appreciation Rotary Internat., Kiwanis and other service orgns., 1970—; Richard N. Friedman Week held in his honor, City of Homestead, Fla., 1978. Mem. Unified Bar D.C. Club: Tiger Bay (Miami). Featured performer motion picture Lenny, 1974, other TV and theatrical films. Office: 100 N Biscayne Blvd Miami FL 33132

FRIEDRICHS, ANDREW VALLOIS, JR., zoologist, educator; b. Metairie, La., Apr. 20, 1924; s. Andrew V. and Anna (Crawley) F.; B.S., Tulane U., 1946; postgrad. La. State U., 1955; m. Catherine Estelle Planche, Dec. 28, 1952; children—Andrew Vallois III, Maurice Pierre, Marie Planche, Catherine Slattery. Salesman, Lederle Labs., Nashville, 1946-50; high sch. tchr., Covington, La., 1952-53; marine biologist La. Wildlife and Fisheries Commn., Grand Isle, 1955-57, asst. chief marine biologist, 1957-61; asst. prof. zoology Southeastern La. U., Hammond, 1961-64, asso. prof., 1964-79, prof., 1979—; cons. to oyster and petroleum industries in La. coastal area. Active Boy Scouts Am., United Givers Fund. Mem. AAAS, La. Acad. Sci., La. Cattlemen's Assn., Sigma Xi. Roman Catholic. Contbr. articles to profl. jours. Home: Route 2 Box 26 Covington LA 70433 Office: PO Box 702 Univ Sta Hammond LA 70402

FRIEDRICHS, ARTHUR MARTIN, former mfg. co. exec.; b. N.Y.C., May 8, 1911; s. Arthur C. and Olga A. (Knoepke) F.; student Union Coll., 1930-31; B.S., N.Y. U., 1935; m. Juanita Elizabeth Barrett, Nov. 2, 1968. Bookkeeper, Corn Exchange Bank, N.Y.C., 1935-37; with E. H. & A.C. Friedrichs Co., 1937-71, pres., 1958-71. Bd. dirs. Wartburg Home and Orphan Farm Sch., Mt. Vernon, N.Y., Hackley Sch. Alumni Assn., Fredrix Artists Canvas, Inc., Lawrenceville, Ga.; life mem. Imperial Point Hosp. Aux., Ft. Lauderdale; mem. Norwalk Hosp. Vols. Served with USCGR, 1944-45. Mem. Pompano Beach Power Squadron, Fraternal Order Police (asso.), Artists Fellowship, Weston Hist. Soc., Met. Opera Guild (contbg.), Art Material Mfrs. Assn. N.Y. (past pres.). Clubs: Salmagundi (life) (N.Y.C.); Lighthouse Point Yacht and Racquet (Fla.); Quiet Birdmen. Home: 2510 NE 35th St Lighthouse Point FL 33064

FRIEND, GEORGE CLAUDE, social worker; s. Eric and Else (Marcus) F.; B.A., Marietta Coll., 1949; M.S.W., Tulane U., 1953; m. Sept. 2, 1950; 1 son, Michael Claude. Mem. staff VA Hosp., Richmond, Va., 1953-59, supr. VA Richmond Regional Office, Roanoke, Va., 1959-68, supr./officer in charge, Salem Va., 1968-70, program supr. VA Med. Center, Richmond, 1970—; instr. sociology Va. Commonwealth U., 1968-70. Bd. dirs., chmn. personnel com. Adult Devel. Center, 1969-79. Served with U.S. Army, 1943-46. Recipient Award of Appreciation for activities as hearing officer, VA, 1978. Mem. Nat. Assn. Social Workers, Va. Council Social Welfare. Episcopalian. Office: VA Med Center Richmond VA 23249

FRIES, CHARLES THOMAS, psychologist; b. Ft. Worth, June 13, 1940; s. Charlie T. and Evelyn (Old) F.; B.A., Asbury Coll., 1966; M.Div., Asbury Theol. Sem., 1968; M.Ed., Stephen F. Austin State U., 1972; Ed.D., E. Tex. State U., 1975; m. Janis Ruth Jackson, May 2, 1959; children—Jerry Marshall, Kathy Lynn. Ordained to ministry Evang. Methodist Ch., 1968; minister Evang. Meth. Ch., Jacksonville, Tex., 1968-75; psychologist Travis Clinic Assn., Jacksonville, 1975—; instr. Tex. Eastern U., Tyler; cons. to pub. schs. and industry. Bd. dirs. Jacksonville Sch. Vocat. Nursing, 1976-77, Youth in Action, 1971-72; treas. Cherokee County Child Welfare Bd., 1977. Licensed psychologist and social psychotherapist, Tex.; approved health care provider, Tex. Mem. Am., Tex. psychol. assns., Am., Tex. assns. marriage and family counselors. Home: 906 Meadowbrook St Jacksonville TX 75766 Office: PO Box 870 Hwy 204 Jacksonville TX 75766

FRIES, HELEN SERGEANT HAYNES (MRS. STUART G. FRIES), civic leader; b. Atlanta; d. Harwood Syme and Alice (Hobson) Haynes; student Coll. William and Mary, 1935-38; m. Stuart G. Fries, May 5, 1938. Bd. mem. Community Ballet Assn., Huntsville, Ala., 1968—; mem. nat. nurses aid com. ARC, 1958-59; dir. ARC Aero Club, Eng., 1943-44; supr. ARC Clubmobile, Europe, 1944-46; mem. women's com. Nat. Symphony Orch., Washington, 1959—, chmn. residential fund drive for apts., 1959; bd. dirs. Madison County Republican Club, 1969-70; mem. nat. council Women's Nat. Rep. Club N.Y., 1963—, chmn. hospitality com., 1963-65; bd. mem. League Rep. Women, 1952-61. Recipient certificate of merit 84th Div., U.S. Army, 1945. Mem. Nat. Soc. Colonial Dames Am., D.A.R., Nat. Trust for Historic Preservation, Va., Nat., Valley Forge (Pa.), Eastern Shore Va., Huntsville-Madison County hist. socs., Assn. Preservation Va. Antiquities, Greensboro Soc. Preservation, Tenn. Valley Geneal. Soc., AIM, Nat. Soc. Lit. and Arts, English Speaking Union, Turkish-Am. Assn. Clubs: Army-Navy, Washington, Capitol Hill, Army-Navy Country (Washington); Garden (Redstone Arsenal), Redstone (Ala.) Yacht. Home: 409 Zandale Dr Huntsville AL 35801

FRIES, HERBERT CHRISTIAN, engring. exec.; b. Vienna, Austria, Jan. 19, 1917; s. Egon and Rosa Renee Fries; chem. engring. diploma Tech. U. Vienna, 1940; postgrad. U. Nacional de Ingenieria, Lima, Peru, U. Tulsa; m. Helga Fischer, Sept. 12, 1942; children—Christiane, Margaret Rose, Norbert Christian. Came to U.S., 1957, naturalized, 1962. Engr., Nova Refinery, Vienna, 1940-44; mgr. Ebensee Refinery, Austria, 1944-48; mgr. Eastern div. Empresa Petrolera Fiscal, Lima, 1948-57; v.p. Portable Gasoline Plants, Inc., Tulsa, 1957—; dir. Process Equipment Internat., Inc., Tulsa, Pressurre Vessel Handbook Pub., Inc., Tulsa. Gen. chmn., nomads coordinator Internat. Petroleum Exposition. Mem. Nat., Okla. socs. profl. engrs., Nat. Oil Equipment Mfrs. Soc. (pres. 1967, regent 1968-70), Gas Processors Assn. Clubs: Kiwanis, Internat., Philcrest Hills Tennis. Contbr. articles on oil and gas industries. Home: 4308 S Braden Ave Tulsa OK 74135 Office: 412 Phil Tower Bldg Tulsa OK 74103

FRIESE, HARRISON LEONARD, city ofcl.; b. L.I., N.Y., July 17, 1904; s. Herman A. and Marie Louise (Elcholtz) F.; grad. St. Paul's Sch., 1923; A.B. in Econs. and Banking, Colgate U., 1927; m. Grace M. Fellows, May 6, 1933 (dec. Oct. 1966); children—Harrison Leonard, John Frank; m. 2d, Bette H. Hinsdale, June 29, 1968. With Fellows Engring. & Constrn., Hollis, N.Y., 1934-37; v.p. Fellows and Friese Constrn., 1938-42; planning Grumman Aircraft, Bethpage, L.I., 1942-47; owner, operator Sunrise Nursery, landscape constrn. and design, Fort Lauderdale, Fla., 1948-68; vice mayor, Fort Lauderdale, 1967-69; city commr. Fort Lauderdale, 1963-71. Vice chmn. Fort Lauderdale Planning and Zoning Bd., 1961-63; mem. Fort Lauderdale-Hollywood Internat. Airport Zoning Bd,, 1965-67; mem. area planning bd. Community Shelter Com. Broward County, 1969-71; mem. Broward County Erosion Prevention Bd., 1967-71; mem. Ft. Lauderdale Little Yankee Stadium Com. Republican precinct committeeman, Ft. Lauderdale, 1961-63. Bd. dirs. Fort Lauderdale Mus. Arts, 1967-71, Fort Lauderdale Symphony Orch., 1967-71; bd. dirs. Fla. Dist. 5 Mental Health Bd., 1973-77, sec., mem. exec. com., 1975, treas., 1976; bd. dirs., v.p. Fla. Dist. 3 Mental Health Bd., 1977—; trustee Ft. Lauderdale Parker Play House, 1967-69. Recipient V.I.P. award Little League Baseball League, 1970. Mem. Fla. League Municipalities (legis. com. 1967-69), Taxpayers League Broward County (v.p. 1960), Fla. Nurserymen and Growers Assn. (charter), Phi Kappa Psi. Methodist. Clubs: Masons Shriners, Elks, Rotary, Colgate Gold Coast Alumni (pres. 1962), Harbor Beach Surf (pres. 1963-65); Gainesville (Fla.) Golf and County, Turkey Creek Golf and Racquet. Home: Route 2 Box 185 Trenton FL 32693 also 150 NE 15th Ave Fort Lauderdale FL 33308

FRIESEN, MERLE ROYSTON, psychologist; b. Madrid, Nebr., Apr. 20, 1933; s. Edward M. and Leona Marie (Wiens) F.; B.S., Mich. State U., 1954, Ed.S., 1969; M.S., So. Ill. U., 1963; Ed.D., Auburn U., 1976; postdoctoral study A.U.M., 1977; m. Dolores Goldie Nelson, Sept. 24, 1955; children—Gary, Julie, Susan, Gregory, Jeffrey. Served with U.S. Navy, 1954-59; commd. 2d lt. USAF, 1959, advanced through grades to lt. col., 1973; security police officer various mil. bases, 1954-66; asst. prof. aerospace sci. Mich. State U., 1966-69; coordinator Drug Abuse Prevention Programs, USAF, Vietnam, 1969-70; chief of social action Maxwell AFB, 1970-75; ret., 1975; psychologist Ala. Bd. Corrections, Montgomery, 1976—; adj. prof. Troy State U., 1973-75. Elder, Presbyterian Ch., 1977—; pres. PTA, Wiesbaden, Germany, 1964-65, Head Sch. Parent Tchr. Orgn., Montgomery, 1975-76. Decorated Meritorious Service medal, Airmen's medal, Bronze Star medal, Air Force Commendation medal. Mem. Am. Correctional Assn., Am. Personnel and Guidance Assn., Am. Psychol. Assn., Am. Assn. Correctional Psychologists, Phi Delta Kappa. Home: 613 Bellehurst Dr Montgomery AL 36109

FRINK, BETTYE JEAN, state ofcl.; b. Crossville, Ala., Feb. 19, 1933; d. Lester Love and Edna Leora (McMillian) Haynes; m. William David Frink, July 7, 1951; children—Victor Farrell, William David, Bettye Lynn, Leigh Ellen. Proofreader, Dept. Treasury, 1955-57; with IRS, 1957-59; sec. state Ala., 1959-63; auditor State of Ala., Montgomery, 1963-67, 75—; mem. Ala. Bd. Edn., 1971-75. Mem. Nat. Assn. State Auditors, Comptrollers and Treasurers. Home: 1943 Talbot Terr Montgomery AL 36106 Office: State Capitol Montgomery AL 36130

FRISBIE, SAYER LOYAL, newspaper publisher; b. Biloxi, Miss., Mar. 6, 1915; s. Sayer Lloyd and Marguerite Elizabeth (Bernard) F.; A.B., Fla. So. Coll.; m. Mildred Louise Kelley, June 30, 1937; 1 son, Sayer Loyal IV. Mng. editor Polk County Democrat, Bartow, Fla., 1937-46, editor, 1946-64, pub., 1964—; editor Citrus Industry mag., 1964—; v.p. Frisbie Pub. Co., Bartow, 1946-64, pres., 1964—; sec.-treas. Asso. Publs. Corp., 1946—. Chmn. Bartow Bicentennial Com., 1973-77; mem. Fla. Council on Research and Tng. in Mental Health, 1955-66, chmn., 1964-65. Served with AUS, 1944-46; ETO. Decorated Purple Heart, Combat Inf. Badge, Bronze Star. Mem. Fla. Press Assn. (pres. 1947-48, numerous awards), Sigma Delta Chi (pres. West Coast Fla. profl. chpt. 1955-56). Methodist. Club: Rotary. Home: 290 E Hooker St Bartow FL 33830 Office: PO Box 120 Bartow FL 33830

FRISON, LEE ANDERSON, coll. bus. ofcl.; b. LaFayette County, Miss., June 9, 1941; s. Lester M. and Lydia M. Frierson; B.S. in Bus. Adminstrn., Miss. Valley State U., 1963; M.B.A., Jackson State U., 1979; postgrad. Inst. for Ednl. Mgmt., 1968, Harvard U., 1974; m. Luxie M. Greene, Sept. 16, 1963; children—Jacqueline M., Lee A., Luxie Lynette. Bookkeeper, Miss. Valley State U., Ittabena, 1966-67, bus. mgr., 1977—; asst. v.p. fiscal affairs Jackson (Miss.) State U., 1969-77; bus. mgr. Coahoma Jr. Coll., Clarksdale, Miss., 1967-69. Served with U.S. Army, 1963-66. Recipient Service award Jackson State U., 1977, Miss. Valley State U., 1977. Mem. Omega Psi Phi (keeper of fin. 1973-77), So. Assn. Colls. Bus. Officers. Baptist. Clubs: Shriners, Masons (33 deg.) (grand treas. 1973—). Home: PO Box 20 Miss Valley State U Itta Bena MS 38941 Office: Mississippi Valley State Univ Itta Bena MS 38941

FRITH, DOUGLAS KYLE, lawyer; b. Henry County, Va., Sept. 2, 1931; s. Jacob Ewell and Sally Ada (Nunn) F.; A.B., Roanoke Coll., 1952; J.D., Washington and Lee U., 1957; m. Ella Margaret Tuck, Sept. 10, 1960; children—Margaret Waller, Susan Elaine. Admitted to Va. bar, 1957; since practiced law in Martinsville; asso. firm Taylor & Young, Martinsville, 1959-60; partner Young, Kiser & Frith, 1960-71, Frith, Gardner & Gardner, 1973—. Dir. Va. Nat. Bank/Henry County, Frith Constrn. Co., Inc., Frith Equipment Corp. Substitute judge 21st Gen. Dist. Ct., 21st Juvenile and Domestic Relations Dist. Ct., 1969—. Chmn., March of Dimes, 1960, Brotherhood Week, 1960; capt. profl. div. United Fund, 1971; mem. Martinsville Central Bus. Dist. Commn. Served with AUS, 1952-54. Mem. Va. (com. torts and ins. 1971, 5th dist. com. 1973-75), Martinsville-Henry County (pres. 1970-71) bar assns., Va. Trial Lawyers Assn. (dist. v.p. 1970-71, del.-at-large 1971-77). Baptist (past deacon, mem. adminstrv. com., trustee). Kiwanian (dir. Martinsville). Home: 1409 Whittle Rd Martinsville VA 24112 Office: 58 W Church St Martinsville VA 24112

FRITH, JAMES BURNESS, constrn. co. exec.; b. Va., Jan. 29, 1916; s. Jacob Ewell and Sally Ada (Nunn) F.; B.C.S., Nat. Bus. Coll., Roanoke, Va., 1937; m. Mary Kathryn Nininger, Aug. 21, 1947; children—Shelley Anne (Mrs. Wayne A. Kenas), Jacob Ewell II, James Burness Jr. Gen. bldg. contractor, 1945—; pres., treas. Frith Constrn. Co., Inc., Martinsville, Va., 1956—; v.p. Frith Equipment Corp.; dir. Piedmont Trust Bank, Piedmont Bank Group, Hop-In Food Stores, Tultex Corp. Pres. Patrick Henry Coll. Scholarship Found., Va. Coll. Fund, Richmond, 1973—; trustee Averett Coll., Danville, Va. Served with USAAF, 1942-45. Mem. Asso. Gen. Contractors Am. (state bd. dirs. 1967-72, state exec. com. 1972—), Martinsville-Henry County C. of C. (dir. 1973, sec. 1972—). Kiwanian (pres. 1952, lt. gov. 1955), Elk, K.P. Clubs: Shenandoah (Roanoke, Va.); Chatmoss Country, Forest Park Country (Martinsville). Home: 1127 Cherokee Trail Martinsville VA 24112 Office: PO Box 5028 Martinsville VA 24112

FRITSCHEL, WILLIAM GODFREY, physician; b. Dubuque, Iowa, June 1, 1939; s. Rudolph Herman and Monica Melinda (Meyer) F.; student St. Norbert Coll., 1957-60; B.S., U. Wis., 1961, M.D., 1964; m. Frances Carol Hardgrove, June 20, 1964; children—Gregory William, Jennifer Lynn. Intern, St. Vincent Hosp. and Med. Center, Toledo, 1964, resident in pathology, 1965; resident in phys. medicine and rehab. U. Mich., Ann Arbor, 1966-67; phase I monitor Upjohn Co., Kalamazoo, 1967; asso. dir. profl. relations Pittman-Moore, Zionsville, Ind., 1967-68; health dir. Jackson (Mich.) County, 1968-70; practice medicine specializing in family practice, Albion,

Mich., 1970-75; physician Asheville (N.C.) VA Hosp., 1975—; instr. Albion Ambulance Service, 1971; mem. faculty U. Mich. Med. Center, Ann Arbor, 1966. Served to maj. USAR, 1978—. Recipient AMA Physician's Recognition awards, 1974-77, 80, 81; citation DAV, 1980. Diplomate Am. Bd. Family Practice. Fellow Am. Acad. Family Physicians; mem. Buncombe County Med. Soc., Am. Acad. Family Practice, N.C. Acad. Family Practice, U. Wis. Med. Alumni Assn., Assn. Mil. Surgeons of U.S., Res. Officers Assn. U.S., AMA, Delta Epsilon Sigma, Phi Chi. Roman Catholic.

FRITZ, CARL GEORGE, mech. engr.; b. Poughkeepsie, N.Y., Sept. 8, 1923; s. Carl VerValin and Katherine (Robb) F.; B.M.E., Villanova U., 1946; M.S. in M.E., Purdue U., 1963; m. Grace Eileen Musker, June 16, 1948. Test engr. Stratos Corp., Babylon, L.I., N.Y., 1948-50; head mechanics dept. Musker Engring. Inst., Winnipeg, Man., Can., 1950-53; asst. prof. U. Man., Winnipeg, 1953-60; chief thermodynamics and heat transfer Marshall Space Flight Center, NASA, Huntsville, Ala., 1960—. Mem. ASME (mem. nat. bd. energitics 1967-69, chmn. N. Ala. sect. 1975, Mech. Engr. of Yr. award), Soc. Automotive Engrs., Am. Soc. Engring. Edn. Clubs: Burning Tree Country (Decatur, Ala.), Elks. Home: 135 Millstream Dr Huntsville AL 35806 Office: NASA Marshall Space Flight Center Huntsville AL 35812

FRITZE, CAROL DOZIER, ednl. adminstr.; b. Tulsa, Dec. 20, 1935; d. Laws Harvey and Alma Clara (Sloan) Dozier; B.A., Austin Coll., 1957; M.Ed., N. Tex. State U., 1970; postgrad. Pepperdine Coll., 1970, UCLA, 1971, Tex. Women's U., 1967, E. Tex. State U., 1972; m. Julius Arnold Fritze, May 18, 1973; children—Reed Allen Sprinkel, Sharon Louise Sprinkel, Gregg Baker Sprinkel. Tchr., Carroll Ind. Sch. Dist., Southlake, Tex., 1964-66, Denton (Tex.) State Sch., 1966-67, Dallas Ind. Sch. Dist., 1967-71; counselor Concordia Counseling Center, Dallas, 1969-71; lead tchr. Richardson Ind. Sch. Dist., Tex., 1971-73, cons., 1973-74; asso. dir. Spl. Care Sch., Dallas, 1976-78, exec. dir., 1978—; cons. in field. Cert. tchr., counselor Tex. Mem. Council for Exceptional Children, Nat. Assn. Retarded Citizens, Am. Assn. Mental Deficiency, Coalition of Agys. that Serve Handicapped. Lutheran. Club: Soroptimist. Home: 3240 Lancelot St Dallas TX 75229 Office: Spl Care Sch 3030 Fyke Rd Dallas TX 75234

FRITZE, JULIUS ARNOLD, marriage counselor; b. Albuquerque, Dec. 30, 1918; s. Martin Herman and Mary (Staerkel) F.; student St. Paul's Jr. Coll., 1937-39; diploma Concordia Sem., 1944; B.A., in Edn., U. N.M., 1943; M.S., Central Mo. State Coll., 1969; m. Marion Caroline Becker, June 4, 1944; children—Christine, Timothy; m. 2d, Anita Carol Dozier, May 18, 1973. Ordained to ministry Lutheran Ch., 1944; pastor in Corpus Christi, Tex., 1944-48, Higginsville, Mo., 1948-57; exec. dir. Marriage and Parenthood Center, Dallas, 1957-59; pvt. practice marriage counseling, Dallas, 1959—; indsl. psychologist N. Am. Mktg., 1975-76; mgmt. cons. Concord Systems, Inc., 1978—. Cons. Mo. Snyod, Luth. Ch., St. Louis, 1961, Tex. dist., 1976—; lectr. to profl. and laymen's insts., 1956—; lectr. Dallas County Jr. Coll. Bd. dirs. Dallas area Am. Lung Assn., 1976—. Mem. Am. Assn. Marriage Counselors, Am. Personnel and Guidance Assn., Nat. Vocational Guidance Assn., Nat. Council Family Relations Am., Southwestern, Tex. psychol. assns., Am. Orthopsychiat. Assn., Internat. Platform Assn. Author: The Essence of Marriage, 1969; Mini Manual for Ministers, 1978. Contbr. series of articles to nat. mags. Home: 3240 Lancelot St Dallas TX 75229 Office: Suite 112 2919 Welborn Dallas TX 75219

FRIZZELL, JOHN KEITH, govt. ofcl.; b. Pitts., June 6, 1936; s. John Strangford and Hope Blanche (Lewis) F.; student Otterbein Coll., 1954-55, Pa. State U., summer 1960; B.A., Grove City Coll., 1964; postgrad Fla. Internat. U., 1976; m. Nancy Lee Davis, June 15, 1963; children—John Wesley, Lisa Lyn. Acct., Gen. Telephone Co. Pa., 1964-65; acct. Screw & Bolt Corp. Am., Mt. Pleasant, Pa., 1965-66; comptroller, fin. mgr. Parsons Forest Industries (W.Va.), 1966-67; field audit group mgr. IRS, Orlando, Fla., 1976—; instr. night sch. Dade County Public Schs., 1973-76. Coach, Pop Warner Football, 1976-79; deacon 1st Presbyterian Ch., Miami Springs, 1975. Served with USAF, 1956-59; to capt. USAFR, 1964—. Mem. U.S. Jaycees, Air Force Assn., CAP. Club: Optimists. Home: 1002 Bonita Dr Altamonte Springs FL 32701 Office: 80 N Hughey St Orlando FL 32702

FRIZZELL, RICHARD WELLINGTON, health care exec.; b. Balt., Oct. 5, 1930; s. Richard Wellington and Dorothy K. (Collins) F.; student public schs., Blacksburg, Va.; m. Geneva D. Webb, Mar. 29, 1963; children—Rick, Dan, Jill. Owner, Atlas Constrn., Inc., Sarasota, Fla., 1956-67; partner Steel Enterprises Inc., Blacksburg, 1967-73; partner, pres. Health Care Med. Facilities, Blacksburg, 1973—; dir. First Nat. Bank, Blacksburg. Mem. Va. Gov.'s Bd. for Licensure of Nursing Home Adminstrs., 1979; chmn. United Way campaign, 1979; of Yr., Mem. Blacksburg C. of C. (pres. 1976-78, Disting. Citizen of Yr. 1979). Clubs: Kiwanis, Blacksburg Country (dir. 1970-74). Office: 3610 S Main St Blacksburg VA 24060

FROEHLICH, RICHARD CARL, telephone co. exec.; b. Cleve., Nov. 12, 1935; s. Otto A. and Elsie F.; B.A., Ohio Wesleyan U., 1957; M.A., Kent State U., 1959, Ph.D., 1971; m. Frances J. Frey, Oct. 9, 1961; children—Victoria, Richard, Kurt, Erik, Jennifer. Personnel mgr. Glidden Co., Cleve., 1960-63; spl. agt. FBI, 1963-65; teaching fellow Kent State U., 1965-68; asst. prof. history Radford Coll., 1968-72; mgr. ops. and services Security Systems div. Gould Inc., Cleve., 1972-75; staff mgr. security Southwest Bell Telephone Co., San Antonio, 1975—. Served with U.S. Army, 1959-60. Cert. Protection Profl. Mem. Am. Soc. Indsl. Security, Soc. Former Spl. Agts of FBI, Phi Alpha Theta, Sigma Phi Epsilon. Home: 4810 Los Reyes Dr San Antonio TX 78233 Office: Southwest Bell Tel Co Room 611 PO Box 390 San Antonio TX 78292

FROEHLICH, SUE ANN WERTHEIMER, advt. exec.; b. Dallas, Dec. 28, 1946; d. Jack and Beatrice (Phillips) Wertheimer; student Bennett Coll., 1965-66; B. Journalism, U. Tex. at Austin, 1970; m. Travis Dean Froehlich, May 30, 1970; 1 son, Stephen Brent. Pub. relations asst. Glastron Boat Co., Austin, 1969-70; pub. relations dir. Austin Symphony Orch. Soc., 1970-71; pub. info. dir. Brackenridge Hosp., Austin, 1972-74; creative dir., copywriter Rector-Duncan & Assos., Austin, 1975-77; pres., account exec. FRALIX, Inc., Austin, 1977—; sr. v.p. X-3 Account Group, Inc., 1979—; guest lectr. U. Tex. Recipient Best Outdoor Advertising award Am. Inst. Outdoor Advt., 1975; also local, regional, nat. Addy awards, 1975, 76, 77, 79, 80. Office: 700 W 22d St Austin TX 78705

FROMHAGEN, CARL, JR., obstetrician-gynecologist; b. Tampa, Fla., 1926; s. Carl Frederick and Minnette Gertrude (Douglass) Von Fromhagen; B.S., U. Miami, 1950; student U. Utah, 1949; grad. mil. pilot tng. USAF, 1951; M.S., U. Colo., 1952; M.D., Emory U., 1955; children—Dana Lynn, Carol Leslie, Carl Scott. Intern Baylor U., 1955-56, resident in obstetrics and gynecology, 1956-59; instr. Sch. Medicine U. Miami, Coral Gables, Fla., 1959-62, asso. prof., 1975—; obstetrician, gynecologist, specialist in aviation medicine, FAA sr. med. examiner, Clearwater, Fla., 1960—; pres. Fromhagen Aviation Inc., 1969—; chmn. bd. Navigate Inc., 1970-73; med. cons. Planned Parenthood, 1963-67. Mem. Fla. State Aviation Council, 1966-67. Mem. Com. of 100 Pinellas County, pres. Honduras Relief Soc., 1970. Bd. dirs. Am. Cancer Soc., 1962-68; bd. dirs. Interprofl. Family Council, 1967-68. Served to col. USAFR. Named outstanding resident Baylor U. Med. Sch., 1959; recipient award merit Res. Officers Assn., 1964. Diplomate Am. Bd. Obstetrics and Gynecology. Fellow Am. Coll. Obstetrics and Gynecology, A.C.S., Am. Coll. Abdominal Surgeons; mem. Pan Am. Med. Assn., Fla. Soc. for Preventive Medicine (pres. 1968), Aerospace Med. Assn., Civil Aviation Med. Assn., Flying Physicians (v.p. 1967-68, dir., 1968-74, state pres. 1966-74), Res. Officers Assn. Fla. (Clearwater chpt. pres. 1963-67, state surgeon 1964), N.Y. Acad. Sci., Aviation Maintenance Found., Iron Arrow, Omicron Delta Kappa, Pi Kappa Alpha, Beta Beta Beta. Clubs: Kiwanis, Carlouel Yacht, Ye Mystic Krewe of Neptune. Home: 1666 Robinhood Ln Clearwater FL 33516 Office: 1745 S Highland Ave Clearwater FL 33516

FROMKIN, AVA LYNDA, nurse; b. Toronto, Ont., Can., May 3, 1946; d. Joseph and Sara Ann (Hurovitz) F.; came to U.S., 1948, naturalized, 1953; B.S. in Nursing, U. Miami, 1969, cert. adminstrv. scis., 1975. Nurse, Mt. Sinai Med. Center, Miami Beach, Fla., 1970-71, 73-76; dir. surg. services cedars of Lebanon Health Care Center, Miami, 1976—. Mem. S. Fla. Shared Purchasing Assn. (chairperson operating room adv. com. 1976-79), Assn. Operating Room Nurses (dir. Miami chpt. 1979-80). Home: 150 SE 25th Rd Miami FL 33129 Office: 1400 NW 12th Ave Miami FL 33136

FROMM, STEFAN H., surgeon; b. Vienna, Austria, Dec. 24, 1936; s. Fritz W. and Ilse (Pflanm) F.; B.S., U. P.R., 1955, M.D., 1959; m. Shirley J. Burgy, June 25, 1960; children—Theresa, Stefan, Richard, Michael, Sandra. Intern, San Francisco Gen. Hosp., 1959-60; resident Wayne State U. program Detroit Gen. Hosp., 1961-62, 64-68; practice medicine, specializing in surgery, Detroit, 1968-69, Hato Rey, P.R., 1969—; asst. prof. surgery Wayne State U., 1968, VA Hosp., San Juan, P.R., 1969; attending surgeon Hamilton Meml. Hosp., Dalton, Ga., 1978—; asst. prof. surgery U. P.R. Sch. Medicine, Rio Piedras, 1969-76. Bd. dirs. Pee Wee Football League, 1974-77. Served with AUS, 1962-64. Mem. A.C.S. (chmn. com. trauma 1975, sec. P.R. chpt. 1975), Christian Med. Soc., AMA (del. 1976—), Alpha Omega Alpha. Home: 2235 Rocky Face Circle Dalton GA 30720 Office: PO Box 1969 Dalton GA 30720

FROST, JACK ANDREW, b. Sunset, Tex., Aug. 31, 1926; A.A. in Edn., Weatherford (Tex.) Jr. Coll., 1948; B.S. in Edn., Tex. Wesleyan U., Fort Worth, 1949; M.Ed. in Pub. Sch. Adminstrn., Tex. Christian U., Fort Worth, 1954; postgrad. Baylor U., North Tex. State U., Sul Ross U., S.W. Tex. State U., San Marcos; m. Fran; 6 children. Supt. Alpine (Tex.) Ind. Sch. Dist., 1961-64, Weslaco (Tex.) Ind. Sch. Dist., 1964-69, Georgetown (Tex.) Ind. Sch. Dist., 1969—; statewide guest lectr. Mem. NEA, C. of C. Clubs: Lions, Optimists. Home: PO Box 881 Georgetown TX 78626 Office: 1201 Maple St Georgetown TX 78626

FROST, JONAS MARTIN, congressman; b. Glendale, Calif., Jan. 1, 1942; s. Jack and Doris (Marwil) F.; B.A., U. Mo., 1964, B.J., 1964; J.D., Georgetown U., 1970; m. Valerie Hall, May 9, 1976; children—Alanna Shaw, Mariel Jeanne, Camille Faye. Admitted to Tex. bar, 1970; law clk. U.S. Dist. Ct. judge, 1970-71; individual practice law, Dallas, 1972-79; legal commentator sta. KERA-TV, Dallas, 1971-72; mem. 96th Congress from 24th Dist. Tex. Vice pres. Dallas Democratic Forum, 1976-77; del. Dem. Nat. Conv., 1976; coordinator N.Tex., Carter-Mondale campaign, 1976; bd. dirs. local Am. Cancer Soc., Oak Cliff Conservation League, Am. Jewish Com. Served with USAR, 1966-72. Address: 1238 Longworth House Office Bldg Washington DC 20515

FROST, JUANITA C. CORBITT, orgn. exec.; b. Rockford, Ill., Aug. 4, 1926; d. Mervin Charles and Eva Marie (Moberg) Corbitt; student Little Rock U., 1959-61; m. Thomas Tapenden Frost, Jan. 3, 1954 (dec. Oct. 1966); children—Annemarie, Thomas Tapenden. Med. sec., asst. clin. pathology lab. VA Hosp., Whipple, Ariz., 1951-54; exec. dir. Camp Fire Girls, Temple, Tex., after 1967; now exec. sec. to dir. Nursing Service Scott and White Hosp., also Sherwood and Brindley Found., Temple. Den mother Cub Scouts, 1969; mem. Community Concert Assn., 1954—. Mem. Bell County Med. Aux., Phi Sigma Alpha (charter pres. 1966). Episcopalian. Clubs: Central Texas Dinner, Stillhouse Sailing (sec. 1974). Home: 3001 Las Moras Dr Temple TX 76501 Office: 2401 S 31st St Temple TX 76501

FROST, RILEY LEON, bus. info. co. exec.; b. Johnson County, Ga., Nov. 17, 1928; s. Riley L. and Roma Edith (Norris) F.; student W. Ga. Coll., 1945-47; m. Lanelle Nation, Jan. 25, 1948; children—Sharon, Cynthia, Angela. With Equifax Inc., 1952—, credit mgr., Atlanta, 1970—. Unit chmn. Atlanta United Way, 1978. Cert. adminstrv. mgr. Mem. Adminstrv. Mgmt. Soc. (internat. v.p. mgmt. devel. 1978, pres. Atlanta chpt. 1971-72, Merit award 1971, Diamond Merit award 1974). Baptist. Club: Toastmasters (past pres. Mobile). Home: 3651 N Kimberly Dr Atlanta GA 30340 Office: PO Box 4081 1600 Peachtree St Atlanta GA 30302

FROST, SIDNEY WAYNE, computer scientist; b. Austin, Tex., Dec. 6, 1936; s. Sidney Henry and Eva Lee (Williams) F.; student (Jesse Jones Naval scholar) U. Tex., 1955; B.A. in Math., U. Calif., 1967; M.S. in Computer Sci., U. Houston, 1975; m. Gale Sullivan, Nov. 16, 1962 (div. Jan. 1980); children—Eva, David, Julie. Data processor TRW Systems, Redondo Beach, Calif., 1959-67, Houston 1967-69; criminal justice cons. Symbiotics Internat., Inc., Houston, 1969-71, Ultrasystems, Inc., San Antonio, 1972-73; systems mgr. for Harris County, Tex., 1973-76; planning coordinator for Tex. State Comptroller, Austin, 1976—; teaching fellow, research asst., instr. U. Houston, 1969; mem. Tex. Gov's Subcom. on Criminal Justice Standards and Goals, 1974. Clk. of vestry St. Barnabas Episcopal Ch., Houston, 1975-76, del. to Diocesan Council, 1976. Served with USMC, 1956-59. Mem. Am. Judicature Soc., Tex. Criminal Justice Info. Users Group (sec. 1974). Author: A Jury Selection System, 1969; also articles in trade and profl. jours. Home: Star Route A Box 1015 Austin TX 78737 Office: 111 E 17th St Austin TX 78711

FROSTE, EDWARD ELMO, JR., state ofcl.; b. Richmond, Ky., Feb. 27, 1952; s. Edward Elmo and Phyllis Ann (Pearson) F.; student U. Ky., 1970-72; A.A. in Computer Sci., Ky. State U., 1976, A.A. in Acctg., 1978; m. Deborah Ann Pulliam, Oct. 15, 1969; children—Edward Elmo, Candace Lorea. Computer operator Ky. Dept. Finance, Frankfort, 1972-73; programmer Cowden Mfg. Co., Lexington, Ky., 1973-74, Ky. Dept. Human Resources, Frankfort, 1974-75; mgr. data processing services Ky. Div. Air Pollution Control, Frankfort, 1975—. Mem. Ky. Info. Processing Adv. Com., 1974—. Democrat. Author: Short-Term Air Pollution Modeling User Guide, 1976. Home: 115 Valley View Frankfort KY 40601 Office: 1050 US 127 By-Pass S Frankfort KY 40601

FRUITERMAN, JAN PAUL, physician; b. N.Y.C., Aug. 24, 1946; s. Howard Edward and Adele Lucille (Lee) F.; B.A., U. Pa., 1968; M.D., Georgetown U., 1972; m. Catherine Cameron, June 21, 1969; 1 dau., Erica Lee. Intern, Hosp. of U. Pa., 1972-73, resident in obstetrics and gynecology, 1973-76; asst. instr. obstetrics and gynecology U. Pa., 1975-76; chief infertility clinic Naval Regional Med. Center, Camp Lejeune, N.C., 1976-78; pvt. practice medicine specializing in obstetrics and gynecology, Fairfax, Va., 1978—. Served with USNR, 1976-78. Diplomate Am. Bd. Obstetrics and Gynecology. Fellow Am. Coll. Obstetrics and gynecology, Am. Fertility Soc.; mem. Am. Assn. Gynecol. Laparoscopists, Obstet. Soc. No. Va., Med. Soc. Va., Fairfax County Med. Soc. Contbr. articles to profl. jours. Home: 9800 Vertain Ct Fairfax VA 22032 Office: 8996 Burke Lake Rd Suite 204 Burke VA 22015

FRY, DAVID DONALD, civil engr.; b. Canton, Ohio, Oct. 4, 1924; s. Don David and Mary J. (Petch) F.; student Kans. State Coll., 1943-44; B.S.C.E., Case Inst. Tech., 1949; m. Ann Selden Nicholson, Apr. 25, 1958; 1 dau., Constance Louise. Engr., Ohio Dept. Hwys., Ravenna, 1949-53; engr. Peter Kiewit Sons Co., Portsmouth, Ohio, 1953-54; area engr. Arabian Am. Oil Co., Dhahran, S.A., 1954-56; design engr. M. H. Connell & Assoc., Inc., Miami, 1956-60; asst. dir. pub. works City of Coral Gables (Fla.), 1960-67; v.p. charge Fla. office Brighton Engring. Co., 1967-69; project engr. Clarkeson, Kononoff & Smith, Inc., Coral Gables, 1970-71; chief engr., gen. mgr. Pavlo Engring. Co., Inc., Coral Gables, 1971—. Registered profl. engr., Ohio, Fla. Mem. Theta Chi. Presbyterian. Home: 6001 SW 81st St South Miami FL 33143 Office: 2012 Ponce de Leon Blvd Coral Gables FL 33134

FRY, LEO MARCUS, JR., hosp. adminstr.; b. Pampa, Tex., July 31, 1948; s. Leo M. and Eva Louise (Young) F.; B.S., Abilene Christian Coll., 1970; M.S., Trinity U., 1975; m. Paula Gayle Cox, Aug. 24, 1968. Bus. mgr. Central Cath. Sch. Dist., Abilene Tex., 1970; adminstrv. resident R.E. Thomason Gen. Hosp., El Paso, Tex., 1972, asst. adminstr., 1973, ad interim adminstr., 1973; adminstr. Merced (Calif.) Community Med Center, 1973-75; adminstr. Sierra Med. Center, El Paso, Tex. 1975—; regional v.p. Nat. Med. Enterprises, 1978—. Bd. dirs. El Paso Center for Mental Health, 1976-78, chmn., 1977-78. Mem. Am. Hosp. Assn., Tex. Hosp. Assn. (mem. ho. of dels. 1978-79), Am. Coll. Hosp. Adminstrs., El Paso Hist. Soc. Mem. Christian Ch. Home: 826 Marimba St El Paso TX 79912 Office: 1625 Medical Center Dr El Paso TX 79902

FRY, LLOYD VERN, veterinarian, ret. state ofcl.; b. Kalona, Iowa, Apr. 12, 1913; s. Harry John and Mabel Lena (Taylor) F.; D.V.M., Iowa State U., 1937; m. Lorna Virginia Haight, June 11, 1939; children—Sharon Jan. (Mrs. Thomas A. Markle), Karen Ann (Mrs. Richard H. Boytz), Kyle Kristine (Mrs. John Bremmer). Pvt. practice vet. medicine in Kalona and Winfield, Iowa, 1937; commd. 1st lt. U.S. Army, 1937, advanced through grades to col., 1960; ret. 1968; asst. chief S.C. Meat-Poultry Inspection Service, Columbia, 1968, chief, 1972-78. Instr., U.S. Army Vet. Sch., Chgo., 1947-50; cons. to surgeon gen. U.S. Army Vet. Service, Washington, 1950-52. Decorated Legion of Merit. Mem. Am., S C. vet. med. assns., Alpha Sigma Phi (pres. Phi chpt. 1936-37), Presbyterian (elder Clarendon Hills, Ill. 1953-55). Elk, Lion (pres. 1974-75). Home: 7717 Loch Ln Columbia SC 29206

FRY, THOMAS BOYD, transp. co. exec.; b. Hammond, Ind., Mar. 30, 1942; s. Edwin G. and Lucille (Wilson) F.; B.A. with honors, Princeton U., 1964; M.B.A. with honors, U. Chgo., 1965; postgrad. Johann Wolfgang Goethe U. (Germany), 1965-66; m. Susan Ann Elkins, June 13, 1964; children—Peter Alan, Christina Ann. Brand mgr. Procter & Gamble, Germany, 1969-70, Venezuela, 1970-72, group mgr., 1972-77; pres., owner Electrastart of Houston, Inc., 1978—, A Mobile Car Doctor, Houston, 1979—. Club: Wimbledon Racquet. Home: 16118 Yorkminster Dr Spring TX 77373 Office: 14200 Stuebner Airline Space B Houston TX 77069

FRYBURGER, L(AWRENCE) BRUCE, lawyer; b. Cin., Apr. 7, 1933; s. Lawrence W. and Norma C. (Hunsicker) F.; B.A. (Sutphin law scholar), U. Cin., 1956, LL.B., U. Tex., 1958; children—Craig William, Lawrence Kent. Admitted to Tex. bar, 1959, U.S. Supreme Ct. bar, 1963; specialist in labor relations law for mgmt., San Antonio, from 1959; prin. Law Offices of L. Bruce Fryburger, Inc.; spl. prof. on labor relations law San Antonio Coll., 1968—. Originator Ann. Tex. Young Lawyers Inst., 1964. Chmn. lawyers div. United Fund, San Antonio and Bexar County, 1967-68; mem. Bd. Adjustment, City of San Antonio, 1969-72. Served with USAF, 1958-59. Cert. in labor law, Tex. Bd. Legal Specialization; recipient Law Week award Bur. Nat. Affairs, Washington, 1958. Mem. State Bar of Tex. (grievance prosecuting com. 1967-70, spl. com. lawyers' referral service 1973-75, program chmn. Current Devels. in Labor Law 1978, mem. council labor law sect. 1978—), State Jr. Bar of Tex. (dir. 1964-66), Am. (mem. labor com., equal employment opportunity com. of adminstrv. law sect. 1976—, mem. equal employment opportunity com. of labor relations law sect. 1976—), San Antonio (chmn. lawyer reference plan 1970-72), San Antonio Jr. (pres. 1963-64, Outstanding Young Lawyer of San Antonio award 1967) bar assns., Phi Delta Phi, Sigma Chi. Presbyterian (bd. deacons). Club: San Antonio German. Contbr. articles to profl. jours. Mem. editorial bd. Tex. Lawyers Practice Guide, 1964. Office: 1661 Frost Bank Tower San Antonio TX 78205

FRYE, ALVA LEONARD, chem. co. exec.; b. Gray, Okla., July 19, 1922; s. John Leonard and Flora (Appling) F.; student John Tarleton A & M Coll., 1940-41; B.S. in Chem. Engring., Iowa State U.; m. Evelyn Mae De Booy, Dec. 9, 1943; children—Katherine Frye Ellstrom, Susan. With 3M Co., 1944-68, tech. dir. paper products div., 1962-68; v.p. research and devel. Inmont Corp., 1968-70; with Aladdin Industries, Inc., Nashville, 1970—, v.p. research and devel.; dir. ALH, Inc. Mem. Am. Chem. Soc., Am. Inst. Chem. Engrs., Am. Mgmt. Assn. (mem. council 1970—). Home: 6210 Bridlewood Ln Brentwood TN 37027 Office: 703 Murfreesboro Rd Nashville TN 37210

FRYE, CHARLES ELBERT, paper mfg. co. exec.; b. Pilot Mountain, N.C., Aug. 1, 1935; s. Howard L. and Ronnie I. (McKinney) F.; grad. Oak Ridge Mil. Acad. Jr. Coll., 1957; B.A. in Acctg. and Bus. Adminstrn., Elon Coll., 1963; m. Dorothy Mae Stone, July 15, 1961; children—Susan Carole, Lisa Kay. Dispatcher, Western Electric Co., Greensboro, N.C., 1958-63; asst. office mgr. Pet, Inc., Greensboro, 1963-65; credit mgr. Sc. Elevator Co., Greensboro, 1965-66; corp. credit mgr. Dillard Paper Co , Greensboro, 1966—. Mgmt. advisor Jr. Achievement of Greensboro, 1967-68; vol. United Way Campaigns, 1963-69; chmn. stewardship campaign Muirs Chapel United Meth. Ch., 1974-75, mem. bldg. com. 1974-79, lay leader, 1978-79; bd. dirs. Guilford Coll. Community YMCA, 1974-79, capt. joint capital funds drive, 1978-79, asst. chmn. golf tournament, 1979; bd. dirs. Guilford Primary-Elem. Sch. PTA, 1971—. Recipient Disting. Service to Youth award YMCA, 1975. Mem. Piedmont Paper Credit Assn., Exec. Info. Guild. Democrat. Clubs: Elks, Civitan (pres. 1969-70, Disting. Pres. award 1969, Disting. Internat. Lt. Gov. 1976-77, Internat. Honor Key 1979). Home: 1703 New Garden Rd Greensboro NC 27410 Office: 3900 Spring Garden St Greensboro NC 27407

FRYE, DONALD LEE, mgmt. cons.; b. Washington, Pa., Nov. 8, 1927; s. John Albert and Gertrude McNeill (Bebout) F.; B.A., Bucknell U., Lewisburg, Pa., 1952, M.A., 1953; M.Th., Garrett Theol. Sem., Evanston, Ill., 1960; Ph.D., Northwestern U., 1961; m. Helen Jackson, Aug. 17, 1957 (dec. Dec. 1958); m. 2d, Louise Newton, Aug. 19, 1972; children—Karen, Jeanne, John, Mark. Asst. dean students U. Wis., River Falls, 1951-65; dean students N.C. Wesleyan Coll., Rocky Mount, 1965-66; assoc. prof. U. N.D., Grand Forks, 1966-67; dean students Blue Ridge Coll., Weyers Cave, Va., 1967-68; asso. prof. edn. Radford (Va.) Coll., 1968-69; dir. profl. services Career Mgmt.,

Inc., Atlanta, 1969-77; acad. dean Life Chiropractic Coll., Marietta, Ga., 1977-79; sr. v.p. career mgmt. Organizational Resource Devel., Inc., Savannah, Ga., 1979—. Mem. Inman Sch. Dist. Mental Health Bd., 1970-73; bd. govs. Savannah Little Theater. Served with USNR, 1946-48. Faculty grantee U. N.D., 1968; fellow Northwestern U., 1959-61, Menninger Found. Mem. Ga. Psychol. Assn., Assn. Counselor Educators and Supervisors, Am. Personnel and Guidance Assn., Am. Coll. Personnel Assn. Republican. Episcopalian. Clubs: Atlanta Northwestern U. (dir.), West Paces Ferry Racquet. Contbg. author: Guidelines for Guidance, 1966. Home: 211 W Wayne St Savannah GA 31401 Office: CMI-ORD 2018 1/2 Abercorn St-In Sisters' Ct Savannah GA 31401

FRYE, EVELYN MCCRARY, psychologist; b. Nashville; d. Robert and Lillian (Benson) McCrary; B.S., Midd. Tenn. State U., 1963; M.A., Peabody Coll., 1967; Ed.S., 1971, Ph.D., 1976; div., 1 dau., Ashley Ann. Tchr. psychology Met. Nashville Public Schs., 1963-77; adj. asst. prof. George Peabody Coll., Nashville 1975-77; asso. prof. U. Tenn., Nashville, 1977-79; asso. prof. Tenn. State U., Nashville, 1979—; individual practice psychology, Nashville, 1979—. Bd. dirs. Crisis Call Center Nashville. Mem. Am. Psychol. Assn., Southeastern Psychol. Assn., Tenn. Psychol. Assn. Episcopalian. Home: 1051 Nesbitt Dr Nashville TN 37207 Office: Doctors Bldg Nashville Meml Hosp Madison TN 37115

FRYE, JACK RICHARDSON, architect; b. Montgomery, Ala., Apr. 3, 1922; s. John Richardson and Inez Vivian (Eiland) F.; ed. pvt. tutoring; m. Mary Elizabeth Baxter; children—Margaret Frye Miller, Ann Frye Bondurant. Architect various archtl. firms, 1938-61; pvt. practice gen. architecture, Atlanta, 1961—; works include banks, regional hdqrs. of Scott-Foresman Co., nat. office of Weathers Bros. Transfer, public housing, public and sch. libraries, S.L. Lewis Elem. Sch., Gilmer County Recreational and Emergency Facilities. Mem. North Atlanta Zoning Bd. Appeals, 1953-56. Served with C.W.S., AUS, World War II. Mem. AIA, Am. Arbitration Assn. (panel arbitrators). Presbyterian (deacon, elder). Clubs: Masons, Lions. Home: 900 Woodstock Rd Roswell GA 30075 Office: Profl Bldg Suite 203 Ellijay GA

FRYE, PAULINE LEACH, lawyer; b. Chillicothe, O.; d. Omer and Marietta (Moats) Leach; student Am. Inst. Banking; grad. Nat. U. Law (now merged with George Washington U.), 1950; m. Roger Ellis Frye, Dec. 29, 1951; children—Peggy Ann, Judy Maria. Admitted to D.C. bar, 1951, U.S. Supreme Ct. bar, 1959; practiced in Washington, 1951—; asso. firm Murphy & Nelson, 1957-67; atty. Econ. Stablzn. Agy., 1951-53. Parliamentarian, N.C. Fedn. Republican Women, 1968-77, pres. elect, 1970-71; women's coordinator 8th Congl. Dist. of N.C., Nat. Rep. Congl. Com., 1968; candidate Rep. primary U.S. Congress, 1968; chmn. Pinehurst sect. N.C. Com. for Responsible Legislation, 1971. Mem. N.C., D.C. bar assns., George Washington U. Law Assn., Supreme Ct. Hist. Soc., Phi Alpha Delta. Home: Polrog Farm Box 322 Pinehurst NC 28374

FRYE, WESLEY CURTIS, fast food co. exec.; b. Franklin, Ky., June 30, 1949; s. Benjamin Moss and Donelda Clara (Buell) F.; B.S. in Zoology, Okla. State U., 1970; M.S. in Natural Sci., 1973; m. Donna Ruth McAfee, May 23, 1971; children—Brian, Nathaniel. Area supr. Jim Dandy Fast Foods, Dallas, 1973-75; area supt. Long John Silvers, Lawton, Okla., 1975-78, dist. dir., 1978—. Mem. Am. Mgmt. Assn., Tex. Restaurant Assn. Republican. Home and Office: 5501 2d Pl Lubbock TX 79416

FRYER, JOHN STANLEY, educator; b. Park City, Ky., July 12, 1937; s. John Harvey and Carrie Enola (Beckner) F.; B.S., U. Evansville, 1959; M.B.A., Ind. U., 1969, D.B.A. in Prodn. Mgmt., 1971; m. Sara Lee Coleman, June 18, 1960; children—Mark Edward, David Joseph. Systems and project engr. Nav. Satellite Program, U.S. Naval Avionics Facility, Indpls., 1962-65, chief satellite systems engring. br., 1965-66, dep. program mgr. Walleye Weapons System, 1966-67; asso. instr. mgmt. Ind. U., Bloomington, 1968-70, vis. faculty lectr. in mgmt., 1970, vis. asst. prof., 1971; asst. prof. mgmt. U. S.C., Columbia, 1971-73, asso. prof., 1973-76, prof., 1976—, chmn. mgmt. dept., 1975-78, dir. div. research, 1978—. Bd. dirs., treas. Columbia Swimming League, 1977-79; coach in youth baseball and basketball programs, 1974—; mem. planning div. United Way of Midlands, 1978—. Served with USAF, 1959-62. Mem. Acad. Mgmt. (chmn. prodn./ops. mgmt. div. 1978-79), Am. Inst. for Decision Scis. (nat. council 1976-78, S.E. council 1978-79, v.p. for membership S.E. 1974-75), So. Mgmt. Assn., Inst. Mgmt. Sci., Am. Prodn. and Inventory Control Soc., Alpha Iota Delta, Beta Gamma Sigma, Sigma Iota Epsilon, Omicron Delta Epsilon, Phi Beta Chi, Sigma Pi Sigma. Contbr. articles to profl. jours. Home: 414 Leton Dr Columbia SC 29210 Office: Coll Bus Adminstrn U SC Columbia SC 29208

FRYER, WILLIAM NEAL, psychologist; b. Cin., Mar. 10, 1920; s. Roy Charles and Alice (Carson) F.; B.A., Harding Coll., 1948; M.A., Columbia U., 1953, Ed.D., 1965; m. Dorothy Elizabeth McClain, May 11, 1942; children—Bonnie Jean, Debra Lynn. Aircraft painter Aero. Corp. Am., Cin., 1937-39; salesman Sears, Roebuck & Co., Covington, Ky., 1940-41; minister Bklyn. Ch. of Christ, 1948-56; asst. prof. psychology Abilene (Tex.) Christian Coll., 1956-65, asso. prof., 1965-68, part-time tchr. psychology, 1968-70; chief psychologist Abilene State Sch., 1968—. Mem. Mayor's Com. on Mental Retardation, Abilene, 1964-65; mem. exec. com., profl. adviser Abilene Suicide Prevention Service. Bd. dirs., mem. profl. adv. com. Abilene Assn. for Mental Health, pres., 1958-59; past bd. dirs. Tex. Assn. for Mental Health. Served to capt. USAAF, 1941-46. Mem. Am., Southwestern, Tex., Abilene (pres. 1978-79) psychol. assns., AAAS, N.Y. Acad. Sci., Am. Assn. Mental Deficiency, Phi Delta Kappa, Kappa Delta Pi. Mem. Ch. of Christ. Kiwanian. Author: (with Orval Filbeck, Max Leach) College, Classroom, Campus, and You, 1959. Home: 833 East North 10th St Abilene TX 79601 Office: Box 451 Abilene TX 79604

FUDENBERG, HERMAN HUGH, immunologist, educator; b. N.Y.C., Oct. 24, 1928; s. Nathan and Frances F.; A.B., UCLA, 1949; M.D., U. Chgo., 1953; M.A. in Immunology, Boston U., 1956; m. Betty S. Roof, Nov. 23, 1955; children—Drew, Brooks, David, Haskell. Intern, U. Utah Hosp., Salt Lake City, 1953-54; trainee with Dr. William Dameshek, dir. hematology Tufts Med. Sch., Boston, Dr. R.E. Rosenfield, dir. Rh Lab., N.Y.C. Bd. Health, Dr. Fred H. Allen, Jr., Harvard Blood Grouping Lab., Boston, Dr. William Boyd, Boston U., 1954-56; resident Mt. Sinai Hosp., N.Y.C., 1956-57, Peter Bent Brigham Hosp., Boston, 1957-58; research asso. Rockefeller Inst., N.Y.C., 1958-60; asst. prof. medicine U. Calif. Sch. Medicine, San Francisco, 1960-62, asso. prof., 1962-66; asso. prof. immunology U. Calif., Berkeley, 1965-66; prof. medicine U. Calif. Sch. Medicine, San Francisco, 1966-75; prof. bacteriology and immunology U. Calif., Berkeley, 1966-75; prof., chmn. dept. basic and clin. immunology and microbiology Med. U. S.C., Charleston, 1974—; adj. prof. Sch. Public Health, U. Calif., Berkeley, 1974-77; adj. prof. epidemiology U. N.C. Sch. Public Health, Chapel Hill, 1977—; mem. adv. com. personnel for research Am. Cancer Soc.; cons. ARC; mem. expert adv. panel on immunology WHO, 1962-67, 68-73, 73-78, 78—, expert com. on genes, genotypes, and phenotypes, 1966—, expert com. genetics on immune response, 1967—, expert com. immunologic deficiency states, 1970, 73; mem. various panels NRC, Council, 1974—; mem. VA Nat. Study sect. on Oncology. Recipient Pasteur medal Inst. Pasteur, Paris, 1962; Robert A. Cooke Meml. medal Am. Acad. Allergy, 1967; Disting. Service award U. Chgo. Med. Alumni, 1973; Petrov medal, USSR, 1976; many noted lectureships. Fellow AAAS; mem. Am. Acad. Microbiology, Am. Assn. Cancer Research, Am. Assn. Immunologists, Am. Fedn. Clin. Research, Am. Rheumatism Assn., Am. Soc. Clin. Investigation, Am. Soc. Hematology, Am. Soc. Human Genetics, Assn. Am. Physicians, Council Biology Editors, Genetics Soc. Am., Internat. Soc. Hematology, Internat. Union Immunol. Socs., Reticuloendothelial Soc., Royal Soc. Medicine, S.E. Cancer Research Assn. (pres. elect), Swiss Soc. Sci., Transplantation Soc., Sigma Xi; hon. mem. Netherlands Soc. Immunology, Internat. Platform Assn. Club: Commonwealth Am. Mem. numerous editorial bds. including: Am. Jour. Human Genetics, 1968-71, Blood, 1968-71, 76—, Clin. Immunology and Immunopathology (chief editor), 1972—, Excerpta Medica, 1973—, Immunochemistry, 1965-71, 73—, Jour. Irreproducible Results, Transfusion, 1966-74; author: (with Pink, Douglas and Wang) Basic Immunogenetics, 1972, 77; (with Stites, Wells and Caldwell) Basic and Clinical Immunology, 1976, 78, 80; (with Melnick) Biomedical Science and Public Policy, 1977, 78; editor: Phagocytic Mechanisms in Health and Disease, 1972; Disorders of Lymphopoiesis and Lymphoid Function, 1977; The American Biomedical Network, 1977; contbr. over 600 articles, reviews and editorials to profl. jours. Home: 675 Fort Sumter Dr Charleston SC 29412 Office: Medical Univ South Carolina 171 Ashley Ave Charleston SC 29403

FUDGE, RUSSELL OLIVER, univ. adminstr.; b. Sulphur, Okla., Dec. 22, 1910; s. Russell Oliver and Ruth Francis (Dunlavy) F.; B.J., U. Mo., 1933; M.A., George Washington U., 1949, postgrad., 1962; grad. U.S. Army War Coll., 1954; m. Betty Ann Morrison, Dec. 5, 1936; children—John D., Linda Ann Fudge Taylor, Jane Olivia Fudge Rinehart. Commd. capt. U.S. Army, 1941; advanced through ranks to col., 1955; ret. 1962; div. chief Internat. Relations and U.S. Fgn. Policy, U.S. Army War Coll., Carlisle Barracks, Pa., 1958-62; dean and asso. prof. polit. sci. Douglas MacArthur Acad. Freedom, Howard Payne U., Brownwood, Tex., 1962—, Carr P. Collins, Jr. prof. internat. affairs, 1965—. Gen. chmn. Am. Revolution Bicentennial Com., Brownwood, 1974-76; grand marshall Brown County Rodeo and Celebration, 1971. Mem. Am., So., Southwestern polit. sci. assns., Am. Acad. Polit. and Social Sci., U.S. Army Assn., U.S. Army Ret. Officers Assn., Kappa Tau Alpha, Sigma Delta Chi, Pi Gamma Mu. Baptist. Author: Pocket Guide to Turkey, 1953; The Foreign Policy Process, 1961; Nation-State System, 1962; Douglas MacArthur Academy of Freedom, 1969; The Campaigns of Gen. Douglas MacArthur, 1979. Contbr. articles to profl. jours. Home: 3904 Oakdale Dr Brownwood TX 76801

FUENTES, FLORINE GONZALES, counselor; b. San Antonio, Feb. 27, 1927; d. Richard and Flora (Garza) Gonzales: A.A., San Antonio Coll., 1946; B.S., Trinity U., 1947, M.Ed., 1956; children—Florine Diana, Maria Suzanna, Elena Patricia, Anita Alicia. Tchr., San Antonio Ind. Sch. Dist., 1949-68; counselor Sidney Lanier High Sch., San Antonio, 1968-71; counselor St. Philip's Coll., San Antonio, 1971-75, asst. dir. guidance and counseling, 1975—; mem. adv. com. Tchr. Corps, 1970-72. Mem. San Antonio Women Deans and Counselor Assn. (treas. 1975-76), Am., Tex., S. Tex. personnel and Guidance assns., Am. Coll. Personnel Assn., Jr. Coll. Student Personnel Assn. Tex., Tex. Assn. Chicanos in Higher Edn. Methodist. Home: 158 Rosemont San Antonio TX 78228 Office: 2111 Nevada St San Antonio TX 78203

FUGATE, JOHN LETCHER, educator; b. Richmond, Va., Jan. 11, 1941; s. John Banner and Anna May (Letcher) F.; B.A., U. Richmond, 1963, M.A. (Univ. fellow), 1968; m. Judith Ray Butler, Dec. 26, 1970; 1 son, John Letcher. Tchr., Richmond public schs., Bainbridge Jr. High Sch., 1963-70; instr. Va. Community Coll. System, Lord Fairfax Community Coll., Winchester, 1970-74; asst. prof. English J. Sargeant Reynolds Community Coll., Richmond, 1974—. Vice-pres. Broad Meadows Civic Assn., 1977-78; umpire Amateur Softball Assn. Am., 1971-74, Little League Baseball, 1975-78. Mem. AAUP, Southeastern Conf. Tchrs. English in Two-Year Colls., Va. Assn. Tchrs. English, Assn. Curriculum Devel., Va. Hist. Soc., Phi Delta Theta. Mem. Ch. of Christ. Club: Spider. Home: 9317 Coleson Rd Glen Allen VA 23060 Office: PO Box 12084 Richmond VA 23241

FUGAZZI, HELEN ALEXANDER, telephone co. exec.; b. Belleville, Pa.; d. Joseph A. and Harriet Alice (Freet) Alexander; grad. Moody Bible Inst., Chgo., 1968; student Manatee Jr. Coll., 1978—; m. William H. Fugazzi, Aug. 23, 1958; children—Susan, Ernest. Long distance operator Gen. Telephone Co., Sarasota, Fla., 1953-60, service observer, 1961-62, supr., 1963-69, mgr. operator services, 1969—; founder People for Christ, Inc., family and marriage counseling, Sarasota, 1969—; condr. seminars for women; writer, radio broadcaster. Pres., Sarasota Christian Bus. and Profl. Women's Council, 1973-75; organist, Bible tchr. Faith Baptist Ch., Sarasota, 1972—. Named Citizen of Yr., Gen. Telephone of Fla., 1972. Mem. Ind. Telephone Pioneers Am. Home: 2840 Arlington St Sarasota FL 33579 Office: Gen Telephone Co 1701 Ringling Blvd Sarasota FL 33577

FUJISHIRO, KATAKAZU KENNETH, cons. planner, engr.; b. Cambridge, Mass., Sept. 25, 1932; s. Shinji F. and Yasu (Matsudaira) F.; B.S. in C.E., U. S.C., 1964; postgrad. Rensselaer Poly. Inst., 1969, Ga. Inst. Tech., 1970, Mich. Tech. Inst., 1972; m. Jane Foster Eubanks, Nov. 22, 1973; 1 child, Joni. Casualty underwriter Am. Internat. Underwriters Corp., Tokyo and N.Y.C., 1948-57; engr./expeditor Charles J. Craig Constrn. Co., Columbia, S.C., 1958-65; planner/engr. Lyles Bissett Carlisle and Wolff, Columbia, 1965-73; environ. planner, acting dir. Berkeley-Charleston (S.C.)-Dorchester Regional Planning Council and Charleston County Planning Bd., 1973-76; chief water pollution control and prin. planner Met. Washington Council Govts., 1976-79; sr. program analyst, group mgr. resources tech. group Planning Resources and Energy Directorate, Advanced Tech., Inc., McLean, Va., 1979—; course dir. architects and engrs. profl. devel. program Def. Civil Preparedness Agy., 1967-73; evening div. instr. Midlands Tech. Coll., Columbia, 1965, 66. Served with Adj. Gen. Corps, U.S. Army, 1954-56. Recipient ASCE award U. S.C., 1963; Mich. Tech. U. fellow, 1972. Mem. Am. Planning Assn. (service award Nat. Capitol area chpt. 1979), Am. Inst. Cert. Planners. Contbr. articles to profl. jours. Home: 5804-81 Merton Ct Alexandria VA 22311 Office: Advanced Tech Inc 7923 Jones Branch Dr McLean VA 22102

FULBRIGHT, GARLAND W., state ofcl.; b. nr. Hillsboro, Tex., Nov. 30, 1909; s. Edward H. and Maude B. (Barnes) F.; student Southwestern Jr. Coll., 1926-27; m. Marjorie Ruth Trimble, Apr. 27, 1935; children—Donald G., Larry Ray, Linda Jean. With San Antonio Fire Dept., 1929-42, 47-71, fire marshall, 1952-63, 1st asst. fire chief and exec. officer, 1963-71; exec. dir. Tex. Commn. on Fire Protection Personnel Standards and Edn., Austin, 1971—; 1st asst. chief in charge crash fire fighting Kelly AFB, San Antonio, 1942-47; dir. 8th Service Command Crash Fire-fighting Sch., 1942; instr. Tex. A. and M. Coll. Fire Sch., 1939—; mem. fire ins. rate study com. Tex. Municipal League, San Antonio; pres. bd. dirs. Tex. Arson Conf., Inc., Austin, 1958-68; fire cons. for Hemisfair, 1967-68; project dir. organizational design for fire tng. in Tex., Nat. Fire Acad., 1976. Dir., treas. San Antonio Fed. Credit Union, 1948-70, pres., 1971; pres. Highland Park Little League Stadium, Inc., San Antonio, 1950-64; safety chmn, Bob Hill dist. Boy Scouts Am., 1951-53, advancement chmn., 1953-57; chmn. formation and control Fiesta Flambeau, San Antonio, 1948-71; pres. Northwood Elementary Sch. PTA, 1960-62; coordinator San Antonio Civil Def., 1958-60, chief staff, 1960-71. Bd. dirs. Nat. Found., San Antonio (exec. com. county chpt., chmn. ednl. com.), Firemen's Benevolent Fund, San Antonio; Bexar County campaign dir. March of Dimes. Recipient various awards San Antonio Civil Def., 1958, Tex. Civil Def., 1958, Tex. A. and M. Coll., 1958, Treasury Dept., 1944; Guy Cude award for fireman making most outstanding contbn. to community and civic projects. Exchange Club, 1961; named Outstanding Fireman of Year, 1962. Mem. Internat. Assn. Firefighters, Nat. Fire Protection Assn. (chmn. subcom. useful statistics 1963—, mem. fire reporting com., mem. steering com.), Fire Marshalls' Assn. N.A., Tex. Firemen's and Fire Marshall's Assn. (pres. 1970-71), San Antonio C. of C. (mem. fire prevention com. 1947-71, certificate of merit 1951), Hermann Sons Tex., San Antonio Power Squadron. Methodist (mem. ofcl. bd. 1949-61). Mason (Shriner). Developer fire demonstration equipment. Home: 605 Turtle Ln Seguin TX 78155 Office: 510 S Congress Suite 406 Austin TX 78704

FULCHER, JOHN HOWARD, business exec.; b. Orpington, Kent, Eng., Jan. 26, 1922; s. Howard Charles and Hilda (Pinner-Cook) F.; student Inst. Engring. Tech., Cairo, 1945, U. Ottawa 1959; m. B. Sharkey, June 21, 1941; children—Simon John Howard, Michael Hugh, John Paul, David Robin. Asst. plant engr. ITT Standard Telephones, Cables Ltd., Eng., 1943-45; prodn. plant engr. Anglo-Iranian Oil Co., Kuwait Oil Co., 1945-48; exec. engr. J. Birch & Co. Ltd., Baghdad, Iraq, 1948-53; sr. engr. designer to chief mech. engr. Canadian Army Fed. Govt. of Can., 1953-62; mktg. mgr., controller, gen. comml. mgr., dir. Jas. Howden & Parsons of Can. Ltd., Toronto, 1962-68; dir. P.M.C. Insurors Inc., Sea Shells Inc., Pick Everard U.S. Inc., Cons. Engrs., John Fulcher & Sons; tech. cons. Govt. Ont., 1969—; gen. mgr. proposals dept. comml. div. Atomic Energy Can. Ltd., Mississauga, Ont.; pres. Harbor Bluffs Waterfront Condominium, Inc., 1978—. Served with Brit. Mcht. Navy, 1939-43. Mem. ASME, Canadian Soc. Mech. Engrs., Am. Petroleum Inst., Inst. Mktg. and Sales Mgmt., Engring. Inst. Can., Bd. Trade, Nat., Fla. socs. profl. engrs. Club: Bath (Redington Beach, Fla.). Home: 1228 11th Circle SE Largo FL 33541 Office: Atomic Energy of Can Ltd Sheridan Park Research Community Mississauga ON L5K 1B2 Canada

FULKERSON, JOHN ROGERS, psychologist; b. Goose Creek, Tex., Nov. 23, 1941; s. Roy L. and Mildred Louise F.; B.S. Psychology, Tex. A. and M. U., 1964; Ph.D. Psychology, Baylor U., 1969; m. Judith Ann Robinson, July 24, 1965; children—Jonathan, Jennifer. Research asst. Baylor U., 1964-67; field dir. assessment services Edn. Service Center, Waco, Tex., 1967-69; assessment psychologist CIA, Washington, 1970-73; prin. psychologist LWFW, Inc., Dallas, 1973-79; v.p. human resource devel. S.W. Bancshares, Houston, 1979—; dir. Gulf Freeway Nat. Bank; instr. U. Va., Fairfax, 1972-73, U. Tex., Dallas, 1978. Bd. dirs., v.p. Dallas Girls Clubs. Mem. Am. Psychol. Assn., Am. Mgmt. Assn., Houston Indsl./Organizational Psychol. Assn., Baylor U. Grad. Students Orgn. (pres.), Sigma Xi. Clubs: Houston, Wimbledon Racquet, Chantilly Homeowners Va. (pres.). Home: 6811 Wimbledon Estates Spring TX 77373 Office: SW Bancshares PO Box 2629 Houston TX 77001

FULLEN, RAY SANDERS, JR. (JACK), mfg. co. exec.; b. Bristol, Va., June 28, 1950; s. Roy Sanders and Marjorie (Roller) F.; student East Tenn. State U., 1972; m. Diane Elizabeth Davenport, Sept. 13, 1969; children—Aaron Robert, David Maxwell. Sales rep. Falconer Security Printers, Balt., 1972-75, dist. sales mgr., 1975-78; div. sales mgr. Clarke Checks, Atlanta, 1978-80, regional sales mgr., 1980—. Pres., Windwood Homeowners Assn., Inc., Douglasville, Ga., 1978—. Mem. Sales and Mktg. Execs., Atlanta Jaycees. Republican. Methodist. Club: Atlanta City. Home: 6667 Windwood Circle Douglasville GA 30135 Office: PO Box 3001 Atlanta GA 30301

FULLEN, ROBERT EDWARD, nurse, educator; b. Ft. Ritner, Ind., Oct. 6, 1920; s. Emma (Freeman) F.; R.N., Queen of Angels Coll. Nursing, Los Angeles, 1951; B.S. in Nursing, Ind. U., 1956; M.S., Butler U., 1956; M.S. in Nursing, U. Pa., 1967; Ph.D., Laurence U., 1978. Adminstrv. nursing positions with various hosps., Calif., 1951-53; adminstrv. positions Ind. Dept. Mental Health Hosps., 1953-61; state cons. mental health nursing Mo. Div. Mental Diseases, Jefferson City, 1961-64; mem. faculty, chmn. sec. of nursing Purdue U. North Central, Westville, Ind., 1965-68; chmn. dept. nursing Coll. of Ablemarle, Elizabeth City, N.C., 1969-72; asso. dean nursing Troy State U., Montgomery, Ala., 1972-73; dept. head in nursing Northwestern State U., Shreveport, La., 1974—. Mem. Am. Nurses Assn., Nat. League for Nursing, La. Nurses Assn., Sigma Theta Tau. Club: Elks. Office: Northwestern State U 1427 Kings Hwy Shreveport LA 71103

FULLER, DAVID WAYNE, telecommunications equipment mfg. ofcl.; b. Burlington, N.C., Sept. 23, 1950; s. Wayne D. and Jonlyn K. (Murray) F.; B.S. in Indsl. Engring., N.C. State U., 1972; M.B.A., U. Richmond, 1978; m. Judith L. Collier, Aug. 5, 1972; 1 son, Andrew D. With Western Elec. Co., 1971—, indsl. engr., Winston-Salem, N.C., product engr., Greensboro, N.C., process engr., Richmond, Va., plant and safety engr., Richmond, sec. chief ops., Richmond, 1976-79, sect. chief printed circuit phototools, Richmond, 1979—; cons. bus. adminstr.; corp. univ. rep. U. Richmond. Project bus. cons. Jr. Achievement of Richmond, Inc., also bd. dirs.; instr. CPR and advanced 1st aid ARC. Recipient Outstanding Community Service award Western Elec. Co., 1976. Mem. Am. Inst. Indsl. Engrs. (sr.), Am. Soc. Safety Engrs., Nat. Fire Protection Assn., N.C. State Student Aid Assn., N.C. State Alumni Assn., U. Richmond Alumni Assn. Republican. Club: Order of DeMolay (life). Home: 1323 Mintawood Ln Mechanicsville VA 23111 Office: 4500 Laburnum Ave Richmond VA 23231

FULLER, GERALD RALPH, veterinarian; b. Chandler, Ariz., Sept. 8, 1919; s. Horace Ralph and Hortense (McClellan) F.; student Ariz. State U., 1937-39; B.S. in Dairy Husbandry, U. Ariz., 1941; M.S. in Dairy Mfg., Tex. A. and M. U., 1943, D.V.M., 1954; m. Glenda Richardson, June 6, 1941; children—Gerald Ralph, Gilbert R., Barbara Ann (Mrs. Melvin Doyle Shurtz), Glen R., Gordon R., Gene R., Grant R. Instr. agrl. sci. Ariz. State U., Tempe, 1946-50; fed. veterinarian U.S. Dept. Agr., Animal and Plant Health Inspection Service-Meat and Poultry Inspection Program Tex., Ark., Okla., 1953—. Served to 1st lt. AUS, 1943-46, lt. col. Vet. Corps, Res. Mem. Nat. Assn. Fed. Veterinarians (pres. Okla. chpt. 1974-79), Ariz. Aggie Club (pres. coll. chpt. 1940-41), Ariz. State Future Farmers Am. (pres. 1936-37), Alpha Zeta, Lambda Delta Sigma. Democrat. Mem. Ch. of Jesus Christ of Latter Day Saints. Author: Hoop(e)s Genealogy Book, 1979; Adamic Lineage, 1968; Ancestors and Descendants of Andrew Lee Allen, 1952. Home: 6612 N Grove Ave Oklahoma City OK 73132 Office: Wilson Co PO Box 24001 Oklahoma City OK 73124

FULLER, GLORIA JUNE, ednl. adminstr.; b. Purcell, Okla., Nov. 27, 1931; d. Raymond Ralph and Myrtle Lorraine (Taylor) Jones; B.S., U. Scis. and Arts of Okla., 1951; M.S., Okla. State U., 1972, postgrad. 1978-79; postgrad. Northeastern State U., 1968-69, Kans. State U., 1973, Central State U., 1979; m. William Wade Fuller, June 7, 1952; children—Michael Wade, William Kurt. With Claremore (Okla.) Public Schs., 1976—, now dir. sch. food service; mem. adv. bd. Area Vocat. Tech. Sch., Pryor, Okla., 1978-79; adv. County Sch. Food Service chpt., 1978—; speaker Kans. State Vocat. Home Econs. Tchrs. Conf., 1972. Bd. dirs. Boy Scouts Am., Muskogee, Okla., 1968-70; sec. United Meth. Women, 1968-69; active Heart Fund. Recipient Appreciation award Boy Scouts Am., 1969. Mem. Rogers County Sch. Food Service Assn., Okla. Sch. Food Service Assn., Am. Sch. Food Service Assn., Phi Upsilon Omicron, Phi Kappa Phi. Republican. Methodist. Clubs: City Booster (sec. 1973), Extension Homemakers (pres. elect 1969-70). Home: 1513 W Valley View Dr Claremore OK 74017 Office: 325 N Owalla St Claremore OK 74017

FULLER, JAMES HOWE, surgeon; b. Bardwell, Ky., Oct. 14, 1939; s. J. Virgil and Frances Virginia (Mabry) F.; A.B., Murray State Coll., 1961; M.D., U. Ky., 1965; m. Rena Joyce Morris, June 29, 1958; children—James Howe, Steven Bradley, Kimberley Lynn, Jennifer Michelle, Jeffrey Michael, David Patrick. Intern, Duval Med. Center, Jacksonville, Fla., 1965-66; resident in gen. surgery Jacksonville Hosps. Ednl. Program, 1966-67; resident in otolaryngology Case-Western Res. U. Hosps., Cleve., 1967-70; practice medicine specializing in otolaryngology, Ft. Myers, Fla., 1972—; mem. staff Lee Meml. Hosp., Ft. Myers, Fort Myers Community Hosp., Cape Coral (Fla.) Hosp. Chmn. bd. dirs. First Christian Ch., Ft. Myers, 1976-79. Served as maj. M.C., U.S. Army, 1970-72. Diplomate Am. Bd. Otolaryngology, Nat. Bd. Med. Examiners. Fellow ACS, Am. Acad. Ophthalmology and Otolaryngology; mem. Am., Fla. med. assns., Lee County Med. Soc., Am. Council Otolaryngology. Republican. Home: 2858 McGregor Blvd Fort Myers FL 33901 Office: 3677 Central Fort Myers FL 33901

FULLER, JAMES WALKER, surgeon; b. Dyersburg, Tenn., Jan. 5, 1945; s. David Walker and Mary Francis (Lockhart) F.; B.S., U. Tenn., 1969, M.D., 1970; m. Suzanne Fuller, June 22, 1968; children—Dana Michelle, Kevin Walker. Intern, U. S. Fla., Tampa, 1971-72, resident in gen. surgery, 1972-76; practice medicine specializing in surgery, Inverness, Fla., 1978—; mem. staff Citrus Meml. Hosp. Served with USAF, 1976-78. Diplomate Am. Bd. Surgery. Fellow Internat. Coll. Surgeons, ACS; mem. Am. Soc. Colon and Rectal Surgeons. Methodist. Patentee Fuller-Elliot Sump. Office: 411 W Highland St Inverness FL 32650

FULLER, JOHN FLEMING, aerospace co. ofcl.; b. Pennington Gap, Va., Nov. 23, 1928; s. Clifford Marion and Gladys Lee (Trinkle) F.; B.S., East Tenn. State U., 1958; M.B.A., Rollins Coll.. 1963; m. Hadley Jean Shaw, Nov. 25, 1965; stepchildren—Michael, Shawn; 1 son, Richard. Planning analyst, sr. planner, planning chief Martin Marietta Aerospace Co., Orlando, Fla., 1958-62, NATO planning cons., Oslo, 1962-63, planning chief, Orlando, 1963-79, navy guided projectile planning mgr., 1979—. Mem. Orange County Democratic Exec. Com., 1960-62; Sunday sch. tchr. 1st Bapt. Ch., Orlando, 1970-79. Served with USN, 1946-48, 50-56. Mem. Am. Inst. Indsl. Engrs., Am. Ordnance Assn., Am. Legion, DAV, Martin Marietta Mgmt. Club (Outstanding Mgmt. award 1977). Club: Toastmasters (cert. of achievement 1962). Contbr. articles to profl. publs. Home: 610 MacArthur Dr Orlando FL 32809 Office: PO Box 5837 (MP354) Orlando FL 32855

FULLER, JOSEPH DORCAS, III, coll. ofcl.; b. Baytown, Tex., Aug. 30, 1947; s. Joseph Dorcas and Elizabeth Josephine (King) F.; B.A. cum laude (Mpls.-Star scholar), Tex. Christian U., 1969; M.A., U. Tex., 1971, postgrad., 1974—; m. Charlotte Ann Smith, July 14, 1967; 1 son, Joseph Edward. Instr., dir. student publs. Seguin (Tex.) High Sch., 1970-71; instr., adviser daily campus newspaper Tex. Christian U., Fort Worth, 1971-76; dir. public relations Austin Coll., Sherman, Tex., 1976—; reporter Fort Worth Star-Telegram, 1972-76; editor Tarrant County Hosp. Dist. mag., 1976—. Mem. Sherman Conv. and Visitors Bur., 1976—. Recipient Ft. Worth Press award, 1969. Mem. Council for Advancement and Support of Edn., Ind. Colls. and Univs. Tex. (public info. task force 1976—), Inter-Univ. Council, Sigma Delta Chi (Outstanding Grad. 1969, Mark of Excellence award 1975). Baptist. Club: Lions. Office: Austin Coll 900 N Grand Ave Sherman TX 75090

FULLER, JOYCE THOMAS, educator; b. Atlanta, Sept. 29, 1929; d. Brower Bernard and Charlotte (Burnett) Thomas; A.B. cum laude, U. Ga., 1951; M.A.T. (Ford Found. fellow), Vanderbilt U., 1956; postgrad. U. N.C., Chapel Hill, 1959-60; m. Justin Fuller, Nov. 23, 1960; 1 dau., Elizabeth Oliver. Field sec. Kappa Kappa Gamma, 1952-53; tchr. English Westminster Schs., Atlanta, 1953-55, 57-59; teaching fellow U. N.C., 1959-60, asst. dir. placement bur., 1960-62; asst. prof. English, U. Montevallo (Ala.), 1966-80, asso. prof., 1980—; counselor, head counselor Camp Greystone, Tuxedo, N.C., 1950-78. Jr. warden St. Andrew's Episcopal Ch., Montevallo. Mem. Nat. Council Tchrs. English, Am. Dialect Soc. (new words com.), Phi Beta Kappa, Kappa Kappa Gamma (nat. scholarship chmn.), Phi Kappa Phi (founder, pres. U. Montevallo chpt.). Republican. Home: 133 Tecumseh Rd Montevallo AL 35115 Office: Sta 151 U Montevallo Montevallo AL 35115

FULLER, KERMIT, accountant; b. Feds Creek, Ky., Jan. 16, 1936; s. Elsie and Mandy (Fuller) F.; student Ashland Sch. Commerce, 1957; B.S. in Bus. Adminstrn., S.W. Va. Coll., 1971; postgrad. U. Ky., 1967, Clinch Valley Coll., 1972, W.Va. Tax Inst., 1974—, U. Louisville, 1971; m. Doris Elkins, July 6, 1979; 7 children by 1st marriage. Bookkeeper, Matney Ins. Agy., Grundy, Va., 1957-61; accountant Clevinger Ins. Agy., Vansant, Va., 1962-64; pvt. practice acctg., Grundy, 1964—; registered investment advisor, Grundy, 1964—; tax cons.; dir. various small corps. Served with USMC, 1953-56. Mem. Inst. Fed. Taxation, Nat. Assn. Accountant, Am. Mgmt. Assn., W.Va. U. Alumni Assn., S.W. Va. Community Coll. Alumni Assn., U. Louisville Alumni Assn., Mem. Ch. of Christ. Club: Odd Fellow. Author: Coal Productions Statistics, 1972; Coal Mining Individual Employment Statistics: Personal Attitudes, 1971; editor various coll. publs. Home: Route 83 Slate Creek Rd Grundy VA 24614 Office: US 460 E Grundy VA 24614

FULLER, MARILYN KAY TRIBBEY, accountant; b. Maud, Okla., July 1, 1934; d. Tom Henry and Ruth Marguerite (Dodson) Tribbey; B.S., Okla. State U., 1955; M.B.A., U. Ark., 1965; divorced; children—John Stephen, Carole Ann. Pub. accountant, 1956-64, part-time, 1971—; part-time instr. U. Ark., 1965-66; instr., pub. accounting Paris Jr. Coll., Blossom, Tex., 1968—. H.B. Earhart fellow, 1966. C.P.A., Okla., Tex. Mem. Am. Accounting Assn., Tex. Jr. Coll. Tchrs. Assn., Tchrs. Accounting at Two Year Colls., Am. Women's Soc. C.P.A.'s, Women's Bowling Assn. (sec. Larmar County 1968). Creator electronic printing calculator, 1972. Home: Route 1 Blossom TX 75416 Office: Paris Jr Coll Paris TX 75460

FULLER, MAYNARD GERALD, ret. civil engr.; b. Ft. Cobb, Okla., Apr. 21, 1907; s. Martin Luther and Christina Barbara (Patten) F.; B.S. in Civil Engring., Okla. U., 1930; m. Ethel Mae Munson, June 6, 1931 (dec. Feb. 1972); children—Maynard Gerald, Alen Munson, Ingrid Ellen (Mrs. Michael Hogue); m. Bonnie Hartley Wade, June 2, 1973. Surveyor, Gypsy Oil Co., Tulsa, 1928; resident engr. Okla. Hwy. Dept., 1930-38, 40-41; constrn. engr. Holway & Neuffer, cons. engr. Grand River Dam Authority, 1938-40; sr. engr. C.E., Tulsa Dist., 1941-44, Hdqrs. 8th Service Command, Dallas, 1944-46; sr. engr., chief rds., r.r.'s runways-engr. sect. hdgrs. 4th Army, San Antonio, 1946-54; sr. engr., civilian asst. post engr. U.S. Army, Ft. Sill, Okla., 1954-58; contractor hwy. and heavy Freeman, Inc., Lawton, Okla., 1958-61; co-founder, partner Dambold & Fuller, Cons. Engrs., 1961-64; cons. civil engr., founder, owner M.G. Fuller and Assos., Inc., Cons. Engrs., Lawton, Okla., 1964-74, chmn. bd., 1974-76. Co-promoter registration law for profl. engrs. in Okla., 1934-35. Co-founder Christian Serviceman's Center, San Antonio, dir., 1951-54; co-founder Christian Serviceman's Center, Lawton, Okla., dir., 1959—, pres. bd., 1959. Recipient certificate appreciation for civilian war service with war dept. Sec. War, 1946; certificate achievement U.S. Army Arty. and Missile Center, 1958. Registered profl. engr., Okla. Mem. Okla. Soc. Profl. Engrs. (co-founder, charter mem., dir., sec.-treas. 1942, v.p. 1943, pres. 1944), Sigma Tau. Democrat. Baptist (deacon 1944—, tchr. Bible 1945—). Author: Focal Paths of Revelation, 1969. Contbr articles to profl. jours. Home: 2221 SW 69th St Oklahoma City OK 73159

FULLER, PARRISH, lumber mfr.; b. Madison, Wis., May 21, 1892; s. William Wilson and Minnie Liza (Parrish) F.; student Wabash Coll., 1910-11, M.A., 1949, LL.D., 1954; m. Hester Porter, Oct. 18, 1919; children—Mary Margaret (Mrs. James D. Voorhees), William Porter. Gen. mgr. J. O. Parish Lumber Co., Shelbyville, Ind., 1914-18; asst. to pres. Hillyer Deutsch Edwards, Inc., Oakdale, La., 1919-20, v.p., gen. mgr., 1920-68; v.p. Hillyer Edwards Fuller, Inc., Glenmora, La., 1923-40; gen. partner King Edwards-Fuller Co., St. Francisville, La., 1940-47, Avoyelles Timber Co., Bordelonville, La., 1940-64; v.p. King Lumber Industries, Canton, Miss., 1946-50, Canton (Miss.) & Carthage R.R. Co., 1946-53, Heflands, Inc., 1961-68, Porter Steel Specialties, Inc., Shelbyville, Ind., 1946-51; dir., chmn. forest lands and products Celotex Corp., Chgo., 1946-66; pres. J. O. Parrish Lumber Co., Shelbyville, Ind.; gen. partner Fuller Farms, Shelbyville, 1930-72, Edwards & Fuller, Oakdale, La., 1938-70; former dir. Nat. Bank of Commerce, New Orleans, South Shore Oil and Devel. Co., New Orleans, Lower Coast R.R. Chmn., Citizens Adv. Com. on La. Edn., 1964. State Salvage chmn. 1942-45, United War Fund, 1943-45; pres. Pub. Affairs Research Council La., Inc., 1958; mem. Coordinating council La. State Colleges and La. State U., 1948-52; mem. La. State Bd. Edn., 1929-52, pres., 1952; vice chmn. La. Commn. Higher Edn., 1955-56. Bd. visitors Tulane U., 1953; bd. govs. Ochsner Med. Found., New Orleans; trustee Wabash Coll.; chmn. bd. dirs. St. Frances Cabrini Hosp., Alexandria, La. Served as 2d lt. aviation sect. O.R.C., 1919. Decorated Benemerenti medal (Pope John Paul II); recipient Citizenship Citation, La. div. V.F.W. (14th Good Citizenship medal for pub. service in a vital war effort); pub. service citations So. U., 1952, La. Council Coll. Pres., 1953; award merit Wabash Coll., 1960; Silver Beaver award Boy Scouts Am., 1974; named Humanitarian of Yr., Abbeville, La., 1960. Mem. Sigma Chi. Presbyn. Clubs: The Chicago; Boston, International House, Plimsoll (New Orleans). Address: Box 663 Oakdale LA 71463

FULLER, PETER MCAFEE, educator; b. Grand Rapids, Mich., Jan. 24, 1943; s. Edson Hemingway and Elizabeth (McAfee) F.; B.A., Olivet Coll., 1966; Ph.D., U. Va., 1974; m. Sarah Davis, Jan. 17, 1970; 1 dau., Rachel. Research asso. Hwy. Safety Research Inst., U. Mich., Ann Arbor, 1967-70; asst. prof. anatomy U. Louisville, 1974—. NASA grantee, 1975—. Mem. Am. Assn. Anatomists, So. Soc. Anatomists, Soc. Neurosci., Am. Assn. Automotive Medicine, Aerospace Medicine Soc., Am. Soc. Zoologists. Contbr. articles to profl. jours. Home: 411 Browns Ln Louisville KY 40207

FULLER, WILLIAM NORMAN, architect; b. Savannah, Ga., Feb. 17, 1948; s. Harvey and Dorothy May (Baxter) F.; B.Arch., Ga. Inst. Tech., 1973; m. Carolyn Watson, June 7, 1969; children—Marcia, Norman. Draftsman, I.E. Saporta, Architect, Atlanta, 1966-67; archtl. designer Jova/Daniels/Busby, Architects, Atlanta, 1971-73; architect The Austin Co., Atlanta, 1973-74; pres. The Fuller Group, Atlanta, 1974-78; v.p. Brockway & Co., Architects and Engrs., Atlanta, 1978—. Mem. Zoning Rev. Bd., City of Atlanta, 1976-79; mem. S.W. Community Groups, Atlanta, 1973—; bd. dirs. Friends of the Library, Atlanta, 1979—. Mem. AIA. Democrat. Roman Catholic. Contbr. articles to profl. jours. Home: 2444 Poole Rd SW Atlanta GA 30311 Office: 1626 E Virginia Ave College Park GA 30337

FULLERTON, BETTY JANE, computer services exec.; b. Los Angeles, Mar. 29, 1925; d. Melvin and Louise Katherine (Kuntz) Woldstad; B.A. cum laude, U. So. Calif., 1946, postgrad. in Asiatic studies, 1946-47; m. Hal Bradford Fullerton, Sept. 7, 1944 (dec. 1974); children—Hal, Frances, Lorraine, Scott, Kent, Rhonda. Corp. sec. and dir. Kern Drilling Co. Internat., Ltd., Whittier, Calif., 1963-66, United Drilling Services, Inc., Whittier, 1964-75; local advt. rep. The Christian Science Monitor, 1967-70; staff asst. Brown & Root, Inc., Houston, 1975-77, office mgr. personnel tng. and devel. dept., 1977-78, industry rep. computer services div., 1978—. Dist. precinct chmn. Republican Central Com. of Los Angeles County, 1960-64; mem. Republican State Central Com. of Calif., 1962-64; bd. dirs. Whittier area council Girl Scouts U.S., 1962-64, v.p. personnel, 1962-63; v.p. youth activities Freedom Found., Valley Forge women's div., Los Angeles County, 1964-66; bd. dirs. 1st Ch. of Christ, Scientist, Whittier, 1971-73; bd. dirs. Family YMCA, East Whittier, Calif., 1973-75; 1st reader 9th Ch. of Christ, Scientist, Houston, 1976-79, trustee, 1979—. Named Republican Woman of Yr., Whittier, 1972. Mem. Am. Soc. Tng. and Devel., Assn. Systems Mgmt., Engrs. Council of Houston (tech. careers com. chmn.). Home: 17406 Anvil Circle Houston TX 77090 Office: PO Box 3 Houston TX 77001

FULMER, JAMES SIDNEY, gynecologist; b. Spartanburg, S.C., June 23, 1932; s. Sidney Cohen and Martha Carolyn (Waters) F.; B.S., Wofford Coll., 1957; M.D., Emory U., 1959; m. Lenna MacLean Moore, Jan. 10, 1969; 1 son, James Sidney. Resident in Ob-Gyn, U. Va., 1960-64; partner Fleming, Fleming & Fulmer, Spartanburg, 1964—; mem. staffs Spartanburg Gen., Drs. Meml., Mary Black hosps.; gynecol. cons. Converse Coll.; clin. prof. Ob-Gyn, Med. U. S.C., 1964—. Bd. dirs. Spartanburg Music Found., 1977—, pres., 1976-77; v.p. Spartanburg Girls Home, 1979-80; trustee Spartanburg County Found., 1978—; bd. dirs. Spartanburg Little Theatre, 1973-75, pres., 1974-75; bd. dirs. Spartanburg Arts Council, 1970-74; pres. Vis. Nurses Assn., 1965-66. Served to lt. USN, 1958-60; PTO. Recipient Eben J. Carey Anatomy award Phi Chi, 1953. Diplomate Am. Bd. Ob-Gyn. Mem. Spartanburg County Med. Soc. (past pres.), S.C. Med. Assn. (2d v.p. 1978-80), So. Med. Assn., Am. Coll. Ob-Gyn, Am. Fertility Soc., Phi Beta Kappa. Episcopalian. Clubs: Spartanburg Country, Piedmont. Contbr. articles to med. jours. Home: 167 Ivy Ct Spartanburg SC 29302 Office: 1 Catawba St Spartanburg SC 29303

FULMER, RICHARD STEPHEN, psychologist; b. Orlando, Fla., Sept. 29, 1943; s. Judson and Shelley Marie (Todd) F.; B.S.B.A. (Fla. Alumni scholar), Carson-Newman Coll., 1966; M.Religious Edn., So. Bapt. Theol. Sem., 1968; M.A. in Psychology, Middle Tenn. State U., 1969; Ph.D. in Psychology, George Peabody Coll. for Tchrs., 1972; children—Stephen Judson, Nancy Elizabeth. Religious edn. dir. various chs., Tenn., Fla., Ind., 1965-69; grad. asst. Middle Tenn. State U., 1969; manpower cons. U. Tenn. Center for Tng. and Career Devel., 1969; research asst. learning theory research lab. George Peabody Coll. for Tchrs. Inst. on Mental Retardation and Intellectual Devel., 1970-71, postdoctoral research asso., 1971-72; instr. psychology Belmont Coll., 1969-71, asst. prof., 1971-72; asst. prof. psychology Middle Tenn State U., 1972-73; postdoctoral intern dept. med. psychology U. Oreg. Med. Sch., 1973-74; dir. psychol. services Bristol (Tenn.) Regional Mental Health Center, 1974—; with East Tenn. State U. Sch. Medicine, 1978-79; personnel cons., 1969-73. Pres. Haynesfield Sch. PTA, Bristol, Tenn., 1976; 2d v.p., dir. SW Va. Lung Assn., 1977. Mem. Am., Southeastern, Tenn., Intermountain (dir.) psychol. assns., Assn. Advancement Psychology. Democrat. Baptist. Contbr. articles to profl. jours. Home: 2407 Broad St Bristol TN 37620 Office: 225 Midway St Bristol TN 37620

FULTON, JAMES WAYTE, JR., clergyman; b. Stuart, Va., Feb. 23, 1911; s. James Wayte and Mary Ward (King) F.; B.A., Davidson Coll., 1933; B.A., Union Theol. Sem., 1936; D.D., Belhaven Coll., 1956; m. Jerry Liddell, Mar. 9, 1946; children—Alyce, Christine, Frances Anne, Jerry Virginia, Kathleen Bell. Ordained to ministry Presbyterian Ch., 1937; pastor First Ch., Gloucester, Va., 1937-39, Bishopville, S.C., 1939-41, Royal Oak Ch., Marion, Va., 1946-49; dir. Christian Edn., Synod La., New Orleans, 1949-52; pastor Shenandoah Ch., Miami, Fla., 1952-69, Meml. Presbyn. Ch., West Palm Beach, Fla., 1969—; moderator Synod of Fla., 1978. Trustee Davidson Coll.; bd. dirs. Christianity Today. Served with Chaplains' Corps, USNR, 1941-46, capt. Res. ret. Mem. U.S. Naval Inst., S.A.R. Kiwanian. Home: 200 Ellamar Rd West Palm Beach FL 33405 Office: 1300 S Olive Ave West Palm Beach FL 33401

FULTON, LEROY MARCUS, coll. pres.; b. Jenkins, Ky., Nov. 13, 1931; s. William Mark and Esther (Hermean) F.; B.A., Anderson (Ind.) Coll., 1953, M.Div., 1960, D.D., 1977; m. Beverly Jean Wilson, Sept. 9, 1951; children—W. Douglas, Kevin Neale, Mark Eric. Ordained to ministry Ch. of God, 1955; pastor in Anderson, 1953-57, Drexel, N.C., 1957-66 Sarasota, Fla., 1966-71; pres. Warner So. Coll., Lake Wales, Fla., 1969—. Mem. State Bd. Independent Colls. and Univs. Fla. Mem. exec. council Ch. of God in Fla., 1966—; mem. commn. Christian higher edn. Ch. of God, 1969—, rec. sec. Gen. Assembly, also mem. exec. council. Bd. dirs. Lake Wales Band. Mem. Am. Assn. for Higher Edn., Fla. Assn. Evangelicals (pres.). Rotarian. Address: Warner Southern Coll Lake Wales FL 33853

FULTON, RICHARD WAYNE, physicist; b. Detroit, May 17, 1933; s. Marvin Lewis and Catherine Mary (Brown) F.; A.B., Eastern Mich. U., 1958; m. Greta Ann Hellum, Aug. 29, 1957; children—Duane Alan, Linda Catherine. Physicist research and devel. night vision Dept. Army, Fort Huachuca, Ariz., 1958-66, physicist night vision and electrooptics labs., Fort Belvoir, Va., 1966—. Served with USNR, 1952-54. Mem. Optical Soc. Am., Soc. Photooptical Instrumentation Engrs., Tech. Transfer Soc. Home: 5410 Ellzey Dr Fairfax VA 22032 Office: Night Vision and Electro Optics Labs Fort Belvoir VA 22060

FULTZ, SUE CAROL, advt. agy. exec.; b. Conroe, Tex., July 15, 1946; d. Kelton Benton and Harriett Sue (Woodson) F.; B.A., U. Houston, 1967. Sec., Houston Post, 1968; v.p. Lloyd G. Jakeway Advt. & Public Relations, Houston, 1968-74; dir. press relations First Mktg. Group, Houston, 1974-77; pres. Suzy Fultz Advt. & Public Relations, Houston, 1974—. Vol., Pin Oaks Charity Horse Show, Houston Livestock Show and Rodeo, St. Joseph Benefit, Monte Carlo Ball, Inst. Hispanic Culture, Achievement Rewards for Coll. Scientists. Recipient Franklin award U. Houston, 1964-67. Mem. Houston Advt. Fedn. (dir. 1977-78, editor newsletter, 1977—), Am. Women in Radio and TV (past dir.), Houston Assn. Broadcast Execs. in Tex., Art Dirs. Club Houston, Press Club Houston, Delta Zeta. Office: 2041 Westcreek St #111D Houston TX 77027

FUNCHESS, LAURIE BROWN, telephone co. exec.; b. Birmingham, Ala., Apr. 12, 1943; d. Joseph Morris and Eula Mae (Pope) Brown; B.M., Samford U., 1965, postgrad, 1972; postgrad U. Ala., 1967-68; m. Dennis Voss Funchess, Sept. 1, 1974; children—Warren Scott, Dennis Voss, Stephanie Lynn. Mktg. and TV prodn. asst. So. Baptist Radio-TV Commn., Ft. Worth, 1965-66; tchr. Birmingham City Schs., 1966-67; minister music First Presbyterian Ch., Marion, Ala., 1967-68; tchr. music, Marion, 1967-68; public relations/advt. supr. S. Central Bell Telephone Co., Birmingham, 1971-74, ednl. relations supr., 1974-76, staff mgr. bus. systems, 1976—. Dir. promotion and publicity Mountain Brook Baptist Ch., Birmingham, 1973, 75. Mem. Am. Mgmt. Assn., AAUW, Delta Omicron. Club: Pine Harbor Yacht. Home: 4417 Overlook Rd Birmingham AL 35222 Office: 600 N 19th St Birmingham AL 35201

FUNK, CHARLES SILAS, instrument mfg. co. exec.; b. New Tazewell, Tenn., Aug. 23, 1941; s. Basil Lee and Edith Lucille (Green) F.; A.A. in Chem. Engring., U. N.C., Charlotte, 1961; B.S. in Chem. Engring., N.C. State U., 1964; children—Carol Alane, Charles Silas (dec.), Karen Leigh, Angela Gayle. Engr., Union Carbide Corp., Cleve., 1964-65; area engr. E.I. DuPont Co., Kinston, N.C., 1965-69; research and devel. engr., group supr. Thiokol Fibers, Waynesboro, Va., 1964-71; sales mgr. Chromalox Instrument and Controls, E.L. Wiegand div. Emerson Electric Co., La Vergne, Tenn., 1972—. Mem. Instrument Soc. Am. (past pres. Nashville), Mensa. Contbg. editor Fiber Producer mag., 1974-77; contbr. articles to profl. jours. Office: Chromalox Instrument & Controls 100 Heil Quaker Blvd LaVergne TN 37086

FUNKE, FRANCIS JOSEPH, educator; b. Indpls., June 11, 1915; s. Anthony and Caroline A. (Reimer) F.; A.B. magna cum laude (Liberal Arts scholar 1936-37), Butler U., 1937; M.A. (Legis. scholar 1937-38), U. Wis., 1938 postgrad. U. Pa., 1940, George Washington U., 1953-54; Ph.D., Fla. State U., 1964; m. Bertha Julia Sainz, Aug. 20, 1941; 1 son, John Anthony (dec.). Tchr. modern lang. Riverside Mil. Acad., Gainesville, Ga., 1938-41; Spanish tchr. Reitz High Sch., Evansville, Ind., 1941-43; tchr., Culver (Ind.) Mil. Acad., 1943-45; pharm. translator Eli Lilly Internat. Corp., Indpls., 1945-50; translator, interpreter U.S. Govt., Washington, 1950-55; adult edn. tchr. Good Neighbor Sch., Washington, 1951-53; tchr., North Miami High Sch., 1955-60; prof. Spanish-French, Miami-Dade Community Coll., 1960—. Past v.p. and pres. Instituto de Cultura Hispanica de Miami. Mem. Mayor's Hispanic Culture Com., Miami. Mem. Am. Assn. Tchrs. Spanish and Portuguese, Am. Assn. for Advancement of Humanities, Nat. Hist. Soc., Fla. Fgn. Lang. Assn., So. Atlantic Modern Lang. Assn., Dade County Spanish Tchrs. Assn. (pres. 1960-61), Fla. State Alumni Assn. (sec. bd. Dade County 1967—), Kappa Delta Pi (past counselor, pres. Miami alumni chpt. 1974-75), Phi Kappa Phi, Sigma Delta Pi, Pi Delta Phi, Alpha Mu Gamma. Home: 7146 Ballantrae Ct Miami Lakes FL 33014

FUNKHOUSER, A. PAUL, railroad exec.; b. Roanoke, Va., Mar. 8, 1923; s. Samuel King and Jane Harwood (Cocke) F.; B.A., Princeton U., 1945; LL.B., U. Va., 1950; m. Eleanor Rosalie Gamble, Feb. 4, 1950; children—John Paul, Eleanor Kent. Admitted to Va. bar, 1951; asso. firm Hunton, Williams, Anderson, Gay & Moore, Richmond, 1950-51; from solicitor to asst. gen. counsel Norfolk & Western Ry. Co., 1951-63; from asst. v.p. to sr. v.p. sales and mktg. Pa. R.R., and successor Penn Central Transp. Co., Phila., 1963-75; sr. v.p., pres., then exec. v.p. Seaboard Coast Line Industries, Inc., 1975-78, pres., Jacksonville, Fla., 1978—, also dir.; dir. Seaboard Coast Line R.R.

Co., Louisville & Nashville R.R. Co., Atlantic Land & Improvement Co., Universal Leaf Tobacco Co., Richmond, Va., Flagship Banks, Inc., Miami, Fla. Chmn. Jacksonville U.S. Savs. Bond campaign, 1979; trustee Hollins (Va.) Coll., 1962—; bd. dirs. United Way, Jacksonville. Served with AUS, 1943-46. Mem. Jacksonville C. of C. (gov.), Phi Beta Kappa, Order of Coif, Delta Psi, Phi Delta Phi, Omicron Delta Kappa. Episcopalian. Clubs: Laurel Valley Golf (Ligonier, Pa.); Princeton, Union League (N.Y.C.); Metropolitan (Washington); Ponte Vedra (Fla.); Timuquana Country, Fla. Yacht, River (Jacksonville). Home: 4258 Ortega Forest Dr Jacksonville FL 32210 Office: 500 Water St Jacksonville FL 32202

FUQUA, BENJAMIN THOMAS, savs. and loan assn. exec.; b. Dickson, Tenn., Apr. 1, 1922; s. Benjamin Franklin and Ethel (Baker) F.; diploma Bowling Green Bus. U., 1946. Payroll clk. fuel dept. N & W Rwy., Williamson, W.Va., 1946-50; personnel dir. Red Jacket Coal Co., Red Jacket, W.Va., 1952-55; with First Fed. Savs. & Loan Assn., Dickson, Tenn., 1955—, exec. v.p., mng. officer, 1966-71, pres., 1971—. Dist. chmn. Boy Scouts Am., 1958-62, mem. exec. bd. Middle Tenn. Council, 1958-78; chmn. Dickson County Adv. Com., Dept. Pub. Welfare, 1958. Bd. dirs. Tenn. Savs. and Loan League, 1972-75. Served with AUS, 1942-45, 51. Decorated Bronze Star medal; recipient Silver Beaver award Boy Scouts Am., 1963, Long Rifle award, 1971. Mem. Dickson County C. of C. (pres. 1969), VFW, Am. Legion. Methodist (chmn. adminstrn. bd. 1966-69; treas. 1966-79). Kiwanian (sec. 1956-58, pres. 1959). Home: Box 404 Route 1 Dickson TN 37055 Office: 611 E College St Dickson TN 37055

FUQUA, DON, congressman; b. Jacksonville, Fla., Aug. 20, 1933; s. J.D. and Lucille (Langford) F.; B.S. in Agrl. Econs., U. Fla., 1957; children—Laura, John. Mem. Fla. Ho. of Reps. from Calhoun County, 1958-62; mem. 88th-96th Congresses, 2d Dist. Fla. Trustee Fla. Sheriffs Boys Ranch, Rodeheaver Boys Ranch. Served with AUS. Named one of five outstanding young men in Fla., Fla. Jr. C. of C., 1963; recipient Disting. Alumnus award U. Fla., 1971. Mem. Future Farmers Am. (pres. Fla., 1950-51), Jr. C. of C., Red Cross Constantine, Am. Legion, Fla. Blue Key, Fla. Gold Key, Alpha Gamma Rho. Presbyn. (elder). Elk, Woodman of the World, Mason (32 deg., Shriner, Jester), Rotarian (sec. Blountstown, Fla.). Office: 2268 Rayburn House Office Bldg Washington DC 20515*

FUQUA, JOHN BROOKS, diversified conglomerate exec.; b. Prince Edward County, Va., June 26, 1918; s. John Brooks and Ruth (Fuqua) Elam; student pub. schs., Va.; m. Dorothy Champman, Feb. 10, 1945; 1 son, J. Rex. Chmn., chief exec. officer Fuqua Industries, Inc., Atlanta, 1965—; chmn. bd. Fuqua TV, Inc., Fuqua Nat., Inc.; dir. Central of Ga. R.R. Mem. Ga. Ho. of Reps., 1957-62, chmn. banking com., 1959-62; mem. Ga. Senate, 1963-64, chmn. banking and fin. coms., 1963-64; chmn. Democratic Exec. Com. Ga., 1962-66; trustee Duke U., Hampden-Sydney Coll., Ga. State U. Found. Recipient Golden Plate award Am. Acad. Achievement, 1974; named Boss of Year, Augusta Jr. C. of C., 1960, Broadcaster Citizen of Year, Ga. Assn. Broadcasters, 1963; Ga. Pioneer in Broadcasting award, 1979. Mem. Ga. Bus. and Indsl. Assn. (dir.), World Bus. Council, Chief Execs. Forum, Augusta (past pres.), Atlanta (past dir.) chambers commerce. Club: Augusta Exchange (past pres.). Home: 3574 Tuxedo Rd Atlanta GA 30305 Office: 3800 First Nat Bank Tower Atlanta GA 30303

FUQUA, MITCH PERVIS, computer microfilm co. exec.; b. Eastman, Ga., Jan. 7, 1938; s. Herbert Wayne and Kathryn (Pervis) F.; B.A., Emory U., 1960; postgrad. Ga. State U., 1960-62; 1 son, Mitch Pervis. Computer systems project leader Lockheed Ga. Co., Atlanta, 1964-69; mgr. computer services So. Airways, Atlanta, 1969-72; data center mgr. Nat. Service Industries, Atlanta, 1972-73; gen. mgr. Computer Microfilm Internat. Corp., Atlanta, 1973—. Mem. Nat. Micrographics Assn. (bd. dirs.). Baptist. Clubs: Mensa, Atlanta Ski. Home: 293 Young Deer Dr Route 9 Cumming GA 30130 Office: Suite 300C 1874 Piedmont Rd NE Atlanta GA 30324

FURFARI, TONY ANGELO, restaurant exec.; b. Phila., Apr. 20, 1947; s. Salvatore J. and Rita A. (Guglielomo) F.; student Drexel U., 1965-67, Inst. Applied Sci., 1968-69, Strayer Coll., 1969-70; m. Elizabeth J. Ewing, Feb. 26, 1977. Nat. dir. ops. McDonald's Corp., Oakbrook, Ill., 1970-77; dir. ops. systems Burger King Corp., Miami, Fla., 1977-78; v.p. restaurant ops. Burger Queen Enterprises, Louisville, 1978—. Served with USN, 1967-69. Mem. Nat. Restaurant Assn., Am. Mgmt. Assn. Republican. Roman Catholic. Mem. adv. panel Restaurant Bus. Mag., 1979—. Author: The Exciting and Rewarding World of Fast Food, 1979. Office: 4000 DuPont Circle Louisville KY 40206

FURGIUELE, MARGERY WOOD, educator; b. Munden, Va., Sept. 28, 1919; d. Thomas Jarvis and Helen Godfrey (Ward) Wood; B.S., Mary Washington Coll., 1941; postgrad. U. Ala., 1967-68, Catholic U. Am., 1974-76; m. Albert William Furgiuele, June 19, 1943; children—Martha Jane Furgiuele MacDonald, Harriet Randolph Furgiuele Carpenter. Advt. and reservations sec. Hilton's Vacation Hide-A Way, Moodus, Conn., 1940; sec. TVA, Knoxville, 1941-43; adminstrv. asst., ct. reporter Moody AFB, Valdosta, Ga., 1943-44; tchr. bus. Edenton (N.C.) High Sch., 1944-45; tchr. bus., coordinator Culpeper (Va.) County High Sch., 1958—; tchr. Piedment Tech. Edn. Center, 1970—. Co-leader Future Bus. Leaders Am., Culpeper, mem. state bd., 1979-80, 80-81; state advisor 1978-79, Va. Bus. Edn. Assn. Com. chmn., 1978-79. Certified geneal. record Searcher. Mem. Nat., Va. bus. edn. assns., Am., Va. vocat. assns., Smithsonian Assos. Club: Country (Culpeper). Home: 2 Stonybrook Ln Culpeper VA 22701 Office: 475 Achievement Dr Culpeper VA 22701

FURINO, ANTONIO, economist, educator; b. Rome, Italy, May 7, 1931; J.D., U. Rome, 1955; M.A., U. Houston, 1965, Ph.D., 1972. Free lance writer, Rome; asst. prof. St. Mary's U., San Antonio, 1966-67; asst. prof. to asso. prof. econs. St. Edwards U., Austin, Tex., 1967-70; dir. regional analysis Alamo Area Council Govts., San Antonio, 1970-73; prof. econs., dir. Center for Studies in Bus., Econs. and Human Resources, U. Tex., San Antonio, 1973-78, prof. econs., dir. Human Resources Mgmt. and Devel. program, 1978—; sr. partner, dir. Devel. Through Applied Sci., San Antonio, 1972—; econ. cons. Tex. Nat. Bank of Commerce, 1966-68, Cattedra di Techniche di Richerche di Mercato, U. Rome, 1972-79, others. Mem. Am. Econ. Assn., So. Econ. Assn., Urban Regional Info. Systems Assn., Omicron Delta Epsilon. Home: 8915 Data Point 48-D San Antonio TX 78229

FURNISS, JAMES PINE, bus. cons.; b. Pelham, N.Y., Feb. 1, 1920; s. Henry Dawson and Ruth (Pine) F.; A.B., Yale U., 1941; m. Laleah Adams Sullivan, June 15, 1948; children—Laleah Furniss, James Pine. Reporter, Atlanta Constitution, 1941, 45-49; with Citizens & So. Nat. Bank, Atlanta, 1949-69; sr. v.p. Unicapital, Atlanta, 1969-75; chmn. Gt. Am. Mortgage Investors, Atlanta, 1969-75; pres. Furniss & Assos., Atlanta, 1975—, Wakefield Co., Atlanta, 1975—; dir. S.E. Aviation Underwriters, Atlanta. Pres. High Mus. Art, Atlanta, 1974-78; chmn. Community Council, Atlanta, 1965-67. Served with U.S. Army, 1941-46. Decorated Silver Star, Bronze Star with oak leaf cluster. Democrat. Episcopalian. Clubs: Piedmont Driving, Peachtree Golf, Commerce (Atlanta). Home and Office: 147 15th St NE Atlanta GA 30361

FURNIVAL, GEORGE EDWARD, psychotherapist; b. Munhall, Pa., Oct. 25, 1929; s. George Edward and Catherine Elizabeth (Schweinberg) F.; B.A., Mount Union Coll., 1951; M.Div., Drew U., 1955; M.A., Pacific Sch. Religion, 1975; m. Patricia Ann Smith, Feb. 15, 1967; children—George Edward III, Charles Steven, Barbara Lynn. Ordained to ministry Methodist Ch., 1955; pastor United Meth. Chs., N.Y. Conf., 1953-65; pastor United Meth. Ch., Pearl City, Ill., 1967-72; clin. supr. Bowling Green (Fla.) Inn, Inc., 1973-79, dir., 1979—; teaching asso. U. South Fla., Tampa, 1978—. Mem. Nat. Assn. Social Workers, Assn. Profl. Alcoholism Specialists. Democrat. Home: PO Box 1761 Avon Park FL 33825 Office: PO Box 337 Bowling Green FL 33834

FURST, ALEX JULIAN, thoracic and cardiovascular surgeon; b. Augusta, Ga., Dec. 21, 1938; m. George Alex and Ann (Segall) F.; student U. Fla., 1963; M.D., U. Miami, 1967; m. Elayne Kobrin, Aug. 11, 1962; children—James Andrew, Jeffrey Michael, Joseph Robert. Intern, U. Miami Hosp., 1967-68, resident, 1968-72, clin. instr. dept. surgery, 1974—; chief resident in thoracic and cardiovascular surgery Emory U. Hosp., Atlanta, 1972-73; sr. surg. registrar of thoracic unit Hosp. for Sick Children, London, 1973-74; practice medicine specializing in thoracic and cardiovascular surgery, Miami, Fla.; mem. staff Mercy Hosp., Miami. Served with U.S. Army, 1958-60. Fellow Am. Coll. Cardiology, Am. Coll. Chest Physicians, A.C.S.; mem. Dade County Med. Assn., Fla. Med. Assn., Heart Assn. Greater Miami. So. Thoracic Surg. Assn. Office: 3661 S Miami Ave Suite 509 Miami FL 33133

FUSELIER, LOUIS ALFRED, lawyer; b. New Orleans, Mar. 26, 1932; s. Robert Howe and Monica (Hanemann) F.; B.S., La. State U., 1953; LL.B., Tulane U., 1959; m. Eveline Gasquet Fenner, Dec. 27, 1956; children—Louis Alfred, Henri de la Claire, Elizabeth Fenner. Admitted to La. bar, 1959, Miss. bar, 1964, U.S. Supreme Ct. bar, 1965; trial atty. NLRB, New Orleans 1959-62; pres. firm Fuselier, Ott, McKee & Flowers, P.A., and partner in predecessors, Jackson, Miss. Served as pilot and squadron comdr. USAF, 1953-56. Mem. Am., La. (past chmn. labor law sect.), New Orleans, Hinds County, Fed. bar assns., Miss. Bar Found., Am. Judicature Soc., Am. Law Inst., Miss. Def. Lawyers, Miss. Wildlife Fedn. (pres. 1975-76), Jackson C. of C. Clubs: Rotary, Round Table, Boston (New Orleans); Country of Jackson, Capital City Petroleum, Univ. (Jackson). Home: 3804 Old Canton Rd Jackson MS 39216 Office: 2100 Deposit Guaranty Plaza Jackson MS 39201

FUSELIER, MARY ANN, speech and lang. cons.; b. Jennings, La., Aug. 10, 1949; d. Walter J. and Mabel Gay Fuselier; B.A., U. Southwestern La., 1971, M.S., 1977. Speech therapist St. Landry Parish (La.) public schs., 1971-77; pvt. practice speech and lang. pathology, Opelousas, La., also Lafayette, La., 1977-78; speech and lang. cons. U. Southwestern La., Lafayette, 1978—. Mem. Am. Speech and Hearing Assn., La. Speech and Hearing Assn. Roman Catholic. Home: PO Box 41130 USL Lafayette LA 70504 Office: PO Box 40515 USL Lafayette LA 70504

FUSON, CHARLES RAY, indsl. designer; b. Prairie Grove, Ark., Mar. 26, 1945; s. James Author and Lahoma Cora (Painter) F.; B.S. in Indsl. Tech., Northeastern State U., 1979; 1 son, Christopher Bryce. Engring. draftsman Okla. Natural Gas Co., Tulsa, 1968-76; instrument designer Williams Bros. Engring. Co., Tulsa, 1979—. Served with U.S. Army, 1964-67. Home: Route 4 Box 137 Stillwell OK 74960 Office: 6600 S Yale St Tulsa OK 74177

FUSS, KAREN GATES, counselor; b. Milville, N.J., Mar. 31, 1951; d. Charles Carter and Edith Marguerite (Wallace) Gates; Mus.B., Westminster Choir Coll., 1973; M.Music Edn. (fellow), Miss. U. for Women, 1977; m. John Robert Fuss, July 20, 1973. Tchr. music Sch. for Little Children, Longview, Tex., 1973-74; with Longview Nat. Bank, 1974; pvt. tchr. voice and piano, Columbus, Miss., 1975-77; fin. aid counselor, student consumer info. officer Miss. U. for Women, Columbus, 1977—, soloist Chorale; choir accompanist, substitute organist 1st United Methodist Ch., 1975—, sec. commn. on worship, 1978, 79, 80, chmn. flower com., 1979—. Mem. Nat. Assn. Student Fin. Aid Adminstrs., So. Assn. Student Fin. Aid Adminstrs., Miss. Assn. Student Fin. Aid Adminstrs., United Meth. Women, AAUW, Sigma Alpha Iota. Club: Columbus Music Study. Home: 1106 9th Ave N Columbus MS 39701 Office: Office Fin Aid Miss U for Women College St Columbus MS 39701

FUSSELMAN, WILLIAM FRANK, telephone co. exec.; b. Orange, N.J., Oct. 11, 1941; s. Wilbur Frank and Catherine Schaeffer (Gunn) F.; B.S. in Mgmt., No. Ill. U., 1976; m. Sandra Dianne Lewis, Aug. 1, 1964; 1 son, William Charles. Programming counselor Bell Telephone Labs., Whippany, N.J., 1965-70, computer ops. mgr., 1970-76; computer ops. mgr. So. Bell Tel. & Tel., Atlanta, 1976—; cons. in employee motivation and computer center ops. Served with USAF, 1961-65. Mem. Internat. Platform Assn., Data Processing Mgmt. Assn., Aircraft Owners and Pilots Assn., Sigma Iota Epsilon, Beta Gamma Sigma. Baptist. Home: 2400 Riverglenn Ct Dunwoody GA 30338 Office: 100 Perimeter Center Pl Chamblee GA 30346

FUTCH, GEORGE PEYTON, JR., accountant; b. Henderson, Tex., Mar. 12, 1920; s. George P. and Loma (Barton) F.; B.B.A., Sam Houston State U., 1941; M.S., Tex. A. and M. U., 1947; m. Marie Ford, May 8, 1959. Auditor Sears Roebuck & Co., Dallas, 1948-53; self-employed as accountant, 1953—. Sec., treas. Wood Automatic Gas Co., Henderson, 1955—. Chmn. Henderson Community Chest, 1954—, Rusk County (Tex.) chpt. March of Dimes, 1956—. Chmn. Rusk County Democratic Exec. Com., Henderson, 1966-75, Rusk County Vol. Parole Bd., 1957-77. Served to lt. (s.g.) USNR, World War II. Mem. Nat. Soc. Pub. Accountants, Tex. Assn. Pub. Accountants. Presbyn. (deacon 1965-68). Lion (pres. 1959-60, extension award 1972, dist. gov. 1976-77), Mason (Shriner). Home: 711 S Main Henderson TX 75652 Office: 705 S Main Henderson TX 75652

FUTRAL, CATHRYN, educator; b. Wadley, Ga., July 7, 1928; d. John Watson and Mary Elizabeth (Sheppard) F.; A.B., Tift Coll., 1949; M.R.E., New Orleans Bapt. Theol. Sem., 1952; M.A. in English, U. So. Miss., 1962, Ph.D. (Nat. Teaching fellow), 1980. With Tift Coll., 1953—, asso. prof. English, 1953-79, asso. dean, 1980—. Danforth asso., 1973—. Mem. South Atlantic Modern Lang. Assn., AAUP, AAUW, Alpha Psi Omega, Kappa Delta Pi, Delta Kappa Gamma, Phi Delta Kappa. Democrat. Baptist. Home and Office: Tift College Forsyth GA 31029

FUTRELL, GLENN ELIOTT, engring. co. exec.; b. Wayne County, N.C., May 30, 1941; s. Graham Codgell and Aileen Rose (Best) F.; B.S. in Civil Engring., N.C. State U., Raleigh, 1963, M.S., 1965; m. Phyllis Rose Jernigan, Nov. 3, 1958; children—Jan Rose, Glenda Aileen. Soils engr. Charlotte (N.C.) br. Soils & Material Engrs., Inc., 1965-66, br. mgr., Raleigh, 1966-73, pres., 1973—; treas. Cons. Engrs. Council N.C., 1977—. Registered profl. engr., N.C. Mem. ASCE, Nat. Soc. Profl. Engrs., Constrn. Specifications Inst. (pres. 1977), Profl. Engrs. N.C. Democrat. Home: 4809 Elizabeth Rd Raleigh NC 27604 Office: PO Box 58096 3109 Spring Forest Rd Raleigh NC 27658

FUTRELL, JOHN WILLIAM, lawyer; b. Alexandria, La., July 6, 1935; s. J.W. and Sarah Ruth (Hitesman) F.; B.A., Tulane U., 1957; Fulbright scholar, Free U. Berlin, 1958; LL.B., Columbia U., 1965; m. Iva Macdonald, Aug. 13, 1966; children—Sarah, Daniel. Admitted to La. bar, 1966; atty. firm Lemle & Kelleher, New Orleans, 1966-71; prof. law U. Ala. Law Sch., 1971-74, U. Ga. Law Sch., 1974—; Woodrow Wilson fellow Smithsonian Instn., 1979-80; dir. Environ. Law Inst., Washington, 1976—; lectr. Dept. State in Japan and India, 1978. Pres., Sierra Club, San Francisco, 1977-78, nat. dir., 1971—; del. UN Conf. on Water, 1977, White House Conf. Inflation, 1974. Served as officer USMCR, 1957-62. Mem. Am. Bar Assn., AAAS, Phi Beta Kappa, Order of Coif. Address: 115 Tillmann Ln Athens GA 30606

FUTRELL, KATHLEEN HUNT, educator; b. N.Y.C., Jan. 13, 1926; d. Robert Emmett and Margaret Mary (Fitzgerald) Hunt; B.A., Ladycliff Coll., 1947; student Goddard Coll., 1977; Primary Diploma, Washington Montessori Inst., 1965, Elem. Diploma, 1973; m. Alvin Franklin Futrell, June 5, 1946; children—Jonathan, David, Alison, Daniel. Dir., Aquinas Montessori Children's House and Elem. Sch., Alexandria, Va., 1965—; pedagogical staff asso. Washington Montessori Inst., 1975—. Mem. N.Am. Montessori Tchrs. Assn., Assn. Montessori Internationale. Roman Catholic. Author: The Normalized Child, 1971. Home: 3007 Cunningham Dr Alexandria VA 22309 Office: 8334 Mount Vernon Hwy Alexandria VA 22309

FUTRELL, ROBERT FRANK, historian; b. Waterford, Miss., Dec. 15, 1917; s. James Chester and Sarah Olivia (Brooks) F.; B.A. with distinction, U. Miss., 1938, M.A., 1939; Ph.D. in History, Vanderbilt U., 1950; m. Marie Elizabeth Grimes, Oct. 8, 1944. Spl. cons. U.S. War Dept., Washington, 1946; historian USAF Hist. Office, Washington, 1946-49; asso. prof. mil. history Air U., Maxwell AFB, Ala., 1950-51, prof., 1951-71, sr. historian, 1971-74, prof. emeritus mil. history, 1974—; professorial lectr. George Washington U., 1963-68; guest lectr. Air U. Squadron Officer Sch., Air War Coll., 1951—; hist. advisor to USAF project Corona Harvest, 1969-74. Served from pvt. to capt. USAAF, 1941-45, lt. col. Res. ret. Recipient Meritorious Civilian Service award Air Force, 1970, Exceptional Civilian Service decoration Sec. Air Force, 1973. Mem. Ala. Hist. Assn., SAR (pres. Montgomery County chpt. 1971-74), So. Hist. Assn., Air Force Hist. Found. (mem. editorial advisors 1969—), Inst. Mil. Affairs, Phi Eta Sigma, Pi Kappa Pi. Methodist. Author: Ideas, Concepts, Doctrine: A History of Basic Thinking in the United States Air Force, 1907-1964, 2 vols., 1971; The United States Air Force in Korea, 1950-53, 1961; (with Wesley Frank Craven, James L. Cate) The Army Air Force in World War II, 1948-58; contbr. chpts. to hist. books, articles to scholarly publs. Address: 1871 Hill Hedge Dr Montgomery AL 36106

FUZEK, JOHN FRANK, chemist; b. Knoxville, Tenn., Dec. 21, 1921; s. John and Maria (Pucher) F.; B.S., U. Tenn., 1943, M.S., 1945, Ph.D., 1947; m. Bettye Lynn Bean, May 31, 1943; children—Mary Ann, Mark Lynn, Martha Elizabeth. Chemist Hercules Powder Co., Wilmington, Del., 1943-44; research chemist North Am. Rayon Corp. subs. Beaunit, Elizabethton, Tenn., 1948-55; head physics lab. Beaunit Fibers, Elizabethton, 1956-66; sr. research chemist Tenn. Eastman Co., Kingsport, 1966-70, research asso., 1970—. Recipient Hercules Powder Co. Research fellowship, 1944-47; Office Naval Research Postdoctoral fellowship, 1947-48; Oak Ridge Inst. Nuclear Studies Sci. Research award, 1950. Fellow Am. Inst. Chemists (state pres. 1971-72; chmn. com. 1972-74), AAAS; mem. Am. Chem. Soc. (sec., treas. 1955-56; sect. chmn. 1957-58; nat. councilor 1964-66, alt. councilor 1977—), ASTM (subcom. chmn. 1972—), Fiber Soc., Am. Assn. Textile Chemists and Colorists, Am. Crystallographic Assn., N.Y. Acad. Sci., Coblentz Soc., Sigma Xi (sec., treas. 1973-74, chmn. 1976-77), Phi Eta Sigma, Phi Kappa Phi, Tau Beta Pi, Alpha Chi Sigma. Presbyn. (deacon 1949-61; elder 1961—). Home: 4603 Mitchell Rd Kingsport TN 37664 Office: Tenn Eastman Co Kingsport TN 37662

GABARD, WILLIAM MONTGOMERY, educator, historian; b. Lewisburg, Tenn., Aug. 17, 1922; s. William Montgomery and Nell Melvina (Haynes) G.; A.B., Tenn. U., 1947; M.A. (Hearst Found. fellow), Northwestern U., 1949; Ph.D. (Carnegie Found. fellow), Tulane U., 1963; m. Lougenia Gillis, Nov. 18, 1961. Instr. history Northwestern U., Evanston, Ill., 1949, Tulane U., New Orleans, 1955; asst. prof. history Valdosta (Ga.) State Coll., 1948-57, asso. prof., 1957-62, prof., 1962—, dir. internat. studies, 1974—; exec. dir. The Ga. Consortium, Valdosta, 1973-78; dir. grants to India, Office of Edn., Valdosta, 1971, 1972; dir. Ga. Consortium Seminar in India, 1974; participant numerous profl. seminars, 1974-77. Trustee, So. Center for Internat. Studies, Atlanta, 1977-78. Faculty fellow Duke U., Durham, N.C. 1967, Ford Found. fellow Duke U. and U. N.C., 1968-69. Mem. Assn. for Asian Studies, South Atlantic States Assn. for South Asian and African Studies (mem. exec. com. 1974-78), AAUP, Am. Assn. State and Local History, Nat. Trust for Hist. Preservation, Orgn. Am. Historians, S., Ga., Tenn., Iowa, Lowndes County (Ga.), Marshall County (Tenn.) hist. socs., Ga. Assn. Historians. Episcopalian. Clubs: Rotary, Elks. Contbr. numerous articles in field to profl. jours. Home: 116 E Moore St Valdosta GA 31601 Office: Valdosta State Coll Valdosta GA 31601

GABELER, LANE REED, lawyer; b. Louisville, June 14, 1937; d. Robert Buren and Rachel (Faulkner) Reed; B.A., Hollins Coll., 1959; J.D., U. Ky., 1970; postgrad. in labor negotiations, wills and estates, family law CSC Sch., 1976; m. Charles Pierce Gabeler, Aug. 4, 1974; 1 son, George E. Ward. Tchr. elementary schs., Lexington, Ky. and Roswell, N.Mex., 1959-62; accountant to firms, Lexington, 1967-70; admitted to Tex. bar, 1970, U.S. Supreme Ct. bar, 1975, D.C., Va. bars, 1976; legal cons. to adminstr. EPA, Washington, 1971, asst. dir. legis., Washington, 1972-74, dir. exec. secretariat, 1974-75; adminstrv. counsel Dept. Justice, Washington, 1975; exec. dir., Occupational Safety and Health Rev. Commn., Washington, 1977-79; partner firm Gabeler & Gastley, McLean, Va., from 1979, now sr. partner; dir. hearing and appeals commodities FTC, Washington, 1976; research asst. Ky. Crime Commn., 1968. Bd. dirs. Roswell Heart Assn., Eastern N.Mex. Med. Center Aux., Roswell, 1962-67; supt. Sunday sch. St. John's Episcopal Ch., McLean, Va., 1976-77, St. Andrews Episc. Ch., Roswell, 1961-67. Decorated Bronze medal; recipient Spl. Achievement award EPA, 1973; Moot Ct. award, 1969. Mem. Tex., Va., D.C., Fed., Am., Fairfax, McLean bar assns., Roswell Assistance League, Kappa Beta Pi, Nat. Lawyers Club, McLean Lawyers Assn. (v.p.). Club: Langley Swim and Tennis. Editor, author; EPA Compilation, 40 vols., 1971-75; EPA Current Laws, 1971-75; Synopsis of Environmental Law, 1971-75; EPA Legal Authority Index, 1971-75; Primer on EPA's Statutory Authority, 1971-75. Home: 904 Lawton St McLean VA 22101 Office: 6623 A Old Dominion Dr McLean VA 22101

GABLE, ELLEN MORPHONIOS, circuit ct. judge Fla.; b. Ponzer, N.C., Sept. 30, 1929; d. Wesley and Lydia (Winfield) James; J.D., U. Miami, 1957; m. Alex G. Morphonios, 1950 (div. 1971); children—Dale, Dean; m. 2d, John Rowe, Mar. 20, 1972 (div. 1974); m. 3d, Vincent Louis Gable. Admitted to Fla. bar, 1958, U.S. Supreme Ct. bar; practiced in Miami, 1958-61; asst. state's atty. Fla., 1961; trial atty., chief prosecutor Criminal Ct., 1961-70; judge Criminal Ct. Record in and for Dade County, Miami, 1971-73, Circuit Ct., 1973—, adminstrv. judge, 1977—. Mem. Fla. Bd. Bar Examiners, 1968; lectr. Police Acad.; mem. com. criminal ct. relief Fla. Supreme Ct., 1971; commentator Sta. WKAT, Miami, 1968-72; mem. jud. sect., tenure and discipline com. Conf. Fla. Circuit Judges, 1974—; mem. corrections task force Gov.'s Commn. on Criminal Justice Standards and Goals, 1974—. Recipient Gen. McArthur Meml. award League Am. Ideals, 1970, Good Citizenship award Dept. Fla. Ladies Aux., Jewish War Vets. U.S.A., 1971; named Lady of Year, Miami Beach Democratic Club, 1972, Outstanding Woman Dade County, 1972, Citizen of Yr., Dade County Police Benevolent Assn., 1978. Mem. Am., Fla. bar assns., Am. Judicature Soc., Nat. Assn. Women Lawyers, NOW, Bus. and Prof. Women's Club. Home: 8640 SW 84th Ave Miami FL 33143 Office: 1351 NW 12th St Miami FL 33125

GABLE, ROBERT ELLEDY, real estate investment co. exec.; b. N.Y.C., Feb. 20, 1934; s. Gilbert E. and Paulina (Stearns) G.; grad. Deerfield (Mass.) Acad.; B.S., Stanford U., 1956; m. Emily Brinton Thompson, July 5, 1958; children—James, Elizabeth, John. With Stearns Coal & Lumber Co. Inc. (Ky.), 1958—, asst. to pres., 1958-60, sec., 1960-70, treas., 1961-62, v.p., 1962-70, chmn. bd., 1970—, pres., 1975-78, also dir.; chmn. bd., dir. Ky. & Tenn. Ry., Stearns; chmn. bd. Lumber King Inc., Stearns; dir., mem. audit com. Kuhn's-Big K Stores Corp., Nashville, 1979—; dir., mem. fin. com., long-range planning com. Ky. Blue Cross and Blue Shield Plan; dir. McCreary County Bank. Commr. Ky. Dept. Parks, 1967-70; mem. pub. lands com. Interstate Oil Compact Commn., 1968-70; mem. adv. com. Ky. Ednl. TV, 1971-75; former mem. Breaks Interstate Park Commn. Past pres., past dir. McCreary County Indsl. Devel. Corp.; former trustee Stearns Recreational Assn., Inc.; mem. S.E. regional adv. com. Nat. Park Service, 1973-78, sec., 1977-78; bd. dirs. Ky. Mountain Laurel Festival Assn., v.p., 1974-75; mem. McCreary County Air Bd., 1967—; mem. adv. bd. U. Ky. for Somerset Community Coll., 1965-73. Republican candidate for U.S. Senate from Ky., 1972; Ky. co-chmn. Finance Com. for Re-election of Pres., 1972; mem. Rep. Nat. Finance Com., 1971-76; Rep. state finance chmn., 1973-75; mem. Ky. Rep. Central Com., 1974—; Rep. nominee for gov. Ky., 1975; trustee George Peabody Coll. for Tchrs., Nashville, 1970-79, mem. exec. com., 1976-79, chmn. bd., 1979; former trustee Capital Day Sch., Frankfort, Ky.; trustee Vanderbilt U., Nashville, 1979—; bd. dirs., past chmn., past pres., founder Ky. Council on Econ. Edn., Inc.; trustee Ky. State U. Found., 1979—; past mem. bd. dirs. Ky. Better Roads Council, Inc., vice chmn., 1976-79. Served to lt. (j.g.) USNR, 1956-58. Named Ky. Col., Mr. Coal of Ky., 1970. Mem. Ky. Coal Assn. (dir. 1972—, exec. com. 1974-78, sec. 1979—), Ky. C. of C. (regional v.p., 1971-72, 76-80, exec. com. 1971-72, 76-80, dir. 1971-80, fin. com. 1978-79), McCreary County Devel. Assn., McCreary County Jaycees (past pres.), Tau Beta Pi, Alpha Kappa Lambda (past chpt. pres.). Episcopalian. Clubs: Stearns (Ky.) Golf; Frankfort (Ky.) Country; Keeneland, Lafayette, Bluegrass Auto (dir.) (Lexington); Pendennis (Louisville); Capitol Hill (Washington). Home: 1715 Stonehaven Dr Frankfort KY 40601 Office: The Stearns Co 303 McClure Bldg Frankfort KY 40601

GABRIEL, PAT (MRS. GENE F. GABRIEL), club woman; b. Rock Island, Ill., May 2, 1922; d. Max Voyle and Faye (Crist) Wolfe; grad. Canterbury Sch. Fine Arts, 1939; m. Gene Floyd Gabriel, Mar. 8, 1941; 1 dau., Patricia Gene. Society columnist, drama critic Coral Gables Times-Guide. Drama chmn. Morgan Park Jr. Woman's Club, Chgo., 1952-54, 3d Dist Jrs., 1952-54; children's theatre dir. Beverly Hills Jr. Woman's Club, Chgo., 1954; dist. coordinator Mothers March of Dimes, Chgo., 1952-55, Coral Gables, Fla., 1956-61; publicity chmn. woman's com., pres. woman's com. Variety Children's Hosp., pres. women's com., 1968-70; pres. Theatre Arts League, Inc., 1971-73; pres. Dade County Com. for Project Hope, 1973-74; chmn. Com. of Allied and Performing Arts of City of Coral Gables; 2d v.p. Dade County Women's Com. Project Hope; public relations dir. Coral Gables Country Club, 1979. Women's campaign mgr. Senator Doyle Carlton, Jr. for Gov., Coral Gables, 1960. Mem. D.A.R. (rec. sec. 1962-64), Fla. Fedn. Women's Clubs (drama co-chmn. 1960-62), Women in Communications, Sigma Delta Chi. Methodist. Clubs: Coral Gables Senior Women's (1st v.p. 1962-64), Coral Gables Garden (pres. 1980—). Author: Outstanding Homes of Greater Miami, 1975; society columnist Neighbors Miami Herald. Home: 3915 Monserrate St Coral Gables FL 33134

GABRIELE, VINCENZO, restaurateur; b. Palermo, Sicily, Jan. 17, 1948; s. Carmelo and Rosa Eleonora (Romeo) G.; came to U.S., 1969; student Mcht. Marine Sch. for Capt., 1962-68; m. Patricia Ann Tansey, July 3, 1972; 1 dau., Rosa. Asst. capt., then dining room dir. Tony's Restaurant, St. Louis, 1969-75; with Grisanti Inc., corp. of Casa Grisanti and Mamma Grisanti, Louisville, 1976—, gen. mgr., 1977-78, exec. v.p., co-owner, 1978—; cons. Jefferson Community Coll. Bd. dirs. Phoenix Hill Assn., 1978—; mem. spl. com. evaluation dept. modern langs. U. Louisville. Recipient award Jefferson County public schs. Mem. Italian-Am. Assn. Roman Catholic. Home: 11203 Darlington Pl Louisville KY 40243 Office: 1000 E Liberty St Louisville KY 40204

GADD, WILLIAM LEE, chemist; b. Reader, W.Va., Feb. 25, 1934; s. Harvey Lee and Mary Irene (Tennant) G.; student Trevecca Coll., Nashville, 1952-54, Ohio Valley Hosp. Sch. Med. Tech., Steubenville, Ohio, 1955-56; B.S. in Biology and Chemistry, West Liberty (W.Va.) State Coll., 1967; spl. courses Carnegie-Mellon U., Bur. Mines, Environ. Health Service Tng. Inst., Am. Indsl. Hygiene Assn.; m. Delores Jean Rhoades, June 25, 1957; children—Dawn, Kimberly, Shanah, Jodie, Matthew. Asst. chief technologist Ohio Valley Hosp. Assn., Steubenville, 1959-64; technician, chemist, research chemist, sr. research chemist, mgr. indsl. hygiene Nat. Steel Corp., Pitts., 1964—. Mem. Brooke County Bd. Health, 1971-76, Brooke County Republican Exec. Com., 1966—, Brooke County Environ. Com., 1971-76, Brooke County 4-H Leaders Council, Brooke County 4-H Found., 1976-77; pres. Region XI Brooke/Hancock County Comprehensive Health Planning Commn., Hooverson Heights Sch. P.T.A., 1970-73; denominational rep. World Bible Quiz Assn., 1976-80, sec., 1977—, v.p., 1978—. Served with AUS, 1957-59. Recipient W.Va. 4-H Alumni award, 1975; certified emergency med. technician W.Va. Dept. Health, in respirable dust sampling Bur. Mines, in noise control and measurement Bur. Mines. Mem. Am. Indsl. Hygiene Assn., Water Pollution Control Fedn., W.Va., Ohio water pollution control assns., Am. Soc. Med. Technologists, Am. Soc. Clin. Pathologists (affiliated, registered), Am. Iron and Steel Inst., Nat. Coal Assn., Nat. Safety Council, Brooke Band Boosters Assn., Nat. Rifle Assn. Republican. Mem. Ch. of the Nazarene. Club: Brooke County Sportsmen. Home: 151 Loretta Ave Follansbee WV 26037 Office: 2800 Grant Bldg Pittsburgh PA 15219

GADE, MARVIN FRANCIS, paper co. exec.; b. Clinton, Iowa, Nov. Calif., Bernhardt Henry and Anna Mae (Jessen) G.; B.S. in Engring., U. Iowa, 1952; postgrad. exec. program U. Calif. at Los Angeles, 1960-61; m. Lorraine F. McDonald, Dec. 2, 1944; children—Michael David, Patricia Ann (Mrs. Alonzo Conn), Steven Dennis, Laura Jean (Mrs. Neal Stevens), Mary Kay (Mrs. Barry McIntyre), Karen Lynn (Mrs. Darryl Smith), Jeffrey Scott. Process instrumentation engr. Standards Brands Co., Clinton, 1946-50; with Kimberly-Clark Corp., hdqrs. Neenah, Wis., 1952—, sr. v.p., group exec., 1974-77, exec. v.p., 1977—, also dir. Bd. dirs. Calif. Water Quality Control Bd., 1964-67, S.C. Tech. Edn. Bd., 1968-70; pres. Fullerton C. of C., 1964-65; chmn. bd. adv. com. St. Jude's Hosp., Fullerton, Calif., 1962-67. Served as aviator USNR, 1943-46. Home: Coosa Pines AL 35044 Office: Kimberly-Clark Corp Coosa Pines AL 35044

GADSON, MELVIN FRANKLIN, educator; b. Cuthbert, Ga., Oct. 11, 1944; s. Rushiel Woodrow and Rosa Lee Scott G.; B.S., Albany State Coll., 1966; M.A., Fisk U., 1970; postgrad. Oak Ridge Associated Univs., 1970, Fla. State U., 1970-71; Ed.D. (Univ. fellow), Am. U., 1974; m. Narrest Hunter, July 24, 1965; 1 son, Rodney Gerard. Tchr. biology, chemistry and physics A.S. Clark High Sch., Cordele, Ga., 1966-69; instr. chemistry and phys. sci. Fla. A&M U., Tallahassee, 1970-72, asst. prof. sci. edn. and ednl. research, 1973—; asso. prof. phys. geography and math. Washington Tech. Inst., 1972-73; state sci. supr. State of Fla., 1975—; cons. metric edn. Asst. coach Little League Baseball, Tallahassee Recreation Dept., 1974—, coach Little League Football, 1974—. Multicultural Edn. certificates Fla. State Sci. Suprs.; Ga. Bd. Regents scholar, 1963, 64; NSF fellow, 1969-70. Mem. Nat. Sci. Tchrs. Assn., Fla. Ednl. Research Assn., Phi Delta Kappa, Alpha Phi Alpha (pres. Gamma Mu Lambda chpt.). Democrat. Baptist. Home: 3116 Brandywine Dr Tallahassee FL 32312 Office: Gore Edn Center Fla A&M U Tallahassee FL 32307

GAETAN, MANUEL, publishing co. exec.; b. San Juan, P.R., July 17, 1937; s. Libertad and Ida (Rivera) G.; B. in Mgmt. Engring. (P.R. Dept. Edn. scholar), Rensselaer Poly. Inst., 1958; M.S. in Indsl. Engring., Cleve. State U., 1970; m. Elizabeth Hochgertel, Dec. 19, 1964; children—Michele, Linda. Indsl. engring. officer Econ. Devel. Adminstrn. P.R., 1958-62; engring. dir. internat. div. Van Heusen Co., Pottsville, Pa., 1962-65; chief engr. Joseph & Feiss Co., Cleve., 1965-70; v.p., editorial dir. Bobbin Publs., Inc., Columbia, S.C., 1970—; dir. PBI, Columbia, Glendee Assos., Columbia, Gerber Garment Tech., Inc.; instr. Midlands Tech. Coll., Columbia, 1973; cons. to U.S. Dept. Commerce, 1979—. Served to capt., AUS, 1959-70. Registered profl. engr. Ohio, Pa., P.R. Mem. Am. Inst. Indsl. Engrs. (sr.), Profl. Photographers Am., Am. Bus. Press, Am. Apparel Mfg. Assn. Author: The Supervisory Development Handbook for the Sewn Products Industry, 1971; Sewing Machine Operator's Training Handbook, 1972. Compiler, editor The Sewn Products Engineering and Reference Manual, 1977. Home: 3708 Shallow Pond Rd Columbia SC 29206 Office: 1110 Shop Rd Columbia SC 29202

GAETZ, EDWARD FRANCIS, educator; b. N.Y.C., Sept. 20, 1925; s. Edward Francis and Dorathy Eileen (Ehrlick) G.; student N.W. Mo. State Tchrs. Coll., 1943, Whitman Coll., 1944; B.S., U. Wash., 1946; postgrad. Navy Postgrad. Sch., 1958; M.S. with distinction, Air Force Inst. Tech., 1963; postgrad. Ga. State U., 1976-80; m. Viola Mary Evans, June 9, 1949; children—Timothy Edward, Catherine Sue, Lori Anne. Served as enlisted man U.S. Navy, 1943-46, commd. ensign, 1946, advanced through grades to capt., 1967; supply officer on U.S. Navy Pacific Fleet Comdrs. Staff, 1964-67; dir. ops. Navy Electronics Supply Office, 1967-70; sr. navy supply officer, chief of staff for supply Naval Forces, Vietnam, 1970-71; comdg. officer Navy Supply Corps Sch., Athens, Ga., 1971-73, ret., 1973; asso. prof. bus. adminstrn., coordinator programs Ga. Coll., Warner Robins and Robins AFB, Ga., 1973—. Past pres. parish council Sacred Heart Roman Catholic Ch. Decorated Legion of Merit, Bronze Star. Mem. So. Mgmt. Assn., Soc. Logistic Engrs., Ga. Assn. Mktg. Educators, Ret. Officer Assn. Ga. (state auditor), Navy Supply Corps Alumni Assn. (exec. dir.), Warner Robins Tennis Assn. (pres.). Roman Catholic. Clubs: Internat. City Saddle, K.C., Moose, Robins AFB Officers. Home: 509 Navarro Dr Warner Robins GA 31093 Office: Bldg 1675 Robins Resident Center Robins AFB GA 31098

GAFFORD, FRANK HALL, ret. educator; b. Afton, Okla., Jan. 11, 1903; s. Benjamin Ford and Elizabeth Newman (Payne) G.; B.A., U. Tex., 1925, M.A., 1927, Ph.D., 1940; m. Anita Marguerite Engerrand, Dec. 28, 1926; children—Eleanor Marguerite (Mrs. Ernest Owen Bransford, Jr.), Frank Hall, Jeanne Engerrand. Instr. history U. Miss., 1927-29, asst. prof., 1929-31; asst. prof. history Coll. of Charleston, S.C., 1931-32, asso. prof., 1932-41, prof., 1941-49; asso. prof. history North Tex. State U., 1949-51, prof., 1951-73, prof. emeritus, 1973—, chmn. dept., 1951-52, dir., 1952-65, dean Coll. Arts and Scis., 1953-73; instr. U. of South, summer 1944, Tulane U., summer 1949. Mem. Am. Hist. Assn., AAUP, Phi Alpha Theta, Pi Sigma Alpha, Pi Kappa Alpha. Home: 2520 Royal Ln Denton TX 76201

GAGE, GEORGE RAYMOND, JR., physician; b. Bklyn., Feb. 13, 1919; s. George R. and Mary A. (Green) G.; B.A., Columbia U., 1938, M.D., 1942; m. 2d, Doris Jean Robbins, Aug. 25, 1972; children—Mary, Joanne, Janice, Kathleen, Margaret, George III, Richard. Practice obstetrics and gynecology, Coral Gables, Fla., 1950-78; asst. prof. obstetrics and gynecology U. Miami; med. dir. Group Health, Inc., Coral Gables. Served lt. M.C. USNR, 1943-47. Diplomate Am. Bd. Obstetrics and Gynecology. Fellow A.C.S., Am. Coll. Obstetricians and Gynecologists, South Atlantic Assn. Obstetrics and Gynecology, Internat. Coll. Surgeons; asso. Royal Soc. Medicine; mem. Fraternal Order of Police Assos. K.C. Office: Group Health Inc 1320 S Dixie Hwy Coral Gables FL 33146

GAGE, TOMMY WILTON, dentist, pharmacologist; b. Stamford, Tex., Oct. 6, 1935; s. Carl and Mildred (Hughes) G.; student McMurry Coll., 1953-54; B.S., U. Tex. Austin, 1957; D.D.S., Baylor U., 1961, Ph.D., 1969; m. Loyce M. Voss, June 2, 1956; children—Sharon, Stephen, Susan, Stacey. Gen. practice dentistry, Munday, Tex., 1963-66; prof., chmn. dept. pharmacology Baylor Coll. Dentistry, Dallas, 1969—. Served with USAR, 1961-63. Nat. Inst. Dental Research postdoctoral fellow, 1966-69. Mem. ADA, Tex. Dental Assn. (Cooley trophy 1976), Dallas County Dental Assn., Internat. Assn. Dental Research, Am. Assn. Dental Schs., S.W. Soc. Oral Medicine, Rho Chi, Sigma Xi, Omicron Kappa Upsilon. Methodist. Contbr. chpts. to textbooks. Office: 3302 Gaston St Dallas TX 75246

GAHAGAN, THOMAS GAIL, obstetrician, gynecologist; b. Brush Valley, Pa., Apr. 14, 1938; s. Ben D. and Zula G. (Brown) G.; B.A., Washington and Jefferson Coll., 1960; M.D., U. Pa., 1964; m. Mary A. Miller, Dec. 23, 1960; children—David, Diane, Kevin, Keith. Intern, U. Ky. Med. Center, Lexington, 1964-65; resident in obstetrics and gynecology, 1965-68; practice medicine specializing in obstetrics and gynecology, Newark, Ohio, 1970-71, Naples, Fla., 1971—. Bd. dirs. Fla. div. Am. Cancer Soc.; chmn. Prevent-A-Care Health Exposition, 1975-79. Served to capt. USAF, 1968-70. Recipient Physicians Recognition award AMA, 1977. Fellow Am. Coll. Obstetricians and Gynecologists; mem. AMA. Republican. Presbyterian. Home: 855 18th Ave S Naples FL 33940 Office: 775 1st Ave N Naples FL 33940

GAILLARD, EDSEL LAMAR, indsl. supplies co. exec.; b. Anderson County, S.C., Aug. 3, 1929; s. Lawrence Guyton G.; student public schs., Pelzer, S.C.; children—Joy Patrice, Gordon Lee. With Rembert Co., Inc., Anderson, S.C., 1960—, v.p., 1975—. Served with U.S. Army, 1951-53. Mem. Gideons Internat. Baptist. Home: Route 1 Box 214 Williamston SC 29697 Office: 1821 S McDuffie St Anderson SC 29624

GAINER, RUBY JACKSON (MRS. HERBERT P. GAINER), educator, civic leader b. Buena-Vista, Ga.; d. William B. and Lovie (Jones) Jackson; student Miles Meml. Coll.; B.S., Ala. State Tchrs. Coll.; M.A. in English and Social Studies, Atlanta U.; postgrad. Fla. A. and M. Coll., Western Wash. State Coll., U. Conn., Okla. State U.; H.H.D. (hon.), Selma U., Daniel Payne Coll., 1971; LL.D., Birmingham Bapt. Coll.; Ph.D. (hon.), Colo. State Christian Coll., 1973; LL.D. (hon.), Faith Coll., Birmingham; L.H.D. (hon.), Bishop Coll., Dallas; m. Herbert P. Gainer; children—Ruby Paulette, James H., Cecil F. Tchr., J. B. Turner High Sch., Milton, Fla., pub. schs., Birmingham, Ala., Washington Jr. High Sch., Pensacola, Fla., prior to 1968; guidance counselor Wedgewood Jr.-Sr. High Sch., Pensacola; English tchr. Woodham High Sch., Pensacola. Brought 2 successful legal cases against Jefferson (Ala.) County Sch. Bd. for equalization of Negro tchr. salaries, 1946-47, re-instatement Negro tchrs. under Tchr. Tenure Act in 1960's; organized 1st tchrs. union, Birmingham; also organized local high sch. chpt. Future Tchrs. Am., local tchr. aide and teen service groups, local and county assns. edn.; local capt. Heart Fund, Mothers March of Dimes, Cancer Fund; active local P.T.A., chmn. Fla. P.T.A. Workshop; participant Gov. Fla. Conf. Edn., Tallahassee, Nat. conf. Profl. Rights and Responsibilities, Arlington, Tex.; participant chmn. numerous profl. ednl. confs. So. U.S.; mem. Escambia County Guidance Council; mem., past officer Fla. Guidance Council; mem., bd. dirs. Partners for Progress. Bd. dirs. Escambia County Tb Assn. Recipient Tchr. of Year Award Dist. 1 Fla. State Tchrs. Assn., also award meritorious service, Distinguished Service award, 1966, DuShane Outstanding Service award; recipient DuShane Outstanding Dir. award Escambia County Tchrs. Assn., 1967, Distinguished Service award civil, human, profl. rights, 1965; recipient Outstanding Tchr. and Leader award Fla. Edn. Assn., honor award N.E.A. and Fla State Tchrs. Assn., 1966, Centennial Service to Mankind award Ala. State U., 1974, also numerous awards distinguished service youth, community orgns.; cited newspapers, NAACP; honored as alumnus Ala. State U. with meml. tablet in Academic Mall of Univ., 1975. Mem. Jefferson County (past sec., past pres.), Escambia County (past sec., past pres.), Fla. State (past bd. dirs. dist. 1, past pres. dist. 1, mem. tchr. edn. and profl. standards commn. and evaluation com., bd. advisers dept. classroom tchrs.), Ala. (past chmn. secondary sch. tchrs.), Am. tchrs. assns., AAUW, Jefferson County Tchrs. Union (past pres.), N.E.A., Assn. Classroom Tchrs. (v.p. 1969), Nat. Council English Tchrs., Nat. Council Social Studies Tchrs., Escambia County League Justice, Future Tchrs. Am. Advisers Council, City-Wide Fedn. Women's Clubs (past officer), LWV, Top Ladies Distinction (organizer, 1st pres. Pensacola chpt., Top Lady of Year), Alpha Kappa Alpha (Am. Woman's Service award 1974). Baptist (mem., pres. Bd. Ushers). Democrat. Mem. Order Eastern Star. Clubs: Mary M. Bethune (officer); New Idea Art and Study (officer). Composer: God Planted You Here, Talking to the Moon, It Is Better Not to Know, In the Quiet of the Day. Contbr. articles, poems, publs. Address: 1516 W Gadsden St Pensacola FL 32501

GAINES, CLARENCE EDWARD, coll. adminstr.; b. Paducah, Ky.; B.S., Morgan State Coll., Balt.; 1948; M.A., Columbia U., 1949; m. Clara Berry; children—Lisa Gaines McDonald, Clarence E. Coach football Winston-Salem U., 1946-50, coach track, 1961-62, coach basketball, 1946—, chmn. dept. phys. edn., athletic dir. and coordinator phys. edn. program Parochial Sch.; 1960—; cons. in field. Co-founder Winston-Salem Youth Baseball League, in 1960; bd. mgmt. Patterson Ave. YMCA, Winston-Salem, 1968-71, Winston-Salem Boys Club; bd. dirs. Winston-Salem Little League Baseball; bd. dirs. Winston-Salem Found.; bd. mgmt. Amos Cottage. Named Nat. Coll. Athletic Assn. Coll. div. Basketball Coach of Yr., 1967; named to N.C. Sports Hall of Fame, 1978. Mem. Central Intercoll. Athletic Assn. (Football Coach of Yr. 1948, Basketball Coach of Yr. 1957, 61 63, 70, 75), Nat. Assn. Intercoll. Athletics (dist. chmn. 1966-72), AAHPER, NEA, N.C. Assn. Health, Phys. Edn. and Recreation, Nat. Assn. Basketball Coaches, Nat. Assn. Coll. Dirs. Athletics. Office: Station A Winston-Salem U Winston-Salem NC 27182

GAINES, STANLEY FRANCIS, JR., petroleum distbr.; b. Cleveland, Miss., Feb. 6, 1940; s. Stanley Francis and Scottie (Polk) G.; B.A., Davidson (N.C.) Coll., 1961; m. Caroline Suzanne Laudig, Dec. 29, 1962; children—Caroline Laudig, II, Stanley Laudig (dec.), Stanley Francis, III. Salesman, Goodyear Tire & Rubber Co., 1960; pres. Gaines Oil Co., Inc., Boyle, Miss., 1962—, Gaines Enterprises, Inc., Boyle, 1968—; dir. Central Delta Warehouse, Inc. Chmn., Miss. Library Com., 1972-79, Bolivar County Library, 1968—; vice chmn. Miss. Library Assn., 1972; charter pres. Crosstie Arts Council, 1969-71; pres. Cleveland-Bolivar County Indsl. Devel. Found., 1978-79; bd. dirs. Delta Council, 1970-71, Bolivar County Farm Bur., 1968; chmn. adminstrv. bd., trustee First United Methodist Ch., Cleveland, 1968-71. Served with AUS, 1962-64; capt. Res., 1964-68. Decorated Army Commendation medal. Mem. Nat. Oil Jobbers Assn., Miss. Petroleum Marketers Assn., ALA, Omicron Delta Kappa, Cleveland-Bolivar County C. of C. (v.p. 1970-71, 78-79). Club: Exchange (pres. 1968). Home: 705 Farmer St St Cleveland MS 38732 Office: Gaines Oil Co Gaines Hwy Boyle MS 38730

GALASSI, JOHN PAUL, JR., psychologist, educator; b. Stamford, Conn., Jan. 22, 1945; s. John P. and Anna Marie (Pace) G.; A.B., Middlebury Coll., 1966; Ed M., Harvard U., 1967; Ph.D., U. Calif., Berkeley, 1971; m. Merna Dee Posner, June 16, 1967. Clin.-counseling psychologist Student Counseling Service, W.Va. U., Morgantown, 1971-73, also adj. asst. prof. guidance and counseling; asst. prof. edn., counseling and guidance U. N.C., Chapel Hill, 1973-76, asso. prof. edn. (counseling psychology), 1976—; cons. to Moore County (N.C.) Pub. Schs., EPA, Durham, Berlin Bros. Valley Sch. Dist., Sommerset, Pa., Fayette County (Pa.) Assn. for Retarded Children, Meredith Coll., Raleigh, N.C., N.B. Psychol. Assn. NIMH grantee, 1972-73. Clin. fellow Behavior Therapy and Research Soc.; mem. Am. Psychol. Assn., Assn. for Advancement of Behavior Therapy, Am. Personne and Guidance Assn., Am. Coll. Personnel Assn., N.C. Personnel and Guidance Assn., Assn. for Counselor Edn. and Supervision, Phi Delta Kappa. Co-author: Assert Yourself! How to be Your Own Person. Contbr. articles on counseling and psychotherapy to profl. jours. Mem. editorial bd. Behavior Therapy; Jour. Behavior Therapy and Exptl. Psychiatry. Office: 113 Peabody Hall University of North Carolina Chapel Hill NC 27514

GALBRAITH, RUTH LEGG, univ. dean; b. Lecompte, La., Nov. 5, 1923; d. Byron S. and Dora Ruth (Lindley) Legg; B.S., Purdue U., 1945, Ph.D., 1950; m. Harry W. Galbraith, June 16, 1950; 1 son, Allan Legg. Chemist, E. I. duPont de Nemours, Waynesboro, Va., 1945-46; textile chemist Gen. Electric Co., Bridgeport, Conn., 1946-47; teaching asst. in chemistry Purdue U., 1947-48, research fellow, 1948-50; prof. textiles U. Tenn., Knoxville, 1950-55; asso. prof. textiles U. Ill., Urbana, 1956-64, prof., 1964-70, chmn. div. textiles and clothing, 1962-70; prof. consumer affairs, head dept. consumer affairs Auburn U., 1970-73, dean Sch. Home Econs. and head home econs. research, 1973—; mem. task force on quality of living Dept. Agr., 1967-68; mem. Nat. Adv. Com. Flammable Fabrics Act, 1971-73; mem. Carpet and Rug Inst. Consumer Action Panel, 1975; mem. home econs. sub-com. Agrl. Expt. Sta. Com. on Policy, 1975-79, sec., 1977-79. Recipient Disting. Alumni award Purdue U., 1970. Fellow Am. Inst. Chemists; mem. Am. Home Econs. Assn. (chmn. agy. mem. unit 1975-76, chmn. research sect. 1978-80), Ala. Home

Econs. Assn., Am. Assn. Textile Chemists and Colorists, Am. Chem. Soc., ASTM (3d v.p. com. D-13 Textiles 1976-79), Assn. Coll. Profs. Textiles and Clothing, Assn. Adminstrs. Home Econs., AAUW, Sigma Xi, Omicron Nu, Phi Kappa Phi. Contbr. articles on textiles to profl. publs.; editorial bd. Research Jour. Home Econs., 1973-77, chmn. policy bd., 1978-80. Office: Sch Home Econs Auburn U Auburn AL 36849

GALBREATH, JOYCE CONDRAY, interior designer; b. Birmingham, Ala., Mar. 11, 1940; s. Marvin Walto and Leota Frances (Cochran) Condray; B.S., U. Ala., 1961; postgrad. Sorbonne U., Paris, 1962. Accountant, Infants Diaper Service, Birmingham, 1962-63; interior designer Galbreath Interiors Co., Huntsville, Ala., 1965-76, Nashville, 1977—; lectr., cons. in field. Mem. Am. Inst. Interior Designers. Republican. Baptist. Club: Bell Meade Country. Home: 743 Longhunter Ct Nashville TN 37217

GALE, STEVEN HERSHEL, educator; b. San Diego, Aug. 18, 1940; s. Norman Arthur and Mary Louise (Wilder) G.; B.A., Duke U., 1963; M.A., U. Calif., Los Angeles, 1965; Ph.D., U. So. Calif., 1970; m. Kathy L. L. Johnson, May 20, 1973; children—Shannon Erin, Ashley Alyssa. Reading asst. English Los Angeles Met. Coll., 1965-66; teaching asst. U. So. Calif., 1966, instr., 1967-68; asso. U. Calif. at Los Angeles, 1968-70; asst. prof. U. P.R., Rio Piedras, 1970-73; Fulbright prof. U. Liberia, Monrovia, 1973-74; asso. prof. U. Fla., Gainesville, 1974—, dir. MLA Spl. Session Grad. Program and Curriculum Devel.; dir. Univ. Players, Monrovia Players; author lecture series Am. Film History for USIS, Liberia, 1974; spl. advisor Liberian Ministry Edn., 1973-74; cons. Nat. Endowment Humanities, Fla. Fine Arts Council. Mem. alumni admissions com. Duke U.; participant NEH Humanities Perspectives on Professions; USIS cultural exchange tour, India, 1964. Grantee U. Puerto Rico, 1971, 72, U. Fla. Humanities Council, 1975, 77; Danforth asso., 1976—. Mem. Modern Lang. Assn., Am. Theatre Assn., African Studies Center (U. Fla.), AAUP, Am. Film Inst., So. Assn. Africanists, Fulbright Alumni Assn., Nat. Ret. Tchrs. Assn., Conf. on Coll. Composition, Coll. Eng. Assn., Fla. Track Ofcls. Assn., Mid-Fla. Ofcls. Assn., Fla. High Sch. Activities Assn., Chi Delta Pi. Author: Butter's Going Up, 1977; Harold Pinter: An Annotated Bibliography, 1978; also short stories, dramas, poetry. Editor: Reading for Today's Writers, 1980. Contbr. articles to profl. jours.; reviewer Garland Press, John Wiley & Sons, St. Martin's Press, Modern Drama, Pacific Quar.; referee Theatre Jour. Home: Route 4 Box 190-G Gainesville FL 32601 Office: Dept English U Florida Gainesville FL 32611

GALINDO, RAMIRO ANZE, developer-industrialist; b. Cochabamba, Bolivia, Oct. 5, 1938; s. Eudoro Q. and Blanca G. (Anze) G.; came to U.S., 1956, naturalized, 1977; student Villanova U., 1957; B.S., Tex. A. and M. U., 1962, C.E., 1960, M.S., 1962; children—Cid, Kim, Lis. Pres., Galindo Cons. Engrs., Cochabamba, 1965-73, Galco Engring. Co., Nassau, Bahamas, 1970—, The Braver Corp., Inc., Bryan, Tex., 1974—, Bera de Bolivia S.Am., tin alloys factory, 1972—; dir. Citizens Bank, Bryan; cons. in field. Hon. consul from Denmark to Bolivia, 1970—. Registered profl. engr., Tex.; decorated knight Royal Order of Danebrog (Denmark). Mem. ASCE, Nat., Tex. socs. profl. engrs., Amateur Athletic Union, Civil Engring. Nat. Honor Soc. Club: Optimist. Contbr. articles to profl. jours. Home: 3015 Hummingbird Circle Bryan TX 77801 Office: PO Box 3322 Bryan TX 77801

GALINSKY, GOTTHARD KARL, educator; b. Strassburg, Alsace, Feb. 7, 1942; s. Hans Karl and Edith (Margenburg) G.; came to U.S., 1961, naturalized, 1971; A.B., Bowdoin Coll., 1963; M.A., Princeton U., 1965, Ph.D., 1966; m. Susan Plume, Sept. 17, 1976; children by previous marriage—Robert Charles, John Anthony. Instr. classics Princeton, 1965-66; asst. prof. U. Tex., Austin, 1966-68, asso. prof., 1968-72, prof. classics, 1972—, chmn. dept., 1974—, chmn. grad. assembly, 1977-79; lectr. U.S.-U.K. Ednl. Commn., 1973; adv. council Am. Acad. in Rome, 1968—, prof. in residence, 1972-73. State dir. Tex. Fathers for Equal Rights, 1977-79. Trustee Vergilian Soc. Am., 1972-76, v.p., 1977-78. NEH grantee, 1967, Fulbright grantee, 1972-73, ACLS fellow, 1968-69, Guggenheim fellow, 1972-73; recipient Teaching Excellence award U. Tex., 1970, 76. Mem. Am. Philol. Assn., Archeol. Inst. Am., Classical Assn. Midwest and South (pres. 1980—). Roman Catholic. Author: The Herakles Theme, 1972; Ovid's Metamorphoses, 1975. Contbr. articles to profl. jours. Mem. editorial bd. Classical World, Vergilius. Home: 2729 Trail of Madrones Austin TX 78746

GALL, WILLIAM ROLFE, mech. engring. cons.; b. Portland, Oreg., May 20, 1913; s. Charles Love and Myra Billings (Rolfe) G.; B.S. in Mech. Engring., U. Tenn., 1936; M.E., Yale U., 1947; m. Edith Marie Beltram, Dec. 12, 1969; children—William Robert, Boyd J. Jones, Mary Eleanor, Nancy Victoria. Research asst. U. Cin., 1939-41; asst. prof. mech. engring. U. Louisville, 1941-44; sr. design engr. Clinton Engr. Works, Oak Ridge, 1944-47, reactor design engr., 1947-64, cons. engr., 1964—. Registered profl. engr., Tenn. Fellow ASME (J. Hall Taylor medal 1972); mem. Nat. Soc. Profl. Engrs., Am. Nuclear Soc., ASTM, Tenn. Soc. Profl. Engrs., Tau Beta Pi, Phi Kappa Phi. Methodist. Contbr. articles to profl. jour. Home and Office: PO Box 334 Oak Ridge TN 37830

GALLACHER, JAMES JOHN, biochemist; b. Detroit, July 14, 1928; s. Patrick Joseph and Catherine Helen (Boyle) G.; B.S., U. Detroit, 1950, M.S., 1954; m. Mary Lou Currier, Aug. 26, 1950; 1 son, James Anthony. Clin. chemist Children's Hosp. Mich., Detroit, 1953-55; clin. chemist Mt. Carmel Hosp., Detroit, 1955-57; dir. med. edn. Mercy Coll., Detroit, 1955-57; pres., biochemist BEL Research and Testing Labs., Plymouth, Mich., 1957-67; clin. biochemist Peoples Community Hosp. Assn., Wayne, Mich., 1967-76; sr. analytical chemist Coulter Diagnostics, Hialeah, Fla., 1976—. Mem. Am. Chem. Soc., AAAS, Am. Assn. Clin. Chemists, Soc. Nuclear Medicine, Am. Inst. Chemists, Latin Am. Soc. Pathology. Elk. Contbr. articles to profl. jours. Home: 2829 NE 33d Ct Ft Lauderdale FL 33306 Office: 740 W 83d St Hialeah FL 33014

GALLAGHER, BERNARD THOMAS, govt. ofcl.; b. N.Y.C., Jan. 28, 1922; ed. U. Ala.; diploma Command Staff Coll. Air U., 1962; diploma Nuclear Weapons Def. Atomic Support Agy., 1963, U.S. Army Dugway Proving Ground, 1964, Indsl. Coll. Armed Forces. Commd. officer USAAF, 1942, advanced through grades to col. U.S. Air Force, 1965; comdr. test squadron Olmstead AFB, Pa., 1958-62; chief spl. flight br. USAF hdqrs., Washington, 1963-64; chief USAF Disaster Preparedness Program, Washington, 1964-65; ret. 1965; chief plans and programs br. Office Emergency Preparedness, Exec. Office Pres., 1965-66, dep. chief div., 1966-68, chief div. nuclear biology and chem. warfare Office Emergency Preparedness, 1968-75; dir. Western Va. ops. office Fed. Preparedness Agy., 1975-79, Fed. Emergency Mgmt. Agy., 1979—; U.S. mem., chmn. Quadrapartite Standardization Coordinating Com., 1964; tech. adv. to U.S. rep. NATO, 1964, mem. interservice nuclear biol. chem. procedures com., 1964; mem. U.S. Govt. Sr. Exec. Service; cons. in nuclear biol. and chem. warfare defensive measures. Mem. Mensa. Home: 112 Sydnor Dr Route 2 Leesburg VA 22075 Office: Fed Emergency Mgmt Agy Premier Bldg Washington DC 20472

GALLAGHER, EARLE FLOYD, airplane pilot, safety cons.; b. Atlanta, Jan. 26, 1908; s. Michael and Pearl Eunice (Ivey) G.; student Southwestern U., Memphis, 1947-48, Pan-Am. U., Edinburg, Tex., 1965-67; m. Marion Leona Renfroe, Dec. 30, 1949; children—Theresa, Earle Floyd. Dist. sales mgr. Remington-Rand Corp., Tampa, Fla., 1939; dep. collector IRS, West Palm Beach, Fla., 1941; civilian flight instr. U.S. Air Force, Columbus, Miss. and Mission, Tex., 1953-61; exec. dir. Donna (Tex.) Urban Renewal, 1961; sales mgr. Reynolds Mfg. Co., McAllen, Tex., 1963; pilot U.S. Dept. Agr., Mission, 1963—. Vice pres. bd. dirs. Hidalgo Fed. Credit Union, McAllen, 1976—. Served with AUS, 1944-46; PTO. Cert. flight instr.; registered real estate broker, Tex. Club: Masons. Address: 2704 N 6th St McAllen TX 78501

GALLAGHER, FRANCIS JOSEPH, mfrs. rep.; b. Scranton, Pa., Mar. 2, 1920; s. Peter Joseph and Lorena Theresa (Eckenrode) G.; student U. Pa., 1938-40; m. Josie Ruth Collins, Nov. 6, 1943; children—Patricia Colleen, Maureen Michele, Francis Joseph. With United Metal Box Co., 1940-41; salesman kitchen cabinets, self-employed mfrs. rep. Boro Wood Proudcts Co., Bennettsville, S.C., 1947-76; mfrs. rep. L-Co Cabinet Corp., Raleigh, N.C., 1976—. Active Rex Hosp. Found., Raleigh, N.C. Democratic Party, YMCA, Boys Club, Raleigh, N.C. State Student Aid Assos. Served with USMC, 1941-46. Mem. Home Builders Assn., Nat. Kitchen Cabinet Assn., Nat. Assn. Home Builders, Sales Exec. Club. Democrat. Roman Catholic. Clubs: Carolina Country, N. Ridge Country, Downtown (Richmond, Va.); Cavalier (Norfolk, Va.); Wolfpack. Home: 1305 Westfield Ave Raleigh NC 27607

GALLAGHER, JAMES FRANCIS, ins. co. exec.; b. Pitts., Aug. 25, 1945; s. James Francis and Gertrude Helen (Hando) G.; B.A., Duquesne U., 1967; M.B.A., So. Meth. U., 1975; m. Barbara Ann Dugan, Sept. 30, 1967; children—Brian Keith, Kevin Patrick, Eric Paul. Sr. claims rep. Conn. Gen., 1969-73, asst. claims mgr., 1973-75, asst. v.p., 1975-76, v.p., 1976-78, asst. dir. ops., 1978; sr. v.p., dir. ops. World Service Life Ins. Co., Fort Worth, 1978—. Exec. com. Jr. Achievement, 1978-79; vice chmn. St. Bartholomew's Parish Council, 1977-79, chmn., 1979-80; corp. coordinator United Way campaign, 1978-79. Served with U.S. Army, 1967-69. Mem. Am. Mgmt. Assn., Internat. Found. Employee Benefits, Life Office Mgmt. Assn., Dallas Soc. Claimsmen (exec. com., dir.). Democrat. Roman Catholic. Home: 4613 Saldana Dr Fort Worth TX 76133 Office: 307 W 7th St Fort Worth TX 76102

GALLAGHER, JOHN CURRIER, pathologist; b. Phila., June 21, 1933; s. James Roswell and Constance Ruby (Dann) G.; B.S. magna cum laude, Yale U., 1954, M.D. cum laude, 1958; m. Elizabeth Susan Brailsford, June 29, 1954; 1 son, James Harrison Roswell. Intern, Yale-Grace New Haven Hosp., 1958-59, resident, 1959-60; resident in pathology West Haven (Conn.) VA Hosp., 1960-62; asso. pathologist pulmonary-mediastinal-ear, nose, throat br. Armed Forces Inst. Pathology, Washington, 1964-65, chief otolaryngic pathology, 1965-68; asst. chief lab. service VA Med. Center, Bay Pines, Fla., 1968-75, chief lab. service, 1975—; asso. clin. prof. pathology U. South Fla., Tampa, 1975—. Chmn. bd. trustees Pilgrim Congregational Ch., St. Petersburg, Fla., 1979, moderator, 1978, chmn. bd. Christian edn., 1974-77. Served with USN, 1962-64. Fellow Coll. Am. Pathologists, Am. Soc. Clin. Pathologists; mem. AMA, Fla. Med. Assn., Suncoast Archaeol. Soc., St. Petersburg Shell Club. Contbr. articles in field to profl. jours. Home: 12250 6th St E Treasure Island FL 33706 Office: VA Med Center Bay Pines FL 33504

GALLAGHER, PATRICIA CECILIA, author; b. Lockhart, Tex.; d. Frank Joseph and Martha Leona (Rhody) Bienek; student Trinity U., 1951; 1 son, James Craig. Novels include: The Sons and the Daughters, 1961, Answer To Heaven, 1964, The Fires of Brimstone, 1966, Shannon, 1967, Shadows of Passion, 1971, Summer of Sighs, 1971, The Thicket, 1974, Castles in the Air, 1976, Mystic Rose, 1977; No Greater Love, 1979. Mem. Women in Communications, San Antonio Mag. Council. Office: Scott Meredith Literary Agency Inc 845 3d Ave New York City NY 10019

GALLAGHER, PHIL C., ins. exec.; b. Miami, Fla., Nov. 10, 1926; s. Phil J. and Blonda (Burrow) G.; B.B.A., U. Miami, 1949; children—Pamela Robertson, Vivien Elizabeth. With D.R. Mead & Co., Miami, 1949-72, exec. v.p., 1958-72; partner Gallagher-Cole Assos., Miami, 1972—; dir. Skylake State Bank, North Miami Beach, Fla.; underwriting mem. Lloyd's of London; past instr. Lindsey Hopkins Edn. Center. Bd. dirs. Grand Jury Assn. Fla., J. Edwin Larson Found. for Ins. Edn. Served with USNR, 1944-46. Mem. Ind. Ins. Agts. Am. (former nat. dir., past chmn. agy. mgmt. com.), Ind. Ins. Agts. of Dade County (past pres.), Nat. Assn. Ins. Brokers, Profl. Ins. Agts. Fla. and the Caribbean, Profl. Ins. Agts. Dade County, Am. Risk and Ins. Assn., Nat. Assn. Casualty and Surety Agts., Fla. Surplus Lines Assn., Nat., Fla., Miami assns. life underwriters, Fla. Assn. Ins. Agts. (past pres.), Greater Miami C. of C., Econ. Soc. South Fla. Clubs: Palm Bay, Jockey, Bankers (Miami); Ocean Reef, Surf, La Gorce Country. Home: 1 Palm Bay Ct Miami FL 33138 Office: 4700 Biscayne Blvd Miami FL 33137

GALLANDER, CATHLEEN SPARKS, museum ofcl.; b. San Antonio, Feb. 4, 1931; d. Walter Charles and Lyra Millicent (Haisley) Sparks; A.A., Stephens Coll., 1950; B.A. in Sociology, U. Tex., Austin, 1952; postgrad. Del Mar Coll., (scholar) Harvard U., summer 1964, Inst. for Arts and Adminstrs., Harvard Bus. Sch., 1971; 1 dau., Melissa Hope. Dir., Art Museum of South Tex., Corpus Crhisti, 1961—; panel mem. Tex. Commn. on Arts and Humanities, Nat. Endowment for Arts. Mem. Coll. Art Assn. Am., Am. Assn. Museums, Am. Fedn. Arts, Western Assn. Art Museums, Tex. Museums Assn. (trustee), Assn. Art Museum Dirs. (trustee). Office: Art Museum of South Tex PO Box 1010 Corpus Christi TX 74803

GALLANT, KENNETH ADRIAN, assn. exec.; b. Berlin, N.H., May 25, 1939; s. Earl and Joyce (Shields) G.; B.S., U. Cin., 1976; m. Margaret Ann Snow, Aug. 19, 1961; children—Pamela Joy, Deborah Lynn. With Brown Co., Berlin, 1957-58; officer Salvation Army, various locations, 1958-71; exec. dir. Warren County United Appeal, Lebanon, Ohio, 1971-76; exec. dir. Hopkinsville (Ky.) United Way and exec. dir. United Services Council, 1976—. Mem. Inter-Agy. Council of Social Service Agencies, Lebanon, Ohio, 1971-76, Pennyrile Players Drama Group, Lebanon, 1976-80; mem. Ohio Citizens Council, Columbus, 1971-76. Mem. Nat. Assn. Social Workers, Ky. Assn. United Way Execs. Methodist. Club: Rotary. Office: 1202 S Virginia St Hopkinsville KY 42240

GALLE, WILLIAM PRESTON, JR., educator; b. New Orleans, Nov. 19, 1942; s. William Preston and Lillian (Welch) G.; B.S., La. State U., 1967, M.B.A., 1969; Ph.D., U. Ark., 1972; m. Julia Ann Williams, June 25, 1966; children—Julie Michelle, William Preston III. Instr. mgmt. U. Ark., 1969-71, asst. prof. 1971-73; asst. prof. E. Tenn. State U., Johnson City, 1973-79, dir. grad. studies Coll. Bus., 1977—, asso. prof., 1979—; mgmt. communications cons.; mem. standing com. on personnel Tenn. Bd. Regents. Recipient Outstanding Young Man award Nat. Jaycees, 1977. Mem. Acad. Mgmt., Am. Bus. Communications Assn., Adminstrv. Mgmt. Soc. Methodist. Home: Route 5 Johnson City TN 37601 Office: Dept Mgmt E Tenn State U Johnson City TN 37601

GALLEGOS, CARL MICHAEL, forester; b. Silverton, Colo., Nov. 6, 1943; s. Max A. and Cora (Gurule) G.; B.S. (scholar) Doane Coll., 1965; M.Forestry, Duke U., 1969; Ph.D., N.C. State U., 1978; m. Joy L. Walker, Mar. 27, 1976; 1 stepdau., Kimberly Ann Gray. Research asst. Duke U., Durham, N.C., 1967-69; prof. forest genetics and tree improvement (Peace Corps vol.), Universidad Austral de Chile, Valdivia, 1969-72; research asst. N.C. State U., Raleigh, 1973-76; sr. research forester Central and S. Am. species Internat. Paper Co., Mobile, Ala., 1976—. Mem. Soc. Am. Foresters, Soil Sci. Soc. Am., Forest Farmers Assn., Xi Sigma Pi. Republican. Contbr. articles to profl. jours. Home: 5818 Innsbruck Dr Mobile AL 36608 Office: PO Box 2328 Paper Mill Rd Mobile AL 36601

GALLETTE, RUSSELL F., banker; b. Toledo, Nov. 4, 1918; s. Russell C. and Ora Ada (Harmon) G.; B.S., U. Toledo, 1942; m. Lucille Elinora Rupley, May 10, 1956; 1 son, Russell F. Vice-pres. First Nat. Bank, Lake Worth, Fla., 1959-63; v.p., Litchfield State Savs. Bank, (Mich.), 1963-68; exec. v.p., sec. Citizens Trust Co., Portsmouth, Va., 1968—; pres., chmn. bd. Portsmouth Local Devel. Co., Inc., 1970—; sec., dir. Citizens Trust Co., 1968—; pres. Citizens Trust Bank, 1976—. Chmn. Hillsdale County (Mich.) chpt. OEO, 1964-65; council mem., finance dir., fire commr. Village of Palm Springs, Fla., 1959-61; mem. Portsmouth Planning Commn., 1973, Portsmouth TV Cable Commn., 1973, Va. Port Authority, 1974, Portsmouth Municipal Fin. Commn., 1976, Portsmouth Parking Authority, 1977; chmn. Portsmouth Bd. Equalization, 1974; bd. dirs. United Fund, Portsmouth, treas., 1970-71, exec. com., 1970-75, v.p., 1973-75, pres., 1976—; bd. dirs. Jr. Achievement Tidewater, 1977—. Served with USAAF, 1943-46. Mem. Am. Inst. Banking, Bank Adminstrn. Inst., Portsmouth C. of C. (dir. 1976, state and local legis. com., chmn. indsl. devel. com.), Retail Mchts. Assn. Portsmouth (dir. 1977—), Aircraft Owners and Pilots Assn., Clubs: Cedar Point, Elizabeth Manor Golf and Country (Portsmouth). Home: 135 Yorkshire Rd Portsmouth VA 23701 Office: 355 Crawford St Portsmouth VA 23704

GALLIANO, VERNON FREDERICK, univ. pres.; b. Cut Off, La., Apr. 26, 1923; s. Emile D. and Josephine (Vega) G.; B.S. (Univ. acad. scholar), U. Southwestern La., 1947; M.S., La. State U., 1954, Ph.D. (Univ. fellow), 1960; m. Josephine Bennett, Apr. 13, 1945; children—Vernon Frederick, Timothy, Gregory, Jonathon. Tchr. vocat. agr. Larose-Cut Off High Sch., Lafourche Parish, La., 1947-54; supervising tchr. Southwestern La. Inst. (now U. Southwestern La.), Lafayette, 1948-54, prof. agrl. edn., dir. tchr. tng., 1954-60; dean edn. Nicholls State Coll., Thibodaux, La., 1960-63, pres. Nicholls State U., Thibodaux, 1963—. Dir. Citizens Bank & Trust Co., Thibodaux; trustee Gulf S. Research Inst. Mem. adv. com. La. State Supt. Edn., 1965-66; chmn. adv. council for vocational and tech. edn. La. Bd. Edn., 1969-72; mem. adv. council for federally assisted programs La. Dept. Edn., 1967-72; mem. La. Gov.'s Legislative Com. Study Coordination Higher Edn., 1968-69, La. Indsl. Adv. Com., 1968-69, Council for Devel. French-Speaking La., 1968—; mem. commn. on colls. So. Assn. Colls. and Schs., 1974—, also mem. program planning com., 1975—; mem. La. state adv. council Title IV ESEA. Dist. finance campaign chmn. Boy Scouts Am., 1965; mem. La. Sci. Found., 1964-70, v.p., 1967-68, pres., 1969-70; mem. com. community action and crime La. Commn. Law Enforcement and Adminstrn. Criminal Justice, 1968—, citizens adv. com. Greater Lafourche Port Commn., 1969, adv. com. Lafourche Parish Airport Dist., 1964-65; chmn. St. Charles-St. John the Baptist Bridge and Ferry Authority, 1968-70; mem. So. Regional Edn. Bd., 1972—, La. Sea Grant Adv. Council, 1974—. Bd. dirs. St. Joseph Hosp., Thibodaux, 1965-69; past mem. bd. advisers St. Joseph Sem., St. Benedict, La.; bd. commrs. Hosp. Service Dist. 3 Lafourche Parish; mem. adv. bd. Nat. Ocean Industries Assn. Served to lt. USNR, 1943-45, 61-62; lt. comdr. Air Res. ret. Recipient Hon. State Farmer degree La. Assn. Future Farmers Am., 1955, commendation Houma-Terrebonne C. of C., 1966; Best Educator award River Parishes Chem. Indsl. Council, 1972. Mem. So. Educators Corp. (bd. govs. 1968—), Gulf S. (Athletic) Conf. (pres. 1971-72), Am. Assn. State Colls. and Univs. (environment com. 1970—, com. on sea grant programs 1969-70, dir. 1977—), La. State Colls. and Univs. Presidents' Council (chmn. 1964-66), La. Tchrs. Assn. and Dept. Higher Edn., Thibodaux C. of C., Am. Legion, VFW, John Henry Cardinal Newman Hon. Soc., Blue Key, Phi Kappa Phi, Phi Delta Kappa, Delta Tau Alpha, Delta Mu Delta. Democrat. Roman Catholic. K.C., Rotarian (pres. Thibodaux club 1966-67). Club: Propeller of the U.S. (Port of Orleans). Contbr. articles to ednl. jours. Home: President's Home Nicholls State University Thibodaux LA 70301 Office: Box 2001 Nicholls University Station Thibodaux LA 70301

GALLMAN, DAVID CLINTON, ins. exec.; b. Resaca, Ga., Feb. 27, 1922; s. Dennis J. and Mamie (Hall) G.; student Ga. Tech. U., 1942, N.C. State Coll., 1943; div.; children—Sharon Nelle (Mrs. Robert L. Bramblett, Jr.), Gary C., David Christopher; m. 2d, Maria de Noronha. Owner, operator photog. studio, Calhoun, Ga., 1946-51; asst. factory rep. Advance Aluminum Castings Corp., Ga., 1951-55; dist. supr. state circulation Atlanta Newspapers, Inc., 1955-60; supr. agts. David C. Gallman Ins. Agy., Monroe, Ga., 1960—. Cons. auto financing. Pres. Monroe PTA, 1963-64; bd. dirs. and co-chmn. Ga. Partner Cities and Penambuco, Brazil, Partners of the Americas, 1980—. Served to sgt. USAAF, 1943-45. Decorated Air medal with 2 oak leaf clusters; recipient Distinguished Leadership award Boy Scouts Am., 1961. Mem. Life Underwriters Assn. (sec.), Internat. Platform Assn., Monroe Assn. Life Underwriters (pres. 1967-68, 76-77), Monroe C. of C. Baptist (deacon). Clubs: Masons, Shriners, Rotary (local pres. 1962-63, worldwide fellowship dist. chmn. 1979-80, cert. of leadership award 1963, zone chmn. dist. gov.'s staff 1964), Toastmasters (pres. 1969-70). Home: 4202 Riverclub Dr Lilburn GA 30247 Office: 414 E Spring St Monroe GA 30655

GALLOWAY, DAN CROSS, radiologist; b. Electra, Tex., Feb. 11, 1943; s. Paul Rhea and Louise (Cross) G.; B.A., Hardin Simmons U., 1965; M.D., ll. Okla., 1969; m. Leanne Pierson, Jan. 11, 1977. Resident in diagnostic radiology U. Okla. Health Scis. Center, 1970-73; fellow in neuroradiology Montreal Neurologic Inst., 1974-75; asso. prof. radiology U. Okla. Health Sci. Center, Oklahoma City, 1977—, head sect. spl. procedures, dept. radiology, 1977—. Served to lt. cmdr. M.C., USN, 1976-77. Diplomate Am. Bd. Radiology. Mem. Am. Coll. Radiology, Radiol. Soc. N.Am., Assn. Univ. Radiologists, AMA, Am. Soc. Neuroradiology, Okla. Med. Assn., Alpha Omega Alpha. Mem. Christian Ch. Contbr. articles to profl. jours. Home: 8617 Lakehurst St Oklahoma City OK 73120 Office: 800 NE 13th St Oklahoma City OK 73125

GALLOWAY, DOCK ROSCOE, accountant; b. Transylvania County, N.C., July 12, 1915; s. Samuel Roscoe and Laura (Owen) G.; B.S. in Bus. Adminstrn., U. S.C., 1955; m. Lileree Mary Tanner, Sept. 28, 1949; children—Vera Lynn, Roxanne Elizabeth (dec.). Income tax auditor S.C. Tax Commn., Columbia, 1955-61; field auditor Agrl. Stablzn. and Conservation Service, U.S. Dept. Agr., Atlanta, 1961-62; pub. accountant L.C. Dodge, C.P.A., Spartanburg, S.C., 1962-65; plant accountant Spartan Mill, Spartanburg, 1965-67; forester and farmer, Spartanburg, 1967-69; dept. supr. Butte Knitting Mills, Spartanburg, 1969—. Served in U.S. Army, 1939-45. Mem. Nat. Mgmt. Assn. (chpt. cert. of appreciation 1979), U. S.C. Alumni Assn.,

Delta Sigma Pi. Democrat. Methodist. Home: 641 Overhill Dr Spartanburg SC 29303

GALLOWAY, LOUIE ALTHEIMER, III, physicist; b. Pine Bluff, Ark., Feb. 3, 1936; s. Louie Altheimer and Jessie Nina (Laws) G.; A.B., Hendrix Coll., 1958; M.S., Case Inst. Tech., 1961, Ph.D., 1966; m. Harriett Allen Laws, June 7, 1958; children—Nina Victoria, Louie Altheimer IV, Mack Laws. Asst. prof. William and Mary U., 1963; asso. prof. physics Centenary Coll. of La., Shreveport, 1966-69, prof., 1969-78, chmn. dept., 1967-78, Keen prof., 1972-78, dir. Computing Center, 1968-74; chief engr. Petroleum Assos. of Lafayette, Inc., 1978—; pres. Foremost Cons., Shreveport, 1966—, Legal Data Systems, Shreveport, 1972-74; aerospace technologist NASA Manned Spacecraft Center, Houston, 1967; lectr. VA Hosp., Shreveport, 1972-78. NSF fellow, 1967-68, NASA grantee, 1968-70 Mem. Am. Phys. Soc., Am. Assn. Physics Tchrs. Republican. Methodist (adminstrv. bd. 1973). Clubs: Elks, Rotary. (Shreveport). Home: 410 Elmwood Dr Lafayette LA 70503 Office: Box 52449 Lafayette LA 70505

GALLOWAY, REX FARMER, educator; b. Murray, Ky., May 11, 1936; s. Harding and Hattie Lee (Farmer) G.; B.S., Murray State U., 1963; M.B.A., Memphis State U., 1966; D. Bus. Adminstrn., Miss. State U., 1970; m. Frances Inez Taylor, July 9, 1966; children—Andrea Kaye, John Harding. Self-employed automobile sales, Murray, 1954-58; sales mgr. Ralston Purina Co., St. Louis, 1963-65; research asso. Miss. Research and Devel. Center stipendiary Miss. State U., 1966-67, vis. prof. bus. adminstrn., extension div., 1967-69; asst. prof. Murray State U., 1969-71; asso. prof., 1971-78, prof., 1978—, coordinator Fed. Title I Program, 1974—, adminstr. pub. service tng. Coll. Bus. and Pub. Affairs, 1975—, chmn. dept. mgmt., 1976—. Mgmt. cons. to indsl. and govtl. orgns.; rep. nat. meeting Nat. Tax Assn.-Tax Inst. Am., 1976, 77, 78. Served with AUS, 1958-59. Mem. Acad. Mgmt., Four Rivers Mfrs. Assn. (v.p. 1978-79, pres. 1980), So. Mgmt. Assn., Am. Inst. Decision Scis., Data Processing Mgmt. Assn., Ky. Acad. Computer Users Assn., Beta Gamma Sigma, Phi Kappa Phi, Sigma Lambda Iota, Pi Sigma Alpha, Alpha Tau Omega (pres. chpt. housing corp. 1969-70, chmn. bd. dirs. chpt. housing corp. 1970-72, Outstanding Alumnus of chpt. 1971). Baptist. Contbr. articles to profl. jours. Home: 308 Oak Dale Dr Murray KY 42071

GALLUP, RUSSELL DAVID, JR., real estate corp. exec.; b. Norfolk, Va., Nov. 10, 1950; s. Russell David and Anna Eloise (Seal) G.; student Va. Poly. Inst. and State U., 1969-72; B.S. in Mgmt., Bob Jones U., 1976. Forestry laborer, Continental Can Co., Hopewell, Va., 1970; revenue agt. trainee, IRS, Norfolk, Va., 1971; metal punching machine operator, Guille Steel Products Co., Virginia Beach, Va., 1972; auto parts deliveryman, Indian River Auto Parts, Chesapeake, Va., 1973; pres. R AND R Corp., Norfolk, 1975—. Mem. John Birch Soc., Concerned Citizens for Constl. Govt., Bob Jones U. Alumni Assn. (life). Am. Party. Baptist. Home and Office: 4411 Princess Anne Rd Virginia Beach VA 23462

GALOS, ANDREW JOHN, musician, educator; b. Kassa, Hungary, Feb. 18, 1918; s. Maximilian Steiner and Margaret (Geller) G.; came to U.S., 1928, naturalized, 1928; B.S. (scholar), Juilliard Sch. Music, 1942, M.S., 1950; M.A., Columbia U., 1952, Ed.D., 1958; m. Ruth Fishberg, Nov. 1, 1945; 1 son, Michael Jonathan. First violinist NBC Symphony, N.Y.C., 1946; asst. concertmaster Balt. Symphony, violin tchr. Peabody Conservatory Music, 1948-50; asst. concertmaster Radio City Music Hall, 1st Violin City Center Opera, N.Y.C., 1950-56; prof. violin and orch. Utah State U., Logan, 1956-60, U. N.H., Durham, 1960-66; head music dept., prof. violin and orch. dir. Columbus (Ga.) Coll., 1969—; concertmaster Columbus Symphony, 1969—, Portland (Maine) Symphony, 1956-60, Youngstown-Akron Symphonies, 1963-69; soloist Boston Pops, New Orleans Symphony, Portland Symphony; mem. Mischakoff, Galimir and Chautaugua string quartets. Served with USAF, 1942-45. Mem. Am. Fedn. Musicians, Music Educators Nat. Conf., Am. String Tchrs. Assn. (pres. Ga. chpt.), Phi Delta Kappa, Phi Mu Alpha. Contbr. articles to profl. jours. Home: 5525 Southlea Ln Columbus GA 31904 Office: Music Dept Columbus Coll Columbus GA 31907

GALPERIN, SIMON HIRSCH, JR., state senator; b. Charleston, W.Va., Aug. 5, 1931; s. Simon Hirsch and Fan (Lavenstein) G.; B.S. in Commerce, Washington U., St. Louis, 1953; m. Maureen Fahey Supcoe; children—Stephen, Gregory. With Galperin Music Co., Charleston, 1956-71, pres., 1963-71; realtor Old Colony Co., Charleston, 1973—, dir., 1976—; past pres. Nat. Assn. Young Music Mchts.; past dir. Nat. Assn. Music Mchts.; mem. W.Va. Ho. of Dels. from Kanawha County, 1967-70, W.Va. Senate from 17th Dist., 1971—. Served with USNR, 1954-56. Mem. Am. Bus. Club. Democrat. Jewish. Home: 632 Gordon Dr Charleston WV 25314 Office: 1210 Kanawha Blvd E Charleston WV 25301

GALT, BARRY JACK, lawyer; b. Ardmore, Okla., Dec. 14, 1933; s. Monroe S. and Ethelyn (Barry) G.; B.A. (Naval ROTC scholar), U. Okla., 1955, LL.B., 1960; m. Mary Kathryn Moore, Aug. 14, 1954; children—Terri Kathryn, Carol Ann, Gayle Lyn. Admitted to Okla. bar, 1960; asso. Conner, Winters, Ballaine, Barry & McGowen and predecessor firm, Tulsa, 1960-65, partner, 1966-75; sr. v.p., gen. counsel Williams Cos., 1975-77, exec. v.p., 1977-78, pres., chief operating officer, 1979—. Com. chmn. 1977 U.S. Open Championship. Bd. dirs. Salvation Army, Hillcrest Med. Center Assos., St. John Med. Center. Served to lt. USNR, 1955-58. Mem. Am., Okla., Tulsa County bar assns., U. Okla. Assn. (dir.), Order of Coif, Phi Delta Theta, Phi Alpha Delta. Presbyterian (elder). Clubs: So. Hills Country, Tulsa. Home: 6730 S Evanston St Tulsa OK 74136 Office: One Williams Center Tulsa OK 74172

GALT, ELEANOR, mus. dir.; b. Mansfield, Ark., Dec. 22, 1928; d. John Carney and Eleanor (DeVault) Galt; B.S., Tex. Coll. Arts and Industries, 1950. Sec., Gen. Electric Apollo Systems, Houston, 1964-71; sec. pub. relations dept. Stran Steel Corp., Houston, 1971-73; dir. Rio Grande Valley Mus., Harlingen, Tex., 1973—. Publicity chairperson Cameron County Red Cross. Mem. Rio Grande Valley Mus. Assn., Zonta, City Fedn. Women's Clubs, Valley Arts and Craft Club. Home: 421 D N 3d Harlingen TX 78550 Office: Industrial Air Park Harlingen TX 78550

GALYA, THOMAS ANDREW, geologist; b. New Brunswick, N.J., July 11, 1947; s. Andrew Peter and Geraldine Rose G.; B.S., W.Va. U., 1971; M.S., N.E. La. U., 1975; Ph.D., Miami U., Oxford, Ohio, 1980; m. Lanora Lucille Bucklew, Jan. 8, 1970. Geologist, coal group Pittston Co., Nettie, W.Va., 1972, chief geologist, Dante, Va., 1978—; teaching asst. Northeast La. U., Monroe, 1973-75; teaching fellow Miami U., Oxford, Ohio, 1975-77, dissertation fellow, 1977-78. Mem. Am. Assn. Petroleum Geologists, Soc. Econ. Paleontologists and Mineralogists, Mineral. Soc. Am., Sigma Xi, Sigma Gamma Epsilon. Democrat. Roman Catholic. Home: Westwood Colonial Circle Apt 12 Abingdon VA 24210 Office: Pittston Co Clinchfield Coal Dante VA 24237

GAMACHE, GERALD LEE, psychotherapist, mem. naval staff; b. Des Moines, Dec. 30, 1942; s. Joseph Elmer and May Louise (Kolb) G.; B.A., U. N.Fla., 1975, M.A., 1976; m. Mildred Emmelene Nichols Koger, Dec. 14, 1974; children—David Anthony, Kimberly Kay, Erik Terrance, Sarah Michele. Enlisted as Seaman U.S. Navy, 1963, advanced through grades to 1st class petty officer, 1968; mem. adj. staff, clin. psychologist Naval Regional Med. Center, Jacksonville, Fla., 1975-77; dir. drug/alcohol edn. and program devel. Naval Air Sta., Jacksonville, 1975-77; counselor U.S. Navy, 1974—; pres. N.E. Fla. Counseling Services, Jacksonville; also pvt. practice, 1974—; lectr. Fla. Jr. Coll., 1974—, U. North Fla., 1975—, Jacksonville U., 1975—; asst. prof. psychology Jones Coll., Jacksonville, 1976-77; asst. prof. psychology, dept. continuing edn. Old Dominion U., Norfolk, 1977—; instr. Fla. Jr. Coll., 1979—; cons. Jacksonville Drug Abuse Program, 1974-75. Mem. exec. com. Muskogee dist. Boy Scouts Am., 1974-76; mem. N.E. Fla. Mental Health Bd., 1974-77. Decorated Navy Commendation medal, Navy Achievement medal, Gross Gallantry; recipient numerous certificates appreciation. Mem. Am. Psychol. Assn., Am. Personnel and Guidance Assn., Assn. Counselor Edn. and Supervision, Assn. Specialists in Group Works, AAAS, Internat. Transactional Analysis Assn., U.S. Capitol Hist. Soc. Democrat. Roman Catholic. Author: A Handbook for Drug Education Facilitators, 1974; A Systematic Approach to Client Assessment, 1975. Devel. mosaic-self concept in psychotherapy. Address: 901 F Armfield Circle Norfolk VA 23505

GAMBACORTA, MARY ADRIANNA, bldg. products co. ofcl.; b. Buffalo, Mar. 18, 1922; d. Salvatore and Michelina (Costa) Russo; Asso. Bus. Adminstrn., Erie Community Coll., 1973; student SUNY, Buffalo, 1977; m. Joseph A. Gambacorta (div.). Mgr. dental office, Buffalo, 1951-58; supr. employee benefits Gold Bond Bldg. Products, Charlotte, N.C., 1958—. Bd. dirs. Nat. Gypsum Employees Credit Union, 1976—. Roman Catholic. Club: Christopher Columbus of Carolinas (Charlotte). Office: 2001 Rexford Rd Charlotte NC 28211

GAMBLE, ALFRED JAMES, retail co. exec.; b. Lansing, Mich., July 18, 1921; s. Alfred F. and Rebecca B. (Woodward) G.; student Mich. State U., 1939-42; children—Alfred T., Ernest Mark. Exec. v.p. Hartley Boiler Works, 1946-61; pres. Gamble's, Montgomery, Ala., 1957—; partner Woodland Hills Mobile Home Park; dir. Trinity Industries, Inc. Past bd. dirs. Montgomery Little Theater. Served to 1st lt. USAAF, 1941-45. Mem. Sales and Mktg. Execs. of Montgomery, So. Assn. Steel Fabricators (past pres.), Montgomery C. of C. (past dir.), Men of Montgomery. Republican. Episcopalian. Elk, Mason (Shriner). Clubs: Montgomery Country. Home: 6315 Kathmoor Dr Montgomery AL 36117 Office: 1401 N Decatur St Montgomery AL 36195

GAMBLE, JESS FRANKLIN, hematologist; b. Pollock, Mo., Feb. 14, 1914; s. Shelby Vale and Jessie Alma (Garrett) G.; student U. Omaha, 1936; B.S., U. Nebr., 1938, M.D., 1940; m. Eleanor Winifred McNulty, Mar. 30, 1942; children—John Franklin, Eleanor Ann, William Raymond. Intern, Walter Reed Gen. Hosp., Washington, 1940-41; resident internal medicine and hematology Ohio State U. Hosps., Columbus, 1946-49; instr. Ohio State U., 1948-49; asst. chief medicine VA Hosp., Houston, 1949-52, chief medicine, 1952-53; asst. prof. clin. medicine Baylor U. Coll. Medicine, Houston, 1949-65; practice medicine specializing in hematology and internal medicine, Houston, 1954-65; internist, prof. medicine U. Tex.-M.D. Anderson Hosp., Houston, 1965—. Served to col. M.C., AUS, 1941-46. Diplomate Am. Bd. Internal Medicine. Decorated Bronze Star. Fellow A.C.P.; mem. Internat. Soc. Exptl. Hematology, Am. Assn. Cancer Research, Am. Soc. Hematology, Am., Tex., Houston socs. internal medicine, Am., Tex., Harris County med. assns., So. Med Assn. Home: 5118 Queensloch St Houston TX 77035 Office: 6723 Bertner St Houston TX 77030

GAMBLE, LYNE STARLING, ophthalmologist; b. Greenville, Miss., Sept. 12, 1912; s. Hugh Agnew and Katharine Innes (Starling) G.; B.A., Davidson (N.C.) Coll., 1934; M.D., Vanderbilt U., 1938; postgrad. Grad. Sch. Medicine, U. Pa., 1940-41; m. Cynthia Pauline Black, July 10, 1945; children—Hugh Agnew II, Paula Innes, Lyne Starling, William Gaston, Innes Paul. Intern, Charity Hosp., New Orleans, 1938-39, resident in ophthalmology Tulane service, 1939-42; partner Gamble Bros. and Archer Clinic, Greenville, Miss., 1942—; mem. attending staff King's Daus. Hosp., Delta Med. Center; clin. instr. ophthalmology U. Miss. Med. Center (Jackson); dir. Miss. Found. Med. Care, 1975—, Blue Cross and Blue Shield of Miss., 1973-76, 76—; med. adv. to local Selective Service System. Diplomate Am. Bd. Ophthalmology. Mem. Miss. Med. Assn. (pres. 1976-77, past trustee), AMA, Miss. Eye, Ear, Nose and Throat Assn., La.-Miss. Ophthal. and Otolaryn. Soc. (pres. 1976-77), Am. Acad. Ophthalmology, Delta Med. Soc. Presbyterian. Home: 1108 East Dr Gamwyn Park Greenville MS 38701 Office: 344 Arnold Ave Greenville MS 38701

GAMBLE, ROY JACKSON, forester; b. nr. Hanceville, Ala., June 5, 1924; s. Ota K. and Ivela (Parsons) G.; B.S., Auburn U., 1951; m. Mary Jane Duren, Apr. 18, 1953; children—David Jackson, Steven Roy, Julia Dale, John Neil, Barbara Jane. Asst. forester Gulf States Paper Corp., 1951-52, asst. dist. forester, 1952-54, dist. forester, 1954-61, dist. supt., 1961-66; intermittent cons.-dist. chmn. Ala. Tree Farm Com., 1962-66; now pulpwood dealer, Cullman, Ala. Active Boy Scouts Am. Vice chmn. Bibb County Republican Com., 1964—. Bd. dirs. Auburn Forestry Found., 1966—, pres., 1976—. Served with USMCR, 1944-46. Recipient Valley Scouter award. Mem. Soc. Am. Foresters, Forest Farmers Assn., Ala. Registered Foresters. So. Methodist. Clubs: Masons, Shriners (pres. Cullman 1977-78). Contbr. articles to co. jours. Home: 741 Scenic Dr NE Cullman AL 35055 Office: PO Box 253 Hanceville AL 35077

GAMBLE, SAMUEL JAMES REEVES, chemist; b. Pennsauken, Twp., N.J., Dec. 15, 1916; s. John Robert and Bessie Blanche (Hammer) G.; student Lynchburg Coll., 1933-34, U. Va., 1936-38; B.S., Va. Poly. Inst. and State U., 1947, M.S., 1951; m. Louise Gordon Daniel, July 5, 1943; children—Margaret Virginia, Marion Daniel, William Reeves. Instr. bacteriology Va. Poly. Inst. and State U., Blacksburg, 1949-52; instr. math. Staunton (Va.) Mil. Acad., 1947-48; research microbiologist Merck & Co., Rahway, N.J., 1952-58; asso. prof. chemistry Lynchburg (Va.) Coll., 1958—; research asso. Harvard U. lysine fortification program, Tunisia, N. Africa, 1970-71; NIH fellow Pasteur Inst., Paris, France, 1964-65. Served in inf. U.S. Army, 1941-46; ETO. Mem. Phytochem. Soc. N.Am., Va. Acad. Sci., Sigma Xi, Phi Sigma, Chi Beta Phi. Presbyterian. Home: 1366 Timberlake Dr Lynchburg VA 24502 Office: Lynchburg Coll Lynchburg VA 24501

GAMBLE, WILLIAM BELSER, JR., physician; b. Andrews, S.C., Apr. 17, 1925; s. William Belser and Anna (Moyd) G.; B.S., U. S.C., 1945; M.D., Med. Coll. S.C., 1948; M.P.H., U. N.C., 1972; m. Margaret Florence DuBose, June 7, 1947; children—William Belser III, Richard Ervin, Heather Moyd. Intern, Roper Hosp., Charleston, S.C., 1948-49; resident pediatrics, teaching fellow Med. Coll. S.C., Charleston, 1953-56, asso. prof. pediatrics; practice medicine specializing in pediatrics and allergy, Charleston, 1956-71; state epidemiologist State Bd. Health, also dir. div. epidemiology State Dept. Health and Environ. Control, Columbia., S.C., 1972—; mem. staffs Med. Coll., Roper, St. Francis hosps., Charleston. Pres., Coastal Carolina Tb. and Health Assn. Dist. dir. S.C. Bd. of Health, 1972. Bd. dirs. Charleston County Mental Health Assn., Charleston County Tb Assn., Charleston. Served with M.C., U.S. Army, 1951-53. Diplomate Am. Bd. Pediatrics, Am. Bd. Allergy and Clin. Immunology. Fellow Am. Acad. Allergy, Am. Acad. Pediatrics; mem. A.M.A., Am. Acad. Pediatrics, Southeastern Allergy Assn., Phi Beta Kappa, Alpha Kappa Kappa, Kappa Sigma, Alpha Omega Alpha, Delta Omega. Methodist (mem. ofcl. bd.). Rotarian (past pres.). Contbr. articles to profl. jours. Address: 3251 Seabrook Island Rd Johns Island SC 29455

GAMBONE, VICTOR EMMANUEL, JR., physician; b. Phila., Aug. 28, 1949; s. Victor Emmanuel and Eleanor Joyce (Porambo) G.; B.S., Pa. State U., 1971, M.D., 1975. Intern and resident in internal medicine U. S. Fla., Tampa, 1975-78; practice medicine specializing in internal medicine, Clearwater, Fla., 1978—. Diplomate Am. Bd. Internal Medicine. Mem. AMA, A.C.P., Am. Soc. Internal Medicine. Author: Post Operative Recall of Intra-Operative Events, 1975 (research award U. Miami Med. Sch.). Office: 3231 McMullen-Booth Rd Clearwater FL 33519

GAMBRELL, BARMORE PEPPER, lawyer; b. Belton, S.C., Jan. 27, 1894; s. Enoch Pepper and Macie (Latimer) G.; B.A., Furman U.; Washington and Lee U.; LL.B., Georgetown U. Clk. office of sec. of U.S. Senate, 1 1/2 years; in practice of law, Atlanta, 1920—; mem. law firm Arnold, Arnold & Gambrell, 1930-33, Arnold, Gambrell & Arnold, 1933-52, Arnold & Gambrell, 1952-57; now in individual practice. Served with U.S. Navy, World War I. Recipient Distinguished Alumnus award Furman U., 1968. Fellow Am. Coll. Trial Lawyers, Am. Bar Found.; mem. Am., Atlanta bar assns., State Bar Ga., Am. Judicature Soc., Lawyers Club Atlanta, Am. Legion (comdr. Atlanta post 1922-23). Democrat. Baptist. Clubs: Capital City, Piedmont Driving (Atlanta). Home: 2025 Peachtree Rd NE Apt 1227 Atlanta GA 30309 Office: 504 William-Oliver Bldg Atlanta GA 30303

GAMBRELL, JAMES BRUTON, lawyer, educator; b. Rochester, Minn., Jan. 17, 1926; s. James Bruton and Martha Judson (Corley) G.; student UCLA, 1943-44; B.S. in Mech. Engring., U. Tex., 1949; M.A. in Econs., Columbia U., 1950; LL.B., N.Y. U., 1957; m. Helen Jeanette Roddy, Aug. 12, 1950; children—Jamey, Gretchen, James Bruton IV. Mem. staff Tex. legislative Council, Austin, 1950; instr. econs. Baylor U., Waco, Tex., 1950-51; mem. tech. staff (engr.) Bell Telephone Labs., Murray Hill, N.J., 1951-53, mem. patent staff N.Y.C., 1953-57; admitted to practice before U.S. Patent Office, 1954; admitted to D.C. bar, 1957, Okla. bar, 1958, Calif. bar, 1961, N.Y. bar, 1967, Tex. bar, 1976; asst. patent atty. Well Surveys, Inc., Tulsa, 1957-59; asso. firm Townsend & Townsend, San Francisco, 1959-61; spl. asst. to commr. patents, dir. office legislative planning U.S. Patent Office, Washington, 1961-63; partner firm Fowler, Knobbe & Gambrell, Santa Ana, Calif., 1963-66; prof. law N.Y. U., N.Y.C., 1966-76, U. Houston, 1976—; patent counsel N.Y. U., 1967-76; partner firm Pravel, Wilson & Gambrel, Houston, 1976—. Cons. to Practising Law Inst., N.Y.C., 1966-71, Com. Revision Fed. Ct. Appellate System, 1974; commr. patents Patent Adv. Commn., 1968-72. Served as lt. (j.g.) USNR, 1943-46. Mem. Am., Calif., Tex. bar assns., Assn. Bar City N.Y., Am., N.Y. patent law assns. Author: (with Donald R. Dunner, Martin J. Adelman) Patent Law Perspectives, 9 vols., 1970—. Home: 807 Chowning Rd Houston TX 77024 Office: 1177 West Loop S 10th Floor Houston TX 77027

GAMBRELL, RICHARD DONALD, JR., reproductive endocrinologist; b. St. George, S.C., Oct. 28, 1931; s. Richard Donald and Nettie Anzo (Ellenburg) G.; B.S., Furman U., 1953; M.D., Med. U. S.C., 1957; m. Mary Caroline Stone, Dec. 22, 1956; children—Deborah Christina, Juliet Denise. Intern, Greenville (S.C.) Gen. Hosp., 1957-58, resident, 1961-64; flight surgeon, Hickam AFB, Hawaii, 1958-61; chief obstetrics and gynecology, Tinker AFB, Okla., 1964-66; chmn. dept. obstetrics and gynecology, also cons. to surgeon gen. USAF Hosp., Wiesbaden, Germany, 1966-69; fellow endocrinology Med. Coll. Ga., Augusta, 1969-71; chief gynecologic endocrinology Wilford Hall USAF Med. Center, Lackland AFB, Tex., 1971-78; mem. staff Westlawn Baptist Mission Med. Clinic, San Antonio, 1972-78; asso. clin. prof. obstetrics and gynecology U. Tex. Health Sci. Center, San Antonio, 1971-78, Med. Coll. Ga., Augusta, 1978—. Served to col. M.C., USAF, 1958-78. Recipient Chmn.'s Best Paper in Clin. Research from Teaching Hosp. award Armed Forces Dist. of Am. Coll. Obstetrics-Gynecology, 1972, Host award, 1977, Chmn.'s award, 1978, Purdue-Frederick award, 1979. Diplomate Am. Bd. Obstetrics and Gynecology (div. reproductive endocrinology). Fellow Am. Coll. Obstetricians and Gynecologists; mem. Am. Fertility Soc., Tex. Assn. Obstetrics and Gynecology, San Antonio Obstetrics-Gynecology Soc (v.p. 1975-76), Chilean Soc. Obstetrics and Gynecology (hon.), Internat. Soc. Reproductive Medicine (program chmn. 1980), Internat. Family Planning Research Assn., Internat. Menopause Soc., Am. Geriatric Soc., Nat. Geog. Soc., Phi Chi, Am. Philatelic Soc., Alpha Epsilon Delta. Baptist (deacon, Sunday sch. tchr. 1971-78). Contbr. chpts. to med. books, articles to profl. jours.; author: (with R. Greenblatt) The Menopause: Indications for Estrogen Therapy, 1979. Home: 3542 National Ct Augusta GA 30907 Office: 903 15 St Augusta GA 30901

GAMMON, JAMES EDWIN, clergyman; b. San Diego, Jan. 23, 1944; s. Jack Albert and Thalia Gammon; B.A., Tex. Christian U., 1970, postgrad., 1971-72; m. Sharon Elaine Head, June 27, 1965; children—John Paul, James Edwin, Jeffrey David. Ordained to ministry Ch. of Christ, 1965; minister Carter Park Ch., Ft. Worth, 1966-69, Scotland Hills Ch., Ft. Worth, 1969-70, Northside Ch., Dallas, 1970-73, Central Ave Ch., Valdosta, Ga., 1973-78; debate coach Christian Coll. S.W., Dallas, 1971-73; pres. So. Bible Inst., Valdosta, 1977-78; minister Trinity Oaks Ch. of Christ, Dallas, 1978—. Served with U.S. Army, 1963-66. Republican. Club: Lions of Oak Cliff. Home: 716 Cottonwood Circle DeSoto TX 75115 Office: 7200 S Hampton Rd Dallas TX 75232

GAMMON, JOSEPH ALLEN, conglomerate exec.; b. Bowling Green, Ky., Apr. 13, 1922; s. Lelie S. and Lela (Bray) G.; ed. pub. schs., Bowling Green; m. JoAnn Glenn, Sept. 20, 1974; 1 son by previous marriage, John Scott. Propr. retail liquor bus., Indpls., 1944-47; pres., part owner Service Transport Co., Bowling Green, 1948-52; exec. v.p. Gasoline Transport Co., Louisville, 1953-56; pres. So. Tank Lines, Louisville, 1957-66; pres., stockholder Ala. Tank Lines, Birmingham, Ala., 1957-64; pres., stockholder Yellow Cab-Louisville, 1957-75, chmn. bd., 1975—; pres., stockholder Yellow Cab-Birmingham, 1957-66; pres., stockholder Yellow Cab-Memphis, 1957-75, chmn. bd., 1975—; pres., stockholder Yellow Cab-Atlanta, 1957-66, Yellow Cab-Tampa (Fla.), 1957-66; exec. v.p. South Atlantic Co., Tampa, 1962-66; v.p. transp. Nat. Industries, Louisville, 1967-70, exec. v.p., chief operating officer, 1971-75, pres., chief exec. officer, 1975—; pres., dir. Cott Corp., Nat. Recreation Products Inc. Mem. Ky AEC, 1960-66; chmn. Louisville Tourist Council, 1972; dir. Louisville Area Safety Council, 1973. Served with USNR, 1942-44. Named Ky. Col. Mem. Nat. Tank Truck Carriers Assn. (dir. 1958-66), Internat. Taxicab Assn. (dir. 1970), Ky. Motor Transp. Assn. (pres. 1963-65, chmn. 1966-67, dir. 1961-65). Clubs: Standard Country, Pendennis, Jefferson (Louisville), Masons. Home: 5100 Brownsboro Rd Apt 1222 Louisville KY 40222 Office: 510 W Broadway Louisville KY 40202

GAMMON, NATHAN, JR., educator; b. Cheyenne, Wyo., June 22, 1914; s. Nathan and Mabel Agnes (Fair) G.; B.S., U. Md., 1936, M.S., 1938; Ph.D., Ohio State U., 1941; m. Dorothy Verna Allen, Mar. 25, 1941; children—Nathan Allen, Penelope Gay (Mrs. Daniel Webster). Asst. in agronomy U. Md., College Park, 1936-38; asst. in corn investigations Ohio Agrl. Exptl. Sta., Wooster, 1938-42; faculty dept. soil sci. U. Fla., Gainesville, 1946—, prof. soil chemistry, 1946-79, prof. emeritus, 1979—. Served to lt. USNR, 1942-46. Fellow AAAS; mem. Am. Chem. Soc., Am. Soc. Agronomy, Soil Sci. Soc. Am., Soil and Crop Sci. Soc. Fla. (pres. 1955-56, asso. editor procs. 1972-78), Fla. Hort. Soc., S.E. Pecan Growers Assn., Gainesville Rose Soc., Sigma Xi, Alpha Chi Sigma, Phi Lambda Upsilon, Phi Upsilon Phi, Gamma Alpha, Gamma Sigma Delta. Presbyterian (deacon). Contbr. articles to profl. jours. Home: 1403 NW 11th Rd Gainesville FL 32605

GAMSON, ALVIN NORMAN, counselor mental health; b. N.Y.C., June 4, 1930; s. William Victor and Joyce Edith G.; B.S., N.Y. U., 1952, M.A., 1958; postgrad. Family Studies Inst. of Bronx Psychiat. Center, 1974-78; m. Alice Hoffman, May 2, 1954; children—Andrew Stuart, Jonathan Neil, Maren Eve. Tchr., Mt. Vernon (N.Y.) Public Schs., 1952-59, counselor, 1959-70; family and edn. counselor Family Relations Center, White Plains, N.Y., 1961-63; adj. lectr. edn. Hebrew Union Coll.-Jewish Inst. Religion, N.Y.C., 1970-72; asst. prof. counseling, also dir. counseling center Bronx (N.Y.) Community Coll., 1970-78; dir. edn. Free Synagogue Westchester, Mt. Vernon, 1967-78; exec. dir. Jewish Family Service, Orlando, Fla., 1978—. Bd. dirs. Mt. Vernon Mental Health, 1953-55, Youth Bd. Adv. Council Mt. Vernon, 1968-70; chmn. program evaluations Met. Alcoholism Council, Orlando, 1978—; spiritual leader Temple Shalom, Deltona, Fla., 1978—. Served with USAF, 1952-56. Recipient Shofar award Boy Scouts Am., 1972; grantee Jewish Assn. Coll. Youth, 1973—. Mem. Nat. Assn. Temple Educators (exec. bd., chmn. ethical practices com. 1976-78), Am. Mental Health Counselors Assn., Am. Personnel and Guidance Assn., Kappa Phi Kappa, Kappa Delta Pi. Jewish. Club: B'nai B'rith. Editor: Career Search, 1957.

GANDARILLAS, MANUEL P., surgeon; b. Pinar del Rio, Cuba, Dec. 29, 1926; s. Hilario P. Presmanes and Pilar G. Valdes; came to U.S., 1968, naturalized, 1974; B.S., Alcorta Inst., Cuba, 1944; M.D., Havana U., 1951; m. Isabel Jover, May 6, 1956; children—Manuel, Jose, Isabel. Intern, U. Hosp., Havana, 1951-52, resident in surgery, 1952-55; intern in pathology VA Hosp., Miami, Fla., 1968-69; pvt. practice surgery and family practice, Silsbee, Tex., 1969, Cleveland, Tex., 1969—; gen. surgeon Children's Hosp., Pinar del Rio, 1955-63, State Hosp., Pinar del Rio, 1955-68, chief of surgery, 1966-68; cons. gen. surgery San Martin Anti-Tb Hosp., Guanito, Cuba, 1955-59; chief of surgery Leggett Meml. Hosp., 1970—; guest lectr. various profl. orgns., Cuba, 1954-65, U.S., 1972-76. Diplomate Am. Bd. Family Practice, Am. Bd. Abdominal Surgery. Fellow Am. Acad. Family Practice; mem. Tex. Med. Assn., Am. Soc. Abdominal Surgery, Liberty County Med. Soc. (pres. 1977-78), Am. Geriatric Soc., AMA (Recognition award 1974-77), Cleveland C. of C., Am. Cancer Soc. (chmn. of local chpt. 1971-77). Roman Catholic. Club: Rotary. Contbr. articles on surgery and oncology to profl. jours. Home: 704 Jefferson St Cleveland TX 77327 Office: PO Box 1149 Cleveland TX 77327

GANDIN, WILLIAM BAILOUS, SR., auditor; b. Houston, July 17, 1921; s. Jacob William and Leona Stone G.; B.B.A., U. Houston, 1957, postgrad., 1957-59; postgrad. Rice U., 1946-49; hon. grad. Indsl. Coll. Armed Forces, 1970; m. Mildred Snowden, July 17, 1942; children—William B., Paul Snowden, David Lee. With Exxon Co. U.S.A., 1941—, head spl. studies for controller, 1966-67, field auditor nine states, 1967-74, hdqrs. controllers staff auditor, 1967—. Cub and scout unit leader Boy Scouts Am., 1959-66, scouting coordinator for Country of Libya, 1966-67, asst. dist. chmn., 1963-65, 67-76, dist. fin. chmn., 1967-76, dist. commr., 1969-72, 76-79; loaned exec. United Way, 1977; team mgr. Little League, 1961-64. Served with USAAF, 1942-45, USAF, 1950-52; col. Res. (ret.). Decorated Air Force Meritorious Service medal; recipient Silver Beaver award, also dist. award of merit Boy Scouts Am., 1974; Outstanding Service award Shriners Hosp., 1950-70; Outstanding Loaned Exec. award United Way, 1977; named Commd. Flying Col., Delta Airlines, 1975, Continental Statesman, 1976. Mem. Houston C. of C., Air Force Assn., Res. Officers Assn., Assn. Loaned Execs.-United Way, PTA (Tex. life mem.), U. Houston Alumni Orgn., Rice U. Alumni Assn. Methodist. Clubs: Masons, Shriners. Home: 1927 Viking Dr Houston TX 77018 Office: Exxon Co USA 4500 Dacoma St Houston TX 77018

GANDY, EDYTHE EVELYN, lt. gov. Miss.; b. Hattiesburg, Miss., Sept. 4, 1922; d. Kearney C. and Abbie (Whigham) Gandy; student U. So. Miss., 1939-40; LL.B., U. Miss., 1944. Admitted to Miss. bar, 1944; legis. asst. to Senator Theodore G. Bilbo, Washington, 1944-46; practiced in Hattiesburg, 1947-55; mem. Miss. Ho. of Reps., 1948-52; atty. Miss. Dept. Pub. Welfare, Jackson, 1953-58, commr., 1964-67; asst. atty. gen. State of Miss., Jackson, 1959; treas. State of Miss., 1960-64, 68-72; commr. ins. State of Miss., 1972-76, lt. gov., 1976-80; former mem. Miss. State Bd. Savs. and Loan Assns., Miss. Ins. Commn.; mem. Commn. Budget and Acctg., Bldg. Commn., Agrl. and Indsl. Bd., Keep Miss. Beautiful. Del., Miss. Democratic Convs., 1948-60; former bd. dirs. Miss. Hosp. and Med. Service. Recipient Jackson Woman of Year award, 1964; named One of Top Ten Women of Sixties in a 3-state area Comml. Appeal Memphis. Mem. Am., Miss. bar assns., Am. Judicature Soc., Miss. Cabinet Women in Pub. Affairs, Miss. Econ. Council, Am. Assn. Women Accountants, Miss. Conf. Social Welfare, Miss. Fedn. Bus. and Profl. Women's Clubs (pres. 1953-54), Congress Parents and Tchrs. Democrat. Baptist. Club: Altrusa (Jackson). Home: 727 Arlington St Jackson MS 39202 Office: Central High Bldg Jackson MS 39205

GANDY, GERALD LARMON, educator, counselor, psychologist; b. Thomasville, Ga., Feb. 9, 1941; s. Larmon Brinkley and Ruby Wylene (Vickers) G.; student Jacksonville U., 1959-61; B.A., Fla. State U., 1963; M.A., U. of S.C., 1968, Ph.D., 1971; m. Patricia Kay Haltiwanger, Jan. 22, 1966. Counselor, U. of S.C. Counseling Bur., Columbia, 1968-70; counseling psychologist VA Regional Office, Columbia, 1970-75, chief counseling and rehab. sect., 1974-75; coordinator undergrad. program, asso. prof. dept. rehab. counseling Va. Commonwealth U., Richmond, 1975—; mem. state and fed. govt. advisory coms. Served to capt. U.S. Army, 1963-66. Licensed counseling psychologist, S.C.; licensed profl. counselor, Va.; certified rehab. counselor. Mem. Am. Psychol. Assn., Am. Personnel and Guidance Assn., Am. Rehab. Counseling Assn., Nat. Rehab. Assn., Nat. Rehab. Counseling Assn., Psi Chi, Phi Delta Kappa, Alpha Kappa psi. Democrat. Clubs: Sigma Alpha Epsilon, Toastmasters Internat. Contbr. articles to profl. jours. and textbooks. Home: 300 Southern Ct Richmond VA 23075 Office: 812 W Franklin St Richmond VA 23284

GANDY, JAMES HARRELL, architect; b. Lake City, S.C., May 11, 1939; s. James Harrell and Gertrude Pauline (Lee) G.; A.A. in Civil Engring., S.C. U., 1959; B.S. in Architecture, Clemson U., 1963; m. Vera Marie Allen, Apr. 12, 1962; children—Allen Darius, Harrell Clayton, Aaron Brett. Staff, Daniel Constrn. Co., Greenville, S.C., 1964-66, Lucas & Stubbs, Charleston, S.C., 1966-72; owner, architect J. Harrell Gandy, Architect, Charleston, 1972—. Cert., Nat. Council Archtl. Registration Bds.; lic. architect, S.C., N.C., Ga. Mem. AIA Charleston Council Architects, Home Builders Assn., Constrn. Specifications Inst. Charleston C. of C. Democrat. Baptist. Home: 2059 Cheraw Dr Charleston SC 29412 Office: J Harrell Gandy Architect 122 Meeting St Charleston SC 29401

GANDY, THOMAS WHITNEY, coll. dean; b. Foley, Ala., Oct. 18, 1919; s. John William and Amye (Daniel) G.; B.S., Berry Coll., 1942; B.S., Auburn U., 1947, M.S., 1950; Ed.D., U. Ill., 1953; m. Theodora H. Nettles, Oct. 25, 1944; 1 dau., Suzanne Nettles. Tchr. vocat. agr., Opelika, Ala., 1945-46, 47-50; instr. agrl. edn. Auburn (Ala.) U., 1950-51, asso. prof., 1953-61; research asst. U. Ill., Urbana, 1951-53; adminstrv. asst. to pres. Womans Coll. Ga., Milledgeville, 1961-63; v.p. Berry Coll. and Berry Acad., Mt. Berry, Ga., 1963-69, acad. dean Berry Coll., 1969-71; dean Sch. Edn., Valdosta (Ga.) State Coll., 1971-73, dir. pub. services, 1971—. Pres. Lee County (Ala.) Mental Health Assn., 1958-59; drive dir. Auburn Community Chest, 1959-61. Trustee, Berry Coll., 1954-56; devel. dir. Found. Womans Coll. Ga., 1961-63. Served with USNR, 1942-45. Mem. Berry Alumni Assn. (nat. pres. 1954-56), Ala. Vocat. Assn. (sec.-treas. 1959-61), Phi Kappa Phi, Gamma Sigma Delta, Phi Delta Kappa, Kappa Delta Pi. Rotarian. Editor: The Agrl. Edn. Mag., 1961-62. Address: 2128 Lakeshore Dr Valdosta GA 31601

GANN, GARY RUFUS, dental lab. technologist; b. Guin, Ala., Nov. 13, 1950; s. Milton Rufus and Sula Lee (Homer) G.; grad. USAF Sch. Dental Tech., 1971; m. Cynthia Martinez, Oct. 6, 1973. Partner, Gulf Coast Dental Studio, Inc., New Port Richey, Fla., 1974-76, owner, 1976—, also dir., sec.-treas. Mem. Hidden Lake Community Assn., Inc. Served with USAF, 1970-74. Mem. Nat. Assn. Dental Labs. (cert. in dentures, crown and bridge, ceramics. Fla. Dental Lab. Assn., New Port Richey C. of C. Baptist. Home: 7409 Luscombe Ct New Port Richey FL 33553 Office: 909 South Blvd New Port Richey FL 33552

GANN, RONNY DALE, hosp. ofcl.; b. Mobile, Ala., Sept. 14, 1948; s. Willie Robert and Grace Lee (Hill) G.; cert. George C. Wallace Community Coll., 1976; m. Judy Carol Burton, Oct. 12, 1968; children—Anthony, Sean, Heath, Jennifer. Laborer, Internat. Paper Co., Mobile, Ala., 1970-71; agt. United Ins. Co., Mobile, 1971-72; dir. phys. plant operations Good Samaritan Hosp., Selma, Ala., 1974—. Served with AUS, 1967-70; Vietnam. Decorated Purple Heart, Air Medal with 2 oak leaf clusters. Mem. Internat. Solar Energy Soc., Am. Soc. Hosp. Engrs., Am. Soc. Indsl. Security. Democrat. Baptist. Club: Woodman of the World. Home: Rt 1 Box 33 Tyler AL 36785 Office: 1107 Voeglin Ave Selma AL 36701

GANTER, BERNARD J., bishop; b. Galveston, Tex., July 17, 1928; s. Bernard J. and Marie L. (Bozka) G.; student Tex. A. and M. Coll., 1944-45, St. Mary's Sem., LaPorte, Tex., 1945-52; J.C.D., Cath. U. Am., 1955; Ordained priest Roman Catholic Ch., 1952; adminstr. to Sacred Heart Parish, Conroe, Tex., 1955; sec. to Bishop W.J. Nold, pastor Sacred Heart Co-Cathedral, Houston, 1966-73; officialis Diocesan Matrimonial Tribunal, Houston, 1958-66; became monsignor, 1969; bishop Diocese of Tulsa, 1973-78, Diocese of Beaumont (Tex.), 1979—. Bd. dirs. St. Gregory's Coll., Shawnee, Okla., Tulsa chpt. Nat. Conf. Christians and Jews; mem. health affairs com. Nat. Conf. Cath. Office: PO Box 3948 Beaumont TX 77704

GANTNER, ROSE KARLO, marriage and family therapist, educator; b. Pitts., Dec. 16, 1943; d. Milan and Laura (Mamula) Karlo; B.S. in Health Edn., Slippery Rock State Coll., 1965; M.Ed., U. Pitts., 1968, postgrad., 1970-71; Ed.D., Auburn U., 1976; certificate in counseling Ga. State U., 1973; m. Charles John Gantner, Jr., Aug. 14, 1971. Instr. edn. U. Pitts., 1967-69; asst. dir. ARC, Vietnam, 1969-70; asst. prof. Washington and Jefferson Coll., Washington, Pa., 1970-71; tchr. Brookstone Sch., Columbus, Ga., 1971-73; psychology intern VA Hosp., Tuskegee, Ala., 1973-75; individual practice as marriage and family counselor, Columbus, 1975—; asst. prof. psychology, asst. dir. grad. studies Troy U., Phenix City, Ala. and Ft. Benning, Ga. extensions, 1976—. Vol. ARC, 1967—, recipient Service award, 1976; mem. Columbus Mayor's Commn. on Status of Women, 1977—. Recipient Civilian Service award Dept. Def., 1970; named Career Woman of Yr., Chattahoochee Valley Bus. and Profl. Women's Club, 1977. Mem. Am. Personnel and Guidance Assn., Assn. Counselor Edn. and Supervision, Ga. Assn. Counselors, Am. Assn. Marriage and Family Therapists, Am. Psychol. Assn. Democrat. Eastern Orthodox. Home: 6801 Trapper Way Midland GA 31820 Office: Cross Country Office Park Bldg 2607 Columbus GA 31906

GANTT, JAMES DALE, ops. research analyst; b. Murray, Ky., Aug. 11, 1949; s. Wilson and Virginia (Collie) G.; B.S., Murray State U., 1971; M.S., U. Mo., 1972; Ed.S., Ball State U., 1978; m. Alice Kay Thompson, Aug. 7, 1971; 1 dau., Heather Marie. Grad. teaching asst. U. Mo., Rolla, 1971-72; computer specialist Army Inst. Adminstrn., Indpls., 1976-78; ops. research analyst Army Inst. for Research in Mgmt. Info. and Computer Sci., Atlanta, 1978—; faculty Ind. U.-Purdue U., Indpls., 1973-74, Butler U., 1977-78, Vincennes U., 1977; cons. Data Resources Mgmt. Cons., Inc., 1977-78. Mem. adv. bd. Shults-Lewis Childrens Home, Valparaiso, Ind., 1977-78. Served with U.S. Army, 1973-76. Decorated Army Commendation medal. Named Disting. Educator, U.S. Army, 1978, cert. of achievement, 1976. Mem. Am. Mgmt. Assn., Soc. for Computer Simulation, Phi Kappa Phi, Gamma Beta Phi. Democrat. Ch. of Christ. Contbr. to Systems Analysis Handbook, 1976. Home: 5986 Dana Dr Norcross GA 30093 Office: 313 Calculator Bldg Ga Tech Atlanta GA 30332

GANTT, JAMES RAIFORD, surgeon; b. Texarkana, Tex., Mar. 5, 1930; s. James Emmett and Nettie (Wren Raiford) G.; B.A., Baylor U., 1953; M.D., Johns Hopkins, 1957; m. Joan Durstine, Aug. 18, 1968. Intern, Charity Hosp., New Orleans, 1957, resident in internal medicine, 1958; resident in gen. and thoracic surgery Tulane U. Charity Hosp., 1962-65; resident in thoracic surgery U. Kans. Med. Center, 1966; practice medicine specializing in thoracic surgery, Dallas, 1966—; mem. staffs Presbyn., Irving Community hosps. Instr. U. Tex. Southwestern Med. Sch. at Dallas, 1966—. Served with USN, 1960-62. Tulane surg. fellow, 1959; NIH fellow, 1959-60. Diplomate Am. Bd. Surgery, Am. Bd. thoracic Surgery. Fellow A.C.S.; mem. So. Thoracic Surg. Assn., Soc. Thoracic Surgeons, Am. Coll. Chest Physicians, So., Tex. med. assns., AMA. Home: 3512 Lexington St Dallas TX 75205 Office: 2007 W Park Dr Irving TX 75061

GANZ, CHARLES ROBERT, chem. co. exec.; b. Bklyn., Dec. 20, 1942; s. Hyman and Irene (Friedman) G.; B.A., N.Y. U., 1963; M.A., City U. N.Y., 1966; Ph.D., Adelphi U., 1969; m. Joan Newman, Dec. 15, 1963; children—Steven, Keith. Research asso. Pfizer, Inc., Bklyn., 1963-66; teaching asst. Adelphi U., 1968; staff scientist environ. and analytical research services Ciba-Geigy Corp., Ardsley, N.Y. and Greensboro, N.C., 1969-76; pres. En-Cas Analytical Labs., Winston-Salem, N.C., 1976—; tech. dir., cons. in field. NASA research fellow, 1966-67, Petroleum Research Fund fellow, 1968-69. Mem. Am. Chem. Soc. (analytical and environ. divs.), Water Pollution Control Fedn., Am. Assn. Textile Chemists and Colorists, AAAS. Editorial bd. Toxic Substances Jour., 1978—. Office: En-Cas Labs 1409-J S Stratford Rd Winston-Salem NC 27103

GARCIA, CARMELO ATANGAN, physician; b. Rosario, Cavite, P.I., July 16, 1937; s. Gerardo Estrella and Dorotea Trias (Atangan) G.; came to U.S., 1969, naturalized, 1974; A.A., U. Santo Tomas (P.I.), 1957, M.D., 1963; m. Marietta Lacson Gonzales, Dec. 8, 1961; children—Azalea Marie, Patrick Arnold, James Anthony. Pvt. practice medicine, Baguio City, P.I., 1964-69; co. physician, head med. dept. Benguet Exploration and Black Mountain Mining Cos., P.I., 1965-68; physician U. St. Louis, 1965-67; staff Ky. State Hosp., Danville, 1970-71; physician-chief emergency and house staff services St. Anthony Hosp., Louisville, 1971-79; practice medicine specializing in family practice, Dallas, 1979—; mem. staff Lakewood Gen. Hosp., Pleasant Grove Hosp., Dallas, S.W. Jefferson Hosp., Suburban Hosp., Louisville, Drs. Hosp., Bristol Gen. Hosp., Mesquite Meml. Hosp., Dallas; lectr. St. Louis U., Baguio City, P.I., 1965-67. Fellow Am. Coll. Internat. Physicians; mem. Baguio-Mountain Med. Soc. (councilor), Holy Name Soc. (1st v.p.), Philippine Med. Assn., Dallas County Med. Soc., Tex. Med. Assn., Jefferson County Med. Soc., Ky. Med. Assn. Philippine Fedn. Pvt. Med. Practitioners, Am. Coll. Emergency Physicians (charter mem.), Am. Acad. Family Practice, Dallas Acad. Family Practice, So. Med. Assn., Filipino Am. Soc. Ky. and So. Ind., Philippine Jaycees. Roman Catholic. Home: 9327 Moss Farm Ln Dallas TX 75243 Office: Lakewood Profl Bldg Suite 104 1616 Abrams Rd Dallas TX 75214

GARCIA, LINO, JR., educator; b. Brownsville, Tex., Jan. 7, 1934; s. Lino and Felipa (Lopez) G.; B.A., St. Mary's U., San Antonio, 1959; M.A., N. Tex. U., 1966; postgrad. Tulane U., 1973-76; m. Amalia Garcia, Sept. 2, 1957; children—Cynthia, Linus. Tchr., Peacock Mil. Acad., 1959-66, Our Lady of Lake U., 1966-67; prof. Spanish, Pan Am. U., Edinburg, Tex., 1967—, dean of men, dir. placement, 1971-72. Mem. Edinburg City Commn., 1977—; chmn. Bicentennial Com., 1976; pres. St. Joseph Sch. Bd.; chmn. Community Devel. Council. Served with USNR; Korea. Mem. South Central Modern Lang. Assn., Am. Assn. Tchrs. Spanish and Portuguese (past pres. Alamo Valley chpt.), Spanish Heritage Assn. Democrat. Roman Catholic. Author: Carlos Fuentes-Imagen Ideal de Mexico, 1970; El Tema Religioso en al filo del agua, 1974. Home: 1723 W Smith St Edinburg TX 78539 Office: 1201 W University St Edinburg TX 78539

GARCIA-MENENDEZ, ALBERTO AUGUSTO, educator; b. Cienfuegos, Cuba, Aug. 15, 1923; naturalized, 1970; s. Augusto C. Garcia-Castro and Josefina L. Menendez-Palacios; Licenciate Diplomatic and Consular Law, Havana U., 1943, LL.D., 1946, D.Philosophy and Letters, 1953; M.A. in History, U. P.R., 1978. Admitted to Cuba bar, 1946; individual practice law, Cienfuegos, 1946-60; prof. prins. of econs. and fgn. and domestic trade Profl. Bus. Coll., Cienfuegos, 1955-60; prof. bus. and criminal law Masonic U. Jose Marti, br. Cienfuegos, 1956-58; prof. econs. and bus. adminstrn. Interam. U., Barranquitas, P.R., 1961-67, prof. history, Met. Campus, Hato Rey, P.R., 1967—; lectr. Latin Am. history, U. P.R., 1970-72; adv. council La Fortaleza Lecture Series, Office Cultural Affairs of Gov. P.R., 1978-80. Nat. Endowment for Humanities summer grantee, 1975, reviewer for grant proposals, 1978-80. Mem. AAUP, Grupo Cubano de Estudios Historicos, Assn. Caribbean Historians (editorial com., 1978-79), Caribbean Studies Assn., Sociedad Bolivariana de P.R. (sec.), Latin Am. Studies Assn., Unesco P.R., Academia Interamericana de P.R., Phi Alpha Theta. Roman Catholic. Author books, articles in field. Home: 16 Bajos Ruiz Belvis St Floral Park Hato Rey PR 00917 Office: Interamerican University Social Sciences Dept 117 Eleanor Roosevelt St Hato Rey PR 00919

GARCÍA OLLER, JOSÉ LUIS, neurosurgeon; b. San Juan, P.R., Mar. 17, 1923; s. Jose Leocadio and Laura (Oller) Garcia; B.S. with honors, U. P.R., 1942; M.D., Jefferson Med. Coll., 1945; M.M.Sc., Tulane U., 1950; m. Mary Ann Balsley, Oct. 1, 1949; children—Maria, José, Ana, Antonio, Teresita, Margarita. Rotating intern Jefferson Med. Coll. Hosp., Phila., 1945-46; preceptorship in gen. surgery with Drs. Devine and Devine, Lynchburg, Va., 1946-47; fellow in neurosurgery Ochsner Clinic, New Orleans, 1947-50; chief resident in neurosurgery Charity Hosp., New Orleans, 1950-51, head ind. neurosurgery service, 1952-63; instr. physiology Tulane U., New Orleans, 1951-59; practice medicine specializing in neurosurgery, New Orleans, 1950—; chief staff, head intensive care and neurosurgery, EEG, EMG and neuroradiology Mercy Hosp., New Orleans, 1952—; founder, exec. pres. Pvt. Drs. of Am., New Orleans, 1968—; lectr. in field. Bd. dirs. New Orleans Area Health Planning Council, 1969-76. Served to lt. USAR, 1938-45; to comdr. M.C., USN, 1954-56. Recipient Ochsner award, 1950; Best Sci. exhibit award La. State Med. Soc., 1961; Anatomy prize, Jefferson Med. Sch., 1943. Mem. Am. Assn. Neurosurgeons, So. Neurosurg. Soc., So. Med. Assn., Congress of Neurosurgeons, Am. Acad. Neurology, La. Med. Soc., Orleans Parish Med. Soc., So. Electroencephalography Soc., Am. Assn. Electromyography and Electrodiagnosis, Am. Soc. Assn. Execs. Contbr. articles in field to profl. jours.; patentee in field; author: PSRO, 1973; PSRO-II, 1974. Address: 3422 Bienville St New Orleans LA 70119

GARCIA SANABRIA, RAUL, accountant; b. Lajas, P.R., Nov. 19, 1920; s. Innocencio Garcia Toro and Juanita Sanabria; B.B.A. in Acctg., U. P.R., 1950; postgrad. N.Y. U., 1976; m. Mercedes Dorta, June 5, 1946; children—Jose Raul, Lourdes Mercedes, Linda M. Accountant for various firms, Arecibo, P.R., 1950-79; owner, mgr. Accts. Supply House, Arecibo, 1977—. Bd. dirs. Universidad Hispanoamericana, 1979—. Served with inf. U.S. Army, 1943-47; PTO. C.P.A., P.R. Mem. P.R. Assn. C.P.A.'s (pres. 1978-79), Alumni Assos. U. P.R., Newspaper Assos. P.R., P.R. Coll. C.P.A.'s. Club: Optimists (pres. Arecibo chpt. 1973-75). Pub. newspapers Morivivi, 1977—, Impacto, 1975-76. Home: Ocean View Calle 2 G-9 Arecibo PR 00612 Office: Edificio Oliver Suite 305 Arecibo PR 00612

GARDINE, JUANITA CONSTANTIA FORBES (MRS. CYPRIAN A. GARDINE), educator; b. St. Croix, V.I., Aug. 6, 1912; d. Alphonso Sebastian and Petrina (Actien) Forbes; B.A., Hunter Coll., 1934; M.A., Columbia, 1940; postgrad. U. Chgo., 1950, N.Y. U., 1960-66; m. Cyprian A. Gardine, Apr. 23, 1942; children—Cyprian A., Vicki Maria Camilla, Letitia Theresa, Richard Whittington. Tchr. elementary schs., 1934-35; tchr. math. high sch., 1935-41, 48-49; acting asst. high sch. prin., 1941; jr. high sch. prin., 1941-47; substitute tchr. math., physics, Montclair, N.J., 1947-48; asst. supt. edn., 1949-55; asso. dean Community Colls., 1955-57; high sch. prin., 1957-58; supr. ednl. statistics, 1958-62; social worker Dept. Welfare, 1962-63; prin. Christiansted (St. Croix) Pub. Grammar Sch., 1963-74; tchr. math. evening session extension classes Cath. U. P.R., 1961; part-time instr. math. Coll. Virgin Islands, 1974-76. Past sec. bd. dirs. St. Croix Fed. chpt. ARC; mem. bd., chmn. supervisory com. St. Croix Fed. Credit Union; past sec. St. Croix Sch. Health Com.; past mem. and pres. St. Croix (V.I.) Mental Health Assn. Pres., Tchrs. Assn., 1940, Municipal Employees Assn., 1942. Sch. named in her honor, 1974. Mem. Am. Statis. Assn., NAESP, V.I. Fedn. Bus. and Profl. Women's Clubs (past sec.), Episcopal Ch. Women of V.I. (past chmn. world affairs com.), Christiansted Bus. and Profl. Women's Club (past pres.; Woman of Year 1966), Daus. King (sec.), Christiansted Bus. and Profl. Club (past historian). Episcopalian (past pres. women's group). Home: 142 Whim Estate Frederiksted St Croix VI 00840 Mailing address: Box 1505 Christiansted St Croix VI 00820

GARDINER, PAULINE SUSAN, artist, nurse; b. Salem, Oreg., Oct. 27, 1947; d. Paul Shedrick and Josie Laura (Allan) Wolfe; B.S. R.N., U. Portland and Portland Community Coll., 1968; children—Douglas Aldwin, John Paul. Mem. colonial service group Brit. Govt., Brit. Solomon Islands, W. Pacific, 1970-72; exhibited paintings numerous art shows, 1974-76; group shows in Seattle, Houston, Solomon Islands; represented in permanent collections in Eng., Australia, N.Z., Solomon Islands, Ireland, Tex., Ala., Ark., Fla., Oreg., also numerous pvt. collections; paintings include: Morafic, 1974, Sir Seyn, 1976, Mary Gale at Seabrook, 1978; staff lectr. photography, dept. physics U. Warwick, Coventry, Eng. 1970-72; lectr. in field to art classes and groups. Active Seabrook (Tex.) city politics; v.p. Concerned Residents of Seabrook, 1977; mem. Galveston Bay Conservation and Preservation Assn., 1978—; mem. Houston C. of C., 1978—, agribus. com., 1978—. Recipient numerous awards in art, photography, speech and as breeder of Arabian horses; licensed real estate agent, Tex. Mem. Clear Creek Art League, Oreg., Tex. State bds. nursing, Gulf Coast Arabian Horse Club, Alpha Tau Delta. Republican. Episcopalian. Home: 3613 N Meyer St Seabrook TX 77586

GARDNER, BILLY DEAN, univ. ofcl.; b. Wellington, Tex., Sept. 29, 1936; s. Troy William and Grace (Johnson) G.; B.B.A., West Tex. State U., 1960, M.B.A., 1970; m. Jewell Carline Uselton, Sept. 4, 1955; children—Kathy Lynn, Jeffery Douglas. Accountant Leon L. Hoyt & Co., C.P.A.'s, Amarillo, Tex., 1960-63; adminstrv. staff West Tex. State U., 1963-73; partner firm Holcomb & Gardner, C.P.A.'s, Canyon, Tex., 1973; chief fiscal officer Corpus Christi State U., 1973—. Former bd. dirs. Randall County Little League; bd. dirs. Randall County Kids, Inc.; mem. exec. com. Tex. Assn. State Sr. Coll. and Univ. Bus. Officers. C.P.A., Tex. Mem. Tex. Soc. C.P.A.'s, Am. Inst. C.P.A.'s. Kiwanian (past dir.). Home: 405 Frio St Portland TX 78374 Office: 6300 Ocean Dr Corpus Christi TX 78412

GARDNER, DONALD ANGUS, architect; b. Portchester, N.Y., June 2, 1944; s. Angus John and Mary (Shaw) G.; B.Arch., Clemson U., 1968; m. Gloria Orr, Dec. 27, 1966; children—Angela Renee, Donald Angus, Sonia Dale. Draftsman, J.B. Lindsay, Clemson, S.C., 1970-74; project architect Vickery Allen Bashor, Greenville, S.C., 1974-75; partner Gardner, Edelblut & Assos., Seneca, S.C., 1975-76; project architect Daniel Internat./Daniel Engrs., Greenville, S.C., 1976-79; pres., Donald A. Gardner, Architect, Inc., Greenville, 1978—, also dir. Served to 1st lt. C.E., U.S. Army, 1968-70. Decorated Army Commendation medal. Mem. AIA. Methodist. Home: 104 Westover Place Greenville SC 29615 Office: PO Box 16045 Station B Greenville SC 29606

GARDNER, EARL ROBERT, counselor, educator; b. Johnson City, N.Y., Aug. 9, 1940; s. William Jay and Eleanore (Loder) G.; B.S., SUNY, Oswego, 1962, M.S., 1967; Ph.D., Fla. State U., 1979; m. Barbara L. Merritt, Aug. 21, 1966; children—Kimberly Allison, Gregory Alan. Elem. sch. counselor, Cazenovia, N.Y., 1966-68; Oneonta, N.Y., 1970-73; dir. clin. tng. and treatment team leader Brevard County Mental Health Center, Rockledge, Fla., 1974-77; research asso. Tex. Research Inst. Mental Scis., Houston, 1977-78; asst. prof., research asso. U. Tex. Med. Sch., Houston, 1978—, psychiat. consultation liaison service dept. psychiatry; cons. Brevard Community Coll. Lab Sch., 1974-76, Fla. Tech. U. Sch. Social Work, 1976-77. Chmn. clin. div. Fla. Council Community Mental Health, 1975-77; Fla. Mental Retardation Human Rights Advocacy Council, 1976-77; mem. Brevard County Coalition for Responsible Funding in Edn., 1976-77. Mem. Am. Acad. Psychosomatic Medicine, Am. Mental Health Counselors Assn., Am. Personnel and Guidance Assn., Soc. Behavioral Medicine. Contbr. articles to pubs. Home: 16223 Tibet Rd Friendswood TX 77546 Office: 6431 Fannin St PO Box 20708 Houston TX 77025

GARDNER, FRANCIS EUGENE, JR., physiologist; b. Wichita, Kans., Dec. 13, 1938; s. Francis Eugene and Liberty Belle (Merryman) G.; B.A., Ottawa (Kans.) U., 1965; M.S., Wichita State U., 1968; Ph.D., U. Ill., Champaign-Urbana, 1973; m. Ann Adams Baker, June 4, 1975; children—Kelly Wayne, Stephanie Suzanne, Holly Ann. NIH postdoctoral fellow U. Ga., Athens, 1973-74; asst. prof. biology Columbus (Ga.) Coll., 1974-77, asso. prof., 1977—. Served with USN, 1959-61. USPHS grad. fellow U. Ill., 1968-72; recipient Dean's award Columbus Coll., 1974. Mem. AAAS, Am. Inst. Biol. Scis., Assn. Southeastern Biologists, Am. Coll. Sports Medicine, Ga. Acad. Scis., Gold Key. Home: 7588 Nature Trail Columbus GA 31904 Office: 202 Faculty Office Bldg Columbus Coll Algonquin Dr Columbus GA 31907

GARDNER, JACQUELINE, guidance counselor; b. St. Paul, Feb. 23, 1922; d. John and Arabelle (Retherford) Bergman; B.A., U. Minn., 1943, M.A., 1971; cert. advanced studies Old Dominion U., 1977; m. Walter John Gardner, Mar. 2, 1945; children—Lee Camille, Scot Gregory, Kip Geoffrey. Guidance counselor, work study coordinator Portsmouth (Va.) City Sch. System, 1969—; adj. instr. Old Dominion U.; presenter workshops on communication skills; demonstrator group work with mentally retarded adolescents; vol. counselor and cons. Portsmouth Juvenile Ct.; mem. adv. bd. AFL-CIO Human Relations Devel. Inst. Del. Republican Party State Conv., 1977, 79; bd. dirs. Tidewater Vocat. Center, 1975-79, Effingham YMCA. Served as lt. (j.g.), WAVES, USNR, 1943-45. Recipient citizens award Nat. Assn. Retarded Citizens, 1977. Mem. Council Exceptional Children, Nat. Assn. Physically Handicapped, Am. Personnel and Guidance Assn., Va. Personnel and Guidance Assn., Hampton Roads Personnel and Guidance Assn., Va. Assn. Specialists in Group Work, Psi Chi. Republican. Unitarian. Home: 1501 Sleepy Lake Pkwy Suffolk VA 23433 Office: 2323 Portsmouth Blvd Portsmouth VA 23704

GARDNER, LAWRENCE GALE, physician; b. Knoxville, Tenn., Nov. 23, 1930; s. Gale and Mary Ellen (Hitch) G.; B.S., U. Tenn., 1955, M.D., 1955; m. Carol Hartsfield, Aug. 13, 1971; children—Lauren Ann, Angeline Eliza, Charlotte Emerson, David Bryan. Intern, Confederate Meml. Med. Center, Shreveport, La., 1955-56; resident John Peter Smith Hosp., Ft. Worth, 1959-60; resident in surgery Kennedy VA Hosp., Memphis, 1964-65; resident in otolaryngology City of Memphis Hosp., 1963-64, 65-67; fellow in otology Los Angeles Found. of Otology, 1968-69; practice medicine specializing in otology, Memphis, 1969—, in otolaryngology, Memphis, 1963-64, 65-67; mem. cons. med. staff Meth. Hosp., 1967—, VA Hosp., 1969—; mem. active staff City of Memphis Hosp., 1974—, Memphis Eye and Ear Hosp., 1974—, Bapt. Meml. Hosp., 1978—; asst. prof. dept. otolaryngology and maxillofacial surgery U. Tenn. Center for the Health Scis., Memphis, 1974—; guest lectr. to various univs. and profl. groups. Served to capt. M.C., USAF, 1957-59. Recipient Meritorious Service award Phi Rho Sigma, 1975; diplomate Am. Bd. Otolaryngology. Fellow Am. Acad. Ophthalmology and Otolaryngology; mem. So. Med. Assn., Tenn. Acad. Otolaryngology (chmn. ethics and peer rev. com. 1974—), Memphis Soc. Otolaryngology and Maxillofacial Surgery (sec. treas. 1973-75, v.p. 1977, pres. 1978), Memphis and Shelby County Med. Soc., Nat. Hearing Aid Soc. (med. adv. 1979), Mid South Med. Assn., Tenn. Med. Assn., AMA, Pan-Am. Assn. of Oto-Rhi-nolaryngology and Bronchoesophagology, Better Hearing Inst. (chmn. adv. bd. 1976—), Centurion Club of Deafness Research Found., Soc. of Univ. Otolaryngologists, Soc. for Ear, Nose and Throat Advances in Children, Nat. Rehab. Assn., Nat. Assn. for Hearing and Speech Action, Mid-South Med. Assembly, U. Tenn. Otolaryngology Alumni Assn. (sec.-treas. 1974-76). Contbr. numerous articles on otology to med. jours.; producer ednl. films in field. Office: 899 Madison Ave Suite 602A Memphis TN 38103

GARDNER, LELA MARSHALL, speech pathologist; b. Wymore, Nebr., June 2, 1908; d. Virgil Ralph and Jeanie Mae (Warriner) Marshall; B.S. in Edn., U. Nebr., 1930; M.S. in Public Adminstrn., Washington U., St. Louis, 1932; postgrad. Columbia U., 1958-59, 60-61; m. John Hall Gardner, June 7, 1932; 1 dau., Marvel Jean Gardner. Speech pathologist Toledo Hearing League, 1959-60; grad. asst. Bowling Green (Ohio) State U., 1959-60; speech pathologist Bd. Edn., Newark, 1960-63; speech pathologist Johnstone Tng. Sch., Bordentown, N.J., 1963-66; speech pathologist Bd. Edn., Frederick County, Md., 1966-76; speech pathologist Western Md. Center, Hagerstown, 1976-77; free lance writer weekly Letters on nat. and internat. affairs, 1976—; cons. speech pathology State Home for Boys, Jamesburg, N.J., 1964-67. Mem. nat. adv. bd. Am. Security Council, 1973; life mem. Am. Conservation Union, 1973, John Birch Soc., 1973; founder Center for Internat. Securities Studies, 1977; sponsor Am. Council for World Freedom, 1972; pres. W.Va. Panhandle chpt. Eagle Forum, 1977; active Coalition for Peace Through Strength, Com. to Restore the Constn., 1974, Found. of Law and Soc., 1978; mem. bd. policy Liberty Lobby, 1973—. bd. dirs. Northampton County (Pa.) Soc. for Crippled Children and Adults, 1951-55, dir. public relations, 1953-55. Recipient Tchrs. cert., N.J., 1960, life cert., 1965, Advanced Profl. cert. in speech and hearing, Md., 1969. Mem. Am. Speech and Hearing Assn. (life mem., cert. clin. competence), AAUW (arts chmn. Easton, Pa. br., dir.), Pi Lambda Theta. Republican. Club: Women's (music chmn. Easton). Home: Route 1 Box 240 Jefferson Terr Charles Town WV 25414

GARDNER, PAMELA FOGELMAN, credit union exec.; b. London, Oct. 12, 1940; came to U.S., 1960; d. Jack and Jenny (Rowley) Fogelman; student London Sch. Bus., 1957, U. London, 1957, Patrick Henry Jr. Coll., 1975-76; children—Martyn Dale, Jenny Denise. Asst. mgr. overseas claims dept. Pearl Ins. Co., London, 1956-60; asst. bookkeeper, teletype operator Hornady Bros. Trucking Co., Monroeville, Ala., 1965-67; asst. treas., mgr. Allied Credit Union, Jackson, Ala., 1969—. Mem. Credit Union Mgrs. Assn., Jackson C. of C. Methodist. Home: 701 Edgewood Circle Jackson AL 36545 Office: Allied Credit Union 1225 Forest Ave Jackson AL 36545

GARDNER, PAUL MILLS, coll. adminstr.; b. Sistersville, W.Va., Apr. 5, 1943; s. Lester Oral and Ruby Albertine (Barnhouse) G.; B.A., Harding Coll., Searcy, Ark., 1965; M.S., W.Va. U., 1968; Ph.D., Ohio U., Athens, 1975; m. Mary Cronin, Dec. 29, 1967. Instr., coach Ohio Valley Coll., Parkersburg, 1966-68; dir. devel. Harding Acad., Memphis, 1968-69; dir. ann. giving Harding Coll., 1971-75; v.p. Ohio Valley Coll., 1975—. Chmn. bd. Vienna (W.Va.) Christian Nursery Sch. Mem. Am. Assn. Higher Edn., Council Advancement and Support Edn., Phi Delta Kappa. Republican. Mem. Ch. of Christ. Club: Rotary. Home: 1019 51st St Vienna WV 26105 Office: Ohio Valley Coll College Pkwy Parkersburg WV 26101

GARDNER, RICHARD CALVIN, sch. supr.; b. Indpls., Sept. 21, 1931; s. Selby A. and Mary E. (Armstrong) G.; B.S., Butler U., 1951; M.A., East Tenn. U., 1955; postgrad. U. Del., 1959, U. Tenn., 1960, 72, U. Wis., 1965; m. Dorothy Faye Fleenor, Aug. 25, 1951; children—Sylvia Jeannine, Kirby Hunter, Trevor Christian. Tchr. elementary sch., Kingsport (Tenn.) Pub. Schs., 1951-55; asst. prof. edn. U. N.Y., Oneonta, 1955-57; elementary sch. supr. Kingsport City Schs., 1957-61, asst. supt. schs., 1961-65, 69-71; supr. curriculum devel. Tenn. State Dept. of Edn., Nashville, 1966-67, coordinator div. of instrn., 1972; supt. of schs. Norton (Va.) City Schs., 1972-79; supr. elem. edn. Wise County (Va.) Public Schs., 1979—. Extension instr. East. Tenn. State U., Johnson City, 1959-65, U. Va., Charlottesville, 1967—, U. Tenn., Knoxville, 1967-72, Va. Poly. Inst. and State U., Blacksburg, 1973—; vis. prof. St. Mary of the Plains Coll., Dodge City, Kans., summer, 1971; mem. tchr. edn. adv. council Clinch Valley Coll., U. Va., 1974—; mem. adv. council Wise Speech and Hearing Clinic, 1975; cons. to Day Care Services, Tenn. Dept. of Pub. Welfare, 1959-71. Bd. dirs. Regional Child Devel. Center, 1974—, Appalachian Regional Lab., 1971-72, Kingsport Community Chest; bd. dirs. Dilenowisco Ednl. Co-op, chmn., 1972—. Recipient Good Citizenship award Jaycees, 1962. Mem. Nat., Va., Norton edn. assns., Nat. Soc. for Study of Edn., Am. Assn. Sch. Adminstrs., Phi Delta Kappa, Kappa Delta Pi, Phi Kappa Phi. Mem. Universalist Ch. (trustee 1955-57, ch. sch. dir. 1955-57). Kiwanian (dir. 1972-75, v.p. 1974-75). Home: Route 6 Abington VA 24210 Office: PO Box 1217 Wise VA 24293

GARDNER, ROBERT HAMILTON, savs. and loan exec.; b. Plainfield, N.J., Mar. 15, 1922; s. Thompson and Jennie (Knight) G.; student Hofstra Coll., 1941-43; B.A., Rutgers U., 1948; m. June R. Scott, Mar. 30, 1946; children—Kathleen (Mrs. Robert P. Johnson), Scott, Robert. Spl. agt. FBI, 1948-52; self-employed, 1952-68; dir. insuring office HUD, Tulsa, 1969-78; loan officer State Fed. Savs. & Loan Assn., Tulsa, 1979—. Served to capt. USMCR, 1943-46. Decorated Purple Heart. Rotarian (pres. southside Tulsa club). Mem. Tulsa Homebuilders Assn. (dir. 1979). Clubs: Cedar Ridge Country, Oaks Country (pres. 1968). Home: 6131 S Hudson Tulsa OK 74136 Office: 610 S Boston St Tulsa OK 74119

GARDNER, RUSSELL MENESE, lawyer; b. High Point, N.C., July 14, 1920; s. Joseph Hayes and Clara (Flynn) G.; A.B., Duke U., 1942, LL.B., 1948; m. Joyce Thresher, Mar. 7, 1946; children—Winthrop Gillet, Page Stansbury, June Thresher. Admitted to Fla. bar, 1948; asso. McCune, Hiaasen, Crum, Ferris & Gardner, and predecessor firms, 1948-50, partner, 1950—. Dir. Thellian Co., Inc. Charter revision com. City of Fort Lauderdale, 1957; mem., chmn. info. and edn. subcom. Ft. Lauderdale Citizens Adv. Com.; mem. adv. bd. Nova U., also bd. govs. Law Sch.; pres., chmn. bd. Jack and Jill Nursery, Inc.; bd. dirs. United Fund Broward County; trustee Ft. Lauderdale Museum Arts, pres. bd., 1964-67; bd. dirs. Boys Clubs of Broward County Cultural Council Greater Ft. Lauderdale, Inc.; trustee Broward County affiliate Am. Heart Assn. Served from ensign to lt. Supply Corps, USNR, 1942-46. Fellow Am. Coll. Probate Counsel; mem. Fla. Bar (mem. grievance com.), Am., Broward County (chmn. cts. com.) bar assns., Am. Judicature Soc., Ft. Lauderdale Hist. Soc. (trustee, pres. 1975—), U.S. Navy League (dir. Ft. Lauderdale council), Phi Delta Phi, Omicron Delta Kappa. Democrat. Presbyterian (trustee, deacon, elder). Clubs: Drummer; Kiwanis, Coral Ridge Country; Lauderdale Yacht (dir., vice commodore 1977, commodore 1978). Home: 2412 NE 14th St Fort Lauderdale FL 33304 Office: Century Nat Bank Bldg Fort Lauderdale FL 33301

GARDNER, WARREN SANDERS, JR., mfrs. agt.; b. Chattanooga, Dec. 5, 1924; s. Warren Sanders and Virginia (Charlton) G.; B.Mgmt. Engring., Rensselaer Poly. Inst., 1949; m. Barbara Lee, Sept. 18, 1949; children—Warren Sanders III, William Lee, David Louis, Virginia Lee. Regional mgr. Comer Avondale Mills, Chattanooga, 1949-52; pres. Gardner and Meredith, Inc., Chattanooga, 1960—, Gardner-Southeast, Inc., Chattanooga, 1975—. Trustee McCallie Sch.; bd. dirs. United Fund; elder Signal Mountain Presbyterian Ch. Served to 1st lt. USAAF, 1943-45. Decorated Air medal with oak leaf cluster. Mem. Mfrs. Agts. Nat. Assn., Nat. Welders Supply Assn., Nat. Assn. Small Bus. Clubs: Mountain City, Signal Mountain Golf and Country. Home: 7 Stone Point Ln Signal Mountain TN 37377 Office: 820 Hamilton Ave Chattanooga TN 37405

GARDNER, WILLIAM ALBERT, JR., pathologist; b. Sumter, S.C., Aug. 2, 1939; s. William A. and Betty Lee (Kennedy) G.; B.S., Wofford Coll., 1960; M.S. in Anatomy, Med. Coll. S.C., 1963, M.D., 1965; m. Kathryn Ann Medlin, June 30, 1960; children—Mary Elizabeth, Kathryn Lee, William Dylan. Intern, Johns Hopkins Hosp., Balt., 1965-66, asst. resident, 1966-67, fellow in pathology, 1965-67; asst. resident Duke U., Durham, N.C., 1967-68, chief resident, 1968-69, instr. pathology, 1968-69; acting chief lab. service VA Hosp., Charleston, S.C., 1969, chief, 1969; asst. prof. of pathology Med. U. S.C., 1969-72, asso. prof., 1972-76; prof. pathology Vanderbilt U., Nashville, 1976—, also vice chmn. dept. pathology; chief lab. service VA Hosp., Nashville, also mem. clin. exec. bd. Recipient Cert. of Appreciation for Outstanding Teaching, Med. U. S.C., 1975; named Boss of Yr., Secretaria Assn., Charleston, 1975. Diplomate Am. Bd. Pathology. Fellow Am. Soc. Clin. Pathologists, Coll. Am. Pathologists (del. for govtl. pathology) mem. Internat. Acad. Pathology, Acad. Clin. Lab. Physicians and Scientists, Tenn. Med. Assn., AMA, Alpha Omega Alpha. Methodist. Contbr. articles on oncology and pathology to profl. jours. Home: 776 Greeley Dr Nashville TN 37205 Office: 1310 24th Ave South Nashville TN 37203

GARDNER, WILLIAM BEVERLY, JR., cons. petroleum engr.; b. San Antonio, Tex., Sept. 20, 1926; s. William Beverly and Thelma (Van Riper) G.; B.S., U. Tex., Austin, 1950, LL.B., 1957; m. Yvonne Gebhard, Jan. 28, 1956; children—Sharon Clare, Melanie Jane. With Humble Oil and Refining Co., Houston, Tex., 1945; petroleum engr. Union Oil of Calif., Midland, Tex., 1950; formation logging engr. Rotary Engring. Co., Midland, 1951-54; cons. petroleum engr., Austin, Tex., 1954—; owner, dir. 3G Land and Cattle Co. Inc., 1965—; pres. Gardner-Leander Co., 1969—; vis. prof. dept. petroleum engring. U. Tex., Austin, 1977; Precinct chmn. Republican Party, 1960-71; del. State Rep. Conv., 1960-70. Served with USNR, 1944. Mem. Am. Petroleum Inst., Nat. Soc. of Profl. Engrs., Soc. of Petroleum Engrs. (chmn. Balcones sect. 1965-66), Tex. Soc. of Profl. Engrs. (chpt. pres. 1967), Pi Kappa Alpha. Episcopalian. Clubs: Austin, Headliners. Home: 4500 Deepwoods Dr Austin TX 78731 Office: PO Box 1867 Austin TX 78767

GARERI, DAN JAMES, cons. in aerospace scis.; b. Bovey, Minn., Apr. 14, 1922; s. James and Frances (Coppoletti) G.; B.S., U. Minn., 1947, M.S., 1949; M.B.A., U. Chgo., 1962; M.S. in Internat. Affairs, George Washington U., 1965; postgrad Air War Coll., 1964-65; m. Lucille Venetucci, June 18, 1949; children—Danita, Gina. Commd. lt. USAF, 1947, advanced through grades to col., 1974; chief aircraft div. and chief plans Wright-Patterson AFB, O., 1961-68, chief tech. div. DIA, Pentagon, 1971-74, ret., 1974; cons. in aerospace scis., Annandale, Va., 1974—. Served with USAAF, 1942-45. Decorated Legion Merit, D.F.C., Air medal with 5 oak leaf clusters. Asso. fellow Am. Inst. Aeros. and Astronautics; mem. tech. history com. 1973-75), Assn. Old Crows, Smithsonian Asso., Nat. Geog. Soc., Tau Omega, Sigma Xi. Contbr. to profl. jours. Address: 4111 Turkey Creek Ct Annandale VA 22003

GARFIELD, WARREN, hosp. personnel adminstr.; b. Milw., Aug. 4, 1922; s. James Albert and Edna Katherine (Bahling) G.; student Ark. State Coll., 1944, Oklahoma City U., 1955, Troy State Coll., 1956, North Tex. State U., 1957-58, U. Md., 1958-59, San Antonio Coll., 1962-63, St. Marys U., 1963-64; B. Gen. Edn. in Bus., U. Nebr., Omaha, 1965. Served as enlisted man AC, U.S. Army, 1942-46, advanced through grades to lt. col.; Service in Korea, 1951-52, Germany, 1958-61; asst. ops. officer Surgeon's Office, 8th Army, Korea, 1965-66; sec. Army Primary Helicopter Sch., Ft. Wolders, Tex., 1966-67; ret., 1967; dir. personnel Presbyterian Hosp., Dallas, 1967—. Decorated Bronze Star, Legion of Merit, Army Commendation medal; accredited exec. in personnel. Mem. Am. Soc. Hosp. Personnel Adminstrn. (dir. 1976-79), Tex. Soc. Hosp. Personnel Adminstrn. (pres. 1975-76, dir. 1968-74), Dallas Personnel Assn., Metro Hosp. Personnel Assn. Baptist. Clubs: Exchange (pres. 1974-75, dir. 1977-78), Masons, Shriners. Home: 9936 Mill Tr Dr Dallas TX 75238 Office: 8200 Walnut Hill Ln Dallas TX 75231

GARLAND, GLADYS EARLENE, cons. dietitian; b. Lubbock, Tex., June 14, 1926; s. Earl William and Gladys May (Bell) Judd; B.S., Tex. Tech. U., Lubbock, 1950; m. Thomas Mack Garland, Feb. 22, 1946; children—Brenda Kay, Thomas Earl, Ronald Carl, Larry Allen. Student dietitian Lubbock Gen. Hosp., 1947-50; dietician St. Joseph Hosp., Wichita, Kans., 1953-55; asst. dietitian Wichita Falls (Tex.) Gen. Hosp., 1955-56; chief dietitian Wichita Falls State Hosp., 1956-69; cons. nursing homes and hosps., Tex., 1968—. Mem. Am. Dietetic Assn., Tex. Dietetic Assn., Dallas Dietetic Assn., Am. Dietetic Cons. Interest Group, Dallas Dietetic Cons. Interest Group (chmn. 1976-77), Nutrition Today. Methodist. Address: 135 Classen Dr Dallas TX 75218

GARLAND, JACK RICHARD, univ. spl. services dir.; b. Erwin, Tenn., Dec. 22, 1943; s. Frank Newland and Tilda (Courtney) G.; B.A., Emory and Henry Coll., 1969; M.A., E. Tenn. State U., 1974, doctoral fellow, 1979; m. Carole Evonne Crabtree, Apr. 17, 1965; children—Brett Ryan, Vaughn Whitney, Holley Beth. Social studies tchr. John S. Battle High Sch., Washington County, Va., 1969-76; doctoral asst. Office of Spl. Services, E. Tenn. State U., Johnson City, 1977-77, acting dir., 1977-79, dir. Office of Spl. Services, 1979—. Dist. officer Va. Democratic Party. Served with AUS, 1963-65. Nominated Outstanding Tchr. of Year, Washington County Edn. Assn., 1970-71. Mem. Am. Personnel and Guidance Assn., Tenn. Assn. Spo. Programs, S.E. Assn. Spl. Programs Personnel, Am. Hist. Assn., Washington County Hist. Assn., NEA, Washington County Edn. Assn., Va. Edn. Assn., Phi Delta Kappa, Pi Gamma Mu. Democrat. Baptist. Club: Glade Springs (Va.) Lions (sec.-treas. 1970-75). Author: (with others) Seminar in Supervision, 1977, Seminar in Curriculum, 1977. Home: PO Box 53 Emory VA 24327 Office: PO Box 23920A ETSU Johnson City TN 37601

GARLAND, JAMES EDWARD, architect; b. Tilman, Fla., Mar. 17, 1918; s. Edward Oliver and Verda (Thompson) G.; B.A. in Architecture, U. Fla., 1941; M.Ed., U. Miami, 1953; postgrad. Sorbonne; m. Marian Freeling, June 20, 1942; children—James Edward, G. Jeffery. Mem. faculty Sch. Architecture, U. Fla., 1946-48; state sch. architect State of Fla., 1948-49; sch. architect Dade County, Miami, 1949-56; prin. Cornell, Pierce, Garland and Friedman, architects, engrs., Miami Fla., 1956-75, Carr Smith and Assos. Inc., engrs., architects, planners, Coral Gables, Fla., 1976—; adj. prof. U. Miami, 1970—; pres. Gov. Fla. Art Commn., 1961-67; mem. Fla. Bd. Architecture, 1963-75, pres., 1972. Served to maj., C.E., AUS, 1941-46; ETO. Decorated Bronze Star, Purple Heart; recipient Pullara award Fla. Assn. Architects, 1970. Mem. AIA. Democrat. Baptist. Clubs: Royal Palms Tennis, Coral Gables Country, Progress (pres. 1972). Prin. works include Fla. Presbyn. Coll., Fla. Meml. Coll., Martin Marietta Co. plant, Orlando, Fla., Bayfront Center, St. Petersburg, Fla., Am. 1st Fed. Savs. and Loan Bldg., Miami, Fla. Keys Community Coll. Art Center. Home: 7795 SW 79th St Miami FL 33143 Office: 123 Almeria Ave Coral Gables FL 33134

GARLAND, LARETTA MATTHEWS, ednl. psychologist, nurse, educator; b. Jacksonville, Fla.; d. Wilburn L. and Clyde-Marian (Chamberlin) Matthews; diploma Fla. State Sch. Nursing, 1942; B.S.N., Emory U., 1950, M.Ed., 1953; B.A. in Edn., U. Fla., 1951; cert. cardiologist nurse specialty Tex. Med. Center, 1965; Ed.D., U. Ga., 1975; postgrad. in counseling and guidance Ga. State U., 1969; m. John B. Garland, Mar. 2, 1946; children—John Barnard, Brien Freeling, Amy-Gwin. Office and staff nurse, Lakeland, Fla., 1942, 45; nurse ARC, Buffalo, 1956; asst. prof. nursing Med. Coll. Ga., 1965-67; instr. Emory U., 1952-54, asso. prof., 1967-71, prof., 1972—, ednl. psychologist, dir. gerontol. nurse practitioner program, 1978—. Served with Nurse Corps, U.S. Army, 1942-45. Decorated Bronze Star; recipient Outstanding Teaching award Emory U. Sch. Nursing Grad. Srs., 1977; HEW fellow, 1967-68. Mem. Am. Psychol. Assn., Am. Personnel and Guidance Assn., Am. Nurses Assn., Nat. League Nursing, Alpha Chi Omega, Sigma Theta Tau, Kappa Delta Pi. Methodist. Author: (with Carol Bush) A Coping Text for Health Care Professionals, 1980; contbr. articles to profl. jours. Office: Nell Hodgson Woodruff Sch Nursing Emory U Atlanta GA 30322

GARMAN, GEORGE BAKER, elec. engr.; b. Balt., Sept. 15, 1949; s. George Byerly and Winifred Mae (Baker) G.; B.S.E.E., N.C. State U., 1971; m. Donna Kay Phillips, Sept. 20, 1975; children—George Phillips, Kelly Dawn. Jr. engr. design engring. dept. Duke Power Co., Charlotte, N.C., 1971-73, asso. engr., 1973-74, supv. quality assurance design, 1974-77, asst. design engr., 1977—. Advisor Explorer post 229, Boy Scouts Am., 1977—. Served with U.S. Army, 1971-72. Registered profl. engr., N.C., S.C. Mem. IEEE (publicity chmn. Charlotte sect.; Outstanding Service award Charlotte 1978, N.C. 1978), Power Engring. Soc. (chpt. rep. S.E. region), Charlotte Engrs. Club, Nat. Soc. Profl. Engrs., Profl. Engrs. N.C. Democrat. Mem. Wesleyan Ch. Club: Gaston County Wildlife. Home: 502 Ridgeway Dr Belmont NC 28012 Office: 422 S Church St Charlotte NC 28242

GARMAN, RONALD EUGENE, artist/designer; b. Pekin, Ill., Apr. 26, 1940; s. O. E. and Ruth M. (Haasis) G.; B.F.A., U. N.Mex., 1965; m. Maureen Jeri Mangold, Nov. 25, 1961; children—Christopher Ronald, Kevin Paul. Sr. book designer Better Homes and Gardens, Des Moines, 1966-70; book and gift products designer Hallmark Cards, Inc., Kansas City, Mo., 1970-76; asst. art dir. Word, Inc., Waco, Tex., 1976—. Recipient Addy '77 for best use of photography, also 1979; Type Dirs. Club award, 1979. Mem. Am. Inst. Graphic Arts. Methodist. Home: 2224 Lake Ridge Circle Waco TX 76710 Office: 4800 W Waco Dr Waco TX 76703

GARNER, ALTO LUTHER, educator; b. Dothan, Ala., Dec. 10, 1916; s. Albert Early and Martha (DeBardeleben) G.; A.B., U. Ala., 1944; postgrad. So. Baptist Theol. Sem., 1944-45, U. Tex., Austin, 1947; M.A., N.Y. U., 1947; Ed.D., U. Ky., 1954; m. Katie Mae Sanders, Oct. 5, 1945; 1 son, Robert Edward Lee. Ordained to ministry So. Bapt. Conv., 1942; instr. history and polit. sci. Georgetown Coll., 1947-49, asst. prof., 1949-53; asso. prof. edn. Howard Coll., 1953-54; prof. edn. Samford U., Birmingham, 1954—, chmn. div. tchr. edn., 1964-66, head dept. edn., 1964-66, dean Sch. Edn., 1966—. Served with AUS, 1941. Hon. lt. col. a.d.c., Ala. State Militia, 1972; hon. adm. Ala. Navy, 1978. Mem. Kappa Phi Kappa, Kappa Delta Pi, Phi Alpha Theta, Phi Kappa Phi. Home: 3325 Misty Ln Birmingham AL 35243 Office: 800 Lakeshore Dr Birmingham AL 35209

GARNER, CICERO, JR., lawyer; b. Waynesboro, Ga., Dec. 1, 1936; s. Cicero and Bernice (Welch) G.; A.B., Emory U., 1959; J.D. cum laude, U. Ga., 1961; m. Laurie Geiger, Mar. 17, 1975; children—Caroline Belle, Evan Cicero. Admitted to Ga. bar; asso. firm Gambrell, Harlan, Russell, Moye & Richardson (now Gambrell, Russell & Forbes, Atlanta, 1962-65; partner firm Hurt, Richardson, Garner, Todd & Cadenhead and predecessors, Atlanta, 1965—, Mem. Atlanta Bar Assn., State Bar Ga., Am. Bar Assn., Am. Law Inst., Lawyers Club Atlanta (pres. 1979-80). Methodist. Clubs: Lions, Commerce, Capital City. Office: 1100 Peachtree Center Harris Tower 233 Peachtree St NE Atlanta GA 30303

GARNER, GERALDINE MARIE, ednl. researcher; b. Lynn, Mass., June 10, 1946; d. John J. and Geraldine Marie (Sowers) O'Donnell; A.B. in Edn., Coll. William and Mary, 1968, Ed.M. in Counseling, 1976; Ed.D., Va. Poly. Inst. and State U., 1980; m. Jerry Lawrence Garner, June 15, 1968; children—Lauren Christine, Adrian Derek. Tchr., Fairfax County (Va.) Public Schs., 1968; researcher Forera Corp., Washington, 1969; research specialist Am. Personnel and Guidance Assn., Washington, 1972; founder and dir. Clearinghouse for Women's Career Info., Alexandria, Va., 1972-74; staff editor Bur. Nat. Affairs, Washington, 1973-74; program planner Williamsburg-James City County Community Action Agy., Williamsburg, Va., 1975-76; coordinator coop. edn. Va. Poly. Inst. and State U., Blacksburg, 1976-78, research asst., 1978-79; research intern Appalachia Ednl. Lab., Charleston, W.Va., 1979—; cons. Montgomery County (Md.) Public Schs., 1979; lt. gov.'s rep. to Vocat. Guidance Conf., 1978. Bd. dirs. New River Valley Community Action Agy., 1977-78. Recipient Cert. of Service, Williamsburg-James City County Community Action Agy., 1976. Mem. Am. Personnel and Guidance Assn., Nat. Vocat. Guidance Assn., Am. Ednl. Research Assn., Va. Personnel and Guidance Assn., Co-op Edn. Assn., Am. Soc. Engring. Edn., AAUW, William and Mary Fellowship, Phi Kappa Phi, Phi Delta Kappa, Kappa Delta Pi. Home: 802 Toms Creek Rd Blacksburg VA 24060

GARNER, LEE ELTON, mktg., mgmt. cons.; b. Ivan, Ark., Aug. 24, 1931; s. Iverson Lee and Cynthia Elizabeth (McAllister) G.; B.S. Ed., So. State Coll., 1952; M.R.E., Southwestern Baptist Theol. Sem., 1958, D.R.E., 1966, Ed.D., 1975; m. Billie Joyce Barr, Apr. 17, 1953; children—Steven Lee, Cynthia Joyce, Craig Andrew. Staff, Kroger Grocery Co., Fordyce, Ark., 1948-52; acctg. and mktg. clk. Lion Oil Co., El Dorado, Ark., 1955-56; dir. youth and recreation Gambrell St. Baptist Ch., Ft. Worth, 1957-58; youth dir. Broadway Baptist Ch., Ft. Worth, 1958-60; asso. dir. tng. dept. Baptist Gen. Conv. Tex., Dallas, 1961-65; cons. vocat. guidance Baptist Sunday Sch. Bd., Nashville, 1965-68, cons. communication staff, 1968-70, cons. gen. adminstrn., ch. tng. dept., 1970-73, coordinator mktg., planning, 1973-77, specialist promotion and products, 1977-79; instr. Vol. State Coll., Gallatin, Tenn., 1979, Evelyn Wood Reading Dynamics Inst., 1978-79; freelance cons. mktg., mgmt., tng., Nashville, 1979—. Vol., Crisis Call Center, 1970-71. Served with U.S. Army, 1952-54. Mem. Am. Mktg. Assn. (pres. Middle Tenn. chpt. 1976). Home: 782 Rhonda Ln Nashville TN 37205

GARNER, WARNER, sprinkler co. exec.; b. Booneville, Ark., Sept. 27, 1927; s. Dixon and Rebecca Jane (Pointer) G.; B.S., U. Central Ark., 1950; postgrad. U. Ark., 1950-51; m. Bobbie Jean Thompson, Apr. 5, 1953; children—Gail, Lance. Asst. br. mgr. Tex. Automatic Sprinkler, North Little Rock, Ark., 1951-55; mgr. L.D. McCraw Sprinkler Co., North Little Rock, 1955-69; pres. Masco, Inc., North Little Rock, 1969—. Served with USNR, 1946-48. Mem. Constrn. Specifications Inst., Asso. Gen. Contractors, U. Central Ark. Alumni Assn. (pres. 1956-57), Sigma Tau Gamma. Baptist. Clubs: Optimist, Rotary. Home: 52 Heritage Park Circle North Little Rock AR 72116 Office: Buckeye and Arkansas Ave North Little Rock AR 72115

GARNES, RONALD VINCENT, computer co. exec.; b. Washington, Mar. 7, 1947; s. Kenneth Richard and Vauda Mason (Hall) G.; student U. Dayton, 1965-68; B.S., U. Md., 1975; postgrad. Am. U., 1980. Adminstrv. mgr. Western Union Electronic Mail, Inc., McLean, Va., 1976; dir. mktg. Communications Cons., Inc., Silver Spring, Md., 1977; partner CAC, Washington, 1977; account mgr. PRC Computer Center, Inc., McLean, Va., 1978-79, sr. account mgr., 1979—; prin. Ronald V. Garnes Assos. Cons. Mem. Fairfax County Republican Com. Mem. Nat. Assn. Market Developers, Greater Washington Bd. Trade, Fairfax County C. of C. Republican. Roman Catholic. Clubs: Lincoln; U.S. Senatorial. Office: PRCf Computer Center Inc 7670 Old Springhouse Rd McLean VA 22102

GARNETT, CHARLES COX, clin. social worker; b. Charlottesville, Va., Aug. 5, 1949; s. Edgar Nottingham and Ruby Christina (Cornett) G.; B.A., Emory and Henry Coll., 1971; M.S.W., Va. Commonwealth U., 1976; m. Linda Kay Cox, Apr. 1, 1973; 1 dau., Christina Erin. Vol., Peace Corps, India, 1971-72; recreation aide, houseparent Holston Meth. Home, Greeneville, Tenn., 1972-73, intake officer, case worker, 1973-74, social worker, 1976-79; clin. social worker adolescent unit Southwestern State Hosp., Marion, Va., 1979—; instr. Emory (Va.) and Henry Coll., 1977-79. Mem. Appalachians for Clean Energy; bd. dirs., mem. personnel com. Highlands Home. Mem. Nat. Assn. Social Workers, Va. Council Social Welfare. Lutheran. Home: Rt 4 Box 392 Abingdon VA 24210 Office: Southwestern State Hosp Marion VA 24354

GARNETT, ROBERT EUGENE, sales exec.; b. Grinnell, Ia., Aug. 25, 1943; s. Robert Tompkins and Louise (Nuckolls) G.; B.B.A., Memphis State U., 1970; m. Mary Alison Cooke, Dec. 19, 1964; children—Robert Eugene, Eben Christopher. Product mgr. orthopedic soft goods Richards Mfg., Memphis, 1970-71; ter. mgr. Baxter Travenol Labs., Little Rock, 1972-73, nat. advt. mgr., Deerfield, Ill., 1973-74, parenteral specialist, Atlanta, 1974-76; area sales mgr. med. sales Span Am., Inc., Hernando, Miss., 1976-79; mfrs. rep. Wright-Jones Enterprises, 1980—. Served with USNR, 1966-68. Mem. Am. Mktg. Assn., Am. Mgmt. Assn., Pharm. Drug Mfrs. Assn. Republican. Episcopalian. Club: Advt. (Memphis). Patentee in field. Home: 169 Commerce St Hernando MS 38632 Office: PO Box 5231 Greenville SC 29606

GARNSEY, CLARKE HENDERSON, artist, art historian; b. Joliet, Ill., Sept. 22, 1913; s. Charles Bushniell and Sibyl Mary (VanPelt) G.; grad. Cleve. Inst. Art, 1947; B.S., Western Res. U., 1947, M.A., 1948, Ph.D., 1962; postgrad. U. Colo., W. Tex. State; m. Jean Sharpless Shoemaker, Oct. 21, 1943. Ednl. staff Cleve. Mus. Art, 1947-49, 57-59; instr. Cleve. Inst. Art, 1957-59; dept. chmn. art. Amarillo Coll., Tex., 1949-63; prof., chmn. dept. art Wichita State U., 1963-66; chmn. dept. art U. Tex., El Paso, 1966-79, emeritus, 1979—; cons. El Paso Div. Upward Bound. Bd. dirs. Wichita Art Mus., 1964-66, El Paso Art Mus., 1967-71. Served with USAAF, 1941-46. Mem. Coll. Art Assn., Am., Soc. Archtl. Historians, Rio Bravo Watercolorists, El Paso Designer Craftsmen. Home: 221 Carnival Dr El Paso TX 79912

GARRETSON, CARROLL CURRY (GARY), pvt. investigator; b. Eakly, Okla., Aug. 24, 1917; s. George Washington and Ruth (Curry) G.; B.S., Okla. A&M Coll., 1941; A.S. in Agr., Central Fla. Jr. Coll., 1971; m. Anne, June 18, 1943; children—Don Gary, Karen Ruth. Commd. 2d lt. U.S. Army, 1941, advanced through grades to maj., 1945, served OSS, PTO; ret., 1959; supt. recreation Clearwater, Fla., 1960-66; pvt. investigator, 1949—; founder, dir. The Investigation Agy., Clearwater, 1969—; profl. animal hunter, Africa, C. Am., S. Am., 1949-66; Served with N.G., 1934-41. Mem. Fla. Assn. Pvt. Investigators, Nat. Investigator's Council, World Assn. Investigators. Club: Masons. Address: PO Box 4085 Clearwater FL 33518

GARRETT, CAROL ANN, speech-lang. pathologist; b. Danville, Va., June 24, 1940; d. James Claude Swanson and Hilma May (Hall) G.; A.A., Averett Coll., 1960; B.S. magna cum laude, Miss. U. for Women, 1962; M.Ed., U. Va., 1966. Speech-lang. pathologist Lynchburg (Va.) Public Schs., 1962—; pvt. practice speech-lang. pathology Lynchburg, 1963—; cons. in field. Mem. Am. Speech-Lang.-Hearing Assn., Speech and Hearing Assn. Va., AAUW, Spl. Edn. Adv. Com. Lynchburg Public Schs., Beta Sigma Phi (pres. Lynchburg Council 1964-65, pres. chpt. 1965-66, 69-71, 73-75, girl of yr. award 1969-71, 73-75), Methodist. Home: 723 Custer Dr Lynchburg VA 24502 Office: Lynchburg Public Schs 10th and Court Sts Lynchburg VA 24504

GARRETT, CHARLES THOMASSON, advt. exec.; b. Carrollton, Ga., July 8, 1954; s. David Clyde and Lu Waters (Thomasson) G.; B.A., Mercer U., 1977. Mental health asso. in state and pvt. instns., 1973-77; TV producer Burke Dowling Adams, advt., Atlanta, 1978—. Office: 3290 Northside Pkwy Atlanta GA 30322

GARRETT, DAVID CLYDE, JR., airline exec.; b. Norris, S.C., July 6, 1922; s. David Clyde and Mary H. Garrett; B.A., Furman U., 1942; M.S., Ga. Inst. Tech., 1955; m. Lu Thomasson, Sept. 11, 1947; children—David, Virginia, Charles. With Delta Air Lines, Inc., Atlanta, 1946—, pres., 1971—, also chief exec. officer, dir.; dir. Travelers Corp. Served with USAAF, 1943-46. Mem. Soc. Automotive Engrs. Office: Delta Air Lines Atlanta Airport Atlanta GA 30320

GARRETT, DONALD LYNN, pub. utilities co. exec.; b. Crawfordsville, Ind., Nov. 30, 1948; s. Harry T. and Verna (Spragg) G.; B.S. in Civil Engring., Purdue U., 1971; postgrad. U. Tenn.; m. Corliss J. Ellis, June 21, 1969; children—Todd, Ryan. Civil engr. TVA, Knoxville, Tenn., 1971-74, personnel officer engring. design div., 1974-76, tng. officer, 1976-77, supr. manpower mgmt. and devel., 1977, supr. civil engring. and design br., staff services, 1977—; lectr. U. Tenn., 1976, 77, 78. Key man leader United Way, Knoxville, 1976—. Registered profl. engr. Tenn. Mem. ASCE (mem. nat. subcom. on tech. curricula and accreditation 1978—, sec.-treas. 1979, v.p. 1980, nat. coordinator energy initiative program 1980—), Am. Soc. Tng. and Devel., Nat. Mgmt. Assn. (membership chmn. Knoxville br. 1976, mgmt. devel. com. 1977, youth program chmn. 1979), Assn. Cooperation in Engring. (mem. coordinating com. on energy 1980—). Home: 5607 Aster Ln Knoxville TN 37921 Office: TVA 400 Commerce Ave Knoxville TN 37902

GARRETT, FRANKLIN MILLER, historian; b. Milw., Sept. 25, 1906; s. Clarence Robert and Ada (Kirkwood) G.; LL.B., Woodrow Wilson Coll. Law, 1941; L.H.D., Oglethorpe Coll., 1970; m. Frances Steele, 1978; children by previous marriage—Patricia Abbott, Garrett Wise, Franklin Miller. Br. mgr. Western Union Telegraph Co., Atlanta, 1934-38; salesman Ward Wight & Co., Atlanta, 1939-40; mem. exec. staff pub. relations, historian Coca-Cola Co., Atlanta, 1940-68. Chmn., Fulton County (Ga.) Civil Service Bd., 1955-72; ofcl. historian City of Atlanta, 1973—, Fulton County, 1975—. Bd. dirs. Children's Center Met. Atlanta, 1958-70. Served with AUS, 1942-45. Named a City Shaper, Atlanta Mag., 1976. Mem. Nat. Ry., Va., Ga., Atlanta (chmn. bd. trustees 1967-68, dir. 1968—), DeKalb County hist. socs., Newcomen Soc. N.Am., Atlanta Art Assn., Atlanta Civil War Round Table, Grand Jurors Assn. Fulton County, Ga. Geneal. Soc. Presbyterian. Clubs: Rotary, Commerce, Piedmont Driving. Author: Atlanta and Environs I-III, 1954, rev. edit., 1969; Yesterday's Atlanta, A picture history, 1974. Home: 3433 Roxboro Rd NE Atlanta GA 30326 Office: 3101 Andrews Dr NW Atlanta GA 30305

GARRETT, JAMES HERSCHEL, hosp. adminstr.; b. Stillwater, Okla., Nov. 26, 1943; s. Raymond Cleaver and Helen Dean (Connell) G.; B.A., Tex. Christian U., 1966, M.A., 1969; M.H.A., Washington U., 1971; m. Wilda Lee Reeves, Aug. 3, 1974; children—Kyle Connell, Kristin Brooke. Asst. dir. grad. program health care adminstrn. Washington U. Sch. Medicine, St. Louis, 1971-73; dir. edn. Sparks Regional Med. Center, Fort Smith, Ark., 1973-74, asst. to pres., 1974-75, dir. devel., 1974-75, dir. Sparks Manor, 1974-76, asso. adminstr., 1975-76; dir. edn. Harris Hosp.-Meth., Fort Worth, 1976-77, asso. dir., 1977—. Pres., Fort Smith Symphony, 1975-76; v.p. Art Center Fort Smith, 1975-76. Served with M.C., U.S. Army, 1966-68. Decorated Bronze Star with oak leaf cluster, Air medal. Mem. Am. Soc. Tng. and Devel., Nat. League Nursing, Am. Hosp. Assn., Am. Soc. Hosp. Edn. and Tng., Tex. Hosp. Assn., Tex. Soc. Hosp. Educators (pres.), Jr. C. of C. Democrat. Methodist. Clubs: Optimist (pres.), Rotary (v.p.), Lions, Kiwanis, Leadership, Masons, Amirita Grotto, Eastern Star. Home: 4508 Foxfire Way Fort Worth TX 76133 Office: 1300 W Cannon St Fort Worth TX 76104

GARRETT, JERRY WAYNE, chem. co. exec., educator; b. Poseyville, Ind., Sept. 28, 1946; s. George Edward and Veda Merle (Rippy) G.; stepson Raymond T. Curtis; student Ark. State U., 1976-77, Lain Tech. Inst., 1970-72; m. Anita Sue Rouse, July 17, 1971; children—Mike, William, Jerry Wayne, Steven, Margaret, Richard. Draftsman, Internat. Steel Co., Evansville, Ind., 1967-70, Mid South Mfg. Co., Marked Tree, Ark., 1972, Structural Steel Inc., Memphis, 1973; sr. draftsman Velsicol Chem. Corp., Memphis, 1973-75; designer Transvaal Chem. Co., Jacksonville, Ark., 1975-77; designer Humko Products, Memphis, 1977-79; tchr. drafting Crowley's Ridge Vocat.-Tech. Sch., Forrest City, Ark., 1979—. Served with USAF, 1964-65. Mem. Am. Inst. Design and Drafting (chmn. com. South Central region), Am. Inst. Chem. Engrs., DAV, Am. Legion. Mem. Christian Ch. (deacon). Club: M-Club. Patentee in field. Home: Route 2 Box 884 Marion AR 72364

GARRETT, JOHN MAXWELL, JR., ret. retail trade exec.; b. Greensboro, N.C., Sept. 14, 1924; s. John Maxwell and Nellie Victoria (Leonard) G.; B.A., Elon Coll., 1948; m. Jean Marie Abell, Dec. 25, 1949; children—Victoria Marie (Mrs. Norman Paul Kaneklides), John Keith. Asst. mgr. Western Auto Supply Co., Knoxville, 1948-49, mgr., 1949-50, Raleigh, N.C., 1950-51, Winston-Salem, N.C., 1951-52, retail sales mgr., Atlanta, 1952-57; mgr. Lowe's Cos., North Wilkesboro, N.C., 1957-73, regional v.p., 1973-76, sr. v.p. ops., 1976. dir. Wilkes Savs. and Loan. Mem. Profit Sharing Investment Com., 1970—. Bd. dirs. Alcoholic Beverage Control, 1971—. Served with AUS, 1943-45. Decorated Bronze Star. Mem. Alpha Phi Delta. Democrat. Presbyterian (deacon 1970—). Elk. Club: Oakwoods Country. Home: 1114 Brookwood Dr Wilkesboro NC 28697

GARRETT, LARRY VICK, ice cream mfg. co. exec.; b. St. Louis, Sept. 14, 1946; s. Marion Vick and Mary Lois (Graham) G.; B.S. in Bus. Adminstrn., S.E. Mo. State U., Cape Girardeau, 1972; m. Nancy Ann Bullard, Aug. 30, 1969; children—Angela Christine, Larry Shaun. Mgr. self-service gas stas., Cape Girardeau, 1970-73; shift foreman Kroger Egg Plant, Jackson, Mo., 1972-73; successively area mgr., dist. mgr., regional mgr. Autotronic Systems, Inc., Dallas, 1973-76; dir. franchise sales Polar Bear Ice Cream Co., Dallas, 1976—. Served with USAR, 1967-68; Vietnam. Decorated Bronze Star. Home: 2717 Hilldale Blvd Arlington TX 76016 Office: 400 S Zang St Suite 1216 Dallas TX 75208

GARRETT, RICHARD CARL, state ofcl.; b. Battle Creek, Mich., Sept. 11, 1940; s. Carl Sanford and Gertrude Maragret G.; B.S. in Law Enforcement Eastern Ky. U., 1974, M.S. in Criminal Justice, 1976; m. Charlene Ann Boston, Jan. 5, 1967; 1 son, Richard Carl. Enlisted in U.S. Navy; service in Greenland, 1963, Vietnam, 1965-67; sr. patrolman Battle Creek (Mich.) Police Dept., 1967-72: with Ky. Dept. Justice, Richmond, 1974—, instr., coordinator basic police tng., 1974-77, program supr. spl. agys. tng., 1977—; adj. prof. Eastern Ky. U., 1974—. Adv. explorer post Blue Grass council Boy Scouts Am., Richmond. Mem. Nat. Assn. State Dirs. Law Enforcement Tng., Am. Soc. Indsl. Security, Nat. Rifle Assn. Mem. Christian Ch. Club: Mason. Homes: University Mobile Home Park #57 Richmond KY 40475 Office: 313 Stratton Bldg Eastern Ky U Richmond KY 40475

GARRETT, RICHARD EDWARD, educator; b. Roanoke, Va., Feb. 17, 1922; s. James Paul and Elizabeth Marie (Craig) G.; B.S., Roanoke Coll., 1942; M.S., Ga. Inst. Tech., 1950; Ph.D. (Dupont fellow), U. Va., 1953; m. Gene Alice Harvath, June 4, 1947. Instr. to asst. prof. physics, math. Roanoke Coll., 1942-43, 46-48; instr. physics Ga. Inst. Tech., 1948-50, U. Va., 1950-53; asso. prof. physics Hollins Coll., 1953-63; research asso. U. Va., 1962-63; asso. prof. physics U. Fla., 1963-70, prof., 1970—. Vis. lectr.; editorial cons. to pubs. Served with USNR, 1943-46; PTO. Mem. Am. Phys. Soc., Am. Assn. Physics Tchrs. (sec.-treas. Fla. sect. 1966-70), AAAS, Fla. (pres. 1971-73), Va. (chmn. 1961) acads. sci., Sigma Xi, Sigma Pi Sigma. Home: 537 NW 34th Terr Gainesville FL 32607 Office: U Fla Gainesville FL 32611

GARRETT, ROSA MARTIN, occupational therapist; b. Belfast, No. Ireland, June 18, 1949; d. William Head and Maureen (Baird) Martin; came to U.S., 1949, naturalized, 1958; B.S., Tex. Woman's U., 1972; m. James Francis Garrett, Jr., Dec. 30, 1970. Rehab. occupational therapist Dallas Home Jewish Aged, 1972-74, dir. occupational therapy, 1974—; adj. faculty Tex. Woman's U., N.E. La. State U., U. Tex. Med. Br., Galveston; mem. workshop faculty U. Tex. Health Sci. Center, Dallas, 1973. Mem. Am. (commn. on edn. 1979), Tex. (chmn. by-law com. 1977-79, conf. chmn. 1977, gerontology liaison 1977-79), Trinity N. Tex. (chmn. continuing edn. 1974-75) occupational therapy assns. Home: 1506 Englecrest Richardson TX 75801 Office: 2525 Centerville Rd Dallas TX 75228

GARRIS, STEVE CALHOUN, ednl. adminstr.; b. Kingstree, S.C., Sept. 10, 1946; s. Scenus Berry and Ann Neal (Martin) G.; A.B., Erskine Coll., 1968; M.Ed., U. S.C., 1971, M.B.A., 1975; m. Sarah Elizabeth Richardson, Aug. 28, 1972; children—Sally Sue, Robert. Supr., insp. S.C. Dept. Edn., 1971-72; mgr. personnel services U. S.C., Columbia, 1972-79, asst. dir. Daniel Mgmt. Center, 1979—, lectr., 1976—. Served with AUS, 1969-71. Mem. Am. Soc. Personnel Adminstrs., Coll. and Univ. Personnel assn., S.C. Assn. Higher Continuing Edn., Carolina Soc. Tng. and Devel., Columbia Personnel Assn. Methodist. Club: De Bordian Colony. Editor: Personnel Jour. Am. Soc. Personnel Adminstrs., 1978—; contbr. articles to profl. jours. Home: 6007 Woodvine Rd Columbia SC 29206 Office: Daniel Mgmt Center Coll Bus Adminstrn U SC Columbia SC 29208

GARRISON, ROBERT EDWARD, II, finance co. exec.; b. Freeport, Tex., Mar. 25, 1942; s. Robert Edward and Berneice Agnes (Hammar) G.; A.A., Lon Morris Coll., 1962; B.B.A., U. Tex., 1964, M.B.A., 1965; m. Carol Jane Morrison, Nov. 28, 1964; children—Melanie, Claire. Security analyst, portfolio mgr. Equitable Life Assurance Soc. N.Y., N.Y.C., 1965-69; v.p., Bus. Devel. Services, Inc. subs. Gen. Electric Corp., N.Y.C., 1969-71; v.p., dir. research Underwood Neuhaus & Co., Houston, 1971—; lectr. in field; dir. Avant Inc., Vital Assits, Matcon. Chartered fin. analyst, Tex. Mem.

N.Y., Houston socs. security analysts, Fin. Analyst Fedn., Inst. Chartered Fin. Analysts. Clubs: Houston, Westside Tennis. Home: 12127 Mossycup St Houston TX 77024 Office: 724 Travisat Rusk St Houston TX 77002

GARRISS, PHYLLIS WEYER (MRS. W. P. GARRISS), educator; b. Hastings, Neb., Dec. 25, 1923; d. Frank Elmer and Mabelle (Carey) G.; A.B., Hastings Coll., 1945, Mus.B., 1945; Mus.M., Eastman Sch. Music, U. Rochester, 1948; m. William Philip Garriss, Aug. 28, 1954; children—Daniel Weyer, Meredith Carey, Margaret Elizabeth. Instr. mus. theory, violin DePauw U., Greencastle, Ind., 1948-51; vis. prof. violin Ball State Coll., Muncie, Ind., summers, 1951, 53; asst. prof. violin, theory Meredith Coll., Raleigh, N.C., 1951—. Mem. Tri-City Chamber Symphony, 1951—, Roanoke Symphony, 1954—, Duke U. Symphony, 1954—; tchr. Cannon Music Camp, Appalachian State U., Boone, N.C., summers 1971—. Mem. Raleigh Civic Council, 1958-60. Mem. Raleigh Chamber Music Guild (dir.), N.C. Art Soc., N.C. Fedn. Music Clubs, Nat. Assn. Amateur Chamber Music Players, A.A.U.W., A.A.U.P. (sec. chpt. 1961), Am. String Tchrs. Assn. (corr. sec. 1950-54), Music Educators Nat. Conf., Music Tchrs. Nat. Assn., Raleigh Concert Music Assn. (dir.), Am. Fedn. Musicians (dir. local), P.E.O., Mu Phi Epsilon, Pi Kappa Lambda. Presbyterian. Home: 3400 Merriman Ave Raleigh NC 27607

GARRITY, THOMAS ANTHONY, JR., lawyer, geophysicist; b. New Orleans, Aug. 17, 1925; s. Thomas Anthony and Viola Louisa (Roser) G.; Geophys. Engr., Colo. Sch. Mines, 1952; LL.B., U. N.Mex., 1964, J.D., 1968; m. Betty Jean Greenlee, May 1, 1953; 1 son, Thomas Anthony. Div. review geophysicist Pure Oil Co., Tulsa, 1952-57; chief seismic interpretations Creole Petroleum Co., Lake Maracaibo, Venezuela, 1957-61; admitted to N.Mex. bar, 1964, Tex. bar, 1977, U.S. Supreme Ct. bar, 1968; atty. advisor Albuquerque Field Solicitor's Office, U.S. Dept. Interior, 1964-73, field solicitor, Tex., Amarillo, 1973—; spl. asst. to U.S. Atty., N.Mex., 1969—; geophys. cons., 1964-76. United Fund rep. at various times, 1967-75. Served with USAAF, 1942-46. Recipient spl. achievement award U.S. Dept. Interior, 1973-74; registered profl. engr., N.Mex. Mem. Soc. Exploration Geophysicists (treas. Venezuela chpt. 1960), Panhandle Geologic Soc. Tex., N.Mex. (editorial bd. Jour. 1968-69), Amarillo, Fed. (pres. N.Mex. chpt. 1969) bar assns., Albuquerque Lawyers Club. Mem. coms. U. N.Mex.; Indian Law Seminar, 1967, Geothermal Seminar, 1966; chmn. Water Quality Seminar, 1968; active Law Days, 1966-67, 69-70, 71; author: Water Law Atlas, 1967; research editor Natural Resources Jour., 1963-64; patentee analog computer; contbr. research writings to profl. publs. in field. Home: 3706 Rutson Dr Amarillo TX 79109 Office: Box H-4393 Herring Plaza Amarillo TX 79101

GARTEN, VERL RANDOLPH, electronic engr.; b. Keota, Okla., Apr. 24, 1934; s. Theodore Elmer and Beulah Mae (Davis) G.; A.S. in E.E., Tulsa Tech. Coll., 1957; M.R.E., Am. Bible Inst., 1964; E.E., Cleve. Inst. Electronics, 1974; M.S. in Psychology, Northwestern U., 1974; Ph.D. in Psychology, Neotarian Coll., 1978. TV repairman Garten TV Service, 1958-60, Gem TV Service, 1960-64, Garten, Eagleberger, Moore, 1960-64, White City Truck Stop, 1964-68; electronics engr., test equipment supr. Zenith Electronics, McAllen, Tex., 1968—. Leader Boy Scouts Am, 1959—, recipient award of merit, Silver Beaver award, others; former gov. Am. Health Alliance; former v.p. Muscular Dystrophy Assn.; mem. Am. Heart Assn., Cerebral Palsy Assn.; vol. counselor Women Together; public relations, counselor Parents Without Partners; former fund raiser United Fund; instr., donor ARC; pres., speaker Unitarian Fellowship. Home: 316 Daffodil St McAllen TX 78501 Office: 6601 S 33d St McAllen TX 78501

GARTMAN, MAX DILLON, educator; b. Mobile, Ala., May 3, 1938; s. Noah Christopher and Edna Olga (Schwartzauer) G.; B.A., Samford U., 1960; M.A., U. Ala., 1962, Ph.D., 1973; m. Marcia Ann Hubbard, Aug. 31, 1962; children—Noel Don, Polly Antoinette, Paul Dillon. Instr., grad. fellow U. Ala., Tuscaloosa, 1960-65; instr. Stillman Coll., Tuscaloosa, 1964; prof. Romance langs. Samford U., Birmingham, 1965—, head dept. fgn. langs., 1974; minister of music Vestavia Hills Bapt. Ch., Birmingham, Ala., 1965-69, Boyles Bapt. Ch., Birmingham, 1969-72, Raleigh Ave. Bapt. Ch., Birmingham, 1972—. Mem. Birmingham Com. on Fgn. Relations, 1976—. NDEA fellow, 1960-64; U. Ala. Grad. fellow, 1961-64. Mem. Ala. Assn. Fgn. Lang. Tchrs. (pres. 1971-72), Ala. Assn. Tchrs. French (v.p. 1970), Am. Assn. Tchrs. French, So. Conf. Lang. Teaching (chmn. 1976), S. Atlantic Modern Lang. Assn., Am. Assn. Tchrs. Spanish and Portuguese, Phi Kappa Phi, Tau Kappa Alpha, Theta Alpha Phi, Phi Alpha Theta, Pi Delta Phi, Sigma Delta Pi, Omicron Delta Kappa. Republican. Baptist. Club: Kiwanis. Editor Faculty Forum Annual, 1969-74, Am. Assn. Tchrs. French Newsletter, 1969-73, Dimension: Languages, 1976. Home: 1121 Crest Ave Birmingham AL 35209 Office: Dept of Fgn Lang Samford U Birmingham AL 35209

GARTON, CHARLES EUGENE, real estate broker and developer; b. Jane Lew, W.Va., Dec. 25, 1921; s. George Mertz and Christina Catherine (Mason) G.; student U. Okla., 1945; m. Opal Mae Dunham, May 3, 1941; children—Stephen S., Deborah Garton Gibson, Melissa Garton Wilson, Charles Gregory. Pres., gen. mgr. Garton Real Estate, Inc., Weston, W.Va., 1962—; pres. Garton Real Estate & Constrn., Inc., Weston, 1978—, GCH Devel., Inc., Weston, 1973—. Served with USNR, 1944-46. Mem. W.Va. Assn. Realtors, Lewis County C. of C., Nat. Homes Corp. (adv. com.), Am. Legion. Republican. Roman Catholic. Clubs: Deerfield Country, Moose, K.C. Home: PO Box 747 421 Main Ave Weston WV 26452 Office: PO Box 747 467 Main Ave Weston WV 26452

GARTRELL, FRANCIS EUGENE, cons. engr.; b. Nesbitt, Miss., July 21, 1913; s. Francis Eugene and Gladys Estelle (Williamson) G.; B.S. in Elec. Engring., Miss. State U., 1933; M.S. (Gordon McKay scholar), Harvard U., 1935; M.P.H. (Rockefeller Found. fellow), Johns Hopkins U., 1944, Dr.P.H., 1954; m. Mabel Louise Lee, Mar. 28, 1934; 1 dau., Frances Lee Gartrell Brabston. Engring. and adminstrv. positions TVA, 1936-51, asst. dir. health, Chattanooga, 1951-69, dir. environ. research and devel., 1969-72, dir. environ. planning, 1972-73; cons. engr., Chattanooga, 1974—; cons. WHO, Geneva, TVA, Knoxville; air pollution panel U.S.-Japan Coop. on devel. natural resources, 1965-70; mem. U. Tenn. Environ. Com., 1970-73; atomic indsl. forum com. on environment, 1972-73. Recipient award Nat. Coal Assn., 1974; diplomate Am. Acad. Environ. Engrs. Mem. AAAS, Am. Mosquito Control Assn., Air Pollution Control Assn., Nat., Tenn. socs. profl. engrs. Baptist. Contbg. author: Air Pollution, 1962, 68, 77; contbr. tech. publs. in fields of malaria control, insecticides, stack gases, water resource devel., pollution control, environ. protection. Home and Office: 3114 Colyar Dr Chattanooga TN 37404

GARVER, LOUIS RALPH, advt. exec.; b. New Orleans, Sept. 24, 1924; s. Thomas Earl and Albertine (Leon) G.: B.B.A., Tulane U., 1949; m. Audrey Rosemary Prindle, Sept. 1, 1951; children—Susan, Steven, John, Scott. Acct., So. Bell Telephone Co., 1949-51; editor Gilmore Sugar Manuals, 1951-54; dist. mgr. John Budd Co., New Orleans, 1955-60; dist. mgr. Branham Co., New Orleans, 1960-67; v.p., dir. George H. Lehleitner & Co., Inc., New Orleans, 1968—. Served with USNR, 1943-46. Mem. La. Assn. Broadcasters, La. Assn. Appliance Dealers, Beta Gamma Sigma. Episcopalian. Home: 4009 N Labarre Rd Metairie LA 70002 Office: PO Box 52409 New Orleans LA 70152

GARVEY, CHARLES CARTER, newspaper exec.; b. New Orleans, Aug. 22, 1916; s. Walter M. and Nadine Beatrice (Carter) G.; B.S. in Bus. Adminstrn., La. State U.; m. Mary Lollie Brousseau, Feb. 10, 1942; children—Charles Garvey, Mary Garvey Frye, Mike, Anne, Jim. With Sta. WJBO, 1947-54, gen. mgr., 1954; retail advt. mgr. State-Times & Advocate, Baton Rouge, 1954-61, advt. dir., 1961-67, bus. mgr., 1967-77, v.p. bus. and advt., 1977—; dir. Capital Savs. Assn. Served with USNR, 1941-45. Mem. Baton Rouge Advt. Club (Pres.), Midwest Newspaper Advt. Execs. Assn. (past pres.), Baton Rouge Sales and Mktg. Execs. Club (past pres.). Democrat. Roman Catholic. Club: City (Baton Rouge). Home: 8371 Highland Rd Baton Rouge LA 70808 Office: 525 Lafayette St Baton Rouge LA 70821

GARVIN, BARNEY WILLARD, oil co. exec.; b. New Holland, S.C., Aug. 15, 1904; s. Ernest Luther and Annabel (Courtney) G.; student Clemson (S.C.) U., 1924-25; B.S., N.C. State U., Raleigh, 1925. Dist. mgr. S.C. Electric & Gas Co., Florence, 1935-42; engr. S.C. Public Service Authority, Columbia, 1943; cotton broker, Aiken, S.C., 1944-45; farmer Wagener, S.C., 1932—; owner, operator Garvin Oil Co., Inc., Wagener, 1958—. Bd. dirs. Shriners' Children's Hosp., Greenville, S.C. Mem. Sigma Chi. Democrat. Baptist. Clubs: Palmetto (Columbia); Houndslake Country (Aiken); Masons, Shriners (pres. Florence 1937-39), Jesters, Rotary (pres. Florence 1939-40). Home and Office: Route 1 Box 352 Wagener SC 29164

GARWOOD, THOMAS CHASON, JR., lawyer; b. Jacksonville, Fla., July 12, 1944; s. Thomas Chason and Anna (McCracken) G.; B.A. with honors in Internat. Affairs, Fla. State U., 1965; J.D., Stetson U., 1971; m. Brenda Kay Borders, Sept. 17, 1977; children by previous marriage—Thomas Chason, Shara Christiansen, Whitney Walker. Admitted to Fla. bar, 1971; partner firm Akerman, Senterfitt & Eidson, Orlando, Fla., 1974—; adj. prof. Rollins Coll., 1980—; atty. Orlando Civil Service Bd., 1976—. Served with USN, 1966-69; Vietnam. Mem. Am. Bar Assn., Fed. Bar Assn., Fla. Bar Assn., Orange County Bar Assn. Republican. Presbyterian. Club: Bay Hill Country. Contbr. articles to legal publs. Home: 4352 Player Circle Orlando FL 32804 Office: PO Box 231 Orlando FL 32801

GARY, ALBERT LEE, psychologist; b. Hamilton County, Tenn., Apr. 20, 1935; s. Hal B. and Sarah (Lee) G.; A.B., Ga. State U., 1967, M.Ed., 1969; Ed.D., U. Tenn., 1973; scholar Stanford U. Sch. Social Research, 1978; m. Dorothy Thomas, July 1, 1954; children—Albert Scott, Kandace, Erika. Co-founder, corp. officer Area Psychiat. Clinic, Chattanooga, 1975-76; asso. prof. counseling edn. U. Tenn., Chattanooga, 1974-77, Found. prof., 1975—; pvt. practice psychology, Hixson, Tenn., 1977-79, Orlando, Fla., 1979-80, Dayton, Tenn., 1980—; psychologist Tepper Hosp.; cons. HEW; dir. Team Evaluation Center; psychol. rep. on child abuse Tenn. Rev. Bd. Mem. Am. Personnel and Guidance Assn., Am. Psychol. Assn., Southeastern Psychol. Assn., Chattanooga Psychol. Assn. Club: Masons. Contbr. articles to internat. psychol. jours. Research in behavior modification and personality theory. Office: Rhea County Med Center Dayton TN 37321

GARZA, CARLOS ROMEO, ofcl. Dept. Energy; b. Edinburg, Tex., Nov. 4, 1931; s. Jose G. and Tomasa (DeLaGarza) G.; B.A., U. Tex., 1958, J.D., 1960; m. Marlena Leticia, Aug. 4, 1957; children—Marla, Monica, Katy, Laura, Jose. Admitted to Tex. bar, 1960; asst. dist. counsel C.E., U.S. Army, Galveston (Tex.) Dist., 1960-66; asst. counsel Johnson Space Center, NASA, Houston, 1966-70, chief, contractor equal opportunity programs, 1970-72, chief counsel, equal opportunity officer Flight Research Center, Edwards, Calif., 1972-76; mem. bd. contract appeals ERDA, Washington, 1976-77; mem. bd. contract appeals Dept. Energy, Washington, 1977—; vice chmn., 1979, mem. invention lic. appeals bd., 1978—, mem. fed. assistance appeals bd., 1979—. Active YMCA, P.T.A.; area 4 mem. Greater L.A. Community Action Agy.; v.p. Lancaster (Calif.) council League United Latin Am. Citizens, 1973-74; chmn. bd. dirs. Antelope Valley Community Action Center, 1973—; mem. Hispanic ad hoc energy com., 1976—. Served with USAF, 1950-54. Recipient Equal Employment Opportunity award NASA, 1972. Mem. Tex., Bar Assn., Fed. Bar Assn. (dir. 1978—), D.C. Bar Assn., Hispanic Bar Assn. (dir. 1978—), Nat. Conf. Bd. of Contract Appeals Mems. (sec. 1979). Home: 2411 Riviera Dr Vienna VA 22180 Office: 4040 N Fairfax Dr Rm 1009 Arlington VA 22203

GARZA, PETER DELEON, banker; b. Asherton, Tex., Nov. 7, 1948; s. Antonio Chapa and Josefina Deleon G.; student Tex. Tech. U., 1968-72, Amarillo Coll., 1974-77, Advanced Sch. Banking, Tex. Tech. U., 1977; m. Dominga Cuevas, Dec. 31, 1971; 1 son, Michael. Drug salesman Sav-A-Stop, Lubbock, Tex., 1972; public relations officer First State Bank, Dimmitt, Tex., 1972-73, asst. cashier, 1973—, now installment loan officer. Pres., Dimmitt United Lions, 1973-74, Tex. Panhandle Community Action Corp., 1979; bd. dirs. Dimmitt United Way, 1976; scoutmaster Boy Scouts Am., 1973—, mem. exec. bd. S. Plains council, 1979; com. chmn. Mexican-Am. community Re-Elect Jimmy Davis for Dist. Atty., 1978, Elect Kent Mance as Congl. Rep., 1978. Named Outstanding Young Man of Am., Jr. C. of C., 1976. Mem. Am. Bankers Assn., Tex. Bankers Assn., Dimmitt Jr. C. of C. (treas. 1972-73). Home: Box 571 404 NW 3d St Dimmitt TX 79027 Office: Box 929 Dimmitt TX 79027

GARZA, REYNALDO G., fed. judge; b. Brownsville, Tex., 7, 1915; s. Ygnacio and Zoila (Guerra) G.; B.A., LL.B., U. Tex.; LL.D. (hon.), U. St. Edwards, Austin, Tex., 1965; m. Bertha Champion, June 9, 1943; children—Reynaldo G., David C., Ygnacio Damiel, Bertha Victoria, Monica Bernadette. Admitted to Tex. bar, 1939; pvt. practice, 1939-42, 46-50; partner firm Sharpe, Cunningham & Garza, 1950-60, Cunningham, Garza & Yznaga, 1960-61; U.S. dist. judge So. dist. Tex., Brownsville, 1961—, chief judge, 1974-79; judge U.S. 5th Circuit Ct. of Appeals, 1979—; Treas. Cameron County Child Welfare Bd., 1950-52; mem. Tex. Good Neighbor Commn., 1957-61. Commr., City Brownsville, 1947-49. Trustee Brownsville Ind. Sch. Dist., 1941-42. Served with USAAF, 1942-45. Recipient Pro Ecclesia et Pontifica medal Pope Pius XII, 1952; decorated knight Order St. Gregory the Great, Pope Pius XII, 1954. Mem. Am., Cameron County bar assns., State Bar Tex. Office: PO Box 1129 Brownsville TX 78520*

GASKINS, AUBREY SYLVESTER, assn. exec.; b. Norfolk, Va., Dec. 3, 1921; s. Benjiman Sylvester and Nettie May (Horne) G.; B.S., U. Md., 1957; student Air Command and Staff Coll., 1960, Air War Coll., 1971; m. Graham Conway Atkinson, May 1, 1942; children—Mary Graham Hundley, Ann Forbes Wright, Susan Conway. Staff, Chesapeake & Potomac Telephone Co., 1940-42; commd. 2d lt., A.C., U.S. Army, 1943, advanced through grades to col., combat tour 58 missions, Korea, 1948-51, dir. maintenance Air Force Communications Services, 1956-60, European Communications Area, 1960-64, Air Staff, 1964-68, Joint Command Vietnam, 1969, wing comdr. Air Force Communications Service, Kansas City, Mo., 1970-72, staff Joint Chiefs Staff, Washington, 1973; ret., 1973; exec. dir. public affairs No. Va. Bd. Realtors, Merrifield, 1973—; exec. v.p. Virginia Beach (Va.) Bd. Realtors, Inc., 1979—. Decorated Legion of Merit with 2 oak leaf clusters, D.F.C., Air medal with 9 clusters, Meritorious Service medal, Joint Service medal. Mem. Am. Soc. Assn. Execs., Air Force Assn., Ret. Officers Assn. Republican. Methodist. Club: Army-Navy Country (Arlington, Va.); Masons (32 deg.), Shriners Home: 1269 Southfield Pl Virginia Beach VA 23452 Office: Virginia Beach Bd Realtors Inc 222 Mustang Trail Virginia Beach VA 23452

GASKINS, WILLIAM JOHN, logging contractor; b. New Bern, N.C., Sept. 11, 1916; s. Daniel and Elizabeth (Potter) G.; student pub. schs., Bridgeton, N.C.; m. Marie Fulcher, Oct. 9, 1936; children—Sara Lou Gaskins Bass, William John. Logging contractor, pulpwood producer and dealer, N.C., 1938-57; contractor Weyerhaeuser Co., New Bern, 1957—; chmn. bd., pres. W. J. Gaskins & Son, Inc., New Bern, 1971—; partner Gaskins Saw & Equipment Co., 1966—. Mem. N.C. Forestry Assn., Eastern N.C. Assn. Loggers (sec. treas. 1965-68), New Bern C. of C. Democrat. Baptist. Home: Bil-Rie Acres PO Box 1614 New Bern NC 28560

GASPERONI, EMIL, real estate exec.; b. Hillsville, Pa., Nov. 13, 1926; s. Attico and Rose Mary (Sarnicola) G.; diploma real estate, U. Pitts., 1957; m. Ellen Jean Lias, May 28, 1955; children—Samuel Dale, Emil Attico, Jean Ellen. Owner, pres. Gasperoni Real Estate, New Castle, Pa., 1956-63, Ft. Lauderdale, Fla., 1970—; founder, chmn. bd. Fill-R-Up Auto Wash Systems Inc., Ft. Lauderdale, 1967-70; pres. Investment Property Adv. Corp., Ft. Lauderdale, 1975—. Mem. com. 100, Broward Inds 1. Bd., Ft. Lauderdale. Served with U.S. Army, 1945-46; ETO. Mem. Nat. Inst. Real Estate Brokers, Internat. Real Estate Fedn., Nat. Soc. Fee Appraisers, Fla. Assn. Mortgage Brokers. Clubs: Coral Ridge Golf and Country (Ft. Lauderdale); Lake Toxaway (N.C.) Country. Home: 4201 NE 25th Ave Fort Lauderdale FL 33308 Office: 2501 E Commercial Blvd Fort Lauderdale FL 33308

GASQUE, MARVIN KENNETH, advt. exec.; b. Charlotte, N.C., Dec. 21, 1943; s. Thomas Baker and Hallie Marjory (Huntley) G.: student E. Carolina U., 1962-67; m. Jeanne Hough, Feb. 14, 1967 (div.); children—Marelyn Renee, Thomas Baker II. Creative dir. Jefferson Standard Broadcasting Co., Charlotte, 1967-72; art dir. Hellems-McKnight Advt. Agy., Columbia, S.C., 1972-73; pres., creative dir. Ken Gasque & Assos. (formerly M.G. Graphics), Columbia, 1973—; adv. graphic art Central Piedmont Community Coll.; instr. U. S.C. Sch. Journalism. Recipient numerous profl. awards. Mem. Columbia Soc. Communicating Art, Charlotte Soc. Communicating Arts. Club: Lake Murray Sail. Office: M G Graphics Inc Box 32 Columbia SC 29202

GASS, ROBERT LOUIS, JR., furniture co. exec.; b. Murray, Ky., Jan. 8, 1943; s. Robert Louis and Mildred (Childers) G.; student Broward Community Coll., 1961-62, Murray U., 1962-63, Am. Inst. Banking, 1967-72; m. Victoria Fuhrer, Aug. 21, 1965; children—Kimberly Ann, Kelly Elizabeth. With finance div. Gen. Electric Co., West Palm Beach, Fla., 1965-66; with trust dept. Landmark First Nat. Bank, Ft. Lauderdale, Fla., 1967-72; pres. Mar-Tec Corp., Ft. Lauderdale, 1972—. Group leader United Fund of Broward County, 1973. Mem. Ft. Lauderdale Young Republican Club, Ft. Lauderdale C. of C., S.Fla. Mfg. Assn. (chmn.). Kiwanian. Home: 1752 NE 1st St Fort Lauderdale FL 33301 Office: 900 SW 20th Way Fort Lauderdale FL 33312

GASSET, ANTONIO RAMON, physician; b. Havana, Cuba, Feb. 8, 1936; came to U.S., 1961, naturalized, 1969; s. Antonio and Maria (Rossello) G.; B.S., Colegio de Belen, Cuba, 1954; postgrad. U. Havana, 1955-61; M.D., Boston U., 1966; m. Gloria M. Perez-Subirats, Nov. 4, 1961; children—Anthony, Carin, Edward. Intern, St. Elizabeth's Hosp., Boston, 1966-67; corneal fellow Retina Found., Boston, 1967; resident in ophthalmology Shands Teaching Hosp., U. Fla., Gainesville, 1967-71; practice medicine specializing in ophthalmology, Miami, Fla.; asst. prof. ophthalmology, chief Contact Lens Clinic, Shands Teaching Hosp., U. Fla., 1971—; mem. staff Miami Eye Inst., 1979—; chmn. dept. ophthalmology Am. Hosp. Recipient Lincoln-Marti award HEW, 1973, Juan J. Remos award, 1972, Rudolph Ellender Med. Found. award, 1971; diplomate Am. Bd. Ophthalmology. Mem. Am. Assn. Ophtalmology, Assn. Research in Ophthalmology, Cuban Soc. Surgeons, Am. Soc. Contemporary Ophthalmology, Pan-Am. Assn. Ophthalmology, Contact Lens Soc. of Ophthalmologists (Hunter H. Romain Meml. award 1968), Dade County Med. Soc., Fla. Soc. Ophthalmology, AMA (award 1969), Fla. Med. Assn., AAAS, Mexican Ophthalmologists Soc. (hon. mem.), Boston U. Alumni Assn., U. Fla. Dept. Ophthalmology Alumni. Contbg. author to chpts. for books on ophthalmology; (with M.H. Uotila) Fitting Manual in Soft Lens Symposium, 1972; contbr. numerous articles in field to profl. jours.; editor Soft Contact Lens Symposium, 1972. Home: 11860 SW 47th St Miami FL 33175 Office: Miami Eye Institute Inc 11880 Bird Rd Miami FL 33175

GASTON, GRGGORY DAVID, advt. agy. exec.; b. Okmulgee, Okla., Feb. 7, 1949; s. Dale Leon and Minnie Jo (Gregory) G.; student Northeastern State Coll., Tahlequah, Okla., 1967-69; B.A. in Journalism, U. Okla., 1978; m. Vicki Ann Jamison, July 1, 1973; children—Stacy Heather, Matthew Gregory. Reporter, feature writer Okla. Daily, Norman, 1969-70, acct. mgr., 1970; sales rep. McAlester (Okla.) News Capital, 1970; account exec. Sta. WNAD, Oklahoma City, 1973-74; promotion asst. WKY Radio and TV, Oklahoma City, 1974-75; creative dir., account exec. Gordon-Keitzman-Dennis, Inc., Oklahoma City, 1976, v.p. consumer/retail div., 1976-77; field account exec. N.Y. Ayer ABH Internat., Brandon, Miss., 1977—. Served with USNR, 1971-72. Recipient 1st pl. Addy awards Oklahoma City Ad Club, 1976, 77; award of excellence 19th Dist., Am. Advt. Fedn., 1977. Mem. Am. Advt. Fedn., Memphis Advt. Fedn., Greater Jackson Advt. Club, Sigma Delta Chi. Home and Office: 48 Sagewood Dr Brandon MS 39042

GASTON, PATRICIA MAE, sociologist, educator; b. Birmingham, Ala., Apr. 8, 1949; d. Arthur George and Sally Dean (Robinson) G.; B.A., Miles Coll., 1970; M.A., Atlanta U., 1972. Sociol. researcher U. Ala., Birmingham, 1970-72; instr. sociology Lawson State Community Coll., Birmingham, 1972—. Mem. Ala. Ednl. Assn., NEA, Nat. Urban League, Am. Assn. Women in Community and Jr. Coll., So. Sociol. Soc. Lutheran. Home: PO Box 2401 Birmingham AL 35201 Office: Lawson State Community Coll 3060 Wilson Rd Birmingham AL 35221

GASTON, ROBERT OTIS, computer co. exec.; b. Fort Worth, Tex., Apr. 12, 1942; s. Winfred Robert and Thelma (Vance) G.; student U. Tex. at Austin, 1960-61, Baylor U., 1963-64; B.B.A., Midwestern U., 1967; m. Linda Lou Shaw, Mar. 1, 1968; children—Jeffery Scott, Emily Ann. With IBM, Dallas, 1967-69; v.p. systems Omnis Corp., Dallas, 1969-70, pres., 1970-72; v.p. systems and services Tres Computer Systems, Dallas, 1972-77, sr. v.p., 1977—, also dir., mem. exec. com. Bd. dirs. Edna Gladney Home, Fort Worth, 1971-75. Mem. Am. Mgmt. Assn., Assn. Computer Machinery, Beta Alpha Psi, Alpha Chi. Home: 3220 Forester Way Plano TX 75075 Office: 4255 LBJ Freeway Dallas TX 75234

GASTON, WARREN EDWARD, univ. adminstr., educator; b. Dallas, Oct. 14, 1930; s. Charlie Ray and Gladys (Murphy) G.; B.A., Columbia Bible Coll., 1953; postgrad. U. Algiers, 1954-56, Hartford Sem. Found., 1958-59, U. Pa., 1968-69; M.A., U. Tenn., 1968, Ed.D., 1974; m. Mildred Louise Stout, May 28, 1951; children—Warren Edward, John Steven, Charles Alan. Instr. Missionary Training Sch., Tunis, Tunisia, 1957-58; dir. ext. div. N. Africa Mission, Tunis, 1961-63, Marseille, France, 1963-67, adminstrv. sec. N. Am., Phila., 1968-69; instr. dept. foreign langs. U. Tenn., Knoxville, 1969-74, asst. prof., 1974-78, asso. prof., 1978—, asst. dean admissions and records, 1974—; cons. Oak Ridge Schs., 1973, Chattanooga Sch. Dist., 1972, 73. Mem. Modern Lang. Assn., S. Atlantic Modern Lang. Assn., Tenn. Philological Assn., Am. Council Teaching Fgn. Langs., Tenn. Fgn. Lang. Tchrs. Assn., Am. Assn. Tchrs. Arabic, Tenn. Consortium Asian Studies, AAUP, Nat. Assn. Self-instructional Lang. Programs (dir., pres. 1978-79), Phi Kappa Phi, Pi Delta Kappa, Phi Delta Kappa. Democrat. Home: 224 Druid Dr Knoxville TN 37920 Office: 305 Student Services Bldg U Tenn Knoxville TN 37916

GASTON, WILLARD FORREST, hosp. exec.; b. O'Donnell, Tex., Aug. 4, 1929; s. William Forrest and Katie (Lawson) G.; cert. in Personnel Mgmt., LaSalle U., 1966; student UCLA, 1948-51, U. Richmond, 1967-69; m. Carolyn Russell, Feb. 18, 1956; children—Larry Gene, Michael Forrest. Enlisted in U.S. Navy, 1948; resigned, 1963; personnel dir. Maryview Hosp., Portsmouth, Va., 1963—; minister Bowers Hill Ch. of Christ, 1972-78. Mem. adv. bd. Tidewater Community Coll., 1975-79, Lic. Practical Nurse Sch., 1968-78; chmn. panel of budget com. United Fund, 1977-78. Mem. Am. Hosp. Assn., Am. Soc. Hosp. Personnel Adminstrn., Va. Assn. Hosp. Personnel Adminstrn., Tidewater Assn. Hosp. Personnel Adminstrn., Tidewater Hosp. Council. Democrat. Mem. Ch. of Christ. Home: 3522 Forest Haven Ln Chesapeake VA 23321 Office: 3636 High St Portsmouth VA 23707

GATCHEL, JOSEPH ANDREW, educator; b. Winterset, Iowa, May 6, 1914; s. Manning Andrew and Goldie (Evans) G.; student Moody Bible Inst., 1942-44, New Tribes Missionary Center, Chgo., 1944; B.S., So. Bible Coll., 1964, Th.B., 1967, D.D. (hon.), 1979; m. Eliza May Lattin, Aug. 12, 1936; children—Ronald Andrew, Lois Mae. Ordained to ministry Pentecostal Ch. of God, 1942; pastor, Kansas City, Mo., 1940-42; pioneer missionary for orgn., Kona, Hawaii, 1946-56; founder, supt., dir. Pentecostal Bible Inst., San Fernando, La Union, Philippines, 1958-63; chmn. div. ministries, mem. bd. adminstrn. So. Bible Coll., Houston, 1964—, prof. dept. missions, 1964—, dir. summer overseas missionary work for students, 1970—; mem. adv. bd. World Missions Bd., Pentecostal Ch. of God, 1965—. Mem. Assn. Evangelical Profs. of Missions. Office: So Bible Coll 10950 Beaumont Hwy Houston TX 77078

GATELY, STEVEN FRANK, artist, educator; b. West Palm Beach, Fla., Nov. 24, 1946; s. George Henry and Isobel Doris (Castiglioni) G.; A.A., Palm Beach Jr. Coll., 1966; B.F.A., Fla. Atlantic U., 1968; M.F.A., Fla. State U., 1971. Asst. prof. art Francis Marion Coll., Florence, S.C., 1973—; one-man shows include: Coker Coll., Hartsville, S.C., 1974, Florence Mus., 1975; group shows include: High Mus. Art, Atlanta, 1969, Hunter Mus. Art, Chattanooga, 1976, Mint Mus. Art, Charlotte, N.C., 1977, 79; represented in permanent collections: Fine Arts Mus. of the South, Mobile, Ala., Columbia (S.C.) Mus. Art, Gibbes Art Gallery, Charleston, S.C., Art Collection State S.C., Southeastern Center Contemporary Art, Winston-Salem, N.C. Recipient Purchase award Columbia Mus. Art, 1977; S.C. Arts Commn. fellow, 1977. Mem. Guild S.C. Artists. Office: Francis Marion Coll Florence SC 29501

GATENBEE, ELIZABETH ROBBINS, bearings co. exec.; b. Louisville, Feb. 24, 1916; d. Orlando Douglass and Elizabeth (Holtzhauer) Robbins; spl. student Tarkio Coll., 1955-56; m. Robert James Gatenbee, Sept. 11, 1934; children—Robert James, John Douglass. Sec., Ky. Bearings Service, Inc., Louisville, 1934-48, 57-60, exec. v.p., 1973—, also dir.; dir. So. Bearings Service, Inc., Knoxville/Kingsport, Tenn., Ky. Bearings Service Eastern Div., Inc., Lexington. Mem. D.A.R., Daus. Founders and Patriots. Home: PO Box 336 Pewee Valley KY 40056 Office: 1524 Algonquin Pkwy Louisville KY 40210

GATENS, BARBARA ELIZABETH, audiologist; b. Charleston, W.Va., Sept. 22, 1952; d. Maurice Edward and Janette Elizabeth (Popp) Gatens; B.S. in Speech and Hearing Sci., Ohio U., 1974, M.A. in Audiology, 1975. Med. audiologist Otolaryngol. Consultants, West Chester, Pa., 1975-76; audiology cons. La Motte Clinic, Hilton Head Island, S.C., 1976-78; dir. audiology St. Joseph's Hosp., Savannah, Ga., 1977—; condr. local lipreading classes, sign lang. course, 1976—; vol. lectr. for service groups on speech and hearing problems, 1977—. Vol. various service projects. Lic. pvtvpvt. pilot. Mem. Am. Speech, Hearing and Lang. Assn. (cert. clin. competance), So. Audiological Soc., Savannah Speech and Hearing Study Group, Aircraft Owners and Pilots Assn., Ladies Golf Assn. Clubs: Volleyball, Racquetball. Home: 5502 Treetops Hilton Head Island SC 29928 Office: St Joseph's Hosp 11705 Mercy Blvd Savannah GA 31406

GATES, DAVE LOWRY, JR., univ. adminstr.; b. Houston, Jan. 6, 1942; s. Dave Lowry and Frances Elizabeth (Lyles) G.; B.S. magna cum laude, U. Houston, 1962; M.A., U. So. Calif., 1966; LL.D., U. Tex., San Antonio, 1969; Ph.D., Tex. A&M U., 1973; children—Caton Merrill, Ian David. Prof., Alvin Jr. Coll., 1963-65; asst. to pres. Sam Houston State U., 1967-70; asst. to pres. U. Tex., San Antonio, 1970-72; asst. provost U. Houston at Clear Lake City, 1973-76; v.p. for mgmt. Tex. Woman's U., Denton, Tex., 1976-77, v.p. for acad. affairs, 1977—; mem. nat. bd. advisors Am. Inst. Fgn. Study. Democrat. Home: 1721 Teasley Ln 161 Denton TX 76201 Office: Tex Woman's Univ Denton TX 76204

GATES, JESSE LAMAR, JR., jr. retail store exec.; b. Jackson, Miss., Feb. 7, 1940; s. Jesse Lamar and Juanita (Van Zandt) G.; student Hinds Jr. Coll., Jackson, 1957-58, Miss. State U., 1959-61; m. Peggy S. Prisk, Apr. 18, 1971; 1 son, Jason Lamar. Mgmt. trainee Midland Container Corp., Jackson, 1966-67, dir. personnel, then dir. personnel and safety, 1967-72; employment mgr. Jitney Jungle Stores Am., Jackson, 1972-76, dir. employment and EEO, 1976—; curriculum adv. to mgmt. dept. Hinds Jr. Coll., 1976—. Active local Jr. Achievement, 1975—, United Way; mem. adv. council Urban League, 1978—; mem. Pvt. Industry Council, 1978—. Served with USAR, 1961-66. Mem. Am. Soc. Personnel Adminstrn., Am. Soc. Tng. and Devel., Mid-South Mgmt. Conf., Central Miss. Mgmt. Assn. Methodist. Club: Masons. Home: 64 Sumac Dr Madison MS 39110 Office: 453 N Mill St Jackson MS 39205

GATES, LESLIE CLIFFORD, cons. engr.; b. Dorothy, W.Va., Nov. 17, 1918; s. Lauren Adolphus and Lillian (Sandburg) G.; B.S. in Civil Engring., Va. Poly. Inst., 1940; m. Martha Rose Shrewsbury, Dec. 21, 1940; children—Ellen Elaine Gates Anderson, Leslie Allen. Field party Solvey Process Co., Hopewell, Va., 1940-41; asso. Gates Engring. Co. (formerly Ferguson-Gates Engring. Co.), cons. engrs., 1946-54, partner, 1955-58, owner, 1958-62, pres., 1962-79, chmn., chief exec. officer, 1979—; dir. Cardinal State Bank. Mem. W.Va. Registration Bd. Profl. Engrs., 1965—, pres., 1969-70, 74-75; trustee Engring. Index Inc. Mem. advisory bd. Salvation Army, 1956-59; pres. Beckley Bus. Devel. Corp., 1965, Raleigh County United Fund, 1965, Raleigh County Citizens Scholarship Assn., 1966; mem. advisory bd. W.Va. U., 1970—. Served from 2d lt. to maj. U.S. Army, 1941-46: ETO. Registered profl. engr. W.Va., Ky., Ohio, Pa., Ill., Tenn., Wyo., Utah, Va., Mont., Ind., Ariz., Colo., Wash., N.Mex., N.D. Fellow ASCE; mem. Am. Rd. Builders Assn. (dir. planning and design div. 1970-73), W.Va. C. of C. (v.p. 9th dist. 1972—, pres. 1978-79), Beckley-Raleigh County C. of C. (pres. 1953), Flat Top Lake Assn. (pres. 1965), Nat. (pres. 1974-75, v.p. Central region 1967-69, chmn. policy rev. com. 1971-72), W.Va. (pres. 1951) socs. profl. engrs., Am. Inst. Mining Engrs. (chmn. Central Appalachian sect. 1965-66), Am. Mining Congress, Am. Water Works Assn., W.Va. Coal Mining Inst., Colo. Mining Assn., Ill. Mining Inst., Am. Concrete Inst., Am. Arbitration Assn., Nat. Coal Assn., Am. Soc. Engring. Edn. Presbyn. (elder). Rotarian (pres. 1962-63). Home: 21 Flat Top Lake Ghent WV 25843 Office: PO Drawer AF Beckley WV 25801

GATES, MAC STUART, clergyman, sch. adminstr.; b. Romeo, Mich., June 24, 1914; s. Ernest E. and Mary (Stuart) G.; student Moody Bible Inst., 1942-44; B.A. cum laude, Ouachita Bapt. U., 1948; student U. Ark., 1950, 53; M.S. in Edn., Henderson State Tchrs. Coll., 1956; m. Mary E. Brown, Jan. 21, 1949; step-children—Mary P. (Mrs. Jerry Howell), Rual T. Lee. Ordained to ministry Baptist Ch., 1945; pastor-evangelist, 1940-48; pastor Glenwood (Ill.) United Ch., 1944-45, 1st Bapt. Ch., Bingen, Ark., 1945-49, Walnut Valley Ch., 1950-56, Riverside Ch., Donaldson, Ark., 1956-59; adminstr. Malvern (Ark.) pub. schs., 1948—, fed. coordinator, dir. early childhood edn., 1975—; mission pastor 1st Bapt. Ch., Malvern, 1959-65; prin. Malvern Jr. High Sch., 1952-75; pastor 2d Bapt. Ch., Bryant, Ark., Salem Bapt. Ch., Benton, Ark., 1970-72, Mountain Valley Bapt. Ch., Hot Springs, Ark., 1972-75, Hurricane Lake Bapt. Ch., 1975—; lectr. series, Edn., Now, 1965—. Mem. Hot Spring County Library Bd., 1955-57; sec., publicity dir. Malvern City Planning Commn., 1952-65; mem. State Com. Guidance and Selection Audio-Visual Materials; chmn. Malvern Housing Authority, 1966—; chmn. Malvern Civil Service Commn., 1973. Mem. Photographers Internat. Assn., Nat., Ark., Hot Spring County (pres. 1956-57) edn. assns., Ark. Hist. Assn., Ouachita Valley Schoolmasters Assn. (past pres.), Ams. United for Separation of Ch. and State (Malvern pres. 1973), Phi Delta Kappa (historian Henderson State Coll. chpt. 1970). Home: 2017 Wilson Malvern AR 72104 Office: 404 N Banks St Malvern AR 72104

GATEWOOD, WILLARD BADGETT, JR., historian; b. Pelham, N.C., Feb. 23, 1931; s. Willard Badgett and Bessie Lee (Pryor) G.; B.A., Duke U., 1953, M.A., 1954, Ph.D., 1957; m. Mary Lu Brown, Aug. 9, 1958; children—Willard Badgett, III, Elizabeth Ellis. Asst. prof. history East Tenn. State U., 1957-58, East Carolina U., 1958-60; asso. prof. N.C. Wesleyan Coll., 1960-64; prof. U. Ga., 1964-70; Alumni Distinguished prof. history U. Ark., 1970—. Recipient Parks Excellence in Teaching award, Phi Alpha Theta, 1970, Michael Research award, 1967. Truman Library fellow, 1963; Acad. Arts, Scis. grantee, 1962. Mem. Am., So., Ark. hist. assns., Orgn. Am. Historians, Assn. Study Afro-Am. Life and History, Phi Beta Kappa. Presbytgrian. Author books including: Theodore Roosevelt and the Art of Controversy, 1970; Smoked Yankees, 1971; Black Americans and the White Man's Burden, 1975; bd. editors Ga. Rev., 1968-70, Jour. Negro History, 1972-74. Home: 1651 Cleveland St Fayetteville AR 72701 Office: Ozark Hall U Ark Fayetteville AR 72701

GATHERCOLE, PATRICIA MAY, linguist, educator; b. Erie, Pa., Oct. 5, 1920; d. John William Gathercole and Iris (Beech) Gathercole Thompson; B.A., U. B.C., 1941, M.A., 1942; Ph.D., U. Calif., Berkeley, 1950. Instr., U. B.C., 1950-53, U. Oreg., 1953-56; asst. prof. fgn. langs. Roanoke Coll., Salem, Va., 1956-57, asso. prof., 1957-65, prof., 1965—, chmn. dept., 1970—; panelist fellowships Nat. Endowment Humanities, 1975-77. Lay reader Episcopal Ch. Fulbright fellow, 1955; Southern U. fellow, 1958-60; Mellon fellow, 1977-79. Mem. AAUW (past pres. Roanoke br.), Am. Assn. Tchrs. French, MLA, Mediaeval Acad., Internat. Arthurian Soc., Dante Soc., Am. Assn. Tchrs. Italian, Fgn. Lang. Assn. Va. Republican. Author: Laurent de Premierfait's Des Cas, 1969; Tension in Boccaccio, 1975; contbr. articles to profl. jours. Home: 423 Highfield Rd Salem VA 24153 Office: Dept Fgn Langs Roanoke Coll Salem VA 24153

GATHINGS, JOHN MILTON, accountant; b. Bastrop, La., Aug. 8, 1953; s. Marion Milton, Jr. and Trudy Mae (Williamson) G.; B.B.A., N.E. La. U., 1974; m. Wanda Gail Patrick, Dec. 1972; 1 son, John Milton, II. Pvt. practice acctg., Oak Grove, La., 1974-75, 77—; asst. liason ofcl. fed. employment program West Carroll (La.) Parish Police, 1975-76; jr. acct. H.C.H., C.P.A.'s, New Iberia, La., 1976-77. Mem. Oak Grove Jaycees (dir.). Democrat. Baptist. Clubs: Lions (chmn. fin. com. 1979), Moose (sec. 1974-76), Masons (Oak Grove). Address: PO Box 791 Hwy 2 E Oak Grove LA 71263

GATLIFF, BEN FRANKLIN, physician; b. Macon, Ga., Jan. 19, 1922; s. Benjamin and Mellie (Corley) G.; B.S., U. Ga., 1948; M.D., Med. Coll. Ga., 1952; m. Marion Hays, Aug. 19, 1950; children—Gary Edwin, Eda Marie, Laural Francis. Intern, Orange Meml. Hosp., Orlando, Fla., 1952-53; pvt. practice medicine specializing in gen. practice, Plant City, Fla., 1953—; staff mem. South Fl. Bapt. Hosp., Plant City, chief of staff, 1959-60. Served from pvt. to T/5, AUS, 1943-45. Mem. AMA, Fla. Med. Assn., Theta Kappa Psi. Episcopalian. Named Ky. col. Home: 716 Pinedale Dr Plant City FL 33566 Office: 402 Dort St Plant City FL 33566

GATTIS, ELVIS FRANKLIN, sheet metal contractor; b. Jacksonville, Tex., Aug. 21, 1932; s. Arnett M. and Bertha A. (Yancy) G.; student U. Houston, 1972-73; m. Annie Joyce Ermel, June 20, 1953; children—Elvera, Gary, Lera, Jerry. With Straus-Frank Co., Houston, 1951-53, 1954-58, A & M Sheet Metal, Houston, 1958-59; owner E.F. Gattis Sheet Metal, Houston, 1959-66; pres., chief exec. officer Gattis Inc., Houston, 1966—. Mem. Houston Sheet Metal Contractors Assn. (dir. 1969-70, 78-79, pres.-elect 1980), Am. Soc. Heating, Refrigerating and Air-Conditioning Engrs., Nat. Assn. Sheet Metal and Air-Conditioning Contractors, Tex. Environ. Balancing Bur., Gideons Internat., Internat. Biog. Centre (Eng.) Baptist (deacon). Woodman of World. Home: 746 Sue Barnett Houston TX 77018 Office: 1615 Keene Houston TX 77009

GATTIS, JOHN EDWARD, electronic engr.; b. Paris, Ark., Mar. 29, 1934; s. Clark Edward and Jewell Linda (Titsworth) G.; student Ark. Tech. Coll., 1953-54; B.S. Elec. Engring., U. Ark., 1961; m. Alma Dean Dorrough, Mar. 13, 1955; 1 dau., Pamela Kay. Electronic engr. Western Electric Co., Inc., Winston-Salem, N.C., 1961-63; aerospace engr. Saturn IB, Saturn V, Apollo, Skylab and Space Shuttle space programs NASA, Marshall Space Flight Center, Huntsville, Ala., 1963—. Served with AUS, 1954-57. Recipient Apollo achievement award, 1969, Outstanding Performance award, 1972, Dir.'s commendation for Skylab, 1973, Skylab Achievement award, 1974, Space Shuttle Group Achievement award, 1976 (all NASA). Registered profl. engr., Ala. Baptist. Home: 10117 Dunbarton Dr SE Huntsville AL 35803 Office: EF 12 Marshall Space Flight Center AL 35812

GATTON, ROBERT LAURENCE, ednl. adminstr.; b. Ft. Wayne, Ind., Sept. 21, 1937; s. James Walter and Virginia Evelyn (Geyer) G.; B.A., Union Coll., 1960, M.A. (Nat. Def. Edn. Act fellow), 1963; postgrad. U. Ky., 1964-65; Ed.D. (U.S. Office Edn. fellow, W.K. Kellogg Found. fellow), U. Fla., 1971; m. Christine Dale Banks, Jan. 22, 1960; children—Robert Earl, Melissa Anne. Tchr. English and social studies Cumberland (Ky.) High Sch., 1960-61, Whitesburg (Ky.) High Sch., 1961-64; prin. Eolia (Ky.) Consol. Sch., 1966-69; dean Brenau Acad., Gainesville, Ga., 1971-72; headmaster Wilkes Acad., Washington, Ga., 1972-74; prin. Cowen Sch., Whitesburg, Ky., 1974—. Sec. Letcher County (Ky.) United Way Fund; adv. bd. Union Coll., Barbourville, Ky.; bd. dirs. U. Ky. S.E. Center, Cumberland. Named hon. Ky. col. Mem. Am. Assn. Sch. Adminstrs. (life), NEA, Ky. Assn. Elem. Sch. Prins. (regional rep. to state bd.), Pi Gamma Mu, Kappa Delta Pi, Phi Delta Kappa. Home: Box 460 Cowan Creek Whitesburg KY 41858

GAUDIERI, ALEXANDER VINCENT JOSEPH, museum dir.; b. Columbus, Ohio, Apr. 23, 1940; s. Alexander V. and Olga A. G.; student Ohio State U., 1958-62, Sorbonne, U. Paris, 1962-63, Colgate U., 1963, (Barton Kyle Young scholar) Am. Grad. Sch. Internat. Commerce, 1964-65, N.Y. U., 1972-76; m. Millicent Hall, June 10, 1967; 1 son, Alexandre Barclay Everson. Internat. banking officer Marine Midland Bank, N.Y.C., 1965-72; dir. Telfair Acad. Arts and Scis., Inc., Savannah, Ga., 1977—; vis. lectr. Armstrong State Coll. Chmn., Nat. Council, Young Concert Artists; chmn. jr. com. Harlem Sch. of Arts. Mem. Am. Assn. Museums, Assn. Art Mus. Dirs., Soc. Archtl. Historians, Appraisers Assn. Am. Club: Rotary. Office: Telfair Acad Arts and Scis Inc 121 Barnard St Savannah GA 31401

GAUDIN, HOMER CHARLES, judge; b. New Orleans, July 14, 1930; s. Regis B. and Inez C. (Grenier) G.; student La. State U., 1947-50; B.A., U. Southwestern La., 1952; LL.B., Loyola U., New Orleans, 1958; postgrad. U. Pa., 1967, U. Nev., 1970, U. Colo., 1975, U. N.H., 1976; m. Myra Elizabeth Altman, June 8, 1956; children—Melanee Anne, Monique Grenier, Charles Altman. Head football and basketball coach St. Paul's Coll., Covington, La., 1954-55; sports columnist New Orleans States-Item newspaper, 1956-66; admitted to La. bar, 1958; practiced in New Orleans and Gretna, La., 1958-66; dist. judge 24th Jud. Dist. Ct., Gretna, 1966—, chief judge, 1976-78. State pres. Nat. Cystic Fibrosis Research Found. Served with USAF, 1952-54. Mem. Am., La., Jefferson Parish bar assns., La. Dist. Judges Assn. (dir.), Am. Judicature Soc., N. Am. Judges Assn., Fourth Circuit Judges Assn. (pres.), VFW, Am. Legion, Amvets, Delta Theta Phi. Roman Catholic. Lion. Club: New Orleans Country. Home: 28 Farnham Pl Metairie LA 70005 Office: New Parish Courthouse Gretna LA 70053

GAUNCE, JAMES RICHARD, ednl. adminstr.; b. Shelbyville, Ind., June 19, 1932; s. Herman Francis and Helen Marie (Young) G.; B.A., Asbury Coll., 1957; M.A., Western Carolina U., 1973; m. Avanelle Gravley, June 28, 1952; children—Deborah, Carol, Belinda, Teresea. Tchr., Whitfield County, Ga., 1958-65; ordained to ministry Evang. Meth. Ch., 1956, Baptist Ch., 1973; minister Evang. Meth. Ch., Dalton, Ga., 1958-65; tchr. Mobile County, Ala., 1965-68; minister Evang. Meth. Ch., Bayou La Batre, Ala., 1965-68; tchr. Spartanburg (S.C.) Sch. Dist. 6, 1968-74, prin., 1974—; pres. South Mobile Ministries, 1966-68. Bd. dirs. Westview Athletic Assn. Served with AUS, 1952-54. Mem. NEA, S.C. Assn. Sch. Adminstrs., Assn. Supervision and Curriculum Devel., S.C. PTA (hon.). Democrat. Clubs: Lions, Ruritan (v.p. 1972). Research on mental health and elem. student. Home and Office: Box 195 Pauline SC 29374

GAUNCE, JUDITH COMBS, retail furniture co. exec.; b. Nov. 15, 1943; d. J. Gordon and Martha (Hollon) Combs; R.N., Good Samaritan Hosp. Sch. Nursing, 1964; m. David Gaunce, Apr. 3, 1964; children—Brennan, Chad. Staff nurse Eastern State Hosp., Lexington, Ky., 1964-65; staff nurse VA Hosp., Lexington, 1965-66; indsl. nurse Hoover Ball Bearing Co., Georgetown, Ky., 1966-70; owner, mgr. Gaunce's Hearth & Patio Shop, Lexington, Ky., 1974—. Democrat. Home: 940 Turkey Foot Rd Lexington KY 40502 Office: 2350 Woodhill Center Lexington KY 40509

GAUSMAN, HAROLD WESLEY, physiologist; b. Morris, Minn., Dec. 23, 1921; s. Emil Henry and Kate Emma (Heick) G.; B.S. with distinction, U. Maine, 1949; M.S., U. Ill., 1950, Ph.D., 1952; m. Laura Ellen Davis, Feb. 3, 1945; 1 son, Donald Harris. Research asst. U. Ill., Urbana, 1949-52; scientist Tex. A. and M. U., College Station, 1952-54; research specialist Rutgers U., New Brunswick, N.J., 1954-55; faculty U. Maine, Orono, 1955-67, prof. soil chemistry, 1957-67; research leader U.S. Dept. Agr., Agrl. Research Service, Weslaco, Tex., 1967—; radiation protection officer U. Maine, Orono, 1956-60, chmn. grad. faculty Coll. Agr., 1965-66. Served with USAAF, 1942-45. NSF Research fellow, 1964. Mem. Am. Soc. Agronomy, Am. Inst. Biol. Scis., Am. Soc. Plant Physiology, AAAS, Am. Soc. Photogrammetry, Societas Physiologiae Plantarum Scandinavia, Sigma Xi, Phi Kappa Phi, Alpha Zeta, Gamma Sigma Delta, Phi Sigma. Contbr. articles in field to books and profl. jours. Home: 502 W 11th St Weslaco TX 78596 Office: Box 267 Weslaco TX 78596

GAUSTER, CHRISTIAN BELRUPT, assn. exec.; b. St. Gilgen, Austria, Dec. 30, 1945; came to U.S., 1950, naturalized, 1954; s. Wilhelm Friedrich and Marietta (Belrupt) G.; B.A., U. Tenn., 1966, M.A., 1972; M.S.I.M., Ga. Inst. Tech., 1977. Teaching fellow U. Tenn., 1966-68; lectr., devel. coordinator dept. modern langs. Ga. Inst. Tech., 1968-75; spl. courses instr. Lockheed-Ga. Co., Marietta, Ga., 1975-76; meetings adminstr., adminstr. profl. devel. ops. council TAPPI, Atlanta, 1979—. Mem. Ga. Soc. Assn. Execs., Am. Soc. Tng. and Devel., TAPPI, Atlanta Hist. Soc., Mems. Guild of High Mus. Art. Democrat. Roman Catholic. Clubs: Cath. Alumni, Alumni Ga. Inst. Tech., Alumni of U. Tenn. Home: 3660 Shadow Ln Atlanta GA 30319 Office: One Dunwoody Park Suite 130 Atlanta GA 30338

GAUT, JIMMY LEE, oil co. exec.; b. Wann, Okla., Dec. 14, 1939; s. Anderson Byrne and Mildred Mary G.; B.A., U. Okla., 1962; student U. Tulsa Law Sch., 1964, 65; m. Brenda Lynette Nelson, May 28, 1977; children—Michelle Leigh, Kristie Morgan, Kerrie Morgan, Greg Morgan. File clk., roustabout Cities Service Co., Bartlesville and Walter Okla., 1958-62; credit rep. Internat. Harvester Co., Oklahoma City, 1962-64; contract analyst Cities Service Co., Bartlesville, 1964-67, joint interest rep., Houston, 1968-72, region officer mgr., 1973-78, region services mgr., 1978—; treas. Prode Inc., Houston, 1972-74; owner, mgr. J. L. Gaut Real Estate Investments, Houston, 1973—. Cities Service rep. United Way, 1973-78. Served with U.S. Army, 1963-69. Mem. Houston C. of C., Tex. Assn. Bus. Republican. Baptist. Home: 13238 Rain Lily Ln Houston TX 77083 Office: 5100 Southwest Freeway Houston TX 77027

GAUTHIER, THOMAS RUGG, cons. metallurgist; b. Waterloo, Iowa, Apr. 15, 1918; s. Thomas Louis and Alice Edna (Rugg) G.; B.S. in Chem. Engring., Iowa State U., 1940; M.S. in Metall. Engring., Case Inst. Tech. (name changed to Case-Western Res. U.), in advanced mgmt. Princeton U., 1972, 1941; postgrad. Allegheny Coll., 1973-78, Sandhills Community Coll., 1978-79; m. Phyllis Irene Peterson, Aug. 23, 1941; children—Sherry Irene Gauthier Slawski, Gwedolyn Lucille Gauthier Weller. Staff metallurgist Aluminum Co.

Am., Cleve., 1940-45, chief control metallurgist, Pitts., 1945-51, chief metallurgist of forgings, Cleve., 1951-57, chief metallurgist Cleve. ops., 1957-62, chief metallurgist Tenn. ops., 1962-65, chief staff metallurgist, Pitts., 1965-69, chief metallurgist and exec. sec. research and devel., 1965-78; cons. non ferrous metallurgy, 1975—; lectr. U. Tenn., 1962-65; adv. dept. metallurgy Vanderbilt U., 1962-65; metall. adv. Service Corps Ret. Execs. Adv. for Jr. Achievement, Pitts., 1967-75; elder First Presbyn. Ch., Northfield, Ohio, 1955-67; bd. visitors U. Pitts., 1967-75, U. Pa., 1967-75; bd. dirs. Renaissance for Gifted Children, Pitts., 1975-80; chmn. Am. Cancer Soc., Pinehurst, 1980. Mem. Am. Inst. Mining and Metall. Engrs., Am. Soc. for Metals, Metals Properties Council (dir., exec. com.), Brit. Inst. Metals, Navy League, Nat. Geog. Soc., Wilderness Soc., World Golf Hall of Fame (exec. sponsor), U.S. Golf Assn. (patron), Audubon Soc., Sigma Xi, Phi Delta Theta. Republican. Presbyterian. Clubs: Duquesne, St. Clair Country (Pitts.); Cleve. Athletic, Boston Heights Country (Cleve.); Green Meadow Country (Alcoa, Tenn.); Pinehurst (N.C.) Country. Contbr. numerous articles on metallurgy to sci. publs.; pioneer in forging of beryllium and titanium for space capsules and inventor of several aluminum and magnesium casting methods. Home: 228 Gingham Ln PO Box 953 Pinehurst NC 28374

GAUTREAUX, MARCELIAN FRANCIS, JR., chem. co. exec.; b. Nashville, Jan. 17, 1930; s. Marcelian Francis and Mary Eunice (Terrebonne) G.; B.S. in Chem. Engring. magna cum laude, La. State U., 1950, M.S. in Chem. Engring., 1951, Ph.D. in Chem. Engring., 1958; m. Mignon Alice Thomas, Apr. 26, 1952; children—Marcelian Francis, Marian, Kevin, Andrée. Chem. engr. process design Ethyl Corp., Baton Rouge, 1951-55, head engring. and math. scis. dept., 1958-59, asst. dir. process devel., 1959-62, dir. chem. engring., 1962-66, tech. dir., research and devel. dept., 1966-68, gen. mgr. research and devel. dept., 1968-69, v.p., 1969-74, sr. v.p., 1974—, also dir.; Instr. chem. engring. La. State U., Baton Rouge, 1955-56, asst. prof., 1957-58. Bd. dirs. Baton Rouge Community Concerts Assn., 1974—; trustee La. Arts and Sci. Center, 1974-77. Recipient PACE award, 1968; Charles E. Coates Meml. award, 1976; Chem. Mktg. Research annual Meml. award, 1978; charter mem. La. State U. Engring. Hall of Distinction, 1978. Mem. Nat. Acad. Engring., Am. Inst. Chem. Engrs., Soc. Chem. Industry, Soc. Engring. Sci. (bd. dirs. 1972-75). Roman Catholic. Clubs: Baton Rouge Country, Baton Rouge City, Baton Rouge Camelot. Patentee numerous items; contbr. articles to profl. jours. Home: 1662 Pollard Pkwy Baton Rouge LA 70808 Office: PO Box 341 Baton Rouge LA 70821

GAUTREAUX, MICHAEL SIDNEY, ins. agt.; b. Attleboro, Mass., Jan. 11, 1949; s. Lawrence J. and Annette G.; B.S. in Indsl. Engring., U. R.I., 1972; M.B.A., U. Ga., 1974. Comml. acct. exec. Pruden Ins. Agy., Inc., Dalton, Ga., 1972-73; v.p., comml. account exec. Athens Insurers Inc., (Ga.), 1973—. C.P.C.U. Mem. Ind. Ins. Agts. Ga., Ind. Ins. Agts. Athens (past pres.), Phi Kappa Phi, Beta Gamma Sigma. Home: PO Box 761 Athens GA 30603 Office: PO Box 626 Athens GA 30603

GAY, BIRDIE SPIVEY, librarian; b. Atlanta, Mar. 13, 1918; d. Charlie Warren and Bertha (Harris) Spivey; A.B., Morris Brown Coll., 1939; M.S. in L.S., Atlanta U., 1962; m. Howard Donald Gay, Nov. 24, 1943. Mem. staff, faculty E.R. Carter Elementary Sch., Atlanta, 1946—, librarian, 1959-70, media specialist, 1970—. Mem. com. on adminstrn. YWCA, Atlanta, 1969-72; neighborhood chmn. fund drive Easter Seal Drive, 1968-71. Named Tchr. of Year, E.R. Carter Elementary Sch., 1961. Mem. A.L.A., Ga. Library Assn., Am. Assn. Sch. Librarians, N.E.A., Ga., Atlanta assns. educators, Morris Brown Coll. Alumni Assn., United Negro Coll. Fund, NAACP, Am. Bus. Women's Assn., Beta Phi Mu, Sigma Gamma Rho (Distinguished Service plaque 1970). Club: Nancy Bridge (Atlanta). Home: 1874 Penelope Rd NW Atlanta GA 30314 Office: 80 Ashby St NW Atlanta GA 30314

GAY, DAVID EDWARD RYAN, economist; b. Bryan, Tex., Sept. 19, 1945; s. John Gordon and Emma Louise (Ryan) G.; B.A., Tex. A&M U., 1968; Ph.D. (NDEA fellow), 1973; postdoctoral Kans. U., 1974, U. Chgo., 1979, U. Miami, 1980. Asst. prof. econs. U. Ark., Fayetteville, 1973-77, asso. prof., 1977—; vis. scholar U. Glasgow (Scotland), 1975, Hoover Instn. Stanford U., 1975. Bd. dirs. N.W. Ark. Community Concerts, 1975-76, Tex. A&M Opera and Performing Arts Soc., 1972-73; bd. govs. Ark. Union, 1977-79. Mem. Am. Econ. Assn., Am. Fin. Assn. (life), Eastern Econ. Assn. (founding, life), Public Choice Soc., Royal Econ. Soc. (life), So. Econ. Assn. (life), Western Econ. Assn. (life), Beta Gamma Sigma, Alpha Kappa Psi, Omicron Delta Epsilon, Western Social Sci. Assn. (exec. council), Mid-South Acad. Economists (exec. council). Republican. Methodist. Editorial bd. Ark. Bus. and Econ. Rev., 1976—; contbr. articles to profl. jours. Office: Dept Econs U Ark Fayetteville AR 72701

GAY, JACQUELYN BLOCKER, nurse, hosp. ofcl.; b. Savannah, Ga., Sept. 21, 1927; d. Joseph Jackson and Margaret Alwilda (Davis) Blocker; R.N., Warren A. Candler Hosp. Sch. Nursing, 1945-48; student Armstrong State Coll., 1953-54; m. Robert Earl Gay, Jan. 28, 1948; children—Rebecca Lynn, Robert Daniel, Jack Michael. Staff nurse Candler Hosp., Savannah, 1948-49, head nurse, 1950-52, instr. nursing at sch. nursing, 1953-60, dir. spl. edn., 1964-66, dir. surg. services, 1966-73, dir. nursing service Telfair unit, 1973—; lectr. in field. Recipient Boss of Year award Grace Anne chpt. Am. Bus. Women Assn., 1979. Mem. SE Ga. Health Systems, Ga. Nurses Assn., Ga. Hosp. Assn. (exec. bd. 1977—), Am. Soc. Nursing Service Adminstrs., Ga. Soc. Nursing Service Adminstrs., Am. Operating Room Assn., Candler Alumni Council on Nursing for Ga., Nursing Service Adminstrs. SE Dist. (pres. 1977), Nursing Service Adminstrs. for Ga. (pres. 1979). Home: 2004 Bacon Park Dr Savannah GA 31406 Office: Candler Hosp Telfair Unit 17 E Park Ave Savannah GA 31402

GAY, JAMES FERBEE, lawyer, solar energy co. exec.; b. Norfolk, Va., Dec. 9, 1942; s. Milton F. and Thelma (Henderson) G.; B.S., Norfolk State Coll., 1965; J.D., U. Va., 1968; m. Marilynn Miller; 1 son, James Ferbee. Admitted to Va. bar, 1968; market analyst, legal officer Allied Chem. Internat., N.Y.C., 1968-69; asst. to pres. Nat. Bus. League, Washington, 1969, gen. counsel, 1973—; pres. Coastal Pharm. Co., Inc., Norfolk, Va., 1970-77, Energy Dynamics Ltd., Norfolk, 1977—; pres. Ghent Arms Corp., Aqua Dynamics, Ltd., Global Dynamica Ltd. Pres., Va. Coll. Young Democrats, 1967; pres. Tidewater Area Bus. League, 1971. Bd. dirs. Planned Parenthood, United Front for Christian Brotherhood, Norfolk Soc. for Prevention Cruelty to Animals; trustee Norfolk State Coll. Found. Recipient Pres.'s award Tidewater Area Bus. League, 1972; Phi Beta Lambda Bus. Leadership award, 1973. Mem. Am., Va., Old Dominion, Norfolk-Portsmouth bar assns., Am. Judicature Soc., Alpha Phi Alpha. Mem. Ch. of Christ (trustee). Co-author: Rhodes Directory of Black Dentists in the U.S., 1973. Home: 237 Lucian Ct Norfolk VA 23502 Office: 2624 Nevada Ave Norfolk VA 23513

GAY, JAMES ROWLAND, neurologist, neurosurgeon; b. Dunmore, Pa., June 23, 1914; s. Owen W. and Ruth (Lenington) G.; B.S. in Biol. Scis., Va. Poly. Inst., 1935; M.D., Johns Hopkins U., 1939; M.S. in Neurosurgery, U. Minn., 1959; m. Lillian Cabell, July 2, 1940. Intern, Johns Hopkins Hosp., Balt., 1939-41; resident in neurosurgery Mayo Found., Rochester, Minn., 1941-42, 46-49; pvt. practice neurol. surgery, Columbus, Ohio, 1949-53, White Plains, N.Y., 1953-54, Bethlehem, Pa., 1954-61, Albuquerque, 1961-68; asst. dean U. N.Mex. Sch. Medicine, 1968-74, dir. Regional Med. Program, 1971-74; vice chancellor U. Tenn. Center for Health Scis., 1974-77, asso. v.p. for health affairs, 1977—. Served with M.C., U.S. Army, 1942-46; ETO. Decorated Bronze Star; Croix de Guerre with Star, Medal de Reconnaissance Francais (France); diplomate Am. Bd. Psychiatry and Neurology, Am. Bd. Neurol. Surgery. Mem. AMA, A.C.S., Congress Neurol. Surgeons (founder, pres. 1954), Am. Acad. Neurology, Internat. Coll. Surgeons, Am. Assn. Neurol. Surgeons, AAAS, Assn. Am. Med. Colls., Am. Med. Writers Assn., Royal Coll. Surgeons (Eng.), World Fedn. Neurosurg. Socs., Pan Am. Med. Assn., Tenn. Med. Assn., Memphis and Shelby County Med. Soc., Sigma Xi, Phi Kappa Phi. Contbr. articles to profl. jours. Home: 2384 Holly Grove Dr Memphis TN 38138 Office: 62 S Dunlap St Memphis TN 38163

GAY, LEONARD OMAR, retail furniture exec.; b. Georgetown, Ga., Mar. 13, 1919; s. Lee Omar and Emmelle (Hammack) G.; B.B.A., Emory U., 1941; m. Augusta Hixon, June 10, 1942; children—Emily June, Leonard O. Sr. accountant Ernst & Ernst, Atlanta, 1941-47; sr. v.p., treas. Haverty Furniture Cos., Inc., Atlanta, 1947—, dir., 1961—; mem. mgmt. devel. faculty Northwestern U., 1972-77. Dir. Atlanta Better Bus. Bur., 1974-77. Bd. dirs. Atlanta council Camp Fire Girls, Inc., 1971-75; trustee Tift Coll., 1973-78; mem. parents adv. council Wofford Coll., Spartanburg, S.C., 1970-73; bd. visitors Emory U., Atlanta, 1972—; bd. dirs. Am. Furniture Acad. and Hall Fame, 1976, 79. Served as ensign USNR, 1941. Mem. Fin. Execs. Inst. (treas. 1966-67), Am. Retail Fedn. (dir., treas. 1972—), Ga. Soc. C.P.A.'s, Nat. Assn. Cost Accountants (asso. dir.), Nat. Home Furnishings Assn. (dir., pres. 1977-78, chmn. govtl. affairs com. 1972-76, chmn. exec. com. 1978-79), Atlanta Tax Club, C. of C., DeKalb County Grand Jurors Assn., Alpha Kappa Psi. Baptist (chmn. bd. deacons 1967). Kiwanian (trustee found.). Home: 1534 Victoria Falls Dr NE Atlanta GA 30329 Office: 866 W Peachtree St NW Atlanta GA 30308

GAY, RICHARD CALDWELL, ins. co. exec.; b. Takoma Park, Md., Dec. 23, 1934; s. Henry Caldwell and Evelyn (Glenn) G.; A.A., Montgomery Jr. Coll., 1954; B.A., Am. U., 1958; M.A., George Washington U., 1961; m. Barbara Lee Melton, June 19, 1976; children—Brian, Cloanne, Kevin, Cathy, Kim (by previous marriages). Asst. personnel dir., training officer George Washington U., Washington, 1958-62; personnel dir. Washington Hosp. Center, 1962-64; personnel mgr. Intertype Co., Winchester, Va., 1964-66, Stackpole Components Co., Farmville, Va., 1966-67; personnel supr. Fiber Industries, Inc., subsidiary of Celeanese Corp., Salisbury, N.C., 1967-71; pres. Ins. Personnel Resources, Inc., Atlanta, 1971—. Mem. Ga. State Employment Agy. adv. council, 1974-80, vice chmn., 1978-80. Mem. Am. Soc. Personnel Adminstrn., Am. Compensation Assn., Adminstrv. Mgmt. Soc., Nat. Assn. Personnel Cons. (bd. dirs. 1979-80, area dir. 1979-80), Ga. Assn. Personnel Cons. (pres. 1974, dir. 1974—). Republican. Methodist. Home: 4795 Longchamps Dr NE Atlanta GA 30319 Office: 1155 Hammond Dr Suite 5250 Atlanta GA 30328

GAY, WILLIAM WALLACE, telephone co. exec.; b. Meridian, Miss., Jan. 18, 1928; s. William Raymond and Lula Mae (Lucy) G.; B.S., U. So. Miss., 1951, M.A., 1953; m. Mary Elizabeth Trussell, Aug. 21, 1949; 1 son, William Alan. Tchr., Forrest County (Miss.) Schs., 1951-52; instr. extension dept. U. So. Miss., 1951-53; jr. engr. So. Bell Telephone Co., Jackson, Miss., 1953-55, statis. accountant, Atlanta, 1955-59, staff statistician, 1959-65, supervising statistician, 1965-68; bus. research mgr. S. Central Bell Telephone Co., Birmingham, Ala., 1968—. Precinct leader DeKalb County (Ga.) Republican Party, 1966-68; mem. DeKalb County Rep. Exec. Com., 1967-68; mem. 4th Congl. Dist. Ga. Rep. Exec. Com., 1967-68. Served with USAAF, 1945-48. Mem. Am. Mktg. Assn. (v.p., dir. Birmingham chpt.). Club: Optimist of Shades Valley (pres. Homewood, Ala. 1971-72). Home: 3273 Brashford Rd Birmingham AL 35216 Office: PO Box 532 Birmingham AL 35201

GAYAO, LAURENCE TABANAO, physician; b. Kalasungay, Malabalay, Bukidnon, Philippines, Feb. 23, 1946; s. Anastacio Berial and Vivencia (Tabanao) G.; B.A., Philippine Union Coll., 1966; M.D., U. of the East, 1971; m. Edith Cabus, Feb. 13, 1972; children—Lorraine, Lawrence, Lorena Mae, Chester. Med. resident Mindanao Sanitarium and Hosp., Iligan City, Philippines, 1971-73; gen. practice medicine, McCamey, Tex., 1973-74; resident family practice physician Tex. Tech. U., Lubbock, 1974—; practice family medicine, Clyde, Tex., 1975—; chmn. bd. Callahan Gen. Hosp., 1975—, Comfort Community Hosp., 1979—; city health officer Clyde, 1976—. Diplomate Am. Bd. Family Practice. Mem. AMA (Physician's Recognition award 1977), Tex. Med. Assn., Am. Acad. Family Practice, Tex. Assn. Family Physicians, Gospel Music Assn. Republican. Seventh-day Adventist. Composer gospel song I'm in Love, True Happiness, 1979. Home: North Village Baird TX 79504 Office: 216 Oak St Clyde TX 79504

GAYLE, JOHN BEN, mgmt. scientist, educator; b. Scottsboro, Ala., May 26, 1924; s. John B. and Sallie Ruth G.; B.S., U. Ala., 1949, M.S., 1951, Ph.D., 1954; m. Jean Elizabeth Wallace, Sept. 23, 1945; children—Jacqueline Sue, Sandra Louise, Barbara Lucille. With Bur. Mines, Tuscaloosa, Ala., 1946-61, chief coal research lab., 1954-61; chief phys. chemistry sec. Marshall Space Flight Center, 1961-66; chief Reliability and Quality Assurance Office, Kennedy Space Center, 1966-70, chief contract adminstrn., 1970-72, chief lab. div., 1972-78; asso. prof. mgmt. sci. Fla. Inst. Tech., Melbourne, 1978—. Mem. Am. Inst. Decision Scis., Sigma Xi. Democrat. Methodist. Contbr. articles to profl. jours. Home: Route 2 Box 63E10 Titusville FL 32780 Office: Dept Mgmt Sci Fla Inst Tech Melbourne FL 32901

GAYLE, JOHN MARSHALL, textile machinery co. exec.; b. Houston, Mar. 5, 1909; s. John Marshall and Mazyck Lillian (Walker) G.; Textile Engr., Ga. Sch. Tech., 1931; m. Marie Fowler, Oct. 30, 1931; children—Beverly Fowler, Glenda Marie. Plant mgr. Ross Fabrics, Morganton, N.C., 1947-51, Brookline Fabrics, Greenville, S.C., 1951-53; gen. mgr. Gastonia Weaving Co. (N.C.), 1953-60; v.p. Watson & Desmond Machinery Co., Charlotte, N.C., 1960-73; pres. JMG Textile Machinery, Inc., Gastonia, 1973—. Served with USN, 1943-45. Democrat. Baptist. Clubs: Rotary, Masons, Shriners, Elks. Home: 520 Hawthorne Ln Gastonia NC 28052 Office: JMG Textile Machinery Inc 625 E 2d Ave Gastonia NC 28052

GAYLORD, EDWARD LEWIS, pub. co. exec.; b. Denver, May 28, 1919; s. Edward King and Inez (Kinney) G.; B.A., Stanford U., 1941; postgrad. Harvard Bus. Sch., 1942; LL.D., Oklahoma City U., 1966, Okla. Christian Coll., 1968; m. Thelma Feragen, Aug. 30, 1950; children—Christine Elizabeth, Mary Inez, Edward King II, Thelma Louise. Chmn., pres., dir. Gaylord Broadcasting Co. and affiliated stas., Oklahoma City, Mistletoe Express Service, Oklahoma City, 1948—; pres., gen. mgr., dir. Okla. Pub. Co., Oklahoma City, 1955—; editor, pub. Daily Oklahoman, Oklahoma City Times; pres. Colo. Springs Sun, OPUBCO Resources, Inc., Dallas, OPUBCO Devel. Co., Oklahoma City; chmn. Gayno, Inc., Denver, Gaylord Production Co., Los Angeles, Farmer-Stockman Pub. Co., Dallas; dir., mem. exec. com. First Okla. Bancorp. Chmn., trustee Okla. Industries Authority; pres. Okla. State Fair, 1961-71. Chmn. president's council, adv. bd. Okla. Christian Coll. Bd. dirs., trustee Cowboy Hall of Fame, Western Heritage Center, bd. dirs. Dean A. McGee Eye Inst., Oklahoma City, Southwest Research Inst.; vice chmn., bd. govs. Am. Citizenship Center. Served with AUS 1942-46. Mem. Oklahoma City C. of C. (dir., treas. 1963-69, pres. 1960), So. Newspaper Pubs. Assn. (pres. 1965-66, chmn. bd.). Conglist. Home: 1506 Dorchester Dr Oklahoma City OK 73120 Office: Okla Pub Co PO Box 25125 Oklahoma City OK 73125

GAYNOR, JAY IRVIN, dentist; b. Chgo., May 13, 1924; s. Sam and Frieda (Dorman) G.; student Theodore Herzl Jr. Coll., 1941-42; B.S., U. Ill. at Urbana, 1943 D.D.S., U. Ill. at Chgo., 1947; m. Elaine Ruth Shure, Oct. 12, 1947 (dec. Dec. 1965); children—Richard, Mitchell; m. 2d, Barbara Legrande Beene, May 15, 1968; stepchildren—Gordon Beene, Debra (Mrs. Ricky White Hamby). Pvt. practice dentistry, Chgo., 1947-56, Hale Center, Tex., 1956-64, Plainview, Tex., 1964—; mem. staff Hi-Plains Hosp. Hale Center, Tex., 1956—, Central Plains Gen. Hosp., Plainview, 1964—; internat. lectr. dentistry, 1977—. Mem. Hale Center (Tex.) City Council, 1959-63. Trustee, Tex. Tech. U. Dads Assn. Served with U.S. Army, 1942-45. Mem. Acad. Gen. Dentistry, Am., Tex. dental assns., Internat. Assn. Orthodontia, Am., European orthodontic socs., Soc. Dentistry for Children, Internat. Acad. Gnathology, Am. Equilibration Soc. Lion. Home: 1106 Holiday Dr Plainview TX 79072 Office: 701 Houston St Plainview TX 79072

GAYNOR, LEAH, radio program host; b. Irvington, N.J., Dec. 22, 1931; d. Jack and Sophia Kamish; A.A., Miami Dade Community Coll., 1970; B.A., Fla. Internat. U., 1975, postgrad., 1975—; m. Robert Merrill, Mar. 27, 1954; children—Michael David, Lisa Heidi, Tracy Lynn. Owner, operator Lee Gaynor Assos., pub. relations, Miami, Fla., 1970-72; exec. dir. Ft Lauderdale (Fla.) Jaycees, 1970-71; host interview program Sta. WGMA, Hollywood, Fla., 1971-73, stas. WWOK and WIGL-FM, Fla., 1973-79; occupational specialist Lindsey Hopkins Edn. Center Dade County Pub. Schs., publicity-pub. relations, Miami, 1971—. Mem. NE Citizens Adv. Com. Career and Vocat. Edn., 1973—; mem. adv. com. North Miami Beach High Sch., 1977-79; communications com. Council Continuing Edn. Women Miami, 1972—. Mem. Women in Communications, Am. Women in Radio and TV (dir. publicity Goldcoast chpt. 1974-76), Internat. Assn. Bus. Communicators, Public Relations Soc. Am. Democrat. Home: 1255 NE 171 Terr North Miami Beach FL 33162 Office: 1410 NE 2d Ave Miami FL 33132

GEAN, CYNTHIA GREER, educator, counselor; b. Madison, Tenn., Oct. 22, 1954; d. Leo Curtis, Sr., and Evelyn (Dickens) Greer; B.A., David Lipscomb Coll., 1976; M.Ed., Ga. State U., 1978; m. Gilbert Farrell Gean, Dec. 8, 1972. Counselor/sec., Ga. State U., Atlanta, 1976-77; counselor, English tchr. secondary level Greater Atlanta Christian Sch., Norcross, Ga., 1977-79; sports editor Babbler Newspaper, adminstrv. asst. Backlog Publs., 1979-80; free lance model, Nashville and Atlanta, 1976-80; dir. placement David Lipscomb Coll., Nashville, 1980—; communications cons. Vol. Nurses Aid Service; active Ladies Assn. for Christian Edn., Civitan. Named Miss Tennessee, 1972; finalist Miss USA, 1972. Mem. Coll. Placement Council, So. Coll. Placement Council, Am. Soc. Personnel Adminstrn., Am. Personnel and Guidance Assn., Sigma Tau Delta (v.p.), Pi Delta Epsilon. Home: 3624 Robin Rd Nashville TN 37204 Office: David Lipscomb Coll Nashville TN 37203

GEARIN, LOUISE MURPHY, social worker; b. Vernon, Ala., May 10, 1924; d. Robert Lewis and Hattie Belle (Clearman) Murphy; B.A., Huntingdon Coll., 1952; M.S. in Social Work, U. Tenn., 1961; m. 2d, Carroll Gordon Gearin, June 26, 1953; 1 dau., Virginia Carol; children by previous marriage—Richard Murphy Spring, Stephen Howard Spring. Acting dir. Montgomery County Mental Health Center, Montgomery, Ala., 1962-63; psychiat. social worker VA Hosp., Memphis, 1964-68; chief social worker Children and Youth Project, Memphis, 1968-69; exec. dir. Episcopal Ch. Home for Girls, Memphis, 1969-70; dir. med. social services Meth. Hosps., Memphis, 1973—; field instr. grad. social work students U. Tenn.; bd. dirs. Vis. Nurse Assn. Mem. Nat. Assn. Social Workers, Acad. Cert. Social Workers, Soc. for Hosp. Social Work Dirs. Methodist. Club: Zonta (corr. sec. 1979—). Office: Meth Hosps 1265 Union Ave Memphis TN 38104

GEBOFF, I. STEWART, clin. lab. scientist; b. Phila., Mar. 29, 1945; s. Abraham H. and Shirley (Letteau) G.; B.A., George Williams Coll., 1971; m. Michele S. Burday, Mar. 25, 1979; children—Joshua David, Amy Elizabeth, Samantha Robyn. Asso. dir., chem. supr. Caribbean Labs. Internat., Inc., St. Thomas, V.I., 1966-67; staff technologist Gottlieb Meml. Hosp., Melrose Park, Ill., 1969-71; radio-immunoassay supr., asst. toxicologist Oak Park (Ill.) Hosp., 1971-72; tech. rep. Curtis Nuclear Corp., Los Angeles, 1972-74; Q.A. lab. supr. Wellcome Reagents div. Burroughs Wellcome Co., Research Triangle Park, N.C., 1974—. Served with USAF, 1963-67. Mem. Am. Soc. for Med. Tech., Clin. Lab. Mgmt. Assn. (dir. 1975-78, pres. 1977), Am. Soc. Clin. Pathologists, Am. Assn. Clin. Chemistry, Am. Bd. Bioanalysis, Internat. Soc. Clin. Lab. Technologists. Democrat. Jewish. Home: 40 Laurel Ridge Apts Chapel Hill NC 27514 Office: Wellcome Reagents Div 3030 Cornwallis Rd Research Triangle Park NC 27709

GEENTIENS, GASTON PETRUS, JR., constrn. engring. exec.; b. Garfield, N.J., Apr. 6, 1935; s. Gaston Petrus and Margaret (Piros) G.; B.S. in Civil Engring., The Citadel, 1956; m. Barbara Ann Chamberlain, Oct. 14, 1960; children—Mercedes Frith, Faith Piros. Plant engr. Western Elec. Co., Inc., Kearny, N.J., 1956-58, owner's rep., N.Y.C., 1960-64; v.p. Gentyne Motors, Inc., Passaic, N.J., 1958-60; project engr. Ethyl Corp., Baton Rouge, 1964-65; mgr. Timothy McCarthy Constrn. Co., Atlanta, 1965; asst. to v.p. A.R. Abrams, Inc. and Columbia Engring., Inc., Atlanta, 1965-66; supr. engring. and constrn. Litton Industries, N.Y.C., 1966-71; pres. G.P. Geetiens, Jr., Inc., Charleston, S.C., 1971—. Mem. Ramapo (N.Y.) Republican Com., 1961-64. Served to 1st lt. C.E., AUS, 1956-58. Registered profl. engr., 13 states. Mem. ASCE, Soc. Profl. Engrs. Clubs: Country of Charleston, Charleston Yacht. Home: 7 Fort Royal Dr Charleston SC 29407 Office: 4 Carriage Ln Charleston SC 29407

GEER, WILLIAM MONROE, ednl. adminstr., historian; b. Jonesville, S.C., Mar. 11, 1915; s. Soloman Haddon and Mary Malvina (Southard) G. A.B., The Citadel, 1935; M.A., Emory U., 1936; m. Elizabeth Dantzler Grayson, Dec. 20, 1945 (dec.); children—Sarah Southard, Anne Dantzler, Frederick Bates. Tchr. history, Charleston, S.C., 1936-38, U.S. Mil. Acad., West Point, N.Y., 1942-46; historian U.S. Dept. State, Washington, 1946-47; lectr. modern civilization, dept. history U. N.C., Chapel Hill, 1947—, dir. student aid, 1966—; pres. Morgan Creek Land Co., Chapel Hill, N.C., 1970-75; v.p. Homestead Devel., Inc., 1975—; trustee Coll. Entrance Exam. Bd., 1977—. Precinct chmn. Dem. Party of Orange County, N.C. Served to col. Mil. Intelligence, USAR, 1936-67. Recipient Danforth Tchr. fellowship, 1955-56; Tanner award U. N.C., 1957, 63; honored in TV documentary NET, 1967. Mem. Nat. (v.p. nat. council 1977-78), So. (pres. 1977-78) assns. student fin. adminstrs., Nat. Inst. Fin. Aid Adminstrn. (trustee 1975-77), Soc. for Advancement of Fin. Aid Mgmt., Sigma Alpha Epsilon. Democrat. Clubs: St. Cecelia Soc. of Charleston. Author: The Govts. of the Major Fgn. Powers, 1944; Contemporary Fgn. Govts., 1946. Home: 1506 Michaux Rd Chapel

Hill NC 27514 Office: 300 Vance Hall Univ NC Chapel Hill NC 27514

GEERDES, JAMES DIVINE, indsl. co. exec.; b. Davenport, N.D., Apr. 13, 1924; s. William A. and Martha M. (Buchholoe) G.; B.S., N.D. State U., 1949, M.S., 1950; Ph.D., U. Minn., 1953; m. Patricia Carolyn Seney; children—Andrew, John, Laura, Margaret. Instr. biochemistry U. Minn., Mpls., 1950-53; research chemist E.I. du Pont de Memours & Co. Inc., Richmond, Va. and Seaford, Del., 1954-58, group supr., 1958-60, tech. supr., 1960-62, research asso., 1962-64; dir. research Entoleter Inc., Hamden, Conn., 1964-65, exec. v.p., 1965-66, pres., 1966-67; asst. to v.p. fibers div. Allied Chem. Corp., N.Y.C., 1967, asst. to pres., 1967-68, exec. v.p., 1968, pres., 1968-71; pres., dir. Alrac Corp., Stamford, Conn., 1971-73; pres. Geerdes Indstries, Richmond, Va., 1973—; dir. Action Concepts Tgch. Inc. Rochester, N.Y., Trans Ecology Inc., Richmond, Photo Chem. Industries Inc., Meriden, Cbnn. Bd. dirs. Richmond Children's Mus. Sgrved to 1st lt., C.E., AUS,1943-46. Mem. Textile Inst., Del. Acad. Sci., Am. Chem. Soc., AAAS, Sigma Xi, Phi Kappa Phi, Gamma Sigma Delta, Gamma Alpha. Contbr. articles to profl. jours.; contbg. editor Fiber Producer mag. Patentee in field. Office: 3223 Hawthorne Ave Richmond VA 23222

GEERY, VIRGINIA BOYD ROGERS, copying service exec.; b. Rockford, Ill., Dec. 11, 1942; d. Frederick Tilghman and Jeannette Marian (Dresser) Boyd; student Fla. State U., 1960-63; m. Patric Geery, Sept. 2, 1978; children by previous marriage—David Andrew Rogers, Carrie Elizabeth Rogers. Partner, Triple B Day Camp, Ft. Lauderdale, Fla., 1960-62; clk. in state agencies, 1962-63; sec., office mgr. law offices, N.C., Fla. and Calif., 1964-70; owner typing service, Ann Arbor, Mich., 1970-71; pres., founder Ginny's Copying Service, Inc., Austin, Tex., 1971—; cons. to quick printers. Bd. dirs. Jr. Achievement of Central Tex., 1979; active Austin C. of C., Better Bus. Bur. Mem. Printing Industries of Am. (best sr. paper exec. devel. program 1977, pres. Austin chpt. 1979), Nat. Assn. Quick Printers (dir.), Internat. Electronic Facsimile Users Assn. (chmn. bd. 1979). Mem. Baha'i Faith. Office: 108 Congress Ave Austin TX 78701

GEESLIN, DORINE HAWK (MRS. ROBERT JONES GEESLIN), educator; b. Priceville, Ky., June 22, 1918; d. Benjamin Franklin and Rosa (Avery) Hawk; B.A., Western Ky. U., 1938; M.Ed., U. Louisville, 1959; D.Ed., Fla. State U., 1967; m. Robert Jones Geeslin, May 19, 1938; children—Robert Hawk, Franklin Andrew, Melanie Rose. Tchr., Versailles (Ky.) City Schs., 1950-52, Jefferson County Schs., Louisville, 1952-56; supr. of instrn. Elizabethtown (Ky.) City Schs., 1956-64; research asst. Fla. State U., Tallahassee, 1964-65; dir. reading inst. N. Fla. Jr. Coll., Madison, summer 1965; asst. prof. edn. and human devel. Valdosta (Ga.) State Coll., 1965-67; reading cons. DeKalb County Schs. Reading Center, Clarkston, Ga., 1967-70; instr. dept. psychology, prof. tchr. edn. Western Ky. U., Bowling Green, 1970—. Mem. AAUW, AAUP, Delta Kappa Gamma (state pres. 1977-79), Phi Kappa Phi, Kappa Delta Pi. Presbyterian. Democrat. Home: Upton KY 42784 Office: Dept Edn Western Ky U Bowling Green KY 42101

GEFFRE, AMBROSIA MARIE, dietitian; b. Union City, Okla., Dec. 7, 1929; d. Joseph A. and Alosia Elizabeth (Novosad) Michalicka; B.S., St. Scholastica, 1952; m. Sebastian Geffre, June 27, 1955; children—John, Johanna, Cecilia, Cynthia, David, Roseann. Intern, U. Kans., 1953, pediatric dietitian, 1953; camp dietitian Diabetic Camp for Children, Kansas City, Kans., 1953; dietitian Central State Hosp., Norman, Okla., 1954-56; dietitian Lindsay Mcpl. Hosp., 1965—. Active Lindsay PTA. Mem. Okla. Dietetic Assn., Am. Dietetic Assn. Democrat. Roman Catholic. Office: Lindsay Municipal Hosp Box 127 Lindsay OK 73052

GEHRING, DONALD DAVID, educator; b. Trenton, N.J., Oct. 9, 1937; s. Phillip Francis and Elsie Evelyn (Jackson) G.; B.S. in Indsl. Mgmt., Ga. Inst. Tech., 1960; M.Ed., Emory U., 1966; Ed.D., U. Ga., 1971; m. Elizabeth Groover, Aug. 6, 1960; children—Lisa Jaye, David Ellis. Resident counselor Emory U., 1962-63, dir. student center, 1963-64, supr. men's housing, asst. to dean men, 1964-66; dir. housing W. Ga. Coll., Carrollton, 1966-69; dean student devel., asst. prof. edn. Mars Hill (N.C.) Coll., 1971-78; asso. prof. higher edn. U. Louisville, 1978—; mem. adv. bd. Council Advancement Small Colls. Chmn. fund drive ARC, Carroll County, Ga., 1967-68, Cancer Crusade, 1968-69; lay leader, mem. adminstrv. bd. United Meth. Ch. Served with USN, 1960-62. Mem. Am. Assn. Higher Edn., Nat. Orgn. Legal Problems of Edn., So. Coll. Personnel Assn., AAUP, Assn. Coll. and Univ. Housing Officers, Nat. Entertainment and Campus Activities Assn., Am. Philatelic Soc., Phi Delta Kappa, Kappa Delta Pi. Home: 8609 Charing Cross Rd Louisville KY 40222 Office: Dept Adminstrn U Louisville Louisville KY 40208

GEIGER, ALBERT JAMES, JR., radiologist; b. Elberton, Ga., Dec. 22, 1929; s. Albert James and Sara Frances (Asbury) G.; A.B., Princeton U., 1951; M.D., Emory U., 1955; m. Laura Marvine Gillespie, June 10, 1956; children—Albert James, III, Laura Elizabeth, Suzanne Catherine. Intern, Grady Meml. Hosp., Atlanta, 1955-56; resident in radiology Emory U. Hosp., Atlanta, 1958-61, instr. radiology, 1961-62; individual practice medicine specializing in radiology St. Petersburg, Fla., 1962-77; dir., Suncoast Med. Clinic, Inc., St. Petersburg, 1962-79, chmn. bd. dirs., 1976-77. Pres., Fla. Gulf Coast Symphony, Inc., 1976-77, chmn. bd., 1977-78; pres. Suncoasters, Inc., St. Petersburg, 1978-79, v.p., 1975-77; exec. bd. Pinellas Area Council, Boy Scouts Am., 1975-77; mem. Com. of 100 of Pinellas County Fla., 1972-77; bd. dirs. Pinellas Assn. Retarded Children, 1967-75, Suncoast Goodwill Industries, 1972-73, S. Pinellas chpt. ARC, 1974-77, United Way of Pinellas County, 1978; mem. St. Petersburg Arts Commn., 1976-77. Diplomate Am. Bd. Radiology. Fellow Nat. Cancer Inst., NIH, 1959-61. Mem. Pinellas County Med. Soc. (bd. gov. 1974-77), Fla., Am. med. assns., Am. Coll. Radiology, Fla. Radiol. Soc., Southern Med. Assn., Fla. W. Coast Radiol. Soc., Radiol. Soc. of N. Am., Golden Triangle Civic Assn. Republican. Methodist. Clubs: Rotary (St. Petersburg, pres. 1970-71), Polywogs, Dragons (pres. 1979-80). Home: 1233 Snell Isle Blvd NE Saint Petersburg FL 33704 Office: 1833 9th St N Saint Petersburg FL 33704

GEIGERMAN, CLARICE FURCHGOTT, pub. relations, ins. and real estate agt.; b. Charleston, S.C., Sept. 24, 1916; d. Melvin and Doreta (Brown) Furchgott; student Draughon Sch. Commerce, 1934-35, U. Ga., 1935-36, Am. Inst. Banking, 1936-41; m. Henry David Geigerman, July 4, 1941 (dec. Nov. 1967); children—Henry David, Robert M. Sec. to v.p. investment dept. Citizens & So. Nat. Bank, Atlanta, 1935-41; personnel dir., payroll chief Atlanta Ordnance Dept., 1941-43; pub. relations counselor, 1944—; agt. Nat. Life Ins. Co. Vt., Atlanta, 1968—; agt. First Atlanta Equity Corp., 1972-76; real estate agt. Barton and Ludwig, 1976—. Bd. dirs. So. Regional Opera, 1969—, chmn. women's com., 1969—, v.p. exec. com., 1972—; bd. dirs., parliamentarian Shoestring Opera Co.; pres. Atlanta Civic Ballet Assos., 1962-64; adv. bd. Muscular Dystrophy Assn., 1968—; bd. sponsors Atlanta Symphony Guild, 1969—, v.p. women's bd., 1966-68, mem. policy bd., 1966—; bd. dirs. Active Voters, 1965—, Youth Symphony Met. Atlanta; mem. High Mus. Art; mem. women's com. Brandeis U., Alliance Theatre; mem. Atlanta Fund Appeals Rev. Bd.; pres. Atlanta Playhouse Theatre. Mem. Am. Women in Radio and TV, Pub. Relations Soc. Am. Women's C. of C., English-Speaking Union, Nat. Acad. TV Arts and Scis., Italian Cultural Soc., Victorian Soc. Am. Nat. Council Jewish Women, Atlanta Music Club (dir., co-editor newsletter). Jewish religion. Clubs: Atlanta Press, Georgia Writers, Standard, Oaks (Atlanta). Contbg. editor Arts mag., So. Israelite, TV Guide, Seydell Quar., Nat. Messenger. Home and Office: 620 Peachtree St NE Atlanta GA 30308

GEISERT, GENE A., ednl. adminstr.; b. Toledo, Ohio, July 22, 1927; s. George and Cora (LeConte) G.; B.A., U. Toledo, 1951, M.A., 1955; Ph.D., U. Mich., 1965; m. Glenna Jane Withrow, Dec. 23, 1952; children—Jeanne, Ann. Asst. supt. Bd. Edn., Alpena, Mich., 1963-65, supt., 1965-68; supt. Wilmington (Del.) Pub. Schs., 1968-72; supt. New Orleans Pub. Schs., 1972—. Bd. dirs. Urban League Greater New Orleans, 1972-74, 76-79 v.p., 1974-75; bd. dirs. ARC; chmn. Nat. Assessment Ednl. Progress; bd. dirs. Mental Health Assn. Greater New Orleans; bd. dirs. Am. Found. Negro Affairs; mem. bd. govs. Mayor's Econ. Council. Served with USNR, 1945-46. Mem. Am. Assn. Sch. Adminstrs., La. Assn. Sch. Adminstrs., Supts. Large City Schs., Council Greater City Schs., Nat. Community Schs. Assn., La. Assn. Supts. Schs., Phi Delta Kappa. Democrat. Unitarian. Home: 29 Hawk St New Orleans LA 70124 Office: 4100 Touro St New Orleans LA 70122

GEISLER, MARK MATTHEW, state ofcl.; b. Jersey City, May 22, 1945; s. Samuel and Dorothy (Chonovsky) G.; B.S., Fla. State U., 1967; M.S.W., Ohio State U., 1970. Social worker Fla. Dept. Public Welfare, Jacksonville, 1967-68; community orgn. cons. Div. Family Services, Jacksonville, 1970-73; asst. region dir. Pensacola (Fla.) Div. Family Services, 1973-75; region dir. Fort Myers Div. Family Services, 1975-76; dep. dist. adminstrn. Fla. Dept. Health and Rehab. Services, Fort Myers, 1976-79, sub-dist. adminstr., 1979—; mem. faculty Edison Community Coll. Vice chmn. bd. govs. Fla. Alcoholism Treatment Center, G. Pierce Wood Meml. Hosp. Mem. Acad. Cert. Social Workers, Nat. Assn. Social Workers, Am. Public Welfare Assn., Fed. Exec. Inst. Alumni Assn. Jewish. Home: 4720 West Dr Fort Myers FL 33907 Office: 3949 Evans Ave Fort Myers FL 33901

GELDART, DONALD BLAIR, physician; b. Moncton, N.B., Can., Oct. 5, 1940; s. William and Margaret (Arsenault) G.; student Oshawa Missionary Coll., 1960; M.D., Dalhousie U., 1968; m. Ruth Alice Brace, July 18, 1960; children—Michael David Donald, Crystal Lillian Ruth, Kimberley Rose Florynce. Intern, Victoria Gen. Hosp., Halifax, N.S., Can., 1967-68; practice medicine specializing in family practice, Moncton, 1968-76, Avon Park, Fla., 1976—; mem. staff family practice residency program Fla. S. Hosp., Orlando. Bd. dirs. Highlands County Environ. Soc. Diplomate Am. Bd. Family Practice. Mem. AMA, Am. Acad. Family Practice, Highlands County Med. Soc., Am. Geriatric Soc. Seventh-Day Adventist. Home: Route 2 Box 188A Avon Park FL 33825 Office: 105 E Main St Avon Park FL 33825

GELWICKS, EARL O., III, aluminum co. exec.; b. Louisville, July 20, 1948; s. Earl Oscar and Pauletta Jane (Rich) G.; B.A., U. Louisville, 1970; m. Susan Elizabeth Brooks, Aug. 7, 1971. Sr. programmer/analyst Sears Co., Louisville, 1969-74, Cybernetics & Systems, Inc., Louisville, 1974-75; cons. Info. Processing, Inc., Louisville, 1976; projects adminstr. Anaconda Aluminum Corp., Louisville, 1977—. Mem. Data Processing Mgmt. Assn. (v.p. edn. 1976-77, treas. 1977—). Methodist. Home: 10416 Edgewater Rd Louisville KY 40223 Office: 1st Nat Tower Louisville KY 40202

GEMMER, H. ROBERT, civic worker, clergyman; b. Indpls., Apr. 4, 1923; s. Hiram Conrad and Edith May (Miller) G.; B.S., Ind. U., 1944; certificate Yale Sch. Alcohol Studies, 1945; B.D., Chgo. Theol. Sem., also U. Chgo., 1947; postgrad. Christian Theol. Sem., 1950; M.A., Western Res. U., 1960; m. Myrna Jean Flory, June 11, 1949; children—David Robert, Jean Annalee (Mrs. Larry J. McCutchan). Ordained to ministry Christian Ch. (Disciples of Christ), 1947; asst. minister, dir. youth activities First Friends Ch., Indpls., 1948-49; pastor First Ch. of Brethren, Cleve., 1951-55; asst. to dir. student activities and guidance Fenn Coll. (now Cleve. State U.), 1955-56, acting dir. student activities, 1956-57; dir. social welfare dept. Cleve. Area Ch. Fedn., 1957-63; exec. dir. Council Chs. Mohawk Valley Area, Utica, N.Y., 1963-67, Council Chs. Greater St. Petersburg (Fla.), 1967-70; sales rep. Wholesale Tours Internat. N.Y., 1972—, Ednl. Opportunities, Inc., 1977—; dir. Dean Mohr Plaza Apts., Inc., St. Petersburg, 1976—, sec., 1979—; dean Bapt. Disciples Brethren Sch. Christian Living, 1954, 55; mem. adv. com. WLCY-TV, 1968-74, commentator, 1967-70, corr. at World Council Chs. Assembly, 1975. Mem. nat. council Fellowship of Reconciliation, 1955-65; mem. bd. social welfare and dept. ednl. devel. Nat. Council Chs., 1961-67; sec. Downtown Neighborhood Center, Goodrich House Bd., Cleve., 1962-63; chmn. Adirondack-Mohawk Regional Planning Commn., 1965-67, Utica Area Interreligious Commn. on Religion and Race, 1964-66; pres. Council Human Relations of Greater St. Petersburg, 1968-80; sec. Religions United in Action for Community, 1968-69, mem. exec. com., 1969-70, observor Pinellas County (Fla.) Sch. Bd., 1971-76; mem. Minority Relations Goals Com., City of St. Petersburg, 1970-73; mem. adv. com. Pinellas County Charter Commn., 1971-72; chmn. Pub. Health Council, Utica, 1966-67; treas. Suncoast Progress, 1968, Pinellas Opportunity Council, 1969; v.p. Lakewood Property Owners (now Lakewood Civic) Assn., 1972, pres., 1974, 75, bd. dirs., 1976—, sec., 1979; mem. Nat. Ch. Commn. on Scouting, 1963-70; pres. H.C. Gemmer Family Christian Found., 1956—; edn. chmn., bd. dirs. St. Petersburg br. NAACP, 1969—, treas., 1974-76, v.p., 1976—, edn. chmn. Fla. state conf., 1976-78; mem. Shalom Task Force, Dist. of Fla. and P.R., Ch. of Brethren, 1977—, chmn., 1977-78; mem. UN Day Com., St. Petersburg, 1969—; active numerous other orgns. Republican candidate Pinellas Sch. Bd., 1968, chmn. bi-racial adv. com., 1969-70, sec.-treas., 1970-71, alt., 1971-75, voting mem., 1975—, chmn., 1980—, chmn. zoning com., 1976—, vice chmn., 1977—, vice chmn. Sch. Facilities Task Force, 1977-78; non-partisan candidate St. Petersburg City Council, 1970. Bd. dirs. Found. Religious Studies Indpls., 1973—, N.Y. Council Chs., 1963-67, Baptist Children's Home, Oneida, N.Y., 1965-67, St. Petersburg chpt. UNA-U.S.A., 1969—, Suncoast Goodwill Industries, 1969-72, Nat. Neighbors, Washington, 1978-80; bd. dirs. Urban Devel. Corp., St. Petersburg, 1976—, sec., 1979—; bd. dirs. Habitat for Humanity, Inc., 1976—, program devel. and evaluation com. 1976—; exec. bd. Pinellas Suncoast Urban League, 1976—, sec., 1977-78. Recipient citation U.S. Sec. HEW, 1962. Mem. Acacia. Contbg. editor Peace Action, 1955-68. Contbr. articles to mags. Address: 1863 Lakewood Dr S St Petersburg FL 33712

GENAWAY, DAVID C., librarian; b. Elmira, N.Y., May 29, 1937; s. Wilbur Daniel and Helen Louise (Andrews) G.; B.A., Atlantic Union Coll., 1960; M.A., Andrews U., 1964; M.A.L.S., U. Mich., 1965; Ph.D., U. Minn., 1975; m. C. Inez Travis, Aug. 16, 1979; 1 dau., Sharon E. Tchr., Flint (Mich.) Jr. Acad., 1961-62; spl. edn. tchr. Niles (Mich.) Exceptional Sch., 1961-62; catalog librarian Andrews U., Berrien Springs, Mich., 1963-64; instr. Central Wash. State U., Ellensburg, 1965-67; asst. prof. George Peabody Coll. Tchrs. Library Sch., Nashville, 1967-69; library dir. Dakota State Coll., Madison, S.D., 1969-71; librarian Waite Library Dept. Agrl. and Applied Econs., U. Minn., 1972-76; asso. dean of libraries Eastern Ky. U., Richmond, 1976—; cons. in field. NEH grantee, 1969-71. Mem. Am. Soc. Info. Sci., ALA, Spl. Libraries Assn., Ky. Library Assn., Southwestern Library Assn., Mountain Plains Library Assn. Contbr. articles to profl. jours. Home: Rt 10 Stateland Richmond KY 40475 Office: Crabbe Library Eastern Ky Univ Richmond KY 40475

GENIUS, JEANNETTE MORSE (MRS. HUGH FERGUSON MCKEAN), artist; b. Chgo.; d. Richard Millard and Elizabeth (Morse) Genius; student Dana Hall and Pine Manor Jr. Coll.; D.F.A., Rollins Coll., 1962; m. Hugh Ferguson McKean, June 28, 1945. Pres. Winter Park (Fla.) Land Co.; owner, mgr. Center St. Gallery; one man shows: Maitland (Fla.) Research Studio, 1951, Contemporary Arts Gallery, N.Y.C., 1953, 56, 64, Pen and Brush Club, N.Y.C., 1959, Morse Gallery of Art, Winter Park, 1968, Fla. Fedn. Art, DeBary, 1970, Art Center, Daytona Beach, Fla., 1971, Longboat Key (Fla.) Art Center, 1974, James Hunt Barker Galleries, Palm Beach, Fla., 1975-78, Fla. So. Coll., 1975; group shows include Allied Artists of Am., N.Y., Norton Gallery, Palm Beach, Currier Gallery, Manchester, N.H., Delgado Mus., New Orleans, Contemporary Arts Gallery, N.Y.C., Butler Art Inst., Youngstown, Ohio, Pioneer Gallery, Stockton, Calif., Am. Embassy Gallery, Athens, Greece, Kunst Mus., Berne, Switzerland, Royal Scottish Acad. Galleries, Edinburgh, Royal Birmingham So. Artists, Eng., Museo des Bellas Arts, Argentine, U. Central Fla., Orlando, 1976, many others; represented in permanent collections at Ga. Mus. Art, Columbus Mus. Arts and Crafts, many pvt. collections; mem. adminstrv. bd. Winter Park office Sun 1st Nat. Bank of Orlando. Trustee emeritus Rollins Coll.; dir. Morse Gallery Art. Decorated Order Hosp. St. John of Jerusalem; recipient 1st prize Fla. Fedn. Arts, 1948; 2d prize Soc. Four Arts, 1950; Algernon Sydney Sullivan medallion, 1954; 2d prize Pen and Brush Club, N.Y.C., 1953, 1st prize, 1959, 3d, 1962; Cervantes medal Hispanic Inst. Fla., 1952; Holiday Mag. Citation of Merit for a beautiful Am., 1968; Fla. Gov.'s award for arts, 1973; others. Mem. Am. Soc. Interior Designers, Nat. Assn. Women Artists (hon. v.p.), Fla. Artists Group, N.H. Art Assn., Nat. Arts Club, Artists Equity. Clubs: Junior League (N.Y.C.); Women's Athletic (Chgo.); Women's (Winter Park, Fla.); Rosalind (Orlando, Fla.); Cosmopolitan, Pen and Brush (N.Y.C.); Wonalancet Outdoor (N.H.). Address: PO Box 40 Winter Park FL 32790

GENN, MORDECAI HALEVI, clergyman; b. N.Y.C., Dec. 6, 1946; s. Bernard and Fannie (Kusher) G.; B.A., Yeshiva U., 1968, B.R.E., 1968, M.S. in Ednl. Adminstrn., 1971; M.A. in Hebrew Lit., Brandeis U., 1975, Ph.D. in Near Eastern Studies, 1978. Ordained rabbi, 1971; rabbi Temple Emmanuel of Wakefield, Mass., 1971-73; asst. prin. Schechter Day Sch., Westchester, N.Y., 1973-74; prin. Hebrew Day Sch., Pelham Pkwy., Bronx, N.Y., 1975-77; rabbi Temple Israel, Daytona Beach, Fla., 1977—. Mem. Pelham Pkwy. Community Council, 1975-77; trustee Greater Daytona Federated Jewish Charities, 1977-80. N.Y. State Regents scholar, 1964. Mem. Assn. Univ. Instrs. Jewish Studies, Assorted Clergy and Interfaith Councils, Arista Honor Soc., Educators Assembly of United Synagogue, N.Y. State Assn. Hebrew Prins., Mass. Bd. Rabbis, Sigma Tau Delta, Psi Chi, Pi Gamma Mu. Address: PO Box 1341 Daytona Beach FL 32015

GENSEL, RICHARD LLOYD, county ofcl.; b. St. Paul, Mar. 19, 1934; s. Lloyd and Berniece (Elliott) G.; B.B.A., U. Ga., 1954; M.B.A., Ga. State U., 1972, M. Govtl. Adminstrn., 1976; m. Linda Damon, Apr. 22, 1961; children—Grace Dean, Damon Lloyd. Gen. mgr./part owner Aircraft Hardware & Marine Supplies Co., East Point, Ga., 1960-62; contract adminstr., coordinator bids and proposals, rep. customer relations Lockheed-Ga. Co., Marietta, 1962-70; program dir. Cobb County C. of C., Marietta, 1970-72; coordinator govt. projects Cobb County, Marietta, 1972-75, mgr. projects control, 1976—; mem. Law Enforcement Coordinating Com. Cobb County, 1970—. Pub. service M. Govtl. Adminstrn. Alumni adv. council Ga. State U.; chmn. Supervisory com. C-Mar Credit Union, 1976—. Served with USNR, 1955-59; capt. Res. Mem. Nat. Mgmt. Assn., Naval Res. Assn., Ga. State U. Alumni Assn., Water Pollution Control Fedn., Am. Pub. Works Assn., Municipal Fin. Officers Assn., Adminstrn. Mgmt. Soc., Southeastern Airport Mgrs. Assn., Res. Officers Assn., Beta Gamma Sigma. Office: PO Box 649 Marietta GA 30061

GENTILE, JOHN JOSEPH, security investigator; b. Bklyn., Nov. 18, 1947; comml. degree N.Y. Inst. Photography, 1967; m. Judith Gentile, Dec. 10, 1970. Pvt. cons. for in-house security Wells Fargo, 1970-72; pres. Business-Residential Security Corp., N.Y.C., 1972-74; with Fla. Dept. Rehab. and Corrections until 1980. Recipient Legion of Valor award Am. Police Acad., Washington, 1979; elected to Internat. Acad. Criminology, 1980. Club: K.C. (officer). Home: 265 NW 80th Ave Pompano Beach FL 33063

GENTRY, DWIGHT LONNIE, educator; b. Roxboro, N.C., Nov. 16, 1919; s. Lonnie B. and Nancy (Davis) G.; A.B., Elon Coll., 1941; M.B.A., Northwestern U., 1947; Ph.D., U. Ill., 1952; m. Alice Louise McGirt, Mar. 24, 1946; children—Dwight Lonnie, Nancy Liles. Asst. prof. U. Miami at Coral Gables, 1947-49; asso. prof. Wake Forest Coll., 1951-54; prof., asso. dean Sch. Bus. and Pub. Adminstrn., U. Md., College Park, 1954-70; prof. bus. adminstrn., dir. grad. program bus. U. N.C. at Greensboro, 1970—. Mktg. cons., Washington Gas Co., 1959-70; mem. mktg. adv. bd. Kal, Ehrlich & Merrick Advt., 1960-64; lectr. Sch. Consumer Banking, Charlottesville, 1955-75. Mem. Town Council, University Park, Md., 1961-70. Served to capt. AUS, 194146. Decorated Bronze Star, Purple Heart, Silver Star. Found. for Econ. Edn. fellow, 1953, 59; Ford Found. fellow, Williams Coll., 1957; Mem. Am. Mktg. Assn., Beta Gamma Sigma. Republican. Author: (with Charles Taff) Business Enterprise, 1961, 66, 71; (with High Wales) Advertising Copy, Layout and Typography, 1958; (with Donald Shawver) Fundamentals of Managerial Marketing, 1964. Contbr. to profl. jours. Home: 226 E Avondale Dr Greensboro NC 27403 Office: Sch Bus Univ NC Greensboro NC 27412

GENTRY, WILLIAM NORTON, telephone co. exec.; b. Greenwood, Ark., May 29, 1908; s. William Fred and Lola (Caudle) G.; B.S. in Bus. Adminstrn., U. Ark., 1929; m. Margaret Sue Whaley, May 25, 1938; children—Susan Margaret, William David. Wire chief SW Bell Telephone Co., Hope, Ark., 1932-34, constrn. foreman, 1935-40, exchange engr., 1940-42, 46-50, plant tng. supr., 1950-57, plant personnel and tng. supr., 1958-67, plant tng. and employment supr., 1967-73. Div. leader Community Chest, Little Rock, 1949-52; pres., del. from Ark., Pres.'s Conf. on Occupational Safety, 1958; organizing pres. United Cerebral Palsy of Central Ark., 1959-60; chmn. Little Rock Safety Commn., 1970-71, mem., 1966—; bd. dirs. Little Rock Central YMCA, 1972-74; worker, mem. organizing bd. Contact Inc., Crisis Prevention Center, Little Rock, 1968-76; mem. Gov.'s Com. on Employment of Handicapped, Ark., 1973—; del. to Pres.'s Conf. on Employment of Handicapped, Washington, 1977. Served with Signal Corps, U.S. Army 1942-46. Recipient W.H. Sadler trophy Community Chest of Little Rock, 1950, 51, Service award United Cerebral Palsy of Central Ark., 1969, Safety award of commendation Ark. Dept. Labor, 1973. Mem. Am. Soc. Safety Engrs. (charter mem. Ark. chpt., sec. 1974—, vice chmn. 1959-60, gen. chmn. 1960-61, chmn. annual safety inst. 1972-76), So. Safety Conf. (pres. 1968-69, exec. dir. 1969-72, dir. 1962—). Democrat. United Methodist. Club: Hilltop Kiwanis. Only hearing mem. of Kiwanis Club for the deaf. Address: 12524 Colleen Dr Little Rock AR 72212

GEOFFROY, KEVIN EDWARD, educator; b. Milford, Mass., Nov. 1, 1932; s. Frank Anthony and Dorothy Veronica (Cahill) G.; B.A., Tufts U., 1955; M.Ed., Boston U., 1960; Ed.D., Ariz. State U., 1966; m. Shirley Jo Chilcoat, Apr. 17, 1959; children—Leigh-Ann, Mark. Counselor, Littleton (Mass.) High Sch., 1961-63; fellow Ariz. State U., Tempe, 1963-65; vis. prof. U. Miami, 1968-69; prof., div. chmn. dept. edn. Coll. William and Mary, Williamsburg, Va., 1965—. Bd. dirs. Eastern State Hosp.; mem. Williamsburg Community Theatre. Recipient citation Assn. Specialists in Group Work, 1979; NDEA fellow, 1963-65. Mem. Am. Personnel and Guidance Assn., Assn. Specialists in Group Work, Assn. Counselor Edn. and Suprs., Peninsula Personnel and Guidance Assn. (pres.), Va. Personnel and Guidance Assn. Clubs: Civil War Round Table, Porsche, William and Mary Faculty (pres.). Founding editor Va. Personnel and Guidance Jour., 1973-75, Jour. Specialists in Group Work, 1975-79. Home: 106 Little John Rd Williamsburg VA 23185 Office: Sch Edn Coll William and Mary Williamsburg VA 23185

GEORGE, DEVERAL D., journalist; b. Dallas, Nov. 23, 1939; s. Jack Weldon and LLeen Lelia (Hume) G.; student U. Tex., 1958-61; B.A., N. Tex. State U., 1964; P.B.A., U. Houston, 1974. Copywriter advt. agys., Houston, Dallas, 1964-70; free lance journalist, 1970-73, 75-76; copy and creative dir. Schey Advt., Houston, 1973, Bruce Advt., Houston, 1973-75; editor-in-chief, v.p. Bus. and Energy Internat., Houston, 1976—. Del. Democratic Conv., 1972. Mem. Soc. Internat. Devel., N.Am. Congress on Latin Am., Amnesty Internat., Internat. Platform Assn., Center for Study of Dem. Instns., Asia Soc., World Expeditionary Assn., Soc. Profl. Journalists-Sigma Delta Chi. Club: Houston Press. Author: Cathedrals of Mexico, and Other Poems, 1963; The Erratic Pilgrimage, 1973; The Whole World Cookbook, 1976. Home: 230 W Alabama #910 Houston TX 77006 Office: 4040 Milam Suite 105 Houston TX 77006

GEORGE, DREW THERON, broadcasting exec.; b. Colorado Springs, Colo., Sept. 21, 1945; s. Lloyd R. and Frances J. (Hopkins) G.; B.S., Stephen F. Austin State U., 1968; m. Diana Sue Williams, Nov. 11, 1974; 1 dau., Victoria Leigh. Acct. exec. Sta. KULF, Houston, 1972-75; local sales mgr. Sta. KYND, Houston, 1975-77, gen. sales mgr., 1977-79; nat. sales mgr. Sta. KULF/KYND, Houston, 1979—. Mem. Houston Assn. Broadcasting Execs., Assn. Broadcasting Execs. Tex. Republican. Methodist. Clubs: Scuba Divers of Houston, Masons, Shriners. Home: 5618 Valkeith St Houston TX 77096 Office: 2100 Travis St 600 Houston TX 77002

GEORGE, ERNEST THORNTON, III, ins. exec.; b. Charleston, S.C., Dec. 29, 1950; s. Ernest Thornton and Bettye (Long) G.; student U. Miss., 1969-71; B.S. in Mktg., Miss. State U. 1973; estate planning cert. La. State U., 1975; student U. Southwestern La. and Inst. of Ins. Mktg. Dynamics Lab., 1975; m. Frances Thomson, Sept. 30, 1977; children—Andrew Neal, Ernest Thornton. With Mutual of N.Y., Mississippi State, Miss., 1974—, ins. and investment counselor, 1977—; pres. Ernie George & Assos., Fin. Services Co., Mississippi State, 1977—. Chmn. mchts. solicitation com. United Fund, Starkville, Miss., 1977-78; exec. membership com. Boy Scouts Am., Starkville, 1975-77; adv. bd. Pace Setter Agy. of Miss., 1977-80. Recipient Nat. Quality award Nat. Assn. Life Underwriters, 1977-80, Nat. Sales Achievement award, 1977-80, Health Ins. Quality award, 1976-80. Mem. Nat. Assn. Life Underwriters, Miss. Assn. Life Underwriters, Internat. Assn. Fin. Planners, Nat. Assn. Security Dealers, Sigma Chi, Pi Sigma Epsilon. Republican. Presbyterian. Clubs: Men of Ch. (pres.), Rotary, 100, Pres., Million Dollar Round Table. Contbr. articles to profl. jours. Home: 502 N Montgomery St Starkville MS 39759 Office: PO Box 1033 Mississippi State MS 39762

GEORGE, FRANCES LABORDE, taxpayer service specialist; b. Columbia, S.C., Sept. 3, 1949; d. Pierre Fabian LaBorde and Virginia Adams LaBorde Cheatham; B.A. in English cum laude, U. S.C., 1971; m. Rick George, July 14, 1973. Substitute tchr., 1971-72; taxpayer service rep. IRS, Columbia, S.C., 1972-75, taxpayer service specialist, Columbia, 1975-79, Atlanta, 1979—; appeared on pub. service and TV and radio programs; instr. vol. tax assisters; pub. speaker. Recipient Spl. Achievement award IRS, 1977. Mem. Phi Beta Kappa. Episcopalian. Home: 3160 Buford Hwy Apt H-6 Atlanta GA 30329 Office: 275 Peachtree St NE Atlanta GA 30043

GEORGE, HENRY HOWARD, metal co. exec.; b. Pitts., Oct. 27, 1914; s. Arthur and Edith (Hall) G.; B.S. in Physics and Engring., U. Pitts., 1935, M.S. in Physics, 1939, Postgrad., 1939-41; m. Alice Jessie Blinn, Nov. 16, 1939; children—Henry F., Carolyn George Wilkirson, Cynthia George. Engr. color motion pictures Technicolor, Inc., Hollywood, Cal., 1935-36; engr. water purifying Scaife Co., Oakmont, Pa., 1936-40; physicist Jones & Laughlin Steel Corp., Pitts., 1940-44; v.p. engring., tube turns div. Chemetron Corp., Louisville, 1944—. Active Boy Scouts Am., 1956-60. Registered profl. engr., Ky. Mem. Am. Gas Assn., ASME, Am. Petroleum Inst., Am. Nat. Standards Inst., Mfrs. Standardization Soc. of the Valve and Fittings Industry (treas. 1970—, mem. exec. com. 1970—, chmn. com. on wrought welding fittings 1967—), Pi Kappa Alpha, Sigma Pi Sigma. Republican. Presbyterian (deacon 1950-55). Contbr. articles on pipe fittings to profl. jours. Patentee in field. Home: 2727 Wickham Rd Melbourne FL 32935 Office: PO Box 32160 Louisville KY 40232

GEORGE, JESSE L., JR., oil co. exec.; b. Stephens County, Tex., Apr. 3, 1921; s. Jesse L. and Lois Lee (Brooks) G.; student U. Tex., 1939-40; B.S., Tex. Tech. U., 1947; m. Ann Jeanette Davis, Nov. 24, 1971; children—Stephen L., Richard L., David L. Div. geologist Sohio Petroleum Co., 1947-55; mgr. exploration, Rutherford Oil Co., Houston, 1955-64; v.p., gen. mgr. Newmont Oil Co. and subsidiaries, Houston, 1964-75; pres. Williams Exploration Co., Tulsa, 1975—, also dir.; pres., dir. La. Resources Co., Rainbow Resources, Inc. Councilman, Bunker Hill, 1962-67, mayor, 1967-68. Pres., chmn. bd. Houston Inst. for Cancer Research, Detection and Treatment, 1973. Served to maj. USAAF, 1942-46: ETO. Mem. Houston (pres. 1967), Lafayette (pres. 1951), Tulsa geol. socs., Am. Assn. Petroleum Geologists, Am. Inst. Profl. Geologists, Am. Petroleum Inst., Am. Assn. Petroleum Landmen, Ind. Petroleum Assn. Am., Energy Advocates, Okla. Petroleum Assn. Clubs: So. Hills Country, Tulsa, Petroleum. Office: PO Box 3102 Tulsa OK 74101

GEORGE, JOSEPH DAVID, educator; b. Lorain, Ohio, Oct. 28, 1942; s. Leo Joseph and Kathrine (Namey) G.; B.F.A., Ohio U., 1966; M.A.Ed., Akron U., 1970, Ph.D., 1973; m. Linda Rose Wagner, June 15, 1968; 1 dau., Christine Lynn. Community planner Electronic Products Co., Cleve., 1966-67; spl. edn. tchr. Clearview Bd. Edn., Sheffield Twp., Ohio, 1967-69; dir. Spl. Edn. Instrn. Materials Center, Parma (Ohio) Bd. Edn., 1969-71, Strongsville (Ohio) Bd. Edn., 1971-72; grad. asst. Akron U., 1972-73; asso. prof. edn. Columbus (Ga.) Coll., 1973—; dir. Title VI Handicapped Personnel Preparation; cons. to mil., schs., industry; bd. dirs. Listening Eyes Sch. for Deaf, 1976—. Bd. dirs., chmn. long-range planning Chattahoochie Valley, Goodwill of Am., 1975—; bd. mgrs. Ga. State PTA, 1975-79. Recipient Spoke award Jaycees, 1967, Most Valuable Chmn. of Yr. award, 1967; Title VI grantee, 1979-81. Mem. Council Exceptional Children, Assn. for Children with Learning Disabilities, Phi Delta Kappa, Kappa Delta Phi. Club: Kiwanis (chmn. local Younger Year's 1975-77) (Columbus). Contbr. articles to profl. jours. Home: 4041 Twilight Dr Columbus GA 31904 Office: Sch Edn Columbus Coll Columbus GA 31907

GEORGE, LEE ROY, urban planner; b. Ft. Stockton, Tex., June 14, 1934; s. Olan and Lula (Carrier) G.; B.S. in Parks Adminstrn., Tex. Tech U., 1962; M.S. in Urban Planning, Tex. A. and M. U., 1970; m. Gwendolyn George, Apr. 20, 1957; children—Tina George, Wade, Trace. Planner, City of Lubbock (Tex.), 1962-64, City of Wichita Falls (Tex.), 1964; chief planner City of Columbus-Muscogee (Ga.), 1965; sr. planner City of Abilene (Tex.), 1966-68, dir. planning, 1970—; part-time prof. transp. McMurry Coll., Abilene, 1971—. Served with USN, 1952-55. Mem. Am. Inst. Cert. Planners, Am. Planning Assn., City Planners Assn. Tex. (pres. 1973-75), Tau Sigma Delta, Phi Kappa Phi. Mem. Ch. of Christ. Club: Key City Kiwanis (past v.p.). Home: 2541 Madison St Abilene TX 79601 Office: 555 Walnut St Abilene TX 79604

GEORGE, LILA-GENE PLOWE KENNEDY (MRS. RICHARD PAINTER GEORGE), composer; b. Sioux City, Iowa, Sept. 25, 1918; d. Eugene Preston and Lila Mae (Pickle) Plowe; B.A., U. Okla., 1939, Mus.B., 1940; postgrad. Northwestern U., 1950, Columbia U., 1963-65; pvt. study piano with Egon Petri, Silvio Scionti, Herbert Ricker, Edward Steuermann, 1942-63; pvt. study composition with Nadia Boulanger, Fountainebleau, summers 1971, 72, 73; m. Richard Painter George, Sept. 11, 1941; children—Eugenia (Mrs. Edward N. Haley), Richard Painter. Solo pianist Okla. Little Symphony, 1935-37, Houston Symphony, 1956; pvt. piano tchr. Latin Am., 1948-52, N.Y., 1961-65, Houston, 1955-60, 71—. Adjudicator contests, Okla., 1940. Recipient Composers award Sigma Alpha Iota Okla., 1969. Mem. Am. Music Center, Am. Musicological Soc., Tuesday Mus. Club (pres. 1960), Pan Am. Round Table, D.A.R., Sigma Alpha Iota, Chi Delta Phi. Episcopalian. Composer: Horn Trio, 1963; Violin and Piano Sonata, 1964; Madrigals, 1966; Children's pieces, 1964, 73; Organ Preludes, 1965, 73. Home: 2301 Reba Dr Houston TX 77019

GEORGE, LINDA KAYE, social services adminstr.; b. Mangum, Okla., July 24, 1948; d. Floyd Allen Denton and Shirley McCleery; B.A., Southwestern State Coll., 1970; M.S.W., U. Ark., 1973; student Menninger Found., 1978; cert. tng. VA Patient Rep., Oklahoma City, 1979; m. Douglas William George, June 14, 1969; children—Douglas Denton, Olivia Nicole. Counselor, Upward Bound, Southwestern State Coll., 1968; social work asso. VA Hosp., North Little Rock, Ark., 1971-72; dir. Nat. Council Sr. Citizens, Memphis, 1974; instr. Armstrong State and Savannah State Coll., 1976-77; dir. social service Grady Meml. Hosp., Chickasha, Okla., 1978—; co-owner Papa G's Restaurant, Chickasha. Bd. dirs. United Way, Chickasha; bd. dirs., officer Chisholm Trail Mental Health Center. Am. Cancer Soc. scholar. Mem. Nat. Assn. Social Workers, Soc. Hosp. Social Work Dirs., Okla. Restaurant Assn. Mormon. Home: PO Box 272 Chickasha OK 73018 Office: Grady Meml Hosp 2220 Iowa St Chickasha OK 73018

GEORGE, MICHAEL LOUIS, mfg. co. exec.; b. South Gate, Calif., Dec. 22, 1939; s. Nick and Mary Eileen (Jessen) George; A.B. in Physics, U. Calif. at Los Angeles, 1962; M.S. in Physics, U. Ill., Urbana, 1964; m. Jacqueline Jones, Nov. 2, 1968; children—Mark, Michael, Susan, Kim, Shelly. Sales trainee Tex. Instruments Corp., Dallas, 1964-65, sales engr., 1965-67, dist. sales mgr., 1967-69; v.p. mktg. Internat. Power Machines Co., Dallas, 1969-71, pres., 1971—, also dir. Mem. Am. Phys. Soc. Home: 4450 Cedarbrush St Dallas TX 75229 Office: 3328 Executive Blvd Mesquite TX 75149

GEORGE, RICK ALLEN, regional arts orgn. exec.; b. Princeton, Mo., May 15, 1943; s. Harold Eugene and Betty (Scott) G.; B.S. in Edn., N.E. Mo. State U., 1964, M.A. in Edn., 1967; m. Mary Frances LaBorde, July 14, 1973. Tchr. music Princeton High Sch., 1964-66; instr. music Culver-Stockton Coll., 1966-67, asst. prof., 1969-72; asst. dir. Mo. State Council on the Arts, St. Louis, 1967-68; chmn. dist. music faculty Francis Howell Sch. Dist., St. Charles, Mo., 1968-69; dir. div. profl. arts devel. S.C. Arts Commn., Columbia, 1972-74, exec. dir., 1974-80; exec. dir. So. Arts Fedn., Atlanta, 1980— Vice chmn. So. Arts Fedn., 1976-78, chmn., 1978-79; exec. v.p. S.C. Arts Found., 1974-80; mem. State Programs Advisory Panel, Nat. Endowment Arts. Mem. Nat. Assn. for Regional Ballet (dir. 1974—), Partners of the Americas (dir. S.C. chpt. 1975-79), Blue Key, Kappa Delta Pi. Contbr. articles to profl. jours. Home: 827 Poinsettia St Columbia SC 29205 Office: 225 Peachtree St NE Suite 712 Atlanta GA 30303

GEORGE, VICTOR FRANK, landscape architect; b. N.Y.C., May 6, 1904; s. Daniel and Pauline (Salvia) G.; student ed. pub. schs.; m. Lucille May Fisher, July 21, 1934; 1 dau., Marilyn (Mrs. Salvatore Pinzone). Draftsman Westchester County Park Commn., Bronxville, N.Y., 1924-32; landscape architect N.Y.C. Parks Dept., 1934, Shreve, Lamb & Harmon, Architects, N.Y.C., 1934-35, Madigan & Hyland, Cons. Engrs., N.Y.C., 1935-40, Clarke & Rapuano, Cons. Engrs. and Landscape Architects, N.Y.C., 1940—. Mem. Am. Soc. Landscape Architecture. Home: 12461 SW 106th Terr Miami FL 33186 Office: 215 Lexington Ave New York City NY 10006

GEORGE, WILLIAM BROOKS, indsl. co. exec.; b. Stuart, Va., Dec. 21, 1911; s. T.J. and Minnie Lou (Handy) G.; B.S., Coll. William and Mary, 1932, L.H.D., 1972; postgrad. Va. Mechanics Inst., 1935-36, T.C. Williams Sch. Bus. Adminstrn., 1937-38; m. Elizabeth Harman Simmerman, Nov. 24, 1934; children—William Brooks, Henry H. Asst. to auditor Larus & Brother Co., Inc., Richmond, Va., 1937-39, controller, 1939-51, asst. to pres., 1951-54, exec. v.p., 1954-62, pres., 1962-66, pres., chief exec. officer, 1966-68, chmn. bd. Larus & Brother Co., Inc., 1968—; v.p. Rothmans of London, Inc., 1970—; dir. T/A House of Edgeworth, Richmond, 1968—, Bank of Va. County, Bank of Va.-Central, Lawyers Title Ins. Corp., Life Ins. Co. Va. Bd. dirs. Tobacco Tax Council, Asso. Tobacco Mfrs., Tobacco Inst., Inc., Richmond Symphony, Central Va. Ednl. TV.; mem. Nat. Tobacco Adv. Com., 1967—; mem. devel. council Coll. William and Mary, 1976—; mem. bd. govs. Richmond, Henrico and Chesterfield United Givers Fund, 1973—; elder First Presbyterian Ch., Richmond, 1950-77. C.P.A., Va. Mem. Tobacco Mchts. Assn. (pres. 1977-80, dir. 1960-80), Phi Beta Kappa, Beta Gamma Sigma, Kappa Sigma, Omicron Delta Kappa. Clubs: Commonwealth, Forum, Newcomen Soc., Country of Va. Established Elizabeth Herman Simmerman scholarship fund, Coll. William and Mary. Home: 106 Berkshire Rd Richmond VA 23221

GEORGE, WILLIAM ROBERT, II, physician; b. West Palm Beach, Fla., Nov. 29, 1943; s. William Robert and Alice Mary (Shehan) G.; B.S. in Chemistry, U. Fla., 1965; M.D., U. Miami, 1970; m. Lynda Carol De Cell, Nov. 15, 1970; children—William Robert III, Kimberly Lyn. Intern, Jackson Meml. Hosp., Miami, Fla., 1970, resident in family medicine, 1970-73; practice family medicine, Boca Raton, Fla., 1973—; mem. staff Boca Raton Community Hosp.; clin. instr. family medicine U. Miami Sch. Medicine, 1973—; asst. med. dir. Model Cities of Miami, 1973. Recipient Anatomy Book award Sch. Medicine, U. Miami, 1966. Diplomate Am. Bd. Family Practice. Mem. Fla. Med. Soc., Fla. Acad. Family Physicians, Palm Beach County Med. Soc., Phi Delta Epsilon. Democrat. Roman Catholic. Office: 5741 N Federal Hwy Boca Raton FL 33432

GEORGIADE, NICHOLAS GEORGE, physician; b. Lowell, Mass., Dec. 25, 1918; s. George Nicholas and Stephanie C. (Englisch) G.; student Fordham U., 1937-40; D.D.S., Columbia, 1944; M.D., Duke, 1949, B.S., 1950; m. Ruth Catherine Sauer, Sept. 21, 1942; children—Greg, Robert, Nancy. Intern oral surgery Kings County Hosp. Med. Dept., 1944; intern Duke Med. Sch. Dept. Surgery, 1949-50, asst. resident, 1950-52, resident plastic and maxillofacial surgery, 1952-54; cons. plastic, maxillofacial and oral surgery Durham's VA Hosp., U.S. Army, Air Force, NIH, 1956; practice medicine, specializing in plastic and maxillofacial surgery, Durham, N.C.; mem. staff Duke U. Med. Center; prof. plastic, maxillofacial and oral surgery Duke U. Med. Center, Durham, 1954—, now chmn. div. plastic, maxillofacial, reconstructive and oral surgery. Dir. Liberty Bank and Trust Co. Served with AUS, 1944-46. Diplomate Am. Bd. Plastic Surgery (mem. exec. com.). Fellow A.C.S. (chmn. adv. com. plastic and maxillofacial surgery); mem. Am. Soc. Maxillofacial Surgeons (pres. 1965-66), Am. Assn. Plastic Surgeons (v.p. 1975-76, pres.-elect 1976-77, pres. 1977-78), Am. Soc. Plastic and Reconstructive Surgery (mem. exec. com. 1967-68), Am. Cleft Palate Assn. (trustee 1967-71), A.M.A. (chmn. sect. plastic surgery 1968, now del.), Am. Burn Assn., So. Surg. Assn. Contbr. to books on plastic and reconstructive surgery, burns, and aesthetic surgery, numerous articles to profl. jours.; editor 4 textbook in field. Office: Duke Univ Med Center Durham NC 27710

GERATO, ERASMO GABRIELE, educator; b. Formia, Italy, Mar. 24, 1943; s. Mario and Natalina Cristina (Capogrosso) G.; came to U.S., 1956, naturalized, 1962; B.S. with honors, Coll. City N.Y., 1966; M.A., U. Wis., 1968, Ph.D. (Fulbright scholar), 1974. Teaching asst. U. Calif. at Los Angeles, 1966-67, U. Wis. at Madison, 1967-70; asst. prof. dept. modern langs. Fla. State U., 1970-77, asso. prof., 1977—. Mem. Assn. Am. Tchrs. of Italian, S. Atlantic, S. Central, Rocky Mountain modern lang. assns., Am. Assn. Univ. Profs. Italian, Mountain Interstate Fgn. Lang. Assn., Pi Delta Phi, Gamma Kappa Alpha. Roman Catholic. Author: A Critical History of the Life and Works of Alessandro Poerio 1975; contbr. articles on lit. history and criticism to lit. jours. Home: 2016 Ted Hines Dr Tallahassee FL 32308 Office: Dept Modern Lang Fla State U Tallahassee FL 32306

GERBER, CLARENCE R., JR., dentist; b. Akron, Ohio, Feb. 8, 1921; s. Clarence R. and Marie E. (Foust) G.; student W.Va. U., 1939-41; D.D.S., U. Md., 1944; postgrad. in oral surgery Ohio State U., 1950; m. Bonna Buffington Bray, Oct. 17, 1947; children—Jay William, Clarence Richard. Individual practice dentistry, St. Marys, W.Va., 1946—; mem. staff St. Joseph Hosp., Camden Clark Hosp., both Parkersburg, W.Va. Chmn. Pleasants County Welfare Soc., 1953-56, Pleasants County T.B. Assn., 1958, City Planning Commn., St. Mary's, 1960; pres. P.T.A., St. Mary's, 1960. Served with Dental Corps, USNR, 1944-46. Mem. Am. Legion, Internat. Acad. Orthodontics, Am. Inst. Orthodontics, Am. Dental Assn., W.Va., Blennerhassett dental socs. Presbyterian (elder). Elk, Odd Fellow, Mason (32 deg., Shriner), Kiwanian. Home: 316 Barkwill St Saint Marys WV 26170 Office: 314 Barkwill St Saint Marys WV 26170

GERELDS, JAMES KENNETH, JR., draftsman; b. Montgomery, Ala., Aug. 19, 1933; s. James Kenneth and Joe Alice (Williams) G.; student Auburn U., 1952-54; m. Delilah Edith Conley, Dec. 29, 1953; children—Patrick Kenneth, Donna Elizabeth, Christopher Kenneth. Structural steel draftsman Strickland & Assos. cons. engrs., Birmingham, Ala., 1956-58, McGimsey & Assos., 1958-60, Menefee & Smith Engrs., 1960-64; chief draftsman Stricland & Assos., 1964-67; design draftsman Planet Corp., 1967-68; structural steel checker United Fabricators, 1968-70; structural design draftsman Rust Engring. Co., Birmingham, 1970-72; pres. Profl. Drafting Services Inc., 1972—(all Birmingham); mem. occupational adv. com. Bessemer State Tech. Coll., vocat. adv. com. Jefferson County Bd. Edn. Asst. scoutmaster Boy Scouts Am. Served with AUS, 1954-56. Mem. Nat. Soc. Profl. Engrs., Am. Inst. Design and Drafting, Am. Soc. Certified Engring. Technicians, Nat. Inst. Steel Detailers (pres.). Roman Catholic. Clubs: Pine Harbor Country, K.C., The Club. Home: 2443 Gawain Dr Birmingham AL 35226 Office: 11 W Oxmoor Rd Suite 205 Birmingham AL 35209

GERGEN, JOHN ANDREW, psychiatrist; b. Cambridge, Mass., Aug. 7, 1932; s. John Jay and Aubigne (Lermond) G.; B.S. magna cum laude, Yale, 1953; M.D. (Earl H. Kirkland fellow), Harvard, 1957; m. Jacqueline Dunn, Aug. 1, 1970; children by previous marriage—Peter, Mark, James, Michael, Constance; stepchildren—Elizabeth Kennedy, James Kennedy, Susan Kennedy-Gergen, Stephanie Kennedy. Intern Duke, 1957-58, resident neurology, 1958-59, resident psychiatry, 1968-71, asst. prof. psychiatry, 1971-72; asst. prof. physiology Bowman Gray Sch. Medicine, Winston-Salem, N.C., 1962-67, asso. prof., 1967-68, lectr. 1968-70; med. examiner Durham County, N.C., 1969-72; cons. psychiatrist Durham County Community Mental Health Center, Durham, N.C., 1971-72; asso. prof. psychiatry, dir. div. community and liaison psychiatry U. Ala., Birmingham, 1972-74; dir. Comprehensive Community Mental Health Center, 1973-74; program dir. Mental Health Services Merced County, Kings View Community Services, Merced, Calif., 1974-75; dep. commr. Bur. Health Services, Ky. Dept. Human Resources, Frankfort, 1975-77, cons. psychiatrist, 1977—; asso. prof. dept. psychiatry and behavioral scis. U. Louisville, 1975—. Served with USPHS, 1959-62. Diplomate Am. Bd. Psychiatry and Neurology, Am. Electroencephalographic Soc. Mem. Am. Psychiatric Assn., AMA, Ky. Psychiat. Assn., Am. Physiol. Soc., Phi Beta Kappa, Sigma Xi. Contbr. articles in field to profl. jours. Home: Box 572 1033 Kimbel Dr Frankfort KY 40601 Office: 309 Shelby St Frankfort KY 40601

GERIES, DICKIE GLENN, banker; b. Clovis, N.Mex., Dec. 3, 1943; s. Raymond Douglas and Pauline G.; B.S., West Tex. State U., 1966; M.Agr., 1976; postgrad. N.Mex. State U., 1966-67; m. Glenda Taylor, Jan. 21, 1966; children—Tammy, Greg. Grad. asst. N.Mex. State U., 1966-67; mgr. Monsanto Agr. Center, Hereford, Tex., 1969-71; installment loan officer First Nat. Bank of Hereford, 1971-74, agr. rep., 1974-75, v.p., comml. loan officer, 1975—. City commr. City of Hereford, 1978-79; pres. Hereford Indsl. Found., 1979. Served as officer U.S. Army, 1967-69. Mem. Am. Inst. Banking. Baptist. Club: Lions. Home: Route 4 Hereford TX 79045 Office: 300 N Main St Hereford TX 79045

GERLOFF, EDWIN ADOLPH, educator; b. Dallas, Oct. 4, 1929; s. Ernest A. and Myrtle (Battle) G.; B.B.A., U. Tex., Arlington, 1964; M.B.A., N. Tex. State U., 1966; Ph.D., U. Tex., Austin, 1971; m. Shirley M. Wainscott, Nov. 20, 1954; children—Anthony August, Rhonda Renee. Organizational research analyst, cons. Def. Contract Adminstrn., Dallas, 1972— asst. prof. dept. bus. adminstrn. U. Tex., Arlington, 1970-73, asst. dean of Grad. Sch., 1973, asso. prof., 1973—, chmn. dept. of bus. adminstrn., 1973-78. Cons. mgmt. orgn., behavior and communication, 1970—. Served with Signal Corps, AUS, 1951-53. Recipient Prize Paper award IEEE, 1973. Mem. Acad. of Mgmt. (3d v.p. S.W. div. 1979—), So. Mgmt. Assn., Southwest Fedn. Adminstrv. Disciplines, Beta Gamma Sigma, Phi Kappa Phi. Baptist. Author: (with others) Organizational Communication: The Keystone to Managerial Effectiveness. Asso. editor Gen. Systems Bull., 1972-73. Home: 1502 Juneau St Grand Prairie TX 75050 Office: Dept of Mgmt Univ of Texas Arlington TX 76019

GERSH, SAMUEL RAY, aerospace engring. and land devel. co. exec.; b. N.Y.C., Oct. 8, 1932; s. Morris M. and Nettie Gay (Sherman) Gershberg; M.S. in Systems Engring., So. Methodist U., 1971; married; children—Aaron Richard, Deborah Ellen, Linda Emily, David Marc. Engr., Presdl. Team on Nuclear Detection Systems, 1962-72; v.p. The Highliner, Dallas, 1972-78, pres., 1978—. Served with U.S. Army, 1952-54; Korea. Decorated Purple Heart. Mem. IEEE, Tex. Contracts Adminstrs. Soc. Republican. Methodist. Clubs: Lions, Mason, Toastmasters. Home: 4610 Royal Ln Dallas TX 75229 Office: 500 S Ervay St Dallas TX 75229

GERSHON, STANTON ARTHUR, ins. exec.; b. Atlanta, Mar. 10, 1946; s. Sylvan and Terry (Goldman) G.; A.B., U. Ga., 1969; m. Rose Raskin, July 18, 1971; children—David Ervin, Brian Scott. Advt. copywriter Rich's Inc., Atlanta, 1971-73; sales rep. Life of Ga., Atlanta, 1973—. Fund raiser United Negro Coll. Fund, 1975; bd. dirs. B'nai B'rith, 1973-77, Cliff Valley Sch., 1976-77; mem. state rep. re-election campaign com., 1978. Served with USAR, 1970. C.L.U. Mem. Nat. Assn. Life Underwriters, Million Dollar Round Table, Life Ins. Leaders Ga., Pres.'s Club Life of Ga. Jewish. Home: 2715 Lange Ct Marietta GA 30062 Office: 600 W Peachtree St Atlanta GA 30308

GERSTUNG, KATHERINE MARIE, hosp. ofcl.; b. Birmingham, Ala., Jan. 15, 1925; d. Elbert Clemons and Laura Talulah Grosskopf; children—Ann Katherine Miller, Paul Thomas Gray, Allison Marie Gray. Dir. vols. Children's Hosp. Louisville, 1961-63; dir. public relations, vol. services and patient reps. Doctors Hosp., Lake Worth, Fla., 1973—. Mem. Am. Soc. Dirs. Vol. Services of Am. Hosp. Assn., Fla. Assn. Dirs. Hosp. Vol. Services, Am. Soc. Hosp. Public Relations Dirs., Fla. Hosp. Assn. of Public Relations Council, Fla. Public Relations Assn., So. Public Relations Fedn. Office: Doctors Hosp of Lake Worth Inc 2829 10th Ave N Lake Worth FL 33460

GERTNER, BERNARD WILLIAM, bus. exec.; b. N.Y.C., July 25, 1944; s. Samuel and Edith G.; B.S. in Mktg., N.Y. U., 1969. With H. Friedman & Sons, N.Y.C.; now v.p. ops. Edward Don & Co., Miami, Fla., Democrat. Jewish. Office: Edward Don & Co 1550 N Miami Ave Miami FL 33136

GERTZ, JOSEPH BARRY, investments exec., fin. cons., philanthropist, state ofcl.; b. Detroit, May 7, 1942; s. Harold Morris and Geneva Rice (Skirvin) G.; A.B., Stanford U., 1964; M.B.A., UCLA, 1966, C.Phil., 1970; m. Dorinda Donohoe DeWitt, Dec. 31, 1978; 1 dau., Lindsey Dene. Investment analyst Bank of Am., Los Angeles, 1961-63; officer tng. program Shearson Hammill & Co., Los Angeles, 1965; research asso. fin. U. Calif. at Los Angeles, 1966-68; asst. prof. fin. U. Tex., 1968-71; owner J.B. Gertz & Co., N.Y.C., 1969—, Faubion Ranch, Leander, Tex., 1970-73, Town Lake Apts., Austin, 1971-73; pres. Combined Deposits Fund, Inc., Los Angeles, 1974—, No. Trust Co., Panama, 1973—, Am. Land Investors Corp., Columbia, S.C., 1973—; chmn. bd., chief exec. officer Columbia Nat. Cons.'s Alaska, Inc., Anchorage, 1978—, AMTAX Cons.'s Palm Springs, Calif., 1977—, Carolina Nat. Cons., Inc., Carolina Tax Planning, Inc., Desert Oil Corp., Nat. Resources Corp., and predecessor firms, 1977—; dir. S.C. Energy Crisis Assistance Program, 1979-80; chief planning and budgeting S.C. Dept. Corrections, 1980—. Cons. Competitive Capital Corp.; editorial cons. on investments to pubs.; lectr. mergers and acquisitions, fin. investment banking and portfolio mgmt.; dir. Innovation Research Assos. of Prescott (Ariz.) Coll. Trustee Endowment for Commonwealth, Gertz Found. Ky. col. Mem. Econometric Soc., Am. Econ. Assn., Am. Fin. Assn., Am. Mgmt. Assn., Inst. Mgmt. Sci., Los Angeles World Affairs Council, Am. Judicature Soc., Ephebian Soc. Los Angeles (past pres.), Beta Gamma Sigma, Delta Sigma Pi. Clubs: Los Angeles Athletic, Town Hall, Rotary (past chief fin. officer). Author publs. on mergers, acquisitions, investments, fin. Home: PO Box 4051 Columbia SC 29240 Office: PO Box 860 Palm Springs CA 92263

GESSELL, JOHN MAURICE, clergyman, educator; b. St. Paul, June 17, 1920; s. Leo Lancien and Mabel Aseneth (Wing) G.; B.A., Yale U., 1942, B.D., 1949, Ph.D., 1960. Ordained priest Episcopal Ch., 1951; rector Emmanuel Episcopal Ch., Nottoway Parish, Southampton County, Va., 1951-53; asso. rector Grace Ch., Salem, Mass., 1953-61; mem. faculty Sch. Theology, U. of South, Sewanee, Tenn., 1961—, now prof. Christian ethics, editor St. Luke's Jour. Theology; priest-in-charge Otey Meml. Ch., Sewanee, 1977-78; mem. nat. exec. com. Episcopal Pace Fellowship; bd. dirs. Absalom Jones Theol. Inst., Atlanta, Mid-South Career Devel. Center, Nashville. Bd. dirs., pres. Multi-County Comprehensive Mental Health Center, Tullahoma, Tenn., 1972-74, Sewanee Civic Assn. and Community Chest, 1967-68. Dwight fellow Yale U., 1949-50; Coll. of Preachers fellow, Washington, 1953. Mem. Am. Soc. Christian Ethics, AAUP, Am. Assn. Theol. Schs. (faculty fellow 1967-68), Phi Beta Kappa. Contbr. articles to theol. books and jours. Home: Carruthers Rd Sewanee TN 37375 Office: Univ of South Sewanee TN 37375

GETTE, TIMOTHY JOSEPH, helicopter co. exec.; b. San Bernardino, Calif., Apr. 11, 1946; s. Joseph Eugene and Phyllis Ruth (Cole) G.; B.A., Angelo State U., San Angelo, Tex., 1968; M.S., U. Ark., 1974; m. Kristi Diane Barton, Oct. 15, 1977; 1 son, Brent Timothy. Asst. to pub. San Angelo Standard-Times, 1974-75; public relations rep. Bell Helicopter Internat., Tehran, Iran, 1975-77; public relations staff asst. Bell Helicopter Textron, Ft. Worth, 1977-79, sr. market research analyst, 1979—; instr. advt. and mktg. Tarrant County Jr. Coll. Served with USAF, 1970-74; Vietnam. Decorated Air Force Commendation medal. Mem. Tex. Public Relations Assn. (Silver Spur award 1979), Aviation and Space Writers Assn., Am. Soc. Personnel Adminstrs., Assn. U.S. Army, Am. Helicopter Soc., Arlington Jaycees, Lambda Chi Alpha. Republican. Presbyterian. Clubs: San Angelo Press, Lions. Author: Iran Medical Handbook, 1976; Life in Iran, 1977. Home: 2300 Country Green Ln Arlington TX 76011 Office: PO Box 482 Fort Worth TX 76101

GETTIG, CARL WILLIAM, optometrist; b. Cleve., June 15 1928; s. Edmund Elmer and Arlie (Williams) G.; O.D., No. Ill. Coll. Optometry, 1949; student U. Ala., 1952-53, Spring Hill Coll., 1957; A.B., Oberlin Coll., 1962, B.M., 1962; attended Mozarteum, Salzburg, Austria, 1959-60. Individual practice optometry, Norwalk, Ohio, 1949-50, Mobile, Ala., 1952-58, Foley, Ala., 1963—; part-time music tchr., Foley and Robertsdale, Ala., 1955—. Co-founder Performing Arts Assn., Foley, 1967, pres., 1968-69, 72-73. Organist, choirmaster Christ Episcopal Ch., Mobile, 1972—. Served with U.S. Army, 1950-52. Mem. Am. Optometric Assn., Am. Optometric Found., Coll. Optometrists in Vision Devel., Am. Pub. Health Assn., Am. Guild Organists, ALA, Am. Forestry Assn. Composer piano sonata, 1961. Home: 1608 N Alston St Foley AL 36535 Office: 1605 N McKenzie St Foley AL 36535

GEWIN, EDWARD MURFEE, real estate broker; b. Montgomery, Ala., May 26, 1943; s. Edward Murfee and Dorothy Elizabeth (McDowell) G.; B.S. in Commerce, U. Ala., 1965; m. Helen Foster. Analyst, Dun & Bradstreet Inc., Birmingham, Ala., 1966-69, Nashville, 1969-70, cons., 1970-71; bank examiner State of Ala., Montgomery, 1970-71; pres. E.M. Gewin Agy., Inc., real estate, Montgomery, 1971—. Mem. Nat. Rifle Assn., Ala. Rifle and Pistol Assn., Montgomery Bd. Realtors, Nat., Ala. assns. realtors, Coosa River Gun Club, SCV, Fraternal Order Police, Nat. Wild Turkey Fedn. Club: Whitehall Hunt. Presbyterian. Home: 1818 Shoreham Dr Montgomery AL 36106 Office: 609 S Hull St Montgomery AL 36104

GHOLSON, HUNTER MAURICE, lawyer; b. Columbus, Miss., Feb. 19, 1933; s. Leon Carter and Marie (McDoniell) G.; B.A., U. Miss., 1954, LL.B., 1955, J.D. 1968; m. Hortense Jones, June 3, 1961; children—Emily Jones, William Webster. Admitted to Miss. bar, 1955, U.S. Supreme Ct. bar, 1974, D.C. bar, 1976; practiced in Columbus, 1955—; mem. firm Gholson, Hicks & Nichols, and predecessor firms; sec., dir., exec. com. Nat. Bank Commerce Miss. Sec., dir. Realty Rentals Corp., Meml. Leasing Co., Quality Products, Inc., Egger's dept. store. Chmn., Lowndes County Republican Party, 1960-64. Pres., dir. Columbus Ednl. Found., 1965-70; founder, dir. Stephen D. Lee Found. Served to lt. USNR, 1956-59. Mem. Am., Miss., Lowndes County (pres. 1973-74), D.C. bar assn., Lowndes County Hist. Soc. (pres. 1964-65), Columbus C. of C. (dir. 1969—), Ole Miss. Alumni Assn. (chpt. pres. 1964-65), Claiborne Soc., Phi Delta Theta, Phi Delta Phi. Episcopalian. Kiwanian (v.p. 1964, dir. 1960-64). Home: 1100 N 6th St Columbus MS 39701 Office: Court Square Towers 605 N 2d Ave Columbus MS 39701 also 1629 K St NW Washington DC 20006

GIACOMAZZI, ALLYN LEE, hosp. personnel adminstr.; b. Salinas, Calif., July 3, 1944; s. Elmer Francis and Annie Bell (Norred) G.; student Hartnell Jr. Coll., 1963-64; B.B.A. in Personnel Mgmt., E. Tex. State U., 1972; m. Cheryl Lou Hahn, Sept. 3, 1966. Quality control technician Varo Inc., Garland, Tex., 1967-70; personnel dir. Meml. Hosp. of Garland, 1972—. Bd. dirs. Garland unit Am. Heart Assn., 1973—, pres., 1975-76. Served with USNR, 1964-67; Vietnam. Recipient Meritorious Service award Am. Heart Assn., 1976. Mem. Am. Soc. Personnel Adminstrn. (accredited personnel mgr.), Am. Soc. Hosp. Personnel Adminstrn., Tex. Soc. Hosp. Personnel Adminstrn., Dallas Met. Hosp. Personnel Assn., Garland Personnel Assn. Democrat. Home: 1127 Southgate Circle Garland TX 75041 Office: Meml Hosp of Garland 2300 Marie Curie Dr Garland TX 75042

GIAM, CHOO-SENG, educator; b. Singapore, Apr. 2, 1931; s. Chong-Hing and Eng-Keow (Tan) G.; came to U.S., 1964, naturalized, 1970; M.Sc., U. Sask., 1961, Ph.D., 1963; m. Mun-Yung Ng, Feb. 25, 1956; children—Benny Y.B., Patrick Y.Y., Michael Y.K. Research chemist Imperial Oil, Sarnia, Can., 1963-64; postdoctoral fellow Pa. State U., State College, 1964-65; research asso. U. Calif. at Irvine, 1965-66; asst. prof. Tex. A. and M. U., College Station, 1966-70, asso. prof., 1970-72, prof. chemistry dept., 1972—. Mem. Am., Can. chem. socs., Royal Inst. Chemistry, N.Y. Acad. Scis., Sigma Xi, Phi Lambda Upsilon. Contbr. articles to profl. jours. Patentee in field. Home: Route 3 Box 225 E Bryan TX 77801 Office: Chemistry Dept Tex A and M U College Station TX 77843

GIANCARLO, SAMUEL SALVATOR, corp. exec.; b. Buffalo, June 11, 1942; s. Guy Paul and Josephine Helen (Alessi) G.; student Cleve. State U., 1960-62; B.S. in Chem. Engring., State U. N.Y., Buffalo, 1965, M.B.A., 1968; m. Heather Andrea Murphy, Jan. 15, 1966; children—John Paul, Matthew Christopher. Engr. trainee Rep. Steel Corp., Buffalo, 1961-63; devel. engr. Allied Chem. Corp., Buffalo, 1965-67; mgr. engring., asst. sales mgr. Luwa Corp., Charlotte, N.C., 1968-73; contract engr. engring. and constrn. J.F. Pritchard & Co., Kansas City, Mo., 1973; project mgr. M.W. Kellogg Co., Houston, 1973-74; engring. and constrn. sales exec. A.G. McKee & Co., Houston, 1974-79; v.p., gen. mgr. GKN Birwelco (U.S.) Inc., Houston, 1979—. Pack exec. com. Boy Scouts Am.; cub master Cub Scouts, leader Webelos, 1975-77; active YMCA Indian Guide Program, 1973-77. Licensed profl. engr., Tex. Mem. Am. Inst. Chem. Engrs., Nat., Tex. socs. profl. engrs., U. Buffalo Alumni Assn., Beta Gamma Sigma, Tau Kappa Epsilon. Roman Catholic. Club: Univ., Houstonian (Houston). Home: 12927 Taylorcrest St Houston TX 77079 Office: 4801 Woodway Suite 251 W Houston TX 77056

GIARRUSSO, ZONA TURNOY, employment security counselor; b. Fargo, N.D., Oct. 17, 1923; d. Isaac and Celia (Leivenstein) Turnoy; B.A., U. New Orleans, 1969, M.Ed., 1980; m. Alfred Peter Giarrusso, Sept. 29, 1945; children—Jerel Monté, Joel Iver, Peter James. File clk. U.S. Treasury Dept., Chgo., 1942-43; sales analyst Continental Distbrs. Corp., Chgo. and New Orleans, 1945-46; med. photographer La. State U. Sch. Medicine, New Orleans, 1947-50; employment security master counselor La. Office Employment Security, New Orleans, 1969—. Served with Waves, USNR, 1943-45. Mem. Am., La. personnel and guidance assns., Nat., La. employment counselors assns., Nat. Council Jewish Women, Kappa Delta Pi, Phi Delta Kappa. Clubs: Friends of the Cabildo, Tikvat Shalom Sisterhood, Krewe of Minerva, Delgado Coll. Faculty Wives. Home: 7943 Edgelake Ct New Orleans LA 70126 Office: 120 E Solidelle St Chalmette LA 70043

GIASOLLI, ROSE MARIE ANTOINETTE LEVATO, real estate co. exec.; b. Chgo., Mar. 14, 1939; d. Rosario A. and Carmella (D'Ambrose) Levato; student Chgo. Sch. of Music, 1957, Santa Monica City Coll., 1960, South West Coll., 1965, student U. Hawaii, 1970, El Paso Community Coll., 1973-77; cert. U. Tex., 1975; grad. Real Estate Inst., 1979; m. Mero V. Giasolli, Aug. 10, 1957; children—Vincent S., Michael J., Anthony R., Robert M. Real estate sales agt. PDC Realty, El Paso, Tex., 1975-77; real estate broker DeWitt & Rearick Inc., El Paso, 1977-79; partner and prin. broker White-Giasolli-Hary Inc., El Paso, 1979—, dir., 1979—. Active performing mem. Ballet Folklorica, El Paso, 1978—; founder Ladies Mission Group, Kwajalein Island, Marshall Islands, 1968, pres., 1968-70. Cert. residential specialist. Mem. Tex. Assn. Realtors (mem. profl. standards com.), Nat. Assn. Realtors, El Paso Bd. Realtors, Women's Council of Realtors (founder El Paso chpt. 1979, pres. 1979-81), El Paso C. of C., Soc. Arts and Letters, St. Matthews Guild. Roman Catholic. Clubs: Amici Italian (founder, pres. 1977-78), Tex. A&M Mothers (pres. 1979-80). Office: 6520 N Mesa St El Paso TX 79912

GIBBES, WILLIAM HOLMAN, lawyer; b. Hartsville, S.C., Feb. 25, 1930; s. Ernest Lawrence and Nancy (Watson) G.; student Coker Coll., 1947-48; B.S., U. S.C., 1952, LL.B., 1953; postgrad. U. Va., 1954; m. Frances Virginia Hagood, May 1, 1954; children—Richard H., William Holman, Lynn. Admitted to S.C. bar, 1953, U.S. Ct. Mil. Appeals bar, 1954, U.S. Dist. Ct. bar, 1956, U.S. Supreme Ct. bar, 1959, U.S. Ct. Appeals bar, 1965; asst. atty. gen. S.C., Columbia, 1957-62; mem. firm Berry, Lightsey & Gibbes, Columbia, 1962-71; pvt. practice law, Columbia, 1971-79; partner firm Gibbes & Powell, 1979—; sec., gen. counsel S.C. Credit Ins. Assn., Columbia, 1963—; chief judge U.S. Army Legal Services Agy. Chmn., trustee U. S.C. YMCA, pres., 1952; chmn., trustee Columbia, 1958-62. Served as 1st lt. AUS, 1954-57; now brig. gen. Res. Mem. Am., S.C. (exec. com. 1961-62, chmn. com. on lawyer referral 1975-78), Richland County (chmn. memls. com. 1976) bar assns., Euphradian Soc. (pres. 1951), U. S.C. Alumni Assn. (counselor-at-large 1959-60), Columbia C. of C., Omicron Delta Kappa, Kappa Sigma Kappa (James Patterson award), Pi Kappa Alpha (pres. 1951). Episcopalian. Kiwanian (dir. 1973-74, 78-79). Clubs: Young Lawyers (pres. 1960-61); German; Forest Lake; Summit; Tarentella; Caprician (all Columbia). Home: 6143 Martha's Glen Rd Columbia SC 29209 Office: 1518 Washington St Columbia SC 29201

GIBBON, SAMUEL YOUNG, investment banker; b. Phila., Apr. 8, 1905; s. John Heysham and Marjorie Gwendolyn (Young) G.; B.A., Princeton U., 1924; m. Virginia Newbold, Apr. 29, 1930; children—Samuel Young, Virginia G. (Mrs. J. Daniel Nyhart). With Am. Tube & Stamping Co., Bridgeport, Conn., 1924-26, Battles & Co., investment bankers, Phila., 1926-32; with W.H. Newbold's Son & Co., mem. N.Y. Stock Exchange, Phila., 1933-42, partner in charge trading and investment counsel div., 1936-42, ltd. partner, 1967-74; founder, pres., chmn. Air-Shields, Inc., Hatboro, Pa., 1946-66. Mayor Town of Longboat Key (Fla.), 1969-74, mem. Longboat Key Town Commn., 1968-76; pres. Longboat Key Art Center, 1978—. Served to capt. USAAF, 1942-45. Clubs: Princeton (N.Y.C.); Philadelphia; Sarasota (Fla.) Yacht, University (Sarasota). Patentee in field infant incubators, other breathing equipment. Home: 641 Rountree Dr Sarasota FL 33577 Office: 10 S Adams Dr PO Box 908 Sarasota FL 33578

GIBBONS, ASHTON FRANK ELEAZER, physiologist; b. Guyana, S.Am., Apr. 20, 1935; came to U.S., 1958, naturalized, 1974; s. Eleazer Samuel and Ettie Henrietta (Reece) G.; B.A., Atlantic Union Coll., 1962; M.A., Boston U., 1967, Ph.D., 1970; m. Devalie McDonald, Nov. 3, 1963; children—Michael Christopher, Ashlie Conrad. Research asst. Worcester Found. for Exptl. Biology, Shrewsbury, Mass., 1963-66, sr. research asst., 1967-70, research asso., 1970-72, asst. to sci. dir., 1973-78, staff scientist, 1975-78; asso. prof. physiology Oakwood Coll., Huntsville, Ala., 1978—. NIH summer research fellow, 1979-80. Mem. N.Y. Acad. Scis., Soc. Study of Reproduction, Soc. Study of Fertility (Eng.), Am. Soc. Zoologists, Radiation Research Soc., Sigma Xi. Contbr. articles to profl. jours. Home: 4607 Lakeview Dr Huntsville AL 35810 Office: Biology Dept Oakwood Coll Huntsville AL 35806

GIBBONS, CELIA VICTORIA TOWNSEND (MRS. JOHN SHELDON GIBBONS), editor, publisher; b. Fargo, N.D. d. Harry Alton and Helen (Haag) Townsend; student U. Minn., 1930-33; m. John Sheldon Gibbons, May 1, 1935; children—Mary Vee, John Townsend. Advt. mgr. Hotel Nicollet, Mpls., 1933-37; contbg. editor children's mags., 1935—; partner Youth Assos. Co., Mpls., 1942-65; pub., art dir. Mines and Escholier mags., 1954-65; founder Bull. Bd. Pictures, Inc., Mpls., 1954, pres., 1954—; founder pres. Periodical Litho Art Co., Mpls., 1962-65. Republican chairwoman Golden Valley, Minn., 1950; alternate del. Hennepin County Rep. Conv., 1962. Mem. Mpls. Inst. Arts, Ft. Lauderdale Mus. Arts, Art Guild of Boca Raton, Delta Zeta. Clubs: Woman's, Minikahda. Home: 1416 Alpine Pass Tyrol Hills Minneapolis MN 55416 Office: 1057 Hillsboro Mile Hillsboro Beach FL 33062

GIBBONS, JOSEPH JOHN, former mill equipment co. exec.; b. Wheatland, Wyo., Mar. 18, 1906; s. Michael and Edith (D'Arcy) G.; student Crane Jr. Coll., 1925-26; Ph.B., U. Chgo., 1930; postgrad. Northwestern U., 1931-33, De Paul U., 1933-35; m. Hazel Bisson, Jan. 1, 1930; children—Betty Louise Gibbons Smith, Albert J., Robert J. Tax supr. U.S. Steel Corp., Duluth, Minn. and Pitts., 1941-50; mgr. tax and ins. dept. Mine Safety Appliances Co., 1950-52; with Blaw-Knox Co., Pitts., 1952-69, treas., 1967-68, v.p. finance, 1968-69; treas. Corde Co., Pitts., 1962-68, pres., 1968-69; controller Cleve. Builders Supply Co., 1969-71. Mem. Am. Inst. C.P.A.'s, Tau Kappa Epsilon, Alpha Kappa Psi. Presbyn. (elder). Club: Boca Raton Country. Home: Hillsboro Colonnade 1161 A1A Hillsboro Beach FL 33062

GIBBONS, MICHAEL FRANCIS, constrn. co. sales exec.; b. Warren, O., Dec. 31, 1941; s. William Amedeus and Mary Jane Gibbons; B.S., U.S. Air Force Acad., 1963; M.B.A., So. Meth. U., 1973; m. Sharon Kay Deffner, June 6, 1967; children—Christopher, Brian, Jason. Sales, Tremco Mfg. Co., Cleve. and Dallas, 1969-73; real estate broker Good Financial Corp., Dallas, 1973-74; constrn. sales Ward & Capers, Dallas, 1974-77; pres. Archtl. Systems, Inc., Dallas, 1977—. Active Am. Diabetic Assn. Served with USAF, 1963-69. Mem. Constrn. Specifications Inst. (regional dir. 1978—). Asso. Gen. Contractors. Office: 7824 El Pensador Dr Dallas TX 75248

GIBBONS, SAM MELVILLE, congressman; b. Tampa, Fla., Jan. 20, 1920; s. Gunby and Jessie Kirk (Cralle) G.; LL.B., U. Fla., 1947; LL.D., U. So. Fla., 1969; m. Martha Hanley, Sept. 14, 1946; children—Clifford, Mark, Timothy. Admitted to Fla. bar, 1947; mem. Fla. Ho. of Reps. from Hillsborough County, 1952-58, Fla. Senate, 1958-62; mem. 88th-89th Congresses from 10th Fla. Dist., 90th-93d Congresses from 6th Fla. dist., 95th-96th Congresses from 7th Fla. dist. Bd. dirs. Hillsborough County Heart Assn., Hillsborough County Guidance Center, Fla. Mental Health Assn.; founder, 1st pres. U.S. Fla. Found., 1958. Served to maj. U.S. Army, 1941-45; ETO. Decorated Bronze Star medal; named Outstanding Young Man, Tampa Jr. C. of C., 1954; recipient Pres.'s award Tampa C. of C., 1955. Mem. Tampa (dir.), Hillsborough (dir.) bar assns., Greater Tampa C. of C. (dir.), U. Fla. Hall of Fame, Fla. Blue Key. Democrat. Presbyn. (deacon). Office: 2206 Rayburn House Office Bldg Washington DC 20515*

GIBBS, FREDERICK H., educator; b. Knoxville, Tenn., Mar. 31, 1902; s. William Ary and Lena Margaret (Durham) G.; student U. Tenn., 1920-21; B.S., U. Md., 1958; M.H.A., U. Minn., 1959; m. Ivy Lois Brooks, May 1, 1931; children—Frederick William, Thomas Cecil, Helen Lois (Mrs. John J. Justy), Mary Barbara. Salesman, asst. supt. Cosmopolitan Life Ins. Co., Nashville, 1921-25; joined U.S. Army, 1925, advanced through grades to col.; with Transport Service, 1930-32, hosp. insp. 4th Service Command, 1943-45, exec. office surgeon Far East Command, 1945-48, exec. officer plans and operations Div. Surgeon Gen., 1948-52, organizer Surgeon Gen.'s Hosp. Mgmt. Research Program, 1948-52, dir. dept. adminstrn. Army Med. Service Sch., San Antonio, 1952-56; ret., 1957; dir. grad. program in hosp. adminstrn. Baylor U., 1952-56; dir. Interagy. Insts. for Fed. Hosp. Adminstrs., Washington, 1956-70; prof. hosp. adminstrn., coordinator-dir., chmn. dept. health care adminstrn. George Washington U., Washington, 1959-67, founder grad. program in health care adminstrn., 1959, Gordon A. Friesen prof. health care adminstrn., 1969-72, emeritus, 1972—; ednl. cons., 1957—; cons. Cath. Hosp. Assn., 1956-57, Office Def. Moblzn., 1960-61, Columbia U.'s Health Care Continuation Studies, 1956-67; vis. prof. U. San Paulo, 1964, Trinity U., San Antonio, 1973; operational adviser H.W. Durham Found. and Meml. Home for Aged, Memphis, 1977—. Pres. Assn. Univ. Programs in Hosp. Adminstrn., 1964-65, mem. long term care task force, 1965-72; cons. chief med. dir. VA, 1961-68; mem. adv. council Med. Service Internat., 1966-71. Recipient awards for outstanding ednl. contbns. Surgeon Gen.'s Fed. Med. Services, 1965, 1970, Distinguished Service award George Washington U., 1974. Fellow Am. Coll. Hosp. Adminstrs. (life, book awards com., policy com. 1960-68, adv. editorial bd. 1970—, chmn. on long term care 1972-74), Am. Coll. Nursing Home Adminstrs. (hon., com. on ethics 1970-71, chmn. jour. com. 1971-73, cons. editor 1973—); mem. Inter-Agy. Insts. Alumni Assn. (pres. 1953, distinguished service award 1968), Am. Hosp. Assn. (life, council on adminstrv. practice 1951-55, chmn. com. on methods improvement 1954-55), Am. Health Care Assn. (hon.; trustee ednl. trust, Better Life award for lasting contbns. to instns. for health care of aged, 1970), AAUP, Am. Pub.

Health Assn. Contbr. to mags. Address: PO Box 1991 Holmes Beach FL 33509

GIBBS, JAMES ALANSON, geologist; b. Wichita Falls, Tex., June 18, 1935; s. James Ford and Clovis (Robinson) G.; B.S., U. Okla., 1957, M.S., 1962; m. Judith Walker, June 18, 1966; children—Ford W., John A. Geologist, Calif. Co., New Orleans, 1961-63, Lafayette, La., 1963-64; cons. geologist, oil producer, Dallas, 1964—. Served with USNR, 1957-59. Certified profl. geologist. Mem. Dallas Geol. Soc. (past pres.), Am. Assn. Petroleum Geologists, Am. Inst. Profl. Geologists, Geol. Info. Library of Dallas (v.p.), Soc. Ind. Profl. Earth Scientists (past chmn. Dallas chpt.), Sigma Xi, Sigma Gamma Epsilon, Phi Delta Theta, Petroleum Engrs. Clubs: Dallas, Dallas Petroleum. Republican. Methodist. Home: 3514 Caruth Blvd Dallas TX 75225 Office: One Energy Sq Dallas TX 75206

GIBBS, JEANNE OSBORNE, editor, poet; b. Stone Mountain, Ga., June 1, 1920; d. Virgil Waite and Daisy Hampton (Scruggs) Osborne; B.A., Agnes Scott Coll., 1942; divorced; children—Robert Allan, Marilyn Osborne. Mem. editorial staff Atlanta Constitution, 1942; feature writer New London (Conn.) Day, 1943; book reviewer Atlanta Constitution, 1940-42, Atlanta Jour., 1945-48; poetry editor Banner Press, Emory U., 1957-59; book editor Georgia Mag., Decatur, 1957-73. Pres., Newton class Druid Hills Baptist Ch., 1973-74. Recipient Robert Martin, Burke, Otto awards N.Y. Poetry Forum, 1973, 79; Westbrook award Ky. Poetry Soc., 1976. Mem. Ga. Writers Assn. (lit. achievement award 1971), Poetry Soc. Ga. (John Clare prize 1955, Katharine H. Strong prize 1975, Eunice Thomson prize 1976, Jimmy Williamson prize 1977), Atlanta Writers Club (pres. 1949-50, named Aurelia Austin Writer of Year in poetry 1971), Phi Beta Kappa. Author: The Other Side of the Water (Author of Year in Poetry award Dixie council of Authors and Journalists), 1970; Unravelling Yarn, 1979; co-author: Noel!, 1979; contbr. poems to mags. Home: 809 Pinetree Dr Decatur GA 30030

GIBBS, KAYE LOUISE, therapist; b. Moscow, Idaho, Nov. 9, 1943; d. Paul Frank and Roberta Lavra (Morgan) Prior; B.E., U. Idaho, 1965; M.Ed., Northeastern U., 1969; postgrad. Humanistic Psychology Inst., San Francisco, 1977—. Tchr. Augusta (Ga.) schs., 1965-66, Los Angeles, 1966-67, Acton, Mass., 1967-68; editor Houghton Mifflin Pub. Co., Boston, 1968-69; fin. and career counselor U. Miami, 1969-72; counselor Div. Vocat. Rehab., Mental Health Unit, Miami, 1973-74; family therapist Village South, Inc., Miami, 1974-76; pvt. practice family therapy, Miami, 1973—. Mem. Am. Assn. Marriage and Family Counselors, Am. Personnel and Guidance Assn., Am. Psychol. Assn. Home: 2715 Tigertail Ave Apt PH7 Miami FL 33133 Office: Mercy Profl Bldg Suite 303 3661 S Miami Ave Miami FL 33133

GIBBS, MEADA, bus. educator; b. Pamplico, S.C., Mar. 25; d. Hosea and Mary Liza (Robinson) G.; B.S., Allen U., Columbia, S.C.; M.S., U. Wis., Madison, Ph.D., 1973. Instr. bus. Allen U.; teaching asst. bus. U. Wis., Madison; asst. prof. bus. Allen U.; project dir. Tuskegee (Ala.) Inst.; asst. prof. bus., then asso. prof. Winston-Salem (N.C.) U.; chairperson dept. bus. edn. and adminstrv. services N.C. Agrl. and Tech. State U., Greensboro, 1974—; cons. in field. Chairperson, Greensboro Commn. on Status of Women, 1976-77, vice-chairperson, 1977-79; bd. dirs. Greensboro, YWCA, 1977-79; mem. Greensboro/Guilford County/High Point Manpower Planning Consortium, 1978—; mem. Adv. Com. for Devel. Public Mgrs. Programs in N.C., 1979—. Mem. Nat. Bus. Edn. Assn., Am. Bus. Communication Assn., Internat. Word Processing, Am. Vocat. Assn., N.C. Bus. Edn. Assn., Nat. Collegiate Assn. Secs., Pi Omega Pi, Delta Sigma Sigma, Sigma Gamma Rho (pres. chpt. 1977—). Club: Bus. and Profl. Women's (rec. sec. chpt. 1979-80). Home: 2619 Pinelake Dr Greensboro NC 27407 Office: Dept Bus Edn and Adminstrv Services NC Agrl and Tech State U 312 N Dudley St Greensboro NC 27411

GIBBY, MABEL ENID KUNCE, psychologist; b. St. Louis, Mar. 30, 1926; d. Ralph Waldo and Mabel Enid (Warren) Kunce; student Washington U., St. Louis, 1943-44, postgrad., 1955-56; B.A., Park Coll., 1945; M.A., McCormick Theol. Sem., 1947; postgrad. Columbia U., 1948, U. Kansas City, 1949, George Washington U., 1953; M.Ed., U. Mo., 1951, Ed.D., 1952; m. John Francis Gibby, Aug. 27, 1948; children—Janet Marie (Mrs. Kim Williams), Harold Steven, Helen Elizabeth, Diane Louise, John Andrew, Keith Sherridan, Daniel Jay. Dir. religious edn. Westport Presbyn. Ch., Kansas City, Mo., 1947-49; tchr. elementary schs., Kansas City, 1949-50; high sch. counselor Arlington (Va.) Pub. Schs., 1952-54; counselor adult counseling services Washington U., 1955-56; counseling psychologist Coral Gables (Fla.) VA Hosp., 1956—, Miami (Fla.) VA Hosp., 1956—. Recipient Meritorious Service citation Fla. C. of C., 1965, President's Com. on Employment of Handicapped, 1965; commendation for meritorious service Com. on Employment of Physically Handicapped Dade County, 1965, named outstanding rehab. profl., 1966; named Profl. Fed. Employee of Year, Greater Miami Fed. Exec. Council, 1966; Outstanding Fed. Service award Greater Miami Fed. Exec. Council, 1966; Fed. Woman's award U.S. Civil Service Commn., 1968, Community Headliner award Theta Sigma Phi, 1968, Outstanding Alumni award Park Coll., 1968; certificate of appreciation Bur. Customs, U.S. Treasury Dept., 1969, Fla. Dept. Health and Rehab. Services, 1970. Mem. Am., Dade County (past sec.) psychol. assns., Nat., Fla. (past dir. Dade County chpt.) rehab. assns., Nat. Rehab. Counseling Assn. (past sec.). Patentee. Home: 4501 Granada Blvd Coral Gables FL 33146 Office: 1201 NW 16th St Miami FL 33125

GIBLIN, THOMAS RICHARD, plastic surgeon; b. Utica, N.Y., May 6, 1930; s. Thomas Richard and Mary Warfield (Bayley) G.; B.S. in Medicine, Emory U., 1951, M.D., 1955; m. Elena del Carmen DelMonte, July 23, 1954; children—Cecilia E., Thomas R., Gregg H., Michael G. Intern, Grady Meml. Hosp., Atlanta, 1955-56; resident Emory U., Atlanta, 1959-60, VA Hosp., Atlanta, 1969-62; resident in plastic surgery Duke U., Durham, N.C., 1963-65; practice medicine specializing in plastic surgery, Charlotte, N.C., 1965—; mem. staff Mercy Hosp., 1965—, chief plastic surgery service, 1976—; mem. staff Presbyn. Hosp.; v.p., sec. Altany and Giblin, P.A.; sec. bd. dirs. Metrolina Nat. Bank. Served in USAF, 1956-59. Mem. AMA, Am. Soc. Plastic and Reconstructive Surgery, Southeastern, N.C. plastic surgery socs., J.C. Thurman Soc., Kenneth Pickrell Soc. Home: 2301 Cortelyou Rd Charlotte NC 28211 Office: 2027 Randolph Rd Charlotte NC 28207

GIBSON, CHARLES HUGH, JR., univ. adminstr.; b. Richmond, Ky., July 17, 1927; s. Charles Hugh and Emma Margaret (Davison) G.; B.S. with distinction, Eastern Ky. U., 1953, M.A., 1959; Ph.D., U. Ky., 1968; m. Shirley Ann Carson, Mar. 7, 1954; children—Margaret Ann, Rebekah Ellen, Charles Hugh, III. Instr. in indsl. arts Madison County (Ky.) Schs., 1955-62; asst. prof. indsl. arts Eastern Ky. U., 1962-66, asst. dean, 1968-69, asso. dean, 1969-73, grad. dean, 1973—; research asst. U. Ky., 1966-67; cons. pub. schs.; workshop lectr.; accreditation reviewer; dir. 1st Fed. Savs. and Loan Assn., 1977—. Troop leader, dir. Blue Grass Council Boy Scouts Am., 1968-75; vice chmn., sec. Richmond (Ky.) Bd. Zoning Adjustments, 1970—. Served with USN, 1945-49. Recipient Outstanding Alumnus award, Eastern Ky. U., 1974. U. Ky. research fellow, 1966. Mem. Nat. Soc. Profs. Ednl. Research, Am. Ednl. Research Assn., Nat. Soc. Study Edn., Council Grad. Schs. in U.S. (instl. rep.), Phi Delta Kappa, Kappa Delta Pi. Home: 211 Magnolia Dr Richmond KY 40475 Office: Eastern Ky U Grad Sch Richmond KY 40475

GIBSON, DALE LYNN, coll. pres.; b. Jenks, Okla., Dec. 4, 1932; s. Lynn R. and Freda P. (Dole) G.; A.A., Coffeyville (Kans.) Jr. Coll., 1952; B.S., Emporia (Kans.) State Coll., 1957, M.S., 1959; Ed.D., U. Tulsa, 1968; m. Carol Dean Williams, Aug. 8, 1954; children—Scott Dale, Mark Carroll, Lynn Dean. Tchr., coach Leavenworth (Kans.) High Sch., 1957-60; counselor, coach Owasso (Okla.) Public Schs., 1960-62; dir. guidance and counseling Jenks Public Schs., 1962-64; asst. dean of men in charge of residence halls Okla. State U., Stillwater, 1964-66; dean of students Panhandle State Coll., Goodwell, Okla., 1966-68; dean of instruction Seward County Community Coll., Liberal, Kans., 1968-69, pres., 1969-74; pres. S. Oklahoma City Jr. Coll., 1974—; chmn. pres.'s council Kans. Dept. Edn., mem. various commns.; mem. Mid-Continent Community Coll. Leadership Consortium; cons. Lee Coll., Baytown, Tex., Carl Albert Jr. Coll., Poteau, Okla., N.Mex. Jr. Coll., Hobbs, N.Mex. Jr. Coll. Assn. Mem. various adv. coms. to Oklahoma City Mayor; trustee, chmn. master planning com. Hillcrest Osteo. Hosp. Served with U.S. Army, 1933-35. Mem. Am. Mgmt. Assn., Am. Assn. Community and Jr. Colls., Assn. Community Coll. Trustees, Am. Council on Edn., Council N. Central Community and Jr. Colls., N. Am. Consortium, Okla. Personnel and Guidance Assn. (pres.), Kans. Assn. Community Colls. (legis. chmn.), Oklahoma City C. of C., S. Oklahoma City C. of C. (dir.). Club: S. Oklahoma City Rotary (dir.). Office: 7777 S May St Oklahoma City OK 73159

GIBSON, DAVID BAILEY, electronic devel. co. exec.; b. N.Y.C., Aug. 9, 1913; s. David Derrick and Florence Anna (Bailey) G.; B.S., Auburn U., 1936; postgrad. Syracuse U., 1955-56; m. Sally Estelle Watson, Dec. 23, 1936; children—David Bailey, Kirkwood W., Charlotte E. Pres., chief exec. officer Unitron Corp., Dade City, Fla., 1954—. Named hon. citizen of Boys Town. Registered profl. engr., Fla. Mem. Auburn U. Alumni Assn. (life), Fla. Sheriffs Assn. (hon.). Methodist. Patentee in field. Home: 1607 Fort King Hwy Dade City FL 33525 Office: PO Box 235 Dade City FL 33525

GIBSON, EDWINA CAMPBELL, counselor; b. Monticello, Ky., Apr. 10, 1927; d. Charles Homer and Clara (Mercer) Campbell; A.A., Cumberland Coll., 1946; B.S. in Elem. Edn., Eastern Ky. U., 1967, M.A. in Edn., 1972, Rank 1 in Guidance and Counseling, 1978; m. Joseph Brook Gibson, Apr. 6, 1947; children—Joseph Brook, Dana Lynn. Tchr., Wayne County (Ky.) schs., 1947-52; tchr. Monticello (Ky.) Ind. Schs., 1959-70, guidance counselor, 1971—. Recipient award for most outstanding entire guidance program for dist. Ky. Assn. Coll. Adminstrs. and Suprs., 1978. Mem. NEA, Nat. Vocat. Guidance Assn., Am. Sch. Counselors Assn., Am. Personnel and Guidance Assn., Ky. Edn. Assn., Monticello Edn. Assn., Ky. Sch. Counselors Assn., Mid-Cumberland Guidance Assn., Ky. Personnel and Guidance Assn., Ky. Elem.-middle Sch. Counselors Assn., DAR (organizing regent, 1st and 2d regent Nicholas Mercer chpt.), Phi Delta Kappa. Republican. Baptist. Home: 308 S Main St Monticello KY 42633 Office: Monticello Ind Sch 135 Cave St Monticello KY 42633

GIBSON, ELIZABETH GERRALD, biologist; b. Mullins, S.C., July 23, 1928; d. William Tolar and Sadie (Mishoe) Gerrald; B.A., Coker Coll., 1950; M.A.T., U. N.C., Chapel Hill, 1963; m. Bentley G. Gibson, June 16, 1951. Tchr., Lancaster (S.C.) High Sch., 1950-51, Paris High Sch., Greenville, S.C., 1951-55, Norview Jr. High Sch., Norfolk, Va., 1955-57, Columbia High Sch., Lake City, Fla., 1957-64; instr. microbiology, botany, biology St. Johns River Community Coll., Palatka, Fla., 1964—. NSF grantee, 1960-62; recipient Tchr. of Yr. award St. Johns River Community Coll., 1970. Mem. Alpha Delta Kappa. Democrat. Methodist. Home: Drawer A 115 Mulholland Park Palatka FL 32077 Office: Dept Biol Sci St Johns River Community Coll Palatka FL 32077

GIBSON, EVERETT KAY, JR., space scientist, geochemist; b. Seagraves, Tex., May 13, 1940; s. Everett Kay and Lillie Gertrude (Ivey) G.; B.S., Tex. Tech. U., Lubbock, 1963, M.S., 1965: Ph.D., Ariz. State U., 1969; m. Mary Morgan Shott, Oct. 13, 1973; 1 son, Bradford Pierce Gibson. Instr. Tex. Tech. U., 1963-65; research asst. Ariz. State U., Tempe, 1965-69; postdoctoral research asso. NASA Johnson Space Center, Houston, 1969-70, space scientist, geochemist, 1970—; mission sci. advisor Apollo 14; test dir. Lunar Receiving Lab., NASA, 1971; prin. investigator Lunar Sample Analysis Program, NASA, 1971—, planetary geology program, 1978—, mem. Lunar Sample Analysis and Planning Team, 1974-77; adj. prof. geology U. Houston, 1975—, lectr. Sch. Continuing Edn., 1976-78; vis. program mgr. NSF, Washington, 1979; cons. The Economist (London), BBC (London). Bd. dirs. Clear Creek Basin Authority, Harris County, Tex., 1974-75. Recipient outstanding performance rating NASA-Johnson Space Center, 1970-71, sustained performance award, 1971-72, group award for lunar sci. team participation, 1974, group award for preliminary exam. team for lunar samples, 1973; named outstanding lectr. S.E. region Am. Astron. Soc., 1976; NASA-Nat. Research Council postdoctoral fellow, 1969-70. Mem. Meteoritical Soc. (sec. 1974—), Am. Chem. Soc., Geochem. Soc., Internat. Assn. Geochemistry and Cosmochemistry, AAAS, Am. Geophys. Union, Mineralogical Soc. Am., Am. Astron. Union, Sigma Xi, Phi Lambda Upsilon. Democrat. Baptist. Asso. editor 5th, 6th, 7th and 8th Proceedings Lunar Sci. Conf., 1974-77. Contbr. articles sci. jours. Home: 1015 Trowbridge Dr Houston TX 77062

GIBSON, FRANCIS EWING, III, ins. agt.; b. Greenville, S.C., Apr. 17, 1947; s. Francis Ewing and Hazel (Sanders) G.; B.S. in Bus. Adminstrn., The Citadel, 1969; m. Shera Lynn Carter, Aug. 23, 1975; children—Christopher H., Shera Lynne. With Bankers Trust of S.C., 1969-72; loan officer, asst. sec. S.C. Fed. Savs. and Loan Assn., Columbia, S.C., 1972-75, office mgr. Beaufort, S.C., 1975-76; owner, operator Ins. Services of Beaufort (S.C.), 1976—; partner Gibson Ins. Agy., Allendale, S.C., 1976—. Bd. dirs. Contact Help, Columbia, 1970-71; mem. speakers bur. United Fund; active, membership campaign YMCA, 1972-74. Mem. Ind. Ins. Agts., So. Coll. Football Ofcls. Assn., S.C. High Sch. Football Ofcls. Assn., S.C. N.G. Assn., Columbia Jr. C. of C. (dir. 1970-72). Episcopalian. Clubs: Rotary (past dir.), Sertoma (past dir.)(Beaufort). Home: 2609 Boyer St Beaufort SC 29902 Office: Ins Services of Beaufort 145 A Ribaut Rd Beaufort SC 29902

GIBSON, FRANK LESLIE, surgeon; b. Thomasville, Ga., July 17, 1922; s. Frank Leslie and Willie (Martin) G.; B.S., Emory U., 1942, M.D., 1944; m. Elizabeth Teaver, Mar. 24, 1946; children—Kathrine Martin, Elizabeth Teaver, Frank Leslie. Intern, Grady Meml. Hosp., Atlanta, 1944-45, resident in gen. surgery, 1947-51; pvt. practice gen. surgery Bainbridge, Ga., 1951—; mem. staff Meml. Hosp., Bainbridge; dir. Citizens Bank & Trust Co. Bainbridge, 1972—. Mem. City of Bainbridge Planning and Zoning Bd., 1963—. Served with USNR, 1945-46, 53-54. Diplomate Am. Bd. Surgery. Fellow A.C.S.; mem. Decatur-Seminole County, 2d Dist. (pres. 1974-76) med. socs., Med. Assn. Ga., AMA, Southeastern Surg. Soc. Presbyterian. Home: 1245 Lake Douglas Rd Bainbridge GA 31717 Office: PO Box 525 1506 E Evans St Bainbridge GA 31717

GIBSON, G. RUTH, educator; b. Phila., Oct. 13, 1927; d. Eberhard and Florence (Miller) Sommer; B.S. in Edn., Manchester Coll., 1949; M.Ed., West Ga. Coll., 1969: specialist in Edn., U. Ga., 1972; postgrad. Ga. State U., 1975—; m. Daniel Priser, Jan. 2, 1949; children—David Bruce Priser, Joseph Patrick Priser; m. 2d, James Leslie Gibson, June 30, 1967. Tchr. phys. edn. and English, Coesse, Ind., 1949-50, Attica, Ind., 1950-51, Bradenton, Fla., 1959-64, Burlington, N.J., 1964-66: program dir. YWCA, Decatur, Ill., 1955-58, Binghamton, N.Y., 1966-67; vocat. coordinator for spl. needs Gwinnett County (Ga.) pub. schs., 1969-75; tchr. educator, vocat. dept. Ga. State U., Atlanta, 1975—; cons. vocat. spl. needs Ga. Dept. Edn., 1975—. Active local Girl Scouts U.S.A., YWCA. Named Ga. Vocat. Guidance Tchr. of Year, Ga. Vocat. Assn., 1975. Mem. Am., Ga. personnel and guidance assns., Am. (life), Ga. vocat. assns., Nat., Ga. vocat. guidance assns., Am., Ga. sch. counselors assns., Nat. Assn. Vocat. Edn. Spl. Needs Personnel (v.p. 1979-80), Ga. VOCA Youth Club (life), Coordinated Vocat. Acad. Edn. Assn., Phi Kappa Phi, Kappa Delta Pi (life). Contbr. articles to profl. jours. Home: 1185 Winterberry Ct Lawrenceville GA 30245 Office: Vocational and Career Devel Dept Ga State U Atlanta GA 30303

GIBSON, GEORGE ALLEN, univ. adminstr.; b. Joplin, Mo., June 22, 1924; s. William Arthur and Mary Luticia (Pugh) G.; B.S., U. Md., 1961; postgrad. U.S. Naval War Coll., 1961, Canadian Nat. Def. Coll., 1970; m. Gertrude Frances Archung, Mar. 11, 1949; children—George Allen, Gregory Arthur. Commd. 2d lt. U.S. Marine Corps, 1944, advanced through grades to col., 1967, ret., 1972; designated planner Joint Chiefs of Staff, Washington, 1970-72, U.S. del. to Conf. of Com. on Disarmament, Geneva, 1972; bus. mgr. U. S.C. at Aiken, 1972-75, dean adminstrn., 1975-79, asso. chancellor for bus. affairs, 1979—. Served with USNR, 1942-44. Decorated Bronze Star, Air medal, Legion of Merit. Recipient U. Md. Disting. Scholarship award, 1961. Mem. S.C. Assn. of State Planning and Constrn. Ofcls. (sec.-treas. 1979-80), U.S. Marine Corps Aviation Assn., Ret. Officers Assn., Nat. Assn. Coll. and Univ. Bus. Officers, So. Assn. Coll. and Univ. Bus. Officers. Baptist. Home: 2063 Lorraine Ave Aiken SC 29801 Office: 171 University Pkwy Aiken SC 29801

GIBSON, GEORGE MURRAY, mfg. co. exec.; b. Lassater, Tex., Oct. 18, 1933; s. Vance Loyed nd Margaret Rose (Beauchamp) G.; student E. Tex. State U., 1951-52, Abilene Christian U., Dallas, 1980—; m. Mayon Watkins, Sept. 27, 1952; children—Murralyn, Mark Wayne, Gina Michelle. Asst. mgr. classified advt. Tyler (Tex.) Courier Times Telegraph, 1953-55; sr. labor relations rep. Lone Star Steel Co. (Tex.), 1955-71; personnel mgr. Rogers Mustang Co., Garland, Tex., 1971-73; mgr. div. indsl. relations Howmet Aluminum Corp., Mesquite, Tex., 1973—. Recipient Meritorious Service in Employing Handicapped award Gov. Briscoe, 1973. Mem. Tex. Assn. Bus. Republican. Methodist. Mem. adv. staff So. Meth. U. Inst. Mgmt., 1978-79. Home: Rt 2 Box 214-4 Wylie TX 75098 Office: 227 Towneast Blvd Mesquite TX 75149

GIBSON, GRAEME ELLIOTT BOSSON, electronics co. exec.; b. Detroit, May 29, 1951; s. James Elliott and June (Bosson) G.; A.S. in Mgmt., Indian River Coll., 1969-71; student Duke U., 1971-72; m. Susan Louise Glave, Jan. 3, 1976. Partner, Grosse Pointe Photographers, Detroit, 1967-69; radio programmer WGYL-FM, Vero Beach, Fla., 1971; gen. mgr. Vetrol Tech. Inc., Audio div., Vero Beach, 1972-73, corporate sec. Service Bur., Vetrol Data Systems Co., 1973-74, pres. Vetrol Tech. Inc., 1975—; pres. Diversified Investment Service Corp., Vero Beach, 1976-78, Diversity Inc., Vero Beach, 1975—; v.p. Perq Corp., Vero Beach, 1976—; tech. dir. Page Theatre and Vero Beach Community Theater, Vero Beach, 1971—; asso. Sta. WAXE, Vero Beach; lectr. in field. Recipient Award of Merit Indian River Coll., 1971. Certified advanced ground instr. FAA, comml. pilot. Mem. Fla. Electronic Service Assn. (v.p. 1971-75), Soc. Audio Cons.'s (certified), Airplane Owners and Pilots Assn., Nat. Pilots Assn., Vero Beach Amateur Radio Club, Amateur Radio Relay League, Aviation Consumers Group. Episcopalian. Club: Exchange. Home: 2475 20th Ave Vero Beach FL 32960 Office: Waxe South US 1 Vero Beach FL 32960

GIBSON, HENRY WRIGHT, physician; b. Batesburg, S.C., June 18, 1924; s. William Thornwell and Kate Bates (Wright) G.; B.S., Wofford Coll., 1946; M.D., Med. U. S.C., 1950; m. Janet Yvonne Gilliland, June 6, 1953; children—Yvonne Kinsley, Amy Susan, Rosalyn Bates, Katherine Wright. Intern Columbia Hosp. Richland County, 1950-51; gen. practice medicine, Barnwell, S.C., 1951—; chief staff Barnwell County Hosp.; surgeon So. Ry. System, Seaboard-Coastline R.R.; med. dir. Allied Gen. Nuclear Services, Barnwell S.C., Barnwell Woolen Mills. Dir. Palmetto Savs. and Loan Assn. Served with USAAF, 1943-45. Decorated Air medal with four oak leaf clusters. Mem. AMA, Am. Acad. Gen. Practice, S.C., So. Barnwell County med. assns., Am. Legion, Kappa Sigma, Alpha Kappa Kappa. Home: 2015 Simms Ave Barnwell SC 29812 Office: 1802 Wren St Barnwell SC 29812

GIBSON, JOHN HENRY, coll. adminstr.; b. Selma, Ala., June 20, 1933; s. Conner and Maggie (Fincher) G.; A.A., Immanuel Luth. Coll., 1953; B.S. in B.A., Roger Williams Coll., 1977; M.S., Central Mich. U., 1980; m. Naomi G. Williamson, Dec. 25, 1957; children—Byron J., Valeria M., Paula R. Commd. U.S. Army, 1953, advanced through grades to maj., 1973, ret., 1973; personnel asst. Ga. Inst. Tech., Atlanta, 1973-76, asst. to v.p. for bus./fin., 1976—. Bd. dirs. S.W. Atlanta Law Enforcement Adminstrn. Assn., 1978—; mem. Southeastern Luth. Synod Commn. on Profl. Leadership, 1977—, Met. Atlanta W. Point Parent Assn., 1978—, S.W. Atlanta Polit. Action Assn., 1978—. Decorated Legion of Merit, Bronze Star, Army Commendation medal. Mem. Coll. and Univ. Personnel Assn., Atlanta Black Adminstrs./Personnel Assn. Lutheran. Address: 225 N Ave NW Atlanta GA 30332

GIBSON, JOHN SEVIER, aircraft co. exec.; b. Louisville, Dec. 10, 1934; s. Bryon Hall and Alberta Moore (Lotspeich) G.; B.S., Stetson U., 1956; m. Martha Diane Smith, June 23, 1956; 1 dau., Lisbeth Randol. With Lockheed-Georgia Co., Marietta, 1959—, asso. engr., 1959-60, engr., 1960-62, sr. engr., 1962-65, group engr., 1965-76, staff scientist, 1976-79, dep. advanced internat. program mgr., 1979—; tech. cons. Pres., Nat. Sevier Family Assn., 1973-77. Served as officer U.S. Army, 1956-58. Asso. fellow AIAA (chmn. Atlanta sect. 1976-77, nat. dir. 1978—); mem. Acoustical Soc. Am. (chmn. Ga. chpt. 1969-70), Internat. Council Aero. Scis. (U.S. mem. council 1978-80), Ga. Acad. Scis., So. Center Internat. Studies. Home: 813 Parkway Dr Smyrna GA 30080 Office: Dept 97-13 Zone 19 Lockheed-Georgia Co Marietta GA 30063

GIBSON, JOHN THOMAS, educator; b. Montgomery, Ala., Sept. 19, 1948; s. Herman F. and Lillian Gibson; B.S., Tuskegee Inst., 1970, Ed.M., 1971; Ed.S., U. Colo., 1972, Ph.D., 1973; m. Mayme Voncile Pierce, Jan. 31, 1970; children—John Thomas, Jerard Trenton. Instr. phys. edn. Tuskegee Inst., 1970-71; adminstrv. asst. Smiley Jr. High Sch., Denver, 1971-72; dir. lab. experiences Ala. State U., Montgomery, 1973-75, coordinator fed. relations, 1975-76, asso. prof., area coordinator edn. fin. and adminstrn., 1976—. Chmn. affirmative action com. Elmore and Montgomery Manpower Consortium, 1976-79; mem. Bellingrath Exec. Community Council; treas., trustee First Congregational Ch. Served to capt. U.S. Army,

1970-78. Mem. Urban League, Ala. Edn. Assn., NEA, Am. Edn. Fin. Assn., Am. Assn. U. Adminstrs., AAUP, Kappa Alpha Psi. Democrat. Clubs: Elks, Masons, Shriners. Home: 43 N Anton Dr Montgomery AL 36105 Office: Councill Hall Ala State U Montgomery AL 36101

GIBSON, JON LEE, social scientist; b. Urania, La., Mar. 22, 1943; s. Claude Lee and Kathren (Maxwell) G.; B.A., Northwestern State U., 1965; M.A., La. State U., 1968; M.A., So. Meth. U., 1970, Ph.D., 1973; m. Mary Beth Sellers, Feb. 8, 1965; 1 dau., Erin Lea. Research archeologist So. Meth. U., Dallas, 1967-69; asst. prof. anthropology U. Southwestern La., Lafayette, 1969-75, asso. prof., 1975-79, prof., 1979—, head dept. social studies, 1975—; pres. Archaeology, Inc., Lafayette, 1978—. Recipient Disting. Prof. award U. Southwestern La., 1975, Disting. Alumni award, 1975; NSF trainee, 1968-69. Mem. Soc. Am. Archeology, Soc. Prof. Archeologists, Southeastern Archeol. Conf., So. Anthropol. Soc., La. Archaeol. Soc. Baptist. Author: The Culture of Acadiana, 1975; editor La. Archaeology, 1974—; contbr. articles to profl. jours. Home: 120 Beta St Lafayette LA 70506 Office: Box 40198 U Southwestern La Station Lafayette LA 70504

GIBSON, RALPH DODGE, plastics co. exec.; b. Melrose, Mass., Oct. 1, 1924; s. Robert and Jane Lydia (Bartlett) G.; A.B., Bowdoin Coll., 1950; m. Sarah Hollenbeck Mitchell, June 15, 1951; children—Marden, Christopher, Robert, Daniel, Ralph. Traveling internal auditor Gen. Motors Corp., Detroit, 1950-55; sales mgr. Gen. Tire and Rubber Co., Lawrence, Mass., 1955-69; v.p., gen. mgr. Ind. Plastic Sheet div. Schott Industries, Elkhart, Ind., 1969-73; gen. mgr. Paragon Plastics Co., Mansfield, Tex., 1973—. Served with USAAF, 1943-47. Decorated Air medal. Mem. Soc. Plastics Engrs., Soc. Plastics Industry, Nat. Rifle Assn., Amateur Trapshooting Assn. Republican. Presbyterian. Club: Ft. Worth Gun. Home: 4201 Sparkford Ct Arlington TX 76013 Office: 1500 E Dallas St Mansfield TX 76063

GIBSON, RAY ALLEN, obstetrician and gynecologist; b. Webster County, Ky., Jan. 15, 1941; s. Curtis Ray and Mildred J. (Allen) G.; B.S., Berea Coll., 1962; M.D., U. Louisville, 1968; m. Nancy Sue Bailey, Nov. 28, 1963; 1 dau., Rachel Janel. Intern, U. Louisville Hosps., 1968-69, resident in obstetrics and gynecology, 1969-72; sr. obstetrician-gynecologist Howard Clinic, Glasgow, Ky., 1974—; chief of staff T.J. Samson Hosp., Glasgow, 1975, dir. med. edn., 1976—. Deacon, Glasgow Bapt. Ch. Served with U.S. Army, 1972-74. Diplomate Am. Bd. Obstetrics and Gynecology. Mem. AMA, Ky. Med. Assn., Barren County Med. Soc., Am. Coll. Obstetricians and Gynecologists, Am. Fertility Soc., So. Seminar Obstetrics and Gynecology, Glasgow C. of C. Club: Masons (32 deg). Home: 112 Cranbrook St Glasgow KY 42141 Office: Howard Clinic Washington St Glasgow KY 42141

GIBSON, TRINI STOVALL, educator; b. Minden, La., Apr. 3, 1941; d. Jesse and Sallie (Williams) Stovall; B.S., Grambling State U., 1960; M.Ed. in Guidance and Counseling, So. U., 1970; m. Everett D. Gibson, Sept. 27, 1956; children—Andrea, Kiwanii, Everett D. II, Tamue Lyn Dea. Elem. sch. tchr. and counselor, 1960-76; asst. prof. early childhood edn. So. U., Baton Rouge, 1976—, also supr. student tchrs.; mem. textbook adoption com. La. Dept. Edn., 1976. Chmn. Day Care Center, St. Rest Baptist Ch., Baton Rouge, 1964-71; sec. Parkwood Terr. Improvement Orgn., 1972-74; active local Girl Scouts, United Fund, March of Dimes; asst. den leader Cub Scouts, 1979-80. Mem. Am. Personnel and Guidance Assn., NEA, La. Edn. Assn., Women in Politics, Phi Delta Kappa (Found. rep. 1979—), Delta Sigma Theta (Mother of Yr. 1978). Home: PO Box 10140 Baton Rouge LA 70813 Office: 771-3870 Southern Univ Baton Rouge LA 70813

GIBSON, WAYNE ALLEN, ins. co. exec.; b. Fairmont, W.Va., Feb. 6, 1947; s. James and Gloria Joyce (Lorenz) G.; B.S., Youngstown State U., 1969; M.B.A., Ohio U., 1979; m. Ilona Barbara Kantor, Apr. 20, 1968; 1 dau., Dawn Michelle. Mktg. cons. Internat. Harvester Co., Youngstown, Ohio, Pitts., 1969-70; mktg. rep INA, Pitts., 1970-74; sr. mktg. rep., 1974-78, br. mgr., Charleston, W.Va., 1978—. Rep., Jr. League Baseball League, 1973-77. Mem. W.Va. Ins. Assn. (pres. 1980), Ohio U. Alumni Assn., Youngstown State Alumni Assn. Methodist. Clubs: Mountain State Sportsmans Assn., Greenmont Racquet. Home: 3505 River Rd Vienna WV 26105 Office: 400 Allen Dr Charleston WV 25302

GIBSON, WILLIAM EDWIN, mining engr.; b. Weeksbury, Ky., Sept. 16, 1930; s. Edwin Joseph and Irene (Depew) G.; B.S. in Mining Engring., Va. Poly. Inst., 1955; m. Gwenda Jean Wicker, Dec. 15, 1954; children—James Edwin, Barbara Ann, Deborah Irene. Indsl. engr. U.S. Steel Co., Lynch, Ky., 1956-62; mining engr. Evans Elkhorn Coal Corp., Wayland, Ky., 1964-66; indsl. engr. Eastern Coal Corp., Stone, Ky., 1962-64, mining engr., 1966-70; mining engr. Ky. Carbon Corp., Phelps, 1970-74, Beth Elkhorn Corp., Jenkins, Ky., 1974-77, Va. Iron, Coal & Coke Co., Coeburn, 1978—. Registered profl. engr. Mem. Nat., Ky., Va., W.Va. socs. profl. engrs., AIME. Club: Masons. Home: 596 Mudtown PO Box 179 Jenkins KY 41537 Office: PO Drawer C Coeburn VA 24230

GIDEON, WILLIAM PATRICK, obstetrician and gynecologist, educator; b. Oklahoma City, June 16, 1943; s. A. C. and Rose Catherine (McCormick) G.; B.S., Okla. State U., 1964; M.D., U. Okla., 1969. Intern, U. Okla., Tulsa, 1969-71; resident in Ob-Gyn, Tulsa Obstetrical and Gynecol. Ednl. Found., 1971-73; commd. med. officer USPHS, 1973, advanced through grades to col.; chief Ob-Gyn, Indian Hosp., Claremore, Okla., 1973-75, chief of staff, 1974-75; maternal and child health br. chief Oklahoma City Area Indian Health Service, 1975—; asst. prof. Ob-Gyn, U. Okla., Tulsa Med. Coll., 1977—; mem. Okla. Mortality Com., 1978, Okla. Com. on Perinatal Health, 1977. Decorated USPHS Commendation medal. Fellow A.C.S., Royal Soc. Health, Royal Soc. Medicine, Am. Coll. Obstetricians and Gynecologists; mem. Central Assn. Obstetricians and Gynecologists, Assn. of Mil. Surgeons, U.S. Commd. Officers Assn., So. Med. Assn., AMA, Okla. Med. Assn., Tulsa County Med. Soc., Assn. Am. Med. Colls., Assn. Profls. of Ob-Gyn, Okla. Public Health Assn., Am. Public Health Assn., Am. Fertility Soc., Am. Assn. Sex Educators, Counselors and Therapists, AAAS. Democrat. Roman Catholic. Contbr. articles in field to profl. jours.; contbr. Merck Manual, 1977. Office: 2727 E 21st St Suite 408 Tulsa OK 74114

GIECK, JOE HOWARD, athletic trainer, phys. therapist; b. Hollis, Okla., Dec. 15, 1938; s. Ralph Herman and Clarice Pearl (Coots) G.; B.S. in Phys. Therapy, U. Okla., 1961; M.Ed. in Phys. Edn., U. Va., 1965, Ed.D. in Counselor Edn., 1975; m. Sally DeJarnette Grymes, Mar. 19, 1966; children—Elizabeth DeJarnette, Katherine Wentworth. Asst. trainer U.S. Mil. Acad., West Point, N.Y., 1961-62; head trainer dept. athletics U. Va., Charlottesville, 1962—, instr. Grad. Edn. Sch., 1965—, dir. Adapted Service Edn. Program, 1962—, dir. Athletic Tng. Masters Program, 1975—; trainer U.S. Olympic Basketball Devel. Camp, 1971, U.S. Pan Am. Games, 1971; pvt. practice phys. therapy, Charlottesville, Va., 1961—; cons. to Fed. Exec. Inst., 1974—. Bd. dirs. Central Va. Red Cross, 1971-73. Recipient Distinguished Service award Va. High Sch. Coaches Assn., 1976. Mem. Am. Coll. Sports Medicine, Am., Va. phys. therapy assns., AAUP, Am. Personnel and Guidance Assn., Nat. Athletic Trainers Assn. (dir. 1968-73, chmn. 1969-70, editorial bd. 1976—), Am. Orthopedic Soc. for Sports Medicine, Phi Delta Kappa. Episcopalian. Contbr. articles on phys. therapy and sports medicine to profl. jours. Home: Wentworth Farm Route 6 Box 147 Charlottesville VA 22901 Office: PO Box 3785 Charlottesville VA 22903

GIENGER, DONALD KARNS, II, computer corp. exec.; b. Cumberland, Md., June 14, 1949; s. Donald Karns and Wilma B. G.; B.A., U. S. Fla., 1971; m. Rebecca Pepple, June 25, 1970; 1 dau., Jennifer Dawn. Sales exec. Xerox Corp., Central Fla., 1972-77; sales mgr. A.B. Dick Co., Atlanta, 1978-79; br. mgr. Nixdorf Computer Corp., Atlanta, 1979; major accounts mgr. Micom Data Systems Inc., Atlanta, 1979—. Mem. Internat. Word Processing Assn. Mem. Christian and Missionary Alliance Ch. Home: 4924 Kings Valley Dr Roswell GA 30075 Office: Micom Data Systems Inc 12700 Park Central Pl Dallas TX 75251

GIESEN, HERMAN MILLS, indsl. mgmt., engring. cons.; b. San Antonio, Sept. 22, 1928; s. Herman Iglehart and Emeline Barbara (Frey) G.; student Tex. A. and M. U., 1946-47; B.S. in Engring., U.S. Naval Acad., 1951; M.S. in Elec. Engring., USAF Inst. Tech., 1960; M.S. in Ops. Mgmt., U. So. Calif., 1966; m. Linda Berger Williams, Aug. 9, 1979; children—John Herman, David Douglas, Amy Lynn, Jonathan. Commd. 2d lt, USAF, 1951, advanced through grades to maj., 1966; served as aircraft maintenance mgr., 1954-56, flight instr., 1957-59, research and devel. program officer, 1960-63, aircraft, flight comdr., 1963-64, elec. engr.-analyst, 1964-66, resigned, 1966, now col. Res.; exec. adviser in program control McDonnell-Douglas Corp., Huntington Beach, Calif., 1966-68; sr. bus. planner E-Systems, Inc., Greenville, Tex., 1968-71; pres. Giesen & Assos., Inc., mgmt. engring. cons., Dallas, 1971-72, 78—; plant engr. Dixie Metals of Tex., Dallas, 1972-73; plant engr. Murph Metals Div., R.S.R. Corp., Dallas, 1973-74, ops. maintenance/engring. mgr., 1974-76; mfg. mgr. Ferguson Industries, Dallas, 1976-78; cons., 1978—. Decorated Air medal USAF Commendation medal. Registered profl. engr., Tex.; certified flight instr., advanced instrument ground aircraft instr. FAA, Mem. Nat., Tex. socs. profl. engrs. Home: 3636 Shenandoah Ave Dallas TX 75205 Office: 5319 N Central Expressway Dallas TX 75205

GIFFEN, JAMES KELLY, lawyer; b. Knoxville, Tenn., Nov. 30, 1942; s. Lowell Lorimer and Mary Hartley (James) G.; B.S., U. Tenn., 1966, J.D., 1967; m. Joan Phyllis Meyer, Sept. 4, 1965; children—James Eric, John Gregory. Admitted to Tenn. bar, 1967; asso. Fowler, Rowntree, Fowler & Robertson, Knoxville, 1967-68, partner, 1968-79, partner firm Fowler & Robertson, 1979—. Bd. dirs., treas. Knoxville Housing Corp. of Kappa Sigma, 1972—, Fox Den Village Homeowners' Assn., 1978-79. Mem. Am., Tenn., Knoxville bar assns., Knoxville Jr. C. of C. (treas. 1968-69), Scarabbean Sr. Soc., Phi Delta Phi, Kappa Sigma, Omicron Delta Kappa, Phi Kappa Phi, Beta Gamma Sigma. Clubs: Knoxville City; LeConte; Fox Den Country (dir., sec. Concord, Tenn. 1970-74, 76-78, pres. 1974-76). Presbyn. (deacon 1969-72). Home: 12428 Hound Ears Point Concord TN 37922 Office: 700 First Tenn Bank Bldg Knoxville TN 37902

GIFFORD, KENNETH ALBERT, landscape architect; b. Troy, N.Y., Oct. 4, 1945; s. Kenneth Harold and Evelyn Jeanette (Swankey) G.; B.Landscape Arch., Syracuse (N.Y.) U., 1971; postgrad. SUNY, Syracuse, 1964-71; m. Nancy Louise Moore, July 28, 1979. Asso. landscape architect Schumm Assos., Syracuse, 1971-75; dir. planning Walter Taft Bradshaw & Assos., Lauderdale-by-the-Sea, Fla., 1973-75; sr. asso. Barton Aschman Assos., Washington, 1975-77; exec. dir. downtown revitalization City of Charleston (S.C.), 1977—; adv. bd. George Washington U. Sch. Continuing Edn.; cons. cities grants program Nat. Endowment Arts; past mem. Broward County (Fla.) Planning Adv. Bd. Mem. Am. Soc. Landscape Architects. Landscape architect for Boca Del Mar, Fla., Doral Country Club, Miami, Fla., Onondaga Lake Park, Syracuse. Home: One King St Charleston SC 29401 Office: 205 King St Charleston SC 29401

GIGLIO, FRANCIS ANTHONY, obstetrician, gynecologist; b. Beaumont, Tex., Dec. 29, 1928; s. Charles Samuel and Antoinette Cecilia (Cuchia) G.; B.A., U. Tex., 1950, M.D., 1955; m. Marcia May Frey, June 25, 1955; children—Joan Marie, Suzanne. Intern, Providence Hosp., Washington, 1955-56; resident in obstetrics and gynecology U. Ala., 1958-61, asst. prof. U. Ala. Med. Center, Birmingham 1963-65; practice medicine specializing in obstetrics and gynecology, Beaumont, Tex., 1965—; clin. asst. prof. U. Tex. Med. Br., 1977—. Served with M.C., U.S. Army, 1956-58. Diplomate Am. Bd. Obstetrics and Gynecology. Mem. Central Assn. Obstetricians and Gynecologists, Tex. Assn. Obstetricians and Gynecologists, Am. Fertility Soc., Tex. Med. Assn., AMA, Jefferson County Med. Soc., Beaumont Acad. Medicine, Soc. Gynecol. Laparoscopists. Roman Catholic. Club: Beaumont Country. Contbr. articles to med. jours. Home: 1265 Nottingham Ln Beaumont TX 77706 Office: 2625 Laurel St Beaumont TX 77702

GILBERT, BENJAMIN FRANCIS, public utility ofcl.; b. Havana, Cuba, Feb. 13, 1941; s. Gabriel G. and Winifred F. (Walton) G.; student Ga. Inst. Tech., 1959-63; B.S. in Mech. Engring., U. Miami, 1964; m. Maria Estela Leon, June 18, 1965; children—Benjamin Francis, Winifred C., Alfredo G. Plant engr. Fla. Power & Light Co., Miami, 1965-72, supervising engr., asst. project mgr., project mgr., power plant engr., 1972-77, coordinator fossil fuels sect. fuel resources dept., 1977—; cons. power plant design, operation, and maintenance. Mem. ASME, Assn. Cuban Engrs. (sr.). Republican. Methodist. Clubs: MG Car (Eng.); New Eng. MG T Register; Classic MG of Fla. (past pres.). Office: PO Box 529100 Miami FL 33152

GILBERT, FREDERICK EMERSON, physician; b. Birmingham, Ala., June 1, 1941; s. Frederick E. and Mary Ethel (Spivey) G.; B.S., Birmingham So. Coll., 1963; M.S., U. Ala., 1965, M.D., 1968; children—Robert, Patrick. Intern, Birmingham Baptist Hosp., 1969; resident Birmingham Med. Center, 1971-73; chief cytopathology lab. HEW, Center for Disease Control, Atlanta, 1971-73; lab. dir. Coweta Gen. and Newnan (Ga.) Hosp., 1973—; cons. HEW Medicare Cytology Adv. Com., 1973-77. Served with USPHS, 1970-73. Recipient U. Ala. Research award, 1968; So. Med. Research award, 1965. Mem. Coweta County Med. Soc. (sec.-treas. 1978-80), Am. Soc. Clin. Pathologists, Coll. Am. Pathology, Am. Assn. Clin. Chemists, Am. Assn. for Med. History, N.Y. Acad. Sci., Ala. Acad. Sci., Internat. Acad. Pathology, Am. Soc. Cytology. Methodist. Author numerous articles on cytology and clin. chemistry. Home: 2 Pinehollow Dr Newnan GA 30263 Office: PO Box 1301 Newnan GA 30264

GILBERT, GEORGE RONALD, educator; b. Phila., Nov. 12, 1939; s. John Ralph and Miriam (Wagner) G.; B.S., U. Oreg., 1962; M.S.W., Calif. State U., 1967; M.P.A., Ph.D., U. So. Calif., 1973; m. Janet Louise Abercrombie, Sept. 30, 1961; children—Jennifer Lynn, Stephen Abercrombie. Adminstr., Lockheed Missiles & Space Co., Vandenberg AFB, Calif., 1962-65; parole agt., psychiat. social worker State of Calif., 1965-67; dir. war on poverty programs urban and migrant populations in San Joaquin Valley, Calif., 1967-69; sr. research asso., mem. faculty U. So. Calif., 1969-74, asso. dir. dual masters degree program, 1973-74; prof. pub. adminstrn. Fed. Exec. Inst., Charlottesville, Va., 1974-77, Fla. Internat. U., North Miami, 1977—; lectr. U. Va., George Washington U., U. So. Calif.; cons. to govt. Mem. exec. bd. Community Council, Hanford, Calif., 1967-69; judge Miss. Black Am., Hanford, 1969; mem. charter bd. City of North Miami, 1977—. Grantee Law Enforcement and Assistance Adminstrn., 1972-75. Mem. Am. Soc. Pub. Adminstrn. (nat. bd. mgmt. sci. sect.), Am. Acad. Polit. and Social Sci., Acad. Certified Social Workers, Nat. Assn. Social Workers, Research Soc. (a founder), Phi Kappa Phi. Co-author: Evaluation Management: A Sourcebook of Readings, 1977. Home: 13240 Coronado Ln North Miami FL 33181 Office: Fla Internat Univ North Miami FL 33181

GILBERT, GORDON BRAZIL, JR., mortgage banker; b. Stillwater, Okla., Feb. 5, 1947; s. Gordon B. and Lillian (Freeman) G.; B.B.A., Okla. State U., 1969, M.S., 1971; m. Mary E. Rink, July 6, 1968; children—Stacey Kristen, Tiffany Lynn. With Peat, Marwick, Mitchell & Co., Houston, 1971-76; controller Sam Houston Mortgage Corp., Houston, 1976-79, v.p., 1977-79, fin. v.p., 1979—. Treas. Christ Meml. Lutheran Ch., Houston, 1979—. Mem. Am. Inst. C.P.A.'s, Tex. Soc. C.P.A.'s, Okla. Soc. C.P.A.'s. Office: PO Box 53536 Houston TX 77052

GILBERT, HAROLD WENDELL, record co. exec., social worker; b. Murray, Ky., Jan. 24, 1939; s. Vernon and Martha (Walls) G.; student Miss. Vocational Coll., 1956-58, Wayne State U., George Peabody Coll., Austin Peay State U.; B.S., Tenn. A. and I. U., 1958-62; m. Jean Farley, Sept. 7, 1958; children—Kenneth, Keith, King, Kim, Kleetha. Tchr. Hampton High Sch., Dickson, Tenn., 1960-65; pres. Hitsburgh Music Co. & Rec. Co., Gallatin, 1964—; chmn. bd. Hal and Jean Enterprises, Inc.; pres. So. City Records, 7th Day Music Co.; staff songwriter Cape Ann Music Co., 1971-72, Moss Ross Music Co., 1963, Tree Pub. Co., 1962-63; resource specialist Clarksville-Montgomery Sch. System, Clarksville, Tenn. Work Adjustment coordinator Tenn. Div. Vocat. Rehab.; magistrate 4th dist. Sumner County (Tenn.). Served with USAF, 1958-60. Named Mid-Tenn. High Sch. Band Dir. of Yr., 1969. Mem. Nat. (del. conv. 1977), Tenn. (del. to rep. assembly 1977), Clarksville Montgomery, Sumner County (legis. chmn. 1976-77) edn. assns., Union Hist. Soc. (chmn.), Council for Exceptional Children, U.S. Olympic Soc. Clubs: Mystery Men Soc. (treas.); Elks (del. grand lodge conv. 1977, exalted ruler lodge 1977-78, state dir. civil liberties, del. grand lodge conv. 1978-79). Author: A History of Black American Music. Home: 157 Ford Ave PO Box 195 Gallatin TN 37066 Office: Hitsburgh Music Bldg Ford Ave Gallatin TN 37066

GILBERT, JAMES HAROLD, musician, univ. adminstr.; b. El Dorado, Ark., June 7, 1920; s. James Rankin and Clara Ursula (McCuin) G.; student Baylor U., 1938-40; B.A., La. Tech. U., 1946; B.Mus.Edn., Am. Conservatory of Music, 1952; M.M., Northwestern U., 1955; m. Eleanor Ann Wortham, June 16, 1963; children—Timothy Clark, Steven Todd. Profl. musician, Chgo., 1946-54; band dir. Billings (Okla.) High Sch., 1954-55; band and orch. dir. Horace Mann Jr. High Sch., Amarillo, Tex., 1955-66; arts adminstr. La. Tech. U., 1966—; violinist Amarillo Symphony, 1955-66; condr. Ruston Civic Symphony, 1969-73. Served with AUS, 1942-46. Mem. Assn. Coll., Univ. and Community Arts Adminstrs., Internat. Soc. Profl. Arts Adminstrs., Nat. Sch. Orch. Assn., NEA, Phi Mu Alpha Sinfonia, Pi Kappa Alpha, Phi Beta. Democrat. Baptist. Home: 408 Forest Circle Ruston LA 71270

GILBERT, JOSEPH FRANKLIN, trucking co. exec.; b. Staunton, Va., Aug. 30, 1928; s. Robert Franklin and Myrtle Guinn (Carr) G.; grad. Dunsmore Bus. Coll., 1947; m. Nancy Katheryn Parker, Apr. 17, 1948; children—Jeffery Parker, Jill Nanette. With Smith's Transfer Corp., Staunton, 1947—, div. mgr., Wallingford, Conn., 1959-64, regional v.p., Staunton, 1964-74, pres., chief operating officer, 1974—; dir. Va. Nat. Bank, Staunton. Bd. dirs. United Way Staunton and Augusta County, Salvation Army Staunton. Mem. Trucking Mgmt. Inc. (dir.), Va. Hwy. Users Assn., Trucking Employers Labour Council, Am. Trucking Assn., C. of C. Staunton and Augusta County (dir.). Club: Verona Kiwanis. Home: 406 Rainbow Dr Staunton VA 24401 Office: PO Box 1000 Staunton VA 24401

GILBERT, JOSEPH GATLIFF, clin. psychologist; b. Pineville, Ky., Nov. 21, 1920; s. Thomas Joseph and Eva (Gatliff) G.; B.A. cum laude, U. S.C., 1951, M.A., 1952; Ph.D. in Clin. Psychology, U. Tenn., 1954; m. Katherine Armida Jennings, Aug. 30, 1948; children—Armida Jennings, Arthur Herbert, Robert Joseph, Katherine Elizabeth. Clin. psychologist Regional Office VA, St. Petersburg, Fla., 1954-55; chief clin. psychologist VA Mental Health Clinic, Pensacola, Fla., 1955-59, VA Gen. Med. and Surg. Hosp., Fayetteville, N.C., 1959-60; clin. and research psychologist State Hosp., Yankton, S.D., 1960-61; chief clin. psychologist Richland County Mental Health Clinic, Columbia, S.C., 1961-63, Child Devel. Center, S.C. Med. Coll. Hosp., Charleston, 1963-64; chief clin. psychologist Mental Health Center, Anderson, 1964-66; clin. psychologist VA Hosp., Charleston, 1966-69; clin. psychologist S.C. State Hosp., Columbia, 1969-75, key psychologist unit IV, 1975—. Served with U.S. Mcht. Marine, 1942-46. Mem. Phi Beta Kappa. Author: Clinical Psychological Tests in Psychiatric and Medical Practice, 1969; Interpreting Psychological Test Data, Vol. I, 1978, Vol. II, 1979. Research and publs. in field. Home: 1624 Romain Dr Columbia SC 29210 Office: SC State Hosp Columbia SC 29201

GILBERT, JOSEPHINE DOROTHY, educator; b. Fairfield, Conn., Dec. 31, 1913; d. Peter J. and Eva Gill; B.A., Tex. A&I U., Kingsville, 1950, M.A., 1955; spl. courses U. Tex., 1954, U. Houston, 1955; m. Robert L. Gilbert, Sept. 2, 1939. Sales rep. Bookhouse for Children, 1937-40; clearance officer Simsbury (Conn.) Airport, 1941-44; citrus grower, Rio Grande Valley, Tex., 1945-51; tchr., coordinator distributive edn., Robstown, Tex., 1952-59, Miller High Sch., Corpus Christi, 1959-72; tchr., coordinator W.B. Ray High Sch., Corpus Christi, 1972—. Life cert. tchr., coordinator distributive edn., Tex. Mem. Corpus Christi Classroom Tchrs., Tex. Tchrs. Assn., NEA, Tex. Vocat. Tchrs., Nat. Vocat. Tchrs., Tex. Assn. Distributive Edn. Tchrs., Nat. Assn. Distributive Edn. Tchrs., AAUW, Aux. VFW, Am. Legion Aux., Tex. Aviation Assn., Aux. World War I Assn., Distributive Edn. Tchrs. S. Tex. (pres. 1964). Methodist. Clubs: Afflatus (pres. 1950), Valley Garden. Author: Communications for Distribution, 1962. Home: 4258 Dody St Corpus Christi TX 78411 Office: 1002 Texan Trail Corpus Christi TX 78411

GILBERT, LEONARD HAROLD, lawyer; b. Hutchinson, Minn., Apr. 3, 1936; s. Sidney and Clara (Franzblau) G.; B.A., Emory U., 1958; LL.B., Harvard Law Sch., 1961; m. Jean Buchman, Apr. 21, 1963; children—Jonathan Stuart, Suzanne Elaine. Admitted to Fla. bar, 1961; atty. firm Carlton, Fields, Ward, Emmanuel, Smith & Cutler, Tampa, 1961—. Chmn. Arts Council of Tampa, 1973-74; mem. Hillsborough County (Fla.) Bicentennial Commn., 1973-76; mem. charter revision com. City of Tampa, 1975. Bd. dirs. Gasparilla Sidewalk Festival, Tampa, 1970-74. Served with USCGR, 1961-69. Fellow Am. Bar Found.; mem. Am. Bar Assn. (chmn. gen. practice sect. 1979-80), Fla. Bar (bd. govs. 1975—, chmn. corp., banking and bus. law sect. 1970-71, chmn. gen. practice sect. 1972-73, pres.-elect 1979-80), Bar Assn. Hillsborough County (pres. 1974-75). Club: Kiwanis (pres. 1972). Home: 926 Golfview Tampa FL 33609 Office: PO Box 3239 Tampa FL 33601

GILBERT, MILDRED OPAL, nurse; b. Dry Fork, W.Va., Oct. 19, 1919; d. Leon Hulver and Grace Victoria (Mongold) Judy; diploma Capital City Sch. Nursing, 1944; m. Earl Edward Gilbert, Oct. 11, 1968. Charge nurse Washington D.C. Gen. Hosp., 1944-45; civilian nurse USAF, Md., 1945-49; civilian staff nurse U.S. Army, Japan, 1949-52, USPHS, Washington, 1952-53; commd. 1st lt. USAF, 1952, advanced through grades to maj., 1965; staff nurse, charge nurse, flight nurse, various posts, 1953-73; ret., 1973. Awarded Flight Nurse Wings U.S. Air Force; registered nurse, D.C., Tex. Mem. Am., Tex. nurses assns., Capital City Sch. Nursing Alumnae Assn., Am. Heart Assn., Am. Assn. Ret. Persons. Democrat. Methodist. Clubs: Daus. of Nile (San Antonio); Nile of the Hills (pres. 1978) (Boerne, Tex.); Question Mark. Home: Route 5 Box 5227 Boerne TX 78006

GILBERT, PHILIP HENRY, med. assn. exec.; b. Walpole, N.H., Sept. 15, 1939; s. Bernard Simmons and Ada (Brown) Smalley (guardians); B.S. in Social Welfare, Fla. State U., 1965; postgrad. in Vocat. Rehab., 1966-68; postgrad. in vocat. rehab. So. Ill. U., 1967; Hon. degree, So. Coll. Bus., Orlando, Fla., 1969; m. Carole Frances Roberts, Nov. 26, 1971; 1 son, Kevin Austin. Counselor vocat. rehab. Bur. Blind Services, State of Fla., Jacksonville, 1966-67, state placement specialist, 1967-68, state supr. social security trust fund program, 1968-71, dist. dir., 1971-72; dir. rehab. Gateway Hope Center, Inc., Jacksonville, 1971; exec. dir. Fla. Council on Aging, Jacksonville, 1972-73; chief Bur. Grants Devel. and Monitoring, Div. of Aging, State of Fla., Tallahassee, 1973-74; dir. med. edn. and services dept. Fla. Med. Assn., Jacksonville, 1974-75; asso. dir. Fla. Med. Found., Jacksonville, also dir. found. dept., 1975-77; exec. dir. Fla. Med. Polit. Action Com., Tallahassee, 1977-78, dir. govt. program dept., 1979—. Mem. steering com. First Internat. Conf. on The Blind in Computer Programming, 1968; mem. Pres.'s Com. on Employment of Handicapped, 1969—; mem. Fla. Gov.'s Com. on Employment of Handicapped, 1969—; bd. govs. Gateway Hope Center, Inc., 1972-74; cons. first blind computer programmer tng. project So. Coll. Bus., 1968-69; cons. placing the blind in competitive employment So. Ill. U., 1968; cons. employment of handicapped Disney World, 1972. Recipient Outstanding Service award Fla. Council on Aging, 1973. Mem. Am. Assn. Workers for the Blind (dir. 1968), Nat., Fla. rehab. assns. Home: 2731 Blairstone Rd Apt 8 Tallahassee FL 32301 Office: PO Box 10269 100 E College St Tallahassee FL 32302

GILBERT, RAYMOND MC CUIN, educator; b. El Dorado, Ark., July 20, 1922; s. James R. and Clara Ursula (McCuin) G.; B.Mus., Am. Conservatory Music, 1949, M.Mus., 1951; Ed.D., Northwestern State U. La., 1970; m. Ida Sampson, Aug. 10, 1946; children—Diane Gilbert Lawhon, Deborah Ann. (dec.). Tchr., El Dorado Pub. Schs., 1951-68; asst. prof. edn. Northwestern State U., Natchitoches, La., 1970-74, asso. prof., 1974-79, prof., 1979—; cons. in field. Dir. El Dorado Choral Soc., 1964-68; mem. Pres.'s Com. Traffic Safety, 1958. Served with U.S. Army, 1942-45. Recipient Pres.'s Scholarship award Northwestern State U. La., 1970. Mem. Ark. Jr. High Sch. Vocal Music Assn. (pres. 1964), Lions (pres. El Dorado chpt. 1966-67), Assn. Ednl. Communications and Tech., United Fedn. Coll. Tchrs., Assn. Supervision and Curriculum Devel., Nat., La. assn. tchr. educators, U.S. Jaycees (nat. dir. 1957-58), Phi Delta Kappa, Phi Mu Alpha Sinfonia. Democrat. Presbyterian. Contbr. articles in field to profl. jours. Home: 111 S Williams Ave Natchitoches LA 71457 Office: Dept Secondary Edn Northwestern State U Natchitoches LA 71457

GILBERT, STEVEN JOHN, lawyer; b. Freeport, Tex., Sept. 5, 1947; s. William Drew and Josephine (Inamouretti) G.; B.A., Stephen F. Austin U., 1969; J.D., U. Houston, 1975; m. Phyllis Fenerarily, May 23, 1970; children—Steven Drew, Emily Clair. Tchr., Huntington (Tex.) Ind. Sch. Dist., 1969-70, Ft. Bend Ind. Sch. Dist., 1970-75; admitted to Tex. bar, 1975; asst. dist. atty., Richmond, Tex., 1976-77; mem. firm Van Slyke & Gilbert, Richmond, 1977—. Mem. State Bar Tex., Houston Bar Assn., Ft. Bend Bar Assn. (dir.), Tex. Criminal Defense Lawyers Assn. Democrat. Baptist. Club: Lions (dir. Sugar Land 1976-77). Office: 500 Morton St Richmond TX 77469

GILBERT, WALTER RANDOLPH, JR., ophthalmologist; b. Dalton, Ga., Oct. 16, 1936; s. Walter Randolph and Betty Lynn (Prater) G.; B.S., Emory U., 1958; M.D., Duke U., 1963; m. Aimee Elizabeth Sparks, Apr. 6, 1967; children—Elizabeth Lynn, Walter Randolph III. Intern in medicine Osler Med Service, Johns Hopkins Hosp., Balt., 1963-64; resident in ophthalmology Wilmer Eye Inst., Johns Hopkins Hosp., 1964-67; fellow in ophthalmology Bascom-Palmer Eye Inst., Miami, Fla., 1967-68; practice medicine specializing in ocular surgery, Jacksonville, Fla., 1968—; mem. staff St. Vincent's Med. Center, 1968—, chief sect. ophthalmology, 1976—; mem. staffs Riverside Hosp., St. Lukes Hosp., Bapt. Hosp., Univ. Hosp.; clin. asst. prof. ophthalmology Sch. Medicine, U. Fla. Diplomate Am. Bd. Ophthalmology. Mem. Am. Acad. Ophthalmology and Otolaryngology, Am. Intraocular Lens Implant Soc., Phacoemulsification and Cataract Methodology Soc., A.C.S., AMA, Fla. Med. Assn., Duval County Med. Assn., Duval County Soc. Ophthalmology, Alpha Omega Alpha. Mem. editorial bd. Jour. Ophthalmic Surgery, 1970—. Home: 5161 Yacht Club Rd Jacksonville FL 32210 Office: 2535 Riverside Ave Jacksonville FL 32204

GILCHRIST, WILLIAM RISQUE, JR., economist; b. Lexington, Ky., July 16, 1944; s. William Risque and Susan (McLemore) G.; B.B.A., U. Miami, 1966, M.B.A., 1970; postgrad. Northwestern U., 1973—; m. Peggy Linder Gardner, Mar. 20, 1968; children—William Risque, Shannon Linder, Heather Susan. Asso. dir. conf. services div. continuing edn. U. Miami, Coral Gables, Fla., 1966-71; asst. dir. edn. and tng. Mortgage Bankers Assn. Am., Washington, 1971-73; pres. Ventura Fin. Corp., Fort Lauderdale, Fla., 1973-76; pres. Gilchrist and Assos., Pompano Beach., Fla., London, Eng., and Basel, Switzerland, 1976—; dir. Cafe Embajador, Fort Lauderdale and Bogota, Colombia; cons. in field. Recipient Certificate of Achievement, Savs. and Loan Execs. Seminar, 1971. Mem. Miami-Dade County (Fla.) C. of C., NAB, Econ. Soc. South Fla., Mortgage Bankers Assn. Republican. Episcopalian. Clubs: Kiwanis. Marina Bay, Mutiny. Author: International Monetary Systems—Alternatives, 1969; Eurodollar Outlook-OPEC and the LDC's, 1978. Home: 1341 SE 9th Ave Pompano Beach FL 33060

GILES, HERMAN HASCAL, newspaper exec.; b. Big Stone Gap, Va., July 30, 1922; s. Harrison Oliver and Clara (Rose) G.; grad. pub. high sch.; m. Ruth Miller, Sept. 21, 1942; children—Kay, Eric, Amanda. With Bristol Virginia-Tennessean newspaper, Bristol, Va., 1949-50, 53—, asso. pub., 1961-64, pub., 1969—; pub. Bristol Herald Courier, 1974—; asst. news editor Nashville Tennessean, 1950-51; make-up editor Louisville Times, 1951-53; v.p. Bristol Newspaper Printing Co., 1953; pres. Bristol Newspapers, Inc., 1978—; v.p., dir. Sullivan County News, Blountville, Tenn.; dir. Hi-Riser Publs., Ft. Lauderdale, Fla., 1978—, Dominion Nat. Bank, Bristol, Va. Chmn. Bristol (Tenn.) Indsl. Devel. Commn., 1969—. Recipient N.W. Ayer award Kingsport News, 1944; news writing award Va. Press Assn., 1954. Mem. Bristol C. of C. (pres. 1963). Baptist. Author: Kansas Trail, 1956; also adventure stories in popular publs. Home: 100 Stonecroft Circle Bristol TN 37620 Office: 320 Morrison Blvd Bristol VA 24201

GILES, JERRY WILL, artist; b. Birmingham, Ala., Jan. 7, 1949; s. Sterlin Perry and Zula Marie (Hearn) G.; student Athens Coll., 1967-68, Memphis State U., 1968-70; B.F.A., U. Tex., Austin, 1973; m. Patricia Anne Siegfreid, Sept. 25, 1971. Artist, Dallas Stage Scenery, 1973-74, scenic artist, 1975-79; design artist Party Time, Inc., Dallas, 1974-75; prin. Jer Giles Scenic Artist, Lancaster, Tex., 1979—; prodn. design cons. to colls. Mem. United Scenic Artists, Lancaster Hist. Soc., Alpha Psi Omega. Home and Office: 102 W 7th St Lancaster TX 75146

GILES, JOHN MICHAEL, facilities planner; b. Oak Ridge, July 13, 1951; s. Thomas Clarence and Jeanette (Beaudion) G.; B.S., Ga. Inst. Tech., 1976; m. Mary Jo Swenson, June 15, 1974. Plant mgr. Dettelbach Chem. Corp., Atlanta, 1973-75; facilities planning mgr. Tex. Instruments Corp., Dallas, Tex., 1976—. Bd. dirs., v.p. Texins Activity Center. Mem. Am. Inst. Indsl. Engrs., Tex. Soc. Profl. Engrs., Ga. Inst. Tech. Alumni Assn. Roman Catholic. Club: Sierra. Home: 4521 Fargo Dr Plano TX 75075 Office: PO Box 5474 M/S 207 Dallas TX 75222

GILES, JOHN ROBERT, social worker; b. Tabiona, Utah, Oct. 3, 1923; s. Draper and Nellie Chelatta (Casper) G.; B.S. in Secondary Edn., Brigham Young U., 1954; M.S.W., U. Utah, 1956; cert. Pan Am. U., Tex., 1975; m. Helen Geneva Moubray, Mar. 10, 1948; children—Roaney, Bobi, Dirk, Kelly, Peggy. Foster home cons. Hidalgo County Child Welfare Dept., Edinburg, Tex., 1956-57; supr. of adoptions Childrens Home Soc. of Idaho, Boise, 1957-59; exec. dir. Family Counseling Service, McAllen, Tex., 1959-62; chief psychiat. social worker Tex. Adult Mental Health Clinic, Harlingen, Tex., 1962-67; program dir. Mental Health-Mental Retardation Center, Edinburg, 1967-71; instr. Pan Am. U., Edinburg, 1971; program adminstr. Lower Valley Youth Service Bur., McAllen, 1972-74; planner Area Agy. on Aging Lower Rio Grande Valley Devel. Council, McAllen, 1975-77; psychiat. social worker Tropical Tex. Center for Mental Health and Mental Retardation, Edinburg, 1977—. Mem. community adv. council McAllen Sch. Dist., 1975-77; bd. dirs. Image Youth Services System, Inc., 1973-78, co-chmn., 1975-78. Mem. Acad. Cert. Social Workers, Nat. Assn. of Social Workers. Contbr. articles on social work to profl. jours. Home: Route 1 Box 133D Mission TX 78572 Office: Tropical Tex Center for Mental Health and Mental Retardation 1409 S 9th St PO Drawer 1108 Edinburg TX 78539

GILES, MARTIN LOUIS, fire sprinkler co. exec.; b. Danville, Va., Dec. 20, 1944; s. Roland Carter and Louise (Towler) G.; certificate, Richmond Profl. Inst., 1965; m. Patricia Kaye Hoffler, July 19, 1979; children—Matthew Jason, Jeffrey Martin. Engr., Va. Sprinkler Co., Ashland, 1965-66, v.p., 1968-71, pres., 1971—, also dir.; dir. Va. Pipe & Supply Co., Ashland. Served with U.S. Army, 1966-68. Mem. Nat. Fire Protection Assn., Soc. Fire Protection Engrs., Va. Fire Prevention Assn., Nat. Automatic Sprinkler and Fire Control Assn. Home: 1708 Cloister Dr Richmond VA 23233 Office: PO Box 986 Atlee Elmont Exit I95 Ashland VA 23005

GILES, N(ORMA) JANE, profl. counselor; b. Coles County, Ill., Oct. 2, 1935; d. Leonard A. and Erica R. Anderson; B.S. in Edn., Eastern Ill. U., 1970, M.S. in Ednl. Psychology, 1972; m. Emory L. Giles, Feb. 2, 1974; children by previous marriage—James Michael Shoot, Larry Alan Shoot. Speech therapist Arcola (Ill.) Community Sch., 1970-72; grad. asst. Eastern Ill. U., Charleston, 1972-73; speech therapist and counselor Stewardson-Strasburg (Ill.) Community Schs., 1973-74; counselor Eastmont Jr. High Sch., Salt Lake City, 1974-76; counselor Dhahran (Saudi Arabia) Acad., 1976-78; profl. counselor, 1978—. Youth group leader 1st Christian Ch., Charleston, 1969-72. Recipient citation Champaign (Ill.) Services for Crippled Children, 1972. Mem. Am. Personnel and Guidance Assn., Am. Sch. Counselor's Assn., NEA, Near East South Asia Assn., Kappa Delta Pi, Sigma Eta Lambda (chpt. pres. 1970). Republican. Presbyterian. Home and Office: 429 Alpine St E Altamonte Springs FL 32701

GILES, THOMAS D., physician; b. Greenwood, Miss., Feb. 24, 1938; s. John Thomas and Aliece (Davis) G.; A.A., East Central Jr. Coll., Decatur, Miss., 1957; postgrad. Millsaps Coll., 1957-58; M.D., Tulane U. Sch. Medicine, 1962; m. Helene Marie Rowley, June 9, 1961; children—Helene Marie, Denise Marie, Lizette Marie. Intern, Charity Hosp. of La., New Orleans, 1962-63, resident internal medicine Tulane Service, 1963-66, chief resident, 1965-66, cardiology fellow, 1966, 68-70; instr. dept. medicine Tulane U. Sch. Medicine, 1964-70, asst. prof. medicine, 1970-73, asso. prof., 1973-74, 76-77, clin. asso. prof. medicine, 1974-76, prof., 1977—; sr. vis. physician Tulane div. Charity Hosp. of La., New Orleans, 1970—, asso. dir. La. Heart Center, 1974, dir. Quality Assurance Program, 1974-76; dir. quality assurance program Tulane Med. Center-Hosp. and Clinic, 1976—; chief of medicine New Orleans VA Hosp., 1976—; adviser high blood pressure control La. Health and Human Resources Adminstrn., 1977—; cons. USPHS Hosp., New Orleans, 1977—. Served with MC AUS, 1968-69. Gillentine fellow, Tulane U. Sch. Medicine, 1969. Fellow Am. Coll. Cardiology, A.C.P.; mem. Am. Soc. Echocardiography, Am. Fedn. Clin. Research, Am., La. heart assns., Musser-Burch Soc. (sec.-treas. 1964—), New Orleans Acad. Internal Medicine, So. Soc. Clin. Investigation, Orleans Parish Med. Soc., Phi Theta Kappa, Alpha Epsilon Delta. Contbr. numerous articles to med. jours. Home: 3433 St Charles Ave Apt F New Orleans LA 70115 Office: 1430 Tulane Ave Room 7714 New Orleans LA 70112

GILFORD, MARYE BLAND, educator; b. Hot Springs, Ark.; d. Clarence Theodore and Naomi Frances (Hill) Andrews; B.A., Wiley Coll., Marshall, Tex., 1957; M.B.A., U. Tex., 1960; postgrad. St. Mary's U., 1964-65, Our Lady of Lake U., 1966, North Tex. State U., 1975, 76, 79, S.W. Tex. State U., 1974, Tex. U., 1977; m. Murrene Gilford, Feb. 18, 1961; children—Dexter Earl, Muriel Yvonne. Mgr., Pythian Bath House, Hot Springs, 1949-55; sec. Grand Ct. Order of Calanthe of Tex., 1955-58; tchr. bus. Austin and San Antonio public schs., 1959-70; instr. St. Philip's Coll., San Antonio, 1970-74, asst. prof., 1974—, chmn. dept. acctg. tech. and real estate, 1977—. Chmn. supervisory com. Black Unity Coordinating Council Fed. Credit Union, 1976—. Mem. Am. Acctg. Assn., Tex. Jr. Coll. Tchrs. Assn., Tex. Bus. Edn. Assn., Bus. Edn. Tchrs. Assn., Nat. Bus. Edn. Assn., Delta Pi Epsilon, Zeta Phi Beta, Alpha Wives Aux. Home: 3802 Willowwood St San Antonio TX 78219 Office: St Philip's Coll 2111 Nevada St San Antonio TX 78203

GILKESON, JAMES WILLIAM, JR., constrn. co. exec.; b. Fisherville, Va., Oct. 9, 1925; s. James William and Zanie Julia (Winchester) G.; B.S. in Civil Engring., Va. Poly. Inst., 1950; m. Emily Thomas Scott, June 27, 1953; children—J. Scott, Julia R., David T., Emily Page. Foreman, Va. Asphalt Paving Co., Inc., 1950-55, mgr. no. dist., 1955-56; v.p. engring., safety dir. Nielsen Constrn. Co., Inc., Harrisonburg, Va., also dir.; dir. Shen Valley Corp., 1968-71. Mem. gen. adv. com. Massenutten Vocation Tech. Center, 1970—; mem. exec. com. bldg. div., constrn. sect. Indsl. Dept., Nat. Safety Council, 1970—; chmn. activities com. Stonewall Jackson Area council Boy Scouts Am., 1970-75, dir. 1970—, v.p. scouting, 1975—; mem. local Price Stblzn. Bd., 1970—; mem. Christian edn. com. Lexington Presbytery, Va., 1959-67, pres. ch. sch. supts., 1961-62, with Christian edn. com. Synod of Va. Presbyn. Ch., 1961-63, with ministry group Synod of Vas., 1977; commr. Gen. Assembly Presbyn. Ch. U.S., 1965; missions leader Desmios Community House Ch., 1972-73, pastoral leader, 1973-76; mem. corrections adv. com. Va. State Crime Commn., 1973-74; mem. corrections subgroup Va. Task Force on Criminal Justice Goals and Objectives, 1975—. Mem. Planning Commn., City of Harrisonburg, Va., 1969-76, vice-chmn., 1971-72, chmn., 1973-76. Bd. dirs. Va. Safety Assn., Inc., 1970—. Bd. dirs. Homes Found. Served with USNR, 1943-46. Recipient dist. award merit Stonewall Jackson area council Boy Scouts Am., 1971, Silver Beaver award, 1973. Mem. ASCE (asso. mem.; mem. exec. council, program chmn. Blue Ridge chpt. Va. sect. 1971), Asso. Gen. Contractors Am. (co-chmn. safety com. Va. br. 1967), Harrisonburg Rockingham C. of C. (chmn. safety com. 1968-73), Va. Poly. Inst. Alumni Assn. (v.p. Massanutten chpt. 1967-68), Order Arrow Boy Scouts Am. (Vigil honor 1972). Presbyn. (elder 1961). Home: 1048 S Dogwood Dr Harrisonburg VA 22801 Office: Route #1 PO Box 591 Harrisonburg VA 22801

GILKEY, HERBERT TALBOT, trade assn. exec.; b. Boulder, Colo., Nov. 27, 1924; s. Herbert James and Mildred Virginia (Talbot) G.; B.S. in Mech. Engring., Iowa State U., 1947, M.S., 1949; postgrad. U. Ill., 1950-53; m. Romona Marie Olsen, June 28, 1946 (dec. 1970); children—Virginia Anne, Herbert David, Edele Christine, Arthur Talbot, Martha Olive; m. 2d, Mary Louise Tucker Brown, Apr. 26, 1974. Research asso. in mech. engring. U. Ill., Urbana, 1949-55; dir. tech. services Nat. Warm Air Heating and Air Conditioning Assn., Cleve., 1955-67; research dir. Waterloo Register div. Dynamics Corp. of Am., Cedar Falls, Iowa, 1967-70; dir. of govt. and consumer affairs Air Conditioning and Refrigeration Inst., Arlington, Va., 1971-77, exec. dir. pub. affairs, 1977—. Scoutmaster Greater Cleve. council Boy Scouts Am., 1964-67, commr. Wapsipinicon and Nat. Capital Area councils, 1967—; mem. Bd. Zoning Appeals, Cedar Falls, 1969-70; mem. Energy Conservation Task Force, Fairfax County, Va., 1977-78; elder Presbyn. Ch., Cleveland Heights, Ohio, 1960-62, Cedar Falls, 1968-70. Served with C.E., U.S. Army, 1943-45. Recipient Award of Merit, Boy Scouts Am., 1974; registered profl. engr., Ohio, Iowa. Fellow Am. Soc. of Heating, Refrigerating and Air-Conditioning Engrs. (Distinguished Service award 1970, chmn. research and tech. com. 1971-72, chmn. govt. affairs com. 1975-76, chmn. energy conservation com. 1976-77); mem. ASME, Nat. Fire Protection Assn. (mem. air-conditioning com. 1960-67), Uniform Boiler and Pressure Vessel Laws Soc. (mem. council). Contbr. articles on heating and air-conditioning engring. to profl. jours.; editor various air-conditioning design and installation manuals, 1955-67. Home: 2606 E Meredith Dr Vienna VA 22180 Office: Air Conditioning and Refrigeration Inst 1815 N Ft Meyer Dr Arlington VA 22209

GILL, EUGENE LAVERNE, accountant; b. Kansas City, Kans., Jan. 2, 1929; s. Carl and Anna (Sambol) G.; student La. State U., 1953-59, U. Ala., 1960; m. Mary Alita Williams, Sept. 9, 1967; children—Alita Ann, Carla Gene, Mary Kristin. Partner firm Carl Gill & Son, Mercantile, New Roads, La., 1950-63; pub. accountant Eugene L. Gill, C.P.A., New Roads, 1962-66; partner Gill & Kendrick, New Roads, 1966—; pres. 104 West End Drive, Inc., Ben Morgan Furniture Co., Poor Boy's Friend, Inc., Gill Land Co., Ltd.; v.p. Liberty Oil & Gas Corp. Chmn. bd. dirs. Pointe Coupee Gen. Hosp., 1969-70; conferee La. Regional Citizens Conf. on Criminal Justice, 1973. Life mem. Lions League for Crippled Children, La. Scottish Rite Found. C.P.A., La., Miss., Ark. Mem. Am. Acctg. Assn., Nat. Assn. Accts., Am. Inst. C.P.A.'s Soc. La. C.P.A.'s (mem. com. to secure C.P.A. problems 1962-69, chmn. 1963-66, vice chmn. consultation com. 1966-67, mem. profl. devel. council 1967-71), La. Civil Service League, Am. Bus. Law Assn., Am. Judicature Soc., Public Affairs Research Council La. (trustee 1968-78), Nat. Soujourners, Am. Hort. Soc., Farm Bur. Fedn., Assn. Am. Indian Affairs, Am. Radio Relay League. Democrat. Episcopalian (warden, vestryman, lay reader, del. diocesian conventions 1975—). Clubs: Masons (32 deg.), Shriners (knight comdr. Ct. Honor), Lions (past pres., past treas. New Roads); Order Eastern Star; Shrine (Baton Rouge); False River Country. Contbr. articles to profl. jours. Home: Waterloo Pl Ventress LA 70783 Office: 104 W End Dr New Roads LA 70760

GILL, LAWRENCE EDWARDS, air force officer; b. San Antonio, Aug. 23, 1940; s. John Edwards and Ruth (Scammahorn) G.; B.A., Tex. Tech. U., 1964; postgrad. Air Command and Staff Coll., 1977; M.S., Abilene Christian U., 1980; m. Mary Eleanor Murphy, Apr. 24, 1965; children—Lawrence Edwards II, Michael Murphy, Marla Ruth. Commd. 2d lt. Air Force, 1964, advanced through grades to lt. col., 1980; squadron pilot, dep. chief current ops. Cam Rahn Air Base, Viet Nam, 1971-72; instr., course dir. U.S. Air Force Acad., 1972-76; chief 463TAW Safety Div., Dyess AFB, Tex., 1978-80. Decorated D.F.C. with 1 oak leaf cluster, Air medal with 4 oak leaf clusters. Mem. Air Force Assn. (mem. jr. officer adv. council exec. com. 1974-76), Airlift Assn., Am. Security Council, Order of Daedalians, Phi Delta Theta. Republican. Roman Catholic. Home: 3117 Ivanhoe Abilene TX 79605 Office: 463TAW Dyess AFB TX 79607

GILL, RALPH WELCH, chem. co. exec.; b. Glenmora, La., Mar. 23, 1943; s. Stamps Clay and Tessa (Welch) G.; student La. Coll., Pineville, 1963-64; A.A. in Bus. Adminstrn., Pensacola Jr. Coll., 1977; m. Dovie Slaughter, Aug. 10, 1963; children—Donna, Gina, Randall. Signalman, Mo.-Pacific Ry., St. Louis, 1961-63; control lab. technician Tenneco Chems. Inc., Oakdale, La., 1963-66, shipping supr., 1966-71, freight specialist Pensacola, Fla., 1971-73; fleet mgr. Reichhold Chem. Co. Inc., Pensacola, 1973-75, traffic mgr., 1975-77, procurement mgr., 1977—. Loaned exec. Escambia County United Way, 1978-79. Recipient Disting. Service award Escambia County, 1978. Mem. Pulp Chems. Assn., TAPPI, Pensacola Traffic Club (pres. 1978-79), Pensacola Jaycees (dir. 1978-79), Aircraft Owners and Pilots Assn. Democrat. Baptist. Home: 3746 Bayou Blvd Pensacola FL 32503 Office: PO Box 1433 Pensacola FL 32596

GILL, RAYMOND ALEXANDER, architect; b. Dallas, July 20, 1946; s. Raymond Alexander and Louise Deel G.; B.Arch., U. Tex., Austin, 1970; m. Carolyn Kay Smith, Nov. 30, 1945. With Page Southerland Page, archtl. firm, Austin, Tex., 1968-71; constrn. mgr. Nat. Homes Constrn. Corp., Lago Vista, Tex., 1971-73; gen. mgr. constrn. services Nat. Resort Communities, Lago Vista, 1973-74; owner R. Gill & Assos., Round Rock, Tex., 1974—. Mem. Round Rock Preservatives Commn., 1978—. Mem. AIA, Nat. Council Archtl. Registration Bds., Tex. Soc. Architects, Tex. Bd. Archtl. Examiners, Round Rock C. of C. (dir. 1978), Round Rock Jaycees (state dir. 1975). Methodist. Home and Office: PO Box 217 Round Rock TX 78664

GILLAM, DAVID EARL, elec. engr.; b. Orangeburg, S.C., Nov. 19, 1941; s. David Hydrick and Edith (Inabinet) G.; B.S. in E.E., U. S.C., 1965; m. Harriet Alice Smith, Aug. 22, 1964; children—Kenneth David, John Christopher. Senate page, S.C. State Senate, Columbia, 1963; elec. engr. Dept. Public Utilities, City of Orangeburg (S.C.), 1965-77, supt. Electric Div., 1978—. Notary public, S.C.; registered profl. engr., S.C. Mem. Internat. Assn. Elec. Inspectors. Methodist. Clubs: Kiwanis, Elks. Home: 694 Heyward St NW Orangeburg SC 29115 Office: PO Box 1057 Orangeburg SC 29115

GILLANDERS, J. DAVID, elec. engr.; b. Schenectady, May 18, 1939; s. Donald Clarke and Cathrine (Schauber) G.; B.S.E.E., U. Mich., 1962, M.S. in Elec. Engring., 1963, M.S. in Physics, 1969,

Ph.D. in Elec. Engring., 1972; m. Barbara Lois Lanehart, Aug. 11, 1962; children—Kendra Maria, Tara Zabrina. Design engr. Lear Seigler Co., Ann Arbor, Mich., 1963; research asso. U. Mich., Ann Arbor, 1966-69; systems engr., systems analyst Interface Systems, Inc., Ann Arbor, 1969-73; asst. prof. elec. engring. Tex. A&I U., Kingsville, 1973—. NASA/Am. Soc. Engring. Edn. summer faculty fellow, 1975, 77, 79. Office: Campus Box 192 Kingsville TX 78363

GILLEAN, WILLIAM OTHO, JR., physician, psychiatrist; b. Stamford, Tex., Jan. 24, 1935; s. William Otho and Esther Lillie (Parish) G.; B.A., U. Tex., 1957, M.D., 1961; m. Doris Milan, Nov. 8, 1964; children—William Otho III, Julia Rebecca, Martha Amelia, Anne Elizabeth. Intern, U. Tex. Med. Br., Galveston, 1961-62, resident psychiatry and neurology, 1962-65; practice medicine specializing in psychiatry, Corpus Christi, Tex., 1965, San Antonio, 1968—; chief psychiatry dept. Bapt. Meml. Hosp., San Antonio, 1969, Luth. Gen. Hosp., San Antonio, 1969-72; chief psychiatry service Brooke Gen. Hosp., San Antonio, 1967; cons. psychiatry VA Mental Hygiene Clinic, San Antonio, 1969-74; chmn. psychiat. policy com., vice-chmn. psychiatry dept. Villa Rosa unit Santa Rosa Med. Center, 1973, chmn. utilization review psychiat. dept., 1975; clin. asst. prof. psychiatry U. Tex. Health Sci. Center, San Antonio, 1968—; chief psychiatrist, Bexar County Mental Health Center, San Antonio, 1973—; cons., Patrician Movement Program, San Antonio, 1971-74. Bd. dirs. Halfway House, San Antonio, 1970-72. Served to capt., M.C., AUS, 1966-68. Mem. A.M.A., Am. Psychiat. Assn., Tex., So. med. assns., Titus Harris Psychiat. Soc., Bexar County Med. Soc. (mem. mental health and mental retardation com. 1975), Phi Beta Pi. Baptist. Gillean family genealogist. Office: 2415 W South Cross San Antonio TX 78211

GILLELAND, ROY RAYMOND, retail store owner; b. Tracy, Tex., July 17, 1913; s. Robert Alexander and Daisey Modena (Crantrell) G.; m. Dorothy Mae Ray, Sept. 7, 1935; children—Dorothy Ann, Richard Barton, Cathie Sue. With F. W. Woolworth Co., 1929-45; pres. Roy R. Gilleland, Inc. DBA Martins, Longview, Tex., 1980—; dir. Corpus Christi Savs. & Loan Assn., 1948-49. Pres., Downtown Devel. Corp., Longview, 1977; trustee Corpus Christi Ind. Sch. Dist., 1947-58. Baptist. Clubs: Masons, Kiwanis. Home: 515 Ruthlyn Dr Longview TX 75601 Office: 127 E Tyler St Longview TX 75601

GILLENWATER, ANNE RIDINGS, systems design engr.; b. Mich., Apr. 23, 1936; d. James Clarence and Mary Sue (Hughes) Ridings; B.S. in Bus. Adminstrn. (F.T. Bonham scholar), U. Tenn., 1971. Various secretarial positions ALCOA, Alcoa, Tenn., 1962-71, adminstrv. analyst, 1971-73, indsl. engr., 1973-75, systems analyst, 1975-76, systems design engr., 1976—. Chmn., Ops. Savs. Bond, 1972; mem. Tenn. Commn. Status of Women, 1974-81, chmn., 1975, 80; treas. Laurel Lake Youth Camp, 1977—; co-sponsor White House Conf. on Domestic and Econ. Affairs, 1975; bd. dirs. Blount County Girls' Club, 1980. adv. Alcoa Jr. Achievement. Cert. profl. sec. Mem. Am. Inst. Indsl. Engrs., Soc. Women Engrs. (sec. 1976, S.E. student activities coordinator 1977-79, pres. Knoxville 1979, nat. chmn. new student sects. 1979-80), Nat. Secs. Assn. (pres. 1972-74), Am. Soc. Tng. and Devel. (sec. 1980), Tenn. Valley Personnel Assn., AAUW, Delta Zeta. Republican. Home: 720 Chester Circle Maryville TN 37801 Office: ALCOA PO Box 9158 Alcoa TN 37701

GILLESPIE, MYRTLE LOU EDDINS, audiologist; b. Atmore, Ala., Dec. 29, 1938; d. Clifford Eddins and Rachel (Steadham) Eddins; B.S., U. So. Miss., 1960; M.A., Ohio State U., 1961; m. Marion Ray Gillespie, July 13, 1963; children—Andrea Clare, Marion Boyd, Allen Ray. Audiologist, Audiology and Speech Center, Walter Reed Gen. Hosp., Washington, 1961-65; audiologist Anderson (S.C.) Public Schs., 1978—; bd. dirs., vice chmn. profl. review Anderson-Oconee Speech and Hearing Services, 1975—. Bd. dirs. Anderson County Arts Council, treas., 1975-76, sec., 1977-78. Mem. Anderson County Med. Aux. (pres. 1977-78), S.C. Med. Aux. (corr. sec. 1973-74, rec. sec. 1978-79), Am. Speech and Hearing Assn. (cert. clin. competence). Baptist. Clubs: McCants Study, Garden Trail Garden (pres. 1979-80). Contbr. articles to profl. jours. Home: 108 Carter Oaks Dr Anderson SC 29621 Office: Anderson Public Schs Sch Dist 5 PO Drawer 439 Anderson SC 29622

GILLESPIE, ROBERT GILL, ret. chief justice Miss. Supreme Ct., educator; b. Madison, Ala., Sept. 17, 1903; s. Philander M. and Flora (Gill) G.; student Huntsville Jr. Coll., 1923-24; law student U. Ala., 1924-26; m. Margaret Griffith, June 30, 1930 (dec.); children—Robert Gill, Virgil Griffith; m. 2d, Alice Wells McIlwaine, July 29, 1975. Admitted to Miss. bar, 1927, practiced in Meridian, 1927-33; spl. agt. FBI, 1934-35; partner firm Bailey & Gillespie, 1939-43, Gillespie & Minniece, 1945-48, Gillespie, Huff & Williams, 1948-54; chancellor 2d Chancery Ct. Dist. of Miss., 1939; justice Miss. Supreme Ct., 1954-66, presiding justice, 1966-71, chief justice, 1971-77; vis. prof. law Miss. Coll., Clinton, 1977—. Mem. Miss. Council State Govts., 1944-48. Bd. dirs. Southwestern Coll., 1952-60. Mem. Am. Bar Assn., Miss. State Bar, Am. Judicature Soc., Delta Tau Delta. Presbyn. Home: 1355 Belvoir Pl Jackson MS 39202 Office: Miss Coll Sch Law Clinton MS 39058

GILLETTE, LYNDA BYRD, counselor; b. Durham, N.C., Mar. 20, 1946; d. William Figgatt and Frances Lavenia (Byrd) Lovell; B.A. in English, Converse Coll., 1967; cert. in lang. arts and social studies, U. N.C., 1971; M.Ed. in Counseling, Xavier U., 1973; m. Thomas Fredrick Gillette, Apr. 27, 1976; children—Kassi Brittain, Krysten Lynne. Emergency room ombudsman, child care worker St. Elizabeth Hosp., Covington, Ky., 1973-74; cons., edn. coordinator, therapist Mental Health Services East, Cin., 1973-75; treatment dir. Lucas County Mental and Mental Retardation Bd., Ruth S. Ide Center, Toledo, 1975-78; pvt. practice counseling, Columbia, S.C., 1978—; coordinator schs. program Lexington/Richland Alcohol and Drug Abuse Council, Columbia, 1978—; instr. counselor edn. Xavier U., 1974-75; ednl. cons. Boone County Citizens for youth; facilitator Nat. Social Seminar; community mental health cons.; project dir. Boone County Drug Abuse Com.; mem. Columbia Council Child Abuse and Neglect; active PTA. Cert. rehab. counselor; lic. parent effectiveness tng. instr. Mem. Am. Personnel and Guidance Assn., Am. Rehab. Counselor Assn., Nat. Assn. Social Workers. Home: 9824 Bonnyridge Rd Columbia SC 29206 Office: 2020 Washington St Columbia SC 29204

GILLEY, RUBY TACKETT, hosp. food service adminstr.; b. Sabathany, Tex., Feb. 11, 1910; d. Houston and Emma Lee (Davis) Tackett; student public schs., Bromide, Okla., Electra, Tex.; m. Carl A. Gilley, Nov. 1, 1925; children—Joyce Modena, Carl Adrian, Vaneel Vaughn, Mary Maxine, Mona Jean. Farm worker, Sabathany, 1926-42; meat packer Armour & Co., 1942-44; wing riveter Gen. D. Co., 1944-45; with food processing plant Gt. Western Foods, Ft. Worth, 1945-61; dir. dietary Eagle Mountain Area Suburban Hosp. (formerly Community Hosp.), Azle, Tex., 1961-72, dietary supr., 1972—. Sec. Sunday Sch. class First Methodist Ch., Azle. Mem. Hosp. Instl. Edn. Food Service Soc. (state treas. 1972-74, pres. local chpt. 1975-76), Azle Hist. Soc. Clubs: Azle Woman's (pres. 1971-72), Rebekah (noble grand 1967-68, 77-78, dist. dep. pres. 1980-81, Decoration of Chivalry 1977). Research on cookbooks and recipes. Home: Route 1 Box 120 Weatherford TX 76086 Office: 108 Denver Tr Azle TX 76020

GILLHAM, JOHN FRANKLIN, JR., real estate agt.; b. Edwardsville, Ill., Sept. 24, 1928; s. John Franklin and Doris (Early) G.; A.B., Washington U., St. Louis, 1950; m. Von Whitener, Oct. 9, 1964; 1 dau., Carol Whitener. Instr. English, Western Mil. Acad., Alton, Ill., 1963-66; broker A.G. Edwards & Sons, East St. Louis, Ill., 1966-69; salesman Steele Realty, Inc., Indialantic, Fla., 1978—. Served with U.S. Army, 1952-54. Address: 519 S River Oaks Dr Indialantic FL 32903

GILLIAM, DARRELL KAY, physician; b. Wise, Va., Nov. 11, 1928; s. Franklin William and Mary Virginia (Bevins) G.; student Marshall U., 1946-48; B.A., U. Richmond, 1950; M.D., Med. Coll. Va., 1959; m. Nancy Evelyn Giannotti, Mar. 25, 1951; children—Darrell Kent, Shelley Lynn, William Anthony. Rotating intern Stuart Circle Hosp., Richmond, Va., 1959-60, now mem. staff; gen. practice medicine, Richmond, 1960—, former mem. staff St. Luke's Hosp., Richmond, Retreat for the Sick, Richmond; mem. staff Johnston-Willis Hosp., Richmond, Grace Hosp., Richmond, Chippenham Hosp., Richmond; dir. Chesterfield Family Practice Center; clin. instr. dept. family practice, health sci. div. Va. Commonwealth U., 1970-71; asso. clin. prof. dept. family practice Med. Coll. Va.-Va. Commonwealth U., 1975—. Served with AUS, 1951-53; ETO. Diplomate Am. Bd. Family Practice. Fellow Am. Acad. Family Physicians; mem. AMA, Med. Soc. Va., Va. (del. 1971, sec. 1972-76), Richmond (pres. 1969-70) acads. family physicians, Richmond Acad. Medicine (sec. 1968-70), Manchester Med. Soc., Alumnus U. Richmond, Theta Kappa, Sigma Phi Epsilon. Methodist (chmn. bd. trustees 1966-71). Club: Beulah Recreation Assn. (Richmond). Home: 5110 Monza Ct Richmond VA 23234 Office: 2500 Pocoshock Pl Richmond VA 23235

GILLIAM, GEORGE HARRISON, lawyer; b. Alexandria, Va., July 26, 1942; s. Robert Skelton and Delia Bryan (Harrison) G.; student Princeton U., 1960-61; B.S., Columbia U., 1965; LL.B., U. Va., 1968; m. Sara Wilson Brown, May 29, 1964; children—Louise Bell, Sara Carter. Admitted to Va. bar, 1968; asst. commonwealth's atty., Charlottesville, Va., 1968-70; asso. Paxson, Marshall & Smith, Carlottesville, 1968-70; mem. firm Paxson, Smith, Boyd, Gilliam & Gouldman, Charlottesville, 1970—; pres. Sotico Corp.; dir. Fidelity Am. Bank, Charlottesville, 1977—; dir. So. Title Ins. Corp. Pres., Family Service of Charlottesville-Albemarle, Va., 1970-71; Charlottesville-Albemarle Mental Health Assn., 1968-70; treas. Va. Assn. for Mental Health, 1970; pres. Camp Holiday Trails, Charlottesville, 1971-74. City councilman City of Charlottesville, 1972-76; mem. Charlottesville Democratic Com., 1969—; Dem. candidate for Ho. of Reps., 1974; Va. campaign coordinator Carter-Mondale Campaign, 1980. Recipient Disting. Service award Charlottesville-Albemarle Jaycees, 1972. Mem. Va., Charlottesville-Albemarle bar assns., Phi Alpha Delta. Episcopalian. Home: 1409 Foxbrook Ln Charlottesville VA 22901 Office: PO Box 1151 Charlottesville VA 22902

GILLIAM, ROBERT LINDSAY, III, lawyer; b. Lynchburg, Va., Dec. 13, 1937; s. Robert Lindsay and Kathaleen Kimball (Snyder) G.; student U. Miss., 1955-58; LL.B. summa cum laude, Washington and Lee U., 1961; m. Marie Annette Whitaker, May 29, 1957 (div. June 1973); children—Marie Kimball, Robert Lindsay IV; m. 2d, Lois Lynn Doleman, Feb. 20, 1975. Admitted to Va. bar, 1961; asso. Wilbur C. Hall, Leesburg, Va., 1961-62; partner firm Hill, Dizerega & DeButts, Leesburg, 1961-64; asso. firm Cohen, Cox & Kelly, Richmond, Va., 1964; individual practice in Montross, Va., 1964—; Commonwealth's atty. Westmoreland County (Va.), 1964-75. Fund dr. chmn. Red Cross, Westmoreland County, 1965. Sec., Westmoreland Dem. County Com., 1964-78. Bd. dirs. Woodland Acad., 1970-75, chmn. 1971-72. Served with USAF, 1961-62. Mem. Am., Va., No. Neck bar assns., Order of Coif. Home: Box 277 Montross VA 22520

GILLILAND, FRANK MARSHALL, JR., lawyer; b. Memphis, Nov. 27, 1927; s. Frank Marshall and Elizabeth (Jordan) G.; B.A., Vanderbilt U., 1949, LL.B., 1951; m. Tandy A. Jones, Dec. 27, 1958; children—Tandy Elizabeth, Mary Josephine, Carol Jordan, Frank Marshall III. Admitted to Tenn. bar, 1951, since practiced in Memphis; law clk. U.S. Dist. Judge, Memphis, 1955-56; mem. firm Merrill, Gilliland & Wilson; sec.-treas. Gilliland Farms; sec.-treas. DeSoto Properties, Inc. Gen. counsel Memphis Cotton Carnival Assn., 1959—. Trustee Webb Sch., Bell Buckle, Tenn., 1961—. Served to lt. (j.g.) USNR, 1951-54; capt. Naval Res. Intelligence Program. Mem. Vanderbilt Law Rev., Navy League U.S., Order of Coif, Phi Beta Kappa, Omicron Delta Kappa, Phi Delta Theta, Phi Delta Phi. Clubs: Memphis Country, Memhis Univ. Home: 4008 N Galloway Dr Memphis TN 38111 Office: Sterick Bldg Memphis TN 38103

GILLILAND, JOHN DOUGLAS, lawyer; b. Dallas, Sept. 28, 1935; s. Arvin Douglas and Dorothy Nanette (Fenner) G.; B.A., Baylor U., 1959, J.D., 1969; m. Carol Ann McCall, Mar. 28, 1959; children—John Douglas, Patrick Edward, Paul Christopher. Admitted to Tex. bar, 1959; lease analyst Humble Oil & Refining Co., 1959-60; asst. city atty., Dallas, 1960-64; pvt. practice, Dallas, 1964-72; partner firm Gilliland, Cates & Flagg, Dallas, 1972—; dir. Carlocke/Langden, Inc., Dallas. Chmn., Dallas Motion Picture Classification Bd., 1967-71; mem. Dallas Parks and Recreation Bd., 1971-75, v.p., 1973-75; chmn. bd. trustees First Baptist Acad., Dallas, 1977—; Democratic precinct chmn., 1963-70; mem. Dallas County Dem. Exec. Com., 1963-70. Mem. Am., Tex., Dallas bar assns., Am. Judicature Soc., Phi Alpha Delta. Home: 6208 Highgate Ln Dallas TX 75214 Office: 2001 Bryan Tower Suite 2663 Dallas TX 75201

GILLILAND, ROY ALEXANDER, JR., air force officer; b. Charlestown, W.Va., July 10, 1943; s. Roy Alexander and Margaret (Kunkle) G.; B.A., Allegheny Coll., 1965; M.B.A., Auburn U., Montgomery, Ala., 1977; m. Suann Edwards, June 25, 1965; children—Roy Alexander, John Edwards, Robyn Ann. Commd. 2d lt. U.S. Air Force, 1965, advanced through grades to maj.; co-pilot Air Refueling Squadron, Seymour-Johnson AFB, N.C., 1966-68; pilot Tactical Airlift Squadron, Taiwan, 1969-70; pilot/instr./evaluator Air Refueling Wing, Rickenbacker AFB, Ohio, 1970-74; pilot/evaluator Combat Evaluation Group, Barksdale AFB, La., 1974-76; faculty instr. Air Command and Staff Coll., Maxwell AFB, Ala., 1976—. Cubmaster pack 307 Tuckabatchee council Boy Scouts Am., 1976-79; v.p. Southeastern League Dixie Youth Baseball, Montgomery, 1976-79; coach youth soccer, basketball SE Montgomery YMCA, 1979. Decorated D.F.C., Air Medal with 6 oak leaf clusters. Mem. Air Force Assn., Air Command and Staff Coll. Faculty Assn. (sec./treas.), Delta Tau Delta. Episcopalian. Clubs: Univ., Masons, Shriners. Home: 2064 Edinburgh Dr Montgomery AL 36116 Office: Air Command and Staff College EDO 2 Maxwell AFB AL 36112

GILLILAND, WILLIAM ELTON, lawyer; b. Hood County, Tex., May 8, 1919; s. Albert Floyd and Rosa Lee (Wood) G.; student Tex. Technol. Coll., 1937-39, U. Tex., 1939-41; LL.B., U. Tex., 1947; m. Garlan Nita Thomas, May 17, 1947 (dec. 1977); children—Chloe Ella, John Marshall; m. 2d, Frances Lindsey Esmond, Jan. 27, 1979. Admitted to Tex. bar, 1947; county atty. Martin County, Tex., 1947-48, Howard County, Tex., 1948-49; dist. atty. 118th Jud. Dist. Tex., 1949-54; mem. firm Little & Gilliland, Big Spring, Tex., 1954-59, firm McDonald, Shafer & Gilliland, Odessa, Tex., 1959-62, Shafer Gilliland Davis McCollum & Ashley, Odessa, 1962—. Served to capt. Signal Corps, AUS, 1942-46. Mem. Am. Coll. Trial Lawyers, Am. Law Inst., Tex. Bar Found., State Bar Tex., Am. Bar Assn., Internat. Assn. Ins. Counsel, Am. Judicature Soc., Tex. Assn. Def. Counsel. Home: 11 Chimney Hollow Odessa TX 79762 Office: First Nat Bank Bldg Box 1552 Odessa TX 79760

GILLIS, CHARLES TOD, real estate appraiser; b. San Antonio, Sept. 24, 1950; s. Donelson Caffery and Patricia Theresa (Huth) G.; B.A., Okla. U., 1972; B.S., St. Marys U., 1977; grad. Tex. Realtors Inst., 1975, Am. Coll. Real Estate, 1975; m. Gloria Lucinda Urrutia, Aug. 27, 1978. Project mgr. Padre Island Investment Corp. (Tex.), 1972-74; v.p. Walter Goodwin & Assos., Inc., San Antonio, 1976—; staff appraiser Nelson Cory Co., San Antonio, 1976-77; staff appraiser, cons. Love & Dugger Co., San Antonio, 1977—; dir. Hood Gillis Bldg. Co.; cons. Homequity, Inc. Recipient Chgo. Tribune award, 1968. Mem. Soc. Colonial Wars, Magna Carta, DAR, Nat. Assn. Realtors (chmn. real estate fin. com.), Am. Inst. Real Estate Appraisers, Soc. Real Estate Appraisers, San Antonio Indsl. Econ. Found., Nat. Assn. Realtors, Tex. Assn. Realtors (community revitalization com. 1980—), San Antonio Bd. Realtors, Tex. Com. on Natural Resources. Republican. Roman Catholic. Contbr. articles to trade mags. Office: 802 Main Plaza Bldg San Antonio TX 78205

GILLIS, EVERETT ALDEN, educator, author; b. Cameron, Mo., Mar. 4, 1914; s. Earle Adrien and Pearle (Owens) G.; B.A., Tex. Christian U., 1936, M.A., 1939; Ph.D., U. Tex., 1948; m. Ona Louise Cline, Nov. 18, 1978. Asst. prof. English, Tex. Coll. Arts and Industries, Kingsville, 1947-49; prof. English, Tex. Tech U., Lubbock, 1949-79, prof. emeritus, 1979—, chmn. dept., 1964-69. Served with AUS, 1942-46. Fellow Ford Found., 1955-56. Mem. Modern Lang. Assn., Am. Folklore Soc., Nat. Council Tchrs. English, Tex. Inst. Letters, Poetry Soc. Tex. (v.p. 1951), Tex. Folklore Soc. (pres. 1961). Nat. Writers Club, Southwestern Am. Lit. Assn. (pres. 1970), Internat. Poetry Soc., Poetry Soc. London. Author: Sing Your America, 1954; A College Forum, 1963; Oliver La Farge, 1967; (verse) Hello the House, 1944; Who Can Retreat, 1944; Sunrise in Texas, 1949; Angles of the Wind, 1954; Heart Singly Vowed, 1980; (music lyrics) Ballads for Texas Heroes, 1964; The Waste Land as Grail Romance, 1974; contbg. author: The Enemy Gods, 1975; (lyrics) West Texas Suite, 1976; also articles. Home: 3209 26th St Lubbock TX 79410

GILLIS, SAMUEL PETERS, surgeon; b. Knoxville, Tenn., July 10, 1935; s. Malcolm Elisha and Rose (Peters) G.; B.S., Miss. State Coll., 1957; M.D. U. Tenn., 1959; m. Sandy Phyfer, Dec. 18, 1955; children—Benjamin Knox, Daniel Paul. Intern, Holston Valley Community Hosp., Kingsport, Tenn., 1959-60; surg. fellow Mayo Clinic, Rochester, Minn., 1961-65; practice medicine, specializing in surgery, Birmingham, 1968—; asst. prof. surgery U. Ala., Birmingham, 1967-68, clin. asst. prof. surgery, 1969—. Served with AUS, 1965-67. Decorated Bronze Star, Commendation medal; recipient Mayo Staff award, 1965. Diplomate Am. Bd. Surgery. Fellow A.C.S. Baptist. Home: 212 Yelton Ln Birmingham AL 35216 Office: St Vincent's Professional Bldg Suite 735 2660 10th Ave S Birmingham AL 35205

GILLMORE, GEORGE GILBERT, ins. co. exec.; b. Fort Lupton, Colo., Oct. 11, 1922; s. Clyde Gilbert and Opal (Arnhold) G.; B.S., Millikin U., 1949; m. Imogene M. Isringhausen, June 22, 1952; children—Diana Lee and Deborah Lynn (twins). Sales engr. Met-L-Wood Corp., Chgo., 1949-50, Indpls., 1950-54, Cleve., 1954-57; sales staff Am. Gen. Life Ins. Co., Denver, 1958-60, agy. mgr., Houston, 1960-62, San Antonio, 1962-67; v.p. Rebsamen Ins. Co., Little Rock, 1967—. Served with USAF, 1943-46; ETO. Decorated Bronze Star (2). Mem. Life Underwriters Assn. (pres.), Gen. Agts. and Mgrs. Assn. (pres.), Ark. Underwriters Assn., Nat. Underwriters Assn., Million Dollar Round Table (life). Elder, Presbyterian Ch., 1973—. Clubs: Masons, Sertoma (founder, chmn. bd. communicative disorder centers Ark. 1976-78, exec. com. 1976—, Ark. dist. gov. 1973-75). Home: 2924 Shenandoah Valley Dr Little Rock AR 72212 Office: 1500 Riverfront Dr Little Rock AR 72202

GILLOGLY, DAVID BRANT, state ofcl.; b. Ponca City, Okla., Feb. 15, 1947; s. Elwin Clay and Dorothy Mae (Phillips) G.; B.A. in Econs., U. Okla., 1972; M.B.A., 1973; m. Millicent Perry, Sept. 27, 1969; 1 dau., Erin Joy. Asst. to v.p. ops. and mktg. Bray Lines, Inc., Cushing, Okla., 1974-76; mgmt. analyst Okla. Gov.'s Div. Planning and Mgmt. Analysis, Oklahoma City, 1976-77; adminstrv. asst. to gov. State of Okla., Oklahoma City, 1977; commr. Okla. Ins. Fund, Oklahoma City, 1977—; dir. Agape Industries; guest lectr. Oklahoma City U. Pres. bd. dirs. Cushing United Fund, 1975-76; sec. bd. deacons, treas. Council Road Bapt. Ch.; dist. chmn. Explorer Scouts, Boy Scouts Am. Served with U.S. Army, 1970-72. Mem. Nat. Council on Compensation Ins. (chmn. Okla. classification and rating com.), Am. Assn. State Compensation Ins. Funds (v.p.), So. Assn. Workers Compensation Adminstrs. (dir.). Home: 5805 NW 31st Terr Oklahoma City OK 73122 Office: 410 N Walnut St Oklahoma City OK 73152

GILLS, JACQUELYN TREADWELL, state grant adminstr.; b. Morrilton, Ark., Nov. 29, 1940; d. Marion Weldon and Edith Evelyn (Funkhouser) Treadwell; m. James Orvel Gills, Aug. 22, 1964; children—Michael Lewis, James Steven, Traci Michelle, Kristi Lynn. Legal sec., legal div. State Hwy. Dept., Little Rock, 1961-68; comml. artist Ind. Grocers Assn., 1968; med. sec. Dr. Alfred Kahn, Little Rock, 1969-70; reporter, sportswriter, graphic artist Cabot (Ark.) Star Herald, 1970-75; mng. editor newspaper Carlisle (Ark.) Ind., 1976; adminstrv. asst., media coordinator State Dept. Fin. and Adminstrn., Little Rock, 1977-79, subgrant adminstr., 1979-80; planning specialist State Dept. Local Services, Little Rock, 1980—; mem. Gov.'s Rural Fire Task Force Com., 1978. Recipient Cert. of Recognition, Gov. Ark., 1978. Mem. Ark. Info. Coordinators Assn. Democrat. Baptist. Home: 901 Eastern Ave Cabot AR 72023 Office: 1 Capitol Mall DLS Outreach Program Little Rock AR 72203

GILLUM, GAY, med. technologist; b. Farmerville, La., Jan. 23, 1940; s. J.D. and Emma Maxine (Crow) G.; B.S., La. Poly. Inst., 1962; med. technologist Charity Hosp. Sch., 1962-63. Staff technologist Stanocola, Baton Rouge, 1963-65; hematology supr. J.L. Goforth Labs., Dallas, 1965-68; lab. supr. Good Shepherd Hosp., Longview, Tex., 1968-70; adminstrv. technologist in hematology Med. Coll. Va., Richmond, 1970—. Mem. Am. Soc. Clin. Pathologists, Am. Soc. Med. Technologists. Home: 1108 Ironington Rd Richmond VA 23227 Office: Medical College of Virginia Box 597 MCV Station Richmond VA 23298

GILMAN, LAUREN CUNDIFF, educator; b. Bozeman, Mont., Nov. 24, 1914; s. Ralph Webster and Pearl (Cundiff) G.; A.B., Baker U., 1936; Ph.D., Johns Hopkins U., 1940. Asst. prof. zoology U. S.D., Vermillion, S.D., 1946-47; asso. prof. zoology U. Miami, Coral Gables, 1947—. Mem. corp. Marine Biol. Lab., Woods Hole, Mass., 1949—. Served from pvt. to capt. AUS, 1941-46. Fellow AAAS (council 1967-73); mem. Am. Inst. Biol. Scis., Am. Genetic Assn., AAUP, Assn. Southeastern Biologists, Assn. Acads. Sci. (pres. 1975), Soc. Protozoologists (mem. exec. com. 1957-62), Phi Beta Kappa (pres. Greater Miami assn. 1964), Sigma Xi (treas. Miami chpt. 1959-65), Alpha Delta Sigma, Beta Beta Beta, Gamma Alpha. Democrat. Research in mating types and syngens in Paramecium caudatum; morphol. and physiol. differences among syngens. Home: 423 Majorca St Coral Gables FL 33134

GILMER, JESSE BENTON, equipment co. exec., state ofcl.; b. Rocksprings, Tex., June 15, 1910; s. Jesse W. and Frankie Inez (Benton) G.; B.S. in Civil Engring., N.Mex. State U., 1934; children—Terese Inez Ray, Jessie A. With U.S. Dept. Agr., Washington, 1934-48, adminstr., Prodn. and Marketing Adminstrn., pres. Commodity Credit Corp., 1944-48; sec. Tri State Equipment Co., El Paso, Tex., 1948-53, pres., 1953-65, chmn. bd., 1965—; pres. Gilmer Cattle Co., 1965—. Commr., Rio Grande Compact, State of Tex., El Paso, 1969—. Registered profl. engr., Tex. Mem. Am. Soc. of Profl. Engrs. Democrat. Methodist. Clubs: Masons (Scottish Rite), Shriners. Home: 341 Clariemont St El Paso TX 79912 Office: PO Box 771 El Paso TX 79945

GILMORE, HARRY FREDERICK, JR., hosp. adminstr.; b. New Orleans, Aug. 30, 1937; s. Harry Frederick and Dorothy Lloyd (LeBlanc) G.; A.A., Pearl River Jr. Coll., 1963; B.S., U. So. Miss., 1967; m. Sylvia Ann Dronet, May 25, 1958; children—Richard Allen, Kenneth Troy, Donna Lynne. Med. technologist, X-ray technologist L.O. Crosby Meml. Hosp., Ricayune, Miss., 1961-67, Gen. Electric, Bay St. Louis, Miss., 1967; adminstr. Pearl River County Hosp. and Nursing Home, Poplarville, Miss., 1967-77, Hancock Gen. Hosp., Bay St. Louis, 1977—. Bd. dirs. S.E. Miss. Air Ambulance, 1974-77; sec. Poplarville-Pearl River County Airport Bd., 1970-77; bd. dirs. Pearl River County United Givers Fund, 1975; dist. chmn. Boy Scouts Am., Poplarville; pres. Poplarville Boys and Girls Club, 1974. Served with USAF, 1957-61. Mem. Registry of Med. Technologists, Am. Soc. Clin. Pathologists, Am. Registry of Radiologic Technologists, Am. Hosp. Assn., Miss. Hosp. Assn. Roman Catholic. Rotary. Home: 312 Ramoneda St Bay Saint Louis MS 39520 Office: 725 Dunbar Ave Bay Saint Louis MS 39520

GILMORE, HUGH REDLAND, lawyer, ret. govt. ofcl.; b. Bristol, Vt., Aug. 13, 1916; s. John R. and Rubie (Rathbun) G.; Ph.B. magna cum laude, U. Vt., 1937; J.D., Columbia U., 1941; m. Marjorie V. Havens, May 8, 1942; children—Douglas H., Anne C., Joan L. Admitted to Vt. bar, 1946, N.Y. State bar, 1948; asso. firm Sylvester & Ready, St. Albans, Vt., 1946-47; atty.-adviser Office Gen. Counsel Air Force, Office Sec. Air Force, Washington, 1949-54, asst. gen. counsel Air Force for personnel and adminstrn., 1954-74, asst. gen. counsel Air Force for personnel and fiscal matters, 1974-75; ret., 1975. Served to maj. AUS, 1942-46, 47-49; col. Air Force Res. Decorated Asiatic-Pacific ribbon with 3 bronze stars, Phillippine Liberation ribbon with 1 bronze star; recipient Exceptional Civilian Service award U.S. Air Force 1965; certificate of spl. recognition Sec. Air Force, 1969. Mem. Phi Beta Kappa, Pi Gamma Mu. Mason. Clubs: Overlee Community Assn., Arlington Forest (past dir.). Home: 3020 N Nottingham St Arlington VA 22207

GILMORE, JAMES HERBERT, JR., clergyman; b. Rutledge, Tenn., Jan. 7, 1925; s. James Herbert and Mabel Lorena (Doyal) G.; B.A., Carson-Newman Coll., 1945; M.A., Peabody Coll., 1949, B.D., 1950, Th.M., 1951; Ph.D., The So. Bapt. Theol. Sem., 1959; postgrad. Yale U. 1970, (Merrill fellow) Harvard U., 1978; m. Joyce Marie Wade, June 17, 1946; children—Victor Alan, Dale Temple, James Winston, Joy Marie. Ordained to ministry Bapt. Ch., 1944; minister First Bapt. Ch., Marshall, Mo., 1953-56, Deer Park Bapt. Ch., Louisville, 1956-60; vis. prof. homiletics So. Bapt. Theol. Sem., Louisville, 1958-60; prof. applied Christianity, Carver Sch. Missions and Social Work, Louisville, 1960-63; minister Chevy Chase Bapt. Ch., Washington, 1963-68, First Bapt. Ch., Birmingham, Ala., 1968-70, The Bapt. Ch. of the Covenant, Birmingham, 1970-76. Vis. prof. philosophy U. Ala. at Birmingham, 1971-72; vis. prof. theology, preaching, Nigerian Bapt. Theol. Sem., Ogbomosho, Nigeria, W. Africa; adj. prof. preaching, worship, Midwestern Bapt. Theol. Sem., Kansas City, Mo., 1977; lectr. in field. Mem. Downtown Action Com., Birmingham, 1968-76; mem. Ala. Heart Assn., 1969-76; Trustee Midwestern Bapt. Theol. Sem., Kansas City, Mo., 1969-76. Mem. Acad. Parish Clergy, Soc. Bibl. Lit., Soc. Sci. Study Religion, Am. Acad. Religion, Am. Soc. Christian Ethics, The Acad. Polit. Sci., Am. Acad. Polit. and Social Sci., Birmingham C. of C., 1968-76. Author: When Love Prevails, 1971, They Chose to Live, 1972, Devotions for the Home, 1972; The Cross of Love, 1979; The Church and The Nation, 1979. Home: PO Box 706 Gatlinburg TN 37738

GILMORE, JERRY RONALD, paper co. exec.; b. Enterprise, Ala., Mar. 10, 1949; s. James Adron and Lillie Bell (Hatcher) G.; B.S. in Bus. Adminstrn. and Acctg., Troy State U., 1972, postgrad., 1979—; m. Linda Cheryl McCall, Mar. 27, 1970. Acct./auditor Richmond C. McClintock, C.P.A., Dothan, Ala., 1972-75; subs. acct. Gt. So. Paper Co., Cedar Springs, Ga., 1975-76, supr. subs. acctg., 1976-77, supr. fin. acctg., 1977-78, mgr. acctg., 1978-80; controller Nekoosa Papers, Inc., Ashdown, Ark., 1980—; chmn. supervisory com. Cedar Springs Fed. Credit Union. Cert. mgmt. acct. Mem. Nat. Assn. Accts., Inst. Mgmt. Acctg. Baptist. Home: 1400 E 35 St Texarkana AR 75502 Office: PO Box 496 Ashdown AR 71822

GILMORE, MARJORIE HAVENS (MRS. HUGH REDLAND GILMORE), lawyer, club woman; b. N.Y.C., Aug. 16, 1918; d. William Westerfield and Elsie (Medl) Havens; A.B., Hunter Coll., 1938; J.D., Columbia, 1941; m. Hugh Redland Gilmore, May 8, 1942; children—Douglas Hugh, Anne Charlotte (Mrs. George Decker), Joan Louise. Admitted to N.Y. bar, 1941, Va. bar, 1968; research asst. N.Y. Law Revision Commn., 1941-42; asso. firm Spence, Windels, Waiser, Hotchkiss & Angell, N.Y.C., 1942, Chadbourne, Wallace, Parke & Whiteside, N.Y.C., 1942-43; atty. U.S. Army, Washington, 1948-53. Sec., Thomas Jefferson Jr. High Sch. P.T.A., 1956-58; parliamentarian Wakefield High Sch. P.T.A., 1959-60, chmn. citizenship com., 1960-61; publicity chmn. Patrick Henry Sch. P.T.A., 1963-64, sec., 1964-65; parliamentarian Nottingham P.T.A., 1966-69; troop leader Girl Scouts U.S.A., 1963-70; mem. extra-curricular activities com. Arlington County Sch. Bd.; area chmn. fund drive Cancer Soc., 1955-56. Recipient Constl. Law award Hunter Coll., 1938. Mem. Arlington Fedn. Women's Clubs (rec. sec. 1979-80), Columbia Law Sch. Alumni Assn., Alpha Sigma Rho. Presbyterian. Club: Williamsburg Women's (publicity chmn. 1969-70, corr. sec. 1970-72, 1st v.p. 1972-74, pres. 1974-76, chmn. consumer affairs 1977—). Home: 3020 N Nottingham St Arlington VA 22207

GILMORE, PHILLIP KING, hosp. ofcl.; b. Lena, Miss., Sept. 15, 1949; s. Rufus Huellis and Zelma (King) G.; student Millsaps Coll., 1968; A.A., Holmes Jr. Coll., 1969; B.S., U. So. Miss., 1971, M.S. (fellow), 1973; postgrad. Southwestern Bapt. Theol. Sem., 1975, U. Tex., 1976; M.H.A., Washington U., St. Louis, 1978; m. Frances Valeria Townsend, Nov. 16, 1974; 1 dau., Ginger Michelle. Adminstrv. resident VA Hosp., San Francisco, 1977-78; adminstrv. asso. Univ. Hosp., U. Miss. Med. Center, Jackson, 1978—. Outreach leader, mem. bldg. steering com. Day Star Bapt. Ch., 1979-80. Served with U.S. Army, 1973-75; 1st lt. Res., 1975—. Mem. Miss. Young Hosp. Adminstrs. Forum (charter pres.), Am. Coll. Hosp. Adminstrn., Res. Officers Assn., Am. Hosp. Assn., Omicron Delta Kappa. Home: Route 1 Box 224A Florence MS 39073 Office: University Hospital 2500 N State St Jackson MS 39216

GILMORE, STUART IRBY, educator; b. N.Y.C., July 24, 1930; s. Charles Theodore and Henrietta (Kohn) Goldman; B.A., State U. N.Y., 1950, M.A., 1951; Ph.D., U. Wis., 1962; m. Jewel Louise Pollak, June 19, 1950 (dec. Mar. 1969); children—Harmony (Mrs. Thomas Weston Miller), Barry, Christopher, Megan, Eric, Ford. Instr., Talladega (Ala.) Coll., 1952-53; dir. Jr. League Speech and Hearing Clinic, Columbia, S.C., 1954-60; asst. prof. Vanderbilt U. Med. Sch., Nashville, 1960-62; asst. prof. U. Wis., Madison, 1962-65; prof. speech La. State U., Baton Rouge, 1965—. Cons. La. State Dept. Hosps., 1970—, State Bd. Health, 1965—, State Dept. Edn., 1967-71, Belle Chasse State Sch., 1971—. Recipient Distinguished Faculty award La. State U. Alumni Fedn., 1974. Vocat. Rehab. Adminstrn. research grantee, 1959-61, U.S. Office Edn. tng. grantee, 1966—, Social and Rehab. Services Adminstrn. tng. grantee, 1967—. Mem. Am. Assn. Mental Deficiency (regional speech pathology-audiology chmn. 1973-76, v.p. for speech pathology and audiology 1977—), Am. Cleft Palate Assn. (internat. relations com. 1966-69), Am. (fellow, state chmn. congl. action contact network 1972-77, legis. councillor 1976—), La. (pres. 1971, adv. com. to agys. and orgns. 1972—, comprehensive health planning com. 1972—, chmn. continuing edn. com. 1975—) speech and hearing assns., So. Speech Assn. (program com. 1967-68), Sigma Xi. Democrat. Mem. Soc. of Friends. Editorial cons. Jour. Speech and Hearing Disorders, 1967-68, 77—. Home: 240 Leeward Dr Baton Rouge LA 70808 Office: Speech and Hearing Clinic La State U Baton Rouge LA 70803

GILREATH, ANNE CAMERON, personnel exec.; b. Fairview, N.C.; d. William P. and Octavia B. Cameron; student Berea Coll., 1951-52; bus. degree Blanton's Bus. Coll., 1955; m. James Ralph Gilreath, May 4, 1955; children—Cynthia Anne, Melanie Jane. Exec. sec., office adjuster Md. Casualty Co., Asheville, N.C., 1959-66; job developer Manpower Devel. Program, Asheville, 1970-73; counselor Jobs 70 Program, Asheville, 1973-74; personnel and safety dir. J. L. deBall-Girmes of Am., Asheville, 1974—; mem. Employer Adv. Com., Western region, 1978—. Mem. N.C. Personnel Club. Baptist. Home: Star Route Fairview NC 28730 Office: PO Box 9097 Asheville NC 28805

GILSTRAP, JOE JACKSON, ins. exec.; b. Pickens, S.C., Apr. 21, 1923; s. Luther Hubbard and Ethel Bulah (Massey) G.; B.A., Furman U., Greenville, S.C., 1948; m. Esterlene Burroughs, Dec. 22, 1945; children—Carol, Donald. Asst. treas. Liberty Life Ins. Co., Greenville, 1948—; v.p. Hampton Ins. Agency, 1969; ins. mgr. Liberty Corp., Greenville, 1970—, asst. v.p., 1975—. Served with USNR, 1943-46. Fellow Life Office Mgmt. Assn., Risk and Ins. Mgmt. Soc. (v.p. Carolinas chpt.). Methodist (chmn. coms., tchr.). Mason (Shriner). Home: 34 Lockwood Ave Greenville SC 29607 Office: PO Box 789 Greenville SC 29602

GILSTRAP, MICHELLE, editor; b. Oklahoma City, Oct. 19, 1951; d. Donald Ross and Anne Dorothy (Feeko) G.; B.A. in Journalism, Central State U., Edmond, Okla., 1973. Feature writer, reporter Tinker Take-Off, Tinker AFB, 1973-74; indsl. editor Am. Fidelity Assurance Co., Oklahoma City, 1974-75; dist. advisor Girl Scouts U.S.A., Lubbock, Tex., 1975-76, Red Lands Council, Oklahoma City, 1976-78; editor Okla. Bankers Assn., Oklahoma City, 1978—; cons. Red Lands Council Girl Scouts U.S.A. Mem. Internat. Assn. Bus. Communicators (treas. Central Okla.), Public Relations Soc. Am., Bank Mktg. Assn. (dir. Okla. chpt.). Clubs: Bus. and Profl. Women (pres.), Town (Oklahoma City). Office: 643 NE 41st St Oklahoma City OK 73105

GINDY, BENJAMIN LEE, ins. co. exec.; b. Detroit, July 23, 1929; s. Roy E. and Anne M. Gindy; B.S., U. Fla., 1951; m. Judith Youngerman, Dec. 20, 1953; children—Deborah, Daniel, David. Field rep. Penn Mut. Ins. Co., 1957-59; brokerage mgr. Mass. Indemnity Co., Miami, Fla., 1959-68; gen. agt. Guardian Life Ins. Co. Am., Miami, 1968—; instr. Life Underwriter Tng. Council, C.L.U. diploma course U. Miami; past columnist Miami Rev.; guest speaker Fla. State U., Notre Dame U. Recipient Nat. Health Ins. award Guardian Life Ins. Co. Am., 1977. C.L.U. Mem. Am. Soc. Chartered Life Underwriters (past pres. Miami chpt.), S.Fla. Inter-Profl. Council (pres.), Gen. Agts. and Mgrs. Assn. (past pres.), Miami Assn. Life Underwriters (past pres., Man of Year award). Home: 1018 Aduana Ave Coral Gables FL 33146 Office: 1401 Brickell Ave Suite 803 Miami FL 33131

GINGRICH, NEWTON LEROY, Congressman; b. Harrisburg, Pa., June 17, 1943; s. Robert Bruce G.; B.A., Emory U., 1965; M.A., Tulane U., 1968, Ph.D., 1971; m. Jacquelyn Battley, June 19, 1962; children—Linda Kathleen, Jacquelyn Sue. Mem. faculty dept. history W. Ga. Coll., Atlanta, 1970-78; mem. 96th Congress from 6th Ga. Dist., mem. public works and transp. com., house adminstrn. com., exec. com. Clearinghouse on the Future. Mem. AAAS, Ga. Conservancy, World Futurist Soc. (com. on anticipatory democracy). Republican. Baptist. Clubs: Kiwanis, Moose. Home: Howell Ln Carrollton GA 30117 Office: 417 Cannon House Office Bldg Washington DC 20515

GINN, JOHN CHARLES, newspaper publisher, communications co. exec.; b. Longview, Tex., Jan. 1, 1937; s. Paul S. and Bernice C. (Coomer) G.; B.J., U. Mo., 1959; M.B.A., Harvard U., 1972; m. Diane Kelley, Jan. 2, 1976; children by previous marriage—John Paul, Mark Charles, William Stanfield. Chief copy editor Charlotte Observer, Charlotte, N.C., 1959-64; editor Kingsport (Tenn.) News, 1964-65; city editor Charlotte News, 1965-67; mgr. of advt. and pub. relations Celanese Corp., Louisville, 1967-70; dir. of corporate devel. Des Moines Register and Tribune, 1972; editor and publisher Jackson (Tenn.) Sun, 1972-74; pres. and publisher Anderson (S.C.) Independent and Daily Mail, 1974—; pres. Century group Harte-Hanks Communications, 1979—, corp. v.p., 1978—; mem. Pulitzer Prize Journalism Jury, 1976, 77, 78. Pres., Anderson YMCA, 1975-76; bd. dirs. United Way, Anderson, 1974—. Recipient Outstanding Editorial award Tenn. Press. Assn., 1965, 73, 74. Mem. Am., So. (vice-chmn. editorial com. 1979-80) newspaper pubs. assns., S.C. Press Assn., Anderson Area C. of C. (pres. 1977). Club: Rotary. Home: Route 1 Anderson SC 29622 Office: PO Box 2709 Anderson SC 29622

GINN, RONALD (BO), congressman; b. Morgan, Ga., May 31, 1934; student Abraham Baldwin Agrl. Coll., 1951-53, Ga. So. Coll., 1953-56; m. Gloria Averitt, 1956; children—Kacy, Julie, Bryan. Tchr.; businessman; farmer; adminstrv. asst. to Rep. G. Elliott Hagan, 1961-66, Sen. Herman E. Talmadge, 1967-71; congressman from 1st Dist. Ga. Democrat. Baptist. Address: 317 Cannon House Office Bldg Washington DC 20515

GINSBURG, MERRILL STUART, geophysicist; b. Chgo., July 20, 1935; s. William Joseph and Ethel (Geller) G.; B.S., Mass. Inst. Tech., 1959, M.S., 1960; Ph.D., U. Utah, 1963; m. Margaret Patricia Myers, Apr. 9, 1971; children—Jason Ross, Caryn Marie. Sr. geophys. engr. Mobil Oil Corp., Dallas, 1963-65, sr. geophys. interpreter, 1965-70, asso. geophysicist, 1970-74, geophys. specialist, 1974-77, staff geophysicist, 1977—. Mem. Am. Geophys. Union, Soc. of Exploration Geophysicists, European Assn. Exploration Geophysicists, Dallas Geophys. Soc., N.Y. Acad. Scis., Sigma Xi, Phi Kappa Phi. Mem. B'nai B'rith (2d v.p. lodge 1978-80). Home: 2918 Country Place Circle Carrollton TX 75006 Office: Mobil Oil Corp Exploration and Producing Services Box 900 Dallas TX 75221

GINTAUTAS, JONAS, neuroscientist, research adminstr., educator; b. Justinava, Lithuania, Oct. 3, 1939; s. Jonas and Elena (Zaveckaite) Sinsinas; came to U.S., 1967, naturalized, 1970; M.D., Moscow Med. Inst., 1967; Ph.D., Northwestern U., 1975; m. Kristina Zebrauskaite, June 13, 1970; 1 dau., Pasaka. Physician in pediatric neurology Cook County Hosp., Chgo., 1968-1969; asso. prof. speech pathology and psychology, 1975-1977, dir. research grants, 1975-1977, research asso. Brain Research Labs., Health Scis. Center, 1977-1978, dir. research, asso. prof., anesthesiology, 1979—; cons. in field. NIH fellow, 1968-1970; Inst. Biomed. Research grantee. Mem. Am. Heart Assn., Am. Speech and Hearing Assn., Internat. Assn. Logopedics and Phoniatrics, Soc. Neuroscis., AAAS, Soc. for Research Adminstrs. Methodist. Contbr. articles to profl. jours. Research in higher cortical function disorders, neuropathologies of neuromuscular functioning and neurophysiology of brainstem-spinal cord. Home: 2126-67th St Lubbock TX 79412 Office: Health Sci Centers Tex Tech U Sch Medicine Lubbock TX 79430

GIOVANELLA, BEPPINO CARLO, biologist; b. Merano, Italy, June 12, 1932; s. Clemente and Maria Francesca (Felicelli) G.; Laurea in Biol. Scis. magna cum laude, U. Rome (Italy), 1956; postgrad. (post doctoral fellow), U. Wis., 1960-62; m. Wendy Ann Lohman, June 18, 1971; children—Corrado Francesco, Micol Danielle. Came to U.S., 1960, naturalized, 1973. Research fellow Regina Elena Cancer Inst., Rome, 1956-60; research asso. McArdle Lab. for Cancer Research, Madison, Wis., 1962-70; lab. dir. Stehlin Found. for Cancer Research, Houston, 1970—; clin. asso. prof. oncology, dept. obstetrics and gynecology Baylor U. Coll. Medicine, Houston, 1975—. Internat. fellow USPHS, 1960; Damon Runyon Found. fellow, 1960, Libera Docenza in gen. pathology, Rome, 1962. Mem. Am. Assn. Cancer Research, AAAS, N.Y. Acad. Sci., Am. Assn. Pathologists, Tissue Culture Assn., Bioelectro-magnetic Soc. Home: 6030 Yarwell St Houston TX 77096 Office: St Joseph Profl Bldg Houston TX 77002

GIPSON, ROBERT MALONE, chemist; b. Odessa, Tex., Apr. 9, 1939; s. Felix Claude and Mary Dell (Butler) G.; B.S., Abilene Christian Coll., 1961; M.A. (Rosalie B. Hite fellow), U. Tex., Austin, 1963, Ph.D., 1965; m. Annette Foster, Jan. 28, 1961; children—Michael, Paul. Research chemist Jefferson Chem. Co., Austin, Tex., 1965-68, sr research chemist, 1968-71, project chemist, 1971-74, project leader, 1974-75, supr. applied chem. research, 1975—. Mem. Am. Chem. Soc. (chmn. Central Tex. sect. 1972-73), S.W. Catalysis Soc. Patentee in field. Office: PO Box 4132 Austin TX 78765

GIRARD, CHARLES MARTIN, research and tng. exec.; b. Detroit, Feb. 3, 1943; s. Charles G. and Meta Ann (Geschwend) G.; B.A., Park Coll., 1965; M.Govtl. Adminstrn., Wharton Sch., U. Pa., 1967; Ph.D., Wayne State U., 1971; m. Roberta C. Jeorse, June 6, 1965; 1 son, Charles John. Analyst personnel and labor relations Ford Motor Co., 1965-66; asst. to city mgr. City of Port Huron (Mich.), 1966-67; instr., tng. coordinator dept. polit. sci. Wayne State U., Detroit, 1967-69; asst. dir. S.E. Mich. Council of Govt., Detroit, 1969-71; chmn. bd. pres. Internat. Tng., Research and Evaluation Council, Fairfax, Va., 1971—; curriculum advisor to Commn. on Police Officer Standards and Tng., State of Calif., 1975-79; adj. prof. Am. U., 1977-78; mem. Nat. Crime Prevention Inst.; adv. bd. U. Louisville, 1975-77; reviewer Nat. Criminal Justice Reference Service, Law Enforcement Assistance Adminstrn., Washington, 1978—. Chmn. budget and fin. com. Villa-Lee Community Assn., 1973—, chmn. archtl. com., 1974—. Recipient 1st Disting. Service award Mass. Crime Prevention Officers Assn., 1978; named Hon. Col., Salt Lake City Police Dept., 1978; Fels scholar, 1965-67. Mem. Am. Soc. Public Adminstrn., Am. Polit. Sci. Assn., Am. Mgmt. Assn., Internat. Soc. Law Enforcement and Criminal Justice Instrs., Am. Soc. Tng. and Devel., Nat. Assn. Dirs. Law Enforcement Tng., Nat. Assn. Clock and Watch Collectors, Wilsonian Asso., Nat. Geog. Soc., Internat. Assn. Chiefs Police, Phi Sigma Alpha. Author: A Short Course in Crime Prevention, 1975; contbr. articles profl. publs. Office: 10500 Sager Ave Fairfax VA 22030

GIRDNER, ALWIN JAMES, assn. exec.; b. Albuquerque, Oct. 10, 1923; s. Glen Clark and Marie Ellen (Holcomb) G.; B.S., U. Ariz., 1948, M.A., 1950; m Marjorie Jo Wilson, Sept. 1, 1946; children—Allen James, Sharon Girdner Magee, Kennan, Mari Jo Honeycutt. With RCA Victor, Camden, N.J., 1952-53, Temco Aircraft, Dallas, 1954-58; asst. dir. edn. Tex. Credit Union League, Dallas, 1958-61; asst. mng. dir. N.Mex. Credit Union League, Albuquerque, 1961-64, mng. dir., 1964-73; pres. Tenn. Credit Union League, Chattanooga, 1973—. Treas. N.Mex. Central Credit Union, Albuquerque, 1963-73; pres. N.Mex. Credit Union League Service Corp., Albuquerque, 1966-73, Tenn. Credit Union League Service Corp., Chattanooga, 1973—; instr. Peace Corps program, U. N.Mex., 1965-66. Mem. Credit Union Nat. Assn. (dir. 1966, legis. forum rep. 1973-77), Internat. Assn. Mng. Dirs. (sec. 1968-72), Nat. Platform Assn., Am. Soc. Assn. Execs., U. Ariz. Alumni Assn. (pres. Dallas-Ft. Worth club 1959-60), Founders Club. Republican. Methodist. Author: Credit Union Information Manual, 1960; Chapter Leaders Handbook, 1959; Navaho-U.S. Relations, 1950. Home: 7829 Parkshore Circle Chattanooga TN 37343 Office: Box 21524 1817 Hickory Valley Rd Chattanooga TN 37421

GIRGUS, SAMUEL DANIEL, investment co. exec.; b. Elizabeth, N.J., Mar. 21, 1932; s. Nicholas and Mary (Makara) G.; A.A., Union Coll., N.J., 1955; B.S. in Elec. Engring., Rutgers U., 1957; m. Lequetta Sue Tacker, Sept. 7, 1952; children—Mark Daniel, Glen Samuel, Todd John. Lab. dir. Avionics div. ITT, Nutley, N.J., 1957-70; v.p. intelligence Kuras-Alterman Corp., Fairfield, N.J., 1970-74; pres. mfg. K-A South, San Antonio, 1974-79; chmn. bd. Shield Investment Corp., San Antonio, 1979—; dir. Competitive Bus. Forms, Mil-Com Electronics Corp., Community Nursery. Elder, Bethany Presbyn. Ch., Bloomfield, N.J. Served with USAF, 1948-52. Mem. AIM (pres.'s council), Am. Inst. Indsl. Engrs. (sr.), Air Force Assn., Soc. Logistics Engrs., Electronic Def. Assn., San Antonio C. of C. (chmn. govt. contracting task force 1976-78, mem. econ. devel. steering com. 1978), North San Antonio C. of C. (charter), Rutgers U. Alumni Assn., Assn. Old Crows. Contbr. articles on electronic intelligence to classified publs.; developer Aero Gate complex, San Antonio, 1978, Energy Plaza, San Antonio, 1979. Home: 600 Paseo Canada San Antonio TX 78232 Office: 8820 Broadway San Antonio TX 78217

GIRTANNER, ROBERT EDUARD, JR., oncologist; b. Tex., July 24, 1945; s. Robert E. and Doris G.; B.A., Upsala Coll., 1958; M.D., U. Basel (Switzerland), 1969. Intern, Jackson Meml. Hosp., Miami, Fla., 1969-70; resident in Ob-Gyn, Baylor Coll. Medicine, Houston, 1970-71; resident in gynecologic oncology U. Miami, 1971-73, 73-75; practice medicine specializing in gynecologic oncology, Galveston, Tex., 1975-77, Miami, 1977—; asso. dir. Gynecol. Oncology div. U. Tex. Med. Br., Galveston, 1975-77; asso. prof. gynecologic oncology U. Miami, 1977—; cons. UPSHS Hosp., St. Marys Hosp., Galveston. Served with USAF, 1953-55. Am. Cancer Soc. prof., Galveston, 1975-76. Fellow A.C.S., Am. Coll. Obstetricians and Gynecologists, Western Assn. Gynecologic Oncologists, Internat. Soc. Study Vulvar

Disease. Contbr. articles to profl. jours. Office: PO Box 016960 Med Sch U Miami Miami FL 33101

GITTESS, RONALD MARVIN, dentist; b. Nyack, N.Y., Nov. 10, 1937; s. David and Mildred (Levin) G.; B.S., Columbia, 1959, D.D.S., 1963; postgrad. U. Pa., 1964-66; m. Carol May Block, Apr. 6, 1963; children—Robert Andrew, Leslie Ellen. Intern, Mt. Sinai Hosp., Miami, Fla., 1963-64, now attending dental surgeon; pvt. practice dentistry specializing in endodontics, Miami, 1966—; mem. staff Variety Children's Hosp., VA Hosp., Miami, Mt. Sinai Hosp.; cons. Dade County Dental Research Clinic. Asst. coordinator dental div. United Fund Campaign, 1968. Recipient certificate of recognition Jarvie Honor Soc., 1961. USPHS fellow, 1962-63. Diplomate Am. Bd. Endodontics. Mem. Am. Dental Assn., Am. Assn. Endodontics, AAAS, Fedn. Dentaire Internationale, Fla., Miami, Miami Beach, South Dade, East Coast dental socs., So. Endodontic Study Group. Alpha Omega. Home: 14520 SW 84th Ave Miami FL 33158 Office: 7400 N Kendall Dr Miami FL 33156

GITTINGER, EUGENE AUGUST, ins. agt.; b. San Antonio, Aug. 24, 1926; s. Frank C. and Albie (Rutta) G.; B.B.A., St. Mary's U., San Antonio, 1948; m. Emily Lane, June 25, 1952; children—Frank C., Richard E., Jeanmarie, Paul A., John J. With Gittinger Agy., San Antonio, 1948—, partner, 1956-76, owner, operator, 1976—; tchr. ins. St. Mary's U. Former pres. Woman's Shelter of Bexar County; former chmn. bd. placement com. City of San Antonio, also former chmn. ins. adv. com. Served with USNR, 1944-46. Mem. Ind. Ins. Agts. San Antonio (past pres., now regional v.p.), Nat. Assn. Ind. Agts., Ind. Agts. Assn. Tex., Builders Exchange of Tex. (dir.). Club: K.C. Home: 214 Five Oaks Dr San Antonio TX 78209 Office: 518 Petroleum Commerce Bldg San Antonio TX 78205

GIVHAN, THOMAS BARTRAM, lawyer, state legislator; b. Lexington, Ky., Sept. 24, 1926; s. Thomas Holman and Eva Mae (Beck) G.; student Iowa State Coll., 1947; LL.B., U. Ky., 1951; m. Sharon Rose Richard, June 11, 1949; children—Elise Charles, Ellen Foster, Aaron Todd. Admitted to Ky. bar, 1951; practice law, Shepherdsville, Ky.; city atty., Shepherdsville, 1953-58; county atty. Bullitt County, 1959-62, 66-73. Mem. Ky. Ho. of Reps., 1974—, chmn. judiciary com., 1976. Served with USMC, 1945-46. Mem. Ky. Bar Assn. (ho. of dels.), Am. Bar Assn., Am. Trial Lawyers Assn., Ky. Acad. Trial Attys. Sigma Chi. Baptist. Clubs: Masons, Jefferson Club (Louisville). Home: 5406 East Hwy 44 Shepherdsville KY 40165 Office: Professional Bldg Shepherdsville KY 40165

GIVIDEN, GEORGE MASSIE, JR., psychologist; b. Lexington, Ky., Apr. 3, 1929; s. George Massie and Edith L. (Hootman) G.; B.S., U.S. Mil. Acad., 1951; M.A., Vanderbilt U., 1957; postgrad. Columbia U., 1959-61; m. Betty June Hudson, Dec. 23, 1951; children—Deborah Ann, George Massie, John Richard, Kathryn, James Michael. Commd. 2d. lt. U.S. Army, 1951, advanced through grades to capt., 1956; psychologist U.S. Mil. Acad., 1957-60; mem. faculty N.Y. U., 1960-62; human factors psychologist, pres., chmn. Tri-State Parachute Co., Flemington, N.J., 1962-63; exec. dir. U.S. Parachute Assn., Monterey, Calif., 1963-64; research psychologist, ops. analyst, project dir. Stanford Research Inst., Calif., 1965-66; mgr. ops. analysis dept., mgr. applied tech. lab. Litton Industries, Monterey, 1966-71; chief Army Research Inst., Fort Hood, Tex., 1971—; cons. in field. Bd. trustees Monterey Peninsula Unified Sch. Dist., 1970-71; mem. city council, Copperas Cove, Tex., 1976—, mayor pro-tem, 1977-78. Served with USMC, 1945-47. Decorated DSC, Silver Star, 5 Purple Hearts. Mem. DAV (comdr. chpt.), VFW, Exchange Club, Am. Psychol. Assn., Ops. Research Soc. AM., Human Factors Soc., Hon. Order Ky. Cols., Am. Legion, Commonwealth Club Calif. Home: 702 S Main St Copperas Cove TX 76522

GLADDEN, RICHARD DAWSON, ins. co. exec.; b. Little Rock, Sept. 2, 1934; s. Harry Blake and Elizabeth Jane G.; B.S. in Bus. Adminstrn., U. Ark., 1957; m. Patsy Courtney, Aug. 26, 1956; children—Gail, David. Agt. Prudential Ins. Co., Shreveport, La., 1959-63, mgr. staff, 1963-65; sales rep. Hartford Ins. Group, Shreveport, 1965-67; ins. agt. Hargrove Ins. Agy., Shreveport, 1967-68; life mgr. Southland Ins. Agy., Hot Springs, Ark., 1968-69; Ark. Bank & Trust Co. Ins. Agy., Hot Springs, 1969—. Instr. bus. adminstrn. Garland County Community Coll., 1974—. Vice pres. bd. dirs. Boys Club, Hot Springs, 1971-72; pres. bd. dirs. Hot Springs YMCA, 1974-77; pres. elect Ouachita Area Council, 1978. Served with AUS, 1957-59. Recipient Nat. Sales Achievement award Nat. Assn. Life Underwriters, 1973, 74, 75, 76, 77, 78, 79. C.L.U. Mem. Leading Producers Club of Occidental Life, Central Assn. Am. Coll. Chartered Life Underwriters (pres. 1977-78), Hot Springs Assn. Life Underwriters (pres. 1972-73), Sigma Alpha Epsilon. Democrat. Baptist. Optimist, Elk. Home: 207 Hermlee Dr Hot Springs AR 71901 Office: Ins Agy Ark Bank & Trust Co Hot Springs AR 71901

GLADDING, EVERETT BUSHNELL, exec., writer; b. New Haven, June 27, 1917; s. Daniel Henry and Grace A. (Brown) G.; B.A., Wesleyan U., 1938; M.A., Johns Hopkins, 1946; m. Harriet Allen Clark, June 7, 1941; children—Nicholas Clark, Brenda Bushnell (Mrs. Scott Alexander). Commd. ensign USN, 1941, advanced through grades to capt., 1960; staff SACLANT, 1956-59; chief Nat. Security Agy., Pacific, 1960-63; comdg. officer Naval Communications Sta., Adak, Alaska, 1963-64; chief staff officer Naval Security Group, 1964-66, dir. Naval Security Group, Pacific, 1966-68; ret., 1968; planning specialist LTV Electrosystems, Inc., Greenville, Tex., 1968-70; mgmt. analyst Conn. State Welfare Dept., 1970-72; pub. relations asst. Air Kaman, Inc., 1971-75; editor Flight Line Times, 1974-75; pres. Majors Aviation Service, Inc., 1975—. Judge dog obedience trials, 1957-74. Mem. I.E.E.E. (sr.), Armed Forces Communications-Electronics Assn., CAP, Am. Radio Relay League, Nat. Pilots Assn., Aircraft Owners and Pilots Assn., various dog clubs. Episcopalian. Clubs: Quinnipiack (New Haven); Rotary. Home: 24 Mullaney Rd Greenville TX 75401 Office: Box 1907 Greenville TX 75401

GLADSTEIN, MICHAEL FALK, distbn. cos. exec.; b. McAlester, Okla., Jan. 27, 1935; s. Irvin A. and Margaret (Falk) G.; B.B.A., U. Okla., 1957; m. Bobett Beatus, Dec. 23, 1956 (div.); children—Mark Beatus, Margaret Rose. Pres., Economy Housing Developers, McAlester, 1968—; v.p., sec. Welding Supplies, Inc., McAlester, 1964—, also dir.; v.p., sec. Gladstein Co. and Gladstein Co. of Ada, Inc., McAlester, 1966-72, pres., 1972—, also dir.; v.p., sec. Out Products, Inc., Hominey, Okla., 1970-73, also dir.; mng. partner Gladco Devel., McAlester, 1966—, M & G Properties, 1979—; pres. M & D Devel. Co., Tulsa, 1966-70; pres. the Gladstein Co. of Shawnee (Okla.), 1978—; partner G & M Properties, 1979—; chmn. Okla. Aeros. Commn. Treas., Citizens for Better McAlester; active United Fund; chmn. active Indian Nations council Boy Scouts Am.; mem. Okla. Aeros. Commn., vice chmn., 1978; mem. Interstate Commn. Airport Authority; mem. McAlester Mayor's Com. for Handicapped Workers; trustee Okla. Trauma Research Com.; mem. Task Force Com. City of McAlester, 1977-78. Mem. Am. Supply Assn., Nat. Assn. Wholesale Distbrs., McAlester Jaycees (pres., Leadership award), McAlester C. of C. Jewish. Clubs: Navy League, McAlester Country, Elks, Okla. Alumni of Pittsburg County (dir.). Home: 1837 S 14th St McAlester OK 74501 Office: 403-25 S Main St McAlester OK 74501

GLADSTEIN, MIMI REISEL, educator; b. Leon, Nicaragua, Feb. 14, 1936; d. Emil and Regina (Rosen) Reisel; came to U.S., 1938, naturalized, 1955; B.A., U. Tex., El Paso, 1959, M.A., 1966; Ph.D., U. N.Mex., 1973; m. Jay Stephen Gladstein, Aug. 18, 1956; children—Clifford, Denise, Alfred. Instr., Hebrew Sch., El Paso, 1959-66; tchr. phys. edn., El Paso, 1960; mem. faculty U. Tex., El Paso, 1966—, asst. prof. English, 1974-79, asso. prof., 1979—; teaching asst. U. N.Mex., 1970-71. Bd. dirs. B'nai Zion Synagogue; adv. bd. Rape Crisis Center, El Paso Hebrew Day Sch. Named Woman of Year in Edn., El Paso Women's Polit. Caucus, 1975. Mem. Modern Lang. Assn., Nat. Council Tchrs. English, Rocky Mountain Modern Lang. Assn., AAUP, Coll. Conf. Tchrs. English, Coordinated Campus Ministry, AAUW, Hadassah, B'nai B'rith Women. Jewish. Contbr. articles to profl. jours. Home: 430 Crown Point El Paso TX 79912 Office: English Dept U Tex El Paso TX 79968

GLANCE, BILL DOW, pub. relations exec.; b. Leicester, N.C., June 7, 1930; s. John Marvin and Paron J. (Meadows) G.; B.S., Western Carolina U., 1952; m. Bette Lou Winchester, Oct. 23, 1955; children—William Jeffrey, Jonathan Carlyle, Jason Dow. Reporter, Asheville (N.C.) Citizen, 1952-56; sports editor Charleston (S.C.) Evening Post, 1956-62; dir. pub. relations Bowman Gray Sch. Medicine, Wake Forest U. and N.C. Bapt. Hosp., Winston-Salem, 1962—; vis. lectr. Babcock Grad. Sch. Mgmt., Wake Forest U., Winston-Salem, 1976. Bd. dirs. Forsyth County Heart Assn., 1972-75, Health Care Info., Inc., 1974-76. Recipient S.C. Press award, 1958; award for Excellence in Med. Edn. Pub. Relations, Assn. Am. Med. Colls., 1971; Compleat Communicator award Internat. Assn. Bus. Communicators, 1976, 79. Mem. Group on Pub. Relations, Assn. Am. Med. Colls. (nat. chmn. 1975), Winston-Salem Pub. Relations Round Table (pres. 1973). Republican. Moravian. Clubs: Kiwanis (dir. 1967-70); Pine Brook Country. Home: 3120 Burkeshore Rd Winston-Salem NC 27106 Office: Bowman Gray Sch Medicine 300 S Hawthorne Rd Winston-Salem NC 27103

GLASER, JOHN SIMON, social welfare exec.; b. Rochester, N.Y., May 23, 1939; s. Jerome and Frances Sarah (Kauffmann) G.; B.A., Cornell U., 1961; M.S.W., Boston U., 1965; m. Rochelle Sosne, July 4, 1965; children—Matthew, Leah. With Am. Friends Service Com., Haiti, 1961-63; br. dir. Elizabeth Peabody House, Somerville, Mass., 1965-69; dir. community services div. United Way of Dade County, Miami, Fla., 1969-71; v.p. United Way Internat., Alexandria, Va., 1972—; v.p. services outreach div. United Way of Am., 1978—; dir. Internat. Standing Conf. on Philanthropy, 1972—. NSF fellow, 1961; cert. Acad. Cert. Social Workers. Mem. Nat. Assn. Social Workers. Home: 1713 Hollinwood Dr Alexandria VA 22307 Office: 801 N Fairfax St Alexandria VA 22314

GLASGOW, JAMES ARCHIE, coll. adminstr.; b. Belgreen, Ala., May 16, 1926; s. Kemper Talmadge and Lela (Thompkins) G.; B.S., Florence State Coll., 1949; M.A., George Peabody Coll., 1953; LL.D., Jacksonville State U., 1968; m. Ruby Mae Britton, July 9, 1947; children—Jane Elizabeth, James Britton. Tchr., Phil Campbell (Ala.) High Sch., 1950-56; entomologist U.S. Dept. Agr., 1952-53; prin. Belgreen (Ala.) High Sch., 1956-59, Phil Campbell High Sch., 1959-63; pres. N.W. Ala. State Jr. Coll., Phil Campbell, 1963—; mem. adv. bd. 1st Nat. Bank of Russellville (Ala.). Mem. Franklin County Democratic Exec. Com., 1978—, Pres.'s Com. on Employment of Handicapped, 1977-79, Citizens Adv. Bd. on Rural and Agrl. Devel. for Ala., 1972-79; chmn. public employees div. United Fund Drive, Franklin County, 1975. Served with USNR, 1944-46. Mem. Ala. Assn. Coll. Adminstrs. (pres. 1970), NEA, Am. Assn. Jr. Colls., Ala. Council Jr. Coll. Pres.'s (pres. 1973-74), Ala. Farm Bur., Ala. Assn. Jr. Colls. Methodist. Clubs: Lions, Masons. Home and Office: Rt 3 Phil Campbell AL 35581

GLASGOW, VAUGHN LESLIE, mus. curator; b. Portland, Ind., Apr. 23, 1944; s. Leslie Lloyd and Garnet Lucile G.; B.A., La. State U., 1967; M.A., Pa. State U., 1970. Instr. dept. art history Pa. State U., 1970-71; asst. prof. art history Middle Tenn. State U., 1972-73; arts mgr. La. Council for Music and Performing Arts, 1973-75; chief curator La. State Mus., New Orleans, 1975—; lectr. modern art Tulane U., 1975-79. NDEA fellow, 1968-72, NSF grantee, 1971. Mem. Southeastern Mus. Conf., La. Crafts Council (dir.), La. Alliance for Arts Edn. (dir.). Contbr. articles to profl. jours. Office: 751 Chartres New Orleans LA 70116

GLASS, GEORGE JEAN, air force officer; b. Hamlet, N.C., Mar. 12, 1935; s. James Hunter and Catherine Regina (Stewart) G.; B.S. in Occupational Edn., So. Ill. U., Carbondale, 1977; M. Mgmt., Webster Coll., 1978; m. Frances Carolyn Farrer; children—Mary Katherine Glass Williams, David George. Served as enlisted man U.S. Air Force, 1954-57; commd. 2d lt. U.S. Air Force, 1957, advanced through grades to col., 1978; command instructional system devel. program mgr. Hdqrs. Mil. Airlift Command, Scott AFB, Ill., 1972-75; comdr. 443 Tech. Tng. Squadron, Altus AFB, Okla., 1975-78; 34 Tactical Airlift Tng. Group., Little Rock AFB, Ark., 1978—. Decorated D.F.C., Bronze Star, Air medal with 3 oak leaf clusters. Mem. Assn. for Edn. and Communications Tech., Air Force Assn., Order Daedelians. Home: 300 N Beverly St Sherwood AR 72116 Office: 34 Tactical Airlift Tng Group/Comdr Little Rock Air Force Base AR 72076

GLASS, JAMES DALE, oil co. exec.; b. McLean, Tex., Nov. 8, 1934; s. John Raymond and Lura Viola (Back) G.; student W. Tex. State U., 1953-56; m. Mary Lou Miller, Aug. 17, 1958; children—MariDale, Sherry Kay, JamieLou, Terri Gaye, John David, Angela Ruth. With Phillips Petroleum Co., Borger, Tex., 1958-79; owner J.R. Glass Oil Co., McLean, 1979—. City alderman, City of McLean, 1974-79. Served with U.S. Army, 1957-58. Mem. Tex. Oil Jobbers, Nat. Oil Jobbers. Republican. Baptist. Club: Lions (pres. 1973-74, Lion of Yr. 1974). Address: Box 28 McLean TX 79057

GLASS, JAMES MADISON, III, digital communications specialist; b. Parkersburg, W.Va., Jan. 1, 1949; s. James Madison and Betty Jeanne (Briscoe) G.; B.S. in Math., U. N.C., 1971. Programmer/analyst 7th Army Hdqrs., Heidelberg, W. Ger., 1971-73; lead programmer/analyst Hamilton County Data Processing, Chattanooga, 1974-76; head microcomputer devel. Data Communications Corp., Memphis, 1976-78; mgr. node software Cylix Communications Network, Memphis, 1978—. Mem. Phi Beta Kappa. Home: 3681 Winchester Park Circle Apt 1 Memphis TN 38118 Office: 3000 Directors Row Memphis TN 38131

GLASS, ROBERT JAMES, apparel mfg. co. exec.; b. Detroit, July 3, 1934; s. Roy Burns and Lois Margaret (Soldal) G.; B.S., Central Mich. U., 1956; postgrad. U. Detroit, 1960; m. Barbara Wisser, May 22, 1971; children—Robert, Kirk, Gavin, Darin, Arin. Sales mgr. Cosmetic div. Chesebrough Ponds, Inc., N.Y.C., 1961-69; region mgr. Philip Morris U.S.A., N.Y.C., 1969-72; sr. v.p. No Nonsense Fashions div. Kayser Roth, N.Y.C., 1972-79; pres. Kayser Roth Branded Products, Greensboro, N.C., 1979—. Served with arty. U.S. Army, 1957-59. Mem. Nat. Assn. Chain Drug Stores, Food Mktg. Inst., Sigma Tau Gamma. Club: Sedgefield Country. Home: 4602 Trailwood Dr Greensboro NC 27407 Office: PO Box 7057 Greensboro NC 27407

GLASS, RONALD WAYNE, chem. engr.; b. Cardwell, Mo., Nov. 9, 1943; s. F. T. and Jameszenia (Reed) G.; B.S.Ch.E., U. Ark., 1965; M.S.Ch.E., Clemson U., 1967, Ph.D. in Chem. Engring., 1970; 1 son, Brian Kelly. NSF research participant U. Ark., 1962-65; engr. Esso Refinery, Baton Rouge, 1965; engr., group leader, sect. head Oak Ridge Nat. Lab., 1970—, sect. head, engring. coordination and analysis sect., chem. tech. div., 1976—, fossil energy program mgr. engring. evaluations, 1977—. Active Boy Scouts Am. Mem. Am. Inst. Chem. Engrs., Nat. Soc. Profl. Engrs., Tenn. Soc. Profl. Engrs., Sigma Xi, Tau Beta Pi, Pi Mu Epsilon, Phi Kappa Phi, Omega Chi Epsilon. Office: Oak Ridge Nat Lab PO Box X Bldg 4500N Room 232 Oak Ridge TN 37830

GLASS, THOMAS REAKIRT, newspaper pub.; b. Lynchburg, Va., May 13, 1928; s. Carter and Ria (Thomas) G.; student Va. Mil. Inst., 1945-46; B.A. in Journalism, Washington and Lee U., 1949; m. Julia Marguerite Thomason, Sept. 29, 1951; children—Julia Eastham, Mary Byrd, Laura Binford, Blair Thomas. Co-pub., exec. editor The News and The Daily Advance, Lynchburg, 1955-77, pub., exec. editor, 1977-79; pres. Carter Glass & Sons, Pubs., Inc., Lynchburg, 1977-79, v.p., asso. pub., 1979-80; pub. emeritus, v.p. Carter Glass Newspapers, Inc., 1980—; dir. Fidelity Am. Bank NA, Central Fidelity Bank. Mem. Va. Commn. on Pub. Edn., 1960-62; mem. Va. State Boating Commn., 1962-63; mem. exec. com. Va. State Commn. on Tourist Trade and Travel, 1965-66, Va. State Hwy. Commn., 1969-79; vice chmn. Va. Bd. Community Colls., 1966-68; mem. Lynchburg Naval Adv. Bd., 1960; charter mem., chmn. Lynchburg Tri-Partite; mem. Com. for Cooperation Between Retail Mchts., Chamber and Central Va. Industries; mem. pub. relations com. Community Chest, Lynchburg, 1955-56; charter mem. bd. dirs. Lynchburg Safety Com., 1955; bd. dirs. Lynchburg chpt. Va. Mental Health, 1954-56, vice-chmn., fund chmn., 1956; bd. dirs. Lynchburg Salvation Army, 1956—; vice chmn. Va. State Salvation Army Adv. Bd.; bd. dirs. Lynchburg chpt. A.R.C., 1955-56; mem. adv. com. Va. chpt. Ams. for Effective Law Enforcement, Inc., 1971—. Mem. Va. Ho. of Dels., 1958-66; chmn. Va. Jefferson-Jackson Day Dinner for Democratic Party, 1964. Trustee Lynchburg Coll., 1972—. Served to 1st lt. USAF, 1951-53; Korea. Recipient Outstanding Young Man of the Year award Lynchburg Jaycees, 1956; Cross of Mil. Service, United Daus. of Confederacy, 1962, Spl. Certificate of Recognition award Roanoke Regional Blood Program; named Outstanding Young Man of Am., Nat. Jaycees, 1964. Mem. Va. Press Assn. (treas. 1955-57), Va. AP (chmn. freedom of info. com. 1962), Nat., So. (dir. 1975-78) newspaper pubs. assns., Lynchburg Retail Mchts. Assn. (dir. 1953-56), Greater Lynchburg C. of C. (dir. 1957-60, 77—, pres. 1960-61), Newcomen Soc. N.Am., Lynchburg Hist. Soc., Phi Delta, Sigma Delta Chi. Episcopalian. Mason (32 deg., Shriner), Elk, Lion, Odd Fellow. Clubs: Boonsboro Country (Lynchburg); Commonwealth (Richmond). Home: 3130 Landon St Lynchburg VA 24503 Office: Wyndale Dr Lynchburg VA 24506

GLASSCOCK, KIRBY D., III, travel agy. exec.; b. Muskogee, Okla., Mar. 15, 1947; s. Kirby D. and Mona Rose (Thomas) G.; student Okla. State U., 1965-69; children—Kelly Dawn, Kacey Diane. With Webster Mfg. Co., Tulsa, 1966-68, Beneficial Fin. Co., Kansas City, Mo., 1968-69; with Holiday Travels, Inc., Stillwater, Okla., 1969—, now sec.-treas.; bd. dirs. State of Okla. Dept. Tourism. Bd. dirs. Stillwater Airport Adv. Com. Mem. Am. Soc. Travel Agts., Okla. C. of C., Stillwater C. of C. Democrat. Roman Catholic. Office: Holiday Travels Inc 1134 Hall of Fame Ave Stillwater OK 74074

GLASSMAN, ARMAND BARRY, physician; b. Paterson, N.J., Sept. 9, 1938; s. Paul and Rosa (Ackerman) G.; B.A., Rutgers U., 1960; M.D. magna cum laude (Johnson Found. scholar), Georgetown U., 1964; m. Alberta C. Macri, Aug. 30, 1958; children—Armand P., Steven B., Brian A. Intern, Georgetown U. Hosp., Washington, 1964-65; resident Yale-New Haven Hosp., West Haven VA Hosp., 1965-69; asst. prof. pathology U. Fla. Coll. of Medicine, Gainesville VA Hosp.; practice lab. and nuclear medicine, 1969-71; dir. clin. labs. Med. Coll. Ga., Augusta, 1971-76; cons. physician in pathology VA Hosp., Augusta, 1973-76; cons. physician in nuclear medicine U. Hosp., Augusta, Ga., 1973-76; med. dir. clin. labs. Med. U. Hosp., Med. U. S.C., Charleston, 1976—, attending physician in lab. and nuclear medicine, 1976—; med. dir. clin. labs. Charleston County (S.C.) Hosp., 1976—; cons. VA Hosp., Charleston, 1976—; prof., chmn. dept. lab. medicine Med. U. S.C., 1976—, asso. dean Coll. Medicine, 1979—, also dir. clin. labs. Served with USMC, 1956-64. Diplomate Am. Bd. Pathology, Am. Bd. Nuclear Medicine. Fellow Coll. Am. Pathologists, A.C.P., Assn. Clin. Scientists, Am. Soc. Clin. Pathology; Am. Coll. Nuclear Medicine; mem. Internat. Acad. Pathology, Am. Assn. Pathologists and Bacteriologists, Soc. Nuclear Medicine (acad. council 1979—), Soc. Nuclear Medicine (chmn. membership com. SE chpt. 1972-74, chmn. edn. com. 1973-77), Ga. Radiol. Soc., AMA (physician's recognition award), So. Med. Assn., Am. Geriatric Soc., Am. Soc. Microbiology, Ga. Heart Assn., Am. Assn. Blood Banks (chmn. cryobiology com. 1974—), S.E. Area Blood Bankers (pres. 1980-81), Assn. Schs. Allied Health Professions (editorial bd. Jour. Allied Health 1979—), Soc. Cryobiology, AAAS, N.Y. Acad. Scis., Acad. Clin. Lab. Physician and Scientists (exec. council 1978—), Sigma Xi (program chmn., pres. elect Med. Coll. Ga. chpt. 1975-76), Alpha Eta, Alpha Omega Alpha. Club: Charleston Tennis. Contbr. articles on lab. medicine to profl. jours. Home: 167 Broad St Charleston SC 29401 Office: 171 Ashley Ave Charleston SC 29403

GLASSMAN, MICHAEL, educator; b. Fastov, Russia, Oct. 12, 1899; s. Meyer Joseph and Frieda (Kaganovsky) G.; came to U.S., 1908, naturalized, 1924; B.A. (Tremaine scholar 1921), Coll. City N.Y., 1923, M.S. in Edn., 1932; J.D., N.Y. U., 1926; m. Miriam Frantz, Aug. 24, 1935; children—Rhoda, Judith M. Admitted to N.Y. bar, 1927; tchr., adminstr. N.Y.C. Bd. Edn., 1923-69, asst. examiner personnel dept., 1944, prin. Benjamin Franklin Jr. High Sch., 1955-60, prin. Parsons Jr. High Sch., 1960-69; adj. instr. polit. sci. Bklyn. Coll., 1944-47; adj. asst. prof. edn. emeritus Pace Coll., 1970—; lectr., prof. emeritus Inst. New Dimensions, Palm Beach Jr. Coll., 1978—; ednl. adviser, journalist N.Y. Herald Tribune, N.Y.C., 1955-58. Trustee Friends of Public Broadcasting in Palm Beach County; co-organizer, v.p. Chamber Music Soc. of the Palm Beaches. Mem. N.Y. Tchrs. Guild (co-organizer; mem. exec. bd.), Am. Fedn. Tchrs. (del. nat. conv. 1934), Jr. High Sch. Prins. Assn., Council Suprs., Adminstrs. N.Y.C., Ret. Tchrs. Assn. Jewish. Author: New York State: Its History and Its Constitution, 1949, rev. title New York State: Geography, History, Government, 1965; Barron's Social Studies Regents series, 1949-70; Pollution of the Environment: Can We Survive?, 1974. Address: 7228 Pine Park Dr W Lake Worth FL 33463

GLASSON, JOHN, orthopaedic surgeon; b. Durham, N.C., June 5, 1918; s. William Henry and Mary Beeler (Park) G.; A.B., Duke U., 1939; M.D., Cornell U., 1943; m. Ella Eddins, Dec. 26, 1942; children—John, Mary Park, George Eddins, Joel Collins, Jean Kent, Jenny Gray. Gen. surg. intern N.Y. Hosp., N.Y.C., 1943-44, asst. resident in surgery, 1946-50; resident in orthopaedic surgery Shriner's Hosp., Greenville, S.C., 1950-52; practice medicine specializing in orthopaedic surgery, Durham, 1952—; pres. Med. Group, Inc.,

Durham, 1968-77, Triangle Orthopedic Assos., Durham, 1977—; attending orthopaedic surgeon Watts Hosp., Durham, 1951-76, Durham County Gen. Hosp., 1976—; cons. surgeon Lincoln Hosp., Durham, 1951-76; mem. med. staff Lenox Baker Cerebral Palsy Hosp., Durham, 1970—; co-dir. Henderson Crippled Children's Clinic, State of N.C. Crippled Children's Program, 1954—; cons. in orthopaedic surgery Durham VA Hosp., 1952—; asst. in surgery Cornell Med. Coll., 1947-50; clin. asso. in orthpaedics Duke U. Med. Center, Durham, 1969-72, asso. clin. prof. orthopaedics, 1972—. Bd. dirs. N.C. Med. Peer Review Found., 1974-78, Arthritis Found., 1972-74; mem. exec. com., bd. dirs. Am. Cancer Soc., 1972-73; mem. external adv. com. Health Services Research Center, U. N.C., 1979—; mem. adv. com. on Medicaid Program, N.C. Dept. Human Resources, 1978—; mem. N.C. Steering Com. on Cost Containment in Med. Care, 1978—; mem. Durham City Bd. Edn., 1960-64; mem. Duke U. Athletic Council, 1965-68; chmn. Duke Loyalty Fund, Class of 1939, 1966; chmn. ofcl. bd. and bldg. com. Duke Meml. United Meth. Ch., 1966-67; bd. trustees Duke Meml. Ch., 1970—, mem. fin. com., 1974—. Served to capt. M.C., U.S. Army, 1944-46. Diplomate Am. Bd. Orthopaedic Surgery. Fellow Nat. Found. for Infantile Paralysis, Am. Acad. Orthopaedic Surgeons; mem. Am. Orthopaedic Assn., AMA, N.C. Med. Soc. (exec. council 1964—, pres. 1972-73), N.C. Orthopaedic Assn. (pres. 1965-66), Piedmont Orthopaedic Soc., So. Med. Assn., Durham-Orange County Med. Soc., Durham C. of C., Sigma Xi. Democrat. Methodist. Clubs: Kiwanis, Hope Valley Country. Home: 615 Swift Ave Durham NC 27701 Office: 2609 N Duke St Durham NC 27704

GLEASON, DEAN LAWRENCE, machine products co. exec.; b. Norfolk, Nebr., Feb. 22, 1925; s. Lawrence A. and Mary Opal (McCartney) G.; student Long Beach State Coll., 1950, UCLA, 1950; m. Charlotte Johansen Glanville, May 30, 1943; children—Alice, Janet, James, Patrick. Tool and die maker Douglas Aircraft, Los Angeles, 1944-49; gen. mgr. Falco Machine Tool Co., Los Angeles, 1953-58; gen. mgr. South Gate Aluminum (Calif.), 1958-59; staff asst. to pres. Precision Screw Products, Dallas, 1959-65, v.p., gen. mgr., 1965—; pres. Precision Machine Products, Inc., Precision Measurement, Inc., Dallas, 1978—, also dir. Mem. Am. Soc. Mfg. Engrs. Home: 3795 Cripple Creek Dr Dallas TX 75224 Office: 2020 W Clarendon Dr Dallas TX 75208

GLEICHAUF, JOHN GEORGE, ophthalmologist; b. Rochester, N.Y., Mar. 21, 1933; s. George William and Cecelia Frieda (Lehner) G.; A.B., U. Rochester, 1955; M.D., U. Buffalo, 1962; m. Barbara Helen Warm, Aug. 20, 1960; children—Kurt and Karin (twins). Intern, Milw. Hosp., 1962-63; resident St. Mary's Hill Hosp., Milw., 1963-64; resident ophthalmology Jefferson Med. Coll., 1964-67; practice medicine specializing in ophthalmology, Santa Fe, N.Mex., 1967—; active staffs St. Vincents Hosp., Santa Fe, Espanola (N.Mex.) Hosp.; grad. instr. Eastern N.Mex. U., 1968; cons. Holloman AFB Hosp., 1968, N.Mex. State Penitentiary, 1970-74, N.M. Sch. for the Visually Handicapped, 1968-74; supervising ophthalmologist Crippled Children's Services, State of N.Mex., 1971—. Served to lt. USMCR, 1955-58. Diplomate Nat. Bd. Med. Examiners, Am. Bd. Ophthalmology. Fellow Am. Acad. Ophthalmology and Otolaryngology, A.C.S.; mem. AMA, Am. Intraocular Implant Soc., Santa Fe Med. Soc., N.Mex. Med. Soc., Internat. Platform Assn., Nu Sigma Nu, Theta Delta Chi. Home: 7 Jacana Rd Hilton Head Island SC 29928 Office: Saltaire Plaza Hilton Head Island SC 29928

GLEITER, THEODORE PAUL, county ofcl.; b. Alma, Wis., Nov. 26, 1921; s. Paul Fred and Johanna Marie (Aeppler) F.; student Eau Claire State Tchrs. Coll., 1938-39; B.S., River Falls State Tchrs. Coll., 1942; postgrad. U. Chgo., 1943-44; M.A., Am. U., 1952, postgrad., 1952-57; m. Marcia Karine Healy, May 16, 1942 (dec. July 1971); children—Karin Jill, Jan Elizabeth, Thomas Glen, Martha Johanna; m. 2d, Caroline F. Davis, Jan. 4, 1975. Civilian instr. USAAF, 1942-43; meteorologist Weather Bur., Commerce Dept., 1947-57, budget and mgmt. div. chief, 1957-63, resources mgmt., 1963-66, asst. adminstr. for adminstrn. NOAA, Rockville, Md., 1966-79; personnel analyst Fairfax County (Va.), 1979—. Pres., Annandale (Va.) Christian Community for Action, 1969, 78. Served from ensign to lt. USNR, 1943-46. Mem. Internat. Personnel Mgmt. Assn., Am. Soc. Public Adminstrn. Home: 3809 Foxwood Nook Falls Church VA 22041 Office: 4101 Chainbridge Rd Fairfax VA 22030

GLEITZ, GEORGE PHILLIP, lawyer; b. Louisville, July 11, 1943; s. Elmer Louis and Pauline Sophia (Reinhardt) G.; B.A., Western Ky. U., 1966; J.D., U. Louisville, 1972; m. Nancy Marie Rupp, Oct. 14, 1967; 1 son, Geoffrey Phillip. Admitted to Ky. bar, 1972, Fla. bar, 1975, U.S. Supreme Ct. bar, 1976; legal aid advisor, asst. to pub. defender Bowling Green-Warren County Legal Aid, 1973-74; pvt. practice law, Bowling Green, Ky., 1974-75; partner Huddleston Bros., Gleitz & Duncan, Law Firm, Bowling Green, Ky., 1975—; chmn. bd. Cumberland Trace Legal Services, Inc., Bowling Green, 1977—. Served with U.S. Army, 1967-69. Mem. Bowling Green-Warren County Jaycees, C. of C., Am., Fla., Ky., Bowling Green-Warren County bar assns., Ky. Acad. Trial Lawyers, Pi Kappa Alpha, Delta Theta Phi. Democrat. Lutheran. Home: 918 Elm St Bowling Green KY 42101 Office: 1032 College St Bowling Green KY 42101

GLENDY, ROBERT EARLE, cardiologist; b. Columbus, Ohio, Sept. 21, 1902; s. Cloyd Darst and Elizabeth Louise (Gardner) G.; B.S. in Chem. Engring., Va. Mil. Inst., 1925; M.D., U. Va., 1931; m. Margaret Elizabeth Moriarty, Aug. 16, 1933; children—Robert, David, Elizabeth. Intern, U. Hosp., Charlottesville, Va., 1930-31; med. house officer Peter Bent Brigham Hosp., Boston, 1931-33; asst. physician Middlesex Tb Hosp., Waltham, Mass., 1933; asst. resident physician Mass. Gen. Hosp, Boston, 1933-34, Dalton scholar, 1934-35, research fellow in cardiology, 1935-36; instr. medicine Harvard Med. Sch., 1936-41; pvt. practice cardiology, Boston, 1936-41, Roanoke, Va., 1945-68; dir. cardiology Roanoke Meml. Hosps., 1968-77, dir. emeritus, cons. cardiology, 1977—. Pres., Roanoke Valley Heart Assn., 1953-54, Va. Heart Assn., 1956-57. Served to lt. col. M.C., AUS, 1941-45. Clin. scholar internal medicine U. Va. Sch. Medicine, 1976—. Diplomate Am. Bd. Internal Medicine. Fellow A.C.P.; mem. AMA, Am. Heart Assn., Mass., Va., S.W. Va. med. socs., Roanoke Acad. Medicine (pres. 1962-63). Contbr. articles to profl. jours. Home: 3806 Heatherton Rd SW Roanoke VA 24014

GLENN, ALFRED HILL, meteorology and oceanography cons.; b. Yonkers, N.Y., June 3, 1921; s. Earl Rouse and Mary Elizabeth (Easley) G.; student Ind. U., 1938-39, Calif. Inst. Tech., 1939-40; B.S. in Civil Engring., U. Wis., 1942; M.S. in Meteorology, N.Y. U., 1943; postgrad. in oceanography, U. Calif., Los Angeles, 1943, in math. Tulane U., 1950; m. Gladys Norris Glenn, Sept. 12, 1947. Engr., Chgo. Bridge and Iron Co., 1942; meteorologist USAAF, Washington, 1946; pres. A.H. Glenn Assos., New Orleans, 1946—. Served to capt. USAAF, 1943-45; PTO. Decorated Air medal; recipient Applied Meteorology award, Am. Meteorol. Soc., 1962, Outstanding Service to Meteorology award, 1970, Distinguished Alumnus citation N.Y. U., 1955. Registered civil engr., La., Tex. Fellow ASCE, Royal, Am. meteorol. socs.; mem. Soc. Petroleum Engrs., Am. Soc. Limnology and Oceanography, AAAS, Am. Geophys. Union, N.Y. Acad. Scis., Tau Beta Pi. Contbr. articles in field to profl. jours. Home: 60 Wren St New Orleans LA 70124 Office: New Orleans Lakefront Airport New Orleans LA 70126

GLENN, DEAN ARTHUR, advt. exec.; b. Bklyn., Dec. 22, 1947; s. David and Marian Baratt G.; B.A., Johns Hopkins U., 1969; M.B.A., U. Va., 1971; m. Charlotte Carr, Aug. 26, 1972; 1 son, Adam Lawrence. Pres., Nat. Advt. and Publishing Corp., Fairfax, Va., 1971-76, 77—; pres. Brazil Imports Ill., Chgo., 1976-77; dir. Ervin Assos., Inc., Learning Resources Corp., Nat. Publs. Center, Sandcastles, Wash. Real Estate Weekly. Home: 8521 Minerva Ct Vienna VA 22180 Office: 2820 Dorr Ave Fairfax VA 22031

GLENN, DONALD TAYLOR, JR., mgmt. consulting co. exec.; b. Farmville, Va., Aug. 21, 1948; s. Donald Taylor and Agnes (Cook) G.; B. Indsl. Engring., Ga. Inst. Tech., 1971; m. Sally Joan Steele, Mar. 20, 1971. Systems analyst Fulton Nat. Bank, Atlanta, 1969-71; indsl. engr. Litton Industries, Florence, Ky., 1971-72; pres. GlennCo. Services Inc., Ft. Lauderdale, Fla., 1972—; dir. Glenn Properties Inc. Mem. S. Fla. Mfrs. Assn., Inst. Mgmt. Cons., Am. Inst. Indsl. Engrs., Execs. Assn. Ft. Lauderdale. Methodist. Clubs: Lauderdale Yacht, Rotary. Office: 509 NE 3d Ave Fort Lauderdale FL 33301

GLENN, JOE DAVIS, JR., civil engr.; b. Fair Play, S.C., Aug. 12, 1921; s. Joe Davis and Elise M. G.; B.S. in Civil Engring., Clemson U., 1942; M.S. in Civil Engring., U. Tenn., 1956; m. Margaret Glenn, Feb. 21, 1946; children—Joe D. III, William Harry, Diane Elizabeth, Mary Kathryn. Asst. prof. civil engring. Clemson U., 1946-56; structural engr. Tidewater Constrn. Corp., Norfolk, Va., 1956-60; owner, mgr. Joe D. Glenn, Jr. & Assos., Norfolk, 1960-76, (merged with A.E. Rollins and Assos. now Glenn-Rollins and Assos., Inc.), pres., 1976—. Former elder Coleman Pl. Presbyterian Ch., Norfolk. Served with C.E., U.S. Army, 1942-46. Decorated Bronze Star. Mem. ASCE, Va. Soc. Profl. Engrs. (pres. 1975-76, named Engr. of Yr. 1976), Nat. Soc. Profl. Engrs. (nat. dir. Va. 1976-80), Cons. Engrs. Council Va., Engrs. Club Hampton Rds. (pres. 1974), Soc. Am. Mil. Engrs., Va. Assn. Professions. Home: 1204 Pascal Pl Norfolk VA 23502 Office: #5 Koger Executive Center Suite 112 PO Box 12154 Norfolk VA 23502

GLENN, NORVAL DWIGHT, sociologist, educator; b. Roswell, N.Mex., Aug. 13, 1933; s. William N. and Mary E. (Cochrain) G.; B.A., N.Mex. State U., 1954; Ph.D., U. Tex., 1962; m. Grace G. Gonzalez, Sept. 18, 1978. Instr., Miami U., Oxford, Ohio, 1960-61; instr. U. Ill., 1961-63, asst. prof., 1963-64; asst. prof. U. Tex., Austin, 1964-65, asso. prof. sociology, 1965-70, prof. sociology, 1970—. Served to 1st lt. AUS, 1954-56. Mem. Am. Sociol. Assn. Author: (with Leonard Broom) Transformation of the Negro American, 1965; Cohort Analysis, 1977. Editor: (with Charles Bonjean) Blacks in the United States, 1969; Contemporary Sociology, 1977—; compiler: (with Jon Alston and David Weiner) Social Stratification: A Research Bibliography, 1969. Home: 2308 Matador Circle Austin TX 78746

GLENN, THOMAS MICHAEL, pharmacologist; b. Detroit, July 20, 1940; s. Spencer Smith and Mary Catherine (Snell) G.; A.B., Rockhurst Coll., 1962; M.S., U. Mo., 1965, Ph.D. (NIMH fellow), 1968; m. Patricia Ann Ross, Aug. 25, 1962; children—Thomas, Timothy P., Christine D. Asso. prof. pharmacology N.D. State U., Fargo, 1966-68, Fla. A&M U., Tallahassee, 1968-69; vis. asso. prof. pharmacology U. Miss., Oxford, summer, 1969; prof. dept. pharmacology U. Pa., Phila., 1971-73; prof. dept. pharmacology U. S.Ala. Coll. Medicine, Mobile, 1973—, chmn. dept. pharmacology, 1973—, acting chmn. dept. microbiology, 1976-77; cons. to Merck, Sharpe & Dohme Corp., 1971-73; manuscript referee Circulation Research, 1969-73, Science, 1975—, Life Scis., 1975—, Circulatory Shock, 1973—. Coach, mgr. Little League Baseball, 1974-78; explorer post adv. Mobile council Boy Scouts Am., 1975-78; pres. Mobile County div. Am. Heart Assn., 1978-79, chmn. com. for youth, 1979-80; mem. Catholic Bd. Edn., Diocese of Mobile, 1979—; bd. dirs. Marriage Encounter, Mobile, 1978-80. NIH fellow, 1969-71. Mem. Am. Chem. Soc., Am. Soc. for Pharmacology and Exptl. Therapeutics, Soc. for Exptl. Biology and Medicine, Assn. for Med. Sch. Pharmacology, Ala. Acad. Sci., N.Y. Acad. Sci., AAAS, Am. Heart Assn., Ala. Heart Assn., Internat. Study Group in Heart Research, Sigma Xi, Rho Chi. Roman Catholic. Contbr. articles on pharmacology to sci. jours.; editorial bd. Circulatory Shock, 1973-80. Home: 1458 Fern Valley Rd Mobile AL 36609 Office: Univ of South Alabama College of Medicine Dept Pharmacology Mobile AL 36688

GLENN, WILLIAM ALLEN, former educator, research historian; b. Logan, Ala., Mar. 28, 1925; s. Columbus Grady and Arletta Gertrude (Entrekin) G.; A.B., U. Ala., 1951, M.A., 1965; postgrad. Am. U., summer 1967, Samford U., summer 1976; m. Ruth Evangeline McClendon, Sept. 10, 1949; children—Phyllis Ann, Bryan Cleveland. Civilian research analyst U.S. Air Force and U.S. Army, 1952-58; tchr., prin. Morgan County Schs., Decatur, Ala., 1959-64; tchr., counselor, prin., dir. fed. aid projects Jefferson County Schs., Birmingham, Ala., 1965-77, ret., 1977; researcher Abraham Lincoln family Bible with Nat. Park Service, 1977—, geneal. background of Ala. governors with Ala. Hist. Commn., 1977—; part time lic. minister So. Bapt. Ch. Chaplain, Ala. Rep. Inaugural Ceremonies for Pres., Nixon, 1969; mem. Ala. Commn. in Intergovtl. Cooperation, 1972-74; cons. Cullman County Mus., 1978-79; deacon So. Bapt. Ch.; mem. Pineywood Baptist Ch., Gardendale, Ala. Served with USN, 1943-46. Recipient awards from Freedoms Found., Valley Forge, Pa., Schoolmen medal, 1967, awards, 1969, 70. Mem. Ala. Edn. Assn., Ala. Ret. Tchrs. Assn., Nat. Ret. Tchrs. Assn., Birmingham-Jefferson Hist. Assn., Ala. Hist. Assn., Nat. Hist. Soc., N. Jefferson Hist. Soc. (v.p. 1979-80), Internat. Platform Assn., Alpha Kappa Delta, Phi Delta Kappa, Kappa Phi Kappa. Republican. Club: Internat. Lions. Author biog. sketches for radio broadcast Freedoms Found., 1968-70; co-author History of the Jefferson County Schools (Ala.), 1967-68; editor script for filmstrip series History of South Carolina, 1968-69; contbr. articles to profl. jours. and newspapers; writer speeches for govs. and U.S. senators; scholar Shroud of Turin. Home: 1319 Columbia Ave Gardendale AL 35071

GLICK, ROBERTA JO, ednl. adminstr.; b. West Frankfort, Ill., Dec. 25, 1922; d. Virgil J. and Constance S. (Newman) Coale; student So. Ill. U., 1941-43; B.S., U. Ill., 1949; M.S., UCLA, 1952; postgrad. Pa. State U., 1958-59, Fla. State U., 1962-71; m. Richard E. Glick, May 20, 1947; children—D'Ann, Randy, Debbie, Dan. Elem. tchr. Mt. Vernon (Ill.) public schs., 1943-46; tchr., Champaign (Ill.) Sch. Bd., 1949-52, Culver City (Calif.) public schs., 1952-54; elem. tchr. Patchogue (L.I.) Sch. Bd., 1955-56, Brookline (Mass.) public schs., 1956-57; asst. prof. edn. Pa. State U., University Park, 1957-60, Fla. State U., Tallahassee, 1960-64; tchr., supr., coordinator program devel. Leon County (Fla.) Sch. System, Tallahassee, 1964—; lang. arts cons., Taylor County Schs., Fla., 1967-68; Jr. League ednl. cons., 1976-78; flexible staffing cons. State of Fla., 1974-75. Mem. Fla. Gov.'s Task Force on Status of Women, 1976-77; adv. bd. Fla. Volunteers in Edn., 1966-67, 74-76; bd. dirs. Voluntary Action Assn., Inc., 1974-76; sec. bd. dirs. Tallahassee Jr. Mus., 1968-70. So. Ill. U. Music scholar, 1941-42. Mem. Leon Edn. Assn. (bd. dirs. 1965-68, pres. 1974-76), Childhood Edn. Internat., Assn. for Supervision and Curriculum Devel., Reading Assn. Internat., Delta Kappa Gamma, Kappa Delta Phi. Home: 1909 Chowkeebin Ct Tallahassee FL 32301 Office: 2757 W Pensacola St Tallahassee FL 32304

GLISSON, CHARLES HERBERT, med. contract services co. exec.; b. Portsmouth, Va., Feb. 17, 1946; s. Charles Edward and Dorothy Mae (Harrell) G.; B.A., U. Richmond, 1968; 1 dau., Lauren Laine. Regional mgr. Am. Hosp. Supply Co., Atlanta, 1970-71, Johnson & Johnson, Atlanta, 1971-72, Dow Chem. Corp., Atlanta, 1972; founder, v.p. Med. Contract Services, Inc., Winter Park, Fla., 1972—; bd. advs. Mass. Life Ins. Co., Orlando, Fla., 1979-80. Bd. dirs. Tangerine Bowl Assn., Orlando, 1976-79. Served with U.S. Army, 1969. Recipient Pres.'s award U. Richmond, 1968. Mem. Am. Mgmt. Assn., Fla. Real Estate Assn. Democrat. Baptist. Home: 341 Raintree Dr Casselberry FL 32807 Office: 290 Purlieu Pl Winter Park FL 32792

GLOCKER, THEODORE WESLEY, JR., lawyer; b. Knoxville, Tenn., Aug. 10, 1925; s. Theodore W. and Julia (McClarty) G.; student U. of South, 1943-44, U. Tex., 1944-45; B.S., U. Tenn., 1947; J.D., Harvard U., 1950; m. Eleanor Julia Glocker, Nov. 30, 1950; children—Theodore William, Margaret McClarty, Eleanor Julia, David Hansen. Admitted to N.Mex. bar, 1951, D.C. bar, 1953, Fla. bar, 1956; practiced in Albuquerque, 1950-51, Jacksonville, Fla., 1956—; mem. firm Buck & Drew, 1956-57, Buck, Drew & Glocker, 1958-75; individual practice, 1975—; trial atty., lands div. Dept. of Justice, Washington, 1952-53; atty. Tax Ct. of U.S., 1953-56. Mem. Spl. Liaison Tax Com. Southeastern Region, Jacksonville, 1956-57, 59-60, 65-67. Chmn. bd. Duval County Beaches Hosp., 1959-63; v.p., bd. dirs. Riverside Presbyn. House, Inc., 1970-74. Served with USNR, 1943-46. Mem. Am., N.Mex., Jacksonville bar assns., Bar Assn. of D.C., Fla. Bar (chmn. tax sect. 1963-64). Sigma Chi, Tau Beta Pi, Beta Gamma Sigma, Phi Kappa Phi. Presbyterian. Home: 949 Elder Ln Jacksonville FL 32204 Office: Atlantic Bank Bldg Jacksonville FL 32202

GLOSSER, ROBERT, physicist; b. Johnstown, Pa., Dec. 14, 1937; s. Frank and Beatrice (Werfel) G.; B.S., Mass. Inst. Tech., 1959; M.S., U. Chgo., 1962, Ph.D., 1967; m. Joan Kathleen Thorn, Aug. 4, 1963; 1 son, Jeremy David. Lectr., U. Calif., Santa Barbara, 1969-71; asst. prof. U. Md., College Park, 1971-75; asso. prof. U. Tex., Dallas, 1975—. Served to capt. AUS, 1966-69. Recipient grant U. Md., 1972. Mem. Am. Phys. Soc., Sigma Xi. Jewish. Contbr. articles to profl. jours. Home: 2909 Deep Valley Trail Plano TX 75075 Office: U Texas PO Box 688 Richardson TX 75080

GLOTFELTY, JOHN WILLIAM, physician; b. Libertyville, Iowa, Sept. 28, 1928; s. Galen Floyd and Mary Susan (Boley) G.; B.Sc., Parsons Coll., 1948; postgrad. State U. Iowa, 1948-49; M.D., U. Louisville, 1953; m. Bonnie Jeanne Dunnock, May 27, 1949; children—Robert, John David, Emma Jeanne, Michael, Neal, Randy. Intern, USPHS, Norfolk, Va., 1954-55, resident in eye, ear, nose, throat, S.I., 1955-60, chief eye, ear, nose, throat, Norfolk, 1960-61; practice medicine Lake and Eye Clinic (Fla.), 1961—; mem. staff Lakeland Gen. Hosp., pres., 1976; clin. instr. ophthalmology U. Fla., 1975—; mem. Fla. Vocat. Rehab. Adv. Com. Dist. chmn. Fla. Polit. Action Com., 1971-73, pres., 1977; bd. dirs. Polk County Learning Disability Assn. Recipient Med. Achievement award Sunshine State Assn. for Blind, 1975. Fellow A.C.S., Internat. Coll. Surgeons; mem. AMA, Am. Acad. Ophthalmology and Otolaryngology, Intraocular Lens Assn., Contact Lens Assn., Am. Assn. Ophthalmology (v.p. 1976), So. Med. Assn., Fla. Med. Assn. (del. 1964—), Fla. Soc. Ophthalmology (pres. 1976) Polk County Med. Assn. (pres. 1977), Phi Beta Kappa, Alpha Omega Alpha. Clubs: Torch, Kiwanis (dir.). Home: 2233 Nottingham Rd Lakeland FL 33803 Office: 1247 Lakeland Hills Blvd Lakeland FL 33801

GLOVER, DORTHA LOU, county ofcl.; b. Red Oak, Okla., Oct. 30, 1924; d. Charles L. and Georgia (Briggs) Dennis; grad. Texarkana Bus. Coll., 1946; m. Bobby Ray Glover, Feb. 25, 1972; stepchildren—Mary Ellen Livingston, Shirley Ann Green, Judy Arlene Chapel, Mollie Virginia Jack, Kathy Louise Shinn. Bookkeeper, McAlester (Okla.) Tobacco & Candy Co., 1946-47, Taylor Mfg. Co., Tulsa, 1947-48; auditor John A. Brown Co., Oklahoma City, 1948; legal sec., legal asst. John B. Baument, Atty., McAlester, 1949-74; ct. clerk Pittsburg County (Okla.), 1975—. Mem. County Officers Assn. Okla., Okla. Ct. Clks. Assn., Bus. and Profl. Women's Club, Pittsburg County Legal Secs. Assn., Okla. Assn. Legal Secs., Nat. Assn. Legal Secs., Nat. Assn. Legal Assts. Democrat. Baptist. Home: 804 S 9th St McAlester OK 74501 Office: PO Box 460 McAlester OK 74501

GLOVER, DOUGLAS DENNIS, physician; b. Rowlesburg, W.Va., Feb. 7, 1929; s. Douglas and Iva (Wix) G.; B.S. in Pharmacy, W.Va. U., 1951, B.S. in Medicine, 1959; M.D., Emory U., 1961; m. Barbara Anne Brady, Sept. 6, 1958; children—Joseph Brady, William Howard, Donald Francis, Geoffrey Gordon, Robert Grady. Pharmacist, H-H Drug Co., Fairmont, W.Va., 1954-56; intern Grady Meml. Hosp., Atlanta, 1961-62; resident Grady Meml. Hosp. and Crawford W. Long Hosp., Atlanta, 1962-65; practice medicine specializing in obstetrics and gynecology, Marietta, Ga., 1965—; mem. staff Kennestone Hosp., Marietta, dir. tumor service, 1968—; chief pharmacist Our Lady of Perpetual Help Home for Cancer, Atlanta, 1976—; bd. dirs. Ga. Cancer Mgmt. Network, regional dir. tumor services, 1969—. Served with 45th Inf. Div., U.S. Army, 1951-53; Korea. Decorated Bronze Star, Purple Heart. Fellow Am. Soc. Pharm. Law, Am. Coll. Obstetricians and Gynecologists, Am. Fertility Soc.; cancer liaison fellow A.C.S.; mem. Am., Ga., Cobb County (dir.), 7th Dist. Ga. pharm. assns., Am. Soc. Hosp. Pharmacists, AMA, Med. Assn. Ga., Cobb County Med. Assn., W.Va. U. Sch. Pharmacy Alumni Assn. (past pres.). Am. Cancer Soc. (regional profl. ednl. dir.). Republican. Presbyterian. Club: Masons (32 deg.). Home: 526 Heyward Circle NW Marietta GA 30064 Office: 653 Cherokee St NE Marietta GA 30060

GLOVER, EDWIN EUGENE, univ. ofcl.; b. Stillwater, Okla., Mar. 29, 1922; s. William Earl and Grace Althea (Andrews) G.; B.S., Okla. State U., 1947; m. Mary L. Hall, Jan. 18, 1941; children—Linda (Mrs. John S. Mahar), Thomas E. Acct., Okla. State U., 1947-50, asst. chief acct., 1950-58, internal auditor, instl. rep. for grants and contracts, 1958-65, asst. bus. mgr., internal auditor, instl. rep. for grants and contracts, 1965-69, dir. internal audits, instl. rep. for grants and contracts, 1969-78, dir. internal audit, 1978—. Sec., treas. Scabbard and Blade Endowment and Resources, Inc., 1965-75. Served with AUS, 1943-46. Decorated Purple Heart, Bronze Star; recipient citations Inst. Internal Auditors, 1972, Oklahoma City chpt. Inst. Internal Auditors, 1975. Certified internal auditor. Mem. Inst. Internal Auditors (past pres. Oklahoma City chpt. 1965-71, 75—), Assn. Coll. and Univ. Auditors (nat. pres. 1976, Stanley C. Smith award 1979), Okla. State U. Alumni Assn. (life), Ret. Officers Assn., Am. Legion, Scabbard and Blade (past nat. comdr.). Democrat. Lion (past pres. Stillwater). Club: Red Red Rose. Home: 1111 W Knapp St Stillwater OK 74074 Office: Oklahoma State University Stillwater OK 74074

GLOVER, KATHLEEN DEBORAH BROWN, advt. cons., artist; b. New Orleans, Nov. 7, 1952; d. Willie Leo and Kathleen Norris (Wilson) Brown; B.A.J., La. State U., 1974; m. John Armand Glover, Jr., July 26, 1974. Advt. mgr. Daily Reveille, La. State U., 1973-74; asst. buyer Halsey, Stakelum & Brown, Inc., New Orleans, 1975; asst. buyer Media Investment Service/McCann-Erickson Inc., Metairie, La., 1975-76, media buyer media investment service, 1976—. Mem.

jr. opera com. New Orleans Opera Assn., 1974—; com. mem. New Orleans Area council Boy Scouts Am., 1977-79. Mem. Women in Communications (treas. New Orleans profl. chpt. 1975-76, pres. La. State U. chpt. 1973-74), Metairie Art Guild, Crescent City Needlework Guild, Board Soc. (v.p.), U.D.C. (3d v.p. 1980—), Candlelighters. Democrat. Baptist. State Dept. grantee World Congress Women Journalists and Writers, Israel, 1973. Home: 1521 Haring Rd Metairie LA 70001 Office: 901 Papworth St Metairie LA 70005

GLOVER, LYNN, III, geologist, educator; b. Washington, Nov. 29, 1928; s. Lynn and Winifred (Mears) G.; B.S., Va. Poly. Inst. and State U., 1952, M.S. in Geology, 1953; Ph.D. in Geology, Princeton, 1967; m. Ellen Fielder Waters, Nov. 4, 1950. Geologist, U.S. Geol. Survey, southeastern U.S. and P.R., 1953-70; prof. geology Va. Poly. Inst. and State U., Blacksburg, 1970—. NSF grantee, 1971, 73, 76; Nuclear Regulation Commn. awardee for geol. research in atomic power plant siting, 1974-80; Dept. Energy awardee, 1976-80. Fellow Geol. Soc. Am.; mem. Am. Assn. Petroleum Geologists, Soc. Econ. Petrologists and Mineralogists, Sigma Xi. Club: Cosmos (Washington). Contbr. articles on geology of Caribbean and Appalachian regions to sci. jours. Home: 914 Mason Dr Blacksburg VA 24060

GLOVER, NATHANIEL BANKS, JR., mgmt. cons.; b. West Point, N.Y., Mar. 12, 1947; s. Nathaniel Banks and Margaret (Wilson) G.; B.S. in Bus. Adminstrn., The Citadel, 1969; M.B.A. in Mgmt., Ga. State U., 1975. Plant mgr. Lunsford Wilson Co., Atlanta, 1969-72; asst. plant mgr. Kaufman & Broad Home Systems, LaGrange, Ga., 1972-73; v.p. prodn., dir. purchasing Unadilla Homes, Inc. (Ga.), 1973-75; sec. Sumac Corp., 1974-75; cons. engr. Alexander Proudfoot Co., Chgo., 1975-77; mgr. installations, asso. analyst A.T. Oxford, Inc., Coral Gables, Fla., 1977—. Republican. Baptist. Smyrna GA

GLOVER, WILLIAM PEYTON, physician; b. San Antonio, Jan. 16, 1911; s. Sidney Peyton and Pauline (Rieden) G.; B.S., Tex. Arts and Industries U., 1932; M.D., U. Colo., 1950; m. Frances Winborne Boyce, Mar. 2, 1974; 1 dau., Claire (Mrs. Jack Anchick). Joined U.S. Army, 1932, advanced through grades to lt. col., 1964; intern Crawford Long Hosp., Atlanta, 1950-51; resident Albuquerque VA Hosp., 1954-57; preventive medicine officer 45th Inf. Div., Korea, 1951-52; gen. surgeon, 1958-65, ret., 1965; practice medicine, specializing in gen. surgery, Wise, Va. and Middleboro, Ky., 1965-69, Virginia Beach, Va., 1969—. Club: Optimist. Home: 5333 Academy Rd Virginia Beach VA 23462 Office: 5261 Challedon Dr Virginia Beach VA 23462

GLOWCZWSKI, ROBERT VINCENT, mfg. co. ofcl.; b. St. Louis, June 18, 1931; s. Lawrence Wellington and Gladys (Tucker) G.; B.S. in Aero. Engring., St. Louis U., 1955, M.S., 1963; m. Maxine Lee Burris, Mar. 2, 1973; children—David, John, Alan, Lisa, Mark, Susan, Melinda. Design engr. McDonnell Aircraft Co., St. Louis, 1955-56, aerodynamist, 1956-58, tech. integration engr., 1958-64; systems engr. McDonnell Douglas Astronautics Co., St. Louis, 1965-66, dynamics engr., 1966-68, program mgr., 1969-72, mgr. tech. integration, 1973-74; mgr. new bus. devel. McDonnell Douglas Tech. Service Co., Houston, 1975-79, mgr. program control and adminstrn., 1980—. Pres., Walker Elem. Sch. PTA, 1961-62; deacon, elder Florissant Presbyn. Ch., 1964-68; chief Indian Guides, Bay Area YMCA, 1970, bd. dirs., 1969-72. 74-75, mgr. bd. dirs., 1976. Served with USMCR, 1950-52; Korea. Fellow AIAA (asso.; treas. Houston chpt. 1978-79, Nat. Membership Chmn. of Yr. award 1977, Sect. Service award Houston sect. 1978); mem. Am. Mgmt. Assn., Nat. Contract Mgmt. Assn., Parks Coll. Alumni Assn. (pres. 1960). Democrat. Club: Houston Mgmt. Home: 16407 Larkfield Houston TX 77059 Office: 16441 Space Center Blvd Houston TX 77058

GLOYER, STEWART EDWARD, chem. co. exec.; b. Milw., May 23, 1942; s. Stewart Wayne and Dorothy A. (Johnson) G.; B.S. Chemistry, U. Rochester, 1964; Ph.D. in Chemistry, U. Mich., 1969; M.B.A., U. Chgo., 1977; m. Marilyn Ann Schmoekel, June 24, 1967; children—Karen, Paul. Chemist, research and devel. Kraft, Inc., Glenview, Ill., 1969-70, group leader, 1971-76; mgr. commercial devel. Humko Sheffield Chem. Co. div. Kraft, Inc., Memphis, 1977, tech. dir., 1978—. Bus. instr. Jr. Achievement project, 1978. Nat. Dairy fellow, 1968. Mem. Am. Chem. Soc., Am. Oil Chemists Soc., Soc. Automotive Engrs., Phi Lambda Upsilon, Beta Gamma Sigma. Patentee in field. Home: 1880 Grenville Dr Germantown TN 38138 Office: PO Box 398 Memphis TN 38101

GLUCROFT, STEPHEN HENRY, orthopedic surgeon; b. Jamaica, N.Y., Feb. 3, 1924; s. Sheppard and May (Gertz) G.; B.S., Union Coll., Schenectady, 1943; M.D., L.I. Coll. Medicine, 1947; m. Doris Kohn, June 15, 1945; children—Ann, James. Intern, Queens Gen. Hosp., N.Y.C., 1947-49, resident in orthopedics, 1949-51; mem. orthopedic staff VA Hosp., Fort Hamilton, N.Y., 1954-57; practice medicine specializing in orthopedic surgery, Miami, 1957—; clin. instr. State U. N.Y., 1956-57, U. Miami, 1966-71; dir. Mfrs. Nat. Bank, Parkway Gen. Hosp., Miami, 1977—; sec. bd. trustees Caduceus Self Insured Med. Liability Trust, 1976—. Served with M.C., U. S. Army, 1952-54. Diplomate Am. Bd. Orthopedic Surgery. Fellow A.C.S.; mem. Am., Dade County, Fla. med. assns., Am. Acad. Orthopedic Surgeons, Fla. Orthopedic Soc. Office: 16501 NW 2d Ave Miami FL 33169

GOAD, BARRY STEPHENS, banker; b. Smith County, Tenn., Apr. 22, 1930; s. Harvey Cyrus and Polly Frances (Patterson) G.; B.S., David Lipscomb Christian Coll., 1954; m. Linda Gayle Brown, Mar. 20, 1959; children—Angela, Anita, Alisa, Adrian. Trust ops. officer Commerce Union Bank, Nashville, 1956-69; v.p., trust ops. officer 3d Nat. Bank, Nashville, 1969—. Served with U.S. Army, 1954-56. Mem. Am. Inst. Banking. Republican. Mem. Chs. of Christ. Office: 201 4th Ave N Nashville TN 37244

GOAD, WILLIAM RAY, mfr.'s rep.; b. Scottsville, Ky., May 29, 1926; s. Francis Roark and Anna Laura (Kemp) G.; student Western Ky. U., 1946-49; m. Elena Victoria Reynolds, July 2, 1948; children—William Ray II, Stanton R., Patrick N. Partner, mgr. 5 small dept. stores, Ky., Tenn., 1950-58; operator J.L. Turner & Son, Nashville, 1958-70; owner, operator 7 Dollar Gen. Stores, 1 clothing store, Ky., Tenn., Ala., 1960-70; treas. Mid-South Life Ins. Co., pres., dir., 1966-67; treas. Crusade Bible Co., Nashville, 1972-74; pres., dir. Southeastern Pub. Co., Nashville, 1974-78; sec., dir. Regal Pub. Co., Nashville, 1975-78; pres. Bill Goad Co., Inc., Madison, Tenn., 1971—. Parade marshall/mgr. Nashville-Madison Hillbilly Day Parade, 1967. Served with USAAF, 1944-46. Mem. hon. gov.'s staffs: Ala., Ark., Ind., Ill., Ky., La., Md., Miss., Nebr., Ohio, Tenn., Tex., Wyo.; named Salesman of Yr., U.S. Caster Corp., 1971, Sales and Mktg. Execs. Assn., 1972, 73, Blisscraft of Calif., 1976, Panasonic Corp., 1976-79. Mem. Retail Mchts. Assn. (pres. 1957). Democrat. Baptist. Clubs: Lions (pres. 1971-72), Masons, Order Eastern Star. Home: 118 S Graycroft St Madison TN 37115 Office: PO Box 4387 Madison TN 37115

GOBELMAN, ROBERT CARL, lawyer; b. East St. Louis, Ill., July 7, 1927; s. Carl John and Daisy Emmaline (Baylor) G.; B.A. cum laude, Wittenberg U., 1955; J.D., U. Chgo., 1958; divorced; 1 son, David Leslie. Admitted to Fla. bar, 1958, since practiced in Jacksonville; partner firm Mathews, Osborne, Ehrlich, McNatt, Gobelman & Cobb, 1963—. Chmn. bd. Gobelman Enterprises, Inc., Jacksonville, 1971—. Mem. Zoning Bd., City of Jacksonville, 1968-72, chmn., 1968-70; pres. Duval County Legal Aid Assn., 1972-73. Served with USNR, 1945-49, AUS, 1950-52. Mem. Am., Fla., Jacksonville bar assns., Jacksonville Assn. Def. Counsel (pres. 1971-72), Fla. Def. Lawyers Assn. (dir. 1972-73, 77—), Am. Judicature Soc., Am. Arbitration Assn. (nat. panel), Phi Delta Phi. Clubs: San Jose Country, Ponte Vedra, River, Timuguana Country, Sawgrass. Home: 6A Broadview Towers 1596 Lancaster Terr Jacksonville FL 32204 Office: 1500 Am Heritage Bldg Jacksonville FL 32202

GOBER, HENRY FRED, lawyer; b. Gainesville, Ga., Apr. 30, 1917; s. John Y. and Leila (Johnson) G.; A.B., Columbia U., 1939, LL.B., 1942; m. Margaret Carolyn Maddox, Feb. 19, 1948; children—Henry Fred, James Alan, Carolyn Jean, Elisabeth Ann. Admitted to Ga. bar, 1945; asso. Dunaway, Riley & Howard, Atlanta, 1946-50; gen. counsel Atlanta Legal Aid Soc., 1950-55; asso. Arnall, Golden & Gregory, 1955-58, partner, 1959—; lectr. in law Emory U., 1950—. Mem. Fulton County Ct. Revision Commn. Bd. dirs. YMCA, 1959. Served from pvt. to staff sgt., CIC, U.S. Army, 1942-46. Mem. Am. Ga. (legal aid com. chmn. 1959), Atlanta bar assns., Lawyers Club of Atlanta, Am. Judicature Soc., Legal Aid Assn. (chmn. com. on policies standards and statistics 1955-56); Southeastern Law Tchrs. Assn., P.T.A. (chmn. edn. com. 1959), Phi Alpha Delta, Sigma Chi. Methodist (ofcl. bd.). Clubs: East Lake Civic (pres. 1958), Atlanta Social Workers (dir. 1954-56), Masons, Shriners. Editor: Supplement Code of the City of Atlanta, 1949; (Ga. sect.) Compendium of Laws-Armed Forces, 1954. Home: 4358 Northside Dr NW Atlanta GA 30327 Office: Fulton Fed Bldg Atlanta GA 30303

GOBER, LEWIS LARON, mech. engr.; b. Madison, Miss., June 5, 1917; s. Thomas Henry and Stella Ray (Culley) G.; B.M.E., Miss. State U., 1940; B.S., The Citadel, 1942; m. Esther Smith, June 5, 1941. Design engr. U.S. Navy, Charleston, S.C., 1942-46, 46-50; staff engr. Maxwell AFB, Ala., 1948-50, The Pentagon, Washington, 1950-56; engring. mgr. Redstone Arsenal, Ala., 1956-67; chief engr. troop support command U.S. Army, St. Louis, 1967-72; cons. engr., Kosciusko, Miss., 1972-77; dir. engring. Sheller Globe, Kosciusko, 1977-79. Served with U.S. Army, 1943-46. Mem. Soc. Am. Mil. Engrs., Soc. Automotive Engrs., Nat. Soc. Profl. Engrs. Presbyterian (elder 1967-72). Club: Masons. Home: Route 2 Box 390E Kosciusko MS 39090 Office: Sheller Globe Corp Kosciusko MS 39090

GOBLE, ROSS LEE, engring. research adminstr., mech. engr.; b. Richmond, Ind., Mar. 27, 1931; s. Samuel M. and Rose (Ross) G.; B.S. in Mech. Engring., Clemson U., 1959; M.S., N.Y. U., 1964; Ph.D., Va. Poly. Inst. and State U., 1970; m. Mabel Fimple, Feb. 26, 1954; children—Deborah Lee, Pamela Gail, Gregory Ross. Mem. tech. staff Bell Telephone Labs., Whippany, N.J., 1959-60; sr. exptl. engr. Pratt and Whitney Aircraft Co., West Palm Beach, Fla., 1960-63; head systems analysis sect. NASA-Langley Research Center, Hampton, Va., 1963-70, head design and structural integration sect., 1970, structures mgr., advanced transport tech. office, 1970-72, head research facilities planning office, 1972-73, chief research facilities engring. div., 1973-78; v.p. Advex Corp., 1978—; instr. engring. Hampton Inst., 1971; instr. pub. adminstrn. Golden Gate U., 1973—. Pres. P.T.A., Riverside Elementary Sch., Newport News, Va., 1971; pres. James River Civic League, 1970-71, treas., 1971-72; chmn. scout com. Newport News council Boy Scouts Am., 1972-73; program chmn. Peninsula Beautification/Ecology Council, Va., 1975-76; civic adviser Jr. League of Hampton Roads, 1975—; vice chmn. Newport News City Planning Commn., 1975-78, chmn., 1978—; bd. dirs. Council for Environ. Quality, 1970-74, pres., 1970-71; trustee Peninsula Nature Sci. Center, 1971-75, 1st v.p. finance, 1972-73. Served with USN, 1951-55; Korea. Recipient Lunar Orbiter Project Group Achievement award NASA, 1968, Apollo Achievement award, 1969. Fellow AIAA (asso.); mem. ASME, Am. Nuclear Soc., Am. Soc. Planning Ofcls., Engrs. Club of Va. Peninsula (pres. 1975-76). Contbr. articles to profl. publs. Home: 37 Meade Dr Newport News VA 23602 Office: Advex Corp PO Box 7263 121 Floyd Thompson Dr Hampton VA 23666

GOBLE, STEVEN CRAIG, mgmt. cons.; b. Terre Haute, Ind., Mar. 23, 1949; s. Robert Wood and Charlotte Elaine (Newlin) G.; B.S., Rose-Hulman Inst. Tech., 1971; M.B.A., U. Chgo., 1974. Design engr. Inland Steel Co., East Chicago, Ind., 1971-72, process control engr., 1972-74; fin. analyst FMC Corp., Chgo., 1974-75, staff asst., Houston, 1975-76, mgr. materials, 1976-79; mgmt. cons. Booz, Allen & Hamilton, Dallas, 1979—. Cert. fellow Am. Prodn. and Inventory Control Soc. Republican. Methodist. Home: 15539 Preston Rd Dallas TX 75248 Office: 1700 One Dallas Center Dallas TX 75201

GODARD, JOHN ELLINGTON, ophthalmologist; b. Moultrie, Ga., Nov. 23, 1942; s. Jencie Bryan and Frances (Baker) G.; B.A., Emory U., 1964; M.D., Med. Coll. Ga., 1968; m. Mildred Peniston Fokes, June 10, 1967; children—John E., Robert F., Mary L. Intern, Med. Coll. Ga., 1968-69, resident, 1973-76; practice medicine specializing in ophthalmology, Carrollton, Ga., 1976—; pres. Carrollton Eye Clinic P.C. chief surgery Tanner Meml. Hosp.; cons. in field. Served to maj. USAF, 1969-73. Diplomate Am. Bd. Ophthalmology. Fellow Am. Acad. Ophthalmology; mem. Carroll-Haralson Med. Soc. (pres.-elect), Med. Assn. Ga., AMA, Ga. Soc. Ophthalmology, Am. Assn. Ophthalmology. Republican. Episcopalian. Club: Rotary. Home: Colonial Dr Carrollton GA 30117 Office: 160 Clinic Ave Carrollton GA 30117

GODBEY, JOHN KIRBY, research engr., b. Cisco, Tex., Nov. 14, 1921; s. Josiah Jernigan and Emma Lee (Taylor) G.; B.S. in Elec. Engring. with honors, So. Meth. U., 1944; M.S. in Elec. Engring., U. Tex., 1947; m. Jo Fay Harrison, Nov. 20, 1943; children—John Kirby, Gayle Harrison (Mrs. Daniel Arthur Morgan III). Teaching fellow U. Tex., Austin, 1946-47; research technologist field research lab. Magnolia Petroleum Co., Dallas, 1947-58; sr. research engr. in petroleum prodn. Mobil Research & Devel. Corp., Dallas, 1958—. Served to lt. (j.g.) USNR, 1944-46. Registered profl. engr., Tex. Mem. Tex. Mid-Continent Oil and Gas Assn. (Outstanding Performance award 1964, chmn. oil information com. 1961-69), IEEE (chmn. Dallas-Ft. Worth sect. 1952-53), Soc. Petroleum Engrs., Measurements and Data Soc., U.S., Tex. socs. profl. engrs., Dallas Petroleum Engrs.' Club. Contbr. articles to profl. jours. Patentee in field petroleum prodn., exploration. Home: 4339 Hockaday Dr Dallas TX 75229 Office: PO Box 900 Dallas TX 75221

GODBOLD, JAKE MAURICE, city ofcl.; b. Jacksonville, Fla., Mar. 14, 1934; s. Charles B. and Irene Noegel (Whitfield) G.; ed. public schs.; m. Jean Jenkins, Feb. 16, 1957; 1 son, Ben. With Ind. Life Ins. Co.; owner, operator Gateway Chem. Co., from 1969; now mayor City of Jacksonville (Fla.). Mem. Jacksonville City Council, from 1967, pres., 1971, 78; bd. dirs. Gator Bowl Assn., Muscular Dystrophy Assn.; pres. Big. Bros. Served with U.S. Army, 1951-53; Korea. Recipient Disting. Service award Jacksonville Area C. of C., 1968. Mem. Nat. League of Cities, U.S. Conf. of Mayors, Fla. League of Cities. Democrat. Methodist. Clubs: Rotary, Northside Businessmen's, Springfield Businessmen's. Office: City Hall Office of Mayor 220 E Bay St Jacksonville FL 32202

GODDARD, DAVID WATSON, surgeon; b. Portsmouth, Ohio, Nov. 19, 1914; s. Rodney Watson and Mary Margaret (Williams) G.; B.A., Duke U., 1936, M.D., 1940; m. Jeanne Molyneaux, July 1, 1939; children—Mary Margaret Goddard Thompson, Susan, Jane Goddard Akin. Intern, dept. pathology Duke U. Hosp., 1940-41, intern dept. medicine, 1941-42, asst. resident dept. urology, 1943-44, 46-47, resident urologist, 1947-48; asst. resident dept. surgery Johns Hopkins Hosp., Balt., 1942-43; practice medicine specializing in urology, Daytona Beach, Fla., 1948—; attending urologist Halifax Dist. Hosp., 1948—, chief of staff, 1957-58; cons. urologist Fish Meml. Hosp., Deland, Fla., Fish Meml. Hosp., New Smyrna Beach, Fla., West Volusia Meml. Hosp., Deland; attending urologist Ormond Beach (Fla.) Meml. Hosp.; clin. asso. prof. dept. urology U. Miami (Fla.) Sch. Medicine, 1968—. Commr. Daytona Beach Housing Authority, 1963-70; trustee Fla. Internat. Music Festival, 1969; bd. dirs. Valleylab, Inc., Boulder, Colo., 1972—. Served to lt. USNR, 1944-46. Diplomate Am. Bd. Urology, Nat. Bd. Med. Examiners. Fellow A.C.S., Southeastern Surg. Congress; mem. Am. Assn. Clin. Urologists, Am. Urol. Assn. (pres. southeastern sect. 1968-69), Fla., So., Pan Am. med. assns., Volusia County Med. Soc., Fla. Urol. Soc. (pres. 1954-55), Flying Physicians Assn., Pan Am. Cancer Cytology Soc., Societe Internat. D'Urologie, Daytona Beach C. of C., Isaak Walton League Am. Democrat. Presbyterian. Clubs: Masons (32 deg.), Daytona Beach Quarterback. Contbr. articles to profl. jours., chpts. to med. texts. Home: 602 Riverside Dr Ormond Beach FL 32074 Office: 1012 Volusia Ave Daytona Beach FL 32014

GODDARD, FRANCES BYRD, clin. social worker; b. Greensboro, N.C., Aug. 11, 1939; d. Henry Davis and Blanche Newton (Leavell) Blake; B.A. with honors, Converse Coll., 1961; M.S.W., U. N.C., 1963; m. Anthony Edward Goddard, Oct. 10, 1964; 1 dau., Caroline Stuart. Sr. social worker Children's Home Soc. Va., Richmond, 1963-71; supr. services Culpeper County Dept. Social Services, Culpeper, Va., 1971-74; dir. Culpeper Mental Health Clinic, 1974-76; dir. Culpeper Family Counseling Service, 1976—; mem. Va. Bd. Social Workers, 1978—, chmn., 1980; cons. Va. State Dept. Welfare on Child Abuse. Pres., Culpeper County Mental Health Assn., 1973. Fellow Am. Orthopsychiat. Assn.; mem. Nat. Assn. Social Workers (pres. Va. chpt. 1978), Otto Rank Assn., Va. Council on Social Welfare, Acad. Certified Social Workers, Va. Soc. Clin. Social Workers. Episcopalian. Author: A Social Profile of a Southern Community, 1961; Difference Without Distance: Identification with Function in the Helping Process, 1963. Home: Quant Acres Boston VA 22713 Office: 110 N East St Culpeper VA 22703

GODDARD, JOHN IRVING, mgmt. cons. exec.; b. Detroit, July 7, 1916; s. Karl Blake and Ethel H. (Green) G.; B.A., Albion Coll., 1941; m. Mary Elizabeth Bradley, Mar. 12, 1941 (dec.); children—Priscilla Anne, Mary Elizabeth; m. 2d; Annette B. Johnson, 1979. Dist. mgr. Formica Co., Cin., 1947-56; pres. William and Mary Nursing Hotel, St. Petersburg, Fla., 1956-63, Bixby Bus. Coll., St. Petersburg, 1964-68; v.p. in charge bus. devel. St. Petersburg Fed. Savs. & Loan Assn., St. Petersburg, 1972-73; specialist in continuing edn. St. Petersburg Jr. Coll., 1970-72; asst. to pres. St. Leo (Fla.) Coll., 1977; cons. Russell F. Scott Co., Mortgage Bankers, Pensacola, Fla., 1977—; dir. Gulfport Bank, Treasure Island Bank, St. Petersburg Fed. Savs. and Loan Assn. Past mem. exec. com. St. Petersburg Community Welfare Council: founder mem. Gov. Fla.'s Commn. on Aging; mem. St. Petersburg Com. of 100; treas., past v.p. chpt. S. Pineallas County Mental Health; past v.p. Pineallas County Mental Health Soc. Served as lt. USNR, 1944-46; NATOUSA, ETO. Named Man of Yr. for Fla., Southeastern Bus. Schs. Assn., 1967. Republican. Presbyterian. Club: St. Petersburg Yacht. Home: 2001 Shady Lane Dade City FL 33525 Office: PO Box 2580 Saint Leo FL 33574

GODFREY, AGNES MULVEY, ednl. adminstr.; b. N.Y.C., July 24, 1915; d. Charles Watt and Mary Elizabeth (Whalen) Mulvey; B.A., Columbia U., 1937, M.A., 1938; postgrad. SUNY, Buffalo, George Washington U., UCLA, Rollins Coll., Fla. State U., U. Fla., U. Hawaii, Fla. Tech. U.; m. Raymond V. Godfrey; children—James Terrance, Lynn Ellen Godfrey Kelada, Raymond Michael, Susan Marie. Teaching fellow Lincoln Sch., Columbia U., 1936-37; research asst. ERPI Ednl. Films and Sci. Sch. of the Air, 1937-38; tchr. schs., Cranford, N.J., 1938-41; mem. staff Div. Cultural Relations, Dept. State, 1942; mem. staff Nat. Cathedral Sch., Washington, 1943-44; Burroughs Sch., China Lake, Calif., 1947-50; area reading clinician dir. of inst., dir. curriculum and materials center, curriculum coordinator Brevard County Schs., 1958-77. Dir. Little Theatre, Conn. State Tchrs. Coll.; mem. Friends of Library Bd., Melbourne; bd. dirs. PTA. Named Tchr. of Yr., Melbourne, Fla., 1961. Mem. AAUW, Internat. Reading Assn., Assn. for Supervision and Curriculum Devel., Fla. Reading Assn., Red Cross Motor Corps, Delta Kappa Gamma. Club: Eau Gallie Yacht. Author: Reference Guides of Reading, and Lang. Arts Guidelines, Brevard County Schools. Home: 736 W Espanola Way Melbourne FL 32901 Office: Sch Bd of Brevard County S Area Office 1948 Pineapple Ave Melbourne FL 32935

GODFREY, J(AMES) FIKE, co. exec., rancher; b. Dallas, June 5, 1923; s. W. F. and Katherine G. (Boykin) G.; B.S. in Indsl. Engring., Tex. Tech. U., 1944; m. Naomi Frances Sweeney, Mar. 13, 1948; children—David, Jan. Research engr. Phillips Petroleum Co., Phillips, Tex., 1947-48; pres. Godfrey Motor Co., Spur, Tex., 1948-69; owner Godfrey Ranch, Kent County, Tex., 1951—; dir. public affairs Western Co. of N. Am., 1978—; exec. v.p. West Tex. C. of C., Abilene, 1971-77. Sec. West Tex. Chamber Found., 1973-77; area chmn. Cattleman's Roundup for Crippled Children, Abilene, 1960—. Gov. Region Beautify Tex. Council; bd. overseers Ranch Heritage Center. Served to lt., j.g., USNR, 1944-47. Named Hon. Citizen of El Paso, Tex., 1975; recipient Rural Service award U.S. Dept. Agr., 1968, Freedom Found. medal for speechs. West Tex. (pres. 1969) chambers commerce, Soc. Am. Mil. Engrs., Soc. Range Mgmt., Am. Soc. Assn. Execs. (Grand award mgmt. achievement 1976), Tex. Contbr. articles to profl. jours. Pub. This Is West Tex. mag., 1971-78, West Tex. Action newsletter, 1971-78. Office: 6100 Western Place Fort Worth TX 76101

GODFREY, JOHN MUNRO, economist; b. San Antonio, Mar. 20, 1941; s. George Phillips Godfrey and Frieda (Allen) Godfrey Dearing; A.A., Armstrong State Coll., 1964; B.B.A., U. Ga., 1964, Ph.D., 1976; m. Nancy Porter, June 4, 1966 (div. 1976); 1 son, John Munro. Instr., U. Ga., 1967-69; fin. economist Fed. Res. Bank of Atlanta, 1969-75, sr. fin. economist, 1975-77, research officer, 1978—. NDEA fellow, 1964-67. Mem. Am. Econ. Assn., So. Econ. Assn., Nat. Assn. Bus. Economists, Atlanta Econs. Club (v.p. 1979), Chi Phi. Episcopalian. Author: Monetary Expansion In the Confederacy, 1978; contbr. articles to bank publ. Home: 200 26th St NW Atlanta GA 30304 Office: Fed Res Bank Atlanta GA 30303

GODFREY, WILLIAM RUFUS, mgmt. analyst; b. Gay, Ga., May 18, 1948; s. John Will and Iula G.; B.S., Clark Coll., 1970; M.B.A., SUNY, Buffalo, 1973; m. Joyce Lincoln, Dec. 23, 1970; children—William Runako, Kenan Anderson, Sarah Nyasha. Banking services officer Wells Fargo Bank, San Francisco, 1970-71; market analyst Ford Motor Co., Atlanta, 1974-75; mgmt. analyst U.S. GAO, Atlanta, 1976—. Mem. Assn. M.B.A. Execs., Am. Mgmt. Assn.

GODKE, ROBERT ALAN, physiologist; b. Kewanee, Ill., Sept. 9, 1944; s. Robert August and Marcelene Edith (Krause) G.; B.S., So. Ill. U., 1966, M.S., 1968; Ph.D., U. Mo., 1974; m. Nancy Lynn Ebbert, Sept. 5, 1965; children—Elizabeth Ann, Jennifer Lynn, John Robert. Asso. prof. reproductive physiology La. State U., Baton Rouge, 1973—; mem. La. Cattle Reproductive Improvement Council; mem. Speakers and Artists Bur. for Ednl., Vocat. and Cultural Exchange with Community, 1977-79. Served to capt. U.S. Army, 1968-70. Recipient Phi Kappa Phi Faculty Research award La. State U., 1977; named Outstanding Tchr., Outstanding Research Scientist of Yr., Coll. Agr., La. State U., 1979. Mem. Am. Soc. Animal Sci., Internat. Embyro Transfer Soc., Internat. Soc. Study Animal Reprodn., Nat. Assn. Coll. Tchrs. Agr., La. Acad. Sci., Am. Legion, Magnolia Woods PTA, Kenilworth Civic Assn., Sigma Xi, Phi Kappa Phi, Gamma Sigma Delta, Alpha Zeta, Omicron Delta Kappa. Methodist. Home: 7623 Amesbury Circle Baton Rouge LA 70803 Office: Animal Sci Dept La State Univ Baton Rouge LA 70803

GODOY, ALBERT, personnel exec.; b. San Antonio, Mar. 29, 1946; s. Stanley and Julia (Gonzalez) G.; B.S. in Gen. Engring., Tex. A. and I. U., 1971, M.B.A., 1974; m. Sylvia Gonzalez, Apr. 5, 1975; 1 dau. Selena Janette. Math. instr. Bee County Coll., 1971-73; tng. coordinator Brown & Root, Inc., Houston, 1975-78, personnel records mgr., 1979—. Served with Tex. N.G., 1970-76. Mem. Assn. Records Mgrs. and Adminstrs., Am. Soc. Tng. and Devel. Democrat. Roman Catholic. Home: PO Box 57094 Webster TX 77598 Office: PO Box 3 Houston TX 77001

GODSEY, FRANK WALDMAN, cons.; b. Beaumont, Tex., Sept. 14, 1906; s. Frank Waldman and Martha Evelyn (Wilkerson) G.; B.S., Rice U., 1927; M.S., Yale, 1929, E.E., 1933; m. Helen Anita Kjoss, Dec. 12, 1929; children—Anne (Mrs. Robert J. Stinnett), Sally Goshen, Frank Waldman III, William J. Devel. engr. safety car H & L Co., New Haven, 1928-34; chief elec. engr. Sprague Electric Co., North Adams, Mass., 1934-40; v.p. Westinghouse Electric Co., Pitts. and Balt., 1940-56; pres. Electronic Communications, Inc., St. Petersburg, Fla., 1956-61; owner, pres. Advanced Tech. Corp., Towson, Md., 1964-68; cons. in mgmt. and tech. cons., Washington and St. Petersburg, 1961—; cons. NASA, 1961-71, Dept. Transp., 1969-72. Mem. Sci. Center Pinellas County; pres. Suncoast Heart Assn. Fellow IEEE; mem. Nat. Security Indsl. Assn. (life), Sigma Xi. Author: Gas Turbines for Aircraft, 1949. Patentee in field. Home: 4038 12th St N St Petersburg FL 33703

GODSMAN, KATHERINE GULOS, sch. psychologist; b. West, Tex., June 21, 1922; d. Bill and Frances (Chronin) Gulos; B.A., Baylor U., 1942, M.A. with honors (Grad. fellow 1943), 1943; m. Mitchell Sidney Godsman, Oct. 16, 1944; children—Frances Charlotte, Paul Bromley, II, Cornelia Mitchell, Elizabeth Allen, William Pickett, Thomas Gregory. Asst. to dean men Waco (Tex.) High Sch., 1943-44; asst. to geophysicist Shell Oil Co., Houston, 1944; tchr. College View Sch., Denver, 1950; ct. psychologist juvenile div. Berrien County, Mich., 1956-60; psychologist Title I, ESEA and acting dir. ednl. measurement Grand Haven (Mich.) pub. schs., 1965-72; sch. psychologist Richmond (Va.) pub. schs., 1972—. Precinct co-chmn. Grand Haven Republican Party, 1964-72; mem. Henrico Rep. Com.; chmn. Cancer Crusade, N. Lincoln Twp., Mich., 1957; pres. region XII Episcopal Ch. Women, Diocese of Va., 1977-79; mem. worship com. Region XII Diocese of Va., Episcopal Ch., 1977-79; mem. women's com. Richmond Symphony, Va. Mus. Mem. Am., Richmond psychol. assns., Va. Assn. Sch. Psychologists, Am. Acad. Human Services (hon.), PTA, AAUW, League Women Voters, Am. Legion Aux., VFW Aux. Home: 1504 Westshire Ln Richmond VA 23233 Office: 301 N 9th St Richmond VA 23219

GODSMAN, MITCHELL SIDNEY, pump mfg. co. exec.; b. Burlington, Colo., Mar. 25, 1923; s. Sidney Paul and June(Mitchell) G.; B.S. in Civil Engring., U. Denver, 1949; m. Katherine Gulos, Oct. 16, 1944; children—Frances Charlotte, Paul Bromley II, Cornelia Mitchell, Elizabeth Allen, William Pickett, Thomas Gregory. Engr., then sales Standard Oil Co. (Ind.), 1949-57; spl. agt. Prudential Ins. Co., 1958-61; service mgr. Bennett Pump Co., Muskegon, Mich., 1961-72, dist. mgr., Richmond, Va., 1972—; chmn. asso. membership com. Nat. Conf. Weights and Measures, 1971. Pres. Central-Elliott Sch. PTA, Grand Haven, Mich., 1964; del. county and state Republican convs., 1962—; asst. Ottawa (Mich.) dist. chmn. Boy Scouts Am., 1963-67. Served with USAAC, 1942-45, USAF, 1951-52; ETO. Decorated Air medal; recipient honor award Mat. Conf. Weights and Measures, 1971, 78, spl. recognition award Western Conf. Weights and Measures, 1973. Mem. Va. Oil Men's Assn., Va. Weights and Measures Assn. (chmn. industry relations com. 1979-80), N.C. Oil Jobbers Assn., Md. Petroleum Council, VFW, Am. Legion. Republican. Episcopalian. Clubs: Masons, Kiwanis (pres. 1961, 67). Home: 1504 Westshire Ln Richmond VA 23233 Office: 1501 Santa Rosa Rd Suite B-14 Richmond VA 23288

GODWIN, DAVID HOUSTON, hosp. adminstr.; b. East Tallassee, Ala., Oct. 8, 1936; s. Loveth Herd and Vera Jane (Hale) G.; B.S., U. Ala., 1964, postgrad., 1964, 70; m. Judith Elizabeth Jordan, June 13, 1964; children—Denise, Lisa, Darren. Bioresearch technician VA Hosp., also Univ. Hosp., Birmingham, Ala., 1966-70; head gastroenterology dept. St. Vincent Hosp., Birmingham, 1970-72; hosp. adminstr. Macon County Hosp., Tuskegee, Ala., 1972-75; adminstr. Bledsoe County Hosp. and Nursing Home, Pikeville, Tenn., 1975-79, Ridgecrest Med. Center, Inc., Clayton, Ga., 1979—. Mem. Tuskegee Action Council, Tuskegee Area Planning Com. Pres.-elect Mason County Cancer Soc.; counselor Health Careers in Ala. Served with U.S. Army, 1956-59. Presbyterian. Clubs: Rotary (pres.); Lions (pres.) (Pikeville). Contbr. articles to profl. jours. Home: Wheeler Subdiv Pikeville TN 37367 Office: Hwy 30 West Pikeville TN 37367

GODWIN, MILLS EDWIN, JR., former gov. Va.; b. Nansemond County, Va., Nov. 19, 1914; s. Mills Edwin and Otelia (Darden) G.; LL.B., U. Va., 1938; LL.D. (hon.), Elon (N.C.) Coll., 1954, Coll. William and Mary, 1966, Roanoke Coll., 1969, Washington and Lee U., 1970, Elmira Coll., 1972, Hampden-Sydney Coll., 1973, U. Richmond, 1974, Bridgewater Coll., 1974; m. Katherine Beale, Oct. 26, 1940; 1 dau., Becky (dec.). Admitted to Va. bar 1937; practice in Suffolk, 1938-62, 70-73; spl. agt. FBI, 1942-46; mem. Va. Ho. Dels. from Suffolk-Nansemond County, 1947-52, senate, 1952-61; lt. gov. Va., 1962-66; gov. State of Va., Richmond, 1966-70, 74-78. Chmn. So. Regional Edn. Bd., 1968-69, 76-77; chmn. Appalachian Govs. Council, 1968-69; vice chmn. So. Govs. Conf., 1968-69, chmn., 1975-76; mem. exec. com. Nat. Govs. Conf., 1968-69, 75-76, 76-77. Trustee Va. Wesleyan Coll. Named Suffolk and Nansemond County First Citizen, 1956, 59. Mem. Raven Soc., Omicron Delta Kappa, Phi Delta Phi. Republican. Mem. Christian Ch. K.P., Mason (33, Shriner), Rotarian, Moose, Ruritan (nat. pres. 1952).

GODWIN, PAUL MILTON, musician; b. Hot Springs, Ark., June 18, 1942; s. Walter Franklin and Mamie Viola (Meek) G.; B.A., Ark. Tech. U., 1964; M.A., Ohio State U., 1969, Ph.D., 1972; m. Mary Mae Wolfe, July 22, 1967; children—Katherine Elizabeth, Kimberly Ann, Jeremy Wolfe. Band dir. Lewisville (Ark.) Sch., 1966-67, Lee Sr. High Sch., Marianna, Ark., 1972-73; teaching asso. Ohio State U., 1970-71; mem. faculty Belmont Coll., Nashville, 1973—, asso. prof. music, 1975-80, prof., 1980—, coordinator music theory, 1973—, band dir., 1973-79; choir dir. Crievewood United Methodist Ch., Nashville, 1973-74; dir. Middle Tenn. Jr. High Clinic Honors Band, 1979. Served with USAR, 1964-66. Mem. Soc. Music Theory, Coll. Music Soc., Middle Tenn. Sch. Band and Orch. Assn., Music Educators Nat. Conf., Tenn. Music Educators Assn., Phi Mu Alpha Sinfonia. Methodist. Club: Elks. Home: 15459 Old Hickory Blvd Nashville TN 37211 Office: Music Dept Belmont Coll Nashville TN 37203

GOEBEL, JEROME ANTHONY, architect; b. Detroit, Mar. 28, 1932; s. Francis Lawrence and Anne Marie (Martin) G.; B.Archtl. Engring., U. Detroit, 1956; m. Ruth Cristina Rivas, Oct. 22, 1968; children—Ruth Cristina, Mary Ann. Project mgt. archtl. firm William Lindhout, Livonia, Mich., 1959-67; architect charge hosp. div. firm James M. Hartley, Hollywood, Fla., 1967-76; propr. Jerome A. Goebel, AIA, Hollywood, 1976—. Mem. Broward County Community Devel. Com., 1977-79. Served with U.S. Army, 1956-58. Recipient cert. appreciation Broward County, 1979. Mem. AIA, Nat. Fire Protection Assn., Constrn. Specifications Inst. Office: 1720 Harrison St Suite 1735 Hollywood FL 33020

GOELL, JAMES EMANUEL, electronics co. exec.; b. N.Y.C., Oct. 13, 1939; s. Milton Jacob and Amy (Jacob) G.; B.E.E., Cornell U., 1962, M.S., 1963, Ph.D., 1965; m. Tamara Greenberg, Sept. 11, 1960; children—Lisa Sue, Fredric Scott. Mem. tech. staff Bell Labs., Holmdel, N.J., 1965-74; v.p., dir. fiber optics lab. Electro-Optical Products div. ITT, Roanoke, Va., 1974—. Vice pres. Middletown Twp. (N.J.) Bd. Edn. Fellow IEEE; mem. Optical Soc. Am., Am. Phys. Soc., Sigma Xi, Eta Kappa Nu, Tau Beta Pi, Phi Kappa Phi. Home: 5420 Linda Ln Roanoke VA 24018 Office: ITT Box 7065 Roanoke VA 24019

GOERTZ, RICHARD JOHN, chem. co. exec.; b. Newton, Kans., Sept. 8, 1925; s. John P. and Elizabeth (Flaming) G.; B.S. in Chemistry, U. Kans., Lawrence, 1948; m. Mary Constance Banowetz, Nov. 6, 1954; 1 son, Steven Richard. Mgr. product devel., research and devel. dept. Phillips Petroleum Co., 1948-63; mgr. project devel., comml. devel. dept. Mobil Chem. Co., N.Y.C., 1963-66, v.p. mktg. indsl. chems. div., Richmond, Va., 1966-74, v.p., gen. mgr. crop chems. group, 1974-77, mgr. bus. devel. phosphorus div., 1977—. Served to 2d lt. USAAF, 1943-46, 1st lt. USAF, 1951-52. Named Outstanding Grad., Sch. Chemistry U. Kan., 1948. Mem. Comml. Devel. Assn., Am. Chem. Soc., Alpha Chi Sigma. Presbyterian. Club: Bull and Bear (Richmond). Home: 4 N Mooreland Rd Richmond VA 23229 Office: PO Box 26683 Richmond VA 23261

GOERTZ, ROGER LAMAR, sch. counselor; b. Freer, Tex., Apr. 24, 1938; s. Albert F. and Dorothy (Martin) G.; student San Angelo Coll., 1957-60; B.A., Southwest Tex. State Coll., 1964; postgrad. U. Tex., 1969-70; M.Ed., Sul Ross State U., 1974; married. Coach, tchr. public schs., Knippa, Tex., 1964-65, Sanderson, Tex., 1965-69, Big Spring, Tex., 1969-76; spl. edn. counselor 5 elem. schs., Plainview, Tex., 1976-78; vocat. counselor Eden (Tex.) High Sch., 1978—. Mem. NEA, Am. Personnel and Guidance Assn., Am. Vocat. Assn., Tex. Tchrs. Assn., Tex. High Sch. Coaches Assn., Tex. Personnel and Guidance Assn., Phi Delta Kappa. Republican. Presbyterian. Clubs: Lions, Optimist, Plainview Fork and Knife, Toastmasters. Home: 1801 Industrial Ave San Angelo TX 76901 Office: Eden High School PO Drawer X Eden TX 76837

GOETHE, SAM PAUL, cons. engr.; b. Jacksonville, Fla., Feb. 18, 1914; s. Hugh McTeer and May Conners (Paul) G.; B.S. in Mech. Engring., U. Fla., Gainesville, 1936, M.S. in Engring., 1938, M.E., 1949; m. Virginia Marie Andes, Sept. 12, 1944; children—Camilla Goethe McKinney, Patricia Goethe Marwick. Air conditioning engr. Tampa Armature Works, 1938-39; partner Goethe-Wilson Lumber Co., Jacksonville, Fla., 1939-42; chief mech. engr. War Research Labs., Gainesville, Fla., 1943-45; liaison engr. Nat. Def. Research Commn., 1945; research engr. Fla. Engring. and Indsl. Experiment Sta., U. Fla., 1945-47, prof. mech. engring., 1947-49, dir. phys. plant, campus engr., 1949-50; cons. engr., 1946—; v.p. Ebaugh & Goethe, Inc., cons. engrs., Gainesville, 1950-75; sec. Big Bend Engring. Co., Tallahassee, 1965-70; v.p., treas. Nesadale, Inc., Gainesville, 1960-73. Elder, past deacon First Presbyterian Ch., Crystal River, Fla. Recipient Exceptional Service award Naval Bur. Ordnance, 1945; award OSRD, 1945; registered profl. engr., Fla. Fellow ASME (life mem.; chmn. Fla. sect. 1949); mem. ASHRAE, Sigma Tau, Beta Theta Pi. Home: 226 NW Magnolia Circle Crystal River FL 32629

GOETTEE, JAMES HENRY, ret. ednl. adminstr.; b. Carmona, Tex., July 18, 1907; s. Francis Marion and L. Catherine (Welch) G.; B.S., Sam Houston U., 1933; M.Ed., U. Tex., 1937; D.Ed., U. Houston, 1959; m. Edna Mae Survant, Aug. 23, 1933; 1 son, James Lee. Teaching prin. county schs., Trinity County, Tex., 1927-30; teaching prin. Field's Store Sch., Waller, Tex., 1930-33; supt. Spring (Tex.) Ind. Sch. Dist., 1933-38; tchr. Oates Jr. High Sch., Houston, 1938-42, acting prin., 1942-44; asst. prin. Stephen F. Austin Sr. High Sch., Houston, 1944-49, prin., 1949-66; dir. secondary edn. Houston Ind. Sch. Dist., 1966-68, asst. supt., 1968-72. Mem. Tex. Tchrs. Assn. (past v.p.), Houston Council Edn. (past pres.), Houston Assn. Sch. Adminstrs. (past pres.), So. Assn. Coll. and Schs. (Tex. com.), Nat. (life), Tex. (life) congresses parents and tchrs., Nat. Assn. Drs. in U.S., S.A.R., San Houston State Coll. Ex-Students Assn. (past pres.), Nat. Assn. Secondary Sch. Prins., Phi Delta Kappa, Delta Kappa Pi. Democrat. Baptist. Mason (33 deg., Shriner); mem. Order Eastern Star (past grand patron Tex.), Clubs: Knife and Fork (Houston), Southeastern Houston Kiwanis (past pres.). Contbr. to profl. publs. Home: 8106 Beverly Hill Lane Houston TX 77063

GOFF, DOYLE ROGER, clergyman; b. Miami, Fla., June 19, 1950; s. Vernon Harry and Elizabeth Amanda (Bostick) G.; student Lee Coll., 1968-71; B.A. in Humanities, Fla. Internat. U., 1974, M.S. in Counseling, 1979; m. Terrie Lane Roberts, May 16, 1970; children—David Roger, Duane Richard. Ordained to ministry Church of God, 1974; served as new field evangelist, 1974-75; pastor at Carrabelle, Fla., 1975-76; minister Ch. of God, Chokoloskee, Fla., 1977—; dist. dir. youth and Christian edn. Ch. of God, 1977—. Scoutmaster, Boy Scouts Am., 1973-75; campaign chmn. Cystic Fibrosis Found., 1978, 80. Mem. Am. Personnel and Guidance Assn., Am. Sch. COunselor Assn., Am. Mental Health Counselors Assn., Lee Coll. Alumni Assn. (sec.-treas. Fla. chpt. 1976—). Republican. Home: PO Box 54 Everglades City FL 33929 Office: 100 Demere Ln Chokoloskee FL 33925

GOFF, EDITH ELLIS, med. technologist; b. Pascagoula, Miss., June 26, 1945; d. Gwyn C. and Silvis (Davidson) Goff; B.S., U. So. Miss., 1967, M.S., 1970; med. technologist St. Dominic Sch. Med. Tech., 1975. Clin. chemistry technician Univ. Hosp., Jackson, Miss., 1969-70; supr. clin. microbiology St. Dominic-Jackson Meml. Hosp., 1970-75; cons. microbiologist and rotating med. technologist West Paces Ferry Hosp., Atlanta, 1975-76, chief med. technologist, 1975—. NSF fellow, 1968. Mem. Am. Soc. Clin. Pathologists, Am. Inst. Biol. Scis., Am. Soc. Microbiology, Am., Ga. socs. med. tech., Am. Acad. Microbiology, Beta Sigma Phi. Home: 9 Independence Pl NW Atlanta GA 30318 Office: 3200 Howell Mill Rd Atlanta GA 30327

GOFF, WAYNE HULEN, educator; b. Imboden, Ark., May 1, 1922; s. Washington Esro and Ruth Etta (Abee) G.; B.S. in Physics and Math., U. S.W. La., 1955; M.A. in Pub. Adminstrn., U. Okla., 1967; Ph.D. in Mgmt., N. Tex. State U., 1972; m. Julia Elizabeth Sanford, Sept. 2, 1943; children—Sandra Janice, Larry Wayne, Ronald Keith, Susan Lynn, Elizabeth Ann, Rebecca Kay. Electronics specialist CAA, Lafayette, La., 1947-58; dep. dist. supr. FAA, 1958-59, dist. supr., 1959-63, chief tech. staff, Ft. Worth, 1963-65, chief engring. br., 1965-67, chief plans and programs br., 1967-68, chief facilities and equipment br., 1968-70, chief electronics engring. br., 1970-72; prof. mgmt. Ark. State U., 1972-75, Sch. Bus., Tex. Eastern U., 1975—. Instr. physics U. S.W. La., also Centenary Coll., 1958-59. Served with USN, 1940-46. Mem. Am. Inst. for Decision Scis., Am. Soc. for Pub. Adminstrn., Inst. Mgmt. Scis., Ops. Research Soc. Am., Acad. Mgmt., Soc. for Gen. Systems Research. Home: 8217 Purdue Dr Tyler TX 75701 Office: Tex Eastern U Sch Bus Tyler TX

GOFORTH, HUGH MAXEL, mech. engr.; b. Oxford, Miss., July 1, 1933; s. Joseph Slate and Marie Higdon G.; B.S. in Mech. Engring., U. Miss., 1958; m. Ruth Kerr, Aug. 24, 1952; children—Hugh Maxel, Kristina, Anne Marie. Test engr. Boeing Aircraft Co., Wichita, Kans., 1958, Lockheed Co., Marietta, Ga., 1958-60; sr. project engr. Brown Engring Co., Huntsville, Ala., 1960-72; dir. phys. plant N. Miss. Retardation Center, Oxford, 1972—; instr. plant engring. Oxford-Lafayette Vocat.-Tech. Sch. Recipient 1st Saturn V Launch Achievement award G C. Marshall Space Flight Center, 1967, award of achievement for 1st manned lunar landing, 1969; Apollo Achievement award NASA, 1969; registered profl. engr., Miss., Ala. Served with U.S. Army, 1955-57. Mem. Nat. Mgmt. Assn., Nat. Soc. Profl. Engrs. Baptist. Home: 240 St Andrews Circle Oxford MS 38655 Office: PO Box 967 Hwy 7 South Oxford MS 38655

GOFORTH, JAMES ALTON, civil engr.; b. Asheville, N.C., July 17, 1915; s. James Alton and Elizabeth (Savage) Goforth; student Berea Coll.; B.S., U. Ky., 1938; m. Charline Adams, Sept. 13, 1940; children—Betty (Mrs. James M. Horton), James Adams, John L. Project engr., FSA Western Ky., 1938-42; stress engr. Bristol Aircraft Div. (Va.), 1942-43; constrn. engr. Clinchfield R.R. Co., Erwin, Tenn., 1943-48, maintenance engr., 1951-68, chief engr., 1968-73; city engr., Johnson City, Tenn., 1973-76; cons. engr., Johnson City, 1976—; pvt. practice as consulting engr., Erwin, 1948-51; cons. city engr., Erwin, 1947-65. Bd. dirs. Tenn. Conservation League. Registered profl. engr. Mem. Nat., Tenn., socs. profl. engrs., Am. Ry. Engring. Assn., (chmn. engring. div. com. roadway and track), Assn. Am. Railroads (Tenn. chmn. grade crossing com.), Am. Ry. Bridge and Bldg. Assn. (pres. 1970). Presbyn. (deacon, elder). Clubs: Erwin Kiwanis (past pres.), Unicoi County Rod and Gun (Distinguished Service award 1962, past pres.). Home: 743 N Elm St Erwin TN 37650 Office: First Security Bank Bldg Erwin TN 37650

GOGGANS, TRAVIS PAUL, accountant; b. Littlefield, Tex., Nov. 11, 1929; s. William C. and Cora Elizabeth (Hukill) G.; B.B.A., U. Okla., 1957, M.B.A., 1958, Ph.D., 1963; m. Ann Nell Tew, July 18, 1975; 1 dau. by previous marriage, Paula Sue. Mem. faculty U. Okla., Norman, 1958—, asso. prof. acctg., 1965-67, prof., 1967—. Served with USAF, 1950-54. Mem. Am. Acctg. Assn., Okla. Soc. C.P.A.'s, Hosp. Fin. Mgmt. Assn. Baptist. Clubs: Touchdown, Order Eastern Star, Masons. Contbr. articles to profl. jours. Address: 742 Terrace Pl Norman OK 73069

GOGGINS, HORACE, dentist; b. Hodges, S.C., May 14, 1929; s. Ulysses and Mattie Lou (Butler) G.; B.S., S.C. State Coll., 1950; D.D.S., Howard U., 1954; m. Juanita Willmon, May 13, 1961; 1 son, Horace Willmon. Individual practice dentistry, Rock Hill, S.C., 1956—. Mem. Mayors' Citizens Adv. Com., So. Regional Council, 1965-71. Bd. dirs. Carolina Community Actions, 1965-67. Served to capt., Dental Corps, AUS, 1954-56. Mem. NAACP (sec. Rock Hill br. 1960-67), Am. Soc. Analgesia, Nat., Palmetto dental assns., Beta Kappa Chi, Alpha Phi Alpha. Democrat. Baptist. Home: 1635 W Main St Rock Hill SC 29730 Office: 425 Dave Lyle Blvd Rock Hill SC 29730

GOGGINS, JUANITA W., state legislator; b. Pendleton, S.C., May 11, 1934; d. Willie and Lillian (Aikens) Willmon; m. Horace Goggins, May 13, 1961; 1 son, Horace Willmon. Tchr. public schs., S.C.; now mem. S.C. Ho. of Reps. Del., Dem. Nat. Conv.; mem. nat. com. S.C. Dem. Party; founder Rock Hill Sickle Cell Anemia Found. Mem. Alpha Kappa Alpha. Baptist. Club: Links.

GOGONELIS, ALEXANDER GEORGE, educator; b. Cairo, Egypt, Dec. 15, 1929; s. George and Helen (Constantine) G.; came to U.S., 1959, naturalized, 1963; B.S., Photios Coll., Egypt, 1950, London Inst. Tech., 1957; m. Georgia Argus, Oct. 4, 159; children—George, Paul. Asst. prof. bus. and accounting Shelby State Community Coll., Memphis, 1973—; pvt. practice pub. accounting, Memphis, 1971-73; chief internal auditor Internat. Tel. & Tel., Milan, Tenn., 1969-71. Cert. internal auditor; C.P.A. Mem. Nat., Tenn. (past gov.) socs. pub. accts., Nat. Assn. Accts., Tenn. Soc. C.P.A.'s, Inst. Internal Auditors, Tenn. State Soccer Referee Assn. (sec.-treas.). Mem. Greek Orthodox Ch. Club: Holly Hills Country. Home: 1799 Teddington Germantown TN 38138

GOINGS, STELLA ALICE JONES, physician, epidemiologist; b. Phila., May 2, 1945; d. David Greene and Grace (Sasportas) Jones; A.B., Rutgers U., 1972; M.D., U. Pa., 1975; m. Milton Conwell Goings, May 24, 1964 (div. June 1968); 1 son, Christopher David. Intern, Mass. Gen. Hosp., Boston, 1975-76, resident in medicine, 1976-77; epidemic intelligence service officer Hosp. Infections br. Center for Disease Control, Atlanta, 1977—; clin. fellow in medicine Harvard U., 1975-77, Emory U., Atlanta, 1977-79. Mem. AMA, Pa. Med. Alumni Assn., Harvard Med. Alumni Assn., Commd. Officers Assn. USPHS, Internat. Platform Assn., Alpha Omega Alpha. Office: 1600 Clifton Rd Atlanta GA 30333

GOINS, JAMES BERNARD, plastic fabrication co. exec.; b. Knoxville, Tenn., Aug. 5, 1939; s. James Hoyle and Charlotte Pauline (Holloway) G.; student in engring. U. Toledo, 1962-63, Henry Ford Community Coll., 1965; m. Charlotte A. Anderson, Nov. 15, 1958; children—Bradford Scott, Marsha Lynn, Marla Leigh. Sales engr. Centri-Spray, Inc., Livonia, Mich., 1965-69; ops. mgr. Centri-Spray Can. Ltd., Windsor, Ont., 1969-71; pres., gen. mgr. Designers Plastics, Inc., Clearwater, Fla., 1971—; pres. Designers Laminates, Inc., Clearwater. Pres., Dunedin Am. Little League, 1973, Dunedin Babe Ruth Baseball, 1975, Dunedin Youth Festival Com., 1975-77; exec. dir. Dunedin Bi-Com Com., 1976. Served with USAF, 1958-62. Republican. Methodist. Mason, Rotarian. Home: 1726 Great Brikhill Rd Clearwater FL 33515 Office: 4740 126th Ave North Clearwater FL 33520

GOINS, JAMES HOWARD, clergyman, missionary; b. Decatur, Ark., Mar. 14, 1909; s. James Thomas and Sarah E. (Gardener) G.; student Okla. Bapt. U., 1945-46, Southwestern Bapt. Sem., Ft. Worth, 1948-49; m. Claire Katherine Campbell, July 18, 1932; children—Verla Lee, Ruby Laverne (Mrs. Robert E. Sutton). Ordained to ministry Bapt. Ch., 1946; with Sequoyah Bapt. Ch., Claremore, Okla., 1945-46, Easton Heights Bapt. Ch., Tulsa, 1946-47; pastor Bellview Bapt. Ch., Midland, Tex., 1949-57, North Tucson

(Ariz.) Bapt. Ch., 1959-63, Mission Dr. Bapt. Ch., Phoenix, 1963-68; missionary Chickasaw (Okla.) Bapt. Assn., 1947-49, Ariz. So. Bapt. Conv., Globe, Airz., 1957-59, 68-76; also missionary Home Mission Bd. So. Bapt. Conv., 1968-76; pastor Vigo Park Bapt. Ch., 1976-80. Pres., Ariz. Bapt. Children's Home, Phoenix, 1964-65; moderator Permian Basin Assn., Midland, 1955-56, Catalina Bapt. Assn., Tucson, 1962-63; dir. missions Little Colo. Assn. and White Mountain Assn., Show Low, Ariz., 1968—; chaplain Midland Police Dept., 1950-57; mem. Mo.-Australian Crusade, Mo. Bapt. Conv., 1964. Mem. Internat. Platform Speakers Am. Democrat. Mason, Lion. Composer religious songs. Address: Vigo Park Rural Station Box No 1 Tulia TX 79088

GOINS, JOSEPH LEWIS, JR., food chain exec.; b. Tulsa, Nov. 27, 1947; s. Joseph Lewis and Patricia Anne (Studer) G.; student U. Okla., 1965-66, U. Houston, 1971-74; m. Jean Arlene Faour, Sept. 20, 1974; children—Joseph Lewis, Jennifer Ann. With Hickory Farms of Ohio, Inc., 1971—, regional gen. mgr. for Tex., Kans., Mo. and Colo., Houston, 1979—. Mem. adv. bd. Distributive Edn. Clubs Am. Served with USMC, 1967-71. Decorated Air medals (12). Mem. Meyerland Plaza Merchants Assn. (dir. 1979-80), VFW, Marine Corps Assn. Republican. Roman Catholic. Home: 5003 Porter Ridge Houston TX 77053 Office: 1022 Wirt Rd Suite 320 Houston TX 77055

GOKEE, DONALD LEROY, clergyman; b. Lansing, Mich., Aug. 8, 1933; s. Richard Alden and June Elizabeth (Colenso) G.; B.A., Mich. State U. and Temple U., Chattanooga, 1958; postgrad. (A. Morehouse and William Walker scholar) George Washington U., 1960-64, Washington Sch. Psychiatry, 1964, Va. Theol. Sem., 1964-65, Columbia Theol. Sem., 1968, New Coll., U. Edinburgh (Scotland), 1975, Frankfurt U. (Germany), 1977, U. Athens (Greece), 1978; m. Maxine Pawlik Adkins, Apr. 21, 1974; children—Douglas Richard, Charles Jeffrey, Mary Beth, Jessica Lynn. Ordained to ministry Presbyn. Ch., 1965; dir. Christian edn. Central Presbyn. Ch., Chattanooga, 1958-59, Fairlington Presbyn. Ch., Alexandria, Va., 1959-66; asso. pastor Pine Shores Presbyn. Ch., Sarasota, Fla., 1966-69; pastor Conway Presbyn. Ch., Orlando, Fla., 1969—; chaplain Orange County Juvenile Ct., 1969-73; mem. Council Synod Fla., 1972—; mem. ecumenical coordinating team as rep. Presbyn. Ch. U.S., 1977—; guest lectr. Goshen (Ind.) Coll.; vis. prof. So. Coll. Mem. Nat. Task Force on Criminal Justice and Prison Reform, 1976—. Recipient certificate of merit for distinguished service to Christ, ch. and community, 1970; In-God-We-Trust award Family Found. of Am., 1980. Home: 3026 Carmia Dr Orlando FL 32806 Office: 4300 Lake Margaret Dr Orlando FL 32806

GOLAN, FLOYD ALLEN, poultry scientist; b. Kenney, Tex., Aug. 29, 1939; s. Jesse and Edna May (Lyons) G.; A.A., Blinn Jr. Coll., 1958; B.S., Sam Houston State U., 1960, M.Ed., 1961; Ph.D., Tex. A&M U., 1965; m. Mary Ann Quebe, Sept. 3, 1960; children—Brian Allen, Mandy Elizabeth. Instr., Sam Houston State U., 1959-60; research asst. Tex. A&M U., 1961-65, supr. Nat. Poultry Improvement Plan, 1965-77, supr. Nat. Poultry Improvement Plan and mandatory pullorum typhoid program, 1977—. Bd. dirs. 2-S3 Eye Bank, 1975-77. Mem. Poultry Sci. Assn., Am. Inst. Biol. Sci., Tex. Poultry Fedn., Sigma Xi, Phi Tau Sigma. Baptist. Club: Lions (dep. dist. gov.). Home: 106 Greenway Dr Bryan TX 77810 Office: Kleburg Center Tex A&M U College Station TX 77843

GOLD, ALLEN JAY, apparel co. exec.; b. Newark, Aug. 23, 1927; s. Bernard Leon and Shirley (Brodofsky) G.; student So. Meth. U., 1945-47. Partner, Nardis of Dallas, 1948-65; pres. Nardis of Dallas, Inc., 1965—, also dir. Bd. dirs. Dallas Civic Opera. Served with USCGR, 1945-46. Mason (32 deg., Shriner). Home: 5205 Royal Lane Dallas TX 75229 Office: 1300 Corinth St Dallas TX 75215

GOLD, DAVID, mfg. co. exec.; b. Russia, Sept. 2, 1907; s. Israel and Molly (Coleman) G.; student Academy High Sch., Erie, Pa.; m. Leah Weiss, Feb. 15, 1931; children—Arnold Z., Ivan L. Propr., Ace Oil Co., Meadville, Pa., 1934-41; sales mgr. Rack Engrng. Co., Connellsville, Pa., 1941-46, exec. v.p., 1947—. Nat. v.p. Zionist Orgn. Am., nat. exec. com.; pres. Pitts. Zionist Dist., 1964-66; 1st pres. N.W. Pa. council B'nai B'rith, 1940; v.p. Coll. Jewish Studies, 1958-60, Pitts.; bd. dirs. United Jewish Fedn., Jewish Chronicle Bd.; v.p. Sch. Advanced Jewish Studies, Pitts., 1972-74. Recipient Israel Service award, 1967. Mem. Material Handling Inst., Am. Def. Preparedness Assn. Pres., Beth Shalom Congregation, 1973-75. Clubs: Concordia, Masons. Home: 1912 S Ocean Dr Tower 1 Apt 19C Hallandale FL 33009

GOLD, KENNETH RAY, computer industry exec.; b. Providence, Ky., Aug. 9, 1934; s. Vernon R. and Irene Frances (Mitchell) G.; B.A., Wayne State U., 1960; M.B.A., Fla. State Christian U., 1971; m. Olga Ann Szakacs, Aug. 23, 1958; children—Victoria, Rebecca, Jennifer. Tech. and mktg. positions IBM, 1960-69; With Latin Am. Computer Mktg. and Cons. Mgmt., 1969-79; Infodata Systems Inc., Miami, Fla., 1979—; mem. faculty U. Toledo, 1967-69. Served with USN, 1952-56. Certified data educator. Mem. Brazilian Computer Soc. Republican. Presbyterian. Contbr. articles to profl. jours. Home: 17230 SW 90th Ave Miami FL 33157 Office: 17891 S Dixie Miami FL 33157

GOLDABER, IRVING, sociologist; b. N.Y.C., Nov. 24, 1925; s. Harry Louis and Minnie (Brown) G.; B.A., Bklyn. Coll., 1948; M.A., Columbia, 1951; Ph.D., N.Y. U., 1965; m. Marilyn Edith Marinoff, Dec. 23, 1951; children—Kenneth Gordon, Richard Scott. Asst. dir. Mayor's Com. on Unity of N.Y.C., 1951-53; asst. to nat. coordinator Nat. Community Relations Adv. Council, N.Y.C., 1953-57; dep. exec. dir. N.Y.C. Commn. on Human Rights, 1957-66; cons. govtl. bodies, pvt. orgns. on social conflict resolution, 1966—; adj. prof. sociology Bklyn. Coll. City U. N.Y., 1955—. Served with AUS, 1944-46. Rockefeller Found. grantee, 1976. Mem. Am. Sociol. Assn., Soc. for Study of Social Problems, Internat. Soc. for Research on Aggression, NEA, AAAS, AAUP. Home and office: 2451 Brickell Ave Miami FL 33129

GOLDBERG, LEE DRESDEN, physician; b. Point Pleasant, N.J., July 29, 1937; s. Milton J. and Maude (Dresden) G.; B.S. summa cum laude, Yale U., 1959, M.D., 1963; m. Lana Ditchek, July 23, 1967; children—Marissa Julie, Sara Amy, Rachel Sherry. Intern, Mt. Sinai Hosp., N.Y.C., 1963-64; resident in internal medicine Montefiore Hosp., N.Y.C., 1964, 66-68; fellow in endocrinology Albert Einstein Coll. Medicine, N.Y.C., 1968-69, Bellevue Hosp.-N.Y. U. Med. Center, N.Y.C., 1969-70; practice medicine specializing in endocrinology, Miami Beach, Fla., 1970—; mem. staff South Shore Hosp., 1970—, chief internal medicine, 1975-79; mem. staff Mt. Sinai Hosp., 1970—, co-chief endocrinology, 1974—; mem. staff St. Francis Hosp., asso. chmn. medicine, 1977-78; mem. staff Miami Heart Inst.; clin. asst. prof. medicine Sch. Medicine, U. Miami, 1971—. Bd. dirs. Landow Yeshiva Center, 1974-78; bd. dirs. Hebrew Acad. Greater Miami, 1975—, v.p., 1978—. Served with USNR, 1964-66. Recipient Physicians Recognition award AMA, 1969, 72. Diplomate Am. Bd. Internal Medicine, Nat. Bd. Med. Examiners. Fellow A.C.P.; mem. Am. Diabetes Assn., Endocrine Soc., Am. Fedn. Clin. Research, Am. Physicians Fellowship for Israel Med. Assn., Phi Beta Kappa, Sigma Xi. Jewish. Club: Yale (Miami). Contbr. articles on endocrinology to profl. jours. Home: Miami Beach FL Office: 1674 Meridian Ave Suite 505 Miami Beach FL 33139

GOLDBLATT, BARRY ARTHUR, communications software cons.; b. Abilene, Tex., Nov. 26, 1949; s. Leonard L. and Gertrude E. G.; B.A., U. Tex., Arlington, 1972, postgrad., 1976—; m. Janet Delle Ray, June 17, 1976. Media relations cons., Tex., Washington, 1967-72; public affairs commentator Sta. KFMN, Abilene, 1975; owner, operator multi-unit retail bus., 1972-77; cons., guest lectr. colls., univs. West Tex., 1976-77; cons. audio visual industry; dir. audio visual services Color Tile Supermart, Inc., Fort Worth, Tex., 1976-79; mgr. audio visual services Electronic Data Systems, Dallas, 1979—. Mem. Assn. for Multi-Image, Alpha Epsilon Pi. Office: 7171 Forest Ln Dallas TX 75230

GOLDEN, KENNETH STEVEN, state ofcl.; b. N.Y.C., Mar. 9, 1944; s. Jack and Ruth (Friedman) G.; B.C.E., Rensselaer Poly. Inst., 1964; M. City Planning, Yale U., 1966; m. Anne Leff Warwick, Aug. 26, 1965; children—Melissa, Jared. Community planner S.C. State Devel. Bd., Columbia, 1966-68; state planner S.C. State Planning and Grants Div., 1968-69; sr. asso. Harold F. Wise & Assos., Planning Cons., Washington, 1969-70; asso. dir. Div. State Planning and Community Affairs, Richmond, Va., 1970-73; dep. dir. Commn. on State Govtl. Mgmt., Richmond, Va., 1973-77; exec. dir. Commn. State Govtl. Mgmt., Richmond, 1977-78; asst. sec. adminstrn. and fin. Commonwealth of Va., 1978—; lectr. city planning U. Va. County council rep. Henrico (Va.) PTA, 1975; mem. planning com. Richmond Jewish Community Fedn. Mem. Am. Soc. Pub. Adminstrn. (council (Council chpt.), ASCE, Tau Epsilon Phi. Club: Raintree Swim and Racquet. Office: Ninth St Office Bldg Richmond VA 23219

GOLDEN, ROGER LEE, mech. engr.; b. Orange, Tex., Mar. 26, 1947; s. Lee Roy and Francine Carolyn (Rogers) G.; A.A., Fla. Coll., 1967; B.M.E., Auburn U., 1971. Mech. engr. So. Co. Services, Birmingham, 1969—. Registered profl. engr., Fla., Ga., Miss., Ala. Mem. Nat. Mgmt. Assn., ASME. Home: 2117 3d St NW Birmingham AL 35215 Office: PO Box 2625 Birmingham AL 35202

GOLDEN, WILLIAM MICHAEL, JR., merchandising co. exec.; b. Lima, Peru, Dec. 5, 1948 (parents Am. citizens); s. William Michael and Jane Ruth (Faber) G.; B.A., U. South Fla., 1970; m. Gwendolyn Lutrell Brown, Dec. 30, 1978. Sec., Touche Ross & Co., Jacksonville, Fla., 1971-77; Southeastern regional controller Modern Merchandising, Inc., Jacksonville, 1977—. Mem. agy. rev. com. United Way Jacksonville, 1978. Served with USMC, 1970-71. Recipient Nat. award Pianist Guild, 1962. Mem. Fla. Inst. C.P.A.'s (asso.), Phi Delta Theta (pres. 1969-70). Presbyterian.

GOLDENBERG, ALAN LEE, surgeon; b. Bklyn., Sept. 7, 1939; s. Morris H. and Pauline L. (Zelony) G.; B.S., Franklin and Marshall Coll., 1960; M.D., State U. N.Y. Downstate Med. Sch., 1963; m. Sandra D. Zavidow, June 27, 1965; children—Roger, Evan, David. Intern Downstate Med. Center of N.Y., Bklyn., 1963-64, resident surgery, 1964-69, asst. instr. surgery, 1964-69; practice medicine specializing in surgery, Lauderdale Lakes, Fla., 1971—; mem. staff Fla. Med. Center Hosp., chief of surgery, 1974-77; mem. staffs Plantation (Fla.) Gen. Hosp., U. Community Hosp., Tamarac, Fla., Bennett Community Hosp., Plantation. Served to maj. M.C., USAF, 1969-71. Diplomate Am. Bd. Surgery. Fellow Am. Cancer Soc., A.C.S.; mem. Am., So., Fla., Broward County (Fla.) med. assns., Phi Beta Kappa. Home: 7220 SW 5th St Plantation FL 33317 Office: 4900 W Oakland Park Blvd Lauderdale Lakes FL 33313

GOLDMAN, ELLEN MYNETTE EASON, lawyer; b. Kosciusko, Miss., Apr. 11, 1921; d. Van Vernon and Nellie Clayton (Vaughan) Eason; B.A., Miss. State Coll. for Women, 1941; M.A., U. Miss., 1960, J.D., 1970; m. James Oswald Goldman, July 31, 1947; 1 son, James Oswald. Admitted to Miss. bar, 1970; with E & J Enterprises, Marks, Miss., 1965—, v.p., 1965—; practiced in Marks, 1970—; judge 11th Jud. Dist. Miss., 1978; vice chmn. bd. bar admissions State of Miss., 1974-79. Sec., City Beautification, Marks, 1971-73; docent Brooks Meml. Art Gallery, Memphis, 1973; bd. dirs. Brooks Meml. Art Gallery Found., Memphis, Tenn., Northwest Miss. Girl Scout Council, Inc.; mem. Gov.'s Adv. Com. for Legal Services of Miss. Mem. Am. Trial Lawyers Assn., Am. Judicature Soc., Am. (mem. practice-handbook com., real property div. com.), Miss., Quitman County (sec. 1970—) bar assns., Mensa, Herb Soc. Am. Embroiderers Guild Am., Practising Law Inst., Internat. Platform Assn., Alumni Assn. U. Miss. (dir.), Law Alumni Assn. U. Miss. (dir.), Marks C. of C. (pres. 1970-73), Kappa Beta Pi, Delta Kappa Gamma. Methodist. Home: 551 Lamar St Marks MS 38646 Office: 231 Chestnut St Marks MS 38646

GOLDMAN, GERALD CARL, dermatologist; b. Boston, Jan. 2, 1941; s. Arthur L. and Charlotte (Katz) G.; B.A., Harvard U., 1962; M.D., Boston U., 1966; m. Raida Ann Levine, June 23, 1963; children—Heather Meryl, Elizabeth Sara. Intern, Mary Hitchcock Meml. Hosp., Hanover, N.H., 1966-67; resident in dermatology, teaching fellow Harvard U. and Mass. Gen. Hosp., Boston, 1967-69; instr. dermatology Washington U., St. Louis, 1970-72; practice medicine specializing in dermatology, St. Petersburg, Fla., 1972—; mem. staff St. Anthony's Hosp., St. Petersburg Gen. Hosp. Served as maj. M.C., U.S. Army, 1970-72. Fellow Am. Acad. Dermatology; mem. AMA, Fla. Med. Assn., Fla. Dermatology Soc., Am. Jewish Com. Home: 7657 133d St N Seminole FL 33542 Office: 501 11th St N St Petersburg FL 33705

GOLDMAN, ROBERT MICHAEL, educator; b. Chgo., Dec. 3, 1945; s. Milton William and Ruth (Levin) G.; student Hiatt Inst., Brandeis U., Israel, 1966; B.A., U. Ill., 1967; M.A., Ph.D., Mich. State U., 1976. Asst. prof. history and polit. sci. Va. Union U., Richmond, 1974—; cons. Met. Richmond Multi-Ethnic Heritage Studies Program. Bd. dirs., 1st v.p. Masada-Hillel of Richmond; mem. community relations com. Jewish Community Fedn., Richmond. Mem. Am. Hist. Assn., Am. Soc. for Legal History, Orgn. Am. Historians, Phi Kappa Phi. Contbr. articles to profl. jours. Home: 2014 Stuart Ave Richmond VA 23220 Office: 1500 N Lombardy St Richmond VA 23220

GOLDNER, HERMAN WILSON, lawyer; b. Detroit, Nov. 12, 1916; s. Michael and Ethel (Wilson) G.; B.S., Miami U., 1939; LL.B., Western Res. U., 1942; M.B.A., Harvard U., 1948; m. Winifred Herlan Munyan, Nov. 3, 1939; children—Brian Early, Michael Herlan. Admitted to Ohio bar, 1942, Mass. bar, 1947, Fla. bar, 1948, U.S. Supreme Ct. bar, 1952; of counsel firm Goldner and Cramer (now Goldner, Reams, Marger, Davis, Piper and Kiernan, P.A.), St. Petersburg, Fla., 1948—; prof. municipal law Stetson Law Sch., 1973-75; dir. Central Plaza Bank & Trust Co.; dir. Home TV, Inc. Mayor City of St. Petersburg, 1961-67, 71-73; bd. dirs. Bayfront Med. Center, St. Petersburg, 1968-70, Sci. Center of St. Petersburg, 1970. Served with USN, 1942-46. Recipient Jaycees Good Govt. award, 1967; Tampa Bay Regional Planning Leadership award, 1963. Mem. U.S. Conf. Mayors, Am., St. Petersburg (bd. govs. 1970-71) bar assns., Fla. Bar, Trial Lawyers Assn., President's Adv. Commn. on Intergovtl. Relations, Am. Legion, Mil. Order World War II. Democrat. Jewish. Clubs: Lakewood Country, St. Petersburg Yacht, Commerce of Pinellas County, Masons, Shriners. Contbr. articles on legal and local govt. topics. Office: 3819 Central Ave PO Drawer 14233 Saint Petersburg FL 33713

GOLDSMITH, JUDITH ANN ADAMS, sch. psychologist; b. Cin., Apr. 30, 1939; d. Harry Wesley and Sarah Elizabeth (Irwin) Adams; B.A. in Psychology, Miami U., 1960; M.Ed. in Counseling, Boston U., 1977; m. Albert Lewis Goldsmith, Jr., Aug. 27, 1961; children—Elizabeth Ann, Christopher Adams. Research psychologist Ames Research Center, NASA, Moffitt Field, Calif., 1963-64; clin. intern Boeblingen Am. Elementary and Jr. High Sch., Stuttgart, W. Ger., 1976-77; spl. edn. placement specialist, sch. psychometrist, sch. psychologist Fairfax County (Va.) Pub. Schs., 1977—. Mem. Am. Personnel and Guidance Assn., Sch. Counselors Assn., Psi Chi, Alpha Kappa Delta. Office: 3011 Memorial St Alexandria VA 22306

GOLDSTEIN, IRWIN OWEN, computer mgmt. cons.; b. N.Y.C., Nov. 18, 1933; s. Joseph Robert and Florence (Sherman) G.; B.B.A., U. Miami, Coral Gables, Fla., 1954; L.L.B., J.D., 1965; postgrad. Wharton Sch., U. Pa., Am. Grad. U., U. Miami, U. Ala.; m. Paulette Iris Goldner, Sept. 13, 1954; children—Bonnie P., Michael J., Shari B. Adminstrv. asst. Wometco-WTVJ, Inc., Miami, 1954-56; controller Jetronic Industries, Inc., Miami, 1958-61; dir. purchasing/contracts corp. make or buy Thiokol Chem. Corp., Huntsville, Ala., 1962-66; corp. exec., officer SCI Systems Inc., Huntsville, 1966-71; v.p. Systems Engrng. Labs., Ft. Lauderdale, Fla., 1971-79; chmn., pres. I.O.G. Assos., Inc., mgmt. cons.; pres. GKD Electronics, Inc., Costa Mesa, Calif.; dir. Afcoa Korea Co., Ltd., Seoul; past pres. SCI Plastics Inc., Decatur, Ala.; past sec. Houston Research, Inc. Served to capt. Signal Corps AUS, 1956-58, 64-65. Cert. profl. contract mgr., 1974, purchasing profl. Mem. Nat. Contract Mgmt. Assn., Air Force Assn., Am. Purchasing Soc., Soc. Plastics Engrs. Home: 1131 S W 69th Ave Plantation FL 33317 Office: 1399 Logan Ave Costa Mesa CA 92626

GOLDSTEIN, JACK CHARLES, lawyer; b. Ft. Worth, May 11, 1942; s. Bennie Harrison and Rae (Shanblum) G.; B.S.M.E., Purdue U., 1964; J.D. with honors, George Washington U., 1968; m. Leslie Paula Silber, July 3, 1965; children—Jason Brent, Jill Paige. Patent examiner U.S. Patent and Trademark Office, Washington, 1964-67; patent adviser Office of Naval Research, Washington, 1967-68; law clk. U.S. Ct. Customs and Patent Appeals, Washington, 1968-69; admitted to Ill. bar, 1968, Tex. bar, 1968, D.C. bar, 1969; mem. firm Arnold White & Durkee, Houston, 1969—; adj. prof. copyright law South Tex. Coll. Law, 1974—; mem. adv. bd. Patent, Trademark and Copyright Jour. Bur. Nat. Affairs, Washington, 1978—. Mem. adv. council The Little Sch. House, Houston, 1975-78. Mem. Am., Fed., Houston bar assns., Am. Patent Law Assn., D.C. Bar, State Bar of Tex., Houston Patent Law Assn. (pres. 1979-80), Internat. Patent and Trademark Assn., Patent Office Soc., Nat. Council Patent Law Assns. (councilman 1978-80), Copyright Soc. U.S.A. (trustee), Order of the Coif, Pi Tau Sigma. Clubs: University (Houston), Chancellors. Contbr. articles to profl. jours. Home: 6231 S Braeswood Blvd Houston TX 77096 Office: Arnold White & Durkee 2100 Transco Tower Houston TX 77056

GOLDSTEIN, LIONEL ALVIN, accountant; b. Bklyn., Oct. 19, 1932; s. Alexander and Ruth (Spitzer) G.; student Tex. A. and M. U., 1950-52, So. Meth. U., 1960-65; M.S. in Adminstrn., U. Dallas, 1977; children—Alex, Sharon; m. Judy Ruth Calk, May 19, 1973. Accountant, Arrow Industries, Inc., Carrollton, Tex., 1965, office mgr., 1966-68, controller, 1968-69, v.p., 1969-76, also dir.; pvt. practice accounting, 1976—. Trustee Rosenberg Brothers Found. Served with C.E., AUS, 1952-54. C.P.A., Tex., La., Ark. Mem. Am. Inst. C.P.A.'s, Tex. Soc. C.P.A.'s, Soc. La. C.P.A.'s, Tex. Soc. C.P.A.'s (Dallas chpt.), Nat. Assn. Accountants, Am. Inst. Indsl. Engrs., Dallas Estate Planning Council, Sigma Iota Epsilon. Jewish. Home: 2861 Parkhaven Plano TX 75075

GOLDSTEIN, NORMAN EDWARD (NED), bldg. contractor; b. Phila., Aug. 7, 1931; s. Albert and Sarah Rose (Miller) G.; B. Commerce, Pa. State Coll., 1953; postgrad. Wharton Grad. Sch., U. Pa., 1953; m. Ruth Lois Gabel, June 16, 1957; children—Karen Sara, Debbie Jenny. Pres., chief operating officer N. Edward Goldstein, Inc., Phila., 1959-79; Served with U.S. Army, 1954-55. Mem. Builders Assn. South Fla. (dir.), Home Owners Warranty Council South Fla. (dir.), Inst. Residential Mktg. Jewish. Home: 4201 North Hills Dr Hollywood FL 33021 Office: 6191 SW 45th St Fort Lauderdale FL 33314

GOLDSTEIN, STANLEY HARVEY, govt. agy. ofcl.; b. Bklyn., Sept. 25, 1931; s. Irving and Hilda K. (Shapiro) G.; B.A. in Sociology, Bklyn. Coll., 1953; M.A. in Labor and Indsl. Relations, U. Ill., 1956; postgrad. U. Colo., 1978—; m. Joan I. Davis, Nov. 3, 1955; children—Jill, Susan. Investigator, N.Y.C. Dept. Hosps., 1953-55; personnel trainee RCA, Camden, N.J., 1956-57; personnel mgmt. specialist U.S. Navy, Great Lakes, Ill., 1957-61; personnel mgmt. specialist, supr. NASA Johnson Space Center, Houston, 1961-67, tng. dir., 1967—. Recipient Outstanding Citizen letter Pres. Nixon, 1970; Superior Achievement award NASA, 1975, Equal Opportunity award, 1978. Mem. Am. Soc. Public Adminstrn., Am. Soc. Tng. and Devel., Clear Lake Personnel Assn. Club: B'nai B'rith. Office: AH 3 Johnson Space Center Houston TX 77058

GOLEMON, HARRY ABBOTT, architect; b. Fairfield, Ala., Feb. 7, 1926; s. James A. and Kate (Cheeseman) G.; B.Arch., Auburn U., 1951; M.Arch., M.I.T., 1952; m. Johanna Baker, Nov. 7, 1975; children—Donna, Kerry, Larry, Jonathan, James. Architect, Golemon & Rolfe, Assos., Inc. Architecture, Houston, 1952—, pres., chmn. bd., 1973—; dir. San Felipe Nat. Bank, 1975—. Mem. fin. council Nat. Dem. Com., 1977—. Served with U.S. Army, 1944-47; col. USAR (ret.). Decorated Meritorious Service award; recipient Algernon Sidney Sullivan award Auburn U., 1951. Fellow AIA; mem. Houston C. of C. (chmn. future studies com. 1978—, bd. dirs. 1980), Tex. Soc. Architects, World Bus. Council. Clubs: Houston, Rotary. Presbyterian. Editor: Financing Real Estate Development, 1973. Home: 10303 Olympia St Houston TX 77042 Office: Golemon & Rolfe Assos Inc Architecture 3000 S Post Oak Rd 12th Floor Houston TX 77056

GOLLHOFER, FRANK RICHARD, civil engr., offshore service and constrn. co. exec.; b. St. Louis, May 19, 1933; s. Frank Henry and Esther Margaret (Maag) G.; B.S.C.E., U. Mo., Rolla, 1955; postgrad. U. Calif., Berkeley, 1973, 75, M.I.T., 1977, U. New Orleans, 1978; m. Marian Anita Hoeh, June 11, 1955; children—Gary Lee, Lynne Carol, Diane Elizabeth, Paul Andrew. Strength engr. McDonnell Douglas, St. Louis, 1956-63, group engr., 1963-68, engrng. mgr., 1968-73; mgr. engrng. and constrn. Kerr McGee, Oklahoma City, 1973-77; pres. Smit Internat. La., New Orleans, 1977—; instr. U.S. Army Reserves. Del., Okla. State Republican Conv., 1977; mem. adv. bd. Congressman Mickey Edwards, 1977. Served with C.E., U.S. Army, 1956. Recipient Recognition of Spl. Achievement award U. Mo., Rolla, 1970. Mem. Am. Mgmt. Assn., Soc. Naval Architects and Marine Engrs., Am. Bur. Shipping (mem. spl. com.), Am. Petroleum Inst. (mem. standardization com.), Nat. Offshore Ops. Industry Adv. Com., Oklahoma City C. of C. (mem. energy council 1977), Pi Kappa Alpha. Home: 56 Park Timbers Ct New Orleans LA 70114

GOLOMB, HERBERT STANLEY, dermatologist; b. N.Y.C., Sept. 6, 1933; s. Morris and Ida (Schwartz) G.; A.B., U. Pa., 1955; M.D., State U. N.Y., Bklyn., 1960; m. Suzanne Nazer, Dec. 20, 1964; children—Meredith, Valerie. Intern, Ohio State U. Hosp., Columbus, 1960-61; resident in dermatology State U. N.Y.-Kings County Med. Center, 1961-62, N.Y. U. Skin and Cancer Unit and Bellevue Hosp., N.Y.C., 1962-64; practice medicine specializing in dermatology, Falls Church, Va., 1964-66, 68—; mem. staff George Washington U., S.E. Community, Fairfax (Va.), Arlington hosps.; instr., then clin. asst. prof. dermatology George Washington U. Sch. Medicine, 1964—; cons. USPHS Dermatology Clinic, 1964-66; chmn. Atlantic Dermatol. Conf., 1978. Bd. dirs. Dermatology Found. No. Va., 1978-79. Served with USPHS, 1966-68. Diplomate Am. Bd. Dermatology. Fellow Am. Acad. Dermatology; mem. AMA, Soc. Investigative Dermatology, Internat. Soc. Tropical Dermatology, Med. Soc. Va., D.C., Fairfax County med. socs., D.C. (pres. 1977-78), Va. dermatol. socs. Clubs: McLean Indoor Tennis, Tuckahoe Swim and Tennis. Home: 1910 Woodgate Ln McLean VA 22101 Office: 6060 Arlington Blvd Falls Church VA 22044

GOLUB, LEIB J(ACOB), obstetrician, gynecologist; b. Roumania, Sept. 8, 1904; came to U.S., 1920, naturalized, 1930; student St. Joseph Coll., 1925-26; B.S., LaSalle Coll., Phila., 1928; M.D., Jefferson Med. Coll., 1930; m. Evelyn Richman Baker, May 6, 1968; 1 son, Franchot. Intern, Mt. Sinai Hosp., Phila., 1930-31, mem. staff, 1931-38; gen. practice medicine, Phila., 1931-34; practice medicine specializing in ob-gyn, Phila., 1934-44, specializing in gynecology, 1944-69; mem. staff St. Luke's-Children's Med. Center, 1938-69, Jefferson Med. Coll. Hosp., 1944-69; dir. oncology-gynecology service Phila. Gen. Hosp., 1964-69; asso. prof. gynecology Hahnemann Med. Coll., 1942-50; hon. asst. prof. ob-gyn Thomas Jefferson U., 1969—; clin. asst. Jefferson Med. Coll., 1934-40, clin. instr., 1940-44, asso., 1944-52, clin. asst. prof., 1952-65, asst. prof., 1965-69; bd. dirs. Phila. div. Am. Cancer Soc., 1944-69, sec., 1962-66, bd. dirs. Dade County (Fla.) unit, 1969-78, hon. life mem., 1979—; co-founder Pelvic Cancer Com. Phila.; founder Breast Cancer Com. Diplomate Internat. Bd. Surgeons, Am. Bd. Ob-Gyn. Fellow A.C.S. (life), Am. Coll. Ob-Gyn (life); mem. Sigma Xi. Contbr. numerous articles on dysmenorrhea and pelvic cancer to profl. jours.; asso. editor in charge cancer concepts Miami Medicine, 1973-78. Home: 9801 Collins Ave Bal Harbour FL 33154

GOMES, NORMAN VINCENT, indsl. engr., Realtor; b. New Bedford, Mass., Nov. 7, 1914; s. John Vincent and Georgianna (Sylvia) G.; B.S. in Indsl. Engring. and Mgmt., Okla. State U., 1950; M.B.A. in Mgmt., Xavier U., 1955; m. Carolyn Moore, June 6, 1942. Asst. chief engr. Leschen div. H.K. Porter Co., St. Louis, 1950-52; staff mfg. cons. Gen. Electric Co., Cin., 1952-57: lectr. indsl. mgmt. U. Cin., 1955-56; vis. lectr. indsl. mgmt. Xavier U. Sch. Bus. Adminstrn., 1956-57; staff indsl. engr. Gen. Dynamics, Ft. Worth, 1957-60; chief ops. analysis Ryan Electronics, San Diego, 1960-64; sr. engr., jet propulsion lab. Calif. Inst. Tech., Pasadena, 1964-67, mgr. mgmt. systems, 1967-71; industry rep. and cons. U.S. Commn. on Govt. Procurement, Washington, 1970-72; adminstrv. officer GSA, Washington, 1973-78, program dir., 1979; investments and real estate enterprises, 1980—. Served as 2d lt. to maj. C.E., AUS, 1941-46; engring. adviser to War Manpower Bd., 1945. Registered profl. engr., Calif., Mo., Tex.; lic. real estate broker, Tex. Mem. Am. Inst. Indsl. Engrs. (nat. chmn. prodn. control research com., 1951-57; bd. dirs. Cin., Fort Worth, San Diego, Los Angeles chpts. 1954-71, pres. Los Angeles 1970-71, nat. dir. community services 1969-73), Nat. Calif. socs. profl. engrs., Soc. Am. Mil. Engrs., Nat. Mgmt. Assn., Soc. Am. Value Engrs., San Antonio Bd. Realtors, Tex. Assn. Realtors, Am. Assn. Realtors, Ret. Officers Assn. U.S. (chpt. pres. 1968-69, recipient Nat. Pres. certificate Merit 1969), Mil. Order World Wars, Nat. Security Indsl. Assn. (mgmt. systems subcom. 1967-69). Republican. Roman Catholic. Club: K.C. Address: 2719 Knoll Tree San Antonio TX 78247

GOMEZ, ALFREDO A., mortgage banker; b. San Diego, Sept. 3, 1932; s. Alfredo and Teresa (Corona) G.; G. Sr. Air Force Supr. Course, 1958, Advanced Career guidance and counseling course, 1970, Vets. Benefits Briefing course, 1971; B.A. in History, Park Coll., 1969; M.A. in Counseling, La. Tech. U., 1973; grad. Collection Theory and Practice, 1975; m. Betty Jane Lynch, Feb. 24, 1954; children—Steven R., Michael D., Betty. U.S. Air Force, 1952, advanced through grades to E-8, 1973; chief personnel Quality Control Div., Barksdale AFB, La., 1970, chief personnel plans and programs, 1971-72, chief personal affairs div., Saigon, Republic of S. Vietnam, 1972; ret., 1973; v.p. First Fidelity Mortgage Co., Monroe, La., 1973—; panel mem. HUD-FHA workshops, 1976. Decorated Bronze Star medal, Commendation medal with two Oak Leaf Clusters, Vietnam campaign medal. Mem. La. Fedn. Housing Counselors (dir.), Am. Personnel and Guidance Assn., Nat. Fedn. Housing Counselors, Exec. Info. Guild. Clubs: Optimists, Ky. Cols. Home: 79 Holiday Dr Monroe LA 71203 Office: 1803 Tower Dr Monroe LA 71203

GOMEZ, HECTOR, social worker; b. Laredo, Tex., Oct. 11, 1943; s. Lorenzo and Conseulo G.; A.A., Tex. A&I U., Laredo, 1969, B.S., Kingsville, 1971; M.S.W. (NIMH grantee), Our Lady of Lake U., 1974. Social worker, The Patrician Movement, San Antonio, 1971-74; dir. Laredo Mental Health Center, 1974-79; probation officer 49th Dist. Ct., Laredo, 1974—; cons. The Mitre Corp.; mem. faculty Laredo Jr. Coll., 1979. Counselor, vol. Crisis Hot Line; mem. Webb County Welfare Bd., 1974—, South Tex. Health Agy. Bd., 1974—, Migrant Council Welfare Bd., 1974—, S. Tex. Devel. Council, 1974—; mem. Pres. Carters 1st Com. on Community, 1974. Mem. Nat. Assn. Social Workers. Home: 2616 Salinas St Laredo TX 78040

GOMEZ, JACQUÉ BETTY, interior designer; b. Bklyn., July 27, 1919; d. George Edward and Emily Kathryn (Clark) Gill; student Annette Dietz Sch. Art, 1936, Drake Bus. Coll., N.Y.C., 1939; m. Walter F. Gomez, June 17, 1939 (dec. 1959); children—Walter F., Jacquelyn K. Gomez Winkler, Glenn G., Gigi B. Legal sec. Gen. Motors Corp., N.Y.C., 1936-44; tchr. in various pvt. schs., 1962-63; tchr. Broward Sch. Bd., Miami, Fla., 1963-64; interior designer, space planner gen. mgr. Pavlow Co., Miami, 1964—. Mem. lay com. Seaford (N.Y.) Sch. Bd., 1952; pres., life mem. PTA, 1957; mem. exec. bd. Miramar Methodist Ch., 1967-77. Republican. Designed office for Pres. Richard Nixon in Key Biscayne, also in Exec. Office Bldg., Washington. Home: 7630 Ramona St Miramar FL 33023 Office: 2801 SW 31st Ave Miami FL 33133

GOMEZ, JULIAN, III, physician; b. Alice, Tex., Apr. 25, 1946; s. Julian and Maria Dolores (Garcia) G.; B.S. in Biology, North Tex. State U., 1969; M.D. with honors, Baylor Coll. Medicine, 1973; m. Maricela Montalvo, Aug. 9, 1969; children—Julian Carlos, Vanessa. Intern, Baylor U. Med. Center, 1973-74, resident in gen. surgery, 1974-78, fellow in peripheral vascular surgery, 1978-79; practice medicine specializing in surgery, McAllen, Tex.; staff McAllen Gen. Hosp., Mission Mcpl. Hosp., McAllen. Diplomate Am. Bd. Surgery. Mem. Student AMA, AMA, Tex. Med. Assn., Hidalgo County Med. Soc. Beta Beta Beta, Tau Kappa Epsilon, Friars. Roman Catholic. Home: 722 S G St McAllen TX 78501 Office: 620 S 12th St McAllen TX 78501

GOMEZ, RAUL, elec. engr.; b. Brownsville, Tex., Dec. 21, 1947; s. Francisco Patricio and Generosa (Gracia) G.; A.A., San Antonio Jr. Coll., 1968; B.S. in Elec. Engring., U. Tex., 1972. Engr. pvt. line design and spl. service engring. Southwestern Bell Telephone Co., San Antonio, 1972-75, engr. plant extension engring. group, 1975, sr. engr., 1975-76, engring. project supr., 1976—. Mem. Kenwood Community Council, also mem. design and rev. com. Registered profl. engr., Tex. Mem. Nat., Tex. socs. profl. engrs., Tex. Soc. Telephone Engrs., San Antonio Jaycees, Jets (past mem. membership com.). Roman Catholic. Home: 427 Millard St San Antonio TX 78212 Office: 1010 N St Mary's St Room 1006 San Antonio TX 78215

GOMEZ, ROBERT, JR., sales exec.; b. Tampa, Fla., Dec. 2, 1952; s. Robert and Dalia S. (Santisteban) G.; B.A. in Mass Communications, U. South Fla., 1978; m. Doria A. Cutro, Mar. 18, 1978. Draftsman, Fla. Steel Corp., Tampa, 1970-74; operator, truck driver Reynolds Aluminum Co., Tampa, 1974-76; dist. sales mgr. Telecredit, Inc., Dallas, 1978—. Served with USAFR, 1971-77. Republican. Roman Catholic. Club: Kiwanis. Home: 1600 Whiteway Dr Arlington TX 76013 Office: 800 W Airport Freeway Suite 301 Irving TX 75062

GOMEZ BERRIOS, NELIDA, ins. cons.; b. Barranquitas, P.R., Nov. 6, 1935; d. Salomon and Josefa (Berrios) Gomez; B.B.A., U. P.R., 1955; M.A.S., World U. P.R., 1979; children—Edmund, Conrado, Norman Luis, Yamira Santiago. With Indsl. Devel. Co., Santurce, P.R., 1955-56; statistician, auditor P.R. Dept. Agr. and Commerce, Santurce, 1956; accountant III Treasury Dept., San Juan, 1956-60; with Flamingo Telefilm Assn., N.Y.C., 1960-61, P.R. Urban Renewal & Housing Corp., Rio Piedras, 1962-66, Commonwealth of P.R. Employees Assn., Santurce, 1966-73; sr. v.p. Coop. Bank of P.R., Rio Piedras, 1973-77; asst. to pres. Almac Enterprises, Inc., Rio Piedras, 1977—; ind. cons., 1977—; dir. Multiples Ins. Coop. of P.R., 1967—, treas. 1970-75. Mem. Nat. Assn. Accountants of Coops. (chpt. dir. 1971—), Assn. Coop. Educators, League Coops. U.S.A. (ins. and fin. com. 1974—). Home: 312 32d Villa Nevarez Rio Piedras PR 00927 Office: 623 Ponce de Leon Ave Rio Piedras PR 00927

GOMEZ BLANCO, JOSE R., mental health worker; b. Santa Clara, Cuba, Mar. 20, 1946; s. Jose R. Gomez and Digna E. Blanco; B.S., Xavier U., 1968; M.S. in Clin. Psychology, Instituto Sicologico de P.R., Hato Rey, 1969; M.P.A., U. P.R., 1979; postgrad. Nova U.; m. Gladys L. Betancourt, June 26, 1973; children—Jocelyn, Alejandro J., Raul. Psychology intern State Psychiat. Hosp., Rio Piedras, P.R., 1968-69; psychol. technician, 1968-69; psychologist Bayamon Community Mental Health Center, 1969-72; psychologist Drug Addiction Prevention Center, Guyama, P.R., 1972-73; cons. Adminstrn. Corrections, San Juan, P.R., 1973-76; dir. Cayey (P.R.) Community Mental Health Center, 1976-79; dir. undergrad. program in mental health Inter Am. U., Hato Rey, 1979—; lectr. psychology, 1968-69, instr. Sch. Law, 1969-72, prof. Criminal Justice Center, 1979—; asst. prof. dept. community health Cayey Med. Sch., 1977—; prof. Caribbean Center Grad. Studies, Santurce, P.R., 1978—; pvt. practice, Bayamon, 1970-74, Cayey, 1977—; cons. vocat. rehab. Bayamon Regional Office, Dept. Social Services, 1970—; lectr. Turabo U.; cons. Head Start, Caguas, P.R., 1973-74; lead cons. mental health Westinghouse Health Service, 1978—; adv. bd. Bayamon Community Mental Health Center, 1969-72, Bayamon Clinic, 1972-76. HEW fellow, 1980-81. Mem. P.R. Psychologists Assn. (officer 1976), Assn. Puerto Rican Profls. (com. on profl. issues 1976), P.R. Public Health Assn., Interam. Assn. Community Psychologists, Nat. Assn. Mental Health, Nat. Council Family Relations, Am. Assn. Mental Deficiency, Council Exceptional Children, Am. Psychol. Assn., Am. Assn. Guidance Counselors, Am. Assn. Mental Health Adminstrs., Am. Group Psychotherapy Assn., Assn. Psychol. Study Social Issues, Am. Mgmt. Assn., Am. Correctional Assn. (exec. mem. 1975—), Am. Soc. Criminology, Am. Public Health Assn., Nat. Council Community Mental Health Centers, Assn. Tchrs. Preventive Medicine, Caribbean Psychologists Assn., Royal Soc. Health (Eng.), Internat. Assn. Psychiat. Treatment Offenders, Villa del Rey Residents Council, Psi Chi. Clubs: Rotary, Exchange. Author publs. in field. Home: 30 LD-11 V del Rey PO Box 5264 Caguas PR 00625 Office: Box 1293 Hato Rey PR 00619

GOMEZ DE TOLOSA, MARIA ELISA, psychologist; b. Ponce, P.R., Sept. 14, 1908; d. Pablo H. and Elisa M. de Gomez; B.S., Coll. Agr. and Engring., U. P.R., Mayaguez, 1928; M.A., Columbia U., 1944; L.H.D. (hon.), World U., P.R., 1977; m. Pedro Tolosa, July 3, 1947; children—Marie L., Pedro, Jose E. Tchr. chemistry, P.R., 1930-43; founder, dir. Instituto Psicopedagogica for mentally retarded, Bayamón, P.R., 1947-74; organizer, dir. P.R. Office of Planning and Coordination in Mental Retardation, San Juan, 1964-68; dir. Children's Commn. Commonwealth P.R., San Juan, 1957-64, dir. P.R. Office of Handicapped, San Juan, 1953-57; pvt. practice psychology, San Juan, 1974—. Named Woman of Yr., Gulf Petroleum Co., 1972. Mem. Am. Assn. Mental Deficiency (life), P.R. Psychol. Assn. (pres. 1968-69), P.R. chpt. Am. Assn. on Mental Deficiency (founder, 1st pres. 1977-78), Alumni Columbia U., N.Y. Alumni Regional Coll. U. P.R., Mayaguez, Pi Lambda Theta, Kappa Delta Pi. Democrat. Roman Catholic. Clubs: Lions, Kiwanis (Eugenio M. de Hostos award 1967-68), Exchange, Altrusa (pres. San Juan 1968-70). Home and Office: St 2 B-18 Parkside-Caparra San Juan PR 00920

GOMEZ-RIVERO, ORLANDO, petroleum reservoir engr.; b. Villa Cuauhtemoc, Mexico, Sept. 7, 1928; s. Fortino Gomez and Guadalupe Rivero; Petroleum Engr., Instituto Politecnico Nacional, Mexico, 1952. Petroleum engr. Petroleos Mexicanos, 1953-57; chief dist. reservoir engr., 1957-66, gen. dept. chief, Mexico, D.F., 1966-73, gen. dept. chief reserves estimates, 1974—; prof. Instituto Politecnico Nacional, 1969-71; co-author study on energy problems for Pardido Revolucionario Institucional, 1969. Petroleos Mexicanos fellow, 1951-52. Mem. Asociacion de Ingenieros Petroleros de Mexico (pres. Coatzacoalcos chpt. 1964, Juan Hefferan award 1967), Colegio de Ingenieros Petroleros de Mexico, Soc. Petroleum Engrs., Tex. Soc. Profl. Well Log Analysts. Author: Book on Well Logs, 1975. Contbr. articles profl. jours. Home: Apdo Postal 71 011 Mexico 3 DF Mexico Office: 329 Marina Nacional Mexico DF 17 Mexico

GOMEZ-RODRIGUEZ, MANUEL, physicist, coll. dean; b. Ponce, P.R., Oct. 15, 1940; s. Manuel Gomez-Acevedo and Lucila Rodriguez; B.Sc., U. P.R., 1962; Ph.D. (AEC fellow), Cornell U., 1968; m. Adele M. Mouakad, June 12, 1975; children—Marisol, Beatriz Cristina. NRC postdoctoral fellow Naval Research Lab., Washington, 1967-69; asst. prof. physics U. P.R., Mayaguez, 1969-71; asso. prof. U. P.R., Rio Piedras, 1971-75, prof., 1979—, chmn. dept. physics, 1971-75, dean Coll. Natural Scis., 1975—. Internat. Union Pure and Applied Physics grantee, 1975; NSF grantee, 1974, 76, 77; Office Naval Research grantee, 1974; Dept. Energy grantee, 1976-78. Mem. Am. Phys. Soc., Sci. Tchrs. Assn. P.R. (hon.; pres. 1973), Sigma Xi. Contbr. articles to profl. jours.; editor Jour. Ferroelectrics, 1977. Office: U PR Rio Piedras PR 00931

GONANO, JOHN ROLAND, physicist; b. Winchester, Va., Jan. 21, 1939; s. Lezelle and Mary (Fuss) G.; B.S. in Physics with honors (Sigma Pi Sigma Freshman scholar), W.Va. U., 1960; Ph.D. in Physics (So. Fellowships Fund fellow), Duke, 1967; m. Joyce E. Dove, Aug. 22, 1959; children—Gina M., Dawn M., John Roland. Postdoctoral fellow U. Fla., 1966-68; physicist Nat. Bur, Standards, Wash., 1968-71; research physicist U.S. Army Mobility Equipment Research and Devel. Command, Ft. Belvoir, Va., 1971—. Served with USAF, 1961-62. Recipient Sci. Conf. Achievement award U.S. Army, 1974; NSF Summer fellow 1960. Mem. Am. Phys. Soc., Mensa, Boyds Civic Assn. (pres.), Sigma Xi, Sigma Pi Sigma. Contbr. articles on magnetism, nuclear magnetic resonance, thermometry, explosive detection to profl. jours. Office: MERADCOM DRDME-N Fort Belvoir VA 22060

GONERKA, TIMOTHY ALLEN, advt. and mktg. exec.; b. Peoria, Ill., Oct. 30, 1951; s. Bernard Anthony and Fyrne Louise G.; B.A., Drake U., 1973; postgrad. Mich. State U., 1975. Copywriter, Bruce Green Advt. Co., Bloomington, Ill., 1973; promotion dir. Northwoods Mall, Peoria, Ill., 1974-75; promotion dir. Salem Mall div. Rouse Co., Dayton, Ohio, 1975-76, dir. advt./mktg. NW Mall div., Houston, 1976-77, Almeda Mall div., 1978—; lectr. in field. Vol. leader Young Life Campaign, teen outreach, 1972—. Recipient Maxi best merchandising award Internat. Council Shopping Centers, 1976, 78, best advt. award, 1977; accredited shopping center promotion dir. Mem. Internat. Council Shopping Centers. Methodist. Home: 1111 S Post Oak St Apt 214 Houston TX 77056 Office: 555 Almeda Mall Inc Houston TX 77075

GONG, EDMOND JOSEPH, lawyer, former state senator; b. Miami, Fla., Oct. 7, 1930; s. Joe Fred and Fayline G.; A.B. cum laude, Harvard U., 1952, student Sch. Law, 1954-55; J.D., U. Miami, 1960; m. Sophie Vlachos, July 25, 1957; children—Frances Fayline, Peter Joseph (dec.), Madeleine, Joseph Fred II, Edmond Joseph. Spl. writer Hong Kong Tiger Standard, 1955-56; staff writer Miami Herald, 1958-59; admitted to Fla. bar; asso. firm Helliwell, Melrose & De Wolf, 1960-61; practice law, Miami, 1962—; vice-chmn. Fla. State Bd. Bus. Regulation, 1976-77; dir. Royal Trust Bank Miami; mem. Fla. Senate, 1966-72. Trustee Fla. Gulf Realty Trust; pres. Inflahedge Resources Fund; chmn. Fla. Land Sales Adv. Council, 1974-76. Asst. U.S. Atty. So. Dist. Fla., 1961-62; mem. Fla. Ho. of Reps., 1963-66. Fellow Inst. Politics John Fitzgerald Kennedy Sch. Govt., Harvard U., 1969-70, asso. dir., 1971-72. Mem. Am., Dade County, Fed. bar assns., Assn. Harvard U. Alumni (dir.-at-large). Methodist. Home: 7751 S W 78th Ct Miami FL 33143 Office: 8585 Sunset Dr Miami FL 33143

GONSOULIN, DEWEY JUDE, lawyer; b. Houston, Dec. 27, 1929; s. Robert Frederic and Elma (Bourgeois) G.; B.A. with distinction, Rice Inst., 1951; LL.B. with honors, U. Tex., 1954; m. Jean E. Johnson, Apr. 25, 1959; children—Jean E., Anne C., Dewey J. Admitted to Tex. bar, 1954; asso. firm Mehaffy, Weber, Keith & Gonsoulin, Beaumont, 1956-62, partner, 1962-72, shareholder employee 1972—. Mem. Beaumont Civil Service Commn., 1971—; dir. Beaumont council Camp Fire Girls, Inc., 1964-70. Served with AUS, 1954-56. Mem. Jefferson County (pres. 1973-74), Am., Tex. bar assns., Tex. Assn. Def. Counsel (pres. 1978-79), Internat. Assn. Ins. Counsel, Assn. Ins. Attys., Phi Beta Kappa, Delta Tau Delta, Phi Delta Phi. Roman Catholic. Clubs: Knife and Fork Club of Beaumont (pres. 1964-65), Beaumont Country (dir. 1975-78). Asso. casenote editor Tex. Law Review, 1953-54. Home: 8185 Evangeline Ln Beaumont TX 77706 Office: 1400 San Jacinto Bldg Beaumont TX 77701

GONYEA, EDWARD FRANCIS, neurologist; b. Plattsburgh, N.Y., Jan. 14, 1932; s. George Herbert and Eleanor (Rausch) G.; B.S. cum laude, Georgetown U., 1953, M.D., 1957; m. Patricia Louise Olson, Sept. 22, 1967; children—Gregory Joseph, Bruce Chandler, Larisa Marie, Carol Nadine. Intern, D.C. Gen. Hosp., Washington, 1957-58; resident in internal medicine Emory U. and VA Hosp., Atlanta, 1958-59, 60-61; resident in neurology Jefferson Hosp., Phila., 1959-60, 63-65; chief neurol. service VA Hosp., Indpls., 1965-67, Gainesville, Fla., 1967-74, Memphis, 1974—; asst. prof. neurology Ind. U. Med. Center, Indpls., 1965-67; asst. prof. medicine, neurology U. Fla., 1967-74; asso. prof. neurology U. Tenn. Center for Health Scis., 1974-78, prof., 1978—; jr. examiner Am. Bd. Neurology, 1970-72. Served with U.S. Army, 1961-63. Fellow Am. Acad. Neurology; mem. AMA, Silver Stick Soc., Ind. Neurol. Soc., Memphis Acad. Neurology, Memphis Neurol. Soc., Assn. Tenn. Neurologists, AAUP, AAAS. Democrat. Roman Catholic. Contbg. author: Baker's Clinical Neurology, 1971, 80. Home: 2445 Dogwood Trail Dr Germantown TN 38138 Office: Veterans Administration Hospital 1030 Jefferson Ave Memphis TN 38104

GONZALES, CHARLES JOHN, architect and planner; b. N.Y.C., Oct. 20, 1941; s. Carlos and Ricarda (Martinez) G.; tech. diploma SUNY and Charles Evans Hughes Sch., 1959; B.S. in Arch., CCNY, 1965, postgrad., 1968-69; M. in Urban and Regional Planning magna cum laude, U. P.R., 1976, postgrad., 1977; m. Leticia Maria Rodriguez de Sevilla, Aug. 24, 1970; children—Carlos Jose Juan, Mari-Angel Catalina, Carlos Manuel Lucien Ricardo. Cons. for Westside/Morningside area P.R. Community Devel. Project, N.Y.C., 1969, Office of Historic Monuments, Inst. P.R. Culture, San Juan, 1969-72; sr. architect Gaumann, Quinones, Spencer, 1972-73; sr. architect and planner Quinones, Spencer & Partners, San Juan, 1973-76; sr. architect and planner, personnel dir. Office of Pablo Quinones Architects, San Juan, 1976—; cons. architect La Casa Del Libro Museum, San Juan, 1972—, Office of Eduardo Figueroa, architects, Ponce, P.R., 1977-79, De Castro, Font, Gaumann, Spencer and Assos., Hato Rey, P.R., 1972-74, InterAm. U. P.R., 1979—; P.R. del. Congress of Interam. Planning Soc., 1976, 79; major works include: Restoration of Convent of Santo Domingo, Old San Juan, 1969-70, Restoration of Casa Suazo, Old San Juan, 1969-71; cons. San Juan Jud. Center, Bayamon Jud. Center, 1974-77, Cuartel Ballaja, Old San Juan, 1976-77, Bell, Book and Candle Bookstore, 1977-79. Spl. asst. to P.R. Sec. of Commerce, San Juan, 1977; bd. dirs. Condominium Washington; advisory bd. P.R. EPA, 1979—; mem. State Recreation Council P.R. Recreational Devel. Agency, 1979—. Served with arty. U.S. Army, 1965-68. Recipient Merit award P.R. Govt. Dept. Instruction, 1972. Mem. P.R. Planning Soc. (pres. 1978-80), Interam. Planning Soc., Am. Planning Assn., Nat. Recreation and Park Assn., Nat. Soc. Park Resources, Mus. Natural History, Met. Assn. Urban Designers and Environ. Planners, Nat. Hist. Soc., Alumni Assn. City Coll., Internat. Platform Assn., P.R. Nat. Coll. Soccer Referees. Roman Catholic. Home: 60 Washington St Santurce PR 00907 Office: 33 Loiza Ave Isla Verde Santurce PR 00913

GONZALES, HENRY ISAAC, indsl. engr.; b. Eagle Pass, Tex., June 3, 1929; s. Santiago and Maria Irma G.; student Eastern N.Mex. U., 1952, San Antonio Coll., 1953-66; B.B.A., U. Tex., 1964; m. Vicky, Nov. 22, 1953; children—Norma, Henry, Sandy, Edward. Tech. staff U. Tex. Elec. Engring. Research Lab., 1957-64; engr. Directorate of Maintenance, Kelly AFB, Tex., 1964-75; mgr. modernization program San Antonio Air Logistics Center, Kelly AFB, 1975-77, mgr. energy conservation program, 1977-79; sr. indsl. engr. U.S. Air Force Logistics Commd., Kelly AFB, 1979—. Pres. St. Dominic Parish Council, San Antonio, 1976-77. Served with USAF, 1948-52. Recipient Gen. Thomas D. White Environ. award, 1975, Internat. Engring. and Sci. award, 1979. Mem. Am. Inst. Indsl. Engrs. (pres. 1973-74, dir. 1974-77), Air Force Assn. Democrat. Roman Catholic. Club: Kelly Mgmt. Home: 157 Camelot Ct Apt C San Antonio TX

78226 Office: US Air Force Logistics Command Jet Engine Div Kelly AFB TX 78241

GONZALEZ, ABEL REYES, petroleum geophysicist; b. Mex., Nov. 3, 1945; s. Marcelino and Emilia (Reyes) G.; came to U.S., 1950; naturalized, 1964; B.S. in Physics, U. Tex., 1975; m. Grace Gloria Anguiano, Sept. 28, 1968; 1 dau., Rebeca Elizabeth. Geophysicist, Mobil Oil Exploration Services Center, Dallas, 1975-76, petroleum geophysicist, 1976—. Served with USN, 1969-74; Vietnam. Mem. Soc. Exploration Geophysicists, Smithsonian Assos. Baptist. Home: 428 Hillview Dr Hurst TX 76053 Office: Box 900 Dallas TX 75247

GONZALEZ, ANTONIO, lawyer, educator; b. Edinburg, Tex., Mar. 14, 1943; s. Manuel and Natalia (Torres) G.; B.A., U. Md., 1971; M.A., U. Tenn., 1973; J.D., Miles Coll., 1979; m. Elma de Luna, Oct. 10, 1975; 1 dau., Julissa Priscilla. Ops. staff 1st. Nat. Bank Atlanta, 1971; dept. asst. Spanish, U. Tenn., Knoxville, 1972-73; research staff Am. Research Bur., Beltsville, Md., 1975; instr. history Tex. A&I U., Kingsville, 1975; law clk. Spitler & Lyon, Pelham, Ala., 1978-79; law clk. Crain, Caton, James & Oberwetter, Houston, 1979—. Served with USAF, 1966-70; Vietnam. Decorated Air Force Commendation medal; Vietnamese Cross of Gallantry. Recipient Law Day award Miles Coll., 1978, Outstanding Student award, 1978, Am. Jurisprudence award, 1979, Corpus Juris Secundum award, 1979. Mem. Am. Bar Assn., Am. Hist. Assn., AAUP, Delta Theta Phi. Democrat. Roman Catholic. Home: 1207 Blalock Rd Houston TX 77055 Office: Crain Caton James & Oberwetter 3300 Two Houston Center Houston TX 77002

GONZALEZ, ANTONIO CARMELO, radiologist; b. Lares, P.R., Dec. 9, 1937; s. Rafael Antonio and Elvira (Lariz) G.; A.B., Duke U., 1958, M.D., 1962. Intern, Grady Hosp., 1962-63; resident, 1966-67; asst. prof., dir. nuclear medicine Tex. Med. Sch., San Antonio, 1972-74; asst. prof., dir. diagnostic ultrasound Emory U. Sch. Medicine, Atlanta, 1974—, asso. prof., 1979—; chief nuclear medicine Atlanta VA Med. Center, 1979—. Served to maj. USAF, 1964-69. Diplomate Am. Bd. Radiology, Am. Bd. Nuclear Medicine. Mem. Ga. Heart Assn., AMA, Ga., Fulton County radiol. socs., Nuclear Med. Soc., Fulton County Med. Soc., So. Med. Assn., Am. Inst. Ultrasound in Medicine. Contbr. articles in field to med. jours. Home: 3094 Peachtree Dr Atlanta GA 30305 Office: 80 Butler St Atlanta GA 30303

GONZALEZ, ARMANDO I., newspaper co. exec.; b. Cardenas, Cuba, Dec. 28, 1939; s. Armando M. and Florinda G.; came to U.S., 1968, naturalized, 1974: B.S., La. State U., 1960; postgrad. U. Havana, 1964-66: m. Teresa Gou, June 17, 1967; children—Silvia, Raul. Asst. constrn. supt. Damuji Paper Mill, Abreu, Cuba, 1960-62; engring. mgr. Cuban Paper Enterprise, Havana, 1962-67; service engr. Combustion Engring., Inc., Windsor, Conn., 1968-73; engring. mgr. Miami (Fla.) Herald Pub. Co., 1973—; owner, cons. Newspaper Engring. Internat. Corp., Miami Lakes, Fla., 1979—. Mem. Interam. Businessmens Assn., Am. Inst. Indsl. Engrs. Roman Catholic. Clubs: Am., Royal Biscayne Racquet. Home: 7313 Loch Ness Dr Miami Lakes FL 33014 Office: Miami Herald Publishing Co 1 Herald Plaza Miami FL 33101

GONZALEZ, AURORA, educator; b. Edcouch, Tex., Apr. 6, 1932; d. Raul M. and Aurora (Saldana) G.; B.S., Tex. Woman's U., 1955, M.Ed., 1959. Tchr., Dallas Ind. Sch. Dist., 1955-59, tchr. spl. edn., 1961-63, sch. counselor, 1972—; tchr. spl. edn. Robstown Ind. Sch. Dist., 1959-61; exec. dir. Children, Inc., sch. for severely retarded, Dallas, 1963-69; nat. field adviser Camp Fire Girls, Inc., N.Y.C., 1969-72. Bd. dirs. Dallas Assn. Retarded Children, v.p., 1964-69; active fund drives United Way, Leukemia Soc.; mem. Dallas Educators Polit. Action Bd., 1976—, vice chmn., 1980—. Recipient service award Dallas Assn. Retarded Children, 1968. Life elementary teaching certificate, Tex.; profl. life counselor certificate, profl. life mental retardation counselor certificate, profl. life mental retardation teaching certificate, Tex. Mem. Am., Tex. personnel and guidance assns., Am., Tex. sch. counselors assns., Council for Exceptional Children, Dallas Assn. Counselors (dir. 1976, 77, treas. 1980—), Classroom Tchrs. Dallas (faculty rep. 1976—, bd. dirs. 1979—), Tex. State Tchrs. Assn., NEA, Assn. Tex. Educators, Oak Cliff Bus. and Profl. Women. Roman Catholic. Club: Altrusa (pres. 1968-69, dir. 1965-72). Home: 1415 Matagorda St Dallas TX 75232 Office: 2300 S Ravinia St Dallas TX 75211

GONZALEZ, CARLOS LUIS, plant breeder, educator; b. P.R., June 28, 1923; s. Juan C. and Juano M. (Molina) G.; B.S.A., U. P.R., 1950; M.S., Iowa State U., 1957, Ph.D., 1964; m. Melba Acevedo, Dec. 17, 1955; children—Nilda, Alma, Melba I, Carlos J. Research agronomist U. P.R., Rio Piedras, 1950-56, asso. plant breeder, 1957-60, plant breeder, 1964—, project leader, 1967—, prof., 1979; prof. Inter Am. U. P.R., Mayaguez, 1979—. Bd. dirs. Am. Cancer Soc., 1977-78. Served with U.S. Army, 1944-46. Mem. Coll. of Agronomy, Am. Soc. Agrl. Sci., Am. Soc. Agronomy, Internat. Soc. Sugarcane Technologists, Sociedad Puertorriquena de Ciencias Agricolas, Sigma Xi, Phi Kappa Phi, Gamma Sigma Delta. Roman Catholic. Clubs: Rotary, Shooting. Contbr. articles to profl. jours. Home: PO Box 586 San Sebastian PR 00755 Office: U PR Mayaguez Campus Mayaguez PR 00708

GONZÁLEZ, DOREEN ETHEL, speech-lang. pathologist; b. Phila., May 5, 1948; d. Junius Elbert and Doreen Mary May Davis; B.A. in Spanish, U. Houston, 1971, B.A. in Speech Pathology and Audiology, 1972, M.A., 1974; m. José J. González, Aug. 24, 1974. Speech pathology trainee VA Hosp., Houston, 1972-74; speech pathologist Channelview (Tex.) Ind. Sch. Dist., 1974-75; clin. instr. div. audiology and speech pathology, dept. otorhinolaryngology Baylor Coll. Medicine, Houston, 1975-77; speech pathologist Klein Ind. Sch. Dist., Spring, Tex., 1977—; staff speech pathologist Meth. and Jefferson Davis Hosps., 1975-77; speech and hearing clinic supr., vis. lectr. Sam Houston State U., summer 1979; pres. Nat. Student Speech and Hearing Assn., U. Houston chpt., 1973-74. Recipient Winfred E. Garrison award in Latin, U. Houston, 1971. Mem. Am. Speech and Hearing Assn. (cert., chmn. directory com., conv., 1976), Tex. Speech and Hearing Assn., Phi Kappa Phi. Contbr. articles to profl. publs. Office: 18035 Kuykendahl Spring TX 77373

GONZALEZ, HENRY B., congressman; b. San Antonio, May 3, 1916; s. Leonides and Genevieve (Barbosa) G.; student San Antonio Jr. Coll.; Student U. Tex.; LL.B., St. Mary's Law Sch., St. Mary's U., San Antonio; m. Bertha Cuellar, 1940; children—Henry, Rosemary, Charles A., Bertha, Stephen, Genevieve, Francis, Anna Maria. Tchr. citizenship adult vocat. class Ladies Garment Workers Union; slum clearance projects San Antonio Housing Authority; translator; pub. relations counselor for ins. co., San Antonio; chief probation officer Bexar County, Tex., 1946; exec. sec. Jr. Deputies of Am. (predecessor Pan Am. Progressive Assn.); councilman, San Antonio, 1953-56, mayor pro-tem, 1955-56; mem. Tex. Senate, 1956-61; mem. 87th-96th Congresses from 20th Tex. Dist., chmn. subcom. on internat. finance Banking, Fin. and Urban Affairs Com., 1972—, mem. Small Bus. Com., 1976—. Past civilian cable and radio censor Mil. and Naval Intelligence, World War II. Home: 238 W King's Hwy San Antonio TX 78212 Office: Rayburn House Office Bldg Washington DC 20515

GONZALEZ, JOAQUIN ANTONIO, tire distbg. co. exec.; b. San Jose de las Lajas, Cuba, Aug. 16, 1943; s. Antonio and Georgina Gonzalez (Perez) G.; came to U.S., 1962, naturalized, 1975; B.A., Inst. Luz Caballero, San Jose de las Lajas, Cuba, 1957, postgrad., 1960; m. Maria A. Carmona, Mar. 19, 1966; children—Antonio Rafael, Georgina Armelia, Joaquin Antonio. Pres., TCM Internat., Inc., Miami, Fla., 1970—, TCM Automotive Center, Miami, 1978—, Toca Inc., Miami, 1972—, Giant Mart, Miami, 1976—, TMF Investment, Miami, 1976—, Wide World Import & Export, Miami, 1978—. Pres., Comite Por Rincon a San Lazaro. Mem. Nat. Tire Dealers Retreaders Assn., Fla. Tire Retreaders Assn., Asociacion Interamericana de Hombres de Empresa, Camacol. Club: Kiwanis. Office: 3466 N Miami Ave Miami FL 33127

GONZALEZ, JORGE AUGUSTO, educator; b. Havana, Cuba, Sept. 2, 1932; s. Justo and Luisa (Garcia) G.; came to U.S., 1961; naturalized, 1969; B.L., Candler Coll., Cuba, 1950; student U. of Havana Law Sch., 1950-52; S.T.B., Matanzas Union Theol. Sem., Cuba, 1955; postgrad. Universidad Central de las Villas, Cuba, 1959; Ph.D., Emory U., 1967; m. Ondina Felicia Santos Diaz, June 27, 1954; children—Jorge Luis, Ondina Ester, Carlos Alberto. Ordained Methodist minister, 1955, deacon, 1955, elder, 1957; pastor Nuevitas Methodist Ch., Cuba, 1955-57, Cienfuegos Methodist Ch., Cuba, 1957-60; prof. Methodism and ch. admnstrn., Matanzas Union Theol. Sem., Cuba, 1959-61; asst. prof. religion Berry Coll., Mt. Berry, Ga., 1962-67, asso. prof., 1967-70, prof., 1970-72, Gund prof. religion, 1972-77, Fuller E. Callaway prof. religion, 1977—. Mem. Cuban Methodist Annual Conf., 1955-66, N. Ga. United Methodist Annual Conf., 1966—, Ga. Methodist Commn. on Higher Edn., 1968-72, N. Ga. Bd. Ministry, United Methodist Ch., 1972-76; bd. dirs. Alfalit Internat., Inc., Miami, Fla., 1976—; faculty N. Central Jurisdiction Lay Pastors Sch., Evanston, Ill., 1974—; adj. prof. McCormick Theol. Sem., Chgo., 1976—. Danforth Tchr. grantee Emory U., 1965-66; recipient Americanism medal, DAR, 1976. Mem. Am. Acad. of Religion, Soc. Biblical Lit., Am. Schs. Oriental Research, N. Ga. Conference of the United Methodist Ch., Alpha Chi (pres. of Region III, 1976-78, nat. council 1979—). Contbr. numerous articles to Methodist publs. Office: PO Box 153 Mt Berry GA 30149

GONZALEZ, JORGE JOSE, physician; b. Valdivia, Chile, Aug. 13, 1945; came to U.S., 1973; s. Manuel and Emma C. (Clasing) G.; M.D., U. Chile, 1971; m. Barbara S. Hayworth, May 22, 1971; children—Carla Andrea, Maria Cristina. Resident in internal medicine Hosp. San Juan de Dios, Santiago, Chile, 1971-73; resident in internal medicine New Hanover Meml. Hosp., Wilmington, N.C., 1973-76; instr. internal medicine, fellow in endocrinology and metabolism Med. U. S.C., Charleston, 1976-78; asst. prof. medicine U. N.C., 1978—; asso. investigator VA, 1976-78. Diplomate Am. Bd. Internal Medicine. Mem. AMA. Episcopalian. Contbr. research and clin. papers to med. publs. Home: 8 Beauregard Dr Wilmington NC 28403 Office: 2131 S 17th St Wilmington NC 28401

GONZALEZ, JOSE MANUEL, psychiatrist; b. Cristo Oriente, Cuba, Dec. 20, 1914; s. Servando and Estelvina (Maceira) G.; B.A., Inst. Secondary Edn., Santiago, Cuba, 1934; M.D., U. Havana, 1943; m. Josefa Lopez Vila, Mar. 16, 1952; children—Jose Manuel, Raul Alberto, Gilberto Jorge. Intern, Hosp. Saturnino Lora, Santiago, Cuba, 1944; resident in ob-gyn Hosp. Saturnino Lora, 1945-48; chmn. obstetric service Hosp. Provicial Orienta, Cuba, 1960-63; rotating intern Athens (Ga.) Ednl. Program, 1964; psychiat. resident Central State Hosp., Milledgeville, Ga., 1965-68, clin. dir. mental retardation div., 1974—. Diplomate Am. Bd. Psychiatry and Neurology. Recipient Physicians Recognition award AMA, 1975, 78; award Am. Psychiat. Assn., 1978. Mem. Baldwin County Med. Soc., Med. Assn. Ga., Am. Psychiat. Assn. Roman Catholic. Contbr. articles to profl. jours. Home: 911 Riverbend Dr Milledgeville GA 31061 Office: Central State Hosp Milledgeville GA 31061

GONZALEZ, MANUEL ENRIQUE, architect; b. Utuado, P.R., Jan. 19, 1919; s. Enrique Gonzalez and Emilia Torres; student City U. N.Y., 1948; B.S. in Archtl. Engring., Ohio U., Athens, 1951; postgrad. Newark Coll. Engring., 1955; m. Ada E. Gonzalez, Feb. 14, 1948; children—Eric M., Wanda E. Pvt. practice architecture, San Juan, P.R., 1957-69; dir., organizer archtl. and constrn. div. Dept. Social Service, Commonwealth of P.R., 1969-73; dir. sch. planning and constrn. Orange County Schs., Orlando, Fla., 1973-76; now prin. firm on design and constrn. schs., chs., instnl. bldgs., Altamonte Springs, Fla.; cons. architect Duval Devel. Corp., Paramus, N.J. Elder, Presbyn. Ch., Sunday Sch. tchr., 1965-72, organizer Spanish bible study group in Orlando, 1975; pres. Bicentennial Com., Bayamon, P.R., 1971. Served with U.S. Army, 1940-45; ETO. Decorated Silver Star medal. Mem. A.I.A. Clubs: Mason, Shriner, Rotary, Order Eastern Star. Contbr. articles to mags. Home: 431 N Maitland Ave Altamonte Springs FL 32701

GONZALEZ, MARY HELEN, counselor; b. Kingsville, Tex., Feb. 14, 1938; d. Santos Z. and Genoveva (Jaramillo) Yzaquirre; B.S., Pan Am. U., 1970; M.Ed., Tex. A&M U., 1972; m. Candelario L. Gonzalez, Dec. 26, 1957; children—Barbara, Larry, Patrick, Charlotte. Elem. tchr. Donna (Tex.) Ind. Sch. Dist., 1966-70, jr. high sch. counselor, 1972-76; counselor Weslaco (Tex.) High Sch., 1976—. Mem. Am. Personnel and Guidance Assn., Tex. Personnel and Guidance Assn., Rio Grande Valley Personnel and Guidance Assn., AAUW, Kappa Delta Phi, Epsilon Sigma Alpha. Democrat. Roman Catholic. Club: Lioness. Home: 824 S Texas St Weslaco TX 78596 Office: Weslaco High School 1005 Pike St Weslaco TX 78596

GONZALEZ-ALCOVER, JOSE CARMELO, chem. and electro mech. co. exec.; b. Lares, P.R., June 1, 1937; s. Antonio Gonzalez-Gonzalez and Ruperta Alcover; B.S. in Mech. Engring., U. P.R., 1962; postgrad. Inter-Am. U., 1975-76; m. Maggie Magraner, Dec. 25, 1961; children—Marga-Mari, Lissette-Marie, Marisol. Student asst., project engr. P.R. Nuclear Center, Mayaguez, 1962; maintenance engr., transp. mgr. Molinos de PR (Conagra), Catano, P.R., 1964-67; prodn. mgr. Phelps Dodge P.R., Inc., Carolina, 1967-68; prodn. mgr. E.L. Mfg. Corp. subs. Econs. Lab., Inc., Dorado, P.R., 1968-70, gen. mgr., 1970—, pres., 1970—, also dir.; officer, dir. E.L. Caribbean, Inc., Elso, Inc. Former bd. dirs. Movimiento por un Mundo Mejor (Movement for Better World). Served as officer U.S. Army, 1962-64. Licensed engr., P.R. Mem. Inst. Engrs., Architects and Surveyors P.R., Am. Mgmt. Assn., Soc. Mfg. Engrs., P.R. C. of C., Phi Sigma Alpha. Roman Catholic. Club: Dorado Beach Gulf and Tennis. Home: 1959 Sauco-San Ramon Rio Piedras PR 00927 Office: PO Box 667 Dorado PR 00646

GONZALEZ-ROMANACE, HECTOR R., banker, diversified co. exec.; b. Ponce, P.R., Dec. 13, 1933; s. Carlos G. and Jacqueline (Romanace) G.; A.B., Holy Cross Coll., 1955; postgrad. in Bus., Columbia U., 1955-56; m. Provita Torres, Aug. 24, 1958; children—Leticia, Hector O., Mike. Clerk part-time Bloomingdale's Dept. Stores, N.Y.C., 1956; v.p. Farmacias Gonzalez, Inc., Ponce, P.R., 1957—; pres., chief exec. officer Gonzalez & Co., Inc., Ponce, 1966—; dir. Banco de Ponce, P.R. and N.Y., 1973—; pres. Alexandria Corp., Ponce, 1975—, Melcor Leasing, Ponce, 1975—; pres., chief exec. officer Teleponce Corp., 1975-79; trustee, mem. fin. and exec. com. Damas Hosp., Ponce, 1977—. Appointed hon. consul France, 1969. Served with U.S. Army, 1956-57. Recipient Youth Devel. Program award Vice Pres. of U.S., 1966. Mem. C. of C. of P.R., Tourist Bd. Ponce, Bankers Assn., Am. Soc. Travel Agts., Nat. Cable TV Assn. Roman Catholic. Clubs: Bankers, Ponce Yacht, Club Deportivo, Ponce Golf, Rotary (pres. Ponce chpt. 1963). Home: 1 Lindaraja La Alhambra Ponce PR 00731 Office: Cristina and Plaza Sts Gonzalez Bldg Ponce PR 00731

GONZALEZ-TEJERA, ENRIQUE, agronomist; b. Utuado, P.R., Jan. 20, 1928; s. Ramon and Paulina (Tejera) G.; B.A.S., U. P.R., 1958; M.S., (P.R. Govt. fellow), U. Rutgers, 1960; m. Emma Morales Casablanca, Nov. 19, 1961; children—Ana Rosa, Enrique J. With Agrl. Expt. Sta., U. P.R., Rio Piedras, 1960—, asso. agronomist, 1967-77, agronomist sugar cane and pineapple, 1977—. Served with AUS, 1951-53. Mem. Am. Soc. Hort. Sci., Caribbean Food Crops Soc., Sigma Xi, Gamma Sigma Delta. Roman Catholic. Home: G-18 Glacier Park Gardens Rio Piedras PR 00926 Office: Agr Ext Sta Box H Rio Piedras PR 00928

GONZMART, CAESAR, JR., coll. adminstr.; b. Apr. 16, 1944; s. Cesar and Claudina (Novoa) G.; A.B., George Washington U., 1966; M.S., Fla. State U., 1968. Asst. to ops. mgr. W.R. Grace & Co., Lima, Peru, 1965; research asso. Center for Advanced Internat. Studies, U. Miami, Coral Gables, Fla., 1968; econ. coordinator Model Cities Program, Tampa, Fla., 1969-70; dir. resource devel. Hillsborough Community Coll., Tampa, 1979—. Vice chmn. Fla. State Commn. on Hispanic Affairs, 1978-79; chmn. Bicentennial Com., Hillsborough County, Fla., 1973-75; advisor Spanish-Am. activities Southeastern Fed. Regional Council, 1972-75. Mem. Nat. Council Resource Devel., Fla. Council Resource Devel., Nat. Image, Inc., Ybor City C. of C. (dir. 1974-78, pres. 1979). Roman Catholic. Office: PO Box 22127 Tampa FL 33622

GOOCH, JOHN PHILLIP, chem. engr.; b. N.Y.C., June 6, 1941; s. Durward Belmont and Ruth (Alexander) G.; B.S., Auburn U., 1963, M.S., 1964; Ph.D., U. Ala., 1971. Asso. chem. engr. So. Research Inst., Birmingham, Ala., 1964-68, research chem. engr., 1970-73, head control device research sect., 1973-77, head control device research div., 1977—; research asst. U.S. Bur. Mines, Tuscaloosa, Ala., 1968-70. Registered profl. engr., Ala. Mem. Am. Inst. Chem. Engrs. (asso.), Phi Kappa Phi, Tau Beta Pi, Phi Lambda Upsilon. Sigma Pi Sigma, Omega Chi Epsilon. Home: 3560 Stonehenge Pl Birmingham AL 35210 Office: Southern Research Inst 2000 9th Ave S Birmingham AL 35205

GOOCH, PATRICIA CAROLYN, cytogeneticist; b. Michie, Tenn., Mar. 28, 1935; d. James Lide and Mary Frances (Hyneman) G.; B.S., U. Tenn., Knoxville, 1957. Tchr. sci. Knoxville (Tenn.) City Sch. System, 1957-58; biologist, biology div. Oak Ridge Nat. Lab., 1958-70, 73—; research asso. Grad. Sch. Biomed. Sci., U. Tex., Houston, 1970; sr. research analyst Northrop Corp., NASA-Johnson Space Center, Houston, 1970-72. Mem. AAAS, Am. Genetic Assn., Genetics Soc. Am., Environ. Mutagen Soc., Sigma Xi. Democrat. Mem. Chs. of Christ. Contbr. articles in field to profl. jours. Home: 226 Tusculum Dr Oak Ridge TN 37830 Office: Biology Div Oak Ridge Nat Lab PO Box Y Oak Ridge TN 37830

GOOD, JOSEPH COLE, JR., lawyer; b. Columbia, S.C., Sept. 18, 1945; s. Joseph Cole and Miriam Virginia (Williams) G.; A.B., Wofford Coll., 1967; J.D., U. S.C., 1970; m. Virginia St. Clair Craver; children—Katharine Steed, Joseph Cole III. Admitted to S.C. bar, 1970; supr. magistrate cts. for law enforcement assistance program, asst. atty. gen. State of S.C., 1970-73; corporate atty. South Carolina Electric & Gas, Columbia, 1973—. Bd. dirs. S.C. ARC; active Boy Scouts Am., Mid-Carolina Council on Alcoholism, United Fund. Served with Q.M.C., U.S. Army, 1970. Mem. Am., S.C., Richland bar assns., Am. Judicature Soc., S.C. Young Lawyers, Columbia (v.p. 1971) Young Lawyers. Democrat. Presbyterian. Clubs: Rotary (pres.) (Columbia); Met., Palmetto, Forest Lake. Home: 1510 Berkeley Rd Columbia SC 29205 Office: 320 S Main St Columbia SC 29218

GOOD, MARY LOWE, chemist, educator; b. Grapevine, Tex., June 20, 1931; d. John W. and Winnie (Mercer) Lowe; B.S. with honors, State Coll. Ark., 1950; M.S., U. Ark., 1953, Ph.D., 1955; m. Bill J. Good, May 17, 1952; children—Billy John, James Patrick. Instr., dept. chemistry La. State U., Baton Rouge, 1954-56, asst. prof., 1956-58, asso. prof., 1958-63, Boyd prof. material sci., 1979—; prof. dept. chemistry U. New Orleans, 1963-74, Boyd prof. chemistry, 1974—. Mem. Joint Sch. Bd. St. Paul-First English Lutheran Sch., 1972. Recipient Agnes Faye Morgan Research award, 1969, Distinguished Alumni citation U. Ark., 1973, Tchr. of Year award Delta Kappa Gamma, 1974; NSF grantee, 1973-76; Maritime Adminstrn. and Sea grantee Dept. Commerce, 1976—; Office of Naval Research grantee, 1976-; Frederick Gardner Cottrell grantee, 1955-57. Fellow Am. Inst. Chemists, Chem. Soc. London; mem. Am. Chem. Soc. (Garvan medal award 1973, Harvey medal 1975, Fla. award 1979; chmn. editorial bd. Chem. and Engring. News 1974-77, chmn. La. sect. 1967-68, nat. dir. 1972—, chmn. bd. 1978), Phi Beta Kappa, Sigma Xi, Alpha Chi, Iota Sigma Pi. Lutheran. Club: Zonta Internat. (pres. New Orleans chpt. 1969-70). Contbr. articles on spectroscopy to sci. jours. Home: Route 1 Box 139 Sorrento LA 70778 Office: Div Engring Research La State U Baton Rouge LA 70803

GOOD, RICHARD STANDISH, geologist, geochemist; b. West Chester, Pa., Sept. 18, 1928; s. Bernard Stafford and Marjorie Payne (Johnson) G.; B.S., Pa. State U., 1950, M.S., 1955; m. Edith Read Brodhead, Oct. 15, 1966. Chem. analyst Foote Mineral Co., 1951; project engr. Aeroprojects Co., West Chester, 1952-53; research asst. Pa. Statg U., 1953-55; geologist Geo-Tech. Devel. Co., Ltd., Toronto, Ont., Can., 1955-56, Hunting Tech. Services, Ltd., London, 1957-58; cons., 1958-60; chem. analyst Kawecki Chem. Co., Boyertown, Pa., 1960-62; teaching asst. Bryn Mawr (Pa.) Coll., 1962-64; self-employed, 1965; head geol. lab. Va. Div. Mineral Resources, Charlottesville, 1966—. NSF fellow, summers 1963, 64. Mem. Geol. Soc. Am., Assn. Exploration Geochemists, Soc. Mining Engrs. of AIME, AIME (mem. geochem. com. 1972-76, chmn. Va. sect. 1979-80). Va. Acad. Sci. Unitarian. Home: 20 Orchard Rd Charlottesville VA 22901 Office: Va Div Mineral Resources PO Box 3667 Charlottesville VA 22903

GOODALL, CECILE ROBERTA, educator; b. Pinch, W.Va.; d. Robert Lee and Julie (Belcher) Goodall; A.B., W.Va. U., 1928, M.A., 1937, postgrad., 1958-64; postgrad. summers Cambridge U., 1938, Am. U., 1942, Oxford, 1948. Tchr., Charleston (W.Va.) High Sch., 1932-70, head history dept., 1957-70; editor W.Va. History, quar. publ., 1941—; instr. history, critic tchr. Morris Harvey Coll., Charleston, part-time, 1962-70. Mem. W.Va. Historic Commn., 1961-69; researcher adv. com. Div. Hwy. Markers, W.Va. Dept. Archives and History, 1970-77. Recipient W.Va. Library Commn. award, 1955. Hon. fellow Truman Library Inst.; mem. Nat. Hist. Soc., Smithsonian Assos., W.Va. State Hist. Soc., NEA, So. Scholastic Press Assn. (mem. area council 1966-70), Am. Assn. U. Women, W.Va. Edn. Assn., Phi Beta Kappa, Kappa Delta Pi, Phi Alpha Theta, Delta Kappa Gamma. Compiler, editor: West Virginia Highway Markers-Historic, Prehistoric, Scenic, Geological, 1967; editorial asst. textbook. Editorial adviser West Virginia Yesterday and Today, 1931. Asso. editor W.Va. Rev., 1931-34. Home: 524 Nancy St Charleston WV 25311

GOODE, CECIL EARNEST, mgmt. cons., former UN ofcl.; b. Glasgow, Ky., Mar. 5, 1915; s. William L. and Lela May (Cary) G.; B.S., Purdue U., 1938, M.S., 1938; m. Dorothy Gene Bryant, Feb. 9, 1941; children—Cecil Earnest, Richard Bryant, Marilyn Gene Goode Lowe. Engaged in personnel adminstrn. State of Ind., FHA, 1938-41, Office Emergency Mgmt., 1941-43; dir. personnel mgmt. staff VA, 1946-51; dir. personnel Fed. CD Adminstrn., 1951-54; staff dir. Hoover Commn. Subcom., 1954-55; spl. asst. to asst. sec. def., Washington, 1955-59; research dir. Pub. Personnel Assn., 1957; exec. dir. Nat. Civil Service League, 1959-60; mgmt. analyst, asst. chief, mgmt. improvement and research br. Bur. Budget, also Office Mgmt. and Budget, Washington, 1960-71; dep. dir. Adminstrv. Mgmt. Service, UN Secretariat, N.Y.C., 1971-76; mgmt. cons., 1976—. Profl. lectr. George Washington U., 1960-71; Trustee Va. Meth. Children's Home. Served to capt. USAAF, 1943-46. Recipient citation for Hoover Commn. work Pres. Hoover, 1955. Mem. Am. Soc. Pub. Adminstrn., Soc. for Personnel Adminstrn. (pres. 1950-51), S. Central Ky. Hist. and Geneal. Soc. (pres. 1978—). Methodist. Club: Rotary. Author: Personnel Research Frontiers, 1958; Kentucky Cousins, 1967; also monographs. Editor: Personnel Adminstrn., 1955-60. Home: 111 Douglas Dr Glasgow KY 42141

GOODE, CLEMENT TYSON, educator; b. Richmond, Va., July 10, 1929; s. Clement Tyson and Bessie Mae (Trimble) G.; A.B., Hendrix Coll., 1951; M.A. (teaching fellow), Vanderbilt U., 1953, Ph.D. (teaching fellow, So. Fellowship Fund grantee), 1959; m. Elizabeth Jane Anderson, Aug. 19, 1952; children—Sara Elizabeth, Robert Clement. Instr. English Vanderbilt U., Nashville, 1954-56; instr. English Baylor U., Waco, Tex., 1957-58, asst. prof., 1958-60, asso. prof., 1960-63, prof., 1963—, dir. freshman English, 1961-64, grad. dir. English dept., 1968—; exchange prof. Seinan Gakuin U., Fukuoka, Japan, 1972-73. Adv. bd. Salvation Army Waco, 1968-69; deacon 1st. Baptist Ch. Waco, 1970—. Mem. Am., S. Central modern lang. assns., Nat. Council Tchrs. English, Coll. Conf. Tchrs. English, Byron Soc., Shelley Soc. Democrat. Author: (with Oscar Santucho) A Comprehensive Bibliography of Secondary Materials in English: George Gordon, Lord Byron with a Review of Research, 1976. Contbr. articles, revs. to profl. publs. Home: 2720 Braemar St Waco TX 76710

GOODE, DAVID HENRY, fabrication co. exec.; b. Covington, Tenn., Feb. 9, 1948; s. W. R. and Wilma LeVerghne (Johnson) G.; m. Linda Melba Creswell, June 1, 1968; children—Terri Michelle, Tammy Denise. Sales/engring. rep. Am. Fabricating Engring., Memphis, 1962-68; welding shop supr. Gen. Machine Works, Memphis, 1968-71; gen. mgr. Fuller & Owens Boiler Works, Memphis, 1971-75, Memphis Boiler & Fabricating, 1975—. Baptist. Office: 1519 Castalia St Memphis TN 38114

GOODE, MARK GIDEON, III, cons. engr.; b. Dallas, Sept. 6, 1950; s. Marquis Gideon and Lucille (McDermott) G.; B.S. in Civil Engring., U. Tex., Austin, 1972, M.S. in Engring. (Nat. Hwy. Inst. fellow), 1974; m. Dianne Helen Diez, Jan. 26, 1974. Research asso. Center for Hwy. Research, U. Tex., Austin, 1972-74, tchr., undergrad. lab. in transp. engring., 1973-74; transp. engr., traffic control dept. City of Dallas, 1974-75; project engr. Young Hadawi DeShazo Inc., Dallas, 1975-76, project mgr., 1976-78, mgr., 1979-80, v.p., 1980—. Registered profl. engr., Tex. Mem. Inst. Transp. Engrs., ASCE, Am. Inst. Planners, Phi Kappa Phi, Tau Beta Pi, Chi Epsilon, Omicron Delta Kappa. Presbyterian. Home: 8043 Moss Meadows Dr Dallas TX 75231 Office: Suite 320 8350 N Central Expressway Dallas TX 75206

GOODE, MARTIN, fin. and mgmt. cons., ret. naval officer; b. Trenton, N.J., Nov. 25, 1928; s. Maurice Joseph and Betty (Cooperman) G.; B.S.I.E., Ga. Tech., 1959; M.S. in Adminstrn., George Washington U., 1971; m. Paula Weishaupt, May 28, 1967; children—Nelege, Cheryl, Francheska. Enlisted U.S. Navy, 1945, advanced through grades to comdr., 1964; exec. officer Operational Test and Evaluation, Norfolk Depot; dept. head U.S.S. Boxer cv-g; sr. mgmt. cons. Laventhol & Horwath, C.P.A.'s, Norfolk, Va., 1972-74; bus. mgr. Goodman & Co., C.P.A.'s, Norfolk, 1974-75; v.p. Physicians Underwriting Co., Virginia Beach, Va., 1975-77; individual practice as mgmt. cons., Virginia Beach, 1977—; adminstr. Chrysler Mus. at Norfolk. Served with USN, 1945-72. Decorated Air medal (3), Meritorious Service medal. Mem. Inst. Mgmt. Accountants, Nat. Assn. Accountants (pres. chpt. 1977-78), Ret. Officers Assn. Jewish. Address: 105 Conference Ct Virginia Beach VA 23462

GOODE, READ FISHER, ins. co. exec.; b. Midlothian, Va., Oct. 12, 1941; s. Isaac Read and Mary (Fisher) G.; student Frederick Coll., 1961-63; B.S. in Finance, U. Richmond, 1965; m. Josephine Ann Sheehy, Oct. 23, 1965; children—Read Fisher, Kimberly Ann. Ins. agent New Eng. Mut. Life Ins. Co., Richmond, Va., 1965-72; v.p. Wheat Ins. Services, Richmond, 1972-73; agent New Eng. Mutual Life Ins. Co., 1973-75; mng. partner Goode, Maguire & Assos. (Life Ins. Co. of Va.), Richmond, 1975-79; pres. Read F. Goode & Assos., Inc., Richmond, 1980—. Active, Central Richmond Assn.; mem. estate planning adv. council U. Richmond; worker campaigns Sen. Harry F. Byrd, 1972, 76, Pres. Ford, 1976. C.L.U.; recipient Nat. Quality and Nat. Sales Achievement awards Nat. Assn. Life Underwriters; various ins. sales awards. Mem. Richmond Assn. Life Underwriters, Estate Planning Council Richmond, Assn. Advanced Life Underwriting, Soc. C.L.U.'s, Life of Va. Mgrs. Assn., Life of Va. C.L.U. Assn., Herman P. Thomas Econ. Soc., Six Million Dollar Forum, U. Richmond Alumni Assn., Nat. Fedn. Ind. Businessmen, SAR, Richmond C. of C. Clubs: Salisbury Country, Princess Anne, Commonwealth, Ducks Unltd., Trouts Unltd., Va. Yacht, Chesapeake, Gen. Soc. Colonial Wars, Jamestowne Soc., Midlothian Ruritan. Home: Millwood Route 2 Box 75 Powhatan VA 23139 Office: Suite 1976 F&M Center Richmond VA 23277

GOODHUE, WILLIAM WALTER, JR., physician; b. St. Louis, Feb. 5, 1945; s. William W. and Rose Marie (Vahousek) G.; B.S. cum laude with honors, Georgetown U., 1966; M.D., Cornell U., 1970. Intern anatomic pathology N.Y. Hosp.-Cornell Med. Center, N.Y.C., 1970-71, resident anatomic pathology, 1971-74; chief resident pediatric anatomic pathology Columbia-Presbyn. Med. Center, N.Y.C., 1974-75; resident clin. pathology Tripler Army Med. Center, Honolulu, 1976-78, chief resident, 1978; practice medicine specializing in pathology, 1975—; instr. pathology U. Hawaii Sch. Medicine, Honolulu, 1975-76; chief dept. pathology U.S. Army Hosp., Ft. Campbell, Ky., 1978—; cons. in pathology Am. Nat. Red Cross, 1978-80. Served to lt. col., M.C., U.S. Army, 1975—. USPHS research fellow, 1971-74. Diplomate Am. Bd. Pathology. Fellow Am. Soc. Clin. Pathologists, Coll. Am. Pathologists, Am. Soc. Abdominal Surgeons; mem. Pediatric Pathology Club, Assn. Mil. Surgeons U.S., Am. Assn. Blood Banks, Nashville Pathology Soc., Hawaii Soc. Pathologists, AAAS, N.Y. Acad. Scis., Soc. Armed Forces Med. Lab. Scientists, AMA (Physician's Recognition award 1976-79), Sigma Xi, Phi Beta Kappa. Republican. Roman Catholic. Clubs: Cornell of N.Y.; Kauai Yacht. Contbr. articles on pathology to profl. jours.; research in clin. pathology. Home: 1137 Madison St Clarksville TN 37040 Office: USAMEDDAC Dept Pathology Fort Campbell KY 42223

GOODING, JESSIE JEWELL SIMS (MRS. ARTHUR RAY GOODING), clubwoman; b. Hartshorne, Okla., May 9, 1902; d. William Poley and Leola (Sullivan) Sims; student Okla. Coll. Women, 1921-22; m. Arthur Ray Gooding, Aug. 16, 1925; children—Jack Bascom, Arthur Gene. Shipping clk. William Volker Wholesale Co., Oklahoma City, 1942-43; bookkeeper, sales clk. Seela Windowshade Co., 1944-51; sales clk. John A. Brown Co., 1957. Recipient Torch award Am. War Mothers, 1966. Mem. Bus. and Profl. Women's Club, Am. War Mothers (charter, chpt. pres. 1955-56, chpt. treas. 1956-62, state treas. 1958-60, chpt. corr. sec. 1963-68, chpt. historian 1969-76, state pres. 1968-70, state hosp. chmn. 1975—; state alt. rep. in Vets. Voluntary Service 1969-71, nat. rep. 1974—), World War One Aux. (chpt. jr. v.p. 1973-74, sr. v.p. 1975-76; pres. 1976-77; 5th dist. guard 1974-75, dist. conductress 1975-76), Am. War Dads Aux. (pres. 1965-66, nat. council woman, Okla. historian, state parliamentarian 1971-74; life mem.), Am. Assn. Ret. Persons. Baptist. Mem. Order Eastern Star. Clubs: Flower (v.p. 1965—), Home Demonstration, Merry Modern Mothers (past v.p.). Home: 508 SW 35th St Oklahoma City OK 73109

GOODKIN, JOANNE MYERS, mag. founder and publisher; b. N.Y.C., July 7, 1941; d. Charles and Clara (Strachman) Kissel; B.A., Syracuse U., 1963; m. Lewis Goodkin, Jan. 1, 1980; 1 dau., Deborah Lynne. Tchr. English pub. schs., Lawrence, N.Y., 1963-65; mem. sales and mgmt. staff various real estate cos., Scarsdale, N.Y., 1965-72; dir. advt. Western News, Davie, Fla., 1973-74; founder, publisher Broward Life, Ft. Lauderdale, Fla., 1974—. Bd. dirs. Jr. Achievement, Ft. Lauderdale Center for the Blind, 1977; div. chmn. United Way, Ft. Lauderdale, 1977. Mem. Greater Ft. Lauderdale Advt. Fedn. (dir. 1975-78, v.p. 1977, 78), S. Fla. Savs. and Loan Mktg. Soc., Nat. Fedn. Bus. and Profl. Women's Club, Women in Communications (Woman of Yr. finalist 1977, Woman of Yr. 1978), W. Broward C. of C. (dir. 1975). Jewish. Clubs: Inverrary Country, Le Club Internat., Marina Bay. Home: 2900 NE 24th Ct Fort Lauderdale FL 33305 Office: 3081 E Commercial Blvd Fort Lauderdale FL 33308

GOODMAN, BARRY MICHAEL, lawyer; b. Los Angeles, Nov. 22, 1946; s. Ralph Arthur and Natalie Bell (Hamburger) G.; B.A. in History, Calif. State U., 1967; J.D., U. So. Calif., 1970; m. Susan Lynn Reigrod, June 18, 1969; children—Gregory, Alison. Admitted to Calif. bar, 1971, D.C. bar, 1972; sr. atty. Office of Chief Counsel, Urban Mass Transp. Adminstrn., Washington, 1971-74; dir. Office of Public Transp., City of Houston, 1974-78; exec. dir. Met. Transit Authority, Houston, 1978-79; pres. Barry M. Goodman & Assos., Houston, 1979—. Mem. Calif. Bar Assn., Washington Bar Assn., Am. Bar Assn., Urban Land Inst., Transp. Research Bd. Jewish. Home: 2702 Valley Manor Kingwood TX 77339 Office: PO Box 61429 Houston TX 77208

GOODMAN, JAMES JACOB, psychiatrist; b. Boston, Mar. 31, 1922; s. Morris and Rosa (Wolfsen) G.; B.A., Boston U., 1943; M.D., Middlesex U., 1945; m. Janice Annabel Stenson, July 11, 1951; 1 dau., Ann Rosalind. Intern St. Mark's Hosp., Salt Lake City, 1946-47; resident St. Vincent's Sanitarium, St. Louis, 1947-48, Western State Hosp., Ft. Steilacoom, Wash., 1948-50; staff psychiatrist VA Hosp., American Lake, Wash., 1950-51; asst. attending physician dept. psychiatry and neurology Jackson Hosp., Miami, Fla., 1954—, also clin. dir. Miami Med. Center; practice medicine specializing in psychiatry, Miami, 1954-65; staff psychiatrist VA Hosp., Indpls., 1966-69, VA Hosp., Miami, Fla., 1969—. Instr. psychiatry U. Miami, 1955-57, clin. asst. prof. neurology, 1957-59, clin. instr. psychiatry, 1969-72, clin. asst. prof. Sch. Medicine, 1972-73, asst. prof. dept. psychiatry, 1973—; instr. psychiatry Ind. U. Sch. Medicine, 1967-69. Bd. dirs. P.L. Dodge Found. and Meml. Hosp., Miami. Served to capt. M.C., U.S. Army, 1951-54. Mem. Am. Psychiat. Assn. A.M.A. So., Fla., Dade County med. assns. Assn. Am. Med. Colls., Am. Assn. U. Profs., Nat. Assn. for Mental Health, Mental Health Soc. S.E. Fla., Assn. Mil. Surgeons, Am. Soc. for Group Psychotherapy and Psychodrama, Acad. Religion and Mental Health, Fla. Council on Aging, Fla. Soc. Neurology and Psychiatry, World Med. Assn. (U.S. com.), Nat. Com. on Alcoholism, N.Y. Acad. Scis., Am. Geriatrics Soc., Am. Acad. Forensic Scis. Home: 6818 Corsica St Coral Gables FL 33146 Office: 1201 NW 16th St Miami FL 33125

GOODMAN, NORA WOOD, nursing adminstr.; b. Morgan County, Ga., Apr. 20, 1940; d. Henry Hughand Emma Estelle Wood; R.N., Ga. Bapt. Sch. Nursing, 1961; cert. registered nurse anesthetist Mayo Clinic Sch. Anesthesia, 1964-66; m. James Barnett Goodman, Sept. 22, 1973; 1 son, John Jeffrey Achter. Head nurse neurosurgery St. Mary's Hosp., Rochester, Minn., 1962-64; nurse anesthetist, Olney, Md., 1964-67, Cannonsbury, Pa., 1967-69; staff nurse anesthetist, instr. Anesthetists Sch., Ga. Bapt. Hosp., Atlanta, 1970-71; anesthetist various hosps., Pitts., 1969-70; chief nurse anesthetist, operating room supr. Paulding Meml. Hosp., Dallas, Ga., 1971—, dir. critical care areas, 1979—. Chmn. Women's Farm Com., Paulding County, 1979-80. Mem. Am. Assn. Nurse Anesthetists, Ga. Santa Gertrudis Assn. (charter pres. 1978-80), Farm Bur. Paulding County (dir.). Republican. Presbyterian. Home: Box 247 Route 2 Temple GA 30179 Office: 600 W Memorial Dr Dallas GA 30132

GOODMAN, WILLIAM WOLF, lawyer; b. Memphis, June 26, 1900; s. Abe and Bobye (Wolf) G.; ed. Memphis U. Sch., Culver Mil. Acad.; B.A., U. Pa., 1920; J.D., Harvard, 1923; postgrad. St. Johns Coll., Cambridge (Eng.) U., 1923-24; Barrister, Lincoln's Inn (London), 1926; m. 1942; 5 children. Chmn. bd. Memphis Cold Storage Warehouse Co., Mid-South Refrigerated Warehouse Co., Commerce Title Bldg. Corp. Sec., Tenn. State Planning Commn., 1932-40; pres., commr. Goodwyn Inst., 1952-75. Served as pvt. U.S. Army, 1918, col. AC, U.S. Army, 1942-45. Decorated Legion of Merit, Army Commendation Ribbon, Am. Theater Ribbon (U.S.); Royal Yugoslav Aviator's Wings, Honoris Causa; Spl. Breast Award order of Yun Hui (Cloud and Banner) (China); knight comdr. Order Orange-Nassau (Netherlands); knight comdr. Royal Order St. Olaf (Norway); chevalier Legion of Honor (France); officer Order Brit. Empire (Eng.). Mem. Am., Tenn., Memphis and Shelby County bar assns., Assn. Bar City N.Y., Brit. Barrister, Memphis Freight Bur. (pres. 1951-60). Clubs: Harvard (N.Y.C.); Army and Navy (Washington); Univ. (Memphis). Home: 159 E Parkway N Memphis TN 38104 Office: Commerce Title Bldg Memphis TN 38103

GOODNER, DWIGHT BENJAMIN, mathematician, educator; b. What Cheer, Iowa, Aug. 15, 1913; s. William Clifford and Myrtle E. (Harbour) G.; B.A. with honors, William Penn Coll., 1934; M.A. (T.Wistar Brown fellow), Haverford Coll., 1935; Ph.D. (Univ. fellow), U. Ill., 1949; m. Mildred E. Wilson, June 29, 1936. Instr. S.D. State Coll., Brookings, 1937-41, asst. prof., 1941-46; faculty Fla. State U., Tallahassee, 1949—, prof. math., 1954—, asso. dean grad. sch., 1953-58. Cons. Commn. on Accreditation of Armed Services Ednl. Experiences, 1950-59, Ednl. Testing Service, Princeton, N.J., 1965-70. Served with USNR, 1942-46. Mem. Am., London, Edinburgh, Indian math. socs., Math. Assn. Am. (gov. 1967-71, cons. 1971—), Sigma Xi, Phi Beta Kappa, Phi Kappa Phi, Pi Mu Epsilon, Phi Delta Kappa, Chi Gamma Iota, Phi Eta. Presbyterian (ruling elder 1957—). Math. editor: Jour. of Communication, 1959-61. Contbr. articles in field to profl. jours. Home: 1317 Lemond Tallahassee FL 32303

GOODNIGHT, CHARLES MERLE, restaurant owner; b. Prosper, Tex., Feb. 27, 1922; s. Fred Hoyle and Eula Blossom (Wells) G.; student public schs., Dallas; m. Claudia Whitter, May 30, 1942; children—Charles Merle, Susan, Dean. Owner, Goodnight Grocery, Dallas, 1946-51; owner, operator Goodnight Motel, Austin, Tex., 1951-72; owner Hills Cafe, Inc., Austin, 1951—; chmn. bd. Southside Savs. & Loan, Austin, 1980—; dir. Bank of Austin. Mem. Parks and Recreation Bd.; bd. dirs. United Way, Austin Citizens League. Served with U.S. Mcht. Marines, 1942-45. Named Hon. Citizen Lubbock (Tex.), 1968, Amarillo (Tex.), 1968. Mem. Tex. Restaurant Assn. (past pres.), Austin Restaurant Assn. (past pres.), C. of C., Austin Civil Service Bd. Presbyterian. Clubs: South Austin Civic, Boys (Austin); Lions, Masons, Shriners. Home: 11001 Onion Creek Ct Austin TX 78745 Office: 4700 S Congress St Austin TX 78745

GOODNIGHT, CHARLES RAY, fraternal lodge exec.; b. Waco, Tex., Nov. 10, 1941; s. John Henry and Lois Mary (Poston) G.; student Durham Bus. Coll., 1961, Baylor U., 1964-65; m. Iris Marlene Patrick, Sept. 17, 1970; children—Kristy Michelle, Jennifer Leigh. Asst. grand sec. Grand Lodge of Tex., A.F. & A.M., 1964—; fed. tax cons. fraternal orgns. U.S. Mem. Bellmead (Tex.) City Council, 1968-72, mayor, 1970. Served with USNR, 1962-64. Republican. Methodist. Clubs: Masons (32 deg., past high priest, past master council royal and select masters, past dist. dep. grand master), Shriners. Home: 104 Countryside Dr Arlington TX 76014 Office: 1111 W Mockingbird Dallas TX 75247

GOODPASTER, HOWARD THOMAS, state ofcl., archivist; b. Winchester, Ky., May 12, 1917; s. Kella Johnson and Rebecca M. (Estes) G.; B.S., U. Ky., 1940; m. Helene Marie Langlois, July 10, 1943 (dec.); children—Diane, Howard, Ronald, Donald; m. 2d, Opal Joy Edwards, June 22, 1974. Commd. 2d lt., U.S. Air Force, 1943, advanced through grades to lt. col., 1964; ret., 1964; dep. state archivist, State of Ky., 1967-71, state archivist, dir. div. archives and records mgmt., 1971—; coordinator State Hist. Records Adv. Bd. Mem. Assn. Records Mgrs. and Adminstrs. (cert. records mgr.; pres. Louisville chpt. 1978-79), Ky. Hist. Soc. (exec. bd.), Soc. Am. Archivists, Nat. Assn. Archivists and Records Adminstrs., Nat. Micrographics Assn., Ky. Council Archivists, Ky. Geneal. Soc., Civil War Round Table. Democrat. Roman Catholic. Clubs: K.C., Am. Legion, Blue Grass Sportsmans. Home: 1 Timberlawn Ln Frankfort KY 40601 Office: 851 E Main St Frankfort KY 40601

GOODRICH, GILLIAN WHITE, civic worker; b. Birmingham, Ala., Nov. 23, 1946; d. William Bew and Gay (Comer) White; A.B., Converse Coll., 1968; M.A., U. Ala., 1974; m. Thomas Michael Goodrich, Dec. 28, 1968; children—Thomas Michael, Braxton Comer, Charles Drennen. Tchr., Tuscaloosa (Ala.) Bd. Edn., 1968-70, Tuscaloosa High Sch., 1968-69, Westlawn Jr. High Sch., Tuscaloosa, 1969-70. Public affairs chmn. Birmingham Jr. League, 1975-76, child advocacy chmn., 1976-77, child abuse project chmn., 1978-79, asst. treas., 1979—; bd. dirs. Family and Child Services, 1974—, sec., 1979—; bd. dirs. Birmingham ARC, 1975—, chmn. Awards Day, 1979; 13th pl. adv. bd. Jr. Womens Com. of 100, 1977-80, pres., 1978-79; mem. exec. bd. Jefferson County Child Devel. Council, 1978-80. Greater Birmingham Found. for research on women's suffrage in Ala. grantee, 1975. Mem. Ala. Hist. Soc., Birmingham Hist. Soc., Child Abuse Edn. Bur., Child Abuse Task Force. Presbyterian. Address: 2862 Surrey Rd Birmingham AL 35223

GOODRICH, SAMUEL MELVIN, obstetrician and gynecologist; b. Milledgeville, Ga., May 4, 1936; s. Ellis and Frieda (Bergman) G.; B.S., U. Ga., 1957; M.D., Med. Coll. Ga., 1961; m. Ellen Schneider, Mar. 31, 1971; children—Jason Alexander, Harriet Schneider. Intern in pathology and medicine Med. Coll. Ga., Augusta, 1961-62, resident in obstetrics and gynecology, 1962-66; practice medicine specializing in obstetrics and gynecology, Milledgeville, Ga., 1969—; asst. prof. obstetrics and gynecology Med. Coll. Ga., Augusta, 1968-69, asst. clin. prof., 1969—; chief surgery Baldwin County Hosp., 1976—, chief staff, 1970-71; cons. Ga. Med. Care Found., 1972—. Advisor to Baldwin County chpts. March of Dimes, 1971-74, Am. Cancer Soc., 1971-74, ARC, 1972—; chmn. profl. div. Baldwin County Heart Fund, 1977; mem. Ga. Task Force on Hosp. Maternity and Newborn Facilities, 1974-75; bd dirs. Health System Agy. Central Ga., 1975—. Served with M.C., U.S. Army, 1966-68. Recipient Sheard Sanford award Am. Soc. Clin. Pathologists, 1961; Physician Recognition award AMA, 1969, 72, 76. Diplomate Am. Bd. Obstetrics and Gynecology. Fellow Am. Coll. Obstetricians and Gynecologists, S. Atlantic Assn. Obstetricians and Gynecologists; mem. AMA, Am. Assn. Gynecologic Laparoscopists, Med. Assn. Ga., Baldwin County Med. Soc., Ga. Obstet. and Gynecol. Soc. (pres. 1979), Phi Beta Kappa, Alpha Omega Alpha, Phi Kappa Phi. Jewish. Contbr. articles to med. jours. Address: PO Box 893 Milledgeville GA 31061

GOODROE, JOSEPH HOLLIS, econ. analyst; b. Jackson, Ga., Aug. 24, 1942; s. Joseph Turner and Josephine Elizabeth (McCorvey) G.; B.S. in Indsl. Mgmt., Ga. Inst. Tech., 1965; m. Nancy Gayle Johnson, Dec. 3, 1965; children—Glenn, Gary. Mfg. engr. Lockheed Aircraft Co., Atlanta, 1965-69; systems analyst Bowles, Andrews & Towne, Atlanta, 1969-70; systems analyst So. Co. Services Inc., Atlanta, 1970-72, prin. econ. analyst, 1972—. Mem. So. Services Profl. Devel. Assn. (charter). Democrat. Methodist. Home: 4783 Luray Dr Dunwoody GA 30338 Office: 64 Perimeter Center Atlanta GA 30346

GOODRUM, WAYNE LOUIS, telephone co. exec.; b. Fort Worth, Tex., Dec. 8, 1934; s. Albert L. and Lillian Elaine (Thompson) G.; student N.Mex. State U., 1953-54; B.B.A., Hardin-Simmons U., 1957; J.D., U. Tex., 1971; m. Arvella S. Powell, Nov. 22, 1973; children—Carolyn Dale, Bryan Wayne, Whitney Leigh. With Gen. Telephone Co. S.W., 1959-76, div. mgr., Seymour, Tex., 1967-69, sr. atty., San Angelo, Tex., 1972-76; gen. counsel Gen. Telephone Co. Ky., Lexington, 1976—. Bd. dirs. Fayette County Legal Aid, Inc. Mem. Am. Bar Assn., Ky. Bar Assn., Tex. Bar Assn., Fayette County Bar Assn. Republican. Baptist. Home: 411 Holiday Rd Lexington KY 40502 Office: 1st Security Plaza PO Box 1650 Lexington KY 40502

GOODWIN, ANDREW WIRT, II, radiologist; b. Oil City, Pa., Feb. 4, 1932; s. Frank B. and Florence Bickford (Green) G.; A.B., Colgate U., 1953; M.D., U. Mich., 1957; children—Andrew, Victoria, Elizabeth, Mark, Martha. Intern, Mary H. Hitchcock Meml. Hosp., Hanover, N.H., 1957-58; resident Mayo Clinic, Rochester, Minn., 1958-62; practice medicine specializing in radiology, Charleston, W.Va., 1962—; mem. dept. radiology Charleston Area Med. Center, 1962-77, chmn., 1972—; dir. Associated Radiologists, Inc., 1969—, pres., 1970—; clin. prof. W.Va. U.; instr. Morris Harvey Coll.; adj. prof. W.Va. State Coll.; adv. com. Sch. X-ray Tech.; exec. com. Charleston Area Med. Center; dir. Blue Cross. Diplomate Am. Bd. Radiology, Am. Bd. Nuclear Medicine. Fellow Am. Coll. Radiology (councillor); mem. AMA, W.Va. Radiol. Soc. (past pres.), Radiol. Soc. N.Am. (past councilor), Kanawha County Med. Soc., W.Va. Med. Assn., Soc. Clin. Radiology (pres.). Clubs: Rotary. Home: 739 Canterbury Dr Charleston WV 25314 Office: 3100 MacCorkle Ave SE Charleston WV 25301

GOODWIN, BYROM ODELL, rehab. counselor; b. Birmingham, Ala., Mar. 31, 1945; s. Henry Odell and Frances Elease (Quick) G.; B.S., U. North Ala., Florence, 1968; M.A., U. Ala., Tuscaloosa, 1972; postgrad. in Edn. U. Tenn., Knoxville, 1973—; Ed.S., George Peabody Coll. for Tchrs., 1978; m. Brenda Joy May, Aug. 23, 1968; 1 son, Griffin Byrom. Park ranger U.S. Dept. Interior, Jackson, Miss., 1967; ins. rep. Am. Gen. Life Ins. Co., Muscle Shoals, Ala., 1967-68; social worker Dept. Pensions, Security, Florence, 1968-69; rehab. counselor deaf Vocat. Rehab. Service, Huntsville, Ala., 1969-79, supervising counselor blind and deaf program, 1979—. Instr. sign lang.; planning cons. Huntsville Hosp. dept. social service, 1971-72; mem. Gov. Ala. Com. on Employment of Handicapped, 1973-75; v.p. Huntsville Registry Interpreters for Deaf, 1974-75, pres., 1975-78. Vice pres. Conf on Aging, Huntsville, 1971-72. Named Hon. Dep. Sheriff, Huntsville, 1972, Hon. Police Officer, Huntsville, 1975. Mem. Am. Personnel and Guidance Assn. (parliamentarian dist. II), Nat., Ala. rehab. assns., Nat. Rehab. Counseling Assn., Ala. Edn. Assn. (sec. state chpt. 1972-73), Space Capital Cheer Club (hon., trustee), North Ala. Waterfowl Assn., Huntsville Inst. Martial Arts, Muscle Shoals Long Rifles Assn., U. No. Ala. Alumni Assn. (life), U. Ala. Alumni Assn. Baptist. Mason. Club: Huntsville Ski. Home: 10027 Nadina Dr SE Huntsville AL 35803 Office: 407 Governors Dr Huntsville AL 35801

GOODWIN, DAVID, ins. cons. firm exec.; b. N.Y.C., May 14, 1926; s. Paul Theodore and Anna (Matz) G.; student (Gooch scholar) Southwestern Coll., Memphis, 1943, U. Tenn. at Knoxville, 1943-44, Duke U., 1944-45; B.B.A., U. Miami, 1949; m. Selma Rabinovitz, Mar. 28, 1960; 1 son, Ari E. Agt., solicitor M. M. Sheldon Ins. Agy., Inc., Miami Beach, Fla., 1949-56; pres. Goodwin Ins. Agy., Inc., Miami, 1956-60; owner Dave Goodwin & Assos., Miami Beach, 1960—; pres. Sound Money Matters, Inc., Miami Beach, 1975—. Instr. ins. Div. Continuing Edn., U. Miami, 1970-71. Vice-chmn. Zionist Youth Council, Miami Beach, 1954-56; mem. bd. edn. Hebrew Acad., Miami Beach, 1974-75; bd. regents Coll. for Financial Planning, Denver, 1971-73; pres. Funds for Charity, Miami Beach, 1977—. Served with USNR, 1944-46. Sr. mem. Internat. Assn. Financial Planners; mem. Am. Risk and Ins. Assn., Miami Beach Taxpayers Assn. (chmn. ins. com. 1969-74), Masada (pres. 1950-52), Zionist Orgn. Am. (southeast regional v.p. 1953-55), Nat. Assn. Hosp. Developers (asso.), Zeta Beta Tau. Democrat. Jewish. Mason. Author: Stop Wasting Your Insurance Dollars, 1969; ins. glossary in A Financial Planner's Guide (Glass and Yurman), 1972; syndicated newspaper column Insurance of Consumers, 1970—. Contbr. articles in field to profl. jours. Chmn. ins. seminar U. Miami-Fla. Internat. U. Consumer Affairs Inst., Miami Beach, 1973. Home: 721 86th St Miami Beach FL 33141 Office: 2301 Collins Ave Room #M23 Miami Beach FL 33139

GOODWIN, EARL, state senator; b. Adger, Ala.; student Howard U., Birmingham, Ala., U. Ala.; m. Geraldine Hubbard; children—Patricia Dale Goodwin Sexton, Sharon Kay Goodwin Alsobrook, Eva Elizabeth Goodwin Davis, Beverly Ann Goodwin Sousoulas. Employee U.S. Govt., 1940-42; formerly pres. Bush Hog, Inc., now cons.; dir. J&G Realty Co., City Nat. Bank, Selma; mem. Ala. Senate, 1976—. Past. pres. Asso. Industries Ala.; past indsl. chmn. local ARC, United Appeal; mem. bd. stewards, past pres. Morgan Bible class Ind. Protestant Ch.; chmn. Ala. div. Am. Cancer Soc. drive, 1964; chmn. Gov. Ala. Com. Hiring Handicapped, 1964-65; mem. Ala. Democratic Exec. com.; del. Dem. Nat. Conv., 1964, 68, 72, 76, chmn., 1972. Served with USAAF, World War II. Recipient Freedom award, 1969. Mem. Dallas County C. of C. (past pres.), Selma C. of C. (past pres.), Howard Coll. Alumni Assn. (past pres.; Alumni of Year award 1965, Athletic Alumni award 1971). Club: Civitan (past pres. Selma, past internat. dir. membership; Honor Key). Address: PO Box 886 Selma AL 36701

GOODWIN, JACK HOWARD, librarian; b. Columbus, O., Mar. 9, 1921; s. Ernest S. and Lucy Rebecca (Hart) G.; B.A., Olivet Nazarene Coll., 1948; M.L.S., U. Ill., 1949; postgrad. U. Edinburgh (Scotland), 1951-52; m. Mary Ellen Wilson, July 25, 1943; children—James Wilson, Jeremy Philip. Librarian, Va. Theol. Sem., Alexandria, 1954—. Served with U.S. Army, 1942-46. Mem. Am. Theol Library Assn. Home: Box 12111 Alexandria VA 22304

GOODWIN, LARRY DARRELL, airline exec.; b. Gainesville, Fla., Apr. 1, 1947; s. Charles Rudolph and Hazel (Wood) G.; B.A., U. N.C., 1969; M.B.A., Ga. State U., 1973. Supr. purchasing Am. Hosp. Supply, Chamblee, Ga., 1972-73; inventory analyst Rich's Inc., Atlanta, 1973-74; mgr. inventory planning and control So. Airways, Atlanta, 1974-77, mgr. material services, 1977-78, dir. prodn. control, 1978—; cons. in field. Served with U.S. Army, 1969-72. Decorated Bronze Star. Mem. Beta Gamma Sigma. Home: 1501 Waterford Ct Marietta GA 30067 Office: Hartsfield Internat Airport Atlanta GA 30320

GOODWIN, MARK ALLEN, music educator; b. Flagstaff, Ariz., Feb. 22, 1948; s. John J. and Norma Lee (Morrison) G.; B.S. in Edn., cum laude, U. Mo., 1970; Ed.M., U. Mo., 1972; postgrad. U. South Fla., 1979—; m. Barbara Sue Redburn, Jan. 24, 1970; children—Scott, Timothy. Instr. music Evangel Coll., Springfield, Mo., 1972-73, Central Mo. State U., Warrensburg, 1973-75; asst. prof., chmn. dept. music Southeastern Coll., Lakeland, Fla., 1975—, also supr. music interns; guest clinician S.W. Mo. Mass Band Festival, 1973; bassoonist Central Mo. State U. Faculty Woodwind Quintet, 1973-75; minister of music Skyview Assembly of God Ch., Lakeland, 1975—, mem. bd. deacons. Mem. Phi Mu Alpha Sinfonia, Phi Eta Sigma, Sigma Rho Sigma, Pi Kappa Lambda. Mem. Assembly of God Ch. Home: 4927 Gachet Blvd Lakeland FL 33803 Office: 1000 Longfellow Blvd Lakeland FL 33801

GOODWIN, NANCY ANN, counselor, educator, coach; b. Pasadena, Tex., Jan. 24, 1949; d. Newton White and Julia Henrietta (Roberts) G.; B.S. in Edn., SW Tex. State U., 1971; M.Ed., Our Lady of Lake, 1977. Tchr. girls' phys. edn. O. Henry Jr. High Sch., Schertz, Tex., 1971-72; tchr. girls' phys. edn., health, sociology, psychology, tennis coach, swimming sponsor, John Marshall High Sch., San Antonio, 1972—, chmn. phys. edn. and health depts., 1974-78, swimming sponsor, 1974-78, Pep Squad sponsor, 1973-74, tennis coach, 1972-73; instr., women's varsity volleyball coach Our Lady of Lake U., 1978—; elementary phys. edn. specialist Colonies North Elem. Sch., Locke Hill Elem. Sch., 1978-80. Winner Intramural, intermediate Fencing Champion, S.W. Tex. State U., 1969-70; named outstanding sr. mem. Sigma Kappa sorority, 1970-71. Mem. Am. Personnel and Guidance Assn., S. Tex. Personnel and Guidance Assn., Am. Fedn. Tchrs., Tex. Assn. Health, Phys. Edn. and Recreation, Sigma Kappa, Phi Epsilon Mu, AAHPER, Tex. Interscholastic Swimming Coaches Assn. Researcher in field. Home: 629 Westwood Dr San Antonio TX 78212

GOODWIN, RAY ALLEN, lawyer; b. Paragould, Ark., Feb. 12, 1938; s. Ray Howard and Helen Louise (Griffin) G.; B.A., Hendrix Coll., 1962; J.D., So. Methodist U., 1965; student U. South, 1957-59; m. Kay Evelyn Monk, May 26, 1963; children—Mark Allen, James Allen. Admitted to Ark. bar, 1965, since practiced in Paragould; asso. firm Kirsch, Cathey & Brown, 1965-68; partner firm Cathey, Goodwin & Hamilton, 1968—. Mem. Greene County Library Bd., 1966-75, chmn., 1970-75; mem. N.E. Ark. Regional Library Bd., 1966-75, chmn., 1970-75; mem. Greene County Law Library Bd., 1973—, chmn., 1973—; mem. Ark. Library Commn., 1976—. Served with AUS, 1956. Baker scholar, 1956-57. Mem. Am., Ark. (various coms.), NE Ark., Greene County (pres. 1973-74), Greene-Clay County (sec. 1967-69) bar assns., Paragould Area C. of C., Barristers, Blue Key, Alpha Tau Omega, Delta Beta Phi, Alumni Assn. Hendrix Coll. (gov. 1973-76). Methodist (adminstrv. bd. 1967-71, 75—). Rotarian. (sec. Paragould 1970-73, v.p. 1974, pres. 1975). Home: PO Box 427 Paragould AR 72450 Office: 206 W Emerson St Paragould AR 72450

GOODWIN, SELMA (SUNNY) RABINOVITZ, audiologist, speech pathologist; b. N.Y.C., May 21, 1936; d. Ephraim and Ruth (Blumstein) Rabinovitz; B.A., Queens Coll., N.Y.C., 1956; postgrad. Bklyn. Coll., 1956-59; m. David Goodwin, Mar. 27, 1960; 1 son, Ari Ephraim. Pvt. practice speech pathology and audiology, Miami Beach, Fla., 1960—; chief speech pathologist Nat. Parkinson Inst., Miami, 1969-77; cons. VA Med. Center, Miami, 1977—. Cert. Porch Index of Communicative Ability examiner. Mem. Am. Speech and Hearing Assn. (cert. clin. competency), Fla. Speech and Hearing Assn., Miami Assn. Communication Scis. Jewish. Home and office: 721 86th St Miami Beach FL 33141

GOOLDY, WILLIAM HALL, speech pathologist; b. Blackwell, Okla., Mar. 23, 1933; s. Joseph Robert and Jennie Ruth (Sullivan) G.; B.A., U. Tulsa, 1955, M.T.A., 1967; m. Frances Joan Aringdale, Feb. 17, 1952; 1 son, Robin. Speech pathologist Tulsa public schs., 1957-63; supr. speech pathologists, 1963-78, speech pathologist, 1978—; pvt. practice speech pathology, Tulsa, 1978—. Mem. Am. Speech and Hearing Assn. Democrat. Methodist. Home and office: 2301 E 4th St Tulsa OK 74104

GOOLSBEE, JOHN WALTER, army officer; b. Camp Pickett, Va., Mar. 22, 1954; s. Daniel Shephard and Marian Ruth (Jones) G.; B.B.A., Ga. State U., 1978; A.A., Clayton Jr. Coll., 1975; m. Renee Jean Tucker, Mar. 30, 1979. Control clk. S. Fulton Hosp., East Point, Ga., 1973-78; commd. 2d lt. U.S. Army, 1978; health materiel officer, storage officer 36th Med. Co., Ft. Bragg, N.C., 1978—. Mem. Am. Hosp. Assn., Res. Officers Assn. U.S., Assn. U.S. Army, Pershing Rifle Honor Soc. Baptist. Home: 40 Nijmegen Fort Bragg NC 28307 Office: 44th Medical Bde 36th Medical Co CER Fort Bragg NC 28307

GOORLEY, JOHN THEODORE, educator; b. Galion, Ohio, Mar. 12, 1907; s. William H. and Emma (Ness) G.; B.S., Ohio State U., 1930; M.S., Purdue U., 1932, Ph.D., 1934; m. Ethel L. Coleman, Nov. 27, 1935; children—John, Alice (Mrs. Harold A. Breard, Jr.), Robert, Richard. Chief control chemist Burroughs Wellcome & Co., Tuckahoe, N.Y., 1933-38; research dir. Labs. Lex, Havana, Cuba, 1939-42, Ben Venue Labs., Bedford, Ohio, 1946-48, Johnson & Johnson de Argentina, Buenos Aires, 1948-50; owner, dir. Labs. Goorley, Buenos Aires, 1950-55; prof. pharm. chemistry Ohio No. U., Ada, 1956-57; v.p., gen. mgr. Inland Alkaloid Co., Tipton, Ind., 1957-58; prof. pharm. chemistry N.E. La. U., Monroe, 1958-68, prof. pharmacognosy, 1968-72; chemist Laboratorios Finlay, S.A., San Pedro Sula, Honduras, 1974-76; prof. chemistry and pharmacy U. Nacional Autonoma de Honduras, Tegucigalpa, 1976. Fulbright prof. U. Honduras, 1966-67, cons., 1967—; vis. prof. U. El Salvador, 1968; cons. pharm. industries. Active Little Theater, Monroe. Served to capt. AUS, 1942-46. Col. staff govs. Ky., La. Mem. Am. Pharm. Assn., Am. Chem. Soc., AAAS, Sigma Xi, Rho Chi, Phi Delta Chi, Tau Kappa Epsilon. Research in pharm. chemistry and biochemistry. Contbr. articles to profl. jours. Patentee in field. Home: 117 Avant Rd West Monroe LA 71291

GOPLEN, DONNELLE, counselor; b. Loco, Okla., Nov. 5, 1936; d. Allen R. and Dorothy R. (Carmichael) Bean; B.A. with honors, U. N.Mex., 1974, M.A., 1977; m. Bruce C. Goplen, Sept. 26, 1969; children—Stephen Harvey, Donald Harvey. State welfare worker State Welfare Agy., N.Mex., 1975-77; counseling intern Presbyn. Hosp., Albuquerque, 1977; social worker State of N.Mex., 1977-78; vol. mental health aide Prince William County (Va.) Community Mental Health Center, 1978-79, coordinator Social Activity Center, 1979—, also mental health counselor, cons. Mem. Am. Personnel and Guidance Assn., AAUW. Home: 18414 Cedar Dr Triangle VA 22172 Office: Prince William Mental Health Center 8807 Sudley Dr Manassas VA 22110

GORAKHPURWALLA, HOMI DHUNJISHAW, elec. engr., educator; b. Hyderabad, India, Aug. 5, 1937; came to U.S., 1957, naturalized, 1971; s. Dhunjishaw H. and Katy D. (Dinshaw) G.; B.S. with honors, Bombay U. (India), 1957; B.S. in Elec. Engring., Purdue U., 1957, M.S., 1961; m. Anita M. Fuegener, Dec. 2, 1963; children—Catherine Anita, Ashley Homi. Instr. elec. engring. Purdue U., 1959-61, U. Toronto (Ont., Can.), 1961-66; asst. prof. elec. engring. S.D. State U., 1966-69; engr. DorRan Electronics, Sioux Falls, S.D., 1969-70; asso. prof. elec. engring. Tex. A&I U., Kingsville, 1970—, chmn. dept. elec. engring., 1977-79, dir. Task Force on Sci. Edn., 1975-76; cons. to TRW, Inc., 1970-71, Entonic, Inc., 1977-79; proposal reviewer NSF edn. programs, 1977-79. U.S. Dept. Agr. grantee, 1971-76; NSF grantee, 1974-77, research fellow, 1979; registered profl. engr., Tex. Mem. IEEE (chmn. Corpus Christi sect. 1979), Am. Soc. Engring. Edn., Internat. Microwave Power Inst., India Students Assn., Sigma Xi, Tau Beta Pi, Eta Kappa Nu. Zorastrian. Club: Kiwanis. Contbr. articles on microwave applications to elec. engring.; patentee in field. Home: 2112 Colorado Ave Kingsville TX 78363 Office: Dept Electrical Engring Texas A&I Univ Kingsville TX 78363

GORBET, BARBARA WHITEHEAD, neurol. clinic ofcl.; b. Refugio County, Tex., Sept. 28, 1931; d. Victor Clyde and Mary Lois (Brownson) Whitehead; student Tex. A&I U., 1948-49, Trinity U., 1949-50; m. Zac Gorbet, Jr., Dec. 4, 1958 (dec.); children—Kelly Kathryn, Zac III. Office mgr. Thomas Spann Clinic and Hosp., Corpus Christi, Tex., 1951-70; C.P.A. asst. J.R. Gibson, Inc., 1971-73; office mgr. Driscoll Found. Children's Hosp., Corpus Christi, 1973-79, The Neurol. Clinic, Corpus Christi, 1979—; owner, mgr. Med. Collection Services; mem. adv. bd. Upjohn Health Care, Inc. Mem. Am. Soc. Profl. and Exec. Women, Am. Mgmt. Assn., Am. Bus. and Profl. Women's Assn. Presbyterian. Club: Pilot Internat. Home: 4249 Sierra St Corpus Christi TX 78410 Office: 1224 3d St Corpus Christi TX 78404

GORDON, BRUCE ALLEN, retail clothing exec.; b. Savannah, Ga., Mar. 16, 1951; s. Robert Leon and Rosalyn (Weiser) G.; B.B.A. in Mgmt. and Mktg., Armstrong State Coll., 1975. Clk., S. & G. Men's Shop, Savannah, Ga., 1965-66; asst. mgr. King and Prince Men's Shop, Savannah, 1966-67; mgr. Bruce Gordon Ltd., Savannah, 1969-73; co-owner Bruce Gordon's, Savannah, 1973-74, owner, 1974—; pres. Gorlev, Inc., Savannah, 1973—. Mem. Young Leadership Group, Savannah Jewish Council; active Better Bus. Bur., Jewish Ednl. Alliance. Mem. Victory Dr. Shopping Plaza Mchts. Assn. (pres. 1975—), Savannah Area C. of C. Democrat. Jewish. Club: Jewish Ednl. Alliance Men's. Home: 1113 E 51st St Savannah GA 31404 Office: 2113-2115 E Victory Dr Savannah GA 31404

GORDON, CATHERINE ANN, constrn. and ins. agy. exec.; b. Jacksonville, Fla., Jan. 16, 1953; d. Robert E. and Annette (Willcox) G.; A.A., Fla. Jr. Coll. Vice pres., partner Gordon Constrn. Co., Inc., Jacksonville; owner, pres. Agri Bus. Ins. Agy., Jacksonville; ind. ins. agt., 1976. Mem. Am. Bus. Women's Assn., Am. Soc. Profl. and Exec. Women, Ga. Forestry Assn., Fla. Forestry Assn., Beta Sigma Phi. Baptist. Home and Office: 17901 Lem Turner Rd Jacksonville FL 32218

GORDON, CRAIG STEPHEN, gastroenterologist; b. Nashville, July 4, 1948; s. Joseph and Juanita Gordon; B.A., Fisk U., 1970; M.D., Boston U., 1974; m. Patricia Denise Irvin, Aug. 22, 1973. Intern, Wilmington (Del.) Med. Center, 1974-77, resident in internal medicine, 1975-77; fellow in gastroenterology Baylor Coll. Medicine, Houston, 1977-79; practice medicine specializing in gastroenterology, Houston, 1979—; mem. clin. faculty Baylor Coll. Medicine, 1979—; clin. instr. St. Joseph Hosp., 1979—; mem. sci. adv. bd. Nat. Found. Ileitis and Colitis, Inc. Mem. Am. Gastroent. Assn., Am. Soc. Gastrointestinal Endoscopy, AMA, A.C.P., Tex. Soc. Gastrointestinal Endoscopy, Harris County Med. Soc. Episcopalian. Office: 2101 Crawford St Suite 203 Houston TX 77002

GORDON, DAVID NEIL, audio-visual equipment co. exec.; b. Bronx, N.Y., Dec. 28, 1947; s. Julius and Rose (Brodkin) G.; A.B., Bucknell U., 1969; m. Leslie Joyce Kayftez, Feb. 5, 1971; children—Nina Ruth, Daniel Isaac. Tchr. public schs., Howard County, Md., 1969-73; account exec. Wometoc Film Labs., Miami, Fla., 1973-77, southeast sales mgr., Atlanta, 1977-79; southeastern regional sales mgr. Fairchild Indsl. Products div. Fairchild Camera and Instrument Corp., Atlanta, 1979—. Bd. dirs. Nat. Jr. Tennis League, Miami, 1972-73. Mem. Soc. Motion Picture and TV Engrs. Home: 3573 Vanet Rd Chamblee GA 30341 Office: Fairchild Indsl Products Div 3 Dunwoody Park Suite 103 Atlanta GA 30338

GORDON, EDWIN FREDERICK ROBERT, metal fabricating co. exec.; b. Oak Park, Ill., Jan. 4, 1921; s. Edwin C. and Alice (Heller) G.; B.S., Concordia Coll., 1942; M.A., Northwestern U., 1945; Ph.D., Purdue U., 1951; children—Dawn Alice, Denise Ann, E. Robert F., Allen D., Roger M., James Adams, John Robin, Jana Amanda. Chmn. bd. dirs. Geuder Paeschke & Frey Co. metal fabricating Milw. 1955—; dir. Gordon-Hoover & Assos. Inc., mgmt. cons., Chgo., Capital Investments Inc., Milw.; chmn. bd. dirs. Boyer-Rosene Moving & Storage Co., Inc., Arlington Hts., Ill., Gordon Studios, Inc., Hillsboro Beach, Fla.; pres. Hillsboro Land Mark Inc., Hillsboro Beach, Fla. Mem. Am. Psychol. Assn., Sigma Xi. Home: 1021 Hillsboro Mile Hillsboro Beach FL 33062 Office: 324 N 15th St Milwaukee WI 53201

GORDON, EUGENE ANDREW, dist. judge; b. Guilford County, N.C., July 10, 1917; s. Charles Robert and Carrie (Scott) G.; A.B., Elon Coll., 1938; LL.B., Duke, 1941; m. Virginia Stoner, Jan. 1, 1943; children—Eugene Andrew, Rosemary Anne. Admitted to N.C. bar, 1941; practice of law, 1946-64; mem. firm Young, Young & Gordon, Burlington, 1947-64; solicitor Alamance Gen. County Ct., 1947-54; county atty., Alamance County, 1954-64; U.S. judge Middle Dist. N.C., 1964—, chief judge, 1972—; mem. U.S. Adv. Com. on Criminal Rules; instr. U.S. Attys. Gen.'s Sch. for New Asst. U.S. Attys. Past chmn. adv. bd. Salvation Army. Past nat. committeeman N.C. Young Democrats; past pres. Alamance County Young Dems.; chmn. Alamance County Dem. Exec. Com., 1954-64. Served to capt. AUS, 1942-46; comdg. officer N.G., Burlington, 1946-47. Mem. Alamance County Bar Assn. (past pres.), Burlington-Alamance County C. of C. (past pres.), Assn. U.S. Dist. Judges (pres. 4th jud. circuit), Phi Delta Phi. Rotarian (past pres.). Club: American Business (Burlington). Home: PO Box 3285 Greensboro NC 27402 Office: Greensboro NC 27402

GORDON, HELMUT ALBERT, med. researcher and educator; b. Malinska, Austria, May 5, 1908; s. Albert John and Cornelia Leopoldina (de Adamich) Gordon-Koniges; came to U.S., 1946, naturalized, 1951; student medicine U. Rome, U. Budapest; M.D.; degree habilitation, U. Budapest, 1944; m. Irene Julianna Rontskevits, Nov. 28, 1942; children—Iretta Celta Gordon Micskey, Brent Helmut. Practicant, asst. prof. Dept. Physiology, U. Budapest, 1932-40, asso. prof., 1940-44; asso. prof. Lobund Labs., U. Notre Dame (Ind.), 1946-62; prof. pharmacology U. Ky., Lexington, 1962—, now emeritus; pres. Acad. Cons., Inc., Lexington, 1979—. Mem. Niles (Mich.) Twp. sch. bd., 1957-60. Served to capt., M.C., Royal Hungarian Air Force, 1934-44. Recipient Cressy-Morrison award, N.Y. Acad. Sci., 1969; Faculty award in biomed. scis., U. Ky., 1970. Rockefeller Research fellow, 1937; Eszterhazy fellow, 1938. Fellow Gerontologic Soc., N.Y. Acad. Sci.; mem. Am. Physiologic Soc., Assn. for Gnotobiotics (pres. 1973-74). Lutheran. Contbr. numerous articles to profl. jours. Home: Morning Glory Farm Route 10 Grimes Mill Rd Lexington KY 40511

GORDON, JERRY CLAY, telephone network exec.; b. Marion, N.C., Apr. 4, 1941; s. Joel Edwin and Virginia Belle (Sprouse) G.; A.A. in Bus. Admnstrn., Blanton Coll., 1977; m. Linda Jane Rice, July 13, 1963; children—Kenneth Scott, Mark Edwin. Asst. accountant P.B. Ward Accountants, Marion, 1965-66; asst. mgr. B.C. Moore & Sons, Inc., Marion, 1966-67; office mgr. Suburban Propane Gas Co., Marion, 1967-68; central office foreman Western Carolina Telephone Co., Weaverville, N.C., 1968-73, central offices supr., 1973-77, network sers. supr., 1977-79, network sers. supt., 1979—. External v.p. Weaverville Jaycees, 1976-77, pres., 1977-78; bd. dirs. North Buncombe Fire Dept., 1978-81, sec., 1979-80. Served with U.S. Army, 1959-62. Mem. Communications Workers Am. (pres. 1965), WWTC Credit Union (chmn. supervisory com. 1975), Contel. N.C. Ind. Telephone Pioneer Assn. (charter pres. 1979-80). Democrat. Baptist. Clubs: Masons, N.C. State Firemen. Home: 29 Wildwood Park Weaverville NC 28787 Office: 15 S Main St Weaverville NC 28787

GORDON, M. MICHAEL, judge; b. San Francisco, Dec. 21, 1911; s. Rudolph and Sarah (Mesinger) G.; B.A., St. Ignatius Coll., 1931; LL.B., U. San Francisco, 1935. Admitted to Tex. bar, 1935, since practiced in Houston; now mem. firm M. Michael Gordon; judge Houston Municipal Ct., 1962—; dir., gen. counsel Sterling Electronics, Inc., Houston. Founder, Teenage Jury System, 1964, judge, 1964—. Pres. Juvenile Delinquency and Crime Commn., Houston 1958-59. Mem. bd. Houston Bd. Pub. Welfare, 1948-56; Bd. dirs. Am. Acad. Jud. Edn., 1970—, Nat. Center for State Cts., 1971—. Served to capt., USAAF, 1942-46. Recipient Disneyland trophy for achievement in reducing juvenile delinquency in U.S. and Can., Nat. Assn. Municipal Judges, 1965. Mem. Am. Judges Assn. (gov. 1965—, treas. 1965-66, pres. 1969-70, award merit 1976), Am., Houston bar assns., State Bar Tex. Am. Judicature Soc. (dir. 1969-70, Centennial jud. award 1972), Am. Acad. Jud. Edn. (pres. 1972-74) Mason (Shriner). Home: 2014 Southgate Houston TX 77025 Office: 5017 Fannin St Houston TX 77004

GORDON, MELVIN TRUSSELL, JR., apparel mfg. co. exec.; b. Atlanta, Feb. 24, 1943; s. Melvin Trussell and Lettie Lenora (Houseworth) G.; E.E., Ga. Inst. Tech., 1963; B.B.A. in Mgmt., Ga. State U., Atlanta, 1967; m. Camille Elizabeth Henderson, Aug. 27, 1966; children—Michael Dennis, Nicole Renee. Adminstrv. staff mdse. specialist Rich's, Inc., Atlanta, 1966-67; adminstrv. mgr., zone sales support Dover Elevator Co., Atlanta, 1967-69; bus. systems analyst Blue Bell, Inc., Greensboro, N.C., 1969-70, adminstrv. services mgr., 1970-73, dir. micrographics systems/services and spl. projects, 1973-79, mgr. data processing adminstrv. support, micrographics systems/ops., 1980—. Mem. Nat. Micrographics Assn. (co-founder chpt., treas. 1977-79, dir. newsletter 1980—), Am. Mgmt. Assn., Internat. Diamond Distbrs. Assn., Am. Entrepreneurs Assn. Republican. Episcopalian. Patentee in pet product field. Home: 5107 Amberhill Dr Greensboro NC 27405 Office: PO Box 21488 Greensboro NC 27420

GORDON, RICHARD EDWARDS, psychiatrist; b. N.Y.C., July 15, 1922; s. Richard and Virginia (Ryan) G.; B.S., Yale, 1943; M.D., U. Mich., 1945; M.A., Columbia U., 1956, Ph.D., 1961; m. Katherine Lowman Kline, Nov. 12, 1949; children—Richard Edwards, Katherine Lowman (Mrs. Stanley F. Reed), Virginia Lamborn, Laurie Lloyd. Intern City Hosp., N.Y.C., 1945-46; resident neurology N.Y. Postgrad. Hosp., N.Y.C., 1946-47; resident in psychiatry N.Y. Psychiat. Inst., N.Y.C., 1947-48, Manhattan (N.Y.) State Hosp., 1948-49; fellow in psychosomatic medicine and child psychiatry Mt. Sinai Hosp., N.Y.C., 1949-51; practice medicine specializing in psychiatry, N.Y.C., 1950-51, Englewood, N.J., 1953-67; mem. staffs Univ. Settlement House, 1950-51, Englewood Hosp., 1953-67, Shands Teaching Hosp., Gainesville, Fla., 1967—, Gainesville VA Hosp., 1967—; sr. research psychiatrist, EEG cons. Rockland State Hosp., Orangeburg, N.Y., 1953-54; founder Englewood Hosp. EEG Clinic, 1953, also dir.; dir. research unit Englewood Hosp., 1954-60; prof. psychology, cons. psychiatrist Wagner Coll., S.I., N.Y., 1960-67; asso. prof. psychiatry, psychology, research dir. multiphasic health testing center U. Fla., Gainesville, 1967—; dir. Fla. Mental Health Inst., Tampa, 1975-79; adj. prof. clin. psychology U.S. Fla., Tampa, 1977—. Founder Mental Health Consultation Center, Hackensack, N.Y., 1956, trustee, 1956-57; founder Community Multiphasic Health Testing Center, Gainesville. Mem. N.J. Mental Health Commn., 1957-61; pres. Kirkwood Environ. Improvement Assn., Gainesville, 1970-75. Served to capt., AUS, 1943-45, 51-53. Grantee in field. Diplomate Am. Bd. Psychiatry and Neurology. Fellow Am. Psychiat. Assn. (life), Soc. Advanced Med. Systems; mem. AAAS, Fla. Psychiat. Soc. (pres.), Sigma Xi. Rotarian. Clubs: Yale of N.Y.C.; Yale of Gainesville. Author: Prevention of Postpartum Emotional Difficulties, 1961; (with K. K. Gordon, M. Gunther) The Split-Level Trap, 1961; (with K. K. Gordon) The Blight on the Ivy, 1963, Closing the Gaps: Integrating Systems of Treatment for the Chronically Ill Mental Patient, 1980; (with B. Franklin et al) Towards Better Mental Health in New Jersey, 1961. Contbr. numerous articles to profl. jours. Home: 4431 Vieux Carre Circle Lutz FL 33549 Office: 1625 SW 6th Terr Gainesville FL 32601

GORDON, ROBERT JAY, communications co. exec.; b. Bklyn., Jan. 30, 1942; s. Irving and Stella (Cohen) G.; m. Elizabeth Peter, Aug. 27, 1978; children—Mark, Bruce, Lori, Carre. Account exec. Sta. WGBB, Merrick, N.Y., 1967-69; account exec. retail devel. Sta. WCBS, N.Y.C., 1969-71; account exec., coordinator coop. advt. Sta. WCBS-TV, N.Y.C., 1971-74; pres. Louisville (Ky.) Prodns., aduiovisuals, 1975—. Jewish. Home: 7502 Shelbyville Rd Louisville KY 40222 Office: Louisville Prodns 520 Chestnut St Louisville KY 40201

GORDON, ROBERT MURRAYE, elec. engr.; b. Corpus Christi, Tex., Jan. 24, 1947; s. Robert Carter and Alice LaBelle (Weeks) G.; B.S. in Elec. Engring., Lamar U., 1970; postgrad. in Indsl. Engring. U. Houston, 1975-76; m. Judith Sue Rogers, June 5, 1970; 1 dau., Kathryn Frances. Jr. engr. Houston Lighting & Power Co., 1970-72, instrument controls engr., 1972-73, engr. power plant engring. and tech. services, 1973-74, sr. engr., 1974-75, supervising engr., 1975—. Registered profl. engr., Tex. Mem. IEEE, Tex., Nat. socs. profl. engrs., ASME, Am. Inst. Indsl. Engrs., Lambda Chi Alpha. Baptist. Home: 11443 Sagevale Houston TX 77089 Office: PO Box 1700 Houston TX 77001

GORDON, RUDOLPH GILES, sch. adminstr.; b. Kingstree, S.C., Oct. 21, 1937; s. Robert L. and Ruth R. (Cooper) G.; B.S., Benedict Coll., 1959; M.S., S.C. State U., 1972; postgrad. U. S.C., 1979—; m. Corine S. Gordon, June 15, 1960; children—Rudolph Giles, Melanie C. Tchr. math. Bryson High Sch., Fountain Inn, S.C., 1959-68, asst. prin., 1968-70; dean student affairs Williamsburg Tech. Edn. Center, Kingstree, 1970-71; asst. prin. S.L. Mann High Sch., Greenville, S.C., 1971-72, prin., 1973-77; prin. Beck Middle Sch., Greenville, 1972-73; S.W. area asst. supt. Sch. Dist. of Greenville County, 1977—. Pres. bd. dirs. Big Bros., 1975-79; mem. commn. Greenville County Mus. Art, 1979—; mem. United Speech and Hearing Bd., Greenville, 1976-79. Served with U.S. Army, 1957-58. NSF grantee, Duke U., 1964, Clemson U., 1968. Mem. Am. Assn. Sch. Adminstrs., Nat. Assn. Secondary Sch. Prins., Assn. Supervision and Curriculum Devel., Alpha Phi Alpha. Methodist. Club: Rotary (bd. dirs. 1977-79). Home: PO Box 607 Fountain Inn SC 29644 Office: 37 Tindal Ave Greenville SC 29605

GORDON, THOMAS EDWIN, JR., dentist; b. Orlando, Fla., Sept. 12, 1925; s. Thomas Edwin and Lillian (Stover) G.; D.D.S., Emory U., 1948; m. Jeanne Love, Nov. 19, 1949; children—Tina Lynne, Thomas Gary, Karen Anne. Pvt. practice dentistry Decatur, Ga., 1948-50, Orlando, Fla., 1951-53, 55—; cons. dentistry in space; attending staff Orange Meml. Hosp., chief laser lab.; mem. Gordon Conf. on Lasers in Medicine and Biology. Bd. dirs. Orange County unit Am. Cancer Soc; trustee Central Fla. Mus. and Planetarium, sec. bd. trustees, 1960-61, chmn. finance com., 1963-72. Served from 1st lt. to capt. USAF, 1953-55. Fellow Royal Soc. Health; mem. Internat. Assn. Dental Research, ADA, Fla. Dental Assn., Orange County Dental Assn., Internat. Assn. for Orthodontics, Acad. Gen. Dentistry, AAAS, Am. Assn. Gnathological Orthopedics, Fed. Prosthodontic Orgn., Am. Equilibration Soc., Soc. Oral Physiology, Am. Practicing Physicians Assn., Am. Acad. Functional Prosthodontics, Am. Acad. Maxillofacial Prosthesis, Orlando C. of C. (chmn. criminal justice com. 1980—), Sigma Chi. Contbr. articles to profl. jours. Research laser in dentistry and med. research; developer 1st laser welding system and technique for dentistry. Home: 1410 N Westmoreland Dr Orlando FL 32804 Office: 550 N Bumby Av Orlando FL 32803

GORDON, VIVIAN VERDELL, sociologist; B.S. in Physics and Gen. Social Scis., Va. State Coll., Petersburg, 1955; M.A. in Sociology, U. Pa., 1957; Ph.D., U. Va., 1974; married; 2 children. Social worker Women's Christian Alliance Child Welfare Agy., Phila., 1956-57; research asst. edn. and pub. welfare div., legis. reference service Library of Congress, 1957, edn. and social sci. analyst, 1957-63; coordinator research spl. study com. edn. and labor U.S. Ho. of Reps., 1963; asst. dir. Upward Bound project U. Calif., Los Angeles, 1966-67; dir. ednl. participation in communities program Calif. State Coll., Los Angeles, 1967-69; mem. faculty U. Va., 1971—, asso. prof. sociology, 1974-80, chmn. dept. Afro-Am. and African studies, 1975-79. Chmn. adv. bd. Area Community Action Program; advisory bd. So. Regional Council, Task Force Abused Women. Mem. Am. Sociol. Assn., So. Sociol. Soc. Author papers, book in field. Address: RFD 2 Box 229 Crozet VA 22932

GORDON, WILLIAM BRICE, banker; b. Lyons, Kans., Feb. 22, 1941; s. William Houston and Helen Jane (Mathews) G.; B.S. in Bus. Adminstrn., U. Kans., 1963, M.P.A., 1973; m. Patricia Jane Ross, Sept. 1, 1963; children—William Ross, Travis Houston. Budget analyst City of Ft. Worth, 1964-67, asst. city mgr., 1970-74, budget dir., 1974-77; v.p. Continental Nat. Bank, Ft. Worth, 1977—; instr. Tex. Christian U., 1973-77. Served as capt. M.S.C., U.S. Army, 1967-70. Decorated Bronze Star, Army Commendation Medal; named Outstanding Young Man, Ft. Worth, 1976. Presbyterian. Club: Ft. Worth Kiwanis (sec., v.p., dir.). Author: Budget Manual for Texas Cities, 1972. Home: 5201 Winifred St Fort Worth TX 76133 Office: Continental National Bank PO Box 910 Fort Worth TX 76101

GORE, ALBERT, JR., Congressman; b. Mar. 31, 1948; s. Albert and Pauline (Lafon) G.; B.A. cum laude, Harvard U., 1969; postgrad. Vanderbilt Sch. Religion, 1971-72, Vanderbilt Sch. Law, 1974-76; m. Mary Elizabeth Aitcheson, 1970; children—Karenna, Kristin, Sarah. Investigative reporter, editorial writer The Tennessean, Nashville, 1971-76; home builder, Carthage, Tenn., 1971-76; owner livestock farm, Carthage, 1973—; mem. 95th to 96th Congresses, from 4th Tenn. Dist. Served with U.S. Army, 1969-71; Vietnam. Mem. Smith County Jaycees, Am. Legion, VFW, Farm Bur. Democrat. Baptist. Office: 1417 Longworth House Office Bldg Washington DC 20515

GORE, CHARLES MINOR, lawyer; b. Johnson City, Tenn., Oct. 26, 1910; s. Benjamin Stone and Helen (Hayward) G.; A.B., Vanderbilt U., 1933; postgrad. Harvard Law Sch., 1933-34; LL.B., U. Tenn., 1936; m. Mildred Anne Smith, June 20, 1937; children—Charles Smith, Anne Hayward. Admitted to Tenn. bar, 1936; mem. firm Gore & Gore, Bristol, Tenn., 1937-54, 63-65, Gore, Gore & McIntyre, Bristol, 1954-63, Gore, Gore and Ladd, Bristol, 1965-68, Gore, Ladd and Gillenwater, Bristol, 1968-75, Gore, Ladd, Gillenwater & Hillman, 1976-77, Gore, Gillen water and Hillman, 1977-78, Gore and Hillman, 1978—; spl. justice Supreme Ct. Tenn., 1976; sec., dir. Appalachian Broadcasting Corp., WCYB-TV, 1946-74, dir., asst. sec., 1977—; sec., dir. Strong-Robinette Bag Co., Inc., 1953—; dir., mem. exec. com. Gen. Shale Products Corp., Johnson City. Mem. Tenn. Democratic exec. com., 1970-74. Bd. dirs. United Fund., 1957-59. Served from lt. (j.g.) to lt., USNR, 1943-46. Mem. Am., Tenn., Bristol bar assns., Jud. Conf. Sixth Circuit (life). Presbyterian. Democrat. Home: 101 Lick Branch Rd Bristol TN 37620 Office: Central Bldg Bristol TN 37620

GORE, DANIEL RAYMOND, mgmt. cons.; b. Phila., Nov. 23, 1945; s. Allen Moore and Marie Elizabeth (Eissler) G.; A.A., Kings Coll., 1967; B.B.A., Oglethorpe U., 1975. Treas., Kale Ruling & Binding, 1967-70; plant acct. Rexham Corp., Charlotte, N.C., 1970-73; controller Meisel Photochrome, Atlanta, 1973-76, Ruralist Press, Atlanta, 1976-79; mgmt. cons. Waters/Trego, Dallas, 1979—; speaker. Active Big Brother Assn. Atlanta, 1975-79. Methodist. Home: 6060 Village Bend 19 Dallas TX 75206 Office: 3117 Routh St Dallas TX 75201

GORE, JOHN HOWARD, health edn. adminstr.; b. Cin., June 30, 1944; s. Howard and Bessie Irene G.; B.A., Marshall U., Huntington, W.Va., 1972, M.A., 1974; m. Carolyn Sue Whetsell, Oct. 22, 1963; 1 dau., Kristy Sue. Alcohol treatment specialist Lansdowne Mental Health Center, Ashland, Ky., 1974-76; clinic dir. Adams County Mental Health Clinic, West Union, Ohio, 1976-77; clin. dir. Elkhorn Mental Health Clinic, Welch, W.Va., 1977-79; dir. McDowell County Health Edn. Program, Gary, W.Va., 1979—; asso. prof. psychology Bluefield State Coll., Welch. Mem. McDowell County Health Action Council. Served with USAF, 1963-67. Recipient letter of commendation Asst. Surgeon Gen. U.S., 1979. Mem. Am. Coll. Personnel Assn., Am. Rehab. Counseling Assn., Am. Personnel and Guidance Assn. Home and Office: PO Box 760 Gary WV 24836

GORE, THOMAS PRYOR, II, med. found. exec.; b. Washington, Nov. 5, 1937; s. Thomas Notley and Mary Elisabeth (Alexander) G.; B.A., The Citadel, 1960; m. Marta Guadelupe Fiallos, Nov. 19, 1976; 1 son, Robert Houston. Dir. public info. United Appeal, Balt., 1964-66; dir. public relations Union Meml. Hosp., Balt., 1966-70; dir. public affairs Md. Hosp. Assn., Balt., 1970-75; v.p. public affairs Alton Ochsner Med. Found., New Orleans, 1975—; cons. in field. Chmn. Greater Balt. Citizens for Clean Air, 1971; pres. Forum Four Democratic Club, Baltimore County, Md., 1969. Served with USAF, 1960-63. Mem. Am. Soc. Hosp. Public Relations, Public Relations Soc. Am., Am. Hosp. Assn., Assn. Am. Med. Colls., Heart Assn. La., Assn. Health Care Communicators. Roman Catholic. Club: New Orleans Press. Home: 9533 Arbor Ln River Ridge LA 70123 Office: 1516 Jefferson Hwy New Orleans LA 70121

GOREN, SHEILA ABBIE, librarian; b. Bklyn., June 24, 1951; d. William and Margaret (Gluck) Glotzer; B.S. in Psychology, Bklyn. Coll., 1972; M.L.S., Pratt Inst., Bklyn., 1973; m. Ira Barry Goren, June 14, 1974; 1 son, Todd Gary. Asst. law librarian firm Proskauer, Rose, Goetz and Mendelsohn, N.Y.C., 1973-75; systems librarian Am. Express Co., Ft. Lauderdale, Fla., 1975—, organized Am. Express Co. Library Consortium, 1980. Mem. Am. Soc. Info. Sci., Spl. Libraries Assn., Broward County Library Assn. Office: 777 American Expy Fort Lauderdale FL 33337

GORGES, HEINZ AUGUST, research engr.; b. Stettin, Germany, July, 22, 1913; s. Gustav and Marga (Benda) G.; M.E., Tech. U. Dresden (Germany), 1938; Ph.D., Tech. U. Hannover, Germany, 1946; m. Sapienza Teresa Coco, Sept. 2, 1957. Came to U.S., 1959. Group leader LFA Aero Research Establishment, Braunschweig, Germany, 1940-45; with Royal Aircraft Establishment, Farnborough, Eng. 1946-49; prin. sci. officer Weapons Research Establishment, Adelaide, South Australia, 1949-59; sci. asst. George C. Marshall Space Flight Center, NASA, Huntsville, Ala., 1959-61; dir. advanced projects Cook Technol Center, Morton Grove, Ill., 1961-62; scientific adviser Ill. Inst. Tech. Research Inst., Chgo., 1962-66; prin. scientist, dir. research Tracor, Inc., Austin, Tex., 1966—, asst. v.p. Environmental and Phys. Scis. div., 1970-72, v.p. Tracor-Jitco, Rockville, Md., 1972-75; pres. Vineta Inc., sci. consultants, 1975—. Prof. Redstone extension U. Ala., 1960. Registered profl. engr., D.C. Fellow Am. Inst. Aeros. and Astronautics (asso.); mem. Am. Geophys. Union, ASME, N.Y. Acad. Scis., Acoustical Soc. Am. Club: Cosmos. Research on thermodynamics, indsl. engring., resource mgmt., system engring. and analysis. Home: 3705 Sleepy Hollow Rd Falls Church VA 22041

GORMAN, CHARLES, coll. pres.; b. Newport, Tenn., July 18, 1917; s. George W. and Queen G.; A.B., Carson-Newman Coll., 1939; m. June Thomason, July 24, 1944; children—Charles Michael, Mary Jane. Prin., basketball coach Mason Hall High Sch., Kenton, Tenn., 1939-42; mgr. Nat. Bus. Coll., Knoxville, Tenn., 1946-49; mgr. Office Tng. Sch., Memphis, 1949-52; pres. Columbia (S.C.) Jr. Coll., 1952—. Served with U.S. Army, 1942-46. Mem. Assn. Ind. Colls. and Schs., Southeastern Bus. Coll. Assn., S.C. Assn. Pvt. Ind. Schs., C. of C. (adminstrv. mgmt. pres. 1964). Club: Rotary (Columbia). Home: 4633 Carter Hill Dr Columbia SC 29206 Office: Columbia Jr Coll 1234 Hampton St Columbia SC 29201

GORR, LOUIS FREDERICK, museum exec.; b. North Platte, Neb., Aug. 1, 1941; s. Ernest Frederick and Bethel Eileen (Green) G.; B.A., U. Neb., Omaha, 1965, M.A., 1967; postgrad. U. Md., 1969-73, U. So. Calif., 1975-76, U. Dallas, 1979; m. Madeleine Zangla, Dec. 8, 1968; 1 dau., Michaela. Lectr. Frince George's Coll., Largo, Md., 1966-67; lectr. U. Md., overseas br., 1967-68, Coll. Park, 1968-73; historian, spl. asst. to dir. Nat. Mus. History and Tech., Washington, 1970-73; dir. museums Fairfax County (Va.) Park Authority, 1973-77; exec. dir. Dallas County Heritage Soc., 1977-79; dir. Dallas Mus. Natural History, cons. Community Museums program Am. Studies Assn., 1974-75; pvt. cons. Mus. Cultural Adminstrn.; mem. security com. Internat. Council Museums; mem. bd. commerce Dallas Nat. Bank. Pres. Fairfax Symphony Orch., 1974-77; mem. exec. com., sec. Prince George's County (Md.) Arts Forum, 1974-75; mem. Fairfax History Adv. Com., 1975-76. Served with USAF, 1963-69. Fellow Smithsonian Instn., 1970-71; grantee Marine Corps Mus., 1972, Naval Inst., 1972. Mem. Tex. (council 1978—, v.p. 1980), Am. (accreditation vis. com. 1976—) assns. museums, Orgn. Am. Historians, Soc. Archtl. Historians, Coll. Art Assn., Am. Mgmt. Assn., Internat. Council Museums, Am. Soc. Pub. Adminstrn., Nat. Recreation and Parks Assn., Assn. Sci. Mus. Dirs., Lambda Chi Alpha. Mason. Editor: Beyond Relevance, 1971; book reviewer Museum News, 1975—. Contbr. articles to profl. jours. Home: 1606 Yale Blvd Richardson TX 75081 Office: Fair Park PO Box 26193 Dallas TX 75226

GORSKI, EDWARD JOSEPH, iron foundry exec.; b. Kansas City, Kans., Feb. 13, 1944; s. Stance C. and Edith Marie (Oberforcher) G.; B.S., U. Kans., 1968. Programmer, Goodyear Tire & Rubber Co., Akron, 1968-72; mgr. data processing Perfect Equipment, Murfreesboro, Tenn., 1972-76; mgr. systems EDP, Cutler Hammer Corp., Cleveland, Tenn., 1976-78; mgr. data processing U.S. Industries Agri-Bus. Co., Atlanta, 1978-79; dir. data processing Columbus (Ga.) Foundries, Inc., 1977—. Served with U.S. Army, 1968-70. Decorated Bronze Star. Lic. pvt. pilot. Mem. Data Processing Mgmt. Assn., Am. Prodn. and Inventory Control Soc., Mensa. Home: 1216 Autumnridge Dr Columbus GA 31904 Office: PO Box 4201 Columbus GA 31904

GORT, JAMES ARTHUR, ins. co. exec.; b. Eau Claire, Wis., Sept. 22, 1928; s. Roy Peter and Mary Margaret (Sugars) G.; B.S., U. Wis., 1950; m. Cordelia Hilfinger, Dec. 28, 1970; children—Michael, Susan, Pamela, Carol, Cynthia, Deirdre. Claims mgr. CNA Ins. Co., Chgo., 1952-68, Fla. Adminstrs. Ins. Co., Miami, 1968-74; v.p. Fla. Gen. Life Ins. Co., Coral Gables, 1974—; mem. ins. rev. com. Dade County Med. Assn. Served with U.S. Army, 1950-52. Mem. Internat. Claims Assn., So. Claims Conf. (chmn. elect), Fla. Claims Assn. (past chmn.). Home: 223 Sidonia Ave Coral Gables FL 33134 Office: Fla Gen Life Ins Co 1550 Madruga St Coral Gables FL 33146

GOSS, KENNETH GEORGE, physician; b. N.Y.C., Dec. 6, 1922; s. Charles Henry and Ruth Colina (Mackenzie) G.; B.A., Alfred U., 1948; M.D., U. Rochester, 1952; m. Dorothy Jean Burdick, Sept. 22, 1946; children—Kenneth Mackenzie, Jeffrey Dean, David Victor, John Charles, Patricia Jean. Intern, Strong Meml. Hosp., Rochester, N.Y., 1952-53; gen. practice medicine, Rochester, 1953-60, New Canaan, Conn., 1963-74; with med. dept. Eaton Labs., Norwich, N.Y., 1960-61; med. dir. Dean L. Burdick Assos., N.Y.C., 1961-63; asso. prof. family practice, chief geriatrics div., med. dir. physician asst. program Med. U. S.C., Charleston, 1974-77; prof. family practice, chmn. dept. family and community medicine U. Ark. for Med. Scis., Little Rock, 1977—. Served with U.S. Army, 1942-45. Diplomate Am. Bd. Family Practice. Fellow Am. Acad. Family Physicians; mem. Soc. Tchrs. Family Medicine, Gerontol. Soc., Am. Geriatric Soc. Home: 1521 Spring St Little Rock AR 72202 Office: 1700 W 13th St Little Rock AR 72202

GOSSETT, DAVID ISAAC, acctg. co. exec.; b. Steubenville, Ohio, Dec. 10, 1946; s. Isaac Watson and Francis Jean (Turrentein) G.; student Ohio U., 1964-66; B.S. in Acctg., Kent State U., 1976; m. Ann L. McMillen, June 10, 1967; children—Christopher David, Nicole Donnelly. Mgr., Steak & Ale Restaurants Am., Houston, 1974; sr. auditor Arthur Andersen & Co., Houston, 1976-78; controller Riviana Foods Inc., Houston, 1979; office adminstr. Price Waterhouse & Co., Houston, 1979—. Second v.p. Bear Creek Parent Tchr. Orgn., 1979-80, 1st v.p., 1980—. Served to capt. U.S. Army, 1968-73. Decorated Bronze Star, Army Commendation medal, Purple Heart. Mem. Inst. Internal Auditors, Am. Acctg. Assn. Roman Catholic. Office: 1200 Milam Suite 2700 Houston TX 77002

GOSSMAN, FRANCIS JOSEPH, bishop, Roman Cath. Ch.; b. Balt., Apr. 1, 1930; s. Frank Michael and Mary Genevieve (Steadman) G.; B.A., St. Mary Sem., 1952; S.T.L., North Am. Coll., Rome, Italy, 1955; Juris Canonici D., Catholic U. of Am., 1959. Ordained priest Roman Catholic Ch., 1955; asst. pastor Basilica of the Assumption, Balt., 1959-68; adminstr. Cathedral of Mary Our Queen, Balt., 1968; named aux. bishop of Balt., also titular bishop of Aguntum, vicar gen. Balt., 1968; aux. bishop St. Peter the Apostle, Balt., from 1968, urban vicar, from 1970; bishop Diocese of Raleigh, N.C., 1975—. Asst. chancellor Archdiocese of Balt., 1959-65, vice chancellor, 1965; pro-synodal judge Tribunal Archdiocese of Balt., 1961, vice officialis, 1962-65, officialis, 1965; papal chamberlain 1965; mem. Nat. Conf. of Cath. Bishops, from 1968, adminstrv. bd. U.S. Cath. Conf., from 1973; mem. Bd. of Consultors of Archdiocese, Balt., 1969. Mem. Balt. Community Relations Commn., 1969; mem. exec. com. of Md. Food Com., Inc., 1969—. Bd. dirs. United Fund of Central Md. Mem. Canon Law Soc. Am. Address: 300 Cardinal Gibbons Dr Raleigh NC 27606*

GOTTIER, RICHARD FRANKLIN, univ. pres.; b. Findlay, Ohio, Mar. 20, 1933; s. Russell F. and Ethel F. (Morehart) G.; A.B., Asbury Coll., Wilmore, Ky., 1955; B.D., Winebrenner Theol. Sem., Findlay, 1961; M.A., Bowling Green (Ohio) State U., 1962, Ph.D., 1968; m. Carol Ann Stauffer, June 14, 1953; children—Denise Linn, Renee Annette, Lisa Kae. Asst. dean students, then asst. prof., asso. prof. psychology Findlay Coll., 1963-69; dean acad. affairs, then v.p. acad. affairs Spring Arbor (Mich.) Coll., 1969-73; successively acad. v.p., v.p., provost, pres. Western New Eng. Coll., Springfield, Mass., 1973-79; pres. CBN U., Virginia Beach, Va., 1979—; dir. Kaman Corp., Bloomfield, Conn. Mem. Am. Assn. Higher Edn., Am. Psychol. Assn., Animal Behavior Soc., Phi Kappa Phi. Home: 4448 Leatherwood Dr Virginia Beach VA 23462 Office: CBN Univ CBN Center Virginia Beach VA 23463

GOTTMAN, LLOYD EUGENE, mfg. co. exec.; b. Memphis, Aug. 25, 1939; s. Dewitt C. and Pauline P. G.; B.S. in Indsl. Mgmt., Ga. Inst. Tech., 1961; M.B.A. with honors, U. Pa., 1966; m. Heidrun Sudeck, May 23, 1964; children—Dirk, Mark. Supr. systems and programming Cummins Engine Co., Columbus, Ind., 1966-68; mgr. systems and programming Aladdin Industries, Nashville, 1968-70; new markets mgr. Aladdin Synergetics, Inc., 1970-74, v.p. adminstrn. and ops., 1974—; dir. Temp-Rite Internat., Inc. Served with U.S. Army, 1961-64. Mem. Planning Execs. Inst., Am. Mgmt. Assn., Strategic Planning Inst. Home: 209 Clearlake Dr W Nashville TN 37217 Office: PO Box 100888 Nashville TN 37210

GOTTSCHALK, OLIVER ALVIN, business broker; b. Roslyn, S.D., Apr. 5, 1922; s. Forrest M. and Helga (Monshaugan) G.; student U. S.D., 1940-42; m. Eunice F. Pachernigg, May 16, 1943; children—Marica, Mark, Maureen. Owner, operator grocery store, Lake Preston, S.D., 1946-47; agt. Equitable Life Assurance Soc., Lake Preston, 1947-50; with Gottschalk Co., Inc., Brookings, S.D., 1950-79, pres., 1957-79; v.p. Brookings Bowling Corp., 1960-79; pres. Am. Bus. Exchange, 1977-79; bus. broker, Sarasota, Fla., 1979—; dir. Area Devel. Corp., Brookings. Mayor, Brookings, 1960-62. Served with USAAF, 1942-46. Decorated Air medal with clusters; named S.D. Realtor of Yr., 1970. Mem. Nat. Assn. Realtors, Nat. Inst. Real Estate Brokers, Nat. Inst. Farm and Land Brokers, Inst. Cert. Bus. Counselors, Am. Legion, Brookings C. of C. (recipient Spl. award of merit 1970). Lutheran. Clubs: Masons, Shriners, Elks, Rotary. Home: 2891 Hardee Dr Sarasota FL 33581 Office: 2700 S Tamiami Trail Sarasota FL 33579

GOTTWALD, BRUCE COBB, chem. co. exec.; b. Richmond, Va., Sept. 28, 1933; s. Floyd Dewey and Anne Ruth (Cobb) G.; B.S., Va. Mil. Inst., 1954; postgrad. U. Va., Inst. Paper Chemistry, Appleton, Wis.; m. Nancy Hays, Dec. 22, 1956; children—Bruce Cobb, Mark Hays, Thomas Edward. With Albermarle Paper Mfg. Co. (became Ethyl Corp. 1962), 1956—, pres., 1970—; dir. First & Mchts. Corp., Richmond Engring. Co., James River Corp. Trustee, Randolph Macon Woman's Coll., Va. Museum; bd. dirs. Richmond Met. YMCA; chmn. edn. Presbyn. Ch., Richmond; chmn. Va. Indsl. Devel. Commn.; bd. visitors Va. Mil. Inst. Presbyterian. Clubs: Chemists (N.Y.C.); Commonwealth, Country of Va. (Richmond). Home: 4203 Sulgrave Rd Richmond VA 23221 Office: 330 S 4th St Richmond VA 23219

GOTTWALD, FLOYD DEWEY, JR., chem. co. exec.; b. Richmond, Va., July 29, 1922; s. Floyd Dewey and Ann (Cobb) G.; B.S., Va. Mil. Inst., Lexington, 1943; M.S., U. Richmond, 1951; m. Elisabeth Morris Shelton, Mar. 22, 1947; children—William M., James T., John D. With Albemarle Paper Co., Richmond, 1943-68, sec., 1956-57, v.p., sec., 1957-62, pres., 1962-68, also dir.; exec. v.p. Ethyl Corp., 1962-64, vice chmn. bd., 1964-68, chmn. bd., 1968—, chief exec. officer, 1970—; dir. Seabord Coast Line R.R. Co. Trustee Va. Mil. Inst. Found., U. Richmond, Va. Inst. Sci. Research. Served to 1st lt. USAR, 1943-46. Decorated Bronze Star, Purple Heart. Mem. Am. Petroleum Inst. (dir.). Home: 300 Herndon Rd Richmond VA 23229 Office: 330 S 4th St Richmond VA 23217

GOUGER, JESSIE SIFFORD, b. N.C.; widowed, 2 children. B.S. in Elem. Edn., Appalachian State U., Boone, N.C., 1940; M.Ed. in Elem. Edn., U. N.C., Chapel Hill, 1952, postgrad. in supervision, 1968. Elem. tchr. Chapel Hill-Carrboro City Schs., Chapel Hill, N.C., 1952-55, elem. prin., 1955-58, supr., 1958-70, dir. elem. edn., 1970—. Active Boy Scouts, Girl Scouts, ARC, cancer edn., Cummunity Fund drives, Art Guild. Mem. Assn. Educators, Delta Kappa Gamma. Home: 1298 Mason Farm Rd Chapel Hill NC 27514

GOUGH, JESSIE POST (MRS. HERBERT FREDERICK GOUGH), educator; b. Nakon Sri Tamaraj, Thailand, Jan. 26, 1907 (parents Am. citizens); d. Richard Walter and Mame (Stebbins) Post; B.A., Maryville Coll., 1927; M.A. in English, U. Chgo., 1928; Ed.D., U. Ga., 1965; m. Herbert Frederick Gough, June 30, 1934; children—Joan Acland (Mrs. Alexander Reed), Herbert Frederick. Tchr. English, Linden Hall, Lititz, Pa., 1930-32; tchr. Fairyland Sch., Lookout Mountain, Tenn., 1955-64; research asst. English curriculum studies center U. Ga., 1964-65; prof. elementary edn. LaGrange (Ga.) Coll., 1965-75. Prof., N.W. Ga. area tchr. edn. services, 1969-71. Mem. Walker County (Ga.) Curriculum Council, 1959-61, Walker County Ednl. Planning Bd., 1958-60. Mem. Am. Ednl. Research Assn., East Tenn. Hist. Soc., Nat., Ga. edn. assns., Delta Kappa Gamma, Kappa Delta Pi. Home: Savannah Hills Dr Ooltewah TN 37363

GOUGH, ORAN DEAN, broadcasting-advt. and production exec.; b. Detroit, Apr. 3, 1937; s. Henry Dean Gough and Gertrude (Schutz) Gough Kidd; m. Sharon Ann Beals, Dec. 12, 1955 (dec. Feb. 1972); children—Laura Ellen Gough Perryman, Oran Dean, Frank Dixon II, Juliann Michelle; m. 2d. Joyce A. Ondo-Southrey, Apr. 12, 1972; m. 3d, Donna Jane Bender Hammond, Dec. 31, 1976. Program dir. WIRK-TV, Palm Beach, Fla., 1953-56; pres., gen. mgr. Eloral Assos., Inc., Pub., 1957-59; production mgr., TV dir. Florino Advt., 1960-62; mgr. Palm Coast Shopping Center, 1963; program dir. WEAT-TV, West Palm Beach, Fla., 1963-66, production mgr., 1966-70, dir. ops., mem. mgmt. com. WEAT-AM-FM-TV, 1970-73; pres. Color Communications Corp., 1967-70, Gough Enterprises of Palm Beach Inc., 1975—; prin. Newera TV Productions., 1976—; production mgr. WPTV, 1978—. Public relations counsel Palm Beach County Republican Exec. Com. Bd., 1968-70. Bd. dirs. Big Bros., 1971-72; trustee Better Bus. Bur. Palm Beach County, 1972-73, bd. dirs., 1974. Recipient Outstanding individual Achievement award 4th dist. Am. Advt. Fedn., 1969. Mem. Palm Beaches Advt. Club (v.p., sec., dir. 1961-64, 69-71, pres. 1972). Clubs: Masons, Moose. Home: 806 9th St Lake Park FL 33403 Office: 622 N Flagler Dr West Palm Beach FL 33401

GOULD, ALFRED RAYMOND, physician; b. New Orleans, May 24, 1928; s. Harley Nathan and Mary (Raymond) G.; B.S., U. Ill., 1950, M.D., Tulane U., 1954; m. Barbara Carolyn Baird, Dec. 24, 1952; children—Alfred Raymond, Phillips Brooks, Harley Nathan II, Hal William, David Wallace. Intern, Touro Infirmary, New Orleans, 1954-55; practice medicine, specializing in family practice, St. Francisville, La., 1957—; coroner W. Feliciana Parish, State La., St. Francisville, 1960—; clin. instr. community medicine Tulane U. Sch. Medicine, New Orleans, 1971—; pres. W. Feliciana Parish Health Council, 1963. Served with USPHS-USCG, 1955-57. Diplomate Am. Bd. Family Practice. Mem. Am. Acad. Family Practice, AMA (Physicians Recognition award 1972, 75), So. Med. Assn., La. Acad. Family Practice, La. State Med. Soc., Bi-Parish Med. Soc., East and West Feliciana Parish Med. Soc. (pres. 1978-79). Democrat. Baptist. Home: Waverly Plantation Bains LA 70713 Office: PO Drawer C St Francisville LA 70775

GOULD, EDWARD RAY, paper co. ofcl.; b. Joshua, Tex., Aug. 17, 1933; s. Clifford Lee and Eula Lee (Brawner) G.; student U. Houston; m. Adria Lee Laird, Nov. 24, 1954; 1 dau., Cathrin Adria. Adminstrv. mgr. Moore Paper Co., Houston, 1953-67; salesman Palmer Paper Co., Houston, 1968—; chmn. graphic arts edn. com. Lee Jr. Coll., Baytown, Tex., 1977-79. Treas., Seton Cath. Jr. High Sch., 1977-79; mem. sch. bd. St. Rose of Lima Cath. Sch., 1977-80, fin. chmn. ch., 1977-80. Mem. Soc. Repro-Graphics Communication (dir. Houston chpt.). Republican. Roman Catholic. Office: PO Box 81 Houston TX 77001

GOULD, KAREN KEEL, art historian, educator; b. Austin, Tex., Sept. 26, 1946; d. John Lewis and Helen Darwin (Kuhn) Keel; B.S., U. Tex., Austin, 1968, M.A., 1970, Ph.D., 1975; m. Lewis L. Gould, Oct. 24, 1970. Instr. dept. art U. Tex., Austin, 1971-73, 75-76; participant Medieval Acad. Summer Insts., 1972, 74. Fellow Duke U. Medieval-Renaissance Summer Inst., 1976. Mem. Coll. Art Assn., Medieval Acad. Am., Internat. Center Medieval Art, Alpha Delta Pi, Phi Kappa Phi, Phi Alpha Theta, Tau Sigma Delta. Methodist. Author: The Psalter and Hours of Yolande of Soissons, 1978. Contbr. to Gothic and Renaissance Illuminated Manuscripts from Texas Collections, 1971; contbr. article to profl. jour. Home: 2602 La Ronde St Austin TX 78731

GOULD, LEWIS LUDLOW, educator; b. N.Y.C., Sept. 21, 1939; s. John Ludlow and Carmen L. (Lewis) G.; A.B., Brown U., 1961; M.A., Yale U., 1962, Ph.D., 1966; m. Karen D. Keel, Oct. 24, 1970. Instr. history Yale U., 1965-66, asst. prof., 1966-67; asst. prof. history U. Tex., Austin, 1967-71, asso. prof., 1971-76, prof., 1976—. Recipient Carr P. Collins award Tex. Inst. Letters, 1973; Nat. Endowment for Humanities Younger Humanist fellow, 1974-75. Mem. Am., So., Tex. hist. assns., Phi Beta Kappa, Phi Kappa Phi. Democrat. Author: Wyoming: A Political History, 1868-1896, 1968, Progressives and Prohibitionists: Texas Democrats in the Wilson Era, 1973; (with Richard Greffe) Photojournalist: The Career of Jimmy Hare, 1977; Reform and Regulation: American Politics, 1900-1916, 1978. Editor: (with James C. Curtis) The Black Experience in America, 1970; The Progressive Era, 1974. Home: 2602 La Ronde St Austin TX 78731

GOULD, MERLE LESTER, energy and chems. cons.; b. Hitchcock, S.D., Mar. 10, 1919; s. Ervin Albert and Minnie Ella (Ingalls) G.; B.S., Nebr. U., 1943; m. Orrie Adeline Watson, Feb. 28, 1942; children—Larry Allen, Shirley Ann, Jeffrey Eugene. Chem. engr. Shell Devel. Co., Emeryville, Calif., 1943-51; chief devel. engr. Vulcan Engring. Co., Cin., 1951-53; devel. and process engr. Ethyl Corp., Baton Rouge, 1953-57, asst. dir. products devel., 1957-59, dir. comml. devel., 1959-64, dir. trade relations, 1964-66, gen. mgr. indsl. chems., 1966-73, dir. corporate research and devel. planning, 1973-75; pres. Fuels Devel. Corp., Baton Rouge, 1975—. Mem. Am. Inst. Chem. Engrs. (dir. petrochem. div. 1965-70), Soap and Detergents Assn. (dir. 1971-72), Am. Chem. Soc., Chem. Devel. Assn., Mfg. Chemists Assn., Drug and Allied Trades Assn., Sigma Xi, Sigma Tau, Phi Lambda Upsilon. Republican. Patentee chem. processing, reactor design, chem. reactions, high velocity mixing. Home and office: 1134 Lee Dr Baton Rouge LA 70808

GOULD, PAUL FREDERICK, physicist; b. Mpls., Jan. 12, 1938; s. Paul Dawson and Cleo Patricia (Kayser) G.; A.A., Grandview Jr. Coll., 1958; B.A., Drake U., 1961; M.S., U. So. Calif., 1974; m. Janet Ann Melhus, Jan. 29, 1960; children—Laura Ann, Scott Fredrik, Cynthia Ann, Robb Kayser. Physicist, task leader Mine Countermeasures dept. Naval Coastal Systems Lab., Panama City, Fla., 1961-75, mgr. Range Data and Control Center, 1975—; cons. Chief of Naval Material for End Sweep Mine Clearance; cons. Suez Canal Authority. Bd. dirs. Woodlawn Community Club; bd. dirs. Rhett Borland Jr. Major League; chmn. Bay County Snapper Bowl Com. Mem. Am. Def. Preparedness Assn., Alpha Tau Omega. Club: Optimist (honor pres.). Home: 123 Woodlawn Dr Panama City FL 32407 Office: Naval Coastal Systems Lab Panama City FL 32407

GOULD, STEPHEN, paper mfg. exec., writer; b. N.Y.C., Dec. 25, 1909; s. Jacob and Fannie (Schwartz) G.; D.F.A. (hon.), Geneva Theol. Coll., 1969; D.Integral Philosophy (hon.), World U., 1969, D.F.A. (hon.), 1972; D.Metaphysics, Am. Bible Inst., 1975; Ph.D. in Psychology, Clayton U., 1979; m. Marlene Ossias, Aug. 24, 1941; children—Phyllis Jane Miller, Roberta Louise Gould, Debra Elaine Gould. Columnist Port & Terminal publs., L.I., N.Y., 1931-36; dir., cons. Stephen Gould Paper Co., Inc. N.J., Bayonne, Stephen Gould Corp. N.J., Bayonne. Artist, violinist; exhbns., concerts; music synthesized Princeton U., 1977; mus. dir. Nova Tamarac Symphonic Assn., 1975. Fellow Am. Assn. Humanistic Psychology, Internat. Coll. Applied Nutrition, Nat. Psychiat. Assn.; mem. Indsl. Packaging and Handling Engrs., Soc. N.Y. Acad. Sci. (life), Nat. Soc. Arts and Letters (life), Artists Equity. Royal Soc. Arts (life). Mason. Home: 4905 Bayberry Ln Tamarac FL 33319

GOULD, SYD S., publisher; b. Boston, Dec. 16, 1912; s. Charles M. and Cecelia (Duke) G.; student Coll. William and Mary, 1934; m. Grace Leich, May 22, 1938; 1 dau., Nancy Hamilton (Mrs. Lucien M. Gex, Jr.). Radio bus., Buenos Aires, Argentina, 1934, 36; advt. dept. Call-Chronicle Newspapers, Allentown, Pa., 1936-42; v.p., adv. dir. Baytown (Tex.) Sun, 1943-55; pub.-owner Cleveland (Tenn.) Daily Banner, 1955—; pres. Cleveland Newspapers, Inc., 1956-67; exec. v.p. Southern Newspapers, Inc., 1963-69; pres. Syd S. Gould Assos., 1966—, Bolivar Newspapers, Inc., 1967—, Ironton Tribune Corp. (O.), Franklin Newspapers, Inc. (La.), Comet-Press Newspapers, Thibodaux, La., Milton Newspapers, Inc. (Fla.). Mem. Regional Small Bus. Adv. Council. Sec., Bradley County (Tenn.) Indsl. Devel. Bd., 1961—; pres. Bradley County Heart Assn., 1960-61; mem. advisory bd. Providence Hosp.; bd. dirs. Mobile Pub. Library. Served with USNR, World War II. Mem. Newspaper Advt. Execs. Assn., Tenn. Press. Assn., Bur. Advt., Am. Newspaper Pubs. Assn., USCG Aux., U.S. Power Squadron, Sigma Delta Chi. Episcopalian. Clubs: Bayou Country, Mobile Big Game Fishing, Isle Dauphine Country, Capitol Hill, Yachting of Am., Internat. Trade, Bienville, Athelstan. Home and Office: Route 1 Box 146 Theodore AL 36582

GOULDING, CLARENCE EUGENE, JR., anesthesiologist; b. Memphis, Nov. 9, 1931; s. Clarence Eugene and Bertha Maude (Tomlinson) G.; student East Tenn. State U., 1949-51; M.D., U. Tenn., 1954; m. Melba Jean Leonard, Dec. 21, 1952; children—Amelia Ann, Clarence Eugene III, Karen Jean, Richard Leonard. Intern, Knoxville (Tenn.) Gen. Hosp., 1955-56; gen. practice medicine Elizabethton, Tenn., 1956-57; resident anesthesiology U. Tenn. Meml. Research Center and Hosp., Knoxville, 1959-61; practice medicine specializing in anesthesiology, Johnson City, Tenn., 1961—; mem. staff Johnson City Meml. Hosp., chmn. med. staff, 1968-69; mem. staff Johnson City Eye and Ear Hosp.; clin. asst. prof. anesthesiology, coordinator unit of anesthesiology Coll. Medicine, East Tenn. State U. Vice chmn. Daniel Boone Dist., Boy Scouts Am., Johnson City, 1967-68. Bd. dirs. Watauga Hist. Assn., 1962-75. Served to lt. comdr. M.C., USNR, 1957-59. Named Kiwanian of the Year, 1966. Diplomate Am. Bd. Anesthesiology. Mem. AMA, Tenn. Med. Assn., Washington, Carter, Unicoi county (pres. 1980) med. socs., So. Med. Assn., Am., Tenn. State Socs. anesthesiologists, Internat. Anesthesia Research Soc., Am. Soc. Regional Anesthetists. Methodist (lay leader 1967-69). Mason, Kiwanian (pres. 1971). Clubs: Am. Philatelic Soc.; Holston Stamp (Johnson City). Home: 1600 Crystal Springs Dr Johnson City TN 37601 Office: Anesthesia Office Memorial Hospital Johnson City TN 37601

GOULSON, JO PINNELL, med. research adminstr., sculptor, musician; b. Birmingham, Ala., July 31, 1926; d. John W. and Frances (Moores) Pinnell; B.S., U. Ala., 1947; postgrad. Yale U. Div. Sch., 1947-48, Woman's Med. Coll. Pa., 1948-50, U. Mich. Med. Sch., 1950, Tulane Med. Sch., 1951; M.S. in Public Health, U. N.C., 1954; m. Hilton Thomas Goulson, Aug. 21, 1954; children—Daniel Thomas, Amy Frances. Free lance editor, Chapel Hill, N.C., 1961-65; research asso. U. N.C. Center for Research in Pharmacology and Toxicology, Chapel Hill, 1965-67; research asso. U. N.C. Dental Research Center, 1968—, head office of communication and edn., 1976—; research asso. dept. parasitology U. N.C. Sch. Public Health, 1977—; wood sculpture tchr., exhibitor Durham (N.C.) Arts Council, 1974-76; percussion tchr., 1955—, performer, 1945—. Vol. wood sculpture tchr. and lectr. Chapel Hill Public Schs., 1970—; vol. percussionist U. N.C. Symphony Orch., 1954-68, U. N.C. Wind Ensemble, 1953-67, Village Band, Chapel Hill, 1974—, Durham (N.C.) Symphony, 1978. Ch. sch. supt. United Ch. Christ, Chapel Hill, 1958-60; vice chmn. United Ch. Women, Raleigh/Henderson dist., 1966-67; v.p. Chapel Hill dist. Ch. Women United, 1971, pres., 1972; chmn. bd. Christian World Missions, 1960-62, chmn. bd. deacons, 1973-74; mem. N.C. Gov.'s Commn. on Edn., 1968-69; bd. dirs. Chapel Hill United Fund, 1975-77, N.C. Symphony Soc., 1970-72, Orange County Mental Health Assn., 1974-76; sec. Inter-Ch. Council for Social Services, 1963, 2d v.p., 1968. Mem. Carolina Designer Craftsmen (sec. 1970-73, 78-80), Nat. Woodcarvers Assn., Am. Crafts Council, Durham Art Guild, S.E. Sculptors Assn., N.C. Crafts Assn., N.C. Fedn. Women's Clubs (pres. dist. 8, 1969-70, chmn. resolutions com. 1973-76, mem. legis. com. 1971-72), U. N.C. Sch. Public Health Alumni Assn. (sec. 1980—), N.Y. Acad. Scis., Sigma Xi, Alpha Epsilon Delta. Democrat. Mem. United Ch. Christ. Club: Chapel Hill Woman's (arts chmn. 1963, pres. 1963-66, trustee 1967-70, chmn. fin. com. 1976—). Home: 52 Oakwood Dr Chapel Hill NC 27514 Office: Dental Research Center 210H Univ of North Carolina Chapel Hill NC 27514

GOURLEY, JAMES LELAND, editor, publisher; b. Mounds, Okla., Jan. 29, 1925; s. Samuel O. and Lodema (Scott) G.; B.L.S., U. Okla., 1963; m. Vicki Graham Clark, Nov. 24, 1976; children—James Leland II, Janna Lynn, Kelly, Brandon. Pres., pub., editor Daily Free-Lance, Henryetta, Okla., 1955-73, Friday newspaper, Oklahoma City, 1973—; pres. Hugo (Okla.) Daily News, 1953-63; chief staff to Gov. Okla., 1959-63; chmn., pres. State Capitol Bank Oklahoma City, 1962-69; pres. KHEN-AM-FM, Henryetta, 1950-71; v.p. KJEM-AM-FM, Oklahoma City, 1962-67, KXOJ-AM, Sapulpa, Okla., 1973-75. Democratic candidate gov. Okla., 1966; vice chmn. U. Okla. Master Plan, 1967; mem. nat. council State Govts., 1960-63; bd. dirs. So. Regional Edn. Bd., 1959-67, Oklahoma City Civic Music Assn., 1976—; dist. chmn. Boy Scouts Am., 1962-64; exec. dir. Gov's. Commn. on Higher Edn., 1960-61, Okla. crusade chmn. Am. Cancer Soc., 1964; chmn. Okla. Lake Redevel. Authority, 1960-63. Bd. dirs. Okla. Symphony Soc., 1976—. Served to maj. AUS, 1942-46. Recipient Best Newspaper Advt. award Suburban Newspapers Am., 1976; Best Weekly Newspaper award Okla. Press Assn., 1977, 78; Best Small City daily award, 13 times; Okla. Heritage Edit. award, 1972; Marshall Gregory award distinguished journalism in edn. Okla. Edn. Assn., 1971. Mem. Oklahoma City C. of C. (dir. 1963—), UPI Editors Okla. (pres. 1958-59), Inter-Am. Press Assn., Suburban Newspapers Am. (dir. 1978—), Okla. Press Assn., Sigma Delta Chi. Mem. Christian Ch. Disciples of Christ (pres. Okla. 1964-65). Clubs: Rotary, Oklahoma City Golf and Country. Home: 1605 W Wilshire Oklahoma City OK 73116 Office: Box 20340 Oklahoma City OK 73156

GRACE, GEORGE HENRY, telephone co. exec.; b. Bartow, Fla., May 20, 1948; s. Dee Cee and Lillie Mae (Colson) G.; cert. Polk Vocat. and Tech. Inst., 1967; B.S., Tuskegee Inst., 1971; cert. Gen. Motors Inst., 1972; middle mgmt. certificate (fellow) U. Miami, 1978; m. Regina Mobley, June 13, 1970; 1 dau., JeRhonda Janee. Prodn. supr. Gen. Motors Co., Pontiac, Mich., 1972-74; mgmt. asst. So. Bell Telephone Co., Miami, Fla., 1974, installation foreman, 1974-75, engr., 1975-78, asso. staff mgr., 1978—. Mem. Richmond Heights Planning Commn.; mem. Miami Citizens Ad-Hoc Com., 1977—; campaign mgr. Clayton Hamilton Campaign Com., 1978; scoutmaster Boy Scouts Am., 1977-79. Mem. NAACP (mem. exec. bd. South Dade 1977—), Tuskegee Alumni Assn. (bus. mgr. 1976-78), Richmond Perrine Jr. C. of C., Omega Psi Phi (Community Service award 1978). Democrat. Methodist. Home: 11250 Washington Blvd Miami FL 33176 Office: So Bell Telephone Co 250 Alhambra Circle Room 106 Coral Gables FL 33134

GRACE, KENNETH MAYNARD, mental health cons.; b. Superior, Wis., May 24, 1924; s. George Washington and Lenora (Jensen) G.; B.A., U. N.D., 1949; M.S.W., U. Denver, 1953; m. Olive C. Krefting, Feb. 7, 1947; children—Keith, Barbara, David, Cathryn. Child welfare worker Benson County (N.D.) Welfare Bd., 1950-52, 53-55; psychiat. social worker Cass County Children's Social Service Center, Fargo, N.D., 1955-60, Western Mental Health Center, Marshall, Minn., 1960-64; exec. dir. Eastside Community Mental Health Center, Bellevue, Wash., 1964-73; dir. mental health Dallas County Mental Health and Mental Retardation Center, 1973-75; mental health cons., Plano, Tex., 1975-77; chmn. bd., pres. Am. Interlocked Mental Services, Seattle, 1975—; mental health cons. HEW/USPHS Alcohol, Drug Abuse and Mental Health Region VI, Dallas, 1977—. Served with AUS, 1943-46; ETO. Recipient award VFW of U.S., Grand Forks, 1949. Mem. Puget Council Mental Health Programs (pres. 1971-73), Nat. Council Community Mental Health Centers (dir. 1971-73). Home: 3812 Yosemite St Plano TX 75023 Office: 18th Floor 1200 Main Tower Dallas TX 75202

GRACE, WILLIAM FRANCIS, ins. co. exec.; b. Louisville, Sept. 10, 1913; s. Albert Clement and Cecile Jeanne (LeBesque) G.; student Tulane U., 1930-32; m. Helen Meyers, July 26, 1941; children—Josephine Grace McCloskey, Cecile Grace Ballard, William Francis, Elizabeth Manning. Loan officer, bank, New Orleans, to 1941; with John Hancock Mut. Life Ins. Co., New Orleans, 1945—, gen. agt., 1953—. Treas. citizens council Pub. Sch. Survey; active United Fund; chief fund raiser Sara Mayo Hosp., 1970; bd. dirs. ARC. Recipient award Juvenile Ct. New Orleans. Mem. New Orleans Life Underwriters Assn. (past pres.), John Hancock Mut. Life Ins. Co. Gen. Agts. Assn. (past pres.), New Orleans Gen. Agts. and Mgrs. Assn. (past pres.), Nat. Assn. Life Underwriters, Million Dollar Round Table. Clubs: Stratford (past pres.), Lake Shore (past pres.), New Orleans Country, Boston, La., Pickwick. Home: 1328 Octavia St New Orleans LA 70115 Office: 809 Howard Ave New Orleans LA 70113

GRACIDA, RENE HENRY, bishop; b. New Orleans, June 9, 1923; s. Henry J. and Mathilde (Derbes) G.; student Rice U., 1942-43; B.S. in Architecture, U. Houston, 1950; postgrad. U. Fribourg, Switzerland, 1950, St. Vincent Coll., Latrobe, Pa., 1951-53, St. Vincent Maj. Sem., 1953-60. Faculty, U. Houston Sch. Architecture, 1948-51; practice architecture with Donald Bartheline & Assos., Houston, 1949-51; ordained deacon Roman Catholic Ch., 1958, priest, 1959, bishop, 1971; asst. pastor Holy Family Parish, North Miami, Fla., 1961-62, St. Coleman Parish, Pompano Beach, Fla., 1962-63, St. Matthew Parish, Hallandale, Fla., 1963-64; adminstr. St. Ambrose Parish, Deerfield Beach, Fla., 1964; asst. pastor Visitation Parish, North Dade, Fla., 1964-65; adminstr. St. Ann Parish, Naples, Fla., 1966-67; pastor Nativity Parish, Hollywood, Fla., 1967-69; rector St. Mary Cathedral, Miami, Fla., 1969-71; St. Patrick Parish, Miami Beach, Fla., 1971-72; pastor St. Kiernan Parish, Miami, 1973-75; bishop Diocese of Pensacola-Tallahassee, 1975—; mem. Archdiocesan Bldg. Commn., Archdiocese of Miami, 1961-75, sec., 1962-65, chmn., 1967—, chmn. West Coast Deanery, Human Relations Bd., 1966-67, senator Priests Senate, 1967-69, archdiocesan consultor, 1967—, chmn. Broward Deanery, Human Relations Bd., 1967-69, chancellor, 1968-72, treas., 1969-72, vicar gen., 1969-75; aux. bishop Archdiocese Miami, 1971-75, supt. edn., 1973-75. Pres. Community Action Fund. Served with USAAF, 1943-45. Decorated Air medal. Mem. Liturgical Arts Soc., Tex., Fla. socs. architects, AIA, Liturgical Conf., Nat. Assn. Community Devel., Guild Religious Architecture. Important archtl. works include remodeling St. Vincent

Archabbey Basilica, Latrobe, Ch. of the Nativity, Hollywood, St. Ambrose Ch., Deerfield Beach. Address: PO Box 2395 Tallahassee FL 32304

GRACY, ROBERT WAYNE, biochemist, educator; b. McKinney, Tex., Dec. 30, 1941; student La. State U., 1960-62; B.S., Calif. State Poly. U., 1964; Ph.D., U. Calif., Riverside, 1968; postgrad. Albert Einstein Coll. Medicine, 1968-70; m. Lynne Hitchcock, 1963; children—Kimberly, Delaney. Research asso. Space Gen., El Monte, Calif., 1963-64; instr. Calif. State Poly. U., Pomona, 1963-64; postdoctoral fellow Albert Einstein Coll. Medicine, Bronx, N.Y., 1968-70; asst. prof. chemistry N.Tex. State U., Denton, 1970-73, asso. prof., 1973-75, prof. chemistry and basic health scis., 1975—, chmn. dept. biochemistry, 1976—; prof., chmn. biochemistry Tex. Coll. Osteo. Medicine, 1976—; vis. prof. U. Wurzburg (W. Ger.), 1975-76. NIH grantee, 1970—; NDEA fellow, 1964-68. Mem. Am. Soc. Biol. Chemists, AAAS, N.Y. Acad. Sci., Tex. Acad. Sci., AAUP, Am. Assn. Chairmen Med. Sch. Depts. of Biochemistry, Tex. Assn. Nutrition, Sigma Xi, Alpha Chi Sigma. Home: 1414 Windsor Denton TX 76201 Office: N Tex State Univ Denton TX 76203

GRADDICK, CHARLES ALLEN, state govt. ofcl.; b. Mobile, Ala., Dec. 10, 1944; s. Julian, Jr. and Elvera (Smith) G.; B.S., U. Ala., 1967; J.D., Samford U., 1970; m. Corinne Whiting, Aug. 19, 1966; children—Charles Allen, Herndon Whiting, Corinne. Admitted to Ala. bar, 1970; clk. Ala. Supreme Ct., 1970; asst. dist. atty., then dist. atty. Mobile County, 1971-79; atty. gen. State of Ala., 1979—. Mem. Ala. N.G. Named Outstanding Young Man Mobile, 1976; recipient cert. appreciation Ala. Peace Officers Assn., 1978, appreciation award Mobile Optimist Club, 1978. Mem. Nat. Assn. Attys. Gen., Am. Trial Lawyers Assn., Am. Bar Assn., Nat. Dist. Attys. Assn., Ala. Bar Assn. Democrat. Episcopalian. Address: 64 N Union St Montgomery AL 36130

GRADEN, MAYNARD A., III, electronics engr.; b. Norwich, Conn., May 23, 1945; s. Maynard A., Jr. and Jacqueline Yvette (Cote) G.; Asso. Sci. in Electronics Engring., Mitchell Coll., 1968; B.S., Ohio Inst. Tech., 1973. Design engr. Am. Computer Communications Co., Columbus, Ohio, 1973-76, North Electric Co. Research Lab., Delaware, Ohio, 1976-78; prin. mem. tech. staff Siemens Corp., Boca Raton, Fla., 1978—; tech. writer Popular Electronics mag., 1977-. Served with C.E., U.S. Army, 1968-70. Mem. IEEE. Contbg. author: Signetics FPLA Applications Manual, 1977. Finalist, Nat. Design Contest sponsored by Intersil Corp., 1976, Tex. Instruments, 1977, Raytheon, 1978, Gen. Instruments, 1979. Home: 942 Lantern Tree Ln Wes Palm Beach FL 33411 Office: care Siemens Corp 5500 Broken Sound Blvd NW Boca Raton FL 33431

GRADY, ANTHONY FRANK, JR., automation specialist; b. Hartford, Conn., Nov. 30, 1935; s. Anthony and Mary Kathleen (Kudrika) G.; A.Engring. Tech., Grantham Coll. Engring., 1977; m. Mary Eugenia Holcomb, Jan. 30, 1976; children—Kim, Anthony Kirk, Kevin Scott, Patricia Eugenia. Flight test technologist Kaman Aircraft Co., Bloomfield, Conn., 1960-63; missile technologist Raytheon Corp., Texarkana, Tex., 1963-64; tech. adviser U.S. Navy Space Surviellance, Lewisville, Ark., 1965-67; sr. ordnance engr. Day & Zimmermann, Inc., Texarkana, Tex., 1967-77; fault analyst Michelin Tire Corp., Greenville, S.C., 1977—. Served with USAF, 1954-58. Recipient various awards Day & Zimmermann, Inc., 1967-77. Mem. Nat. Mgmt. Assn., Am. Def. Preparedness Assn., Am. Security Council. Republican. Roman Catholic. Home: 116 Bangor St Mauldin SC 29662 Office: Z/US-0 Michelin Tire Corp Sandy Springs SC

GRADY, JAMES MARTIN, computer exec.; b. Horatio, Ark., July 2, 1935; s. Paul Elmo and Annie Laurie (Martin) G.; B.A., Rice U., 1958; B.A. in Econs., U. Houston, 1966-67. With Tenneco, Inc., Houston, 1961—, corp. systems mgr. 1975—, pres. Tenneco Fed. Credit Union, 1977—. Explorer area chmn. Sam Houston Council, Boy Scouts Am., 1974—; bd. dirs. Area Cerebral Palsy Center; chmn. bd. Rice U. Wesley Found., 1978—. Served to lt. USNR, 1958-60. Mem. Assn. for System Mgmt., Data Processing Mgmt. Assn., Res. Officers Assn., (mem. mil. affairs com. 1973—), Naval Res. Assn. (pres. Space Center chpt. 1978—). Methodist. Home: 6307 Spruce Forest Houston TX 77092 Office: 1010 Milam Houston TX 77001

GRADY, JOHN EDWARD, JR., investment banker; b. Boston, June 15, 1935; s. John Edward and Catherine Agnes (Connolly) G.; A.B., Harvard U., 1956, M.B.A., 1965; children—John Edward III, Robert Emmet McDonnell, Douglas Anderson. Account exec. Merrill Lynch, Pierce, Fenner & Smith, N.Y.C., 1960-63; sr. asso. Cresap, McCormick and Paget, N.Y.C., 1965-69; v.p., Investment Mgmt. and Research, Inc., St. Petersburg, Fla., 1969-70; v.p. fin., treas. Suncoast Highland Corp., Largo, Fla., 1970-74, v.p. fin. and ops., sec.-treas., 1974-76, dir., 1970-76; v.p. corporate fin. Raymond, James & Assos., Inc., St. Petersburg, Fla., 1976—. Regional chmn. Harvard Bus. Sch. Fund, 1971-74; mem. pres. roundtable Eckerd Coll., 1971—; mem. Tampa Bay Area Com. Fgn. Relations, 1979—. Trustee Canterbury Sch. Fla., 1973—, treas. bd. trustees, 1974-75, chmn., 1975-76; mem. com. social service allocations, City of St. Petersburg, 1978; trustee Fla. Gulf Coast Symphony, St. Petersburg, 1979—, St. Petersburg Boychoir, 1980—. Served to lt. (j.g.) USNR, 1956-60. Clubs: Lakewood Country, Harvard West Coast (sec.-treas. 1973-74, v.p. 1974-75, pres. 1975-78, schs. and scholarships chmn. 1978—), Rotary, St. Petersburg (Fla.) Yacht; Suncoast Tiger Bay, Harvard Bus. Sch. Fla. West Coast (dir. 1976—) (St. Petersburg-Tampa). Home: 5910 Bayou Grande Blvd NE Saint Petersburg FL 33703 Office: 6090 Central Ave Saint Petersburg FL 33707

GRADY, JOHN PAUL, food co. exec.; b. Vandalia, Ill., Nov. 3, 1916; s. Paul Leo and Alleen Collins (Gochenour) G.; A.B., DePauw U., 1938; student Kent Law Sch., 1939, Northwestern U., 1956; m. Alice Margaret Scott, Sept. 17, 1941 (dec.); children—Suzanne (Mrs. William A. Gleason), John Michael, Robert Paul; m. 2d, Betty Grady, Sept. 5, 1974. With Chase Bag Co., Chgo., 1939-46, asst. gen. sales mgr., 1948-57; account exec. Young & Rubicam, Chgo., 1946-48; v.p. marketing Lily-Tulip Cup Corp., N.Y.C., 1957-63; v.p. Permacel div. Johnson and Johnson, New Brunswick, N.J., 1963-65; exec. v.p., chief exec. officer Citrus Central Inc., Orlando, Fla., 1965-71, vice chmn., 1977—, also dir.; pres. Juice Bowl Products Inc., Lakeland, Fla., 1971—; dir. Combank-Pinecastle, Fla. Served with USNR, 1941-45. Mem. Fla. Canners Assn. (dir.), Delta Upsilon. Presbyn. Clubs: Country of Orlando; Lone Palm. Home: 1236 Lakepoint Dr Lakeland FL 33803 Office: Box 1048 Lakeland FL 33802

GRADY, THOMAS J., bishop; b. Chgo., Oct. 9, 1914; s. Michael and Rose (Buckley) G.; S.T.L., St. Mary of Lake Sem., Mundelein, Ill., 1938; student Gregorian U. Rome, 1938-39; M.A. in Engilsh, Loyola U., Chgo., 1944. Ordained priest Roman Catholic Ch., 1938; prof. Quigley Prep. Sem., Chgo., 1939-45; procurator St. Mary of Lake Sem., 1945-56; dir. Nat. Shrine Immaculate Conception, Washington, 1956-67; titular bishop Vamalla, aux. bishop Chgo., 1967-74; pastor St. Hilary Ch., Chgo., 1968-74, St. Joseph Ch., Libertyville, Ill., 1974; bishop of Orlando (Fla.), 1974—; Chgo. Archdiocesan dir. seminaries and post-ordination priestly tng., 1967-74; chmn. Chgo. Archdiocesan Liturgical Commn., 1968-74; dir. program Permanent Diaconate, Chgo., 1969-74; cons. Bishops' Com. on Priestly Formation, 1967—, chmn., 1969-72; mem. Ad Hoc Com. on Priestly Life and Ministry, 1971-73; chmn. Bishops' Com. on Priestly Life and Ministry, 1973—.

GRADY, VIOLA KINNAIRD, ednl. adminstr.; b. Randlett, Okla., Nov. 28, 1919; d. Theodore and Grace Blanceh (Tuel) Kinnaird; B.A., U. Okla., 1941; postgrad. U. Calif., Los Angeles, 1947; M.S., U. So. Calif., 1950; m. Paul Grady, Sept. 7, 1957. Sch. psychologist Los Angeles City Schs., 1953-57; dean of women Midwestern State U. Wichita Falls, Tex., 1958-72, dean of students, 1972—. Bd. dirs. Vol. Services, Wichita Falls, 1972-76, Hopecrest Lodge, Wichita Falls, 1974—, Girl Scouts U.S.A., Wichita Falls, 197, Concern, Wichita Falls, 1973-75. Mem. Tex. Assn. Coll. and Univ. Personnel Adminstrs., Internat. Transactional Analysis Assn., Nat. Assn. Humanistic Psychology, Nat., Tex. (past pres.) Women Deans and Counselors. Democrat. Episcopalian. Home: 2718 Devon Rd Wichita Falls TX 76308 Office: 3400 Taft St Wichita Falls TX 76308

GRAEBER, MAX CHARLES, univ. adminstr.; b. Valparaiso, Ind., Dec. 9, 1928; s. Ralph Gordon and Geneva (Cobb) G.; B.S., Ind. U., 1952; M.S., Bowling Green State U., 1970, Ph.D., 1973; m. Kathy McClain, Aug. 30, 1952; children—Charles, Susan, Jeff, Marainne. Owner, operator Max Graeber, Bowling Green, Ohio, 1955-67; debate coach U. Richmond, 1967-72, dean Univ. Coll., 1972—; speech cons. Served to comdr., USAF, 1948-54. Republican. Methodist. Office: Univ Richmond Richmond VA 23173

GRAF, JOSEPH CHARLES, petroleum co. exec.; b. Jersey City, Sept. 10, 1928; s. John Bernard and Margaret Cecilia (Toomey) G.; B.S., Seton Hall U., 1949; M.B.A., U. Pa., 1954; children—Claire, Joseph Charles, Michelle, Mary Ellen, Thomas, Richard. Trainee, Prudential Ins. Co., Newark, 1954-55, systems analyst, 1955-56, asst. research analyst, 1956-58, research analyst, 1958-61, investment analyst, 1961-63, sr. investment analyst, 1963-64, Houston, 1964-67; v.p. So. Nat. Bank, Houston, 1967-69; financial advisor Quintana Petroleum Corp., Houston, 1969—; dir. Terrain King Corp., Tapco Internat., Inc., Linbeck Constrn. Middle East Ltd., Quintana Oil and Gas Co., Outdoor Leisure Products Inc., Southland Enterprises, Inc., Internat. Bank Fin., Cayman Islands; mem. investment com. trust dept. Cullen Bank & Trust. Cons. research com. Houston C. of C., 1966-71. Exec. sec. Cullen Found., 1974; bd. govs. Center for Retarded Inc., Houston. Served with AUS, 1951-53. Mem. Houston Financial Analysts (pres. 1973-74, dir. 1974-77) Clubs: Houston, Houston Racquet. Home: 11711 Memorial Dr #139 Houston TX 77024 Office: 601 Jefferson St Houston TX 77002

GRAF, RICHARD EDWARD, chem. co. exec.; b. Woodland, Calif., Dec. 25, 1945; s. Charles Edward and Mary Elizabeth (McCoey) G.; B.S., U.S. Mil. Acad., 1971; m. Annette Joan Oliva, June 12, 1971; children—Alyssa Joan, Christiaan Jonas. Tech. rep. E.I. DuPont de Nemours & Co., Inc., Tulsa, 1977-79, sr. tech. rep., Houston, 1979—. Served to capt. U.S. Army 1965-67, 71-77. Decorated Meritorious Service medal, Army Commendation medal with oak leaf cluster. Mem. Am. Soc. Nondestructive Testing, Soc. for Radiol. Engring., West Point Soc. Greater Houston, Army Athletic Assn., West Point Alumni Assn. Roman Catholic. Address: 5411 Coral Gables St Houston TX 77069

GRAFF, JOHN ROBERT, bus. exec.; b. McLoud, Okla., Dec. 14, 1935; s. John Lee and Mary Catherine (Babiak) G.; B.M.E., Okla. U., 1960. Asst. sales engr. Westinghouse Corp., Kansas City, Mo., 1961-64, sales eng., Wichita, 1964-66; pres. Mosehart Schleeter Co., Houston, 1966—; dir. Nat. Assn. Decorative Fabric Distbrs. Served with US Army, 1954-55. Mem. Nat. Assn. Wholesalers, Southwestern Assn. Decorative Fabric Distbrs., Houston C. of C. Republican. Roman Catholic. Home: 2323 Augusta Dr #38 Houston TX 77057 Office: PO Box 8 Houston TX 77001

GRAHAM, BEULAH MAE, hosp. personnel adminstr.; b. Brooksville, Fla., Aug. 27, 1933; d. Nathan Williams and Anna May (Durant) Smith; student Jacksonville Sch. Tech., 1948-49, Hernando Adult Edn., 1972, Pasco Hernando Community Coll., 1974—; m. Emory Earl Graham, Apr. 21, 1950; children—Christy Jean, Thomas Wesley, Nathan William. Cashier, A&P Tea Co., 1955-57, 59-60, 65; acctg. office clk. Edmond Gibbons Ltd., Hamilton, Bermuda, 1961-62; sales store checker CSC, U.S. Navy, San Juan, P.R., 1968-70; accounts clk. Lykes Meml. Hosp., Brooksville, 1973-74, personnel and payroll dir., 1974—; mem. adv. bd. for coop. edn. Paso Hernando Community Coll., 1976; mem. Hernando County Health Facilities Authority, 1978—. Mem. West Central Fla. Hosp. Personnel Dirs. Assn. (treas. 1978), Fla. Hosp. Assn., Personnel Adminstrn. Council, Am. Hosp. Assn., Am. Soc. Hosp. Personnel Adminstrs., Am. Bus. Woman's Assn. (membership chmn. 1979-80). Democrat. Mem. Churches of Christ. Home: 1085 McIntyre Rd Brooksville FL 33512 Office: 100 S State Rd 700 Brooksville FL 33512

GRAHAM, DANIEL ROBERT, gov. Fla.; b. Coral Gables, Fla., Nov. 9, 1936; s. Ernest R. and Hilda (Simmons) G.; B.A., U. Fla., 1959; LL.B., Harvard U., 1962; m. Adele Khoury, 1959; children—Gwendolyn Patricia, Glynn Adele, Arva Suzanne, Kendall Elizabeth. Vice pres., sec. Sengra Devel. Corp., Miami Lakes, Fla.; mem. Fla. Ho. of Reps., 1966-70, Fla. Senate, from 1970; gov. State of Fla., Tallahassee, 1979—. Mem. Nat. Commn. on Reform Secondary Edn., Nat. Found. for Improvement Edn., So. Regional Edn. Bd. Named Outstanding 1st Term Mem. of Senate, Allen Morris, 1971, Most Valuable Legislator, St. Petersburg Times, 1972, Lawmaker-Newsmaker of Yr., Tallahassee Democrat, 1972; recipient conservation award Sierra Club, Fla. Wildlife Fedn., Save Our Bays Assn. Mem. Builders Assn. South Fla., Fla. Blue Key, Phi Beta Kappa, Sigma Nu. Democrat. Mem. United Church of Christ. Office: Office of Governor State Capitol Bldg Tallahassee FL 32304

GRAHAM, DONALD RICHARDSON, physician, epidemiologist; b. Springfield, Ill., Feb. 25, 1949; s. Hugh Joseph Jr. and Edith Mary (Larmon) G.; B.S. cum laude, U. Notre Dame, 1970; M.D., Washington U., St. Louis, 1974; m. Patricia Ann Kienzler, June 17, 1972; children—Hugh Michael, Donald Richardson, Jr., Sarah Elizabeth. Intern, Jewish Hosp., St. Louis, 1974-75, resident in internal medicine, 1975-77; fellow in infectious diseases Washington U., 1977-78, asst. in medicine, 1974-78; epidemic intelligence service officer Center for Disease Control, Atlanta, 1978-80, acting chief epidemic investigations activity Hosp. Infections br., 1980—. Sec., class of 1970 U. Notre Dame, 1970—; bd. dirs. Pruitt-Igoe Men's Progressive Club, Med. Action Center, St. Louis, 1971-74; adult advisor troop 777, Boy Scouts Am., Atlanta, 1979. Served with USPHS, 1978-80. Diplomate Am. Bd. Internal Medicine, Nat. Bd. Med. Examiners. Democrat. Roman Catholic. Club: Notre Dame of Atlanta. Home: 4167 Hambrick Way Stone Mountain GA 30083 Office: 1600 Clifton Rd Atlanta GA 30333

GRAHAM, FLOYD, mfg. co. exec.; b. Lake City, S.C., July 6, 1929; s. Jimmy Clinton and Mattie Bell (Player) G.; student Lee Coll., 1950, Memphis State U., 1963, Broward Community Coll., 1973; m. Dolores Elizabeth Cook, Dec. 6, 1952; children—Richard Allen, Michael Lee, Sandra Ann. Enlisted in U.S. Marine Corps, 1948; ret., 1968; tech. tng. instr. RCA, Palm Beach Gardens, Fla., 1968-71; asso. engr. Photon, Inc., Delray Beach, Fla., 1971-72; tech. pub. specialist Systems Engring. Labs., Inc., Ft. Lauderdale, Fla., 1972—; pres., owner Graham Realty, Ft. Lauderdale, 1977—. Vice pres. Sunrise Taxpayers Assn., 1979—. bd. dirs. Palm Beach Gardens Youth Athletic Assn., 1971. Mem. Am. Mgmt. Assn., Am. Legion, Fleet Res. Assn. Democrat. Contbr. articles to profl. jours. Home: 2291 NW 77 Ave Sunrise FL 33322 Office: 6901 W Sunrise Blvd Fort Lauderdale FL 33313

GRAHAM, GEORGE GRIMSLEY, surgeon; b. Goldsboro, N.C., Dec. 1, 1921; s. William Henry and Lillian (Austin) G.; student Hendrix Coll., Conway, Ark., 1938-41, Cornell U., Ithaca, N.Y., 1943-44; M.D., U. Ark., 1947; M.S. in Surgery, U. Minn., 1952; m. Barbara Ann Holt, Aug. 22, 1972; children by previous marriage—George Grimsley, Larry Lain, Louis Austin. Intern Ancker Hosp., St. Paul, 1947-48; resident, surgery preceptorship Mpls. Gen. Hosp., 1948-49; surgery fellow Mayo Clinic, Rochester, Minn., 1949-52; practice medicine specializing in gen. and thoracic surgery, Little Rock, 1955—; mem. staffs St. Vincent's Infirmary; chief of staff Ark. Bapt. Med. Center, Little Rock, 1967, chief of surgery, 1974-75; chief of staff Ark. Children's Hosp., Little Rock, 1959; chief surgery Meml. Hosp., Little Rock, 1965; clin. prof. surgery U. Ark. Med. Center, Little Rock, 1955—. Med. dir. Union Life Ins. Co., Little Rock, 1974. Served with U.S. Army, 1943-46, M.C., 1st Marine Div., USNR, 1952-54; Korea. Diplomate Am. Bd. Surgery. Mem. A.C.S., Am. Coll. Chest Physicians, Alpha Omega Alpha. Presbyn. (elder, deacon). Home: 18 Sunset Dr Little Rock AR 72207 Office: 990 Med Towers Bldg Little Rock AR 72207

GRAHAM, HUGH ZWINGLE, JR., bank exec.; b. Greenville, S.C., Sept. 5, 1941; s. Hugh Zwingle and Hessie (Morrah) G.; A.B., The Citadel, 1963; J.D., U. S.C. 1966; m. Mary Elliott Ball, Aug. 29, 1965; children—Anne Stuart, Mary Elliott. Admitted to S.C. bar, 1966, U.S. Supreme Ct. bar, 1971; practiced law, Greenville, 1968-70; v.p. S.C. Nat. Bank, Greenville, 1970-75, sr. v.p., dir. trust, 1975—; asst. solicitor 13th Jud. Circuit, S.C., 1968-70. Chmn., S.C. Exchange Bldg. Commn. Served with U.S. Army, 1966-68. Decorated Army Commendation medal. Mem. S.C. Bankers Assn. (pres. trust div.). Office: 1241 Main St Columbia SC 29202

GRAHAM, JIMMY, physician; b. Atlanta, Jan. 14, 1949; s. Luther Jerome and Dorothy Louise (White) G.; B.S. in Chemistry, Emory Coll., 1971; M.D., Columbia U., 1975; m. Vickie Laverne Miller, Apr. 11, 1974; children—Charity Renay, Jimmina Laverne. Intern, Emory U. Affiliated Hosps., Atlanta, 1975-76, resident in internal medicine, 1976-78; fellow in rheumatology/immunology Emory U. Sch. Medicine, 1978-79; practice medicine, specializing in internal medicine and clin. rheumatology, Atlanta, 1979—. Diplomate Am. Bd. Internal Medicine. Asso. A.C.P.; mem. Atlanta Med. Assn., Ga. Rheumatism Soc. Baptist. Office: 777 Cleveland Ave Atlanta GA 30315

GRAHAM, LARRY HUGH, food co. exec.; b. Wayne County, N.C., Aug. 20, 1947; s. Jesse Ervin and Hilda Gray (Westbrook) G.; A.S. in Acctg., Mt. Olive Coll., 1972; B.S. cum laude, U. N.C., 1974; m. Cornelia Wells Powell, Aug. 15, 1970; 1 dau., Susan Alyse. With Mt. Olive Pickle Co., Inc. (N.C.), 1965—, asst. plant mgr., 1974-77, sec., controller, 1977—. Served with U.S. Army, 1967-69. Decorated Bronze Star. Democrat. Mem. Christian Ch. (Disciples of Christ). Club: Masons. Home: Route 2 Box 543 Dudley NC 28333 Office: PO Box 609 Mount Olive NC 28365

GRAHAM, PAUL RONALD, med. supply co. exec.; b. Buffalo, Oct. 10, 1946; s. Paul Edwards and Beatrice Ruth (Glaesner) G.; A.S.D., Sinclair Coll., 1966; B.A., Wright State U., 1970; m. Mary Agnes Beck, Oct. 23, 1971; children—Rebecca Anne, Michael Paul and Timothy Leonard (twins). Phys. dir. Kettering (Ohio) YMCA, 1971-75; sr. program dir. Charleston YMCA, Charleston, W.Va., 1975-77; sales rep. Med-Pak Corp., Charleston, 1977-78, sales mgr., 1978—. Bd. dirs. Charleston Area Heart Assn. Mem. Assn. Profl. Dirs. Nat. Council YMCA, Am. Mgmt. Assn. Democrat. Lutheran. Club: Optimists. Home: 116 Carson St Saint Albans WV 25177 Office: Med-Pak Corp Rock Branch Indsl Park Poca WV 25159

GRAHAM, PHILIP ALAN, engring. co. exec.; b. Ottumwa, Iowa, Nov. 23, 1941; s. Ray Ott and Mildred Bertina (Moore) G.; B.S., Mass. Inst. Tech., 1963; M.S., Rensselaer Poly. Inst., 1965, Ph.D., 1972; m. Kathleen Janet Hay, June 19, 1965 (div. 1979); children—David Scott, Daniel Timothy. Project engr. U.S. Naval Air Propulsion Test Center, 1967-68; research asso. George Washington U., 1970-72; pres. Serv-O-Link Corp., Ft. Worth, 1973-78, Audio Books, Inc., Ft. Worth, 1974—. Served as officer USNR, 1965-67. Mem. Am. Inst. Aeros. and Astronautics, ASME. Author tech. reports, research papers. Home: 2604 W Waggoman St Fort Worth TX 76110 Office: 2600 W Waggoman St Fort Worth TX 76110

GRAHAM, ROY EUGENE, architect; b. Shreveport, La., Aug. 20, 1938; s. Cecil Clare and Lise Picton (Coffey) G.; B.S., La. State U., 1960; M.A., U. Va., 1968; postgrad. U. Tex., Austin, 1973-75; children—Heather, Elizabeth Picton. Asst. prof. Sch. Architecture and Planning, U. Tex., Austin, 1968-72, asso. prof., 1973; instr. Sch. Gen. Studies U. Va., Charlottesville, 1967-68, archtl. coordinator planning dept., 1965-66, vis. prof. archtl. history, 1975—; self-employed as architect, Shreveport, 1965; mem. firm Randle Hand-Claude Franklin, Architects, Shreveport, 1964-65, Butler & Dobson, Architects, Natchitoches, La., 1960-64; resident architect Colonial Williamsburg Found. (Va.), 1973—. Del. Nat. Conservation Adv. Council, 1978-79; treas. Found. Preservation Tech., 1975-79; mem. properties com. Nat. Trust Hist. Preservation, 1979; bd. dirs. 20th Century Gallery, 1975-76. Served to capt. U.S. Army, 1959-60. Recipient award of achievement in archtl. preservation San Antonio Conservation Soc., 1972; Thomas Jefferson Meml. scholar U. Va., 1967, 68, Attingham Adult Coll. scholar, Shropshire, Eng., 1966. Mem. Assn. Preservation Tech. (v.p. 1978-79), AIA (mem. com. on hist. resources 1975-79), Soc. Archtl. Historians (chmn. Attingham scholarship com.), Coll. Art Assn., Nat. Trust Eng., Nat. Trust Scotland, Assn. State and Local History, English Speaking Union, Friends of Cast Iron Architecture, Victorian Soc. Am. (v.p. 1979-80). Author: Progressive Preservation, 1972; Texas Historic Forts, 1968. Home: Ludwell-Paradise House Duke of Gloucester St Williamsburg VA 23185 Office: Colonial Williamsburg Found Drawer C Williamsburg VA 23185

GRAHAM, SHARON SHANKS, audiologist; b. Little Rock, Nov. 18, 1946; d. John W. and Wilda Carson (Barnes) Shanks; B.A. with highest honors, So. Methodist U., 1967, M.A. with highest honors, 1969; m. Nathan Graham, May 24, 1969. Cons. audiology and speech pathology N.E. Tex. Edn. Service Center, 1969-70; instr. spl. edn. U. Ark., 1973-74, adj. clin. supr. communicative disorders, 1972-73, 76-78; clin. audiologist Ear and Nose-Throat Clinic, P.A., Little Rock, 1971—, coordinator hearing prosthetics and rehab. audiology, 1974-78; dir. diagnostic audiology Bailey-Pappas Ear Clinic, P.A., Little Rock, 1971-74, coordinator research and devel., dir. cochlear implant project, 1979—; pres. Ark. Bd. Hearing Aid Dispensers, 1974-75. Mem. Am. Soc. Med. Audiology (pres. 1978-80), Am. Speech and Hearing Assn., So. Med. Audiology Soc., So. Audiological Soc., Ark. Speech and Hearing Assn. Episcopalian. Author papers in field. Home: 8 Racquet Ct Little Rock AR 72207 Office: 1200 Medical Towers Bldg Little Rock AR 72205

GRAHAM, WALTER HOPKINS, thoracic, cardiovascular surgeon; b. Phila., Oct. 27, 1934; s. Walter Hopkins and Metta (Hudgins) G.; B.A., Va. Mil. Inst., 1956; M.D., Med. Coll. Va., 1960; m. Sylvia Ann Smith, June 16, 1956; children—Walter H. III, Ann C., Robert Gary, Cynthia L. Intern, Med. Coll. Va., Richmond, 1960-61, resident in surgery, 1961-65, resident in thoracic surgery, 1967-69, surg. instr., NIH research fellow, 1967-69; now staff thoracic surgeon Riverside Hosp., Newport News, Va.; clin. asst. prof. surgery Eastern Va. Med. Sch. Served with U.S. Army, 1965-67. Diplomate Am. Bd. Surgery, Am. Bd. Thoracic Surgery. Fellow A.C.S.; mem. Soc. Thoracic Surgeons, So. Thoracic Surg. Assn., Humera Soc., Med. Soc. Va., Newport News Med. Soc. (sec.-treas.). Episcopalian. Contbr. articles on thoracic, cardiovascular surgery to med. jours. Home: 114 Dogwood Dr Newport News VA 23606 Office: 11030 Warwick Blvd Newport News VA 23601

GRAHAM, WALTER WAVERLY, III, computer co. exec.; b. Nashville, Apr. 30, 1933; s. Walter Waverly and Irene (Turner) G.; B.S., U.S. Naval Acad., 1955; M.S. (AEC spl fellow), Vanderbilt U., 1960; Ph.D. (AEC spl. fellow), Ga. Inst. Tech., 1965; m. Ann Elizabeth Bennett, June 3, 1955; children—Kerry, Holly. Research and devel. staff asso. Gen. Atomic div. Gen. Dynamics Co., La Jolla, Calif., 1960-62; asso. prof. nuclear engrng. Ga. Inst. Tech., 1965-70; v.p. Tech. Analysis Corp., Atlanta, 1970-73, pres., 1973—; cons. Eberline Instrument Co.; seminar lectr. Am. Mgmt. Assn.; mem. nuclear safeguards com. Ga. Inst. Tech. Mem. organizing com. Friendship Force Flight, Atlanta to Brussels, 1978. Served with USN, 1955-59. Mem. Am. Mgmt. Assn., Sigma Xi. Presbyterian. Co-author: Experiments in Logic Design and Computer Interfacing, 1971; contbr. articles on nuclear reactor kinetics and computers in edn. to profl. jours., 1961-71; patentee digital credit system. Home: 4700 Jett Rd NW Atlanta GA 30327 Office: 120 W Wieuca Rd NE Atlanta GA 30342

GRAHAM, WILLIAM EDGAR, JR., utility co. exec., lawyer; b. Jackson Springs, N.C., Dec. 31, 1929; s. William E. and Minnie A. G.; A.B. in Econs., U. N.C., 1952, J.D. with honors, 1956; m. Jean Dixon McLaurin, Nov. 24, 1962; children—William McLaurin, John McMillan, Sally Faircloth. Admitted to N.C. bar, 1956; law clk. to Chief Judge John J. Parker, U.S. Ct. Appeals, 1956-57; practiced law, Charlotte, N.C., 1957-69; judge N.C. Ct. Appeals, 1969-73; v.p., sr. counsel Carolina Power & Light Co., Raleigh, 1973, now sr. v.p., gen. counsel, group exec. legal, regulatory and communications group. Served with USAF, 1952-54. Mem. Am. Bar Assn., N.C. State Bar, N.C. Bar Assn., Am. Judicature Soc. Presbyterian. Office: PO Box 1551 Raleigh NC 27602

GRAHAM, WILLIAM THOMAS, lawyer; b. Wayneboro, Va., Oct. 24, 1933; s. James Monroe and Margaret Virginia (Goodwin) G.; A.B., Duke U., 1956; postgrad. U. Hawaii, summer 1958, Wake Forest U., summer 1961; J.D., U. Va., 1962; m. Nancy Kent Hill, Feb. 1, 1958; children—William Thomas, Ashton Cannon. Admitted to N.C. bar, 1962; partner firm Craige, Brawley, Horton & Graham, Winston-Salem, N.C., 1965-69; asst. gen. counsel HUD, Washington, 1969-70; partner firm Billings & Graham, Winston-Salem, 1971-75; judge N.C. Superior Ct., Winston-Salem, 1975-79; partner firm Graham, Glenn, Crumpler & Habegger, Winston-Salem, 1979—; mem. N.C. Bd. Corrections, 1976-79; judge trial practice seminar Wake Forest U. Law Sch., 1977—. Chmn., Forsyth County Republican party, 1966-69, 73-75; co-chmn. Com. to Re-Elect the Pres., Forsyth County, Forsyth County Holshouser for Gov. Com., 1972. Served with U.S. Army, 1957-58. Recipient Sr. Party award N.C. Young Reps., 1971. Mem. Am. Bar Assn., N.C. Bar Assn., Va. State Bar, Forsyth County Bar Assn., N.C. Acad. Trial Lawyers. Methodist. Club: Old Town. Columnist Winston-Salem Suburbanite, 1973-74; restaurant editor Triad Mag., 1980—. Home: 1000 Arbor Rd Winston-Salem NC 27104 Office: Graham Glenn Crumpler & Habegger 102 Cherry St Winston-Salem NC 27102

GRAINGER, EDWARD WALTER, chem. engr.; b. Ilion, N.Y., June 13, 1944; s. Edward Joseph and Florence Alberta (Ludwig) G.; B.S., Clarkson Coll. Tech., 1966; m. Janet Lee Church, Aug. 17, 1972; 1 dau., Stephanie Michelle. Process engr. Corning Glass Works, Horseheads, N.Y., 1966-67, Martinsburg, W.Va., 1967-69, quality control engr., Martinsburg, 1969-73, supr. quality control, 1973—. Scoutmaster, Shenandoah area council Boy Scouts Am., 1967-69, explorer post advisor, 1973—. Registered profl. engr., Calif. Mem. Am. Inst. Chem. Engrs., Am. Soc. Quality Control. Home: 1001 Windemere Rd (Stoneleigh) Inwood WV 25428 Office: Corning Glass Works Martinsburg WV 25401

GRAIVIER, LEONARD, pediatric surgeon; b. Chgo., Nov. 5, 1928; s. Solomon and Jennie (Klojz) G.; B.S., U. Ill., 1949, M.S., 1950; M.D., Chgo. Med. Sch., 1954; m. Pauline F. Pierce, July 16, 1954; children—Lisa, Miles, Tracy. Intern, Cook County Hosp., 1954-55, resident in gen. surgery, 1958-62; resident in pediatric surgery Children's Hosp. Pitts., 1963-64; teaching fellow pediatric surgery Sch. Medicine, U. Pitts., 1963-64; practice medicine specializing in pediatric surgery, Dallas, 1964—; clin. asso. prof. pediatric surgery Southwestern Med. Sch., U. Tex., Dallas, 1972—; cons. March of Dimes Birth Defect Center, Dallas, 1964—. Regional vol. chmn. Nat. Found. March of Dimes, 1970—, recipient Leadership award, 1975, 76. Served to capt. USAF, 1956-58. Diplomate Am. Bd. Surgery, Am. Bd. Pediatric Surgery. Fellow A.C.S., Am. Acad. Pediatrics, Southwestern Surg. Congress; mem. Am. Pediatric Surg. Assn. (charter), Am. Trauma Soc. (founding), Phi Delta Epsilon. Jewish. Club: B'nai B'rith (Anti-Defamation League). Contbr. articles on surgery to profl. jours. Home: 5509 Lindenshire Ln Dallas TX 75230 Office: Suite 867 Locke Med Bldg 6011 Harry Hines Blvd Dallas TX 75235

GRAMM, PHIL, congressman; b. Ft. Benning, Ga., July 8, 1942; B.B.A. in Econs., U. Ga., 1964, Ph.D. in Econs., 1967; m. Wendy Lee, 1970; children—Marshall Kenneth, Jefferson Philip. Prof. econs. Tex. A&M U., 1967-78; partner Gramm & Assos., 1971-78; mem. 96th Congress from 6th Congl. Dist. Tex. Named Outstanding Young Man of Yr., Brazos County Jaycees, 1976, One of 5 Outstanding Young Texans, Tex. Jaycees, 1977. Author several books and monographs; contbr. articles to Am. Econ. Rev., Jour. Money, Credit and Banking, Jour. Econ. History. Office: Room 1609 Longworth House Office Bldg Washington DC 20515

GRAMMER, JOHN COLQUITTE, physician; b. Brenham, Tex., June 20, 1925; s. John Colquitte and Elizabeth (Miller) G.; student Tex. A. and M. Coll., 1942-43; M.D., Southwestern Med. Sch., 1947; student U. Pa. Grad. Sch. Medicine, 1953-54; m. Jessica Turpin, May 11, 1956; children—John Miller, Robert Turpin. Intern, City-County Hosp., Ft. Worth, Tex., 1947-48; resident Gen. Hosp., Kansas City, Mo., 1948-50; practice medicine specializing in internal medicine, Midland, Tex., 1954-66; fellow cardiovascular diseases Scripps Clinic and Research Found., La Jolla, Calif., 1966-67; cons. cardiologist, dir. coronary care unit St. Paul Hosp., Dallas, 1967—, also dir. tng. courses nurses and physicians; chief cardiology Med. Arts Hosp., Dallas, 1979—; clin. asso. prof. U. Tex. Southwestern Med. Sch., Dallas. Served with M.C., USMC, 1951-53; lt. USNR Res. Diplomate Am. Bd. Internal Medicine. Fellow Am. Coll. Cardiology, Am. Coll. Chest Physicians, A.C.P.; mem. Tex. Acad. Internal Medicine, Am. Soc. Internal Medicine, Tex. Club Internists, Sigma Nu, Phi Chi. Home: 3809 Stratford St Dallas TX 75205 Office: 5909 Harry Hines St Dallas TX 75235

GRAMS, IRVING JOHN, II, prodn. controller; b. South Bend, Ind., Nov. 4, 1948; s. Irving John and Rose Marie (Zummer) G.; B.S., East Tex. State U., 1970, M.B.A., 1976; m. Carolyn McMichael, May 26, 1970; children—Dawn Marie, April Joanna. Dir. computer sci. dept. Texarkana Bus. Coll., 1973; intern U.S. Dept. Army, Red River Army, Depot, Texarkana, Tex., 1973-74, prodn. controller, 1974-79, chief maintenance plan sect., 1979—. Alderman, Hooks, Tex., 1977-79; pres. East Hooks PTA, 1979—. Served with USAF, 1971-73. Mem. Assn. M.B.A. Execs., Hooks C. of C. Presbyterian. Home: Box 800 Hooks TX 75561 Office: SDSRR-SP (Grams) Texarkana TX 75501

GRAND, JOHN LOUIS ROCHON, architect; b. Washington, Nov. 12, 1909; s. Jean Louis and Reine Agnes (Rochon) G.; student George Washington U., 1926-28; B.S., Cath. U. Am., 1931, A.M., 1932; cert. in architecture Beaux-Arts Inst. Design, 1933; postgrad. U.S. Dept. Agr. Grad. Sch., 1936, Columbia U., summer 1938, Art Students League, 1938; m. Winifred Mary Metcalfe, June 14, 1939; children—Jeanne Metcalfe, Kathleen Rochon. Draftsman, Murphy & Olmsted, Washington, 1929-32; asst. architect with various firms and govt. depts., 1932-35; head exhbns. Housing Div., Public Works Adminstrn., 1935-36; pvt. practice architecture, Washington, 1936-37; mem. faculty U. Fla., Gainesville, 1937-75, prof. architecture, 1947-75, head dept., 1948-56, prof. emeritus, 1975—, dir. Univ. Center of Arts, 1949-56. Served to capt. C.E., U.S. Army, 1942-46. LeBrun scholar, 1940. Mem. AIA (dir. No. Fla. chpt. 1951, 53-55, pres. 1952, sec. 1961-69, treas. S. Atlantic regional council 1957-59, treas. Fla. dist. 1959-61, Dedicated Service award 1970), Soc. Beaux-Arts Architects (asso.), Beaux-Arts Inst. Design (hon.). Democrat. Roman Catholic.

GRANDALSKI, MATTHEW FRANK, air force officer; b. Erie, Pa., Apr. 1, 1945; s. Matthew and Audrey Bell (Palmer) G.; asso. degree Ga. Mil. Coll., 1978; Asso. Applied Sci., Community Coll. of Air Force, 1978; B.B.A. in Mgmt., Tex. Christian U., 1978; m. Judith.A. Steinbaugh, Oct. 30, 1965; children—Michael David, Steven Matthew. Brass moulder Tanner Mfg. Co., Erie, Pa., 1963-65; served as enlisted man U.S. Air Force, 1965-78, commd. 2d lt., 1979, advanced through grades to 2d lt., 1979; tech. instr., Chanute AFB, Ill., 1965-67; maintenance analyst, Takhli, Thailand, 1968, Vandenberg AFB, Calif., 1969; advanced analysis course cons., Chanute AFB, Ill., 1970-73; maintenance analyst Osan AB, Korea, 1974, Carswell AFB, Tex., 1974-78; resource plans officer, Homestead AFB, Fla., 1979—. Coach youth football teams, 1970-73; v.p. Benbrook Girls Soft Ball Assn., 1974-76. Decorated Air Force Commendation medal. Mem. Non-Commd. Officer Acad. Grads. Assn., Jr. Officer Council. Roman Catholic. Club: Homestead AFB Officers. Office: 18450 SW 92 Pl Miami FL 33157

GRANGER, FLOYD RANDOLPH, II, research co. exec.; b. San Pedro, Calif., Dec. 29, 1940; s. Floyd Randolph and Cecelia (Genta) G.; student Anthony Sch. for Gen. Contractors, 1962, Greenville Tech. Sch., 1974; m. Priscilianna Marquez, Aug. 24, 1964; children—Suzanne, Deborah, Kathleen, Floyd Randolph III, Frank. With constrn. firms, Los Angeles area, 1961-63; partner Crane Constrn. Co., Los Angeles area, 1963-65; gen. constrn. supt. in Los Angeles area, 1965-70; pres. F.R. Granger Builders, Greenville, S.C., 1970-74; pres. Helio Thermics Inc., Greenville, 1974—. Served with USNR, 1959-61. HUD grantee. Mem. Internat., S.C. solar energy socs. Democrat. Roman Catholic. Patentee solar collector, solarheating cooling system. Home: 24 Heard Dr Greenville SC 29605 Office: 1070 Donaldson Center Indsl Park Orion St Greenville SC 29607

GRANSTAFF, EDWARD LEE, agrl. scientist; b. Pryor, Okla., Feb. 6, 1921; s. William Hugh and Della Kathryn (Madole) G.; B.S., Okla. State U., 1947, M.S., 1966; m. Marcia Jeanne Livingston, Sept. 24, 1943; children—William Edward, Kristen Jeanne, Michael Pitts. Agrl. agt. Union Equity Coop. Exchange, Enid, Okla., 1947-48; mktg. specialist extension grain Okla. State U., Stillwater, 1948-50, regional grain U.S. Dept. Agr., Stillwater, 1950-53; prof. agr., specialist extension crops Okla. State U., 1953—; chmn. Nat. Certified Alfalfa Variety Rev. Bd., 1976—; adv. com. Certified Alfalfa Seed Council Inc., Bakersfield, Calif., 1974—; mem. variety certification com. Nat. Alfalfa Improvement Conf., 1970—. Served with U.S. Army, 1943-46. Decorated Purple Heart. Mem. Assn. Ofcl. Seed Certifying Agys. (pres. 1972-73), Am. Seed Trade Assn. (program chmn. farm seed ann. conf. 1967), Am. Soc. Agronomy (chmn. div. c-4 1969), Okla. Crop Improvement Assn. (sec.-treas. 1953—), Okla. (sec.-treas. 1970—), So. seedmen's assns., Alpha Zeta, Epsilon Sigma Phi, Farmhouse (nat. dir. 1966-70). Democrat. Methodist. Home: 1501 Fairway Dr Stillwater OK 74074 Office: 368 Ag Hall Okla State U Stillwater OK 74074

GRANT, ALEX, labor rep.; b. Savannah, Ga., July 28, 1940; s. Alexander and Hester Ann (Graham) G.; grad. pub. schs.; m. Albertha Holmes, Oct. 12, 1957; children—Elizabeth, Anthony, Ronald, Sheryl, Yasmin, Donna. Mem. Internat. Exec. Bd., 1972-76, staff rep., 1972—, staff human rights rep., 1977—. Mem. Ad Hoc Labor Com., NAACP, 1977—; mem. operating com. A. Phillip Randolph Inst., 1976—. Democrat. Baptist. Mason. Home: 35 Barrington Circle Savannah GA 31405 Office: 1225 E McMillan St Cincinnati OH 45206

GRANT, ALICE BOYLE, ret. educator; b. Wayne County, Mich., Aug. 18, 1911; d. James Lee Robinson and Rebecca (Hopkins) Boyle; B.A., U. Cin., 1932, Certificate in Journalism, 1947; m. Lloyd Winslow Grant, Sept. 30, 1932; children—Stephen Lloyd, Andrew Merritt. Clinic registrar, social service dept. Children's Hosp., Cin., 1932-40; psychologist in market and consumer research, 1947-50; field supr. U.S. Dept. Agr., Washington, 1947-51; indsl. psychologist RCA Corp., Cin., 1951-52; secondary sch. tchr. Cin. Pub. Schs., 1953-73, curriculum specialist, 1955-73. Mem. Am. Personnal and Guidance Assn., NEA, Nat. Council Tchrs. English, Nat. Council for Econ. Edn., AAUW (group leader for drama Tyler br. 1976-78), Assn. Supervision and Curriculum Devel, Ohio Edn. Assn., Nat. Vocat. Guidance Assn., Piney Woods Personnel and Guidance Assn., Tyler Women's Forum, D.A.R., United Daus. of the Confederacy, Mensa (proctor for E. Tex.), Triple Nine Soc., Chi Delta Phi, Kappa Delta Pi, Alpha Chi Omega. Republican. Episcopalian. Author: Curriculum Guide for Job Training Course, 1960; co-author: Curriculum Guide Newswriting, 1961. Address: PO Box 243 Cumberland Ridge Bullard TX 75757

GRANT, DAVID ALAN, physician; b. Mart, Tex., Nov. 28, 1926; s. Walter Lee and Emma (Reichert) G.; student Tex. Christian U., 1944-45; B.A., U. Tex., 1947, M.D., 1951; m. Alice Louise Inskeep, Dec. 23, 1949; children—Cynthia Lynn, Karen Ann. Intern, Emory U., 1951-52; resident U. Tex. Med. Br., 1954-60; practice medicine specializing in aesthetic and reconstructive plastic surgery, Ft. Worth, 1960—; mem. staffs St. Joseph's, All Saints Episcopal. Ft. Worth Children's, W. I. Cook Childrens', Glenview hosps.; mem. staff, chmn. bd. trustees Med. Plaza Hosp.; chief div. surgery Harris Hosp., 1971-73, surgeon-in-chief, 1975-78; chief div. plastic surgery John Peter Smith Hosp., 1969-74; Pres. bd. dirs. Tarrant County Easter Seal Soc. for Crippled Children and Adults, 1971-72. Served to lt. (j.g.) M.C., USNR, 1952-54. Diplomate Am. Bd. Surgery, Am. Bd. Plastic Surgery. Fellow A.C.S.; mem. AMA, Tex., So. med. assns., Tarrant County Med. Soc., Southwestern Surg. Congress, Ft. Worth Acad. Medicine, Tex., Ft. Worth (v.p. 1977, pres. 1978), Singleton (1st v.p. 1965, 77, pres. 1979) surg. socs., Am. Burn Assn., Tex. Soc. Plastic Surgery (v.p. 1969-70, pres. 1971), Am. Soc. Plastic and Reconstructive Surgery, Am. Assn. for Hand Surgery, Am. Assn. Plastic Surgery, Am. Assn. Physicians and Surgeons, Sigma Xi, Phi Beta Pi, Alpha Epsilon Delta, Alpha Phi Omega. Rotarian (dir. 1964-66). Home: 2736 Colonial Pkwy Fort Worth TX 76109 Office: 800 8th Ave Fort Worth TX 76104

GRANT, GEORGE THOMAS, optometrist; b. Chgo., Oct. 17, 1937; s. George Merton and Juanita (Battistoni) G.; student Ill. State U., 1956-58, Thornton Jr. Coll., 1958-59; D.Optometry, Ill. Coll. Optometry, 1962; children by previous marriage—Jeffrey Thomas, Matthew Thomas, Brynn Elizabeth; m. Donna Jean Grant, July 30, 1975. Practice optometry, Perry, Ga., 1962-63, Hinesville, Ga., 1964-71, Cartersville, Ga., 1972-75, Hinesville, Ga., 1975—. Mem. Liberty County Bd. Health Hinesville, 1964-71; Liberty County rep. Comprehensive Health Planning, 1968-71; mem. Liberty County Title I Adv. Com., 1968-71, Liberty County Recreation Commn., 1970-71; pres. Coastal Areawide Comprehensive Health Planning Council, 1970-71; mem. Ga. Comprehensive Health Planning Council, 1972-76; chpt. chmn. Liberty County chpt. ARC, 1964-66, mem. Bartow County chpt., 1972-75; chmn. plan devel. com., chmn. project rev. com., bd. dirs., v.p. S.E. Ga. Health Systems Agy., 1978—. Liberty County campaign chmn. Jimmy Carter for Gov., 1970. Recipient award of appreciation ARC, 1966; named Ga. Optometrist of Year, 1975; commd. adm. Ga. Navy, 1971. Fellow Am. Acad. Optometry (sec.-treas. Ga. chpt. 1970-72, chpt. pres. 1972-75); mem. Am., Ga. (pres. 1974-75) optometric assns., Ga. Vision Services (dir. 1971-74), So. Council Optometrists (trustee 1975-76), 1st Dist. (pres. 1965-66), 7th Dist. optometric socs., C. of C. (past pres. Liberty County, v.p., dir., past pres. Cartersville-Bartow County), Mensa (proctor SE Ga. area), Tomb and Key, Beta Sigma Kappa. Club: Rotary (pres. 1978-79). Home: PO Box 555 Hinesville GA 31313 Office: 513 Oglethorpe Hwy Hinesville GA 31313

GRANT, GERRY LEE, veterinarian; b. Pine Bluff, Ark., Aug. 30, 1940; s. Otis Edgar and Mary Howard (Suit) G.; B.S., Okla. State U., 1964, D.V.M., 1966; m. Beverly Gale Mc Minn, June 18, 1967; children—Lee Edgar, Craig Mc Minn. Asso. Animal Med. Clinic, Clarksdale, Miss., 1966-67; resident veterinarian Beaver Dam Angus Ranch, Dundee, Miss., 1970-71; owner Animal Med. Clinic, Clarksdale, Miss., 1971—. Served to capt., U.S. Army, 1967-69. Mem. Clarksdale-Coahoma County C. of C. (dir. 1975-78), Am., Miss. vet. med. assns., Am. Animal Hosp. Assn. (hosp. dir.), Am. Assn. Bovine Practitioners, Miss. Cattlemen's Assn., Miss. Farm Bur., Beta Theta Pi. Methodist (ofcl. bd. mem. 1972—, chmn. 1978). Clubs: Rotary (dir. 1975, 79), Clarksdale Country. Home: 309 Maple Clarksdale MS 38614 Office: Hwy 61 S Clarksdale MS 38614

GRANT, HENRY GIGNILLIAT, youth and community devel. extension agt.; b. Westminster, S.C., May 26, 1948; s. Odis and Marie (Henderson) G.; B.S., S.C. State Coll., 1969; M.S., U. Fla., Gainesville, 1972; postgrad. Fla. State U., 1974, Fla. A. and M. U., 1975. Extension agt. youth and community devel. Fla. Cooperative Extension Service of U. Fla., Gainesville, and Fla. A. and M. U., Tallahassee and Quincy, 1973—. Chmn., Community Devel. Block Grant Com., Gretna, Fla., 1975; co-chmn. Gadsden County (Fla.) Citizens Planning and Adv. Com., 1975. Rockefeller Acad. Devel. fellow, 1969-72. Mem. Am. Soc. Microbiology, Nat., Fla. assns. county agr. agts., Fed. Employees Assn. (pres. 1975). Baptist (clk. 1975). Home: PO Box 122 Gretna FL 32332 Office: PO Box 820 Quincy FL 32351

GRANT, JAMES MARSE, editor; b. High Point, N.C., Sept. 13, 1920; s. Lon L. and Elsie (Warren) G.; A.B. with honors, High Point Coll., 1941, L.H.D., 1972; m. Marian Gibbs, June 16, 1942; children—Susan (Mrs. Robert Rawls), Marcia (Mrs. Kenneth Hungate), Carol. With personnel dept. Firestone Textiles, 1943-47; editor Ecusta Paper Corp. (now Olin), Pisgah Forest, N.C., 1947; editor Lincoln County News, Lincolnton, N.C., 1948, News-Herald, Morganton, N.C., 1949; editor Charity and Children for Bapt. Children's Homes, Bapt. State Conv. N.C., Thomasville, N.C., 1950-60, editor Bibl. Recorder, Raleigh, 1960—. Mem. N.C. Good Neighbor Council, 1963-71, exec. com., 1963-71; N.C. chmn. March of Dimes, 1964-67; mem. N.C. Gov.'s Com. Jobs for Ex-Offenders, 1970-74, Gov.'s Com. on Comprehensive Health Planning, 1974-77, So. Bapt. Radio and TV Commn., 1966-76, N.C. Adv. Com. Pub. Edn., 1970-72, Com. to Study N.C. Liquor Laws, 1973-75, chancellor's adv. com. on med. edn. East Carolina U., 1975—. Bd. dirs. N.C. Center for Pub. Policy Research, 1975-77. Mem. So. Bapt. Press Assn. (pres. 1970, chmn. state goals and policy bd. 1977-78). Author: Whiskey at the Wheel, 1970. Home: 1428 Ridge Rd Raleigh NC 27607 Office: Biblical Recorder PO Box 26568 Raleigh NC 27611

GRANT, JOHN G., publisher; b. Chgo., June 11, 1933; s. Gerald and Rosemary G.; B.A. magna cum laude in history, Princeton U., 1957; m. Madelyn A. Stephenson, Dec. 9, 1961; children—Bruce, Gillian. With McGraw-Hill Publs. Co., 1957-76, regional mgr., Houston, 1973-76; publ. mgr. Petroleum Engr. Pub. Co., 1976-78; pub. Petroleum Engr. Internat., Dallas, 1978—; v.p. Energy Publs. div. Harcourt Brace Jovanovich. Served with U.S. Army, 1954-56. Mem. Assn. Petroleum Writers. Clubs: Petroleum Engrs., Dallas Petroleum, N. Dallas Racquet, Nomads (Dallas). Office: Box 1589 Dallas TX 75221

GRANT, ROBERT NEIL, surgeon; b. Old Fort, N.C., Jan. 31, 1937; s. Ewart and Gay (McNeil) G.; M.D., Duke U., 1962; m. Ann Fry, June 21, 1959; children—Robert Neil, Jr., Tina Michelle. Intern, U. Oreg., Portland, 1962-63; resident Letterman Gen. Hosp., San Francisco, 1964-68; practice medicine specializing in surgery, San Angelo, Tex.; pres. Angelo Clinic Assn., San Angelo, 1975—; pres. staff Shannon Hosp., 1974—, chmn. med. bd., 1978—; chief surgery St. John's Hosp., 1973—. Pres., San Angelo chpt. Am. Cancer Soc., 1975-76; v.p. Little League Baseball Assn., 1977—. Served to lt. col. U.S. Army, 1964-71. Decorated Bronze Star. Diplomate Am. Bd. Surgery. Fellow A.C.S.; mem. Am., Tex. med. assns., Southwestern Surg. Soc., Soc. Abdominal Surgeons. Presbyterian. Contbr. articles to profl. jour. Home: 2501 Christoval Rd San Angelo TX 76901 Office: 120 E Beauregard St San Angelo TX 76901

GRANT, SILAS WINTON, physician, univ. adminstr.; b. Ravia, Okla., Mar. 1, 1921; s. William Capers and Nola Ella (Sharp) G.; B.A., U. Tex., Austin, 1942; M.D., U. Tex. Med. Br., Galveston, 1946; m. Bettye Griffiths, May 1, 1942; children—Evelyn (Mrs. Hugh Parmer), Stephen William. Intern John Sealy Hosp., Galveston, Tex., 1946-47; practice medicine, specializing in family practice, Hillsboro, Tex., 1947-72; mem. staffs Grant-Buie Hosp., Hillsboro, Huntsville (Ala.) Hosp., Med. Center Hosp., Huntsville, Crestwood Hosp., Huntsville; vis. asst. prof. family practice U. Ia., Iowa City, 1972-73; asso. dean Sch. Primary Med. Care, U. Ala. in Huntsville, 1973-77, 78—, acting dean, 1977-78. Mem. Am. com. of Superior Sch. of Medicine of Poly.

Inst. of Mexico City, Mexico, 1968-72. Pres. bd. trustees ednl. research Inst. Gen. Medicine, Austin, Tex., also bd. dirs. Diplomate Am. Bd. Family Practice (certification exam panel 1968-74, chmn. recertification com. 1974, 78). Fellow So. Geriatric Assn. (founding), Internat. Coll. Angiology; mem. Am. Acad. Family Practice (commn. on edn. 1964-70), AMA, N.Y. Acad. Sci., Soc. Tchrs. of Family Medicine (dir., chmn. com. publs. 1968-75), AAAS. Mason. Contbg. author: Management Processes, 1968. Editorial bds. Med. Digest, 1964—, Geriatric Digest, 1968—, Jour. Family Practice, 1972-75. Contbr. articles, revs. to profl. jours. Home: 702 Corlett St Huntsville AL 35802 Office: U of Ala in Huntsville Sch Primary Med Care Clin Sci Center 109 Governors Dr Huntsville AL 35801

GRANT, WILLIAM ALEXANDER, JR., coal mining co. exec.; b. Richmond, Va., Nov. 7, 1918; s. William A. and Louise T. (Hooper) G.; B.A., U. Richmond, 1941; m. Marion Louise Bankhead, Aug. 27, 1945; children—William Alexander, Walter. Founder, sec.-treas. Bankhead Mining Co., Jasper, Ala., 1953—; partner Cobb Coal Co.; Jefferson Coal Co., Bankhead Devel. Co. Inc.; pres., dir. Gatorland Broadcasting Co., Chattanooga Sound, Inc., GMC Broadcasting, Inc.; mem. firm Grant-Grant-Brown; dir. Tri W Broadcasting Inc., Franklin Broadcasting Inc., Live Line Inc., Viking Oil Co., Energy Explorations Inc., Realty Property Inc. Served with USNR, 1943-53. Decorated D.F.C., Navy Cross, Air medal with two gold stars. Mem. Jasper Area C. of C. (past dir.), Nat. Assn. Accts. Methodist. Clubs: Mosgrove Country, Birmingham Downtown, North River Yacht. Office: Bankhead Mining Co PO Box 1629 Jasper AL 35501

GRANTHAM, CHARLES EDWARD, broadcast engr.; b. Andalusia, Ala., Mar. 15, 1950; s. J.C. and Geraldine (Brooks) G.; student Enterprise State Jr. Coll., 1968-69; A.A., Lurleen B. Wallace Coll., 1979; m. Sandra J. Mosley, Mar. 9, 1973; 1 son, Christopher Charles. Sales engr., draftsman S.E. Ala. Gas Co., Andalusia, 1968-70; asst. mgr., engr. Sta. WAAO, Andalusia, 1972-78; engr. Ala. Public TV, WDIQ-TV, Dozier, Ala., also chief technician Sta. WAAO, Andalusia, 1978—. Notary public, Ala. Served with inf. U.S. Army, 1970-72. Named Civitan Outstanding Young Am., 1967. Mem. Country Music Assn., Country Music Disc Jockey Assn., Phi Theta Kappa. Mem. Ch. of Christ. Home: Route 5 Box 177A Andalusia AL 36420 Office: WDIQ TV Route 2 Dozier AL 36028

GRANTHAM, DEWEY WESLEY, historian; b. Manassas, Ga., Mar. 16, 1921; s. Dewey W. and Ellen (Holland) G.; A.B., U. Ga., 1942; M.A., U. N.C., 1947, Ph.D. (Waddell Meml. fellow), 1949; m. Virginia Burleson, Dec. 26, 1942; children—Wesley, Clinton, Lauren. Instr. in social sci. U. N.C., 1946-48, vis. asst. prof. history, summer 1950; asst. prof. North Tex. State Coll., 1949-50; asst. prof. U. N.C. Woman's Coll., 1950-52; asst. prof. Vanderbilt U., 1952-55, asso. prof., 1955-61, prof., 1961—, Harvie Branscomb Distinguished prof. history, 1971-72, Holland N. McTyeire prof. history, 1977—; vis. prof. Coe Inst., State U. N.Y., Stony Brook, summer, 1970; dir. Nat. Endowment for Humanities Summer Seminar for Tchrs., Vanderbilt U., summer, 1975. Fellowships in Residence for Coll. Tchrs. Seminar, 1976-77; Fund for Advancement of Edn. faculty fellow Harvard U., 1955-56; fellow Henry E. Huntington Library and Art Gallery, 1968-69; Fulbright-Hays lectr. U. Aix-en-Provence (France), 1978-79. Served with USCG, 1942-46. Recipient Charles S. Sydnor award for best book on So. history So. Hist. Assn., 1959. Social Sci. Research Council fellow, 1951, 59; John Simon Guggenheim Meml. Found. fellow, 1960. Mem. Am. Hist. Assn. (council 1969-71, bd. editors 1975-77, chmn. com. on program 1977), Orgn. Am. Historians (exec. bd. 1965-68, chmn. com. on program 1973), So. Hist. Assn. (pres. 1966-67), Am. Studies Assn. (pres. Ky.-Tenn. chpt. 1962-63), AAUP, Pi Gamma Mu, Phi Beta Kappa. Democrat. Unitarian. Author: Hoke Smith and the Politics of the New South, 1958; The Democratic South, 1963; The United States Since 1945: The Ordeal of Power, 1976; The Regional Imagination: The South and Recent American History, 1979. Home: 3510 Echo Hill Rd Nashville TN 37215 Office: Dept History Vanderbilt U Nashville TN 37235

GRANTHAM, STEVE WILEY, ins. co. exec.; b. Clinton, Iowa, May 4, 1936; s. Vernon Luther and Anna Belle (Ewing) G.; B.BA., U. Miss., 1959; m. Rosemary Flint, Apr. 7, 1958; children—Steve Wiley, Robert V. With Flint Brothers Constrn. Co., Jackson, Miss., 1959-62, Crystal Springs Ins. Agy., (Miss.), 1962-65; pres. Barksdale Bonding & Ins. Co., Jackson, 1965—; dir. Jackson Savs. & Loan Assn., Road Info. Program, Inc., Am. Inst. Mktg. Corp. Bd. dirs. YMCA, Miss. Heart Assn., United Way. Served with USN, 1955-57. Mem. Nat. Assn. Surety Bond Producers, Nat. Assn. Casualty and Surety Agts., Miss. Ins. Agts., Miss. Road Builders Assn., Am. Road and Transp. Builders Assn., Associated Gen. Contractors, Miss. Associated Builders and Contractors, U. Miss. Alumni Assn. Republican. Methodist. Clubs: Country of Jackson, Colonial Country, Capitol City Petroleum, Plimsoll, Mason. Home: 147 St Andrews Dr Jackson MS 39211 Office: PO Drawer 12189 Jackson MS 39211

GRASER, EARL JOHN, indsl. designer; b. Toledo, Dec. 27, 1920; s. Ottomar S. and Irene Olga (Frommer) G.; B.S., U. Cin., 1950; m. Marianne Loveless, Nov. 19, 1942; 1 dau., Cathy Ann. Asso., Edwin W. Fuerst Indsl. Design, Toledo, 1947-50; v.p., asso. Packaging and Product Devel. Inst., Cin., 1958-61; mgr. product devel. Olinkraft, Inc. Subs. Johns-Manville Corp., West Monroe, La., 1961-75, mgr. packaging systems div., 1975-77, dir. indsl. design, 1977—. Set design dir. Miss La. Pageant, 1974; flotilla comdr. USCG Aux., 1958-61; active Monroe Fine Arts Found., CAP, St. Francis Hosp. Bldg. Fund; bd. dirs. Monroe Little Theater. Served with USN, 1942-45. Recipient Inventor of Year award Olinkraft, Inc., 1971, Package of Year award Food and Drug Packaging mag., 1972, Packaging Design mag., 1972, Set Design of Year award Strauss Playhouse, 1974. Mem. Packaging Inst. U.S.A., World Packaging Orgn., Am. Mgmt. Assn., Am. Soc. Innovators in Tech. (dir.), Am. Frozen Food Inst., Nat. Soft Drink Assn., Soc. Indsl. Designers, Nat. Assn. Awareness in Music, Aircraft Owners and Pilots Assn., Soc. Soft Drink Technologists, Alpha Sigma Phi. Republican. Roman Catholic. Club: Aero Nutz, Inc. Contbr. articles on packaging to profl. jours. Patentee in field. Home: 3607 Hanging Moss Ln Monroe LA 71201 Office: PO Box 488 Jonesboro Rd West Monroe LA 71291

GRASER, JUDITH ANN, psychologist; b. Zanesville, Ohio, June 21, 1944; d. Robert W. and Margaret C. (Barnes) Paul; student (scholar) Chico (Calif.) State Coll., 1965-66; B.A., U. Calif., Sacramento, 1967, M.Ed., 1972; M. Counseling, Ariz. State U., Tempe, 1974; Ed.D. in Counseling Psychology (fellow), Ball State U., 1979; m. John C. Graser, May 2, 1970; 1 son, John R. Tchr. Pershing Elementary Sch., Orangevale, Calif., 1968-70; counselor, dept. chmn. spl. edn. Dysart High Sch.; Peoria, Ariz., 1973; counselor, cons. Devereux Sch. for Emotionally Handicapped and Learning Disabled, Tempe, Ariz., 1974; practicum asst. Ball State U.; counselor drug and alcohol abuse clinic, Ramstein Air Base, W. Ger., 1976-77, psychotherapist 2d. Gen. Hosp., Landstuhl, W. Ger., 1977-78; sch. psychologist Alexandria, Va., 1978—; asst. professorial lectr. George Washington U. Mem. Am. Personnel and Guidance Assn. Contbr. research papers to profl. publs. and confs. Home: 7927 Saint George Ct Springfield VA 22153 Office: 3011 Memorial St Alexandria VA 22306

GRASSER, ROBERT EVAR, mgmt. adminstr.; b. Rockford, Ill., Oct. 28, 1941; s. Willard Evar and Marion Helen Grasser; B.S. in Arch., U. Cin., 1965; M.S. in City and Regional Planning, Ohio State U., 1968; M.S. in Public Adminstrn., Auburn U., 1974; m. Linda Carol Hamm, Feb. 13, 1965; children—Terri Lynn, Denise Nikole. Engring. technician City of Cin. Planning Commn., 1960-65; urban planner dept. devel. City of Columbus (Ohio), 1965-68; project planner Urban Cons., Inc., Montgomery, Ala., 1968-70; regional planning coordinator State of Ala., 1970-71; devel. dir. Central Ala. Regional Planning and Devel. Commn., Montgomery, 1971-73, exec. dir., 1973—; instr. grad. urban studies program Ala. A&M U., 1970-71; mem. Urban Planning Adv. Bd., U. Ala., 1979—. Vol., Patch the Pony Child Abuse Program, 1974-78; bd. dirs. SE Ala. Health Systems Agy., 1973—; mem. Antanga-Elmore-Montgomery Manpower Consortium, chmn. program evaluation subcom. and mem. program research subcom., 1976—. Named Hon. Councilman, Town of Carrville, 1975. Mem. Am. Mgmt. Assn., Am. Planning Assn., Internat. City Mgmt. Assn. Home: 1729 Hillhedge Dr Montgomery AL 36106 Office: 808 S Lawrence St Montgomery AL 36104

GRASSIE, JOSEPH ROBERTS, city ofcl.; b. Buenos Aires, Argentina, Oct. 3, 1933 (parents Am. citizens); s. Joseph Flagg and Vida Clarisa (Roberts) G.; B.A., U. Chgo., 1958, M.A., 1960; m. Josette Krespi, Mar. 23, 1958; children—Yvonne, Scott. Staff cons. Pub. Adminstrn. Ser., Chgo., 1960-65, supervising cons., 1965-68, dep. city mgr. Grand Rapids, 1968-69, city mgr., 1970-76; city mgr. City of Miami, 1976—; lectr. public service Grand Valley State Colls., Mich., now mem. adv. bd. Mem. area adv. council Western Mich. U., adv. com. Ferris State Coll., U. Miami, trustee Public Adminstrn. Service, Washington; mem. Gov.'s Adv. Council on Mich. Inter-Govtl. Personnel Act. Trustee Grand Rapids Arts Council. Mem. Internat. City Mgmt. Assn., Am. Soc. Public Adminstrn., Am. Public Works Assn. Home: 2880 SW 33rd Ct Miami FL 33133 Office: 3500 Pan American Dr Miami FL 33133

GRAVEL, CAMILLE F(RANCIS), JR., lawyer, state ofcl.; b. Alexandria, La., Aug. 10, 1915; s. Camille F. and Aline (Delvaille) G.; student Notre Dame U., 1931-35, La. State U., 1935-37, Catholic U. Am., 1937-39; LL.D., Loyola U., New Orleans, 1976; m. Katherine Yvonne David, Nov. 26, 1939 (dec. May 1979); children—Katherine Ann (Mrs. Stephen J. Vanderslice), Mary Eileen (Mrs. Richard B. Cappell), Martha Louise (Mrs. Thomas A. Antoon), Camille F. III, Grady David, Eunice Holloman (Mrs. Joseph A. Mitchell), Virginia Maureen (Mrs. Charles L. Carbo, Jr.), Margaret Lynn, Mark Alan, Charles Gregory. Mem. U.S. Capitol Police Force, 1937-39; admitted to La. bar, 1940, U.S. Supreme Ct. bar, U.S. 5th Circuit Ct. Appeal bar, U.S. Dist. Cts. of La.; practiced in Alexandria, La., 1940—; sr. partner firm Gravel, Roy & Burnes; asst. dist. atty. Rapides Parish, La., 1942, atty. for inheritance tax collector, 1943-45; asst. atty. city of Alexandria, 1946-48; atty. La. Workmen's Compensation Laws and Tax Laws, 1964-65; spl. counsel on medicare to gov. of La., 1966-67, on health, 1967; mem. La. Interdepartmental Health Policy Commn., 1967-68; gen. counsel La. Labor-Mgmt. Commn. Inquiry, 1967; spl. legis. counsel to gov. La., 1972-75, exec. counsel, 1975—; spl. asst. atty. gen. ad hoc La., 1975—; chmn. La. Interim Emergency Bd., 1975—; mem. numerous state adv. panels and commns.; hon. brig. gen. on staff gov. La. Mem. Nat. Citizens Com. for Community Relations, 1964-68, La. Adv. Com. on Civil Rights, 1965-67, Nat. Adv. Bd. on Community Relations, 1965-67; founding mem. Com. on So. Progress; mem. adv. bd. Catholic Youth Orgn., Diocese of Alexandria. Mem. La. Democratic Central Com., 1948-64; presdl. elector, 1952; Dem. nat. committeeman for La., 1954-60; rep. on exec. com. Dem. Nat. Com., 1955-60; chmn. La. delegation Dem. Nat. Conv., 1956, chmn. site selection com., co-chmn. credentials com., mem. arrangements com., 1960, del., 1964, 72; mem. Nat. Adv. Council of Dem. Party, 1956-60; co-chmn. La. Lawyers for Johnson-Humphrey Presdl. Campaign, 1964; founding mem. So. Com. on Polit. Ethics, So. Polit. Edn. Action Com.; bd. dirs. La. Council on Human Relations, 1965-68, Catholic Charities, Diocese of Alexandria; bd. suprs. La. State U. and Agrl. Coll., 1975—. Decorated Knight of St. Gregory; recipient citation for outstanding achievement in field of politics Catholic U. Am., 1962. Fellow Internat. Acad. Trial Lawyers (dir. 1960-69), Internat. Soc. Barristers, Law Sci. Acad.; mem. Am., La. (vice chmn. constl. conv. com. 1953-56, gov. 1969-71, chmn. criminal law sect. 1971—), Alexandria (pres. 1949-50) bar assns., Notre Dame Law Assn. (dir. 1960-66, pres. 1962-63), Am. Judicature Soc., Nat. Assn. Criminal Def. Lawyers, Nat. Diocesan Attys. Assn., Am. Trial Lawyers Assn., Nat. Assn. Compensation Claimant's Attys. (asso. editor Law jour. 1954-68, state v.p. 1958-59), Alexandria-Pineville C. of C., Pub. Affairs Research Council, La. Civil Service League, Am. Legion, Internat. Platform Assn., La. Forestry Assn., La. Wildlife Fedn., L.Q.C. Lamar Soc., Catholic U. Am. Alumni Assn. (nat. gov. 1963-67, 71-72, past pres. Alexandria chpt.), Phi Delta Phi, Kappa Sigma. K.C. (4 deg.), Elk (past exalted ruler Alexandria). Club: City (Baton Rouge). Home: 3214 Carol Ct Alexandria LA 71301 also Apt 1A2 Pentagon Courts Baton Rouge LA 70804 Office: 711 Washington St Alexandria LA 71301 also Office of Gov State Capitol Baton Rouge LA 70804

GRAVEN, LYNDELL STARR, accountant; b. Glasgow, Ky., Nov. 21, 1949; s. Lawrence Garland and Velma (Starr) G.; B.S., Western Ky. U., 1972, M.A., 1974; m. Deborah Kay Johnson, Feb. 26, 1976. Instr. bus. for disadvantaged students Hopkinsville (Ky.) High Sch., 1972-73; distributive edn. coordinator Elizabethtown (Ky.) High Sch., 1974-75; acctg. clk. water-sewer div. Bowling Green (Ky.) Mcpl. Utilities, 1975-76, office mgr., 1976-78, supr. acctg., 1978—; tchr. Bowling Green Bus. Coll., 1975—. Mem. Am. Water Works Assn., Am. Public Works Assn., Mcpl. Fin. Officers Assn., Nat. Assn. Accts. (v.p. edn. and profl. devel. S. Central Ky. chpt.), Ky.-Tenn. Water-Sewer Acctg. and Fin. Assn. (sec.-treas.), Ky. Mcpl. Fin. Officers Assn. (sec.-treas., mem. exec. bd.). Baptist. Clubs: Ky. Mid-State Appaloosa Horse (newsletter editor 1978-79), Warren East Optimists (sec., pres.-elect 1980-81), Bowling Green Noon Lions. Home: Route 1 Box 32 Bowling Green KY 42101 Office: 801 Center St PO Box 478 Bowling Green KY 42101

GRAVES, CURTIS, chem. co. exec.; b. Denmark, S.C., June 15, 1935; s. Booker T. and Genevive (Faust) G.; B.S. in Mech. Engring., U. Wyo., 1971; M.E.A., U. Utah, 1976; m. Ina Arlean Holbrook, May 7, 1960; children—Ronald E., Wanda D., Alan D. Commd. 2d lt. U.S. Air Force, 1959, advanced through grades to col., 1975, ret., 1976; sr. mech. engr. E.I. DuPont de Nemours & Co., Inc., Aiken, S.C., 1976-78, area supr., 1978—; indsl. cons. Edn. Commn. of the States, Denver, 1978-79; rep. Nat. Adv. Council on Minorities in Engring., 1977—. Arbitrater for sch. dists. spl. edn. program, Denmark, S.C., 1978—; exec. com., parlimentarian County Grassroot Com., 1978-79; exec. com. S.C. Dem. Party, 1978, 79. Decorated Air Force Commendation medal, Bronze Star medal. Mem. ASME, Ret. Officers Assn., NAACP, Voorhees Alumni Assn. (pres. 1976-79). Clubs: D-O Band Booster, Viking Booster (v.p. 1979-80). Home: Route 2 Box 187 Denmark SC 29042 Office: E I DuPont de Nemours and Co Inc Savannah River Plant Aiken SC 29801

GRAVES, GORDON EUGENE, mfg. co. exec.; b. Phila., Feb. 10, 1948; s. Robert G. and Shirley Jean (Scudder) G.; student Kings Coll., 1967-68; B.B.A., Stephen F. Austin State U., 1972; m. Shirley Lynn Turner, May 23, 1971; children—Wendy Lea, Gordon Scott. Staff acct. Affiliated Food Stores, Inc., Dallas, 1972-73, Shop Rite Foods, Inc., Dallas, 1973-74, asst. acctg. mgr., 1974-76; asst. controller Jet Fleet Corp., Dallas, 1976—. Republican precinct chmn., Tarrant County, Tex., 1978—, mem. county exec. com. Mem. Nat. Assn. Accts., Credit Mgmt. Assn. Dallas, Credit Mgmt. Assn. Tex., Internat. Consumer Credit Assn., Alpha Kappa Psi. Baptist. Home: 2705 Woodshire Dr Arlington TX 76016 Office: 8605 Lemmon Ave Dallas TX 75209

GRAVES, LAWRENCE P., bishop; b. Texarkana, Ark., May 4, 1916; student St. John's Sem., Little Rock, Ark., North Am. Coll., Rome, Cath. U. Am. Ordained priest Roman Catholic Ch., 1942; titular bishop of Vina and aux. bishop of Little Rock, 1969-73; bishop of Alexandria (see title changed to Alexandria-Shreveport (La.) 1977), 1973—. Office: 2315 Texas Ave Alexandria LA 71306*

GRAVES, MARY JO, landscape contractor; b. Beirne, Ark., Aug. 26, 1928; d. Wells Albert and Stella Mae (Baker) Wright; student Henderson (Ark.) State Tchrs. Coll., 1946-48, La. Landscape Sch., 1968-71; extension student Ark. State Tchrs. Coll. Conway, 1948; m. Cleve Verlon Graves, Mar. 5, 1949; children—Cleve Verlon, Sandra Lyn Graves Sims. Tchr., Glenrose, Ark., 1947-49, England, Ark., 1950; partner N. Caddo Drug Co., Vivian, La., 1954—; propr. N. Caddo Landscape, Vivian, 1973—; horticulturist, beautification mgr. City of Vivian, 1973-78; mem. bd. Caddo-Bossier Conv. and Tourists Bur., 1975—, vice chmn., 1977; chmn. N.W. La., Gov.'s Clean-up and Beautification Com., 1975-76. Chmn. N. Caddo Parish Bicentennial Com., 1973-76, museum renovations furnishings chmn., 1970-76, 79-80; organizer Redbud Festival, 1964, pres., 1965-67; pres. Vivian Garden Club, 1963-65 organizer N.W. La. Wildflower Trail, 1979. Recipient award of appreciation from gov. La., 1974, 75; grantee La. Bicentennial Com., 1973; various other honors. Accredited master flower show judge. Mem. Landscape Design Critics Council, Council State Garden Clubs (pres. 1979-80), La. Garden Club Fedn. (judges council), N.W. La. Hist. Soc. Presbyterian. Club: North Highlands Garden (pres. 1976-78). Co-author: Monterey?, 1973. Home: 311 W Mary St Vivian LA 71082 Office: 144 W Louisiana St Vivian LA 71082

GRAVES, THOMAS DORLAND, lawyer; b. Hollywood, Calif., Mar. 22, 1936; s. George Murphy and Emmy Lou (Dorland) G.; student Orlando (Fla.) Jr. Coll., 1953-55; B.A., Rollins Coll., 1955-57; J.D., Stetson U., 1960; m. Marion Stewart Crislip, June 29, 1957; children—Carolyn, Nancy, George, Linda. Admitted to Fla. bar, 1961, practiced in St. Petersburg, 1968—; estate tax examiner IRS, St. Petersburg, Fla., 1960-68; mem. firm Kalle & Graves, 1968-69, Harris, Barrett & Dew, 1970—. Instr. Fla. Trust Sch., Gainesville, 1974—. Served with USNR, 1961-62. Mem. St. Petersburg, Fla., Am. bar assns., Rollins Key Soc., Pi Gamma Mu. Elk. Home: 6380 26th Av N St Petersburg FL 33710 Office: 600 Fla Nat Bank Bldg St Petersburg FL 33701

GRAVES, WALLACE MORRISON, JR., pathologist; b. Plainfield, N.J., June 20, 1930; s. Wallace Morrison and Emma (Dietz) G.; B.A., Syracuse U., 1952; M.D., U. Va., 1956; m. Henrietta A. Crutcher; children—Candice Joanne, Penelope Sue, Wallace Morrison, Melissa Robyn. Intern, U. Chgo. Clinics, 1956-57; resident in pathology Harrisburg (Pa.) Hosp. 1959-60, Jackson Meml. Hosp., Miami, Fla., 1960-63; practice medicine, specializing in pathology, Miami, 1963-65, Ft. Myers, Fla., 1965—; mem. staffs Ft. Myers Community, Hendry Gen., Lehigh Acres Gen. hosps.; pres. Pathology Assos. Labs., Ft. Myers, 1970—; mem. Fla. Med. Examiners Commn., 1972—, vice-chmn., 1974-79, chmn., 1979—; mem. Fla. Dept. Health and Rehab. Services adv. council, 1976—; dist. med. examiner, Lee, Hendry and Glades counties, Fla., 1973—. Fellow Am. Soc. Clin. Pathologists, Coll. Am. Pathologists, Am. Acad. Forensic Scientists; mem. Nat. Assn. Med. Examiners, N.Y. Acad. Sci., AAAS, Fla. Med. Assn. Office: 3949 Evans Ave Ft Myers FL 33901

GRAVES, WILLIAM LESTER, JR., educator; b. Terry, Miss., Aug. 26, 1915; s. William Lester and Ada Lee (Graves) G.; student Graceland Coll., 1933-36; B.S., N.W. Mo. State Coll., 1945; M.M.Ed., Drake U., 1948; Ed.D. U. Colo., 1963; m. Kathlyn Earlita Cato, Feb. 20, 1938; children—William Lester III, Pamella Kay (Mrs. Joe Rayford Daniel). Instr. music pub. schs., Mo., 1936-45, Ia., 1945-46, Miss., 1953-61; mem. faculty Graceland Coll., Lamoni, Ia., 1946-53; state supr. music Tenn. Dept. Edn., 1961-64; prof. music Miss. U. for Women at Columbus, 1964—. Mem. arts edn. adv. panel Miss. Arts Commn., 1970-73; cons. Miss. Textbook Com., 1966; music cons. community, civic music orgns., 1961—. Bd. reps. Columbus Civic Arts Council, pres., 1975. Mem. Miss. Music Educators Assn. (bd. reps. 1954-57, 58-61, 65-74, 76-80, pres. 1960-61, v.p. 1976-78, pres., 1978-80; editor Miss. Notes 1966-74), Miss. Edn. Assn., Am. String Tchrs. Assn., Nat. Sch. Orch. Assn., Coll. Music Soc., Music Educators Nat. Conf. (instructional advisory bd. 1975—), A.S.C.A.P., Phi Delta Kappa, Lambda Delta Sigma. Mem. Reorganized Ch. of Jesus Christ of Latter-day Saints (elder). Author: A Comparison of Three Methods for Improving Intonation in the Performance of Instrumental Music, 1963. Mus. compositions include Passacaglia and Fugue for Strings, 1962, Hear Us, O Lord, from Heav'n Thy Dwelling Place, 1965, Unto Thee Do We Cry, 1969; Prelude and Fugue, Choral Suite, 1975. Contbr. articles to profl. jours. Home: 1421 College St Columbus MS 39701

GRAVLEE, LELAND CLARK, JR., physician; b. Fayette, Ala., Apr. 10, 1928; s. Leland C. and Mary (Wright) G.; B.S., Auburn U., 1951; M.D., U. Ala., 1955; children—Jan, Luanne, Leland Clark. Intern U. Hosp., Birmingham, Ala., 1955-56, resident in obstetrics and gynecology, 1956-59; practice medicine specializing in obstetrics and gynecology, Birmingham, 1959—; mem. courtesy staff Bapt. Med. Center, Brookwood Hosp.; mem. active staff U. Hosp., Bapt. Med. Center; cons. staff Carraway Meth. Hosp., East End Meml. Hosp.; pres. elect med. staff South Highlands Hosp., 1976-77; asst. clin. prof. medicine U. Ala. Sch. Medicine, Birmingham, 1974-77, clin. prof. obstetrics and gynecology, 1975-77; pres. Cancer Research and Edn. Found., 1974-77; guest lectr. Russian govt. Health Fair and Tumor Inst., 1974, Philippines, 1976, Oxford (Eng.) U. Served with USN, 1946-48. Diplomate Am. Bd. Obstetrics and Gynecology. Fellow Am. Coll. Obstetrics and Gynecology; mem. Med. Assn. of State Ala., Am. Soc. for Study of Sterility, Ala., S. Central, Birmingham obsterical gynecol. socs., AMA, Birmingham Acad. Medicine, Alpha Omega Alpha, Med. Coll. of Ala. Alumni Assn. (pres. 1964-65). Baptist. Clubs: Rotary, Country Club of Birmingham. Editor: Endometrum, 1976, Endometrium, 1977. Contbr. numerous articles in field to profl. jours.; inventor of uterine cancer detecting device and automatic umbilical cord tying device. Office: 1717 11th Ave S Birmingham AL 35205

GRAY, CHARLES WEBSTER, mgmt. cons., cons. engr.; b. nr. Clinton, Mo., Sept. 9, 1914; s. Harvey Gant and Mary (Lay) G.; student Central Coll., 1931-33, U. Mo., 1933-36; Pittsburg (Kans.) State Coll., 1949-50; m. Frances Louise Thomas, Sept. 6, 1936; children—Mary Elizabeth (Mrs. James E. Bolin, Jr.), Charles Webster. Jr. engr., supr., asst. state planning engr. WPA, Jefferson City, Mo., 1936-40; design engr., field engr., asst. maintenance supt. Hercules Powder Co., Radford, Va., Wilmington, Del., 1940-46; maintenance and engring cons., Carthage, Mo., 1946; engr., sr. engr., projects supt. Spencer Chem. Co., Quaker Valley Constructors, Inc. subsidiary, Pittsburg and Kansas City, 1947-53; sr. maintenance engr., maintenance supt. Am. Cyanamid Co., New Orleans, 1953-59; maintenance cons., pres. Gray Equipment, Inc., Metairie, La., 1959-61, chmn. bd., 1959—; resident engr. Barnard and Burk, Baton Rouge, Seneca, S.C., 1961-62; chief planner, project supt., project mgr., cons. Catalytic Inc., Orange, Tex., Toledo, Phila., 1962—; mgmt. and engring. cons. on maintenance, constrn. chem. and petroleum industries and critical path method planning for chem. processing cos., oil refining cos., govt. agys., others, 1961—. Recipient numerous commendations, certificates for distinguished service in engring. planning and mgmt. achievements. Registered profl. engr., Mo., La., Kans. Mem. Internat. Platform Assn., Am. Mgmt. Assn., Nat., Mo. socs. profl. engrs., La. Engring. Soc., Am. Welding Soc. (dir. 1954-55). Democrat. Methodist (ofcl. bd.). Elk. Home: 121 N Livingston Pl Metairie LA 70005 Office: 121 N Livingston Pl Metairie LA 70005 also 1908 Dana Dr Adelphi MD 20783 also care George Butler and Assos City Center Sq 1100 Main St Kansas City MO 64105 also 613 S Patterson St Gibsonburg OH 43431 also care Catalytic Inc Center Sq West 1500 Market St Philadelphia PA 19102

GRAY, CLARENCE JONES, educator, dean; b. Red Bank, N.J., June 21, 1908; s. Clarence J. Sr. and Elsie (Megill) G.; B.A., U. Richmond, 1933, LL.D., 1979; M.A., Columbia U., 1934; postgrad. Centro de Estudios Historicos, Madrid, Spain, summer 1935; Ed.D., U.Va., 1962; m. Jane Love Little, Aug. 25, 1934; children—Frances Gray Mark, Kenneth Stewart. Underwriter Aetna Life Ins. Co., 1925-30; instr. Spanish, Columbia U., 1934-38; gen. sec., mem. exec. council Instituto de las Espanas en los Estados Unidos, 1934-39; instr., sec. dept. Romance langs. Queens Coll., N.Y.C., 1938-46 (on mil. leave 1943-46); dean students U. Richmond (Va.), 1946-68, asso. prof. modern langs., 1946-62, prof., 1962-79, emeritus, 1979—, dean adminstrv. services, 1968-73, dean adminstrn., 1973-79, emeritus, 1979—, spl. cons. to pres., 1979—, editor bull., 1968-74, moderator U. Richmond-WRNL Radio Scholarship Quiz Program, mem. bd. Univ. Assos. Cons., Commn. on Colls., So. Assn. Colls. and Schs. Trustee' Inst. Mediterranean Studies. Served from lt. to lt. comdr., USNR, 1943-46. Mem. Modern Lang. Assn., NEA, Am. Assn. Tchrs. Spanish, Am. Assn. for Higher Edn., Newcomen Soc. N.Am., Inst. Internat. Edn. (cert. meritorius service), Phi Beta Kappa (sec. emeritus), Phi Delta Kappa, Kappa Delta Pi, Omicron Delta Kappa (nat. sec. gen. council 1966-72, Distinguished Service key 1968, nat. chmn. scholarship awards 1972-78), Alpha Psi Omega, Phi Gamma Delta, Alpha Phi Omega. Baptist. Mem. Legion of Honor, Order of De Molay. Clubs: Country of Va., Colonnade, Masons, Rotary. Contbr. to profl. jours. Home: 1 Bostwick Ln U Richmond Richmond VA 23173

GRAY, DORA EVELYN, accountant; b. Smith County, Tex., Mar. 26, 1924; d. H. Esten and Mattie E. (Payne) Clyburn; grad. Fed. Inst., 1944; m. Harvie A. Gray, Dec. 22, 1945 (dec.); children—Dennis H., Ladell L. Gray Green. Treas., asst. mgr. Wagner Office Equipment, 1948-61; asst. treas. Pool. Co., San Angelo, Tex., 1962-72; loan officer, acting mgr. Concho Educators Fed. Credit Union, San Angelo, 1972-75; warehouse accountant M System Food Stores, Inc., San Angelo, 1976—. Precinct del. county convs., 1976—; active various community drives; active in legislation regarding ERA, 1959—. Mem. Bus. and Profl. Women's Club (local pres., dist. chmn. for personal devel., legislative chmn., past state bd. dirs.). Democrat. Mem. Ch. of Christ. Home: 915 N Adams St San Angelo TX 76901

GRAY, DUNCAN MONTGOMERY, JR., bishop; b. Canton, Miss., Sept. 21, 1926; s. Duncan Montgomery and Isabel (McCrady) G.; B.E.E., Tulane U., 1948; M.Div., U. of South, 1953, D.D. (hon.), 1972; m. Ruth Miller Spivey, Feb. 9, 1948; children—Duncan Montgomery, Anne Gray Finley, Lloyd Spivey, Catherine Gilmer. Ordained priest Episcopal Ch., 1953, consecrated bishop, 1974; priest-in-charge Calvary Ch., Cleveland, Miss. and Grace Ch., Rosedale, Miss., 1953-57, Holy Innocents Ch., Como, Miss., 1957-60; rector St. Peter's Ch., Oxford, Miss., 1957-65, St. Paul's Ch., Meridian, Miss., 1965-74; bishop coadjutor Diocese of Miss., Jackson, 1974, bishop, 1974—, chmn. House of Bishops Com. Canons, 1975—, chmn. joint com. on constns. and canons Gen. Conv. of Episcopal Ch., 1977—; chmn. Miss. Religious Leadership Conf., 1977—. Chmn. bd. trustees All Saints Episc. Sch., Vicksburg, Miss., 1975-77; trustee U. of South, 1974—; bd. dirs. Miss. Council on Human Relations, 1962—, pres., 1963-67; mem. Miss. Advisory Com. to U.S. Commn. on Civil Rights, 1975—; bd. dirs. Miss. Mental Health Assn., 1968-73. Named Nat. Speaker of Yr., Tau Kappa Alpha, 1962. Contbr. articles to religious pubs. Home: 3775 Old Canton Rd Jackson MS 39216 Office: PO Box 1636 Jackson MS 39205

GRAY, EDGAR LAUGHLIN, educator; b. Manchester, Ohio, Apr. 28, 1914; s. R.F. and Ella J. (Howard) G.; B.S., Wilmington Coll., 1936; M.A., Ohio State U., 1946, Ph.D. in History, 1951; postgrad. Oxford U., 1958; m. Virginia Pomroy, June 1, 1963. Tchr. pub. schs., Aberdeen, Ohio, 1936-41; asst. Ohio State U., 1949-51; instr. U. Ala., 1951-52, asst. prof., 1952-56; asso. prof. Ohio No. U., 1956-60; prof. Morris Harvey Coll., Charleston, W.Va., 1960—, head dept. history, 1960-73, chmn. social sci. div., 1973—. Mem. W.Va. Antiquities Commn. Served to capt. AUS, 1941-46. Mem. Am., Mississippi Valley, Ohio, W.Va. (past pres.) hist. assns., AAUP, Pi Gamma Mu, Phi Alpha Theta. Methodist. Mason (K.T.). Research in field. Home: 303 McKinley Ave Charleston WV 25314

GRAY, FRED L., fin. services exec.; b. Pelahatchie, Miss., Jan. 7, 1938; s. Paul F. and Alice Lena (Blakney) G.; student U. Tex., Arlington, 1958-61; postgrad. in Banking, So. Meth. U., 1962-73; m. Harla N. Hill, Apr. 16, 1960; children—Carl Allen, Sandra Alice, Carole Ann, Susan Annette. Various positions Republic Nat. Bank, Dallas, 1966-70, mgr. money order and travelers check service sect., 1970-74, v.p. money order and travelers check service sect., 1974-75; v.p., mgr. ops. div. Republic Money Orders, Inc., Dallas, 1975-76, v.p., gen. mgr., 1976-78, sr. v.p., gen. mgr., dir., mem. exec. com., 1978—. Served with USN, 1956-58. Republican. Author: Management by Objectives—A Total Systems Review for the Banking Industry, 1976. Office: Republic Money Orders Inc 1900 Pacific St Dallas TX 75201

GRAY, FREDERICK THOMAS, state senator; b. Petersburg, Va., Oct. 10, 1918; s. Franklin Pierce and Mary Gervase (Pouder) G.; B.A., U. Richmond, 1948, J.D., 1949; m. Evelyn Johnson, Oct. 16, 1943; children—Frederick Thomas, Evelyn Cary. Admitted to Va. bar, 1949; asst. atty. gen. Va., 1949-54, atty. gen., 1961-62; individual practice law, Richmond, 1954—; mem. Va. Ho. of Dels., 1966-71, Va. Senate from 11th Dist., 1972—; mem. Va. Commn. Constl. Govt., 1956; mem. Va. Code Commn., 1970—; mem. So. Regional Edn. Bd., 1961—, chmn. legis. council, 1975; dir. So. Bank Inc., Pioneer Fed. Savs. & Loan Assn. Lay leader, trustee Bermuda Hundred United Methodist Ch., 1943—; bd. dirs. Va. Meth. Found.; trustee Randolph-Macon Coll. Served as 1st lt. USAAF, 1942-46. Named Outstanding Young Man in Chesterfield County, Jaycees, 1954. Fellow Am. Coll. Trial Lawyers; mem. Va. Bar Assn., Richmond Bar Assn., Chesterfield-Colonial Heights Bar Assn. (past pres.; sec.-treas. 1967—), Phi Beta Kappa. Democrat. Club: Chesterfield Country Lions (pres. 1954), Home: 4701 Bermuda Hundred St Chester VA 23831 Office: Courthouse Sq Chesterfield VA 23832 also 510 United Va Bank Bldg Richmond VA 23219

GRAY, FREDERICK THOMAS, JR., state govt. ofcl.; b. Hopewell, Va., Mar. 22, 1951; s. Frederick Thomas Gray and Evelyn (Helms) Johnson; B.A. with distinction, U. Va., 1972, J.D., 1975. Admitted to Va. bar, 1976; law clk., then asso. William, Mullen & Christian, Richmond, Va., 1975-78; sec. Commonwealth of Va., 1978—; mem. Va. Commn. on Interstate Cooperation. Mem. Nat. Assn. Secs. State, Va. Bar Assn., Richmond Bar Assn., Chesterfield Jaycees (sec. 1979, pres. 1980). Republican. Methodist. Home: 11721 S Briarpatch Dr Midlothian VA 23113 Office: PO Box 1-B Richmond VA 23201

GRAY, GEORGE WILLIAM, pub. relations and advt. exec.; b. Jacksonville, Fla., Feb. 28, 1927; s. George Williams and Peggy (Dickey) G.; B.A., U. Ala., 1949; divorced; children—Gretchen, Bradley. Reporter, Scripps-Howard Newspapers, 1950; pres. Gray Advt., Inc., Tampa, Fla., 1960-65; chmn. bd., chief exec. officer Gray Denton & French, Inc., Tampa, 1965-76; pres. Gray & Assos. Pub. Relations, 1976—; adj. prof. mass. communications U. South Fla., 1974—. Bd. dirs. Hillsborough County Heart Assn., Hillsborough-Manatee Mental Health Bd. Served with USCGR, World War II. Named Advt. Man of Year, Tampa Advt. Fedn., 1974, recipient Silver medal, 1978; recipient Distinguished Service award Am. Fedn. Advt., 1968; named Alumnus of Year U. Ala., 1976. Mem. Pub. Relations Soc. Am. (pres. Fla. chpt.), Tampa Advt. Fedn. (past pres.). Episcopalian. Clubs: Tampa Yacht and Country, Tower, N.Y. Publicity. Home: 107 South O'Brien St Tampa FL 33609 Office: Kennedy Center Tampa FL 33609

GRAY, HORTENSE WILLIAMS, counselor; b. Charleston, S.C., Jan. 26, 1919; d. Israel Elias and Arnolta (Johnston) Williams; B.A., Fisk U., 1941; M.A., Columbia U., 1943, profl. diploma, 1948; Ed.D., Nova U., 1978; 1 dau., Charlene Hortense. Asst. dean women Del. State Coll., from asst. dean women to dean women Fisk U.; social group worker Urban League Greater N.Y.; tchr. Duval County (Fla.) Sch. System, Jacksonville, later counselor, dean girls, adminstrv. asst.; now counselor Fla. Jr. Coll., Jacksonville; cons. in field. Mem. Duval County Bd. Library Trustees; mem. governing bd. Health System Agy., N.E. Fla. Regional Planning Council; bd. dirs. Family Consultation Center; mem. exec. com. Epsicopal Diocese of Fla. Recipient Mademoiselle Mag. Merit award, 1948; Camp Fire Girls citation; Nat. Council Negro Women citation; Boy Scouts Am. citation. Mem. Am. Personnel and Guidance Assn., Fla. Assn. Community Colls., Fla. Personnel Assn., Internat. Transactional Analysis Assn., Kappa Delta Pi, Alpha Kappa Alpha. Democrat. Clubs: Links Internat., Criterion Matrons. Author: Make the Most of Yourself, 1950. Office: 3939 Roosevelt Blvd Jacksonville FL 32205

GRAY, JESSIE WILLARD, sch. supply co. data processing exec.; b. De Kalb, Miss., Mar. 12, 1949; s. Clinton Franklin and Ola Mae (Stovall) G.; A.A., East Miss. Jr. Coll., 1969; B.S., Miss. State U., 1971, M.Ed., 1974; m. Elwyn Clair Wright, July 11, 1970. Tchr. math. Florence (Miss.) High Sch., 1971-77; mgr. data processing Miss. Sch. Supply Co., Jackson, 1977—; adv. Hinds Jr. Coll.; condr. edn. workshops. Project bus. cons. Jr. Achievement, 1978; deacon First Baptist Ch., Florence; mem. Rankin County (Miss.) Republican Com. Named STAR Tchr., Miss. Econ. Council, 1976. Mem. Nat. Council Tchrs. Math., Miss. Council Tchrs. Math., Metric Assn., U.S. Jaycees, S.W. Rankin Jaycees (dir. 1975), Phi Kappa Phi, Kappa Delta Pi. Home: Route 5 Box 518 Florence MS 39073 Office: PO Box 1059 Jackson MS 39205

GRAY, JOHN WAYNE, health care adminstr.; b. Oklahoma City, Aug. 8, 1942; s. Johnnie Nathanial and Thelma (Harmon) G.; B.A., Central State U., Edmond, Okla., 1967, M.B.A., 1976; m. Marianne Twedt, May 30, 1964; children—Julianne, Christianne. Asst. office mgr. Oldsmobile div. Gen. Motors Corp., Oklahoma City, 1967-69, dist. mgr., Enid and Tulsa, Okla., 1969-74; gen. mgr., owner Quality Oldsmobile-Cadillac, Inc., McAlester, Okla., 1974-75; adminstrv. asst. to pres. St. Mary's Hosp., Enid, 1976-77, v.p. gen. services, 1977—. Served with U.S. Army, 1962—. Mem. Assn. M.B.A. Execs., Am. Coll. Hosp. Adminstrs., Res. Officers Assn., Okla. Hosp. Public Relations Soc. (pres. bd. 1978-79), Enid C. of C. (capt. Ambassadors 1978-79), Jaycees. Roman Catholic. Clubs: Ambucs, Elks. Home: 913 Quail Creek Dr Enid OK 73701 Office: 305 S 5th St Enid OK 73701

GRAY, LOVIE, food service co. exec.; b. Memphis, June 19, 1951; s. Joseph and Lucy Mae Gray; B.A., Christian Bros. Coll., 1973; m. Patricia Jeans, Dec. 19, 1973; 1 son, Lovie. Unit field mgr. W.T. Grant Co., Madison, Tenn., 1973-74; ops. unit mgr. Denny's Co., Memphis and Houston, 1975-78; SW regional personnel dir. ARASERV Inc., Houston, 1978—. Mem. Am. Soc. Personnel Adminstrn., Houston Jr. C. of C., Am. Mgmt. Assn. Democrat. Roman Catholic. Home: 1414 Gentle Bend Missouri City TX 77459

GRAY, OSCAR EDWARD, III, govt. ofcl.; b. Phila., Dec. 17, 1943; s. Oscar Edward and Josephine Lucille (Hart) G.; B.S., U.S. Naval Acad., 1965; M.S., Ohio State U., 1971; m. Susan Patricia Tate, May 12, 1979; 1 dau., Christine Lee. Commd. ensign USN, 1965, advanced through grades to lt., resigned, 1970; nuclear licensing engr. TVA, Chattanooga, 1971-73, mgmt. staff, nuclear engr., 1974-75, supr. environ. planning sect., 1975-77, asst. chief regulatory br., 1977-79, program coordinator gen. mgr.'s office, 1979, 80, chief spl. projects staff, 1980—; project engr. nuclear reactor licensing AEC, Bethesda, Md., 1973-74. AEC spl. fellow, 1970; registered profl. engr., Tenn. Mem. Nat. Mgmt. Assn., Am. Nuclear Soc., Naval Acad., Ohio State U. alumni assns. Home: 9322 Thrasher Trail Soddy TN 37379 Office: 1000 Chesnut Tower II Chattanooga TN 37401

GRAY, PHYLLIS ANNE, librarian; b. Boston, Jan. 2, 1926; d. George Joseph and Eleanor M. (Morrison) G.; Ph.B., Barry Coll., 1947, M.B.A., 1979; M.S. in Library Sci., Cath. U. Am., 1950. Deptl. librarian Cath. U. Am., Washington, 1950-52; librarian, AFB, Miami, Fla., 1952-53; asst. librarian Brockway Meml. Library, Miami Shores, Fla., 1953-55; head librarian N. Miami Public Library, 1955-59; supervising librarian Santa Clara County Library, San Jose, Calif., 1959-61; library dir. City of Commerce (Calif.) Public Library, 1961-68; adminstrv. librarian Miami-Dade Public Library Service, 1969-76; asst. chief Miami Beach (Fla.) Public Library, 1976-78, chief librarian, 1978—. Councilwoman, Bar Harbour Village, Fla., 1979—. Mem. ALA, Fla. Library Assn., Southeastern Library Assn., Am. Soc. Public Adminstrn., Barry Coll. Alumni Assn., Dade County Library Assn. Democrat. Roman Catholic. Home: 54 Park Dr Bal Harbour FL 33154 Office: 2100 Collins Ave Miami Beach FL 33139

GRAY, RICHARD LAIRD, army officer; b. Honolulu, Feb. 16, 1942; s. Percy Scott and Pauline Ann (Laird) G.; B.S., U.S. Mil. Acad., 1964; M.S. in Mech. Engring., U. Ala., 1972; married; 1 dau., Jerri Marie. Commd. 2d lt. U.S. Army, 1964, advanced through grades to maj., 1979; served in Vietnam, 1966-67, 69-70; company comdr., 1968-70; ops. officer 5th Div., 1977-78; research and devel. coordinator, optics directorate Ballistics Missile Def. Advanced Tech. Center, Huntsville, Ala., 1978—. Decorated Bronze Star with V and 3 oak leaf clusters, Meritorious Service medal, Army Commendation medal with oak leaf cluster. Mem. Assn. U.S. Army, Armor Assn., Sigma Xi. Republican. Roman Catholic. Home: 9000 Cannstatt Dr Huntsville AL 35803 Office: Ballistic Missile Def Advanced Tech Center PO Box 1500 Huntsville AL 35807

GRAY, ROBERT ALAN, JR., ednl. adminstr.; b. Allegan, Mich., Nov. 28, 1929; s. Robert A. and Dorothy May (Palmer-King) G.; A.B., George Washington U., 1956; M.A., Columbia U., 1963; postgrad. U. Va., 1961-62, Coll. William and Mary, 1963-64, U. West Fla., 1977; m. A. Radine Pellegrin, Aug. 7, 1963. Research analyst Insp. Gen. Chief of Staff, USAF, Washington, 1950-53; research analyst Bd. of Geographic Names, Dept. Interior, Washington, 1953-54; tchr., dir. social studies Fairfax (Va.) County schs., 1956-62, counselor, 1963-64; instr. Tchrs. Coll., Columbia U., N.Y.C., 1963; supr. counseling and psychol. services Dependents Edn. Office, Dept. of Navy, Washington, 1964-67, dep. dir. of schs., 1967-68, asso. dir. personnel services, 1969-70; mem. President's Job Evaluation and Pay Rev. Task Force, U.S. Civil Service Commn., Washington, 1970-71; edn. specialist Dept. of Def. Dependents Schs., Atlantic region, Pensacola, Fla., 1972-79, chief exec. sers. div., 1979—; presentor Nat. Conf. on Affective Edn., 1971; instr. Pensacola Jr. Coll., Pensacola, Fla., 1977; mem. Commn. for Edn. of Handicapped, 1967-68. Mem. Citizens Goals for Pensacola-Escambia Arts Council, 1977; life mem. Friends St. Andrews U. (Scotland); bd. dirs. Gulf Coast Festival, 1975. Served with USAAF, 1946-49. Mem. Am. Personnel and Guidance Assn., Nat. Vocat. Guidance Assn. (chairperson ad hoc com. armed forces and dependents edn. 1976-77), Am. Sch. Counselor Assn., Council for Exceptional Children, Assn. for Measurement and Evaluation in Guidance, Assn. for Counselor Edn. and Supervision, St. Andrews Soc. Washington, St. Andrews Soc. Pensacola (pres. 1976-77, dir. 1974—), St. Andrews Soc. Edinburgh (Scotland, life), Harrow Caledonia Soc. (Eng., life), Phi Sigma Kappa, Phi Delta Kappa. Contbr. articles on guidance and counseling to profl. jours. Home: 6334 Harvard Ct Pensacola FL 32504 Office: DODD-AR Block 2 Eastcote APO New York NY 09241

GRAY, ROBERT STEELE, publishing co. exec.; b. Beaumont, Tex., Oct. 6, 1923; s. Fred and Ruth Louise (Lewelling) G.; B.S. in Journalism, U. Houston, 1954; m. Nellie Frances McGuinness, July 3, 1945; children—Robert Steele, Laura Elizabeth, Ruth (Mrs. Paul Lindholm). Newsman radio sta. KPRC, Houston, 1947-48; radio news dir. sta. KNUZ, Houston, 1948-49, KXYZ, Houston, 1949-50; staff writer Citizen Weekly Newspapers, Houston, 1949-50, Houston Post, 1956-59; founder Cordovan Corp., Houston, 1959, pub., gen. mgr., 1959—, pres. Cordovan Pub., 1977—; tchr. TV news reporting U. Houston, 1954. Service with USMCR, 1942-46, 51-52. Mem. Am. Horse Publs. (pres. 1972-73), Sigma Delta Chi (v.p. Gulf Coast chpt. 1973). Author or co-author 5 books on horses and horse tng. Home: 1350 M'Ardi Ln Houston TX 77055 Office: 5314 Bingle Rd Houston TX 77092

GRAY, ROBERT TAYLOR, mgmt. cons.; b. Cuba, Ill., May 14, 1927; s. Ned Taylor and Doris Katherine (Howerter) G.; B.S. in Sci., Kans. State U., 1953, postgrad. (Grad. fellow), 1954; m. Shirley Jean Sapp, July 29, 1969; children—John Stephen, Mark Robert, Todd Douglas; stepchildren—Wendy, Margot, Lori (Peterson). With Kaiser Aluminum and Chem. Corp., 1954-65; dir. labor relations Tex. Instruments Co., 1965-69; corp. dir. indsl. relations Litton Industries, 1969-72; sr. v.p., chief adminstrv. officer Wheelabrator-Frye, Inc., 1972; exec. v.p., dir. Wylain, Inc., Dallas, 1972-76; pres. Gray Enterprises, Inc. and Gray & Assos., Inc., Dallas, 1976—; pres., chief exec. officer Cement Producers Bargaining Assn., Dallas; v.p., treas., dir. Homestead Minerals Corp.; pres., dir. Black Diamond Mining Corp. Mem. N. Tex. Arabian Assn., Sigma Chi. Club: Tanglewood Yacht and Country (Texoma). Home: 6254 Emeraldwood Pl Dallas TX 75240 Office: 2775 Villa Creek Dr Dallas TX 75234

GRAY, ROGER NELSON, food broker; b. Washington, May 23, 1953; s. Robert LeRoy and Mary Ovelton (Zurhorst) G.; student U. of Ams., 1970-71. Sales rep. Sysco-H&R Wholesale Co., El Paso, Tex., 1977-78; area mgr. Kirkpatrick Brokerage Co., El Paso, 1978-79, Westerburg, Farley & Co., El Paso, 1979—. Mem. Tex. Restaurant Assn. (asso.), Nat. Food Brokers Assn. Home: 1101 Baltimore Dr El Paso TX 79902 Office: Box 4741 El Paso TX 79914

GRAY, SAM WILSON, JR., portrait photographer; b. Durham, N.C., Mar. 2, 1947; s. Sam Wilson and Dorothy (Buchanan) G.; student N.C. State U. Extension Service, 1972; m. Donna Elizabeth Hawkins, Oct. 4, 1974; 1 dau., Lisa Marie. Salesman WSSB radio sta., Durham, 1969, Weltron Electronics Co., Durham, 1970; news photographer, reporter WTVD-TV, Durham, 1969-70; owner, portrait photographer Sam Gray, Creative Photography, Durham, 1970—; lectr. in field. Bd. dirs. Allied Arts Found. of Durham, 1973-74. Served with Paratroopers, U.S. Army, 1965-68. Decorated three Commendation medals, Purple Heart, Combat Inf. Badge; recipient photographic awards N.C. Traveling Loan Collection, 1973, 75-79, photographic awards U.S.A. Traveling Loan Collection, 1974. Profl. Photographers asso. fellow, 1974, fellow, 1975. Mem. Profl. Photographers Am. (membership com. 1974-75, vice-chmn. nat. membership council, publs. com. 1978—, nat. ser. award, U.S. Master photographers degree 1979), Profl. Photographers N.C. (chmn. guild 1972, treas. 1973-74, program chmn. 1974-75, budget and fin. com. 1974-75, edn. com. 1974-75, dir. 1974-75), Southeastern Profl. Photographers, Profl. Picture Framers Am., Durham C. of C. (Bus. Beautification award 1973), Better Bus. Bur. Club: Carolina Sailing. Home: 4315 Barbary St Durham NC 27707 Office: 2705 Chapel Hill Rd Durham NC 27707

GRAY, SANFORD, JR., ednl. adminstr., realtor; b. Ft. Payne, Ala., July 14, 1930; s. Rubin S. and Bertheena L. G.; B.S., Carson Newman Coll., 1952; postgrad. U. Tenn., 1955-56; m. Esther S. Gray, Nov. 22, 1952; children—Bridgett, Mary Lu, David. Football coach TMI Acad., Tenn., 1955-65, athletic dir., 1959-69, v.p., 1963-71, pres., owner, 1975—; developer-owner Tellico Mountain Camp, Sweetwater, also pres. Tellico Land Co., Sweetwater, 1963—. Vice-pres. adv. com. Carson Newman Coll., 1976—. Served with U.S. Army, 1952-54. Mem. Am. Camping Assn. (nat. standards bd. 1976—), Camp Horsemanship Assn. (nat. bd. 1975—), Nat. Realtors Assn. Baptist. Home: 1313 Peachtree St Sweetwater TN 37874

GRAY, SCOTT MICHAEL, missionary; b. Lubbock, Tex., Feb. 12, 1953; s. Mays Leroy and Nelda Ramelle (Moore) G.; B.S. in Acctg. and B.S. in Fin., Fla. State U., 1977; m. Julie Theresa Stein, Sept. 4, 1976. Sr. field staff and sr. man Ark. State U., Campus Crusade for Christ, Jonesboro; leadership tng. class coordinator, tchr. Ark. State U. Inst. Bibl. Studies; tchr., Lake Tahoe, Calif., 1979. Baptist. Office: 1620 S Carraway Suite 5 Jonesboro AR 72401

GRAY, WILLIAM NORWOOD, urban and regional planner; b. Glendale, Calif., Jan. 19, 1947; s. Evelyn Ruth Buss; B.D.Arch., U. Fla., 1971; M.S. in Urban and Regional Planning, Fla. State U., 1973; m. Marica Carol Imber, June 29, 1969. Prin., William Gray & Assos., Cons. Planners, Tallahassee, Fla., 1972-73; urban planner, dir. Urban Planning div. Wayne H. Coloney Co., Tallahassee, 1973-74; project dir. Fla. Dept. Gen. Services, Tallahassee, 1974-76; planning dir. Capitol Center Planning Commn. Fla., 1975; prin. William Gray, Inc., Cons. Planners, Tallahassee, 1976—; dir. Communication Designs and Fields Typesetting Service Tallahassee. Ben Novak scholar, 1965-69; Haydon Burns scholar, 1965-69. Mem. Fla. Indsl. Devel.

Council, Fla. Planning and Zoning Assn., Am. Soc. Photogrammetry, Council Planning Librarians, Am. Planning Assn., Am. Inst. Cert. Planners, AIA (asso.), Tau Sigma Delta, Gargole Hon. Soc. Democrat. Jewish (temple bd. dirs.). Office: 233 Office Plaza Suite 2 PO Drawer 6129 Tallahassee FL 32301

GRAYBEAL, HENRY CLAY, educator; b. Damascus, Va., Feb. 1, 1889; s. David and Lydia Florence (Mock) G.; B.A., Emory and Henry Coll., 1913, L.H.D., 1966; postgrad. Vanderbilt U., summer 1916; M.S., Cornell U., 1923; m. June Evangeline McConnell, June 15, 1916; children—David, Charlton, William, Clare (Mrs. Roland Houghton), Burke, Patrick. Prin. high sch., Rogersville, Tenn., 1913-15, Damascus, Va., 1915-18; faculty U. Tenn., 1921-24, Emory and Henry Coll., 1924-32, Radford Coll., 1932-42; asst. supr. secondary edn. Va. Dept. Edn., 1942-58, chmn. Secondary Sch. Evaluation Com., 1955-56; pres. New River Hist. Soc., 1967-74; chmn. Bi-Centennial Commn., Radford, Va., 1972—; chmn. Radford Recreation Commn., 1941-50. Trustee, Emory and Henry Coll., Tenn. Wesleyan Coll., Hiwassee Jr. Coll., 1960-72. Served with U.S. Army, World War I. Recipient Distinguished Service award Emory and Henry Coll. Alumni Assn., 1964; Meritorious Service award Country Life Commn. Hoston Conf. Meth. Ch., 1965; Silver Beaver award Boy Scouts Am., 1944. Mem. Va. Council Chs. (v.p.), Ret. Tchrs. Va. (pres. 1972-74), Am. Legion (chpt. comdr.), World War I Vets. (chpt. comdr.), Phi Delta Kappa. Methodist. Rotarian (Paul Harris fellow). Home: Gilbert and Sullivan Sts Radford VA 24141

GREASON, MURRAY CROSSLEY, JR., lawyer; b. Wake Forest, N.C., Dec. 12, 1936; s. Murray Crossley and Evelyn Elizabeth (Hackney) G.; B.S. magna cum laude, Wake Forest U., 1959, J.D. magna cum laude, 1962; m. Joan Millicent Wilder, June 25, 1960; children—Murray Crossley III, Millicent Wilder, Elizabeth Hillary. Admitted to N.C. bar, 1962, since practiced in Winston-Salem; asso. firm Womble, Carlyle, Sandridge & Rice, 1965-70, mem. firm, 1970—. Dir. Winston-Salem Savs. & Loan Assn. Vis. lectr. Wake Forest U., 1972-74. Pres. Winston-Salem Estate Planning Council, 1973; trustee Denmark Loan Fund, scholarships to Wake Forest U. Served to capt., JAG, AUS, 1962-65. Mem. Forsyth County, Wake Forest U. Alumni Assn. (pres. 1973), N.C., Am. bar assns., Phi Beta Kappa, Omicron Delta Kappa. Episcopalian (past vestryman, sr. warden). Club: Forsyth Country. Home: 745 Arbor Rd Winston-Salem NC 27104 Office: PO Drawer 84 Winston-Salem NC 27102

GREATHOUSE, MYRLE, drilling co. exec.; b. Amarillo, Tex., Sept. 19, 1922; s. Emmons and Mamie Ethyl (Tubbs) G.; B.A., U. Okla., 1949; m. Marcella L. Schubach, June 25, 1965; children—Sharon An, Steve Wayne (dec.), Micah. Former profl. football player Dulaneys, Oklahoma City, then salesman Western Co., Ft. Worth; with Wes-Tex Drilling Co., Abilene, Tex., 1955—, now pres. Bd. dirs. Wes-Tex Rehab. Center. Served with USMC, World War II. Decorated Purple Heart. Mem. AIME, Abilene Petroleum Club (past pres.). Office: Wes-Tex Drilling Co PO Box 2895 Abilene TX 79604

GRECO, MICHAEL ROBERT, journalist; b. Gilroy, Calif., Jan. 30, 1943; s. Angelo Michael and Virginia Dale (Johnson) G.; B.A., San Jose State U., 1968; Ph.D., Johns Hopkins U., 1974; children—Michael Angelo, Matthew Paul. Spl. asst. to Hon. Paul Sarbanes, 1971-72; lectr. history San Jose State U., 1972-75; film editor Marquee Mag., 1975; asst. prof. film and history U. Houston, Clear Lake City, 1976-79; editor Movie Guide mag., 1978; contbg. writer Los Angeles Times, Los Angeles Times Syndicate, Boxoffice, Houston Post, Houston City Mag., The Star, Film Comment, 1979—; contbg. editor Jour. Film/Psychology, Jour. Psychohistory, 1978—. Am. Film Inst. Humanities-Film Inst. fellow, 1978. Mem. Soc. Cinema Studies, Internat. Psychohist. Assn., Am. Hist. Assn., Motion Picture Council Houston (dir.), Phi Alpha Theta. Democrat. Home: 16442 Larkfield Dr Houston TX 77059

GREEAR, YVONNE ETNYRE, librarian; b. Austin, Tex., June 19, 1921; d. Mentor and Caroline Atahlie (Goeth) Etnyre; B.F.A., U. Tex., Austin, 1948, M.L.S., 1962; m. David Edmond Lewis, June 21, 1937 (dec. 1943); children—Yvonne Patricia Lewis Ramage, Kathryn Lynne Lewis Loewenstein; m. 2d, Jimmie Ralph Greear, Feb. 16, 1949 (div. 1958); 1 dau., Julie Greear MacQueen. Continuity writer Sta. KNOW, Austin, 1948, Gilbert Advt. Co., Austin, 1948-50; with public relations dept. El Paso (Tex.) Nat. Bank, 1950; exec. sec. Tex. Western Coll. Library, El Paso, 1950-56; librarian El Paso Natural Gas Co., 1957-62; reference librarian Ft. Bliss, Tex., 1963-64; dir. reference services U. Tex., El Paso, 1964-72, asst. dir. public services, 1972—; vis. lectr. grad. sch. library sci. U. Tex., Austin, summers 1968, 69. Named Librarian of Year, Border Region 1 Library Assn., 1968. Mem. Tex. Library Assn., Spl. Libraries Assn., Am. Name Soc. Episcopalian. Condr. research, contbr. paper on Texas street names, 1971-75. Office: Library University of Texas at El Paso El Paso TX 79968

GREEMAN, NELSON WILLIAM LINTON, JR., optometrist; b. San Antonio, Mar. 26, 1923; s. Nelson William Linton and Edith Mae (Crow) G.; D. Optometry, Ohio State U., 1948; postgrad. U. Houston, 1959-62, Purdue U., 1957; m. Dorothy Ruth Trimble, Dec. 22, 1946 (dec. July 1970); children—Janice (Mrs. Dennis Bryant), Nelson William Linton III; m. 2d, Patsy Ruth Seiler, Oct. 16, 1971; 1 dau., Laura Lee (dec.). Pvt. practice optometry, San Antonio, 1948—. Extern, Gesell Inst. Child Devel., New Haven, 1958; vis. lectr. Coll. Optometry, U. Houston, 1964-65; guest lectr. U. Miss., 1965; clinics chmn. S.W. Congress Optometry, 1960—; dir. SW States Optometric Council, 1974—; lectr. various groups and profl. orgns. Pres. San Antonio Better Bus. Bur., 1957. Served to 2d lt. USAAF, 1943-45. Named Optometrist of Yr., Tex. Optometric Assn., 1972. Fellow Am. Acad. Optometrists; Coll. Optometrists in Vision Devel. Internat. (chmn. bd. 1971-72, dir. region IV 1973-76), Southwest Contact Lens Soc. (pres. 1972-74); mem. Southwest Developmental Vision Soc. (pres. 1969-70), Southwest Optometric Forum, Am. Acad. Optometry (pres. Tex. chpt. 1960-61), Bexar County Dist. Optometric Soc. (past pres.), Am. Legion (post comdr. 1968). Methodist (mem. adminstrv. bd. 1958-64, 70-74, 77—). Club: Optimist (San Antonio). Home: 208 Wyanoke St San Antonio TX 78209 Office: 249 E Hildebrand St San Antonio TX 78212

GREEN, ARTHUR GEORGE, accountant; b. Midland, Tex., June 2, 1937; s. Lymond Darrel and Viona (Grant) G.; Asso. Applied Sci., Odessa Coll., 1960; B.B.A., U. Tex., 1962; m. Marilyn Comstock, June 2, 1977; children by previous marriage—Shane Ann, Sabrina Kay, Amy Suzanne, William Wade. Estimator, Boing Co., New Orleans, 1962-63; staff accountant Main, Lafrentz & Co., Odessa, Tex., 1963-65, Will Faris & Co., Odessa, 1965-67; partner Faris, Sims & Green, Odessa, 1968-73, Griffin & Green, Odessa, 1973—. Govs., treas. Globe of Gt. S.W., 1969—; bd. dirs. Tex. Tech. U. Tax Inst., 1967-70; bd. regents Odessa Coll., 1972—. Served with USAF, 1954-58. Mem. Am. Inst. C.P.A.'s, Tex. Soc. C.P.A.'s (chpt. v.p. 1969—), Data Processing Mgrs. Assn. (chpt. treas. 1970), Odessa Jr. C. of C. Mem. Christian Ch. (dir.) Mason (K.T., Shriner). Home: 4212 Clover St Odessa TX 79760 Office: 2101 N Grandview St Odessa TX 79761

GREEN, BERNARD CLAY, lawyer; b. Shelby County, Ky., Oct. 11, 1904; s. Clarence Evans and Fanny (Baker) G.; student Centre Coll., 1922-25; student Jefferson Sch. Law, 1927-29; LL.B., U. Louisville, 1930; m. Clara Ellen McCammon, Aug. 6, 1936; children—Wanda Mae, Suzette Clay, Earl Mac. Admitted to Ky. bar, 1929; dept. supt. United Merc. Agys., Louisville 1930-36; practiced in Louisville, 1936-40, Owensboro, Ky., 1940—; asst. county atty. Daviess County, Ky., 1953; city prosecutor, Owensboro, 1954-58. Mem. Am., Ky. State, Daviess County (pres. 1970) bar assns., Am. Trial Lawyers Assn., Comml. Law League Am., Am. Judicature Soc., Internat. Acad. Law and Sci., Ky. Hist. Soc. Mem. Christian Ch. (elder, mem. ofcl. bd., past chmn.). Kiwanian (pres. Owensboro 1970-71). Home: 1030 College Dr Owensboro KY 42301 Office: 700 Frederica St Owensboro KY 42301

GREEN, CHARLES STEVEN, life ins. co. exec.; b. Atlanta, Mar. 18, 1946; s. Frank Robert and Marilyn Ruth (Altman) G.; B.S., U. Ga., 1968; LL.B., LaSalle Coll., 1971; m. Linda C. Smith, Feb. 12, 1971; 1 dau., Kimberly M. Insp. agencies Sun Life Assurance Co. Can., 1967-71; asst. v.p. Ga. Internat. Life Ins. Co., 1971-75; exec. v.p. Am. Progressive Life Ins. Co., 1975-77; v.p., dir. mktg. Am. Pioneer Life Ins. Co., 1977-79, sr. v.p., 1979—; dir. DeKalb Travel Agy. Mem. Am. Mgmt. Assn., Nat., Atlanta assns. life underwriters. Home: 501 Sweetwater Cove Blvd S Orlando FL 32750 Office: PO Box 3509 Orlando FL 32802

GREEN, DAVID SPENCER, architect; b. Dallas, Jan. 22, 1943; s. Herbert Spencer and Delma Dorothy (Stephenson) G.; student Arlington State Coll., 1961-63; B.Arch., Tex. A. and M. U., 1968; children—Derek Scott, Lamar Allen. Draftsman, George E. Christensen, Dallas, 1960-63; facilities design specialist, 1970-72; project architect Army and Air Force Exchange Service, Dallas, 1972-76; v.p. architecture Vantage Cos., Dallas, 1976—. Vice chmn. Dallas Area Block Partnership Program. Prin. works: concept planning for shopping centers Ft. Jackson, S.C., Ft. Benning, Ga., Ft. Knox, Ky., Redbird Distbn. Centers I and II. Home: 535 Campana Ct Irving TX 75061 Office: 4445 W Ledbetter Dr Dallas TX 75236

GREEN, DONNA MARIE, army edn. specialist; b. Murdo, S.D., Sept. 9, 1937; d. Henry Andrew and Vera Emogene (Newsam) Anderson; B.S. in Secondary Edn., Black Hills State Coll., Spearfish, S.D., 1969; M.A. in Human Relations, U. Okla., 1977; m. Cameron Cordell Green, Jan. 28, 1956; children—Kirk Morgan, Cory Jon, Clint Patrick, Kris Anderson. Instr., librarian Sch. Dist. 3, Cascade, Mont., 1967-70; instr. lang. C.Z. Schs., Balboa, 1971-74; army edn. specialist 193d Inf. Brigade, Dept. of Army, Ft. Clayton, C.Z., 1974-78, U.S. Army Recruiting Command S.E. Region Beckley (W.Va.) Dist., 1978—; race relations group facilitator; advisor, supr. counselor edn.; counselor Prot. Youth Group, 1966-69. Named Civilian of Year, U.S. Army Recruiting Command, Beckley Dist., 1978. Mem. Am. Personnel and Guidance Assn., Mil. Edn. Counselors Assn., Nat. Adult Edn. Assn., Am. Vocat. Assn., AAUW. Democrat. Methodist. Office: 300 N Kanawha St Beckley WV 25801

GREEN, EDWARD THOMAS, JR., educator; b. Oxford, N.J., Apr. 19, 1921; s. Edward Thomas and Euphemia (Lanterman) G.; B.S. cum laude, Ithaca Coll., 1942; M.S., Syracuse U., 1947, Ed.D., 1965; m. Margaret Evelyn Tuttle, Jan. 30, 1944; children—Marsha, Margaret, Barbara. Music instr. high sch., Palmyra, N.Y., 1942-50, dir. guidance, vice-prin., 1946-50; prin. Palmyra-Macedon Central Sch., 1950-54; supervising prin. New Berlin (N.Y.) Central Sch., 1954-58, Rondout Valley Central Sch., Accord, N.Y., also supt. schs., 1958-66; supt. schs., Oneida, N.Y., 1966-77; asso. prof. edn. Ga. So. Coll., Statesboro, 1977—. Pres., Mid-Hudson Sch. Study Council, New Paltz, N.Y., 1960; vice chmn. CHE-MAD-HER-ON, Inc.; area sec. Central Sch. Study; mem. exec. com. Catskill Study on Small Sch. Design; v.p. N.Y. State Tchrs. Retirement Bd. Vice-pres. Rip Van Winkle council Boy Scouts Am., 1964-66, v.p., then pres. Madison County council, chmn. Madison Dist., pres. Iroquois council; pres. Palmyra Betterment Club 1952; mem. Ulster County Community Action Program; past pres. Ithaca Coll. Alumni Council. Served with AUS, 1942-46; ETO. Mem. N.Y. State Sch. Dist. Adminstrs. (pres.), Am. Assn. Sch. Adminstrs., Assn. for Supervision and Curriculum Devel., Nat. Sch. Pub. Relations Assn., Nat. Orgn. for Legal Problems in Edn., Phi Delta Kappa, Phi Mu Alpha. Clubs: Masons (Shriner), Optimist. Home: RD #1 Merrywood Statesboro GA 30458 Office: Landrum 8143 Ga So Coll Statesboro GA 30458

GREEN, GEORGE FRANKLIN, physician; b. Bostwick, Ga., Sept. 27, 1924; s. Rice Burkitt and Rubye (Riden) G.; B.S., N. Ga. Coll., 1948; M.D., Med. Coll. Ga., 1951; m. Helen Montine Maxwell, June 4, 1944; children—George F., Helen Claudia, Wallace Maxwell. Intern Brooke Army Med. Center, 1951; pvt. practice, gen. practitioner, Sparta, Ga., 1953—; chief staff Hancock Meml. Hosp., Putnam Gen. Hosp., 1978—; asso. prof. clin. medicine Duke; asso. prof. clin. and ambulatory medicine U. Ala. Pres. Oconee Valley Investment Corp.; dir. Bank of Hancock County; pres. Hancock Redevel. Corp., Sparta Med. Clinic. Mayor, Sparta, Ga., 1966-70; past commr. Hancock County Bd. Rds. and Revenue; past chmn. Oconee Area Planning and Devel. Commn. Bd. dirs. local council Boy Scouts Am. Served as capt. inf. AUS, 1943-46; capt. M.C. U.S. Army, 1951-53. Fellow Am. Geriatrics Soc., Am. Acad. Family Physicians (charter), Am. Bd. Family Physicians; mem. Am., So., Ga. med. assns., Oconee Valley Med. Soc., Ga. Acad. Family Practice (past dir. 6th dist.), V.F.W., Gridiron Soc., Alumni Assn. Med. Coll. Ga. (pres. 1974-75), Am. Legion, Delta Sigma Pi (hon.) Baptist (deacon). Mason (Shriner, K.T.), Lion (pres. 1961-62). Club: Civitan (past pres. Sparta br., past lt. gov. Ga. dist.). Home: Route 1 Sparta GA 31087 Office: 325 E Broad St Sparta GA 31087

GREEN, GORDON LUCIUS, otolaryngologist; b. Randolph, Vt., Nov. 12, 1914; s. Gardner Leland and Flora (Humphrey) G.; B.S., Davidson Coll., 1935; M.D., U. Louisville, 1939; m. Glavis Ray Bishop, Dec. 18, 1937; 1 dau., Connie Virginia. Intern, Louisville Gen. Hosp., 1939-40; resident in ear, nose and throat medicine Henry Ford Hosp., Detroit, 1945-48; practice medicine specializing in ear, nose and throat, Louisville, 1949—; asst. clin. prof. otolaryngology U. Louisville, 1950—; mem. staff Methodist, Baptist, Norton, Jewish hosps. Served to lt. col. M.C., USAF, 1941-45. Recipient certificate of merit U. Louisville, 1975; named Ky. col. Diplomate Am. Bd. Ophthalmology and Otolaryngology. Mem. AMA, Am. Acad. Otolaryngology, Am. Soc. Ophthal. and Otolaryn. Allergy, Am. Acad. Facial Plastic and Reconstructive Surgery, Ky., Louisville (pres., founder) otolaryn. socs., Ky., Jefferson County med. socs. Republican. Presbyterian. Club: Louisville Boat. Contbr. articles to med. jours. Home: 2001 Round Ridge Rd Louisville KY 40207 Office: 712 Med Towers Bldg Louisville KY 40202

GREEN, HARRY GEORGE, bus. coll. pres.; b. Harbor Springs, Mich., Aug. 28, 1908; s. Judson Burrows and Ella Agnes (Burdge) G.; Ph.C., U. Wash., 1930, B.S., 1931; m. Martha Jane Hart, Dec. 28, 1935; children—Richard B., Harry George, Rogers H., Barbara (Mrs. H. Murrell McLeod), Judy (Mrs. Claude D. Foster). With Delta Tau Delta Frat., N.Y.C., 1931-33, field sec., editor, asst. to controller, Indpls., 1933-37; bus. mgr. Phillips Bus. Coll., Lynchburg, Va., 1937-44, pres., 1944—. Pres. Lynchburg Met. YMCA, 1968-72. Mem. Lynchburg Sch. Bd., 1948-58, chmn., 1951-58; mem. Lynchburg Interracial Commn., 1960-72, sec., 1962-72. Mem. Assn. Ind. Colls. and Schs. (pres. 1967-68), Va. Council Bus. Colls. (pres. 1971-73), Nat. Secs. Assn. (hon.). Methodist (lay leader 1964-79). Clubs: Lions (local pres. 1946-47, dist. gov. 1950-51), Masons. Home: 1020 Federal St Lynchburg VA 24504 Office: 1112 Church St Lynchburg VA 24505

GREEN, HOLCOMBE TUCKER, JR., lawyer; b. Atlanta, Sept. 29, 1939; s. Holcombe Tucker and Mary Katharine (Woltz) G.; A.B., Yale U., 1961; LL.B., U. Va., 1967; m. Nancy Reade Hall, June 18, 1966. Admitted to Ga. bar 1967; asso. firm Hansell, Post, Branden & Dorsey, Atlanta, 1967-70, mem. firm, 1970—; sec. Independence Mortgage Trust; dir. Collins & Co. Trustee Ga. Conservancy, 1976-79, Atlanta Bot. Garden, 1976—, St. Jude's House, 1977-80; bd. dirs. Save Am.'s Vital Environment, 1973-78, pres., 1974-76; founding dir. Friends of River, Inc.; bd. dirs. Child Service and Family Counseling Center, 1972—; active Leadership Atlanta, 1974-75, You Men's Round Table High Mus. Art, 1976-79. Served to lt. (j.g.) U.S. Navy, 1961-64. Mem. Am., Atlanta bar assns., State Bar Ga., Lawyers Club Atlanta, Atlanta Tax Forum, Raven Soc. of U. Va., Atlanta Hist. Soc. (mus. com. 1975—), Order of Coif. Democrat. Presbyterian. Clubs: Piedmont Driving, Capital City, Commerce, Nine O'Clocks. Decisions editor Va. Law Rev., 1965-67. Home: 3655 Tuxedo Rd Atlanta GA 30305 Office: 3300 First Nat Bank Tower Atlanta GA 30303

GREEN, HOLLIS LYNN, religious assn. exec.; b. Rhea County, Tenn., Jan. 6, 1933; s. Herbert Barton and Grace Irene (Curton) G.; student Beckley Coll., 1952-54, U. Cin., 1957-58; B.A., Southwestern Coll., 1962; B.D., Luther Rice Sem., 1965, M.R.E., Th.D., 1968; Ph.D., Walden U., 1978; m. Peggy Jean Lane, Dec. 8, 1951; children—Barton Lynn, Brian Lane; m. 2d, Gloria Gail Parks, 1974. Ordained to ministry, 1955; pastor various churches Ohio, S.C., Ind., Fla., 1958-64; state dir. Christian edn. W.Va., 1952-58; mem. gen. youth and Christian Edn. Bd., Ch. of God, 1958-62; dir. pub. relations Ch. of God Exec. Offices, 1964-72; pres. Aid, Ltd., Atlanta, 1966—; founder, pres. Greenleaf Found., Jacksonville, Fla., 1973—; dir. Provident Investment Corp., Atlanta. Cons., Time Life Books, Protestant Armed Forces Field Rep. Mem. U.S. Postal Forum II, III, 1968-69, Inter-Racial Study Commn. of the South, 1962-64, Dr. King's List of 200, 1966-68. Trustee Luther Rice Sem., 1968-74, v.p., 1974-79, prof. evangelism and ch. growth. Served as res. chaplain (maj.) CAP, USAF, 1964-74. Recipient pub. service award U.S. Postal Service, 1968. Fellow Program and Platform Techniques div. Internat. Platform Assn.; mem. Pub. Relations Soc. Am., Religious Pub. Relations Council, Evange. Press Assn., Soc. Pentecostal Scholars, Nat. Sunday Sch. Assn. (bd. dirs. 1958-62), Internat. Pub. Relations Assn. Republican. So. Baptist. Kiwanian. Author: Hitching Your Star to a Wagon, 1958; Dynamics of Christian Discipleship, 1962, Christian Education Cyclopedia, 1965; Marchings As to War, 1969; Understanding Pentecostalism, 1970; Where in the World are you Going, 1971; Why Churches Die, 1972; Why Wait Till Sunday, 1975. Home: 6236 Pinelock Dr Jacksonville FL 32211 Office: 1820 Monument Rd Jacksonville FL 32225

GREEN, J. FORREST, state legislator Tex.; b. Kirvin, Tex., Dec. 11, 1921; s. J.F. and Pauline (Norman) G.; student U. Tex., Arlington, 1940-42. With P.O. Dept., Arlington, Tex., 1947-55; postal insp., Des Moines, 1955-59; contracts adminstr. Bell Helicopter, Hurst, Tex., 1960-63; rancher, Corsicana, Tex., 1964—; dir. Corsicana Fed. Land Bank, 1965—, Am. Bank of Arlington, 1979—; mem. Tex. Ho. of Reps. from 27th Dist., 1972—, chmn. agr. and livestock com., 1979—. Served as pilot AAC U.S. Army, World War II, maj. USAF Res. Mem. Sons of Republic of Tex. Democrat. Baptist. Clubs: Rotary, Masons. Home: Route 2 Box 39 Corsicana TX 75110 Office: PO Box 2910 Austin TX 78769

GREEN, JAMES COLLINS, lt. gov. N.C.; b. Halifax County, Va., Feb. 24, 1921; s. John Collins and Frances Sue (Oliver) G.; ed. Washington and Lee U.; m. Alice McAulay Clark, 1943; children—Sarah Frances, Susan Clark, James Collins. Mem. N.C. Ho. of Reps., 1961-65, 69-73, speaker, 1975-76; mem. N.C. Senate, 1967; lt. gov. State of N.C., 1977—. Precinct vice-chmn., then chmn. Democratic Com.; mem. Bladen County (N.C.) Bd. Edn., 1955-61; deacon Clarkton (N.C.) Presbyterian Ch. Served with USMC, 1944-46. Recipient Labor award Organized Labor and Workmen's Circle, 1975. Clubs: Masons, Shriners. Office: Office Lt Gov State Legis Bldg Raleigh NC 27611

GREEN, JAMES DON, banker; b. Lawrence County, Tenn., July 22, 1943; s. Herbert Lee and Kathleen Ada (Crews) G.; B.S., U. North Ala., 1967; m. Elizabeth Mitchell Green, June 29, 1968; children—Lisa Dawn, Johnathan Lee, James Lance. Teller, bookkeeper Bank of Loretto (Tenn.), 1962-65; asst. cashier, loan officer First Nat. Bank, Florence, Ala., 1966-70; pres. Am. Bank, St. Joseph, Tenn., 1970—; dir. Elk River Devel. Assn. Bd. dirs. Lawrence County Mental Health Assn. Mem. Lawrence County C. of C. (past pres.), U. North Ala. Nat. Alumni Assn. (past pres.). Democrat. Methodist. Club: Lions. Home: PO Box 86 Saint Joseph TN 38481 Office: PO Box 97 Saint Joseph TN 38481

GREEN, JANIE (MARY JANE), pianist, educator; b. Siloam Springs, Ark., Sept. 25, 1922; d. William H. and Roxanna (Edmiston) Stowell; B.A., William Jewell Coll., Liberty, Mo., 1945; M.R.E., Southwestern Baptist Sem., Ft. Worth, 1948; m. Joseph F. Green, May 8, 1949; children—Mary Green Vickrey, Carol Green Butler. Pvt. tchr. of piano, Nashville, 1958—. Mem. Nat. Guild Piano Tchrs. (chmn. Irl Allison Center 1968-72), Music Tchrs. Nat. Assn. (mem.-at-large So. div. 1976-78), Tenn. (dir. Middle Tenn. 1970-72, 74-76, pres. 1979—), Middle Tenn. (pres. 1975-77) music tchrs. assns., Nashville Music and Arts Tchrs. Guild (pres. 1973-75). Baptist. Club: Oak Hill Home Demonstration. Co-author: God Wants You, 1966. Address: 419 Barrywood Dr Nashville TN 37211

GREEN, LARRY ALEXANDER, travel agt.; b. Huntsville, Ala., Apr. 11, 1948; s. Clarence and Shirley G.; B.A., N. Tex. State U., 1969; M.B.A., Pepperdine U., 1980. Pres., Green Assos., Inc., Dallas, 1972-73; account exec. Merrill, Lynch, Pierce, Fenner & Smith, Dallas, 1973-75; tour mgr. Bible Land Tours, Cairo, 1975-77; exec. v.p. Middle East Travel Center, Inc., Houston, 1977—; partner TVL Agy.; exec. v.p. Nabil Al-Hashim Trading Establishment, Jeddah, Saudi Arabia. Mem. Harris County Democratic Exec. Com., 1978-79. Served to capt. USMC, 1969-72; Vietnam. Mem. Assn. Retail Travel Agts., Nat. Assn. Cons., Delta Sigma Phi. Baptist. Club: Houston City. Office: 3800 Buffalo Speedway Houston TX 77098

GREEN, MARION ETHEL, editor; b. Mpls., Apr. 15, 1937; d. Raymond Lloyd and Doris Marion (Pincoe) Green; B.A., George Washington U., 1959. Tchr., Highlands High Sch., San Antonio, 1959-60; founds. asst. Trinity U., San Antonio, 1961-63; editor tech. pubs. USAF Sch. Aerospace Medicine, Brooks AFB, Tex., 1963-69, chief editor, 1969—. Mem. Am. Med. Writers Assn., Phi Beta Kappa, Pi Lambda Theta. Episcopalian. Home: 258 Pinewood Ln San Antonio TX 78216 Office: USAF Sch Aerospace Medicine Brooks AFB TX 78235

GREEN, ROBERT LAMOYNE, mgmt. and postal cons.; b. Bellaire, Ohio, Sept. 19, 1916; s. Walter Allen and Ruth (Simpson) G.; student Ohio State U., 1934-36, Western Res. U., 1946; B.S., Fla. So. Coll., 1947, postgrad., 1947-48; postgrad. George Washington U., 1960; m. Mary Elizabeth Barksdale, Sept. 7, 1946; children—Allen Barksdale, Marion Elizabeth. Supr., Postal Transp. Service, Cin., 1936-39, Pitts., 1939-40, Cleve., 1940-41; postal insp. Postal Inspection Service, Chgo. and Atlanta divs., 1951-58; dir. distbn. procedures br. Post Office Dept. Hdqrs., Bur. Ops. and Transp., Washington, 1958-68; sr. mgmt. edn. specialist Postal Service Mgmt. Inst., Washington, 1968-73; mgmt. and postal cons., Springfield, Va., 1973—. Served to maj. AUS, 1941-46; MTO, NATOUSA; ret. col. Res. Decorated Army Commendation medal with oak leaf cluster; numerous commendations Postal Service. Mem. Res. Officers Assn., Fed. Exec. Inst. Alumni Assn., Direct Mktg. Club Washington. Episcopalian. Contbr. numerous articles on army postal service and U.S. postal service to tech. publs. Address: 7711 Elgar St Springfield VA 22151

GREEN, RONALD WILLIAM, hosp. adminstr.; b. East St. Louis, Ill., July 2, 1944; s. William Merritt and Jesse Blanche (Bowles) G.; B.S., So. Ill. U., 1966; M.H.A., St. Louis U., 1971; m. Barbara R. Graebner, Dec. 21, 1970; children—William J., Jason A. Adminstrv. asst. St. Louis U. Hosps., 1971, asst. adminstr., 1972-73, asso. dir., 1973-77; adminstr. Tulane Med. Center Hosps. and Clinics, New Orleans, 1977—; instr. Tulane U., St. Louis U.; adj. prof. Webster Coll.; chmn. hosp. adminstrv. service com. Cardinal Ritter Inst. Served with U.S. Army, 1966-68. Mem. Met. Hosp. Assn. (bd. dirs.), Am. Coll. Hosp. Adminstrs., Am. Trauma Soc. Lutheran. Home: 5828 MacArthur Blvd New Orleans LA 70114 Office: 1415 Tulane Ave New Orleans LA 70112

GREEN, SHARI HELENE, services co. exec.; b. Newark, May 4, 1943; d. Irving and Tillie L.; student Miami Dade Jr. Coll., 1962-63, U. Miami, 1975-78; m. William C. Green, June 25, 1967; children—Pamela Jill, Spencer Keith. Mem. staff U. Miami, Coral Gables, Fla., 1965-78, adminstrv. asst. to asso. dean Grad. Sch. Marine and Atmospheric Sci., 1968-72, adminstrv. asst. to v.p. Univ., 1972-74, adminstrv. dir. fin. affairs, 1976-78; owner, mgr. Word Processing Center, Inc., Miami, 1978—, Word Processing Service Bur., Inc., 1979—. Mem. Am. Bus. Women's Assn. (Woman of Year 1979—, chpt. pres.), Internat. Word Processing Assn. (v.p., treas. 1979-80), Nat. Assn. Women Bus. Owners. Home: 2124 SW 98th Ave Miami FL 33165 Office: 7875 SW 40th St Suite 222 Miami FL 33155 also 8390 NW 53 St Suite 110 Miami FL

GREEN, THOMAS EDWARD, social worker; b. Plumerville, Ark., Mar. 30, 1948; s. Harvey and Rebecca Louise (Brigance) G.; B.A., Philander Smith Coll., 1970; M.S.S.W., U. Tenn., 1972; m. Carol Bernita Smith, Sept. 14, 1974; children—Ebonye Nicole, Tene LaCarole. Social worker Porter-Leath Children Center, 1970-71; dir. summer camp Little Rock AFB, summer 1971; asst. dir. Planned Parenthood Knox County, 1971-72; family adv. social worker E. Little Rock Community Complex, 1972—. Chair Region V Ark. Conf. on Children and Youth, 1976-77, cert. merit, 1978; chair Com. to Improve Mental Health Services to Blacks, 1978-79. Recipient cert. of merit Community Council Central Ark., 1978. Mem. Nat. Caucus on Black Aged, Nat. Assn. Black Social Workers (pres. 1975-79, founder, bd. mem. Ark. chpt.), Nat. Assn. Social Workers, ACLU, Alpha Phi Alpha. Baptist. Home: 2313 W 12th St Little Rock AR 72202 Office: 2500 E 6th St Little Rock AR 72202

GREEN, WILLIAM LAWRENCE, C.P.A.; b. Tulsa, June 15, 1942; s. Robert Lee and Dorothy Sue (Porter) G.; B.B.A., U. Houston, 1966; m. Patricia Ann Ellis, Aug. 6, 1965. Staff accountant Arthur Young & Co., Houston, 1966-68; with Weller, Jeffery & Green, Inc., C.P.A.'s Houston, 1968-78, v.p., sec., 1971-78, Green, Wheeler & Co., C.P.A.'s, Houston, 1978—. Capt., Pin Oak Charity Horse Show, Houston, 1972. Mem. dean's adv. bd. U. Houston Coll. Bus., 1974—, bd. dirs. U. Houston Coll. Bus. Alumni Ednl. Found., 1974-76, v.p., 1975, pres., 1976. Served with AUS, 1960-63. Recipient dean's award of appreciation Coll. Bus., U. Houston, 1977. Mem. Am. Inst. C.P.A.'s. Tex. Soc. C.P.A.'s, U. Houston Coll. Bus. Alumni Assn. (dir. 1971-74, 76—, pres. 1973-74), Beta Alpha Psi. Club: Rotary. Home: 3106 Lawrence St Houston TX 77018 Office: 4111 Directors Row Suite 100 Houston TX 77092

GREEN, WILLIAM PAUL, educator; b. Rayne, La., Sept. 7, 1930; s. Murphy Joseph and Verl Russia (Butler) G.; B.S. in Bus. Adminstrn., U. Colo., 1963, M.B.A. in Fin., 1964; Ph.D. in Bus. Adminstrn., U. N.C., Chapel Hill, 1968; m. Margaret Phyllis Lapleau, July 9, 1961; children—Philip Lee, Larre Paul, Sara Margaret. Mgmt. trainee Johns-Manville Corp., Denver, 1951-52; owner, mgr. Green's Hardware and Machinery Co., Inc., Crowley, La., 1952-63; prof. finance U. Tex., Arlington, 1967—; chmn. bd. Bramlett Telecom, Inc. Mem. Am. Fin. Assn., Fin. Mgmt. Assn., Am., Inst. Decision Scis., Southwestern Fin. Assn., Fin. Execs. Inst., MBA Assn., So. Fin. Assn., Beta Gamma Sigma. Methodist (adminstrv. bd.). Home: 4000 Fairway Ct Arlington TX 76013 Office: 602-B Coll Bus Adminstrn U Texas Arlington TX 76019

GREEN, WILLIAM SHELANDER, investment banker; b. Tulsa, Aug. 30, 1942; s. Wilson O. and Doris S.; B.I.E., Ga. Inst. Tech., 1964; M.B.A., Harvard U., 1969; m. Debra Kent Glidden, May 27, 1972. With Paine Webber, Inc., 1969—, sr. v.p. Blyth Eastman Paine Webber, Inc. (Atlanta), in charge Southeast investment banking, 1975—; dir. Mktg. Systems Inc., Southeast Tire Assos., Inc. Served to 1st lt. USAR, 1965-66. Mem. Atlanta Roundtable, Commerce Club of Atlanta. Clubs: Algonquin, Union Boat (Boston). Home: 4249 Dykes Dr Atlanta GA 30342 Office: 3340 Peachtree Rd #1685 Atlanta GA 30326

GREEN, WILLIAM WELLS, civil engr.; b. Sioux City, Iowa, Nov. 26, 1911; s. Thomas William and Jessie Eadie (Wells) G.; B.S., U. Notre Dame, 1934; m. Patricia Cecille Gregory, Jan. 10, 1944; children—William Joseph, Mary Teresa. Asst. engr. Iowa Hwy. Commn., Cherokee, 1935-40; asst. engr. City Corpus Christi, Tex., 1940-44; asst. office county surveyor, Nueces County Tex., 1944-54, county surveyor, 1955—. Past mem. Tex. Bd. Registration Pub. Surveyors. Past bd. dirs. Carmelite Day Nursery; regional bd. dirs. Lay Carmelites. Life mem. ASCE; mem. Am. Congress Surveying Mapping, Tex. Surveyors Assn. (bd. dirs.). Democrat. Roman Catholic. K.C. Home: 3149 Topeka St Corpus Christi TX 78404 Office: Room 102 County Courthouse 901 Leopard St Corpus Christi TX 78401

GREENBERG, FRANK S., corp. exec.; b. 1929; ed. U. Chgo.; married. Pres., Charm Tred Mills (acquired by Burlington Industries Inc. 1959), 1953-59; v.p. Charm Tred Mills div. Burlington Industries Inc., Greensboro, N.C., 1959-61, pres., 1961-62, pres. Monticello Carpet Mill div., 1962-70, group v.p., 1970-72, exec. v.p., mem. mgmt. policy com. parent co., 1972-78, pres., chief operating officer, 1978—, also dir. Served with U.S. Army, 1951-53. Office: Burlington Industries Inc 3330 W Friendly Ave Greensboro NC 27420

GREENBERG, HANK, assn. exec.; b. Cleve., Mar. 25, 1934; s. Max and Charlotte (Wallens) G.; grad. high sch.; m. Joan Roth, Feb. 17, 1974; children—Marcie, Lorie, Debra. Pres. Miami Local, United Fedn. Postal Clks., AFL-CIO, 1965-66, editor, 1961-69; editor Fla. Fedn. Postal Clks., Miami, 1967-68; editor Dade County central labor council AFL-CIO, Miami, 1969-80, mem. exec. bd., 1974-80; nat. pres. Am. Postal Workers Union Labor Press Assn., Miami, Fla., 1969-81. Bd. dirs. Dade County (Fla.) chpt. Am. Lung Assn., 1965-76. Served with USAF, 1953-57. Mem. Nat. Jewish Civil Service Employees, Jewish Vets. Fgn. Wars. Club: Am. Legion. Home: 8281 SW 128th St Miami FL 33156 Office: Box 560606 Miami FL 33156

GREENBERG, MICHAEL JOHN, educator; b. N.Y.C., Sept. 28, 1931; s. Abraham S. and Lena (Kirsch) G.; A.B., Cornell U., 1953; M.A., Fla. State U., 1955; Ph.D., Harvard U., 1958; m. Rima Robbins, June 10, 1954; children—Peter A., John K., Karl P. Instr. zoology U. Ill., Urbana, 1958-60, asst. prof., 1960-64; asso. prof. biol. scis. Fla. State U., Tallahassee, 1965-73, prof., 1973—, dir. marine lab., 1978—; vis. prof. Hiroshima U. Med. Sch., 1978. Instr. exptl. invertebrate zoology Marine Biol. Lab., Woods Hole, Mass., summers 1969-73, course dir., 1975-77. Mem. Gov.'s Task Force on Narcotics, Dangerous Drugs and Alcohol Abuse, 1970-72, adv. screening com. Internat. Exchange of Scholars, 1976-78. Recipient grants Fla. State U. Research Council, 1965-67, AEC, 1967-72, Am. Cancer Soc., 1967, Nat. Heart and Lung Inst. NIH, 1960-80; NSF sr. postdoctoral fellow U. Melbourne (Australia), 1964-65, Misaki Marine Lab., Japan, 1965. Mem. Am. Soc. Zoologists (div. program officer 1969-70, div. chmn. 1976-77, co-chmn. joint task force with Am. Physiol. Soc. 1977-78, assn. fellow), Am. Physiol. Soc., Soc. Gen. Physiologists, AAAS, Marine Biol. Lab. Woods Hole, Soc. Exptl. Biology (U.K.), Tallahassee, Sopchoppy and Gulf Coast Marine Biol. Assn. (pres. 1967—), Sigma Delta Chi. Mem. editorial bd. Jour. Exptl. Zoology, 1974-78, Comparative Gen. Pharmacology, 1970—, Physiol. Zoology, 1975—, The Physiology Tchr., 1977-78, Marine Biology Letters, 1978—, Molecular and Cellular Neurobiology, 1978—. Home: 221 Westridge Tallahassee FL 32304

GREENBERG, PETER DAVID, mech. engr.; b. N.Y.C., Apr. 24, 1942; s. Abraham S. and Lena K. G.; B.S. in Engring., U.S. Naval Acad., 1964; M.S. in Bus. Adminstrn., Va. Commonwealth U., 1975; m. Leta L. Fogel, Dec. 26, 1966; children—Rebecca, Joshua. Staff engr. process engring. Philip Morris U.S.A., Richmond, Va., 1970—. Served with USN, 1964-69. Mem. ASME, U.S. Naval Acad. Alumni Assn. Home: 10100 Stonemark Ct Richmond VA 23233 Office: Philip Morris USA PO Box 26603 Richmond VA 23261

GREENBERG, RICHARD NEIL, physician; b. Washington, Oct. 16, 1947; s. Herman and Betty (Saks) G.; A.B., Cornell U., 1968; M.D., Tufts U., 1972; m. Kathy Ann Frey, June 16, 1979. Med. intern Ind. U. Med. Center, Indpls., 1972-73, resident in medicine, 1973-74; resident in medicine La. State U. Med. Center, New Orleans, 1976-77, fellow in clin. infectious disease, 1977-79; research fellow in infectious disease U. Va. Med. Center, Charlottesville, 1979—; smallpox cons. WHO, 1974-75. Served with USPHS, 1974-76. Diplomate Am. Bd. Internal Medicine. Mem. A.C.P., Am. Soc. Microbiology, Am. Fedn. for Clin. Research. Jewish. Contbr. articles to med. jours. Home: 1745 Easy Ln Charlottesville VA 22901 Office: Box 485 U Va Hosp Charlottesville VA 22908

GREENBERG, STANLEY, pharmacologist; b. Bklyn., Sept. 14, 1945; s. Louis Meyer and Anna (Pinckosowitz) G.; B.S. magna cum laude, L.I. U., 1968; M.S., U. Iowa, 1970, Ph.D., 1972; m. Patricia Ann Powers; children—Jonathan Michael, Kristen Amy. Trainee pharmacology dept. U. Iowa, 1968-72, fellow internal medicine dept., 1972-73; fellow physiology dept. U. Mich., 1973-74; instr. cell biophysics Baylor U. Coll. Medicine, 1974-75, instr. pharmacology, 1974-75; asst. prof. pharmacology Ohio State U., 1975-77; asso. prof. pharmacology U. S.Ala., Mobile, 1977—; co-chmn. smooth muscle IV Internat. Congress Pharmacology, 1975; v.p., mem. exec. bd. Mobile Area High Blood Pressure Council. Active Mobile Jewish Community Center. Recipient Research Career Devel. award Hypertension br. Nat. Heart, Lung and Blood Inst., 1976, 78; NIH fellow, 1973-74. Mem. Am. Heart Assn. (high blood pressure council 1972—, basic sci. council 1974—, cardiopulmonary council 1973—), Am. Soc. Pharmacology and Exptl. Therapeutics (Travel Grant awardee 1975-76), Am. Physiol. Assn., Am. Fedn. Clin. Research, Internat. Research Study Group in Cardiac Metabolism, Western Pharmacology Soc., AAAS, Internat. Shock Soc., Microchem. Soc., N.Y. Acad. Scis., Soc. Exptl. Biology and Medicine, Rho Chi. Contbr. sci. articles to profl. jours. Home: 2009 Burnt Oak Ct Mobile AL 36609 Office: Dept Pharmacology Coll Medicine 2025 Med Sci Bldg U South Ala Mobile AL 36688

GREENE, ANDREW FRANK, orthopedic surgeon; b. Montclair, N.J., Feb. 10, 1942; s. Irving Lewis and Harriet (Altschul) G.; B.A., Amherst Coll., 1963; M.D., Harvard U., 1967; children—Robin, Karen, Scott. Intern, Med. Coll. Va., Richmond, 1967-68; resident in orthopedic surgery N.Y. Orthopedic Hosp. at Columbia Presbyn. Med. Center, N.Y.C., 1971-74; practice medicine specializing in orthopedic surgery, Stuart (Fla.), 1977—. Served with M.C., USN, 1969-70. Diplomate Am. Bd. Orthopedic Surgery. Fellow A.C.S., Am. Acad. Orthopedic Surgeons; mem. Eastern Orthopedic Soc., Fla. Orthopedic Soc., Fla. Med. Assn., Martin County Med. Soc. Office: Orthopaedic Clinic of Stuart 725 E Osceola St Stuart FL 33494

GREENE, ANTHONY, apparel mfg. co. exec.; b. Balt., Dec. 13, 1940; s. Albert Walter and Bertha Eva G.; B.S., U. Md., 1962; m. Nancy E. Anderson, Nov. 11, 1961; children—Anthony Edward, Laura Beth. Mgmt. trainee Proctor & Gamble, Washington, 1962-63; prin. Kurt Salmon Assos., Atlanta and Nashville, 1968-74; pres. Stevens Sportwear, Taylorsville, Miss., 1974—, also dir. Served to lt. USN, 1963-67. Mem. Am. Apparel Mfrs. Assn., Miss. Mfrs. Assn., Omicron Delta Kappa, Beta Gamma Sigma. Republican. Roman Catholic. Clubs: Racquet Club of Hattiesburg (Miss.), Hattiesburg Country (v.p.). Office: 587 Fellowship Rd Taylorsville MS 39168

GREENE, BRUCE MITCHELL, telephone co. exec.; b. Macclesfield, N.C., Apr. 26, 1947; s. Raymond Jackson and Mary Mitchell (Edwards) G.; B.S. in Bus. Adminstrn., East Carolina U., 1978; m. Judy Carolyn Walston, Aug. 11, 1966; children—Raeford Mitchell, Joseph Walston. Central office repairman Carolina Telephone & Telegraph Co., Greenville, N.C., 1966-79, coin telephone mktg. supr., 1979-80, communications cons., 1980—. Mem. Pitt County Fair Bd.; membership chmn. Pitt County Young Reps., 1978-79. Served with AUS, 1966-69. Decorated Army Commendation medal. Mem. Beta Gamma Sigma. Baptist. Home: 1603 Beaumont Dr Greenville NC 27834 Office: 901 Fairfiew Rd Rocky Mount NC 27801

GREENE, DALLAS WHORTON, JR., city ofcl.; b. Shreveport, La., June 29, 1923; s. Dallas Whorton and Eunice (Lester) G.; student Centenary Coll., 1941; m. Alice Whittington, Oct. 4, 1947; 1 dau., Valerie (Mrs. David Randall Rockett). With La. Fire Dept., Shreveport, 1942—, fire chief, 1965—. Mem. State Fire Marshal's Fire Safety Rev. Bd.; advisory mem. U.S. Senate Veterans Affairs com. Mem. Shreveport Assn. for Blind, 1966—, YMCA; mem. governing com. Arthritis Found., 1968—; bd. dirs. Sports for Boys; mem. Gov.'s Com. on Emergencies, 1978—. Served with C.E., AUS, 1943-45. Recipient Friendship award Fraternal Order Police; Dictograph Salutes award Internat. Assn. Fire Chiefs, 1973. Mem. Internat. Assn. Fire Chiefs (pres. Southwestern div. 1971-72, dir. 1972—), La. State Fire Chiefs Assn. (dir.), La. Firemens Assn. (life), Fraternal Order Fire Fighters (hon.), 40 and 8, Nat. Fire Protection Assn., Am. Legion (post comdr.), VFW, Am. Ordnance Assn. Mem. Christian Ch. Lion. Home: 8826 Stonelake Pl Shreveport LA 71108 Office: PO Box 1143 Shreveport LA 71163

GREENE, DAVID LOUIS, educator; b. Middletown, Conn., Sept. 24, 1944; s. George Louis and Margaret Elsie (Chindahl) G.; B.A., U. South Fla., 1966; M.A. (Woodrow Wilson fellow 1966-67), U. Pa., 1967, Ph.D. (4 year fellow), 1974; m. Elizabeth Larrabee Johnson, Nov. 30, 1974; children—Jennifer Helen, Christopher Douglas. Mem. faculty Piedmont Coll., Demorest, Ga., 1970—, asso. prof. English, 1973-75, prof., 1975—, chmn. dept., 1972—, chmn. humanities div., 1975—, chmn. ann. conf. lit. aspects of children's lit., 1975-77, co-chmn., 1978—. Mem. Modern Lang. Assn. Am., Am. Soc. 18th Century Studies, S. Atlantic Modern Lang. Assn., Children's Lit. Assn. Democrat. Conglist. Author articles, revs., introductions. Editor: (L. Frank Baum) The Purple Dragon and Other Fantasies, 1976; co-author: The Oz Scrapbook, 1977; book rev. editor Children's Lit., 1980—. Address: 460 Piedmont Coll Circle PO Box 368 Demorest GA 30535

GREENE, E(RNEST) LONZO, architect; b. Greenville, S.C., Apr. 8, 1931; s. Ernest W. and Gertrude P. (Pitts) G.; B.S., Clemson U., 1952; m. Laura B. Clyborne, July 10, 1976; children by previous marriage—Lon, Lynn. Co-owner, A/E, Inc., Greenville, S.C., 1965-70, exec. v.p., 1965-70; partner Greene, Bankes & Lee, Greenville, S.C., 1970-72; owner E. Lonzo Greene Architect, Greenville, S.C., 1972; pres. E. Lonzo Greene & Assos., Greenville, S.C., 1972—. Served with AUS, 1953-55. Mem. A.I.A., Greenville Council of Architects (pres. 1968-69). Baptist (deacon 1964-71). Rotarian (dir. 1969-70). Architectural works include K-Mart Shopping Centers, Kannapolis, N.C., Anderson, S.C., Lynchburg, Va., Mauldin, S.C., and Montgomery, Ala., Greenville (S.C.) Jr. High Sch., Sans Souci Jr. High Sch., Greenville, S.C., Presbyn. Ch., Baptist Ch., Ranch House Restaurant, Greenwood, S.C., Masonic Temple, Holmesview Rehab. Center, Carolina Fed. Savs. & Loan Assn., Monarch Foods Data Processing Center, 1st Bapt. Ch., Gaffney, S.C., Baptist Book Store, Oakmont Nursing Home, Wade Hampton Fire Sta., bank of travelers rest Mitchell Rd. Presbyn. Ch., new clubhouse Pebble Creek Country Club, phase III addition Luth. Ch. of Our Saviour (all Greenville), Activities Bldg., Trinity United Meth. Ch., Anderson, S.C., Anderson Orthopaedic Clinic, Mt. Pleasant United Meth. Ch., Anderson, Trinity Presbyn. Ch., Spartanburg, S.C., others. Home: 115 Howell Circle Greenville SC 29615 Office: PO Box 5559 Greenville SC 29606

GREENE, HENRY VINCENT, accountant; b. Newton, Mass., Aug. 9, 1946; s. Henry V. and May (Hewitt) G.; B.S., Utica Coll., 1969; M.B.A., Western Carolina U., 1979; m. Madeleine A. Rudy, Sept. 27, 1969. Auditor, Coopers & Lybrand, White Plains, N.Y., 1971-75, Talley Industries, Inc., Stamford, Conn., 1975-76; gen. mgr. Stencel Aero. Engring. Corp. subs. Talley Industries, Asheville, N.C., 1976—. Served as pilot USN, 1969-71. Mem. Nat. Assn. Accts. Republican. Roman Catholic. Home: 312 Vanderbilt Rd Asheville NC 28803 Office: PO Box 1107 Arden NC 28704

GREENE, JAMES ALLEN, psychiatrist; b. Sneedville, Tenn., Mar. 15, 1939; s. Ambrose Kyle and Martha Argelene (Surgenor) G.; B.S., U. Tenn., 1959, M.D., 1963; m. Rebecca O'Connor, Sept. 18, 1970; 1 son, John Robert. Intern, U. Tenn. Hosp., Knoxville, 1963-64; resident Dorothea Dix Hosp., Raleigh, N.C., 1964-67, asst. dir. forensic unit, 1968-69; asso. med. dir. Oak Ridge (Tenn.) Regional Mental Health Center, 1969-70; practice medicine specializing in psychiatry, Birmingham, Ala., 1970—; mem. staff Hillcrest Hosp., Birmingham, Ala., pres. 1973—; asso. prof. psychiatry U. Ala., Coll. Medicine, Birmingham, 1970—. Mem. profl. activities com. Salvation Army Hosp., Birmingham, Ala., 1973—. Served with USAF, 1967-68. Recipient Physicians Recognition award A.M.A., 1969, 72, 75. Fellow Acad. Psychosomatic Medicine, Am. Psychiat. Assn.; mem. So. Psychiat. Assn., AMA, Ala. (vice chmn. reference com. 1973—, del. 1973), So. med. assns., Ala. Acad. Neurology, Birmingham Acad. Medicine, C. of C. Methodist. Club: Kiwanis. Contbr. articles to profl. publs. Home: 10123 Woodsong Way Tampa FL 33618 Office: 12901 N 30th St Tampa FL 33612

GREENE, JEROME GEORGE, lawyer, labor arbitrator; b. N.Y.C., June 7, 1919; s. Emil and Ann (Sommers) G.; student Cornell U., 1937; A.B., N.Y. U., 1939; J.D., Harvard U., 1943; postgrad. New Sch. for Social Research, 1943-45; m. Isabel Marshall, Oct. 15, 1955; 1 dau., Adrienne F. Admitted to N.Y. bar, 1943, Fla. bar, 1949; asso. Greenbaum, Wolff & Ernst, N.Y.C., 1943-44; exec. CBS, N.Y.C., 1944-46, Mut. Broadcasting System, N.Y.C., 1946-47; asso. atty. Meyer, Weiss & Rosen, Miami, Fla., 1949-50, Price, Zaring & Florence, Miami, 1950-52; partner Pallot, Silver & Malloy, Miami, 1952-54, Botts & Greene, Miami, 1954-66; pvt. practice, Miami, 1966—. Guest lectr. arbitration Fla. Internat. U., U. Fla., Dade Community Coll., Am. Arbitration Assn., Fla. Bar Assn. and Dade League of Cities seminars. Spl. dep. atty. gen. N.Y., 1947; spl. hearing officer New York Rent Commn., 1948; mem. Mayor's Safety Commn., Miami Beach, 1950-51; city committeeman Boy Scouts Am., 1954-56; div. chmn. ARC, 1957; mem. adv. bd. Central and So. Fla. Flood Control Dist., 1961; mem. Dade Youth Council, 1962; mem. Commn. for Community Improvement Met. Dade County, 1962-64; chmn. Save Urban Renewal Campaign, 1963; vice chmn., commr. Met. Dade County Urban Renewal Agy., 1964-67; mem. Met. Dade County HUD Bd., 1967-69; commr. City of Miami Beach, 1969-73. Mem. adv. bd. League Women Voters, 1961. Pres. Govt. Research Council of S.Fla., 1967-69, Miami Beach Taxpayers Assn., 1962; bd. dirs. Dade League of Cities, 1971-73; bd. govs. Greater Miami Jewish Fedn., 1959-66; mem. regional bd. Anti-Defamation League, 1960-72; v.p. Jewish Vocat. Service, 1964-66; mem. exec. bd. Am. Jewish Com., 1957-67; chmn. bd., pres. Fla. Fedn. B'nai B'rith Lodges, 1960-62. Mem. Fla., Dade County bar assns., Harvard Law Sch. Assn. of Fla. (dir. 1965), Am. Judicature Soc., Estate Planning Council S.Fla., Am. Arbitration Assn. (S.E. adv. council 1969—), Nat. Acad. Arbitrators. Mem. B'nai B'rith (bd. govs. Dist. 5, 1959-61), Elk. Clubs: Harvard; Bankers. Home: 5161 Collins Ave Miami Beach FL 33140 Office: Suite 310 19 W Flagler St Miami FL 33130

GREENE, MONICA CYNTHIA, pediatrician; b. Trinidad, W. Indies, Feb. 17, 1944; d. Donald Obediah and Elsa Mary (Dennis) Grant; came to U.S., 1967, naturalized, 1977; B.S. with honors, West Ham Coll. Tech. (London), 1966; M.S. in Biochemistry, Howard U., 1969, M.D., 1973; m. James Phillip Greene, July 15, 1967; children—James Phillip, Eva Adenike. Jr. technician Radiol. Protection Service, Med. Research Council, Sutton, Surrey, Eng., 1962-63; asst. clin. biochemist Willesden Gen. Hosp., London, 1966-67; research asst. biochemistry Howard U., Washington, 1967-70, tutor, 1970-72; pediatric intern Howard U. Hosp., Washington, 1973-74, resident, 1974-75; fellow ambulatory pediatrics Johns Hopkins Hosp., Balt., 1975-76; staff Jackson Obstet. Profl. Corp., Washington, 1976-77; practice medicine specializing in pediatrics, Aiken, S.C., 1977—; cons. pediatrician Margaret J. Weston Health Center, Clearwater, S.C.; cons. dept. fed. employee health clin.

Services br. USPHS, Washington, 1975-77; clin. instr. dept. pediatrics Johns Hopkins Hosp., Balt., 1977. Active various fund raising campaigns United Way, March of Dimes, Kidney Found.; local campaign worker Democratic Party, 1977. Recipient First John B. Johnson award for outstanding performance in cardiovascular disease Howard U., 1973, Charles H. Garvin award in Obstetrics and Gynecology, 1973, Community Health Practice award, 1973; Certificate of for Acad. Scholarship, Am. Med. Women's Assn., 1973. Licentiate Inst. Biology (London); mem. Nat. Inst. Sci., St. George Soc., Med. Soc. D.C., Aiken County Med. Soc., Nat. Med. Assn., Stony Med.-Dental Pharm. Assn., LWV, AAUW, Alpha Omega Alpha. Democrat. Episcopalian. Club: Toastmasters Internat. Home: Chukker Creek Rd Aiken SC 29801 Office: Kalmia Mall Aiken SC 29801 also 905 15th St #D Augusta GA 30902

GREENE, RANDALL FREDERICK, real estate co. exec.; b. Palatka, Fla., Apr. 17, 1949; s. Vernon F. and Betty E. (Bould); A.A., U. Fla., 1972; m. Debra Marie Holder, Dec. 11, 1976. Regional mgr. Realty Resource Inc., 1972-75; dir. property mgmt. Bos & Assos., Jacksonville, Fla., 1976; v.p. Charter Mortgage Co., Jacksonville, 1976-77; pres., dir. Coastland Corp. Fla., Ft. Myers, 1977—; pres. Greene Realty Inc.; tchr. various real estate courses. Bd. dirs. Fla. Apt. Assn., 1974-75; pres. Gainesville (Fla.) Apt. Assn., 1975; bd. dirs., pres. Big Bros. Lee County (Fla.), 1979, Lee County YMCA. Mem. Am. Land Devel. Assn., Inst. Real Estate Mgmt., Ft. Myers Assn. Realtors, Fla. Assn. Realtors, Nat. Assn. Realtors, Fla. Jaycees, Fla. Blue Key, Omicron Delta Kappa, Phi Kappa Tau (pres. chpt. 1972-73). Republican. Club: Rotary. Home: Route 22 Box 2014 B Fort Myers FL 33908 Office: Route 11 Box 1000 Fort Myers FL 33908

GREENE, RAY JOSEPH, advt. exec.; b. Twin Falls, Idaho, Feb. 4, 1933; s. Charles Estus and Anna Marie (Pfieufauf) G.; ed. Sacred Heart Acad., Salem, Oreg., 1948-51; m. Carol Marie Meier, July 12, 1952; children—Tom, Tim, Terry, Cheryl, Kevin, Kerry, Kris, Jenny, James, John, Jeff, Darrin, Heather. Copy boy, retail sales, mgr. classified advt. Oreg. Statesman, Salem, 1951-53, Statesman and Jour., 1953-66; mgr. classified and real estate advt. Balt. News-Am., 1966-73; v.p. Newspaper Advt. Bur., N.Y.C., 1973-76; pres., chief exec. officer Classified Internat. Advt. Services Inc., Hialeah, Fla., 1976—; pres. Greene House of Printing, Hialeah, 1977—. Active Boy Scouts Am., 1956-66; bd. dirs. Exec. Search Program. Mem. Assn. Newspaper Classified Advt. Mgrs. (hon. life mem.; pres. 1970, Disting. Service award 1963), Pacific N.W. Classified Advt. Mgrs. (pres. 1954), Internat. Newspaper Advt. Execs., Western Classified Advt. Mgrs. Assn. (dir. 1954-59), So. Classified Advt. Mgrs. Assn., Northeastern Classified Advt. Mgrs. Assn. (dir. 1968—). Democrat. Roman Catholic. Club: K.C. (grand knight 1961-63). Aughor: How To Double The Payoff of Your Real Estate Advertising, 1974; contbg. author real estate manuals Oreg., Md. Home: 4701 Monroe St Hollywood FL 33021 Office: Classified Internat Advt Services Inc 1345 E 10th Ave Hialeah FL 33010

GREENE, RAYMOND HOUSTON, newspaper publisher, reporter, editor; b. Houston, July 23, 1925; s. Cullum Ethridge and Leah Jean (Kermickle) G.; student in chemistry Tex. Christian U., 1942-43; B.J., U. Tex. at Austin, 1949; m. Sarah Jane Laschinger, Apr. 12, 1952; children—Sarah Lee, William Russell. Wire editor AP, Dallas, 1949; night police reporter, gen. assignment Dallas Morning News, 1950-51, Ft. Worth Star Telegram, 1951-53; reporter, editor, co-pub., gen. mgr. The Gilmer (Tex.) Mirror, 1953—; dir., adv. bd. Robroy Industries, Gilmer, 1962—. First chmn. Gilmer City Planning Commn., 1965-74; chmn. Upshur County Library Bd. for spl. fund dr., Gilmer, 1965-66. Served to lt. j.g. USNR, 1943-46. Recipient highest student hon. Friars Soc., U. Tex. at Austin, 1948, outstanding citizen award, Upshur County, Gilmer, 1966 and numerous service awards through Gilmer Mirror. Mem. Gilmer Indsl. Found. (pres. 1971—), Tex., NE Tex. (dir. 1960-61) press assns., Nat. Newspaper Assn. Clubs: Rotary, Gilmer Country. Home: 1200 Greeneway St Gilmer TX 75644 Office: 214 E Marshall St Gilmer TX 75644

GREENE, ROBERT EDWARD LEE, JR., mfg. co. exec., engr.; b. Raleigh, N.C., Apr. 18, 1941; s. Robert Edward Lee and Lucy Davis (Fortescue) G.; B.M.E., U. Fla., 1963; postgrad. Gordon Jr. Coll., 1976-77; M.B.A., Columbus Coll., 1979; m. Linda Ruth Edenfield, Dec. 27, 1962; children—Amy Noel, Robert Edward. Plant engr. Western Electric Co., Atlanta, 1969-71; staff engr. Thomaston Mills (Ga.), 1971-72, corp. chief engr., 1972—. Mem. bd. elders, supt. Sunday Sch., 1st Presbyn. Ch., Thomaston, 1975-77; mem. certified cities evaluation com. City of Thomaston, 1976-77. Served with USN, 1963-69. Registered profl. engr., Ga. Mem. Am. Textile Managerial Engring. Soc., Am. Textile Mfrs. Inst., Ga. Textile Mfrs. Assn., Naval Res. Assn. Clubs: Thomaston Country, Thomaston Kiwanis (dir. 1975-77, com. chmn. 1975-78, pres. 1979-80). Home: Route 4 Box 167-D Thomaston GA 30286 Office: 115 E Main St Thomaston GA 30286

GREENE, ROBERT THOMAS, clergyman; b. Vance County, N.C., Aug. 28, 1919; s. Edward Jones and Iola (Gooch) G.; B.A., Wake Forest Coll., 1944; B.D., So. Baptist Theol. Sem., Louisville, 1948; spl. grad. studies Syracuse U., summer 1963, Fla. State U., 1978; m. Grace Carolyn Bailey, Dec. 24, 1939; children—Ruth Adams, Robert Thomas. Ordained to ministry Bapt. Ch., 1942; pastor Bapt. Center Bapt. Ch., Clayton, N.C., 1942-44, Olive Branch Bapt. Ch., Dillsboro, Ind., 1945-48, Beech Grove Bapt. Ch., Owenton, Ky., 1948-49, Riverside Bapt. Ch., Merry Hill, N.C., 1949-52; missionary for West Chowan Bapt. Assn., Ahoskie, N.C., 1952-53, Cabarrus Bapt. Assn., Concord, N.C., 1953-60; dir. retirement Bapt. State Conv. N.C., 1960-61, sec. dept., stewardship devel., 1963-70, dir. coop. program promotion, 1971-73, dir. dept. stewardship, 1973-77, asso. dir. div. bus., 1977—; sec. Christian Education Advance, 1962-63. Pub. relations dir. for denominational work in Bapt. assns. in N.C., 1957-58; writer Bible. Column for newspapers called Biblical Series, 1952-57. Active in ARC. Recipient citation from Editorial Conf. of N.C., 1953. Democrat. Co-author: How To Write and Use a Few Words for an Effective Harvest, 1967. Contrbr. over 1300 articles to Bapt. publs., over 300 to jours. and newspapers. Home: 2700 St Marys St Raleigh NC 27609 Office: PO Box 26508 Raleigh NC 27611

GREENE, SHELDON, motel-hotel brokerage co. exec.; b. Bklyn., June 25, 1933; s. Morris and Jean (Kessler) G.; B.B.A., City Coll. N.Y., 1954; m. Lila Marilyn, Apr. 2, 1960 (dec.); children—Susan Dana, Joel Mathew. Vice-pres. Futterman Corp., N.Y.C., 1956-63; v.p. Elk Realty, Inc., N.Y.C., 1964-66; v.p. Keyes Nat. Investors, Miami, Fla., 1968-70; pres. Sheldon Greene & Assos., Inc., Miami, 1971—. Served with U.S. Army, 1954-56. Mem. Motel Brokers Assn. Am., Fla. Motel Brokers (pres.), Miami Beach Bd. Realtors (dir.), Nat. Assn. Ind. Fee Appraisers, Nat. Innkeeping Assn. Jewish. Club: Elks. Home: 7441 Wayne Ave Miami Beach FL 33141 Office: 1720 79th St Causeway Miami FL 33141

GREENE, VIRGIL KEITH, food co. exec.; b. Kansas City, Mo., Apr. 24, 1942; s. Sherman Olen and Phyllis Mae Greene; student public schs., Kansas City, Mo.; m. Edna Marie Arnold, May 16, 1963; children—Michael Keith, William Sherman. With U.S. Post Office Dept., 1964-68; with dairy and poultry dept. Wilson & Co., Kansas City, Kans., 1973; with Crystal Lake Foods, Inc., div. Peterson Industries, 1971-73, 73—, br. mgr., Decatur, Ill., 1976-77, dir. br. ops. home office, Decatur, Ark., 1977—. Served with U.S. Army, 1961-64. Mem. Southeastern Polutry Assn., Ga. Poultry Fedn., Ark. Poultry Fedn. Baptist. Club: Decatur Kiwanis. Home: Route 1 Box 75 A Decatur AR 72722 Office: Peterson Industries PO Box 248 Decatur AR 72722

GREENFIELD, CHARLES THOMAS, mfg. co. exec.; b. Toronto, Ont., Can., Jan. 9, 1920; s. Albert Edgar and Emily (Smith) G.; came to U.S., 1920, naturalized, 1946;; student U. Cin., 1951-52; m. Martha Jeannetta Connor, June 29, 1941; children—Janet Kay (Mrs. Ronald Hanock), Richard Duane, Susan Carol (Mrs. Michael Julius), Judith Ann (Mrs. Thomas Ward). Tool maker Union Carbide & Carbon Co., 1941-48, Fostoria Machine & Tool Co., 1948-51; tooling supr. Gen. Tire & Rubber Co., 1951-52; chief tool engr. Aerojet-Gen. Corp., Cin., 1952-54; gen. foreman Ex-Cell-O Corp., Lima, Ohio, 1954-57, plant supt., New Breman, Ohio, 1957-60, asst. plant mgr., Elwood, Ind., 1960-63, div. project mgr., Lima, 1963-64, gen. mgr., Black Mountain, N.C., 1964-66; dir. mfg. Duff-Norton Co., Charlotte, N.C., 1966-70; plant mgr. Kay Mfg. Corp., High Point, N.C., 1970—. Served with USAAF, 1942-45. Decorated Air medal. Mem. Am. Ordnance Assn., Am. Rocket Soc., Am. Soc. Tool Engrs., Am. Inst. Aeros. and Astronautics. Republican. Address: 1422 Grantham Dr High Point NC 27260

GREENHILL, JOE ROBERT, chief justice Tex. Supreme Ct.; b. Houston, July 14, 1914; s. Joe Robert, Jr. and Violet (Stanuell) G.; B.A., U. Tex., 1936, B.B.A., 1936, LL.B., 1939; LL.D. (hon.), So. Meth. U., 1977; m. Martha Shuford, June 15, 1940; children—Joe Robert IV, William Duke. Admitted to Tex. bar, 1938; partner firm Bryan, Suhr, Bering, and Bell, Houston, 1939-41, Graves, Dougherty & Greenhill, Austin, 1950-57; briefing atty. Supreme Ct. Tex., 1941-42, 46, asso. justice, 1957-72, chief justice, 1972—; asst. atty. gen. Tex., 1947-48, 1st asst. gen. Tex., 1948-50. Served from ensign to lt. USNR, 1942-46. Named Distinguished Alumnus, U. Tex. Mem. Am. Judicature Soc. (past dir.), Am. Bar Assn., State Bar Tex. (chmn. mineral sect. 1957-58, chmn. jud. sect. 1970-71), Philos. Soc. Tex., Phi Beta Kappa, Phi Delta Theta, Order of Coif. Episcopalian. Mason (33 degree). Home: 3204 Bridle Path Austin TX 78703 Office: Supreme Ct Tex Austin TX 78711

GREENHOUSE, BARRY DAVID, engring.-planning firm exec.; b. Bklyn., Feb. 16, 1946; s. Morton Melvyn and Harriet (Bokor) G.; B.A., City Coll. of N.Y., 1969; M.S. in Planning, Pratt Inst., 1972; m. Meryl Lynn Jurgrau, Aug. 2, 1969; children—Matthew Myles, Marshall Neal, Melissa Beth. Sci. tchr. West Hempstead, N.Y., 1969-72; dir. planning McIntosh Trail Area Planning & Devel. Com., Griffin, Ga., 1972-74; regional dir. Murray-McCormick, Inc., Atlanta, 1974-75; exec. v.p. and partner, dir. mktg. Soil Systems, Inc., Marietta, Ga., 1975—; instr. Gordon Jr. Coll., W. Ga. Coll., 1973-74; advisor local mun. and county planning commns. Mem. Am. Planning Assn., Am. Clean Water Assn. (dir.), High Mus. of Art (Atlanta), Am. Inst. Cert. Planners, Am. Def. Preparedness Assn. Republican. Jewish. Contbr. publs. in field of planning to Nat. Tech. Info. Service, Springfield, Va. Home: 205 Brandon P NW Atlanta GA 30328 Office: 525 Webb Industrial Dr Marietta GA 30062

GREENLEE, BETTY JOAN, fin. co. exec.; b. Reform, Ark., Apr. 8, 1920; d. Harold Hyde and Mabel (Warren) Bailey; student Hot Springs Bus. Coll., 1943; grad. Savs. and Loan Grad. Sch., Bloomington, Ind., 1972; m. Elmer H. Greenlee, Oct. 9, 1958. With First Fed. Savs. of Hot Springs (Ark.), 1943—, sr. v.p., 1976, exec. v.p. and chief fin. officer, 1977—, dir., 1960-78; dir. Ark. Savs. & Loan League, 1955-57, treas., 1959-65. Treas., United Fund Campaign of Garland County (Ark.), 1957-58. Mem. Inst. Fin. Edn., Nat. Assn. Fin. Mgrs. (steering com. southwestern regional conf. 1969-78), Alumni Grad. Sch. Savs. and Loan, Hot Springs Iris Soc., Garland County Hist. Soc., Asso. Women of Harding U. Republican. Mem. Ch. of Christ. Clubs: Pilot of Hot Springs (pres. 1956-57), Sabina (pres. 1954-55). Author various tech. manuals on fin. procedures. Home: 108 Woodridge Dr Hot Springs AR 71901 Office: 1 Market Pl Hot Springs AR 71901

GREENLEE, (MARY) ELYSIA, conservation ranger; b. Dallas, Jan. 1, 1950; d. Paul Calvin, Sr., and Anne J. (Stapp) Greenlee Raven; B.A. in English (scholar), Presbyn. Coll., Clinton, S.C., 1971; M.Ed., U. Ga., Athens, 1976, postgrad. in law enforcement, 1975-76. Tchr. English and reading, Athens, Ga., 1971-74; conservation ranger Ga. Game and Fish div. Dept. Natural Resources, Calhoun, 1974-79, conservation cpl., Clayton County, Walton Dist., 1979—. Named Ranger of Year for Calhoun Dist., 1979; cert. tchr., guidance counselor, peace officer, Ga. Mem. NOW, Peace Officer Assn. Ga., Am. Personnel and Guidance Assn., Am. Coll. Personnel Assn., Southeastern Assn. Fish and Wildlife Agencies, Women's Sports Found. Democrat. Presbyterian. First woman ranger in Ga. Home: 8904 Dorsey Rd Riverdale GA 30274 Office: Dept of Natural Resources Game and Fish Div Rt 2 Box 119B Social Circle GA 30279

GREENSPAN, MICHAEL M., air force officer; b. N.Y.C., Jan. 19, 1940; s. Alexander and Ruth Greenspan; B.S., Ball State U., Muncie, Ind., 1969; M.P.A., Golden Gate U., San Francisco, 1974; grad. Air Command and Staff Coll., 1969, Indsl. Coll. Armed Forces, 1973, Air War Coll., 1976; m. Joanne B. Ivey, Feb. 13, 1966; children—Amy, Daniel. Commd. 2d lt. U.S. Air Force, 1960, advanced through grades to lt. col., 1977; service in Vietnam; insp., staff analyst, chief programs and analysis br. Office Insp. Gen., Air Tng. Command, Randolph AFB, Tex., 1976-79; dep. comdr. Brooks AFB, Tex., 1979—. Liaison officer Boy Scouts Am., Loring AFB, Maine, 1963-66; chmn. Youth Activities Bd., Mather AFB, Calif., 1971-72; vol. counselor DeWitt Nelson Tng. Center, Stockton, Calif., 1973-74. Decorated D.F.C., Meritorious Service medal with 2 oak leaf clusters, Air medal with 9 oak leaf clusters, Air Force commendation medal. Mem. Air Force Assn., Assn. Old Crows, Inst. Navigation, Ret. Officers Assn., Nat. Sojourners, Heroes of '76, B-58 Hustler Assn. Clubs: Masons, Shriners. Editor The Navigator mag., 1973-74. Home: 8302 Athenian Dr Universal City TX 78148 Office: 6570th Air Base Group Brooks AFB TX 78235

GREENSPAN, MYRON JONAS, dietitian; b. N.Y.C., Jan. 9, 1944; s. Milton and Adelyne (Block) G.; B.A. (Howard Johnson food scholar 1963), U. N.H., 1965; M.A., N.Y. U., 1967; m. Arlene Lynn Cohen, Jan. 28, 1967; children—Dara Cheri, Mark Jared. Sch. lunch mgr. Bur. Sch. Lunches, Bd. Edn., City of N.Y., 1967-68; asst. dir. dietetics Bapt. Med. Center, Jacksonville, Fla., 1970-72, dir. dietetics, 1972—; cons. in field. Bd. trustees Leukemia Soc., 1979—. Served to lt. USPHS, 1967-70. Named Outstanding Young Dietetian, State of Fla., 1973. Mem. Fla. Dietetic Assn. (pres. 1977-78), Jacksonville Dietetic Assn. (pres. 1971-72), Hosp. Food Service Adminstrs. (pres. 1972-73, 75-76), Am. Dietetic Assn. (registered dietitian), Am. Hosp. Assn. Jewish. Club: Jacksonville Racquetball. Home: 2955 Bernice Ct Jacksonville FL 32217 Office: 800 Prudential Dr Jacksonville FL 32207

GREENSTEIN, STANLEY GEORGE, retail co. exec.; b. N.Y.C., Aug. 26, 1925; s. Harry and Ray (Cohen) G.; B.B.A., Coll. City N.Y., 1948; M.B.A., Harvard, 1951; children—Amy, Robin, Steven. Pub. acct., N.Y.C., 1947-49; mdse. exec. R.H. Macy & Co., N.Y.C., 1951-58; pres. Carnaby Shops of Fla., Inc., N.Y.C., 1960—; cons. Harvard Bus. Sch. Minority Consulting Program. Mem. nat. commn. domestic affairs Am. Jewish Com.; past mem. adv. bd. Great Neck (N.Y.) Bd. Edn.; mem. exec. bd. Miami region Am. Jewish Com., v.p. Jewish Community Centers S. Fla. Served to 2d lt., USAAF, 1943-45. Mem. Mus. Modern Art. Democrat. Jewish. Club: Harvard Business School (Fla.); Harvard (N.Y.C.). Office: 1345 NE 163d St North Miami Beach FL 33162

GREENWAY, CHERYL ANN, accountant; b. Atlanta, Oct. 2, 1952; d. Aubrey Eugene and Frances (Webb) Greenway; A.B., Kennesaw Jr. Coll., 1972; B.B.A., Ga. State U., 1974. Mgr., Deloitte Haskins & Sells, Atlanta, 1974—. C.P.A., Ga. Mem. Ga. Soc. C.P.A.'s, Am. Inst. C.P.A.'s, Feminist Action Alliance, Parents Anonymous, Phi Kappa Phi, Beta Gamma Sigma, Beta Alpha Psi, Phi Chi Theta. Office: Suite 1800 100 Peachtree St Atlanta GA 30303

GREENWAY, ZELMAR CARVEY, fire chief; b. Swainsboro, Ga., Nov. 16, 1919; s. Arlie Thomas and Mattie (Davis) G.; student Tampa Bus. Coll., 1938, St. Petersburg Jr. Coll., 1961, 68-69; m. Donnie Mae Thomas, Mar. 12, 1943; 1 dau., Donnie Jean (Mrs. Alan C. Brown). With St. Petersburg (Fla.) Fire Dept., 1946—, fire capt., 1957, tng. officer, 1958-61, fire chief, 1962—. Dir. rescue Pinellas County, 1961; exec. dir. St. Petersburg Civil Def., 1969. Pres. Greater Sun Coast chpt. Muscular Dystrophy Assn. Am.; mem. adv. council Medic Alert. Served with USNR, 1942-45. Recipient Pub. Service citation of merit Muscular Dystrophy Assn., 1963-68; Service Appreciation award ARC, 1961. Mem. Internat., Southeastern, Fla. assns. fire chiefs. Democrat. Methodist. Rotarian. Home: 4574 8th Ave N Saint Petersburg FL 33713 Office: 1429 Arlington Ave N Saint Petersburg FL 33705

GREENWOOD, KENNETH RENNAU, educator; b. Brainard, Minn., July 29, 1923; s. William R. and Helen (Rennau) G.; B.A., U. Nebr., 1948; m. Marian Jean Coombs, July 21, 1944; children—Gil Jay, Sharon Louise, Jody Jill. With Swanson Broadcasting, Tulsa, 1961-72, pres., 1965-72, now dir.; head communication dept. U. Tulsa, 1972—; cons. communication cos.; chmn. bd. Radio Index. Pres. bd. dirs. Children's Med. Center; pres. Tulsa chpt. NCCJ, 1969-71; bd. dirs. Gilcrease Mus. Served with USAAF, 1941-45. Mem. Tulsa C. of C. (dir. 1969-72), Okla. Broadcasters Assn. (pres. 1970-71), Southwestern Legal Inst., Tulsa Advt. Club, Okla. Wildlife Fedn. Episcopalian. Producer: Conversation with Will Rogers, radio series. Home: 3130 S Utica St Tulsa OK 74105 Office: 600 S South College Tulsa OK 74104

GREER, DONALD MERRILL, JR., plastic and reconstructive surgeon, educator; b. Chgo., Nov. 14, 1936; s. Donald Merrill and Mary Elizabeth (Adams) G.; student Deep Springs Coll., 1954-55; B.S., U. Chgo., 1958; M.D., U. Cin., 1962; children—Donald Merrill, William Wright. Mixed intern U. Chgo. Hosps., 1962-63, resident in gen. surgery, 1963-66, 68-69, instr. in surgery, 1969-70; resident in plastic surgery U. Mich., Ann Arbor, 1970-72; asst. prof. div. plastic and reconstructive surgery Sch. Medicine U. Fla., Gainesville, 1972-75; asso. prof., head div. plastic and reconstructive surgery U. Tex. Health Sci. Center San Antonio, 1975—. Active Boy Scouts Am. Served to lt. comdr. M.C., USN, 1966-68. Diplomate Am. Bd. Plastic Surgery. Mem. AMA, Tex. Med. Assn., Bexar County Med. Soc., Am. Burn Assn., Am. Cleft Palate Assn., Am. Soc. Plastic and Reconstructive Surgery (instructional com. of Ednl. Found.). Club: Flying Ten (sec.). Contbr. articles to profl. jours., presentations to profl. confs. U.S. and Can. Office: Plastic Surgery Univ Texas Health Science Center 7703 Floyd Curl Dr San Antonio TX 78284

GREER, FRED JONES, JR., ins. co. exec.; b. Baton Rouge, Dec. 31, 1916; s. Fred Jones and Nannie Austin (Stephenson) G.; student La. State U., 1935-39; m. Phyllis Miriam Rosiere, Jan. 18, 1941; children—Jacqueline, Joyce, Fred Jones III, Phyllis Ann. With Union Nat. Life Ins. Co., Baton Rouge, 1939—, sr. v.p., 1975—, sec., 1946—, treas., 1975—, editor, 1948—. Mgr., chmn. United Givers Drive, 1967. Served as sgt. Armed Forces, World War II; PTO. Mem. La. Home Office Life Underwriters (past pres.), Baton Rouge Assn. Indsl. Editors (past pres.), Baton Rouge C. of C. (treas. 1944, 45, 46). Democrat. Methodist. Home: 2330 Olive St Baton Rouge LA 70806 Office: 8282 Goodwood Blvd Baton Rouge LA 70806

GREER, MACK VARNEDOE, physician; b. Valdosta, Ga., July 29, 1927; s. Lloyd Barton and Julie Winn (Varnedoe) G.; A.B., Emory U., 1951; postgrad. Valdosta State Coll., 1955-56; M.D., Med. Coll. Ga., 1960; m. Betty Dame English, Dec. 27, 1951; children—Betty June, Mack Varnedoe. Adjuster, Crawford & Co., ins. adjusters, Atlanta, 1951-52; high sch. math. and sci. tchr., football coach Clinch County (Ga.) and Waycross (Ga.) High Sch., 1952-55; rotating intern Bapt. Meml. Hosp., Jacksonville, Fla., 1960-61; gen. practice medicine and surgery, Homerville, Ga., 1961-72; mem. staff South Ga. Med. Center, chief staff, 1980; Coll. athletic physician; coll. physician, also asso. prof. biology Valdosta State Coll., 1972—. Bd. dirs. Valdosta (Ga.) Girls Club. Served with USMCR, World War II, Korea. Diplomate Am. Bd. Family Practice. Mem. AMA, So., Ga. med. assns., S.Ga. Med. Soc., Clinch County Bd. Health, Am. Coll. Emergency Physicians, Pi Kappa Alpha, Alpha Kappa Kappa. Methodist. Club: Valdosta (Ga.) Touchdown, Exchange. Home: PO Box 2196 Valdosta GA 31601 Office: Farber Health Center Valdosta State Coll Valdosta GA 31601

GREGERSON, PETER VALJEAN, JR., advt agy. exec.; b. Davenport, Iowa, Aug. 1, 1952; s. Peter Valjean and Janet Emelyn (Dyke) G.; student public schs., Gadsden, Ala.; m. Susan Ann Warren, Apr. 1, 1972; children—Jennifer Gay, Michelle Kay, Nicole Sue. Gen. mdse. mgr. Warehouse Groceries Mgmt. Inc., Gadsden, Ala., 1970-76, dir. advt., 1976-79; pres. Mediacom Mktg., Gadsden, 1979—; dir. Coosa Warehouse Groceries, Inc., Carrollton Warehouse Market Inc. Mem. Audit Bur. of Circulations, Super Market Inst., Am. Mgmt. Assn., Internat. Entrepreneurs Assn., Nat. Free Lance Photographers Assn. Mem. Jehovah's Witnesses. Home: Box 31P Country Club Dr Centre AL 35960 Office: PO Box 2095 Gadsden AL 35903

GREGG, ETHELMAE (EFFIE) HELMS, hosp. ofcl.; b. Richmond, Va., June 16, 1923; d. Carlos and Frances Amilea (Rikard) Helms; student Limestone Coll., 1942, Francis Marion Coll., 1977; m. Walter Gregg, May 25, 1946; children—Sandra, Frances M., Walter, Helen E. Exec. sec. C&WC R.R., Spartanburg, S.C., 1942-46, Sta. WBTV, Channel 13, Florence, S.C., 1963-66, Cayce Co. Inc., Florence, 1966-71; adminstrv. sec. Bruce Hosp. Inc., Florence, 1971-75, personnel dir., 1975—. A founder Health Facilities Credit Union, 1977, chmn. credit com., 1977-78. Mem. Greater Florence C. of C., Am. Hosp. Assn., S.C. Hosp. Assn. (sec. personnel club 1978-79). Democrat. Presbyterian. Home: 838 Congaree Dr Florence SC 29501 Office: Bruce Hosp Inc 514 Dargan St Florence SC 29501

GREGG, MICHAEL ALAN, publishing co. exec.; b. Fostoria, Ohio, Nov. 4, 1946; s. Alan Frank and Donna Louise (Bradner) G.; B.A., Tiffin (Ohio) U., 1971; m. Judy Kay Birkmire, Aug. 9, 1964; children—Linda Raye, Wendy Sue, Michael Andrew. Read stock dept. Foodtown, Fostoria, 1963-67; service mgr. Goodyear Tire & Rubber Co., Fostoria, 1967-68; gen. mgr. RKM Corp., Tiffin, 1968-76;

sales mgr. Hillsboro News Co., Tampa, Fla., 1976—. Mem. Am. Mgmt. Assn. Republican. Home: 8225 Drycreek Dr Tampa FL 33615 Office: 2102 N Stering Ave Tampa FL 33607

GREGG, PAUL CHARLES, naval flight surgeon; b. N.Y.C., Ma. 8, 1925; s. Benjamin Paul and Catherine Jane (Fales) G.; B.S., Union Coll., Schnectady, 1947; M.D., Johns Hopkins U., 1951, M.P.H., 1967; m. Ann Taylor Garner, June 11, 1949; children—Paul Charles, Katherine Ann (Mrs. Richard L. Quinn), Patricia Ann, Janice Taylor, Michael Benjamin, Elizabeth Lucette. Joined U.S. Navy, 1943; served in Pacific, 1945-46, commd. lt. (j.g.), 1951, served active duty, 1951-53, 62—, advanced through grades to capt., 1968; intern U.S. Naval Hosp., St. Albans, N.Y., 1951-52; practice gen. medicine, Levittown, Pa., 1953-62; sr. med. officer U.S.S. Essex, 1962-64; asst. dir. tng. Naval Aerospace Med. Inst., Pensacola, Fla., 1964-66, resident aerospace medicine, 1967-69; sr. med. officer Naval Air Sta., Corpus Christi, Tex., also med. officer Chief Naval Aviation Advanced Tng., 1969-71; comdg. officer Naval Hosp., med. officer Second Marine Air Wing, med. officer Marine Air Bases, East Cherry Point, N.C., 1971-73; dep. comdg. officer Naval Aerospace and Regional Med. Center, Pensacola, Fla., 1974-76; comdg. officer Naval Regional Med. Center, New Orleans, 1976-78, Naval Hosp., Roosevelt Roads, P.R., 1978—. Diplomate Am. Bd. Preventive Medicine (in aerospace medicine). Fellow Am. Coll. Preventive Medicine, Aerospace Med. Assn. (asso.); mem. Assn. Mil. Surgeons, Johns Hopkins Med., Surg. Assn., Phi Delta Theta, Phi Chi. Home: 5 FDR US Naval Sta FPO Miami FL 34051 Office: US Naval Naval Hosp FPO Miami FL 34051

GREGG, ROSEMARY ROBINSON, hosp. adminstr.; b. Gadsden, Ala., Mar. 11, 1948; d. Roy Robert and Cleophas Josephine (Brosemer) Robinson; B.S., U. Ala., 1970, postgrad., 1978—; m. John Robert Gregg, May 31, 1969; children—Phillip Michael Robert, Thomas Neil. Clin. dietitian Crawford W. Long Hosp., Atlanta, 1973-74, adminstrv. dietitian, 1974-75; dir. dietary services Med. Center Hosp., Huntsville, Ala., 1977—. Recipient Black Friar award U. Ala. Theater, 1967; Silver Trivet award Stokely Van Camp, 1970; Mead Johnson scholar, 1970-71; registered dietitian, Ala. Mem. N.Ala. Dietetic Assn. (pres. 1979—, treas. 1978-79), Atlanta Dist. Dietetic Assn. (chmn. food adminstrn. sect. 1970-71, chmn. community nutrition sect. 1973-74), Lehigh Valley Dietetic Assn. (chmn. food adminstrn. sect. 1975-77). Republican. Roman Catholic. Home: 2605 Valley Brook Circle NE Huntsville AL 35811 Office: 911 Big Cove Rd Huntsville AL 35801

GREGORCYK, WALLIS JAMES, fin. co. exec.; b. Beeville, Tex., Sept. 23, 1937; s. Albert Hubert and Irene Minnie (Mussman) G.; B.B.A., Tex. A&I U., 1960; m. Frances Carol Sralla, Aug. 25, 1958; children—Michael Scott, Vicky Ann, Sharon Gaye. Br. mgr. Gen. Electric Credit Corp., Corpus Christi and Beaumont, Tex., 1961-68; pres. Conn Credit Corp., Beaumont, 1968—, also dir.; treas. Conn Applieances, Inc., Beaumont, 1968—, dir., 19—. Mem. Soc. Cert. Consumer Credit Execs. (cert.), Credit Mgmt. Assn. Beaumont, Credit Mgmt. Assn. Tex., Internat. Consumer Credit Assn., Retail Mchts. Assn. Port Arthur (dir.), Credit Mgmt. Assn. Beaumont (pres. 1972), Bus. and Profl. Women's Club, Young Men's Bus. League. Roman Catholic. Home: 5920 Tangledahl St Beaumont TX 77706 Office: Conn Credit Corp 195 N 11th St Beaumont TX 77702

GREGORIO, PETER ANTHONY, retail grocer, artist; b. Chgo., July 29, 1916; s. Frank and Teresa (Marotta) G.; grad. pub. schs., Chgo., 1942; m. Marie Blanton, Mar. 17, 1945; children—Frank Allen, Carole Teresa. Owner, operator Davis Island Supermarket, Tampa, Fla. 1949—; dir. Ellis Nat. Bank of Davis Island, Tampa 1977-78; exhibited in one man show Islands Gallery, 1976-77; group shows Am. Bicentennial, Paris, 1976, Rochester (N.Y.) Religious Art Festival, 1972, Tampa Bay Art Center, 1979, Hillsborough Art Festival, 1976, 77, 78, award of merit, 1979, represented in permanent collections Vatican Library, Rome, also numerous pvt. collections. Served to capt. USAF, 1941-46. Decorated Air medal with 6 clusters. Mem. Am., Internat. socs. artists, Graphic Soc. Roman Catholic. Home: 149 Bosphorus Ave Tampa FL 33606 Office: 304 E Davis Blvd Tampa FL 33606

GREGORY, ANN YOUNG, newspaper editor-publisher; b. Lexington, Ky., Apr. 28, 1935; d. David M. and Pauline A. Young; B.A. with high distinction, U. Ky., 1956; m. Allen Gregory, Jan. 29, 1957; children—David Young, Mary Peyton. Traffic mgr. Sta. WVLK, Lexington, 1956-61; tchr. adult basic edn. Wise County (Va.) Sch. Bd., St. Paul, Va., 1967-73; adminstrv. asst. Appalachian Field Services of Children's TV Workshop, St. Paul, 1971-74; editor-pub. Clinich Valley Times, St. Paul, 1974—; tchr. journalism for high sch. students S.W. Va. Community Coll., 1976. Mem. Wise County Sch. Bd., 1975—; trustee Lonesome Pine Regional Library, 1972—, 1972-78, chmn., 1978—; chmn., organizer establishment St. Paul Pub. Library, 1975; chmn. St. Paul Bicentennial Com., 1976, St. Paul Cancer Drive, 1966-73; pres. St. Paul Band Boosters, 1974-78; adv. bd. Wise County YMCA, 1976—; pres. Wise County Humane Soc., Inc. Ky. Broadcaster Assn. scholar, 1955; named Clubwoman of Year, St. Paul Jr. Woman's Club, 1964, 66; S.W. Va. Citizen of Yr., Va. Fedn. Women's Clubs, 1968; recipient art awards for oils. Mem. Women in Communications, Va. Press Assn. (1st place editorial writing 1976), Nat. Newspaper Assn. (asso.), Nat., Va. press women, Va. Sch. Bds. Assn. (dir.), Nat. Sch. Bds. Assn., U. Ky. Alumni Assn., Wise County, St. Paul chambers commerce, Mortar Bd., Phi Beta Kappa, Alpha Delta Pi, Alpha Lambda Delta, Theta Sigma Phi, Chi Delta Phi, Alpha Epsilon Rho. Democrat. Methodist. Clubs: Lake Bonaventure Country, Saintly Squares Sq. Dance (pres.). Editor, textwriter Flood of '77, 1977; editor privately printed cookbook. Home: Longview Dr PO Box 303 St Paul VA 24283 Office: PO Box 817 Russell St St Paul VA 24283

GREGORY, ARTHUR, lawyer; b. Savannah, Ga., Mar. 22, 1940; s. Euthemious Athan and Sophie (Christopher) G.; A.B., Duke, 1963; J.D., U. S.C., 1968. Admitted to Ga. bar, 1969; asso. firm Candler, Cox, McClain & Andrews, Atlanta, 1968-70; asso. firm McClain, Mellen, Bowling & Hickman, Atlanta, 1970-73, partner, 1973—. Lectr. law Atlanta Law Sch., 1969—. Mem. U. S.C. Alumni Council, 1975-77; chmn. Peach Bowl Team Selection Com., 1979—. Served to lt. (j.g.) USNR, 1963-65. Recipient Certificate of Appreciation award Ga. Heart Assn., 1974, U. S.C. Alumni Assn., 1976. Mem. Duke U. (pres. Atlanta chpt. 1975-76), U. S.C. (pres. Atlanta chpt. 1975-76) alumni assns., Duke U. Loyalty Fund (chmn. Atlanta region 1974-75), The Touchdown Club of Atlanta, Inc. (pres. 1976-77), Nine O'Clocks Club, Lawyer's Club of Atlanta, Iron Dukes Booster Club, Ahepa Greek Am. Fraternal Order. Mem. Greek Orthodox Ch. Home: 898 Wesley Dr NW Atlanta GA 30305 Office: PO Drawer 56505 Atlanta GA 30343

GREGORY, EDWARD MEEKS, clergyman; b. Richmond, Va., Sept. 30, 1922; s. George Craghead and Constance (Heath) G.; grad. St. Christopher's Sch., Richmond, 1941; A.B., U. Va., 1947; M.Div., Episcopal Theol. Sch., Cambridge, Mass., 1954; postgrad. George Washington U., 1949; D.Min., U. of South, 1977. Ordained to ministry Episcopal Ch., 1954; instr. Staunton (Va.) Mil. Acad., 1947-48; master Episcopal High Sch., Alexandria, Va., 1948-51; curate St. Mark's Episcopal Ch., Richmond, Va., 1954-69; vicar St. Peter's Episcopal Ch., Richmond, 1969-79; chaplain Christchurch Sch., 1980—; dean East Richmond, 1974-78; diocesan youth dir., 1956-60; diocesan del. Va. Council Chs., 1967-73; spiritual adviser Dignity-Integrity/Richmond, 1976-79. Mem. Diocesan Dept. on Social Relations, 1970-72, Diocesan Lit. Commn.; 1973—; pres. Religious Edn. Council, Richmond, 1961-62, Richmond Episcopal Clericus, 1972-73. Bd. dirs. Vol. Service Bur., Richmond, 1960-63, Ednl. Therapy Center, 1964-79, Multiple Sclerosis, 1961-66, Va. Community Devel. Orgn., 1968-75, Va. chpt. ACLU, 1970-71, 76-77, Internat. Council; bd. dirs. Va. Council on Human Relations, 1965-70, treas., 1972-73; bd. dirs. Richmond Planned Parenthood, 1969-74, Richmond chpt. ARC, 1973-79, Richmond United Neighborhoods, 1977-79, Met. Area Resources Clearing House, 1977-79, Ch. Hill Revitalization Team, 1979; bd. govts. Christchurch Sch., Va., 1978-79; pres. Richmond Council Human Relations, 1960-62; pres. Friends' Assn. for Children, 1967-70, bd. dirs., 1975-79; mem. adv. bd. Richmond Model Neighborhood, 1971-73; bd. dirs. Richmond Community Sr. Center, 1975-78, Daily Planet, 1974-79, Alcohol and Drug Abuse Prevention and Tng. Services, 1978-79; vice chmn. Richmond Health Occupations, 1979. Served with M.C., AUS, 1942-46. Mem. Richmond Clergy Assn., Jamestown Soc. (gov. 1951-54), Mayflower Soc. (elder Va. co. 1963—), Va. Hist. Soc., Episcopal Soc. Cultural and Racial Unity (chmn. Richmond 1964-66), Assn. for Preservation Va. Antiquities, Va. Mus. Fine Arts, Chi Phi. Clubs: James River Catfish, 2300, Home and Office: Christchurch Sch Christchurch VA 23031

GREGORY, EDWARD WADSWORTH, JR., educator; b. Chase City, Va., Sept. 29, 1903; s. Edward Wadsworth and Kate Winn (Cleveland) G.; A.B., U. Va., 1925, M.A., 1926, Ph.D., 1931; m. Margaret Louise Jeffreys, Aug. 28, 1934; 1 son, Allen Wadsworth. Instr. sociology U. Va., 1925-28; asst. prof. sociology U. Ala., 1928-29, asso. prof., 1929-35, prof., 1935-45; prof. sociology U. Md., 1946; prof. sociology U. Richmond (Va.), 1946-72, emeritus, 1972—. Chmn. Tuscaloosa Co. (Ala.) Bd. Pub. Welfare, 1940-43; pres. Ala. Conf. Social Work, 1941-42; pres. Va. Council Social Welfare, 1950-51; mem. Va. Commn. on Aging, 1962-68, Bd. Welfare and Instns. Va., 1963-71. Chmn. adv. bd. Pub. Welfare, Richmond, 1953-55; pres. Richmond Area Community Council, 1951-53. Mem. War Price and Rationing Bd. of Tuscaloosa County, 1942-43; mem. commn. of Reorgn. State Govt., Va., 1947. Commd. lt. USNR, Jan. 1943, lt. comdr., Oct. 1945 (on active duty, Feb. 1943-Jan. 1946). Mem. Am. Sociol. Soc., So. Sociol. Soc. (pres. 1939), Nat. Council Family Relations (nat. adv. council 1939-42). Am. Assn. U. Profs., Va. Social Science Assn. (pres. 1951-52), Family and Children's Service Richmond (bd. dirs.), Delta Sigma Phi, Delta Sigma Rho, Phi Beta Kappa, Phi Delta Kappa, Alpha Kappa Delta. Raven. Methodist. Club: Country of Va.; Torch. Author: Introductory Sociology (with Lee Bidgood), 1939. Co-author: Social Control, 1947, rev. ed., 1956. Contbr. articles to jours. Address: University of Richmond Richmond VA 23173

GREGORY, LOWELL DEAN, aerospace co. exec.; b. Chickasha, Okla., Feb. 19, 1918; s. Simeon Roscoe and Pearl (Robinson) G.; B.A. in English, U. Okla., 1940, M.A. in Math., 1950; Ph.D. in Math. Statistics (Ling-Temco-Vought fellow), So. Meth. U., 1968; m. Marian Gavin, May 27, 1939; children—Gavin George, Lynn. Instr. math. U. Okla., Norman, 1947-51; sr. analyst Chance Vought Aircraft, Dallas, 1951-55, devel. project engr., 1955-57, supr. advanced weapon systems analysis, 1957-59, chief reliability astro. div., 1959-62; mgr. reliability engring. astro. div. Ling-Temco-Vought Dallas, 1962-64, supr. operations analysis, 1964—. Spl. lectr. Nat. War Coll., 1972. Served to 1st lt. F.A., AUS, 1940-42, to capt. USAAF, 1942-45. Mem. Aerospace industries Assn. (mem. reliability com. 1964-66), Am. Astronautical Soc. Assn. (sr.), Ops. Research Soc. Am., North Tex. Operations Research Soc. (dir.), Sigma Xi, Pi Mu Epsilon. Home: 1300 W 2d St Arlington TX 76013 Office: PO Box 5907 Dallas TX 75222

GREGORY, VIRGINIA LOIS SULLENGER, agri-bus. exec.; b. Crittenden County, Ky., Mar. 29, 1912; d. William David and Mary Lee (Paris) Sullenger; A.B., U. Ky., 1933; M.A., Murray State Coll., 1960; M.L.S., George Peabody Coll., 1968; m. James Lee Gregory, June 4, 1932; children—Lucy Lee (Mrs. John Daniel Quertermous), James William, Richard Davis, John Scott, Rose Marie. Sec. to county judge Crittenden County, Marion, Ky., 1935-39; high sch. librarian Crittenden County Bd. Edn., 1955-68; reference librarian Murray (Ky.) State U., 1968-77; pres. Gregory Inc., 1977—. Mem. Ky. Adv. Com. on Tchr. Edn. and Certification, 1967-68. Mem. Am., Southeastern, Ky. library assns., Ky. Assn. Sch. Librarians (pres. 1967-68), NEA, Ky. Edn. Assn., Ky. Hist. Soc., Beta Phi Mu, Kappa Delta Pi. Republican. Mem. Disciples of Christ Ch. Author: Afro-Americans, 1972; Natural Resources and Environment, 1973. Home: 108 Broach Ave S Murray KY 42071

GREGORY, WALTON CARLYLE, II, computer corp. exec.; b. Cookeville, Tenn., May 10, 1941; s. Walton Carlyle and Margaret (Pfluge) G.; B.S., N.C. State U., 1963, M.Sc., 1966, Ph.D., 1970; m. Mary Sue Wilking, Feb. 20, 1971; children—Carol Diane, James Franklin, Charles Edward, Laura Jane, Ellen Marie. Cons. statistician Procter & Gamble Co., Cin., 1966-70; v.p. IMSL, Inc., Houston, 1970-77, pres., dir., 1977—; vis. lectr. math. scis. dept. Rice U., 1973-75; co-prin. investigator software portability research NSF, 1974-76. Mem. Am. Statis. Assn., Assn. for Computing Machinery. Home: 7734 Romney St Houston TX 77036 Office: IMSL Inc 7500 Bellaire Blvd Houston TX 77036

GREGORY, WILLIAM THOMAS, III, nuclear engr.; b. Greenville, S.C., Aug. 4, 1945; s. William Thomas and Virginia (Ricker) G.; B.S., U. N.Mex., 1967; M.B.A., Lamar U., 1976; m. Melanie Martin; 1 son, Brian Allen. Power engr. Stone & Webster Engring. Corp., Boston, 1972; nuclear staff asst. Gulf States Utilities Co., Beaumont, Tex., 1974-77; mgr. nuclear applications Luwa Corp., Charlotte, N.C., 1977-79; mgr. tech. mktg. Chem-Nuclear Systems, Inc., Columbia, S.C., 1979—. Served with USN, 1967-72; mem. Res. Mem. ASME (asso.), Am. Nuclear Soc. Republican. Home: 234 Shoreline Dr Columbia SC 29210 Office: 240 Stoneredge Dr Columbia SC 29210

GREIDER, JOHN CALHOUN, educator; b. Atlanta, Dec. 26, 1928; s. William Fredrick and Nadine (Calhoun) G.; B.A., U. Ga., 1953; M.A., George Peabody Coll., 1956; B.D., New Orleans Bapt. Theol. Sem., 1955; postgrad. U. Heidelberg, W. Ger., 1959-61, U. Chgo., 1961-63, (Fulbright scholar) U. Thessaloniki, Greece, 1963-64; Ph.D., U. Liverpool, Eng., 1966; m. Marilyn J. Muench, Aug. 1, 1964; children—Wendel C., Courtney Ann. Instr. English, DePaul U., Chgo., 1961-63; asso. prof. Kennesaw Coll., Marietta, Ga., 1966-72, prof., 1973—, chmn. div. humanities, 1966—; photographer; owner Devonshire Photography Ltd. Bd. dirs. Cobb County Youth Museum, March of Dimes. Mem. Modern Lang. Assn., S. Atlantic Modern Lang. Assn., Philos. Soc., Medieval Assn., Classical Assn., So. Baptist. Club: Civitan Internat. (dir., pres. 1978-79 Outstanding Citizenship award Marietta chpt. 1975, Outstanding Pres. award 1980). Author: The Teaching of English, 1964; American Literature: A Critical Bibliography, 1966; The New Renaissance, 1971. Office: Kennesaw Coll Marietta GA 30061

GREIFE, ALICE LEE, indsl. hygienist; b. Kansas City, Mo., Dec. 7, 1953; d. Karl W. and Mary Ann (Carnahan) G.; B.S. in Biology and Chemistry, Central Mo. State U., 1975, M.S. in Indsl. Hygiene, 1976; m. John N. Zey, Feb. 12, 1977. Commd. 2d lt. USPHS, 1976, advanced through grades to capt., 1979; project officer Nat. Inst. Occupational Safety and Health, Morgantown, W.Va., 1976—. Mem. Am. Indsl. Hygiene Assn., Am. Conf. Govt. Indsl. Hygienists, Microbeam Analysis Soc., Soc. Environ. Health. Office: Nat Inst Occupational Safety and Health 944 Chestnut Ridge Rd Morgantown WV 26505

GREINER, MORRIS ESTY, JR., TV exec.; b. Mpls., Nov. 7, 1920; s. Morris Esty and Irene Marie (O'Connell) G.; A.B., Duke U., 1942; m. Dorothy J. Carter, May 23, 1946; 1 son, Derek Carter. Promotion mgr. Sta. WHB, Kansas City, Mo., 1946-50; editor Swing mag., 1946-50; copy dir. Rogers & Smith, advt. agy., Kansas City, Mo., 1950-51, radio and TV dir., 1951-53; mgr. Sta. WHB-TV, Kansas City, Mo., 1953-54, Sta. KMBC-TV, Kansas City, Mo., 1954-64; mgr. Sta. WMC-TV, Scripps-Howard Broadcasting Co., Memphis, 1964-66, v.p. Scripps Howard, 1966—, also dir.; gen. mgr. stas. WMC-TV, WMC, WMC-FM, Memphis, 1966—; dir. NBC TV Affiliates Bd. Dels., 1969-73; faculty Memphis State U., 1968-70. Pres. Red Ballon Players, 1969-70, bd. dirs., 1968-75; pres. Greater Memphis State, 1970-72, bd. dirs., 1966—; bd. dirs. Memphis Speech and Hearing Center, 1968-79, pres., 1973-77; steering chmn. United Memphis, 1970-71; trustee Memphis State U. Found., Memphis Acad. Arts; bd. dirs. United Way Memphis, 1964-78, chmn., 1977-78; bd. dirs. Mid-South Fair Assn., Memphis Community Planning Council, Memphis Vol. Placement Program; mem. chancellor's round table U. Tenn. Med. Units, LeMoyne-Owen Coll., Pres.'s Club Christian Bros. Coll., Pres.'s Council Memphis State U.; adv. council Memphis Cotton Carnival Assn. Served to lt. USNR, 1942-46. Named Boxer Breeder of Year 1955; Regional Emmy winner Nat. Acad. TV Arts and Scis., 1971. Mem. Nat., Tenn. assns. broadcasters, Maximum Service Telecasters. Home: 18 Morningside Park Memphis TN 38104 Office: 1960 Union Ave Memphis TN 38104

GREINKE, EVERETT DONALD, govt. electronics ofcl.; b. Elmhurst, Ill., Oct. 31, 1929; s. Herman and Marie (Kline) G.; B.S., No. Ill. U., 1951, M.S., 1956; postgrad. U. Wis., 1956; m. Clara Plasil, Sept. 29, 1951; children—Donald, David, Mark. Asst. head photo research and devel. br. Bur. Aeros., Washington, 1956-61; adviser automatic data processing, asst. dir. for command and control Office Dep. Chief of Naval Ops., 1961-67; staff specialist for tactical command and control Office, Office of Dir. Def. Research and Engring., Office of Sec. of Def., Washington, 1967-75, asst. dir. combat support, 1975-77, dir. combat support, 1977—; dir. European affairs NATO, 1980—. Troop scoutmaster Nat. Capital Area council Boy Scouts Am., 1968-77, com. chmn. Explorer post, 1970-74; pres. W.T. Woodson PTA, 1974. Served to comdr. USNR, 1951-55. Fellow Am. Inst. Chemists. Lutheran (pres. ch. vestry 1970-71, elder 1974—). Home: 8315 Toll House Rd Annandale VA 22003 Office: Room 3E1081 Pentagon Arlington VA 20301

GRENINGER, EDWIN THOMAS, educator; b. Montoursville, Pa., Apr. 12, 1918; s. Fred R. and Martha (Cutler) G.; student Susquehanna U., 1936-38; A.B., Gettysburg Coll., 1941; M.A., Temple U., 1947; Ph.D., U. Pa., 1958; m. Jane Torbert, June 26, 1948 (dec. Mar. 1963); m. 2d, Gem Kate Taylor, Oct. 26, 1968. Instr. history Valparaiso U., 1948-49, Pa. State U., Ogontz, 1950, 52-53, Wilkes Coll., 1951-52; asst. prof. history E. Tenn. State U., Johnson City, 1958-61, asso. prof. 1961-64, prof. history, 1964—. Writer ann. travelogue, 1963—. Mem. com. on higher edn. Synod Va., United Luth. Ch. Am., 1959-63, Southeastern Synod, 1963-77. Served with AUS, 1942-46. Mem. Luth. Hist. Conf., So. Hist. Assn. (European sect.), Lexington Group, AAUP (chpt. v.p. 1969-70, pres. 1970-72), Phi Delta Kappa, Pi Kappa Alpha, Pi Gamma Mu (treas. local chpt. 1961—, gov. Tenn. province, 1975—). Author: Fifteen Days in Russia, 1966. Book rev. editor: Social Science, 1961-62. Home: 2210 Wyndale Rd Johnson City TN 37601

GRENITZ, ROBERT, gynecologist; b. N.Y.C., May 3, 1935; s. Paul and Dorothy (Shapiro) G.; B.S., Ursinus Coll., 1957; M.D., Albert Einstein Coll. Medicine, 1961; m. Sheila Mildred Grossman, Dec. 22, 1957; children—Mark, Sherrie. Intern, Fitkin Meml. Hosp., Neptune, N.J., 1960-61; resident in gynecology Albert Einstein Coll. Medicine, Bronx Mcpl. Hosp. Center, N.Y.C., 1961-66; chief dept. Ob-Gyn, Broward Gen. Med. Center, Ft. Lauderdale, Fla., 1976—; active staff Plantation (Fla.) Gen. Hosp., 1968—; clin. asst. prof. U. Miami Sch. Medicine. Trustee N. Broward Hosp. Self Ins. Trust; bd. dirs. Jewish Fedn. Greater Ft. Lauderdale, 1975—. Served with M.C., USAF, 1966-68. Diplomate Am. Bd. Ob-Gyn. Mem. Assn. Profs. of Ob-Gyn, Fla. Med. Assn., Broward County Med. Assn., Ft. Lauderdale Ob-Gyn Soc., So. Med. Assn. Office: 2100 S Andrews Ave Fort Lauderdale FL 33316

GRESHAM, CHARLES RUSSELL, clergyman, educator; b. Erie, Ill., Mar. 20, 1928; s. Fred Earl and Sara Jane (Duncan) G.; A.B., Manhattan (Kans.) Christian Coll., 1949; M.R.E., Southwestern Bapt. Theol. Sem., Ft. Worth, 1956, D.R.E., 1958, Ed.D., 1970; m. Virginia Ruth Smith, Aug. 3, 1947; children—Michael, Barbara (Mrs. Michael Bundy), Timothy, Janelda. Ordained to ministry Christian Ch., 1947; minister Christian Chs., Kans., 1945-50, McKinney, Tex., 1951-56; interim pastorates, 1957-75; sr. minister First Christian Ch., Elizabethton, Tenn., 1975-77; prof. Dallas Christian Coll., 1951-56, Midwest Christian Coll., Oklahoma City, 1956-60, Manhattan Christian Coll., 1960-66, Emmanuel Sch. Religion, Johnson City, Tenn., 1966-73, 75—; dean Ky. Christian Coll., Grayson, 1973-75, prof., dir. ch. relations, 1977—. Exec. sec. Chaplancy Endorsement Commn. Christian Chs., Chs. of Christ, 1967—. Mem. Phi Alpha Theta, Theta Phi, Sigma Delta Psi. Rotarian. Author: Recent Baptismal Discussions, 1954; The Adult Department, 1965. Editor Christian Quar., 1952-58, Consultation Internal Unity Reports, 1961-66, Christian Educators' Jour., 1968—. Contbr. numerous articles to profl. jours. Home: Lansdowne St Grayson KY 41143 Office: Box 530 KCC Grayson KY 41143

GRESHAM, FURMAN ALLEN, JR., data processing exec.; b. Spartanburg, S.C., May 11, 1947; s. Furman Allen and Carolyn (Groce) G.; A.A., N. Greenville Coll., 1967; A.S., Greenville Tech., 1969; m. Sandra Joan Broad, June 21, 1969; children—David Allen, Gregory James. Computer programmer, systems analyst S. Atlantic Life Ins. Co., Charleston, S.C., 1969-73, asst. data processing mgr., 1973-76, data processing mgr., personnel mgr., 1977—; partner S. & G. Enterprises. Mem. Data Processing Mgmt. Assn. (internat. dir.). Baptist (deacon). Club: Masons. Home: 834 Targave Rd Charleston SC 29412 Office: PO Box 2546 Charleston SC 29403

GRESSETTE, LAWRENCE MARION, lawyer, state senator; b. nr. St. Matthews, S.C., Feb. 11, 1902; s. J. T. and Rosa (Wannamaker) G.; J.D., U. S.C., 1924, LL.D. (hon.), 1977; m. Florence Howell, Aug. 18, 1927; 1 son, Lawrence Marion. Practiced in St. Matthews; partner firm Gressette & Gressette; mem. S.C. Senate, 1937—, chmn. jud. com., 1953—, chmn. rules com., 1959-75, pres. pro tem, 1972—, chmn. hwys. com., 1972-75. Chmn., S.C. Sch. Com., 1951-64, Com. Interstate Coop., 1972—; vice chmn. S.C. Reorgn. Com. Mem. S.C. Democratic Exec. Com., 1948—, chmn., 1953-54; mem. S.C. Ho. of

Reps., 1925-28, 31-32. Mem. governing bd. Council State Govts. Fellow Am. Coll. Trial Lawyers; mem. Blue Key, Phi Kappa Phi. Baptist. Mason. Home: PO Box 346 St Matthews SC 29135 Office: State House Columbia SC 29201

GREY, REX BURTON, mfg. co. exec.; b. El Paso, Tex., Oct. 27, 1920; s. Rex and Georgie Mary (Ferris) G.; student Tex. A&M U., 1937-41; B.S., U. Houston, 1945; M.B.A., Harvard U., 1952; m. Matalie Tandy, May 2, 1942; 1 son, Rex. Oliver. Mgr. distbn. div. Gen. Electric Co., 1945-50; pres. Tex. Apparatus Co., Houston, 1950-56; mgr. control div. Dresser Co., 1956-59; v.p. ITT N.Y., 1960-75; mng. dir. ITT/Standard Telephone and Cable U.K., 1960-65; pres. ITT Africa and Middle East, 1965-75; chmn. Fisk Telephone Systems Inc., Houston, 1975—; chmn., chief exec. officer Environ. Control Products Co., Service Tool & Supply Co.; chmn., pres. Internat. Flux Co.; chmn. Greyco, Janssen Bros.; dir. Fayetteville Bank, Mountain View Estates. Chmn., Center for Edn. and Research in Free Enterprise, Tex. A&M U. Served to maj. USAAF, 1941-45. Decorated D.F.C.; named Disting. Alumnus, Tex. A.&M. U., 1972. Episcopalian. Home: Route 4 Box 209A La Grange TX 78945 Office: 3102 Milam St Houston TX 77006

GRIBBLE, JOE CARROLL, univ. dean; b. Guymon, Okla., July 24, 1930; s. Joe and Marog (Zerker) G.; B.S., Panhandle State U., Goodwell, Okla.; M.Ed., Adams State Coll.; m. Lecnene Valdez, June 2, 1953; children—Roger, Carol Lee. Tchr., coach high schs. in Okla., Tex. and Colo.; coach Adams State Coll., Huron (S.D.) Coll.; coach Panhandle State U., now dean students. Address: Panhandle State Univ Goodwell OK 73939

GRICE, LYLE MARVIN, helicopter co. exec.; b. Laurens, Iowa, May 25, 1935; s. Harold Marvin and Lois Crisman G.; B.S. in Bus. Adminstrn. (fellow), Denver U., 1957. Sect. head Hughes Aircraft Co., Culver City, Calif., 1958-66; mgr. adminstrn. Litton Data Systems Co., Van Nuys, Calif., 1966-73; acctg. supr. Bell Helicopter Textron, Ft. Worth, 1973—. Served with U.S. Army, 1958-60. Home: 6529 Amundson Rd North Richland Hills TX 76180 Office: Box 482 Fort Worth TX 76101

GRIER, PAUL LIVINGSTON, librarian; b. Clover, S.C., May 26, 1914; s. William Pressly and Nellie Brownlee (Bigham) G.; A.B., Erskine Coll., 1936; A.B. in L.S., U. N.C., 1938; A.M., U. Mich., 1947; m. Eleanor Jane Meacham, Aug. 16, 1947. Library asst., Washington Pub. Library, 1936-40; librarian Hampden-Sydney (Va.) Coll., 1940-42, 46-79. Mem. evaluating coms. So. Assn. Schs. and Colls. Served from ensign to lt. USNR, 1942-46. Mem. ALA, Southeastern, Va. library assns., Assn. for Preservation Va. Antiquities, Assn. Am. Museums, English-Speaking Union, Sigma Upsilon, Omicron Delta Kappa. Presbyterian (elder). Home: PO Box 85 Hampden-Sydney VA 23943

GRIEVE, BONNIE-JO MCLEAN, physician; b. N.Y.C., Jan. 1, 1949; d. Jesse Terry and Josephine (Stanton) G.; B.S., Cornell U., 1969; M.D., U. Utah, 1973; M.S., U. Wis., 1979. Intern, U. Wis., Madison, 1973-74, resident in pediatrics, 1974-76, Stetler Found. postdoctoral fellow in clin. genetics, 1976-78, NIH fellow in molecular genetics, 1978-79; asst. prof. human genetics and pediatrics Med. Coll. Va., Richmond, 1979—. Diplomate Am. Bd. Pediatrics. Mem. AMA, Am. Med. Women's Assn., Am. Soc. Human Genetics, AAAS, Richmond Acad. Medicine, Phi Kappa Phi. Office: Box 33 MCV Station Richmond VA 23298

GRIFFETH, RONALD CLYDE, lawyer; b. Athens, Ga., Jan. 5, 1935; s. Alton White and Lilly Clyde (Silvey) G.; A.B., U. Ga., 1957; J.D., Augusta Law Sch., 1972; m. June Mellosan Duffie, Feb. 16, 1963; children—Robin Audrey, Elaine Lilly. Adjuster, br. mgr. Gen. Adjustment Bur., Inc., West Palm Beach, Fla., Augusta, Ga., 1958-66; v.p., claims counsel First of Ga. Ins. Group, Augusta, 1966-77; admitted to Ga. bar, 1972; asso. firm Allgood and Childs, and predecessor firm, Augusta, 1977-78, partner, 1979—. Chmn. adminstrv. bd. Grace United Methodist Ch., North Augusta, 1980. Served to capt. Armored Div., U.S. Army Res., 1957-65. Mem. Am., Ga., Augusta bar assns., Assn. Trial Lawyers Am., Ga. Trial Lawyers Assn., Christian Legal Soc. Home: 1848 Bolin Rd North Augusta SC 29841 Office: PO Box 1895 Augusta GA 30903

GRIFFIN, ALAN NASH, clin. psychologist; b. Dallas, Oct. 23, 1943; s. Jack Forrest and Mary Helen (Nash) G.; B.A., N. Tex. State U., 1965, M.A., 1966; Ph.D., U. Fla., 1971. Pvt. practice clin. psychology, Dallas, 1973—; asst. prof. psychology N. Tex. State U., 1973-74; staff psychologist Hillsborough County Guidance Center, 1972; cons. Plano (Tex.) Sch. System, 1974-79, Richland Coll., 1974-76. Dir. Suicide Prevention Center, Dallas, 1975-78, pres., 1978—. Democratic precinct chmn., 1969. Recipient award of merit Richardson (Tex.) Jaycees, 1974. Lic. psychologist, Tex. Mem. Am., Southwestern, Tex., Dallas psychol. assns., Am. Assn. Marriage and Family Counselors, Am. Soc. Clin. Hypnosis. Home: 13309 Kit Ln Dallas TX 75240 Office: 12110 Webbs Chapel Rd Dallas TX 75234

GRIFFIN, JERRY EDWARD, social worker, educator; b. Wilcox, Ala., Jan. 1, 1934; s. Randolph Simpson and Linnie (Barrett) G.; B.S., U. Ala., 1956, Ph.D., 1974; M.S.W., Boston Coll., 1963; m. Jeanne Franklin, July 19, 1959; children—Julia, Christopher. Exec. dir. Greater Boston Assn. Retarded Children, 1958-60; child welfare supr. Mass. Div. Child Guardianship, 1960-65; exec. dir. Community Action Agy., Tuscaloosa, Ala., 1965-67; prof. social work U. Ala., University, 1975—, mem. doctoral program faculty, 1976—; condr. accreditation surveys of social work degree programs Council Social Work Edn., 1977—; chmn. profl. adv. bd. Indian Rivers Mental Health Center, 1978. Cert. Acad. Cert. Social Workers; lic. social worker, Ala. Mem. Nat. Assn. Social Workers, Council Social Work Edn. Unitarian. Contbr. articles profl. jours., chpts. in books. Home: 23 Valley View Ln Tuscaloosa AL 35405 Office: PO Box 1935 University AL 35486

GRIFFIN, JO ANN THOMAS, coll. adminstr.; b. Dallas, July 20, 1933; d. John Baxton and Joan Marion (Ament) Thomas; B.A., U. Miss., 1955; B.S. magna cum laude, Lamar U., 1964; M.Ed. (AAUW scholar), U. Del., 1972: m. Thomas Reese Griffin, Jan. 25, 1976; children by previous marriage—John Barrett Brown, Jr., Daniel Thomas Brown; stepchildren—Gregory Crawford Griffin, Kevin Bradley Griffin. Asst. buyer, bridal cons. Neiman Marcus Co., Dallas, 1955-57; coordinator student activities So. Meth. U., Dallas, 1957-58; asst. women's editor Beaumont (Tex.) Enterprise, 1958-61; therapist, dir. outpatient counseling service Alcoholism Services, Wilmington, Del., 1972; statewide rehab. coordinator Del. Alcohol Safety Action Project, Wilmington, 1972-74; tchr., counselor Wilmington Public Schs., 1974-76; site mgr. Motivatonal Center, Inc., Wilmington, 1976-78; asst. dir. Indochinese social services Asso. Cath. Charities of New Orleans, Inc., 1978-79; dir. continuing edn. St. Mary's Dominican Coll., New Orleans, 1979—; cons. New Orleans Public Schs. Docent New Orleans Mus. Art, 1978—; lay reader Episcopal Ch., 1971—; exec. bd. Jr. League of Wilmington, 1968-70; mem. exec. com. Outreach div. Episc. Diocese of Del., 1977-78. Mem. Am. Personnel and Guidance Assn., Bus. and Profl. Women, Connections II, La. Assn. Women Adminstrs., Deans and Counselors, DAR, New Orleans C. of C., Jr. League of New Orleans, Mortar Board, Delta Delta Delta. Democrat. Home: 1210 Marengo St New Orleans LA 70115 Office: 7214 St Charles Ave New Orleans LA 70118

GRIFFIN, JOHN BUNYAN, JR., psychiatrist, educator; b. Mt. Airy, Ga., Sept. 24, 1931; s. John Bunyan and Ella Mae (Loudermilk) G.; M.D., Emory U., 1956; m. Lavinia Ann Jones, Sept. 10, 1960; children—John Bunyan III, Richard Steven. Intern Grady Meml. Hosp., Atlanta, 1956-57; resident in psychiatry St. Christopher's Hosp. for Children, Phila., 1957-59; practice medicine specializing in pediatrics, Decatur, Ga., 1961-63; resident in psychiatry Emory U., Atlanta, 1964-65, resident in child psychiatry, 1966-67; acting chief children's unit Ga. Mental Health Inst., Atlanta, 1967-68; asst. prof. psychiatry Emory U., Atlanta, 1967-74, asso. prof., 1974-79, prof., 1979—, dir. med. student tng., 1974—; child psychiatry cons. North Ga. Community Mental Health Center, 1967—, Newton County Mental Health Clinic, 1967—; site visitor NIMH, 1973-74. Served with USAF, 1959-61. Career Tchr. Tng. grantee NIMH, 1968-70, Career Tchr. Tng. grantee NIDA, 1973—. Mem. AMA, Med. Assn. Ga., Am., Ga. psychiat. assns., DeKalb County Med. Soc., Assn. Acad. Psychiatry, Alpha Tau Omega, Alpha Omega Alpha, Alpha Kappa Kappa. Home: 5666 Redcoat Run Stone Mountain GA 30087 Office: 1256 Briarcliff Rd Atlanta GA 30306

GRIFFIN, JOHN MICHAEL, plastic surgeon; b. Utica, N.Y., Jan. 2, 1938; s. Francis Stanley and Genevieve Agnes (Shea) G.; A.B., Hamilton Coll., 1959; M.D., Harvard U., 1963; m. Kathleen Anne Hanlon, June 26, 1965; children—Molly Elizabeth, Jennifer Susan, Julianna. Intern, Strong Meml. Hosp., Rochester, N.Y., 1963-64; resident in surgery Peter Bent Brigham Hosp., Boston, 1964-65, 67-68, St. Louis U., 1968-70, resident in plastic surgery, 1970-72; practice medicine specializing in plastic and reconstructive surgery, partner Drs. Hamm, Schatten, Hartley and Griffin, Atlanta, 1972—; asst. clin. prof. surgery-plastic surgery Emory U., 1973—. Bd. sponsors Atlanta Arts Alliance Theater, 1976-79, exec. com., 1977; mem. Leadership Atlanta, 1977; pres. Atlanta Virtuosi Found., 1978-79. Served with USAF, 1965-67. Christine Kleinert fellow in hand surgery U. Louisville, 1972. Diplomate Am. Bd. Surgery, Am. Bd. Plastic Surgery. Fellow A.C.S.; mem. Am., Southeastern, GA. socs. plastic and reconstructive surgeons, Am. Assn. Hand Surgery, AMA, Med. Assn. Ga., Med. Assn. Atlanta, Atlanta Clin. Soc., Phi Beta Kappa. Democrat. Roman Catholic. Clubs: Harvard of N.Y., Harvard of Atlanta (pres. 1975-76), Harvard of Boston, Governor's of Ga., Asso. Harvard Alumni (regional dir.). Contbr. articles on gen. and plastic surgery to profl. jours. Home: 5585 Whitner Dr NW Atlanta GA 30327 Office: 3280 Howell Mill Rd NW Atlanta GA 30327

GRIFFIN, JOHN TOOLE, wholesale grocery co. exec.; b. McAlester, Okla., May 3, 1923; s. John Taylor and Ada (Toole) G.; B.S. in Bus., U. Okla., 1947; m. Martha Louise Watson, Apr. 25, 1959; children—John, David. Pres., Griffin Grocery Co., Muskogee, Okla., 1944—; chmn. bd. Griffin TV, Inc., Oklahoma City, 1945—; dir. Citizens Nat. Bank, Muskogee, Okla. Gas & Electric Co. Pres. bd. dirs. Five Civilized Tribes Museum; bd. dirs. Okla. Heritage Assn. Served with AUS, 1943-45. Mem. World Bus. Council. Home: 600 Robb St Muskogee OK 74401 Office: 111 S Cherokee St Muskogee OK 74401

GRIFFIN, LARRY PAUL, obstetrician, gynecologist; b. Louisville, June 19, 1947; s. Elmer Paul and Emma Ann (Woehler) G.; B.A., U. Louisville, 1969, M.D. (student fellow Am. Soc. Anesthesiologists 1972), 1973; m. Gloria Jean Craig, July 18, 1964; children—Eric Paul, Craig Alan. Intern, U. Louisville, Louisville Gen. Hosp., 1973-74, resident in Ob-Gyn, 1973-76, chief resident, 1976; Samuel McMurtry fellow in maternal/fetal medicine, U. Louisville, 1976-77, clin. instr. dept. Ob-Gyn, 1976—, asst. prof. dept. family practice, 1977—; practice medicine specializing in Ob-Gyn, Louisville, 1977—, partner Oberst & Griffin, P.S.C. Bd. dirs. Planned Parenthood of Louisville; mem. profl. adv. com. Kentuckiana Chpt. March of Dimes; physician mem. Ky. Athletic Commn., 1974—. Diplomate Am. Bd. Ob-Gyn. Recipient cert. of merit March of Dimes, 1978. Jr. Fellow Am. Coll. Obstetricians and Gynecologists (nat. chmn. 1979, asst. sec.-treas. dist. V, 1974-75, sec.-treas. 1975-76, vice chmn. 1976-77, chmn. 1977-78, Mead-Johnson award 1975), Ky. Ob-Gyn Soc. (W.O. Johnson prize paper 1976), Louisville Ob-Gyn Soc., AMA, Ky. Med. Assn. (del. 1979), Jefferson County Med. Soc., So. Perinatal Assn., Am. Fertility Soc., Am. Assn. Gynecologic Laparoscopists, Alpha Kappa Kappa, Alpha Epislon Delta. Republican. Clubs: Jefferson, Plantation Country, Jefferson Racquetball. Co-author 9 articles pub. in med. jours. Home: 1907 Daleview Ln Louisville KY 40207 Office: 404 Medical Towers N Louisville KY 40202

GRIFFIN, MARK ALEXANDER, JR., psychiatrist: b. Asheville, N.C., Mar. 15, 1922; s. Mark Alexander and Penelope Cleary (Brothers) G.; B.S., U. N.C., 1943; M.D., U. Pa., 1946; m. Dorothy Wilson Griffin, Oct. 12, 1945; children—Mark Alexander, III, Susannah Carroll, Michael Jeffries. Intern, Del. Hosp., Wilmington, 1946-47; resident in neurology U. Pa. Hosp., 1947-49; resident, fellow in psychiatry Pa. Hosp., Phila., 1949-52; staff psychiatrist Appalachian Hall, Asheville, 1952-68, med. dir., bd. dirs., 1968—; mem. N.C. Med. Rev. Panel, 1969—. Served as ensign USNR, 1943-44. Diplomate Am. Bd. Neurology and Psychiatry. Fellow Am. Psychiat. Assn., So. Psychiat. Assn. (pres. 1969); mem. AMA, N.C. Neuropsychiat. Assn. (pres. 1963), N.C. Med. Soc., Southeastern Psychiat. Assn. (pres. 1965), Buncombe County Med. Soc., Rhododendron Royal Brigade Guards, Order Long Leaf Pine. Republican. Episcopalian. Club: Biltmore Forest Country. Home: 11 Forest Rd Asheville NC 28803 Office: PO Box 5534 Caledonia Rd Asheville NC 28803

GRIFFIN, NEWTON BRAMBLETT, obstetrician, gynecologist; b. Nashville, June 7, 1932; s. George Allen and Della Evangeline (Bramblett) G.; B.A. magna cum laude, Vanderbilt U., 1954, M.D., 1957; m. Betty Caroline Stroud, Apr. 9, 1960. Intern surgery Vanderbilt U. Hosp., 1957-58, resident obstetrics and gynecology, 1960-63; practice medicine specializing in obstetrics and gynecology, Nashville, 1965-66, Raleigh, N.C., 1968—; asst. prof. obstetrics and gynecology Vanderbilt U., 1966-68; chief service obstetrics and gynecology Metropolitan Nashville Gen. Hosp., 1966-68; instr. obstetrics and gynecology Vanderbilt U., 1962-63. Served to capt. USAF, 1958-60. Recipient Physicians Recognition award AMA, 1969, 72, 77; Advanced Clin. fellow in Gynecology Am. Cancer Soc., M.D. Anderson Hosp. and Tumor Inst., Houston, 1963-64. Diplomate Am. Bd. Obstetrics and Gynecology. Fellow Am. Coll. Obstetrics and Gynecology, Am. Fertility Soc.; mem. S. Atlantic Assn. Obstetricians and Gynecologists, AMA, So. Med. Assn., N.C., Wake County med. socs., Raleigh Acad. Medicine, Phi Beta Kappa. Baptist. Lion. Home: 3910 Stratford Ct Raleigh NC 27609 Office: 3803 Computer Dr Raleigh NC 27609

GRIFFIN, OSCAR O'NEAL, JR., oil well service co. exec.; b. Daisetta, Tex., Apr. 28, 1933; s. Oscar O'Neal and Myrtle Ellen (Edgar) G.; B.J., U. Tex. at Austin, 1958; m. Patricia Lamb, July 28, 1955; children—Gwendolyn Ann, Amanda Karen, Gregory O'Neal, Marguerite Ellen. Editor, Canyon (Tex.) News, 1959-60, Pecos (Tex.) Ind., 1960-62; reporter Houston Chronicle, 1962-66, White House corr., 1966-69; asst. dir. pub. affairs U.S. Dept. Transp., Washington, 1969-74; pres. Griffin Well Service, Inc., El Campo, Tex., 1974—, Griffin Supply, Inc., 1976—; chmn. bd. dirs., sec.-treas. Cross Roads Oil Field Supply, Inc., El Campo, 1980—. Bd. dirs. Museum Soc. El Campo. Served with U.S. Army, 1953-55. Recipient award for investigative reporting S.W. Journalism Forum, 1963; Pulitzer prize for local reporting, 1963; Courage in Journalism award Des Moines chpt., 1963, distinguished service award, nat. orgn., 1963 (both Sigma Delta Chi); award for journalistic reality Tex. Headliners Club, 1964. Mem. Assn. Oilwell Servicing Contractors (dir.), El Campo C. of C. (v.p.). Roman Catholic. Club: Nat. Press (Washington). Home: PO Box 1301 El Campo TX 77437 Office: PO Box 1239 El Campo TX 77437

GRIFFIN, RICHARD ALLEN, telephone service co. exec.; b. Rocksdale, W.Va., Feb 22, 1938; s. Clarence Everett and Louise Alberta G.; student Manchester (Ohio) Pub. Schs.; m. Mary Jane Sifritt, Oct. 29, 1966; stepchildren—Donna Brodsky, Gail Rice, Jack Rice; 1 dau., Virginia Louise. Contractor, 1957-69; pres. Underground Service Co., 1969-75; mgr. W.Va., S.E. Ohio, Ky. area High Voltage Systems Inc., Toledo, 1975; pres., chmn. bd. Telecom Corp., Bridgeport, W.Va., 1975—, Tuner Leasing Co., Inc., Meadowbrook, W.Va., 1977—; master plumber and electrician. Chmn. Northampton Twp. Water Bd.; active polit. campaigns. Mem. N.Am. Telephone Assn., U.S. C. of C. Methodist. Home: 799 Long St Bridgeport WV 26330 Office: Route 19 N Meadowbrook WV 26404

GRIFFIN, ROBERT JAMES, physician; b. Cane Valley, Ky., Nov. 15, 1904; s. William Sherrod and Mary Elizabeth (Miller) G.; A.B., U. of Ky., 1927; M.D., U. of Pa., 1931; m. Charlotte Marjorie Craig, Nov. 5, 1934; children—Robert James, Jr., Suzanne Craig, Barbara Louise. Intern, Chestnut Hill Hosp., Phila., 1931-32; resident in obstetrics, gynecology, Kensington Hosp. for Women, Phila., 1932-34; health officer Scott County, Ky., 1935-37; acting dir. Div. Maternal and Child Health, Ky. State Dept. Health, 1937-38; asst. prof. hygiene, public health, U. of Ky., Lexington, 1938-41; practice medicine specializing in obstetrics, gynecology, Lexington, 1946-76; med. dir. Plasma Derivatives, Inc., Lexington, 1976-79; attending physician Alpha Therapeutic Corp., Lexington, 1979—; chmn. dept. obstetrics, gynecology Central Baptist Hosp., 1954-55, St. Joseph Hosp. 1959-63; mem. com. for study of maternal mortality, Ky., 1950-76. Served to col. as commanding officer M.C., U.S. Army, 1941-46. Decorated 4 Battle Stars for Italian Campaign; recipient John G. Clark award for research, U. Pa. Sch. Medicine, 1928. Diplomate Am. Bd. Obstetrics, Gynecology, Nat. Bd. Med. Examiners. Mem. Ky., Southern, Am. med. assns., Ky., Lexington obstetrical & gynecological socs., Fayette County Med. Soc., U. Ky. Alumni Assn. (life), Phi Sigma Kappa, Alpha Chi Sigma, Phi Chi. Presbyterian. Clubs: Spindletop Hall. Contbr. numerous articles, papers in field. Home: 280 Swigert Ave Lexington KY 40505 Office: 313 E Short St Lexington KY 40507

GRIFFIN, RODNEY LEVERETT, telecommunication engr.; b. Houston, Nov. 4, 1946; s. William Lewis and Margaret Louise (Riggins) G.; B.A. in Math., U. Tex., Austin, 1970; m. Jan Faye West, Mar. 13, 1979; children—Elizabeth Ann, William Leverett, Omari Akil. Curriculum writer S.W. Edn. Devel. Lab., Austin, Tex., 1970-72; div. head City of Austin, 1972-73; mng. editor Black Registry Pub. Co., 1973-76; legis. aide Tex. Ho. of Reps., Austin, 1975; producer Radio KHFI, Austin, 1975; mktg. rep. Southwestern Bell Telephone Co., Houston, 1976-77, facilities supr. engring. div., 1977-78; engring. coordinator Cable Tech. Services Corp., Houston, 1978—. Permanent chmn. Democratic Party Precinct 127, Travis County, Tex., 1972; mem. Travis County Democratic Credentials Com., 1972; alt. del. at large Dem. State Conv., Tex., 1972; bd. dirs. Human Opportunities Corp. Travis County, 1971-72; bd. dirs. Central Tex. Legal Services Corp., 1971-76; chmn. subcom. Rosewood Med. Clinic, Austin, 1972-73; chmn. Nat. Clients Council Tex., 1976—; bd. dirs. Nat. Clients Council Inc., Washington, 1976-77, vice chmn. S.W. U.S., 1977-79; bd. dirs. Nat. Consumer Law Center Inc., Boston, 1976-78. Recipient Community Service award Human Opportunities Corp., 1971, 72; Jesse H. Jones scholar, 1965-69; Hogg Found. grantee, 1968-69. Mem. Am. Mgmt. Assn., Tex. Soc. Telephone Engrs. Baptist. Home: 735 Stephanie Dr Missouri City TX 77459 Office: Cable Tech Services Corp 800 W Belt S Houston TX 77003

GRIFFIN, ROLAND GERALD, athletic dir.; b. Martin County, N.C., Jan. 5, 1938; s. Roland C. and Minnie Katherine G.; B.S., U. N.C., 1960, M.S., 1962. m. Sandra Beth Forney, June 17, 1962; children—Clay, Pam, Minda. Profl. baseball player Phila. Phillies Club, 1961-65; baseball coach St. Andrews Presbyn. Coll., Lauringburg, N.C., 1965-72; athletic dir., baseball coach Francis Marion Coll., Florence, S.C. 1972—; mem. athletic com. Florence YMCA, 1974. Mem. Am. Assn. Coll. Baseball Coaches, Nat. Assn. Athletic Dirs., Nat. Baseball Coaches Assn., Nat. Collegiate Athletic Dirs. Assn. Presbyterian. Club: Kiwanis (dir. 1978, 79). Home: 1890 Westmoreland Ave Florence SC 29501 Office: Francis Marion Coll Florence SC 29501

GRIFFIN, SHIRLEY MAE, educator; b. Milw., May 30, 1944; d. Andrew and Daisy (Smith) Fumphrey; Ed.D., U. Ark., 1979. Tchr., research specialist Opportunities Industrialization Center, Little Rock, 1970-73; adv. specialist Ouachita Baptist U., 1973-75; asst. prof. elem. edn. U. Ark., Little Rock, dir. Sex Discrimination Inst., 1975-76. Mem. Child Abuse Aux. Bd., 1979. Mem. Assn. Supervision and Curriculum Devel., Phi Delta Kappa, Kappa Delta Phi. Lutheran. Home: 7215 Apache Rd Little Rock AR 72205 Office: Dept Elem Edn U Ark Little Rock 72205

GRIFFIN, VILLARD STUART, JR., educator; b. Birmingham, Ala., May 19, 1937; s. Villard Stuart and Myra (Justice) G.; B.A., U. Va., 1959, M.S., 1961; Ph.D., Mich. State U., 1965; m. Raija Tuulikki Nikander, June 12, 1966; children—Victoria Sirkka, Elizabeth Roosa-Maria, Anna Kristina. Grad. asst. U. Va., Charlottesville, 1960-61, Mich. State U., E. Lansing, 1961-63; geologist Little Bob Mining Co., Marietta, Ga., summer 1960; geologic aide Roland F. Beers, Inc., Alexandria, Va., summer 1960, Va. Div. Mineral Resources, Charlottesville, summers 1961, 62, 64; faculty Clemson (S.C.) U., 1964—, prof. geology, 1975—; vis. research investigator Geol. Survey Finland, Helsinki, 1975; project geologist S.C. Geol. Survey, Columbia, 1965—; cons. S.C. Electric and Gas Co., 1973-76, E. D'Appolonia Engrs., Inc., 1973, John Wiley & Sons, Pub. Co., 1971, Bechtel Corp., 1966, Chevron Corp., 1976, E.I. duPont de Nemours Co.-Dept. Energy, 1978; lectr. Geologisk-Mineralogisk Museum and Institut, Oslo, Norway, 1975, Mineralogical Soc. Stockholm, Sweden, 1975, Geologiska-Mineralogiska Inst. Uppsala, Sweden, 1975, Turku (Finland) U. Geol. and Mineralogical Inst., 1975, others; asso. investigator U.S. Office Water Resources Research, 1965-66; participant N.E. Section Geol. Soc. Am. symposium, 1973, UMR-DNR Conf. Energy, Rolla, Mo., 1979. Recipient W.A. Tarr award, Sigma Gamma Epsilon, 1960; J.K. Roberts Geology Dept. award, U. Va., 1961. Mich. State U. scholar, 1961-63; Philip Francis du Pont fellow, 1960-61; Sigma Xi grantee, 1963; NSF grantee, 1968, 70, 72. Licensed profl. geologist, Ga. Fellow Geol. Soc. Am.; mem. AAAS, Geol. Soc. Finland, Carolina Geol. Soc. (v.p. 1968), Ga. Geol. Soc., Nat. Geographic Soc., Am. Inst. Profl. Geologists, Sigma Xi. Cons. editor: Rocks and Minerals, 1976-79; editorial bd. Geologic

Notes, 1976-80. Contbr. articles to profl. jours. Home: PO Box 1204 Clemson SC 29631

GRIFFIN-SWINK, MARSHA, counselor; b. Charlotte, N.C., July 2, 1946; d. Martin Luther and Margaret Lucille (Patterson) Griffin; B.A., Western Carolina U., 1975, M.A. in Edn., 1977; 1 dau., Angelia Courtney. Grad. asst. Dean's Office, Sch. of Edn. and Psychology, Western Carolina U., Cullowhee, N.C., 1975-76, mem. dean's grant adv. com., 1979; adult vocat. counselor Mountain Projects, Inc., Waynesville, N.C., 1976-78; asst. dir./vocat. evaluator Jackson County Sheltered Workshop, Webster, N.C., 1978—. Counselor, R.E.A.C.H. (woman's crisis intervention), 1978—; mem. Council on Appalachian Woman, 1978—. Mem. Nat. Rehab. Assn., Vocat. Evaluation and Work Adjustment Assn., Am. Personnel and Guidance Assn. Democrat. Methodist. Club: Woodmen of the World. Home: PO Box 193 Webster NC 28788 Office: PO Box 220 Webster NC 28788

GRIFFIS, JAMES TRUMAN, rancher, ret. educator; b. Bonham, Tex., Aug. 1, 1909; s. James Arthur and Minnie (Magouirk) G.; B.A., Austin Coll., 1941; B.S., U. Corpus Christi, 1952; M.A., Tex. Coll. Arts and Industry, 1950; Ed.D., U. Houston, 1955; m. Billye Florine Snow, June 5, 1931; 1 son, Bill J. Tchr., prin. rural schs., Fannin County, Tex., 1937-41; field exec. Boy Scouts Am., Corpus Christi, Tex., 1941-48; elementary prin. Flour Bluff Schs., Corpus Christi, 1948-52; instr., research asst. U. Houston, 1953-55; asst. supt. N.E. Houston schs., 1955-59; prof., head dept. edn., dean men Coll. Ozarks, Clarksville, Ark., 1961-64; prof., head dept. elementary edn. Panhandle State Coll., Goodwell, Okla., 1964-75; now engaged in ranching, Bonham. Summer sch. faculty Troy (Ala.) State Coll., 1963-65, Okla. State U., Stillwater, 1966; research cons. Hugoton (Kan.) Schs., 1966—, Okla. Commn. on Tchr. Edn. and Certification, 1965—. Participant 1st World Congress on Reading, Paris, 1966, 2d congress, Copenhagen, 1968. Recipient Hornaday award for distinguished service to wild life, 1940. Mem. Phi Delta Kappa, Kappa Delta Pi. Presbyterian (elder). Mason (Shriner, 32 deg.), Kiwanian (past pres.), Author monograph: Education at Three Cost Levels, 1955. Home: Rt 2 Box 200 Bonham TX 75418

GRIFFIS, WILLIAM KEARLEY, cons. engr.; b. Paris, Tex., Mar. 29, 1915; s. William Edward and Lassie Jane (Kearley) G.; A.A., Schreiner Inst., Kerrville, Tex., 1934; B.S., U. Tex., 1938, M.S., 1950; m. Mary Louise Parks, July 30, 1944; children—Kathleen, John Quincy, Eleanor Schofield. Asst. supr. Crane Mfg. Co., Chgo., 1938-42; asso. mech. engr. St. Louis Ordnance Dist., Omaha, 1942-43; asst. prof. mech. engring. U. Tex., Austin, 1946-51; research engr., systems devel. specialist U. Tex., 1951-58; research scientist Electro-Mechanics Co., Austin, 1958-61; cons. mech. engring., Austin, 1961—. Bldg. mgr. Tchr. Retirement System Tex., 1971-76. Served with USNR, 1943-46. Decorated Bronze Star. Registered profl. engr., Tex. Mem. Nat., Tex. socs. profl. engrs., Pi Tau Sigma. Presbyterian. Clubs: Rotary Internat., Austin Yacht. Home: 2502 Bowman Ave Austin TX 78703

GRIFFITH, BENJAMIN FRANKLIN, JR., communication co. exec.; b. Minden, La., Aug. 27, 1927; s. Benjamin Franklin and Inez (Gladden) G.; student mech. engring. La. Poly. Inst., 1948-50; m. Quay Crutsinger, Oct. 19, 1954; 1 son, Benjamin Paul. Petroleum reservoir engr. Core Labs., Inc., Dallas, 1952-70; pres. Data Com Inc., New Orleans, 1970—; dir. The Offshore Telephone Co., New Orleans, 1971—. Served with USMCR, 1945-48. Mem. Gulf Coast Geol. Soc., Am. Inst. Mining, Metall. and Petroleum Engrs., Am. Legion. Democrat. Methodist. K.P. Club: Lakewood Country, New Orleans Petroleum, Lamplighter. Home: 6130 Shetland Dr New Orleans LA 70114 Office: 1010 Common St New Orleans LA 70112

GRIFFITH, BENJAMIN WOODWARD, JR., coll. dean; b. Lanett, Ala., Mar. 30, 1922; s. Benjamin W. and Mary Lula Norman G.; A.B., Mercer U., 1944; M.A., Northwestern U., 1948, Ph.D., 1952; m. Betty Irvine, Aug. 29, 1948; children—Mary Eugenia Griffith Dupell, Benjamin Woodward, III. Chmn., English dept. Tift Coll., 1950-55; prof., chmn. English dept. Mercer U., Macon, Ga., 1955-70; prof., chmn. English dept. W. Ga. Coll., Carrollton, 1970-73, dean grad. sch., 1973—; mem. governing bd. Atlanta Area Tchr. Edn. Services, 1974—. Trustee, Mercer U. Served with USN, 1943-46; PTO. Northwestern U. univ. scholar grantee, 1949-50, So. Fellowship Found. research grantee, 1957, Duke U. vis. scholar, 1955. Mem. Conf. So. Grad. Schs., S. Atlantic MLA, Alpha Tau Omega. Democrat. Baptist. Club: Rotary. Author: A Simplified Approach to Wuthering Heights, 1966; A Simplified Approach to Silas Marner, 1967; A Simplified Approach to Huckleberry Finn, 1969; Preparing for the Graduate Record Examination in Literature, 1969; Editor: All for Love (John Dryden), 1961; The Beggars Opera (John Gay), 1962; Knight of the Burning Pestle (Beaumont and Fletcher), 1963; co-editor Notes on Contemporary Lit., 1971—. Home: 215 Dixie St Carrollton GA 30117 Office: Grad Sch W Ga Coll Carrollton GA 30118

GRIFFITH, ELSIE INGRAM, assn. exec.; b. Dallas, July 9, 1925; d. Michael Herschel and Vivian Cecelia (Eidt) Ingram; B. Nursing, U. Wash., Seattle, 1962; M. Nursing Adminstrn., 1965. Dir. vol. bur. Council Social Agys., Washington, 1952-56; supr. Vis. Nurses Assn., St. Louis, 1956-61, exec. dir., Dallas, 1970—; asst. dir. Dept. Community Health, Nat. League Nursing, N.Y.C., 1965-69; dir. health planning Community Council of Dallas, 1969-70; chmn. Council of Home Health Agys. N.Y.C., 1976-77; faculty grad. sch. nursing Tex. Women's U., 1974; chmn. phys. health task force Health Systems Agy. N. Tex., 1975-78. Recipient Lois C. Lillick award, 1979. Roman Catholic. Researcher service delivery methods for home health agys. Home: 6256 Lupton Dr Dallas TX 75225 Office: Vis Nurse Assn Dallas 4606 Greenville Ave Dallas TX 75206

GRIFFITH, JACK WILLIAM, med. librarian; b. Rockwell City, Iowa, Dec. 19, 1929; s. William J. and Nell J. Griffith; B.A., U. Md., 1966; M.S. in Geography, U. Nebr., 1969; M.A. in Library Media, U. S.D., 1975; m. Lydia Griffith; children—Mary A., Anna B. Served with U.S. Air Force, 1950-70; tchr., Lewis Central High Sch., Council Bluffs, Iowa, 1970-72, librarian, 1972-75; librarian Def. Systems Mgmt. Sch., Ft. Belvoir, Va., 1975; med. librarian Archbishop Bergan Mercy Hosp., Omaha, 1976-78; now med. librarian VA Med. Center, North Little Rock, Ark. Mem. ALA, Am. Assn. Sch. Librarians, Med. Library Assn. NEA, Iowa, Lewis Central edn. assns. Certified dir. library services, tchr., librarian, Iowa; tchr., ednl. media specialist, Nebr. Club: Masons. Home: 5713 N Cedar North Little Rock AR 72116 Office: Med Library VA Med Center Little Rock AR 72114

GRIFFITH, LUTHER BAILEY, accountant; b. Mansfield, La., June 25, 1901; s. William Jasper and Elizabeth (Bailey) G.; student Soule Coll., 1922; B.C.S., YMCA Coll., 1931; m. Louie Barnard, Apr. 25, 1931; children—Emilia Gay Griffith Means, Louie Griffith Chalfant. Vice pres. Griffith Lumber Co., Mansfield, 1922-27; clk. La. Oil Co., Shreveport, 1927-34; bookkeeper Haynes Oil Corp., Shreveport, 1934-41; sr. accountant Colbert & Pasquier, C.P.A.'s, 1935-41; partner Griffith and Hettler, C.P.A.'s, Shreveport, 1941-77. Mem. La. Soc. C.P.A.'s, Am. Inst. C.P.A.'s, Internat. Lightning Class Yachting Assn. (life; v.p. 1960-61, co chmn. selection 1st site yacht races 1960-61, commodore So. dist. 1963-64), De Soto Parish Hist. Soc., S.A.R., Ga. Geneological Soc. Episcopalian (vestryman). Mason. Clubs: Shreveport Country, Shreveport Yacht; Northwood Country. Home: 3255 Old Mooringsport Rd Shreveport LA 71107 Office: PO Box 7393 LaBank Bldg Shreveport LA 71101

GRIFFITH, MARION SHERMAN, JR., airline pilot and exec.; b. Austin, Tex., Oct. 19, 1930; s. Marion Sherman and Myrtle Agusta (Birkelbach) G.; B.A. in Music, U. Tex., Austin, 1952, M.A. in Music, 1954; m. Mary Lynn Puckett, Feb. 16, 1958; children—Marion Sherman III and Sheryl Lynn (twins). Pilot, Braniff Internat. Airways, Inc., Dallas, 1957—, tng. pilot, 1968—, dir. tech. standards, 1975-77, dir. flight standards, 1977-79. Mem. Nat. Com. for Aviation Exploring, 1973—. Active Boy Scouts Am. Served with USAF, 1954-57. Mem. Air Transport Assn. (simulator subcom. 1973-75), Dallas Gliding Assn., Inc. (sec.-treas. 1968—), Soaring Soc. Am. (pres. 1973-74, dir.-at-large 1970—; exceptional Service award 1974), Nat. Aero. Assn. (Certificate of Appreciation 1974). First U.S. pilot lic. to fly Concorde Supersonic transport, 1978. Home: 4031 Fawnhollow St Dallas TX 75234 Office: Box 35001 X-17 Dallas TX 75335

GRIFFITH, MELVIN EUGENE, govt. ofcl.; b. Lawrence, Kans., Mar. 24, 1912; s. George Thomas and Estella (Shaw) G.; A.B., U. Kans., 1934, A.M., 1935, Ph.D. (fellow in entomology), 1938; postgrad. U. Mich., summers, 1937-40; m. Pauline Sophia Bogart, June 23, 1941. Instr. zoology N.D. Agrl. Coll., Fargo, 1938-39, asst. prof., 1939-41, asso. prof., 1941-42; malaria control entomologist USPHS, La., 1942-43, Okla. 1943-46; Okla. communicable disease center entomologist USPHS-Okla. Dept. Health, 1946-50; communicable disease center rep. Ark.-White-Red River Basins investigations USPHS, Ark., Colo., Kans., La., Mo., N.Mex., Okla., Tex., 1950-51; chief malariologist ICA, USPHS, Thailand, 1951-60; asso. dir. Malaria Eradication Tng. Center, Jamaica, 1960; regional malaria adviser S.E. Asia, Agy. Internat. Devel., USPHS, New Delhi, India, 1960-62, regional malaria adviser Near East and So. Asia, 1962-64, dep. chief malaria eradication br., Washington, 1964-67, chief, 1967-71; ret., 1971; cons. Office of Health, AID, Washington, 1971-75. Asso. prof. zool. scis. U. Okla., Norman, 1946-52, prof., 1952-56. Recipient citation for distinguished ser. U. Kans., 1962. Mem. AAAS, Am. Pub. Health Assn., Am. Soc. Tropical Medicine and Hygiene, Am. Mosquito Control Assn., Am. Soc. Limnology and Oceanography, Entomol. Soc. Am., USPHS Commd. Officers Assn., Siam Soc., Phi Beta Kappa, Sigma Xi. Contbr. articles and monographs on entomology, malaria control, pub. health. Address: PO Box DG Williamsburg VA 23185

GRIFFITH, PATSY REEVES, govt. ofcl.; b. Elberton, Ga., Dec. 31, 1934; d. Ralph Rodney and Addie Mary (Seymour) Reeves: student Clemson (S.C.) Coll., 1954-55; children—Maria Lee, Patricia Grace, Paul Frank. Sec. athletic dept. Clemson Coll., 1954-57; clk., stenographer Southeastern Power Adminstrn., U.S. Dept. Energy (formerly U.S. Dept. Interior), Elberton, 1957-68, adminstrv. asst., 1968-74, office sers. supr., 1974—. Active PTA, Elberton, 1960—; treas. Elbert County (Ga.) Little League Aux., 1978—. Recipient U.S. Dept. Interior Superior Service award, 1976. Mem. Federally Employed Women. Presbyterian. Club: Elberton Elks Aux. (yearbook chmn.). Home: 128 Lake Forest Dr Elberton GA 30635 Office: Samuel Elbert Bldg Elberton GA 30635

GRIFFITHS, SUSAN BATES, psychiat. social worker; b. Miami, Fla., June 7, 1944; d. Edward Hugh and Gretchen (Washburn) G.; B.S Psychology, U. Miami, 1966; M.S.W. (Silverman scholar), Hunter Grad. Sch. Social Work, 1969; postgrad. U. Miami, 1974—. Trainee, Children's Home Soc., Miami, 1967-68, Bronx (N.Y.) State Hosp., 1968-69, Juvenile Ct., Miami, 1977; research trainee fellow City of N.Y. Health Services, 1969; clin. social worker Miami VA Hosp., 1969-77, psychiat. social worker, 1977—; pvt. practice marriage and family counseling, Miami, 1978—; field instr. Fla. State U. Sch. Social Work, Miami, 1971-72; clin. faculty, field instr. Fla. Internat. U. Sch. Social Work, Miami, 1972—, Barry Coll. Sch. Social Work, Miami, 1972—; clin. faculty psychiatry U. Miami Sch. Medicine, 1978—; counselor alcoholic employees VA Hosp., 1973-75. Mem. Nat. Assn. Social Workers, Acad. Cert. Social Workers, Am. Assn. Sex Educators, Counselors and Therapists, Am. Personnel and Guidance Assn., Am. Assn. Marriage and Family Therapy. Office: 2525 SW 27th Ave Miami FL 33133

GRIGALIS, ZIGURDS EDGAR, architect; b. Riga, Latvia, June 9, 1934; came to U.S., 1950, naturalized, 1956; s. Janis and Lidija (Milmanis) G.; student U. Queensland, Brisbane, Australia, 1957-58; U. Calif., Berkeley, 1962-63; B.A., U. Ill., 1958; postgrad. U. Ky., 1975-76; M.B.A., Xavier U., Cin., 1979; m. Amelitta N. T. Linde, Sept. 21, 1956; children—Delilah, Edgar, Robert, Zigurds Michael, Steven. Owner, Grigalis Constrn. Co., Aurora, Ill., 1959-64; with Ranka Land Co. and Imperial Real Estate Co., Aurora, 1961-64; staff Systems Constructors, Ltd., Chgo., 1968-70; owner, operator Grigalis & Assos., Lexington, Ky., 1971—. Served with USMCR, 1953-56; Korea. Registered architect Ill., Ky., Ga., Ala., Tenn. Mem. AIA, Constrn. Specification Inst. (pres. chpt. 1979), Ky. Soc. Architects (sec. 1976), E. Ky. chpt. AIA (pres. 1975). Home: 858 Glendover Rd Lexington KY 40502 Office: Grigalis & Assos 342 Waller Ave Lexington Ky 40504

GRIGGS, FRANKLIN KEITH, educator; b. Haw River, N.C., Jan. 12, 1937; s. Ralph Frank and Marcie Ellen (Rudd) G.; B.S., Appalachian State U., 1960, M.A., 1964; M.Ed., U. N.C., 1975; Ed.D., Highland U., 1977; Ed.S., Western Carolina U., 1978; m. Nell Self, Nov. 27, 1959; children—Margaret Lynn, Gregory Keith. Tchr. bus. Crest High Sch., Boiling Springs, N.C., 1960-64; instr. bus. Chowan Coll., Murfreesboro, N.C., 1964-65; asst. prof. bus. Gardner-Webb Coll., Boiling Springs, 1965—; computer cons. Vice pres. Delview Acres Corp., Cherryville, N.C., 1975-76; dir. Gaston Parks and Recreation, 1975-77, Cherryville Day Care, 1977-79; nat. bd. advisors Am. Security Council, 1978-79; Gaston County rep. Jud. Com. Dem. Party, 1975-77. Mem. N.C. Research Assn., Data Processing Mgmt. Assn., Honeywell Users Group, Phi Delta Kappa. Democrat. Methodist. Club: Lions. Home: PO Box 311 Cherryville NC 28021 Office: PO Box 554 Boiling Springs NC 28017

GRIGGS, JIMMY GLENN, utility co. exec.; b. Woodburn, Ky., July 1, 1933; s. Walter J. and Anne (Watkins) G.; student U. Evansville, 1973-75, Ky. Wesleyan Coll., 1974, Brescia Coll., 1976—; m. Kay S. Mitchell, June 15, 1956; children—Donna Lynn, Jimmy Glenn. With TVA, 1953-65, unit operator, Gallatin, Tenn., 1961-65, Kingston, Tenn., 1962; shift supr. S.C. Public Service Authority, Conway, 1965-67, mech. maintenance supr., 1967-69; with Big Rivers Electric Corp., Henderson, Ky., 1969—, acting plant supt., 1971, supt. plants ops., 1972-75, dir. tng. and safety, 1975-77, mgr. corp. services, 1977—; instr. power plant tng. Owensboro Vocat. Tech. Sch., 1979—. Served with U.S. Army, 1950-52. Mem. Am. Soc. Tng. and Devel., Coop. Edn. Assn. Ky. Democrat. Mem. Ch. of Christ (deacon). Home: 2216 Reid Rd Owensboro KY 42301 Office: 201 3d St Henderson KY 42420

GRIGGS, JOSEPH, III, architect; b. Virginia Beach, Va., Nov. 24, 1932; s. Joseph, Jr., and Irene (Masters) G.; B.Arch., Va. Poly. Inst., 1967; m. Joanne Carolyn Jones, Aug. 25, 1957; children—Adrienne, Victoria. With Mills, Petticord & Mills, 1956-57, Heery & Heery, Atlanta, 1957-61, Mills, Petticord & Mills, Norfolk, Va., 1961-62, Oliver & Smith, Norfolk, 1962-63; pvt. practice architecture, Christiansburg, Va., 1963-66; partner Clay & Griggs, Roanoke, Va., 1966-72; prin. Joseph Griggs Assos., Roanoke, 1972-75, pres., 1975—; pres. Sugarloaf-Highlands Corp., Sugarloaf Devel. Corp., Contract Carpets, Inc., Falcon Properties, Inc., Victoria Properties, Inc., Oak Grove Properties, Inc., Acad. Park Assos., Inc., 1000 Oaks, Inc., Flagship Properties, Inc., Internat. Solar Energy Corp., Internat. Solar Energy Distbrs. Ltd.; partner Mark Cos., CMP Co., Western Co., Bear Run Assos., Back Bay Co., Union Manor, Nashville Equities, Bent Tree Partnership, English Wood Partnership, Summer Hill Partnership, Center Point Co., Dickson Co., Oak Tree Co. Works include Grant Plaza Shopping Center, Sugarloaf Highlands Apts., Heritage Hall Nursing Homes, Camelot Hall Nursing Homes. Mem. Roanoke Sci. Mus. Assn. Served with USAF, 1952-56. Mem. AIA, YMCA. Home: 4909 Buckhorn Rd SW Roanoke VA 24014 Office: 3130 Chaparral Dr SW Roanoke VA 24018

GRIGGS, THOMAS MCKAY, physician; b. New Orleans, Mar. 17, 1941; s. Orvis Bass and Lilliam May (McKay) G.; B.A., U. Va., 1963, M.D., 1968; m. Barbara Dale Boatwright, Aug. 4, 1962; children—Christopher, Amy, Randall. Intern, U. Fla., 1968-69, resident, 1969-73; practice medicine specializing in otolaryngology, Huntsville, Ala., 1975—. Served with U.S. Army, 1973-75. Fellow Am. Acad. Otolaryngology; mem. AMA, Am. Council Otolaryngology. Mem. Disciples of Christ Ch. Home: 1009 Brookridge Circle Huntsville AL 35801 Office: 205 Saint Clair Ave Huntsville AL 35801

GRIGSBY, ROBERT L., coll. adminstr.; b. Saluda, S.C., Jan. 25, 1924; s. Robert L. and Juell G. (Gregory) G.; B.S., Clemson U., 1947; M.S., N.C. State U., 1952; m. Martha Callahan, Mar. 25, 1978; 1 son, Robert L. Tchr. public schs., Gilbert, S.C., 1947-51, Irmo, S.C., 1952-56; mfg. supr. Gen. Electric Co., Irmo, 1956-62; chief adminstrv. officer Midlands Tech. Coll., Columbia, S.C., 1962-74, pres., 1974—. Sec., Lexington County Bd. Edn., 1961-74; trustee Commn. on Colls., 1968-74. Served with AUS, 1942-45. Decorated Purple Heart. Mem. Am. Assn. Community and Jr. Colls., Am. Council Edn., Am. Soc. Engring. Edn., Nat. Tech. Edn. Assn., Assn. Community Coll. Industries, Phi Kappa Phi, Kappa Sigma, Kappa Phi Kappa. Clubs: Rotary, Summit. Home: Rt 2 Box 344 Leesville SC 29070 Office: PO Box 2408 Columbia SC 29202

GRIGSBY, RONALD DAVIS, educator; b. Tulsa, Feb. 28, 1936; s. Logan Charles and Helen Dorothy (Davis) G.; B.S., U. Okla., 1958, Ph.D. in Chemistry, 1966; m. Nancy Jane Hampton, Apr. 20, 1962; children—Lynn E., Brian P., Debra C., David R., Steven A., Jonathan C., Sara J. Research chemist Continental Oil Co., Ponca City, Okla., 1964-68; asst. prof. biochemistry and biophysics Tex. A. and M. U., College Station, 1968-74, asso. prof., 1974—; propr. Mass Spectrometer Accessories, 1972-77; pres. Masspec, Inc., 1977—; vis. scientist NRC Can., Halifax, N.S., 1973-74. Mem. Am. Chem. Soc., Am. Soc. Mass Spectrometry, SW Sci. Forum, Sigma Xi, Alpha Chi Sigma, Phi Lambda Upsilon. Home: 3707 Warren Circle Bryan TX 77801 Office: Dept Biochemistry and Biophysics Tex A and M U College Station TX 77843

GRIMES, FRANCES SELLS, bus. cons. co. exec.; b. Johnson City, Tenn., Feb. 8, 1930; d. Samuel Hayward and Helen (Milligan) Sells; student Agnes Scott Coll., 1948-50; B.S., E. Tenn. State U., 1952; m. Alton Barger Grimes, Mar. 24, 1979; children—Helen Doss, Dorothy Doss, Robert McB. Doss. Vice pres. Farnsworth Cannon, Inc., McLean, Va., 1970-77; dir. King's Inc., Johnson City, 1968—, Gen. Shale Products Corp., Johnson City, 1977—. Bd. dirs. Sells Found., 1973—. Mem. Daus. Am. Colonists, DAR, Nat. Soc. So. Dames of Am., Colonial Dames XVII Century. Republican. Presbyterian (elder).

GRIMES, JOAN MOBLEY, educator; b. Birmingham, Ala.; B.S., U. Ala., 1968, M.S., 1972; postgrad. U. London, 1978; m. Robert Franklin Grimes Jr., Aug. 5, 1950; children—Emily, Mark, Jeffery, Melanie. Tchr. English and history Springdale Jr. High. Sch., Birmingham, 1968-70; tchr. English, Gardendale (Ala.) High Sch., 1971-75, 76—. Mem. Nat. Council Tchrs. English, Jefferson County Edn. Assn., Ala. Edn. Assn., NEA, U. Ala. Alumni Assn., Alpha Phi. Baptist. Home: 327 Minor Rd Gardendale AL 35071

GRIMES, JOHN FRANK, III, forensic chemist; b. Dallas, Aug. 22, 1947; s. J. F. and Pearl Elsie (Schwadlenak) G.; B.S. (Robert Welch Found. fellow 1971-72), Abilene Christian U., 1972, postgrad., 1972-74; postgrad. North Tex. State U., 1978-79; m. Jennifer Susan Buck, July 7, 1967; children—John Frank, Kiah Michelle. Research asst. Abilene Christian U., 1968-69; corrections supr. Abilene Police Dept., 1969-71; chemist Dallas Water Utilities, 1973-76; group leader research Mary Kay Cosmetics Co., Dallas, 1976-79; tech. supr. Tex. Dept. Public Safety, Wichita Falls, 1979—. Unit commr. N.W. Tex. council Boy Scouts Am., 1979—. Cert. breathalyzer operator, Tex.; cert. tech. supr., Tex.; cert. water operator, class B., Tex. Mem. Assn. Ofcl. Analytical Chemists, S.W. Assn. Forensic Chemists, S.W. Assn. Toxicologists, N. Tex. Chromatography Forum (sec.-treas.), Am. Chem. Soc. Democrat. Home: 5804 Greentree Wichita Falls TX 76306 Office: PO Box 2529 Wichita Falls TX 76307

GRIMES, JOYCE METTS, state ofcl.; b. Columbia, S.C., Dec. 6, 1946; d. Carlisle Eusebuis and Ruth Elisabeth (Cannon) Metts; continuing edn. cert. Clemson U., 1977, U. N.C., Chapel Hill, 1978; student U. S.C., Columbia, 1978—; m. Jimmy W. Grimes, Apr. 24, 1971; children—Jarrett Bartley, James Reid. Sec.-bookkeeper Eastern States Serum Co., Columbia, 1965-67; legal asst., office of legal counsel S.C. Dept. Health and Environ. Control, Columbia, 1967-69, asst. to commr., 1969-78, exec. asst. to commr., 1978—. Bd. dirs., program chmn. Ballentine (S.C.) Civic Assn., 1979—. Mem. Am. Public Health Assn., Am. Acad. Health Adminstrs. (dir.), S.C. Public Health Assn. (exec. sec.). Methodist. Home: PO Box 25 Ballentine SC 29002 Office: SC Dept Health and Environ Control 2600 Bull St Columbia SC 29210

GRIMES, SHERRILL DEANE, savs. and loan exec.; b. Pascagoula, Miss., Apr. 11, 1947; d. George Mallison and Lizzie Kate (Haden) Rose; A.A., Hinds Jr. Coll., 1967; student Ga. Inst. Tech., 1970, U. So. Miss., 1972-73, Miss. Coll., 1979—; m. Eddie Grimes, June 26, 1971. Dir. personnel and public relations Rankin Gen. Hosp., Brandon, Miss., 1969-76; adminstrv. asst., dir. staff devel. Miss. State Hosp., Whitfield, 1976-79; asst. v.p., dir. personnel Unifirst Fed. Savs. & Loan Assn., Jackson, Miss., 1979—; cons. public relations and staff devel. Miss. State Hosp.; dir. guidance dept. Jackson State U. Bd. dirs. Mental Health Assn. Miss.; vice chmn. adv. council Hinds Jr. Coll. Notary public Rankin County. Mem. Inst. Fin. Edn., Nat. Assn. Nurse Recruiters, Am. Soc. Personnel Adminstrs. (accredited), Am. Hosp. Soc. for Personnel Adminstrn., Miss. Hosp. Assn. Soc. Personnel Adminstrs., Am. Hosp. Soc. Edn. and Tng. Methodist. Office: PO Box 1818 Jackson MS 39205

GRIMES, TERRY KEITH, educator; b. Lexington, Ky., Apr. 8, 1951; s. George Taylor and Jacquelyn (Jackson) G.; B.S., Ky. State U., 1973; M.A., Ohio State U., 1974; postgrad. Ind. U., 1979. Waste control coordinator Am. Can Co., Lexington, 1974-75; instr. music edn., voice Ky. State U., Frankfort, 1975—; adj. faculty Capital U., Dayton, Ohio, 1977-79, Berea (Ky.) Coll. Gospel Ensemble, 1978—; applied vocal and instrumental chairperson Gospel Music Workshop Am., 1976, asso. dean curriculum and instrn., 1977, free lance actor; music cons. Mem. Ky. Music Educators Assn., Music Educators Nat. Conf., Nat. Assn. Tchrs. Singing, Alpha Phi Alpha. Baptist. Author: Choir Directing, 1979. Home: 945 Waverly Dr Lexington KY 40505 Office: Dept Music Ky State Univ Frankfort KY 40601

GRIMES, URBAIN FABER, social worker; b. Goldsboro, N.C., Nov. 19, 1941; s. Braxton Allison and Neta (Chestnutt) G.; B.S., E. Tenn. State U., 1967; M. in Sociology, N.C. State U., 1973; m. Hilda Porter, Oct. 3, 1964; children—James Braxton, William Ashley. Social worker N.C. Dept. Corrections, Raleigh, 1969; counselor GROW, Inc., Raleigh, 1967-69; clin. social worker Cherry Hosp., Goldsboro, 1969—; pvt. practice individual and group therapy, Goldsboro, 1977—; instr. Wayne Community Coll., Goldsboro, 1979—; cons. in field. Mem. Nat. Assn. Social Workers, Internat. Transactional Analysis Assn. Democrat. Methodist. Home: Route 1 Box 201 Faison NC 28341 Office: Caller Box 8000 Cherry Hospital Goldsboro NC 27530

GRIMLAND, JOHN MARTIN, JR., accountant, orgn. ofcl.; b. Clifton, Tex., May 11, 1917; s. John Martin and Mayme (Gollihar) G.; B.S. in Commerce, Tex. Christian U., 1939, LL.D. (hon.), 1979; m. Phyllis Miss Montgomery, Nov. 1, 1947; children—Diane, Donna Jean, Norma Gayle. With Universal C.I.T. Corp., 1940-42, Internal Revenue Service, 1946-47; pub. accountant, Midland, Tex., 1947-51, C.P.A., 1951—; partner Main Hurdman & Cranstoun, 1968—. Mem. Optimist Internat., 1949—, gov. Dist. 7, 1957-58, internat. v.p., 1958-59, chmn. internat. pub. relations com., 1959-62, internat. pres., 1962-63, chmn. internat. community service com., 1966-69; treas. Midland Symphony Assn., 1960-62, pres. 1963-65; pres. Midland United Fund, 1969, Indsl. Found. of Midland, 1971-74. Trustee, Tex. Christian U., 1972—, Midland Meml. Hosp., 1977—; pres. Midland YMCA, 1980—. Served to lt. USNR, World War II. C.P.A., Tex. Mem. Am. Inst. C.P.A.'s, Tex. Christian U. Alumni Assn. (pres. 1965-66), Midland C. of C. (pres. 1970). Methodist (chmn. bd. 1961-62, trustee 1974—). Home: 1605 Country Club Dr Midland TX 79701 Office: HBF Bldg Midland TX 79701

GRIMM, DEAN FRANKLIN, aero. engr.; b. Argonia, Kans., May 28, 1930; s. Ralph Albert and Laura MayBelle (McIntyre) G.; B.S., U. Kans., 1958; m. Eunice M. Mull, Nov. 22, 1955; children—Deana Lynne, Gregory Scott. Flight test engr. Convair-Gen. Dynamics, Ft. Worth, 1958-60; aerodynamic engr. Boeing Co., Renton, Wash., 1960-61; flight test engr. FAA, Oklahoma City, 1961-63; chief flight crew integration div. NASA Johnson Space Center, Houston, 1963-74, chief expt. systems div., 1974—. Asst. scout master Boy Scouts Am., Nassau Bay, Tex., 1973—. Bd. dirs. All Play Football, Nassau Bay. Served with USAF, 1950-54. Recipient Exceptional Service medal NASA, 1973. Registered profl. engr., Okla. Mem. Am. Inst. Aeros. and Astronautics. Presbyterian. Mason (32 deg.). Home: 18638 Prince William Ln Houston TX 77058 Office: NASA Johnson Space Center (ED) Houston TX 77058

GRIMM, RODGER ALAN, hosp. food service dir.; b. Decatur, Ill., Aug. 14, 1950; s. Robert Allen and Virginia Dorene G.; B.S., Belmont Coll., 1974. Mgr., Morrison Food Service Accounts for frats., Auburn, Ala., 1975-78; mgr. food service Decatur Gen. Hosp., 1978-79, Coffee Gen. Hosp., Douglas, Ga., 1979-80, A.B. Donelson (Tenn.) Hosp., 1980—. Mem. Am. Soc. Hosp. Food Service Adminstrs. Home: Laurel Hills Apts G206 3417 Lebanon Rd Hermitage TN 37076 Office: AB Donelson Hospital Donelson TN

GRINDELL, ALBERT GORDON, nuclear engr.; b. Balt., Apr. 25, 1917; s. Thomas Edward and Norma Wilhelmina (Tolson) G.; B.S., Carnegie Inst. Tech., 1949; M.S., U. Tenn., 1957; m. Mary Edwardine Davin, Nov. 2, 1940; children—Maureen Ellen, Don Kevin. Simplex telegrapher, clk. asst., office mgr. Balt., 1934-36; boilermaker helper, machinist, clk. B & O R.R., Balt., 1936-42; mech. engr. designer homogeneous reactor experiment (HRE-1), Oak Ridge Nat. Lab., 1950-51, exptl. engr. developing components, systems for nuclear reactors, 1951—, Served with USAAF, 1942-46; ETO. Mem. ASME, Am. Nuclear Soc., ASTM, Sigma Xi. Registered profl. engr., Tenn.

GRINSTEAD, WILLIAM CARTER, JR., coal co. exec.; b. Houston, Aug. 8, 1930; s. William Carter and Lee Menefee (Tevis) G.; student Rice Inst., 1948-50; B.S. in Petroleum Enging., U. Tex., 1953; m. Linda Ruth Rowe, Oct. 24, 1953; children—Cindy, Carter. With Exxon Co., 1957—, engr., 1957-68, mem. staff supply dept., 1968-69, enging. mgr., ops. mgr. western div., Los Angeles, 1969-72, div. ops. mgr. southeastern div., New Orleans, 1972-73, mgr. govt. relations pub. affairs dept., Houston, 1973-76, div. mgr. E. Tex. div., 1976-78, sr. v.p., dir. Carter Oil Co., 1978-80, pres. Exxon Coal U.S.A., Inc., 1980—. Served to lt. j.g., USNR, 1953-57. Registered profl. engr. Tex. Mem. Am. Inst. Mining and Metall. Engrs., Tex. Soc. Profl. Engrs., Am. Petroleum Inst., U.S. C. of C., Delta Kappa Epsilon. Episcopalian. Clubs: Petroleum, Allegro, Houston Country (Houston). Office: PO Box 2180 Houston TX 77001

GRISE, JERRY WADE, radiologist; b. Ft. Smith, Ark., Apr. 25, 1933; s. Strauther Wade and Mary Beth (Thurman) G.; B.S., E. Tenn. State U., 1953; M.D., U. Tenn., 1956; m. Betty Lunati, Feb. 14, 1959; children—Jeffrey Wade, John David. Intern, D.C. Gen. Hosp., Washington, 1957; resident radiology Strong Meml. Hosp., Rochester, N.Y., 1958-60; practice medicine specializing in radiology Bapt. Hosp., Nashville, 1964-65, Meth. Hosp., Memphis, 1965—. Served to capt. M.C., USAF, 1960-64. Mem. Am., Tenn. med. assns., Radiol. Soc. N.Am., Am. Roentgen Ray Soc., Tenn. Radiol. Soc. (sec.-treas. 1975-77, pres. 1979-80), Memphis Roentgen Soc. (pres. 1971-72). Home: 4822 Fleetview Memphis TN 38117 Office: Dept Radiology Meth Hosp 1265 Union Ave Memphis TN 38104

GRITZ, JACK LINTON, clergyman, writer, editor; b. Okmulgee, Okla., Dec. 31, 1916; s. Harry Vernon and Katie (Houston) G.; student Phillips U., 1935-37; A.B., Okla. Bapt. U., 1939; Th.M., Southwestern Bapt. Theol. Sem., 1942; Th.D., So. Sem., Louisville, 1947; m. Veva Chloe Hammack, June 29, 1947; 1 son, Paul Linton. Asso. sec. dept. religious edn. Bapt. Gen. Conv. Okla., 1944-47; pastor First Bapt. Ch., Tahlequah, Okla., 1947-49; editor Bapt. Messenger, Oklahoma City, 1949-79. Mem. So. Bapt. Press Assn. (pres. 1968-69). Home: 1419 N Drexel St Oklahoma City OK 73107

GRIVSKY, EUGENE MICHAEL, chemist; b. Pskov, Russia, Dec. 20, 1911; s. Michael Theodore and Alexandra Yakovlevna (Gemchuzhina) G.; M.S. summa cum laude, Brussels U., 1938, D.Sc. summa cum laude, 1940; m. Helen Vlassova, Oct. 27, 1935; children—Michael, Tatiana Grivsky-Berls; came to U.S., 1957, citizen. Research fellow Internat. Bur. Standards, Brussels U., 1939-41; group leader Organic Research Labs., Pharm. div. Union Chimique Belge, Brussels, 1941-57; sr. research chemist Wellcome Research Labs., Burroughs Wellcome Co., Tuckahoe, N.Y., 1957-70, Research Triangle Park, N.C., 1970-78. Served with Estonian Army, 1931-33, Belgian Army Res., 1950-62. Fellow Am. Inst. Chemists; mem. Am. Chem. Soc., Soc. Chimique de Belge, Soc. Chimique de France, Pharm. Soc. Japan, Chem. Soc. Eng., Gesellschaft Deutscher Chemiker, N.Y. Acad. Scis., Royal Netherlands Chem. Soc. Research, publs. in organic and medicinal chemistry, mechanism of reactions, syntheses of novel anti-histamines, anti-cancer, anti-bacterial, anti-epileptic, chemotherapeutic and various medicinal agts. Patentee in field. Home and office: 4407 Eastwood Ct Fairfax VA 22032 also Georgetown U Washington DC 20037

GROBEN, RICHARD LOUIS, frozen bacteria cultures mfg. co. exec.; b. Evansville, Ind., Sept. 21, 1926; s. Edmund and Alvina Mary (Loeffler) G.; B.Ch.E., Purdue U., 1950; m. Jeannette Glenn, Apr. 11, 1953; children—Sharon Lynne, Carol Ann, Deborah Jean. Prodn. supt. Container Corp. Am., Phila., 1950-51; process engr. Internat. Harvester Corp., Evansville, Ind., 1951-52; v.p. sales Pfizer Inc., N.Y.C., 1952-73; v.p. sales, partner Microlife Technics, Sarasota, Fla., 1973—. Co-chmn. fund drive Greater N.Y. Councils Boy Scouts Am., 1970. Served with USNR, 1944-46. Mem. Drug, Chem. and Allied Trades Assn. (dir. 1971-73), Calorie Control Council (dir. 1970-73), Sales Exec. Club N.Y., Inst. Food Technologists. Republican. Clubs: Univ. (Sarasota), Bent Tree Golf and Racquet. Home: 1014 Contento St Sarasota FL 33581 Office: Box 3917 Sarasota FL 33578

GROCHOLA, CHESTER WALTER, psychologist, mental health center exec., educator; b. Jamaica, L.I., N.Y., July 20, 1918; s. Joseph and Leokadia (Dzienisiewicz) G.; A.B., U. N.C., 1941; A.M., N.Y. U., 1953; m. Marjorie Stoothoff, Apr. 13, 1943; children—Jean E. Sterner, William J. S. Psychologist U. N.C., 1945-46; rehab. counsellor Dept. Hosps. N.Y.C., 1946-47; adminstr., psychologist, instr. phys. medicine and rehab. N.Y. U.-Bellevue Med. Center, 1947-48, asst. to dir., 1947-55; instr. N.Y. State Sch. Indsl. and Labor Relations Cornell U., 1953-54; dir. Madison Park Hosp., Bklyn., 1955-61; asst. prof. psychology Adelphi U., Garden City, N.Y., 1955-61, prof. psychology, dir. Inst. Behavioral and Social Scis., 1962-65; asst. to pres. Adelphi U., 1965-68; dir. Comprehensive Mental Health Center, Nassau County Med. Center, East Meadow, L.I., N.Y., 1968-73; exec. dir. Hope for Youth, Rockville Center, L.I., 1973-75; adminstr., program coordinator adminstr. dept. family practice Southside Hosp., Bay Shore, N.Y., 1975-77. Bd. dirs. Nassau County Health and Welfare Council. Mem. Nassau County Adv. Com. on Edn. Served from pvt. to maj. USAAF, 1941-46. Licensed psychologist, N.Y. State. Mem. Am. Psychol. Assn., Am. Pub. Health Assn., Am. Coll. Pub. Relations Assn., Am. Hosp. Assn. Club: University of Long Island. Contbg. author: The Community Mental Health Center. Home: Route 7 Box 601 Chapel Hill NC 27514

GROCHOWSKA, CLARA LETITIA, educator, nun; b. Mt. Carmel, Pa., Oct. 29, 1910; d. Ignatius and Helene (Ambrosiewicz) G.; B.A., Catholic U. of Am., 1935, M.A., 1942; Ph.D., Universidad de Santo Domingo, 1959. Joined religious order, 1935; tchr. Nazareth Acad., Phila., 1935-47, Holy Family Acad., Chgo., 1947-50, Colegio Espiritu Santo, Hato Rey, P.R., 1951-55; prof. dept. modern langs. Holy Family Coll., Phila., 1955-69; prof. Jackson (Miss.) State U., 1969—, chmn. dept. modern langs., 1955-69, head humanities div., 1955-69. Recipient Award of Merit, Am. Assn. of Colls. for Tchr. Edn. Mem. MLA, Miss. Modern Lang. Assn., Assn. for Advancement of Polish Studies, Nat. Coalition of Am. Nuns. Author: The Assessment of William Faulkner in Poland: An Annotated Bibliography; editor: Centennial History of Jackson State U., 1O77-1977. Home: 1661 Lynch St Jackson MS 39203 Office: Jackson State Univ Jackson MS 39217

GROGAN, HIRAM JOHN, lawyer, psychologist; b. Ball Ground, Ga., Aug. 21, 1925; s. Paul and Lila (Stamper) G.; student Oglethorpe U., 1942-43, Ga. So. Coll., 1946; A.B. cum laude, Piedmont Coll., 1948; M.Ed., U. Ga., 1949, Ed. S., 1972; J.D., Woodrow Wilson Coll., 1958; D.Min., Luther Rice Sem., 1976; m. Ruth Carney, Oct. 2, 1948. Tchr., prin. Etowah Sch., Cherokee County, Ga., 1950-51; tchr., coach Blackwell Sch., Cobb County, Ga., 1951-52; accountant Ga. Hwy. Dept., Atlanta, 1952-56; chief probation officer, Marietta, Ga., 1956-69, area probation supr., 1969-73, psychologist, 1973—; admitted to Ga. bar, 1958; since practiced in Marietta. Part-time instr. sociology Marietta Center, U. Ga., 1964. Apptd. lt. col. gov.'s staff, 1967. Served with USNR, 1944-46. Mem. Am., Ga., Cobb bar assns., Nat. Council on Crime and Delinquency, Ga. Probation and Parole Assn., Soc. Psychotherapy Research, Soc. Police and Criminal Psychology, Am. Mental Health Counselors Assn., Am., Ga. psychol. assns. Clubs: Civitan, Marietta Art. Author: Modern Bow Hunting, 1958; also monographs numerous articles in profl. jours., mags. Home: 3420 Lee St Smyrna GA 30080 Office: 514 Gloner St Suite 202 Marietta GA 30060

GROLL, ELKAN WILEY, architect, landscape architect, city planner; b. Mpls., Feb. 15, 1914; s. Sirach and Rachel (Cohn) G.; B.S. in Architecture, U. Minn., 1936; M.L.A., Harvard U., 1939; C.E. in City Planning, George Washington U., 1942; m. Jessie A. Jacobson, Oct. 22, 1939; children—Sharon Lynn, Gail Allison, Gary Steven. Architect, Resettlement Adminstrn., 1936-37; architect, site planner Office Chief of Engrs., U.S. Dept. Army, Washington, 1939-43; chief architect Atomic Bomb Project, Hanford, Wash., 1943-45; urban devel. specialist Nat. Housing Agy., Washington, 1945-47; prin. Elkan W. Groll & Assos., Silver Spring, Md., 1947-73; cons. architect, city planner, 1973—; cons. architect Dept. Army, 1948-58; spl. project coordinator Broward County (Fla.); mem. Planning Bd., Pompano Beach, Fla. designer numerous army, navy and air force installations, also internat. airports in Iceland, Azores, Bermuda and Hawaii. Recipient Civilian Service award War Dept., 1943, Sec. War Service award, 1945. Mem. AIA, Am. Soc. Landscape Architects, Am. Inst. Cert. Planners, Am. Soc. Planning Ofcls. Author publs. on zoning, sub-div. regulations, site planning, airfield planning, recreation. Home and office: 3100 N Course Ln Pompano Beach FL 33060

GRONER, FRANK S(HELBY), hosp. adminstr.; b. Stamford, Tex., Sept. 25, 1911; s. Frank S. and Laura (Wyatt) G.; B.A., Baylor U., 1934; LL.D., Tex. Bapt. Coll., 1946, Union U., 1952, Baylor U., 1969; m. Daisy Amanda McFearin, Dec. 12, 1936. Dean sch. bus. Coll. of Marshall (Tex.), 1934-36; asst. adminstr. So. Bapt. Hosp., New Orleans, 1936-43, adminstr., 1943-46; adminstr., pres. Bapt. Meml. Hosp., Memphis, 1946—. Cons. USPHS; cons. Div. Hosp. and Med. Facilities, also Bur. Family Services on Med. Matters, HEW; exec. dir. Health, Edn. and Research Found. Mem. Surgeon Gen.'s adv. com. on Nat. Health Survey. Bd. govs., exec. com. Blue Cross; bd. dirs. ARC, Am. Cancer Soc. Memphis Community Chest, Memphis Theol. Sem., 1975-78. Dollar-a-Year Man, Washington, 1942-45. Recipient Justin Ford Kimball award, 1964, Distinguished service award Am. Hosp. Assn., 1966, Memphis and Shelby County Med. Soc. Distinguished Service award, 1967, gold medal Am. Coll. Hosp. Adminstrs., 1968, Vocat. Service award Memphis Rotary, 1975, Rotary Club Vocat. Service award, 1975, Memphis Civitan Club Outstanding Citizen award, 1976, L.M. Graves Meml. Health award Mid-South Med. Center, 1977, Brotherhood award NCCJ, 1980. Mem. Am. (pres. chmn. council hosp. planning and plant operation, chmn. hosp. architects qualifications, trustee, past pres.) La. (past pres., now hon. mem.), Tenn. (past pres,) hosp. assns., Southeastern Hosp. Conf. (past pres.), Southwide Bapt. Hosp. Assn. (past pres.), So. Inst. Hosp. Adminstrs. (dir.), Am. Coll. Hosp. Adminstrs. (pres., dir.), Internat. Hosp. Fedn. (del.); hon. mem. Miss. Hosp. Assn., Future Memphis, Inc. Baptist. Home: 3170 Southern Ave Memphis TN 38111 Office: 899 Madison Ave Memphis TN 38146

GRONINGER, CAROLE PERRY, counselor; b. Akron, Ind., Nov. 9, 1932; d. Artie Worden and Esther (Murphy) Perry; student U. Kans., 1965, U. Hawaii, 1965-67, U. Va., 1967-68, George Washington U., 1968; B.A. in Edn., Purdue U., 1970; M.A., Rollins Coll., 1974; m. Dwight L. Groninger, Dec. 17, 1951; children—Keith Lynn, Ann Kimberly. Tchr. social studies Am. Sch., Teheran, Iran, 1971-72; counselor Columbia Elementary Sch., Orlando, Fla., 1974-75, tchr. emotionally disturbed children, 1975-76; counselor Engelwood Elementary Sch., Orlando, 1976—; tchr. continuing edn. Valencia Community Coll. Mem. Am., Orange County personnel and guidance assns., Orange County Guidance Assn., Mental Health Assn. Republican. Presbyterian. Home: 435 Mallard Circle Winter Park FL 32789 Office: 900 Engle Dr Orlando FL 32807

GROSS, CHARLES MERRILL, artist; b. Cullman, Ala., Sept. 18, 1935; s. Robert Merrill and Delma Jane (Hesterley) G.; B.F.A., Atlanta Coll. Art, 1967 M.F.A., U. Guanajuato (Mex.), 1968; m. Rosalie Westbrook, July 4, 1956; 1 son, Robert Mark. Instr., Miss. Coll., Clinton, 1968-69; prof. art U. Miss., Oxford, 1969—; one-man exhbns. include Miss. Art Assn., Jackson, 1969, U. Miss., 1976, U. N.Ala., Florence, 1977; exhibitioner in numerous juried exhbns., 1969—. Recipient award merit Mid-South Exhbn., Memphis, 1969, Nat. Arts and Crafts Exhbn., Jackson, 1969, Holiday Arts Festival, McComb, Miss., 1969, Miss. Artists Juried Exhbn., Hattiesburg, 1979, Southeastern Competition, Rome, Ga., 1979. Mem. So. Assn. Sculptors (v.p. 1972-74), Nat. Art Edn. Assn., Coll. Art Assn. Democrat. Baptist. Home: 300 Longest Rd Oxford MS 38655 Office: Art Dept Univ Miss University MS 38677

GROSS, EMILY GERTRUDE LOWREY, pianist; b. Lenoir City, Tenn., Apr. 12, 1925; d. William Alex and Alma Gertrude (Ghormley) Lowrey; A.A., Tenn. Wesleyan Coll., 1944; Mus.B., U. Tenn., Chattanooga and Cadek Conservatory, 1946; Mus.M., Baylor U., 1974; m. Francis Burcett Gross, Dec. 22, 1946; children—Ronald Burdett, Timothy Lowrey. Organist, choir dir. First Meth. Ch., Morristown, Tenn., 1945; music supr. pub. schs., Athens, Tenn., 1946-47; pvt. tchr. piano, Chickamauga, Ga., 1948-49, Waco, Tex., 1953—; tchr. piano Memphis Coll. Music Southwestern U., 1952-53; organist, choir dir. Westminster Presbyn. Ch., Waco, 1963-66; organist Lake Shore Hills Presbyn. Ch., Waco. Finalist tchrs. div. Internat. Piano Rec. Competition, 1972. Certified Music Tchrs. Nat. Assn. Mem. Nat., Tex. (theory com. 1977-78), Waco (pres. 1974—) music tchrs. assns., Tex. Student Affiliate Tchrs., Nat. Guild Piano Tchrs., DAR, United Daus. Confederacy. Club: Waco Euterpean. Contbr. articles to profl. jours. Home and Studio: 104 Turtle Creek Dr Waco TX 76710

GROSS, FRANK BLACKBURN, JR., physician; b. Des Moines, Nov. 22, 1921; s. Frank Blackburn and Esther Irene (Walkup) G.; B.S., Wake Forest U., 1942; M.D., Bowman Gray Sch. Medicine, 1945; m. Ann Mendenhall Kanoy, June 22, 1944 (dec. Jan. 1970); children—Diana (Mrs. George Antonini), Janet (Mrs. William Underwood), Frank B., Christopher Spencer. Intern, St. Louis U. Hosp., 1945-46; resident N.C. Bapt. Hosp., Winston-Salem, 1948-50; fellow psychosomatic medicine Duke U., 1950; practice medicine specializing in internal medicine, Asheville, N.C., 1951-60, Harlan, Ky., 1960-67, Winter Haven Fla., 1967-70, Bartow, Fla., 1970—; med. dir. Polk Gen. Hosp., Bartow, 1970—, treas. bd. dirs. Polk Gen. Hosp. Found., 1972—; faculty U.S. Fla. Sch. Medicine. Served with AUS, 1945-47. Mem. Am. Acad. Med. Dirs., Am. Soc. Internal Medicine, Winter Haven Sertoma (chmn. bd. dirs. 1968), Am., Fla., Polk County (Fla.) (bd. censors 1972—) med. assns., So. Golf Assn. (dir. 1967—). Home: 700 Mirror Terr Winter Haven FL 33880 Office: Polk Gen Hosp Bartow FL 33830

GROSS, GARY NEIL, physician; b. Ft. Lewis, Wash., July 25, 1944; s. Norman Harold and Dorothy Naomi (Bercu) G.; B.A., U. Tex., Austin, 1967, M.D., Southwestern, Dallas, 1969; m. Elaina Wee, Mar. 23, 1974. Intern, U. Utah Hosps., Salt Lake City, 1969-70, resident in internal medicine, 1970-71; fellow in allergy and clin. immunology Nat. Jewish Hosp. and U. Colo. Med. Center, Denver, 1971-74; practice medicine specializing in allergy, Dallas, 1974—; mem. staff Med. City, Dallas, Presbyterian, Parkland Meml., Baylor hosps.; clin. asst. prof. internal medicine U. Tex. Health Sci. Center. Mem. Tex. Area 5 Environ. Health Task Force. Diplomate Am. Bd. Allergy and Immunology, Am. Bd. Internal Medicine. Mem. Am. Coll. Physicians, Am. Thoracic Soc., Am. Acad. Allergy, Am. Lung Assn. (dir. Dallas). Jewish. Home: 3529 Rankin Ave Dallas TX 75205 Office: 8335 Walnut Hill Ln Dallas TX 75231

GROSS, JOHN C(HARLES), broker, industrialist; b. N.Y.C., Apr. 2, 1904; s. Edward H. and Anna Catharine (Muelhaus) G.; student pub. schs. N.Y.C.; m. Helen Victoria Newman, Sept. 26, 1926; 1 dau., Jean Anne. Pres., treas., dir. John C. Gross, Inc.; treas., dir. Gen. Automation Fla., Metrodynamics Corp.; pres., treas., dir. Yacht Club Island Corp., Yacht Club Island Apts.; pres., treas. Ponce de Leon Corp., Artifacts Recovery Corp.; pres., dir. New Smyrna Subcontractors Corp., Yacht Club Island Estates. Mem. Com. of 100 of New Smyrna Beach; mem. Edgewater (Fla.) Planning Bd.; chmn. S.E. Volusia Area Devel. Council; pres. Edgewater Civic Assn.; mem. Edgewater Indsl. Bd. Mem. Nat. Assn. Security Dealers, New Smyrna Beach C. of C. Lutheran (council). Rotarian. Home: 404 N Riverside Dr Edgewater FL 32032 Office: 404 N Riverside Dr Edgewater FL 32032

GROSSEL-ROSSI, MARION NICHOLAS, lawyer, corp. exec.; b. New Orleans, June 22, 1931; s. Arthur and Helen G. (Troyanovich) G-R; B.S., Tulane U., 1955, LL.B., 1962, J.D., 1977; m. Sandra Sue Cason, Nov. 30, 1975. Geologist, Forest Oil Corp., Lafayette, La., 1955-59; admitted to La. bar, 1962; with firm Jackson & Hess, New Orleans, 1962-63; partner firm Leach & Grossel-Rossi, New Orleans, 1963-68, Leach, Grossel-Rossi & Paysse, 1968-77; of counsel firm Leach, Paysse & Baldwin, 1977—; exec. v.p. Tex. Sch. Book Depository, Inc., Dallas, 1977—. sec.-treas. Elisan Corp., New Orleans. Bd. govs. Southeastern Admiralty Law Inst. Mem. Fed., Am., La. bar assns., Maritime Law Assn. U.S., Am. Judicature Soc., La. Hist. Soc., Upper Audubon Assn. (pres. 1971-72), Audubon Soc., Nat. Rifle Assn. (life), Internat. Oceanographic Found., Friends of Cabildo, Am. Arbitration Assn. (panel arbitrators), La. Assn. Def. Counsel. Clubs: Dallas Woods and Waters, Dallas Gun, Brookhaven Country, Essex, Sports Car of America (pres. Delta region 1965). Home: 8901 Douglas Dallas TX 75225 Office: 8301 Ambassador Row Dallas TX 75247

GROSSMAN, MAURICE SIDNEY, physician; b. Corpus Christi, Tex., June 1, 1927; s. Edward and Sarah (Mushlin) G.; B.A., U. Tex., 1948, M.D., 1952; m. Ann Dea Donovon, Sept. 29, 1974; children—Carla, Daryl, Sandor, Dallas. Intern medicine, asst. resident internal medicine St. Louis City Hosp., 1953-54; sr. resident internal medicine New Eng. Center Hosp., Boston, 1954-55; chief fellow gastroenterology Lahey Clinic, Boston, 1955-56; mem. staff New Eng. Bapt. Hosp., also New Eng Deaconess Hosp., Boston, 1955-56; pvt. practice internal medicine and gastroenterology, Corpus Christi, 1957—; chief dept. medicine Spohn Hosp.; hon. staff Meml. Hosp.;

lectr. med. groups. Served to maj., AUS Res., 1965-61; served with USNR, 1945-46. Diplomate Am. Bd. Internal Medicine. Fellow A.C.P., Am. Coll. Gastroenterology (exec. council 1973-75); mem. AMA, So. Med. Assn., Am. Soc. Internal Medicine, Am. Gastroenterol. Assn., Tex. Acad. Internal Medicine, Corpus Christi Acad. Internal Medicine (pres. 1969), Sigma Alpha Mu, Alpha Epsilon Delta. Jewish. Contbr. articles to profl. jours. Home: 321 Bayshore Dr Corpus Christi TX 78412 Office: 1001 Louisiana Pkwy Corpus Christi TX 74804

GROSSMAN, ROBERT GEORGE, physician, educator; b. N.Y.C., Jan. 24, 1933; s. Ferenc and Vivian (Isenberg) G.; B.A., Swarthmore Coll., 1953; M.D., Columbia, 1957; m. Ellin Friedman, June 26, 1955; children—Amy, Kate, Ruth. Intern, Strong Meml. Hosp., Rochester, N.Y., 1957-58; resident Presbyn. Hosp., Columbia, 1960-63; practice medicine specializing in neurol. surgery, Galveston, Tex., 1973—; instr., asso. prof. neurosurgery U. Tex. S.W. Med. Sch., 1963-68; asso. prof., prof. neurol. surgery Albert Einstein Coll. Medicine, 1969-73; prof., chmn. div. neurol. surgery U. Tex. Med. Br., Galveston, 1973—. Chmn. neurology B study sect. USPHS, NIH, 1972-74. Served with AUS, 1958-60. Diplomate Am. Bd. Neurosurgery. Mem. Am. Assn. Neurol. Surgeons, A.C.S. Author: (with W.D. Willis) Medical Neurobiology, 1973, 1977. Home: 18723 Point Lookout Dr Nassau Bay TX 77058 Office: U Tex Med Br Galveston TX 77550

GROSSO, CAMILLE MARIE, nurse; b. Geneva, N.Y., Sept. 28, 1938; d. Frank Leo and Gaetana Nicolina (Luongo) Balistreri; diploma Willard State Hosp. Sch. Nursing, 1959; B.S. in Nursing, George Mason U., 1976; M.S. in Nursing, Cath. U., 1978; m. Gerard M. Grosso, Apr. 8, 1961; children—Gerard M., Gina M. Staff nurse Univ. Hosp., Syracuse, N.Y., 1959-61; head nurse, care coordinator Project Hope, Saigon, S. Vietnam, 1961-62; vol. Am. Red Cross, Colorado Springs, Colo. and No. Va., 1963-71; staff nurse and head nurse The Fairfax Hosp., Falls Ch., Va., 1973-76; cons. mental health and alcoholism nursing, Va., 1976—; mental health nursing clin. specialist Arlington (Va.) Hosp., 1978—, asst. dir. nursing; adj. faculty mem. U. Va. Continuing Edn. Center, Falls Church. Chairperson advisory council Fairfax Community Action Alcoholism Program; bd. dirs. Fairfax Community Action Program, 1976-78. NIMH traineeship, 1976-78; named Dist. 8 Outstanding Nurse, Va. Nurses Assn., 1975; recipient Service award, George Mason U., 1976. Mem. Am., Va. (chmn. com. on profl. nursing practice, bd. dirs. Dist. 8) nurses assns., Nat. Council on Alcoholism, Council on Alcoholism for Fairfax County, Nat. Nurses Soc. on Alcoholism, Alumni Assn. Cath. U., Alumni Assn. George Mason U., Va. Nurses Coalition for Action in Politics (chairperson 1978 annual meeting), Sigma Theta Tau, Alpha Chi. Club: Italian Cultural Soc. of Washington. Home: 7853 Danby Dr Annandale VA 22003 Office: 1701 N George Mason Dr Arlington VA 22205

GROTE, RICHARD CHARLES, mgmt. cons.; b. Bklyn., N.Y., Dec. 14, 1941; s. Charles Henry and Muriel (Steele) G.; B.A. with honors, Colgate U., 1963; m. Evelyn Owings, Oct. 11, 1963 (div.); children—Cord Carl, Natasha Marie. Personnel mgr. Gen. Electric Co., Schenectady, N.Y., 1965-67; mgr. mgmt. edn. United Air Lines, Chgo., 1967-72; mgr. of tng. and devel. Frito-Lay Inc., Dallas, 1972-77; pres. Performance Systems, Dallas, 1977—; adj. prof. mgmt. U. Dallas; instr. Richland Coll.; cons. U.S. State Dept., HEW, Am. Heart Assn. Trustee Schaumburg Pub. Library, pres., 1970-72; trustee Countryside Unitarian Ch., 1969-72, pres., 1971-72; trustee First Unitarian Ch., Dallas, 1974—; bd. dirs. Dallas Theater Center, 1978—; mem. bd. rev. Inst. Mus. Services. Mem. Am. Soc. for Personnel Adminstrn., Woodlands Group, Am. Mgmt. Assn., Assn. for Humanistic Psychology, Am. Soc. for Tng. and Devel., The 500 Inc., Dallas Print and Drawing Soc., Alpha Chi Epsilon. Democrat. Unitarian. Author: Solving Managerial Problems, Positive Discipline, others. Home: 3744 Brookhaven Club Dr Dallas TX 75234

GROTEFEND, MARY EMERY, nurse, educator, sociologist; b. Wetmore, Kans., Dec. 1, 1910; d. Edward Henry Herbert and Lucy (Ward) Emery; R.N., Bethany Hosp. Sch. Nursing 1931; B.A., Baker U., 1934; M.S., Catholic U. Am., 1944; postgrad. U. Md., 1948-51; Ph.D. in Sociology, Am. U., 1966; m. Ralph L. Grotefend, July 1, 1937 (dec. Mar. 1963); 1 son, Edward Emery. Sci. instr. Jameson Hosp. Sch. Nursing, New Castle, Pa., 1934-35, Columbia Hosp. Sch. Nursing. Milw., 1935-37; ednl. dir. Burge Hosp. Sch. Nursing, Springfield, Mo., 1938-40; sci. instr., asst. div. dir. Sch. Nursing and Nursing Service. W. Balt. Gen. Hosp., 1941-47; social sci. instr., asst. prof. pub. health nursing U. Md., College Park and Balt., 1947-65, asso. prof. pub. health nursing, 1965-68; project dir. Facilitation of Student Learning through Meaningful Use of Community Resources, also asso. prof. Med. Coll. Ga., Augusta, 1968-71; asso. prof., chmn. nursing div. South Ga. Coll., Douglas, 1971-73; now pvt. practice nursing also research and writing. Chmn. social sci. com. Md. Bd. Examiners of Nurses, 1946-47; chmn. case finding Diabetes Assn. Atlanta, 1977—. Mem. Am., Md. (sec. dist. 2, 1946-48, mem.-at-large exec. com. pub. health sect. 1958-60), Mo. (pres. dist. 4, 1940) nurses assns., Nat., Md. (chmn. membership com. 1945-47) leagues for nursing, Am. Sociol. Assn., Mental Health Assn., Am. Pub. Health Assn., Women's Soc. Christian Service (pres. 1969-71), United Meth. Women, League Women Voters, Dalmatian Club Am., Zeta Tau Alpha, Sigma Theta Tau (organizer, counselor Pi chpt., faculty adviser 1957-60). Methodist (local bd. stewards 1956-59, chmn. commn. on missions 1956-60). Contbr. articles to profl. jours. Home: 5917 Hillside Dr PO Box 47114 Doraville GA 30362 Office: 1365 Peachtree St NE Atlanta GA 30309

GROUT, E. DEAN, hosp. adminstr.; b. McPherson, Kans., July 20, 1928; B.A., Bethany Nazarene Coll., 1951; M.H.A. with honors, Northwestern U., 1956; m. Elsie Browning, June 1, 1948; children—Randall L., Victor K. Tchr., prin., coach Okarche (Okla.) Public Schs., 1953-54; asst. adminstr. Wesley Med. Center, Wichita, Kans., 1956-60; adminstr. William Newton Hosp., Winfield, Kans., 1960-65, Swedish-Am. Hosp., Rockford, Ill., 1965-69; pres. Meth. Evang. Hosp., Louisville, 1976—. Trustee, Christ Meth. Ch., Louisville. Fellow Am. Coll. Hosp. Adminstrs.; mem. Louisville Hosp. Council (pres. elect). Republican. Club: Rotary. Office: Box 843 Louisville KY 40202

GROVDAHL, DAVID LLOYD, transp. engr.; b. Faribault, Minn., Aug. 10, 1941; s. Lloyd W. and Lillian M. (Schatz) G.; B.A., St. Olaf Coll., 1963; M.S., Fla. State U., 1973; m. Elba J. Castrillo, Nov. 23, 1973; 1 son, David F. Transp. planner E. Central Fla. Regional Planning Council, Winter Park, 1973-77, dir. transp. planning div., 1977—. Served with USAF, 1963-70. Decorated Bronze Star. Mem. Nat. Acad. Scis. (Transp. Research Bd.), Am. Planning Assn., Res. Officers Assn. U.S. (sec. Central Fla. chpt. 1977-78, v.p. 1978-79), Air Force Assn., Air Commando Assn. Republican. Lutheran. Clubs: Sports Car, Austin-Healey, Pacific Centre. Home: 7411 Portside Ct Orlando FL 32807 Office: 1011 Wymore Rd Winter Park FL 32789

GROVE, EDWARD RYNEAL, artist, sculptor; b. Martinsburg, W.Va., Aug. 14, 1912; s. Harry Muth and Bertha Mae (Sigler) G.; art studies Nat. Sch. Art, Washington, 1933-34, Corcoran Sch. Art, Washington, 1934-37, 40-45, Robert Brackman, 1946; m. Jean Virginia Donner, June 24, 1936; children—David Donner, Eric Donner. Die sinker, 1936-40; vignette and portrait engraver Bur. Engraving and Printing, Washington, 1940-47, Security-Columbian Banknote Co., Phila., 1947-62; sculptor-engraver U.S. Mint, Phila., 1962-65; free lance artist, West Palm Beach, Fla., 1965—; works exhibited one man shows Nat. Philatelic Mus., Phila., 1954, Phila. Art Alliance, 1960, Norton Gallery Art, West Palm Beach, 1971; works exhibited Cayuga Mus. History and Art, Auburn, N.Y., 1964, Episcopal Acad. Gallery, Phila., 1966, nat. and regional annual exhibits; works represented in permanent collections Met. Mus. Art, Carnegie Inst., Corcoran Art Gallery, U. Pa. Div. Grad. Medicine, Pangborn Corp., Hagerstown, Md., Pa. Hist. Soc., Phila., Am. Bag & Paper Corp., Phila., U.S. Dept. Navy, Smithsonian Instn., Rehab. Inst. Chgo., The Citadel, Charleston, S.C., Washington Cathedral, Ch. of Bethesda-by-the-Sea, Palm Beach, Fla., Coventry (Eng.) Cathedral, Imperial Palace, Tokyo, Miami Heart Inst., Mus. Medallic Art, Breslau, Poland; instr. drawing and portraiture Flagler Art Center, West Palm Beach, 1972-73; works include Congl. gold medal for Bob Hope, 1963, World War II medal series, 1966-70, mural Ch. of Holy Comforter, Drexel Hill, Pa., 1952-58, four coin set for Knights of Malta, 1965, alphabet medal Soc. Medalists, 1973, imperial Japanese visit medal, 1975, Am. Legion armed forces bicentennial medal series, 1975, Soyuz-Apollo medal, 1975, bronze Bicentennial monument, Palm Beach, Fla., 1976, E. Sterling Nichol Meml. plaque, 1977, John Paul Jones Nat. medal, 1979, 2d prize Brookgreen Gardens Soc. Medalists sculpture competition, 1979. Pres. Animal Rescue League Palm Beaches, Inc., 1979-80. Recipient bronze medals Washington Landscape Club, 1945, 53, Grumbacher watercolor award Cumberland Valley Art Exhibit, Hagerstown, 1965, Lindsey Morris meml. prize Nat. Sculpture Soc., 1967, Bennett meml. prize, 1971, gold medal Am. Numis. Assn., 1969. Fellow Nat. Sculpture Soc.; asso. N.A.D.; mem. Artists Equity Assn. (nat. v.p. 1965-67), Engravers Guild, Steel and Copper Plate Engravers League Phila. (pres. 1957-59), Phila. Sketch Club, Am. Numis. Assn. (Heath Lit. cert. 1979), Art Mus. Palm Beaches, Soc. Four Arts, English Speaking Union, Mensa, Knights Malta (chevalier). Republican. Episcopalian. Club: Poinciana (Palm Beach). Contbr. articles to profl. jours. and books. Home and studio: Sea Lake Studio 3215 S Flagler Dr West Palm Beach FL 33405

GROVE, JEAN DONNER (MRS. EDWARD R. GROVE), sculptor; b. Washington, May 15, 1912; d. Frederick Gregory and Georgia V. (Gartrell) Donner; student Cornell U., 1932, Hill Sch. of Sculpture, 1934-35, Corcoran Sch. of Art, 1935-37, 42-44, Cath. U. Am., 1936-37, Phila. Mus. Art Sch., 1967; B.S., Wilson Tchrs. Coll., 1939; m. Edward R. Grove, June 24, 1936; children—David Donner, Eric Donner. Exhibited in one-man shows at Wilson Tchrs. Coll., Washington, 1939, Cayuga Mus. History and Art, Auburn, N.Y., 1964, Episcopal Acad. Gallery, Phila., 1966; exhibited in group shows at Pa. Acad. Fine Arts, Phila., 1947, 48, 51, 53, N.A.D., N.Y.C., 1949, Nat. Sculpture Soc. at Archtl. League, N.Y.C., Topeka, 1957 and Lever House, N.Y.C., 1974, 75, 76, Art U.S.A., Madison Sq. Garden, N.Y.C., 1958, Corcoran Gallery Art, Washington, 1943-47, Internat. Gallery, Washington, 1946, Phila. Mus. Art, 1955, 59, 62, Phila. Art Alliance, 1957, 60, 66, Phila. Civic Center, 1968, Flagler Art Center, West Palm Beach, Fla., 1972, Norton Gallery Art, West Palm Beach, 1974; represented in permanent collections at Rosenwald Collection, Phila., Ch. of Holy Comforter, Drexel Hill, Pa., Fine Arts Commn., City Hall, Phila. Sculptor numerous portrait commns., garden figures and fountains, 1940—. Recipient 1st prize sculpture met. reg. Nat. Mus. Washington, 1946; 1st prize Sculpture Arts Club, 1946, Portrait prize, 1947; Morris Goodman award John Herron Art Mus., Indpls., 1957; Competition prize for design and sculpture of Artists Equity Phila. Award, 1960; Tallix Foundry award NSS Bicentennial Exhbn. Equitable Mall Gallery, N.Y.C., 1976, others. Mem. Nat. Sculpture Soc., Artists Equity Assn. (dir. Phila. chpt. 1964-66), Phila. Art Alliance, Soc. of Four Arts, Norton Gallery Art, Soc. Washington Artists, English Speaking Union, Animal Rescue League of Palm Beaches (com. chmn. 1972—, dir. 1975—), St. Mary's Guild of Episcopal Ch. Women (v.p. 1974-76), Kappa Delta Pi. Club: Poinciana (Palm Beach). Address: Sea-Lake Studio 3215 S Flagler Dr West Palm Beach FL 33405

GROVE, PAUL ELLSWORTH, electronic technologist, educator; b. Martinsburg, W.Va., Feb. 20, 1927; s. Nelson Hines and Pauline Cynthia (Byers) G.; student Marshall U., 1971-74, W.Va. Inst. Tech., 1975—; m. Anna Lee Cheek, Apr. 21, 1950; children—Paul Lee, Nelson R. Served in U.S. Navy, 1945-64; electronic technician Tech. Materiel Corp., Mamaroneck, N.Y., 1964-71; instr., field engr., head engring. documentation James Rumsey Vocat. Tech. Center, Martinsburg, 1971—, instr. electronic technology, 1971—; adviser Vocat. Indsl. Clubs Am. Mem. Fleet Res. Assn., VFW, Nat. CB Assn., Am. Vocat. Assn., NEA, Am. Security Council, Nat. Electronic Technicians Assn. Methodist. Contbr. articles to profl. jours.; writer tech. manuals. Home: Route 1 Box 103 Inwood WV 25428 Office: Route 6 Box 268 Martinsburg WV 25401

GROVE, RUSSELL SINCLAIR, JR., lawyer; b. Marietta, Ga., Dec. 25, 1939; s. Russell Sinclair and Miriam (Smith) G.; B.S., Ga. Inst. Tech., 1962; LL.B. with distinction, Emory U., 1964; postgrad. (Fulbright scholar-Hays Act Research grantee) U. Melbourne (Australia) Faculty Law, 1965; m. Charlotte Mariam Glascock, Jan. 9, 1965; children—Farion Smith Whitman, Arthur Owen Sinclair. Admitted to Ga. Bar, 1964, since practiced in Atlanta; asso. atty. firm Smith, Currie & Hancock, 1966-67; asso. firm Hansell, Post, Brandon & Dorsey, 1968—, mem. firm, 1972—; lectr. IBM Exec. Edn. Program. Served with USMCR, 1960-65. Mem. Am., Ga., Atlanta bar assns., Am. Judicature Soc., Omicron Delta Kappa, Phi Delta Phi. Episcopalian. Clubs: Commerce, Lawyers of Atlanta, Dunwoody Country. Author: Word Processing and Automatic Data Processing in the Modern Law Office, 1978. Editor-in-chief Jour. Pub. Law, 1964. Office: 3300 First Nat Bank Tower Atlanta GA 30303

GROVER, ANIL KUMAR, geophysicist; b. Lahore, India, Aug. 15, 1945; s. Shiv Raj and Subhag (Arora) G.; came to U.S., 1967, naturalized, 1971; Sc.B. with honors, Indian Sch. Mines, 1966, M.Sc., 1967; M.S. in Seismology (U.S. Air Force fellow), St. Louis U., 1971; m. Susann Duggal, Mar. 23, 1972. Research asso. St. Louis U., 1967-71; geophysicist TransOcean Oil Co., Houston, 1971-73; cons. geophysicist Amerada Hess Petroleum Corp., Houston, 1973-75; sr. geophysicist, geoscientist Gulf Oil Corp., Houston, 1975—. Founding dir. India Culture Center, Houston, 1974-75. Mem. Soc. Exploration Geophysicists, Am. Geophys. Union, Seismol. Soc. Am. Home: 9702 S Petersham St Houston TX 77031 Office: Gulf Oil Corp Exploration and Geosci Div PO Box 1635 Houston TX 77001

GROVES, DAVID UPDEGRAFF, trade assn. exec., mgmt. newsletter publisher, cons. co. exec.; b. Lexington, Mo., Nov. 10, 1926; s. William Lester and Adelaide Rebecca (Updegraff) G.; B.A., U. Md., 1950; M.A., Johns Hopkins, 1951; m. Nancy Jane Bustamante, June 23, 1951; children—Nancy Alice, Patricia Rebecca. Cartoonist, Stars & Stripes, 1946, Washington Post, 1947-48; artist, researcher syndicated newspaper feature Spotlight on Bus., 1949-51; cons. mgmt., pub. relations and indsl. relations Washington, 1951-54, Guatemala City, Guatemala, 1954-58, Havana, Cuba, 1958-60; gen. mgr. pub. and indsl. relations Relaciones Publicas Interamericanas S.A., Mexico City, Mexico, 1960-72; Midwest regional dir. Internat. Mgmt. Center, Cleve., 1973-78; pres. David U. Groves and Assos., Cleve., 1977-79, Washington, 1979—; sr. cons. The Silver Inst. and The Gold Inst., Washington, 1978—; pub. Stamp Research Report, 1980—. Bd. dirs. Mexican Devel. Found., 1969-72, Fomento Educacional Found., Mexico City, 1971-72. Served with AUS, 1944-46. Mem. Am. C. of C. of Mexico (chmn. communication adv. com. 1971-72), Pub. Relations Soc. Am., Internat. Assn. Bus. Communicators, Shaker Heights (pres., dir. 1973-79), Potomac (dir. 1980—), Am. philatelic socs., Newsletter Assn. Am., Greater Cleve. Public Relations Soc., Am. Acad. Polit. and Social Sci., Phi Theta Kappa. Roman Catholic. Clubs: Univ. (Mexico City); U. Md. (College Park). Home: 9321 Reach Rd Potomac MD 20854 Office: PO Box 34478 Washington DC 20034

GROVES, IVOR DURHAM, JR., physicist, govt. ofcl.; b. Bowling Green, Ky., Dec. 30, 1919; s. Ivor Durham and Jane Robinson (Atkinson) G.; B.S., Rollins Coll., 1948, M.B.A., 1964; student Oak Ridge Inst. Nuclear Studies, 1949-50; m. Marjorie Louise Lee, Aug. 5, 1944; children—Ivor D., Carol (Mrs. Richard Noland), Gail. Engr. Orlando (Fla.) Broadcasting Co., Inc., 1941-42, 45-48; electronic engr. Union Carbide Co., Oak Ridge, Tenn., 1948-51; physicist, asso. supt. underwater sound reference div. Naval Research Lab., Orlando, 1951—. Guest lectr. Tex. A. and M. U., College Station, 1973, U. Fla., Orlando, 1970. Served to capt. USAF, 1943-45. Recipient Sec. Navy Cost Reduction Program award, 1971, Naval Research Lab. Ann. Research Publ. award, 1971, 73, 74. Fellow Acoustical Soc. Am. (mem. tech. com. engring. acoustics 1969-77); mem. Audio Engring. Soc., Fla. Acoustical Soc. (treas. 1973-79), Delta Chi. Baptist (deacon 1952—). Home: 518 Baxter Ave Orlando FL 32806 Office: PO Box 8337 Orlando FL 32806

GROVES, SIDNEY KEPLER, ret. elec. engr.; b. Rome, Ind., Jan. 26, 1917; s. Sidney Kepler and Dessa (Ramsey) G.; B.S. with distinction, Purdue U., 1937 m. Virginia Leonore Lehman, June 14, 1941; 1 dau., Anne Leonore. Tchr. sci. and mathematics Cannelton (Ind.) High Sch., 1937-42; factory engr. Ken-Rad and Gen. Elec. Co., Tell City, Ind., 1942-51; sect. engr. Gen. Elec. Co., 1951-56; specialist process engring., 1956-60, sr. engr. product design, Owensboro, Ky., 1960-75, ret., 1975. Registered profl. engr., Ind., Ky. Mem. Nat., Ky. socs. profl. engrs., IEEE, Nat. Rifle Assn., Sigma Pi Sigma. Republican. Home: 1612 Ford Ave Owensboro KY 42301

GROZEA, PETRE NICOLAE, physician; b. Comana-Romania, Apr. 19, 1923; naturalized U.S. citizen, 1978; s. Nicolae Ilie and Sultana (Soare) G.; B.A., Sf. Sava Nat. Coll., Bucharest, Romania, 1941; M.D., U. Bucharest, 1949; m. Rodica Viorica, Jan. 17, 1953. Intern in medicine U. Bucharest, Romania, 1948-50, resident and clin. asst. medicine, 1950-52, asst. prof., 1952-54; investigator Inst. Internal Medicine, Romanian Acad. Scis., Bucharest, 1954-56, prin. investigator, 1956-63, sci. sec., 1960-64, asst. coordinator Ministry of Health and Welfare and head clin. hematology-chemotherapy sect. Inst. Internal Medicine, 1963-67; vis. scientist fellow Eleanor Roosevelt Found./Am. Cancer Soc./Internat. Union Against Cancer, Institute de Recherches Sur les Maladies du Sang, Paris, 1967-69; vis. research asso. Foundation Curie, Paris, 1967-69; vis. scientist Burroughs-Wellcome Found. grantee Chester Beatty Cancer Research Inst., London, 1968; vis. scientist and research asso. cancer sect. Okla. Med. Research Found., Oklahoma City, 1969-74; asst. prof. research medicine U. Okla. Coll. Medicine, Oklahoma City, 1972-76, asso. prof. research pathology, 1973—, asst. prof. medicine, 1975-76, asso. prof. medicine, 1976—; asst. mem. cancer research program Okla. Med. Research Found., 1974-77, asso. mem., 1977—; physician VA Hosp., Oklahoma City, 1975-79; vis. scientist fellow WHO, Institute de Recherches Sur les Maladies du Sang, Paris, 1964-65; attending staff Okla. Med. Research Found., Okla. Children's Meml. Hosp., U. Okla. Health Scis. Center, Oklahoma City VA Hosp., Presbyn. Hosp., Oklahoma City. Mem. Alliance Internationale (council 1967—), Assn. des Anciens de la Cité Internationale de l'Université de Paris, Comité International, Brit. Assn. Cancer Research, Internat. Soc. Hematology (exec. bd. counselors 1968-72), Romanian Acad. Scis. (editorial bd. Studies and Researches in Internal Medicine 1960-67), Société Française d'Hematologie, Union Socs. Med. Scis. Romania (council hematology sect. 1962-67), Am. Soc. Clin. Oncology, Am. Assn. Cancer Research, AMA, Am. Soc. Hematology, Okla. Med. Assn., Oklahoma County Med. Soc., N.Y. Acad. Scis., S.W. Oncology Group (lymphoma coordinating com., lung cancer coordinating com.), Sigma Xi. Christian Orthodox. Contbr. numerous articles to profl. jours. Home: 1221 Devonshire Ct Edmond OK 73034 Office: 825 NE 13 St Oklahoma City OK 73104

GRUBB, ROBERT LYNN, computer system designer; b. Knoxville, Tenn., Nov. 23, 1927; s. William Henry and DoLores Alfisi (Pierucci) Hollinshead; B.S., Central State Coll., Edmond, Okla., 1972; m. Donna Jean Chicado, May 28, 1973; children—Robert Lynn, Werner, Luke, Jubal. Air traffic controller FAA, Ft. Worth, 1955-62; engr. Philco-Ford Corp., Oklahoma City, 1962-65; service co. exec. Lear-Siegler Inc., Oklahoma City, 1965-67; computer specialist U.S. Navy, Corpus Christi, Tex., 1967-71, U.S. Army, Petersburg, Va., 1971-77, U.S. CSC, Washington, 1977-79, U.S. Dept. Justice, San Antonio, 1979—; cons. Durham Bus. Coll., Corpus Christi; cons. Corpus Christi Pub. Sch. Bd. Committeeman Boy Scouts Am., 1963-64; bd. dirs., athletic coach Southside Youth League, 1970. Served in USNR, 1945-46; PTO. Mem. Western Writers Am., Am. Hist. Soc. (charter). Author: Conversion and Implementation of CS3 Computer System, 1973; Economic Analysis of Automated System-TOPS, 1977. Contbr. articles and stories on Western history to various periodicals. Home: Route 1 Box 1068 Wetmore TX 78163 Office: INS Room A-305 727 E Durango San Antonio TX 78206

GRUBBS, BILL GENE, communications corp. exec.; b. Waco, Tex., Dec. 14, 1929; s. Howard C. and Thelma (Scott) G.; student Central City Comml. Coll., Waco, Tex., 1948; B.B.A., Baylor U., 1952; diploma Criswell Bible Inst., 1974; m. Ripple Ann Braden, May 5, 1950; children—Sheri, Bill, Tex, Paula. European mgr. service burs. IBM, Paris, France, 1956-67; v.p. Univ. Computing Co., Dallas, 1967-70; chmn. bd. dirs., chief exec. officer Communications Corp. Am., Dallas, 1970—; dir. First Security Nat. Bank of Dallas, Am. Diversified Properties Corp. Trustee, Golden Gate Baptist Theol. Sem., Mill Valley, Calif., 1969-78, Criswell Bible Inst., Dallas, 1973-77; mem. advisory and long range planning bd. Baylor U., 1968, Dallas Bapt. Coll., 1968—, So. Bapt. Annuity Bd., 1969, Criswell Found., 1973-75; adv. bd. Southwestern Bapt. Theol. Sem., Ft. Worth; chmn. bd. deacons 1st Bapt. Ch., Dallas. Served as pilot USAF, 1953-56; Korea. Recipient Key to City of New Orleans award Mayor of New Orleans, 1969. Mem. Dallas Antiques and Fine Arts Soc. (officer). Baptist. Clubs: Maranatha Garden (officer); Bent Tree Country of Dallas. Home: 6810 Gateridge St Dallas TX 75240 Office: 6767 Oakbrook St Dallas TX 75235

GRUBBS, WILLIAM EUGENE, minister; b. Foley, Ala., Dec. 4, 1924; s. Walter D. and Fbra Elizabeth (Younce) G.; B.A., Stetson U., 1949; B.D., New Orleans Bapt. Theol. Sem., 1952, Th.D., 1957; m. P. Anne Coffman, May 30, 1946; children—Walter, Paul Alan, Joseph Dennis, Laura Catherine. Ordained to ministry Baptist Ch., 1947; pastor chs., Ala., Mo., Miss., Calif., 1948-60; mem. faculty Philippine Bapt. Theol. Sem., 1960-63; dir. dept. evangelism So. Bapt. Gen. Conf. of Calif., 1964-68; exec. dir. N.W. Bapt. Conv. (Oreg.-Wash.), 1968-71; cons. for Laymen Overseas and Relief Ministries Fgn.

Mission Bd., So. Bapt. Conv., Richmond, Va., 1971—. Bd. dirs. Ch. World Service, 1976—; mem. nat. com. CROP, 1979—; mem. spl. adv. com. World Hunger, 1980—, mem. U.S. spl. com., 1976—. Served with USN, 1973-76. Mem. Soc. for Internat. Devel., Bread for the World, IMPACT. Contbr. articles in field to profl. jours. Home: 1404 Cloister Dr Richmond VA 23233 Office: Bapt Fgn Missions Bd 3806 Monument Ave Richmond VA 23222

GRUBER, ELLEN JOAN, educator; b. N.Y.C., June 21; d. Henry H. and Mary A. (Ashkalony) Carlish; B.S., Boston U., 1958; M.Ed., Ga. State U., 1972, Ph.D., 1974; J.D., Woodrow Wilson Coll. Law, 1979; m. Morton M. Gruber, June 15, 1958; children—Lee, Lloyd, Lane. Follow through cons. Ga. State U., Atlanta, 1972-74; prof. dept. edn. W. Ga. Coll., Carrollton, 1974—; pvt. practice marriage and family therapy, Atlanta, 1978—; charter mem. Sees Corp., edn. cons., 1975—; pub. Gruber Assos., Atlanta, 1977—. Vol. Heart Fund, 1970-78. Ford Found. grantee, 1970, 71. Mem. Assn. Humanistic Edn. (charter), Assn. Family Conciliation Cts., Am. Assn. Marriage and Family Therapists, Assn. Supervision and Curriculum Devel., Assn. Childhood Edn. Internat. Author: Creative Fun for Everyone, 1976; Learning Can Be Fun, 1979; Could I Speak to You About This Man Piaget?, 1979; mem. publ. com. Jour. Humanistic Edn., 1975-78. Office: 233 Peachtree Center Atlanta GA 30303 also Suite 350 Prado North 5600 Roswell Rd Atlanta GA

GRUEMER, HANNS-DIETER FRIEDERICH, clin. chemist; b. Bochum, Germany, May 25, 1924; came to U.S., 1955, naturalized, 1960; M.D., Goethe U., Frankfort-on-Main, W.Ger., 1949. Research asso. physiol. chemistry Goethe U., 1949, 54-55; lab. physician Charité Hosp., Berlin, 1950-54; research asso., sr. instr. medicine Tufts U. Med. Sch., Boston, 1956-63; prof. physiol. chemistry and pathology Ohio State U., Columbus, 1963-77; prof. clin. pathology Med. Coll. Va., 1977—. Mem. Am. Chem. Soc., Acad. Clin. Lab. Physicians and Scientists, AMA, Am. Soc. Biol. Chemists, Am. Assn. Clin. Chemistry (bd. diplomate, recipient Bernard J. Katchman award 1976, award for Outstanding Efforts in Edn. and Tng. 1978). Contbr. articles in field to profl. jours. Office: Med Coll Va MCV Station Box 597 Richmond VA 23298

GRUETZMACHER, JOYCE ELAINE SIMON, musician; b. Port Neches, Tex., July 4, 1933; d. Alphe and Lola Rose (Landry) Simon; B.Mus., North Tex. State U., 1952, M.S. in Music Edn., 1953; m. Clifton F. Gruetzmacher, Feb. 27, 1954. Tchr. Calhoun (Tex.) pub. schs., 1953-57; tchr. piano, owner Gruetzmacher Piano Studio, Port Lavaca, Tex., 1956—; mem. faculty Am. Coll. Musicians, 1966—, adjudicator for Nat. Guild auditions, 1975—. Organist, dir. choir Our Lady of the Gulf Roman Catholic Ch., Port Lavaca, 1954—; vol. tchr. in music and phys. coordination Calhoun Tng. Center for Retarded, 1962-72. Chmn. Port Lavaca Parks and Recreation Commn., 1975—, Port Lavaca Fine Arts Series, 1976; Calhoun County chmn. Gov.'s First Ladies Vol. Porgram, 1976—. Mem. Nat. Guild Piano Tchrs. (adjudicator), Am. Coll. Musicians, Port Lavaca Art Guild, Jr. League Port Lavaca (pres. 1975-76), North Tex. State U. Alumni Assn., Sigma Alpha Iota, Pi Kappa Lambda. Democrat. Club: Am. Sportsman. Writer music revs. Calhoun Citizen, 1973-76. Home: 717 Westwood St Port Lavaca TX 77979

GRUND, CLARENCE B., JR., elec. utility exec.; b. Portland, Oreg., July 31, 1925; s. Clarence B. and Frances (Eckert) G.; B.E.E., Ala. Poly. Inst., 1951, M.E.E., 1952; m. Marilyn Grace Hornsby, May 2, 1948. Engr. system planning Ala. Power Co., Birmingham, 1953-58; engr. rate dept. So. Services, Inc., Birmingham, 1958-63; supr. research rate dept., 1964-67, asst. mgr. rate dept., 1967-69, mgr. rate dept., 1969-72, asst. v.p., 1972—; instr. Ala. Poly. Inst., 1951-52, extension center U. Ala., 1952. Pres., Rocky Ridge Vol. Fire Dept., 1957-58, bd. dirs., 1956-62. Served with USAAF, World War II. Registered profl. engr., Ala., Miss. Mem. IEEE, Nat. Soc. Profl. Engrs., Birmingham Soc. Engrs., Newcomen Soc. N. Am., Internat. Platform Assn., Am. Legion, Phi Kappa Phi, Tau Beta Pi, Eta Kappa Nu. Contbr. articles to profl. jours. Home: 3421 Cruzan Dr Birmingham AL 35243 Office: Southern Services Inc 64 Perimeter Center E PO Box 720071 Atlanta GA 30346

GUBER, DONALD, ophthalmologist; b. N.Y.C., Dec. 29, 1935; s. Philip and Mildred (Ruderman) G.; B.A., N.Y. U., 1956; M.D., Bowman Gray Sch. Medicine, 1960; m. Ann Harrelson, June 26, 1960; children—Alison Robin, Susan Danette, David Sandler. Intern, Roosevelt Hosp., N.Y.C., 1960-61; resident in ophthalmology Yale U. Coll. Medicine, 1963-66; fellow in pediatric ophthalmology Baylor U., Houston, 1966-67; practice medicine specializing in ophthalmology, Orlando, Fla., 1968—; mem. staff Orange Meml. Hosp., Holiday Hosp.; asst. prof. ophthalmology Baylor U. Coll. Medicine, 1967-68. Served as capt. M.C., USAF, 1961-63. Diplomate Am. Bd. Ophthalmology. Mem. AMA, Fla., Orange County med. assns., Am. Acad. Ophthalmology and Otolaryngology, Contact Lens Assn. Am. Contbr. articles to ophthal. jours. Home: 145 Oakleigh Ln Maitland FL 32751 Office: 1021 E Robinson St Orlando FL 32801

GUBITZ, STEPHEN PAGE, banker; b. Glens Falls, N.Y., Mar. 6, 1935; s. Edwin R. and Viola P. G.; B.A., U. Rochester, 1957; postgrad. U. Rochester, Northwestern U., U. Wis., Harvard Bus. Sch., Am. Inst. Banking; m. Susan Steele, Nov. 30, 1974; children—Christian Steele, Carrie Ray. Bonding rep. Glens Falls Ins. Co. (N.Y.), 1957-60; mktg. dir. Marine Midland Bank, Rochester, N.Y., 1960-72; sr. v.p., dir. mktg. Houston Nat. Bank, 1972—; instr. Am. Inst. Banking. Exec. bd. communications chmn. Sam Houston Area council Boy Scouts Am.; mem. steering com. Camp Fire Girls; mem. Go Texan gen. activities com. Houston Livestock Show and Rodeo, 1980. Mem. Am. Bankers Assn., Tex. Bankers Assn., Bank Mktg. Assn. (past dir.), Am. Mktg. Assn., Houston Advt. Fedn., Houston C. of C., Tex. Arts Alliance, NAM. Club: Brae-Burn Country. Office: Houston Nat Bank PO Box 299001 1010 Milam St Houston TX 77299

GUDE, NANCY CARLSON, systems and programming mgr.; b. Kane, Pa., Aug. 5, 1948; d. Edward Walter and Theo Alberta (Herzog) Carlson; B.A. in History, Pa. State U., 1969; postgrad. U. Central Fla., 1975—; m. Alberto Gude, Jr., June 30, 1973. Programmer, Group Hospitalization, Inc., Washington, 1969-70; programmer analyst Space Age Computer Systems, Washington, 1970-73, Ky. Fried Chicken, Louisville, 1973-75; systems analyst Sentinel Star Co., Orlando, Fla., 1975-77, programming supr., 1977-78, systems and programming mgr., 1978-80, asst. dir. data processing, 1980—; mem. pension/profit sharing adminstrv. com., 1978. Mem. Assn. Systems Mgmt., Assn. Computer Programmers and Analysts. Methodist.

GUDE, WILLIAM D., histology lab. supr.; b. Balt., Feb. 27, 1914; s. William D. and Mary C. (Mullikin) G.; A.B., Tulane U., 1940; M.S. in Zoology, U. Tenn., 1952, M.S. in Indsl. Mgmt., 1959; m. Mary Stebbins, Feb. 14, 1942; children—Patricia L. Gude Creekmore, Katie Lee Gude Dripps. Clin. lab. technician Hotel Dieu Hosp., New Orlenas, 1940-42; histology technician dept. anatomy Sch. Medicine, Tulane U., New Orleans, 1946-48; supr. histology labs. biology div. Oak Ridge (Tenn.) Nat. Lab., 1948—. Active, Rec. for the Blind, Oak Ridge. Served with U.S. Army, 1942-46. Decorated Purple Heart, Bronze Star; mem. AAAS, Tenn. Acad. Scis., Sci. Research Soc., Gerontol. Soc., Assn. Southeastern Biologists, N.Y. Acad. Scis. Lutheran. Author: Autoradiographic Techniques: Localization of Radioisotopes in Biological Material, 1968; researcher aging, glomerulosclerosis, radiation injury. Office: Biology Div PO Box Y Oak Ridge TN 37830

GUDELL, HOWARD ALLEN, city ofcl. Columbus (Ga.); b. Newark, Nov. 5, 1942; s. Siegbert and Etta (Reiss) G.; B.A., Temple U., 1965, M.A., 1968; M. in Urban Planning, N.Y. U., 1970; m. Naomi Gail Berkman, June 23, 1974; children—Seth Evan, Melissa Robin. Intern, N.Y. State Pub. Adminstrn., 1966; urban planner N.Y. State Div. Housing, N.Y.C., 1967; asso. urban planner, N.Y. State Dept. Transp., 1967-70; dir. Model Cities Agy., Cohoes, N.Y., 1970-74; dir. Columbus (Ga.) Dept. Community Devel., 1974-79, exec. dir. Office Econ. Devel., 1979—; cons. Ga. State U. Coll. Urban Affairs, Atlanta, 1979; exec. dir. Valley Council Local Govts., Columbus, 1974-76; project dir. Columbus (Ga.)-Phenix City (Ala.) Transp. Study, 1974—; lectr. Russell Sage Coll., Union Coll., Columbus Coll. Mem. N.Y. State Manpower Planning Bd., 1972-74; mem. United Way, Columbus, 1974—, Shearith Israel Synagogue, Columbus, 1974—, Columbus Arts Council. Mem. Am. Soc. Planning Ofcls., Am. Inst. Planners. Club: B'nai B'rith. Home: 4021 Timbalier Dr Columbus GA 31907 Office: Govt Center PO Box 1340 Columbus GA 31902

GUDGER, LAMAR, Congressman; b. Asheville, N.C., Apr. 30, 1919; s. Vonno Lamar and Elizabeth (Wilson) G.; A.B., U. N.C., Chapel Hill, 1940, LL.B., 1942; m. Eugenia Reid, Oct. 24, 1947; children—Carol Eugenia, Martha Elizabeth, Vonno Lamar, III, Eugene Reid. Admitted to N.C. bar, 1942; mem. firm Gudger & McLean, Asheville; mem. N.C. Ho. of Reps., 1951-52; solicitor 19th Dist., N.C., 1951-54; mem. N.C. Senate, 1971-76; mem. 95th and 96th Congresses from 11th N.C. Dist.; permanent mem. judiciary for 4th Circuit. Bd. stewards Central Meth. Ch.; state sec. N.C. Democratic Party, 1962-63, mem. council, 1965-66. Served to capt. USAAF, 1942-45. Decorated D.F.C., Air medal with 5 oak leaf clusters. Mem. N.C., Buncombe County bar assns., N.C. Jud. Council, Asheville C. of C., VFW. Clubs: Biltmore Forest Country; Mountain City; Asheville City. Office: 428 Cannon House Office Bldg Washington DC 20510

GUDMUNDSEN, ANNE MYERS, nurse, educator; b. Waukegan, Ill., Apr. 18, 1940; d. Glen Isenhour and Grace Alberta (Maier) Myers; B.S. (Harding-Ky Kendall scholar 1958-60), Tex. Woman's U., 1962; M.S., U. Colo., 1967; Ph.D., U. Denver, 1975; children—Richard Andrew, Kathryn Lynne. Instr. Tex. Woman's U., Denton, 1965-66, asso. prof., 1976-77, coordinator doctoral program, 1977-78, asso. dean for grad. studies Coll. Nursing, 1977-78, dean Coll. Nursing, 1978—, provost Inst. Health Scis.; asst. prof. U. Colo., 1967-73; cons. Colo. Dept. Health, 1975-76; grant reviewer div. nursing HEW. Block chmn. March of Dimes, 1967-70; active Another Mother for Peace, 1967—, ARC. Served as lt. (j.g.) Nurse Corps, USN, 1962-65. Mem. Am., Tex. nurses assns., Am. Heart Assn., Sigma Theta Tau, Phi Kappa Delta, Kappa Delta Pi. Author: (with Peggy L. Chinn) Child Health Maintenance, 1974; also articles, book revs., audiovisual prodns. Office: Texas Woman's U Denton TX 76204

GUERRA, FERNANDO AMADO, pediatrician; b. San Antonio, Aug. 11, 1939; s. Fernando P. and Eva V. (Vela) G.; B.S., U. Tex., Austin, 1960; M.D., U. Tex., Galveston, 1964; children—Alicia, Catalina, Roberto, Luis. Intern San Francisco Gen. Hosp., 1964-65; resident in pediatrics U. Tex. Hosp., Galveston, 1967-69; chief resident in pediatrics U. Tex. Health Scis. Center, San Antonio, 1969-70, instr. dept. pediatrics, 1970-71; founder, med. dir. Barrio Children's Clinic, San Antonio, 1971—; practice medicine specializing in pediatrics, San Antonio, 1971—; mem. staff Santa Rosa Children's Hosp., 1969—, vice chmn. dept. pediatrics, 1973—; mem. staff Bapt. Hosp., 1971—, chmn. dept. pediatrics, 1974-76; regional cons. Head Start, 1975—; cons. Early Childhood Edn. for Handicapped, 1971—. Trustee Bexar County Mental Health/Mental Retardation Center, 1971-74, vice chmn., 1974; bd. dirs. Foster Grandparent Project, 1973—, Santa Rosa Med. Center, 1975—. Served to capt. M.C., U.S. Army, 1965-67. Decorated Air medal, Army Commendation medal, Bronze Star medal. Diplomate Am. Bd. Pediatrics. Fellow Am. Acad. Pediatrics; mem. AMA, Am. Pub. Health Assn., Tex. Pediatric Soc. Roman Catholic. Office: 343 W Houston St Suite 406 San Antonio TX 78205

GUERRA, MIRTHA, accountant; b. Havana, Cuba, Mar. 11, 1946; d. Jose R. and Mirtha (Regalado) Guerra; came to U.S., 1961, naturalized, 1970; B.B.A., U. Miami, 1972. Accountant, Ernst & Ernst, Miami, 1972—. Active United Way Dade County. Mem. Am. Soc. Women Accountants (pres.), Am., Fla. insts. C.P.A.'s, Am. Woman Soc. C.P.A.'s. Office: 1 Biscayne Tower Suite 2700 Miami FL 33131

GUERRA, ROLANDO ANTONIO, automobile parts distbg. co. exec.; b. Laredo, Tex., Sept. 15, 1934; s. Armengol and Leandra (Castano) G.; student pub. schs., Laredo; m. Felipa Arriaga, Mar. 14, 1954; children—Rolando, Patricio, Adolfo, David, Ana, Melida, Bernadette, Raquel. Credit mgr. Guerra Hardware Co., Laredo, 1954-60; sales mgr. Laredo Hardware Co., 1960-62, dir., 1960—; sec., treas. Laredo Motor Mart, 1963-73, v.p., store mgr., 1973—, also dir.; gen. partner Armengol & Guerra Investments. Chmn. Webb County Republican Party, 1971-72, vice chmn. exec. com., 1972-77; dist. v.p. Tex. PTA, 1974-78; mem. dist. adv. council SBA, 1971-72. Named Man of Year, Laredo Times, 1973. Mem. Automotive Service Industry Am., Automotive Wholesalers Tex., Laredo C. of C. Roman Cath. Club: Laredo Noon Optimist (past v.p.). Home: 2302 Elm St Laredo TX 78040 Office: 1202 Houston St Laredo TX 78040

GUERRERO, MICHAEL C., mech. engr.; b. Havana, Cuba, Dec. 6, 1941; s. Leandro M. and Fredesvinda R. (Calonge) G.; came to U.S., 1961, naturalized, 1969; B.S. in Mech. Engring., U. Miami (Fla.), 1965; M.S. in Mech. Engring., U. Mo., 1968; m. Alina de los Reyes, Aug. 31, 1963; children—Alina M., Lisa A. Research engr. Shell Oil Co., Wood River, Ill., 1965-69; design and devel. engr. div. computer systems RCA, Palm Beach Gardens, Fla., 1969-71; mgr. instrument mfg. engring. instrument mfg. Dade div. Am. Hosp. Supply Corp., Miami, Fla., 1971—. Cons. engr. and gen. contractor. Alumni asso. Sch. Engring. U. Miami. Recipient DADE Sci. award, 1975. Registered profl. engr., Fla. Mem. ASME, Nat. Soc. Profl. Engrs., Fla. Engring. Soc., Tau Beta Pi, Pi Mu Epsilon. Republican. Roman Catholic. Patentee in field. Home: 10240 SW 84th Ave Miami FL 33156 Office: 9750 NW 25th St Miami FL 33122

GUGINO, HILAH A., psychiat. nurse; b. North Tonawanda, N.Y., Jan. 3, 1940; d. Henry O. and Ann (Sebold) Smith; grad. Mercy Hosp. Sch. Nursing, Buffalo, 1960; student U. Ga., 1965, U. Md., 1966-67; B.S.N., Med. Coll. Ga., 1977; M.S.N., Emory U., 1978; children—Lisa Ann, John Louis. Nursing supr. Brooks Meml. Hosp., Dunkirk, N.Y., 1961-64; pvt. duty rehab. nurse, Athens, Ga., 1969; psychiat. nurse, coordinator Clarke County Alcoholism and Drug Abuse Clinic, Athens, 197—72; psychiat. nurse clinician Manatee County Guidance Center, Inc., Bradenton, Fla., 1972-73; head nurse psychiat. unit Athens Gen. Hosp., 1973-74, unit dir., 1974-77; instr. psychiat. nursing Med. Coll. Ga., Augusta, 1978-79, clin. instr. continuing edn., 1979—; psychiat. clin. nurse specialist Avalon Psychiat. Clinic and Center for Personnel Growth, Athens, 1979—; nurse educator Ga. Retardation Center, Athens, 1979—. Home: 130 Woodlands Rd Watkinsville GA 30677

GUGLIELMINO, PAUL JOSEPH, mktg. and mgmt. cons.; b. Bklyn., May 19, 1942; s. Carl and Rose (Loreto) G.; B.A. in English, The Citadel, 1964; M.A. in Advt., U. Ga., 1970, Ed.D. in Adult and Continuing Edn., 1978; m. Lucy Margaret Madsen, June 31, 1965; children—Joseph Allen, Margaret Rose. Mktg. analyst Shell Chem. Co., N.Y.C., 1966-67; asst. dir. pub. relations The Citadel, Charleston, S.C., 1967-69; propr. Cobblestone Tours, Charleston, 1970-71; pres. Communica Inc., Savannah, Ga., 1970—; asst. prof., dir. Center for Mgmt. and Profl. Devel., Fla. Atlantic U., Boca Raton, 1977—. Served to capt. AUS, 1964-66. Mem. Adult Edn. Assn. U.S., Am. Mktg. Assn., Am. Soc. Tng. and Devel., Nat. Univ. Extension Assn. Contbr. articles to profl. jours. Home: 734 Marble Way Boca Raton FL 33431 Office: Center Mgmt and Profl Devel Fla Atlantic U Boca Raton FL 33431

GUIDRY, LAWRENCE SAL, psychologist, educator; b. New Orleans, Aug. 20, 1937; s. Gillis Everett and Thelma Francis (Kurtz) G.; Ph.D., U. So. Miss., 1973; m. Brynn Ann Kessler, June 8, 1972; 1 son, Brett Lawrence. Instr., U. New Orleans, 1965-68; staff psychologist Loyola U. Counseling Center, New Orleans, 1972-73; staff psychologist VA Hosp., New Orleans, 1973—; clin. asst. prof. psychiatry neurology Tulane U. Med. Sch., New Orleans, 1975—; clin. asst. prof. psychiatry and neurology in psychology La. State U. Med. Sch., 1978—. Lic. psychologist, La. Clin. fellow Behavior Therapy Research Soc. Contbr. articles in field to research jours. Home: 4716 Bissonet Dr Metairie LA 70003 Office: 433 Metairie Rd Metairie LA 70005

GUIHURT, ORLANDO FEDERICO, engring. exec.; b. Colombia, Oct. 8, 1941; came to U.S., 1964, naturalized, 1978; s. Federico and Maria (Diaz) G.; B.S. in Mech. Engring., U. P.R., 1966; m. Blanca Perez, Aug. 30, 1969; children—Orlando, Glorimar, Brenda, Betsy. Engr. inspection office Mayaguez (P.R.) Med. Center, 1966-70; engr. Rexach Constrn. Co., Ponce, P.R., 1970-72; dir. plant services Hosp. Damas, Ponce, 1972-77, Auxilio Mutuo Hosp., Hato Rey, P.R., 1977-78, Mcpl. Hosp. of Ponce, 1977-79; engring. mgr. Travenol Labs., Carolina, P.R., 1979—; cons. safety and sanitation engr. Hosp. Fernandez-Garcia, Hato Rey. Mem. Colegio de Ingenieros de P.R., Mech. Engring. Inst. (sec. bd. dirs.), P.R. Soc. Hosp. Engring. (v.p.), Am. Soc. Hosp. Engring, ASHRAE. Club: Lions (Ponce). Home: Cond Hato Rey Plaza 9B Hato Rey PR 00918 Office: Box 1374 Hato Rey PR 00919

GUILARTE, PEDRO MANUEL, utility co. exec.; b. Cuba, May 19, 1952; s. Miguel G. and Emma G.; B.S. in Indsl. Engring. (scholar), Northwestern U., 1975; M.B.A., Washington U., St. Louis, 1977; cert. systems dynamics MIT, 1978; m. Zulima Piedra, May 26, 1979. Market analyst Cummins Engine Co., Columbus, Ind., 1976; planning analyst Fla. Power & Light Co., Miami, 1977—. Consortium for Grad. Study in Bus. fellow, 1975-77. Mem. Northwestern U. Alumni Admission Council (dir. S. Fla. region 1979—), Planning Execs. Inst. Republican. Methodist. Home: 13232 SW 12th Ln Miami FL 33184 Office: PO Box 529100 Miami FL 33152

GUILFORD, ROGER ELLORY, engr.; b. Enterprise, Ala., July 14, 1943; s. Mark and Nunnie Rebecca (Grimes) G.; B.E.E., Auburn U., 1965; children—Roger Ellory, William Mark, Jennifer Lee. Engr., Plantation Pipe Line Co., Baton Rouge, 1965-69, Atlanta, 1969-74, project mgr.-automation, Atlanta, 1974—; project engr., Ratliffe and Assos., Atlanta, 1974; instr., Internat. Sch. Hydrocarbon Measurement, Norman, Okla., 1974. Registered profl. engr., Ga. Mem. IEEE, Am. Petroleum Inst. (com. on dynamic measurement, com. on pipeline cybernetics). Club: Theta Chi. Home: 2087 Capehart Circle Atlanta GA 30345 Office: 3390 Peachtree Rd NE PO Box 18616 Atlanta GA 30326

GUILLEN, WANDA VAUGHN, med. records adminstr.; b. Chatsworth, Ga., Nov. 3, 1935; d. Winfred Ray and Bertha Inez (Hickey) Vaughn; A.A. with honors, Dalton Jr. Coll., 1973; B. Med. Sci., Emory U., 1975; m. Efrain Guillen, Aug. 23, 1969; children—Ricky, Kinmia, Kara, David. Health record analyst Meml. Hosp., Chattanooga, 1973-75; review coordinator Tenn. Found. for Med. Care, Inc., 1975-77; clin. instr. Sch. of Allied Health, U. Ala., Birmingham, 1977—; affiliate dir. Center for Health Scis., U. Tenn., Memphis, 1977—; dir. med. records Baroness Erlanger Hosp., T.C. Thompson Children's Hosp., Chattanooga, 1977—; clin. instr. Emory U. Sch. Medicine, Atlanta, 1977—; cons. Tri-County Hosp., Fort Oglethorpe, Ga., 1975—, Dodson Ave. Health Center, Chattanooga, 1977—, Alton Park Health Center, Chattanooga, 1977—. Recipient Meritorious award Am. Cancer Soc. Mem. Am. Med. Record Assn., Tenn. Med. Record Assn., Chattanooga Area Med. Record Assn. (chmn. edn. com. 1975-76), Tenn. Assn. for Rev. Coordinators (dir., treas. 1976-77), Bus. and Profl. Women's Orgn., Phi Theta Kappa. Baptist. Home: Route 5 Dogwood Circle Cleveland TN 37311 Office: 975 E 3rd St Chattanooga TN 36403

GUILLORY, JOSEPH ARNOLD, audiologist; b. Opelousas, La., Feb. 25, 1948; s. Alcide J. and Pearl (Fruge) G.; B.A., U. Southwestern La., 1967, M.S., 1973, M.S., 1978; m. Peggy Ann Meullion, Aug. 21, 1971; 1 son, Brandon. Speech therapist St. Landry Parish Sch. Bd., Opelousas, 1969-70, audiologist, 1970—, dir. speech lang. and hearing program, 1977—; cons. in field. Mem. Am. Speech and Hearing Assn. (cert. clin. competence), La. Speech and Hearing Assn., Am. Auditory Soc., Soc. Ear, Nose and Throat Advancement in Children, NEA, Alpha Phi Alpha. Roman Catholic. Home: 441 N Walnut St Opelousas LA 70570 Office: 251 Blair St Opelousas LA 70570

GUIN, J(UNIUS) FOY, JR., judge; b. Russellville, Ala., Feb. 2, 1924; s. Junius Foy and Ruby (Pace) G.; student Ga. Inst. Tech., 1940-41; J.D., U. Ala., 1947; LL.D., Magic Valley Christian Coll., 1963; m. Dorace Jean Caldwell, July 18, 1945; children—Janet Elizabeth Smith, Judith Ann Mullican, Junius Foy III, David Jonathan. Admitted to Ala. bar, 1948; practiced in Russellville; sr. partner firm Guin, Guin, Bouldin & Porch, Russellville, 1948-73; fed. dist. judge, Birmingham, Ala., 1973—; pres. Abstract Trust Co., Inc.; sec. Iuka TV Cable Co., Inc., Haleyville TV Cable Co., Inc.; dir., gen. counsel First Nat. Bank Russellville, Franklin Fed. Savs. & Loan Assn. Russellville. Mem. adv. com. civil practice and procedure Supreme Ct. Ala., 1971—; chmn. Ala. Jud. Commn., 1972—; Commr. Ala. Bar, 1965-73, 2d v.p., 1969-70, active World Peace Through Law Center. Chmn. Russellville City Planning Com., 1954-57; county chmn. Republican party, 1954-58, 71—, state fin. chmn., 1972—; candidate for U.S. Senator from Ala., 1954. Served to 1st lt., inf. U.S. Army, 1943-46. Mem. Am. Radio Relay League, Am. Counsel Assn., Assn. Ins. Attys., Am. Bar Assn. (mem. spl. com. on residential real estate transactions 1972—), Ala. Bar Assn. (com. chmn. 1965—), Franklin County Bar Assn., Ala. Law Inst. (dir. 1969—), Am. Trial Lawyers Assn., Ala. Def. Lawyers Assn., Ala. Plaintiffs Lawyers Assn., Farrah Law soc. Farah Order jurisprudence, Phi Beta Kappa, Delta Chi. Mem. Ch. of Christ (elder 1969—). Club: Rotary. Home: 3308 Overton Rd Birmingham AL 35223 Office: Fed Courthouse Birmingham AL 35203

GUINN, DAVID CRITTENDEN, engr., drilling and exploration co. exec.; b. Port Arthur, Tex., Nov. 29, 1926; s. Leland Lee and Corrie Andrews (Avery) G.; A.A., Lamar Inst. Tech., 1948; B.S. in Petroleum Engring., U. Tex. at Austin, 1951; m. Marguerite V. Guinn, Oct. 7, 1966; children—Susan, David, Jay, Jeffrey. Engr. trainee Dowell, Inc., Alice, Tex., 1949; petroleum engr. Calif. Co., Lafayette, La., 1951-52, area prodn. and drilling engr., Venice, La., 1952-54, evaluation engr., New Orleans, 1954-55; dist. engr. Republic Natural Gas Co., 1955-56, div. drilling engr., 1956-57; div. engr. Shaffer Tool Works, Inc., 1957-63, sales mgr., Midcontinent div., Beaumont, 1963-65; div. mgr. Mid-Continent-Gulf Coast div., 1965-67; pvt. practice as cons. petroleum engr., New Orleans, 1957, Houston, 1967—; owner of Guinn and Assos., Engrs., Guinn Internation, Inc.; founder Internat. Subsea Devel. Corp., Atlantic Ocean Service Center, Inc., Mission Drilling and Exploration Corp., Tropic Drilling and Exploration Co.; pres. Consol. Offshore Corp., 1978—; part-owner drill ship Tainaron. Served from pvt. to cadet USAAF, 1943-46. Registered profl. engr., La., Tex. Mem. Nat., Tex. socs. profl. engrs., ASME, Am. Inst. Mining and Metall. Engrs., Soc. Petroleum Engrs., Internat. Assn. Drilling Contractors, Houston Engring. and Sci. Soc., Marine Tech. Soc., Am. Soc. Oceanology, Nomads, Internat. Oceanographic Found., SAR. Clubs: Pine Forest Country, Houston (Houston). Lakeway Country (Austin, Tex.). Contbr. articles to profl. jours. Pioneer, patentee in domestic and fgn. offshore and floating vessel drilling, offshore petroleum subsea prodn. systems. Home: 7910 Beverly Hill Ln Houston TX 77063 Office: Suite 400 2650 Fountainview Houston TX 77057

GUINSBURG, PHILIP FRIED, clin. psychologist; b. N.Y.C., Sept. 13, 1946; s. Theodore and Elena (Fried) G.; B.A., Columbia U., 1968; M.A., U. N.D., 1970, Ph.D., 1973; m. Debrah Josias, June 15, 1968; children—Mark Jeffrey, Michael Scott. Staff psychologist, then clin. dir. Nashville Drug Treatment Center, 1973-77, out-patient coordinator, asso. dir. center, 1977—; practice with firm Bell, Stepbach, Guinsburg & Cooper, Nashville, 1974—; instr. Vol. State Community Coll., Gallatin, Tenn., 1973-77; oral examiner Licensing Bd. Healing Arts in Psychology, 1974—; bd. dirs. Nashville Child Care Center, 1975-76, Crisis Intervention Center, 1977—. N.D. Bd. Edn. scholar, 1971, NIMH fellow, 1972. Mem. Am. Psychol. Assn., Tenn. Psychol. Assn., Am. Acad. Psychotherapists, Nat. Register Health Service Providers in Psychology. Jewish. Author papers. Home: 8121 Maryland Ln Brentwood TN 37027 Office: 1918 Church St Nashville TN 37203

GUITTAR, LEE JOHN, newspaper exec.; b. St. Louis, May 4, 1931; s. LeRoy and Edna Mae (Johnston) G.; A.B., Columbia U., 1953; M.B.A., U. Mass., 1962; m. Joan Mayo, Sept. 13, 1952 (div. Aug. 1979); children—David Lee, Stephen Joseph, Mitchell John, Jeanne Marie, Richard Laughran. With Gen. Electric Co., Schenectady, 1955-63, mgr. community and govt. relations programs, N.Y.C., 1963-65; mgr. employee and public relations Tidewater Oil Co., N.Y.C., 1965-66; dir. personnel, circulation dir. Miami (Fla.) Herald Pub. Co., 1967-72; v.p., bus. mgr. Detroit Free Press, Inc., 1972-74, v.p., gen. mgr., 1974-75, pres., dir., 1975-77; pub. Dallas Times Herald, 1977—. Bd. dirs. Dallas Citizens Council, Goals for Dallas, ARC, United Way, Central Bus. Dist. Assn. Served to lt. (j.g.) USNR, 1953-55. Mem. Nat. Press Club, Am. Press Inst., Am. Newspaper Pubs. Assn., Dallas C. of C. (dir.), Phi Beta Kappa. Republican. Roman Catholic. Clubs: City, Lancers, Bent Tree Country (Dallas). Office: 1101 Pacific St Dallas TX 75202

GULAK, MORTON BLUM, architect; b. Pitts., Sept. 21, 1938; s. Meyer J. and Bessie (Isack) G.; B.Arch., Pa. State U., 1961; M.Urban and Regional Planning, Va. Poly. Inst., 1972; postgrad. U. Pa., 1974-76; m. Paula S. Paster, May 28, 1967; children—Loren, Misha. Archtl. apprentice various firms, Pitts., Arlington, Va., 1964-68; partner Twitchell, Allen, Gulak, Sarasota, Fla., 1968-70; asso. prof. urban studies and planning Va. Commonwealth U., Richmond, 1972—; cons. in architecture, planning, urban design. Mem. Richmond Urban Design Com., 1979—. Served to lt. USN, 1961-64. Mem. Am. Inst. Planners (chmn. awards com. Va. 1978), AIA, Nat. Council Archtl. Registration Bds., Alpha Epsilon Pi, Phi Kappa Phi, Tau Sigma Delta. Democrat. Jewish. Home: 1509 Grove Ave Richmond VA 23220 Office: 812 W Franklin St Richmond VA 23284

GULATI, JAGJIT, EDP adminstr.; b. Lahore Pakistan, Oct. 8, 1939; s. Mithe Shah and Sita Devi (Subo Bhab) G.; came to U.S., 1969; M.A. in English, U. Delhi, 1964; M.A. in Lit., Panjabi U., 1966; B.E., Darbhanga U., 1968; asso. ins., Chartered Inst. Ins., 1967; grad. programming tech. Control Data Inst., 1970; m. Margaret Pruett, Apr. 11, 1971; 1 dau., Annita Belle. Ins. underwriter Oriental Ins. Co., New Delhi, 1961-69; ops. mgr. Control Data Corp., Beltsville, Md., 1970-73; EDP mgr. N.C. A. and T. State U., Greensboro, 1974—; tchr. computer sci.; cons. EDP. Home: 2704 W Market St Greensboro NC 27403 Office: 313 Dudley St Greensboro NC 27411

GULDE, ROBERT EMMETT, cardiologist; b. Amarillo, Tex., May 10, 1934; s. John Fidelis and Philippina Marie (Lutz) G.; B.S., U. Notre Dame, 1956; M.D., St. Louis U., 1960; children—Lauri, Marjorie, Robert, Michele, Michael. Intern, St. Joseph's Hosp., Denver, 1960-61, resident, 1961-62; resident Hermann Hosp., Houston, 1962-64, Tex. Children's Hosp.-St. Luke's Hosp., Houston, 1963-64; spl. fellow in cardiovascular disease Cleve. Clinic, 1964-66; instr. dept. cardiology Naval Med. Sch., Bethesda, Md., 1966-68; staff cardiologist Nat. Naval Med. Center, 1966-68; staff cardiologist St. Anthony's Hosp., Amarillo, 1968—, chief cardiopulmonary lab., 1968-72; staff cardiologist High Plains Baptist Hosp., Amarillo, 1968—; staff cardiologist Northwest Tex. Hosp., Amarillo, 1968—; cons. cardiologist VA Hosp., Amarillo, 1972-77, chief cardiology, 1977, 78; asso. clin. prof. U. Tex., Lubbock, 1972— dir. The Heart Inst., CARE, Amarillo, 1975—. Served as lt. comdr. USNR, 1966-68. Diplomate Am. Bd. Internal Medicine. Fellow Am. Coll. Chest Physicians, Am. Coll. Cardiology, Soc. Cardiac Angiography; mem. AMA, Tex. Med. Assn., Potter-Randall County Med. Soc., A.C.P., Tex. Soc. Internal Medicine, Amarillo Soc. Internal Medicine. Roman Catholic. Club: Rotary. Contbr. articles to profl. jours. Home: 1601 Rusk St Amarillo TX 79102 Office: 1901 Medi-Park St Suite 1010 Amarillo TX 79106

GULLAHORN, JACK WALLACE, lawyer; b. Austin, Tex., Jan. 15, 1948; s. Wallace Sentell and Nan Marie (Smith) G.; B.A., Trinity U., 1970; J.D., U. Tex., 1973; m. Patricia Ann Hogan, Dec. 30, 1971; children—Ryan Sentell, Andrew Hogan, Daniel Jackson. Admitted to Tex. bar, 1973; com. counsel Tex. House Interim Com. on Water, 1973-75; legal counsel, exec. asst. to Speaker of Tex. Ho. of Reps., Austin, 1975-78; pres. Roan & Gullahorn, P.C., Austin, 1978—; com. counsel Tex. Ho. of Reps. Impeachment Com., 1975; dir. Tex. Navy, Inc. Mem. Travis County Bar Assn., Tex. Bar Assn. Roman Catholic. Home: 3902 Cresthill Austin TX 78731 Office: San Jacinto Bldg Suite 407 Austin TX 78701

GULLATT, V(ICTOR) REID, physician; b. Cochran, Ga., Jan. 26, 1923; s. Victor Reid and Mary (McVay) G.; B.S., U.S. Naval Acad., 1945; M.D., Med. Coll. Ga., 1955; m. Margie Carlton, June 9, 1945; children—Mary Burdick, Pam Triay, Betsy McDonald, Victor Reid, Sally. Intern, Univ. Hosp., Augusta, Ga., 1955-56; gen. practice medicine, Cochran, Ga., 1956-62; physician VA med. centers, Bay Pines and Gainesville, Fla., 1962-79; chief med. officer VA Ambulatory Care Clinic, St. Petersburg, Fla.; clin. asst. prof. medicine U. Ga., 1959-62, U. Fla., 1971-77, U. South Fla., 1978—; VA leadership, 1979; sr. aviation med. examined and accident investigator FAA, 1974—. Served to capt. USN, 1945-50, with M.C., USNR, 1941—. Diplomate Am. Bd. Family Practice. Mem. Fla. Med. Assn., Pinellas County Med. Soc. Contbr. articles to med. jours. Home: 5671 Bayview Dr N Seminole FL 33542 Office: VA Medical Center Bay Pines FL 33504

GULLICKSON, JOHN CHARLES, mfg. co. exec.; b. Chattanooga, Oct. 5, 1940; s. Charles Henry and Florence Virginia (Higgins) G.; B.S., Ga. Inst. Tech., 1964; LL.D., Emory U., 1966; m. Nancy Ann Bowen, June 25, 1966; children—Jay Weldon, Christine Lee. Indsl. engr. Sweetheart Plastics, Conyers, Ga., 1970-72; adminstrv. asst. to exec. v.p., corp. counsel Owen of Ga., Inc., Lawrenceville, 1972—; arbitrator nat. panel Am. Arbitration Assn. Chmn. adv. com. Gwinnett County (Ga.) United Way; bd. dirs. Atlanta Met. United Way, 1976-78, Mental Health Assn. Met. Atlanta. Served with U.S. Navy, 1966-69. Decorated Bronze Star; recipient NASA Apollo Achievement award, 1969; Atlanta Met. United Way Appreciation award, 1978. Roman Catholic.

GULLY, DONNA MAYRELOYD PAYNE, speech pathologist; b. Austin, Tex., Feb. 13, 1944; d. Lloyd W. and Milda (Vasterling) Payne; B.S. in Edn., S.W. Tex. State U., 1963; divorced; children—Kent Lloyd, Lauren Larie. Speech therapist Austin Ind. Sch. Dist., 1964-68, 69—; laryngologist LBJ Human Opportunities Corp., Austin, 1969; office speech therapist for laryngologist, 1969. Methodist. Home: 2702 Cedarview St Austin TX 78704 Office: Cannuth Annex 6101 Dillard Circle Austin TX 78752

GUMMELT, ELWYN FREDERICK, educator; b. Hallettsville, Tex., Oct. 15, 1920; s. Gustave Emil and Emily Christine (Kaase) G.; B.S., Colo. State U., 1947; B.S., Concordia Tchrs. Coll., 1948; M.L., U. Houston, 1954; Ph.D., Tex. A. and M. U., 1974; m. Mattie Pearl Fegette, Jan. 29, 1945; children—James E., Barbara S., Mary B., William L. Tchr., Trinity Luth. Sch., Houston, 1948-49; asst. prin., tchr. Houston Luth. High Sch., 1949-58; faculty Concordia Coll., Austin, Tex., 1958-59; research ship radio officer, oceanographer Tex. A. and M. U., Galveston, 1959-60; faculty Victoria (Tex.) Coll., 1968—, counselor, 1970—. Mayor, Veterans Village (Colo.), 1946-47. Served with USMC, 1941-45, 50-51, Tex. State Guard, 1979—. Mem. Tex. Jr. Coll. Tchrs. Assn., Jr. Coll. Student Personnel Assn. Tex., Internat. Reading Assn., Tex. State Guard Assn., N.G. Assn. Tex., Am. Physics Tchrs. Assn. Democrat. Lutheran. Clubs: Lions, Deutsche Heimat. Author: Physical Science: A Simple Survey, 1963; contbr. articles to profl. jours. Home: 111 Sussex Dell St Victoria TX 77901 Office: 2200 Red River St Victoria TX 77901

GUMNICK, JAMES LOUIS, research inst. adminstr.; b. Balt., Oct. 5, 1930; s. Michael and Mary Rose (Schap) G.; B.S. summa cum laude, Loyola Coll., Balt., 1953; Ph.D., U. Notre Dame, 1958; m. Jean Kathleen Lawler, Oct. 30, 1959; children—John, Anne, Edward, Mary, Jane, Elizabeth. Teaching fellow U. Notre Dame, 1954-57; chmn. dept. physics Loyola Coll. and prin. scientist Martin Marietta Corp., Balt., 1957-64; dir. research ITT Indsl. Labs., Ft. Wayne, Ind., 1964-68; dir. elec. engring. dept. Franklin Inst., Phila., 1968-72, dir. system sci. dept., 1970-72; v.p. programs University City Sci. Center, Phila., 1972-76; dir. research devel. U. Houston, 1976-80; gen. mgr. Gulf Univs. Research Consortium, Houston, 1980—; chmn. bd. Asso. Western Univs., 1979-80; Martin-Loyola prof. physics, 1957-64; chmn. govt. programs com. Pa. Gov.'s Energy Council, 1973-74; exec. dir. Nat. Council Energy Conservation, 1973-76. cons. in field. Vice pres. Russell Elem. Parent Tchr. Orgn., Phila. 1974-75; mem. Radnor-Marple-Haverford Townships (Pa.) Sewer Authority, 1975-76; mem. parish council St. Anastasia Parish, Phila., 1974-76; chmn. social ministry com. Holy Ghost Parish, Houston, 1979—. Danforth fellow, 1953-55. Mem. Am. Phys. Soc., AAAS, Nat. Council Univ. Adminstrs., Am. Mgmt. Assn., Soc. Research Adminstrs., Soc. Univ. Patent Adminstrs., Sigma Xi, Alpha Sigma Nu. Club: Marilyn Estates Swim (pres. 1977-78). Discovered cyclic migration of cesium on refractory metals, 1962; invented multiple reflection photocathode efficiency enhancement, 1966. Office: Gulf Univs Research Consortium 5909 W Loop S Bellaire TX 77401

GUMPRECHT, DONALD LAMBERT, chemist, chem. co. mktg. exec.; b. Fresno, Cal., Nov. 10, 1923; s. Henry H. and Doris E. (Lambert) G.; student Quincy (Ill.) Coll., 1945; B.S. in Chemistry, U. N.C., 1949; m. Blanche B. Condon, July 3, 1970; children from previous marriage—Nancy (Mrs. Eugene Barnes), Mary (Mrs. Robert Culwell), Donna (Mrs. Robert Wilson), Carol (Mrs. Ronnie Miller). Research chemist Shell Chem. Corp., Houston, 1949-54; chief chemist Alkydol Labs., Cicero, Ill., 1954-56; mgr. specialty resins mktg. So. div., Market Devel. Lab. mgr. Reichhold Chems. Inc., Tuscaloosa, Ala., 1956—. Served with USAAF, 1943-45. Fellow Am. Inst. Chemists (accredited profl. chemist); mem. Ala. Acad. Sci. Am. Chem. Soc. (program chmn. 1962-65), (treas. chpt. 1965-69). Methodist (treas. 1975-80). Reviewer Forest Products Jour., 1970—. Contbr. articles to profl. jours. Patentee in field. Home: Route 4 Box 99 Tuscaloosa AL 35405 Office: Reichhold Chems Inc Tuscaloosa AL 35403

GUNBY, WILLIAM RICHARDSON, JR., constrn. co. exec., educator; b. Tampa, Fla., Feb. 20, 1931; s. William Richardson and Violet (Eversole) G.; student Centre Coll., 1950; B.Bldg. Constrn., U. Fla., 1953; M.B.A., Stetson U., 1972; m. Ethelind North Roberts, 1960 (div. 1974); children—Robert, Richard, Greer, Adrienne. Archtl. engr., Atlanta, 1957-59; archtl. engr., Jacksonville, Fla., 1960-69, constrn. mgr., 1970-71, constrn. cons., 1971-75; pres. Fla. North Central Co., Inc., Gainesville, 1979—; v.p. Black Forest Builders, Inc., Gainesville, 1978—; partner Gunby-Halperin Properties, Gainesville, 1977—; prof. Sch. Bldg. Constrn., U. Fla., Gainesville, 1973—. Served to capt. USAF, 1953-68. Named Tchr. of Yr., Coll. Architecture, U. Fla., 1978. Mem. Am. Inst. Constructors, Asso. Schs. Constrn. (dir. S.E. region), Soc. Cincinnati, Kappa Alpha Order. Episcopalian. Clubs: Univ. (Jacksonville); Ponte Vedra. Home: 2313 Costa Verde Blvd Jacksonville Beach FL 32250 Office: Sch Bldg Constrn U Fla Gainesville FL 32611

GUNKEL, FRANCES MARIE, nurse; b. Elk City, Okla., Jan. 11, 1952; d. Jack Elvin and Ada Marie (Weiss) G.; A.D. in Nursing, Odessa (Tex.) Coll., 1972; B.S.N., W.Tex. State U., 1975. Charge nurse Midland (Tex.) Meml. Hosp., 1972-73; inservice dir., infection control nurse, public relations dir. Women's and Children's Hosp., Odessa, 1975—; leader workshops. Mem. Shakespeare Festival Com. Odessa, 1978—. Mem. Am. Diabetes Assn., Am. Heart Assn., Am. Cancer Soc., Assn. Infection Control Practitioners, Am. Soc. Tng. and Devel. (nat. liason del. 1975-77), Am. Bus. Women's Assn., Tex. Perinatal Assn., Tex. Soc. Hosp. Educators, Tex. Soc. Infection Control Practitioners, Tex. Hosp. Assn., Globe of Gt. S.W. Juliet Soc. Democrat. Lutheran. Club: Altrusa. Home: 1709 Beverly St Odessa TX 79761 Office: 520 E 6th St Odessa TX 79760

GUNN, EDWARD MANSFIELD, physician, med. cons.; b. Providence, Oct. 25, 1913; s. Stanley Morton and Emily (Mansfield) G.; student R.I. State Coll., 1935; M.D., Syracuse U., 1939; m. Audrey R. Hopson, May 30, 1936; children—Wendy (Mrs. Herbert Arthur John Wickenden), Edward Mansfield. Physician-educator Civil Service, Dept. Army, 1946-52; intern Charles V. Chapin, Providence Lying-In, R.I. hosps., Providence, 1939-40; med. dir. Sonoco Products Co., 1952-55; cons. occupational medicine, 1955—. Served from 1st lt. to col. M.C., AUS, 1940-46. Fellow Am. Occupational Med. Assn.; mem. Am. Acad. Occupational Medicine, Mil. Surgeons Assn. U.S., Beaufort County Med. Soc., S.C. Med. Assn., USCG Aux. (comdr. flotilla), Am. Assn. Sr. Physicians, AMA, S.C. Hist. Soc., Navy League. Clubs: Yacht (Hilton Head Island, S.C.); U.S. Yacht Racing Union. Travelled, profl. cons. in Africa, Near, Middle and Far East. Home: 10 Marsh Wren Rd Sea Pines Plantation Hilton Head Island SC 29928

GUNTER, JOSEF KARL, inventor, textile machinery co. exec.; b. Durham, N.C., June 29, 1930; s. Elbert Colie and Swanie Blanch (Mims) G.; student N.C. State Coll., 1951-52; grad. Army Intelligence Sch., Balt., 1954; grad. Artillary Officers Sch., Fort Sill, Okla., 1955; short course for execs. of the textile industry, N.C. State Coll.; m. Betty Maness, Mar. 27, 1954; children—3 daus. Prospected for gold, held various jobs, Alaska, 1950-51; v.p., gen. mgr. Engring. Reproduction & Services, Inc., Durham, N.C., 1952-53; sales engr. Triangle Electric Motor Co., Durham, 1957-59, Deutsch Co., Banning, Calif., 1959-60; pres., chmn. bd. Gunter & Cooke, Inc., Durham, 1960—; mem. U.S. Dist. Export Council, 1978—. Served to 1st lt. U.S. Army, 1953-57. Mem. Am. Soc. Inventors, So. Textile Assn., Durham Engrs. Club. Contbr. articles in field to profl. jours.; presented tech. papers at conferences; invented Gunter's Card Drive, co-inventor Super Card High Production Carding System. Home: 5205 Sourwood Rd Durham NC 27712 Office: 3333 Industrial Dr Durham NC 27704

GUNTHARP, PATRICIA ANN, nurse; b. Decatur, Ala., Nov. 12, 1944; d. William Bryant and Virginia Mae (Brady) Moses; student Birmingham Bapt. Hosp. Sch. Nursing, 1963-65, U. Ala., 1963-65; R.N., Meth. Hosp., 1968; B.S., Athens (Ala.) State Coll., 1976; m. Grady Elvis Guntharp, Jr., Apr. 21, 1967; children—Anthony Todd, Angelia Michelle. Staff nurse to head nurse Bapt. Meml. Hosp., Memphis, 1968-71; pediatric supr. Decatur (Ala.) Gen. Hosp., 1971-77; pediatric nursing care coordinator Parkland meml. Hosp., Dallas, Tex., 1977—; lectr. Calhoun Community Coll.; tchr. mother's aide classes ARC, also bd. dirs. Morgan County chpt. Mem. Am., Ala., Tex., Dist. nurses assns. Baptist. Home: 604 Cypress Dr Euless TX 76039

GUPTA, SURINDER NATH, neurol. surgeon; b. Patiala, India, July 30, 1938; came to U.S., 1968, naturalized, 1978; s. Ishwar C. and Maya G.; M.B., B.S., Patiala Med. Coll., 1961; m. Urmil Mirchia, Dec., 1966; children—Tina, Ramona, Suneel. Intern, Deaconess Hosp., Cleve., 1968-69; resident in neurosurgery U. Ark. Med. Center, Little Rock, 1970-73; practice medicine specializing in neurol. surgery, Hot Springs, Ark., 1973—; mem. staff St. Joseph Hosp., Ouchita Meml. Hosp. Mem. Garland County Med. Soc., Ark. Med. Assn., Congress of Neurol. Surgeons, Internat. Congress of Neurol. Surgeons, Am. Assn. Neurol. Surgeons. Clubs: Rotary, Hot Springs Country. Office: 606 Central Tower Hot Springs AR 71901

GUPTA, VISHNU DAS, pharm. analyst, educator; b. Kalyanpur, India, Nov. 6, 1931; s. Anant Ram and Devki Devi (Goel) G.; M.S., U. Tex., 1961; Ph.D., U. Ga., 1967; m. Kanta Kumari Goel, Sept. 2, 1957; children—Alka, Varun. Asst. prof. pharmaceutics U. Houston, 1967-71, asso. prof., 1971-77, prof., 1977—; cons. in field. Mem. Am. Pharm. Assn., Acad. Pharm. Scis., Sigma Xi, Kappa Psi. Contbr. articles to profl. jours. Home: 9010 Sterlingame Dr Houston TX 77031 Office: U of Houston Coll Pharmacy Houston TX 77004

GUPTON, GUY WINFRED, JR., engr.; b. Atlanta, Nov. 15, 1926; s. Guy Winfred and Mary Alice (Barron) G.; B.B.A., Ga. State U., 1967; m. Dorothy Egan Temple, Apr. 17, 1948; children—Guy W., Mary Alice, Isabel Temple, Walter Temple. Asso. Newcomb & Boyd, Atlanta, 1952-73; partner Peters-Gupton & Assos., Atlanta, 1973-76; pres., chief engr. Gupton Engring. Assos., Inc., Atlanta, 1976—; instr. Ga. Tech. Sch. Mech. Engring. Served with USAAF, 1944-45. Fellow Am. Soc. Heating, Refrigerating and Air Conditioning Engrs.; mem. Constrn. Specification Inst., Nat. Fire Protection Assn. Republican. Presbyterian. Contbr. articles in field to profl. jours. Home: 2405 Woodward Way Atlanta GA 30305 Office: 3109 Maple Dr Atlanta GA 30305

GURNSEY, RONALD ALLEN, elec. engr.; b. Automba, Minn., Oct. 31, 1931; s. Grant Oliver and Ina Margaret (Karjala) G.; B.S.Engring., U.S. Naval Acad., 1953; M.S.E.E., U.S. Naval Postgrad. Sch., 1960; married; children—Stephanie Ann, Eric Brian. Commd. ensign U.S. Navy, 1953, advanced through grades to lt. comdr. resigned 1965; tech. dir. Stanwick Corp., Norfolk, Va., 1965-69; staff engr. Sigma Systems, Inc., Washington, 1969-70; pres. Ron Gurnsey Assos., McLean, Va., 1971-72; exec. v.p. Senkow Assos., Inc., Falls Church, Va., 1972-73; dir. Indsl. Technol. Assos., Inc., Bethesda, Md., 1973-77; project mgr. Tracor Inc., Rockville, Md., 1977—. Mem. Am. Inst. Indsl. Engrs., IEEE, Am. Soc. Naval Engrs., Soc. Logistics Engrs. Baptist. Home: 1746 Westwind Way McLean VA 22102 Office: 1601 Research Blvd Rockville MD 20850

GÜRTLER, MARTIN MATHIAS, II, civil engr.; b. New Orleans, May 3, 1916; s. Martin Mathias and Louisa Benedicta (Rieth) G.; B.S. in Civil Engring., Tulane U., 1937; m. Audrey May Salzer, Apr. 15, 1944; children—Martin Mathias III, Linda Anna, Friedrich W. L., Michael K. A. Indsl. engr. Engring. Splty. & Mfg. Co., New Orleans, 1937-39; chief engr. LeMieux Bros., Inc., foresters and piledriving contractors, 1939-41; constrn. engr. Doullut & Ewin, Inc., civil engrs., gen. contractors, 1944-46; v.p. Bernard & Byrd, Inc., gen. contractors, 1946-51; pres. Gürtler, Hebert & Co., Inc., civil engrs., gen. contractors, New Orleans, 1951—; pres., dir. Am. Thrift & Finance Plan, Inc.; partner K.W. Salzer & Co., City Park Ave. Floral Co., Gürtler & Bro. Bd. dirs. New Orleans Opera House Assn.; trustee Geneal. Research Soc. New Orleans, Mem. La. Engring. Soc., Nat. Soc. Profl. Engrs., Nat. Geneal. Soc., Swiss Am. Soc. New Orleans, France-Amerique de la Louisiane, Westdeutsche Gesellschaft für Familien Kunde, La. Hist. Soc., Tau Beta Pi. Roman Catholic. Clubs: Pendennis, Round Table, Internat. House (New Orleans); Metairie (La.) Country; City (Baton Rouge). Home: 1320 2d St New Orleans LA 70130 Office: 4334 Earhart Blvd St New Orleans LA 70185

GUSTAFSON, DAVID JALMAR, accountant; b. Waterville, Maine, July 18, 1936; s. Maynard John and Eleanor (Wilson) G.; B.A., Baldwin-Wallace Coll., 1958; postgrad. U. Maine, 1960-62; m. Margaret Anne Woods, June 21, 1958; children—Nanci Anne, Bruce J. Accountant, Fairmont Foods Co., 1958-60, Ruberoid Co., 1965-67, Gen. Telephone Co., 1967-68; tchr. public sch., Augusta and Waterville, Maine, 1960-64; chief accountant Multi-Line Cans, Inc., Tampa, Fla., 1968-70; office mgr., adminstrv. mgr. Lykes Food Products, Inc., Tampa, 1970-74; budget mgr. U.S. Home of Fla., Inc., Clearwater, 1974; controller, sec.-treas. Am. Aluminum Distbrs., Inc., Clearwater, 1975-79; prin., owner Gustafson's Acctg. Service, Clearwater, 1979—; dir. Gottenstrate & McClain C.P.A.'s. Mem. Nat. Assn. Accountants. Republican. Methodist. Club: Rotary. Home: 616

College Hill Dr Clearwater FL 33515 Office: 2189 Cleveland St Bldg J Suite 266 Clearwater FL 33515

GUSTAFSON, FRANCES D., hosp. ofcl.; b. Lynchburg, Va., Aug. 7, 1928; d. Frank and Mattie Isabel (Dunn) Decker; student Bklyn. Coll., 1945-47; m. Norman Albert Gustafson, Dec. 29, 1950; children—Carl, Paul, Norma Jean. Exec. sec. to editor-in-chief MacFadden Publs., N.Y.C., 1945-51; dir. dir. vol. services Bapt. Meml. Hosp., San Antonio, 1975—. Mem. Am. Bus. Women's Assn., San Antonio Council Dirs. Vol. Services, Am. Soc. Dirs. Vol. Services, Am. Hosp. Assn. Republican. Baptist. Clubs: Women's Fedn., San Antonio Opti-Mrs. (scholarship chmn. 1975—). Home: 5214 Newcome Dr San Antonio TX 78229 Office: Baptist Memorial Hospital 111 Dallas St San Antonio TX 78286

GUSTAFSON, GEORGE ROBERT, assn. exec.; b. Austin, Tex., May 19, 1928; s. Fred W. and Nell V. (Wheless) G.; student U. Tex., Austin, 1948-51, 59; m. Norma June Windsor, July 22, 1950; children—Cynthia Ann, Deborah Kay, Tami Lynn. With Tex. Dept. Public Safety, 1949-50; gen. mgr. Tex. Safety Assn., Austin, 1950—; dir. Nat. Safety Council; mem. Citizens Traffic Safety Comm. Corp. charter mem. Boys Club of Austin. Mem. Am. Soc. Assn. Execs. (pres.-elect), Assn. Safety Council Execs. (cert.), Tex. Soc. Assn. Execs. Club: Austin Civitan (past pres.). Home: 6510 Auburn Hill Austin TX 78723 Office: PO Box 9345 Austin TX 78766

GUSTE, ROY FRANCIS, lawyer, banker, planter, restaurateur; b. New Orleans, Nov. 28, 1923; s. William Joseph and Marie Louise (Alciatore) G.; B.A., Loyola U. at New Orleans, 1943, LL.B., 1948; m. Beverly Taylor, July 1, 1948; children—Roy Francis, Taylor, Colette, Robert, Beatrice, Michael. Admitted to La. bar, 1948, since practiced in New Orleans; asso. firm now Guste, Barnett & Shushan and predecessor firm, New Orleans, 1948-56, mem. firm, 1956—; owner, dir. Antoine's Restaurant, New Orleans, 1972—, Guste Island Plantation, Madisonville, La.; dir. Continental Savs. & Loan Assn., New Orleans, 1966—, v.p., 1977—. Pres. Young Men's Bus. Club, New Orleans, 1955-56, Pres.'s Council Loyola U., 1973-77. Mem. adv. bd. Delgado Trade Sch., New Orleans, 1955-56; bd. dirs. Internat. House, New Orleans, 1955-56, Nat. Cath. Conf. for Interracial Justice, 1974—; trustee Loyola U., 1980—. Served with USNR, 1943-46. Mem. New Orleans, La. State, Am. bar assns., Am. Judicature Soc., St. Thomas More Law Club, Alpha Delta Gamma, Delta Theta Phi. Democrat. Roman Catholic (pres. archdiocese human relations com., 1971-73). K.C. (4 deg.). Home: 1707 Palmer Ave New Orleans LA 70118 Office: 1624 Nat Bank of Commerce Bldg New Orleans LA 70112

GUSTE, WILLIAM JOSEPH, JR., atty. gen. La.; b. New Orleans, May 26, 1922; s. William Joseph and Marie Louise (Alciatore) G.; A.B., Loyola U., New Orleans, 1942, LL.B., 1943, LL.D., 1974; m. Dorothy Schutten, Apr. 17, 1947; children—William Joseph III, Bernard Randolph, Marie Louise, Melanie Ann, Valerie Eve, Althea Maria, Elizabeth Therese, James Patrick, Anne Duchense, John Jude (dec.). Admitted to La. bar, 1943; practice in New Orleans, 1943-72; mem. firm Guste, Barnett & Colomb, 1970-73; atty. gen. La., 1972—. Chief counsel New Orleans Housing Authority, 1957-71; pres. New Orleans Met. Crime Commn., 1956-57; chmn. Juvenile Ct. Adv. Com. Orleans Parish, 1961-63; mem. New Orleans St. Paving Study Commn., 1965-66. Co-owner, Antoine's Restaurant, New Orleans, 1944—. Pres. New Orleans Cancer Assn., 1960-62, United Cancer Council, 1965-67, Asso. Catholic Charities New Orleans, 1960-62, La. Housing Council, 1965-66; chmn. Nat. Housing Conf., 1963-64; sec. United Fund Greater New Orleans. Mem. La. Senate from 21st Dist., 1968-72. Trustee Xavier U., New Orleans, 1957—, chmn. bd. lay regents, 1956. Served with AUS, 1942-46. Named Outstanding Young Man U.S. Jaycees, 1955; recipient John F. Kennedy Leadership award Young Democrats La. State U., 1973; Gautrelet award Springhill Coll., Mobile, Ala., 1977; Nat. Penology award State of La., 1979. Mem. New Orleans Bar Assn., St. Thomas More Cath. Lawyers Assn., Am. Assn. Small Bus. (dir.), Nat. Assn. Housing and Redevel. Ofcls. (dir., Man of Year 1976), Nat. Conf. Dem. State-wide Elected Ofcls. (chmn.), Am. Judicature Soc., Legal Aid Bur., Blue Key, Sigma Alpha Kappa. Democrat. Clubs: K.C. (state dep. 1965-66); Internat. House, Pickwick, Bienville (New Orleans). Office: 234 Loyola Ave New Orleans LA 70112

GUTERMUTH, CLINTON RAYMOND, conservationist, naturalist; b. Fort Wayne, Ind., Aug. 16, 1900; s. Henry Christian and Alice Virtue (Zion) G.; student Notre Dame, 1918-19; grad. Am. Inst. Banking, 1927, postgrad., 1927-28; D.Sc., U. Idaho, 1972; m. Ila Bessie Horm, Mar. 4, 1922 (dec. Dec. 1975); m. 2d, Marian S. Happer, Mar. 21, 1977. Asst. cashier St. Joseph Valley Bank, Elkhart, Ind., 1922-34; dir. div. of edn., Ind. Dept. of Conservation, Indpls., 1934-40, dir. div. fish and game, 1940-42; Ind. rent dir. OPA, Indpls., 1942-45; exec. sec. Am. Wildlife Inst., Washington, 1945-46; v.p. Wildlife Mgmt. Inst. 1946-71. Sec., trustee N.A. Wildlife Found., Inc., 1946-74; pres., trustee Stronghold, Inc., 1947—; former chmn., hon. mem. Natural Resources Council Am., 1946-72; pres., dir. Wildfowl Found., 1956—; pres., dir. Urban Wildlife Research Center, 1976; hon. pres., dir. World Wildlife Fund (U.S.), 1961-71; trustee, mem. exec. council World Wildlife Fund (Internat.), 1971-75; hon. life mem. Am. Com. Internat. Wildlife Protection, 1973—; sec.-treas. Citizens Com. for Natural Resources Found., 1974-77. Recipient Leopold medal Wildlife Soc., 1957; Nat. Service award Keep Am. Beautiful, 1965; Gold medal of honor N.Y. Camp Fire Club Am., 1977; Albright medal Am. Scenic and Historic Preservation Soc., 1971; Order Golden Ark, Netherlands, 1972; Conservation award African Safari Club, 1977; elected to Fishing Hall Fame, 1958, Hunting Hall Fame, 1975. Fellow AAAS; mem. Nat. Rifle Assn. (life mem., life dir., exec. council, past pres.), Izaak Walton League Am. (life), Outdoor Writers Assn. Am., Wildlife Soc. (hon. life, trustee), Am. Forestry Assn. (hon. life mem.), Am. Soc. Range Mgmt., Nat. Audubon Soc., Nat. Parks Assn., Wilderness Soc. (life), Am. Fisheries Soc., Internat. Assn. Game, Fish and Conservation Commrs. (hon. life), Soil Conservation Soc. (hon. life mem.), Arctic Inst. N.Am., Zool. Soc. (N.Y.), Mason (32 deg., K.T.). Clubs: Cosmos, Univ., Nat. Press (Washington); Explorers, Boone & Crockett, Camp Fire (N.Y.C.): (hon.) Booneville (Ind.) Press. Elkhart (Ind.) Conservation. Miami (Fla.) Sailfish. Tanana Valley (Alaska) Sportsmen's. Author: Where to Go in Indiana, Official Lake Guide, 1938; Quips and Queries page on natural history, Outdoor Indiana, 1934-42; W.M.I. bi-weekly Outdoor News Bull., 1947-50; co-author: The Fisherman's Encyclopedia; The Standard Book of Fishing. Author numerous articles on natural resource conservation. Home: 2111 Jefferson Davis Hwy Arlington VA 22202

GUTHRIE, A. MAXEEN DANSBY, educator, coll. admnstr.; b. Payner, Tex.; d. D.W. and Angeline (Douglas) Dansby; B.A., U. of Tex. at Austin, 19—; M.Edn., Clemson U., 1975; m. Rufus Kent Guthrie, Aug. 8, 1948; children—Annie Lynn, R. Kent. Exec. sec. Shell Oil Co., Houston, 1950-54; case mgr. S.C. Dept. of Social Services, Pickens, 1971-74; dir. coop. edn. and career placement, instr. human development N. Harris County Coll., Houston, 1975—; cons. continuing edn. contempory woman's series, U. of Houston, 1975—. Mem. Am. Personnel and Guidance Assn., Nat. Vocat. Guidance Assn., Nat. Cooperative Ednl. Assn., Tex. Coop. Ednl. Assn., SW Placement Assn., Tex. Jr. Coll. Tchrs. Assn. Mem. Palmer Episcopal Ch. Home: 5811 Portal St Houston TX 77096 Office: 2700 WW Thorne Dr Houston TX 77073

GUTHRIE, BETTY JUNE, clin. social worker; b. Clinton, Okla., June 4, 1926; d. David G. and Laura (Simpson) G.; student Christian Coll., Columbia, Mo., 1944-45; B.A., U. Okla., 1948; M.S.W., Tulane U., 1956. Child welfare worker Okla. Child Welfare Div., Oklahoma City, 1949-56; dist. child welfare supr. Okla. Child Welfare Div., Ponca City, 1957-67; clin. social worker Bi-State Mental Health Found., Ponca City, 1967-74, chief clin. social worker, 1974—; pvt. practice psychotherapy Fair Clinic, Inc., Ponca City, 1968—; asso. prof. Okla. U.; regional vice chmn. White House Confs. Children and Youth, 1960, regional sec., 1970; pres. Kay Council Community Services, 1964-67; exec. bd. Kay County Youth Shelter, 1972-77; mem. Kay County Child Welfare Adv. Bd., 1967—. Mem. Mayor's Com. on Drug Abuse, chmn., 1976-77. Mem. Acad. Certified Social Workers, Registered Social Workers in Okla., Nat. Registry Health Care Providers in Clin. Social Work, Nat. Assn. Social Workers, Okla. Health and Welfare Assn., Delta Delta Delta. Methodist. Home: 2413 Prospect St Ponca City OK 74601 Office: Fair Clinic Doctor's Park 404 Fairview Ponca City OK 74601

GUTIERREZ, FRANCISCO LUIS, II, physician; b. Havana, Cuba, Dec. 2, 1920; s. Francisco and Maria Luisa (Fernandez) G.; came to U.S., 1963, naturalized, 1969; M.D., U. Havana, 1950; m. Ada Isabel Vinjoy, Dec. 5, 1947; children—Francisco Luis III, Ada Ines. Intern, St. Joseph Hosp., St. Louis, 1963-64; mem. staff Clinica Santa Maria Cotorro, Havana, 1951, Policlinico Santa Maria Rosario, Havan, 1951-58, Clinica Accion Medica, Havana, 1953-63, Winfield (Kans.) State Hosp., 1964-70, Suffolk State Tng. Sch., N.Y.C., 1970-74, NE Fla. State Hosp., Macclenny, 1974—; practice medicine Macclenny, 1974—. Certified Kans. State Bd. Healing Arts, Fla. State Bd. Med. Examiners. Mem. Colegio Medico Municipal de Santa Maria del Rosario, Colegio Medico Nacional Cuba, Circulo Medico de Cuba, Cuban Med. Assn. in Exile, Miami, Am. Profl Practice Assn. Republican. Roman Catholic. K.C. (3d deg.). Club: Lehigh Acres Country (Fla.). Office: NE Fla State Hosp Macclenny FL 32063*

GUTIÉRREZ-MAZORRA, JUAN FRANCISCO, anesthesiologist; b. Veracruz, Mex., May 12, 1944; s. Francisco Alberto and Rissett Mazorra (Vega) Gutiérrez-Pelaez; came to U.S., 1960; naturalized, 1969; B.S. in Chem. Engring., Northeastern U., 1965; M.D., W.Va. U., 1969; m. Candy Eleanor Snyder, Dec. 26, 1967; children—Lara Alicia, Jana Francesca. Intern, W.Va. U. Med. Center, Morgantown, 1969-70; resident U. Ala., Birmingham, 1970-72; pediatric anesthesia fellow The Children's Hosp., Birmingham, 1972-73; chief anesthesiologist Naval Submarine Med. Center, Groton, Conn., 1973-75; practice medicine specializing in anesthesiology, 1975—; asso. prof. anesthesiology, dir. operating room W.Va. U. Med. Center, Morgantown, 1975-78; asso. prof., dir. pediatric anesthesia U. Ala., Birmingham, 1978—; anesthesiologist in chief, co-dir. respiratory therapy The Children's Hosp., Birmingham, 1978—. Served to lt. comdr. USNR, 1973-75. Mem. Am. Soc. Anesthesiology, Internat. Anesthesiology Research Soc., Am. Acad. Pediatrics, Am. Coll. Chest Physicians, Am. Inst. Chem. Engrs., Am. Lung Assn. (bd. dirs. W.Va. branch 1977) Am. Heart Assn. (bd. dirs. W.Va. branch 1977). Roman Catholic. Contbr. articles to med. jours. Home: 2208 Baxter Circle Birmingham AL 35216 Office: 1601 6th Ave S Birmingham AL 35233

GUTMANN, ROGER CARL, social services adminstr.; b. Fort Wayne, Ind., Jan. 4, 1947; s. Arthur Carl and Louanna (Rapp) G.; B.A., Wartburg Coll., 1969; M.S.W., Washington U., St. Louis, 1974; m. Carol Louise Grunke, Dec. 28, 1968; children—Laura Louise, Daniel Alan. Coll. admissions counselor Wartburg Coll., Waverly, Iowa, 1970-72; dir. child protective services S.C. Dept. Social Services, Columbia, 1976-79; program adminstr. human services Richland County Dept. Social Services, Columbia, S.C., 1979—. Chmn. sunbelt mobilization project Lutheran Social Service Systems, 1979—. Served with USAF, 1973-76. Mem. Acad. Cert. Social Workers, Nat. Assn. Social Workers (dir.), Am. Public Welfare Assn. Home: 1819 Omarest Dr Columbia SC 29210 Office: 2020 Hampton St Columbia SC 29202

GUTOWSKI, EDWARD PAUL, physician; b. Brandenburg, Germany, Aug. 3, 1943; came to U.S., 1949, naturalized, 1954; s. Franz and Anna G.; B.S., U. N.D., 1965; M.D., Harvard U., 1969; m. Lourdes Galvan, June 9, 1969; children—Eddie, Alex. Intern, St. Francis Hosp., Honolulu, 1969-70; chief of staff Med. Center Hosp., Punta Gorda, Fla., 1979—, pres. staff, 1980—; air med. examiner FAA. Served with USPHS, 1970-72. Diplomate Am. Bd. Family Practice. Fellow Am. Acad. Family Physicians; mem. AMA (Physicians Recognition award 1976, 79), Charlotte County Med. Soc. (pres. 1980). Republican. Roman Catholic. Home: 335 Orchid Dr Punta Gorda FL 33950 Office: 350 Mary St Punta Gorda FL 33950

GUTTENSOHN, ARTHUR ERNST, JR., telecommunications co. exec.; b. Chgo., Sept. 24, 1936; s. Arthur Ernst and Rose Francis (Schuler) G.; B.S. in Elec. Engring., Northwestern U., 1959, M.S. (HEW fellow), 1961, postgrad. (Applied Research Projects Assn. fellow), 1961-65; m. Lila J. Karger, July 27, 1963; children—Eric, Laurel, Kurt, Mark. Lectr. info. engring. dept. U. Ill., Chgo., 1965; with GTE, 1965—, research and staff engr. thin films GTE Automatic Electric, Northlake, Ill., 1965-70, research and devel. staff engr. electromech. design, 1970-73, devel. group leader thick films, 1973-77, supervising staff engr. thick film mfg. GTE Lenkurt, Albuquerque, 1977, supr. mfg. engring thick film mfg. GTE Telcom, Huntsville, Ala., 1977—; evening instr. Triton Coll., Harper Coll., Chgo., 1966-77, Calhoun Coll., Decatur, Ala., 1979—. Judge com. Chgo. public sch. sci. and math. conf., 1968-77; mem. parish council Holy Spirit Cath. Ch., Huntsville, 1978—. Recipient Charles Schneider award, 1976. Fellow Coll. Relay Engrs.; mem. Am. Vacuum Soc., Internat. Soc. for Hybrid Microelectronics, Am. Ceramic Soc., Sigma Xi, Eta Kappa Nu, Pi Mu Epsilon. Club: K.C. Review com. Plating Jour.; contbr. articles to tech. publs. Home: 7706 Treeline Dr SE Huntsville AL 35802 Office: GTE Telcom 13000 Memorial Pkwy S Huntsville AL 35803

GUTTMAN, JOHN ROBERT, civil engr.; b. Manitowoc, Wis., Apr. 13, 1944; s. Robert Arthur and Lucille G.; B.S. in Biology, Marquette U., 1967, B.S. in Civil Engring., 1971, M.S. in Environ. Engring., 1972; m. Jeanne Marie Tremblay, June 15, 1968; children—Kristin, Kari, Robert. Research asso. Marquette U., Milw., 1967-71; project engr. Donohue & Assos., Sheboygan, Wis., 1971-72; project engr. Connell Assos., Inc., Miami, Fla., 1972-73; project mgr. Connell Metcalf & Eddy, Inc., Coral Gables, Fla., 1973-75, dir. environ. engring., 1975-78, v.p., 1978—. Mem. Fla. Engring. Soc., Fla. Pollution Control Assn., Greater Miami C. of C., Marine Council Greater Miami, Chi Epsilon. Home: 7440 SW 174th St Miami FL 33157 Office: PO Box 341939 Coral Gables FL 33134

GUY, DAVID PAUL, physical therapist, rehab. adminstr.; b. Rockville Centre, N.Y., Feb. 15, 1944; s. Paul A. and Dorothy Marie (Sachse) G.; B.S. in Physical Therapy, Marquette U., Milw., 1967; M.S., U. Ariz., 1976; m. Karen Louis Rutz, Sept. 27, 1969; children—Christian Paul, Stephen Peter, Joseph Patrick. Chief phys. therapist Ariz. Tng. Program Mentally Retarded, 1974; phys. therapist, arthritis counselor U. Ariz. Med. Center, 1975-76; dir. phys. therapy and rehab. services Providence Meml. Hosp., El Paso, Tex., 1977—. Served with U.S. Army, 1967-74. Decorated Army Commendation medal, Meritorious Service medal; grantee Rehab. Services Adminstrn., 1966-67. Mem. Am. Phys. Therapy Assn., Nat. Rehab. Assn., Am. Personnel and Guidance Assn., Nat. Rehab. Counselors Assn., Vocat. Evaluation and Work Adjustment Assn., Am. Congress Rehab. Medicine. Democrat. Roman Catholic. Club: K.C. Author papers. Inventor shoulder brace for hemiplegics, 1967, spl. crutch for upper extremity amputees, 1970. Home: 6632 Mesa Grande St El Paso TX 79912 Office: 2001 N Oregon St El Paso TX 79902

GUY, LOUIS LEE, JR., san. engr.; b. Norfolk, Va., Apr. 26, 1938; s. Louis Lee and Grace Baxter (Mayo) G.; B.S.C.E., Va. Poly. Inst., 1959; postgrad. George Washington U., 1972-73; m. Suzanne Penn West, Oct. 9, 1965; children—James Thornton, Louis Lee, Francis West. Project engr. Norfolk Dredging Co., Va., Md., 1959; design engr. Wiley & Wilson, Lynchburg, Va., 1962-66; civil engr. George, Miles & Buhr, Salisbury, Md., 1966-68; san. engr. Langley, McDonald & Overman, 1969-70; asst. mgr. tech. services Water Pollution Control Fedn., Washington, 1970-73; prin. Patton, Harris, Rust & Guy, Fairfax, Va., 1973—; mem. Va. Water Study Commn., 1977—. Treas., Nat. Soc. Profl. Engrs. Edn. Found.; 2d. v.p. Fairfax County Fedn. Citizens Assns., 1974-75; adv. bd. WNVT. Served to lt. U.S. Army, 1959-62. Named Citizen of Year, Annandale C. of C., 1977. Registered engr., Va., Md., Del., W.Va., N.C., D.C.; certified san. engr. Environ. Engring. Intersoc. Bd. Fellow ASCE; mem. Nat. Soc. Profl. Engrs. (trustee, treas. 1975-80), mem. polit. action com. 1980—, Young Engr. of Year award 1973), Va. Soc. Profl. Engrs. (officer 4 chpts., Engr. of Year award 1978), Am. Acad. Environ. Engrs. (trustee), Water Pollution Control Fedn., Am. Water Works Assn., Am. Cons. Engrs. Council (trustee, mem. polit. action com.), Fairfax County C. of C. Presbyterian (elder 1979—). Club: Rotary. Contbr. numerous articles to tech. and profl. jours. Home: 8330 Queen Elizabeth Blvd Annandale VA 22003 Office: 10523 Main St Fairfax VA 22030

GUYTON, JAMES OPLE, JR., ins. mgr.; b. Tuscumbia, Ala., Mar. 8, 1929; s. James O. and Lottie M. G.; B.S., U. Ala., 1956, M.A., 1967; postgrad. George Peabody Coll., Nashville, 1960; m. Jo Nell Guyton, July 1, 1950; children—Jane Marie, Susan Elizabeth. High sch. football coach, Nocona, Weimar and Rosenberg, Tex., 1957-65; dist. mgr. James Guyton & Assos., Rosenberg, 1965—. Served with AUS, 1950-52. Recipient numerous ins. sales awards. Mem. Nat. Assn. Life Underwriters, Tex. Assn. Life Underwriters, Houston Assn. Life Underwriters, Tex. Leaders Roundtable. Democrat. Baptist. Club: Rotary. Home: 3832 Ave O Rosenberg TX 77471 Office: 1919 Ave H Suite 209 Rosenberg TX 77471

GUYTON, JAMES TERRY, clergyman; b. Cartersville, Ga., Oct. 23, 1948; s. Leonard Milow and Mary Frances (Shelton) G.; B.S. cum laude, Ga. Southwestern Coll., 1975; m. Iris Anita Lawson, June 6, 1978; children—Chadwick, Brandon, Javan. Ordained to ministry Chs. of God, 1972; pastor Adel (Ga.) Ch. of God, 1970-73, Albany (Ga.) Ch. of God, 1973-76 Buford (Ga.) Ch. of God, 1976—, also dist. supt.; chaplain City of Buford, 1976—. Chmn. fund dr. Cystic Fibrosis Found., Buford. Mem. State Council Chs. of God in N. Ga. (chmn. bd. edn.). Democrat. Home: 378 W Park Buford GA 30518 Office: 225 Lee Buford GA 30518

GUZMAN, ALBERTO PORRATA, hosp. supplies co. exec.; b. Ponce, P.R., Oct. 30, 1942; s. Virgilio Porrata and Raquel (Guzman) Porrata; B.B.A., Cath. U. P.R., 1965; grad. Antilles Detective Acad., 1979; m. Carmen Gloria Roda Rodriguez, June 19, 1970. With Thom McAn, Atocha St. Ponce, 1960-65; accountant Amstel Brewing Co., Ponce, 1965-67; comptroller St. Luke's Episcopal Hosp., Ponce, 1967-74; v.p. Island Med. and Hosp. Supplies, Inc., Ponce, 1974—; pres. Ponce Rental Equipment Corp., 1979—. Adminstr. of shelters S. Coast, P.R. Civil Def., Voluntary Corps., 1972—. Mem. Real Estate Inst. P.R., React Internat., P.R. Shooting Assn. Mem. New Progressive Party P.R. Roman Catholic. Clubs: William's Shooting, Ponce Country. Home: Urb Las Delicias St 17 T 25 Ponce PR 00731 Office: Urb Mercedita 83 PO Box 7606 Ponce PR 00731

GWALTNEY, EMMA CAROLYN, educator; b. Prescott, Ark., May 16, 1922; d. Cohen Christy and Gladys Mae (Teeter) Calhoun; B.S.E., Ark. State Tchrs. Coll., 1944; M.A., U. Ark., 1951; m. Francis I. Gwaltney, Aug. 19, 1947; children—Mary Lee, Francis Irby. Public sch. tchr. English, Fayetteville, Ark., 1947-63; instr. English, La. Tech. U., Ruston, 1963-70; asst. prof. English, Ark. Poly. Coll., Russellville, 1970—, dir. Freshman English studies, 1977—. Mem. AAUP, MLA, Ark. Tchrs. of Coll. English. Democrat. Episcopalian. Home: W 23d St Russellville AR 72801 Office: Ark Poly Coll Russellville AR 72801

GWALTNEY, FRANCIS IRBY, educator, author; b. Traskwood, Ark., Sept. 9, 1921; s. Francis Boulanger and Mary Effie (Irby) G.; B.A., U. Ark., 1949, M.A., 1951; m. Emma Carolyn Calhoun, Aug. 19, 1947; children—Mary Lee, Francis Irby. Prof. English and creative writing Ark. Poly. Coll., Russellville, 1970—. Author novels, television plays. Served with Cavalry, AUS, 1942-46. Author: The Yeller-Headed Summer, 1954; The Day the Century Ended, 1955; A Moment of Warmth, 1957; The Numbers of Our Days, 1959; A Step in the River, 1960; The Quicksand Years, 1965; Destiny's Chickens, 1973; Idols and Axle Grease, 1974. Home: W 23rd St Russellville AR 72801

HAACK, DAVID ARNO, geologist; b. St. Louis, Dec. 21, 1931; s. Arno John and Florence (Reppert) H.; A.B., Washington U., St. Louis, 1954, M.A., 1955; m. Katherine Ann Vanston, June 6, 1953; children—William James, Robert David. Teaching asst. Washington U., 1954-55; geologist, dist. devel. supr. Texaco, Inc., Corpus Christi, Tex., 1957-67, div. staff geologist, well log analyst, devel. supr., Houston, 1967-69; dist. geologist Clark Oil Producing Co., Corpus Christi, 1969-71; chief geologist Normandy Oil and Gas Co., Corpus Christi, 1971-72; sr. exploration geologist Mitchell Energy & Devel. Corp., Houston, 1972-75, dist. geologist So. div., 1975-77; exploration geologist Kilroy Co. of Tex. Inc., Houston, 1977—. Served to 1st lt. AUS, 1955-57. Mem. Am. Assn. Petroleum Geologists, Houston, Corpus Christi geol. socs., Sigma Xi, Tau Kappa Epsilon. Clubs: Imperial Point Civic (exec. bd. 1967-69), Alief Band Boosters (v.p. 1968-69) (Houston). Home: 12003 Chessington Dr Houston TX 77031 Office: Kilroy Co of Tex Inc 1908 First City Nat Bank Bldg Houston TX 77002

HAAR, CAROLYN MCCANN, speech pathologist; b. New Orleans, Jan. 13, 1950; d. Wesley David and (M.) Therese (Martin) McCann; B.S. in Speech Pathology, Dominican Coll., 1971; M.S. in Speech Pathology, Tulane U., 1975; m. Michael Paul Haar, Aug. 21, 1971; children—Jeanne Marie, Peter Michael. Itinerant speech-lang. pathologist New Orleans Public Schs., 1972; lang. specialist, Title I Oral Lang. Program, Orleans Parish, 1972-75, coordinator Title I lang. devel. program, 1975-76; speech/lang. pathologist New Orleans Public Schs., 1976-78; tchr. severely lang. impaired children Orleans Parish, 1978-79. Mem. Am. Speech and Hearing Assn., La. Speech and Hearing Assn., Adoptive Couples Together. Roman Catholic. Home: 616 Harang Ave Metairie LA 70001

HAAR, HERBERT RAYMOND, JR., state ofcl.; b. Alexandria, Va., Apr. 14, 1923; s. Herbert Raymond and Geraldine Fairfax (Davis) H.; B.C.E., Va. Poly. Inst., 1943; M.S. in City Planning, U. Ill., 1964; m. Dorothy Bromley, July 16, 1946; children—Herbert Raymond, Susan F. Haar Gordon. Commd. 2d lt. C.E., U.S. Army, 1943, advanced through grades to col., 1966; officer in charge Nicaragua Canal Survey, 1949-52; asst. engr. commnr. urban devel. City Govt. D.C., 1965-66; U.S. army engr., Thailand, 1967-68; New Orleans dist. engr. U.S. Army C.E., 1968-71; ret., 1971; asso. dir. planning and engring. Port of New Orleans, 1971—; chmn. bd. Nat. Waterways Conf., 1974-76; bd. dirs., exec. com. Gulf Intercoastal Canal Assn.; pres., Met. Safety Council New Orleans Area, 1976; nat. commr. Am. sect. Permanent Internat. Assn. Nav. Congresses, 1977—. Decorated Legion of Merit; recipient Meritorious Pub. Service award D.C. Govt., 1966; Order Ayachucho (Peru), 1962; certificate of merit Gov. La., 1972; registered profl. engr., D.C., La. Fellow Soc. Am. Mil. Engrs. (past pres. La.); mem. Am. Inst. Planners, AAPA (chmn. ad hoc com. dredging), Mid Am. Ports Steering Com. (chmn.). Democrat. Episcopalian. Clubs: Internat. House, Plimsoll, World Trade, Propeller (New Orleans). Author papers, reports. Home: 933 Vintage Dr Kenner LA 70062 Office: PO Box 60046 New Orleans LA 70160

HAAS, ROBERT LANCE, oral surgeon; b. N.Y.C., Oct. 7, 1933; s. Kalman and Ruth (Soloway) H.; B.S., Ohio State U., 1953; D.D.S., Columbia U., 1957, M.P.H., 1973; Certificate in Oral Surgery, N.Y. U., 1959; m. Lois Natalie Feldman, April 14, 1957; children—Kara Lyn, Robyn Laurie, Bradley Nathan, Felice Sharon. Intern in oral surgery Harlam Hosp., N.Y.C., 1958; resident in oral surgery Grasslands Hosp., Valhalla, N.Y., 1960; pvt. practice oral surgery, Tampa, Fla., 1975—; asso. attending oral surgeon Fordham Hosp., Bronx, 1965, Bronx-Lebanon Med. Center, 1963, Grassland Hosp., Valhalla, 1970; attending oral surgeon Royal Hosp., Bronx, 1960, Newark Beth Israel Med. Center, 1973, chief of dental services, 1973, dir. out-patient dept., 1973, mem. exec. med. bd., 1974, also mem. joint pharmacy com.; asso. clin. prof. oral surgery, anesthesiology and hosp. dentistry Coll. of Medicine and Dentistry of N.J., Newark, 1974; asst. adj. prof. oral surgery, Columbia, N.Y.C., 1971, lectr. in dentistry and oral medicine, 1971; cons. for Fla. Regional Med. Program (name changed to So. Health Found.), 1975; vice chmn. Fla. High Blood Pressure Coordinating Council, 1977—; adj. prof. U. S.Fla. Pres. bd. edn. Port Chester, Rye, N.Y., 1968; mem. Newark Dental Coordinating Council of Newark Dept. Health Planning, 1974. Served to capt., USAR, 1958-73. HEW grantee, 1972; NIH grantee, 1975; licensed dentist, N.Y., Md.; diplomate Am. Bd. Oral and Maxillofacial Surgery, Pan-Am. Med. Assn. Fellow Am. Dental Soc. of Anesthesiology, Internat. Soc. Oral Surgeons of the Royal Coll. of Surgeons, Royal Soc. Health, Am. Coll. Oral and Maxillofacial Surgery (founding); mem. ADA, Am. Hosp. Assn., Am. Pub. Health Assn., Am., N.Y. (chmn. pub. health com., legis. com.) socs. oral surgeons, Internat. Assn. Dental Research, Internat. Assn. Maxillo-Facial Surgeons, Internat. Assn. for Study of Pain (founder), West Coast Dist. Dental Soc., Fla. Dental Assn., Bronx County Dental Soc. (exec. com.), N.J. Dental Assn. (chmn. workshop on dental residency programs of N.J. council on hosp. dental services), Alpha Omega. Contbr. articles in field to profl. jours. Home: 5104 San Jose St Tampa FL 33609 Office: 5104 San Jose St Tampa FL 33609

HAAS, THELMA ROBERTS SUMNER (MRS. CHARLES ELMER HAAS), ret. ednl. adminstr.; b. Dade City, Fla., Feb. 28, 1910; d. Jefferson Davis and Mittie (Roberts) Sumner; B.A., Fla. State U., 1931; postgrad. Duke U., summers 1935-36; M.Ed. in Personnel Services, U. Fla., 1963; m. Charles Elmer Haas, June 11, 1938; children—Donald Victor, Edith Douglas (Mrs. Stanley W. Hill). Tchr. English and history Benjamin Franklin Jr. High Sch., Tampa, Fla., 1931-34, Andrew Jackson Sr. High Sch., Jacksonville, Fla., 1939-45; tchr. English, H. B. Plant Sr. High Sch., Tampa, 1934-38; tchr. sci. and health North Shore Elementary-Jr. High Sch., Jacksonville, 1954-57; tchr. history Andrew Jackson Sr. High Sch., Jacksonville, 1957-61, guidance counselor, 1961-69, dean girls, 1970-75; dean of girls Oceanway Jr. High Sch., Jacksonville, 1969-70. Sec. Marigold Circle Garden Club, 1953-54, v.p., 1954-55, 76-78, horticulture chmn., 1975-78; mem. Civic Music Assn., Friends of Pub. Library, Jacksonville, Fedn. Garden Clubs, 1952-56; vol. St. Luke's Hosp. Aux., 1976-78. Mem. NEA, Fla. Edn. Assn., Am. Personnel and Guidance Assn., Fla. Deans and Counselors Assn., AAUW (pres. Tampa br. 1936-38, pres. Jacksonville br. 1939-40, Fla. treas. 1936-37), Mortar Bd., Delta Kappa Gamma (chpt. pres. 1966-68, chmn. coordinating council 1968-70, chaplain 1974-76), Alpha Chi Alpha, Pi Lambda Theta, Kappa Delta Pi (corr. sec. 1968-70), Phi Mu. Democrat. Baptist. Club: Marigold Garden Circle (pres. 1978-80). Home: 332 W 69th St Jacksonville FL 32208

HAAS, WILLIAM JOSEPH, phys. scientist; b. Gary, Ind., July 7, 1938; s. Vernon Vinton and Fern Marie (Oliver) H.; B.E.E., Purdue U., 1961; student George Washington U., 1964-68; m. Eva Elizabeth Cruikshank, Jan. 5, 1963; children—Cynthia, Kristin, Theresa. Design engr., San Diego (Calif.) Gas & Electric Co., 1961; project engr. U.S. Army Mobility Equipment Research and Devel. Command, Fort Belvoir, Va., 1961-65, project group leader, 1965-69, div. chief, 1969-75, lab. chief, 1975—. Served with AUS, 1961-63. Mem. Research Soc. Am., Am. Def. Preparedness Assn., Sigma Xi. Roman Catholic. Club: Amateur Softball Assn. Home: 12209 Oakwood Dr Woodbridge VA 22192 Office: US Army MERADCOM Fort Belvoir VA 22060

HABAL, MUTAZ BILLAH, plastic surgeon; b. Damascus, Syria, Apr. 27, 1938; came to U.S., 1964, naturalized, 1977; s. Mounier Said and Rabia (Rickaby) H.; M.D., Am. U. Beirut, 1964; m. Randa Dabbagh, June 21, 1964; children—Rula, M. Bassam. Intern, Am. U. Beirut, 1964; resident in surgery SUNY, Syracuse, 1964-69, Harvard U., 1969-72; prof. surgery, chief plastic and reconstructive surgery U. South Fla., Tampa, 1978—; chief plastic surgery VA Hosp. Fellow A.C.S.; mem. Royal Coll. Surgeons, Internat. Coll. Surgeons, Am. Trauma Assn., AMA (Physicians Recognition award). Republican. Moslem. Contbr. numerous articles to med. and sci. jours. Home: 4211 Carollwood Village Dr Tampa FL 33606 Office: 12901 N 30th St Tampa FL 33612

HABEISHI, FARID GABRIEL, project mgr.; b. Latakia, Syria, July 26, 1945; s. Gabriel John and Olivia (Tatar) H.; B.S. in Civil Engring., Auburn U., 1965; m. Glenda Sue Washington, Apr. 26, 1965; 1 son, Christopher Farid. Jr. structural engr. Rust Engring. Co., Birmingham, Ala., 1965-67, design engr., 1967-70, sr. design engr., 1970-72, project engr., 1972-76, project mgr., 1976—. Mem. ASCE, TAPPI. Methodist. Home: Route 1 Box 204 Springville AL 35146 Office: Rust Engring Co PO Box 101 Birmingham AL 35201

HABER, LEE LOUIS, hosp. adminstr.; b. N.Y.C., Mar. 21, 1942; s. Herman L. and Marion D. Haber; B.A., N.Y. U., 1963; M.B.A., George Washington U., 1971; m. Karen E. Rae, Aug. 27, 1967; children—Todd Michael, Joshua Scott. Supr. group and medicare claims Aetna Life & Casualty Co., N.Y.C., 1965-68; coordinator spl. projects Am. Medicorp. Inc., Los Angeles, 1971; asst. adminstr. Sherman Oaks Community Hosp., Los Angeles, 1971-72; adminstr. dept. psychiatry Bronx (N.Y.) Mcpl. Hosp., 1972-73; adminstr. Hudson County Meadowview Hosp., Secaucus, N.J., 1973-75; asst. adminstr. French and Polyclinic Med. Sch. and Health Center, N.Y.C., 1975-76; adminstr. Grant Center Hosp., Miami, Fla., 1976—; exec. v.p. Grant Assos., Inc., Miami. Chmn. Fla. Assn. Pvt. Psychiat. Hosps., 1979—; bd. dirs. Grant Sch. of Miami Inc. Served with U.S. Army, 1964-65. Mem. Assn. Mental Health Adminstrs. Office: Grant Center Hosp 20601 SW 157th Ave Miami FL 33187

HABERECHT, ROLF REINHOLD, electronic co. exec.; b. Germany, June 4, 1929; came to U.S., 1956, naturalized, 1962; Ph.D., U. Berlin, 1956; M.B.A., So. Meth. U., 1967; m. Ute Schwarz, Aug. 18, 1961; children—Michael, Caroline. Dept. head research and devel. P.R. Mallory & Co., Indpls., 1956-61; with Tex. Instruments Inc., Dallas, 1962—, v.p. mgr. U.S. semicondr. group, 1975—. Trustee St. Mark's Sch., Dallas, Episcopal Sch., Dallas. Mem. Electrochem. Soc., Beta Gamma Sigma. Contbr. articles in field to profl. jours. Home: 10984 Crooked Creek Dr Dallas TX 75229 Office: 13500 N Central Expressway Dallas TX 75265

HABERMAN, MICHAEL ALLEN, psychiatrist; b. N.Y.C., Oct. 31, 1947; s. Harvey Hyman and Sylvia (Blecker) H.; B.S. with distinction, U. Wis., 1969; M.D., SUNY, Buffalo, 1973; m. Judith Lynn Sajowitz, June 22, 1969; 1 dau., Alison Melanie. Intern, resident in psychiatry SUNY, Buffalo, 1973-74; resident Emory U., Atlanta, 1974-76; staff physician Fulton County Alcoholism Treatment Center, Atlanta, 1975-77; asst. prof. psychiatry Emory U. Sch. Medicine, Atlanta, 1976—; staff psychiatrist Grady Meml. Hosp., Atlanta, 1976—; practice medicine specializing in psychiatry, Atlanta, 1976—; cons. Disability Adjudication Sect., State of Ga., Dept. Human Resources, 1979; med. dir. dept. psychiatry W. Paces Ferry Hosp., 1979—, sec. dept. psychiatry, 1978; mem. psychiatry specialty panel Metro. Atlanta Found. for Med. Care, Inc., 1977—. VA fellow, 1970; Am. Cancer Soc. summer fellow, 1971; diplomate Am. Bd. Psychiatry and Neurology. Mem. Atlanta Hypnosis Soc. (treas. 1978—), James A. Gibson Anatomical Soc., Am. Psychiat. Assn., Ga. Psychiat. Assn., Med. Assn. Ga., Med. Assn. Atlanta, Am. Soc. Clin. Hypnosis, Internat. Soc. Hypnosis, Atlanta Hypnosis Soc. Contbr. articles in field to profl. jours. Office: 1938 Peachtree Rd NW Suite 404 Atlanta GA 30309

HACKERMAN, NORMAN, univ. pres., chemist; b. Balt., Mar. 2, 1912; s. Jacob and Anne (Raffel) H.; A.B., Johns Hopkins, 1932, Ph.D., 1935; m. Gene Allison Coulbourn, Aug. 25, 1940; children—Patricia Gale, Stephen, Sally, Katherine. Asst. prof. Loyola Coll., Balt., 1935-39; research chemist Colloid Corp., 1936-40; chemist USCG, S.I., 1939-41; asst. prof. Va. Poly. Inst., Blacksburg, 1941-43; research chemist Kellex Corp., 1944; asst. prof. chemistry U. Tex., 1945-46, asso. prof., 1946-50, prof., 1950-70, chmn. dept., 1952-61, dir. corrosion research lab., 1948-61, dean research and sponsored programs, 1960-61, v.p., provost, 1961-63, vice chancellor acad. affairs, 1963-67, pres., 1967-70; prof. chemistry Rice U., Houston, 1970—, pres., 1970—; chmn. Gordon Corrosion Research Conf., 1950; cons. in corrosion, 1946—; chmn. Inter Soc. Corrosion Com., 1956-58; chmn. Gordon Research Conf. on Chemistry, 1959; mem. nat. sci. bd. NSF, 1968—, chmn., 1974-77; mem. Def. Sci. Bd., 1978—. Mem. Nat. Bd. on Grad. Edn., 1971-75; chmn. bd. on energy studies Nat. Acad. Scis./NRC/Commn. on Natural resources, 1974—. Recipient Whitney award Nat. Assn. Corrosion Engrs., 1956; Joseph J. Mattiello Meml. lectr. Fedn. for Socs. of Paint Tech., 1964; Gold medal Am. Inst. Chemists, 1978. Fellow AAAS, Am. Acad. Arts and Scis.; mem. Am. Chem. Soc. (bd. editors, 1956-62, exec. com. colloid div. 1955-58, 1965 S.W. Regional award), Electrochem. Soc. (pres. 1957-58, Palladium medal 1965), Faraday Soc., Nat. Corrosion Engrs. (dir. 1952-55, chmn. com. on edn. Corrosion Research Council 1957-60, Argonne Univs. Assn. (chmn. bd. trustees 1969-73), Nat. Acad. Scis., Am. Philos. Soc., Sigma Xi, Phi Lambda Upsilon, Alpha Chi Sigma, Phi Kappa Phi. Editor Jour. Electrochem. Soc., 1969—; mem. editorial bd., mem. adv. edn. bd. Corrosion Sci., 1969-73; mem. editorial bd. Catalysis Rev. Home: President's House Rice Univ PO Box 1892 Houston TX 77001

HACKETT, CHARLES WILSON, JR., educator; b. Austin, Tex., Oct. 26, 1921; s. Charles Wilson and Jean (Hunter) H.; B.A., U. Tex., 1942, M.B.A., 1948; Ph.D., U. Wash., 1955; m. Ruby E. Bloomquist, July 25, 1953; children—Jean Elizabeth, Ruth Christina. Instr., Air Activities Tex., Corsicana, 1942-44, Schreiner Inst., Kerrville, Tex., 1946; mgmt. engr. Gulf Oil Corp., Port Arthur, Tex., 1948-50; instr., research bus. adminstr. U. Wash., Seattle, 1950-55; asst. prof. bus. orgn. Ohio State U., Columbus, 1955-56; industry financial analyst, credit rep. U.S. Steel Corp., Pitts., 1956-64; asst. dist. credit mgr., Houston, 1964-66; asst. prof. finance U. Tex. at Austin, 1966-69, asso. prof., 1969—. Trustee St. Andrew's Episcopal Sch., Austin. Served with USAAF, 1944-46. Recipient Exec. award Dartmouth Coll. Grad. Sch. Credit and Financial Mgmt., 1964. Mem. Am., Southwest (pres. 1975-76) finance assns., Financial Mgmt. Assn., Phi Beta Kappa, Beta Gamma Sigma, Phi Kappa Sigma, Alpha Kappa Psi, Sigma Iota Epsilon, Pi Sigma Alpha, Sigma Delta Pi, Phi Eta Sigma. Episcopalian. Author: A Techno-Fundamental Portfolio Management Simulation with Computer Applications, 1967. Home: 102 W 33d St Austin TX 78705 Office: Dept Finance U Tex Austin TX 78712

HACKLEY, LLOYD VINCENT, ret. air force officer, univ. ofcl.; b. Roanoke, Va., June 14, 1940; s. David Walton and Ernestine H. Hackley; student Northwestern Mich. Coll., 1962-63; B.A. magna cum laude, Mich. State U., 1965; postgrad. U. Colo., 1966-67; Ph.D. with honors, U. N.C., 1975; m. Brenda Stewart, June 12, 1960; children—Dianna M., Michael R. Enlisted U.S. Air Force, 1958, commd. 2d lt., 1965, advanced through grades to maj., 1976; comdr. 3436 Student Squad, Lowry AFB, 1966-67; exec. officer 20th Spl. Ops. Squad, Vietnam, 1967-68; analyst for Middle East, North Africa, NATO South Flank, Hdqrs. USAF in Europe, 1968-71; asso. prof. internat. relations U.S. Air Force Acad., 1974-78, ret., 1978; asst. v.p. U. N.C., Chapel Hill, 1978—. Counselor, treas. Denver Area council Boy Scouts Am., 1966-67; instr. AAU, 1976-78, Pres.'s Council on Phys. Fitness, 1975—; coach USAF Acad. men's and women's cross-country and track, 1975-78; bd. dirs. United Fund, Chapel Hill, 1979—; mem. exec. com. Triangle World Affairs Center, 1978—. Decorated Bronze Star, Vietnam Cross of Gallantry, Meritorious Service medal. Mem. Polit. Sci. Assn. N.C., Phi Beta Kappa, Phi Kappa Phi, Pi Sigma Alpha. Home: 104 Highland Dr Chapel Hill NC 27514 Office: Univ NC Gen Adminstrn PO Box 2688 Chapel Hill NC 27514

HACKMAN, EDWARD MERRILL, mfg. co. exec.; b. Denver, Sept. 13, 1929; s. Andrew Walter and Gaye Frances (Steele) H.; B.A., El Camino Coll., 1962; M.B.A., Calif. Western U., 1978; m. Vera Gean Pattinson, Sept. 4, 1970. Data processing analyst United Ins. Co., Los Angeles, 1953-56; data processing mgr. TRW, Inc., Redondo Beach, Calif., 1956-70; dir. corp. data processing and communications Commonwealth Oil Refining Co., Ponce, P.R., 1970—. Vice pres. Humane Soc. Ponce, 1974-75. Mem. Soc. Cert. Data Processors, Data Processing Mgmt. Assn., Am. Mgmt. Assn. Clubs: Ponce Country (dir. 1974-79), Exchange (pres. 1979), Ponce Exec. (pres. 1980), Cerromar Golf. Home: A-12 Jardines de Ponce Ponce PR 00731 Office: Firm Delivery Ponce PR 00731

HACKMAN, JOHN EDWARD, neurosurgeon; b. Covington, Ky., Dec. 24, 1940; s. MatthewRobert and Virginia Marie (Gautsch) H.; B.S. in Mech. Engring., U. Cin., 1963; M.D. magna cum laude, U. Ky., 1970; m. Jeanne Frances Leighton, Aug. 28, 1964; children—Jennifer Jeanne, Jonathan Leighton. Intern, U. Ky., Lexington, 1970-71, resident in neurosurgery, 1971-75; staff neurosurgeon Wausau (Wis.) Hosp., 1975-76; pvt. practice neurosurgery, Montgomery, Ala., 1976—; mem. staff Jackson Hosp., Bapt. Med. Center, St. Margarets Hosp., Montgomery. Bd. dirs. Arthritis Found. Diplomate Am. Bd. Neurol. Surgery. Fellow A.C.S., Internat. Coll. Surgeons; mem. Med. Assn. Ala. (interspity. council), Montgomery County Med. Soc., Montgomery Surg. Soc., Ala. Neurosurg. Soc., So. Med. Assn., So. Neurosurg. Soc., AMA, Congress Neurol. Surgeons, Am. Assn. Neurol. Surgeons, Alpha Omega. Alpha. Roman Catholic. Clubs: Montgomery Country, Capital City, Unity, Rotary. Home: 3230 Thomas Ave Montgomery AL 36106 Office: 1722 Pine St Suite 504 Montgomery AL 36106

HACKNEY, HUGH EDWARD, lawyer; b. McGregor, Tex., July 17, 1944; s. Hoyle Edward and Louise Witte H.; B.A. magna cum laude, So. Meth. U., 1966, J.D., 1969; student U. Coll. N. Wales, 1966-67; m. Janet Louise Tate, Oct. 7, 1967; 1 dau., Tate Louise. Admitted to Tex. bar, 1970; partner firm Fulbright & Jaworski, Houston, 1977—. Bd. dirs. Gulf Coast chpt. Leukemia Soc. Mem. Am. Bar Assn., State Bar Tex. (cert. specialist in family law and labor law), Houston Bar Assn., Phi Beta Kappa. Methodist. Clubs: Athletic (Houston); Big Bros. Office: 800 Bank SW Bldg Houston TX 77002

HACKWORTH, WILLIAM THOMAS, printing co. exec.; b. Charleston, W.Va., Nov. 15, 1927; s. William Newton and Gladys (Bailey) H.; student public schs., Charleston; m. Eleanor Dodd, Oct. 13, 1945 (dec.); children—Larry Wayne, Deborah Lynn; m. 2d, Pauline Dotson Whitten, Jan. 25, 1975; stepchildren—James, Jill, Joy, Katrina. With Jarrett Printing Co., Charleston, 1945-58, pressroom foreman, 1955-58; pres. Dunbar Printing Co., (W.Va.), 1958—; dir. Printing Industries of the Virginias, Charlottesville, Va. Pres. Dunbar Democratic Club, 1967-68. Served with USMC, 1945-46, 50-51. Named to W.Va. Printing Hall of Fame, 1971. Mem. Dunbar C. of C. (pres. 1965), Printing Industries Am., W.Va. Mfrs. Assn., W.Va. Safety Council, W.Va. Retailers Assn. Methodist. Clubs: Lions (pres. 1978-79), Masons, Shriners (treas. Mid-Atlantic Shrine Clown Assn.), Moose. Home: 5147 Brookside Dr Charleston WV 25313 Office: 1310 Ohio Ave Dunbar WV 25064

HADDAWAY, JAMES DAVID, ins. exec.; b. Louisville, July 25, 1933; s. Charles Montgomery and Viola (Sands) H.; B.Sc., U. Louisville, 1961; M.B.A., Xavier U., 1973; m. Myrna Lou Harris, June 5, 1954; children—Peggy Ann, Robert Marshall, Susan Gayle. Ins. cons. Met. Life Ins., Louisville, 1955-59; supt. Byck Bros. & Co., Louisville, 1959-61; dir. purchasing Liberty Nat. Bank, Louisville, 1961-63; v.p., mgr. gen. services adminstrn. Citizens Fed. Bank, Louisville, 1963-79; personnel mgr. Ky. Farm Bur. Ins. Co., 1979—. Founder, chmn. emeritus Kentuckiana Expn. of Bus. and Industry, 1973—. Served with U.S. Army, 1953-55. Named Boss of Year, Louisville chpt. Nat. Secs. Assn., 1978, 79. Cert. adminstrv. mgr., purchasing mgr. Mem. Assn. M.B.A. Execs., Internat. Adminstrv. Mgmt. Soc. (dir. 1979—), Adminstrv. Mgmt. Soc. Louisville (past pres.), Purchasing Mgmt. Assn. Louisville (past pres.), Louisville Personnel Assn. Baptist. Clubs: Masons, Shriners. Home: 4015 Wimpole Rd Louisville KY 40218 Office: 120 S Hubbard Ln Louisville KY 40207

HADDOCK, PENNY WILLIAMSON, educator; b. Birmingham, Ala., Oct. 1, 1953; d. Marcos Johnson and Pearl Irene (Lovett) Williamson; B.A., Birmingham-So. Coll., 1975; M.A. in Elem. Edn., U. Ala., 1978; m. Steven E. Haddock, June 7, 1975. Elem. tchr. Holy Spirit Sch., Tuscaloosa, Ala., 1974-78, Decatur (Ala.) City Schs., 1978—. Active Birmingham Mus. Art, Ala. Hist. Soc. Mem. Decatur Area Profl. Educators, Ala. Talented and Gifted, AAUW, Kappa Delta Pi, Kappa Delta. Methodist. Home: 1826 Eastmead Ave SE Decatur AL 35601

HADDOCK, R(EYBURN) PHILIP, lawyer; b. Astoria, Oreg., Jan. 8, 1919; s. Walter Hill and Jamie (Wilson) H.; A.B., Coll. William and Mary, 1942, student law sch., 1945-46, J.D., Stetson U., 1947; m. Doris Helen Hussell, June 12, 1948; 1 son, Randolph Reyburn. Admitted to Fla. bar, 1947, since practiced in Lakeland; atty. City of Mulberry, 1950-61; municipal judge, Lakeland, Fla., 1963-64. Dir. Attys. Title Services, 1971—. Trustee Polk County Law Library; bd. dirs. Polk County Blood Center, pres., 1962-76; bd. dirs. Polk County Drug Counseling Center, 1975—, pres., 1975; bd. dirs. Fla. Assn. Blood Banks, Lakeland Boys Club, Polk County Legal Aid Soc., mem. Prepaid Legal Sers. Com., Real Property and Trust Law Session. Chmn. Polk County Draft Bd., 1948-76, chmn., 1963-76. Served as sgt. inf. AUS, 1942-45. Decorated Bronze Star medal. Mem. Am., Fla., 10th Jud. Circuit (pres. 1957-58), Lakeland (pres. 1960) bar assns., Acad. Fla. Trial Lawyers, Am. Trial Lawyers Assn., Polk County Criminal Def. Attys. Assn. (pres. 1972-73), Lake Region Audubon Soc. (dir.), C. of C. (pres. 1962), Stetson Alumni Assn. (past pres. Polk County chpt., dir. 1975-77), Stetson Lawyers Alumni Assn. (pres. 1975-77), Am. Legion, V.F.W., 36th Div. Assn., Phi Alpha, Delta Kappa Alpha. Democrat. Methodist (bd. stewards; pres. bd. trustee Fla. Conf. 1966-68). Kiwanian (pres. 1957), Mason (32 deg.). Home: 1610 Reynolds Rd Lakeland FL 33801 Office: 601 E Lime St Lakeland FL 33802

HADGOPOULOS, SARALYN DE HAVEN POOLE, educator, author; b. Atlanta, Aug. 31, 1931; d. George Grady Poole and Sarah (Wimberly) Shaw; student Vassar Coll., 1949-51, Sorbonne, Paris, 1951, U. Ga., 1952; B.S., Columbia, 1955; M.A., N.Y. U., 1961; Ph.D., Emory U., 1965; m. Kerim Onder, 1953 (div. 1954); m. William E. Campbell III, 1960 (div. 1960); m. George John Hadgopoulos, Nov. 23, 1963 (div. 1978); 1 son, John George de Haven. Promotion asst. TV Programs Am., N.Y.C., 1955-56; asst. to fashion and beauty editor Am. Weekly Mag., N.Y.C., 1956-57; tchr. Miami Edison Sr. High Sch., Fla., 1958-60; asso. prof. English, Slippery Rock (Pa.) State Coll., 1967-69; asso. prof., lectr. George Washington U. Tidewater Center, Hampton and Norfolk, Va., 1972-79, PACE prof., 1973-75. Mem. Modern Lang. Assn. Am., Nat. Council Tchrs. English. Author: Poems of North Africa, 1973; Poems of Greece, 1975; The Crystal Mandala, 1976; Imagination's Wine, 1977. Home: 2309 Treasure Island Dr Virginia Beach VA 23455

HADLER, LYLE MILTON, clergyman; b. Moose Jaw, Sask., Can., Jan. 25, 1923; s. Frank Mathews and Annie Sophia (Hanson) H.; diploma South Eastern Bible Inst., 1950; B.A., Fla. So. Coll., 1951; M.A., Middle Tenn. State U., 1959; M.A.T., Rollins Coll., 1975; m. Helen Louise Haymond, Oct. 5, 1952; children—Sonja Louise, Paula Suzanne. Ordained to ministry Assemblies of God Ch., 1955; pastor chs., Murfreesboro, Tenn., 1953-59, Knoxville, 1959-61, Spartanburg, S.C., 1961-64; asso. prof. social sci. Southeastern Bible Coll., Lakeland, Fla., 1965—. Served with USAF, 1942-46. Mem. Psi Epsilon, Sigma Tau Delta. Republican. Contbg. editor state newsletter Tenn. dist. Assemblies of God, 1954-61. Home: 521 Queen's Loop Lakeland FL 33803 Office: 1000 Longfellow Blvd Lakeland FL 33801

HADLEY, DONNA SUE, mfg. co. exec.; b. Fort Worth, July 9, 1945; d. Adelbert Berry and Rose Alice (Keith) C.; student Hill Jr. Coll., 1963; children—Ellen Yvonne, Joe Bruce. Collection mgr. Credit Bur. Cleburne (Tex.), 1969-70; sec., bookkeeper Creative Marble Co., Fort

Worth, 1972-73; pres. A.B.C., Small Assemblies, Inc., Alvarado, Tex., 1973—. Mem. Burleson C. of C., Nat. Assn. Female Execs., Am. Mgmt. Assn., Am. Def. Preparedness Assn., Tex. Assn. Realtors, Nat. Assn. Realtors, Fort Worth Bd. Realtors. Mem. Ch. of Christ. Clubs: Mountain Valley Country, Ladies Golf Assn. Home: 813 Barkridge Trail Burleson TX 76028 Office: Route 3 Box 125 Alvarado TX 76009

HADLOCK, CHANNING MACGREGOR, pub. co. exec.; b. Mason City, Iowa, Feb. 25, 1923; s. Frank D. and Pauline M. Hadlock; B.A. in Journalism, U. N.C., 1948; postgrad. UCLA, New Sch. Reporter, Durham (N.C.) Morning Herald, 1947, telegraph editor, 1948; continuity dir. Sta. WDUK, Durham, 1946-47; press news editor NBC, Hollywood, Calif., 1948-51; TV writer-producer Cunningham & Walsh Advt., N.Y.C., 1951-53; account supr. Quality Bakers, N.Y.C., 1953-56; v.p., account supr. Rose/Martin Advt., N.Y.C., 1956-60; v.p., account supr., dir. radio/TV Chirurg & Cairns Advt., N.Y.C., 1960-66; v.p. Mktg. Innovations, N.Y.C., 1966-67; dir. mktg. Paramount Pictures, N.Y.C., 1967-68; sr. v.p. W. Kendall Brown, N.Y.C., 1968-70; dir. mktg. services Ogilvy & Mather, Houston, 1970-73; dep. nat. dir. Foster Parents Plan R.I., 1973-76; mktg. mgr. Time-Life Books, Alexandria, Va., 1976—. Served with AUS, 1942-46; PTO. Mem. Writers Guild Am. East, Dirs. Guild Am. Clubs: Lambs, Nat. Press, Anglo-Belgian (London). Contbr. articles to advt. publs.

HADSELL, CARL DONALD, ednl. adminstr.; b. Wheeling, W.Va., Mar. 25, 1947; s. William Miller and Mary Louise (Robinson) H.; B.S., W.Va. U., cum laude, 1969, M.B.A., 1970, postgrad., 1972; m. Antonia Lynn McGinley, June 7, 1969. Ops. research analyst U.S. Mgmt. Systems Support Agency, Office of Asst. Vice-Chief Staff, U.S. Army, Washington, 1970-72; asst. dean office admissions and records W.Va. U., Morgantown, 1972—, instr. EDP, 1972—; pres. Computer Corner Inc., Morgantown, 1977—; cons., lectr. in field. Adminstrv. asst. to chmn. Monogalia County Cancer Crusade, 1975-76. Served with U.S. Army, 1970-72. Mem. Am. Assn. Collegiate Registrars and Admissions Officers, Assn. Computer Machinery, W.Va. U. Alumni Assn., Beta Gamma Sigma, Phi Delta Kappa. Presbyterian. Contbr. articles to profl. jours. Home: 101 Jackson Ave Morgantown WV 26505 Office: 100 ARC Admission and Records WVa U Morgantown WV 26506

HAEHNEL, WILLIAM OTTO, JR., public relations mgr.; b. San Antonio, July 30, 1924; s. William Otto and Marie Helena (Fricke) H.; B.B.A., U. Tex., Austin, 1950; M.B.A., Tulane U., 1952; m. Mildred Engelken, June 25, 1947; children—William Otto III, Nancimarie. With Southwestern Bell Telephone Co., 1952—, public info. mgr., San Antonio, 1979—. Former trustee Freedoms Found., Valley Forge, Pa., recipient award; bd. govs. Internat. Summer Spl. Olympics. Served with AUS, 1942-46. Recipient numerous awards from cities, states and civic orgns. Republican. Lutheran. Club: Austin Civitan (internat. pres. 1972, recipient dist. and internat. honor keys). Home: 2607 Greenlawn Pkwy Austin TX 78757 Office: Room 1321 1010 N Saint Marys St San Antonio TX 78292

HAESLER, JOHN NEAL, architect; b. Ft. Belvoir, Va., Nov. 21, 1950; s. John Detrich Walter and Geraldine (McIlhaney) H.; B. Environ. Design with honors, Tex. A&M U., 1972, M. Arch., 1974; m. Janice Anne Zak, Dec. 21, 1974; children—Aaron Andreas, John Michael. Grad. asst. in architecture Tex. A&M U., Bryan, 1973-74; engr., gen. architect's office Southwestern Bell Telephone Co., St. Louis, 1974-75, archtl. asso., area architect's office, Little Rock, 1975-77, project architect, 1977-79, mgr. architecture, office of dist. mgr. real estate and architecture, 1979—. Cert. Nat. Council Archtl. Registration Bds. Mem. Am. Arbitration Assn., AIA (corp.). Home: 140 McMurtrey Dr North Little Rock AR 72118 Office: Southwestern Bell Telephone Co Room 598 1111 W Capitol Ave Little Rock AR 72203

HAEUSSLER, CHARLES LOUIS, govt. ofcl.; b. N.Y.C., Feb. 1, 1938; s. Ernest F. and Frieda (Erdmann) H.; B.A., Dickinson Coll., 1960; M.Govt. Adminstrn., U. Pa., 1962; m. Judith L. Dymock, Mar. 20, 1964; children—Linda, John. Exec. dir. Lebanon County (Pa.) Planning and Zoning Commn., 1962-68; account exec. McDonnell & Co., N.Y.C., 1968-69; mgr. Kendree & Shepherd, Jamestown, N.Y., 1969-71; chief planner N.W. Pa. Planning and Devel. Commn., Oil City, Pa., 1971-74; exec. dir. 5th Planning Dist., Roanoke, Va., 1974—; lectr. Alliance Coll., Cambridge Springs, Pa., 1972. Fels fellow, 1960-61. Mem. Am. Inst. Cert. Planners. Presbyterian. Club: Elks. Home: 2510 Avenham St Roanoke VA 24014 Office: Box 2569 Roanoke VA 24010

HAFELY, G. DOUGLAS, JR., publishing co. exec.; b. Garden City, N.Y., Feb. 23, 1933; s. Girard D. and Eugenie M. (Cronk) H.; B.B.A., Hofstra U., 1953; grad. USN Sch. Journalism, 1949, RKO Inst. Radio and TV Technique, 1951; Ph.D. in Philology, Taurus U., 1979; m. Kay Baker, June 28, 1975. Partner, Vickers Bros., N.Y.C., 1952-61; pres. First Gulf Coast Corp. of Tex., Houston, 1961-65, Houston Securities Systems, Inc. (Tex.), 1965-70, Tex-A-Que, Inc., 1970-72; dir., gen. mgr. Majestic Corp., Tampa, Fla., 1972-75; exec. dir. Cashco, 1975—, exec. editor of newsletter, 1975—, syndicated fin. columnist Trans-World News Service, Inc., 1976—; partner W. Coast Litho, 1977—; instr. mgmt. and fin. Pasco-Hernando Community Coll., 1980. Lic. psychologist, Fla. Mem. Fla. Press Assn., Sales and Mktg. Execs. Club, Hernando County C. of C. (exec. dir. 1979—). Republican. Episcopalian. Clubs: Downtown Athletic; Riverbend Country; Cork, Lions. Author: The Road-Map to Easy Riches, 1976. Address: PO Box 1999 Brooksville FL 33512

HAFER, W(ILLIAM) KEITH, marriage and family counselor; b. Gettysburg, Pa., Jan. 16; s. Warren Lavere and Helena Himes (Keith) H.; J.D., George Washington U., 1941; M.A., N.Y. U., 1973; Ph.D., Walden U., 1976; postgrad. Harvard U., 1968-69, U. Va., 1972-73, U. Ga., 1973, U. Tex., 1974-75; m. Joyce Pennington, Aug. 19, 1978; children by previous marriage—Lindsay Burgoyne Hafer Carpenter, Alexander Keith. U.S. fgn. service officer Am. embassy, Paris, 1945-46; dir. personnel Internat. Cellucotton Products Co., Chgo. and partner Sadler, Hafer & Assos., 1946-50; supt. indsl., public relations Internat. Minerals & Chem. Corp., Carlsbad, N.Mex., 1950-52; dir. human relations and communications, corp. dir. Fischer & Porter Co., Hatboro, Pa., 1952-54; pres. Chalfont Crafts, Inc., Bucks County, Pa., 1954-58; bus. devel. mgr., account group supr. N.W. Ayer, Phila., N.Y.C., San Francisco, Los Angeles, 1958-64; v.p. Silton Co., Boston, 1965-70; faculty mem. U. P.R., 1970-72, U. Va., 1972-73, U. Ga., 1973, U. Tex., 1974-76, Norfolk State Coll., 1976-79; pvt. practice marriage and family counseling, St. Petersburg, Fla., 1979—. Co-founder Family Service Assn., Bucks County, 1953; bd. dirs. Family Service of Santa Monica, Calif., 1958-63, Tri-Counties Mental Health Clinics, Norristown, Pa., 1953-56, Big Bros./Sisters, Norfolk, Va., 1978-79; trustee Family Service of Greater Boston, 1965-70. Served from to lt. col. Gen. Staff Corps, AUS, 1942-45; lt. col. (ret.) USAFR. Mem. Am. Acad. Advt., Nat. Assn. Social Workers, Nat. Council on Family Relations, Am. Psychol. Assn. Author: Psalm of Life, 1962; History of Our Presidents, 1964; Things I Love, 1968; Advertising Writing, 1977; editor: Understanding Texas Politics, 1975. Address: 6296 39th Ave N Saint Petersburg FL 33709

HAFF, RODERICK CANAVAN, surgeon; b. Panama, Canal Zone, July 10, 1936; s. Alexander O. and Blanche (Canavan) H.; B.A., Yale U., 1958, M.D., 1962; m. Veronica Ling, June 2, 1962; children—Alexander, Christopher S., William O. Intern Barnes Hosp., St. Louis, 1962, asst. resident in surgery, 1962-69, resident in surgery, 1969-70; practice medicine specializing in surgery, 1970—; commd. capt. U.S. Air Force, 1962, advanced through grades to col., 1977; asst. surgeon USAF Hosp., March AFB, Calif., 1964-66; surgeon USAF Hosp., Clark AFB, Philippines, 1970-72, chief of gen. surgery, 1971-72; comdr. 657th Tactical Hosp., Clark AFB, 1970-72; staff surgeon Wilford Hall USAF Med. Center, Lackland AFB, Tex., 1972-77, asst. chief of gen. surgery service, 1972-77; clin. asst. prof. surgery U. Tex. Health Center, San Antonio, 1972-77. Vestryman St. Thomas Episcopal Ch., San Antonio, 1974-76, sr. warden, 1976. Diplomate Am. Bd. Surgery. Fellow A.C.S.; mem. Soc. Surgery of Alimentary Tract, Soc. Air Force Clin. Surgeons, Assn. for Acad. Surgery, San Antonio Surg. Soc., Southwestern Surg. Congress, Alpha Omega Alpha. Contbr. articles in field to profl. jours. Home: 15060 Cadillac Dr San Antonio TX 78248 Office: 8601 Village Dr San Antonio TX 78217

HAFFNER, GEORGE LESLIE, optometrist; b. Pittsfield, Mass., Oct. 8, 1932; s. Harold Richard and Maude (Barnum) H.; A.A., U. Fla., 1953; B.S., So. Coll. Optometry, 1958, Dr. Optometry, 1958; m. Marjorie Newsom, Dec. 30, 1956; children—Marjorie Gail, April Charlene, Kimberlee Anne, George Leslie. Practice optometry, Tampa, Fla., 1959—. Dir. Mineral Resources, Inc. Sec., dir. Vision Care, Inc. of Fla., 1969-75; mem. Fla. Health Manpower Council, 1969-74; mem. profl. staff Easter Seal Soc. Crippled Children, 1967-69; mem. adv. staff optometric assistance course Hillsborough County Sch. System, 1971-76. Chmn. optometry div. United Fund, 1966, 70-80; mem. Pres.'s council Fla. So. Coll. Trustee Hillsborough Vision Care Found., 1964—, Fla. Kiwanis Found., 1974-76. Served to capt. AUS, 1954-56. Recipient Distinguished Service award Key Club Internat., 1967, Outstanding Service certificates and awards Greater Tampa Lions Sight Fund, Inc., 1961—. Fellow Am. Acad. Optometry; mem. Am. (chmn. career guidance com. 1972-74, 75-76, chmn. com. assistance to grads. and undergrads. 1977-80, Outstanding Service pin 1970), Fla. (trustee 1971-73, chmn. career guidance 1965-74, sec.-treas. 1973-74, pres. 1976-77) optometric assns., Hillsborough Soc. Optometrists (pres. 1964-66), So. Council Optometrists (trustee 1976-77). Democrat. Methodist (lay speaker). Mason (32 deg., Shriner), Kiwanian (lt. gov. Div. 8 Fla. dist. 1973-74; trustee Fla. dist. Kiwanis Internat. 1973-74). Home: 408 Lakewood Ave Tampa FL 33612 Office: 4515 S Manhattan Ave Tampa FL 33611

HAGAN, RALPH SEMANS, chemist; b. Uniontown, Pa., May 22, 1931; s. Ralph Semans and Sara Frances (Minehart) H.; B.S., Bucknell U., 1953; m. Carol Lee Childress, Nov. 3, 1969; children (by previous marriage)—Mark, Phillip Stuart; children—Kara, Kristi. Personnel interviewer, mfg. tng. program Gen. Electric Co., Louisville, 1956-58, plastics evaluation chemist, Louisville, 1958-62, polymer rheologist, 1962-64, mgr. polymer research, 1964-68, mgr. plastics lab., 1968-78, plastics lab. and applications center, 1978—. Lectr., U. Louisville, Stevens Inst. Tech. Mem. com. on life cycles of materials Fedn. Materials socs. Bd. dirs. Plastics Edn. Found. Served with AUS, 1953-56. Mem. Soc. Plastics Engrs. (chmn. Kentuckiana sect. 1965-66, mem. exec. council 1968-70, chmn. internat. awards com. 1972—), Soc. Rheology, Appliance Engrs. Soc., Plastics Edn. Found., Fedn. Materials Socs., Sigma Xi. Contbr. articles to profl. jours. Patentee in field. Home: 3100 Tremont Dr Louisville KY 40205 Office: Appliance Park Bldg 35 Louisville KY 40225

HAGANS, JOE WILLIAM, county ofcl.; b. Hosford, Fla., Mar. 26, 1912; s. Isom and Etta (Nickols) H.; student FBI Nat. Acad., 1956; m. Oveda Keene, Nov. 16, 1941; children—Joe W., Jack D., Sherod O., Oveda K. Patrolman, Lake City (Fla.) Police Dept., 1938-39; with Fla. Hwy. Patrol, 1939-73, capt., 1957-73; supt. Palm Beach County Park Rangers, Lake Worth, Fla., 1974—; tchr. Fla. Hwy. Patrol Acad., 1940-57. Mem. FBI Nat. Acad. Assn., Internat. Chiefs Assn., Palm Beach County Chiefs Assn., Nat. Sheriffs Assn., Fla. Peace Officer Assn., Frat. Order Police. Democrat. Clubs: Masons, Shriners, Kiwanis, Elks. Home: 608 29th St West Palm Beach FL 33407

HAGBERG, ROBERT DAVID, physician; b. Nelson, N.Z., Dec. 5, 1945; s. Robert Leonard and Noreen Lucy H.; came to U.S., 1945, naturalized, 1945; A.B., Miami U., 1968; postgrad. (Rockefeller Bros. fellow) Yale U., 1969; M.D., Ohio State U., 1973; m. Carol Sutton Miller, Dec. 28, 1968; 1 son, Jesse David. Resident in family practice, U. N.C., 1973-76; gen. med. officer Cherokee (N.C.) Indian Hosp., 1973—; cons. Fellow Am. Bd. Family Practice; mem. Acad. Family Practice. Home: Box 226 Route 3 Sylva NC 28779 Office: Cherokee Indian Hosp Cherokee NC 28719

HAGE, RAYMOND JOSEPH, cons. co. exec.; b. Huntington, W.Va., Nov. 28, 1943; s. Raymond and Cathleen Eleanor (Allport) H.; student U. Ky., 1961-63; B.B.A., Marshall U., 1966; exec. program, U. Va. Colgate Darden Grad. Bus. Sch., 1971; m. Susan Lee McCray, June 27, 1964; children—Shari Lynn, Raymond Joseph, Amy Elizabeth. Pres., chief exec. officer Am. Benefit Corp., Huntington, W.Va. Vestryman, St. John's Episcopal Ch.; mem. adv. com. 4th Congressional Dist. W.Va.; trustee Huntington Galleries; bd. dirs. Big Bros.-Big Sisters; registered health underwriter. Mem. Internat. Found. Employee Benefit Plans, Am. Mgmt. Assn., Nat. Assn. Life Underwriters, Nat. Assn. Health Underwriters, Am. Assn. Mus. Trustees (com. mem.), Sigma Nu. Democrat. Clubs: Rotary, Regency, Guyan Golf and Country, Masons, Elks. Home: 2105 Wiltshire Blvd Huntington WV 25701 Office: 401 Eleventh St Huntington WV 25701

HAGEN, RAOUL O'NEIL, army officer; b. Sioux Falls, S.D., Aug. 24, 1934; s. Albert O. and Theresa (Haugo) H.; B.A., U. Iowa, 1955; M.D., U. Iowa, 1958; children—Steve, Mike, Mark, Susan, Elizabeth. Intern, St. Benedict's Hosp., Ogden, Utah, 1958-59; commd. 1st lt. M.C., U.S. Army, 1959, advanced through grades to col., 1973; resident radiology Tripler Gen. Hosp., Honolulu, 1963-65, Walter Reed Gen. Hosp., Washington, 1965-66; chief profl. services 93d Evacuation Hosp., Vietnam, 1968-69; chief dept. radiology Brooke Army Med. Center, Fort Sam Houston, 1970—, dir. radiology residency tng. program, 1970—; cons. in radiology Health Services Command, 1975—; Army regional cons. in radiology for SW, 1976—; program coordinator radio logic tech. Acad. Health Scis., 1973—; chmn. Radiology Goals and Mgmt. Conf. U.S. Army, 1976; clin. prof. radiology U. Tex. Med. Sch., San Antonio, 1973—; team physician Robert G. Cole High Sch., San Antonio, 1973-75; cons. in radiology to surgeon gen., 1978—. Coach, commr. many youth baseball and basketball teams Fort San Houston, 1967—. Diplomate Am. Bd. Radiology. Mem. Am. Coll. Radiology, Radiol. Soc. N.Am. (Magna Cum Laude award 1971), San Antonio Mil. Civilian Radiology Soc. (pres. 1971-72), Bexar County Med. Soc., Long Binh Radiol Soc. Club: Fort Sam Houston Officers. Home: 1172 Garraty St San Antonio TX 78209 Office: Brooke Army Med Center Fort Sam Houston TX 78234

HAGENDOORN, WILLEM JACOB, mech. engr.; b. Rotterdam, Netherlands, July 13, 1932; s. Jan and Adriana (Boender) H.; came to U.S., 1957, naturalized, 1965; Mech. Engr., U. Delft (Netherlands), 1953; B.A., U. Louisville, 1965, postgrad., 1965-68; m. Barbara Jo Chaddic, Sept. 30, 1972; children—Tanja, Michelle, Lee. Research and devel. engr. Am. Air Filter, Inc., 1957-65; design engr. Gen. Electric Co., Louisville, 1965-68; mgr. engring. and sales Fisher-Klosterman Inc., dust control and pneumatic conveying, Louisville, 1968-79; pres., chmn. bd. Air Action Systems Internat., Inc., Louisville, 1979—; dir. Packaging Services Corp., Inc., Louisville. Served to 1st lt. Dutch Army, 1953-56. Registered profl. engr., Ky., Miss. Patentee in field. Home: 1219 Constitution Dr Louisville KY 40214 Office: PO Box 1204 Louisville KY 40211

HAGER, CHARLES WILLIAM, psychologist; b. Mancos, Colo., June 28, 1918; s. Ben W. and Tina E. (Wright) H.; B.A., So. Meth. U., 1944; B.D., S.W. Bapt. Sem., 1951; Ph.D., U. Tex., Austin, 1961; m. Beverly Benson, Jan. 17, 1959; children—John Floyd, W. Allen, Bryan Henry, David Wayne. Dir. guidance services Williamson County Schs., 1955-60, Georgetown Public Schs., 1960-61; dir. testing and counseling Tex. Wesleyan Coll., Fort Worth, 1961-75, asso. prof. psychology, 1961—; cons. psychologist Tex. Rehab. Commn., 1962—, Tex. Dept. Mental Health, 1963—. Mem. Planning and Zoning Commn., North Richland Hills, Tex., 1970-74. Recipient Citizen's Cert. of Recognition, Fort Worth Police Assn., 1975. Mem. Am. Psychol. Assn., AAAS. S.W. Psychol. Assn. Episcopalian. Club: Masons. Home: 4832 Wedgvew St Hurst TX 76053 Office: Tex Wesleyan Coll Fort Worth TX 76105

HAGER, PAUL CALVIN, coll. ofcl.; b. East Point, Ky., Oct. 15, 1931; s. Harry Homer and Priscilla (Baldridge) H.; A.B. with Distinction, Eastern Ky. State Coll., 1954, A.M. in Guidance and Counseling, 1962; Ph.D., U. Ky., 1974; m. Martha Joyce May, Aug. 16, 1959; children—Julie, Edward. Instr. music Prestonsburg-Floyd County Schs., Ky., 1954-56, 58-59, Community Unit Schs., Springfield, Ill., 1959-6 ; dir. counseling and testing service Berea (Ky.) Coll., 1962-71, testing and spl. services, 1971-75, asso. dean acad. affairs, 1975—, dean summer session, 1975—; teaching asst. human relations Ohio U., 1966-67; participant Coll. Entrance Exam. Bd. Conf., N.Y., 1968. Served with U.S. Army, 1956-58. Mem. Am. Psychol. Assn., Am. Assn. Higher Edn., Scientists and Engrs. for Appalachia, Am. Philatelic Soc., Phi Kappa Delta, Phi Kappa Phi, Kappa Delta Pi. Democrat. Methodist. Editor: Jour. of the Croatian Philatelic Soc., 1972-75 Home: 113 Lorraine Ct Berea KY 40403 Office: CPO Box 2315 Berea KY 40404

HAGERTY, CHARLOTTE KERR, educator; b. Anniston, Ala., Mar. 16, 1928; d. John Morgan and Myrtle Lee (Perry) Kerr; B.S., Jacksonville State U., 1948, M.S., 1968; postgrad. Emory U., U. Ala.; m. Julius P. Hagerty, Jr., Nov. 28, 1968; children by previous marriage—Dale R. Mintz, Kathleen Mintz Bowling, Elaine Mintz Scarbrough, Elizabeth Mintz Dear. Tchr., Munford (Ala.) High Sch., 1949-50, Mechanicsville Jr. High Sch., Anniston, 1953-54; lang. arts instr. U.S. Air Force, Reese AFB, Tex., 1955; tchr., chmn. dept. English, Oxford (Ala.) High Sch., 1958-67; instr. Gadsden (Ala.) State Jr. Coll., 1967—. Mem. NEA, Nat. Council Tchrs. English, Assn. Coll. English Tchrs. Ala., Southeastern Conf. English in Two-Year Colls., South Atlantic Modern Lang. Assn., Ala. Edn. Assn., Kappa Delta Pi. Democrat. Baptist. Club: Anniston Country. Home: 1809 Michael Ln Anniston AL 36201 Office: Lang Arts Div Gadsden State Jr Coll Gadsden AL 35903

HAGGARD, LLOYD RANDOLPH, state govt. ofcl.; b. Ft. Worth, Mar. 31, 1948; s. Roy Cecil and Billie (Purselley) H.; B.S., Baylor U., Waco, Tex., 1971; M.P.H., U. Tex.; m. Linda Jean Haynes, Aug. 9, 1969 (div.); children—Brandon Winthrop, Miranda Lynn. With Tex. Dept. Health, 1971—, microbiologist, lab. evaluator, Austin, 1971-75, lab. dir., sr. lab. evaluator, Port Arthur, 1975—; dir. Port Arthur's Women, Infants and Children Nutritional Food Supplement Program, 1976—. Registered med. technologist. Mem. Am., Tex. (sect. council 1977—) public health assns., Soc. Am. Med. Technologists. Democrat. Episcopalian. Home: 6439 Jefferson Blvd Groves TX 77619 Office: 431 Beaumont St Port Arthur TX 77640

HAGGARD, RUDOLPH LESLIE, broadcasting exec.; b. San Angelo, Tex., Apr. 2, 1933; s. Raymon Leslie and Ina E. (Byers) H.; grad. Tex. Tech. U.; m. Robbie Ann Easterwood, June 17, 1950; children—Chery Ann, Susan Gail. Mgr. City of Lubbock (Tex.); salesman Sta. WSEZ-AM-FM, Lubbock, 1964-67; salesman Sta. KCLU, Clovis, N.Mex., 1967-71; with Sta. KDJW, Amarillo, Tex., 1971-77; gen. mgr. Sta. KTEZ, Lubbock, 1977—. Mem. Tex. Assn. Broadcasters (dir.), N.Mex. Assn. Broadcasters. Baptist. Office: Suite 276 5002 University St Lubbock TX 79413

HAGGERTY, PATRICK EDWARD, hosp. adminstr.; b. New Orleans, Aug. 24, 1948; s. Daniel Bernard and June Katherine (Elliott) H.; R.N., Fitzsimmons Gen. Hosp., 1973; B.A., Loyola U. of South, 1975, M.B.A., 1977; m. Mary Jo Komodowski, Aug. 26, 1972. Staff nurse Hotel Dieu Hosp., New Orleans, 1972-73; intensive care nurse St. Charles Gen. Hosp., New Orleans, 1973-75; adminstr. West St. James Hosp., Vacherie, La., 1975—. Dir., Profl. Staffing of La., Inc. Mem. Health Planning Adv. Council, Nicholls State U., 1977—. Mem. Hosp. Fin. Mgmt. Assn., La. Hosp. Assn., Young Adminstrs. Forum, New Health Care Mgrs. Assn., Beta Gamma Sigma. Roman Catholic. Home: 2212 Country Club Dr Laplace LA 70068 Office: PO Box 128 Hwy 20 Vacherie LA 70090

HAGIN, T. RICHARD, lawyer; b. Thomasville, Ga., Sept. 13, 1941; s. Wesley Richard and Mildred Elizabeth (Skinner) H.; B.A., Fla. State U., 1962; LL.B., Stetson U., 1964; children—John Wesley, Grace Elizabeth. Admitted to Fla. bar, 1964; practiced in Bushnell, Fla., 1964—; mem. firm Davis & Hagin, 1964-65; individual practice, 1966-67; mem. firm Getzen & Hagin, 1967—; city atty. City of Coleman, Fla., 1969-72; gen. counsel Fla. Bank, Bushnell, 1967—; local counsel Fla. Nat. Bank at Lakeland, 1973—; county atty., Sumter County, Fla., 1969-76, pros. atty., 1969-73; atty. Sumter County (Fla.) Zoning Commn., 1973-76. Mem. Fla. Traffic Ct. Rev. Com. of Supreme Ct., 1971-72; chmn. Sumter County Subdiv. Adv. Com., 1973-76; vice-chmn. Withlacoochee Regional Planning Council Fla., 1973-75, chmn. 1975-76; chmn. Fifth Jud. Circuit Grievance Com. A., 1973-76; gen. counsel City of Webster (Fla.), 1966—, Lake Panasoffkee Water Assn., 1967—, Sumter County Hosp. Authority, 1967-76; local counsel Seaboard Coast Line R.R. Co., 1967—. Mem. city council, Bushnell, 1967-69. Mem. Nat. Assn. County Civil Attys. (dir. 1974-75), Nat. Dist. Attys. Assn., Nat. Criminal Defense Lawyers Assn., Am., Lake-Sumter (pres. 1969-70), Tri-County (sec. 1971-73, pres. 1973-74), bar assns., Fla. County and City Prosecutors Assn. (pres. 1969-72), Acad. Fla. Trial Lawyers, Fla. County Attys. Assn. (pres. 1973-74, 74-75), Delta Theta Phi. Mason (Shriner), Kiwanian. Home: 400 E Dade Ave Bushnell FL 33513 Office: PO Box 248 224 Bushnell Plaza Bushnell FL 33513

HAGINS, BRUCE LARRY, fin. mgr.; b. Woodruff, S.C., Dec. 23, 1950; s. Finley B. and Helen (Adams) H.; B.A. in Econs., Davidson Coll., 1972; M.B.A. in Fin. (fellow), Tulane U., 1974; m. Jan Kathryn Lanford, May 20, 1973; 1 son, Brannon. Laminates controller, prodn. control adminstr. Cryovac div. W.R. Grace & Co., Simpsonville, S.C., 1974-77, sr. fin. analyst Cryovac div., Duncan, S.C., 1977-78, fin. planning group leader, 1978-79, fin. planning mgr., 1979—; sec., dir. Cryovac Credit Union, 1978, pres., 1979. Mem. adv. bd. Simpsonville Welcome Center, 1977-78; adviser Jr. Achievement. Mem. Am.

Prodn. and Inventory Control Soc., Tulane Bus. Alumni Assn., Beta Gamma Sigma, Beta Alpha Psi. Republican. Methodist. Club: Kiwanis (treas.). Home: Route 3 Box 195-B Woodruff SC 29388 Office: PO Box 464 Duncan SC 29334

HAGLER, JOHN CARROLL, III, iron works exec.; b. Augusta, Ga., Feb. 14, 1923; s. John Carroll and Susan (Barrett) H.; B.S., U. Ga. 1946; m. Mary Anne Tyler, Oct. 16, 1948; children—Mary Anne, John Carroll IV, Richard Belton, Katharine Waterman, Elizabeth Tyler. Chmn. bd. Ga. Iron Works Co., 1947—; chmn. bd. GIW Industries, Inc., pres., treas. H & T Brass & Aluminum Foundry, Inc., Thomson, Ga., 1965—, Winfield Hills, Inc., Augusta, Ga., 1967—. Mem. Augusta Aviation Commn., 1962-72, 73—. Trustee, Historic Augusta, Inc., pres., 1971-74; bd. dirs. Richmond County Hist. Soc.; bd. dirs., mem. exec. com. Ga. Trust for Hist. Preservation. Served with A.C., AUS, 1943-45. Mem. Am. Foundrymen's Soc., Am. Inst. Mining, Metall. and Petroleum Engrs., ASTM, Am. Soc. for Metals, Nat. Assn. Mfgrs., Aircraft Owners and Pilots Assn., Quiet Birdmen, Ducks Unltd. (former chmn. Augusta area), Sigma Alpha Epsilon. Republican. Roman Catholic. Rotarian. Clubs: Augusta Country, The Pinnacle, Ponte Vedra, Highlands Country; World Trade Center (N.Y.C.). Home: 999 Highland Ave Augusta GA 30904 Office: PO Box 626 Grovetown GA 30813

HAGUE, JOHN FRANKLIN, III, newspaper publisher; b. Jacksonville, Fla., June 20, 1940; s. John Franklin, Jr. and Julia Ann (Jeter) H.; student LaGrange (Ga.) Coll., 1959-60, Middle Ga. Coll., 1969-70; B.A. in Bus., Robins Residence Center, 1972; m. Paula Edith Walter, Apr. 7, 1961; children—William Franklin, Sheri Lyn. Classified ad salesman Atlanta Newspapers, Inc., 1961-62; advt. mgr. Houston Home Jour., Perry, Ga., 1962-65, Daily Sun, Warner Robins, Ga., 1965-71; owner, pub., chmn. bd. Enterprise Newspapers, Inc. (Ga.), 1971-75; owner, pub., chmn. bd., pres. Oxford Sun Pub. Co., Inc. (Ala.), 1975—. Publicity chmn. Heart Assn., 1976; bd. dirs. Salvation Army. Served with U.S. Army, 1959-61. Recipient certificate of appreciation for patriotic civilian service U.S. Army, 1977. Mem. Nat. Editorial Assn., Ala. Press Assn., Ga. Jaycees (past dir.), Oxford C. of C. (dir.). Democrat. Roman Catholic. Clubs: Oxford Kiwanis (dir.); Byron (Ga.) Lions (pres. 1972). Editor Houston Home Jour., 1962-65, Claxton Enterprise, 1971-75, Peach County Enterprise, 1971-75, Warner Robins Enterprise, 1971-75, Oxford Sun, 1975—. Office: PO Box 3388 Oxford AL 36203

HAHN, JOHN WILLIAM, ins. co. exec.; b. N.Y.C., July 12, 1940; s. Ferdinand J. and Evelyn H. H.; B.A., Queens Coll., 1962; P.M.D., Harvard Bus. Sch., 1973; m. L. Dale Mazza; children—Nancy, John. With Atlantic Mut. Ins., N.Y.C., 1963—, v.p. adminstrv. services, 1974-78, Roanoke, Va., 1978—. Served with USMCR, 1959-66. Mem. Am. Mgmt. Assn., Ins. Acctg. Statis. Assn. Clubs: Harvard Bus. Sch. (N.Y.C.); Roanoke Country. Office: PO Box 4657 Roanoke VA 24015

HAHN, LOUISE O'CONNOR, psychotherapist; b. Astoria, N.Y., June 26, 1941; d. Daniel Francis and Louise (Kolarik) O'Connor; B.A. in Psychology, Coll. New Rochelle (N.Y.), 1963; M.A. in Counseling, Appalachian State U., Boone, N.C., 1976; m. Robert A. Hahn, July 8, 1967; children—Pamela Patricia, Jennifer Kathleen. Pre-kindergarten tchr. N.Y.C. Bd. Edn., 1967; elem. sch. music tchr. Okaloosa County (Fla.) Bd. Edn., 1970-71; adult basic edn. tchr. Wilkes Community Coll., Wilkesboro, N.C., 1973-75; staff therapist New River Mental Health Center, Wilkesboro, 1976-78; founder, 1978, since dir. Counseling Assos., Wilkesboro. Mem. Am. Personnel and Guidance Assn., Am. Rehab. Counselors Assn., AAUW, N.C. Personnel and Guidance Assn., N.C. Rehab. Counselors Assn. Author weekly newspaper column. Home and Office: 1903 Elwood Ave Greensboro NC 27403

HAHN, RICHARD BALSER, chemist, cons., author; b. Detroit, July 6, 1913; s. Balser Paul and Hattie (Liebau) H.; B.S., Wayne State U., 1935, M.S., 1936; Ph.D., U. Mich., 1948; m. Constance Lake, June 25, 1938; children—Paul B., Thomas E. Prof. chemistry Wayne State U., Detroit, 1942-78; research chemist Oak Ridge Nat. Lab., 1950-51; vis. scientist U.K. Atomic Energy Research Inst., Harwell, Eng., 1969; individual practice as cons., Oak Ridge, 1979—; cons. to USPHS, 1955-60. Mem. Detroit Nuclear Council, 1955-60. Recipient Excellence in Teaching award Wayne State U., 1978. Mem. Am. Chem. Soc., AAUP, Assn. Analytical Chemists (award 1977), Sigma Xi, Phi Kappa Phi, Gamma Alpha, Alpha Chi Sigma, Phi Lambda Upsilon. Lutheran. Co-author: Semi Micro Qualitative Analysis, 1955; Inorganic Qualitative Analysis, 1970; Quantitative Analysis, 1977; mem. editorial bd. Talanta, 1965-68. Home and office: 894 W Outer Dr Oak Ridge TN 37830

HAIDUSEK, MARY MARTIN, educator; b. West, Tex., Aug. 6, 1916; d. Louis Rehor and Mary Zofie (Cocek) Haidusek; B.A., Our Lady of Lake U., 1945, M.Ed., 1954, M.S. in L.S., 1970, M.A. in Guidance and Psychology, 1975; postgrad. U. Okla., 1952-53, 62-64, U. Tex., 1969. Entered Sisters of Divine Providence, Roman Catholic Ch., 1931; tchr. public schs. various locations, 1937-55; prin. various public schs., Tex., La., Calif., Okla., 1937-67; summer instr. Grad. Sch. Edn., Our Lady of Lake U., San Antonio, 1955-62, instr., reference librarian, 1967-68, grad. sch. edn. instr., cons., acad. advisor and counselor supr., 1968—. Asst. supr. Democratic Voting Poll, 1976. NSF grantee U. Okla., 1952-53, 62-63, 63-64; Higher Edn. Media Inst. grantee U. Tex., 1969; cert. profl. elem. tchr., Tex., Calif., La., Okla.; profl. elem. prin., Tex., Calif.; profl. counselor, Tex. Mem. AAUP, Am. Personnel and Guidance Assn., Tex. Assn. Counselor Educators and Suprs., Tex. Personnel and Guidance Assn., S. Tex. Personnel and Guidance Assn., Tex. Tchrs. Assn., Nat. Ret. Tchrs. Assn., Our Lady of Lake U. Alumni Assn., San Antonio Choral Soc. Democrat. Club: Mastersingers of San Antonio Symphony. Office: 411 SW 24 St San Antonio TX 78285

HAIR, MATTOX STRICKLAND, state senator Fla.; b. Coral Gables, Fla., Jan. 18, 1938; s. Henry Horry and Frances Alberta (Strickland) H.; B.S., Fla. State U., 1960; J.D., U. Fla., 1964. Admitted to Fla. bar, 1964, practice as partner Marks, Gray, Conroy & Gibbs, Jacksonville; asst. atty. gen., Fla., 1964-65; mem. Fla. Ho. of Reps. from 22d Dist., 1972-74, Fla. Senate from 9th Dist., 1974—. Served as 1st lt. U.S. Army, 1962. Mem. Am. Bar Assn., Fla. Bar Assn., Jacksonville Bar Assn. (bd. govs. 1968-72), Jacksonville C. of C., West Duval C. of C. (legal counsel), Fellowship Christian Athletes. Democrat. Baptist. Home: 2950 St Johns Ave Jacksonville FL 32205 Office: PO Box 447 Jacksonville FL 32201

HAIRE, CAROL DIANE, speech pathologist; b. Littlefield, Tex., June 24, 1949; d. Lloyd F. and Martha Vera (Smith) H.; B.A., Tex. Tech. U., 1970, Ed.D., 1976; M.A., N.Tex. State U., 1971. Speech pathologist Cooke County (Tex.) Schs., 1972; speech pathologist Muleshoe (Tex.) Schs., 1973-74; instr. Tex. Tech. U., Lubbock, 1974-76; clin. supr. speech pathology Howard Payne U., Brownwood, Tex., 1976-77; dir. speech pathology and audiology Hardin-Simmons U., Abilene, Tex., 1977—; cons. speech pathology, ednl. diagnostician W. Tex. Rehab. Center, Abilene, 1977—. Cert. profl. supr. speech and hearing therapy, profl. ednl. diagnostician, lang./learning disabilities Tex. Edn. Agy. Mem. Am. Speech and Hearing Assn. (cert. clin. competence), Tex. Speech and Hearing Assn., Big Country Speech and Hearing Assn. (pres. 1979—), Council for Exceptional Children, Phi Delta Kappa, Phi Kappa Phi. Baptist. Home: 4810 Stonehedge Rd Abilene TX 79606 Office: Hardin-Simmons U Box 1292 Abilene TX 79698

HAIRE, HENRY MADISON, physician; b. Auburndale, Fla., May 4, 1943; s. Henry Haywood and Jewell (Dyal) H.; B.A., Fla. State U., 1965, M.S., 1967; M.D., U. Miami, 1971; m. Ilze G. Gueiros, 1971; children—Alexander, Sonya. Intern, Harborview Hosp., Seattle, 1971-72; resident in medicine U. Wash., Seattle, 1972-75, fellow in nephrology, 1975-77; chief resident USPHS, Seattle, 1974-75; practice medicine, specializing in internal medicine and nephrology, Seattle, 1975-77, Orlando, Fla., 1978-79; mem. med. staff Central Fla. Artificial Kidney Center, Orlando, 1977-79; mem. staff Orlando Reginal Med. Center, Fla. Hosp., Holiday Hosp., Lucerne Gen. Hosp., Kissimmee Community Hosp., South Lake Meml. Hosp., Mercy Hosp.; nephrologist Watson Clinic, Lakeland, Fla., 1980—; tchr. Orlando Regional Med. Center, 1977-79. Diplomate Am. Bd. Internal Medicine. Mem. A.C.P., Am. Soc. Internal Medicine, Orange County Med. Soc., Fla. Acad. Family Physicians, Fla. Soc. Nephrology, Renal Physicians Assn., Fla. Med. Soc., Alpha Omega Alpha, Alpha Epsilon Delta. Contbr. articles to profl. jours. Office: Watson Clinic 1600 Lakeland Hills Blvd Lakeland FL 33802

HAJIAN, GERALD, biostatistician; b. Newark, Jan. 15, 1940; s. Zakar and Rose (Bakalian) H.; B.S. in E.E., Newark Coll. Engring., 1961; M.S., Rutgers U., 1965; Ph.D., Columbia U., 1972; m. Christina Langadinos, June 12, 1966; 1 dau., Eleanore. Asso. programmer IBM, Poughkeepsie, N.Y., 1961-63; sci. programmer Princeton (N.J.) U., 1963-64; asst. prof. math. King's Coll., Wilkes-Barre, Pa., 1971-73; biostatistician Am. Cyanamid Co., Princeton, 1973-76; head preclin. stats. Burroughs Wellcome Co., Research Triangle Park, N.C., 1977—. Mem. Am. Statis. Assn., Am. Math. Soc., Biometric Soc., Sigma Xi. Office: Burroughs Wellcome Co 3030 Cornwallis Rd Research Triangle Park NC 27709

HAKE, DON FRANKLIN, psychologist, educator; b. St. Louis, June 28, 1936; s. Wesley Franklin and Flora Haline (Sechrest) H.; B.A., DePauw U., 1958; M.A., So. Ill. U., 1962, Ph.D., 1963; m. Elaine Bicknell, Sept. 18, 1960; children—Lisa, Holly. Psychology intern Anna (Ill.) State Hosp., 1960-61, research scientist IV, 1961-74; prof. So. Ill. U., Carbondale, 1965-74; dir. research Regional Inst. for Children, Balt., 1974-76; prof. W.Va. U., Morgantown, 1976—. Fellow Am. Psychol. Assn.; mem. Midwest Assn. Behavior Analysis (mem. council 1978—), Soc. Exptl. Analysis Behavior (bd. dirs. 1970-78), Psychonomic Soc. Mem. editorial bd. Jour. Exptl. Analysis, 1966-69, 71-72, 77-80, asso. editor, 1973-77, Jour. Applied Behavior Analysis, 1972-74, 76-77. Home: 140 Poplar Dr Morgantown WV 26505 Office: Oglebay Hall West Virginia U Morgantown WV 26506

HALABY, RAOUF JAMIL, educator; b. Jerusalem, Nov. 22, 1945; s. Jamil Tanas and Katrina Hilane (Halabi) H.; came to U.S., 1965, naturalized, 1976; B.A., Ouachita Bapt. U., 1968, M.S., 1970; Ed.D., E. Tex. State U., 1973; m. Rachel Dell Lollar, Dec. 26, 1970; 1 son, Ramzy Truman. Teacher English, French and speech Magnet Cove (Ark.) Public Schs., 1970; asst. instr. English, E. Tex. State U., 1970-73; asst. prof. English and linguistics Ouachita Bapt. U., 1973—. Mem. S. Central Onomastics Assn., Ark. Coll. Tchrs. of English. Baptist. Club: Lions. Home: 123 Evonshire Arkadelphia AR 71923

HALBERSTEIN, ALEX, indsl. engr., banker; b. Vienna, Austria, Oct. 28, 1933; came to U.S., 1974; s. Isaac Leon and Clara (Weinraub) H.; B.S., U. Colo., Boulder, 1954; m. Elsie Eskenazi, July 31, 1955; children—Eduardo, Daniel, Jennifer, Cecilia, Ariela. Founder tin can mfg. plants, real estate corps., liquor bottling and mfg. plant, Lima, Peru, 1956-74; pres. Pan Amco Fin. Corp., North Miami Beach, Fla., 1974—, Argentinian Fin. and Investment Corp., Miami, Fla., 1978—, Fabrica Nacional de Envases, Lima, Peru, 1957—; dir. Capital Bank, Miami; bd. adv. Sunshine State Bank, Miami, others. Active Jewish orgns., sports, philanthropic orgns., Peru. Office: 1550 NE Miami Gardens Dr Suite 307 North Miami Beach FL 33179

HALBERT, DAVID DEAN, med. products mfg. and metal fabrication co. exec.; b. San Antonio, Dec. 19, 1955; s. David Stafford and Jo Ann (Walling) H.; B.B.A., Abilene Christian U., 1978; m. Kathryn Ann Gay, Aug. 25, 1979. Chief operating officer Sabian Corp., Abilene, Tex., 1977—. Mem. Republican Nat. Com., 1978—. Recipient cert. of merit SBA, 1977. Mem. Am. Mgmt. Assn. Mem. Ch. of Christ. Club: U.S. Senatorial. Office: Sabian Corp 5301 N 1st St Abilene TX 79603

HALBKAT, JAMES EVERETT, JR., transp. co. exec.; b. Denver, Dec. 19, 1934; s. James Everett and Eleanor Ware (Baldwin) H.; B.S., Yale, 1957; m. Sandra Gordon Hartshorn, June 14, 1957; children—James Everett III, Lucinda, Amanda, Stanley, Sarah. Investment banker Alex, Brown & Sons, Balt., 1959-65; mgr. diversification planning Continental Can Co., Inc., 1965-69, asst. treas., 1969; v.p. corporate devel., mem. mgmt. com. Liberty Corp., Greenville, S.C., 1969-72; pres., Intertruck Corp., Greenville, S.C., 1972—; dir., chmn. audit com. Rowe Price New Horizons Fund, Balt.; dir. T. Rowe Price Growth Stock Fund, T. Rowe Price Assos., Inc., Investment Counsel. Bd. dirs. Greenville (S.C.) Symphony. Served with USNR, 1957-59. Mem. Financial Analysts Assn. Wilmington, Del. Episcopalian. Clubs: Pequot Yacht (Southport, Conn.); Green Valley Country (Greenville, S.C.); Poinsett (Greenville, S.C.); Merchants (Balt.); Yale (N.Y.C.). Home: RFD 7 Foothills Rd Greenville SC 29609 Office: PO Box 6999 Greenville SC 29606

HALBOUTY, MANAH ROBERT, ret. air force officer; physician; b. Beaumont, Tex., Apr. 28, 1914; s. Tom C. and Sodia (Monolley) H.; M.D., Tulane U., 1937; grad. Sch. Aviation Medicine, 1940, Med-Field Service Sch., 1941, Army Air Staff Command and Gen. Staff Sch., 1944; m. Gracye Collinsworth, Mar. 23, 1940; 1 son, Michel Robert William. Intern, St. Paul's Hosp., Dallas, 1937-38, resident internal medicine, 1938-39; house doctor Mo.-Kans.-Tex. R.R. Hosp., Denison, Tex., 1939-40; commd. 1st lt., M.C., U.S. Army Air Force, 1940, advanced through ranks to col., 1951; aviation med. examiner, sr. flight surgeon chief flight surgeon and med. aircraft observor; research aviation medicine Mayo Clinic, 1941; asst. chief med. processing center SAACC, Tex., 1942; hosp. comdr., Ohio and Fla., 1943-44; troop carrier wing surgeon, Italy, Germany, 1945-46, comdr. hosps., wing and base surgeon, N.Y. State, Alaska, Ariz., Tex., 1956-57; div. surgeon 43d Air Div., comdr. 8th Tactical Hosp., also 6160th USAF Hosp., Itazuke AFB, Japan, 1957-60; chief flight surgeon, div. surgeon 819th Air Div., dir. base med. services hosp. and 819th Med. Group, Comdr. Dyess AFB, Abilene, Tex., 1960-66, also chief preventive medicine and comdr. USAF Hosp.; mem. phys. evaluation bd. USAF Hdqrs., 1966-68; USAF surgeon gen.'s staff med. rep. on USAF Phys. Rev. Council, Hdqrs. USAF Mil. Personnel Center, Randolph AFB, Tex., 1968-74; ret., 1974; chief Med. Bd. Rev. Service, Wilford Hall, USAF Med. Center, San Antonio, 1974—; practicing med. clinician Randolph AFB Hosp. and Wilford Hall USAF Med. Center. Decorated Legion of Merit with oak leaf cluster, Purple Heart. 2 Army and 3 Air Force Commendation medals; Gold Flight Surgeon's Wings with citation from Comdg. Gen. Chinese Nationalist Air Force. Mem. AMA, Assn. Mil. Surgeon's U.S., Aerospace Med. Assn. U.S., Am. Acad. Family Practice, Civil Aviation Med. Assn., Japanese-Am. Med. Assn. (founder), Assn. U.S. Flight Surgeons. Contbr. numerous articles to mil. and profl. med. jours. Home: 6002 Wildwind Dr San Antonio TX 78239 Office: Wilford Hall USAF Med Center (SGHF) San Antonio TX 78236

HALBOUTY, MICHEL THOMAS, geologist, petroleum engr., ind. producer, operator; b. Beaumont, Tex., June 21, 1909; s. Tom Christian and Sodia (Monnelly) H.; B.S., Tex. A. and M. Coll., 1930. M.S., 1931, Profl. Degree in Geol. Engring., 1956; E.D., Mont. Coll. Mineral Sci. and Tech., 1966;; m. Fay Renfro, June 22, 1945. Geologist, petroleum engr. Yount-Lee Oil Co., Beaumont, Tex., 1931-33, chief geologist, petroleum engr., 1933-35; v.p., gen. mgr., chief geologist and petroleum engr. Glenn H. McCarthy, Inc., Houston, 1935-37; owner firm of cons. geologists and petroleum engrs. in Houston, 1937—; discoverer numerous oil fields La. and Tex.; pioneer ind. to discover gas field Alaska. Chmn. bd. North Side State Bank, Houston, First Nat. Bank, West Side Nat. Bank, both San Angelo, Tex., First Nat. Bank, Paris, Tex., First Nat. Bank, Deport; dir. Allied Bank of Tex., Post Oak Bank, Houston. Served as lt. col. AUS, 1942-45. Mem. many tech. and sci. socs. Episcopalian. Clubs: Houston, Petroleum, River Oaks Country (Houston); Eldorado Country (Palm Desert, Cal.); Dallas Petroleum; New Orleans Petroleum; Broadmoor Golf (Colorado Springs, Colo.); Cosmos (Washington). Author: Petrographic and Physical Characteristics of Sand from Seven Gulf Coast Producing Horizons, 1937; Salt Domes—Gulf Region, United States and Mexico, 1967; co-author: Spindletop, 1952, The Last Boom, 1972; also numerous tech. and sci. papers on geology and petroleum engring. Home: 3630 Willowick Rd Houston TX 77019 Office: The Halbouty Center 5100 Westheimer Rd Houston TX 77056

HALDEMAN, LLOYD H., orch. exec.; b. Columbia, Pa., July 28, 1933; s. Lloyd H. and Hilda Haldeman; B.S. in Music Edn., Westchester State Coll.; m. Jeanene Haldeman, July 12, 1958; 1 dau., Janet. Gen. mgr. orchs. in Fresno, Calif., Vancouver, and Cin.; pres. Ednl. Mgmt. Corp., N.Y.C.; now pres., mng. dir. Dallas Symphony Orch., also dir.; mem. music adv. panel Tex. Arts Council; dir. North Park Nat. Bank, Dallas. Served with AUS. Named Entrepreneur of Year, So. Methodist U. Sch. Bus., 1977; Man of Year, N. Dallas C. of C., 1979. Presbyterian. Home: 10840 Strait Ln Dallas TX 75229 Office: 14580 Midway Rd Dallas TX 75234

HALE, ARNOLD WAYNE, army officer, ednl. specialist; b. Colome, S.D., Sept. 2, 1934; s. Archiebald William and Alvena Lucille (Williams) H.; A.B., U.S.D., 1959; M.Ed., Our Lady of the Lake Coll., 1971, M.Ed., 1973; B.S., SUNY, 1976; m. Mary Alice Mauricio, Nov. 30, 1962; 1 son, Alexander; children by previous marriage—Colleen, Zola; stepchildren—Charles, Marlow. Infantryman, U.S. Army, 1953-55, commd. lt., 1959, advanced through grades to maj., 1973, served in various staff and mgmt. positions with Med. Service Corps, 1959-67, Mil. Assistance Command, Vietnam, 1967-68, ednl. tng. officer, U.S. Army Med. Tng. Center, Ft. Sam Houston, Tex., 1968-73, hosp. comdr., Ft. Campbell, Ky., 1973-75, med. advisor Tex. Army N.G., Austin, 1975-77, ret., 1977; learning resources specialist, Thorndale/Milano Independent Sch. Dists., Milam County, Tex., 1977—; tchr. secondary schs., S.D., 1959, Tex., 1977; instr. psychology Austin Community Coll., 1977—. Decorated Bronze Star. Recipient Duke of Paducah award, 1975. Mem. Am. Personnel and Guidance Assn., NEA, Tex., Milam County, Tex. Jr. Coll. tchrs. assns., Ret. Officers Assn. (life), N.G. Assn. Tex. (life), Assn. U.S. Army, U.S. Armor Assn. Democrat. Club: Masons (W. Ger.). Home: 10412 Firethorn Ln Austin TX 78750

HALE, JAMES WALTER, III, transp. co. exec.; b. Pulaski, Va., Jan. 3, 1943; s. James J. and Janannie A. (Miller) H.; B.S. in English, Fla. Meml. Coll., 1965; postgrad. in Human Resource Mgmt., Nova U., 1978-80; children by previous marriage—Andrea Renee, Jai Lea. Spl. agt. Essex County Prosecutor's Office, Newark, 1965-66; instr. English, Broward County (Fla.) Sch. Bd., 1966-67; alumni dir. Fla. Meml. Coll., Miami, 1967-69; reporter Sta. WPLG-TV, ABC, Miami, 1969-70; program analyst Manpower and Econ. Devel. Div., Model City Program, Miami, 1970-71, dir. Citizen Participation div., 1971-73; adminstrv. officer Community Devel. Div., Met. Dade County, 1972-74; asst. dir. public involvement div. Kaiser Engrs./Kaiser Transit Group, Miami, 1974—. Bd. dirs. Tri-City Community Agy., 1979—. Named Outstanding Alumnus, Fla. Meml. Coll., 1976; Rockerfeller fellow, 1974-76. Mem. Public Relations Soc. Am., Internat. City Mgmt. Assn., Am. Soc. Public Adminstrn., Miami-Dade C. of C., NAACP, Northwest Jaycees, Alpha Phi Alpha (chmn. polit. action com. 1978-79). Democrat. Methodist. Home: 3061 NW 186 Terrace Miami FL 33055 Office: 44 W Flagler St Miami FL 33131

HALE, JOSEPH P., data processing cons.; b. Kansas City, Mo., Mar. 18, 1946; s. George C. and Dorothy E. (Burgess) H.; certificate in data processing Inst. for Certification Computer Profls., 1977; m. Judy M. Lanier, Sept. 15, 1979; children by previous marriage—Pat, Ted, Shannon. Project leader City of Kansas City (Mo.), 1967-68, Yellow Freight Co., Kansas City, Mo., 1968-69; data processing mgr. United Telephone Co. Fla., Ft. Myers, 1969-72; mgr. systems Decatur (Ga.) Fed. Savs., 1973-76; founder, owner, pres. Hale Systems, Inc., Decatur, 1976—; co-founder, co-owner, v.p., sec. Micro Acctg. Systems, Inc., 1979—; cons. security com. SE telephone cos. Mem. Ga. Savs. and Loan Assn., Data Processing Mgmt. Assn. (v.p. Atlanta chpt.), Jaycees. Roman Catholic. Home and Office: 1952 Scarbrough Dr Stone Mountain GA 30083

HALE, MARGIE NORNHAUSSER, chem. co. exec.; b. Carlsbad, N.Mex., Oct. 20, 1921; d. Muryl Marshall and Lena Florence (Witthauer) N.; B.S. U. Texas, 1942, M.S. Purdue U., 1948; m. Cecil Harrison Hale, May 6, 1945; children—Bryan M., Connie M., Chris A. Analytical chemist Esso Labs., Standard Oil Devel. Baton Rouge, 1942-45, patent contact, 1948-49, research chem. 1949-50; teaching asst. U. Tex., 1945-46, Purdue U., 1946-48; owner Southwestern Analytical Chems. Austin, Tex., 1950-65; v.p. Southwestern Analytical Chems., Inc. Austin, 1965—. Judge Austin area Sci. Fair, 1977, 78. Mem. Am. Chem. Soc. (exec. com., reporter Central Tex. sect. 1972-73, treas. regional meeting, 1979), AAAS, Sigma Xi., Methodist (steward 1960—). Contbr. articles to prof. jours. Home: 1300 Windsor Rd Austin TX 78703 Office: 821 E Woodward Austin TX 78704

HALE, SELDON HOUSTON, automobile sales exec.; b. Jefferson, Tex., June 11, 1948; s. Woster Seldon and Geraldine Leston (Sacra) Hale, Jr.; student U. Tex., Arlington, 1972-76; m. Kay Ellen Moler, Aug. 7, 1970; children—Emily Michelle, Denise Kathleen. Asst. mgr. service center Phillips Petroleum Co., San Antonio, 1968-69; asst. youth dir. N.W. YMCA, San Antonio, 1969-70; youth dir. Greenville (Tex.) YMCA, 1970-71; asst. mgr. men's and boy's dept. Watson's Arlington, 1971-76; gen. mgr. Pate's San Antonio, 1976-77; bus. mgr. Bruce Lowrie Chevrolet, Ft. Worth, 1977—. Vice chmn. Greenville 4th of July Celebration, 1971; chmn. youth com. Arlington YMCA, 1973-75, sec. bd., 1976. Recipient Dedicated Service award Arlington Fellowship of Christian Athletes, 1975-76, Membership Producer award, 1975; Dedicated Service award, Arlington YMCA, 1976; Outstanding Service award Tex. State Youth and Govt. Program, 1970-71. Mem. Am. Mgmt. Assn., U.S. Golf Assn., Arlington

Fellowship of Christian Athletes (pres.-elect 1976), Chevrolet Soc. Sales Execs. Methodist. Home: 111 Hidalgo Ln Arlington TX 76014 Office: 711 SW Loop 820 Fort Worth TX 76116

HALES, A(LBERT) QUINCY, JR., aerospace mfg. co. exec.; b. Akron, Ohio, Sept. 4, 1928; s. Albert Quincy and Jessie (Narron) H.; B.S. in Econs., Kent State U., 1953; M.B.A., U. Akron, 1964; m. Aug. 10, 1951; children—Lynne, Brian, Bruce. With Goodyear Tire & Rubber Co., 1950-74; s.w. dist. mktg. mgr. Goodyear Aerospace Corp., Dallas, 1974—. Past chmn. Summit County (Ohio) Mental Retardation Bd.; past pres. Summit County Council Retarded Children; past mem. adv. com. Summit County Child Welfare Bd.; mem. Ariz. Democratic State Com., also dist. treas. Served with USN, 1945-49. Mem. Am. Mgmt. Assn., Nat. Contract Mgmt. Assn. Clubs: Goodyear Foreman's, U. Akron Alumni, Kent State U. Alumni. Home: 700 Hurst Dr Bedford TX 76021 Office: PO Box 226004 7301 Ambassador Row Dallas TX 75266

HALES, JACK, JR., accountant; b. Chillecothe, Tex., Nov. 8, 1933; s. Jack and Frances Esto (Burch) H.; B.B.A. in Acctg. and Econs., Pan Am. U., 1957; m. Lula Mae Ivey, Oct. 8, 1954; children—Jack Robert, Pat Lawrence, Lynn Candise, Richard Allen. Staff accountant R.J. Welch, C.P.A., Weslaco, Tex., 1956-60; partner Welch, White & Co., Weslaco, 1961—; v.p., dir. Seal Produce Co., Pharr, Tex., 1975—. Treas., bd. dirs. Mid Valley Elem. Sch., Weslaco, 1979; bd. dirs. United Fund, 1963. Served with USAF, 1951-53. Named Boss of Yr., Weslaco Jaycees, 1979. Mem. Weslaco C. of C., Aircraft Owners and Pilots Assn., Am. Inst. C.P.A.'s, Tex. Soc. C.P.A.'s, Am. Acctg. Assn., Am. Taxation Assn. Republican. Baptist. Home: 415 Westgate St 15 Weslaco TX 78596 Office: 322 S Missouri Ave Weslaco TX 78596

HALEY, GERALD JOHN, mfr.'s rep.; b. Bradford, Pa., June 3, 1927; s. George Philip and Gertrude Theresa (Henretty) H.; student parochial schs., Bradford, 1933-45; m. Kathleen Marie Crutchfield, Nov. 17, 1956; children—Daria, Cecelia, Theresa. Trainee to br. mgr. Bond Plumbing Supply Co., Miami, Fla., 1947-52; Fla. mgr. Lewin-Mathes Co., St. Louis, 1952-53; mfr.'s rep., Osteen, Fla., 1953—. Founder, Fla. plumbing industry Student Loan Fund, Inc., also ann. golf tournament, 1972. Served with USAAF, 1945-46. Mem. Mfrs. Agts. Nat. Assn., Assn. Industry Mfrs. Democrat. Roman Catholic. Clubs: Rotary, K.C. Home and office: PO Box 70 Doyle Rd Osteen FL 32764

HALEY, JAMES KENNETH, urban devel. ofcl.; b. Elberton, Ga., Dec. 1, 1928; s. William Harris and Ruby M. (Ginn) H.; A.B., Wofford Coll., Spartanburg, S.C., 1952; m. Margaret Kennette, June 13, 1953; children—Julia Lee, Margaret Anne. With Procter and Gamble Co., 1954-56; realtor H.Y. Dunaway Co., also Allen Tate Co., Charlotte, N.C., 1956-62; with HUD, 1962-63; asst. exec. dir. Redevel. Commn. Winston-Salem, N.C., 1963-70; exec. dir. Housing Authority/Redevel. Commn. Winston-Salem, 1970-78, exec. dir. Housing Authority, Winston-Salem, 1978—; lectr. Inst. Govt., U. N.C., Chapel Hill. Bd. dirs. Winston-Salem C. of C., 1974-79, Piedmont Repertory Co., 1977-80, Rural Urban Coalition, 1974-77, N.C. Housing Fin. Agency, 1978—. Served with USMC, 1946-48. Recipient certificate appreciation HUD, 1975; named Exec. Dir. of Year, N.C. Turnkey III Homebuyers Assn., 1975. Mem. Nat. Assn. Housing and Redevel. Ofcls. (bd. govs., past regional pres.), Carolinas Council Housing, Redevel. and Codes Ofcls. (past pres.). Democrat. Presbyterian. Club: Winston-Salem Stratford Rotary (pres. 1977-78). Home: 2873 Fairmont Rd Winston-Salem NC 27106 Office: 901 Cleveland Ave Winston-Salem NC 27101

HALEY, MARGUERITE JANE, artist; b. Memphis, Mar. 5, 1946; d. Albert Jago and Annie Laurie (Tyler) Crawford; B.S. in Edn., Ark. State U., 1968; m. Richard Eugene Haley, Aug. 19, 1967; children—Richard Forrest, Marguerite Suzanne. Tchr. art K-12 grades, supr. art K-8, Newport (Ark.) Pub. Schs., 1968-69; tchr. English, Judsonia (Ark.) Pub. Schs., 1971-74, 77-79, Title I tutor, 1979-80; proofreader, secy., bookkeeper White County Record newspaper, Judsonia, Ark., 1975-76; pvt. instr. art, Judsonia, 1975-76; teller Judsonia Water & Sewer Co., 1977; tchr. English, yearbook sponsor Judsonia Schs., 1977—; one person shows banks and libraries in Newport, Tuckerman and Judsonia, 1967-76; group shows: Ark. State U. Alumni, 1975, White County Fair, 1977; paintings include: Day's End, 1970, Memories, 1970, Symphony, 1976, Grand Canyon Relics, 1978. Sec. Jaycee Aux., Judsonia, 1974-75; active justice of peace campaigns White County Democratic Party, 1976—; active with Cystic Fibrosis Fund Dr., Judsonia, 1978, Heart Fund Dr., Judsonia, 1977, March of Dimes campaign, Judsonia, 1977-78, N.G. activities, 1976—, Boy Scouts Am., Judsonia, 1976-77, Ark. Arthritis Found., 1978. Recipient appreciation award for artwork U.S. Army, 1969; citizenship award DAR, 1964; numerous others. Mem. Internat. Soc. Artists, Ark., Nat., Judsonia edn. assns., Beta Sigma Phi (Zeta Delta chpt. photographer, historian 1979), Alpha Omicron Pi (ritual doorkeeper). Democrat. Methodist. Clubs: White County Justice of Peace Wives, Am. Legion Aux. Subject of articles Jackson County Ind. Newspaper, Newport, 1970. Address: Star Route Judsonia AR 72081

HALEY, MARLIN ELROY, ins. exec.; b. Kingsdown, Kans., May 27, 1921; s. Olin Rutledge and Pearl (Smith) H.; student Kans. State U., Pittsburg, 1938-40, U. Houston, 1959-60, Tex. Christian U., 1966-69; m. Dorothy Alta Lincoln, Mar. 23, 1941; children—Nancy Marlene, Cheryl Sue. Agt., Am. Nat. Ins. Co., Galveston, Tex., 1948-50, staff mgr., 1950-55, dist. mgr., 1955-59; agt. supr. Combination Agencies Home Office, 1959-65; v.p., dir. agencies, dir. Family Security Ins. Co., Ft. Worth, 1965—. Bd. dirs. Multiple Sclerosis Assn. of Tarrant County, 1978-79; speakers bur. United Way. Served with U.S. Maritime Service, 1943-45. C.L.U. Mem. Am. Soc. C.L.U.'s. Republican. Presbyterian. Clubs: Ridglea Country, Masons. Home: 508 Oak Hollow Fort Worth TX 76112 Office: 1200 Pennsylvania Ave Fort Worth TX 76104

HALEY, SUZANNE, speech pathologist; b. Waco, Tex., Jan. 20, 1953; d. Edmond Milton and Gloria Lorraine (Kaul) H.; B.A. in Edn., U. Miss., 1975, M.Communicative Disorders, 1976. Speech pathologist Jackson (Miss.) Speech and Hearing Clinic, 1976—, Home Health Care Miss., Jackson, 1978—. Jones scholar, 1971-75; U. Miss. non-service fellow, 1975-76. Mem. Am. Speech and Hearing Assn., Miss. Speech and Hearing Assn., Phi Kappa Phi. Roman Catholic. Home: 164 A Grove Circle Jackson MS 39206 Office: 1510 N State St Jackson MS 39202

HALFORD, JAKE HALLIE, elec. engr., educator; b. Columbia, S.C., Nov. 26, 1941; s. James Dorman and Mary (Jaudon) H.; B.S. in Elec. Engring., U. S.C., 1965; M.S. in Elec. Engring., Duke U., 1968, Ph.D. in Elec. Engring., 1973; m. Celia Childress, Sept. 11, 1965; children—Jonathan Jacob, Blair Kenneth, Spencer Jaudon. Instr. math. Guilford Coll., Greensboro, N.C., 1966-67; asst. prof. elec. engring. U.S. Naval Acad., Annapolis, Md., 1973-78; asst. to acad. dean, asso. prof. elec. engring. The Citadel, Charleston, S.C., 1978—; adj. prof. Anne Arundel Community Coll., Arnold, Md., 1975-78. Elder, Seventh-Day Adventist Ch., 1975—, organizer, bd. chmn. Martin Barr Seventh-Day Adventist Sch., 1974-77. Mem. IEEE (vice chmn. Annapolis 1975-76, chmn. 1976-77), Sigma Xi, Eta Kappa Nu, Tau Beta Pi. Republican. Author papers on amorphous thin films; developer amorphous thin film non-volatile memory device. Office: Dept Elec Engring The Citadel Charleston SC 29409

HALL, ANDREW CLIFFORD, lawyer; b. Warsaw, Poland, Sept. 16, 1944; came to U.S., 1949, naturalized, 1954; s. Edmund and Maria (Hahn) H.; B.A., U. Fla., 1965, J.D. with high honors, 1968; m. Patricia Ann Hall, Aug. 14, 1966 (div. 1980); children—Michael Ian, Adam Stuart. Admitted to Fla. bar, 1968, Ga. bar, 1971, U.S. Supreme Ct., 1973; law clk. U.S. Dist. Ct. So. Dist. Fla., 1968-70; asso. firm Haas, Holland, Levison & Gilbert, Atlanta, 1970-72, firm Frates, Floyd, Pearson & Stewart, Miami, Fla., 1972-75; partner firm Storace, Hall and Hauser, Miami, 1975-79, firm Hall & Hauser, Miami, 1979—. Mem. Am. Bar Assn., Am. Judicature Soc., Acad. Fla. Trial Lawyers, Am. Trial Lawyers Assn., Phi Kappa Phi, Phi Alpha Delta, Order of Coif. Democrat. Jewish. Home: 600 NE 36 St Miami FL 33137 Office: 1401 Brickell Ave Miami FL 33130

HALL, ANNA WHITLOCK, educator; b. Edgefield, S.C., May 28, 1919; d. Charles Milledge and Lila (Logan) Whitlock; B.S. in Elem. Edn., U. Ga., 1956, M.S., 1960, Ed.S. in Elem. Edn., 1965; divorced; children—James Battle, Jr., Judy Ann Hall Summerford. Elem. sch. tchr. in Ga., 1939-72; asst. prin. S. Rome (Ga.) Sch., 1972-74; asst. prof., coordinator student teaching Berry Coll., Mt. Berry, Ga., 1974—. Ga. State grantee, 1962-65. Mem. AAUW, NEA, Internat. Reading Soc., Ga. Edn. Assn., Berry Assn. Educators, Leona Clements Porcelain Art Guild, Phi Kappa Pi, Kappa Delta Pi, Delta Kappa Gamma (pres.). Democrat. Baptist. Club: Spade and Trowel Garden. Home: 31 Maplewood Sq Rome GA 30161 Office: Berry Coll Mount Berry GA 30161

HALL, CHARLES WORTH, educator, former soldier; b. Louisville, Dec. 18, 1946; s. Worth Leroy and Gertrude Omega (Greenwell) H.; A.A., Hartnell Coll., 1975; B.S., U. So. Miss., 1976; postgrad. S.D. State U., 1977; M.Ed., U. Louisville, 1979; m. Maryann Doris Pillatzki, July 15, 1972; 1 dau., Charlotte Ann Hall. Enlisted in U.S. Army, 1963; specialist personnel mgmt. U.S. Army, various locations Europe and Asia, 1963-73; advanced through grades to sgt. 1st class, 1975; systems analyst for personnel, mgmt. info. systems, Ft. Campbell, Ky., 1973-74; field recruiter U.S. Army Res., Southwestern Miss., 1976-77; res., 1978; counselor, instr. human relations, admissions counselor, asst. dir. student services Ivy Tech-South central, Sellersburg, Ind., 1979—; chmn., pres. Personnel Services Co. Inc., Jackson, Miss., 1976—; founder, pres., dir. New Horizons Devel. Co., Louisville, 1978—. Mem. Voters Registration Com., Hattiesburg, 1974-75; del. Forrest County (Miss.) Democratic conv., 1975; chmn. Pinecrest Conservative Precinct Caucus, 1975; pres. Young Dems. U. So. Miss., 1975-76; dist. commr. Monterey Bay council Boy Scouts Am., 1971-72, asst. dist. commr. Pine Burr council, 1972-75; mem. Beauvoir Devel. Found. Decorated Vietnam Cross of Gallantry, Mil. Service Cross; recipient Eagle Scout award, 1963, Commr's. Tng. Key, 1969, Disting. Service Key, 1976; Disting. Recruiting Cup, 1977; hon. Ky. Col. Mem. Am. Soc. Personnel Adminstrs., Am. Coll. Personnel Assn., Am. Personnel and Guidance Assn., Nat. Assn. Student Personnel Adminstrs. (affiliate), Am. Mensa Soc., Kadets of Am./Internation (lt. gen., state comdr. Ky. 1964-68; CAP (lt., squadron comdr. 1968-69), Sons Confederate Vets. (comdr. 27th Miss. regtl. camp 1975-76), Mil. Order Stars and Bars (adj. gen. Ky. 1979-80), Confederate Meml. Lit. Soc., Res. Officers Confederate Alliance (col.-at-large), Nat. Eagle Scout Assn., Am. Legion, VFW, Alpha Phi Omega (pres. Kappa Eta chpt. 1976-77), Phi Delta Kappa, Phi Kappa Phi, Omicron Delta Kappa, Pi Gamma Mu (chpt. v.p. 1976-77), Epsilon Delta Chi. Roman Catholic. Club: K.C. (3 deg.). Home: Gen Delivery Hattiesburg MS 39401 also 1800 S 2d St Apt 27-B Louisville KY 40208 Office: Ind Vocat Tech Coll South Central 8204 Hwy 311 W Sellersburg IN 47172

HALL, CLAUDE HAMPTON, educator; b. Proffit, Va., Sept. 29, 1922; s. Robert Montgomery and Josephine (Wood) H.; B.A., U. Va., 1947, M.A., 1949, Ph.D., 1954; m. Mary Inez Wingfield, Aug. 19, 1951; children—Claude Hampton, David Bruce. Asst. ref. librarian U. Va., 1947-51; instr. history Tex. A. and M. U., College Station, 1951-55, asst. prof., 1955-59, asso. prof., 1959-64, prof., 1964—; vis. asso. prof. U. Mo., 1964. Served with AUS, 1942-45. Recipient Distinguished Achievement in Teaching award Tex. A. and M. U., 1958. Mem. AAUP, ACLU, Am., So., Tex. (H. Bailey Carroll award 1968), E. Tex. (pres. 1977) hist. assns., Va. Hist. Soc., Am. Acad. Polit. and Social Sci., Phi Kappa Phi (pres. local chpt. 1973). Baptist. Author: Abel Parker Upshur: Conservative Virginian, 1964. Contbr. articles to profl. jours. Home: 2515 Memorial Dr Bryan TX 77801 Office: Dept History Texas A and M University College Station TX 77843

HALL, DENNIS RAY, realtor, developer, rancher; b. Boswell, Okla., May 18, 1946; s. Robert Lee and Ester (Holland) H.; B.A. in Bus. Adminstrn., Troy State U., Dothan, Ala., 1973; postgrad. in edn. Southeastern Okla. State U., Durant, 1973-75; m. Vivian Gayle Dancer, Sept. 5, 1964; children—Wendy Danae, Dennis. Enlisted in U.S. Army, 1966, advanced through grades to capt., 1969; aviator-pilot, 1968-71, comdg. officer troop co., 1971-72, brigade staff officer, 1972-73; realtor G H & M Realty, Durant, 1973-77; developer Sunny Meadow Devel. Co., Durant, 1977—; rancher, Durant, 1970—; owner Hall Enterprises; cons. real estate and fin. Decorated D.F.C., Bronze Star, Air medal (21). Baptist. Home: Star Route Durant OK 74701 Office: 400 W Main St Durant OK 74701

HALL, DONALD LEROY, ophthalmologist; b. Vicksburg, Miss., Apr. 1, 1940; s. John Evans and Audrey (Lard) H.; B.S., Miss. State U., 1962; M.D., U. Miss., 1965; m. Mary Jane Ray, Oct. 14, 1966; children—Mary Ashley, Courtney Brooke, Donald Clayton. Intern, U. Miss. Hosp., 1965-66, resident in ophthalmology, 1968-71; Heed fellow in retinal diseases Presbyn. Hosp. of Pacific Med. Center, San Francisco, 1971-72; clin. instr. ophthalmology U. Tex., Houston, Galveston, 1972-73; practice medicine specializing in ophthalmology, Shreveport, La., 1973—; clin. asst. prof. ophthalmology Med. Sch., La. State U., 1978—. Bd. dirs. St. Mark's Day Sch., 1975—; vestryman Episcopal Ch. of Holy Cross, 1975-78. Served to capt. M.C., USAF, 1966-68. Diplomate Am. Bd. Ophthalmology (asso. examiner 1976, 77, 80). Fellow Am. Acad. Ophthalmology and Otolaryngology (chmn. practitioner advisory com. 1979-80), A.C.S.; mem. AMA, La. Med. Soc., Am. Assn. Ophthalmology (council long range planning and devel. 1976-77), La. Ophthal. Assn. (councilor 1975-80), Tristate Ophthal. Soc. (pres. 1974-80), Alpha Omega Alpha, Sigma Chi. Club: Ambassadors of Shreveport. Democrat. Contbr. sects. on ophthalmology to basic and clin. sci. course, med. articles to profl. lit. Home: 6611 Gilbert Dr Shreveport LA 71106 Office: 2751 Virginia Ave Shreveport LA 71103

HALL, DONALD MYERS, lawyer; b. Negritos, Peru, June 7, 1934; s. John Dale and Ruby Garnet (Parsons) H.; B.A., U. Miami (Fla.), 1955; LL.B., Tulane U., 1958; m. Belen Valentin, Sept. 23, 1966; children—John Dale, Christopher Lee, Layne Allender, Rachel Jennifer, Sarah Amanda. Admitted to La. bar, 1958, Fla. bar, 1960, P.R. bar, 1964; mem. firm Fowler, White, Gillen, Humkey & Trenam, Tampa and Miami, 1959-62, Kullman & Lang, New Orleans, 1962, McConnell, Valdes, Kelley, Sifre, Griggs & Ruiz Suria, San Juan, P.R., 1962—, partner, 1966—, Miami (Fla.) Office, 1978—. Home: 14100 SW 81st Ave Miami FL Office: 904 Greater Miami Fed Bldg 200 SE 1st St Miami FL 33131

HALL, E. EUGENE, univ. pres.; b. Mansfield, La., June 19, 1932; s. Alvin and Rose Marie (White) H.; B.A., La. Coll., 1953; B.D., So. Baptist Theol. Sem., 1956; M.A., La. State U., 1959, Ph.D., 1963; m. Reba Frances Hobby Dec. 27, 1955; children—David, Laurie, Steven. Asst. prof. speech Georgetown (Ky.) Coll., 1962-65, asso. prof., chmn. dept. speech, 1968-71; staff asst. to dean Coll. Arts and Humanities, asso. prof. Western Ky. U., 1971-73; asso. prof., chmn. dept. speech La. Coll., 1965-68, dean of coll., 1973-76, interim adminstrn., 1974-75, v.p. acad. affairs, 1976-77; pres. Okla. Bapt. U., 1977—. Served with Chaplain Corps, USN, 1956-58. Recipient Disting. Alumni award La. Coll., 1978. Mem. Am. Assn. Univ. Adminstrs., Assn. So. Bapt. Coll. and Univs. Pres.'s, Am. Assn. Higher Edn., Nat. Collegiate Honors Council, Assn. Gen. and Liberal Studies, AAUP, Phi Mu Alpha Sinfonia. Baptist. Club: Rotary. Contbr. articles to communications and denominational jours.; editor Ky. Jour. Communication Arts; contbg. editor La. Bapt. Message, 1974-75. Office: 500 W University Shawnee OK 74801

HALL, ELVAJEAN, librarian; b. Hamilton, Ill.; d. Henry Nelson and Nellie (Hyer) Hall; A.B., Oberlin Coll., 1930; certificate U. Wis. Library Sch., 1932; M.L.S., Columbia, 1941. Asst. librarian Milw.-Downer Coll., 1932-33; librarian high sch., Elgin, Ill., 1934-37, Milw. U. Sch., 1937-42, Stephens Coll., Columbia, Mo., 1944-46; supr. sch. libraries, Jackson, Mich., 1942-44, Newton, Mass., 1946-75. Instr. Mass. Dept. Edn., 1948; cons. Sch. Library Jour., 1958-63, Grolier Soc., 1959; cons. sch. library expert Library Services br. U.S. Office Edn., Washington, spring 1960; cons. library program Chung Chi Coll., Hong Kong, 1962-63; lectr. Nat. U. of Ireland, summers 1967-69. Mem. ALA, Am. Assn. Sch. Librarians (nat. recruitment chmn. 1956), NEA, Mass. (chmn. 1948-49), New Eng. sch. library assns., Assn. for Supervision and Curriculum Devel., Women's Nat. Book Assn. (pres. Boston chpt. 1957-59, nat. dir. 1957-62, nat. sec. 1960-62), Authors Guild Am., Nat. League Am. Pen Women (pres. Boston br. 1970-72, nat. dir. librarian 1980—), AAUW, Kappa Delta, Delta Kappa Gamma. Republican. Author: Books To Build On, 1955; Land and People of Argentina, 1960, 72; Pilgrim Stories, 1962; Argentina Pueblo y Costumbres, 1962; Land and People of Norway, 1963, rev. edit., 1973; Pilgrim Neighbors, 1964; The Volga: Lifeline of Russia, 1965; Land and People of Czechoslovakia, 1966; Hong Kong, 1967; The Psalms, 1968; Picture Map Geography of Eastern Europe, 1968; The Proverbs, 1970; (with R.J. Houlehen) The Battle for Sales, 1973; Jobs in Marketing and Distribution 1974; Today in Old Boston, 1975; Today in Old New York, 1975; Today in Old Philadelphia, 1976. Contbr. articles to edn. and library jours. Home: 4010 Camelot Dr Apt C-2 Raleigh NC 27609

HALL, GEORGE WANDA, accountant; b. Lake Creek, Tex., Feb. 1, 1921; s. George Washington and Lottie Elizabeth (Reed) H.; B.C.S., Okla. Sch. Acctg., 1953; m. Ida Nell Goodacre, Oct. 4, 1943; 1 son, George Wayne. With Seismograph Service Corp., Athens, Tex., 1948—, supr. gen. acctg., 1954-72, internal auditor, 1972-78, adminstrv. asst. drilling div., 1978—. Bd. dirs. Rainbow Girls, Boy Scouts Am. Served with U.S. Army, 1942-46; CBI. Mem. Jr. C. of C., Adminstrv. Mgmt. Assn. Methodist. Clubs: Masons, Order Eastern Star, DeMolay. Home: Route 5 Box 76 Athens TX 75751 Office: PO Box 1862 Athens TX 75751

HALL, JAMES, III, architect, urban planner; b. Chickasha, Okla., May 13, 1934; s. James and Lella Mae (Bogney) H.; B.S., Hampton Inst., 1959; M.S., Ill. Inst. Tech., 1966; M.City Planning, Harvard U., 1974; m. Shirley Maria Sullivan, July 11, 1965; children—Sandra Maria, Marisa Annette, James IV. Designer, draftsman Henry L. Livas & Assos., Hampton Norfolk, Va., 1957-59; archtl. cons. Ken L. Freeman, Bethesda, Md., 1963; designer, draftsman PACE Assos., Chgo., 1964-66; project architect Tidewater Design Group, Hampton, Va., 1967-70; asst. prof. architecture Hampton Inst., 1966-72, asso. prof., 1974-77, prof., 1977—; prin. staff planner Roxbury Action Program, Inc., Boston, 1972-74. Served with U.S. Army, 1959-63. NSF fellow, 1968. Mem. AIA, Am. Inst. Planners, Alpha Phi Alpha. Home: 5 Gatewood St Hampton VA 23668

HALL, JAMES BRUCE, III, elec. engr.; b. Abbeville County, S.C., Jan. 16, 1939; s. James Bruce, Jr. and Doris Vivian (Sternenberg) H.; student Clemson U., 1955-56, U. Ga. at Athens, 1970-71, U. Ala. at Huntsville, 1972; m. Wilma Mae Awtry, Jan. 6, 1957; children—Charlton Bruce, Sheila Victoria, Candace Moscelia, Sanford Lane. Electrician, Monsanto Co., Greenwood, S.C., 1965-70, engring. technician, 1970-71, project engr., Guntersville, Ala., 1971-78, sr. project engr. 1978; systems engr. Instrument Control Service, Pensacola, Fla., 1978, systems engring. supr., 1978—; instr. electronics Piedmont Tech. Edn. Center, Greenwood, 1969-71. Certified engr.-in-tng., Ala. Mem. Instrument Soc. Am., ASME (asso.). Baptist. Clubs: Masons, Shriners. Home: 7670 Le Jeune Dr Pensacola FL 32504 Office: PO Box 7126 Pensacola FL 32504

HALL, JAMES WILLIAM, JR., univ. adminstr.; b. Montgomery, Ala., Dec. 23, 1931; s. James William and Hazel (Kemp) H.; student Huntington Coll., 1950; B.A., U. Ala., 1958, M.A., 1968; postgrad. Tulane U., 1964; m. Martha Faye George, Aug. 31, 1958. Gen. assignment reporter Montgomery Advertiser, 1956-57; with So. Bell Telephone Co., New Orleans, 1958-66, directory compilation mgr., 1963-64, pub. relations mgr., 1965-66; exec. dir. Ala. Press Assn., University, 1966-74; asst. to pres. Troy (Ala.) State U., 1974-79, dean Hall Sch. Journalism, 1977-79; lectr. journalism dept. U. Ala., Tuscaloosa, 1966-72; pres. Quest. Inc., Tuscaloosa, 1968-71; v.p. Ala. News Service, Tuscaloosa, 1969-71; pres. Leader Enterprises, 1979—. Mem. Ala. Safety Coordinating Com., 1968-74, Ala. Farm-City Week Com., 1970-74; 2d v.p. New Orleans Floral Trail, 1966; chmn. Nat. Newspaper Week, 1973. Sec. Ala. Press Assn. Journalism Found., 1968-74. Served with USAF, 1951-54. Named Outstanding Indsl. Editor, Greater New Orleans Area United Fund, 1966; Hon. Blind Man Ala. Sch. for Deaf and Blind, 1967; Distinguished Alumnus, U. Ala. Dept. Journalism, 1972. Mem. Troy Council Arts and Humanities (sec.), Jasons, Phi Beta Kappa, Omicron Delta Kappa, Phi Kappa Phi, Phi Eta Sigma Chi Phi, Sigma Delta Chi (pres. 1970). Presbyterian. Mason (32 deg.), Rotarian. Clubs: Troy Country, Capital City, Troy C. of C. Home: The Abattoir Troy AL 36081

HALL, JESSIE RAY, educator; b. Carroll County, Galax, Va., Feb. 5, 1924; s. Alonzo Alexander and Clara Jane (Crissman) H.; B.S. in Bus. Adminstrn., Va. Poly. Inst. U., 1950, M.S. in Bus. Edn., 1951; m. Lois I. Taylor, May 4, 1946; children—Karren Rae Hall Lingle, Gordon Taylor. Tchr., Woodrow Wilson High Sch., Portsmouth, Va., 1951-52; head bus. dept. Woodrow Wilson Tech. Inst., Fishersville, Va., 1952-56; asst. cashier Planters Bank & Trust Co., Staunton, Va., 1956-64; chmn. bus. dept. Catawba Valley Tech. Inst., Hickory, N.C., 1964-75, instr., 1975—; instr. Am. Inst. Banking, 1957-72. Served with U.S. Army, 1943-46. Mem. Am. Vocat. Assn., NEA, Nat. Bus. Edn. Assn., So. Bus. Edn. Assn., N.C. Vocat. Assn., N.C. Assn. Educators, N.C. Bus. Edn. Assn., Alpha Kappa Psi (life), Delta Pi Epsilon. Democrat. Methodist. Clubs: Newton-Conover Kiwanis (dir., pres.), Fishersville Ruritan (pres.). Home: 211 5th St NE Conover NC 28613 Office: Hwy 64-70-321 E Hickory NC 28601

HALL, JOANN, publishing co. exec.; b. Auburn, Ky., Apr. 2, 1927; d. Everett Bluford and Geneva Mae (Maxwell) H.; student public schs., Detroit; m. Dec. 15, 1945 (div. 1964); 1 son, Mark Stephen Rudolph. With Daily News Broadcasting Co., Bowling Green, Ky., 1950-73, women's dir., dir. music and public affairs, 1960-70, ops. mgr., 1970-73; bus. mgr. Cockrel Corp., Bowling Green, 1974—. Hon. Ky. col.; recipient public service award USAF, 1971, Distbv. Edn. Clubs Am., 1970. Mem. Am. Bus. Women's Assn. (pres. 1967, Woman of Year award 1967), Bowling Green C. of C. Cumberland Presbyterian. Home: 2148 Walnut Ln Bowling Green KY 42101 Office: Rt 9 Box 79EE Bowling Green KY 42101

HALL, JOE BEASMAN, basketball coach; b. Cynthiana, Ky., Nov. 30, 1928; s. Charles Curtis and Ruth Marshall (Harney) H.; student U. Sewanee, 1950-51; B.A., U. Ky., 1955; M.A., Colo. State Coll., 1963; m. Katharine Roberta Dennis, Oct. 25, 1951; children—Judy M., Kathy Jo, Stephen D. Salesman, H. J. Heinz, 1951-53; with Kawneer, Cynthiana, Ky., 1955-56; coach Shepherdsville (Ky.) High Sch., 1956-58; coach basketball, baseball, athletic dir. Regis Coll., Denver, 1958-64; coach basketball Central Mo. State U., Warrensburg, 1964-65; asst. coach basketball U. Ky., Lexington, 1965-71, coach, 1971—; dir. The Nat. Bank, Cynthiana. Named Coach of Year, Southeastern Conf., 1973, 75, 78. Mem. Nat. Assn. Basketball Coaches. Democrat. Office: Univ of Ky Basketball Office Lexington KY 40506

HALL, JOHN HOWLAND, dermatologist; b. N.Y.C., Aug. 7, 1938; s. Harvey and Mary Emily (Allen) H.; B.A. with distinction, U. Okla., 1960; M.D., Duke U., 1964; m. Jane Ardelle Weisiger, Feb. 16, 1957; children—John Howland, Kimberly Willis, Mark Allen. Intern, Duke Hosp., Durham, N.C., 1964, resident, 1965-68, chief resident, 1967; instr. Duke U. Sch. of Medicine, 1967; clin. asst. Mass. Gen. Hosp., 1968-70; instr. dermatology Boston U. Sch. of Medicine, 1968-70; v.p. Drs. Lupton and Hall, Greensboro, N.C., 1970—; clin. asso. Duke U. Sch. Medicine, U. N.C. Sch. of Medicine. Dir., Eastern N.C. Citizens for Goldwater, 1964; vice-chmn. 6th Dist. Rep. Exec. Com., 1972-77, N.C. Del. to GOP Conv., 1976. Served with USN, 1968-70. Diplomate Am. Bd. Dermatology; recipient Physicians Recognition award AMA, 1969, 72, 76. Mem. AMA, N. Am. Clin. Dermatol. Soc. (dir. 1979-82), So. Med. Assn., Guilford County Med. Soc. (pres. 1980). Republican. Episcopalian. Clubs: Civitan. Contbr. articles to med. jours. Home: 3 Anson Circle Greensboro NC 27407 Office: 1100 Olive St Greensboro NC 27401

HALL, JOHN PATRICK, lawyer; b. Dallas, Oct. 11, 1936; s. John Patrick and Maurine (Still) H.; student U. Tex., 1954-55; B.B.A., So. Methodist U., 1957, LL.B., 1960; postgrad. U. Brussels (Belgium), 1963-64, Hague Acad. Internat. Law, 1964; Diploma Internat. Faculty for Study of Comparative Law (Strasbourg, France), 1964; m. Carol Anne Fraser, May 5, 1962; children—John Patrick III, Jessica Elizabeth. Admitted to D.C. bar, 1963; Tex. bar, 1960; atty. Corp. Finance div. SEC, Washington, 1960-63; practiced in Brussels, Belgium, 1963-64, Dallas, 1964—; partner firm Stroud & Smith, Dallas, 1964—. Mem. Environmental Quality Com. City of Dallas, 1971-74. Bd. dirs. Dallas chpt. Nat. Conf. Christians and Jews. Mem. Am., Tex., D.C., Dallas bar assns., Sigma Chi, Delta Theta Phi, Beta Alpha Psi. Clubs: City, Brook Hollow Golf, Idlewild, Terpsichorean (Dallas). Home: 6032 DeLoache St Dallas TX 75225 Office: 1407 Main St Dallas TX 75202

HALL, JOHN RANDOLPH, JR., physician; b. Napton, Mo., June 20, 1913; s. John Randolph and Ferda (Roberts) H.; A.B., Central Mo. Meth. Coll., 1935; B.S. in Medicine, U. Neb., 1938; M.D., Washington U., St. Louis, 1939; M.S. in Pharmacology, U. Chgo., 1949; M. Pub. Health, Johns Hopkins, 1954, Nat. War Coll., 1959; m. Josephine Miles, Nov. 24, 1938; children—John Randolph III, Sarah (Mrs. William Thompson Garcelon), M. Bruce, Rogers. Commd. lt. U.S. Army, 1934, advanced through ranks to col. M.C., 1946, retired, 1964; intern St. Louis City Hosp., 1939-40; partner Kelsey-Seybold Clinic, Houston, 1964-69, chief occupational medicine, 1964-69; pres. Space Center Med. Assos., Houston, 1969-73, v.p., 1973—; mem. staffs Methodist, St. Lukes, Galveston County Meml., Clear Lake hosps.; acting dean, organizer Sch. Pub. Health, U. Tex., Houston, 1968-69, adj. prof., 1969—. Bd. dirs. Houston Community Welfare Assn., 1964-70, mem. exec. com., 1968-70; bd. dirs. Family Service Centers, Houston, 1971-73. Decorated Silver Star, Legion of Merit (2), Bronze Star medal (3), Air medal, Purple Heart; recipient Andreas Vesalius medal Augsburg Fortbilding, Augsburg, Germany, 1969. Diplomate Am. Bd. Preventive Medicine. Fellow A.C.P., Am. Coll. Preventive Medicine, Am. Pub. Health Assn.; mem. Assn. Mil. Surgeons U.S., AMA, Tex. Med. Assn., Harris County Med. Soc., C. of C. Clear Lake (dir. 1971-74), C. of C. Dickinson, Nu Simga Nu. Mason (32 deg., K.T., Shriner). Contbr. to publs. in field. Home: 741 Winfield Circle San Antonio TX 78239

HALL, JOHN ROBERT, coll. ofcl.; b. Waterloo, Iowa, Jan. 21, 1942; s. John Martin and Alice Geraldine H.; A.A., Freed-Hardeman Coll., 1962; student Harding Coll., 1962-63, George Peabody Coll., 1963-64; B.A., Morehead State U., 1966, M.A., 1966; postgrad. U. Miss., 1970—, Brigham Young U., 1971; m. Freda Marie Skelton, July 22, 1962; children—Alissa Cheree, Anna Lynn, Andrea Leigh. Student asst. ednl. broadcasting Morehead State U., 1964-66; dir. broadcasting radio sta. Freed-Hardeman Coll., Henderson, Tenn., 1966-73, condr. a cappella singers, 1966-78, partner audio recording bus., 1971-76, dir. alumni affairs, 1976-78, dir. public and alumni relations, 1978—, exec. sec. alumni assn., 1972—. Mem. exec. com. Chester County Democratic Party, 1980—; bd. dirs. West Tenn. Cerebral Palsy Assn., 1979. Named Boss of Year, Nat. Collegiate Assn. Secs., 1979; recipient Dirs. award Freed-Hardeman Alumni Assos., 1977. Mem. Am. Choral Dirs. Soc., Council for Advancement Edn. (dist. conf. com. 1980), Chester County C. of C. (dir. 1979), Iota Beta Sigma. Mem. Ch. of Christ. Clubs: Civitan, Chester County Lions (3d v.p. 1979). Home: 514 White Ave Henderson TN 38340 Office: Box 712 Freed-Hardeman College Henderson TN 38340

HALL, KATHRYN EVANGELINE, author, lectr.; b. Biltmore, N.C.; d. Hugh Canada and Evangeline Haddon (Jenkins) Hall; B.A., U. N.C., 1946, M.A., 1951; diploma Adams Sch. Music, Montreat, N.C., 1948; postgrad. Yale, 1950-54, U. London, 1961, Fla. Atlantic U., 1967. Author: The Papal Tiara, 1952, History of the Episcopal Church of Bethesda-By-The-Sea, 1964, The Architecture and Times of Robert Adam, 1969, The Pictorial History of the Episcopal Church of Bethesda-By-The-Sea, 1970-71, Joseph Wright of Derby, A Painter of Science, Industry, and Romanticism, 1974, A History of English Architecture, 1976-78; lectr. history, art and architecture, U.S., Eng. and Scotland, 1961—. Vice pres. The Jr. Patronesses, Palm Beach, Fla., 1964. Mem. Nat. League Am. Pen Women (Owl award 1972, 76, 77, pres. Palm Beach chpt. 1975—), Palm Beach Quills (historian), Palm Beach County Hist. Soc. (gov.), Internat. Platform Assn., Soc. Four Arts, Cum Laude Soc., Palm Beach Civic Assn. Episcopalian. Clubs: Everglades (Palm Beach); English Speaking Union (Palm Beach and London). Home: Acadie PO Box 648 Palm Beach FL 33480

HALL, MARGARET JEAN, chemist; b. Boston, Mar. 25, 1942; d. Robert King and Margaret (Wheeler) H.; A.B., U. N.C., 1964, Ph.D.; M.S., U. Denver, 1971. Med. technician U. N.C. Med. Center, Chapel Hill, 1963-68, research asst., 1971—; research asst. chemistry U. Colo. Med. Center, Denver, 1970-71. Mem. Am. Chem. Soc., Am. Soc. Med. Tech., Sigma Xi, Iota Sigma Pi. Republican. Club: Ballet. Home: 22 Braddock Circle Parkwood Durham NC 27707 Office: U NC Med Center Dept Pathology 703 PCE Chapel Hill NC 27514

HALL, MILES LEWIS, JR., lawyer; b. Ft. Lauderdale, Fla., Aug. 14, 1923; s. Miles Lewis and Mary Frances (Dawson) H.; A.B., Princeton, 1947; J.D., Harvard, 1950; m. Muriel M. Fisher, Nov. 4, 1950; children—Miles Lewis III, Don Thomas. Admitted to Fla. bar, 1951, since practiced in Miami; partner Hall & Hedrick, 1953—; admitted to U.S. Supreme Ct. bar, 1959. Mem. nominating com. Dade County Met. Ct., 1969-72; chmn. nominating com. Dist. Ct. Appeals, 3d Dist. Fla., 1972-75. Vice-pres., Orange Bowl Com., 1961-63, pres., 1964-65, dir., 1950—; vice chmn. Fla. Council of 100, 1961-62, mem., 1971-72, 73—; exec. bd. S. Fla. council Boy Scouts Am., 1966-67; vice chmn., dir. Dade County chpt. ARC, 1961-62, chmn., 1963-64, dir., 1967-73, nat. fund cons., 1963, 66-68; mem. adv. bd. Salvation Army, 1968—; bd. dirs. Coral Gables War Meml. Youth Center, 1967—, v.p., 1968-69, pres., 1969-72; mem. citizens bd. U. Miami, 1961-66; pres. Ransom Sch. Parents Assn., 1966; chmn. S. Fla. Gov.'s Scholarship Ball, 1966; bd. visitors Coll. Law, Fla. State U., 1974—. Served to 2d lt. USAAF, 1943-45. Mem. Am. (Fla. co-chmn. membership com., sect. corp. banking and bus. law), Dade County (dir. 1964-65, v.p. 1966-67, pres. 1967-68) bar assns., Fla. Bar, Am. Judicature Soc., Miami-Dade County C. of C. (v.p. 1962-64, dir. 1966-68), Harvard Law Sch. Assn. Fla. (dir. 1964-66), Alpha Tau Omega. Methodist (steward). Clubs: Kiwanis; Princeton So. Fla. (past pres., dir.); Harvard of Miami, Cottage, The Miami. Author: Titles, Ejectment and Election of Remedies, Vol. VIII, Fla. Law and Practice, 1958. Home: 2907 Alhambra Circle Coral Gables FL 33134 Office: 200 SE 1st St Suite 1104 Miami FL 33131

HALL, MONTAGUE COCRAM, contracting stevedoring exec.; b. McComb, Miss., Aug. 28, 1907; s. James Thomas and Emmie Gertrude (Guyton) H.; grad. accounting Chenier Bus. Coll., Beaumont, Tex., 1932; m. Wilma Olive Little, June 25, 1937; 1 dau., Frances Anne (Mrs. Bair Clyde Stoker). Salesman, So. Drug Specialty Co., McComb, Miss., 1925-30; asst. dist. auditor Lykes Brothers Steamship Co., Inc., Beaumont, Tex. and Lake Charles, La., 1932-37; payroll and prodn. clk. Stanolind Oil Co., Lake Charles, 1937-39; mem. staff traffic and pub. relations Port of Lake Charles, 1939-41; supt., 1941-42, 47-49; v.p. Lake Charles Stevedores, Inc. and Lake City Stevedores, Inc., 1949—, also dir. both. Treas., Lake Charles Dock Bd., 1971—; commr. La. Pilots Fee Commn., 1967—. Bd. dirs. Campfire Girls, 1952-56. Served as maj., Transp. Corps, AUS, 1942-46. Mem. Nat. Assn. Stevedores (nat. dir. 1974—), Lake Charles Pilots Assn. (commr. 1964—), Lake Charles Maritime Assn. (pres. 1967—). Presbyterian. (elder). Mason. Clubs: Lake Charles Traffic, Pioneer, Lake Charles Country; Port Sabine Propeller (dir.); Kiwanis, Lions. Home: 3916 Buccaneer Ln Lake Charles LA 70605 Office: Port Lake Charles Lake Charles LA 70601

HALL, PHILIP ADKINS, social worker; b. Boston, June 20, 1941; s. Robert Anderson and Frances Love (Adkins) H.; B.A., Cornell U., 1964; M.S.W., Washington U., St. Louis, 1966; Ph.D., U. Chgo., 1980; m. Sue Elaine McCoy, June 19, 1965; children-Rebecca Lane, Stephen Anderson. Community organizer St. Louis Housing Authority, 1966; asst. adminstr. Patrician Movement, San Antonio, 1972-77; asst. prof. Worden Sch. Social Service, Our Lady of Lake U., San Antonio, 1977—; cons. in adoptions Tex. Cradle Soc.; instr. San Antonio Coll. Bd. dirs. Beacon Hill Neighborhood Assn., 1978-79. Served with AUS, 1967-70. Mem. Acad. Cert. Social Workers, Nat. Assn. Social Workers, Council Social Work Edn. Home: 1005 W Agarita St San Antonio TX 78201 Office: 411 SW 24th St San Antonio TX 78285

HALL, RAY COWAN, advt. exec.; b. Searcy, Ark., July 22, 1940; s. Maurice M. and Pansy Lucile (Cowan) H.; B.A., U. Okla., 1962, M.A., 1965; m. Janet Susan Cooper, Nov. 27, 1965; children—Lauren Elise, Julie Steele, Nancy Elizabeth. Mem. public relations staff Southwestern Bell Telephone Co., Oklahoma City, 1965-66, St. Louis, 1966-68, Austin, Tex., 1968-71; advt. account exec. Neal Spelce Assos., Austin, 1971-72; pres. Ray Hall Advt. & Public Relations, Inc., Austin, 1973—; part-time instr. U. Tex., Austin, 1977—. Exec. v.p. Austin Symphony, 1973-78; pres. Center Stage Theater, 1979—; vice commodore Austin Aqua Festival, 1971-73; vice chmn. Parks and Recreation Bd., 1978—; bd. dirs. March of Dimes, Am. Cancer Soc. Recipient awards Am. Advt. Fedn., Art Dirs. Club Houston, Outdoor Advt. Inst. Mem. Am. Mktg. Assn. (pres. 1979-80), Austin Advt. Club (pres. 1973-74), Am. Advt. Fedn., Public Relations Soc. Am., Tex. Public Relations Assn., Am. Acad. Advt., Delta Tau Delta. Republican. Baptist. Clubs: Headliners, Westwood Racquet, Onion Creek Golf and Country. Home: 4004 Edgemont St Austin TX 78731 Office: 221 W 6th St #1150 Austin TX 78701

HALL, RICHARD CLAYTON, psychologist; b. Pitts., Apr. 29, 1931; s. Clayton LeClaire and Genevieve Hanley (Gorman) H.; B.S., Trinity Coll., Hartford, Conn., 1948-52; M.S., U. Pitts., 1959, Ph.D., 1963; m. Doris Margaret Bjorkland, Aug. 26, 1963; children—Karen Elizabeth, Janice Lee, Dorothy Evelyn. Research asso. U. Pitts., 1963; research psychologist, dir. behavior tng. programs Polk (Pa.) State Sch. and Hosp., 1963-75; ind. research, 1975—. Served with U.S. Army, 1953-55. NSF coop. grantee, 1959-60. Mem. Am., Pa. psychol. assns., Sigma Xi, Pi Gamma Mu, Delta Phi. Contbr. articles to profl. jours. Address: 1331 Sunset Dr Key West FL 33040

HALL, RICHARD CLYDE, JR., religious exec.; b. Florence, Ala., Apr. 13, 1931; s. Richard Clyde and Annie Hazel (Darrah) H.; B.A., U. Fla., Gainesville, 1953; M.R.E., Southwestern Baptist Theol. Sem., Ft. Worth, 1958, D.R.E., 1966, Ed.D., 1975; m. Mildred Denham, May 19, 1957; children—Richard D., Darralyn M., Kevin C., Edward E. Youth dir. So. Bapt. chs. in Fla. and Tex., 1953-54; dir. Bapt. Student Union, Fla. Bapt. Conv., Jacksonville, 1954-57; minister edn. chs. in Tex. and Tenn., 1957-65; asso., then sec. ch. tng. dept. Bapt. Gen. Conv. Tex., 1965-73; mgmt. cons. Pro, Inc., San Diego, 1973-74; with ch. tng. dept. Bapt. Sunday Sch. Bd., Nashville, 1974—, cons. adult and gen. adminstrn., 1974-76, supr. youth sect., 1976—. Mem. Internat. Religious Edn. Assn., Am. Soc. Tng. and Devel., Adult Edn. Assn., So. Bapt. Religious Edn. Assn., Eastern Bapt. Religious Edn. Assn. (pres. elect 1979), Southwestern Bapt. Religious Edn. Assn. Author curriculum materials. Office: 127 9th Ave N Nashville TN 37234

HALL, ROBERT BRUCE, bishop; b. Wheeling, W. Va., Jan. 27, 1921; s. Kent Bruce and Mary Ellen (Hazlett) H.; B.A., Trinity Coll., Hartford, Conn., 1943, D.D., 1967; S.T.B., Episcopal Theol. Sem., Cambridge, Mass., 1949; D.D., Seabury Western Theol. Sem. 1966, Va. Theol. Sem., Trinity Coll., 1967, Kenyon Coll., 1969; m. Dorothy Varner Glass, Jan. 26, 1949; children—Ellen Lynn, Kent Bruce II, Elizabeth Hazlett, Anne Louise, Susan Glass. Ordained to ministry Episcopal Ch., 1949; asso. minister, Huntington, W. Va., 1949-53; rector, Huntington, 1953-58, Chgo., 1958-66; bishop coadjutor Episcopal Diocese Va., Richmond, 1966-73, bishop, 1974—. Trustee Va. Theol. Sem., 1967—, Blue Ridge Sch., Dyke, Va., 1968—. Served with AUS, 1943-46. Fellow Coll. of Preachers, Delta Phi, Pi Gamma Mu. Home: 11 River Rd Richmond VA 23226 Office: 110 W Franklin St Richmond VA 23220

HALL, ROBERT E., retail exec.; b. Heavener, Okla., Jan. 26, 1939; B.S., Okla. State U., 1961; m. Donna Ann Rogers, Mar. 7, 1964; 1 dau., Robin Christine. With Conn. Mut. Life Ins. Co., Kansas City, Mo., 1964-67; with IBM, Kansas City, Mo. and Tulsa, 1967-74; owner, pres. Salutation, Inc., Tulsa, 1974—; pres. Hall Investment Co., bus. cons.; dir. State Nat. Bank, Heavener. Served with AUS, 1961. Republican. Methodist. Home: 7425 S College St Tulsa OK 74136 Office: 3200 S Elm Pl Broken Arrow OK 74012

HALL, ROBERT HARDY, JR., ins. co. exec.; b. Petersburg, Va., July 5, 1928; s. Robert Hardy and Kathryn Marie H.; student Va. Commonwealth U., 1946-47, U. Richmond, 1960-63; m. Evelyn McFarland, Nov. 5, 1949; children—Linda Evelyn, Robert Wayne, Brenda Gail, Mark Kevin. With Equitable Life Assurance Soc. U.S., 1954—, agy. mgr., Springfield, Ill., 1965-70, Charleston, W.Va., 1970—. Bd. dirs. ARC, Petersburg, Va., 1963-65, United Fund, Petersburg, 1962-65. Recipient President's Trophy, Equitable Life Assurance Soc., 1975, 78, Silver award, 1979, numerous other awards. Mem. Charleston Life Underwriters Assn., Nat. Assn. Life Underwriters, Am. Soc. C.L.U.'s (past pres.), Charleston Estate Planning Council (pres. 1972-73), Charleston Area C. of C. Republican. Mem. Christian Ch. Club: Kiwanis (pres. Springfield 1969-70). Home: 6 Birch Tree Ln Charleston WV 25314 Office: 1110 Commerce Sq Charleston WV 25301

HALL, ROBERT LARRY, retail exec.; b. Houston, Nov. 12, 1945; s. Herman Delois and Virgie Kathryn (Alexander) H.; student U. Houston, 1965-69. With Weiner's Stores, Inc., Houston, 1967—, advt. mgr., 1972-74, dir. advt., 1974—. Served with USAFR, 1965-71. Mem. Houston Advt. Fedn., Retail Mchts. Assn., Am. Mktg. Assn., Houston Assn. Broadcast Execs. Office: 6005 Westview St Houston TX 77055

HALL, ROGER FISHER, ins. agency exec.; b. Lumber Bridge, N.C., Oct. 17, 1910; s. John Wesley and Sarah Lula (Bullard) H.; B.S., Davidson Coll., 1932; postgrad. U. N.C., 1932-33, Tulane U., 1937; m. Mary Hodgin, Oct. 7, 1950; children—Caroline Walters Shook, Roger, Elise Hall McIntosh, Sally Lou Overton. Dir. pub. welfare, High Point, N.C., 1933-34, Houston County, Ala., 1935, Lauderdale County, Ala., 1936-41; chmn. bd., pres. S.E. Butane Co., Lumber Bridge, N.C., 1946—; chmn. bd., pres. Third Century Water Corp., 1971-73; chmn., pres. Safety Ins. Agency, Inc., Parkton, N.C., 1974—. Councilman, town of Lumber Bridge (N.C.), 1964-65; mem. Robeson County Indsl. and Agrl. Devel. Commn., 1965—, chmn., 1969-70; mem. N.C. Gen. Assembly, 1970-71; mem. Democratic Exec. Com. Lumber Bridge Twp., 1960—. Served with AUS, 1941-46. Decorated Silver Star, Bronze Star, and others. Mem. N.C. Liquefied Petroleum Gas Assn., Ind. Ins. Agents N.C. Presbyn. Clubs: Shriners, Masons, Elks, Scottish Rite, York Rite, Scothurst Country, Fort Bragg Officers. Home: 192 Raeford Rd Lumber Bridge NC 28357 Office: PO Drawer 100 Lumber Bridge NC 28357

HALL, ROLAND MEREDITH, Realtor, gen. contractor, real estate developer; b. Shreveport, June 20, 1947; s. Charles Thaxter and Ruth Lucille (Bouanchaud) H.; B.S., La. State U., Baton Rouge, 1969; m. Phyllis Charlene Felts; children—Roland Meredith, Allison Courtney, Jennifer Mason. Pres., Hall & Co., real estate, Hall-Robi Constrn. Co. Inc.; v.p. Hall Devel. Corp.; sec. 70th Jewella Corp.; appraiser various cos. Mem. Nat., La. realtors assns., Shreveport-Bossier Bd. Realtors, Metal Bldg. Dealers Assn., Sigma Chi (life). Republican. Baptist. Clubs: Shreveport Racquet/Tennis Indoor; Pierremont Oaks Tennis. Home: 7515 Millbrook Dr Shreveport LA 71105 Office: 1941 E 70th St Shreveport LA 71105

HALL, SAM BLAKELEY, JR., Congressman; b. Marshall, Tex., Jan. 11, 1924; grad. Coll. of Marshall, 1942; student Law Sch., U. Tex., 1942-43; LL.B., Baylor U., 1948; m. Madeline Segal, 1946; children—Linda Rebecca Hall Palmer, Amanda Jane Hall Wynn, Sandra Blake. Admitted to Tex. bar, 1949; practice law, Marshall; mem. 94th-96th Congresses from 1st Tex. Dist. Deacon, Eastern Hills Ch. of Christ, Marshall; bd. devel. Baylor U., Waco, Tex. Served with USAF, 1943-45. Named Outstanding Citizen, City of Marshall, 1970. Mem. Baylor U. Ex-Students Assn. (dir.). Democrat. Office: 318 Cannon House Office Bldg Washington DC 20515*

HALL, SUSAN ANN HINDERER, phys. therapist; b. Ft. Wayne, Ind., Jan. 5, 1950; d. Robert Frederick and Mary Katherine (Gilliam) Hinderer; B.S., U. Mich., 1972, certificate in phys. therapy Med. Sch., 1972; M.Ed., U. So. Ala., 1976; m. Theodore Leslie Hall, Jan. 6, 1973. Staff phys. therapist Mt. Carmel Mercy Hosp., Detroit. 1973-74; bedside rover phys. therapist Providence Hosp., Mobile, Ala., 1974-75; dir. phys. therapy Gulf Coast Home Health Agy., Mobile, 1975; owner, operator Home Phys. Therapy Service, Mobile, 1977—; mem. State of Ala. Ind. Living Program, 1979; cons. in field; chmn. wheelchair basketball game Mott Children's Hosp., Ann Arbor, Mich., 1971. Bd. dirs. U. So. Ala. Alumni, 1977. HEW phys. therapy grantee, 1971-72, 77. Mem. Am. Phys. Therapy Assn., Am. Personnel and Guidance Assn., Mobile Phys. Therapists (sec. 1974), Am. Bus. Women's Assn., LWV, Mobile Bar Aux., Alpha Omicron Pi. Presbyterian. Club: Timberlane Garden. Home: 5360 Larchmont Dr Mobile AL 36609 Office: Vocat Rehab Ser 1870 Pleasant Ave Mobile AL 36617

HALL, TOMMY GEORGE, sch. system adminstr.; b. Cooke County, Tex., Apr. 26, 1931; s. Frank B. and Jane (Terry) H.; B.S., Tex. A. & M. U., 1954; M.Ed., U. Houston, 1961; postgrad. U. Houston, 1962-73; m. Bettye Anne Curson, Dec. 26, 1957. Teacher mathematics Houston Ind. Sch. Dist., 1957-65, counselor, 1965-66, coordinator group testing, 1966-71, asst. dir., 1971-75, dir. group testing, 1975—. Served with USMCR, 1954-56. Mem. Nat. Council on Measurement in Edn., Houston Prins. Assn. (exec. bd. 1979—), Houston Council Teachers Mathematics (pres. 1963-64, treas. 1961-62), Tex. State Teachers Assn., NEA, Phi Delta Kappa (pres. Houston area chpt. 1976-77). Episcopalian (treas. 1975-78). Clubs: Highland Village Lions Club of Houston (pres. 1974-75). Home: 3839 Prudence Dr Houston TX 77045 Office: 3830 Richmond Ave Houston TX 77027

HALL, WILLIAM LLOYD, surgeon; b. Wichita Falls, Tex., Aug. 25, 1925; s. Lloyd Lorenso and Frankie (Hodges) H.; M.D., Southwestern Med. Coll., 1947; student N. Tex. State U., 1942-44; m. Ann Carolyn Short, July 11, 1947; children—Marc William, Michael Steven, Lisa Merenith, Jay Jonathan. Intern George Washington U. Hosp., 1947-48; resident Gt. Lakes Naval Hosp., 1948-49, Baylor U. Hosp., 1953-56; practice medicine specializing in surgery, Dallas, 1956—; mem. staff Meth. Hosp.; chief of surgery Kessler Hosp., 1961-80. Served as lt. M.C., USN, 1948-53. Diplomate Am. Bd. Surgery. Mem. Am., Tex. med. assns., Dallas County Med. Soc. Home: 1419 Yakimo Dr Dallas TX 75208 Office: 122 W Colorado Dallas TX 75208

HALLAS, DAVID JACKSON, educator; b. Enfield, Conn., July 17, 1924; s. David Milford and Dorothy Elizabeth (Clayton) H.; B.A., Am. Internat. Coll., 1948; M.Ed., U. Va., 1963; m. Priscilla M. Mellor, Aug. 30, 1947 (div. Aug. 1976); children—Jacqueline, Jill, John, Jeff,

Wendi, Staci, Laura; m. 2d, Gail P. Ghigna, Oct. 28, 1976. Social worker, Juvenile ct. counselor Pasco County (Fla.), 1950-54; chmn. dept. sci. Seminole High Sch., Pinellas County, Fla., 1963-66; tchr. sci., middle schs., Pasco and Pinellas Counties, Fla., 1954-62; TV instr. Sta. WEDU, Channel 3, Tampa, Fla., 1966-68; prof. dept. natural scis. St. Petersburg (Fla.) Jr. Coll., 1968-79; dir. edn. Fla. Health Edn. Assn., St. Petersburg, 1976—; cons. metric edn./metrication. Chmn. legis. com. Health Care Cost Containment, 1979—. Served with M.C., U.S. Army, 1943. Mem. AAAS, Fla. Nat. Ret. Tchrs. Assn., Nat. League Nurses, Phi Delta Kappa. Republican. Club: Sertoma Internat. (recipient Outstanding Sec. award 1976, Centurion award 1976). Editor: The Rheumatoid Arthritis Patient, 1979; contbr. to Fla. Marine Sci. Handbook, 1965-67, Biophys. Scis. Lab. Manual, 3d edit., 1970—. Office: 1400 66th St N Suite 240 Saint Petersburg FL 33710

HALLECK, CONSTANCE JOYCE, advt. specialty co. exec.; b. Dayton, Ohio, May 23, 1944; d. Curtis Woodrow and Ruth Marjorie (Gray) Harvey; A.S., St. Petersburg Jr. Coll., 1964; B.S., U. Fla., 1965; m. Thomas Michael Halleck, Feb. 23, 1975; 1 son, John Robert. Sec./treas., v.p. Trans Global Corp., Atlanta, 1973-75; sales mgr. NFC Mktg. Assn., Dallas, 1975-76; sales rep. Ran Specialties, Houston, 1976-77; chmn. bd., pres. CHAS, Atlanta and Houston, 1977—. Mem. Splty. Advt. Assn. Internat. (grad. distbr. mgmt. inst. 1979, grad. mgmt. devel. seminar 1980, cert. advt. specialist 1980, mem. speakers bur.), Splty. Advt. Assn. Am., Nat. Assn. Female Execs., Am. Bus. Women's Assn. (chpt. v.p.), Atlanta Women Bus. Owners Assn. (hospitality chmn.), Atlanta Network. Office: 4741 Pine Acres Ct Dunwoody GA 30338

HALLECK, MARK, advt. agy. exec.; b. Chgo., Nov. 10, 1925; s. Mandel and Louise (Lehrer) H.; B.S. in Agrl. Engring., Tex. A&M U., 1947; m. Dorothy R. Levy, Aug. 10, 1947; children—Steven, Donald. Announcer, Sta. WTAW, College Station, Tex., 1947; sports and farm dir. Sta. WLEX, Lexington, Ky., 1947-50, Sta. WKLO, Louisville, 1950-53; free-lance radio and TV announcer, Louisville, Lexington, 1953-67; regional sales mgr. Gay-Bell Broadcast Group, Lexington, 1967-69; pres. Mark Halleck Advt., Inc., Lexington, 1969—. Mem. adv. bd. Good Samaritan Hosp., Lexington; bd. dirs. Blue Grass Area Comprehensive Care, Lexington. Served with USAAF, 1943-45. Recipient various profl. awards; Ky. col. Mem. Lexington Advt. Club, Lexington Sales and Mktg. Execs. Club. Club: Kiwanis. Home: 1165 Indian Mound Rd Lexington KY 40502 Office: Mark Halleck Advt Inc 342 Waller Ave Lexington KY 40504

HALLEN, E. DONALD, utility co. exec.; b. Belvidere, Ill., Apr. 10, 1930; s. Carl Terry and Elizabeth Alva (Bring) H.; B.S. in Indsl. Mgmt., U. Ill., 1960; m. Susanne L. Erickson, July 14, 1956; children—Bradley J., Ross D., Katherine B. With Gen. Telephone Co. Ill., Bloomington, 1960-72, gen. plant mgr., 1969-72; supply adminstr. Gen. Telephone & Electronic Co., Stamford, Conn., 1972-77; dir. supply and transp. Gen. Tel. Co. Ky., Lexington, 1977—. Vice pres. Kewanee (Ill.) Jaycees, 1964-65; cubmaster, treas., sec., com. chmn. Boy Scouts Am., Bloomington, 1965-72. Served with USN, 1947-56; Korea. Presbyterian. Club: Shriners. Home: 1348 Strawberry Ln Lexington KY 40502 Office: PO Box 1650 Lexington KY 40511

HALLIBURTON, JOHN ROBERT, communications and electronics co. exec.; b. Shreveport, La., July 31, 1934; s. Ralph Eloe and Mary Katherine (Smith) H.; B.S., Centenary Coll., 1955; J.D., So. Meth. U., 1964, postgrad., 1968-70; LL.M. in Internat. Law, George Washington U., 1974; m. Julia Ella Bateman, Dec. 17, 1955; children—Cherie Ann, John Robert II, Rhonda Marie. Admitted to Tex. bar, 1964, U.S. Supreme Ct. bar, 1967, D.C. bar, 1970; engr. Chrysler Corp., Huntsville, Ala., 1959-60; engr. Collins Radio Co., Dallas, 1960-66, contract mgr., 1966-68, tactical data sales mgr., 1968-69, dir. contract policy, dir. govt. relations and contract policy, 1969-74; gen. mgr. Collins Radio Limitada, Brazil, 1974-75; v.p. Collins Systems Internat., 1974-75; mgr. internat. contracts and dealer adminstrn. Collins Group, Rockwell Internat. Corp., 1975-76, dir. govt. relations, 1976—; mem. telecommunications tech. adv. com. Dept. Commerce, 1973-74. Served with U.S. Army, 1955-59. Mem. Electronic Industries Assn., State Bar Tex. (sec.-treas. internat. law sect.), Nat. Security Indsl. Assn., Nat. Aviation Club, Omicron Delta Kappa, Alpha Sigma Pi, Kappa Alpha, Phi Delta Phi. Roman Catholic. Club: K.C. Composer: Absence, 1953. Contbr. articles to profl. jours. Home: PO Box 278 Rockwall TX 75087 Office: Electronic Systems Group Rockwell International Corp PO Box 10462 Dallas TX 75207

HALLIGAN, JAMES EDMUND, univ. dean; b. Moorland, Iowa, June 23, 1936; s. Raymond Anthony and Ann Margaret (Crawford) H.; B.S., Iowa State U., 1962, M.S., 1965, Ph.D. in Chem. Engring., 1967; m. Ann E. Sorenson, June 29, 1957; children—Michael, Patrick, Christopher. Process engr. Humble Oil and Refining Co., 1962-63; postdoctoral fellow Iowa State U., 1967-68; mem. faculty Tex. Tech. U., Lubbock, 1968-76, chmn. dept. chem. engring., 1976-77; dean of engring. U. Mo., Rolla, 1977-79, U. Ark., Fayetteville, 1979—; cons. to industry. Mem. Gov. Tex. Energy Adv. Council, 1975-77. Served with USAF, 1954-58. Recipient Disting. Teaching award Tex. Tech. U., 1972, 73, Disting. Research award, 1973, 74; Outstanding Teaching award U. Mo., Rolla, 1977. Mem. Am. Inst. Chem. Engrs., Am. Chem. Soc., Ark. Soc. Profl. Engrs., Tau Beta Pi. Contbr. articles to profl. jours. Office: Coll Engring U Ark Fayetteville AR 72701

HALONEN, ROBERT JOHN, fin. exec.; b. Virginia, Minn., Mar. 18, 1940; s. Edward and Martha Elizabeth (Hervi) H.; B.S., U. Minn., 1963; M.B.A., U. Chgo., 1966; Ph.D., U. Ariz., 1975. Orderly, Meth. Hosp. Mpls., 1963; prodn. coordinator instrument sect. aero. div. Honeywell, Inc., Mpls., 1963-64; adminstrv. resident Iowa Meth. Hosp., Des Moines, 1965-66, adminstrv. asst., 1966-68; instr. Grandview Jr. Coll., Des Moines, 1967-68; staff asst. to adminstr. Ariz. Med. Center, Tucson, 1968-73; asst. prof. hosp. and health adminstrn. Sch. Allied Health Professions, Med. Coll. Va., Richmond, 1973-75; v.p. for fin. Charleston (W.Va.) Area Med. Center, Inc., 1975—; asst. prof. grad. studies W.Va. U., Charleston, 1977-79. Bd. dirs. Family Services of Kanawha Valley, 1978-79, W.Va. Heart Assn., 1979—; ednl. adv. Jr. Achievement of Kanawha Valley, 1977-79. Mem. Hosp. Fin. Mgmt. Assn., W.Va. Hosp. Fin. Mgmt. Assn., Am. Fin. Assn., W.Va. Hosp. Assn., Fin. Mgmt. Assn., Eastern Fin. Assn., Beta Gamma Sigma. Lutheran. Contbr. articles to profl. jours. Home: 12 Roller Rd Charleston WV 25314 Office: 1210 Elmwood Ave Charleston WV 25326

HALPERIN, DON AKIBA, educator; b. Cleve., Jan. 22, 1925; s. Moses Phillips and Sara (Allen) H.; B.S.C.E., Case Inst. Tech., 1945; B.S. in Archtl. Engring., U. Ill., 1948, M.S., Va. Poly. Inst., 1957, Ph.D., 1960; m. Elsa Mildred Paul, June 18, 1949; children—Philip M., Kenneth M. Civil engr., U.S. Navy, Washington, 1945-46; architect Braverman & Halperin, Cleve., 1948-53; prof. U. Fla., Gainesville, 1953—, dir. sch. of bldg. constrn., 1976—. Cons. architecture, United Synagogues Am., 1970—, Easter Seal Soc., 1971-73. Mem. Pres.'s Com. to Employ Handicapped, 1969-71, Bur. Standards Modular Coordination, Washington, 1971-73; chmn. Gov.'s Com. on Archtl. Accessibility, 1968-70; trustee Am. Council Constrn. Edn., 1977—. Served with U.S. Army, 1948-49. Am. Philos. Soc. grantee, 1967, Wolfson Found. grantee, 1968. Mem. Assn. Schs. Constrn. (nat. chmn. grad. study and research 1966-72), Assn. Gen. Contractors (nat. edn. com.). Mem. B'nai B'rith. Author: Building with Steel, 1967; Ancient Synagogues of Iberia, 1969; Construction Funding, 1975; Statics and Strength of Materials, 1976.

HALPERIN, SANFORD BERYL, educator; b. Newark, July 14, 1923; s. Clement J. and Bertie Viola (Hollander) H.; B.S., N.Y. U., 1947; M.A. (Huebner Found. scholar), U. Pa., 1948; Ph.D., Mich. State U., 1972; diploma U.S. Army Command and Gen. Staff Coll., 1961; m. Joan Lenore Friedman, Aug. 27, 1948; children—Jack Lee, Jill Halperin Roberts. Teaching fellow SUNY, Buffalo, 1948-49, instr., 1949-50; ins. agt., 1950-66; asst. prof. ins. and bus. adminstrn. Ferris State Coll., Big Rapids, Mich., 1966-69, asso. prof., 1969-74; cons. ins. personnel, 1948—; prof. ins. Northeast La. U., Monroe, 1974—; asst. prof. mil. sci. Mich. State U., 1969; instr. C.L.U. program, C.P.C.U. program. Instr., ARC, 1947; bd. dirs. Grad. Sch. Ins. of South, 1976—; trustee Little Theatre of Monroe, 1975-78, chmn., 1977-78. Served in inf. U.S. Army, 1943-46, Res., 1942-43, 46-78. Decorated Bronze Star, Meritorious Service Medal, Purple Heart; C.L.U., C.P.C.U. Mem. Am. Soc. C.L.U.'s, Am. Risk and Ins. Assn., Soc. Ins. Research, Ins. Co. Edn. Dirs. Soc., Fed. Emergency Mgmt. Agy., Soc. C.P.C.U.'s, Delta Sigma Pi, Delta Pi Epsilon, Phi Kappa Phi, Beta Gamma Sigma. Jewish-Unitarian. Contbr. numerous articles on ins. to profl. jours. Home: 26 Lakeview Dr Monroe LA 71203 Office: Dept Econs and Finance Coll Bus Adminstn Northeast La Univ Monroe LA 71209

HALPIN, DANIEL WILLIAM, civil engr.; b. Covington, Ky., Sept. 29, 1938; s. Jordan William and Gladys (Moore) H.; B.S., U.S. Mil. Acad., 1961; M.S.C.E. (NDEA Title IV fellow), U. Ill., Urbana, 1969, Ph.D., 1973; m. Maria Kirchner, Feb. 8, 1963; 1 son, Rainer. Vis. scholar Tech. U. Munich, 1967-68; grad. fellow U. Ill., 1968-70; operations research analyst U.S. Army Constrn. Research Lab., Champaign, Ill., 1970-72; research prof. U. Ill., 1972-73; asso. prof. civil engring. Ga. Inst. Tech., Atlanta, 1973—; cons. constrn. mgmt. Served to capt. U.S. Army, 1961-67; Vietnam. Decorated Bronze Star. Mem. ASCE (Huber research prize 1979), Am. Soc. Engring. Edn., Sigma Xi. Republican. Methodist. Author: Design of Construction and Process Operations, 1976; (with others) Planung und Kontrolle von Bauproduktionsprozessen, 1979. Home: 1655 Harbour Oaks Dr Tucker GA 30084 Office: Sch Civil Engineering Ga Inst Tech Atlanta GA 30332

HALSEY, JIM, theatrical producer, talent mgr.; b. Independence, Kans., Oct. 7, 1930; s. Harry Edward and Carrie Lee (Messick) H.; student Independence Community Coll., 1948-50, also U. Kans.; children—Sherman Brooks, Gina. Producer shows for auditoriums, fairs, rodeos, celebrations in various cities throughout world, 1950—; pres. Thunderbird Artists, Inc., Independence, 1952—, Jim Halsey Co., Inc., Jim Halsey Lighting & Sound Co., Jim Halsey Agy., Jim Halsey Radio Mgmt., James Halsey Property Mgmt., Silverline-Goldline Music, Inc., Proud Country Entertainment (stas. KTOW Tulsa, KGOW-FM Tulsa), Cyclone Records, Tulsa Records; gen. partner Parker Ranch, Tulsa; pres. Otter Creek Music, Pencil Music, Quill Music, Palo Duro Music, Brazos Valley Music, Parker Lane Music, Open Air Music, Town Crier Music, Fish Music, Palo Mesa Music; producer Tulsa Internat. Music Festival; dir., producer Kans. Celebration Neewollah, Independence, 1958—; v.p. country and Western div. Gen. Artists Corp., Beverly Hills, Calif., 1966-67, Singin' T Prodns., NERECO Prodns.; dir. Mercantile Bank & Trust, Tulsa, Farmers & Mchts. Bank, Mound City, Kans., Roy Clark Celebrity Golf Classic; personal mgr. various entertainment personalities. Mem. Kans. Centennial Commn., 1960-61; mem. Independence Park Bd., 1969-72; trustee Philbrook Art Center, Tulsa; bd. dirs. Thomas Gilcrease Mus. Assn., Tulsa Philharm. Served with AUS, 1954-56. Recipient Distinguished Service award U.S. Jr. C. of C., 1959; Ambassador of Country Music award SESAC Corp., 1978. Mem. Independence C. of C. (dir. 1958-61), Country Music Assn. (v.p. 1979-80, dir. 1963-64, 70-71), Acad. Country Music (Jim Reeves Meml. award 1977; dir. 1969-70, 73-74, v.p. 1975-76, 79-80), Downtown Tulsa Unltd. Episcopalian. Clubs: Rotary, Elks (trustee). Home: 801 W Beech St Independence KS 67301 Office: Penthouse Corporate Pl 5800 E Skelly Dr Tulsa OK 74135

HALSEY, WILLIAM MCCLURG, oil co. exec.; b. Independence, Kans., June 23, 1924; s. Cyrus B. and Carrie Lee (Messick) McClurg; B.S., U. Kans., 1950; m. Billie Jean Rotermund, Sept. 5, 1948; children—Susan Kay Archer, Kevin McClurg. Asst. mgr. Halsey's Dept. Store, Independence, Kans., 1952-60; adminstrv. asst. to U.S. Congressman from 3d Dist. Kans., Washington, 1960-61; indsl. relations mgr. Sinclair Pipeline Co., Independence, 1961-66, Sinclair Oil and Gas Co., Tulsa, 1967-68; labor relations mgr. Arco Oil and Gas Co., Dallas, 1969—. Served with AUS, 1943-45; ETO. Decorated Bronze Star medal. Diplomate Am. Soc. Personnel Adminstrn. (mem. labor relations com. Personnel Accreditation Inst.). Mem. VFW, Kans. U. Alumni Assn., Alpha Tau Omega. Republican. Episcopalian. Home: 3335 Dothan Ln Dallas TX 75229 Office: PO Box 2819 Dallas TX 75221

HALSTEAD, FREDERICK ARTHUR, mgmt. cons.; b. Chgo., Jan. 22, 1943; s. Edward Grey and Eleanor (Stromer) H.; B.A., Wabash Coll., 1965; grad. Grad. Sch. Mgmt., Northwestern U., 1966; M.S. in Bus., U. Tex., 1976; m. Donna M. Daughety, Dec. 13, 1970; children—Frederick Arthur, Juliet Marhea. Staff controller Container Corp. Am., Chgo., 1971-73; fin. mgr. E-Systems, Inc., Dallas, 1973-76; controller, dir. fin., tax and adminstrn. Prior Products, Inc., Dallas, 1976-78; pres. Halstead & Assos., Inc., mgmt. cons. and exec. search, 1978—; instr. Wayne Community Coll., Goldsboro, N.C. Served to capt. USAF, 1967-71. Republican. Episcopalian. Clubs: Kiwanis (pres. Dallas chpt.), Goldsboro Jaycees (dir.). Home: 9728 Edgepine St Dallas TX 75238 Office: 3131 Turtle Creek Blvd Dallas TX 75219

HALTER, EDMUND JOHN, mech. engr.; b. Bedford, Ohio, May 10, 1928; s. Edmund Herbert and Martha (Demske) H.; student Akron U., 1946-48; B.S. in Mech. Engring., Case Inst. Tech., Cleve., 1952; M.S. in Mech. Engring., So. Meth. U., 1965; m. Carolyn Amelia Luecke, June 29, 1955; children—John Alan, Amelia Katherine, Dianne Louise, Janet Elaine. Flight test engr., analyst Chance Vought Aircraft, Dallas, 1952-59; chief research and devel. engr. Burgess-Manning Co., Dallas, 1959-68; engring. specialist acoustics Vought div. LTV Aerospace Corp., Dallas, 1968-69; mgr. continuing engring. Maxim Silencer div. AMF Beaird, Inc., Shreveport, La., 1969-72; chief research and devel. engr. Burgess-Manning div. Burgess Industries, Dallas, 1972-79; chief engr. Vibration & Noise Engring. Corp., Dallas, 1979—; cons. Organizer Citizen Noise Awareness Seminar. Served with USNR, 1946-49. Registered profl. engr., Tex., Ohio; certified fallout shelter analyst. Mem. Inst. Environ. Scis. (pres. S.W. chpt.), Indsl. Silencer Mfrs. Assn. (chmn. 1975-77), Acoustical Soc. Am., Nat., Tex. socs. profl. engrs., Inst. Noise Control Engrs. Republican. Lutheran. Contbr. articles to profl. jours. Patentee in field. Home: 200 Hillcrest Ct Irving TX 75062 Office: 2655 Villa Creek Dr Dallas TX 75234

HALVERSTADT, DONALD BRUCE, urologist, univ. ofcl.; b. Cleve., July 6, 1934; s. Lauren Oscar and Lillian Frances (Jones) H.; B.A. magna cum laude, Princeton U., 1952-56; M.D. cum laude, Harvard U., 1960; m. Margaret Ann Marcy, Aug. 4, 1956; children—Donna, Jeffrey, Amy. Intern, Mass. Gen. Hosp., Boston, 1960-61, resident in surgery, 1961-62, resident in urology, 1964-67; practice medicine specializing in urology, Oklahoma City, Okla., 1967—; chief pediatric urology service Oklahoma Children's Meml. Hosp., Oklahoma City, 1967—, chief of staff, 1974—; clin. prof. urology U. Okla., 1975—, provost Health Scis. Center, 1979—. Served with USPHS, 1962-64. Fellow A.C.S.; mem. AMA (recipient physician recognition award 1969, 72, 77, 79), Am. Urol. Assn., Inc., Am. Acad. Pediatrics, Soc. Pediatric Urology, Okla. State Med. Assn., Okla. County Med. Soc., So. Med. Assn., Am. Soc. Nephrology, Soc. Univ. Urologists. Presbyterian. Contbr. articles in field to profl. jours. Home: 2932 Lamp Post Ln Oklahoma City OK 73120 Office: 711 Stanton L Young Blvd Oklahoma City OK 73104

HAM, ADRIENNE CAMILLE, educator; b. St. Louis, Nov. 14, 1943; d. Vincent F. and Erma (Clemons) Balaty; B.S., No. Ill. U., 1965; M.A., U. Iowa, 1972; m. Russell Allen Ham, Aug. 21, 1965. Tchr. kindergarten, Huntley, Ill., 1965-66; tchr. home econs. West Branch (Iowa) Public Schs., 1966-70; asst. prof. home econs. McNeese State U., Lake Charles, La., 1972—; workshop leader for home economists in El Salvador, 1978; adv. student home econs. hon. soc., 1976—; mem. U.S. del. Hemispheric Conf. of Internat. Fedn. Home Economics, 1976. Iowa Home Econs. Assn. scholar, 1969-70. Mem. La. Home Econs. Assn. (chmn. internat. sect. 1978-80, chmn. art sect. 1974-76, dist v.p. 1977-78), Am. Home Econs. Assn., Internat. Fedn. Home Econs., Omicron Nu, Kappa Omicron Phi, AAUW, Partners of Americas. Club: McNeese U. Faculty Wives. Home: 4321 Hearth St Lake Charles LA 70605 Office: McNeese Univ Home Economics Dept Lake Charles LA 70609

HAM, OSCAR EMERSON, JR., neurologist; b. Atlanta, Feb. 22, 1940; s. Oscar Emerson and Ruth Roan (McCarry) H.; B.A., Emory U., 1960, M.D., 1964; m. Mary Schofield, Sept. 12, 1964; children—Oscar Emerson III, Stephen Barry. Intern, U. Fla. Teaching Hosp., Gainesville, Fla., 1964-65; resident in neurology Mayo Clinic, Rochester, Minn., 1965-68; clin. instr. neurology U. Tex. Med. Sch., San Antonio, 1969-70; practice medicine specializing in neurology, pres. Neurologic Assos. Savannah, 1970—; dir. Candler Gen. Hosp. Stroke Unit, Savannah, 1972-78; chief staff Meml. Med. Center, Savannah, 1980—; chief neurology sect. Meml. Med. Center, Savannah, 1972—. Served with USAF, 1968-70. Mem. Ga. Med. Soc. (pres. 1977), Med. Assn. Ga., AMA, So. Med. Assn., Am. Acad. Neurology, Am. EEG Soc. Episcopalian. Clubs: Savannah Yacht, Oglethorpe, Debtors, Cotillion, Rotary. Home: 9000 Ferguson Ave Savannah GA 31406 Office: 4 Jackson Blvd Savannah GA 31405

HAM, ROBERT ELLIS, nuclear power plant exec.; b. Covington, Va., Mar. 7, 1940; s. Cleon Audley and Lucille Eva (Smith) H.; M.E., Internat. Corr. Schs., 1966-71; m. Goldie Smith, Mar. 12, 1960; children—Jeffrey Mark, John Michael. Systems engr., aux. systems Babcock & Wilcox Co., Lynchburg, Va., 1969-73, unit mgr., RCS mech. integration, 1973-76, project engr., internat. projects, 1976-78, product line mgr. engring. services, 1978—. Served with N.G., 1957-63. Mem. ASME, Methodist. Home: Route 1 Goode VA 24556 Office: Babcock & Wilcox Co PO Box 1260 Lynchburg VA 24505

HAM, WAYNE ALBERT, educator; b. Toronto, Ont., Can., May 13, 1938; s. Albert Alfred and Edna Frances (Dempster) H.; B.A., Graceland Coll., 1959; M.A., Brigham Young U., 1961; postgrad. Coll. of Siskiyous, 1962; M.Div., St. Paul Sch. Theology Meth., 1969; postgrad. Central Mo. State Coll., 1969-70; Ph.D., U. Fla., 1972-77; m. Marliene Margaret Miller, Dec. 24, 1959; children—Terry Russell, Brian Neal. Tchr. langs. Dunsmuir (Ca.) High Sch., 1961-62; asst. prof. English, U. Valle, Cali, Colombia, 1962-63; dir. Adult Materials dept. religious edn. The Auditorium, Independence, Mo., 1963-70; curriculum dir. Wildwood (Fla.) Middle Sch., 1970-73; supr. Sumter County Schs., 1973—; faculty Sch. of Restoration, Independence, 1964-69. Ordained to ministry Reorganized Ch. of Jesus Christ of Latter Day Saints, 1956; cir. religious edn. Santa Fe Stake, 1965-68. Mem. United Teaching Profession, Nat. Council Tchrs. English, Civitan. Author: Enriching Your New Testament Studies, 1965; Man's Living Religions, 1965; Faith and the Arts, 1968; The Call to Covenant, 1969; Publish Glad Tidings, 1970; The First Century Church, 1971; Where Faith and World Meet, 1972; Listening for God's Voice, 1973; On The Growing Edge, 1973; Yesterday's Horizons, 1975; More Than Burnt Offerings, 1977. Editor, founder Dimensions, jour. young leadership devel.; editorial bd. Courage, A Jour. of Thought and Action. Home: Route 1 Box 174T Wildwood FL 32785

HAMBLEN, LAPSLEY WALKER, JR., lawyer; b. Chattanooga, Dec. 25, 1926; s. Lapsley Walker and Libbie (Shipley) H.; B.A., U. Va., 1949, LL.B., 1953; m. Martha O'Hagan Murdock, Apr. 15, 1950 (div. Oct. 1970); children—Lapsley Walker III, Allen Murdock, William Shipley; m. 2d, Claudia R. Terrell, Mar. 20, 1971. Admitted to W.Va. bar, 1954, Ohio bar, 1955, Va. bar, 1957; law asso. Spilman, Thomas, Battle & Klostermeyer, Charleston, W.Va., 1953-54; asso. Smith, Schnacke & Compton, Dayton, Ohio, 1954-55; trial atty. Office Chief Counsel, IRS, Atlanta, 1955; atty.-adv. to judge Tax Ct. U.S., 1955-56; partner Caskie, Frost, Davidson & Hobbs, 1957-69, Caskie, Frost, Hobbs & Hamblen, 1969—; v.p., dir., gen. counsel Carter Glass & Sons Pubs., Inc., Lynchburg, 1974-79; sec., dir. Staunton Foods, Inc., Lynchburg Steel & Splty. Co., 1976—; organizer, dir. Jefferson Nat. Bank (now Va. Nat. Bank), Lynchburg; co-dir. U. Va. Ann. Conf. Fed. Taxation, 1970—. Trustee So. Fed. Tax Inst., Atlanta, 1973—. Served with USNR, 1945-46. Fellow Am. Coll. Probate Counsel; mem. Am., Fed., Va., Lynchburg bar assns., Va. State Bar, U. Va. Alumni Assn., Greater Lynchburg C. of C. (pres., dir. 1971-72), Raven Soc., Order of Coif, Omicron Delta Kappa. Contbr. articles to profl. jours. Home: 3708 Manton Dr Lynchburg VA 24503 Office: 2306 Atherholt Rd Lynchburg VA 24501

HAMBRICK, KEITH SHELDON, educator; b. Westlake, La., Oct. 7, 1943; s. Joseph Eugene and Seva Elizabeth (Knight) H.; B.A. in History, McNeese State U, 1967, M.A. in History, 1971. Mem. faculty dept. history McNeese State U., Lake Charles, La., 1971—. Mem. Orgn. Am. Historians, So. Hist. Assn., La. Hist. Assn., Am. Hist. Assn. Baptist. Contbr. book reviews to hist. jours; research in outlaws and vigilantes in La. during 19th century. Home: PO Box 475 Westlake LA 70669

HAMBY, LESLIE DEION counseling psychologist; d. Eddie Gene and Martha Jeanine (White) H.; B.S., Appalachian State U., 1976, M.A., 1979. English tchr. Avery High Sch., Newland, N.C., 1976; CETA counselor, dir. Head Start CAFI Agency, LaGrange, Ga., 1976-77; instructional developer, adminstrv. asst. Appalachian State U., Boone, N.C., 1977-78; human resource therapist Cumberland Psychiat. Hosp., Fayetteville N.C., 1979; counseling psychologist E. Ala. Mental Health Dept., Valley, 1980—. Fed. edn. grantee, 1973-76. Mem. Am. Personnel and Guidance Assn., N.C. Personnel and Guidance Assn., Am. Psychol. Assn., Kappa Delta Pi. Democrat. Baptist. Home: PO Box 477 Valley AL 36872 Office: E Ala Mental Health Dept Valley AL 36854

HAMBY, PHILIP WAYNE, realtor, contractor, land developer; b. Greenville, S.C., Aug. 13, 1944; s. Richard Manning and Sylvia Juanita (Waddell) H.; student Furman U., 1969, U. S.C., 1963; m. Jama Lynn McDaniel, Jan. 30, 1976; children—Melissa Lynn, Phyllis Melissa, James Alan. Pres., Phil Hamby Constrn. Co., Inc., Knoxville, Tenn., 1971—; v.p. KXB & B, Inc., Knoxville, 1976—. Served with U.S.Army, 1967-68. Decorated Bronze Star. Mem. Nat., Tenn. (area v.p.), Greater Knoxville (dir.) assns. home builders, Nat., Tenn. assns. Realtors, Knoxville Bd. Realtors, Knoxville Multiple Listing Service, Knoxville Apt. Council, Knoxville C. of C. Baptist. Club: Pres.'s (U. Tenn.). Home: 1910 Matthew Ln Knoxville TN 37919 Office: 6620 Pine Bluff Blvd Knoxville TN 37919

HAMDEN, RAYMOND HARRY, psychotherapist; b. Princeton, W.Va., Aug. 26, 1949; s. Harry and Najla (Bahmad) H.; B.A., Concord Coll., 1972; M.A., Radford Coll., 1975; Ph.D., Heed U., 1977; postgrad. Phila. Sch. Psychoanalysis, 1977—; m. Kathy J. Safady, Aug. 26, 1978. Dean of asso. degree W.Va. Career Coll., Charleston, 1975-76; clin. psychologist Kanawha County Bd. Edn., Charleston, 1976-77; physician asst. R. G. Wanderman, M.D., Charleston, 1976-78; founder, pres., psychotherapist Human Relations Clinic, Washington and Charleston, 1976—. Registered hypnotherapist Am. Guild Hypnotherapy; cert. clin. mem. Nat. Alliance Family Life. Mem. Nat. Accreditation Assn. Psychoanalysis (Am. Exam. Bd. Psychoanalysis), Nat. Assn. Arab-Ams., Nat. Alliance Family Life, Am. Assn. Sex Educators, Counselors and Therapists, Am. Psychol. Assn., Assn. Humanistic Psychology, Jaycees, Am. Druze Soc. Club: Elks. Contbr. articles to profl. jours. Address: People's Bldg Suite 402 Charleston WV 25301 also 2317 Pennsylvania Ave NW Suite 11 Washington DC 20037

HAMES, CARL MARTIN, educator, sch. adminstr.; b. Birmingham, Ala., July 12, 1938; s. William Geda and Mary Anna (Martin) H.; B.A., Birmingham-So. Coll., 1958; M.A., Samford U., 1971, M.Ed. Tchr., Birmingham Public Schs., 1958-64; tchr. Birmingham U. Sch., Altamont, 1964-75, asst. headmaster, chmn. English dept. Altamont (merger), 1975—; dir. Town Hall Gallery. Pres., Birmingham Music Club, 1978—, Connoisseur Concerts, 1974, 75, 76; bd. dirs. Birmingham Festival of Arts, Birmingham Art Assn. (editor newsletter), Birmingham Festival Theatre; curator Eye Found. Hosp. Art Collection; catalogue author and coordinator Spain Rehab. Hosp. Art Collection. Recipient Freedom Found. Classroom Tchr. award; Hackney Lit. prize for poetry, 1969, 79; Silver Bowl award Festival of Arts, 1971, 63. Mem. Ala. Hist. Soc., Birmingham Hist. Soc., Birmingham Mus. Art (men's com.), NEA, Nat. Council Tchrs. English, Ala. Council Tchrs. English (dir.), Soc. 18th Century Studies, English Speaking Union, Birmingham Mus. Art Edn. Council, Ala. Mus. Photography (dir.), Alliance Française. Democrat. Roman Catholic (Sunday sch. tchr.). Club: The Club. Contbr. to Andover Rev. Home: 3317-D Old Montgomery Hwy Birmingham AL 35209 Office: 4801 Altamont Rd Birmingham AL 35222

HAMFF, LEONARD HARVEY, physician; b. West Blocton, Ala., Nov. 22, 1913; s. Christian F. and Meri (Harvey) H.; A.B., Emory U., 1932, M.D., 1938; m. Elizabeth Anne Babington, Dec. 22, 1936; children—Mary Anne McClemens, Catherine Willis. Intern, Univ. Hosp., Ann Arbor, Mich., 1938-39, asst. resident, 1939-40, resident in internal medicine, 1940-41, instr., 1941-42; practice medicine specializing in internal medicine, Atlanta, 1942—; dir. diabetic service Grady Meml. Hosp., 1945-68; clin. prof. medicine Emory U. Sch. Medicine, 1965—. Fellow Am. Coll. Physicians, Am. Coll. Chest Physicians; mem. Ga. Diabetes Assn., Diabetes Assn. Atlanta, Am. Diabetes Assn., Ga. Rheumatism Assn., AMA, Med. Assn. Ga., Am. Heart Assn., So. Med. Assn., Fulton County Med. Soc., Atlanta Clin. Soc. Methodist. Clubs: Capital City, Piedmont Driving. Office: 478 Peachtree St NE Atlanta GA 30308

HAMILL, PATRICK JAMES, physicist; b. Salt Lake City, Apr. 29, 1938; s. Frank Anthony and Jane (McCollom) H.; B.S., St. Edwards U., 1959; postgrad. U. Tex., 1959-61; M.S., U. Ariz., 1968, Ph.D., 1971; Nat. Center Atmospheric Research, postdoctoral fellow U. Chgo., 1971-72; m. Elsa Li Che, Jan. 14, 1966; children—Carla Alexandra, Candace Joy. Aerospace engr. NASA Lewis Research Center, Cleve., 1961-63; vol., Peace Corps, Peru, 1963-66; asst. prof. physics Clark Coll., Atlanta, 1972-74; research scientist NASA Ames Research Center, Moffett Field, Calif., 1974-78; research scientist Systems and Applied Sci. Corp., NASA Langley Research Center, Hampton, Va., 1978—. NASA summer faculty fellow, 1974, 75; NRC sr. postdoctoral fellow, 1978; grantee NASA, EPA, CONICIT. Mem. Am. Meteorol. Assn., Am. Phys. Soc., Am. Assn. Physics Tchrs., Sigma Xi. Contbr. articles to profl. jours.; research in air pollution. Home: 116 C Pinewood Crescent Hampton VA 23666 Office: MS 233-A NASA Langley Research Center Hampton VA 23665

HAMILTON, CHARLES GRANVILLE, clergyman; b. Homestead, Pa., July 18, 1905; s. Augustus William and Mary Catherine (Frey) H.; A.B., Berea Coll., 1925; B.D., Columbia Sem., 1928, M. Div., 1971; D.D., Ministerial Coll., 1941; M.A., U. Miss., 1947; Ph.D., Vanderbilt U., 1958; postgrad. U. S.C., Butler U., Columbia U., Emory U., Ind. U., Miss. State U., Temple U., Tulane U., U. Wis., others; m. Mary Elizabeth Casey, May 23, 1939. Ordained to ministry Episcopal Ch., 1929; rector Mid-South field, 1928—; chaplain, prof. religious edn. Okolona Coll., 1933-40, prof. Wood, Furman, Memphis State, Vanderbilt and other univs., 1942-73; Danforth fellowships, 1955-60; fellowships St. Augustine's, Canterbury, England, 1961, Ford, 1962, Truman Library, 1963, Bell Telephone 1964, Am. Philos. Soc., 1969; minister Quiet Hour radio broadcast, 1942—; commentator The World Goes On, 1934—; pres., v.p., sec. Miss. Council for Christian Social Action, 1938—; v.p., dir. Rural Fellowship, 1955-63; sec., dir., pres. Crossroads Fellowship, 1964—; columnist Aberdeen (Miss.) Examiner, 1933-47. Del. Province of Sewanee, 1935, 36, 38, 39, 53, 54; sr. reporter Episcopal Convs., 1937—, World Council Chs., 1963. Mem. Miss. Ho. of Reps., 1940-44, floor leader, 1942; del. Democratic Nat. Convs. 1940, 44, 48, 52, 56, 60, 64, 68, 72, mem. credentials com. 1952; chmn. Miss. Vols. for Stevenson, 1952, 56, for Humphrey, 1968; pres., sec., sponsor Young Democrats, 1944-60; mem. White House Traffic Safety Commn., Tenn. Constn. Conv. Commn. Bd. dirs. Family Protection League. Served as 1st lt., chaplain AUS, 1940-42. Named Miss. Minister of Year, 1953; recipient research award Acad. Sci., 1955, Distinguished Alumnus of Year award Berea Coll., 1972; Ky. col. Mem. Am., So., Miss. hist. socs., Am., So. polit. sci. socs., Eugene Field Soc., Soc. Sacred Songwriters, Sons Confederate Vets. (chaplain gen.), Order Stars and Bars (chaplain gen.), New Orleans Civil War Roundtable (sec.), Pi Sigma Alpha, Phi Kappa Phi. Author many works, 1936—, including: Within Whose Memories Abide, 1935; South, 1935; There Came One Running, 1937; Mississippi I Love You, 1941; These United States, 1942; The Prophet in Wartime, 1947; Negro Education in Mississippi, 1952; Lincoln and the Know Nothings, 1954; 48 in '48, 1956; Democratic America, 8th edit., 1969; You Can't Steal First Base, 1971; Mississippi I Still Love You, 1975; The Flag Was Flame, 1976; Justice Standeth Afar Off, 1978; Holy, 1977; Progressive Mississippi, 1977. Liberty and Justice to All, under God, 1979; Mississippi, Mirror of the 1920's, 1979, also booklets. Editor: Brave Voyage, 1936; Lyric Monroe, 1937; Basic Relationships of Science, 1939; Those Precious Years, 1941; Preaching is Flame, 1961; Singing Spirit, 1962; Moments of Meditation, 1963; Music of Eternity, 1964; Grass on the Mountains, 1966; God of the Years, 1968; Our Yesterdays (Mary C. Hamilton), 1969; Christianity in 52 Words, 1970; Life's Benediction, 1971; The North Wind Comes, 1972; Afterglow, 1973; Touchstones of Right, 1974. Contbr. Poems of Justice, Master of Men, Poems for Life, others. Editor Jour. Miss. History, 1941-52. Editor: Anglican Outlook, 1952-57, Christian Outlook, 1957-60, Crossroads, 1957-70, Churchman, 1958—, Jour. Monroe County History, 1974—. Home: Gregg-Hamilton Meridian Monroe and Maple Aberdeen MS 39370

HAMILTON, DAGMAR STRANDBERG, educator, lawyer; b. Phila., Jan. 10, 1932; d. Eric Wilhelm and Anna Elizabeth (Sjöström) Strandberg; A.B., Swarthmore Coll., 1953; J.D., U. Chgo. Law Sch., 1956; J.D., Am. U., 1961; m. Robert W. Hamilton, June 26, 1953; children—Eric Clark, Robert Andrew Hale, Meredith Hope. Admitted to Tex. bar, 1972; atty., civil rights div. U.S. Dept. Justice, Washington, 1965-66; asst. instr. govt. U. Tex., Austin, 1966-71; lectr. Law Sch. U. Ariz., Tucson, 1971-72; editor, researcher Asso. Justice William O. Douglas, U.S. Supreme Ct., 1962-73, 75-76; editor, research Douglas autobiography Random House Co., 1972-73; counsel Judiciary Com., U.S. Ho. of Reps., 1973-74; asst. prof. L.B.J. Sch. Pub. Affairs, U. Tex., Austin, 1974-77, asso. prof., 1977—. Mem. steering com. Westlake Neighborhood Assn.; bd. dirs. ACLU. Mem. So., Am. polit. sci. assns., Tex. Bar Assn. Democrat. Quaker. Home: 403 Allegro Ln Austin TX 78746 Office: LBJ Sch Public Affairs U Tex Austin TX 78712

HAMILTON, DALE RICHARD, marketing exec.; b. Dallas, June 23, 1938; s. Charles Curtis and Elsie Madalyn (Baynes) H.; B.S., A&M Coll. Tex., 1961; m. Shirley Frances Marlow, June 16, 1961; children—Linda Suzanne, Mark Richard. Checker, Great Atlantic and Pacific Tea Co., Dallas, 1954-56; engr. Stewart Engring. & Equipment Co., Inc., Richardson, Tex., 1961-64, estimator, 1963-68, asst. sales mgr., 1968-73, product mgr., 1973-75, sales mgr., 1975-78; mgr. mktg. services Stewart Systems Inc., Plano, Tex., 1978—; bd. dirs. Baking Industry Sanitation Standards Com., 1976-78. Asst. scoutmaster Boy Scouts Am., 1965-66, scoutmaster, 1966-67, service clan adv., 1967-68, commr., 1967-68. Mem. Am. Soc. Bakery Engrs., Jaycees (internat. senator), Tex. Jaycees (state treas. 1974-75, Outstanding Appointed Officer 1974, 75), Richardson Jaycees (dir. 1969-70). Methodist. Home: 745 Loganwood Ave Richardson TX 75080 Office: 808 Stewart Ave Plano TX 75074

HAMILTON, DALTON EARL, civil engr.; b. Dalhart, Tex., Aug. 14, 1930; s. William E. and Verna (Miller) H.; B.S. in Civil Engring., Tex. Tech. U., 1951; m. Anita Reynolds, Oct. 20, 1951; children—Cheryl Annette Hamilton Huck, Mary Anna. Constrn. engr. CAA, Fort Worth, 1951-52; hwy. engr. U.S. Army Corp Engrs., Tulsa, 1952-55; constrn. engr. City of Abilene, Tex., 1955-59; v.p. Trinity Engring. Testing Corp., Austin, Tex., 1959—; vis. profl. Tex. A. and M. U., 1972—. Scoutmaster Boy Scouts Am., 1952-58. Mem. C. of C., Am. Council Ind. Labs., Tex. Soc. Profl. Engrs. (regional v.p., Engr. of Yr. 1980), Nat. Soc. Profl. Engrs. Tex. Constrn. Council, Am. Welding Soc., Tex. Council Engring. Labs. (past pres.), Am. Concrete Inst. Methodist (trustee). Home: 12507 Silver Spur St Austin TX 78758 Office: PO Box 572 Austin TX 78767

HAMILTON, HOLMAN, historian, educator; b. Ft. Wayne, Ind., May 30, 1910; s. Dr. Allen and Helen (Knight) H.; A.B., Williams Coll., 1932; Ph.D., U. Ky., 1954, Litt.D., 1977; L.H.D., Franklin Coll., Ind., 1966; LL.D., Lincoln Meml. U., 1973; LL.D., Ind. U., 1976; m. Suzanne W. Bowerfind, Oct. 7, 1939; 1 dau., Susan C. Reporter, Ft. Wayne Journal-Gazette, 1932-34; editorial writer, 1935-42, 46, 47-50; asst. prof. history U. Ky., Lexington, 1954-57, asso. prof., 1957-65, prof., 1965—, Hallam prof., 1969-71; Guggenheim fellow, 1946; Fulbright prof. U. Chile, Santiago, 1966. Trustee Lincoln Meml. U., 1957-63. Served from pvt. to maj. AUS, 1942-46. Recipient Pelzer prize Miss. Valley Hist. Assn., 1954; faculty research award U. Ky., 1965, Great Tchr. award, 1968, 75, Disting. Prof. award Coll. Arts and Scis., 1971. Mem Am., So. (pres. 1979) hist. assns., Orgn. Am. Historians, Soc. Am. Historians, Ind., Ky. hist. socs. Clubs: Nat. Press (Washington); Idle Hour (Lexington); Williams (N.Y.C.). Author: Zachary Taylor: Soldier of the Republic, 1941; Zachary Taylor: Soldier in the White House, 1951; White House Images and Realities, 1958; Prologue to Conflict, 1964; The Three Kentucky Presidents: Lincoln, Taylor, Davis, 1980. Co-author: The Democratic Experience, 1963, rev. edit., 1977. Contbr. to Dictionary of American History, 1940; Major Crises in American History, 1962; Notable American Women, 1971; History of American Presidential Elections, 1971; Encyclopedia of American Biography, 1974. Co-editor: Indianapolis in the Gay Nineties, 1964. Editor: Three American Frontiers, 1968. Home: 220 Barrow Rd Lexington KY 40502

HAMILTON, HOWARD LAVERNE, educator; b. Lone Tree, Iowa, July 20, 1916; s. Harry Stephen and Gertrude Ruth (Shibley) H.; B.A., State U. Iowa, 1937, M.S., 1938; postgrad. U. Rochester, 1938-40; Ph.D., Johns Hopkins U., 1941; m. Alison Phillips, Dec. 22, 1945 (dec. 1972); children—Christina Helen, Phillips Howard, Martha Jayne; m. 2d Elizabeth Burnley Bentley, June 18, 1975; children—Elizabeth Marshall, Catherine Randolph. Asst. prof. to prof. zoology Iowa State U., 1946-62, acting head, 1960-61, chmn. dept. zoology and entomology, 1961-62; prof. biology U. Va., 1962—. Mem. Am. Soc. Zoologists, Am. Soc. Naturalists, Soc. Devel. Biology, Internat. Inst. Devel. Biology, Am. Inst. Biol. Sci., Sigma Xi., Phi Beta Kappa, Phi Kappa Phi, Phi Sigma. Author: Lillie's Development of the Chick, 1952. Cons. editor: McGraw-Hill Encyclopedia of Science and Technology, 1962-78. Mng. editor: The American Zoologist, 1965-70. Author: (with Viktor Hamburger) Citation Classic: A Series of Normal Stages in the Development of the Chick, 1951. Home: Jumping Branch Farm Route 5 Box 401 Charlottesville VA 22901 Office: Department of Biology Gilmer Hall University of Virginia Charlottesville VA 22901

HAMILTON, HUDSON BRANTLEY, state ofcl.; b. Belleville, Ala., July 23, 1922; s. William Irving and Essie Kate H.; student pub. schs., Repton, Ala.; m. Marie Wasalski, June 13, 1945; children—Kathleen, Linda Diane. Clk.-typist Cowan Irving Ins. Co., Mobile, Ala., 1941-47, real estate appraiser, 1946-47; with Gulf Mobile & Ohio R.R. Co., Mobile, 1947-66; dep. dir., traffic rate mgr. Miss. State Port Authority, Gulfport, 1966—; mem. Dist. Export Council, Southeastern Shippers Adv. Bd. Served with USCGR, 1942-45, U.S. Army, 1950-52. Mem. Nat. Def. Transp. Assn. (past pres.), Gulf Coast Traffic Club (past pres.), So. Traffic League, Gulf Ports Assn. Baptist. Home: 110 Pimlico St Long Beach MS 39560 Office: Miss State Port Authority PO Box 40 Gulfport MS 39501

HAMILTON, JOHN FREDERICK, acctg. co. exec.; b. Columbia, S.C., Sept. 13, 1945; s. J.M. and J.M. (Pledger) H.; B.S. in Bus. Adminstrn., U. S.C., 1967; m. Jean R. Adkins, Oct. 26, 1963; children—James, Leslie. Acct., Finch Kight & Jackson, C.P.A.'s, Columbia, 1966-71; supr. Ernst & Whinney, C.P.A.'s, Columbia, 1971-73; partner Finch, Hamilton, Oxner, Yochum & Co., C.P.A.'s, Columbia, 1973—. Mem. S.C. Bd. Examiners for Nursing Home Adminstrs. Mem. Am., S.C. assns. C.P.A.'s, Nat. Assn. Accts., NACPAF (SE chmn.), SCACPA (chmn. auditing standards com.), Columbia C. of C., U. S.C. Alumni Assn. (dir. Richland County chpt.). Republican. Methodist. Home: 209 Garden Springs Rd Columbia SC 29209 Office: PO Box 11625 Columbia SC 29211

HAMILTON, JOHN WILLIAM, indsl. psychologist; b. Janesville, Wis., Nov. 15, 1943; s. Ray Henry and Marjorie Alice (Leng) H.; B.S. summa cum laude, Colo. State U., 1971, M.S. in Indsl. Psychology, 1974, Ph.D., 1977; m. Bonnie Marie Swenson, June 22, 1966; children—Tyler Leng, Terra Lynn. Lab. technician, Systems analyst Woodward Gov. Co., 1965-69; research asst. Colo. State U., Ft. Collins, 1974, mktg. supervisory tng. program, 1974-75; instr. U. Colo., Denver Center, 1974; asst. prof. psychology, Va. Poly. Inst. and State U., Blacksburg, 1976-80; sr. psychologist Mich. div. Dow Chem. Corp., Midland, 1980—; cons. Police Dept. Ft. Collins, 1971-75, Battelle Human Affairs Research Center, Seattle, 1972-73, Rocky Mountain Inst. Community Relations and Adminstrn. of Justice, Denver, 1972-73, Police Dept. Colo. State U., Ft. Collins, 1973-75, Project Go, 1974-75, Police Dept. Town of Blacksburg, 1976-80, Ednl. Communications. Va. Poly. Inst. and State U., 1977-78, Tex. Instruments, Inc., Dallas, 1977-78, Manpower, Inc., Norfolk, 1979-80, U.S. Geol. Survey, 1979; condr. seminar for profl. assn., workshops for Commonwealth of Va., 1977-78. Served with USAF, 1961-65, Project dir. grant, Town of Blacksburg, 1978-80. Mem. Rocky Mountain Psychol. Assn., Southeastern Psychol. Assn., Am. Psychol. Assn., Acad. Mgmt., Southeastern Indsl./Organizational Psychol. Assn., Sigma Xi, Phi Kappa Phi. Contbr. articles to profl. publs., papers to profl. confs. Home: 3606 Mary Jane Dr Midland MI 48604 Office: 47 Bldg Dow Mich Div Midland MI 48604

HAMILTON, KATHY SUE, ednl. counselor; b. Dallas, Dec. 23, 1950; d. Carroll Maurice and Sara Katherine (Corpier) Hamilton; B.S. in Edn., U. Tex., Austin, 1973; M.Ed., N.Tex. State U., 1975. Tchrs. aide, substitute tchr. Austin Ind. Sch. Dist., 1973-74; office sec. Nat. Chemsearch Corp., 1974-75; dir. counseling services YMCA Urban Services, Dallas, 1976—, also program dir. for sponsors ednl. opportunity and satellite dir. YMCA Ednl. Opportunity Center, tng. coordinator YMCA CETA project, 1979-80, named sr. dir., 1979; cons. Action Line, Dallas Times Herald, Dallas King and Dye Founds., Engrs. Club Dallas. Co-chmn. exec. com. Sponsors for Ednl. Opportunity, 1976—; corr. sec. Tex. Assn. for Services to Children, 1977—; mem. resource com. Urban Career Edn. Project, 1977; vol. DIS D Letot Alternative Sch., 1979-80. Cert. tchr., Tex. Mem. Am. Personnel and Guidance Assn., S.W. Assn. Student Assistance Programs (asso.), Nat. Vocat. Guidance Assn., Ex-Students Assn. U. Tex. (life), AAUW, Tex. Coalition Juvenile Justice. Democrat. Methodist. Home: 3820 Spring Valley #4115 Dallas TX 75234 Office: 901 Ross Ave Room 309 Dallas TX 75202

HAMILTON, LINDA GAIL, state ofcl.; b. Miami, Fla., Nov. 24, 1939; d. Hebert W. and Adeline (Lindsey) H.; A.A., Miami Dade Jr. Coll., 1973; B.S., Fla. Internat. U., 1975; diploma Gradwohl Sch. Lab. Technique, 1960. Med. technologist lab. services Dade County (Fla.) Kendall Hosp., 1960-61, VA Hosp., Miami, 1961-77, asst. supr. transfusion service, 1966-74, supr., 1964-66; lab. cons. Fla. Dept. Health and Rehab. Services, 1977-78; lab. cons. Health Care Financing Adminstrn., Region III, Phila., 1978-79, Fla. Office of Licensure and Cert., Miami, 1979—. Recipient Superior Performance award Fla. VA Hosp., 1967. Mem. Am. Soc. Med. Technologists, Am. Med. Technologists, Am. Assn. Blood Banks, Am. Soc. Clin. Pathologists, Am. Bd. Bioanalysts, Phi Theta Kappa. Democrat. Methodist. Home: 4250 SW 67th Ave Miami FL 33155 Office: Palmetto Lakes Office Bldg 5190 NW 167th St Miami FL 33014

HAMILTON, LUTHER MYLES, JR., ret. mech. engr.; b. Crystal Springs, Miss., Aug. 19, 1912; s. Luther M. and Elizabeth L. (Davidson) H.; B.S. in Mech. Engring., Miss. State U., 1938; postgrad. Princeton U., 1944, Harvard U., 1944, U. Ala., 1946, 47, Spring Hill Coll., 1960, Ohio State U., 1961; m. Josephine Morris, Jan. 20, 1939. Engring. draftsman Miss. Hwy. Dept., Jackson, 1938, soils technician, 1939; jr. engr. Signal Corps Gen. Devel. Lab., Ft. Monmouth, N.J., 1941-42, asst. mech. engr., 1942-43, asso. engr., 1943-44; coordinator Trade and Indsl. Edn., Coffee County High Sch., Enterprise, Ala., 1946-49; office mgr. Gulf Oil Distributor, Enterprise, 1950-53; planning estimator E.I. duPont de Nemours & Co., Pensacola, Fla., 1953-54; mech. engr. Brookley AFB, Mobile, Ala., 1954, supervisory mech. engr., 1955, supervisory gen. engr., 1958-66; gen. engr. Naval Ship Research and Devel. Lab., Panama City, Fla., 1966-71, ret., 1971. United Fund coordinator Brookley AFB, 1955-66. Served to lt. USNR, 1944-46; PTO. Registered profl. engr., Ala., Mem. Panama City Art Assn., Panama City Music Assn. Baptist. Mason, Lion. Author: Guide to Uniformity in Specification Preparation, 1970. Address: 1100 W 10th St Panama City FL 32401

HAMILTON, NANCY CAROL, hosp. ofcl.; b. Albemarle, N.C., Apr. 24, 1949; d. Max C. and Frances Delores (Cranford) Frye; student Rowan Tech. Inst., 1968; m. Robert Worth Hamilton Jr., June 23, 1973; children—Robert Worth, Catherine Elizabeth. Sec., Richfield (N.C.) Mfg., 1967-68; exec. sec. Stanly County Hosp., Albemarle, N.C., 1968-73; dir. personnel services Rex Hosp., Raleigh, N.C. Mem. Nat. League Nursing, Am. Hosp. Assn., N.C. Hosp. Personnel Assn. Home: Route 4 Box 156A Apex NC 27502 Office: Rex Hospital 1311 Saint Marys Saint Raleigh NC 27603

HAMILTON, ROBERT WILLIAM, acctg. scientist, educator; b. Anson, Tex., July 24, 1923; s. William Enoch and Verna Powell (Miller) H.; B.B.A., Tex. Technol. U., 1953, M.B.A., 1954; B.S., E. Tex. State U., 1975; m. Helen Marie Keese, June 4, 1944; children—William Morris, Sue Marie. Customer service mgr. Sears Roebuck & Co., Lubbock, Tex., 1946-51; owner, operator Hamilton Booking and Tax Service, Lubbock, 1951-70; pres. Electronic Tabulating Inc., Lubbock, 1964-70; instr. acctg. and EDP and computer sci. Tex. Technol. U., Lubbock, 1963-66; dir. EDP, South Plains Coll., Levelland, Tex., 1966-70; chmn. dept. computer info. systems Amarillo (Tex.) Coll., 1970—. Served with USAAF, 1942-46. Mem. Nat. Assn. Ednl. Data Systems, Tex. Jr. Coll. Tchrs. Assn. (chmn. data processing group 1979—), Tex. Assn. Ednl. Data Systems (sec. 1978—). Methodist. Clubs: Lions, Kiwanis, 20/30 Internat. Office: PO Box 447 Dept Data Processing Amarillo Coll Amarillo TX 79178

HAMLET, RICHARD MCDOWELL, savs. and loan exec.; b. Norfolk, Va., Nov. 8, 1948; s. Ernest Benjamin and Verdelma Anderson H.; B.A., Va. Mil. Inst., 1970; postgrad. U. Va., 1971; M.A., Old Dominion U., 1976; m. Darrellyn Dee Hamlet, Aug. 7, 1971; children—Benjamin Harrison, Elizabeth Wetherbee. With Atlantic Permanent Savs. & Loan Assn., Inc., Norfolk, 1972—, asst. v.p., 1975-77, v.p., 1977-78, sr. v.p. savs. and investments, 1979—; pres. Tidewater Profl. Services; instr. Tidewater Community Coll. Chmn. fin. com. Tidewater March of Dimes; bd. dirs. Lions Club Found. Served with U.S. Army, 1971-72. Mem. Am. Soc. Personnel Adminstrs., Fin. Mgrs. Soc., Urban League Tidewater (dir.), Va. Mil. Inst. Alumni Assn. (pres.). Republican. Roman Catholic. Club: Va. Mil. Inst. Keydet. Home: 1977 Irish Bank Virginia Beach VA 23454 Office: Atlantic Permanent Savs & Loan Assn Inc 740 Boush St Norfolk VA 23510

HAMLIN, GUY ANDREWS, lawyer, state ofcl.; b. Brushton, N.Y., Oct. 31, 1923; student U. Vt., 1941-43, 46-47; LL.B., Duke U., 1950; m. Gloria Livingston, June 30, 1950; 1 son, Bradley. Served with inf. U.S. Army, Europe, 1943-46; admitted to N.C. bar, 1950, U.S. Supreme Ct. bar, 1962; commd. 1st lt. Judge Adv. Gen.'s Corps., U.S.

Army, 1950, advanced through grades to lt. col., 1964; staff judge adv. 82d Airborne Div., Ft. Bragg, N.C., 1963-66; sr. legal adv. to Vietnamese Armed Forces in Vietnam, 1966-67; ret., 1967; asst. atty. gen. State of N.C., 1967—. Decorated medal of Honor 1st class (Vietnam). Mem. Ret. Officers Assn., N.C. Bar Assn., N.C. State Bar, Airborne Assn., Delta Theta Phi, Sigma Phi. Club: Airborne Century. Office: Suite 207 20 S Spruce St Asheville NC 28801

HAMM, RAYMOND PETERS, theol. sem. ofcl.; b. Carter County, Tenn., Oct. 13, 1936; s. Raymond Harrell and Pauline (Peters) H.; student East Tenn. State U., 1955—; m. Deanna, July 4, 1963; 1 dau., Joy Michele. Br. mgr. Gen. Electric Credit Corp., Johnson City, Tenn., 1967-74; bus. mgr. Emmanuel Sch. Religion, Johnson City, 1975—. Bd. dirs., pres. East Tenn. Educators Credit Union, Johnson City. Served with USAF, 1956-60. Mem. Am. Mgmt. Assn. Mem. Chs. of Christ. Club: Masons. Home: 303 N Gilmer Park Johnson City TN 37601 Office: Emmanuel Sch Religion Route 6 Box 500 Johnson City TN 37601

HAMMACK, VIRGINIA COLLINS, med. clinic adminstr.; b. Edgefield County, S.C., Dec. 9, 1929; d. Daniel Self and Lela Mae (Dorn) Collins; Asso. in Bus. Adminstrn., Columbia Coll. Commerce, 1948; m. Leslie Perry Hammack, June 24, 1949; 1 son, James Leslie. Acct., Milliken Co., McCormick, S.C., 1948-54; adminstrv. sec. to plant mgr., Johnston, S.C., 1956-58, adminstr. sec. to minister Edgefield (S.C.) Methodist Ch., 1963-66; office mgr. Edgefield Med. Clinic, P.A., 1966—. Cert. notary public, S.C. Republican. Methodist. Home: Route 2 Box 153 Edgefield SC 29824 Office: 409 Simpkins St Edgefield SC 29824

HAMMAKER, WILBUR KIRACOFE, ins. exec.; b. Libertytown, Md., Feb. 26, 1928; s. Wilbur Foard and Bernice (Kiracofe) H.; B.S. in Bus. Adminstrn., Johns Hopkins U., 1950; grad. Command and Gen. Staff Coll., 1969; m. Mollie Jo Thomas, July 10, 1966; children—Michael Kirk, Jeffrey Beckh, Frederick Karl. Unit salesman Procter and Gamble Distbg. Co., Balt., 1950-53; fuel oil mgr. Crown Central Petroleum Corp., Balt. and Richmond, Va., 1953-57; retail sales supr. Va., Tidewater Oil Co., Richmond, 1957-62; pres. Parham Gen. Agy. Inc., Norfolk, Va., 1962-69, Towels & Stuff, Virginia Beach, Va., 1969-72; sr. v.p. Pembroke Ins. Agy. Inc., Virginia Beach, 1972—. Chmn. ins. com. Neptune Festival. Served to lt. col. U.S. Army, 1945-50, 60-62. Mem. Ind. Ins. Agts. Assn., Profl. Ins. Agts. Assn., Insurors Group, Ins. Mktg. Services, Res. Officers Assn., Assn. U.S. Army, Va. Assn. Realtors (chmn. ins. com.), Virginia Beach Bd. Realtors (chmn. ins. com.). Office: Pembroke Insurance Agency 281 Independence Blvd 101 Virginia Beach VA 23462

HAMMER, EDSON GEORGE, educator; b. Galesville, Wis., July 5, 1922; s. Nels John and Josephine Delia (Brenegan) H.; B.S., U. Wis., 1948; M.A., George Washington U., 1959, D.B.A., 1973; m. Eileen Merlin Borhofen, June 23, 1951; children—Nikki Ann, Nancy Marie. Commd. 2d. lt. U.S. Air Force, 1949, advanced through grades to lt. col., 1964, ret., 1968; dir. counseling and info. services Coll. Gen. Studies, George Washington U., Washington, 1968-73; asso. prof. sch. bus. U. Tenn., Chattanooga, 1973—; cons. to dir. personnel City of Chattanooga. Decorated Legion of Merit; U. Chattanooga Found. research grantee, 1977, 79. Mem. Acad. Mgmt., Acad. Internat. Bus., So. Mgmt. Assn. Republican. Roman Catholic. Clubs: Lions, K.C. (dir. Mental Retardation Found. Tenn.), Am. Legion, Air Force Assn. Author: Survey of Graduates' Attitudes Toward Curriculum Course Requirements, 1977. Home: 804 Brynwood Park Ln Chattanooga TN 37415 Office: 615 McCallie Ave Chattanooga TN 37402

HAMMER, JOHN WILLIAM, JR., dentist; b. Charleston, W.Va., June 1, 1945; s. John William and Mary George (Spangler) H.; D.D.S., W.Va. U., 1969; postgrad. periodontology Temple U., Phila.; m. Linda Lee Burton, Nov. 8, 1968; children—Jennifer Lee, Kristen Lee, Susan Elizabeth. Residency USPHS Hosp., Balt., 1970-71; gen. practice dentistry, Martinsburg, W.Va., 1971—. Served with USPHS, 1969-71. Fellow Acad. Gen. Dentistry; mem. ADA, W.Va. Dental Assn., W.Va. U. Sch. Dentistry Alumni Assn., Potomac Valley Dental Soc., Eastern Panhandle, No. Va., Appalachian dental study clubs, N.G. Assn. W.Va., N.G. Assn. U.S., Acad. Air NG Dentists (treas.). Home: 1002 Mill Race Rd Martinsburg WV 25401 Office: 111 Tavern Rd Martinsburg WV 25401

HAMMER, WADE BURKE, oral surgeon, educator; b. Lakeland, Fla., Apr. 21, 1932; s. Orval Seown and Lilly Pearl (Wade) H.; A.A., U. Fla., 1956; D.D.S., Emory U., 1960; postgrad. U. Pa., 1962; m. Betty Dean Webb, June 22, 1956; children—Robert Burke, Joanna Wade. Practice dentistry, Orange Park, Fla., 1960-61; resident in oral surgery Grady Hosp., Emory U., Atlanta, 1963-65; active staff Eugene Talmadge Meml. Hosp., Augusta, Ga., 1968—; cons. Univ. Hosp., Augusta, 1968—, VA Complex, Augusta, 1968—, Ft. Gordon Army Hosp., 1969—; clin. asst. prof. oral surgery Emory U., 1966-68; asst. prof. oral surgery and surgery Med. Coll. Ga., Augusta, 1968-71, asso. prof. oral surgery, 1971-75, prof., 1975—. Active Boy Scouts Am. Bd. govs. Dental Found. Ga., 1974-77, pres., 1976-77. Served with USN, 1950-54; oral surgeon, comdr. USAR. Diplomate Am. Bd. Oral Surgery. Fellow Am. Dental Soc. Anesthesiology; mem. Am., Ga., Eastern Dist. dental assns., Augusta Dental Soc., Am., Southeastern, Ga. socs. oral surgeons, Internat. Assn. for Dental Research, Am. Assn. Dental Schs., Omicron Kappa Upsilon. Contbr. articles to profl. jours. Home: 3020 Vassar Dr Augusta GA 30904 Office: Med Coll Ga Augusta GA 30902

HAMMERBECK, AL WALTER, tng. and devel. program exec.; b. Duluth, Minn., Sept. 14, 1936; s. Walter A. and Mabel H. (Dehli) H.; B.S. in Psychology, U. Nebr., 1971; grad. U.S. Army Command and Gen. Staff Coll., 1972; M.A., Central Mich. U., 1974; children—Robert, Charles and Mark (twins). Commd. 2d lt. U.S. Army, 1958, advanced through grades to lt. col., 1975; aviator; ret., 1978; prof. mil. sci., chmn. dept. Wofford Coll., 1977-78; human relations officer Army Hawaii, 1972-75; pvt. practice counseling, Spartanburg, S.C., 1976—; partner Hammerbeck Assos., Spartanburg, 1978—; public speaker; instr. U. LaVern. Active Mental Health Assn., PTA. Decorated D.F.C., Bronze Star, Army Commendation medal, Purple Heart, Meritorious Service medal. Mem. Am. Mental Health Counselors Assn., Am. Personnel and Guidance Assn., Bus. Men's Assn., Army Aviators Assn., Scabbard and Blade. Republican. Baptist. Contbr. articles to mil. jours. Home: 113 Westhaven Ct Spartanburg SC 29301 Office: 430 Oak Grove Rd Spartanburg SC 29301

HAMMERSCHMIDT, JOHN PAUL, congressman; b. Harrison, Ark., May 4, 1922; s. Arthur Paul and Junie (Taylor) H.; student The Citadel, 1938-39, U. Ark., 1940-41, Okla. State U., 1945-46; m. Virginia Sharp; 1 son, John Arthur. With Hammerschmidt Lumber Co., Harrison, 1946—, pres., 1959—; dir. Harrison Fed. Savs. & Loan Assn.; mem. Harrison City Council, 1948, 60, 62; mem. 90th-96th Congresses, 3d Dist. Ark. Served as pilot USAAF, World War II; CBI. Decorated Air medal with 4 oak leaf clusters, D.F.C. with 3 oak leaf clusters. Mem. Ark. Lumber Dealers Assn. (past pres.), Southwestern Lumbermens Assn. (past pres. Kansas City), Nat. Lumber and Bldg. Material Dealers (dir.), Harrison C. of C. (named Man of Yr. 1965), Am. Legion, V.F.W. Presbyn. (elder) (deacon). Mason (32 deg., Shriner), Elk, Rotarian (past pres. Harrison). Home: PO Box 999 Harrison AR 72601 Office: Rayburn House Office Bldg Washington DC 20515

HAMMETT, BOBBY LYNN, computer installation cons.; b. Sherman, Tex., Mar. 16, 1935; s. William Henry and Leola (Gurley) H.; student various IBM Data Processing Schs., 1960-75; student Lamar U., 1977—; m. Dorene Yvonne Gantt, June 6, 1958; children—Susan Alysia, Deena Marque. With Levingston Shipbuilding Co., Orange, Tex., 1953-77, planner, 1961-65, mgr. data processing, 1965-77; cons. computer installations, 1977—. Councillor, Jr. Achievement, 1967-72; master Three Rivers Council Boy Scouts, Am., 1954-55; res. dep. sheriff, Orange County, Tex. Mem. data processing com. Lamar U., 1971-73. Mem. COMMON, HASU (computer users groups), Am. Numismatic Assn., Data Processing Mgrs. Assn., Citizens Radio Assistance Corp. Home: 3106 Western Ave Orange TX 77630 Office: 3106 Western Ave Orange TX 77630

HAMMOCK, MARCUS DANIEL, JR., petroleum distbg. co. exec.; b. Washington County, Ga., Oct. 4, 1929; s. Marcus Daniel and Trudie Belle (Parker) H.; ed. high sch., Sandersville, Ga.; m. Jean Holton, Feb. 13, 1955; 1 son, Marcus Daniel. Pres., M.D. Hammock Oil Co., Sandersville, 1971—; pvt. pilot. Served with C.E., U.S. Army, 1951-53. Mem. Ga. Oilmen Assn. Methodist. Clubs: Civitan (bus. mgr., dir. 1973—), Twin City Country. Home: 616 Woodland Dr Sandersville GA 31082 Office: M D Hammock Oil Co 428 Industrial Dr Sanderville GA 31082

HAMMON, CARL KONRAD, cons. engr.; b. Fuerth, Germany, Jan. 13, 1909; s. Lorenz and Kunigunda (Griesgau) H.; came to U.S., 1926, naturalized, 1936; student Engring. Coll. (Germany), 1928-29; student Newark Coll., 1931-35; m. Mary Louise Eggerding; children—Lorenz Karl, Andreas Otto; m. 2d, Miriam Elizabeth McPherson, Apr. 17, 1965. With Singer Mfg., Elizabeth, N.J., 1926-27, Mack Truck, Plainfield, N.J., 1927-28, draftsman, 1929-37; designer Watson-Stillman, Roselle, N.J., 1937-47, mgr. new design devel., 1947-53; mgr. hydraulic press dev., chief engr. Erie Foundry Co., Erie, Pa., 1953-71; cons. engr. in pvt. practice on hydraulic presses and machinery on new developments, Morehead, City, N.C., 1972—; lectr. in field. Dir., pres. Pine Knoll Assn., Pine Knoll Shores, N.C., 1972-74, chmn. com. for inc., 1973. Mem. Am. Def. Preparedness Assn. Republican. Presbyterian. Contbr. articles in field to profl. jours. patentee in field. Address: Oakleaf Dr Pine Knoll Shores Morehead City NC 28557

HAMMOND, BRENDA HURLEY, ednl. counselor; b. Mouthcard, Ky., Dec. 8, 1947; d. James L. and Goldie M. H.; B.S., Concord Coll., 1971; M.S., Radford U., 1976; children by former marriage—Tina, Brian. Tchr., Mercer Sch., Princeton, W.Va., 1972-77, counselor elem. guidance, 1977—; research asso. Appalachia Ednl. Lab., Charleston, W.Va., 1979—. Dir. spiritual life 1st Ch. God, Princeton, 1977-78, dir. missionary edn., 1979—; bd. dirs. CDC Inc., 1978—. Mem. NEA, W.Va. Edn. Assn., Am. Personnel and Guidance Assn., Am. Sch. Counselors Assn. Home: 411 Gayle St Princeton WV 24740 Office: Mercer Sch 1200 Mercer St Princeton WV 24740

HAMMOND, EARLE B., JR., steel co. exec.; b. Dayton, Tex., May 26, 1927; s. Earle B. and Ola Mae (Griffin) H.; B.B.A., U. Houston, 1950; m. Alice Nell White, June 28, 1948; children—Patricia Kay, Donna Gayle. Acct., Houston Works, ARMCO, 1953-66, supr. cost acctg., 1966-69, works controller Armco Butler Works (Pa.), 1969-75, mgr. plant acctg. Nat. Supply Co. div., Houston, 1975-78, mgr. fin. planning and analysis, 1978-79, mgr. bus. strategy Western Steel div., 1979—. Served with USCG, 1944-45. C.P.A., Tex.; cert. mgmt. acct. Mem. Nat. Assn. Accts. (pres. Butler area chpt. 1973-74), Inst. Mgmt. Accts., Planning Exec. Inst., Tex. Soc. C.P.A.'s. Republican. Methodist. Club: Masons. Home: 10918 Candlewood Dr Houston TX 77042 Office: 1455 West Loop South Houston TX 77027

HAMMOND, GEORGE ROBERT, chiropractor; b. Porterdale, Ga., Sept. 10, 1925; s. George Gibson and Anne Mae (Coley) H.; D.C., Lincoln Coll., Indpls., 1949; P.T., Nat. Coll. Chiropractic, 1958; m. Eleanor Emilie Maurer, Dec. 27, 1947; children—Carol Ann Hammond Reaves, Jody Hammond Bissette, Robin, Allyson. Practice chiropractic, Wilson, N.C., 1950—. Pres. N.C. Bd. Chiropractic Examiners, 1969-75. Trustee Boys' Home at Lake Macamaw (N.C.), 1957-60, Civitan Found., 1960-64, Nat. Coll. Chiropractic. Served with AUS, 1943-44. Decorated Purple Heart; recipient Sci. Journalism award N.C. Chiropractic Assn. Jour., 1960. Fellow Internat. Coll. Chiropractors; mem. N.C. Chiropractic Assn. (pres. 1962), Wilson Civitan Club (pres. 1957-58), Civitan Internat. (lt. gov. dist. 1960-61), Delta Tau Alpha. Democrat. Episcopalian. Home: 212 Wilshire Blvd Wilson NC 27893 Office: 605 Fairview Ave Wilson NC 27893

HAMMOND, LYN HORTON, physician; b. Greenville, S.C., Dec. 30, 1948; s. Robert Newton and Emogene (Horton) H.; B.S., Wofford Coll., 1970; M.D., Med. U. S.C., 1973; children—Christopher Lyn, Heather Victoria. Intern, Greenville Hosp. System, resident in family practice, 1974-76; practice medicine specializing in family medicine, Greenville, 1976—; mem. staff Greenville Hosp. System, St. Francis Hosp., Greenville. Mem. Greenville County Health Planning Council, 1979-80. Diplomate Am. Bd. Family Practice. Fellow Am. Acad. Family Physicians; mem. Greenville County Med. Soc. Baptist. Home: 38 Fieldstone Pl Greenville SC 29615 Office: 410-B Pelham Rd Greenville SC 29615

HAMMOND, RALPH CHARLES, real estate exec.; b. Valley Head, Ala., Feb. 1, 1916; s. William Bleve and Alice Corina Jane (Holleman) H.; student Snead Jr. Coll., 1938-39, Berea Coll., 1940-41; A.B., U. Ala., 1945; m. Myra Leak, June 20, 1954; children—James, Ben. Press sec. to gov. Ala., Montgomery, 1946-50, exec. sec., 1955-59; gen. rep. ARC, Greensboro, N.C., 1950-54; mayor of Arab, Ala., 1963-69; pres. City Center, Inc., Arab, 1959—. Commr. from Ala., U.S. Study Commn. S.E. River Basins, 1958-64. Dir. Ala. Tb Assn., 1956—, pres., 1972-74; hon. Christmas Seal chmn., Ala., 1974. Served with AUS, 1941-45. Mem. Ky. Hist. Soc., Phillip Hamman Family Assn. Am. (pres. 1972—), Filson Club. Democrat. Methodist. Mason. Author: My GI Aching Back, 1945; Ante Bellum Mansions of Alabama, 1951; Philip Hamman, Man of Valor, 1976. Contbr. short stories and feature articles to jours., mags. Home: Guntersville Rd Arab AL 35016 Office: Box 486 Arab AL 35016

HAMMOND, RONNIE LYNNEL, systems engr.; b. Tyler, Tex., July 17, 1948; s. George Author and Nathell Miller (Beck) H.; student (scholar) St. Phillip's Jr. Coll., 1966-68, (scholar) Huston-Tilloston Coll., 1968-70; B.A. in History, St. Mary's U., 1977; m. Carmen Yvette Richardson, Aug. 18, 1975. Dietary worker Bapt. Meml. Hosp., 1966-68; with So. Pacific R.R., 1970-72; computer operator St. Mary's U., San Antonio, 1973-74, ops. mgr. Computer Center, 1974-79; systems engr. NCR Corp., 1979—; data processing clk. San Antonio Ind. Sch. Dist., 1974. Mem. Omega Psi Phi, Phi Alpha Theta (historian). Mem. Churches of Christ. Home: 8711 Townpark Dr Apt 2161 Houston TX 77036 Office: NCR Corp 6808 Hornwood Houston TX 77074

HAMMOND, THERESA MARIE, librarian; b. Wilmington, Del., Jan. 26, 1944; d. Michael M. and Laura S. (Mateusczyk) Marroni; B.S., Villanova U., 1966, M.S., 1971; postgrad. U. Md., 1970-71; m. Thelbert R. Hammond, Jan. 7, 1967; children—Thelbert R., Christopher M. Br. librarian J. Lewis Crozer Library, Chester, Pa., 1965-67; adult services librarian Jervis Library, Rome, N.Y., 1968-69; librarian Prince George's County Meml. Library System, Hyattsville, Md., 1970-72; head tech. services Auburn U., Montgomery, Ala., 1972-74; asst. librarian Va. Inst. Marine Sci., Gloucester Point, Va., 1975-77; dir. library services The Daily Press, Inc., Newport News, Va., 1977—. Mem. ALA, Spl. Library Assn., Am. Soc. Info. Specialists, Nat. Micrographics Assn., Va. Spl. Library Assn. Roman Catholic. Home: 107 Leslie Dr Newport News VA 23606 Office: 7505 Warwick Blvd Newport News VA 23607

HAMMOND, WAYNE LAVERNE, builder, Realtor; b. Augusta, Ga., Jan. 4, 1935; s. Thurmond Henry and Amanda Gertrude (Phagan) H.; student USAF Inst. Coll., 1964; m. Marian Elizabeth Guy, Nov. 23, 1956; children—Gregory Wayne, Cheryl Dianne, Anthony Russell. Enlisted U.S. Navy, 1954, served to 1974; owner, mgr. Hammond Builders & Realty, Charleston, S.C., 1974—; owner Coastal Carolina Glass Insulators, Charleston. Bd. dirs. Forest Lakes Civic Club, 1976, pres. 1976. Mem. Nat. Bd. Realtors, S.C. Bd. Realtors, Charleston Bd. Realtors, Nat. Assn. Home Builders, Greater Charleston Home Builders, S.C. Residential Home Builders Commn. Clubs: Sertoma, Elks. Office: 1325 Ashley River Rd Charleston SC 29407

HAMMONS, DONALD RAY, indsl. research engr.; b. Frederick, Okla., Mar. 16, 1922; s. Philip Hayden and Cecile Lee (Stewart) H.; B.S., Tex. Technol. U., 1951 m. Genevieve Sophia Litteken, Nov. 9, 1943; children—Carolyn (Mrs. E.M. McMahon), Katherine (Mrs. Gary Earl Adams), Donald Ray II, Brenda Ann (Mrs. Richard Hays), Phillip Martin. Indsl. engr. Red River Arsenal, Texarkana, Tex., 1952-54, Redstone Arsenal, Huntsville, Ala., 1954-56; indsl. engr. meats research U.S. Dept. Agr. at Tex. A. and M. U., College Station, 1956-62, research leader meats industry engring. research Okla. State U., Stillwater, 1962-75, research leader meat handling and facilities research, College Station, 1975—. Cons. meat plant design and requirements, 1962—. Served with AUS, 1942-46. Registered profl. engr., Tex., Okla. Mem. Nat. Okla. socs. profls. engrs., Am. Soc. Agrl. Engrs., Food Distbn. Soc. Democrat. Home: 2604 Arbor Dr Bryan TX 77801 Office: PO Box EC College Station TX 77840

HAMMONS, EDWARD PARNELL, physician; b. Jackson, Tenn., July 17, 1941; s. Otis Parnell and Evelyn (Pierce) H.; B.S., Baylor U., 1962; M.D., U. Tenn., 1966. Intern, St. Francis Hosp., Honolulu, 1966-67; resident in surgery Meth. Hosp., Memphis, 1967-68, VA Hosp., San Juan, P.R., 1968-70; practice medicine, specializing in family practice, Forrest City, Ark., 1972—; med. dir. Paramedic Curriculum, E. Ark. Community Coll., 1975—; clin. instr. family practice U. Ark. Med. Sch., Little Rock, 1976-78; chmn. Gov. Adv. Com. on EMT Tng., 1976—; chief of staff Forrest Meml. Hosp., 1975-77. Served with USAF, 1970-72. Mem. Am. Coll. Emergency Physicians (state pres. 1979—), Ark. Acad. Family Practice (state dir. 1978—), Am. Coll. Family Physicians, Am. Coll. Cryosurgery, Ark. Med. Soc. Baptist. Home: 132 Rose Ln Forrest City AR 72335 Office: 328 Kittel Rd Forrest City AR 72335

HAMON, RICHARD GRADY, lawyer; b. Corpus Christi, Tex., Dec. 30, 1937; s. Richard Paul and Dorothy Ileen (Norris) H.; A.A., Del Mar Jr. Coll., 1957; B.B.A., Baylor U., 1959, J.D., 1962; m. Mary Lynn Farmer, Mar. 2, 1963; children—Leigh Ann, Clark Everett. Admitted to Tex. bar, 1962, since practiced in Dallas; mem. firm Blanchette, Hamon, Tabor & Coke, predecessor firms, 1962-76; mem. firm Winstead, McGuire, Sechrest & Trimble, 1976—. Mem. State Bar Tex., Am., Dallas bar assns. Baptist (deacon). Rotarian. Home: 9619 Brentgate Dr Dallas TX 75238 Office: 1700 Mercantile Dallas Bldg Dallas TX 75201

HAMPTON, CAROL CUSSEN MCDONALD, historian; b. Oklahoma City, Sept. 18, 1935; d. Denzil Vincent and Mildred (Cussen) McDonald; B.A., U. Okla., 1957, M.A., 1973; m. James W. Hampton, Feb. 22, 1958 children—Jaime Jennifer, Clayton Christopher, Diana Elizabeth, Neal McDonald. Instr. philosophy U. Okla., Norman, 1973—, grad. asst. in history, 1976—; mem. Caddo Tribal Council, 1976—, tribal historian, 1979—. Mem. Nat. Congress Am. Indians, 1978—; active women's com. Oklahoma City Symphony Orch., Jr. League Oklahoma City; bd. dirs. Oklahoma City chpt. Am. Cancer Soc.; mem. Oklahoma City Area Indian Health Service Bd., 1977—. Mem. Phi Alpha Theta. Episcopalian. Clubs: Oklahoma City Golf and Country, Faculty House Oklahoma City. Researcher Am. Indian history, Native Am. ch., peyote, chronicles of Caddo tribe. Home and Office: 1414 N Hudson St Oklahoma City OK 73103

HAMPTON, CHARLES, social worker; b. Bklyn., Mar. 21, 1949; s. Charles Everette and Gloria June (Sweetapple) H.; B.S., Abilene Christian U., 1971; M.S. in Social Work, U. Tex., Arlington, 1973; m. Madaline Faye Hyde, July 4, 1969; children—Derek, Leslie, Brooke. Dir. planning and placement Foster Home for Children, Stephenville, Tex., 1973-75, dir. children's services, 1975-78, dir. profl. services, 1978—; instr. social work Tarleton State U., Stephenville, Tex., 1974-75. Lic. child care adminstr. Mem. Acad. Cert. Social Workers, Nat. Assn. Social Workers (chpt. registrar 1974-75), Stephenville C. of C., Erath County Assn. Civic and Social Orgns. (co-founder, pres. 1978-79), Group Child Care Cons. Democrat. Ch. of Christ. Club: Optimist (dir. 1979—). Home: 1215 N Dale St Stephenville TX 76401 Office: PO Box 978 Stephenville TX 76401

HAMPTON, DALE ALAN, utility adminstr.; b. Charlotte, N.C., Oct. 26, 1945; s. William Alexander and Lucile C. H.; B.S. in Adminstrv. Mgmt., Clemson U., 1972; m. Patricia Ann Lewis, Sept. 12, 1964; 1 dau., Kimberly Nicole. Asst. store mgr. Belk Simpson Co., Easley, 1972-76; office mgr. Ft. Hill Natural Gas Authority, Easley, 1976—. Commr., Easley Housing Authority. Served with USN, 1967-69. Named to Outstanding Young Men of Am., U.S. C. of C., 1979. Mem. Nat. Assn. Accts., Easley C. of C. (dir.). Club: Rotary (Easley). Home: Route 1 Albertson Estates Easley SC 29640 Office: 307 S Pendleton St Easley SC 29640

HAMPTON, GEORGE LEO, III, educator; b. Topeka, July 10, 1937; s. George Leo and Helen Louise (Hess) H.: B.S., Trinity Coll., 1959; M.A., U. Ariz., 1966, Ph.D., 1969; children—George Leo, April Elizabeth. Asst. prof. Edinboro (Pa.) State Coll., 1966-67; chmn. dept. psychology Drury Coll., Springfield, Mo., 1967-70, Miss. U. for Women, Columbus, 1970-76 chmn. div. behavioral scis. and asso. prof. U. Houston - Downtown Coll., 1976—. Mem. Miss. Gov.'s Adv. Com. on Children, 1974, Gov.'s Com. on Compulsory Edn., 1976. Served with U.S. Army, 1959-62. Named Tchr. of Year, Drury Coll., 1969. Mem. Southwestern Psychol. Assn. Republican. Episcopalian. Editor: Readings in the Development of Personality, 1968; Psychology Doing Its Thing, 1971; Readings for Psychology and You, 1979; contbr. articles to profl. jours. Home: 3015 Walnut Bend #33 Houston TX 77042 Office: 1 Main Pl Houston TX 77002

HAMPTON, HERMAN LESTER, surgeon, educator; b. Shreveport, La., Dec. 15, 1935; s. Herman Lester and Doris (Beckham) H.; B.S., Baylor U., 1958; M.D., U. Tenn., 1961. Intern, Parkland Meml. Hosp., Dallas, 1961-62, resident surgery, 1966-69; resident in surgery Southwestern Med. Sch., Dallas, 1962-64; practice medicine specializing in peripheral vascular and gen. surgery, Dallas, 1969—; mem. staff Presbyn. Hosp., Dallas; asst. clin. prof. surgery U. Tex. Southwestern Med. Sch., Dallas, 1972—. Served with M.C., USAF, 1964-66. Diplomate Am. Bd. Surgery. Fellow A.C.S.; mem. Southwestern Surg. Congress, Pan-Pacific Surg. Assn., Soc. Clin. Vascular Surgery. Home: 5805 Colhurst St Dallas TX 75230 Office: 8210 Walnut Hill Ln Dallas TX 75231

HAMPTON, LAWRENCE HERBERT, III, hosp. devel. co. exec.; b. Maxton, N.C., Nov. 11, 1944; s. Lawrence Herbert and Mary Lou (Britton) H.; B.B.A., U. Tex., 1967; m. Nancy Lee Melton, June 3, 1979; 1 dau. by previous marriage, Laura Dawn. Prodn. supr. Johnson & Johnson, Wichita Falls, Tex., 1967-68; contract rep. Am. Hosp. Supply Co., Dallas, 1968-70; contract mgr. Am. Health Facilities Co., Dallas, 1971-73; mgr. equipment planning Hosp. Affiliates internat. Co., Nashville, 1973-78; v.p. equipment planning Hosp. Facilities Devel. Corp., 1979—; lectr. hosp. interior design. Recipient Spl. Appreciation award City of Grand Prairie (Tex.), 1972. Mem. Nat. Assn. Purchasing Mgrs., Fedn. Am. Hosps., Delta Sigma Pi. Methodist. Home: Route 8 Highland Dr Brentwood TN 37027 Office: Hosp Affiliates Internat Co 4525 Harding Rd Nashville TN 37205

HAMPTON, LEROY BERTRAM, accountant; b. Phila., Apr. 20, 1942; s. George Leroy and Frances H.; cert. in accountancy Bank's Bus. Coll., Phila., 1963; student Temple U., 1965-66; B.S. in Accountancy, Oakwood Coll., Huntsville, Ala., 1969; M.B.A., Ala. A. and M. U., 1977; m. Geroice Robinson, Apr. 19, 1970; children—Jayneen, Darryl. Agt., IRS, Lancaster, Pa., 1969-71; asst. treas. Allegheny East Conf., Pine Forge, Pa., 1971-72; fin. aid officer Oakwood Coll., Huntsville, Ala., 1972-79, asst. to bus. mgr., 1977—; treas. Oakwood Credit Union, 1978-79. Mem. Nat. Assn. Accts., Internal Auditors Assn., Am. Mgmt. Assn., Assn. M.B.A. Execs. Seventh-day Adventist. Office: Oakwood Rd Ord 5765 Huntsville AL 35806

HAMPTON, MAXINE HALFORD, nurse; b. St. Charles, Va., Apr. 30, 1917; d. Charles Hugh and Dora Elizabeth (Napier) H.; L.P.N., Kingsport Vocat. Sch. Practical Nursing, 1951; student Whitneys Sch. Bus., 1952. With Tenn. Eastman Co., Oak Ridge, 1945-47; with Holston Valley Community Hosp., Kingsport, Tenn., 1950—, scrub nurse, operating room, 1952-75, asst. supr. central sterile supplies, 1975—. Lic. practical nurse, Tenn. Mem. Tenn. Lic. Practical Nurses Assn., Sterile Supplies Suprs. Democrat. Baptist. Home: 2032 Granby Rd Kingsport TN 37665 Office: Holston Valley Community Hosp Ravine St Kingsport TN 37662

HAMPTON, MERLIN, elec. engr.; b. Hawthorne, Nev., Jan. 1, 1947; s. Lester Cirk and Esther Irene (Stroud) H.; student Okla. Baptist U., 1965-66; B.S., U. Tex., Arlington, 1970; m. Janet Kay Hall, Nov. 20, 1970; children—Michael Brian, Mindy Lynn. Jr. engr. Tex. Electric Service Co., Ft. Worth, 1970-71; engr. Love, Friberg & Assos., Inc., cons. engrs., Ft. Worth, 1971-78; v.p. elec. engring. Walter Cash and Partners, Dallas, 1979—. Mem. Ft. Worth Elec. Code Bd. Appeals. Registered profl. engr., Tex. Mem. Illuminating Engring. Soc., IEEE, Nat., Tex. socs. profl. engrs., Epsilon Nu Gamma. Home: 7312 Vanessa Fort Worth TX 76112 Office: 3011 Hood St Dallas TX 75219

HAMPTON, PEGGY, librarian; b. Newport, Tenn., Sept. 2, 1914; d. John Erwin and Emmeline Candice (Cogdill) Hampton; student Biltmore Jr. Coll., 1933-35; A.B., U. N.C., 1937, A.B., in L.S., 1938. County librarian Mecklenburg County Library, Boydton, Va., 1939-42; regional librarian Southside Regional Library, Boydton, 1945-48; head circulation and reference librarian E. Carolina U. Library, Greenville, N.C., 1948-54; hosp. librarian Spl. Services Hosp. Library, Ft. Bragg, N.C., 1954-57, USAF Med. and Spl. Services Hosp. Library, Wiesbaden, Germany, 1957-60; young adult and reference librarian Los Angeles Pub. Library, 1961-68; extension librarian, publicity coordinator U.S. Army Post Library System, Ft. Bragg, 1968—. Chmn. Nat. Library Week Luncheon, Ft. Bragg, 1979. Recipient awards for library publicity scrapbooks, 1958-59, John Cotton Dana Publicity Scrapbook award, 1971, Toastmistress Club Scrapbook award, 1975. Mem. Calif. (past dist. chmn. So. Calif.), Am. (membership com. 1967) library assns., AAUW (treas. Fayetteville, N.C. 1969-71), Chi Omega. Episcopalian. Club: Toastmistress (sec. Ft. Bragg 1974-75, community rep. 1975-76, winner speech contest 1978). Home: PO Box 70032 Fort Bragg NC 28307 Office: Library Br Bldg AT-2747 Fort Bragg NC 28307

HAMPTON-KAUFFMAN, MARGARET FRANCES, banker; b. Gainesville, Fla., May 12, 1947; d. William Wade and Carol Dorothy (Maples) Hampton; B.A. summa cum laude with honors, Fla. State U., 1969; student U. Nice (France), summer 1969; M.B.A., Columbia U., 1974; m. Kenneth L. Kauffman, May 12, 1973. Bd. govs. Fed. Res. System, Washington, 1974-75; asst. v.p., banking industry specialist, corp. fin. dept. Mfrs. Hanover Trust Co., N.Y.C., 1975-76; v.p., dir. corp. planning and research, sec. asset and liability mgmt. and strategic planning coms. Nat. Bank Ga., Atlanta, 1976—; dir. Accent Enterprises, Inc., Atlanta; guest lectr. Ga. Inst. Tech.; dir. TOMAK, Inc., Atlanta. Comptroller, Angel Flight, 1967-68, liaison officer, 1966-67, del. area and nat. conclaves, 1966-68. Alcoa Found. fellow, 1973: Dorothy Shaw Leadership award finalist. Mem. Planning Execs. Inst., Inst. Mgmt. Scis., Am. Inst. Banking, Inst. Fin. Edn., Am. Fin. Assn., Phi Beta Kappa, Beta Gamma Sigma, Mortar Board, Garnet Key, Phi Kappa Phi, Alpha Lambda Delta, Pi Delta Phi (v.p.), Alliance Française, Alpha Delta Pi (exec. bd., efficiency chmn., scholarship chmn.), Kappa Sigma (treas. Little Sisters, pres., snow ball queen). Democrat. Episcopalian. Home: 1065 W Paces Ferry Rd NW Atlanta GA 30327 Office: 34 Peachtree St Atlanta GA 30301

HAMRICK, JOHN ASA, coll. adminstr.; b. Fountain Inn, S.C., Jan. 17, 1916; s. Clarence Thomas and Myrtle (Esmer) H.; B.A., Coll. Charleston, 1937; Th.B., So. Baptist Theol. Sem., 1939, Th.M., 1940; D.D., Furman U., 1953; LL.D., Atlanta Law Sch., 1965; m. Margaret Clare Kelly, Jan. 11, 1939; children—Margaret Clare Hamrick Hollingsworth, John Asa. Ordained to ministry, So. Bapt. Conv., 1935; pastor 1st Bapt. Ch., Charleston, S.C., 1940-68; pres. Bapt. Coll. at Charleston, 1964—; pres. S.C. Bapt. Conv., 1951-52, S.C. Bapt. Pastors Conf., 1949-50, Charleston Higher Edn. Consortium, 1977-78. Pres., Bapt. Hist. Soc., 1945-51; trustee Furman U.; bd. dirs. Charleston YMCA, Salvation Army. Mem. Am. Assn. Pres.'s Ind. Colls., Am. Council Edn., Nat. Assn. Ind. Colls. and Univs., S.C. Found. Ind. Colls., Assn. So. Bapt. Colls. and Schs., S.C. Council Bapt. Coll. Pres.'s, S.C. Assn. Colls. Home: 2267 Ashley River Rd Charleston SC 29407 Office: Baptist Coll at Charleston Charleston SC 29407

HAMROCK, MARILYN ANGELA, speech pathologist; b. Youngstown, Ohio, Dec. 21, 1946; d. Aloysius Thomas and Angela Marie (Salreno) H.; B.S., Kent State U., 1968; M.A. in Speech Pathology, Northwestern U., 1969. Dir. speech and hearing clinic Great Oaks Center, Silver Spring, Md., 1970-73; speech pathologist Children's Hosp. Nat. Med. Center, Washington, 1973-74; co-owner, adminstr., speech pathologist Speech Pathology Assos., South Miami, Fla., 1974—. Mem. Am. Speech, Lang. and Hearing Assn., Fla. Speech, Lang. and Hearing Assn., Dade County Assn. Retarded Citizens, Internat. Assn. Logopedics and Phoniatrics, Kappa Delta Pi. Home: 10931 SW 177th St Miami FL 33157 Office: 6201 SW 70th St Suite 305 South Miami FL 33143

HAMSA, CHARLES FREDRICK, librarian; b. Omaha, July 17, 1938; s. William R. and Anna Marie (Brodegaard) H.; B.A., U. Nebr., Omaha, 1965; M.A., U. Nebr., Lincoln, 1969; M.L.S., Kans. State Tchrs. Coll., 1969; m. Sara Boyden, June 11, 1966; 1 son, Michael Boyden. Acquisitions librarian U. Southwestern La., Lafayette, 1969—; owner G & C Photography, Lafayette, 1974—. Pres., Lafayette Assn. Retarded Citizens, 1976; bd. dirs. La. Assn. for Retarded Citizens, 1977—, recipient award for outstanding service, 1973. Served with USN, 1959-63. Mem. Southwestern Library Assn., La. Library Assn. Republican. Presbyterian. Club: Civitan (named Civitan of Yr., South La. 1971, Outstanding Civitan 1974, lt. gov. dist. S. La. 1975). Author: (with J. Norman Heard) Bookman's Guide to Americana, 1977. Home: 612 Alonda Dr Lafayette LA 70503 Office: PO Box 40199 Lafayette LA 70504

HAN, SOO WOONG, psychiatrist; b. Seoul, May 25, 1942; s. Kyok Boo Han and Kwi Boon Kang; came to U.S., 1969, naturalized, 1977; M.D., Cath. Med. Coll., Seoul, 1968; m. Sung Yim Cho, Mar. 27, 1968; children—Darow, Donna, Luna. Intern, Salem (Mass.) Hosp., 1970-71; resident in psychiatry Warren (Pa.) Hosp., 1971-73, unit dir., 1973-75; child psychiatrist Children's Hosp., Washington, 1975-77; practice medicine specializing in psychiatry, Alexandria, Va., 1977—. Diplomate Am. Bd. Psychiatry and Neurology. Mem. Am. Acad. Child Psychiatry, Am. Psychiat. Assn., AMA, Md. Med. Soc., Korean Med. Assn. Greater Washington. Home: 8006 Garlot Dr Annandale VA 22003 Office: 6395 Little River Turnpike Alexandria VA 22309

HANAHAN, JAMES LAKE, life ins. co. exec.; b. Burlington, Iowa, Aug. 27, 1932; s. Thomas J. and Clarice P. (Lorey) H.; B.S., Drake U., 1955; postgrad. George Williams Coll., 1956; m. Marilyn R. Lowe, Dec. 27, 1952; children—Bridget Sue Bahlke, Erin Rose Hoff. Phys. dir. Monmouth (Ill.) YMCA, 1955-56; mem. community relations staff Caterpillar Tractor Co., Peoria, Ill., 1956-57; rep. Conn. Gen. Life Ins. Co., Des Moines, 1957-59, asst. mgr., 1959-63, mgr. group ins. ops., Tampa, Fla., 1963-80; pres. WHAPCO, Inc., 1980—; instr. certified property casualty underwriters courses; seminar leader C.L.U. workshop; cons. ins. seminar Fla. State U. Bd. dirs. Jr. Achievement. Recipient Double D award Drake U., 1978. Mem. Sales Mktg. Execs. Tampa (pres.), Tampa Commerce Club, Nat. Assn. Life Underwriters, Greater Tampa C. of C. (gov.), Minerat Soc. U. Tampa, Tampa Sports and Recreation Council (dir.), Com. of 100. Democrat. Roman Catholic. Clubs: 7th Inning (chmn.), Nat. D (Drake U.) (v.p., dir.). Home: 8012 W Hiawatha St Tampa FL 33615

HANBURY, GEORGE LAFAYETTE, II, city mgr.; b. Norfolk, Va., Sept. 20, 1943; s. Emmette Cecil and Adah Christine (Nelligar) H.; B.S. in Pub. Adminstrn., Va. Poly. Inst., 1965; M.Pub. Adminstrn., Old Dominion U., 1977; m. Diana Bernadette Lee, July 30, 1966; children—George Lafayette III, Melissa Lee. Asst. to city mgr., Norfolk, 1967-70; asst. city mgr., Virginia Beach, Va., 1970-74, city mgr., 1974—. Named Outstanding Young Man of Virginia Beach, 1975, Outstanding Young Man of Va., 1976. Mem. Internat. City Mgmt. Assn., Am. Mgmt. Assn., Am. Soc. Pub. Adminstrs., Am. Soc. Planning Ofcls. Home: 1792 Upper Chelsea Reach Virginia Beach VA 23454 Office: Municipal Center Virginia Beach VA 23456

HANCE, KENT R., state govt. ofcl.; b. Dimmitt, Tex., 1944; s. Raymond L. and Beral (Cole) H.; B.B.A., Tex. Tech. U., 1965; LL.B., U. Tex., 1968; m. Carol Hays, 1964; children—Ron, Susan. Admitted to Tex. bar 1968; individual practice law, Lubbock, Tex., 1968—; prof. bus. law Tex. Tech. U., 1968-73; Tex. state senator, 1974—, U.S. Congressman 19th Dist. Tex., 1978—, mem. Fin., State Affairs, Natural Resources coms., chmn. Water subcom. on Natural Resources. Regent, W.Tex. State U., 1972-74; mem. agrl., sci. and tech. coms. U.S. House of Reps., consent calendar com., chmn. 96th new mems. Congressional Caucus; mem. Tex. Citizens Advisory Council; founder men. Tex. Boys' Ranch, Lubbock; Tex. chmn. March Dimes, 1972-73. Mem. Am., Tex., Lubbock bar assns. Democrat. Baptist. Clubs: Rotary, Lions, Tex. Tech., Century. Office: 1039 Longworth Bldg Washington DC 20515

HANCHEY, JONATHAN KEITH, pharmacist: b. DeRidder, La., Dec. 4, 1947; s. Graydon Alton and Edith Louise (Comeaux) H.; B.S. in Pharmacy, N.E. La. U., 1970; m. Janet L. Hood, May 25, 1974. Pharmacy mgr. Lakeshore Pharmacy, Lake Charles, La., 1970-72; hosp. pharmacy resident Harris Hosp., Ft. Worth, 1972-73; asst. dir. pharmacy Santa Rosa Med. Center, San Antonio, 1972-78; dir. pharmacy services Meth. Hosps. of Dallas, 1978—: regional mgr. The Owen Co., 1978—. Mem. Am. Soc. Hosp. Pharmacists, Tex. Soc. Hosp. Pharmacists (Service award 1977, pres. 1979-80), Central Tex. Soc. Hosp. Pharmacists (pres. 1978-79). Democrat. Roman Catholic.

HANCOCK, JAMES EDWARD, radiation therapist; b. Ripley, Tenn., Mar. 7, 1927; s. William Christopher and Mary Isabel (Gilmore) H.; B.S., U. Tenn., 1952, M.D., 1961. Intern, Methodist Hosp., Memphis, 1961-62, resident, 1964-66; resident Oak Ridge Inst. Nuclear Studies, 1963; radiation therapist St. Jude Childrens Research Hosp., Memphis, 1968, Bapt. Meml. Hosp., Memphis, 1968-75; med. dir., radiotherapist Mary Bird Perkins Radiation Center, Baton Rouge, 1975—; mem. cons. staff Woman's Hosp., Drs. Meml. Hosp., Baton Rouge Gen. Hosp., Our Lady of the Lake Hosp., Earl K. Long Meml. Hosp. (all Baton Rouge); asst. clin. prof. Coll. Medicine U. Tenn., Memphis, 1968-75; mem. faculty La. State U. Med. Sch., Baton Rouge, 1975—. Bd. dirs. Am. Cancer Soc., 1971-75. Served with USNR, 1945-46. Fellow, U. Tex. M.D. Anderson Hosp., 1967-68. Diplomate Am. Bd. Therapeutic Radiology. Mem. AMA, Am. Coll. Radiology, Mid South Med. Soc., Tenn. Radiologic Soc., Sports Car Club Am. Home: 12814 Pecos St Greenwell Springs LA 70739 Office: 9042 Airline Hwy Baton Rouge LA 70815

HANCOCK, JOHN HOWARD, ins. agy. exec.; b. Dothan, Ala., Jan. 17, 1943; s. Howard E. and Mary F. Hancock; A.S., Gulf Coast Community Coll., 1962; div.; children—Bryan H., John W. Life ins. agt. Ind. Life Ins. Co., Panama City, Fla., 1963-68; life agt., property and casualty agt., br. mgr.-ins., asst. sec., asst. v.p. Commonwealth Corp., Panama City, 1968-75; owner, mgr. John Hancock Ins. Agy., Panama City, 1975—. Mem. Resort Council of 100, 1978—. Named Boss of Yr., Ins. Women of Panama City, 1979. Mem. Nat. Assn. Ind. Agts., Fla. Assn. Ind. Agts., Bay County Assn. Ind. Agrs. (pres. 1971-72), Bay County C. of C. (mil. affairs com. 1972—). Democrat. Episcopal. Home: 2405 Petty Dr Lynn Haven FL 32444 Office: 810 W 11th St Panama City FL 32401

HANCOCK, WILLIAM GEREMAIN, JR., lawyer; b. Charlotte, N.C., July 29, 1943; s. William Geremain and Lucille Annette (Wiley) H.; A.B., U. N.C., 1965; J.D., Duke, 1968. Admitted to N.C. bar, 1971; asso. firm Patterson, Belknap & Webb, N.Y.C., 1968-70; asst. dir. devel. health affairs Duke U., Durham, N.C., 1970-71, spl. asst. to univ. pres. in devel. So. Growth Policies Bd., 1971; campaign coordinator Bowles for Gov., Raleigh, N.C., 1971-72; partner firm Everett, Everett, Creech & Craven, Durham and Raleigh, 1972—. Chmn. N.C. Center for Pub. Policy Research, 1976—; vice chmn. N.C. Bd. Ethics; mem. steering com. The Children's 100, 1975-77; mem. Wake County Mental Health Assn.; bd. dirs. Fount, Inc., 1975—; mem. N.C. Democratic State Exec. Com., 1977—. Mem. Am., N.C., Wake County, Durham County bar assns., Common Cause (chmn. N.C. 1974-76), L.Q.C. Lamar Soc., Phi Delta Phi. Democrat. Methodist. Home: 923 W Markham Ave Durham NC 27701 Office: PO Box 586 Durham NC 27707

HANCOX, WILLIAM ARTHUR, JR., optometrist; b. Maryville, Tenn., Oct. 3, 1929; s. William Arthur and Mildred Blanche (Morton) H.; B.S., Tenn. Tech. U., 1954; O.D., So. Coll. Optometry, 1957; m. Daisey Jarrett Martin, Sept. 15, 1957; children—William Arthur III, Amy Leigh. Pvt. practice optometry, Fayetteville, Tenn., 1957—. Budget com. Lincoln County Quarterly Ct., 1976-77, magistrate, 1969-78; bd. dirs. Elk Valley Home Health Center, 1976—, Elk River Devel. Assn., 1980—. Served with USN, 1950-52. Recipient Cert. of Merit, Lincoln County Quarterly Ct., 1978; Kiwanis Leadership award, 1960. Mem. Tenn. State Optometric Soc., S.E. Optometric Assn., Am. Optometric Assn., S. Central Tenn. Optometric Assn. (pres. 1969-70), Armed Forces Optometric Assn., Am. Public Health Assn., Nat. Fedn. Ind. Bus. Republican. Baptist. Clubs: Kiwanis, Masons. Office: 201 E Washington St Fayetteville TN 37334

HAND, DONALD EDMUND, constrn. co. exec.; b. West Palm Beach, Fla., Jan. 10, 1925; s. Fred William and Lessy Estelle (Thomas) H.; B.C.E. with honors, U. Fla., 1951; m. June Claire Cone, Aug. 20, 1945; children—Susan Claire, Donna Rhea, Donald Edmund. With Batson Cook Co., Jacksonville, Fla., 1951—, field supt., 1953-61, project mgr., 1959—, br. officer asst. mgr., asst. v.p., 1973—; chmn. Constrn. Trades Qualifying Bd. for Duval County, Fla. Deacon, Riverside Baptist Ch. Served with USN, 1943-48. Registered profl. engr., Fla. Mem. Assn. Gen. Contractors Am. (past pres., dir. N. Eastern Fla. chpt.), N. Fla. Carpenters (trustee), ASCE, U. Fla. Alumni Assn. Democrat. Clubs: Rotary, Masons. Home: 4407 Travelers Rd Jacksonville FL 32210 Office: PO Box 4963 Jacksonville FL 32201

HANDEL, ALEXANDER FREDERIC, accreditation cons.; b. St. Joseph, Mo., Dec. 15, 1909; s. Harry G. and Ethel H.; Ph.B., U. Chgo., 1931, M.A., 1941; m. Marguerite A. Wilks, Jan. 15, 1944; children—Richard, Jeffrey, Todd. Dean, prof. Adelphi U., Garden City, N.Y., 1948-54; dir. community services Am. Found. for Blind, N.Y.C., 1954-67; exec. dir. Nat. Accreditation Council, N.Y.C., 1967-75; cons. in accreditation, 1975—. Pres. Rahway River Civic Assn., 1968-71; pres., treas. Social Work Vocat. Bur., N.Y.C., 1969-72. Served with U.S. Army, 1943-45. Recipient Migel medal Am. Found. for Blind, 1974; Alumni medal U. Chgo., 1977. U.S. Children's Bur. fellow, 1940-41. Mem. Nat. Assn. Social Workers, Acad. Cert. Social Workers, Nat. Rehab. Assn. Author: The Comstac Report, 1966. Home: 23099 Barwood Ln Boca Raton FL 33433

HANDLEMAN, CHESTER, educator; b. Worcester, Mass.; s. Bertram L. and Bessie T. (Shafner) H.; A.B., Clark U., M.A., 1961; M.Ed., Mass. State Coll., 1951; 6th yr. profl. diploma U. Conn., 1957; Ed.D., Nova U., 1975; postgrad. U. N.C., Chapel Hill, 1975-78; m. Mildred G. Engel. Asst. mgr. family bus., Worcester, 1946-50; tchr. secondary schs., Mass., 1950-57, Worcester, 1955-57; faculty history and polit. sci. Broward Community Coll., Ft. Lauderdale, Fla., 1961—, mem. faculty senate, sec., 1978-80, sec. faculty, 1975-76, mem. acad. affairs com, vice chmn., 1977-78, mem. various faculty coms., speakers' bur.; faculty sponsor Phi Theta Kappa, 1967—; part time lectr. Barry Coll., Miami, Fla., Nova U., Fla. Internat. U., Ft. Lauderdale; speaker on nat. and internat. current topics. Mem. Hollywood Youth Council Bd. Served in U.S. Army, 1942-45. Mem. Fla. Polit. Sci. Assn. (exec. com. 1978—), Clark U. Alumni Assn. (nat. chmn. alumni fund 1956-57), Phi Theta Kappa (faculty sponsor awards), Phi Delta Kappa (officer, historian), Phi Alpha Theta. Clubs: Masons, Scottish Rite, Shriners. Editorial bd. Community Coll. Social Science Jour.; contbr. numerous articles, book revs., abstracts to profl. publs. Home: 3701 Jackson St Apt 212 Hollywood FL 33021 Office: Dept History and Polit Sci Broward Community Coll Central Campus Fort Lauderdale FL 33314

HANDLER, FRANCES CLARK (MRS. FRANK STEVENSON HANDLER), educator, writer, assn. exec.; b. Maplewood, N.H., Feb. 28; d. Frank J. and Marie (Jamia) Clark; B.S. in Bus. Machine Teaching, Boston U., B.B.S. in Accounting, A.B. in Banking and Finance, Ph.D., 1977; Litt. D., Internat. Research Socs., U. Asia, Pakistan, 1968; m. Frank Stevenson Handler, Sept. 21, 1946. Instr. accounting Burroughs Sch., Boston, later collaborating writer poetry books, hist. novels, autobiographies, children's books. Lectr. on women's vocations Barry Coll., Miami, Fla., 1965—; founder, nat. dir. Fla. Nat. Poetry Day Com., 1965—; founder Am. Coalition Poets br. World Congress Poets; sponsor San Antonio Poetry Festival. Named hon. poet laureate UN Day, Philippines, 1967; recipient over 100 awards and prizes, including King Journalism award, 1972, 1st award Clover Poetry Assn., 1976, 1st prize San Antonio Poetry Festival; named hon. mayor San Antonio. C.P.A., Mass. Mem. United Poets Laureate Internat. (award, 1967, membership chmn. 1968—), World (internat. dir., adviser 5th World Congress, coordinator conv. 1981), Fla. (founder, sec., treas. 1965—, editor, pub. Flamingo 1969), Nev. (hon. life) poetry socs., Fla. Arts Council, Iowa Poetry Day Assn. (hon. life), Nat. League Am. Pen Women (treas. Coral Gables, Fla. br. 1963—), Hotel Accountants Assn. (pres. 1947-51). Author: Reina Mercedes, 1956; Canberra, 1957; Turns On The Spiral, 1971; Beyond The Silent River, 1972; Nobel Goes To Heaven, 1972; Nurses Notes, 1973; Devastators, 1973. Contbr. to Ency. of Jazz, 1955, Selected Poems, 1969-74, Memorial Award Books, 1966-71, 72-73. Editor, designer International Hall of Fame Poets, 4 books, 1969-72, Governor's Book, 1971-72, 9 Muses I and 9 Muses II, 1971. Home: 1110 N Venetian Dr Miami Beach FL 33139

HANDLOS, STEVEN ARTHUR, forester; b. Milw., Sept. 7, 1944; s. Alphonse Anthony and Lucile (Frommell) H.; B.S., U. Mich., 1966, M.B.A., 1967; m. Agnita Marie Knapp, Nov. 25, 1966; children—Agnita Ann, Sandra Marie, Steven Arthur. Dist. forester Westvaco Corp., Summerville, S.C., 1968-69, staff asst., 1969-71, systems analyst, forest analyst, 1971-74, comml. mgr., 1974-76, adminstrv. projects mgr., 1976—. Bd. dirs. Quail Arbor Civic Club, 1976-77, 79-80. Profl. forester, S.C. Mem. Soc. Am. Foresters. Roman Catholic. Club: K.C. Home: 406 Grouse Rd Summerville SC 29483 Office: Westvaco Corp PO Box WV Summerville SC 29483

HANDWERK, JOSEPH HENRY, ceramic engr.; b. Joliet, Ill., Oct. 19, 1920; s. Joseph and Katherine (Bittermann) H.; B.S., U. Ala., 1942, M.S., 1946; m. Marianna Shepherd, May 13, 1942 (dec.); 1 son, Joseph Henry. Engr., AC Spark Plug div. Gen. Motors Corp., Flint, Mich., 1942-46; supt. Stephenson Brick Co., Birmingham, Ala., 1946-49; asso. prof. ceramics U. Ala., University, 1949-54; group leader ceramic engring. Argonne Nat. Lab., 1954-69; exec. v.p. Beckwith Carbon Corp., Van Nuys, Calif., 1969-71; supervisory ceramic engr. U.S. Bur. Mines, Tuscaloosa, Ala., 1971—; cons., Tuscaloosa, 1974—. Fellow Am. Ceramic Soc., ASTM, Nat. Inst.

Ceramic Engrs., Keramoes (hon.). Contbr. articles to profl. jours. Patentee in field. Address: 2817 14th St E Tuscaloosa AL 35401

HANDWERKER, EARL HOWARD, hosp. adminstr.; b. Columbus, Ohio, Apr. 23, 1946; s. Benjamin J. and Celia (Einbinder) H.; A.B., Columbia U., 1968, M.S. in Hosp. Adminstrn., 1973. Teaching asst. Northeastern U., Boston, 1972-73; cons. Am. Hosp. Assn., N.Y.C., 1973-74; planning coordinator Beth Israel Med. Center, N.Y.C., 1974-76; fin. analyst Health Maintenance Orgn. program USPHS, Chgo., 1976-78; dir. USPHS Outpatient Clinic, San Juan, P.R., 1978—. Served to lt. (j.g.) USNR, 1968-69. Mem. Am. Coll. Hosp. Adminstrs., Am. Hosp. Assn. Office: USPHS Outpatient Clinic Box 3788 San Juan PR 00904

HANDY, JOHN WILLIAM, JR., educator; b. Harrisburg, Pa., Jan. 10, 1918; s. John Wesley and Cora Myrtle (Shirley) H.; B.S. in Chemistry, Shaw U., 1941, postgrad., 1942; postgrad. Drew U. Sem., 1942-43; M.Ed., U. Colo., 1959, Ed.D., 1971; M.A., N.Y. U., 1961; m. Lois Elizabeth Reed, June 18, 1954. Ordained to ministry Methodist Ch., 1942; pastor St. James Meth. Ch., Oriole, Md., 1942-43; commd. 1st lt., AUS, 1943, advanced through grades to col., 1966; served as staff chaplain Camp Shanks, N.Y., 1946, Camp Kilmer, N.J., 1948-49, Kobe Base, Japan, 1950, Ft. Eustis, Va., 1952-54, Ft. Carson, Colo., 1956-57, 58, Fitzsimons Gen. Hosp., Denver, 1961-63, Hawaii, 1965-68; dep. CONARC staff chaplain, Ft. Monroe, 1968-69; ret., 1969; asst. prof. psychology and guidance, dir. psychol. services Hampton (Va.) Inst., 1969-70, dir. psychol. services, acting chmn. dept. psychology, 1970-71, dir. psychol. services, 1971-73, asso. prof. psychology, chmn. dept. psychology, 1971-73, prof. psychology and guidance, 1973—, dir. div. grad. studies, 1973-76, acad. dean, 1976—. Trustee Peninsula Drug Abuse Council, Hampton, 1970-74; mem. Adv. Council Ednl. TV, State of Va., 1971-75; mem. bd. Heritage Girl Scout Council, 1972-75; bd. dirs. Inst. Indsl. and Comml. Ministry, 1972-75; evaluation com. Peninsula Manpower Commn., 1974-75. Del. Republican Nat. Conv., 1972. Sec. bd. visitors VA. Sch., Hampton, 1974—. Decorated Bronze Star, Legion of Merit with oak leaf cluster, Army Commendation medal with 3 oak leaf clusters; named Alpha Man of Year Alpha Phi Alpha, 1972; Urban League fellow Jones and Laughlin Steel Corp., summers 1972, 73; Randolph Peyton lectr., 1974. Mem. Mil. Chaplain Assn. U.S., Res. Officers Assn. U.S., Va., Am. personnel and guidance assns., Am., Va. psychol. assns., AAUP, Nat. Geog. Soc., Acad. Religion and Mental Health, Alpha Phi Alpha, Phi Delta Kappa, Psi Chi. Home: 124 Diggs Dr Hampton VA 23666

HANEMANN, ARDLEY RAYMOND, JR., corp. publ. editor; b. New Orleans, Mar. 7, 1943; s. Ardley Raymond and Thecla Louise (Whalen) H.; B.A., Loyola U., New Orleans, 1966; student TV Prodn. Workshop, Miami, Fla., 1971; m. Maureen Michael Blount, June 18, 1966; children—Ardley Raymond III, Christophe Lyle. Asst. publs. editor Kent (O.) State U., 1966-67; asst. alumni dir. Loyola U., New Orleans, 1967-69; sr. publs. editor B.F. Goodrich, Akron, Ohio, 1969-72; publs. editor J. Ray McDermott & Co., Inc., New Orleans, 1972—, asst. dir. public relations, 1978—; instr. journalism So. U., Baton Rouge, La., also St. Mary's Dominican Coll., New Orleans, 1977. Mem. fund raising com. Jesuit High Sch., also mem. alumni exec. com.; bd. dirs. Country Club Homes Recreation, 1977; pres. New Orleans Right to Life, 1977-79, Country Club Homes, 1978-80. Recipient awards Best Design-Booklet Nat. Am. Collegiate Pub. Relations Assn., 1969, Best Indsl. Publ., 1971—, Best Feature Writing, 1971, Best Black and White Photography, 1970. Mem. Internat. Assn. Bus. Communicators (Best Editorial Writing award 1970), Art Dirs. Designers Assn., Loyola U. Alumni, Blue Key, Upsilon Beta Lambda. Clubs: Carte, Lotus, Gentily Social. Home: 4817 Purdue Dr Metairie LA 70003 Office: PO Box 60035 1010 Common St New Orleans LA 70160

HANES, ROBERT CARPENTER, sch. supt.; b. Charlotte, N.C., July 26, 1928; s. Robert David and Ida (Carpenter) H.; student Mars Hill Coll., 1945-47; B.A., U. N.C. at Chapel Hill, 1949, M.A., 1954, Ph.D., 1956; m. Nancy Hoover Root, June 23, 1951; 1 dau., Nancy Jean. Tchr. Jr. High, Gastonia, N.C., 1949-50; tchr., asst. prin. Gray High Sch., Winston-Salem, N.C., 1956-57; asst. prof. Wake Forest Coll., Winston-Salem, 1957-58; dir. secondary edn. Winston-Salem City Schs., 1958-62; asst. supt. Charlotte-Mecklenburg (N.C.) Schs., 1962-72; supt. Chapel Hill-Carrboro City Schs., 1972—. Served to 1st lt., USAF, 1950-53. Mem. NEA, Nat. Assn. Core Curriculum (dir.), Assn. Supervision and Curriculum Devel. (dir.), N.C. Assn. Supervision and Curriculum Devel. (pres. 1970-71), Phi Delta Kappa. Episcopalian (lay reader). Kiwanian. Contbr. articles in field to profl. jours. Home: 712 Churchill Dr Chapel Hill NC 27514 Office: Merritt Mill Rd Chapel Hill NC 27514

HANGER, BOB GRANT, pub. relations exec.; b. Huntington, W.Va., May 18, 1934; s. Theodore Otis and Percie Lee (Tucker) H.; student Marshall U., 1951, U. Va., 1962-64; m. Ruth Ann Suiter, Nov. 24, 1960; children—Pamela Diane, Robert, Connie Sue, Robbie Lee, Rhonda Lynn, Roni Lea. Broadcaster, exec. WINA radio-TV, Charlottesville, Va., 1960-73; sales and pub. relations exec., 1960—; rep. Nat. Chemsearch Corp., 1974—; group talent mgr. Bee-Gee Enterprises, Charlottesville, 1961-70; nat. sales mgr. Bee-Gee Prodns., Charlottesville, 1961-71; pres. Bee-Gee Records Div., 1963-70, Music Div., 1962-70; cons. Dogwood Festival, 1962-65, Hillbilly Pub. Co., 1964-71; dir. Bee-Gee Prodns. Talent Agy., Cottonhill Pub. Co.; cons. Cherry River Festival, Richwood, W.Va., 1969-71. Nat. sec. U. Hard Knocks, Inc., 1965-68. Mem. adv. bd. Charlottesville Youth Action Commn., 1971—; mem. adv. bd. Albemarle High Sch., 1979-80; bd. dirs. YMCA. Named Ky. Col.; recipient Top Quality and Sales achievement awards, 1977, 78, 79; Nat. Chemsearch Pres.'s Club award, 1976, 77, 78. Mem. East Coast Talent Soc. (dir. 1964-71), Va. Soc. Country and Folk Music, Nat. Assn. Broadcasters, Am. Soc. Notaries, Jaycees (hon.). Republican. Presbyterian. Kiwanian (dir. 1963-70). Club: Ruritan (pub. relations dir. Earlysville 1972, sec. 1975, pres. 1976—, zone gov. 1977). Home: 3405 Indian Spring Rd Charlottesville VA 22901

HANKE, DAN HENRY, acct.; b. San Antonio, Dec. 8, 1941; s. William F. and Evie (Jackson) H.; B.B.A. with honors, U. Tex., Austin, 1963, postgrad. in accounting, 1963-64; m. Genie Garrett, Nov. 9, 1963; children—Dan William, Diane G. Partner, Hanke & Hanke, 1963, gen. sers. partner, 1963-70, tax matters and gen. sers. partner, 1970-74, mng. partner, 1974-75; partner Alford, Meroney & Co., San Antonio, 1975-79; partner, office dir. taxes Arthur Young & Co., 1979—; lectr. U. Tex. (San Antonio). Pres. S. Central Tex. chpt. Arthritis Found., 1971-76; admission and allocations com. United Way; bd. dirs. San Antonio Literacy Council. Served to lt., Fin. Corps, AUS, 1964-65. Named Young C.P.A. of Year, Tex. Soc. C.P.A.'s, 1976; recipient E.W. Sells and J.B. Allred Merit awards, 1963. Mem. Tex. Soc. C.P.A.'s (past pres. San Antonio chpt., dir., State v.p., 1979-80), Am. Inst. C.P.A.'s, Petroleum Accts. Soc. San Antonio (past pres.), Nat. Council Petroleum Acctg. Beta Gamma Sigma, Beta Alpha Psi. Episcopalian (trustee). Clubs: Bexar Kiwanis, 730 of San Antonio, Oak Hills Country. Contbr. articles to profl. jours. Home: 10407 Mt Marcy St San Antonio TX 78213 Office: 1700 Frost Bank Tower San Antonio TX 78205

HANKINS, KEITH MILTON, occupational therapist; b. Parsons, Kans., Mar. 10, 1951; s. Roger Howard and Norma Jean (Shank) H.; A.A., State Fair Community Coll., 1971; B.S., U. Tex. Med. Br., 1974; postgrad. N. Tex. State U., 1971-72; M.S., Baylor U., 1977; m. Sharon Gay Witte, Sept. 13, 1975. Chief occupational therapy Central Tex. Rehab. Center, Waco, 1974-78; occupational therapy cons. Robinson (Tex.) Developmental Center, 1976-78; adminstrv. dir. Baylor Health Center, Baylor U., Waco, 1978—; rehab. cons. to sch. dist., Waco, 1976-78; therapy cons. health dept., 1975-77. Adv. com. Health Dept. and County Arthritis Assn., 1975-77. Registered occupational therapist, 1975. Mem. Dist. Occupational Therapy Assn. (sec. 1976-77), Am. Occupational Therapy Assn., Tex. Occupational Therapy Assn. Baptist. Home: 1924 Casa Linda Waco TX 76708 Office: 1121 S 7 St Waco TX 76703

HANKINSON, COE FOGLE LONG, mfg. co. exec.; b. St. Matthews, S.C., Aug. 5, 1938; d. John Robert and Kathryn McLain (Smoak) Fogle; student (scholar) Columbia Coll., 1956-57; B.S. in Bus. Adminstrn., U. S.C., 1976; m. John Crimmins Hankinson, Jr., Sept. 6, 1975; children—Mary Kathryn Long, George Robert Long. Sec. to personnel dir. S.C. Dept. Mental Health, Columbia, 1957-66; asst. to pres. The State-Record Co., Columbia, 1966-72; asst. corp. sec. Shakespeare Co., Columbia, 1972-78, corp. sec., 1978—, corp. risk mgr., 1972—; chmn. S.C. mktg. assistance S.C. Ins. Commn., 1977—. Mem. Hist. Columbia Found., 1968-70, Richland County Preservation Commn., 1968-70; sec. S.C. Gov.'s Hwy. Adv. Com., 1969-70; div. chmn. United Way, 1976, chmn. agy. relations, mem. exec. com., 1977-80; pres. bd. dirs. Carolina Ballet Co., 1971-72; rep. Miss S.C. Pageant, 1956. Mem. Am. Soc. Corp. Secs., Risk and Ins. Mgrs. Soc. (nat. chmn. govtl. affairs), S.C. C. of C., S.C. Textile Mfrs. Assn. (legis. com.). Presbyterian. Clubs: Palmetto, Spring Valley Country. Home: 5 Sims Alley Columbia SC 29205 Office: 1801 Main St Columbia SC 29201

HANKINSON, JOHN CRIMMINS, JR., banker, state ofcl.; b. Waynesboro, Ga., Oct. 14, 1933; s. John Crimmins and Sara (Blount) H.; B.S., Clemson U., 1955; grad. Sch. Banking of South, La. State U., 1964, S.C. Bankers Sch., 1965, Am. Bankers Assn. Nat. Comml. Lending Grad. Sch., U. Okla., 1979; m. Coe Fogle; children—Mona Lane, Ann Crimmins. Mgmt. trainee S.C. Nat. Bank, Greenville, 1957-59, adminstrv. asst., Sumter, 1959-60, asst. cashier, Cheraw, 1960-63, asst. v.p., sr. officer, Bennettsville, 1963-67, v.p. internat. banking div., Columbia, 1967-71, v.p. adminstrn. nat. banking div., 1971-80; dep. dir. S.C. State Devel. Bd., Columbia, 1980—. Pres., Bennettsville Parking and Devel. Co., 1965-67. Chmn. Pee Dee Area chpt. Nat. Found. March Dimes, 1966-67; chmn. S.C. edn. funds crusade S.C. div. Am. Cancer Soc., 1969-70, treas. S.C. div., 1970-75; vice chmn. S.C. Regional Export Expansion Council, 1969-73. pres. Young Bankers div. S.C. Bankers Assn., 1973-74. Served with AUS, 1956. Cert. comml. lender. Presbyterian. Home: 5 Sims Alley Columbia SC 29205 Office: PO Box 927 Columbia SC 29202

HANKINSON, RISDON WILLIAM, chem. engr.; b. St. Joseph, Mo., Dec. 11, 1938; s. William Augusta and Rose Mary (Thompson) H.; B.S., U. Mo., Rolla, 1960, M.S., 1962; Ph.D. (Am. Oil fellow), Iowa State U., 1972; m. Lyla Pollard, June 4, 1960; children—Kenneth, Michelle, Michael, Mark. Instr. chem. engring. U. Mo., Rolla, 1960-62; instr. chem. engring. Iowa State U., 1964-67; engr. Phillips Petroleum Co., Bartlesville, Okla., 1967-69, group leader, 1969-70, cons., 1970-78, unit dir., 1976—, prin., 1978—; adj. prof. math. Okla. State U., 1967-75, Bartlesville Wesleyan Coll., 1969-71. Vice pres. Tech. Careers Adv. Com., 1972-73, pres., 1973-74; v.p. Vol. Okla. Overseas Mission Bd., 1970-71; cub scout leader; tchr. religious edn., minister of Eucharist, lector, Roman Cath. Ch., 1976—. Served from 2d lt. to 1st lt. AUS, 1962-63. Recipient Outstanding Alumnus Achievement award Ia. State U., 1971; named Outstanding Young Engr. in Okla., 1970. Registered profl. engr., Okla. Mem. Am. Inst. Chem. Engrs. (dir., past pres. Bartlesville sect.), Soc. Profl. Engrs. (Young Engr. of Year Bartlesville chpt. 1970), Am. Petroleum Inst. (chmn. phys. properties com. static measurement 1979—). Clubs: Elks, K.C. Contbr. articles to profl., sci. jours. Home: 701 Sooner Park Dr Bartlesville OK 74003 Office: TRW Bldg Phillips Petroleum Co Bartlesville OK 74004

HANKS, JOANNA DAVIS, educator; b. Warsaw, Va., Mar. 25, 1948; d. Lawrence Hall and Leona (Packett) D.; B.S., Longwood Coll., 1969; M.S., Va. Commonwealth U., 1974; postgrad. Va. Poly. Inst. and State U., 1978—; m. William Roger Hanks, 1968; children—Leann Davis, Lawrence Ryland. Coop. office edn. coordinator and tchr. Hermitage High Sch., Henrico County, Va., 1969-74; asso. prof., program head secretarial sci. J. Sargeant Reynolds Community Coll., Richmond, Va., 1974—; cons., editor Media Systems, Inc., Southwestern Pub. Co., John Wiley Pub. Co. Mem. choir, chmn. ch. publicity Cool Spring Bapt. Ch. Mem. Va. Bus. Edn. Assn., Va. Edn. Assn., Delta Pi Epsilon. Home: 216 Santa Maria Dr Mechanicsville VA 23111 Office: PO Box 12084 Richmond VA 23241

HANLEY, MARGARET VIRGINIA, hosp. ofcl.; b. Rutherford, N.J., Oct. 1, 1933; d. John Francis and Anna (Mahoney) H.; B.S. in Nursing, Cath. U. Am., 1955, M.S., 1966. Staff nurse, head nurse, supr., dir. nursing Providence Hosp., Washington, 1957-64; dir. nursing service De Paul Hosp., Norfolk, Va., 1966-71, Community Hosp. Roanoke Valley, Roanoke, Va., 1971—. Bd. dirs. Health Systems Agy. III of Va., 1976—, Roanoke Health Council, 1977—. Mem. Nat. League Nursing, Am. Soc. Nursing Service Adminstrs. (chpt. pres. 1979—), Va. League Nursing, Va. Hosp. Assn., Va. Nurses Assn. (dir. 1972-74, pres. 1974-76), Roanoke Valley Mental Health Assn. (dir. 1971-77), Mental Health Assn. Va. (dir. 1979—), Sigma Theta Tau. Roman Catholic. Home: 4707 Easthill Dr SW Roanoke VA 24018 Office: Community Hospital of Roanoke Valley PO Box 12946 Roanoke VA 24029

HANLEY, WAYNE STEWART, chemist; b. Edinburgh, Scotland, Oct. 30, 1945; s. Wayne William and Jane Lawrence (Stewart) H.; B.A., Tarkio Coll., 1966; Ph.D., Vanderbilt U., 1971; m. Mary Catherine Wehrle, Feb. 28, 1979; children—Elizabeth, Laura. Research asso. medicinal chemistry dept. U. Minn., Mpls., 1970-71, dept. chemistry Vanderbilt U., Nashville, 1971-72; asst. prof. chemistry Georgetown (Ky.) Coll., 1972-77; dir. research and devel. Conwood Corp., Memphis, 1977—. Shell Found. fellow, 1966-67, NSF grantee, 1976-77. Mem. Am. Chem. Soc. (grants 1974-77), Inst. Food Technologists, Sigma Xi. Contbr. articles to profl. jours. Home: 1456 Tutwiler St Memphis TN 38107 Office: 46 Keel Ave Memphis TN 38107

HANLIN, HUGH CAREY, JR., life ins. co. exec.; b. Chattanooga, Mar. 16, 1925; s. Hugh Carey and Irene (Thompson) H.; student Emory U., 1942-44, 46-47; B.A., U. Mich., 1948; m. Wilma Jean Deal, June 23, 1951; children—Timothy Carey, Chris Allan. With Provident Life & Accident Ins. Co., 1948—, exec. v.p., 1973-77, pres., 1977-79, pres., chief exec. officer, 1979—, dir., 1973—; dir. Am. Nat. Bank & Trust Co., Chattanooga, 1978—; Provident Gen. Ins. Co. Bd. dirs. Chattanooga Opera Assn., pres. 1973-74; mem. resource group of opera adv. panel Tenn. Arts Commn., 1974-76; trustee U. Chattanooga Found., 1977—; past pres. Chattanooga-Hamilton County Speech and Hearing Center; bd. dirs. Allied Arts Fund of Chattanooga, v.p., 1975-76; bd. dirs. Moccasin Bend council Girl Scouts, 1971-75, Girls' Club Chattanooga, 1976-77, Tenn. Council Economic Edn., 1978—, United Fund, 1979, Tenn. Ind. Colls. Fund, 1979. Served to lt. (j.g.) USNR, 1943-46. Fellow Soc. Actuaries; mem. Southeastern Actuaries Club (pres. 1956-57), Chattanooga C. of C., Phi Beta Kappa, Alpha Tau Omega. Clubs: Mountain City (bd. govs.), Chattanooga Golf and Country, Rotary. Home: 7472 Preston Circle Chattanooga TN 37421 Office: Provident Life and Accident Ins Co Chattanooga TN 37402

HANLON, ANDREA WHITSON, learning disabilities specialist; b. Nashville, Dec. 10, 1950; d. Fred and Verdie (Canady) Whitson; B.A. in Speech, David Lipscomb Coll., Nashville, 1971; M.A. in Teaching, Learning Disabilities, The Citadel, Charleston, S.C., 1975; m. Cary Hanlon. Hard-of-hearing specialist Charleston (S.C.) County Schs., 1971-72; learning disabilities specialist Berkeley County Schs., Moncks Corner, S.C., 1972-78, Knox County Schs., Knoxville, Tenn., 1979—. Mem. NEA, Tenn. Edn. Assn., Knox County Edn. Assn., Assn. Childhood Edn. Certified in learning disabilities edn., Tenn., S.C., Ky. Home: 1611 Laurel Ave #607 Knoxville TN 37916 Office: Route 2 Strawberry Plains TN 37871

HANNA, JAMES RICHARD, accountant; b. Ticonderoga, N.Y.; s. James Albert and Effie May (Martell) H.; B.C.S., N.Y. U., 1928; m. Joan Hebert, May 31, 1940; children—Kathleen, James Richard, Regis. Staff, H.F. Farrington & Co., 1922-24, Harris, Kerr & Cook, 1924-27; with Rankin & Co., 1927-33, partner, 1935-44; v.p., treas. Tillier-Thompson, Inc., Importers, 1933-35; ind. practice acctg., N.Y.C., 1944-47; sr. partner J.R. Hanna & Co., N.Y.C. and Bronxville, N.Y., 1947-74, Boca Raton, Fla., 1975—; chmn. bd. Wright & McGill Co., Denver, 1963—, Wright & McGill Internat. Ltd., Denver, 1972—; v.p. J.R. Hanna & Co., P.C., Ardmore, Pa. Pres., Lincoln Park (N.J.) Bd. Edn., 1947-50; chmn. budget com. Bronxville-Eastchester Community Fund, 1965-66, bd. dirs., 1964-66. C.P.A., N.Y., Ill. Mem. Am. Inst. C.P.A.'s, N.Y. State Soc. C.P.A.'s, Beta Gamma Sigma, Sigma Phi Epsilon, Beta Alpha Psi. Roman Catholic. Club: Deerfield Country.

HANNA, PHILIP KOLB, mktg. exec.; b. Rochester, N.Y., May 3, 1947; s. Adrian M. and Blanche (Kolb) H.; B.S., Eastern N.Mex. U., 1969; m. Mary R. Hennahane, Aug. 24, 1968; children—Maureen C., Anne Clarke and Courtney Mackenzie (twins). With Gannett Rochester (N.Y.) Newspapers, 1969-73, Ithaca (N.Y.) Jour., 1973-76, Today Newspaper, Cocoa, Fla., 1976-78; v.p. consumer mktg. N.Y. Times, Lakeland, Fla., 1978—; lectr. N. Tex. State U., Denton, 1977-79, Am. Press Inst., Reston, Va., 1975. Served with U.S. Army, 1970-71. Decorated Bronze Star, Army Commendation medal. Mem. Internat. Circulation Mgrs. Assn., So. Circulation Mgrs. Assn. Club: Lakeland Yacht and Country. Home: 6361 Cedar Ln Lakeland FL 33803 Office: PO Box 408 Lakeland FL 33803

HANNA, RONALD EDWARD, prin.; b. New Kensington, Pa., July 14, 1931; B.S. in Phys. Edn., The Citadel, Charleston, S.C., 1956; M.A. in Adminstrn., Appalachian State U., Boone, N.C., 1970; m. Charlotte; 5 children. Dir athletics, head coach, Bishop England, Charleston, S.C., 1956-64; dir., YMCA, Spartanburg, S.C., 1964-66; mgr., Hickory Farms, Asheville, N.C., 1966-68; prin. Stiles Point Elementary Sch., Charleston, S.C., 1968—. Mem. exec. bd. YMCA. Mem. Charleston County Prins. Assn. (pres. 1975-77), Nat. S.C. assns. elementary sch. prins., NEA, Am. Assn. Sch. Adminstrs. Certified as elementary, secondary prin., tchr., sci., phys. edn., health. Home: 876 Quail Dr Charleston SC 29412 Office: 883 Mikell Dr Charleston SC 29412

HANNA, RONALD FREDERIC, airline pilot, flight exec.; b. Takoma Park, Md., June 20, 1934; s. Fred Greer and Seona Estelle (Shenk) H.; B. of Aero Engring., Ga. Inst. Tech., 1957; m. Margaret Ann Ripley, Nov. 10, 1962; children—Christine, Michael, Kyle. With American Airlines, 1965—, co-pilot, N.Y.C., 1965-69, capt., test pilot, Tulsa, 1969-74, capt., Chgo., 1974-76, Dallas-Ft. Worth, 1976—, also mgr. flying engring. Chmn. Tulsa Young Life Bd., 1970-73, recipient Distinguished Service award, 1974. Served as pilot, USN, 1957-64. Recipient Symons Wave Meml. award, 1971. Mem. Allied Pilot's Assn. (domicile chmn. 1970-74), Navy League U.S., Am. Inst. Aero. and Astronautics. Methodist. Clubs: Tulsa Skyhawks Soaring (pres. 1970-73), Centre Tennis, Arlington Yacht, Arlington Young Life (chmn. 1977—), Tex. Soaring Assn. Home: 806 Loch Lomond Dr Arlington TX 76012 Office: Am Airlines Flight Acad Am Airlines Plaza Fort Worth TX 76125

HANNAFORD, THOMAS DIXON, music pub., rec. co. exec.; b. Jackson, Miss., Sept. 15, 1952; s. Cecil Wendell and Mary Joe (Pettit) H.; B.S. In Bus., Samford U., 1975. Staff acct. Haskins & Sells, C.P.A.'s, Birmingham, Ala., 1975-77; theater technician Opryland, Nashville, 1978; fin. mgr. Paragon Assos., Inc., Nashville, 1978—; fin. cons. Land Ho, Nashville, 1978—, Magnecom, Inc., Nashville, 1978—. Mem. Nat. Acad. Rec. Arts and Scis., Am. Mgmt. Assn., Gospel Music Assn. Baptist. Home: 300 Bakertown Rd Apt 25-G Antioch TN 37013 Office: 1816 Hayes St Nashville TN 37203

HANNAH, JAMES GUESS, hosp. adminstr.; b. Muskogee, Okla., Sept. 10, 1944; s. Joseph England and Myrtle Evelyn (Leininger) H.; A.A., Westark Community Coll., 1965; student Harding Coll., Searcy, Ark., 1965-67; m. Donna Ray Cook, Aug. 9, 1969; children—Laura Kay, Sarah Renee. News dir. KWHN/KMAG, Fort Smith, Ark., 1972-74; news editor, news dir. public affairs KFPW-TV, Fort Smith, Ark., 1974-77; dir. communications and devel. St. Edward Mercy Med. Center, Fort Smith, 1977—, mem. adminstrv. council, 1977—; exec. dir. St. Edward Devel. Corp., Fort Smith, 1977—. Pres., Fort Smith Vol. Action Center, 1975: founder, chmn. Fort Smith Regional Air Show, 1976—; chmn. Ft. Smith Housing Assistance Bd., 1976-80, mem. governing bd., 1980. Mem. Aviation/Space Writers Assn. (writing citation 1975), Nat. Assn. Hosp. Devel., Fort Smith C. of C. (chmn. aviation com.). Mem. Chs. of Christ. Club: Noon Exchange (Fort Smith). Home: 4708 N 31st St Fort Smith AR 72904 Office: 7301 Rogers Ave Fort Smith AR 72903

HANNAH, JOHN DAVID, historian, educator, clergyman; b. Elmer, N.J., Aug. 9, 1945; s. Milo Wilbur and Violet Naomi (Todd) H.; B.S., Phila. Coll. Bible, 1967; Th.M. cum laude, Dallas Theol. Sem., 1971, Th.D., 1974; postgrad. So. Meth. U., 1978-80; m. Carolyn Ruth Lupole, July 20, 1968; children—Rebecca, Nancy. Ordained to ministry Ind. Baptist, 1972; pastor Granbury (Tex.) Bible Ch., 1970-72; prof. history Plano (Tex.) U., 1972-73; instr., asst. prof. hist. theology Dallas Theol. Sem., 1972-77, asso. prof., 1978-80, prof., chmn. dept. hist. theology, 1980—; interim pastor Trinity Bible Ch., Richardson, Tex., 1977; speaker bible confs.; tchr. Inst. Bibl. Studies, Campus Crusade for Christ. Recipient Charles Nash award in ch. history Dallas Sem., 1969, 70, 71. Mem. Am. Hist. Assn., Dallas Hist. Soc., Orgn. Ch. Historians, Ch. History Soc., Am. Hist. Soc. Contbr. paper Oxford U. Research and Reading Seminar, 1976; articles to profl. publs. Home: 9118 Lynbrook St Dallas TX 75238 Office: 3909 Swiss St Dallas TX 75204

HANNAMAN, ROSE FAILLA, painter; b. Los Angeles, Mar. 30, 1919; d. Tony and Concetta (Faso) Failla; B.A.B.A., Fresno State Coll., 1941; postgrad. in art Panama Canal Coll., 1969-79; m. John

Hannaman, Sept. 7, 1956. In various civilian personnel mgmt. positions U.S. Govt., 1941-66, program analyst U.S. Army Forces So. Command, C.Z., 1964-66, ret., 1966; exhibited paintings in one-woman shows at Adminstrn. Bldg., Balboa Heights, Panama, 1977, USIA, Panama, Panama, 1978; exhibited in group shows Nat. League Am. Pen Women Traveling Slide Art Show, 1976, 76, 80, Kennedy Center, Washington, 1976; represented in pvt. collections. Recipient numerous prizes Panama's Internat. Fishing Tournament, 1971-76; honorable mention Pictorial Art Contest, 1972. Mem. Internat. Soc. Artists, Nat. League Am. Pen Women (nat. art bd. 1976-78, pres. C.Z. and Panama br. 1976-78, state pres. for former C.Z. and Panama 1978-80; art editor Pen Woman Mag. 1978—), Instituto Panameno de Arte. Democrat. Roman Catholic. Clubs: Inter-Am. Women's of Panama (editor bull. 1969-70, pres. 1975-76), Isthmian Coll., Quarry Heights and Ft. Amador Officers' Wives, Altar-Bible Rosary Soc. Editor So. Cross, 1971-75 (1st Place Nat. award 1976).

HANNAN, PHILIP MATTHEW, archbishop; b. Washington, May 20, 1913; s. Patrick F. and Lilian Louise (Keefe) H.; student St. Charles Coll., 1931-33; A.B., Cath. U., 1935, M.A., 1936, J.C.D., 1949; student North Am. Coll., 1936-40; S.T.B., S.T.L., Gregorian U., Rome, 1940. Ordained priest Roman Catholic Ch., 1939; clerical appointment St. Thomas Aquinas Ch., Balt., 1940-42; student Cath. U., 1946-49, vice chancellor, 1948-51, chancellor, 1951-62, vicar gen., 1960-65; archbishop of New Orleans, 1965—; adminstr. St. Patrick's Ch., Washington 1951-56, pastor, 1956-65; aux. bishop Archdiocese of Washington, 1956-65; editor-in-chief Cath. Standard, 1951-65. Mem. administrv. bd. U.S. Cath. Conf., chmn. dept. communications. Mem. White House Conf. on Children and Youth. Chmn. bd. trustees Cath. U. Am., 1973—; trustee United Way New Orleans. Served as chaplain USAAF, 1942-46. Address: 7887 Walmsley Ave New Orleans LA 70125

HANNIGAN, JOSEPH FRANCIS, physicist; b. Ft. Sill, Okla., July 10, 1926; s. Francis Hugh and Ava Lodema (Wilson) H.; B.S., Okla. State U., 1950; M.Teaching Sci., Cath. U. Am., 1971; m. JoAnn Young, Nov. 5, 1955; children—Michael Kevin, Patrick Sean, Mary Kathleen. Physicist, U.S. Army Engr. Research and Devel. Lab., Ft. Belvoir, Va., 1953-60, U.S. Army Engr. Topographic Labs., Ft. Belvoir, 1960—. Served with USAAF, 1944-46, U.S. Army, 1950-52. Recipient Army Sci. Conf. Outstanding Sci. Achievement award, 1978; Army Research and Devel. Achievement award for tech. achievement, 1973; Spl. Act Service award, 1972, 74, 75, 76, 77. Mem. IEEE, Sigma Xi. Roman Catholic. Contbr. articles to profl. jours.; patentee in field. Home: 6018 Meriwether Ln Springfield VA 22150 Office: Research Inst US Army Engr Topographic Labs Bldg 2592 Fort Belvoir VA 22060

HANRAHAN, ROBERT JOSEPH, chemist; b. Chgo., Jan. 7, 1932; s. James Richard and Lucille Florence (Granger) H.; B.S., Loyola U. (Chgo.), 1953; Ph.D., U. Wis., Madison, 1957; m. Mary Ellen Hogan, Oct. 28, 1957; children—Ann Marie, Sheila Frances, Robert Joseph, Margaret Evyleen. Research chemist Pure Oil Co., Crystal Lake, Ill., 1953; teaching asst., research asst., Monsanto research fellow U. Wis., Madison, 1953-57; U.S. NSF postdoctoral fellow Leeds (Eng.) U., 1957-58; asst. prof. phys. chemistry U. Fla., 1958-64, asso. prof., 1964-71, prof., 1971—, chmn. phys. chemistry div., 1977-79; vis. sci. Hahn-Meitner Inst. for Nuclear Research, Berlin, 1976; cons. in field. U.S. AEC research grantee, 1963-74; ERDA grantee, 1975—. Mem. Am. Chem. Soc., Am. Phys. Soc., Radiation Research Soc., AAAS, Am. Soc. Mass Spectrometry, Inter-Am. Photochem. Soc. Democrat. Roman Catholic. Research on chem. effects of nuclear radiation, 1954—; contbr. articles to profl. jours. Home: 3730 NW 16th Pl Gainesville FL 32605 Office: Dept Chemistry U Fla Gainesville FL 32611

HANSARD, JAMES WILLIAM, librarian; b. Charleston, Ark., May 2, 1936; s. J. D. and Emma (Collier) H.; B.S.E., U. Central Ark., 1958; M.S. in Library Sci., La. State U., 1966; m. Ruth Avery Bishop, June 1, 1962; children—Will, Sharon, Rebecca. Librarian, tchr. history Corning (Ark.) High Sch., 1958-59, librarian, choral dir., band dir., 1959-62; dir. libraries Presbyterian Day Sch., Memphis, 1960-62; dir. libraries Memphis Univ. Sch., 1960-62, librarian, tchr. geography, 1962-64; acquisitions librarian Ark. State U., 1964-65, asst. librarian for tech. processing, 1965-77, asso. librarian, 1977-78, head librarian, 1978—, chmn. dept. library sci., 1965—. Mem. Ark. Library Assn., Southwestern Library Assn., N.E. Ark. Library Assn., Crowley's Ridge Ednl. Media Assn., Council on Library Edn. Baptist. Club: Civitan. Office: PO Box EEEE State University AR 72467

HANSARD, LOUIS LAWSON, constrn. equipment co. exec.; b. Thornberry, Tex., Nov. 11, 1920; s. Stephen Lester and Mary Jane (Sears) H.; student U. So. Calif., 1946-47, Midwestern State U., 1949-51; m. Elizabeth Jane Van Buskirk, Mar. 14, 1944; children—Louis Lawson, Dale Jerry, Charles David. Corp. mgr. Safway Scaffolds Co., Wichita Falls, Tex., 1952-63, Material Sales Inc., Wichita Falls, 1955-63, Hiway Concrete Sawing Co. Inc., Wichita Falls, 1957-63; owner Constrn. Equipment & Splty. Co. (CESSCO), Wichita Falls, 1964—. Mem. Wichita Falls Bd. Commerce and Industry. Served with AUS, 1942-46. Decorated Silver Star. Mem. Am., Tex. rental assns., N. Tex. Home Builders Assn. Republican. Methodist. Clubs: S.W. Rotary of Wichita Falls (charter mem., dir.), Masons, Wichita (Wichita Falls). Home: 2606 Amherst Dr Wichita Falls TX 76308 Office: 703 E Scott St PO Box 238 Wichita Falls TX 76302

HANSEN, HAROLD JOHN, artist; b. Chgo., June 18, 1942; s. Harold Melborne and Florence Marion (O'Connell) H.; B.F.A. with honors, U. Ill., 1964; M.F.A., U. Mich., 1966; m. Martha Dianne Lyon, May 8, 1965; children—Daniel Charles, Susan Elizabeth. Instr. art, chmn. founds. program Kendall Sch. Design, Grand Rapids, Mich., 1966-69; asst. prof. Ferris State Coll., Big Rapids, Mich., 1969-70; mem. faculty U. S.C., Columbia, 1970—, asso. prof. arts, 1975, dir. grad. studies in art, 1975-76, head div. art studios, 1976—; sec.-treas. S.C. Guild Artists, 1974. Grantee S.C. Arts Commn., 1974-75, Nat. Endowment Arts, 1974-75. Mem. Coll. Art Assn. Am., Southeastern Coll. Art Assn. Contbr. articles profl. jours. Office: Art Dept Univ SC Columbia SC 29208

HANSEN, HERBERT EDWIN, oil co. exec., lawyer; b. Cleve., Oct. 29, 1920; s. Marius and Romaine (Christman) H.; B.A. summa cum laude, Oberlin Coll., 1942; M.B.A. with distinction, Harvard U., 1946, J.D., 1949; m. Marietta Grider Hewitt, Jan. 5, 1946; children—Marian Romaine, Donna Hewitt, David Christman. Admitted to Mo. bar, 1949; asso. firm Dietrich, Tyler and Davis, Kansas City, Mo., 1949-52; zone landman Gulf Oil Corp., Tulsa and Wichita, Kans., 1952-56; adminstrv. asst. to gen. mng. dir. Iranian Oil Operating Co., Tehran, 1956-62; coordinator govt. agreements Eastern Hemisphere, Gulf Oil Co., London, 1962-69; v.p. Gulf Oil Corp., Pitts., 1969-75, Gulf Oil Exploration & Prodn. Co., Houston, 1975—; speaker, panelist at seminars and confs. Mem. adv. bd. program internat. bus. diplomacy Georgetown U. Served to lt. comdr. USNR, 1943-46; PTO. Mem. Mo. Bar Assn., Houston Com. Fgn. Relations, Houston World Trade Assn., Conf. Bd., Asia Soc., Center Internat. Bus., Middle East Inst. and ANERA of Washington (bd. govs.), Harvard Law Sch. Assn., Phi Beta Kappa. Republican. Methodist. Clubs: Houston, Harvard of Houston. Home: 11839 Durrette St Houston TX 77024 Office: Box 2100 Houston TX 77001

HANSEN, KIM DANIEL, chem. co. sales rep.; b. Bogota, Colombia, Jan. 20, 1950; s. Ole Daniel and Grete Heide (Jensen) H.; came to U.S., 1971, naturalized, 1974; B.S. in Bus. Adminstrn., Babson Coll., Wellesley, Mass., 1974; m. Susan M. Mackinnon, July 8, 1972; 1 dau., Kristina Marie. Salesman, Nat. Mdsg. Co., Natick, Mass., 1974; sales rep. Dun & Bradtreet, Inc., Boston, 1974; export mgr. Arne Vittrup Cia Ltda., Bogota, 1975; sales rep. Dow Chems. U.S.A., Dallas, 1976—. Soccer coach Plano (Tex.) Sports Authority, 1978—. Served with Danish Marines, 1969-71. Mem. Soc. Petroleum Engrs., Soc. Paint and Coating Tech., Dallas Paint and Coatings Assn. Lutheran. Clubs: Los Rios Country, Toastmasters (chpt. v.p. 1976-77). Home: 2605 Lemmontree Ln Plano TX 75074 Office: 12700 Park Central Dallas TX 75251

HANSEN, NILS ERLING, cons. engr.; b. New Orleans, July 28, 1931; s. Hans Trygve and Hanna (Hansen) H.; B.S., Tulane U., 1953; m. Johanna Reinetta Wristers, May 13, 1960; children—Norman Trygve, Helen Reinetta, Jon Erling. Chief engr. T. Hansen Constrn., Inc. New Orleans, 1956-62; design engr. Prescott Follett & Assos., New Orleans, 1962-66; prin. N. E. Hansen & Assos., Cons. Engrs., New Orleans, 1966-70; chief engr. Petro-Marine Engring., Inc., 1970-74; gen. mgr. Ocean Oil Internat. Engring. Corp., 1975, v.p. CE Crest Engring., Inc., 1975—. Chmn. bd. trustees Norwegian Seamen's Mission, New Orleans. Served to lt. (j.g.) USCG, 1953-56; capt. Res. Decorated St. Olav's medal (Norway); recipient Achievement medal U.S. Coast Guard, 1970, Commendation medal, 1973. Mem. Am. Soc. C.E., Nat. Soc. Profl. Engrs., Am. Soc. Mil. Engrs., Mil. Order World Wars, U.S. Naval Inst., Am. Scandinavian Found., Norwegian Am. Hist. Assn., USCG Acad. Alumni Assn., Norwegian Am. Sesquicentennial Assn., U.S. Coast Guard Officers Assn., Norseman's League, Sons of Norway, Soc. Tulane Engrs., La. Engring. Soc., Res. Officers Assn. (pres. 1969-71). Clubs: Army-Navy (Washington); Petroleum. Home: 6707 Canal Blvd New Orleans LA 70124 Office: 3000 S Post Oak Houston TX 77027

HANSEN, PAUL TRAVIS, physician; b. Ponca City, Okla., May 24, 1939; s. Bernhardt Frode and Helga Marie (Nelsen) H.; B.A., Rice U., 1961; M.D., Baylor U., 1965; M.P.H., U. Calif., 1968; m. Mary Louise Deady, Dec. 28, 1968; children—Stephanie, David. Intern, Wilford Hall USAF Med. Center, 1965-66; resident in aerospace medicine USAF Sch. Aerospace Medicine, 1967-70; practice medicine specializing in occupational and preventive medicine, San Antonio, 1977—. Pres. Windcrest (Tex.) Fire Dept., 1975-76; health dir. City of Windcrest, 1976—. Served to lt. col., USAF, 1964-77. Decorated Bronze Star. Diplomate Am. Bd. Preventive Medicine, Am. Bd. Family Practice. Fellow Am. Coll. Preventive Medicine; mem. AMA, Am. Coll. Emergency Medicine, Soc. USAF, Flight Surgeon Assn. Lutheran. Home: 5919 Northgap St San Antonio TX 78239 Office: 215 M and S Tower San Antonio TX 78205

HANSER, SISTER JULIE, hosp. adminstr.; b. East St. Louis, Ill., July 5, 1941; d. Forrest Fredrick and Isabel Cecilia (Saunders) H.; B.S. in Nursing, Marillac Coll., 1965; masters with high distinction in health adminstrn. Ind. U., 1976. Nursing service adminstr. St. Mary's Hosp., Evansville, Ind., 1970-74; adminstrv. resident St. Mary's Hosp., Saginaw, Mich., 1976; asst. adminstr. Providence Hosp., Mobile, Ala., 1976-78, adminstr., 1978—; bd. dirs. S.W. Health Planning Agy.; health coordinator Diocese of Mobile; mem. health commn. Daus. of Charity. Bd. dirs. St. Marys Home for Children, Mobile, 1976—; trustee St. Vincent's Hosp., Birmingham, Ala. Registered nurse, Mo., Ala. Mem. Hosp. Fin. Mgmt. Assn., Ala. Assn. Hosp. Execs., Ind. U. Sch. Medicine Alumni, C. of C. Mobile. Roman Catholic. Home: 156 N Catherine St Mobile AL 36604 Office: Providence Hosp 1504 Springhill Ave PO Box 3201 Mobile AL 36601

HANSON, BERNOLD MORRIS, corp. exec.; b. Mayville, N.D., May 7, 1928; B.S. in Engring. Geology, U. N.D., 1951; M.A. in Geology, U. Wyo., 1954; m. Marilyn Miller, Oct., 1951; children—Karen, Gretchen, Eric. Geologist, Magnolia Petroleum Co., Midland, Tex., 1951-52; instr. grad. sch. and petrology lab. U. Wyo., Laramie, 1953-54; dist. geologist Humble Oil and Refining Co., New Orleans, project supr., Alaska, dist. geologist, Midland, 1955-60; pvt. practice cons. geologist, ind. oil operator, Midland, 1960—; pres. Hanson & Allen, Inc., Midland, 1966-74, Hanson Exploration Co., Inc., Midland, 1971-75, Hanson Corp., Midland, 1974—. Capt., United Fund, 1960-62; football and basketball coach YMCA, 1965-66; active Boy Scouts Am., 1940—, asst. scoutmaster Elks troop, Laramie, 1953, asst. scoutmaster troop 51, 1967-69, instl. rep., 1966, scoutmaster, 1969-70, camping and activities chmn. Buffalo Trail counsil, 1970, Philmont leader, 1970, scoutmaster World Jamboree in Japan, 1971, canoe trail leader, 1972, O-A Indian Dance Team asst., council pres., 1972, 73, chmn. S. Central region World Jamboree Com., World Jamboree in Norway, 1975, participation chmn. World Jamboree in Sweden, 1979; mem. Pres.'s Council, U. Wyo., 1979. Recipient Sioux award U. N.D., 1978, awards Boy Scouts Am., Order of Arrow, 1944, Vigil Honor in Order of Arrow, 1970, Silver Beaver award, 1973, Disting. Eagle Scout, 1974, Silver Antelope award, 1976. Mem. Am. Assn. Petroleum Geologists (sec. 1973-74, sec. profl. sect., mem./chmn. coms.) AIME, Am. Inst. Profl. Geologists (fin. adv.), Soc. Econ. Paleontologists and Mineralogists (pres. sect. 1962-63), W. Tex. Geol. Soc. (pres. 1965-66, hon. life mem.), S.W. Fedn. Geol. Socs., Soc. Ind. Profl. Earth Scientists, All-Am. Wildcatters (charter), Sigma, Sigma Gamma Epsilon. Republican. Episcopalian. Author: Permian Limestone on Pacific Side of Alaska Peninsula, 1956; Geology of Elkhorn Ranch Area, North Dakota, 1954; West Texas Oil and Gas Fields, 1965; Oil and Gas Development Paper, West Texas and Southeastern New Mexico, 1958; Geology of the Bar-Mar Devonian Field, West Texas, 1966. Home: 1613 W Pecan St Midland TX 79701 Office: 1302 First National Bank Bldg Midland TX 79701 PO Box 1212 Midland TX 79702

HANSON, BERTIL LENNART, educator; b. Chgo., Sept. 8, 1932; B.Sc., Northwestern U., 1953; M.A., U. Chgo., 1956, Ph.D., 1959. Mem. faculty Okla. State U., Stillwater, 1959—, prof. polit. sci., 1976—; vis. prof. U. Oslo, 1965-66, Uppsala (Sweden) U., 1973-74. Fulbright scholar, 1965, 73. Mem. Am. Polit. Sci. Assn. Home: PO Box 270 Route 5 2808 Sangre Rd Stillwater OK 74074 Office: Dept Polit Sci Okla State U Stillwater OK 74074

HANSON, CLARENCE BLOODWORTH, JR., publisher; b. Augusta, Ga., Nov. 7, 1908; s. Clarence Bloodworth and Harriet (Pinkham) H.; student Richmond Acad., Augusta, Ga., 1921-25; B.S., U. Va., 1930; Litt.D. (hon.), U. Ala., 1974; m. Elizabeth Fontaine Fletcher, Sept. 9, 1929; 1 son, Victor Henry II. Advt. dept. Indpls. Star, 1929-30; with advt. dept. Birmingham (Ala.) News, 1930-34, nat. advt. mgr., 1934-37, asst. advt. dir., 1937-42, pub., 1945; chmn., dir., mem. exec. com. The Birmingham News Co. (pubs. Birmingham News, Huntsville Times, Huntsville News, Agent, Birmingham Post-Herald); v.p., dir. Mercury Express, Inc.; dir., mem. exec. com. First Nat. Bank Birmingham, Ala. Bancorp.; chmn. exec. com., dir. Royal Crown Cola Co. Bd. dirs. Birmingham Mus. of Art; trustee Eye Found. Hosp. Served as maj. AC, AUS, 1942-45. Mem. AP (v.p. 1952-56), Am., So. (pres. 1950) newspaper pubs. assns., Ala. Press Assn. (pres. 1951), Phi Gamma Delta. Episcopalian. Clubs: Mountain Brook County, Birmingham Country, Shoal Creek Country, Relay House (Birmingham); Hon. Co. of Edinburg Golfers (Muirfield, Scotland). Home: 4055 Old Leeds Rd Mountain Brook Birmingham AL 35213 Office: 2200 4th Ave N Birmingham AL 35203

HANSON, DONALD FARNESS, elec. engr.; b. Urbana, Ill., Mar. 5, 1946; s. Alfred Olaf and Elizabeth Marie (Miller) H.; student Iowa State U., 1964-67; B.S. in Elec. Engring. with honors, U. Ill., 1969, M.S., 1972, Ph.D., 1976. Systems programmer ILLIAC IV project U. Ill., Urbana, 1968-69, research asst. in computer sci., 1969-71, teaching asst. elec. engring., 1971-73, lectr. in architecture, 1973-74, instr. in elec. engring., 1974-76; asst. prof. elec. engring. Iowa State U., Ames, 1976-77; asst. prof. elec. engring. U. Miss., University, 1977—. Mem. IEEE, Illuminating Engring. Soc. (affiliate), Sigma Xi (asso.). Home: PO Box 4166 University MS 38677 Office: 314 Anderson Hall Dept Elec Engring University MS 38677

HANSON, GORDON ALBERT, social work exec.; b. Gowanda, N.Y., Apr. 5, 1927; s. Gordon Martin and Marjorie Ann (Wing) H.; student Rutgers U., 1944-45; B.A., U. N.C., 1953, M.S.W., 1955; m. Ella Rose McEachin, Jan. 15, 1948; children—Dianne, Larry Gordon, Gregory Arthur. Chief med. social worker McCain (N.C.) Sanitorium, 1955-57; clin. social worker VA, Winston-Salem, N.C., 1957-59; sec. div. health and welfare Gen. Assembly, Presbyterian Ch. U.S., Atlanta, 1959-72; pres. Evergreen Presbyn. Vocat. Sch., Minden, La., 1972—; prof. U. London, 1967. Pres. Goodwill Industries, 1958, P.T.A., 1961-62; dir. United Fund, 1964; chpt. pres. U. N.C. Alumni Assn., 1976—; mem. bd. annuities and relief Presbyn. Ch. U.S. Served with AUS, 1945-47. Recipient Outstanding Service award Presbyn. Assn. Homes for Aging, 1973; cert. Acad. Cert. Social Workers; cert. social worker, La. Mem. Nat. Conf. Social Welfare, Nat. Assn. Social Workers, Nat. Assn. Retarded Citizens. Republican. Club: Masons. Author: Your Neighbor As Yourself, 1962. Home: 8606 W Wilderness Way Shreveport LA 71106 Office: PO Box 6217 Shreveport LA 71106

HANSON, HOWARD HENRY, assn. exec.; b. White River, S.D., May 4, 1924; s. Otto Theodore and Margaret (Bramer) H.; diploma S.D. Sch. for Blind, 1942; B.S., S.D. State Coll., 1947, M.S., 1948; postgrad. U. Mich., 1949; m. Phyllis Marie Geis, Apr. 23, 1954; 1 son, Phillip Gerald. Owner, operator Coffee Shop, Brookings, S.D., 1948-49; counsellor, home tchr. S.D. Service to Blind, Pierre, 1949-52, dir. agy., 1952-77; exec. dir. Ark. Enterprises for Blind, Little Rock, 1978—. Adviser, N.W. Rehab. Center for Blind, Mpls.; teaching cons. Inst. for Home Tchrs., Little Rock, Ark. Cons., founder S.D. Lions Sight and Service Found.; U.S. del. to World Council on Welfare Blind, New Delhi, India; mem. Nat. Task Force Geriatric Blindness, 1969—; chmn. first session on blindness, World Congress Rehab. Internat., Sidney, Australia, 1972; v.p. Nat. Accreditation Council Agys. Serving the Blind and Visually Handicapped, 1973-78, also mem. nat. accreditation commn. Trustee Am. Found. for Blind (mem. service com. on geriatric blindness); chmn. subcom. capital fund drive YMCA, 1976-77. Named Outstanding Handicapped Citizen of S.D., 1963; recipient Distinguished Alumnus award S.D. State U., 1972. Mem. Am. Assn. Workers for Blind (pres. 1968-69), Nat. Council Execs. Agys. for Blind (pres. 1972-73), S.D. Assn. for Blind (Gus Zachte award 1974), S.D. Social Welfare Conf. (pres. 1964), S.D. Rehab. Assn. (pres. 1967), Council State Adminstrs. Vocational Rehab. (pres. 1967), Dirs. Vocational Rehab. (pres. region 6 1967), Nat. Planning Commn. Rehab. Blind, Nat. Rehab. Assn. (pres. 1970), Phi Kappa Delta. Lutheran. Mason, Elk, Lion (internat. counsellor, life mem. Pierre, dist. gov. 1957-58, state chmn. capital fund dr. to expand workshop for blind 1977). Home: 416 Shamrock Little Rock AR 72205 Office: Ark Enterprises for Blind 2811 Fairpark Little Rock AR 72204

HANSON, PHYLLIS MARIE GEIS (MRS. HOWARD H. HANSON), Realtor; b. Sioux Falls, S.D.; d. William H. and Jane Irene (Manley) Geis; student Nettleton Bus. Coll., 1943; grad. Realtors Inst. S.D., 1972; m. H.S. Eidy, Mar. 8, 1942 (div. 1947); m. 2d, Howard H. Hanson, Apr. 23, 1954; 1 son, Phillip G. Co-owner, mgr. hotel, 1942-43; asst. mgr. State Theatre, asst. to dir. for Eastern S.D., Minn. Amusement Co., 1943-45; owner, operator Brunch House Cafe, 1947; founder home econs. dept. L.C. Lippert Co., Sioux Falls, 1948, dir., 1949-54; salesman Dorothy Poulos, Real Estate, Pierre, S.D., 1959; partner Poulos & Hanson, Real Estate, Pierre, 1961—. Mem. Central S.D. Bd. Realtors, 1959—, sec., 1961, treas., 1962, pres., 1963, chmn. state real estate conv., 1963, named Realtor of Year, 1963, 73; mem. S.D. Bd. Realtors, 1959—, state bd. dirs., 1971—. Mem. S.D. Assn. for Blind, 1954—. Recipient Outstanding Service award S.D. Lions Internat., 1970. Mem. Nat. Assn. Real Estate Bds. (mem. Women's Council), Nat. Brokers Inst., S.D. Realtors Assn. (dir. 1971-75), Pierre C. of C. (dir. 1966-69, treas. 1967-69, exec. bd. 1967-69, dir. 1973-76, pres. 1976-77, pres. Ambassador Club 1977-78), U.S. C. of C. (mem. tourist and conv. com. 1964-65), Beta Sigma Phi (host pres. state conv. 1966, 1st pres. Pierre City council 1968). Roman Catholic (pres. band 1963). Club: Pierre Lioness (charter mem.). Home: 416 Shamrock St Little Rock AR 72205

HANSON, VICTOR HENRY, II, newspaper exec.; b. Augusta, Ga., Aug. 17, 1930; s. Clarence Bloodworth and Elizabeth (Fletcher) H.; student U. Va.; B.A., U. Ala., 1954; m. Elizabeth Stallworth, Dec. 29, 1953; children—Clarence B., Victor H., Elizabeth M., Mary Fletcher, Robert S. With The Birmingham News, 1946-54, 59—, asst. sec.-treas., 1959-61, pres., gen. mgr., dir.; pres., dir. Mercury Express, Inc., 1971—; dir. First Nat. Bank Birmingham. Trustee, Ala. Sch. Fine Arts, Gordon Coll., Wenham, Mass.; bd. dirs. So. Research Inst., Birmingham. Served to capt. USAFR, 1955-59. Mem. Birmingham Area C. of C., So. Newspaper Pubs. Assn. (dir.), Ala. Press Assn. (v.p. 1963-64), Am. Newspaper Pubs. Assn., Kappa Alpha, Sigma Delta Chi. Presbyterian. Clubs: Mountain Brook, Birmingham Country, Relay House, Downtown, Rotary. Office: 2200 4th Ave Birmingham AL 35203

HANSSON, KENNETH SIGURD, coll. adminstr.; b. Chgo., June 23, 1929 (parents Swedish citizens); s. Henning Engelbrekt and Elvira Astrid (Johansson) H.; came to Sweden, 1931, came to U.S., 1952, naturalized, 1954; B.S., So. Ill. U., 1960; M.Ed., U. Mo., 1964, Ph.D., 1966; m. Evelyn Fay Daniels, Dec. 21, 1955; children—Karen Beth, Kristena Ann. Constrn. worker Hanson Contracting Co., Chgo., 1952-53; tchr. indsl. arts Dundee (Ill.) Community Sch., 1960-63; instr. U. Mo., Columbia, 1964-65; chmn. Ky. Sch. Crafts Eastern Ky. U., 1966-69, chmn. dept. indsl. tech., 1969-73, asso. dean Coll. Applied Arts, Tech., 1973-75, dean, 1975—. Served with Swedish Air Force, 1948-52, USAF, 1953-57. Nat. Def. Service fellow, 1963-66. Mem. Nat. Assn. Indsl. Tech. (pres. 1977-78, editor conv. procs. 1977-78), Nat. Assn. Indsl. Tech. Tchr. Edn., Am. Vocat. Assn., Am. Council Indsl. Arts Tchr. Edn., Ky. Indsl. Edn. Assn., Phi Delta Kappa, Iota Lambda Sigma, Kappa Delta Pi. Methodist. Prin. writer Curriculum Guides for Indsl. Arts in Ky., 1974; contbr. articles to profl. jours. Home: Route 9 Hillcrest Richmond KY 40475 Office: Eastern Ky U Richmond KY 40475

HANZEL, MARSHA WEINSTEIN, writer; b. Columbus, Ohio, Oct. 3, 1947; d. Marcus Leroy and Eleanor Frances (Reich) Weinstein; B.J., U. Mo., 1969; postgrad. U. Va., 1970-71; m. Jeffrey Sheldon Hanzel; children—Michael Brian, William Stephen. Staff writer Norfolk (Va.) Virginian-Pilot, 1969-70; editor Norfolk Naval Sta. newspaper, 1972-73; staff writer Hartford (Conn.) Courant, 1973-74; free-lance writer and photographer, 1974—. Vol., Bur. Child Protective Services, Va. Dept. Welfare. Mem. Women in Communications, Nat. Fedn. Press Women, League Women Voters. Club: Bon Air Jr. Woman's. Home: 1613 Robindale Rd Richmond VA 23235

HARAGAN, DONALD ROBERT, meteorologist, engr.; b. Houston, Apr. 15, 1936; s. Donald William and Mary Louise (Thompson) H.; B.S., U. Tex., Austin, 1959; M.S., Tex. A&M U., 1960, Ph.D., 1970; m. Willie Mae O'Berry, July 2, 1966; children—Shannon, Shelley. Research scientist U. Tex., Austin, 1960-65, instr., 1965-69; asst. prof. atmospheric sci. Tex. Tech. U., Lubbock, 1969-72, asso. prof., 1972-79, prof., chmn. dept. atmospheric scis., 1979—; cons. to bus. and industry applied meterology and climatology. Registered profl. engr., Tex. Mem. Am. Meteorol. Soc., Tex. Acad. Sci., Nat. Soc. Profl. Engrs., Tex. Soc. Profl. Engrs., Weather Modification Assn., Sigma Xi, Phi Kappa Phi, Omicron Delta Kappa, Chi Epsilon Pi. Contbr. articles to profl. jours. Home: 3204 53d St Lubbock TX 79413 Office: PO Box 4320 Lubbock TX 79409

HARALICK, JOY GOLD, educator; b. Binghamton, N.Y.; d. Harold Kenneth and Sara (Shapiro) G.; B.A., George Washington U., 1958, M.A., 1960; Ph.D., U. N.C., 1964; 1 dau., Tammy-Beth. Research asso. dept. sociology Duke U., Durham, N.C., 1963-64; asst. prof. sociology U. Kans., Lawrence, 1964-68; sociologist, 1968-72; adj. asst. prof. sociology, div. continuing edn. U. Kans., Lawrence, 1972-76, project coordinator Project RETOOL, spl. edn. dept., 1976, research fellow Bur. Child Research, 1976-78: asst. prof. sociology U. Ala., Huntsville, 1978—; cons. Centron Ednl. Film Corp., Lawrence, 1976-78. Originator/chairperson, Parent-Tchr. Resource Com., Lawrence, 1975; v.p./sec. Lawrence PTA permanent adv. com. on curriculum, 1975-76; bd. dirs. Day Care Assn. Huntsville-Madison County, 1979—, Douglas County (Kans.) Mental Health Assn., 1970-76. Nat. Inst. Child Health and Devel. research fellow, 1976-78. Mem. Am. Sociol. Assn., So. Sociol. Soc., AAAS, Council Exceptional Children, Am. Assn. Mental Deficiency, Soc. Research in Child Devel., Assn. Childhood Edn. Internat., Ednl. Resources Info. Center, Chess Nat. Acquisitions. Author book. Contbr. articles to profl. jours. Office: Dept Sociology Box 1247 Univ of Ala Huntsville AL 35807

HARB, MITCHELL ABRAHAM, inventor, metal craftsman; b. Greensboro, N.C., Oct. 15, 1919; s. Fareed J. and Catherine Mae Hannah H.; student U. Wis., 1942-45; m. Marilee Cruse, Oct. 25, 1941; children—Mitchell Joseph, Marille Priscilla. Propr., owner Harb Tire Service, mgr. Foundry, Lexington, N.C., 1949—; patent cons., 1957—; instr. Nat. Rifle Assn., 1957—; designer patterns and molds for plaques and medals, 1949—; created a Silver Jubilee medallion for Queen of Eng., 1977; minature models of Am. ships and cannons represented in permanent display at Mariners Mus. Monitor and Merrimac, Beauford, N.C., various Davidson County libraries and state museums. Served with U.S. Army, 1942-44, USAF, 1944-45. Recipient Presdl. Sports award (Rifle), 1977; nominated to Nat. Inventors Hall of Fame, 1979. Mem. Nat. Rifle Assn. (life), High Rock Lake Assn. Democrat. Baptist. Club: Eagle Coin (charter). Inventor daul tire cutting machine; patentee in field. Home: 1 Harb Dr Lexington NC 27292 Office: 8 Conrad St Lexington NC 27292

HARBERT, HUGH PARKER, III, soil scientist; b. Lubbock, Tex., Aug. 26, 1946; s. Hugh P. and May Jean (Faulkner) H.; B.S. in Agronomy, Tex. Tech. U., 1973; M.S. in Soil Sci., Colo. State U., 1975; m. Lou C. Wulfjen, June 26, 1971. Technician, Soil Physics Research Group, Tex. A&M U. Research and Extension Center, Lubbock, 1967-73; grad. research asst. dept. agronomy Colo. State U., Fort Collins, 1973-75, research asso. disturbed land research group Colo. State U., 1975-77; research asso. Tex. Agrl. Expt. Sta., Tex. A&M U. Research and Extension Center, Lubbock, 1977-79; soil scientist surface mining and reclamation div. R.R. Commn. Tex., Austin, 1980; mined reclamation specialist/soil scientist Central & S.W. Services, Inc., Dallas, 1980—; tour adv. to Pres. Ford on disposal of spent oil shale, Anvil Points Oil Shale Facilities, 1975; mem. Pres. Carter's oil shale adv. panel on Terrestrial Effects of Oil Shale Devel., 1978. Served with USN, 1964-67. Cert. Soil Scientist. Mem. Soil Sci. Soc. Am., Am. Soc. Agronomy, Soil Conservation Soc. Am., Soc. Range Mgmt., AAAS, Sigma Xi, Alpha Zeta. Republican. Episcopalian. Contbr. articles on soil sci. to sci. jours. Home: 620 Glenwood Trail Forney TX 75126 Office: 2700 One Main Pl Dallas TX 75250

HARBIN, WAYNE DEWITT, mfg. co. exec.; b. Donna, Tex., Apr. 29, 1925; s. Jesse Mathuews and Lela (Bettes) H.; B.B.A., U. Tex., 1949; grad. Advanced Mgmt. Program, Harvard, 1962; m. Elinor Victoria Tolish, Apr. 17, 1946; children—Kenneth Wayne, Richard Wayne. With Arthur Young & Co., C.P.A.'s, N.Y.C. and Houston, 1949-68, adminstrv. partner, 1959-68; pres., chmn. bd. Marathon Mfg. Co., fabricated metal products, Houston, 1968-73; pres., chmn. bd., chief exec. officer Richmond Tank Car Co., 1973—; dir. Crutcher Resources Corp., Houston, 1971—. Mem. adv. council U. Tex. Bus. Sch., 1963—, also mem. chancellor's com.; mem. pres.'s council U. Baylor. Served with USN, 1942-46. Recipient Distinguished Alumni award U. Tex. Bus. Sch. Mem. Tex. Soc. C.P.A.'s, Am. Inst. C.P.A.'s. Baptist. Mason. Clubs: River Oaks Country, Petroleum, Coronado (Houston); Harvard Business (Cambridge, Mass.). Home: 3994 Inverness St Houston TX 77019 Office: 1700 W Loop St Suite 1500 Houston TX 77027

HARBORDT, CHARLES MICHAEL, forest products co. exec.; b. Houston, Apr. 8, 1942; s. Charles and Mary Lydia (Shumard) H.; B.S., Stephen F. Austin U., Nacogdoches, Tex., 1963; M.S., So. Methodist U., Dallas, 1965; Ph.D. (Grad. fellow), Tex. A. and M. U., College Station, 1970; m. Jackie Ruth Ward, June 23, 1960; children—Michelle, Katherine, Julie. Asso. chemist, then sr. chemist Texaco, Inc., Bellaire, Tex., 1965-71; dir. environ. control Temple Industries, Inc., Diboll, Tex., 1971-75; dir. environ. affairs Temple-Eastex, Inc., Diboll, 1975—. Vice pres. United Fund Angelina County, Tex., 1976; pres. Diboll Jaycees, 1972, dir., 1974; mem. adminstrv. bd. First Meth. Ch., 1979-82. Robert A. Welch fellow, 1963-65, 70. Mem. TAPPI, Tex. Forestry Assn. (dir. 1978—), Air Pollution Control Assn., Am. Bd. Products Assn., Water Pollution Control Fedn., Angelina Ducks Unltd. (dir. 1979—), Angelina County C. of C. (chmn. bus. com. 1979), Phi Kappa Phi, Phi Lambda Upsilon. Methodist. Clubs: Masons, Tex. A. and M. (v.p. 1975-76). Contbr. articles to profl. jours. Home: 708 Lazy Ln Lufkin TX 75901 Office: PO Drawer N Diboll TX 75941

HARDEE, BILLIE CHARLENE, nurse, hosp. ofcl.; b. Williamson County, Tex., July 26, 1934; d. Robert Newton Gaines and Madge Leola (Fisher) Gaines Neal; student Huston-Tillotson Coll., Austin, 1952-58; L.V.N., Sid Peterson Sch. Vocat. Nurses, 1967; m. Raymond Julius Hardee, Aug. 20, 1958: children—Julius Earl, Todd Ray, Lateesha Charlene. With Sid Peterson Meml. Hosp., Kerrville, Tex., 1962—, head nurse central service, 1970—. Mem. Alpha Kappa Alpha. Methodist. Club: Home Demonstrators Civic. Home: 320 Pearl St Kerrville TX 78028 Office: Sid Peterson Meml Hosp 710 Water St Kerrville TX 78028

HARDEE, JOHN NORTON, outdoor advt. co. exec.; b. Loris, S.C., July 19, 1947; s. Leston V. and Thelma M. (Brown) H.; student U. S.C., 1966-67. Salesman, Combined Ins. Co. Am., 1970; salesman electric div. Tyson & Co., Myrtle Beach, S.C., 1970-71, leasing agt., outdoor div., 1971-73, mgr., Walterboro, S.C., 1973-74, mgr., Florence, S.C., 1974-78; v.p. Creel Outdoor Advt., Inc., Florence, 1978—. Mem. adv. bd. Boy Scouts Am., Horry County, 1971-72; adv. bd. Salvation Army, Florence, vice chmn., 1980-81; mem. adv. bd. Pee Dee Regional Nutrition Program for Elderly, chmn., 1979-80. Served with U.S. Army, 1967-69. Mem. Am. Legion (1st vice comdr. Loris post 41, 1971), Walterboro Jaycees (treas.). Baptist. Club: Lions (Pres.'s award 1978)(Florence). Home: 1402 S Lakeside Dr Florence SC 29501 Office: PO Box 3985 Florence SC 29502

HARDEE, LAURANCE ASHLEY, savs. and loan exec.; b. Madison, Fla., Sept. 18, 1950; s. James Edward and Ashley Fraleigh H.; A.A., Oxford Coll. of Emory U., 1970; B.S., Fla. State U., 1972; m. Faye Hollingsworth, Feb. 17, 1973; 1 dau., Kimberly. Exec. sec. Greater Madison County C. of C., Madison, 1972-73; v.p. 1st Fed. Savs. and Loan Assn., Perry, Fla., 1973-78; asst. v.p. Freedom Fed. Savs. and Loan Assn., Panama City Beach, Fla., 1978-79; exec. v.p., mng. officer Security Fed. Savs. and Loan Assn., Panama City, 1979—. Treas., 1st Meth. Ch., 1978. Mem. Inst. Fin. Edn., Fla. Savs. and Loan League, Nat. Assn. Home Builders, Panama City Bay County Homebuilders Assn., Bay County C. of C. Democrat. Clubs: Lions, Beach Businessmen's Assn., Elks, Jaycees. Home: 4405 Pine Tree Rd Lynn Haven FL 32444 Office: 800 Harrison Ave Panama City FL 32401

HARDEN, DAVID THEODORE, city adminstr.; b. Ft. Pierce, Fla., Nov. 11, 1942; s. Charles D. and Mary Ealnor (Caraway) H.; B.A., Emory U., 1964; M.C.P., Ga. Inst. Tech., 1968; m. Andrea Lea Koleda, June 10, 1972; children—Jeremy Whitfield, Charles David. Planner III, Orange County (Fla.), 1971-74; city planner City of Winter Park (Fla.), 1974-77, city mgr., 1977—; chmn. Orlando (Fla.) Urban Area Transp. Tech. Com., 1974-77. Served with USN, 1967-71; Vietnam. Decorated Navy Achievement medal; Mellon fellow, 1965-67. Mem. Am. Inst. Cert. Planners, Internat. City Mgmt. Assn., Fla. City and County Mgmt. Assn., Fla. Planning and Zoning Assn. (v.p. Central Fla. chpt. 1977), Naval Res. Assn. Baptist. Club: Rotary (Winter Park). Office: 401 Park Ave S Winter Park FL 32789

HARDEN, DOYLE BENJAMIN, import-export co. exec.; b. Banks, Ala., Oct. 15, 1935; s. J.C. and Gladis C. (Romine) H.; student pub. schs.; m. Bertha Garcia, Oct. 7, 1975; 1 child by previous marriage—Janet Denice. Salesman, Gordon Foods, Atlanta, 1955-64; pres. Kwik Shop Markets, Columbus, Ga., 1964-73, Exportaciones Chico, S.A., Juarez, Mex., 1973-76, Chico Arts, El Paso, Tex., 1976—, Transp. Interoceanica, S.A., Honduras, C.Am., 1975—. Office: 1045 Humble Dr El Paso TX 79915

HARDEN, JIMMIE WALTER, hosp. adminstr.; b. Kimberly, Ala., Apr. 11, 1928; s. Walter Harry and Hattie Snow (Hughes) H.; student U. Ala., 1953-55, Jacksonville U., 1955, U. North Fla.; m. Carley Jeanette Caradine, Feb. 20, 1953; 1 dau., Deborah Jean. Head bookkeeper Birmingham Trust Nat. Bank, 1946-48, 50; cost and prodn. controller U.S. Steel Co., Fairfield, Ala., 1951-53; sales account exec. U.S. Pipe & Foundry, Birmingham, Ala., 1953-55; chief acct. Presdl. Ins. Co., Jacksonville, Fla., 1955-57; auditor Fla. State Prison, Raiford, 1958-61; controller, asst. adminstr. Baptist Meml. Hosp., Jacksonville, Fla., 1961-73; asso. adminstr. Bapt. Med. Center, Jacksonville, 1973—. Treas., bd. dirs. Duval Assn. Retarded Citizens, 1967-75; bd. dirs. Leukemia Soc. Am., 1977—. Served with U.S. Army, 1948-51. Fellow Am. Coll. Hosp. Adminstrs.; mem. Hosp. Fin. Mgmt. Assn. (advanced mem., pres. Fla. chpt. 1969-70), N.E. Fla. Hosp. Council. Democrat. Baptist. Club: Masons. Home: 1122 Marco Pl Jacksonville FL 32207 Office: 800 Prudential Dr Jacksonville FL 32207

HARDEN, JOHN WILLIAM, publicist; b. Graham, N.C., Aug. 22, 1903; s. Peter Ray and Nettie Cayce (Abbott) H.; A.B., U. N.C., 1927; m. Josephine Holt, June 13, 1928 (dec. 1951); children—Glenn Abbott, John William, Holmes Plexico and Mark Michael (twins), Jonathan Holder; m. 2d, Sarah Plexico, Oct. 5, 1953. Circulation mgr., advt. mgr. Burlington (N.C.) Daily Times-News, 1922, editor Graham news dept., 1922; classified advt. mgr. Raleigh (N.C.) News and Observer, 1923; with U. N.C. News Bur., Chapel Hill, 1923-28; reporter, columnist Charlotte (N.C.) News, 1928-37; news editor Salisbury (N.C.) Evening Post, 1937-44, Greensboro (N.C.) Daily News, 1944; pvt. sec. Gov. R. Gregg Cherry, Raleigh, 1945-48; state campaign mgr. U.S. Senator William B. Umstead, 1948; dir. public relations Burlington Industries, Greensboro, 1948-58, asst. v.p., 1948, v.p., 1949-58; public relations counselor and cons. John Harden Asso., Greensboro, 1958—; dir. public relations Cannon Mills Co., Kannapolis, N.C., 1972-73, asst. to pres., 1973-74; v.p., dir. Rowan Corp., Salisbury, N.C., 1970—. Mem.-at-large Greensboro council Boy Scouts Am., 1958; mem. visitors com. Guilford Coll., 1969; bd. dirs., mem. exec. com. Episcopal Home for Aging, 1964; bd. dirs. N.C. Bus. Found., 1970, Carolina Regional Theatre, 1975, N.C. Historic Preservation Soc.; trustee Crossnore (N.C.) Sch., 1970. Recipient Charlotte Public Relations Soc. Infinity award, 1977. Mem. Greensboro C. of C., Public Relations Soc. Am., Gen. Alumni Assn. U. N.C. (pres. 1955). Democrat. Episcopalian. Clubs: Greensboro City, Rotary (dir. 1948, pres. 1960-61, dist. gov. 1962-63), Greensboro Country, Carolina Motor (dir. 1975, exec. com. 1976), Grandfather Golf and Country (dir. 1971-74), Grandfather Mt. Lake (pres. 1972-73), Linville Golf. Author: Alamance County: Economic and Social, 1928; The Devil's Tramping Ground and Other North Carolina Mystery Stories, 1949; Tar Heel Ghosts, 1954; North Carolina Roads and Their Builders, 1966; Cannon, 1977; contbr. articles to profl. jours. Home: 2700 Twin Lake Dr Greensboro NC 27407 Office: PO Box 21408 Greensboro NC 27420

HARDESTY, GEORGE RAYMOND, dept. store exec.; b. Memphis, Tenn., Sept. 13, 1936; s. Gabriel Leonard and Zada Mae H.; Mech. Engrng. Technician, State Tech. Inst., Memphis, 1978; m. Ester Lillian Olive, Mar. 18, 1960; children—Wendy Michel, David Alan, Heather Lynn. Broadloom carpet sewer Sears Roebuck & Co., Memphis, 1954-56, customer goods repairer, 1956-58, maintenance electrician, 1962-68, asst. bldg. mgr., 1968-73, bldg. mgr., Jacksonville, Fla., 1973—. Served with U.S. Army, 1958-61. Mem. Bldg. Owners and Mgrs. Assn. Lutheran. Club: Kiwanis (v.p.) (North Jacksonville, Fla.). Home: 10459 Tulsa Rd Jacksonville FL 32218 Office: 1 Imeson Park Blvd Jacksonville FL 32297

HARDEWAY, GRANT ULYSESS, SR., lawyer; b. Houston, Sept. 15, 1945; s. Arthur R. and Flora Dell (Gaynor) H.; B.B.A., Tex. So. U., 1969, J.D., 1973; m. Verna Mae Boatner, Dec. 17, 1965; children—Grant Ulysess, Gabrielle Uyvette, Gretchen Undria. Acct., IBM, Greencastle, Ind., 1966, systems operator, Houston, 1966-67, asso. programer Houston Sci. Project, 1968-72; supr. Houston Data Center, 1972-74; admitted to Tex. bar, 1973, U.S. Supreme Ct. bar, 1976; individual practice law, Houston, 1973—. Dir. Tex. So. U. Ex Student Assn.; active Houston Legal Found. Recipient Congressional cert. appreciation, 1964. Mem. Houston Jr., Houston bar assns., Nat., Tex. (dir.), Houston assns. criminal def. lawyers, Am. Trial Lawyers Assn. Home: 9630 Highmeadow St Houston TX 77063 Office: 202 Travis Suite 222 Houston TX 77002

HARDIMAN, RICHARD LAWRENCE, former oil co. ofcl.; b. Cheviot, Ohio, May 16, 1912; s. Randolph Lawrence and Bertha Celesta (Henderson) H.; A.A., Ashland Jr. Coll., 1948; B.S., Morehead State U., 1972; m. Ella Louise Stafford, May 18, 1941; children—Jane (Mrs. Charles E. Patterson), Martha (Mrs. George M. Prout). With Ashland Oil, Inc. (Ky.), 1933-77, tech. ser. engr. product application dept., 1958-77. Served with USNR, 1944-46; PTO. Mem. Am. Soc. Lubrication Engrs. (chmn. 1974-75), Soc. Automotive Engrs., Presbyterian (deacon 1955-57, treas. 1955-57, 69-70, ruling elder 1959-61, 64-66, 74-76, trustee 1965—). Home: 108 Bellefonte Dr Ashland KY 41101

HARDIN, GEORGE CECIL, JR., petroleum cons.; b. Oakwood, Tex., Oct. 6, 1920; s. George Cecil and Pearl (Moore) H.; B.S. in Geology and Petroleum Engring., Tex. A. and M. U., 1941; Ph.D. in Geology (Van Hise fellow 1941), U. Wis., 1942; m. Virginia Howard, Nov. 21, 1942; children—George Howard, Susan. Mining engr. Victory Fluorspar Mine, Cave in Rock, Ill., 1942; geologist U.S. Geol. Survey, 1942-45, party chief, 1944-45; geologist Carter Gragg Oil Co., Palestine, Tex., 1945-46; geologist, petroleum engr. M. T. Halbouty Cons. Firm, Houston, 1946-51; exploration and prodn. mgr. M.T. Halbouty Oil and Gas Interests, Houston, 1951-59, gen. mgr., 1959-61; exec. v.p. Halbouty Alaska Oil Co., 1957-61, gen. mgr., 1959-61, dir., 1957—; partner Hardin and Hardin, cons. geologists, Houston, 1961-65; mgr oil and gas exploration Kerr-McGee Oil Ind., Inc., 1964-65; v.p. N.Am. Oil & Gas Exploration, 1965-67; v.p. oil, gas and mineral exploration, Kerr-McGee Argentina, 1967-68, Kerr-McGee Can., Ltd., 1967-68, Kerr-McGee Australia, Ltd., 1967-68; pres. Royal Resources Corp., 1968-70; pres. Ada Exco; v.p. Ada Oil Exploration Co., 1970-71; pres. Ashland Exploration Co., 1971-80; sr. v.p. Ashland Oil, Inc., 1971-80; dir. Allied Bank of Tex., Houston, 1956-77, mem. exec. com., 1956-62, chmn. auditing com., 1962—; dir. North Side State Bank, Houston; owner Poverty Ridge Farm, Okla. City, 1966—. Registered profl. engr., Tex., Okla. Fellow Geol. Soc. Am., AAAS; mem. Houston Geol. Soc. (pres. 1961-62), Soc. Econ. Paleontologists and Mineralogists, New Orleans, South Tex. geol. socs., Gulf Coast Assn. Geol. Socs. (pres. 1959), Am. Assn. Petroleum Geologists (sec.-treas. 1964-66; chmn. house dels. 1971-72), Soc. Exploration Geophysicists Am. Inst. Profl. Geologists. Clubs: Petroleum (dir. 1956-58), Terra (dir. 1958-59); Brazos River Hunting and Fishing (dir. 1961-64), Columbia Lakes Country (West Columbia, Tex.); River Oaks Country, Plaza (Houston). Author articles in field. Home: 204 Arborway Houston TX 77057 Office: 1115 Barkdull Houston TX 77006

HARDIN, JAMES NEAL, educator; b. Nashville, Tenn., Feb. 17, 1939; s. James N. and Ina M. (Anderson) H.; A.B., Washington and Lee U., 1960; postgrad. U. Berlin (Fulbright scholar), 1960-61; Ph.D., U. N.C., 1967. Instr., U. N.C., Chapel Hill, 1961-67; prof. German lit., U. S.C., Columbia, 1969—. Served to capt. Field Artillery, U.S. Army, 1967-69. Recipient Alexander von Humboldt award, 1974-75. Mem. Modern Lang. Assn. of Am., Am. Assn. of Tchrs. of German, S. Atlantic Modern Lang. Assn., Am. Soc. for German Lit. of the 16th and 17th Centuries, Internationaler Verein fuer Germanistik. Author: Die Heilige Johanna, 1975; editor Der Verliebte Oesterreicher, 1977; contbr. articles on German Lit. to jours. and mags. Home: 132 Norse Way Columbia SC 29206 Office: Dept of Foreign Languages Univ South Carolina Columbia SC 29208

HARDIN, JAMES THOMAS, coal co. exec.; b. Paintsville, Ky., Feb. 18, 1951; s. Sheldon Arthur and Helen (Pinson) H.; B.B.A., Eastern Ky. U., 1972; m. Henrietta Adkins, July 20, 1974; 1 dau., Russella. Banquet dir Holiday Inns, Lexington, Ky., 1973-74; equipment operator Yankee Clipper Mining Co., Inez, Ky., 1974-75; adminstrv. mgr. Pontik Coal Corp., Lovely, Ky., 1975—. Mem. Big Sandy Mining Inst., Ky Coal Assn., Martin County Jr. C. of C. (pres. 1975). Republican. Club: Coal Country Bassers (pres. 1979). Home: Box 96D Route 5 Inez KY 41224 Office: Box 57 Lovely KY 41231

HARDIN, LUCILE (MRS. SIDNEY LANIER HARDIN), book reviewer; b. Fate, Tex., Sept. 26, 1899; d. Thomas Preston and Ina Pearl (Davidson) McGraw; student So. Meth. U., 1919-20, 36, 50, U. Dallas, 1959-60; m. J. B. Hill, Sept. 26, 1920 (dec. 1949) children—Peggy Lucille (Mrs. John C. Taylor), J.B., Joy Hill (Mrs. Charles Flach), Martha (Mrs. Tommy Prince), Thomas, David; m. 2d, Sidney Lanier Hardin, Aug. 31, 1957. Profl. reviewer books for book clubs, civic clubs and pubs., 1949—. Mem. Delphians, Dallas Story League, Internat. Platform Assn., Bus. and Profl. Women's Club. Baptist. Rebekah, Maccabees; mem. Order Eastern Star. Office: 6362 Malcolm St Dallas TX 75214

HARDIN, ROBERT SCOTT, ins. exec.; b. Ft. Worth, Mar. 4, 1917; s. John Alpha Scott and Gela Laura (Galiher) H.; C.L.U., Am. Coll., 1974; m. Josephine Myers, Apr. 2, 1966; children—Kathleen, Lynne, John, Christopher, Heidi, Mark. With S. H. Kress Co., Tulsa and Sapulpa, Okla., Anaheim, Calif., 1935-50; pres. Henson Hardin Shoes, Oklahoma City and Temple, Tex., 1950-61; C.L.U., registered rep. Phoenix Cos., Oklahoma City, 1962—. Served to maj. U.S. Army, 1941-46. Mem. Nat. Assn. Life Underwriters, Oklahoma City Assn. Life Underwriters, Oklahoma City Estate Planning Council, Nat. Assn. Security Dealers, Phoenix Hall of Fame. Republican. Episcopalian. Club: Phoenix Pres.'s. Home: 5024 NW 19 Ter Oklahoma City OK 73127 Office: 4201 N Classen St Oklahoma City OK 73118

HARDIN, SIDNEY LANIER, lawyer, lectr., commentator; b. Prairie Hill, Tex., Nov. 16, 1894; s. Lee P. and Clementine (Mitchell) H.; grad. Sam Houston State Coll., 1914; student U. Tex., summers 1914-19; Columbia U. seminar, 1920; U. Calif. at Berkeley, seminars, 1921-22, U. Tex. Law Sch., summer 1929; m. Lucille Mason, Oct. 12, 1935 (dec.); children—Sidney Lee, Margaret Francis, John C.; m. 2d, Lucile Hill. Supt. city schs., Mission, Tex., 1917-32; admitted to Tex. bar, 1930; dist. atty., Edinburg, Tex., 1932-35; pvt. practice law, Edinburg, 1935—; city atty., Edinburg, 1950-54, radio commentator covering Southwestern States, 1940—; lectr., after-dinner speaker, 1924—; coordinator incentive export program U.S. Dept. Agr., Tex. Citrus Industry and European Importers Tex. Citrus Fruit. Polit. speaker nat. campaigns, 1940—; mem. speakers staff of Lifeline Seminars, N.C., Washington. Mem. nat. adv. bd. Am. Security Council. Bd. dirs. Jackson-Todd Meml. Cancer Found., San Antonio. Recipient Congress of Freedom Liberty award Alcalde of San Antonio (hon. mayor for life), 1963; Silver medal award S.A.R.; George Washington Honor Medal award Freedoms Found., 1970; Gold plaque Tex. Citrus Growers and Shippers, 1976. Mem. Inter-Am. Bar Assn., State Bar Tex., Internat. Platform Assn., U.S.C. of C. Democrat. Baptist. Rotarian (gov. 47th dist., hon. life mem.). Home: 121 Austin Blvd Edinburg TX 78539 Office: First State Bank Bldg Edinburg TX 78539

HARDING, DELORES ARAMENTA, educator; b. Norfolk, Va., June 8, 1923; d. Birt Brown and Devetta Wills Brown; student Va. State Coll., 1941-43; B.A. Va. Union U., 1945; M.Ed., U. Va., 1972; m. June 25, 1947; children—Carolyn, Beverly, Phylicia, Milton, Junior. Tchr. English public schs., Farmville, Va., 1945-47, Victoria, Va., 1955-57, 66-76; tchr. grade 4, Kenbridge (Va.) Grade Sch., 1957-66; instr. in English, Va. State U., Petersburg, 1976—; chmn. vis. com. for English, Va. Dept. Edn. Recipient Leader's award 4-H Club, 1968. Mem. Nat. Council Tchrs. English, Va. Assn. Tchrs. English, Coll. Lang. Assn., South Atlantic MLA, NEA, Va. Edn. Assn., Va. State U. Edn. Assn. (faculty rep.). Baptist. Club: Order Eastern Star (past worthy matron chpt.). Editor: Voices Above the Appomattox, 1979. Office: PO Box 484 Va State U Petersburg VA 23803

HARDING, EDWARD LLOYD, real estate broker; b. Washington, N.C., Feb. 22, 1953; s. Henry Champion and Dorothy Ann (Lloyd) H.; B.S., Atlantic Christian Coll., 1976. Spl. rep. Pilot Life Ins. Co., Washington, 1977—. Fund raising chmn. Beaufort County Heart Fund, 1976-77. Mem. Washington Jr. C. of C. (Presdl. award of Honor, 1976-77, dir. 1977-78, sec. 1979-80). Democrat. Episcopalian. Home: 615 Bank St Washington Park Washington NC 27889 Office: 107 Union Dr Suite 102 Washington NC 27889

HARDINGE, BYRON CANTINE, engring. co. exec.; b. Albany, N.Y., Feb. 8, 1921; s. Harlowe and Florence Cummings (Donnelly) Hardinge; student U. Pa., 1948-53, U. Mo.-Rolla, 1955-57; m. Alberta Conner, Mar. 1961. Asst. prodn. mgr. York Shipley Inc., York, Pa., 1945-48; devel. engr. Hardinge Co. Inc., York, 1948-55, now dir.; chief metallurgist Dresser Minerals Co., Houston, 1957-61; metall. cons. 1961-64; dept. mgr. engring. Brown & Root Inc., Houston, 1964—. Served with USAAF, 1942-45. Registered profl. engr., Calif., N.H., N.B., Can. Mem. N.Y. Acad. Scis., Am. Soc. Safety Engrs., Am. Inst. Mining, Metall. and Petroleum Engrs., Am. Inst. Chem. Engrs., Nat., Tex., Calif. socs. profl. engrs., Houston Engring. and Sci. Soc., Theta Xi. Clubs: El Dorado Country, Briar. Contbr. articles in mineral processing field to profl. publs. Home: 7603 Skyline Dr Houston TX 77063 Office: PO Box 3 Houston TX 77001

HARDISON, ROBERT RAY, mech. engr.; b. New Bern, N.C., Oct. 4, 1940; s. Curtis Ray and Addie Lee (Bennett) H.; B.S., Old Dominion U., 1967, M.B.A., 1979; m. Sharon Stewart, June 15, 1973; 1 dau., Jennifer Brandy. Engr., Newport News Shipbuilding Co. (Va.), 1967-69, sr. staff supr., 1969, mgr. nondestructive testing sect., 1969-73, mgr. nondestructive testing dept., 1973—. Profl. engr. Mem. Am. Soc. Nondestructive Testing (dir., vice chmn. coms., level III certification), ASTM (vice chmn. com.), Theta Xi. Home: 2452 Eastchester Dr Virginia Beach VA 23454 Office: 4101 Washington Ave Dept X03 Newport News VA 23607

HARDMAN, PATRICIA KIRVEN, sch. adminstr., researcher; b. Florence, S.C., May 6, 1944; d. Wilds Wallace and Stella (Davis) Kirven; B.S., U. S.C., M.Ed., The Citadel, 1976; Ph.D., Walden U., 1980. Tchr., Dentsville High Sch., 1st Bapt. High Sch., 1966-69; dir. Reading Clinic Charleston (S.C.), 1969-72; founder, headmistress Trident Acad., Mt. Pleasant, S.C., 1970-72; founder, dir. Reading Research Found. S.C., 1972—, Woodland Hall Academics, Mt. Pleasant, Tallahassee and Maitland, Fla., Macon and Albany, Ga., 1972—; founder, pres. Dyslexia Research Inst., Laurel Oak, 1977; academic adminstr. Killearn Acad., Tallahassee, 1978—; cons., learning disabilities Crestwood Hall, N.C., 1975—. Recipient Danforth award, 1962. Mem. Orton Soc., Am. Personnel and Guidance Assn., Internat. Reading Assn. Presbyterian. Author profl. publs. in field. Home: Route 1 Box 25 Maitland FL 32751

HARDWICK, CHARLES SIDNEY, univ. adminstr.; b. Lubbock, Tex., Oct. 27, 1931; s. Paul Moore and Ida Mae (Dunwoody) H.; B.A., Tex. Technol. Coll., 1952, M.A., 1959; Ph.D., U. Tex., Austin, 1967; m. Carlyn Sue Haynie, Mar. 12, 1954; children—Kem, Kay, Karen. With Lubbock Savs. and Loan Assn., 1954-60; mem. faculty Tex. Tech. U., Lubbock, 1960—, v.p. acad. affairs, 1976—. Served with U.S. Army, 1952-54. Mem. Am. Assn. Higher Edn., Charles S. Peirce Soc., Southwestern Philos. Soc. Author: Semiotic and Significs: The Correspondence Between Charles S. Peirce and Victoria Lady Welby, 1977. Home: 6205 Indiana Lubbock TX 79413 Office: PO Box 4609 Tech Station Lubbock TX 79409

HARDWICK, CHARLES VINCENT, judge; b. Kinsale, Va., Sept. 1, 1910; s. Vincent Branson and Willie (Unruh) H.; student U. Va., 1929-32; LL.B., George Washington U., 1937; m. Mary Elizabeth McBirney, July 3, 1937; children—Charles Vincent, Ann McBirney; m. 2d, Harriet Lowry Atwill, June 30, 1979. Admitted to Va. bar, 1937; practice law, Tappahannock, Va., 1937-58; judge, county, juvenile and domestic relations cts., Essex, Richmond and Westmoreland counties, Tappahannock, 1958-72; judge 11th Regional Juvenile and Domestic Relations Ct., 1972-73; chief judge 15th Dist. Juvenile and Domestic Relations Cts., 1973—. Served to 2d lt. inf. AUS, 1945. Mem. Va., No. Neck bar assns., Delta Upsilon. Democrat. Methodist. Lion. Club: Ruritan. Home: Hwy 17 Tappahannock VA 22560 Office: 215 Queen St Tappahannock VA 22560

HARDWICK, GALLY JEFF, JR., architect; b. Little Rock, Oct. 25, 1922; s. Gally Jeff and Charlotte Elizabeth (Barber) H.; student Ark. Poly. Coll., 1940-42, U. Ark., 1942, 46-47; m. Flo E. Parchman, May 15, 1944; children—Jeff Norman, John C. Sr. draftsman Swaim & Allen, architects, 1947-59; asso., Swaim-Allen-Wellborn & Assos., architects, Little Rock, 1959-73; partner Welborn-Hardwick-Henderson, architects, Little Rock, 1974—. Mem. Spl. Com. on Edn., North Little Rock, Ark., 1966-67. Served to maj. USAAF, 1943-46; ETO, PTO. Mem. AIA, Constrn. Specifications Inst. (dir. Little Rock chpt. 1967-70), Little Rock, North Little Rock chambers commerce. Democrat. Baptist (mem. planning com. 1970-77). Lion. Club: North Hills Country (North Little Rock, Ark.). Prin. archtl. works include Park Hill Bapt. Ch., North Little Rock, Ark., Vocational-Music Bldg. and Fine Arts Bldg., Ark. Sch. for the Blind, Little Rock, addition to St. Vincent Infirmary, Little Rock. Home: 1508 Northline Dr North Little Rock AR 72116 Office: 212 Center St Little Rock AR 72201

HARDWICK, LAWSON HUGH, III, banker; b. Nashville, Oct. 20, 1951; s. Lawson Hugh and Montelle Joyce (Carson) H.; B.A. in Music and Theology, Gateway Coll., 1973; B.B.A. in Fin. Belmont Coll., 1975; postgrad. U. Tenn., 1976-78; m. Ronda Liles, June 5, 1976. Loan officer Guaranty Mortgage Co., Nashville, 1975-76; real estate officer First Am. Nat. Bank, Nashville, 1977, asst. v.p., 1978—. Vol. worker with underprivileged children Christ Ch., 1972, Boy Scouts Am., United Way, others. Mem. Nashville Young Mortgage Bankers Assn., Nashville Mortgage Bankers Assn., Nashville Jr. C. of C., Phi Sigma Nu. Club: Lions (program chmn.). Home: 424 Ocala Ct N Nashville TN 37311 Office: First Am Nat Bank First Am Center Nashville TN 37237

HARDY, CLYDE THOMPSON, JR., med. adminstr.; b. Norfolk, Va., Nov. 10, 1917; s. Clyde Thompson and Nora (Morris) H.; B.A., U. Richmond, 1938; cert. in hosp. adminstrn. Duke U., 1941; m. Elaine Marjorie Fleischer, June 10, 1941; children—Sharon Hardy Brondos, Clyde Thompson III. Trainee, Vick Chem. Co., N.Y.C., 1938-39; asst. bus. mgr. pvt. clinic Duke Hosp., Durham, N.C., 1941; faculty Bowman Gray Sch. Medicine, Winston-Salem, N.C., 1941—, asso. dean for patient services, 1964—; dir. First Union Nat. Bank. Mem. Med. Group Mgmt. Assn. (pres. 1962-63), Am. Coll. Med. Group Adminstrs. (pres. 1972-73), Omicron Delta Kappa. Methodist. Club: Rotary (pres. 1968-69). Author: Your Roles as a Medical Assistant, 1975; contbr. articles to profl. jours. Home: 521 Buckingham Rd Winston-Salem NC 27104 Office: Bowman Gray Sch Medicine Winston-Salem NC 27103

HARDY, GERALD NEIL, tax cons.; b. Solon Mills, Ill., June 22, 1917; s. Clay Grow and Alice Effie (Reading) H.; B.S., U. Ill., 1942; M.S., U. Denver, 1948; m. Elinor Elaine Scheib, Aug. 4, 1940; children—Thomas George, Robert Gerald. Exec. dir. Tax Research Assn., Houston, 1952-54; pub. adminstrn. adviser U.S. Embassy, Rio de Janeiro, Brazil, 1954-56; dir. field service Tax Found., N.Y.C., 1956-63; tax adviser U.S. Embassy, Amman, Jordan, 1963-65; dir. field service Nat. Municipal League, N.Y.C., 1965-68; dir. univ. devel. Western Carolina U., Cullowhee, N.C., 1968-70; asst. dir. Nat. Municipal League, N.Y.C., 1970-76, field cons., 1976—; tax cons. property tax div. Alexander & Alexander, Inc., N.Y.C., 1976-77. Served with USNR, 1943-46. Recipient U.S. Meritorious Service award, Brazil, 1956. Alfred P. Sloan Found. fellow U. Denver, 1942-43. Mem. Am. Soc. Pub. Adminstrn., Govtl. Research Assn. (sec.-treas. 1974-78), Western Govtl. Research Assn. Presbyterian. Editor GRA Reporter, 1974-78. Home and office: Route 3 Box 73-A Littleton NC 27850

HARDY, JAMES B., JR., ednl. adminstr.; b. Mobile, Ala., Aug. 17, 1932; s. James B. and Hermie (Gray) H.; B.S., Tuskegee Inst., 1961; M.Ed., Temple U., 1971; postgrad. U. S.C., summers 1967, 72, 73; m. Mary Marie Richardson, Dec. 23, 1957; children—James B. IV, Jolanda Marie. Tchr. Fairwold Middle Sch., Columbia, S.C., 1961-70; adminstrv. asst. Booker T. Washington High Sch., Columbia, 1970-71; asst. prin. Alcorn Middle Sch., Columbia, 1971-77; prin. McCants Elementary Sch., Columbia, 1977—; lectr., cons. in field; field rep. Kirschner Assos., Columbia, 1974—. Chmn. sch. bd. Cardinal Newman High Sch., 1969-71; bd. dirs. St. Peters Elementary Sch., 1971-73; commr., pres. Columbia Pop Warner Jr. Football, 1973—; mem. supervisory bd. Richland County Tchrs. Fed. Credit Union, 1969-73, dir., 1977—; mem. exec. com. Richland County Democratic party, 1976—; regional dir. Cath. Youth Orgn., 1977—; mem. Central Midlands Regional Planning Council, 1979-81. Served with inf. U.S. Army, 1956-59. Mem. NEA (life), S.C., Richland County edn. assns., Richland County Adminstrs. Assn., Nat., S.C. assns. elementary sch. prins., Assn. Supervision and Curriculum Devel., Kappa Alpha Psi (Southeastern bd. 1977—), Phi Delta Kappa (pres. chpt. 1973-75). Roman Catholic (deacon). Clubs: Townsmen's (chmn. bd. 1969-73), K.C. (4 deg.). Home: 1616 Frye Rd Columbia SC 29203 Office: 3501 Lyles St Columbia SC 29201

HARDY, JAMES LEE, chemist; b. Louisville, Oct. 21, 1950; s. James F. and Margaret E. (Ramsier) H.; student U. Ky., 1968-72; B.A. in Chemistry, U. Louisville, 1975; m. Eileen Morgan, Nov. 24, 1979. Exploratory research technician Celanese Coatings & Spltys. Co., 1972-75; chemist gravure research and devel. Flint Ink Corp., New Albany, Ind., 1975-76; chemist, group leader product control Porter Paint Co., Louisville, 1976—. Lic. pvt. pilot. Mem. Louisville Soc. Coatings Tech. Home: 4303 Sunflower St Louisville KY 40216 Office: 400 S 13th St Louisville KY 40201

HARDY, PAUL JUDE, sec. of state La.; b. Lafayette, La., Oct. 18, 1942; s. Florent and Agnes (Angelle) H.; B.A., U. Southwestern La., 1965; J.D., Loyola U., New Orleans, 1966; m. Sandra Gatlin, 1965; children—Gregory Paul, Yvette Rachelle. Admitted to La. bar, 1966; mem. firm Willis & Hardy, St. Martinville, La., 1966—; mem. La. Senate, 1971-76, judiciary com., natural resources com., legislative council, drug abuse com., com. reorgn. levee dists., Atchafalaya Basin Commn., chmn. Pipeline Rt. of Way subcom.; sec. of state La., Baton Rouge, 1976—. Vice pres., Evangeline Area Guidance Soc., 1969-70; mem. Pub. Affairs Research Council, 1969—; trustee Tchrs. Retirement System, La. Sch. Employees Retirement System, Tourist Devel. Commn., La. Workmen's Compensation. Recipient Kay Man award St. Martinville Jaycees, 1970; named Outstanding Senate Newcomer, Baton Rouge (La.) State Times, 1972. Mem. Am. Bar Assn., La. Bar Assn., St. Martin Parish Bar Assn., Am. Judicature Soc., St. Martinville Jr. C. of C. (pres. 1968-69), N.R.A., U. Southwestern La. Alumni Assn., Internat. Platform Assn. Democrat. Club: K.C. (mem. council). Home: 1721 Sherwood Forest Blvd Baton Rouge LA 70815 Office: State Capitol Baton Rouge LA 70804

HARE, GEORGE ARTHUR, respiratory therapist; b. Balt., May 8, 1939; s. Carvel Albert and Nellie J. (Croft) H.; ed. U. Chgo. 1974, Sch. Med. and Respiratory Tech., 1975; P.A. certificate, 1972; R.T., 1975; m. Joann Krutz; children—Stephanie Laura, Kimberly Robyn, Roshanna Leigh. Asst. chief respiratory dept. Md. Gen. Hosp., Balt., 1962-66; internat. cons. Arthur Jennings Assn., Balt., 1962-68; mem. staff respiratory dept. Seminole Meml. Hosp., Sanford, Fla., 1970—, dir. pulmonary services, 1974—, clin. instr. respiratory therapy. Mem. Am. Assn. Physicians Assts. (nat. exec. v.p. 1977-78), Am. Thoracic Soc., Am. Assn. Respiratory Therapy, Am. Heart Assn., Muscular Dystrophy Assn. Am. (past mem. exec. bd.), Am. Lung Assn., Internat. Union Against Tb, Profl. Photographers Am., Internat. Platform Assn. Home: 508 Satsuma Dr Sanford FL 32771 Office: Seminole Meml Hosp 1101 E 1st St Sanford FL 32771

HARE, ROBERT LEE, JR., evangelist; b. McKinney, Tex., Jan. 12, 1920; B.A., Harding Coll., Searcy, Ark., 1950, M.A., 1956; m. Ruth Bradley, June 4, 1949; children—Reggy Lynn Hare Hiller, Mary Lee, Linda Jean. Served Chs. of Christ in Ark., 1946-50; missionary, Munich, Ger., 1950-55; 1st missionary to Salzburg (Austria), 1952-55, Vienna, 1956-73, Yugoslavia, 1958, Czechoslovakia, 1960, Hungary, 1960, E. Ger., 1961, Poland, 1962, Bulgaria, 1964, Romania, 1964; asst. to pres. European Christian Coll., 1979—. a co-organizer Ch. of Christ, Wiener Neustadt, Austria, 1974; mem. Com. Furtherance and Preservation Religious Freedom in Austria, 1973—. Home: 411 E Vine St Searcy AR 72143 also Schrattensteingasse 50 A-2700 Wiener Neustadt Austria

HARE, WILLIAM CLEVELAND, III, ins. co. exec.; b. Plainfield, N.J., Aug. 11, 1943; s. William Cleveland and Dorothy Elizabeth (Higgins) H.; B.S. in History, Polit. Sci., Spring Hill Coll., Mobile, Ala., 1966; m. Mary Catherine Shea, Aug. 26, 1966; children—William Michael, Laura Elizabeth. Div. supr. Allstate Ins. Co., Sacramento, 1971-73, San Diego, 1973-74; dir. policyholder services Res. Life Ins. Co., Dallas, 1974—. Treas., Pioneer Cemetery Assn., Plano, Tex., 1979—; Eucharistic minister St. Elizabeth Seton Ch., Plano, 1976-78, chmn. fin. com., 1976—. Served with USAF, 1966-71. Mem. Life Office Mgmt. Assn., Southwest Ins. Assn., Am. Mgmt. Assn., Tex. Policyholders Service Assn. Home: 2621 Winfield Dr Plano TX 75023 Office: 403 S Akard St Dallas TX 75202

HAREN, JAMES HARRISON, bus. exec.; b. Denton, Tex., Mar. 25, 1935; s. William Harrison and Effie E. (Jones) H.; B.S., Va. Poly. Inst. and State U., 1955; M.A., N.Mex. State U., 1968; postgrad. Tex. Tech. U., 1958-59; children—James Harrison II, David M., Susan J., Jeffrey W., Gregory P., Jamie L. Tchr., coach Washington Lee High Sch., Arlington, Va., 1958-60; pres. Safe Baby Products Co., Washington and Pitts., 1960-72; pres. Internat. Inventors, Inc. East, Alexandria, Va., 1972—; pres. Internat. Bartending Inst., Alexandria, 1977—. Served with U.S. Army, 1956-58. Mem. Va. Assn. Pvt. Career Schs., Better Bus. Bur., Washington C. of C. Home: 3701 S George Mason Dr Falls Church VA 22041 Office: 4900 Leesburg Pike Alexandria VA 22302

HARGER, GLENN RAY, assn. exec.; b. Decatur, Ala., July 20, 1947; s. Grady Lanier and Geraldine Belmont (Biles) H.; student U.S. Ala., 1965-66; grad. Ala. Police Acad., 1973; m. Gloria Annette Glenn, Aug. 24, 1968; children—Gregory Glenn, Andrea Lynn. Engring. asst. Ala. State Hwy. Dept., Mobile, 1966-71; mgr. Home Pest Control Co., Mobile, 1971-73; patrolman Prichard (Ala.) Police Dept., 1973-76; rep., lobbyist Ala. State Employees Assn., Montgomery, 1977; field rep. U.S. Jaycees, Boise, Idaho, 1977-79, tng. coordinator, Tulsa, 1979—. Mem. Jaycees (past pres. chpt., regional dir., pres. Ala. 1976-77, chmn. bd. 1977-78). Republican. Baptist. Home: 104 E Kent Ave Broken Arrow OK 74012 Office: PO Box 7 Tulsa OK 74121

HARGETT, STEPHEN ANDREW, hosp. controller; b. Memphis, Dec. 24, 1952; s. George Welch and Winifred Joan (Schadrack) H.; B.B.A., Memphis State U., 1974; student U. Ark., 1979—; m. Rebecca McGill, May 19, 1973. Acct., Baptist Meml. Hosp., Memphis, 1974-76; bus. mgr. U. Tenn. Hosp., Memphis, 1976-79, asst. controller, 1979—, rep. to Mid-South Data Council, 1978—. Mem. Hosp. Fin. Mgmt. Assn., Memphis State Bus. Alumni Assn., Memphis Jaycees (asso. dir. community and govtl. affairs 1978). Home: 247 S Reese St Memphis TN 38111 Office: 951 Court St Memphis TN 38103

HARGRODER, CHARLES MERLIN, journalist; b. Franklin, La., Sept. 5, 1926; student La. State U., 1943-47. Writer, Baton Rouge Morning Advocate, 1947-50, Monroe (La.) Morning World, 1952-53; exec. asst. to gov. La., 1953-56; public relations sec. to Congressman Hale Boggs, 1956-57; regional rep. Inter-Industry Highway Safety Com., 1957-58; writer New Orleans Times-Picayune, 1959—, polit. writer, columnist, 1961—. Served with U.S. Army, 1950-52. Republican. Methodist. Home: 10157 Runnymede Ave Baton Rouge LA 70815 Office: PO Box 44122 Capitol Station Baton Rouge LA 70804

HARGROVE, JOSEPH EARLE, ins. agt., real estate broker; b. Birmingham, Ala., Dec. 20, 1925; s. William Earle and Bonnie (Huff) H.; B.A., U. Ala., 1950; LL.B., Birmingham Sch. Law, 1959; m. Annie M. Moore, Dec. 14, 1957; children—Joey, Bonnie Ann. Grad. asst. U. Ala., 1953; mgr. mortgage loan dept. Molton Allen & Williams, Birmingham, 1960-63; spl. agt. Md. Casualty Co., State of Ala., Birmingham, 1965-68; owner Leeds Ins. and Real Estate Agy., Leeds, Ala., 1969—. Served with USNR, 1944-46. Mem. Ala. Ind. Agts. Assn., Birmingham Bd. Realtors, C. of C. (dir.). Baptist. Clubs: Civitan, Terry Walker Golf and Country. Office: 106 N 9th St Leeds AL 35094

HARGROVE, JOSEPH LEONARD, JR., lawyer; b. Beeville, Tex., May 5, 1949; s. Joseph Leonard and Martha Delacour (Dean) H.; B.A., U. Tex., 1971; J.D., La. State U., 1975; m. Nancy Katherine Green, May 22, 1971; children—Robert Green, Reginald Joseph. Admitted to La. bar, 1975; asso. firm Hargrove, Guyton, Ramey & Barlow, Shreveport, La., after 1975, now partner; dir. Kemerton Energy, Inc. Mem. Am., La., Shreveport bar assns. Republican. Episcopalian. Club: Shreveport. Home: 587 Oneonta Shreveport LA 71106 Office: PO Drawer B Shreveport LA 71161

HARITUN, ROSALIE ANN, educator; b. Johnson City, N.Y., May 30, 1938; d. George and Helen (Ternosky) Haritun; B.Mus., Baldwin-Wallace Conservatory, 1960; M.S., U. Ill., 1961; Profl. Diploma, Columbia U. 1966, Ed.D., 1968; Music tchr. Union Free Sch. Dist., Patchogue, N.Y., 1961-63, jr. high sch. instr., 1963-65; teaching fellow Columbia U. Tchrs. Coll., 1966-68; instr. music edn. Temple U. Sch. Music, 1968-71; asst. prof. music edn., clarinet instr. East Carolina U. Sch. Music, 1972—, asst. dir. summer string camp, 1976-78; adjudicator Eastern N.C. Instrumental Choral Solo and Ensemble Contests, 1973—; cons. curriculum devel. programs, N.C.; choir dir. Landmark Bapt. Ch., Greenville, N.C., 1975—; mem. Summer Sunday-in-the-Park Concert Band, 1974—. Mem. N.C. Music Educators Conf., Music Educators Nat. Conf., Sigma Alpha Iota (pres. chpt.), Pi Kappa Lambda (pres. E. Carolina U. 1977—). Democrat. Baptist. Contbr. articles to profl. jours. Home: 206 N Oak St Apt 8 Greenville NC 27834 Office: 204 Sch Music East Carolina U 10th St Greenville NC 27834

HARKEY, CATHERINE ADELE, educator, adminstr.; b. Charlotte, N.C., Jan. 7, 1949; d. Harold Walker and Rosemary Cecelia (Phelan) H.; B.A. in Spl. Edn., U. N.C., Chapel Hill, 1971; M.Ed., U. Va., 1974. Instr. learning disabled children Charlotte Country Day Sch., summer 1971; tchr. educable mentally retarded children Landsdowne Sch., Charlotte-Mecklenburg Schs., 1971-72, team tchr. enrichment program, summer 1972, coordinator model program, learning lab., 1972-73; student team tchr. S.W. Va., 1973; spl. edn. coordinator Developmental Evaluation Center, Duke U. Med. Center, 1974-77; part-time lectr. edn. Duke U., 1975—; developer, dir. Learning Devel. Center, Durham (N.C.) Acad., 1977—; pres. Orange County Assn. Children with Learning Disabilities, 1976-77, adviser, 1977—; cons. in field; chmn. conf. N.C. Assn. Children with Learning Disabilities, 1977-78, 78-79, v.p., 1979. Danforth scholar, 1967. Mem. Assn. Children Learning Disabilities, Internat. Reading Assn., Council Exceptional Children, Council Adminstrs. Spl. Edn. Roman Catholic. Home: 227 McCauley St Chapel Hill NC 27514 Office: Learning Devel Center 3130 Pickett Rd Durham NC 27705

HARKNESS, RICHARD ARTHUR, cable co. exec.; b. Jackson, Mich., Nov. 15, 1932; s. Forrest B. and Dorothy May (Alden) H.; student Data Processing Inst., 1965-66, IBM Sch., 1964; m. Jeannette Hollar, Jan. 9, 1954; 1 dau., Kathryn. Enlisted in USMC, 1952, ret., 1974; project mgr. Superior Cable Corp., Hickory, N.C., 1974-76, dir. data systems, 1976—. Decorated Navy Commendation medal. Mem. Data Processing Mgmt. Assn. Baptist. Club: Optimist. Address: PO Box 489 Hickory NC 28601

HARLAN, ARTHUR SCOTTY BYRON, merchant; b. Valparaiso, Ind., Sept. 12, 1926; s. Arthur Brian and Dorothy Fay (Shaffer) H.; B.S., Ind. U., Bloomington, 1950; m. Nancy Joan Wilhelm, July 1, 1950; children—Rebecca Scott, Toby Kay, Anthony Bradford, Eve Andrea. With Bruning div. Addressograph Multigraph, Los Angeles, 1950-67, dir. mktg., 1967; pres., chmn. bd. Scotty's Inc., Fort Lauderdale, Fla., 1969—. Served with USMC, 1944-46; PTO. Recipient George Washington award Freedom Found., Valley Forge, Pa., 1977. Republican. Unitarian. Home: 1501 E Broward Fort Lauderdale FL 33301 Office: 1102 E Las Olas Fort Lauderdale FL 33301

HARLAN, VERNIE ELIJAH, farm implement co. exec.; b. Batesville, Miss., Nov. 14, 1904; s. Luther Montgomery and Jessie Lawrence (Legge) H.; student Warren Bus. Coll., 1929, LaSalle Extension U., 1932; m. Sarah Elizabeth Watson, Oct. 15, 1933;

children—Dowell Brooks, Carolyn Drew (Mrs. Cecil Knight Province, Jr.), Ronald Kent (dec.). Prodn. clk. Bradley Lumber Co., Warren, Ark., 1923-29; payroll clk. Lee Wilson & Co., Wilson, 1929-32; office mgr. Keiser Supply Co., Keiser, 1932-37, Lee Wilson & Co., Victoria, 1937-40; treas. Missco, Inc., Osceola, Ark., 1940—, Missco Implement Co., Inc., Monette, 1951—; Missco Implement Co. of Blytheville, Inc., 1941—; registered rep. Consumer-Investor Planning Corp., St. Louis, 1960-71. Treas. Osceola chpt. ARC, 1942-45. Mem. C. of C. Osceola. Baptist (treas. 1953-66, sec. bd. deacons 1971). Clubs: Masons (32 deg.), Shriners. Home: 404 E Johnson Ave Osceola AR 72370 Office: 501 S Walnut St Osceola AR 72370

HARLESS, JAMES WARREN, univ. adminstr.; b. Charleston, W.Va., Nov. 27, 1937; s. Bernard Lewis and Grace Irene (Bradshaw) H.; B.S., Morris Harvey Coll., 1959; M.A. (NDEA fellow), Marshall U., 1962; Ed.D., Nova U., 1976; m. Harriet Ann Javins, June 19, 1959; children—Robin Lynn, Daniel Joseph. Tchr., Man (W.Va.) High Sch., 1959-63; dir. Logan (W.Va.) br. Marshall U., 1963-67; asst. dir. admissions Marshall U., Huntington, W.Va., 1967-70, dir. admissions, 1970—; mem. corp. Am. Coll. Testing Program. Named Young Man of Year, Logan Jaycees, 1966. Mem. Am., W.Va. personnel and guidance assns., Am., W.Va. (pres.) assns. collegiate registrars and admissions officers, Am. Coll. Personnel Assn. Republican. Presbyterian. Club: Optimist (pres. Huntington chpt. 1974, 79-80). Home: 40 Simpson Dr Huntington WV 25705 Office: 4th Ave and 16th St Huntington WV 25705

HARLIN, SAM HUGH, JR., diversified co. exec.; b. Nashville, Oct. 8, 1939; s. Sam Hugh and Alyne Gill H.; B.S., Athens Coll., 1965; m. Elizabeth Gregg, June 24, 1960; children—Stephen Gregg, Dana Elizabeth, Stuart Andrew. Mathematician, NASA advanced systems Brown Engring. Corp., Huntsville, Ala., 1960-64; systems engr. Sci. Data Systems, Huntsville, 1964-65, br. mgr., Dallas, 1965-66; mgr. Dallas Computing Center, Data Automation Computing Corp., 1966-71; sr. analyst Electronic Data Systems, Atlanta, 1971-72; ind. cons., Atlanta, 1972; dir. data processing services Terminal Transport Co., Atlanta, 1972-77; v.p. mgmt. systems Watking Associated Industries, Inc., Atlanta, 1977—; instr. acctg. and data processing Atlanta Tech. U., 1973; instr. DeKalb Coll., 1974. Mem. Data Processing Mgmt. Assn., Am. Trucking Assn. Mem. Ch. of Christ. Home: 1593 Bent River Dr Lilburn GA 30247 Office: 1958 Monroe Dr NE Atlanta GA 30301

HARLOW, CHARLES ALTON, educator; b. New Boston, Tex., Mar. 14, 1940; s. Aubrey and Geneva (Perry) H.; B.S. in Elec. Engring., U. Tex., 1963, Ph.D., 1967; m. Elaine Kenas, Aug. 19, 1961; children—Raelon Jil, Janda Lea. Asso. prof. elec. engring. U. Mo., 1970-72, prof., 1972-78; prof. elec. engring. La. State U., Baton Rouge, 1978—, dir. Remote Sensing and Image Processing Lab., 1978—; vis. prof. U. Calif., Berkeley, 1974. Mem. IEEE, Assn. for Computing Machinery, Sigma Xi, Tau Beta Pi, Eta Kappa Nu. Contbr. articles to profl. jours. Home: 6649 Sandstone Ave Baton Rouge LA 70808

HARLOW, RICHARD FESSENDEN, biologist; b. Boston, Dec. 16, 1919; s. William Bleakie and Harriet (Lailer) H.; B.S., U. Maine, 1947, M.S., 1948; M.S., Va. Poly. Inst., 1971; m. Margaret Findlay, Feb. 14, 1942; children—William, David, Dana. Game technician Me. Inland Fisheries and Game, Brewer, 1948-49; soil conservationist Soil Conservation Service, Ebensburg, Pa., 1950-52; asst. chief, game mgmt. div. Fla. Game and Fresh Water Fish Commn., Tallahassee, 1952-66; research wildlife biologist Southeastern Forest Exptl. Sta., U.S. Forest Service, Blacksburg, Va., 1966-75, Clemson, S.C., 1975—. Acting asso. prof. U. Fla., Gainesville, 1972. Served with USCGR, 1941-45. Mem. Sigma Xi, Phi Sigma, Kappa Sigma. Contbr. articles to profl. jours. Home: 100 Ft Rutledge Rd Clemson SC 29631 Office: Southeastern Forest Sta Dept Forestry Clemson U Clemson SC 29631

HARM, RODNEY HARRY, city ofcl.; b. Union Hill, N.J., Apr. 9, 1926; s. William and Mabel Bernardine (Paseler) H.; student Phila. Textile Inst., 1946-49, Inst. Govt., U. N.C., Chapel Hill, 1976-77, U. Nev., Las Vegas, 1978-79; m. Virginia Florence Carsley, May 8, 1947; children—Rodney Harry, David Carsley. Plant tng. dir. Burlington Industries, Greensboro, N.C., 1968-70, area tng. mgr., 1970-74, human resources research mgr., Greensboro, 1974-75; city tng. dir. City of Charlotte (N.C.), 1975—; cons. to industry; cons. S.E. U.S., CSC; vis. lectr. U. N.C. Inst. Govt. Served with USMC, 1944-46. Mem. Am. Soc. Tng. and Devel. (past pres. N.C./Va. chpt., founding pres. Piedmont chpt.), Internat. Personnel Mgrs. Assn., Am. Soc. Personnel Adminstrs. Lutheran. Home: 1501G Lansdale Dr Charlotte NC 28205 Office: 600 E Trade St City Hall Annex Charlotte NC 28202

HARMAN, JAMES WILLIAM, JR., lawyer; b. Richmond, Va., Sept. 29, 1922; s. James William and Coralie (Laird) H.; student Lynchburg Coll., 1940-41; B.S. in Bus. Adminstrn., Washington and Lee U., 1947, LL.B., 1949; m. Evelyn R. Herring, Mar. 29, 1949; children—James William III, Jonathan H.; m. 2d, Joan Brown, Dec. 6, 1972. Partner Harman & Burgess Co., Tazewell, Va., 1946—; admitted to Va. bar, 1949; since practiced law in Tazewell; partner firm Harman & Harman, 1949—; atty. Town of Tazewell, 1956-61; commonwealth's atty. Tazewell County, 1952-56; sec., treas., dir., gen. counsel Coal Creek Coal Co., Tazewell, 1951—; partner Edwards & Harman, Welch, W.Va., 1959-76; gen. counsel S.W. Va. Nat. Bank, Bluefield, 1963-76; dir. Doran Devel. Corp., 1976—, Black Diamond Savs. & Loan Co., 1977—. Recorder Town of Tazewell, 1949-51, mayor, 1961-67. Pres., bd. dirs. Tazewell Community Hosp., 1968-72. Served with AUS, 1943-46. Mem. Am., Va. (dist. com. 1957-60, chmn. 1960), Tazewell County (pres. 1960-61) bar assns., Phi Beta Kappa, Omicron Delta Kappa, Phi Delta Phi. Republican. Episcopalian. Rotarian (pres. Tazewell club 1962-63). Club: Fincastle Country. Home: Sunset Hills Tazewell VA 24651 Office: 116 W Main St Tazewell VA 24651

HARMAN, MARYANN WHITTEMORE, artist, educator; b. Roanoke, Va., Sept. 13, 1935; d. John Weed and Clifford (Kelly) Whittemore; B.A., Mary Washington Coll., 1955; M.A., Va. Poly. Inst., 1974; m. Roy Phillip Harman, July 26, 1955; children—Mary Kelly, John Whittemore, Phillip Mears. One-woman shows include: Andre Emmerich Gallery, N.Y.C., 1976, 78, Allen Rubiner Gallery, Detroit, 1977, 78, Meredith Long Gallery, N.Y.C., 1980, others; group exhbns. include: Butler Inst. of Art, Youngstown, Ohio, 1969, 72, Gallerie Ariadne, N.Y.C., 1974, 75, Southeastern Center for Contemporary Art, 1969-77, Va. Mus., 1972, 74, 75, 79, Osuna Gallery, Washington, 1979, others; represented in permanent collections: 3M Co., Phillip Morris Corp., Boston Mus. Fine Arts, Hunter Mus., Chattanooga, Am. Can.; asso. prof. art Va. Poly. Inst., 1972-76, asso. prof., 1977—. Recipient awards Hunter Mus., 1974, Va. Mus., Richmond, 1973, 74, others. Mem. Am. Fedn. Arts, Coll. Art Assn., AAUP, Va. Mus. Fine Arts, Tau Sigma Delta. Episcopalian. Home: 602 Landsdowne Dr Blacksburg VA 24060 Office: Art Dept Va Polytechnic Inst Blacksburg VA 24061

HARMON, (LOREN) FOSTER, art dealer; b. Judsonia, Ark., Nov. 5, 1912; s. Alfred Roscoe and Mae (Foster) H.; student Ind. U., 1930-32, Ohio U., 1932-33; B.A., State U. Iowa, 1935, M.F.A., 1936; m. Martha Rowles Foster, July 25, 1943. Dir. Univ. and Exptl. Theatre, Ind. U., Bloomington, 1936-42; pub. relations mgr. WKBN Broadcasting Corp., Youngstown, Ohio, 1943-48; owner, developer, dir. Pine Shores Park, Sarasota, Fla., 1950-54 v.p., dir. Players, Sarasota, 1955-57; pub. relations dir. Ringling Mus. Art, 1958-59; dir. Oehlschlaeger Galleries, Sarasota, Fla., 1961-70; v.p. Vandium Tool Co., Athens, Ohio, 1954-64; founder, owner, dir. Harmon Gallery, Naples, Fla., 1964-79, dir. emeritus, 1979—; owner, dir. Foster Harmon Galleries Am. Art, Sarasota, 1979—. Adviser, Ohio U. Collection Am. Art. Mem. Asolo Theater Angels, 1970—, Ringling Mus. Mems. Council, 1957—; adviser Fla. Artists Group Mus./Gallery, 1974—; corp. mem. Naples Community Hosp., 1966-79. Recipient Certificate of Merit, Ohio U., 1970. Mem. Am. Ednl. Theatre Assn. (founder), Am. Fedn. Arts, Sarasota Art Assn. (pres. 1959-60), Fla. League Arts, Smithsonian Inst., Archives Am. Art, Am. Fedn. Arts, St. Armands Assn. (pres. 1957-58), Internat. Platform Assn. Methodist. Clubs: Sarasota Yacht, University, Players of Sarasota. Home: PO Box 6187 Sarasota FL 33578 Office: Foster Harmon Galleries Am Art 1415 Main St Sarasota FL 33577

HARMON, FREDERICK INGERSOLL, engring. and equipment co. exec.; b. Waukesha, Wis., Feb. 15, 1923; s. John Neal and Louise (Ingersoll) H.; B.S., U. Tex., 1946; m. Marjorie Elfreda Hanna, Dec. 27, 1944; children—Scott Ingersoll, Keith Hanna, Cynthia Lynn. Process engr. Gasoline Plant Constrn. Corp., Corpus Christi, 1945-46; v.p., chief engr. Gulf Engrs., Houston, 1946-49; founder Southwestern Engring & Equipment Co., Dallas, 1949, v.p., 1949-64, owner, pres., 1964—; v.p. Hanna Devel. Co.; dir. Analytica, Inc. Judge, Sci. Fairs, 1971-80. Mem. adv. council Engring. Found., U. Tex., Austin; mem. adv. council, sci. div. Skyline Tex. Center, Dallas. Served as 2d lt. USAAF, World War II. Named Distinguished Grad. Coll. Engring., U. Tex., 1975. Registered profl. engr., Tex., N.Mex. Asso. fellow Am. Inst. Aeros. and Astronautics; mem. I.E.E.E., Inst. Environmental Scis., A.A.A.S., Nat., Tex. socs. profl. engrs., Instrument Soc. Am. Home: 1009 Waterford Dr Dallas TX 75218 Office: 6260 E Mockingbird Ln Suite 201 Dallas TX 75214

HARMON, GEORGE MARION, coll. pres.; b. Memphis, Aug. 12, 1934; s. George M. and Madie P. (Foster) H.; B.A., Southwestern U., Memphis, 1956; M.B.A., Emory U., 1957; D.B.A. (research asso. 1960-63), Harvard U., 1963; m. Bessie W. Porter, Dec. 27, 1958; children—Nancy R., Mary K., Elizabeth T., George Marion, III. Market research analyst Continental Oil Co., Houston, 1957; asst. prof. Coll. Bus. Adminstrn., dir. Salzberg Meml. Transp. Program, Syracuse (N.Y.) U., 1963-66; sr. asso. systems econs. div. Planning Research Corp., Washington, 1966-67; prof., chmn. dept. econs. and bus. adminstrn., dir. continuing edn. program in econs. and bus. adminstrn. Southwestern U., Memphis, 1967-74; prof., dean div. bus. and mgmt. W.Va. Coll. Grad. Studies, Charleston, 1974-75; prof., dean Sch. of Bus. and Mgmt., Saginaw Valley State Coll., University Center, Mich., 1975-78; pres. Millsaps Coll., Jackson, Miss., 1979—; mem. cons. staff Logistics Research, Inc., 1967—; dir. cons. staff Ramcon, Inc., 1968—; mem. faculty fin. Sch. of Banking of the South, La. State U., 1968-72; dir. Audio Visual Systems, Inc., Tenn., 1970-72; v.p., treas. Allen Industries, Inc., Tenn., 1970-72; co-founder, v.p. Computer Survey Systems, Inc., Tenn., 1972-73. Mem. bd. edn. Fayetteville-Manlius (N.Y.) Central Sch. Dist., 1961-63; trustee, chmn. personnel and labor relations com. Saginaw Osteo. Hosp., 1977-78. Served with U.S. Army, 1958-59. Mem. Acad. of Mgmt., Am. Mktg. Assn., Midwest Bus. Adminstrn. Assn., Midwest Fin. Assn., Phi Beta Kappa, Beta Gamma Sigma, Omicron Delta Kappa. Clubs: Rotary, Scenic Hills Recreation (pres. 1971-74), Jackson Country. Contbr. articles on bus. adminstrn. to profl. jours. Home: 1837 Peachtree St Jackson MS 39202 Office: 1701 N State St Jackson MS 39210

HARMON, HARVEY C., physician; b. San Antonio, Aug. 25, 1946; s. Norman Harvey and Luella (Hanshew) H.; student U. Hawaii, 1964-68; M.D., U. Tenn., 1971; m. Dorothy West, Oct. 15, 1976; children—Erich August, Laura Ashley. Resident in surgery U. Tenn., 1972-76, asst. prof. surgery, 1976—; staff cons. U. Tenn. Med. Center, City of Memphis Hosps., Memphis VA Hosp. Am. Cancer Soc. fellow. Diplomate Am. Bd. Surgery. Fellow A.C.S., Southeastern Surg. Soc.; mem. Assn. Acad. Surgeons, AMA, Memphis and Shelby County Med. Soc., Harwell Wilson Surg. Soc. (exec. sec.), Mid South Renal Transplant Assn. (asst. dir.), Omicron Delta Kappa. Home: 1481 Hollow Fork Cove Memphis TN 38138 Office: 951 Court Ave Memphis TN 38163

HARMON, JUDSON SPENCER, conservationist, ret. educator; b. Pine Knot, Ky., Oct. 9, 1904; s. John Lawrence and Minnie (Spencer) H.; diploma Eastern Ky. State Tchrs. Coll., 1924; A.B., Eastern Ky. U., 1928; M.A., U. Ky., 1969; m. Rova Henry, Apr. 13, 1924; children—Judson Spencer, John Joseph. Tchr., prin. McCreary County (Ky.) pub. schs., 1923-33; prin. Prestonsburg (Ky.) schs., 1933-34; Ky. rep. of Ginn & Co., ednl. publishers, 1934-69; instr. Cumberland Coll., Williamsburg, Ky., from 1969, ret.; chmn. McCreary County Bd. of Edn., 1970—; pres. Cumberland Green Lakes Resource Conservation and Devel.; pres. McCreary Apts. Inc. Recipient Ky. Col. award, Ky. State Tax Revision Commn., 1945-49; Dist. Service award, profl. Bookmen of Am., 1961; Ky. Statesman award, 1963; Dist. Service award, Cumberland Resource Conservation and Devel. and Commonwealth of Ky., 1974; Dist. Service award Lake Cumberland Area Devel. Dist., 1976; dist. Alumni award Eastern Ky. U., 1976. Mem. Ky. Ho. of Reps., 1934-36; mem. Senate, Ky. Gen. Assembly, 1944-48. Bd. dirs. McCreary County Farm Bur., McCreary County Conservation Dist., 1944—; McCreary County Devel. Assn., Lake Cumberland Area Devel. Dist.; mem. Baptist state bd. of missions, 1942-46. Mem. Ret. Tchrs. Assn. Republican. Mason. Home: 133 Route 1 Whitley City KY 42653

HARMON, PAUL A., educator; b. Evansville, Ind., July 12, 1935; s. Paul Adams and Georgia Helen (Colvin) H.; B.A., U. Evansville, 1967; M.S.W., Tulane U., 1970. Ordained to ministry Ch. of Christ, 1957; minister Ch. of Christ, Warrington, Fla., 1959-63; supr. Family Ct., Pensacola, Fla., 1963-67; casework supr. Youth Counsel Bur., N.Y.C., 1967-68; dir. social welfare Dillard U., New Orleans, 1970—; individual practice therapy, New Orleans, 1975—; cons. to social welfare agys. Named Youth Worker of Yr., Optimist Club, 1967. Mem. Acad. Cert. Social Workers, La. Bd. Cert. Social Workers, Council on Social Work Edn., Nat. Assn. Social Workers. Contbr. articles to profl. jours. Home: 716 Dumaine St New Orleans LA 70116 Office: Dillard U 2601 Gentilly Blvd New Orleans LA 70122

HARMON, RITA P., city ofcl.; b. Eglin AFB, Fla., Sept. 23, 1948; d. Samuel Joseph and Mildred M. (Missal) Palmetera; A.S., Amarillo Jr. Coll., 1968; B.A., Tex. Tech. U., 1970, M.Ed., 1977; m. Michael D. Harmon, July 19, 1968; 1 dau., Kimberly Anne. Instr. adult edn. Lubbock (Tex.) city schs., 1970-72; dir. fin. aid Draughon's Bus. Coll., Lubbock, 1972-73, dir., 1973-76; asst. personnel dir. City of Lubbock, 1976—; lectr. in field. Mem. pub. relations com. City of Lubbock, 1977—; mem. loan com. City of Lubbock Employees Credit Union, 1979—; vol. United Way, Lubbock, 1977—; mem. personnel com. YWCA. Named Outstanding Profl. Woman of Yr., Women in Communications, 1979. Mem. Am. Soc. Personnel Adminstrs. Roman Catholic. Home: 4416 80 St Lubbock TX 79424 Office: 916 Texas Ave Lubbock TX 79401

HARMON, SUSAN PETTY, marriage and family therapist; b. Tryon, N.C., Sept. 9, 1945; d. John Lawson and Mildred Ella (McComb) Petty; B.A., Winthrop Coll., 1967; M.S.W., Tulane U., 1969; m. John Cannon Harmon, Sept. 20, 1969; 1 son, John Cannon. Marriage and family therapist Family Service, Greensboro, N.C., 1969-75; pvt. practice marriage and family therapy, Greensboro, 1976—; supr. of grad. students in social work U. N.C., 1973-74; mem. sex edn. com. Family Life Council, Greensboro, 1973-75. Bd. dirs. Greensboro Civic Ballet, Greensboro Symphony Guild, Presbyn. Personal and Family Center, Eastern Music Festival Aux., Vols. to the Ct., Greensboro, 1973-76, Jr. League. Mem. Acad. Cert. Social Workers, Am. Assn. Marriage and Family Counselors, N.C. Group Behavior Soc., Mental Health Assn. Greensboro, Nat. Assn. Social Workers. Presbyterian. Clubs: Greensboro Country, Sherwood Swim and Racket. Address: 621 Myers Ln Greensboro NC 27408

HARMS, KENNETH IRVIN, police chief; b. Miami, Fla., June 11, 1938; s. Walter I. and Frances H. (Hudson) H.; B.A., Fla. Internat. U., 1974; M. candidate Biscayne Coll., 1980; grad. various FBI acads.; m. Magaly C. Villa, Apr. 11, 1958; children—Kenneth Charles, Paige Alison, Lisa Jean. Mem. Miami Police Dept., 1959—, capt., 1975-78, chief, 1978—. Bd. dirs. D.U.I. Countermeasures. Mem. Internat. Assn. Chiefs Police, Fla. Assn. Police Chiefs, Dade County Police Chiefs Assn. (treas. 1979), Police Found., Police Exec. Research Forum, Dade County Criminal Justice Council. Baptist. Clubs: Rotary, Tiger Bay Polit., Masons, Shriners. Office: 400 NW 2 Ave Miami FL 33128

HARMS, LOUISE IVIE (MRS. WILLARD DANIEL HARMS), librarian; b. Birmingham, Ala., June 25, 1924; d. Henry J. and Lola (Hicks) Ivie; B.S., U. Ala., 1944; B.S. in L.S., George Peabody Coll. for Tchrs., 1946; m. Willard Daniel Harms, Oct. 17, 1955; children—Dennis Leon, Daniel Lee (dec.), Willard Daniel. Asst. librarian Coll. Edn. Library, U. Ala., 1944-45; night reference asst. George Peabody Coll. Tchrs., Nashville, 1945-46; cataloger Allegheny Coll. Library, Meadville, Pa., 1946-47; 1st asst. cataloging dept. U. Ark. Library, Fayetteville, 1947; head cataloger Coll. Edn. Library, U. Ala., 1948-51; spl. services librarian U.S. Army, Europe, 1951-55, library adminstr. spl. activities div., 1958-63; tchr. English, Sweetwater (Tenn.) High Sch., 1963-64; asst. librarian Merner-Pfeiffer Library, Tenn. Wesleyan Coll., Athens, 1964-65, head librarian, 1965—. Mem. A.L.A., Southeastern, E. Tenn., Tenn. library assns., NEA, AAUP, Kappa Delta Pi, Alpha Beta Alpha. Presbyn. Home: 112 Hickory Ln Sweetwater TN 37874 Office: Tenn Wesleyan Coll Athens TN 37303

HARNED, HORACE HAMMERTON, JR., state legislator Miss.; b. State College, Miss., July 27, 1920; s. Horace Hammerton and Harriet McFarland (Rice) H.; B.S., Miss. State U., 1942; m. Nellie Jean Howell, June 19, 1949; children—Margaret Ann Harned Chandler, Helen, Alice, Horace H. Mem. Miss. Senate, 1952-56; mem. Miss. Ho. of Reps., 1960—, chmn. Univ. and Colls. com., 1964-76, chmn. Select Com. for Higher Edn., 1972-73. Served to capt. USAF, 1942-46. Recipient Women for Constl. Govt. Patriots award, 1975; named Outstanding Dairyman, 1970; recipient Outstanding Beef Cattle award, 1975. Mem. Am. Jersey Cattle Club, Miss. Cattlemens Assn., Blue Key, Omicron Delta Kappa, Kappa Sigma. Democrat. Baptist. Clubs: Rotary, Forty & Eight, Am. Legion, Farm Bur., Masons. Home: Route 1 Box 259 Starkville MS 39759

HARNER, CHARLES EMORY, editor; b. N.Y.C., Aug. 27, 1901; s. Lloyd Charles and Anna (Webster) H.; A.B., U. Ill., 1923; m. Zofia Wasilewska, July 27, 1935; 1 son, Michael James. Reporter, Hinsdale (Ill.) Doings, 1917-19, Ill. State Jour., Springfield, 1923-24, Chgo. Tribune, 1924-25, Champaign (Ill.) News-Gazette, 1925-28; editor A.P., Chgo., Washington, S.Am., N.Y.C., 1928-41; pub. relations counselor N.W. Ayer & Son, Hill & Knowlton, N.Y.C., 1944-48; dir. pub. relations Nat. Retail Mchts. Assn., N.Y.C., 1944-48; owner, operator advt. agy., Oceanside, Calif., 1948-52; pub. affairs officer Am. embassies, San Salvador, El Salvador, 1952-56, La Paz, Bolivia, 1956-60, Caracas, Venezuela, 1960-64; editor Fla. Trend Mag., Tampa, 1965-68. Served from capt. to maj. USAAF, 1942-44. Mem. Tau Kappa Epsilon, Sigma Delta Chi. Episcopalian. Mason (32 deg.). Author: Florida's Promoters: The Men Who Made It Big; A Pictorial History of Ybor City. Home: 3632 Meyer Pl Sarasota FL 33579

HARNER, JOSEPH WINFRED, JR., physician; b. Frederick, Md., June 6, 1918; s. Joseph Winfred and Ida Belle (Hendry) H.; B.S., U. Ga., 1940; M.D., Med. Coll. Ga., 1943; m. Helen Louise Childs, Dec. 25, 1943; children—Mary Helen (Mrs. Bill M. Strickland), Martha Jane (Mrs. Jackson Kiper), Joseph Winfred III, Bonnie Lynn (Mrs. Michael E. Brown). Intern, Grady Meml. Hosp., Atlanta, 1943; resident in pathology Univ. Hosp., Augusta, Ga., 1944; preceptorship in surgery, Dr. C. H. Watt, Thomasville, Ga., 1944-48; mem. surg. staff Regional Med. Center, Anniston, Ala., 1949—, Stringfellow Meml. Hosp., Anniston, 1957—. Bd. dirs. Ala. div. Am. Cancer Soc., also chmn. state service com., v.p., pres., 1975-77, nat. del., 1977—, dir. nat. del., 1979—; adminstrv. v.p., bd. dirs. Choccolocco council Boy Scouts Am., pres., 1976—. Recipient Silver Beaver award Boy Scouts Am., 1970. Diplomate Am. Bd. Surgery. Fellow A.C.S.; mem. AMA, Med. Assn. Ala., Calhoun County Med. Soc. (pres. 1953), So. Med. Assn., Am. Soc. Gastrointestinal Endoscopy. Methodist (adminstrv. bd. mem. 1953—, ch. sch. supt. 1959-61, chmn. adminstrv. bd. 1962-64, chmn. commn. on edn. 1967-69, leader mission team to Kapanga, Zaire, Africa, 1972, chmn. commn. on missions 1973-75). Home: 1401 Glenwood Dr Anniston AL 36201 Office: 720 Leighton Ave Anniston AL 36201

HAROLD, RICHARD WESLEY, applications engring. adminstr.; b. Louisville, Jan. 5, 1944; s. John Wesley and Dorothy (Jones) H.; B.S. in Chemistry, U. South Fla., Tampa, 1965, postgrad. in organic chemistry, 1965-67. NSF researcher, teaching asst. in chemistry U. South Fla., Tampa, 1965-67, also research chemist Mary Carter Paint Co., Tampa; color control coordinator Harshaw Chem. Co., Louisville, 1967-70; quality assurance mgr. Hunter Assos. Lab., Inc., Fairfax, Va., 1970-75, applications engring. mgr., 1976—. Mem. Inter Soc. Color Council (chmn. com. on determination of strength of colorants 1970-75), Am. Assn. Textile Chemists and Colorists, U. South Fla. Alumni Assn. (scholarship com. 1975—), Delta Tau Delta Alumni Assn. Republican. Baptist. Contbr. article to profl. jour. Office: 9529 Lee Hwy Fairfax VA 22031

HARPAVAT, GANESH LAL, office systems co. exec.; b. Udaipur, India, May 13, 1944; came to U.S., 1965, naturalized, 1969; s. Dadam Chand and Najar (Devi) H.; Ph.D., U. Rochester, 1968; M.B.A., U. Dallas, 1978; m. Singhvi, Dec. 6, 1970; children—Manisha, Sanjiv. Asso. scientist Xerox Corp., Rochester, N.Y., 1968-70, scientist, 1970-75, sr. scientist, Dallas, 1975—. Mem. ASME, Am. Soc. Aeros. and Astronautics, Soc. Photog. Sci. and Engring., IEEE, Sigma Xi, Sigma Iota Epsilon. Contbr. articles to profl. jours. Home: 3601 Brookshire Dr Plano TX 75075 Office: Xerox Corp 1341 W Mockingbird Ln Dallas TX 75247

HARPER, CHARLES FLOYD, architect; b. Bonham, Tex., Nov. 15, 1929; s. Charles Floyd and Donna Gertrude (Coonrod) H.; B.Arch., Tex. Tech. U., 1955; m. Catherine Elisabethe Fonville, July 1, 1955; children—Charles Martin, Jon Mark. Apprentice architect Harris &

Killebrew, architects and engrs., Wichita Falls, Tex., 1955-57; chief designer Butler-Kimmel Co., architects and engrs., Lubbock, Tex., 1957-61; asso. James R. Killebrew & Assos., architects and engrs., Wichita Falls, 1961-62; partner Harper, Martin & Assos., architects, engrs., Wichita Falls, 1962-69; prin. architect Charles Harper Assos., architects, engrs., planners, Wichita Falls, 1969—. Pres., Concern, 1969-70; treas. Concerned Ams. for Responsible Edn., 1971; chmn. Wichita Falls Common Cause, 1973-75, Reconstruction and Redevel. Task Force for Tornado, 1979; co-chmn. Disaster Action Task Force, AIA, 1977—; mem. exec. com. Goals for Wichita Falls; chmn. Wichita Falls Planning Commn., 1976-77; v.p. Midtown NOW, 1977—; del. Democratic state conv., 1972. Bd. dirs. Southside Girls' Club, 1962, Golden Cross Found.; bd. dirs. Child Care, Inc., pres., 1975; bd. dirs. Wichita County Heritage Soc., treas., 1975-79. Recipient Citizen of Yr. award LWV, 1978. Mem. AIA (pres. Wichita Falls chpt. 1967), Human Resources Council, Urban Planning and Design Com., Tex. Soc. Architects (v.p. 1972), Tech. Execs. Assn. (dir. Wichita Falls 1964-72, pres. 1972, dir. region 9 1978), Interfaith Forum on Religion, Art and Architecture, Guild Religious Architects. Methodist (dist. treas. 1970-71, North Tex. Conf. bd. Young adults and campus ministries, lay leadership devel., dist. lay leader North Tex. Conf., 1977—, vice chmn. N. Tex. Conf. council on ministries, del. Jurisdictional Conf.). Mason (Shriner). Club: Red Raider (Wichita Falls). Prin. archtl. works include Classroom/Office Bldg. Tex. Tech. U., Evans Elementary Sch., Bonham, Tex., Bethania Hosp., Wichita Falls, Univ. United Meth. Ch., Wichita Falls, Nocona Sch., Midtown Manor, Wichita Falls, Electra Meml. Hosp., Burkburnett Schs., N. Tex. Savs. and Loan. Home: 2501 Amherst Dr Wichita Falls TX 76308 Office: 4724 Old Jacksboro Hwy Wichita Falls TX 76302

HARPER, CLINTON EDWARD (CLINT), office furniture mfg. co. exec.; b. Maud, Tex., May 14, 1943; s. Otis Edward and Bertha Winfred (Teague) H.; student Texarkana Jr. Coll., 1961-63; B.A., Ouachita Baptist U., 1963-65; m. Neta Faye Dupree, Oct. 19, 1962; children—Steven Edward, Cheryl Faye. Customer service rep. Comml. Credit Corp., Dallas, 1965; sales rep. IBM, Dallas, 1965-67; buyer Day & Zimmermann, Inc., Texarkana, Tex., 1967-69, sr. buyer, 1969-71; materials control supr. Rockwell Internat., Texarkana, Ark., 1971-73, sr. buyer, 1973-76, purchasing mgr., 1976-80; materials mgr. Anderson Hickey Co., Henderson, Tex., 1980—. Mem. Maud (Tex.) City Council, 1975-76. Mem. E. Tex. Purchasing Mgmt. Assn., Four States Area Purchasing Mgmt. Assn. Baptist. Clubs: Maud Athletic Booster, Maud Band Booster. Home: PO Box 329 Maud TX 75567 Office: PO Box 80 Henderson TX 75652

HARPER, DIXON LADD, publisher; b. Ames, Iowa, Nov. 29, 1922; s. Harlan Howard and Mary Joan (Parsons) H.; student Mich. State U., 1943; B.S., Iowa State U., 1948; m. Shirley Thevenin, Mar. 22, 1947; children—Susan Shirley, Tod Dixon. Vice pres. broadcast Aubrey, Finlay, Marley & Hodgson, Chgo., 1956-63; account supr. Foote, Cone & Belding, Inc., Chgo., 1963-70; v.p. Lennen & Newall, Inc., Chgo., 1970-72; mgmt. supr. Clinton E. Frank, Inc., Chgo., 1972-75; pub. Specialized Agrl. Publs., Raleigh, N.C., 1975—; cons. Nat. Project in Agrl. Communications. Bd. dirs. North Bend Townhouse Homeowners Assn. Served with USAAF, 1943-44. Mem. N.C. Assn. Farm Writers and Broadcasters (pres.), Nat. Agrl. Mktg. Assn. (dir.), Nat. Assn. Farm Broadcasters (Meritorious Service award 1959), Fla. Mag. Assn., Sigma Delta Chi. Democrat. Methodist. Office: PO Box 95075 Suite 300 3000 Highwoods Blvd Raleigh NC 27625

HARPOLE, TONY HESS, merchant; b. Clinton, Ky., Feb. 26, 1926; s. Homer Hess and Sarah (Cunningham) H.; grad. pub. schs.; m. Margaret Elizabeth Costello, June 23, 1946; children—Jan Hess, Mark Aden. Mgr., owner Harpole Supply Co., Clinton, 1946—. Asst. fire chief Clinton Fire Dept., 1953-68, chief, 1968-74, chmn. bd., 1974—; dir. Hickman County Civil Def., 1956-70; safety services chmn. Clinton chpt. A.R.C., 1968—; mem. Ky. Pub. Safety Adv. Com., 1971-72. Bd. dirs. Four Rivers council Boy Scouts Am., 1973-75. Served with AUS, World War II. Mem. Nat. Assn. Fire Investigators, Am. Legion, I.E.E.E., Am. Radio Relay League, Internat. Platform Assn., Clinton C. of C., Am. Hort. Soc. Mem. Christian Ch. (deacon 1968—, chmn. bd. 1975-77). Clubs: Brigadier; Oak Hill Country. Home: 407 N Washington St Clinton KY 42031 Office: 115-119 N Washington St Clinton KY 42031

HARPSTER, JAMES ERVING, lawyer; b. Milw., Dec. 24, 1923; s. Philo E. and Pauline (Daanen) H.; Ph.B., Marquette U., 1950, LL.B., 1952. Admitted to Wis. bar, 1952, Tenn. bar, 1953; dir. info. services Nat. Cotton Council Am., Memphis, 1952-55; dir. pub. relations Christian Bros. Coll., 1956; mgr. govt. affairs dept. Memphis C. of C., 1956-62; exec. v.p. Rep. Assn. Memphis and Shelby County, 1962-64; individual practice law, Memphis, 1965; partner Rickey, Shankman, Blanchard, Agee & Harpster, and predecessor firm, Memphis, 1966-80, Harpster & Baird, 1980—. Mem. Shelby County Tax Assessor's Adv. Com., 1960-61; editor, asst. counsel Memphis and Shelby County Charter Comm., 1962; mem. Shelby County Election Commn., 1968-70; mem. Tenn. State Bd. Elections, 1970-72, sec., 1972; mem. Tenn. State Election Commn., 1973—, chmn., 1974—, sec., 1975-79. A founder Lions Inst. for Visually Handicapped Children, 1954, chmn. E. H. Crump Meml. Football Game for Blind, 1956; pres. Siena Student Aid Found., 1960; bd. dirs. Memphis Pub. Affairs Forum; mem. Civic Research Com., Inc., Citizens Assn. Memphis and Shelby County. Republican candidate Tenn. Gen. Assembly, 1964; v.p. Nat. Council Republican Workshops, 1967-69; pres. Rep. Workshop Shelby County, 1967, 71, 77, 78, Rep. Assn. Memphis and Shelby County, 1966-67. Chmn. St. Michael the Defender chpt. Catholics United for the Faith, 1973, 75. Served as sgt. USAAF, 1942-46. Mem. Am., Tenn., Wis. bar assns., Navy League U.S., Am. Conservative Union, Conservative Caucus, Cardinal Mindszenty Found., Am. Security Council, Catholics United for the Faith (pres. local chpt. 1973, 75), Am. Cause, Am. Legion, Latin Liturgy Assn. Roman Catholic. Lion (dir. Memphis 1955-62). Clubs: Tenn., Capitol (Nashville). Home: 3032 E Glengarry Rd Memphis TN 38128 Office: Suite 3217 100 North Main Bldg Memphis TN 38103

HARRAL, HARRIET BRISCOE, educator; b. San Antonio, June 28, 1944; d. Joe Edmund and Gene Aubrey (Hargis) Briscoe; B.A., Baylor U., Waco, Tex., 1966, M.A., 1967; Ph.D., U. Colo., 1973; m. Paul K. Harral, Aug. 6, 1966; 1 son, Huard Briscoe. Teaching asst. Baylor U., 1966-67; tchr. Dallas Ind. Sch. Dist., 1967-69, Jefferson County, Colo., 1969-70; teaching asso. U. Colo., 1970-72; instr. Northeastern Ill. U., 1972; asst. prof. communication U. Ill., Chgo. Circle, 1974-78; adj. prof. communication U. No. Fla., Jacksonville, 1978—; cons. in field, 1972—. Mem. planning com. Chgo. Baptist Assn., 1977-78; vice chmn. adv. com. Hendricks Ave. Elem. Sch., Jacksonville, 1979-80. Fellow Clark Found., 1967; grantee U. Ill., 1978, Fla. Dept. Edn., 1979. Mem. Speech Communication Assn., Internat. Communication Assn., Central States Speech Assn., Ill. Speech and Theatre Assn. Democrat. Author articles in field. Address: 925 Alhambra Dr N Jacksonville FL 32207

HARRAWOOD, PAUL, univ. dean; b. Akin, Ill., Aug. 28, 1928; s. Raymond E. and Verdie Alma (Galbraith) H.; B.S., U. Mo. at Rolla, 1951, M.S., 1956; Ph.D. (NSF fellow), N.C. State U., 1967; m. June Anne Harris, Nov. 28, 1953; 1 dau., Laura Anne. Instr. civil engring. U. Mo. at Rolla, 1954-56; asst. prof. civil engring. Duke, 1956-67, asst. dean engring., 1961-62; asso. prof. civil engring. Vanderbilt U., Nashville, 1967-70, prof., 1970—, asso. dean engring., 1967-69, acting dean engring., 1970-71, dean engring., 1979—; test engr. McDonnel Aircraft Corp., 1957; constrn. mgmt. engr. U.S. Army C.E., 1958. Served with USNR, 1951-54. Mem. ASCE, Soc. Am. Mil. Engrs., Am. Soc. Engring. Edn., Am. Assn. Higher Edn., AAAS, Sigma Xi, Tau Beta Pi, Chi Epsilon. Home: 5314 Camelot Ct Brentwood TN 37027 Office: Vanderbilt U Box 1607 Sta B Nashville TN 37235

HARRELL, DAVID LYNN, utility exec.; b. Sandersville, Ga., May 7, 1953; s. Ivey Duane and Shirley Frances (Page) H.; A.A., Hillsboro Community Coll., 1973; B.S. in Mech. Engring., U. South Fla., 1978; m. Carmen Valentin, Apr., 1973; 1 dau., Chyrisse Lynette. Sec., inventory clk. Bay Sportswear, Tampa, Fla., 1971-73; inventory clk. Spartan Slacks, Tampa, 1973-74; balance clk. 1st Nat. Bank Data Processing Center, Tampa, 1974-74; tech. engring. asst. Westinghouse Electric Corp., Tampa, 1974-75, quality control technician, 1975-78; asso. piping engr. Pullman Kellogg, Houston, 1978-79; asso. engr. power plant engring. Houston Light & Power, 1979—. Registered engr.-in-tng. Mem. ASME, ASHRAE. Republican. Baptist. Home: 12220 Sapling Way #1904 Houston TX 77031 Office: PO Box 1700 Energy Devel Center Houston TX 77001

HARRELL, GEORGE PETTIGREW, steel joist co. exec.; b. Florence, S.C., May 1, 1936; s. George Pettigrew and Cynthia Lou (Severance) H.; student Clemson Coll., 1955-56, 56-57; m. Susan Price, Dec. 21, 1958; children—George Pettigrew III, Steve, Mark, Sarah Beth, Pam, Susan. Detailer, Nucor, Florence, 1960-61, sales engr., 1961-65, sales mgr., Norfolk, Nebr., 1966-70; sales mgr. M.S. Churchman Co., Indpls., 1965-66; asso. McDonald Co., Phoenix, 1970-72; sales mgr. Socar Inc., Florence, 1976—. Served with USNG. Mem. Am. Mgmt. Assn. Republican. Baptist. Club: Florence Country. Home: 1327 3d Loop Florence SC 29501 Office: Socar Inc PO Box 671 Florence SC 29503

HARRELL, JAMES ALFRED, chem. co. exec.; b. Broken Arrow, Okla., Oct. 4, 1941; s. Alfred Emanuel and Dorothy Mae (Smith) H.; student in Chem. Engring., U. Okla., 1959-61, Okla. State U., 1962-64; m. Helen Jennifer Timbers, Mar. 4, 1972; children—James Bradley, Jennifer Adrienne. Researcher drilling fluids Amoco Prodn. Co., Tulsa, 1964-67; mktg. rep. Indsl. Solvents div. Apco Oil Corp., Tulsa, 1967-69, various mgmt. positions, 1969-78; br. mgr. Okla. Solvents & Chems. Co., Tulsa, 1978—. Mem. City of Broken Arrow (Okla.) Sts. and Hwys. Commn., 1976—. Mem. Propeller Club. Republican. Methodist. Home: 904 Twin Oaks Dr Broken Arrow OK 74012 Office: Okla Solvents & Chems Co PO Box 6007 Tulsa OK 74106

HARRINGTON, ARNOLD WHITMAN, elec. engr.; b. Winter Haven, Fla., Dec. 3, 1931; s. Elizur Whitman and Doris (Bartlett) H.; B.S. in E.E., Ga. Tech., 1953; m. Joyce Marie Johnson, July 30, 1954; 1 dau., Pamela Jean. Engring. mgr. Turner Electric Works, Jacksonville, Fla., 1955-71; head elec. dept. for power generation Reynolds, Smith & Hill, Jacksonville, 1971-74; dir. power and system engring. Jacksonville Electric Authority, 1974-77, asso. mng. dir. engring. and ops., 1977-79; v.p. engring. Tampa (Fla.) Armature Works, Inc., 1979—; mem. Fla. Bd. Profl. Engrs. and Land Surveyors, 1976-79. Served to lt. (j.g.) USNR, 1953-55. Registered profl. engr., Fla., Ga., Ala., Va. Mem. IEEE (sr.; chmn. 1973-74), Fla. Engring. Soc. (sr.), Nat. Soc. Profl. Engrs. (sr.), Am. Guild Organists, Eta Kappa Nu, Tau Beta Pi, Phi Kappa Phi, Beta Gamma Sigma, Alpha Tau Omega. Republican. Episcopalian. Home: 8615 Cattail Dr Tampa FL 33617 Office: 440 S 78th St Tampa FL 33601

HARRIS, ANTHONY CHARLES, air force officer; b. Atlanta, Ga., Sept. 19, 1946; s. Charles R. and Helen I (Egan) H.; A.B. in History, U. Ga., 1968; M.S. in Mgmt., U. Ark., 1974; student Air U.; grad. Squadron Officer Sch., 1975, Air Command and Staff Coll., 1979; m. Kay Lynn Skelton, Mar. 1, 1969; children—Jennifer Elizabeth, Michelle Angela. Commd. 2d lt., U.S. Air Force, 1968, advanced through grades to maj., 1979; dir. adminstrn. 3826th Command and Control Group, Maxwell AFB, Montgomery, Ala., 1968-70; chief postal ops. USAF Europe/Mid-East Postal and Courier Region, Rhein-Main Air Base, Frankfurt, W. Ger., 1971-74; chief central base adminstrn. 4787th Air Base Group, Duluth Internat. Airport, Minn., 1974-76; asst. prof. aerospace studies Air Force ROTC Detachment 930, U. Wis., Superior, 1976-79; assigned Hdqrs. Air Tng. Command, Randolph AFB, Tex., 1979—; dir. Duluth (Minn.) AFB Fed. Credit Union, 1975-78. Trustee United Meth. Ch., Duluth, 1977—, choir mem., 1975-79, mem. adminstrv. bd., 1978-79, chmn. fin. com., 1978-79. Named Outstanding Adminstrn. Officer, Hdqrs. Command USAF, 1974. Mem. Air Force Assn., Res. Officers Assn. U.S., Nat. Geog. Soc., U. Ga. Alumni Assn. Club: Kiwanis (pres. 1978-79). Home: 4422 Grantilly San Antonio TX 78217 Office: Hdqrs Air Tng Command Randolph AFB TX

HARRIS, ARNOLD FREDRICK, hosp. ofcl.; b. Chapel Hill, N.C., June 27, 1937; s. Thelbert T. and Garnell (Horton) H.; B.S., Morgan State U., 1959; cert., N.Y. U., 1964; m. Barbara Jacqueline Brown, July 19, 1975; children by previous marriage—Bryan Arnold, Michael Clayton, Kimberly, Allyson. Enlisted in U.S. Army, 1959, advanced through grades to maj., 1967, ret., 1973; dep. supt. Mass. Dept. Corrections, Boston, 1974-75; corporate dir. safety and security Durham County Hosp. Corp., Durham, N.C., 1975—. Pres., N.C. Safety and Security Health Care Council, 1979-80. Decorated Bronze Star, Army Commendation medal. Mem. Internat. Assn. Hosp. Security, Am. Soc. Indsl. Security, Omega Psi Phi. Democrat. Methodist. Club: Masons. Contbr. articles to profl. jours. Home: 200 Seven Oaks Rd Durham NC 27704 Office: 3643 N Roxboro St Durham NC 27704

HARRIS, ARTHUR LEE, retail exec.; b. Shreveport, La., Nov. 12, 1940; s. Arthur Lee and Odessa (Black) H.; student pub. schs., Shreveport; m. Minnie Pearl Thomas, May 15, 1965; children—Casundra Tess D'Ann, Keidra Monique, LaShana Evette. Owner, mgr. Mr. Swiss on Hollywood restaurant, Shreveport, 1969—; owner Fil-A-Sak Grocery, Shreveport, 1972—; v.p. Black Asso. Bus., Shreveport. Baptist. Home: 2909 W Maple St Shreveport LA 71109 Office: 4158 Hollywood Ave Shreveport LA 71109

HARRIS, BENJAMIN HARTE, realty co. exec.; b. Mobile, Ala., Dec. 22, 1908; s. Robert O. and Mary (Mighell) H.; grad. cum laude Davidson Coll., 1931; m. Mary Cade Aldridge, June 21, 1934; children—Ben Harte, John Aldridge, Russell Mighell, Frank. Mem. firm Thames, Jackson Harris Co., Inc., Mobile, 1948—, v.p., 1969—. Vice chmn. United Fund Mobile County (Ala.), 1965-68; chmn. Gordon Smith Bldg. Fund, 1967-68; co-chmn. Searcy Hosp. Chapel Fund, 1977-78; elder Government St. Presbyn. Ch., Mobile, 1952-79, mem. bd. deacons, 1940-79; bd. dirs. Boys Clubs Am., 1960-79, Mobile Community Chest, 1969-72, Cerebral Palsy, 1960-63; bd. dirs. Gordon Smith Health Center, 1965-79, pres., 1965-70; bd. dirs. America's Jr. Miss, 1960-79; trustee YWCA, 1965-79; chmn. bd. trustees U.M.S. Prep. Sch., 1951-76. Named Mobilian of Year, 1978, Ala. Realtor of Yr., 1962; gen. council Presbyn. Ch. U.S., 1966-72. Mem. Mobile County Bd. Realtors (pres. 1952), Mobile C. of C. (treas. 1962-65), Scabbard and Blade, Phi Delta Theta. Clubs: Rotary, Athelstan. Home: PO Box 416 Point Clear AL 36564 Office: 60 Saint Francis St Mobile AL 36602

HARRIS, CHARLES EDGAR, wholesale distbg. co. exec.; b. Englewood, Tenn., Nov. 6, 1915; s. Charles Leonard and Minnie (Borin) H.; m. Dorothy Wilson, Aug. 20, 1938; children—Charles Edgar, William John. With H.T. Hackney Co., Knoxville, Tenn., 1948—, dir., 1962—, pres., treas., chief adminstrv. officer, 1971-72, pres., chief exec. officer, 1972—; chmn. bd., dir. Hackney Carolina Co., Murphy, N.C., Hackney Jellico Co., Harlan, Ky., Haywood Wholesale Grocery Co., Waynesville, N.C., Dale San. Supply Co., Jellico Wholesale Grocery Co., Oneida and Elizabethton, Tenn., Corbin and Somerset, Ky., Tri-State Wholesale Co., Middlesboro, Ky., Brink's, Inc., Knoxville, Park Oil Co., Alcoa, Tenn., Knoxoil Co., Knoxville, Valley Oil Co., Athens, Tenn., Testoil Co., Harlan, Carolina Oil & Gas Co., Bryson City, N.C., Pride Markets, Inc., Knoxville, Foodser. Distbrs., Inc., Knoxville, Central Oil Co., Mid-State Investment Corp., McMinnville, Tenn.; chmn. bd., dir. Appalachian Realty Corp.; dir. Park Nat. Bank. Treas., Knox County Baptist Assn., 1964-67, chmn. fin. com., mem. exec. bd., 1973-77; deacon, trustee Central Bapt. Ch.; mem. exec. bd. Tenn. Bapt. Conv., 1976—; asso. chmn. Laymens Nat. Bible Com., Inc., 1977; bd. dirs. Met. YMCA of Knoxville, 1971-77, mem. exec. com., 1971-76, treas., 1975; dir. exec. bd. Gt. Smoky Mountain council Boy Scouts Am., 1956-57; bd. dirs. Downtown Knoxville Assn., v.p., 1979; bd. dirs. Tenn. Taxpayers Assn., 1976—; bd. dirs. U.S. Indsl. Council, 1975—, mem. exec. com., 1977. Recipient Outstanding Community Leadership award Religious Heritage Am., 1978, YMCA Red Triangle award, 1979. Mem. Greater Knoxville C. of C. (dir. 1973-76, v.p. 1975-76), Knoxville Wholesale Credit Assn. (pres. 1956-57), Nat. Assn. Wholesalers-Distbrs. (trustee 1977—). Club: Rotary of Knoxville (dir. 1973-76, v.p. 1975-77). Home: 7709 Westland Dr Knoxville TN 37919 Office: Fidelity Bldg Gay St PO Box 238 Knoxville TN 37901

HARRIS, CHARLES MINIARD, educator; b. Seminole, Okla., Apr. 22, 1936; s. Raymond and Mary Loneta (Thompson) H.; B.A., Bob Jones U., 1960, M.A., 1961, B.D., 1964; Ph.D., Ohio State U., 1970; m. Rosetta Ann Walton, Aug. 2, 1957; children—Kevin Shawn, Dana Walton. Acquisition specialist Center for Vocat. Edn., Ohio State U., Columbus, 1966-68, document analyst, 1968-70; asst. prof. psychology James Madison U., Harrisonburg, Va., 1970-71, asso. prof., 1971-77, prof., 1977—. Served with USMC, 1954-57. Licensed counselor, Va. Mem. Am., Va. personnel and guidance assns., Nat., Va. (pres. 1977-78) vocat. guidance assns., Assn. Counselor Educators and Supervisors, Phi Delta Kappa (pres. Shenendoah Valley chpt. 1975-76). Mem. Ch. of the Brethren. Contbr. developmental task resource guide, handbook in field; editor Va. Personnel and Guidance Jour., 1976-79. Home: 109 S Pope St Bridgewater VA 22812 Office: Psychology Dept James Madison U Harrisonburg VA 22801

HARRIS, CHARLES WILLIS, JR., sales exec.; b. Snyder, Tex., June 19, 1951; s. Charles Willis and Nell Raye (Delcore) H.; B.S., Southeastern State U., 1972; M.B.A., Pepperdine U., 1979; m. Deborah J. McClain, Aug. 31, 1973; 1 son, Charles Willis. Instr. pilot Kerr Aviation Co., Oklahoma City, 1972-73; co. pilot/test pilot Tri-Air Corp., Artesia, N.Mex., 1973-74; sales/service rep. NL Atlas Bradford, Houston, 1974-76; sales rep. Ft. Worth Pipe & Supply div. Whittaker Corp., Houston, 1976-78, sales mgr. Gulf Coast, Tex., 1978—; pres. Tex. Pup, Inc., 1980—. Leader, Explorer Scouts, Artesia, 1972-73; active Big Bros., 1972-73. Mem. Am. Petroleum Inst., Internat. Aikido Assn., Internat. Karting Assn., Alpha Eta Rho. Clubs: Sports Car Am., Elks.

HARRIS, CHRYS JAY, sch. dist. psychologist; b. Camp Le Jeune, N.C., Feb. 3, 1948; s. William Arnold and Gayle Conkey (Harris) H.; B.S. in Psychology, Wofford Coll., 1973; M.A. in Edn., Wake Forest U., 1975; m. Judith E. Buohl, Mar. 25, 1979. Psychologist, Beaufort (S.C.) County Sch. Dist. Advisory chmn. Beaufort Jasper Comprehensive Health Home Care Service. Served with U.S. Army, 1967-68. Mem. Nat., Am., S.C. assns. sch. psychologists, Am. Personnel, Guidance Assn., Paralyzed Vets. Assn., Profl. Assn. Diving Instructors (divemaster), Psi Chi. Democrat. Research in field. Home: Stuart Towne 3-B Port Royal SC 29935 Office: Beaufort County Sch Dist Drawer 309 Beaufort SC 29902

HARRIS, D. QUILLIAN, III, surgeon; b. Savannah, Ga., Jan. 23, 1945; s. D. Quillian and Dorothy Eunice (Calhoun) H.; B.S., U. Ga., 1967; M.D., Med. Coll. Ga., 1971; m. Mary Josephine Wood, June 1, 1969; children—Jere Eunice, Neville Lynn. Intern, Med. Coll. Ga., 1971-72; resident in orthopedic surgery U. Louisville, 1972-76; emergency rm. physician Palmyra Park Hosp., Albany, Ga., 1979-80; practice orthopedic surgery, Moultrie, Ga., 1978-79, 80—; mem. staff Colquitt County Meml. Hosp., Moultrie. Served with AUS, 1976-78. Diplomate Am. Bd. Orthopedic Surgery. Mem. Moultrie Track Club. Home: Quiet Cove Moultrie GA 31768 Office: 1414 S Main St Moultrie GA 31768

HARRIS, DANNY MAC, accountant; b. Albemarle, N.C., May 30, 1951; s. Edgar Milton, Sr., and Mary Evelyn (McManus) H.; A.B. in Acctg., Pfeiffer Coll., 1973; m. Mary Annette Isenhour, Sept. 15, 1973. Teller, loan officer 1st Nat. Bank, Albemarle, 1971-74, loan officer, br. mgr., 1974, asst. cashier, internal auditor, 1974-78, asst. cashier, 1978—. Former mem. adminstrv. bd., council ministries New London United Methodist Ch., now organist. Home: PO Box 158 New London NC 28127 Office: PO Box 309 Albemarle NC 28001

HARRIS, DAVID, JR., clergyman; b. Apr. 12, 1932, Dallas; s. David and Annie Mae. B.S., Wiley Coll., 1957; B.D., M.R.E., Southwestern Sem.; attended Princeton U., Harvard U. Founder, minister 2d Corinthian Ch., Dallas, 1974—; lectr. various audiences and chs. Active Community Chest, Dallas, Big Bros. Dallas, Dallas Voters League, World Neighborhood Center for World Peace. Recipient Internat. Lang. award Southwestern Baptist Theol. Sem., 1967, Outstanding Service award Commrs. Ct. Dallas, 1977, Outstanding Minister's award 2d Corinthian Ch., 1980. Mem. NAACP, Dallas Black C. of C., Dallas Urban League, Dallas Interdenominational Ministers Alliance, Greater Dallas Community Chs., NCCJ, Epsilon Delta Chi. Council on World Affairs, Fellowship of Christian Atheletes, Mason. Office: 1803 Browder St Dallas TX

HARRIS, DAVID MICHAEL, accountant; b. Houston, Mar. 14, 1947; s. Edwin Fleener and Mary Gayle (McKinney) H.; B.B.A., U. Tex., Austin, 1970; M.S. Accountancy, U. Houston, 1971; m. Rachel Anne Williams, June 6, 1970; 1 son, Matthew Edwin. Mem. audit staff and tax staffs Arthur Andersen & Co., Houston, 1971-73; mem. Exxon Co. U.S.A. controllers dept. at Friendswood Devel. Co., Houston, 1973-75, at Exxon Minerals Co. U.S.A., Houston, 1976-79; mem. market research staff Friendswood Devel. Co., Houston, 1975-76; staff fin. analyst supply controllers Exxon Co. U.S.A., Houston, 1979; v.p., controller Eden Corp. subs. Gen. Homes Consol. Cos., Houston, 1979—; pvt. practice acctg., 1971—. Vol. worker U. Houston Excellence Campaign Fund, 1975—. C.P.A., Tex. Mem. Am. Inst. C.P.A.'s. Republican. Episcopalian. Club: Kingwood Runners (founder, team capt.). Home: 3778 Georgetown St Houston TX 77005 Office: 4434 Bluebonnet Dr Stafford TX 77477

HARRIS, DONALD LEE, geol. design draftsman; b. Medford, Okla., Oct. 23, 1928; s. Otto Lee and Mardie Faye H.; A.S., No. Okla. Jr. Coll., 1948; m. Patricia McIntire Veros, Dec. 14, 1974; children by previous marriage—Terry, Robert. Gen. mgr. Early Hardware, Medford, 1949-56; jr. draftsman Sunray D-X, Oklahoma City, 1956-58; chief corp. drafting design div. exploration Kerr-McGee Corp., Oklahoma City, 1958—; instr. in geol. drafting Okla. State U. Extension, 1976—, drafting adviser, 1967—; condr. slide symposiums, speaker, slide adviser Am. Assn. Profl. Geologists. Active Last Frontier council Boy Scouts Am., 1959-73. Recipient Slide Service award Nat. Am. Assn. Profl. Geologists, 1968, 78, cert. for design of display Okla. Dept. Energy, 1976-78. Mem. Kerr-McGee Golf Assn., Oklahoma City Jaycees. Democrat. Methodist. Club: Westbury Country. Author: Geological Map Drafting, 1977, rev. edit., 1979; designer geol. model of Gulf of Mexico, 1973; research on color slide artwork and materials effects, 1964—. Home: 2021 Norwich Pl Yukon OK 73099 Office: PO Box 25861 Oklahoma City OK 73125

HARRIS, ERLE WARFIELD, JR., psychiatrist; b. Shreveport, La., Apr. 23, 1924; s. Erle Warfield and Annie West (Stevens) H.; student Centenary Coll., 1941-43; M.D., Tulane U., 1946; m. Billye F. Loveladdy, Aug. 18, 1945; children— Erle Gregory, Madeline Harris, Daniel Robert. Intern, Shreveport Charity Hosp., 1946-47; resident in psychiatry Sheppard and Enoch Pratt Hosp., 1950-52, staff psychiatrist, 1952-53; dir. psychiat. edn. Spring Grove State Hosp., Balt., 1953-54; staff psychiatrist Confederate Meml. Med. Center, Shreveport, 1954-57; practice specializing in psychiatry, Shreveport, 1957—. Served with M.C., U.S. Army, 1947-49. Diplomate Am. Bd. Psychiatry and Neurology. Fellow Am. Psychiat. Assn.; mem. Am. Group Psychotherapy Soc., La., Shreveport med. socs., Caddo Dixie Cruising Assn., U.S. Power Squadron. Club: Pierremont Oaks Tennis. Home: 8351 E Wilderness Way Shreveport LA 71106 Office: 713 Southfield Rd Shreveport LA 71106

HARRIS, EWING JACKSON, lawyer; b. Sylvia, Tenn., Mar. 17, 1901; s. John Chastain and Sarah Frances (Walker) H.; ed. pub. schs. Tenn. and Detroit; LL.B., Cumberland U., 1928; m. Lena Sue Hartman, Mar. 28, 1931; children—Frances Ann Harris (Mrs. Frank Avent), Marjorie Sue Harris (Mrs. Dean Lucht), Ewlene Harris. Admitted to Tenn. bar, 1928 and practiced in Bolivar, 1932—; city atty., Bolivar, 1942—; county atty. Hardeman County, 1942-70; dir. Bank of Bolivar. Pres. State Bd. of Elections, 1949-53, Tenn. Democratic Exec. Com. 1949-51, 1953-55; mem. Tenn. State Senate, 1937-39; del. Tenn. Constl. Conv., 1965. Fellow Am. Coll. Probate Counsel; mem. Am., Tenn. (bd. govs. 1959-62, mem. Ho. Dels. 1973-75, mem. spl. joint com. on ct. modernization), Hardeman County bar assns., Am. Judicature Soc., C. of C. (pres.1958), Phi Beta Gamma. Methodist (trustee). Mason, Elk, Rotarian (Paul Harris fellow). Home: 608 S Union St Bolivar TN 38008 Office: Bank of Bolivar Bldg Box 148 Bolivar TN 38008

HARRIS, FOREST DELBERT, pediatrician; b. Barbados, W.I., Feb. 23, 1923; s. Delbert Hutson and Violet Inez (Foster) H.; came to U.S., 1943, naturalized, 1947; M.D., Washington U., 1951; m. Gabye June Bell, Oct. 5, 1961; children—Paul Delbert, Raymond Hutson. Intern, St. Louis City Hosp., 1951-52; resident Children's Hosp., St. Louis, 1952-54; practice medicine specializing in pediatrics, Ardmore, Okla., 1954-57, Lawton, Okla., 1957—; mem. staff Comanche County Meml. Hosp.; mem. staff Southwestern Hosp., chief of pediatrics, 1975—; vis. staff Okla. Children's Meml. Hosp., 1977—; med. dir. Alcoholic Detoxification Centers, Lawton, 1974—; med. adv. Head Start Program of Comanche County, 1974—; cons. in field. Vestryman, St. Andrews Episcopal Ch., Lawton, 1974-77, Sunday Sch. tchr., 1973—; del. Episcopal Diocesan Conv., 1977. Served with U.S. Army, 1944-47. Recipient Outstanding Citizen Service award, Optimists Club, Ardmore, 1957; diplomate Am. Bd. Pediatrics. Fellow Am. Acad. Pediatrics; mem. Am., Okla. mem. assns., Comanche-Cotton & Tillman Counties Med. Soc. (pres. 1973), Am. Fedn. Physicians and Dentists, Okla. Pediatrics Soc. Democrat. Episcopalian. Contbr. articles to med. jour. Home: 304 NW 35th Lawton OK 73505 Office: 1930 Ferris Lawton OK 73501

HARRIS, FRANK MALCOLM, tobacco corp. exec.; b. Washington, June 5, 1946; s. Frank Howard and Margaret (Kelley) H.; B.S., U. S.C., 1969; children—Barbara Winfield, Kathryn Steele; m. 2d, Susan McGillicuddy. Prodn. supr. Burlington Industries, 1969-70; with Brown & Williamson Tobacco Corp., 1970—, staff asst. to factory mgr., Petersburg, Va., 1974, prodn. supt., 1975-76, mgr. corp. recruiting, 1977, mgr. corp. employment, Louisville, 1978, personnel mgr., Petersburg, 1978—; guest speaker on recruiting, personnel mgmt. skills to coll. classes. Mem. adv. bd. Tri-City Info. and Referral Service, 1978—; 1st v.p., bd. dirs. United Way of Southside Va., 1978-79, chmn. campaign, 1979-80, pres. elect, 1980-81, bd. dirs., mem. exec. com. United Way of Va., 1979—. Recipient numerous certs. of appreciation for speaking engagements, civic services; Outstanding Young Man of Yr. award Petersburg Jaycees, 1980. Mem. Am. Mgmt. Assn., Va. Mfrs. Assn., Petersburg C. of C. (dir. 1979—), Va. C. of C., Phi Kappa Sigma. Republican. Episcopalian. Clubs: Country of Petersburg, Rotary. Home: 226 High St Petersburg VA 23803 Office: Brown & Williamson Tobacco Corp 325 Brown St Petersburg VA 23803

HARRIS, FRANK ODELL, JR., research chemist; b. Mebane, N.C., July 5, 1944; s. Frank Odell and Marjorie Jenny (Bradley) H.; B.S., N.C. State U., 1966, M.S., 1973, Ph.D., 1973; m. Sylvia Anne Hakanson, Dec. 2, 1967; children—Andrea, Melissa, David. Chemist, Eastman Chem. Products, Inc., 1966; chemist Dye Tech. Service Lab., 1967; with Tenn. Eastman Co., Kingsport, 1968—, sr. research chemist fibers research lab., 1975—. Mem. Am. Assn. Textile Technologist, Am. Assn. Chemists and Colorists, Sigma Xi. Club: Jaycees (pres. Kingsport). Home: 945 Meadow Ln Kingsport TN 37663

HARRIS, GEORGE CHRISTIE, JR., writer; b. Wilmington, Del., Sept. 29, 1947; s. George C. and Luise (Peratsakis) H.; B.A., U. Del., 1973; tchr.'s cert. Western Carolina U., 1975; m. Cathy Jean Hogsed, Dec. 24, 1976; 1 son, Andrew George. Tchr. elem. sch., Brevard, N.C., 1973-77; tech. writer Olin Corp., Pisgah Forest, N.C., 1977—. Mem. county sch. supt.'s steering com., 1975-76, editor county sch. system monthly newsletter, 1974-76; adv. Jr. Achievement, 1978-79. Served with USAF, 1966-70; S.E. Asia. Episcopalian. Home: Route 1 Box 224C Brevard NC 28712 Office: Olin Corp PO Box 200 Pisgah Forest NC 28768

HARRIS, HERBERT E., II, congressman; b. Kansas City, Mo., Apr. 14, 1926; student Mo. Valley Coll., U. Notre Dame; B.A., Rockhurst Coll.; J.D., Georgetown U.; m. Nancy F. Harris; children—Herbert III, Frank, Susan, Sean, Kevin. Admitted to Mo. D.C. bars; individual practice law; congressman from 8th Va. dist. Mem. Fairfax County (Va.) Bd. Suprs., 1968-74, vice-chmn., 1971-74, chmn., 1972; commr. No. Va. Transp. Commn., 1968-74; bd. dirs. Washington Met. Area Transit Authority, 1970-74, 1st vice-chmn., 1971, 74, 2d vice-chmn., 1973; pres. Fairfax County Fedn. Citizens Assns. Mem. D.C., Mo. bar assns. Roman Catholic (past chmn. parish adv. com.). Home: 9106 Old Mt Vernon Rd Alexandria VA 22309 Office: US House of Reps Washington DC 20515

HARRIS, IMOGENE HARRELL, lawyer; b. Dunbar, Okla., Jan. 9, 1930; d. J.C. and Janie (Watkins) Hairell; LL.B., J.D., U. Tulsa, 1959; 1 son, John Jason Harrell-Harris. Admitted to Okla. bar, 1959; partner firm Howard, Larkin & Harris, 1960-66; atty. Sun Oil Co., 1966-70; asst. prof. law U. Tulsa, 1970-73; asst. city atty. City of Tulsa, 1973—; judge alt. City of Broken Arrow (Okla.). Sec., Met. Tulsa Transit Authority; v.p. Citizens for Transit; mem. Leadership Tulsa. Mem. Am., Okla., Tulsa County bar assns., Am. Pub. Transit Assn. (legal com.), Bus. and Profl. Women, Okla. Municipal Lawyers, Okla. Women Lawyers (past pres.). Democrat. Unitarian. Clubs: Tulsa Ski, Photography. Editor The Tulsa Lawyer, 1969-72. Contbr. articles to legal jours.

HARRIS, JACK HOMER, radio sta. exec.; b. Waverly, Va., Nov. 2, 1917; s. George Harvey and Mabel J. (Brooker) H.; student William and Mary Coll., 1936, Columbia U., 1944; m. Margaret Virginia Ives, Dec. 27, 1944; children—Margaret Lealand, Linda Mae, Jackie Anne. Sports writer Norfolk (Va.) Ledger Dispatch, 1941, UP Radio, N.Y.C., 1945; sports announcer Sta. WNOR, Norfolk, 1949-53, gen. mgr., v.p., 1956-66; exec. v.p., gen. mgr. Sta. WVAB, Virginia Beach, Va., 1967—. Mem. Tidewater Assn. Radio Broadcasters. Democrat. Presbyterian. Club: Kempsville Meadows Golf & Country.

HARRIS, JACK RONDAL, lawyer; b. Detroit, Feb. 12, 1928; s. Walter Lee and Pinkey Marbell (Meetze) H.; B.S. in Bus. Adminstrn., U. N.C., 1952; LL.B., 1955, J.D., 1969; m. Paulette Henderson, Sept. 23, 1972; children—Mary J., Jack R. Admitted to N.C. bar, 1955; asso. firm Scott, Collier, and Nash, Statesville, N.C., 1955-59, partner firm Collier, Harris & Homesley, Statesville, 1959-64; sr. partner firm Collier, Harris, Homesley & Jones, Statesville, 1964-76, Harris & Pressley, 1976—; judge Statesville Recorders Ct. 1959-64; city atty. Statesville, 1959-71. Counsel, state lobbiest N.C. Electric Cities, 1969-72. Trustee Iredell Meml. Hosp., Statesville. Served with AUS, 1946-58, 50. Mem. N.C., Dist., Iredell County bar assns., Am. Legion (judge adv. 1972—), Phi Alpha Delta. Mason (Shriner). Home: Route 10 Box 365A Statesville NC 28677 Office: Suite 207 Spainhour Bldg Statesville NC 28677

HARRIS, JAMES DOUGLAS, JR., lawyer; b. Tallassee, Ala., Feb. 12, 1943; s. James Douglas and Edna Marie (Flournoy) H.; A.B., U. Ala., J.D., 1967; m. Sara Jean Brooks, May 7, 1966; children—Jennifer Brooks, James Douglas III, Stewart Katherine. Admitted to Ala. bar, 1967, U.S. Supreme Ct. bar, 1971; mem. firm Harris & Harris, Montgomery, Ala., 1967—. Active United Appeal. Mem. Ala. Ho. of Reps., 1970—. Bd. dirs. YMCA Youth Legislature. Served with AUS, 1967-69. Decorated Bronze Star medal. Mem. Am. Legion, VFW, Phi Alpha Delta, Sigma Chi. Democrat. Baptist. Club: Kiwanis. Home: 3243 Bankhead Ave Montgomery AL 36106 Office: 200 S Lawrence St Montgomery AL 36104

HARRIS, JAMES EDWARD, JR., govt. ofcl.; b. Farmville, Va., May 15, 1943; s. James Edward and Nell (Fitzpatrick) H.; B.A., U. Va., 1966; postgrad. Va. Commonwealth U., 1978—; m. Caryl Gray Shepard, Mar. 23, 1973; children—James, Julie Elizabeth. Newspaper reporter Farmville Herald, 1970-72; civil def. planner Piedmont Planning Dist. Commn., Farmville, 1972-73; criminal justice planner Lord Fairfax Planning Dist. Commn., Front Royal, Va., 1973-76; pub. safety planner Piedmont Planning Dist. Commn., Farmville, 1976-79; adminstrv. asst. to exec. asst. dir. Va. Dept. Corrections, Richmond, 1979—; chem. warfare def. instr. U.S. Air Force Res., 1980. Served with USAF, 1966-70, USAFR, 1972-80. Recipient commendation Piedmont Planning Dist. Commn., 1972, 77. Mem. So. States Correctional Assn., Air Force Assn. Presbyterian. Contbr. articles to profl. jours. Office: PO Box 26963 4615 W Broad St Richmond VA 23261

HARRIS, JESSIE G. (MRS. HUBERT LAMAR HARRIS), ret. ednl. adminstr.; b. Athens, Ga., May 12, 1909; d. Wiley Jackson and Dora (Hilley) Ginn; B.B.A., U. Ga., 1956; A.B., Ga. State Coll., 1960; m. Hubert Lamar Harris, Nov. 25, 1930; children—Mary Ann Harris (Mrs. William Wallace Holley), Hubert Lamar, Dorothy Elizabeth (Mrs. Ronald Zazworsky), Martha Susan (Mrs. R.R. McCue, Jr.). Various secretarial positions, ins. and law offices, 1923-30; sec. div. of gen. extension U. Ga., 1930-35, asst. dir. div. gen. extension, 1935-47; asst. compilation survey Univ. System, Ga., 1949-50, adminstrv. asst. to regents, 1951-63, asst. exec. sec., 1963-67, asso. exec. sec., 1967-73, asst. vice chancellor personnel, 1973-74, asst. exec. dir. and asst. vice chancellor emeritus, 1974—; ret., 1974. Asst. exec. dir. State Scholarship Commn., 1965-66. Mem. AAUW (chmn. study group 1964-66, treas. 1972-74), Crimson Key Honor Soc., Mortar Board, So. Hist. Assn., Atlanta Hist. Soc., Phi Chi Theta, Delta Mu Delta, Psi Chi. Club: Atlanta Writers. Home: 765 Douglas Rd NE Atlanta GA 30342

HARRIS, JOHN WOODS, banker; b. Galveston, Tex., Sept. 23, 1893; s. John Woods and Minnie (Hutchings) H.; LL.B., U. Va., 1920; m. Eugenia Davis, June 14, 1917; children—Eugenia (Mrs. Archibald Rowland Campbell, Jr.), Anne (Mrs. Donald C. Miller), Joan (Mrs. Alvin N. Kelso), Florence (Mrs. Marshall McDonald, Jr.) (dec.). Admitted to Tex. bar, 1920; practiced as atty., mng. agt. oil, farm, ranch properties in Tex., 1922—; dir. Hutchings Sealy Nat. Bank, 1930-58; chmn. exec. com., chmn. bd. First Hutchings Sealy Nat. Bank (merged into First Internat. Bancshares 1974), Galveston, 1960—; pres. Hutchings Joint Stock Assn., 1936—; dir. Galveston Corp., Cotton Concentration Co., Gulf Transfer Co., Tex. Fibreglas Products, Inc., Galveston; sr. v.p., chmn. land com. The Sealy and Smith Found. for John Sealy Hosp.; pres. Galveston Found. Inc.; v.p. Ball Charity Found.; pres. bd. Rosenberg Library, Galveston Orphans Home; trustee Galveston Ind. Sch. Dist., 1927-30. Served as aviator USN, 1918. Mem. Sons Republic of Tex., Am. Legion, Early and Pioneer Naval Aviators Assn., Delta Kappa Epsilon. Episcopalian. Clubs: Galveston Artillery; Farmington Country (Charlottesville, Va.); Bob Smith Yacht. Home: 2603 Ave O Galveston TX 77550 Office: First Hutchings Sealy Nat Bank Bldg Galveston TX 77550

HARRIS, JOSEPH HERBERT, headmaster; b. Birmingham, Ala., Aug. 18, 1918; s. Herbert H. and Nannetta M. (Ellis) H.; A.B., Birmingham-So. Coll., 1941; postgrad. U. Ala., Fairleigh-Dickinson U., Madison, N.J.; m. Rosa M. Stewart; children—Lynne H. Rachal, Stewart H. Indsl. engr. Tenn. Coal, Iron and R.R. Co., Birmingham, 1941-46; tchr. Birmingham Univ. Sch., 1947-52, headmaster, 1952-57; headmaster Mead Hall Sch., Aiken, S.C., 1957—. Served with U.S. Army, 1941-46. Mem. Nat. Assn. Episcopal Schs. (dir.), Episcopal Schs. Assn. (diocesan chmn. 1965—), Writer's Club Am., Nat. Soc. Lit. and Arts, World Poetry Soc. Contbr. numerous poems and short stories to mags. and jours. Home: 194 Dogwood Rd Aiken SC 29801 Office: 129 Pendleton St Aiken SC 29801

HARRIS, LANE FRANK, mgmt. cons.; b. Waco, Tex., Apr. 14, 1941; s. Manuel Frank and Ida Lee (Wolkoff) H.; B.A., U. Tex., Austin, 1963, M.B.A., 1970; postgrad. Northwestern U.; m. Henrietta Cohen, Aug. 27, 1941. Systems rep. IBM Corp., Houston, 1970-73; mgr. systems research and planning Bank of Southwest, N.A., Houston, 1973-75; mgmt. cons. Lifson, Herrmann, Blackmarr & Harris, mgmt. cons., Dallas, 1975—; instr. data processing, adviser Jr. Achievement. Served to capt. USAF, 1963-67. Barker fellow, 1970; NASA fellow, 1971; Wilton Park participant, London. Mem. Assn. EDP Auditors, Data Processing Mgmt. Assn., Beta Gamma Sigma, Tau Delta Phi, Phi Kappa Phi, Sigma Iota Epsilon. Jewish. Office: One Turtle Creek Village Dallas TX 75219

HARRIS, LEWIS KARL, mech. engr., clergyman; b. Sand Springs, Okla., Feb. 9, 1924; s. Lewis Russell and Jennie June (West) H.; ed. 1941-43, 49-52; m. Bonita June Lingo, Dec. 28, 1941 (dec. July 1949); children—Richard Karl, Robert Clinton. Ordained to ministry Evangelical Ch. Alliance, 1952; minister various chs.; machinist Walter O'Bannon Co., Tulsa, 1941-43, Franks Mfg. Co., Tulsa, 1952-57; draftsman C-E Natco, Tulsa, 1957-63; engr. C-E Invalco div. Combustion Engring. Inc., Tulsa, 1963—; watercolors exhibited Tulsa Public Library, 1980. Recipient Plant Design award Materials Handling Inst. Am., 1956. Registered profl. engr., Okla. Mem. Nat. Hist. Soc., Mensa (chmn. exec. bd. chpt. 1975-76). Republican. Author: Five Seasons and Other Poems, 1973. Contbr. numerous articles on religious, math., phys., paleoanthropol., psychol. subjects to profl. publs. Patentee in field. Home: PO Box 50255 Tulsa OK 74150 Office: C-E Invalco PO Box 556 Tulsa OK 74101

HARRIS, MARGARET PARSONS (MRS. JOHN MALCOLM HARRIS), civic worker; b. Tampa, Fla.; d. William H., Jr. and Bonnie (Crews) Parsons; student Fla. State U.; B.A., U. N.C., 1945; m. John Malcolm Harris, Aug. 16, 1946; children—John Malcolm, William D., Donna M. Mem. women's com. Houston Symphony Soc. Bd. dirs. Gulf Coast Arthritis Found., Houston Grand Opera Assn.; trustee Houston Mus. Fine Arts; mem. nat. women's bd. Northwood Inst. Mem. Harris County Heritage Soc., Women's Inst. Houston, Mus. Fine Arts, Friends of Bayou Bend, Alley Theater Guild, Houston Ballet Guild, Delta Delta Delta. Episcopalian. Clubs: River Oaks Country, University, Champions Golf (Houston). Home: 2928 Del Monte Dr Houston TX 77019

HARRIS, MARGO BULLOCK, guidance counselor; b. Durham, N.C., Feb. 23, 1943; d. McCoy and Mary Elizabeth Bullock; B.S., N.C. Coll., 1965; M.S., N.C. Central U., 1974; m. July 30, 1967 (div.); 1 son, William McCoy Harris. Tchr., Henry Grove Sch., Lilesville, N.C., 1965-66, Darden (N.C.) High Sch., 1966-67; tchr., dir. kindergarten Morris Coll., Sumter, S.C., 1969-70; tchr. St. Anne Inst., Albany, N.Y., 1971-72; elem. guidance counselor Estes Hills Sch., Chapel Hill, N.C., 1975—, facilitator parent group. Vol., Durham (N.C.) Community Guidance Clinic for Children and Youth, Trent dr., 1978—. Named outstanding tchr. Upward Bound, U. N.C. Chapel Hill, summer 1977. Mem. Am. Personnel and Guidance Assn., N.C. Pupil Personnel Assn., NEA. Democrat. Baptist. Home: 59A Colonial Apts Durham NC 27707 Office: Estes Hills Elementary Sch Estes Dr Chapel Hill NC 27150

HARRIS, MARTIN HARVEY, aerospace co. exec.; b. N.Y.C., Mar. 14, 1932; s. Leo and Gertrude (Litt) H.; B. Aero. Engring., N.Y. U., 1953; M.S. in Systems Mgmt., U. So. Calif., 1973; m. Patricia Ann Franklin, Apr. 27, 1970; children—Lori Kathryn, Barbara Ann. Test engr. Curtis-Wright Corp., Woodbridge, N.J., 1952-53; staff engr. Martin Marietta Corp., Denver, 1957-58, program mgr., Orlando, Fla., 1958—. Trustee, Aerospace Edn. Found. Served with USAF, 1953-57; col. Res. Mem. Air Force Assn. (nat. sec. 1972-77, nat. dir. 1965—, Nat. Man of Year 1972), Am. Def. Preparedness Assn. (nat. v.p. 1977-79), AIAA, Res. Officers Assn., Orlando Area C. of C. Patentee in field. Home: 2845 Summerfield Rd Winter Park FL 32792 Office: PO Box 5837 Orlando FL 32855

HARRIS, MICHAEL ALAN, psychiatrist; b. Washington, Oct. 25, 1937; s. Christopher Cleo and Charlotte (Nelson) H.; B.S., U. Tenn., M.D., 1962; m. Martha Marie Healey, Dec. 17, 1967; children—Charlotte Ann Marie, Daniel Martin. Intern, Chelsea Naval Hosp., Boston, 1962-63; commd. lt. U.S. Navy, 1962, advanced through grades to capt., 1978—; tng. in flight surgery, 1963-64; assigned Marines, Japan and Viet Nam, 1964-66; flight surgeon, Nfld., Can., Argentina, 1966-68; resident in psychiatry Naval Hosp., Oakland, Calif., 1968-71; chief psychiat. clinic Treasure Island and interim commanding officer San Francisco Dispensary, 1973; staff psychiatrist Charleston (S.C.) Naval Regional Med. Center, 1973—; cons. Charleston County Youth Program, 1977-79. Decorated Air medal. Mem. Orthopsychiat. Assn., AMA, Assn. Mil. Surgeons U.S., Naval Inst., Phi Rho Sigma. Baptist. Clubs: Army-Navy, Officers. Office: Box 143 NRMC Charleston SC 29408

HARRIS, NADA ROCHELLE, speech pathologist; b. Flora, Ill., Jan. 5, 1939; d. Marshall Foster and Novice (Charlie) Ebeling; A.R.E., Southwestern Baptist Theol. Sem., 1970; B.S., Tex. Woman's U., 1974, M.A., 1975; m. Donald Keith Harris, Dec. 29, 1955; children—Michelle Delynn, Steven Dane, Kyle Alan. Speech-lang. pathologist Ft. Worth Ind. Sch. Dist., 1974-77, 79—; speech-lang. pathologist High Plains Spl. Edn. Coop. (Kans.), 1977-79; cons. Care Homes in Western Kans. Mem. AAUW, Am. Speech and Hearing Assn., Speech and Hearing Assn. N.Tex., NEA, Tex. Edn. Assn., Classroom Tchrs. Ft. Worth, Gen. Fedn. Women's Clubs, Beta Sigma Phi. Democrat. Baptist. Home: 800 Newport St Fort Worth TX 76112 Office: 5533 Whitman St Fort Worth TX 76133

HARRIS, OLLIE, state senator; b. Anderson, S.C., Sept. 2, 1913; s. John Frank and Jessie Mae (Hambright) H.; grad. Gupton-Jones Coll. Embalming, Nashville, 1935; m. Abbie Wall, May 4, 1936; children—Ollie, Jane Wall. With Lutz-Austell Funeral Home, Shelby, N.C., 1928-47; pres., treas. Harris Funeral Home, Kings Mountain, N.C., 1947—; dir. First Union Nat. Bank, Kings Mountain; past pres. N.C. Bd. Embalmers; coroner Cleveland County, 1946-70; mem. N.C. Senate, 1971—. Served with AUS, 1943-45. Decorated Bronze Star; recipient Valand award N.C. Assn. Mentally Ill and Mentally Retarded, 1979; Disting. Service award N.C. Public Health Assn., 1979. Mem. N.C Funeral Dirs. and Embalmers Assn. (past pres.). Democrat. Baptist. Clubs: Lions, Shriners. Home: 921 Sharon Dr Kings Mountain NC 28086 Office: 108 S Piedmont St Kings Mountain NC 28086

HARRIS, OREN, judge; b. Belton, Ark., Dec. 20, 1903; s. Homer and Bettie Lee (Bullock) H.; B.A., Henderson State Coll., Arkadelphia, Ark., 1929; LL.B., Cumberland U., 1930; m. Ruth Ross, May 9, 1934; children—Carolyn Marie, James Edward. Admitted to Ark. bar, 1930; U.S. Supreme Ct. bar, 1943; dep. pros. atty. Union County, Ark., 1933-36; pros. atty. 13th Judicial Circuit, 1936-40; mem. 77th-89th Congresses from 4th Dist. Ark., 1957-66, chmn. com. on interstate and fgn. commerce, 1957-66, chmn. spl. investigatory com. on regulatory agys., 1957-60; now judge U.S. Dist. Ct. Eastern and Western dist. Ark., El Dorado. Recipient Saturday Rev. award, 1960; Public Service award Air Freight Forwarders Assn., 1960; award of Merit, Air Traffic Control Assn., 1962; Disting. Public Service citation Western Ry. Club, 1962; Nat. Transp. award Nat. Def. Transp. Assn., 1962; Presdl. citation Pioneer Nat. Broadcasting Assn., 1963; Albert Lasker Service award, 1964; George Washington award Am. Good Govt. Soc., 1965. Mem. Am. Bar Assn., Ark. Bar Assn. Democrat. Baptist. Clubs: Lions (dist. gov. Ark. 1939-40), Masons, Shriners. Office: 219 Federal Bldg El Dorado AR 71730

HARRIS, PAT I., hosp. adminstr.; b. Liberty Hill, Tex., June 12, 1923; d. James Edward and Ethel Gertrude (Hunt) Isaacks; A.S. in Nursing, El Centro Coll., 1972; m. Dec. 1, 1944; children—Paul W.,

Patricia Dianne. Sec., Adjutant Gen. Dept., Austin, Tex., 1940-42; to post comdr., Port of Embarkation, Charleston, S.C., 1942-43; sec. to dir. Magnesium Plant, Austin, 1943-44; sec. Tex. Employers Ins. Co., Dallas, 1944-45; dir. vols. Presbyterian Hosp. of Dallas, 1968—; participant profl. seminars. Mem. Am. Soc. Dirs. Vols. (charter), Am. Hosp. Assn. (charter), Tex. Hosp. Assn., Dirs. Vols., Tex. Nurses Assn. Office: Presbyn Hosp Dallas 8200 Walnut Hill Ln Dallas TX 75231

HARRIS, RICHARD FOSTER, JR., ins. co. exec.; b. Athens, Ga., Feb. 8, 1918; s. Richard Foster and Mai Audli (Chandler) H.; B.C.S., U. Ga., 1939; m. Virginia McCurdy, Aug. 21, 1937 (div.); children—Richard Foster, Gaye Karyl Harris Law; m. 2d, Kari Melandso, Dec. 29, 1962. Bookkeeper, salesman 1st Nat. Bank, Atlanta, 1936-40; agt. Vol. State Life Ins. Co., Atlanta, 1940-41; asst. mgr. N.Y. Life Ins. Co., Atlanta and Charlotte, N.C., 1941-44; mgr., agt. Pilot Life Ins. Co., Charlotte and Houston, 1944-63; mgr., agt., bus. planning div.; city agy. Am. Gen. Life Ins. Co., Houston, 1963—; dir. Fidelity Bank & Trust Co., Houston, 1965-66. Chmn. fund drive Am. Heart Assn., Charlotte, Mecklenburg County, 1958-59, chmn. bd., 1959-61; gen. chmn. Shrine Bowl Promotion, Charlotte Shriners, 1955; v.p., dir. Myers Park Meth. Ch. Men's Class, 1956-59, bd. stewards, Charlotte, 1959-61. Recipient Pres.'s Cabinet award Am. Gen. Life Ins. Co., 1964-67, 69, 71, 77, 78, 79; Disting. Salesman award Charlotte Sales Exec. Club, 1955, 57-59; Bronze Medallion award Am. Heart Assn., 1959; Nat. Quality award Life Ins. Agency Mgmt. Assn. and Nat. Assn. Life Underwriters, 1976-79; C.L.U. Mem. Assn. Advanced Life Underwriters, Am. Soc. C.L.U.'s, Nat. Assn. Life Underwriters, SAR (sec. chpt. 5, Tex. Soc. 1974—), Sertoma Internat. (life, v.p., dir. Charlotte chpt.), Life Underwriters Polit. Action Com. (life), Ky. Cols., Houston Estate and Fin. Forum, English Speaking Union, Mensa Internat., Houston Assn. Life Underwriters, Lone Star Leaders Club, Tex. Leader's Round Table (life), Million Dollar Round Table, Tex. Assn. Life Underwriters, Am. Security Council (nat. adv. bd. 1979—), Tex. Crime Prevention Assn., Nat. Platform Assn., Pi Kappa Phi. Republican. Episcopalian. Clubs: Warwick, Napoleon, 100, Kiwanis (dir. 1979—), Houston Knife and Fork, Masons (32 deg.), Shriners. Contbr. articles to profl. jours. Home: 2701 Westheimer Rd Houston TX 77098 Office: Am Gen Bldg 2727 Allen Parkway Suite 500 Houston TX 77019

HARRIS, ROBERT SANDERSON, land surveyor, civil engr.; b. Miami, Fla., June 22, 1938; s. Harry Lee and Gertrude (Sanderson) H.; student U. Miami, 1956-58, Internat. Corr. Sch., 1963-65; grad. Dade County Surveying Sch., 1958-60; student Alexander Hamilton Inst., 1967-69; m. Margie Ann Cashion, June 27, 1972; children-by previous marriage—John C., Debra M., Daniel S.; 1 stepson, Michael A. Rodman, instrumentman G.B. Adams & Assos., Miami, Fla., 1953-57; instrumentman, party chief H.C. Schwebke & Assos., Miami, 1957-62; party chief, chief of surveys Post, Buckley, Schuh & Jernigan, Inc., Miami, 1962-73, regional mgr., Homestead, Fla., 1973—, prin. asso., 1970—; chmn. Fla. Public Land Survey Adv. Bd., 1977-79. Named Fla. Land Surveyor of Year, 1976. Fellow Am. Congress Surveying and Mapping; mem. Soc. Am. Mil. Engrs., Am. Soc. Photogrammetry, Fla. Soc. Profl. Land Surveyors (state pres. 1976-77), Homestead C. of C., South Dade C. of C., Hist. Assn. So. Fla. Democrat. Methodist. Club: Rotary. Contbr. articles in field to profl. jours. Office: Post Buckley Schuh & Jernigan Inc 10 Palms Plaza Homestead FL 33030

HARRIS, SARAH LONG, sch. counselor; b. Lexington, N.C., Sept. 17, 1932; d. Richard Ottis and Thelma (Sowers) Long; B.A., Bennett Coll., 1955; postgrad. Western Carolina U., 1972, U. N.C., Greensboro, summers 1974-75; M.S., A&T State U., 1978; children—Carl Edward II, Richard Delos. Music and reading tchr. Columbus High Sch., 1955-58; lang. arts and music tchr. Lee Holt Sch., 1958-61, Lucy S. Herring Sch., 1962-68, David Millard Jr. High Sch., 1969-71; sch. counselor South French Broad Jr. High Sch., Asheville, N.C., 1971—. Mem. NEA, N.C. Assn. Educators, N.C. Personnel and Guidance Assn., N.C. Sch. Counselor Assn., N.C. Assn. Non-White Concerns, Am. Personnel and Guidance Assn., Am. Sch. Counselor Assn. Democrat. Roman Catholic. Club: Leisurette Civic and Social. Home: 36 Avon Rd Asheville NC 28805 Office: 197 S French Broad Ave Asheville NC 28801

HARRIS, SHELBY LANE, educator; b. Union, Miss., Jan. 11, 1938; s. Onon and Nettie (Talbert) H.; A.A., E. Central Jr. Coll., 1956; B.S., U. So. Miss., 1959; M.Ed., Miss. State U., 1963; Ed.D., U. So. Miss., 1975. Tchr., Newton County (Miss.) Schs., 1959-61, Kemper County (Miss.) schs., 1961-63; faculty E. Central Jr. Coll., Decatur, Miss., 1963—, prof. math., 1963—, chmn. dept. math. and sci., 1977—; faculty Extension U. So. Miss., Meridan, 1965-73, Miss. State U., Meridian, 1973-77; cons. Miss. Dept. Edn., 1977-78. NSF fellow, 1963-64, 65-66. Mem. E. Central Jr. Coll. Faculty Assn., Miss. Jr. Coll. Faculty Assn., Miss. Edn. Assn., NEA, Miss. Tchrs. Coll. Math., Miss. Council Tchrs. Math., Math. Assn. Am., Phi Theta Kappa, Lambda Iota Tau, Kappa Mu Epsilon, Kappa Delta Pi. Mem. Ch. of God. Home: 109 5 Ave Decatur MS 39327 Office: PO Box 41 Decatur MS 39327

HARRIS, STEPHEN ROBERT, psychologist; b. Bklyn., Nov. 16, 1940; s. Claud R. and Paula T. (Kohlhepp) H.; B.S., Tulane U., 1962; M.S., N.C. State U., 1965; Ph.D., U. N.C., 1974; m. Julie Ann Williams, June 5, 1965; children—Erin Lee, David Fredric. Research asso. in child devel. Inst. for Child Devel., U. N.C., Greensboro, 1965, instr. psychology extension div., 1972-73; instr. edn. and psychology N.C. A&M State U., Greensboro, 1965-66; instr. psychology N.C. State U., Ft. Bragg, 1969; asst. prof. psychology Coll. of Steubenville (Ohio), 1973-75; research cons. Brooke, Hancock and Jefferson Regional Planning Commn., Steubenville, 1975; cons. psychologist, Jonesboro, Ark., 1976-79, Harrison, Ark., 1979—. Mem. Craighead County (Ark.) Republican Com., 1978-79. Served with U.S. Army, 1966-69. Mem. Soc. for Psychophysiol. Research, Am. Psychol. Assn., Ark. Psychol. Assn., Soc. for Neurosci., Ark. Biofeedback Assn., Psi Chi (pres. local chpt. 1970-71). Episcopalian. Club: Elks. Home: 315 N PIne Harrison AR 72601 Office: PO Box 1770 Harrison AR 72601

HARRIS, THOMAS LEE, indsl. engr.; b. Florence, Ala., Nov. 13, 1941; s. John Pearson and Bertha Viola (Townsend) H.; A.A. in Gen. Sci., Pensacola Jr. Coll., 1967; B.S. in Indsl. and Systems Engring., U. Ala., Huntsville, 1973; m. Lynn Marie Sharpless, Dec. 31, 1962; children—Thomas Lee, Johanna Lynn, Elizabeth Juanita, Margaret Pauletta. Devel. technician Am. Cyanamid, Pace, Fla., 1962-66; lab. technician Escambia Treating Co., Pensacola, Fla., 1966-67; sr. computer operator and acting ops. mgr. UNIVAC, Huntsville, Ala., 1967-70; indsl. engr. Huntsville Hosp., 1973, U.S. Army Missile Research and Devel. Command, Redstone Arsenal, Ala., 1974—; acting chief spl. projects and planning div. Programs Mgmt. Office, U.S. Army Missile Command, 1975-77. Co-chmn. Santa Rosa County (Fla.) Scott Kelly for Gov., 1966, Barry Goldwater for Pres., 1964. Served with USNR, 1959-64. Recipient letters of commendation Gov. George C. Wallace, 1970, Sen. Edward M. Kennedy, 1975, Comdr. U.S. Army Missile Research and Devel. Command, 1977; aide-de-camp Ala. State Militia, 1978. Mem. Soc. Children's Book Writers (Los Angeles), The Franklin Mint Collectors Soc. (Phila.), Huntsville Sci. Fiction Assn., Am. Legion; hon. mem. Calhoun's Collectors Soc. (Mpls.). Democrat. Mem. Ch. of Christ. Author: The Little Lady Wore A Glove, 1976; composer: Memory Lane, 1966, rec., 1980; actor Army tng. films and local theatre groups. Home: 6515 Marsh Ave Huntsville AL 35806 Office: US Army MICOM DRSMI-HP Redstone Arsenal AL 35809

HARRIS, THOMAS RAYMOND, biomed. engr.; b. San Angelo, Tex., Feb. 19, 1937; s. Loyd Franklin and Rubye Pearl (Mitchell) H.; B.S., Tex. A. and M. U., 1958, M.S., 1962; Ph.D., Tulane U., 1964; M.D., Vanderbilt U., 1974; m. Carol Ann Cox, June 1, 1963; children—Calvin Thomas, Andrew Mitchell. Design engr. Standard Oil Calif., San Francisco, 1958-60; asst. prof. chem. engring. Vanderbilt U., 1964-67, asso. prof. chem. and biomed. engring., 1967-75, prof. biomed. and chem. engring., 1975—, asst. prof. medicine, 1974—, dir. biomed. engring. services Sch. Medicine, 1974—, dir. biomed. engring. program Sch. Engring., 1976—. Served to 2d lt. arty. U.S. Army, 1958-59. Mem. Biomed. Engring. Soc., Am. Inst. Chem. Engrs., Am. Heart Assn., Am. Soc. Engring. Edn., Am. Fedn. Clin. Research. Baptist. Contbr. numerous articles on biomed. engring., chem. engring., circulatory physiology and investigative medicine to profl. jours. Office: Box 1724 Sta B Nashville TN 37240

HARRIS, VANDER E., phys. plant dir.; b. Nashville, Tenn., Dec. 27, 1932; s. Adolphus A. and Sarah (Smith) H.; B.A., Fisk U., 1957, student urban planning grad. sch., 1975; student Tenn. State U., 1957-58; m. Janie Greenwood, Nov. 15, 1960; children—Vander (Jody) E., Jason Greenwood. With A. D. Harris, Contractor, Nashville, 1946-60; supt. bldgs. and grounds Fort Valley State Coll., 1960-66; archtl. design instr. Vocat. Tech. Sch., Macon, Ga., 1966-67; coordinator phys. facilities Ala. A. & M. U., 1967-69; dir. phys. facilities Fisk U., Nashville, 1969-76; asst. dir. phys. plant U. Tenn., Nashville, 1975-76; dir. Plant Benedict Coll., Columbia, S.C., 1976—. Served with AUS, 1953-55. Mem. Nat. Soc. Profl. Engrs., Soc. Coll. and Univ. Planning, Assn. Phys. Plant Adminstrs. Univs. and Colls., Am. Inst. Plant Engrs., VFW. Methodist. Home: 1417 Pine St Columbia SC 29204 Office: Benedict Coll Columbia SC 29204

HARRIS, VINCENT MADELEY, bishop; b. Conroe, Tex., Oct. 14, 1913; s. George Malcolm and Margaret (Madeley) H.; student St. Mary's Sem., La Porte, Tex., 1932-34, Pontifical N.Am. Coll., Rome, 1934-39; S.T.B., Pontifical Gregorian U., Rome, 1936, J.C.B., 1939; J.C.L., Cath. U. Am., 1940. Ordained priest Roman Catholic Ch., 1938; prof. St. Mary's Sem., La Porte, 1940-51; sec.-treas. St. Mary's Sem., Houston, 1952-66; chancellor Diocese of Galveston-Houston, 1948-66, diocesan consultor, 1950-66; 1st bishop of Beaumont, Tex., 1966-71; coadjutor bishop, Austin, 1971, 2d bishop, Austin, 1971—. Made domestic prelate with title Rt. Rev. Msgr., 1956. Decorated knight grand cross Equestrian Order of Holy Sepulchre of Jerusalem. Mem. Alumni Assn. N.Am. Coll. in Rome, Sons Republic of Tex. Club: K.C. (Tex. chaplain 1967-69). Home: 4007 Balcones Dr Austin TX 78731 Office: 1600 N Congress Ave Austin TX 78701

HARRIS, WALLACE GLENN, state ofcl.; b. Welch, W.Va., June 11, 1947; s. Walter Conner and Clara Catherine (Dominici) H.; B.A., U. Richmond, 1969, M.B.A., 1977; m. Nancy Allen McGrath, May 15, 1976; 1 son, David Glenn. Adminstrv. analyst Va. Dept. Taxation, Richmond, 1972-76, asst. personnel officer, 1976-77; ops. mgr. Va. Supplemental Retirement System, Richmond, 1977-79, asst. dir. for benefit programs and services, 1979—; adj. faculty in econs. J. Sargeant Reynolds Community Coll., Richmond, 1973-77. Lay minister, fin. chmn. Redeemer Catholic Ch., Mechanicsville, Va., 1979—. Served with USAF, 1969-72. Mem. Am. Soc. Personnel Adminstrn. Home: 619 Stuart Dr Mechanicsville VA 23111 Office: Virginia Supplemental Retirement System 11 N 6th St Richmond VA 23219

HARRIS, WILLIAM BURLEIGH, geologist; b. Norfolk, Va., July 2, 1943; s. Roy Solomon and Emily (Kasey) H.; B.S. in Geology, Campbell U., 1966; M.S. in Geology, W.Va. U., 1968; Ph.D. in Geology, U. N.C., Chapel Hill, 1975; m. Sharon Jones, Aug. 25, 1965; children—Daniel Wyatt, Timothy Roy. Petroleum geologist Texaco, Inc., Tulsa, 1968-70; econ. geologist Va. Div. Mineral Resources, Charlottesville, 1970-72; asst. prof. geology U. N.C., Wilmington, 1976—; cons. DuPont-Savannah River Lab., 1978, 79. N.C. Bd. Sci. and Tech. grantee, 1976-77. Mem. Am. Assn. Petroleum Geologists, Carolina Geol. Soc., Soc. Econ. Paleontologists and Mineralogists, Sigma Xi. Presbyterian. Author articles on coastal plain stratigraphy, radiometric dating, carbonate mineralogy. Home: 213 Dallas Dr Wilmington NC 28405 Office: Dept Earth Sciences University of North Carolina Wilmington NC 28403

HARRIS, WILLIAM DEAN, mfg. co. exec.; b. North Andover, Mass., July 15, 1927; s. John Leon and Gertude Mable (Steele) H.; student U. Houston, 1955; m. Mary Louise Yarbrough, Dec. 2, 1950; 1 dau., Deborah L. Personnel mgr. FMC Corp., Houston, 1951-73; dir. indsl. relations Reed Tool Co., Sherman, Tex., 1973-76; personnel mgr. Hydril Co., Houston, 1976-78; dir. personnel Pritchett Engring. & Machine Inc. div. Eagle Picher Industries, Houston, 1978—. Chmn. vocat. edn. dept. Sherman Sch. Dist., 1973-76. Served with USN, 1945-46, U.S. Army, 1950-51. Mem. Tex. Mfg. Assn. (chmn. indsl. relations), Houston Personnel Assn., Am. Soc. Personnel Adminstrn., Am. Mgmt. Assn., Nat. Tool and Die Assn. Republican. Methodist. Club: Masons. Home: 12323 Steeple Ln Houston TX 77039 Office: 8122 Hillsboro St Houston TX 77020

HARRIS, WILLIAM MADISON, banker, cons.; b. Farmville, Va., Feb. 28, 1932; s. William Madison and Ann (Thackston) H.; B.S., Coll. William and Mary, 1953; m. Marian Leonie Burks, July 27, 1957; children—Ann Holladay, William Claiborne, Elizabeth Madison, John Spencer Randolph. Dist. traffic supr., traffic engr., traffic supr.-personnel Chesapeake & Potomac Telephone Co. of Va., Richmond, Norfolk, Lynchburg, 1953-63; personnel dir. Central Nat. Bank of Richmond, 1963-71; v.p. personnel Planters Nat. Bank, Rocky Mount, N.C., 1971—; lectr. U. Richmond, 1965-71; adv. bd. Booke & Co., 1978—. Mem. subscriber adv. council Blue Cross and Blue Shield N.C., vice chmn., 1975-77. Mem. Henrico County Republican Com., 1964-66. Mem. exec. bd. Va. Coll. Placement Assn., 1968-69; bd. dirs. Richmond Senior Center, 1970-71. Served as lt. USNR, 1953-56. Mem. Am. Soc. Personnel Adminstrn. (accredited exec. in personnel; pres. Richmond 1965, mem. nat. compensation com. 1975—), S.R. (sec. Va. chpt. 1970-71), Rocky Mount C. of C., Order White Jacket, Sigma Epsilon Pi, Kappa Alpha, Republican. Presbyn. (elder). Rotarian. Clubs: Cosmopolitan (pres. 1958) (Lynchburg); Fishing Bay Yacht (commodore 1970) (Deltaville, Va.); Benvenue Country, Belmont Farms Racquet and Swim (Rocky Mount); Pamlico Yacht (Washington). Home: 210 Gravely Dr Rocky Mount NC 27801 Office: 131 N Church St Rocky Mount NC 27801

HARRIS, WILLIAM STEPHEN, II, steel co. exec.; b. San Diego, Mar. 24, 1931; s. William Stephen and Virginia (Powell) H.; B.S. in Aero. Engring., Ala. Poly. Inst., 1955; m. May 8, 1953; children—William Stephen, Marcus Edward. With Opelika (Ala.) Welding Machine & Supply, Inc., 1954—, v.p., 1965—. Mem. Opelika Indsl. Devel. bd. 1976—. Served with USN, 1950-51. Mem. ASTM, Assn. Iron and Steel Engrs. Clubs: Country, Elks. Home: 813 Shelby Ave Opelika AL 36801 Office: 1200 Steel St Opelika AL 36801

HARRISON, BARBARA SIMPKINS, nurse; b. Radford, Va., Dec. 8, 1950; d. Thomas Jefferson and Marjorie Maxine (Jacobs) Simpkins; A.A.S. in Nursing, Thomas Nelson Community Coll., 1971; B.S. in Nursing, Hampton (Va.) Inst., 1973, M.A. in Guidance and Counseling, 1975; m. Earl Wayne Harrison, Sept. 4, 1971. Pub. health nurse Portsmouth (Va.) Health Dept., 1971-72; nurse coordinator Peninsula Child Devel. Clinic, Va. Health Dept., 1972-73; instr. nursing, project coordinator Hampton Inst., 1973—. Mem. Am., Va. nurses assns., Am. Personnel and Guidance Assn., Am. Coll. Personnel Assn., Am. Pub. Health Assn., Postal Commemorative Soc. Mem. Ch. of Christ. Home: 1921 Long Bridge Ln Virginia Beach VA 23454 Office: PO Box 6517 Hampton Institute Hampton VA 23668

HARRISON, DALE STEPHEN, biomed. engr.; b. Cleve., Jan. 26, 1953; s. Dale Ellesworth and Mary Louise (Orne) H.; B.S.E., Duke U., 1975; M.B.A., Vanderbilt U., 1977. Accoustic engr. Gulf Oil Co., Pitts., 1976; process engr. Glasrock Products, Fairburn, Ga., 1977-78, project mgr. biomed. group, 1978-80, product mgr. biomed. group, 1980—. Mem. Am. Mgmt. Assn., Biomed. Mktg. Assn. Clubs: Atlanta Ski, Marietta (Ga.) Scuba. Home: 4012 Cove Pl Atlanta GA 30339 Office: 7380 Bohannon Rd Fairburn GA 30213

HARRISON, DAVID FRANCIS, data processing co. exec.; b. St. Louis, Aug. 1, 1936; s. Horace Earl and Lottie Ruth (Moore) H.; Mus.B., St. Louis Inst. Music, 1961; Mus.M., U. Nebr., 1966; postgrad. U. Iowa, 1966-70; m. Susan Jean Luttringhaus, May 13, 1979; children—Bryon Scott, Grant David. Music supr. North Andrew R-VI Schs., Rosendale, Mo., 1961-62, Keya Paha County Schs., Springview, Nebr., 1962-64; mgr., electronic repair shop Dietze Music House, Lincoln, Nebr., 1964-66; music dir. Sta. WSUI-KSUI, Iowa City, 67-71; Sta. WKAR-FM, East Lansing, Mich., 1971-74; asso. producer Nat. Public Radio, Washington, 1974; systems analyst Geico and Affiliates, Washington, 1974-76; sr. systems analyst Control Data Corp., Alexandria, Va., 1976—. Mem. Am. Mgmt. Assn., Pi Kappa Lambda. Home: 5111 Lavery Ct Fairfax VA 22032 Office: Control Data Corp 1800 N Beauregard Alexandria VA 22311

HARRISON, DONALD RICHARD, state senator; b. Montgomery, Ala., Nov. 24, 1947; s. Vernon Richard and Margaret Virginia (McLain) H.; B.S., Auburn (Ala.) U., 1970; J.D., Cumberland Sch. Law, Birmingham, Ala., 1973; m. Christry Lockett, Aug. 8, 1970; children—Donald Richard, Jackson Brett, Matthew David. Law clk. Ala. Ct. Criminal Appeals, Montgomery, 1973; admitted to Ala. bar, 1973; legal counsel Gov. Ala. Office Consumer Protection, 1973-75; practice in Montgomery, 1975—; individual practice, 1977—; mem. Ala. Senate from 26th Dist., 1978—; mem. Ala. Permanent Jud. Study Com.; mem. com. urban affairs So. Legis. Conf. Mem. Am. Bar Assn., Am. Trial Lawyers Assn., Ala. Bar Assn., Ala. Trial Lawyers Assn., Montgomery County Bar Assn., Ala. Peace Officers Assn., Ala. Cattlemen's Assn., Phi Alpha Delta, Tau Kappa Epsilon. Democrat. Baptist. Clubs: Lions, Shriners. Author articles in field. Home: 3723 Malabar Rd Montgomery AL 36116 Office: 516 S Perry St Montgomery AL 36104

HARRISON, ERNEST, JR., physicist; b. Jackson, Miss., Aug. 8, 1929; s. Ernest McAllister and Mary Bernice (McCoy) H.; B.S. in Physics, Millsaps Coll., 1951; M.S. in Physics, N.C. State U., 1964, Ph.D. in Materials Sci., 1974; m. Mary Jo Williams, June 6, 1951; children—Linda Gale, Ernest Barton. Sr. tech. writer Bendix Radio Corp., Towson, Md., 1952-55, project engr., 1957-61; research asso. dept. engring. research N.C. State U., Raleigh, 1961-67; research engr. engring. and environ. sci. div. Research Triangle Inst., Raleigh, 1967-74; dir. biomed. engring. dept. Miss. Meth. Rehab. Center, Jackson, 1974—. Served with AUS, 1955-57. Mem. Assn. Advancement Med. Instrumentation (recognition for accomplishments Bd. Examiners Clin. Engring. Certification), Phi Kappa Phi, Sigma Pi Sigma, Theta Nu Sigma. Research on impact forming of metallic materials, elec. conduction in lead monosilicate glass, tech. transfer mechanisms, biomed. engring. Patentee in field. Home: Cedar Hill Rd PO Box 566 Madison MS 39110 Office: 1350 E Woodrow Wilson Dr Jackson MS 39216

HARRISON, EUGENE TALBOT, III, computer systems scientist; b. Macon, Ga., Apr. 1, 1937; s. Eugene Talbot and Minnie Amerson (Pringle) H.; B.E.E., Ga. Inst. Tech., 1960, M.S. in Elec. Engring., 1962; postgrad. U. Va., 1967; m. Carol Anne Rollins, June 10, 1962; children—Dawn Victoria, Ansley Rollins, Shelley Reeves. Engr., Shell Chem. Co., Deer Park, Tex., 1961-62; electronics engr., data processing engring. mgr. WRAMA Service Engring., Warner Robins, Ga., 1962-70; systems analyst, clin. info. systems devel. mgr. Med. Coll. Ga., Augusta, 1970—. Bd. dirs. Augusta Art Assn., 1973-74; deacon, elder Covenant Presbyterian Ch.; chmn. SWAP Med. Spl. Interest Group, 1976—. Stained glass master craftsman. Fellow Nat. Inst. Pub. Affairs; mem. Electronics Computing Health Oriented, Hosp. Info. Systems Sharing Group, Assn. Computer Users, Tau Beta Pi, Eta Kappa Nu, Phi Kappa Phi. Club: Exchange (pres.). Home: 2807 Kipling Dr Augusta GA 30909 Office: Med Coll Ga Augusta GA 30901

HARRISON, FRANK RUSSELL, III, educator; b. Jacksonville, Fla., Mar. 11, 1935; s. Frank Russell, Jr. and Annye Mae (Blackwelder) H.; B.A. in Philosophy with honors, U. South, Sewanee, Tenn., 1957; M.A., U. Va., 1959, Ph.D., 1961; m. Dorothy Louise Gordy, Sept. 10, 1966. Grad. asst. U. Va., 1958-61; instr. philosophy Roanoke Coll., Salem, Va., 1961-62; mem. faculty U. Ga., Athens, 1962—, prof. philosophy, 1972—; vis. prof. U. N.C., Chapel Hill, summer 1963, Emory U., summer 1965, Sch. Info. and Computer Sci., Ga. Inst. Tech., 1965-66. Mem. nat. bd. examining chaplains Episcopal Ch., 1974-78. Mem. Ga., Am. philos. assns., Soc. Philosophy Religion (sec.-treas. 1965—), So. Soc. Philosophy and Psychology (chmn. program com. 1973, sect. chmn. 1965, 74, 75, 76, 78, council 1973-75), Metaphys. Soc. Am., Am. Guild Scholars (pres. 1968-69), AAAS, Gridiron Secret Soc., Phi Kappa Phi, Phi Sigma Tau. Author: Deductive Logic and Descriptive Language, 1969; also monographs, articles, chpts. in books. Mng. editor Internat. Jour. Philosophy Religion, 1972—. Home: 310 Cedar Creek Dr Athens GA 30605 Office: Dept Philosophy and Religion Univ Ga Athens GA 30602

HARRISON, JAMES HARVEY, JR., computer systems mgmt. cons.; b. Shelbyville, Tenn., Sept. 13, 1927; s. James Harvey and Mary Berniece (Orr) H.; B.S., Middle Tenn. State U., 1951; M.S., Am. U., 1975; m. Dolores May Hansen, Nov. 23, 1957; children—James Harvey III, Elizabeth Ann. Served as enlisted man U.S. Army, 1945-46; commd. ensign, U.S. Navy, 1951, advanced through grades to lt. comdr., 1972; asst. project officer, command ship data systems project and ops. officer U.S. Navy Electronics Lab., San Diego, 1963-64; exec. officer U.S.S. Maddox, 1964-66; project mgr. DLG26 class ships operational program Fleet Program Center, Virginia Beach, Va., 1966-69; dir. mgmt. info. systems Comdr. in Chief U.S. Navy Europe Hdqrs., London, 1969-72, ret., 1972; computer systems cons. Raytheon Co., Arlington, Va., 1972-78; program mgr. Japanese and German programs Internat. Systems div. Sperry Univac, Arlington, 1978—. Bd. dirs., chmn. schs. com. Taxpayers Alliance of Alexandria; mem. Alexandria Sch. Bd., 1979—; active Boy Scouts Am. Decorated Navy Commendation medal. Mem. Assn. Computing Machinery, Data Processing Mgmt. Assn., Soc. Mgmt. Info. Systems, Am. Soc.

for Info. Sci. Democrat. Methodist. Club: Masons. Home: 303 Aspen Pl Alexandria VA 22305 Office: RCA Bldg 1901 N Moore St Arlington VA 22209

HARRISON, JAMES WILLIAM, banker; b. Winder, Ga., June 18, 1939; s. James Thomas and Kathryn Marjie (Jones) H.; B.S., Ga. Inst. Tech., 1962; M.B.A., Ga. State U., 1967; m. Ina Sue Hunter, Sept. 1, 1962; children—James William, Mark Hunter, Amy Lynn. Sales rep. Burroughs Corp., 1962-63; sr. adminstr. Trust Co. Ga., 1964-65; sr. mktg. research analyst Lockheed-Ga. Co., 1966-70; asst. prof., chmn. undergrad. studies Calif. State U., Sacramento, 1971-75; asst. v.p. Bank of Barrow, Winder, 1975—. Deacon, vice chmn., chmn. 1st Christian Ch., Winder. Served with U.S. Army, 1960-66. Democrat. Clubs: Pine Shore, N.Am. Hunting. Home: 107 Olevia St Route 1 Sherwood Forest Winder GA 30680 Office: PO Drawer 627 Winder GA 30680

HARRISON, KENNETH GERALD, investment co. exec.; b. Chgo., Aug. 5, 1940; s. Harold Jack and Betty (Fretzin) H.; B.S., U. Ill., 1962; M.B.A., DePaul U., 1964; m. Jacqueline Zaffos, Apr. 20, 1968; children—Suzanne Melissa, Robert Martin. Account exec. E.F. Hutton & Co., Chgo., 1965-67; trust portfolio mgr. Harris Trust & Savs. Bank, Chgo., 1967-68; sr. investment analyst Central Nat. Bank Cleve., 1968-72; investment v.p. Am. Gen. Capital Mgmt. Co., Houston, 1972-79, v.p. A.G. Income Fund, Provident Fund for Income, Houston, 1973-79; with Highland Investment Corp., Memphis, 1980—; lectr. finance Cleve. State U., 1970-72. Served with Air N.G., 1964-70. Mem. Am. Fin. Assn., Houston Soc. Security Analysts, U. Ill. Alumni Assn., DePaul U. Alumni Assn. Jewish. Contbr. articles to Christian Sci. Monitor, Wall St. Transcript. Home: 2364 Dogwood Trail Dr Germantown TN 38138 Office: PO Box 11087 Memphis TN 38111

HARRISON, MANNIE PASCAL (PAT), clergyman; b. Atlanta, May 5, 1931; s. Mannie Pascal and Beulah Mae (Jordan) H.; A.A., Norman Coll., 1950; A.B., Mercer U., 1952; B.D., So. Baptist Theol. Sem., 1955, Th.M., 1956, D.Min., 1979; m. Gloria Jean Malcom, Aug. 3, 1953; children—Patti, Dodi, Jack, Jenni. Pastor, First Baptist Ch., Jefferson, Ga., 1956-58, Beech Haven Baptist Ch., Athens, Ga., 1958-66, First Baptist Ch., Hazlehurst, Ga., 1966-69, Beecher Hills Baptist Ch., Atlanta, 1969-72, First Baptist Ch., Mobile, Ala., 1972—; tchr. Extension Center Mercer U., 1956-69. Mem. Mayor's Commn. on Progress, Mobile, 1973-77; staff mem. lt. gov. State of Ala., 1976. Mem. Mobile Ministerial Assn., Bay Area Theol. Soc., Denominational Leadership Assn. Club: Rotary. Contbr. articles to denominational jours. Home: 4159 N Spring Valley Dr Mobile AL 36609 Office: 806 Government St Mobile AL 36602

HARRISON, PATRICIA GREENWOOD, historian; b. Monticello, Ark., Jan. 2, 1937; d. Howard Walter and Lorene (Stewart) G.; B.S.Ed., Henderson State Coll., 1959; M.A., So. Meth. U., 1964; postgrad. U. Wis., Madison, 1965-67; m. Edward Lindsay Harrison, Aug. 7, 1960; children—Gregory Edward, Rebecca Lindsay, Laura Patricia. Tchr. history Richardson (Tex.) High Sch., 1964-65; instr. Eastfield Coll., Dallas, 1972-74, Richland Coll., Dallas, 1972-74; instr. U. South Ala., Mobile, 1977—, Spring Hill (Ala.) Coll., 1979—. Mem. AAUW, Am. Hist. Assn., So. Hist. Assn., So. Assn. Women Historians, Soc. History Edn., Ala. Assn. Historians, Phi Alpha Theta. Methodist. Home: 413 Stirrup Ct Mobile AL 36608 Office: Dept History U South Ala Mobile AL 36688

HARRISON, ROBERT BRENT, radiologist; b. Greer, S.C., Mar. 17, 1938; s. Claudo Wilson and Janeie Louvenia (Hudson) H.; B.A., Duke U., 1959, M.D., 1962; m. Mary Susan Stretch, June 9, 1962; children—Sean Wilson, Scott Edwin, Travis O'Neal, Matthew Brent. Intern, St. Anthony Hosp., Denver, 1963; resident Norfolk (Va.) Gen. Hosp., 1966-69, radiology fellow U. Va., 1970; practice medicine specializing in radiology, Charleston, W.Va., 1970-73, Charlottesville, Va., 1973—; asst. prof. radiology, U. Va. Hosp., 1973-78, asso. prof., 1978-80; prof., chmn. dept. radiology U. Miss. Med. Center, Jackson, 1980—. Served with USN, 1964-66. Diplomate Am. Bd. Radiology. Mem. Am. Coll. Radiology, Am., Va. med. assns. Club: Boar's Head Sports. Contbr. articles, chpts. to med. jours. and texts. Office: Dept Radiology U Miss Med Center 2500 N State St Jackson MS 39216

HARRISON, STANLEY EARL, profl. services exec.; b. Northup, Ohio, Nov. 19, 1930; s. Stanley Mervin and Helen Mildred (Northup) H.; B.S. in Elec. Engring., Ohio State U., 1958; M.S. in Elec. Engring., U. N.M., 1962; m. Doris Ann Powell, June 21, 1953; children—Brenda Kay (Mrs. Peter Anthony Ruysen), Anne Elizabeth, David Stanley, Anita Lynn. Mem. tech. staff Sandia Corp., Albuquerque, 1958-63; supr., program mgr. nuclear div. Martin-Marietta Corp., Balt., 1963-68; dir. western operations BDM Corp., Albuquerque, 1968-72, v.p. ops., Vienna, Va., 1972-74, exec. v.p., 1974-78, exec. v.p., chief operating officer, dir., McLean, Va., 1978—, also dir., exec. v.p. BDM Services Co., McLean, 1971—; pres., dir. ZAPEX Corp., McLean, 1974-79. Chmn. Com. for Tomorrow, Ohio State U.; bd. dirs. Wolf Trap Found. Served with USAF, 1948-52. Named Distinguished Alumnus, Ohio State U. Registered profl. engr., Ohio. Mem. Assn. U.S. Army, IEEE (sr. mem.), Ohio State U. Assn. (life), Am. Mgmt. Assn., U.S. Air Force Assn., Nat. Council Tech. Services Industries (dir. 1976—), Armed Forces Communications and Electronic Assn., Am. Def. Preparedness Assn. (dir. Washington chpt. 1979—), Navy League U.S., Smithsonian Assos., Eta Kappa Nu, Pi Mu Epsilon. Methodist (chmn. stewardship commn.). Mason (Shriner); mem. Order Eastern Star. Clubs: Westwood Country (Vienna); International (Washington); Presidents (Ohio State U.). Contbr. articles to profl. jours. Home: 1417 Montague Dr Vienna VA 22180 Office: 7915 Jones Branch Dr McLean VA 22102

HARRISON, THOMAS COLLINS, mental health exec.; b. Nashville, July 5, 1948; s. Thomas Collins and Marylou (Wright) H.; B.A., Furman U., 1971; postgrad. Fla. State U., 1975-76; M.Ed., U. Fla., 1980, Ed.S., 1980; m. Linda Lanier, Aug. 20, 1976. Account exec. King Broadcasting Co., Seattle, 1971-72; pres. Grendel Maintenance, Inc., Seattle, 1972-75; grad. teaching asst. English Lang. Inst., U. Fla., Gainesville, 1979; dir. Day Treatment Center, Tri-County Mental Health Center, Palatka, Fla., 1979—; vol. tchr. Summit Alternative High Sch., Seattle, 1973-74. Mem. Counselor Edn. Student Assn. (co-founder 1976), U. Fla. Counselor Edn. Student Assn. (sec. 1976-77), Am. Personnel and Guidance Assn., Fla. Personnel and Guidance Assn., Fla. Assn. Counselor Edn. and Supervision. Founder, pub., editor-in-chief Caesura, 1976-78. Home: 2346 SW 34 Pl Apt C Gainesville FL 32608 Office: 421 St John's Ave Palatka FL 32077

HARRISON, WILLIAM GROCE, III, chem. co. exec.; b. Jacksonville, Fla., Jan. 19, 1934; s. William Groce and Mabel Ruth (Hopson) H.; student U. Va., 1951-53, U. Colo., 1953, Midwestern U., 1954; m. Jane Grace Napier, Jan. 20, 1953; children—Katherine J., Cynthia L., Susan L., William Groce IV. With Dowell, Inc., Wichita Falls, Tex., 1954-57; founder Select Industries, Inc., Wichita Falls, 1957, pres., dir., 1957—; officer dir. Lynn Chem. Co., Lubbock, Tex.; officer, dir. Select Chem., Wichita Falls. Christian Scientist. Mason (32 deg., Shriner). Home: 6901 Peoria St Lubbock TX 79413 Office: Box 4126 Wichita Falls TX 76308

HARRISON, WINNIE MYRTLE BROADWAY (MRS. JULIUS C. HARRISON), clubwoman; b. Madisonville, Tex.; d. Issac Newton and Eugenia (Stafford) Broadway; student Acad. Collegiate Inst., 1910-11, Bryan Bapt. Acad., 1912-13; m. Julius C. Harrison, Dec. 30, 1914; children—Ina Eugenia (Mrs. Ferrell Keefer), Barbara Avis (Mrs. Samuel Franklin Hiser), Myrtle Lee, Martel Wayne, Gloria June. Pres. of women Oak Cliff Christian Ch., Dallas, 1932-33, Magnolia Christian Ch., Ft. Worth, 1935-36; supt. Vacation Bible Schs., 1946-48, Black Presbyn. Missions 1946-50; pres. Aeolian Music Club, Spartanburg, S.C., 1953-54, Woman's Club, Spartanburg, 1954, 62, Glad Gardeners Garden Club, 1962. Homemakers Garden Club, 1964, Jubal Music Club, Spartanburg, 1954-56, 61-65, 68-69, Past President's Assembly, Spartanburg, 1964-65; bd. mem. S.C. Fedn. Music Clubs, 1950—, chaplain, 1968—, bd. mem.-at-large, 1979-81; mem. com. for nat. past pres. scholarship fund Nat. Fedn. Music Clubs, also life mem.; hon. mem. Philharmonic Music Club, Spartanburg; sponsor Spartanburg Little Theatre, Music Found. of Spartanburg; bd. dirs. Music Found. Spartanburg; state chmn. Blind and Deaf Coll. Spartanburg; mem. pres.'s club Converse Coll., Spartanburg, Christian Coll., Tulsa. Served with USAAF, 1944-45. Presbyterian (asst. organist 1969-70). Mem. Order Eastern Star.

HARRY, ROSELYN BERGER, chem. engr.; b. Lafayette, La., Aug. 30, 1936; d. Lewis Andrew and Agnes Rose (Comeaux) Berger; B.S. in Chem. Engring., U. So. La., 1958; m. Van Cleve Harry, Nov. 4, 1972; 1 son, Van Cleve III. Chem. engr. PPG Industries, Inc./Chem. Div. U.S., Lake Charles, La., 1958-68, chem. engr.-librarian, 1968-71, tech. info. coordinator, 1971—; chmn. com. ways and means PPG Employees Credit Union. Licensed chem. engr., La. Mem. Soc. Women Engrs., Spl. Libraries Assn., Am. Inst. Chem. Engrs., Internat. Mgmt. Council, PPG Recreation Assn., Ducks Unltd. Democrat. Roman Catholic. Home: 402 Ward Ln Sulphur LA 70663 Office: PO Box 1000 Lake Charles LA 70602

HART, CHARLES JOSEPH, mgmt. cons., accountant; b. Shreveport, La., Apr. 1, 1949; s. Charles Minter and Louise (Martin) H.; B.A. in Econs., Rice U., 1971; M.B.A. in Fin., U. Pa., 1973; m. Irene Alarcon, Mar. 18, 1977. Mgr. adminstrv. services div. Arthur Andersen & Co., Houston, 1973—. Bd. dirs. Bellfort Place Community Assn., 1978—. Mem. Rice Alumni Assn., Planning Execs. Inst., Tex. Soc. C.P.A.'s (data processing com. Houston chpt. 1980—), Am. Inst. C.P.A.'s, Pres.'s Club of Rice U. Greater Houston Builders Assn., Wharton Club Houston. Clubs: Athletic of Houston, Clear Lake Sports Car, Houston Racquetball. Office: Arthur Andersen & Co 711 Louisiana Suite 700 Houston TX 77002

HART, CLYDE LEWIS, computer programmer; b. Mayville, N.Y., Apr. 3, 1922; s. Lloyd F. and Ruth (Kidder) H.; B.S., N.Y. State Coll. Agr., Ithaca, 1946; M.S., Cornell U., 1960; m. Audry Woodall, June 29, 1979; 1 stepdau., Sharon Woodall Beard; children by previous marriage—Kathy M. Hart Faben, Cindy K. Hart Snyder. Asst. mgr. Seed Improvement Coop., Ithaca, 1955-64; computer programmer, dairy records processing lab. Cornell U., Ithaca, 1964-69; asst. prof. computer sci. tech. Tex. State Tech. Inst., Waco, 1969-78, computer programmer, 1978—. Mem. Village Planning Bd. Dryden (N.Y.), 1967-69. Served with USAAF, 1943-45. Decorated Air medal. Mem. Assn. Computing Machinery, Tex. Tech. Soc. Club: Kiwanis. Office: Computer Services Tex State Tech Inst Waco TX 76705

HART, DABNEY GARDNER, environ. analyst; b. Jackson, Miss., Dec. 3, 1940; d. Malcolm Everett and Nancy Elizabeth (Parrish) Gardner; A.B., Bryn Mawr Coll., 1962, M.A., 1970; m. Charles Willard Hart, June 9, 1962. Biologist/statistician Acad. Natural Scis., Phila., 1962-64, research biologist, 1964-70, spl. projects editor, 1970-75; sr. writer, editor MITRE Corp., McLean, Va., 1975-76, mem. tech. staff Metrek div., 1976—; mem. sci. adv. bd. EPA; cons. Mediterranean Marine Sorting Center, Khereddine, Tunisia; participant Archbold-Bredin-Smithsonian Expdn. to Dominica, W.I., 1964, 66; participant program in investigations in shallow-water eco-systems Smithsonian Instn., Carrie Bow Cay, Belize, 1976. NSF grantee, 1963-68. Mem. AAAS, Assn. Southeastern Biologists, Assn. Women in Sci., DAR, Sigma Xi. Clubs: Ninety Nines, Jr. League, Bryn Mawr (Washington). Author: (with C. W. Hart, Jr.) Ostracod Family Entocytheridae, 1974; contbr. articles to profl. publs. Office: 1820 Dolley Madison Blvd McLean VA 22102

HART, DOROTHY, actress, internat. affairs speaker; b. Cleve.; d. Walter C. and Mabel (Keister) H.; B.A. with honors, Flora Stone Mather Coll., Case-Western Res. U., 1948; 1 son, Douglas Hart. Starred in 24 movies including The Naked City, 1949, Gunfighters, 1949, Take One False Step, 1949, The Story of Molly X, 1950, Loan Shark, Down to Earth, I Was a Communist for the FBI, Outside the Wall, Raton Pass, Second Dawn, 1953; also many TV dramas including Omnibus, Suspense, Playhouse 90, Medallion Theatre, Studio One, Robert Montgomery Presents, Kraft Theater, Four Star Playhouse; TV panel shows include Pantomine Quiz, Stump the Stars, 1954-64, I've Got a Secret, Take a Guess, To Tell the Truth, Girl Talk, 1969; portrait artist; apptd. U.S. observer UN Conf., Geneva; speaker Motion Picture Producers Assn., Zonta Internat., UN 10th anniversary, Am. Assn. UN; ofcl. hostess reception com. N.Y.C. Mayor's Gracie Mansion, 1958-64; active USO, United Theatrical War Activities Com., ARC, Vis. Nurses Assn., work for retarded children. Recipient Golden Key award for outstanding actress Screenplay Motion Pictures Arts and Scis. Mem. Kappa Alpha Theta. Author poetry and prose. Home: 43 Martindale Rd Asheville NC 28804

HART, FRANK EDWARD, hosp. adminstr.; b. Clyde, Miss., May 17, 1915; s. Edward Soloman and Dora (Moore) H.; B.Sci. and Commerce, U. Miss., 1939; grad. Am. Coll. Hosp. Adminstrs., 1972; m. Margaret Walker, Aug. 28, 1937; 1 son, Frank Edward. Coach, athletic dir. public high sch., Crosby, Miss., 1939-41; rep. Gen. Motors Corp., 1941-42; owner, operator retail bus., Picayune, Miss., 1946-59; asst. dir. Univ. Hosp., Jackson, Miss., 1960-78; v.p. for hosp. affairs Miss. Meth. Hosp. and Rehab. Center, Jackson, 1978—, a founder, 1968, sec. bd. trustees, 1970-78, disaster chmn., 1976—; cons. health affairs; pres. Progressive Health Care Inst. Mem. health and welfare ministry Miss. Conf. United Meth. Ch., 1967; trustee Southeastern Meth. Agy. for Retarded, 1970-77. Served as officer USNR, 1942-46. Cert. lic. nursing home adminstr. Fellow Am. Coll. Hosp. Adminstrs.; mem. Jackson/Vicksburg Hosp. Council, Miss. Hosp. Assn., Southeastern Hosp. Conf., Am. Hosp. Assn., Am. Protestant Hosp. Assn., U. Miss. M Club, U. Miss. Alumni Assn., Blue Key, Omicron Delta Kappa. Republican. Clubs: Civitan (pres. club 1977, Honor Key 1978, Internat. Pres. award 1978), Colonial Country, Yellow Bird, Central Miss. M. Home: 3556 Edmar Pl Jackson MS 39216 Office: 1350 E Woodrow Wilson Dr Jackson MS 39216

HART, GARY RAY, physician; b. Fort Worth, May 29, 1949; s. Marlyn Ray and Betty Anne (Walton) H.; B.A., U. Tex., Austin, 1971; M.D., Southwestern Med. Sch., Dallas, 1975; m. LuAnn Logan, July 16, 1971. Intern, Parkland Meml. Hosp., Dallas, 1975-76, resident in internal medicine, 1976-78; asst. prof. dept. internal medicine Southwestern Med. Sch., 1978—, asso. dir. div. ambulatory care, 1978—. Diplomate Am. Bd. Internal Medicine. Mem. A.C.P., Tex. Med. Assn., Phi Beta Kappa, Alpha Omega Alpha, Pi Kappa Alpha. Republican. Home: 3323 Princess St Dallas TX 75229 Office: Dept Internal Medicine U Tex Health Sci Center 5323 Harry Hines Blvd Dallas TX 75235

HART, GEORGE EDWARD, mortgage co. exec.; b. Madison, Ind., May 11, 1945; s. Alvin B. and Catherine L. Shipley; student Hanover (Ind.) Coll., 1967-70; B.A., U. South Fla., 1971; postgrad. Sch. Mortgage Banking, Notre Dame U., 1977; m. Shirley Gail Stinnett, June 13, 1971; children—Catherine E., Paul E. Asst. to pres. Green River Constrn. Co., Altamonte Springs, Fla., 1971-75; loan officer Citizens Fidelity Bank & Trust Co., Louisville, 1975-78; loan officer Am. Fletcher Mortgage Co. of Indpls., Louisville, 1978—, asst. v.p., 1979—; instr. Am. Inst. Banking, Louisville, 1979—. Served with USAF, 1963-67. Mem. Sigma Pi Sigma. Home: 819 Foxwood Ave Louisville KY 40223 Office: 1941 Bishops Ln Louisville KY 40218

HART, JACQUELINE SPOERER, physician; b. Balt., July 11, 1934; d. Paul M. and Lillian (Spoerer) Hart; B.S., Rice Inst., 1956; M.D., U. Tex., Galveston, 1961. Intern, John Sealy Hosp., Galveston, 1961-62, resident internal medicine, 1962-65, internal medicine fellow endocrinology and metabolism, 1965-66; internal medicine fellow oncology and hematology M.D. Anderson Hosp. and Tumor Inst., Houston, 1966-67, asst. prof. medicine, 1969—; practice medicine specializing in internal medicine, Houston, 1967—. Exec. sec. Lymphoma Task Force, Nat. Cancer Inst., Washington, also mem. breast cancer com. Fellow Royal Soc. Health; mem. A.M.A., Am. Soc. Internal Medicine, So., Tex. med. assns., World, Harris County med. socs., Postgrad. Med. Assembly South Tex., S.W. Cancer Chemotherapy Group for Cancer Research, Leukemia Soc. Am., Am. Soc. Clin. Oncology, Internat., Am. socs. hematology, Am. Med. Women's Assn. N.Y. Acad. Scis., Doctors Club, Sigma Xi, Mu Delta, Alpha Epsilon Iota. Club: University Faculty (Houston). Home: 5301 Brae Burn Dr Bellaire TX 77401 Office: MD Anderson Hospital and Tumor Institute 6723 Bertner Ave Houston TX 77030

HART, JOHN WALLACE, utilities exec.; b. Anderson, S.C., Sept. 2, 1930; s. James Luther and Lola Irene (Rhouda) H.; B.E.E., Clemson U., 1958; m. Barbara Jean Kline, Nov. 24, 1955; children—John Kline, Stephanie Charlene, Angela Jeannine. With Fla. Power & Light Co., 1958—, emergency service supr., Sarasota, 1969, dist. supr., 1969-72, No. div. transmission and distbn. mgr., Daytona Beach, 1972-79, mgr. eastern div., W. Palm Beach, Fla., 1979—. Organizer, Miami Home Assn., 1963; Palmetto rep. Dade County Sch. Bd., 1964-65; Cotillion sponsor, 1968-69; active Ringling Art Mus., 1970-72, Sarasota Playhouse, 1970-72, Mus. Arts and Scis., 1972—, Daytona Symphony Soc., 1972-74, Civic Mus., 1972-74, Daytona Playhouse, 1972—. Served with USN, 1950-54; PTO. Recipient Dir. of Year award FBC of Daytona Beach, 1975. Mem. IEEE. Democrat. Baptist. Home: 12763 Westport Circle West Palm Beach FL 33411 Office: Drawer D West Palm Beach FL 33402

HART, LARRY EDWARD, data processing co. exec.; b. Deland, Fla., Jan. 28, 1945; s. Clarence William and Gladys Mary (Rodgers) Ludlow; B.S. in Elec. Engring., Ohio State U., 1969; m. Carol Lee Byer, July 17, 1972. Communications specialist UNIVAC/Sperry Rand Co., Blue Bell, Pa., 1969-72; dir. ops. Ednl. Telefilms, Blue Bell, 1972-75; mgr. performance services CACI, Washington, 1975-77; dir. mktg. and product design Xicron, Inc., McLean, Va., 1976-77; dir. Tesdata-MSB, Tesdata Systems Corp., Washington, 1977—; lectr. Dept. Def. Computer Inst., 1973—; lectr. in field. Bd. dirs. Big Bros. Assn., Phila., 1970-73. Named Big Bro. of Year, Phila., 1970. Mem. Am. Mgmt. Assn., Assn. Computing Machinery, Computer Measurement Group, Assn. Systems Mgmt. Presbyterian. Contbr. articles to profl. jours.; co-inventor micro processor based measurement device; co-designer measurement ser. bur. concept. Home: 2222 Wheelwright Ct Reston VA 22091 Office: 7291 Jones Branch McLean VA 22101

HART, LLOYD ANDREW, mfg. co. exec.; b. Houston, Sept. 23, 1947; s. J.T. and Georgie Lee (Lacy) H.; B.Arch., U. Houston, 1972; m. Lawanna Delores Stubblefield, Jan. 23, 1971; 1 dau., Tiffanie Lynn. Draftsman, Wilson, Morris, Crain & Anderson, Houston, 1966-72; with Si Morris Asso., Architects, Houston, 1972-73; founder Southwestern Symbols, Inc., Houston, 1971—, pres., chmn. bd., 1973—; project architect Hedrick Architects, Houston, 1977; office mgr. John S. Chase, Architect, Houston, 1978. Mem. AIA, Nat. Orgnl. Specialty Vendors Assn., (founding mem.), Omega Psi Phi (founder chpt., pres. 1970-71). Democrat. Baptist. Inventor automatic circle sanding machine, 1977. Home: 3902 Cheryl Lynne St Houston TX 77045 Office: 2615 Calumet Dr Houston TX 77004

HART, MAXWELL MORRIS, II, educator; b. Brownsville, Tex., Feb. 13, 1940; s. (Maxwell) Morris and (Elizabeth) Jeannette (Watson) H.; student Ottawa U., 1958-60, Kans. State U., 1960-61; B.A., Baylor U., 1963, M.A., 1966; postgrad. U. Tex., Austin, 1966-70; m. Nancy June Millegan, Dec. 17, 1966; children—Richard Allan, Ronald Aaron, Robert Andrew. Tchr. math. and physics LaFeria (Tex.) Ind. Sch. Dist., 1963-64, Waco (Tex.) Ind. Sch. Dist., 1964-66; teaching asst. U. Tex., Austin, 1966-68; asst. prof. math. and physics U. Mary Hardin-Baylor, Belton, Tex., 1968—, dir. career planning/placement center. Asst. scoutmaster Heart of Tex. council Boy Scouts Am., asso. post advisor, 1963-70; part time ch. music dir., children's choir dir., youth handbell choir dir.; Royal Ambassador counselor 1st Baptist Ch., Belton, dir., 1970—; associational brotherhood dir. Bell Assn. Bapt. Chs., Bell County, Tex., 1979. Eagle Scout; NSF fellow, 1971. Mem. Central Tex. Council Tchrs. of Math., AAUP, Math. Assn. Am., Coll. Placement Council, Southwestern Placement Assn., Sigma Pi Sigma. Baptist. Club: Hist. Phila. Soc. (sponsor). Composer musical arrangements for handbell ringers. Home: 503 E 12th St Belton TX 76513 Office: 9th at College St Belton TX 76513

HART, PATRICIA ECK-DAKE, educator; b. Hattiesburg, Miss., Jan. 16, 1942; d. Millard Eugene and Mary Frances (Pollitt) Eck; B.A. with honors, Purdue U., 1965; M.B.A. in Fin., Ga. State U., 1976; m. John Fincher Hart, June 17, 1978; children—Christopher, Karen, Wendy, Pam. Teaching fellow dept. real estate Ga. State U., Atlanta, 1977—; v.p. Independence, Inc. Am. Inst. Real Estate Appraisers grantee, 1979-80; Ga. Real Estate Commn. grantee, 1979-80. Mem. Nat. Assn. Corp. Real Estate Execs., Am. Real Estate and Urban Econs. Assn., Phi Chi Theta (officer), Rho Epsilon (v.p. 1977—), Phi Alpha Theta. Office: Dept Real Estate Suite 750 Lawyers Title 1 University Plaza Ga State U Atlanta GA 30303

HART, ROY JAMES, JR., aero. engr.; b. Elizabethton, Tenn., Dec. 29, 1927; s. Roy James and Charlsey Lee (Lacy) H.; B.S., E. Tenn. State U., 1950; postgrad. U. Calif., Los Angeles, 1956-57; m. Ethel Feathers, Nov. 24, 1954; 1 son, Gary Lee. Engr., N.Am. Aviation, Los Angeles, 1955-57; sr. engr. Lockheed Ga. Co., Marietta, 1957-68, group engr., 1968-72, aircraft devel. engr. specialist, 1972—; cons. Air Research, 1975-76; co-dir. aerospace edn. workshops, Ga. and Tenn. Scoutmaster, Boy Scouts Am., 1949-50, 74-76, asst. scoutmaster, 1977, com. chmn., 1972-79; bd. dirs. East Marietta Christian Ch., 1966-77, adult Bible sch. tchr., 1970-77; active Wheeler High Sch. PTA and Booster Club. Served with USAF, 1951-55; Korea; lt. col., regional comdr. Res. FAA certified flight instr. Mem. Lockheed Mgmt. Club, CAP, Order of Arrow. Author engring. reports; pub.

Principles and Theory of Flight, History of Aviation. Home: 12 Old Farm Rd Marietta GA 30067 Office: 86 S Cobb Dr Marietta GA 30060

HART, WILSON REESE, chemist; b. Binghamton, N.Y., Sept. 16, 1916; s. Wilson Taylor and Erma Marie (Reese) H.; m. Elva Elizabeth Drake, July 14, 1943. Owner, Columbia Labs. (S.C.), 1943-65, Coastal Labs., Pawleys Island, S.C., 1965—. Lectr., U. S.C., 1949-57. Chief devel. S.C. State Devel. Bd., 1949-57; dir. S.C. Regional Blood Center, Columbia, 1957-64; chmn. com. Georgetown County Office Econ. Devel. Named Man of Year, Columbia Jaycees, 1947. Mem. Georgetown C. of C. (pres. 1967), Internat. Brotherhood Magicians' Order of Merlin. Mason (33 deg.). Home: PO Box 242 Pawleys Island SC 29585 Office: Coastal Labs US Hwy 17 Pawleys Island SC 29585

HARTGRAVES, TRAVIS MILLER, lawyer; b. Sweetwater, Tex., Aug. 30, 1948; s. Ellis Elwood and Beulah Pearl (Miller) H.; B.B.A. in Finance, McMurry Coll., 1970; postgrad. Tex. Tech. U. Sch. Law, 1970-72; J.D., Oklahoma City U., 1974; m. Kay Galbraith, June 17, 1972; 1 dau., Tiffany Kate. Admitted to Tex. bar, 1974; individual practice law, Aspermont, Tex., 1974—; asst. county atty. Stonewall County, Tex., 1974-76, county atty., 1977—. Sec., Stonewall County Indsl. Found., 1975—; mem. housing subcom. West Central Tex. Council Govts., 1976—; bd. dirs. Stonewall County Cancer Soc. Unit, 1976—; bd. govs. Tex. Arts Alliance, 1977—; chmn. bd. govs. Gibson Meml. Nursing Home, Aspermont, Tex. Mem. Am., Tex. bar assns., Am. Judicature Soc., Tex. Dist., County Attys. Assn., Jaycees (charter pres. Aspermont chpt. 1975-76, sec.-treas. 1976-77, dist. dir. 1979-80, state dir. 1980-81, named Outstanding Young Man 1977), Delta Theta Phi. Democrat. Baptist. Club: Masons. Home: 3209 Westchester Abilene TX 79606 Office: PO Box 726 309 Hickory St Abilene TX 79604

HARTGROVE, BILLY RAY, ins. co. exec.; b. Beaumont, Tex., Sept. 10, 1931; s. L.B. and Virginia (Ledenham) H.; student McNeese State Coll., Lake Charles, La., 1949-52, U. Houston, 1959-60; m. Evelyn Summers, Mar. 31, 1955; children—Billy Ray, Brian Lee. Vice pres. Great Midwest Life Ins. Co., Oklahoma City, 1962-64; v.p., sec. Security Brokers Investment Corp., Oklahoma City, 1964-66, Great Midwest Life Ins., 1967-69; v.p., sec. United Investors, Inc., 1969-73, pres., 1974—; v.p., sec. Mid-American Investors Life Ins. Co., Oklahoma City, 1969-71, pres., 1971-72 (merged into Investors Life), pres. Investors Life, 1973-75, Liberty Investors Life, 1975—; dir. City Nat. Bank, Oklahoma City, Republic Bank, Oklahoma City. Served to lt. (j.g.) USNR, 1952-57. Club: Oak Tree Golf. Home: Villa 27 3101 Castle Rock Rd Oklahoma City OK 73120 Office: 4001 Lincoln Blvd Box 18839 Oklahoma City OK 73154

HARTIS, WILLIAM HARLEY, elec. design engr.; b. Aquilla, Tex., Nov. 17, 1937; s. William Martin and Clara Mae (McCain) H.; A.S., Arlington State Coll., 1959; B.S.E.E., U. Tex., Arlington, 1974; m. Sharon Ruth Johnson, July 24, 1964; children—Kelly Shawn, William Keith. With Dallas Power & Light Co., 1959—, engr., 1974-76, sr. engr., 1976—. Sports commr. Seagoville (Tex.) Sports Assn., 1975-76, pres., 1977-78; chmn. Seagoville United Way, 1977; mem. Seagoville City Council, 1977—, mayor pro tem, 1980—; mem. Seagoville A.R.C., 1979-80; bd. dirs. Dallas Girls Chorus, 1979—. Served with U.S. Army, 1961-63. Registered profl. engr., Tex. Mem. IEEE, Seagoville C. of C. Mem. Chs. of Christ. Club: Masons. Home: 600 Shady Ln Seagoville TX 75159 Office: 1506 Commerce St Dallas TX 75201

HARTLAGE, LAWRENCE CLIFTON, neuropsychologist, educator; b. Portsmouth, Ohio, May 11, 1934; s. Clifton Paul and Mary Louise (Pierron) H.; B.S., Ohio State U., 1959; M.A., U. Louisville, 1962, Ph.D., 1968; postgrad. Ind. U. Med. Center, 1972; m. Patricia Louise Hughes, Jan. 21, 1967; 1 dau., Mary Beth. Dir. psychology Central State Hosp., Louisville, 1966-68; clin. dir. Asso. Psychol. Services, Louisville, 1968-70; head clin. psychology sect. pediatric neurology Ind. U. Med. Center, 1970-72; head neuropsychology sect., prof. neurology and pediatrics Med. Coll. of Ga., Augusta, 1972—; cons. HEW, VA; vis. faculty Ind. and Ga. univs. Served with AUS, 1956-58. Rehab. Service Adminstrn. research grantee, 1970-72. Fellow Internat. Acad. Forensic Psychology, Am. Psychol. Assn.; mem. Nat. Acad. Neuropsychology (pres. 1978), Nat. Rehab. Tng. Inst. (pres. 1973-74), Nat. Rehab. Assn. (dir. 1972-73), Am. Soc. Human Genetics, Council for Exceptional Children, Sigma Xi. Author: Mental Development Evaluation of the Pediatric Patient, 1973; Anthology of Theory, Practice and Research in Learning Disabilities, 1974. Cons. editor Internat. Jour. of Forensic Psychology; Rehab. Psychology; Psychology in the Schs. Home: Route 3 Box 395 Evans GA 30809 Office: Med Coll Ga Augusta GA 30912

HARTLEY, ELLEN RAPHAEL, writer, social worker; b. Dortmund, Germany, Jan. 1, 1915; d. Gustave and Elizabeth (Steinweg) Raphael; grad. Schiller Lyceum, 1932; B.Social Work, Fla. Internat. U., 1976; m. William Brown Hartley, Oct. 7, 1957. Arrived in U.S., 1951, naturalized, 1962. Asst. advt. prodn. mgr. Sales Mgmt., N.Y.C., 1952-53, head records and research dept. 1954-55; prodn. control mgr. Grant Advt. Agy., Inc., Miami, Fla., 1956; billing supr. So. Advt. Inc., Miami, 1956-57; journalist, Miami, 1957—, author, 1957—; social worker dept. family medicine U. Miami Sch. Medicine, 1975-76, Fellowship House, Psycho-Social Rehab. Center Dade County, 1977—. Founder and adminstrv. asst. Southeastern Writers Conf., 1970, 71. Served with WAAF, 1943-46. Mem. Am. Soc. Journalists and Authors, Nat. Assn. Social Workers. Author: The Ellen Knauff Story, 1952, reprinted 1974; (with William B. Hartley) Your Important Years, 1962; Young Living, 1963; A Woman Set Apart, 1963; Eine Tapfere Frau, 1964; Osceola-The Unconquered Indian, 1973; The Alligator—King of the Wilderness, 1977. Contbr. articles to popular mags. Address: 5747 SW 82d St South Miami FL 33142

HARTLEY, JACK HUBERT, state health exec.; b. Middleport, Ohio, Feb. 6, 1926; s. Albert Elijah and Goldie (Greenway) H.; B.S. in Engring., U.S. Naval Postgrad. Sch., Monterey, Calif., 1964, M.S. in Mgmt., 1971; m. Jean Ann Board, Feb. 24, 1951; children—Susan Jane, James Douglas. Commd. 2d lt. U.S. Navy, 1943, advanced through grades; ret., 1973; dir. adminstrv. services W.Va. Health Dept., Charleston, 1973—. Decorated Air medal. Mem. Am. Public Health Assn., Electronic Computing Health Oriented Assn., W.Va. Public Health Assn. (exec. council), Fleet Res. Assn., Ret. Officers Assn. (pres. Mountain State chpt. 1975). Clubs: Masons, Shriners. Office: 1800 Washington St E Charleston WV 25305

HARTLEY, JAMES MITCHELL, architect; b. Macon, Ga., Dec. 5, 1922; s. James Mitchell and Ethel Claire (Cadenhead) H.; student North Ga. Coll., 1941-43, The Citadel, 1944; student Shrivenham Am. U. (Eng.), 1945; B.Arch., U. Fla., 1950; m. Edith Sneidar, July 2, 1951; children—Jan, James Mitchell, Karen. Architect, owner, mgr. James M. Hartley, Architect, Hollywood, Fla., 1955—; chmn. bd. dirs. Hollywood Fed. Savs. & Loan Assn., 1977—; pres. Beverly Hills, Inc., 1966—; dir. S.E. Bank of Broward County. Pres., Broward County Opportunity Center for the Handicapped, 1962; pres. Hollywood Pioneer Club, 1964; chmn. Com. of 100 of Hollywood, 1971; vice-chmn. Hollywood Restoration and Redevel. Authority, 1977—; chmn. Broward County Bd. Rules and Appeals, 1979. Served with U.S. Army, 1944-46. Mem. AIA, Fla. Assn. Architects, Fla. Alumni Assn., Delta Chi. Club: Kiwanis. Home: 3452 Pierce St Hollywood FL 33021 Office: 4600 Sheridan St Hollywood FL 33021

HARTLEY, ROBERT HAYWARD, ret. govt. ofcl.; b. Glen Ridge, N.J., May 28, 1929; s. James Leonard and Elizabeth (Gunn) H.; B.E.E., U. Fla., 1960, M.S.E., 1964; m. Verna Jo Stovall, Apr. 1, 1977; children from previous marriage—Martha Leigh, Laurie Celeste, Lisa Ann. Asst. in research dept. nuclear engring. U. Fla., Gainesville, 1960-65; nuclear engr. U.S. Army Nuclear Def. Lab., Edgewood Arsenal (Md.), 1965-66; project engr. High Voltage Engring. Corp., Burlington, Mass., 1966-70; tax examiner IRS, Andover, Mass., 1971-72, Memphis, 1972-73, engr., revenue agt., field audit, Atlanta, 1973-75, Jacksonville, Fla., 1975-78, Tampa, Fla., 1978-79. Served with USMC, 1948-56. Mem. IEEE, Am. Nuclear Soc., Tau Beta Pi, Sigma Tau, Phi Kappa Phi. Home: 1851 Juarez Way S Saint Petersburg FL 33712

HARTLEY, WILLIAM CADENHEAD, surgeon; b. Macon, Ga., July 16, 1924; s. James M. and Claire C. (Cadenhead) H.; B.S., Emory U., 1945, M.D., 1949; m. Barbara Conti, Aug. 26, 1973; children by previous marriage—William Miller, John; 1 dau., Kristen. Rotating intern Brooke Gen. Hosp., San Antonio, 1949-50, straight surg. intern Grady Meml. Hosp., Atlanta, 1950-51; resident in surgery Vanderbilt U. Hosp., Nashville, 1953-55, Jackson Meml Hosp., Miami, Fla., 1955-57; practice medicine specializing in surgery, Hollywood, Fla., 1957—; mem. staff Meml. Hosp., Hollywood, 1957—, chief of staff, 1967-69, chief surgery 1962-63, 75—; clin. instr. surgery U. Miami, (Fla.) 1957-65. Bd. dirs. YMCA, Hollywood, 1970-77; mem. City of Hollywood Adv. bd., 1971-72; Served to capt. MC, U.S. Army, 1951-53. Diplomate Am. Bd. Surgery. Mem. Am., Fla., Broward County (v.p. 1977, pres. 1979-80) med. assns., Southeastern Surg. Congress, So. Med. Assn., ACS, Fla. Assn. Gen. Surgeons, Pan. Am. Med. Assn., Kiwanis (dir.), Com. of 100 (chmn. 1977), Hollywood C. of C. (dir.). Republican. Presbyterian. Home: 600 N 35th Ave Hollywood FL 33021 Office: 3714 Johnson St Hollywood FL 33021

HARTMAN, BART PAUL, educator; b. Chgo., Aug. 18, 1943; s. Bart Paul and Rose Ann (Correra) H.; B.B.A., U. Wis., 1966; M.B.A., No. Ill. U., 1967; D.B.A., U. Ky., 1975; m. Elizabeth Anne Gilday, Aug. 16, 1969; 1 son, Bart Paul III. Asst. prof. acctg. No. Mich. U., Marquette, 1967-72; grad. asst. U. Ky., Lexington, 1972-75; asso. prof. acctg. La. State U., Baton Rouge, 1975—. Recipient Lybrand Gold medal, 1977; C.P.A., La. Mem. Nat. Assn. Accountants (Dir. of Yr. 1976-77, 77-78), Am. Inst. C.P.A.'s, Am. Acctg. Assn., Am. Inst. Decision Scis., La. Soc. C.P.A.'s, Evans Scholar Alumni Assn., Beta Alpha Psi (Outstanding Faculty Vice-Pres. 1979), Beta Gamma Sigma, Alpha Kappa Psi, Sigma Iota Epsilon. Contbr. articles to profl. jours. Office: Dept Acctg Coll Bus Adminstrn La State U Baton Rouge LA 70803

HARTMAN, JAMES PAUL, mech. engr.; b. Hannibal, Mo., June 21, 1937; s. Bert Emerson and Alta Lucille (Agnew) H.; B.S., U. Mo., Rolla, 1959, M.S., 1963; postgrad. N.C. State U., 1964-66; postgrad. Calif. State U., 1967-73; grad. Command and Gen. Staff Coll., 1977; postgrad. E. Tenn. State U., 1978, U. So. Miss., 1979; m. Ingrid Winfriede Stenzenberger; children—Susan, Nancy, Peter, Andrea. Engr., Lockheed Calif. Co., Burbank, 1962-63, Space Gen. Corp., El Monte, Calif., 1963-64; instr. N.C. State U., Raleigh, 1964-66; mech. engr. Aerojet Nuclear Co., Sacramento, 1966-74, TVA, Knoxville, 1974—; partner, Systems Engring., Knoxville, 1975—. Served with AUS, 1959-62. Registered profl. engr., Tenn. Mem. ASME, Nat. Rifle Assn. (life), Appalachian Zool. Soc., Assn. U.S. Army, Res. Officers Assn., Sigma Phi Epsilon. Republican. Home: 1217 Glencliff Rd Kingsport TN 37663 Office: PO Box 938 Kingsport TN 37662

HARTMAN, RENATE KATHARINA, personnel co. exec.; b. Solingen, W.Ger., June 7, 1940; d. Mathias Wilhelm and Frieda Emma (Kapraun) Krapp-Williams; came to U.S., 1955, naturalized, 1962; B.A., Barry Coll., Miami Shores, Fla., 1962; M.A., Fla. Atlantic U., 1971; m. James E. Hartman, June 15, 1968 (dec. Feb. 1974). Tchr., Dade County schs., Miami, Fla., 1962-65, 66-70; stewardess Northeast Airlines, Boston, 1965-66; v.p., gen. mgr. Hartman Personnel Enterprises, Inc., Miami, 1971-74, pres., 1974—; pres., founder Hartman Services, Inc., Miami, 1977—, offices also in Miami, Ft. Lauderdale, Dallas and Austin; v.p. Hartman & Assos., exec. search, 1968-76, pres., 1979—; dir. Plaza Bank, Miami, Federated Services, Inc. Adv. council Sch. Bus., Barry Coll., Miami Shores, Fla. Mem. Nat. Assn. Temporary Services, Ind. Office Services Inst. Republican. Roman Catholic. Home: 1 Palm Bay Plaza Miami FL 33138 Office: 3550 Biscayne Blvd Miami FL 33137

HARTMAN, WILLIAM HENRY, guidance and counseling dir.; b. Houston, Oct. 28, 1946; s. Henry H. and Marie Jeanne (Boulian) H.; B.A., Holy Redeemer Coll., Waterford, Wis., 1969; M.A., U. St. Thomas, Houston, 1972; M.Ed., Loyola U., New Orleans, 1974; m. Sylvia Marie Rezzoffi, Aug. 5, 1972; children—Alexander Henry, Jacquelyn Roselle. Seminarian, tchr., youth dir., vice-province New Orleans, Redemptorist Fathers, 1966-70; counselor New Orleans Mental Health Inst., 1973-74; dir. guidance and counseling services Catholic Schs. Galveston-Houston Diocese, 1974—; family counselor. Mem. Am., Tex., Houston (dir. 1975-76, 77—) personnel and guidance assns., Am. Sch. Counselor Assn. Democrat. Roman Catholic. Club: North Spring Civic. Contbr. articles to religious publs. Home: 23803 English Oaks Spring TX 77373 Office: 2401 Holcombe Houston TX 77021

HARTMANN, DONALD H., business exec.; b. 1927; B.S. in Mech. Engring., 1949. Dir. diesel engine div. Gen. Motors Corp., 1949-51; mgr. govt. and indsl. products and planning, Packard Motor Car Co., 1951-57; v.p. Dura Corp., 1957-61; exec. v.p. Heath div. Daystrom Electric, Inc., 1961-63; with Dresser Industries, Inc., Dallas, Tex., 1963-71, pres. Lane Wells div., 1963-66, pres. Magcobar div., 1966-67, v.p. petroleum and minerals group, 1967-69, exec. v.p., 1969-71, also dir.; pres., chief exec. officer Crutcher Resources Corp., Houston, 1971-75, pres., chief exec. officer Ramteck Industries, Inc., Houston, 1975—, also subs. F-H Maloney Co., Houston, The Rochester Corp., Culpeper, Va.; dir. Peninsula Resources Corp., Corpus Christi, Tex. Served with USNR, 1945-47. Office: 1212 Main St Suite 1500 Houston TX 77002

HARTON, THOMAS GORDON, water resources cons.; b. Phila., Apr. 12, 1909; s. Horace Decatur and Alice Vera (Yarbrough) H.; B.S. in C.E., U. Tenn., 1933; m. Margaret Isabelle Burch, June 22, 1960; m. Eddie Ruth Horton, Apr. 25, 1942 (div. 1949); 1 son, Thomas Dean. With TVA, Knoxville, 1933-41, 46; prin. engr. U.S. Bur. Reclamation, Washington, 1946-47; commd. maj. C.E., U.S. Army, 1947, advanced through grades to col., 1958; ret., 1964; dir. planning div., office water and air resources Dept. Natural and Econ. Resources N.C., Raleigh, 1964-75, ret., 1975; now cons. Alt. mem. Ohio River Basin Commn., 1971—, S.E. Basins Inter-Agy. Com., 1967—. Served to lt. col. AUS, 1941-46; CBI. Registered profl. engr., Tenn. Fellow ASCE (life); mem. Soc. Am. Mil. Engrs., Am. Soc. Photogrammetry (life), A.A.A.S., Phi Kappa Phi, Tau Beta Pi, Sigma Phi Epsilon. Rotarian. Supervisory editor Wise Management of North Carolina Water Resources, 3 vols., 1966-67. Home: 404 College St Eastman GA 31023

HARTSON, MAURICE JOHN, JR., ins. agt.; b. New Orleans, Jan. 20, 1906; s. Maurice J. and Marguerite (Calongne) H.; grad. Loyola U. of South, 1922-26; m. Elizabeth Freret, June 6, 1929; children—Liseanne (Mrs. J. Parham Werlein), Maurice J. III, Elizabeth. In ins. bus., 1924—; pres. M.J. Hartson, Inc., New Orleans, 1937—; dir. Lafayette Ins. Co.; dir., v.p. Columbia Homestead Assn. Past chmn. New Orleans Fire Prevention Bd.; pres. New Orleans Community Chest, 1952, 73; pres. United Fund Greater New Orleans, 1962-63; pres. adv. com. Convent of Good Shepherd; pres. St. Marys Boys Orphan's Asylum; chmn. Civic Affairs Com.; pres., organizer New Orleans Area Health Planning Council. Bd. dirs. St. Mary's Dominican Coll., New Orleans Speech and Hearing Center; mem. pres.'s council Jesuit High Sch. Recipient Weiss award NCCJ, medallion Order St. Louis, Archdiocese New Orleans; named One of 10 Outstanding Persons, Inst. Human Understanding, 1977, Knight of St. Gregory; named to Vol. Activists, 1976. Mem. Nat. Assn. Ins. Agts. (dir., mem. exec. com.), War of 1812 Soc., Blue Key (elected hon. mem. 1963), Sigma Alpha Epsilon. Catholic. Most loyal gander Blue Goose, Knight of St. Gregory. Clubs: Pickwick (past pres.); Serra (pres. New Orleans; dist. gov.); Stratford, New Orleans Country, Southern Yacht. Home: 1528 Webster St New Orleans LA 70118 Office: 332 Carondelet St New Orleans LA 70130

HARTUNG, RODERICK L., refinery exec.; b. Albion, Mich., July 25, 1935; s. Clarence Robert and Evelyn Anna (Young) H.; B.S. in Chem. Engring., U. Mich., 1958; M.S. in Chem. Engring., 1959; postgrad. exec. program Stanford U., 1976; m. Stella Evelyn Ludy, Jan. 3, 1959; children—Kathy, Victoria, Robert. Project engr. Standard Oil of Calif. Corp., asst. supt., supt. mfg. ops. Richmond Refinery and Hawaiian Refinery; dir. Refinería Conchán-Chevron-Latin Am., Lima, Peru; refinery mgr., Salt Lake Refinery, Chevron-West; asst. chief engr. corp. engring. dept. Standard Oil of Calif., San Francisco; now refinery gen. mgr. Chevron U.S.A. Inc., Pascagoula, Miss. Exec. bd., v.p., chmn. long-range planning com. Pine Burr area council Boy Scouts Am.; bd. dirs., chmn. allocation com. United Way of Jackson County (Miss.); bd. dirs., chmn. prospect com. Jackson County Econ. Devel. Found.; chmn. task force on rapid transit Jackson County; bd. dirs. E.H. Bacot Found. of Jackson County; bd. dirs., v.p. Community Concerts Assn.; mem. Am. Enterprise-M.B. Swayze Found.; adv. bd. Nat. Alliance Bus. Recipient Gold award Nat. Petroleum Refiner's Assn., 1977. Named Outstanding Citizen in Jackson County, 1980. Mem. Pascagoula-Moss Point Area C. of C. (exec. bd. dirs., treas. 1978-79, pres.-elect 1979), Indsl. Mgrs. Assn. Jackson County, Clubs: Pascagoula Rotary (pres. 1980-81 dir., chmn. budget and allocation com., chmn. scholarship program), Chevron Speaker's (Golden award for service to community 1979). Office: PO Box 1300 Pascagoula MS 39567

HARTWELL, WILLIAM GERSHAM, III, musician, educator; b. Spokane, Wash., Mar. 20, 1939; s. William Gersham and Barbara (Parker) H.; B.A., Whitman Coll., 1961; Mus.M., Ind. U., 1964; m. Leilani Lu Fillhard, Sept. 23, 1972; children—William, Susanne, Ronda, Leslie. Instr. music Eastern Wash. State Coll., Cheney, 1963-66, Whitworth Coll., Spokane, Wash., 1967-68; chmn. dept. music St. George's Sch., Spokane, Wash., 1964-69; asso. instr. music Ind. U., 1969-71; asst. prof. music Alma (Mich.) Coll., 1971-72; asso. prof. music Tex. Tech. U., Lubbock, 1973—; vocal clinician and adjudicator, dir. ch. choirs, 1963—. Contributing mem. Lubbock Symphony Orch., 1974—; dir. music St. John's United Meth. Ch., Lubbock, Tex., 1974—; bd. dirs. Lubbock Community Concert Assn., 1976—. Mem. Nat. Assn. Tchrs. Singing, Nat. Soc. for Lit. and Arts, AAUP, Tex. Assn. Coll. Tchrs., Phi Mu Alpha, Phi Delta Kappa, Beta Theta Pi. Methodist. Bass-baritone soloist with symphony orchestras throughout U.S. and Canada; premiered role of Rogozhin in opera Myshkin, Pub. Broadcasting Service TV, 1973. Home: 3204 68th St Lubbock TX 79413 Office: Dept Music Texas Technical University Lubbock TX 79409

HARVARD, BEVERLY JOYCE, city ofcl.; b. Macon, Ga., Dec. 22, 1950; d. Arcelious and Irene (Perkins) Bailey; B.A., Morris Brown Coll., 1972; M.S., Ga. State U., 1980; m. Jimmy C. Harvard, July 30, 1972. Police officer City of Atlanta, 1973-75; affirmative action specialist City of Atlanta, 1975-80; dir. Office Public Info., Atlanta Dept. Public Safety, 1980—; crime prevention cons., security cons. Mem. Am. Bus. Women's Assn., Am. Mgmt. Assn., Am. Soc. Profls. and Exec. Women, Bur. of Nat. Affairs Personnel Policy Forum, Delta Sigma Theta. Club: United Youth-Adult Conf. Home: 3541 Cumberland Rd East Point GA 30344 Office: 175 Decatur St Atlanta GA 30303

HARVEY, EDWIN MALCOLM, mfg. co. exec.; b. Hattiesburg, Miss., July 23, 1928; s. Clarence C. and Ezilda (Pegues) H.; B.S. in Chem. Engring., La. State U., 1950; m. Charlotte Trewolla, July 7, 1951; children—Sylvia Jane, Sharon Ann, Rebecca Lynn. With Ethyl Corp., 1950—, dir. econ. evaluation, N.Y.C., 1960-66, pres. William L. Bonnell Co. Inc. subs. Ethyl Corp., Newnan, Ga., 1966—, also dir., v.p. aluminum Ethyl Corp., Richmond, Va., 1975—; pres., dir. Capitol Products Corp. subsidiary Ethyl Corp.; dir. First Nat. Bank in Newnan. Bd. dirs. Newnan Hosp. Mem. Ga., Newnan-Coweta chambers commerce. Episcopalian (sr. warden 1968). Home: PO Box 636 Newnan GA 30264 Office: 25 Bonnell St Newnan GA 30263

HARVEY, JAMES DOUGLAS, ednl. adminstr.; b. Tupper Lake, N.Y., Mar. 7, 1947; B.S., State U. N.Y., Buffalo, 1970, Ed.M., 1971, Ed.D., 1978. Tchr. phys. edn. Robert Lynde Sch., Williamsville, N.Y., 1969-70, asst. prin., 1972-76; instr. State U. N.Y., Buffalo, 1970-71; tchr. health edn. East Aurora (N.Y.) High Sch., 1971-72; dir. Catholic Charities Youth Programs, Erie County, N.Y., 1976-78; asst. prof., chmn. dept. health, phys. edn. and recreation Miami-Dade Community Coll., Miami, Fla., 1978—; cons. preceptual motor problems; lectr. in field; research technician Buffalo Bills; recreation cons. ARC; mem. Erie County Youth Adv. Council, 1976-78; mem. steering com. N.Y. State Edn. Dept.'s Telecommunications Project, 1975-78. Mem. Assn. Supervision and Curriculum Devel., State U. N.Y. at Buffalo Alumni Assn., Am. Personnel and Guidance Assn., AAHPER, Council Exceptional Children, Amateur Softball Assn., Boys' Club Am. (hon. life), Sigma Phi Epsilon (pres. local chpt. 1968-69, del. 1968-69). Home: 10501 SW 108th Ave Apt 204A Miami FL 33176 Office: 11011 SW 104th St Miami FL 33176

HARVEY, RAYMOND CHESTERFIELD, JR., educator; b. Tyler, Tex., Dec. 14, 1934; s. Raymond Chesterfield and Eula Mae (Cromwell) H., Sr.; B.A., Baylor U., 1956; B.D., Southwestern Sem., 1960; M.S., E. Tex. State U., 1967, Ph.D., 1971; m. Mary Powell Garton, Oct. 16, 1956; children—Mary Grace, Raymond, III. Ordained to ministry Baptist Ch., 1956; pastor Hopewell Bapt. Ch., Tyler, Tex., 1956-57, First Bapt. Ch., Bullard, Tex., 1958-62, Winnsboro, Tex., 1962-67, Shady Grove Bapt. Ch., Greenville, Tex., 1967-69; instr. sociology E. Tex. State U., Commerce, 1967, instr. psychology, 1968-71; owner, operator Day Car Center, Commerce, 1969-71; prof. psychology, counseling Samford U., Birmingham, Ala., 1971—; cons. family affairs Iron & Steel Credit Union, Birmingham, 1972—. Voted Friendliest Prof. by Samford U. student body, 1975.

Mem. Am. Psychol. Assn., Am. Personnel and Guidance Assn., Am. Coll. Personnel Assn., Student Personnel Assn. for Tchr. Edn., Assn. for Counselor Edn. and Supervision, Phi Delta Kappa. Baptist. Clubs: Rotary, Shriners, Masons. Contbr. research paper and article. Home: 2360 Hackberry Ln Birmingham AL 35226 Office: 800 Lakeshore Dr Birmingham AL 35226

HARVEY, RICHARD MCEUEN, real estate and constrn. co. exec.; b. Durham, N.C., July 4, 1935; s. Arthur Lester and Mary (McEuen) H.; B.S. C.E. and Constrn., N.C. State U., 1959; m. Ann Craven, Dec. 22, 1957 (dec.); 1 dau., Lane. Constrn. project mgr. L.S. Bradshaw Corp., Salisbury, N.C., 1959-66; gen. mgr. Gray Constrn. Co., Inc., Lexington, N.C., 1966-69; v.p., project mgr. Gates Constrn. Co., Inc., Mooresville, N.C., 1969-72; pres. Harvey Constrn. & Craven Properties, Salisbury, 1972—; dir., sec. Padgett Investments, Inc., Salisbury. Served with U.S. Army, 1954-56. Mem. Kappa Alpha Order. Republican. Presbyterian. Home: 1310 E Colonial Dr Salisbury NC 28144 Office: 1917 W Innes St Salisbury NC 28144

HARVEY, WILLIAM BRANTLEY, JR., former lt. gov. S.C.; b. Walterboro, S.C., Aug. 14, 1930; s. William Brantley and Thelma (Lightsey) H.; A.B., in Polit. Sci. (2d honor grad.), The Citadel, 9151, LL.D. (hon.), The Citadel, 1978; J.D. magna cum laude, U. S.C., 1955; m. Helen Coggeshall, Dec. 30, 1952; children—Eilen L., William Brantley III, Helen C., Margaret D., Warren C. Admitted to S.C. bar; practiced in Beaufort, S.C., 1955—; sr. partner firm Harvey, Battey & Bethea; mem. S.C. Ho. of Reps. from Beaufort County, 1958-75; lt. gov. S.C., Columbia, 1975-78; mem. exec. com. Nat. Lt. Govs. Conf., 1977-78; local dir. Citizen & So. Nat. Bank S.C.; dir. Tidewater Investment & Devel. Corp., S.C. Devel. Corp. Commr. Coastal Carolina council Boy Scouts Am.; trustee Allen U., Coker Coll. Served to lt. U.S. Army, 1952-54. Mem. Am., S.C., Beaufort County bar assns., Beaufort County C. of C. (dir.), Am. Legion, Phi Beta Kappa, Kappa Alpha, Phi Delta Phi, Omicron Delta Kappa. Democrat. Presbyterian (elder; tchr. Sunday sch.). Office: 1001 Craven St PO Box 1107 Beaufort SC 29902

HARVEY, WILLIAM BYRON, lawyer; b. Quitman, Miss., July 7, 1942; s. Lucian Alston and Mary Florence (Patton) H.; B.S., Miss. State U., 1964; J.D., U. Miss., 1967; LL.M., N.Y. U., 1969; m. Sylvia Nelle Abernethy, Oct. 8, 1967; 1 son, William Byron. Admitted to Miss. bar, 1967; U.S. Supreme Ct. bar, 1971, Ala. bar, 1971; atty. advisor to chief judge U.S. Tax ct., Washington, 1969-71; mem. firm Armbrecht, Jackson & DeMouy, Mobile, Ala., 1971—, partner, 1975—; dir. Harvey Constrn. Co. Sec., atty. John M. Will Scholarship Found. of Sigma Delta Phi. Served to capt. AGC, U.S. Army, 1967-68. Mem. Am., Miss. State, Ala. State, Am. bar assns., Phi Alpha Delta, Sigma Chi. Methodist. Clubs: Touchdown, Asst. Coaches, U.S. Ala. Basketball Booster (pres. 1976-77). Mem. Miss. Law Jour. Home: 5514 Nassau Dr Mobile AL 36608 Office: Box 290 Mobile AL 36601

HARVEY, WILLIAM ROBERT, ednl. inst. pres.; b. Brewton, Ala., Jan. 29, 1941; s. Willie D.C. and Mamie Claudis (Parker) H.; B.A., Talladega Coll., 1961; Ed.D., Harvard U., 1971; m. Norma Baker, Aug. 13, 1966; children—Kelly Renee, William Christopher. Asst. to dean Harvard Grad. Sch. Edn., 1969-70; adminstrv. asst. to pres. Fisk U., 1970-72; v.p. student affairs, dir. planning Tuskegee Inst., 1972-75, v.p. adminstrv. services, 1976-78; pres. Hampton (Va.) Inst., 1978—; dir. United Va. Bank, Newport News Savs. and Loan Assn.; chmn. Pres.'s Nat. Adv. Council Elem. and Secondary Edn. Act. Bd. dirs. United Way, Peninsula Econ. Devel. Council; mem. alumni council Harvard U. Served with U.S. Army, 1962-65. Woodrow Wilson Found. Martin Luther King fellow; Harvard U. Higher Edn. Adminstrv. fellow; Woodrow Wilson Found. intern fellow. Mem. Am. Council Edn., Am. Assn. Higher Edn., Va. Assn. Higher Edn., Nat. Assn. Equal Opportunity in Higher Edn., Peninsula C. of C. (dir.), Omega Psi Phi. Baptist. Club: Peninsula Rotary. Author articles in field. Office: Hampton Inst Hampton VA 23668

HARVIE, EDWIN JAMES, JR., physician; b. Winston-Salem, N.C., Sept. 22, 1932; s. Edwin James and Mary Henderson (Roane) H.; B.A., U. Va., 1954, M.D., 1958; m. Katherine Elizabeth Wickre, Sept. 1, 1956; children—Elizabeth Roane, Edwin James III. Intern, Kans. U. Med. Center, Kansas City, 1958-59; resident in medicine Bowman Gray Sch. Medicine, Winston-Salem, 1961-64; practice medicine specializing in internal medicine, Danville, Va., 1964—; mem. staff Meml. Hosp. Pres. Danville Concert Assn., 1971-74. Served with M.C., U.S. Army, 1959-61. Diplomate Am. Bd. Internal Medicine. Fellow A.C.P.; mem. AMA, Am. Soc. Internal Medicine, Med. Soc. Va., Danville Pittsylvania Acad. Medicine. Episcopalian. Clubs: Rotary, Danville Golf, German of Danville. Office: 101 Holbrook St Danville VA 24541

HARVILL, HALBERT, state senator; b. Tottys Bend, Tenn., Nov. 28, 1893; B.S., Middle Tenn. State U.; M.A., George Peabody Coll., Nashville; married. Commr. of edn. State of Tenn.; pres. Austin Peay State Coll., 1946-62; past pres. Tenn. Coll. Assn.; mem. Tenn. Senate. Mem. Montgomery County Equalization Bd. Served with mil., World War I, World War II. Mem. Am. Legion (past comdr. Tenn.), VFW, C. of C., Montgomery Conservation Club, 101st Airborne Div. Assn. (hon.), Ret. Officers Assn. (life). Democrat. Methodist. Clubs: Moose, Civitan. Address: 136 N Meadow Circle Clarksville TN 37040

HARVILLE, JAMES M., govt. ofcl.; b. Middlesboro, Ky., Aug. 9, 1940; s. John and Cora Bell (Robbins) H.; B.S., Eastern Ky. U., 1963; postgrad. U. Ky., 1963-64, U. Louisville, 1965-66; m. Jerry Ann Gonyer, Feb. 13, 1964; children—Jon, Jayme, Matthew. Adminstrv. intern Ky. Dept. Transp., Frankfort, 1964-65, personnel adminstr., 1965-69, exec. officer, 1969-72, dir., 1972—. Recipient award YMCA, 1976. Mem. Am. Soc. Public Adminstrn. Home: Rural Route 2 S Benson Rd Frankfort KY 40601 Office: High St Frankfort KY 40620

HARVIN, JAMES SHAND, plastic surgeon; b. Sumter, S.C., Dec. 19, 1929; s. Harry Lewis and Gladys Alice Mary (Shand) H.; student The Citadel, 1946-48; A.B., Duke, 1951; M.D., Med. Coll. S.C., 1953; m. Abbie Leah Bradham, Sept. 1, 1951; children—Gail Stephanie, James Shand, Steven Lewis, Carol Ann. Intern, Wayne County Gen. Hosp., Eloise, Mich., 1953-54; commd. 1st lt. USAF, 1954, advanced through grades to lt. col., 1966; resident gen. surgery Barnes Hosp., St. Louis, 1956-58, fellow plastic surgery, 1959-60, resident plastic surgery, 1960-61; fellow hand surgery Passavant Meml. Hosp., Chgo., 1959; preceptor gen. surgery Wright-Patterson USAF Hosp., 1961-63, asst. chief plastic surgery service, staff surgeon gen. surgery service, 1961-62; asst. chief plastic surgery service Wilford Hall USAF Hosp., Lackland AFB, Tex., 1962-63, chief plastic surgery service, 1963-67; asso. prof., head div. plastic and maxillofacial surgery Med. U. S.C., Charleston, 1967—; cons. VA Hosp., Charleston, 1967—; staff mem. Charleston County Hosp., 1967—; cons. staff St. Francis Hosp., Charleston; cons. Charleston Naval Hosp. Diplomate Am. Bd. Plastic Surgery, Am. Bd. Surgery. Fellow A.C.S.; mem. Am., Southeastern socs. plastic and reconstructive surgeons, Mil. Assn. Plastic Surgeons, Soc. Air Force Clin. Surgeons, Assn. Mil. Surgeons, Soc. USAF Flight Surgeons, Am. Cleft Palate Assn., Soc. Head and Neck Surgeons, AMA, S.C. Med. Assn., Charleston County Med. Soc., S.C. Surg. Soc., Pi Kappa Alpha, Phi Chi. Contbr. articles to profl. jours. Home: Route 5 Box 367 Bohicket Rd Johns Island SC 29455 Office: 171 Ashley Ave Charleston SC 29403

HARVLEY, DAVID L., chemist; b. Nacogdoches, Tex., Jan. 24, 1933; s. Vernon L. and Susan (Watson) H.; student Stephen F. Austin Coll., 1954-55; B.S., U. Houston, 1970; m. Janet Rubottom, 1 dau., Julie Christine. Lab. technician Humble Oil and Refining Co., Houston, 1957-58; chem. asst. to mng. engr. Keystone Engring. Co., Houston, 1958; sales rep. Field Enterprises Corp., Houston, 1958-59; sr. lab technician Devoe and Raynolds Paint Co., Houston, 1959-77; mgr. quality control Devoe Prufcoat div. Grow Group, Inc., Baton Rouge, 1977-79; tech. mgr. automotive div., 1979-80; tech. dir. Guardsman Chem., Inc., Thomasville, Ga., 1980—. Mem. Harris County Exec. Com., Houston, 1962-77; election judge, Houston, 1962-77; co-founder West University Place Civic Club, Houston, 1973. Served with U.S. Army, 1955-56. Mem. Am. Chem. Soc., Soc. for Paint Tech. Home: 307 Tuxedo Dr Thomasville GA 31792 Office: 631 Campbell Rd Thomasville GA 31792

HARWAY, MAXWELL, real estate exec.; b. N.Y.C., Mar. 7, 1913; s. Samuel and Esther (Steinbook) H.; B.S. in Econs., Coll. City N.Y., 1940; grad. Indsl. Coll. Armed Forces, 1951; M.A. in Internat. Relations, Georgetown U., 1952; m. Georgette Nadelar, Dec. 1, 1945 (dec.); children—Michele, Philip A., Danielle S. Tchr., econs. research dir. WPA, 1935-38; wage hour insp. Dept. Labor, 1941, economist, 1941; chief econs. processed food rationing OPA, 1942; dir. transp. div. Nat. Housing Authority, 1946; fgn. affairs officer Dept. State, 1947-53; owner import-export bus. N. Africa, 1954-56; corr. for mags., 1954-57; fgn. corr. McGraw Hill World News, 1956-59; asst. to pres. Continental Ore Corp., 1959-65; program officer SBA, 1965; cons. Office Econ. Opportunity, 1965; internat. economist Commerce Dept., 1966; with AID, 1967-78; chief comml. import div. Supporting Assistance Bur., 1967-78; pres. Warrenton Realty Co., Inc., N.Y.C., Waterloo (Va.) Enterprises, 1978—; Served with USAAF, 1942-46. Mem. Pres.'s Task Force on War Against Poverty, 1964. Mem. Nat. Assn. Bus. Economists, Soc. Internat. Devel., LVW, Overseas Press Club. Home: 132B Fairfield Dr Warrenton VA 22186 Office: 301 E 45th St New York NY 10017

HARWELL, KENNETH EDWIN, educator; b. Kellyton, Ala., Nov. 22, 1936; s. Kelly Edwin and Etta Antionette (Sasser) H.; B.S. (Anchor Rome Mills scholar), U. Ala., 1959; M.S. (Tau Beta Pi fellow 1959-60, Calif. Tech. scholar 1959-63), Calif. Inst. Tech., 1960, Ph.D., 1963; m. Betty Ruth Miller, June 12, 1959 (dec. Nov. 1966); 1 dau., Kathryn Ruth; m. 2d, Sharon Elizabeth Hilton, Aug. 18, 1968; children—Karen Elizabeth, Kenneth Hilton. Asso. engr. Gen. Dynamics, Ft. Worth, 1959; grad. research and teaching asst. Calif. Inst. Tech., Pasadena, 1959-63; engr. Jet Propulsion Lab., Pasadena, 1960; prof. dept. aeronautics Auburn (Ala.) U., 1963-76; dir. gas diagnostics div. U. Tenn. Space Inst., Tullahoma, 1976—; vis. research prof. Research and Devel. and Engring. Lab. U.S. Army Missile Command, Redstone Arsenal, Ala., 1973-74; cons. Hayes Internat. Corp., Birmingham, 1965-67, Ballistic Research Lab., Aberdeen, Md., 1969, U.S. Air Force, Eglin AFB, Fla., 1972-73, U.S. Navy, 1976—, Army Research Office, 1976—; mem. U.S. Army missile sci. adv. group, 1974—. Recipient Ford Found. Resident fellowship Am. Soc. Engring. Edn., 1973-74. Mem. Am. Inst. Aeronautics and Astronautics, Am. Phys. Soc., Baptist Alumni Assn. U. Ala. (v.p. 1972-73, pres. 1973-74, dir. 1969-72), Capstone Engring. Soc., Sigma Xi, Tau Beta Pi, Theta Tau, Sigma Tau, Sigma Pi Sigma. Contbr. articles to profl. jours. Home: Route 2 Box 327 Tullahoma TN 37388

HARWOOD, JOHN SAMUEL, counselor; b. Ft. Leonard Wood, Mo., Apr. 26, 1951; s. Arthur James and Theresa (Dennehy) H.; B.S., N. Tex. State U., 1974, M.Ed., 1977; m. Benita Ellen Bock, Feb. 2, 1974. Dir., Denton (Tex.) Free U., 1972-73; resident asst. N. Tex. State U., Denton, 1973; counselor aide Richland Coll., 1974, counselor, mem. faculty, 1977—; coordinator 3D project Dallas County Community Coll. Dist., Dallas, 1974-76; coordinator career guidance Eastfield Coll., Mesquite, Tex., 1976-77; coordinator testing and Center for Choice, counselor, faculty Richmond Coll., 1978—; cons. team mem. Counselor Accountability Tng. Systems, 1976—. Mem. Am. Coll. Personnel Assn., Am. Personnel and Guidance Assn., Nat. Vocat. Guidance Assn., Jr. Coll. Student Personnel Assn. Tex. Author publs. in field. Home: 8523 Forest Hills Blvd Dallas TX 75218 Office: Richland Coll 12800 Abrams Rd Dallas TX 75149

HASELWOOD, SCOTT, electronics engr.; b. Thomas, Okla., Oct. 14, 1921; s. William Earl and Ruth Elmira (Scott) H.; student U.S. Naval Acad., 1941-44; B.S., U. Okla., 1956; M.S., St. Louis U., 1966; m. Betty Jane Schneider, Dec. 9, 1944; children—Glenna Jane (Mrs. John Blackford), William Scott, Elaine Marie and Ellen Lee (twins). Electronic engr. McDonnel Aircraft Corp., St. Louis, 1956, electronic group engr., 1956-64; sr. group engr. Conductron Co., St. Charles, Mo., 1964-66; chief Guidance Devel. Center, Martin-Marietta Corp., Orlando, Fla., 1966-69, project engr. antenna tracking system NASA, 1969-71, tech. dir. electro-optical simulation system, 1971-73, program engr. Atlas laser fire control system, 1974-76, program engr. tactical weapons systems, 1977-79, dept. mgr., tech. dir., 1979—; instr. elec. lab., research asst. U. Okla., 1954-56. Served with USNR, 1944-46. Lic. pvt. pilot. Mem. IEEE. Democrat. Mem. Christian Ch. (trustee, elder). Mason (32 deg.). Contbr. articles to profl. jours. Home: 2671 Vine St Orlando FL 32806 Office: PO Box 5837 Orlando FL 32805

HASSAN, ZUBAIR UL, cardiologist; b. Mardan, Pakistan, Dec. 5, 1938; s. Mian Abdul Majid and Saeeda Shujauddin; came to U.S., 1962, naturalized, 1975; F. Sc., Islamia Coll., Lahore, Pakistan, 1955; B.S., King Edward Med. Coll., Lahore, Pakistan, 1960, M.B., 1960; m. Loretta Boxley, May 19, 1968; children—Sameena Shireen, Aalya Mehrin, Sabrina Yasmin. House surgeon Mayo Hosp., Lahore, 1961-62; intern St. Mary's Hosp., Phila., 1962-63; resident in internal medicine Med. Coll. of Va., Richmond, 1963-66, research fellow in cardiopulmonary physiology, 1966-68; resident in medicine Queen Mary VA Hosp., Montreal, Can., 1968-69; cardiologist, dir. coronary care unit VA Hosp., Richmond, 1972-79; dir. cardiac catherization lab., 1979—, acting chief cardiovascular section, 1976-77; asst. prof. medicine Med. Coll. of Va., Va. Commonwealth U., 1975-79, asso. prof., 1979—; cons. cardiologist Blackstone (Va.) Family Practice Clinic; bd. dirs. Am. Heart Assn. Fellow ACP, Am. Coll. Cardiology, Am. Coll. Chest Physicians, Am. Heart Assn. (Council on Cardiology), Royal Coll. of Physicians of Can.; mem. Richmond Acad. Medicine. Mem. Islamic Center of Va. Clubs: Avalon. Contbr. numerous articles to profl. jours. Home: 9507 Carterwood Rd Richmond VA 23229

HASSELL, JERRY GLENN, educator; b. Oklahoma City, Dec. 7, 1928; s. William Henry and Thada Allene (Holder) H.; B.S. Gallaudet Coll., 1951; M. Ed., U. Tex., 1959; m. Dovie Lee McGaugh; children—Sandra Ann, Sharon Lynn. Counselor Cal. Sch. for Deaf, Berkeley, 1952-54; tchr. Tex. Sch. for Deaf, Austin, 1954—; extension instr. U. Tex. at Austin, 1973-77. Pres. Tex. Bapt. Conf. of Deaf, 1967-70. Mem. Nat., Tex. (pres.) assns. of the deaf, Nat. Fraternal Soc. of the Deaf, Tex. State Tchrs. Assn., Austin Club of Deaf (v.p.). Home: 2204 Laramie Trail Austin TX 78745 Office: 1102 S Congress Ave Austin TX 78704

HASSELL, MORRIS WILLIAM, lawyer; b. Jacksonville, Tex., Aug. 9, 1916; s. Alonzo Seldon and Cora (Rainey) H.; A.A., Lon Morris Coll., 1936; LL.B., U. Tex., 1942; m. Mauriete Watson, Sept. 3, 1944 (div. Sept. 1975); children—Morris William, Charles Robert; m. 2d, Beatrice Mercado Wade; 1 son, Donald Eugene Wade. Tchr. Cherokee County Public Schs., 1937-38; admitted to Tex. bar, 1942; pvt. practice since 1946, mem. firm Norman, Hassell, Spiers & Thrall; sec. The S.W. Title and Guaranty Co. of Tex.; dir. First State Bank of Rusk; chmn. bd. Swift Oil Co.; sec. H & I Oil Co., I, H & I, Inc.; v.p., dir. Citizens Indsl. Life Ins. Co. Tex. County atty. Cherokee County, Tex., 1943-46 mayor of Rusk, 1959-63, 73—; judge 2d Jud. Dist. Tex., 1978—. Scoutmaster, Boy Scouts Am., 1944-45; Dem. nominee for County atty., 1942 and 1944; v.p. Jr. Bar of Tex., 1944. Mem. state adv. com. Wesley Found., Austin, Tex.; bd. devel., trustee, chmn. exec. com. bd. trustees Lon Morris Coll. Mem. C. of C. (pres.), Am., E. Tex. (dir. 1964-65) bar assns., State Bar Tex. (dir.; chmn. gen. practice sect. 1967-68 chmn. profl. ethics com. 1970—). Methodist (steward, trustee Tex. Conf. 1976—, trustee found. 1978—). Odd Fellow, Mason, Kiwanian (dist. lt. gov.). Office: 335 W Park Houston TX 77027

HASSLER, WEDDIE HOWARD, pharmacist; b. Crossville, Tenn., Jan. 7, 1924; s. John Thomas and Edna Ruth (Cox) H.; B.S., U. Tenn., 1949; M.S., Purdue U., 1952; m. Gena Anne Deal, Aug. 5, 1972; 1 dau., Pamela Elizabeth. Asst. prof. U. Tenn., 1949-57; cons. Mead-Johnson Co., 1952-54; chief pharmacist West Tenn. Chest Disease Hosp., Memphis, 1949-71; owner, mgr. Hassler's Aopthecary, Memphis, 1957-71, Hassler's Drugs, Spring City, Tenn., 1975—. Served with USAAF, 1942-46. Mem. Am. Sci. Soc., Rho Chi, Kappa Psi. Contbr. articles to profl. jours.; research on suppository bases. Home: PO Box 476 New Lake Rd Spring City TN 37381 Office: PO Box 476 Spring City TN 37381

HASTEY, JOEL ALBERT, cons. engring. co. exec.; b. Donalsonville, Ga., June 7, 1948; s. Luther Henry and Martha Ann (Goodwin) H.; B.E.E., Auburn U., 1970; M.B.A., Ga. State U., 1974; m. Carol Ann Hensley, Sept. 11, 1971; children—Stephen Todd, Scott Tyler. Electronic engr. trainee FAA, 1970; div. substation engr. Ala. Power Co., 1971; project engr. Hensley-Schmidt, Inc., Chattanooga, 1972-74, asst. to v.p., 1974-75, asst. to pres., 1975-77, mgr. ops., 1977-78, v.p. ops., 1978—; lectr. in field. Chmn., Re-elect Sen. Howard Baker Com. 1978. Mem. Inst. Transp. Engrs., Nat. Soc. Profl. Engrs., Am. Cons. Engrs. Council, Chattanooga Engrs. Club, Eta Kappa Nu, Tau Beta Pi, Beta Gamma Sigma. Republican. Presbyterian. Club: Kiwanis. Home: 906 Kentucky Ave Signal Mountain TN 37377 Office: 817 Broad St Chattanooga TN 37402

HASTINGS, DAVID CARTER, banker; b. Richmond, Va., Jan. 28, 1948; s. Allen Erman and Jane (Gorman) H.; B.S., Va. Commonwealth U., 1972. Acct., A.M. Pullen & Co., Richmond, 1972; sr. acct. Peat Marwick Mitchell & Co., Richmond, 1973-74, sr. tax specialist, 1974-76; tax compliance mgr. First & Mchts. Corp., Richmond, 1976-77, v.p., dir. taxes, 1977—; adj. faculty J. Sargent Reynolds Community Coll., 1979-80. Auditor, Lutheran Ch., 1975-77. C.P.A., Va. Mem. Am. Bankers Assn. (taxation com.), Va. Bankers Assn. (ad hoc tax com. 1978-80), Bank Adminstrn. Inst. (tax commn. 1980—), Va. Commonwealth U. Collegiate Jaycees (state dir., v.p.), Am. Inst. C.P.A.'s, Tax. Execs. Inst., Am. Inst. Banking, Southeastern Bank Tax Assn. Clubs: Hermitage Country, Va. Commonwealth U. Rams (dir. 1977-80). Office: PO Box 27025 Richmond VA 2326

HASTINGS, EDMUND STUART, ret. naval officer, petroleum geologist; b. New Orleans, Jan. 2, 1924; s. James Stuart and Winnie Dorothy (Miller) H.; student U.S. Naval R.O.T.C., U. Tex., 1943, Command Staff Course Naval War Coll., 1959; B.S., U. So. Cal., 1950; m. Elizabeth Theresa Dean, June 21, 1947; children—Theresa Christine (Mrs. Aaron R. Folse), Margaret Elizabeth, James Stuart. Commd. ensign USN, 1943, advanced through grades to comdr., 1971; with weapons tng. unit NAS, Dallas; with Naval Ammunition Depot, Pusan, Korea; ret.; spl. projects geologist Phillips Petroleum Co., Lafayette, La., 1955-59, dist. div. geologist, 1959-62, regional staff geologist, Bartlesville, Okla., 1962-64, petroleum geologist, Houston, 1964-70, 1973—, petroleum geologist, Lafayette, 1970-73. Expert witness petroleum exploration, devel., drilling prodn. opns., onshore offshore. Vice pres. Hastings Properties, Gautier, Miss., 1967-75. Recipient commendations U.S. Dept. Def., 1962, 68, 69. Mem. Explorers Club, Am. Inst. Profl. Geologists (state v.p. 1972-73), Am. Assn. Petroleum Geologists (silver cert. for 25 yrs.), Naval Res. Assn., Soc. Exploration Geophysicists (silver cert. for 25 yrs.), SAR, Phi Kappa Tau. Elk, Optimist. Home: 8414 Braesmeadow Dr Houston TX 77071 Office: PO Box 1967 Phillips Bldg Houston TX 77001

HASTINGS, JOHN HARRY, automobile dealer; b. Sylva, N.C., May 20, 1929; s. Harry R. and Queen (Duvall) H.; B.S. in Bus. Adminstrn., U. Richmond (Va.), 1951; m. Joyce Rivembark, Nov. 22, 1969. Automobile dealer, 1957—; pres. Hastings Ford, Inc., Greenville, N.C., 1970—; dir. Wachovia Bank & Trust Co., Greenville, 1979; chmn. Mid-Atlantic region Ford Dealer Council; mem. Ford Nat. Dealer Council, 1979-80; v.p. Richmond dist. Ford Dealer Advt. Fund. Mem. N.C. Automobile Dealers Assn. (dir.). Democrat. Methodist. Clubs: Elks, Moose. Home: 207 York Rd Greenville NC 27834 Office: 3013 E 10th St Greenville NC 27834

HASTINGS, PETER COLEMAN, chem. co. exec.; b. Columbia, S.C., Dec. 12, 1940; s. Coleman Livingston and Locri (Pachelis) H.; B.S. in Chem. Engring., U. S.C., 1964, M.S. in Chem. Engring., 1972; M.B.A., Va. Commonwealth U., 1979; m. Linda Watts, Nov. 17, 1964; children—Monica Lynn, Peter Coleman. Prodn. supr. Allied Chem. Co., Columbia, 1965-66 tech. asst. to plant mgr. Exide Power Systems div. ESB, Inc., Sumter, S.C., 1966-68; process/project engr. Mobil Chem. Co., Charleston, S.C., 1968-70, engring. group leader, Richmond, Va., 1973-79, gen. supt., Ft. Meade, Fla., 1979—; project engr. Marbon div. Borg Warner, Parkersburg, W.Va., 1972-73; adj. instr., head dept. nuclear engring. Midlands Tech. Edn. Center, Columbia, 1971-73 instr. Parkersburg Community Coll., 1973. Mem. Am. Inst. Chem. Engrs., Indsl. Mgmt. Club, Sigma Xi. Republican. Episcopalian. Clubs: Hanover Country, Imperial Lakes Country. Home: 85 Country Club Ln Mulberry FL 33860 Office: PO Box 311 Nichols FL 33863

HASTINGS, ROBERT CLYDE, research physician, pharmacologist; b. Tipton County, Tenn., Apr. 23, 1938; s. Robert Simpson and Margaret Marie (Peterson) H.; student Vanderbilt U., 1956-59; M.D., U. Tenn., 1962; Ph.D., Tulane U., 1971; children—Cynthia Margaret, Robert Clyde, Jeffrey. Med. intern City of Memphis Hosps., 1963-64; commd. sr. asst. surgeon USPHS, 1964, advanced through grades to med. dir., 1976; staff physician and dep. chief clin. br. USPHS Hosp., Carville, La., 1964-68, staff physician, 1971—, chief pharmacology research dept., 1971—; instr. dept. medicine La. State U., New Orleans, 1966—; adj. instr. dept. pharmacology Tulane U. Sch. Medicine, New Orleans, 1970-71, asst. prof., 1971-74, asso. prof., 1974—, clin. asso. prof. dept. medicine, 1976—; asso. med. staff Tulane Med. Center Hosp., New Orleans, 1977—, chmn. com. for use of humans in med. research, 1977—; mem. U.S. Leprosy Panel, U.S.-Japan Coop. Med. Sci. Program, NIAID, NIH, 1977—. Recipient Physicians Recognition award

AMA, 1972, 76; Kellersberger Meml. Lecture, Addis Ababa, Ethiopia, 1979. Fellow Am. Coll. Clin. Pharmacology; mem. USPHS Commd. Officers Assn., Internat. Leprosy Assn., Am. Soc. Tropical Medicine and Hygiene, AAAS, Reticuloendothelial Soc., Am. Chem. Soc., Am. Fedn. Clin. Research, Am. Soc. Pharmacology and Exptl. Therapeutics, Soc. Exptl. Biology and Medicine, N.Y. Acad. Sci., Am. Soc. Microbiology, Am. Soc. Clin. Pharmacology and Therapeutics, Sigma Xi. Democrat. Methodist. Contbr. articles to profl. jours.; editor Internat. Jour. Leprosy, 1978—. Office: USPHS Hosp Carville LA 70721

HASTY, GERALD RICHARD, educator, ret. army officer; b. Pekin, Ill., Apr. 12, 1926; s. Leslie Parke and Bernice Arthene (Brown) H.; B.S., Bradley U., 1952; M.B.A., 1954; postgrad. Harvard, 1961; M.A., Am. U., 1962; Ph.D., Northwestern U., 1963; LL.B., Blackstone Sch. Law, 1968; postgrad. summers U. Toledo, 1958, U. Maine, 1963, State U. N.Y. at Buffalo, 1963, Armed Forces Staff Coll., 1968, Air War Coll., 1965, Harvard Law Sch., 1976; D.D. (hon.), Am. Fellowship Ch., 1977; m. Betty Anne Osmundson, June 23, 1951; children—Grant Rutledge, Mark Osmund, Deborah Anne. Commd. 2d lt. U.S. Army, 1954, advanced through grades to lt. col., 1966; chief Q.M. Supply div. 7th Logistical Command, Korea, 1961-62; comdg. officer 34th Supply and Service Bn., Vietnam, 1966, also dir. adminstrn. 58th Field Depot; exec. asst. joint logistics rev. bd. Office Sec. Def., Washington, 1969-70; comdg. officer Charleston (S.C.) Army Depot, 1970-72; joint logistics plans officer on staff comdr.-in-chief UN Command, 1972-73; logistics staff officer Joint and Strategic Forces Directorate, Army Concepts Analysis Agy., Bethesda, Md., 1973-74, ret.; asst. prof. pub. adminstrn. George Washington U., Washington, 1964-65, 67, asso. prof., 1968-69, 73; vis. prof. polit. sci. Bapt. Coll., Charleston, 1970-72, now asso. prof.; tchr., lectr., various colls., U.S. Korea, Vietnam; vis. Prof. Central Mich. U., 1974—. Counselor, Boy Scouts Am., 1968—; mem. citizen's adv. and action council to gov. Coastal Carolina Community Pre-release Center, S.C. Dept. Corrections. Bd. dirs. Charleston Safety Council; apptd. spl. envoy by gov. for Commonwealth of Pa., 1970. Served AUS, 1944-50. Decorated Legion of Merit with oak leaf cluster, Purple Heart with oak leaf cluster; Nat. Endowment for Humanities fellow U. Ga., summer 1978. Mem. Charleston Trident C. of C., La. Societe Francaise deBienfaisance de Charleston, Navy League, Mil. Order Purple Heart, Fed. Exec. Assn. (com. on govt.-wide policy areas), Armed Forces Mgmt. Assn., S.C. Law Enforcement Officers Assn., Nat. Def. Transp. Assn., Am. Bar Assn., S.C. Polit. Sci. Assn. (exec. council, v.p.), Pi Sigma Alpha, Tau Kappa Epsilon, Pi Gamma Mu. Lutheran. Mason (32 deg., Shriner), Kiwanian. Home: 1282 Winchester Dr Charleston SC 29407

HATCH, MARY GIES, educator; b. Omaha, Feb. 17, 1913; d. Charles George and Jane Elizabeth (Sturman) Gies; A.B., Vassar Coll., 1935; postgrad. (Vassar fellow) U. Heidelberg (Germany), 1935-36; M.A., U. Mich., 1937; Ph.D. (Univ. scholar), Syracuse U., 1952; m. David Lincoln Hatch, Aug. 24, 1940; children—Charles Winthrop, Mary Abby Hatch Cleland, Faith Winslow Hatch Mann, Elizabeth Ann Hatch Dimmery. Tchr., Lincoln High Sch., Detroit, 1937-38, Montclair (N.J.) High Sch., 1938-40, Dana Hall, Wellesley, Mass., 1940-42; prof., head German dept. Columbia (S.C.) Coll., 1960—; profl. translator. Columbia Coll. Faculty research grantee, 1964; So. Assn. Ind. Colls. research grantee, 1968. Mem. MLA, Am. Assn. Tchrs. of German, Am. Sociol. Assn., AAUP, AAUW, S.C. Conf. Fgn. Lang. Tchrs., S. Atlantic MLA, Phi Beta Kappa. Episcopalian. Author: (with David Hatch) Under the Elms, Yesterday and Today, 1948; contbr. articles to profl. jours. Home: 2420 Terrace Way Columbia SC 29205 Office: Columbia Coll Columbia SC 29203

HATCHER, HAROLD AMOS, JR., ophthalmologist; b. Cookeville, Tenn., Jan. 7, 1945; s. Harold Amos and Minnie (Pippin) H.; B.S., Tenn. Tech. U., 1967; M.D., Vanderbilt U., 1970; m. Patricia Ann Curtis, Aug. 5, 1967; children—Kristin Kathleen, Andrew Curtis. Intern, U. Fla., Gainesville, 1970-71; resident in ophthalmology U. Tex., Southwestern Med. Sch., Dallas, 1971-74; practice medicine, specializing in ophthalmology, Montgomery, Ala., 1974—; mem. staff Bapt. Med. Center, Jackson's Hosp., Univ. Med. Center, St. Margaret's Hosp. Mem. exec. com. Boy Scouts Am., Montgomery, 1977—; bd. dirs. YMCA, Montgomery, 1977—. Served with USAF, 1974-76. Recipient Physician Recognition award AMA, 1980; diplomate Am. Bd. Ophthalmology. Mem. AMA, ACS, Am. Assn. Ophthalmology, Research to Prevent Blindness, Ala. Acad. Ophthalmology, Physicians Edn. Network, Montgomery County Med. Soc., Am. Intra Ocular Implant Soc. Presbyterian. Club: Rotary. Contbr. articles to profl. jours. Home: 2315 Midfield Dr Montgomery AL 36111 Office: 2020 Normandie Dr Montgomery AL 36111

HATCHER, JOHN HENRY, archivist; b. Prestonburg, Ky., Dec. 10, 1924; s. William Boone and Dora (Meador) H.; student U. Ky., 1942-43, U. Va., 1943-44; B.G.E., U. Md., 1962; M.A., Hardin Simmons U., 1963, Ph.D., U. Cin., 1967; m. Hildegard Ostermeier, Feb. 19, 1961; children—Eva-Marie Elizabeth, John Henry III. Enlisted in U.S. Army, 1943, advanced through grades to col. USAF, 1971; combat crew mem., communications staff officer, adminstr.; ret., 1971; prof. U. Md., Stuttgart, Ger., 1967-72; German and mil. specialist Nat. Archives, Washington; adj. prof. Am. U., Washington, 1977-79; archivist U.S. Army, Washington, 1979—; vis. prof. Kultus Ministerium, Baden-Wurttember State Govt., 1968-69. Decorated knight of grace Order St. John Jerusalem; Legion of Merit, Air medal, Joint Services Commendation medal; Dept. Army medal meritorious civilian service, 1979. Mem. Assn. Records Mgrs. and Adminstrs., Nat. Classification Mgmt. Soc., Orgn. Am. Historians, Am. Hist. Assn., W. Tex. Hist. Assn., Filson Club, Ky. Hist. Soc., Order Ky. Cols., Air Force Hist. Found., AAUP, Am. Cath. Fedn. Austrian, German and Swiss U. Profs., ACLU, Air Force Sgts. Assn., Air Force Assn., U.S. Army Assn., Soc. Am. Archivists, Ky. Soc. of Washington, Wolf Trap Assn., Smithsonian Asso., Nebraska of Washington, Acad. Polit. Sci., Am. Acad. Polit. and Social Sci., Assn. Records Mgrs. and Adminstrs., Nat. Classification Mgmt. Soc., Phi Alpha Theta. Republican. Lutheran. Author: US Army Combat Units of the War in Vietnam, 1965-73, 1979; Select Bibliography: The War in Vietnam, 1977; Users' Guide to Sources on the War in Viet Nam, 1975. Home: 5251 Rolling Rd Springfield VA 22151 Office: Dept Army Records Mgmt Div Adjutant Gen Center Washington DC 20314

HATCHER, JOSEPH CARROLL, chem. engr.; b. Glasgow, Ky., Jan. 15, 1939; s. J.C. and Tressie Ree (Britt) H.; B.S., Purdue U., 1961, M.S., 1964; m. Rosemary Helen Shaw, June 3, 1961; children—James Carroll, Robert Lloyd, Christopher Lee. Chem. engr. E.I. DuPont deNemours & Co., Louisville, 1962—. Precinct capt. Republican Party, 1974—. Mem. Am. Inst. Chem. Engrs., Gideons Internat. Baptist. Home: 4012 Goldstein Ln Louisville KY 40272 Office: PO Box 1378 Louisville KY 40201

HATCHER, LARRY WAYNE, ins. co. exec.; b. Dallas, Apr. 30, 1947; s. John H. and Mary C. (Sandle) H.; B.B.A., E. Tex. State U., 1969. Staff, Nat. Old Line, Dallas, Denver, 1970-72, Liberty Mortgage Ins. Co., Dallas, 1972-74; with Ticor Mortgage Ins. Co., Dallas, 1974—, Los Angeles, 19—, Houston, 1977—, sr. v.p., 1976—; lectr. in field. Mem. Mortgage Brokers Assn. Washington, U.S. Savs. and Loan League, Tex. Savs. and Loan Assn., Tex. Mortgage Bankers Assn., Houston Home Builders Assn., Sigma Phi Epsilon (v.p. chpt. 1968—). Republican. Methodist. Home: 13211 Mission Valley Houston TX 77069 Office: 2719 Main St Houston TX 77001

HATCHER, MARTHA OLIVIA TAYLOR (MRS. FRANK PRIDGEN HATCHER, SR.), educator; b. Birmingham, Ala., Feb. 17, 1920; d. Sanford Allia and Mary (McCullough) Taylor; B.S., Howard Coll., 1936-40; M.Ed. in Sci. Edn., U. Ga., 1966, Ed.D., 1973; tchrs. certificate Breanu Coll., 1964; m. Frank Pridgen Hatcher Sr., Nov. 7, 1941; children—Frank Pridgen, Martha Elizabeth, Nancy Louise. Chief bacteriologist vet. div. Ga. Dept. Agr., Atlanta, 1943-45; supr. surg. pathology lab. Jefferson Hillman Hosp., Med. Coll. Ala., Birmingham, 1945-46, research asst. in pathology, 1945-46; mgr. offices Fran Mar Farms, Inc., Gainesville, Ga., 1957-66; instr. biology Gainesville Jr. Coll., 1966-67, asso. prof. biology, 1967, chmn. div. natural scis. and maths., 1968-74, chmn., 1974—, prof. biology; accompanist music dept. Brenau Coll., Gainsville, 1959-61. Chmn. Gray Ladies Vol. Services, Gainesville chpt. A.R.C., 1957-62; sec. Yohah council Girl Scouts U.S.A., 1959-61; bd. dirs. Community Concert Assn. Gainesville, 1968-70. NSF sci. faculty fellow in microbiology, 1970-71. Mem. AAUP, AAAS, Am. Guild Organists, Am. Inst. Biol. Scis., Nat. Assn. Biology Tchrs., Assn. S.E. Biologists, Nat. Assn. Research Sci. Teaching, Ga. Acad. Sci. Nat. Sci. Tchrs. Assn., Am. Legion Aux. (pres. 1948-50), Am. Soc. Zoologists, UDC (chpt. pres. 1949-51), Am. Soc. Microbiology, AAUW, Kappa Delta Pi, Alpha Epsilon Delta, Delta Kappa Gamma, Phi Delta Kappa, Delta Zeta. Clubs: Music (pres. 1950-52), Federated Music (sec. 1957-58) (Gainesville), Phoenix Soc. Home: 840 Memorial Dr NE Gainesville GA 30501 Office: PO Box 1358 Gainesville Jr Coll Gainesville GA 30501

HATCHER, ROBERT LEE, endocrinologist; b. Dallas, Jan. 14, 1941; s. Maxey Manvel and Leita May (Chrisman) H.; A.B., Columbia Coll., 1962; M.D., Baylor U., 1966; m. Carol Jean Schoonover, Sept. 12, 1964; children—Reed Chrisman, Leita Catherine. Rotating intern Royal Victoria Hosp., McGill U., Montreal, Que., Can., 1966-67, resident in internal medicine, 1969-71; fellow in endocrinology and metabolism Mayo Clinic, Rochester, Minn., 1971-73, instr. in medicine, 1973-74; physician specialist in endocrinology and metabolism Valley Diagnostic Clinic, Harlingen, Tex., 1973—; chief of medicine Valley Baptist Med. Center, Harlingen, 1977-79; v.p. Cameron Willacy County (Tex.) Med. Soc.; bd. dirs. Rio Grande Home Health Agency, Rio Grande Radiation Treatment Center, McAllen, Tex., 1974—; dir. poison control Valley Baptist Med. Center, 1974-79. Bd. dirs. St. Alban's Episcopal Sch., 1976-80, ch. layreader, vestry. Served with USPHS, 1967-69. Diplomate Am. Bd. Internal Medicine with subsplty. in internal medicine and endocrinology. Mem. Cameron Willacy County Med. Soc., Tex., Am. med. assns., A.C.P., Am. Diabetes Assn. (1st v.p. S. Tex. Affiliate), Phi Gamma Delta, Phi Chi. Republican. Episcopalian. Clubs: Rotary, The Argyle Club (San Antonio); Tower (McAllen); Rancho Viejo Country. Contbr. articles to profl. jours. Home: Rural Route 3 PO Box 440 A Harlingen TX 78550 Office: Valley Diagnostic Clinic 2121 Pease St Suite 1A Harlingen TX 78550

HATCHER, WILLARD LYNWOOD, clin. social worker; b. Marianna, Fla., Mar. 7, 1940; s. A. W. and Pearl E. (Neel) H.; B.S. in Criminology, Fla. State U., 1964, M.S.W., 1969; m. Barbara E. Dupont, Aug. 16, 1960; 1 son, Willard Lynwood. Probation and parole officer, Sarasota and Quincy, Fla., 1964-67; clin. social worker Fla. State Hosp., Chattahoochee, Fla., 1969-79, clin. social services standard specialist, 1979—; field instr. Fla. State U. Served with USAF, 1958-62. Mem. Nat. Assn. Social Workers. Democrat. Baptist. Club: Chattahoochee Lions (pres. 1974-75, 77-78, zone chmn. internat. 1975-76). Home: Route 1 Box 240 Chattahoochee FL 32324 Office: Social Service Dept Florida State Hospital Chattahoochee FL 32324

HATCHER, WILLIAM JULIAN, JR., educator; b. Augusta, Ga., July 21, 1935; s. William Julian and Norvell (Kelley) H.; B.Ch.E. with honors Ga. Inst. Tech., 1957; M.Ch.E., La. State U., 1964, Ph.D., 1968; m. Sharon Lynn Hancock, Jan. 18, 1958; children—Jeffrey Craig, Rebecca Lynn, Michael William. Research engr. Esso Research Labs., Baton Rouge, La., 1960-66; research asso. La. State U., 1966-68; sr. research engr. Esso Research Labs., Baton Rouge, La., 1968-69; asso. prof. chem. engring. U. Ala., 1969-76, prof., 1976—, dept. head, 1973—; cons. U.S. Bur. Mines, 1972—. Served to lt. USMC, 1957-60. NSF Research grantee, 1970-72, 77-80. Mem. Am. Inst. Chem. Engrs., Am. Soc. Engring. Edn., Phi Kappa Phi, Tau Beta Pi, Phi Eta Sigma, Omega Chi Epsilon, Phi Lambda Upsilon. Methodist. Contbg. author: Environmental Engineering Handbook, 1973, Computer Programs for Chemical Engineering Education, Vols. II and IV, 1972. Research in petroleum processes, 1960-66; air pollution control, 1968-69; catalysis, 1970—. Home: 30 Woodland Hills Tuscaloosa AL 35401 Office: PO Box G University AL 35486

HATCHETT, CAPRES STRIPLING, JR., radiologist; b. Dalhart, Tex., Nov. 14, 1918; s. Capres Stripling and Aleene (Smith) H.; M.D., U. Tex., 1943; m. Martha Bell Clayton, Mar. 21, 1973; children by previous marriage—Nancy Paul, Capres, Dana Marie. Intern, Parkland Hosp., Dallas, 1943, resident in radiology, 1944, U. Nebr., 1948; practice medicine specializing in radiology, Amarillo, Tex., 1949—; med. dir. radiology Northwest Tex. Hosp., Amarillo, 1949—, chief of staff, 1970, mem. exec. com., 1980—; clin. instr. radiology U. Nebr., 1948, U. Tex., 1949; clin. asso. prof. Tex. Tech. U., 1973—; cons. in field. Dir. Amarillo Symphony Bd.; bd. dirs. Amarillo United Way; treas. Potter-Randall County Child Welfare Bd.; v.p. Tex. Panhandle Health Services Agy., 1976—; mem. Tex. Statewide Health Coordinating Com., 1977—. Served with AUS, 1944-46. Diplomate Am. Bd. Radiology. Fellow Am. Coll. Radiology, Am. Coll. Nuclear Medicine; mem. Radiol. Soc. N. Am. (councilor 1971-75), Potter-Randall County Med. Soc. (pres. 1958), AMA, Tex. Med. Assn., Tex. Radiol. Soc., Soc. Nuclear Medicine, Rocky Mt. Radiol. Soc., Am. Assn. Med. Educators. Republican. Unitarian. Clubs: Amarillo Country, Amarillo, Garden of God. Contbr. articles to profl. jours. Home: 6212 Belpree St Amarillo TX 79106 Office: 2209 W 7th St Amarillo TX 79106

HATCHETT, JOSEPH WOODROW, fed. judge; b. Clearwater, Fla., Sept. 17, 1932; s. John Arthur and Lula Gertrude (Thomas) H.; A.B., Fla. A&M U., Tallahassee, 1954; J.D., Howard U., 1959; m. Betty Lue Davis, Aug. 20, 1956; children—Cherly Nadine, Branda Audrey. Admitted to Fla. bar, 1959; pvt. practice, Daytona Beach, 1959-66; spl. asst. to city atty., Daytona Beach, 1964; cons., mem. staff Daytona Beach Urban Renewal Dept., 1963-66; asst. U.S. atty., Jacksonville, 1966-70, U.S. magistrate, 1961-75; justice Fla. Supreme Ct., 1975-79; judge 5th circuit U.S. Ct. Appeals, Tallahassee, 1979—; seminar lectr. Fed. Jud. Center, Washington; coordinator legal ethics seminar, U. Fla. Served as officer USAR, 1954-56. Mem. Am. Bar Assn., Nat. Bar Assn., Nat. Council Fed. Magistrates, Am. Judicature Soc., Fed. Bar Assn., Fla. Bar Assn., Jacksonville Bar Assn., D.W. Perkins Bar Assn., Lawyers Title Guaranty Fund Fla. Baptist. Office: PO Box 10429 Tallahassee FL 32302

HATCHETT, SHARI, artist; b. Houston, June 11, 1940; d. Albert Frederick and Gene (Aufricht) Metzler; student S.W. Tex. State Coll., 1958-60, U. Houston, 1962-63; m. Robert L. Hatchett, III, Oct. 31, 1967; children—Mark S., Kelly Lynn, Robert L. Exhibited in one man shows Bright Shawl Gallery, San Antonio, 1976, Midland (Tex.) Community Theatre, 1977, 78; represented in permanent collections Zeta Sorority House, U. Tex., Austin, Houston Country Club, Majestic Hotel, Hot Springs, Ark., Hyatt Regancy Hotel, San Francisco, also 4000 pvt. collections in U.S.; represented by Robert Rice Gallery, Brownstone, Houston, Boen Gallery, Cape Girardeau, Mo., Ginger Bread Square Gallery, Key West, Fla.; juried art and craft fairs, Laguna Gloria Fiesta, Austin, 1973-78, Kermezaar, El Paso, 1973-78, Septemberfest, Midland, Tex., 1973-79, Fiesta del Arte, Odessa, Tex., 1974-79, Mayfest, Ft. Worth, 1975-78, Jr. League Christmas Affair, Austin, 1976-78, San Antonio Jamboree, 1973-77, Dallas 500, 1975-76, Tex. State Arts and Crafts Fair, Kerrville, 1977, New Orleans Jazz and Heritage Festival, 1977, Kaleidoscope, Beaumont, Tex., 1977, 78, Bayfest, Corpus Christi, Tex., 1976-77, Vero Beach Winter Fair, 1979, Coconut Grove Art Fair, Miami, Fla., 1979, Oklahoma City Arts and Humanities Fair, 1979, Fine Art Mus. of South, 1978, 79, Chgo. Gold Coast Art Fair, 1978, 79, Piedmont Park, Atlanta, 1979. Episcopalian. Home: 2213 Staples Ave Key West FL 33040

HATFIELD, AUDREY ROBERTS, accountant; b. Harriman, Tenn., Feb. 2, 1930; d. William Bert and Ethel Landreth Roberts; student Oklahoma City U., 1952-54, U. Tenn., Knoxville, 1961-63; m. Franklin Eugene Hatfield, Feb. 12, 1950. Control bookkeeper A. B. Long Constrn. Co., Harriman, 1956-68; adminstrv. asst., office mgr. So. Athletic, Inc., Knoxville, Tenn., 1968-72; chief acct. Environ. Systems Corp., Knoxville, 1972-80, Elk River Resources, Inc., 1980—. Mem. Nat. Assn. Accts. (pres. Knoxville chpt.). Baptist. Club: Order Eastern Star (past matron). Home: 10205 El Pinar Dr Knoxville TN 37922 Office: PO Box 10388 Knoxville TN 37919

HATFIELD, BENJAMIN FRANK, pub. utility cons.; b. Livermore, Ky., July 31, 1906; s. Henry and Katie Corinne (Scholl) H.; B.S. summa cum laude in Elec. Engring., U. Tenn., 1930, B.S. summa cum laude in Mech. Engring., 1930; m. Ada Ella Hatcher, June 11, 1930; children—Ada Joyce (Mrs. James Edward Coleman), Benjamin Frank Jr. (dec.). With Western Electric Co., Memphis, 1924-25, 28, Cumberland Tel. & Tel. Co., Memphis, 1925-26; engr. U.S. Bur. Pub. Rds., Selmer, Tenn., 1929; instr. hydraulics U. Tenn., 1929-30; with So. Bell Tel. & Tel. Co., 1930-71, La. chief engr., New Orleans, 1949-53, asst. v.p., 1953-71; faculty mem. Bell System Center for Tech. Edn., Lisle, Ill., 1971-72; tech. mem. Steinhauer, Hatfield & Good, Assos., Atlanta, 1971—; v.p. A.L. Groce Assos., Charlotte, N.C., 1972—. Trumpet player Memphis Symphony Orch., 1924-25, Atlanta Philharmonic Orch., 1931-36; v.p., trumpet player Atlanta Concert Band, 1957-64; trumpet player, sec. Yaarab Temple Shrine Band, 1969—; counselor YMCA, 1953-60; committeeman, treas., camping chmn. Boy Scouts Am., 1953-60; treas., pres. High Sch. Band Parents Assn., 1953-63; pres. Land O'Lakes Civic Club, 1960, dir., 1961-64; v.p. 8th Ward Civic Assn., 1967-69. Served from capt. to lt. col., AUS, 1941-45; to col. Res., 1946-60. Decorated Bronze Star medal. Fellow Internat. Inst. Community Service; mem. I.E.E.E., Am. Inst. E.E. (dir. New Orleans sect. 1952-53), La. Engring. Soc., Ga. Archtl. and Engring. Soc., Armed Forces Communications and Electronics Assn., Res. Officers Assn., Mil. Order World Wars, Telephone Pioneers of Am., N.C. Independent Telephone Assn., Phi Kappa Phi, Tau Beta Pi. Methodist (trustee). Mason (32 deg., Shriner). Address: 3916 Land O'Lakes Dr NE Atlanta GA 30342

HATFIELD, CAROL SUTHERLAND, editor, writer; b. McCamey, Tex., Apr. 10, 1935; d. Thomas Shelton and Lois Peyton (Hartley) Sutherland; B.J., U. Tex., Austin, 1956, postgrad., 1962-64, 73-75; m. Thomas Marvin Hatfield, Oct. 24, 1959; children—Thomas Sutherland, Alice Elizabeth, Sara Carol. Editorial asst. Nat. Geog. Soc., 1957-59; ednl. writer News Service, U. Tex., 1964-66; pub. info. dir. John Tyler Coll., Chester, Va., 1967-69; info. dir., bd. trustees workshop U. Calif., Los Angeles, 1970; ednl. writer and coordinator children's folklore program S.W. Ednl. Devel. Lab., Austin, 1971-76; editor Discovery Mag., U. Tex., Austin, 1976—. Tex. del. Nat. Women's Conf., 1977; mem. state coordinating com. Tex. Women's Meeting, 1977; mem. nat. adv. com. Women and Stress, 1976—; mem. exec. council nat. families and stress project Harvard U., 1977—; mem. Univ. Council on Status of Women and Minorities, 1976-78. Mem. Women in Communications (pres. Austin chpt. 1973-74), Austin Mental Health Assn. (dir. 1973-75). Contbr. articles to profl. jours. Home: 3404 Northwood Circle Austin TX 78703 Office: Main Bldg 303 U Tex Austin TX 78712

HATFIELD, JOHN DEMPSEY, chemist; b. Sneedville, Tenn., Aug. 18, 1919; s. George Harrison and Della Mae (Livesay) H.; A.B., U. Tenn., 1938, M.S., 1939; Ph.D., Purdue U., 1942; m. Mary Wills Hollingsworth, Oct. 14, 1943; children—Elizabeth (Mrs. Charles Edmond Baddley), Mary (Mrs. Thomas Gail LeCroy), John, Kemper. Chemist, E.I. duPont de Nemours & Co., Richmond, Va., 1939; fellow, asso. chemist Purdue U., 1940-42; research chemist TVA, Muscle Shoals, Ala., 1943—. Chmn. Gordon Research Conf., 1968. Chmn. Lauderdale County chpt. A.R.C., 1960-61. Served with USNR, 1944-46. Recipient Environmental Protection Agy. grants, 1967, 70. Mem. Am. Chem. Soc. (sect. chmn., chmn., councilor, Outstanding Chemist award Wilson Dam sect. 1977, Charles H. Stone award Carolina-Piedmont sect. 1977). Presbyn. (elder). Rotarian. Contbr. articles to profl. jours. Home: 1224 Sorrento Rd Florence AL 35630 Office: Div Chem Devel TVA Muscle Shoals AL 35660

HATFIELD, THOMAS MARVIN, coll. adminstr.; b. San Antonio, Tex., Mar. 5, 1935; s. Marvin Adolphus and Lucille Elizabeth (Smith) H.; B.S., Trinity U., San Antonio, 1960; M.A., U. Tex., 1965, Ph.D., 1966; m. Carol Hartley Sutherland, Oct. 24, 1959; children—Thomas, Alice, Sara. Tchr., San Antonio Schs., 1959-61, Brown Sch. Exceptional Children, Austin, Tex., 1961-62, St. Stephen's Episcopal Sch., 1962-63; tchr. dept. history U. Tex., 1963-64, dean continuing edn., asso. prof., 1977—; founding pres., prof. history John Tyler Community Coll., Chester, Va., 1966-69; postdoctoral fellow U. Calif., Los Angeles, 1970; state adminstr. community colls. Tex. Coordinating Bd. for Colls. and Univs., 1970-71, head academic program devel. div., 1971-73; founding pres. Austin (Tex.) Community Coll., 1973-77; v.p., dir. Physicians and Surgeons Pharmacy, Inc.; dir. Central Va. Ednl. Television, Inc., 1967-70, Capitol-Eye TV, 1974-77; lectr. and cons. in field. Bd. dirs. Brackenridge Hosp., Austin, 1979—, Wesley Found., 1979—. Served with U.S. Army, 1957-65. W. K. Kellogg Found. fellow, 1964-66; recipient Jaycees Distinguished Service award, 1967. Mem. Nat. Univ. Continuing Edn. Assn., Am. Assn. Community and Jr. Colls., Phi Delta Kappa, Phi Alpha Theta, Phi Kappa Phi. Methodist. Clubs: Rotary, Town and Gown, Delta Tau Delta. Contbr. chpts. to books, articles to profl. jours. Office: Main Bldg 2500 U Texas Austin TX 78712

HATFIELD, WILLIAM EMERSON, chemist; b. Ransom, Ky., May 31, 1937; s. Emerson B. Hatfield and Pricy (Gardner) Hatfield Wallen; B.S., Marshall U., Huntington, W.Va., 1958, M.S., 1959; Ph.D., U. Ariz., 1962, postgrad. U. Ill., 1962-63; m. Peggy Ransom, 1955 (div. 1967); children—Timothy, Robert, Maryan, Julia, Ellen; m. 2d, Jane Cheek, 1967 (div. 1973). Mem. faculty U. N.C., Chapel Hill, 1963—, prof. chemistry, 1972—; Nat. Acad. Sci. exchange scientist to USSR, 1977; participant Am. specialist program State Dept., 1977; external examiner U. Sierra Leone, 1976-78; dir. NATO

Advanced Research Inst., 1978; vis. scholar Cambridge U., 1978. Recipient award Cahn Instruments Co., 1965; named Disting. Alumnus, Marshall U., 1975. Mem. AAAS, Am. Chem. Soc. (chmn. inorganic exam. subcom. exam. com. 1974—), Chem. Soc. London, U. Ariz. Alumni Assn. (pres. N.C. chpt. 1977—), Sigma Xi, Phi Lambda Upsilon. Democrat. Author: Problems in Structural Inorganic Chemistry, 1971; Symmetry in Chemical Bonding and Structure, 1974; also research articles; editor Molecular Metals, 1978; adv. bd. Jour. Inorganic and Nuclear Chemistry. Home: 400 Wesley Dr Chapel Hill NC 27514 Office: A406 Kenan Labs Univ NC Chapel Hill NC 27514

HATHAWAY, AMOS TOWNSEND, naval officer, educator; b. Pueblo, Colo., Dec. 5, 1913; s. James Amos and Nina (North) H.; B.S., U.S. Naval Acad., 1935; postgrad. U.S. Naval War Coll., 1947-48; M.A. in Teaching, Duke, 1965-66; m. Marianne Langdon Train, June 10, 1937 (dec. Dec. 1972); children—Joan Langdon, Marianne Train, Melinda North (dec.), Barbara Spencer, Sarah Townsend; m. 2d, Gay Johnson Blair, Jan. 2, 1979. Commd. ensign U.S. Navy, 1935, advanced through grades to capt., 1954; exec. officer, navigator destroyer minesweeper Zane, Guadalcanal, 1942; command destroyer Heermann, Battle off Samar, 1944; mem. faculty U.S. Naval Acad., 1945-47, U.S. Naval War Coll., 1951-53; mem. war staff Gen. MacArthur, Korea, 1948-50, writer theater logistic plan Inchon Landing, 1950; exec. officer cruiser St. Paul, 1950-51; command Destroyer Div. 92, 1953-54, command attack transport Okanogan, 1958-59; command cruiser Rochester, 1959-60; mem. joint staff Joint Chiefs of Staff, 1961-63, dir. logistic plans Office Chief of Naval Operations, 1963-65, ret., 1965; asst. prof. math. The Citadel, Charleston, S.C., 1966-79. Decorated Navy Cross, Legion of Merit (2), Bronze Star (2), Mem. Math. Assn. Am., U.S. Naval Acad. Alumni Assn., U.S. Naval Acad. Athletic Assn. (dir. 1945-47), U.S. Naval Inst., Kappa Delta Pi. Club: Army Navy (Washington). Home: 11 Sayle Rd Charleston SC 29407 also PO Box 5463 Charlottesville VA 22905

HATHAWAY, ARTHUR JUSTIN, printing co. exec.; b. Dallas, Jan. 11, 1953; s. Herbert Hoover and Dawn (Leggett) H.; student S.W. Tex. State U., 1976-77; m. Delia Sanchez, Mar. 31, 1977; 1 son, Brian Patrick. Print shop mgr. BBA Advt., San Antonio, 1969-72; prodn. mgr. Pacesetter Pub. Co., San Antonio, 1972-73; print shop mgr. Sherwood Van Lines, San Antonio, 1973-75; vocat. printing instr., supr. Gary Job Corps., San Marcos, Tex., 1975-78; prodn. mgr. Bennett Printing Co., Dallas, 1978—; coordinator graphic communications Woodcreek Resort, Wimberly, Tex., 1977-78. Bd. dirs. Miss. Black San Antonio Beauty Pagent, 1976-77. Recipient cert. of Achievement, Eastman Kodak Co., 1979, Dallas Sch. Printing Papers, 1979. Mem. Internat. Graphic Arts Edn. Assn., Council Reprographics Execs., Graphic Arts Tech. Found., Am. Printing History Assn. Democrat. Baptist. Club: Dallas Litho. Home: 5615 Mercedes St Dallas TX 75206 Office: 7411 Hines Pl Dallas TX 75235

HATHCOAT, DARYL FRANKLIN, civil engr.; b. Harrison, Ark., Mar. 1, 1952; s. Leslie Franklin and Peggy Ann (Evans) H.; student Ark. Poly. Coll., 1970-72; B.S. in Civil Engring., U. Ark., 1974; m. Teresa Jo Hankins, Dec. 27, 1974; 1 dau., Kimberly Elaine. Engr. and design engr. Brown & Root, Houston, 1975-80, sr. engr., to 1980; partner Tech. Offshore Designs and Engring. Cons.'s, Inc., Houston, 1980—. Registered profl. engr., Tex., Calif. Mem. ASCE, Chi Epsilon. Home: 16814 Bonnie Sean St Spring TX 77373 Office: 654 E N Belt Dr Suite 256 Houston TX 77060

HATHWAY, CHARLES WILSON, shipyards co. exec.; b. Sycamore, Ill., Aug. 7, 1931; s. George Wilson and Dorothy Louise (Counsell) H.; student No. Ill. State Tchrs. Coll., DeKalb, 1949-50; B.S.M.E., Bradley U., Peoria, Ill., 1953; m. Mardell Ann Roth, Dec. 20, 1952; children—Craig Wilson, Jefferson Roth, Georgia Mardell. Design engr. Gen. Electric Co., Schenectady, 1953-54, reactor supr., San Jose, Calif., 1955-60; nuclear supt. Nuclear div. Todd Shipyards Corp., N.Y.C., 1960-61, supt. adminstrv. dept., Galveston, Tex., 1961-66, div. mgr. research and tech. div., 1966—; pres. SAFE, Inc., Galveston, Tex., 1967-71; mem. nuclear tech. adv. com. Tex. State Tech. Inst., dir. 1st Nat. Bank of LaMarque. Served to 1st lt. USAF, 1954-56. Mem. ASME, Am. Nuclear Soc., Soc. Naval Architects and Marine Engrs., Tex. Soc. Profl. Engrs. Home: 2511 Meadow Ln LaMarque TX 77568 Office: PO Box 1600 Galveston TX 77553

HATLEY, LARRY J., elec. engr.; b. Tahlequah, Okla., Aug. 4, 1946; s. Jerome Edward and Otha Josephine (Hubbard) H.; B.S. in Physics and Math., Northeastern Okla. State U., 1969; m. Kathleen Anne Ogden, Apr. 10, 1971. Results engr. Okla. Gas and Electric Co., Horseshoe Lake, 1969-73, sr. results engr., Muskogee, 1973—. Registered profl. engr., Okla. Mem. Eta Kappa Nu. Home: 2105 Boston Ave Muskogee OK 74401 Office: PO Box 1270 Muskogee OK 74401

HATTAWAY, GERALD TERRY, advt. agy. exec.; b. Columbus, Ga., June 7, 1953; s. Gerald Bennett and Jean K. H.; student Columbus Coll., 1971-73, 78; m. Rhonda Dilleshaw, Aug. 16, 1975. Chief videotape operator WRBL-TV, Columbus, 1969-74; prodn. technician Video Systems Group, Sea Pines Co., Hilton Head Island, S.C., 1974-75; prodn. mgr. WKAB-TV, Montgomery, Ala., 1975-77; pres. Hattaway Advt. Inc., Columbus, 1977—; producer, dir. Miss. Columbus Pageant, 1980. Mem. Columbus C. of C. (public relations-publicity com.). Chmn. TV com., chmn. publicity com. Edgewood Baptist Ch. Clubs: Met. Sertoma, Columbus Advt. Home: 6328 Fox Chapel Dr Columbus GA 31904 Office: 3026 Cody Rd Columbus GA 31907

HATTIER, MAURICE JOSEPH, accountant; b. New Orleans, Dec. 17, 1947; s. Victor Gustave and Cecile Marie (St. Pierre) H.; student Tulane U., 1975-77; m. Sharon Frey, Aug. 24, 1968; children—Maurice Joseph, Kim Marie, Beth Anne. Accounting clk. Carl E. Woodward, Inc., New Orleans, 1965-71, asst. controller, 1971-76, controller, head acctg. dept., 1976—, head computer ops., 1976-79. Treas. local pack Boy Scouts Am., 1978; mem. adv. council Meraux Sch., 1977; youth activity coach Versailles Park, 1975-78. Served with U.S. Army, 1968-71; Vietnam. Decorated Bronze Star. Mem. Am. Mgmt. Assn., Honeywell Users Assn., New Orleans C. of C. Democrat. Roman Catholic. Club: Jefferson Racquet. Home: 263 Oak Alley Pearl River LA 70452 Office: 1019 S Dupre St New Orleans LA 70185

HAUCH, RUTHADELE LATOURRETTE, educator; b. Muscatine, Iowa, Apr. 16, 1914; d. Arthur James and Annamay (Hendriks) LaTourrette; B.A. magna cum laude, U. Iowa, 1935; M.A., U. Chgo., 1939; Edn. Specialist, George Washington U., 1967; m. Charles C. Hauch, Jan. 1, 1941; children—Priscilla Hauch Peters, Charlotte Hauch Hall, Valerie. Tchr. Muscatine (Iowa) Pub. Schs., 1935-38, Whitefish Bay (Wis.) Pub. Schs., 1938-39; asst. prof. edn. Western Ill. Coll., Macomb, 1939-40; tchr., asst. dir. Am. Sch. Santo Domingo, Dominican Republic, 1941; counselor continuing edn. for women George Washington U., Washington, 1973—; cons. in field. Mem. Arlington (Va.) Com. Sch. Improvement, 1948-51; Arlington Health Welfare Council, 1965-70; Arlington County United Way Council, 1974—. Mem. Nat. Assn. Women Deans, Adminstrs., Counselors, Am. Personnel and Guidance Assn., Iowa Alumni Assn. (life), George Washington Alumni Assn., Columbian Women, Mt. Vernon Baptist Assn. (bd. 1972-75), Phi Beta Kappa, Pi Lambda Theta, Phi Delta Gamma (chpt. pres. 1974-75). Baptist. Home: 5418 N 21st St Arlington VA 22205

HAUG, SCOTT ANDREW, audiologist; b. Houston, June 29, 1950; s. Clarence Olaf and Margaret Ann (Scott) H.; student S.W. Tex. State U., 1968-69; B.A., U. Tex., 1972, M.A., 1974; m. Constance Marie Ries, Aug. 10, 1974; stepchildren—Rob Cowman, Rusty Cowman. Tchr. asst. audiology U. Tex., Austin, 1972; clin. audiologist Med. Center Ear Nose and Throat Clinic, Houston, 1973-75; clin. instr. audiology Baylor Coll. Medicine, Houston, 1974-76; clin. audiologist Austin Ear Nose and Throat Clinic, 1975—. Named outstanding clinician U. Tex., 1972. Mem. Am. Speech and Hearing Assn. (cert. of clin. competency), Tex. Speech and Hearing Assn., Acad. Dispensing Audiologists, Soc. Med. Audiology, So. Audiological Soc. Club: Centurion. Contbg. author book Help for the Hard-of-Hearing, 1977. Home: 4803 Sage Hen Dr Austin TX 78759 Office: Austin Ear Nose and Throat Clinic 401 Medical Park Tower Austin TX 78705

HAUGH, JACK ALBERT, retail exec.; b. Mannington, W.Va., Mar. 2, 1927; s. Tolbert Oscar and Esther (Sybert) H.; A.B., Fairmont State Coll., 1949; postgrad. W.Va. U., 1952-53; m. Patricia Ann Lolos, Aug. 27, 1948; children—Jack, Linda, Judith, Barry, Michael, Mark. Coach athletics public schs., Fairmont, 1949-55; sales mgr. Barr Thomas Lumber Co., Fairmont, 1955-60; v.p. ops. Bauer Home Centers, Fairmont, 1960-72; v.p., gen. mgr. Browns Lumber & Supply Co., Fairmont, 1973—; mem. home center adv. com. Weyerhaeuser Corp., 1979—. Elder, 1st United Presbyterian Ch., 1961—. Served with USN, 1945-46. Mem. W.Va. Bldg. Supply Assn. (v.p.), Lumbermans Merchandising Corp. Republican. Clubs: Fairmont Field, Lakeview Country. Home: 1 Holly Hill Fairmont WV 26554 Office: PO Box 1589 Fairmont WV 26554

HAULENBEEK, ROBERT BOGLE, JR., govt. ofcl.; b. Cleve., Feb. 24, 1941; s. Robert Bogle and Priscilla Valerie (Burch) H.; B.S., Okla. State U., 1970; m. Rebecca Marie Talley, Mar. 1, 1965; children—Kimberly Kaye, Robert Bogle, III. Micro paleontological photographer Pan Am. Research Co., Tulsa, 1966-67; flight instr. Okla. State U., 1970; air traffic control specialist FAA, Albuquerque, 1970-73, Farmington, N.Mex., 1973-78, flight service specialist, Dalhart, Tex., 1978—; staff officer CAP, Albuquerque, 1970-73, Farmington, 1974-78. Served with U.S. Army, 1964-65. Recipient Meritorious Service award CAP, 1978. Mem. Profl. Air Traffic Controllers Orgn. Republican. Presbyterian. Home: 1221 Sagebrush Rd Dalhart TX 79033 Office: FAA Flight Service Sta PO Box 1431 Dalhart TX 79022

HAUN, LOUIS EUGENE, JR., ophthalmologist; b. Memphis, July 23, 1940; s. Louis Eugene and Jane (Gray) H.; B.S., U. Tenn., 1964, M.D., 1964; m. Katherine Cartwright Alden, June 24, 1963; children—Louis Eugene, Alden Kirkpatrick, Christopher Cartwright. Intern Vanderbilt U. Hosp., 1965-66; resident in ophthalmology U. Cin. Gen. Hosp., 1968-71; postgrad. trainee Stanford U., 1971; practice medicine specializing in ophthalmology, Maryville, Tenn., 1971—; mem. staff U. Tenn. Meml. Research Center and Hosp., Children's Hosp., Blount Meml. Hosp. Served with M.C., USAF, 1966-68. Diplomate Am. Bd. Ophthalmology and Otolaryngology. Mem. AMA, Tenn. Med. Assn., Blount County Med. Soc., Am. Assn. Ophthalmology, Am. Acad. Ophthalmology and Otolaryngology. Presbyterian. Club: Cherokee Country. Home: Route 2 Lakeside Acres Louisville TN 37777 Office: Chilhowee Med Park Maryville TN 37801

HAUN, WILLIAM PATRICK, coll. adminstr.; b. Huntington, W.Va., Feb. 28, 1948; s. Horace Lee and Sarah Jane (Haley) H.; B.A., Salem Coll., 1971; M.A., W.Va. U., 1978; m. Catherine Mary Alk, June 26, 1976. Dist. scout exec. Boy Scouts Am., Ashland, Ky., 1971-74; dir. alumni affairs Salem Coll., 1974, dir. admissions, 1974—. Mem. Nat. Assn. Coll. Admissions Counselors, W.Va. Personnel and Guidance Assn., Am. Assn. Coll. Registrars and Admissions Officers. Democrat. Roman Catholic (pres. parish council). Clubs: Masons, Shriner (Ashland). Participant local theatrical productions. Home: Lakeview Terr Salem WV 26426 Office: Office Admissions Salem Coll Salem WV 26426

HAURI, BECKY ANN, coll. adminstr.; b. Midland, Mich., May 27, 1949; d. Lawrence D. and Barbara Jean (Ames) Hauri; B.A., Western Mich. U., 1970, M.A., 1971; m. Alan Dodge Dehnke, June 12, 1971. Counselor, Alternative Drug Abuse Program, Houston, 1971-73, lead counselor, 1973-75, supr. outpatient services, 1975-76; counselor Houston Community Coll., 1975-77, outreach specialist, 1977—; speaker before profl. groups; cons. LULAC nat. meeting, Webster, Tex., 1979. Mem. Am. Personnel and Guidance Assn., Tex. Assn. Women Deans, Adminstrs. and Counselors (2d v.p. 1979—), Tex. Personnel and Guidance Assn., Tex. Assn. Drug Abuse Services (sec. 1976-77). Office: Houston Community Coll 22 Waugh Dr Houston TX 77002

HAURI, DAVID JOHN, service co. exec.; b. West Palm Beach, Fla., July 6, 1951; s. John F. and Joan E. H.; B.A. in Psychology U. Tex., Austin, 1973; M.A. in Psychology, U. Tex., San Antonio, 1975; m. Sharyn Elaine Hauri, May 20, 1977; 1 dau., Kimberley Lynne. Mem. mktg. staff 3M Co., 1973-75; regional sales mgr. ITT Services, Detroit, 1975-77; v.p. Oxford Services div. Consol. Foods Corp., Atlanta, 1977—. Mem. Am. Mgmt. Assn., Bldg. Services Contractors Assn. Ga. (treas.), Atlanta C. of C. Home: 840 Lost Creek Circle Stone Mountain GA 30083 Office: 1445 Marietta Blvd NW Atlanta GA 30318

HAUSE, EDITH COLLINS, ednl. adminstr.; b. Rock Hill, S.C., Dec. 11, 1933; d. Ernest Orell and Violet (Smith) Collins; A.B., Columbia Coll., 1956; postgrad., U. S.C., 1971-75; m. James Luke Hause, Sept. 3, 1955; children—Stephen Mark, Felicia Gaye. Tchr. Holly Hill (S.C.) Acad., 1970-71, Dent Jr. High Sch., Columbia, S.C., 1971-74; dir. alumnae affairs, Columbia (S.C.) Coll., 1974—. Charter mem. Jr. Women's Club, Melbourne, Fla., 1962-64; mem. Service League, N.C. Named Outstanding Teacher of Year, Dent Jr. High Sch., 1973-74. Mem. Council for Advancement and Support Edn., Alpha Delta Kappa. Republican. Methodist. Clubs: Garden (Melbourne, Fla., Burlington, N.C.). Office: Alumnae Office Columbia College Columbia SC 29203

HAUSEMAN, DAVID PEGUES, investment advisor; b. Port Clinton, Ohio, Aug. 22, 1924; s. David Nathaniel and Rosa Rowan (Pegues) H.; B.S., Washington and Lee U., 1946; M.B.A., Temple U., 1948; m. Jeanette Arnett, Sept. 10, 1946 (div. Apr. 1971); children—Susan, Jeanette, Davida, Carolyn, David Nathaniel II; m. 2d, Jane McLean, May 23, 1973. Gen. mgr. Westmoreland Metal Co., Phila., 1950-56; pres. Hathaway Co., Narberth, Pa., 1956-62; v.p. N.Am. Steel Corp., Lakeland, Fla., 1962-65; pres. D.P. Hauseman Co., Lakeland, 1965—; tchr. investments, fin., mktg. Fla. So. Coll., Lakeland, 1965-66. Served with U.S. Army, 1942-45. Republican. Episcopalian. Mem. Am. Contract Bridge League (life master player), Alpha Tau Omega. Club: Bala Golf. Contbr. articles to profl. jours. Patentee bldg. specialty products. Home and Office: 2611 Jonila Ave Lakeland FL 33803

HAUSER, MICHAEL FRANCIS, social worker; b. Winston-Salem, N.C., May 7, 1944; s. Wilbur Woodrow and Doris (Stimson) H.; B.S. in Indsl. Relations, U N.C., 1966, M.S.W., Charleston, 1972; m. Susan Kay Poe, Aug. 15, 1970; children—Jason Michael, Zachary David, Jessica Susanna. Social worker Rockingham County Dept. Public Welfare, Reidsville, N.C., 1967; social worker Forsyth County Dept. Social Service, Winston-Salem, 1969-70, social work supr., 1972-77; dir. social work Bapt. Children's Home of N.C. Inc., Thomasville, 1977—. Active Boy Scouts Am., 1978—; Democratic precinct committeeman, 1978—. Served with USNR, 1967-68. Mem. Acad. Cert. Social Workers, Nat. Assn. Social Workers, Assn. Couples for Marriage Enrichment. Clubs: Lions, Internat. Management. Home: 225 Jones Circle Thomasville NC 27360 Office: PO Box 338 Baptist Children's Home Thomasville NC 27360

HAUSSMANN, JOHN GEORGE, cons. engring. co. exec.; b. Bronx, N.Y., Nov. 24, 1946; s. John George and Dorothy Agnes (Johnson) H.; B.S.C.E., Newark Coll. Engring., 1968; m. Carol Ann Stietz, Oct. 24, 1968; children—Michele, Christopher. Project engr. hwy. and mass transp. projects Gannett Fleming Corddry and Carpenter Inc., Harrisburg, Pa., 1968-79, mgr. Detroit regional office, 1975-79; div. mgr. Soilstone Engring. Testing Lab., Inc., Atlanta, 1979—. Mem. Ga. Soc. Profl. Engrs., Nat. Soc. Profl. Engrs., ASCE. Club: Berkeley Hills Golf. Home: 6053 Wandering Way Norcross GA 30093 Office: 600 Virginia Ave NE Atlanta GA 30306

HAUTH, FLOYD FRANCIS, air force officer; b. River Falls, Wis., Apr. 20, 1939; s. Frank Edward and Dorothy Catherine (Roller) H.; student U. Wis., 1955-58, M.S., 1968; B.S., Pa. State U., 1962; m. Janet Veronica Malicki, Dec. 15, 1962; children—Clara M., Kathryn J., Tanya N., Rachel A. Enlisted in U.S. Air Force, 1958, advanced through grades to lt. col., 1979; weather officer Offutt AFB, Nebr., 1963-66; weather detachment comdr., Vietnam, 1968-69; team chief Latin Am. Forecast Center, Charleston AFB, S.C., 1969-70; weather detachment comdr. Vance AFB, Okla., 1970-74; operations officer Air Force Global Weather Central, Offutt AFB, 1974-78; chief operations 5th Weather Squadron, Ft. McPherson, Ga., 1978—; instr. Okla. State U., 1973 cons. mil. meteorologist, 1978—. Pres., Vance AFB Chapel Fund Council, 1972-73. Decorated Air Force Commendation medal, Bronze Star. Mem. Am. Meteorol. Soc. (vice chmn. 1978), Air Force Assn. Democrat. Roman Catholic. Clubs: Ind. Order Foresters, Vance AFB OK Officer's (council mem. 1972-73), Mt. McPherson Officer's. Author: Forecaster's Handbook, 1970. Home: 1085 Redan Trail Stone Mountain GA 30088 Office: 5th Weather Squadron Fort McPherson GA 30330

HAUXWELL, GERALD DEAN, chem. engr.; b. Indianola, Nebr., Sept. 24, 1935; s. Lawrence F. and Mildred E. (Wing) H.; A.A. in Engring., McCook Coll., 1955; B.S. in Chem. Engring., U. Colo., 1958; M.S. (NROTC Scholar) in Chem. Engring., U. Idaho, 1960; Ph.D. in Chem. Engring. (Dow fellow, Shell Oil Co. fellow), Oreg. State U., 1971; postgrad. U. Del., San Jose State U.; m. Ingrid M.D. Postner, Dec. 20, 1964. Program engr. Gen. Electric Co., San Jose, Calif., 1962-64; research engr. E. I. du Pont de Nemours & Co., Wilmington, Del., 1964-68, devel. asso., Richmond, Va., 1971; cons.; mem. adj. faculty U. Va., Va. Commonwealth U. Pres., bd. dirs. Newberrytowne Assn., 1975-76; active United Givers Fund, 1976; elder Wilmington Christian Ch., 1968. Served to lt. (j.g.) USN, 1959-62. Registered profl. engr., Oreg., Va., Md. Mem. Am. Chem. Soc., Am. Inst. Chem. Engrs., Nat. Soc. Profl. Engrs., Alpha Chi Sigma, Phi Theta Kappa, Phi Kappa Phi, Phi Rho Pi, Sigma Tau. Home: 2915 Ennismore Ct Richmond VA 23224

HAVELOS, SAM GEORGE, restaurant exec.; b. Pavlpoulon, Greece, Dec. 4, 1915; s. George D. and Spyridoula G. (Kanavos) H.; student Distributive Edn., Wytheville, Va., 1955-60, Parkwood Bus. Coll., Marion, Va., 1961, Statesville (N.C.) Coll., 1963, Zanerian Coll. Penmanship, Columbus, Ohio, 1964; m. Dina K. Karageorge, Sept. 12, 1953. Owner, Presto Restaurant, Winston-Salem, N.C., 1932-34; mgr. Central Restaurant, Fayetteville, N.C., 1934-38, owner, 1940-52; mgr. San. Restaurant, Winston-Salem, 1938-40; owner Washington Restaurant, Wytheville, Va., 1952-61, Reynolda Manor Cafeteria, Winston-Salem, 1962-64; mgr. Sam's Gourmet, Winston-Salem, 1965-69, Greeks Cellar, Blacksburg, Va., 1969—; treas. Wytheville Twins baseball team, 1960. Active ARC. Recipient certificate of meritorious service Nat. Soc. SAR, 1973. Mem. Restaurant Assn. Cumberland and Robinson Counties (pres.), N.C. Restaurant Assn. (dir.), Am. Numismatic Assn., Nat. Geog. Soc., Evrytanian Assn., Calhoun's Collectors Soc., Am. Helenic Edn. Progressive Assn., F.M. Philatelic Assn., Smithsonian Inst., C. of C., Three Hundred Knights of Thermophylae (responsible for financing constrn. meml. monument 1951), Patriots of Am. Bicentennial, Nat. Wild Life Fedn., Nat. Flag Found. Greek Orthodox. Clubs: K.P., Dram Order Knights of Korassan, Quarterback, Execs. Am., Moose. Calligraphist; designed suggested new U.S. flag at Hawaii statehood, 1959. Address: Drawer E Blacksburg VA 24060

HAVENS, DOLORES DRAEGER, speech pathologist; b. Del Rio, Tex., Jan. 19, 1938; d. Ernest J. and Rosalia (Rosas) Draeger; B.S., S.W. Tex. State U., 1959, M.Ed. (grantee Bur. Edn. Handicapped), 1972; Ph.D. (U.S. Office Edn. grantee), U. Wis., 1975; m. Rudolph E. Havens, Feb. 10, 1962; children—Ralph Charles, Frances Yvonne. Speech pathologist Del Rio Ind. Sch. Dist., 1959-71; pvt. practice speech pathology, Del Rio, 1975—. Mem. Am. Speech and Hearing Assn., Am. Acad. Pvt. Practice Speech Pathology and Audiology, Tex. Tchrs. Assn. (life). Author papers in field. Address: 207 W Strickland St Del Rio TX 78840

HAVERKORN, GARY WAYNE, accountant; b. Houston, May 24, 1955; s. Alvah Arthur and Lillian Haverkorn; B.B.A., U. Tex., 1975; m. Marion Elizabeth Kipp, Mar. 25, 1978. Asst. county auditor Harris County (Tex.), 1976-77; accounts payable supr. Zapata Off-Shore Co., Houston, 1977-78, sr. acct., 1978—. Mem. U. Tex. at Austin Ex Student Assn. Republican. Baptist. Home: 4138 Windrift Dr Houston TX 77066 Office: PO Box 4240 Houston TX 77001

HAVILAND, LEONA, librarian; b. Stamford, Conn., Nov. 10, 1916; d. Howard Brush and Ada Grace (Jewell) Haviland; B.S., U. Ala., 1940; M.S., U. Ill., 1951; postgrad. Columbia, 1943, 56-60; m. Warren John Burke, Sept. 10, 1973. Jr. asst. Ferguson Library, Stamford, 1936-37, summers 1938-39, sr. asst., 1940-44; student asst. U. Ala., 1937-40; asst. to cataloguer U.S. Nat. Mus. Library, Washington, 1944-48; librarian Arts and Industries Mus., Smithsonian Instn., Washington, 1948-50; reference librarian U.S. Mcht. Marine Acad., Kings Point, N.Y., 1952-77. Mem. council YWCA, Washington, 1945-47. Mem. A.L.A., Spl. Libraries Assn. (past group membership chmn.), L.I. Hist. Soc., N.Y. Geneal. and Biog. Soc., Smithsonian Assos., South Street Seaport Mus., Alpha Beta Alpha, Alpha Lambda Delta. Home: 809 Pennsylvania Ave Saint Cloud FL 32769

HAWK, WALTER, II, coll. counselor; b. Jacksonville, Fla., Nov. 23, 1950; s. Walter and Mattie Bell (Simmons) H.; B.S. in Psychology, Oakwood Coll., 1973; M.Ed. in Counseling, U. N.C., Charlotte, 1975; m. Sylvia Denise Sumpter, Mar. 4, 1971; children—Walter III, Shawna Denise, Wesley Deltwan, Warren Edward. Salesman, Sears, Roebuck & Co. Huntsville, Ala., 1972-73; sales rep. Met. Life Ins. Co., Charlotte, N.C., 1973-74; counselor Barber-Scotia Coll.,

Concord, N.C., 1975-76, Livingstone Coll., Salisbury, N.C., 1976—. Mem. Am. Personnel and Guidance Assn. Democrat. Adventist. Home: PO Box 541 Salisbury NC 28144 Office: Livingstone Coll Salisbury NC 28144

HAWKINS, ELINOR DIXON (MRS. CARROLL WOODARD HAWKINS), librarian; b. Masontown, W.Va., Sept. 25, 1927; d. Thomas Fitchie and Susan (Reed) Dixon; A.B., Fairmont State Coll., 1949; B.S. in L.S., U. N.C., 1950; m. Carroll Woodard Hawkins, June 24, 1951; 1 son, John Carroll. Children's librarian Enoch Pratt Free Library, Balt., 1950-51; head circulation dept. Greensboro (N.C.) Pub. Library, 1951-56; librarian Craven-Pamlico Library Service, New Bern, N.C., 1958-62; dir. Craven-Pamlico-Carteret Regional Library, 1962—; storyteller children's TV program Tele-Story Time, 1952-58, 63—. Mem. New Bern Hist. Soc., 1973—, Tryon Palace Commn., 1974—. Mem. N.C. Assn. Retarded Children, N.C. Library Assn. Baptist. Club: Pilot (pres. 1957-58, v.p. 1962-63). Home: PO Box 57 Cove City NC 28523 Office: 400 Johnson St New Bern NC 28560

HAWKINS, ELMER JOHN, physician; b. Jayton, Tex., July 8, 1922; s. Elmer and Arlis (Cunningham) H.; B.S., McMurry Coll., 1942; M.D., Baylor U., 1945; m. Gabie Smallwood, June 19, 1943; children—Lou Ann (Mrs. C. Richard Bullock), James Earl, Sharon Kay, Jonathan Lewis. Intern, Meth. Hosp., Madison, Wis., 1945-46. practice gen. medicine, Roby, Tex., 1948-49, Hamlin (Tex.) Hosp. & Clinic, 1949-72, Stamford (Tex.) Clinic, 1972—; mem. staffs West Tex. Hosp., Hendricks Hosp., Abilene, Tex., Stamford Meml. Hosp. Served to capt. AUS, 1946-48. Mem. Am., Tex. med. assns., Am., Tex. acads. family physicians, Taylor-Jones County Med. Soc. Methodist. Club: Petroleum (Abilene). Home: PO Box 23 Stamford TX 79553 Office: Stamford Clinic Stamford TX 79553

HAWKINS, GEORGE ELLIOTT, JR., nutritionist; b. Caldwell County, Ky., July 26, 1919; s. George Elliott and Mary Elizabeth (Rodgers) H.; B.S., Western Ky. U., 1941; M.S., U. Ga., 1947; Ph.D., N.C. State U., 1952; m. Mary Elizabeth Cline, Apr. 6, 1946; 1 dau., Mary Anne Murray. Teaching asst. U. Ga., 1946-47, instr., asst. prof., 1947-49; research asst. N.C. State U., 1949-51; asst. prof. dairy sci. Auburn U., 1952-53. asso. prof., 1954-59, prof. animal and dairy sci., 1959—. Served with AUS, 1942-46. Decorated Bronze star, Purple Heart. Mem. Am. Dairy Sci. Assn. (past pres. So. div.), Am. Inst. Nutrition, Am. Soc. Animal Sci., So. Assn. Agrl. Scientists, Council Agrl. Sci. and Tech., Coll. Dairy Feed Conf. Bd., Sigma Xi, Phi Kappa Phi, Gamma Sigma Delta. Roman Catholic. Clubs: Saugahatchee Country, Dairy Shrine. Home: 601 Auburn Dr Auburn AL 36830 Office: Animal and Dairy Sci Dept Auburn U Auburn AL 36830

HAWKINS, HERMAN HERBERT, design engr.; b. Borger, Tex., May 7, 1954; s. Calvin Sidney and Alice Blanch (Hill) H.; A.A., Frank Phillips Coll., 1973; B.S.M.E., Tex. Tech. U., 1975; postgrad. W. Tex. State U., 1978-80. Engr., Mason & Hanger, Silas Mason Co., Inc., Amarillo, Tex., 1975-79, sr. engr., 1979—. Mem. ASME (vice chmn. subsect), Pi Tau Sigma, Tau Beta Pi. Home: 1221 Cooley Dr Borger TX 79007 Office: Box 30020 Amarillo TX 79177

HAWKINS, JAMES ARTHUR, hosp. adminstr.; b. St. Joseph, Mo.; s. Clarence Arthur and Blanche (Wood) H.; B.A., U. Chgo., 1974, M.B.A., 1975. Evening adminstr. Christ Hosp., Oak Lawn, Ill., 1975-76; computer cons. Rex Hosp., Raleigh, N.C., 1972-77; asst. adminstr. Martin Gen. Hosp., Williamston, N.C., 1977-79; adminstr. Robersonville Twp. Hosp. for Martin County Hosp., Inc., 1977-79; adminstr. Dist. Meml. Hosp., Andrews, N.C., 1979—. Bd. dirs. Eastern Area Health Edn. Center, Greenville, N.C., 1977-79. Mem. Am. Coll. Hosp. Adminstrs. Baptist. Home and Office: PO Box E Andrews NC 28901

HAWKINS, JOHN MORGAN, personnel and labor relations cons.; b. Winfield, Ala., June 22, 1935; s. John Morgan and Bertie (Beasley) H.; A.B., U. Ala., 1957; M.S., Ga. Inst., Tech., 1974; m. Marianne Scifres, Sept. 11, 1976; 1 son, Roland Bernard. Govt. intern Center for Disease Control, Atlanta, 1957-62; adminstv. asst. Ga. Power Co., Atlanta, 1962-65; labor relations rep. Lockheed-Ga. Co., Marietta, 1965-72; personnel dir. Haverty Furniture Cos.. Inc., Atlanta, 1972-74; prin. John Morgan Hawkins, personnel and labor relations cons., Atlanta, 1974—. Mem. Ga. Ho. of Reps., 1975—. Served to capt. USAR, 1957-68. Recipient Friend of Children award Child Advocacy Coalition, 1979—. Mem. Am. Soc. Tng. Dirs., Am. Arbitration Assn. (advisory council 1978—), Am. Soc. Personnel Adminstrn. Democrat. Presbyterian. Club: Druid Hills Kiwanis. Home: 1360 Harvard Rd NE Atlanta GA 30306

HAWKINS, ROBERT A., coll. adminstr.; b. Anabelle, W.Va., Aug. 21, 1924; s. Lawrence R. Hawkins and Grace O. (Lauer) Glover Hawkins; B.A., Abilene Christian Coll., 1948, M.A., 1967; Ed.D., Tex. Tech U., 1974; m. Nina Jo Milton, June 6, 1943; children—Paul C., Sheila Ann. Adminstr. youth camps, 1949-64; tchr., adminstr. Denver schs., 1953-56; instr. Abilene (Tex.) Christian Coll., 1965-68; instr., registrar Lubbock (Tex.) Christian Coll., 1968-74; dir. guidance Midland (Tex.) Coll., 1974—, instr. behavioral and social sci. depts., 1974—. Recipient Outstanding Tchr. award Lubbock Christian Coll., 1971. Mem. Am., Tex., Permian Basin personnel and guidance assns., Jr. Coll. Student Personnel Assn. Tex., Tex. Assn. Collegiate Registrars and Admissions Officers, Tex. Jr. Coll. Tchrs. Assn., Phi Kappa Phi, Alpha Chi. Author, translator: Bible Student's New Testament, 19—. Contbr. articles to profl. jours. Home: 3305 Providence Dr Midland TX 79703 Office: 3600 N Garfield St Midland TX 79701

HAWKINS, ROWLAND SPECK, physician, ophthalmologist; b. Memphis, Mar. 18, 1941; s. Rowland Dale and Martha Helen (Speck) H.; B.S. in Chem. Engring., U. Tenn., 1963, M.D., 1967. Intern, City of Memphis Hosps., 1967-68; resident in ophthalmology Baylor Coll. Medicine, Houston, 1968-71; individual practice medicine, specializing in ophthalmology, Houston, 1971—; asso. dir. Inst. Ophthalmology, Houston, 1977—. Fellow Am. Acad. Ophthalmology and Otolaryngology, A.C.S.; mem. Harris County Med. Soc., Tex. Med. Assn. Office: Inst Ophthalmology 4126 SW Freeway Suite 500 Houston TX 77027

HAWKINS, WILLIAM BLEDSOE, JR., lawyer; b. Lynchburg, Va., Aug. 27, 1912; s. William Bledsoe and Nellie W. (Rangeley) H.; A.B., Davidson Coll., 1932; LL.B., U. S.C., 1935; m. Sarah Nell Hestle, Dec. 1, 1945; children—Diana (Mrs. David L. Bailey), William Bledsoe III, Melissa A. Admitted to S.C. bar, 1935, since practiced in Dillon; partner firm Hawkins & Bethea, 1935-41, 46-57, Hawkins & McInnis, 1969—. Dir. 1st Citizens Bank & Trust Co., Dillon. Fed. election commr., 1938-40; chmn. Dillon County Democratic Com., 1948-54; mem. S.C. Dem. Exec. Com., 1954-58; mem. S.C. Ho. of Reps., 1967-72. Bd. dirs. Dunbar Meml. Library, Dillon, St. Eugene Community Hosp., Dillon; trustee U. S.C., 1972—. Served to lt. col. USAAF, 1941-46. Mem. Am., S.C., Dillon County bar assns., Am. Legion, V.F.W., Phi Delta Theta, Phi Delta Phi. Presbyn. (elder, deacon, trustee). Mason, Woodman of World. Club: Twin Lakes Country. Chmn., Dillon County Devel. Bd., 1972—. Home: 310 Johnson Dr Dillon SC 29536 Office: 302 W Harrison St Dillon SC 29536

HAWLEY, JEFFREY LANCE, mortgage banker; b. Shreveport, La., Aug. 28, 1948; s. Eugene Elvin and Opal Marie (Hitchcock) H.; B.S., La. Tech. U., 1970; M.B.A., Northeast La. U., 1978; m. Pamela Haley, Mar. 7, 1970; children—Suzanne Marie, Allison Jean. Sr. acct. Peat, Marwick, Mitchell & Co., Houston, 1970-74; fin. planner Olinkraft Inc., Monroe, La., 1974-77; v.p., treas. Palomar Financial, Monroe, La., 1977—; dir. First Fidelity Mortgage Co. subs. Palomar, dir. other subs.'s; co-founder, co-owner The Stitchery, Monroe, 1976—. Leader, Houston Jr. Achievement, 1972-73. C.P.A., La., Tex. Mem. Am. Inst. C.P.A.'s, Tex. Soc. C.P.A.'s, La. Soc. C.P.A.'s. Republican. So. Baptist. Clubs: Chauvin Racquet, Optimist (sec.-treas., dir.). Home: 3023 River Oaks Dr Monroe LA 71201 Office: 1803 Tower Dr Monroe LA 71203

HAWLEY, MARY BARBARA, librarian; b. Ludlow Center, Mass., Aug. 25, 1925; d. Charles Arthur and Barbara Dickinson (Kimball) H.; B.A., Park Coll., 1947; M.A., Syracuse U., 1950; M.S. in Library Sci., Columbia U., 1960. Tchr. English, Madison (Kans.) High Sch., 1947-48; tchr. jr. high sch. United Presbyn. Ch. U.S.A., Holman and Santa Fe, N.Mex., 1949-51, 52-55, sec. bd. nat. missions, N.Y.C., 1955-59; librarian Hartford (Conn.) Sem. Found., 1960-62; reference librarian Coe Coll., Cedar Rapids, Iowa, 1962-70; head librarian Damavand Coll., Tehran, Iran, 1970-72; acquisitions librarian, asst. prof. library sci. Berea (Ky.) Coll., 1973—; library cons. Yonsei U., Seoul, 1972. Mem. ALA, Southeastern Library Assn., Ky. Library Assn., AAUW. Republican. Presbyterian. Home: CPO 835 Berea KY 40404 Office: Hutchins Library Berea Coll Berea KY 40404

HAWS, GARY LEWIS, educator; b. Vernal, Utah, Apr. 12, 1935; s. Glen Asael and Ellen Mae (Soderquist) H.; A.B., Brigham Young U., 1959; Ph.D., U. N.Mex., 1967; m. Silvia B. Valle, Mar. 6, 1959; children—Nadine, Shane, Cindy, Marcelo Gary, Johnathan, Summer, Heather; m. 2d, Rebecca Jean Johnston, Dec. 28, 1978. Mem. staff Peace Corps Tng. Center, U. N.Mex., 1961-63; chmn. dept. modern langs. Adams State Coll., Alamosa, Colo., 1963-64; dir. lang. labs. Weber State Coll., Ogden, Utah, 1964-67; prof. Latin Am. lit. Murray (Ky.) State U., 1967—, dir. Latin Am. studies program, 1970-79. Pres., Paris br. Ch. of Jesus Christ of Latter-Day Saints, 1977-78, mem. Hopkinsville (Ky.) stake high council, 1978-80. Nat. Def. Title IV fellow, 1959-62; Murray State U. Found. research grantee, 1967-70. Mem. Am. Assn. Tchrs. Spanish and Portuguese, Latin Am. Studies Assn., MLA, Ky. Edn. Assn., Nat. Geog. Soc., Instituto Internacional de Literatura Iberoamericana, Sigma Delta Pi. Author: Carlos Sabat Ercasty y la poesía uruguaya del siglo XX, 1967; El Prometeo Uruguayo, 1969; Florencio Sánchez y el teatro rioplatense, 1980. Office: PO Box 3187 University Station Murray State U Murray KY 42071

HAWS, RONALD WILLIAM, ins. co. exec.; b. Bay City, Mich., Mar. 25, 1941; s. Ernest Robert and Clara Louise (Schieber) H.; B.S., U. Tampa, 1965; M.A., U. South Fla., 1970; C.L.U., Am. Coll., 1978; m. Rebecca Lynne Wright, Mar. 15, 1974; children—Matthew Lloyd, Heather Leigh. Mng. owner Gen. Agency Operation, Tampa, Fla., 1975-76; dir. mktg. and tng. Founders Life, Tampa, 1976-79; dir. sales devel. and tng. Profl. Ins. Corp., Jacksonville, Fla., 1979—. Mem. Nat. Assn. Life Underwriters, Am. Soc. C.L.U.'s, Sales and Mktg. Execs. Internat. Home: 3875 Fernglen Dr Jacksonville FL 32211 Office: Professional Insurance Corp 135 Riverside Ave Jacksonville FL 32202

HAWTHORNE, JOHN DAVID, retail hardware mcht.; b. Abingdon, Va., Apr. 30, 1923; s. Arthur Hopkins and Beulah (Crenshaw) H.; student King Coll., 1940-42, Wittenberg Coll., 1943, U. Richmond, 1946-47; m. Dorothy Jane Montgomery, May 28, 1955; children—David Malcom, Mary Elizabeth, Nancy. With George E. Failing Supply Co., 1947-49; partner Mut. Warehouse Inc., Enid, Okla., 1950-57, owner, 1957-58; partner Walker Truck Lines, Enid, 1955-57, owner, 1957-60; with Montgomery Oil Co., Enid, 1959-63; owner Rude & Co. Hardware, Enid, 1963—. Mem. Met. Area Planning Commn., Enid, 1963-67; Enid rep. Okla. Soc. Crippled Children, 1954—. Served to 1st lt. USAAF, 1943-45. Decorated Air medal with five oak leaf clusters. Mem. Okla. Assn. Realtors, Nat. Assn. Real Estate Bds., Enid Bd. Realtors, Air Force Assn., Kappa Sigma. Presbyn. (elder 1966-69). Rotarian (sec.-treas. 1964-69). Home: 425 N Oakwood Rd Enid OK 73701

HAY, EDWARD WALTER, marine and indsl. supply co. exec.; b. Franklin, La., Nov. 2, 1948; s. Laurie Madison and Emma Adalade (Bodin) H.; B.S. in Acctg., Nicholls State Coll., 1970, M.B.A., 1971; m. June Anne Maureaux, Aug. 23, 1969; children—Shelly, Alyssia, Russell. Internal auditor, asst. cashier Guaranty Bank, Morgan City, La., 1973-74; controller Marine Industries Co., Morgan City, 1974-75; controller Morgan City Supply of La., 1975—. Served with USAF, 1971-73. Mem. La. Assn. Credit Mgmt., Nat. Assn. Credit Mgmt., Delta Sigma Pi. Club: Sertoma Internat. Home: 3228 Wytchwood St Morgan City LA 70380 Office: 1529 Hwy 90 E Morgan City LA 70380

HAY, RAYMOND A., corp. exec.; b. L.I., N.Y., July 13, 1928; B.S. in Econs., L.I. U., 1949; M.B.A., St. John's U., 1960; m. Grace Mattson; children—John Alexander, Susan Elizabeth. Salesman, Nat. Cash Register, 1954-58; regional mgr. Northeastern div. Monroe Calculating Machine Co., 1958-61; with Xerox Corp., Rochester, N.Y., 1961-75, br. mgr., N.Y.C., 1961-62, zone mgr. Western Region also asst. dir. sales ops., dir. mktg., 1962-68, group v.p. and gen. mgr. info. systems, 1968, exec. v.p., to 1975, also pres. U.S. ops.; pres., chief operating officer LTV Corp.; bd. dirs. First City Bancorporation of Tex., Houston, Diamond Shamrock Corp., Dallas, Dallas Civic Opera. Bd. govs. Dallas Symphony Orch., Performing Arts at Kennedy Center; trustee Dallas Mus. Fine Arts, St. Mark's Sch. Tex. Office: LTV Corp PO Box 225003 Dallas TX 75265

HAY, ROBERT DEAN, educator; b. La Porte, Ind., Nov. 17, 1921; s. Carl Roy Hay and Almetta Diedrich; student Ind. U., 1940-42; B.S., U. Okla., 1949, M.B.A., 1950; Ph.D., Ohio State U., 1954; m. Margaret Appelman, 1944; children—Sue Ann, Carol Lynn. Teaching asst. dept. bus. communications U. Okla., 1947-49; instr. dept. acctg. Ohio State U., Columbus, 1952-54; instr. mgmt. Coll. Bus Adminstrn., U. Ark., Fayetteville, 1949-51, asst. prof., 1951-55, asso. prof., chmn., 1955-59, prof., 1959—; v.p. Uark Credit Union, 1977—. Served to capt. USAAF, 1943-47. C.P.A., Okla. Fellow Am. Bus. Communication Assn. (pres. 1967); mem. Case Research Assn., Acad. of Mgmt., Ozarks Econ. Assn., Beta Gamma Sigma, Delta Pi Epsilon, Beta Alpha Psi, Sigma Iota Epsilon. Author books including: Business and Society (with Ed Gray) 1976; (with Frank Broyles) Athletic Administration: A Managerial Approach, 1979; contbr. articles to profl. jours. Office: Dept Mgmt U Ark Fayetteville AR 72701

HAY, RUSSELL EARL, JR., ret. univ. adminstr.; b. Dayton, Ohio, Jan. 5, 1918; s. Russell Earl and Harriet Ellen (Lillis) H.; A.B., Miami U., 1940; M.S., U. Nebr., 1942; Ph.D., U. Ill., 1948; m. Patriica Aull, Jan. 28, 1943; children—Nancy Hay Cadwallender, Susan Hay Dawson, Katherine Ann. Agronomist, plant physiologist U.S. Army Chem. Corps., Biol. Warfare Labs., Md., 1948-50; asst. supr. Agrl. Research, Battelle Meml. Inst., Columbus, Ohio, 1950-53; research plant physiologist C. F. Kettering Lab., Yellow Springs, Ohio, 1953-55; asso. dir. program devel. div. Ohio State U. Research Found., Columbus, 1955-67; dir. research devel. Wright State U., Dayton, Ohio, 1968-76; v.p. Aaron's Flowers & Gifts, Dayton, 1970-75; tchr. Miami U., 1938-40, U. Nebr., 1941, Ohio State U., 1955-67. Mem. Grandview Height Bd. Health, 1964-67; bd. dirs. Miami Valley Heart chpt. Am. Heart Assn., 1969-76; trustee Nat. Ch. Residences, Inc., 1960-67, Franklin County chpt. Arthritis Found., 1962-64. Served with C.E., U.S. Army, 1942-46; PTO; lt. col. Res. ret. Mem. Am. Chem. Soc., AAAS, Am. Inst. Biol. Scis., Am. Soc. Plant Physiology, Nat. Council Univ. Research Adminstrs., Nat. Rifle Assn., Sigma Xi, Phi Sigma, Gamma Sigma Delta, Phi Kappa Tau. Presbyterian. Clubs: Masons, Shriners. Author: (with others) Cereal Rusts: Epidemiology, Losses and Control, 1952. Home: Route 2 Box 314 Carthage NC 28327

HAY, WILLIAM WINN, educator; b. Dallas, Oct. 12, 1934; s. Stephen John and Avella (Winn) H.; student Universitaet Muenchen (Germany), 1953-54; B.S., So. Meth. U., 1955; postgrad. Universitaet Zuerich (Switzerland), 1955-56; M.S., U. Ill., 1958; Ph.D., Stanford U., 1960. NSF fellow Universitaet Basel (Switzerland), 1959-60; asst. prof. U. Ill., Urbana, 1960-63, asso. prof., 1963-68, prof., 1968-73; prof. marine geology and geophysics Rosenstiel Sch. Marine & Atmospheric Sci., U. Miami (Fla.), 1968—, dean, 1977—. Bd. govs. JOI, Inc., 1976—, pres., 1979-80; mem. ocean sci. bd. NAS/NRC, 1977—. Fellow Geol. Soc. Am., Geol. Soc. London; mem. AAAS, Am. Assn. Petroleum Geologists, Am. Geophys. Union, Internat. Assn. Math. Geologists, Internat. Assn. Sedimentologists, Nat. Assn. Geol. Tchrs., Paleontol. Assn., Paleontol. Research Inst., Phi Beta Kappa, Sigma Xi, Omicron Delta Kappa, Phi Eta Sigma, Delta Phi Alpha. Clubs: Cosmos (Washington); Whitehall (Chgo.); Coral Reef Yacht, Key Biscayne Yacht, Ocean Reef. Contbr. articles in field to profl. jours. Home: 881 Ocean Dr Key Biscayne FL 33149 Office: 4600 Rickenbacker Causeway Miami FL 33149

HAYDEN, GLENN RICHARD, educator; b. Newark, Dec. 5, 1947; s. Herman William and Edith June (Perry) H.; student U. Fla., 1965-67, Valencia Community Coll., 1968; B.A. cum laude, Fla. Tech. U., 1970; M.A., U. Ky., 1973. Instr. English, U. Ky., Lexington, 1970-73, Valencia Community Coll., Orlando, Fla., 1973—; communications course Red Lobster Inns, Inc., 1974-78; instr. auto maintenance Valencia Open Campus, 1975—. Mem. Fla. Assn. Community Colls. Author: How Your Central Florida Government Works for You, 1975. Home: Box 245 Windermere FL 32786 Office: PO Box 3028 Orlando FL 32802

HAYDEN, JULIUS JOHN, JR., coll. pres.; b. Pass Christian, Miss., May 19, 1920; s. Julius John and Forrest (Spring) H.; A.A., Perkinston Jr. Coll., 1940; B.S., Miss. State U., 1949, M.S., 1950; Ed.D., U. So. Miss., 1966; m. Lillian R. Aschbacher, Apr. 23, 1943; children—Julius John III, Glover Richard, Susie Stafford. Tchr., coach Lee Road Sch., Tammany Parish, La., 1949-50; instr. history Perkinston Jr. Coll., 1950-52, dean, 1952-53, pres., 1953-62; pres. Miss. Gulf Coast Jr. Coll., 1962—. Served with USAAF, 1940-41, USCG, 1941-45. Named King, Biloxi Revelers, 1972; Boss of Yr., Gulfport Jaycees, 1976. Mem. Miss. Econ. Council (edn. com.), Miss. Coast Power Boat Squadron, Navy League, Phi Theta Kappa (dir.), Kappa Delta Pi, Phi Alpha Theta, Phi Theta Kappa, Omicron Delta Kappa. Clubs: Rotary, Biloxi Cavaliers (King 1965). Office: Miss Gulf Coast Jr Coll Perkinston MS 39573

HAYDEN, WILBURN, JR., educator/social work adminstr.; b. Darlington, S.C., Sept. 23, 1949; s. Wilburn and Willie Mae (Dargan) H.; B.A., St. Andrews Coll., 1971; M.S.W. (NIMH correctional fellow), U. N.C., Chapel Hill, 1973; postgrad. U. Toronto, 1975—; m. Virginia Hill Lahiff, Mar. 5, 1977; stepchildren—Joe Hill, Shayna Hill. Counselor, N.C. Dept. Correction, 1970-71; instr. Clinch Valley Coll., Wise, Va., 1973, U. N.C., Greensboro, 1973-75, U. Toronto, 1976-77; cons., 1975-78; dir. Chapel Hill Dept. Human Services, 1978—; photographer Durham (N.C.) Arts Council. Bd. dirs. Chapel Hill-Carrboro United Fund, 1977-80; vice chmn. bd. dirs. N.C. Council Internat. Program, 1978-80; v.p. St. Andrews Coll. Alumni Council, 1980-81. Whitney Young fellow, 1975-76. Mem. Nat. Assn. Social Workers (treas. N.C. chpt.), Nat. Conf. Social Welfare, Am. Public Welfare Assn., Council Social Work Edn., ACLU. Democrat. Baptist. Creator photog. essay exhibit of blacks in Central Appalachian Region, 1975. Home: 410 Brookside Dr Chapel Hill NC 27514 Office: Dept Human Services Town of Chapel Hill 306 N Columbia St Chapel Hill NC 27514

HAYEK, MARY ANNIE, psychotherapist; b. Paterson, N.J., Feb. 13, 1925; d. Anthony T. and Mary N. (Sara) Haddad; A.A., Miami Dade Jr. Coll., 1972; B.A. with distinction in Psychology, Fla. Internat. U., 1975, M.S. in Counselor Edn., 1978; Ph.D., Heed U., 1980; m. James Paul Hayek, Aug. 12, 1945; children—George Anthony, James Paul, Joanne Cristine. Trainee/intern Alcohol Treatment program South Miami Hosp., 1977-78; pvt. practice psychotherapy, Miami, 1978—. Masters and Johnson fellow, 1979; recipient cert. of Achievement, U.S. Treasury Dept., 1944. Mem. Am. Personnel and Guidance Assn., Mental Health Assn., Nat. Rehab. Assn., Fla. Assn. Profl. Hypnosis, Phi Theta Kappa, Psi Chi, Phi Lambda Pi. Home: 1801 SW 84th Ct Miami FL 33155

HAYES, CAROLYN FLORENCE, educator; b. Auburn, N.Y., Oct. 10, 1941; d. Walton Edward and Evelyn Ina (Townsend) Krell; A.A.S. Auburn Community Coll., 1961; B.S., N.Y. State U., Albany, 1965; M.S., Coll. St. Rose, Albany, 1969; m. James Henry Hayes, Jr., Aug. 17, 1968; children—James Walton, Bradley William. Instr., Albany (N.Y.) Bus. Coll., 1965-67, Sullivan County Community Coll., South Fallsburg, N.Y., 1967-68, Skidmore Coll., Saratoga Spa, N.Y., 1968-71, So. Vt. Coll., Bennington, 1971-73; prof. Polk Community Coll., Winter Haven, Fla., 1974—, advisor Phi Beta Lambda chpt., 1977—. Calling chmn. Welcome Wagon Internat., Bennington, Vt., 1973-74; sec. Elbert Elementary Sch. PTA, 1975, pres., 1977—. Mem. Nat., Fla. bus. edn. assns., Eastern, N.Y. State, Vt. bus. tchrs. assns. Presbyterian. Home: 405 Flagler Rd Winter Haven FL 33880 Office: Polk Community Coll Winter Haven FL 33880

HAYES, GAYNELLE HASSELMEIER, coll. adminstr.; b. Galveston, Tex., Feb. 14, 1943; d. Allison Gale and Nellie (Hanicak) Hasselmeier; B.A. in English, Lamar U., Beaumont, Tex., 1965; M.Ed., U. Houston, 1969; Ed.D. in Community Coll. Edn., Nova U., Ft. Lauderdale, Fla., 1977; 1 dau., Anne-Marie. Tchr. English and history Ball High Sch., Galveston, 1965-68; counselor, then chief counselor Galveston Coll., 1968-77, coordinator counseling and placement, 1977—. Recipient resolution Tex. Senate, 1979. Mem. Am., Tex. (program chmn. conv. 1971) personnel and guidance assns., Jr. Coll. Student Personnel Assn. Tex. (dir. 1975—, sec.-treas. 1977, pres. 1977—, program coordinator 1980 conf.), Tex. Jr. Coll. Tchrs. Assn. (vice chmn. counseling and student personnel sect. 1977-78, chmn. 1978-79, sec. 1979-80), Tex. Assn. Coll. and Univ. Student Personnel Adminstrs. (exec. com. 1978-80), Nat. Assn. Student Personnel Adminstrs., Delta Kappa Gamma (chpt. pres. 1976-78; chpt. Achievement award 1979; White-Arrington scholar 1974), Delta Zeta. Roman Catholic. Club: Pilot Internat. (sec. Galveston 1976-80, 2d v.p. 1980—). Home: 4811 Woodrow Galveston TX 77550 Office: Galveston Coll 4015 Ave Q Galveston TX 77550

HAYES, GEORGE ROY, JR., state ofcl.; b. Shreveport, La., July 5, 1920; s. George Roy and Florence Hazel (Row) H.; student U. Ill., 1938-39; B.S., La. Tech. U., 1942; M.S., U. Ark., 1951; m. Marie Lane St. John, July 10, 1943; 1 dau., Susan Leslie (Mrs. George Virgo). Commd. lt. (j.g.) USPHS, 1943, advanced through grades to capt., 1968; various assignment including State Pub. Health entomologist, Little Rock, 1947-54; tech. cons., asst. chief and chief state aids sect., Atlanta, 1951-59; research entomologist on toxicology of pesticides, Phoenix, 1959-64; project officer Aedes Aegypti Eradication Program, New Orleans, 1964-69; vector control cons., Atlanta, 1969-72; adminstr. solid waste and vector control La. Dept. Health and Human Resources, New Orleans, 1972—; vis. lectr. Tulane U., 1964-69, U. New Orleans, 1972—, Delgado Jr. Coll., 1973—; mem. La. Mosquito Control Adv. Bd. Chmn. adv. com. urban pest mgmt. Delgado Jr. Coll., 1974-77, mem. adv. com. environ. health, 1975-77. Recipient Phi Sigma award U. Ark., 1951. Mem. Entomol. Soc. Am., Am., La. (pres. 1975) mosquito control assns., Nat. Vector Control Conf. (chmn. 1974-76), Gulf State Council on Fisheries, Wildlife and Mosquito Control (pres. 1975), Nat. Assn. State Solid Waste Mgmt. Ofcls. (dir. 1975), Lambda Chi Alpha. Contbr. numerous articles to profl. jours. Home: 2411 Comet St New Orleans LA 70114 Office: PO Box 60630 New Orleans LA 70160

HAYES, ISABELLA MALLORY (MRS. WALTER HAROLD HAYES), civic worker; b. Kewanee, Ill., Mar. 27, 1908; d. George Adelbert and Ella Bowie (Swayze) Mallory; B.A., Knox Coll., 1930, B.L.S., U. Wis., 1931; postgrad. U. Md., 1953; m. Walter Harold Hayes, Nov. 9, 1935; 1 dau., Anne (Mrs. Dixon L. Hume). With Kewanee Pub. Library, 1926-30; head reference dept., pub. library, Roanoke, Va., 1931-43; instr., asst. reference librarian U. Md. Library, College Park, 1949-58, head Md. and rare book room, also in charge displays and pub. relations, 1958-69, editor Library News, 1952-69. Exec. dir. Nat. Library Week in Md., 1962; chmn. First Citizens Conf. on Libraries in Md., 1965. Mem. State Adv. Com. on Day Care to Md. Dept. Social Services, 1962-72; chmn. Health and Welfare Council Prince Georges County, 1965-68. Bd. dirs. Health and Welfare Council Nat. Capital Area, Washington, 1964-68, Md. Com. for Day Care of Children, Balt., 1964-69, Prince George's County Retarded Day Care Center, 1962-69, St. Johns County (Fla.) ARC, 1975-78. Recipient Community Service award Health and Welfare Council Nat. Capital Area, Washington, 1968. Mem. League Women Voters (county pres. 1957-58, mem. state bd. 1958-62), AAUW (2d v.p. 1973-77, dir. 1978—), Mothers Club Kappa Alpha Theta, Alpha Delta Pi (patroness). Author: Ethics of Advertising: a Selected Bibliography, 1931; Financing Presidential Campaigns, A Selected Bibliography, 1953. Home: 70 Willow Dr Saint Augustine FL 32084

HAYES, JACK DEE, ins. co. exec.; b. Hutchinson, Kans., June 22, 1940; s. Elmer William and Margaret (Dondlinger) H.; B.A., Wichita U., 1962, M.A., 1964; m. Jeanne L. Franks, July 20, 1959; children—Terry, Mischelle, Jackie, Dana. Football coach Derby (Kans.) High Sch., 1963-64; agt. Fidelity Union Life Ins., Wichita, Kans., 1964-65, gen. agt., Omaha, 1965-66, regional dir., Kansas City, Kans., 1965-66, supt. of agencies, Midwest Region, 1967-68, asst. v.p., Atlanta, 1968-70, v.p. sales, Dallas, 1970—. Mem. Nat. Assn. Life Underwriters, Tex. Assn. Life Underwriters, Gen. Agts. and Mgrs. Assn. Democrat. Roman Catholic. Home: 305 Summit Ridge Dr Rockwall TX 75087 Office: 1506 Pacific St Dallas TX 75221

HAYES, KATHY PERDUE, hosp. vol. services adminstr.; b. Thomaston, Ga., Apr. 3, 1941; d. James Seay and Fan (Britt) Perdue; B.S., Auburn U., 1962; m. Ellis Lee Hayes, June 9, 1963; children—Brent Seay, Kristen Lee. Tchr., St. Elmo Elem. Sch., Columbus, Ga., 1962-64; tchr. Avondale Elem. Sch., Birmingham, Ala., 1964-65; vol. coordinator Shallowford Hosp., Atlanta, 1973-75; activities dir. Great Oaks Nursing Home, Roswell, Ga., 1977-78; dir. vol. services DeKalb Gen. Hosp., Decatur, Ga., 1978—; speaker, leader vol. workshops. Named One of Outstanding Young Women of Am., 1974. Mem. Council on Auxiliaries Bd. Mgmt. (corr. sec. 1974-76, rec. sec. 1976-78, state teen chmn. 1978—), Am. Soc. Dirs. Vol. Services, Southeastern Conf. Soc. Dirs. Vol. Services (sec. 1979), Ga. Soc. Dirs. Vol. Services (edn. chmn.), Shallowford Hosp. Aux. (pres. 1973-75). Methodist. Clubs: Peachtree Woman's (corr. sec.), Jr. League of DeKalb County Inc. Home: 4825 Village Creek Dr Dunwoody GA 30338 Office: 2701 N Decatur Rd Decatur GA 30033

HAYES, LARRY JOHN, chemist, electronics co. ofcl.; b. Houston, Nov. 24, 1941; s. Allen Joseph and Erna (Frels) H.; B.S., Sam Houston State U., 1966, M.S., 1968; Ph.D., U. Va., 1971; m. Katherine Eriksson, Dec. 27, 1965; children—Erik Chandler, James Allen. Asst. prof. Sul Ross State U., Alpine, Tex., 1971-72; research chemist Air Products and Chems. Inc., Allentown, Pa., 1972-77; cost center mgr. Recognition Equipment Inc., Dallas, 1977—. Ch. vestryman, 1975-77. Served with U.S. Army, 1960. DuPont fellow, 1969-71; recipient IR-100 award, 1978. Mem. Am. Chem. Soc., Sigma Xi. Contbr. articles to profl. publs.; patentee in field. Home: 109 Ridgewood Circle Roanoke TX 76262 Office: 2701 E Grauwyler St Irving TX 75061

HAYES, MARGARET SMITHEY, retail co. exec.; b. Wilkesboro, N.C., Aug. 11, 1911; d. Nikeard Bruce and Hattie Eudora (Little) Smithey; student Lenoir Rhyne Coll., Hickory, N.C., 1928-30; m. Raymond Kyle Hayes, Nov. 10, 1932. Sec.-treas., dir. N.B. Smithey Stores Co., North Wilkesboro, 1954—, N.B. Smithey Stores of Wilkesboros, Inc., 1954—, N.B. Smithey Auction Co., North Wilkesboro, 1954—; pres., dir. N.B. Smithey Mountain Stores Co., North Wilkesboro, 1954—; mem. Coop. Office Occupations program Wilkes Central High Sch., 1971-72. Past treas., trustee, Sunday sch. tchr., mem. fin. com. Wilkesboro United Methodist Ch., 1941—, pres. Wesleyan Service Guild, 1952, life mem. Women's Soc. Christian Service; mem. bd. Old Wilkes, Inc., Wilkes County, N.C. Republican. Club: Order Eastern Star (worthy matron 1944). Home: 604 E Main St Wilkesboro NC 28697 Office: 319-321 10th St North Wilkesboro NC 28659

HAYES, MARTHA BELL, cosmetologist; b. Fayetteville, N.C., Oct. 20, 1943; d. Otha James and Earlean (Williams) Bell; m. Daniel A. Hayes, Jan. 9, 1974 (separated); children—Wilfred, Henry, Gwendolyn, Daniel A. Owner Martha's Enterprises Ltd., Fayetteville, 1969—, Martha's Discount Beauty Salon, Fayetteville, 1976—, Martha's Beauty Salons 1, 2, and 3, Fayetteville, 1978—; dean Cape Fear Beauty Inst. and Hair Weaving, 1978; mgr. Shade's of Beauty Modeling Club, 1979. Recipient numerous awards and certs. Mem. Nat. Beauty Culturists League, Nat. Hairdressers and Cosmetologists Assn., Internat. Ind. Hairweaving Assn., NAACP, Fayetteville C. of C., Fayetteville Bus. and Profl. League, Beauticians Club (v.p., historian Fayetteville). Baptist. Club: Order Eastern Star. Author hairweaving booklet. Address: Cape Fear Beauty Inst PO Box 1811 Fayetteville NC 28302

HAYES, OTIS CALVIN, chemist, govt. agy. adminstr.; b. Forest Green, Mo., Aug. 3, 1928; s. Otis and Jane Lee (White) H.; B.S. in Chemistry, Washington U., 1958; M.S. in Chemistry, Roosevelt U., 1963; m. Delores LaVonne Hall, June 14, 1949; children—Karen, Keith, Kimberly, Kristi. Analytical chemist U.S. Dept. Agr., Meat and Poultry Inspection, St. Louis, 1956-58, instrumental chemist, Chgo., 1958-67, chemist-in-charge, Omaha, 1967-74, lab. dir. food safety and quality, Athens, Ga., 1974—. Mem. Am. Chem. Soc., Inst. Food Technologists, Am. Mgmt. Assn. Baptist. Clubs: Optimists, Toastmasters. Home: 120 Hickory Ln Watkinsville GA 30677 Office: US Dept Agr Lab College Station Rd Athens GA 30604

HAYES, WAYLAND JACKSON, JR., toxicologist; b. Charlottesville, Va., Apr. 29, 1917; s. Wayland J. and Mary L. (Turner) H.; B.S., U. Va., 1938, M.D., 1946; M.A., U. Wis., 1940, Ph.D., 1942; m. Barnita Donkle, Feb. 1, 1942; children—Marie Hayes Sarneski, Maryetta Hayes Hacskaylo, Lula Hayes McCoy, Wayland, Roche del Moser. Intern, USPHS Marine Hosp., N.Y.C., 1946-47; individual practice as toxicologist, Savannah, Ga., 1949-60, Atlanta, 1960-68, Nashville, 1968—; chief Vector Transmisson Investigations Br., Savannah, 1947-48; chief toxicology sect. USPHS, Savannah, 1949-60, Atlanta, 1960-67, chief toxicologist, 1967-68; prof. biochemistry Vanderbilt U. Sch. Medicine, Nashville, 1968—; cons. WHO, 1950—, NRC, 1964-76, various govt. agys. and profl. orgns., 1953-76. Served with U.S. Army, 1943-46. Recipient Meritorious Service medal USPHS, 1964. Mem. Am. Soc. Pharmacology and Exptl. Therapeutics, Am. Soc. Tropical Medicine and Hygiene, Soc. Toxicology (pres. 1971-72). Club: Univ. Author: Clinical Handbook on Economic Poisons, 1963; Toxicology of Pesticides, 1975; contbr. articles to sci. jours.; mem. editorial bd. Jour. Pharmacology and Exptl. Therapeutics, 1962-64, Archives of Environ. Health, 1965-72, 76—, Food and Cosmetics Toxicology, 1967-78. Home: 2317 Golf Club Ln Nashville TN 37215 Office: Vanderbilt U Nashville TN 37232

HAYES, WILLIAM TIMOTHY, pathologist; b. Hazleton, Ind., Oct. 25, 1937; s. William Thomas and Margie (Sears) H.; B.S. with honors, U. Ill., 1959; M.D., U. Tenn., 1963; m. Charlotte Conant, Sept. 8, 1962; children—William T., Thomas C., Terrence S. Intern, Meth. Hosp., Memphis, 1963-64; resident VA Hosp., Memphis, 1964-67, U. Tenn., Memphis, 1967-68, Children's Hosp., Boston, 1968-69; pathologist St. Francis Hosp., Memphis, 1970—. Diplomate Am. Bd. Pathology. Mem. AMA, Am. Assn. Blood Banks. Republican. Methodist. State level soccer referee; contbr. articles to med. jours. Home: 2306 Kimbrough Woods Pl Germantown TN 38138 Office: 5959 Park Ave Lab Memphis TN 38117

HAYHURST, MARY LEA, ednl. adminstr.; b. Benton, Ark., Aug. 3, 1940; d. Chester Aven and Oma Lea (Hudgins) Mitchell; A.A., Central Tex. Coll., 1974; B.S. in Bus., Am. Tech. U., 1976; div.; children—Owen W., Jill S., Karl J., Cynthia Lea. Sec. to data processing mgr. Central Tex. Coll., Killeen, 1974-75; sec. for computer services Research Inst. for Advanced Tech., 1975-76; supr. records Am. Preparatory Inst., Killeen, 1976-77; adminstrv. trainee Am. Ednl. Complex, Killeen, 1977; bookstore mgr. Central Tex. Coll., 1979—. Mem. Am. Bus. Women's Assn., Assn. U.S. Army, Altrusa Internat., Epsilon Delta Pi. Club: Las Damas of Central Tex. Coll. Home: 1106 Ridgeway Dr Killeen TX 76541 Office: Hwy 190 W Killeen TX 76541

HAYMES, EDWARD RANDOLPH, educator; b. Lynchburg, Va., Dec. 15, 1940; s. Carter Edward and Jeannette (Randolph) H.; B.A., Lynchburg Coll., 1965; M.A., U. Va., 1966; Ph.D., U. Erlangen (Germany), 1969; m. Winifried Christine Schneider, Aug. 17, 1963; children—Thomas Harmon, David Carter. Asst. prof. German, Va. Commonwealth U., Richmond, 1969-72; asst. prof. German, U. Houston, 1973-76, asso. prof., 1976—. Served with U.S. Army, 1960-63. Woodrow Wilson fellow, 1965. Mem. Modern Lang. Assn., S. Central Modern Lang. Assn., Mediaeval Acad., Am. Assn. Tchrs. of German. Author: Mündliches Epos in mittelhochdeutscher Zeit, 1975; Das mündliche Epos, 1977. Home: 1731 Indiana St Houston TX 77006 Office: Dept German U Houston Houston TX 77004

HAYNES, EFFIE GILLIS, ret. clin. social worker; b. Excelsior, La., Nov. 9, 1906; d. Joseph Benjiman and Ada Helen (Phillips) Gillis; student La. Coll., 1949-50; B.A., Tex. U., 1950-53; M.S.W., Wordens Sch. Social Service, 1958; m. Wiley J. Gremillion, Feb. 4, 1928 (div. Mar. 1947); children—Barbara Margaret (Mrs. Linton Bowman III), Dona Madrice (Mrs. William Weaver Harris), Effie Jeanne (Mrs. Jack L. Paris, Jr.); m. 2d, Henry M. Haynes, Dec. 29, 1976. Social worker Austin State Hosp., 1954-57; clin. social worker VA Hosp., Shreveport, La., 1958-65, mem. intensive psychiat. staff, 1965-76, dir. psychodrama, 1968-76, ret. Treas., Austin-Travis County Assn. Mental Health, 1956-57. Bd. dirs. Cadd-Bossier chapt. La. Assn. Mental Health, 1958-76. Mem. Nat. Assn. Social Workers, Acad. Certified Social Workers, Moreno Acad. World Center Psychodrama, Sociometry and Group Psychotherapy. Methodist. Home: 4016 Fawnhollow Dr Dallas TX 75234

HAYNES, GEORGE EDWARD, artist; b. Hinton, W.Va., Apr. 29, 1910; s. Julian Alexander and Cora Mae (Williams) H.; student Phoenix Art Inst., N.Y.C., Lockwood Sch. Art, Kalamazoo, Art Inst. Pitts.; m. Bessie Newton, Oct. 17, 1936; children—Mary Ellen, George Edward. Free lance artist, Pitts., 1931-35, Portsmouth, Va., 1967, Richmond, Va., 1967—; dir. Portsmouth Artists Guild, 1967; artist, tchr., gallery dir. James River Art League, Richmond, 1967—; bus. cons. on arts. Recipient numerous awards in art shows, locally and nationally. Mem. Internat. Platform Assn. Baptist. Club: Torch Internat. Home: 1521 Avondale Ave Richmond VA 23227

HAYNES, GEORGE HENRY, JR., elec. engr.; b. Montgomery, Ala., Aug. 5, 1944; s. George Henry and Sarah Ruth (Gaines) H.; student Miss. State U., 1962-63; B.E.E., Auburn U., 1967; M.S. in Mgmt., Troy State U., 1980; m. Patricia Ann Puckett, Dec. 15, 1967; children—Wendy Ladonna, Stephanie Nicole, Derek Christopher. Electronic engr. U.S. Air Force Ground Electronics Engring. Installation Agency, Brookley AFB, Ala., 1967-68; elec. engr. Naval Air Rework Facility, Pensacola, Fla., 1968-74, supr. elec. engr., 1974—. Registered profl. engr., Fla. Democrat. Mem. Ch. of Christ. Home: 2800 Venetian Way Gulf Breeze FL 32561 Office: US Navy Naval Air Rework Facility Pensacola FL 32508

HAYNES, JAMES ALAN, sporting goods co. exec.; b. Tyler, Tex., Oct. 23, 1939; s. James Sidney and Edith (Allen) H.; B.B.A., U. Tex., 1961; postgrad. U. Tex. Law Sch., 1961-64; M.B.A., E. Tex. State U., 1970. Prof. bus. and acctg. Tyler (Tex.) Jr. Coll., 1969-73; pres. The Sportster, Inc., Tyler, 1973—; fishing tackle buyer, adv. dir. Nat. Buying Syndicate, Ft. Worth. Mem. Safety Commn. City of Tyler, 1972-74. Recipient Leadership award as ind. retailer of the yr. Sporting Goods Dealer mag., 1978. Mem. Nat. Sporting Goods Assn., Tyler C. of C., Delta Upsilon (past dep.). Democrat. Baptist. Home: 1317 E Elm St Tyler TX 75701 Office: 4220 Timms St PO Box 7250 Tyler TX 75711

HAYNES, JIM, public relations exec.; b. Van Zandt County, Tex., Dec. 26, 1937; s. James Milton and Clause Indiana (Winn) H.; B.J., U. Tex., Austin, 1959; postgrad. U. Houston, 1964-65; m. Nelda B. Boenig, Jan. 13, 1962; children—Amy, Bert, Evan. Dir. public info., adminstrv. asst. to exec. dir. Tex. Rehab. Center, Gonzales, 1959-62; public relations supr. Tex. Eastern Corp., Houston, 1962-68; dir. public relations Tracor, Inc., Austin, 1968-73, Media Communications, Inc., Austin, 1973-75; pres. La Mancha Group, Inc., Austin, 1975-77; owner Jim Haynes, public relations cons., Austin, 1975-77; sr. v.p., dir. public relations Kerss Chapman, Bua & Norsworthy, Inc., 1977-78, exec. v.p., gen. mgr. div. KCBN Public Relations, Dallas, 1978—; mem. adj. faculty U. Tex., Austin, Tex. Christian U.; cons., internat. speaker in field. Bd. dirs. Goodwill Industries Dallas. Mem. Internat. Assn. Bus. Communicators, Public Relations Soc. Am. (dir. 1980—), Public Relations Found. Tex. (chmn. bd. 1978—), Tex. Public Relations Assn. (pres. 1975). Lutheran. Author articles, book revs. Office: 3434 Fairmount St Dallas TX 75219

HAYNES, LEONARD L., JR., educator; b. Austin, Tex., Mar. 16, 1923; s. Leonard L. and Thelma (Watkins) H.; A.B., Huston Tilloston Coll., 1942; B.D., Gammon Theol. Sem., 1945; Th.D., Boston U., 1948; m. Leila Davenport, Nov. 21, 1945; children—Leonard L. III, Walter Lafayette, Angeline Thelma, Leila Anne. Ordained to ministry Methodist Ch., 1948; pastor Wesley United Meth. Ch., Baton Rouge, 1960—; dean students prof. philosophy Philander Smith Coll., Little Rock, 1948-52; dir. humanities Ark. State Coll., Pine Bluff, 1952-54; dean of coll. Claflin Coll., Orangeburg, S.C., 1952-57; pres. Morristown Jr. Coll., 1957-59; prof. philosophy and edn. Wiley Coll. Marshall, Tex., 1959-60, So. U., Baton Rouge, 1963—. Mem. Human Relations Council, Baton Rouge, 1967. Recipient Distinguished Alumnus award Boston U. Sch. Theology, 1971. Mem. Ministerial Assn. Baton Rouge, Alpha Kappa Mu, Omega Psi Phi, Mason (33 deg.). Author: The Negro Community within American Protestantism, 1619-1844, 1952. Home: 1798 77th St Baton Rouge LA 70821

HAYNES, MELVIN, JR., coll. counselor; b. Fruitland Park, Fla., Mar. 21, 1940; s. Melvin and Chessie Lee (Hunley) H.; B.S., Fla. A&M U., 1963; M.Ed. (NDEA fellow), U. Ga., 1968, Ed.S. (Gen. Electric Co. fellow), 1970, Ed.D., 1973; m. Yvonne Antoinette Young; children—Antony Kahlil, Malcolm Gibran, Matthew Melvin, Wendy Melva. Tchr. math. high schs. in Fla., 1964-67; sch. counselor, then dir. guidance Clarke County Jr. High Sch., Athens, Ga., 1968-70; asst. dir. Southeastern Tchr. Corps, Athens, 1970-73; dir. counseling and self-devel. center S.C. State Coll., Orangeburg, 1973—; bd. dirs. Athens Family Counseling Service, 1970-71; adv. bd. Tri-County Commn. Alcohol and Drug Abuse, Orangeburg, 1975-76; public relations adv. bd. Orangeburg Regional Hosp., 1978—. Bd. dirs. Orangeburg chpt. Am. Cancer Soc., 1976—. Mem. Am. Personnel and Guidance Assn., Internat. Transactional Analysis Assn., S.C. Personnel and Guidance Assn. (Outstanding Adminstr. award 1977), Phi Delta Kappa, Kappa Delta Pi, Omega Psi Phi.

HAYNES, WALTER GEORGE, neurol. surgeon; b. Marseilles, Ill., Mar. 21, 1913; s. Walter Abel and Jessie (Bogle) H.; B.S., U. Ill., 1936; M.D., U. Ill., 1938; m. Peggy Marcus, Nov. 7, 1953; children—Susan H. (Mrs. Robert A. Borden, Jr.), Walter G., Peter. Intern St. Luke's Hosp., Chgo., 1938-39; resident neurosurgery U. Ill. Research Ednl. Hosps., Chgo., 1939-41; practice medicine, specializing in neurol. surgery, Birmingham, Ala., 1945—; chmn. depts. surgery and neurosurgery Bapt. Med. Center, Birmingham, 1960—, chmn. Center Neurol. Scis., 1972—; cons. neurosurgeon Carraway Meth. Hosp., East End Meml. Hosp., Birmingham, South Highlands Infirmary, 1945—. Dir. Bapt. Hosps. Found., Birmingham. Served to lt. col., cons. neurosurgeon, AUS, 1941-45. Decorated Bronze Star medal. Diplomate Am. Bd. Neurosurgery. Fellow A.C.S.; mem. Congress Neurol. Surgery, So. Ala., Pan-Pacific neurol. socs., Am., So. med. assns., Ala., Jefferson County (Ala.) med. socs., Sigma Xi, Phi Kappa Sigma, Nu Sigma Nu. Republican. Episcopalian. Clubs: The Club, Vestavia Country, Shoal Creek Country, Wildcat Cliffs, Country of Saphire Valley. Author: Textbook of Neurosurgical Nursing, 1952. Editor Bull. of Surg. Forum, Bapt. Med. Center. Contbr. articles to profl. jours. Home: 3805 Forest Glen Dr Birmingham AL 35213 Office: Suite 505 800 Princeton Ave Birmingham AL 35211

HAYNIE, JOHN JAMES, educator, musician; b. Ralls, Tex., Dec. 14, 1924; s. James Stephen and Lelia Virginia (Benedict) H.; B.S. with highest honors, U. Ill., 1949, M.S., 1950; m. Marilyn Louise Hindsley, Aug. 26, 1951; children—Melinda Haynie Zeagler, Mark Stephen. Instr. music, N. Tex. State U., Denton, 1950-54, asst. prof., 1954-60, asso. prof., 1960-68, prof., 1968—; guest clinician, soloist; adjudicator. Mem. Denton C. of C., 1960-64. Served with U.S. Army, 1943-45. Decorated battle ribbons for Bulge, Seigried, Central Europe, certificate of merit; recipient A.A. Harding award, U. of Ill., 1949, Outstanding Educators of Am. award, N. Tex. State U., Denton, 1971. Mem. Tex. Assn. Coll. Tchrs., AAUP, Tex. Music Educators Assn., Music Educators Nat. Conference, Nat. Assn. Wind Tchrs., Kappa Kappa Psi, Phi Mu Alpha, Phi Eta Sigma, Pi Kappa Lambda. Republican. Presbyterian. Club: Kiwanis. Trumpet recordings, articles in field, faculty research study. Home: 115 Alan-a-Dale Circle Denton TX 76201 Office: Sch Music N Tex State U Denton TX 76203

HAYNSWORTH, CLEMENT FURMAN, JR., fed. judge; b. Greenville, S.C., Oct. 30, 1912; s. Clement Furman and Elsie (Hall) H.; ed. Darlington Sch. Rome, Ga.; A.B., Furman U., 1933; LL.B., Harvard, 1936; LL.D., Furman U., 1964; m. Dorothy Merry Barkley, 1946. Admitted to S.C. bar, 1936: mem. firm Haynsworth, Perry, Bryant, Marion & Johnstone, Greenville, until 1957; judge U.S. Ct. Appeals 4th Circuit, 1957-64, chief judge 4th Jud. Circuit U.S., 1964—. Advisory council Furman U., 1961—. Served with USNR, 1942-45. Mem. Am., S.C., Greenville bar assns., Am. Law Inst. (mem. council), Am. Judicature Soc. (past dir.). Episcopalian. Home: 111 Boxwood Ln Greenville SC 29601 Office: Fed Bldg Greenville SC 29603

HAYS, EMMETT LEROY, airline pilot, export co. exec.; b. VanBuren, Ark., Nov. 24, 1921; s. Fred Nathan and Adda Laura (Seger) H.; m. Anne Gavrilkin, Oct. 16, 1948; children—Richard Lee, George Eric. Commd. 2d lt. U.S. Air Force, 1944, advanced through grades to col., 1965; service as fighter squadron comdr., Japan and Vietnam, 1962-66; vice base comdr. Luke AFB, Ariz., 1966; ret., 1968; pilot for exec. Jet Aviation, Inc., Columbus, Ohio, 1969-70; pilot Internat. Air Bahama, 1970-78; capt. Air Jamaica, 1978—; pres. E. L. Hays, Inc., Miami, 1978—. Decorated D.F.C. with oak leaf cluster, Air medal with 13 oak leaf clusters, Bronze Star. Mem. Air Force Assn., Hump Pilots Assn., P-40 Warhawks Assn., Combat Pilots Assn. Republican. Club: Homestead Officers.

HAYS, JACK RUFE, asphalt co. exec.; b. Parsons, Tenn., May 30, 1931; s. James Rufus and Birdie Opal (Carrington) H.; student Bethel Coll., 1953-56; m. Bettie Lou Reed, Feb. 2, 1954; children—Deborah Diane, Jacqueline Jeanette, Jack Reed, Lucien Thomas. Owner, operator J.R. Hays Constrn. Co., Paris, Tenn., 1950-51, 55-65; with Tenn. Asphalt Co. Inc., Paris, 1965—, v.p., 1974—; pres. Henry County Investment Corp., Paris, 1975—. Bd. dirs. Henry County Fair Assn., 1977—. Mem. Greater Paris and Henry County C. of C. (dir. 1971-74, 76—), Tenn. Asphalt Pavement Assn., Tenn. Crushed Stone Assn., Tenn., Am. rd. builders assns. Methodist; Clubs: Henry County Saddle (pres. 1974-75), Buchanan Saddle, Big Sandy Saddle. Served with USAF, 1951-55. Home: Route 6 Hwy 79 S Paris TN 38242 Office: PO Box 1327 Hwy 79 E Paris TN 38242

HAYS, PATRICK HENRY, lawyer; b. Little Rock, Jan. 8, 1947; s. Arthur Henry and Linnea Marie (Lindahl) H.; B.A., U. Ark., 1970, postgrad. Sch. Polit. Sci., 1970-71, J.D., 1973. Admitted to Ark. bar, 1974; staff asst. to U.S. senator from Ark., 1971-73; legal clk. Law

Enforcement Assistance Adminstrn., U.S. Dept. Justice, 1972; mem. staff U.S. Senate, 1973; asst. city atty., North Little Rock, Ark., 1974-75; individual practice law, North Little Rock, 1974-75, 1977—; legal adviser Ark. sec. of state, Little Rock, 1975-77. Former adviser explorer troop Boy Scouts Am., North Little Rock, now mem. dist. com.; del. Ark Constl. Conv., 1979-80. Mem. Am. (past chmn. bd. govs. law student div., past pres. div., mem. com. on nat. inst. justice, spl. com. on law students), Ark., Pulaski County, North Pulaski County bar assns., Jaycees (dir.), Sigma Chi, Phi Alpha Delta. Presbyterian (elder, bldgs. and grounds com.). Club: Rotary. Home: 409 West H St North Little Rock AR 72207 Office: Suite 711 TCB Bldg North Little Rock AR 72114

HAYS, ROBERT WILLIAM, educator; b. Atlanta, Oct. 17, 1925; s. Calvin Samuel and Elizabeth (Green) H.; student Duke, 1943-44; A.B., Presbyn. Coll., 1947; M.Ed., Emory U., 1957; m. Rebecca Guy Copeland, June 15, 1950; children—Michael Stephen, David, William. Comml. mgr. Sta. WSFT, Thomaston, Ga., 1947-48, Sta. WLBG, Laurens-Clinton, S.C., 1948; co-owner Clinton Plastic Co. (S.C.), 1948-49; instr. So. Tech. Inst., 1950-51, asst. prof., 1952-57, head dept. English, 1953-73, asso. prof., 1958-60, prof., 1960—; supr. tng. course devel. Lockheed Aircraft Corp., Marietta, Ga., 1951-52. Communications cons. Served from apprentice seaman to lt. (j.g.), USNR, 1943-46. Recipient 2d place nat. Arthur Williston award for contbns. to lit. of engring. tech., 1967; award Internat. Tech. Communications Conf., 1979. Mem. Soc. for Tech. Communications, Am. Bus. Communications Assn. Author: Pacific Parodies, 1947; Principles of Technical Writing, 1965; Practically Speaking in Business, Industry and Government, 1969; Guide to Technical Writing, 1970; also numerous articles pub. in profl. and trade jours. Research on tech. communication ednl. methodology. Home: 2741 Benson Dr Marietta GA 30062

HAYWARD, OLGA LORETTA HINES (MRS. SAMUEL E. HAYWARD), librarian; b. Alexandria, La.; d. Samuel James and Lillie (George) Hines; A.B., Dillard U., 1941; B.S. in L.S., Atlanta U., 1944; M.A., U. Mich., 1959; M.A. in History, La. State U., 1977; m. Samuel E. Hayward, July 12, 1945; children—Anne Elizabeth, Olga Patricia. Tchr., Marksville (La.) High Schs., 1941-42; head librarian Grambling (La.) Coll., 1944-46; br. librarian br. nine New Orleans Pub. Library System, 1947-48; reference librarian So. U., Baton Rouge, 1948-73, prof. library sci., social scis. librarian, 1973—. Bd. dirs. La. Diocese Episcopal Community Services. Mem. Am., La. library assns., AAUP, Spl. Libraries Assn. (pres. La. chpt. 1978-79). Episcopalian. Author: Graduate Theses of Southern University 1959-71; A Bibliography of Literature By and About Whitney Moore Young, Jr., 1929-71, 1972; The Influence of Humanism on Sixteenth Century English Courtesy Texts, 1977; also other bibliographies. Contbr. articles to profl. jours. Home: 1632 Harding Blvd Baton Rouge LA 70807

HAYWOOD, H(ERBERT) CARL(TON), psychologist; b. Taylor County, Ga., July 2, 1931; s. Howard Chapman and Rosebud (Smith) H.; student West Ga. Coll., 1948-50; A.B., San Diego State Coll., 1956, M.A., 1957; Ph.D., U. Ill., 1961; m. Nancy Patricia Roberts, Oct. 5, 1951 (div. Mar. 1971); children—Carlton, Terence, Elizabeth, Kristin. Staff psychologist VA Hosp., 1961-62; mem. faculty George Peabody Coll. (merged with Vanderbilt U. 1979), 1962—, dir. mental retardation research tng. program 1968-70, dir. Inst. on Mental Retardation and Intellectual Devel., 1970-73, dir. Office Research Adminstrn., 1974-76, dir. John F. Kennedy Center for Research on Edn. and Human Devel., 1971—, asst. prof. psychology, 1962-65, asso. prof. psychology, 1965-66, Kennedy asso. prof. psychology, 1966-69, Kennedy prof. psychology, 1969-75, prof. psychology and spl. edn., 1975—, prof. neurology Sch. Medicine, 1971—; vis. prof. U. Toronto, 1965-66; mem. adv. bd. Tenn. Dept. Mental Health, 1964—, Ill. Inst. Developmental Disabilities, Chgo., 1970—, Eunice Kennedy Shriver Center for Mental Retardation, Waltham, Mass., 1973—; cons. Pres's. Com. on Mental Retardation, 1968-73; mem. sci. rev. com. health research facilities NIH, 1967-71. Served with USN, 1950-54. Licensed psychologist, Tenn. Fellow Am. Assn. Mental Deficiency (v.p. for psychology 1975-77), Am. Psychol. Assn. (pres.-elect div. 33 1977-78); mem. Soc. Research in Child Devel., Nat. Acad. Scis. Inst. Medicine, Psychonomic Soc. Democrat. Episcopalian. Contbr. articles to profl. publs.; editor: Brain Damage in School Age Children, 1968; Social-Cultural Aspects of Mental Retardation, 1970; editor Am. Jour. Mental Deficiency, 1969—. Office: Box 40 Peabody Coll Nashville TN 37203

HAYWOOD, JOHN DAVIS, lawyer; b. Charleston, S.C., Apr. 26, 1945; s. Egbert Lynch and Margaret (Davis) H.; A.B., U. N.C., 1967, J.D., 1970; m. Mary Edmunds, June 6, 1970. Admitted to N.C. bar, 1970; partner firm Haywood Denny Miller, Durham, N.C., 1978—. Served with USN, Judge Advocate Gen.'s Corps, 1970-73. Mem. Am. Bar Assn., N.C. Bar Assn., N.C. Def. Attys. Assn., Def. Research Inst. Democrat. Episcopalian. Clubs: Hope Valley Country, Cotillion, Durham Kiwanis (dir. 1977—). Home: 4032 Nottaway Rd Durham NC 27707 Office: 200 Wachovia Bldg 201 W Main St Durham NC 27701

HAZELIP, EDWINA KAY, nurse; b. Louisville, Ky., Jan. 25, 1952; d. Edwin O'Neil and Lorraine Esta (Nicols) H.; grad. High Point (N.C.) Hosp. Sch. Nursing, 1975. Nurses aide Wilkes Gen. Hosp., North Wilkesboro, N.C., 1971-72; day care center worker Child's Kingdom, Wilkesboro, N.C., 1971-72; head nurse coronary and intensive care unit Wilkes Gen. Hosp., North Wilkesboro, 1972—, pres. nursing staff, sec. coronary care staff; instr. basic life support, cardiac defibrillation. Mem. Am. Nurses Assn., N.C. Nurses Assn. Baptist. Home: 1120 Myers Park North Wilkesboro NC 28659

HAZELRIGG, WILLIAM REUBEN, III, accountant; b. DeGraf, Minn., Dec. 30, 1936; s. William Reuben and Rosalyn (Newell) H.; B.S., U. Louisville, 1970, M.B.A., 1974; m. Susan Ann Hunn, Dec. 3, 1955; children—Katherine Ann, Charles Anthony, Karan Elizabeth, Janet Eileen, Richard Louis. Computer operator, relief supr. L. & N. R.R., Louisville, 1966-76; corp. controller John Conti Vending Co., Louisville, 1976; instr. Spencerian Bus. Coll., Louisville, 1977—; pres., accountant, tax cons. S-W Assos., Inc., Louisville, 1966—. Recipient Sponsor award Louisville Heart Assn. Bike-a-thon, 1979. Mem. Am. Mgmt. Assn., Nat. Soc. Public Accountants, Am. Soc. Profl. Cons.

HAZELWOOD, CARROLL THOMAS, pulp mill exec.; b. Richmond, Va., Oct. 27, 1941; s. Howell P. and Ruth (Walls) H.; B.S., N.C. State U., Raleigh, 1971; m. Katherine Lee Russell, Dec. 30, 1961; children—Thomas Marchant, Holly Ann. With Chesapeake Corp. Va., 1972-74, Union Camp Co., 1974-76; tech. dir. Boise So. Co., DeRidder, La., 1976-77, pulp mill supt., 1977-79, prodn. mgr. Calcasieu Paper Co. div., Elizabeth, La., 1979—. Grantee State of Va., 1970, 71. Mem. TAPPI, Pulp Mill Supts. Assn. (sect. chmn. 1978), Phi Kappa Phi. Address: 1210 Mohawk St DeRidder LA 70436

HAZELWOOD, GARY WAYNE, sales account exec.; b. Dallas, Apr. 30, 1948; s. William Aubry and Myrtle Odessa (Coleman) H.; B.Career Arts, Dallas Bapt. Coll., 1979; m. Karla Jeannine Steger, Apr. 12, 1969 (div., 1978); 1 dau., Christina Lynn; m. 2d, Vickie L. Berry, Feb. 14, 1980. Dist. mgr. Jim Walter Homes Inc., Dallas, 1972-73; sales mgr. Burke Concrete Accessories, Dallas, 1973-77; sales account mgr. Symons Inc., Dallas, 1977—. Served with USAF, 1968-72. Lic. pvt. pilot. Mem. Asso. Gen. Contractors, Aircraft Owners and Pilots Assn. Republican. Mem. Assembly of God Ch. Clubs: Chimeras, Presidents Health. Home: 9452 Amberton Pkwy Dallas TX 75243 Office: 1839 W Commerce St Dallas TX 75208

HAZEN, RALPH EDWARD, govt. ofcl.; b. Albion, Pa., May 15, 1915; s. James Mead and Bessie Rosemond (Shellito) H.; B.A., Coll. William and Mary, 1960; M.A., George Washington U., 1962; m. Helen Elizabeth Ticknor, Oct. 5, 1935; children—Lois Darline, Robert Wade. Tchr., Clarks Corner (Ohio) Schs., 1935-37; prodn. engr. Rogers Bros., Albion, Pa., 1937-39, Reed Roller Bit Co., Houston, 1939-41; commd. ensign U.S. Navy, 1941, advanced through grades to comdr., 1956, ret., 1964; with GSA, Washington, 1965-66; mgr. U.S. Atlantic Fleet, Naval Air Force, Norfolk, Va., 1967—; asst. prof. George Washington U. Grad. Sch., 1967—. Mem. Meadowbrook Terr. Civic League. Mem. Am. Soc. Mil. Comptrollers, Tidewater Automatic Data Processing Fed. Council, Ret. Officers Assn. Republican. Mason (32 deg.). Home: 1621 Longdale Dr Norfolk VA 23518

HAZEN, STEVEN JOEL, navy officer, physician; b. Boscobel, Wis., Aug. 13, 1943; s. Floyd Willard and Margie Marilyn (Rice) H.; student Jacksonville (Fla.) U., 1961-63; B.S., U. Fla., Gainesville, 1965; M.D., U. Miami (Fla.), 1969; m. Mavis Mary Stokke, June 24, 1967; children—Tara Dawn, Mahryah Rae, Joshua Garhett Moors. Commd. ensign U.S. Navy, 1966, advanced through grades to comdr., 1977; surg. intern. Phila. Naval Hosp., 1969-70, flight surgeon HAL-3, Vietnam, 1971-72; flight surgeon HSL-31, dir. local alcohol abuse control program San Diego, 1972-73; resident in family practice Jacksonville (Fla.) Naval Hosp., 1973-75; chief clin. br. dept. family practice Naval Regional Med. Center, Jacksonville, teaching staff residency, dir. physician asst. tng. program, 1975-78; dir. family practice residency tng. program, asst. chmn. dept. family practice Naval Aerospace Regional Med. Center, Pensacola, Fla., 1978—; clin. instr. community health and family medicine U. Fla., 1975-76, clin. asst. prof., 1976-78; clin. asso. Sch. Allied Health Professions, Med. Center, U. Nebr., 1976-78. Decorated Bronze Star with Combat V, Air Medal with 9 clusters; Republic of Vietnam Gallantry Cross with gold star. Diplomate Am. Bd. Family Practice. Fellow Am. Acad. Family Physicians; mem. Acad. Family Practice, Am. Coll. Emergency Physicians (pres. Govt. Services chpt. 1979), Soc. Tchrs. Family Medicine, Soc. Tchrs. Emergency Medicine, Aerospace Med. Assn., Assn. Mil. Surgeons, Soc. Naval Flight Surgeons. Office: Naval Aerospace Regional Med Center Pensacola FL 32512

HAZENBERG, CARL FREDERICK, agronomist, educator, crop specialist; b. Gulpen, The Netherlands, Nov. 23, 1919; s. Carel F. and Alberdine (Pape) H.; came to U.S., 1954, naturalized, 1959; B.S., State Coll. Tropical Agr., Netherlands, 1944, M.S., 1945, Ph.D. in Agronomy, 1954; m. Derkje Tervelde, Sept. 25, 1946; children—Marjory Maya, Yolanda Yvonne, Carl Anthony. Field mgr. Deli-Batavia Rubber My., Deli, Sumatra, Indonesia, 1948-53; dir. research Fla.-Ga. Research Found., Quincy, Fla., 1955-64; head exptl. sta. Philip Morris Internat., Valencia, Venezuela, 1965-66; cons. agronomist U.S. AID, Guyana, 1966-69, Latin Am. Devel. Corp., Coral Gables, Fla., 1968-72; cons. agronomist crop prodn. and research Na-Churs Plant Food Co., San Antonio, 1970-78; dir. research and devel. St. Lawrence Corp., Grand Rapids, Mich., 1978—. Served with Dutch Intelligence Service, 1946-48. Decorated Royal Disting. Cross (Netherlands); recipient Recognition award Govt. of Guyana, 1969; named Ky. Col., 1975; cert. cons. agronomist and crop specialist. Mem. Am. Soc. Agronomy, Crop Sci. Soc. Am., Soil Sci. Soc. Am., Council Agrl. Sci. and Tech., Nat. Fertilizer Solution Assn. (agronomy com. 1980), Am. Hort. Soc. Republican. Methodist. Club: Rotary. Contbr. numerous articles on crop sci. to profl. publs. Home: 1261 Hillcrest Dr New Braunfels TX 78130 Office: 2505 Ardmore St Grand Rapids MI 49506

HAZLEHURST, FRANKLIN HAMILTON, educator; b. Spartansburg, S.C., Nov. 6, 1925; s. Robert Purviance and Lottie Lee (Nicholls) H.; B.A., Princeton U., 1949, M.F.A., 1952, Ph.D. (Charlotte Elizabeth Proctor fellow), 1956; m. Carol Foord, Aug. 26, 1950; children—Franklin Hamilton, Robert Purviance, II, Mary Hadley, Abigail Norris. Asst. instr. dept. art and archaeology Princeton U., 1951-53, instr., 1954-56; lectr., research asst. Frick Collection, N.Y.C., 1956-57; lectr. Princeton Theol. Sem., 1956-57; asso. prof. art history U. Ga., 1957-63; asso. prof. fine arts Vanderbilt U., 1963-67, prof., 1967—, chmn. dept. fine arts, 1963—. Trustee Harpeth Hall Sch., Nashville. Served with Combat Engrs. U.S. Army, 1944-46. Recipient Madison Sarratt prize Vanderbilt U., 1970; Fulbright fellow, 1953-54; Sarah H. Moss fellow, 1961-62; Am. Council Learned Socs. grantee, 1967; Am. Philos. Soc. grantee, 1967. Mem. Am. Archaeol. Soc., Coll. Art Assn., Southeastern Coll. Art Assn., Société de l'histoire de l'art français, Soc. Archtl. Historians. Episcopalian. Clubs: Univ. (Nashville); East Chop (Mass.) Tennis. Author: Jacques Boyceau and the French Formal Garden, 1966; contbr. articles to profl. jours. Home: 4430 Shepard Pl Nashville TN 37205 Office: Dept Fine Arts Vanderbilt U Nashville TN 37235*

HAZLETT, ROBERT LEE, psychologist; b. Wheeling, W.Va., Jan. 29, 1946; s. Robert Sheldon and Mildred Lorraine (Davis) H.; B.S. (Union Carbide scholar), W.Va. U., 1967, M.A., 1973; Ed.D., U. Va., 1980; m. Janet Emily Siebert, Jan. 27, 1973; children—Jacqueline Erin, Amanda Christine. Tchr., counselor, adminstr. Roane County (W.Va.) Schs., 1967-69; vocat. evaluator Va. Dept. Rehab. Services, Williamsburg, 1969-70, tng. coordinator, 1970-71, rehab. counselor, 1970-71, supr., 1971-73, rehab. program dir., 1973-75; developmental disabilities project dir. Va. Dept. Mental Health, Gloucester, 1973; adminstr., prof., cons. Human Services Tng. and Research Council, Inc., Charlottesville, Va., 1975—; cons. various social agys. and orgns. Recipient Outstanding Young Tchr. award Roane County Edn. Assn., 1967; lic. profl. counselor and tchr. Mem. NEA, Nat. Rehab. Assn., Nat. Rehab. Adminstrn. Assn., Nat. Rehab. Counseling Assn., Vocat. Evaluation and Work Adjustment Assn., Va. Rehab. Assn., Va. Council Social Welfare. Methodist. Home: 3990 William Ct Charlottesville VA 22901 Office: Human Services Tng and Research Council Inc 7 Elliewood Ave Charlottesville VA 22903

HAZZARD, MARY ELIZABETH, nurse, educator; b. Evansville, Ind., Mar. 2, 1941; d. John Warren and Lucille Elizabeth H.; B.S. in Nursing, Nazareth Coll., 1963; A.M., N.Y. U., 1965, Ph.D., 1970; 1 dau., Mary Lucille. Staff nurse Caldwell County War Meml. Hosp., Princeton, Ky., summers 1962, 63, 65; teaching fellow N.Y. U., 1965-66, instr., 1966-68; asst. prof. U. Va., 1966-70, asso. prof., 1970-74, dir. learning resource, 1970-74; asso. prof. nursing Sangamon State U., Springfield, Ill., 1974-79; prof., head dept. nursing Western Ky. U., Bowling Green, 1979—; doctoral research adviser Walden U., 1975—. Chmn. nursing com. VA, 1969-74; mem. nursing com. Task Force on Cardiac Rehab., 1976-79, Ill. Cancer Soc., 1975-79; bd. dirs. Va. Heart Assn., 1971-73, Colonnade Club at U. Va., 1971-74: mem. mobile intensive care adv. bd. Ill. Heart Assn., 1976-77. Fellow Am. Acad. Nursing; mem. Am. Nurses Assn., Nat. League for Nursing, Health Edn. Media Assn., AAAS, AAUP, Soc. for Gen. Systems Research, Am. Heart Assn., Am. Cancer Soc., W. Central Ill. Health Systems Agy., Sigma Theta Tau, Pi Lambda Theta. Democrat. Roman Catholic. Author: An Investigation of Bioelectric Potential in Non-pregnant and Pregnant Rabbit, 1970; Review of Medical Surgical Nursing, 1976; Nursing Outline Series: Critical Care Nursing, 1978. Contbr. articles to profl. jours. Home: 2465 Grider Pond Rd Bowling Green KY 42101 Office: Western Ky U Bowling Green KY 42101

HEACOCK, GEORGE THOMAS, indsl.-govt. cons.; b. Sylacauga, Ala., June 21, 1920; s. John Warren and Mexie (McDowell) H.; student U. Ala., 1939-40; B.C.S., Benjamin Franklin U., 1963; m. Marie Terese Baltes, Oct. 23, 1948; children—Thomas Michael, Mark Alan, David Andrew. Intelligence officer, specialist CIA, various locations, 1947-69; prin. firm Heacock Govt. Marketing Agy., Falls Church, Va., 1969—. Asst. scoutmaster, mem. exec. com. Nat. Capital Area council Boy Scouts Am., 1962-72, chmn. fund drive, 1972; bd. dirs. Sleepy Hollow Recreation Assn., 1971-72. Served with M.I., USNR, 1942-46. Recipient letter merit Dir. CIA, 1953. Mason. Address: 6711 Rolfs Rd Falls Church VA 22042

HEAD, WILLIAM IVERSON, chem. co. exec.; b. Tallapposa, Ga., Apr. 4, 1925; s. Iverson and Ruth Britain (Hubbard) H.; B.S. in Textile Engring. with honors, Ga. Inst. Tech., 1950; m. Mary Helen Ware, June 12, 1947; children—William Iverson, Connie Suzanne, Alan David. Research and devel. engr. Tenn. Eastman Co., Kingsport, 1949-56, quality control-mfg. sr. engr., 1957-67, dept. supt., 1968-74; supt. acetate yarn Chems. div. Eastman Kodak Co., Kingsport, 1975—; personnel cons., 1975—. Div. labor coordinator radiol. unit Sullivan County CD, 1962—. Served with USN, 1943-46; capt. Res. Mem. Am. Assn. Textile Tech., Internat. Soc. Philos. Enquiry (internat. v.p., personnel cons. 1978-79), Internat. Platform Assn., Naval Res. Assn., Mil. Order World Wars, Res. Officers Assn. (Tenn. v.p.), VFW, Mensa (pres. Upper East Tenn.), INTERTEL. Republican. Unitarian. Clubs: Kiwanis, Elks, Eagles. Patentee textured yarns tech. in U.S. and Gt. Britain. Home: 2026 Bruce St Kingsport TN 37664 Office: PO Box 511 Bldg 59 Kingsport TN 37662

HEADLEY, ELWOOD JEAN, physician; b. Atlantic City, July 22, 1939; s. Elwood Alverson and Elizabeth Louise (Glatterer) H.; student U. of South, 1957-59; A.B., Vanderbilt U., 1962, M.D., 1966. Intern internal medicine Vanderbilt U. Hosp., Nashville, 1966-67, resident internal medicine, 1967-68; resident internal medicine Ohio State U. Hosp., Columbus, 1968-69, fellow hematology, 1969-70; fellow hematology U. Fla., Gainesville, 1972—, chief resident internal medicine, 1975-76, now asst. prof. medicine; asso. chief of staff for edn. Gainesville VA Hosp. Prin. investigator Gainesville (Fla.) Methodone Program, 1972; mem. Region III Drug Abuse Adv. Council, 1972. Served to maj., M.C., AUS, 1970-72. Episcopalian. Home: 2220 SW 34th St Apt 176 Gainesville FL 32608 Office: Div Hematology U Fla Gainesville FL 32610

HEALEY, CATHERINE BURKHART, social worker, govt. ofcl.; b. Athens, Ga., May 27, 1919; d. Walter C. and Pearl P. (Pennington) Burkhart; B.S. in Math. and Chemistry, U. Ga., 1939; M.S.W., Tulane U., 1941; m. Charles Shepard Healey, Dec. 28, 1940; children—Charles Shepard II, William Walter. Case worker Children's Bur. of New Orleans, 1942; vol. worker ARC, 1943-50; supr., dir. of maternity home and adoption service Protestant Home for Babies, New Orleans, 1950-60; supr. of case work Methodist Home Hosp., New Orleans, 1960-61, 61-63; dir. community vol. service Social Welfare Council, New Orleans, 1963-69; sub-profl. officer Ga. State Dept. of Family and Children Services, 1969-71, vol. adminstrn. cons., 1971-72; coordinator older Am. Vol. program ACTION, region IV, Atlanta, Ga., 1972-74, tng. officer, 1974—; cons. to various social and health service orgns., 1960—, Gov.'s Commn. on Voluntarism for State of Ga., 1973. Recipient Spl. Commendation award ACTION, 1975. Mem. Acad. Cert. Social Workers, Nat. Assn. Social Workers, Ga. Adult Edn. Council, Ga. Gerontol. Soc., Psi Chi, Phi Mu Epsilon. Methodist. Author: (manual) Guidelines, 1964; contbr. articles to jours. on social welfare. Home: 289 S Colonial Homes Circle NW Atlanta GA 30309 Office: ACTION 101 Marietta St Atlanta GA 30303

HEALY, KEITH EUGENE, hosp. adminstr.; b. Effingham, Ill., May 11, 1933; s. Tilman Alonzo and Lillian Matilda (Petzing) H.; B.A., Ga State Coll., 1964; M.B.A., So. Ill. U., 1973; m. Patricia Eileen Lauck, Jan. 9, 1955; children—Candace Suzette, Catherine Eileen, Keith Eugene, David Tilman. Commd. airman U.S. Air Force, 1951, advanced through grades to maj., 1975, ret., 1975; distbn. mgr. Sommers Drug Stores Co., San Antonio, 1975-77; adminstrv. asst. St. Mary Hosp., Port Arthur, Tex., 1977—; cons. risk mgr. Sister's of Charity Hosps., 1978—. Chmn., Port Arthur Disaster Com., 1978; bd. dirs.-at-large El Dorado Homes Assn., San Antonio, 1976; pub. chmn. San Antonio Ballet Guild, 1976; pres. Swing Squares Square Dancers, 1979—. Decorated Air medal (4), Bronze Star, Meritorious Service medal. Mem. Tex. Hosp. Assn., Tex. Safety Assn., Nat. Fire Protection Assn., Nat. Safety Council, Risk and Ins. Mgrs. Soc., Nat. Def. Driving League. Republican. Methodist. Author Health Care Series, Base Newspaper, Chanute AFB, Ill., 1970. Home: 657 Birchwood Dr Port Neches TX 77651 Office: PO Box 3696 Port Arthur TX 77651

HEALY, ROBERT EDWARD, advt. agy. exec.; b. Bklyn., Aug. 15, 1904; s. Walter F. and Florence E. (Davis) H.; grad. Dwight Prep. Sch., N.Y.C., 1924; student Pace Inst., N.Y.C., 1924-26; D.S.C. (hon.), Pace Coll., 1961; m. Lille Rose, Aug. 3, 1927; children—Lilie Jane, Patricia Anne, Robert E. (dec.); m. 2d, Wayne Clark, Jan. 11, 1957; children—Edward W., James D. Salesman, T.J. Adikes, Jamaica, N.Y., 1926, Hoover Co., 1927-28; asst. to v.p. charge sales promotion Johns-Manville Co., 1929-33; mgr. prodn. sect. advt. dept. Colgate-Palmolive Co., Jersey City, 1934-36, asst. advt. mgr. 1936-39, brand advt. mgr., 1939-42, gen. advt. mgr., 1942-46, v.p. charge advt., 1946-52; v.p., treas., dir., mem. exec. com. McCann-Erickson, Inc., 1952-53, v.p., gen. mgr., dir., mem. exec. com., 1953-54, gen. mgr. N.Y. office, 1954, exec. v.p., 1955-58, vice chmn. bd., 1958-60, chmn. bd., 1960-62, mem. finance com., 1957-61; chmn. bd. McCann-Erickson Corp. (Internat.), 1956-58; pres. Interpublic, S.A., Geneva, Switzerland, 1962-65; exec. v.p. Interpublic Group Cos., Inc., 1965-67, pres., 1967-71, chief exec. officer, 1967-71, chmn. bd., 1968-73, hon. chmn. bd., 1973—, mem. fin. com., 1968-77. Mem. adv. council Pace Coll. Clubs: N.Y. Athletic; Ocean Reef; Confrerie de la Chaine des Rotisseurs; Paris American. Home: 1111 Crandon Blvd Key Biscayne FL 33149 Office: 1271 Ave of Americas New York City NY 10020

HEALY, ROBERT LEO, psychologist; b. Arlington, Mass., Aug. 25, 1925; s. Richard Michael and Anne Veronica H.; M.A., Goddard Coll., 1976; Ph.D., Clayton U., 1978; m. Juliana Marie Tinker, Aug. 1, 1970; children—Richard M., Toni A., Robyn J., Tara G., Monica. Mfrs. rep., S.W., 1957-70; dir. Paseo Drug Center, Tulsa Psychiat. Center, 1970-73; state coordinator drug abuse programs Okla. Atty. Gen.'s Office, 1973-75; pvt. practice psychotherapy, hypnotherapy Oklahoma City, 1975—; trainer in clin. hypnosis; pres. Personal Growth Center, Oklahoma City. Served with USN, 1942-45; PTO. Recipient award for service to troops Australian Govt., 1944, Man of Yr. award K.C., 1973, award Tulsa Mental Health Assn., 1974. Mem. Nat. Assn. Social Workers, Am. Humanistic Psychology Assn., Southwestern Psychol. Assn. Club: Sportsman's (Oklahoma City). Office: 6161 N May Ave Suite 270 Oklahoma City OK 73112

HEARD, GLADYS MAE CAREY, educator; b. Lexington, Miss., Nov. 1, 1938; d. Sam Gwin and Lillian Doris (Wadlington) Carey; student Tougaloo (Miss.) Coll., 1955-57; A.B., Fisk U., 1959; M.A. in Teaching, Ind. U., 1961; Ed.D., Rutgers U., 1975; m. Robert Alvin Heard, Dec. 26, 1961; 1 son, Bradley Erik. English tchr. N. Dade Jr.-Sr. High Sch., Opa-Locka, Fla., 1960-62; instr. English, Miss. Valley State U., Itta Bena, 1962-66, N.C. Central U., Durham, 1966-69; instr. English, Norfolk (Va.) State Coll., 1969-74, asst. prof., 1974-75, asso. prof., 1975-76, coordinator transitional English program, 1977—. Advanced Instnl. Devel. Program grantee, 1973-75. Mem. Nat. Concil Tchrs. of English, Conf. Coll. Composition and Communication, Coll. Lang. Assn., Alpha Kappa Alpha. Democrat. Baptist. Contbr. article to profl. jour. Home: 6259 Drew Dr Virginia Beach VA 23464 Office: Norfolk State Coll Norfolk VA 23504

HEARD, VIRGIL GALE, educator; b. Willow, Okla., May 2, 1943; s. Ira Rutherford and Elbie (Harris) H.; student Amarillo Jr. Coll., 1962-64; B.S. in Biology, W. Tex. State U., 1965; M.Ed., N. Tex. State U., 1973, Ph.D., 1975; m. Patricia Ann Scroggs, Aug. 18, 1973; children—John Kevin, Alston Bradford. Tchr. phys. scis. Ft. Worth Schs., 1966-70; secondary sci. methods asst. N. Tex. State U., Denton, 1971-72, elem. sci., 1972-73; sci. chmn. Trinity Sch., Midland, Tex., 1973-75; biology instr. N.E. Miss. Jr. Coll., Booneville, 1975—; program dir. N. Miss. Environ. Edn. Center; water quality cons. U.S. Geol. Survey, Three Rivers Ednl. Consortium. Edn. chmn. Prentiss County chpt. Am. Cancer Soc. Served with U.S. Army, 1968-70. Decorated Air medal; Dallas-Tarrant County Council Sci. Socs. grantee, 1966, 67. Mem. AAUP, Miss. Jr. Coll. Faculty Assn. (pres.), NEA, Miss. Assn. Educators, Phi Delta Kappa, Beta Beta Beta, Alpha Chi. Democrat. Episcopalian. Contbr. article to profl. jour. Home: 102 7th St Booneville MS 38829 Office: Box 1805 NE Miss Jr Coll Booneville MS 38829

HEARIN, WILLIAM JEFFERSON, publishing co. exec.; b. Mobile, Ala., Aug. 27, 1909; s. William Jefferson and Mary Lou (Luddington) H.; m. Louise Chamberlain, Oct. 7, 1936; 1 dau., Ann Bartlett. Classified and retail advt. solicitor Mobile News-Item, 1927-32; retail advt. solicitor, retail advt. mgr., nat. advt. mgr., circulation mgr., advt. dir., bus. mgr. Mobile Press Register, 1932-44, gen. mgr., exec. v.p., 1944-65, co-pub., 1965-70, pub., pres., 1970—, also dir.; dir. Mobile Gas Service Corp., First Nat. Bank Mobile. Bd. dirs. United Fund, YMCA; mem. adv. bd. Salvation Army, Jr. Achievement; pres. Mobile Assn. Blind; bd. regents Spring Hill Coll. Named Hon. Col., Salvation Army, 1974; Lion of Year, 1975; Mobilian of Year, 1977. Mem. Am. Newspaper Pubs. Assn., So. Newspapers Pubs. Assn., Ala. Press Assn., Sigma Delta Chi. Office: 304 Government St PO Box 2488 Mobile AL 36630

HEARN, CLAUDE DAVID, surgeon; b. Chattanooga, May 27, 1939; s. Claude Daugherty and Mary Mildred (MacKenzie) H.; A.B., Birmingham-So. Coll., 1961; M.D., Med. Coll. Ala., 1965; m. Cynthia Clair Ford, June 10, 1962; children—Cynthia Denise, Rebecca Alyse, Heather Leigh, Laurie Elizabeth. Intern, Carraway Meth. Hosp., Birmingham, Ala., 1965-66; resident surgery La. State U., 1968-72; practice medicine, specializing in gen. surgery, Houston, 1972—; mem. staff Clear Lake Hosp., Houston, 1972—, chief surgery, 1974, 77; surg. cons. Apollo-Soyuz Mission, Johnson Space Center, 1975. Served with USAF, 1966-68. Decorated Air Medal. Diplomate Am. Bd. Surgery. Fellow A.C.S.; mem. Tex. Med. Assn., Harris County Med. Soc., Houston Surg. Soc., Omicron Delta Kappa, Sigma Alpha Epsilon. Methodist. Contbr. articles to profl. jours. Home: 11 Windcreek Dr Friendswood TX 77546 Office: 200 Medical Center Blvd Webster TX 77598

HEARTWELL, CHARLES MONROE, JR., dentist; b. Lawrenceville, Va., Aug. 27, 1908; s. Charles Monroe and Elva Antenette (Dortch) H.; student Hampden-Sydney Coll., 1925-27, U. Va., 1927-28; D.D.S., Med. Coll. Va., 1932; m. Marjorie Coleman Elmore, July 25, 1933; 1 son, Charles Monroe. Intern in prosthodontics U.S. Navy Dental Clinic, Norfolk, Va., 1951; gen. practice dentistry, South Hill, Va., 1932-36; pvt. practice prosthodontics, 1936-40; commd. lt. j.g. U.S. Navy Dental Corps, 1940, advanced through grades to capt., 1953, ret., 1961; faculty Med. Coll. Va. Dental Sch., Richmond, 1961-73, prof., 1962-73; cons. dept. oncology Med. Coll. Va. Hosps., 1964-73; cons. VA Hosp., Richmond, 1972-77; guest lectr. VA Hosp. and depts. anatomy and oral pathology Va. Commonwealth U., 1973-77. Licensed dentist, Va.; diplomate Am. Bd. Prosthodontists. Fellow Am. Coll. Maxillo Facial Prosthetics, Va. Dental Assn., Am. Coll. Dentists; mem. Va. Commonwealth U. Alumni Assn., Richmond Dental Soc., ADA, Southeastern Acad. Prosthodontics, Soc. Oral Physiology and Occlusion (v.p. 1969), Am. Coll. Prosthodontists, Am. Prosthodontic Soc., Fedn. Prosthodontic Orgns., Full Gospel Bus. Men's Fellowship Internat., Theta Chi, Psi Omega, Omicron Kappa Upsilon. Methodist. Republican. Club: Century. Author: (with Arthur O. Rahm) Syllabus of Complete Dentures, 1968, 2d edit., 1971. Address: 16 Ralston Rd Richmond VA 23229

HEATH, BOBBY JERRELL, cardiac surgeon; b. Grenada, Miss., Feb. 19, 1943; s. Ernest and Louise (Corder) H.; student Holmes Jr. Coll., 1961-63; M.D., U. Miss., 1968; m. Linda M. Cowan, Sept. 30, 1967; 1 dau., Ashley Milligan. Intern, Parkland Meml. Hosp., Dallas, 1968-69; resident in gen. surgery U. Miss. Hosp., Jackson, 1972-76, resident in thoracic-cardiac surgery, 1976-78; asst. prof. cardiac surgery Univ. Med. Center, Jackson, Miss., 1978—. Served with USAF, 1970-72. Decorated Air Force Commendation medal; diplomate Am. Bd. Surgery, Am. Bd. Thoracic Surgery. Mem. AMA, Am. Coll. Chest Physicians, Alpha Omega Alpha, Phi Kappa Phi. Presbyterian. Contbr. articles to profl. jours. Home: 5150 Shirlwood Dr Jackson MS 39211 Office: Univ Med Center 2500 N State St Jackson MS 39216

HEATH, CHARLES CHASTAIN, mgmt. cons.; b. Sapulpa, Okla., Sept. 7, 1921; s. Connie Clifton and Keren (Boyd) H.; student U. N.C., 1945-47; m. Doris Roe, Nov. 10, 1979; children—Janice Heath Chuk, Brian Neal, Eric Scott. Mgr., Shelby Gas, Inc., Shelbyville, Ill., 1946-49; supt. gas Ill. Power Co., Decatur, Ill., 1950-54, City of Shelby (N.C.), 1954-59; pres. Heath & Asso., Shelby, 1959—; pres., dir. Minex, Inc., Shelby, 1973-77, Energy Resources, Inc., Shelby, 1977-79; officer, dir. N.C. R.R. Co., 1960-62. Charter mem. N.C. Indsl. Devel. Found., 1960-62; bd. dirs. N.C. Conservative Union, 1978-79, 10th Dist., The Conservative Caucus, 1976. Served with USMC, 1942-46. Recipient Disting. Service award Jaycees, 1957. Mem. Am. Gas Assn., Southeastern Gas Assn. Republican. Baptist. Clubs: N.C. Congressional, Cleve. Country. Author: You Can Save America, 1972; The Golden Egg, the Goose and Us, 1976. Home: 97-3 Edgemont Ave Shelby NC 28150 Office: 7 N LaFayette St Shelby NC 28150

HEATH, THOMAS ALFRED, transp. co. exec.; b. Bellmore, N.Y., July 21, 1929; s. Sam Leo and Gertrude Katherine (Woodington) H.; B.S., La. State U., 1954; m. Mary Ann Davis, Oct. 10, 1954; children—Thomas Alfred, Lisa Ann. Operations mgr. Madisonville Terminal Co., Baton Rouge, 1969; v.p., personnel and safety dir. Bulk Transport, Baton Rouge, 1969-73; personnel and safety dir. Comml. Carrier Corp. and Clay Hyder Trucking Lines, Inc., Auburndale, Fla. Chmn., La. Motor Transport Council of Safety Suprs., 1968-69; so. regional chmn. Am. Trucking Assn. Council of Safety Suprs., 1979—. Served with U.S. Army, 1951-53. Mem. Fla. Trucking Assn., Am. Trucking Assn., Heartland Safety Soc., Nat. Com. for Motor Fleet Tng., Am. Soc. Personnel Adminstrn., Internat. Soc. Stress Analysts. Republican. Episcopalian. Home: 538 W Coleman Dr Winter Haven FL 33880 Office: 502 E Bridgers Ave Auburndale FL 33823

HEATHCOCK, JOHN HERMAN, JR., children's apparel mfg. co. exec.; b. Anniston, Ala., June 20, 1943; s. John Herman and Fallie Mae (Ford) H.; B.A., Jacksonville State U., 1965; postgrad. U. So. Calif., 1969-70; m. Janice Carol McCrary, Dec. 31, 1974; 1 son, Deven Scott. In-charge accountant Ernst & Whinney, Chattanooga, 1970-72; asst. auditor Hamilton Bancshares, Inc., Chattanooga, 1972-73; acctg. mgr. Skyland Internat. Corp., Chattanooga, 1973-76, asst. controller, 1976-79, controller, 1979—. Adviser, Jr. Achievement, Chattanooga, 1974. Served with U.S. Army, 1965-70. Decorated Bronze Star, Army Commendation medal, Air medal with 7 oak leaf clusters; C.P.A., Tenn. Mem. Am. Inst. C.P.A.'s, Tenn. Soc. C.P.A.'s, Nat. Assn. Accts. Home: 7370 McCormack Dr Hixson TN 37343 Office: PO Box 5008 Chattanooga TN 37406

HEBDEN, JAMES H., loan co. exec.; b. Providence, Oct. 6, 1950; s. Lael Aubrey Wharton and Muriel Avis H.; student Tenn. Tech. U., 1968-70, U. Tenn., Nashville, 1970-73; m. Janice Diane Turnbow, June 1, 1973. Mgr., Avco Fin. Services, Lexington and Louisville, Ky., Knoxville, Tenn., 1972-75; mgr. CIT Fin. Services, Smyrna, Tenn., 1975-77; asst. v.p., loan officer First Nat. Bank Rutherford County, Smyrna, 1977-78; mgr. CIT Fin. Services, Lebanon, Tenn., 1978—. Vice-pres. Rutherford County Heart Unit, 1977-78, 78-79; chmn. N. Rutherford County Heart Fund Drive, 1977, 78, 79. Mem. Smyrna C. of C. Episcopalian. Clubs: Rotary (dir. 1976-78), Lions, Exchange. Home: 1706 N Tennessee Blvd Murfreesboro TN 37130

HEBERT, CAROLYN ST. AMANT, cardiologist; b. New Orleans, Dec. 21, 1939; d. Julius Clement and Marie Pauline (Martin) St. Amant; B.S., Dominican Coll., 1961; M.D., La. State U., 1965; m. Leo P. Hebert, Jr., Aug. 2, 1969; children—Anne Marie, Catherine, Elizabeth, Leo P. III, Maria Pauline, Julie. Intern, Charity Hosp., New Orleans, 1965-66, resident in internal medicine, 1966-69, resident in cardiology, 1969-71; cardiologist, dir. intensive care unit Thibodaux (La.) Gen. Hosp., 1971—. Diplomate Am. Bd. Internal Medicine. Mem. AMA, Lafourche Parish Med. Assn., Am. Soc. Internal Medicine, Alpha Omega Alpha, La. Heart Assn. (ednl. com.), Phi Kappa Phi. Democrat. Roman Catholic. Office: Suite N-2 1101 Audubon St Thibodaux LA 70301

HEBERT, CARROLL FRANCIS, chemist; b. Houma, La., Jan. 14, 1942; s. Clifford Louis and Eugenie (Savoie) H.; student Nicholls State U., 1963-64; B.S., Southeastern La. U., 1966; Ph.D., Notre Dame U., 1970; m. Lua Maria Fanguy, July 20, 1968. Data processing mgr. Radiation Lab. Notre Dame U., 1971-73; pres. Sci. Computer Services, New Orleans, 1971-73; founder, pres. Quantum Tech. Labs., Harvey, La., 1973—. Mem. Am. Phys. Soc., AAAS, Sigma Xi. Democrat. Roman Catholic. Home: 24 Sievers Dr Marrero LA 70072 Office: Quantum Tech Labs 1732 4th St Harvey LA 70058

HEBERT, PAUL LINDEN, food service co. exec.; b. Thibodeaux, La., Feb. 1, 1927; s. Joseph Issadore and Ruby (Cappel) H.; B.S., La. State U., 1950; m. Jacqueline Mary Rauch, Nov. 25, 1950; children—Ann, Gayle, Sue, Paul Linden, Lori. With Ponchartrain Stores, Inc., Slidell, La., 1950-70, pres., 1960-70; nat. sales mgr. Frosty Acres, Frozen Food Forum, Atlanta, 1970-75; mgr. Instl. Supply Co. for Consol. Cos., Inc., New Orleans, 1975-79; v.p. sales Sunbelt Food Service, Metairie, La., 1979—. Served with U.S. Army, 1945-46. Mem. Food Service Exec. Assn., Nat. Food Brokers Assn., La. Restaurant Assn. Roman Catholic. Clubs: K.C. (4 deg.), Traffic and Transp. of New Orleans. Home: 6420 Marshal Foch St New Orleans LA 70124 Office: PO Drawer 9248 Metairie LA 70005

HEBERT, PETER WILLIAM, urologist; b. Erie, Pa., Apr. 2, 1934; s. Francis Willard and Frances Elen (Wood) H.; B.S., Allegheny Coll., 1956; M.D., Jefferson Med. Coll., Phila., 1960; m. Patricia A. Serritella Smith, Nov. 1, 1971; children—Leslie C., Melanie L. Intern, St. Vincent's Hosp., Erie, 1960-61; commd. lt. U.S. Navy, 1961, advanced through grades to comdr., 1969; resident in surgery and urology Naval Med. Center, San Diego, 1967-71; chief urology Bremerton (Wash.) Naval Med. Center, 1971-73; ret., 1973; practice medicine specializing in urology, pres. Hebert & Stephenson Urology Assos., Corpus Christi, Tex., 1973—; mem. staff Meml. Med. Center, Spohn, Drs., Physicians and Surgeons hosps. Diplomate Am. Bd. Urology. Fellow A.C.S.; mem. AMA, Tex. Med. Assn., Am. Urologic Assn., Am. Fertility Soc. Republican. Clubs: Town (Corpus Christi); Taylor Hose (Meadville, Pa.); Elks. Office: 1201 19th St Corpus Christi TX 78405

HECHT, MANFRED HERMANN, surgeon; b. Greifswald, Germany, Oct. 2, 1929; s. Curt Karl and Felicitas Minna-Luise (Koberger) H.; came to U.S., 1949, naturalized, 1955; student U. Philippines, 1948-49, U. Calif., Berkeley, 1949-50; B.S., Columbia U., 1953; postgrad. Heidelberg U., 1956-62; M.D., Duke U., 1964; m. Virginia Marie Daugherty, Oct. 29, 1955; children—Karen, Monica, Susan, Manfred C. Enlisted in U.S. Army, 1954, advanced through grades to col., M.C., 1979; intern Brooke Gen. Hosp., Tex., 1964-65; resident in surgery Womack Army Hosp., Ft. Bragg, N.C., 1965-66; resident in orthopedics Tripler Med. Center, Hawaii, 1966-69; chief profl. services and orthopedics 67th Evacuation Hosp., Vietnam, 1969-70, Dewitt Army Hosp., Ft. Belvoir, Va., 1970-72, 2d Gen. Hosp., Landstuhl, Germany, 1972-75; dep. comdr., chief profl. services U.S. Mil. Acad. Hosp., West Point, N.Y., 1975-78; chief dept. surgery, chief orthopedic service and dir. residency program Gorgas Hosp., Balboa Heights, C.Z., 1978—; prof. mil. hygiene U.S. Mil. Acad.; cons. 1st U.S. Army Orthopedic Surgeon, Dept. Def. Med. Rev. Bd. Vice pres. PTSA, Europe, 1974-75. Decorated Bronze Star, Meritorious Service medal with oak leaf, Army Commendation medal, Republic of Vietnam Gallantry Cross; recipient Republic of Vietnam Ministry Edn. certificate of appreciation, 1970. Diplomate Am. Bd. Orthopedic Surgeons. Fellow A.C.S., Am. Acad. Orthopedic Surgeons; mem. AMA (Physicians Recognition award), Eastern Orthopedic Assn., Assn. Mil. Surgeons U.S., Soc. Mil. Orthopedic Surgeons, Pan Am. Med. Assn., Royal Soc. Medicine (London), Am. Orthopedic Soc. for Sports Medicine. Clubs: Masons (32 deg.); Shriners (Ft. Worth); Sojourner (West Point). Author: Large War Wounds in Extremities, 1968; Women Assimilation in the Armed Forces, 1976; Sport Conditions in Military Cadets, 1978. Office: Gorgas Army Hosp MEDDAC Panama APO Miami FL 34004

HECHT, MITCHELL NEIL, speech pathologist; b. Bklyn., Dec. 16, 1954; s. Arnold Chick and Gloria Bernice Hecht; B.A. magna cum laude, Bklyn. Coll., 1975; M.A., U. Miami (Fla.), 1977. Speech and lang. pathologist Holy Cross Hosp., Ft. Lauderdale, Fla., 1977-78; pvt. practice speech and lang. pathology, Coral Springs, Fla., 1978—; speech and lang. pathologist Bright Horizon Sch. for Exceptional Children, 1979-80. Recipient Dr. Letita Rubencheck Meml. award Assn. Chairmen of Speech/Bur. Speech Improvement, 1972. Mem. Am. Speech and Hearing Assn., Fla. Speech and Hearing Assn., Broward County Speech and Hearing Assn. Address: 4111 NW 88th Ave Coral Springs FL 33065

HECK, GLENN EUGENE, cable TV exec.; b. Mondovi, Wis., Apr. 11, 1929; s. Oscar August and Mae Charlotte (Moy) H.; B.Mus., U. Redlands, 1952; m. Margaret Lois Stephens, Sept. 19, 1953; children—David Stephens, Rebecca Ann, Karen Margaret. Sales rep. Bibb Music Center, Macon, Ga., 1956-58; band dir. pub. schs., Warner Robins, Ga., 1958-60; mgr. Jackson-Oetter Co., Macon, 1960-63; mgr. Robins Telecable, Warner Robins, 1963—. Cubmaster, Boy Scouts Am., 1964-68, dist. chmn., 1968-70; campaign chmn. United Givers Fund, 1965; mem. Warner-Robins Library Bd., 1972-74; trustee Houston County Library System, 1974—; bd. dirs. Houston County Pub. Sch. System, 1971—; Christian Sci. minister Robins AFB, 1956-76. Served with USAF, 1952-56. Named Civic Leader of Yr., Jr. C. of C., 1970; Silver Beaver award Boy Scouts Am., 1971; Dist. Bd. Mem. of Yr., Ga. Sch. Bds. Assn., 1976. Mem. Ga. Cable TV Assn. (founder, pres. 1971-72), Warner Robins C. of C. (pres. 1968, 70), Ga. Sch. Bds. Assn. (pres. 1978-79), So. Region Cable TV Assn., Nat. Cable TV Assn., So. Sch. Bds. Assn., Nat. Sch. Bds. Assn. Democrat. Christian Scientist. Club: Optimist (pres. 1973). Contbr. articles to profl. jours.; composer, pub. songs; composer words and music Warner Robins' ofcl. Bicentennial Song, 1975. Home: 116 Briardale Ave Warner Robins GA 31093 Office: PO Box 2288 Warner Robins GA 31093

HECK, WILLIAM ROSS, acct., educator; b. Columbus, Ga., Nov. 28, 1925; s. Harry Roswell and Myrtle Ann (Turner) H.; B.S., Auburn U., 1954, M.S., 1955; Ph.D., La. State U., 1960. Instr. accounting La. State U., Baton Rouge, 1956-59; prof. acctg. Fla. State U., Tallahassee, 1959—; sr. acct. Arthur Andersen & Co., Atlanta, 1967-68. Ednl. cons. Seidman & Seidman, N.Y.C., 1970. Served with USN, 1943-47, USNR, 1950-52. Decorated Bronze Star medal, Sec. Navy Commendation pendant. Named Outstanding Prof. Coll. Bus. Fla. State U., 1964, 74; named among Outstanding Educators Am., 1975. C.P.A., La., 1959. Mem. Am., Fla. (v.p. Tallahassee chpt.) insts. C.P.A.'s, La. Soc. C.P.A.'s, Am. Acctg. Assn., Gold Key, Beta Gamma Sigma, Phi Kappa Phi, Omicron Delta Kappa, Pi Kappa Alpha, Delta Sigma Pi, Beta Alpha Psi. Mem. editorial adv. bd. Prentice-Hall Federal Tax Course-Students Edition, 1967-80. Home: 420 E Park Ave Tallahassee FL 32301 Office: College Business Florida State Univ Tallahassee FL 32306

HEDGE, GEORGE ALBERT, physiologist; b. St. Louis, June 7, 1939; s. George Calvin and Elsie Margaret (Metz) H.; B.S. in Biology, U. Mo., 1961, M.A. in Pharmacology, 1963; Ph.D. in Physiology, Stanford U., 1966; m. Jacqueline Stake McMillan, Aug. 31, 1963; children—Naomi C., David T. Research fellow dept. pharmacology U. Utrecht (Netherlands), 1966-68; asst. prof. dept. physiology Coll. Medicine, U. Ariz., Tucson, 1968-72, asso. prof., 1972-77; prof., chmn. dept. physiology and biophysics Sch. Medicine, W.Va. U., Morgantown, 1977—; ad hoc cons. NIH; reviewer manuscripts for profl. jours. Served with U.S. Army, 1957. NIH research grantee. Mem. Am. Physiology Soc., Endocrine Soc., Internat. Soc. Neuroendocrinology, Assn. Chmn. Depts. Physiology, Am. Thyroid Assn. Author numerous abstracts and sci. papers. Home: 673 Nueva Morgantown WV 26505 Office: WVa Univ Med Center Dept Physiology Morgantown WV 26506

HEDGECOCK, JOHN PHILLIP, chem. engr., govt. ofcl.; b. North Little Rock, Ark., Nov. 6, 1933; s. Charles Arthur and Bessie Louise (Stevens) H.; B.S. in Chem. Engring., U. Ark., 1960; m. Ila Trene Kelley, Jan. 24, 1959; children—Kelley Leigh, John Keith, Cathryn Anne, Eric Andrew. Chem. engr. Stauffer Chem. Co., Houston, 1960-64; chem. engr. Pine Bluff (Ark.) Arsenal, 1965-72; chem. engr. Nat. Center Toxicological Research, Jefferson, Ark., 1972—. Served with USN, 1953-55. Recipient Exemplary Civilian Service award U.S. Army Munitions Command, 1972. Registered profl. engr., Ark., Tex. Mem. U.S. Judo Assn. (life). Club: River City Rugby (pres.). Contbr. articles to sports mags. Home: 105 Coronado Pl North Little Rock AR 72116 Office: Nat Center Toxicological Research Jefferson AR 72079

HEDGES, WILLIAM ALMUS, mfg. co. exec.; b. Cleve., July 7, 1941; s. Norman William and Margaret Francis (Wynne) H.; B.S. in Indsl. Mgmt., U. Ala., 1968; m. Doris Ann Hilliard, May 13, 1961; children—Mark, Tim, Brent. Ops. analyst, quality control foreman, systems analyst GTE Automatic Electric Co., Huntsville, Ala., 1968-73; prodn. and inventory control mgr. Hyster Co., Sulligent, Ala., 1973-75; prodn. and inventory control mgr. Clark Equipment Co., Lima, Ohio, 1975-76; materials mgr. Cutler Hammer Co., Cleveland, Tenn., 1976-77; mfg. mgr., prodn. and inventory control mgr. EG&G ORTEC, Inc., Oak Ridge, 1977—; speaker profl. confs. Recipient Charles R. Scott award Soc. Advancement Mgmt., 1968. Am. Prodn. and Inventory Control Soc. (dir. chpt., cert. practitioner), Inst. Mgmt. Sci., Internat. Material Mgmt. Soc. (chmn. software internat. MRP steering com., cert. profl.), Alpha Kappa Psi. Methodist. Clubs: Optimist. Home: 705 Pine Valley Rd Knoxville TN 37923 Office: 100 Midland Rd Oak Ridge TN 37830

HEDRICK, ADDIE MAE, poet; b. Black Rock, Ark., Aug. 22, 1903; d. William Henry and Mary Elizabeth (Lunsford) Underwood; student pub. schs.; m. Joseph A. Hedrick, Nov. 21, 1920; children—Louise (Mrs. Leonard Caranna), Joseph A. Author collections of poetry Sentient Dust, 1952; Mumbaloo, and other Poems, 1967; A Cup of Stars, 1969; contbr. numerous poems to various publs. Mem. Nat. League Am. Pen Women, Poetry Soc. Tenn., Ark. Authors and Composers, World Poetry Soc. Intercontinental. Baptist. Home: 2810 Earle Dr Winnsboro LA 71295

HEEBE, FREDERICK JACOB REGAN, fed. judge; b. Gretna, La., Aug. 24, 1922; s. Bernhardt and Marguerite (Reagan) H.; B.A., Tulane U., 1943, LL.B., 1949; m. Willie Dee Barnes, Aug. 29, 1947; children—Frederick Riley, Adrea Dee. Admitted to La. bar, 1949; practice in Gretna, 1949-60; dist. judge B. 24th Jud. Dist. Ct., Jefferson Parish, La., 1961-66; U.S. dist. judge Eastern Dist. La., 1966—. Charter mem. Community Welfare Council Jefferson Parish, 1957—; chmn. Jefferson Parish Bd. Pub. Welfare, 1953-55. Mem. Jefferson Parish Council, 1958-60, vice chmn., 1958-60. Bd. dirs. Social Welfare Planning Council New Orleans, New Orleans Regional Mental Center and Clinic, W. Bank Assn. for Retarded. Served to capt. inf., AUS, World War II. Decorated Purple Heart, Bronze Star. Mem. Am., La., New Orleans, Fed. bar assns., Am. Judicature Soc., Phi Beta Kappa. Office Chamber C-525 500 Camp St New Orleans LA 70130*

HEELAN, GEORGE, coll. adminstr., bus. cons.; b. Danbury, Conn., Aug. 31, 1940; s. George and Mary N. (Nassara) H.; A.A.S., Norwalk Community Coll., 1966; B.S., U. Bridgeport, 1967, M.B.A., 1969; Ed.D., U. S.C., 1979; m. Carol Julia Baucom, Aug. 5, 1978. Grad. asst. U. Bridgeport, 1968-69; dir. bus. affairs, asst. prof. Prairie View A&M, Ala. State U., U. S.C., 1969-73; dir. bus. affairs Morris Coll., Sumter, S.C., 1973—. Mem. Head Start Policy Council. Served with AUS, 1958-59. Mem. Nat. Assn. Coll. and Univ. Bus. Ofcls., S.C. Acctg. Instrs. Assn., Am. Mgmt. Assn., Phi Delta Kappa. Eastern Orthodox. Author: Public Employees and the Right to Strike, 1969; A Critical Analysis of the South Carolina Tuition Grants Program, 1979. Home: 671 Pringle Dr Sumter SC 29150 Office: Morris College N Main St Sumter SC 29150

HEEMANN, PAUL WARREN, univ. adminstr.; b. Balt., July 27, 1933; s. Paul Adolph and Loretta Marie (Lange) H.; A.B., U. N.C., 1956, M.A., 1959; postgrad. U. Md., 1959-62; m. Mary Ellen Placht, Aug. 15, 1958; children—Eve Anne, Lori Barbara, Paul Joseph. Exec. trainee Van Sant Dugdale, Balt., 1956-57; mem. faculty dept. English Coll. William and Mary, Williamsburg, Va., 1962-79, asst. prof., 1965-73, dir. instnl. resources, 1967-69, asst. v.p., 1969-71, v.p., 1973-79, dir. Va. Associated Research Center, 1969-71; v.p. Ga. Inst. Tech., Atlanta, 1979—; chmn. research and devel. adv. com. State Council for Higher Edn. in Va.; chmn. com. on nat. gift and cost reporting standards Council for Advancement and Support of Edn. Bd. dirs. Peninsula Assn. Retarded Children, 1965-72, Va. Peninsula Indsl. Devel. Com., 1970-71, Williamsburg Community Hosp., 1979. Editor: Cost-Effectiveness Analysis in Fund-Raising for Colleges and Universities, 1979. Home: 1115 Terramont Rd Atlanta GA 33076 Office: Ga Inst Tech Atlanta GA 30332

HEFFLER, PAUL MARK, lawyer; b. Bronx, N.Y., Nov. 22, 1953; s. Abraham Solomon and Selma (Cohen) H.; B.S.S.W., U. Ala., 1975; J.D., Samford U., 1979. Admitted to Ala. bar, 1979; social worker Ala. Dept. Pensions and Security, Birmingham, 1975-76; clk. to Hon. G. Ross Bell, Judge Family Ct. of Jefferson County, Ala., 1979; legal intern Legal Aid Soc. Family Ct. Div., Birmingham, 1978-79; individual practice law, Birmingham, 1979—; cons. atty. Birmingham Urban League, Project Hope. Proctor in admiralty Cumberland Sch. Law, 1979; named Cadet of Year, NROTC, 1971. Mem. Am. Bar Assn., Ala. Bar Assn., U.S. Naval Inst., Assn. Trial Lawyers Am., Ala. Trial Lawyers Assn., Am. Judicature Soc., Phi Alpha Delta, Alpha Epsilon Pi. Jewish. Home: 1157 C 14th Ave S Birmingham AL 35205 Office: 4 Office Park Circle Suite 114 Birmingham AL 35223

HEFFNER, DIANE, pharm. co. ofcl.; b. Shelby, N.C., Aug. 3, 1947; d. Moses Dan and Mae (Davis) Scruggs; student East Carolina U., 1965-66, East Tenn. State U., 1967-68; 1 dau., Angela Christine. Tchr., Cowan (W.Va.) Elem. Sch., 1969; sales rep. Manpower, Inc., Durham, N.C., 1971-73; mgmt. tng. specialist Burroughs Wellcome Co., Research Traingle Park, N.C., 1973—; seminar adv. Duke U., 1979. Loaned exec. United Way, 1979; co-chmn. task force N.C. Gov.'s Conf. on Mental Health, 1979. Mem. Am. Soc. for Tng. and Devel. (pres. Triangle chpt. 1976, dir. 1976-79, chmn. nat. awards com. 1979-80, nat. dir., regional v.p. 1980-81). Home: 615 Chalice St Durham NC 27705 Office: 3030 Cornwallis Rd Research Traingle Park NC 27709

HEFFNER, RICHARD LOUIS, mgmt. cons.; b. St. Louis, Apr. 9, 1933; s. Edward Louis and Esther (Herter) H.; A.B., Columbia U., 1955; M.B.A. cum laude, U. Tenn., 1965; m. Charlotte Anne Maclellan, Sept. 2, 1961; children—Richard Louis, Thomas Maclellan. Asst. advt. mgr. Richardson-Merrell, Inc., N.Y.C., 1957-60; new products market mgr. Chattem Drug & Chem. Co., 1960-64; v.p. mktg., corp. planning Dorsey Corp., Chattanooga, 1964-69, v.p., asst. sec., 1970-73; dep. adminstr. Bus. and Def. Services Adminstrn., Dept. Commerce, Washington, 1969-70, mem. nat. marketing adv. com., 1971—; pres., chief exec. officer, dir. Chattanooga Glass Co. subs. Dorsey Corp., 1970-73; trustee Glass Container Industry Research Corp. U.S., 1971-73; exec. v.p., exec. com. Hamilton Bancshares, Inc., Chattanooga, 1973-75; regional rep. sec. commerce Southeastern states U.S. Dept. Commerce, 1975-77; mem. Fed. Regional Council, 1975-77; mgmt. cons., Atlanta, 1977—. Mem. Nat. Def. Exec. Res., 1969-77; vice chmn. Regional Export Expansion Council, 1971-74; mem. Ky.-Tenn. Dist. Export Council, 1974-75. Mem. allocations com. Chattanooga United Fund, 1961-72; bd. dirs. Chattanooga Tb and Respiratory Diseases Assn., 1962-76, pres., 1969-70; v.p. Chattanooga Allied Arts Fund, 1969-70; bd. dirs. Chattanooga Family Service Agy., Chattanooga Travelers Aid Soc., 1968-69, Jr. Achievement, 1971-74, Chattanooga Symphony Assn., 1973-74; bd. dirs., mem. exec. com. YMCA, 1974-76; regional chmn. Republican Nat. Fin. Com., 1979—. Served to lt. USNR 1955-57. Mem. NAM (mktg. com. 1967-70), Nat. Alliance Businessmen (metro chmn. 1970-71), Newcomen Soc. N.Am., Chattanooga C. of C. (dir. 1971-74), Sigma Alpha Epsilon. Presbyterian. Clubs: Rotary; Sea Island (Ga.) Cottage; Capital City. Home: 3655 Randall Hall NW Atlanta GA 30327

HEFLIN, HOWELL THOMAS, U.S. senator, former chief justice Supreme Ct. Ala.; b. Poulan, Ga., June 19, 1921; s. Marvin Rutledge and Louise D. (Strudwick) H.; A.B., Birmingham Sc. Coll., 1942; J.D., U. Ala., 1948; LL.D. (hon.), U. No. Ala.; m. Elizabeth Ann Carmichael, Feb. 23, 1952; 1 son, Howell Thomas. Admitted to Ala. bar, 1948, practiced in Tuscumbia; mem. firm Heflin, Rosser and Munsey; chief justice Supreme Ct. Ala., 1971-77; chmn. Nat. Conf. Chief Justices, 1976-77; U.S. senator from Ala., 1979—. Bd. dirs. Meth. Pub. House, 1952-64; lectr. U. Ala., 1946-48; lectr. Florence State Tchrs. Coll., 1949-52; Tazewell Taylor vis. prof. law Coll. William and Mary, 1977. Mem. Ala. Edn. Commn., 1957-58; chmn. Colbert County A.R.C., 1950; Ala. field dir. Crusade for Children, 1948; pres. Ala. Com. Better Schs., 1958-59; chmn. Tuscumbia Bd. Edn., 1954-64; chmn. Ala. Tenure Commn., 1959-64; pres. U. Ala. Law Sch. Found., 1964-66; co-chmn. Nat. Conf. Christians and Jews, Tri-Cities area; chmn. Brotherhood Week. Bd. dirs., v.p. Nat. Center for State Cts.; hon. pres. Troy State U. Served to maj. USMCR, 1942-46. Decorated Silver Star, Purple Heart; recipient Ala. Citizen of Yr. award Ala. Cable TV Assn., 1973; Outstanding Alumnus award U. Ala. and Birmingham So. Coll., 1973; Herbert Lincoln Harley award Am. Judicature Soc., 1973; Ala. Citizen of Year award Ala. Broadcasters Assn., 1975; mem. Ala. Acad. Honor; named Outstanding Appellate Judge in U.S., Assn. Trial Lawyers Am., 1976; recipient Highest award Am. Judges Assn., 1975. Fellow Internat. Acad. of Law and Scis., Internat. Acad. Trial Lawyers, Internat. Soc. Barristers, Am. Coll. Trial Lawyers; mem. Ala. Law Inst. (v.p.), Am., Ala. (pres. 1965-66), Colbert County (past pres.) bar assns., Ala. Bar Found. (past pres.), Am. Judicature Soc. (v.p.), Ala. Law Sch. Alumni Assn. (past pres.), Ala. Plaintiff Lawyers Assn. (past pres.), V.F.W., Am. Legion, 40 and 8, D.A.V., Third Marine Div. Assn., C. of C., Omicron Delta Kappa, Phi Delta Phi, Tau Kappa Alpha, Lambda Chi Alpha. Methodist. Office: Dirksen Senate Office Bldg Rm 3203 Washington DC 20510*

HEFNER, W.G. (BILL), congressman; b. Elora, Tenn., Apr. 11, 1930; s. Emory James and Icie Jewel (Holderfield) H.; grad. high sch.; m. Nancy Louise Hill, Mar. 23, 1952; children—Stacye Hugh, Shelly Gay. Congressman from 8th N.C. dist.; pres. WRKB Radio Sta., Kannapolis, N.C. Democrat. Optimist. Office: Room 328 Cannon House Office Bldg Washington DC 20515

HEGAR, KATHRYN NADINE (WEIGE), educator; b. Holland, Tex., Mar. 13, 1938; d. Lessie William and Laura Ester (Koonsen) Weige; B.B.A., N. Tex. State U., 1962, M.B.E., 1964, Ph.D., 1977; m. Henry Wallace Hegar, Nov. 9, 1960; children—Sonya Michelle, Jill Andrea. Various secretarial and acctg. assignments Tex. Hwy. Dept., Austin, 1956-57, Ft. Worth, 1957-59; office mgr. Allied Fence Co., Temple, Tex., 1959; sec., office asst. Kelly Girl Service, Dallas, 1960; instr. bus. El Centro Coll., Dallas, 1966-70, Mountain View Coll., Dallas, 1970—; partner H & A Cons. Assos., 1978—; condr. supervisory workshops for pvt. bus. firms, 1969—; cons. in bus. edn., 1969—. Vol. worker CARIH, asthma assn., 1966-78, Juvenile Diabetes Assn., 1977—; Sunday sch. tchr. Walnut Hill Lutheran Ch., 1964-66, Bible sch. tchr., 1965, sec. to congregation, 1964-65. Named Goodwill Ambassador for State of Tex., 1978; recipient Hon. Cert., Seneca Coll., Toronto, Ont., Can., 1978. Mem. Nat. Bus. Edn. Assn., Tex. Bus. Edn. Assn. (Coll. Tchr. of Year Dist. X, 1980, also for State of Tex. 1980), Mountain-Plains Bus. Edn. Assn., Southwestern Mktg. Assn., Internat. Soc. Bus. Edn., Internat. Congress for Individualized Instrn., Tex. Jr. Coll. Tchrs. Assn., Phi Delta Kappa, Delta Pi Epsilon. Author: Study Guide for It's Everybody's Business, 1975, 77, 79; (telecourse) It's Everybody's Business, 1975; Understanding Business Today: A Study Guide, 1980; Course Management in Individualized Instruction, 1978; contbr. chpt.: Faculty Personnel Adminstration in Higher Education: A Systems Approach, 1977. Home: 13220 Shahan Dr Dallas TX 75234 Office: 4849 W Illinois Ave Dallas TX 75211

HEGSTROM, WILLIAM JEAN, educator; b. Macomb, Ill., Oct. 21, 1923; s. Carl William and Thelma (Canavit) H.; student Western Ill. U., 1941-42; B. Sc., Rutgers U., 1949, Ed.M. 1952; M.A. Teaching, Purdue U., 1964; postgrad. U. Fla., 1961, Fla. Atlantic U., 1965-68; Ed.D., U. Miami, 1971; m. Grace Ann Paladino, May 3, 1944; children—Elizabeth Louise (Mrs. Edward Cook), William Jean II, Jean. Tchr. jr. high sch., South Plainfield, N.J., 1949-52, high sch., Bernardsville, N.J. 1952-54, Oak St. Sch., Bernard's Twp., N.J., 1954-55, high sch., Summit, N.J., 1955-58, jr. high sch., Delray Beach, Fla, 1958-65; chmn. math. dept. John I. Leonard High Sch., Lake Worth, Fla., 1965-68, dir. Palm Beach County research project, 1966-68; adj. prof. Fla. Atlantic U., 1965-69, asso. prof., 1969-70; counselor coordinator John Leonard Adult Center, Lake Worth, 1965-68; supr. research and evaluation Palm Beach County Sch. Bd., West Palm Beach, Fla., 1970-74; now math. tchr. Boca Raton (Fla.) High Sch. Served with USAAF, 1942-46. Mem. AAUP, NEA, Nat. Council Tchrs. Math., Math. Assn. Am., Fla. Ednl. Research Assn., Am. Ednl. Research Assn., Phi Delta Kappa. Contbr. articles to profl. jours. Home: 225 NE 22d St Delray Beach FL 33444 Office: Boca Raton Community High Sch Boca Raton FL 33432

HEHN, MERLIN DALE, educator; b. Scotland, S.D., Aug. 1, 1935; s. Rueben H. and Lula C. (Fisher) H.; B.S. with honors, U. So. Miss., 1977, M.S., 1979; m. Eloise Ann Fuentus, Mar. 31, 1957; children—Terry Lee, Debra Ann, Betty Jean, Elizabeth Ann. Enlisted in U.S. Air Force, 1954, ret., 1974; faculty Jones County Jr. Coll., Ellisville, Miss., 1974—, chmn. div. tech. edn., instr. electronics tech., 1974—. Mem. Miss. Assn. Tech. Edn. (pres. 1979—), NEA, Miss. Assn. Educators, Am. Tech. Edn. Assn., Am. Vocat. Assn., Nat. Assn. Tchrs. Electronics, Nat. Assn. Instructional Leaders in Tech. Edn., Vocat. Indsl. Club Am., C. of C. Democrat. Roman Catholic. Club: Rotary (dir. 1976-77, sec. 1977-79). Home: PO Box 296 Ellisville MS 39437 Office: Jones County Jr Coll Ellisville MS 39437

HEIBERG, HAROLD WILLARD, musician; b. Minn., Feb. 6, 1922; s. Andreas Severin and Gerda Clarissa (Olson) H.; Mus.B., St. Olaf Coll., 1943; M.A., Columbia U., 1949; m. Eva Margrethe Lundberg, Sept., 1957. Organist-choirmaster Our Saviour's Luth. Ch., Bklyn., 1947-49, East Cleveland Congl. Ch., 1954-56, Trinity Luth. Ch., Bklyn., 1956-71. Orchestral, ensemble and solo piano recitalist, Western Europe, U.S., 1948—; asso. prof. vocal coaching and accompanying North Tex. State U., 1971—; mem. faculty Cleve. Music Sch. Settlement, 1952-56, N.Y. Theol. Sem., 1959-68, Am. Inst. Mus. Studies Summer Vocal Inst., Graz, Austria, 1970—; workshop condr. in field; ofcl. accompanist Opera Am. auditions, Ann. J.B. Dealey Awards, Dallas. Served with Signal Corps, U.S. Army, 1943-45. Recipient Distinguished Alumnus award St. Olaf Coll., 1974. Mem. Music Tchrs. Nat. Assn., Tex. Music Tchrs. Assn., Pi Kappa Lambda. Lutheran. Translator opera: Il Prigioniero (Dallapiccola), 1951; translator numerous choral work and art song texts, including: Laud to the Nativity (Respighi), 1958, Stabat Mater (Poulenc), 1958, Songs of Nature (Dvorak), 1952, Execution of Stepan Razin (Shostakovich), 1968. Home: 2111 N Locust St Denton TX 76201 Office: Sch of Music North Tex State U Denton TX 76203

HEIDBRINK, VIRGIL EUGENE, paper co. exec.; b. Ireton, Ia., Dec. 4, 1925; s. Edward H. and Luella (Dittmer) H.; A.B., U.S.D., 1949; B.F.T., Am. Inst. Fgn. Trade, 1950; postgrad. Hunter Coll., 1952-53, Coll. City N.Y., 1953-54, N.Y. U. Grad. Sch. Bus., 1954-56. Export asst. fgn. trade, various firms, N.Y.C., 1951-56; with Hammermill Paper Co., Erie, Pa., 1956, Chgo., 1956-57, dist. sales mgr. SW ter., Dallas, 1958—. Del. Tex. Republican Conv., 1964, 70, 72, 74, precinct chmn. Served with Med. Dept., AUS, 1944-46, 50-51. Decorated Bronze Star. Mem. Dallas Advt. League, Dallas Club Printing House Craftsmen (sec. 1976-77), Dallas Council on World Affairs, Alianza Cultural de Artes y Letras de Mexico, Internat. Good Neighbor Council, Internat. Trade Assn. Dallas, Dallas Fgn. Visitors Bur., Phi Beta Kappa. Lutheran. Clubs: Toastmasters (pres. 1965, dist. gov. 1968-69), Brookhollow Rotary. Home: 2623 Hudnall St Dallas TX 75235 Office: 1545 W Mockingbird Ln Suite 5038 Dallas TX 75235

HEIDEMAN, DALE H., govt. ofcl.; b. Owosso, Mich., Mar. 15, 1946; s. Harold Burdette and Olive Aldine (Hatfield) H.; B.S. in Police Sci., Mich. State U., 1968; m. Barbara Jean Murrow, Dec. 27, 1968. Crime lab. analyst Fla. Dept. Law Enforcement, Tallahassee, 1968-76, crime lab. supr., Sanford, Fla., 1976-77, crime lab. supr., 1977—; mem. Nat. Forensic Microscopy Workshop Steering Com., 1978-79. Active Boy Scouts Am. Mem. Am. Acad. Forensic Scis., Am. Soc. Crime Lab. Dirs., Assn. Ofcl. Analytical Chemists, ASTM, So. Assn. Forensic Scientists. Methodist. Clubs: U.S. Power Squadron (Past comdr.), St. Mary's Yacht. Home: 7482 Hanging Vine Way Tallahassee FL 32301 Office: 420 N Adams St Tallahassee FL 32301

HEIDEMANN, CLARA DAISY WUEST, tourist industry exec.; b. Newkirk, N.Mex.; d. Hillard Joseph and Clara Catherine (Oebel) Wolfe; student Alamo City Bus. Coll., 1934-36, San Antonio Coll., 1964; m. Hilmar Wuest, June 16, 1937 (dec. 1956); children—Reginald Dennis, Trudy Carol Wuest Soechting; m. 2d, Harry Heidemann, Jan. 21, 1961. Mgr., Clara Wuest Ranch, Natural Bridge Caverns, Tex., 1956-74; pres., gen. mgr., treas., gift shop buyer Natural Bridge Caverns, Inc. (Tex.), 1964—; supt. in charge Natural Bridge Caverns Rural Br. Post Office, 1969—. Dir. tourism chpt. Tex.-Mex. Internat. Good Neighbor Council; 1st pres. Faith Circle of First Protestant Faith Ch., New Braunfels, Tex. Recipient Human Relations award Dale Carnegie, 1958; cert. of appreciation City Council San Antonio, 1978; named Outstanding Range Conservationist of Comal County, Comal County Farm Bur., 1960. Mem. Nat. Caves Assn. (regional dir. 1966-71, pres. 1971-73, chmn. bd. 1973-74, cave cons. 1965—), Discover Tex. Assn. (dir. 1971-74), Discover Am. Travel Orgn. (com. mem. nat. council travel attractions), Nat. Tour Brokers Assn., Nat. Speleogical Soc., Roadside Bus. Assn., Hotel Sales Mgmt. Assn., New Braunfels C. of C., Am. Luth. Ch. Women. Lutheran. Author Tex. cavern conservation law, 1977. Home and Office: Route 3 PO Box 515 Natural Bridge Caverns TX 78218

HEIDT, GARY ALLEN, educator; b. South Bend, Ind., May 20, 1942; s. Vernice W. and Doris B. H.; student Rose Poly. Inst., 1960-61; B.S., Manchester Coll., 1964; M.S., Mich. State U., 1968, Ph.D., 1969: m. Robin G. Goslee, Mar. 6, 1976; children—Deborah, Scott, Nora, Brian. Asst. prof. Mich. State U., 1969-70; asst. prof. biology U. Ark., Little Rock, 1970-74, asso. prof., 1974-79, prof., 1979—, dir. basic animal service unit, 1974—; cons. in field. Trustee Little Rock Mus. Sci. and History, 1973-79, pres., 1974-75, v.p., 1976-77; bd. dirs. Friends of Zoo, 1975-77; mem. Ark. Endangered Species Tech. Com., 1976—. Mem. Am. Soc. Mammalogists, Southwestern Assn. Naturalists, Wildlife Soc., Ecol. Soc. Am., Am. Assn. Lab. Animal Sci. (pres. Ark. chpt. 1978-79), Ark. Acad. Sci. (editor 1977—). Presbyterian. Home: 12106 Teton Forest St Little Rock AR 72212 Office: Dept Biology U Ark at Little Rock 33d and University St Little Rock AR 72204

HEILMAN, EARL BRUCE, univ. pres.; b. La Grange, Ky., July 16, 1926; s. Earl Bernard and Nellie (Sanders) H.; diploma Campbellsville Jr. Coll., 1948; B.S., Peabody Coll., 1950, M.A., 1951, Ph.D., 1961; postgrad. U. Tenn., 1951-52, U. Omaha, summers 1953, 55, U. Ky., summers 1954, 56, LL.D., Wake Forest U., 1967; H.H.D., Campbell Coll., 1971; m. Betty June Dobbins, Aug. 27, 1948; children—Bobbie Lynn, Nancy Jo, Terry Lee, Sandra June, Timothy Bruce. Instr. bus. Peabody Coll., Nashville, 1950-51, bursar, 1957-60, adminstrv. v.p., 1963-66; instr. accounting Belmont Coll., Nashville, 1951-52; auditor Albert Maloney Co., Nashville, 1951-52; asst. prof. accounting, bus. mgr. Ky. Wesleyan Coll., Owensboro, 1952-54; treas. Georgetown (Ky.) Coll., 1954-57; treas. housing project City of Louisville, 1955-57; coordinator higher edn. and spl. schs. State of Tenn., Nashville, 1960-61; v.p. dean Ky. So. Coll., Louisville, 1961-63; pres. Meredith Coll., Raleigh, N.C., 1966-71, U. Richmond (Va.), 1971—. Dir., Central Fidelity Bank, N.A., Fidelity Bankers Life Ins. Co., A.H. Robins Co. Cons. instl. studies in edn. and adminstrn., 1954—; dir., cons. long range planning confs. Fund for Advancement Edn., 1960—; cons. Acad. Ednl. Devel., 1966—. Mem. steering com. Baptist Ednl. Study Task. Bd. advisers Bapt. Hosp. Sch. Nursing, 1959-60, 64—; mem. adv. bd. Richmond Ballet, Marine Mil. Acad.; bd. dirs. Bill Wilkerson Speech, Hearing Center, Richmond Symphony, United Givers Fund. Served with USMCR, 1944-47. Recipient Merit award Owensboro Jr. C. of C., 1953, Service award Agrl. and Industry U. Nashville, 1961. Mem. Nat. Fedn. Bus. Officers, Nat. Fedn. Bus. Officers Cons. Service, So. Assn. Colls. for Women (pres. 1970), Tenn. Edn. Assn., Ky. Ednl. Buyers Assn., Ky. Assn. Acad. Deans, Peabody Alumni Assn. (exec. com.), Nat., So. assns. colls. and univs. bus. officers, N.C. Assn. Colls. and Univs. (pres.-elect), Internat. Platform Assn., Richmond C. of C. (dir.), Richmond Council Year 2000, Phi Beta Kappa, Pi Omega Pi, Kappa Phi Kappa, Kappa Delta Pi, Omicron Delta Kappa, Beta Gamma Sigma, Lambda Chi Alpha, Delta Pi Epsilon. Democrat. Baptist (deacon). Rotarian. Club: Downtown (Richmond). Author: (with others) Sixty College Study, 1954. Contbr. articles to profl. publs. Developer uniform financial accounting and reporting program for Tenn. instns. higher edn. Home: 7000 River Rd Richmond VA 23229 Office: Office of Pres U Richmond Richmond VA 23173

HEIMANN, KERMIT HARRY, supt. schs.; b. Fredericksburg, Tex., Mar. 10, 1935; s. Harry Otto and Rubie Bertha (Danz) H.; B.S., Tex. A&M U., 1961; M.Ed., S.W. Tex. State U., 1964; postgrad. U. Tex., 1964-68; m. Antonette Meta Hartmann, Oct. 31, 1954; children—Jeffrey, Debra, Brenda. Coach, tchr. sci. Spring Branch High Sch., Houston, 1961-62, Seguin (Tex.) High Sch., 1962-64; tchr. S.F. Austin High Sch., Austin, Tex., 1964-65, prin., 1975; tchr., coach Reagan High Sch., Austin, 1965-67, dean, 1968-70; asst. prin. Webb Jr. High Sch., Austin, 1970-71; prin. Lamar Jr. High Sch., Austin, 1971-74; supt. schs. Pflugerville (Tex.) Ind. Sch. Dist., 1975—; mem. bd. Travis County Coop. Coordinating Com. for Adult Edn. First aid and water safety instr. ARC, 1960-70. Served with USAF, 1954-58. Mem. Nat. Assn. Supervision and Curriculum Devel., Nat. Assn. Profl. Educators, Tex. Assn. Supervision and Curriculum Devel., Tex. Assn. Sch. Adminstrs., Tex. PTA (life), U.S. Tennis Assn., Tex. Tennis Assn., Am. Security Council, Phi Kappa Phi. Lutheran. Home: 11404 Indian Head Dr Austin TX 78753 Office: Pflugerville Ind Sch Dist PO Box 778 Pflugerville TX 78660

HEIN, PAUL RICHARD, chem. co. exec.; b. N.Y.C., May 16, 1941; s. Paul G. and Mary (Litauer) H.; B.S. in Chemistry, Bklyn. Poly. Inst., 1963; M.S. in Chemistry, Stevens Inst. Tech., 1968; 1 child, Alyson Gene. Research chemist Inmont Corp., Clifton, N.J., 1964-68; group leader Nopco Chem. div. Diamond Shamrock Co., Harrison, N.J., 1968-70; research and devel. mgr. W.R. Grace Co., Atlanta, 1970—. Mem. Am. Chem. Soc., Soc. Photog. Scientists and Engrs., Flexographic Trade Assn., Am. Pub. Health Assn., Inter-Am. Photochem. Soc., Am. Assn. Textile Chemists and Colorists, Zool. Soc. Atlanta. Patentee in field. Office: W R Grace Co 5210 Philip Lee Dr Atlanta GA 30336

HEINE, LARRY LITTLETON, bank mgmt. cons.; b. Ft. Wayne, Ind., Oct. 19, 1938; s. Elwood Littleton and Mary Ruth (Logue) H.; student Ind. U., 1957-59, Millikin U., 1961; m. Lorraine F. St. George, Dec. 19, 1969; children—Timmothy, Tammera L. Dist. mgr. Comml. Credit Corp., Ft. Wayne, 1962-66; loan officer Ind. Bank & Trust Co., Ft. Wayne, 1966-67; pres. Howard J. Blender Co., Dallas, 1967-74, Larry Heine & Assos., Inc., Dallas, 1975—; cons. cost control programs. Home: 3406 Town Bluff Plano TX 75075 Office: 312 N Central Suite 219 Dallas TX 75080

HEINEMANN, SOL, urologist; b. Jenkes, Okla., Dec. 17, 1914; s. Charles and Hattie (Heinemann) Brasch; B.S., U. Ark., 1935; M.D., U. Tenn., 1939; M.S., St. Louis U., 1950; m. Katherine Arnstein, July 8, 1950; 1 dau., Katherine Heinemann Taucher. Intern, John Gaston Hosp., Memphis, 1939-41; resident in urology St. Mary's Group Hosps., St. Louis U., 1948-50; practice medicine specializing in urology, St. Louis, 1950-55, Carlsbad, N.Mex., 1955-60, El Paso, Tex., 1960—; mem. staff Providence Meml. Hosp., chief of staff, 1965; mem. staff Hotel Dieu Sisters Hosp., Sun Towers Hosp., Sierra Med. Center; cons. urology Ft. Bayard (N.Mex.) VA Hosp., 1958-65. Bd. dirs. Carlsbad chpt. ARC; mem. El Paso Drive-A-Meal Council, 1965-66, El Paso County Bd. Devel., 1962-64. Served with M.C., AUS, 1941-45. Diplomate Am. Bd. Urology. Fellow A.C.S.; mem. AMA, AM., S. Central urol. assns., Tex. Med. Assn., N.Mex., El Paso County med. socs., Am. Soc. Archeology, El Paso Archeol. Soc. (pres. 1971-72), Soc. Am. Archaeology. Jewish. Club: Rotary (dir. 1965-66, v.p. 1968-69). Contbr. articles to med. and archeol. jours. Home: 4252 Ridgecrest Dr El Paso TX 79902 Office: 1900 N Oregon St El Paso TX 79902

HEINS, JAMES EDWARD, telephone co. exec.; b. Lee County, N.C., Nov. 17, 1930; s. Max Thomas and Eunice (Blue) H.; B.S. in Bus. Adminstrn., U. N.C., 1953, M.B.A., 1959; m. Carroll Butts, July 9, 1960; children—James Edward, Cooper Corinne. Sales rep. Anaconda Wire & Cable Co., 1959-60; product mgr. Whitney Blake Co., 1960-63; exec. v.p. Heins Telephone Co., Sanford, N.C., 1963-71, pres., 1971—; dir., mem. exec. com. Carolina Bank, Sanford; active in formation and devel. N.C. Sch. Telephone, Sanford; commr. N.C. Agy. Public Telecommunications. Past chmn. bd. dirs. and chmn. fund raising com. N.C. Heart Assn.; past chmn. Sanford community guidance com. N.C. Dept. Corrections; mem. Lee County Recreation Commn., 1964-68, chmn., 1970-76; pres. Lee County Young Democratic Club, 1964-65; bd. dirs. N.C. Citizens Assn.; deacon, mem. planning council 1st Presbyn. Ch., Sanford. Served with U.S. Army, 1955-56. Named Young Man of Yr., Sanford Jaycees, 1964, Sanford Citizen of Yr., Sanford Herald, 1977. Mem. U.S. Ind. Telephone Assn. (pres. 1979-80, chmn. advt. and public relations com. 1975-79), N.C. Ind. Telephone Assn. (dir., pres. 1969-70), Sanford C. of C. (pres. 1967), R.R. House Hist. Assn. (pres. 1968-69). Club: Sanford Rotary. Home: 1906 Windmill Dr Sanford NC 27330 Office: 106 Gordon St PO Box 1209 Sanford NC 27330

HEINTGES, JOHN ARNOLD, JR., real estate co. exec.; b. Manila, Philippines, Sept. 6, 1938 (parents Am. citizens); s. John Arnold and Betty L. (Lovejoy) H.; B.S. in Civil Engring., U.S. Mil. Acad., 1961; m. Mary Kay Holmes, Nov. 22, 1971; 1 son, Milton Paul. Ops. dir. Klingbeil Mgmt. Co., Columbus, Ohio, 1972-74; property mgr. Daniel Investment Co., Dallas, 1974-75; v.p. Murray Mgmt. Corp., Dallas, 1974-79; pres. Asset Property Mgmt. Corp., Dallas, 1979—; tchr. Sch. Continuing Edn., So. Meth. U. Served with inf. U.S. Army, 1955-56, 61-62. Mem. Nat. Assn. Home Builders, Home and Apt. Builders Assn., Nat. Apt. Council, Nat. Apt. Assn. (dir.), Tex. Apt. Assn. (dir.), Dallas Bd. Realtors, Dallas Apt. Assn. (v.p., dir.). Republican. Presbyterian. Office: 4230 LBJ Suite 104 Dallas TX 75234

HEISERMAN, ALBERTA ELIZABETH NARDI, educator; b. Balt., Oct. 6, 1931; d. Albert Alfred and Teresa Josephine (Crimy) Nardi; R.N., Sinai Hosp., Balt., 1952; B.S., Okla. State U., 1959, M.S., 1978; postgrad. spl. edn. Syracuse U., 1955, McCoy Coll., 1955, Leslie Coll., 1971-72; m. Russell Lee Heiserman, Aug. 19, 1956; children—Scott, Alan, Christa. Nurse, Sinai Hosp., Balt., 1952-54, Okla. State U. Infirmary, 1956-58; tchr. spl. edn., Balt., 1955-56; phys. edn. tchr. St. Mary's Sch., Winchester, Mass., 1968-69; spl. edn. tchr. trainable, Winchester, 1970-74; graphic arts aide Sheltered Workshop, Stillwater, Okla., 1974-75; Title VI B spl. edn. tchr. Stillwater Schs., 1975-76; Title I resource tchr. Oilton Schs., Okla., 1976-77; tchr. spl. edn. of pre-sch. multi-handicapped Cushing (Okla.) Schs., 1977—, supervising tchr. E.C.I. Coop., 1978—. Bd. dirs. Rayne County Sheltered Workshop, 1980. Registered nurse, Okla.; cert. tchr. visually handicapped, physically handicapped, learning disabilities and mental retardation, elem. sch. Democrat. Roman Catholic. Home: Box 42F Route 1 Stillwater OK 74074 Office: Wilson School 1140 E Cherry St Cushing OK 74023

HEISLER, WILLIAM JOHN, educator; b. Livingston Manor, N.Y., Dec. 28, 1942; s. William A. and Fay M. (Sherwood) H.; B.M.E., Union Coll. (N.Y.), 1964; B.S. in Mgmt., U. Ark., 1969; M.B.A., Syracuse U., 1970, Ph.D., 1972; m. Patricia Elaine Novak, Sept. 1, 1963; children—Jamie Leigh, John Daniel. Mech. design engr. Pa. Power & Light Co., Allentown, 1964; instr. Sch. Mgmt., Syracuse (N.Y.) U., 1970-71, asst. to dir. M.B.A. program, 1971-72; asst. prof. mgmt. U. Notre Dame, 1972-76; asso. prof. mgmt. Babcock Grad. Sch. Mgmt., Wake Forest U., Winston-Salem, N.C., 1976—, dir. M.B.A. exec. program, 1978—; cons. numerous bus., govtl., non-profit orgns., 1972—. Served with USAF, 1965-69. U. Notre Dame Faculty grantee, 1973, 75; AACSB-Fed. Faculty fellow, 1974; S&H Found. lectr., 1975. Mem. Am. Psychol. Assn., So. Mgmt. Assn., Acad. Mgmt. Democrat. Presbyterian. Contbr. articles on mgmt. to profl. jours.; editor books. Home: 4931 Lombardy Ln Winston-Salem NC 27103 Office: Babcock Grad Sch Mgmt Wake Forest U Winston-Salem NC 27109

HEITZMAN, HARRY BRADLEY, physician; b. Biloxi, Miss., Oct. 26, 1943; s. Harry McMillan and Shirley Ann (Redding) H.; A.S., Miss. Gulf Coast Jr. Coll., 1963; B.S., U. Miss., 1965, M.D., 1969; m. Vivian Ann McNair, Dec. 23, 1965; children—Brandy Alesia, Hunter McMillan. Intern, Roanoke (Va.) Meml. Hosp., 1969-70; resident U. Hosp. Jackson, Miss., 1973; internist Coastal Med. Center, Biloxi, Miss., 1973-75, Gulf Coast Surg. and Diagnostic Center, Ocean Springs, Miss., 1975—, also dir.; pres., chmn. bd. Community Home Health Nursing Service; chief medicine Ocean Springs Hosp., 1976, 78—. Mem. Miss. Thoracic Soc. Republican. Episcopalian. Home: 3405 Nottingham Rd Ocean Springs MS 39564 Office: Medical Plaza Van Cleave Rd Ocean Springs MS 34564

HEJTMANCIK, MILTON RUDOLPH, physician, educator; b. Caldwell, Tex., Sept. 27, 1919; s. Rudolph Joseph and Millie (Jurcak) H.; B.A., U. Tex., 1939, M.D., 1943;; m. Myrtle Lou Erwin, Aug. 21, 1943 (dec. June 1975); children—Kelly Erwin, Milton Rudolph, Peggy Lou; m. 2d, Myrtle M. Granberry, Nov. 27, 1976. Resident internal medicine U. Tex., 1946-49, instr. internal medicine, 1949-51, asst. prof. internal medicine, 1951-54, asso. prof. internal medicine, 1954-65, prof. internal medicine, 1965—, dir. heart clinic, 1949—, dir. heart station, 1965—; chief staff John Sealy Hosp., 1957-58; chief staff U. Tex. Med. Br. Hosps., 1977-79. Served from 1st lt. to capt. M.C., AUS, 1944-46, ETO. Diplomate in cardiovascular diseases Am. Bd. Internal Medicine. Fellow A.C.P., Am. College Chest Physicians, Am. Coll. Cardiology; mem. Am. (fellow council clin. cardiology), Tex. (chmn. med. and sci. com. 1976-78, pres. 1979-80), Galveston Dist. (pres. 1956) heart assns., AMA (Billings Gold medal 1973), Am. Fedn. Clin. Research, AAAS, Tex. Acad. Internal Medicine (gov. 1971-73, pres. 1976), Tex. Club Cardiology (pres. 1972-73), Tex. (del. 1972-79), Galveston County (pres. 1971) med. assns., N.Y. Acad. Sci., AAUP, Phi Beta Kappa, Sigma Xi, Alpha Omega Alpha, Phi Eta Sigma, Mu Delta. Contbr. numerous papers on cardiovascular disease to profl. jours. Home: 118 Marlin St Galveston TX 77550 Office: U Tex Med Br Galveston TX 77550

HELBLING, GILES HAROLD, income tax and bookkeeping service co. exec.; b. Fort Smith, Ark., Sept. 22, 1932; s. Emil Felix and Esther H.; student Westark Jr. Coll., 1960-65; m. N. Susan Atchley, Aug. 30, 1968; children—Paul David, John Daniel. Pres., chief operating officer Amtax Corp., Fort Smith, 1969—. Ch. tng. dir. Oak Cliff Baptist Ch., 1978—. Served with U.S. Army, 1950-54. Mem. Nat. Assn. Tax Consultors. Republican. Club: Flightmasters. Home: 5200 Poplar St Fort Smith AR 72904 Office: 2310 N B St Fort Smith AR 72901

HELD, BEREL, obstetrician, gynecologist; b. Bklyn., Dec. 31, 1938; s. David and Rose (Sternberg) H.; student Hamilton Coll., 1958; M.D., Tulane U., 1962; m. Linda Prager, June 18, 1962; children—Lawrence, Theodore, Kenneth, Karla. Rotating intern Charity Hosp. of La., New Orleans, 1962-63; jr. asst. resident dept. obstetrics and gynecology Boston City Hosp., 1965-66, sr. asst. resident, 1966-67, chief resident, 1967-68; teaching fellow dept. obstetrics and gynecology Harvard U.-Tufts U.-Boston U., 1967-68; asst. prof. dept. obstetrics and gynecology Coll. Medicine, U. Fla., Gainesville, 1972, asso. prof., 1972; prof., chmn. dept. obstetrics and gynecology Med. Sch., U. Tex., Houston, 1972—; mem. staff Hermann Hosp., M.D. Anderson Hosp. and Tumor Inst. Served to capt. MC, USAF, 1963-65. Diplomate Am. Bd. Obstetrics and Gynecology. Fellow Am. Coll. Obstetricians and Gynecologists; mem. Am. Assn. Planned Parenthood Physicians, AMA, Assn. Profs. of Gynecology and Obstetrics, So. Perinatal Assn., Tex. Med. Assn., Harris County Med. Soc., Houston Surg. Soc., Houston Gynecol. and Obstet. Soc., Tex. Assn. Obstetricians and Gynecologists. Jewish. Home: 818 Chowning Rd Houston TX 77024 Office: Obstetrics/Gynecology U Tex Med Sch at Houston 6431 Fannin St Houston TX 77030

HELD, EDWARD CARLISLE, JR., oil co. exec.; b. Okmulgee, Okla., Nov. 15, 1925; s. Edward Carlisle and Caroline (Mills) H.; B.S. in Chem. Engring., U. Okla., 1950; m. Latita Ann Wittmer, June 17, 1944; children—Steven Edward, John David, Jennifer Held Knode, Karen Held Daniel. Refinery product blend chemist Phillips Petroleum Co., Kansas City, Kan., 1950-53, process evaluation supr. rocket fuels div., Waco, Tex., 1954-58, tech. service engr. plastics, Bartlesville, Okla., 1958-64, supr. new plastic fabrication techniques, 1964-68, mgmt. cons. exec. dept., 1969—. Vice chmn. profl. devel. and staffing Bartlesville Edn. Council, 1972, local govt. and finance com. Bartlesville Goals Study, 1974-75. Served with AUS, 1943-46. Registered profl. engr., Okla. Mem. Soc. Plastics Engrs. Presbyn. Contbr. articles to profl. jours. Patentee in field. Home: 2200 Parkway Dr Bartlesville OK 74003 Office: Phillips Petroleum Co Bartlesville OK 74004

HELDMAN, JULIUS DAVID, oil and chem. co. exec.; b. Cleve., May 9, 1919; s. Nathan and Lottie (Weisberg) H.; B.A., UCLA, 1939, M.A., 1940; Ph.D. in Chemistry, Stanford U., 1942; m. Gladys Vivian Medalie, June 15, 1942; children—Carrie Medalie, Julie Medalie. Instr. chemistry U. Calif., Berkeley, 1943-44; with Shell Oil Co., 1945—, v.p. Shell Devel. Co., Houston, 1969—; dir. SES, Inc.; mem. U.S. Com. for World Petroleum Congresses. Woodrow Wilson vis. fellow, 1978-79, 79-80. Mem. Am. Petroleum Inst., Am. Chem. Soc., Am. Inst. Chem. Engrs., AAAS, Nat. Assn. Mfrs., Houston Solar Energy Soc., Internat. Photochemistry Soc., Indsl. Research Inst. Clubs: Houston, Univ., Met. Racquet, Houston Racquet. Home: 109 Timberwilde Ln Houston TX 77024 Office: PO Box 2463 Houston TX 77001

HELGANZ, BEVERLY BUZHARDT, telephone co. exec.; b. Tampa, Fla., June 7, 1941; d. M. Owain and Virginia Jeanne Myers (Crabb) Buzhardt; B.A., Jacksonville U., 1974; m. Charles F. Helganz, Jr., June 26, 1964 (dec.). Operator, So. Bell Telephone and Telegraph Co., Jacksonville, Fla., 1959-63, assignment clk., 1963-64, service rep., 1964-66, bus. office supr., tng. supr., 1966-76, employee relations supr., 1977-78, staff supr. equal employment opportunity, 1978-79, asst. mgr. real estate, 1979—. Mem. Am. Bus. Women's Assn. (past pres.), Jacksonville U. Alumni Assn., Jacksonville Alumnae Panhellenic Assn. (rec. sec.), Beta Sigma Phi (past pres.), Zeta Tau Alpha (past pres., dist. pres.). Methodist. Home: 5000 San Jose Blvd Apt 77 Jacksonville FL 32207

HELGESON, NORMAN GORDON PHELPS, pathologist; b. Mpls., Jan. 6, 1931; s. Gail Phelps and Jean Margaret (Spiers) H.; B.A., U. Minn., 1952; M.S., U. Wis., 1958, M.D., 1961; m. Mary Louise Hammer, Sept. 25, 1964; children—Sara Louise, Matthew Gail Phelps. Intern, Receiving Hosp., Detroit, 1961-62; resident in pathology Mass. Gen. Hosp., Boston, 1962-66; pathologist Baylor U. Med. Center, Dallas, 1966—, dir. clin. pathology, 1969—, asso. dir. labs., 1971—; pathologist Gaston Episcopal Hosp., Dallas, 1966—, George J. Race and Assos., Dallas, 1966—; cons. clin. pathology Dallas Med. and Surg. Clinic, 1969—; prof. Baylor Coll. Dentistry, Dallas, U. Tex. Health Sci. Center, Dallas; adj. prof. biology So. Methodist U., Dallas. Diplomate Nat. Bd. Med. Examiners, Am. Bd. Pathology. Fellow Am. Soc. Clin. Pathologists, Coll. Am. Pathologists; mem. Acad. Clin. Lab. Physicians, Scientists, AMA, Am. Soc. Microbiology, Am. Soc. Cytology. Club: Lakewood Country. Author: (with others) A Review of Microbiology, 1976. Asso. editor for microbiology Laboratory Medicine, 1975—. Home: 6725 Avalon Ave Dallas TX 75214 Office: Baylor University Medical Center Dallas TX 75246

HELLAMS, CHARLES HOWARD, advt. exec.; b. Greenville, S.C., Sept. 12, 1941; s. Charles Edwin and Daisy Catherine (Smith) H.; A.B., U. S.C., 1963; m. Brenda Joyce Williams, Aug. 17, 1963; children—Paige Elizabeth, Charles Harper. News editor The State daily, Columbia, S.C., 1962-64; asst. dir. advt. S.C. Devel. Bd., Columbia, 1964-67; pres. Harper, Hellams & Paige, Inc., Columbia, 1967—; adj. prof. advt. U. S.C., 1974-77. Bd. dirs. Indian Waters council Boy Scouts Am., 1977-79. Recipient Addy awards (45) Am. Advt. Fedn., also Andy awards (15); Advt. Club N.Y., Clio award, 1979, 80; N.Y. Soc. Illustrators award, 1978; Internat. Broadcasting award Hollywood Radio and TV Soc., 1979. Mem. Columbia Advt. Club (pres. 1978), Columbia Communicating Arts Soc. (pres. 1977), Am. Advt. Fedn., Advt. Club N.Y., Am. Inst. Graphic Arts, Sigma Delta Chi. Presbyterian. Club: The Summit. Home: 6509 Olde Knight Pky Columbia SC 29209 Office: PO Box 50425 Columbia SC 29250

HELLER, BARBARA JANE, ret. educator; b. Abilene, Kans., July 17, 1924; d. Samuel Raymond and Dorothy (Tanke) Heller; student Kans. State U., 1942-44; B.A., U. Kans., 1946; M.A., Columbia, 1947, Ed.D., 1955. Asst. prof. Ohio State U., Columbus, 1947-53, Sam Houston State U., Huntsville, Tex., 1954-57; chmn. women's phys. edn. St. Stephen's Episcopal Sch., Austin, Tex., 1957-60; asst. prof. U. Calif. at Davis, 1960-64, supr., 1965-73, ref., 1973, faculty research fellow, 1964, summer research grantee, 1963, also adviser and supr. student tchrs. phys. edn., 1970-73; prof. emergency med. tech. Daytona Beach (Fla.) Community Coll., 1973—, prof. criminal justice program, 1977-78. Adviser community health and biol. scis., 1965—. Bd. dirs. Yolo County ARC; v.p. Volusia County Mental Health Assn.; pres. Volusia County Drug Council; v.p. Volusia County Women's Republican Club. Recipient resolution Calif. Senate. Mem. Am., Calif. (del. to advisers com. to Calif. State Dept. Pub. Sch. Health 1970-73, v.p., chmn. health div., 1971-72) assn. health, phys. edn. and recreation, Am. Pub. Health Assn., Nat. Assn. Phys. Edn. for Coll. Women, Am. Coll. Quill Club, Calif. Accreditation Com., USCG Aux. (career candidate officer), Kappa Delta Pi, Pi Lambda Theta, Kappa Kappa Gamma. Republican. Episcopalian. Home: 3869 S Atlantic Ave Daytona Beach FL 32019 Office: Dept Applied Sci Daytona Beach Community Coll Volusia Ave Daytona Beach FL 32014

HELLER, GEORGE LOUIS, chem. engr.; b. Albany, N.Y., Dec. 5, 1908; s. Frederick Louis and Christine Catherine (Dorn) H.; Ch.E., Rensselaer Poly. Inst., 1931, M.Ch.E., 1933; m. Marguerite Rose Hoffman, Oct. 12, 1935; children—Richard L., Robert G., Frederick L., George E., Thomas P. Asst. bridge engr. D&H R.R., 1929-30; air conditioning and heating engr. M.W. Co., 1931-32; dir. research Gen. Atlas Carbon Co., Pampa, Tex., 1933-41; dir. devel. Cities Service Co., Monroe, La., 1941-74, ret., 1974; cons. engring. to carbon black industry, Monroe, La., 1974—. Mem. bishop's adv. com. Roman Catholic Diocese of Alexandria, 1948-52; chmn. bldg. com. Our Lady of Fatima Parish, Monroe, 1951-77. Recipient Tech. Achievement award State of La., 1974, Outstanding Creativity award Cities Service Co., 1973. Mem. Am. Chem. Soc. (life; chmn. 1935-39), Am. Inst. Chem. Engrs. (life; chmn. 1952-54), Nat. Soc. Profl. Engrs., La. Engring. Soc. (life; chmn. 1970-71), Sigma Xi (life). Club: K.C. (Order of Merit 1977). Contbr. articles to profl. jours., bulls.; U.S. fgn. patentee in field. Home and Office: 4710 Bon Aire Dr Monroe LA 71203

HELLER, PEARL BAILIE (MRS. RAYMOND J. HELLER), manpower cons.; b. Turtle Creek, Pa., Aug. 12, 1918; d. John Langfitt and Hannah (Boord) Bailie; B.S., Columbia U., 1949, M.A., 1950; R.N., Mt. Sinai Hosp., N.Y.C., 1943; m. Raymond J. Heller, Apr. 9, 1955. Supr. surg. wards Mt. Sinai Hosp., 1946-48; rehab. counselor Queensboro (N.Y.) Tb and Health Assn., 1950-54; program dir. Hartman Area Neighborhood Centers Assn., Houston, 1954-63, asst. to city program dir., 1963-67; now pvt. practice as manpower cons., program specialist; instr. creative writing St. Luke's Sch. Continuing Edn. Bd. dirs., treas. Neighborhood Ednl. Center; bd. dirs., mem. personnel com., treas. Sickle Cell Disease Research Found. Tex., 1976—; bd. dirs. Forty Plus of Houston, 1978. Mem. AAUW (dir., chmn. pub. info. com. 1972-74), Nat. Assn. Social Workers, Acad. Certified Social Workers Author: An Outreach Demonstration, 1967; (with Malcolm S. Host) Day Care Administration, 1971. Home: 4106 Tennyson Houston TX 77005

HELLING, SUSAN GAIL, retail mgr.; b. Rochester, N.Y., Apr. 6, 1940; d. Francis Stanley and Helen Shirley (Keeler) DeVoy; student Simmons Coll., 1958-59, Rochester Inst. Tech., 1959-62; children—Stephen R., Kenneth S. With E.W. Edwards, Sibley Lindsey & Curr, Rochester, 1957-61, J.C. Penney Co., Rochester, 1964-70; with M.C. Topps Co., Ruskin, Fla., 1977—, retail buyer, store mgr., 77-78, supr. 5 stores, 1978—. Named M.C. Topps Mgr. of Year, 1978. Mem. Am. Assn. Bus. Women (v.p. 1979—), Nat. Retail Mcht. Assn., S. Hillsborough C. of C. Republican. Baptist. Home: 705 1st Ave NE Ruskin FL 33570 Office: PO Box 158 Ruskin FL 33570

HELM, BOYD EDWARD, cardiologist; b. New Orleans, Jan. 28, 1942; s. James Boyd and Helen (Friloux) H.; B.S., Loyola U. of South, 1964; M.D., La. State U., 1967; m. Barbara Mahoney, July 2, 1966; children—Shannon, Boyd, Eric. Intern, Charity Hosp. La., New Orleans, 1967-68, resident in internal medicine, 1968-71: NIH fellow in cardiology U. Tenn., 1973-75; cons. cardiologist, invasive cardiologist Cardilogy Clinic, Baton Rouge, 1975—; practice medicine specializing in cardiology, Baton Rouge, 1975—; mem. staff Baton Rouge Hosp., Our Lady of Luke Hosp., Drs. Hosp.; mem. teaching staff U. Tenn., 1973-75, E.K. Long Hosp., 1975. Tchr., advisor Mended Heart Assn., 1977—; bd. dirs. Am. Heart Assn. La. Served to lt. comdr. USN, 1971-73. Cancer Assn. grantee, 1962-63; Am. Heart Assn. grantee, 1964. Fellow Am. Heart Assn., Am. Coll. Cardiology, Am. Coll. Chest Physicians; mem. AMA, La. Med. Assn., East Baton Rouge Parish Med. Soc., So. Med. Soc. Republican. Roman Catholic. Club: K.C. Office: 4045 North Blvd Baton Rouge LA 70806

HELM, DEWITT FREDERICK, JR., consumer products co. exec.; b. Charlotte, N.C., Apr. 24 1933; s. DeWitt F. and Blanche Buchanan (DeBusk) H.; B.S. in History, Davidson Coll., 1956; m. Mary McNair Jones, Oct. 5, 1957; children—DeWitt Frederick III, Mary McNair. Advt. mgr. Vick Chem. Co., N.Y.C., 1956-63; consumer products mgr. labs. div. Pfizer, Inc., N.Y.C., 1963-66; mgr. consumer product devel. A.H. Robins Co., 1966-69; exec. v.p. Miller-Morton Co., Richmond, Va., 1969-72, pres., 1972—, also dir.; v.p. Miller-Morton Co. of Can. Ltd., 1969-72, pres., 1972—. Mem. exec. com. trustees council Union Theol Sem. Va., 1975-77; bd. dirs. Nat. Tobacco Festival, 1977—; deacon, elder Presbyterian Ch. Served to 1st lt. U.S. Army, 1956-58. Mem. Proprietary Assn. (dir. 1975—, mem. public relations com. 1970-71, spl. com. on drug abuse 1971-72, chmn. exec. com. 1973-75), Cosmetic, Toiletry and Fragrance Assn. (dir. 1977—), Young Pres.'s Assn., N.C. Soc. N.Y., Omicron Delta Kappa, Davidson Coll. Nat. Alumni Assn. (v.p. 1974-75). Clubs: Hermitage Country, Bull and Bear (Richmond); Wintergreen (Va.). Home: 2503 Kensington Ave Richmond VA 23220 Office: 2007 N Hamilton St Richmond VA 23230

HELM, HUGH BARNETT, judge; b. Bowling Green, Ky., Dec. 27, 1914; s. Hugh Barnett and Ermine (Cox) H.; B.A., Vanderbilt U., 1935, postgrad. law sch., 1936-37, 52-53, Stanford U., 1953-56; m. Vivian Loreen Downing, June 5, 1943; children—Beverly, Hugh B. III, Nathaniel Henry. Admitted to Ky. bar, 1938, Tenn. bar, 1938, U.S. Supreme Ct. bar, 1942; atty. Trade Practice Conf., FTC, Washington, 1938-42; asso. counsel U.S. Internat. Prosecution Sect. G.H.Q., SCAP, Tokyo, Japan, 1946; practiced in Nashville, 1946-53; bond specialist Swett & Crawford, San Francisco, 1956-57; resident mgr. Totten & Co., San Francisco, 1958, v.p. gen. mgr., 1959-60; sr. trial atty. Bur. Restraint of Trade, FTC, Washington, 1961-66, chief div. of advisory opinions, 1966-70, acting dir. Bur. Industry Guidance, 1969-70, atty. adviser FTC Bur. Consumer Claims, until 1971; adminstrv. law judge Bur. Hearing and Appeals, Social Security Adminstrn., HEW, Chattanooga, 1971-73, adminstrv. law judge charge Western Ky. and So. Ill., Paducah, Ky., 1973-76, Louisville, 1976-78; adminstrv. law judge in charge Miami (Fla.) office Hearings and Appeals, 1979—; mem. regional jud. council Social Security Adminstrn. Pres. Surety Claims Assn. No. Calif., 1957-58. Mem. Tenn. Ho. of Reps., 1949-50. Served with inf. USAAF, 1941-45; served to capt. U.S. Army, 1950-52. Decorated Bronze Star, Combat Infantry Badge; recipient Founders medal for oratory Vanderbilt U., 1935, Distinguished Service Commendation FTC, 1969. Mem. Am. (com. on civil service law), Ky., Tenn. bar assns., Am. Acad. Polit. and Social Sci., Am. Acad. Polit. Sci., Nat. Lawyers Club, Pi Sigma Alpha, Tau Kappa Alpha. Presbyterian (deacon). Club: Jefferson. Home: 23301 Lago Mar Circle Boca Raton FL 33433 Office: 150 SE 2d Ave 4th Floor Miami FL 33131

HELME, JAMES BUCKELEW, physician; b. Port Chester, N.Y., Apr. 27, 1924; s. James Buckelew and Mary DeHaven (Van Deren) H.; grad. Choate Sch., 1942; A.B., Princeton U., 1947; M.D., U. Wash., 1952; m. Josephine Coleman Douglas, May 22, 1953 (div. Sept. 1974); children—Susan Van Deren, Catherine Douglas, Martha Buckelew, John Franklin. Intern, Kings County Hosp., Bklyn., 1952-53; intern Johns Hopkins Hosp., 1953-54, resident, 1954-55; resident Vanderbilt U. Hosp., Nashville, 1955-56; practice medicine, specializing in pediatrics, Nashville, 1956-68; instr. pediatrics and community health Meharry Med. Coll., 1968-71; pediatrician Davidson County Health Dept., 1971-72; med. dir. Nashville Drug Treatment Center, 1972-78, Tenn. State Prison and Hosp., 1978—; chief pediatrics service Nashville Gen. Hosp., 1956-60. Cons., Tenn. Fine Arts Commn., 1968-70. Pres. Nashville Arts Council, 1963-65; bd. dirs. Tenn. Fine Arts Mus., 1963-65, Theatre Nashville Mgmt., 1973-74. Served to 1st lt. USMCR, 1943-45. Mem. Nashville Acad. Medicine, Tenn. Med. Assn., Tenn., Davidson County pediatric socs., Am. Philatelic Soc. (expert com. and writers unit), Middle Tenn. Princeton Alumni Assn. (pres. 1962-65). Clubs: Princeton, Collectors (N.Y.C.); Colonial (Princeton). Contbr. to The Yucatan Affair, 1974. Home: 3704 Estes Rd Nashville TN 37215 Office: Station A West Nashville TN 37203

HELMS, JESSE U.S. senator; b. Monroe, N.C., Oct. 18, 1921; s. Jesse A. and Ethel Mae (Helms) H.; student Wingate Jr. Coll., 1936-37, Wake Forest Coll., 1937-40; LL.D., Bob Jones U., Greenville, S.C.; m. Dorothy Jane Coble, Oct. 31, 1942; children—Jane (Mrs. Charles R. Knox), Nancy (Mrs. John C. Stuart), Charles. City editor Raleigh (N.C.) Times, 1945-46; adminstrv. asst. to N.C. senators Smith and Lennon, Washington, 1951-53; exec. dir. N.C. Bankers Assn., Raleigh, 1953-60; exec. v.p., vice chmn. bd., asst. chief exec. officer Sta. WRAL-TV, Sta. WRAL-FM and Tobacco Radio Network, Raleigh, 1960-72; U.S. senator from N.C., 1973—, asst. minority whip, mem. Fgn. Relations com. Mem. Raleigh City Council, 1957-61, chmn. law and finance com., 1957-61. Bd. dirs. N.C. Cerebral Palsy Hosp., United Cerebral Palsy N.C., Wake County Cerebral Palsy and Rehab. Center, Raleigh; founder, bd. dirs. Camp Willow Run, Littleton, N.C.; trustee Meredith Coll., John F. Kennedy Coll., Campbell Coll., Wingate Coll. Recipient Freedoms Found. award, 1962, 73; So. Bapt. Nat. Award, 1972; awards V.F.W., 1970, Am. Legion, 1971, Raleigh Exchange Club, 1971; Golden Gavel award, 1973, 74; Man of the Year award Women for Const/Govt.,

1978. Baptist (deacon, Sunday sch. tchr.). Clubs: Rotary (past pres.), Raleigh Execs. (past pres.), Masons. Editor, Tarheel Banker, 1953-60; author newspaper, radio, TV editorials, 1960-72. Office: Dirksen Office Bldg Washington DC 20510

HELMS, JOHN BENJAMIN, furniture accessories mfg. co. exec.; b. Monroe, N.C., June 18, 1946; s. Lester Lee and Mary Emiline (Smith) H.; B.S. in Bus. Adminstrn., U. N.C., Chapel Hill, 1968, postgrad. Young Execs. Inst., 1973; postgrad. small co. mgmt. Harvard U., 1980; m. Anne Bonnell Rushing, July 17, 1976; 1 son, Paul Christopher. With MaLeck Industries, Inc., Wingate, N.C., 1968—, exec. v.p. ops., 1973-75, pres., chief exec. officer, 1975—; dir. N.C. Nat. Bank, Monroe; instr. Mgmt. Devel. Inst., U. N.C., Chapel Hill; del. White House Conf. Small Bus., 1980. Mem. United Community Services Social Planning Council; v.p. Central N.C. council Boy Scouts Am.; adv. bd. Wingate Elem. Sch. and Career Center; bd. overseers, bus. com. Wingate Coll. Mem. USAR, 1968-74. Recipient Silver Beaver award Boy Scouts Am., 1978. Mem. Pres.'s Assn., Am. Mgmt. Assn., N.C. Citizens Assn., U. N.C. Chapel Hill Alumni Assn., Charlotte Sales and Mktg. Execs., Mensa, Phi Kappa Sigma. Clubs: Rotary; Lake Norman (N.C.) Yacht. Home: PO Box 305 Wingate NC 28174 Office: PO Box 247 Wingate NC 28174

HELMS, NANCY ANNE EDDINS, guidance counselor; b. Rockingham, N.C., Feb. 12, 1937; d. Edward Birch and Hettie Pearl (Smith) Eddins; student Eastern Carolina U., 1956-57; A.B., Coll. William and Mary, 1959, M.Ed., 1972, advanced cert., 1980; m. Billy Charles Helms, Dec. 25, 1956; children—Kyle Edward, Kendell Craig. Social studies tchr. Newport News (Va.) Sch. System, 1959-72, counselor, 1972-79, dir. guidance Dozier Intermediate Sch., 1975—; cons. tchr. advisor program; tchr., trainer Tchr. and Parent Effectiveness Tng. Mem. City Planning Com. for Youth, 1977. Mem. Va. Personnel and Guidance Assn. (sec.), Peninsula Personnel and Guidance Assn. (Outstanding Chpt. mem. 1978, past pres.), Am. Personnel and Guidance Assn. (cert.), Va. Assn. Specialists in Group Work, Va. Vocat. Guidance Assn., Delta Kappa Gamma, Kappa Delta Pi. Democrat. Baptist. Home: 112 Three Point Ct Yorktown VA 23692 Office: 432 Industrial Park Dr Newport News VA 23602

HELTON, GERALD, human resource specialist; b. Carrollton, Ga., Jan. 25, 1949; s. Leamon and Laura Mae (Kirby) H.; B.A. (scholar), Morehouse Coll., 1970; M.A., U. Chgo., 1975; m. Carol Ann Norton, Jan. 25, 1979. Social work psychology specialist U.S. Army, Ft. Bragg, N.C., 1970-73; psychiat. nursing asst. U. Chgo., Billings Hosp., 1973-75; manpower counseling supr. City of Atlanta CETA Program, 1976-77; human resource specialist Forest Service, U.S. Dept. Agr., Atlanta, 1977—. Vice chmn. bd. dirs. West End Community Health Center, 1979—. Served with U.S. Army, 1970-73. Mem. NAACP, Am. Mgmt. Assn. Methodist. Home: 476 Larchmont Circle NW Atlanta GA 30318 Office: 1720 Peachtree Rd NW Suite 712 Atlanta GA 30309

HELTON, JOSEPH EARL, educator; b. St. Louis, Jan. 21, 1925; s. Carl and Ruth Winifred (Williams) H.; B.S. in C.E., So. Meth. U., 1950; m. Betty Jane Stalcup, Dec. 20, 1948; children—Beverly Karen, Stephen Carl, Dwight Robert, Joseph Earl. Civil engr. Arabian Am. Oil Co., Dhahran, Saudi Arabia, 1951-60; sr. field rep. Am. Plywood Assn., Ft. Worth, 1960-76; master instr. Tex. State Tech. Inst., Waco, 1976—; cons. structural engring. Served with USN, 1942-46. Decorated Bronze Star; registered profl. engr., Tex.; registered land surveyor; cert. bldg. insp., So. Bldg. Code Congress. Mem. Tex. Soc. Profl. Engrs., ASCE. Democrat. Baptist. Club: McClennan County Chess. Author: Estimating Principles and Techniques. Inventor modified spacer clip. Home: 210 Carswell St Waco TX 76705 Office: TSTI Jas Connally Campus Bldg 4-6 Waco TX 76705

HELTON, WILLIAM LEGRAND, supt. schs.; b. Washington County, Va., May 22, 1936; B.A. cum laude, Emory and Henry Coll., 1961; M.A., U. Md., 1968, Ph.D., 1975; m. Cynthia Dalton, Apr. 26, 1970; children—Mollie Monecia, William LeGrand. Tchr., Lancaster (Va.) High Sch., 1961-63, Graham Park Jr. High Sch., Dumfries, Va., 1963-65; asst. prin. Rippon Jr. High Sch., Woodbridge, Va., 1966-68; supr. social studies and staff devel. Prince William Schs., Manassas, Va., 1968-73, supr. community relations, 1973-74, adminstrv. asst. to supt., 1974-75, dir. instructional services, 1975-76, asso. supt. sch. services, 1976-77, div. supt. schs., 1977—. Bd. dirs. Prince William United Way Campaign, 1977-79, Prince William Heart Assn., 1977—. Served with USAF, 1954-58. Mem. Prince William Edn. Assn. (pres. 1966), Orgn. Am. Historians, History of Edn. Soc., Am. Assn. Sch. Adminstrs., Prince William Assn. Sch. Execs. (pres. 1973), Am. Hist. Assn., Phi Delta Kappa, Sigma Mu. Episcopalian. Club: Lions. Home: PO Box 281 Woodbridge VA 22194 Office: Prince William County Schs PO Box 389 Manassas VA 22110

HELVESTON, WILFRED CAROL, county ofcl.; b. Mobile, Ala., Dec. 26, 1926; s. Henry Phillip and Lula Rona (Ball) H.; student U. Ala., 1953-54, Spring Hill Coll., 1954-57; m. Ethel Mae Mead, Oct. 31, 1947; children—Bonnie (Mrs. Donald Frisch), Ronald. Various clerical positions Louisville & Nashville R.R., 1942-61, 62-69; adminstrv. asst. Mobile City Commn., 1961-62; dep. adminstr. Mobile County, 1969-71, adminstr., 1971—. Loaned exec. Mobile County United Fund, 1962; shelter mgr. Mobile County CD; charter mem., past v.p. Mobile County Civic Speakers Bur.; past exec. bd., chmn. speakers bur., chmn. membership com. Mobile County Mental Health Assn. Past pres. Mobile County Young Democrats. Mem. Spring Hill Coll. Alumni Assn., Toastmasters Internat. (past pres. Port City, past pub. relations chmn. dist. 29). Mason (Shriner). Home: 2605 Venaro Ct Mobile AL 36609 Office: PO Box 1443 Mobile AL 36601

HELVIE, CARL O., nurse, educator; b. Gouverneur, N.Y., Aug. 13, 1932; s. Charles A. and Georgia (Forrest) H.; R.N., St. Lawrence State Hosp. Sch. Nursing, Ogdensburg, N.Y., 1954; B.S., N.Y. U., 1958; M.S., U. Calif. at San Francisco, 1961; M.P.H., Johns Hopkins, 1966, Dr. P.H., 1969. Staff nurse Monroe County (N.Y.) Hosp., Rochester, 1954-55; staff nurse Bellevue Hosp., N.Y.C., 1955-56, head nurse, 1956-58; staff pub. health nurse Oakland (Calif.) Health Dept., 1958-59; staff pub. health nurse San Francisco Health Dept., 1959-60; instr. U. Calif. at San Francisco, 1961-65; research asso. pub. health Johns Hopkins, 1968-69; asso. prof. Duke U., 1969-72; prof. Old Dominion U., Norfolk, Va., 1972—, acting chmn. dept. nursing, 1972-73. Named Eminent Scholar Old Dominion U., 1974-75. Mem. Am., Va. nurses' assns., Nat., Va. leagues for nursing, Internat. Platform Assn., Am. Pub. Health Assn. Author: Self Assessment of Current Knowledge in Community Health Nursing, 1975; Community Health Nursing, Theory and Process, 1980; contbr. articles to profl. publs. Home: 421 Lake Dr Virginia Beach VA 23451 Office: Old Dominion U Hampton Blvd Norfolk VA 23508

HELWIG, FREDERICK WILLIAM, govt. ofcl.; b. Burlington, N.C., Apr. 8, 1942; s. Lewis Lloyd and Mabel Helen H.; B.A., U. South Fla., 1963; M. Comml. Sci., Rollins Coll., 1970; m. Victoria Ann Duncan, July 13, 1971; 1 son, Duncan. Contract negotiator U.S. Air Force, Warner Robins, Ga., 1964-66, U.S. Navy, Orlando, Fla., 1966-74; procurement analyst U.S. Army, Petersburg, Va., 1974-77, contract specialist, Orlando, 1977-79; head research and gen. procurement br. U.S. Naval Tng. Equipment Center, Orlando, 1979—; adj. instr. contract mgmt. courses, masters degree program Fla. Inst. Tech., Melbourne. Registered real estate broker Fla. Dept. Profl. Regulation. Mem. Nat. Contract Mgmt. Assn. (award 1975, cert. profl. contract mgr.), Air Force Assn., Res. Officers Assn., Phi Kappa Phi. Methodist. Home: 1250 Alexa Dr Winter Park FL 32789 Office: Naval Tng Equipment Center Code N-62 Orlando FL 32813

HEMBREE, HUGH LAWSON, III, holding co. exec.; b. Ft. Smith, Ark., Nov. 16, 1931; s. Raymond N. and Gladys (Newman) H.; B.S. in Bus. Adminstrn., U. Ark., 1953, LL.B., 1958; m. Sara Janelle Young, Sept. 1, 1956; children—Hugh Lawson IV, Raymond Scott. In middle mgmt. Ark.-Best Freight System, Inc., Ft. Smith, 1958-61; dir. finance 1961-65, v.p., 1965-67; pres., dir. Ark.-Best Corp., Ft. Smith, 1967-73, dir., 1973—; chmn. bd. CEO, 1973—; pres. Sugar Hill Farms, Inc., Ft. Smith, 1962—; dir. Nat. Bank of Commerce, Dallas, 1968—; Riverside Furniture Corp., Mid-Am. Industries, Merchants Nat. Bank, First Fed. Savs. and Loan Assn. (all Ft. Smith), Scheduled Skyways Airlines, Fayetteville, Ark.; nat. adv. bd. Comml. Nat. Bank of Little Rock. Pres., Westark Area council Boy Scouts Am., 1966-67, mem. nat. council, mem. regional exec. bd., 1967—, chmn. regional sustaining membership com., 1974-75, U.S. staff mem. World Boy Scout Jamboree, Norway, 1975; treas. Endowment Trust Fund, U. Ark., bd. dirs., mem. dean's adv. com. Sch. Bus., 1969-73; chmn. bd. devel. St. Edward Community Med. Center, 1972-73. Sec., Ft. Smith-Sebastian County Joint Planning Commn., 1959-72; mem. Ark. Legislative Tax Study Commn., 1969; pres. Sebastian County Mental Health Assn., 1964. Justice of peace Sebastian County, 1959—; mem. Ark. Democratic Central Com., 1968—. Bd. dirs. Jr. Achievement of Ft. Smith, Coalition for Rural Am., 1971, Ark. Council on Econ. Edn., 1964—; chmn. Ark.-Okla. Edn. and Livestock Found., 1974—; trustee Hendrix Coll.; chmn. bd. trustees St. Edwards Mercy Med. Center, 1970—; mem. Ark. Bd. Higher Edn., 1975—. Served to 1st lt. USAF, 1953-55. Recipient Silver Beaver, Silver Antelope awards Boy Scouts Am., Distinguished Service award Ft. Smith Jr. C. of C., 1965, Leadership award State of Ark., 1970, Distinguished Alumni award U. Ark., 1977; named Ark. Outstanding Young Man of Year, 1965. Mem. Nat. Assn. Devel. Orgns. (chmn. adv. com.), Ark. (v.p. 1969-73, pres. 1973-75, chmn. bd. 1976—), Ft. Smith (pres., dir. 1970-73) chambers commerce, Young Pres.'s Orgn., U. Ark. Alumni Assn. (dir., bldg. com.), Am. Trucking Assn. (nat. accounting and finance council), NAM (nat. dir. 1971-74), Ark. Arts Center, Delta Theta Phi, Sigma Alpha Epsilon. Episcopalian (vestryman, co-chmn. ch. fin. com.). Mason (32 deg.). Clubs: Chapperell, Lancers, Economics (Dallas); Town, Fianna Hills Country, Ft. Smith Hardscrabble Country (Ft. Smith); Capital (Little Rock); N.Y. Athletic; Presidents (dir.) (Hendrix Coll., Conway, Ark.). Home: 3220 Park Ave Fort Smith AR 72901 Office: 1000 S 21st St Fort Smith AR 72901

HEMBREE, OSCAR ELI, JR., civil-hydraulic engr.; b. Porum, Okla., Jan. 23, 1926; s. Oscar Eli and Clara Effie (Seney) H.; A.A., Muskogee Jr. Coll., 1950; B.B.A., U. Okla., 1955; m. Lillie Irene Pitts, Sept. 3, 1948; children—DiAnne Kaye, Clara Evelyn. Coll. trainee Skelly Oil Co., Oklahoma City, 1955-56; dispatcher, Okla. Miss. River Products Pipeline, Inc., Tulsa, 1956-59; civil-hydraulic engr. U.S. Dept. Energy, Southwestern Power Adminstrn., Tulsa, 1959—. Mem. adv. bd. Internat. Order Rainbow for Girls, 1974-75. Served with USNR, 1944-46; PTO. Recipient Certificate of Merit awards Southwestern Power Adminstrn., 1965, 71, 72, 73, 77. Mem. Am. Legion, Am. Mil. Engrs., Soc. of Petroleum Engrs. of Am. Inst. Mining Engrs., Engrs. Soc. Tulsa, U. Okla. Alumni Assn. (life). Baptist. Mason (32 deg.). Home: 8242 E 114th St S Bixby OK 74008 Office: PO Drawer 1619 Tulsa OK 74101

HEMMER, JOHN LEE, JR., orthopedic surgeon; b. Oak Ridge, Dec. 24, 1945; s. John Lee and Dorothy Hill H.; B.S., N. Ga. Coll., 1967; M.D., Med. Coll. Ga., 1971; m. Jane Reynolds, Aug. 31, 1968; children—John Lee III, Mary Reynolds. Intern, William Beaumont Gen. Hosp., El Paso, Tex., 1971-72; resident in orthopedics Greenville (S.C.) Hosp. System and Shriner Hosp., 1974-77; practice medicine specializing in orthopedic surgery, Gainesville, Ga., 1977—; mem. staffs Northeast Ga. Med. Center, Lanier Park Hosp. Served as capt. M.C., U.S. Army, 1971-74. Certified Am. Acad. Orthopedic Surgery. Mem. AMA, Med. Assn. Ga., Hall County Med. Soc. Presbyterian. Club: Kiwanis. Home: White Sulphur Farm Route 10 Airline Rd Gainesville GA 30501 Office: 710 Broad St Gainesville GA 30501

HEMNESS, RAY LESLIE, hosp. adminstr.; b. Milltown, Wis., Oct. 28, 1926; s. Louis H. and Maria (Ruud) H.; B.C.S., Strayer Coll., 1948; m. Peggy Ann Sims, Feb. 14, 1947; 1 dau., Deborah Kay. Treas., Standard Engring. Co., Washington, 1956-61; asst. adminstr. No. Va. Doctors Hosp., Arlington, 1961-62, adminstr., dir., 1962—, sec., 1970—, exec. v.p., 1977—; sec. Va. Doctors Properties, Arlington, 1969—; dir. Seven Corners Med. Bldgs., Inc., Falls Church, Va., 1962-71. Chpt. chmn. ARC, Arlington, 1967-70, now bd. dirs.; bd. dirs. No. Va. Heart Assn. Mem. Internat. Underwater Explorers Soc., C. of C. Arlington (v.p. 1980). Mason (32 deg.), Rotarian (pres. Arlington 1976-77). Home: 3027 Hazelton St Falls Church VA 22044 Office: 601 S Carlyn Springs Rd Arlington VA 22204

HENAULT, RICHARD ALAN, hosp. adminstr.; b. Providence, Mar. 18, 1948; s. Nora Anne H.; B.S., U. R.I., 1970; M.P.H., Tulane U., 1974. Adminstrv. resident Ochsner Found. Hosp., New Orleans, 1973-74, asst. adminstrn., 1974-76, asst. hosp. dir., 1976-78; asso. hosp. dir., 1978—; asst. prof. grad. program health adminstrn. U. Ala., 1977—. Mem. exec. com. bd. dirs. New Orlanes Blood Bank. USPHS grantee, 1972-74. Mem. Am. Coll. Hosp. Adminstrs., Am. Hosp. Assn., New Health Care Mgrs. Assn. (pres.), La. Hosp. Assn., C. of C., Carrollton Businessmen's Assn., New Orleans Met. Bus. Orgn. Roman Catholic. Office: 1516 Jefferson Hwy New Orleans LA 70118

HENCK, MARTHA MCCOLLUM, legal adminstr.; b. Hartford, Conn., Sept. 13, 1923; d. Charles Adelbert and Elsie (Bemont) McCollum; B.A., Rice U., 1944; m. Frederick Seymour Henck, July 3, 1944; children—Charles Seymour, Frederick Hollister, Douglas Curry. Office mgr., bookkeeper Continental Investment Corp., Atlanta, 1961-66; acct. Smith, Currie & Hancock, attys., Atlanta, 1966-68; adminstr. Weil, Gotshal & Manges, N.Y.C., 1968-73, Kilpatrick & Cody, Atlanta, 1973—; cons. Ga. State Bar Services Coms., Atlanta Bar Secretarial Placement Com. Mem. Assn. Legal Adminstrs. (past pres. Atlanta chpt., regional v.p.), Am. Soc. Personnel Adminstrn. Episcopalian. Home: 1041 N Jamestown Rd Apt G Decatur GA 30033 Office: 3100 Equitable Bldg 100 Peachtree St Atlanta GA 30303

HENDERSHOTT, CHARLES HENRY, JR., educator; b. Marked Tree, Ark., Oct. 13, 1923; s. Charles Henry and Bertya Mae (Scott) H.; B.S.A., U. Ark., Fayetteville, 1951, M.S., 1952; Ph.D., N.C. State U., 1959; m. Ollie Virginia Layne, May 5, 1944 (div. Feb. 1960); children—Charles Larry, David Lynn, Carol Ann Hendershott Hallack, Ronald Wayne, Barbara Kay Hendershott Neal; m. 2d, Mary Edith Young, June 24, 1960. Asst. prof. agr. U. Ark., 1952-57; asst. prof. Fla. Citrus Commn., Lake Alfred, 1959-63, asso. prof. 1963-64; asso. prof. U. Fla., 1964-67, prof., 1967—; head dept. hort. U. Ga., Athens, 1967-75, prof. hort., 1975—; cons., research adv. Agrl. Expt. Sta., Aguadulce, Panama, 1954-57. Served with AUS, 1942-46; MTO, ETO, PTO. AID grantee, 1969-70, 70-71, 71-72. Mem. Am. Soc. Hort. Sci. (Gourley award for Outstanding Paper 1955), Am. Soc. Plant Physiologists, Am. Inst. Biol. Sci., Sigma Xi, Gamma Sigma Delta, Alpha Zeta. Contbr. articles to profl. jours.

HENDERSON, ARNOLD GLENN, architect; b. Shawnee, Okla., Nov. 10, 1934; s. Henry Glenn and Pearlalee H.; B.Arch., U. Okla., 1961; B.S. in Archtl. Engring., 1961; M.S. Arch., Columbia U., 1964; children from previous marriage—Eric Neal, Alex Jon. Asst. prof. architecture U. Ill., Urbana, 1964-68; asso. prof. U. Okla., Norman, 1968-73, prof., 1973—; pvt. archtl. practice, Norman, 1975—. Chmn., Norman Housing Authority 1972-77; co-chmn. Norman Community Devel. Steering Com., 1974; mem. Hist. Preservation Commn. Guthrie (Okla.), 1979—. Served with AUS, 1953-55. Grantee NSF, Nat. Endowment Arts, AIA. Mem. AIA, Soc. Archtl. Historians, Sigma Tau. Democrat. Presbyterian. Recipient award excellence AIA Okla., 1976. Author: Document for an Anonymous Indian, 1974; The Surgeon General's Collection, 1976; (with others) Architecture in Oklahoma, 1978. Home: 1208 Barkley Ave Norman OK 73071 Office: Sch Arch U Okla Norman OK 73019

HENDERSON, BRADFORD WILLIAM, mgmt. cons., lectr.; b. Detroit, July 28, 1941; s. Ernest W. and Mildred (Wickham) H.; B.S. in Math., Central Mich. U., 1966; M.B.A. in Indsl. Mgmt., U. Oreg., 1967; m. Margery Mae Gill, Nov. 30, 1963; children—Cherie, Brent. Civil engr. Postiff Co., Detroit, 1960-66; cost analyst Ford Motor Co., San Jose, Calif., 1967-69, cons. world hdqrs., Detroit, 1969-71; gen. mgr. systems div. Otid Elevator Co., Cleve., 1971-74; mgr. cons. group Arthur Young & Co., Dallas, 1974-78, Alexander Grant & Co., Dallas, 1978—. Mem. Am. Inst. Indsl. Engrs., Am. Prodn. and Inventory Control Soc., Project Mgmt. Inst. Methodist. Home: 9140 Whitehurst Dallas TX 75243 Office: 1800 One Dallas Centre Dallas TX 75250

HENDERSON, CLARENCE SYLVESTER, ins. agt.; b. Bronx, N.Y., Dec. 31, 1948; s. David Lee and Roxie H.; B.B.A., Tex. So. U., 1976; second year diploma Underwriting Tng. Council, 1978; m. Vinez Singletary, June 17, 1972; 1 son, Curtis. Combination agt. Golden State Mut. Life Ins. Co., Houston, 1971-73, 75—; life agt. Bankers Life & Casualty, Houston, 1973; pres. Hend's Ins. Agy.; Salesman Highams Cadillac/Rolls Royce, 1980—. Asst. Democratic precinct del., 1977. Recipient Million Dollar Round Table award Golden State Mut. Life Ins. Co., 1977; Skipper's award Bankers Life & Casualty Co., 1973. Mem. Nat. Assn. Life Underwriters, U.S. Jr. C. of C. Mem. Ch. of God in Christ. Home and Office: 15610 Golden Eagle Humble TX 77338

HENDERSON, COLIN MAXWELL, banker; b. San Mateo, Calif., Oct. 21, 1948; s. Emanuel and Stella Maris (Lapraik) H.; B.B.A., U. Tex., Arlington, 1975; postgrad. So. Meth. U., 1977-79; m. Cynthia Taylor, Sept. 2, 1967; children—Laurie Gayle, Jeffrey Colin. Trust officer Nat. Bank Commerce, Dallas, 1968-73; asst. v.p. Bank Okla., Tulsa, 1973-75; v.p. Fourth Nat. Bank, Tulsa, 1976—; mem. faculty Sch. Bank Adminstrn., U. Wis., 1978—. Bd. dirs. Mohawk Nature Center Devel., Inc., Tulsa, Tulsa Speech and Hearing Assn.; treas. N.E. Tulsa Soccer Assn. Mem. Am. Bankers Assn., Okla. Bankers Assn. (vice chmn. ops. com. 1978-79). Roman Catholic. Club: Meadowbrook Country (Tulsa). Home: 7518 E 55th Pl Tulsa OK 74145 Office: 515 S Boulder St Tulsa OK 74103

HENDERSON, DARRELL LANE, surgeon; b. Selmer, Tenn., May 28, 1936; s. Roy Wilson and Annie Lee (Beadle) H.; M.D., U. Tenn., 1959; m. Peggie Mize, Dec. 20, 1959; children—Deborah Lee, Darrell Lane, Daniel Lynn. Intern, Baylor U. Med. Center, Dallas, Tex., 1960; resident in gen. surgery Mayo Clinic, Rochester, Minn., 1961-64, resident plastic surgery, 1964-67; practice medicine specializing in plastic surgery, Lafayette, La., 1969—; med. dir. S.W. La. Rehab. Center, 1974—; staff Our Lady of Lourdes Hosp., Lafayette, Lafayette Gen. Hosp., Surgery Center, Inc., Lafayette; clin. instr. dept. surgery La. State U., 1970—, Tulane U., 1977—. Served to comdr. USN, 1967-69. Diplomate Am. Bd. Plastic and Reconstructive Surgery. Fellow A.C.S.; mem. Am. Soc. Plastic and Reconstructive Surgeons, Southeastern Soc. Plastic and Reconstructive Surgeons, Am. Assn. Hand Surgery, Cleft Palate Assn., La. Surg. Assn., Am. Soc. Aesthetic Plastic Surgery, Assn. Mil. Plastic Surgeons of U.S., Internat. Soc. Clin. Plastic Surgeons, So. Med. Assn., La. Med. Assn., AMA, Lafayette Parish Med. Soc., Flying Physicians Assn., Mayo Alumni Assn. Home: 213 Miller St Lafayette LA 70503 Office: 1101 S College St Lafayette LA 70503

HENDERSON, EDWARD MCCRADY, JR., constrn. engr.; b. Columbia, S.C., Dec. 5, 1941; s. Edward McCrady and Amarinthia Lowndes (Webb) H.; B.S.C.E., U. S.C., 1964; M.S.C.E., Stanford U., 1974, Engr., 1976; m. Mary Fulton Green, Aug. 2, 1969. Civil engr. field constrn. power plants S.C. Elec. & Gas Co., 1968-73; with Bechtel Constrn., summer 1974; engr. oil refinery constrn. R.M. Parsons, 1975-76; resident engr. nuclear power Civil Ebasco Services, Killona, La., 1976—; tchr. industry constrn. Stanford U. Served to maj. USMC, 1964-68. Registered profl. engr., S.C., Calif. Mem. ASCE. Episcopalian. Author: The Use of Scale Models for Construction Management, 1976. Home: 5201 MacArthur Blvd New Orleans LA 70114 Office: Ebasco Services PO Box 70 Killona LA 70066

HENDERSON, GEORGE, educator; b. Hurtsboro, Ala., June 18, 1932; s. Kidd Large and Lula Mae (Crawford) H.; student Mich. State U., 1950-52; B.A., Wayne State U., 1957, M.A., 1959, Ph.D., 1965; m. Barbara Ann Beard, Aug. 9, 1951; children—George, Michele Alicia, Faith Elaine, Lea Ann, Joy Lynn, Lisa Gaye, Dawn Noel. Social caseworker Ch. Youth Service, Detroit, 1957-59; social economist Detroit Housing Commn., 1960-61; community services dir. Detroit Urban League, 1961-63; program dir. Mayor's Com. Community Action for Detroit Youth, 1963-64; asst. dir. Wayne State U. Juvenile Delinquency Program, 1964-65; asst. dir. intercultural relations Detroit Pub. Schs., 1965-66, asst. to supt., 1966-67; asso. prof. sociology and edn. U. Okla., 1967-69, S.N. Goldman prof. human relations, prof. edn., asso. prof. sociology, chmn. dept. human relations, 1969—; cons. Dept. Def., FAA, NAACP. Bd. dirs. Urban League of Oklahoma City, 1968-75, St. Gregory Jr. Coll., 1969-74. Served with USAF, 1953-55. Recipient Edn. award Prince Hall Free and Accepted Masons of Detroit, 1966, Superior Teaching award U. Okla. Regents, 1971; Charles Kelly Labor research scholar, 1957-58; Am. Fedn. Tchrs. grantee, 1969. Mem. Am. Sociol. Assn., Assn. Black Sociologists, Nat. Council Social Studies, Assn. Supervision and Curriculum Devel., AAUP, Am. Assn. Higher Edn., Social Sci. Edn. Consortium, Kappa Alpha Psi. Democrat. Baptist. Author books, the most recent being: Human Relations, 1974; Human Relations in the Military, 1975; A Religious Foundation of Human Relations, 1977; Introduction to American Education, 1978; Understanding and Counseling Ethnic Minorities, 1979. Home: 2616 Osborne Dr Norman OK 73069 Office: Dept Human Relations U Okla Norman OK 73019

HENDERSON, HAROLD DALE, pub. relations co. exec.; b. Callaway, Nebr., Oct. 24, 1921; s. Ashton Fremont and Ada E. (Bybee) H.; B.J., U. Mo., 1947; m. Claudine Laverne Lester, Dec. 22, 1946; children—Jeffrey Scott, Susan Kay, Sandra Jean. Editor, Winner (S.D.) News & Colome Times, 1947-49; fund raiser Haney &

Assos., Newtonville, Mass., 1950-53; v.p., mgr. pub. relations Ketchum, Macleod & Grove, Inc., Houston, 1954-65; owner, pres. Dale Henderson, Inc., Houston, 1965—; guest lectr. communications various colls. U. Houston. Scoutmaster, Winner council Boy Scouts Am., committeeman Houston council; trustee Upper St. Clair Presbyterian Ch., Pitts. Served with U.S. Army, 1942-45. Mem. Pub. Relations Soc. Am. (past pres. and dir. Houston chpt.; Silver Anvil award 1973), Tex. Pub. Relations Soc. (Silver Spur award 1977-80). Clubs: Masons, Shriners. Home: 222 Stoney Creek Dr Houston TX 77024 Office: 2200 N Loop W Houston TX 77018

HENDERSON, JERRY DON, assn. exec.; b. Brownfield, Tex., Mar. 9, 1927; s. J.D. and Ethel May (Carter) H.; B.A., Tex. Technol. U., 1950; 1 dau., Paula (Mrs. Dennis Ray Jones); m. Burnis Marie Lyles, June 8, 1964; children—Donna George, Jacqueline George, David. With KFYO Radio, Lubbock, Tex., 1950-56; copy dir. Buckner Advt. Agy., Lubbock, 1956-60; partner Henderson Buckner Pub. Relations, Lubbock, 1960-62; with Brain Radio Promotions, Lubbock, 1962-66; pub. relations dir. United Fund, Lubbock, Tex., 1966—; pres. Brain Bag, Lubbock, 1969—. Pres., Lubbock Jaycees, 1961-62. Served with USNR, 1946-48. Named Hon. adm. Tex. Navy. Mem. Nat. Communications Council United Way of Am., Pub. Relations Soc. Am., Pub. Relations Student Soc. Am. (profl. sponsor Tex. Technol. U. chpt., now called Sellmeyer-Henderson chpt.), Am. (dir. 10th dist. 1975-76), Lubbock (pres. 1970-71, Silver medal award 1976) advt. fedns. Episcopalian (vestryman 1968-71, lay reader 1967—). Rotarian. Clubs: Press (dir. Lubbock), Reveliers Dance (pres. 1973-74). Pub: Sales Pitches on Tape (Jerry D. Henderson), 1971; COMICmercials, 1975. Home: 5214 17th St Lubbock TX 79416 Office: 2201 19th St Lubbock TX 79401

HENDERSON, JOSEPH HARRISON, III, lawyer; b. Alexandria, La., Aug. 13, 1946; s. Joseph Harrison and Constance Randolph (Wilbur) H.; B.S. in Bus. Adminstrn., Citadel, 1968; J.D., Tulane U., 1971. Admitted to La. bar, 1971; with firm Guste, Barnett & Shushan, New Orleans, 1971—; partner Pro Sports, Inc., athletes reps. Bd. dirs., treas. Am. Lung Assn. of La. Inc. Served to capt. USAR, 1968. Democrat. Active renovation, restoration old houses. Home: 820 3d St New Orleans LA 70130 Office: 1624 1st Nat Bank of Commerce Bldg New Orleans LA 70112

HENDERSON, KAYE NEIL, civil engr., bus. exec.; b. Birmingham, Ala., June 10, 1933; s. Ernest Martin and Mary (Head) H.; B.S., Va. Mil. Inst., 1954; B.A. with honors, U. South Fla., 1967; m. Betty Jane Belanus, June 26, 1954; children—David Scott, Alan Douglas, Helen Kaye. Mgmt. trainee Gen. Electric Co., Schenectady, 1954; sales engr. Fla. Prestressed Concrete, Tampa, 1956-57; field engr. Portland Cement Assn., Tampa, 1957-63; gen. mgr. residential and comml. sales Tampa Electric Co., 1963-66; v.p. Watson & Co., architects and engrs., Tampa, 1966-69; v.p. Reynolds, Smith & Hills, architects, engrs. and planners, Jacksonville, Fla., 1969-78, sr. v.p., 1978—, dir., 1976—; dir. Environ. Sci. and Engring., Gainesville, Fla., RSH Internat. Vice chmn. Temple Terrace Planning and Zoning Bd., 1962-67; pres. Guidance Center Hillsborough County, 1969; mem. adv. bd. Multi-State Transp. System, 1976—; mem. Duval County Republican Exec. Com., 1970-72; bd. dirs. Salvation Army Home and Hosp. Council, 1964-69. Mem. found U. South Fla. Served to 1st lt. USAF, 1954-56. Recipient Service awards Greater Tampa C. of C., 1964-66; named Outstanding Young Man of Tampa Jr. C. of C., 1965; Outstanding Young Man of Am., U.S. Jr. C. of C., 1967; Boss of Year award Am. Bus. Women's Assn., 1978; registered profl. engr., Fla., N.C. Mem. Fla. Engring. Soc., Fla. Inst. Cons. Engrs. (dir.), Navy League U.S., Tau Beta Pi, Phi Kappa Phi. Republican. Episcopalian. Clubs: Ye Mystic Revellers, Timuquana Country, River, St. Johns Dinner, University, Rotary (Jacksonville). Home: 4606 Yacht Club Rd Jacksonville FL 32210 Office: 4019 Blvd Center Dr Jacksonville FL 32207

HENDERSON, LORRIE (LEORA FOSTER), psychiat. social worker; b. Cedar Rapids, Iowa, July 30, 1924; d. Floyd Percy and Rosetta Mae (Bair) Foster; student Cornell Coll., Iowa, 1942-44; B.A. in Psychology, U. Tex., Austin, 1964, M.S.W., 1967; m. Charles Perry Henderson, Sept. 15, 1945; children—Charles Timothy, Jane Ann Henderson Herrin. Psychiat. social worker Austin State Hosp., 1964-65; foster home finder, licensing worker Austin-Travis County Child Welfare, 1967-68; successively psychiat. social worker, program dir. Title IVA, sr. therapist social work Austin Guild Guidance Center, 1968-76; dir. social services children's psychiat. unit Austin State Hosp., 1976—; asso. prof. practicum Worden Sch. Social Work, 1975—; field instr. U. Tex. Grad. Sch. Social Work, Austin, 1980, St. Edwards U., 1980—; cons. in field. Bd. dirs. Austin Christmas Bur., 1973-75, v.p., 1974-75; mem. Regional Network for Children, 1979—. Served with WAVES, 1945. Alfred Noyes scholar, 1943-44, 63-64, 65-67; recipient Franklin Lindsay student loan 1963-64, 65-67; NIMH grantee, 1965-66, TDPW Student stipent, 1966-67. Mem. Acad. Certified Social Workers, Nat. Assn. Social Workers, Am. Assn. for Marriage and Family Therapy (approved supr. 1977—; exec. com. 1968-72, 1st v.p. 1971-72), Austin Group Therapy Assn., U. Tex. Austin Exes (life, newsletter editor Sch. Social Work 1972-73, mem. at large exec. com. 1976—), Austin Mental Health Assn. Methodist. Club: Balcones Country (Austin). Office: 4110 Guadelupe St Austin TX 78751

HENDERSON, MARYLEA, sociologist, counselor; b. Coleman, Tex., May 4, 1929; d. Clyde M. and Audrey (Lane) H.; B.A., Howard Payne U., 1950; M.R.E., Southwestern Baptist Theol. Sem., 1952; Ed.D., Tex. Technol. U., 1969; M.S., U. Oreg., 1978; m. Richard Wood, Dec. 18, 1954 (div.); 1 dau., Margaret Lane. Tchr. English and Bible, Lubbock (Tex.) High Sch., 1963-65; instr. sociology South Plains Coll., Levelland, Tex., 1966-67; asst. prof. sociology Campbellsville (Ky.) Coll., 1967-69; asst. prof. sociology Sul Ross State U., Alpine, Tex., 1969-71; asso. prof. sociology Howard Payne U., Brownwood, Tex., 1971-73; asso. prof. edn. Grand Canyon Coll., Phoenix, 1973-74; prof. sociology Paul Quinn Coll., Waco, Tex., 1976—; dir. Community Career Center for Displaced Homemakers, Waco, 1979—. Mem. AAUW, Gerontol. Soc., Am. Personnel and Guidance Assn., Delta Kappa Gamma, Kappa Delta Pi. Republican. Author: Persons, Not Things, 1972. Home: 601 N 33d St Waco TX 76707 Office: 1020 Elm St Waco TX 76704

HENDERSON, ROBBYE ROBINSON, librarian; b. Morton, Miss., Nov. 10, 1937; d. Robert and Aljuria Myers Robinson; B.A., Tougaloo (S.C.) Coll., 1960; M.S.L.S., Atlanta U., 1966; Ph.D., So. Ill. U., 1976; 1 child, Robreka Aljuria. Tchr., Patton Lane High Sch., Batesville, Miss., 1960-66; librarian Utica Jr. Coll., 1966-67; librarian Miss. Valley State U., Itta Bena, 1968-69, univ. librarian, 1972—; cons. Office of Health Resources Opportunity, 1976-78. Mem. ALA, Southeastern Library Assn., Miss. Library Assn., AAUP, Nat. Council Negro Women. Baptist. Home: PO Box 42 Miss Valley State Univ Itta Bena MS 38941 Office: James Herbert White Library Itta Bena MS 38941

HENDERSON, ROBERT LEE, air force officer; b. Morgantown, W.Va., Aug. 12, 1940; s. Ray and Edna Opal (Park) H.; B.S. in Journalism, W.Va. U., 1962; M.A. in Pub. Adminstrn., Ball State U., 1975; grad. Air Command and Staff Coll., 1978; m. Linda Gayle Hoerner, Dec. 18, 1970. Commd. 2d lt. U.S. Air Force, 1965, advanced through grades to maj., 1977; squadron sect. comdr. 93d Security Police Squadron, Castle AFB, Calif., 1967; assigned Vietnam, 1968-69, Armed Forces Police of San Francisco, 1970, 60th Security Police, Travis AFB, Calif., 1971-72; chief security police Zaragoza Air Base, Spain, 1973-77, England AFB, La., 1978—. Pres., Protestant Fund Council, 1978, Protestant Men of Base, 1979. Decorated Bronze Star, USAF Commendation medal. Mem. Nat. Assn. Chiefs Police, Air Force Assn. Republican. Methodist. Home: 3705 Royce Dr Alexandria LA 71301 Office: 23d Security Police Squadron England AFB LA 71301

HENDERSON, SHARON WARD, artist, fine art conservator; b. Mobile, Ala., Dec. 18, 1938; d. Gordon Bert and Mary Caroline (Nash) Ward; student Lindenwood Coll. for Women, 1956-57, U. Ark., 1957-58; m. Donald Henderson, Sept. 25, 1976; children—Lisa Ward, Anne Richmond. One-woman shows Vestavia Country Club, Tavern Gallery, Cobb Lane Gallery, Downtown Club; exhibited in group shows Studio One Painters, Circle Painters, Birmingham Festival of Arts; represented in permanent collections So. Natural Gas Co., Birmingham Trust Nat. Bank, Vestavia Country Club; mem. Studio One, Birmingham, 1970-71; founder, Cobb Lane Gallery, Birmingham, 1971-72; mem. Circle Painters, Birmingham, 1973-74; owner Terrace Gallery, Birmingham. Pvt. art tchr., Birmingham, 1972-73. Chmn. Cobb Lane Christmas Open House, 1971-72. Recipient first prize Still Life Realists Tuscaloosa, 1974, 75. Mem. Arlington Hist. Assn., Nat. Audubon Soc., Birmingham, Vestavia art assns., Nat. Penwomen's Assn., Cousteau Soc., Birmingham Mus. Art, Antiquarian Soc., Bluff Park Art Assn. Clubs: Vestavia Country (pres. art com. 1972); Christian Women's (pres. 1970), Alea Literary (pres. 1974—), Inverness Country (Birmingham). Art editor Village Post mag. Home: 5010 Applecross Rd Birmingham AL 35243 Office: Henderson's Fine Arts Inc Birmingham AL 35223

HENDERSON, WARREN S., state senator; b. Exeter, N.H., Nov. 14, 1927; B.A., Denison U., 1951; m. Polly Ann Schurr; children—Warren C., Susan D., Wendy L. Investment, financial exec.; mem. Fla. Senate, 1963—. Mem., chmn. Sarasota County (Fla.) Commn., 1960-63; chmn. Manatee/Sarasota Airport Authority, 1961-63; chmn. West Coast Inland Nav. Dist., 1962-63; mem. Fla. Energy Com.; mem. U.S. Assay Commn., 1972, 76. Mem. Gov.'s Commn. on Property Rights, 1974. Del. Republican nat. conv., 1968, 72; mem. Fla. Rep. com., 1970—. Served with USNR, World War II. Recipient awards Am. Alligator Council, 1971, Water Resources Conservation, 1973, Fla. Conservation League, 1973, Fla. Pediatrics award, 1975, Distinguished Alumni citation Denison U., 1976, Patriot award Sarasota County, 1976; Fla. Wildlife Spl. Service award, 1977, Physicians for Children award, 1978; Legis. award Fla. Home Builders, 1979; Allen Morris award 1979. Mem. Am. Numis. Assn., Internat. Oceanographic Found., Nat. Wildlife Fedn., Conservation 70's, Fla. Hist. Soc. C. of C., Phi Delta Theta. Presbyterian. Elk, Mason. Address: PO Box 1358 Venice FL 33595

HENDERSON, WILLIAM DONALD, antiquarian, surveyor; b. Bluefield, W.Va., June 20, 1914; s. Thomas Ewell and Cordie Ethel (Nelson) H.; B.S.E.E., Va. Poly. Inst., 1936, postgrad. in Mech. Engring., 1938-39; postgrad. in Bus. Adminstrn., U. Pa., 1937, in Edn., U. Md., 1939-40; m. Edythe May Edwards, 1957. Instr., lectr., demonstrator in driver edn. Am. Automobile Assn., Washington, 1939-40; jr. engr. Washington Inst. Tech., College Park, Md., 1940-41; civilian electronics engr. Airborne Communications and Navigation, Design Br., Navy Dept., Washington, 1941-46; pvt. practice real estate mgmt., Cleveland, Ga., 1946-52, 54—; owner, mgr. comml. timberlands; field service rep. nav. electronics Glenn L. Martin Co., Essex, Md., 1953; surveyor White County, Ga., 1961—. Lic. pvt. pilot. Mem. AAAS, Am. Def. Preparedness Assn., US Naval Inst. (asso.). Developer surveying techniques. Office: PO Box 164 Cleveland GA 30528

HENDRICK, ROBERT SMITH, physician; b. Shreveport, La., June 23, 1923; s. John Alexander and Lois May (Smith) H.; B.S., Tulane U., 1948, M.D., 1951; m. Norma Ann McCook, June 17, 1954; children—Robert Jr., Virginia, Walter. Intern Duke Univ. Hosp., Durham, 1951-52; fellow in otolaryngology Mayo Clinic, Rochester, Minn., 1952-55; practice medicine specializing in otolaryngology, Shreveport, 1955—; asst. prof. otolaryngology La. State Med. Sch., Shreveport, 1970—. Vice chmn. Hendrick Lloyd Found.; vice-chmn. bd. trustees Highland Hosp. Diplomate Am. Bd. Otolaryngology. Mem. Am. Acad. Ophthalmology and Otolaryngology, A.C.S., AMA, La. State Med. Soc., Phi Delta Theta, Phi Chi. Democrat. Baptist (chmn. bd. deacons). Clubs: Shreveport, Shreveport Country. Home: 586 Sherwood Rd Shreveport LA 71106 Office: 1035 Creswell Shreveport LA 71101

HENDRICK, ZELWANDA, educator; b. Rusk, Tex., Nov. 28, 1925; d. Lloyd Irvin and Viola Alice (McGuire) Hendrick; A.A., Lon Morris Coll., 1945; B.S., N. Tex. U., 1947; M.A., So. Meth. U., 1958. Tchr. theatre arts Overton (Tex.) High Sch., 1947-49, Nacogdoches (Tex.) High Sch., 1949-50, Boude Storey Sch., Dallas, 1950-53, Kimball High Sch., Dallas, 1953-62; tchr. theatre arts H. Grady Spruce High Sch., Dallas, 1962-78, chmn. fine arts dept., 1963-78; tchr. Alexander Sch., 1979—. part time tchr. John Robert Powers Finishing Sch., 1951—; teaching fellow North Tex. U., 1964-65. Active Tyler (Tex.) Civic Symphony, 1949-50, Tyler Civic Theatre, 1949-50, Dallas Theatre Center, 1960-61; mem. advisory com. Smithsonian Instn., 1975. Mem. Internat. Thespians (state dir.), Tex. Speech Assn. (sec. 1973—), Am. Assn. Ednl. Theatre, Dallas Ind. Sch. Dist. Assn. Speech and Drama, Tex. Tchrs. Assn., Parents & Tchrs. Assn. (hon. mem. Tex. br.), Nat. Forensic League, AAUW, Classroom Tchrs. Dallas, Dallas Drama Tchrs. Assn. (bd.), N. Tex. Collie Club, Internat. Platform Assn., Ednl. Arts Assn., Daus. Republic of Tex., Dalta Kappa Gamma. Mem. Order Eastern Star. Contbr. to A Guide to Student Teaching in Music, 1968-70. Home: 3016 Westminster St Dallas TX 75205 Office: 13999 Goldmark Dallas TX 75240

HENDRICKS, NATHAN VANMETER, III, lawyer; b. Decatur, Ga., Dec. 16, 1943; s. Nathan VanMeter and Ella L. (Ward) H.; B.A., Washington and Lee U., 1966, LL.B., 1969; m. Kathryn A. Barnes, Aug. 19, 1972. Admitted to Ga. bar, 1970; practiced in Atlanta, 1969—; asso. firm Swift, Currie, McGhee and Hiers, 1969-70, Henning, Chambers and Mabry, 1970-71; asso. firm Redfern, Butler and Morgan, 1971-73, partner 1973-77; partner firm Cobb, Hyre & Hendricks, Atlanta, 1978—. Chmn. Younger Lawyers Com., Campaign for mayor, Atlanta, 1972. Mem. High Mus. of Art, group leader ann. fund-raising campaign, 1973-75, chmn. young career's group, 1972-73, sec. young men's round table, 1974-75; active ann. fund raising campaign Atlanta Symphony Orch. Assn., 1977-78, Atlanta Arts Alliance, 1977-79; bd. dirs. Atlanta Hunter-Jumper Classic, 1978-79, pres., 1979; bd. dirs. Save America's Vital Environment, sec. 1971-74; bd. dirs. Merrie-Woode Found., v.p., 1978-79. Mem. Am., Atlanta (mem. real estate sect. 1972—, comm. 1978) bar assns., State Bar of Ga. (mem. real estate sect. 1972—), Lawyers Club Atlanta, Washington and Lee U. Alumni Assn. (dir. 1972—, pres. Atlanta chpt. 1973-75), Beta Theta Pi, Phi Delta Phi. Episcopalian. Clubs: Ansley Golf, Piedmont Driving, Wildcat Cliffs Country, The Nine O'Clocks. Home: 230 The Prado Atlanta GA 30309 Office: Suite 427 C&S Bank Bldg Roswell Rd Atlanta GA 30328

HENDRICKS, WILLIAM ANDREW, surgeon; b. Dallas, Apr. 30, 1928; s. Barnard A. and Mary (Anderson) H.; B.S., B.A., So. Meth. U., 1950, B.S., 1950; M.D., U. Tex. Med. Br., 1957; m. Sally Armitage, June 29, 1956; children—William Andrew, Mary Evelyn. Intern, Baylor U. Hosp., Dallas, 1957-58; resident in gen. surgery Baylor Med. Center, Dallas, 1958-59, Dallas VA Hosp., 1959-62; asst. Baylor U. Dental Sch. dept. anatomy, 1959; practice medicine specializing in gen. surgery, Irving, Tex., 1963—; mem. staffs Irvington Community Hosp., St. Paul Hosp., Dallas, Meth. Hosp., Dallas. Served to U.S. Army, 1950-52. Diplomate Am. Bd. Surgery. Fellow A.C.S.; mem. Dallas County, Tex., Am. med. socs. Methodist. Club: Lions (dir. and chmn. sight com. local club 1963—, alt. dir. Tissue Found.). Home: 100 Colony Ct Irving TX 75061 Office: 1430 MacArthur St Suite 102 Irving TX 75061

HENDRICKSON, HARVEY SIGBERT, educator; b. Mpls., July 23, 1928; s. Sigbert and Hilma Margaret (Johnson) H.; B.B.A., U. Minn., 1957, M.B.A., 1962, Ph.D., 1963; m. Rosanne Cecilia Maddy, Aug. 18, 1962; children—Mary, Erik, Elise. Instr. acctg. U. Minn., Mpls., 1958-61; asst. prof. acctg. SUNY, Buffalo, 1963-66; asso. prof. acctg. Fla. State U., Tallahassee, 1968-69; vis. asso. prof. U. Minn., Mpls., 1969; asst. dir. exams. Am. Inst. C.P.A.'s, N.Y.C., 1970-72; chmn. fin. and acctg. div., prof. acctg. Fla. Internat. U., Miami, 1972-77, prof. acctg., 1972—. Mem. adv. com. Dade County Public Schs., Miami. Served with U.S. Army, 1950-52. Haskins and Sells Found. scholar, 1957; Ford Found. predoctoral fellow, 1961-62; Arthur Andersen & Co. Found. doctoral dissertation fellow, 1962-63. C.P.A., Minn. Mem. Am. Acctg. Assn., Am. Inst. C.P.A.'s, Minn. Soc. C.P.A.'s, S. Fla. Assn. Accountants for Public Interest (bd. dirs. 1976—), Beta Alpha Psi, Beta Gamma Sigma, Delta Sigma Pi. Democrat. Author: (with T.J. Burns) The Accounting Primer, 1972; editor: (with T.J. Burns) The Accounting Sampler, 1967, 72, 76; mem. editorial bd. The Acctg. Rev., 1976—. Home: 7865 SW 158th Terr Miami FL 33157 Office: Sch Bus Fla Internat U Tamiami Trail Miami FL 33199

HENDRICKSON, JEROME ORLAND, assn. exec., lawyer; b. Eau Claire, Wis., July 25, 1918; s. Harold and Clara (Halvorson) H.; student Wis. State Coll., 1936-39; J.D., U. Wis., 1942; m. Helen Phoebe Harty, Dec. 27, 1948; children—Jaime Ann, Jerome Orland. Admitted to Wis. bar, 1942, U.S. Supreme Ct. bar, 1956; pvt. practice, Eau Claire, 1946; sales and advt. mgr. Coca-Cola Bottling Co., Inc., Eau Claire, 1947-48; exec. sec. Eau Claire Community Chest, 1948-49; in charge dist. office Am. Petroleum Inst., Kansas City, Mo., 1950-53, Chgo., 1953-55; exec. dir. Nat. Assn. Plumbing-Heating-Cooling Contractors, Washington, 1955-64; exec. v.p. Cast Iron Soil Pipe Inst., Washington, 1964-74; pres. Valve Mfrs. Assn., McLean, Va., 1975—; sec. Joint Apprentice Text, Inc., 1955-64. Treas. Wis. Community Chest, 1948-49. Treas. All-Industry Plumbing and Heating Modernization Com., 1956-57; co-sec. Joint Industry Program Com., 1958-64; sec. Nat. Conf. Plumbing-Heating-Cooling Industry, 1962-66; chmn. nat. conf. Plumbing-Heating-Cooling Conf., 1967-69. Served from ensign to lt. USNR, 1943-46. Mem. Am., Wis. bar assns., Am. Soc. Assn. Execs., U. Wis. Alumni Assn., Wis. Law Alumni Assn. (pres. Washington chpt. 1970-73), Bldg. Ofcls. Conf. Am., Internat. Assn. Plumbing and Mech. Ofcls., Wis. State Soc. Washington (pres. 1966-68), NAM, U.S. C. of C., Gamma Eta Gamma (pres. Upsilon chpt. 1941-42). Episcopalian. Clubs Washington Golf and Country; Internat. (Washington); Masons (32 deg.), Shriners. Home: 4621 33d St N Arlington VA 22207 Office: Drawer II Suite 711 6845 Elm St McLean VA 22101

HENDRIX, DON COLE, city ofcl.; b. Coffeyville, Kans., Aug. 15, 1934; s. L. Clark and Josephine Elizabeth (Cole) H.; B.A., Kans. U., 1956, M.P.A., 1963; m. Carol Harshbarger, June 10, 1956; children—Stephen, Scott, Mark. Adminstrv. asst. City of San Angelo, Tex., 1958-59; city mgr. Marceline, Mo., 1959-61, Gladstone, Mo., 1961-64; dir. personnel, Kansas City, Mo., 1964-67, asst. city mgr., 1967-69, exec. dir. Law Enforcement Planning Commn., 1969-71; city mgr., Charlottesville, Va., 1971—. Served with AUS, 1957-58. Named Outstanding Grad., Kans. U., 1956. Mem. Internat. City Mgmt. Assn. Home: 1946 Michael Pl Charlottesville VA 22901 Office: PO Box 911 Charlottesville VA 22902

HENDRIX, JAMES ROBERT, investment banker; b. Birmingham, Ala., May 5, 1905; s. William Robert and Sarah Amanda (Coburn) H.; B.S. in Bus. Adminstrn., Washington and Lee U., 1926; m. Marion Calhoun, Apr. 27, 1973; children by previous marriage—James Coburn, Virginia (Mrs. Richard T. Scruggs, Jr.). Investment officer Birmingham Trust Nat. Bank, 1930-35, br. mgr., 1935-38; partner King, Mohr & Hendrix and predecessor co., Birmingham, 1938-42; v.p. Hendrix & Mayes, Inc., Birmingham, 1942-48, pres., 1948—; pres., chmn. bd. Hendrix, Mohr & Yardley, Inc., Birmingham, 1960—; mem. Indsl. Securities Adv. Council State of Ala., 1974-78; chmn. advisory com. Ala. State Retirement Systems, 1976-77. Chmn., Mountain Brook (Ala.) Bd. Edn., 1959-70. Served from lt. to lt. comdr. USNR, 1942-45. Clubs: Mountain Brook Country, Birmingham Country, Redstone, Downtown, The Club, Relay House. Home: 37 Ridge Dr Birmingham AL 35213 Office: First Nat Southern Nat Bldg Birmingham AL 35203

HENDRIX, LESLYE BRUCE, data processing exec.; b. Atlanta, Aug. 27, 1927; s. Cleveland and Johnnie Marcellous (Jackson) H.; student Howard U., 1946-49; m. Mar. 26, 1950; children—DeJerris K., Roderick M., Reginald K., Leslynn C., Juan B. With Dept. Def., Ft. McPherson, Ga., 1953-68; project leader Western Union Corp., Mahwah, N.J., 1969-77; mgr. data processing, Rock-Tenn Co., Norcross, Ga., 1977—. Served with USN, 1943-46; U.S. Army, 1950-53. Mem. Data Processing Mgmt. Assn., Assn. System Mgmt. Baptist. Home: 1256 Shoreham Dr College Park GA 30349 Office: 504 Thrasher St Norcross GA 30071

HENDRIX, MARTHA JAN, psychologist; b. Spartanburg County, S.C., Mar. 14, 1951; d. Everette Wilson and Martha (Ballenger) Hendrix; student Lenoir Rhyne Coll., 1969-70; B.A. in Psychology and Sociology, Appalachian State U., 1973, M.A. in Counseling and Psychology, 1974, advanced cert. of study in sch. psychology, 1980. Regional sch. psychologist Stanly County, Anson County and Albemarle City Schs., 1974-76, Stanly County, Cabarrus County, Concord City and Albemarle City Schs., 1976—; instr. Stanly Tech. Inst.; psychologist Western Correctional Center, 1979—. Mem. Stanly County Child Abuse Team, Burke County Task Force Battered Women. Certified sch. psychologist, N.C. Mem. Nat. Assn. Sch. Psychologists (co-chmn. research com., nat. conv.), Am. Personnel and Guidance Assn., N.C. Sch. Psychologist Assn., League Women Voters, Beta Psi, Kappa Delta Alumnae. Methodist. Club: Burke County Tennis. Home: Box 957 Morganton NC 28655 Office: Western Correctional Center PO Box 1439 Morganton NC 28655

HENDRIX, THOMIE WAYNE, advt. and public relations co. exec.; b. Lawton, Okla., June 28, 1945; s. Wayne Clifford and Hanna Faye (Phillips) H.; A.A., U. Houston, 1965; B.F.A., U. Okla., 1967; postgrad. UCLA, 1969; m. Sandra Jacquline Susan Robinson, Dec. 24, 1974; children—James Phillip Wayne Robinson, Michael Christopher. Creative dir. KFOX Radio, Los Angeles, 1969-72; asst. radio-TV dir. Brooks, Johnson Zausmer Advt., San Antonio, 1972-73;

mng. editor Non-Commd. Officers Assn., San Antonio, 1973; mng. editor S.W. Airlines Mag., San Antonio, 1973-74; asso. editor St. Mary's U., San Antonio, 1974-75; asst. dir. public relations Trinity U., San Antonio, 1975-78, tchr. fine arts, 1975-79; dir. public relations Pitluk Group, San Antonio, 1978-79; public info. officer San Antonio Housing Authority, 1979—. Recipient Addy awards San Antonio Advt. Fedn., 1976, 77, 78; Golden Quill awards Internat. Assn. Bus. Communicators, 1977, 78. Mem. Public Relations Soc. Am., San Antonio Advt. Fedn., Sigma Delta Chi. Office: PO Drawer 1300 400 Labor St San Antonio TX 78295

HENDRIX, WILLIAM GRADY, advt. agy. exec.; b. Dallas, Mar. 9, 1946; s. Grady John and Willie Irene (Thomas) H.; B.B.A. in Econs., U. Tex., Arlington, 1972; postgrad. U. Dallas, 1972-73, U. Tex., Dallas, 1975; m. Janet Lynn Wells, Apr. 11, 1976; children by previous marriage—Cara Michelle, Kayla Charisse. Mktg. and sales analyst Snap Shots, Inc., Dallas, 1972-75; mktg. analyst, new product devel. Camsco, Inc., Richardson, Tex., 1975-76; advt. account exec. The Mktg. Group, Dallas, 1976-77; v.p. Hendrix Melugin Advt., Dallas, 1977—, also dir. Served with U.S. Army, 1966-69; Vietnam. Recipient cert. of merit Def. Communications Agy./Western Hemisphere, 1969. Mem. Dallas Advt. League, Dallas C. of C., North Dallas C. of C. Methodist. Club: Pier 121 Yacht Racing. Home: 8509 Richardson Branch Trail Dallas TX 75243 Office: Hendrix Melugin Advt 5121 McKinney St Dallas TX 75205

HENDRY, CLIFFORD SAMUEL, electronics mfg. exec.; b. Greene County, Tenn., Nov. 2, 1922; s. William Edward and Alma Eula (Seneker) H.; student Tusculum Coll., Greeneville, Tenn., 1944; m. Dorothy Elizabeth Bird, Oct. 10, 1943; children—Allen Bird, Roger Senker. East Tenn. circulation mgr. Knoxville Jour., 1943-44; bookkeeper, gen. mgr. Tenn. Toy House, 1944-47; with Magnovox Co. of Tenn., Greeneville, 1947—, v.p. indsl. relations Tenn. ops., 1974—; dir. labor relations Magnavox Consumer Electronics Co., 1979—. Former chmn., bd. dirs. Greene County Service Assn. Recipient certificate of recognition for service to mentally retarded Gov. of Tenn., 1975; commd. Ky. col., 1975. Mem. Am. Soc. Personnel Adminstrn., Accredited Exec. in Personnel (dir., charter mem. Upper East Tenn. chpt.), Tenn. Mfg. Assn., Am. Mgmt. Assn. Rotary (past pres. Greenville chpt.) Home: PO Box 512 Greenville TN 37743 Office: PO Box 479 Greeneville TN 37743

HENDRY, JAMES E., lawyer, automobile club exec.; b. Perry, Fla., Nov. 7, 1912; s. Wesley Alonzo and Mae (Weaver) H.; student St. Petersburg Jr. Coll., 1930-32; J.D., U. Fla., 1935; m. Frances Swope, June 25, 1948; children—James E., Jayne L., Thomas S., John W., David F. Vice pres. Hendry Lumber Co., 1935-42, sec., treas., 1946-60; partner, mgr. Hendry Bldg. Co., 1946-60; practice law as James E. Hendry, atty., 1961—; pres. Gulf Housing Corp., 1946; sec.-mgr. St. Petersburg A.A.A. Motor Club, 1962-67, exec. v.p., gen. mgr., 1967—; v.p. Club Ins. Agy., Inc., 1962—; pub. Suncoast Motorist; dir. Guardian Bank, Dr. Chatelier's Plant Food Co. Admitted to Supreme Ct. bar. Mem. City Planning and Zoning Bd., 1948-57, Pinellas County Sch. Bd., 1957-66; mem. Pinellas Co. Airport Com., 1952; mem. St. Petersburg Planning Commn., 1974-75. Mem. citizens adv. com. St. Petersburg Jr. Coll., 1948-68, bd. govs., 1938-48, chmn. dist. bd. trustees, 1968-75; pres. bd. dirs. YMCA, 1951; mem. Mound Park Hosp. Bd., 1951-52; mem. bd. Pinellas County chpt. Am. Cancer Soc., chmn. Cancer Drive, 1962; mem. Civil Def. Council; pres. Fla. Sch. Bd. Assn., 1964; sec.-treas. Southeastern Conf. AAA Motor Clubs, 1964, v.p., 1965, pres., 1966, treas. Eastern Conf. AAA Motor Clubs, 1970-71, vice chmn., 1972-75, chmn., 1975-77; exec. com. Continuing Ednl. Council Fla., 1964; mem. Nat. Com. Support Pub. Schs., 1964; mem. Pinellas Com. of 100, State Community Coll. Council, 1970-75; past pres., St. Petersburg Jr. Coll. Found. Lt. comdr. USCG Res. Mem. Am., St. Petersburg bar assns., Fla. Bar, Am. Judicature Soc., Fla. C. of C., C. of C. U.S., St. Petersburg C. of C. (gov.), Nat. Assn. Home Builders (past dir.), Contractors and Builders Assn. of Pinellas County (pres. 1953), Fla. Home Builders Assn. (v.p. 1955), Phi Delta Theta, Phi Alpha Delta. Democrat. Methodist. Clubs: Rotary, St. Petersburg Yacht, Quarterback, Commerce, Skal, Feathersound Country. Home: 409 Snell Isle Blvd Saint Petersburg FL 33704 Office: 1211 1st Ave N Saint Petersburg FL 33705

HENEGAR, ROBERT MICHAEL, dairy exec.; b. Columbia, S.C., June 16, 1949; s. Richard and Catherine (Wehrheim) H.; B.B.A., U. Ga., 1972. With collections dept. C&S Banks Ga., Athens, 1973-74; credit mgr. Coble Dairies, Athens, 1974-76, asst. controller, 1976-79, controller Florence (S.C.) div., 1979—. Community dir. Clarke County region Action Inc., 1978—. Office: PO Box 3438 Florence SC 29501

HENICAN, CASWELL ELLIS, lawyer; b. New Orleans, Feb. 10, 1905; s. Joseph Patrick and Alice (Boning) H.; LL.B., Tulane U., 1926; m. Elizabeth Cleveland, June 18, 1930; children—Alice (Mrs. Claude V. Perrier, Jr.), Caswell Ellis Jr., Margaret (Mrs. F. Gordon Wilson, Jr.), Dorothy (Mrs. Charles E. Heidingsfelder), Joseph Patrick III. Admitted to La. bar, 1926, since practiced in New Orleans; asso. firm Lemle, Moreno & Lemle, 1926-33; sr. partner firm Henican, Carriere & Cleveland, 1933-40, Henican, James & Cleveland, 1940—. Chmn. La. Bd. Pub. Welfare, 1940-47; pres. New Orleans Community Chest, 1940, Council Social Agys., 1939, Asso. Catholic Charities New Orleans, 1938, Archidiocesian Vocation Devel. Commn. Chmn. adv. bd. Mercy Hosp., Retreat House of Cenacle for Women; bd. dirs., trustee, pres. Magnolia Sch. Decorated Knight of St. Gregory, Order of St. Louis King of France; recipient medal as most outstanding young man New Orleans Jr. C. of C., 1940, F. Edward Hebert award as most outstanding alumnus of Jesuit High Sch., 1960. Mem. Am., La., New Orleans (pres. 1958) bar assns., Soc. Hosp. Attys. (charter), Nat. Health Lawyers Assn., Tulane U. Hall of Fame. Club: Serra (chpt. pres. 1960). Home: 1831 Octavia St New Orleans LA 70115 Office: 4440 One Shell Sq New Orleans LA 70139

HENING, JAMES HAMILTON, JR., architect; b. Hopewell, Va., Feb. 25, 1939; s. James Hamilton and Beatrice Zenobia (Carico) H.; student Va. Poly. Inst., 1957-58, Va. Commonwealth U., 1958, 77-78; B.Arch., U. Va., 1963; postgrad. U. Richmond, 1970, Central Piedmont Community Coll., 1971; children—Rhonda Gayle, James Hamilton III. Designer, Rawlings & Wilson, Richmond, Va., 1963-66; architect C.W. Huff, Jr., Richmond, 1966-68, Leary and Ciucci, Richmond, 1968, Marcellus Wright and Partner, Richmond, 1968-70; architect-asso. William Ward Moseley, AIA, Richmond, 1970-71; architect-v.p., sec.-treas. Moseley-Hening Assos., Inc., Richmond, 1971-79, exec. v.p., sec.-treas., 1979—, trustee, dir., 1971—. Pres., Birchett Estates Recreation Corp., 1966-67, Carillon Civic Assn., 1973—. Registered architect, Va., N.C. Mem. AIA (corp. mem., honor award for design 1970, 74, 78), Constrn. Specification Inst., Scarab Archtl. Hon. Soc. (pres. 1962-63), Raven Soc., Alpha Rho Chi. Co-editor archtl. sect. Va. Record mag., 1977—. Home: 514 S Sheppard St Richmond VA 23221 Office: Moseley-Hening Assos Inc 601 Southlake Blvd Richmond VA 23235

HENKE, EMERSON OVERBECK, accountant, educator; b. Stendal, Ind., Feb. 20, 1916; s. George A. and Sarah (Overbeck) H.; B.S. in Bus. Adminstrn., Evansville Coll., 1937; M.S. in Acctg., Ind. U., 1939, D.B.A., 1953; m. Beatrice Arney, June 6, 1939; children—Michael, Pamela Henke Bailes. Acct., Iglehart Milling Co., 1937-38, Hoosier Lamp & Stamping Co., 1939-40; instr. acctg. Evansville (Ind.) Coll., 1940-41, asst. prof., 1941-43, asso. prof., 1943-45, prof., 1945-48; teaching fellow Ind. U., 1951-52; prof., chmn. dept. acctg. Baylor U., Waco, Tex., 1948-67, prof., 1977-78, disting. prof. Hankamer Sch. Bus., 1977-78, disting. prof. acctg., 1978—, dean Hankamer Sch. Bus., 1967-77; vis. prof. U. Tex., Austin, 1966. Sunday sch. tchr., deacon, elder Presbyterian Ch., Waco. Recipient Alumni Cert. of Excellence award U. Evansville, 1978; named Most Popular Bus. Prof., Baylor U., 1964-65, Outstanding Prof., 1980; C.P.A., Ind., Tex. Mem. Am. Inst. C.P.A.'s (research cons. 1959-63), Am. Acctg. Assn. (past nat. com. chmn. research com., vice chmn. public sector sect. 1977-78, chmn. 1978-79), Tex. Soc. C.P.A.'s (past pres. Central Tex. chpt.), Beta Gamma Sigma, Beta Alpha Psi. Clubs: Rotary, Waco Philosopher's. Author: (with Walstein Smith, Jr.) CPA Review Outline, 1969; Introduction to Accounting, 1974; Accounting for Non-profit Organizations, 1977; (with Roderick L. Holmes and Lucian G. Conway) Managerial Use of Accounting Data, 1978; Introduction to Non-Profit Organization Accounting, 1980; contbr. articles on bus. and acctg. to profl. jours. Home: 3317 Lake Shore Dr Waco TX 76708 Office: Baylor Univ Waco TX 76706

HENKEL, JOHN HARMON, educator; b. Kentwood, La., Aug. 14, 1924; s. William Hatton and Margaret Gwendolyn (Watson) H.; student Southeastern La. Coll., 1941-43; B.S., Tulane U., 1947, M.S., 1948; Ph.D., Brown U., 1954; m. Sara Ernestine Saucier, Apr. 23, 1948; children—Wendolyn Elizabeth, Sally Lee (Mrs. Howard Barry Bone Jr.) (dec.), Jenny Saucier, Margaret Loraine, Pamela Ann. Jr. research technologist Magnolia Petroleum Co., Dallas, 1948-51, sr. research technologist, 1954-55; research asst. Brown U., Providence, 1951-54; asst. prof. U. Ga., Athens, 1955, asso. prof., 1958-64, prof. physics, 1964—. Dir. 19th Ann. Ga. State Sci. Fair, 1967; adviser Ga. chpt. Circle K Internat., 1966-72. Co-pres. Barrow Sch. PTA, Athens, 1964-66; area chmn. Tulane Alumni Found., 1970-76; bd. dirs. Wesley Found., Athens, Ga., 1966-72, pres., 1971-72. Served with USNR, 1943-46. NSF fellow, 1959-60; NSF grantee, 1962-69; NRC sr. research asso., 1973-74. Fellow AAAS; mem. Am. Phys. Soc., Ga. Acad. Sci. (fellow editorial bd. 1964-77, council mem. 1964-67, pres. 1968), Sigma Xi, Sigma Chi. Methodist. Clubs: Green Hills Country (pres. bd. dirs. Athens 1967-71), Kiwanis. Home: 395 Hampton Ct Athens GA 30601

HENLEY, SALLIE HAMLET, artist, deaf interpreter; b. Norfolk, Va., Sept. 29, 1933; d. Charles McDowell and Sarah Speight (White) Hamlet; student pub. schs., Norfolk; m. William Franklin Henley, Jr., July 21, 1951; children—William Franklin III, Robert Matthew. Pub. speaker, Milw., 1968-71, Houston, 1971—; book dramatist, Milw., 1969-71, Houston, 1971-72; interpreter for deaf, Milw., 1969-71, Houston, 1971—; free-lance artist, Atlanta, 1963-65, Houston, 1975—; exhibited Sportsmans Gallery, The Galleria, Houston. Interpreter to deaf Elmbrook Ch., Brookfield, Wis., 1969-70; vol. tchr. deaf retardate Fairview North Elementary Sch., Brookfield, 1970; narrator, interpreter Deaf Olympics, 1969; sec. Quail Valley Civic Assn., 1974-75; bd. dirs. Ephphatha, Inc., Milw., 1969-70. Mem. Registry Interpreters for Deaf. Republican. Home: 2806 E Pebble Beach Dr Missouri City TX 77459

HENN, SHIRLEY EMILY, librarian; b. Cleve., May 26, 1919; d. Albert Edwin and Florence Ely (Miller) Henn; A.B., Hollins Coll., 1941; M.S., U. N.C., 1966; m. John Van Bruggen, July 14, 1944 (div. May 1947); 1 son, Peter Albert (dec.). Library asst. Hollins (Va.) Coll., 1943-44, 61-64, reference librarian, 1965—; advt. mgr. R.M. Kellogg Co., Three Rivers, Mich., 1946-47; exec. sec. Hollins Coll. Alumnae Assn., 1947-55; real Intern, estate salesman Fowlkes & Kefauver, Roanoke, Va., 1955-61. Pres. Soc. for Prevention Cruelty to Animals, 1959-61, 69-72, bd. dirs., 1972—. Mem. Am. Alumni Council (dir. 1952-54, dir. women's activities 1952-54), Am., Va. (membership chmn. coll. and univ. sect. 1969—) library assns., Pub. Documents Forum Va., Nat. D.A.R., Collie Club Am., Roanoke Bird Club, Roanoke Kennel Club. Club: Quota (chpt. pres. 1958-60) (Roanoke). Author and illustrator: Adventures of Hooty Owl and His Friends, 1953. Editor: Hollins Alumnae Bull., 1947-56. Home: 6915 Tinkerdale Hollins VA 24019 Office: Fishburn Library Hollins College VA 24020

HENNECY, BOBBIE BOBO, educator; b. Tignall, Ga., Aug. 11, 1922; d. John Ebb and Lois Helen (Gulledge) Bobo; A.B. summa cum laude, Mercer U., Macon, Ga., 1950; postgrad. Oxford (Eng.) U., 1961; M.A. (NDEA fellow), Emory U., 1962; m. James Howell Hennecy, Dec. 28, 1963; 1 dau., Erin. Mem. faculty Mercer U., 1950—, asst. prof. English, 1976—; a founder Tattnall Sq. Acad., Macon, 1968, sec., 1968-73, dir., 1968-78. Mem. AAUW (chpt. pres. 1965), MLA, S. Atlantic MLA, So. Comparative Lit. Assn., Nat. Assn. Tchrs. English, Ga. Assn. Tchrs. English, English Speaking Union, LWV, Nat. Soc. So. Dames, Nat. Soc. Dames Magna Charta, DAR, Mid. Ga. Hist. Soc., Cardinal Key, Sigma Mu (past pres.), Alpha Psi Omega, Chi Omega. Baptist. Home: 1347-B Adams St Macon GA 31201 Office: Mercer Univ Macon GA 31207

HENNECY, JAMES HOWELL, govt. ofcl.; b. Marion, S.C., Mar. 10, 1913; s. Gabriel Marion and Annie Laurie (Boatwright) H.; student Mercer U., 1948-51; J.D., Walter F. George Sch. Law, 1953; m. Bobbie Helen Bobo, Dec. 28, 1963; 1 dau., Ardith Erin. Plant cashier Bordens Milk Co., Macon, Ga., 1953-55; contract specialist Dept. Air Force, Robins AFB, 1955-58, contract negotiator, 1964-74, contracting officer, 1975—; law librarian, instr. in law Walter F. George Sch. Law, Mercer U., Macon, 1958-63. Active Boy Scouts Am.; spokesman Macon Citizens for Better Hwy. Planning, 1959-62. Adviser, Young Democrats Club, 1960-63. Served with AUS, 1942-45; ETO, MTO. Mem. VFW, Young Americans for Freedom (asso.), Marion (S.C.) Jr. C. of C. (charter), Am. Ordnance Assn., Am. Legion, Air Force Assn., Internat. Platform Assn., Alpha Tau Omega, Delta Theta Phi, Alpha Psi Omega. Baptist (deacon). Clubs: Toastmasters (local pres. 1965, dist. edn. chmn. 1959-60), Lions. Home: 1347-B Adams St Macon GA 31201 Office: Directorate Procurement and Prodn WRALC Robins AFB GA 31093

HENNEN, ALBERT EARL, JR., advt. exec.; b. Wheeling, W.Va., Sept. 16, 1916; s. Albert Earl and Florence (Kirkland) H.; B.A. in Bus., Pa. State U., 1938; m. Anne Nolan Mathison, Oct. 22, 1946; children—Kathleen, Albert Earl III, John, David, Mary, Robert. Mich.-Ohio rep. Wesco Waterpaints Co., Matteson, Ill., 1946-47; advt. salesman Hearst Advt. Services, 1947-53; mgr. sales office George A. McDevitt Co., Pitts., 1953-54; mgr. retail advt. Ogden Newspapers, Inc., Wheeling, 1954-62, dir. advt., 1962—. Mem. Urban Renewal Authority, 1960-70, Wheeling Transp. Authority, 1975-77, Zoning Bd. Appeals, 1977—. Served with inf. U.S. Army, 1941-45; PTO. Mem. Wheeling C. of C. (exec. com.), Downtown Wheeling Assos. (sec., v.p.), Internat. Newspaper Advt. Execs. (state v.p. 1972-78), W.Va. Press Assn., Phi Delta Theta. Republican. Roman Catholic. Club: Symposiarchs. Home: 3 Lynwood Ave Wheeling WV 26003 Office: 1500 Main St Wheeling WV 26003

HENNESSY, JOHN J., lawyer; b. Savannah, Ga., Dec 20, 1905; s. James W. and Lucy (Downing) H.; A.B. magna cum laude, U. Ga.; postgrad. Harvard U.; J.D., Georgetown Law Sch., LL.M. with highest distinction. Admitted to Ga. bar, 1931, since practiced in Savannah; mem. firm Hennessy & Hennessy, 1942-65; spl. hearing officer Dept. Justice, 1948-67. Grand marshal Armed Forces Day parade. 1970, speaker Maritime Day Observance, 1973-77; commentator, lector Chapel Hunter AAF, 1973-79, including Scriptures in Spanish. Served from lt. to lt. comdr. USCGR, 1942-46; capt. Res., 1961—. Mem. Am., Ga., Savannah bar assns., Harvard Law Sch. Assn., Georgetown U., U. Ga. alumni socs., Am. Legion, Mil. Order World Wars, VFW (past post comdr., dist. judge adv.), Maritime Law Assn. U.S., Res. Officers Assn. (past state pres.), Navy League, Coast Guard League, Southeastern Admiralty Law Inst., Hibernian Soc., Phi Beta Kappa, Phi Kappa Phi, Delta Theta Phi. Elk (hon. life, past exalted ruler). Mem. editorial staff Georgetown U. Law Jour., 1930-31. Home: 233 E 52d St Savannah GA 31405 Office: PO Box 1114 Savannah GA 31402

HENNESY, GERALD CRAFT, artist; b. Washington, June 11, 1921; s. Gerald Craft and Frances Lee (Moore) H.; student Corcoran Sch. Art, 1939, George Washington U., 1940; B.S., U. Md., 1948; m. Elizabeth Ann Lovering, Mar. 4, 1950; children—Kathleen, Paul, Brian, Shawn, Hugh, Craig. Artist advt. dept. Times Herald newspaper, Washington, 1941-42; commd. ensign U.S. Navy, 1942; active duty, 1942-46, 52-54; advanced through ranks to comdr., 1956; artist USAF Hdqrs., Pentagon, Washington, 1948-52, AEC, Washington, 1956-72, asst. dir. orgn. and mgmt., 1969-72; dir., artist Studio of Hennesy, Clifton, Va., 1972—; one-man shows: PLA Gallery Fine Art, McLean, Va., 1967, Leo Gallery, Washington, 1970, Gallery of the Sea, Crystal City, Va., 1977; group shows: Corcoran Gallery Art, Washington, 1957, 59, 67, Smithsonian Inst., Washington, 1962, 64, Allied Artists Am., N.Y.C., 1975, 76; represented in permanent collections: Nat. Hdqrs. Am. Legion, Washington, Md. State Exec. Mansion, Annapolis, Fed. Dist. Ct. Bldg., Alexandria, Va.; also numerous pvt. collections; works include: series oil paintings Great Moments of History in Fairfax County, 1974; Boothbay Harbor, 1975; White House South Portico, 1976. Served with USN, 1942-46; to comdr. USNR, 1952-54, 56. Decorated Air medal with star, Presdl. unit citation. Mem. Artists Equity Assn., Fairfax County Council Arts, Landscape Artists Washington (treas. 1973-77). Republican. Address: 6811 White Rock Rd Clifton VA 22024

HENRICH, LEE PERKINS, public relations counselor; b. Memphis, Sept. 26, 1913; s. John Walter and Mary Katherine (Singleton) Perkins; B.S. in Bus., Miami U., Oxford, Ohio, 1936; m. Elaine Medick, June 20, 1960; 1 son, Daniel Lee Henrich. With Hoover Co., N. Canton, Ohio, 1936-41; sr. account exec. W.L. Stensgaard & Assos., Inc., Chgo. and N.Y.C., 1941-47; dir. advt. and public relations, mem. exec. com. Hart Schaffner & Marx, Chgo., 1947-53; mdsg. dir. narrow fabrics Burlington Industries, N.Y.C., 1953-56; advt. dir. Rogers Peet Co., 1956-59; propr. Lee P. Henrich, counselor for public relations, Ft. Lauderdale, Fla., 1960—. Vestryman, All Saints Episcopal Ch., Ft. Lauderdale, 1968—. Served to lt. comdr. USNR, 1942-45. Mem. Am. Public Relations Assn. (dir.), Public Relations Soc. Am., Human Engrs. Assn. (dir.), Sigma Chi. Republican. Author articles in field. Address: 2539 NE 26th Terr Fort Lauderdale FL 33305

HENRY, CLIFFORD HUGH, JR., former state legislator Tenn., ins. exec.; b. Rockford, Tenn., July 15, 1928; s. Clifford Hugh and Bennie (Clark) H.; B.S., Maryville Coll., 1950; M.B.A., Am. U., 1960; m. Shirley Brown, July 6, 1957; children—Stephen Brown, Julie Anna, Jodi Lynn, Holly Leigh. Tchr., Blount County, Tenn., 1950-51, prin., 1956-57; with Applied Physics Lab., Johns Hopkins, Balt., 1958-60; stockbroker Abbott, Proctor & Paine, Knoxville, Tenn., 1961-62; v.p. Bank of Maryville (Tenn.), 1963-64; with Paine, Webber, Jackson & Curtis, Richmond, Va., 1965-67, v.p., Maryville, 1968—; pres., dir. Blazer Ins. Co., Maryville, 1972—; pres. Nebbhett Ins. Agy., Ins. Service & Assos.; mem. Tenn. Ho. of Reps. from 20th Legis. Dist., 1975-76, mem. com. on edn., 1975-76, com. on commerce, 1975-76; mem. exec. com. Blount County, 1972-76. Served with U.S. Army, 1952-55. Mem. Soc. of Sons of the Revolution. Republican. Methodist. Clubs: Green Meadow Country, Mason (Shriner), Highlands (N.C.) Country. Home: 1202 S Heritage Dr Maryville TN 37301 Office: Blazer Bldg Maryville TN 37801

HENRY, DONALD POMEROY, machinery and pump mfg. co. exec.; b. Cin., Mar. 19, 1928; s. George Dunbar and Emma Ethel (Pomeroy) H.; B.S. in Mech. Engring., Purdue U., 1949; m. Dorine Beulah Neil, Sept. 26, 1953; children—Deborah Anne, Donald Neil, Diane Lynn, David Deming. Asst. plant mgr. Yuba Power Products Co., Cin., 1954-59; gen. mgr., power tool plant Rockwell Mfg. Co., Bellefontaine, Ohio, 1959-67; mfg. mgr. John Bean div. FMC Corp., Lansing, Mich., 1967-69; v.p. mfg. Jacuzzi Bros., Inc., Little Rock, 1969—. Mem. Soc. Mfg. Engrs., Theta Xi. Presbyterian. Home: 32 Huntington Rd Little Rock AR 72207 Office: 11511 New Benton Hwy Little Rock AR 72203

HENRY, ELIZABETH ANDERSON, dietitian; b. Bluefield, W.Va., Oct. 30, 1922; d. James Marvin and Evie Maude (Lazenby) Anderson; B.S., Winthrop Coll., Rock Hill, S.C., 1944; R.D., Watts Hosp., Durham, N.C., 1945; m. Robert Randolph Henry III, Oct. 9, 1954; 1 son, Robert Randolph IV. Head dietitian Meml. Hosp., High Point, N.C., 1945-48; therapeutic and teaching instr. Meml. Hosp., Charlotte, N.C., 1948-49; head dietitian St. Luke's Hosp., Bluefield, 1949-57; dietitian Bluefield Community Hosp., 1970—; lectr. nutrition and family living; cons. dietitian affiliated hosps. Mem. Am. Dietetic Assn., N.C. Dietetic Assn. (pres.-elect, editor), W.Va. Dietetic Assn. (pres., del.), Am. Diabetic Assn. (asso.), AAUW. Republican. Methodist. Clubs: Little Garden, DAR. Home: 930 Heatherwood Rd Bluefield WV 24701 Office: Bluefield Community Hosp 500 Cherry St Bluefield WV 24701

HENRY, JOHN JAMES, physicist; b. White Pine, Tenn., Feb. 12, 1929; s. Herbert Holloway and Clara (Spurgeon) H.; student U. Fla., 1946-48; B.S., Lincoln Meml. U., 1954; m. Audrey Duffield, Sept. 14, 1954; children—Mark Stephen, Claudia Alexandra, John James. Instrument technician Carbide & Carbon Chem. Co., Oak Ridge, 1954-56; asso. physicist Union Carbide Corp., Oak Ridge, 1956-61, physicist nuclear div., 1961-74, devel. specialist, 1974-76, devel. staff I, 1976—. Instr. transistor circuit theory Oak Ridge Adult Edn. Program, 1962-65. Scoutmaster, Boy Scouts Am., Oak Ridge, 1960-62; tympanist Oak Ridge Symphony Orch., 1965-73, publicity chmn., 1966-67, v.p., 1968-69. Served with USMC, 1949-52. Recipient IR-100 award Industrial Research Mag., 1979. Mem. Instrument Soc. Am. (sr.), AAAS, IEEE. Episcopalian (vestryman 1974-76, chmn. music and worship com. 1974-75, chmn. outreach com. 1976). Patentee in field. Home: 639 Pennsylvania Ave Oak Ridge TN 37830 Office: Y12 Plant Oak Ridge TN 37830

HENRY, MARION, educator; b. Dallas, Mar. 23, 1927; s. Dewey and Mary Lee H.; B.S., So. U., 1952; M.S., Bradley U., 1953; Ph.D., Syracuse U., 1972; m. Mary Delores Grant, Oct. 23, 1953; children—Byron Timothy, Sharon Lynn Marie. With U.S. Govt., Dallas, 1953-56; prof. Prairie View (Tex.) A&M U., 1956—, dir. Learning Resources Center, chmn. dept. ednl. tech.; cons. United Bd. for Coll. Devel. and NSF Workshop. Trustee, sec. Waller Sch. Dist.; trustee Prairie View Fed. Credit Union. Served with U.S. Army, 1946-49. Mem. Assn. Tchr. Educators, Assn. for Ednl.

Communicationa Tech. (definition and terminology com.), Tex. Assn. Ednl. Tech., ALA, Tex. Library Assn. (intellectual freedom com.), Phi Delta Kappa, Epsilon Pi Tau, Omega Psi Phi. Democrat. Roman Catholic. Co-author: Certification of School Media Specialists. Home: PO Box 2730 Prairie View TX 77445 Office: Prairie View A&M U Prairie View TX 77445

HENRY, MARTHA FRANCES SHOCK, dietitian; b. Columbia, Mo., Sept. 19, 1920; d. James William and Martha Frances (Robinson) Shock; B.S., U. Mo., 1941; postgrad. Iowa State U., 1940, Tex. A. and M. U., 1972-74; m. Walter K. Henry, Feb. 13, 1943; children—Stephen A., Dale Lee, Carl B. Adminstrv. dietitian Bryan (Tex.) Hosp., 1972-74; cons. dietitian Sherwood Health Care Facility, Bryan, 1974-76; adminstrv. dietitian St. Joseph Hosp., Bryan, 1976-78; pvt. cons. diet and nutrition, College Station, 1978—. Mem. Brazos County Hist. Survey Com., 1970—; sec. Brazos County Bicentennial com.; bd. dirs. United Fund, 1975-78; den mother Boy Scouts Am.; pres. Band Boosters; mem. College Station Recreation Council. Registered dietitian. Mem. Brazos Valley Home Econs. Assn., Am. Dietetics Assn., Cons. Nutritionists, Tex. Dietetic Assn., Mid-East Tex. Dietetic Assn., Am. Diabetes Assn., DAR (state Organizing sec., state lineage research chmn.), Daughters Am. Colonists (organizing regent), U.S. Daus. 1812 (registrar, sec.), Magna Charta Dames, Brazos Valley Geneal. Soc., Nat. Geneal. Soc. Methodist. Address: 1202 Caudill St College Station TX 77840

HENRY, WALTER KEITH, meteorologist; b. Moberly, Mo., Jan. 9, 1919; s. Walter R. and Ruth (Parsons) H.; student Missouri Valley Coll., 1936-38; B.S. in Chem. Engring., U. Mo., 1941; M.S. in Meteorology, U. Chgo., 1949; m. Martha Frances Shock, Feb. 13, 1943; children—Stephen Allen, Dale Lee, Carl Bruce. Jr. engr. Mo. Hwy. Dept., Jefferson City, 1941-42; 46; served in USAAC, 1942-45; recalled to active duty USAF, 1947, advanced through grades to lt. col., 1957; chief USAF Weather Forecasting Sch., Chanute AFB, 1954-56; ret., 1957; prof. meteorology Tex. A&M U., College Station, 1957—; guest lectr. Universidad Central, Caracus, Venezuela, 1977, 78. Scoutmaster Boy Scouts Am., 1964-70. Recipient grants U.S. Army, NSF. Mem. Am. Meteorol. Soc., Nat. Weather Assn., AAAS, Am. Geophys. Union, Sigma Xi, Nat. Geneal. Soc., Mo. Hist. Soc., Ohio Geneal. Soc. Methodist. Clubs: Masons (32 deg.), Shriners, Heroes of 76, Sojourner. Contbr. articles to profl. jours. Home: 1202 Caudill St College Station TX 77840 Office: Dept Meteorology Tex A&M U College Station TX 77843

HENRY, WILLIAM RAY, educator; b. Russellville, Ark., Dec. 20, 1925; s. Mace Leon and Violet May (Shinn) H.; B.S. in Agrl. Bus., U. Ark., 1948, M.S. in Agrl. Econs., 1952; Ph.D. in Econs., N.C. State U., 1957; m. Norma Talmadge Wright, Nov. 27, 1954; children—William Ray, Lisa Carolyn, Linda Carol, Lara Carleen. From asst. prof. to prof. N.C. State U., Raleigh, 1956-70; prof. bus. adminstrn. Ga. State U., Atlanta, 1970—. Served with USAAF, 1944-45. Recipient award of merit for published research Am. Agrl. Econs. Assn., 1957, 61. Co-author: Managerial Economics, 4th edit., 1978. Contbr. articles to profl. jours. Home: 4101 Carlisle Pl Stone Mountain GA 30083 Office: Univ Plaza Atlanta GA 30303

HENRY, ZACHARY ADOLPHUS, agrl. engr.; b. Stockbridge, Ga., Apr. 25, 1930; s. Walter R. and Annie L. (Flake) H.; B.S. in Agrl. Engring., U. Ga., 1951; M.S. in Agrl. Engring., Clemson U., 1959; Ph.D., N.C. State U., 1962; m. Norma Rae Taylor, Dec. 19, 1953; children—Zachary Adolphus, Lydia Carol, Vera Lynn, Nathan Lee, Stephen Taylor. Constrn. engr. E.I. DuPont de Nemours Inc., Augusta, Ga., 1951; irrigation engr. Fla. Steel Corp., Decatur, Ga., 1955-57; research fellow Clemson (S.C.) U., 1957-58; research asst. N.C. State U., Raleigh, 1958-61; asst. prof. agrl. engring. U. Tenn., Knoxville, 1961-67, asso. prof., 1967—, faculty adv. to Student Agrl. Engring. Club, 1963—, leader Chinese Christian students, 1965-72. Local leader 4-H Club, 1965—; deacon Corryton (Tenn.) Baptist Ch., 1966—, Bible tchr., 1963—; bd. dirs. West End Learning Center, 1971—, chmn., 1971—. Served with USN, 1952-55. Nat. Found. for Cotton Research fellow, 1957-58; registered profl. engr., Tenn. Mem. Am. Soc. Agrl. Engrs. (chmn. electric power and processing div. 1979—), Am. Soc. Engring. Edn., Sigma Xi, Gamma Sigma Delta. Contbr. articles on instrumentation and agrl. engring. to profl. jours.; editor Instrumentation and Measurement for Environmental Sciences, 1977—. Home: Route 2 Chiles Rd Corryton TN 37721 Office: Univ Tenn Dept Agricultural Engineering Knoxville TN 37916

HENSEL, LEN, radio broadcasting exec.; b. Phila., Mar. 30, 1926; s. John and Jean (Cedar) H.; B.S., Auburn U., 1948; m. Patricia Ann Rhodes, Sept. 15, 1951; children—Patricia Lynn, Janie Sue. Program dir. WOWL Radio, Florence, Ala., 1949-52; account exec. WAPI-TV, Birmingham, Ala., 1952-54; account exec., regional sales mgr. ZIV-TV Programs, 1954-62; nat. sales mgr., gen. sales mgr. WSM Radio, Nashville, 1962-71, v.p., gen. mgr., 1972—, also dir. Served with USNR, 1943-45; PTO. Mem. Sales and Mktg. Execs., Nat. Assn. Broadcasters (chmn.), Nashville C. of C., Pi Kappa Alpha. Presbyn. Kiwanian. Clubs: Hillwood Country, City (Nashville). Home: 6600 Fox Hollow Rd Nashville TN 37205 Office: PO Box 100 Nashville TN 37202

HENSEL, WILBER MARSH, JR., petroleum engr.; b. Dallas, Oct. 2, 1927; s. Wilber Marsh and Mabel (Johnson) H.; student Dallas Coll. of So. Methodist U., 1956; m. Flo McCommas, Aug. 20, 1946; children—Annette Hensel O'Leary, Janette Hensel Kittrell, Marsha Hensel Johns, Christine, Hensel Josey. Salesman, Titchegoettinger Co., Dallas, 1948-49; service/sales staff Ventahood Co., Dallas, 1949-51; technician Core Analysis Lab., Sun Oil Co., Dallas, 1951-55, supr. lab., 1955-73; staff specialist Reservoir Rock Properties, Sun Oil Co., Richardson, 1973—. Chmn. Democratic precinct com., 1967—; election judge Dallas County, City of Richardson; chief election judge Richardson Ind. Sch. Dist., 1967—. Served with USCG, 1945-48. Mem. Soc. Petroleum Engrs., Soc. Profl. Well Log Analysts (asso.). Episcopalian. Home: 10138 Deermont Trail Dallas TX 75243 Office: Box 936 Richardson TX 75080

HENSGENS, LEONARD JOSEPH, farmer, equipment co. exec.; b. Acadia Parish, La., Oct. 7, 1929; s. Christian J. and Elizabeth (Thevis) H.; student parochial schs., Crowley, La.; m. Sarah Ann Smith, July 11, 1950; children—Mary, Sarah. Farmer, Acadia Parish, St. Landry Parish, La., Arkansas County, Ark., 1960—; owner H & H Equipment Co., Crowley, La.; dir. Plaquemine Bank & Trust Co., Plaquemine, La., Growers Elevator Co., DeWitt, Ark., Am. Liberty Fin. Corp., Baton Rouge; past mem. rice adv. com. U.S. Dept. Agr.; bd. dirs. La. Herbicide and Pesticide Commn., 1976—; bd. dirs. New Orleans Futures Exchange, New Orleans. Squadron comdr. CAP. Served in AUS, 1954-55. Named Farmer of Year in Acadia Parish, 1967. Mem. Am., La., Acadia Parish (dir., past pres.) farm burs. Republican. Roman Catholic. Home: 223 E Hutchinson Crowley LA 70526 Office: 405 S Ave H Crowley LA 70526

HENSHAW, ANDY LORENZO, rehab. counselor; b. Jackson County, Ala., Jan. 25, 1943; s. Henry Franklin and Oza (Fowler) H.; student Middle Tenn. State U., 1965-66; B.S. in Edn., U. Ga., 1969, M.S. in Edn. (Automotive Safety Found. fellow), 1970; M.S. in Vocat. Rehab., Memphis State U., 1979; m. Elizabeth Donaldson Bennett, Mar. 14, 1964; 1 dau., Lisa. Machine operator Genesco, Tullahoma, Tenn., 1961-62; timekeeper P.R. Mallor Capacitor Co., Huntsville, Ala., 1962-65; tchr., coach Dougherty County Bd. Edn., Albany, Ga., 1970-72; vocat. rehab. counselor III, div. vocat. rehab. Tenn. Dept. Edn., Nashville, 1972—; sec.-treas. Franklin County Land Co., Winchester, Tenn., 1974—. Pres. Clark Meml. Parent Tchr. Orgn., 1975-76; chmn. Franklin County chpt. ARC, 1975-76; mem. Indsl. Devel. Bd., City of Decherd (Tenn.), 1975—; pres. North Jr. High Sch. P.T.O., 1978-79. Recipient Outstanding Young Man of Year award Franklin County Jr. C. of C., 1976, Outstanding C. of C. Citizen award, 1978. Mem. Nat. (certified), Vol. State rehab. assns., Nat. Rehab. Counseling Assn., Tenn. Guidance and Personnel Assn. Presbyterian. Club: Rotary (dir. 1973-76, sec. 1974-75) (Winchester). Home: Route 1 Tammy Dr Decherd TN 37324 Office: Box 512 Winchester TN 37398

HENSLEY, ALTON LEON, internal auditor; b. Burleson, Tex., July 11, 1933; s. Claude Franklin and Lillian (Harper) H.; student N. Tex. State U., 1955-56; B.S., Tex. Christian U., 1958, postgrad., 1959-60; m. Carol Jean Holm, Aug. 27, 1955; children—Barbara Cathleen, Laura Candace. Asst. mgr. Kresge's, Joplin, Mo., 1958; auditor McCammon, Morris, Pickens & Mayhew, Ft. Worth, 1959-60; internal auditor Tex. Christian U., Ft. Worth, 1960-67, asst. to vice chancellor, 1967-72, controller, 1972-75; internal auditor Ft. Worth Ind. Sch. Dist., 1975—. Served with USAF, 1950-54. Mem. Inst. Internal Auditors, Tex. Assn. Sch. Bus. Ofcls. Republican. Baptist. Home: 2009 Bettibart Fort Worth TX 76134 Office: 3210 W Lancaster Fort Worth TX 76107

HENSLEY, LEE RASBURY, educator; b. Austin, Tex., Dec. 11, 1929; s. Alexander Lee and Christine Yvonne (Rasbury) H.; B.A., Baylor U., 1950; M.A., George Peabody Coll., 1951; Ed.D., E. Tex. State U., 1975; m. Sanoa Julon Falmlen, Jan. 24, 1959; children—Alexander Lee, Heather Helene, Frederick Grant, Sanoa Julon. Tchr. English, Plainview Jr. High Sch., 1956-57; cost engr. Tex. Instruments Co., 1959-62; mgr. Sherwin-Williams store, Dallas, 1962-65; asst. prof. English, Dallas Bapt. Coll., 1965-68, Jarvis Christian Coll., Hawkins, Tex., 1970-74, asso. prof., chmn. dept. English, 1975-76, prof. English, chmn. div. humanities, 1976-78, dean academic sers., 1978—; adj. prof. E. Tex. State U., Commerce, 1975—. Served with USNR, 1953-56. Mem. Modern Lang. Assn., Nat., Tex. Joint councils tchrs. of English, Coll. Conf. Composition and Communication, Conf. Coll. Tchrs. of English, AAUP. Baptist. Home: 4252 Norwich Dr Fort Worth TX 76109 Office: Dean Academic Sers Jarvis Christian Coll Hawkins TX 75765

HENSLEY, REUBEN BRUCE, broadcaster; b. Columbus, Ga., June 16, 1943; s. Reuben B. and Minnie B. H.; B.S., Hampton Inst.; 1 dau., Kermelle D. Tchr., Muscogee County (Ga.) Bd. Edn., 1967-70; art dir. WTVM, Columbus, 1970—; host Both Sides, 1975—, Mr. Play-like and Friends, 1978—, Kids Are People Too, 1979—; mem. art faculty Columbus Coll. Mem. Columbus Mayor's Council; bd. dirs. CD, YMCA, Columbus. Recipient various community service awards. Mem. Columbus Jaycees, Alpha Phi Alpha. Home: 1257 Boxwood Blvd Columbus GA 31906 Office: 1909 Wynnton Rd Columbus GA 31902

HENSON, CLARANCE EDWARD, JR., radio sta. exec.; b. Louisville, July 16, 1951; s. Clarance Edward and Cora Bradford (Buins) H.; B.A., Johns Hopkins U., 1972; m. Gail Clark Ritchie, May 25, 1974; 1 dau., Elizabeth Anne. Pres. Ky. Tech. Inst., Inc., Louisville, 1973—; v.p. Electronic Labs., Inc., Louisville, 1973—; v.p. Electrocast, Inc., Louisville, 1973—; pres. Sta. WLRS-FM, Louisville. Mem. Nat. Radio Broadcasters Assn., Ky. Broadcasters Assn. Democrat. Presbyterian. Office: Suite 2002 800 S 4th St Louisville KY 40203

HENSON, GENE ETHRIDGE, legal adminstr.; b. Lawrenceville, Ga., Sept. 26, 1924; d. Fred Golden and Cora Jewell (Smith) Ethridge; student public schs., Lawrenceville; m. James Arthur Henson, May 2, 1948 (dec.); 1 dau., Gena Arlene. With Smith, Currie & Hancock, Atlanta, 1959—, adminstr., 1965—. Ofcl. hostess for State of Ga., So. Gov.'s Conf., Atlanta, 1971; past adult tchr. First Bapt. Ch., Lawrenceville. Mem. Assn. Legal Adminstrs. (nat. v.p. 1979—, dir. 1979—), Atlanta Assn. Legal Execs. (1st pres. 1975). Home: 74 Scenic Hwy Lawrenceville GA 30245 Office: Smith Currie & Hancock 2600 Peachtree Center Harris Tower Atlanta GA 30303

HENSON, JERRY B., mus. ofcl.; b. Anniston, Ala., July 1, 1922; s. Court L. and Mary (Baker) H.; student Jacksonville State U., 1948; m. Mary Higginbottham, June 29, 1959; 1 son, Jerry Ray. Patrolman, Oxford (Ala.) Police Dept., 1947-68; mem. Anniston Police Dept., 1956-68, ret., 1968; with Anniston (Ala.) Mus. Natural History, 1956—, curator, 1968—, also chief security officer. Served with C.E., AUS, 1943-46. Mem. Am. Radio Relay League, Nat. Rifle Assn., Am. Meteorol. Soc., Nat. Model R.R. Assn. Home: PO Box 1113 Anniston AL 36201 Office: 4301 McClellan Blvd Anniston AL 36201

HENSON, PAUL LOGAN, utility co. exec.; b. Blytheville, Ark., June 6, 1951; s. James Elmer and Nettie Nell (Moore) H.; B.S., Ark. State U., 1973; postgrad. U. Ark., 1978—. Accountant, Mike Isom & Co., C.P.A.'s, Memphis, 1973-75; mgr. internal auditing Ark.-Mo. Power Co., Blytheville, Ark., 1975-77, dir. budgets, forecast and planning, 1977—. Treas., mem. exec. bd. Mississippi County Bapt. Assn., 1977—. Mem. Southeastern Electric Exchange, Blytheville C. of C. Democrat. Club: Optimist (Blytheville). Democrat. Home: 1515 N 6th St Apt 1B Blytheville AR 72315 Office: Ark-Mo Power Co 405 W Park St Blytheville AR 72315

HENTHORN, STEPHEN PERRY, public health ofcl.; b. Anderson, Ind., Oct. 8, 1949; s. Robert E. and Gene L. (Gibbs) H.; B.S., Union Coll., 1971, M.A., 1973; m. Nika Rose Stallard, Jan. 19, 1974; 1 dau., Nikaya Dahn. Dir. dept. community services Sue Bennett Coll., London, Ky., 1974; salesman Royal Crown Bottling Co., Whitesburg, Ky., 1974-75; research analyst Ky. River Dist. Health Dept., Hazard, 1975-78, health planner, 1978—, program mgr., 1975—; spl. cons. Dilce Combs Jr. High and Sr. High Drama Clubs, 1976—. Mem. Hazard City Recreation Commn., 1977—, Hazard/Perry County Drug Edn. Council, 1976-78, evaluation subcom. Statewide Family Planning Task Force, 1978—; mem. Ky. Statewide Family Planning Conf. Com., 1978-80. Recipient Best Actor award Union Coll., 1973, 74. Mem. Ky. Public Health Assn., Alpha Psi Omega, Delta Delta Upsilon. Methodist. Home: 129 Oak St Hazard KY 41701 Office: Kentucky River Dist Health Dept 825 High St Hazard KY 41701

HENTON, WILLIS RYAN, bishop; b. McCook, Nebr., July 5, 1925; s. Burr Milton and Clara Vaire (Godown) H.; B.A., Kearney State Coll., 1949; S.T.B., Gen. Theol. Sem., N.Y., 1952, S.T.D., 1972; D.D., U. of South, 1972; m. Martha Somerville Bishop, June 7, 1952; 1 son, David. Ordained priest Episcopal Ch., 1953, consecrated bishop, 1971; missionary, Mountain Province, P.I., 1952-57; asst. pastor, N.Y.C., 1957-58; rector ch., Mansfield, La., 1958-61, Baton Rouge, 1961-64; archdeacon of La., 1964-71; bishop coadjutor of N.W. Tex., 1971-72, bishop 1972—. Trustee U. of South. Office: Tex Commerce Bank Bldg PO Box 1067 Lubbock TX 79408

HENTZ, WALTER DARDEN (BO), communications co. ofcl.; b. Birmingham, Ala., Jan. 2, 1950; s. Walter Thurston and Elizabeth Ann (Darden) H.; student U. Ala., 1973; 1 son, Walter Sean. Radio telephone sales rep., account exec., Eastern mgr. Motorola Communications Co., Birmingham, 1972-75; So. sales mgr. Amcor, Inc., Birmingham, 1975-77; sales mgr. terminal products Harris Corp., Birmingham, 1977—, Mid-So. regional sales mgr., 1978—. Mem. Ala. Assn. Radio Utilities (pres.), Ala.-Miss. Ind. Telephone Assn., Ala. Assn. Radio Common Carriers (dir.), Phi Theta Kappa. Home: 909 Ryecroft Rd Birmingham AL 35124 Office: 1776 Independence Ct Birmingham AL 35216

HEPNER, LEON WILBURNE, educator; b. Coffeyville, Kans., May 11, 1915; s. Edgar Grant and Iva Christine (Parsons) H.; A.B., Kans. U., 1938, A.M., 1939. Ph.D., 1946; m. Ada Lillian Reiter, Jan. 3, 1942; children—Larry, Paula, Patricia, Leon Wilburne. Mem. faculty Ft. Hays Kans. State Coll., 1946-58; mem. faculty Miss. State U., 1958—, prof. entomology, 1962—. Served with U.S. Army, 1943-45. NSF grantee, 1962-72; U.S. Dept. Agr. grantee, 1965-68. Mem. Entomol. Soc. Am., Kans., Ga., Fla., Miss. entomol. socs. Research on cicadellid systematics. Office: Dept Entomology Miss State U Mississipi State MS 39762

HEPWORTH, SAMUEL WILSON, advt. exec.; b. Topeka, 1909; s. Llewellyn G. and Bertha Beall (Wilson) H.; student Rockhurst Coll., 1930-34; spl. courses U. Okla., 1940-41; m. Ivanola Mozelle Palmer, 1939; 1 son, Wesley Wilson. Worked for various newspapers, Chgo., Oklahoma City and Jackson, Miss., 1934-43; v.p., mgr. Grant Advt., Inc., Dallas, 1943-52; pres., treas. Hepworth Advt. Co. since founded 1952. Mem. Soc. Indsl. Editors, Dallas Hist. Soc., Dallas Advt. League, Dallas Council World Affairs, Nat. Indsl. Advt. Assn. Democrat. Mem. Christian Ch. (deacon). Clubs: Dallas Athletic, Dallas Country, Forth Worth Petroleum, Rotary, Order Eastern Star (worthy patron 1977—), Masons (32 deg.), Shriners. Home: 3700 Amherst Dallas TX 75225 Office: 3403 McKinney Dallas TX 75204

HERBERT, DAMON CHARLES, anatomist; b. N.Y.C., Apr. 15, 1945; s. Bruce Morrison and Helen Catherine (Ebert) H.; A.B. in Biol. Scis., Chico State Coll., 1967; Ph.D. in Anatomy, U. Calif., San Francisco, 1973; m. Marjorie Ellen Gloden, Aug. 20, 1967; children—Garrick Todd, Michelle Lorraine. Instr. anatomy Univ. Tex. Health Sci. Center, San Antonio, 1973-74, asst. prof. anatomy, 1974-78, asso. prof. anatomy, 1978—. Sunday Sch. tchr. St. Andrew Presbyn. Ch., San Antonio 1976-78, dean Ch. Sch., 1978—, bd. dirs. early learning center, 1979—. Coach baseball and football YMCA, 1979—. Edith Claypole Fellow, 1970-72; NIH research grantee, 1977—. Mem. Am. Assn. Anatomists, Endocrine Soc., Am. Soc. Cell Biology, Histochem. Soc., Soc. for Study Reproduction, Am. Soc. Andrology, AAAS, Blue Key, Sigma Xi, Delta Sigma Pi. Asso. editor Anatomical Record; contbr. sci. articles and abstracts to profl. jours. Office: Dept Anatomy Univ Texas Health Science Center San Antonio TX 78284

HERBERT, KEITH JOHN, chem. engr.; b. Madison, Wis., Sept. 19, 1950; s. Clifford Wayne and Elva Mae (Klug) H.; B.S. in Chem. Engring., U. Tulsa, 1972; m. Janet Diane Whaley, June 9, 1968; 1 son, Ronald Keith. Design engr. Pollution Research div. John Zink Co., Tulsa, 1969-72, mgr. project engring., 1972-74; project mech. process engr. Ralph M. Parsons Co., Pasadena, Calif., 1974-75; project mgr. Flare div. John Zink Co., Tulsa, 1975-77; design engr. pollution control sect. Crest Engring., Tulsa, 1978-79; mgr. combustion products McGill, Inc., 1979—. Registered profl. engr., Okla. Mem. Am. Inst. Chem. Engrs. Republican. Home: 5932 S 73d E Ave Tulsa OK 74145 Office: 7477 E 46th Pl Tulsa OK 74145

HERBERT, WILLIAM FIELD, petroleum cons.; b. N.Y.C., June 27, 1899; s. Henry Arthur and Mary Grace (Waterman) H.; B.M.E., Mass. Inst. Tech., 1925; m. Elizabeth Caroline O'Niell, Aug. 29, 1928 (dec. Dec. 1979); children—Patricia Herbert Cook, William Field, John Henry. Various engring. assignments in raw sugar mfg., Cuba and La., 1918-33; with Texaco, Inc., Houston, Ft. Worth and London, 1933-64, asst. div. mgr., 1955-64; cons. Lufkin Industries, 1965-71; pvt. practice petroleum cons., Houston, 1971—. Registered profl. engr., Tex. Mem. Soc. Petroleum Engrs. (honor certificate Gulf Coast chpt.), Am. Petroleum Inst. (certificate appreciation), Houston Engring. and Sci. Soc., Engrs. Council Houston, Houston C. of C., SAR, Mayflower Descs. Republican. Episcopalian. Home: 3739 Darcus St Houston TX 77005 Office: 3630 Wakeforest St Houston TX 77098

HERBST, HARVEY RAYMOND, univ. ofcl., broadcasting adminstr.; b. Dallas, Nov. 21, 1922; s. Frederick Charles and Gertrude (Dorcey) H.; B.A. in Speech, Radio and Drama, U. Denver, 1944; postgrad. Northwestern U., 1947-48, N.Y. U., 1951-52; M.A. in Radio and TV Broadcasting, Syracuse U., 1949; Ed.D., U. Tex., 1967; m. Dean Finley, Aug. 5, 1955; children—Frederick, Marian. Radio program dir. Sta. KHUZ, Borger, Tex., 1946-47; advt. supr. Speigel, Inc., Chgo., 1947-48; writer, producer (part-time) Sta. WFBL, Syracuse, N.Y., 1948; instr. dept. drama U. Tex., Austin, 1949-51, asst. prof. drama, 1956-60, asst. prof. radio-TV, Sch. Journalism, 1960-62, TV program dir., 1956-61, asso. dir. Communication Center, 1956-78, acting dir., 1977—, mgr. Sta. KLRN-TV, 1962-77, sr. v.p., 1977—; mem. TV prodn. staff Sta. WFAA-TV, Dallas, 1953-54; account exec. in TV, Sta. KTBC-TV, Austin, 1954-56; dir. radio and TV broadcasting Nat. Music Camp, Interlachen, Mich., summer, 1956; mem. Ednl. TV Sta. Copyright Commn., 1972-77. Pres., Austin Council for Adult Advancement, 1964; mem. public info. com. Tex. div. Am. Cancer Soc., 1972-76; ruling elder Session of Covenant Presbyn. Ch., 1964-68; mem. Value of Life Com., Tex. Conf. Chs., 1977; bd. dirs. Nat. Cystic Fibrosis Research Found., 1957-67, So. Ednl. Network, 1963-72; trustee Center Stage of Austin, 1977-78. Recipient George Washington medal Freedoms Found., 1958, Ohio State U. award for Excellence in Production, 1951, 56, 62; Sears Roebuck Found. grantee, 1967. Mem. Tex. Ednl. TV Assn., Tex. Audio-Visual Assn., So. Ednl. Communications Assn. (dir. 1968-72), NEA, Phi Delta Kappa, Pi Kappa Alpha, Pi Epsilon, Pi Epsilon Delta, Alpha Epsilon Rho. Club: Rotary (pres. 1975-76). Contbr. articles on ednl. TV to profl. pubs.; editor The Schedule mag., 1962-72; producer (film) Vision Across Texas, 1960. Home: 5705 Bullard Dr Austin TX 78731 Office: Communication Center U Tex PO Box 7158 Austin TX 78712

HERBST, ROY ROGER, elec. engr.; b. Denver, Oct. 5, 1934; s. Claude Edward and Loreen Matilda (Blomsten) H.; B.S. in E.E., Colo. State U., 1958; m. Jane E. Nottingham, Jan. 22, 1977. Sales engr., Bailey Meter Co., Cleve., 1958-67; design engr. Rust Engring. Co., Birmingham, Ala., 1967-71; project engr. Southern Co. Services Inc., Birmingham, 1971-77, prin. engr., 1977—. Mem. IEEE, AAAS, Nat. Mgmt. Assn. Club: Elks. Patentee in black liquor boiler equipment. Office: PO Box 2625 Birmingham AL 35202

HERBSTMAN, DONALD, food co. exec.; b. Bklyn., May 30, 1934; s. Herman and Shirley H.; B.C.E., City Coll. N.Y., 1957; M. in Indsl. Safety, N.Y. U., 1970; m. Sylvia Glassman, Aug. 10, 1957; children—William, Robert, Amy. Supt. dept. public protection N.Y. Fire Ins. Rating Orgn., N.Y.C., 1958-66; dir. constrn. safety/security World Trade Center-Port Authority of N.Y. and N.J., 1966-73; group dir. Facilities adminstrn. constrn. and safety Burger King Corp., Miami, 1973—; guest lect. U. Miami; cons. in field. First v.p. Dade County (Fla.) Citizens Safety Council, 1979—; mem. exec. bd. Dade Clean County Com. Served with U.S. Army, 1957. Registered profl. engr., Fla., N.Y., N.J. Mem. Am. Soc. Safety Engrs. (pres. S. Fla. chpt. 1976-77), Soc. Fire Protection Engrs. (recipient cert. appreciation 1976), Nat. Fire Protection Assn., Nat. Safety Council, Am. Soc. Indsl. Security. Contbr. articles in field to profl. jours. Office: PO Box 520783 GMF Miami FL 33152

HERD, JAMES ROBERT, motel and restaurant exec.; b. Easley, S.C., Feb. 2, 1939; s. Elmer Don and Jamie (Spearman) H.; student Anderson Jr. Coll., 1959; B.S., Erskine Coll., 1961; m. Linda Mamahan, Jan. 17, 1959; children—Cindy, Joey, Pat, Michael. Inter-plant coordinator Saco Lowell Shops, Easley, S.C., 1959-69; gen. mgr. Howard Johnson Motor Lodge, Greenville and Columbia, S.C., 1970-71; food and beverage dir. Holiday Inn, Marietta, Ga., 1971-73; gen. mgr. Ramada Inn, Atlanta, 1973-75; food and beverage mgr. Journey Inn, Marietta, Ga., 1975-79, South of the Border, Dillon, S.C., 1979—; salesman Capital Food Co., Atlanta. Mem. Ga. Restaurant Assn., Cobb County Restaurant Assn., Ga. Tourist Assn. Methodist. Home: 1581 Pine St Marietta GA 30060 Office: South of the Border Dillon SC 29536

HERGE, HENRY CURTIS, SR., ret. educator; b. Bklyn., June 29, 1905; s. Henry John and Theresa (Maaz) H.; B.S., N.Y. U., 1929, M.A., 1933, Ed.D., 1942; M.A. (hon.), Wesleyan U., 1946; Ph.D., Yale U., 1956; m. Josephine E. Breen, July 2, 1931 (dec. 1975); children—Joel Curtis, Henry Curtis; m. 2d, Alice V. Wolfram, 1976. Tchr. English high sch., Port Washington, N.Y., 1928-38; dist. prin., Bayville, N.Y., 1938-41, Bellmore, N.Y., 1941-45; asst. dir. study on Armed Services edn. programs Am. Council Edn., Washington, 1945-46; dir. higher edn. and tchr. certification Conn. Dept. Edn., 1946-53; dean, prof. edn. Rutgers U., 1953-64, prof., 1964-75, prof. emeritus, 1975—, program asso. Rutgers Internat. Center, 1968-75; vis. prof. edn. U. So. Calif., summer 1964, N.Y. U., 1964-65. Del. White House Conf. Edn., 1957; dir. nationwide survey edn. Ministry Edn., Asuncion, Paraguay, 1961; team leader Rutgers-U.S. AID field survey, Zambia and Malawi, 1961-62; chief edn. devel. officer AID mission to Jamaica, 1966-68; repporteur Italian U. Rectors' Ednl. Exchange Project, 1969-70; Fulbright scholar Italian Univs., summer 1970. Trustee Shadow Lake Assn. (Vt.), 1975-76, pres., 1976-78. Served as lt. comdr. USNR, 1942-48. Recipient certificates of recognition NCCJ, 1958, N.J. Congress Parents and Tchrs., N.J. Vo-Tech. Sch. Dirs., N.J. Secondary Sch. Tchrs. Assn. Mem. Naval Res. Assn. (life), Internat. Study Assn., Am. Assn. Higher Edn., N.J. Congress Parents and Tchrs. (hon. life), Greater New Brunswick Urban League (former trustee), N.J. Schoolmasters Club, Phi Delta Kappa, Epsilon Pi Tau (laureate trustee), Kappa Delta Pi (compatriot in edn. 1976). Republican. Presbyterian. Author: Wartime College Training Programs of Armed Services, 1948; The College Teacher, 1965; Disarmament in Western World, 1969; Common Concerns in Higher Edn.; An Italian-American Universities Project, 1971. Contbr. articles to profl. publs. Home: 39 Pineland Rd Hilton Head Island SC 29928

HERLONG, BYRON EDWARDS, fruit producing, shipping co. exec.; b. Sumterville, Fla., Sept. 2, 1913; s. Albert Sydney and Cora (Knight) H.; B.S.A., U. Fla., 1936; m. Frances Letton, Apr. 18, 1937; children—Nancy McMullin, Byron Edwards II, David Letton, Philip Knight. Produce mgr. A.S. Herlong & Co., Leesburg, Fla., 1936-63, pres., 1963—; dir. Fla. Power Corp., Tampa So. R.R. Chmn., Lake County United Appeal; chmn. Ocklawaha Basin (Fla.) Water Authority, 1955—; chmn. Fla. Water Resources Study Commn., 1955—; bd. dirs. Lake-Sumter Dist. Mental Health, 1968—, U. Fla. Found. Served with USNR, 1944-45; PTO. Recipient Disting. Alumnus award U. Fla., 1977. Mem. Fla. Council of 100, Fla. Prodn. Mgrs. Assn., Am. Legion (comdr. post 1948), VFW, Gamma Sigma Delta. Democrat. Methodist. Clubs: Kiwanis (pres. Leesburg 1947-48, lt. gov. Fla. 1957), Country of Silver Lake, Deerwood Country (Jacksonville, Fla.), Elks, Masons, Shriners. Office: A S Herlong & Co 102 Meadow St Leesburg FL 32748

HERLONG, JAMES HERBERT, citrus processing co. exec.; b. Leesburg, Fla., Feb. 15, 1922; s. Albert Sydney and Cora (Knight) H.; student The Citadel, 1939-43; m. Ruby Elizabeth Prevatt, Feb. 21, 1946; children—Cora Nelle, James Herbert. With A. S. Herlong & Co., Leesburg, Fla., 1946—, field mgr., 1948-50, asst. sales mgr., 1950-52, mgr. Fresh Fruit and Processing div., 1952—; pres. Herlong Industries, Inc., Leesburg, 1959—; sec. A.S. Herlong & Co., 1967-78, pres., 1978—; dir., mem. exec. com. B & W Canning Co., Groveland, Fla., 1963—; dir. 1st Fed. Savs. & Loan Assn., Leesburg, Sun 1st Nat. Bank of Leesburg, Lake County Service Corp. Served to capt., inf., AUS, 1943-46. Methodist. Elk. Club: Silver Lake Golf and Country (pres. 1974, dir.) (Leesburg). Home: 6526 N Silver Lake Dr Leesburg FL 32748 Office: 2d and Meadow Sts Leesburg FL 32748

HERLT, BERNARD GEORGE, JR., electronics engr.; b. Muncy, Pa., Aug. 21, 1930; s. Bernard George and Nora Virginia (Hall) H.; student Lycoming Coll., 1952-54; B.E.E., Pa. State U., 1956; m. Bernadine Wilmarth, Aug. 7, 1954; children—Stephen Michael, Carole Virginia, Kimberly Michelle. Staff engr. HRB-Singer, State College, Pa., 1955-68; mgr. electronic systems E-Systems, Greenville, Tex., 1968—. Dist. activities chmn. Circle Ten council Boy Scouts Am., 1969-72; instr. water safety, small craft ARC, 1970—; bd. dir. Greenville Entertainment Series, 1972—, Symphony, 1976—. Served with USMC, 1949-52. Registered profl. engr., Pa. Presbyterian. Researcher instrumentation for complex signal environment testing. Home: 2303 Terrell Rd Greenville TX 75401 Office: Box 1056 Greenville TX 75401

HERMAN, ALEX CHARLES, mfg. co. exec.; b. Ellwood City, Pa., Sept. 14, 1946; s. Alex and Edith Irene (Maffei) H.; B. Mech. Engring., Youngstown (Ohio) State U., 1969; postgrad. Fairleigh Dickinson U., Rutherford, N.J.; m. Lora Jane Guesman, May 13, 1972; 1 son, Alex William. Project and application engr. Mathews conveyor div. Rexnord, Inc., Ellwood, 1970-74, sales engr., Memphis, 1974-77; dist. sales mgr. Litton Unit Handling Systems, Florence, Ky., 1977-78, gen. sales mgr. pre-engineered products, 1978—. Roman Catholic. Club: Summit Hills Country. Home: 8840 Valley Circle Dr Florence KY 41042 Office: 7100 Industrial Rd Florence KY 41042

HERMAN, BERTHA ELIZABETH, former telephone co. exec.; b. Franklin County, Ohio, Oct. 2, 1899; s. David Alfred and Hettie Elizabeth (Williams) Farrand; ed. Ohio State U.; m. Henry R. Herman, Oct. 30, 1918; children—Eleanor, David. Supr., instr. Ohio Bell Telephone Co., Columbus, until 1957, now ret.; cons. in field. Tchr. first aid ARC; past chmn. Lee County Disaster Preparedness; now coordinator Lehigh Acres Disaster Preparedness Program. Recipient Freedoms Found. award, 1976, 77, also awards for service to community; trustee Lehigh Acres Gen. Hosp., past pres. hosp. Aux. Mem. Am. Assn. Ret. Persons, Council Sr. Citizens, Fire Belles, Telephone Pioneers Am. (past pres.). Methodist. Club: Columbus Bus. and Profl. Women (past pres.). Home: 302 Penn Rd W Lehigh Acres FL 33936 Office: 2140 Broadway Fort Myers FL 33901

HERMAN, CHARLES ROBERT, opera assn. exec.; b. Glendale, Calif., Feb. 24, 1925; s. Floyd Caves and Anna (Merriken) H.; A.B. in German summa cum laude, U. So. Calif., 1949. Asst. to head opera dept. U. So. Calif., 1949-53; asst. mgr., artistic adminstr. Met. Opera Co., N.Y.C., 1953-72; gen. mgr. Greater Miami (Fla.) Opera Assn., 1973—; mem. Fine Arts Council Fla., 1977—; mem. grants panel opera-mus. theatre program Nat. Endowment Arts, 1979—; mem. quality of arts action com. Greater Miami C. of C., 1979—. Served as officer AUS, 1944-46; ETO. Decorated Army Commendation ribbon; cavaliere Order Merit (Italy); officers cross Order of Merit (W. Ger.). Mem. Opera Am. (treas., dir. 1977—), Cultural Execs. Council Dade Country (sec. 1978—), Phi Beta Kappa. Clubs: Com. of 100, Bath. Home: 3441 Poinciana Ave Miami FL 33133 Office: 1200 Coral Way Miami FL 33145

HERMAN, DONALD WESLEY, air force officer; b. Ft. Collins, Colo., Nov. 20, 1927; s. Henry Gerhart and Pauline (Laudick) H.; student Ariz. State U., 1947-49; m. Vicki Cook, Oct. 27, 1951; children—Kathy, Pamela, Tracy, Michele. Aviation cadet U.S. Air Force, 1950-51, commd. 2d lt., 1951, advanced through grades to lt. col., 1967; comdr. transp. squadron, 1968-70; mil. adviser to Vietnamese base comdr. Tan Son Nhut, Saigon, 1970-71; dir. adminstrn. maj. air command hdqrs., 1971-73; exec. officer to chief of staff maj. allied hdqrs., Europe, 1973-76; adminstr. USAF Air Ground Ops. Sch., Hurlburt Field, Fla., 1976—. Decorated D.F.C., Bronze Star, Air medal. Mem. Air Force Assn., Ret. Officers Assn. Home: 335 Jonquil Circle Ft Walton Beach FL 32548

HERMAN, LUTHER RUSSELL, educator; b. Hickory, N.C., Mar. 13, 1922; s. Sidney Thruman and Rancie Dorthula H.; B.S., Lenoir Rhyne Coll., 1948; M.S.E.E., N.C. State U., 1951; m. Nan Potter Jones, Aug. 22, 1948; children—Luther Russell, Frederick Eli, Nancy Sue, Ted Walter, David Allen. Engr., Western Electric Co., Winston-Salem, N.C., 1950-53; engr. Gen. Electric Co., Evandale, Ohio, 1953-55, Hendersonville, N.C., 1955-62; engr. The Western Co. of N.Am., Ft. Worth, 1963; asst. prof. elec. engring. N.C. State U., 1964—; part-time cons. engr. Booth & Assos., Raleigh, N.C., 1965—; instr. Va. Electric and Power Co., Richmond, 1965, 66; mem. N.C. State Bd. Examiners of Elec. Contractors, 1978—, chmn. exam. com., 1979—. Served with USNR, 1942-46. Registered profl. engr., N.C., Ohio. Mem. IEEE, Am. Soc. Engring. Edn., N.C. Acad. Sci., Sci. Research Soc., Eta Kappa Nu, Sigma Xi. Lutheran. Home: 306 Brooks Ave Raleigh NC 27607 Office: PO Box 5275 Raleigh NC 27650

HERMANN, CHARLOTTE ELAINE, ednl. adminstr.; b. Oak Park, Ill., Oct. 10, 1946; d. Richard Milton and Will Tom (Nelson) H.; B.A., St. Andrews Presbyterian Coll., 1968; M.A.C.T., U. N.C., Chapel Hill, 1970, now postgrad. Project coordinator for internat. program dept. environ. sci. and engring. Sch. Public Health, U. N.C., 1971-74, asst. dir. for adminstrn. SENIC project, dept. biostats., 1977-79, adminstrv. mgr. dept. bacteriology Sch. Medicine, 1979—; asst. dir. for program devel. Nat. Assn. Fgn. Students Affairs, Washington, 1974-76; guest lectr. St. Andrews Coll., 1969, 70. Mem. St. Andrews Presbyn. Coll. Alumni Council, 1968-69, 79-80; charter mem., mem. inaugural flight N.C. Friendship Force, 1979; docent West Point on the Eno Park, at the Old Mill and House, Durham, N.C. Recipient cert. appreciation Dept. Environ. Sci. and Engring. Sch. Public Health, U. N.C., 1974, cert. cooperation Office Internat. Edn., AID, Dept. State, 1976. Editor: (with Ron Sims) International Program in Environmental Aspects of Industrial Development, 1973; (with Jill Duvall) Global Issue: Hunger, Is It Ingenuity or Wisdom Which Has Failed?, 1975. Home: 18 Cedar Ct Carrboro NC 27510

HERMELEE, LAURENCE STEPHAN, savs. and loan exec.; b. N.Y.C., Dec. 22, 1937; s. Harold Benjamin and Hermine (Wolfson) H.; B.S. in Econs., U. Pa., 1959; postgrad. N.Y. U., 1960-62; m. Mary Beth Moore, June 15, 1972; children—Noelle, Harold, Rory. Sr. fin. planner Pitney Bowes, Stamford, Conn., 1962-67; subs. pres. Litton Industries, N.Y.C., 1967-70; v.p. fin. McCall Pattern Co. subs. Norton Simon, Inc., N.Y.C., 1970-72; exec. v.p. Biscayne Fed. Savs. & Loan Assn., Miami, Fla., 1973—; instr. Inst. Fin. Edn.; fin. cons. Mem. Com. Ecology and Beautification. Served with USAR, 1960-66. Mem. Fin. Mgrs. Soc., Am. Mgmt. Assn., Arabian Horse Assn. Fla. Home: 6487 SW 92d St Miami FL 33156 Office: 1790 Biscayne Blvd Miami FL 33132

HERN, LISA ANN, sales exec.; b. Valdese, N.C., Apr. 25, 1953; d. Joseph Albright and Ann (Long) H.; B.S., Ga. Inst. Tech., 1975. Sales, Honeywell, Inc., Atlanta, 1976-77; alt. program mgr. sales Pyrotronics, Atlanta, 1978—. Active Atlanta Symphony Orch. fund drive. Recipient Merit award Pyrotronics, 1978. Mem. Am. Soc. Indsl. Security, Atlanta Hist. Soc., Nat. Trust Hist. Preservation. Presbyterian. Home: 3703 Peachtree Rd NE Atlanta GA 30319 Office: 3070 Presidential Dr Suite 114 Atlanta GA 30340

HERNANDEZ, ALMA GARZA, ednl. diagnostician; b. San Antonio, Mar. 2, 1927; d. Eusebio Z. and Carolina (Sepulveda) Garza; A.A., San Antonio Coll., 1958; B.S., Our Lady of Lake Coll., 1963, M.Ed., 1972; certificate Trinity U., 1977; m. Ernesto V. Hernandez, Mar. 13, 1970; children—William Larry Carrera, Robert Gary Carrera. Elementary tchr. Edgewood Ind. Sch. Dist., 1958-61, Bonham Elementary Sch., San Antonio Ind. Sch. Dist., 1961-70; bilingual counselor San Antonio Ind. Sch. Dist., 1970-71; bilingual spl. edn. counselor, ednl. diagnostician Northside Ind. Sch. Dist. Pupil Appraisal Center, 1972—; prof. Spanish, U. Md., 1961; tchr. adult basic edn., 1964-65. Cert. provisional elementary tchr., spl. edn. counselor, profl. counselor, ednl. diagnostician, lang. learning disabilities tchr. Mem. Am., Tex. personnel and guidance assns., Tex. State Tchrs. Assn., Council Exceptional Children, Tex. Assn. Children with Learning Disabilities, Tex. Assn. Ednl. Diagnosticians. Democrat. Roman Catholic. Home: 103 City St San Antonio TX 78204 Office: 1827 Westedge San Antonio TX 78227

HERNANDEZ, JOSE YOLANDO BALAGTAS, physician; b. Candaba, Pampanga, Philippines Dec. 30, 1938; s. Pablo and Leoncia (Balagtas) H.; M.D., U. St. Thomas, 1962; m. Minerva R. Cuadrante, Dec. 17, 1966; children—Jay, Myra, Maureen. Intern, St. Clare's Hosp., Schenectady, 1964-65; resident in surgery Springfield (Mass.) Hosp. Med. Center, 1965-66, Trumbull Meml. Hosp., Warren, Ohio, 1966-68; resident in colon-rectal surgery Allentown (Pa.) Hosp., 1968-70; practice medicine specializing in gen. and colon-rectal surgery, Quincy, Fla., 1973—; attending sr. surgeon Gadsden Meml. Hosp., Quincy; staff surgeon Maryview Hosp., Portsmouth Gen. Hosp., Portsmouth, Va., 1977-79, Tallahassee Meml. Regional Med. Center and Capital Med. Center, 1979—. Recipient Physicians Recognition award AMA, 1970. Diplomate Am. Bd. Surgery, Am. Bd. Colon and Rectal Surgery, Internat. Bd. Proctology. Fellow Internat. Coll. Surgeons, Internat. Acad. Proctology, Am. Soc. Abdominal Surgeons, Am. Soc. Colon Rectal Surgeons (asso.); mem. Am. Coll. Emergency Physicians, Panhandle, Fla., Va. med. assns., AMA, Royal Soc. Medicine, Portsmouth Acad. Medicine. Roman Catholic. Home: 3053 Carlow Circle Tallahassee FL 32303 Office: Eastwood Med Plaza 1605 Eastwood Plaza Dr Suite 3 Tallahassee FL 32308

HERNANDEZ, PEDRO, JR., pub. relations exec.; b. Comerio, P.R., Jan. 5, 1922; s. Pedro M. and Carmen R. (Santiago) H.; student spl. courses U. P.R., U. Chgo.; m. Ramonita Santan, Aug. 3, 1942; children—Aida Iris, Pedro Ivan, Yolanda, Carlos. Press officer, Gov. Roberto Sanchez Vilella, San Juan, P.R., 1965-66; asst. press officer Gov. Luis A. Ferre, San Juan, 1974; reporter El Mundo Newspaper, San Juan, 8 yrs.; dir. pub. relations P.R. chpt. A.R.C., 1958; dir. pub. relations Dept. Pub. Works, Santurce, P.R., 1963; dir. pub. relations P.R. Hwys. Authority, Santurce, 1966; dir. pub. relations Dept. Commerce, Commonwealth P.R., San Juan, 1973; news editor U.P.I., San Juan, 1972; owner Hernandez Pub. Relations, Hato Rey, P.R., 1975—. Active PTA. Mem. Am. Newspaper Guide, Pub. Relations Soc. Am., Am. Newspaper Guild, Pub. Relations Soc. P.R., Asociacien Relacionistas Pufesinales de P.R., Fedn. de Periodistas, Asociacien de Periodistas de P.R. Club: Overseas Press. Editor, Bohemia weekly mag., 1974. Home: PP 2 Febe St Reparto Apolo Guaynabo PR 00657 Office: Squire Bldg Suite 501B Hato Rey PR 00917

HERNANDEZ, RAMON FRANCISCO, linguist, educator; b. Matamoros, Tamaulipas, Mex., Oct. 10, 1935; came to U.S., 1942, naturalized, 1956; s. Prisciliano and Josefina G. H.; m. Esther Rodriguez, Aug. 21, 1967; children—Ramon Francisco, Esther, Josefina, Prisciliano, Teresa. Research analyst Def. Intelligence Agy., 1963-66; instr. Spanish, Fgn. Service Inst., Dept. State, 1966; asst. pub. relations officer Latin Am. div. Voice of Am., 1967: interpreter, property officer Superior Ct. of D.C., 1968-69; equal employment counselor-at-large, property officer Dept. Gen. Services Govt. of D.C., 1969-71; veteran's rep., dir. veteran's project Dept. Labor, 1973-74; owner, dir. Internat. Sch. Langs., Brownsville, Tex., 1974—; interpreter for Immigration and Naturalization Service and U.S. ct. system, 1974-79. Dir. plans and research Anti-Povery Agy., Brownsville, 1971-72. Served with USAF, 1953-61. Mem. Am. Soc. Internat. Law, Soc. Fed. Linguists, Am. GI Forum, Alpha Mu Gamma (hon.). Democrat. Roman Catholic. Home: 655 Villa Verde Dr Brownsville TX 78521 Office: Internat Sch of Langs 1144 E Washington St Suite 10 Brownsville TX 78520

HERNANDEZ, SANDRA KAY, nurse; b. Elgin, Ill., Oct. 7, 1946; d. William and Grace Marie Mabel (Holtz) Kethcart; student U. Wis., 1965-67; grad. Mercy Hosp. Sch. Nursing, 1968; m. Ramon A. Hernandez, Jr., Aug. 5, 1974; 1 dau., Sandra. Supr., Rock County Nursing, Jonesville, Wis., 1968; staff nurse St. Mary's Hosp., Madison, Wis., 1968-70; supr. medicare Meml. Med. Nursing Home, San Antonio, 1972-73; medicare supr. Four Seasons Nursing Home, San Antonio, 1973-75; dir. geriatric Poteet (Tex.) Nursing Home, 1975-76; geriatric ward staff nurse San Antonio State Hosp., 1976-78, geriatric ward supr., 1978—. Served to 1st lt., Nurses Corps, USAF, 1970-72. Lutheran. Home: 112 Barrett Ave San Antonio TX 78214 also PO Box 23310 Highland Hills Station San Antonio TX 78223

HERNANDEZ-AVILA, MANUEL LUIS, phys. oceanographer; b. Quebradillas, P.R., Apr. 15, 1935; s. Manuel and Luisa Avila Hernandez; B.S., U. P.R., 1967, M.S. in Marine Scis., 1970; Ph.D. in Phys. Oceanography, La. State U., 1974; m. Evangelina Fradera, Dec. 8, 1956. Research asst. dept. marine scis. U. P.R., Mayaguez, 1963-67, asst. prof. dept. marine scis., 1974-76, chmn., asso. prof., 1976—, dir. sea grant program, 1980—; research asst. Coastal Studies Inst., La. State U., Baton Rouge, 1967-70; sec.-treas., cons. MHR Research Assos., Inc., Mayaguez, 1975-78; 2d v.p. Island Marine Labs. Caribbean Assn., 1978. Served with USAF, 1954-58. NOAA grantee, 1978-79, Dept. Energy grantee, 1978-79, Dept. Agr. grantee, 1975-78. Mem. Am. Meteorol. Soc., Am. Geophys. Union, Internat. Oceanographic Found., AAAS, Marine Tech. Soc., Assn. Island Marine Labs. Caribbean, Estuarine Research Assn., Am. Acad. Arts and Scis., Smithsonian Instn., Oceanic Soc., N.Y. Acad. Scis., Sigma Xi, Phi Sigma Alpha. Roman Catholic. Club: Lions (sec. 1978-79). Home: L-19 Riverside St San German PR 00753 Office: Dept Marine Scis U PR Mayaguez PR 00708

HERNDON, MARY AUREA BALFAY, savs. and loan assn. exec.; b. Atchison, Kans., Nov. 4, 1918; d. Edmond Paul and Eva Muriel (Tilford) Balfay; grad. Am. Savs. and Loan Inst., Chgo., 1964; student Sch. Exec. Devel., U. Athens (Ga.), 1964-65; m. Glenn L. Bingham, Sept. 11, 1937 (dec. 1971); m. 2d, George M. Herndon, May 13, 1974. Bookkeeper Deeb Constrn. Co., St. Petersburg, Fla., 1951-52; bookkeeper, cashier Shaver & Co., securities, St. Petersburg, 1952-54; v.p. comml. loan dept. Fla. Fed. Savs. and Loan Assn., St. Petersburg, 1954—. Bd. dirs. St. Petersburg YWCA, 1969-70, 72-74, adv. bd., 1974—; active United Way Pinellas County, 1974—. Mem. Inst. Fin. Edn. (pres. chpt. 1963). Mem. Christian Ch. Clubs: Nat. Fedn. Bus. and Profl. Womens (pres. Suncoast club 1963-64, 70-71, dist. dir. Fla. Fedn. 1974-75), Women in Constrn. (pres. St. Petersburg chpt. 1962-63), Zonta Internat. (pres. St. Petersburg club 1971-73). Home: 200 55th Ave NE St Petersburg FL 33703 Office: Central at 4th St St Petersburg FL 33701

HERNDON, WANDA ROSANNA, educator; b. Brownwood, Tex., Oct. 22, 1930; d. Richard Henry and Eula E. (Woods) Taylor; B.A., Baylor U., 1951; M.A., Tex. Christian U., 1968; Ph.D., So. Ill. U., 1973; m. Doyle Preston Herndon, June 22, 1968; children—Cecilia Miller, Richard E. Miller. Tchr., White Oak (Tex.) public schs., 1951-52; program dir. Little Rock YWCA, 1952-55; tchr. Texas City (Tex.) public schs., 1955-58; instr. Tex. Christian U., Ft. Worth, 1966-68, 77-78, So. Ill. U., Carbondale, 1968-69; prof. So. Meth. U., Dallas, 1970-77, U. Tex., Arlington, 1977-78; prof., chmn. dept. communications and theatre Hardin-Simmons U., Abilene, Tex., 1978—; cons. Perkins Sch. Theology, So. Meth. U., Dallas, 1972-78; campaign cons. Mem. Tex. Speech Communication Assn. (life), Speech Communication Assn., So. Speech Communication Assn., Ky. Hist. Soc., Ft. Worth Geneal. Soc., Nat. Assn. for Preservation and Perpetuation of Storytelling, Assn. for Communication Adminstrn., Tex. Folklore Soc., AAUW, AAUP. Republican. Presbyterian. Author: Interviewing for Genealogists and Oral Historians, 1978; contbr. articles to profl. jours. Home: 90 Bay Shore Ct Abilene TX 79602 Office: Dept Communication Theatre Hardin-Simmons Univ Abilene TX 79698

HEROD, THOMAS MACK DAVID, JR., film maker; b. Slaton, Tex., Feb. 25, 1947; s. Thomas M.D. and Florence Elizabeth (Cooley) H.; B.A. in Govt., N.Tex. State U., 1969; M.A. in Film Prodn., U. Tex., 1973. Producer, Tex. & Pacific Film Co., Austin, 1974; instr. broadcast film So. Meth. U., Dallas, 1974-76; dir., producer films including: An Evening at Threadgills, 1972; Inner Face, 1972 (Judges award Sinking Creek Film Celebration); The Give and Take of It (honorable mention Chgo. Film Festival); asso. producer for Five Star Prodns. Wheels of Fire, 1979; 2d asst. dir. for TV film Ruby and Oswald, Dallas, 1977; location mgr. Honeysuckle Rose, 1979; prodn. mgr., asst. dir. commls. N. Lee Lacy & Assos., Myers & Griner/Cuesta, Pfeiffer, Bruce Israelson, EUE Screen Gems, Silvertree, others; 1977—; producer, dir. Collection Theater Ensemble's N.Y. prodn. Kennedy's Children, 1979. Mem. Tex. Assn. Film Profls. (founding mem. 1976—, pres. 1977-78), Dirs. Guild Am. Club: Variety. Address: 4042 Hawthorne Dallas TX 75219

HEROLD, HAL DOUGLAS, JR., counselor; b. Harrisonburg, Va., Aug. 31, 1949; s. Curtis Howard and Elsie Browne (Hiner) Terry; B.S., Va. Commonwealth U., 1973; M.Ed., James Madison U., 1977; m. Barbara Paige Taylor, June 2, 1973. Counselor, Va. Div. Corrections, Linville, 1973-74; houseparent Rivendale, Inc., Harrisonburg, Va., 1974-75, asst. dir., 1975, treatment supr., family cons., 1975-79, program dir., 1979—; cons. Childrens Center, Roanoke, Va., DeJarnette Center for Human Devel. Mem. Am. Personnel and Guidance Assn., Va. Council Children with Behavioral Disorders. Contbr. articles to profl. jours. Home: 525 W Gay St Harrisonburg VA 22801 Office: Route 4 Box 62-B Harrisonburg VA 22801

HEROY, DAVID B., computer co. exec.; b. Carlsbad, N.Mex., June 29, 1942; s. William Bayard, Jr. and Dorothy Marie (Meincke) H.; B.A. in Math., Dartmouth Coll., 1964; Ph.D., Tex. Christian U., 1972; m. Joanne Poltorak, July 9, 1966; 1 dau., Kimberly Ayn. Vice pres. systems and ops., treas., dir. Benefit Tech. Inc., Dallas, 1972-77; pres., chmn. bd., dir. Automated Mgmt., Inc., Dallas, 1977—; pres., dir. Benefit Reports Co., Dallas, 1979—, AMI Timesharing, Dallas, 1979—. Grantee NSF, NEDA, NASA. Mem. Am. Phys. Soc., Am. Assn. Physics Tchrs., Assn. Computing Machinery, IEEE, IEEE Computer Soc., Sigma Xi. Author papers in field. Home: 6610 Southpoint St Dallas TX 75248 Office: 12000 Ford Rd Suite 170 Dallas TX 75234

HERREN, LINDA SIMPSON, biophysicist; b. Birmingham, Ala., July 7, 1927; d. Michael Raymond and Gladys (Anderson) Simpson; B.S., U. Ala., 1948; m. Thomas Christian Herren, July 18, 1963; 1 son, Thomas Christian. Instr., U. Ala., Birmingham, 1948; physicist So. Research Inst., Birmingham, 1948-69, sr. physicist, 1969-71, head cell and tissue kinetics sect., 1971—. Bd. dirs. Homewood PTO, 1980—; pres. Homewood High Band Parents, 1979—. Mem. Am. Assn. Cancer Research, Southeastern Assn. Cancer Research, Health Physics, Cell Kinetics Soc. (pres. 1978-89, governing council 1979—), AAAS, Sigma Xi. Club: The Club. Editor for N.Am., Cell and Tissue Kinetics, 1978—; contbr. articles to profl. jours. Home: 1613 Barry Ave Homewood AL 35209 Office: 2000 9th Ave S Birmingham AL 35205

HERRIMAN, ERNEST DONALD, educator; b. Hazel Park, Mich., Apr. 1, 1933; s. Holfred Ernest and Mabel Irene (Svacha) H.; B.S., Tex. A&I U., 1959; M.A., Eastern Mich. U., 1963; Ed.D., U. Mass., 1971; postgrad La. State U., 1973; 1 son, Jeffrey Lynn. Tchr., Banquete (Tex.) Ind. Sch. Dist., 1959-60, Littleton (Colo.) public schs., 1960-61, Walled Lake (Mich.) Consol. Schs., 1961-63; asst. prin. Jefferson County public schs., Golden, Colo., 1963-68; supt. Pawnee public schs., Grover, Colo., 1968-70; asso. prof. edn. Tex. A&I U., Kingsville, 1971—; cons. Kooneys X-ray Service, San Diego Ind. Sch. Dist., Lysord Ind. Sch. Dist., Orange Grove Ind. Sch. Dist. (Tex.). Served with USN, 1952-56. Ford. Found. grantee, 1970; State of Fla. fellow, 1970-71. Mem. Tex. Assn. Coll. Tchrs., NEA, Tex. Tchrs. Assn., Am. Soc. Clin. Hypnosis, Phi Delta Kappa. Democrat. Baptist. Club: Lions. Home: Star Route Box 26 Sandia TX 78383 Office: Dept Edn Tex A&I U Kingsville TX 78363

HERRIN, RAY LYMAN, health care adminstr.; b. Cin., Nov. 19, 1932; s. Lyman Ballard and Mable (Lamb) H.; Asso. Nursing, Sandhills Community Coll., Southern Pines, N.C., 1974; student U. N.C., Chapel Hill, 1976; m. Merle Louise White, Apr. 28, 1951; children—Kathy Ann Fitzpatrick, Theresa Gae Downs, Elizabeth Mable. Staff nurse VA Hosp., Fayetteville, N.C., 1974-75; dir., practitioner East Bend (N.C.) Community Health Center, 1976-78; health planner Clarke County, Quitman, Miss., 1978; clinic dir. primary care services E. Central Miss. Health Care, Inc., Newton, Miss., 1978-79, clin. coordinator, 1979—. Served with USMC, 1949-57; with USAF, 1958-70. Mem. Miss. Nurses Assn., Miss. Council Nurse Practitioners (rep. on exec. bd. 1979). Home: PO Box 466 Newton MS 39345 Office: PO Box 89 Newton MS 39345

HERRING, DAVID M(AYO), engr.; b. Rockport, Tex., Jan. 18, 1929; s. James Clark and Edith Esther (Sneed) H.; B.S., U. Tex., Austin, 1955, M.S. in Structures, 1960; m. Nell Adams, Sept. 10, 1955; children—Clark, John, Scott. Cons. engr. W.P. Moore & Co., Houston, 1955; cons. engr. Chgo. Bridge & Iron Co., Ltd., Caracas, Venezuela, 1956, supt., 1957, asst. mgr. ops., 1958-60, mgr. ops., 1960-64; mgr. internat. ops. western hemisphere CBI Co., Oak Brook, Ill., 1964-68, asst. mgr. CBI NUclear Co., Memphis, 1968-72; constrn. mgr. S.E. div. CBI Co., Birmingham, Ala., 1973-78; pres., dir. Sea-Con Services Inc., Port Iberia, La., 1978—; dir. Thermal Designs Inc., Houston. Served with C.E., U.S. Army, 1950-52; Korea. Mem. ASCE (Featured Engr. award 1971), Am. Concrete Inst., Colegio de Ingeneros, Arquetectos and Agrimensores de P.R., Chi Epsilon, Tau Beta Pi. Episcopalian. Contbr. articles to profl. jours. Invented World's largest revolving derrick. Office: Box 9308 New Iberia LA 70560

HERRING, GROVER CLEVELAND, lawyer; b. Nocatee, Fla., Dec. 9, 1925; s. Joseph I. and Martha (Selph) H.; J.D., U. Fla., 1950; m. Dorothy L. Blinn, Apr. 17, 1947; children—Stanley T., Kenneth Lee. Admitted to Fla. bar, 1950; asso. firm Haskins & Bryant, Sebring, 1950-52; practiced in West Palm Beach, Fla., 1952-60, 64—, mem. firm Blakeslee, Herring & Bie, and predecessor firm, 1953-60, Warwick, Paul & Herring, 1964-70, Herring & Evans, 1970, now Herring & Fulton; atty. City of West Palm, 1960-63, City of Atlantis, 1959-61, Town of Ocean Ridge, 1953-61, 1964-66, Village of Royal Palm Beach, 1964-72, Town of South Palm Beach (Fla.), 1966-72; spl. master-in-chancery 15th Jud. Circuit in and for Palm Beach County, 1953-54; judge ad litem Municipal Ct., West Palm Beach, 1954-55. Field rep. Lawyers Title Guaranty Fund, 1955-60, 64—; dir. Lawyers Title Services, Inc., West Palm Beach. Active PTA, Family Service Agy., Palm Beach County Mental Health Assn.; chmn. profl. sect. A.R.C., 1960; mem. Charter Revision Com. West Palm Beach, 1960-65, Palm Beach County Resources Devel. Bd., 1959—; apptd. mem. Govtl. Study Commn. by Fla. Legislature. Bd. dirs. Community Chest. Mem. Democratic Exec. Com., 1965-70. Served with USNR, 1944-46. Mem. Am., Palm Beach County (treas. 1960), John Marshall bar assns., Fla. Bar, Am. Judicature Soc., Lawyer's Title Guaranty Fund, East Coast Estate Planning Council, Nat. Inst. Municipal Law Officers, Law-Sci. Acad., Am. Trial Lawyers Assn. (asso. editor 1960—), Lawyers Lit. Club, Nat. Municipal League, U. Fla. Law Center Assn., World Peace Through Law Center, Fla. Sheriff's Assn. (hon.), U. Fla. Alumni Assn., VFW, Am. Legion, West Palm Beach C. of C., Civic Music Assn., Palm Beach County Hist. Soc. (pres. 1969-72), New Eng. Hist. Geneal. Soc. Boston. Mason (32 deg.), Elk, Moose. Clubs: West Palm Beach Country (hon.); Airways (N.Y.C.); History Book (Stamford, Conn.). Contbr. legal articles to profl. revs. Home: 3515 Australian Ave West Palm Beach FL 33407 Office: Forum III Bldg Tower B West Palm Beach FL 33401

HERRING, JACK WILLIAM, educator; b. Waco, Tex., Aug. 28, 1925; s. Benjamin Oscar and Bertha K. Elizabeth (Shiplet) H.; A.B., Baylor U., 1947, M.A., 1948; Ph.D., U. Pa., 1958; m. Daphne L. Norred, June 10, 1944; children—Penny Elizabeth, Paul William. Instr. in English, Howard Coll., Birmingham, Ala., 1948-50; asso. prof., acting chmn. dept. English, Grand Canoyon Coll., 1951-55; asst. prof. English, Ariz. State U., 1955-59; prof. English, Baylor U., 1959—; Margaret Root Brown prof. Robert Browning Studies, 1973—, dir. Armstrong Browning Library, 1959—. Served with U.S. Army, 1944-46. Mem. Modern Lang. Assn. Baptist. Club: Kiwanis (pres. Waco 1976-77). Author: Old School Fellow (Browning), 1972; editor: Studies In Browning, 1973. Home: 200 Guittard Ave Waco TX 76706 Office: PO Box 6336 Waco TX 76706

HERRING, MICHAEL MORRIS, lumberman, miner, quarryman, financier; b. Clarksville, Ark., Oct. 15, 1922; s. Michael Eugene and Josephine (Overby) H.; student Eastern A. and M., 1940-41, U. Okla., 1942; B.S., Oklahoma City U.. 1948; m. Dorothy Eleene Evans, Nov. 19, 1948. Owner, M. Herring Slate Mines, Inc., 1946—. Luxury Homes, Inc., 1959—, Mineral Devel. Corp., Diamond Marble Corp., M. Herring Wholesale Lumber, Inc., 1946—; originator, designer Belle Femme, world's most beautiful salon; pres., owner Trouble Shooter, Internat. Internat. cons. on bldg. specifications and materials. Served with USAAF, 1942-45, ETO. Decorated Silver Star, Air medal; recipient N. Atlantic Command award, 1943, Infantile Paralysis and Crippled Children's awards, named Outstanding Businessman, USN, 1961; hon. adm., commodore of navy, hon. col. army State of Okla., hon. dep. sheriff. Mem. Internat. Platform Assn., Nat. Geog. Soc., Mensa (asso.) Nat. Soc. Lit. and Arts, Am. Heritage Research Assn. (mem. Library Human Resources), Beta Beta Beta, Delta Psi Omega, Kappa Alpha. Mason (32 deg., Shriner). Club: Okla. University Touchdown and Recruiting. Home: 4309 NW 61st Terr Oklahoma City OK 73112

HERRITAGE, JAMES MICHAEL, real estate co. exec.; b. Jacksonville, N.C., Aug. 28, 1949; s. James William and Gloria (Crane) H.; B.A., The Citadel, 1972; grad. S.C. Realtors Inst., 1973. Sales asso. Max L. Hill Co., Inc., Charleston, S.C., 1972-74, sales mgr., 1974—; lectr. in field. Mem. Charleston County (S.C.) Bicentennial Com., 1976; mem. citizens adv. com. Charleston Area Transp. Study, 1977-79; bd. dirs. Charleston chpt. Am. Cancer Soc.; sect. chmn. Charleston United Way, 1979—. Mem. Charleston Trident C. of C. (chmn. transp. com. 1977), Nat. Assn. Realtors, S.C. Assn. Realtors (dir.), S.C. Realtors Edn. Found. (dir.), Greater Charleston Bd. Realtors. Republican. Episcopalian. Producer play Freedom Is Never Free, for Charleston Bicentennial, 1976. Home: 1102 Ventura Pl Mount Pleasant SC 29464 Office: Max L Hill Co Fairfield Park Charleston SC 29407

HERRMANN, JAMES ANDREW, fin. analyst; b. Dallas, Aug. 28, 1950; s. Frederick Alvin and Alicemarie (Collins) H.; B.S. in Engring. Mgmt., U.S. Air Force Acad., 1972; M.B.A. in Fin., Ga. State U., 1975. Research fellow Logistics Mgmt. Inst., Washington, 1977-78; fin. analyst Harris Corp., Melbourne, Fla., 1978-80, supr. contract pricing practices Harris Semicondr. Programs div., 1980—. Pres. Condominium Homeowners Assn., 1975. Served from 2d lt. to capt. USAF, 1972-77. Decorated Air Force Commendation medal with oak leaf cluster. Mem. Fin. Mgmt. Assn., Nat. Contract Mgmt. Assn., Assn. M.B.A. Execs. Republican. Roman Catholic. Home: 2308 Colonial Dr S Melbourne FL 32901 Office: Harris Corp Semicondr Group PO Box 883 Melbourne FL 32901

HERRMANN, RONALD JOSEPH, bowling ball mfg. co. exec.; b. San Antonio, Dec. 21, 1934; s. Albert and Helen (Luthy) H.; B.A., St. Mary's U., 1957, J.D., 1959; m. Karen Heizer, Oct. 1, 1977; children—Karin, Carol, Helen, David. Admitted to Tex. bar, 1959; individual practice law, 1959—; sr. v.p. Am. Grain Corp., 1962-66; farmer, rancher, Kans. and Tex., 1952—; pres., dir., co-owner Columbia Industries, Inc., San Antonio, 1961—; pres., owner FM Liquors, Inc., San Antonio, Houston, El Paso, Pasadena and Victoria, Tex., 1969—; dir. Tex. Trust. Co. Mem. devel. com. St. Mary's U. Served with USAR, 1952-61. Recipient Disting. Law Alumni award St. Mary's U., 1978. Mem. San Antonio Bar Assn., Tex. Bar Assn., Tex. Hist. Soc., Tex. and Southwestern Cattle Raisers Assn., Kans. Hist. Soc. (life), Ducks Unltd. Democrat. Roman Catholic. Restored two-story rock home in Fredericksburg Tex., originally built in 1850 (Tex. Hist. Soc. Commemorative Plaque 1973). Office: 5005 West Ave San Antonio TX 78213

HERRON, EDWIN HUNTER, JR., energy cons.; b. Shreveport, La., June 7, 1938; s. Edwin Hunter and Helen Virginia (Russell) H.; B.S. in Chem. Engring., Tulane U., 1959, M.S., 1963, Ph.D. (NSF fellow, 1963-64), 1964; m. Frances Irvine Hunter, June 27, 1959; children—Edwin, David, Ashley. Research engr. Exxon Research & Engring. Co., Linden, N.J., 1959-61; sr. research engr. Exxon Production Research Co., Houston, 1964-66; corp. planning advisor Esso Europe, London, Eng., 1966-74; fin. analyst Exxon Corp., N.Y.C., 1974-78; v.p. Gruy Fed. Inc., Arlington, Va., 1978—. Recipient Levey award, Tulane U., 1970. Mem. Soc. Petroleum Engrs. of AIME, Am. Inst. Chem. Engrs., Sci. Research Soc., Am. Mgmt. Assn., Soc. Tulane Engrs., Tau Beta Pi. Contbr. articles to profl. publs. Office: Gruy Federal Inc 2001 Jefferson Davis Highway Suite 701 Arlington VA 22202

HERSCH, PAUL JAY, physician; b. Bklyn., Feb. 11, 1934; s. Edward and Lillian (Silverstein) H.; B.A., Bklyn. Coll., 1955; M.D., U. Louvain (Belgium), 1961; m. Judite Israel, Apr. 16, 1967; children—Ira A., Nina C. Intern, Univ. Hosp., Louvain, 1960-61, Meadowbrook Hosp., East Meadow, N.Y., 1961-62; resident in internal medicine Brookdale Hosp., Bklyn., 1962-63, Kings County Hosp.-SUNY, Bklyn., 1963-65; practice medicine specializing in internal medicine, Queens, N.Y., 1966-74, Tamarac, Fla., 1974—; mem. staff Margate Gen. Hosp., Fla. Med. Center, Univ. Community Hosp., Cypress Community Hosp. instr. dept. medicine SUNY, Bklyn., 1965-66; instr. CPR, 1976—; community lectr., 1974—. Diplomate Am. Bd. Internal Medicine. Fellow Am. Coll. Angiology; mem. A.C.P., Am. Heart Assn., Am. Soc. Internal Medicine, Fla. Med. Assn., Broward County Med. Assn., Med. Soc. County of Queens, Am. Physician's Fellowship. Jewish. Office: 4959 N State Rd 7 Tamarac FL 33319

HERSEY, GEORGE WILLIAM, judge; b. Bar Harbor, Maine, Feb. 11, 1930; s. George William and Mary Laura (Carter) H.; B.A., U. Maine, 1952; LL.B., Boston U., 1957; m. Andrea Anderson, Sept. 3, 1972; 1 dau., Laura Therese; 1 step-son, Scott Anderson. Admitted to Maine bar, 1957, Fla. bar, 1960; teaching and research fellow Rutgers U., N.J., 1957-58; individual practice law, Bar Harbor, Maine, 1958-59; partner firm Gunster, Yoakley, Criser, Stewart & Hersey, Palm Beach, Fla., 1959-79; judge 4th Dist. Fla. Ct. Appeal, 1979—; dir. Mall Bank. Bd. dirs. Palm Beach Community Found., Palm Beach County Community Mental Health Center; chmn. bd. dirs. Palm Beach Community Chest, 1972—; bd. dirs. The Salvation Army. Named Outstanding Profl. Bus. Man of Year, Palm Beach Daily News, 1975; Man of Year, City of Hope, 1977. Mem. Palm Beach C. of C. (dir.). Club: Palm Beach Kiwanis (dir.). Contbr. articles to legal jours. and manuals. Home: 154th Rd N Jupiter FL 33458

HERSEY, HERMAN LAWRENCE, religious exec.; b. Chgo., Jan. 1, 1926; s. Samuel Freeman and Ruth (Behnke) H.; tchr.'s cert., St. Louis Inst. Music, 1944; A.B., Bob Jones U., 1949; postgrad. Pa. State U., 1973, U. So. Calif., 1979; m. Vernie L. Hood, June 1, 1952; 1 dau., Patricia Ann. Ordained to ministry Free Will Baptist Ch., 1949; pastor Free Will Baptist Ch., Gastonia, N.C., 1949-51, First Free Will Bapt. Ch., Raleigh, N.C., 1952-62; evangelist, 1962-64; pastor Free Will Bapt. Ch., Garner, N.C., 1964-74; dir. bd. retirement Nat. Assn. Free Will Baptists, Nashville, 1974—. Mem. Am. Philatelic Soc. (Speakers Bur.), Nashville Philatelic Soc., (pres. 1977—). Club: Kiwanis. Home: PO Box 17680 Nashville TN 37217 Office: PO Box 1088 Nashville TN 37202

HERSHEY, GERALD LEE, educator; b. Lancaster, Pa., Oct. 6, 1943; s. Isaac and Esther Amanda (Burkhart) H.; B.S., Shippensburg State Coll., 1964; M.S., Ind. U., 1967, Ph.D., 1971; m. Cherry K. Nell, Aug. 14, 1965; children—Debra Louise, Eric Michael. Lectr., Ind. U., Bloomington, 1968-71, asst. prof., 1971-74; asso. prof. So. Ill. U., Edwardsville, 1974-76; asso. prof. U. N.C., Greensboro, 1976-79, prof. Sch. Bus. and Econs., 1979—; cons. office systems, personnel and word processing; speaker on mgmt. and office systems, U.S. and Can. Mem. Internat. Word Processing Assn., Am. Mgmt. Assn., Adminstrv. Mgmt. Soc., Nat. Bus. Edn. Assn. Presbyterian. Contbr. articles to profl. jours. Office: Rm 480 Sch Business and Econs U NC Greensboro NC 27412

HERSKOWITZ, ALLAN, neurologist; b. Bronx, N.Y., May 22, 1942; s. Harry and Rose (Neuman) H.; B.S., U. Fla., 1963; M.D., U. Miami, 1967; m. Marilyn Kornstein, June 12, 1965; children—Kim, Brad, Greg. Intern, Boston City Hosp., 1967-68; resident in neurology Albert Einstein Coll. Medicine, Bronx, 1968-71; chief neurologist Ft. Gordon Hosp., Augusta, Ga., 1971-73; practice medicine specializing in neurology, North Miami Beach, Fla., 1973—; asst. prof. neurology Med. Coll. Ga., Augusta, 1971-73; clin. instr. neurology U. Miami Sch. Medicine, 1977—; cons. neurologist Forest Hills VA Hosp., 1971-73; chief of neurology Cedars of Lebanon Hosp., Miami, 1977—; dir. Am. Service Corp., Miz Tennis Creations. Served with U.S. Army, 1971-73. Mem. Fla. Soc. Neurology (pres. 1977-78), AMA, Am. Acad. Neurology, Dade County, Fla. (editorial bd. jour.) med. assns., Am. EEG Soc., A.C.P., Assn. Research in Nervous and Mental Disease, Am. Assn. for Study Headache, Phi Delta Epsilon, Pi Lambda Phi, Alpha Omega Alpha. Republican. Jewish. Contbr. articles to med. jours. Office: 155 NW 167th St North Miami Beach FL 33169

HERTAN, WILLIAM ALBERT, JR., counselor; b. Hackensack, N.J., Sept. 10, 1953; s. William A. and Harriet P. H.; B.B.A., Stetson U., 1975; M.S., George Peabody Coll. Tchrs., 1979. Salesman, Adams-Cameron Realty, Daytona Beach, Fla., 1975-78; physiologist technician Vanderbilt U., Nashville, 1978-79; cons. Exec. Manning Corp., Ft. Lauderdale, Fla., 1975-79; counselor Embry-Riddle Aero. U., Daytona Beach, Fla., 1979—. Mem. Am. Personnel and Guidance Assn. Republican. Episcopalian. Home: 643 Princewood Dr Deland FL 32720 Office: Embry-Riddle Aero U Regional Airport Daytona Beach FL 32014

HERTH, KAYE ANN, educator; b. Oak Park, Ill., Sept. 9, 1945; d. Donald James and Martha Alice (Kent) H.; diploma, St. Lukes Hosp. Sch. Nursing, 1966; B.S. with honors, No. Ill. U., 1968; M.S. with honors, U. Minn., 1973; cert. phys. assessment, Hartwick Coll., 1974; m. Leonard Alvin Herth, June 19, 1971; children—Wendy Joye, Randy Scott. Nursing team leader Trinity Meml. Hosp., Cudahy, Wis., 1966-67; pediatric staff nurse Geneva (Ill.) Hosp., 1967-68; instr. nursing Milwaukee County Hosp., 1968-69; nursing coordinator United Hosp., St. Paul, 1969-71; med.-surg. instr. Luth. Deaconess Hosp., Mpls., 1971-73; asst. prof. nursing East Tenn. State U., Johnson City, 1973-77; asst. prof. nursing U. Tenn., Memphis, 1977-78; asst. prof. nursing U. Tex., Houston, 1978—; cons., lectr. in field. Advisor, mem. Memphis chpt. Make Today Count, 1977-78; coordinator, instr. ARC—Preparation for Parenthood, 1974-76. Named Outstanding Graduating Sr., No. Ill. U., 1968. Mem. Nurses Christian Fellowship (advisor 1975-77), Johnson City C. of C., AAAS, Am. Nurses Assn., Alexander Graham Bell Assn. for Deaf, Sigma Theta Tau. Methodist. Contbr. articles to profl. jours. Home: 1509 Bayram St Houston TX 77055

HERTZ, ARTHUR HERMAN, bus. services co. exec.; b. Bklyn., Sept. 10, 1933; s. Edwin Carl and Blanche H.; B.B.A., U. Miami (Fla.), 1955, postgrad., 1955-56; children—Stephen R., Andrew P. Acct., Aetna Mortgage Co., Miami, Fla., 1955; acct. Wometco Enterprises, Inc., Miami, 1955-60, controller, v.p., 1960-72, sr. v.p., chief fin. officer, 1971—, also dir.; dir. SE 1st Nat. Bank of Miami. C.P.A. Mem. Am. Inst. C.P.A.'s, Broadcasting Fin. Mgmt. Assn., Greater Miami C. of C. (gov. 1975-78), U. Miami Alumni Assn. (pres. 1979), Phi Kappa Phi, Omicron Delta Kappa, Beta Gamma Sigma. Club: Kiwanis. Home: 610 Fluvia Ave Coral Gables FL 33134 Office: Wometco Enterprises Inc 316 N Miami Ave Miami FL 33128

HERTZ, KENNETH THEODORE, ballet co. exec.; b. Flushing, N.Y., Aug. 19, 1951; s. Irwin R. and Dorothy S. Hertz; B.A. in Spl. Studies, SUNY, Fredonia, 1974. Mgr., Cape Cod (Mass.) Symphony, 1974-75; mng. dir. Tulsa Philharm., 1975-78; pres., gen. mgr. Atlanta Ballet, 1979—; mktg. cons. regional workshops Am. Symphony Orch. League. Mem. Nat. Assn. Regional Ballet, Assn. Am. Dance Cos., Am. Symphony Orch. League, Alpha Phi Omega. Office: 1404 Spring St NW Atlanta GA 30309

HERTZ, LEON, newspaper exec.; b. Perth, Western Australia, Aug. 1, 1938; s. Abraham and Rose (Weintraub) H.; came to U.S., 1975; grad. U. Western Australia; m. Gloria Mignon Wynne, Apr. 18, 1970; 1 dau., Monique Mignon. With News Ltd. Australia, K.R. Murdoch, 1962—, dir. Mirror Newspapers, Sydney, Australia, 1968—, dir., gen. mgr. Nationwide News, 1970, group advt. dir., 1970—, v.p., bus. mgr. Express News Corp., San Antonio, 1975—. Home: 130 Aylesbury Hill San Antonio TX 78209 Office: Ave E at 3d St San Antonio TX 78297

HERVEY, LESLIE DAVID, JR., sales and mktg. co. exec.; b. Greenville, Miss., Sept. 12, 1940; s. Leslie David and Sara Anne (Jackson) H.; B.B.A., U. Miss., 1963; cert. Am. Inst. Banking, 1965; m. Kaffie Elizabeth Mallette, July 18, 1964; children—Dawn Douglas, Leslie David III. Asst. v.p First Nat. Bank, Jackson, Miss., 1963-67; dist. mgr. McGraw-Hill Book Co., N.Y.C., 1967-70; nat. sales mgr. Ednl. Innovations, Inc., Jackson, 1970-75; owner, pres. Hervey & Assos., Jackson, 1976—; v.p. Highland Colony Realty, Inc. Mem. Amway Distbrs. Assn. (Emerald Direct Distbr. 1979), Sunflower Triad Investment Club (pres.). Baptist. Clubs: River Hills Tennis (Jackson). Home and Office: 4330 Deer Creek Dr Jackson MS 39211

HERZOG, RICHARD B., ins. co. exec.; b. Cin., May 21, 1937; s. Arthur E. and Bessie Lois (Berger) H.; cert. Hamilton County (Ohio) Police Acad., 1969; cert. Mktg. Devel. Inst., Purdue U., 1979; m. Sally Annette Bell, Nov. 24, 1956; children—Cindy Sue, Shelly Lynn, Matthew Barrett. Draftsman, Avco, Cin., 1955-56, Kettcorp., Cin., 1956-57, Trailmobile, Inc., Cin., 1957-62; prin. Allied Film Agy., Cin., 1962-63; enrollment rep. Blue Cross of S.W. Ohio, Cin., 1963-68, mgr. mktg., 1968-72; mgr. regional mktg. Blue Cross Assn., Atlanta, 1972-77, dir. mktg., 1977-78; sr. dir. mktg. S.E. region Blue Cross and Blue Shield Assns., Atlanta, 1978—. Bd. dirs. Jr. Achievement, Cin., 1965-66, Cin. chpt. Cystic Fibrosis Research Found., 1963-64; bd. dirs. Carriage Cluster Civic Assn., 1975-76, pres., 1979-80; minister Dekalb Christian Ch. Atlanta, 1974-78; co-chmn. Aronoff campaign for state senate, 1966-72. Recipient various awards Jaycees. Office: Blue Cross and Blue Shield Assns 4488 N Shallowford Rd Atlanta GA 30338

HESS, DELBERT COY, agrl. co. exec.; b. Sweetwater, Tex., May 5, 1936; s. Orval Coy and Opal Louise (Jackson) H.; B.S., Tex. Technol. U., 1958; M.S., U. Wis., 1960, Ph.D., 1965; m. Patricia A. Curry, Aug. 30, 1958; children—Kenneth, Valinda, Kirkland. Sorghum breeder Acco Seed Co. (now div. Anderson, Clayton & Co.), Plainview, Tex., 1965-68, dir. cotton research, 1968—. Chmn., Cotton Improvement Conf., 1977-78. Served with USAF, 1960-63. Mem. Tex. Seed Trade Assn. (dir. 1979—), Am. Soc. Agronomy, Crop Sci. Soc. Am., Sigma Xi. Methodist. Clubs: Plainview Knife and Fork (v.p. 1973-74), Lions (pres. Plainview 1973-74). Dir. devel. cotton varieties. Home: 1311 Holiday St Plainview TX 79072 Office: Acco Seed div Anderson Clayton & Co PO Box 1630 Plainview TX 79072

HESS, MARVIN JAMES, accountant; b. Graceville, Minn., May 20, 1928; s. Albert Plummer and Jessie Ethel (Hess) H.; B.S. in Acctg., Our Lady of the Lake Coll., 1971; M.S. in Mgmt., Trinity U., 1972; m. Jeraldyne Jacobs, July 8, 1956; children—Murray, Marshall. Enlisted in U.S. Air Force, 1947, commd. 2d lt., 1949, advanced through grades to lt. col., 1966; served in Korea, Vietnam; ret., 1970; instr. Incarnate Word Coll., San Antonio, 1972-73; asst. v.p. Broadway Nat. Bank, San Antonio, 1973-76; controller 1st Nat. Bank, San Antonio, 1976-77; controller Govt. Personnel Mut. Life Ins. Co., San Antonio, 1977—. Chmn., Taxpayer Edn. Com., 1979. C.P.A. Mem. Am. Inst. C.P.A.'s, Tex. Soc. C.P.A.'s, Am. Mgmt. Assn., Ins. Acctg. and Statis. Assn. Club: Optimist. Home: 9903 Gemini Dr San Antonio TX 78217 Office: 800 NW Loop 410 San Antonio TX 78216

HESSE, MICHAEL BERNARD, communications scientist, educator; b. Cin., Sept. 24, 1942; s. Melvin Jacob and Hilda (Marcus) H.; A.B., U. Cin., 1965; M.A., Am. U., 1967; Ph.D., U. Wis., 1974; m. Shelley Audia, Sept. 6, 1969; children—Heidi Lyn, Michael Julian. Staff, Sta. WTOP-TV and Washington Post, 1966-67, Public Relations Soc., Am., N.Y., 1966; tchr. Aiken High Sch., 1967-68; staff Blue Cross SW Ohio, 1969, Avco Broadcasting Co./Sta. WLWD, 1969-70; asso. dir. info. services and public relations U. Wis., Whitewater, 1970-74; asst. prof. advt., public relations U. Md., College Park, 1974-77; chmn., asso. prof. advt., public relations U. Ala., University, 1977—. Named Outstanding Jaycee, Wis. Jaycees, 1971-72; grantee Found. Public Relations Research and Edn., 1976-77; U. Wis. Doctoral fellow, 1972-73. Mem. Internat. Communication Assn., Assn. Edn. in Journalism (pres., chmn. public relations div. 1979—), Public Relations Soc. Am. (dir. educators sect. 1979—), Sigma Delta Chi, Pi Delta Epsilon. Home: 113 Vestavia Hills Northport AL 35476 Office: 303 Carmichael Hall U Ala University AL 35486

HESSELBART, SUSAN CAROL, educator; b. Detroit, May 30, 1946; d. Rubin and Naomi Lois (Hendelman) Losh; B.A., U. Mich., 1968, M.A., 1971, Ph.D., 1973; m. John Hesselbart, July 30, 1966. Asst. prof. sociology Fla. State U., Tallahassee, 1973-78, asso. prof., 1978—; dir. Project TAL, Opinion Survey of Tallahassee area, 1974—; cons. on social research Navy Human Goals Project, Leon County Planning Dept., various civic groups, pvt. corps.; survey research cons. legal cases. Recipient Rackham prize, Hopwood Writing award U. Mich., 1965. Mem. Am. Sociol. Assn., Am. Assn. for Pub. Opinion Research, So. Sociol. Soc. (com. status of women 1978-79, exec. com. 1979—), Sociologists for Women in Soc. (newsletter editor so. region 1976-78), Nat. Council on Family Relations, Phi Beta Kappa, Alpha Kappa Delta. Contbr. articles in field to profl. jours.; head sociology editor Sex Roles: A Jour. of Research, 1977—; asso. editor Social Forces, 1978—; editorial bd. Social Sci. Quar., 1979—. Home: 1124 Alachua Ave Tallahassee FL 32308 Office: Dept of Sociology Fla State U Tallahassee FL 32306

HESSLER, FLOYD WAYNE, educator; b. Scottsbluff, Nebr., Mar. 12, 1933; s. Henry A. and Alice (Hagen) H.; A.A., Nebr. Western Coll., 1958; B.Th., Platte Valley Bible Coll., 1959, B.A., 1957; M.S., Fort Hays State U., 1959; Ed.D., Nova U., 1975; m. Anna Marie Frischholz, July 28, 1960; 1 son, Wayne Alan. Tchr., Cheltenham Twp. (Pa.) Schs., 1961-62, Anchorage Schs., 1957-59; prin. Minatare and Henry (Nebr.) Schs., 1955-57, USAF Dependent Overseas Schs., Azores and France, 1959-61, Hampton City (Va.) Schs., 1962-64; instr. Brevard Community Coll., Cocoa, Fla., 1966-70; adminstr. Brevard County Sch. Bd., Rockledge, Fla., 1964—, dir. adult and community edn., 1977—; adj. prof. edn. Grad. Div. Nova U., 1976-80. Vice pres. Spaceport area Fla. Lung Assn.; sec. Brevard County Dem. Exec. Com.; chmn. North Brevard Dem. Com.; pres. Imperial Estates Civic Assn.; deacon Sun Valley Christian Ch. Mem. Am. Assn. Sch. Adminstrs., Nat. Sch. Public Relations Assn., Assn. Supervision and Curriculum Devel., Phi Delta Kappa. Mem. Christian Ch. Home: 5685 Barna Ave Titusville FL 32780 Office: 1274 S Florida Ave Rockledge FL 32955

HESTER, ALCIA MARGUERITE, oil co. exec.; b. McAdoo, Tex., Nov. 17, 1924; d. Robert Alcieus and Jeffie DeLula (Martin) Butler; student Tex. Tech. Coll., 1943-44, U. Tex. at Arlington, 1961; m. Kenneth Latrell Hester, June 13, 1953; 1 son, Robert Latrell. Asst. sec., mgr. land dept. Longhorn Prodn. Co., Dallas, 1965-69, Prudential Minerals Exploration Co., Dallas, 1969-70; owner, operator Alcia Enterprises, Richardson, Tex., also cons. land records systems design, 1970—; mgr. land dept. Pitts Oil Co., Dallas, 1972—; lectr. in field. Active Boy Scouts Am. Mem. Am. Assn. Petroleum Landmen, Ind. Petroleum Assn. Am. (asso.). Club: Eisenhower Yacht. Home: 526 Salem Dr Richardson TX 75280 Office: 133 Meadows Bldg Dallas TX 75206

HESTER, CAWTHON BELL, JR., tax commr.; b. Climax, Ga., Feb. 25, 1937; s. Cawthon Bell and Lota (Allen) H.; B.S., Ga. Inst. Tech., 1959; m. Betty Sue Merritt, Aug. 4, 1962; children—Tammy Kay, Sandy Michelle. With Cole-Layer-Trumble Co., Dayton, Ohio, 1960-61; br. mgr. Universal C.I.T. Credit Corp., Bainbridge, Ga., 1961-66; partner Martin & Son Auto Sales, Bainbridge, 1966-67; office mgr. Gas & Chems. Inc. Attapulgus, Ga., 1967-68; asst. plant supt. Elberta Crate & Box Co., Bainbridge, 1968-69; plant mgr. ITT Thompson Industries, Cairo, Ga., 1969-73; tax commr., Decatur County, Ga., 1973—. Chmn. Decatur County Easter Seals, 1974, 75; chmn. Decatur Heart Fund, 1973; mem. Ga. Dem. Com., 1976—; chmn. Decatur County United Way, 1978. Served with Army N.G., 1959. Mem. Ga. Assn. Tax Ofcls. Democrat. Methodist. Clubs: Lions, Masons (Shriner). Home: 1020 Julia Circle Bainbridge GA 31717 Office: PO Box 246 Bainbridge GA 31717

HESTER, JAMES A., data systems analyst; b. Sigourney, Iowa, June 16, 1949; s. William A. and Mary L. (Barron) H.; B.S. in Bus., Okla. State U., 1976; m. Sandra K. Hester, Mar. 19, 1965; children—Phillip A., Laura E., Steven A., Brian A. With Wilson Foods Corp., Oklahoma City, 1968—, data processing mgr. Oklahoma City plant div., 1976-77, systems analyst corp. hdqrs., 1977—. Mem. Data Processing Mgmt. Assn. Republican. Roman Catholic. Club: Jaycees. Home: 11605 Sagamore Dr Yukon OK 73099 Office: 4545 Lincoln Blvd Oklahoma City OK 73105

HESTER, JOAN MICHELLE HUDDLESTON, educator; b. Miami, Fla., Mar. 13, 1948; d. Mitchill W. and Sallie (Broxson) Huddleston; B.A., U. Fla., 1971; M.A., Western Carolina U., 1975; m. Donald Wayne Hester, Sept. 25, 1970. Headstart tchr./supr. Qualla Indian Boundry Projects, Cherokee, N.C., 1973; speech pathologist Burke Co. Dept. Social Services, Morganton, N.C., 1975, Catawba County Schs., Hickory, N.C., 1975-76, Gracewood State Sch. and Hosp., Augusta, Ga., 1976-78; speech pathologist/instr./supr. U. Tenn., Knoxville, 1979—. Lic. speech pathologist, Ga., N.C. Mem. Am. Speech and Hearing Assn. (cert. of clin. competence), Tenn. Speech and Hearing Assn., Council for Exceptional Children, Pi Lambda Theta. Office: U Tenn Hearing and Speech Center Stadium Dr at Yale Ave Knoxville TN 37916

HESTER, THOMAS ROY, anthropologist; b. Crystal City, Tex., Apr. 28, 1946; s. Jim Tom and Mattie Laura (Umphres) H.; B.A. with honors, U. Tex., Austin, 1969; Ph.D., U. Calif., Berkeley, 1972; m. Lynda Sue Broadway, July 2, 1966; children—Lesley Elise, Amy Lynne. Acting asst. prof. anthropology U. Calif., Berkeley, 1972-73; asst. prof. U. Tex., San Antonio, 1973-75, asso. prof., 1975-77, prof. anthropology, 1977—, dir. Center for Archaeol. Research, 1974—; cons. S.W. Research Inst., San Antonio, 1975—. Woodrow Wilson fellow, 1969-70. Fellow Tex. Archeol. Soc.; mem. Soc. Am. Archaeology, Assn. Field Archaeology (mem. exec. council), Assn. Borderland Scholars (mem. exec. bd.), Tex. Archeol. Soc., Sigma Xi (pres. Alamo chpt.). Methodist. Author: (with R. Heizer and J.A. Graham) Field Methods in Archaeology, 1975. Editor Tex. Archeol. Soc. Bull., 1974-78. Contbr. articles to profl. jours. Home: 105 Country Club Ln San Antonio TX 78232 Office: Center Archaeol Research Univ of Tex San Antonio TX 78285

HETHCOX, ALBERT HARTSELLE, JR., mortgage co. exec.; b. Talladega, Ala., Oct. 14, 1944; s. Albert Hartselle and Sarah Lillian (Nabors) H.; B.S., Jacksonville State U., 1967; M.B.A., Samford U., 1979; m. Marianne Margaret Fisher, Apr. 15, 1968; children—Albert Hartselle III, Jonathan, Cassidy. Exec. dir. Boy Scouts Am., Birmingham, Ala., 1970-72; asst. v.p. Jackson Co., Birmingham, 1972-76; asst. v.p. Mortgage Corp. of South, Birmingham, 1976; v.p. Engel Mortgage Co., Inc., Birmingham, 1976—. Served to capt. U.S. Army, 1967-70. Decorated Bronze Star. Mem. Am. Mgmt. Assn., Nat. Mortgage Bankers Assn., Ala. Mortgage Bankers Assn., Ala. Mortgage Loan Adminstrn. Group. Methodist. Clubs: Exchange (dir. 1979—). Home: 5072 Juiata Dr Birmingham AL 35210 Office: Engel Mortgage Co Inc 501 John Hand Bldg Birmingham AL 35201

HETHCOX, JAMES MALCOLM, pharmacist, pharm. services adminstr.; b. Hattiesburg, Miss., Oct. 27, 1948; s. James Gurnis and Annette (Sumrall) H.; B.S. in Pharmacy with distinction, U. Miss., 1972; postgrad. U. Okla., 1972-77; m. Kathleen Blackburn, May 31, 1970; children—Joshua Matthew, Julie Kaye. Resident in hosp. pharmacy Presbyn. Hosp., Oklahoma City, 1972-73, dir. pharmacy, 1973—, dir. ambulatory care, 1975-80; clin. instr. Coll. of Pharmacy, U. Okla. Health Scis. Center, Oklahoma City, 1973—; instr. pharmacology Okla. State Dept. of Vo-Tech Edn., Oklahoma City, 1976-77; hosp. pharmacy cons. Bristol Labs., Syracuse, N.Y., 1978—; instr. pharmacology health occupations div. Oscar Rose Jr. Coll., Midwest City, Okla., 1972-76. Recipient Geigy Leadership award, 1978; E.R. Squibb President's award, 1978; Roche Hosp. Pharmacy Research grantee, 1973; registered pharmacist, Miss., Okla. Mem. Am. Assn. Colls. Pharmacy, Am. Pharm. Assn., Acad. Pharmacy Practice, Am. Soc. Hosp. Pharmacists, Drug Info. Assn., Okla. Soc. Hosp. Pharmacists (dir. 1977-79, pres. 1977-78), Am. Soc. for Parenteral and Enternal Nutrition, Am. Assn. for Intravenous Therapists, Sigma Xi, Phi Eta Sigma, Phi Kappa Phi, Rho Chi. Republican. Baptist. Contbr. articles to profl. jours. Home: 3924 Coventry Ln Norman OK 73069 Office: NE 13th at Lincoln Blvd Oklahoma City OK 73104

HEWETT, ROBERT JOSEPH, SR., accountant, fin. cons.; b. Kaufmann County, Tex., July 17, 1933; s. Wilber Douglas and Ola Mae (Carroll) H.; B.B.A., Washburn U., 1962; m. JoAnn Jordan, Sept. 3, 1953 (div. June 1971); children—Douglas Edward, Michael Scott, Karen Kay, Jeffrey Robert; m. 2d, Martha Vowels Roemele, Sept. 3, 1971; 1 son, Robert Joseph; stepdaughter Sally Marie. Asst. mgr. Savs. Bond and Mktg. Co., Topeka, Kan., 1959-60; asst. office mgr., asst. div. controller Fleming Co., Topeka, Kan., 1960-62; auditor Office of Insp. Gen. U.S. Dept. Agr., 1962-68, 69-70; controller, personnel mgr. Fixtures Mfg. Corp., Kansas City, Mo., 1968-69; resident examiner Farm Credit Adminstrn., Louisville, 1970-72, comptroller, Washington, 1972-75, asst. dir. review div., 1975-76; pres., co-owner Agrl. Resources Corp. of Am., Washington, 1976-78; pres., owner Hewitt Fin. Services, Inc., Fairfax, Va., 1978—, Robert J. Hewett & Assos., Agrl. Consultants, Fairfax, 1978—. Served with U.S. Army, 1953-58. Mem. Nat. Soc. Accountants for Cooperatives, Fairfax C. of C., Fairfax Hosp. Assn., Delta Sigma Pi. Baptist. Home: 11400 Fairfax Dr Great Falls VA 22066 Office: 9864 Main St Fairfax VA 22031

HEWITT, DEAN JAY, mfg. co. exec.; b. Milw., Dec. 11, 1929; s. Dean J. and Evelyn M. (Danielson) H.; student Northwestern U., 1947-49; B.J., U. Mo., 1953, M.A., 1956; postgrad. Drake U., 1958-59; m. Alice Ann Arntzen, Dec. 27, 1952; children—Thomas Randall, Jeffrey John, Dana Jean. Reporter, San Diego Union, 1956-58; copy and make-up editor Des Moines Register, 1958-59; mgr. product publicity Kimberly-Clark Corp., Neenah, Wis., 1959-68, dir. pub. relations, 1969-73; dir. pub. relations Bendix Corp., Southfield, Mich., 1973-76; v.p. mktg. Facet Cycle Inc., Tulsa, 1978-79; dir. corporate relations Facet Enterprises, Inc., Tulsa, 1976—. Mem. indsl. com. Tulsa Area United Way, 1979; mem. fin. com. Mich. United Way, 1975-76; chmn. Winnebago County (Wis.) Republican Party, 1970-72. Served with USN, 1953-56. Mem. Pub. Relations Soc. Am., Navy League U.S., Res. Officers Assn., Acacia Frat., Sigma Delta Chi. Republican. Episcopalian. Club: Tulsa Press. Home: 5816 E 64 St Tulsa OK 74136 Office: 7030 S Yale Ave Tulsa OK 74177

HEWITT, GERALD NEAL, hosp. adminstr.; b. Maiden, N.C., Oct. 21, 1931; s. Artis Clifton and Ella Coleen (Tuttle) H.; B.A., Wake Forest U., 1958; M.Div., Southeastern Bapt. Theol. Sem., 1962; M.A., Appalachian State U., 1976; m. Phyllis Marion Beattie, Apr. 16, 1952; children—Timothy Neal, Scott Beattie, Angela Denise. Ordained to ministry So. Bapt. Ch., 1957; pastor First Bapt. Ch., Welcome, N.C., 1962-65; bus. mgr. N.C. Bapt. Hosp., Winston-Salem, 1965-71, controller, 1971-73, v.p. patient fin. services, 1973—; lectr. hosp. adminstrn. Bowman Gray Med. Sch., 1975—. Chmn. Bapt. State Conv. Com. on Aging, 1976-80; pres. Southwest Forsyth Community Assn., 1979—; pres. Griffith PTA, 1969, Anderson High Sch. PTA, 1971; trustee N.C. Bapt. Homes, 1978. Served with USAF, 1951-55. Mem. Hosp. Fin. Mgmt. Assn. (advance mem. Follmer award 1974, Reeves award 1978), pres. N.C. chpt. 1977-78), Am. Coll. Hosp. Adminstrs. Home: 3060 Brookhill Dr Winston Salem NC 27107 Office: 300 S Hawthorne Rd Winston Salem NC 27103

HEWITT, NATHANIEL EDRINGTON, geneticist; b. St. Croix, V.I., May 2, 1943; s. Nathaniel and Theolinda Edmonier (Joseph) H.; B.S. Howard U., 1964, M.S., 1970, Ph.D., 1972; m. Minnie Louise Christian, Oct. 13, 1964; children—Nathaniel Edrington III, Denise Edmonier, Michele Elena, Christopher Eric. Tchr. sci. Central High Sch., St. Croix, 1967-68; postdoctoral fellow Oak Ridge Nat. Lab., 1972-74; asst. prof. biology Winston Salem (N.C.) U., 1974—; vis. research fellow Swiss Fed. Inst., Zurich, summer 1971. Mem. parents adv. council Winston-Salem Forsyth County Schs., 1977-79; v.p. PTA Moore Sch., 1978-79; mem. task force bd. Forsyth County Cancer Soc., 1979-80. NSF trainee, 1968-72; Lucy Moten fellow, 1971; Nat. Inst. Gen. Med. Scis fellow, 1972-74. Mem. Genetics Soc. Am., Am. Genetics Assn., AAAS, N.C. Acad. Scis., Am. Soc. Microbiology, Southeastern Drosophilists, Gerontol. Soc., N.Y. Acad. Scis., Sigma Xi, Beta Kappa Chi. Contbr. articles to profl. jours. Office: Dept Biology Winston Salem State U Winston-Salem NC 27102

HEWITT, ROBERT LEE, surgeon, educator; b. Paducah, Ky., Nov. 2, 1934; s. Lee A. and Donis (Brown) H.; student U. Louisville, 1952-55; M.D., Tulane U., 1959; m. Patricia M. Stewart, May 1, 1965; children—Heather Edgeworth, Robert Stewart, Whit Butler, Brooke Lee. Intern, Charity Hosp., Tulane U., New Orleans, 1959-60, resident, 1960-65, faculty Sch. Medicine, 1960—, asst. prof. surgery, 1968-70, asso. prof., 1970-75, prof. surgery, 1975-76, clin. prof. surgery, 1976—; mem. staff Charity, So. Bapt., Tulane U. hosps., Touro Infirmary (all New Orleans); cons. several hosps. Mem. leadership forum Met. Area Com. New Orleans, 1971. Served with M.C., AUS, 1966-68. Diplomate Am. Bd. Surgery, Am. Bd. Thoracic Surgery. Fellow A.C.S.; mem. Soc. Univ. Surgeons, Am. Assn. Thoracic Surgery, So. Surg. Assn., Oscar Creech, Alton Ochsner, New Orleans surg. socs., Southeastern Surg. Congress, Soc. Vascular Surgery, Soc. Thoracic Surgeons, Internat. Cardiovascular Soc., Southeastern Assn. Vascular Surgery, Assn. Acad. Surgeons, AMA, La., Orleans Parish med. socs., Assn. Mil. Surgeons, New Orleans Grad. Med. Assembly, Alpha Omega Alpha, Omicron Delta Kappa, Phi Kappa Tau, Phi Chi. Episcopalian. Contbr. articles to profl. jours. Home: 1207 Webster St New Orleans LA 70118 Office: 4440 Magnolia St New Orleans LA 70115

HEYCK, GERTRUDE PAINE DALY (MRS. THEODORE R. HEYCK), club woman; b. Houston, Nov. 30, 1910; d. David and Gertrude (Paine) Daly; student Wellesley Coll., 1929, Pembroke Coll., 1931-34; B.A., Brown U., 1934; m. Theodore R. Heyck, May 1, 1935; children—Jane Peel (Mrs. Donald H. Gaucher), Theodore Daly. Dir., Union Stock Yards, San Antonio, 1961-64. Sustaining mem. Jr. League, Houston. Club: Brown-Pembroke. Home: 1907 Bolsover St Houston TX 77005

HEYMAN, STEPHEN JOSHUA, oil co. exec.; b. N.Y.C., Apr. 30, 1939; s. George I. and Bess (Weiner) H.; B.S. in Econs., Wharton Sch., U. Pa., 1959; m. Barbara Gussman, June 23, 1963; children—Alexandra, Claudia. With Oscar Heyman and Brothers, Inc., N.Y.C., 1959-65; asso. and partner Nadel and Gussman, Tulsa, 1965—; mng. partner Head Oil Co., Tulsa, 1966—; pres. Res. Drilling Co., Inc., Tulsa, 1967—; dir. Sonic Devel. Corp., Upper Mahwah, N.J., 1968—. Trustee, Undercroft Sch., 1972-75, Children's Med. Center, 1975—, Holland Hall Sch., 1978—; mem. Holland Hall Sch. Endowment Assn., 1976. Republican. Jewish. Clubs: Tulsa, Tulsa Tennis. Home: 2530 E 30th St Tulsa OK 74114 also 45 East End Ave New York NY 10028 also Ocean Ave East Hampton NY 11937 Office: 32nd floor First National Tower Tulsa OK 74103

HIBBERT, WILLIAM ANDREW, JR., surgeon; b. Pensacola, Fla., June 15, 1932; s. William Andrew and Blanche Marie (Blair) H.; B.S., U. of South, 1953; M.D., Emory U., 1957; married; children—Andy III, Blair, Reb Stuart. Intern, Duval Med. Center, U. Fla., Jacksonville, 1957-58; resident in gen. surgery Grady Meml. Hosp., Atlanta, 1958-62; fellow in colon-rectal surgery Ochsner Found. Hosp., New Orleans, 1962-63, Baylor U. Med. Center, Dallas, 1964-65; practice medicine specializing in colon-rectal surgery, Austin, Tex., 1965—; mem. staff St. David, Seton, Brackenridge, Holy Cross hosps; cons. U. Tex. Student Health Center. Served with USPHS, 1963-64. Fellow A.C.S., Am. Soc. Colon and Rectal Surgeons; mem. Pan Am. (chmn. colon-rectal sect.), So., Tex. med. assns., Tex. Colon-Rectal Soc. (pres.), Pan Pacific Surg. Soc., Royal Soc. Medicine (hon.). Clubs: Masons, (Shriner, Jester), Rotary, Austin Downtown. Asso. editor So. Med. Jour., 1973-75. Contbr. articles to med. jours. Home: 3900 Stoneridge St Austin TX 78746 Office: 4210 Medical Pkwy Austin TX 78756

HIBBETT, IRA KNEELAND, sporting goods chain exec.; b. Florence, Ala., Feb. 9, 1931; s. Rufus Gleason and Anne Lee (Lester) H.; m. Barbara Absher, Dec. 23, 1961; children—Leigh Ann, Whitney Jean, Ira Kneeland. Pres., Hibbett Sporting Goods, Inc., Florence, 1952—; adv. Riddell Corp., 1976-77; dir. Shoals Nat. Bank of Florence. Commr. Florence Housing Authority, 1971—. Served with USNR, 1946-49. Mem. Ala. Sporting Goods Dealers Assn. (pres. 1958, now sec.-treas.), Ala. Jaycees (state v.p. 1955), Florence C. of C. (pres. 1975). Mem. Ch. of Christ. Clubs: Saddle-n-Spur (pres. 1961), Rotary, Turtle Point Country. Adv. bd. Sporting Goods Dealer mag., 1965. Home: 1914 Monticello St Florence AL 35630 Office: PO Box 130 Florence AL 35630

HIBBISON, ERIC PAUL, educator; b. Omaha, Jan. 15, 1948; s. George Edward and Mary Miriam (Berens) H.; B.A., Regis Coll., 1969; M.A. (EPDA fellow), U. Ariz., 1971, M.Ed., 1972; m. Elleanor Carol Olmstead, Sept. 4, 1976; 1 son, Mark Brian. Instr., Auburn (N.Y.) Community Coll., 1971-73; asso. prof. J. Sargeant Reynolds Community Coll., Richmond, Va., 1973—; cons. editor developmental composition Prentice-Hall, 1979—. Mem. Nat. Council Tchrs. English, Internat. Reading Assn. Author: (with Kenneth M. Symes) The Apprentice Writer, 1981. Home: 5213 Wythe Ave Richmond VA 23226 Office: PO Box 12084 Richmond VA 23241

HIBBS, BETTY ELLIS, correctional facility adminstr.; b. Macon, Ga., Nov. 5, 1938; d. Ernest Crawford and Williemae (Smith) Ellis; B.A., Wesleyan Coll., 1975; M.Ed., Ga. State U., 1977; children—Ray III, Dana Elizabeth, Pamela Virginia. Mgr., Aero Club, Moody AFB, Valdosta, Ga., 1967-68; probation officer Ft. Valley Office, Macon Jud. Circuit, 1975-77, probation office mgr. Peach and Crawford Counties, 1977-78; dir. Macon Diversion Center Dept. Offender Rehab., 1978—. Named Probation Officer of Yr. for State of Ga., 1978; lic. pvt. pilot. Mem. Ga. Probation and Parole Assn., Am. Personnel and Guidance Assn., Am. Correctional Assn., Pi Gamma Mu. Unitarian. Home: 5072 Pine Ridge Dr Macon GA 31210 Office: 1232 Jeffersonville Rd Macon GA 31201

HIBBS, WILLIE ESTHEL, hosp. adminstr.; b. Hopkins County, Ky., Oct. 1, 1912; s. Ben and Mary May (Tucker) H.; diploma Gupton-Jones Coll. Mortuary Sci., 1937; m. Effie Lorene Gibbons, Sept. 1, 1940; children—Eddie Forrest, Willie Esthel. With Barnett Funeral Home, Madisonville, Ky., 1933-39, Harris Funeral Home, Madisonville, 1939-42, Johnson Funeral Home, Hazard, Ky., 1946-47, Boyd Funeral Home, Salem, Ky., 1947-77; hosp. adminstr. Livingston County Hosp. Inc., Salem, Ky., 1977—. Bd. dirs. Ky. Higher Edn. Served with Q.M.C., U.S. Army, 1942-45; PTO. Lic. embalmer, funeral dir., Ky. Mem. VFW, Am. Legion. Democrat. Mem. Disciples of Christ. Clubs: Masons, Order Eastern Star, Lions. Home: Route 1 Box 2 Salem KY 42078 Office: Livingston County Hosp Inc Box 138 Salem KY 42078

HIBDON, JAMES EDWARD, educator; b. McAlester, Okla., Sept. 1, 1924; s. William Wesley and Minnie Irene (McBride) H.; student Okla. Bapt. U., 1942-43, Syracuse U., 1943; B.A., U. Okla., 1948, M.A., 1949; Ph.D., U. N.C., 1957; m. Mina Mae Gilreath, Aug. 20, 1944; children—Mary Ann, Jennifer Lee. Asst. prof. econs. Ga. State U., 1954-57, asso. prof., 1957-59; asso. prof. Tex. A. and M. U.,

1959-61; asso. prof. U. Okla., Norman, 1961-67, prof., 1967—, chmn. econs. dept., 1971—; vis. scholar U.S. Dept. Commerce, 1977-78. Trustee annuity bd. So. Bapt. Conv. Served with AUS, 1943-46, 50-51. Mem. Am., So., Midwest econ. assns., S.W. Econs. Assn. (pres. 1977-78), Southwestern Social Sci. Assn., Rocky Mountain Social Sci. Assn., Beta Gamma Sigma, Omicron Delta Epsilon. Author: Price and Welfare Theory, 1969; also articles; editor Okla. Bus. Bull., 1970-71, Rev. Regional Econs. and Bus., 1975—. Home: 1501 Leslie Ln Norman OK 73069

HIBSCHMAN, JAMES DEE, mfg. co. exec.; b. Hammond, Ind., Aug. 18, 1947; s. Max Harding and Wanda Mae (Hibschman; grad. Lake Land Coll., 1971; m. Bonnie Smith, Mar. 7, 1970; children—Kara Lindsay. Purchasing agt., personnel mgr. Celotex Corp. div. Jim Walter Corp., Charleston, Ill., 1971-73; employment and salary mgr. Crest Container Corp. div. Continental Group, Inc., Shelbyville, Ill., 1973-77; personnel dir. Rudy's Farm Co. div. Consol. Foods Corp., Nashville, 1977—. Served with U.S. Army, 1967-69. Mem. VFW, Am. Legion, Indsl. Personnel Assn. Nashville, Am. Mgmt. Assn. Democrat. Mem. 1st Christian Ch. Clubs: Lions, Elks, Moose. Home: 438 Neelys Bend Rd Madison TN 37115 Office: 2424 Music Valley Dr Nashville TN 37214

HICKEY, JOHN KING, lawyer; b. Mt. Sterling, Ky., Oct. 15, 1920; s. John Andrew and Anna Christine (King) H.; LL.B., U. Ky., 1948; M.A., George Washington U., 1964; postgrad. Air War Coll., 1964; m. Elizabeth Jane Pattavina, Nov. 23, 1944; children—Roger Dennis, Patricia Elizabeth (Mrs. William H. Corsini, Jr.), John King II. Commd. 2d lt. USAF, 1942, advanced through grades to col., 1964; bombardier, 1942-45; judge advocate, 1948-70, assignments in U.S., Japan, Spain included chmn. bd. review, 1964-66, chief Internat. Law Div. OJAG, Washington, 1966-68; admitted to Ky. bar, 1949; dir. legal and judicial adminstrn. Council State Govts., Lexington, Ky., 1971-73; dir. continuing legal edn. Coll. Law, U. Ky., Lexington, 1973—. Decorated D.F.C. with oak leaf cluster, Air medal with 3 oak leaf clusters, Bronze Star medal. Mem. Am., Ky. bar assns., Phi Delta Phi. K.C. Club: Spindletop (Lexington, Ky.). Home: 3340 Nantucket Rd Lexington KY 40502 Office: Coll of Law Univ of Ky Lexington KY 40506

HICKEY, NORMAN WILBUR, city mgr.; b. Belleville, N.J., Aug. 31, 1927; s. John E. and Jeannette (Gebhard) H.; B.A., Pa. State U., 1954; M. Governmental Adminstrn. (Fels scholar, fellow) U. Pa., 1957; m. Dolores F. Jacobs, Oct. 17, 1956; one son, Christopher N. Mem. staff office of city mgr. City of Windsor (Conn.), 1955; asst. city mgr. City of Ft. Lauderdale (Fla.), 1956-58, 61-62; city mgr. City of Titusville (Fla.), 1958-62, City of Daytona Beach (Fla.), 1962-66; city sr. adviser, dir. devel. ops., chief field ops. land reform, Vietnam, Saigon, 1967-70; chief mission HUD/AID to Columbia, Bogota, 1970-72; dep. city mgr., cons. City of Hollywood (Fla.), also exec. dir. Daytona Beach (Fla.) Downtown Devel. Authority, 1972-73; city mgr. City of Titusville (Fla.), 1973—. Vice-pres. Fla. United Fund, 1960—, chmn., 1964—. Served with USMCR, 1945-49, 50-51. Recipient Good Govt. award Jaycees Titusville, 1960, 76, Daytona Beach, 1965; State of Fla. Good Govt. and Outstanding Contbn. awardee, 1965; Meritorious Honor award AID/Dept. State, 1969; Sertoma Service to Mankind award, 1979. Mem. Internat., Fla. (pres.) city and county mgrs. assns., Fla. League Cities (dir. Titusville), Am. Pub. Works Assn. Episcopalian. Clubs: Civitan, Optimist, Rotary. Home: 1550 Riverside Dr Titusville FL 32780 Office: 555 S Washington Ave PO Box Y Titusville FL 32780

HICKMAN, DEWEY CAUL, hosp., health adminstr.; b. Bklyn., Aug. 10, 1951; s. Prestible Fitzhugh and Edythe Harriet (Caul) H.; A.B., Harvard, 1973; M.B.A. (Michael C. Rockefeller Meml. Travel fellow 1973-74), U. Chgo., 1976; m. Paula Mahone, May 3, 1980. Adminstrv. asst. to exec. v.p. Affiliated Hosps. Center, Inc., Boston, 1976-78; confidential asst. Health Care Financing Adminstrn., Dept. HEW, Washington, 1978-80; asso. dir. Med. Coll. Va. Hosps., Richmond, 1980—. Active Congl. Black Caucus Health Brain Trust, 1979—. Mem. Nat. Assn. Health Service Execs., Am. Coll. Hosp. Adminstrs. Democrat. Baptist. Office: Med Coll Va Sta 510 Richmond VA 23298

HICKMAN, HOYT LEON, clergyman; b. Pitts., May 22, 1927; s. Leon Edward and Mayme (Hoyt) H.; B.A. magna cum laude, Haverford Coll., 1950; M. Div. cum laude, Yale U., 1953; S.T.M., Union Theol. Sem., 1954; D.D., Morningside Coll., 1978; m. Martha Jean Whitmore, Dec. 16, 1950; children—Peter, John, Stephen, Mary. Ordained to ministry, Meth. Ch., 1953; pastor 1st Meth. Ch., Windber, Pa., 1954-57; pastor Claysville and Stony Point Meth. Chs., Claysville, Pa., 1957-59; pastor Coll. Hill Meth. Ch., Beaver Falls, Pa., 1959-64; pastor Cascade United Meth. Ch., Erie, Pa., 1964-72; dir. office local ch. worship, bd. discipleship United Meth. Ch., Nashville, 1972-78, asst. gen. sec. bd. discipleship, 1978—. Exec. sec. Commn. Worship, United Meth. Ch., 1968-72; mem. Commn. Worship, World Meth. Council, 1971—; mem. Nat. Program Com. Christian Family Movement, 1969-73; pres. Erie County Council Chs., 1970-71. Bd. dirs. Liturgical Conf., 1973-80. Served with USN, 1945-46. Mem. Phi Beta Kappa. Democrat. Contbr. numerous articles to mags. Home: 2034 Castleman Dr Nashville TN 37215 Office: PO Box 840 Nashville TN 37202

HICKMAN, JAMES BLAKE, educator; b. Charleston, W.Va., Nov. 29, 1921; s. James Howard and Bessie (Barnsgrove) H.; B.S. in Chemistry, W.Va. U., 1942, M.S., 1943; Ph.D., Pa. State U., 1950; m. Martha Louise Hornor, June 25, 1948. Chemist, Carbide and Carbon Chem. div. Union Carbide and Carbon, South Charleston, W.Va., 1943-45; instr. chemistry W.Va. U., 1946-49, 50-51; asst. prof. chemistry, 1951-56, asso. prof., 1956-62, prof. chemistry, 1962—, dir. NSF Summer Insts., 1959-65; dir. NSF Academic Year Insts., 1961-65. Fellow AAAS, Am. Inst. Chemists; mem. Am. Chem. Soc., Chem. Soc. London (Eng.), Photographic Soc. Am., W.Va. Acad. Sci. (pres. 1968-69), Phi Beta Kappa, Sigma Xi, Phi Lambda Upsilon. Republican. Baptist. Author: Physical Science, 1966; The Nature of Science, 1970. Research on behavior of mixtures non-electrolytes. Home: 145 Waitman St Morgantown WV 26505

HICKS, DOROTHY JANE, obstetrician-gynecologist; b. Cleve., Apr. 18; d. Arnell R. and Marvel M. (Hale) Hicks; A.B., Case-Western Res. U., 1941; M.D., Temple U., 1944. Intern, St. Luke's Hosp., Cleve., 1944-46; resident in obstetrics-gynecology Univ. Hosps., Cleve., 1951-54; practice medicine specializing in obstetrics-gynecology, Cleve., 1954-67; faculty dept. obstetrics-gynecology Sch. Medicine, U. Miami, Fla., 1967—, asso. prof., 1975—, dir. pediatric gynecology clinic, 1967—, dir. Rape Treatment Center, Jackson Meml. Hosp., 1974—; coordinator Maternal and Infant Health Care Project Dade County, 1970-74. Mem. Dade-Monroe Profl. Standards Rev. Orgn. Diplomate Am. Bd. Obstetrics and Gynecology. Mem. Am. Coll. Obstetrics-Gynecology, Fertility Soc., Fla., Miami obstetrical and gynecol. socs., Fla., Dada County med. socs. Clubs: La Gorce Country, Zonta. Contbr. chpts. to books, articles to med. jours. Office: PO Box 016960 Dept Obstetrics and Gynecology Sch Medicine U Miami Miami FL 33101

HICKS, GEORGE EDWARD, museum dir.; b. Hopewell, Va., Sept. 5, 1946; s. Carman Theodore and Barbara Ann (Buren) H.; B.A., Va. Poly. Inst. and State U., 1969, M.A. 1978; m. Sis Hagen, Sept. 2, 1967; children—Jon Kenneth, Carman Theodore II, James Robertson. Mus. dir. Don F. Pratt Mus., Fort Campbell, Ky., 1974-75, Casemate Mus., Fort Monroe, Va., 1975-79, NASA-Langley Visitor Center, Hampton, Va., 1979—; instr. U. Ky., Hopkinsville, 1974-75; mus. mgmt. cons., 1977—. Served to 1st lt. F.A., U.S. Army, 1971-74. Recipient Civilian Outstanding Performance award 1975. Mem. Peninsula Museums Forum (chmn. 1976, 77), Va. History Museums Fedn. (gov. council 1976, 77, sec. 1978, 79, v.p. 1980), Am. Assn. Museums, Am. Hist. Assn., Am. Assn. State and Local History, Va. History and Museums Fedn., Council Abandoned Mil. Posts, Hist. and Archeol. Soc. Fort Monroe. Presbyterian. Club: Model A Ford Am., (pres. chpt. 1979). Home: 19 N Wedgewood Dr Newport News VA 23601 Office: NASA-Langley Visitor Center MS 480 Hampton VA 23665

HICKS, JAMES JOHNSTON, otorhinolaryngologist; b. Washington, Apr. 19, 1920; s. Julius W. and Thelma (Norton) H.; A.B., Emory U., 1940; M.D., Tulane U., 1944; Ph.D. (hon.), Auburn U., 1969; m. Joan Ludington, Sept. 21, 1948; children—Jane L., Kathryn H. Hicks Porter, Leslie. Intern, So. Pacific Hosp., San Francisco, 1944-45; resident in otorhinolaryngology U. Ala., Birmingham, 1946-48, clin. prof., head dept. surgery, div. otorhinolaryngology Sch. Medicine, 1962—, also chmn.; chief of service VA Hosp., Birmingham, 1962—, Children's Hosp., Birmingham, 1974—, Cooper-Green Hosp., Birmingham, 1974—; head ear, nose and throat State Crippled Children's Service, 1970—; mem. staffs Birmingham Hosps., Bapt. Med. Centers, Hillcrest Hosp., St. Vincent's Hosp., S.Highlands Hosp., Univ. Hosp. Pres. Indsl. Santa Agape, S.A., 1960—, New Haven Corp., Ltda., St. Annes Village, Belize, Central Am.; bd. visitors Tulane U., 1973—; bd. dirs., chmn. resources council Gallaudet Coll., 1973—; bd. advisors Ala. Sheriff's Boys Ranch, 1960—; bd. dirs. Ala. Council Arts, 1971-73; pres. Birmingham Festival Arts, 1966; chmn. health affairs com. Ala. Partners of the Alliance, 1975—; mem. bus. adv. council U. South Ala., 1973—; mem. mayor's com. expansion of Med. Center, Birmingham, 1974—; mem. citizens adv. bd. on health and environ. quality State of Ala. Served with U.S. Army, 1945-46, with USAF, 1955-56. Recipient Nat. Sertoma award, 1968; Nat. Disting. award Future Farmers Am., 1968; named hon. lifetime mem. Fla. Sheriff's Boys Ranch Assn.; honored James J. Hicks, M.D., Day, Enterprise, Ala., 1972; recipient award Huehuetenango, Guatemala, 1973; named Man of Yr., Birmingham Area C. of C., 1973. Diplomate Am. Bd. Otolaryngology. Fellow A.C.S., Am. Acad. Ophthalmology and Otolaryngology, AMA; mem. Am. Council Otolaryngology (del. 1962—), Portmann Internat. Found. (France), AAUP, Med. Assn. State Ala., Birmingham Surg. Soc., Birmingham Acad. Medicine, Ear, Nose and Throat Soc. Birmingham, Birmingham Clin. Soc., Centurion Club, So. Med. Assn., Jefferson County Med. Assn. Contbr. articles to profl. publs. Home: 2732 Abingdon Rd Birmingham AL 35243 Office: 924 S 18th St Birmingham AL 35205

HICKS, LILLIE MARIE, newspaper exec.; b. Sweetwater, Tex., Mar. 17, 1934; d. James William and Mary Della (Horrell) Pickett; m. Kenneth Hicks, Sept. 1, 1950. Telephone operator Southwestern Bell Telephone Co., Harlingen, Tex., 1951-53; posting machine operator Valley Baptist Hosp., Harlingen, 1954-56; gen. mgr. Northside Recorder, San Antonio, 1958—, sec.-treas., 1974—. Chmn. recreation com. Leon Springs Mobile Home Villa, 1976—; bd. dirs. San Antonio chpt. ARC. Mem. Tex. Community Newspaper Assn. (sec.-treas. 1975—), Am. Bus. Women's Assn. (pres. 1966—, Woman of Year 1976-77), Nat. Credit Mgrs. Assn., Northside, San Antonio chambers commerce, Nat. Assn. Advt. Pubs. (dir.), Better Bus. Bur. Democrat. Baptist. Club: Order Eastern Star. Home: 25326 Danna Marie Dr San Antonio TX 78257 Office: 3907 Blanco Rd San Antonio TX 78212

HICKS, MARYELLEN WHITLOCK, judge; b. Odessa, Tex., Mar. 10, 1949; d. Albert G. and Kathleen Margaret (Durham) Whitlock; B.A., Tex. Woman's U., 1970; J.D., Tex. Technol. U., 1974; m. Arvid Hicks, Oct., 1971 (dec.); 1 dau., Kathleen. Admitted to Tex. bar, 1972; mem. firm Mitchell & Bonner, Ft. Worth, 1974-75, Bonner & Hicks, Ft. Worth, 1975-77; judge Mcpl. Ct., City of Ft. Worth, 1977-78, chief judge, 1978—; adj. instr. bus. Law Tarrant County Jr. Coll., 1977—. Bd. dirs. W. Tex. Legal Services, 1978-79. Mem. State Bar of Tex., Am. Bar Assn., Nat. Bar Assn., Tarrant County Bar Assn., Tarrant County Black Lawyers Assn., Jud. Council, Am. Judges Assn., Nat. Council Negro Women (v.p. 1977-78). Democrat. Roman Catholic. Clubs: Odessa Social and Civic, Zonta. Office: City of Fort Worth 1000 Throckmorton Fort Worth TX 76102

HICKS, WILLIAM TROTTER, ret. economist; b. Enterprise, Miss., Mar. 15, 1907; s. William Wooten and Matilda (Trotter) H.; B.S. and M.S., U. Fla., 1928; Ph.D., Northwestern U., 1937; postgrad. Harvard U., 1955-56; m. Za-Ida Moore, June 15, 1930; children—William Trotter, Colquitt Keeling, Beverly Ann (Mrs. Edward West Mullen). Asst. prof. econs. and mktg. U. Fla., 1928-37; economist U.S. Depts. Commerce and Agr., chief mil. requirements div. War Food Adminstrn., 1937-47; prof., dir. bur. bus. research U. Ga., 1947-50; chmn. dept. econs., bus. adminstrn. U. Miss., 1950-66; regional supervisory economist U.S. Army Corps Engrs., Vicksburg, Miss., 1966-76; chief econs. br. Mississippi River Commn., 1966-77. Recipient Disting. Ser. award Alpha Kappa Psi, 1939, Ford Found. fellow, 1956. Mem. Am., So. econs. assns., Permanent Internat. Assn. Nav. Congresses (Belgium), Soc. Am. Mil. Engrs. (post v.p. 1969-71). Episcopalian (vestryman). Home: 43 Chapel Hills Vicksburg MS 39180

HIDALGO, CHESTER PAUL, design engr.; b. Opelousas, La., Dec. 19, 1926; s. Archange Leo and Mary Lilla (Briley) H.; student La. State U., 1944; B.S. in Agri. Engring., U. of S.W. La., 1951; student Tex. Christian U., 1963-66; m. Mary Louise Childress, July 18, 1953; children—LeRoy, Casey, Michael, Paula, Melody, James. Engr. Halliburton Co., Lafayette, La., 1953-55; farmer, rancher Lockney, Tex., 1955-62; design engr. Gen. Dynamics, Ft. Worth, Tex., 1962-73; owner, mgr. Granbury Stone and Nursery, Granbury, Tex., 1970-75; pres. ADAL Corp., Granbury, 1975—; sr. design engr. Gen. Dynamics, Ft. Worth, 1975—. Mem. sch. bd. S. Plains, Tex., 1958-62; del. Democratic Party, Floyd County, Tex., 1960; v.p. Granbury C. of C., 1974-76; mem. Met. Hwys. Com. for Hood County, Tex., 1973-76; mem. parks bd. Granbury City, 1975-80; mem. planning bd. Hood County, 1976-80, bicentennial bd., 1976-80. Served with USN, 1944-46, as 1st. lt. with USAF, 1951-53. Recipient Hood County Bicentennial Civic award, 1978. Registered landscape architect, landscape irrigation specialist, Tex. Mem. Am. Mgmt. Assn. (Ft. Worth chpt.), Am. Nurserymen Assn., Tex. Assn. Nurserymen, Internat. Platform Assn. Republican. Roman Catholic. Clubs: Optimist, Lion, Knight of Columbus. Home: 1106 Gifford St Granbury TX 76048

HIDAY, HENRY RUBEN, JR., security co. exec.; b. Norfolk, Va., Jan. 18, 1945; s. Henry Ruben and Virginia Hiday; B.S. cum laude, Fla. State U., 1976; A.A., Fla. Jr. Coll., Jacksonville, 1973; grad. FBI Nat. Acad., 1974; m. Patricia Ginn, Aug. 4, 1973; children—Michael Scott, Jeffrey Douglas. With Jacksonville Electric Authority, 1965-68; lt. Office Sheriff, Jacksonville, 1968-75; exec. v.p. Enforcement Security Corp., Jacksonville, 1975—. Bd. commrs. Cross Fla. Barge Canal Dist., 1978—; bd. dirs. Bethel Bapt. Instl. Ch. Served with USN, 1963-69. Mem. FBI Nat. Acad. Assn., Fla. FBI Acad. Assn., Am. Soc. Indsl. Security. Republican. Episcopalian. Clubs: Propeller, Shriners, Masons. Home: 1301 1st St S Jacksonville Beach FL 32250 Office: 1600 Talleyrand Ave Jacksonville FL 32206

HIEGEL, JAMES EDWARD, mech. engr.; b. Memphis, Oct. 28, 1940; s. Edward Peter and Aileen Louise (Covington) H.; B.S. in Mech. Engring., U. Tenn., 1963; M.S. (Ethyl Corp. fellow, Atlantic Steel Co. fellow 1963-64), Ga. Inst. Tech., 1965, Ph.D., 1968; m. Beverly Anne Maloof, Sept. 19, 1965; children—James Jason, Justin Robert. Grad. teaching and research asst. Ga. Inst. Tech., 1964-67; sr. engr., scientist McDonnell-Douglas Corp., Douglas Aircraft div., Long Beach, Calif., 1968-74; mgr. design and tech. devel., yarn machinery div. Rockwell Internat. Co., Charlotte, N.C., 1974-75; mgr. engring. research and devel. Levi Strauss and Co., Richardson, Tex., 1975—; mem. part-time faculty Pepperdine U., El Toro, Calif., Long Beach State U., U. N.C., Charlotte. Mem. ASME, Am. Soc. Metals. Roman Catholic. Club: K.C. Home: 1704 Lake Side Ln Plano TX 75023 Office: 900 N Dorothy Dr Richardson TX 75081

HIETT, LOUIS ALDEN, paper co. exec.; b. Memphis, Oct. 2, 1925; s. Louis Alden and Mable Ruth (Nourse) H.; B.Chem. Engring., Ga. Inst. Tech., 1949; m. Virginia Scott Wingfield, Dec. 29, 1948; children—Alden Scott, Virginia Lou, Susan Shaw. Process engr. Buckeye Cellulose Corp. subs. Procter & Gamble Co., Memphis, 1949-55, sect. head, 1955-60, asso. dir. tech. div., 1960-61, plant mgr., 1961-64, mgr. product devel., 1964-70, mgr. spl. projects, 1970-72, mgr. tech. div., 1972-76, v.p., 1976—. Mem. exec. com. Chickasaw council Boy Scouts Am., 1963. Bd. dirs. Jr. Achievement, Memphis, 1961-64, pres., 1963; bd. dirs. Shelby United Neighbors, 1962-64; bd. dirs. Memphis Met. YMCA, 1965—, v.p., 1972-73. Served with AUS, 1943-45. Decorated Purple Heart. Mem. Am. Inst. Chem. Engrs., TAPPI, Memphis C. of C. (mem. exec. com., indsl. council 1961-64). Presbyterian (ruling elder 1957—). Rotarian. Patentee in field. Home: 5700 Sycamore Grove Ln Memphis TN 38117 Office: PO Box 8407 Memphis TN 38108

HIGDON, EARL DILLS, JR., mfg. co. exec.; b. Alamance County, N.C., Feb. 14, 1942; s. Earl Dills and Nelle (Hood) H.; B.S. in M.E. with honors, N.C. State U., 1964, postgrad., 1964-65; M.B.A., Harvard U., 1967; m. Gail Marie Taylor, Feb. 26, 1970; 1 dau., Robbie Leigh. Project engr. Ethyl Corp., Baton Rouge, 1967-69; project engr. Anderson Hosiery, Clinton, S.C., 1969-71, sales and prodn. coordinator, 1971-74, div. controller, 1974—. Home: PO Box 236 Clinton SC 29325 Office: PO Box 525 Clinton SC 29325

HIGGINBOTHAM, HUGH OLIVER, JR., ednl. cons., counselor, sch. prin.; b. Memphis, Jan. 19, 1937; s. Hugh Oliver and Mary Kathryn (Sullender) H.; B.S., Memphis State U., 1967, M.Ed., 1969; postgrad. Vanderbilt U., 1972. Tchr., St. Michael Sch., Memphis, 1963-68; tchr., counselor Christian Bros. High Sch., Memphis, 1968-76; prin., counselor St. Anne Sch., Memphis, 1976-79; prof. Latin, Christian Bros. High Sch., Memphis, 1979—. Served with U.S. Army, 1960-62. Recipient Service awards St. Peters Home for Children, 1966; NSF grantee, 1972. Mem. Nat. Catholic Edn. Assn., Nat. Assn. Secondary Sch. Prins., Nat. Assn. Elem. Sch. Prins., Tenn. Personnel and Guidance Assn. Clubs: Memphis Petroleum, Moose. Co-author competency act for certification sch. counselors, State Tenn., 1975. Home: 777 Mt Moriah Rd 22 Memphis TN 38117 Office: 670 S Highland St Memphis TN 38111

HIGGINBOTHAM, PRIEUR, JR., librarian; b. Pascagoula, Miss., July 16, 1937; s. Prieur Jay and Vivian Inez (Perez) H.; B.A., U. Miss., 1960; postgrad. Am. U., 1956, 75, CCNY, 1959; m. Alice Louisa Martin, June 27, 1970; children—Jeanne-Felicie, Denis Prieur, Robert Findlay. Asst. clk. Miss. Ho. of Reps., 1955-58; tchr. history public schs., Mobile, Ala., 1962-73; instr. U. S. Ala., 1973-74; head local history dept. Mobile Public Library, 1974—. Bd. dirs. Neighborhood Improvement Council, City of Mobile, 1973-79, Mobile Community Orgn., 1977-79, Old Dauphin Way Assn., 1975-78. Recipient Gilbert Chinard prize Soc. for French Hist. Studies, 1979; Ala. Library Assn. award, 1979. Mem. Ala. Hist. Assn., La. Hist. Assn. Democrat. Methodist. Author: The Mobile Indians, 1966; The Pascagoula Indians, 1967; The Journal of Sauvole, 1969; Brother Holyfield, 1972; Old Mobile, 1977, others. Home: 60 N Monterey Mobile AL 36604 Office: 704 Government Mobile AL 36604

HIGGINS, DAVID LAWRENCE, police officer; b. Birmingham, Ala., Nov. 8, 1940; s. Samuel Joshua and Clara Martha (Wagner) H.; certificate So. Police Inst., U. Louisville, 1969, Blood Stain Inst., 1974, FBI Nat. Acad., 1975; student numerous spl. courses at various colls. and univs.; m. Doris Ann Lummus, Jan. 6, 1962; 1 son, David Lawrence. With Birmingham Police Dept., 1962—, sgt., 1969—, comdg. officer evidence collection unit, 1970—; tchr. law enforcement acads. in Ala., Jefferson State Jr. Coll.; guest lectr. criminal justice area univs. Mem. Profl. Photographers Am., Inc., Evidence Photographers Internat. Council. Lutheran. Research on police arms and ammunition. Home: 613 Tambay Dr Birmingham AL 35217 Office: 710 N 20th St Birmingham AL 35203

HIGGINS, JOHN JOSEPH, lawyer; b. N.Y.C., Mar. 18, 1934; s. Joseph John and Edna Katherine (Kolish) H.; student Pa. State U.; B.A., Moravian Coll., Bethlehem, Pa., 1958; J.D., U. Va., 1961; m. Sally Ann Longenbach, June 21, 1958; children—Allison Lee, John Thomas. Admitted to Fla. bar, 1963; practice law, Jacksonville, Fla., 1963-68, 70-74; asst counsel Office Gen. Counsel, City of Jacksonville, 1968-70; atty. Fla. East Coast Ry. Co., St. Augustine, 1974-76; practice law, Jacksonville, 1976—. Lay reader Episcopal Ch.; mem. Jacksonville Community Relations Commn., 1978—, 1st vice chmn., 1979, chmn., 1980; mem. wills and bequests com. N.E. Fla. chpt. Cystic Fibrosis Found.; senator Jr. Chamber Internat., 1970. Mem. Jacksonville Bar Assn., NE Fla. Safety Council, Gator Bowl Assn., U.S. Jaycees (dir. 1970), Am. Bar Assn., Fla. Bar Assn., Am. Judicature Soc., Ye Mystic Revellers, Delta Phi. Democrat. Club: Jacksonville Exchange. Home: 2110 Sweet Briar Ln Jacksonville FL 32202 Office: 220 E Forsyth St Jacksonville FL 32202

HIGGINS, KENNETH RAYMOND, landscape architect; b. Holyoke, Mass., Nov. 2, 1915; s. Alfred and Lillie (Ritter) H.; student R.I. State Coll., 1934; B.S. Mass. State Coll., 1937, B.Landscape Architecture, 1939; m. Mary Douthat Smith, Sept. 5, 1942; children—Kenneth Hewlett, Ralph Barton, Janie Lyle (Mrs. Frederick C. Levering Jr.). Landscape architect, site planner Richmond (Va.) Field Office Pub. Housing Adminstrn., 1948-51; pvt. practice landscape architecture, Richmond, 1951-76; prin. Higgins Assos., 1976—. Instr. Richmond Profl. Inst., evenings 1956; cons. in field. Chmn., Richmond Beautification Com., 1954-64; treas. River Rd Citizens Assn., 1956; chmn. Monument Av. Commn., 1969-76. Bd. dirs. Berkeley Thanksgiving Fest. Served to capt. USAAF, 1942-46. Recipient Landscape award Am. Assn. Nurserymen, 1969; Richmond Urban Design award, 1970; Masonry Contractors Assn. Va. award, 1977. Mem. Am. Soc. Landscape Architects (past Va. chmn., Pres.'s award Potomac chpt. 1968), Landscape Architects Va., U. Mass. Landscape Archt. Assn., Va. Hist. Soc., Soc. Archtl. Historians, Nat.

Trust for Historic Preservation, Eastern Nat. Park and Monument Assn., Assn. for Preservation Va. Antiquities (life), Am. Arbitration Assn. Lambda Chi Alpha. Episcopalian (former vestryman). Club: Country of Virginia. Address: 908 S Gaskins Rd Richmond VA 23233 Office: 908 S Gaskins Rd Richmond VA 23233 also 8501 Patterson Ave Richmond VA 23229

HIGGINS, LAWRENCE ERNEST, social work exec.; b. New Orleans, Oct. 2, 1907; s. Lawrence Ambrose and Marie (Jaunet) H.; B.S., Tulane U., 1928; student La. U. Sch. Social Welfare, 1931, certificate social work, 1955; m. Carolyn Belle Cresap, Oct. 20, 1933; children—Kathleen, Laureen. Welfare visitor dept. pub. welfare, New Orleans, 1937-42; asst., acting commr. La. State Bd. Pub. Welfare, 1942-48, commr., 1948-50; exec. sec. La. Youth Commn., 1950-73. Mem. ten-man survey team, IRO, Geneva, Switzerland and U.S. State Dept. to work on welfare and displaced persons problems in Germany and Austria, 1950; adminstr. Interstate Crime Compact, 1948-50; mem. La. State Bd. of Parole, 1945-48; Sec.-treas. Juvenile Ct. Commn., 1948-50; mem. state com. on planning for White House Conf. on Children and Youth, also chmn. pub. welfare sect., vice chmn. La. State adv. com., 1960, del., cons. conf. staff, 1960; dir. Nat. Council State Coms. Children and Youth, 1957-62, pres. So. States Probation and Parole Conf., 1960-61; coordinator Nat. Council Juvenile Ct. Judges Spl. Tng. Project; sec.-treas. La. Displaced Persons Commn.; pres. La. PTA; adv. com. Nat. Soc. Crippled Children and Adults; chmn. La. State Inter-deptl. Com.; cons., mem. adv. com. Family Ct. East Baton Rouge Parish, La. Council for Evaluation Center Exceptional Children; adv. com. on edn. exceptional children, State Dept. Edn.; spl. adviser Pres.'s Com. on Juvenile Delinquency and Youth Crime; chmn. Gov.'s Juvenile Delinquency Adv. Bd., 1976—; cons. on juvenile delinquency Nat. Conf. of Govs.; mem. Nat. Conf. of Juvenile Agys.; dir. La. Conf. Social Welfare (past pres.), Family Service Soc. Baton Rouge; pres. La. Conf. Correctional workers with Juveniles; nat. com. to develop standards for police service in handling juveniles, U.S. Children's Bur.; mem. nat. com. apptd. by Nat. Probation and Parole Assn. for developing revised standards for juvenile cts., vice chmn. profl. council; sec. So. States Probation and Parole Assn.; dir. La. Council Handicapped Children; exec. com. La. Conf. Retarded Children; chmn. profl. council Nat. Council Crime and Delinquency; mem. state com. White House Conf. Children and Youth, 1970, Nat. Joint Commn. Correctional Manpower and Tng.; field cons. Nat. Survey Corrections for Pres.'s Crime Commn., 1967; mem. La. Commn. Law Enforcement and Adminstrn. Criminal justice; mem. adv. council on law enforcement tng. La. State U., now coordinator. Lectr. Tulane U., La. State U., U. Wis., Fla. State U., U. New Orleans, U. Ala., U. Okla., So. Meth. U., others. Recipient Nat. Juvenile Ct. Judges Meritorious service award, La. Juvenile Officers service award, La. Council Juvenile Ct. Judges service award, La Youth Commn. service award. Mem. Nat. Assn. Social Workers, Internat., La. juvenile officer's assns., Am. Pub. Welfare Assn. (nat. com. protective services for children), Nat. Conf. Social Work, Am. Acad. Polit, and Social Scis., Nat. Adult Edn. Assn., Acad. Certified Social Workers, Alpha Chi Sigma, Sigma Pi. K.C. Contbr. articles to profl. jours. Home: 3410 Hyacinth Ave Baton Rouge LA 70808

HIGGS, WILLIAM REGINALD, geologist; b. Cardiff, Wales, Mar. 16, 1913; came to U.S., 1919, naturalized, 1925; s. William Joseph and Marjorie Emma (Green) H.; B.S. in Mining Engring., U. Ala., 1937, M.S. in Geology, 1949; postgrad. U. N.C., summer 1948, Mo. Sch. Mines, 1951-55; m. Catherine Virginia Covington, Nov. 1, 1941; children—William Robert, Kathleen Louise. Mining engr. Woodward Iron Co., 1937-41; engr. Carter Oil Co., 1944-46; instr. in geology and geography U. Ala., 1946-51; geologist Mo. Geol. Survey, summers 1952-54; instr. Mo. Sch. Mines, 1951-55; asst. prof. geology La. Tech. U., 1955-62, asso. prof., 1962-77, prof., 1977—; researcher Fla. State U., summer 1959; geologist U.S. Forest Service, summer 1966. Elder, John Knox Presbyterian Ch., Ruston, La. Served as 1st lt. C.E., U.S. Army, 1941-44. Recipient cert. merit La. Sci. Tchr.'s Assn., 1962; lic. prof. engr., La. Mem. Paleontol. Research Inst., Paleontol. Soc., Soc. Econ. Paleontologists and Mineralogists, Nat. Assn. Geology Tchrs., Sigma Xi, Lambda Chi Alpha, Sigma Gamma Epsilon (nat. sec.-treas. 1951-66). Republican. Author: Alabama Past and Future, 1950. Home: 906 Maple St Ruston LA 71270 Office: PO Box 4338 Tech Sta Ruston LA 71272

HIGGS, WILLIAM ROBERT, cardiovascular and thoracic surgeon; b. Birmingham, Ala., Apr. 10, 1943; s. William Reginald and Catherine (Covington) H.; B.S. summa cum laude, La. Tech. U., 1965; M.D., Baylor U., 1969; m. Marilyn E. Hester, July 26, 1974; children—Lauren Meredith, Meagan Caroline. Intern, City of Memphis Hosps., U. Tenn., 1969, Baylor Coll. Medicine, Houston, 1969, resident in gen. and vascular surgery, 1970-74; resident in thoracic and cardiovascular surgery Sch. Medicine, Emory U., Atlanta, 1974-76; practice medicine specializing in cardiovascular and thoracic surgery, Mobile, Ala., 1976—; clin. asst. prof. U. South Ala.; active staffs Mobile Infirmary, Providence Hosp., Springhill Meml. Hosp., Doctors Hosp., U. South Ala. Hosp.; bd. advisors cardiac rehab. U.S. Sports Acad. Served to maj. inactive res. U.S. Army, 1969-79. Diplomate Am. Bd. Surgery, Am. Bd. Thoracic Surgery. Fellow A.C.S., Am. Coll. Cardiology, Am. Coll. Chest Physicians, Soc. Thoracic Surgeons, So. Thoracic Soc.; mem. AMA, Am. Heart Assn., Am. Thoracic Soc.. Am. Trauma Soc., Mobile C. of C. Republican. Episcopalian. Club: Kiwanis. Contbr. sci. papers to pubs. Home: 3909 McGregor Ct Mobile AL 36608 Office: 185 Louiselle St Mobile AL 36607

HIGHFIELD, KATHLEEN KENNEDY, sch. adminstr.; b. Los Angeles, July 16, 1931; d. Michael Joseph and Winifred Marie (Bray) Kennedy; B.S., U. So. Calif., 1961, M.S., 1966; m. Edward Frederick Highfield, Mar. 12, 1955 (div. 1970). Tchr., Los Angeles Unified Sch. Dist., 1961-66; prin. Shalimar (Fla.) Elementary Sch., 1968-69, Ft. Walton Beach (Fla.) Kindergarten Center, 1969-74; asst. prin. Max Bruner Jr. High Sch., Fort Walton Beach, 1974—. Mem. AAUW, Fla. Assn. Sch. Adminstrs., Okaloosa County Adminstrv. and Supervisory Assn., Mental Health Assn. Okaloosa County, Ft. Walton Beach Ballet Assn., Okaloosa County Humane Soc. Office: 322 Holmes Blvd Fort Walton Beach FL 32548

HIGHSTONE, HARRY ROBERT, indsl. sales co. exec.; b. E. Meadowbrook, N.Y., Jan. 29, 1936; s. Harry Moss and Muriel Josephine (Laughlin) H.; B.S. in Physics, Calif. State U., 1972; m. Jacquelynn Carol Hall, June 18, 1966; children—Harry Robert, Timothy Jay, Sherri, Joel Creighton. Systems sales rep. Data Processing div. Singer Corp., 1964-66; supr. Apollo ops. Bendix Corp., 1966-69; computer/telemetry devel. engr. Calif. Inst. Tech., 1970-73; control systems engr. C & I Girdler Inc., Louisville, 1974-75; sr. control systems engr. Vitok Engrs., Inc., Louisville, 1975-78; pres. Highstone Industries, Inc., Louisville, 1974—; chmn. bd. Primary Devices, Inc., Louisville, 1976-79. Served with USAF, 1953-57. Mem. Instrumentation Soc. Am., Health Physics Soc., Internat. Radiation Protection Assn. Republican. Methodist. Clubs: Kosair Boat, Scottish Rite Cast, Masons, Shriners, Elks. Home: 4404 Upper River Rd Louisville KY 40222

HIGHTOWER, JACK ENGLISH, congressman; b. Memphis, Tex., Sept. 6, 1926; s. Walter T. and Floy (English) H.; B.A., Baylor U., 1949, LL.B., 1951; LL.D., Howard Payne U., 1971; m. Colleen Ward, Aug. 26, 1950; children—Ann, Amy, Alison. Admitted to Tex. bar, 1951; practiced in Vernon, 1951-74; dist. atty. 46th Jud. Dist., 1955-61; mem. 94th-96th Congresses from 13th Tex. dist.; mem. appropriations com.; mem. Tex. Law Enforcement Study Commn., 1957. Bd. dirs. Baptist Standard; mem. exec. bd. and Human Welfare Commn., Bapt. Gen. Conv. Tex.; deacon, Sunday Sch. tchr. First Bapt. Ch., Vernon; mem. Tex. Ho. of Reps., 1953-54, Tex. Senate, 1964-74, pres. pro tem, 1971, chmn. adminstrn. com.; trustee Baylor U.; vice chmn. bd. regents Midwestern U., Wichita Falls, Tex., 1962-64. Served with USNR, 1944-46. Mem. Tex. Dist. and County Attys. Assn. (pres. 1958, Outstanding Dist. Atty. 1959), Tex. Jr. Bar Assn. (v.p. 1958), Vernon C. of C., Am. Legion, Phi Alpha Delta (Outstanding Alumni award 1972). Clubs: Mason (grand master Tex. 1972), Lions. Home: 2719 Mansard St Vernon TX 76384 Office: 120 Cannon House Office Bldg Washington DC 20515

HIGHTOWER, JESS M., mfg. co. exec.; b. Kirksville, Mo., Feb. 9, 1922; s. Jesse Moss and Grace (Renfrow) H.; B.A., U. Tulsa, 1950, postgrad., 1951-52; m. Bette Jean Blackburn, Feb. 21, 1943; children—Jere Jean, Jess Vince, Jami Jean. Pres. Herb-O-Tone Medicine Co., Tulsa, 1946-48; free lance writer, 1949-50; reporter Tulsa Daily World, 1950-51: with McDonnell Douglas Corp., Tulsa, 1951—, mgr. external relations, editor div. publs., 1957—, mgr. pub. relations Douglas Aircraft Southeastern plant, Melbourne, Ark., 1969—. Guest lectr. U. Okla., 1969, U. Tulsa, 1970-71. Mem. Okla. Air Pollution Council, 1967-75, vice chmn. Gov's Link Com., 1970—, Indian Nations Area council Boy Scouts Am., 1968—; vice chmn. pub. relations com. Ark. Basin Devel. Assn., 1969—; chmn. housing com. Mayor's Com. Tulsa Model Cities Program, 1966-67. Trustee, Destination Discovery, Inc., 1980—, Children's Med. Center, Tulsa, 1969-75; vice chmn. Tulsa Charity Horse Show, 1965—, Tulsa Met. Zoo, 1971—. Served with AUS, 1943-45. Decorated Bronze Star medal. Mem. U. Tulsa Alumni Assn. (trustee 1965—), Nat. Mgmt. Assn., Pub. Relations Soc. Am. (dir. 1964-67), UN Assn. (dir. 1969—), Met. Tulsa C. of C. (chmn. alternative edn. task force 1973-74). Episcopalian. Mason. Clubs: Oaks Country, Tulsa Press. Author (some with pseudonym Jim Grant) articles, stories in mags., 1961—. Author, producer, dir. movie Course of Action for Okla. Retarded Childrens Assn., 1957. Home: 5345 E 22d Pl Tulsa OK 74114 Office: 2000 N Memorial Dr Tulsa OK 74115

HIGHTOWER, JOHN ROBERT, communications skills cons.; b. Natchez, Miss., Oct. 9, 1951; s. Lynwood and Mary Julia (Edgecombe) H.; B.A., Miss. State U., 1972; J.D., U. Miss., 1975. Program dir. Sta. WSSO/WSMU-FM, Starkville, Miss., 1972, Sta. WSUH/WOOR-FM, Oxford, Miss., 1973-75; instr. Communications Skills Co., Huntsville, Ala., 1975-77, office mgr., 1978-79. Ch. rep. United Methodist Service Center, Huntsville, 1975-76; lay speaker N. Ala. Conf. United Meth. Ch., 1978-79. Mem. Miss. Bar Assn. Author: Effective Briefings: Course Materials, 1978. Home: PO Box 1352 Huntsville AL 35807 Office: 2225 Briarcliff Rd SE Huntsville AL 35801

HILBURN, WILLIAM GRANT, JR., architect; b. Denver, Dec. 29, 1944; s. William Grant and Catherine J. (Thorwald) H.: B. Arch., U. Tex., Austin, 1970; m. Denise Lynn Mott, Feb. 14, 1967; children—Matthew Clay, Georgia Lynn, Meagan Ilyne. Draftsman, Edgar James & Assos., Dallas, 1970, R.E. Velten, Dallas, 1971; project architect Greener & Sumner, Architects, Dallas, 1972-74, IBS Architects, Dallas, 1972-74; project architect Southeastern Region, Zale Corp. Property Devel. Div., Dallas, 1974-76; pres. Archtl. Designers Inc., Dallas, 1976—. Served to 1st lt., Arty., U.S. Army, 1966-69. Mem. AIA, Tex. Soc. Architects, Constrn. Specifications Inst., Nat. Council Archtl. Registration Bds. (cert.). Office: Archtl Designers Inc PO Box 34355 3333 Golfing Green Dallas TX 75234

HILDEBRANDT, THEODORE WARE, computer scientist; b. Ann Arbor, Mich., Dec. 8, 1922; s. Theophil Henry and Dora Edith (Ware) H.; A.B., U. Mich., 1942, A.M., 1947, Ph.D. in Math., 1956; postgrad. Princeton U., 1947-48; S.M., Mass. Inst. Tech., 1951; m. Ruth Eleanor Stein, Oct. 16, 1953 (dec. Nov. 1961); m. 2d, Mary Kathryn Babcock, June 16, 1962; children—Sarah Catherine, Paul Richard, Thomas Henry, Mary Lise, Peter Warren. Design engr., electronic computer project Inst. for Advanced Study, Princeton, N.J., 1947-48; with project Whirlwind, Mass. Inst. Tech., 1948-49, teaching asst. math., 1949-51; grad. fellow Oak Ridge Inst. Nuclear Studies, 1955-56, asso. scientist, 1956-57; asst. dir. computer center Ohio State U., 1957-66, asst. prof. math., 1957-62, asso. prof., 1962-67, prof. computer and info. sci., 1967-68; dir. computer center, prof. math. Kans. State U., 1968-69; dir. computing facility Nat. Center Atmospheric Research, Boulder, Colo., 1969-73, cons. to dir., 1973-74; expert cons. in computer software Inst. for Telecommunication Scis., Dept. Commerce, Boulder, 1974-75; dir. acad. computer center, prof. math. U. N.C., Greensboro, 1976—. Served with USNR, 1944-46, 51-53. Recipient Computer Pioneer award Nat. Computer Conf., 1975. Mem. Assn. Computing Machinery, Am. Math. Soc., Math. Assn. Am., Phi Beta Kappa, Sigma Xi. Democrat. Episcopalian. Home: 1109 Pebble Dr Greensboro NC 27410 Office: Acad Computer Center U NC-G Greensboro NC 27412

HILES, WILLIAM GAYLE, JR., coll. adminstr.; b. Danville, Ky., Sept. 2, 1945; s. William Gayle and Virgie O'Neil (Freeman) H.; A.B., Transylvania Coll., 1967; M.A., U. Durham (Eng.), 1968; m. Janet F. Smith, Aug. 4, 1979. Staff writer Nashville Tennessean, 1971-74; interim pastor Brookmeade Congregational Ch., Nashville, 1973-74; dir. public info. George Peabody Coll. for Tchrs., Nashville, 1974-79; dir. Univ. News ser. Tenn. State U., Nashville, 1979—. Pres. Tenn. Spl. Olympics, 1977-79; chairperson Citizens in Corrections, Nashville, 1975-76; chairperson bd. dirs. Tennesseans in Corrections, Inc., 1977-78; pres. bd. dirs. Am. Youth Hostel, Nashville, 1977-78; bd. dirs. Travellers Aid of Nashville, 1975—. Mem. AAUP, Nat. Sch. Pub. Relations Assn., Nat. Council Coll. Publs. Advisers, Tenn. Coll. Pub. Relations Assn. (sec.), Phi Delta Kappa. Mem. Disciples of Christ Ch. Home: 1705 Cedar Ln Nashville TN 37212 Office: Public Relations Office Tenn State U 3500 Centennial Blvd Nashville TN 37203

HILL, ADA DANCE, educator; b. Richmond, Va.; B.A. in Social Studies, St. Augustine's Coll., Raleigh, N.C., 1944; M.S. in Spl. Edn., Va. State Coll., Ettrick, 1969; Ed.D. in Spl. Edn., Am. U., Washington, 1976; widowed. Tchr., Va. Dept. Welfare and Instns., Hanover, 1949-52, Hanover County Sch. Bd., Ashland, Va., 1953-63, Richmond Pub. Schs., 1963-69; asst. prof. edn. Va. Commonwealth U., Richmond, 1969—. Mem. adv. com. for exceptional children Richmond Pub. Schs.; chmn. adv. edn. com. Southside Va. Tng. Center. Mem. Council Exceptional Children, Nat. Assn. Retarded Citizens, AAUP, Phi Delta Kappa, Eta Phi Beta. Certified in elementary, secondary and spl. edn., Va.; specialist in lang. arts for mentally retarded, spl. edn. Named vol. tchr. of year, Richmond Pub. Schs., 1965. Author: Time Out for Baseball, the Slow Learner Workshop, 1974; The Mini Grocery Store, 1973; Snack Time is Fun Learning Time, 1973; The Effects of Social Reinforcers on the Task Persistance of MR Children, 1977; co-author chpt. in Recreation Programming for Developmentally Disabled Persons, 1978. Home: 2000 Nevada Ave Richmond VA 23220 Office: Va Commonwealth U 2104 Oliver Hall Richmond VA 23284

HILL, ALLEN WALTER, publishing co. exec.; b. Atlanta, Jan. 9, 1919; s. Clarence J. and Virginia H. (Jones) H.; B.B.A., Emory U., 1939; m. Opal Virginia Baker, Feb. 17, 1965. Mktg. rep. The Coco-Cola Co., Atlanta, 1939-49; pres. Allen W. Hill Pub. Co., Atlanta, 1949-58; sec., treas. So. Indsl. Distbrs. Assn. and So. Wholesalers Assn., Atlanta, 1958-65; pres. Walter W. Brown Pub. Co., Inc., Atlanta, 1965-70, Ernest H. Abernethy Pub. Co., Inc., Atlanta, 1965—. Clubs: Piedmont Driving, Capital City, Shakerag Hounds Hunt (Atlanta). Home: 10 W Andrews Dr NW Atlanta GA 30305 Office: 75 3d St NW Atlanta GA 30308

HILL, ANITA O'NEAL, nursing adminstr.; b. Center Ridge, Ark., May 14, 1924; s. Homer Clayton and Nora Edna (Milam) H.; R.N., Ark. Bapt. Sch. Nursing, 1944; postgrad. Johns Hopkins Hosp., 1947-48. Head nurse surgery Bapt. Hosp., Little Rock, 1944; indsl. nurse Naval Ordnance Plant, Camden, Ark., 1945; head nurse med. and surgery Baptist Hosp., Little Rock, 1946-47, head nurse surgery, 1947; instr. operating room technique to student nurses Bapt. Hosp. Sch., Little Rock, 1948-49, supr. surgery, 1949-51, acting dir. nursing service, 1951-52, supr. surgery, 1952-58, supr. emergency room, 1960-61; supr. surgery Midland (Tex.) Meml. Hosp., 1961-67; supr. surgery, recovery room, day surgery and recovery room Med. Center Hosp., Tyler, Tex., 1967—. Mem. Am. Nurses Assn., Assn. Operating Room Nurses, Tex. Assn. Operating Room Nurses, East Tex. Assn. Operating Room Nurses. Republican. Baptist. Mem. Order Eastern Star. Office: 1000 S Beckham St Tyler TX 75701

HILL, BRYCE DALE, sch. adminstr.; b. Seminole, Okla., Mar. 5, 1930; s. Charles Daniel and Ollie (Nichols) H.; B.S., East Central State Coll., 1952, M.Teaching, 1957; postgrad. U. Okla., 1959-70; profl. adminstrs. certificate, 1969; m. Wilma Dean Carter, Aug. 16, 1956; children—Bryce Anthony, Brent Dale. Tchr. pub. schs., New Lima, Okla., 1952-56, supt. pub. schs., 1956—; owner New Lima Gas Co., 1958—. Chmn. bd. dirs. Seminole County chpt. ARC, 1969—; v.p. bd. dirs. Redland Community Action Program, 1968-71; mem. Seminole County Rural Devel. Council. Chmn. Seminole County Democratic Central Com., 1962-64, 70-72, 74—. Mem. NEA, Okla. Edn. Assn., Am., Okla. (exec. com. 1976-78, 79-81) assns. sch. adminstrs., Seminole County Tchrs. Assn. (pres. 1964-65, 71-72, 79-80), Seminole County Sch. Adminstrs. Assn. (chmn. 1969-70), Seminole County Schoolmasters Club (pres. 1963-64, 69-70, 77-78), Seminole Hist. Soc. (v.p. 1971-73, 74-76). Baptist. Home: Box 97 New Lima OK 74858

HILL, CECIL JAMES, judge, lawyer; b. Asheville, N.C., Nov. 20, 1919; s. Burton H. and Vallie (Staton) H.; A.A., Mars Hill Coll., 1941; B.S., U. N.C., 1943, J.D., 1945; m. Elizabeth T. Richardson, Dec. 15, 1945; children—Elisabeth Hartsfield, James Harrison. With W. Bowen Henderson, C.P.A., Asheville, 1941-43; admitted to N.C. bar, 1945; since practiced in Brevard; mem. firm Ramsey, Hill, Smart, Ransey & Hunt, 1959—; mem. N.C. State Senate, 1975-79; judge N.C. Ct. Appeals, 1979—; dir. First Union Nat. Bank of N.C., Brevard. Chmn., Brevard Housing Authority; v.p. Brevard Music Festival Assn., 1949. Bd. dirs. Moorehead Sch. for Blind, 1965—; chmn. bd. dirs. Gov. Morehead Sch. Mem. N.C. State Bar (pres. 29th jud. dist. 1975-76), Transylvania County Bar Assn. (pres. 1950-51), Brevard C. of C. (pres. 1957), Delta Sigma Pi. Democrat. Baptist. Clubs: Masons (32 deg.), Lions (pres. 1949). Home: Woodside Dr Brevard NC 28712 Office: Legal Bldg Brevard NC 28712

HILL, CLARENCE KENNETH, JR., coll. adminstr.; b. Cowan, Tenn., Nov. 10, 1916; s. Clarence Kenneth and Sarah Roxanna (Borin) H.; student Edmonson Sch. Bus., 1938; B.A., Hardin-Simmons U., 1948; m. Mildred Elizabeth Loveless, May 27, 1939; children—Sarah Elizabeth Hill Mulkey, Susan Evelyn Hill Waldrep. Office mgr. Dow Griscom Engraving and Electrotype Co., Chattanooga, 1936-39; engring. draftsman TVA, Chattanooga, 1939-42; dir. alumni relations Hardin-Simmons U., 1947-55, dir. fin. aid and recruitment, 1962-66, univ. relations asso., 1966-72, dir. alumni affairs, 1972—; minister music edn. First Baptist Ch. of Littlefield, Tex., 1955-57; dir. activities First Baptist Ch. of Lubbock, Tex., 1957-62; cons. in field. Served to maj. USAF, 1942-45. Mem. Council Advancement and Support of Edn., Tex. Baptist Pub. Relations Assn., Baptist Pub. Relations, Abilene C. of C., Tex. Council Alumni Dirs., Independent Coll. and Univs. of Tex. Club: Lions (Abilene). Editor: Range Rider, 1948-55, 72-77. Home: 2705 Southwest Dr Apt 103 Abilene TX 79605 Office: Hardin Simmons Univ Drawer K Abilene TX 79601

HILL, DONALD M., mathematician; b. Knoxville, Iowa, Oct. 28, 1942; s. D. Merle and Virginia June (Lindly) H.; B.S., Iowa Wesleyan Coll., 1962; M.A., Dartmouth Coll., 1964; French cert., Ecole d'Administration de Bruxelles (Belgium), 1965; Ph.D., Fla. State U., 1972; m. Kandace Marguerite Carpenter, May 26, 1968; children—Rebecca Marguerite, D. Matthew. Prof. math. Ecole de Wembo Nyama (Congo), also adj. prof. Universite Libre du Congo, 1965-67; asst. dean Coll. Sci. and Tech., Fla. A&M U., Tallahassee, 1974-76, asso. prof. math., 1974—. Vice pres. Fla. A&M U. High Sch. PTA, 1974; mem. steering com. Leon County Sch. Vols., 1974-76; mem. dist. adv. com. Leon County Sch. Bd., 1976-78; bd. dirs. Camping Opportunities for Children, 1975. Nat. Acad. Sci. travel grantee, 1976. Mem. Nat. Council Tchr. of Math., Math. Assn. Am., Fla. Council Tchrs. of Math. Democrat. Methodist. Home: 3017 Godfrey Pl Tallahassee FL 32308 Office: Math Dept Fla A&M U Tallahassee FL 32307

HILL, ED, publisher; b. El Paso, Tex., June 23, 1937; s. Maurice E. and Una Hill; B.A. in English Lit., U. Tex., El Paso, 1962; m. Sandra Thacker, Feb. 7, 1979; 1 son, Matthew Edward. Propr., Ed Hill Edits., pubs. of fine prints and dealer in contemporary original prints, El Paso. Served with USNR, 1955-57. Office: 4120 Rio Bravo Dr Suite 205 El Paso TX 79902

HILL, GUY LANDRUM, bank exec.; b. Sherman, Tex., Nov. 28, 1946; s. L.C. and Lucille Clara (Holman) H.; B.B.A., East Tex. State Coll., 1969; student Am. Inst. Banking, 1974-76, Intermediate Banking Sch. Bank Mgmt. and Credit Adminstrn., 1978; married; children—Roger, Rachael. Asst. mgr. Allied Fin. Co., Ft. Worth, 1969-72; v.p. in charge of loans Gateway Nat. Bank, Ft. Worth, 1972—. Mem. Am. Inst. Banking, Bankers Adminstrn. Inst., Crowley Jaycees. Baptist. Club: Lions (treas. local club 1975). Office: 3532 Joyce Fort Worth TX 76116

HILL, HARLEY RICHARD, wholesale distbg. co. exec.; b. Madison, W.Va., Jan. 21, 1939; s. Harley and Rachel Ina H.; B.S., Morris Harvey Coll., 1960; m. Carolyn Sue Vickers, Sept. 16, 1960; 1 dau., Leah Denise. Mem. staff Mountain State Coll., Parkersburg, W.Va., 1960-62; acctg. and data processing instr. Wood County Schs., Parkersburg, 1964-65; mgr. data processing Gravely Tractors div. Studebaker Corp., Dunbar, W.Va., 1965-68; dir. mgmt. info. systems McJunkin Corp., Charleston, W.Va., 1968—; instr. U. Charleston, 1977—. Served with AUS, 1962-64. Mem. Data Processing Mgmt. Assn. (pres. 1960—), Charleston Jaycees (pres.). Club: Elks. Home:

1325 W Virginia Ave Dunbar WV 25064 Office: 1400 Hansford St Charleston WV 25301

HILL, HAROLD NELSON, JR., asso. justice Ga. Supreme Ct.; b. Houston, Apr. 26, 1930; s. Harold N. and Emolyn Eloise (Geeslin) H.; B.S. in Commerce, Washington and Lee U., 1952; LL.B., Emory U., 1957; m. Betty Jane Fell, Aug. 16, 1952; children—Ward, Douglas, Nancy. Admitted to Ga. bar; asso., then partner firm Gambrell, Harlan, Russell, Moye and Richardson, Ga., 1957-66; asst. atty. gen. State Law Dept., State of Ga., 1966-68, exec. asst. atty. gen., 1968-72; partner firm Jones, Bird and Howell, Ga., 1972-74; asso. justice Supreme Ct. Ga., 1975—; adj. prof. Emory U. Law Sch. Served with Ordnance Corps, U.S. Army, 1952-54. Mem. State Bar Ga., Am., Atlanta bar assns., Lawyers Club Atlanta, Old War Horse Lawyers Club. Democrat. Methodist. Home: 455 Forest Valley Rd Atlanta GA 30342 Office: 533 State Judicial Bldg Atlanta GA 30344

HILL, HAROLD PERSHING, constrn. exec.; b. Canton, S.D., Nov. 13, 1918; s. Frank A. and Calla (Tucker) H.; student Chillicothe Bus. Coll., 1936-38; m. Nina Lee Fore, June 25, 1941; children—Wayne, Nancy, Shirley. Builder, 1946—; pres. Masterpiece Homes, Houston, 1954—, Gulf Port Lumber & Hardware Co., Inc., Houston, 1951—; dir. Inwood Commerce Bank. Pres., Big Fifty Club. Served with C.E., AUS, 1941-45. Decorated Bronze Star. Mem. Greater Houston Builders Assn. (dir., Builder of Year 1967), Tex. Assn. Builders (dir.), Nat. Assn. Home Builders (dir., exec. com.). Methodist. Home: 5418 Cedar Creek Dr Houston TX 77056 Office: 10403 Heather Hill Houston TX 77037

HILL, HEAGER LEVOYD, govt. ofcl.; b. Phila., Mar. 13, 1934; s. Clarence G. and Maggie C. Miller (Bell) H.; B.S., Morehouse Coll., 1956; postgrad. L.I. U., 1959, Samford U., 1972; m. Yvonne Marie Smith; children—Deborah A., Heager LeVoyd, Jonathan LeVoyd. Agt., U.S. Treasury, N.Y.C., 1958-60; sec. dist. 8 Nat. Alliance Postal Employees, P.O. Dept., N.Y.C., 1963-65; dir. community services and programs Urban Renewal Program, High Point, N.C., 1965-68; dir. VISTA, Miles Coll., Birmingham, Ala., 1968-70; dir. fair housing and equal opportunity div. HUD, Ala. area office, Birmingham, 1970—; mem. task force for model cities application City of High Point (N.C.), 1966; pres. Birmingham (Ala.) Frontiers Internat., Inc., 1975; HUD chmn. U.S. Savs. Bond campaign, 1975; mem. Ala. State adv. com. U.S. Commn. Civil Rights, 1975—. Del. Republican state conv., 1970; mem. nat. Rep. Com., 1975—; bd. dirs. Voter Edn. Project, Inc., Atlanta, 1975—, membership chmn., 1978-79; bd. dirs. Mental Health Assn. of Jefferson County; bd. mgmt. 4th Ave. YMCA, Birmingham, 1975; state chmn. Ala. United Negro Coll. Fund, 1977, recipient Distinguished Vol. Service award, 1977; bd. assos. St. Augustine Coll., Raleigh, N.C., 1979—. Served with AUS, 1956-58. Recipient Man of Year award Ala. State Fedn. Civic Leagues, 1974, certificate of spl. achievement HUD, 1975, community Service award Emancipation Assn. Birmingham. Mem. NAACP (edn. chmn. 1960-65), Am. Soc. Pub. Adminstrn. (dir. Central Ala. chpt.), Alpha Phi Alpha (life). Episcopalian. Home: PO Box 3053 Huntsville AL 35810 Office: HUD 15 S 20th St Birmingham AL 35233

HILL, HUGH STANLEY, fin. planning cons.; b. Wilkinsburg, Pa., July 17, 1929; s. Thomas W. and Gladys H.; B.S., Fla. State U., 1952, M.S., 1954; m. Marilyn J. Hart, Aug. 29, 1952. Sr. account exec. Merrill Lynch & Co., St. Petersburg, Fla., 1954-75; cons. in mktg. and fin., St. Petersburg, 1975-76; mgr. capital planning Merrill Lynch & Co., Atlanta, 1976-78; supr. personel fin. mgmt. So. region E.F. Hutton Co., Atlanta, 1978—. Cert. fin. planner; C.L.U. Mem. Inst. Cert. Fin. Planners, Internat. Assn. Fin. Planners, Am. Soc. C.L.U.'s. Mem. Ch. of God. Home: 4100 Clubview Terr Marietta GA 30067 Office: E F Hutton 3340 Peachtree Rd NE Atlanta GA 30326

HILL, IRVINE BYRD, radio sta. exec.; b. Norfolk, Va., July 2, 1927; s. Herman Roddick and Madaline Carrie (Irvine) H.; student Coll. William and Mary, Harvard U.; m. Elizabeth Stewart, July 30, 1949; children—Robin Hill Anderson, Anne Hill Hughes. Pres., gen. mgr. Sta. WCMA AM/FM, Norfolk. Mem. city council City of Norfolk, 1972-74, mayor, 1975-76. Served with USNR. Mem. Norfolk Radio Broadcasters Assn. (past pres.). Democrat. Roman Catholic. Clubs: Norfolk Yacht and Country, The Harbor. Office: 5600 Curlew Dr Norfolk VA 23502

HILL, JAMES MARK, physician; b. Water Valley, Miss., Oct. 7, 1918; s. Martin Luther and Lillian (Addington) H.; B.A., U. Miss., 1940, M.A., 1942, B.S., 1945; M.D., Jefferson Med. Coll., 1948. Intern, then resident Bapt. Hosp., Memphis, 1949-54; prison physician Miss. State Penitentiary, Parchman, 1950; practice medicine specializing in surgery, Memphis, 1954-74, ret., 1974; mem. staff Bapt. Meml. Hosp.; instr. anatomy U. Miss., 1943, 44, 47, asso. prof., 1951-55, prof. surg. anatomy, 1955—. Mem. adv. bd. Continental Bankers Life Ins. Co. of the South. Served with USNR, 1945, served to lt M.C., 1955-57. Fellow A.C.S.; mem. AMA, So. Med. Assn., Tenn., Memphis and Shelby County med. socs., Memphis Surg. Soc., Phi Chi. Mason (32 deg., K.T., Shriner). Home: 1222 Dovecrest Memphis TN 38134

HILL, JOE DENNIS, carbon graphite co. adminstr.; b. Tyler, Tex., July 29, 1939; s. Denman Carroll and Mary Jo (Crane) H.; B.B.A., So. Meth. U., 1961; m. Janis Elizabeth Branscum, Sept. 1, 1974; children—Jennifer Dee, Joe Dennis, Johnathan Duane. Comml. mgr. Southwestern Bell Telephone Co., Dallas, 1965-70; sales mgr. John Watson Lighting Co., Dallas, 1971-73, Tex. Bronze Mfg. Co. div. Anadite, Ft. Worth, 1974-76, Poco Graphite, Inc. div. Union Oil Co. Calif. subs., Decatur, Tex., 1977—; tech. lectr. indsl. socs.; pvt. pilot. Founder, chmn. bd. Wise County (Tex.) United Fund, 1979—; chmn. Decatur Service unit Salvation Army, 1977—; bd. dirs. Navarro County (Tex.) United Fund, 1967-69. Served to comdr. USNR, 1961-65; Vietnam. Decorated Meritorious Service medal. Mem. Soc. Mfg. Engrs., Decatur C. of C. (dir.). Baptist. Clubs: Shriners, Decatur Rotary (pres., Rotarian of Year 1979). Home: Rt 1 Box 81 1 Decatur TX 76234 Office: 1601 S State St Decatur TX 76234

HILL, JOHN FRANCIS, state ofcl.; b. Marengo, Ill., Dec. 16, 1920; s. Charles Willard and Myrtle Elizabeth (Naylor) H.; B.Philosophy, U. Chgo., 1947; m. Sarah Eleanor Guilford, Feb. 18, 1949; children—Karl Naylor, Cavitt Lucas, John Francis. Commd. 1st lt. USAF, 1948, advanced through grades to lt. col., 1961; sr. pilot, sr. navigator, Italy, 1944-45, Japan and Korea, 1948-50, France and Ger., 1952-57; phys. scis. adminstr. USAF Research and Devel. Command, 1959-64; ret., 1965; employment office mgr. Fla. Employment Service, Perrine, 1969—. Chmn., South Dade Resources Council, 1969-76; bd. dirs. Redlands Christian Migrant Assn., 1971-76. Served with USAAF, 1943-45. Decorated Air medal with 9 clusters, D.F.C., Purple Heart. Republican. Home: 18801 SW 89th Rd Miami FL 33157 Office: 840 Perrine Ave Perrine FL 33157

HILL, JOHN VINCENT, diversified service contract exec.; b. Kansas City, Mo., July 18, 1943; s. John Vincent and Beatrice J. Hill; B.B.A., U. Houston, 1972; children—Troy Vincent, Steven Bradley. Contract adminstr. Dynalectron Corp., NASA Johnson Space Center, Houston, 1965-73; gen. mgr. Dryden Flight Research Center operations Serv-Air, Inc., Edwards, Calif., 1973-75, v.p. mktg., Houston, 1975-76, v.p., gen. mgr. West Coast ops., Houston, 1976-77, v.p. ops. and bus. devel., Greenville, Tex., 1977—. Served with USAF, 1961-64. Mem. Nat. Contract Mgmt. Assn. (past chpt. pres.), Air Force Assn., Greenville C. of C., Lancaster Bd. Trade, Midwest City C. of C., Lancaster C. of C. Republican. Roman Catholic. Club: Elks. Home: 4505 Palos Verdes Dr Mesquite TX 75150 Office: PO Box 1669 Greenville TX 75401

HILL, KAREN NELSON, speech pathologist; b. New Orleans, Jan. 5, 1953; d. Willie and Barbara Elizabeth (Blackwell) Nelson; B.S., St. Mary's Dominican Coll., 1975, cert. deaf edn., 1977; M. Communication Disorders, La. State U., 1978; m. Ronald Alfred Hill, Dec. 27, 1975. Speech pathologist Orleans Parish Sch. System, 1975-77, tchr. hearing impaired, 1977-78, speech pathologist, 1978-79; total communication specialist Child Study Center, Ft. Worth, 1979—. lectr. Xavier U., New Orleans, 1978. Mem. Nat. Soc. Autistic Children, Am. Speech and Hearing Assn., Alexander Graham Bell Assn. for Deaf, Kappa Delta Pi, Zeta Phi Beta. Democrat. Methodist. Home: 1300 Lamar Blvd E #1307 Arlington TX 76011 Office: 1300 W Lancaster Fort Worth TX 76102

HILL, KATHLEEN JONES, legal secretarial co. exec.; b. Rockford, Ill., Aug. 24, 1945; d. Donald E. and Martha (Niman) Jones; B.S., Fla. State U., 1970; m. Frank Denman Hill, III, Aug. 8, 1964; children—Frank Denman, Martha Elizabeth, Cheryl Ann. Various accounting and secretarial positions, 1965-77; paralegal and office mgr. firm Thompson, Wadsworth, Messer & Rhodes, Tallahassee, 1970-77; owner-mgr. Capitol Services, Tallahassee, 1977—; part-time instr. Lively Vocat.-Tech. Sch., 1975. Mem. Nat. (dir.), Fla. (dir., treas.) assns. legal assts., Tallahassee C. of C., Nat. Assn. Legal Adminstrs., Nat., Fla., Tallahassee (past pres.) legal secs. assns., Gamma Alpha Chi (past pres.). Republican. Roman Catholic. Home: 1045 Merritt Dr Tallahassee FL 32301 Office: 201 S Monroe St Suite 108 Tallahassee FL 32301

HILL, KERMIT F., city ofcl.; b. Mars Hill, N.C., Apr. 18, 1932; s. Alvin C. and Edna (Shook) H.; children from previous marriage—Cheryl, Richard, Randall; student Clemson U., 1949-51, Gaston Coll., 1975-77. Mem. Hwy. Patrol Columbia (S.C.), 1956-57; mgr. Roses Stores, Williamson, N.C., 1957-62, Eckerd Drugs, Gastonia, N.C., 1962-67; gen. mgr. Gastonia Alcoholic Beverage Control Bd., 1967—. Served with USN, 1952-55; Korea. Mem. Gastonia C. of C., N.C. Assn. Alcoholic Beverage Control Bds., Nat. Alcoholic Beverage Control Assn., VFW, Am. Legion. Democrat. Home: 40 Paradise Circle Belmont NC 28012 Office: 1840 S York Rd Gastonia NC 28052

HILL, LEWIS BRENT, communications co. exec.; b. Wadesboro, N.C., Sept. 21, 1939; s. John Lewis and Victor Maude (Braswell) H.; student U. Miami, 1958-59, U. S.C., 1959-60; m. Rachel M. Douglas, Dec. 11, 1960; children—Vicki, Michelle. Program dir. sta. WSB, Atlanta, 1964-69; with Cosmos Broadcasting Corp., Columbia, S.C., 1969-80, sr. v.p. radio, also gen. mgr. sta. WIS, 1977-79, corp. dir., 1971-80; chmn., pres. chief exec. officer Interstate Communications, Columbia, 1980—. Mem. S.C. Broadcasters Assn. (dir.), Columbia C. of C. Episcopalian. Clubs: Summit, Kiwanis (Columbia). Office: PO Box 21567 Columbia SC 29221

HILL, MARY CASSANDRA, anthropologist; b. Tuscaloosa, Ala., June 1, 1951; d. Joseph Howard and Mary Virginia (Huckabee) H.; A.B., U. Ala., 1971; M.A., U. Tenn., 1979; postgrad. U. Mass., 1979—. Instr. anthropology Wake Forest U., Winston-Salem, N.C., 1976-77, coordinator edn. Mus. of Man, 1977-78; research cons. phys. anthropology C.E., U.S. Army, other instns. Mem. Southeastern Archaeol. Conf., Am. Assn. Phys. Anthropologists, Soc. for Am. Archaeology, Am. Anthrop. Assn., AAAS, Sigma Xi (asso.), Lambda Alpha. Home: 222 Woodland Hills Tuscaloosa AL 35405

HILL, MAX LLOYD, JR., realtor; b. Belleville, Ill., Aug. 15, 1927; s. Max L. and Leora (Jacobs) H.; student Purdue U., 1944-47; B.S., U.S. Naval Acad., 1951; postgrad. Harvard Law Sch., 1955-56; m. Jane Olivia Evatt, June 23, 1951; children—Larkin Payne, Max Lloyd III, Naomi Evatt. Sales engr. indsl. equipment Indsl. Welding Supplies, Inc., 1957-59; real estate salesman Simmons Realty Co., Inc., Charleston, S.C., 1959-63; pres. Max L. Hill Co., Inc., realtors, Charleston, 1963—; Charleston dir. Citizens & So. Nat. Bank S.C. Lectr. S.C. Realtor's Inst., 1967-73, U. S.C. Sch. Gen. Studies and Extension, 1962-64. Pres. Greater Charleston YMCA, 1965-67; mem. Charleston Planning and Zoning Commn., 1969-74; mem. Charleston Zoning Bd. Adjustment, 1971-74; sec. Charleston County Bd. Assessment Control, 1972-75. Bd. dirs. Edn. Found., 1966-74; bd. dirs. S.C. Assn. Realtors, 1966—, pres., 1976. Served with AUS, 1945-46, USNR, 1946; to 1st lt. USAF, 1951-55. Mem. Nat. (dir. 1976—), S.C. (dir.) assns. realtors, Greater Charleston Bd. Realtors (pres. 1970), St. Andrews Soc., Phi Gamma Delta. Methodist (ofcl. bd. 1964-76). Mason. Clubs: Carolina Yacht, Charleston, Seabrook Island. Home: 109 Tradd St Charleston SC 29401 Office: 33 Broad St Charleston SC 29401

HILL, PEGGY RICHARDSON, banker; b. Nettleton, Miss., Dec. 19, 1937; d. Grady Lee and Trudie Lee (Whitlock) Richardson; m. Aaron B. Hill, May 18, 1957; children—Cynthia Lynn, David Wayne, Andrew Burton. With Bank of Nettleton (Miss.), 1956, Citizens Nat. Bank, Nettleton and Tupelo, 1957-58; with First Columbus (Miss.) Nat. Bank, 1960—, asst. v.p., 1976—; v.p. H & J Quality Builders, Inc., Columbus, 1974—. Active Heritage PTA, 1964-65; treas. Ladies Aux. Home Builders Assn., 1978-79; sec.-treas. welcome com. Miss. U. for Women, 1979—. Mem. Nat. Assn. Bank Women, C. of C. Ch. of Christ. Home: Route 4 305 Jamestown Rd Columbus MS 39701 Office: 231 710 Main St Columbus MS 39701

HILL, RICHARD LEE, engr., educator; b. Nashville, Feb. 25, 1935; s. Lee Bruce and Thelma May (Eldridge) H.; B.S., U. Tenn., Knoxville, 1959; M.E., U. South Fla., 1967; m. Mary Evelyn Teffeteller, Aug. 26, 1956; children—Richard Lee II, Anne Elizabeth. Sr. estimator, estimator Sperry Rand Corp., Bristol, Tenn., 1959-64; mgr. personnel devel., indsl. engr. IMC, Bartow, Fla., 1964-66; mgr., indsl. engring., sr. indsl. engr. IRC div. TRW, Boone, N.C., 1966-68; mgr. indsl. engring. Magnavox Co., Greeneville, Tenn., 1968-70; supt. prodn. control, mgr. indsl. engring., staff indsl. engr., Kingsport Press, Arcata Corp., Kingsport, Tenn., 1970-75; asst. prof. extension div., extension specialist tech. resources Va. Poly. Inst. and State U., Abingdon, 1975—. Bd. dirs. S.W. Va. 4-H Ednl. Center; mem. adv. bd. Scott County Vocat. Center, Tri-Cities Tech. Center, Va. Highlands Community Coll., Polk Jr. Coll.; asso. adviser Explorer Scouts; asst. scoutmaster Boy Scouts Am. Served with U.S. Army, 1954-56. Recipient Unit Superior Service award U.S. Dept. Agr., 1978. Mem. Am. Inst. Indsl. Engrs. (sr., regional v.p., trustee, named Regional Outstanding Indsl. Engr. 1973), Nat. Assn. County Agrl. Agts. (Pub. Info. award 1978), Va. Extension Service Assn., Va. Assn. Extension Agts., Epsilon Sigma Phi. Presbyterian. Clubs: Optimist (dir.), Masons, Shriners, Eagles. Home: PO Box 434 Abingdon VA 24210

HILL, ROSEMARY AUGUSTA, speech pathologist; b. Andalusia, Ala., Dec. 19, 1952; d. Robert Perry and Avalo Gray (Donovan) H.; B.S., U. Ga., 1974; M.A., Western Carolina U., 1975. Speech and lang. pathologist public schs., Atlanta, 1975-78; speech pathologist deaf and orthopedically handicapped E. area Charlotte-Mecklenburg Schs., Charlotte, N.C., 1978—; grad. asst. speech pathology Western Carolina U., Cullowhee 1974-75. Mem. Am. Speech and Hearing Assn. (cert. clin. competence). Methodist. Home: 7709 Byrum Dr Charlotte NC 28210 Office: E Area Charlotte Mecklenburg Schs PO Box 30035 Charlotte NC 28230

HILL, ROY LEEUWENHOEK, author, educator; b. Laurens, S.C., Apr. 26, 1934; s. Clarence B. and Chular McDaniel (Yeargin) H.; B.S., A&T State U., N.C., 1949; M.S. in Journalism, Boston U., 1950; M.A., Mich. State U., 1958; Ed.D., Rutgers U. Mem. faculty dept. English, So. U., Baton Rouge, 1950-52, Grambling (La.) State U., 1956-58, Fort Valley (Ga.) State Coll., 1954-55, U. Denver, 1963-68, Kans. State U., 1967-69, S.C. State Coll., Orangeburg, 1961-63; asso. prof. English and journalism Ala. State U., Montgomery, 1976—; reader poetry to various colls., univs., community groups and churches, 1946—. Served with USN, 1952-54. Mem. World Poetry Soc., Coll. Lang. Assn., Coll. English Assn., Western Speech Assn., Speech Assn. Am., Assn. for Study of Negro Life and History, Sophist Soc., Phi Delta Kappa, Kappa Alpha Psi. Democrat. Roman Catholic. Author: Tuskegee, Montgomery and Other Poems, 1977; Traffic Lights and Other Poems, 1969; Booker T's Child: Memoirs of Portia Marshall Washington Pittman, 1972; Rhetoric of Racial Hope, 1954-64, 1964; Piedmont Ballads (poetry), 1965; Arete and Other Poems, 1966; Corrie J. Carroll and Other Poems, 1963; Light for the Blind (A Biographical Sketch of the Fabulous Booker T. Pittman), 1974, others; recs. of poetry. Home 334 S Jackson St Montgomery AL 36104 Office: Tullibody Hall Alabama State Univ Montgomery AL 36104

HILL, RUSSELL EDWIN, personnel cons.; b. Greenville, Tex., Oct. 10, 1939; s. Irvin Pate and Carrol Nadyne (English) H.; B.A., Tex. A. & M. U., 1962; M.S., 1965; div.; children—Russell Steven, Dallas Kaye. Systems mgr. IBM, Houston, 1964-69; owner Gulf Coast Computer Services, 1970-71, Direct Dial Data Systems, 1971-73; data processing mgr. Info. Processing Corp., Houston, 1973-74; mgr. data processing div. Uptrend Assos., Inc., Houston, 1974—; part-time instr. U. Houston, 1976-77. Mem. Lang. Arts Com., Houston, 1978—. Mem. Data Processing Mgmt. Assn., Am. Prodn. and Inventory Control Soc. Republican. Unitarian. Clubs: Tex. Soc. Rugby Referees, Tex. A. & M. U. Letterman's Club. Office: Uptrend Assos Inc 4120 SW Freeway 114 Houston TX 77027

HILL, RUSSELL LANGSTON, JR., aluminum co. exec.; b. Richmond, Va., Nov. 17, 1933; s. Russell Langston and Gladys (Patron) H.; student Va. Union U., 1958-61; m. Ida M. Johnson, Aug. 18, 1962. With Reynolds Aluminum Co./Reynolds Metals Devel. Corp., Richmond, 1962—, personnel mgr., 1977-79, asst. div. personnel dir., 1979— Served with USAF, 1953-57; Korea. Recipient Merit award Nat. Safety Council, 1974-75, Honor award, 1976. Home: 9921 Salem Church Rd Richmond VA 23234 Office: 6601 W Broad St Richmond VA 23261

HILL, SANDRA STROPE, newspaper exec.; b. Sayre, Pa., June 21, 1938; d. Mahlon Brewster and Margaret Mary (Jones) Strope; B.A. magna cum laude, Pfeffer Coll., 1960; m. William Ross Hill, Dec. 31, 1960; 1 dau., Heather Margaret. Reporter, Charlotte (N.C.) News, 1960-73, asst. city editor, 1973-78, day city editor, 1978, mag. editor, 1979—; instr. journalism U. N.C. at Charlotte, part-time 1978-80. Bd. dirs., pub. relations Hornets Nest council Girl Scouts, 1977. Recipient Service award Mecklenburg Assn. for Blind, 1971-72. Mem. Women in Communications (treas. 1976-77, chmn. freedom of press 1979—, sec. 1980—), Women's Polit. Caucus, Women Execs., Mensa, U.S. Figure Skating Assn. Ice Skating Inst. Am. Republican. Methodist. Home: 5201 Farmbrook Dr Charlotte NC 28210 Office: Charlotte News PO Box 30308 Charlotte NC 28230

HILL, THOMAS AUSTIN, med. mfg. co. exec.; b. Pryor, Okla., Feb. 8, 1943; s. Thomas Austin and Lois Jean (Bavinger) H.; B.E.E., Okla. State U., 1971; m. Kay Kimmell, July 29, 1963; children—Thomas Austin, David Kimmell, Karen. Enlisted in U.S. Marine Corps, 1961, advanced through grades to 1st lt., 1968; resigned, 1968; engr. Kimray, Inc., Oklahoma City, 1971-73, exec. v.p., 1978—; pres., chmn. bd. Kimray Med. Assos., Inc., Oklahoma City, 1973-78. Decorated Air medal with 1 silver, 2 bronze oak leaf clusters. Mem. Assn. Advancement Med. Instrumentation, IEEE, Sigma Tau, Eta Kappa Nu. Lutheran. Inventor method of estimating area of thermal curve, 1977. Home: 2645 NW 26th St Oklahoma City OK 73107 Office: 53 NW 42d St Oklahoma City OK 73118

HILL, THOMAS GLENN, III, dermatologist; b. Atlanta, Dec. 15, 1942; s. Thomas Glenn, Jr. and Wilella (Burns) H.; B.A. in History, Emory U., 1964; M.D., Med. Coll. Ga., Augusta, 1968; m. Peggy Jane Simms, Nov. 9, 1974; children—Elizabeth Burns, Jennifer Michelle, Thomas Glenn IV Intern, USAF Med. Center, Keesler AFB, 1968-69; resident in dermatology Med. Coll. Va., 1972-75; practice medicine specializing in dermatology and cutaneous surgery, Decatur, Ga., 1975—; mem staff DeKalb Gen., Grady Meml., Rockdale County, Newton County hosps.; clin. instr. dermatology Emory U. Med. Sch., 1975—. Served as officer M.C., USAF, 1967-72. Decorated Disting. Service award; diplomate Am. Bd. Dermatology. Mem. AMA (Physician Recognition award 1975), Am. Acad. Dermatology, Am Soc. Dermatologic Surgery, Internat. Soc. Dermatologic Surgery, Am. Dermatologic Soc. Allergy and Immunology, So. Med. Assn., Ga. Soc. Dermatologists, Atlanta Dermatologic Assn. Republican. Presbyterian. Author papers in field. Office: 5040 Snapfinger Woods Dr Decatur GA 30035

HILL, WILLIAM OSCAR, JR., postmaster; b. Richmond, Va., Sept. 14, 1926; s. William Oscar and Pearle Cornelia (May) H.; student Strayer Bus. Coll., 1942-44, U. Philippines, 1945; m. Ruth Floyd, Oct. 28, 1948. With office of treas. B. & O. R.R., Balt., 1942-43; postmaster Brandy Station, Va., 1947—. Dir. Brandy Vol. Fire Co., 1970-76; radiol. monitor CD Served with U.S. Army, 1944-46. Recipient Cross of Mil. Honor, UDC, 1977. Mem. Nat. League Postmasters (state pres. Va. br. 1973, named Postmaster of Year 1973, Past Pres.'s Club), Grand Lodge of Va. (dist. dep. grand master 1961-62), SCV (comdr. Camp 1311), SAR Gen. Soc. Order Stars and Bars, Nat. Rifle Assn. (life), Am. Def. Preparedness Assn. (life). Clubs: Masons (local sec.), Brandy Station Ruritan. Baptist. Home: PO Box 7 Brandy Station VA 22714 Office: Postmaster Brandy Station VA 22714

HILLER, E. A. STURGIS, JR., business cons.; b. Foxboro, Mass., Jan. 20, 1928; s. Edward Abbott Sturgis and Ruth Helen H.; cert. FAA, 1958, 59, U.S. Dept. Agr. Grad. Sch., 1959, 60, 70, Office CD, 1962; children—Wyatt T.M., Christine M. LaGarde, Susan R. Buchanan, James R. With FAA, 1958-64; office mgr. Martinsburg Veneer Corp., 1964; owner Martinsburg Bus. Services, 1965-66; spl. project officer FAA, 1965; dir., mgr. telecommunications, mail processing, micrographics, printing mgmt., distbn. programs FDA, 1965-78; pres. People & Orgns., Inc., Merritt Island, Fla., 1978—. Served with USCG, 1945-57. Recipient Outstanding Performance awards FAA, 1959, FDA, 1966. Mem. Adminstrv. Mgmt. Soc., Am. Soc. Public Adminstrn., Am. Soc. Tng. and Devel., Am. Mgmt. Assn., Soc. Advancement Mgmt., Internat. Word Processing Soc., Nat. Small Bus. Assn., Internat. Entrepreneurs Assn. Republican. Clubs: Lions, Fraternal Order Policemen, CD Communications Unit, Opequon Amateur Radio Soc. Author: Leadership Skills for Office

Supervisors, 1977; Managing the Administrative Services Function, 1978; Effective Management of Mail, 1979; Personnel Management for Supervisors/Managers, 1979, others. Home: 205 S Courtenay Pkwy 206 Merritt Island FL 32952 Office: 262 E Merritt Island Causeway 11 Merritt Island FL 32952

HILLEY, LARRY LEE, elec. engr.; b. Gorman, Tex., Mar. 5, 1937; s. Ira Lee and Catherine Verline (Waggoner) H.; student Mass. Inst. Tech., 1955-57; B.A., Tex. Christian U., 1960, postgrad., 1963-72; m. Leona Diane Rutland, Apr. 26, 1958; children—Terry Lee, Timothy Paul, Sherri Lynn. Elec. engr. Univac, St. Paul, 1960-61, San Diego, 1961-62, Dallas, 1962-64; group leader E-Systems, Greenville, Tex., 1964-66, group supr., Garland, Tex., 1966-69; mgr. spl. products Internat. Computer Products, Dallas, 1969-72; prin. engr. Recognition Equipment Inc., Dallas, 1972—; cons. in field. Mem. Am. Phys. Soc., IEEE, Sigma Pi Sigma. Mem. Ch. Christ. Home: 1110 Vicksburg St Garland TX 75041 Office: PO Box 222307 Dallas TX 75222

HILLIARD, DICK LEE, sales exec.; b. Harrisburg, Ill., June 21, 1943; s. James P. and Gaynell W. (Wise) H.; A.A., Southeastern Ill. Coll., 1963; B.A., So. Ill. U., 1966, M.B.A., 1970; m. Margaret Ann Kellerstrass, June 17, 1967; 1 dau., Amy Elizabeth. Tech. rep. Union Carbide Corp., N.Y.C., 1970-73; sales rep. Mobil Chem. Co., Chgo., 1973-75, sr. sales rep., Richmond, Va., 1975-77, planning analyst, 1978-79, regional sales mgr., 1979—. Adv., Jr. Achievement, 1978. Served with U.S. Army, 1966-68. Home: 3513 Walkers Ferry Ct Midlothian VA 23113 Office: Mobil Chem Co PO Box 26683 Richmond VA 23261

HILLIARD, WILLIAM GERALD, leasing co. exec.; b. Milford, Pa., Feb. 14, 1947; s. Barton Villiers and Josephine Elizabeth (Muller) H.; B.S. in Agrl. Econs., U. Ariz., 1970 postgrad. Wharton Sch. of Bus., U. Pa., 1976; m. Janet Newton McBride, Feb. 2, 1980. Asst. leasing mgr. Jim Click Ford Leasing, Inc., Tucson, 1970-73; account exec. Trans-Nat. Leasing, Inc., Dallas, 1974-76; account exec. Comml. Credit/McCullagh Leasing, Inc., Dallas, 1976-77, regional sales mgr., Houston, 1977—; fin. v.p. Gerrod, Inc., Houston, 1979—; treas. Orme Sch., Mayer, Ariz., 1968-71, bd. dirs., 1968—. Mem. Republican Precinct Com., Tucson, 1971-73. Mem. Am. Mktg. Assn., Sigma Phi Epsilon. Republican. Episcopalian. Home: 9851 Meadowglen Ln Apt 90 Houston TX 77042 Office: 8700 Commerce Park Dr Suite 101 Houston TX 77036

HILLIER, GEORGE THOMAS, broadcasting co. exec.; b. San Francisco, June 19, 1930; s. George Robert and Thelma Laura (Lowery) H.; student Coll. William and Mary Extension, 1949-51; m. Etta Louise Stender, Aug. 19, 1955; children—Bruce Thomas, Paul Thomas. With Norfolk (Va.) Broadcasting Corp., 1958-64; chief engr. Peninsula Broadcasting Corp., Hampton, Va., 1964—; course cons. Norfolk Tech. Vocat. Sch., 1973—. Served with USAF, 1950-53. Decorated Purple Heart. Mem. Soc. Broadcast Engrs., Soc. Motion Picture and TV Engrs., Exptl. Aircraft Assn., Aircraft Owners and Pilots Assn. Baptist. Home: 1064 W Ocean View Ave Norfolk VA 23503 Office: 110 N 3d St Norfolk VA 23510

HILLS, LEE, newspaperman; b. Granville, N.D., May 28, 1906; s. Lewis Amos and Lulu Mae (Loomis) H.; student Brigham Young U., 1924-25, U. Mo., 1927-29; LL.B., Oklahome City U., 1934; Sc.D. in Bus. Adminstrn., Cleary Coll., 1958; L.H.D. (hon.), U. Utah, 1969; LL.D., Eastern Mich. U., 1969; m. Leona Haas, Dec. 25, 1933 (dec.); 1 son, Ronald Lee; m. 2d, Eileen Whitman, June 4, 1948 (dec. 1961); m. 3d, Tina S. Ramos, Oct. 31, 1963. News reporter News-Adv., Price, Utah, 1924-25, editor, 1926; reporter Oklahoma City Times, 1929-32; polit. writer Okla. News, 1932-35, editor, 1938-39; reporter, copyreader Cleve. Press, 1935-36, news editor, 1940-42; chief editorial writer, asso. editor Indpls. Times, 1936-37; asso. editor Memphis Press-Scimitar, 1939-40; mng. editor Miami (Fla.) Herald, 1942-51, exec. editor, 1951-66, asso. pub., 1966-69, pub., 1970-79, editorial chmn., 1979—; exec. editor Detroit Free Press, 1951-69; leave as war corr., Europe, 1945; pub. Detroit Free Press, 1963-79, pres., 1967-73, editorial chmn., 1979—; exec. editor Knight Newspapers, Inc., 1959-66, exec. v.p., 1966-67, pres., 1967-73, chmn. exec. com., 1969-73, chmn. ops. com., 1973-74; chmn. bd., chief exec. officer Knight-Ridder Newspapers, Inc., 1973-76, editorial chmn., 1976—, chmn. bd., 1976-79. Admitted to Okla. bar, 1935. Pres., Detroit Arts Commn., 1966-79; trustee Founders Soc., Detroit Inst. Arts. Recipient Maria Moors Cabot Gold medal for distinguished contbn. inter-Am. relations, Columbia, 1946; Pulitzer prize in journalism, 1956. Mem. Internat. Press Inst., Inter-Am. (dir., pres. 1967-68), Mich. press assns., Am. Soc. Newspaper Editors (pres. 1962-63), Am. Newspaper Pubs. Assn., AP Mng. Editors Assn. (past pres.), Fla. AP Assn. (past pres.), Washington Press Club, United Found. (dir.), Sigma Delta Chi (past pres.). Clubs: National Press; Renaissance, Detroit, Grosse Pointe (Detroit); Miami, Bath and Surf (Miami, Fla.); Bankers. Home: 4450 Banyan Lane Miami FL 33137 Office: 1 Herald Plaza Miami Herald Miami FL 33101 also Detroit Free Press 321 W Lafayette Blvd Detroit MI 48231

HILLSTEAD, ROBERT AVERILL, cons.; b. Big Falls, Minn., Jan. 16, 1915; s. Bert Adolph and Ida Ella (Gowdy) H.; B.B.A., U. Miami, 1940; m. Mattie Lee Wheat, Feb. 22, 1941; children—Gary Alan, Richard Averil. Comptroller Embry-Riddle Co., Miami, Fla., 1940-44; pres. Averil, Inc., Miami, 1946-79; cons., 1979—. Served with USNR, 1944-46.

HILLYER, GEORGE VANZANDT, immunologist/parasitologist, educator; b. San Juan, P.R., Dec. 8, 1943; s. William VanZandt and Ruth Lillian Hillyer; B.S., U.P.R., Rio Piedras, 1967; Ph.D., U. Chgo., 1972; m. Josefina Gomez-Piza, June 15, 1968; children—George VanZandt, Julian Federico. Dir. SUBE research program Faculty of Natural Scis., U. P.R., Rio Piedras, 1974—, asso. prof. pathology Med. Scis. Campus, 1976—, asst. prof. immunology and parasitology, 1972-75, asso. prof., 1975—; adj. asso. prof. tropical medicine Tulane U. Sch. Public Health and Tropical Medicine, New Orleans, 1979—; cons. immunology and parasitology NIH, Edna McConnell Clark Found., Ministry of Health (Egypt), VA Hosp., San Juan, InterAm U., San Juan. NIH grantee, 1973—; Edna McConnell Clark Found. grantee, 1979—. Mem. Am. Assn. Immunologists, Am. Soc. Tropical Medicine and Hygiene, Am. Soc. Parasitologists, Royal Soc. Tropical Medicine and Hygiene, Am. Soc. Microbiology, Soc. Microbiologists P.R. (pres. 1979), Soc. Exptl. Biology and Medicine, Sigma Xi (pres. San Juan 1979). Roman Catholic. Contbr. articles to profl. jours. Home: 254 Himalaya Monterrey Urb Rio Piedras PR 00926 Office: Lab Parasite Immunology Dept Biology U PR Rio Piedras PR 00931

HILTON, ERIC MICHAEL, hotel industry exec.; b. Dallas, July 1, 1933; s. Conrad N. and Mary (Barron) H.; student U. Tex., 1950-51, Cornell Hotel Sch., 1953-54; m. Patricia Skipworth, Aug. 14, 1954; children—Eric Michael, Beverly, Linda, Joseph B. Various exec. positions Dallas Statler Hilton, 1955-59; resident mgr. Dreshler Hilton, Columbus, Ohio, 1959-60; gen. mgr. Aurora (Ill) Hilton, 1960-61; resident mgr. Shamrock Hilton, Houston, 1961-66; southwest sales mgr. Hilton Hotels Corp., Houston, 1966-69; southwest regional mgr. Hilton Inns, Inc., Houston, 1969-72; divisional v.p. Hilton Inns, Inc., Houston, 1972—; dir. Greenspoint Bank, Houston. Pres. North Braes Bayou Little League, 1963; exec. v.p. Houston Trade and Travel Fair, 1963; chmn. Sponsors Club, Pin Oak Horse Show, 1964; bd. dirs. Harris County (Tex.) Cancer Soc., 1964, Houston Livestock Show and Rodeo, 1964, Conrad N. Hilton Found., Beverly Hills, Calif., 1968—, Fun Football, 1963, Lifemark Corp., 1978—; bd. dirs. Am. Contract Bridge League, 1973, pres. dist. 16, 1974; trustee Allen Acad., Bryan, Tex., 1970—, Little League Found., 1977—. Served with U.S. Army, 1953-55. Mem. Airline Passengers Assn. (mem. nat. adv. bd. 1970—), Future Business Leaders Assn., Phi Beta Lambda. Office: One Greenway Plaza East Houston TX 77046

HILTON, RALPH, editor and publisher; b. Mendenhall, Miss., Sept. 10, 1907; s. R.T. and Mary Myrtis (Cruise) H.; A.B., George Washington U., 1929; m. Mary Jane Kendall, Feb. 20, 1935 (dec. 1970); 1 dau., Mary Jane Field; m. 2d, Dorothy M. Asnip, Apr. 27, 1972. Reporter, Jackson (Miss.) Daily News, 1930; newspaper corr., Mexico City, 1931-32; staff writer, membership rep., editor A.P., New Orleans, N.Y.C., Dallas, Richmond, Va., Washington, 1933-43; exec. sec. Coordination Com., Office Inter-Am. Affairs, Lima, Peru, 1943-45; press attache Am. embassy, San Jose, Costa Rica, 1946; pub. affairs officer Am. embassy, Buenos Aires, Argentina, 1947-49; with Mut. Def. Assistance, Dept. State, 1950; pub. affairs adviser to asst. sec. state, 1951; program insp. Fgn. Service, 1952-53; chief Am. Republics area Office Policy and Programs, USIA, 1954; career fgn. service officer, pub. affairs adviser asst. sec. state for Inter-Am. Affairs, 1955-57; counselor Am. embassy, Asuncion, Paraguay, 1957-58; dir. UNESCO relations staff Dept. State, 1959; consul gen., spl. asst. to adminstr. Bur. Security and Consular Affairs, Dept. State, 1960; exec. sec. Joint Bd. Examiners, USIA, 1962-64; cons. Hilton Head Co., Hilton Head Island, S.C., 1966-70; co-founder, editor The Island Packet, Hilton Head Island, 1970-76; co-pub. Savannah (Ga.) Jour.-Record, 1975-77; pres., editor So. World, Hilton Head Island and Atlanta, 1978—. Mem. Am. Fgn. Service Assn., Diplomatic and Consular Officers Ret. Clubs: Nat. Press, Overseas Press. Author: Worldwide Mission, 1971. Editor: The Gentlemanly Serpent, 1974; Tales of the Foreign Service, 1977. Home: 6 Heritage Rd Hilton Head Island SC 29928

HIMEL, CHESTER MORA, entomologist; b. Des Plaines, Ill., Mar. 10, 1916; s. Charles Maurice and Mary Eleanor (Mora) H.; B.S. in Chemistry, U. Chgo., 1938; Ph.D. in Organic Chemistry, U. Ill., 1942; m. Ann Walter, June 21, 1943; children—Barbara Holly Himel Pietrowski, Shelley Jeanne. Research chemist E.I. duPont de Nemour & Co., Inc., Wilmington, Del., 1942-43; Allied Chem. Co., N.Y.C., 1943-44; research group leader Phillips Petroleum Co., Bartlesville, Okla., 1944-49; sr. organic chemist, dir. organic research div. Stanford Research Inst., 1949-65; research prof. entomology U. Ga., Athens, 1965—; indsl. cons. Intra-Sci. Research Found. fellow, 1968—; grantee NIH, Office Naval Research, Dept. Agr., EPA, Army Med. Research and Devel. Command. Mem. Entomol. Soc. Am., Am. Chem. Soc., AAAS, Ga. Entomol. Soc., Sigma Xi, Gamma Sigma Delta. Episcopalian. Contbr. articles to sci. jours., chpt. in book. Holder numerous patents. Home: 165 Xavier Dr Athens GA 30606 Office: Dept Entomology U Ga Athens GA 30602

HIMMELFARB, ELLIOT HARVEY, radiologist; b. Bklyn., Nov. 20, 1942; s. Hyman and Sarah (Blumkin) H.; student Rensselaer Poly. Inst., 1959-62; M.D. summa cum laude, State U. N.Y. Downstate Med. Center, 1966; m. Cynthia Friedman, June 14, 1970. Intern, VA Hosp., Bklyn., 1966-67; resident Kings County Hosp., Bklyn., 1967-69, Bklyn. Cumberland Med. Center, 1969-70; asst. prof. radiology State U. N.Y. Downstate Med. Center, 1971; attending radiologist Long Beach (N.Y.) Meml. Hosp., South Shore Hosp., Far Rockaway, N.Y., 1972-73; asso. prof. U. Tenn. Center for Health Scis., Memphis, 1974-76; dir. radiology Williamson County (Tenn.) Hosp., Franklin, 1977—; clin. asst. prof. radiology Vanderbilt U., 1979—. Served to lt. comdr. USN, 1974-75. Diplomate Am. Bd. Radiology. Mem. Am. Coll. Radiology, Tenn., Williamson County med. assns., AMA, Radiologic Soc. N.Am., Am. Roentgen Ray Soc., Am. Heart Assn., Middle Tenn. Radiologic Soc. Clubs: Woodmont Country (Franklin); Maryland Farms Country. Contbr. articles to med. publs. Home: 228 Franklin Rd Franklin TN 37064 Office: PO Box 745 Franklin TN 37064

HINCKLE, THOMAS WENDELL, educator, counseling psychologist, mgmt. cons.; b. Brunswick, Md., Mar. 22, 1929; s. Thomas Franklin and Eva (Bohrer) H.; B.S. in Psychology, U. So. Miss., 1969, M.S. in Clin. Psychology, 1973; Ed.D. in Counselor Edn., Miss. State U., 1975; m. Susie May Armstrong, July 6, 1956; children—Thomas W., Carrie Lynn; 1 stepson, Charles T. Served as enlisted man U.S. Air Force, 1948-57; supr. Miss. Employment Service, 1961-66; mgr. Wiggins Clinic, 1966-73; staff asst. Miss. State U., 1973-75; psychologist VA, 1975; asso. prof. dept. mgmt. Miss. State U., Mississippi State, 1975—; pvt. practice counseling and family therapy, 1975—; mgmt. cons., 1975—; trainer and cons. to med. clinics, nat. and internat. indsl. orgns., govtl. orgns. Recipient Merit award Internat. Assn. Personnel in Employment Security; cert. rehab. counselor Nat. Commn. Rehab. Counselor Cert. Mem. Acad. Mgmt., Am. Psychol. Assn., Acad. Psychologists in Marital and Family Therapy, Internat. Transactional Analysis Assn., Miss. Assn. Counseling Psychologists, Miss. Psychol. Assn., Southeastern Psychol. Assn., Orgn. Devel. Network, Phi Kappa Phi, Phi Delta Kappa, Delta Sigma Pi. Methodist. Club: Masons. Home: Route 4 Box 128 Starkville MS 39759 Office: PO Drawer MG Miss State U Mississippi State MS 39762

HINCKLEY, CAROLYN GAY, journalist; b. Houston, Aug. 8, 1949; d. Kenneth Rodger and June Marie (Benefield) H.; B.J., U. Tex., Austin, 1971, postgrad., 1977—. Edit. asst. Tex. Outlook mag., Austin, 1971-74; ednl. writer, Dept. Occupational Edn. and Tech., Tex. Edn. Agy., Austin, 1974—; cons. Nat. Center for Research in Vocat. Edn., Columbus; mem. adv. bd. Travis County Cts. at Law. Mem. Am. Vocat. Assn. (pres. public info. sect. 1978-79), Nat. Assn. Vocat. Tech. Edn. Communicators (pres. 1977-79), Women in Communications, Nat. Sch. Public Relations Assn., Tex. Sch. Public Relations Assn., Tex. Vocat. Tech. Assn. Democrat. Episcopalian. Author: (with others) Promoting Vocational Education, 1978. Home: 3611-C Las Colinas Austin TX 78731 Office: 201 E 11th St Austin TX 78701

HINDERER, BYRON FREDERICK, cons.; b. Dallas, Sept. 11, 1935; s. Byron Frederick and Marion Elizabeth (Barth) H.; B.S. in Engring., U. Tex., Austin, 1958, M.S. in Mech. Engring., 1971; m. Betty Loyce Kirkland, Dec. 7, 1973; children—Robin Elena, Byron Frederick, Robert Scott, Jeffrey John; stepchildren—Zetta Loyce, Joetta Still, Kelvin Gene. Engr. N.Am. Aviation, Los Angeles, Calif., 1959-60, McGregor, Tex., 1960-67; project mgr. Tracor, Inc., Austin, Tex., 1967—; cons. in mgmt. and engring., Austin, 1971—; lectr. statistics U. Tex., Austin, 1975-78. Mem. sch. bd. and vestry St. George's Episcopal Ch., Austin, 1968-72, chmn. sch. bd., 1971-72. Registered profl. engr., Tex. Mem. Tex., Nat. socs. profl. engrs., Am. Mgmt. Assn. Democrat. Author tech. bulls., reports, and studies in engring., mgmt., statistics, traffic safety and electronics. Contbr. articles in field to profl. jours. Home and Office: 8900 Viking Dr Austin TX 78758

HINDERMANN, RICHARD LANE, ins. co. exec.; b. New Orleans, Apr. 1, 1923; s. Franz Joseph and Inez Lucille (Ellis) H.; student Tulane U., 1941-42, U.S. Coast Guard Acad.; m. Mary Ann Andry, Sept. 6, 1947; children—Mary Inez, Cheryl Lane. With Pan-Am. Life Ins. Co., New Orleans, 1941—, v.p., 1955-62, sr. v.p., 1962—, mem. exec. com., sr. mgmt. com., fin. com., 1961—, also dir.; pres. Pan Am. Securities Co., Seminole Securities Co.; dir. Security Homestead Assn.; pres. New Orleans Bd. Trade. Pres. Internat. House, New Orleans, 1967—; hon. Turkish consul for La. Served to lt. j.g. USCG, 1942-46. Mem. Pub. Relations Soc. Am. (pres. New Orleans chpt. 1965-66), Life Ins. Advertisers Assn. (pres. 1965-66), Navy League U.S. Democrat. Roman Catholic. Clubs: Pickwick, New Orleans Country, Plimsoll. Home: 426 Vincent Ave Metairie LA 70005 Office: 2400 Canal St New Orleans LA 70119

HINDERSTEIN, MAYER S., property mgmt. co. exec.; b. N.Y.C., July 1, 1921; s. Herman Bernard H.; B.A., N.Y. U., 1947; m. Juliette Wilder, June 19, 1947; children—Ruth, Andrew, Randolph, Karen, Jason. Asst. v.p. Dwelling Mgrs., N.Y.C., 1963-69; v.p. A.P.I. Mgmt. Inc., Miami, Fla., 1969-71; gen. mgr. Maison Grande, Miami Beach, Fla., 1971-73; pres. Point Mgmt. Inc., Delray Beach, Fla., 1973-76; asst. v.p. Hollywood Land Co., Inc. (Fla.), 1976—. Served with USAAF, 1942-45. Decorated D.F.C., Air medal.

HINDMAN, ROBERT EUGENE, JR., univ. ofcl.; b. Greenville, S.C., May 18, 1942; s. Robert Eugene and Gladys Marie (Brown) H.; B.S. in Bus. Adminstrn., The Citadel, 1964; m. Janice Sue Boley, Nov. 26, 1964; children—Laura Elizabeth, Robert Eugene III. Customer services rep. Monsanto Chem. Co., Greenville, 1964-65; asst. treas. Furman U., Greenville, 1969-70, bus. mgr., treas., 1971—; trustee Furman U. Found.; cons. univ. bus. affairs. Bd. dirs. Greenville-Furman Fine Arts Series, 1971-76, John Knox Presbyterian Ch. Kindergarten, 1972-75, Foxcroft Recreation Assn., 1979—. Served to capt. USAF, 1965-68. Mem. So. Assn. Coll. and Univ. Bus. Officers, Nat. Assn. Coll. and Univ. Bus. Officers, Adminstrv. Mgmt. Soc. Baptist. Club: Kiwanis. Home: 108 W Queen Ann Rd Greenville SC 29615 Office: Poinsett Hwy Greenville SC 29613

HINDMARSH, JAMES WESLEY, mfg. co. exec.; b. Denver, Sept. 30, 1946; s. Darrell Wesley and Ruth Ellen (Simmons) H.; student Westark Community Coll., 1977; dip., Internat. Accountants Sch., 1975; m. Roberta Darlene Scroggins, Nov. 13, 1965; 1 son, Darrell Ray. Material expediter Norge div. Borg-Warner, Ft. Smith, Ark., 1964-65; with Arkhola Sand & Gravel Co., Ft. Smith, 1966—, adminstrv. coordinator, 1977—; mktg. cons. Horizens Unltd., Ft. Smith, 1978—. Chmn., Western Ark. Postal Customer Council, 1976—. Mem. Nat. Assn. Accountants, Internat. Accountants Soc. Baptist. Club: Exchange. Editor, The Mailroom Messenger, 1976—. Home: 3106 Kendall St Fort Smith AR 72903 Office: 523 Garrison Ave Ward Garrison Bldg Room 808 Fort Smith AR 72901

HINDS, CHARLES FRANKLIN, state ofcl.; b. Henderson, Ky., Oct. 31, 1923; s. Charles Fretwell and Ruth Alice (Carson) H.; A.B., U. Ky., 1950, M.A., 1958, M.S. in L.S., 1968, postgrad., 1968; postgrad. U. Louisville, 1950-52, 54-56, Am. U., 1961; m. Doris May Rooney, June 8, 1946; 1 son, Joseph James. Account and rate clk., auditor freight accounts L & N R.R., Louisville, 1941-53; tchr. Male High Sch., Louisville, 1953-56; dir. Ky. Hist. Soc., Frankfort, 1956-59; state historian, Ky., 1956-59; field rep. U. Ky. Libraries, Lexington, 1959-60; state archivist, records adminstr. State Archives and Records Commn., Frankfort, 1960-67; head librarian Murray (Ky.) U., 1967-73; state librarian Ky., 1973-77; prin. asst. State Edn. and Arts Cabinet, 1977—; pres. HAE, Inc., 1979—; lectr., U. Ky., 1960-67; instr. Ky. State U., 1966-67, 74—, asso. prof. Murray State U., 1967-73. Sec., mgr. Ky. Hist. Markers Program, 1956-62; chmn. State Records Control Bd., 1956-58; mem. State Archives and Records Commn., 1958-60, 67-77, sec., 1960-61, chmn. State Archives and Records Commn., 1973-77; mem. Civil War Centennial Commn., 1958-65, Ky. Heritage Commn., 1972-77; Ky. Internat. Year of the Child Commn., 1978—. Served with AUS, 1941-45. Decorated Bronze Star. Mem. Ky. Tennis Assn. (sec.-treas. 1958-65, pres. 1967-68), Ky. Microfilm Assn. (pres. 1973-75), SAR (pres. Ky. chpt. 1969-70), Soc. Am. Archivists (chmn. state archives com. 1965, 66), Bluegrass Library Assn. (pres. 1975-76), Ky. Geneal. Assn. (pres. 1978-79), Phi Beta Kappa, Phi Alpha Theta, Beta Phi Mu. Democrat. Episcopalian (vestryman 1967-68, 76—, clk. of vestry 1976-78, sr. warden 1972-73). Rotarian (1st v.p. 1977—, archivist, historian 1976—), Optimist (1st v.p. 1963), Toastmaster (pres. 1964-65, lt. gov. So. div. dist. 11 1968-69). Editor: Register, state hist. quar., 1956-59; Checklist of Ky. State Publs., 1963-67; Ann. Catalog of Federal Programs, Kentucky Education and Arts Cabinet, 1977—. Contbr. weekly news column. Home: 320 Meadow Ln Frankfort KY 40601

HINDS, J. C., ednl. adminstr.; b. Jamestown, Tenn., May 23, 1938; s. Carson and Beuna H.; B.S., Tenn. Tech. U., 1969; M.A., Western Ky. U., 1972, rank I cert., 1976; m. Anne Hutchinson, June 24, 1962; 1 son, James Ross. Supr., Warner-Gear Co., Muncie, Ind., 1961-65, foreman, 1965-67; tchr. Jefferson County (Ky.) Bd. Edn., 1969-77, adminstrv. asst., 1977—. Coach, Little League Baseball, Louisville, 1969-71. Served with USAF, 1957-61; ETO. Named Tchr. of Year for Ky., Driver Edn. Div., 1973; Hon. Ky. Col. Mem. Unified Teaching Profession, Jefferson County Coaches Assn. (sec. 1972), Ky. High Sch. Athletic Assn., PTA, Ky. Real Estate Assn., Ky. Edn. Assn. (conv. del.), NEA (conv. del.), Jefferson County Tchrs. Assn. (profl. rep.). Club: Moose. Home: 10204 Eve Dr Valley Station KY 40272

HINDSMAN, BILLIE FAYE, nurse, hosp. adminstr.; b. Vivian, La., Oct. 17, 1934; d. Jack D. and Dessie D. (Crumpler) Parker; grad. Schumpert Sch. Nursing, 1955; m. Franklin D. Hindsman, Jan. 27, 1956 (div. 1975); children—Debra, Rebecca, Sherri. Head obstetrical nurse Schumpert Meml. Hosp., Shreveport, La., 1955, 1957-60, head nurse recovery room, 1960-65; staff nurse VA Hosp., Shreveport, La., 1955-57; dir. nurses North Caddo Meml. Hosp., Vivian, 1965—. Mem. Am. Nurses Assn., Shreveport Dist. Assn. Nursing Services Adminstrn., La. Soc. Nursing Services Dirs., Operating Room Nurses, Am. Heart Assn. Baptist. Clubs: Am. Legion Aux. (sec. local club), L'Allegro, Fed. Women's. Office: North Caddo Meml Hosp PO Box 792 Vivian LA 71082

HINDSON, EDWARD E., clergyman, educator; b. Detroit, Dec. 21, 1944; s. Edward J. and Helen L. (Snyder) H.; B.A., U. Detroit, 1966; M.A., Trinity Evang. Div. Sch., 1967; Th.M., Grace Theol. Sem., 1970; Th.D., Trinity Grad. Sch. Theology, 1971; D.Min., Westminster Theol. Sem., 1978; m. Donna Jean Currie, Aug. 6, 1966; children—Linda, Christy, Jonathan. Ordained to ministry, Baptist Ch., 1966; pastor Fulton (Ind.) Bapt. Ch., 1967-69; asso. dir. Life Action Ministries, St. Petersburg, Fla., 1970-74; prof. religion Liberty Bapt. Coll., 1974—, dir. counseling, 1974—; minister Thomas Road Bapt. Ch., Lynchburg, Va., 1974—. Mem. Evang. Theol. Soc. Author: Philistines and Old Testament, 1972; Glory in the Church, 1975; Introduction to Puritan Theology, 1976; Isaiah's Immanual, 1978, others. Home: 1711 Laxton Rd Lynchburg VA 24502 Office: Box 1111 Lynchburg VA 24514

HINES, CARL RICHARD, city ofcl.; b. Louisville, Mar. 23, 1931; s. Fred Richard and Ruth Lory (Johnson) H.; student U. Ill., 1949-50, B.S., U. Louisville, 1962; m. Teresa M. Churchill, Mar. 5, 1960; children—Carl Richard, Keith, Cheryl, Cory. Staff mgr. Mammoth Ins. Co., 1963-65, dist. mgr., 1965-70; city dir. Housing Opportunity Centers, Inc., Louisville, 1970-72, exec. dir., 1972-80; mem. Ky. Ho. of Reps., 1980—; real estate broker. Mem. Jefferson County Sch. Bd. Exec. sec. Louisville Community Action Commn., 1969-70; vice chmn. Louisville Chestnut St. YMCA, 1970-75. Mem. Louisville Bd. Edn., 1968-74, vice chmn., 1970, chmn., 1971; mem. Jefferson County Bd. Edn., 1974-76. Served with USAF, 1951-53. Decorated Air medal, D.F.C. Optimist. Club: Just Mens. Home: 635 Southwestern Pkwy Louisville KY 40211 Office: 1111 W Broadway Louisville KY 40203

HINES, JAMES HERMAN, banker; b. Jackson, Miss., Sept. 8, 1914; s. Hulon H. and Ava (Odom) H.; student Jackson Sch. Law, 1935-36, Sch. Banking of South, 1950-53; grad. Advanced Mgmt. Program, Harvard U., 1966; m. Martha Hamilton, Dec. 25, 1942; children—Martha H., Linda Hines White, Julia G. Hines Ditmore. With Deposit Guaranty Nat. Bank, Jackson, 1936—, pres., 1973-75, chmn., chief exec. officer, 1975—; dir. Miss. Power & Light Co., Mchts. & Planters Bank, Tchula, Mississippi Valley Title Ins. Co. Co-chmn. capital funds campaign Miss. Coll., 1976-77; treas., bd. dirs. Millsaps Coll.; vice chmn, trustee Piney Woods Country Life Sch.; bd. dirs. Jackson State U. Found., Jackson Ballet Guild, Jackson YMCA, Miss. Econ. Council; adv. bd. St. Dominic Jackson Meml. Hosp.; disaster chmn. for Miss., A.R.C.; treas. Episcopal Diocese Jackson, 1954-74. Served to maj. U.S. Army, 1941-46. Mem. Mid-Continent Oil and Gas Assn. (dir.). Club: Kiwanis (past lt. gov.). Home: 3909 Cambridge St Jackson MS 39216 Office: 1 Deposit Guaranty Plaza Jackson MS 39205

HINES, JAMES RICHARD, hosp. adminstr.; b. Many, La., Nov. 19, 1945; s. Lonnie Jefferson and Alice Martha H.; B.S. in Acctg., Northwestern State Coll., Natchitoches, La., 1969; B.S. in Health Care Adminstrn., Okla. Baptist U., 1979; m. Janice Faye Wedgeworth, Sept. 12, 1948; children—Pamela Jean, Tracey Lynn. Controller, Natchitoches Parish Hosp., 1969-75; asst. adminstr. Mission Hill Meml. Hosp., Shawnee, Okla., 1975-78, adminstr., 1978—. Served with U.S. N.G., 1963-69. Mem. Okla. Hosp. Fin. Mgmt. Assn., Shawnee C. of C. Democrat. Baptist. Office: 1900 Gordon Cooper Dr Shawnee OK 74801

HINES, MERRILL ODOM, surgeon; b. Jackson, Miss., Nov. 17, 1909; s. Hulon Hunter and Ava Ione (Odom) H.; B.S., Millsaps Coll., 1931; M.D., Tulane U., 1936; m. Margaret McLaurin Davis, Aug. 24, 1937; children—Margaret Anne, Merrill Odom. Intern, Baroness Erlanger Hosp., Chattanooga, 1936-37, surg. resident, 1937-38, chief surg. resident, 1938-39; staff surgeon Tylertown (Miss.) Hosp., 1939-42; fellow Ochsner Clinic, New Orleans, 1944-45, staff mem., 1945—, chmn. div. colon and rectal surgery, 1945-62, asst. med. dir., 1954-60, bd. mgmt., 1960-75, med. dir., 1960-75; staff Ochsner Found. Hosp., 1945—, pres. staff, 1951-52; asst. prof. clin. surgery Tulane U. Med. Sch., New Orleans, 1949-62, asso. prof. clin. surgery, 1962-64, prof., 1964—; staff surgeon Touro Infirmary, New Orleans, 1953-64; staff Sara Mayo Hosp., New Orleans, 1954-70, Flint-Goodridge Hosp., New Orleans, 1959-70; sr. surgeon La. State Charity Hosp., New Orleans, 1956—; cons. proctologist Ill. Central Hosp., New Orleans, 1960-70. Trustee Alton Ochsner Med. Found., New Orleans, 1966—, pres., 1970-74, chmn. exec. com., 1974-80; bd. dirs. Boy Scouts Am., New Orleans, 1965—; adv. bd. Control Data Corp., 1976—; charter mem. Coordinating Council on Med. Edn., 1972-76; cons. on group practice of medicine Dept. HEW, 1966-70, nat. adv. drug com., 1972-74; mem. Health Ins. Benefits adv. council, 1968-71; bd. regents Inst. for Profl. Standards, 1974-76; chmn. La. Council for Statewide Planning for Physician Manpower, 1977—; mem. La. State Bd. Nurse Examiners, 1962-66, 71-72; mem. La. Statewide Health Coordinating Council, 1976—. Served with USAAF, 1942-44. Recipient Disting. Alumnus award Millsaps Coll., 1967; Disting. Med. Alumnus award Tulane U., 1974; diplomate Am. Bd. Colon and Rectal Surgery (pres. 1961-63). Fellow ACS (chpt. pres. 1972-73); mem. Alton Ochsner Med. Found. Fellows Assn. (1st pres. 1954-56), Alton Ochsner Surg. Soc., Am. Assn. Colon and Rectal Surgeons (pres. 1961-62), Am. Cancer Soc. (dir. 1957—, state dir. 1961—, sec. 1966-67, chpt. pres. 1961-62), Am. Group Practice Assn. (trustee 1966-70), AMA (del. 1972—), C. of C., La. Med. Soc., La. Surg. Soc., Midwest Proctologic Soc., New Orleans Surg. Soc. (dir. 1976-79), Orleans Parish Med. Soc., Pan Am. Med. Assn., Pan-Pacific Surg. Assn., Societe Internationale de Chirurgie, Southeastern Proctologic Soc. (pres. 1954), Southeastern Surg. Congress, So. Med. Assn. Methodist. Clubs: La., Boston, Roundtable. Contbr. articles to med. jours.; editorial bd. Jour. Diseases Colon and Rectum, 1957-77. Home: 1634 Robert St New Orleans LA 70115 Office: 1514 Jefferson Hwy New Orleans LA 70121

HINES, RUBEN LEMUEL, historian; b. Chgo., July 26, 1925; s. William and Bernice (Dixon) H.; B.A., Fayetteville State U., 1973; M.A., N.C. Central U., 1975; m. Carey Newton Jenkins, Jan. 31, 1965. Served to sgt. U.S. Marine Corps, 1949-69, ret., 1969; instr. St. Paul's Coll., Lawrenceville, Va., 1974-75, Fayetteville (N.C.) State U., 1975-76; instr. history and polit. sci. Johnson C. Smith U., Charlotte, N.C., 1977—. Decorated Air medal; J.W. Seabrook scholar, 1972-73. Mem. AAUP, Am. Hist. Assn., Assn. Study Afro-Am. Life and History, NAACP, Afro-Am. Cultural Center, Pi Gamma Mu. Democrat. Baptist. Clubs: Masons, Shriners. Home: 1301 Burnwick Ct Charlotte NC 28213 Office: Johnson C Smith U 100 Beattisford Rd Charlotte NC 28216

HINES, WILLIAM THOMAS, JR., electric co. exec.; b. Neosho, Mo., Nov. 24, 1924; s. William Thomas and Irene C. (Igert) H.; student Abilene Christian U., 1942-43; m. Magenta Embry, June 24, 1945; children—Ilea Kay Hines Reat, William Thomas III. Observer, United Geophys. Co., Pasadena, Calif., 1946-50, Seismic Engring. Co., Dallas, 1951-52; account receivable supr. South Plains Electric Coop., Lubbock, Tex., 1952-65, supr. data processing, 1969—; computer operator lead Clark Equipment Co., Lubbock, 1966-69. Trustee at large Central Tex. Area Museum. Served in U.S. Mcht. Marine, 1943-46. Mem. Data Processing Mgmt. Assn. (pres. W. Tex. chpt. 1972), House of Gordon, South Plain Scottish Soc. (pres.). Democrat. Mem. Ch. of Christ. Home: 228 E 6th St Idalou TX 79329 Office: 110 N Amarillo Rd Lubbock TX 79329

HINESLEY, JOSEPH DOCK, space flight contract specialist; b. Corsicana, Tex., Jan. 29, 1919; s. Dock Shundy and Annie Virginia (Martin) H.; student Tex. A. and M. U., 1936-39, Schreiner Inst., 1940-41; m. Lena Grace Flesher, Apr. 27, 1941; children—Norma Anne, Joseph Dock. Served as enlisted man, U.S. Army, 1941-43, commd. lt., 1943, ret. as maj., 1962; contract specialist NASA, Marshall Space Flight Center, Ala., 1962—. Past deacon, vice chmn. bd. First Christian Ch., Huntsville, Ala., 1954. Mem. Nat. Defense Preparedness Assn., Assn. U.S. Army, Reserve Officers' Assn. (sec. chpt. 20, 1954), Ret. Officers' Assn., Nat. Contract Mgmt. Assn. Democrat. Club: Redstone Arsenal Officers. Home: 5819 Criner Rd SE Huntsville AL 35802

HINKINS, CLYDE ERVIN, pharmacist; b. St. Louis, Sept. 6, 1931; s. Stuart G. and Bernice (Davis) H.; A.A., Jones County Jr. Coll., 1959; student U. Miss., 1959-60; B.S. in Pharmacy, Howard Coll., 1962; m. Abbie Wilkins, Oct. 1, 1955; 1 dau., Dianna Hinkins Loftis. Pharmacist, 1960-76; staff pharmacist Byran W. Whitfield Meml. Hosp., 1976-77, dir. pharm. services, 1977—; preceptor Ala. State Pharmacy, 1977-79; chmn. clin. services com. Hosp. Inservice Ednl. Teaching Staff, 1976-79. Served with USMC, 1947-51. Mem. Am. Pharm. Assn., Ala. Pharm. Assn., Am. Soc. Hosp. Pharmacists, Ala. Hosp. Pharmacists Assn., Am. Legion, Kappa Psi. Baptist. Clubs: Jaycees, Moose. Home: 1611 Greenwood Circle Demopolis AL 36732 Office: Bryan W Whitfield Meml Hosp PO Box 890 Demopolis AL 36732

HINKLE, ALLEN OSCAR, JR., oil co. exec.; b. Lockhart, Tex., Aug. 22, 1919; s. Allen Oscar and Rena Kate (Hearne) H.; B.B.A., U. Tex., 1941; postgrad. Northwestern U., Chgo., 1943, Harvard, 1945; m. Margaret Mae Langham, Apr. 12, 1941; children—Ann Hinkle Cox, Mary Linda Hinkle Cain, Joan Ellen Hinkle McClendon. Auditor, State Tex., 1941-42; with Humble Oil & Refining Co. (name now Exxon Co.), Houston, 1946—, asst. controller, 1974-77, gen. auditor, 1977—; accounting faculty adviser North Tex. U., 1969-72. Mem. Pres. Council, Houston Bapt. Coll., 1968-73; active YMCA. Precinct committeeman, del. Democratic party, Harris County, Tex., 1950-52. Served with USNR, 1943-46. Named Distinguished Alumni, U. Tex. Coll. Bus., 1969. C.P.A., Tex. Mem. Financial Execs. Inst., Am. Inst. C.P.A.'s, Inst. Internal Auditors (mem. research com. 1960-74), Am. Petroleum Inst., Tex. Mid-continent Oil and Gas Assn., Tex. Soc. C.P.A.'s (dir. Houston chpt. 1952-55), Houston C. of C. Baptist (deacon 1957—). Clubs: Petroleum, Racquet (Houston); Lakeway Yacht (Austin, Tex.). Home: 439 Brown Saddle Rd Houston TX 77057 Office: 4031 Exxon Bldg Houston TX 77001

HINKLE, WALTER C., JR., banker; b. Trinity, Miss., Apr. 1, 1936; s. Walter C. and Effie M. (Pratt) H.; B.S. in Indsl. and Personnel Mgmt., Miss. State U.; grad. La. State U. Sch. Banking; grad. comml. bank mgmt. program Columbia U., also Sch. Banking Adminstrn., U. Wis.; advanced cert. Am. Inst. Banking; m. Sharon Bay, Oct. 17, 1958; children—Scott, Leslie. Mgmt. trainee Hancock Bank, Gulfport, Miss., 1958-64, mgr. data processing center, 1964-68, v.p. in charge ops., 1968-77, exec. v.p., adminstr. brs., 1977—. Active United Way. Served to sgt. USMC, 1954-56. Mem. Gulfport C. of C. Methodist. Club: Civitan. Office: 2500 14th St Gulfport MS 39501

HINMAN, STEPHEN MONTGOMERY, pharm. co. exec.; b. Quincy, Calif., June 19, 1932; s. Gage Justus and Gladys Dorothy (Montgomery) H.; student Oakland Jr. Coll., 1956-57; B.S., U. N.D., 1960; m. Carol Ann Schmitz, June 6, 1955; children—Stephen Michael, Elizabeth Ann, David Mark, Alice Irene. Tchr. public schs., Crystal, N.D., 1960-62, St. Theresa's Acad., Boise, Idaho, 1962-63, Borah High Sch., Boise, 1963-64; sales rep. B.F. Ascher, Boise, 1964-67, Smith Miller & Patch Corp., Fresno, Calif., 1967-70; sales rep. USV Pharm. Corp., Fresno, 1970-74, New Orleans, 1974—. Served with USN, 1951-55. Pres., St. Vincent de Paul Soc., 1971-73. Republican. Roman Catholic. Club: K.C. Home: 2157 Holiday Dr New Orleans LA 70114 Office: 1 Scarsdale Rd Tuckahoe NY 10707

HINSEY, VALERIE KORP, educator; b. Watertown, N.Y., June 2, 1925; d. Victor John and Marguerite Amelia (Pecott) Viau; B.A. magna cum laude, Trinity U., 1976, M.Ed. (univ. scholar), 1980; m. Henry John Korp, Apr. 22, 1947; children—Susan Alison, James Douglas; m. 2d, Norris Bruce Hinsey, Jr., Dec. 29, 1976. Tchr. deaf and hard of hearing Regional Day Sch. for the Deaf, San Antonio Ind. Sch. Dist., 1976—, tchr. of deaf and health, sci., career edn. and math., 1978—; interpreter for deaf. Mem. San Antonio Conservation Soc., San Antonio Art League, Alexander Graham Bell Assn. for Deaf, Am. Orgn. for Edn. of Hearing Impaired, NEA, Tex. Tchrs. Assn., San Antonio Tchrs. Council, Am. Personnel and Guidance Assn., Tex. Personnel and Guidance Assn., Mensa. Presbyterian. Clubs: Blue Bird Aux. S.W. Meth. Hosp., Women's Aux. San Antonio Symphony Soc. Home: 7103 Oakridge Dr San Antonio TX 78229 Office: Sam Houston High Sch 4702 E Houston St San Antonio TX 78220

HINSON, ARLIS CLARENCE, JR., clergyman; b. Crystal Springs, Miss., May 20, 1931; s. Arlis Clarence and Susie Etta (Joyner) H.; B.A., Miss. Coll., 1955; M.R.E., So. Bapt. Theol. Sem., 1963; m. Georgia Louise Herrin, May 24, 1959. Ordained to ministry Baptist Ch., 1955; dir. Christian edn. First Bapt. Ch., Elizabethton, Tenn., 1958-59; dir. Rockridge Bapt. Assembly, Franklin, Ga., 1964-68; ch. adminstr. Calvary Bapt. Ch., Washington, 1968-71; mgr. Cedamore Bapt. Assembly, Bagdad, Ky., 1971-77; bus. adminstr. First Bapt. Ch., Shreveport, La., 1977—. Served with U.S. Army, 1951-52. Mem. Nat. Assn. Ch. Bus. Adminstrs. (pres. Ark-La-Tex chpt. 1979—), So. Bapt. Bus. Officers Conf. (ch. chmn. 1979, gen. chmn. 1980), So. Bapt. Assn. Ch. Bus. Adminstrs. (pres. 1979-80). Home: 555 Longleaf Rd Shreveport LA 71106 Office: First Bapt Ch 543 Ockley Dr Shreveport LA 71106

HINSON, DERL JASON, electric co. exec.; b. Loris, S.C., Feb. 2, 1933; s. A. Trenton and Lois Esther (Cox) H.; B.S. in Agrl. Econs., Clemson U., 1959; m. Angelyn Grainger, June 23, 1957; children—Angelyn, Penelope. Field rep. Swift & Co., Greensboro, N.C., 1959-60; staff asst., member service dir. Pee Dee Electric Co-op, Darlington, S.C., Marion dist. mgr. Pee Dee Elec. Membership Corp., 1960-67; dist. mgr. Jackson Electric Membership Corp., Gainesville, Ga., 1967-69; gen. mgr. Morgan County Rural Electric Membership Co-op, Martinsville, Ind., 1969-74; gen. mgr. Lumbee River Electric Membership Corp., Red Springs, N.C., 1974—; pres. Tarheel Electric Membership Assn.; pres. Rural Electric Action Program; chmn. Rural Electric Mgmt. Devel. Council. Chmn. Morgan County United Fund. Recipient Gov.'s Cert. for leadership in energy conservation. Mem. Am. Soc. Agrl. Engrs., C. of C. Robeson County. Democrat. Baptist. Clubs: Masons, Elks; Toastmasters (charter; 1st pres.) (Martinsville). Home: 26 Trinity Dr Lumberton NC 28358 Office: Lumbee River Electric Membership Corp PO Box 830 Red Springs NC 28377

HINSON, HOWARD HOUSTON, petroleum co. exec.; b. Fletcher, Okla., Mar. 3, 1913; s. Jasper Lafayette and Dana (Wunsch) H.; B.S., Tex. Tech Coll., 1934, M.S., 1947; postgrad. Harvard Bus. Sch., 1952-53; m. Louise Lawson, 1934 (dec.); children—Barbara Hinson Brightwell, Larry H.; m. 2d, Doris Lloyd Findley, Feb. 17, 1976. With U.S. Bur. Mines, Amarillo, Tex., 1936-48; chief prodn. engr. Continental Oil Co., Ponca City, Okla., 1948-50, asst. mgr. prodn., 1950-52, v.p. exploration, Houston, 1953-57, v.p., gen. mgr. fgn. ops., N.Y.C., 1957-58, v.p., dir., mem. mgmt. exec. com., 1958-66; pres. Imperial-Am. Mgmt. Co., Houston, 1967-68, dir., 1968-69; cons. Hinson, Hall, Internat. Investments & Cons., Houston, 1967-68, Joseph E. Seagram & Sons., 1971-72; pres., chief exec. officer Tex. Pacific Oil Co., Dallas, 1972-79, chmn., 1979—, dir. fgn. subs. and Am. subs. Recipient Distinguished Engr. award, 1975, Distinguished Alumni award, 1976 (both Tex. Tech U.); registered profl. engr., Tex. Mem. Soc. Petroleum Engrs., Am. Assn. Petroleum Geologists, Am. Petroleum Inst., Petroleum Assn. Am., Mid-Continent Oil and Gas Assn., Dallas Council World Affairs (dir.), Pres.'s Assn. N.Y. Methodist. Clubs: Dallas Petroleum, City, Ramada, Fort Worth. Home: 15625 Preston Rd #1030 Dallas TX 75248 Office: 1700 One Main Pl Dallas TX 75250

HINSON, JON CLIFTON, Congressman; b. Tylertown, Miss., Mar. 16, 1942; B.A., U. Miss., 1964. Adminstrv. asst. to Rep. Charles Griffin, 1968-73, to Rep. Thad Cochran, 1973-77; mem. 96th Congress from 4th Congl. Dist. Miss. Served with USMCR, 1964-70. Republican. Office: Room 1512 Longworth House Office Bldg Washington DC 20515

HINTON, CHARLES ANDERSON, oil and gas co. exec.; b. Humble, Tex., July 1, 1923; s. Will Benton and Clara (Griffin) H.; B.S. in Geol. Engring., Tex. A. and M. U., 1948, B.S. in Petroleum Engring., 1948; m. Margaret Elizabeth Ross, Apr. 14, 1951; children—Charles Anderson, Ross W., David D., Margaret Ann. A founder, chief exec. officer Hinton Prodn. Co., Hinton Drilling Co., Mt. Pleasant, Tex., 1957—; dir. Guaranty Bond State Bank, Mt. Pleasant. Served with C.E., U.S. Army, 1943-46. Decorated Bronze Star. Mem. Am. Assn. Petroleum Geologists, Internat. Assn. Drilling Contractors (dir.), Soc. Ind. Earth Scientists. Episcopalian. Clubs: Mt. Pleasant Country, Dallas Petroleum, Masons, Jesters. Office: 1805 N Jefferson St Mount Pleasant TX 75455

HINTON, DANIELLE MARGARET, spl. edn. tchr.; b. Manhattan, N.Y., Sept. 10, 1942; d. William and Louise (Herman) Hinton; B.A., Dillard U., 1963; M.Ed., U. New Orleans, 1972. Tchr. Headstart New Orleans, 1966-67; elementary tchr. Paul L. Dunbar Sch., New Orleans, 1967, tchr. educable mentally retarded, 1970—; tchr. adult edn., New Orleans, 1967-70. Active Animal Protection Inst. ASPCA. Mem. Council Exceptional Children. Democrat. Roman Catholic. Home: 6973 Salem Dr New Orleans LA 70127 Office: 9330 Forshey St New Orleans LA 70118

HINTON, THOMAS EARL, musician; b. Clarksville, Tenn., July 3, 1925; s. Edgar and Myra (Bumpas) H.; B.Music, George Peabody Coll., 1951, M.Music, 1954, Ph.D., 1969; m. Nora Gardner Smith, Apr. 11, 1953; children—Kem G., Keith E. Mgr. Nashville Symphony Assn., 1952-54; instr. music Nashville pub. schs., 1954-60; prof. music Middle Tenn. State U., Murfreesboro, 1960—; cons. to area schs.; dir. U.S. Office Edn. ESEA Title III project in music, 1971-75; researcher in field. Magistrate, Rutherford County (Tenn.) Ct., 1964-66. Served with U.S. Army, 1946-47. Mem. NEA, Music Educators Nat. Conf., Tenn. Music Educators Assn. (pres. 1978-80), Tenn. Alliance Arts Edn. (chmn. 1977-81). Methodist. Home: 1814 Riverview Dr Murfreesboro TN 37130 Office: Middle Tenn State U Murfreesboro TN 37132

HINZ, REINHOLD H., physician; b. Danzig, Free State of Danzig, Sept. 23, 1930; came to U.S., 1965, naturalized, 1970; m. Franz Ludwig and Margarethe (Kirschnick) H.; M.D., Hamburg U., 1958; M.P.H., U. Calif., Berkeley, 1972; m. Mittie D. Poling, Feb. 23, 1963; children—Michael S., Kristian W. Intern, Heidberg, Hamburg, W. Ger., 1956-58; rotating intern, resident pathology and obstetrics-gynecology Meth. Hosp., Dallas, 1960-63, Parkland Meml. Hosp., Dallas, 1961-62; practice medicine, specializing in obstetrics-gynecology, Lubbock, Tex., 1975—; asst. prof. Tex. Tech. U. Med. Sch., Lubbock, 1976—. Served to col. M.C., U.S. Army, 1967-75. Diplomate Am. Bd. Obstetrics and Gynecology. Fellow Am. Coll. Obstetrics and Gynecology; mem. Am. Public Health Assn., Tex. Med. Assn. Office: 4432 SW Loop 289 Lubbock TX 79413

HINZE, VIRGINIA TAYLOR, counselor; b. Evanston, Ill., Feb. 16, 1932; d. John Taylor and Ethel Irene (Parks) Booz; B.S., U. Houston, 1957, M.Ed., 1961; postgrad. Prairie View A&M U., 1974-79, U. Tex., Austin, 1960-61; m. Victor L. Hinze, Apr. 22, 1960; children—Keith Wayne, Kimberly Anne. Tchr. geography Houston Ind. Schs., 1961-64; reservationist Braniff Airways, 1956-61; vocat. counselor Houston Indsl. Coop. Schs., 1975—; instr. vocat. counseling and supr. Coll. Indsl. Edn., Prairie View (Tex.) A&M U., 1974—. Lay reader Episcopal Ch. Served with USAF, 1951-55, USAFR, 1961-79. Mem. Am. Vocat. Assn., Tex. Indsl. Vocat. Assn., Am. Personnel and Guidance Assn., Iota Lambda Sigma, Gamma Sigma Sigma (nat. v.p.). Home: 8818 Birdwood Rd Houston TX 77074 Office: 1906 Cleburne St Houston TX 77004

HIPP, BETTY JEANE, educator; b. Konawa, Okla., Dec. 27, 1929; d. Jack William and Geneva M. (Miller) Walters; B.S., E. Central U., Ada, Okla., 1950; M.Ed., Central State U., 1967; m. Roy William Hipp, July 27, 1958; 1 son, Mark Wayne. Elementary sch. tchr. Stinnett (Tex.) Sch. Dist., 1950-53; learning disabilities tchr., elementary sch. tchr. Midwest City-Del City Sch. Dist., Okla., 1954-77, prescriptive tchr., 1977—. Certified elementary, home econs. and learning disabilities tchr. Mem. NEA, Okla. Edn. Assn., Assn. Classroom Tchrs., Central Okla. County, Okla. assns. children with learning disabilities. Democrat. Mem. Ch. of Christ. Club: Garden. Home: 3204 Woodlane St Midwest City OK 73110 Office: 607 W Rickenbacker St Midwest City OK 73110

HIPP, DENVER LEE, banker; b. Petersburg, W.Va., May 23, 1945; s. Vernis Carl and Clara (Hanlin) H.; student W.Va. U., 1963-66; m. Patsy Ann Omps, Aug. 15, 1970; children—Christopher Lee, Stacey Diane. Credit mgmt trainee, mgr. loan dept. Md. Nat. Bank, Balt., 1969-71, mgr. Western Med. regional loan offices, Hagerstown, 1971-74; cashier, chief exec. officer Jefferson Security Bank, Shepherdstown, W.Va., 1974—. Served with USN, 1966-69; Vietnam. Decorated Navy Commendation medal. Mem. W.Va. Bankers Assn. (past chmn., group rep. Group IX), Am. Inst. Banking, W.Va. Bd. Realtors. Democrat. Methodist. Clubs: Kiwanis, Masons. Home: PO Box 7 Shepherdstown WV 25443 Office: PO Box 35 Shepherdstown WV 25443

HIPP, HOWELL EDSEL, sch. adminstr.; b. Saluda, S.C., Mar. 2, 1925; s. Wilbert Ariel and Willie Mae (Fulmer) H.; A.B., Wofford Coll., 1949; M. Edn., Furman U., 1956; postgrad. U. Ga., summers 1963-66; m. June Annise Cloyd, Jan. 1, 1950; children—Rodney, Stanley. Prin., Inman (S.C.) Elem. Sch., 1950-53, prin. high sch., 1953-54; prin. Inman Jr. High Sch., 1954-55, Chapman High Sch., Inman, 1955-56; dir. instrn. Dist. One Schs., Spartanburg County, S.C., 1956-68, supt. schs., 1968—. Cons. S.C. Migrant Edn., 1970-72; mem. S.C. Textbook Com., 1967-69; counselor Epworth Children's Home, 1949-50; mem. Spartanburg County White House Conf. on Children and Youth, 1970; mem. S.C. Com. for Funding under Title 6, Elementary Sch. Edn. Act, 1970-74; chmn. edn. Spartanburg County United Fund, 1967, 78; 2d v.p. Region XII PTA Council; mem. S.C. adv. com. for tchr. certification S.C. Dept. Edn., 1973-77. Bd. dirs. Charles Lee Center for Handicapped Children, Spartanburg County Speech and Hearing Clinic, Spartanburg County Tech. Edn. Center; mem. Spartanburg County Bd. Developmental Disabilities and Mental Retardation, 1978—, Spartanburg United Council, 1979—. Served with USNR, 1943-46. Mem. Spartanburg County Supts. Assn. (chmn., 1971-72, 78-79), S.C. Instrnl. TV Adv. Council (chmn. 1971-72, regional chmn. 1967-73), Nat., S.C., Spartanburg County (pres. 1955-56) edn. assns., Am., S.C. assns. sch. adminstrs. Methodist (chmn. bd. 1971-72, lay speaker 1970—; bd. pensions 1974—). Rotarian (pres. local club 1973-74). Home: 25 W Miller St Inman SC 29349 Office: Box 218 Campobello SC 29322

HIPP, WILLIAM HAYNE, ins. co. exec.; b. Greenville, S.C., Mar. 11, 1940; s. Francis Moffett and Mary Matilda (Looper) H.; B.A., Washington and Lee U., Lexington, Va., 1962; M.B.A., Wharton Sch.,

U. Pa., 1965; grad. program mgmt. devel., Harvard U., 1971; m. Anna Kate Reid, June 14, 1963; children—Mary Henigan, Francis Reid, Anna Hayne. With Met. Life Ins. Co., 1965-69; with Liberty Life Ins. Co., Greenville, S.C., 1969—, exec. v.p., 1977-79, chmn. bd., 1979—; chmn. exec. com., dir. United Fidelity Life Ins. Co., Dallas, 1979—; vice chmn., chief exec. officer Liberty Corp., 1979—; dir. Cosmos Broadcasting Co., Columbia, S.C., 1977, Greater Ariz. Savs. & Loan Assn., Phoenix, 1979—, S.C. Nat. Bank, Columbia, Textile Hall, Greenville. Trustee, vice chmn. Nat. Urban League, 1979—; chmn. Greenville County Devel. Bd., 1978—; trustee Greenville County Found., 1978—, Greenville County Sch. System, 1975—; pres. Greenville Met. YMCA, 1979—. C.L.U. Home: 1 Bonaventure Dr Greenville SC 29615 Office: PO Box 789 Greenville SC 29602

HIPPERLING, RONALD CHARLES, elec. engr.; b. Englewood, N.J., July 4, 1947; s. Charles Paul and Ruth Maxine (Fischer) H.; B.Engring., Stevens Inst. Tech., 1969; m. Ida Lyvonne Parsons, July 6, 1974; 1 son, Jonathan Paul. Devel. engr. Norden div. United Aircraft Co., Norwalk, Conn., 1969-70; project engr. Martin Marietta Co., Ocala, Fla., 1970-75; with Avionics div. Bendix Corp., Ft. Lauderdale, Fla., 1975—, now sr. quality-reliability engr. Republican. Roman Catholic. Home: 7516 NW 42d Ct Coral Springs FL 33065 Office: Bendix Avionics Div 2100 NW 62d St Fort Lauderdale FL 33310

HIPSCHER, JEROME JAY, govt. ofcl.; b. Bklyn., May 9, 1932; s. Charles and Helen (Blumberg) H.; student Collegiate Bus. Inst., 1954-56; A.A., Queensborough Community Coll., 1978; m. Joan Miller, Nov. 6, 1960; children—Marla, Philip, Hara. Accounting clk. Nat. Screen Service Corp., N.Y.C., 1956-58; clk. N.Y. State Dept. Motor Vehicles, N.Y.C., 1958-59; bulk clk. U.S. Post Office, Jamaica, N.Y., 1959—. With Am. Postal Workers Union, Jamaica, 1959—, adminstrv. aide, 1970—; legis. aide to State Senator John Santucci, N.Y.C., 1972-74; mem. N.Y.C. 208 Council, 1976—. Founder, chmn. Arverne Community Relations Com., N.Y.C., 1968; founder, pres. Rockaway Cultural Soc., N.Y.C., 1969-73, v.p., 1974—; founder, chmn. Rockaway Friends Queensborough Community Coll., N.Y.C., 1973-74; founder, pres. Jamaica Bay Council, N.Y.C., 1968-74; mem. Queens Borough Pres.'s Planning Bd., 1969-71; founder Bay Environ. Action Com., N.Y.C., 1973; mem. Mayors' Subway Watchdog Commn., N.Y.C., 1970-74; chmn. transp. Rockaway Health Council, N.Y.C., 1969-74; adviser Southshore Mental Health Assn., N.Y.C., 1973-74, N.Y. State Dept. Environ. Conservation, 1978; founding mem. Far Rockaway chpt. Am. Cancer Soc., N.Y.C., 1972-74; mem. N.Y.C. Human Resources Devel., 1973-74; founder Rockaway br. Queens Borough Community Coll., Gateway Park E; chmn. Rockaway com. Muscular Dystrophy Assn., N.Y.C., 1974—; founding mem. Rockaway Blood Bank, N.Y.C., 1971-74, treas., 1972-73; founding chmn. Rockaway Transp. Council, N.Y.C., 1968-74; mem. bd. St. Joseph Hosp., N.Y.C., 1970-73; edn. adviser Beach Channel High Sch., N.Y.C., 1973-74; mem. N.Y.C. Citizens Com., 1975—, N.Y.C. Solid Waste Task Force, 1976—, Community Planning Bd., 1976-78; vol. mem. Peninsula Vol. Ambulance Corps, 1975—; N.Y.C. aux. air pollution enforcement patrolman; a founder Gateway Council on Arts, 1975, Council on Prevention Services, 1976; grants writer polit., environ. and arts programs, 1970—; active various environ. projects. Served with AUS, 1950-52. Recipient Spl. award of merit EPA, 1975; Pres.'s Environment award, 1978; N.Y. State Dept. Edn. grantee, 1972; N.Y. Council on Arts grantee, 1970. Mem. Nat. Environ. Health Assn., Inst. Hazardous and Solid Waste, Nat. Geog. Soc., Nature Conservancy, Sierra Club. Democrat. Club: K.P. Home: 20-25 NE 168 St North Miami Beach FL 33162 Office: Gen Post Office Jamaica NY 11431

HIRD, JOHN MEEK, mining exec.; b. Simcoe, Ont., Can., Dec. 18, 1932; came to U.S., 1961, naturalized, 1971; s. James Clifford and Averil Minerva (Meek) H.; mining diploma Haileybury Sch. Mines, 1958; B.S. in Geol. Engring., B.S. in Engring. Adminstrn. Instrs., Mich. Coll. Mining and Tech., 1961; m. Karen Estell, Nov. 19, 1960; children—John, Suzanne, Julie. Geol. engr. Allied Chem. Corp., Syracuse, N.Y., 1961-65; geol. engr. Texasgulf, Inc., Aurora, N.C., 1965-74, mine supt., 1974-77, mgr. mining, 1977—. Chmn. Beaufort County Planning Bd., 1974-75. Registered profl. geologist, N.C. Mem. East Carolina Engring. Club (sec.-treas.), AIME, Am. Inst. Petroleum Geologists. Methodist. Home: PO Box 298 Aurora NC 27806 Office: Box 48 Aurora NC 27806

HIRL, JOSEPH PETER, constrn. co. exec.; b. Mishawaka, Ind., June 22, 1937; s. Joseph Louis and Marie Barbara H.; B.S. in Elec. Engring., U. Notre Dame, 1959; M.S., George Washington U., 1970; m. Margaret Ellen McLemore, June 16, 1962; children—Joseph P., Patrick J., Jeanne Marie (dec.). Engr. instr. Hughes Aircraft Corp., Fullerton, Calif., 1962-64; product engr. Aeronutronics, Newport Beach, Calif., 1964-65; program mgr. Tracor, Inc., Washington, 1965-66; dept. mgr. Westinghouse Electric Corp., Balt., 1966-71, div. mgr., Balt., 1974-75, Middle East area programs mgr. subs. TCOM Corp., Columbia, Md., 1976—; pres. Antares Enterprises Ltd., Fairfax Station, Va., 1971—; div. mgr. Miller and Smith, Inc., McLean, Va., 1971-74. Pres., Summerwind Homes Assn., 1977. Served as officer USN, 1959-62. Holloway scholar, 1955-59; White House fellow, 1971; Dept. Def. Mgmt. fellow, 1971. Mem. IEEE. Roman Catholic. Club: Fairfax Country. Address: 10526 Summerwind Ln Fairfax Station VA 22039

HIRSCH, PHILIP FRANCIS, pharmacologist, research adminstr., educator; b. Stockton, Calif., June 24, 1925; s. Harold and Elsa (Frohman) H.; B.S. in Chemistry, U. Calif., Berkeley, 1950; Ph.D. in Physiology, 1954; m. Eugenia Isaeff, Sept. 21, 1956; children—Steven, Lisa, Kenneth, Nancy. Lectr. physiology U. Calif., Berkeley, 1954-55; instr. pharmacology Harvard U. Sch. Dental Medicine, 1955-57, asso. pharmacologist, 1957-63, asst. prof. pharmacology, 1964; physiologist Lawrence Radiation Lab., U. Calif., Livermore, 1964-66; asso. prof. pharmacology U. N.C. Sch. Medicine, Chapel Hill, 1966-70, prof., 1970—, dir. Dental Research Center, 1975—; USPHS spl. research fellow dept. biochemistry Brandeis U., 1958-59; Kenan leave Faculte de Medecin, Hopital St. Antoine, U. Paris, 1974-75. Served with AUS, 1943-46. Mem. AAAS, Endocrine Soc. Am., Am. Soc. Pharmacology and Exptl. Therapeutics, Am. Soc. Bone and Mineral Research, Internat. Soc. Dental Research, AAUP, Sigma Xi. Home: 2008 S Lake Shore Dr Chapel Hill NC 27514 Office: Dental Research Center 210H U NC Chapel Hill NC 27514

HIRSH, ALBERT, concert pianist; b. Chgo., July 1, 1915; s. Louis and Sonia (Weinberg) H.; studied under Djane Lavoie-Herz; m. Mildred Rigby Wile, May 18, 1937; children—Oliver, Conrad, Ethan. Concert pianist, 1933—; performances throughout U.S., Canada, Mexico, West Indies and Europe; prof. music, artist-in-residence U. Houston, 1950—; mem. faculty Am. Inst. Mus. Studies, Graz, Austria, 1974—. Mem. Municipal Art Commn. Houston, 1966-71; mem. advisory council Miller Theatre, Houston, 1972. Served with U.S. Army, 1944-46. Mem. AAUP, AFL-CIO, Phi Mu Alpha, Phi Kappa Phi. Jewish. Home: 5711 Jackwood St Houston TX 77096 Office: School of Music University of Houston Houston TX 77004

HISEY, FRANZ LAMAR, hosp. adminstr.; b. Cin., July 25, 1927; s. John Paul and Hedy Elizabeth (Hartman) H.; student U. Chattanooga, 1947-48; m. Lollie Peeples, Nov. 8, 1953; children—Haven, Hal. Ch. adminstr. First Cumberland Presbyn. Ch., Chattanooga, Tenn., 1955-70; v.p. John L. Hutcheson Meml. Tri-County Hosp., Ft. Oglethorpe, Ga., 1970—; bd. dirs. Chattanooga/Hamilton County Health Dept., Tb and Respiratory Disease Assn.; chmn. bd., pres. United Cerebral Palsy. Bd. dirs. Chattanooga Conv. and Visitors Bur.; mem., sec. to bd. deacons 1st Cumberland Presbyn. Ch. Served with USNR, 1945-46, USAF, 1950-51. Recipient state and nat. hosp. public relations awards including: Malcolm T. MacEachern Nat. award Acad. Hosp. Public Relations, 1978; fellow in ch. adminstrn. Mem. Am. Hosp. Assn., Nat. Assn. Hosp. Devel. (accredited), Ga. Hosp. Assn. (mem. council on manpower and edn.), Ga. Hosp. Assn. Public Relations Soc. (pres. 1976, 77). Club: Masons. Home: 317 Bass Rd Chattanooga TN 37421 Office: John L Hutcheson Meml Tri-County Hosp 100 Gross Crescent Fort Oglethorpe GA 30742

HISLE, WENDELL LEON, JR., librarian; b. Danville, Ky., Mar. 26, 1950; s. Wendell Leon and Betty Jean (Cundiff) H.; student Ripon Coll., 1967-69; B.A. in English, Berea Coll., 1971; M.S.L.S., U. Ky., 1973; m. Susan Whitson, Nov. 24, 1968; children—Keri Sumiko, Emily Jean. Head librarian, media specialist Henderson Community Coll. Library, Henderson, Ky., 1973-76; library dir. Lexington (Ky.) Tech. Inst. Library, 1976-80; dir. Library Resource Center, Austin (Tex.) Community Coll., 1980—; mem. Task Force on Library Personnel Edn. for Gov.'s Pre-White House Conf. on Libraries and Info. Services, 1978. Mem. ALA, Assn. Ednl. Communications and Tech., Ky. Library Assn. (chmn. acad. library sect. 1980), Ky. Assn. Communications Tech., Southeastern Library Assn., Phi Kappa Phi, Sigma Alpha Epsilon. Home: 363 Transylvania Park Lexington KY 40508 Office: LRC Rio Grande Campus Austin Community College Austin TX 78768

HISSONG, JERRY BRUCE, profl. devel. mgr.; b. Rudolph, Ohio, July 6, 1935; s. Bruce M. and Maude (Wickard) H.; B.A., Bowling Green State U., 1957; M.S.W., Ohio State U., 1961; m. Gloria E. Thurston, Sept. 7, 1957; children—Robin, Andrea, Stephanie, Mark, Courtney. Supt., Woodsbend Boys Camp, West Liberty, Ky., 1964-65; asst. supt. Ky. Village, Lexington, 1965-67; supt. Ormsby Village Treatment Center, Louisville, 1967-73; commr. Ky. Bur. Social Services, Frankfort, 1973-76; project mgr., cons. Am. Public Welfare Assn., Washington, 1976—. Served with U.S. Army, 1957-59; now col. USAR. Mem. Nat. Assn. Social Workers (named Social Worker of Yr. Ky. chpt. 1974), Am. Public Welfare Assn., Nat. Conf. Social Welfare. Baptist. Home: 2335 Riviera Dr Vienna VA 22180 Office: 1125 15th St NW Suite 300 Washington DC 20005

HITCHCOCK, CHARLES HELTON, chem. engr.; b. Alexandria, Va., Jan. 26, 1944; s. Claude Zelmer and Dorothy Elizabeth (Helton) H.; B.S., Va. Poly. Inst., 1967; M.B.A., Golden Gate Coll., 1970; m. Carol Ann Lee, June 11, 1967; children—Susanne Lee, Stephanie Lee, Joanna Lee. Chem. operator Union Carbide Corp., Charleston, W.Va., summer 1964; asst. dept. supt. Tenn. Eastman Co., Kingsport, 1976—. Asst. pastor Ind. Protestant Ch., 1971-77; youth dir. So. Baptist Ch., 1978-79. Served with USAF, 1967-71. Mem. Am. Inst. Chem. Engrs., Chem. Supervisory Club. Club: Moose. Patentee sensitive solid propellant valve. Home: Rt 7 Box 345 Jonesboro TN 37659 Office: Tenn Eastman Co Eastman Rd Kingsport TN 37660

HITCHMAN, CAL MCDONALD, marketing exec.; b. Houston, July 9, 1948; s. Robert McDonald and Isabel Mary (Shugert) H.; B.A. in History, Houston Bapt. U., 1972; cert. U. Houston, 1979; cert. cashiering Western Mich. U., 1976; m. Darlene Ann Cox, Dec. 17, 1969; 1 son, Cal McDonald. Mgr. store Rice Food Markets, Inc., Houston, 1969-72, dist. front end supr., 1972-76, tng. dir., 1976; program mgr. food mktg. Houston Ind. Sch. Dist., 1976—, coordinator distributive edn., 1976—. Mem. Nat. Assn. Distributive Edn. Tchrs., Distributive Edn. Clubs Am., Am. Vocat. Assn., Tex. State Tchrs. Assn., Tex. Assn. Distributive Edn. Tchrs., Alumni Assn. Houston Bapt. U. (dir. 1974-75, chmn. 1975-76), Kappa Alpha, Phi Kappa Epsilon. Methodist. Home: 4907 Falvey St Houston TX 77017 Office: 11625 Martindale Houston TX 77048

HITE, ETHERLENE MCCOY, educator; b. Meridian, Miss., Dec. 23, 1942; d. Floyd and Juanita (Croon) McCoy; B.S. in Edn., Stillman Coll., Tuscaloosa, Ala., 1966; m. Toby Hite III; children—Cherri Elizabeth, Fanita Delorns, Eric Charles, Michael Dean, Christi Lorena. Tchr. elementary sch. phys. edn. East End Elementary Sch., Tuscaloosa, 1966; tchr.-coach Magnolia Jr. High Sch., Meridian, 1966-69, Parrish Jr. High Sch., Hazlehurst, Miss., 1969-73; drug edn. coordinator, tchr. Hazlehurst Municipal Separated schs., 1973—. Adviser, leader Explorer Scouts, 1972—; mem. Copiah County Alcohol Council, 1975—; neighborhood chmn. Girl Scouts, asst. Brownie leader, asst. Cadette troop leader, council trainer; tchr. young adult Sunday sch. class, Bible class. Mem. NEA, Miss. Tchrs. Assn. Recipient Leaders award Boy Scouts Am. Home: 112 Miller St Hazlehurst MS 39083 Office: PO Box 889 Hazlehurst MS 39083

HITE, JANE WALKER SMITH, nurse; b. Frankfort, Ky., Dec. 7, 1942; d. Robert Walker and Katherine (Diamond) Smith; A.D., Georgetown Coll., 1961; B.A. with distinction, Ky. State U., 1977; m. Ronald M. Hunter, Aug. 12, 1961 (dec.); children—Robert Cecil, Rhonda Carol; m. 2d, Jack Keith Hite, Apr. 10, 1976; stepchildren—Hugh Edward, Leigh Ann. Clk., clk. typist, clk. stenographer Commonwealth of Ky., Frankfort, 1961-73; sec., dept. human resources Vol. Services, Frankfort, 1974-75; nosologist Dept. Human Resources Med. Assistance, Frankfort, 1977-78, nurse, drug pre-authorization program, 1978—. Served with N.G., 1973-80. Mem. Ky. Nurses Assn., Am. Bus. Women's Assn. (pres. 1974-75), Enlisted Assn. N.G. Ky., Air Force Sgts. Assn., Air Force Assn. Democrat. Home: 201 Woodhill Ln Frankfort KY 40601

HITT, HAROLD HAMILTON, supt. schs.; b. Burleson, Tex., Sept. 7, 1911; s. Joseph Brown and Elizabeth Ann (Griffith) H.; B.S., N. Tex. State U., 1933, M.S., 1942, Ed.D., 1953; postgrad. U. Tex., 1947-50, So. Meth. U., 1947-50, Columbia U. Tchrs. Coll., summer 1956; m. Veda Elizabeth Trammell, Dec. 25, 1938 (dec. 1972); children—Harold Merritt, Elizabeth Hitt Burks, Warren Trammell; m. 2d, Sara Williamson, June 15, 1974. Tchr. pub. schs., Cotton Center, Tex., 1933-35, Newton, Tex., 1935-36, Mosheim, Tex., 1936-37, Farmers Valley, Tex., 1937-39; area dir. Nat. Youth Adminstrn., Palestine, Tex., 1939-40; coordinator vis. tchr. program Dallas Ind. Sch. Dist., 1941-47; prin. Longfellow Jr. High Sch., Dallas, 1947-53; asst. supt. instrn. Midland (Tex.) Ind. Sch. Dist., 1953-55, supt., 1955-68; supt. San Antonio Ind. Sch. Dist., 1968—. Vis. prof. So. Meth. U., 1949-53; chmn. State Com. for Study Social Studies Curriculum, 1949, State Textbook Com., 1961; mem. Gov.'s Com. on Pub. Edn., 1966. Exec. com. Buffalo Trail council Boy Scouts Am., 1964; bd. dirs. Community Chest, 1963-67, Midland YMCA, 1964-66, United Way, 1961-67. Mem. C. of C. (dir. 1960-63), Nat. Soc. for Study Edn., Tex. Tchrs. Assn., Am., Tex. assns. sch. adminstrs., Phi Delta Kappa. Methodist. Mason, Rotarian. Club: Exchange. Home: 3812 Lomita St San Antonio TX 78230 Office: 141 Lavaca St San Antonio TX 78210

HITT, HERBERT DAN, clergyman; b. Waxahachie, Tex., Feb. 5, 1935; s. James Cleveland and Emily Louisa (Alday) H.; B.A., Baylor U., 1958, Brite Div. Sch., 1958-59; student Perkins Sch. Theology, 1955; m. Hazel LaWanda Sims, June 20, 1953; children—LaWanda Ann, Michael Dan, Janyce Kay. Ordained to ministry Meth. Ch., 1950; pastor chs., Waxahachie, 1950-52, Waco, Tex., 1952-58, Graham, Tex., 1958-59, Breckenridge, Tex., 1959-62, Brownwood, Tex., 1962-64, Ft. Worth, 1968-75, Cleburne, Tex., 1975-77; pastor/adminstr. Saginaw (Tex.) United Meth. Ch., 1977—; owner H. H. Rubber Stamp Service, Saginaw, 1976—. Recipient various awards Lions Clubs and C. of C. of Breckenridge, Saginaw, Waco. Mem. Saginaw C. of C., Central Tex. Ann. Conf. United Meth. Ch. Republican. Club: Lions (v.p. 1979—). Home: 500 Opal St Saginaw TX 76179 Office: PO Box 79100 200 S Bluebonnet St Saginaw TX 76179

HITT, MART NEWMAN, JR., rancher; b. Buckholts, Tex., Oct. 2, 1911; s. Mart N. and Nannie Lynn (Hill) H.; B.S., E. Tex. State U., 1936, M.S., 1942; m. Margy Leopheal McGee, Aug. 22, 1935; children—Raymond William, George Preston. Coach, tchr. Brownsboro (Tex.) High Sch., 1936-38; prin., coach Frisco (Tex.) High Sch., 1938-40; supt. Frisco Ind. Sch. Dist., 1940-42; dean Buckner Orphans Home, Dallas, 1946-47; supt. Wilmer-Hutchins Ind. Sch. Dist., Hutchins, Tex., 1947-64, Pine Tree Ind. Sch. Dist., Longview, Tex., 1964-77; ret., 1977; rancher, Lindale, Tex., 1977—. Mem. Longview Zoning Bd., 1964-77; bd. dirs. YMCA, Longview, 1966-68. Served as lt. comdr. USN, 1944-46. Mem. Tex. Tchrs. Assn., Tex. Assn. Sch. Adminstrs., Am. Assn. Sch. Adminstrs., Am. Red Angus Assn., Tex. and Southwestern Cattle Raisers Assn., Phi Delta Kappa. Baptist. Club: Rotary (pres. 1969-70). Home: Route 4 Box 919 Lindale TX 75771

HIXON, ROBERT CHARLES, ret. army officer; b. Camp Bragg, N.C., Feb. 12, 1922; s. Charles Edward and Edna Grace (Wickham) H.; student Mich. State U., 1942; B.S., U. Md., 1958; M.A., George Washington U., 1960; m. Frances Peele Acree, Dec. 14, 1945; children—Robert Charles, Thomas Edward, James Andrew, William Oliver. Commd. 2d lt. U.S. Army, 1943, advanced through grades to maj. gen., 1972; exec. officer hdqrs. battery comdr. 309 F.A. Bn., Europe, 1943-45; instr. F.A. Sch., Fort Sill, Okla., 1947-49; staff officer, exec. officer 555 F.A. Bn., 5th Regiment Combat Team, Korea, 1953-54; spl. asst. to dep. chief of staff for personnel Dept. Army, 1958-60; comdr. 2d Bn., 16th Arty., 4th Armored Div., Ger., 1961-63; liaison officer, legis. asst. Asst. Sec. Def., 1964-65, exec. officer, 1966-67; comdr. 46th F.A. Group, Fort Carson, Colo., 1967-68; mil. asst. to Sec. Def., 1968-69; comdr. 24th Corps Arty., Vietnam, 1969-70; chief of staff, 1970-71; comdg. gen. Fort Jackson, S.C., 1972-74; comdr. Mil. Assistance Command, Thailand, 1974-75; chief of staff Hdqrs., Army Tng. and Doctrine Command, Fort Monroe, Va., 1975-79; ret., 1979; pres. Assembly Against Hunger and Malnutrition; mem. Va. Task Force on Food and Nutrition Policy. Decorated D.S.M. with oak leaf cluster, Silver Star, Legion of Merit with 2 oak leaf clusters, D.F.C., Air medal with V and 17 oak leaf clusters, Bronze Star with oak leaf cluster; Order of Mil. Merit (Korea); Nat. Order Vietnam (5th Class), Cross Gallantry with palm (Vietnam). Mem. U.S. Parachutist Assn., Assn. U.S. Army, Nat. Rifle Assn., Sigma Alpha Epsilon (pres. local chpt.). Episcopalian. Home: 121 James Landing Rd Newport News VA 23606

HLAVINKA, ANTHONY CHARLES, farmer, farm orgn. exec.; b. East Bernard, Tex., Sept. 1, 1947; s. Frank Charles and Lillian (Poessel) H.; B.S., Tex. A. and M. U., 1970; m. Phyllis Arlt, July 26, 1968; children—Brian Charles, Stephen Jacob, Thomas Frank. Agrl. engr. GS-7, Soil Conservation Service, Rosenberg, Tex., 1970-72, agrl. engr. GS-9, Bryan, Tex., 1972-74; treas. F.C. Hlavinka & Sons, Inc., East Bernard, Tex., 1974—; dir. Am. Rice Inc. Bd. dirs. E. Bernard Farmers Coop.; Registered profl. engr., Tex. Mem. Am. Soc. Agrl. Engrs., Am. Grain Assn., Am. Rice Growers Assn., Tex. Soc. Profl. Engrs., Tex. Farmers Union (pres. Wharton-Lower Colorado County, dir.), S. Tex. Cotton and Grain Assn. (dir.). Democrat. Roman Catholic. Club: K.C. Home: PO Box 27 East Bernard TX 77435 Office: Route 2 Box 36 East Bernard TX 77435

HO, MINH VUONG, physician; b. Mytho, South Vietnam, May 7, 1940; s. Chanh Vanand An Thi (Vuong) H.; Baccalaureate, Lycee Chasseloup Laubat, Saigon, 1958; M.D., U. Saigon, 1965; came to U.S., 1975, permanent resident, 1977; m. Hanh Thi Tran, Dec. 20, 1962; children—Nghiem Uy, Nghi Thanh, Thanh Trang, Trang Xuan. Resident in gen. and hand surgery Cong Hoa Gen. Hosp., Saigon, 1967-69; practice medicine, Saigon, 1965-67, 69-75; practice family medicine, Bronte, Tex., 1977-78, Houston, 1979—; mem. staff West Coke County Hosp., Robert Lee, Tex., Center Pavilion Hosp., Houston, Med. Arts Hosp., Houston. Diplomate Am. Bd. Family Practice. Fellow Am. Acad. Family Physicians; mem. AMA (Physicians Recognition award 1981), Harris Med. Soc., Tex. Med. Assn., Am. Coll. Emergency Physicians, Am. Heart Assn., Am. Acad. Family Practice. Baptist. Office: 1215 Walker St Suite 1024 Houston TX 77002

HO, THOMAS TONG-YUN, geologist; b. Taichung, Taiwan, China, July 2, 1931; s. Chin-tui and Wan-Hsi (Hseih) H.; B.S., Nat. Taiwan U., 1955; M.A., U. Kans., 1961, Ph.D., 1964; m. Yvonne Y.C. Lai, June 1, 1963; children—Anthony C.M., Victor S.P. Came to U.S., 1958, naturalized, 1972. Research asst. U. Kans., Lawrence, 1958-62; research asso. U. Ariz., Tucson, 1964-67; vis. scientist U. Calif. at Los Angeles, 1967; sr. research geologist Exxon Prodn. Research Co., Houston, 1967-75; group leader, sr. research asso. Conoco, Inc., Ponca City, Okla., 1975—. Served to lt. Army Rep. China, 1955-56. Fellow Geol. Soc. Am.; mem. A.A.A.S., Am. Geophys. Union, Geochem. Soc., Am. Assn. Petroleum Geologists (tech. program com. Offshore Tech. Conf.), Sigma Xi. Contbr. articles to profl. jours. Home: 2409 Hummingbird Ln Ponca City OK 74601 Office: PO Box 1267 Ponca City OK 74601

HO, YHI-MIN, educator; b. Nanking, China, Nov. 18, 1934; came to U.S., 1958, naturalized, 1972; s. Yung-Tung and Hsing-In Ho; B.A. in Econs., Nat. Taiwan U., 1955; M.S. in Econs., Utah State U., 1961; Ph.D. in Econs., Vanderbilt U., 1965; m. Shu-Fen Ma, Nov. 23, 1962; children—Andrew M., Katherine. Mem. managerial staff mktg. div. Chinese Petroleum Corp., 1955-58; asst. prof. U. So. Miss., 1963-65, U. Houston, 1965-66, Tulane U., New Orleans, 1966-70; chmn. dept. eccns. and bus. adminstrn. U. St. Thomas, Houston, 1970—, acting dean Cameron Sch. Bus., 1978—. Pres., Assn. Concerned Am.-Chinese Professionals, 1979—; bd. dirs. Chinese Community Center, Inc., Houston, 1979—; mem. Council Chinese Orgns., Houston, 1977—; bd. dirs. United Supporters for Republic of China, 1978-79; mem. adminstrv. bd. Westbury United Meth. Ch., Houston, 1976-79, Houston-Taipei Soc., Inc., 1978—. Ford scholar, 1960-61, Rockefeller fellow, 1961-63, NSF research grantee, 1973-75. Mem. Am. Econ. Assn., So. Econ. Assn., Western Econ. Assn. Author: Agricultural Development of Taiwan, 1903-1960, 1966; contbr. articles in field to profl. jours. Office: Univ St Thomas 3812 Montrose Blvd Houston TX 77006

HOADLEY, FLOYD CROSWELL, oil co. exec.; b. St. Clair Shores, Mich., July 9, 1928; s. Floyd and Ann Wilson (Trice) H.; B.A. in Geology, UCLA, 1951; m. Sheila Adams, June 24, 1953; children—David, Craig, Ann, Steven. Geologist, Mene Grande Oil Co., Venezuela, 1951-60, dist. geologist, 1960-67, exploration mgr., Caracas, 1972-75; exploration mgr. Cabinda Gulf Oil Co., Angola, 1967-68; Argentine Gulf Oil Co., Buenos Aires, 1969-70, Gulf Oil

Co.-Latin Am., Coral Gables, Fla., 1970-72; v.p. regional exploration Africa and Latin Am., Gulf Oil Exploration & Prodn. Co. Internat., Houston, 1975—. Served with U.S. Army, 1954-56. Mem. AIME, Geol. Soc. Am. Republican. Clubs: Houston Plaza, Met. Tennis. Office: 712 Main St Houston TX 77001

HOBBS, BRENDA CASTILLE, speech-lang. pathologist; b. Breaux Bridge, La., Oct. 1, 1950; d. Felix Peco and Elsie (Hollier) Castille; B.A., La. State U., 1971, M.S., 1974; m. William M. Hobbs, Feb. 14, 1975. Speech pathologist Concordia Parish (La.) Sch. Bd., 1972-74; instr., lang./speech diagnostician U. Southwestern La., Lafayette, 1974-76; evaluation specialist Miss. Learning Resources System, Brookhaven, 1976-77; state cons. lang.-speech-hearing services, coordinator univ.-based programs Miss. Dept. Edn., Jackson, 1977—; adj. prof. speech-lang. pathology U. So. Miss., Hattiesburg, 1977—; mem. Adv. Council for Licensure of Speech Pathologists in Miss., 1979—. Adv. com. Community Services Program for Deaf of Miss., 1978-79; coordinator task force Miss. Plan for Deaf, 1978-79; planning com. ann. conf. Services for Deaf Mississippians, 1977—. Clin. cert. in speech pathology Am. Speech and Hearing Assn., 1976—; cert. tchr. deaf edn., Miss., lic. speech and hearing specialist, Miss., La. Mem. Am. Speech and Hearing Assn., Miss. Speech and Hearing Assn. (editor publ. 1977—, exec. bd. 1977—), Council Advs. in Speech Pathology, Council of Exceptional Children, Council of State Dept. Edn. Speech Pathology and Hearing Impaired Consultants. Democrat. Roman Catholic. Clubs: Civitan, Capitol Bus. and Profl. Women's. Office: Spl Edn Sect Miss Dept Edn PO Box 771 Jackson MS 39205

HOBBS, KENNETH BURKETT, museum adminstr.; b. Appalachia, Va., Dec. 18, 1927; s. Earl Kaylor and Mary Katherine (Horner) H.; B.S., Auburn U., 1956, M.S., 1959; postgrad. Ohio State U., 1959-60, U. Wash., 1971; hon. degree, London Inst. Applied Research, 1973; m. Faye Rollins, Oct. 21, 1950; 1 son, G. Bradford. Producer ednl. TV, Auburn (Ala.) U., 1956-59, instr. TV courses in physics, 1957-58; exec. sec. Ohio Acad. Sci., Columbus, 1959-61; chief media devel. NASA, Washington, 1961-63; sr. adminstrv. asst. Battelle Labs., Columbus, Ohio, 1963-66; adminstrv. officer Battelle Research Center, Seattle, 1966-70, staff mgr. adminstrn., 1970-71; dir. Detroit Sci. Center, Inc., 1972-73; exec. v.p. John Young Mus., Orlando, Fla., 1973—. Chmn. Evangeline Residence Bd., Salvation Army, Seattle, 1969-70; mem. adv. council Franklin County Child Welfare Bd., Ohio, 1959-60; trustee Columbus Center of Sci. and Industry, 1960-61, mem. edn. com., 1961-62. Served with USN, 1951-55. Named Disting. Wash. Citizen, Sec. of State, 1971. Fellow AAAS, Ohio Acad. Sci.; mem. Assn. Sci.-Tech. Centers, Council Arts and Scis. for Central Fla. (v.p. 1974-75), Explorers Club, Phi Delta Kappa, Phi Kappa Tau, v.p. 1950-51). Democrat. Author various study guides and pamphlets on audio visual edn. and communications. Home: 2312 Randall Rd Winter Park FL 32789 Office: 810 E Rollins St Orlando FL 32803

HOBBS, MATHEW S., corp. exec.; b. Ga., 1915; married. Pres., Am.-Amicable Life Ins. Co., 1960-74, now dir.; with Gulf Life Ins. Co., 1969—, pres., 1970—, also chief exec. officer, dir.; sr. v.p., dir. Gulf Life Holding Co.; vice chmn., sr. v.p. Gulf United Corp.; dir. Dealers Service Co. Served with USN, 1943-46. Office: Gulf Life Ins Co Gulf Life Center 1301 Gulf Life Dr Jacksonville FL 32207*

HOBBS, MILTON NUEL, JR., bank holding co. exec.; b. Memphis, May 8, 1945; s. Milton Nuel and Euretha (Prevost) H.; B.S.B.A., U. Ark., 1972; m. Mary Katherine Williams, Apr. 5, 1975. Asst., Peat, Marwick, Mitchell & Co., Tulsa, 1972-73, staff acct., 1973-74, sr. acct., 1974-75, supervising acct., 1975; corp. acct., asst. treas. Bancoklahoma Corp., Tulsa, 1975-77, controller, 1977—; mem. Met. Tulsa C. of C. Revenue and Taxation Task Force. Served with USN, 1966-70. C.P.A., Okla. Mem. Am. Inst. C.P.A.'s, Okla. Soc. C.P.A.'s, Bank Adminstrn. Inst., Leadership Tulsa Alumni Assn., U. Ark. Alumni Assn., Sigma Phi Epsilon Alumni Assn., Sigma Phi Epsilon Ednl. Found. Founders. Republican. Presbyterian. Clubs: Tulsa, Tulsa So. Tennis. Office: Bancoklahoma Corp Bank of Okla Tower Tulsa OK 74192

HOBBS, NED PETER, optometrist; b. Worden, Ill., Dec. 26, 1921; s. Kermit Ludolph and Marie (Massa) H.; Dr. Optometry, Ill. Coll. Optometry, 1947; postgrad. U. S.C.; m. Kathryn Louise Stonecypher, Sept. 16, 1941; children—Steven Craig, Karen Susan, Michael Jeffrey. Individual practice optometry, Darlington, S.C., 1947—. Pres. S.C. Bd. Examiners Optometrists and opticians, 1958-63. County commr., Darlington County, S.C., 1964—, coroner, 1969—. Mem. med. adv. bd. Darlington County chpt. Polio Found., 1960-63; internat. chmn. equivalent standards com. Internat. Assn. Bds. Examiners Optometry; pres. Pee Dee Perpetual Care Cemetery Assn.; city chmn. Cystic Fibrosis Campaign, 1977; chmn. Southern 500 Festival Parade, Darlington, 1979. Mem. Darlington City Council, 1950-52. Served from pvt. to capt., Med. Adminstrv. Corps, AUS, World War II; PTO. Named Citizen of Yr., Kiwanis Civic Club, 1950, Optometrist of South, So. Optometrist Jour., 1952, Optometrist of Year in S.C., 1966; recipient Service award So. Cemetery Assn., 1976, S.C. Bd. Examiners in Optometry, 1975. Fellow Am. Acad. Optometry (pres. S.C. chpt. 1959-63); mem. Am., S.C. (pres. 1953-54, named to Hall of Fame 1977) optometric Optometrist So. Council Optometrists (pres. 1958-59), Southeastern Optometry Congress (past sec.), Pee Dee Optometric Assn. (pres. 1975-76, Optometrist of Yr. 1970), V.F.W., Am. Legion, Darlington C. of C., Royal Soc. Health, Optometric Extension Program, Am. Optometric Found. (pres. 1976), S.C. (pres. 1975-76), Pee Dee (Cemetarian of Year 1972) cemetery assns. Baptist. Mason (Shriner), Elk, Lion (pres. 1949-50 Outstanding Lion of Year, Darlington 1950), Toastmaster (pres. Darlington). Home: 420 James St Darlington SC 29532 Office: 161 Cashua St Darlington SC 29532

HOBBS, OLIVER KERMIT, farm equipment mfg. exec.; b. Hobbsville, N.C., Sept. 21, 1918; s. Ephriam J. and Sallie (Brown) H.; student pub. schs., Hobbsville; m. Frances Allsbrook Piland, June 14, 1941; children—Oliver Kermit, Cynthia Russell. Service rep. Sadler Music Co., Suffolk, Va., 1939-42; service mgr. A.E. Sadler Co., Suffolk, 1945-49; gen. mgr. Shotton's Farm Service, Suffolk, 1949-58; dir. research and engring. Benthall Machine Co. Inc., Suffolk, 1958-63, dir., 1959-63; organizer, partner Hobbs Engring. Co., 1963-70; pres. Hobbs-Adams Engring. Co., 1970—; chmn. bd. Pioneer Processors, Inc., 1972—; cons. agrl. mech. devices, 1956—. Mem. exec. com., chmn. trade com. Sudan-U.S. Bus. Council; mem. Suffolk Water Resources Com. Served with USNR, 1942-45; ETO. Recipient Horace Hayden Meml. trophy, 1954; Machinery Design and Mktg. award Forest Products Research Soc., 1974. Mem. So. Farm Equipment Mfrs. Inc., ASME, Va. Farm Equipment Assn., Woodmen of World, Suffolk C. of C., Suffolk-Nansemond Hist. Soc., Va. Mfrs. Assn., Internat. Platform Assn. Baptist. Clubs: Ruritan (Suffolk), Kings Fork (pres. Suffolk 1959). Patentee automotive and agrl. field. Designer mech. sampling devices, peanut harvesting equipment, automatic control devices, power transmission equipment. Home: 1202 West Point Dr Suffolk VA 23434 Office: PO Box 1833 Suffolk VA 23434

HOBBS, SONIA AKOL BLANCO, nurse; b. Iloilo City, Philippines, Feb. 3, 1945; d. Antonio R. and Francisca de Tomas (Akol) Blanco; came to U.S., 1969, naturalized, 1977; diploma in Nursing, U. Philippines, 1966; B.S. in Nursing, Central Philippine U., 1968; m. George Ira Hobbs, June 6, 1970 (dec. 1974); 1 son, Christopher Alan. Pvt. duty nurse, Philippines, 1968-69; exchange visitor nurse Vanderbilt U., Nashville, Tenn., 1969-74; head nurse intensive care unit Meharry Hosp., Nashville, 1974-76; charge nurse intensive care unit Parkview Hosp., Nashville, 1976—. Timawa scholar, 1961-62. Mem. Am., Middle Tenn. heart assns., Am. Assn. Critical Care Nurses. Democrat. Roman Catholic. Home: 480 Sunliner Dr Nashville TN 37209 Office: Parkview Hospital 230 25th Ave N Nashville TN 37203

HOBBS, VAN HUBERT, plumbing co. exec.; b. Cusseta, Ga., Nov. 22, 1937; s. Hubert Ervin and Lorene Elizabeth (Booth) H.; student in Accounting, Perry Bus. Coll., Columbus, Ga., 1959; student Columbus Coll., 1977-78; m. Jane Elizabeth Wallace, Apr. 17, 1960; children—Laura Jane, Van Hubert. Sales rep. Philips Hardware & Supply Co., Columbus, 1959-70; sales rep. W.C. Bradley Co. hardware div., 1970-77, exec. sales mgr., 1977-78; indsl. sales rep. Columbus Plumbing and Mill Supply div. W.C. Bradley Co., Columbus, 1979—. Named Salesman of Year hardware div. W.C. Bradley Co., 1975, 77. Methodist (trustee 1976—, chmn. adminstrv. bd. 1975-76). Club: United Meth. Men. Home: 4544 Gladys Dr Columbus GA 31907 Office: Columbus Plumbing and Mill Supply 5601 Beallwood Connector Columbus GA 31902

HOBBS, WILLARD EARL, physicist; b. Mekinock Twp., N.D., June 13, 1916; s. Charles Andrew and Effie (Deitz) H.; B.A., N.D. State Tchrs. Coll., Mayville, 1938; postgrad. U.S. Naval Acad., 1944-45; A.M., Colo. State Coll. Edn., 1946; M.S., U. Tenn., 1957; m. Hazel Jane Choate, Dec. 24, 1942; children—Willard Earl, Andrew Floyd, Barbara Jane, Elizabeth Ann. Tchr. public schs., Gilby, N.D., 1939-41, Felton, Minn., 1941-42; instr. Trinidad (Colo.) Jr. Coll., 1946-47; instr. physics Va. Poly. Inst. and State U., Blacksburg, 1947-48; physicist Union Carbide Nuclear Co., Oak Ridge, 1948—; instr. U. Tenn., nights 1958-64. Served with USN, 1942-45. Mem. Am. Phys. Soc., Sigma Xi. Republican. Baptist. Patentee preparation of uranium pentafluoride. Home: 103 Uvadle Ln Oak Ridge TN 37830 Office: PO Box P Oak Ridge TN 37830

HOBBY, GRETCHEN CLARK (MRS. WILLIAM M. HOBBY III), civic worker; b. Washington, Apr. 22, 1939; d. Bruce Edmund and Phyllis Bryans (Wilson) Clark; B.A., Mary Baldwin Coll., 1956; m. William M. Hobby III, Oct. 12, 1962; children—Amy, William. Asst. to slide librarian, publs. supr., asst. chief publs. Nat. Gallery Art, summers 1957-59, 60-65; with art dept. Orlando (Fla.) Pub. Library, 1967-68; mgr. Loch Haven Art Center Shop, Orlando, 1969-76, docent, 1966-67. Chmn. teenage vols. Orange Meml. Hosp. Aux., 1968-70; mem. Orlando Opera Gala Guild, 1967-72, Orlando Civic Theatre Guild, 1971-72; rec. sec. Loch Haven Art Center, 1970-71, dir., 1970-72, 75-77, mem. council of 101, asst. v.p. bd. dirs., 1975-77; commr. and corr. sec. Winter Park Sidewalk Art Festival Assn., 1970-79; bd. dirs., curator spl. events, product and shop devel. Maitland Art Center, 1978—. Named Outstanding Woman in the Arts, Orlando Downtown Bus. Assn., 1975. Mem. Orange County Bar Assn. Aux. (corr. sec., bd. dirs. 1975—), Am. Assn. Museums, Mus. Stores Assn. (chmn. conv. 1972, editor newsletter 1973-75, v.p., exec. com. 1973-76, pres. 1976—), Mary Baldwin Coll. Alumnae Assn. (dir. 1974—). Republican. Unitarian. Home: 244 Sylvan Blvd Winter Park FL 32789 Office: Art Center Shop 231 W Packwood Ave Maitland FL 32751

HOBBY, WILLIAM PETTUS, lt. gov. Tex., newspaper exec.; b. Houston, Jan. 19, 1932; s. William Pettus and Oveta (Culp) H.; B.A., Rice U., 1953; m. Diana Poteat Stallings, Sept. 11, 1954; children—Laura Poteat, Paul William, Andrew Purefoy, Katherine Pettus. Asst. sec.-treas. Houston Post, 1957-59, asso. editor, 1959-60, mng. editor, 1960-63, exec. editor, 1963-73, exec. v.p. Houston Post Co., 1963-65, pres. 1965—; vice chmn. Channel Two TV Co., KPRC Radio Co., 1970—; chmn. bd. Channel Five Co., Nashville, 1975—. Parliamentarian, Tex. Senate, 1959; lt. gov. Tex., 1973—; chmn. Nat. Conf. Lt. Govs., 1976-77. Bd. dirs. Child Guidance Center Houston, 1957-63, pres., 1960-62; mem. council overseers Jones Sch. Adminstrn., Rice U. Served to lt. (j.g.) USNR, 1953-57. Mem. Am. Soc. Newspaper Editors, Tex. Hunter and Jumper Assn. (dir. 1953—, pres. 1959-61), U.S. Equestrian Team, Inc. (v.p. 1959-60). Office: PO Box 326 Houston TX 77001 also State Capitol Capitol Sta Austin TX 78711

HOBRATSCH, MELVIN JOHN, real estate investment co. exec.; b. Vernon, Tex., Mar. 29, 1936; s. Alvin Walter and Ella Louise H.; B.B.A., N. Tex. State U., 1960; m. Mary Elyse Mook, Feb. 14, 1978; children—Jana Lynn, Jonathan Emerson. Various positions land investment cos., Dallas-Ft. Worth area, 1968-79; owner, operator Mel Hobratsch Investment Co., Dallas, 1961-75; pres. E. Tex. Properties Inc., Dallas, 1975—; dir. Real Estate Advt. Inc., Hobratsch Ranch Inc. Fin. chmn. Republican party Collin County (Tex.), 1972. Served with U.S. Army, 1958-59, 60-61. Mem. Tex. and Southwestern Cattle Raisers Assn., Dallas Bd. Realtors. Lutheran. Clubs: Bent Tree Country (Dallas); Hot Springs Village (Ark.) Country. Home: 1321 Chesterton St Richardson TX 75080 Office: E Texas Properties Inc 13101 Preston Rd Dallas TX 75240

HOBSON, ANNE GLEN, pharmacist; b. Lawrence, Mass., Apr. 11, 1925; d. William Harvey and Ina (Brown) Sparks; student Radcliffe Coll., 1942-43; B.A., Stanford U., 1946, M.A., 1947; postgrad. U. Houston, 1969-70; Ph.D., U. Tex., 1972, B.S. in Pharmacy, 1974; m. William C. Hobson, Jan. 9, 1960; children—Floyd, Bruce, Scott, William. Research asst. in preventive medicine U. Calif., San Francisco, 1947; research asso. in pharmacology Stanford Med. Sch., San Francisco, 1948; tchr. U.S. Army Dependents Sch., Manila, Philippines, 1949-51, Miss Harker's Sch., Palo Alto, Calif., 1951-53; med. lab. technician Palo Alto Clinic, 1953-54; tchr. Anglo-Am. Sch., Kifissia, Athens, Greece, 1954-56; chief lab. technician Dale County Hosp., Ozark, Ala., 1956-57; tchr. Bloomfield (N.J.) High Sch., 1957-58, Clark (N.J.) High Sch., 1958-59; asst. prof. Hellenika Anglaise Collegion, Athens, Greece, 1959-60; tchr. Molesworth AFB, Eng., 1960-61; asst. prof. Ashton Community Coll., Ashton-under-Lyne, Eng., 1961-62; tchr. Hartshead Sec. Sch., Ashton-under-Lyne, 1962-63, Droylsden (Eng.) Secondary Sch. for Girls, 1963-64; asst. coordinator Trenton (N.J.) Jr. 5 Exptl. Sch. program, for Disadvantaged, 1964-65; tchr. Trenton High Sch., 1965-66; research asso. Princeton (N.J.) U., 1966-67; tchr. Sam Rayburn High Sch., Pasadena, Tex., 1967-70; chief adult councilor Juvenile Drug Addiction, Pasadena, 1970-72; NSF grantee U. Tex., Austin, 1970-74; pharmacist, asst. mgr., mgr. Sommers Drug Stores, Austin, 1974-76; owner, pharmacist Hobson Pharmacy, Pflugerville, Tex., 1976—. Recipient Cert. of Recognition, Am. Inst. History of Pharmacy, 1973; Outstanding Alumna award U. Tex., 1977; registered pharmacist, Tex. Mem. Am. Soc. Hosp. Pharmacists, Am. Pharm. Assn., Tex. Pharm. Assn., Capital Area Pharm. Assn., Am. Inst. History of Pharmacy, Am. Tchrs. Assn., Tex. Tchrs. Assn., AAUW, Bus. and Profl. Women, Better Bus. Bur., Kappa Epsilon. Republican. Episcopal Lutheran. Clubs: Rainbow Girls, Am. Luth. Ch. Women's Assn. Contbr. articles to profl. jours; researcher in RH blood factor and leukemia, possible relationship with epilepsy, and mongolism, possible causal relationship between jaundice and hepatitis, others. Home: 18 Rowe Loop Pflugerville TX 78660 Office: 1 Woodcreek Village Pflugerville TX 78660

HOBSON, CHRISTOPHER GORDON, engr.; b. Westfield, N.J., May 8, 1922; s. Christopher E. and Dorothy C. Maxwell (Crew) H.; B.S., U. Pitts., 1949; m. Sarah Louise Campbell, June 8, 1946 (dec.); children—Christopher G., Hobson, Virginia L., James Wensel. Design engr. Westinghouse Air Brake, Swissvale, Pa., 1947-48; indsl. sales engr. Peoples Natural Gas, Pitts., 1948-53; mfg. rep. Fuel Equipment Co., Pitts., 1953-54; interim mgr. Hauck Mfg. Co. Chgo., 1954-72; sales engr., pres. owner Combustion Tec, Inc., Boxford, Mass., 1970-72; asst. chief engr. Mechtron Internat., Orlando, Fla., 1972-73; exec. v.p. Combustion Tel Inc., Orlando, 1973-76; asst. v.p. Thermal Transer, Winter Park, Fla., 1976-78; divisional v.p. Alpha Glass, El Segundo, Calif., 1978—. Served with USAAF, 1942-45. Decorated Purple Heart, Air medal with 3 clusters, registered prof. engr., Mass. Mem. Am. Ceramic Soc., Canadian Ceramic Soc. Episcopalian. Clubs: Masons, Shriners, Elks. Home and Office: 2628 Cayman Way Winter Park FL 32792

HOBSON, VIRGINIA PRINCE CALVIN, educator; b. Birmingham, Ala.; d. Earle Pegram and Virginia (Robinson) Calvin; student Sullins Coll., 1941-43, George Peabody Coll., Vanderbilt U., 1946-48; A.B., Vanderbilt U., 1948, M.S. in Ednl. Adminstrn., 1978; postgrad. Memphis State U., U. Tenn., 1979; m. John L. Hobson, Sept. 9, 1950 (div. 1974); children—John Lewis, Ginger (Mrs. Thomas E. Watson), Teresa Blaylock. Head gen. cargo for Brit. Ministry, N.Y. Central RR., N.Y.C., 1944; with United Air Lines, N.Y.C., 1945; tchr. Caldwell Sch., Nashville, 1948-50, Venetia Sch., Jacksonville, Fla., 1950-51, Hutchison Sch., Memphis, 1959-65; owner, operator Lee St. Book and Art Shops, Brunswick, Ga., 1970-74, Golden Isles Book Distbr., Brunswick, 1970-74; antiquarian bookman, Far Corners Book Search of Mobile and Bell Buckle, 1970—; mgr., buyer B. Dalton, Bookseller, Mobile, Ala., 1974-78; adminstr., tchr. The Webb Sch., Bell Buckle, Tenn., 1979—; pres. Women Book & Art Travelers, Nashville. Trustee Sullins Coll., 1965, bd. visitors, 1965—; exec. bd. dirs. Jr. League Memphis, 1956-60, chmn. publicity, 1959; pres. YWCA Glynn County (Ga.), 1968, Glynn County Med. Aux., 1970; exec. bd. Women's Aux. Med. Soc. Ga., 1967-71, state v.p., 1971, also state historian; exec. bd. Women of Ch., St. Paul's Episcopal Ch., Mobile, 1977. Mem. English Speaking Union, Am. Booksellers Assn., Antiquarian Bookmen, Mid-S. Sullins Alumnae Assn. (pres. 1964), Ala. Hist. Assn., Nat. Trust Historic Preservation, Allied Arts Council of Ala., Stoneridge Assn. (dir.), Christian Booksellers Assn., Tenn. Hist. Assn., Vanderbilt Art Assn., Daus. Am. Colonists (v.p. Midway, Ga. 1965-75), Assn. Preservation Tenn. Antiquities Jr. League Mobile and Nashville, Friends Museum City of Mobile, Midway (Ga.) Mus. Assn., Smithsonian Assos. Clubs: Pilot, Univ. Memphis. Home: Webb Sch Box 137 Bell Buckle TN 37020

HOCHSTADT, HARRY, health care cons.; b. Bklyn., Apr. 26, 1918; s. Julius and Jenny Hochstadt; student Queens Coll., 1946; m. Meda Lavelle Higgs, Apr. 23, 1945; children—James Layne, Robert Craig, Sharon Lynn, Pamela Renee. Adminstr., All Children's Hosp., St. Petersburg, Fla., 1957-66 nat. hosp. adminstrn. adv. to minister of health Civil Govt. of S. Vietnam, 1966-67; hosp. cons. Ritchie & West, Inc., Boston, 1967-68, Ft. Lauderdale, Fla., 1967-68; exec. v.p. Presbyn. Med. Center, Fort Myers, Fla., 1968-69, Cedars of Lebanon Hosp., Miami, Fla., 1969-74; exec. dir. Surgi-Center of South Fla., Coral Gables, 1974-75; dir. of corp. devel. Med. Computer Scis., Inc., Largo, Fla., 1976; hosp. cons. H. Hochstadt & Assos., Largo, 1976—; guest speaker on hosp. and health care adminstr. at profl. meetings; mem. team for devel. health related tng. programs St. Petersburg Jr. Coll., Fla., 1964; co-preceptor George Washington U. program in hosp. adminstrn., 1970-74. Chmn., Red Cross Com. Pinellas County, Fla., 1963-66; chmn. areawide planning com. State of Fla., 1965-66. Served with USN, 1937-57. Named Outstanding Citizen of Pinellas County, Pinellas County Commn., 1963. Fellow Am. Coll. Hosp. Adminstrs., Soc. for Advanced Med. Systems, Royal Soc. of Health; mem. Am. Mgmt. Assn., East Central Fla. Hosp. Council (hon.). Home: 13810 Kimberly Dr Largo FL 33540 Office: 13810 Kimberly Dr Largo FL 33540

HOCKENBURY, MELVIN RICHARD, environ. engr.; b. Somerville, N.J., Dec. 15, 1950; s. Charles Foster and Marion Phoebe (Porter) H.; B.S. in Civil Engring. with honors, Ohio U., 1973; M.S. in Civil Engring. with honors, Purdue U., 1974 m. Sharon Eileen Flint, Mar. 18, 1973. EPA research trainee Purdue U., 1973-74; environ. engr. Engring.-Sci., Inc., Atlanta, 1974-75, project mgr., 1975—, lab. mgr., 1977—, regional tech. dir., 1978—. Jennie M. Haver Meml. scholar 1969-73. Active DeKalb County (Ga.) YMCA Soccer Program; active DeKalb County Concert Band. Mem. Ga. Water Pollution Control Assn., Water Pollution Control Fedn., ASCE. Author publs. on wastewater treatment. Home: 610 Hillpine Dr NE Atlanta GA 30306 Office: 57 Executive Park S Suite 590 Atlanta GA 30329

HOCKETT, PAUL BRANSON, JR., hosp. devel. exec.; b. Greensboro, N.C., June 24, 1941; s. Paul Branson and Mary Margaret (Waters) H.; B.S. in Med. Tech., La. Coll., 1968; M.A. in Human Resources Mgmt., Pepperdine U., 1977; m. Mary Carolyn Tracy, Aug. 18, 1962; children—Tracy Michelle, Ashley Ann. Staff technologist Huey P. Long Meml. Hosp., Pineville, La., 1968-69; supr. hematology, dept. pathology Rapides Gen. Hosp., Alexandria, La., 1969-72, staff devel. dir., 1972-77, dir. devel. and public relations, 1977—; coll. instr. mgmt., public relations, group dynamics. Div. chmn., speakers chmn. United Givers. Served with USAF, 1959-63. Mem. Am. Soc. for Health Manpower Edn. and Tng., Am. Soc. Clin. Pathologists, Am. Soc. Hosp. Public Relations, Nat. Assn. Hosp. Devel., Alexandria-Pineville C. of C. Democrat. Baptist. Club: Pineville Lions (pres. 1977-78, dist. cabinet sec. 1979—, dist. gov. 1980). Home: 128 Woodcliff Circle Pineville LA 71360 Office: Rapides General Hospital 211 4th St PO Box 7146 Alexandria LA 71301

HOCKETT, ROLAND LEE, artist, educator; b. LaPorte, Ind., Aug. 1, 1938; s. George G. and Wilma H. (Casey) H.; B.S., Ind. U., 1960, M.S., 1962, postgrad., 1963; m. Sydney Sue Hays, Jan. 23, 1965; children—Christopher Lee, Roxanne Leigh. Head dept. art LaPorte (Ind.) High Sch., 1963-66; instr. dept. art Fla. State U., Tallahassee, 1966-69; asso. prof. art Gulf Coast Community Coll., Panama City, Fla., 1969—; design cons. dept. foundational studies in edn. Fla. State U., 1969-70, div. research State Dept., Baton Rouge, 1979-80; art dir. Franceschi Advt. Co., Tallahassee, 1968-69; free lance art designer, 1963-65; one-man shows of painting sculpture include various galleries, museums and public sites in Tallahassee, 1968, 1975, Sarasota, Fla., 1974, Pensacola, Fla., 1972, Panama City, 1968, 72, 77, Miami, Fla., 1970; group shows various galleries and museums, Jacksonville, Fla. and Tallahassee; represented in numerous pvt. collections, Fla. Named Outstanding Allied Artist in N.W. Fla., AIA, 1974. Mem. Fla. Craftsmen, Fla. Art Edn. Assn., Fla. Artists Group, Nat. Art Edn. Assn., Fla. Assn. Community Colls. Methodist. Art editor Jour. of Ednl. Research, 1977-78. Home: 1309 Airport Rd Panama City FL 32405 Office: Gulf Coast Community College W Hwy 98 Panama City FL 32401

HOCOTT, JOE BILL, chem. engr., educator; b. nr. Big Flat, Ark., Sept. 19, 1921; s. Jeiks Edmonds and Frances Clara (Berry) H.; B.S., U. Ark., 1945; M.S., Okla. State U., 1951. Insp. Maumelle Ordnance Works, U.S. Army Ordnance Dept., Little Rock, 1942-43; head sci. dept. Joe T. Robinson High Sch., Little Rock, 1945-46; instr. chemistry U. Tulsa, 1946-47; teaching fellow Okla. A. and M. Coll., Stillwater, 1947-49; research chem. engr. Deep Rock Petroleum Corp., Cushing, Okla., 1950, Kerr-McGee Oil Corp., Stillwater, 1951; chem. engr. cons. Joe Bill Hocott, Little Rock, 1952-55, 63—; med. technician U. Ark. Med. Center, Little Rock, 1955-56, research asso., 1956-57, instr. internal medicine, 1957-62; head chemistry dept. Little Rock Central High Sch., 1963-66; head sci. dept. Met. Vocat.-Tech. High Sch., Little Rock, 1967-73. Asst. scoutmaster Boy Scouts Am., 1945-46, troop committeeman, 1945-46, 57-58, neighborhood commr., 1969-70. Bd. dirs. Ark. Jr. Sci. and Humanities Symposium, 1965-75, asst. dir., 1972. Mem. Am. Inst. Chem. Engrs., Nat. Soc. Profl. Engrs., Ark., Ark. Jr. (dist. dir. 1966-70) acads. sci., Sigma Xi, Phi Lambda Upsilon, Unitarian. Home: 1010 Rice St Little Rock AR 72202

HODEEN, ERIC CARLETON, physician; b. Providence, Aug. 29, 1942; s. Eric and Ruth (Munson) H.; B.S., U. Fla., 1964; M.D. cum laude, Tufts U., 1968; m. Feb. 5, 1965; children—Kristen Lee, Eric Stephen. Intern, R.I. Hosp., Providence, 1968-69; resident in internal medicine U. Mich., Ann Arbor, 1969-70, 73-75, fellow in rheumatology, 1975-77; individual practice medicine specializing in rheumatology, Virginia Beach, Va., 1977-78; practice rheumatology Norfolk (Va.) Diagnostic Clinic, 1978—; mem. staff Norfolk Gen. Hosp., Leigh Meml. Hosp., Norfolk, Bayside Hosp., Gen. Hosp., Virginia Beach, Va.; asso. prof. Eastern Va. Med. Sch., 1979—. Bd. dirs. Tidewater br. Arthritis Found., 1977-80. Served to lt. comdr. M.C., USNR, 1971-73. Diplomate Am. Bd. Internal Medicine. Mem. U. Mich. House Officers Assn. (pres. 1975-76), Am. Rheumatism Assn., Am. Soc. Internal Medicine, A.C.P., Norfolk Acad. Medicine, Va. Med. Soc. Home: 1805 Duke of York Quay Virginia Beach VA 23454 Office: 844 Kempsville Rd Norfolk VA 23502

HODGE, ARTHUR A., utility ofcl.; b. Waxahachie, Tex., Aug. 8, 1931; s. Robert LaFayette and Sallie S. (McCullough) H.; B.B.A., North Tex. State U., 1952; m. Marion Joan Norton, Nov. 23, 1953; 1 dau., Beth Ann. Planner, Gen. Dynamics Co., Ft. Worth, 1952-53; basketball coach Milford (Tex.) Ind. Sch. Dist., 1953-56; trainee Tex. Power & Light Co., Waxahachie, 1956-57, storekeeper, Mineral Wells, 1957-59, jr. acct., Richardson, 1959-60, dist. acct., Irving, 1960-63, safety tng. engr., Dallas, 1962-65, mgr. tng., 1965—; vis. lectr. North Tex. State U., 1979-80, Irving Ind. Sch. Dist., 1974-78, Am. Mgmt. Assn., 1966-70. Accredited personnel specialist Am. Soc. Personnel Adminstrn. Mem. Am. Soc. for Tng. and Devel. (pres. Dallas chpt. 1970), Tng. Dirs. Inst. (Edison Electric Inst.), S.W. Utility Tng. Group, Kappa Sigma. Baptist. Clubs: Cedar Creek Country, Masons, Irving Civitan (pres. 1962). Home: 700 Hillcrest Ct Irving TX 75062 Office: 1511 Bryan St Dallas TX 75201

HODGE, ARTHUR WILEY, dept. store exec.; b. Morgan County, Ala., Sept. 6, 1931; s. Leonard Wiley and Roberta (King) H.; B.B.A., Miss. Coll., Clinton, 1958; m. Betty Joyce Statum, Nov. 25, 1954; children—Arthur Gregory, Lisa Wilette. Salesman, Brown Shoe Co., 1959-64, Butler Mfg. Co., 1964-69; self-employed, 1969-70; pres., owner McAlpin's Dept. Store, Magee, Miss., 1970—; dir. Bank Simpson Co. Bd. dirs. Andrew Council council Boy Scouts Am.; pres. Vision Found., Inc., 1976—; bd. dirs. Nat. Laymen's Bd., Ch. of God, 1968-76, bd. dir. Nat. Radio and TV Bd., 1976—, chmn. Nat. Laymen's Bd., 1976—; bd. dirs. Miss. Methodist Hour, 1976—. Served with USAF, 1950-54. Mem. Miss. Retail Mchts. Assn. (dir.), Magree C. of C. (dir.). Home: 802 S Main St Magee MS 39111 Office: 102 S Main St Magee MS 39111

HODGE, BIRDIA HELEN, counselor; b. Gonzales County, Tex., Dec. 22, 1919; d. Mark and Arilla (Williams) County; B.S., Tex. A&I U., 1961, M.S., 1965; Ph.D. in Edn., U. Nebr., Lincoln, 1978; m. Edward Hodge, Feb. 6, 1942; 1 child, Tonye Rhea. Elem. tchr., Eagle Lake, Tex., 1961, Kingsville, Tex., 1966-74; spl. edn. counselor Kingsville Ind. Sch. Dist., 1974-78; counselor Family Guidance Services, Kingsville, 1978—. Personnel chmn. Community Action Corp of S. Tex. Bd., 1978; bd. dirs. S. Tex. Health Systems, 1978, Community Participation Council, 1978; publicity chmn. NAACP, 1978. Mem. NEA, Tex. Tchrs. Assn., Am. Personnel and Guidance Assn., Tex. Personnel and Guidance Assn. Methodist. Club: Order Eastern Star. Home: 716 W Ragland St Kingsville TX 78363 Office: 729 W Nettie St Kingsville TX 78363

HODGE, CURTIS WILBUR, JR., chem. co. exec.; b. Union, S.C., Aug. 20, 1943; s. Curtiss Wilburn and Mary Elizabeth (Trantham) H.; B.S.B.A., U. S.C., 1966; m. Carolyn Elise Johns, Sept. 18, 1962; children—Susan Elise, Mary Eleanor, David Albert. Offensive guard Phila. Eagles, 1966; with Union Carbide Co., Greenville, S.C., 1966-79, mfg. mgr., 1974-77, plant mgr., 1977-79; v.p. Intex Products, Inc., Greenville, 1979—. Chmn. Simpsonville (S.C.) Recreation Commn., 1976-78. Mem. U. S.C. Bus. Partnership Found., Greenville C. of C. (bd. dirs., chmn. positive mgmt. leadership 1979—). Republican. Methodist. Club: Poinsettia Community (pres. 1968-69). Office: PO Box 6648 Kings Rd Greenville SC 29606

HODGE, DAVID CARROLL, economist; b. Morristown, Tenn., July 25, 1921; s. James Ellis and Georgie Cates (Couch) H.; B.S., U. Tenn., Knoxville, 1949, cert. in crafts, 1950, M.S., 1953; postgrad. U. Ga., 1961-64; m. Alice Arlene Williams, June 14, 1952; children—John David, Alan Andrew. Tchr. indsl. arts Chattanooga pub. schs., 1949-50; carpenter Hodge Constrn. Co., Morristown, 1950-51; research asst., bur. bus. and econ. research U. Tenn., Knoxville, 1952-59; asso. dir. bur. bus. and econ. research U. Ga., Athens, 1959-66; research economist Taylor Murphy Inst., U. Va., Charlottesville, 1966—. Incorporator, Ga. Christian Found. Inc., 1966. Served with U.S. Army, 1942-45; ETO. Mem. Am. Statis. Assn., So. Econ. Assn., AAUP, Beta Gamma Sigma. Mem. Chs. of Christ. Office: Tayloe Murphy Inst U Va PO Box 6550 Charlottesville VA 22906

HODGE, DOROTHY W. (SCOTTIE), gallery exec.; b. Darlington, S.C., Oct. 21, 1940; d. Julian Walter and Elizabeth (Wilson) H.; B.S., Winthrop Coll., 1961; M.A., Furman U., 1973. Performing musician various S.C. locations, 1961-78; owner, dir. Tempo Gallery, Greenville, S.C., 1975—; group shows include: Greenville Artist's Guild, 1978, Guild of S.C. Artists, 1979, Florence (S.C.) Mus., 1980, Spirit Sq. Open Exhbn., Charlotte, N.C.; represented in permanent collection: 1st Fed. Savs. & Loan, Greenville. Mem. Greenville Artist Guild (sec.-treas. 1976-77, pres. 1978-79), Greenville Art Assn. (dir. 1978-79), Guild of S.C. Artists, S.C. Watercolor Soc. (co-founder 1977, adminstrv. asst. 1977—). Office: Tempo Gallery 125 W Stone Ave Greenville SC 29609

HODGE, GAMEEL BYRON, surgeon; b. Spartanburg, S.C., Sept. 16, 1917; s. Charles B. and Mary (Bargot) H.; B.S., Wofford Coll., 1938; M.D., Vanderbilt U., 1942; m. Katie Adams, Sept. 22, 1943; children—Susan, Byron, John Adams. Intern, Duke U. Med. Sch. and Hosp., Durham, N.C., 1942-43, asst. resident, 1943-47, chief resident surgeon, 1947-48; practice medicine specializing in gen., thoracic and cardiovascular surgery, Spartanburg, 1948—; attending surgeon Spartanburg Gen. Hosp.; cons. surgeon St. Luke's Hosp., Tryon, N.C., 1948-58, Cherokee County (S.C.) Meml. Hosp., 1948-74; thoracic surgeon Spartanburg County Tb Hosp., 1948-69; chief of surgery Mary Black Meml. Hosp., 1969-72; asso. clin. prof. surgery Med. U. S.C., Spartanburg, 1970—. Chmn. Spartanburg County Commn. for Higher Edn., 1967—; trustee Spartanburg Day Sch., 1958—. Served to 1st lt. M.C., U.S. Army Res., 1942-53. Diplomate Am. Bd. Surgery. Fellow Am. Coll. Chest Physicians, Internat. Acad. Proctology, N.Y. Acad. Sci., Am. Fedn. Clin. Research, Indsl. Medicine Assn.; mem. Am. Heart Assn., S.C. Med. Assn., S.C. Surg. Soc., S.C. Vascular Surg. Soc., AMA, Spartanburg Med. Soc., Am. Geriatrics Soc., Deryl Hart Surg. Soc., Order of Palmetto, Phi Beta Kappa, Phi Beta Pi. Episcopalian. Clubs: Spartanburg Country, Kiwanis (Citizenship of Year award 1969), Piedmont. Contbr. articles on surgery and gen. medicine to profl. jours. Home: 2500 Old Knox Rd Spartanburg SC 29302 Office: 3 Catawba St Spartanburg SC 29303

HODGES, ALLEN, psychologist; b. Greenville, S.C., Feb. 16, 1925; s. William L. and Estelle (Smith) H.; B.A., U. Minn., 1947; M.A., U. Tenn., 1948, Ph.D., 1953; m. Elizabeth Swanson, June 27, 1944; children—Nancy Elizabeth, Susan Kathleen (Mrs. Charles McDonnell), Sara Louise (Mrs. Gene Juarez), Jane Ellen (Mrs. John Carona). Sch. psychologist, dir. guidance Oak Ridge Pub. Schs., 1948-53; clin. psychologist, dir. So. Minn. Mental Health Center, Albert Lea, 1953-57; cons. psychologist, acting dir. community mental health Minn. Dept. Pub. Welfare, St. Paul, 1957-59; asst. prof., dir. sch. psychology tng. program U. Minn., 1959-61; mental health cons. clin. psychology NIMH, USPHS, HEW, 1961-63, program dir. mental health services, 1964-67, asso. regional health dir., 1967-70, asst. regional dir. planning and evaluation, 1970-78, dir. service delivery assessment, 1978-79; asst. clin. prof. dept. psychiatry U. Colo. Sch. Medicine, 1965-79; lectr. Regis Coll., 1962-79; HEW fellow on loan to Ga. Dept. Human Resources, 1979—. Sec., Minn. Bd. Exam. Psychologists, 1957-61. Served to lt. (j.g.) USNR, 1943-46; PTO. Fellow Am. Psychol. Assn., Am. Pub. Health Assn. Office: PO Box 591 Hinesville GA 31313

HODGES, BRENT, computer scientist; b. Eatontown, N.J., May 22, 1950; s. Allen Thurman and Eleanor Davis (Ravenscroft) H.; B.S. in Computer Sci., N.C. State U., 1972; m. Debra Elaine Bowles, Jan. 1, 1980. Owner, mgr. Datamatic Corp., Fayetteville, N.C., 1973—. Served with U.S. Army, 1972-73. Mem. Assn. Computing Machinery. Mem. Ch. of Christ. Home: 6213 Dixon Dr Raleigh NC 27609 Office: 407 N Churchill Dr Fayetteville NC 28303

HODGES, CHARLES EDWIN, fin. planning co. exec.; b. Norfolk, Va., May 18, 1945; s. Edwin and Margaret R. (Parsley) H.; B.B.A., U. Houston, 1970; m. Minda Shoemaker, Aug. 26, 1967; Sr. analyst Shell Oil Co., Houston, 1967-70; sales mgr. Met. Life Ins. Co., Houston, 1970-76; v.p. Fin. Adv. Clinic, Inc., Houston, 1976—. Mem. Nat., Tex., Houston assns. life underwriters, Inst. Internat. Edn. (unit chmn. host internat. program 1976-77). Home: 5351 Yarwell St Houston TX 77096 Office: 2900 N Loop W Suite 700 Houston TX 77092

HODGES, DAVID BOYD, univ. ofcl.; b. Post, Tex., Aug. 4, 1930; s. Bonnie Boyd and Thelma (Murray) H.; B.S. in Law Enforcement, Hardin-Simmons U., 1978; m. Connie Joyce Veach, June 24, 1951; children—Michael David, Jodi Diane, Timothy Boyd. Enlisted in U.S. Army, 1948, advanced to 1st sgt., 19—; ret., 1968; dep. sheriff Taylor County (Tex.), 1969-72; dir. security, safety mgr. Aileen, Inc., Abilene, Tex., 1972-75; dir. security Hardin-Simmons U., Abilene, 1975—, also instr.; cons. Decorated Silver Star, Bronze Star. Mem. Nat. Assn. Chiefs of Police. Baptist. Club: Civitan. Home: 2041 Anderson St Abilene TX 79601 Office: Box 163 Hardin Simmons U Abilene TX 79601

HODGES, DAVID CLAYTON, kitchen design co. exec.; b. Jacksonville, Fla., July 1, 1945; s. Kenneth Clayton and Edna Earle (Armstrong) H.; B.S. in Bus. Adminstrn., U. Fla., 1967; m. Linda Ann Taylor, Aug. 14, 1971; children—David Clayton, Daniel Wayne, Douglas Taylor. Jr. v.p. Wood Products, Inc., Gainesville, Fla., 1967-68; v.p. West Bldg. Materials, West Palm Beach, Fla., 1973-74; v.p., gen. mgr. Holmes Home Center, Jacksonvillle, 1975-77; pres. Kitchen Design Center, Jacksonville, 1977—. Served to lt. USN, 1968-73. Mem. Shops of Avondale Mchts. Assn. (pres. 1979—), Jacksonville C. of C. (mem. ethics com.), Am. Inst. Kitchen Dealers. Republican. Baptist (dir. 12th grade dept. 1979—, deacon 1979—).

HODGES, JOSEPH HOWARD, bishop; b. Harpers Ferry, W.Va., Oct. 8, 1911; s. Joseph Howard and Edna Belle (Hendricks) H.; student St. Charles Coll., Catonsville, Md., 1928-30; student N.Am. Coll., Rome, 1930-36, D.D. (hon.), 1952. Ordained priest, Roman Cath. Ch., Rome, 1935; asst. Sacred Heart Ch., Danville, Va., 1936-39, St. Andrew's Ch., Roanoke, Va., 1939-45; adminstr. St. Mary's Ch., Richmond, Va., also dir. Diocesan Missionary Fathers, 1945-55; pastor St. Peter's Ch., Richmond, 1955-61; consecrated Titular Bishop of Rusadus and Aux. Bishop of Cath. Diocese of Richmond, 1952; vicar gen. Diocese of Richmond, 1958-61; coadjutor bishop and vicar gen. Diocese of Wheeling, W.Va., 1961, bishop, Wheeling, 1962-74, bishop, Wheeling-Charleston, 1974—. Office: 1300 Byron St PO Box 230 Wheeling WV 26003

HODGES, JOT HOLIVER, JR., lawyer; b. Archer City, Tex., Nov. 16, 1932; s. Jot Holiver and Lola Mae (Hurd) H.; B.S., Sam Houston State U., 1954, B.B.A., 1954; J.D., U. Tex., 1957; m. Virginia Pardue, June 11, 1955; children—Deborah Lee, Jot Holiver III, Darlene Dee. Admitted to Tex. bar, 1958; asst. atty. gen. State of Tex., 1958-62; partner firm Hodges & Kerr, Houston, 1963—. Chmn. bd. Brazoria County Land & Cattle Co., Presidio Devel. Corp. Served to capt. AUS, 1957-58. Mem. Am., Tex., Houston bar assns., Assn. Trial Lawyers Am., Delta Tau Delta, Delta Theta Phi. Clubs: Houston, University. Contbr. articles to profl. jours. Home: 3527 Thunderbird St Missouri City TX 77459 Office: First City Nat Bank Bldg Houston TX 77002

HODGES, RALPH BYRON, state justice; b. Anadarko, Okla., Aug. 4, 1930; s. Dewey E. and Pearl (Emenhiser) H.; A.B., Okla. Baptist U., 1952; LL.B., U. Okla., 1954; m. Janelle Johnson; children—Shari, Mark, Randall. Dist. atty., Bryan County, Okla., 1957-58, dist. judge, 1959-65; justice Okla. Supreme Ct., Oklahoma City, 1965—, chief justice, 1977-78. Baptist. Home: Durant OK 74701 Office: State Capitol Bldg Oklahoma City OK 73105

HODGES, RICHARD EDWARD, advt. and pub. relations exec.; b. Pikeville, Ky., Feb. 9, 1928; s. Richard Edward and Marian (McQueen) H.; student Washington and Lee U., 1946-48; A.B., Emory U., 1950; m. Barbara Burke, Sept. 27, 1951; children—Richard Edward, Burke Vincent. Reporter, Ashland (Ky.) Daily Ind., 1944-48, Atlanta Constn., 1950-51; mem. staff pub. relations dept. Liller, Neal, Battle & Lindsey, Inc., Atlanta, 1951-54, account exec., 1951-56, pub. relations dir. 1956-67, v.p., 1960-67, exec. v.p., 1968-75, pres., 1975-78; chmn. bd. Liller, Neal, Weltin, Inc., 1978—. Pres., Certified Audit of Circulation, 1973-76. Mem. men's adv. com. Atlanta Music Club, 1965-72; chmn. spl. pub. relations adv. com. Atlanta Community Chest-United Appeal, 1966-67, v.p., 1968-72; v.p. United Way Met. Atlanta, 1975; mem. Atlanta Bd. Edn., 1973; bd. dirs. Atlanta area Camp Fire Girls, 1958-60; bd. govs. Pub. Broadcasting Service, 1974-76, bd. dirs., 1977-80; pres. Pub. Broadcasting Council Atlanta and Fulton County Pub. Schs., 1977-79; pres. Pub. Broadcasting Assn. of Greater Atlanta, Inc., 1979—; bd. dirs. North Central Ga. Health Systems Agy., 1976—, Atlanta Consumer Credit Counseling Serivce. Mem. Pub. Relations Soc. Am. (accredited mem., Paul M. Lund Public Service award 1979), So. Indsl. Editors Assn. (pres. Atlanta 1953), Atlanta Advt. Club (pres. 1962-63), Am. Assn. Advt. Agys. (com. for work with students and educators 1965-68, chmn. S.E. council 1968-69), Atlanta C. of C. (dir. 1973, chmn. edn. task force 1974-75), Leadership Atlanta Alumni Assn., Ga. Motor Club (dir.), Inquiry Club, Fulton County Grand Jurors Assn., Sigma Delta Chi, Kappa Alpha, Omicron Delta Kappa. Episcopalian. Clubs: Rotary, Capital City, Commerce. Home: 4615 Brook Hollow Rd Atlanta GA 30327 Office: 1300 Life of Ga Tower Atlanta GA 30308

HODGES, SHIRLEY ANN, artist; b. Big Spring, Tex., Sept. 18, 1940; d. Bernard Cleveland and Lois Elizabeth (Lynn) C.; student Del Mar Coll., 1969-71, E. Central U., Ada, Okla., 1977-79; m. Floyd B. Hodges, Jr., Mar. 29, 1958; children—Resa Lynn, Lavon Reschel. One-woman shows: Naval Air Sta. Officers Club, Corpus Christi, Tex., Another Gallery, Aspen, Colo., also in Phoenix and Oklahoma City; exhibited group shows in Denver, Aspen, Colorado Springs, Colo., Corpus Christi, San Antonio, Houston, Dallas, Taos, Santa Fe, Chgo., N.Y.C.; pvt. instr. painting. Mem. Internat. Soc. Artists (charter). Republican. Mem. Ch. of Christ. Home: 1531 Scenic Dr Ada OK 74820 Office: 117 S Broadway Ada OK 74820

HODGKINSON, ROBERT, obstet. anesthesiologist; b. Bolton, Eng., Feb. 2, 1922; s. Robert and Mary (Shepperd) H.; came to U.S., 1962, naturalized, 1967; M.B., Ch.B., Cambridge (Eng.) U., 1946, M.A. with honours, 1942, M.D., 1956; M.M., Manchester (Eng.) U., 1948, D.R.C.O.G., 1948; m. Ottillia Mathias, Aug. 6, 1975; children—Rima Stella, Sylvia Roxana. Resident in Ob-Gyn, Bolton Hosp., 1946-48; dir. clin. research Parke Davis & Co., Ann Arbor, Mich., 1950-61, Merck & Co., Inc., Rahway, N.J., 1961-70; resident in anesthesiology Albert Einstein Coll. Medicine, Bronx, N.Y., 1970-73; asst. prof. Albert Einstein Sch. Medicine, 1973-76; chief obstet. anesthesiology, prof. anesthesiology U. Tex. Health Center, San Antonio, 1976—. Served as capt. M.C., Brit. Army, 1948-50. Grantee duPont Co., Schering Corp., Bristol Myer Co., Smith, Kline & French Labs. Diplomate Am. Bd. Anesthesiology, Am. Bd. Obstetrics. Fellow Am. Soc. Anesthesiology; mem. Am. Soc. Anesthesia Research, AMA, Royal Soc. Medicine. Episcopalian. Author research papers, chpts. in books. Home: 7527 Wild Eagle St San Antonio TX 78255 Office: Dept Anesthesiology Univ Tex Health Sci Center Floyd Curl Circle San Antonio TX 78255

HODGSON, MORTON STRAHAN, III, broadcasting co. exec.; b. Montevideo, Uruguay, Aug. 12, 1943; came to U.S., 1953; s. Morton Strahan and Alice Steward (Spaulding) H.; B.A. in Econs., Williams Coll., 1965; M.B.A., Emory U., 1967; 1 son, M. Strahan. Comml. lending officer First Nat. Bank of Atlanta, 1971-72; asst. v.p. Charter Investment & Devel. Co., Jacksonville, Fla., 1972-76; v.p., controller Bartell Broadcasting Co., N.Y.C., 1976-77; v.p., gen. mgr. Sta. WMJX-FM, Miami, Fla., 1977—. Served with USNR, 1968-71. Decorated Bronze Star with V. Mem. South Fla. Radio Broadcasters Assn. Clubs: Piedmont Driving, Capital City (Atlanta); Ponte Vedra (Fla.). Office: 825 41st St Miami Beach FL 33140

HODINH, THANH, mech. engr.; b. Quangnam, Vietnam, Sept. 22, 1953; came to U.S., 1972; s. Loi and Chuyen (Le) Ho; B.S. in Mech. Engring., U. Tex., El Paso, 1976; m. Beverly J. Bowen, Mar. 22, 1975; 1 son, Aaron J. Devel. engr. IBM, Austin, Tex., 1976-77, test engr., 1977—. Mem. Tau Beta Pi. Home: 6601 Laurelwood St Austin TX 78731 Office: IBM Corp Dept 163/008 Austin TX 78758

HODNETT, JUDITH VERA, nurse; b. Atlanta, Jan. 23, 1947; d. James Pierce and Mary Sibyl (Bickers) H.; A.D.N., Ga. Southwestern Coll., 1968; postgrad. in Rehab., Ga. Warm Springs Found. Hosp., 1971; B.S.N., Med. Coll. Ga., 1974, M.S.N., 1975. Staff nurse Minnie G. Boswell Meml. Hosp., Greensboro, Ga., 1968-69, head nurse and operating room supr., 1969-70; staff nurse Ga. Warm Springs Found. Hosp., 1970-71, night supr., 1971; sr. staff nurse phys. therapy dept. Central State Hosp., Milledgeville, Ga., 1971-75, clin. specialist med.-surg. center, 1975, clin. specialist dept. planning, evaluation, research and tng. Regional Mental Health Center, 1975-79; coordinator nursing service Ga. War Vets. Home, Milledgeville, 1979—; cons. rehab. care to gen. hosps. and nursing homes. Mem. Am. Nurses Assn., 14th Dist. Ga. Nurses Assn. (2d v.p. 1976—), Nat., Ga. assns. paraplegics. Democrat. Home: RFD White Plains GA 30678 Office: Russell Bldg Ga War Vets Home Milledgeville GA 31062

HOEBER, FRANCIS PACKARD, defense and econs. cons.; b. Whitestone, N.Y., July 15, 1918; s. Paul B. and Catharine P. H.; B.A., Antioch Coll., 1940; postgrad. U. Pa., 1967; m. Ethel Halverson, Sept. 1941; m. 2d, Amoretta Mathes, Aug. 28, 1965; children—Christopher, Richard, Anthony, Mark. Economist, U.S. Govt., Washington, 1940-53; head cost group Ops. Research Office, Johns Hopkins U., Bethesda, Md., 1953-56; mgr. market research, staff economist for pres. Borg-Warner Corp., Chgo., 1956-58; dep. dir. Strategic Studies Center, Stanford Research Inst., Menlo Park, Calif., 1960-68; sr. staff, asso. head social sci. dept., program mgr. def. studies Rand Corp., Santa Monica, Calif., 1968-74; pres. Hoeber Corp., Arlington, Va., 1974—; tchr. U. So. Calif., 1969-70, Cath. U. Am. Grad. Sch., 1979, U.S. Dept. Agr., 1942-45; cons. Dept. Army, 1954-56, Fed. Preparedness Agy., 1977-78, ACDA, 1975-77. Mem. Calif. State Democratic Central Com., 1974-76; mem. bd. Com. on Present Danger, 1976—. Earhart Found. research grantee, 1975-79. Mem. Ops. Research Soc. Am., Mil. Ops. Research Soc., Am. Econ. Assn., Am. Statis. Assn., Am. Ordnance Assn., U.S. Naval Inst., U.S. Strategic Inst., Center Study Democratic Instns. Democrat. Unitarian. Club: Cosmos (Washington). Author: Slow to Take Offense, 1977; Casebook on Military Applications of Modeling, 1978; (with others) Arms, Men and Military Budgets: Issues for Fiscal Year 1977, 1978, 1979, and 1981; asso. editor Comparative Strategy, 1979; contbr. articles to profl. jours. Home and Office: 5151 Williamsburg Blvd Arlington VA 22207

HOEFELMEYER, ALBERT BERNARD, cosmetic co. exec.; b. San Antonio, Mar. 27, 1928; s. Albert H. and Anna Theresa (McMonigal) H.; B.S. in Chemistry, St. Mary's U., San Antonio, 1949; M.A. in Chemistry, U. Tex., Austin, 1950; Ph.D. in Chemistry, Tex. A. and M. U., College Station, 1954. Research chemist Celanese Corp. Am., Clarkwood, Tex., 1953-55; asst. prof. chemistry Tex. A. and I. Coll., Kingsville, 1955-57; sr. nuclear engr., sr. research scientist Gen. Dynamics, Fort Worth, 1957-71; v.p. Burkhart Trailer Mfg. Co., Fort Worth, 1971-74; pres., owner Eagle Labs., Inc., Dallas, 1974—; dir., v.p., sci. cons. Bac Stat Systems, Inc., Dallas, 1976—; adj. prof. chemistry evening coll. Tex. Christian U., Fort Worth, 1958-68. Mem. Soc. Cosmetic Chemists, Am. Chem. Soc., Radiation Research Soc., S.W. Sci. Forum, N.Y. Acad. Scis., Sigma Xi, Phi Lambda Upsilon. Roman Catholic. Home: 7355 Greenacres Dr Fort Worth TX 76112 Office: 3738 W Northwest Hwy Dallas TX 75220

HOERBER, JOHN LEONARD, VI, marine systems mfg. co. exec.; b. Chgo., Mar. 31, 1951; s. John Leonard and Julia (Raia) H.; B.S., U.S. Mcht. Marine Acad., 1973; M.B.A., Pepperdine U., Los Angeles, 1978; m. Jean Marie McDonnell, Sept. 10, 1950. Chief mate research vessel Sperry Star, 1973-74; market devel. rep., then asst. mktg. mgr. for Far East, Sperry Marine Systems, Gt. Neck, N.Y., 1974-77; product mgr. satellite navigation systems and satellite communications systems Magnavox Advanced Products Labs., Torrance, Calif., 1977-79; sales mgr. marine systems Tracor Instruments, Austin, Tex., 1979—; speaker at seminars. Served to lt. USNR, 1973-80; Vietnam. Recipient numerous marine certificates; lic. 3d mate USCG. Mem. U.S. Mcht. Marine Acad. Alumni Assn. (v.p.), Propeller Club U.S., Res. Officers Assn. Republican. Roman Catholic. Author tech. papers. Home: 1505 High Rd Austin TX 78746 Office: 6500 Tracor Ln Austin TX 78721

HOF, CHARLES WILLIAM, ophthalmologist; b. Kansas City, Mo., Jan. 15, 1949; s. Charles Franklin and Olive Louise (Reeder) H.; B.A., U. Calif., Santa Barbara, 1969; M.D., U. Ark., 1973; m. Sallye Ann Lea, Aug. 30, 1970; 1 son, Scott Matthew. Resident in ophthalmology U. Ark., Little Rock, 1977—; practice medicine specializing in ophthalmology, Rogers, Ark.; mem. staffs Rogers Meml., Bates, Springdale Meml. hosps., Washington Regional Med. Center. Mem. Community Sch. Recreation Bd., Rogers, 1979—. Served with N.G., 1974—. N.Y. Life Ins. scholar, 1969-73. Mem. AMA, Am. Acad. Ophthalmology, Am. Intra-Ocular Implant Soc., Ark. Med. Soc., Benton County Med. Soc., Phi Beta Kappa, Alpha Omega Alpha. Baptist. Club: Rotary. Office: 105 S 12th St Rogers AR 72756

HOFF, EDWIN FRANK, JR., chemist; b. Bellville, Tex., Aug. 2, 1938; s. Edwin Frank and Eliza Otto (Bader) H.; B.S. in Math., Central State U., Edmond, Okla., 1960; Ph.D. in Chemistry, N. Tex. State U., Denton, 1970; m. Jean Estell Collum, Apr. 14, 1956; children—Edwin Frank III, Lisa Louise. Research chemist Black Sivalls and Bryson Steel Co., Oklahoma City, 1961-62, Frito-Lay Inc., Dallas, 1962-66; research group head Denka Chem. Corp., Houston, 1970—. Elder Presbyterian Ch. NSF grantee, 1966-69; Welch Found. grantee, 1969-70. Mem. Am. Chem. Soc., N.Y. Acad. Sci., Sigma Xi. Club: Lions (dir., 2d v.p. local club). Contbr. articles to profl. jours. Patentee in field. Home: 3934 Paulette St Pasadena TX 77504 Office: Denka Chem Corp 8701 Park Pl Houston TX 77017

HOFFMAN, GLEN MICHAEL, data processing exec.; b. Herington, Kans., Sept. 26, 1947; s. George Bernard and Della Lorraine (Glessner) H.; student Inst. Computer Systems, 1969; m. Linda Prewitt; children—Kimba, Danka. Programmer, Security Data-center (name Data Resources, Inc. 1980), Ponca City, Okla., 1969-74, asst. mgr., 1974-76, exec. v.p., 1976-80, partner, 1980—. Coach, Girls Softball, Ponca City, 1977—; coach, commr., bd. dirs. Kids Inc., 1980—. Served with USNG. Republican. Roman Catholic. Home: Route 2 Box 377 Ponca City OK 74601 Office: 222 E Grand St Ponca City OK 74601

HOFFMAN, IVAN BRUCE, physician; b. Newport News, Va., Oct. 13, 1949; s. Joe and Sarah (Goldberg) H.; B.A., U. Va., 1971, M.D., 1975; m. Carol Dianne Scholem, Dec. 18, 1976; 1 dau., Adria Rachel. Intern, Spartanburg (S.C.) Gen. Hosp., 1975-76, resident dept. family practice, 1975-78; resident in psychiatry U. Va., Charlottesville, 1978-79, Med. Coll. Va., Richmond, 1979—; vol. lectr. Am. Cancer Soc. Diplomate Am. Bd. Family Practice. Mem. Am. Acad. Family Physicians, Sigma Xi. Jewish. Home: 2602 Pleasant Run Dr Richmond VA 23233 Office: Dept Psychiatry Box 710 Med Coll Va Richmond VA 23298

HOFFMAN, JOSEPH IRVINE, JR., orthopedic surgeon; b. Charleston, S.C., Apr. 14, 1939; s. Joseph Irvine and Ellen Riley (Wiley) H.; A.B., Harvard U., 1960; M.D., Howard U., 1964; m. Pamela Louise Hayling, July 31, 1976; children—Katherine Elaine. Intern, Lenox Hill Hosp., N.Y.C., 1964-65, resident in gen. surgery, 1967-68; resident in orthopedic surgery Hosp. for Spl. Surgery. N.Y.C., 1968-71, fellow in hand and rheumatoid surgery, 1971-72; instr. surgery (orthopedics) Sch. Medicine, Cornell U., N.Y.C., 1970-72; practice medicine specializing in orthopedic surgery, Atlanta, 1972—; mem. staffs S.W. Community, S. Fulton, Crawford W. Long, Physicians and Surgeons Community, Atlanta West hosps. Diplomate Nat. Bd. Med. Examiners, Am. Bd. Orthopedic Surgery. Fellow Am. Rheumatic Assn., Am. Acad. Orthopedic Surgery, Am. Coll. Rheumatology; mem. AMA, Nat. Med. Assn., Med. Assn. Ga., Ga., Atlanta (sec. 1976—) med. assns., Omega Psi Phi (life). Roman Catholic. Home: 3400 Kilby Pl NW Atlanta GA 30327 Office: 2716 Stone-Hogan Rd Atlanta GA 30331

HOFFMAN, LEAH JANE, speech pathologist; b. Charleston, W.Va., June 10, 1953; d. Matt and Betty Jane (Dawson) Fisher; B.S. cum laude, W.Va. U., 1974, M.S., 1975; m. Randall James Hoffman, Mar. 6, 1976. Speech pathologist W.Va. Indsl. Sch. for Boys, Grafton, 1974-75; speech-lang. pathologist Multi-County Action Against Poverty, cons. W.Va. Head Start, Charleston, 1975-76; coordinator speech and hearing services Kanawha County Schs., Charleston, 1976-79; dir. exceptional children Boone County Schs., Madison, W.Va., 1979—; pvt. practice speech-lang. pathology, Charleston, 1978—; adj. instr. W.Va. Coll. Grad. Studies Inst., 1979—. Recipient Grand award W.Va. Indsl. Sch. for Boys, 1974. Mem. Am. Speech and Hearing Assn. (cert. clin. competence), W.Va. Speech and Hearing Assn., Council Exceptional Children. Clubs: Windsor Forest Garden; Newton Cole Dancers; Alumni Chorale; Edgewood Country. Home: 1305 Wychwood Rd Charleston WV 25314 Office: 69 Ave B Madison WV 25130

HOFFMAN, ROBERT JOHN, pharmacist, counselor; b. Jersey City, Sept. 18, 1930; s. John Jacob and Lillian Johanna (Keeble) H.; B.S. in Pharmacy, Mercer U., 1957; M.Ed., Clemson U., 1977; m. Linda Royal Robuck, Sept. 8, 1956; children—Lillian, Robert, Gregory. Lectr. pharmacology Grady Hosp. Sch. Nursing, Atlanta, 1957-58; coordinator attending physician pharmacology program Univ. Hosp., Augusta, Ga., 1967-68; rep. Eli Lilly and Co., 1960—; existential counseling researcher, Anderson, S.C., 1977—; guest lectr. family practice residency tng. program, Anderson. Advisor, S.C. Adoptees Unification Group. Served with USN, 1950-53. Recipient Merck award, 1957. Mem. AAUP, Am. Assn. Sex Educators, Counselors and Therapists, Assn. Humanistic Psychology, Am. Pharm. Assn. Episcopalian. Club: Masons. Home: 1304 Wendover Way Anderson SC 29621

HOFFMAN, WILLIAM WALTER, surgeon; b. Evanston, Ill., July 20, 1928; s. William and Stella (Krygiel) H.; student Loyola U., Chgo., 1945-47; B.S., Northwestern U., 1949, M.D., 1951; m. Doris Rosemary McNamara, Aug. 4, 1956; children—Jo Ann, Virginia, William Walter III. Intern, Cook County Hosp., Chgo., 1951-52; resident Northwestern U., Wesley Meml. Hosp., Chgo., 1952-57; staff urologist Chgo. VA Research Hosp., 1957-58; staff urologist Dallas Med. and Surg. Clinic, 1958—, mem. exec. com., 1969—, chmn. bd. dirs., 1977—; dir. Dallas Med. and Surg. Clinic Investment Co., 1969—, chmn. bd. dirs., 1977—; clin. asst. prof. urology U. Tex. Southwestern Med. Sch., Dallas, 1958—; vice chief urology Baylor U. Med. Center, Dallas, 1975-76, chief urology, 1976—, chmn. med. bd. and its exec. com., 1980—; mem. staffs Children's Med. Center, Dallas, Parkland Meml. Hosp., Dallas, Presbyn. Hosp., Bristol Hosp., Gaston Episcopal Hosp. Served to capt. USAF, 1952-54. Diplomate Am. Bd. Urology, Am. Bd. Med. Examiners. Fellow A.C.S., Internat. Coll. Surgeons, Am. Acad. Pediatrics; mem. AMA (Physicians' Recognition award 1971), Tex. Med. Assn., Dallas County Med. Soc. (treas. 1976—), Soc. Pediatric Urology, Am. Urol. Assn., Intercity Urol. Soc. (pres. 1970-71), Am. Group Practice Assn. (trustee 1973—, pres. South Central sect. 1974—, chmn. accreditation commn. 1976—), Am. Assn. Med. Clinics (commr. accreditation 1970-73). Contbr. articles and chpts. to profl. jours. and books. Home: 6727 Meadow Lake Ave Dallas TX 75214 Office: 4105 Live Oak St Dallas TX 75221

HOFFMANNS, FREDERIC EVERHARDT, mech. and chem. engr.; b. Marion, Ohio, Nov. 5, 1919; s. Johann E. and Anna Rosalie (Feil) H.; B. Chem. Engring., Ohio State U., 1942, Chem. Engr., 1959; M.S., Fla. Inst. Tech., 1969; m. Catherine Elene Mason, Sept. 27, 1952; children—John F., Ann Lynn, Paul Lewis. Dir. engring. J.M. Little & Assos., cons. engrs., Maumee, Ohio, 1956-59; owner Hoffmanns Engring., cons. engr., Tiffin, Ohio, 1959-60, Merritt Island, Fla. 1971—; sr. mech. engr. 1st and 2d Atlas silos Gen. Dynamics-Astronautics, Vandenburg AFB, Calif., 1960-62; engr. in charge ground support equipment, Saturn Apollo program McDonnell Douglas Corp., Kennedy Space Center, Fla., 1962-74; dist. engr. S.W. dist. region Fla. Dept. Environ. Regulation, 1974-79; ret., 1979; lectr. Fla. Inst. Tech., 1969-79. Registered profl. engr., Ohio, Fla. Mem. ASME (chmn. continuing edn. com. 1970-73), Nat. Soc. Profl. Engrs., Amateur Radio Relay League, Am. Fedn. Musicians. Home: 1485 Central Ave Merritt Island FL 32952

HOFMANN, PAUL BERNARD, hosp. adminstr.; b. Portland, Oreg., July 6, 1941; s. Max and Consuelo Theresa (Bley) H.; B.S., U. Calif., Berkeley, 1963, M.P.H., 1965; m. Lois Bernstein, June 28, 1969; children—Julie, Jason. Research asst. in hosp. adminstrn. Lab. Computer Sci., Mass. Gen. Hosp., Boston, 1966-68, asst. dir., 1968-69; asst. adminstr. San Antonio Community Hosp., Upland, Calif., 1969-70, asso. adminstr., 1970-72; dep. dir. Stanford U. Hosp., 1972-74, dir., 1974-77; exec. dir. Emory U. Hosp., 1978—; instr. in computer applications Harvard U., Boston, 1968-69; lectr. in hosp. adminstrn. UCLA, 1970-72, Stanford U. Med. Sch., 1972-77; asso. prof. community health Emory U. Sch. Medicine, 1978—. Served with U.S. Army, 1959. Fellow Am. Coll. Hosp. Adminstrs. (Robert S. Hudgens Meml. award 1976); mem. Am. Hosp. Assn., Assn. Univ. Programs in Health Adminstrn., U. Calif. Alumni Assn. Contbr. articles on hosp. adminstrn. to profl. jours. Office: Emory U Hosp 1364 Clifton Rd NE Atlanta GA 30322

HOFMANN, ROSS ELWOOD, cons. health care and energy recovery; b. Mpls., June 9, 1917; s. Charles Elwood and Jessica Alberta (Ross) Hofmann; honor matriculation Upper Can. Coll., Toronto, Ont., 1935; M.A. cum laude in Econs. and Polit. Sci., U. Toronto, 1939; postgrad. Harvard Bus. Sch., 1941; m. Louisa Anne Simpson, June 10, 1963; children—Gale Elizabeth, Carol Lynette (Mrs. William Lafitte), Anne Bernadette (Mrs. Jeoffrey Craddock), Robert M., Susan Eleanor (Mrs. Robin Wilcox). Asst. to exec. v.p. McGraw-Hill Pub. Co., N.Y.C., 1939-41; pres. So. Cross Trading Co. & Carbosand Corp., Washington, 1946-52, So. Cross Mfg. Corp., Chambersburg, Pa., 1953—, Ross Hofmann Assos., Coral Gables, Fla., 1954—; v.p. Lightval Mines, Toronto, Ont., 1951—, Teddy Bear Mines, Toronto, 1954—; chmn., panelist, lectr. health care and energy prodn. seminars, panels, meetings; cons. in field. Served with USNR, 1941-46. Mem. Am. Hosp. Assn., Hosp. Mgmt. Systems Soc., Am. Pub. Health Assn., Am. Acad. Consultants, Internat. Materials Mgmt. Soc., ASME (solid waste com.), Am. Inst. Biol. Scis., AAAS, Am. Soc. Microbiology, Inst. Indsl. Engrs., Nat. Environ. Health Assn., Theta Delta Chi. Republican. Anglican. Author: (textbook) Automation of Hospital Sterile Processing, 1968. Inventer, developer numerous equipment items, systems in health care delivery, mgmt. and energy prodn., steam and electricity from solid waste. Home: 1104 Malaga Ave Coral Gables FL 33134 Office: 2908 Salzedo Ave Coral Gables FL 33134

HOFMASTER, RICHARD NAMON, entomologist; b. Fostoria, Ohio, Apr. 12, 1915; s. Harry Alpheus and Clara Belle (Sickles) H.; B.Sc., Ohio State U., 1937, M.Sc., 1941, Ph.D., 1948; m. Doris Maude Mears, Aug. 27, 1960. Research asst. Ohio Agr. Expt. Sta., 1936-37; research technician Twin Falls (Idaho) USDA Sugarbeet Leafhopper Lab., 1938-41; instr. entomology Ohio State U., 1938, 46-47; entomologist Va. Truck and Ornamental Res. Sta., Painter, 1947-72, scientist in charge, 1972—. Served with USCGR, 1942-45; CBI. Recipient L.O. Howard Disting. Achievement award Entonol. Soc. Am., 1974. Mem. Va. Acad. Sci. (pres. agr. sect.), Am. Assn. Econ. Entomologists, Va. Acad. Sci., VFW, Am. Legion. Elder, supt. Sunday sch. Presbyn. Ch. Contbr. articles to profl. jours. Home: Box 26 Belle Haven VA 23306 Office: Box 133 Rt 1 Painter VA 23420

HOGAN, EDWARD LEO, neurologist; b. Arlington, Mass., July 26, 1932; s. Patrick Francis and Margaret Mary (McSweeney) H.; B.S. in Biochemistry, Tufts U., 1953, M.D., 1957; m. Gail Manning, July 1, 1961; children—Patrick, Mary Ellen, Timothy, Maura, Michael. Intern, Barnes Hosp., St. Louis, 1957-58; resident in neurology Boston City Hosp., 1959-60; instr. Washington U. Med. Sch., St. Louis, 1957-58; asst. in neurology Harvard U. Med. Sch., Boston, 1965-66; asst. prof. medicine U. N.C. Sch. Medicine, 1966-69, asst. prof. biochemistry, 1966-72, asso. prof. neurology, 1969-73, asso. prof. biochemistry, 1972-73, asso. dir. neurobiology program faculty, 1971-73; prof., chmn. dept. neurology Med. U. S.C., Charleston, 1973—, prof. biochemistry, 1973—; mem. merit rev. bd. for neurobiology Research Service of VA, 1976-79; dir. Muscular Dystrophy Assn. Clinic, Med. U. S.C., 1978—, mem. exec. com. Low Country chpt., 1978—. State chmn. med. fund Tufts U., 1973-79. Served with M.C., U.S. Army, 1961-63. Diplomate Am. Bd. Psychiatry and Neurology. Fellow Am. Acad. Neurology; mem. S.C. Neurol. Soc. (pres. 1978-79), Internat. Soc. Neurochemistry (mem. clin. com.), Assn. Univ. Profs. Neurology, Am. Soc. Biol. Chemists, Am. Soc. Neurochemistry, Assn. Research in Nervous and Mental Disease, So. Clin. Neurol. Soc., Phi Beta Kappa, Sigma Xi, Alpha Omega Alpha. Roman Catholic. Contbr. chpts. to books; contbr. articles to med. jours. Office: 171 Ashley Ave Charleston SC 29403

HOGAN, EUGENE ERNEST, environ. engr.; b. Niagara Falls, N.Y., July 19, 1933; s. Charles Lewis and Catherine Rachael (Dunham) H.; student Erie County Tech. Inst.; A.A., State U. N.Y., 1954; m. Lois Ann Pickens, Nov. 29, 1968; children—Lynn, Mary, Sarah, Robert, Charles. Estimator, Bilmac Iron Works, Buffalo, 1954; welding mgr. Mid Atlantic Industries, Niagara Falls, N.Y., 1955; staff environ. engr. metals div. Union Carbide Corp., Niagara Falls, 1956, Alloy, W.Va., 1956—; adj. prof. environ. engring. U. W.Va.; cons. Mesch Asso., Lockport, N.Y. Mem. Republican Com., Niagara County, 1960, sec. Rep. Party, 1962; chmn. Zoning Commn. City of N. Tonawanda (N.Y.), 1960, alderman, 1966; publicity chmn. Congressman H. Smith, 1964; asst. dir. CD, 1965; elder, fin. sec. United Methodist Ch., 1971; mem. Area Mgrs. Pollution Adv. Com.; chmn. Kanawha Valley Electrostatic Precipitator Seminar. Recipient Union Carbide Corp. Special Merit award, 1966, 1976. Clubs: Masons. Research in design, application of environ. equipment to process, power houses. Home: PO Box 516 Persimmon Rd Gauley Bridge WV 25085 Office: Union Carbide Corp Metals Div Alloy WV 25002

HOGAN, HARL TROY, educator; b. North Little Rock, Ark., Feb. 2, 1930; s. Troy G. and Bertha E. (Voegele) H.; B.S. in Mech. Engring., U. Ark., 1955; m. Dorothy Virginia Meeks, Aug. 31, 1950; children—Michael Har., Deborah Kristina. Plant engr. Pet Milk Co., Kosciusko, Miss., 1958-62; facility design engr. Douglas Aircraft Co., Tulsa, 1961-65; with St. Vincent Infirmary, Little Rock, 1965-67; dir. engring. Harris Hosp., Ft. Worth, 1967-73; maintenance supt. Gen. Cable Co., Bonham, Tex., 1974-75; dir. engring. Mercy Hosp., Muskegon, Mich., 1976; program chmn. plant engring. tech., asso. prof. Tex. State Tech. Inst., Waco, 1976—. Served with USN, 1951-54. Mem. Am. Soc. Hosp. Engrs., Am. Inst. Plant Engrs., Tex. Assn. Hosp. Engrs., Tex. Jr. Coll. Tchrs. Assn. Methodist. Club: Plant Engring. Tech. Home: 5712 Westlawn Dr Waco TX 76710 Office: Bldg 21-13 Tex State Tech Inst Waco TX 76705

HOGAN, JOSEPH THOMAS, chem. engr.; b. New Orleans, Aug. 15, 1917; s. Thomas George and Mary Emelda (McKernan) H.; B.S. in Chemistry, Loyola U., New Orleans, 1957; Ch.E., Tulane U., New Orleans, 1937; m. Alsace-Lorraine Tricon, May 8, 1940; children—Patrick J., Kathleen E. Meterologist, U.S. Weather Bur., New Orleans, 1938-41; chem. engr. So. Regional Research Center, Dept. Agr., New Orleans, 1941-73; engring. cons., Arabi, La., 1973—. Active U.S. Olympic Soc., 1977, Salvation Army Assn., 1973—. Recipient Distinguished Service award Rice Tech. Group, U.S. Dept. Agr., 1974; registered prof. engr., La. Mem. Am. Inst. Chem. Engrs., Inst. Food Technologists, La. Engring. Soc., Smithsonian Assos., La. Folklore Soc., Sigma Xi, Phi Tau Sigma, Alpha Chi Sigma. Democrat. Roman Catholic. Author: Rice and Rice By-Products, 1974; Manufacture of Rice Starch, 1967; contbr. articles to sci. jours. Utilization chem. research and tech. of rice, sweet potatoes, cottonseed and peanuts. Home and office: 7305 O'Neil St Harahan LA 70123

HOGSETT, ROBERT ANDREW, pharm. co. exec.; b. Rainelle, W.Va., Sept. 11, 1930; s. Andrew Wilson and Ruth Laura (Hollandsworth) H.; B.S., W.Va. U., 1954; m. Ruth Ann Russell, May 29, 1954; children—Roberta Ann, Richard Allen, Rebecca Amie, Russell Andrew. Staff rep. for advt. Westinghouse Electric Corp., Staunton, Va., 1955-58; staff Cargill-Wilson & Acree Advt. Agy., Richmond, Va., and Charlotte, N.C., 1958-63; mgr. promotional services dept. A.H. Robins Co., Richmond, 1963—; lectr. in field. Active Boy Scouts Am.; deacon Presbyn. Ch., Richmond, 1969-70. Served from 2d to 1st lt. U.S. Army, 1952-54; Korea; maj. Res. ret. Decorated Meritorious Service medal, Combat Infantryman's badge; recipient 1st place in greeting card design Va. Printers Assn., 1965; 1st place Advt. Regional Competition, 1970; Nat. Diana award Wholesale Druggists Assn., 1973; Nat. Paperboard 1st place packaging award, 1977; Nat. POPAI award for display, 1977. Mem. Advt. Club Richmond (dir. 1976-79), Va. Graphic Prodn. Assn. (pres. 1973-74), W.Va. Alumni Assn., Metro Quarterback Orgn. (dir. Richmond and Chesterfield Counties 1977-80), U.S. Army Res. Assn., Scabbard and Blade. Democrat. Home: 720 Wadsworth Dr Richmond VA 23235 Office: A H Robins Co 1407 Cummings Dr Richmond VA 23220

HOHF, JEROME CHALMERS, surgeon; b. Yankton, S.D., June 17, 1918; s. Julius and Rose Olive (Chalmers) H.; B.A. cum laude, Yankton Coll., 1940; M.D., Case Western Reserve Univ., 1943; m. Dorothy Emma Grunewald, Apr. 17, 1943; children—Judith Kay, Jill Carol. Intern, Univ. Hosps., Cleveland, 1943-44, asst. to resident in gen. surgery, 1944-45; resident in gen. surgery VA Hosp., Des Moines, 1947-49, VA Hosp., Temple, Tex., 1949-52; staff surgeon Buie Clinic, Marlin, Tex., 1952-55; chief surgery Hohf Clinic and Hosp., Victoria, Tex., 1955—; surg. cons. VA Hosp., Marlin, 1952—. Served to capt., M.C., U.S. Army, 1945-47. Diplomate Am. Bd. Surgery, Am. Bd. Abdominal Surgery. Fellow A.C.S.; mem. AMA. Methodist. Club: Masons (Shriner). Home: #9 Tonto Circle Victoria TX 77901 Office: 1404 E Hiller St Victoria TX 77901

HOLBROOK, EDWARD LIONEL, pneumatic control cons.; b. Bristol, Eng., Oct. 27, 1911; s. Frederick Lionel and Eliza Lott (Slade) H.; came to U.S., 1920, naturalized, 1936; student U. Pitts., 1930-34, Carnegie Inst. Tech., 1934-38, Pa. State U., 1938-41, Milw. Sch. Art (correspondence), 1937-38, Alexander Hamilton Inst. Mgmt., 1956-57; m. Annie Lou Gann, Mar. 1, 1941; children—Cynthia Holbrook Counts, Elizabeth Holbrook Shelton, Edward Lionel. Tester, test engr. Westinghouse Air Brake Co., Wilmerding, Pa., 1929-40, dist. mgr. Southeastern ty., Washington, 1940-45, mgr. govt. sales indsl. products div., 1945-54, dir. European ops., Geneva, 1954-56, gen. sales mgr. indsl. products div., Wilmerding, 1956-59; mgr. eastern div., mgr. govt. sales, mgr. fng. sales and licensing Modernair Corp., Cleve., 1959-61; v.p. Barker Air & Hydraulics, Greenville, S.C., 1961-63; dir. research Numatics Co., Highland, Mich., 1963-64; v.p., gen. mgr. Clippard Instrument Lab., Cin., 1964-67; v.p., gen. mgr., dir. Pneucon, Inc., Richmond, Calif., 1967-77; pneumatic control cons., Taylor, S.C., 1977—. Named to Exec. and Profl. Hall of Fame; registered profl. engr., D.C., Ga. Mem. AIM, Naval Architects and Marine Engrs., Nat. Soc. Profl. Engrs., Soc. Am. Mil. Engrs., European Pneumatic Assn., Am. Soc. Tool and Mfg. Engrs., Fluid Power Soc. (Fluid Power Design award 1970), Wash. Soc. Engrs. Contbr. articles to profl. jours. Patentee in field. Address: Route 2 Manley St Taylor SC 29687

HOLBROOK, JAMES MITCHELL, lawyer; b. Mineral Well, Tex., Sept. 9, 1945; s. James R. and Gladys (Denman) H.; B.B.A., U. Tex. at Austin, 1967; J.D., St. Mary's U., 1971; m. Robin Nancy Miller, Sept. 17, 1966; children—Holly Lynn, Tracy Beth. Admitted to Tex. bar, 1971; law clk. to chief judge Western Dist. Tex., U.S. Dist. Ct., San Antonio, 1971-72; partner firm Sawtelle, Goode, Davidson & Troilo, San Antonio, 1972—; lectr. in field. Mem. Am., Tex. bar assns., San Antonio Bar Assn. (sec. treas., dir. 1979-80), St. Mary's Law Sch. Alumni Assn. (dir. 1979-81). Phi Delta Phi. Editor St. Mary's U. Law Jour. Mem. state football and golf champion teams, 1963. Home: 183 Claywell Dr San Antonio TX 78209 Office: 1100 SASA Bldg San Antonio TX 78205

HOLBROOK, M(ARGARET) WILLISIA, coll. dean; b. Asheville, N.C., Jan. 5, 1944; d. Willis L. and Margaret E. H.; B.A. cum laude, Mercer U., 1966; M.Ed., U. Ga., 1971; postgrad. Clemson U., U. S.C., U. Ga. Social studies tchr. Hardoway High Sch., Columbus, Ga., 1966-70; dir. guidance McDuffie High Sch., Anderson, S.C., 1971-76; dean of students Erskine Coll., Due West, S.C., 1976-79; career edn. cons.; chmn. Student Services div. Tri-County Tech. Coll. Adv. Com., 1974-76. Bd. dirs. Anderson County and Abbeville County Am. Cancer Soc., 1975-79. Mem. Am. Personnel and Guidance Assn., Am. Coll. Personnel Assn., Nat. Employment Counselors Assn., Coll. Placement Council, So. Coll. Placement Council, S.C. Coll. Placement Assn. (treas.), S.C. Personnel and Guidance Assn., Anderson County Guidance and Counseling Assn. (sec., pres.). Baptist.

HOLCOMB, LOUISE CRANE, educator; b. Cleveland, Ga., July 19, 1928; d. William Ernest and Lois Marian (Sutton) C.; A.A., Truett-McConnell Coll., 1947; A.B., Piedmont Coll., 1950; M.Ed., U. Ga., 1958, Ed.S., 1972, Ed.D., 1975; m. Jack B. Holcomb, May 4,

1946; 1 dau., Jackie Lynn. Sec., White County Bd. Edn., Cleveland, Ga., 1945-46; sec. to pres. Truett-McConnell Coll., Cleveland, 1946-47, fin. officer, 1947-50, chmn. bus. dept., 1950-67; prof. bus., chmn. div. bus. Gainesville (Ga.) Jr. Coll., 1967—. Mem. Nat. Bus. Edn. Assn., Am. Acctg. Assn., Ga. Assn. Acctg. Instrs. (past state pres.), Ga. Assn. Educators (past local unit pres.), Phi Kappa Phi, Delta Pi Epsilon, Delta Kappa Gamma. Democrat. Baptist. Home: 802 Holly Dr Gainesville GA 30501 Office: Gainesville Jr Coll Gainesville GA 30501

HOLCOMBE, CRESSIE EARL, JR., ceramic engr.; b. Anderson, S.C., Dec. 18, 1945; s. Cressie Earl and Blanche Elizabeth (Keaton) H.; B.S. in Ceramic Engring., Clemson U., 1966, M.S., 1967; postgrad. U. Mo.-Rolla, 1973; m. Catherine Joselyn Brockman, Dec. 27, 1966. Asso. devel. engr. Union Carbide Nuclear Div., Oak Ridge, 1967-72, devel. engr., 1972-76, devel. staff, 1977—. Cabot Corp. Indsl. fellow, 1966. Mem. Am. Ceramic Soc., Keramos, Internat. Platform Assn., Sigma Xi, Tau Beta Pi. Republican. Baptist. Contbr. articles to profl. jours; patentee in field. Home: 1613 Blackwood Dr Knoxville TN 37923 Office: Union Carbide Nuclear Div Oak Ridge Y-12 Plant PO Box Y Oak Ridge TN 37830

HOLCOMBE, TROY LEON, marine geologist; b. Roxton, Tex., Mar. 8, 1940; s. Horace Cleveland and Nellie Estelle (Jenkins) H.; B.A., Hardin-Simmons U., 1961; A.M. (Gregory fellow), U. Mo., 1964; Ph.D. (Higgins fellow, Pres.'s fellow), Columbia U., 1972; m. Janis Eileen O'Neal, Aug. 21, 1971; children—Leigh Harold, Virginia Luce, Terry Estelle. Research oceanographer Ocean Floor Analysis Div., U.S. Naval Oceanographic Office, Chesapeake Beach, Md., 1968-75, marine geologist, br. head and acting div. dir. Naval Ocean Research and Devel. Activity (NORDA), NSTL Sta., Miss., 1976—; participant workshop on marine geology, geophysics of Caribbean and its resources UNESCO/Internat. Decade Ocean Exploration, 1975; convener workshop NORDA and Chief Naval Research, 1979. Mem. Geol. Soc. Am., Am. Geophys. Union, Am. Assn. Petroleum Geologists, Sigma Xi. Democrat. Baptist. Contbr. papers to profl. lit. Home: Route 1 Box 490 Picayune MS 39466 Office: Sea Floor Div Naval Ocean Research and Devel Activity NSTL Sta MS 39529

HOLDEN, ALBERT NASH, coll. adminstr.; b. Fort Worth, Oct. 16, 1922; s. Raymond Nash and Lillian Ruth (McMillan) H.; B.A., So. Meth. U., 1949; M.Ed., U. Tex., Austin, 1950; M. P. H., U. Tex., Houston, 1971; m. Virginia Jane Jacoby, Aug. 30, 1947; children—Mark Raymond, Steven Clark. Asst. dir. Rehab. Services, Tex. Edn. Agy., Austin, 1952-67; dir. Counseling Services, Gary Job Corps Center, San Marcos, Tex., 1965-68; coordinator rehab. services M.D. Anderson Hosp., Houston, 1969-71; div. chmn. Houston Community Coll., 1971—; adv. bd. mem. Coordinating Bd. Tex. Coll. and Univ. System, 1979-80. Served with USAF, 1942-45. Decorated Air medal. Bd. mem. Life Stylers United Vols., 1979. Mem. Am. Soc. Allied Health Professions, Tex. Soc. Allied Health Professions (bd. mem.). Methodist. Home: 5251 Grape St Houston TX 77096 Office: 1205 Holman St Houston TX 77004

HOLDEN, LEONARD PERCY, SR., upholstery shop owner; b. Baton Rouge, Jan. 1, 1926; s. Ben Lewis and Rebecca Beatrice (Washington) H.; Agr. cert. Okinawa U., 1945; m. Ethel Lee Wilson, Aug. 15, 1944; children—Martha Lee, Ethel Mae, Leonard Percy, Helen, James, Calvin, Joe, Linda, Fay, Joseph, Elmer. Farmer, Amite, La., 1938-43; machine operator, 1950-57; owner mgr. Leonard Holden's Upholstery Shop, Amite, La., 1966—. Served with U.S. Army, 1945-46. Mem. Am. Legion, Voters League. Democrat. Baptist. Club: Masons (Independence, La.). Home and Office: Route 3 Box 139 Amite LA 70422

HOLDER, ADOLPHUS DOYLE, educator; b. Winnsboro, Tex., Sept. 9, 1934; s. Adolphus and Cora Ella (Reeves) H.; B.S., Lamar U., 1964; M.Ed., Colo. State U., 1970, Ph.D., 1972; m. Marion Ray St. Clair, May 22, 1959; 1 dau., Madeleine Renee. Dir. middle mgmt. Howard County Jr. Coll., Big Spring, Tex., 1968-70; asst. state supr. distributive edn. Ala. State Dept. Edn., Tuscaloosa, 1972-73; chmn. vocat. edn. div. N. Tex. State U., Denton, 1978—; cons. Tex. Edn. Agy., 1972-78. Served with USMC, 1952-55. Nat. Ednl. Profl. Devel. Act fellow, 1970-72. Mem. Nat. Council Occupational Edn., Nat. Council Distributive Edn. Tchr.-Educators, Nat. Assn. State Suprs. Distributive Edn., Am. Vocat. Assn., Alpha Delta Pi, Phi Delta Kappa, Iota Lambda Sigma. Democrat. Baptist. Home: 1226 Clover Ln Denton TX 76201 Office: Coll Edn N Tex State U Denton TX 76203

HOLDER, HOWARD RANDOLPH, broadcasting corp. exec.; b. Moline, Ill., Nov. 14, 1916; s. James William and Charlotte (Brega) H.; B.A. Augustana Coll., 1939; m. Clementi Lacey-Baker, Feb. 21, 1942; children—Janice Clementi (Mrs. Collins), Susan Charlotte (Mrs. Tom Mason), Marjory Estelle, Howard Randolph. With radio sta. WHBF, Rock Island, Ill., 1939-41, radio sta. WOC, Davenport, Iowa, 1945-47, radio sta. WINN, Louisville, 1947, radio sta. WRFC, Athens, Ga., 1948-56, radio sta. WGAU-WNGC, Athens, 1956—; pres. Clarke Broadcasting Corp., Athens, 1956—, Mid-West Broadcasting Corp., Griffin, Ga., 1965—; dir. Citizens & So. Nat. Bank Athens. Mem. adv. bd. Salvation Army, chmn., 1962, 63; chmn. Athens Parks and Recreation Bd., 1952-62; mem. adv. bd. Athens-Clarke County A.R.C., 1950-70, Clarke County Juvenile Ct., 1960-72; chmn. region IV Am. Cancer Soc., 1968; chmn. Cherokee dist. Boy Scouts Am., 1966, 67, mem. adv. bd. N.E. Ga. Area council; mem. adv. bd. Henry W. Grady Sch. Journalism and Mass Media, U. Ga., 1973-78; bd. dirs. Athens Crime Prevention Com., 1960-70, Augustana Coll. Alumni Assn., 1974-77, Rec. for Blind, 1977—; mem. Model Cities Policy Bd., 1970-71, Georgians for Safer Hwys., 1970; trustee Ga. Rotary Student Fund, 1973—; co-pres. Friends Ga. Mus. Art, 1974-75. Served with AUS, 1941-46; ETO. Recipient Silver Beaver award Boy Scouts Am., 1973; Outstanding Achievement award Augusta Coll. Alumni Assn., 1973, Robert Stolz medaille, 1973; named Boss of Year, Athens Jr. C. of C., 1959; Broadcaster-Citizen of Year, Ga. Assn. Broadcasters, 1962; Employer of Yr., Athens Bus. and Profl. Women, 1969; Ky. col., 1961; Athens Citizen of Year, Athens Woman's Club, 1971; Liberty Bell award Athens Bar Assn., 1977; Paul Harris fellow, 1978; Advocacy award N.E. Ga. Planning and Devel. Commn., 1979. Mem. Res. Officers Assn. (pres. Athens 1962), Ga. Assn. Broadcasters (pres. 1961), Ga. A.P. Broadcasters Assn. (pres. 1963), Internat. Platform Assn., Athens Area C. of C. (pres. 1970), Golden Quill, Sigma Delta Chi, Alpha Delta Sigma, Alpha Psi Omega, Phi Omega Phi, Di Gamma Kappa (Ga. Pioneer Broadcaster of Year award 1971). Rotarian (pres. Athens club 1957-58, dist. gov. 1969-70, Citizen of Yr. award 1971). Clubs: Gridiron, Touchdown (pres. Athens 1963-64). Home: 383 W View Dr Athens GA 30601 Office: 850 Bobbin Mill Rd Athens GA 30604

HOLDER, SIDNEY GEORGE, JR., truck equipment co. exec.; b. Birmingham, Ala., Feb. 19, 1929; s. Sidney George and Fannie Rae (Spiro) H.; B.S., U. Ala., 1950, M.S. in Metallurgy, 1951; M.S. in Indsl. Mgmt., U. Tenn. 1953; postgrad. U. N.C., 1975, Jefferson State Coll., 1976; m. Peggy Israel, Feb. 14, 1969; children—Sidney J., Stephanie A. Sr. metallurgist So. Research Inst., Birmingham, Ala., 1964-70; metallurgist Union Carbide Nuclear Co., Oak Ridge, 1955-64; pvt. cons., 1970-73; with Fontaine Truck Equipment Co., Birmingham, 1973—, mgr. engring. quality and safety, 1973—; lectr. in field. Pres., Greater Birmingham Safety League, 1975-77. Served with Chem. Corps. USAR, 1951-53. Recipient Nat. Safety Council Award of Honor, 1974, 75, 76. Mem. Am. Soc. for Metals (program v.p. 1976-80), Am. Soc. Safety Engrs., Am. Welding Soc. Jewish. Clubs: Good Dogs Ltd., Jewish Community Center, Found. for Christian Living. Contbr. articles on trucking and safety to profl. jours.; author: Quality Control Manual, 1979-80. Home: 3709 Spring Valley Rd Birmingham AL 35223 Office: 1232 N 37 Pl Birmingham AL 35234

HOLDERNESS, HOWARD, life ins. exec.; b. Tarboro, N.C., Nov. 2, 1902; s. George Allen and Harriet (Howard) H.; A.B., U. N.C., 1923; LL.D., U. N.C. at Chapel Hill, 1966, at Greensboro, 1969; M.B.A., Harvard U., 1925; m. Adelaide Fortune, Apr. 4, 1936; children—Adelaide Lucinda, Howard, Alexandra Fortune, Richard Thurston, Pamela Louisa. Former chmn. bd. Jefferson Standard Life Ins. Co., Greensboro, Jefferson-Pilot Corp.; dir. Pilot Life Ins. Co., Jefferson Standard Broadcasting Co., Duke Power Co.; dir. emeritus Carolina Tel. & Tel. Co., Tarbaro; trustee emeritus Wachovia Realty Investments. Civilian aide to Sec. of Army for N.C., 1958-62. Bd. dirs. N.C. Meml. Hosp., Chapel Hill. Recipient Citation for Distinguished Citizenship, N.C. Citizens Assn., 1970. Mem. Inst. Life Ins. (dir., mem. exec. com. 1957-60, chmn. bd. 1959), Life Ins. Assn. Am. (dir. 1957-60). Home: 2000 Granville Rd Greensboro NC 27408

HOLEKAMP, BETTYE JOANNE, interior decorator; b. Waco, Tex., May 10, 1934; d. Wesley Robert and Emma Lille (Bennett) Carolan; B.A. in Edn., U. Tex. at Austin, 1952; m. Lloyd Martin Holekamp, Oct. 3, 1953; children—Paul, Carol. Interior designer, San Antonio, 1957—; owner, operator furniture store, Boerne, Tex., 1976—. Mem. San Antonio Home Builders. Episcopalian. Home: Route 5 Box 5101 Boerne TX 78006 Office: 3735 Colony Dr San Antonio TX 78230 also 265 S Main St Boerne TX 78006

HOLLADAY, CHARLES EDWIN, state supt. edn.; b. Newton, Miss., July 12, 1918; s. Clarence O. and Gladys (Bounds) H.; B.A., Miss. Coll., 1946; M.A., Peabody Coll., 1949; Ed.D., U. Miss., 1969; m. Bess Edward, May 25, 1939; children—Charles E., Stephen E. Tchr. Duncan (Miss.) Pub. Schs., 1941-43, Enochs Jr. High Sch., Jackson, Miss., 1946-49; asst. prin. Central High Sch., Jackson, 1949-53, prin., 1953-58; supt. schs., Tupelo, Miss., 1958-76; state supt. edn. Miss., 1976—. Exec. sec. N.E. Miss. TV Council, 1961—; chmn. Miss. Accrediting Commn., 1963-65; ednl. auditor Fed. project; developer ednl. mgmt. tng. program for adminstrs. N.E. Miss. Trustee Blue Mountain (Miss.) Coll. Served with USAAF, 1942-46. Recipient merit award for outstanding ednl. program Miss. Econ. Council, 1966. Mem. NEA (Pace Maker award for Miss. 1965), Miss. (past pres. adult edn. div.), Tupelo edn. assns., Miss. Secondary Sch. Prins. Assn. (past pres.), Am., Miss. assns. sch. adminstrs., Mental Health Assn. Baptist (deacon). Rotarian (past dir.). Office: PO Box 771 Jackson MS 39205

HOLLADAY, JAMES FRANK, mfg. co. exec.; b. Birmingham, Ala., Apr. 5, 1922; s. Allen Author and Mary Estell (Campbell) H.; B.S., Ga. Inst. Tech., 1950; m. Anne Wedsworth, July 17, 1948; children—James Frank, David Allen, Cynthia Anne. Plant engr. Erwin Mills, Stonewall, Miss., 1950-52, Southwire Co., Carrollton, Ga., 1952-63, v.p., 1963—, dir., 1958—; engring. mgr. Denney-Southwire, Carrollton, 1977—; dir. World of Services, Carrollton. Served to 1st lt., inf., U.S. Army, 1943-47. Named Engr. of Yr., Am. Inst. Plant Engrs., 1966; Engr. of Yr. in Industry, Ga. Soc. Profl. Engrs., 1970; Mr. Industry award, 1972; registered profl. engr., Ga. Fellow Am. Inst. Plant Engrs.; mem. Ga. Safety Council, Wire Assn., Ga. L.P. Gas Assn., Ga. Engring. Found., Order of Engrs. Baptist. Clubs: PTA, Lions (Ga. dist. gov. 1963-64). Home: 305 Kramer St Carrollton GA 30117 Office: Fertilla St Carrollton GA 30117

HOLLAND, ANGE LOUISE NEWBY, speech pathologist; b. Searcy, Ark., June 21, 1953; d. Eugene Riley and Ann Largent Newby; student U. Ark., Fayetteville, 1971-73; B.A. in Speech Pathology, U. Ark., Little Rock, 1974, M.S. in Communicative Disorders, 1979; m. Jimmie Wayne Holland, June 16, 1973; 1 son, Jimmie Wayne. Speech pathologist, tchr. preschool class, early childhood dept. Civitan Center, Benton, Ark., 1976-77; speech pathologist Benton Public Schs., 1977—. Lic. speech pathologist, Ark. Mem. Am. Speech-Lang. and Hearing Assn. (cert. clin. competence in speech pathology), Ark. Speech and Hearing Assn., Saline County Assn. Children with Learning Disabilities, NEA, Ark. Edn. Assn., Benton Edn. Assn., Kappa Delta Pi. Methodist. Clubs: Star Promenaders Square Dance, Bauxite Dance. Office: Benton Pub Schs 536 River St Benton AR 72015

HOLLAND, CHARLOTTE SUE, educator; b. Durham, N.C., Feb. 24, 1937; d. Charles Henry and Maybelle Eudora (Dowdy) H.; B.A., Lynchburg Coll., 1959; M.R.E., Lexington Theol. Sem., 1965. Ordained to ministry Disciples of Christ Ch., 1965; dir. consultation and edn. Central Va. Mental Health Services, Lynchburg, 1974—; part time instr. in sociology Central Va. Community Coll., 1974; group co-counselor. Mem. Am. Personnel and Guidance Assn., Va. Personnel and Guidance Assn., Lynchburg Personnel and Guidance Assn., Internat. Assn. Transactional Analysis, Am. Assn. Creative Change, Am. Soc. Group Work and Psychodrama, Am. Assn. Group Work. Home: 1414 Ashbourne Dr Lynchburg VA 24501 Office: PO Box 2146 1010 Miller Park Sq Lynchburg VA 24501

HOLLAND, CULLEN JOE, educator; b. Blackwell, Okla., Aug. 31, 1915; s. Cullen Gray and Willie Karr (Wells) H.; A.A., No. Okla. Jr. Coll., 1935; B.A., U. Okla., 1937, M.A., 1947; Ph.D., U. Minn., 1956; m. Mary Marie Battle, Dec. 20, 1947; 1 dau., Rebecca Jo. Reporter, Blackwell Daily Jour., 1934-36, sports editor, 1937-38, copy editor, 1940-41; asst. dir. press relations U. Okla., Norman, 1941-43, 46-47, editorial supr. student publs., asst. prof. journalism, 1947-52, asso. prof., 1956-64, prof., 1964—, dir. Sch. Journalism, 1961-69. Served with USAAF, 1943-46. So. fellow, 1955. Mem. Assn. for Edn. in Journalism, Soc. Profl. Journalists. Democrat. Methodist. Home: 1003 Woodland Dr Norman OK 73069 Office: Sch Journalism U Okla Norman OK 73019

HOLLAND, EARL STAFFORD, accountant; b. Windsor, Va., Apr. 1, 1912; s. James Timothy and Ballie (Stephenson) H.; student Coll. William and Mary, 1930-31, Elon Coll., 1933-34; law student U. Va., 1936-37; children—Earl Stafford, Marianne Holland Stern, Phyllis Holland Barton. Tchr. sch., 1931-32; supr. adult edn., 1934-36; real estate broker Earl S. Holland, Franklin, Va., 1954-63; co-owner, corporate sec. Powhatan Corp., 1950-65, Tidewater New, Franklin, 1954-65; tax dir. Baker Equipment Engring. Co., 1967-68; broadcaster various Va. radio stas., 1930-33; pvt. practice accounting as Earl S. Holland, Tampa, Fla., 1970—. Del. Inst. Pub. Affairs, 1934, 35, 36, 37; past pres. PTA; Sunday sch. tchr., Sunday sch. supt. Episcopal Ch.; charter mem. Carrsville Community Center, 1953; instl. rep. Boy Scouts Am., Carrsville, 1954-55. Mem. Internat. Platform Assn., Kappa Psi Nu. Clubs: Lafayett Yacht (Norfolk, Va.); Ruritan (charter mem. Carrsville, lt. gov.); Kiwanis (Tampa, Fla.). Home: 695 Pinewood Dr Dunedin FL 33528 Office: PO Box 397 St Tampa FL 33601

HOLLAND, EDWARD MCHARG, lawyer, state senator; b. Washington, Nov. 28, 1939; s. Edwin Trammell and Elizabeth (McHarg) H.; A.B., Princeton, 1962; LL.B., U. Va., 1965; LL.M., Georgetown U., 1967; m. JoAnn Dotson, Dec. 3, 1966; children—David Ames, Allan Taylor, Lee McHarg. Admitted to Va. bar, 1965; tax law specialist Internal Revenue Service, Washington, 1965-66; partner firm Holland and Dobson, Arlington, Va.; mem. Va. Senate, 1972—; mgr., dir. Tidewater Research Found., Inc., Arlington, 1972—; dir. 1st Va. Banks, Inc. Bd. dirs. Vets. Meml. br. YMCA; mem. Arlington Salvation Army. Mem. Va., Arlington bar assns., Va. Trial Lawyers. Clubs: Princeton (N.J.) Quadrangle; Explorers (N.Y.C.). Home: 3168 N 21st St Arlington VA 22201 Office: 2054 N 14th St Arlington VA 22201

HOLLAND, EVELYN FAUCETTE (MRS. SHERMAN W. HOLLAND, JR.), pub. relations firm exec.; b. Lillington, N.C., Sept. 11, 1927; d. Henry Bethune and Virgina McRorie (Stegall) Faucette; student Charron-Williams Comml. Coll., 1946, U. Miami, 1947, Miami Conservatory of Music, 1945-47; m. Sherman William Holland, Jr., Apr. 28, 1946; children—Karen (Mrs. Charles W. Shaffer, Sr.), Sherman William III, Michael Edward. With Falco Printing, Inc., Miami, Fla., 1962-77, Falco & Assos., Inc., Miami, 1968-77, exec. adminstrv. asst. to state rep. for State of Fla., 1974-77. Commr., Hialeah Housing Authority, 1968-72; mem. Fla. Commn. on Status of Women, 1972-77; chmn. Dade County Personnel Adv. Bd., 1970-77, Model Cities Released Employment Bd., 1972-73; pres. local 11, Graphic Arts Internat. Union, 1965-67; program dir. Spotlite Club, 1977; bd. dirs. Hialeah YMCA, 1978—; mem. Dade County Dem. Exec. Com., 1970-74, treas., 1971-72; mem. Dade County Dem. Com., 1970-74; sec. Northwest Dade County Dem. Club; mem. Fla. Gov.'s Conf. Edn., Fla. Dept. Labor Apprenticeship Adv. Bd. and Apprenticeship Council. Recipient service award VA Hosp., Miami, Fla., 1970, pub. ser. award for sr. citizen service State Vets, Service Office, Hialeah, 1972; Holland Hall sr. citizens' housing project named in her honor, 1972; Citizen's award City of Hialeah, 1977; Housing awards Alcoa Corp., Housing Corp. Am. Mem. Com. of 100, Bus. and Profl. Women's Club Hialeah, Com. for Community Action, Alachua County/Gainesville C. of C. (pvt. industry council). Home: Route 1 Box 148 A Alachua FL 32615

HOLLAND, JAMES CLARENCE, educator, pub.; b. Balt., Nov. 3, 1935; s. Amos Thornton and Cecelia Mary (Gassinger) H.; B.A., U. Md., 1959, M.A., 1965; Ph.D., Cath. U. Am., 1968; m. Mary Griset, July 14, 1968. Systems analyst central charge service Riggs Nat. Bank, Washington, 1961-63; asst. prof. Albertus Magnus Coll., New Haven, 1968-71; asso. prof. history Shepherd Coll., Shepherdstown, W.Va., 1971—; pres., pub. Patmos Press, Inc., Shepherdstown, 1975—; mem. Pres.'s Council, Washington Theol. Union, Silver Spring, Md. Active zoning appeals bd. Corp. of Shepherdstown, 1978—; dir. Hist. Shepherdstown Commn. Served with U.S. Army, 1959-61. Am. Council Learned Socs. grantee for research in U.K., summer 1973. Mem. Am. Acad. Religion, Am. Cath. Hist. Assn. (life), Anglo-Am. Assos., Conf. Brit. Studies, Research Soc. Victorian Periodicals, Soc. Scholarly Publishing (charter), Victorian Studies Assn. Republican. Roman Catholic. Club: Men's (v.p. 1980) (Shepherdstown). Co-author: Lord Acton: The Decisive Decade 1864-1874, 1970; co-editor: The Correspondence of Lord Acton and Richard Simpson, 3 vols., 1971-75. Office: Dept History Shepherd Coll Shepherdstown WV 25443

HOLLAND, JAY WINSTON, audiologist; b. Memphis, Tex., Nov. 29, 1948; s. Billy Bob and Mary Sue (Eddins) H.; B.A., Tex. Tech. U., 1972, M.A., 1974; m. Pamela Anne Fuller, Dec. 28, 1968. Staff audiologist W. Tex. Rehab. Center, Abilene, 1974—, chief audiology services, 1976—; cons. audiologist Abilene Ind. Sch. Dist., Region XIV Day Sch. for Deaf, W. Tex. Services for Deaf. Bd. dirs. Community Recreation Program for Handicapped, 1977—. Served with AUS, 1971. Mem. Big Country Speech and Hearing Assn., Am. Speech Lang. and Hearing Assn., Tex. Speech Lang. and Hearing Assn., Citizens for the Republic. Mem. Lubbock Bible Ch. Club: Kiwanis. Home: 4618 Pamela St Abilene TX 79606 Office: 4601 Hartford St Abilene TX 79605

HOLLAND, JOHN BIRL, obstetrician, gynecologist; b. Albertville, Ala., Jan. 21, 1928; s. Walter Daniel and Margaret Ann (Malone) H.; B.S., Howard Coll., 1949; M.D., Tulane U., 1953; m. Nancy Carol Smith, Sept. 1, 1959; children—John B., Michael R. Intern, Los Angeles Gen. Hosp., 1953-54; resident Alton Ochsner Med. Found., New Orleans, 1954-55, 57-60; practice medicine specializing in obstetrics and gynecology, New Orleans, 1960—; asst. prof. dept. obstetrics and gynecology Tulane U. Med. Sch.; asst. vis. prof. dept. obstetrics and gynecology Charity Hosp., New Orleans. Served with M.C., USAF, 1955-57. Diplomate Am. Bd. Obstetrics and Gynecology. Mem. AMA, La. State, Jefferson Parish med. socs., New Orleans, Southeastern obstet. and gynecol. socs., Am. Coll. Obstetricians and Gynecologists, Am. Fertility Soc., Pi Kappa Alpha, Nu Sigma Nu. Clubs: Beta. Contbr. articles to obstetrical, gynecol. jours. Home: 278 Garden Rd River Ridge LA 70123 Office: 1514 Jefferson Hwy New Orleans LA 70121

HOLLAND, JOHN ROBERT, city ofcl.; b. Stamford, Tex., Apr. 29, 1952; s. Bartlett and Lucy (Moudy) H.; B.S. in Parks Adminstrn. and Landscape Architecture, Tex. Tech. U., 1974; m. Marlene Bowling, Nov. 4, 1978. Dir. grounds maintenance Abilene Christian U., 1974-75; horticulturist City of Winter Park (Fla.), 1975-77, div. chief parks, forestry and cemeteries, 1977-78, parks dir., 1978—; owner, mgr. Planscaping Services, Winter Park, 1978—; pvt. cons. park planning and land devel.; guest lectr. Bd. dirs. United Cerebral Palsy Central Fla., 1979—. Recipient Greening of the Govt. citation Fla. Fedn. Garden Clubs, 1978. Mem. Am. Soc. Landscape Architects, Nat. Recreation and Park Assn., Fla. Inst. Park Personnel (exec. state sec. 1976—, Man of Yr. award 1977). Democrat. Presbyterian. Home: 402 Kilshore Ln Winter Park FL 32789 Office: City of Winter Park 401 S Park Ave Winter Park FL 32789

HOLLAND, KEN L., congressman; b. Hickory, N.C., Nov. 24, 1934; s. James A. and Ruby B. H.; B.A., U. S.C., 1960; LL.B., U. S.C., 1963, J.D., 1970; m. Diane Martin; children—Lamar, Amy, Beth. Admitted to S.C. bar, practiced in Camden; congress man from 5th S.C. dist. Legal counsel S.C. Democratic party, also mem. exec. com. Served with AUS, 1952. Mem. Am., S.C. bar assns., S.C. Trial Lawyers Assn., S.C. Jaycees (past v.p.). Methodist. Kiwanian. Home: Gaffney SC 29340 Office: 103 Cannon House Office Bldg Washington DC 20515

HOLLAND, PETER MARC, ophthalmologist; b. N.Y.C., Apr. 7, 1944. s. George and Estelle H.; B.A., Clark U., 1965; M.D., N.Y. Med. Coll., 1969; m. Merle Susan Lumish, May 26, 1968; children—Matthew David, John Michael. Intern, Montefiore Hosp. and Med. Center, Bronx, N.Y., 1969-70; resident dept. ophthalmology Duke U., Durham, N.C., 1972-75; clin. fellow retinal diseases and surgery Mass. Eye and Ear Infirmary, Harvard Med. Sch., Boston, 1975-76; asst. prof. dept. ophthalmology/retina service George Washington U. Med. Center, Washington, 1976-77; clin. instr. dept. ophthalmology Baylor Coll. Medicine, Houston, 1977—; mem. staff Methodist Hosp., Houston, Hermann Hosp., Houston, Bayshore Hosp., Pasadena, Tex., Southmore Hosp., Pasadena, Clear Lake Hosp., Webster, Tex.; practice ophthalmology specializing in diseases and surgery of the retina, Pasadena, 1977—. Served with USPHS, 1970-72. Diplomate Nat. Bd. Med. Examiners, Am. Bd. Ophthalmology. Fellow Am. Acad. Ophthalmology; mem. Tex. Med. Assn., Tex. Ophthalmol. Assn., Houston Ophthalmol. Assn., Alpha Omega Alpha. Contbr. articles to profl. jours. Office: 3320 Plainview St Pasadena TX 77504

HOLLAND, ROBERT CAMPBELL, anatomist; b. Bushnell, Ill., Aug. 16, 1923; s. Harvey Howard and Lois Sarah (Campbell) H.; B.S., U. Wis., 1948, M.S., 1949, Ph.D., 1955; m. Hilda Pauline Burgi, Sept. 25, 1945; children—Jonathan Robert, Heather Ann. Instr., Northwestern U. Dental Sch., 1949-51; asst. prof. anatomy U. N.D. Sch. Medicine, 1955-60; asso. prof. U. Ark. Sch. Medicine, 1960-66; mem. staff Rockefeller Found. and prof. and chmn. dept. anatomy Mahidol U., Bangkok, Thailand, 1966-76; prof., chmn. dept. anatomy Sch. Medicine, Morehouse Coll., Atlanta, 1976—; Nat. Found. for Infantile Paralysis postdoctoral fellow UCLA Sch. Medicine, 1957-58, vis. prof., 1976. Served with M.C., U.S. Army, 1943-46. Wis. Alumni Research Found. fellow, 1951-54; NIH grantee, 1959-71. Mem. Am. Assn. Anatomists, Am. Acad. Neurology, Soc. Exptl. Biology and Medicine, AAAS, Sigma Xi. Research, publs. on brain. Home: 3653 High Green Dr Marietta GA 30067 Office: Sch Medicine Morehouse Coll Atlanta GA 30314

HOLLAND, ROBERT VANCE, JR., lawyer; b. San Angelo, Tex., Dec. 3, 1946; s. Robert Vance and Jeannie Pauline (Roe) H.; A.A., Schreiner Inst., 1966; B.B.A., U. Tex., 1969; J.D., U. Houston, 1972; m. Dona Lynn Gurtler, Dec. 24, 1973; 1 dau., Kristen Lynn. Asst. sgt. at arms Tex. State Senate, 1969-70; admitted to Tex. bar, 1972; law clk. Bray, Orsburn, Browning & Watson, Houston, 1970-72; partner firm Bray & Watson, Houston, 1974-79; individual practice law, Houston, 1979—. Bd. dirs. March of Dimes, 1978. Mem. Houston Bar Assn., Am. Bar Assn., Tex. Trial Lawyers Assn. (dir.) Am. Trial Lawyers Assn., Mensa. Democrat. Methodist. Home: 2312 Southgate Houston TX 77030 Office: 608 Fannin Houston TX 77002

HOLLAND, WILLIAM MEREDITH, lawyer; b. Live Oak, Fla., Feb. 6, 1922; s. Isaac and Annie E. (Williams) H.; B.A., Fla. A. and M. Coll., 1947; LL.B., Boston U., 1951; children—William Meredith, Maurice, Gian, Gaelim, Shakira. Admitted to Fla. bar, 1951, since practiced in West Palm Beach; now municipal judge, Riviera Beach, Fla. Bd. dirs. Children's Home Soc. Fla. Served with AUS, 1943-46. Mem. Council Human Relations, ACLU; cooperating atty. NAACP Legal Def. Fund. Mem. Am., Palm Beach County bar assns., Am. Judicature Soc., Fla. Municipal Judges Assn., Phi Beta Sigma. Episcopalian. Home: 611 W Kalmia Dr Lake Park FL 33403 Office: 605 Clematis St West Palm Beach FL 33401

HOLLANDER, KENNETH ALLEN, market research co. exec.; b. East Orange, N.J., Aug. 30, 1936; s. Howard Irwin and Elinor Hollander; B.S., Ohio State U., 1958; M.B.A. cum laude, U. Mo., 1964; m. Cynthia Elise Woodruff, Aug. 27, 1960; children—Mark, Todd. Research brand mgr. Procter & Gamble, Cin., 1958-61; asso. research dir. Hallmark Cards, Kansas City, Mo., 1961-64; dir. research Young & Rubicam, Chgo., 1964-70; v.p., dir. Communications Planning Group, Interpublic Cos., Atlanta, 1970-73; pres. Kenneth Hollander Assos., Atlanta, 1973—; lectr. Emory U., cons. SBA. Mem. Am. Mktg. Assn., Am. Statis. Soc., Council Am. Survey Research Orgns., Advt. Research Found., Atlanta Advt. Club (dir.). Contbr. editor: Advertising, 4th edit., 1977. Home: 411 W Wesley Rd Atlanta GA 30305 Office: Kenneth Hollander Assos 400 Colony Square Atlanta GA 30261

HOLLANDSWORTH, THOMAS GREENE, JR., interior and fashion designer, hist. preservation co. exec.; b. Martinsville, Va., Aug. 31, 1947; s. Thomas Greene and June (Forsythe) H.; B.F.A., Va. Commonwealth U., 1970, postgrad., 1970-72; postgrad. Am. U., Athens, 1976, U. for Ams., Perugia, Italy, 1980—. Tchr. art Henry County (Va.) Sch. System, 1971-72; founder Galleries II, Inc., Martinsville, 1971, pres., 1971—; founder Lexington Interiors Ltd. (Va.), rehab. hist. structures, 1979—, Thomas Hollandsworth Ltd., lady's splty. stores, 1979—; chmn. bd. Thomas Hollandsworth Group; tchr. interior design Patrick Henry Coll., Martinsville, 1973; founder Steephill Assos., Augusta County, Va., 1980. Bd. dirs. Govs. Sch. for Gifted, 1973-74. Mem. Va. Mus. Fine Arts, Am. Inst. Interior Designers, Victorian Soc., Am. Soc. for Historic Preservation, Smithsonian Instn., Friends of Met. Mus., Fan Dist. Assn. Club: Country of Staunton. Home: 2301 Hanover Ave Richmond VA 23220 Office: 203 S Jefferson St Lexington VA 24450 also 2E Beverly St Staunton VA

HOLLEMAN, AGNES SMITH, hosp. ofcl.; b. Greenwood, Miss., July 16, 1923; d. George William and Helene (Love) Smith; diploma U. Tenn., 1944; m. Jeremiah Henry Holleman, June 12, 1944; children—Jeremiah Henry, Virginia Ann, Helene Elizabeth. Nurse operating room Greenwood Leflore Hosp., 1945; nurse surg. floor Carraway Meth. Hosp., Birmingham, Ala., 1947-48; head nurse central supply Lowndes (Miss.) Gen. Hosp., 1969, head nurse nursery, 1970-71; inservice dir. Golden Triangle Regional Med. Center, Columbus, Miss., 1973—, adv. com. Nursing Sch.; cons. continuing edn. Active Boy Scouts Am., 1954-56, Girl Scouts U.S., 1956-62; mem. emergency care com. Miss. div. Am. Heart Assn. Mem. Am. Nurses Assn., Dist. 17 Miss. Nurses Assn., Miss. Hosp. Assn. Soc. Hosp. Educators. Methodist. Clubs: Les Amies Study (pres. 1972-73), Galaxy Garden. Home: 1621 Chickasaw Dr Columbus MS 39701 Office: Golden Triangle Regional Med Center 2520 5th St N Columbus MS 39701

HOLLEMAN, WILLIAM DAVIS, mfg. co. exec.; b. St. Louis, Apr. 5, 1953; s. Malcolm Louis and Nancy Benson (Kern) H.; B.S., Auburn U., 1975; M.B.A., U. Miss., 1976. Mgmt. trainee Performance Systems Inc., Nashville, 1969; salesman McRae's Co., Jackson, Miss., 1970; forester's asst. James M. Vardaman Forestry Cons., Jackson, 1971; asst. crew chief Reynolds Engring. Co., Jackson, 1973-74; food service mgr. Interfraternity Co-op, Auburn, Ala., 1975; grad. asst. U. Miss., 1975-76; asst. mktg. rep. IBM, Memphis, 1976-77, asso. mktg. rep., 1978, spl. systems mktg. rep., 1979—. Adv., Jr. Achievement, 1979-80; budget com. United Way, 1980; mem. Memphis-in-May. Mem. Ducks Unlimited Inc., Am. Mgmt. Assn., Am. Mktg. Assn., Omicron Delta Epsilon, Pi Sigma Epsilon, Delta Sigma Pi, Alpha Tau Omega. Episcopalian. Home: 209 Palisade St Memphis TN 38111 Office: 600 Jefferson Ave Memphis TN 38105

HOLLERS, HARDY, lawyer; b. Clarendon, Tex., May 20, 1901; s. James Lemuel and Mattie (Mays) H.; student Southwestern U., 1918-19; LL.B., U. Tex., 1927, J.D., 1927; m. Mildred Bernice Calk, Apr. 18, 1921; children—Hardy Warren, Richard Van, James Carlyle. Admitted to Tex. bar, 1927, since practiced in Austin; asst. county atty., Travis County, 1928-29; asst. dist. atty., Travis County, 1933-34; spl. dist. judge, Travis County, 1935-36. Trial counsel maj. war criminals, Nuremberg, Germany, 1945. Gen. chmn. Greater Austin Assn., 1968-72. Served from maj. to col. AUS, 1941-46; ETO. Decorated Legion of Merit (U.S.); Croix de Guerre with palm (France). Fellow Tex. Bar Found. (life); mem. Nat. Res. Officers Assn. (life), Am. Legion (past post comdr.), Tex. (past dir.), Travis County bar assns. Methodist. Mason (Shriner). Club: Headliners. Home: 2710 Townes Lane Austin TX 78703 Office: Am Bank Tower Austin TX 78701

HOLLIDAY, CHARLES EDWARD, hotel exec.; b. Fayetteville, N.C., Oct. 12, 1942; s. Jasper Talbert and Louise (Price) H.; B.S., Va. Commonwealth U., 1975; m. Judith H., Apr. 10, 1971; children—Charles E., Danielle Nicole. Airline agt. United Airlines, So. Airways, Washington, 1967-70; asst. credit mgr. Washington Hilton Hotel, 1975; front office mgr. John Marshall Hotel, Richmond, Va., 1975; gen. mgr. Boar's Head Inn, Charlottesville, Va., 1975-79; dir. hotel ops. Hotel Mgmt. Corp., Sheraton Salisbury Inn (Md.) and Sheraton Potomac Inn, Rockville, Md., 1979—. Mem. Albemarle County Sign Commn. Served with USAF, 1961-65. Mem. Va. Motel Assn. (dir.), Charlottesville-Albemarle Lodging Assn. (pres.), Charlottesville-Albemarle Tourism Com. Baptist. Home: 1317 Kenwood Ln Charlottesville VA 22901 Office: 3 Research Ct Rockville MD 20850

HOLLIDAY, PATRICIA RUTH, evangelist, microfilm center exec.; b. Jacksonville, Fla., Nov. 17, 1935; d. Robert Irving and Leona Adelle (McKenzie); student Massey Bus. Coll., 1956, Luther Rice Sem., 1975, Coll. Med. Arts and Bus., 1971; m. Vadim Peter Holliday, Jan. 10, 1965; children—Katheryn Patricia, Alexander Vadim, Connie. Owner, pres. The Spa Complex, Inc., Jacksonville, 1964—; v.p. generic drug co., Jacksonville, 1966—; v.p. Gen. Micro-film Corp., Jacksonville, 1974—; sec. Delta Drug Corp., Jacksonville, 1976—. Del. 1st. World Conf. Holy Spirit, Israel, 1974; founder Southeastern Sem. Mem. state com. Republican Party Fla., 1976—, bd. dirs., campaign dir. Richard M. Nixon for Pres., Jacksonville Beach, Fla., 1972. Named lt. col. Ga. Militia, 1971. Mem. Internat. Platform Assn., Ortega Legis. Study Group, Minutewomen Fla., Four Found., Leadership Found., Women's Aglow Fellowship, Eagle Forum. Republican. Clubs: Ponte Vedra; Fine Arts Univ. Jacksonville; Ponte Vedra Women's; Fla. Fedn. Women's Clubs. Author: Scarlet Sins Made White, 1976; A Holiday for the King, 1977; Power Over Satan, 1978. Home: PO Box 368 Ponte Vedra Beach FL 32082 Office: PO Box 10126 1034 Hendrix St Jacksonville FL 32010

HOLLIDAY, PETER OSBORNE, JR., dentist; b. Macon, Ga., July 9, 1921; s. Peter Osborne and Martha Elizabeth (Riley) H.; student N. Ga. Coll., 1939-41, Mercer U., 1941-42; D.D.S., Emory U., 1945; postgrad. U. Mich. Dental Sch., 1947, 48; m. Mary Lucile Dozier, Nov. 12, 1949; children—Peter Osborne, III, Lucy, Lindsay, Mary. Practice gen. dentistry, Macon, 1947—; mem. Gov. Carter's Dental Adv. Com., 1972. Head dental div. United Givers Fund, Macon, 1956. Served to lt. Dental Corps, USNR, 1943-47; China. Fellow Am. Coll. Dentists, Internat. Coll. Dentists, Ga. Dental Assn. (hon., sec.-tres. 1971-76, v.p. 1977, pres. 1978-1979); mem. AAAS, Ga. Acad. Dental Practice, Am. Acad. Gen. Dentistry, Bibb County (Ga.) Dental Soc., Central Dist. Dental Soc. (Dentist of Yr. award 1962, pres. 1963), ADA (alt. del. 1978), Internat. Acad. Preventive Medicine. Democrat. Unitarian. Home: 744 Forest Hill Rd Macon GA 31210 Office: 360 Spring St Macon GA 31201

HOLLIDAY, VADIM PETER, pharm. co. exec.; b. Novocherkas, USSR, Aug. 2, 1920; s. Peter John and Katherine (Kononova) H.; brought to U.S., 1927, naturalized, 1943; B.A., Columbia, 1941; M.B.A., Harvard, 1946; m. Patricia Ruth McKenzie, Jan. 20, 1964; children—Vadim F., Katheryn P., Alexander V. With H.W. Kinney & Sons, Columbus, Ind., 1946-49; div. mgr. Walker Lab., Mt. Vernon, N.Y., 1949-59; pres., dir. Delta Drug Corp. Jacksonville, Fla., 1959—, Direct Devel. Corp., Jacksonville, 1970—; owner Microfilm Center Inc., Jacksonville, 1977—; part-owner Am. Apothecaries, Jacksonville, 1977—. Mem. adv. council SBA, 1969-70; trustee Southeastern Seminary, Savannah, Ga., 1979—. Mem. Republican State Com., 1976-80. Served with USMCR, 1942-45. Decorated Bronze Star, Purple Heart. Named SBA Man of Year Fla., 1967. Mem. Columbia U. Alumni Assn. Mason (32 deg., Shriner). Clubs: River, University (Jacksonville); Ponte Vedra; Columbia Varsity. Home: 301 San Juan Dr Ponte Vedra Beach FL 32082 Office: 1032 Hendricks Ave Jacksonville FL 32207

HOLLING, ARCHIE BAKER, JR., architect, engr.; b. Charleston, S.C., Mar. 30, 1932; s. Archie Baker and Annie Lou (Hart) H.; A.S., So. Tech. Inst., 1959; student Clemson U., 1952-55; m. Sue Walker, Dec. 21, 1957; children—Laura Lee, Archie. Design engr. FAPCO, Summerville, S.C., 1962-63; instr. Cooper River Sch. Dist., North Charleston, S.C., 1963-67; pvt. practice archtl. design, Summerville, 1967-74; architect, engr. So. div. Naval Facilities Engring. Command, Charleston, 1974—. Registered profl. archtl. engr. Lutheran. Home: 116 King Charles Circle Summerville SC 29483 Office: 2144 Melbourne St Charleston SC 29411

HOLLINGER, HELEN WETHERBEE, artist; b. Indpls.; d. Frederic and Madalyn (Brooks) Wetherbee; grad. Herron Sch. Art, Indpls., 1935; m. Harry Mills Hollinger, Oct. 9, 1937 (div. Mar. 1963); 1 son, Drew. Fashion dir. display dept. L.S. Ayres & Co., Indpls., 1935-37; field rep. Merchandising Group, N.Y.C., 1964-66; art dir. Miami Shores Village (Fla.), 1976—; exhibited one man shows Chase Gallery, Miami Shores, Fla., 1967, Bacardi Gallery, Miami, 1968, Burdine's, Miami, 1969-70, Gables Art Gallery, Coral Gables, 1970, exhibited in group shows Granville Gallery, 1964, Mirell Gallery, Coconut Grove, Fla., 1967, 68, 69, Bacardi Gallery, 1967, 68, 70, 73-75, Lever House, N.Y.C., 1970-72, 73-75, Mus. Sci., 1976, 75-79; represented in permanent collections Herron Sch. Art, Meth. Hosp., Indpls., Hist. Assn. S. Fla., Miami, 1st Fed. Savs. & Loan Assn., Coral Gables, Fla.; lectr. in field. Indpls. Marmon scholar, 1930, Art Assn. scholar, 1931-33, 35. Recipient James Whitcomb Riley medal, 1930; 1st Portrait award Palette Club Miami, 1962; 1st prize portraiture Fla. State Art Exhibit, Nat. League Am. Pen Women, 1969; 1st prize Wometco's 2d Ann. Art Competition, 1971; award Bicentennial Exhibit, Miami Shores, 1976; Landscape award Fla. State Art Competition, Nat. League Am. Pen Women, 1979; 1st prize in oils 29th Met. Garden Show, Coconut Grove, 1980. Fellow Am. Artists Profl. League (award of merit Miami chpt., pres. Miami chpt. 1969-71). Mem. Nat. League Am. Pen Women (state art chmn. 1968, 72-73, pres. Miami br. 1970-72, nat. biennial art exhibit chmn., nat. art bd. 1972-74). Republican. Clubs: Miami Shores Woman's, Miami Shores Country. Address: 80 NE 97th St Miami FL 33138

HOLLINGS, ERNEST FREDERICK, U.S. senator; b. Charleston, S.C., Jan. 1, 1922; s. Adolph G. and Wilhelmine D. (Meyer) H.; B.A., The Citadel, 1942; LL.B., U. S.C., 1947; m. Martha Patricia Salley, Mar. 30, 1946; children—Michael Milhous, Helen Hayne, Patricia Salley, Ernest Frederick III; m. 2d, Rita Liddy, Aug. 21, 1971. Admitted to S.C. bar, 1947; mem. S.C. Ho. of Reps., 1948-54, speaker pro tem, 1950-54; lt. gov. of S.C., 1955-59; gov. of S.C., 1959-63; practiced in Charleston, 1963-66; U.S. senator State of S.C., 1966—. Mem. Hoover Comm. on Intelligence Activities, 1954-55; mem. President's Adv. Comm. on Intergovtl. Relations, 1959-63; mem. exec. council Lutheran Ch. Am. Trustee Newberry Coll. Named one of Ten Outstanding Young Men, U.S. Jr. C. of C., 1954. Mem. Assn. Citadel Men, Hibernian Soc., Phi Delta Phi. Democrat. Lutheran. Club: Sertoma (Charleston). Office: Room 115 Russell Office Bldg Washington DC 20510

HOLLINGS, RICHARD WAYNE, psychologist; b. Portsmouth, N.H., Nov. 5, 1945; s. Bertram Alvin and Esther Isabel (Faust) H.; B.A. in Edn., U. Ariz., 1969; M.A. in Clin. Psychology, Austin Peay State U., 1975; m. Nancy Patterson Knox, Apr. 3, 1971. Psychol. examiner Harriett Cohn Mental Health Center, Clarksville, Tenn., 1975-76; child psychologist Cumberland County Mental Health Center, Fayetteville, N.C., 1977-78; individual practice, 1978—; rape counselor Womack Army Hosp., Cape Fear Valley Hosp. Served with U.S. Army, 1969-72. Decorated Bronze Star; certified sch. psychologist, Tenn.; licensed psychol. examiner, N.C., Tenn. Asso. mem. Am., N.C. psychol. assns., Assn. Advancement Behavior Therapy, Am. Assn. Pastoral Counselors, Republican. Baptist. Home: 206 Oakridge Ave Fayetteville NC 28305 Office: Bordeaux Minimall Suite R Fayetteville NC 28304

HOLLINGSWORTH, BOBBY J., mathematician; b. Sunset, Tex. Aug. 17, 1927; s. Ralph E. and Georgia (Davis) H.; B.S. in Civil Engring., La. Poly. Inst., 1949; M.S., Okla. A. and M. Coll., 1951; Ph.D., Kan. U., 1955; m. Bettie Rea Fox, June 8, 1953; children—Rebecca Rea, Lee Ann. With United Gas Corp., Shreveport, La., 1955-68, research mathematician, 1955-61, operations research asso., 1961-63, corporate planning asso., 1963-65, corporate devel. analyst, 1966-68, exec. asst. corporate finance, 1968-71; mgr. fin. analysis Pennzoil Co., Inc., Houston, 1971-78, v.p. mgmt. controls, 1978—; instr. math. evening div. Centenary Coll., 1959-65, La. Poly. at Barksdale AFB, 1965-68. Served with USNR, 1945-46. Mem. Am. Gas Assn. (research com. on transient flow 1962—), Am. Math. Soc., Soc. Indsl. and Applied Math., Canadian Math. Congress, Lambda Chi Alpha, Phi Kappa Phi. Democrat. Methodist. Home: 5339 Tilbury Houston TX 77056 Office: Pennzoil Pl PO Box 2967 Houston TX 77002

HOLLINGSWORTH, JAMES SAM, JR., civil engr.; b. Newton, Miss., Aug. 3, 1928; s. James Sam and Winnie Pauline (Davis) H.; student Spring Hill Coll., 1947-49; B.S., U. Ala., 1959; m. Lois Emily Henderson, May 18, 1953; children—James Stephen, Valla Oleta. Engr., St. Louis-San Francisco R.R., 1949-54; engr., port facilities devel. Ala. State Docks Dept., Mobile, 1954—, facilities engr., 1971—, now chief engr. charge engring. design and constrn. Pres. Docks and Terminals Credit Union, 1967—. Commr., Boy Scouts Am., 1965-69. Served with AUS, 1951-52. Mem. Am. Soc. C.E., Capstone Engring. Soc., Chi Epsilon. Methodist. Home: 209 Patrician Dr Spanish Fort AL 36527 Office: Ala State Docks PO Box 1588 Mobile AL 36601

HOLLIS, ALTON LAVON, oil and gas co. exec.; b. Petal, Miss., June 10, 1928; s. Alvin Columbus and Mattie Leona (Moore) H.; B.S., U. S. Miss., 1950; J.D., U. Miss., 1952; m. Elaine Jenkins, Dec. 22, 1948; children—David, Robert. Landman, Carter Oil Co., Oklahoma City, 1952-57; mgr. land Ada Oil Co., Houston, 1957-58; owner Hollis Oil Co., Houston, 1958-71, pres., 1971—. Mem. Houston, Am. assns. petroleum landmen, Miss. Bar Assn., Tex. Ind. Producers and Royalty Owners Assn. Baptist. Home: 5634 Sylmar St Houston TX 77081 Office: Suite 307 6065 Hillcroft St Houston TX 77081

HOLLIS, CLARENCE OTIS, JR., ins. co. exec.; b. Columbus, Ga., Sept. 9, 1943; s. Clarence Otis and Jane (Jason) H.; B.S., Hampton Inst., 1964; M.B.A., U. Pa., 1966; 1 son, Clarence Otis III. Internal auditor Conn. Gen. Life Ins. Co., Hartford, 1968-73; asst. v.p., controller Pilgrim Health Life Ins. Co., Augusta, Ga., 1973—; part-time instr. bus. Paine Coll., Augusta, 1975—. Chmn. bus. edn. adv. com. Augusta Area Tech. Sch., 1976-77; bd. dirs. A.I.D. of Augusta, 1978—, chmn. bd., 1979—; active Boy Scouts Am.; jr. warden St. Mary's Episcopal Ch., Augusta. Served as fin. officer U.S. Army, 1966-68; Vietnam; maj. USAR. Decorated Army Commendation Medal. Mem. Nat. Assn. Accts., Hampton Inst. Alumni Assn., Omega Psi Phi. Home: 3014 Hummingbird Ln Augusta GA 30906 Office: Pilgrim Health Life Ins Co PO Box 1897 Augusta GA 30903

HOLLOMAN, HASKELL ANDREW, ret. judge, rancher; b. Frederick, Okla., Nov. 12, 1907; s. Andrew Harvey and Dora (Prophit) H.; student Okla. State U., 1926-27, U. Okla. Coll. Law., 1935-38; m. Cornelia Louise Lewis, May 23, 1940. Admitted to Okla. bar, 1938; county atty., Frederick, Okla., 1939-41; atty. for state examiner and insp., Oklahoma City, 1941-42; asst. atty. gen. Okla., 1946; county atty. Frederick, 1946-47, county judge, 1947-49, 52-69; spl. dist. judge Southwestern Okla. Dist., 1969-71. Dir. Tex.-Okla. Fair Assn., Tillman County Mental Health Assn.; dir., past pres. Tillman County Farmers Union Assn. Served from lt. (j.g.) to lt. comdr. USN, 1942-46. Mem. Okla. Assn. County Judges (past pres.), Am. Judicature Soc., Am. Legion, Okla., Caddo County, Tillman County (past pres.) bar assns., Okla. Jud. Conf., Frederick C. of C., Okla.-Texas (director), Okla. (dir.) polled hereford assns., Tex.-Okla. (dir.), Red River Valley (past pres.), Big Pasture (dir.), Shortgrass (dir.) hereford assns., Southwestern Okla. Cattlemen's Assn. (dir.), Tillman County League of Young Democrats (past pres.), V.F.W. Democrat. Methodist. Kiwanian. Club: Frederick Golf and Country. Home: 1501 N 14th St Frederick OK 73542

HOLLOMAN, JAMES HORACE, JR., lawyer; b. Wichita Falls, Tex., May 27, 1946; s. James Horace and Willa Jean (Emenhiser) H.; B.B.A., U. Okla., 1966; J.D., 1969; LL.M. in Taxation, N.Y. U., 1973; m. Lynn Oberlender, Aug. 19, 1967; children—Amy Leah, Erin Lynne, Matthew James, Andrew James. Admitted to Okla. bar, 1969; staff tax accountant Arthur Andersen & Co., Oklahoma City, 1969; partner firm Crowe, Dunlevy, Thweatt, Swinford, Johnson and Burdick, Oklahoma City, 1972—. Served to capt. USMC, 1969-72. C.P.A., Okla. Mem. Oklahoma County, Okla., Am. bar assns. Baptist. Home: 14301 Coles Rd Edmond OK 73034 Office: 1700 Liberty Tower Oklahoma City OK 73102

HOLLOMON, ICILUS C., banker; b. Delight, Ark., July 2, 1929; d. Edwin E. and Bertha Ann (Lee) Steed; student Gonzalez Bus. Coll., 1960, Am. Inst. Banking, 1965, Banking Sch. South, La. State U., 1973; m. Max Hollomon, Nov. 26, 1951 (dec.). With Bank of Gonzales (La.), 1960—, v.p., cashier, security officer, 1972—. Treas., Gonzales Heart Assn., 1965-70. Mem. Am. Inst. Banking, La. Bankers Assn. (chmn. S.E. group 1975-76), Nat. Assn. Bank Women (past chmn. Baton Rouge group), Bank Adminstrn. Inst. (pres. La. 10 Parish chpt. 1978-79), Jambalaya Assn., Greater Gonzales Area Bus. and Profl. Women's Assn. (pres. 1970-71). Democrat. Universalist. Office: PO Box 1097 Worthy and Burnside Gonzales LA 70737

HOLLOWAY, FRED MASTERS, clergyman; b. Black Rock, Ark., Oct. 18, 1903; s. Alfred Elliott and Mattie (Craig) H.; A.B., Hendrix Coll., 1925; B.D., Union Theol. Sem., 1931; A.M., Columbia, 1931; Ed.D., 1958; postgrad. Mansfield Coll., Oxford (Eng.) U., summer 1965, St. Augustine Coll., Canterbury, summer 1969; m. Elizabeth Williamson, Sept. 16, 1931; children—Dianne Elizabeth (Mrs. Ronald C. Chaffee), Fred Masters. Ordained to ministry Meth. Ch., 1932; pastor Pawling (N.Y.) Meth. Ch., 1932-33; pastor First Congl. Ch., Middletown, N.Y., 1933-36; pastor First Presbyn. Ch., Rutherford, N.J., 1936-78; lectr. Fairleigh Dickinson U., Rutherford, 1950-55; lectr. Union Theol Sem. N.Y.C., 1955-70. Bd. dirs. Bloomfield, N.J. Coll. and Sem., 1955-70. Mem. broadcasting and film commn. Nat. Council Chs., 1950-58; chmn. Brit.-Am. Preachers Exchange, 1969—.

Served to capt. as chaplain USNR, 1943-46. Recipient Man of Year award Rutherford C. of C., 1977; Citizen of Year award VFW, 1978. Mem. Mil. Chaplain Assn., Sigma Chi, Alpha Pi. Club: Quill. Author: The Use of Television in Religious Education. Home: 511 Craven St PO Box 1632 New Bern NC 28560

HOLLOWAY, TILMON HENRY, JR., hosp. adminstr.; b. Baton Rouge, July 17, 1939; s. Tilmon Henry and Berta (Price) H.; B.S., N.E. La. State Coll., 1968; M.H.A., Washington U., 1970; m. Beverly, July 24, 1964; children—Mark, Amy, Jennifer. Customer rep. Universal C.I.T. Credit Corp., Waco, Tex., 1963-65; salesman Trailertown of Alexandria, Inc., Monroe, La., 1965-66; postal asst. U.S. Postal Service, Bossier City, La., 1968; asst. adminstr. High Plains Bapt. Hosp., Amarillo, Tex., 1970-76, adminstr., 1977—. Exec. bd. Boy Scouts Am., Amarillo, 1978—; bd. dirs. Amarillo Sr. Citizens Assn., 1975—; trustee Harrington Cancer Center, Amarillo. Served with USAF, 1957-60. Mem. Am. Coll. Hosp. Adminstrs., Tex. Hosp. Assn. (pres. div. 1976), Am. Hosp. Assn., Baptist. Home: 6700 Gainsborough St Amarillo TX 79106 Office: 1600 Wallace Blvd Amarillo TX 79106

HOLLOWAY, VERNON CARYLE, state senator; b. Richmond, Va., Sept. 5, 1919; s. Samuel Lee and Maude Estelle (Powell) H.; grad. Va. Mechanics Inst., U. Miami (Fla.); m. Roberta M. Galbraith, July 28, 1960; children—Jean Estelle Holloway LeDew, Vernon Carlyle, Lee Anthony. Founder, since pres. Interstate Electric Co., Miami; mem. Dade County Mediation Bd., Miami Bldg. Bd. Rules and Appeals; chmn. Met. Dade County Elec. Exam. Bd.; elec. insp. City of Opa Locka, mem. Fla. Ho. of Reps., 1966-74, chmn. transp. com., 1972-74, also speaker; mem. Fla. Senate from 39th Dist., 1974—, chmn. transp. com.; mem. Fla. Energy Com., from 1973, Fla. Council State Housing Goals, from 1974, Gov. Fla. Adv. Com. Transp., 1975-76, Gov. Fla. Hwy. Safety Commn., 1978—, Nat. Com. Uniform Traffic Laws and Ordinances, 1979—; mem. transp. com. Nat. Conf. State Legislators. Past scoutmaster City of Opa Locka Boy Scouts Troop; past pres. council Christ the King Lutheran Ch., Opa Locka. Fellow Acad. Elec. Contracting; mem. IEEE, Fla. Assn. Elec. Contractors (past pres.), Nat. Elec. Contractors Assn. (past pres. Fla.), Fla. Elec. Masters Assn. (past pres.), Nat. Fire Protection Assn. Home: 6255 SW 120th St Miami FL 33156 Office: 6444 NE 4th Ave Miami FL 33138

HOLLOWAY, WILMER OSCAR, radiologist; b. Wellston, Ga., May 8, 1931; s. William J. and Ethel P. H.; A.B., Mercer U., 1953; M.D., Med. Coll. Ga., 1960; m. Idalu Jones, June 14, 1958; children—Thomas Alan, Angela Carole, Charles William, Philip Andrew. Intern, Macon (Ga.) Hosp., 1960-61; resident in radiology to chief resident Talmadge Meml. Hosp., Med. Coll. Ga., 1969-72; gen. practice medicine, Gordon, Ga., 1961-69; chief radiology and nuclear medicine Tift Gen. Hosp., Tifton, Ga., 1972—; radiologist Worth County Hosp., Sylvester, Ga., 1976—. Served with U.S. Army, 1953-55. Fellow Am. Coll. Radiology, Am. Coll. Nuclear Medicine; mem. Radiol. Soc. N. Am., Ga. Radiol. Soc., Med. Assn. Ga., North Fla.-S. Ga. Radiol. Soc., So. Med. Assn., Southeastern Angiographic Soc. (charter), Tift County Med. Soc., AMA (Physicians Recognition award). Republican. Methodist. Home: 302 W 24th St Tifton GA 31794 Office: 212 Victor Dr Tifton GA 31794

HOLLOWELL, DOUGLAS ALBERT, accountant; b. Portsmouth, Va., Apr. 28, 1942; s. Luke and Hulda Marie (Asbell) H.; B.S. in Accounting, Old Dominion U., 1965; M.S., U. Tex., El Paso; m. Ida Francis Edwards, May 3, 1969; children—Donna Lynn, Douglas Albert, Jr. Mgmt. trainee Va. Elec. and Power Co., Norfolk, 1965-66; staff accountant Goodman and Co., C.P.A.'s, Norfolk, 1966-71; fin. mgr. Bush Constrn. Co., Norfolk, 1971-75; individual practice accounting, Portsmouth, 1975—; asst. instr. accounting Old Dominion U., Norfolk, 1975-77; instr. Tidewater Community Coll., Chesapeake, Va., 1974; mem. citizens' adv. com. Vols. of Am., Virginia Beach, Va., 1977-77; mem. accounting adv. com. Tidewater Community Coll., Virginia Beach, 1974; 2d v.p. Cosmopolitan Internat. of Portsmouth, 1978—, treas., 1976-77. C.P.A., Va. Mem. Am. Inst. C.P.A.'s, Va. Soc. C.P.A.'s, Am. Accounting Assn. Baptist. Clubs: Gideons Internat., Corapeake Hunt (pres. 1975-78). Home: 4020 Coffman Blvd Chesapeake VA 23321 Office: 202 Va Fed Bldg PO Box 636 Portsmouth VA 23705

HOLM, JURGEN KURT, civil engr.; b. Hamburg, Ger., Jan. 8, 1930; s. Kurt Peter Leonhard and Erika Margarethe Helene (Buchholtz) H.; came to U.S., 1963, naturalized, 1968; B.S. in Civil Engring., U. Tex., Arlington, 1972; m. Edith Erna Tantau, Jan. 11, 1957; children—Peter Christian Jurgen, Susan Cathleen Edith. Engring. aide Pigott Constrn. Co., Toronto, Ont., Can., 1952-55; surveyor's apprentice Speight & van Nostrand, Toronto, 1955-58; Ont. land surveyor A.M. MacKay & J.A. Lonergan, Timmins, 1958-63; designer, design engr. Forrest and Cotton Inc., Dallas, 1963-67, 70-73; designer M.W. Kellogg Co., Dallas, 1967-70; design and constrn. engr. Ras Shukheir Egypt for Fluor Ocean Services, Houston, 1973-74; sr. design engr. Arecibo Obs. for E-Systems, Garland, Tex., 1974-75; chief engr. Senipah Terminal Handil Project, Borneo, 1975-76; sr. engr. Oasis Oil Co., Tripoli, Libya, 1977—. Mem. Tex. Soc. Profl. Engrs., Chi Epsilon. Home: 9220 Royal Pine Dr Dallas TX 75238 Office: care Oasis Oil Co PO Box 395 Tripoli Libya

HOLMES, ALBERTA, career counselor; B.A., Howard U., 1971, M.Ed., 1975; children—Ronald Kevin, Rhonda Victoria. Adminstrv. asst. Howard U., Washington, 1971-76, admissions recruiter, 1975-78, counselor Office of Career Planning and Placement, 1976-78, budget and fiscal officer, 1976-78; career counselor, instr. Va. State U., Petersburg, 1978—. Mem. Nat. Bus. League, Am. Personnel and Guidance Assn., NAACP, Va. Personnel and Guidance Assn., So. Coll. Placement Assn., Mid-Atlantic Placement Assn., Howard U. Alumni Assn., Nat. Urban League, Nat. Council Negro Women, Smithsonian Assos., Alpha Kappa Alpha. Unitarian. Home: 59 Ivy Ln Petersburg VA 23803

HOLMES, BETTY LANDISS, nurse, hosp. ofcl.; b. Orlando, Fla., July 9, 1927; d. Charles William and Nora (Johnson) Landiss; R.N., Norton Sch. Nursing, 1950; B.A., U. Louisville, 1971, postgrad., 1975—; children—Deborah, Bonnie, Penelope, William. Staff nurse, supr. Southeastern Ky. Baptist Hosp., Corbin, Ky., 1963-68; inservice coordinator Norton Infirmary, Louisville, 1967-72; asso. exec. dir. nursing service Suburban Hosp., Louisville, 1972-80; asso. exec. dir. Lake Cumberland Med. Center, Somerset, Ky., 1980—. Chmn., Louisville and Jefferson County (Ky.) Republican Orgn., 1977-79, pres. Ky. Fedn. Rep. Women, 1978-80; mem. Jefferson County Honest Election Commn., 1979-80. Mem. Ky. Women's C. of C. (charter; dir. 1978—), Am. Nurses Assn., Ky. Nurses Assn., Nat. League Nursing, Ky. League Nursing, Ky. Soc. Nursing Service Adminstrs., Ky. Hist. Soc., English-Speaking Union. Home: 2502 Brighton Dr Louisville KY 40205 Office: Lake Cumberland Med Center Somerset KY 42501

HOLMES, CLARK ROYCE, lawyer; b. Pitts., Sept. 1, 1946; s. Richard Keely and Olive J. Holmes; B.A., U. Fla., 1968, J.D., 1973; divorced; children—Todd R., Tara L. Admitted to Fla. bar, 1974; program participant Center Govtl. Responsibility, 1973-74; clk. Fla. 2d Dist. Ct. Appeals, 1974; atty. firm Shackleford, Farrior, Stallings & Evans, P.A., Tampa, 1974—. Bd. dirs. Tampa YMCA, 1979, Vol. Action Center, Tampa, 1978-79. Served to capt. USAR, 1968-71; Vietnam. Decorated Bronze Star with oak leaf cluster; Vietnamese Cross Gallantry; recipient various Jaycee, YMCA awards. Mem. Am. Bar Assn. (products liability com.), Def. Lawyers Inst., Fla. Bar Assn., Hillsborough County Bar Assn., U.S. Jaycees, Fla. Jaycees, Tampa Jaycees. Editor-in-chief U. Fla. Law Sch. newspaper, 1973. Office: PO Box 3324 Tampa FL 33601

HOLMES, EUGENE THOMAS, lawyer; b. Winona, Miss., May 25, 1948; s. John Barksdale and Suzanne Florence (Harris) H.; B.S. in Chem. Engring., U. Miss., 1970; J.D. with distinction and high honors, 1974; m. Mary Carnathan Mansell, June 21, 1969; 1 dau., Marianne Mansell. Summer project engr. Humble Oil & Refining Co., Harvey, La., 1969; process engr. Union Camp Corp., Savannah, Ga., 1970-72; law clk. EPA, Atlanta, 1974; admitted to Miss. bar, 1974, Ga. bar, 1974, U.S. Patent and Trademark Office, 1975, other fed. cts.; asso. firm Troutman, Sanders, Lockerman & Ashmore, Atlanta, 1974-76; with firm F. Marshall Binford, Atlanta, 1976—; guest lectr. environ. law. U. Miss., 1973, U. Ga., 1975, natural resources law U. Ky., 1977. Carrier scholar. Mem. Internat., Am., Atlanta bar assns., Am. Chem. Soc., Am. Inst. Chem. Engrs., Am. Patent Law Assn., Miss. State Bar, State Bar Ga., TAPPI, Atlanta Com. on Fgn. Relations, Kappa Sigma, Phi Delta Phi, Phi Kappa Phi, Tau Beta Pi, Omicron Delta Kappa. Contbr. articles in field to law jours. Home: 2152 Wood Glen Ln SE Marietta GA 30067 Office: 1380 W Paces Ferry Rd NW Atlanta GA 30327

HOLMES, JACK DAVID LAZARUS, historian; b. Long Branch, N.J., July 4, 1930; s. John Daniel Lazarus and Waltrude Helen (Hendrickson) Holmes; B.A. cum laude, Fla. State U., 1952; M.A., U. Fla., 1953; postgrad. Universidad Nacional Autonoma de Mexico, 1954; Ph.D., U. Tex. at Austin, 1959; m. Anne Elizabeth Anthony, Sept. 6, 1952 (div. Dec. 1965); children—David H., Jack Forrest, Ann M.; m. 2d, Martha Rachel Austin, Feb. 11, 1966 (div. June 1967); m. 3d, Gayle Jeanette Pannell, July 1967 (div. 1970); 1 son, Daniel; m. 4th, Stephanie Pasneker, Apr. 10, 1971. Instr. history Memphis State U., 1956-58; asst. prof. McNeese State Coll., Lake Charles, La., 1959-61; lectr. U. Md. at Constantina, Spain, 1962; asso. prof. U. Ala. in Birmingham, 1963-68, prof., 1968-79. Reading clk. Fla. Ho. of Reps., 1955; reporter-photographer Memphis Press-Scimitar, 1957-58; cons. U.S. Parks Service, 1962, Pensacola (Fla.) Hist. Commn., 1969-70, New Orleans Cabildo Museum, 1968-73, Nat. Endowment Humanities, 1972-79, Miss. Dept. Archives-History, 1978—. Served with inf. AUS, 1951. Created knight, cruz de caballero Royal Order Isabel La Catolica (Spain), 1979; Charles W. Hackett fellow, 1959; Am. Philos. Soc. fellow, 1961, 66; Fulbright fellow, 1961-62; Assn. State and Local History grantee, 1966, award of merit, 1978; U. Ala. grantee, 1964, 66, 68, 72, 74-79; Mexican Govt. grantee, 1954. Mem. Tenn. Squires, So. (life mem.), La. (dir. 1977-78) hist. assns., Miss., Fla. hist. socs., Orgn. Am. Historians, Ala. Acad. Sci., Phi Beta Kappa, Phi Kappa Phi, Sigma Delta Pi, Phi Alpha Theta, Pi Kappa Phi. Author: Documentos ineditos para la historia de la Luisiana, 1963; Gayoso, 1965; Honor and Fidelity, 1965; Jose de Evia, 1968; Francis Baily's Journal, 1969; New Orleans: Facts and Legends, 1970; Luis de Onis Memoria, 1969; Guide to Spanish Louisiana, 1970; New Orleans Drinks and How to Mix Them, 1973; History of the University of Alabama Hospitals and Clinics, 1974; The 1779 Marcha de Galvez: Louisiana's Giant Step Forward in the American Revolution, 1974. Editor, dir. La. Collection Series, 1965—. Contbr. to French in Mississippi Valley, 1965; Frenchmen and French Ways in Mississippi Valley, 1969; Spanish in Mississippi Valley, 1974; Handbook of Texas, Vol. 3, 1978; Cardinales de dos Independencias, 1978; Readings in Louisiana History, 1978; Ency. So. History, 1979, also numerous articles to U.S. and fgn. hist. jours. Home: 520 S 22d Ave Birmingham AL 35205

HOLMES, ROBERT RAYMOND, physicist; b. Granite City, Ill., Mar. 1, 1937; s. Raymond Smith and Dorothy Margaret (McClellan) H.; B.A., Amherst Coll., 1959; M.S., Trinity Coll., Hartford, Conn., 1963; Ph.D. (NSF fellow), Brown U., 1968; m. Elizabeth Holbert Harris, June 6, 1964; children—Deborah Ann, Rebecca Anne. Devel. engr. United Aircraft, 1959-62; research asst. Brown U., 1962-68; mem. tech. staff Bell Labs., Richmond, Va., 1968-74, supr., 1974—. Mem. Randolph Twp. (N.J.) Planning Bd., 1972; pres. Confederate Hills Civic Assn., Highland Springs, Va., 1978—. Mem. IEEE, Sigma Xi. Democrat. Unitarian. Patentee liquid level control; research on radiation damage, printed wiring. Home: 708 Washington St Highland Springs VA 23075 Office: 4500 Laburnum St Richmond VA 23231

HOLMES, SUE, mfg. co. ofcl.; b. Enville, Tenn., Sept. 18, 1932; d. Harold W. and Lucille Tenry; student Memphis Sch. Commerce, 1950; A.S. in Mid-Mgmt., State Tech. Inst., Memphis, 1979; m. Clyde E. Holmes, Feb. 10, 1951; children—Barbara Jean Crowell, Peggy Lou Whitehorn. With Sears Roebuck & Co., Memphis, 1950-52; scheduling clk. Elevator div. Dover Corp., Memphis, 1957-64, sec., v.p., 1965-72, sec., dir. personnel, 1972-73, employment specialist, 1973-77, personnel services mgr., 1977—, mem. credit com. Dover Elevator Credit Union, 1963-67, mem. supervisory com., 1979—; speaker various high and tech. schs., 1973—. Area chmn. March of Dimes, 1965-70; pres. ladies aux. VFW, 1965-68; Sunday sch. tchr. Southaven 1st United Methodist Ch. Mem. Indsl. Personnel Council, Am. Soc. Notaries, Mid South Compensation and Benefits Assn., Tenn. Coll. Placement Assn. Home: 9031 Whitworth St Southaven MS 38671 Office: Elevator Div Dover Corp PO Box 2177 Memphis TN 38101

HOLMES, WILLIAM WALKER, JR., ednl. adminstr.; b. Mobile, Ala., May 20, 1921; s. William Walker and Ada (Warfield) H.; student Edinburg Jr. Coll., 1939-40; B.A., Tex. A&I U., 1943; postgrad. Okla. State U., 1943; M.A., U. Colo., 1949; m. Jean Houston, June 10, 1955; children—William Thomas, Jeananne, Robert Keith. Asst. info. dir., instr. journalism Tex. Coll. Arts and Industries, 1946-49; publs., publicity and journalism dir. McMurry Coll., 1949-51; sports info. dir. Tex. Tech. U., 1951-67; asst. prof. journalism Tex. A&I U., 1967—, dir. info. and news service, 1969-79; mem. selection com. Tex. Sports Hall of Fame, 1977—. Mem. troop com. Gulf Coast council Boy Scouts Am., 1967—; bd. dirs. Kingsville (Tex.) Community Concerts Assn., 1967-75, Kleberg unit Am. Cancer Soc., 1976—; mem. Kingsville Bicentennial Commn., 1975-76. Served with USAAF, 1943-45, F.A., U.S. Army, 1945-46; ret. lt. col. Res., 1973. Recipient Order Golden Quill, Univ. Interscholastic League, 1977, Outstanding Public Relations Publ. award Corpus Christi Press Club, 1978; named to Hall of Fame, Coll. Sports Info. Dirs. Am., 1977. Mem. Council Advancement and Support of Edn. (regional exec. bd. dirs. 1972-73), Football Writers Assn. Am., Tex. Sports Writers Assn. (pres. 1960, chmn. writing awards com. 1953—), Tex. Public Relations Assn., Tex. Assn. Journalism Dirs., Res. Officers Assn., Navy League. Democrat. Methodist. Club: Kiwanis (editor local club bull. 1969—, local dir. 1974-76; Internat. Legion of Honor) (Kingsville). Contbr. articles on public relations to Tex. Coach Mag., 1967—; editor Tusk, 1970-72, Am. Coll. Public Relations Assn. S.W. Regional Newsletter, 1972-73. Home: 1119 Kathleen Kingsville TX 78363 Office: News Service Tex A&I U Kingsville TX 78363

HOLMES, ZACHARY EUGENE, mfg. engr.; b. Columbia, Tenn., Dec. 3, 1951; s. Henry Kerley and Elsie Rabin (Jones) H.; B.S. in Elec. Engring., Vanderbilt U., 1973, M.S. in Elec. Engring. (Gen. Motors fellow), 1974; m. Judy Kay Douglas, Dec. 24, 1971; 1 dau., Monica Renee. Design engr. E.I. DuPont, Old Hickory, Tenn., 1974-76, maintenance supr., 1976-78; mfg. devel. engr. Ford Motor Co., Nashville, 1978—. Mem. IEEE, Sigma Xi. Democrat. Roman Catholic. Home: 161 Country Club Dr Hendersonville TN 37075 Office: Box 1355 Centennial Blvd Nashville TN 37209

HOLST, HOWARD DOUGLAS, broadcasting co. exec.; b. Pierre, S.D., Aug. 6, 1929; s. John Thomas and Rose Angeline (Kramer) H.; B.F.A., U. S.D., 1951; M.A., Memphis State U., 1967; m. Noreen Leone Paulson, July 9, 1954; children—Hollis Helene, Howard Douglas, Heather Angeline. Program content specialist Sta. WOI-TV/AM/FM; Iowa State Coll., 1952-56; prodn. mgr. Sta. WKNO-TV, Memphis, 1956-58, program dir., 1958-61, gen. mgr., 1961—. Mem. Nat. Assn. Ednl. Broadcasters. Club: Rotary (v.p. 1976-77). Office: PO Box 80 000 Memphis TN 38152

HOLT, AMOS EARL, research engr.; b. Grand Canyon, Ariz., Jan. 7, 1940; s. Amos Carl and Willie D. (Kerzee) H.; B.S. in Physics, U. Tex., Arlington, 1963, M.A. in Physics, 1970; m. Carolyn Savage, June 11, 1960; children—Gregory, Karen, Grant, Katherine. Methods and materials research engr. Bell Helicopter Co., Ft. Worth, 1965-72; with Babcock & Wilcox Co., 1972—, sr. research engr. Lynchburg (Va.) Research Center, 1972-75, research specialist, 1975-76, group supr. non-destructive methods and instrumentation sect., 1976—; cons. in field. Elder, Ch. of Christ, Lynchburg, 1977—. Served to 1st lt. U.S. Army, 1963-65. mem. Am. Soc. Non-Destructive Testing (founder Lynchburg chpt. 1973, pres. 1973-74, chmn. bd. 1974-75), Am. Soc. Metals (com. to write holographic exam. sect. in Handbook Vol. II, 1975-76), Sigma Pi Sigma. Club: Ruritan (pres. Lynchburg 1978). Patentee ultrasonic and electromatic devices; presented papers on acoustical holographic imaging in Europe, Japan, Australia. Home: 613 Old Graves Mill Rd Lynchburg VA 24502 Office: PO Box 1260 Lynchburg Research Center Lynchburg VA 24502

HOLT, DOUGLAS EUGENE, utility co. exec.; b. Johnson City, Tenn., Jan. 5, 1925; s. John Henry and Alcyone Carolyn (Tate) H.; B.S., U. Tenn., 1948; m. Elizabeth Ann Henderson, Sept. 21, 1948; children—Douglas Eugene, Lisa Gail, John Timothy, Jeffrey Daniel. With Jellico (Tenn.) Electric and Water System, 1948-54, Johnson City Water & Sewer Dept., 1955-56; with Elizabethton (Tenn.) Electric System, 1956—, office mgr., 1956-74, office mgr., asst. mgr., 1974—, also sec. bd. dirs.; instr. Elizabethton Vocat. Tech. Sch., evenings, 1967—. Bd. dirs. East Tenn. Christian Home, United Fund. Served with USAAF, 1943-44. Recipient Outstanding Citizenship award Carter County C. of C., United Fund. Mem. E. Tenn. Public Power Accts. Assn., Tenn. Valley Public Power Assn., Am. Public Power Assn., Carter County C. of C. (past pres.). Republican. Mem. Ch. of Christ. Club: Rotary. Home: Route 5 Johnson City TN 37601 Office: Sycamore and Hattie Ave Elizabethton TN 37643

HOLT, ESSIE WILLIAMS, ednl. adminstr.; b. Sicily Island, La.; d. Fred and Edna Beatrice (Thomas) Williams; B.S. magna cum laude, Grambling State U., 1965; M.Ed., U. Ark., 1970, ednl. specialist, 1972; Ed.D., U. Tenn., 1978; m. Edwin J. Holt; children—Lisa Michelle, Rachelle Justine. Tchr., Caddo Parish Sch. System, Shreveport, La., 1965-71, guidance counselor, 1971-78, sch. psychologist, 1978-79, prin., 1979—; spl. lectr. psychology La. State U., Shreveport, 1973-76. Mem. NEA, Am. Personnel and Guidance Assn., La. Edn. Assn., Gaddo Edn. Assn., La. Sch. Counselors Assn., Nat. Elem. Sch. Prins. Assn., Caddo Prins. Assn., Phi Delta Kappa, Alpha Kappa Alpha. Baptist. Home: 208 Plano St Shreveport LA 71103

HOLT, JOHN ARNOLD, life ins. co. exec.; b. Ardmore, Okla., May 2, 1930; s. John W. and Jewell (Arnold) H.; student U. Idaho, 1949-52, So. Okla. City Jr. Coll., 1977-78, Am. Coll. Underwriters, 19—; m. Helen Henry, Aug. 15, 1953; children—John Marc, Matthew Thomas, Christopher Paul. Profl. rodeo cowboy, 1949-53; farmer, rancher, N.Mex., 1953-59; ins. sales rep. Prudential, Northwestern Mut. and Great Nat. LIfe Ins., Tex. and N.Mex., 1959-69; v.p., agy. dir. Universal Fidelity Life Ins. Co., Duncan, Okla., 1970—; life office mgmt. instr. Trustee Okla. Missionary Bapt. Coll. Mem. Nat. Assn. Life Underwriters. Baptist. Office: PO Box 700 Duncan OK 73533

HOLT, LARRY, oil co. exec.; b. Buffalo, May 9, 1934; s. Penick S. and Mary (Harrah) H.; B.Sc., Okla. State U., 1957; m. Donna Veillon, June 10, 1961; children—Calvin, Garret. Field engr. Schlumberger Co., Houma, La., 1959-63, dist. mgr., Tripoli, Africa, 1964-69, asst. div. mgr., Far East, 1970-72, Middle East, 1973-75; v.p. Europe, Africa, Middle East, Eastman Whipstock, London, 1976-78, v.p. adminstrn., Houston, 1979—. Served to 1st lt., arty., U.S. Army, 1958. Mem. Soc. Petroleum Engrs., Am. Mgmt. Assn., Gulf AAU. Republican.

HOLT, MARGARET MCCONNELL, artist, writer; b. Gastonia, N.C., July 26, 1909; d. Daniel Edward and Pansy Avery (Traywick) McConnell; B.S. in Music, U. N.C. at Greensboro, 1930; B. Creative Arts, U. N.C. at Charlotte, 1973; m. Donnell Shaw Holt, July 12, 1932. Supr. music Graham (N.C.) Pub. Schs., 1930-32; dir. arts and crafts Concord (N.C.) Dept. Recreation, 1952-55; one-woman shows in area schs., colls. and univs., 1942—; group shows: N.C. Artists Ann., N.C. Mus. Art, 1940, 63, 64, Piedmont Ann., 1960, 63, 65, Mint Mus., Charlotte, 1968, UNICEF, 1971; represented in numerous pub. and pvt. collections; founder, donor D.E. McConnell Art Collection, Gaston-Lincoln (N.C.) Regional Libraries, 1966—; founder Holt Art Collection, Concord, N.C., 1978. Bd. dirs. Friends of Library, U. N.C. at Greensboro, 1967-70, dir. Home Econs. Found., 1967-70; pres. Literary Council, Burlington, N.C., 1949, Cover-to-Cover Book Club, Charlotte, 1979-80, Study Club of Concord, 1972-74; founder Cabarrus-Concord Friends of the Library, 1974; established Holt Scholarship Fund, 1978. Recipient spl. award U. N.C., Greensboro, 1967, alumni award, 1977. Asso. mem. Am. Watercolor Soc., Pi Kappa Lambda; mem. N.C. Hist. Book Club, Guild Charlotte Artists, N.C. Watercolor Soc., Friends Mint Mus., Internat. Soc Artists. Author: How to Build a Kiln, 1953; Chinqua-Penn, 1968; Needlepoint Designs for Church Symbols, 1974. Home: 962 Cherokee Rd Charlotte NC 28207

HOLT, MARY LOUISE, educator; b. Nashville, Sept. 30, 1945; d. Thomas Malone and Mary Louise (Nooe) Holt; B.A., Vanderbilt U., 1967; M.S., U. Tenn., 1972; Ph.D. (Ga. Higher Edn. fellow), U. Ga., 1977. Tchr. math. pub. schs., Nashville Met. Bd. Edn., 1967-72; counselor, asst. prof. psychology Gainesville (Ga.) Jr. Coll., 1972-77; asst prof. edn. Corpus Christi (Tex.) State U., 1977—; pvt. practice clin. psychology; cons. on career devel.; tutor of the disadvantaged, Nashville, 1968-69; speaker in field. Named as favorite tchr. McMurray Jr. High Sch., Nashville, 1971. Cert. and lic. psychologist, Tex. Mem. Am. Personnel and Guidance Assn., Am. Coll. Personnel Assn., Gulf Coast Personnel and Guidance Assn. (pres. 1980-81), Am. Psychol. Assn., Tex. Psychol. Assn. Kappa Delta Pi. Mem. Disciples of Christ Ch. Co-editor manual for master's candidates in student personnel work, 1976-77; contbr. articles, research in field. Home: 6213 Beechwood Dr Corpus Christi TX 78412 Office: 6300 Ocean Dr PO Box 6010 Corpus Christi TX 78411

HOLT, ROBERT LEROI, educator; b. Dixie, Ga., Jan. 1, 1920; s. John G. and Willie (Grimes) H.; A.A., Mars Hill Coll., 1941; A.B., Wake Forest Coll., 1943, M.A., 1946; Ph.D., Duke U., 1951; m. Claire Rebecca Hardin, June 3, 1943; children—James, Becky, Susan. Dir. religious activities East Carolina U., Greenville, N.C., 1950-53, registrar, dir. admissions, 1958-60, dean acad. affairs, 1960-63, v.p., dean of univ., 1964-76, vice chancellor for adminstrn. and planning 1976-79, prof. philosophy, 1979—; v.p. Mars Hill (N.C.) Coll., 1953-58; chmn. N.C. Advisory Council on Tchr. Edn., 1972-75; mem. N.C. Coll. Conf. Exec. Com., 1961. Pres. United Fund for Madison County, N.C., 1957-58; mem. Citizens Awareness Com., Greenville, 1969-70; bd. dirs. Greenville Bicentennial, pres., 1974; trustee Wake Forest U., 1964-68. Mem. N.C. Assn. Colls. and Univs. (mem. com. on standards 1966-67), So. Assn. Colls. and Schs. (chmn. com. on standards and reports 1971—), So. Council on Tchr. Edn., NEA, Assn. Acad. Deans of N.C. Colls., N.C. Edn. Assn., Am. Assn. Colls. for Tchr. Edn., Phi Delta Kappa, Epsilon Pi Tau, Phi Kappa Phi, Pi Omega Pi. Baptist. Clubs: Kiwanis, Rotary, Civitan (dir. 1957, Named Man of Year 1958). Author: Christian Ethics in the Thought of Thomas Traherne, 1951. Home: 1711 Knollwood Dr Greenville NC 27834 Office: 106 Spilman Bldg East Carolina U Greenville NC 27834

HOLTER, WILLIAM HUDSON, mathematician, actor; b. Lock Haven, Pa., Nov. 30, 1929; s. Willard Clyde and Josephine (Tibbins) H.; B.S. magna cum laude, Franklin and Marshall Coll., 1952; M.A., Am. U., 1960; m. Margaret Lawrence, Nov. 24, 1961. Mathematician, sr. scientist, head applied math. computer analysis sect. Atlantic Research Corp., Alexandria, Va., 1953-66; project scientist Booz-Allen Applied Research, Inc., Bethesda, Md., 1966-70; tech. staff Mitre Corp., McLean, Va., 1970-72; sr. analyst Gen. Research Corp., McLean, 1972-76; cons. Control Data Corp., Rockville, Md., 1976—. Actor summer stock, 1953—; actor appearing in The Subcommittee and Uniquecorn Revue, Washington, 1960-63, A Political Party, N.Y.C., 1963. Bd. dirs. Waterford (Va.) Found., 1966—; actor dinner theater circuit, Washington, 1968—. Mem. Ops. Research Soc. Am. (referee), Internat. Platform Assn., Math. Assn. Am., Soc. Indsl. Applied Math., Am. Inst. Aeros. and Astronautics, AFTRA, Am. Ordnance Assn., Phi Beta Kappa. Contbr. articles to profl. jours. Home: Box 146 Waterford VA 22190 also 523 Queen St Alexandria VA 22314 Office: Control Data Corp Rockville MD 20852

HOLTON, HELEN TRUDIE, reading specialist; b. Columbia, Ky., July 3, 1921; d. L.C. and Vara (Jones) Reece; B.A. in English, Wayland Coll., Plainview, Tex., 1955; M.A. in Reading, So. Methodist U., Dallas, 1968; m. Roburn R. Holton; children—Vara Gibbons, Barbara Martinhus. Reading specialist Garland (Tex.) Sch., 1960—; parttime mem. staff So. Meth. U. Reading Clinic. Mem. Tex. PTA (life), Tex. State Tchrs. Assn., NEA, Internat. Reading Assn., Classroom Tchrs. Garland (named Outstanding Tchr. 1975), Garland Assn. Tex. Educators (pres.), Dist. X Assn. Sex Educators (v.p.), Tale Spinners. Home: 1618 Goodwin St Garland TX 75042 Office: 3101 Edgewood St Garland TX 75042

HOLTWICK, PHILIP BARRETT, real estate broker; b. Topeka, Oct. 15, 1921; s. Charles Jansen and Mary M. (Barrett) H.; B.B.A., Ga. State U., 1958; M.B.A., George Washington U., 1968; m. Sarah Estelle Fleming, Apr. 18, 1958. Enlisted U.S. Army, 1940, advanced through grades to col., 1975; exec. officer Frankfurt Army Med. Center, 1972-74, Surgeon's Office, Mil. Dist. Washington, 1974-75; asst. dir. adminstrn. Catawba (Va.) Hosp., 1976-79; real estate broker, Dallas, 1979—; asst. prof. Baylor U. Grad. Sch., Waco, 1968-71. Chmn. bd. dirs. Frankfurt Club System, 1973-74. Decorated Legion of Merit, Iron Cross (Federal Republic of Germany). Mem. Am. Coll. Hosp. Adminstrs. Home: 10108 Branwood Ln Dallas TX 75243 Office: 13031 Coit Rd Dallas TX 75240

HOLTZ, NOEL, neurologist; b. N.Y.C., Sept. 13, 1943; s. Irving and Lillian H.; B.A., N.Y. U., 1965; M.D., U. Cin., 1969; m. Carol Sue Smith, June 9, 1968; children—Pamela Wendy, Aaron David, Daniel Judah. Intern, Cin. Gen. Hosp., 1969-70; resident in internal medicine and neurology Emory U., Atlanta, 1970-71, 73-76; practice medicine specializing in neurology, Marietta, Ga., 1977—; mem. faculty Emory U. Coll. Medicine, Atlanta, 1977—, instr. dept. neurology, 1977—; mem. staffs Kennestone Hosp., Grady Meml. Hosp. Served with USN, 1971-73. Diplomate Am. Bd. Psychiatry and Neurology. Mem. Am. Acad. Neurology, Ga. Neurol. Soc., Atlanta Neurol. Soc., Alpha Omega Alpha. Office: 50 Plaza Way Marietta GA 30060

HOLTZHEIMER, PAUL EDGAR, city ofcl.; b. Bellingham, Wash., Aug. 13, 1947; s. Jack Eugene and Almeta Maxine (Barton) H.; student Oklahoma City U., 1967-71; B.S., Central State U., Okla., 1978; m. Connie Lee Taylor, June 12, 1971; children—Paul Edgar, Taylor Eugene; 1 foster son, Darryl Ray Fraley. Photo aid Roger Myers Comml. Photography, Oklahoma City, 1967-69; freight checker Transcon Lines, Oklahoma City, 1969-70; co-owner, mgr. Almeta Comml. Photography Studio, Bethany, Okla., 1970-72; graphics mgr. Continental Fed. Savs. & Loan Assn., Oklahoma City, 1972-78; mgr. Office Services Div. Oklahoma City, 1978—; drummer Royalaires Dance Band. Precinct chmn. Republican Party, 1977. Cert. graphics communications mgr. Mem. In-Plant Mgmt. Assn. (v.p. Central Okla. chpt.). Mem. Ch. of God (7th Day). Clubs: Masons, Shriners. Home: 2712 NW 21st St Oklahoma City OK 73107 Office: 200 N Walker St Oklahoma City OK 73102

HOM, RICHARD ALAN, microbiologist/immunologist; b. Florence, Ariz., Oct. 13, 1951; s. Bok Him and Pearl (Wong) H.; B.S. (acad. scholar), U. So. Calif., 1973, Ph.D. (univ. research grantee), 1978; m. Nancy Ann Neuenschwander, July 22, 1978. Grad. teaching asst. U. So. Calif., 1973-78; lab. tech. asst. Children's Hosp., Los Angeles, 1973-78; vis. fellow, postdoctoral resident Center Disease Control, USPHS, Atlanta, 1978-80; vis. prof. immunology Ga. State U. Mem. Am. Soc. Microbiology, Amateur Radio Relay League, Atlanta Lawn Tennis Assn., Sigma Xi, Alpha Epsilon Delta. Author articles in field. Home: 6950 Clearlake Ct Doraville GA 30360 Office: Center Disease Control Bldg 1-2385 1600 Clifton Rd Atlanta GA 30333

HOMB, SCOTT MICHAEL, counselor; b. Monroe, Wis., Apr. 13, 1951; s. Wesley C. and Dolores H.; M.A., U. S.Fla., 1972; m. Frances C. Bouman, Oct. 5, 1974. Personal adjustment counselor Goodwill Industries, St. Petersburg, Fla., 1974-75; correctional counselor Fla. Dept. Offender Rehab., Largo, 1976-77; counseling coordinator CETA, Fla. Employment Services, St. Petersburg, 1977-78; employment counseling supr. Fla. Dept. Labor and Employment Security, Tempa, 1978—; instructional cons. St. Petersburg Jr. Coll. Cert. rehab. counselor, cert. employment counselor. Mem. Am. Personnel and Guidance Assn., Fla. Personnel and Guidance Assn., Internat. Assn. Personnel in Employment Security, Fla. Assn. Personnel and Employment Security, Nat. Employment Counseling Assn. Home: 1785 72d Ave NE Saint Petersburg FL 33702 Office: 1441 E Fletcher Ave Suite 2175 Tampa FL 33612

HONAKER, RONALD CLINTON, ins. agt.; b. Huntington, W.Va., Nov. 29, 1938; s. Granville Clinton and Gladys Irene (May) H.; B.A. in Secondary Edn., U. Ill., 1960; postgrad. U. Md., 1961-63, U. Hawaii, 1964; B.A. in Secondary Edn., Shephard Coll., 1973; postgrad. U. Marshall, 1974-76; m. Sandra Lynn Rhodes, June 28, 1964; children—Ronda Leah, Tonya Lynn, Aaron Clinton. Commd. 2d lt. U.S. Army, 1962, advanced through grades to capt. U.S. Army, 1968; ret., 1968; ordained to ministry Ch. of Christ, 1973; agt. Mut. and United of Omaha, Ft. Lauderdale, Fla., 1973—. Chaplain, Young Republicans. Recipient Outstanding Service award U.S. Army, 1967-68; also numerous ins. awards. Mem. Internat. Brotherhood of Magicians, Nat. Assn. Life Underwriters, Huntington Bd. Realtors. Republican. Home: 2506 Cat Cay Ln Lauderdale Isles FL 33312 Office: 2550 W Oakland Park St Fort Lauderdale FL 33312

HONAKER, SHASTA YUVAWN, data processor; b. Lincolnton, N.C., July 4, 1928; d. Richard Monroe and Jessie Beulah (Eplee) Buff; student U. Mo., Kansas City, 1969-74; m. Earl Lee Honaker, Apr. 6, 1969; 1 son, Kevin Smith Hine. Cosmetologist, Rose Beauty Salon, Lincolnton, 1945-47; home economist, credit mgr., salesperson D&W Furniture Co., Abilene, Tex., 1955-63; keypunch operator, billing clk. W. Tex. Utilities, Abilene, billing clk. W. Tex. Utilities, Abilene, 1963-65; keypunch operator, chief verifier McWood Corp., Abilene, 1965-67; programmer Permian Corp., Midland, Tex., 1967-68, Occidental Petroleum Co., Houston, 1968-69, Koch Refrigerators Co., Kansas City, Kans., 1969-74; mgr. data processing POA, Bella Vista, Ark., 1974-76, Crane Co., Rogers, Ark., 1976—. Mem. Data Processing Mgmt. Assn. (pres.), Am. Legion Aux., Beta Sigma Phi. Baptist. Club: Elks. Home: 1318 Rolling Oaks Dr Rogers AR 72756 Office: 1201 N 8th St Rogers AR 72756

HONCHUL, DELBERT, educator; b. Caney, Ky., May 26, 1919; s. Green Berry and Delia (Madden) H.; B.S., U. Md., 1957; postgrad. George Washington U., 1957-58; M.B.A., Ohio State U., 1959, postgrad., 1958-59, 62-65; m. Daris Wandalee Williams, Aug. 10, 1945 (dec.); children—Delbert Dean, Diana Lee, Donna Eugenia, Delaine Beth, Delores Kay, David Wallace; m. 2d, Quava Clark, Aug. 7, 1971. Enlisted USAAF, 1942, commd. 2d lt., 1944, advanced through grades to lt. col., 1963; asst. chief Ready Res. Br., Hdqrs., Pentagon, 1955-58; chief career and quality control Air Force Inst. Tech., 1960-65; instr. Air U., 1965-67; ret., 1967; asso. prof. mgmt. Murray (Ky.) State U., 1967—. Troop committeeman, treas. Boy Scouts Am. Mem. Acad. Mgmt., Orgn. Devel. Inst. Democrat. Contbr. articles to profl. jours. Home: Rt 2 Box 215 Murray KY 42071 Office: Dept Mgmt Murray State U Murray KY 42071

HONEA, WILLIAM MICHAEL, indsl. engr.; b. Camden, Ark., Dec. 23, 1946; s. Grady Garland and Helen Maxine (Voss) H.; B.S., Ark. Tech. U., 1969; M.S., U. Ark., 1979; m. Luciana Kim Jones, Feb. 12, 1977; children by previous marriage—Jonathan Michael, Carolee Elise, Laurel Leigh. Prodn./inventory control supr. Baldwin Electronics, Inc., Little Rock, 1972-73, prodn. mgr., 1973-76, asst. ops. mgr., 1976-78; sr. indsl. engr. Ark. Power & Light Co., Little Rock, 1978—. Served as officer Ordnance Corps, U.S. Army, 1969-72; now mem. Res. Mem. Am. Inst. Indsl. Engrs., Soc. Mfg. Engrs., Am. Mgmt. Assn., Internat. Soc. Hybrid Microelectronics, Nuclear Records Mgmt. Assn. Baptist. Home: 1522 Fair Park Blvd Little Rock AR 72204 Office: PO Box 551 (FNB-25) Little Rock AR 72203

HONEYCUTT, MARY LYNETTE, librarian; b. Alexandria, La., Nov. 5, 1945; d. Obal E. and Birdie Lee (Christy) H.; B.A., Northwestern State Coll., 1967; M.L.S., La. State U., 1974. Tech. services librarian Rapides Parish Library, Alexandria, 1967-71; tchr., librarian Georgetown (La.) Sch., 1971-74; asst. prof./librarian Henderson State U., Arkadelphia, Ark., 1974-79, mem. faculty senate, 1975-77, sec., 1975-76; coordinator state library services Ark. State Library, Little Rock, 1979—. Bd. dirs., sec. Henderson State U. Fed. Credit Union, 1977-79. Mem. ALA, Ark. Library Assn., Southwestern Library Assn., Beta Phi Mu, Phi Delta Kappa, Sigma Tau Delta. Democrat. Baptist. Club: Civitan (dir. 1978-79, sec. 1979—). Home: 1920 Kavanaugh Little Rock AR 72205 Office: Ark State Library One Capitol Mall Little Rock AR 72201

HONG, MOON W., physician; b. Choong-puk, Korea, July 29, 1939; s. Seung D. and Choo-Soon (Song) H.; came to U.S., 1967, naturalized, 1977; M.D., Korea U. Med. Sch., 1964; m. Chung-ja Kim, Apr. 7, 1968; children—Tommy, Eunice, Andy. Intern, St. Joseph Mercy Hosp., Detroit, 1967-68; resident Henry Ford Hosp., Detroit, 1968-72; fellowship tumor pathology St. Jude Hosp., Memphis, 1972-73; asso. pathologist Chattanooga Meml. Hosp., 1974—. Served to lt. Korean Army, 1964-67. Diplomate Am. Bd. Anatomic Pathology, Am. Bd. Clin. Pathology, Am. Bd. Dermatopathology. Mem. AMA, Coll. Am. Pathologists, Chattanooga Med. Assn., Hamilton County Med. Assn., Tenn. Med. Assn., Am. Soc. Clin. Pathologists. Home: 5600 Barrington Country Circle Ooltewah TN 37363 Office: 2500 Citico Ave Chattanooga TN 37404

HONOUR, WALTER WHITAKER, county ofcl.; b. Orange, N.J., Aug. 4, 1920; s. Stanley Whitaker and Carla Marie (Beck) H.; B.S., U.S. Naval Acad., 1943; M.S., George Washington U., 1970, M.S. in Mgmt. Engring., 1972; m. Elaine Lillian Gibson, June 10, 1943; children—Walter W., Craig G., Eric C., Stephen G., Melanie J. Commd. ensign U.S. Navy, 1943, advanced through grades to capt., 1963; ret., 1972; chief bio-environ. services Consol. City-County Govt. of Jacksonville, Fla., 1972—; asso. prof. naval sci. Purdue U., 1953-56. Mem. Fla. Local Environ. Regulation Assn. (chmn. 1975-77), Am. Mgmt. Assn., Air Pollution Control Assn., Mosquito Control Assn., U.S. Naval Acad. Alumni Assn., Navy League, Ret. Officers Assn. Home: 5066 Ortega Forest Dr Jacksonville FL 32210 Office: 515 W 6th St Jacksonville FL 32206

HOOD, ANN KENNEDY, nursing and hosp. adminstr.; b. Beverly, Mass., Mar. 7, 1933; d. David Kennedy and Mary (MacEachern) H.; B.S.N., Cornell U., 1955; M.N., Emory U., 1966. Adminstrv. supr. Lawrence Meml. Hosp., Medford, Mass., 1962-65; asst. dir. patient care Wesley Woods Health Center, Atlanta, 1966-68; adminstrv. asst. nursing Greenville (S.C.) Gen. Hosp., 1968-70, asst. dir. nursing, 1970-72, asso. adminstr. and dr. nurses, 1972—; adj. prof. Clemson U. Bd. dirs. Easter Seal Soc. Anderson County; active Greenville County Mental Health Assn. Mem. Nat. League Nursing, Am. Nurses Assn., Am. Hosp. Assn., S.C. Hosp. Assn., Nat. Forum Adminstrs. of Nursing Services, S.C. Soc. Hosp. Nursing Service Adminstrs., Bus. and Profl. Women's Assn., Cornell and Emory U. alumnae assns. Club: Greenville Country. Home: 207 Ligon Dr Anderson SC 29621 Office: 701 Grove Rd Greenville SC 29605

HOOD, CHARLES C., JR., cable TV system exec.; b. Alabama City, Ala., May 19, 1936; s. Charles C. and Vernia H.; ed. U. Hawaii, Am. River Coll.; m. Shirin George, Jan. 7, 1970; children—Mark Charles, Charles Frank, Robin Denise, Kimberley Michelle. Commd. officer U.S. Navy, 1954, advanced through grades; ret., 1974; western regional mgr. Action Communication Systems, Dallas, 1975-76, nat. mgr. tech. services, 1976-77, dir. field service, 1977-78; mgr. field ops. Tocom, Inc., Dallas, 1978-79; gen. mgr. Woodlands Cable TV, Inc., Woodlands, Tex., 1979—. Mem. Nat. Cable TV Assn. Republican. Lutheran. Home: 2815 Forest Grove Dr Richardson TX 75080 Office: Woodlands Cable TV Inc 2407 Timberlock Pl The Woodlands TX 77380

HOOD, CHARLES HURLBURT, advt. agency exec.; b. Cedar Rapids, Iowa, June 23, 1938; s. Charles Manrose and Pauline B. (Hurlburt) H.; B.J., U. Mo., 1960; m. Judy Drew Frost, Apr. 2, 1977; children by previous marriage—Cindy, Cary, Cathy. Advt. copywriter Sears Roebuck & Co., Chgo., 1960-61; copywriter, account exec. Wilson Advt. Agency, Tulsa, 1962-63; account exec. Whitney Advt. Agency, Tulsa, 1963-66; dir. advt. and pub. relations Unit Rig & Equipment Co., Tulsa, 1967; account supr., account exec. Ackerman Advt. Agency, Tulsa, 1968-69; chmn. bd. Hood-Hope & Assos., Inc., Tulsa, 1970—. Recipient Am. Advt. Fedn. 1st Pl. Nat. award, 1977. Republican. Presbyterian. Clubs: Oaks Country, Tulsa Petroleum, Philcrest Hills Tennis. Office: 6440 S Lewis St Tulsa OK 74136

HOOD, EDDIE A., computer programmer; b. Swansboro, N.C., Mar. 17, 1933; s. Richard Norman and Sallie Luzette (Sullivan) H.; student Albany State Coll., 1974-79; m. Sarah Ann DeLoach, Jan. 19, 1957; children—Eddie Andrew, Jeffery Lynn, Timothy Michael, Richard DeLaney. Enlisted U.S. Air Force, 1950, advanced through grades to tech. sgt., 1967; data automation supt. Webb AFB, Tex., 1967-69; ret., 1971; computer ops. supr. Firestone Tire Plant, Albany, Ga., 1971-77; computer programming instr. S. Ga. Tech., Americus, Ga., 1972—. Mem. Am. Vocat. Assn., Ga. Vocat. Assn. Baptist. Clubs: Elks, Albany High Football Boosters (pres. 1974-75). Author: Computerized Horoscopes, 1975. Home: 1800 Stuart Ave Albany GA 31707 Office: PO Box 1088 Americus GA 31709

HOOD, EDWIN CORNELL, ins. co. exec.; b. Winona, Miss., Apr. 19, 1939; s. Edwin Cornell and Helen Elizabeth (Barry) H.; B.A., U. Md., 1961; m. Phyllis Joan Hughes, Feb. 1, 1969; children—Michael Sheldon, Eric Cornell, Erin Colleen, Amy Nichole. Credit mgr. Family Fin., Kansas City, Mo., 1959-67; credit supr. Nat. Bellas Hess, Kansas City, 1967-68; asst. to pres. Studio Sales & Service, Kansas City, 1968-70; state cir. sales United Cos., Jackson, Miss., 1970-72; banking coordinator new products div. Nat. Found. Life, Baton Rouge, 1972-73; pres. E.C. Hood & Assos., Inc., Baton Rouge, 1973—. Bd. dirs. Shenandoah Homeowners, 1976—. Served with U.S. Army, 1961-64. Mem. Nat. Small Bus. Assn., Nat. Assn. Life Underwriters, La. Assn. Life Underwriters, Ind. Assn. Fin. Planners. Baptist. Clubs: Masons, Shriners, Kiwanis, K.T. Home: 16836 Appomattox St Baton Rouge LA 70816 Office: E C Hood & Assos Inc 12090 S Harrels Ferry Rd Baton Rouge LA 70816

HOOD, JOHN JULIAN, electric utility exec.; b. Newnan, Ga., Aug. 30, 1908; s. Julius C. and Mary Elizabeth (Moore) H.; student Mercer U., 1928; m. Ruth Braden, 1937 (div. 1967); children—Julia Ruth Hood Key, Elizabeth Anne Hood Cox; m. 2d, Margaret Payne, Mar. 11, 1969. Farmer, Newnan, 1943-44; asst. county agt. Coweta County, Newnan, 1944-45; various positions Ga. Dept. Forestry, 1946; organizer Coweta Fayette Electric Membership Corp., Newnan, 1946, mgr. 1946—. Chmn. Coweta County Water Com., 1965—; pres. Cedar Creek Watershed, 1965—; chmn. Chattahoochee Flint Area Planning and Devel. Com., 1964-72; mem. staff, adviser on area planning and devel. Gov. Maddox, 1967-70, Gov. Carter, 1971-74, Gov. Busbee, 1975—. Mem. Am. Right of Way Assn., Nat. Elec. Insps. Assn., Ga., Newnan-Coweta chambers commerce, Sigma Nu. Democrat. Methodist. Clubs: Civitan, Elks. Home: 129A Route 6 Newnan GA 30263 Office: Ga 29 Hwy Newnan GA 30264

HOOD, MARY ELIZA, librarian; b. Sautee, Ga., Jan. 19, 1915; d. William Leonard and Ethel Edna (Lyon) H.; A.B., Piedmont Coll., 1935; postgrad. U. Ga., 1938, 39, 40; B.S. in L.S., George Peabody Library Sch., 1947, M.A. in L.S., 1964; cert. Emory U. and Ga. Dept. Archives and History, 1978. Tchr. English and French, tchr.-librarian Ga. High Schs., 1935-47; tech. services librarian, asso. prof. library sci. Stewart Library, N. Ga. Coll., Dahlonega, 1947—. Mem. Lumpkin Library Bd., 1978—; chmn. Martha Martin Price Circle, Dahlonega Bapt. Missionary Union, 1976—. Mem. Am. Library Assn. (membership drive com.), Southeastern Library Assn., Ga. Library Assn., AAUP, Lumpkin County Hist. Assn. (com. chmn.), Women of N. Ga. Coll. (pres.), Pi Gamma Mu, Delta Kappa Gamma. Democrat. Baptist. Clubs: Dahlonega Woman's (sec., treas.), Faculty Bridge (pres.). Co-author: Handbook for North Georgia College Library, 1965. Home: 405 N Hall Rd Dahlonega GA 30533 Office: N Ga Coll Stewart Library Dahlonega GA 30533

HOOD, MAURICE (MAURY) JOHN, devel. co. exec.; b. Farmington, Wash., Jan 20, 1935; s. Merle Mohr and Margaret Jo (Pine) H.; B.A. in Archtl. Engring. with honors, Wash. State Coll., 1958; m. Shirley Ann Morris, June 13, 1959; children—Julie Lynn, Paul Michael, Marcus Jon. Plant supr., dist. engr. Shell Oil Co., Seattle, 1958-64, Long Beach, Calif., 1964-65, Colton, Calif., 1965-68; asso. partner Bush Roed & Hutching P.S. Inc., Seattle, 1968-72; v.p., regional mgr. Levitt & Sons of Calif., Nashville, 1972-73; regional mgr. Baker Crow Co., Austin, Tex., 1973-74; v.p. Mayfield Cos., Austin, 1974-79; pres. Jester Devel. Corp., Austin, 1979—. Mem. exec. bd. Balconies Civic Assn., Austin, 1976-77, N.W. Austin Civic Assn., 1979—; pres. Cat Mountain Homeowners Assn., Austin, 1977-79; chmn. Austin Environ. Bd., 1978-80; mem. Republican Precinct Com., Seattle, 1966-68; bd. dirs. Bellevue (Wash.) Park Bd., 1971-72. Served to 1st lt. U.S. Army, 1958-60. Recipient Shell Oil award Soc. Golden West, 1965; registered profl. engr., Wash. Mem. Community Assns. Inst., Austin Assn. Builders, Nat. Assn. Home Builders, Austin C. of C., Sigma Phi Epsilon, Tau Beta Phi, Phi Kappa Phi, Sigma Tau. Clubs: Courtyard Tennis and Swim, Lions, Toastmasters. Home: 7804 Heathercrest Circle Austin TX 78731 Office: PO Box 10061 Austin TX 78766

HOOD, WALTER KELLY, painter, art historian; b. Catawba County, N.C., Aug 19, 1928; s. Charles Arthur and Rachel Maude (Clay) H.; student Antioch Coll., 1948-49, Pa. Acad. Fine Arts, 1949-53, Am. Acad. Rome, 1953-55; B.F.A., U. Pa., 1957; M.F.A., U. Hawaii, 1961; Ph.D., Northwestern U., 1966; m. Elizabeth Klaner Welch, July 29, 1967; children—David Walter. Instr. drawing and painting Honolulu Acad. Art, summer 1961; prof. art Catawba Coll., Salisbury, N.C., 1971—, head dept. art, 1971—; one-man shows: La Fontanella, Rome, 1955, Archtl. League, N.Y.C., 1956, Atlanta Fine Arts Gallery, 1967. group shows include: Am. Artists Profl. League, N.Y.C., 1974, 75, 76, Nat. Soc. Painters in Casein and Acrylic, N.Y.C., 1976-78; represented in permanent collections: Pa. Acad., Sandoz Collection Rome; murals St. Peters Ch., Glenside, Pa., 1957-58; fresco panels Honolulu Bd. Engrs., Architects and Land Surveyors, 1961. Served with U.S. Army, 1946-48. Abbey fellow Am. Acad. Rome, 1953-54; recipient awards Am. Artists Profl. League, 1974, Charlotte Whinston award Nat. Soc. Painters Casein and Acrylic, 1976. Mem. Nat. Soc. Mural Painters, Am. Artists Profl. League. Home: 2508 W Innes St Salisbury NC 28144 Office: Catawba Coll W Innes St Salisbury NC 28144

HOOD, WILLIAM ROGERS, electronic engr.; b. Calhoun, Ga., Mar. 2, 1945; s. William Charles and Mary Katherine (Rogers) H.; B.E.E., Ga. Inst. Tech., 1967, M.S., 1968; m. Rita Frances Sewell, May 8, 1967. Grad. teaching asst. elec. engring. Ga. Inst. Tech., Atlanta, 1967; research and devel. staff Lockheed Ga. Co., Marietta, 1967—; instr. electronic engring. tech. So. Tech. Inst., Marietta, 1973—. Mem. IEEE (regional award 1967, del. to China 1979). Home: 1210 Blackwell Rd Marietta GA 30066 Office: D/72 35 Z 316 86 S Cobb Dr Marietta GA 30063

HOOK, ALICE VASQUEZ, bus. adminstr.; b. El Paso, Tex., Dec. 23, 1933; d. Carlos R. and Laura (Torres) Vasquez; student Okaloosa (Fla.) Jr. Coll., 1977—; m. Robert Donald Hook, Jan. 2, 1976; children by previous marriage—Catherine Gurney, Theresa Gurney; stepchildren—Dennis Hook, Denise Hook, Bryan Hook. Various secretarial positions, 1954-64; with U.S. Civil Service, 1964—; word processing mgr. Eglin AFB, Fla., 1977—; Hispanic employment program coordinator EEO adv. council, 1975-77, 79; adv. bd. bus. dept. Okaloosa Walton Jr. Coll.; part-owner Am. Security, security service bus. Recipient Outstanding Performance award USAF, 1967, 71, 72, Sustained Superior Performance award, 1968-70, 74. Mem. Federally Employed Women (chpt. treas. 1977-78), Internat. Word Processing Assn. Home: 505 Virginia St Fort Walton Beach FL 32548 Office: PO Box 802 Shalimar FL 32579

HOOK, DONAL DELOSE, forest scientist; b. Cleveland, Okla., June 21, 1933; s. George C. and Etta J. (Sanders) H.; B.S., Utah State U., 1961, M.S. in Forestry, 1962; Ph.D. (U.S. Forest Service grantee), U. Ga., 1968; m. Eleanor Ann Age, Mar. 16, 1956; children—Karen Linda, Michael Boyd, Kenneth James, Shanna Kay. Silviculturist, plant physiologist Southeastern Forest Expt. Sta., U.S. Forest Service, Dept. Agr., Charleston, S.C. and Athens, Ga., 1963-71; asso. prof. U. Ky., Lexington, 1971-73; prof., dir. Belle W. Baruch Forest Sci. Inst., Clemson U., Georgetown, S.C., 1973—; cons. to pvt. industry. Trustee, Georgetown Hist. Found.; deacon Presbyterian Ch. Served with USNR, 1952-56. Mem. Soc. Am. Foresters (chmn. S.C. div.), Am. Forestry Assn., Forest Farmers Assn., S.C. Forestry Assn., Sigma Xi. Club: Rotary (Georgetown). Editor: (with R.M.M. Crawford) Plant Life in Anaerobic Environments, 1978. Office: Belle W Baruch Forest Sci Inst Clemson U PO Box 596 Georgetown SC 29440

HOOK, HAROLD SWANSON, ins. co. exec.; b. Kansas City, Mo., Oct. 10, 1931; s. Ralph C. and Ruby (Swanson) H.; B.S. in Bus. Adminstrn., U. Mo., 1953, M.A. in Acctg., 1954; m. Joanne T. Hunt, Feb. 19, 1955; children—Karen Anne, Thomas Wesley, Randall Townsend. With Nat. Fidelity Life Ins. Co., Kansas City, Mo., 1957-66, asst. to pres., 1957-60, bd. dirs., 1959-66, adminstrv. v.p., 1960-61, exec. v.p., 1961-63, pres., 1963-66; sr. v.p. U.S. Life Ins. Co., N.Y.C., 1966-67, exec. v.p., 1967-68, pres., 1968-70, dir., 1967-70; pres., chief exec. officer, dir., mem. exec. com. Calif.-Western States Life Ins. Co., Sacramento, 1970-75, chmn., 1975-79, sr. chmn., 1979—; founder, pres. Main Event Mgmt. Corp., Sacramento, 1970—, mem. exec. com., 1975—, dir., 1972—; pres., dir., mem. exec. com. Am. Gen. Ins. Co., Houston, 1975-78, chmn., pres., chief exec. officer, mem. exec. com., 1978—; dir. Delta Calif. Industries, Lloyds Bank Calif., Panhandle Eastern Pipe Line Co., Houston, Trunkline Gas Co., Houston, Past pres. Golden Empire council Boy Scouts Am., exec. bd. Sam Houston Area council; trustee Baylor U. Coll. Medicine, Am. Coll., Bryn Mawr, Pa.; bd. dirs. Houston Symphony Soc., Tex. Research League. Served to lt. USNR, 1954-57. Recipient citation of merit U. Mo., 1965; named Man of Year Delta Sigma Pi, 1969, Silver Beaver award Boy Scouts Am., 1974, Eagle Scout award, 1976; CEO award Fin. World mag., 1979. Served from ensign to lt. (j.g.) USNR, 1954-57. C.L.U. Fellow Life Mgmt. Inst.; mem. Am. Council Life Ins. (dir.), Life Office Mgmt. Assn. (chmn. 1976-77), Life Ins. Mktg. Research Assn., Nat. Assn. Life Underwriters, C.L.U.'s, Houston C. of C. (dir., exec. com.), Philos. Soc. Tex., Young Pres.'s Orgn., Beta Theta Pi, Omicron Delta Kappa, Beta Gamma Sigma. Presbyterian. Clubs: Petroleum, River Oaks Country, Petroleum, Univ. (Houston); Morris County Golf (Morristown, N.J.); Mission Hills Country (Kansas City, Mo.). Home: 2204 Troon Rd Houston TX 77019 Office: 2727 Allen Pkwy Houston TX 77019

HOOK, ROSEMARY LOUISE, nurse, hosp. ofcl.; b. Seymour, Ind., Dec. 16, 1931; d. Frederick John and Emma Mary (Velten) Hunnefeld; diploma St. Elizabeth Sch. Nursing, 1952; student Thomas More Coll., 1975—; m., Feb. 7, 1952; 1 dau., Sharon Marie. Staff nurse, St. Elizabeth Hosp., Covington, Ky., 1953-56, head nurse, 1956-63, staff nurse, 1969-71, supr., 1971-73, asso. dir. patient care, 1973-74, asst. adminstr. nursing, 1974—, adv. bd. pastoral care; office and pvt. duty nurse, Covington, 1963-69. Adv. bds. Home Health Agy., nursing program Thomas More Coll. Mem. Ky. Hosp. Nursing Service Adminstrs. Assn. Democrat. Roman Catholic. Home: 662 Meadow Ln Covington KY 41015 Office: St Elizabeth Hosp 401 E 20th St Covington KY 41014

HOOKER, JOHN PATRICK, neurol. surgeon; b. Frost, Tex., Sept. 5, 1926; s. Rea Ferdinand and Ada (Walker) H.; B.A., U. Tex., 1950; M.D., U. Tex. at Galveston, 1954; m. Mariam Shearin Squires (dec.); m. 2d, Mary Katherine Donahue. Intern, Jackson Meml. Hosp., Miami, Fla., 1954-55, resident gen. surgery, 1955-56; fellow neurol. surgery Mayo Found., Rochester, Minn., 1956-58, Ochsner Found., New Orleans, 1958-61; practice medicine, specializing in neurol. surgery, Midland, Tex., 1961-71, Augusta, Maine, 1971-73, Lumberton, N.C., 1973-77, McAllen Gen. Hosp., 1977—. Bd. dirs. Midland chpt. A.R.C., 1965-71. Served with U.S. Army, 1944-46. Diplomate Am. Bd. Neurol. Surgery. Fellow A.C.S., Internat. Coll. Angiology, Am. Geriatric Assn., Royal Soc. Health (U.K.); mem. Am. Assn. Neurol. Surgeons, Congress Neurol. Surgeons, So. Neurosurg. Soc., Pan-Pacific Surg. Assn., Pan Am. Med. Assn., Robeson County, N.C. med. socs., AMA, Nat. Aero. Assn., Aircraft Owners and Pilots Assn., Royal Soc. Health (U.K.), Order of Quiet Birdmen. Republican. Episcopalian. Rotarian. Club: Ft. Worth. Home: 700 Sunset Apt 205 McAllen TX 78501 Office: 521 W Broadway McAllen TX 78501

HOOKS, EUGENE JAMES, educator, theatre specialist; b. St. Louis, Jan. 1, 1938; s. Eugene Russell and Dorothy Mae (Petway) H.; B.S. in Edn., U. Mo., 1969, M.A., 1970, Ph.D. in Theatre, 1973; m. Marianne Jolly, Jan. 1, 1960; children—James David, Michael Lewis, Jeffrey Quarles, Hugh David. Instr. theatre U. Mo., Columbia, 1970-71, asst. tech. dir., 1970-71, instr., tech. dir., 1971-73; instr. Stephens Coll., Columbia, Mo., 1971; dir. theatre U. Fla., Gainesville, 1973-75, asst. prof., advisor, scene designer, 1973-75, interim chmn., dept. of theatre, asst. prof., advisor, scene designer, 1975-76, chmn. dept., asso. prof., advisor, dir., 1976—; dir. Fla. state play Cross and Sword. Served with USMC, 1956-57. Recipient grants Fla. Arts Council, 1975-79, So. Fedn. of State Arts Agys., 1977, Panama City (Fla.) Civic Music Assn., 1975-76. Mem. Fla. (Univ. and coll. rep. 1977), Southeastern (fin. com. 1977—) theatre confs., Am. Theatre Assn. (conv. planning com. 1977-79), Speech Communication Assn. Am. (chmn. theatre div. 1977-79). Contbr. numerous profl. scene designs, publs. and programs; co-author: (with S. Smiley) Theatre: The Human Art, 1978. Home: 752 NE 22nd St Gainesville FL 32603 Office: 363 ASB U of Fla Gainesville FL 32601

HOOLEY, JOHN STONE, surgeon; b. Hempstead, N.Y., Apr. 11, 1916; s. Francis George and Charlotte Stoddard (Stone) H.; A.B., Cornell U., 1938, M.D., 1942; m. Betty Grunwald, Feb. 26, 1949; children—Deirdra Ellen, John Francis, Priscilla Ann, Richard Martin, Alan Patrick. Intern, Bellevue Hosp., N.Y.C., 1942-43, resident, 1946-48; resident in surgery Meadowbrook Hosp., Hempstead, N.Y., 1948-50; practice medicine specializing in surgery, Rockville Center, N.Y.C., 1950-57, Sigourney, Iowa, 1957-64, Merritt Island, Fla., 1964—; chief staff Keokuk County Hosp., Sigourney, 1959-61; attending surgeon Westhoff Meml. Hosp., Cocoa, Fla., 1965—; courtesy staff Cape Canaveral Hosp., 1965—. Bd. dirs. Community Action Agy., Cocoa, 1972-73, Family Services Bur., Brevard County, 1975-76; v.p. parish council Divine Mercy Parish, Merritt Island, 1971-73. Served to maj. with AUS, 1943-46. Diplomate Am. Bd. Surgery, Nat. Bd. Med. Examiners. Fellow A.C.S., Internat. Coll. Surgeons; mem. Cornell, Cornell Med. Coll. alumni assns., Brevard County, Fla. med. socs., AMA, SAR. Republican. Roman Catholic. Club: Kiwanis. Home: 1793 Rockledge Dr Rockledge FL 32955 Office: 275 Magnolia Ave Merritt Island FL 32952

HOOPER, GLENN SCOBLE, pathologist; b. Bay Minette, Ala., June 28, 1929; s. Leonard John and Lalla Camella (Northcutt) H.; B.S., Auburn U., 1950; M.D., Med. Coll. Ala., 1960; m. Carole Elizabeth King, June 8, 1957; children—James Glenn, John David, Joel Thomas. Process engr. Union Carbide Corp., Oak Ridge and Paducah, Ky., 1951-55; intern St. Vincent Hosp., Birmingham, Ala., 1960-61; resident in pathology Carraway Methodist Hosp., Birmingham, 1961-64, Med. Coll. Va., 1964-65; asst. pathologist St. Joseph Hosp., Lexington, Ky., 1965-66; pathologist Tampa (Fla.) Gen. Hosp., 1966—; asso. pathologist Meml. Hosp. Tampa, 1970—, Women's Hosp. Tampa, 1974; pathologist, dir. labs. Univ. Community Hosp., Tampa, 1968—; asso. clin. prof. pathology U. So. Fla. Coll. Medicine, 1973—. Mem. Am., Fla. med. assns., Am. (dir. 1978—), Fla. (pres. 1978-79) assns. blood banks, Am. Soc. Clin. Pathologists, Coll. Am. Pathologists, Fla. West Coast Assn. Pathologists (pres. 1976—). Democrat. Methodist. Club: Midtown Kiwanis (treas. 1974-75, v.p. 1975-76, pres. 1977-78). Home: 2408 S Dundee Tampa FL 33609 Office: 3100 E Fletcher Ave Tampa FL 33612

HOOPER, IRENE UPSHAW, environ. edn. center adminstr.; b. Miami, Sept. 26, 1935; d. Len William and Florence (Akin) Upshaw; A.A., Mars Hill Coll., 1955; B.A., Hardin-Simmons U., 1957; M.S., Barry Coll., 1972; m. Jackson Holloway Hooper, Sept. 2, 1960 (dec. Oct. 1970). Classroom tchr., Miami, Fla., 1958-60, guidance counselor, journalism tchr., Miami, 1961-69; camp dir. Seacamp, Big Pine Key, Fla., 1964—; exec. dir. Newfound Harbor Marine Inst., Big Pine Key, Fla., 1970—, site adminstr. San Francisco State U. project. Camp dir. Miami Bapt. Assn., 1960; mem. Big Pine Key Civic Assn., 1968—. Mem Mem. Am. Personnel and Guidance Assn., Fla. Edn. Assn., Dade County Classroom Tchrs. Assn. (bldg. rep. 1960-69), Am. Camping Assn. (dir. Fla. sect., pres. Fla. sect. 1976-78). Home: 750 NE 61st St Miami FL 33137 Office: Route 1 Box 170 Big Pine Key FL 33043

HOOTEN, WILLIAM WAYNE, engring. cons., airline transport pilot; b. Dallas, Oct. 30, 1933; s. Francis Nelson and Martha Marie (Greer) H.; B.S., U. Tex., 1956; m. Mildred Ann Hooper, Feb. 16, 1957; children—Sandra Kay, Sheryl Ann. Field engr. IBM Corp., Dallas, 1956-64, tech. support engr., 1964-68, sr. field engr., 1968-71; cons. Comma Corp., Dallas, 1971-77; tech. support engr. Itel Corp., 1977-79; engring. mgr. Mostek Corp., 1979—; flight instr. Dallas Flight Center, 1974-76; instr. Aircrew Tng. Center, 1977—, pilot Astrowing Airlines, 1977, Boardman Aviation, 1977—; pres., partner Tri Inc., 1966—. Served with USN, 1951-54. Mem. Nat. Assn. Flight Instrs. Republican. Methodist. Mason (Shriner, 32 deg.). Contbr. articles on flight instrn. to profl. jours. Home: 3248 Whitehall Dr Dallas TX 75229 Office: 1215 W Crosby Rd Carrollton TX 75006

HOOTMAN, HARRY EDWARD, nuclear engr.; b. Oak Park, Ill., June 5, 1933; s. Merle Albert and Rachel Edith (Atkinson) H.; B.S., Mich. Technol. U., 1959, M.S., 1961; LL.B., LaSalle Extension U., 1971; m. Linda Pearl Smith, Nov. 23, 1963; children—David Ernest, Holly Jean, John Christian. Research asso. Argonne (Ill.) Nat. Lab., 1960-62; reactor engr. Savannah River plant E.I. du Pont de Neumours & Co., Inc., Aiken, S.C., 1962-65, sr. design engr., reactor engring. div., 1965-68, research physicist, theoretical physics div., 1968-74, research staff engr. environ. effects div. Savannah River lab., 1974—. Dir. Central Savannah River Area Sci. and Engring. Fair, Inc.; troop committeeman Boy Scouts Am., Aiken. Served in USAF, 1953-57. Dow Chem. scholar, 1958; registered profl. engr., S.C. Mem. Am. Nuclear Soc., Nat., S.C. socs. profl. engrs., Am. Acad. Environ. Engrs., Augusta Opera Assn., Phi Lambda Upsilon. Baptist. Club: Neptune Dive. Home: 820 Brandy Rd Aiken SC 29801 Office: Savannah River Lab Aiken SC 29801

HOOVER, JIMMIE HARTMAN, librarian; b. Board Camp, Ark., Nov. 5, 1930; s. James Thomas and Alice Victoria (Peters) H.; student Coll. Ozarks, 1948-49; B.A., Ark. Poly. Coll., 1952; M.S., La. State U., 1958; m. Lillian Elaine Fitzgerald, Jan. 2, 1959. With La. State U. Library, Baton Rouge and New Orleans, 1958—, head order dept., Baton Rouge, 1965-67, head govt. documents dept., 1968—, mem. faculty Sch. Library Sci., 1972-73, affiliate faculty Grad. Sch. L.S., 1974—. Served with Security Service, USAF, 1952-56. Mem. La. (bus. mgr. bull. 1964-65), Am., Southwestern library assns., Spl. Libraries Assn. (nat. govt. info. service com. 1969-71), Am. Legion. Author: (with J. Norman Heard) Bookman's Guide to Americana, 6th ed., 1970, 7th edit., 1977; editor Spl. Libraries Assn. Ark., Miss. and La. chpt. Bull., 1970, La. Library Assn. Coll. Sect. Bull., 1968—; govt. documents reviewer Reference Service Rev., 1973—. Home: 1815 Myrtledale Ave Baton Rouge LA 70808

HOOVER, LARRY MARTIN, textiles co. exec.; b. Pine Bluff, Ark., Dec. 6, 1946; s. Richard M. and Martha N. (Womble Vent) H.; B.S., U. Ark., Monticello, 1975; m. Marilyn Reed, Feb. 11, 1966; children—Rhonda, Amy. Indsl. engr. Monticello Carpet Mill (Ark.), 1970-74; tng. mgr. Charm Tred Spinning Plant, Monticello, 1974-75, Burlington House Area Rugs, Monticello, 1975-78; div. tng. mgr. Burlington Industries, Monticello div., 1978—; cons. textiles program Monticello Vo Tech Sch., 1977-80. Mem. funds drive leadership com. Boy Scouts Am. Served with USN, 1967-69. Mem. Am. Mgmt. Assn. Baptist. Club: Kiwanis (Monticello). Home: Route 2 Box 84 Monticello AR 71655 Office: PO Box 120 Monticello AR 71655

HOOVER, RICHARD BRICE, space scientist; b. Sikeston, Mo., Jan. 3, 1943; s. Harry L. and Pansy I. (Rainey) H.; B.S., Henderson State U., 1964; postgrad. (NSF fellow), Duke U., 1964, U. Ark., 1965, UCLA, 1966; m. Miriam Jackson, Aug. 15, 1970. Instr. physics U. Ark., 1965; physicist applied research div. Astrionics Lab., NASA Marshall Space Flight Center, Huntsville, Ala., 1966-70, space scientist solar physics br., 1970-76, space scientist high energy astrophysics br., 1976—; dir. environ. scis. lab. Unidev, Inc., Huntsville, Ala., 1970-72; cons. Grefco Inc., Los Angeles, 1969—, SCI Systems, Inc., Huntsville, 1969-70, Henri Van Heurck Mus., Soc. Royale de Zoologie, Antwerp, Belgium, 1975—. Vice pres. Civic Opera Soc., 1970. Recipient Sustained Superior Performance award NASA, 1975, Achievement award, 1978. Mem. Am. Astronomical Soc., Optical Soc. Am., Von Braun Astron. Assn., Huntsville Gem and Mineral Soc., World Future Soc., Royal Zool. Soc. Am. Unitarian. Contbr. numerous articles on X-ray astronomy, solar physics and X-ray optics to sci. jours. and periodicals; patentee three mirror X-ray telescope and multiplate gamma-ray collimator. Home: 7706 Teal Dr Huntsville AL 35802 Office: High Energy Astrophysics Br ES-62 Space Sciences Lab NASA George Marshall Space Flight Center Huntsville AL 35812

HOOVER, RICHARD LEE, chem. co. exec.; b. South Bend, Ind., Aug. 16, 1949; s. George W. and Mercea M. (Baer) H.; B.S. in Aero. and Mech. Engring., Tri-State U., Angola, Ind., 1971; m. Lee Ann Bryar, Aug. 19, 1972; children—Stacey, Kristin. Sales engr. Trane Co., Pitts., 1971-72; area sales mgr. Nalco Chem. Co., Oak Brook, Ill., 1972—; sales and cons. in water treatment, energy conservation. Mem. membership com. Youngstown (Ohio) YMCA. Named Top Dist. Salesman, Nalco Chem. Co., 1976. Mem. Am. Water Works Assn., Assn. Iron and Steel Engrs., Water Pollution Control Fedn., Youngstown Area Jaycees. Methodist. Club: Masons. Address: 803 Sandness Ct Louisville KY 40243

HOPE, ROBERT EUGENE, profl. baseball club exec.; b. Atlanta, June 12, 1946; s. Eugene Webb and Dorothy Ann (Young) H.; A.B., Ga. State U., 1968; m. Susan Snow, Oct. 9, 1971; children—Alice Elizabeth, Anna Clair. With Atlanta Braves, 1967—, v.p. mktg., 1976—, v.p. mktg. Atlanta Hawks, 1977—. Chmn. fund raising Ga. Spina Bifida Assn., 1979; chmn. fund raising Butler St. YMCA, 1979—; bd. dirs. Muscular Dystrophy Assn., treas., 1978; sec. Ga. Athletic Hall of Fame, 1975—. Mem. Sales and Mktg. Execs. Atlanta. Methodist. Clubs: Atlanta Advt., Kiwanis. Home: 450 S Susan Creek Dr Stone Mountain GA 30083 Office: Atlanta Fulton County Stadium Atlanta GA 30312

HOPE, SAMUEL HOWARD, assn. exec.; b. Owensboro, Ky., Nov. 5, 1946; s. James Russell and Lorraine (Jones) H.; B.Mus., Eastman Sch. Music, Rochester, N.Y., 1967; M. Music Arts, Yale U., 1970; student Nadia Boulanger, France, 1966, 67; m. Judy Bucher, June 24, 1978. Dean, composer-in-residence Atlanta Boy Choir Sch. Music, 1970-73, trustee, 1973—; vis. instr. Lee Coll., 1973-74; exec. dir. music alumni, asso. dir. grad. profl. programs Campaign for Yale, Yale U., 1974-75; exec. dir. Nat. Assn. Schs. Music and exec. dir. Nat. Assn. Schs. Art, Reston, Va., 1975—; exec. dir. Joint Commn. on Dance and Theater Accreditation, 1978—; bd. dirs. Council Specialized Accrediting Agys., 1978—, sec.-treas., 1979—; chmn. Assembly of Specialized Accrediting Bodies Council on Postsecondary Accreditation, 1979—; chmn. govt. relations com. Nat. Music Council, 1976-79, bd. dirs., 1978—, chmn. edn. com., 1979—; mem. exec. com. Am. Soc. Univ. Composers; mem. nat. alumni council Eastman Sch. Music, 1975-78, chmn., 1976-77; bd. dirs. Am. Music Conf., 1978—; composer: Piano Sonata I, 1968, II, 1971; (motet) Solus Ad Victimam Procedis, Domine, 1970, Blessed Be Thou Lord, 1976; Trio for Oboe, Cello and Piano, 1970; Cantata I, 1973, II, 1975; String Quartet I, 1980. Recipient Composition prize Yale U., 1968, 69, 70. Mem. Am. Music Center, Coll. Music Soc., Music Educators Nat. Conf., Music Tchrs. Nat. Assn. Episcopalian. Clubs: Yale (N.Y.C. and Washington). Office: 11250 Roger Bacon Dr Suite 5 Reston VA 22090

HOPKINS, AMY LONGCOPE (MRS. EDWIN BUTCHER HOPKINS), civic worker; b. Lampasas, Tex., Sept. 5, 1887; d. Edmund McLeod and Madeleine (Beall) Longcope; D. Hum. (hon.), Northwood Inst., Dallas, 1978; m. Edwin Butcher Hopkins, June 20, 1913; children—Amy (Mrs. Duke Selig), Jane (Mrs. Jack Munger), Louise (Mrs. Harris Underwood), Madeleine (Mrs. James K. Wade), Edwin Butcher. Past trustee Dallas Mus. Fine Arts, Dallas Symphony Soc.; bd. dirs. Dallas Civic Opera Assn., Found. for Humanities and Scis. of So. Methodist U., Dallas Civic Opera; mem. bd. Friends of Dallas Pub. Library; mem. Assos. of Dallas Mus. Fine Arts; underwriter Dallas Grand Opera; mem. Pres.'s council Tex. Tech U. Found. Mem. Colonial Dames Am., Daus. Barons of Runnemede, Daus. of 1812, Daus. Republic of Tex., Dau. Founders Patriots Am., Order Crown, Magna Charta Dames, Plantagenet Soc., Explorers Club. Episcopalian. Clubs: Brook Hollow Golf, Dallas Petroleum (Dallas). Home: Park Towers 3310 Fairmount Dallas TX 75201

HOPKINS, ANTHONY DUANE, retail exec.; b. Los Angeles, Aug. 29, 1956; s. Walter H. and Annie (Lee) H.; A.S., Dallas Fashion Mdse. Coll., 1976; student Dallas Bapt. Coll., 1976—. Salesman, Neiman Marcus, Dallas, 1973-75; asst. mgr. Kinney Shoe Corp., Dallas, 1975-77; owner, dealership Natural World Candy Co., Dallas, 1977—; pres. Hopco Co., Dallas, 1977—; part owner New World Industries, Inc. Mem. Inst. Logopedics, Nat. Forensic League, Mail Order Assn., Am. Assn. Commodity Buyers, Bradford Exchange, Am. Inst. Banking, Treins Exchange, Unity Buying Service. Democrat. Baptist. Clubs: Commonwealth, Original Print Collectors Group, Nat. Health. Home: 3215 South Blvd Dallas TX 75210

HOPKINS, CARTER BYRD HUNTER, ednl. adminstr.; b. Norfolk, Va., Dec. 8, 1946; d. Henry Blount and Vivian Byrd (Smith) Hunter; A.B., Sweet Briar Coll., 1968; M.Ed., Am. U., 1972; m. Edward Meeks Hopkins, July 30, 1977; 1 son, Edward Hunter. Tech. editor TRW Systems Group, Washington, 1969-70; claims rep. Ins. Mgmt., Inc., Washington, 1970; coll. counselor Stone Ridge Country Day Sch., Bethesda, Md., 1972-76; dir. career planning Sweet Briar (Va.) Coll., 1976—. Chmn. women's legal def. fund com. Jr. League of Washington, 1974-75; vol. Planned Parenthood Clinic, 1975-76. Mem. Am. Personnel and Guidance Assn., So. Coll. Placement Assn., Mid Atlantic Placement Assn., Am. Sch. Counselor Assn., Va. Assn. Student Personnel Adminstrs. Episcopalian. Home: Ridge Dr PO Box 743 Amherst VA 24521 Office: PO Box AT Sweet Briar VA 24595

HOPKINS, CARTER HUNTER, counselor; b. Norfolk, Va., Dec. 8, 1946; d. Henry Blount, Jr., and Vivian Byrd (Smith) Hunter; A.B., Sweet Briar Coll., 1968; M.Ed., Am. U., 1972; m. Edward Meeks Hopkins, July 30, 1977; 1 son, Edward Hunter. Employment counselor Day Personnel, Inc., Washington, 1968; jr. tech. editor TRW Systems Group, Washington, 1969-70; ins. claims clk. Ins. Mgmt., Washington, 1970-71; coll. counselor Stone Ridge Country Day Sch., Bethesda, Md., 1972-76; dir. career planning Sweet Briar (Va.) Coll. 1976—; workshop cons. Bus. and Profl. Women of Lynchburg, Women's Resource Center of Lynchburg, Fidelity Am. Bank. Chair women's legal def. project Jr. League of Washington, 1975; vol. Planned Parenthood, 1976. Mem. Am. Personnel and Guidance Assn., Am. Sch. Counselor Assn., So. Coll. Placement Assn., Middle Atlantic Placement Assn., Va. Coll. Placement Assn., AAUW, Coll. Placement Council. Episcopalian. Clubs: Village Garden (Amherst); Bus. and Profl. Women's (Lynchburg); Va. Fedn. Garden Clubs. Home: Ridge Dr Box 743 Amherst VA 24521 Office: PO Box AT Sweet Briar College Sweet Briar VA 24595

HOPKINS, CHARLES DRENNEN, orthopedic surgeon, army officer; b. El Paso, Tex., Dec. 10, 1945; s. Charles Drennen and Louise (Snyder) H.; B.A., U. Tex., El Paso, 1967; M.D., U. Tex., Galveston, 1971; m. Sherrie Lou Williams, June 13, 1969; children—Amy, Nikki, Kristin. Commd. 2d lt. U.S. Army, 1969, advanced through ranks to lt. col., 1979; intern William Beaumont Army Med. Center, El Paso, 1971-72, resident in orthopedic surgery, 1973-76, mem. pediatric orthopaedic staff, 1980—; chief orthopedic service U.S. Army Hosp., Nurnberg, W. Ger., 1977-79; fellow in pediatric orthopedics Scottish Rite Hosp., Atlanta, 1979-80. Decorated Meritorious Service medal; diplomate Am. Bd. Orthopedic Surgeons. Fellow A.C.S., Am. Acad. Orthopedic Surgeons; mem. Soc. Mil. Orthopedic Surgeons. Roman Catholic. Office: Orthopaedic Service William Beaumont Army Med Center El Paso TX 79920

HOPKINS, JAMES FRANKLIN, historian, cons.; b. Noxapater, Miss., Mar. 28, 1909; s. Samuel Jehu and Vera (Carter) H.; B.A., U. Miss., 1929, M.A., U. Ky., 1938, Ph.D. in History, Duke U., 1949; m. Bernice Rita Hoey, June 12, 1941; children—Vera Kathleen Hopkins

Cudlin, James Hoey. Tchr., Vardaman (Miss.) High Sch., 1929-32; with Louisville (Miss.) Motor Co., 1932-36; agt. Miss. Dept. Public Welfare, 1936-37; instr. to prof. dept. history U. Ky., Lexington, 1940-74, dept. chmn., 1971-73, ret., 1974; editor The Papers of Henry Clay, 1951-74, cons., 1974-79. Served with AUS, 1942-45. Mem. Am. Hist. Assn., So. Hist. Assn., Orgn. Am. Historians, Am. Studies Assn., Agrl. History Soc., Assn. Documentary Editing, Soc. Historians of Early Am. Republic, Ky. Hist. Soc. Democrat. Author: A History of the Hemp Industry in Kentucky, 1951; The University of Kentucky: Origins and Early Years, 1951; editor: The Papers of Henry Clay, 5 vols., 1959-73. Home: 570 Bob-O-Link Dr Lexington KY 40503

HOPKINS, JOSEPH LEE, educator; b. St. Matthews, S.C., Sept. 3, 1933; s. Grover Lee and Hattie (Williams) H.; B.S., Allen U., 1959; M.Ed., S.C. State Coll., 1969; Ed.D., Rutgers U., 1975; m. Alice Hettis Greene, June 5, 1960; children—Tonia Yvette, Beryl Alice, Reginald Gerard, Angela Denise. Math. tchr. St. Matthews (S.C.) Public Schs., 1959-67, Orangeburg (S.C.) City Schs., 1967-68; staff mem. Tchr. Corps, S.C. State Coll., Orangeburg, summer 1968, 69; cons. Region V Ednl. Service Center, Lancaster, S.C., summer 1971; administrv. asst. EPDA Leadership Devel., Rutgers U., New Brunswick, N.J., 1972-74; asst. prof. indsl. edn. S.C. State Coll., Orangeburg, 1974—; vis. asst. prof. indsl. edn. Clemson (S.C.) U., 1975; Mem. HEW Rev. Panel; mem. State Adv. Council Vocat.-Tech. Served with U.S. Army, 1952-55. Recipient EPDA Leadership Devel. award, 1973; Dr. Martin Luther King Jr. fellow, 1971-74; State of N.J. research grantee, 1974. Mem. Am. Vocat. Assn., S.C. Vocat. Assn., Am. Vocat. Ednl. Research Assn., Am. Tech. Edn. Assn., Am. Council Indsl. Arts Tchr. Edn., Nat. Assn. Indsl. and Tech. Tchr. Educators, Phi Delta Kappa, Alpha Phi Alpha. Research on vocat. tchrs. Home: 1911 Atlantic Ave SE Orangeburg SC 29115 Office: PO Box 2015 Orangeburg SC 29117

HOPKINS, LARRY DAVID, state ofcl.; b. Odessa, Tex., July 2, 1949; s. Jack and Dorothy Ella (Butler) H.; student Odessa Jr. Coll., 1967-69; B.A., Howard Payne U., Brownwood, Tex., 1971; m. Vickey Lynn Golden, June 18, 1971; 1 son, David Lynn. Caseworker fin. services div. Tex. Dept. Human Resources, San Angelo, 1971-72, tng. specialist, ednl. dir., 1972-74, unit supr. fin. services programs, 1974—. Mem. Tex. Public Employees Assn. (past pres. local chpt.), Am. Public Welfare Assn., Employees Polit. Action Council Tex. Conservative Democrat. Baptist. Office: PO Box 951 San Angelo TX 76902

HOPKINS, LARRY J., congressman; b. Ky., Oct. 25, 1933; student Murray (Ky.) State U., So. Methodist U., Purdue U.; LL.D. (hon.), Morehead (Ky.) State U., 1975; m. Carolyn Pennebaker, 1956; children—Shae, Tara, Joshua. Mem. brokerage firm J.J.B. Hilliard and W.L. Lyons, Inc., Lexington, Ky., 1978; clk. Fayette County, 1969; mem. Ky. Ho. of Reps., 1972-77, Ky. Senate, 1978; mem. 96th Congress from 6th Ky. Dist. Chmn., Spl. Olympics, Lexington, 1973; mem. Fayette County Crime Council; bd. dirs. Bluegrass Assn. Mental Retardation, Lexington chpt. ARC; adv. council Programs for Exceptional Children. Served with USMCR, 1954-56. Mem. Fellowship Christian Athletes. Republican. Methodist. Clubs: Kiwanis, Shriners, Wildcat, Pyramid. Address: 514 Cannon House Office Bldg Washington DC 20515

HOPKINS, MARJORIE JOHNSON, assn. exec.; b. Potter, Nebr., Oct. 8, 1926; d. Clarence W. and Edith C. (Challburg) Johnson; B.A., Nebr. Wesleyan U., 1949; postgrad. U. Va., 1967-68; m. Don L. Hopkins, Apr. 11, 1953; children—Paula Lynn Hopkins Belt, Lisa Anne, Mark Johnson. Adminstrv. sec. to Ambassador Joseph C. Grew, Washington, 1950-54; supr. performing arts and community services Arlington County (Va.) Dept. Recreation and Parks, 1955-62; dir., co-owner Summer Camp at Mayfield, Herndon, Va., 1962-69; mgr. services Air-Conditioning and Refrigeration Inst., Arlington, 1970—; columnist No. Va. Sun, 1957-60; condr. weekly radio program WEAM, 1956-58; resident dir. Children's Theatre of Arlington, 1967-70. 1st v.p. Va. Recreation Soc., 1961-62; v.p. Arlington Inter-Service Club Council, 1961; mem. steering com. Arlington Jamestown Celebration, 1957. Nominee for Arlington Profl. Woman of 1958. Mem. Washington Soc. Assn. Execs., Nat. Press Club, Asso. Info. Mgrs., Pi Gamma Mu, Psi Chi, Theta Alpha Phi. Republican. Presbyterian. Clubs: Pinehurst (N.C.) Country, Zonta of Arlington (pres. 1960), Jobs Daus. Am. (guardian council 1970-75). Home: 3618 N Potomac St Arlington VA 22213 Office: 1815 N Fort Myer Dr Arlington VA 22209

HOPKINS, ROBERT HOWELL, JR., mortgage banker; b. Dallas, June 29, 1931; s. Robert H. and Pauline (Richardson) H.; B.B.A., Tex. Christian U., 1952; postgrad. Harvard Grad. Sch. Bus., 1952-53; m. Joanne Schneider, Aug. 16, 1952; children—Robert Howell III, Matthew William, Paula. Pres. Nat. Mortgage Corp. Am., Dallas, 1967—; chmn. bd., chief exec. officer Commodore Ins. Co., Dallas. Past pres. Christian Chs. N.Mex.; past chmn. Roswell March of Dimes. Mem. Mortgage Bankers Assn. Am. (nat. com.), Dallas Mortgage Bankers Assn. (pres.), Manufactured Housing Fin. Assn. (past pres.), Tex. Christian U. Letterman's Assn. Mason. Home: 6310 Joyce Way Dallas TX 75225 Office: Box 8046 Dallas TX 75205

HOPKINS, ROY VANVERT, bus. services co. exec.; b. Sneedville, Tenn., July 11, 1928; s. James and Cora H.; grad. in acctg. Morristown (Tenn.) Sch. Bus., 1960; m., Sept. 6, 1952; children—Wanda, Yvonne, Angela. Part-owner, operator Little Dutch Restaurant, Jefferson City, Tenn., 1949-50; meat cutter A & P Co., Morristown, 1954-59; owner, operator Hopkins Meat Market, Morristown, 1961-76; pres. Hopkins Diversified Bus. Services, Morristown, 1976—, Hopkins Ins. and Fin. Services, Inc., 1980—; cons. in field; pres. Add-O-Cycle Corp., Morristown, 1977—. Mem. exec. com. Democratic party Hamblen County (Tenn.), 1975-80. Served with USAF, 1950-54. Mem. Nat. Assn. Life Underwriters, Nat. Fedn. Ind. Bus., Gideons Internat. Baptist. Club: Sertoma (pres. 1967-68). Inventor in field. Home: 404 Spruce St Morristown TN 37814 Office: Hopkins Diversified Bus Services 121 Brown Ave Morristown TN 37814

HOPKINS, SAMUEL FREDERICK, mfg. co. ofcl.; b. Phila., Aug. 1, 1934; s. Francis Courts and Ruth Estelle (Riddell) H.; A.A.S. in Broadcast Engring., Port Arthur Coll., 1956; m. Elaine Eggert Freeman, Apr. 24, 1971; children—David, Clifford, Frances, Kenneth. Tchr. vocat. electronics public schs., Williamsport, Pa., 1960-64; mgr. test equipment dept., Keltec Industries, Springfield, Va., 1964-69; sr. field technician Honeywell, Inc., Springfield, 1969-72, br. service supr., 1972-74, br. service mgr., Orlando, Fla., 1974—, mem. community action com., 1975-79. Mem. adv. com. Brevard County Community Coll.; bd. dirs. Orange County Sheriff's Task Force, 1979. Served with USNR, 1952-54. Mem. Instrument Soc. Am., Assn. for Advancement Med. Instrumentation, Soc. Bio-Med. Equipment Technicians. Home: 500 E Concord St Orlando FL 32803 Office: 1000 Woodcock Rd Orlando FL 32803

HOPPE, LINDA LOUISE, ednl. center adminstr.; b. Corpus Christi, Tex., Nov. 7, 1941; d. Ernest Leonard and Nettie Voncille (Turner) Hudson; B.A., Baylor U., 1962; M.Ed., Tex. A&M U., 1966, supr. cert., adminstr. cert., 1972; m. Charles Allen Hoppe, June 2, 1962. Tchr., Bryan (Tex.) Ind. Sch. Dist., 1962-71; supr. Hearne (Tex.) Ind. Sch. Dist., 1971-73, adminstr., 1973-78; owner, adminstrv. dir. Wonder World Child Care and Ednl. Center, Hewitt, Tex., 1978—; cons. in field. Leader, 4-H Horse Club, Hearne, 1977-78. ESEA Title I grantee, 1973-78; ESAA grantee, 1973-77; Public Law 874 grantee, 1974-78. Mem. Brazos County (Tex.) Tchrs. Assn. (pres. 1967-68), Tex. State Tchrs. Assn. (life), Delta Kappa Gamma. Methodist. Home: Route 3 Box 177 Caldwell TX 77836 Office: 105 Tampico Hewitt TX 76643

HOPPE, SUSAN ANDREA, psychologist; b. Racine, Wis., Sept. 16, 1948; d. Clarence Elmer and Beverly Joyce (Anderson) H.; student Wartburg Coll., 1966-69; B.A., Carthage Coll., 1970; M.S., Purdue U., 1974, Ph.D., 1975. Asst. prof. psychology U. S. Ala., Mobile, 1975—. Womens gymnastics judge U.S. Gymnastics Fedn., 1978—. Mem. Am. Psychol. Assn., Southeastern Psychol. Assn., Ala. Psychol. Assn., Soc. Neuroscience, Sigma Xi, Alpha Chi. Lutheran. Office: Dept Psychology U S Ala Mobile AL 36688

HOPPER, FRANK JAY, painter, illustrator; b. Evansville, Ind., Oct. 15, 1924; s. George and Elizabeth Anne (Pyle) H.; B.F.A., Ind. U., 1942; student Art Inst. Chgo., 1945, Am. Acad. Art, Chgo., 1947; m. Marjorie H. Exhibited group shows Fine Arts Mus. of South, Mobile; Famous Am. Portrait Series Hist. Mus. Washington, 1965; commd. Portrait of Pres. Nixon, 1972; executed murals, Chateau Pyrenees, Denver, 1974, St. Mary Star of Sea, Longboat Key, Fla., 1978; UNICEF commn. Internat. Year of Child; represented in permanent collections, Historic Mus., Washington, Archdiocese of Chgo.; publ., illustrator, co-author, editor, contbr. various publs., including Chicago Tribune, Art Inst. Chgo., Chgo. area Sch. TV. Served with USNR, 1941-45. Mem. Artist's Guild Chgo. Presbyn. Mason (Shriner). Home and Studio: 1050 Ranchero Dr Sarasota FL 33583

HOPPER, HORACE RUSSELL, architect; b. Toccoa, Ga., Jan. 3, 1945; s. James Etsel and Frankie Morene (Holland) H.; B.Arch., Clemson U., 1968, M.Arch., 1975. Architect, Laughlin AFB, Tex., 1975-78, Civil Engring. Directorate of Air Tng. Command, Randolph AFB, Tex., 1978—. Served to capt., pilot, USAF, 1968-74. Decorated D.F.C., Air medal; registered architect, Tex. Mem. AIA, Tex. Soc. Architects. Office: ATC/DEEEA Randolph AFB TX 78148

HOPPER, WILLIAM WALTER, advt. exec., comml. artist; b. Cin., Aug. 29, 1939; s. William Calvin and Lena Irene (McDaniel) H.; B.S., Miami U., 1964; M.S., Xavier U., 1972; m. Shirley Fugate, Nov. 19, 1971; children—Noel R., Erin B., Megan I.; children by previous marriage—William D., Daniel. Artist, Palm Bros Decalomania, 1960; with Kroger Co., 1961-65, advt. mgr., 1965-73; advt. dir. Eastern div. Nat. Bldg. Centers, Miami, Fla., 1973—; owner, pres. Advt. Diversified Services, Ft. Lauderdale, Fla., 1976—. Mem. Advt. Fedn. Ft. Lauderdale, Fine Arts Soc., Soc. Am. Magicians, Internat. Brotherhood Magicians. Democrat. Mormon. Home: 6131 NW 12th St Sunrise FL 33313 Office: 6635 W Commercial Blvd Fort Lauderdale FL 33319

HOPSON, JOANNE WITTE, mktg. rep.; b. Brenham, Tex., Oct. 5, 1950; d. Melvin William and Pearlie Emma (Kramer) Witte; B.A. magna cum laude, U. South Fla., 1973. Adminstrv. asst. Symons Corp., Houston, 1974-77; systems rep. Am. Med. Internat., Houston, 1977-79; systems rep., mktg. rep. Honeywell Info. Systems, Houston, 1979—. Mem. Assn. Systems Mgrs., Nat. Assn. Female Execs., Profl. Women's Exec. Assn. Club: Toastmistress. Home: 5005 Georgi Ln Houston TX 77092 Office: 1535 W Loop S Houston TX 77027

HOPSON, WILLIAM BRIGGS, JR., surgeon; b. Delhi, La., Sept. 20, 1937; s. William Briggs and Mary Jane (Anding) H.; B.S., U. Miss., 1959; M.D., U. Tenn., 1961; m. Patricia Anne Spearman, June 15, 1958; children—Karen Renee, Mary Kathryn, William Briggs III, James Walter. Intern, City of Memphis Hosp., 1961-62; resident in surgery U. Tenn., Memphis, 1962-67; practice medicine specializing in surgery, 1967—; instr. surgery U. Tenn., Memphis, 1966-67; surg. staff St. Clinic, Vicksburg, 1967—, Mercy Regional Med. Center, Vicksburg, 1967—, Vicksburg Hosp., 1975—; med. control dir. Emergency Med. Services, State of Miss., 1975—. Pres., Cath. Home Sch. Assn., 1974-75; trustee Miss Miss. Pageant, 1976—; bd. dirs. Ole Miss. Alumni Assn., 1977—; deans adv. com. U. Miss. Sch. Medicine, 1977—. Diplomate Am. Bd. Surgery. Mem. AMA, A.C.S., Am. Trauma Soc. (chpt. pres. 1973—), W. Miss., Miss. (pres. surg. sect. 1967—), med. assns., Southeastern Surg. Congress. Republican. Methodist. Clubs: Vicksburg Country, Rivertown. Contbr. articles to med. jours. Home: 3320 Indiana Ave Vicksburg MS 39180 Office: Street Clinic 100 McAuley Dr Vicksburg MS 39180

HOPWOOD, STEPHEN ANDREW, export co. exec.; b. Kingston, Jamaica, Oct. 16, 1942; came to U.S., 1974; s. Herbert Donovan and Beryl Grace (Escoffery) H.; student U. Pa., 1960-61; m. Freda Elizabeth Stevens, Jan. 10, 1970; children—Deborah Christine, Stephen Edward, Elizabeth Rebecca Jane. Sales mgr. H.D. Hopwood & Co., Ltd., Jamaica, 1962-74, now dir.; v.p. Hopwood, Inc., Clearwater, Fla., 1974—; dir. Windsor Labs. Ltd. Episcopalian. Club: Countryside Country. Office: 2189 Cleveland St Clearwater FL 33515

HORAN, JOYCE FOSTER, assn. exec.; b. Louisville, Jan. 7, 1928; d. John Phillip and Teresa (Gesenhaus) Foster; ed. high sch.; m. William C. Horan, Jr., Sept. 2, 1950; children—Kathleen, William C., Sharon. Dir. vol. services and community relations Central State Hosp., Louisville, 1968-75; exec. dir. Ky. chpt. Leukemia Soc. Am. Inc., Louisville, 1975—. Pres., Bridgehaven Assos., 1962-64; mem. profl. cert. bd. Ky. Council Adminstrs. Vol. Services; bd. dirs. Bridgehaven Inc. Mem. Ky. Council Dirs. Vol. Services (pres. 1971-75), Assn. Adminstrs. Vol. Services (cert.), Am. Hosp. Assn., Ky. Assn. Mental Health. Democrat. Roman Catholic. Home: 3305 Grandview Ave Louisville KY 40207 Office: Leukemia Soc Am 200 W Broadway Suite 802 Louisville KY 40202

HORCHOW, S(AMUEL) ROGER, mail order exec.; b. Cin., July 3, 1928; s. Reuben and Beatrice (Schwartz) H.; B.A., Yale U., 1950; m. Carolyn Pfeifer, Dec. 29, 1960; children—Regen, Elizabeth, Sally. Buyer, Foley's, Houston, 1953-60; v.p. Neiman-Marcus, Dallas, 1960-68, 69-71; pres. Design Research, Cambridge, Mass., 1968-69, Kenton Collection, Dallas, 1971-73; chmn. Georg Jensen, Inc., N.Y.C., 1971-73; pres. Horchow Collection, Dallas, 1973—. Bd. dirs. Dallas Mus. Fine Arts, Am. Heart Assn., Am. Inst. Public Service, Hockaday Sch.; bd. dirs. Nat. Trust Hist. Preservation. Served to 1st lt., security U.S. Army, 1950-53. Mem. Direct Mail Mktg. Assn., World Wildlife Fund. Clubs: Yale of N.Y.C., Nantucket Yacht. Home: 5722 Chatham Rd Dallas TX 75225 Office: 4435 Simonton Rd Dallas TX 75240

HORGER, EDGAR OLIN, III, physician, educator; b. Eutawville, S.C., May 30, 1937; s. Edgar Olin Jr. and Frances Durant (Jordan) H.; B.S., Furman U., 1959; M.D., Med. Coll. S.C., 1962; m. Polly Jo Collins, May 29, 1960; children—Edgar Olin IV, David Collins, Patricia Bowen. Intern, Med. U. Hosp., Charleston, 1962-63, resident in obstetrics and gynecology, 1963-67; NIH fellow U. Pitts., 1967-68, asst. prof. obstetrics and gynecology, 1968-69; asst. prof. obstetrics and gynecology Med. U. S.C., Charleston, 1969-71, asso. prof., 1971-76, prof., 1976—, prof. radiology, 1978—. Served to capt. AUS, 1963-66. Mem. Am., S.C. med. assns., Am. Coll. Obstetricians and Gynecologists, South Central Obstetrical and Gynecol. Soc., South Atlantic Assn. Obstetricians and Gynecologists, So. Perinatal Assn. (dir. Mid-Atlantic region 1974-76), Soc. Perinatal Obstetricians (dir. 1977-78), Alpha Omega Alpha. Club: Charleston Tennis. Contbr. articles to profl. jours. Home: 712 Angus Ct Mt Pleasant SC 29464 Office: Medical University Hospital Charleston SC 29401

HORN, CARL, JR., utility exec.; b. Rutherfordton, N.C., Oct. 21, 1921; s. Carl and Freda Wagner (Warden) H.; A.B., Duke U., 1942, LL.B., 1947; m. Frances Alice Emmet, Feb. 7, 1948 (dec. 1966); children—Carl III, Claire, Katherine, Thomas E.; m. 2d, Virginia Grey Johnston, Oct. 27, 1967. Admitted to N.C. bar, 1947, practiced in Charlotte until 1953; asst. gen. counsel Duke Power Co., Charlotte, 1954-59, gen. counsel, 1959-63, v.p., gen. counsel, 1963-66, v.p. fin., gen. counsel, 1966-69, exec. v.p., gen. counsel, 1970-71, pres., 1971-75, chmn. bd., chief exec. officer, 1976—; dir. Integon Corp., J.B. Ivey & Co. Bd. dirs. Charlotte Meml. Hosp.; trustee N.C. Found. Ch. Related Colls., S.C. Found. Ind. Colls. Served to capt. AUS, 1942-46; PTO; mem. N.C. N.G., 1953-54. Mem. Am., N.C. bar assns., Edison Electric Inst. (chmn. legal com. 1967—), Duke Univ. Law Alumni Assn. (pres. 1961), Newcomen Soc. N. Am., Order of Coif. Presbyn. (elder). Home: 2111 Wendover Rd Charlotte NC 28211 Office: 422 S Church St Charlotte NC 28202

HORN, JOHN, natural gas co. exec.; b. Mildrow, Okla., Sept. 19, 1918; s. Orien and Eda (Garner) M.; B.S. with honors, Ark. State U., Jonesboro, 1938; m. Lenore E. Schierding, Oct. 20, 1946; children—Chris A., Frances Payton, Scott A., Miriam A. Yeager. With Phillips Petroleum Co., Bartlesville, Okla., 1939—, asst. mgr. natural gas sales, 1957-64, mgr. natural gas and LNG sales, 1964-78, Worldwide mgr. natural gas and LNG sales, 1979—; v.p. Phillips Gas Supply Corp., Kenai LNG Corp.; dir. Arctic LNG Transp. Corp., Polar LNG Shipping; past chmn. gas supply task force, com. U.S. energy outlook Nat. Petroleum Council. Active local Boy Scouts Am. Served with F.A., AUS, 1941-45. Decorated Bronze Star. Mem. Am., So. gas assns., Gas Processors Assn., Ind. Petroleum Assn. Am., Ind. Natural Gas Assn. Am., Soc. Petroleum Engrs. Democrat. Lutheran. Club: Hillcrest Country (Bartlesville). Contbr. papers in field. Home: 3512 Woodland Rd Bartlesville OK 74003 Office: Phillips Petroleum Co Bartlesville OK 74004

HORN, LAWRENCE CHARLES, educator; b. Abilene, Tex., July 7, 1938; s. Alonzo and Isabella (Wheeler) Rhodes; B.A. in Music Edn. (scholar), Langston U., 1961; M.Mus. Edn. (Lew Wentz scholar), U. Okla., 1967; m. Lee Ester Cross, Mar. 6, 1971; children—Kenya, La Dawn. Clarinetist, librarian 2d inf. div. Army Band Ft. Benning, Ga., 1962-64; tchr. math. Abilene (Tex.) Pub. Schs., 1964-65; asst. prof. music Miss. Valley State U., Itta Bena, 1965—, also adv. music chair. Mem. Pan Hellenic Council. Served with U.S. Army, 1962-64. Asst. dir. hon. Braniff Internat. Airline Battle of Bands, 1972. Mem. Music Educators Nat. Conf. (chmn. Lyceum com. 1971-75), Miss. Music Educators Assn. (sec coll. div.), Phi Delta Kappa (sec., reporter), Alpha Kappa Mu, Kappa Kappa Psi, Omega Psi Phi. Mem. Ch. of Christ. Home: PO Box 23 MVSU Itta Bena MS 38941 Office: Dept Music Miss Valley State U Itta Bena MS 38941

HORNBECK, CAROLYN VOSS, hosp. adminstr.; b. Omaha; d. George Otto and Helen (Shuck) Voss; B.S. in Edn., U. Cin., 1943; m. Kenneth Lee Hornbeck, Oct. 19, 1946. Chief ticket agt. Delta Airlines, 1943-46; public relations rep. New Neighbors League, Cin., 1947-63; dir. vol. services S.A. Wm. Booth Meml. Hosp., Florence, Ky., 1963—. Mem. Republican Women's Club, Women of Trinity Ch., Altar Guild. Hon. Ky. col. Mem. Am. Soc. Dirs. Vol. Services, Aux. Wm. Booth Hosp. (life), No. Ky. Heritage League, Chi Omega. Episcopalian. Clubs: Shrine (sec.); Fort Mitchell (Ky.) Country. Home: 1157 Morgan Ct Park Hills KY 41011 Office: 7380 Turfway Rd Florence KY 41042

HORNE, ANNIE PEARL COOKE, mfg. co. exec., civic worker; b. Wayne County, N.C., Nov. 22, 1918; d. Erastus and Pearl (Coley) Cooke; grad. Wilson Tech. Inst., 1971; student Wilson County Tech. Inst., 1972; m. Elmer Lee Horne, 1938; children—Patricia Horne Smith, Elmer Lee, Doris Horne Pruitt, Hadie Cooke. Saleslady, J.C. Penny Co., Inc., Wilson, N.C., 1939-41; sec. Horne Scale & Equipment Co., Wilson, 1942-77, v.p., 1942—. Vol. Wilson County Rescue Squade Aux. 1968-75; vol. Wilson Crisis Center, 1968-75; vol. worker Wilson Meml. Hosp., 1965—; counselor Jr. Garden Club, Wilson, 1966-72; dist. chmn. Jr. Garden Clubs N.C., 1970-75; organized Jr. Garden Club for Eastern N.C. Sch. for Deaf, 1971; mem. Louis Rain Water Extension Homemaker Club, Wilson County, 1968—, pres., 1969-73; vol. Cherry Hosp., Goldsboro, N.C., 1968-70; sec., treas. Democratic precinct Wilson, 1970-75; deaconess First Christian Ch., Wilson, 1965-69, officer Friendship Sunday sch. class, 1938-75; cub scout den mother, Wilson, 1952-77. Recipient Service to Mankind award Sertoma Club, 1973, Green Band award Wilson Dist. Scouting Com., 1968, Silver Tray award Wilson Woman's Club, 1972. Clubs: Altrusa (Merit award 1971), Wilson Woman's (hostess com. 1972-74), Bus. and Profl. Woman's (Merit award 1971). Address: 1107 Anderson St Wilson NC 27893

HORNER, MARKUS LEE, master wood craftsman; b. Dallas, July 27, 1949; s. Parvin Markus and Frances Marjorie (Earles) H.; student U. Tex., 1971-73; m. Judy Kay Clark, Mar. 3, 1973. Quality control insp. Dahlgren Mfg. and Otis Engring., 1971-73; salesman, 1973-76; owner Horner's Custom Furniture, Houston, 1976—, Cambium Creations, 1978—; wood shop cons. Sam Houston High Sch., 1978—. Pres., Corp. for Better Animal Control, 1979—; polit. cons. N. Harris County Homeowners Assn.; asso. mem. Houston Clean City Com.; mem. fund raising and activities com. Leukemia Soc. Houston; organizer rabies vaccination dr.; vol., guest speaker Nursing Clinicians of Houston, 1977—. Served with USN, 1968-71. Named hon. Houston firefighter, 1979. Mem. Houston Jr. C. of C., Woodcarvers Assn. Houston. Episcopalian. Address: 9704 Bauman Rd Houston TX 77076

HORNSBY, WALTER SPURGEON, III, ins. co. exec.; b. Augusta, Ga., Sept. 6, 1941; s. Walter S. and Pauline (Dixon) H.; A.B. in Math., Morehouse Coll., 1961; m. Clara Johnson, Nov. 24, 1964; children—Walter S., Wendel Steven. Statistician, Pilgrim Health & Life Ins. Co., Augusta, 1962-65, asst. actuary, 1965-66, v.p., actuary, 1968-73, sr. v.p., actuary, 1973-75, exec. v.p., actuary, 1975—. Mem. Augusta Port Authority, 1975—; 2d v.p. United Way, 1974, 75, mem. exec. com., 1974—, 1st v.p., 1978, pres., 1979—. Served with AUS, 1966-68. Mem. Augusta C. of C., Southeastern Actuaries Club, Nat. Ins. Assn. (dir. 1971-74, 1976—, actuary 1971-73), Ins. Acctg. and Statis. Assn., Augusta Radio Relay League, Nat. Campers and Hikers Assn., Omega Psi Phi. Baptist. Club: Sportsman's Boat, Shriner, Mason. Home: 1522 Twiggs St Augusta GA 30901 Office: 1143 Laney-Walker Blvd Augusta GA 30901

HORNSTEIN, ROBERT CHARLES, graphic designer; b. Elmhurst, Ill., June 23, 1950; s. Robert Harry and Ruth Catherine H.; B.S. in Advt., So. Ill. U., 1975. Owner, The Gold Mine Restaurant, Carbondale, Ill., 1975-77, cons., 1977—; exec. v.p. Donald M. Medley Inc., Carbondale, 1977-78, cons., 1978-80; design dir. Unigraph Design Inc., Carbondale, 1979-80; graphic designer Handi-Products Corp., Dallas, 1980—. Served with USAR, 1971-73; Vietnam. Decorated Meritorious Service medal. Mem. Pi Sigma Epsilon.

Congregationalist. Home: 8200 Southwestern #1903 Dallas TX 75206 Office: 5800 LBJ Freeway Dallas TX 75240

HOROWITZ, HARRY I., podiatrist; b. Belleair, Fla., Nov. 8, 1915; s. Jacob and Fannie (Singer) H.; student CCNY, 1932-34; Pod.G, First Inst. Podiatry, N.Y.C., 1937; D.Podiatry, L.I. U., 1946; D.P.M., N.Y. Coll. Podiatric Medicine, 1967; m. Sylvia Glaser, Feb. 11, 1940; children—Marc, Susan. Pvt. practice podiatry, Astoria, N.Y., 1937, 76, Belleair, Fla., 1976—; mem. podiatry practice com. Workmen's Compensation Bd. N.Y. State, 1953-66, chmn. com., 1966-76; chief podiatry dept. Queens Hosp. Center-L.I. Jewish Hosp., Jamaica, L.I., 1958-76; dir. Foot Clinics of N.Y., 1970-71; chmn. bd. Suncoast Orthotic Labs., Clearwater, Fla., 1978—; podiatry panel Dept. Welfare N.Y.C. Mem. citizens com. Union Free Sch. Dist. 29, Merrick, N.Y., 1957; mem. library com. dist. 29, 1964; founder Fund for Advancement Podiatry Edn., 1958; hon. pres. Fund for Podiatry Edn. and Research, 1963—, sec., 1963-66; chmn. Task Force on Podiatry, Health and Hosp. Corp., N.Y.C., 1976—; trustee N.Y. Coll. Podiatric Medicine, 1973-74. Recipient award Jour. Podiatry, 1948; Podiatrist of Year Queens County Podiatry Soc., 1956, 71, Podiatry Soc. State N.Y., 1957, 61, testimonial N.Y. Coll. Podiatric Medicine, 1971. Mem. Am. Podiatry Assn. (exec. council, trustee 1955-62, award 1963), Am. Assn. Hosp. Podiatrists, Am. Public Health Assn., N.Y. Public Health Assn., Acad. Podiatry. Clubs: Masons, K.P. Home: 100 Oakmont Ln Belleair FL 33516

HOROWITZ, ROSLYN HAMMER, psychologist; b. N.Y.C., June 1, 1926; d. Benjamin and Minnie (Halpern) Hammer; B.S., City U. N.Y., 1947; M.Ed., U. Miami (Fla.), 1967, Ph.D., 1973; m. Murray Horowitz, Jan. 31, 1948; children—Judith Ellen, Seth Charles. Free lance writer radio, TV commls., 1947-49; editor-in-chief Treasure Island News, North Bay Village, Fla., 1952-57; instr. U. Miami, Coral Gables, 1970-71; pvt. practice psychology, Hollywood, Fla., 1973—; mem. faculty Miami-Dade Community Coll., Broward Community Coll.; cons. Dade County (Fla.), Broward County (Fla.) mental health assns. Mem. Am., Dade County psychol. assns. Home: 7540 Cutlass Ave Treasure Island Miami Beach FL 33141 Office: 2450 Hollywood Blvd Suite 405 Hollywood FL 33020

HORRELL, BILLY BURRES, educator; b. Clarkson, Ky., Apr. 8, 1928; s. C.B. and Lorena (Burres) H.; B.S., Western Ky. U., 1952; M.S., U. Ky., 1958; Ed.S., U. Louisville, 1963; Ed.D., Ind. U., 1969; m. Edna Richardson, June 11, 1949; 1 dau., Pamela Joy. Classroom tchr. Bullitt County (Ky.) Schs., 1953-59, sch. prin., 1959-66, asst. supt., 1966-69; faculty Ky. Wesleyan Coll., Owensboro, 1969—, chmn. dept. edn., 1977—, prof. edn., 1977—. Vice-pres. 2d Dist. Ky. PTA, 1976—, also bd. dirs.; sec. Cliff Hagan Boys Club Bd., 1973-79, v.p., 1977-78, pres., 1978—; moderator Presbytery Western Ky. Union of Presbyn. Ch., 1979—. Mem. NEA (life), Assn. Tchr. Educators, AAUP (v.p. chpt. 1979), Phi Delta Kappa. Democrat. Clubs: Lions (pres. 1961-62), Masons. Home: 1901 Frederica St Owensboro KY 42301

HORSEMAN, MALVIN MILLER, JR., petro-chem. co. exec.; b. Kansas City, Mo., May 31, 1932; s. Malvin Miller and Stella Bertha H.; student La. State U., 1950-52; B.B.A., St. Mary's Coll., 1958; m. Margaret Ann Smith, May 21, 1960; children—Laurie Ann, Lynda Lea, Bonnie Sue, Kevin Andrew, Katrina Lynn. Phys. well logging engr. So. Tech. Service, Baton Rouge, 1954-56; buyer, adminstrv. mgr. State of La., Baton Rouge, 1958-63; materials and contracts mgr. Foster Wheeler Corp., Livingston, N.J., 1964-70, area supt., 1970-74; materials mgr., contracts mgr. Daniel Internat., Greenville, S.C., 1974-75; purchasing and materials control mgr. Champlin Petroleum Co., Corpus Christi, Tex., 1975—; instr. La. State U., Baton Rouge, 1959-60. Chmn., Republican Admendments Com., Country Club Estates, 1976. Served with USAF, 1953-55. Mem. Nat. Purchasing Mgmt. Assn., Am. Inst. Indsl. Engrs., Project Mgmt. Inst., Am. Production and Inventory Control Soc. Republican. Roman Catholic. Home: 4517 Weiskopf St Corpus Christi TX 78413 Office: PO Box 9176 Corpus Christi TX 78408

HORSMAN, DAVID A. ELLIOTT, author, educator; b. Calvert County, Md., June 28, 1932; s. Alvin W. and Bessie L. (Elliott) H.; student U. Chgo.; B.A., San Francisco State U., 1964; M.A., N.Y. U., 1967, Ph.D., 1970. Floor dir., stage mgr. WTOP-TV, Washington, 1959-61; TV writer/producer Insight, Nat. Council Chs., Washington, 1961-62; English master, dir. studies Searing Sch., N.Y.C., 1965-67; asst. prof. humanities Acad. Aeros., Flushing, N.Y., 1967-68; instr. humanities Rensselaer Poly. Inst., Troy, N.Y., 1969-70; asso. prof., founder and coordinator film sequence U. South Fla., Tampa, 1970—; adj. prof. Union Grad. Sch., Yellow Springs, Ohio, 1976—. Served with U.S. Army, 1957-59. Recipient Founders Day award N.Y. U., 1971. Fellow Intercontinental Biog. Assn. (Certificate of Merit 1974); mem. Modern Lang. Assn., Nat. Soc. Hist. Preservation, Univ. Film Assn., Am. Film Inst., Internat. Platform Assn., Soc. Edn. in Film and TV, AAUP, Am. Ch. Union. Episcopalian. Author: The Liturgy as Communication, 1970; (novel and screenplay) Pilgrims on Strange Strands, 1979; Introduction to Structural Description of Liturgical Dromena, 1979. Home: 530 Bosphorus Ave Tampa FL 33606 Office: U S Fla Tampa FL 33620

HORSMAN, THOMAS ALLEN, physician; b. Bim, W.Va., Oct. 26, 1948; s. Anthony and Winnie Loraine (Vance) H.; A.B., W.Va. U., 1970, M.D., 1974; m. JoAnn Vargo, Oct. 3, 1970; children—Thomas Anthony, Amy Lynette. Intern in surgery Charleston (W.Va.) Med. Center, 1974-75, resident in internal medicine, 1975-77, fellow in infectious diseases, 1977-79; practice medicine specializing in internal medicine and infectious disease, Charleston, 1979—; mem. staff Thomas Meml. Hosp., Logan Gen. Hosp.; clin. chief dept. infectious diseases Charleston Area Med. Center, 1980—; cons. Inst. Med. Research and Investigation; clin. asst. prof. medicine W.Va. U., Charleston, 1980—. Bd. dirs. Cross Lanes Ambulance Authority, W.Va. Emergency Med. Services. Diplomate Am. Bd. Internal Medicine. Mem. Am. Soc. Internal Medicine, A.C.P., Am. Coll. Emergency Physicians, Kanawha Med. Soc., Alpha Omega Alpha. Republican. Baptist. Home: 5316 Edgebrook Rd Charleston WV 25313 Office: 3100 MacCorkle Ave Charleston WV 25304

HORTON, ARTHUR MACNEILL, JR., neuropsychologist; b. Alexandria, Va., Jan. 21, 1947; s. Arthur MacNeill and Mary Alice (Carney) Horton; B.A., U. Va., 1969; M.Ed., 1971, Ed.D., 1976; m. Mary Philomena Whitesell, Jan. 31, 1976. Tchr., Albemarle County (Va.) pub. schs., 1969-71; counselor, child devel. cons. Arlington County (Va.) pub. schs., 1971-74; asst. prof. The Citadel, Charleston, S.C., 1976-77; staff neuropsychologist VA Center, Martinsburg, W.Va., 1977—. VA grantee, 1976. Mem. Am., S.C., Charles Area (treas. 1977) psychol. assns. Roman Catholic. Home: 209 W Boscawen St Winchester VA 22601 Office: Neuropsychology Lab VA Center Martinsburg WV 25401

HORTON, GRANVILLE EUGENE, physician, air force officer; b. Jean, Tex., July 2, 1927; s. James Granville and Etna (Boyle) H.; B.A., Tex. Technol. Coll., 1950; M.D., U. Tex., 1954; m. Mildred Helen Veale, June 13, 1953; children—Robert Herman Newlin, Linda Kay, Kevin Bruce, Carson Scott. Intern, Detroit Receiving Hosp., 1954-55; tng. in radioactive isotope techniques Oak Ridge Inst. Nuclear Studies, 1958; practice medicine, Weslaco, Tex., 1955-56; Outlar-Blair Clinic, Wharton, 1956-72; dir. dept. nuclear medicine Nightingale Hosp., El Campo, Tex., 1973-75; mem. staff Horton Med. Clinic, El Campo, 1972-75; part-time research asso. radioisotope dept. Meth. Hosp., Houston, 1961-66; mem. med. adv. com. and sec. med. staff Caney Valley Meml. Hosp., Wharton, 1956-72; clin. dir. Wharton County Tb Assn., 1957-67; commd. lt. col. U.S. Air Force, 1975; postgrad. U.S. Air Force Sch. Aerospace Medicine, 1975; chief aeromed. services Brooks AFB, Tex., 1976—. Bd. dirs. Wharton County div. Am. Cancer Soc., pres,, 1960-61; dist. dir. 8th dist. Tex., Citizens com. for Hoover Report, 1957-58. Served with USN, 1946-47. Diplomate Am. Bd. Nuclear Medicine. Fellow Am. Coll. Angiology (state gov. 1979), Am. Coll. Nuclear Medicine; mem. Am. Coll. Emergency Physicians, Wharton C. of C. (dir., v.p. 1960-61), Am., Tex. (ho. of dels. 1959-61) med. assns., Soc. Nuclear Medicine, Tex. Assn. Physicians Nuclear Medicine, AAAS, Law Enforcement Officers Tex. (asso.), Am. Nuclear Soc., Tex. Med. Found., El Campo C. of C., Phi Chi. Republican. Episcopalian. Club: Elks. Contbr. articles to med. publs. Home: 101 Vinsant Circle San Antonio TX 78235 Office: Chief Aeromedical Services Brooks AFB TX 78235

HORTON, J(OSEPH) REX, cons. acoustical engr.; b. Greeneville, Tenn., Dec. 20, 1908; s. Adolphus Bryan and Rebecca (Marshall) H.; grad. Am. Sch., 1936, Nat. Radio Inst., 1940; m. Mary Charlotte Felix, July 28, 1933; children—Joseph Rex, Robert Earl, Charlotte Anne. With A. B. Horton, bldg. constrn., Knoxville, Tenn., 1928-32; retail service sta. mgr., 1933; retail salesman Pure Oil Co., 1934-35; sta. mgr. Retail Service Orgn., Phoenix, 1936-37; route salesman Radio Sales & Service, Knoxville, 1938-42; chief engr. WBIR-AM-FM-TV, Knoxville, 1943-74; cons. acoustical engr., Knoxville, 1974—. Home and Office: 1715 North Hills Blvd Knoxville TN 37917

HORTON, JANICE FAYE, state senator; b. Barnesville, Ga., Jan. 23, 1945; d. Grover George and Sara Alice (Zellner) Shiver; A.B., Tift Coll., Ga., 1967; postgrad. Woodrow Wilson Law Sch., Atlanta; m. Charles Douglas Horton, Aug. 26, 1967; children—Amy Elaine, Sara Leigh. Tchr. high sch. English, 1967-72; owner Horton Realty & Investment Co., McDonough, Ga., 1975—; mem. McDonough City Council, 1975-78, Henry County Bd. Commrs., 1976-78; mem. Ga. Senate, 1979—. Bd. dirs. local Am. Cancer Soc. Mem. Bus. and Profl. Women (chpt. v.p. 1975—). Democrat. Baptist. Home: 430 Burke Circle McDonough GA 30253 Office: Room 122G State Capitol Atlanta GA 30334

HORTON, KAREN HUTCHINS, counselor; b. Denver, Colo., Sept. 9, 1943; d. Kimball F. and Bonnie I. (Small) Hutchins; B.A., U. Denver, 1965; M.A., George Washington U., 1972; m. Brent Horton, May 29, 1976; 1 son by a previous marriage, Alec. Tchr. English, D.C. Pub. Schs., 1967-69; asst. housing adminstr. George Washington U., Washington, 1970-72; counselor, instr. N.Va. Community Coll., 1972-77; allied health counselor Austin (Tex.) Community Coll., 1977—; assertiveness tng. tchr. for govt. agys., Washington. Den mother Boy Scouts Am., 1975, chmn. troop 678, 1976-77. Mem. Am. Personnel and Guidance Assn., Asso. Specialists Group Work, Columbian Women, Toastmistress Internat., Pi Lambda Theta. Jewish. Editor: Orientation Textbook, 1974-77. Home: 9522 Quail Ct Austin TX 78758 Office: 707 E 14th St Austin TX 78701

HORTON, THOMAS EDWARD, JR., educator; b. Houston, Jan. 12, 1935; s. Thomas Edward and Minnie Tolula (Sloan) H.; B.S., U. Tex., 1957, Ph.D., 1964; M.S. (Caterpillar research fellow), Stanford, 1958; m. Bobbie Jean Newcomb, June 8, 1963; children—Holly Anne, Thomas Edward III. Jr. mech. engr. Shell Devel. Co., Houston, 1957-58; teaching asst., research asst., research scientist U. Tex., Austin, 1959-62; research engr. Jet Propulsion Lab. Calif. Inst. Tech., Pasadena, 1962, sr. research engr., 1963-66; asso. prof. mech. engring., research engr. U. Miss., 1966-71, prof., research engr., 1971—; dir. U.S. Army Laser Sci. Lab., Redstone Arsenal, Ala., 1975-76. Cons. Army Research Office, Durham, N.C., Jet Propulsion Lab., Marathon Oil Co. Asso. fellow Am. Inst. Aeros. and Astronautics (mem. tech. coms.); mem. Am. Soc. M.E. (mem. tech. coms.), Am. Phys. Soc., Am. Soc. for Engring. Edn. (Research award Southeastern sect. 1971), Sigma Xi (pres. local chpt.), Tau Beta Pi (student adviser), Pi Tau Sigma, Phi Eta Sigma. Republican. Methodist. Contbr. articles to profl. jours. Patentee in field. Home: 209 St Andrews Circle Oxford MS 38655 Office: U Miss University MS 38677

HORTON, WILLIAM LAMAR, educator; b. Rock Hill, S.C., Aug. 26, 1935; s. Luther Burns and Ruth (Stogner) H.; Mus.B., Furman U., 1956; M.Sacred Music, So. Bapt. Theol. Sem., 1958, D.Mus. Arts, 1970; postdoctoral study U. Mich., 1968, Paris Académie des Arts Musicaux, 1975; m. Peggy Ann Small, June 16, 1956; children—Richard Lamar, Ronald William, Randall Alan, Julie Anne. Minister music First Bapt. Ch., Taylors, S.C., 1954-56, Broadway Bapt. Ch., Louisville, 1956-58, First Bapt. Ch., Douglas, Ga., 1958-59; instr. music U. Ga., 1958-59, So. Bapt. Theol. Sem., Louisville, 1959-62; prof. music, chmn. dept. ch. music Ouachita Bapt. U., Arkadelphia, Ark., 1963-68; prof. music Okla. Bapt. U., Shawnee, 1968—, chmn. dept. ch. music, 1979—; minister music Univ. Bapt. Ch., Shawnee, 1968-74, 1st Christian Ch., Shawnee, 1977—. Clinician, adjudicator music festivals throughout South and S.W.; baritone soloist various musicals, oratorios, other prodns.; pres. Shawnee Band Parents Assn., 1975-76; mem. State Arts Council Okla., 1977—; pres. Shawnee Community Concerts Assn., 1977-79, Shawnee Arts Council, 1977-79. Trustee B.B. McKinney Music Research Found., 1972—. Named Okla. Musician of the Year, 1975. Mem. Music Tchrs. Nat. Assn., Nat. Assn. Tchrs. of Singing (pres. Okla. chpt. 1973-75), Okla. Music Tchrs. Assn. (3d v.p. 1970-74), A.S.C.A.P., Phi Mu Alpha Sinfonia (Okla. province gov. 1968-78). Mason. Author: Introduction to Singing, 1968; Score Reading, 3 vols., 1975. Contbr. critiques, revs. to profl. jours.; art, music and drama critic Shawnee News-Star. Composer: Song of the Lamb, 1958, Salvation to Our God, 1962, How Excellent is Thy Name, 1962, Praise Ye The Lord, 1963, Cindy, 1977. Home: 18 Mojave Dr Shawnee OK 74801

HORWITZ, STEPHEN THOMAS, gemologist, Orientalist; b. Indpls., Feb. 12, 1950; s. Thomas and Rose H.; A.B. cum laude, Bowdoin Coll., 1972; m. Penelope P. Pilotti, Nov. 13, 1978. Underwriter comml. prodn. Chubb and Sons Inc., Chgo., 1972-73, Atlanta, 1973-74; mktg. agt. ins. agys. based in Atlanta, 1974-75; pres. S.T. Horwitz and Assos. Inc., Atlanta, 1975—; cons. in field. Cert. diamond and colored stones Gemological Inst. Am. Mem. Gemological Assn. Gt. Britain, Atlanta Fed. Statesman's Club. Jewish. Office: S T Horwitz and Assos Inc 1690 N Druid Hills Rd NE Atlanta GA 30319

HOSEA, ADDISON, bishop; b. Pikeville, N.C., Sept. 11, 1914; s. Addison and Alma Eugenia (Bowden) H.; student U. N.C. at Chapel Hill, 1930-31; A.B., Atlantic Christian Coll., 1938; M.Div., U. of South, 1949, D.D., 1970; postgrad. Union Theol. Sem., 1948, Duke U., 1950-53; D.D., Episcopal Theol. Sem. Ky., 1968; m. Jane Eubank Marston, June 24, 1944; children—Nancy Jane, Addison III, Anne Cameron. Tchr. N.C. schs., 1932-34, 38-41; ordained deacon Episc. Ch., 1948, priest, 1949; priest-in-charge St. Gabriel's Ch., Faison, N.C., 1949-51; rector St. Paul's Ch., Clinton, N.C., 1949-54, St. John's Ch., Versailles, Ky., 1954-70; bishop-coadjutor Diocese of Lexington (Ky.), 1970, bishop, 1971—, exam. chaplain, 1964-70; mem. exec. council Diocese of East Carolina, 1951-54, Diocese of Lexington, 1954-70; prof. N.T. lang. and lit. Episc. Theol. Sem. Ky., 1954-59, 65-70; hon. canon Cathedral St. George the Martyr, 1964-70; mem. standing com. Diocese of Lexington, 1957-58, 60-64; dep. to Gen. Conv. Episc. Ch., 1955, 58, 64, 67, 69. Trustee U. of South, 1949-54, 70—. Served to capt. AUS, 1941-46. Mem. Soc. Bibl. Lit. Home: 536 Sayre Ave Lexington KY 40508 Office: 530 Sayre Ave Lexington KY 40508

HOSEMANN, MICHAEL JOSEPH, bank exec.; b. Vicksburg, Miss., May 27, 1940; s. Paul Clement and Rose Mary H.; B.S. in Math., Spring Hill Coll., 1964; M.A. in Math. Edn. (NSF fellow), Ohio State U., 1969; m. Marjorie O'Rourke, Aug. 24, 1968; children—Melissa, Michael. Tchr. math. and sci. St. Aloysius High Sch., New Orleans, 1962-67; systems analyst Fed. Res. Bank Atlanta, 1969-73; staff asst. to cashier La. Nat. Bank, Baton Rouge, 1973-75, v.p., mgr. dept. research and devel., 1975-80, center mgr. Bank Card Center, 1980—; speaker in field; Visa debit card adv.; tchr. in field; mem. exec. com. La.-Ala.-Miss. Automated Clearing House Assn. Chmn. sustaining membership enrollment Audubon council Girl Scouts U.S.A., 1979; chmn. bd. FISH, Inc., Baton Rouge, 1979. Mem. Bank Mktg. Assn. Club: Kiwanis (pres.-elect club 1979). Office: PO Box 3399 Baton Rouge LA 70821

HOSKINS, GODFREY CURTIS, pathologist; b. Reading, Pa., Feb. 8, 1930; s. Godfrey Walter George and Elizabeth Heloise (Curtis) H.; M.D., U. Tex., 1960; m. Betty L. Bruening, June 28, 1957 (div. 1969); children—Betty Kathryn, Kent Eric Courtland. Intern, Meth. Hosp., Houston, 1960-61; fellow Kings Coll., London, 1961-62, Karolinska Inst., Stockholm, 1962-64; practice medicine specializing in pathology, Dallas, 1971—; mem. staff East Dallas Hosp., Presbyn. Hosp., Dallas, Permian Gen. Hosp., Andrews, Tex.; dir. dept. pathology Drs. Hosp., Dallas; asst. prof. anatomy Southwestern Med. Sch., Dallas, 1964-69, clin. asst. prof. pathology, 1972—, clin. asso. prof. anatomy, 1969—; instr. pathology Baylor Dental Sch., Dallas, 1969-71; vis. asst. prof. biology So. Meth. U., Dallas, 1965-66. Served with AUS, 1953-55. Diplomate Am. Bd. Pathology. Fellow Am. Soc. Clin. Pathologists, Coll. Am. Pathologists; mem. Am., Tex. med. assns., AAAS, Am. Soc. Cell Biologists, N. Tex. Soc. Pathologists, Dallas Acad. Pathologists, Dallas So. Clin. Soc., Mensa, Sigma Xi. Formulated geometrically ordered model of ultra structural arrangements of chromosome fiber components and centromere and spindle structure and dynamics to provide geometrically orderly distbn. in mitosis and meiosis of human and animal cells. Home: 2531 Winsted Dallas TX 75214 Office: 10611 Garland Rd Dallas TX 75218

HOSKINS, ROBERT LEE, univ. adminstr.; b. Paragould, Ark., Sept. 24, 1941; s. Ralph Herald and Annamae (Sharp) H.; student Miss. State U., 1959-60; B.J., U. Mo., 1962, M.A., 1963; Ph.D., N. Tex. State U., 1972; m. Andrea Wallace, June 8, 1962; children—Leslie, Charlotte, Zachary. Reporter, editorial writer The Beaumont (Tex.) Enterprise, 1963-65; dir. public relations Alice Lloyd Coll., Pippa Passes, Ky., 1965-68; registrar, dir. admissions Tex. Southmost Coll., Brownsville, 1968-70; dir. community med. manpower project Ark. State U., 1972-73; dean Coll. Communications Ark. State U., 1973—. Mem. Assn. Edn. in Journalism, Soc. Journalism Sch. Adminstrs., Internat. Newspaper Advt. Execs., Ark. Deans Assn., Sigma Delta Chi, Phi Delta Kappa. Presbyterian. Office: Box 24 State University AR 72467

HOSKINS, ROBERT NATHAN, agribus. cons.; b. Keota, Iowa, Feb. 23, 1917; s. Frank A. and Ora E. (Wayman) H.; student U. Mo., 1934-37; B.S., Iowa State U., 1939; m. Julia L. Jones, July 19, 1946; children—Nancy Carol, Mary Susan, Julia Ann, Robert Nathan. Towerman, Sam A. Baker State Forest, Mo. Conservation Commn., 1939, sr. forester, 1940-41; extension forester Fla. Forest Service, 1941-45; indsl. forester Seaboard Air Line R.R. Co. (name changed to Seaboard Coast Line R.R. Co. 1967), Richmond, Va., 1945-46, gen. forestry agt., 1956-64, gen. indsl. and forestry agt., 1964-65, gen. mgr. indsl. devel., 1965-68, asst. v.p. containerization and spl. projects, 1968-69, asst. v.p. forestry and spl. projects, 1969-79; cons. agribus., 1979—. Mem. core com. Keep Fla. Green, 1946-50, Keep N.C. Green, 1947-49; mem. Gov.'s Adv. Com. on Forestry Va. Economy, 1950-53; mem. adv. com. on forestry program in agrl. edn. Va., N.C., S.C., Ga., Fla., Ala., 1950-65; mem. adv. com. vocational edn. Va. State Bd. Edn., 1950-60; mem. profl. adv. group indsl. devel. Commonwealth Va., 1967-68; mem. staff of resources Future, 1949-50; adviser on forestry edn. So. Regional Edn. Bd., 1957-58; southeastern regional chmn. sponsoring com. Nat. Future Farmers Am. Found., 1969-74, state chmn., Va., 1975-76; mem. nat. adv. com. to sec. agr. on state and pvt. forestry, 1970-73; mem. Va. Agri-Bus. Council; vice chmn. publicity centennial com. Va. Dept. Agr. and Commerce, 1977. Pres. Parents' Assn. U. Richmond, 1975-76. Named Norfolk's Outstanding Young Man, Norfolk Jr. C. of C., 1951, recipient certificate of merit, 1952; recipient Distinguished Service award S.C. Agrl. Tchrs., 1953, Alumni Merit award Chgo. Alumni Assn., Iowa State U., 1954, Key to City, Mayor of Cin., 1960, Mayor of Phila., 1961, Merit award Fla. Vocational Agrl. Assn., 1965, Appreciation award Va. Agrl. Tchrs. Assn., 1967, Distinguished Service award S.C. Future Farmers Am. Assn., 1968, Spl. award for distinguished service to sponsoring com. Nat. Future Farmers Am., 1971, Hon. State Farmer degree Tenn. Assn., 1977; Order Palmetto, 1973. Mem. Am. (Merit award 1954, awards chmn. 1949-54, Disting. Ser. award 1978), Ga. (liaison and coordinating com. 1955-56), N.C. (reforestation com. 1951-52), Ala., Fla. forestry assns., Va. Forests, Fla. Forest and Park Assn., Soc. Am. Foresters, Ry. Tie Assn. (chmn. conservation com. 1956-58, mem. pub. affairs com. 1977-78), Forest Farmers Assn. (ednl. com. 1957-58), Am. Vocational Assn. (award merit 1958), U.S. (mem. agribus. and rural affairs com. 1972-75), Fla. State (forestry com. 1952-53), Va. State (indsl. devel. com. 1965-68), Richmond chambers commerce. Methodist (finance com. 1962-63). Clubs: Va. Press (Richmond), Soc. of Va. (dir. 1973-75), Hermitage Country. Author: (with M.D. Mobley) Forestry in the South, 1956. Editor SCL Forestry Bull., 1945-65. Contbr. articles to profl. jours. Home: 7605 Cornwall Rd Richmond VA 23229

HOSSAIN, MOHAMMED NADIR, physician; b. Sikanderpur, India, came to U.S., 1973, naturalized, 1979; s. Mohammed Azimulah and Maimun Nessa H.; MB.B.S., Rajshahi Med. Coll., 1970; m. Shameema Siddique, Oct. 13, 1979. House physician Jinnah Post Grad. Med. Center, Karachi, Pakistan, 1970-72; surg. resident Ali Clinic and Hosp., Karachi, 1972-73; house staff, then chief resident Bklyn.-Cumberland Med. Center, Bklyn., 1973-78; chief surgery USAF Hosp., Dyess AFB, Tex., 1978—. Mem. AMA, Assn. Military Surgeons, Taylor Jones County Tex. Med. Soc. Home: 3217 Heritage Ln Abilene TX 79606

HOSTER, WILLIAM HENRY, JR., steel co. exec.; b. Chillicothe, Ill., Nov. 13, 1912; s. William Henry and Gertrude (Schuenemann) H.; Ph.B., U. Chgo., 1933; m. Eleanor M. Tersip, Dec. 7, 1935; children—William Henry (dec.), Jeffrey Vernon, Karen Barbara, Bruce Richard. Pres., Star Mfg. Co., Oklahoma City, 1945-50; pres., chmn. bd. Okla. Steel Corp., Oklahoma City, 1951-66, Kans. Steel Corp., Wichita, 1958-66, Confederate Steel Corp., Houston, 1959-66, Little Rock, 1962-66, Columbia Steel Co., Magnolia, Ark., 1962-66,

Magnolia Steel Corp., Stamps, Ark., 1963-66; farmer, rancher, Yukon, Okla., 1966-73; v.p., gen. mgr. Lofland Steel Mill, Inc., Oklahoma City, 1973-77; pres. Okla. Steel Mill, Oklahoma City, 1977—, Tulsa (Okla.) REBAR, Inc., Hoster Steel Co., Oklahoma City. Col., Confederate Air Force. Mem. Concrete Reinforcing Steel Inst., Am. Forestry Assn., ASTM, Nat. Hist. Preservation Soc., Aircraft Owners and Pilots Assn., Oklahoma City C. of C. Clubs: Oklahoma City Golf and Country, Petroleum; Internat., Cork (Houston). Home: Oklahoma City OK 73128 Office: 2700 SW 15th St Oklahoma City OK 73108

HOTCHKISS, JOHN FARWELL, JR., aerospace co. exec.; b. San Francisco, June 28, 1931; s. John Farwell and Isabel Montana (Holland) H.; B.S., U.S. Mil. Acad., 1955; student U. So. Calif., 1963; m. Jerra Anne Downey, July 27, 1955; children—Jeffrey, Holly, John. Mktg. engr. Bendix Corp., Teterboro, N.J., Los Angeles, 1960-63; mktg. rep. Sperry Rand Corp., Phoenix, 1963-68; product mgr. Sundstrand Corp., Seattle, 1968-70, mil. sales mgr., avionics sales mgr., 1971-73; dir. govt. avionics sales Collins Radio Co., Cedar Rapids, Iowa, 1973-74, dir. mktg. govt. programs, 1974-75; dir. product devel. ITT Aerospace Optical Div., Ft. Wayne, Ind., 1976; group mktg. mgr. Bendix Aerospace Elec. Group, Arlington, Va., 1976-79, dir. domestic mktg., 1979—. Mem. CAP, Seattle, 1970-71; scoutmaster Boy Scouts Am., Mercer Island, Wash., 1971. Served as pilot USAF, 1955-60. Lic. comml. pilot. Mem. AIAA, Nat. Aeros. Assn., Combat Pilots Assn., Air Force Assn. Republican. Club: Aero of Washington. Home: 5137 38th St N Arlington VA 22207 Office: 1911 N Ft Myer Dr Arlington VA 22209

HOUCHIN, PATRICIA KAY, fin. exec.; b. Radford, Va., Apr. 11, 1946; d. James E. and Pat Anderson; A.A., Mountainview Coll., 1973; B.Career Arts, Dallas Bapt. Coll., 1976; m. Larry W. Sage, June 1, 1975; children—Lori Anne Houchin, Jo Ellen Houchin. Tax cons. H & R Block Income Tax Service, various locations, 1965-70; adminstrv. asst. H & R Block, Washington, 1968-69; v.p. fin., controller Fashions by Mr. Stan, Dallas, 1971—; sec. S.W. Apparel Mfrs. Assn. Controllers and Mgmt. Group, Dallas, 1978-79. Tchr. acctg. YWCA, Irving, Tex., 1977-78. Episcopalian. Club: Toastmasters (adminstrv. v.p. Dist. IV 1979). Home: 210 E Vilbig St Irving TX 75060 Office: 151 Regal Row Suite 116 Dallas TX 75247

HOUCK, EDWARD BERNARD, II, counselor; b. Queens, N.Y., May 13, 1948; s. Edward B. and Evelyn (Seibert) H.; A.A., Broward Community Coll., 1973; B.A., Fla. Atlantic U., 1975, Ed.M. in Guidance and Counseling, 1976. Cons. on handicapped, phys. plant Fla. Atlantic U., 1972-73, peer counselor coordinator Psychol. Counseling Center, 1975-76, staff counselor, 1976-78, vis. lectr. Grad. Sch., Coll. of Edn., 1976-80; instr. psychology, cons. handicapped affairs Prospect Hall Coll., 1979—; pvt. practice counseling, psychotherapy, Deerfield Beach, Fla., 1976—. Acting pres. Coalition for Florida's Disabled Students, 1977-78; speaker Gov.'s Com. on Employment of the Handicapped, State of Fla., 1972. Mem. Am. Personnel and Guidance Assn., Am. Assn. for Marriage and Family Therapy. Office: 809 Robinson Rd Suite 1A Deerfield Beach FL 33441

HOUGH, THOMAS BRYANT, minister; b. Anson County, N.C., Nov. 7, 1903; s. Robert Andrew and Janie (Simpson) H.; B.A., Duke, 1937, postgrad. theology Emory U., 1930-34, Ia. U., 1950; Th.M., Am. Bible Sch., 1950, Th.D., 1952, D.D., 1952; m. Mary Garnett Martin, June 15, 1928; 1 dau., Mary Jane (Mrs. Thoroughgood Fleetwood Hassell). Ordained to ministry United Methodist Ch., 1929; pastor various chs., N.C., 1929-62; supt. Burlington (N.C.) dist., 1962-67; pastor First Ch., Rockingham, N.C., 1967-71; mem. bd. ministerial tng. United Meth. Ch., 1958-62. Del., Jurisdictional Conf., 1964, World Conf. United Meth., London, 1966. Vol. chaplain Richmond County Meml. Hosp., 1967-71, civilian adviser to 3d Army, 1958-70; dist. commr. Cherokee Council Boy Scouts Am., 1948-49. Bd. trustees N.C. United Meth. Conf., 1960-72, Meth. Retirement Homes, 1962-76. Named Citizen of Yr., Rockingham, 1979. Democrat. Kiwanian. Author: Steeple Tones, 1958-62. Contbr. articles to religious jours. and lodge mags. Home and office: 430 Curtis Dr Rockingham NC 28379

HOUGHTON, MARY ALICE, hosp. adminstr.; b. Charleston, W.Va., Mar. 19, 1929; d. John Dixon and Helen Mae (Broyles) Caudill; student Morris Harvey Coll., Charleston, 1950-51; m. William Ernest Houghton, Dec. 24, 1955 (dec. 1959); children—Teresa Elizabeth, Sharon Lee. Pvt. sec. to div. mgr. Appalachian Power Co., Charleston, 1947-51; sec. to atty. Phila. Electric, 1951-53; sect. to advt. mgr. Charleston Daily Mail, 1953-55; pvt. sec. to pres. Charleston Mail Assn., 1961-63; coordinator public relations Princeton Community Hosp., Princeton, W.Va., 1968—, patient rep., 1979—. Mem. Am. Hosp. Assn. Soc. Patient Reps., Am. Soc. Hosp. Public Relations, W.Va. Assn. Hosp. Public Relations. Republican. Baptist. Club: Quota. Editor hosp. newsletter, 1971—. Home: 111 Frederick Ct Princeton WV 24740 Office: Princeton Community Hospital 12th St Princeton WV 24740

HOULDITCH, JIMMY CLAY, electronics co. exec.; b. Hamburg, Ala., Nov. 20, 1935; s. William Clay and Lucille (Smitherman) H.; B.S. in Elec. Engring., Auburn U., 1957; M.B.A. with honors, Pepperdine U., 1976; m. Olivia Champion, July 26, 1958; 1 dau., Tracey Lynn. With Tex. Instruments, Dallas, 1962—, mgr. mfg. radar systems, 1969-73, mgr. printing wiring boards, 1973-76, mgr. quality reliability and product support, 1976-79, mgr. electro optical ops., 1979—; dir. Texins Credit Union; tchr. Dallas U. Pres., PTA Farmers Branch Sch. System. Served with USAF, 1957-62. Mem. IEEE, Am. Soc. Quality Control. Republican. Baptist. Patentee circuit design and mfg. mechanization. Home: 13826 Wooded Creek Dallas TX 75234 Office: Tex Instruments PO Box 6015 Dallas TX 75222

HOUSE, JAMES B(OYD), ins. co. exec.; b. Alicia, Ark., Dec. 4; s. Ora Edward and Lois (Shell) H.; B.S. in Bus. Adminstrn., Harding U., 1966; m. Sue Howarton, Aug. 27, 1965; children—Matthew, Ashley, Jordan. Salesman, Firestone Tire and Rubber Corp., Memphis, 1966-67; with Ark. Blue Cross and Blue Shield, 1967—, gen. sales mgr., Little Rock, 1976-79, v.p. mktg., 1979—. Bd. dirs. Delta Hills Health Systems Agy., 1975—. Served with Army N.G., 1963-69. Named Outstanding Salesman of Yr., Ark. Blue Cross and Blue Shield, 1971, recipient Gen. Sales Mgrs. award, 1973, Regional Mgr.'s Joint Mktg. award, 1974. Mem. Sales and Mktg. Execs. Assn., Searcy (Ark.) C. of C. Democrat. Mem. Churches of Christ. Club: Optimists. Office: Ark Blue Cross and Blue Shield Sixth and Gaines Sts Little Rock AR 72203

HOUSE, WILLIAM CLYDE, educator; b. Comanche, Tex., June 2, 1933; s. William Clyde and Alice Virginia (Halliday) H.; A.S., Tarleton State Coll., 1952; B.B.A., U. Tex., Austin, 1954, M.B.A., 1958, Ph.D., 1965; m. Adrian Musselwhite, June 11, 1961; 1 dau., Melinda Ann. Budget analyst Tex. Eastern Transmission Corp., Shreveport, La., 1958-60; instr. fin. acctg. U. Tex., Austin, 1960-62; asst. prof. bus. Tex. A&M U., College Station, 1962-65, asso. prof., 1966-69; prof. bus. adminstrn. U. Ark., Fayetteville, 1969—. Served with AUS, 1954-56. Nat. Assn. Accts. fellow, 1966. Mem. Inst. Mgmt. Sci., Am. Inst. Decision Scis., Soc. Mgmt. Info. Systems, Assn. Bus. Simulation and Exptl. Learning. Methodist. Club: Elks. Author: (with Gene Dippel) Information Systems, 1969; editor: Data Base Management, 1974; Business Simulation for Decision Making, 1977; Laser Beam Information Systems, 1978; Electronic Communications Systems, 1979. Home: 1833 Rollins Hills Dr Fayetteville AR 72701 Office: Sch Bus Adminstrn U Ark Fayetteville AR 72701

HOUSER, JOHN EDWARD, lawyer; b. Richmond, Va., Dec. 24, 1928; s. Aubrey Alphin and Winnifred (Savage) H.; B.S., U. Va., 1959, LL.B., 1959; m. Rives Pollard; children—Allen Rives Cabell Lybrook, Andrew Murray Lybrook II. Admitted to Fla. bar, Fed. bar, 1959, U.S. Supreme Ct. bar, 1970; practiced in Jacksonville, Fla., 1959—; dir. Wm. P. Poythress & Co., Richmond, Neal F. Tyler & Sons, Jacksonville. Served with AUS, 1953-57. Mem. Internat. Assn. Indsl. Accident Bds. and Commns., Maritime Law Assn. U.S., Jacksonville, Atlanta claimsmen assns., Am., Jacksonville bar assns., Fla. Bar, Fla. Def. Counsel Assn., Am. Judicature Assn., Am. Arbitration Assn., Nat. Trust for Historic Preservation, Fla. Inst. Pub. Affairs, Navy League, Jacksonville Assn. Def. Counsel, Def. Research Inst., Jacksonville U. Council, Jacksonville Symphony Assn., Fla., Jacksonville hist. socs., Cummer Gallery of Art, Jacksonville Art Mus., Jacksonville C. of C., English-Speaking Union (dir. 1970—, pres. 1974-78, nat. regional chmn. 1973-76, nat. dir. 1975—), Thomasville Landmarks, Thomasville Arts Guild, Thomas County Hist. Soc., Theta Delta Chi, Sigma Nu Phi. Clubs: River, Fla. Yacht; Deerwood, Ponte Vedra River, Exchange, German, Ye Mystic Revellers, University; Princeton of N.Y.; Glen Arven (Thomasville); Commonwealth, 2300 (Richmond). Office: Fla Nat Bank Bldg Jacksonville FL 32202

HOUSER, LOUISE KELLEY, health care adminstr.; b. Bowman, S.C., Feb. 22, 1919; d. George Quillie and Byrdie Lucile (Stephens) Kelley; B.S., S.C. State Coll., 1941, M.S., 1959; m. John W. Houser, Jr., Sept. 18, 1943; children—John W., George D. Tchr. pub. schs., Marion County, Ga., 1941-44; tchr. sci. Ga. Sch. for the Deaf, 1959-61; tchr. pub. schs., Rome, Ga., 1961-68; dir. personnel Brentwood (Ga.) Med. Care Home, 1967-71; adminstr. Brentwood Nursing Home, 1972-77; adminstr. Brentwood Park, Three Rivers Health Care Co., Rome, Ga., 1977—. Mem. Rome Council on Human Relations, Ga. Health Care Assn., Am. Health Care Assn., Ga. Soc. Activity Dirs., Ga. Dental Soc. Aux. (past pres.), Am. Cancer Soc. (past pres. Floyd County div.), Aux. Nat. Dental Assn. (past pres., mem. exec. bd.). Home: 121 Jackson St Rome GA 30161 Office: Moran Lake Rd Rome GA 30161

HOUSTON, FRANK MATT, dermatologist; b. New Orleans, Dec. 15, 1939; s. Matt Francis and Amanda Vallie (Welsh) H.; B.S., La. State U., 1960, M.D., 1964; m. Helen Butler, Apr. 24, 1965; children—Frank Matt, Catherine Elizabeth, Amanda Johanna. Intern, Johns Hopkins Hosp., Balt., 1964-65, resident, 1967-70; practice medicine specializing in dermatology, Greensboro, N.C., 1970—; partner Greensboro Dermatology Assos., 1970—; cons. Guilford County (N.C.) Dept. Health, 1973—; asst. prof. dermatology U. N.C., 1973—; mem. staffs Moses Cone Hosp., Wesley Long Hosp., Greensboro. Bd. dirs. Greensboro chpt. Assn. Children with Learning Disabilities, 1974-75; mem. vestry Holy Trinity Episcopal Ch., Greensboro, 1975-78, sec. vestry, 1976-77, sr. warden, 1978; bd. dirs. Greensboro chpt. N.C. Symphony, 1977, also pres.; bd. dirs. Green Hill Art Gallery, Greensboro Hist. Mus., Greensboro chpt. ARC; exec. com. Greensboro Irish Children's Summer Program. Served as capt., M.C., U.S. Army, 1965-67. Diplomate Am. Bd. Dermatology; mem. Am. Acad. Dermatology, Carolina Dermatol. Soc., AMA, N.C., Guilford med. socs., Greensboro Acad. Medicine, Greensboro Preservation Soc., S.A.R., Nat. Trust Historic Preservation, A.C.P., Royal Coll. Physicians, Pi Kappa Alpha, Phi Chi, Phi Eta Sigma, Mu Sigma Rho, Alpha Epsilon Delta, Phi Kappa Phi, Omicron Delta Kappa. Republican. Episcopalian. Clubs: Greensboro City, Sherwood Swim and Racquet. Contbr. articles to med. jours. Home: 3005 Round Hill Rd Greensboro NC 27408 Office: 1030 Profl Village Greensboro NC 27401

HOUSTON, MARCUS CLARENCE, internist; b. Jackson, Tenn., Aug. 14, 1948; s. Rupert and Mary H.; B.A. in Chemistry, Southwestern at Memphis, 1970; M.D., Vanderbilt U., 1974; m. Ellen Sams, 1971; children—Helen Ruth, Marcus. Clerkship in cardiology Crawford Long and Emory U. hosps., Atlanta, 1972; intern U. Calif. Hosps., San Francisco, 1974-75, resident in medicine, 1975-77; chief resident in medicine Vanderbilt U., Nashville, 1977-78; asst. prof. medicine, co-dir. med. ICU, Vanderbilt Med. Center, 1978—, mem. adminstrn. com. Recipient J. William Hillman award for excellence in teaching, 1978. Diplomate Am. Bd. Internal Medicine. Mem. Am. Chem. Soc., Am. Thoracic Soc., A.C.P., San Francisco Heart Assn., Nashville Acad. Medicine, Tenn. Med. Assn., Phi Beta Kappa, Alpha Omega Alpha. Contbr. articles to med. jours. Home: 4436 Sneed Rd Nashville TN 37215 Office: Vanderbilt Med Center Nashville TN 37232

HOUSTON, NEAL BRYAN, educator; b. Dallas, Aug. 7, 1928; s. Neal Bryan and Pauline (Carr) H.; B.S., U. Tex., 1949, M.Ed., 1953, M.A., 1960; Ph.D., Tex. Tech. U., 1965; m. Ellen Joan Norton, Nov. 10, 1956; children—Alan Kyle, Sharon Lee. Lectr. Mitsubishi Chem. Industries, Ltd., Japan, 1952-53; tchr. English Ector County Ind. Sch. Dist., Odessa, Tex., 1953-55, Dallas Ind. Sch. Dist., 1955-57; teaching asst. U. Tex., Austin, 1957-58; prof. Amarillo Coll. (Tex.), 1958-65; asso. prof. Angelo State U., San Angelo, Tex., 1965-66; prof. English, Stephen F. Austin State U., Nacogdoches, Tex., 1966—; vis. prof. U. Hawaii, Hilo, 1970-71. Pres., Episcopal Day Sch., Nacogdoches, Tex., 1974-75; mem. adv. bd. Artes Liberales, 1967-75, editor, 1975—. Served with AUS, 1951-53. Stephen F. Austin State U. faculty grantee, 1966, 68, 75, 79. Mem. Coll. Conf. Tchrs. English, AAUP, Tex. Assn. Coll. Tchrs., Phi Delta Kappa, Sigma Phi Epsilon, Sigma Tau Delta. Democrat. Episcopalian (clk. 1974-75). Author: Phonetikon, 1970; Ross Santee, 1968. Contbr. articles to profl. jours. Home: 2933 Dogwood St Nacogdoches TX 75961

HOUSTON, SHIRLEY MAE (MRS. THOMAS HAROLD HOUSTON), ct. reporter; b. Jasper, Tex., Oct. 4, 1938; d. Walter Louis and Effie Marie (Hulett) Gordon; student U. Houston, 1957, South Tex. Jr. Coll., Houston, 1958; grad. Robert Krippner Sch. Reporting, 1965; m. Thomas Harold Houston, Aug. 3, 1957. Various secretarial positions, 1956-65; ct. reporter, owner Houston Reporting Service, 1965—; owner H-R-S, 1975—, Houston Video Service, 1977—; v.p. Tradewinds Indsl. Park, Inc., 1974—. Vol. juvenile counselor. Registered profl. reporter, Tex. Mem. Greater Houston Ct. Reporters Assn. (pres. 1975), Nat. (dir. 1979-80), Tex. (advt. chmn. conv. 1967) shorthand reporters assns., Nat., Tex., Houston (dir. 1969) assns. legal secs., D.A.R., UDC, Harris County Heritage Soc., Theatre Under the Stars. Baptist. Club: Cotillion (Houston). Address: 609 Fannin St Suite 2121 Houston TX 77002

HOUTMANN, JACQUES, orch. condr. and mus. dir.; b. Mirecourt, France, Mar. 27, 1935; s. Georges and Paule (Saal) H.; came to U.S., 1971; concert license Ecole Normale de Musique, Paris, France, 1962; diploma Santa Caecilia, Rome, Italy, 1963; D. F.A. (hon.), U. Richmond, 1976; m. Yolaine Gerard, July 6, 1967; children—Hélène, Marie-Virginie. Asst. condr. N.Y. Philharmonic, 1965-66; condr. Philharmonic, Lyon, France, 1967-71; music dir., condr. Richmond (Va.) Symphony and Richmond Sinfonia, 1971—; guest condr., Europe, U.S., S.Am. Recipient 1st prize Competition for Condrs., Besançon, France, 1960, Dimitri Mitropoulos competition, 1964. Mem. Am. Symphony Orch. League. Recs. include: 3 Symphonies (F.J. Gossec), 1972 (Belgian Nat. Prize 1972). Office: 15 S 5th St Richmond VA 23219

HOUTZ, DUANE TALBOTT, hosp. adminstr.; b. Kansas City, Mo., Apr. 28, 1933; s. Dudley W. and Helen (Amick) H.; B.S., U. Kans., 1955; M.H.A., Washington U., St. Louis, 1960; m. Margaret McNiel, 1962; children—Jamie, Erik. Resident hosp. adminstrn. Orange Meml. Hosp., Orlando, Fla., 1959, adminstrv. asst., 1960; asst. dir. Shands Teaching Hosp. and Clinics, Gainesville, Fla., 1961-65; asst. prof. Center for Health and Hosp. Adminstrn., U. Fla., Gainesville, 1961-65; adminstr., exec. v.p. Bapt. Med. Center, Montclair, Birmingham, Ala., 1965-75; hosp. dir. Alton Ochsner Med. Found., New Orleans, 1975-77; exec. dir. Morton F. Plant Hosp., Clearwater, Fla., 1977—; cons. div. emergency med. services HEW, 1968-74; adj. asst. prof. George Washington U., 1968-74; adj. asso. prof. Sch. Health Related Professions, U. Ala., Birmingham, 1970-79, adj. asso. prof. Sch. Nursing, 1975-77 Chmn. hosp. div. United Appeal, Birmingham, 1971; mem. adv. com. Red Cross Blood Program, 1967-71; chmn. hosp. div. Birmingham Cancer Crusade, 1972. Fellow Am. Coll. Hosp. Adminstrs. (chmn. com. research and devel. 1972-74); mem. Am. Hosp. Assn. (chmn. com. emergency health services 1974-76, 77-78), Assn. Voluntary Hosps. Fla. (pres. 1979), Fla. League Nursing (treas. 1978-79), Fla. Hosp. Assn. (chmn. com. standards and quality control 1979), Nat. League Nursing (dir. 1975-77), Southeastern Hosp. Assn. (edn. com. 1974), Bay Area Hosp. Council (sec.-treas. 1978-79), Washington U. Alumni Assn. Club: Kiwanis (pres. 1970-71, dir. 1969-72). Contbr. articles on hosp. adminstrn. to profl. pubis. Office: 323 Jeffords St Clearwater FL 33517

HOVEN, ARD, clergyman; b. Athena, Oreg., Oct. 21, 1906; s. Victor and Leona (Bodine) H.; B.A., Eugene Bible Coll., 1930, B.D., 1931; B.A., U. Oreg., 1933; M.A., Cin. Bible Sem., 1937; D.S.T., Milligan Coll., 1954; D.D., Ky. Christian Coll., 1954; m. Dorothy Lillian Harris, Sept. 30, 1938; children—Ardis Dee, Vicki Lee. Ordained to ministry Christian Ch., 1933; minister, Ceres, Calif., 1933-34, Cin., 1934-51, Broadway Christian Ch., Lexington, Ky., 1951-66, First Christian Ch., Columbus, Ind., 1966-78; head dept. Christian ministry Ky. Christian Coll., Grayson, 1978—. Speaker radio program Christians' Hour, 1943—; pres. N.Am. Christian Conv., 1950, mem. continuation com., 1950—; writer weekly Bible Sch. lesson The Lookout, Standard Pub. Co., Cin., 1958—, mem. pub. com., 1957—. Trustee Milligan Coll., Midway Jr. Coll. Republican. Mason, Rotarian. Author: Christ Is All, 1953; Meditations and Prayers for the Lord's Table, 1962. Office: Kentucky Christian College Grayson KY 41143

HOVIOUS, BRADFORD WELDON, athletic dir.; b. Vicksburg, Miss., Jan. 23, 1946; s. John A. and Katherine (Tennant) H.; B.S. in Phys. Edn., U. Miss., 1969, M.Ed., 1970; M.Ed. in Sports Adminstrn., Ohio U., Athens, 1975; Ed.D. in Ednl. Adminstrn., La. State U., 1977; m. Mary Carmille McCulloch, Aug. 24, 1968; children—Mary Katherine, Taylor Camille. Tchr., coach high schs. in Miss. and Ga., 1969-70, 72-74; athletic dir. Delta State U., Cleveland, Miss., 1977—; mem. alumni bd. dirs. Ohio U. Sports Adminstrn. Program; sec.-treas. Delta State U. Booster Club. Served to 1st lt. USAR, 1970-72. Decorated Donsting. Service Award. Mem. Nat. Assn. Collegiate Dirs. Athletics, Coll. Athletic Bus. Mgrs. Assn., Phi Delta Kappa. Presbyterian. Club: Cleveland Rotary. Home: 305 Canal St Cleveland MS 38732 Office: Box A-3 Delta State Univ Cleveland MS 38733

HOWARD, ARTHUR DAVID, geologist; b. N.Y.C., Aug. 9, 1906; s. Louis and Lena H.; B.S., N.Y. U., 1929, M.S., 1931; Ph.D., Columbia U., 1937; m. Julia Salter, Nov. 28, 1910. Instr. geology N.Y. U., 1932-40; cartographic engr. U.S. Coast and Geodetic Survey, 1942-44; tech. rep. Office Strategic Services, China Theater, 1944-46; geologist U.S. Geol. Survey, 1946-48, summers 1948-53; asso. prof. geology Stanford U., 1943-51, prof., 1951-71, emeritus prof., 1971—, chmn. dept. geology, 1959-60, 63-65; vis. prof. emeritus N.C. State U., 1978—; cons. in field Disting. lectr. Am. Assn. Petroleum Geologists, 1950; mem. internat. coms. on erosion surfaces; ofcl. del. Internat. Geologic Congress, Moscow, 1937, Algiers, 1952, Pacific Sci. Congress, Tokyo, 1966. Served with U.S. Army, 1941; CBI. Decorated emblem for meritorious civilian service; recipient A. Cressey Morrison prize N.Y. Acad. Scis., Congl. Antarctic medal, 1970; Antarctic glacier named Howard Glacier, 1961. Mem. Geol. Soc. Am. (chmn. various meetings; pres. geomorphology div. 1969-70), Am. Geol. Inst., Am. Quaternary Assn., Arctic Inst. N.Am., Am. Polar Soc., Sigma Xi. Author books, including: Geology in Environmental Planning, 1978; Geologic History of Middle California, 1979; contbr. numerous articles to profl. jours. Office: Dept Geoscis NC State U Raleigh NC 27650

HOWARD, ARTHUR ELLSWORTH DICK, educator; b. Richmond, Va., July 5, 1933; s. Thomas Landon and Marie Antoinette (Dick) H.; B.A., U. Richmond, 1954; LL.B., U. Va., 1961; B.A. with honors, Oxford U., 1960, M.A., 1965. Admitted to Va., D.C. bars, 1961; asso., Covington & Burling, Washington, 1961-62; law clk. to Justice Hugo L. Black, Supreme Ct. U.S., Washington, 1962-64; asso. prof. law U. Va., Charlottesville, 1964-67, prof., 1967-76, White Burkett Miller prof. law and pub. affairs, 1976—, asso. dean, 1967-69. Counsel, 1969, 1970 sessions Gen. Assembly Va.; cons. Subcom. on Constl. Rights, U.S. Senate Judiciary Com., 1975—. Exec. dir. Va. Commn. on Constl. Revision, 1968-69; mem. Va. Ind. Bicentennial Commn., 1966—; vice-chmn. Magna Carta Commn. Va., 1965-66; Va. sec. Rhodes Scholarship Trust, 1970—. Served with AUS, 1954-56. Fellow Woodrow Wilson Internat. Center for Scholars, Smithsonian Instn., Washington, 1974-75, 76-77, Center for Advanced Studies, U. Va., 1970-71; Rhodes scholar Oxford U., 1958-60. Mem. Va. Bar Assn. (v.p. 1970-71). Episcopalian. Clubs: Cosmos (Washington); Oxford and Cambridge (London, Eng.). Author: State Aid to Private Higher Education, 1977; Commentaries on the Constitution of Virginia, 2 vols. (Phi Beta Kappa prize), 1974; The Road from Runnymede: Magna Carta and Constitutionalism in America, 1968. Bd. editors The American Oxonian, 1968—. Home: 627 Park St Charlottesville VA 22901

HOWARD, BERTIN EDWARD, trust co. exec.; b. Port Arthur, Tex., July 3, 1938; s. Clarence Eral and Josephine Claire (Bertin) H.; B.B.A. in Econs., Lamar U., 1960, B.B.A. in Acctg., 1969, M.B.A. in Acctg., 1970; m. Frances Green, Feb. 2, 1968; children—Justin Eral, Ellen Claire. Tax acct. Peat, Marwick, Mitchell & Co., Dallas, 1970-71; instr. acctg. Stephen F. Austin U., Nacogdoches, Tex., 1971-73; controller Nacogdoches/Irving Community Hosps., Tex., 1973-75; asst. tax mgr. Temple-Eastex, Inc., Diboll, Tex., 1975-78, subs. controller, Austin, Tex., 1978-79; dir. fin. Tex. Med. Liability Trust, Austin, 1979—; mem. faculty Stephen F. Austin U., 1976-78, Austin Community Coll., 1979. Served with USAR, 1961. Cert. Tex. Bd. Public Accountancy. Mem. Nat. Assn. Accts. (past pres. Lufkin/Nacogdoches chpt., nat. com. edn.), Tex. Soc. C.P.A.'s, Am. Inst. C.P.A.'s. Republican. Roman Catholic. Club: Kiwanis. Home: 1706 Cedar Creek Cove Round Rock TX 78664 Office: 1016 La Posada Suite 176 Austin TX 78752

HOWARD, C(LARENCE) EDWARD, geologist; b. Roseboro, N.C., May 31, 1929; s. Hubert Royster and Irene (Britt) H.; student Campbell Coll., 1948-49; B.S., Duke U., 1953; M.S., N.C. State U., 1955; Ph.D., La. State U., 1963; m. Evelyn Kline Baker, Oct. 22, 1955 (div. Feb. 1980); 1 dau., Wendy Gail. Teaching asst. N.C. State U., Raleigh, 1953-55; mining and geol. engr. Tungsten Mining Corp., Henderson, N.C., 1955-57; teaching asst. La. State U., Baton Rouge, 1959-63; asst. prof. geology Campbell Coll., Buies Creek, N.C., 1963-64, asso. prof., 1964-66, chmn. dept. geology, 1964-76, prof., 1966-76; prin. geologist Geotech. Engring. Co., Research Triangle Park, N.C. 1976-78, v.p., 1977-78; pres. Carolina Earth Resources Co., Lillington, N.C., 1977—. Fellow Geol. Soc. Am.; mem. AAAS, Am. Inst. Profl. Geologists, Assn. Engring. Geologists, Am. Inst. Mining Engrs., Carolina Geol. Soc., N.C. Acad. Sci., Sigma Xi, Phi Kappa Phi. Rotarian. Contbr. articles in field to profl. jours. Home: PO Box 11386 Lillington NC 27546 Office: PO Box 1025 Lillington NC 27546

HOWARD, CHARLES, chemist, educator; b. Evanston, Ill., Apr. 2, 1919; s. Marion Boyd and Mary (McLafferty) H.; Ph.D., U. Wis., 1943; postgrad. U. Okla., 1964, Tex. A&M U., 1965; m. Dorothy Thompson, July 16, 1945; children—John, Robert, Margaret. Acting chief chemist Oscar Mayer & Co., Madison, Wis., 1948-50; dir. product control Arbogast & Bastion, Inc., Allentown, Pa., 1950-54; asst. plant supt. Valleydale Packers, Inc., Salem, Va., 1954-59; plant supt. Roegelein Provision Co., San Antonio, 1960; prof., chmn. dept. chemistry San Antonio Coll., 1960-73; prof. chemistry U. Tex., San Antonio, 1973—. Served with USN, 1944-45. Sci. equipment grantee AEC, 1963, 65, 68, NSF, 1967, others. Fellow Am. Inst. Chemists; mem. Am. Chem. Soc., Inst. Food Technologists, Tex. Acad. Sci., Two Year Coll. Chemistry Conf., Sigma Xi. Contbr. articles to ency., lab. textbooks, lab. manuals, audio-visual programs, publs. in sci. jours. Office: Univ Texas at San Antonio San Antonio TX 78285

HOWARD, CHARLES KENNETH, civil engr.; b. Vinita, Okla., Dec. 28, 1939; s. Weldon Hunt and Margaruette Marie (Mc Farland) H.; student Northeastern State Coll., 1961-63; m. Adrienne Beth Swicegood, Feb. 14, 1969; children—Curtis Lee, Christopher Darren, Heather, Sommer. Machine operator Fo-Mac Enterprizes, Tulsa, 1958-61; land surveyor, engring. tech. Breisch Engring. Co., Tulsa, 1963-64, Lansford Engring., Tulsa, 1964-65; engring. tech., engr. Wheeler & Assos., Tulsa, 1965; self-employed Howard Surveying Co. Suburban Engring. Inc., Sapula, Okla., 1966-72; project engr. Max Holloway Engring. Co., Muskogee, Okla., 1972-75; chief engr. Finley Engring. Co., Tulsa, 1975-76; dir. engring. Scott's Assos., Muskogee, 1976—; instr. surveying Tulsa Jr. Coll., 1971—; cons. in field. Surveyor Creek County, Okla., 1969-72. Clk. bd. edn. Osage County, 1974-75. Registered land surveyor, Okla. Democrat. Baptist. Mason. Home: Rt I PO Box 178 Oktaha OK 74450 Office: 901-B Callahan St Muskogee OK 74401

HOWARD, ELIZABETH SIMMONS, civic worker; b. Gadsden, Ala., Sept. 12, 1926; d. John Moses and Ethel (Gilchrist) Simmons; A.B., U. Ala., 1948; m. Max James Howard, Mar. 19, 1948; 1 dau., Beth Elaine. Mem. research dept. U. Ala., 1948-50; tchr. Public Schs., Fort Payne, Ala., 1949-62; trustee, editor Landmarks of DeKalb County, 1972—; dir. Fort Payne Tourist Assn., 1977—; mem. Fort Payne Bicentennial Com., 1975-76; mem. steering com. Ala. Supt. Edn. Com. of 100 for High Sch. Minimum Competency Standards, 1977—; pres. Fort Payne Tchrs. Assn., 1961-62. Mem., sec. adminstrv. bd., trustee 1st United Methodist Ch. Recipient Merit award Ala. Hist. Commn., 1975, Disting. Service award, 1979; Rotary Rose award, 1977; cert. commendation Am. Assn. State and Local History, 1979. Mem. Ala. Hist. Assn., Nat. Hist. Assn., DeKalb County Bar Aux., Am. Polit. Items Collectors, Phi Beta Kappa. Club: DeSoto Country, Fort Payne Study. Author: The Vagabond Dreamer, 1976; editor: The DeKalb Legend; asso. editor Landmarks News. Home: PO Box 128 Fort Payne AL 35967

HOWARD, FRANK SAXON, aerospace engr.; b. Augusta, Ga., July 18, 1938; s. Leonard Evans and Martha (Milligan) H.; B.S. in Mech. Engring., Clemson U., 1956-60; m. Linda Carol Gresham, Jan. 7, 1962; children—Mark, Leah, Carol. Phys. metallurgist Charleston (S.C.) Naval Shipyard, 1960-61, nuclear engr. 1961-65; mech. engr. aerospace technologists, Kennedy Space Center, Fla., NASA, 1965—; ordained minister of the Gospel. Vice pres. Koinonia. Recipient Exceptional Service medal NASA. Registered profl. engr., Fla. Mem. Am. Soc. M.E. Patentee in field. Home: 946 Golden Beach Blvd Indian Harbour Beach FL 32937 Office: Propellants and Gases Br DD-Med-4 NASA Kennedy Space Center FL 32899

HOWARD, GENE CLAUDE, state senator Okla.; b. Perry, Okla., Sept. 26, 1926; s. Joe W. and Nell L. (Brown) H.; LL.B., U. Okla., 1951; div.; children—Jean Ann Howard Peterson, Joseph T. Admitted to Okla. bar, 1950, now partner Howard & Hood, Tulsa; mem. Okla. Ho. of Reps., 1958-62; mem. Okla. Senate, 1964—, pres. pro-tem, 1975—; partner Howard & Rapp, 1980—. Pres., Okla. Jr. Democrats, 1954; del. Dem. Nat. Conv., 1964. Served as officer USAAF, 1944-46, USAF, 1961-62. Mem. Okla., Tulsa County (Outstanding Young Atty. 1963), Tulsa bar assns. Democrat. Mem. Christian Ch. Home: 1742 S Erie Tulsa OK 74112 Office: 1640 S Boston Tulsa OK 74119

HOWARD, GEORGE TURNER, JR., surgeon; b. Harlan, Ky., May 31, 1913; s. George Turner and Nancy (Smith) H.; B.A. U. Ky., 1933; M.D., Harvard, 1937; m. Sue Scott Crizer, July 20, 1946; children—George Turner III, Robert Scott, Edwin Brittain II, Angela Diane. Intern, Boston City Hosp., 1937-39; resident Boston City Hosp., 1940, Meml. Hosp. for Cancer and Allied Diseases, N.Y.C., 1941; mem. surg. faculty Boston U. Med. Sch., 1940-41; practice medicine, specializing in surgery, Knoxville, 1942—; mem. staffs Fort Sanders Presbyn. Hosp., U. Tenn. Meml. Hosp., East Tenn. Bapt. Hosp., St. Mary's Meml. Hosp. Bd. dirs. A.R.C., Knox County, 1956-57, Am. Cancer Soc., State Tenn. and Knox County, 1947-77; bd. dirs. Knoxville Symphony Soc., 1967—, pres., 1969-70. Served with USAAF, 1943-45. Named Ky. col., 1965; recipient Merit certificate Am. Cancer Soc., 1956. Diplomate Am. Bd. Surgery. Fellow A.C.S., Royal Soc. Health (Eng.), Southeastern Surg. Congress, Acad. Internat. Medicine, Pan Pacific Surg. Assn., Internat. Acad. Proctology; mem. A.M.A., So., Tenn., World, Boylston, Pan Am. med. assns., S.A.R., Am. Geriatric Assn., Phi Beta Kappa, Omicron Delta Kappa, Alpha Chi Sigma, Omega Beta Pi, Delta Tau Delta, Nu Sigma Nu. Presbyn. (deacon). Clubs: Knoxville Racquet, Cherokee Country; Tequesta Country, River Edge (Tequesta, Fla.). Home: 1209 Scenic Dr Knoxville TN 37919 Office: 501 20th St Knoxville TN 37916

HOWARD, GORDON EDWARD, educator; b. Columbus, Ohio, Sept. 22, 1941; s. Glenn Willard and Thelma Elizabeth (Akey) H.; B.A., U. N.C., 1963, M.A., 1964; Ph.D., U. Mich., 1968; children—Gordon Edward, Holly. Research technician dept. phys. edn. U. Mich., 1964-67, research technician dept. epidemiology (Tecumseh project), summers 1964-67; asst. prof. dept. recreation and park adminstrn. Clemson (S.C.) U., 1967-71, asso. prof., 1971-77, prof., 1977—. Dir., S.C. Statewide Survey of Outdoor Recreation Facilities, 1968. Mem. leisure resources com. S.C. Appalachian Council Govts., 1970-77, 1st vice chmn., 1973-76. Founder, bd. dirs. Chattooga River Whitewater Canoeing Sch., 1969-78; trustee Clemson Recreation Assn., 1968-71; trustee, pres. Clemson Area Youth Theater, 1969-71. Recipient Gov.'s Phys. Fitness award, 1974. Mem. Am. Alliance for Health, Phys. Edn. and Recreation (life mem.; v.p. recreation div. So. Dist. 1973—), Am. Assn. for Leisure and Recreation (dir.), S.C. Assn. Health, Phys. Edn. and Recreation (v.p. recreation div. 1972-74, Pres.'s award 1978), Nat. Recreation and Park Assn., Soc. Park and Recreation Educators, S.C. Recreation and Park Soc., Am. Coll. Sports Medicine (S.E. chpt.), Phi Delta Kappa. Clubs: Sierra (exec. com. Joseph LeConte chpt. 1970-72, chpt. chmn. 1971-72); Adirondack Mountain. Field dir., coordinating editor Joyce Kilmer Meml. Forest and Slickrock Creek sect. Hikers Guide to the Smokies, 1973. Contbr. articles to profl. jours. Founder, Foothills Trail, S.C., 1969.

HOWARD, JOHN DEWEY, gas measurement service co. mgr.; b. Anadarko, Okla., Nov. 1, 1926; s. Charles Dewy and Bessie Naomi H.; student public schs., Anadarko, 1932-44; m. Marcia Lee Carrell, Apr. 26, 1974; children—Pamula Gayle, Cindy A., Linda K., Larry W. With Mobil Oil Corp., 1949-61, Transwestern Pipeline Co., 1961-69; with Flow Measurement Co., Tulsa, 1969-73, gen. mgr., 1971-73; gen. mgr. John P. Squier Co., Dallas, 1973—. Served with USNR, World War II. Mem. Am. Gas Assn., Tex. Gas Assn., Dallas Engrs. Club, N.E. Tex. Gas Measurement Soc., Oak Cliff C. of C. Republican. Baptist. Home: 103 Greenwood St Route 1 Red Oak TX 75154 Office: PO Box 226100 Dallas TX 75266

HOWARD, LA VOICE HARDISON, pharmacist; b. Duplin County, N.C., Mar. 30, 1944; s. Sam and Louise Cavenaugh H.; student Chowan Bapt. Coll., 1962-64; B.S. in Pharmacy, U. N.C., Chapel Hill, 1968; 1 child. With Jack Eckerd Corp., Charlotte, N.C., 1968-69, Rogers Drug Co., Durham, N.C., 1969-70; pharmacist, mgr. Eckerd Drugs, Inc., Durham, 1970-76; pharmacy area mgr. Jack Eckerds Corp., Durham, 1976—. Mem. N.C. Pharm. Assn., Durham-Orange Pharm. Assn., Sales and Mktg. Assn. Durham, N.C. Pharmacy Polit. Action Com. Home: 4100 Live Oaks 2 Durham NC 27707 Office: 2216 Roxboro Rd Durham NC 27704

HOWARD, LARRY BRUCE, state ofcl.; b. Seattle, Apr. 1, 1928; s. Walter Joseph and Anita (Schnitzlein) H.; B.S., U. Mont., 1950; Ph.D., U. Minn., 1956; postgrad. Emory U., 1956-58; m. Elaine Annette Ungherini, Sept. 20, 1952; children—Randy, Rick, Laure, Lisa. Asst. dir. Ga. Crime Lab., Atlanta, 1956-69, dir., 1969—. Mem. faculty criminology Ga. State U., 1967, mem. faculty anatomy Emory U., 1971—, asst. prof. clin. pathology, 1975—; mem. faculty Ga. Police Acad., 1966—, So. Police Inst. Mem. Ga. Sci. and Tech. Commn., 1969-72; mem. Atlanta YMCA Athletic Council, 1958-59; trustee Forensic Sci. Found., 1977—. Served with AUS, 1945-46. Mem. Am. Acad. Forensic Scis. (chmn. legis. liaison com. 1977-78, mem. toxicology cert. bd., v.p. 1979), AAAS, Soc. Forensic Toxicologists, So. Assn. Forensic Scientists (chmn. 1974), Atlanta Instrument Soc., Am. Soc. Crime Lab. Dirs. (governing bd., treas. 1975-76, pres. 1976-77), Sigma Phi Epsilon. Home: 3106 Lanier Dr NE Atlanta GA 30319 Office: PO Box 1456 Atlanta GA 30301

HOWARD, MARLAND PAUL, sch. adminstr.; b. Dexter, Mich., Jan. 5, 1932; s. Paul James and Luella (Elsasser) H.; B.S., Western Mich. U., 1954, M.A., 1959; Edn. Specialist, Eastern Mich. U., 1968; m. Miriam Anne Roeder, Nov. 21, 1956; children—Mark, Eric. Tchr., coach basketball, track and cross country Covert (Mich.) High Sch., 1956-60; tchr., coach basketball, track and football Bangor (Mich.) High Sch., 1959-61; tchr., counselor, athletic dir. coach basketball, track and football Belleville (Mich.) High Sch., 1961-69; asst. prin., guidance dir. Vicksburg (Mich.) High Sch., 1969-71; curriculum dir. Jones High Sch., Orlando, Fla., 1971-79; asst. prin. Howard Jr. High Sch., 1979—. Served with U.S. Army, 1954-56. Named Southwestern Mich. Basketball Coach of Year 1960; coach Mich. state championship track team, 1957, state championship basketball team, 1960. Mem. Am. Personnel and Guidance Assn., Nat. Coaches Assn., Nat., Fla. assns. secondary prins., Mich. High Sch. Ofcls. Assn., Winter Park C. of C., Winter Park Pony-Colt Baseball League. Democrat. Home: 1570 Elm Ave Winter Park FL 32789

HOWARD, PATRICK MCCOLLOUGH, mining engr.; b. Welch, W.Va., Nov. 8, 1938; s. Clifford Peter and Harriet (Hoge) H.; student Pikeville Coll., 1956-57; U. Ky., 1957-59; m. Mary Elizabeth Cooke, Apr. 8, 1960; children—Marjorie Marie, Patrick McCollough. Jr. designer Electric Elevator div. Dover Corp., Cin., 1959-61; chief engr. Kentland-Elkhorn Coal Corp., Pikeville, Ky., 1961-70, Feds Creek Coal Co., 1967-70; dir. engring. Ky. div. Pittston Co., 1970-71, gen. mgr. Buchanan County Mines Rapoca Resources, 1970-72; owner Mine Tech. Service, Pikeville, Ky., 1965—, Howard Homes Co., Pikeville, 1967—, Howard Enterprises, Pikeville, 1972—; pres. Coal Carriers, Inc., Pikeville, 1974—, Universal Mining Co., 1978—. Scoutmaster Boy Scouts Am. Served with inf. AUS, 1955. Mem. Nat., Ky. (chpt. pres.) socs. profl. engrs., AIME, Big Sandy Elkhorn Mining Inst., Nat. Ind. Coal Operators. Republican. Presbyn. Club: Willow Brook Country. Home: PO Box 228 Grundy VA 24614 Office: Box 2774 Pikeville KY 41501

HOWARD, RHEA, newspaper pub.; b. Wichita Falls, Tex., July 25, 1892; s. Ed and Jettie Lee (Malony) H.; student Trinity U., Waxahachie, Tex., 1910-11, Eastman Coll., Poughkeepsie, N.Y., 1912; m. Kathleen Benson, Oct. 22, 1913; 1 dau., Anna Katherine (Mrs. James B. Barnett). With The Times Publishing Co. (Wichita Daily Times and Wichita Falls Record News) 1913—, pres., 1948—; v.p., dir. Indsl. Devel., Inc.; dir. Burlington Ry. Mem. Wichita Falls Sch. Bd.; mem. nat. adv. council Airline Passengers Assn.; mem. YMCA adv. bd.; active ARC, Wichita Falls Art Museum. Area Health Facility Planning Com.; bd. dirs. Midwestern U. Found., Red River Valley Assn., Wichita Falls United Fund, Wichita Falls Symphony, Wichita Falls Bd. Commerce and Industry Texas Law Enforcement Found. Mem. Tex. State Democratic Exec. Com.; past chmn. senatorial dist.; past del. Nat. Dem. Conv. Served to 1st lt. N.G. U.S. Army, World War I. Named Pub. of Year, Headliners Club, 1960; named Salesman of Year Wichita Falls, 1970. Mem. Am. Soc. Newspaper Editors, N. Tex. Oil and Gas Assn. (dir.), Am., So. (dir.) newspaper pubs. assns., Tex. Daily Newspaper Assn., C. of C. (dir.), Asso. Press, Tex. Council Higher Edn. (charter; exec. com.), Sigma Delta Chi. Presbyterian. Club: President's, Wichita Falls County, Wichita, Nat. Press, Masons (33 deg.), Shriners, K.T. Home: 2105 Berkley Dr Wichita Falls TX 76308 Office: Times Publishing Co PO Box 120 1301 Lamar Wichita Falls TX 76307

HOWARD, ROBERT BRUCE, physician, surgeon; b. Oklahoma City, Mar. 18, 1913; s. Searcy Bennett and Beryl (Ott) H.; B.S., U. Okla., 1934, M.D., 1936; m. Marjorie Mary Newbern, Oct. 21, 1938 (dec. Dec. 1970); children—Diane Howard Appelbaum, Robert M. Intern, Central Dispensary and Emergency Hosp., Washington, 1936-37; resident St. Vincent Hosp., Los Angeles, 1937-38, Okla. U. Hosp., Oklahoma City, 1936; practice medicine specializing in surgery, Oklahoma City, 1938—; mem. staff Mercy Hosp., Presbyn. Hosp., Baptist Hosp., University Hosp., Vets. Hosp., Childrens Meml. Hosp.; sec. of staff St. Anthony Hosp., 1970-75, chief of staff, 1976—; instr. surgery Okla. U., 1940-48, clin. prof., 1958—. Served with M.C., AUS, 1941-46. Decorated Bronze Star medal. Diplomate Am. Bd. Surgery. Fellow A.C.S.; mem. Am. Thyroid Assn., Southwestern Surg. Congress (pres. 1967-68), Am., Okla. med. assns., Oklahoma County Med. Soc., Oklahoma City Clin. Soc., Oklahoma City Surg. Soc. (pres. 1960), Southwestern Soc. Nuclear Medicine, Okla. Surg. Assn., Oklahoma City Acad. Medicine (pres. 1964), Am. Coll. Nuclear Medicine, Soc. Nuclear Medicine. Presbyterian. Clubs: Oklahoma City Golf and Country, Doctors Dinner; Mens Dinner. Office: 544 Pasteur Bldg 1111 N Lee St Oklahoma City OK 73103

HOWARD, ROBERT DAVID, investment banker; b. Toledo, Mar. 18, 1945; s. Herbert Jacob and Beatrice Henriette (Ettinger) H.; B.S., Mass. Inst. Tech., 1967; M.B.A., U. Pa., 1969. Treas., dir. internat. fin. Lang Engring. Co., Coral Gables, Fla., 1971-76; prin. Fla. Cons. Group, Miami, 1976—; pres. N.R.G. Builders Corp., Miami, 1977—; prin. M.G. Lewis & Co., Winter Park, Fla., 1977—; sec.-treas. Besman, Inc., Miami, 1976—. Served with U.S. Army, 1969-71. Mem. Inst. Mgmt. Scis., Nat. Assn. Securities Dealers. Jewish. Home: 9240 W Bay Harbor Dr Bay Harbor Islands FL 33154 Office: 2319 Ponce de Leon Blvd Coral Gables FL 33134

HOWARD, ROBERT EUGENE, banker; b. Greenville, S.C., Dec. 5, 1946; s. Robert L. and Eugenia B. (Jones) H.; B.A., Davidson Coll., 1968; M.B.A., Furman U., 1976; grad. Nat. Comml. Lending Sch., Norman, Okla., 1973; m. Martha Matthews, Sept. 1, 1968; 1 dau., Amy Elizabeth. Br. mgr. Bankers Trust of S.C., Greenville, 1971-73, asst. mgr., then mgr. credit dept., 1973-74, comml. lending officer, 1974-76, sr. comml. lending officer, 1976—; instr. Greenville chpt. Am. Inst. Banking; chmn. Downtown Loan Pool, 1978—. Bd. dirs. Peoples Market, 1977—; asso. deacon 1st Baptist Ch., 1979—. Served to 1st lt. U.S. Army, 1968-71; Vietnam. Decorated Bronze Star; cert. comml. lender Am. Bankers Assn. Mem. Am. Inst. Banking, Greenville Bus. Assn. (1st v.p. 1978-79), C. of C. Club: Greenville Country. Home: 307 McDaniel Ave Greenville SC 29601 Office: Bankers Trust of SC PO Box 608 Greenville SC 29602

HOWARD, TED EMMITT, JR., govt. computer specialist; b. Bristol, Va., Dec. 26, 1941; s. Ted Emmitt and Josephine Elizabeth (Taylor) H.; A.B. in Math., U. Chattanooga, 1967; m. Pauline Kathryn Dickson, June 14, 1969; children—Ted Emmitt, Laura Elizabeth. Bank teller Hamilton Nat. Bank, Chattanooga, 1962-63; with TVA, Chattanooga, 1963—, planning asst., 1973-76, research analyst, 1977—; mem. computer sci. and data processing tech. adv. com. Chattanooga State Tech. Community Coll., 1975-77, instr. dept. bus. and commerce, 1976—. Recipient Citizenship award Am. Legion, 1957. Baptist. Contbr. poems to poetry anthologies. Home: 4223 Forest Plaza Dr Hixson TN 37343 Office: 180 Lupton Bldg Chattanooga TN 37401

HOWARD, THELMA LILLIAN, poet; b. Pitts., Mar. 14, 1925; s. Samuel A. and Hattie G. (Horelick) Yanks; B.S., U. Pitts., 1952, M. Letters, 1958; m. George E. Howard III, June 2, 1962. Works include: (poetry) Thoughts in Winter, 1973, Summer Loves, 1979; poetry reading Folger Library, 1975; tchr. pub. schs., Pitts., 1952, Miami, 1972-74, Washington, 1978—. Recipient Gato award, 1968. Mem. Washington Ind. Writers, Women Writers Assn. Home: 400 King's Point Dr Miami Beach FL 33160

HOWARD, THOMAS EDWARD, SR., real estate broker; b. Delhi, La., Nov. 25, 1913; s. Primous and Lillie Bell (Shelton) H.; B.A., So. U., 1939; M.Ed., Bishop Coll., 1954; postgrad. Concordia Coll., 1965, La. State U., 1970, La. Tech. U., 1971; m. Estella Rebecca Smith, Aug. 15, 1935; children—Thomas Edward, Primous, Edna, Diane (Mrs. Spencer Jordan), Dottie Joe (Mrs. Dennis Kichen), Lindell Howard Anderson, Rebecca, Carl. Prin., Oakhill High Sch., Shreveport, La., 1939-56, Greenmoor Sch., Shreveport, 1956-61, Linear Jr.-Sr. High Sch., Shreveport, 1961-71, Green Oaks High Sch., Shreveport, 1971-73; real estate agt. Burks Real Estate, 1971-75. Bd. dirs. David Raines Recreation Center. Recipient Outstanding Achivement award Kappa Alpha Psi, 1972. Concordia Coll. study grantee, 1965. Mem. N.E.A., Caddo Edn. Assn., La. Edn. Assn., So. U. Alumni Assn. (mem. exec. council 1962-75), Kappa Alpha Psi. Mason (32 deg., Shriner). Kiwanian. African Methodist Episcopal (trustee bd. 1950-75). Home: Route 6 Box 595 Shreveport LA 71109 Office: 2211 Jewella St Shreveport LA 71109

HOWARD, VIRGIL LEE, coal co. exec.; b. Paintsville, Ky., Oct. 6, 1917; s. John Lewis and Rose (Dale) H.; m. Ida Mae Preston, Nov. 25, 1937; children—Bruce, Carolyn, Wilma, Patricia, Vicki, Janie. Various positions Princess Eichorn Coal Co., David, Ky., 1944-65; mine foreman Sewell Coal Co., Richwood, W.Va., 1965-66; with Clinchfield Coal Co., Dante, Va., 1966—, now div. mgr.; ordained minister Baptist Ch., 1961; pastor United Bapt. Ch., Clintwood, Va., 1968—. Named hon. Ky. Col. Mem. Va. Mining Inst. Republican. Club: Masons. Home: Box 297 Clintwood VA 24228 Office: Clinchfield Coal Co Dante VA 24283

HOWARD, WILLIAM RAYMOND, mental health adminstr., ret. navy chaplain; b. South Carrollton, Ky., Feb. 3, 1927; s. Ray Livingston and Ruby Lee (Nicholls) H.; A.B., Georgetown Coll., 1949; B.D., So. Baptist Theol. Sem., 1953, M.Div., 1960; LL.B., La Salle U., 1970; Th.D., Luther Rice Sem., 1973; m. Doris Bernice Schreck, Aug. 27, 1948; children—Sherri Lynn, Sandra Michelle, David Allan. Ordained to ministry, 1948; served with U.S. Navy, from 1944, advanced through grades to capt., 1976; chaplain, U.S., Korea, Vietnam, Japan, 1953-73; mem. staff chief of Naval Tech. Tng. Sch., Memphis, 1974-76, ret., 1976; dir. adminstrn. Collier County Mental Health Clinic, Inc., Naples, Fla., 1976—; lectr. psychology of religion, comparative religion Albany Jr. Coll.; lectr. psychology U. So. Calif. Recipient Distinguished Service medal U.S. Govt., 1976; named Mil. Man of Year, Memphis, 1975; recipient Outstanding Leadership award Mallory Knights of Memphis, 1975. Mem. Coll. Chaplains, Protestant Hosp. Assn., Mil. Order of World Wars, ARC, Navy Relief Soc., Nat. Youth Services, Chaplains Commn., Ministerial Alliance of Collier County, Heroes of 76, Pi Kappa Alpha. Clubs: Masons, Lions. Contbr. articles to So. Baptist, Disciples of Christ publs. Home: 47 Mahogany Dr Naples FL 33940 Office: 4099 Tamiami Trail N Suite 301 Naples FL 33940

HOWARD, WILLIE ABBAY, planter, former state ofcl.; b. Tunica, Miss., June 5, 1891; d. William G. and George Anne Elizabeth (Irwin) Abbay; student U. Miss., summer 1933; m. Thomas Percy Howard, Oct. 12, 1920 (dec.); children—Thomas Percy (dec.), George Anne Irwin (Mrs. Robert Peel Sayle), Elizabeth Irwin (Mrs. Cooper Yerger Robinson). Partner, Howard Plantation, Lake Cormorant, Miss., 1922-55, owner, operator, 1955—. Commr. Yazoo-Miss. Delta Levee Bd., 1955-75; welfare dir. DeSoto County, Miss., 1932-36, DeSoto and Tate counties, 1933-34; organizer, instr. Gulf div. A.R.C., 1917-18; co-organizer, trustee DeSoto County Library Bd., 1946—, chmn. bd. trustees, 1970-75; co-organizer Citizens Library Movement, DeSoto County, Miss., 1947, first Regional Library Miss., 1950, trustee, 1950-63; pres. Miss. Citizen's Library Movement, 1950-52; del. nat. conv. Nat. Rivers and Harbors Congress, Washington, 1964. Trustee Northwest Jr. Coll., Senatobia, Miss., 1943-77. Recipient citation for flood control work Miss. River Commn., 1974, Outstanding Civilian Service medal, 1976; Meritorious Service award Yazoo-Miss. Delta Levee Bd., 1975; Spl. Alumni Assn. award, 1979; honored by naming of Willie Abbay Howard Coliseum, N.W. Jr. Coll., 1979. Mem. Miss. Fedn. Women's

Clubs (state rec. sec. 1920-22), English-Speaking Union, Memphis Execs., Lower Miss. Valley Flood Control Assn. (v.p. 1961, 71), D.A.R., Colonial Dames 17th Century (Woman of Yr. Miss. 1977). Presbyn. Clubs: Memphis Country, Memphis Woman's (pres. 1968-69), Tunica County Woman's (founder 1914, pres. 1916, 1921, 28-29, trustee 1915—). Editor: DeSoto County C.L.M. Handbook, 1946. Address: Howard Plantation Lake Cormorant MS 38641

HOWE, CARROLL LEON, motel and restaurant co. exec.; b. Morgantown, Pa., Dec. 25, 1938; s. Wilkins Brinton and Mary Y. (Yoder) H.; B.S., Bob Jones U., 1961; M.B.A., W.Va. U., 1967; m. Angelyn Karleen Howe, Apr. 27, 1963; children—Kimberly, Kara. Pub. accountant Witschey, Harmon & White, C.P.A.'s, Charleston, W.Va., 1963-67; controller Clayton Industries, Marmora, N.J., 1967-70; controller, treas., dir. Residex Corp. subs. Sun Oil Co., Marmora, N.J., 1970-73; pres., dir. Howe Assos. Inc., Dover, Del., 1973—; fin. cons., 1973—. Pres. Gideons Internat. N.J., 1975-78. Served with U.S.N.G., 1960-67. Recipient Spl. Manuscript award Nat. Assn. Accountants, 1967; C.P.A. Mem. Am. Inst. C.P.A.'s, W.Va., N.J. socs. C.P.A.'s. Republican. Home: Rt 2 Box 122E Inman SC 29349 Office: I-85 & Boiling Springs Rd Spartanburg SC 29303

HOWE, COURTNEY EVERETT, SR., med. services adminstr.; b. Cuba, N.Y., Aug. 30, 1932; s. Everett Erie and Madiline (Taylor) H.; B.S. in Psychology, Pa. State U., 1954; M.S., St. Bonaventure U., 1963; m. Marie Maude Fowler, Apr. 7, 1967; children—Linnea, Karen Annette, Lisa Cross, Courtney E. Personnel supr. Acme Electric Corp., Cuba, 1959-63; employee relations mgr. Celanese Fibers Co., Charlotte, N.C., 1963-65; personnel dir. Rockwell Internat. Corp., Winchester, Ky., 1965-67; pres. Jordan Howe & Associates, Atlanta, 1967-75, 80—; pres., chmn. bd. Cape Coral (Fla.) Med. Clinic, 1976-79. Bd. dirs. YMCA, Lee County, Fla., 1978—. Served to lt. USN, 1956-59. Mem. Am. Coll. Med. Group Mgrs., Med. Group Mgmt. Assn. of Fla. (pres. 1976-77, regional coordinator 1977-78), Med. Group Mgmt. Assn. Republican. Clubs: Sporting (Atlanta); Royal Palm Yacht (Ft. Myers, Fla.). Contbr. articles to publs. on health care. Home: 1479 Ashford Pl Atlanta GA 30319 Office: Suite 171 2971 Flowers Rd Atlanta GA 30341

HOWE, DEBORAH OGLE, telephone co. exec.; b. Benson, Minn., Apr. 29, 1948; d. Howard Daniel and Shirley Marie (Carpenter) Ogle; B.A., Macalester Coll., St. Paul, 1969; m. Thomas Vincent Howe, Apr. 30. Exec. sec. GAC Corp., Miami, 1970-71; communications adviser So. Bell Telephone Co., Miami, 1972-73, supr. area mktg., 1973-74, mgr. bus. services, 1974-77, dir. So. Fla. Communications Center, 1977-79, staff mgr. bus. mktg., 1980—. Recipient Outstanding Service award Vocat. Indsl. Clubs Am., 1976. Mem. Macalester Coll. Alumni Assn. (Fla., Ga., Ala. chmn. recruitment activities 1974—), Internat. Platform Assn., Soc. Advancement Mgmt. (pres. Atlanta chpt.), Nat. Assn. Female Execs. Baptist. Home: 1079 Redan Trail Ct Stone Mountain GA 30088 Office: 316 1st Nat Bank Tower Atlanta GA 30303

HOWE, EVELYN FREEMAN, educator; b. Spartanburg, S.C., Jan. 11, 1929; d. Denver Odell and Tabitha Jane (Bryson) Freeman; A.B., Limestone Coll., 1948; M.A.T., Winthrop Coll., 1967; m. Jack Dean Howe, June 10, 1950; children—Andrew Walter, Angela Jane. Tchr. social studies and civics Whitmire (S.C.) High Sch.; case worker Social Services Bur., Portsmouth, Va.; tchr. Draytonville Elementary Sch., Gaffney, S.C.; prin. Corinth, Draytonville, Alma Elementary Schs., Cherokee County Sch. Dist. I, Gaffney; now tchr. Blacksburg (S.C.) Elementary Sch. No. 2. Pres. Town and Gown Concert Com., Gaffney; pres. S.C. Conf. on Status of Women; pres. women's group Presbyn. Ch. Named Alumna of Decade, Limestone Coll., Gaffney, recipient Alumni Service to Community award; People to People Goodwill Ambassador U.S. to Europe. Mem. Cherokee County (pres.), S.C. (mem. del. assembly) edn. assns., NEA, Cherokee County Literacy Soc., AAUW (past pres. Gaffney br., v.p. S.C. div.), Cherokee Hist. and Preservation Soc. Club: Gaffney Jr. Women's (past pres.). Home: 219 Crestview Dr Gaffney SC 29340 Office: Academy St Blacksburg SC 29702

HOWE, LYMAN HAROLD, III, chemist; b. Wilkes-Barre, Pa., Nov. 5, 1938; s. Lyman Harold and Esther Madeline (Smith) H.; B.S., Duke U., 1960; M.S., Emory U., 1961; Ph.D., U. Tenn., 1966; m. Mary Louise Reinhart, June 16, 1962; 1 dau., Jennifer. Research asso. Emory U., 1960-61; research and teaching asso. U. Tenn., 1962-66; research chemist div. natural resources sers. TVA, Chattanooga, 1966—. Mem. ASTM (water com. results advisor 1976—, chmn. voltammetry task group 1975—, sec. on instrumentation atmospheres subcom.), Am. Chem. Soc., Nat. Mgmt. Assn., AAAS. Presbyterian. Clubs: Torch (2d v.p. chpt. 1980), Signal Mountain CB, The Nost. Co-author publs. in field. Home: 1241 Mountain Brook Circle Signal Mountain TN 37377 Office: 150-401 Chestnut St Chattanooga TN 37401

HOWELL, CHARLES MAITLAND, educator; b. Thomasville, N.C., Apr. 14, 1914; s. Cyrus Maitland and Lilly Mae (Ammons) H.; B.S., Wake Forest U., 1935; M.D., U. Pa., 1937; m. Betty Jane Myers, Feb. 12, 1949; children—Elizabeth Myers, Pamela Jane. Intern, Charity Hosp., New Orleans, 1937-38; resident medicine Burlington County Hosp., Mt. Holley, N.J., 1938-39; sch. physician Lawrenceville (N.J) Sch., 1939-42; resident pathology N.C. Baptist Hosp., Winston-Salem, 1947-48; resident dermatology Columbia Presbyn. Med. Center, N.Y.C., 1948-50; resident allergy Roosevelt Hosp., N.Y.C., 1950-51; practice medicine specializing in dermatology, Winston-Salem, N.C., 1951—; mem. staff N.C. Bapt. Hosp., Forsyth Meml. Hosp.; faculty Bowman Gray Sch. Medicine, Wake Forest U., Winston-Salem, 1951—, prof., head sect. on dermatology, 1961—. Served with M.C., AUS, 1942-46. Fellow Am. Acad. Dermatology, Am. Acad. Allergy; mem. N.Am. Clin. Dermatologic Soc., N.Y. Acad. Scis. Democrat. Baptist. Clubs: Old Town (Winston-Salem); Bermuda Run Country (Clemmons, N.C.). Home: 1100 Kent Rd E Winston-Salem NC 27104

HOWELL, FLOYD, JR., coll. adminstr.; b. Ocean Springs, Miss., Apr. 30, 1921; s. Floyd and Marion Rhea (Miller) H.; B.B.A., Tulane U., 1942; m. Teddy A. Biggers, Jan. 31, 1944; children—Teddy Jean Howell Lamey, Dorothy Marion Howell Moran. Salesman, IBM, Miami, Fla., 1945-50; dir. data processing U. Miami, 1950-67; dir. computer services Miami-Dade Community Coll., 1967-76, fiscal coordinator systems, planning and research, 1976-77, logistic specialist Open Coll., 1977—, asso. prof., 1967—. Deacon, Kendall Presbyterian Ch., Miami. Served to lt. USNR, 1942-45. Named to IBM 100% Club, 1947, 48, 49; recipient Meritorious Service award Miami-Dade Community Coll., 1977. Mem. Data Processing Mgmt. Assn. (chpt. pres. 1955), Fla. Assn. Ednl. Data Systems, Fla. Assn. Community Colls. Clubs: Masons, Shriners. Home: 8030 SW 96th St Miami FL 33156 Office: 11011 SW 104th St Miami FL 33176

HOWELL, FRANK, nutrition program adminstr.; b. Jersey City, July 18, 1916; s. George Edwin and Tillie Collins (Mott) H.; student Am. Inst. Banking, 1952-58; m. G. Alix Denham, July 1, 1938. Asst. to v.p. First Nat. Iron Bank, Morristown, N.J., 1950-61; owner New Haven Motel, Vergennes, Vt., 1961-71; real estate broker, Burlington-Stowe area, Vt., 1971-75; project dir. Nutrition Program for Elderly, Lord Fairfax Planning Dist., Winchester, Va., 1975—. Asst. to v.p. Winchester Apple Blossom Festival, 1975-79; Disaster chmn., bd. dirs. Winchester-Frederick County unit ARC; mem. adminstrv. bd. United Methodist Ch., Winchester, 1975—, steward, 1976—; chmn. continuing edn./community sers. advisory com. Lord Fairfax Community Coll.; public relations chmn. CROP for Hunger. Mem. Nat. Title VII Dirs. Assn. Club: Kiwanis (dir. 1976-79, chmn. communications and pub. relations 1975-79). Home: 812 National Ave Winchester VA 22601 Office: Route 1 Box 329-A Winchester VA 22601

HOWELL, HERBERT LEE, clergyman; b. Red Bay, Ala., Nov. 25, 1909; s. Emmett Presley and Ira Ethel (Johnson) H.; student Berry Coll., 1931; D.Th., Southwestern Bapt. Sem., 1941; postgrad. Miss. State U., 1944-46; m. Coy L.R. Homan, Aug. 28, 1938; children—Dexter, Geard, Gwen, Donald, Stanley, Byron, Janette, Gail, Conrad, Myra, Jerry. Ordained to ministry So. Baptist Conv., 1942; tchr. schs. in Miss., 1942-45; pastor chs., Pontotoc and Tippah counties, Miss., 1948—, Troy Bapt. Ch., Pontotoco, 1976—; chaplain, social service dir. Pontotoc Community Hosp., 1975—. Mem. Pontotoc County Bapt. Assn., Miss. Soc. Hosp. Social Work, Soc. Hosp. Work Dirs. Democrat. Club: Lions. Home: 309 Davis Rd Pontotoc MS 38863 Office: 309 Dack's Rd Pontotoc MS 38863

HOWELL, HUGH HAWKINS, JR., lawyer; b. Atlanta, Aug. 18, 1920; s. Hugh and Ethleen (Horne) H.; student Riverside Mil. Acad., Boys High Sch., Atlanta, Emory U., A.B., U. Ga., 1942; LL.B., John Marshall Law Sch., 1947, LL.M., 1958, J.D., 1959, LL.D., 1960; m. Dorris Callahan; children—Hugh Howell III, James Finn. Admitted to Ga. bar. Dir. Spring Lakes Apts., Inc., Bolton Apts. Mem. Ga. Vets. Service Bd., chmn., 1963-71. Rear adm. USNR. Mem. Judge Advs. Assn. (nat. pres. 1968), Am. Judicature Soc., Fed. (v.p. 5th U.S. Circuit), Am., Ga., Atlanta bar assns., Atlanta Hist. Soc., Am. Legion, Navy League (nat. dir.), Naval Res. Assn. (nat. v.p.), SAR (v.p. dist.), SCV (comdr.), Naval Hist. Found., Old Guard of Gate City Guard (comdt.), Phi Delta Theta, Sigma Delta Kappa. Clubs: Masons (32 deg.), Shrine, Jesters, Athletic, Ansley Golf, Nat. Lawyers, Old War Horse Lawyers. Home: 2811 Ridgewood Rd NW Atlanta GA 30327 Office: 1505 Rock Springs Circle NE Atlanta GA 30306

HOWELL, IRVIN NAPOLEON, telephone co. exec.; b. Chickasaw, Ala., Jan. 3, 1922; s. Irvin N. and Effie (Pierce) H.; B.S. in Elec. Engring., The Citadel, 1951; m. Betty Lou Hinson, July 6, 1943; children—Dorothy Jean, Robert Wayne, Connie. With So. Bell Tel. & Tel., various locations. 1951-53, 55-67, div. staff engr., Memphis, 1963-64, transmission staff engr., Atlanta, 1964-67; with South Central Bell Telephone Co., Birmingham, 1967—, engring. mgr. investment and costs div., 1972-73, engring. mgr. plant extension and costs div., 1973-76, asst. v.p. investment and econs., 1976-78, asst. v.p. rates and economics, 1978—. Served with USCGR, 1940-46. Registered profl. egr., Tenn., Miss. Fellow IEEE; mem. Industry Applications Soc. (past pres., chmn. policy and planning 1973), Inst. Elec. Engrs. (past chmn. student chpt., vice chmn. standards bd.), Nat. Assn. Corrosion Engrs. (past sec.). Home: 2529 Comanche Dr Birmingham AL 35244 Office: PO Box 771 600 N 19th St Birmingham AL 35201

HOWELL, JAMES FOREST, state senator; b. Wewoka, Okla., July 14, 1934; s. Forest F. and Lena (Hand) H.; B.S., Okla. Baptist U., 1956; J.D., Okla. U., 1963; m. Diann Harris, Dec. 21, 1956; children—Cheryl, David, Mark. Tchr., coach high schs. in Okla., 1956-59; admitted to Okla. bar, 1963; practice in Midwest City, 1963—; mcpl. judge, Midwest City, 1964-70; sr. partner firm Howell, Webber & Sharpe, 1969—; mem. Okla. Senate, 1970—. Bd. dirs. Midwest City YMCA, Bapt. Meml. Hosp., Midwest City. Named Man of Year in Midwest City, 1970; recipient Outstanding Legislator award Okla. Sch. Bd., 1974, Friend of Edn. award Okla. Edn. Assn., 1976, Spl. award Okla. Soc. Crippled Children's, 1976, award Phi Delta Kappa, 1977. Mem. Okla. County Bar Assn. (dir.). Democrat. Baptist. Club: Rotary. Home: 3101 Greenoaks St Midwest City OK 73110 Office: 2801 Parklaen Midwest City OK 73140

HOWELL, JENA BEA STONE, nurse, educator; b. Los Angeles, May 28, 1940; d. James McNeil and Frances Elizabeth (Hatchett) Stone; A.S. in Nursing, Texarkana Community Coll., 1962; B.S. in Sociology, Bradley U., 1974; postgrad. Tex. Woman's U., 1977; m. Milton L. Howell, Jr., June 3, 1963; children—Katherine Millee, James Ray, John Wesley. Staff nurse Children's Hosp., Dallas, 1963-64, VA Hosp., Dallas, 1964-66; dir. nursing service Washington (Ill.) Nursing Center, 1966-70; staff nurse II, Zeller Zone Center Comprehensive Community Mental Health Center, Peoria, Ill., 1970-74; instr. nursing, asso. degree nursing program Texarkana (Tex.) Community Coll., 1974—, mem. adv. bd. William Buchanan dept. nursing. Registered nurse, Ark., Tex. Mem. Am. Nurses Assn., Tex. Nurses Assn., Dist. 28 Nurses Assn., Texarkana Community Coll. Faculty Assn., Bradley U. Alumni Assn., William Buchanan Nursing Alumni, Women's Missionary Assn. Baptist. Home: Rural Route 2 Box 140 Fouke AR 71837 Office: Texarkana Community Coll 2600 N Robinson Rd Texarkana TX 75501

HOWELL, JIMMIE SYLVANUS, accountant; b. Forrest County, Miss., July 19, 1940; s. Clayton Eugene and Winnie Eloise (Morgan) H.; B.S. in Accounting, U. So. Miss., 1963; m. Judie Garlane Graham, July 30, 1960; children—Marcus Hunter, Bradley Graham. Pvt. practice masonry contracting, Hattiesburg, Miss., 1959-63; jr. accountant Haskins & Sells, New Orleans and N.Y.C., 1963-65, sr. accountant, 1965-70, prin., 1970-72; v.p., treas. Laitram Corp., New Orleans, 1972—, also dir.; pres., dir. Ryan Ramp, Inc.; v.p., treas., dir. Laitram Machinery, Inc.; sec.-treas., dir. Digicourse, Inc., Intralox, Inc., Tierra-Mar, Inc., Tuna, Inc., dir. Rochelles Inc., Juliette Coture, Inc. Served with USN, 1959. C.P.A., La., Miss., N.Y. Mem. La., New Orleans socs. C.P.A.'s, Am. Inst. C.P.A.'s. Club: Colonial Country. Home: 81 W Imperial Dr Harahan LA 70123 Office: PO Box 50699 New Orleans LA 70150

HOWELL, LEWIS DAVID, JR., educator; b. Macon, Ga., Oct. 30, 1922; s. Lewis David and Dovie Ritchey H.; B.S., U. So. Miss., 1953, M.S., 1961; B.D., Southwestern Bapt. Theol. Sem., 1958; J.D., YMCA Law Sch., 1975; postgrad. Mercer U. Law Sch., 1950-52, U. Houston, 1954, Miss. State U., 1964-67, Ind. State U., 1969-71; m. Beth Alexander, Aug. 31, 1956; children—Lewis David, Lester Daniel, Sarah Ann, Sharon Kay, Lynda Grace. Instr., Auburn U., 1961-63; asst. prof. Miss. State U. for Women, 1963-67; asso. prof. U. Evansville (Ind.), 1967-71, head dept. gen. bus. and fin., 1968-70; asso. prof. bus. law Tenn. State U., Nashville, 1971—; claims adjuster Indemnity Ins. Co., 1953-54; pastor Bapt. chs., Miss., Ala., 1959-67. Served with USN, 1942-48, 51-52. Mem. Am. Bus. Law Assn., Southeastern Bus. Law Assn. Club: Masons. Home: 4444 Andrew Jackson Pkwy Hermitage TN 37076 Office: Tenn State U Centennial Blvd Nashville TN 37203

HOWELL, MABLE SMITH (MRS. BRUCE INMAN HOWELL), former coll. librarian; b. Beaufort County, N.C., Sept. 21, 1942; d. Hyman L. and Thelma (Evans) Smith; B.S., East Carolina U., 1964, M.Ed. in L.S., 1967; postgrad. Duke, 1970; m. Bruce Inman Howell, Aug. 22, 1965; children—Bruce Inman, Virginia Lea. Librarian, Lenoir Community Coll., Kinston, N.C., 1964-76, instr., library tech. asst. curriculum 1970-76. Mem. N.C. State accreditation teams, 1969, 72, N.C. Com. for Edn. Librarianship, 1971. Fund coordinator Sampson County Heart Fund, 1978; Sampson County cookie coordinator Girl Scouts U.S.A., 1979, 80. Mem. Edn. Media Assn. (treas. dept. community colls. N.C. 1968-69, pres. 1969-71; dir. Eastern region N.C. 1967-68), N.C. Library Assn. scholarship com. 1971-75, chmn. 1974-75), Librarians Lenoir County (pres. 1974-75), Am. Assn. U. Women (rec. sec. Kinston br. 1969-71), N.C. Symphony, N.C. Hist. and Lit. Soc., Lenoir County Hist. Assn., N.C. Mus. Assn., Sampson County Arts Council. Club: Clinton Jr. Womans (dir. 1978—). Home: 109 Vista Dr Clinton NC 28328

HOWELL, MARK FRANKLIN, lawyer; b. El Paso, Tex., Nov. 19, 1934; s. Benjamin Randolph and Romaine (Safford) H.; B.A., Stanford U., 1956; LL.B., U. Tex., 1961; m. Linda O'Reilly, Jan. 5, 1973; children—Madeline, Celia, Cara. Admitted to Tex. bar, 1961; since practiced in El Paso; mem. firms Fryer, Milstead & Luscombe, 1961-62, Peticolas, Luscombe & Stephens, 1963-68, pvt. practice, 1969—. Founder, vice chmn., dir. El Paso Legal Assistance Soc., 1969-72; vice chmn. bd. commrs. El Paso Housing Authority, 1970-72; chmn. Mayor's Com. on Housing, 1969; chmn. legal com. Am. Civil Liberties Union, 1974-75. Bd. dirs. El Paso Alternative House, 1974-77. Served with AUS, 1956-58. Mem. Am., Inter-Am., El Paso bar assns., State Bar Tex., Tex. (dir. 1973—), El Paso (dir., pres. 1974—), trial lawyers assns., Sigma Chi, Phi Delta Phi. Democrat. Episcopalian. Editorial staff Tex. Trial Lawyers Forum, 1975. Contbr. articles in field to profl. jours. Home: 1008 Park Rd El Paso TX 79902 Office: 1011 N Mesa St El Paso TX 79902

HOWELL, RALPH RODNEY, pediatrician; b. Concord, N.C., June 10, 1931; s. Fred Lee and Grace Mary (Blackwelder) H.; B.S., Davidson Coll., 1957 M.D., Duke U., 1957; m. Sarah Vosburgh Esselstyn, Nov. 19, 1960; children—Grace Meyer, Elizabeth Eriksson, John Esselstyn. Intern, Duke, 1957-58, resident pediatrics, 1958-59, research fellow in pediatrics and medicine, 1959-60; clin. asso. and staff NIH, Bethesda, Md., 1960-64; asso. prof. pediatrics Johns Hopkins, Balt., 1964-72; pediatrician-in-chief Hermann Hosp., Houston, 1972—, chmn. med. bd. 1972—; prof., chmn. dept. pediatrics U. Tex. Med. Sch., Houston, 1972—; cons. pediatrics M.D. Anderson Hosp. and Tumor Inst. Mem. metabolism study sect. NIH, 1973—; mem. nat. clin. adv. com. Nat. Found. March of Dimes, 1973—. Served to sr. surgeon USPHS, 1960-64. Fellow Am. Acad. Pediatrics; mem. Am. Pediatric Soc., Soc. for Pediatric Research, Houston Pediatric Soc., Tex. Med. Assn., Pi Kappa Alpha. Club: Meml. Forest (Houston). Author: (with G.H. Thomas) Selected Screening Tests for Genetic Metabolic Diseases, 1973. Contbr. articles to profl. jours. Home: 11 Sandalwood Houston TX 77024 Office: Program in Pediatrics University of Texas Medical School at Houston 6400 W Cullen St Houston TX 77025

HOWELL, RONALD THOMAS, musician; b. Bristow, Okla., Jan. 24, 1942; s. Kermit Thurmond and Lillis Lou (Boulware) H.; B. Music Edn., Oklahoma City U., 1963; M. Music Edn., U. Okla., 1968, D. Music Edn., 1976; m. Margaret Jean Graham, Jan. 27, 1967; children—Julie Anne, Jeffrey Graham. Dir. bands Harrah (Okla.) High Sch., 1963-69, Bethel Coll., North Newton, Kans., 1970-72; chmn. dept. instrumental music Okla. Baptist U., Shawnee, 1972—. Mem. Am. Fedn. Musicians, Music Educators Nat. Conf., Nat. Assn. Coll. Wind and Percussion Instrs., Kappa Kappa Psi, Phi Beta Mu, Phi Mu Alpha, Lambda Chi Alpha. Home: 21 Birdie Ln Shawnee OK 74801 Office: Okla Baptist Univ Shawnee OK 74801

HOWELL, WILLIAM HARRY, educator; b. Wilson, N.C., Feb. 14, 1921; s. Harry and Annie Mae (Thompson) H.; A.B., Johnson C. Smith U., 1943; M.A. Atlanta U., 1947; postgrad Western Res. U., 1949-50; Ph.D., Ohio State U., 1957; m. Juanita Brooks, June 3, 1961; 1 dau., Sega Patricia. Instr. sociology Miles Coll., Birmingham, Ala., 1947-49; from asso. prof. to prof. S.C. State Coll., Orangeburg, 1953-61; prof. sociology N.C. Central U., Durham, 1961—, dir. grad. sociology, 1972-78, chmn. dept., 1966-72. Served with AUS, 1943-46. Mem. Am. Sociol. Assn., Alpha Kappa Delta, Nat. Caucus Black Sociologists, Omega Psi Phi. Presbyterian. Home: 314 Wayne Circle Durham NC 27707 Office: Dept Sociology NC Central Univ Durham NC 27707

HOWERTON, JAMES CLIFTON, JR., advt. co. exec.; b. San Antonio, May 23, 1948; s. James Clifton and Joyce E. (Reile) H.; student San Antonio Coll., 1967-69; student U. Tex., 1969-71; m. Carol Ann Hale, Aug. 7, 1971; children—Jenifer, Aubrey, Allison. Advt. mgr. F.W. Woolworth Co., Austin, Tex., 1971-72, San Antonio, 1972-73; account exec. Anderson & Lewis Advt., San Antonio, 1973-76; realtor asso. Deanie Owens Co., San Antonio, 1976—; founder, pres. Heritage Group, San Antonio, 1976—. Mem. Nat. Assn. Realtors, Am. Mktg. Assn., San Antonio Advt. Fedn., S.W. Assn. Advt. Agencies, San Antonio Bd. Realtors, San Antonio Builders Assn., Tex. Assn. Realtors, San Antonio C. of C. Club: Northcliffe Country. Home: 5010 Brookhead Ln Cibolo TX 78108 Office: Heritage Group 901 NE Loop 410 Suite 602 San Antonio TX 78209

HOWETT, JOHN, art historian; b. Kokomo, Ind., Aug. 7, 1926; s. Layke and Ruth (Spurgeon) H.; B.F.A., Herron Inst., Indpls., 1953; M.A. (univ. fellow), U. Chgo., 1962, Ph.D. (Med. and Ren. Inst. fellow), 1968; m. Catherine Mahony, Aug. 17, 1957; children—Meghan, Maeve, Kateri, Ciannat. Asst. prof., curator art U. Notre Dame, 1962-66; mem. faculty Emory U., Atlanta, 1966—, asso. prof. art history, 1969—; bd. govs. High Mus. Art, Atlanta Coll. Art. Served with AUS, 1944-46. Mem. Coll. Art Assn., Southeastern Coll. Art Assn. Roman Catholic. Author: Italian Renaissance Illuminations, 1972, The New Image, 1976. Office: Dept Art History Emory Univ Atlanta GA 30322

HOWEY, JOHN RICHARD, architect; b. New Haven, Jan. 13, 1932; s. Joseph Herman and Dorothy (Good) H.; B.S. in Architecture, Ga. Inst. Tech., 1956, B.Arch., 1957; m. Maria Andrea Hatges, Sept. 8, 1968; children—John, Dorothy. With various archtl. firms in Tampa Bay, Fla., and Atlanta, 1958-61; project architect Harvard & Jolly, Architects, St. Petersburg, Fla., 1961-63; pres. John Howey, Architect, A.I.A., Tampa, Fla., 1963-73; pres. John Howey Asso., Tampa, 1973—. Participant Fla. State Architect's Traveling Show, 1967. Served with C.E., AUS, 1957, 62. Winner St. Petersburg Shelter competition, 1977. Mem. AIA (treas. Fla. Central 1965-66, dir. 1966-68), Sertoma Internat., Tampa Sertoma Club (dir. 1970-71, v.p. 1972-73), Tau Sigma Delta. Episcopalian. Club: Tower (Tampa). Prin. works include: Bierley Residence, Tampa, 1970, McPherson Residence, Orlando, Fla., 1973, Classroom Bldg. A at U. South Fla., 1974, Louis Pappas Restaurant, Tarpon Springs, Fla., 1975, Bay Villa Townhouses, Tampa, 1976, Dr. Albert Davis Office, 1977, Hillsborough County Maintenance Facilities, 1978, Tampa City Hall Plaza, 1979. Home: 1507 Bay Villa Pl Tampa FL 33609 Office: 101 S Franklin St Suite 200 Tampa FL 33602

HOWGATE, DAVID WASHBURNE, research physicist; b. Swedesboro, N.J., Oct. 11, 1932; s. George Washburne and Ann Townsend (Powell) H.; B.S., Marshall U., 1954; M.S., W.Va. U., 1955; Ph.D., U. Ala., 1967; m. Edith Lucille Richardson, Mar. 6, 1964; children—Beverly Kay, Edie Roberta, Erika Leigh. Physicist, U.S. Army Rocket Guided Missile Agy., Redstone Arsenal, Ala., 1959-63, research physicist solid state phys. scis. dir. U.S. Army Missile Command, Redstone Arsenal, 1963-71, research physicist Army High Energy Laser Lab., U.S. Army Missile Research and Devel. Command, 1971-77, research physicist missile research dir., 1977—. Served with U.S. Army, 1957-59. Mem. Am. Phys. Soc., N.Y. Acad. Scis., AAAS, Assn. U.S. Army, Sigma Xi, Sigma Pi Sigma, Phi Eta Sigma. Presbyterian. Clubs: Elks, Toastmasters Internat. Contbr. articles to profl. jours. Patentee in field. Home: 7800 Smoke Rise Rd SE Huntsville AL 35802 Office: DRDMI TRD Bldg 7700 Redstone Arsenal AL 35809

HOWIE, HENRY SANFORD, JR., children's agy. exec.; b. Abbeville, S.C., Oct. 10, 1927; s. Sanford and Anna (Biggers) H.; B.A., Presbyn. Coll., 1950; postgrad. U. Ark., 1953, Furman U., 1954, Winthrop Coll., 1955-56; M.S.W., U. N.C., 1965; m. Betty Jane Shirley, Dec. 20, 1949; children—Lynda Elizabeth, Anna Shirley, Genevieve Sharpe, Henry Sanford III, Robert Marcus. Coach, prin., Norway, S.C., 1949-50; trainee Deering Milliken, 1951-52; sch. prin., Rock Hill (S.C.) Pub. schs., 1952-57; exec. dir. Episcopal Ch. Home for Children, York, S.C., 1957—. Del., White House Conf. on Children, 1970. Bd. mem. S.C. Social Welfare Forum, 1967—, S.C. Com. on Children and Youth, 1966—; chmn. S.C. Com. on Childhood Mental Illness, 1971—; v.p. York County Council on Alcoholism, 1971-72; del. dir. S.C. Mental Health Assn.; chmn. regional adv. com. S.C. Dept. Pub. Welfare; mem. Gov.'s Sub-com. for Social Planning, 1974—; mem. mental health com. Catawba Regional Health Planning Council, 1974—. Bd. dirs. Tri-County Mental Health Center; pres. bd. govs. Group Child Care Cons. Services. Served with USNR, 1945-46. Mem. Nat. Assn. Social Workers, Acad. Certified Social Workers, Southeastern Child Care Assn. (pres. 1966-67), York County Mental Health Assn. (pres. 1968), Pi Kappa Phi (pres. Beta chpt. 1948). Episcopalian (sr. warden 1965-67, vestryman 1955-58). Rotarian (pres. York 1964). Clubs: Springlake Country (York), Crustbreakers (pres. 1966-67). Address: Episcopal Ch Home for Children York SC 29745

HOWISON, JUANITA CARMACK (MRS. CLAUDE F. HOWISON), educator, artist; b. nr. Bristol, Va.; d. Alexander Watson and Lillie (Craig) Carmack; student U. Va., summer 1939, George Washington U., 1945-46, summer 1948, Corcoran Sch. Art, 1951; B.S. in Edn., Madison Coll., 1959; m. Claude Frederick Howison, May 1, 1948. Tchr., Konnarock (Va.) Sch., 1929-36, Highland View Sch., Washington County, Va., 1936-41, Central Sch., Abington, Va., 1941-42, Herndon (Va.) Elementary Sch., 1942-46, Primary Day Sch., Washington, 1946-50, Fairlington (Va.) Elementary Sch., 1950; private tutor, 1950-56; remedial reading tchr., supr. Ft. Myer Elementary Sch., 1957-59; tchr. Potomac Elementary Sch., McLean, Va., 1960-67, tchr. spl. edn. Markham Sch., Ft. Belvoir, Va., 1967—; tchr. Haycock Elementary Sch., Falls Church, Va. Exhibited group shows Smithsonian Instn., 1952, 53, 62, Arts Club, D.C., 1966, 67, No. Va. Artists 1961-68, U. Va., 1966-68, Reston (Va.) Gallery, 1967, others. Mem. Nat. League Am. Pen Women (nat. biennial art exhibit chmn. 1954-56, Va. pres. 1963-64, state art chmn. 1965-66, nat. librarian 1965-66, nat. research chmn. 1966-67, mem. nat. art bd., pres. Alexandria br. 1978-80), NEA, Internat. Reaoing Assn., Greater Washington Reading Council, Arlington Council Spl. Edn., Am. Arts League Washington, McLean Art Club (pres. 1978), Nat. Enamelist Guild, Art Club Washington, No. Va. Art League, Fine Arts Center Roanoke, Delta Kappa Gamma. Presbyterian. Clubs: McLean Women's, Order Eastern Star. Home: 1512 Hardwood Ln McLean VA 22101

HOWLAND, RONALD LLOYD, lawyer; b. Houston, Mar. 27, 1934; s. Aaron Tucker and Ruth Mae (Skinner) H.; B.B.A., U. Okla., 1956; J.D., Oklahoma City U., 1964; m. Ellenmarie Myers, June 17, 1961; 1 dau., Ann Marie. Admitted to Okla. bar, 1964; clk. FBI, Oklahoma City, 1960, district cts., 1960-62, U.S. probation officer U.S. Cts., 1962-65, legal asst. U.S. Dist. Judge, 1965-67; asst. U.S. atty. U.S. Dept. Justice, Oklahoma City, 1967-69; atty. Monnet, Hayes, Bullis, Thompson & Edwards, Oklahoma City, 1969-78; U.S. magistrate Western Dist. Okla., 1978—. Spl. lectr. Oklahoma City U. Sch. w, 1967-69. Bd. dirs., chmn. service to mil. families com. A.R.C., 1972—. Served to lt. col. Okla. N.G., 1956—. Mem. Am., Okla., Oklahoma County (dir.), Fed. bar assns., Legal Aid Soc. (pres. bd. dirs. 1972), Alumni Assn. Oklahoma City U. Sch. Law (pres. 1970-71). Democrat. Methodist (mem. adminstrv. bd. 1968—). Mason (32 deg.), Rotarian. Home: 3104 N Astoria St Oklahoma City OK 73122 Office: 3032 US Courthouse 200 NW 4th St Oklahoma City OK 73102

HOWLETT, GEORGE FRANCIS, JR., builder, land devel. and real estate exec.; b. Bklyn., Oct. 16, 1931; s. George Francis and Helen (Leavell) H.; B.B.A., St. John's U., 1956; postgrad. Hofstra U., 1962; m. Gloria R. Childs, Nov. 3, 1962; children—Drew, Celeste, Brian, Doug. Mktg. dir. pharm. div. Union Carbide Co., N.Y.C., 1967-69; sr. v.p. Sudler & Hennessey div. Young & Rubicam, N.Y.C., 1969-76; mng. partner Grant, Howlett and Moorhead, N.Y., 1976-78; sr. v.p. Mich. Homes, Inc., Naples, Fla., 1978—. Served with U.S. Army, 1953-55. Mem. Pharm. Advt. Club, Pharm. Mfrs. Assn. Republican. Roman Catholic. Clubs: Elks, Rotary, K.C. Home: 1600 Murex Ln Naples FL 33940 Office: 603 5th Ave S Naples FL 33940

HOWLETT, MARLENE SMITH, nurse; b. Wilmington, N.C., Oct. 12, 1947; d. Robert Granville and Zara (Smith) Smith; B.S. in Nursing, Med. Coll. Va., 1969, M.S. in Nursing, 1976; m. Edwin B. Howlett, Jr., Dec. 16, 1967; children—Robert Edwin, Malinda Carrie. Staff nurse St. Marys Hosp., Richmond, Va., 1969-70; staff nurse Petersburg (Va.) Gen. Hosp., part time 1971-78; instr. nursing Petersburg Gen. Sch. Nursing, 1971-73, asst. dir., 1973-76; dir. Sch. Asso. Degree Nursing, John Tyler Community Coll., Chester, Va., 1976—; cons. Va. State U., Petersburg, Va. Nurses Assn. Mem. Va. Nurses Assn. (dist. 13 pres. 1977-79), Am. Nurses Assn., Va. League Nursing, Nat. League Nursing, Sigma Theta Tau. Episcopalian. Home: 13418 Harrowgate Rd Chester VA 23831 Office: 13101 Jefferson Davis Hwy Chester VA 23831

HOWRY, HAMILTON HUBBARD, JR., mfg. co. exec.; b. Oak Park, Ill., Nov. 7, 1922; s. Hamilton Hubbard and Harriet Ruth (Zoller) H.; student Cornell U., 1940-42, Columbia U., 1942-43; m. Jo Ann Muir, Apr. 7, 1945; 1 son, Hamilton H. With Am. Can. Co., 1943-69, commodity mgr., 1962-65, new products project mgr., 1965-69; pres. Howry Assos., Inc., Dallas, 1970—. Pres. Exhibitors Adv. Council, 1956-57. Served with U.S. Army, 1943. Mem. Soc. Packaging and Handling Engrs., Packaging Inst., Soc. Cosmetic Chemists. Presbyterian. Address: 4509 Hockaday Dr Dallas TX 75229

HOWSE, HAROLD DARROW, research inst. adminstr.; b. Poplarville, Miss., Nov. 8, 1928; s. William Jefferson and Artie Mittie (Smith) H.; student Pearl River Jr. Coll., 1945-47; B.S., U. So. Miss., Hattiesburg, 1959, M.S., 1960; Ph.D., Tulane U., 1967; m. Mittie Hazel Gibson, Dec. 18, 1960; children—Trijetta L. (Mrs. Ernest H. Cropp), Claude Demitris Gibson. Instr. zoology Miss. Coll., Jackson, 1960; instr. biology U. So. Miss., 1960-63, prof., 1973—; NIH trainee Tulane U., New Orleans, 1963-67; head sect. microscopy Gulf Coast Research Lab., Ocean Springs, Miss., 1967-79, asst. dir., 1971, acting dir., 1971-72, dir., 1972-79, editor Gulf Research Reports, 1974—; prof. zoology Miss. State U., 1972—, U. Miss., 1972—; mem. Miss. Marine Resources Council, 1971-79. Served with USN, 195-54. Mem. Am. Assn. Anatomists, AAAS, Am. Microscopical Soc., Am. Soc. Zoologists, Am. Soc. Cell Biology, Electron Microscope Soc. Am., Assn. Southeastern Biologists, Gulf Estuarine Research Soc., Herpetologists' League, Internat. Assn. Astracology, Miss. Acad. Sci. (pres. 1973-74), So. Soc. Anatomists, Soc. Research Adminstrs., S.E. Electron Microscope Soc., N.Y. Acad. Scis., Sigma Xi, Beta Beta Beta (Top Upperclass award 1958), Alpha Epsilon Delta, Omicron Delta Kappa, Pi Kappa Pi. Editor (founding) Marine Briefs, 1972-74. Contbr. articles to profl. jours. Home: 4713 Hilma St Moss Point MS 39563 Office: E Beach St Ocean Springs MS 39564

HOWSE, PAUL THOMAS, JR., mech. engr.; b. Birmingham, Ala., Feb. 16, 1931; s. Paul Thomas and Ella Ann (Bowers) H.; B.S.M.E., U. Ala., 1959; m. Ruby Cardin, June 4, 1955; children—Karen Leigh, Lisa Anne. Asso. engr. So. Research Inst., Birmingham, 1959-61; engr. Hayes Internat. Corp., Birmingham, 1962-63; sr. specialist Monsanto Textiles Co., Pensacola, Fla., 1963—. Served with USAF, 1950-52. Recipient award for excellence in machine design Machinery Mag., 1959; registered profl. engr., Fla. Mem. ASME (chmn. N.W. Fla. sect. 1969-70, v.p. Region XI 1974-76), Pi Tau Sigma, Tau Beta Pi. Baptist. Clubs: Krewe of Lafitte (pres. 1979-80), Moose. Patentee field of textile processing and equipment. Home: 3125 Logan Dr Pensacola FL 32503 Office: PO Box 12830 Pensacola FL 32575

HOWSE, WILLIAM LEWIS, III, gerontologist; b. Fort Worth, Nov. 20, 1936; s. William Lewis and Genevieve (Morgan) H.; B.A., Union U., Jackson, Tenn., 1960; M.R.E., Southwestern Bapt. Theol. Sem., Ft. Worth, 1963, Ed.D., 1972; postgrad. North Tex. State U., 1963, Vanderbilt U., 1968-69, U. So. Calif., 1976; m. Annette Craddock, Oct. 19, 1963; children—William Wesley, Annessa Kai. Youth dir. Broadway Bapt. Ch., Fort Worth, 1960-62; caseworker Buckner Bapt. Benevolences, Dallas, 1963-64; ordained to ministry Baptist Ch., 1964; minister of edn. Calvary Bapt. Ch., Garland, Tex., 1964-67; dir. orgn. Christian Life Commn. So. Bapt. Conv., Nashville, 1968-71; dir. alcohol and drug abuse sect. Tenn. Dept. Mental Health, Nashville, 1972-75; dir. Hurt Gerontol. Center, Va. Bapt. Homes, Culpeper, 1975—. Del. White House Conf. on Aging, 1971; dir. Southeastern Conf. Sch. of Drug Studies, 1974; pres. Southeastern Conf. Alcohol, Drug Programs, 1974-75. Bd. dirs. Council State, Territorial Alcoholism Authorities Inc., 1974-75, Dede Wallace Drug Treatment, Rehab. Center, 1974-75, Culpeper Meml. Hosp.; bd. dirs. Mental Health Assn. Culpeper, 1976-79, pres., 1979—; mem. So. Baptist Assn. Ministries with the Aging. Mem. Nat. Council on Aging, Gerontological Soc. Am., Assn. Homes for Aging, Am. Assn. Ret. Persons (asso.), Sigma Alpha Epsilon. Club: Culpeper Optimist (dir. 1976—). Home: 140 Timber Trail Ct Culpeper VA 22701 Office: PO Box 191 Culpeper VA 22701

HOXIT, GARY KELLOGG, elec. engr.; b. Greenville, S.C., Apr. 3, 1946; s. Truman Jones and Nancy Nell (Sharp) H.; B.S. in Elec. Engring., U. S.C., 1971, M.Elec. Engring. (grad. asst.), 1972; m. Carol Ann Hopkins, July 20, 1968; children—Kevin, Melissa. Instr. elec. engring. Midlands Tech. Coll., Columbia, S.C., 1972-79; asst. engr. Duke Power Co., Seneca, S.C., 1979—; cons. in field. Registered profl. engr., S.C. Mem. Nat. Soc. Profl. Engrs., IEEE, S.C. Soc. Profl. Engrs. Methodist. Home: 124 McArthur St Easley SC 29640 Office: Oconee Nuclear Sta Hwy 183 Seneca SC 29678

HOY, MARY CAMILLA, French linguist, educator; b. Clinton, S.C., Jan. 3, 1925; d. William Edwin and Mabel Elizabeth (George) Hoy; A.B., magna cum laude, U. S.C., 1943, M.A., 1944; postgrad. (French Govt. fellow) U. Paris, 1946-47; Ph.D. (resident fellow), Bryn Mawr (Pa.) Coll., 1954. Instr. French and Spanish, Sweet Briar Coll., 1948-50, St. Mary's Coll., Raleigh, N.C., 1952-59; asst. prof. French, Birmingham (Ala.)-So. Coll., 1959-61, asso. prof., 1961-66; asso. prof. French, E. Carolina U., 1966-67; prof. French, chmn. dept. fgn. langs. Greensboro (N.C.) Coll., 1967—. Mem. Am., S. Atlantic modern lang. assns., Am. Assn. Tchrs. French, Am. Council Tchrs. Fgn. Langs., Fgn. Lang. Assn. N.C., Cousteau Soc., Phi Beta Kappa. Republican. Episcopalian. Home: 2906 W Cornwallis Dr Greensboro NC 27408 Office: Greensboro Coll Greensboro NC 27420

HOY, WILLIAM IVAN, educator; b. Mt. Meridan, Va., Aug. 21, 1915; s. William Isaac and Ileta (Saufley) H.; B.A., Hampden-Sydney Coll., 1936; B.D., Union Theol. Sem., 1942; S.T.M., Biblical Sem. in N.Y., 1949; Ph.D., U. Edinburgh, 1945; m. Wilma Lambert, Apr. 29, 1945; children—Doris, Martha. Ordained to ministry Presbyn. Ch., 1942; asst. prin., athletic dir. Virginia High Sch., 1936-39; asst. prof. Bible, Guilford Coll., 1948-49; asst. prof. religion U. Miami, Fla., 1953-57, asso. prof., 1957-60, chmn. dept. religion, 1958-79, prof., 1960—; moderator Presbytery of Everglades, 1960-61, stated clk., 1968-73; mem. bd. Christian edn. Presbyn. Ch. U.S., 1969-73, mem. Gen. Assembly Mission Bd., 1978—; pres. Greater Miami Ministerial Assn., 1964; observer, cons. World Council Christian Edn., Venezuela, Peru, 1971; bd. dirs. Met. Fellowship Chs., 1969—, v.p., 1971-73, interim exec. sec., 1974-77; trustee Davidson Coll., 1975—. Commdr. USNR. Mem. Am. Oriental Soc., Soc. of Biblicial Lit., Acad. of Religion, Am. Soc. of Ch. History, Scottish Ch. History Soc., Religious Research Assn., Studiorum Novi Testamenti Societas, Soc. for the Sci. Study of Religion, Phi Kappa Phi, Omicron Delta Kappa, Lambda Chi Alpha, Alpha Psi Omega, Theta Delta (founder). Clubs: Rotary, Tiger Bay. Contbr. articles and book reviews to religious pubs.; co-author: The History of the Chaplains Corps, 1960; contbr. to Dictionary of Christian Ethics, 1973. Home: 5881 SW 52nd Terr Coral Gables FL 33155 Office: PO Box 248264 University of Miami Coral Gables FL 33124

HOYE, ROBERT EARL, univ. adminstr.; b. Warwick, R.I., Jan. 12, 1931; s. S. Earl and Alice M. (Landry) H.; B.A., Providence Coll., 1953; M.S., St. John's U., 1955: Ph.D., U. Wis., 1973; m. Patricia Buswell, Aug. 20, 1955; children—Robert Earl, Joanne D., Peter M., Kathleen B. Dean, Champlain Coll., 1956-57; supt. schs. Frontier Regional Sch. Dist., Deerfield, Mass., 1958-60; dist. mgr. New Eng., fed. liaison Sci. Research Assos./IBM, 1960-65; nat. dir. Learning Systems div. Xerox Corp., 1965-66; dir. instructional media lab. U. Wis., Milw., 1966-73; asst. v.p. acad. affairs U. Louisville, 1974—; cons. in field. Mem. Dighton (Mass.) Sch. Bd., 1964-65. Cert. tchr., adminstr., R.I., Vt., Mass.; Ky. col. Mem. Am. Psychol. Assn., Ky. Psychol. Assn., Assn. Ednl. Communications and Tech., Am. Assn. Higher Edn. Author: (with A. Wang) Index to Computer Assisted Instruction, 1973; contbr. articles to profl. publs.

HOYLE, JOHN DOUGLAS, hosp. adminstr.; b. Springfield, Ohio, Aug. 27, 1943; s. Paul Vollmer and Elizabeth (Steiner) H.; M.Hosp. Adminstrn., Xavier U., 1967; B.A., Wittenberg U., 1965; m. Janet Lee Weatherspoon, July 24, 1965; children—John D., Christopher, Allison. Chief exec. officer, adminstr. St. Luke Hosp., Ft. Thomas, Ky., 1975—, adminstr., 1972-75, asst. adminstr., 1968-72; evening adminstr. The Christ Hosp., Cin., 1968, adminstrv. asst., 1967; clin. instr. U. Ky., Lexington, 1965—. Vice chmn. disaster services Cin. ARC, 1976—; bd. dirs. Campbell County YMCA, 1975-77; v.p. Ky. Bd. Dentistry and Dental Examiners, 1976—; mem. bd. No. Ky. Emergency Med. Service, 1977—; chmn. disaster and emergency services com. City of Ft. Thomas, 1976—; treas. Greater Cin. Hosp. Council, 1977, exec. com., 1979; class rep. Wittenberg U. Alumni Council, 1970—; scoutmaster Boy Scouts Am., Ft. Thomas, 1978—. Recipient Pfizer award of merit, U.S. CD Council, 1977; Citizenship award, S.A.R., 1960, Am. Legion, 1960. Mem. Ky. Hosp. Assn. (v.p. 1976-77), Ky. Peer Rev. Orgn. (dir. 1976-77), Am. Hosp. Assn., Am. Coll. Hosp. Adminstrs., Royal Soc. Health, Hosp. Fin. Mgmt. Assn., Am. Trauma Soc., Ky. Hosp. Assn., Phi Kappa Psi. Methodist. Club: Optimist. Contbr. articles to profl. jours. Home: 47 Winston Hill Rd Fort Thomas KY 41075 Office: 85 N Grand Ave Fort Thomas KY 41075

HOYT, LA RITA MASON, speech-lang. pathologist; b. Shattuck, Okla., Dec. 13, 1947; d. Byron Stuart and La Veta (Howlett) Mason; B.A. with honors, Phillips U., 1969; M.S., Vanderbilt U., 1970; m. Stephen Lee Hoyt, Aug. 31, 1969. Speech-lang. pathologist Killeen Ind. Sch. Dist. (Tex.), 1970-71; pvt. practice speech-lang. pathology, Lubbock, Tex., 1972—; mem. ancillary profl. staff Meth. Hosp., St. Mary of the Plains Hosp. and Rehab. Center, Univ. Hosp.; cons. W. Tex. Home Health Agy. Mem. Am. Speech-Lang.-Hearing Assn., Tex. Speech, Lang. and Hearing Assn., Tex. S. Plains Speech and Hearing Assn. (past pres.). Mem. Christian Ch. Clubs: Lost Chord, Stroke (Lubbock, Tex.). Home and Office: 2408 Auburn St No 115 Lubbock TX 79415

HOYT, STEPHEN LEE, counselor; b. Fremont, Mich., Feb. 24, 1947; s. William T. and Janet L. (Marvin) H.; student Ferris State Coll., 1965-66; B.A. in Sociology, Phillips U., 1969; M.S., Tex. Tech U., 1974; m. La Rita Mason, Aug. 31, 1969. Instr. psychology South Plains Coll., Levelland, Tex., 1976-77; counselor Planned Parenthood, Inc., Odessa, Tex., 1977-78, Tex. Tech U. Counseling Center, 1978—; pvt. practice marriage and family counseling, Lubbock, Tex., 1978—. Served with U.S. Army, 1970-72. Mem. Am. Assn. Sex Educators, Counselors and Therapists, Am. Assn. Marriage and Family Therapy. Home: 2408 Auburn St Lubbock TX 79415 Office: University Counseling Center Texas Tech U Lubbock TX 79409

HSIEH, HSIANG-CHUAN STEVE, educator; b. Kaohsiung, Taiwan, Dec. 12, 1944; s. Chu-Ray and Shen-Huang (Huang) H.; came to U.S., 1969; B.S., Nat. Taiwan U., 1967; M.S., U. Wis., 1972, Ph.D., 1974; m. Sun-Hua Mary Wei, June 24, 1972; children—Candace, Irene. Teaching asst. dept. chemistry Nat. Taiwan U., Taipei, 1968-69; research asst. dept. nutritional sci. U. Wis., Madison, 1969-74; research asso. dept. chemistry Fla. State U., Tallahassee, 1974-77; investigator Inst. Dental Research, Sch. Dentistry, U. Ala., Birmingham, 1977—, instr. dept. nutrition sci., 1977—. Spl. Dental Research award grantee, 1979—. Mem. Am. Assn. Dental Research, Sigma Xi. Contbr. articles to profl. jours. Home: 520 Windy Ln Birmingham AL 35210 Office: Inst Dental Research U Ala Birmingham AL 35294

HUANG, EDWIN I-CHUEN, physician; b. Hunan, China, Sept. 10, 1933; s. Chu-Ou and Wan-Lan (Chiang) H.; came to U.S., 1970, naturalized, 1976; M.D., Nat. Def. Med. Center, Taipei, Taiwan, 1960; M.P.H., U. Tex., 1971; m. Hwei-Mei Lai, Apr. 4, 1963; children—David, Shaw-Ming, Yaw-Ching. Intern First Army Gen. Hosp., Taipei, 1960-61; resident, staff Taipei Children's Hosp., 1965-67; staff physician Chaiyi Christian Hosp., Taiwan, China, 1962-64, Air Am., Southeast Asia, 1968-70; house officer Kenmore Mercy Hosp., Buffalo, 1973-74; med. officer USPHS Hosp., Clinton, Okla., 1974-77; staff physician Ga. Diagnostic Center, Jackson, 1977-78; practice with Countryside Clinic, DeFuniak, Fla., 1978-80; staff physician Blackwell (Okla.) Hosp., 1980—. Med. examiner, flight surgeon Chinese Civil Aviation Adminstrn., 1967-71. Mem. Aerospace Med. Assn., A.C.P. (asso.), Am. Pub. Health Assn., Chinese Med. Assn., Chinese Aeros. and Astronautics Soc., Chinese-Am. Club of Greater Oklahoma City. Author: Sociocultural Change and Emotional Disorders, 1971; (with others) Taiwan and China, 1972, The Death of Chiang Kai Shek, 1975. Editor: (with others) English-Chinese Glossary of Aerospace Sciences, 1975. Contbr. articles to profl. jours. Home: 2105 Elmwood Dr Blackwell OK 74631 Office: 1009 W Furguson Blackwell OK 74631

HUANG, ENG-SHANG (CLARK), virologist; b. Taiwan, Republic China, Mar. 17, 1940; came to U.S., 1968, naturalized, 1977; s. Jong-Sun and King-fa (Ong) H.; B.S., Nat. Taiwan U., 1962, M.S. in Public Health, 1964; Ph.D., U. N.C., Chapel Hill, 1971; m. Shu-mei Huong, Nov. 7, 1939; children—David Y., Benjamin Y. USPHS fellow U. N.C., Chapel Hill, 1971-73, vis. asst. prof., 1973-78, asst. prof. medicine and bacteriology, 1974-78, asso. prof., 1978—; pres. C.H.W. Corp., Peking Garden Restaurant, 1978—; mem. viriology study sect. NIH, 1979—. Served with Army Republic China, 1964-65. USPHS career devel. awardee, 1978—; grantee EPA, Nat. Inst. Allergy and Infectious Diseases, Nat. Cancer Inst. Mem. Am. Soc. Microbiology, AAAS. Democrat. Contbr. articles to profl. jours. Office: Cancer Research Center U NC Chapel Hill NC 27514

HUANG, JINN-HUIE, chem. engr.; b. Djawa, Indonesia, Sept. 8, 1933; s. Khing Hun and Bie Nio (Tio) H.; B.S., Taipei Inst. Tech., 1955; M.S., U. Tokyo, 1961, Ph.D., 1964; postgrad. U. Va., 1964; D.Sc., London Inst. Tech., 1973; m. Shiu-Chien Lin, July 17, 1937; children—Jen-Wei, Juliana Tjiu-Ling. Research asso. U. Va., 1964-67; research engr. Cities Service Oil Co., Tulsa, 1967-71; sr. engr. Crest Engring., Tulsa, 1971-78, Williams Bros. Engring., 1978—; Mem. Am. Inst. Mining, Metall. and Petroleum Engrs., Am. Geophys. Union, N.Y. Acad. Scis., Sigma Xi. Home: 4812 S 71st East Ave Tulsa OK 74145 Office: 6600 S Yale Ave Tulsa OK 74136

HUANG, RICHARD SHIH-CHIU, mech. engr., engring. co. exec.; b. Peking, China, Feb. 28, 1932; s. Fang-Kang and Viola Johnson (Misner) H.; came to U.S., 1946; naturalized, 1955; B.S. in Mech. Engring., Duke U., 19S5; postgrad. George Washington U., 1974; m. Adele Marie Farren, June 4, 1960; children—William Farren, Michael Edward. Propulsion engr., developer Scout space launch Voight Corp., Dallas, 1955-60, aeroballistics engr. space programs, 1960-66, engring. mgr., 1966—, instr. employee tng., 1961-62. Asso. fellow Am. Inst. Aeros. and Astronautics; mem. Acad. Model Aeronautics (bd. dirs. 1964), Assn. Naval Aviation, Soc. Antique Modelers, Model Engine Collectors Assn. Home: 4032 Deep Valley Dr Dallas TX 75234 Office: PO Box 5907 Dallas TX 75222

HUANG, TED TSUNG-CHE, plastic surgeon; b. Taiwan, China, Oct. 8, 1937; s. M.C. and Y.K. Huang; M.D., U. Tex., Galveston, 1965. Intern, U. Tex. Med. Br. Hosps., Galveston, 1965-66, McLaughlin post-doctoral fellow in surgery, resident in surgery, 1966-70, resident in plastic and reconstructive surgery, 1970-73; instr. to asso. prof. plastic and reconstructive maxillofacial surgery U. Tex. Med. Br., Galveston, 1973—. Am. Cancer Soc. research fellow, 1972; Eaton fellow in plastic surgery, 1973. Mem. AMA, A.C.S., Tex. Med. Assn., Galveston Med. Soc., Am. Soc. Plastic Surgeons, Am. Cleft Palate Soc., Am. Burn Assn., Southwestern Surg. Congress, Tex. Surg. Soc. Contbr. articles in field to surg. jours. Office: Dept Surgery U Tex Med Br Hosps Galveston TX 77550 also 326 Market St Galveston TX 77550

HUBBARD, CARROLL, JR., congressman; b. Murray, Ky., July 7, 1937; s. Carroll and Beth (Shelton) H.; B.A., Georgetown Coll., 1959; J.D., U. Louisville, 1962; m. Joyce Lynn Hall, Aug. 20, 1966;

children—Kelly Lynn, Krista Leigh. Admitted to Ky. bar, 1962; practice law, Mayfield, Ky., from 1962; mem. Ky. Senate from 1st Dist. of Ky., 1967-75; mem. 94th-96th Congresses from 1st dist. Ky. Mem., deacon, moderator 1st Baptist Ch., Mayfield. Served with Air N.G., 1962-67, Army N.G., 1968-70. Named 1 of 3 Outstanding Men of Ky., Ky. Jaycees, 1968; Outstanding Young Democratic Legislator, Ky. Young Democrats, 1970. Office: 204 Cannon House Office Bldg Washington DC 20515

HUBBARD, FRANCES THERESA FERRACCI, educator; b. Shaw, Miss., Aug. 29, 1927; d. Tullio and Elvera P. Ferracci; B.S., Miss. Delta State U., 1950; M. Counseling Edn., Xavier U. La., 1969; postgrad. U. Miami, 1954; m. Gerald Davey Hubbard, June 29, 1957; children—Jacqueline Hubbard Barnhouse, Katherine Hubbard Sevin, Tullio, Joseph, Fanny Hubbard Autin, Gerald Davey. Chmn. health and phys. edn. Coll. and Acad. of Sacred Heart, Grand Coteau, La., 1950-54, Maryville Coll., St. Louis, 1954-56; instr. phys. edn. Trinity Coll., Washington, 1957; asso. prof. health and phys. edn. Xavier U., New Orleans, 1959—. Vol. worker ARC. Recipient longevity service award ARC, 1980. Mem. AAPHER, La. Driver and Traffic Safety Edn. Assn., La. Assn. Health and Phys. Edn. Democrat. Roman Catholic. Office: Dept Phys Edn Xavier U New Orleans LA 70125

HUBBARD, HAMPTON, urologist; b. High Point, N.C., May 19, 1923; s. Robert Clark and Florence Adelaide (Hampton) H.; certificate medicine U. N.C., 1945, postgrad. 1945; M.D., Med. Coll. Va., 1947; m. Florence Anne Holmes, June 12, 1946; children—Margaret Holmes (Mrs. Robert J. Frost, Jr.), John Hampton, Charlotte Elizabeth (Mrs. Gordon Randolph Cox), Anne Fielding, Mark Tigner, Matthew Kevin. Intern, Charlotte (N.C.) Meml. Hosp., 1947-48; resident Watts Hosp., Durham, N.C., 1948-49, U.S. Naval Hosp., San Diego, 1951-54; commd. lt. (j.g.) USNR, 1947, USN, 1948, advanced through ranks to capt., 1964; ret., 1972; practice medicine specializing in urology, Clinton, N.C., 1972—; mem. staff Sampson County Meml. Hosp., Clinton, asso. staff Cape Fear Valley Hosp., Fayetteville, N.C. Pres., Clinton Urol. Assos., Clinton, 1974—; adviser Am. Cancer Soc., Sampson County, N.C., chpt., 1973—. Diplomate, Am. Bd. Urology. Fellow A.C.S.; mem. AMA, So. Med. Assn., Southeastern Sect. Am. Urol. Assn., Am. Urol. Assn., Sampson County Med. Soc. (pres. 1975-77), Pvt. Drs. Am. (treas. 1979—), Royal Soc. Medicine. Republican. Roman Catholic. Lion. Contbr. articles to profl. jours. Home: 102 Country Club Circle Clinton NC 28328 Office: 603 Beaman St Clinton NC 28328

HUBBELL, DAVID SMITH, surgeon; b. Dallas, Aug. 29, 1922; s. Jay B. and Lucinda A. (Smith) H.; A.B., Duke U., 1943. M.D., 1946; m. Barbara M. Baynard, July 3, 1947; children—Katherine A. Hubbell Lawrence, Lawrence B., Daniel B. Intern, Duke Hosp., Durham, N.C., 1946-47; intern Grace-New Haven Community Hosp. (Conn.), 1949-50, resident, 1951-53; Am. Cancer Soc. clin. fellow Yale U., 1951-53, mem. surg. faculty, 1953-54; practice medicine, specializing in surgery and thoracic surgery, St. Petersburg, Fla., 1954—; mem. staffs Bayfront Med. Center, St. Anthony's Hosp.; asso. clin. prof. surgery U. S.Fla., 1974—; chief cancer task force Fla. Regional Med. Programs, 1969-73. Served with U.S. Army, 1943-46, 47-49. USN-Yale research fellow, 1950-51; diplomate Am. Bd. Surgery, Am. Bd. Thoracic Surgery. Fellow A.C.S. (pres. Fla. chpt. 1973-74, nat. gov. 1976—); mem. AMA, Fla. Med. Assn. (del. 1969—), Am. Coll. Chest Physicians, Soc. Thoracic Surgeons, Am. Cancer Soc. (pres. Fla. div. 1968-69, Fla. del. 1973—), Pinellas County Med. Soc. (pres. 1970-71), Am. Heart Assn. (pres. suncoast affiliate 1976-77). Republican. Presbyterian. Clubs: St. Petersburg Tennis, St. Petersburg Yacht, Rotary, Suncoasters. Research on tumors of thymus and lungs, aneurysms of arteries, appendicitis in older people. Home: 1963 Brightwaters Blvd Saint Petersburg FL 33704 Office: 861 6th Ave S Saint Petersburg FL 33701

HUBBELL, ROBERT CARLTON, assn. exec.; b. Johnson City, N.Y., Jan. 4, 1949; s. Andrew George and Ethel (Buchel) H.; B.S., U. Pa., 1970; M. Social Planning (Comprehensive Health Planning fellow), Boston Coll., 1974. Cons., Lab. Statis. and Policy Research, Boston Coll., 1974-75; research specialist Leonard Davis Inst., U. Pa., Phila., 1975-76; dir. communications and program devel. Am. Blood Commn., Arlington, Va., 1976—. Mem. task force on diagnostic and treatment services Health Systems Agy. of No. Va., 1977. Mem. Am. Planning Assn., Internat. Assn. Bus. Communicators. Contbr. articles in field to profl. jours. Home: 809 S Pitt St Alexandria VA 22314 Office: Suite 300 1901 N Ft Myer Dr Arlington VA 22209

HUBBS, LILLIAN GOODEN, museum curator; b. Ft. Worth, May 2, 1923; d. Juewell and Winnifred Hope (Eastus) Gooden; scholarship student Tex. Wesleyan U., 1940-41; student U. Tex., Arlington, 1941-42, Ariz. State U., 1943, U. Wash., 1943; m. Fred Julian Hubbs, June 22, 1946; 1 son, Craig Fred. Asst. curator natural sci. Ft. Worth Mus. Sci. and History, 1959-72; curator natural sci., dir. edn., registrar Heard Natural Sci. Mus. and Wild Life Sanctuary, McKinney, Tex., 1972—; cons. spider identification and classification, TV demonstrator. Mem. Am. Assn. Museums, Mountain Plains Mus. Conf., Tex. Mus. Assn., Am. Mus. Natural History, Nat. Wildlife Assn., Nat. Geog. Soc. Democrat. Presbyterian. Author handbook. Home: 3901 Ashville Dr Garland TX 75041 Office: Route 7 Box 171 McKinney TX 75069

HUBER, ALBERT JOHN, airport mgmt. exec.; b. San Francisco, Sept. 2, 1925; s. Phil and Theresa Beatrice (Dorroh) H.; B.S., U. So. Calif., 1949; m. Barbara Lee Ewy, Mar. 4, 1945 (dec. 1951); children—John Richard, Carla Lee; m. 2d, Ida Mae Howard Saxon, Oct. 2, 1954 (div. 1967); 1 son, Kirt Howard. Civilian in charge base ops. Hobbs AFB, N.Mex., 1945-46; cargo supr. Calif. Eastern Airlines, 1946; asst. airport mgr. Hayward (Calif.) Mcpl. Airport, 1949-57; dir. aviation Kern County, Calif., 1957-62; dir. airports Sacramento County, 1962-72; pres., exec. dir. Met. Nashville Airport Authority, 1972-77; gen. mgr., chief exec. officer Louisville Jefferson County Air Bd., 1977—; chmn. project Intermotal Air Cargo Test (INTACT). Bd. dirs. Internat. Center, U. Louisville. Served with AUS, 1944-45, USAF, 1950-54. Decorated Air medal; recipient Outstanding Contbrn. to Aviation award Bd. Dirs. Met. Nashville Airport Authority, 1977; named hon. Ky. col. Mem. Am. (past dir.), Calif. (past pres.) assns. airport execs., Tenn. Assn. Air Carrier Airports (past pres.), Airports Operators Council Internat. (dir.), Tennesseans for Better Transp. (past dir.), Ky. for Better Transp. (sec.). Club: City (Nashville). Home: 161 Thierman Ln Apt 3A Louisville KY 40207

HUBER, RUDOLPH JOHN, psychologist; b. Cleve., Oct. 26, 1940; s. Rudolph J. and Jenette (Kemper) H.; B.A., Kent State U., 1962; M.A., U. Vt., 1965; Ph.D. (NIMH Fellow, 1969), U. N.H., 1970; m. Pauline Rita Poirier, Aug. 27, 1966; children—Jennifer Ketching, Beth Ely, Emily Atkinson. Resident counselor U. Vt., Burlington, 1962-64, instr. in psychology, 1964-65; instr. psychology State U. N.Y., Plattsburgh, 1965-67; research asst. U. N.H., Durham, 1967-69, lectr. in psychology, 1969-70; asst. prof. psychology Skidmore Coll., Saratoga, N.Y., 1970-74, Skidmore research grantee, 1972; chmn. dept. psychology Meredith Coll., Raleigh, N.C., 1974—. Bd. dirs. Life Enrichment Center, Raleigh. Texasgulf grantee, 1975; Shell asst. grantee, 1976. Mem. Am., Eastern, N.C. (exec. com.) psychol. assns., N.Am. Soc. Adlerian Psychology, Psi Chi, Delta Tau Delta. Republican. Contbr. articles to profl. jours.; panelist at confs. Home: 5413 Maple Ridge Rd Raleigh NC 27609 Office: Dept Psychology Meredith College Raleigh NC 27611

HUBERMAN, JEFFREY ALLEN, architect; b. Boston, Jan. 2, 1942; s. Sidney H. and Miriam (Walker) H.; B.Arch., U. Fla., 1964; m. Barbara Kemp, May 16, 1964; children—Amy Beth, Marc Walker. Partner, Gantt/Huberman Assos., architects and planners, 1971—; exhibited paintings N.C. Mus. Art, Raleigh, Norfolk Mus. Art (Va.), Delgado Mus. Art, New Orleans; represented in permanent collections: Bucknell U., N.C. Nat. Bank, Westinghouse Electric Co., Burlington Industries, Springs Mills, N.C. Mus. Art, Raleigh. Mem. Charlotte-Mecklenburg Community Relations Com., 1974—; chmn. Charlotte Clean City Com., 1975-77; chmn. cultural task force Dimensions for Charlotte-Mecklenburg, 1973-74; mem. Cultural Action Plan for Charlotte-Mecklenburg, 1974-76; bd. dirs. Charlotte-Mecklenburg Arts and Sci. Council, 1975—, campaign chmn. fund dr., 1977, v.p., 1977-79; bd. dirs. Planned Parenthood Greater Charlotte, 1978—; mem. Charlotte Opera Assn., 1966—, pres., 1979-81; bd. dirs., treas. Charlotte Dance Assn., 1973-76; bd. dirs. Charlotte Jr. Soccer Found., 1978-80. Work included in 200 Years of Visual Arts in N.C., N.C. State Mus. Mem. AIA (treas. Charlotte chpt. 1977), Inst. Bus. Designers. Democrat. Jewish (dir. temple 1967—). Contbr. articles to profl. jours. Home: 1607 Dilworth Rd W Charlotte NC 28203 Office: 951 S Independence Blvd Charlotte NC 28202

HUBERT, JOSEPH ARTHUR, lawyer; b. Northport, N.Y., Mar. 22, 1930; s. Joseph F. and Adelyn (Condon) H.; A.B., Centre Coll., 1951; LL.D., U. Miami, Coral Gables, Fla., 1956; m. Marianne Picton Rudd, Apr. 26, 1974; children by previous marriage—Nancy, Lisa, James, Robert, Jean Marie. Admitted to Fla. bar, 1956; partner firm Watson, Hubert, LaSalle & Clark, and predecessor, Fort Lauderdale, Fla., 1956—; dir. Lauderdale Abstract and Title Co., S.E. Bank of Broward. Pres., Community Service Council, 1965, Econ. Opportunity Coordinating Group Broward County, 1965, United Fund of Broward County, 1967. Served with CIC, AUS, Korea, Japan, 1951-53. Mem. Am., Broward County (pres. 1969) bar assns., Fla. Bar, Execs. Assn. Ft. Lauderdale. Home: 2608 NE 37th Dr Fort Lauderdale FL 33308 Office: 3600 N Federal Hwy Fort Lauderdale FL 33308

HUCK, LEWIS FRANCIS, lawyer, real estate cons. and developer; b. Bklyn., Mar. 19, 1912; s. Frank and Jessie (Green) H.; LL.B., St. John's U., 1938, LL.M., 1939; m. Frances M. Love, Jan. 7, 1950; children—Janet Ahearn, L. Frank, William G., Robert L., James J. Admitted to N.Y. bar, 1939, also Tex., Mass. bars; practice law, 1939—; with trust dept. Guaranty Trust Co. N.Y., 1929-41; atty. Gen. Electric Co., Schenectady, 1945-47, chem. counsel, 1947-48, atomic energy counsel, 1948-51, gen. mgr., Richland, Wash., 1951-55; asst. to exec. v.p. Gen. Dynamics Corp., 1955-57; lawyer, real estate cons. and developer, 1957-68, 77; v.p., dir. real estate devel. Eastern Airlines, Inc., 1968-77. Served maj. AUS, 1941-45. Democrat. Home: 15127 Kimberley Ln Houston TX 77079 Office: Exec Office Eastern Airlines Miami Internat Airport Miami FL 33148

HUCKABAY, GARY LOUIS, corporate data processing exec.; b. Monroe, La., Dec. 24, 1937; s. Hilliard L. and Janie L. (McLemore) H.; B.S. in Acctg., N.E. La. State Coll., 1960; M.B.A., U. Denver, 1961; m. Marlene Rumel Bathemess, Sept. 2, 1977; children by previous marriage—Gary Louis, Leslie Ann. Mgr. adminstrv. services Arthur Andersen & Co., Denver, 1961-73; dir. mgmt. info. systems N.W. Pipeline Corp., Salt Lake City, 1973-78; mgr. info. systems Tex. Oil and Gas Corp., Dallas, 1978—. Served to 1st lt. U.S. Army, 1961-63. C.P.A., Colo., Utah. Mem. Am. Inst. C.P.A.'s, Colo. Soc. C.P.A.'s, Nat. Assn. Accts., Data Processing Mgmt. Assn. Democrat. Baptist. Home: 7605 Dunoon St Dallas TX 75248 Office: 2300 Fidelity Union Tower Dallas TX 75201

HUCKABEE, MARTHA CAROLYN, pharmacist; b. Uniontown, Ala., Oct. 13, 1926; d. Thomas Fendley and Carolyn (Blakeney) Huckabee; B.S., Ala. Poly. Inst., 1947. Pharmacist, Jones Drug Co., Anniston, Ala., 1948-49, Bradford Drug Co., 1949-65; owner, pharmacist Huckabee Drugs, Uniontown, 1965—; dir. Central Bank of Uniontown. Instr. first aid A.R.C., 1960—; dir. med. services Civil Def., Perry County, 1961-77; hon. dep. sheriff Perry County, 1962-75. Bd. dirs. Uniontown Community Chest. Mem. Uniontown Mchts. Assn., Nat. Assn. Retail Druggists, Am., Ala. (Perry county dir., Outstanding Pharmacy Grad. award 1947), Perry County (pres.) pharm. assns., Nat. C. of C., D.A.R. (regent Canebrake chpt.), U. D.C., Central Ala., Ala. geneal. socs., Perry County Historic Preservation Soc (dir.), Auburn, Auburn Pharmacy alumni assns., Phi Kappa Phi. Republican. Baptist. Mem. Order Eastern Star. Home: 101 Front St Uniontown AL 36786 Office: 300 N Water St Uniontown AL 36786

HUCKABY, EDWARD EARL, architect; b. Germany, Nov. 11, 1951; s. Edward Vernon and Mary Lou (Hoffman) H. (parents Amo citizens); B. Environ. Design, Tex. A&M U., 1973, M.Arch., 1974; m. Nancy Helen Boehm, Aug. 19, 1972; 1 dau., Erin Elizabeth. With Bernard Johnson, Inc., Architects/Engrs./Planners, 1974-75; with James Falick, The Klein Partnership Health Facilities Group, Inc., Architects/Planners, Houston, 1975—, project architect, 1974—. Registered architect, Tex. Mem. AIA, Tex. Soc. Architects, Phi Kappa Phi, Tau Sigma Delta. Research on health care delivery system for rural Tex. Home: 9802 Westview St Houston TX 77055

HUCKABY, THOMAS GERALD, congressman; b. Hodge, La., July 19, 1941; s. Thomas Milton and Eva (Toland) H.; B.S. in Elec. Engring., La. State U., 1963; M.B.A., Ga. State U., 1968; m. Suzanna Woodard, Dec. 21, 1962; children—Michelle, Clay. With Western Electric Co., 1963-73; owner-operator dairy farm, Ringgold, La., 1973—; mem. 96th Congress from 5th La. Dist., mem. Agr. Com., Interior and Insular Affairs Com. Mem. La. Farm Bur., N.La. Milk Producers Assn., La. Cattlemans Assn. Democrat. Methodist. Home: PO Box 544 Ringgold LA 71068 Office: 228 Cannon House Office Bldg Washington DC 20515

HUDDLESTON, JOHN MCKEAN, architect; b. New Orleans, Apr. 1, 1927; s. John McKean and Emma L. Huddleston, student Tex. A. and M. Coll., 1943-45; B.Arch., Tulane U., 1950; postgrad. Sorbonne U., Paris, 1953-54; m. Beverly Jackson, Aug. 5, 1950 (div.); children—Margaret Louise, Harriet Handa, Johnel Jackson; m. 2d, Betty Ducote, Feb. 12, 1977. Architect, William S. Evans & Assos., 1950-51; partner Stanfield & Huddleston, architects, New Orleans, 1951-54; asst. head archtl. div. of 8th Naval Dist., Pub. Works Dept., New Orleans, 1952-53; prin. John McKean Huddleston, architect, Shreveport, La., 1954-73; architect Huddleston, Emerson, Stiller & Associates, Shreveport; now prin. J. McKean Huddleston, architect, Metairie, La.; v.p. Internat. Cons. Services, Inc. Served with USN, 1946-48. Recipient Fulbright award, 1953. Mem. AIA (mem. nat. housing com. 1968-73), New Orleans C. of C. Episcopalian. Club: Pierremont Oaks Tennis (Shreveport). Patentee in field. Office: 2601 N Hullen St Metairie LA 70002

HUDDLESTON, JOSEPH RUSSELL, lawyer; b. Glasgow, Ky., Feb. 5, 1937; s. Paul Russell and Frances (Martin) H.; A.B., Princeton, 1959; J.D., U. Va., 1962; m. Heidi Lynn Wood, Sept. 12, 1959; children—Johanna Lynn, Lisa Diane, Kristina Lee. Admitted to Ky. bar, 1962; practiced in Bowling Green, Ky., 1962—; mem. firm Huddleston Bros. & Duncan; dir. Nehi-Royal Crown Bottling and Distbg. Co., Houk Ins., Inc. Mem. Ky. Crime Commn., 1972-77; mem. Adv. Com. Criminal Law Revision, 1969-71. Bd. dirs. Princeton U. Fund, 1958-59. Mem. Am., Ky. (ho. dels.), Bowling Green (pres.) bar assns., Am. Assn. Trial Attys., Ky. Acad. Trial Attys. (pres.), Phi Alpha Delta. Clubs: Cap and Gown (Princeton); Jefferson; Port Oliver Yacht. Home: 2626 Smallhouse Rd Bowling Green KY 42101 Office: 1032 College St Bowling Green KY 42101

HUDDLESTON, WALTER DARLINGTON, U.S. senator; b. nr. Burkesville, Ky., Apr 15, 1926; s. Walter Franklin and Lottie (Russell) H.; A.B., U. Ky., 1949; m. Martha Jean Pearce, Dec. 20, 1947; children—Stephen Pearce, Philip Dee. Program-sports dir. WKCT, Bowling Green, Ky., 1949-52; gen. mgr. WIEL, Elizabethtown, Ky., 1952-72; mem. U.S. Senate, 1972—; dir. 1st Fed. Savings & Loan Assn., Elizabethtown, Ky., Radio Sta. WLBN, Lebanon, Ky. Mem. Ky. State Senate, 1966-72, majority leader, 1970, 72; chmn. Democratic Caucus, 1968; Served with U.S. Army, 1944-46: ETO. Mem. C. of C. (pres. 1959), Ky. Broadcasters Assn. (pres. 1958). Methodist. Club: Pendennis (Louisville). Office: 2113 Dirksen New Senate Office Bldg Washington DC 20510

HUDDLESTON, WILLIAM ENNIS, physician; b. Batesville, Ark., Aug. 25, 1928; s. William McKinley and Edna Cecil (Ennis) H.; student Ark. Coll., 1946-48, Ark. State Tchrs. Coll., 1948-49; B.S. in Medicine, M.D., U. Ark., 1953; m. Pauline Maxine Coffman, Sept. 7, 1953; children—Thomas Kevin, Linda Marshaun, Kelly Ennis. Intern, Mo. Meth. Hosp., St. Joseph, 1953-54; practice medicine, specializing in family practice, Iowa Park, Tex., 1956-57, Bridgeport, Tex., 1957—; mem. staff Bridgeport Hosp., chief of staff, 1973-79. Bridgeport City Council, 1960-72. Served with USAF, 1953-56. Diplomate Am. Bd. Family Practice. Fellow Am. Acad. Family Practice (charter), Am. Acad. Family Physicians (charter); mem. Am., Tex. med. assns., Am. Soc. Contemporary Medicine and Surgery, So. Med. Soc. Mason. Methodist (trustee 1962-78). Home: 26 Robinhood Ln Bridgeport TX 76026 Office: 1301 Halsell St Bridgeport TX 76026

HUDDLESTUN, PAUL FRANCIS, geologist; b. Chgo., Jan. 14, 1938; s. Cleal and Aleta Marie (Mathis) H.; B.S., Fla. State U., 1963, M.S., 1965; children—Cleal, Lois Cleaette, Aaron Paul. Micropaleontologist, Shell Oil Co., New Orleans, 1965-68; geologist Ga. Dept. Nat. Resources, Atlanta, 1972—. Mem. Paleontol. Research Inst. Episcopalian. Home: 6355 Memorial Dr Stone Mountain GA 30083 Office: 19 Martin Luther King Jr Dr NW Atlanta GA 30303

HUDGENS, EDWARD BOONE, JR., elec. engr.; b. Nashville, Feb. 19, 1944; s. Edward Boone and Janie Hammet (Leake) H.; B.E.E., Christian Bros. Coll., 1966; postgrad. Memphis State U., 1966-69; m. Abigail Carpenter Sadler, Aug. 28, 1965; children—John Elgin, Lisa Gail. Elec. engr. Office Griffith C. Burr, Cons. Engr., Memphis, 1966-67; elec. and instrumentation engr. Allen & Hoshall, Cons. Engrs., Memphis, 1967-77, chief elec. engr. bldg. dept., 1977-79, asso. of firm and project mgr., 1979—; instr. Herff Sch. Engring. of Memphis State U., 1967-69. Chmn., Memphis Fire Prevention Code Bd. Appeals. Registered profl. engr., Tenn., Ky., La. Mem. IEEE (sr., treas. sect. 1975—, sec. sect. 1976—, pres. sect. 1977—), Instrument Soc. Am. (sr.), Soc. Am. Value Engrs., Illuminating Engring. Soc. (sect. v.p. 1970-71, 75-76), Nat., Tenn., Memphis socs. profl. engrs., Engrs. Club Memphis. Episcopalian (mem. vestry 1971-74, 1976-79). Author: Design and Selection of Hospital Emergency Distribution Systems, 1976. Contbg. editor Elec. Cons. Mag., 1973—. Home: 214 Ridgefield Rd Memphis TN 38111 Office: 2430 Poplar St Memphis TN 38112

HUDGENS, JAMES RONALD, city adminstr.; b. Ada, Okla., Apr. 12, 1944; s. Henry Leo and Lena Lourene (Wooden) H.; B.S. in Sociology, Sam. Houston State U., 1973; m. Frances Margaret Carmichael, July 5, 1967; children—Sherri Lynn, Janie Frances, James Ronald, Robert William. Patrol sgt. Corpus Christie (Tex.) Police Dept., 1966-71; security adminstr. Belin Communities, 1971-73; asst. city mgr. City of Huntsville (Tex.), 1973-78; city mgr. City of La Porte (Tex.), 1978—. Coach, Youth League. Served with USAF, 1962-66. Mem. Internat. City Mgmt. Assn., Tex. City Mgmt. Assn., Mcpl. Fin. Officers Assn. Episcopalian. Clubs: Optimists, Rotary (La Porte); Kiwanis (dir. club) (Huntsville). Office: PO Drawer 1115 La Porte TX 77571

HUDGINS, ARVIN QUINTON, govt. mech. engr.; b. Marshall County, Ala., June 4, 1935; s. Artice Quinton and Mollie (Seay) H.; B.S. in Engring., Auburn U., 1957; diploma Command and Gen. Staff Coll., U.S. Army, 1972; children—Clay Erwin, Gay Patricia. Jr. engr. John Deere Co., Waterloo, Iowa, 1958; engr. Internat. Harvester Co., Memphis, 1960-62, Food Machinery Corp., Lakeland, Fla., 1962; aerospace engr. NASA, Marshall Space Flight Center, Huntsville, Ala., 1962-67, supervisory aerospace engr., 1967-74, aerospace engr. of flight system, 1974—. Served to lt. AUS, 1958-60. Recipient Skylab Emergency Thermal Shield Devel. Team Group Achievement award NASA, 1973, Skylab Twin Pole Sail Certificate of Recognition, 1975; named Hon. Lt. Col. Aide-de-Camp, Gov. State of Ala., 1975; registered profl. mech. engr., Ala. Mem. Nat., Ala. socs. profl. engrs., Res. Officers Assn. U.S. Baptist. Patentee in field. Home: PO Box 1384 Huntsville AL 35807 Office: EP-14 NASA MSFC Huntsville AL 35812

HUDGINS, CATHERINE HARDING (MRS. ROBERT SCOTT HUDGINS, IV), business exec.; b. Raleigh, N.C., June 25, 1913; d. William Thomas and Mary Alice (Timberlake) Harding; B.S., N.C. State U., 1929-33; grad. tchr. N.C. Sch. for Deaf, 1933-34; m. Robert Scott Hudgins, IV, Aug. 20, 1938; children—Catherine Harding, Deborah Ghiselin, Robert Scott. Tchr., N.C. Sch. for Deaf, Morganton, 1934-36; sec. Dr. A. S. Oliver, Raleigh, 1937; tchr. N.J. Sch. for Deaf, Trenton, 1937-39; sec. Robert S. Hudgins Co., Charlotte, N.C., 1949—, v.p., sec., treas., 1960—, also dir. Mem. Jr. Service League, Easton, Pa., 1939; project chmn. ladies aux. Profl. Engrs. N.C., 1954-55, pres., 1956-57; pres. Christian High Sch. PTA, 1963; program chmn. Charlotte Opera Assn., 1959-61, sec., 1961-63; sec. bd. Hezekiah Alexander House Restoration, 1949-52, Hezekiah Alexander House Found., 1975—. Mem. N.C. Hist. Assn., English Speaking Union, Mint Mus. Arts (pres. drama guild 1967-69), Daus. Am. Colonists (state chmn. nat. def. 1973—), DAR (chpt. regent 1957-59, N.C. program chmn. 1961-63, state rec. sec. 1977-79, state chmn. nat. def. 1973-76, state rec. sec. 1977-79, state regent 1979—, mem. state officers club, mem. Nat. Officers Club, Nat. Chairmen's Assn.), Children Am. Revolution (N.C. sr. pres. 1963-66, nat. bd. mgmt. 1963—, hon. sr. state pres. 1968—, nat. DAR vice chmn. Southeastern region, 1965-68, sr. nat. corr. sec. 1966-68, sr. nat. 1st v.p. 1968-70, sr. nat pres., 1970-72, nat. chmn. for DAR 1970-72; 2d v.p. nat. officers club 1975-77, 1st v.p. 1977-79, now mem.), Internat. Platform Assn. Presbyterian (past chmn. home missions, annuities and relief Women of Ch., past pres. Sunday Sch. class). Club: Carmel

Country (Charlotte). Home: 1514 Wendover Rd Charlotte NC 28211 Office: PO Box 17217 Charlotte NC 28211

HUDGINS, EDWARD MORTON, ret. ry. co. exec.; b. Chase City, Va., Dec. 19, 1910; s. Edward Wren and Lucy Henry (Morton) H.; B.S., U. Va., 1933, LL.B., 1935; m. Mary Atherton Howard, Mar. 10, 1945; children—Edward Wren, Frank Howard. Admitted to Va. bar, practiced in Richmond, 1935-40; with law dept. C.& O. Ry. Co., Richmond and Balt., 1940-48, gen. mgr. claims, 1948-71, v.p. casualty prevention, 1971—; dir. Balt. Cement Co., Chesterfield Cablevision, Inc. Mem. Va. Gen. Assembly, 1952-64; mem. Va. Adv. Legis. Counsel, 1956-64; dep. adj. gen. Va., 1964-67. Served brig. gen. AUS, World War II. Decorated Bronze Star. Clubs: Country of Va., Commonwealth (Richmond); Elkridge (Balt.). Home: 8061 Riverside Dr Richmond VA 23225

HUDGINS, JOE LANE, geologist; b. Union City, Tenn., Jan. 12, 1920; s. William Edgar and Mayme Hamblen (Rippy) H.; B.S. in Geology, U. Okla., 1948; m. Martha Grace Stokes, Mar. 25. 1943; children—Linda, Patricia. With Exxon Co. U.S.A., 1948-79, prodn. geologist, Midland, Tex., 1948-50, with exploration dept., 1952-55, div. exploration geologist, Tyler, Tex., 1955-59, div. geologist, New Orleans, 1959-64, area exploration mgr., 1964-68, adminstrv. mgr., Houston, 1968-76, exploration advisor, 1976-79. Served to maj. U.S. Army, 1942-46, 50-52. Decorated Bronze Star. Mem. Am. Assn. Profl. Geologists (pension com. 1975-76), Am. Geol. Inst., Nat. Geog. Soc. Republican. Mem. Ch. of Christ. Home: 13507 Havershire St Houston TX 77079

HUDGINS, MARY DENGLER, writer; b. Hot Springs Nat. Park, Ark., Nov. 24, 1901; d. Jackson Wharton and Ida (Dengler) H.; B.A., U. Ark., 1924; student Rice Sch. of Spoken Word, 1925, U. Chgo., 1940, U. Wis., 1941, Emory U., 1952. Tchr., Waldo (Ark.) High Sch., 1924-25; free-lance writer, 1925-39, 60—; librarian Hot Springs Pub. Library, 1939-43; med. and gen. librarian Army and Navy Gen. Hosp., Hot Springs, 1943-59; writer articles (specializing in Ark. topics) pub. in ency., hist., lit., profl. and popular publs.; dir. Hot Springs Writers' Workshop, 1960-61. Incorporator, dir. Fine Arts Council, Hot Springs, 1960—; local historian YWCA, Hot Springs; active Hot Springs Little Theater, 1928-34. Mem. Ark. Hist. Assn. (dir. 1963-71, v.p. 1972—), Garland County Hist. Soc. (pres. 1962-63), Ark. (sec. spl. libraries div. 1959-60, reporter to S.W. div. ALA 1955), Med. library assns., Ark. Folklore Assn. (1st v.p. 1958-59), AAUW (Ark. 1st v.p. 1929-30, pres. Hot Springs br. 1927, Ark. fellowship chmn. 1959-61), Ark. Geneal. Soc. (dir.), DAR, Altrusa Internat. Presbyterian (historian). Clubs: Hot Springs Music, Fortnightly, Sabina (pres. 1935), Current Book (pres. Hot Springs 1952, 64). Contbr. articles on Ark. music to periodicals; donor Arkansiana to univ. libraries; donor endowments in music and hist. research. Address: 1030 Park Ave Hot Springs National Park AR 71901

HUDGINS, TOM MALONE, accountant; b. Sherman, Tex., June 12, 1925; s. Harry Middleton and Josephine (Malone) H.; B.S., Austin Coll., 1948; postgrad. U. Tex., 1948-49; m. Ruth Wilder, Mar. 5, 1944; children—Josephine Jordan, Kathleen Beale, Tom Malone, Harry Middleton, Bruce W., Ruth Ann. Sr. accountant firm Sproles & Woodard, Midland, Tex., 1950-54; prin. firm Tom M. Hudgins & Co., Sherman, 1955—. Chmn. Sherman Council Drug Edn., 1971-75, Am. Heart Fund, Sherman, 1970-72, Salvation Army, Sherman, 1960-63, USO, Sherman, 1964; pres. Sherman chpt. United Fund, 1955-56; mem. Devel. Bd. div. council Austin Coll., 1956-75. Served with 4th Armored Div., AUS, 1944-45; ETO. C.P.A., Tex. Mem. Tex. Soc. C.P.A.'s (dir., v.p., C.P.A. of Year Dallas chpt. 1974-75, chpt. pres. 1977-78), Am. Mgmt. Assn., Am. Inst. Mgmt., Accounting Principles Bd., Accounting Standards Assn., Am. Accounting Assn., Internat. Platform Assn., Am. Inst. C.P.A.'s. Club: Woodlawn Country (Sherman). Home: 1400 W Washington Ave Sherman TX 75090 Office: 302 M & P Bank Bldg Sherman TX 75090

HUDGINS, WILLIAM HENRY, ret. lawyer; b. Chase City, Va., Nov. 19, 1915; s. Edward Wren and Lucy (Morton) H.; B.J., A.B., Washington and Lee U., 1938; J.D., U. Va., 1941; postgrad. Fgn. Service Inst., Washington, 1947. Admitted to Va. bar, 1953; vice consul Am. embassy, Santiago, Chile, 1947-48; atty. Office Judge Adv. Gen. of Navy and White House aide, 1949-50; aide flag lt. to Comdr.-in-Chief Eastern Atlantic and Mediterranean, London, 1950-51; sr. aide to comdr.-in-chief S. Europe, NATO, Naples, Italy, 1951-53; apptd. to spl. assignments as aide to supreme NATO comdr. (Gen. Eisenhower) and to King Paul of Greece, 1952-53; mil. aide de camp to Va. govs. Tuck, Battle, Stanley and Almond; atty., Chase City, Va., 1953-70; co-owner, partner Marine Transport Assos., Inc., N.Y.C., 1971—; owner Reveille Plantation, Mecklenburg County; world traveller and lectr. on fgn. affairs. Trustee Roanoke River Mus.; trustee Prestwould Found., mem. fin. com., 1979-81. Commd. midshipman USNR, 1940, advanced through grades to comdr., 1953. Decorated commendatore de Italia (Italy); commandeur de l'Ordre du Ouissam Alaouite Cherifien (France). Mem. Assn. Preservation Va. Antiquities, Nat. Trust Historic Preservation, Chase City C. of C. (chmn. civic com., v.p. 1980-81), Soc. Colonial Wars, SAR, Soc. Descs. of Original Knights of the Garter, Magna Carta Barons, Roanoke River Art Assn. (pres. 1979-80), Va. Mus., Phi Alpha Delta, Sigma Delta Chi, Omicron Delta Kappa, Beta Theta Pi. Episcopalian (vestryman 1964-65, gen. chmn. bicentennial commemoration 1966). Club: Univ. (Washington). Home: MacCallum More 500 Walker St Chase City VA 23924 Office: 601 Hudgins St Chase City VA 23924

HUDGINS, WILLIAM ROBERT, physician; b. Ft. Worth, Mar. 10, 1939; s. William Douglas and Nina Blanche (Jones) H.; student U. Okla., 1957-69; M.D., U. Miss., 1964; m. Cynthia Anne Kite, Aug. 20, 1960; children—Catherine, David, Anne, Lauren. Intern, Duke U., Durham, N.C., 1964-65; resident in neurosurgery U. Tenn., Memphis, 1965-69; research fellow in cerebrovascular disease Regional Stroke Center, Memphis, 1968-69; practice medicine specializing in neurosurgery, Jackson, Miss., 1971-73; mem. staff Scott and White Clinic, Temple, Tex., 1973-75; neurosurgeon Dallas Neurosurg. Assn., 1975—; mem. staff Presbyn. St. Paul and Meth. hosps., Dallas, 1975—; clin. instr. neurosurgery U. Tex. Southwestern Med. Sch., Dallas, 1975—; mem. stroke council Am. Heart Assn., 1978. Served with USN, 1969-71. Decorated Vietnamese Cross of Gallantry with Bronze star. Diplomate Am. Bd. Neurol. Surgery. Fellow Am. Coll. Angiology; mem. Am. Assn. Neurol. Surgeons, Congress Neurol. Surgeons, So. Neurosurg. Soc., Tex. Med. Assn. (1st pl. sci. exhibit award 1976), Alpha Omega Alpha. Baptist. Club: Rotary. Asso. editor: Clinical Neurosurgery, 1974. Home: 5111 Park Ln Dallas TX 75225 Office: 5959 Harry Hines Suite 620 Dallas TX 75235

HUDGINS, WILLIAM WAYNE, truck rental co. exec.; b. Houston, Nov. 4, 1942; s. William Andrew and Naomi Hayes (Conway) H.; student Tarleton State Coll., 1961-63; B.S. in Psychology, Tex. A&M U., 1966; m. Patricia Jo Maxwell, Apr. 8, 1966; children—William Kyle, Amy Louise. With Ryder Truck Rental Co., 1970—, dist. controller, Oklahoma City, 1974-76, adminstrv. devel. mgr., Dallas, 1976—. Served with USAF, 1966-70. Decorated Air Force Commendation medal. Republican. Baptist. Home: 6911 Fawn River Spring TX 77373 Office: 9330 Amberton Pkwy Suite 206 Dallas TX 75243

HUDOBA, MICHAEL, author, editor, cons.; b. Struthers, Ohio, Aug. 1, 1913; s. Anthony and Mary (Prochak) H.; m. Frances Ellen Dunken, Nov. 22, 1941. Asso. and Washington editor Sports Afield mag., 1945-71; author column Report From Washington, 1945-71; dir. environ. affairs, mgr. Washington office Braun & Co., 1971—; dir., mem. exec. com., treas. Nat. Press Bldg. Corp., 1975—; chmn. Nash Conservation Awards Com., 1953; mem. adv. com. on conservation to Sec. Interior, 1953-57, chmn., 1957-61; mem. adv. com. on conservation to Sec. Navy, 1957; past mem. exec. bd. Water Resources Council; past chmn. Nat. Clean Streams Award Com.; past chmn. sports and conservation participation of the register, inform yourself and vote program Am. Heritage Found.; past mem. exec. bd. Emergency Com. Natural Resources; charter mem. Aviation Hist. Found., sec.-treas., 1975—; Republican candidate for Ohio Legislature, 1938. Recipient Nat. award Am. Assn. Conservation Info., 1954, Wildlife Soc., 1956. Hon. life mem. Outdoor Writers Assn. Am. (sec. 1946-53, conservation dir. 1953-58), Nat. Assn. Conservation Edn. (past chmn. conservation awards com.), Izaak Walton League Am.; mem. Nat. Parks Assn. (exec. bd.), Internat. Assn. Game, Fish and Conservation Commnrs., White House Corrs. Assn., Sigma Delta Chi. Clubs: Nat. Press (mem. bd. govs. 1962-71, chmn. bd. 1966-68, v.p. 1969, pres. 1970), Circus Saints and Sinners (Washington). Author: Artifact Hunters Handbook. Home: Leeds Manor Hume VA 22639

HUDSON, CHARLES DAUGHERTY, ins. agy. exec.; b. LaGrange, Ga., Mar. 17, 1927; s. J.D. and Janie (Hill) H.; student Auburn U., 1945-48; LL.D., LaGrange Coll.; m. Ida Cason Callaway, May 1, 1955; children—Jane Alice Hudson Cauble, Ellen Pinson, Charles Daugherty, Ida Callaway. Partner, Hudson Hardware Co., LaGrange, 1950-57; partner Hammond-Hudson Ins. Agy., LaGrange, 1957-58, owner, 1958-78; pres. Hammond, Hudson & Holder, Inc., 1978—; dir., mem. exec. com. Citizens & So. Bank West Ga., La Grange, 1963—; acting pres. LaGrange Coll., 1979-80; dir., v.p. LaGrange Industries, Inc., 1956—. Mem. exec. com. Camp Viola, Lagrange, 1956—; v.p., trustee Callaway Found., Inc., 1957—, Fuller E. Callaway Found., 1965—; chmn. LaGrange chpt. United Fund, 1964—; mem. LaGrange Bd. Edn., 1967—, chmn., 1971-74. Chmn. bd. trustees LaGrange Coll., Ga. Baptist Hosp., Atlanta; trustee, pres. West Ga. Med. Center, LaGrange, 1973—; trustee, pres. Ocfuskee Hist. Soc., 1975—. Recipient pres.'s award Colonial Life Ins. Co., 1966, 69, 70, 75, 76, 77, 78, 79, Disting. Alumni award Ga. Mil. Acad., 1971, Respect Law award Optimists Assn., 1967, Public Service award Ga. chpt. AIA, 1977, Leading Producer award Aetna Life & Casualty, 1979. Mem. Ga. Assn. Independent Ins. Agts., Ga. Sch. Bd. Assn. (area dir.), S.A.R., Amicale de Groupe Lafayette (hon.), Chattahoochee Valley Art Assn., Beta Gamma Sigma, Sigma Alpha Epsilon. Baptist (deacon 1953—). Mason, (Shriner), Elk, Rotarian (pres. club 1964-65). Clubs: Highland Country (La Grange); Commerce (Atlanta). Home: Country Club Rd LaGrange GA 30240 Office: 100 Greenville St LaGrange GA 30240

HUDSON, CHARLES HOWARD, plastic co. exec.; b. Winston-Salem, N.C., Aug. 17, 1943; s. Stephen Timothy and Francis (Dagenhart) H.; B.S., U. Va., 1970; m. Vivian Barker Hudson, Dec. 15, 1962; children—Scott Campbell, Kristy Karol. Staff accountant A.M. Pullen & Co., Richmond, Va., 1970-72, Philip Morris Co., Richmond, 1972-73; controller PCL Packaging, Inc., Remington, Va., 1973-75, v.p., 1975—, treas. PCL Industries Ltd., Toronto, Ont., Can., 1976—, PCL Packaging U.K., Stonehouse, Eng., 1976—, Oakville, Ont., 1976—. Served with USN, 1961-64. C.P.A., Va. Mem. Am. Inst. C.P.A.'s. Methodist. Club: Lions. Home: 2380 Fox Hill Rd Culpeper VA 22701 Office: PCL Packaging PO Box 367 Remington VA 22734

HUDSON, DORIS JEAN, furniture co. exec.; b. New Castle, Ind., June 12, 1936; d. Kenneth Leroy and Mary Louise (Jones) Cox; student public schs., Ind.; m. Russell H. Hudson, June 3, 1956; children—Brenda Kay, Russell Brian. Bookkeeper, G.C. Murphy Co., Greensburg, Ind., 1954-57; accounts receivable bookkeeper MoJo Oil Co., Panama City, Fla., 1957-59; head bookkeeper Hall Furniture Co., Inc., Panama City, 1960-74, fin. controller, office mgr., dir. 1974—. Baptist. Home: 2104 E Norwood Dr Panama City FL 32405 Office: Hall Furniture Co Inc 540 Harrison Ave PO Box 266 Panama City FL 32401

HUDSON, JOHN LESTER, chem. engr.; b. Chgo., June 19, 1937; s. John Jones and Linda Madeline (Panozzo) H.; B.S., U. Ill., 1959; M.S. in Engring., Princeton U., 1960; Ph.D. (NSF fellow), Northwestern U., 1962; m. Janette Glenore Caton, June 29, 1963; children—Ann, Barbara, Sarah. Asst. prof. chem. engring. U. Ill., Urbana, 1963-69, asso. prof., 1969-75; mgr. Ill. Div. Air Pollution Control, Springfield, 1974-75; prof., chmn. dept. chem. engring. U. Va., Charlottesville, 1975—; cons. to various industries and govt. agys., 1966—. Fulbright fellow, 1962-63; registered profl. engr., Ill. Mem. Am. Inst. Chem. Engrs., Am. Chem. Soc., Air Pollution Control Assn. Contbr. articles in chem. engring. to profl. jours. Home: 1920 Thomson Rd Charlottesville VA 22903 Office: Thornton Hall U Va Charlottesville VA 22901

HUDSON, JOSEPH WILLIS, business exec.; b. Woodruff, S.C., Feb. 3, 1934; s. Joseph Taylor and Martha Jane (Willis) H.; student U. N.C., 1952-55; m. Elsa Garrow Perlitz, Sept. 1, 1955; children—Elsa Garrow, Joseph Willis. Sales staff Hudson & Co., Inc., Spartanburg, S.C., 1955-59, pres., 1959-73, dir., 1959-73; founder, pres. Willis Brinkman, Ins., Spartanburg, 1960-67; founder Nat. Bank Commerce, Spartanburg, S.C., 1968, chmn. bd., 1968-70 (merged First Citizens Bank & Trust Co. 1970), dir. First Citizens Bank & Trust Co., Columbia, S.C., until 1979; pres. Ward & Hudson Travel Services, Inc. Mem. Small Bus. Adminstrn. Adv. Council for S.C., 1969-70; chmn. S.C. Wildlife and Marine Resources Commn., 1972-78; mem. S.C. Adv. Com. for Environ. Edn. chmn. adv. bd. S.C. Heritage Trust; mem. environ. quality and natural resources com. wildlife adv. com. Coll. Agr., Clemson U., bd. dirs. Game Conversation Internat., 1972—; trustee, mem. exec. com. Ducks Unlimited; trustee African Wildlife Leadership Found.; bd. dirs. S.C. Marine Research and Conservation Found.; adviser marine resources adv. com. Coastal Plains Regional Commn.; pres. Nat. Found. for Conservation and Environ. Officers; bd. dirs. S.C. Wildlife Fedn., 1975—. Served with AUS, 1957-59. Mem. East African Profl. Hunters Assn., Sigma Chi. Clubs: Shikar-Safari Internat.; Explorers of New York, African Safari of New York (N.Y.C.); Boone and Crockett. Home: PO Box 3326 Spartanburg SC 29304 Office: 450 E Henry St Room 315 Spartanburg SC 29304

HUDSON, JUDITH LEE, mfg. co. exec.; b. Columbia, Mo., Apr. 21, 1941; d. Clifford Crim and Bertha Thurlee (Woods) Hough; A.F.A., Columbia Coll., 1961; B.S. in Edn., U. Mo., 1963, M.Ed., 1964; children—Clinton Cain, Brett Alan. Tchr., counselor Sea Gate Elem. Sch., Naples, Fla., 1963-64; tchr. Thomas Jefferson Jr. High Sch., Miami, Fla., 1964-66; resident mgr. El Conquistador Residence Hall, Univ. Inns, Inc., San Diego, 1966-68; personnel rep. Cordis Corp., Miami, 1973-76; employee communications and equal opportunity mgr. Cordis Dow Corp., Miami, 1976-78, corp. mgr. compensation, 1978-80, corp. mgr. compensation and benefits, 1980—. Recipient Appreciation award Regional Purchasing Council ind., 1978. Mem. Am. Soc. Personnel Adminstrs., Am. Compensation Assn. Home: 20030 NE 21st Ave North Miami Beach FL 33179 Office: 999 Brickell Ave Miami FL 33131

HUDSON, LEONARD LESTER, former sch. adminstr.; b. Decatur, Tex., July 23, 1910; s. Harve Hubert and Laura Hilda (Watson) H.; A.S., Decatur Bapt. Coll., 1953; B.S., N. Tex. State U., 1957, M.Ed., 1960; D.D., Kansas City Bible Coll., 1958; Ph.D., Central Christian Coll., 1963; D. Arts-Religion, Internat. U., 1977, Ph.D. 1978; m. Reba Fae Porter, Oct. 16, 1928; children—Robert Lester, Frank L. Clk., asst. mgr. Griffin Grocery, Chickasha, Okla., 1928-43; aircraft foreman Douglas Aircraft Mfg., Oklahoma City, 1943-45; owner Hudson Grocery, Chickasha, 1945-53; instr. Decatur (Tex.) Bapt. Coll., 1953-55, North Tex. State U., Denton, 1955-57; prin. Era (Tex.) Consol. Schs., 1957-61; supt. schs., Beeler, Kans., 1961-66, Ingalls-Alta Vista, Kans., 1966-70, Ford, Kans., 1970-73; adminstr. Bill's Mobile Home Park, Oklahoma City, 1973—. Mem. N.E.A., Assn. Higher Edn., Am. Assn. Higher Edn., Pi Sigma Alpha. Author: Faith, 1948. Inventor in aircraft field. Home: 5945 S Terry Joe Ave Oklahoma City OK 73129 Office: 2145 SE 59th St Oklahoma City OK 73129

HUDSON, MARIAN SUE PARSONS, pharmacist; b. Pinehurst, N.C., Sept. 24, 1951; d. Solomon Lankester and Doris Eva (Bost) Parsons; A.A., Sandhills Community Coll., Southern Pines, N.C., 1971; B.S. in Pharmacy, U. N.C., 1974; 1 son, Stephen Ray. Intern, Duke Med. Center, 1973, Howell Drug Co., Inc., Raeford, N.C., 1974-75; pharmacist Bryan Drug Co., Inc., Aberdeen, N.C., 1975; dir. pharmacy McCain (N.C.) Hosp., 1975—; instr. in field. Vol. fund dr. Heart Assn., Southern Pines; bd. dirs. N.C. PharmPAC. Mem. N.C. Soc. Hosp. Pharmacists, N.C. State Drug Adv. Com. for Purchasing and Contract, Am. Soc. Hosp. Pharmacists, N.C. Pharm. Assn., N.C. State Employees Assn. Democrat. Presbyterian. Office: Hwy 211 McCain NC 28361

HUDSON, MARY GAIL CARNEAL, speech pathologist; b. Dallas, Jan. 4, 1953; d. Virgil Eugene and Mary Sigrid (Lanum) Carneal; B.S. with honors, So. Meth. U., 1974, M.S., 1976; m. Paul William Hudson, Jan. 11, 1975. Speech, hearing and lang. pathologist Richardson Ind. Sch. Dist., Dallas, 1976—; part-time pvt. speech pathologist, 1977—. Recipient cert. clin. competence Am. Speech and Hearing Assn.; cert. tchr., Tex. Mem. Internat. Assn. Logopedics and Phoniatrics, Am. Speech and Hearing Assn., Tex. Speech and Hearing Assn., Assn. Tex. Educators, Richardson Assn. Tex. Educators, Dallas Assn. Speech Pathologists and Audiologists, Richardson Edn. Assn., Dallas Mus. Fine Arts, Smithsonian Asso., Nat. Geog. Soc., Zeta Phi Eta. Republican. Methodist. Home: 3828 Silverstone Plano TX 75023 Office: 7667 Roundrock Rd Dallas TX 75248

HUDSON, RALPH MAGEE, educator; b. Fields, Ohio, Dec. 18, 1907; s. Claude Henry and Agnes Mary (Magee) H.; B.A., Ohio State U., 1930, B.S., 1930, M.A., 1931, fellow Advanced Inst. Art Appreciation, 1966; Ed.D., U. Ala., 1965; m. Louise Dale, Feb. 22, 1929; children—Shirley Hudson Musgrave, Genie Hudson Patrick. Acting chmn., instr. art dept. Morehead (Ky.) State Coll., 1931-32, 33-36; chmn. art dept. U. Ark., 1936-46; prof., chmn. art dept. Miss. State Coll. for Women, 1946-69; prof., chmn. art dept. U. Ala., Huntsville, 1969-74, lectr. art, 1974—; vis. prof. art Instituto Allende, San Miguel de Allende, Mex., 1974; guest curator Huntsville Mus. Art, 1979; lectr. on art and life in various countries. U. Ala. fellow, 1964; Ohio State U. fellow, 1966; Nat. Endowment for Humanities research grantee, 1972-74. Mem. Nat. Art Edn. Assn., Ala. Art Edn. Assn., Southeastern Coll. Art Conf. (Disting. Service award 1974), SAR, Phi Beta Kappa, Phi Kappa Phi, Kappa Delta Pi, Phi Delta Kappa, Kappa Pi. Episcopalian. Club: Rotary. Home: 7102 Criner Rd Huntsville AL 35802

HUDSON, REGGIE LESTER, chemist; b. Newport News, Va., July 23, 1952; s. Everett Lester and Patty Jo (Burleson) H.; A.B., Pfeiffer Coll., 1974; Ph.D., U. Tenn., 1978. Asst. prof. phys. chemistry Eckerd Coll., St. Petersburg, Fla., 1978—. Mem. Am. Chem. Soc., Sigma Xi. Baptist. Contbr. articles to profl. jours. Home: 3651 38th Way S Saint Petersburg FL 33711 Office: Collegium Natural Scis Eckerd Coll Saint Petersburg FL 33733

HUDSON, ROBERT FRANKLIN, JR., lawyer; b. Coral Gables, Fla., Sept. 20, 1946; s. Robert Franklin and Jane Ann (Reed) H.; B.S. in Bus. Adminstrn., U. Fla., 1968, J.D., 1971; postgrad. Univ. Coll., London, 1970; LL.M., N.Y. U., 1972; m. Edith Mueller, June 19, 1971. Admitted to Fla. bar, 1971, N.Y. bar, 1974; law clk. Hon. Don N. Laramore U.S. Ct. Claims, Washington, 1972-73; tax asso. firm Wender, Murase & White, N.Y.C., 1973-77; partner firm Arky, Freed, Stearns, Watson & Greer, Miami, 1977—; asso. prof. econs. U. Fla., 1969-71. Served to 2d lt. U.S. Army, 1972. Mem. Miami Com. Fgn. Affairs, Am. Bar Assn., Fla. Bar Assn., Inter-Am. Bar Assn., Internat. Fiscal Assn., N.Y. State Bar Assn., N.Y. Tax Soc., Greater Miami Tax Inst., Coral Gables C. of C. Democrat. Methodist. Office: 1 Biscayne Tower Suite 2800 Miami FL 33131

HUDSON, SHERRY CARNEY, coll. adminstr.; b. Lake Charles, La., May 30, 1947; d. Payton W. and Theresa R. (Gaisser) Carney; student McNeese State U., 1965-68, U. St. Thomas, 1974-75, N.Y. U., 1977, U. Pa., 1977; m. Donald Wayne Hudson, June 18, 1966; 1 dau., Pamela Cherie. Staff cost acct. PPG Industries, Lake Charles, La., 1968-72; acctg. clk. Pence Constrn. Co., Houston, 1972-73; full charge bookkeeper RHG Constrn. Co., Houston, 1973; sr. adminstrv. asst., dept. cell biology Baylor Coll. Medicine, Houston, 1973—; chmn. supervisory com. Baylor Coll. Medicine Credit Union, 1977—; dir. Houston Biol. Assos. Mem. Nat. Council Univ. Research Adminstrs., Soc. Research Adminstrs., Alpha Delta Pi. Democrat. Roman Catholic. Home: 9203 Montford Dr Houston TX 77099 Office: Dept Cell Biology Baylor College of Medicine 1200 Moursund Ave Houston TX 77030

HUDSON, THOMAS H., state senator; b. Russellville, Ark., Nov. 23, 1946; s. Henry E. and Cecile (Stanford) H.; B.A., La. State U., 1969, J.D., 1971. Admitted to La. bar; spl. asst. to U.S. Senator J. Bennett Johnston, 1972-73; pvt. practice, Baton Rouge, 1973—; mem. La. Senate, 1976—; mem. Commn. Presdl. Scholars, 1977, Capital Econ. Devel. Dist. Council, 1976. Bd. dirs. Baton Rouge Sickle Cell Anemia Found., Community Assn. for Welfare Sch. Children, La. Arts and Sci. Center, La. Physician Manpower, Eden Park Community Center; chmn. profl. div. Baton Rouge Arts and Humanities Council, 1977-78; mem. La. adv. com. EXCEL; meml La. Democratic Central Com. Served to 1st lt. U.S. Army Res., 1972. Mem. Am. Bar Assn., La. Bar Assn., D.C. Bar Assn., Baton Rouge Bar Assn., Baton Rouge Jaycees. Club: Kiwanis. Address: PO Box 65101 Baton Rouge LA 70896

HUDSON, W(ALTER) TAYLOR, utilities co. exec. b. Lexington, Ky., Feb. 24, 1920; s. J. Wood and Beulah (Green) H.; A.B. with distinction, U. Ky., 1949; m. Martha Jean Ireland, Nov. 23, 1952; 1 son, Richard. With Ky. Utilities Co., Lexington, 1951—, automotive fleet mgr., 1953-65, asst. personnel dir., 1965-71, personnel dir., 1971—. Served with AUS, 1941-45. Decorated Bronze Star; recipient Silver Beaver award Boy Scouts Am. Mem. Am. Soc. Personnel Adminstrs. (accredited), Bluegrass Personnel Assn., Central Ky.

Mgmt. Conf. Republican. Methodist. Home: 1039 Della Dr Lexington KY 40504 Office: One Quality St Lexington KY 40507

HUDSPETH, WILLIAM ROY, JR., chem. co. exec.; b. Winston-Salem, N.C., Mar. 21, 1923; s. William Roy and Lee (Wilcox) H.; student Wake Forest Coll., 1942, U. Wis., 1943; B.S., U. N.C., 1948, postgrad., 1948; m. Nancy Webber, Dec. 22, 1944; children—William Broughton, Patricia Lee, Nancy Ann. Control engr. Western Electric Co., Winston-Salem, 1948-49; research engr. Asheville Minerals Research Lab., 1949-51; plant chemist Foote Mineral Co., Kings Mountain, N.C., 1951-52, metall. engr., 1952-54, mill supt., 1954-56, plant supt., Sunbright, Va., 1956-58, gen. supt. 1958, asst. mgr., 1958-59, plant mgr., Cold River, N.H., 1959-60, mgr. spl. project, Exton, Pa., 1960-62, gen. mgr. comml. devel., 1962-65, asst. v.p. mktg., 1965—; asst. to pres. McCall Pattern Co., 1967, v.p. mfg., 1968-71; v.p., gen. mgr. chems. Chattem Drug and Chem. Co. (Tenn.), 1971-76; pres., chief exec. officer Hudspeth Corp., Chattanooga, 1976—. Mem. research adv. bd. N.C. State U., 1956—; mem. Easttown Library Bd., 1964—; mem. council bd. Boy Scouts Am., 1958—; bd. dirs. Johnson Recreational Park Bd., 1959—; trustee Holston Valley Hosp. Served with USAAF, 1942-44. Mem. Am. Inst. Chem. Engrs. (career guidance bd.), Am. Inst. Mining, Metall. and Petroleum Engrs., Am. Ceramic Soc., Am. Chem. Soc., N.H. Edn. Assn., Am. Legion, Jr. C. of C., Alpha Chi Sigma, Phi Kappa Sigma. Republican. Methodist. Clubs: Waynesborough Country, Lions, Rotary. Inventor mica recovery process, mineral analytical technique. Home and Office: 137 Valleybrook Circle Chattanooga TN 37343

HUEBNER, RICHARD ALLEN, assn. exec.; b. Milw., July 31, 1950; s. Otto LeRoy and Audrey Elizabeth (Klabunde) H.; B.B.A., U. Wis., 1972; m. Marsha Kay Lawrence, Sept. 3, 1977; children—Angela Carol, Holly Anne. Grad. asst. U. Wis., 1972-73; cons. Kappa Sigma Fraternity, Charlottesville, Va., 1973-74, tng. dir., 1974-76, exec. dir., 1976—. Lay catechist, youth group adviser St. Marks Lutheran Ch., 1975—. Mem. Am. Soc. Assn. Execs., Internat. Platform Assn., Frat. Execs. Assn., Assn. Frat. Advisers, Edgewater Conf., U.S. Jaycees (dir. Charlottesville-Albemarle chpt., state dir. 1979-80, Key Man award 1979), Kappa Sigma. Home: 2700 Leeds Ln Charlottesville VA 22901 Office: PO Box 5066 Charlottesville VA 22903

HUEG, DONALD CHARLES, savs. and loan exec.; b. Bklyn., June 10, 1928; s. William H. and Anna (Mueller) H.; cert. Hursley Mgmt. Inst., 1974; m. Esther M. Benjamin, Nov. 25, 1978; children—Patricia Gloria, Jean Emilia, Douglas Raymond. With John Walker Letter Service Inc., N.Y.C., 1947-54, prodn. mgr., 1952-54; multilith operator Admiral Photo Offset Co., Inc., N.Y.C., 1954-59, prodn. mgr., 1959-74; mgr. printing, mailing and stores Fla. Fed. Savs. & Loan Assn., St. Petersburg, 1974—. Recipient Reprographic Mgmt. award, 1976; cert. graphics communications mgr. Mem. In-Plant Printing Mgmt. Assn. (v.p. Fla. Gulf Coast chpt. 1975-77, pres. 1977-79), Bus. Forms Mgmt. Assn. Republican. Lutheran. Home: 1201 35th St N Saint Petersburg FL 33713 Office: 16 3d St N Saint Petersburg FL 33731

HUEY, JOHN PETER, hosp. adminstr.; b. Cisco, Tex., Apr. 21, 1915; s. Bell Stephen and Ethel Rhea (Kauffman) H.; student Hardin-Simmons U., Abilene, Tex., 1932-34; m. Mary Elizabeth Montgomery, July 25, 1941; 1 son, Steven Lawrence. Asso. adminstr., comptroller Bexer County Hosp. Dist., San Antonio, 1952-59; adminstr. Collia Meml. Hosp., McKinney, Tex., 1959-71, 72—; adminstr. Physicians and Surgeons Hosp., Corpus Christi, 1971-72. Trustee, chmn. United Fund, McKinney, 1963. Served with USNR, 1942-45. Fellow Am. Coll. Hosp. Adminstrs.; mem. Am. Hosp. Assn., Tex. Hosp. Assn. (trustee 1969-72), Dallas Hosp. Council (pres. 1977, trustee 1974-76). Presbyterian. Club: Rotary (pres. 1962). Contbr. articles to profl. jours. Home: 1913 Wisteria Way McKinney TX 75069 Office: PO Box 370 1800 N Grave St McKinney TX 75069

HUFF, HENRY BLAIR, lawyer; b. Louisville, Aug. 30, 1924; s. Joseph B. and Mattie (Ireland) H.; B.S., J.D., Wake Forest Coll., 1949; M.A., U. Louisville, 1958; m. Mary Anderson, May 24, 1969. Admitted to N.C. bar, 1949, Ky. bar, 1954; law practice, Lenoir, N.C., 1949-54, Louisville, 1954—; dir. OLCO, Inc., Zoeller Co., Inc. Chmn. bd. trustees City of Brownsboro Village, 1958-65; trustee Clear Creek Bapt. Sch., 1967-73; trustee Campbellsville Coll., 1973—, chmn., 1978—; pres. Ky. Bapt. Conv., 1975-76; moderator Long Run Bapt. Assn., 1980—. Served with C.E., AUS, 1943-46. Mem. Am., Ky., Louisville bar assns., Am. Judicature Soc. Home: 170 Westwind Rd Louisville KY 40207 Office: 2110 1st Nat Tower 101 S 5th St Louisville KY 40202

HUFF, KENNETH HARLEN, graphic arts designer; b. Salem, Va., June 16, 1923; s. Howard Harry and Ethel Mae (Dillman) H.; m. Jeanette E. Howell, Jan. 24, 1946; children—Jenny (Mrs. Stephen J. Thomas), Stephen. Art dir. Richmond (Va.) Newspapers Inc., 1952-61; with Hall & Frayser Advt., Richmond, 1961-76; v.p., art dir., prodn. mgr. Robin Frayser Assos., Richmond, 1963—; owner Ken Huff Advt., 1977—; mem. adj. faculty mass communications dept. Va. Commonwealth U., 1957—. Served with AUS, 1943-46. Mem. Ch. of Christ (elder). Home: 2416 Lincoln Ave Richmond VA 23228 Office: Suite 204 2720 Enterprise Bldg Richmond VA 23229

HUFF, LULA ELEANOR LUNSFORD, acct.; b. Columbus, Ga., July 5, 1949; d. Walter Theophilus and Sally Marie (Bryant) Lunsford; B.A. cum laude, Howard U., 1971; M.B.A. with honors, Atlanta U., 1973; m. Charles Efferidge Huff, Jr., June 11, 1972. Election cons. and coordinator Neighborhood Council, Washington, 1967-69; clk. Census Bur., Washington, 1970; tax specialist CSC, Washington, 1970-71; acct. Kennedy, Bussey & Sampson, Atlanta, 1972-73, Ernst & Ernst, Columbus, 1973-76; internal auditor Columbus Consol. Govt., 1976—; instr. acctg. Troy State Coll., Columbus; cons. to small businesses and orgns. Recipient Outstanding Achievement and Service award 1st African Bapt. Ch., Columbus, 1975; Achievement award Link's Inc., 1976; Outstanding Service award St. Benedict Cath. Ch., 1976; Black Excellence award Nat. Assn. Negro Bus. and Profl. Women's Clubs, Inc., 1977; Profl. Woman of Yr. award Iota Phi Lambda, 1977, Outstanding Woman of Yr. award So. region, 1978, Bus. Woman of Yr. award, 1979. Mem. Am. Inst. C.P.A.'s, Ga. State Soc. C.P.A.'s, Inst. Internal Auditors, Am. Women's Soc. C.P.A.'s, Mcpl. Fin. Officers Assn., Howard U. Alumnae, Atlanta U. Alumnae, Nat. Council Negro Women (treas. 1978—), NAACP, Urban League, Delta Sigma Theta (corr. sec. 1972-78). Roman Catholic. Home: 635 Zeron Dr Columbus GA 31907 Office: Columbus Consol Govt PO Box 1340 Columbus GA 31902

HUFF, OZZIE, environ. scientist; b. Marion, Ala., Mar. 30, 1944; s. Emmit and Adelle (Jones) H. B.S., Ala. State U., 1965; M.S., Fisk U., 1972; postgrad. U. West Fla., Oak Ridge Associated Univs., UCLA, Tuskee Inst., U. Detroit; m. Vivian Foster, Dec. 31, 1975; children—LaQuedia Machelle, Vanessa Renee, Gary Bernard. Instr. chemistry R. B. Hudson High Sch., Selma, Ala., 1965-67; chmn. jr. coll. sci. dept. Selma U., 1967-71, asst. basketball coach, dean of men, 1968-71; analytical chemist TVA, Muscle Shoals, Ala., 1972, project mgr., environ. scientist, 1973—. NSF grantee, 1967, 68, 69, 70, 1971-72. Mem. Am. Chem. Soc., TVA Engrng. Assn., AAAS, Air Pollution Control Assn., Black Ednl. Tutoring Assn., Fed. Assn. Blacks. Democrat. Contbr. articles to profl. jours. Home: 3501 Union St Florence AL 35630 Office: EDB Air Quality Branch Muscle Shoals AL 35660

HUFF, WILLIAM JENNINGS, lawyer, educator; b. Summerland, Miss., Mar. 3, 1919; s. William Yancey and Hattie Lenora (Robinson) H.; B.S., Miss. State U., 1956; M.A. (asst. fellow 1956-59), Rice U., 1957, Ph.D. (Tex. Gulf Producing Co. fellow 1960), 1960; LL.B., U. Miss., 1947, J.D., 1968; m. Frances Ellen Rossman, Feb. 26, 1944; 1 son, John Rossman. Admitted to Miss. bar, 1947, Tenn. bar, 1948; closing atty. Commerce Title Guaranty Co., Memphis, 1947-49; atty., adviser FCC, Washington, 1953-54; asso. prof. geology U. So. Miss., Hattiesburg, 1960-65; asst. prof. natural scis. Mich. State U., East Lansing, 1966-68; asso. prof. geology U. South Ala., Mobile, 1968—; practice law, Pascagoula, Miss. Served with USAF, 1941-45, judge adv., 1949-52; lt. col. Res. ret. Decorated Air medal with ten oak leaf clusters. Named Outstanding Grad. Student in Dept. Geology, Rice U., 1959-60. Mem. Miss., Tenn. bars, Am. Assn. Petroleum Geologists, Soc. Econ. Mineralogists and Paleontologists, Paleontol. Research Soc., N.Y. Acad. Sci., Ala. Geol. Soc., AAUP. Mason (Shriner). Contbr. articles to various publs. Home: 5917 Montfort Rd S Mobile AL 36608

HUFFER, MARGARET JEAN, food service adminstr.; b. Rockingham County, Va., Feb. 21, 1929; d. Lester Brunk and Naomi Margaret (Gowl) Shank; m. Arland E. Huffer, Oct. 20, 1946; children—Lester David, Marjorie Arlane, Mary Ellen. Food service supr. Bridgewater (Va.) Home, Inc., 1965-77; food service dir. Shenandoah Lodge, Inc., Harrisonburg, Va., 1977—. Mem. Am. Soc. Hosp. Food Service Adminstrs., Am. Hosp. Assn., Am. Assn. Ret. Persons, Va. Beef Cattle Assn. Mem. Ch. of the Brethren. Club: Home Demonstration. Home: Route 2 Box 240 Dayton VA 22821 Office: Route 6 Box 52 Harrisonburg VA 22801

HUFFMAN, AUDREY BROWN, dietetic asst., hosp. ofcl.; b. Alexander County, N.C., Sept. 9, 1923; d. Jessie Euel and Lillie (Cline) Brown; m. Bruce Houston Huffman, Feb. 5, 1944; children—Patricia Gail, David William, Douglas Eugene, Deborah Leigh. Mgr. sch. lunch St. Stephen's High Sch., Hickory, N.C., 1957-67; mgr. food service Catawba Meml. Hosp., 1967—. Mem. Nutrition Council Catawba County (N.C.), 1978—; sec. Catawba County Nutrition, treas., 1978-79. Mem. Hosp. Food Service Adminstrs., Hosp., Inst., Ednl. Food Service Soc. (past pres. Western N.C. dist.), Bus. and Profl. Women's Club Hickory, Sweet Adolines (pres. chpt. 1977-78). Address: Route 2 Box 321 Conover NC 28613

HUFFMAN, ODELL HAMPTON, state senator W.Va.; b. Wyco, W.Va., Feb. 18, 1923; s. Mitchell Odell and Callie Valerie (Whittington) H.; student Concord Coll., 1940-47; J.D., W.Va. U., 1950; m. Geraldine Cline, Aug. 6, 1950; children—Katherine Ann, David Hampton, William Odell, John Bruce. Admitted to W.Va. bar, 1950; mem. W.Va. Ho. of Dels., 1969-72; mem. W.Va. Senate, 1973—, chmn. health com.; mem. Statewide Health Coordinating Council. Pres. Princeton Planning Commn., 1960-64; mem. Princeton City Council, 1962-66; mayor of Princeton, 1967-68; pres. Princeton Meml. Hosp., 1965-67. Served with USAAF, 1943-46. Mem. Am. Bar Assn., W.Va. Trial Lawyers Assn., Health Research and Ednl. Trust, Princeton Community Hosp. Assn., Princeton C. of C. (dir.), Gt. Lakes to Fla. Hwy. Assn.; affiliate Am. Hosp. Assn. Democrat. Methodist. Clubs: Rotary, Elks, Moose. Home: 1604 W Main St Princeton WV 24740

HUFFMAN, ROBERT TERRY, wetland ecologist; b. San Antonio, June 21, 1950; s. Robert Doyle and Bethel (Havens) H.; B.S.E. in Biology and Edn., Henderson State U., 1971; M.S. in Botany/Community Ecology, U. Ark., 1974, Ph.D., 1976. Team leader-research botanist Wetland Regulatory Criteria Research, U.S. Army Waterways Expt. Sta., Vicksburg, Miss., 1978—. Served as 1st lt. C.E., U.S. Army, 1976-78. NSF research grantee, 1975-76. Mem. Ecol. Soc. Am., Am. Inst. Biol. Scis., Ark. Acad. Scis., Gulf Estuarine Research Fedn., Soc. Wetland Scientists, Sigma Xi. Club: Optimists (v.p. 1979-80) (Vicksburg). Office: USAE Waterways Expt Sta PO Box 631 Vicksburg MS 39180

HUFFMAN, WILLIAM HARRY, pub. sch. counselor; b. Charlestown, W.Va., Dec. 19, 1949; s. Robert Lee and Marion (Lamb) H.; B.A., E. Carolina U., Greenville, N.C., 1971, M.Ed., 1974; m. Jane Gleason, Mar. 6, 1971. Tchr., Sumter (S.C.) Sch. Dist., 1971-73; guidance counselor Pitt County Schs., Greenville, N.C., 1974-79, with dept. counseling psychology Duke U., 1979—; asst. to counseling dept. E. Carolina U., summers 1975-79. Mem. Child Abuse Planning Team, Greenville; cons., lectr., dir. arts and crafts program migrant laborer program, Greenville; active PTA. Mem. Am. Personnel and Guidance Assn., NEA, N.C. Edn. Assn., Psi Chi, Kappa Delta Pi. Democrat. Episcopalian. Home: 2113 Pershing St Durham NC 27705 Office: Duke U West Bldg Durham NC 27705

HUFFORD, GEORGE LUCIAN, state ofcl.; b. Patriot, Ind., June 11, 1934; s. Fletcher Newton and Gertrude Janet (Johnson) H.; student Ind. U., 1961-64, Trinity U., 1955, No. Mich. U., 1957, Columbia State Community Coll., 1974-76; m. Vella Jean Turner, Aug. 9, 1954; children—Charles Richard, Walter Ray, Cynthia Jean. Employment services dir. State Employment Services of Ind., Lawrenceburg, 1959-61; program dir., asst. div. dir. Crippled Children's Services, Ind. State Welfare Dept., Indpls., 1961-64; exec. dir. S.E. Ind. Rehab. Center, Jeffersonville, 1964-69; exec. dir. Mobile (Ala.) Rotary Rehab. Center, 1969-71; adminstr. New Hope Found., Indpls., 1972-73; exec. dir. Tenn. State Easter Seal Soc., Nashville, 1973-75; pres. Hufford Enterprises, Franklin, Tenn., 1976-78; Medicaid investigator Tenn. Dept. Public Health, Nashville, 1979—. Mem. tech. adv. com. on transp. of elderly Tenn. Dept. Transp., 1974-76; chmn. Mobile Com. Employment of Handicapped, 1970-72; program and service design group for comprehensive epilspsy program Vanderbilt U., Nashville, 1974-75; chmn. health rehab. com. Nashville Council Community Services, 1973-74; bd. dirs. S.W. Ala. Regional Health Planning Council, 1970-71. Served with USAF, 1954-58, 62. Lic. nursing home adminstr., Ala., Tenn.; lic. ins. agt., Tenn. Mem. Nat. Assn. Rehab. Services, Tenn. Health Care Assn., Nat. Rehab. Assn., Assn. Med. Rehab. Dirs. and Coordinators, Nat. Easter Seal Exec. Assn., Am. Mus. Natural History, Smithsonian Asso., Nat. Parks and Conservation Assn., Early Am. Soc., Nat. Campers and Hikers Assn., Air Force Assn., Am. Legion. Republican. Methodist. Clubs: Good Sam Recreational Vehicle, Masons. Contbr. articles to profl. jours. Home: Route 2 Hwy 431 Ellington Park Franklin TN 37064 Office: Suite D 283 Plus Park Blvd Nashville TN 37217

HUFFSTETLER, VIRGINIA JEAN, nurse; b. Cleveland County, N.C., Dec. 31, 1931; d. Pressley Casar and Lucy Mabel (Sellers) H.; diploma Shelby (N.C.) Hosp. Sch. Nursing, 1953; postgrad. Baylor U., 1965. Staff nurse operating room Cleveland Meml. Hosp., Shelby, 1953-54, operating supr., 1955—, instr., 1955-58; staff nurse VA Hosp., Durham, N.C., 1955; mem. panel Operating Research Inst. Mem. Assn. Operating Room Nurses (dir. N.C. chpt. 1973-76, pres. elect 1976-77, pres. 1977-78). Democrat. Methodist. Home: Apt 15 811 W Sumter St Shelby NC 28150 Office: 201 Grover St Shelby NC 28150

HUGE, HARRY, lawyer; b. Deshler, Nebr., Sept. 16, 1937; s. Arthur and Dorothy (Vor de Strasse) H.; A.B., Nebr. Wesleyan U., 1959; J.D. (mem. law jour.), Georgetown U., 1963; m. Reba Kinne, July 2, 1960; 1 son, Theodore. Admitted to Ill. bar, 1963, D.C. bar, 1965; asso. firm Chapman & Cutler, Chgo., 1963-65; asso., then partner firm Arnold & Porter, Washington, 1965-76; sr. partner firm Rogovin, Stern & Huge, Washington, 1976—; chmn. trustee United Mine Workers Health and Retirement Funds, 1973-78; dir. DBA Systems, Inc., Melbourne, Fla., 1967-78, Huge Sales, Inc., Gatlinburg, Tenn., 1978—. Mem. President's Gen. Adv. Com. Arms Control, 1977—; trustee Nebr. Wesleyan U., 1978—; pres. Voter Edn. Project, Atlanta, 1974-78. Served with U.S. Army, 1960; mem. D.C. and Ill. N.G., 1960-65. Mem. Am. Bar Assn., D.C. Bar Assn. (bd. profl. responsibility). Contbr. articles to legal jours. Home: 1124 St Stephens Rd Alexandria VA 22304 Office: 1730 Rhode Island Ave NW Washington DC 20036

HUGGHINS, MARCIA LAVERNE, speech pathologist; b. Washington, Apr. 22, 1936; d. Joseph William and Mary LaVerne (McAninch) Greene; B.A., U. Md., 1959; postgrad. UCLA, 1960-61, San Diego State Coll., 1961; M.S.L.S., Cath. U. Am., 1967; postgrad. U. Fla., 1969-72, Fla. State U., 1970, 77-80; m. Harold Terry Hugghins, July 31, 1957. Speech pathologist Public Schs. Loudoun County (Va.), 1958-60, Arlington (Va.) County Schs., 1960, Cajon Valley (Calif.) Union Sch. Dist., 1961-64, Prince George's County, Md., 1964-68, Duval County Schs., Jacksonville, Fla., 1968-70; area specialist speech and hearing Duval County Schs., Jacksonville, 1970-72; speech therapist Berkshire Health Authority, Slough, Eng., 1973-77; speech pathologist for hearing impaired Duval County Schs., Jacksonville, 1977—. Mem. Music Tchrs. Nat. Assn., Actors Equity Assn., Am. Speech and Hearing Assn., Coll. Speech Therapists, Wash. Music Tchrs. Assn., Fla. Speech and Hearing Assn., Beta Phi Mu. Office: 9775 Ivey Rd Jacksonville FL 32216

HUGHES, ANN HANSZEN, psychiatrist; b. Dallas, Sept. 3, 1929; d. Eugene and Gillie May (Whitman) Hanszen; B.A., So. Meth. U., 1955; M.D., U. Tex. Southwestern Med. Sch., 1959; m. John Kinruss-Wright, July 2, 1971; children—Robert Hughes, Ann Louise Hughes. Intern, Baylor Med. Center, Dallas, 1959-60; resident in gen. psychiatry Timberlawn Psychiat. Center, Dallas, 1960-62; resident in child psychiatry U. Tex. Southwestern Med. Sch., Dallas, 1962-64; practice medicine specializing in psychiatry, 1964—; instr. psychiatry U. Tex. Southwestern Med. Sch., 1964-66, asst. prof., 1966-69, clin. asso. prof. dept. psychiatry, 1969-71, dir. Children's Outpatient Psychiat. Clinic, 1967-69; dir. child and adolescent services Tex. Dept. Mental Health and Mental Retardation, Austin, 1969-70; pvt. practice psychiatry, Dallas, 1970-71; prof., head dept. psychiatry Tex. A. and M. Coll. Medicine, 1976-77; med. dir. Bluebonnet Psychiat. Center, Inc., Bryan, Tex., 1973-79; clin. dir. Discovery Land, Inc., Bryan, 1972—. Diplomate Am. Bd. Psychiatry and Neurology. Fellow Am. Psychiat. Assn.; mem Tex. Med. Assn., Am. Assn. Psychiat. Clinics for Children, Tex. Psychiatry Soc., Am. Psychiatric Assn., Tex., Tex. Soc. Child Psychiatry, Brazos-Robertson County med. soc., Am. Acad. Child Psychiatry, Am. Acad. Child Psychiatry (com. for adolescence), Am. Soc. for Adolescent Psychiatry, Houston Soc. for Adolescent Psychiatry, Pi Beta Phi, Psi Chi, Alpha Epsilon Iota. Contbr. articles to profl. jours. Office: PO Box 912 600 E 29th St Bryan TX 77801

HUGHES, ANNE FINKS, occupational therapy adminstr.; b. San Angelo, Tex., Aug. 8, 1934; d. Robert M. and Mary Elizabeth (Huffman) Finks; student Tex. Tech U., 1953-54, So. Meth. U., 1959-60; m. William Jerome Hughes, Apr. 14, 1970; children by previous marriage—Elizabeth Anne, Randal Lee and Robert Donald Roberson. Dir. programs YMCA, San Angelo, 1967-71; exec. dir. Chimney House, BMH Prodns., 1972—; dir. occupational therapy dept., staff services asst San Angelo Center, Tex. Mental Health and Mental Retardation Div., 1972—. Bd. dirs. San Angelo Civic Theatre, 1973—, sec., 1973-74; sec. San-Tex Employee Credit Union, 1977—. Mem. Tex. Pub. Employees Assn. (chpt. pres. 1973-74, 75-76, pres. regional council 1974—, sec.-treas. 1973-74, mem. employees relations council 1974-76, vice chmn. 1975-76). Home: 2609 Hemlock Dr San Angelo TX 76901 Office: San Angelo Center Carlsbad TX 76934

HUGHES, BILLY RAY, coll. adminstr.; b. El Dorado, Ark., Feb. 14, 1932; s. Jesse Gordon and Bonnie Vay (Middlebrooks) H.; B.S.E., Henderson State Coll., 1954, M.S.E., 1957; m. Carolyn Ann Lee, Nov. 30, 1957; children—Barry Ray, Lee Ann. Tchr., Huttig (Ark.) Pub. Schs., 1955-56, McNeil (Ark.) Pub. Schs., 1957-59; tchr., coach Marvell (Ark.) Pub. Schs. 1959-60; dir. spl. edn., Crossett, Ark., 1960-65; news dir. Texarkana Coll. (Tex.), 1965-68, dean students, 1968—. Editorial dir. Wonder State Publs., 1965—. Pres., Texarkana (Tex.) Baseball Assn., 1971, bd. dirs., 1972-73. Mem. Nat. Rifle Assn. (life), Am., Am., S.W., Tex. assns. student personnel adminstrs., Phi Delta Kappa, Theta Alpha Phi. Republican. Presbyn. (deacon 1968-70, 79—). Rotarian. Author: American Handmade Knives of Today, 1972; (with others) Gun Digest Book of Knives, 1973, America's Game Animals and Birds, 1975, Gun Digest Book of Folding Knives, 1977, Modern Handmade Knives, 1980; contbr. articles to profl. jours. Home: 110 Royale Dr Texarkana TX 75501

HUGHES, D. P., police admnstr.; b. Ft. Wayne, Ind., Feb. 5, 1947; s. W.O. and Gala (Studebaker) H.; B.S., Ind. U., 1970; J.D., U. of Miami, 1978; children—Michelle, Jon. Investigator, Allen County (Ind.) Adult Probation Dept., Ft. Wayne, 1968-70; dep. sheriff Dade County (Fla.) Pub. Safety Dept., Miami, 1970-71; staff asst. to chief Miami Shores (Fla) Police Dept., 1971-78, project dir. Burglary/Robbery Control Project, 1976-78; chief investigations Dade County (Fla.) Med. Examiner's Office, Miami, 1978—; participant Fla. Criminal Justice Standards and Goals Conf., Miami, 1975. Certified instr. Fla. Police Standards Council. Mem. Police Benevolent Assn., Am. Assn. Profl. Law Enforcement. Republican. Contbr. article to profl. jour. Home: 250 NE 104th St Miami Shores FL 33138 Office: 1050 NW 19th St Miami FL 33136

HUGHES, EDWIN MCCULLOC, psychologist; b. Coleman, Okla., Feb. 22, 1911; s. Sugar Henry and Epsie Allen (McEachern) H.; B.A., Harding Coll., 1937; M.S., U. Ark., 1942; Ed.D., U. Denver, 1957; m. Ruby Jo McGehee, Sept. 18, 1936; children—Eddy Jo, Philip. Tchr. pub. and pvt. elementary and secondary schs., Ark. and Ky., 1938-52; asst. prof. edn. Harding Coll., Searcy, Ark., 1953-55, asso. prof. psychology, 1956-58; clin. psychologist VA Hosp., North Little Rock, Ark., 1960-77; pvt. practice psychology, Searcy, 1961—; spl. lectr. Little Rock U., evenings 1960-65; mem. Gov.'s Adv. Council on Mental Retardation, 1966-68; mem. Ark. Bd. Examiners in Psychology, 1970-75, exec. sec., 1975—. Fellow Ark. Psychol. Assn., mem. Am. Psychol. Assn, Ark. Soc. Clin. Hypnosis, Assn. Mil. Surgeons U.S., Am. Assn. Suicidology, Internat. Platform Assn., Searcy C. of C., Phi Delta Kappa. Mem. Ch. of Christ (minister). Home and Office: 205 Grand St N Searcy AR 72143

HUGHES, GARY DELL, public adminstr.; b. Lubbock, Tex. Sept. 5, 1946; s. Doyle Eudell and Ella Fay (Norvill) H.; B.B.A., Tex. Tech. U., 1969; M.B.A., S.W. Tex. State U., 1975; m. Karen Sue Brown, Mar. 18, 1978; 1 son, Richard Eric. Unit dir. statewide residential unit Austin (Tex.) State Sch. for Mentally Retarded, 1971-74; dir.

personnel and employee relations, 1974-75, dir. staff services, 1975-79; dir. spl. projects Tex. Dept. Mental Health and Mental Retardation, Austin, 1979; exec. dir. Tex. Public Employees Assn., Austin, 1979—. Mem. Tex. com. United Way, 1978; chmn. U.S. Savs. Bond dr. Tex., 1978-79. Named an outstanding young man Am., U.S. Jaycees, 1977. Mem. Am. Assn. Mental Deficiency (dir. S.W. Region V 1978—), Austin Personnel Assn. (treas. 1978), State Agy. Personnel Adminstrs. Assn. (chmn. 1978), Phi Gamma Delta. Baptist. Contbg. author books; contbr. articles to profl., mgmt. and assn. publs. Home: 1706 Saint Albans St Austin TX 78745 Office: Tex Public Employees Assn Drawer 12217 Capital Sta Austin TX 78711

HUGHES, GEORGE FARANT, JR., safety engr.; b. Roanoke, Va., June 22, 1923; s. George Farant and Pattie (Shafer) H.; B.S., Va. Mil. Inst., 1948; m. Frances Miriam Perdue, July 1, 1950. With roadway maintenance dept. N. & W. Ry. Co., Roanoke, 1948, with Liberty Mut. Ins. Co., Roanoke, Balt., 1949-61, asst. div. mgr., Pitts., 1962-63; safety supr. Westinghouse Electric Corp., Balt., 1963-64; supr. safety and accident prevention, Buffalo, 1965-67; safety dir. U.S. Naval Weapons Sta., Yorktown, Va., 1967-73; head occupational safety U.S. Naval Safety Center, Norfolk, Va., 1973—. Served with AUS, 1943-46, 50-52. Decorated Bronze Star with oak leaf cluster, Purple Heart. Registered profl. engr., Va., Calif.; certified safety profl. Mem. Am. Soc. Safety Engrs. (profl. mem.), Western N.Y. Safety Conf. (dir. 1966-67), Nat. Soc. Profl. Engr., S.A.R., Vets. Safety. Home: 520 Randolph St Williamsburg VA 23185 Office: Naval Safety Center Norfolk VA 23511

HUGHES, HANSEL LEIGH, chemist; b. Kirksey, Ky., Mar. 17, 1917; s. Alford Leigh and Tellie Valarah (Ezell) H.; B.S., Murray State U., 1937; M.S. (fellow), U. Ill., 1946; m. Edith Kathleen Vaden, Mar. 11, 1943; children—Kaye Vaden, David Leigh. Instr. pub. sch., Trenton, Tenn., 1937-38, Sikeston, Mo., 1938-40, Pensacola, Fla., 1940-41; instr. chemistry Murray (Ky.) State U., 1941-42; lab. supr. Hercules Powder Co., 1942-45; instr. chemistry U. Ill., 1945-46; prof. chemistry, chmn. dept. Carthage Coll., 1946-49; asso. prof. chemistry Catawba Coll., Salisbury, N.C., 1949-56, Norfolk (Va.) div. William and Mary Coll. (name now Old Dominion U.), 1956-62; organic chemist Norfolk Naval Shipyard, Portsmouth, 1962—. Fellow Am. Inst. Chemists: mem. AAAS, Am. Chem. Soc., Soc. Am. Mil. Engrs., Nat., Cape Henry Audubon socs., Va. Acad. Sci. Home: 5103 Powhatan Ave Norfolk VA 23508 Office: Norfolk Naval Shipyard Bldg 184 Portsmouth VA 23709

HUGHES, JOHN DAVID, lawyer; b. Lubbock, Tex., Apr. 24, 1935; s. John Alvin and Pauline Goode (Noble) H.; student Kemper Mil. Sch. and Coll., 1953-54; B.B.A., U. Tex., 1958; J.D., Am. U., 1961; m. Karin Lofgren, Apr. 17, 1965; children—John Erik, Stefan David. Admitted to Tex. bar, 1964; practiced in Lubbock, 1964-73; asst. county atty., Lubbock County, Tex., 1964; asst. chief transp. div. Atty. Gen.'s Office of Tex., 1974-76, chief transp. and pub. utilities div., 1976-78, chief energy div., 1979—, asst. atty. gen., 1974—. Instr. comml. law Am. Inst. Banking, Lubbock, 1966-67; lectr. Tex. Tech. Sch. Law, Lubbock, 1970-73. Mem. exec. bd. South Plains council Boy Scouts Am., 1969-73. Bd. dirs. Lubbock Symphony Orch. Served to capt. AUS, 1961-63. Mem. Am., Lubbock County (dir. 1968-71), Travis County bar assns., State Bar Tex. (sec.-treas., chmn. pub. utility, mem. natural resources sects.), Fed. Energy Bar, Assn. ICC Practitioners, Delta Theta Phi. Episcopalian. Contbr. articles to profl. jours. Home: 3133 Honeytree Ln Austin TX 78746 Office: Atty Gen's Office State of Texas PO Box 12548 Austin TX 78711

HUGHES, NETTIE SUE, sch. counselor; b. Ballinger, Tex., Jan. 17, 1931; d. Hubert Edgar and Susie M. (Smith) Cothran; B.S., Centenary Coll. of La., 1951; M.Ed., So. Methodist U., 1971; m. Bennie Dee Hughes, Dec. 16, 1950; 1 dau., Vicki Lynn. Tchr. home econs. Caddo Parish Sch. Bd., Shreveport, La., 1951-54; tchr. elementary and jr. high sch. Refugio (Tex.) Ind. Sch. Dist., 1957-61; tchr. home econs. Assumption Parish, Napoleonville, La., 1962, Lafayette (La.) Parish Sch. Bd., 1963-68; tchr., counselor Richardson (Tex.) Ind. Sch. Dist., 1968—. Mem. Am., Tex., N. Central Tex. personnel and guidance assns., NEA, Tex. State Tchrs. Assn., Richardson Edn. Assn., Richardson Civic Art Soc., Southwest Watercolor Soc., Chi Omega. Baptist. Home: 1217 Ashland Dr Richardson TX 75080 Office: 7630 Arapaho Rd Dallas TX 75248

HUGHES, ROBERT CRITTENDEN, III, comml. collections co. exec.; b. Louisville, Oct. 24, 1945; s. Robert Crittenden and Betty Rose (Simmons) H.; student U.S. Mil. Acad., 1963-64; B.A., U. Louisville, 1967; M.A., Yale U., 1969; student Northrop U. Law Sch., 1977-78; m. Kimberly Craven, Dec. 23, 1978. Pres., Robert C. Hughes and Assos., Louisville, 1972—; pres., chmn. bd. dirs. mfr. Trade Services, Inc., Louisville, 1975—. Republican candidate Ky. State Senate, 1977. Mem. Comml. Law League Am. Republican. Office: 211 Marion E Taylor Bldg Louisville KY 40202

HUGHES, SHELIA PANNELL, thread mfg. co. exec.; b. Batesburg, S.C., July 23, 1953; d. Craig Dennis and Mary Kathleen (Fisher) Pannell; B.A., Western Carolina U., 1973, M.A., 1977. Employment supr. Litton Industries, Murphy, N.C., 1974-78; indsl. relations mgr. Am. Thread Co., Marble, N.C., 1978—; instr. Tri-County Community Coll.; instr. Mars Hill Coll.; cons. indsl., sch.-sponsored tng. Vice pres. Cherokee County United Fund, 1980. Named Cherokee County Young Career Woman, 1978. Mem. Am. Soc. Tng. and Devel. (past v.p.), Western N.C. Safety Council. Baptist. Clubs: Altrusa (ext. chmn.), Cherokee County Women's Assn. Golf. Home: PO Box 171 Lowell Murphy NC 28906 Office: PO Box 269 Marble NC 28905

HUGHES, SUE MARGARET, librarian; b. Cleburne, Tex., Apr. 13; d. Chastain Wesley and Sue Willis (Payne) H.; B.B.A. with highest honors, U. Tex. at Austin, 1949; M.L.S., Tex. Woman's U., 1960, postgrad. Sec.-treas. several privately owned corps., Waco, Tex., 1949-59, asst. in pub. services Baylor U. Moody Library, Waco, 1960-64, acquisitions librarian, 1964-79, librarian, 1980—, mem. univ. senate. Mem. AAUP (chpt. pres. 1979-80), AAUW (pres. Waco br. 1974-76, br. Outstanding Woman of Year 1978, state bylaws chmn. 1977-79), ALA (sec. RTSD Reprinting com., past chmn. duplicates exchange union com.), Southwestern, Tex. (local chmn. dist. 3 meeting 1975) library assns., Library Club (Waco), Tex. Woman's U. Alumnae Assn. (pres. 1979-81), Sigma Delta Pi, Beta Gamma Sigma, Delta Kappa Gamma (rec. sec. 1978-80), Beta Phi Mu. Methodist. Club: Baylor Round Table (treas. 1974-75). Home: 2101 Trinity Dr Waco TX 76710 Office: Box 6307 Waco TX 76706

HUGHES, SUSAN ELIZABETH SIMPSON, educator; b. Toronto, Ont., Can., Dec. 10, 1946; d. James Hamilton and Marian Emily (Leach) Simpson; came to U.S., 1970; A.B., U. Western Ont., 1967; M.A., U. B.C., 1969; m. James Russell Hughes, Dec. 27, 1969. Instr. adult div. St. Louis High Sch., Honolulu, 1972-73: instr. Halton Bd. Edn., Burlington, Ont., Can., 1973-74; instr. communications dept., Danville (Ill.) Jr. Coll., 1974-78; dir. communications programs Individual Devel. Assos., Inc., Woodbridge, Va., 1978—; instr. speech communications dept. Prince George's Community Coll., Largo, Md., 1978; instr. communications and humanities dept. No. Va. Community Coll., Woodbridge, 1978—. Mem. Nat. Council Tchrs. of English. Episcopalian. Home: 15985 Cove Ln Montclair Country Club Lake Dumfries VA 22026 Office: PO Box 1077 Woodbridge VA 22193

HUGHES, VESTER THOMAS, JR., lawyer; b. San Angelo, Tex., May 24, 1928; s. Vester Thomas and Mary Ellen (Tisdale) H.; student Baylor U., 1945-46; B.A. with distinction, Rice U., 1949; LL.B. cum laude, Harvard U., 1952. Admitted to Tex. bar, 1952; law clk. U.S. Supreme Ct., 1952; asso. firm Robertson, Jackson, Payne, Lancaster & Walker (name later changed to Jackson, Walker, Winstead, Cantwell & Miller), Dallas, 1955-58, partner, 1958-76; partner Hughes, Luce, Hennessy, Smith & Castle (now Hughes & Hill), 1976—; dir. Exell Cattle Co. LX Cattle Co., Stewart Engring. Co., Murphy Oil Corp., First Nat. Bank Mertzon (Tex.), Austin Industries, Inc., Memorex Corp., Cornell Oil Co. Tax counsel Dallas Community Chest Trust Fund; bd. dirs. Larry and Jane Harlan Found.; trustee Dallas Bapt. Coll., 1967-77; trustee, exec. com. Tex. Scottish Rite Hosp. for Crippled Children; bd. overseers vis. com. Harvard Law Sch., 1969-75. Served to lt. AUS, 1952-55. Mem. Am. Bar Assn. (council sect. taxation 1969-71), Am. Law Inst. (council 1966—), Phi Beta Kappa, Sigma Xi. Baptist. Clubs: Masons (33 deg.), Order Eastern Star. Home: 1222 Commerce St Dallas TX 75202 Office: 1000 Mercantile Dallas Bldg Dallas TX 75201

HUGHES, WAUNELL MCDONALD (MRS. DELBERT E. HUGHES), psychiatrist; b. Tyler, Tex., Feb. 6, 1928; d. Conrad Claiborne and Bernice Oletha (Smith) McDonald; B.A., U. Tex. at Austin, 1946; M.D., Baylor U., 1951; m. Delbert Eugene Hughes, Aug. 14, 1948; children—Lark, Mark, Lynn, Michael. Intern VA Hosp., Houston, 1951-52; resident Parkland Hosp., Dallas, 1964-67; practiced gen. medicine in Tyler, Tex., 1952-64; acting chief psychiatry service VA Hosp., Dallas, 1967-68, asst. chief, 1968-73, chief Mental Hygiene Clinic and Day Treatment Center, 1973—. Clin. instr. psychiatry Southwestern Med. Sch., U. Tex. Health Sci. Center, Dallas, 1968—. Chmn. pre-sch. vision and hearing program Pilot Club, Tyler, 1960-64. Mem. Am. Med. Women's Assn. (pres. Dallas 1980-81), Am. Psychiat. Assn., Am. Group Psychotherapy Assn., Alpha Epsilon Iota (pres. 1950-51). Home: 3428 University Blvd Dallas TX 75205 Office: 4500 Lancaster Rd Dallas TX 75216

HUGHEY, BOB, city ofcl.; b. Alton, Ill., Mar. 1, 1937; B.S. with honors, Tex. Tech. U., 1960, postgrad., 1960-62; m. Sharon Kay Ramsey, Nov., 1959; children—Vicki Lynn, Kayla Michelle, Robert Shawn. Adminstrv. asst. to city mgr. Lubbock (Tex.), 1960-63; adminstrv. asst. to city mgr. Wichita Falls (Tex.), 1963-66; asst. city-county adminstr. Los Alamos (N.Mex.), 1965-66; asst. city mgr. Wichita Falls, 1966-69; mgr. govtl. services Univ. Computer Co., Dallas, 1969-71; asst. city mgr. for adminstrn. Richardson (Tex.), 1971-74, city mgr., 1974—. Mem. steering com. United Way, 1979. Mem. Internat. City Mgmt. Assn., Mcpl. Fin. Officers Assn., Tex. City Mgmt. Assn., N. Tex. City Mgmt. Assn. (pres. 1978-79), Richardson C. of C. (dir.). Presbyterian. Club: Rotary (dir.). Office: PO Box 309 319 E Main St Richardson TX 75080

HUGIN, ADOLPH CHARLES, lawyer, engr., inventor, educator; b. Washington, Mar. 28, 1907; s. Charles and Eugenie (Vigny) H.; B.S. in E.E., George Washington U., 1928; M.S. in E.E., Mass. Inst. Tech., 1930; certificate in radio communication Union Coll., 1944; J.D., Georgetown U., 1934; LL.M., Harvard U., 1947; S.J.D., Catholic U. Am., 1949; certificate in better bus. mgmt. Gen. Electric Co. Continuing Edn. Program, 1946. Admitted to Mass. bar, D.C. bar, U.S. Supreme Ct. bar, U.S. Ct. Customs and Patent Appeals, U.S. Ct. Claims bars; examiner U.S. Patent Office, 1928; engr. research and devel. instrument lab. West Lynn (Mass.) works Gen. Electric Co., 1928, in charge insulation lab, 1929, engine-electric drive devel. lab., 1929-30, patent asst., Schenectady, 1930, patent investigator, Washington, 1930-33, patent atty., Washington and Schenectady, 1933-46, engr.-in-charge sect. aeros. and marine engring. div., Schenectady, 1942-45, organizer, instr. patent practice course, 1945-46; practiced law in Cambridge, Mass., 1946-47; vis. prof. law Cath. U. Am., 1949-55; practice law, cons. engr., Washington, 1947—. Bd. dirs. St. Margaret's Fed. Credit Union, 1963-67, 1st v.p., 1965-67; mem. Schenectady com. Boy Scouts Am., 1940-42; charter mem., 1st bd. mgrs. Schenectady Cath. Youth League, 1935-38, hon. life mem., 1946; chmn. St. Margaret's Bldg. Fund, 1954; lector St. Margaret's (Md.) Parish, 1966-68, lector-commentator St. Michael's (Va.) Parish, 1969—; mem. St. Margaret's Parish Council, 1969-71; mem. adv. bd. St. Michael's Ch., 1974-77. Registered profl. elect. and mech. engr., D.C.; registered patent atty. U.S. Patent Office. Mem. Holy Name Soc. (parish pres. 1950-52, pres. Prince Georges County (Md.) sect. 1953, pres. Washington archdiocesan union 1953-55), St. Vincent de Paul Soc. (parish conf. pres. 1965—, pres. particular council Prince George County 1959-61, rep. Prince George County on Washington Archdiocesan Central Council Soc. 1961-62, 1st pres. Arlington (Va.) diocesan central council 1975-77, trustee nat. soc. 1975-77), St. Margaret's Parish Confraternity of Christian Doctrine (pres., instr. 1960-61), Archdiocesan Council Cath. Men (pres. So. Prince Georges County deanery 1956-58, 65-68), Men's Retreat League (exec. bd. Washington, 1954-58, St. Margaret's Retreat Group capt. 1965-68), Nocturnal Adoration Soc., John Carroll Soc., Elfun Soc., Nat., D.C. socs. profl. engrs., Am. Bar Assn., Am. Patent Law Assn., Delta Theta Phi. Club: Cath. Men's First Friday. Author: International Trade Regulatory Arrangements and the Antitrust Laws, 1949; editor-in-chief bull. Am. Patent Law Assn., 1949-54; editor notes and decisions Georgetown Law Jour., 1933-34; contbr. articles in fields patents, copyrights, antitrust, radio and air law to profl. jours. Patentee dynamoelectric machines, dynamometers, insulation micrometers, ecology and pollution control, mus. instruments, others. Home: 7602 Boulder St North Springfield VA 22151 Office: Nat Press Bldg Washington DC 20045

HUGULEY, JOHN EARL, retail co. exec.; b. Bessemer, Ala., Jan. 19, 1927; s. Charles Bannon and Hazel A. (Hood) H.; B.B.A., The Citadel, 1951; m. Elizabeth Hanna, Jan. 23, 1948; children—John Earl, Elizabeth Tharin Horres. With John Huguley Co., Inc., books and office products, Charleston, S.C., 1951—, pres., 1959—; chmn. adv. bd. Citizens & So. Nat. Bank. Pres. Charleston United Way, 1970; trustee Historic Charleston Found. Mem. Exchange Club Charleston (pres. 1959), Charleston Retail Mchts. Assn. (pres. 1960-61), Nat. Office Products Assn. (pres. 1971-72), Charleston Trident C. of C. (pres. 1971), S.C. Hist. Soc. (pres. 1973-74), Hiberian Soc., Preservation Soc. Democrat. Methodist (pres. trustees 1969-73). Clubs: Carolina Yacht; Country of Charleston, Arion Soc. Home: 22 Murray Blvd Charleston SC 29401 Office: 269 King St Charleston SC 29401

HULEN, ALFRED CLAYTON, ret. research inst. exec.; b. Mexico, Mo., Jan. 25, 1904; s. Edward Kennan and Blanche (Gillespie) H.; student U. Mo., 1921-23; m. Margaret Worner, Sept. 30, 1931; children—Kennan, Margaret Hulen Huggins, Clayton, Martha Hulen McKenna. Mem. accounting staff Mo. Power & Light Co., Jefferson City, Mo., 1923-40, sr. accounting and fiscal officer, 1941-46; comptroller Slick Airways, Inc., 1946-48; accountant, bus. mgr. Earl F. Slick, 1948-50; controller, asst. treas. Southwest Research Inst., San Antonio, 1950-55, treas., asst. sec., 1955-61, sec.-treas., 1961-69, v.p. fin., sec., 1970-72, sec., cons. to pres., 1973-74. Mem. Nat. Assn. Accountants (emeritus). Baptist. Club: Optimist (life). Home: 2167 NE Loop 410 Apt C-18 San Antonio TX 78217

HULKA, JAROSLAV FABIAN, physician; b. N.Y.C., Sept. 29, 1930; s. Jaroslav Hugo and Milada (Touskova) H.; B.A., Harvard, 1952; M.D., Columbia, 1956; m. Barbara E. Sorenson, Nov. 13, 1954; children—Carol Ann, Gregory Fabian, Bryan Herbert. Intern Roosevelt Hosp., N.Y.C., 1956-57; resident Sloane Hosp. for Women, Columbia-Presbyn. Med. Center, N.Y.C., 1957-60; Josiah Macy, Jr. fellow Columbia-Presbyn. Med. Center, 1960-61; practice medicine specializing in obstetrics and gynecology, 1961—; asst. prof. obstetrics and gynecology U. Pitts. Sch. Med., 1961-66, asso. mem. grad. faculty, 1962-66, acting chmn. dept. obstetrics and gynecology, 1963-64; asso. prof. dept. ob-gyn, dept. maternal and child health Sch. Medicine U. N.C. at Chapel Hill, 1967-76, prof. dept. ob-gyn, dept. maternal and child health, 1976—, asso. dir. Carolina Population Center, 1967-74. Diplomate Am. Bd. Obstetrics and Gynecology. Fellow Am. Coll. Obstetricians and Gynecologists; mem. Soc. for Gynecol. Investigation, Am. Assn. Gynecol. Laparoscopists (pres. 1980), Assn. Profs. Obstetrics and Gynecology, Am. Fertility Soc. Inventor spring clip laparoscopic sterilization. Home: 2317 Honeysuckle Rd Chapel Hill NC 27514 Office: Obstet and Gynecol Dept Meml Hosp Chapel Hill NC 27514

HULL, JAMES DIXON, III, surgeon; b. Mt. Holly, N.J., July 10, 1939; s. James Dixon and Alta Mary (Reagan) H.; B.A., Earlham Coll., 1960; M.D., U. Chgo., 1964; m. Bonnie Gladys Palmer, June 14, 1964; children—Christine Palmer, James Palmer. Intern, Pa. Hosp., Phila., 1964-65, resident, 1967-71; practice medicine specializing in surgery, Morehead, Ky., 1971-79; with Suburban Surg. Assos. P.C., 1979—; mem. staffs Cave Run Clinic, Morehead, St. Claire Med. Center, Morehead, Fleming County (Ky.) Hosp., Flemingsburg, Morgan County (Ky.) Hosp., West Liberty, Douglas Gen. Hosp., Douglasville, Ga., Atlanta West Hosp., Lithia Springs, Ga., 1979—; clin. instr. surgery U. Ky., Lexington, 1971-73, asst. clin. prof., 1973-79. Diplomate Am. Bd. Surgery. Fellow A.C.S., Internat. Coll. Surgeons, Am. Soc. Gastrointestinal Endoscopy; mem. AMA, Ky., So. med. assns., Mensa. Home: 9904 Laurel Dr Douglasville GA 30135 Office: 8954 Hospital Dr Suite 105-C Douglasville GA 30134

HULL, PAUL GARY, physician; b. Tulsa, Nov. 13, 1946; s. Paul G. and Mildred L. (Hall) H.; student U. Tulsa, 1965-68; M.D., U. Okla., 1972; m. Caralea Jane McLure, Jan. 28, 1967; children—Jason Christopher, Tyler Reed, Paul Michael. Intern, St. Francis Hosp., Wichita, 1972-73; family practice medicine, Plano, Tex.; mem. staff Plano Gen. Hosp. Served with USAF, 1971-72, 73-76. Diplomate Am. Bd. Family Physicians. Mem. AMA, Tex. Med. Assn., Collin County Med. Assn. Republican. Mem. Christian Ch. Office: 3900 W 15th St Plano TX 75075

HULL, RICHARD FRANKLIN, ins. brokerage exec.; b. N.Y.C., Nov. 8, 1931; s. Washington and Emily Gloria (Stevenson) H.; student U. Va., Charlottesville, 1949-50; m. Dorothy Dale, Dec. 6, 1963; children—Richard Franklin, David T., Christopher. Underwriter, Crum & Forster Group, N.Y.C., 1953-56; pres. Hull & Co., Washington, 1956-62, Ft. Lauderdale, Fla., 1962—; chmn. bd. Hull & Co. (Calif.), Inc., 1969—; dir. Am. Nat. Bank, Ft. Lauderdale. Served with USMC, 1950-53. Mem. Am. Assn. Mng. Gen. Agts., Nat., Fla. assns. ins. agts., Broward County (Fla.) Insuror's Assn., Fla. Assn. Mut. Ins. Agts., Fla. (pres. 1974-76), Calif. surplus lines assns., Surplus Lines Claims Assn. Republican. Episcopalian. Clubs: Drug and Chem. (N.Y.C.); Balboa Bay (Newport Beach, Calif.); Lauderdale Yacht, Lloyd's Yacht, Ocean Reef, Lago Mar Country, Palm Bay, Tower (Ft. Lauderdale). Home: 201 Fiesta Way Fort Lauderdale FL 33301 Office: 2150 S Andrews Ave Fort Lauderdale FL 33316

HULSE, HERMAN LAWAYNE, educator; b. Wanette, Okla., June 12, 1922; s. James Anderson and Mabel Mildred (Klinglesmith) H.; B.S., So. Meth. U., 1949; M.A., Tex. Christian U., 1967; postgrad. Tex. A. and M. U., 1970-71; m. Vanita Holland, Apr. 10, 1946; children—LaRonna Joyce, James David, Kris Philip, Karen Denise. Newspaperman, Snyder Daily News, Snyder, Tex., 1949-55, San Angelo (Tex.) Standard-Times, 1956-57; Ordained to ministry, Baptist Ch., 1946; pastor rural chs. in Mitchell County, Tex., 1950-54, Belmore Bapt. Ch., San Angelo, Tex., 1955-56, 1st Bapt. Ch., Mason, Tex., 1957-60, Alta Mere Bapt. Ch., Ft. Worth, 1960-64; asst. editor Bapt. Standard, Dallas, 1964-68; prof. Tex. State Tech. Inst., Waco, 1968—. Served with USAAF, 1942-45. Mem. Tex. Tech. Soc. Republican. Author: Meditation Programs, 1968. Home: 2131 Hermanson Dr Waco TX 76710 Office: Dept Tech Communications Tex State Tech Inst Waco TX 76705

HULSE, STEVE LEE, oilfield equipment co. exec.; b. Hayes, Kans., Apr. 25, 1950; s. Verle Lee and Marguerette Ann (Turnbull) H.; B.S., La. Tech. U., 1972; m. Sharon Lou O'Dell, Aug. 21, 1971; children—Angie, Adam, Ashley. Floorman, Jet Drilling Co., Shreveport, La., 1968-72; br. mgr. Peoples Bank & Trust Co., Minden, La., 1972; field salesman, security div. Dresser Industries, Tyler, Tex., 1973-76, area account rep., security div., Shreveport, La., 1977, area sales mgr., security, div., Houston, 1978, area mgr., security div., Houston, 1978—. Mem. Am. Petroleum Inst., Petroleum Equipment Suppliers Assn. Democrat. Methodist. Club: Woodlands Country. Home: 4810 Spanish Oak St Houston TX 77066 Office: Dresser Industries 1656-D Townhurst Dr Houston TX 77043

HULSEY, BURL B., JR., utilities co. exec.; b. Forney, Tex., 1917; married. B.S. in Elec. Engring., Tex. A&M Coll., 1939; with Tex. Electric Service Co., 1939-74, pres., until 1974; pres. Tex. Utilities Co., Dallas, 1975—, also dir. Office: Tex Utilities Co 2001 Bryan Tower Dallas TX 75201*

HUMBER, LUCIE BERTHIER (MRS. ROBERT LEE HUMBER), civic worker; b. Paris, France, Feb. 24, 1895; d. Louis Adolphe and Honorine (Rouxel) Berthier; Brevet Superieur, U. Paris, 1913, Certificate d' Aptitude Pedagogique, 1918, Diplome d'Etudes Superieures, 1927; m. Robert Lee Humber, Oct. 16, 1929; children—Marcel Berthier, John Leslie. Came to U.S., 1940, naturalized, 1944. Tchr. French, pub. schs., Herblay, 1915-19; tchr. pvt. sch., Hinckley, Eng., 1919-22; exec. sec. Am. Univ. Union, Paris, 1922-29. Pres., Greenville (N.C.) Woman's Club, 1945-47; mem. N.C. Gov.'s Com. Rd. and Sch. Program, 1949-50, Gov.'s Adv. Com. Hwy. Safety, 1950-51, N.C. Edenton Hist. Commn., 1972-77; v.p. N.C. Legislative Council, 1952-54, 68—; mem. adv. council N.C. Art Soc.; chmn. UN Week, Greenville; adv. com. Who's Who. Bd. dirs. N.C. Women's Council, N.C. Mental Health Assn., 1951-57. Recipient James Wesley White silver cup for landscape painting N.C. Fedn. Women's Club, 1960. Mem. Am. Assn. U. Women (N.C. pres. 1947-51, mem. exec. com. 1947-63, chmn. civil def. 1951-54, chmn. bldg. fund 1957-62, state bd. mem. 1968—, area chmn. for study world problems 1972—), Nat. Trust for Historic Preservation, Pitt County Democratic Women (mem. state bd. 1968-69), UN Assn., Am. Legion Aux. North Carolina Soc. Preservation of Antiquities, Pitt County Mental Health Assn., Asso. Artists N.C., East Carolina Art Assn., United World Federalists, N.C. Symphony Soc., Pitt County Hist. Assn. Democrat. Mem. French Reformed Ch. Research on history secondary edn. in U.S. Home: 117 W 5th St Greenville NC 27834

HUME, DAVID VANCE, ins. agt.; b. Enid, Okla., July 20, 1949; s. David Ellsworth and Betty Vance (Smith) H.; student Enid Bus. Coll., 1969; m. Barbara Susan Hume, Aug. 1, 1969; children—Susan Claire,

Barbara Elizabeth. Vice-pres. Cansler-Burk Co., Inc., Enid, 1974—. Served with USAF, 1970-74. Mem. Ind. Ins. Agts. of Enid (past pres.), Ind. Ins. Agts. of Okla., Ind. Ins. Agts. Am. Republican. Episcopalian. Home: 2401 Mount Vernon Rd Enid OK 73701 Office: PO Box 1467 Enid OK 73701

HUMENSKY, JOSEPH EDWARD, mech. engr.; b. Cleve., July 8, 1950; s. Joseph John and Anne Marie (Kunovic) H.; B.M.E., Cleve. State U., 1976. Apprentic machinist Balas Collet Co. div. Warner & Swasey, Cleve., 1968-72; mfg. engr. profl. intern program Eaton Corp., Hoist equipment div., Forrest City, Ark., 1976, controls div., Chgo., 1976, transmission div., Kalamazoo, 1976, Kings Mountain, N.C., 1977-79; process engr. TRW, Inc., Greenville, N.C., 1979—. Registered engr.-in-tng., Ohio. Mem. ASME (asso.), Soc. Mfg. Engrs. Roman Catholic. Home: 209 Abbey Ln Greenville NC 27834

HUMPHREY, WILLIAM EDWIN, ins. co. exec.; b. Pauls Valley, Okla., June 19, 1939; s. William Edgar and Mamie Elizabeth (Gooch) H.; A.B., Yale U., 1961; B.S., Okla. State U., 1962; postgrad., Fgn. Service Inst., 1962-63; m. Gay Wells, Mar. 17, 1965; children—Marran Elizabeth, Rebecca Lynn, William Wells. Fgn. service officer, U.S. Dept. State, 1962-74, comml. attache, Managua, Nicaragua, 1963-65, vice consul, Istanbul, Turkey, 1965-67, intelligence analyst for Turkey and Cyprus, 1967-69, asst. to U.S. Ambassador to Mex., 1969-72, consul, Florence, Italy, 1973-74; pres., Loftin and Humphrey, Inc., Pauls Valley, Okla., 1974—; dir. Pauls Valley Nat. Bank, Sea Harvest Packing Co.; v.p., Agee and Humphrey, Ltd. Pres. Pauls Valley C. of C., 1977—, Pauls Valley Hist. Soc., mem. Pauls Valley Bicentennial Commn., 1976. Republican. Clubs: Beacon (Oklahoma City), Whitehall (Oklahoma City), Rotary (Pauls Valley, dir., officer, 1974-77), Elks (Pauls Valley). Home: 1753 S Walnut Pauls Valley OK 73075 Office: 101 S Willow St Pauls Valley OK 73075

HUMPHREYS, HOMER ALEXANDER, educator; b. nr. Waynesboro, Va., Feb. 7, 1902; s. Lewis Greenberry and Annie (Sampson) H.; B.A., Bridgewater Coll., 1928; M.A., U. Va., 1941, research fellow, 1943-44; m. Ruth Elizabeth Gilbert, Sept. 1, 1926; children—Faye (Mrs. Hezekiah Sadler), Joye (Mrs. James Malcolm Hart Harris, Jr.), Anne (Mrs. Richard Edward Talman), Homer Alexander, Jane (dec.), Kaye (Mrs. Ralph Franklin Jones, Jr.). Instr. Moyock (N.C.) High Sch., 1928-29; prin. Darlington Heights (Va.) High Sch., 1929-33, Green Bay (Va.) High Sch., 1934-44; supervising prin. West Point (Va.) High Sch., 1944-65; gen. supr. instrn. Williamsburg-James City County Schools, 1965-67; dir. aviation edn. Mont. State U., Missoula, also Eastern Coll. Edn., Billings, Mont., summers 1954, 55, U. Va., Charlottesville, summers 1956-71; instr. Coll. William and Mary Extension, 1963-68. Coordinator, Civil Def., King William County and Town of West Point, 1950-61. Served from 2d lt. to lt. col. USAF, Civil Air Patrol, 1945—; dir. aviation edn. Va. Wing, Civil Air Patrol, 1956-65. Mem. N.E.A. (past 1st zone v.p. dept. audio-visual instrn.), Va. High Sch. League (chmn. 1955-57), King William-King and Queen Edn. Assn. (pres. 1956-58), Phi Delta Kappa. Kiwanian (pres. West Point 1949, lt. gov. capital dist. div. four 1956). Author: A History of Education in Prince Edward County, Va., 1941; column Wings Over Va., 1956-62; also numerous articles, reports and surveys. Home: 110 Oxford Circle Williamsburg VA 23185

HUMPHREYS, HORACE STEELMAN, food co. exec.; b. Memphis, Oct. 3, 1910; s. Arthur Maurice and Lotti (McAllister) H.; student tech. high sch.; m. Peggy Jean, Dec. 18, 1934; 1 son, Horace Steelman. Meat market mgr. Kroger Co., Memphis, 1926-33, meat supr., 1933-38; pres., gen. mgr. Atlanta Sea Food Co., 1938-40; mgr. rail stock div., trainer salesmen Armour & Co., Atlanta, 1940-42; br. mgr. Booth Fisheries Corp., Chgo. and Louisville, 1942-44; meat buyer Louisville div. Great A & P Co., 1944-46, divisional mgr. fish and poultry sales, 1946-47, meat sales mgr., 1947-48, asst. sales mgr., 1948-50, sales mgr., 1950-53; owner, operator H.S. "Bud" Humphreys Co., Inc., food brokers, Memphis and Jackson, Miss., 1953—; pres. Humphreys-Clower Co., Inc., Jackson. Mem. Memphis, Nat. food brokers assns. Methodist. Clubs: Masons, Chickasaw Country (Memphis). Office: 3798 Premier Ave Memphis TN 38118

HUMPHREYS, JAMES MACK, JR., obstetrician and gynecologist; b. Wilmington, N.C., Feb. 10, 1943; s. James Mack and Barbara Urban (Clark) H.; B.A., Baylor U., 1965; M.D., U. Tex., Dallas, 1969; children—Loyd, Robert, Earl, Adrienne. Intern, resident in ob-gyn Bexar County Hosp. Dist., 1969-73; practice medicine specializing in ob-gyn Midland (Tex.) Women's Clinic, 1973—; asso. acting dir. Midland City/County Health Dept. Bd. dirs. Permian Basin Planned Parenthood, Midland-Odessa Symphony and Chorale, Inc. Served with USAFR, 1970-76. Decorated AF Commendation medal. Diplomate Am. Bd. Ob-Gyn. Mem. Midland County Med. Soc., Tex. Med. Assn., AMA. Baptist. Office: 2009 W Wall St Midland TX 79701

HUMPHREYS, KENNETH KING, academic adminstr., research engr., assn. exec.; b. Pitts., Jan. 19, 1938; s. Meredith Harold and Olga (Adamitis) H.; B.S., Carnegie Inst. Tech., 1959, postgrad., 1961-62; M.S., W.Va. U., 1967; postgrad. Ill. Inst. Tech., 1960, U. Pitts., 1965; m. Harriet Elizabeth Moss, May 6, 1961; children—Kenneth King, Keith Alan, Kevin James, Karen Elizabeth. Tech. asst. U.S. Steel Corp., Applied Research Lab., Chgo., 1959-60, tech. asso., Monroeville, Pa., 1960-62, asst. technologist, Universal, Pa., 1962-63, asso. research engr., 1963-65; cost engr. W.Va. U. Coal Research Bur., Morgantown, 1965-67, sr. staff and cost engr., 1967-71, asst. dir., 1971—; asst. prof. Coll. Mineral and Energy Resources, W.Va. U., Morgantown, 1970-73, asso. prof., 1973-76, prof., 1976—, asst. to dean, 1971-77, chmn. minerals program, 1978—, asst. dean acad. affairs, 1979—; engring. cons. metallurgy and fuel tech., 1963—; exec. dir. Am. Assn. Cost Engrs., 1971—. Leader, Boy Scouts Am., 1961—, dist. commr., 1969-72, dist. tng. chmn., 1972-74, chmn. council tng., 1975-77, vice-chmn. leadership devel. Area 6, E. Central Region, 1977—. Recipient Silver Beaver award, award Merit, Woodbadge award Mountaineer Area council Boy Scouts Am., Het Schaap mit vijf Poten award for distinguished service, Royal Netherlands Industries Fair; named Hon. West Virginian, Gov. of W.Va. Registered profl. engr., Pa., W.Va.; cert. cost engr. Fellow Assn. Cost Engrs. (U.K.); mem. Sociedad Mexicana de Ingenieria Economica y de Costos (Mex.), Soc. Mining Engrs., AIME, Am. Assn. Cost Engrs. (nat. chmn. 1969-71, nat. dir. 1971; mng. editor, pub. Cost Engring. mag.; named Mem. of Moment 1970, award recognition 1979), Internat. Cost Engring. Council (sec.), Nat., W.Va., (pres. Morgantown 1969-70, dir. Morgantown 1970-76, state dir. 1971-76, state v.p. 1980-81) socs. profl. engrs., Am. Assn. Engring. Socs. (bd. govs. 1979—), W.Va. Coal Mining Inst., Sigma Xi, Beta Theta Pi, Alpha Phi Omega. Democrat. Presbyterian (deacon 1968-70, ruling elder 1972-75, pres. congregation 1975-77). Contbr. articles to profl. jours.; author and co-author several books in field. Patentee in field. Home: 305 Lebanon Ave Morgantown WV 26505

HUMPHRIES, FREDERICK S., univ. pres.; b. Appalachicola, Fla., Dec. 26, 1935; s. Thornton and Minnie H.; B.S. magna cum laude in Chemistry, Fla. A&M U., 1957; Ph.D. magna cum laude in Phys. Chemistry, U. Pitts., 1964; m. Antoinette McTurner, June 1960; children—Frederick Stephen, Robin Tanya, Laurence Anthony. Pvt. tutor in sci. and math., 1959-64; asst. prof. chemistry U. Minn., Mpls., 1966-67; asso. prof. chemistry Fla. A&M U., Tallahassee, 1964-67, prof. chemistry, 1967-68, dir. thirteen-coll. curriculum program, 1967-68; dir. innovative instl. research consortium Inst. Services to Edn., Washington, 1972-73, dir. interdisciplinary program, 1973-74, dir. Knoxville Coll. study of sci. capability of the Black Coll., 1972-74, dir. two-univs. grad. program in sci., 1973-74, v.p. ISE, 1970-74; pres. Tenn. State U., Nashville, 1974—; mem. bd. grad. advocates Meharry Med. Coll., 1976; cons. various colls. and univs., 1978-79. Chmn., Fairfax County Anti-Poverty Commn., 1972-74; mem. bd. ethical conduct Met. Govt. of Nashville and Davidson County, 1978—; co-chmn. Reston's Black Focus, 1973; bd. dirs. YMCA, 1975. Served with U.S. Army Security Agy., 1957-59. Recipient Disting. Service award Inst. Services to Edn., 1974; Disting. Edn. and Adminstr. Meritorious award Fla. A&M U., 1975; Human Relations award Met. Human Relations Commn. Nashville, 1978. Mem. Am. Chem. Soc., Am. Council Edn. (dir. 1977-78, sec. bd. 1978-79), Am. Assn. Higher Edn., AAUP, AAAS, NAACP, Nat. Assn. State Univs. and Land-Grant Colls., Nashville Area C. of C. (edn. com. 1975), Fla. A&M Alumni Assn. (Disting. Service award 1976). Roman Catholic. Contbr. articles on edn. in Black Colls. to profl. publs.; Frederick S. Humphries Day declared in his honor by City of Indiana. Home: 2904 Centennial Blvd Nashville TN 37203 Office: Office of Pres Tenn State Univ 3500 Centennial Blvd Nashville TN 37203

HUMPHRIES, JOAN ROPES, educator: b. Bklyn., Oct. 17, 1928; d. Lawrence Gardner and Adele Lydia (Zimmermann) Ropes; B.A., U. Miami, 1950; M.S., Fla. State U., 1955; Ph.D., La. State U., 1963; m. Charles C. Humphries, Apr. 4, 1957; children—Peggy Ann, Charlene Adele. Part-time instr. U. Miami, Coral Gables, Fla., 1964-66; asso. prof. dept. psychology Miami-Dade Community Coll., 1966—. Bd. dirs. Profl. Community Services, Hialeah, Fla., 1977—; bd. dirs., v.p. Inst. Evaluation, Diagnosis and Treatment, Miami, 1975—. Mem. AAUP, Internat. Platform Assn. (gov.), Am. Psychol. Assn., Fla. Psychol. Assn., Dade County Psychol. Assn. Democrat. Clubs: Country of Coral Gables, Jockey. Editorial staff, maj. author: The Application of Scientific Behaviorism to Humanistic Phenomena, 1975; researcher in biofeedback and human consciousness. Home: 1311 Alhambra Circle Coral Gables FL 33134 Office: Miami Dade Community Coll North Campus Miami FL 33167

HUMPHRIES, JOHN EDWARD, oil co. exec.; b. Toledo, Ohio, Mar. 29, 1937; s. John Kern and Phyllis Gertrude (Hadley) H.; B.Sc., Capitol U., 1960; student Ohio State U., 1961-62; m. Mary Sue Morris, Aug. 22, 1959; children—John Kenneth, Steven Edward. Sales rep. Nat. Drug Co., Cin., 1962-63; sales rep. Shell Oil Co., Cin., 1963-66; sales rep. Valvoline Oil Co., Louisville, 1966-71, regional mgr., Cin., 1971-74, mgr. indsl./splty. sales dept., Ashland, Ky., 1974—. Vice-pres. Pleasant Run Farms Youth Recreation Leagues, 1972-73, team mgr., 1972-73. Mem. Am. Soc. Lubrication Engrs., Nat. Assn. Corrosion Engrs. Club: Bellefonte Country. Office: Box 391 Ashland KY 41101

HUMPHRIES, ROBERT LEE, JR., govt. ofcl.; b. Atlanta. Apr. 28, 1930; s. Robert L. and Calhoun (Henderson) H.; student Jr. Coll. Augusta, 1947-49; B.S., U. Ga., 1951, M.S., 1955; m. Susie Davis, Sept. 11, 1955; 1 dau., Susan Alene. Biologist, USPHS, Augusta, Ga., 1951; asst. project leader Ga. Game and Fish Commn., Atlanta, 1951-53; research asst. U. Ga., 1953-55; fisheries research biologist N.C. Wildlife Resources Commn., Hoffman, 1955-64; tech. rep. Curtin Sci. Co.. Atlanta, 1964-68, sales mgr., 1968-72, br. mgr., 1972-73; v.p. Property Research and Devel. Co., Atlanta, 1973-74; environ. info. mgr. Ga. Power Co., Atlanta, 1974-78; dir. Office Congl. and External Affairs EPA, 1978—; chmn. Met. Atlanta Water Resources Study, 1973—; bd. dirs. Ga. Lung Assn.; pres. Save Am's. Vital Environment; v.p. Friends of River; mem. advisory com. to joint water resources com. Ga. Gen. Assembly; chmn. Ga. Council for Clean Air. Mem. AAAS, Am. Inst. Biol. Sci., Ga. Archtl., Engring. Soc., Am. Fisheries Soc., Water Pollution Control Fedn., Am. Soc. Limnology, Oceanography, Am. Soc. Ichthyologists, Herpetologists, Elisha Mitchell Sci. Soc., Ga., S.C., N.C. acads. sci., Ecol. Soc. Am., Izaak Walton League, Ga. Conservancy (trustee) Sierra Club, Nat. Audubon Soc. Contbr. articles to profl., popular publs. Home: 1597 Milford Church Rd Marietta GA 30060 Office: 345 Courtland St Atlanta GA 30308

HUMRICKHOUSE, GEORGE RANDOLPH, lawyer; b. Boydton, Va., Dec. 27, 1909; s. John Johnson and Mary Elizabeth (Pleasants) H.; B.S., U. Va., 1933, LL.B., 1933; D.Cn.L., St. Paul's Coll., 1975; m. Margaret Page Thompson, Apr. 3, 1941; children—Mary Frances, George Randolph. Admitted to Va. bar, 1933; asso. Hutcheson and Hutcheson, Boydton, 1933-42; asst. U.S. atty. Eastern dist. Va., 1942-47, U.S. atty., 1947-51; partner Williams, Mullen, Christian, Pollard & Gray and predecessor firms, Richmond, Va., 1951—. Chancellor, Episcopal Diocese Va., 1958-77, dep. to Gen. Conv. Diocese Va. and So. Va., 1946-73; bd. dirs., treas. Friends of Library, Richmond. Mem. Am., Va., Richmond bar assns., SR. Democrat. Club: Masons. Home: 4504 Seminary Ave Richmond VA 23227 Office: United Va Bank Bldg Richmond VA 23219

HUNGATE, JOSEPH IRVIN, JR., educator; b. Killarney, W.Va., Apr. 30, 1921; s. Joseph Irvin and Nellie (Lickliter) H.; A.B. cum laude, Concord Coll., 1948; M.A., U. Chgo., 1950; Ph.D., U. Tex., 1963; postgrad. St. Louis U., 1948-49; m. Betty Lou Hatzenbuehler, Sept. 11, 1948; children—Ann Elisabeth, Joseph Irvin, Sue Carol. Disaster rep. Chgo. chpt. ARC, 1950; chief psychiat. social work service Valley Forge Army Hosp., Phoenixville, Pa., 1951; psychiat. caseworker Fitzsimons Army Hosp., Denver, 1952-53; chief med. social work service Ft. Jackson, S.C., 1953-55; class dir., social work specialist program Army Med. Sch., San Antonio, 1955-58; asso. prof. social work U. Tex., 1959-68; dean and prof. social work Coll. Social Work, U. S.C., Columbia, 1968-79, dean Coll. Allied Health Professions, 1973-75; teaching cons. Austin State Hosp., 1963-68, William S. Hall Psychiat. Inst., 1972, State of Kans. Social and Rehab. Service, 1974; spl. cons. tech. tng. div. Bur. Family Services, HEW, Washington, 1962-65; mem. profl. adv. com. S.C. Mental Health Assn.; chmn. S.C. Gov.'s Com. on Criminal Justice, Crime and Delinquency, 1968-75; vice chmn. Health Care Adv. Bd., State of S.C., 1974-80; mem. S.C. Gov.'s Health and Welfare Council, 1969-71; chmn. S.C. Merit System Council, 1974-75; cons., faculty mem. multi-regional tng. in mgmt. for social service adminstrn. HEW, 1974-75; mem. com. dependency and state services S.C. State Planning Office, 1976—. Mem. Columbia council USO, 1970—; pres. Arcadia Democratic Precinct, Columbia, 1974-76, exec. com., 1976-78. Served to 1st lt. USAAF, 1942-45, capt. M.S.C., AUS, 1950-58. Decorated Air medal with 3 oak leaf clusters, Purple Heart. Mem. Nat. Assn. Social Workers, Acad. Certified Social Workers, Council on Social Work Edn., AAUP, S.C. Welfare Forum, Greater Columbia C. of C. (community relations council 1972-78). Author: A Guide for Training Public Welfare Administrators, 1965; contbr. articles to profl. jours.; sr. editor Areté, 1971—. Home: 3433 Willow Ridge Rd Columbia SC 29206

HUNNICUTT, JULIAN PERRY, real estate investor; b. Bay City, Tex., June 15, 1927; s. Julian Perry and Theo Irving (Monihan) H.; student U.S. Mil. Acad., 1945-49, B.S. in Mil. Engring., 1949; M.C.E., Tex. A. and M. U., 1959; m. Jennette Mary Jackson, June 15, 1953; children—Julian Perry III, Jennette Mary. Engr., Dow Chem. Co., Freeport, Tex., 1956-58, Tex. Hwy. Dept., Houston, 1959-60; apt. devel., Houston, 1960-63; dir. engring. Jamaica Corp., Houston, 1963-67; pres. Landmark Ventures Inc., Houston, 1968—. Served with U.S. Army, 1949-50, with USAF, 1950-56. Decorated Air medal, Bronze Star. Mem. Tex. (pres. 1964-65), Galveston County (pres. 1975-77), Houston (officer 1962-64) apt. assns., Am. Mgmt. Assn., W.Point Soc. of Houston (pres. 1959-60). Home: 807 S Post Oak Ln Houston TX 77056 Office: PO Box 2841 Houston TX 77001

HUNNICUTT, WARREN, JR., real estate appraiser and broker; b. Columbus, Ga., May 15, 1924; s. Warren P. and Louise S. (Scarbrough) H.; student U. Fla., 1946-48; m. Dorothy M. Barber, Sept. 6, 1947; children—Warren IV, Robert B. With Hunnicutt & Assos., Inc., St. Petersburg, Fla., 1946-74, pres., dir. 1964-74; owner Warren Hunnicut, Jr., Real Estate Appraisers and Consultants, 1974—. Served with USAAF, 1943-46. Mem. Am. Inst. Real Estate Appraisers (chpt. pres. 1972), Soc. Real Estate Appraisers (chpt. pres. 1968), Am. Soc. Real Estate Counselors, St. Petersburg Bd. Realtors (dir. 1974-75, pres. 1976). Home: 7946 9th Ave S St Petersburg FL 33707 Office: 5511 Central Ave St Petersburg FL 33710

HUNSTAD, BERNIE RICHARD, acct.; b. Aberdeen, S.D., June 3, 1951; s. LaVern Bernie and Catherine Agness (Kelly) H.; B.A., Eastern Ky. U., Richmond, 1973; m. Carolyn Ann Jones, Oct. 3, 1976. Plant quality control mgr. Union Underwear Co., Campbellsville. Ky., 1973-74, plant acct., 1974-77, sr. cost acct., Bowling Green, Ky., 1977-78, mgr. accounts receivable, 1978—. Served with AUS, 1973-74. Mem. Campbellsville Jaycees (bd. dirs. 1976). Presbyterian. Office: Box 780 Bowling Green KY 42101

HUNSUCKER, ROBERT DEAN, corp. exec.; b. Winchester, Kans., 1925; ed. Washburn U. With Panhandle Eastern Pipe Line Co., Houston, exec. v.p., 1974, now pres., also dir.; v.p., dir. Trunkline Gas Co. subs.; dir. Gifford Hill Corp. Office: Panhandle Eastern Pipe Line Co 3000 Bissonnet Ave Box 1642 Houston TX 77001*

HUNT, CARLE MANHART, educator; b. Denver, Sept. 14, 1939; s. Carle Clarkson and Mary Wilmina (Manhart) H.; B.B.A., U. Denver, 1962, M.B.A., 1964; D.B.A., U. So. Calif., 1968; m. JoAnna Nelson, Aug. 26, 1961; children—Julia, Annamarie, Carmen, Timothy and Joshua (twins). Asst. prof. mgmt. bldg. industry, real estate U. Denver, 1968-70, asso. prof., 1971-73; v.p. corp. devel. Builders Homes Co., Dothan, Ala., 1970-71; owner C.M. Hunt & Assos., mgmt., real estate cons., Denver, 1973-74; asso. prof. real estate, regional sci. So. Meth. U., Dallas, 1974-76; asso. prof. bus. Oral Roberts U., Tulsa, 1976—, bus. mgr., 1980—. Mem. Am. Real Estate, Acad. Mgmt., Urban Econs. Assn., Nat. Assn. Bus. Economists, Beta Gamma Sigma, Sigma Chi. Presbyterian (elder). Author: Management Simulation of Homebuilding Operations: Players Manual, 1969; (with Richard C. Johanson) Management Simulation of Real Estate Decision Making: Players Manual. Home: 8551 E 31st Pl Tulsa OK 74145 Office: Sch Bus Oral Roberts U Tulsa OK 74102

HUNT, DAVID FORD, lawyer; b. Fort Worth, Apr. 7, 1931; s. John Greffrey and Bernice (Ford) H.; B.S., N. Tex. State U., 1954; LL.B., Vanderbilt U., 1960, J.D., 1960. Admitted to Tex. bar, 1961, law clk. U.S. Dist. Judge, Amarillo, 1960-62; asso. firm Thompson, Knight, Simmons & Bullion, Attys., 1963-67; partner Holloway & Hunt, Attys., Dallas, 1967-70; partner David Ford Hunt, Dallas, 1970-79; partner firm Jenkens & Gilchrist, Dallas, 1980—. Pres. N. Tex. State U. Lambda Chi House Corp., 1965-68; sec., dir. Bootstrap Boys Ranch, Roanoke, Tex., 1972-74; pres. So. Meth. U. Lambda Chi Found., 1972-76, Vanderbilt U. Law Alumni, Dallas, 1972-74; sec. R. Jackson Research Found., 1973—. Served with AUS, 1954-56. Mem. Fed., Am., Tex., Dallas bar assns., Am. Bd. Trial Advocates, Lambda Chi (nat. chancellor 1966-68), Phi Delta Phi. Clubs: Chaparral, Engineers (Dallas). Home: Route 3 Roanoke TX 76262 Office: 2200 First Nat Bank Bldg Dallas TX 75202

HUNT, EARL GLADSTONE, JR., bishop, coll. pres.; b. Johnson City, Tenn., Sept. 14, 1918; s. Earl Gladstone and Tommie Mae (DeVault) H.; B.S., E. Tenn. State U., 1941; M.Div., Emory U., 1946; D.D., Tusculum Coll., 1956, Duke U., 1969, Lambuth Coll., 1978; LL.D., U. Chattanooga, 1957; D.C.L. (hon.), Emory and Henry Coll., 1965; D.H.L., Belmont Abbey Coll., 1976; m. Mary Ann Kyker, June 15, 1943; 1 son, Earl Stephen. Ordained to ministry Methodist Ch., 1944; pastor Sardis Meth. Ch., Atlanta, 1942-44; asso. pastor Broad St. Meth. Ch., Kingsport, Tenn., 1944-45; pastor Wesley Meml. Meth. Ch., Chattanooga, 1945-50, First Meth. Ch., Morristown, Tenn., 1950-56; pres. Emory and Henry Coll., 1956-64; resident bishop Charlotte Area, Meth. Ch., 1964-76, Nashville Area, 1976—; pres. Southeastern Jurisdiction Coll. Bishops, 1973; Willson lectr. S. Central Jurisdiction and Tex. Wesleyan Coll., 1976; Simpson lectr. First United Meth. Ch., Wichita, Kan., 1978; participant Meth. series Protestant Hour, nationwide broadcast, 1956; frequent preacher Chgo. Sunday Evening Club; mem. Meth. Gen. Bd. Edn., 1956-68; del. Meth. Gen. Conf., 1956, 60, 64; del. S.E. Jurisdictional Conf., 1952, 56, 60, 64; chmn. gen. commn. on family life United Meth. Ch., 1968-72, mem. gen. council ministries, 1972-80; exec. com. World Meth. Council; mem. governing bd. Nat. Council Chs., 1972—; Bd. fellows Interpreters' House, Inc.; trustee Scarritt Coll., Emory U., Lambuth Coll., Martin Coll., Rust Coll., Lake Junaluska Meth. Assembly, McKendree Manor, Meth. Hosps., Memphis, A Fund for Theol. Edn.; mem. Com. One Hundred, Emory U. Named Young Man of Year, Morristown Jr. C. of C., 1952. Mem. Blue Key, Newcomen Soc., Pi Kappa Delta. Author: I Have Believed: A Bishop Talks about His Faith, 1980; editor: Storms and Starlight; contbr. articles to mags. and profl. jours. Home: 60 Revere Park Nashville TN 37205 Office: 415 Cavalier Bldg 95 White Bridge Rd Nashville TN 37205

HUNT, ELIZABETH MULLEN, sch. prin.; b. Long Beach, Calif., Dec. 16, 1912; d. William and Anna (Hepp) Mullen; B.A., Occidental Coll., 1934; M.A., U. So. Calif., 1939; postgrad. U. Tex.. 1940; Adminstrs. certificate U. Houston, 1955; m. Andrew W. Hunt, Sept. 3, 1941; children—Lacy H., II, Andrew W., William T.C. Tchr., Calif. Pub. Schs., 1934-41; lectr. in speech, radio, debate Stephen F. Austin U., 1947-49, Hardin Simmon U., 1949-50, McMurry Coll., 1950-55; tchr. Houston Ind. Sch. Dist., 1955—; producer, dir. dramatic prodns., writer Centennial Mus.; prin. Grissom Elementary Sch., 1967—; drama cons., curriculum cons., lectr. childrens creative activities. Recipient Am. Educator medal Freedoms Found. at Valley Forge, 1964. Mem. Nat., Tex. assns. elementary suprs. and prins., Nat., Tex. assns. supervision and curriculum, Am. Assn. Sch. Adminstrs., NEA, Tex. Tchrs. Assn., Houston Prins. Assn., Delta Kappa Gamma. Episcopalian. Club: Freedoms Found. Author numerous childrens plays, operettas and ednl. articles. Home: 5154 Jackwood St Houston TX 77035 Office: 4900 Simsbrook St Houston TX 77045

HUNT, HAROLD EUGENE, ophthalmologist; b. Paris, Tex., June 23, 1924; s. Thomas Ewell and Margaret Edgar (Harper) H.; grad. Paris Jr. Coll., 1943; B.S., Tex. Christian U., 1945; M.D., Southwestern Med. Coll., 1947; m. Sara Agnes Humphries. Feb. 17, 1968; children—Harold Eugene, Michael Griffin. Intern, Charity Hosp., New Orleans, 1947-48; ophthalmology tng. Tulane, 1948-59; ophthalmology resident Baylor Coll. Medicine, Houston, 1949-53;

ophthalmologist Hunt Eye, Ear, Nose and Throat Clinic, Paris, 1953—; mem. staff St. Joseph's Hosp., Paris, past pres. staff, trustee. Dir. Paris Savs. & Loan Assn. Med. adv. bd. 1973—; Commn. for Blind. Past pres. Community Concerts Paris. Bd. regents Paris Jr. Coll., past pres.; past mem. alumni bd. Southwestern Med. Coll., U. Tex.; past mem. adv. bd. Salvation Army; mem. med. adv. bd. Tex. Soc. for Prevention of Blindness; mem. Christian Edn. Coordinating Bd. Bapt. Gen. Conv. Tex., 1978-80. Served with USNR, 1950-52. Recipient Distinguished Service award as outstanding young man Lamar County, 1957. Diplomate Am. Bd. Ophthalmology. Fellow A.C.S., Am. Acad. Ophthalmology; mem. Lamar-Delta Counties Med. Soc. (past pres.), Tex. Med. Assn. (past chmn., sec. eye sect.), Tex. Ophthalmol. Assn. (past pres.), Lamar County C. of C., Tex. Assn. Jr. Coll. Adminstrs. (v.p. 1975-76, pres. 1976-77), Tex. Lions League for Crippled Children (past dir., life mem.), Knife and Fork Club Paris (past pres.). Baptist (past chmn. deacons). Lion (pres. Paris 1953, dist. gov. 1966-67). Home: 595 33d St SE Paris TX 75460 Office: 150 SE 8th St Paris TX 75460

HUNT, J(ULIAN) COURTENAY, artist; b. Jacksonville, Fla., Sept. 17, 1917; s. Julian Schley and Ruth Rosalind (Loftin) H.; student Ringling Sch. Art, 1946-47, Farnsworth Sch. Art, 1948-52. Artist, 1950—; tchr. pvt. classes painting, 1950—; exhibited in one-man shows at Cummer Gallery of Art, Jacksonville, 1963—, Flair Gallery, Palm Beach, Fla., 1970-71; exhibited in group shows at Palm Beach Art Gallery, Soc. Four Arts, Palm Beach, 1968-69, Audubon Artists of Am., N.Y.C., Allied Artists Am., N.Y.C., 1952-56, Atlanta High Mus., 1950-54, St. Augustine (Fla.) Art Assn., 1970-73, Sarasota (Fla.) Art Assn., 1952-56, Fla. Artists Group Show at Norton Art Gallery of the Palm Beaches, 1975; portraits in permanent collections U. Fla., Gainesville, Jacksonville U., City Hall of Jacksonville, Duval County Circuit Ct., Jacksonville, Ind. Life Ins. Co., Jacksonville. Served with USAAF, 1942-46; ETO. Address: 2587 Windwood Ln Orange Park FL 32073

HUNT, JAMES BAXTER, JR., gov. N.C.; b. Greensboro, N.C., May 16, 1937; s. James Baxter and Elsie (Brame) H.; B.S., N.C. State U., 1959, M.S., 1962; J.D., U. N.C., 1964; m. Carolyn Joyce Leonard, Aug. 20, 1958; children—Rebecca Joyce, James Baxter III, Rachel Henderson, Elizabeth Brame. Econ. adviser H.M. Govt. of Nepal for Ford Found., 1964-66; admitted to N.C. bar; mem. firm Kirby, Webb & Hunt, Wilson, N.C., 1966-72; tng. cons. Peace Corps, 1966-67; lt. gov. N.C., 1973, now gov. Past chmn. Democratic Govs.' Conf., Southern Growth Policies Bd., Southern Regional Edn. Bd. Mem. Nat. Govs.' Assn. (chmn. com. criminal justice and public protection, chmn. subcom. small cities and rural devel.). Home: Route 1 Box 138 Lucama NC 27851 Office: Office of Gov State Legis Bldg Raleigh NC 27611

HUNT, JAMES CONRAD, fin. exec.; b. Hickory, N.C., Jan. 30, 1929; s. Bruce Earl and Neva Irene (Eckard) H.; B.A. in Econs. Lenoir Rhyne Coll., 1951; M.B.A. (N.C. Bus. Found. fellow), U. N.C., 1955; m. Dae Ann Turnbull, Nov. 9, 1973; children—James S., Susan C., Lori P. Fin. adminstr. ops. control RCA, Cherry Hill, N.J., 1960-68; with govt. systems group Harris Corp., Melbourne, Fla., 1968—, dir. ops. analysis, 1970-73, asst. controller, 1973, controller, 1973—; adj. prof. Grad. Sch. Mgmt. Sci., Fla. Inst. Tech., 1969-77. Pres., Klnlyn Civic Assn., 1958-60. Served with CIC, U.S. Army, 1951-54. Mem. Nat. Contract Mgmt. Assn., Fin. Execs. Inst., Nat. Security Indsl. Assn. Office: PO Box 37 Melbourne FL 32901

HUNT, JAMES WILLIAM, educator; b. Ellisville, Miss., Dec. 16, 1924; s. James Henry and Thelma (Freeman) H.; grad. Miss. Coll., Clinton, 1950; Ed.D. (HEW fellow in spl. edn.), U. Miss., 1964; m. Alice Margaret Raney, Dec. 24, 1950; children—Elizabeth Ann Hunt Huse, William Daniel. Tchr. math. Yazoo City (Miss.) Pub. Schs., 1950-52, Bailey Jr. High Sch., Jackson, Miss., 1952-54; tchr. French elementary sch., Jackson, 1954-55; prin. Bradley Elementary Sch., Jackson, 1955-58, Green Elementary Sch., Jackson, 1958-61; prof. spl. edn. Miss. U. for Women (formerly Miss. State Coll. for Women), Columbus, 1963—; cons. Miss. Pub. Schs.; cons. spl. edn. div. Miss. Dept. Edn., chmn. Regional Screening Team for Spl. Edn. Bd. dirs. Lowndes County Assn. Retarded Citizens, 1972-76, Work Activity Center for Severely Handicapped, Columbus, Miss. Served with U.S. Army, 1943-45. Decorated Purple Heart. Mem. Am. Assn. Mental Deficiencies, Council Exceptional Children, Am. Assn. Higher Edn., Assn. Children with Learning Disabilities. Methodist. Contbr. articles to profl. jours. Office: W Box 280 Columbus MS 39701

HUNT, JASPER STEWART, physician; b. Winder, Ga., Aug. 21, 1904; s. Henry Robert and Sadie (Stewart) H.; B.S., Emory U., 1924; M.D.-Vanderbilt U., 1929; m. Anne Wright, Dec. 7, 1956; children—Elizabeth B., Steve H., Charles H., Jasper S., Helen P. Intern, U.S. Naval Hosp., Norfolk, Va., 1929-30, Willard Parker Hosp., N.Y.C., 1932; resident Childrens Hosp. of D.C., 1931, chief resident, 1932-33; practice medicine specializing in pediatrics, Charlotte, N.C., 1933-66; chief dept. pediatrics Charlotte Meml. Hosp., 1940-51, hon. mem. med. staff. 1968—; chief pediatrics Mercy Hosp., 1955-57. Mem. mens adv. com. Mobile chpt. Jr. Leagues Am., 1974-77; bd. govs. ARC, Mobile, 1970-74; sr. warden Christ Episcopal Ch., Mobile, 1976-77, vestryman, 1975-77; bd. dirs. Mobile Opera Assn., 1966-69; trustee Wright Girls Sch., Mobile, 1968-70. Served to lt. (j.g.), M.C., USN, 1929-31. Recipient President's Spl. award Mecklenburg County Med. Soc., 1964. Diplomate Am. Bd. Pediatrics. Mem. AMA, N.C. Med. Soc., Am. Acad. Pediatrics, U.S. Navy League (v.p. 1969—), N.C., Charlotte (pres. 1964) pediatric socs., U.S. Power Squadrons, Pi Kappa Alpha. Clubs: Fairhope Yacht; Lakewood Golf (Point Clear, Ala.); Mobile Country. Home and office: 55 Wimbledon Dr Mobile AL 36608

HUNT, JOHN WILLIAMSON, chem. co. exec.; b. Lake Wales, Fla., Nov. 6, 1932; s. Charles Morton and Dorothy Dix (Williamson) H.; B.S. in Agrl. Engring., U. Fla., 1955, M.S. in Animal Nutrition, 1959; m. Kathleen Beatrice Corcoran, Aug. 18, 1956; children—John Williamson, David Corcoran. Asst. county agt. U.S. Dept. Agr., Polk County, Fla., 1959-61; owner Hunt's Ranch and Garden, Bartow, Fla., 1961-63; with Internat. Minerals & Chem. Corp., Lakeland, 1963—, land utilization supr., 1963-67, mgr. cattle ops., 1967-76; sales mgr. for Fla. and Ga., IMC Chem. Corp., 1976—; owner John W. Hunt, Realtor, Bartow, 1973—; dir. Wales Properties, Lake Wales. Pres., chief Alturas Fire Dept., 1972. Served as 2d lt. AUS, 1955-57. Hon. mem. Future Farmers Am., 4-H; U. Fla. fellow, 1957. Mem. Am. Soc. Range Mgmt. (council, 1975), Fla. Soc. Farm Mgrs. and Rural Appraisers, Am. Red Brangus Assn. (dir. 1967-75, pres. 1972), Am., Fla. socs. agrl. engrs., Polk County Soil Conservation Dist. (sec., chmn. 1979-80), Fla., Polk County (dir.) cattlemen's assns., Fla. Assn. Conservation Dists. (pres. 1975, 76), Polk County Farm Bur., Fla. Beef Cattle Improvement Assn. (pres. 1975-76), Nat. Assn. Realtors, Fla. Assn. Realtors, Bartow Bd. Realtors, Fla. Forestry Council, Sigma Nu. Episcopalian. Club: Kiwanis. Patentee chem. feed mixing process. Home and Office: 905 Alturas Rd Bartow FL 33830

HUNT, JOSEPH VICTOR, cons. pub. adminstrn.; b. Phila., July 21, 1905; s. James Francis and Alice (Malone) H.; B.S., St. Joseph's Coll., 1932; A.M., U. Pa., 1941; LL.D., Gallaudet Coll., 1969; m. Dolores Consilia Hede, Oct. 19, 1935; children—Rosemary Dolores, Joseph Michael, Dolores, Cecilia. Asst. dir. Anthracite Industries research in operations of local govt., Schuykill and Northumberland counties, Pa., 1932-36; chmn. dept. bus. adminstrn. St. Joseph's Coll., Phila., 1936-41; sr. bus. economist OPA, Washington, 1941-42; chief div. adminstrv. mgmt. Bur. Old-Age and Survivors Ins., Social Security Bd. (now Social Security Adminstrn., Dept. of Health, Edn. and Welfare), Washington, 1942-43; asso. commr. Vocational Rehab. Adminstrn., Dept. Health, Edn. and Welfare, 1943-67, commr. Rehab. Services Adminstrn., 1967-69, dep. commr. Community Services Adminstrn., 1970-72; cons. pub. adminstrn., 1972—. Recipient Christophers Nat. award, 1953; Superior Service award, Dept. Health, Edn. and Welfare, 1958, Distinguished Service award, 1961; Pres.'s award Nat. Rehab. Assn., 1966, Nat. award Goodwill Industries Am., 1968; named Washington Alumnus of Year, St. Joseph's Coll., 1962. Mem. Am. Assn. Workers for Blind, Internat. Soc. Rehab. of Disabled, Nat. Rehab. Assn., Am. Pub. Welfare Assn., John Carroll Soc., Nat. Soc. Sci. Honor Soc., Pi Gamma Mu. Roman Catholic. Club: Nat. Press (Washington). Home and office: 109 N George Mason Dr Arlington VA 22203

HUNT, SUSANNE CAROL KRAFT, registered nurse; b. Plainfield, N.J., Dec. 25, 1943; d. Rudolph A. and Helen A. (Thomas) Kraft; diploma East Orange Gen. Hosp. Sch. of Nursing, 1964; m. Kenneth G. Hunt, Oct. 29, 1965; children—Kenneth G., Kristen S. Nurse, Overlook Hosp., Summit, N.J., 1965-67; head nurse Woodbine Nursing Home, Alexandria, Va., 1967-68; staff nurse Circle Terrace Hosp., Alexandria, 1969-70; head intensive care Manassas (Va.) Manor Nursing Home, 1976-77, dir. nurses, 1977-79; head nurse Barcroft Inst., Falls Church, Va., 1979, Martin Meml. Hosp., Stuart, Fla., 1979—. Cert. intravenous therapy technician. Mem. Va. Nurses Assn., No. Va. Dirs. of Nursing Assn., United Methodist Women. Home: 1464 NE 24th St Jensen Beach FL 33457 Office: Martin Meml Hosp Hospital Ave Stuart FL 33457

HUNT, WILLIAM DONALD, cosmetic and toiletry co. exec.; b. Pitts., Oct. 3, 1927; s. Everett Kirker and Janet Camille (Wilhere) H.; B.S., Northwestern U., 1950; m. Ovetta Bernice Foster, July 22, 1950; children—Christopher, Gregory, Leslie, Alison, Geoffrey. Sales service mgr. Personal Products Corp., Miltown, N.J., 1950-53; nat. brand mgr. Mennen Co., Morristown, N.J., 1953-55; sr. v.p. mktg. Noxell Corp., Balt., 1955-71, dir., 1963-71; pres., chief exec. officer, dir. Yardley of London, Inc., Atlanta, 1971-78, pres. Yardley & Co. Ltd., Atlanta, 1978—. Served with USNR, 1945-46. Clubs: Balt. Country, Cherokee Town and Country, Commerce (Atlanta); Seaview Country (Absecon, N.J.). Home: 850 Fairfield Rd NW Atlanta GA 30327 Office: 3330 Peachtree Rd NE Atlanta GA 30326

HUNT, WILLIAM FREDERICK, JR., statistician; b. Montclair, N.J., Aug. 22, 1943; s. William Frederick and Elizabeth Catherine (Bridge) H.; B.A. cum laude (N.J. State scholar), Rutgers U., 1966, M.S., 1968; postgrad. Pa. State U., 1972, Calif. Inst. Tech., 1978; m. Janice E. Warsley, May 27, 1967; children—William Frederick, Elizabeth Kathryn. Teaching asst. Rutgers U., New Brunswick, N.J., 1966-67; supervisory math. statistician EPA, Research Triangle Park, N.C., 1970—; co-dir. H&R Assos., Research Triangle Park, 1973—. Served to lt. USPHS, 1968-70. Recipient Bronze award for commendable service EPA, 1976. Mem. Am. Statis. Assn., Air Pollution Control Assn., Am. Soc. Quality Control (program chmn. environ. tech. com. 1975—), Phi Beta Kappa, Sigma Xi. Roman Catholic (pres. parish club, mem. parish council). Contbr. articles to profl. jours. Home: 5821 Williamsburg Way Durham NC 27713 Office: EPA/OAQPS Research Triangle Park NC 27711

HUNTER, CANNIE MAE COX, educator; b. Belton, Tex., July 16, 1916; d. Jesse Daniel and Mary Alice (Hamilton) Cox; B.S., Mary Hardin Baylor Coll., 1940; M.S., San Marcos Tchrs. Coll., 1942; postgrad. U. Tex., 1946-47, Tex. Tech. U., 1956-70, U. San Diego, 1975, St. Mary's U., 1976; m. William Dudley Hunter, June 5, 1938; children—Darline, Bob Roy; m. 2d, Bertrand E. Huggins, Aug. 3, 1979. Tchr. pub. schs., Belton, 1935-38, Galveston, Tex., 1938-42; mem. staff testing dept. U. Ariz., 1942-43; reading cons. Phoenix Pub. Schs., 1943-45; tchr.-counselor pub. schs., Killeen, Tex., 1946-54; classroom tchr., Lubbock, Tex., 1954-74; tchr. first grade bilingual lang. devel. Posey Elementary Sch., Lubbock, Tex., 1974—; pres. CM Corp. First aid chmn. ARC, Lubbock County, 1960-63, first aid instr., 1956—; area dir. March of Dimes, 1958-63; tchr. high sch. dept. First Bapt. Ch., Lubbock, 1960—. Recipient Outstanding Service award ARC, 1966. Certified educator, Tex. Mem. Assn. Childhood Edn. Internat., NEA, Tex. Tchrs. Assn., Tex. Classroom Tchrs. Assn., Nat. PTA, Tex. Edn. Assn., Lubbock Educators Assn., Lubbock Classroom Tchrs. Assn., AAUW, Am. Bus. Women's Assn., S. Plains Writers Guild, YWCA, Lubbock, Killeen chambers commerce. Baptist. Club: University City (Lubbock). Home: 4626 30th St Lubbock TX 79410 Office: 2001 Rancier St Killeen TX 76541

HUNTER, CHARLES EDWIN, mfrs. rep.; b. Oklahoma City, Nov. 8, 1910; s. Charles Edwin and Gertrude (Buchanan) H.; diploma Christian Bros. Coll., 1931; student Memphis State U., 1932-33; m. Marguerite Catledge, May 29, 1954; children—Charles Edwin, Timothy, Kipling, Holly. Salesman Standard Coffee Co., New Orleans, 1933-35, stock clk. Orgill Bros., Memphis, 1935-36; athletic dir. Memphis Park Commn., 1936-37; adjustor Gen. Contract Purchase Corp., 1938-39, unit mgr., 1940-41; salesman Tommy Tucker Co., 1946-47; pvt. bus. as mfrs. rep., Conyers, Ga., 1947—. Served from pvt. to pfc., USMCR, 1942-45. Home: 1955 McCalla Rd SE Conyers GA 30207 Office: PO Box 250 Conyers GA 30207

HUNTER, EMMETT MARSHALL, JR., oil co. exec.; b. Denver, Aug. 18, 1913; s. Emmett Marshall and Pearl Jo (Hubby) H.; LL.B., So. Methodist U., 1936; m. Marjorie Louise Roth, Nov. 21, 1941; children—Marsha Louise Hunter Blanchard, Marjorie Maddin Hunter, Margaret Anne. Admitted to Tex. bar, 1936; practiced law, Dallas, Longview and Houston, 1936-41; with Exxon Co. USA (formerly Humble Oil & Refining Co.), Tyler, Tex., 1945-78, exploration land supr., 1965-78; pres. Internat. Oil Investment Assos., Tyler, 1978—. Served as lt. USNR, 1942-45. Mem. State Bar Tex., Am. Petroleum Inst., Bus.-Industry Polit. Action Com., E. Tex. C. of C., So. Meth. U. Alumni Assn., Hockaday Dads Club, U.S. Naval Inst., SAR (pres. Tyler chpt., registrar Tex. soc., bd. mgrs.), Tex. Hist. Assn., Lambda Chi Alpha, Pi Upsilon Nu. Author: Adventuring Abroad on a Bicycle and $180, 1938; Marinas: A Boon to Yachting, 1948. Home: 2924 Sunnybrook Dr Tyler TX 75701 Office: PO Box 7402 Tyler TX 75711

HUNTER, GORDON COBLE, banker; b. nr. Greensboro, N.C., July 29, 1894; s. Samuel G. and Lalah Vance (Coble) H.; student U. N.C., 1915-17; m. Ethel Gray Wilson, Jan. 26, 1918; children—Rebecca Vance Hunter Vittur, Rachel Gray Hunter Cushwa. With Am. Exchange Nat. Bank, Greensboro, 1919-31; bank examiner FDIC, 1933; exec. v.p. Peoples Bank, Roxboro, N.C., 1933-57, pres., 1957—, chmn. bd., 1960—; chmn. bd. emeritus First Union Nat Bank, Roxboro; dir. Radio Sta. WRXO, Morris Telephone Co., Reinforced Plastic Container Corp., Roxboro Devel. Corp. Treas. Town Bd. of Roxboro, 1934-60; Person County chmn. ARC, 1937-38, USO Drive, 1943-44; N.C. chmn. Nat. Found. 4-H Club, 1955-57; an organizer, bd. dirs. Person County Meml. Hosp.; mem. N.C. Correction and Tng. Bd., 1943-47, N.C. Merit System Bd., 1948-51, N.C. Bd. Conservation and Devel., N.C. Forestry Adv. Com. Served to 2d lt. inf. U.S. Army, 1917-18. Named Citizen of Year, Person County, 1956; recipient citation for 25 year devoted service Nat. Found.; Certificate of Appreciation in recognition 25 years leadership for sales U.S. Savs. Bonds, U.S. Dept. Treasury. Mem. Am. (nat. research council 1955-57, exec. com. 1946-49, regional v.p. 1958-60, N.C. legis. com. 1960-62), N.C. (pres. 1945-46) bankers assns., Roxboro C. of C. (1st pres. 1935), Am. Legion (past comdr. Lester Blackwell post), 40 and 8, Order Long Leaf Pine, Internat. Platform Assn. Methodist (steward). Club: Rotary (past pres. Roxboro). Home: 115 Academy St Roxboro NC 27573 Office: 203 N Main St Roxboro NC 27573

HUNTER, HOWARD JACK, mfg. engr.; b. Moline, Ill., Dec. 29, 1927; s. Howard Shafter and Lyndall Annette (McGehee) H.; bachelors degree Augustana Coll., 1953; m. Lula Grace Mercer, Sept. 11, 1954; 1 son, Howard Kim. Methods and standards engr. Deer & Co., Moline, 1948-54; program analyst Rock Island Arsenal, Rock Island, Ill., 1954-63; program mgr. Def. Indsl. Plant Equipment Center, Def. Logistics Agy., Memphis, 1963—. Bd. dirs. Memphis Cotton Carnival Assn., 1972—, Beale Street Hist. Found., 1974—, Mid-South Fair and Libertyland, 1976—; mem. Memphis and Shelby County Bd. Adjustment, 1977—. Served with USN, 1945-48; PTO. Mem. Soc. Mfg. Engrs. (cert.), Am. Def. Preparedness Assn., Am. Nat. Metric Council, U.S. Metric Assn., Am. Logistics Assn., VFW, Tenn. Squires. Presbyterian. Clubs: Masons, Order of Eastern Star, Shriners, K.T. Home: 1178 Ridgecrest Ct Palm Harbor FL 33563 Office: Def Indsl Plant Equipment Center Memphis TN 38114

HUNTER, JAMES EDWIN, constrn. co. exec.; b. Sumter, S.C., Oct. 22, 1925; s. James Edwin and Sarah DeSaussure (Edmunds) H.; B. Elec. Engring., Clemson U., 1949; m. Lois Catharine Dooley, Aug. 4, 1967; children—James Scott, Caroline Sims. Elec. engr. R. Neal Campbell, Greenville, S.C., 1949-50; chief elec. engr. Deering Miliken Co., Spartanburg, S.C., 1950-52; chief engr. Harrison-Wright Co., Charlotte, N.C., 1952-59; pres. Hunter & Walden Co., Inc., Charlotte, 1959—. Mem. bd. advisors Belmont Abbey Coll., 1976—. Served with USMC, 1943-46. Registered profl. engr., S.C. Mem. Nat. Soc. Profl. Engrs., N.C. Soc. Engrs., Charlotte Engrs. Club, Mensa. Democrat. Episcopalian. Club: Charlotte City. Home: 4600 Sharon View Rd Charlotte NC 28211 Office: PO Box 11756 Charlotte NC 28209 also PO Box 257 Hail Saudi Arabia

HUNTER, LENA VIRGINIA, ch. and civic worker; b. Forsyth County, N.C., Oct. 31, 1914; d. Cicero Gilbert and Ada Jane (Doub) Hunter; Asso. in Bus. Edn., Coll., 1936. Sec. to mgr. Chrysler Plymouth dealership, Winston-Salem, N.C., 1937-57; group rep., account exec. Blue Cross and Blue Shield N.C., Winston Salem, 1957-77; dir. N.C. Grange Mut. Ins. Co. Master, Old Richmond Grange, 1963—; ofcl. N.C. Grange; 7th deg. mem. Nat. Grange; mem. NW Community Concerns Council; tchr., organist, music dir. Pleasant Hill United Meth. Ch., mem. ofcl. bd. Mem. from Forsyth County N.C. Economic Devel. Commn. Named Woman of Year in Service to Agr. N.C. State Grange, 1955, Granger of Year, Farmers and Traders Life Ins. Co., 1972. Home: 6040 Seward Rd Pfafftown NC 27040

HUNTER, MARY DOTY, educator; b. Madison County, Ky., Oct. 11, 1917; d. Joe and Rhoda Russell (Riddle) Hunter; B.S., Eastern Ky. U., 1943, M.A., 1955. Tchr. Madison County Sch. System, 1937-43, Richmond (Ky.) City Sch. System, 1943, tchr. Headstart kindergarten, 1965-69, tchr. Madison High Sch., 1972—. Program chmn. Bellevue Elementary PTA, leader 4-H Richmond, 1965-74; founder annual County-City Schs. Art Exhibit, Richmond, 19S6—. Mem. subcom. Gov.'s Task Force on Edn., 1977—. Mem. Nat., Ky., Central Ky. (v.p., 1975-76, pres. 1977—), Richmond edn. assns., Eastern Ky. U. Alumni Assn. (v.p. 1959-60, dir. 1977—), AAUW (pres. Ky. 1970-72, 73-74), Classroom Tchrs. Assn., Bus. and Profl. Women's Club (past pres.), Beta Sigma Phi. Democrat. Home: 210 S 3d St Richmond KY 40475

HUNTER, MARY JANE BURNS (MRS. JOSEPH LAWTON HUNTER), journalist; b. Atlanta, Oct. 31, 1919; d. Cecil Olney and Mary (Cheves) Burns; student U. Ga., 1935-36, High Mus. Sch. Art, Atlanta, 1937; m. Joseph Lawton Hunter, Oct. 8, 1944; children—Mollie, Ellen. Landscape designer, horticulturist, Fort Lauderdale, Fla., 1960-65, Freeport, Grand Bahama I., 1965-66; writer, garden columns Freeport News, 1966-68, mem. editorial staff, 1968-70, editor weekly entertainment supplement, 1968-70; women's editor Cape Coral (Fla.) Breeze, 1970-74, editor's asst., 1974-76; columnist, reporter Cape Coral Bur., Ft. Myers News-Press, 1976-79, asst. editorial page editor, 1979—. corr. various travel publs., Bahamas, 1969-70. Recipient 2d Pl. Feature Writing award Weekly div. Better Newspaper Contest, Fla. Press Assn., 1970, 2d Pl. Women's News award, 1972, 1st Pl. Women's News Weekly div., 1973; State Media award community service Fla. Easter Seal Soc., 1972, Best of Gannett award, 1978, numerous other awards. Mem. Sigma Delta Chi. Contbr. articles to publs. Office: Fort Myers News-Press Box 10 Fort Myers FL 33902

HUNTER, RICHARD EDMUND, plant pathologist; b. Jersey City, Jan. 26, 1923; s. Frederick William and Margaret (Dahlgren) H.; B.S., Rutgers U., 1949; M.S., Okla. State U., 1951, Ph.D., 1968; m. Edith Earline Clark, June 2, 1946; children—Catherine (Mrs. John Bennett Hays), Margaret Ann (Mrs. Carl D. Roberts), Richard Clark. Asst. in biology N. Mex. State U., State College, 1951-55; instr., research plant pathologist Okla. State U., Stillwater, 1958-68, asst. prof., 1968-71, asso. prof., 1971-72; research plant pathologist Nat. Cotton Pathology Research Lab., College Station, Tex., 1972-75; research plant pathologist Southeast Fruit and Tree Nut Lab., Byron, Ga., 1975-79, research leader Nut Prodn. unit, 1976-79, supervisory research plant pathologist, research leader, location leader W.R. Poage Pecan Field Sta., Brownwood, Tex., 1979—. Served to capt. USAAF, 1943-46. Mem. Am. Phytopath. Soc., Am. Soc. Hort. Scientists, Internat. Soc. Plant Pathologists, Southeast Pecan Growers Assn., No. Nut Growers Assn., Alpha Zeta, Phi Sigma, Sigma Xi. Methodist. Contbr. articles to various jours.; Southeastern regional editor Pecan Quar., 1977—. Home: 3903 Glenwood Dr Brownwood TX 76801 Office: WR Poage Pecan Field St PO Box 579 Brownwood TX 76801

HUNTER, ROBERT KILMER, utility exec.; b. Mantee, Miss., Nov. 11, 1922; s. Leo and Carrie Elvira (Harden) H.; B.S. in Elec. Engring., Miss. State U., 1951; m. Nadine Smith, Aug. 28, 1949; children—Robert Dean, Debra Kaye, Steve Alan. With Miss. Power Co., 1953—, comml. sales mgr., 1962-69, indsl. sales mgr., 1969-79; mgr. indsl. and comml. sales, Gulfport, 1979—; state power liaison rep. Emergency Electric Power Adminstrn., 1970—. Served with AUS, 1941-46, 51-52. Registered profl. engr., Miss. Mem. Nat. Soc. Profl. Engrs., ASHRAE, Nat. Fire Protection Assn., Internat. Assn. Elec. Insps., Southeastern Electric Exchange, Edison Electric Inst., Miss. Engring. Soc. (pres. 1975-76; Engr. of Year award 1979), Gulhan Investment Club. Baptist. Clubs: Gulfcoast Sports Fishing Assn., Gulfport Kiwanis (v.p. 1974-75). Home: 26 E 52d St Gulfport MS 39501 Office: PO Box 4079 Gulfport MS 39501

HUNTER, SUE PERSONS (MRS. CHARLES FORCE HUNTER), cons.; b. Hico, Tex., Aug. 21, 1921; d. David Henry and Beulah (Boatwright) Persons; B.A., U. Tex., 1942; m. Charles Force

Hunter; children—Shelley Hunter Richardson, Mary Hunter McCullough, Margaret Hunter Brown. Air traffic controller CAA (now FAA), San Antonio and Houston, 1942-52; writer Bissonet Plaza News, 1969-72; coordinator Goals for La., 1971-74; adminstrv. dir. Jeff Publs., Inc.; contbg. editor The Jeffersonian, 1975; communications coordinator Jefferson Parish Dist. Atty., 1974-78, adminstr. child support enforcement div., 1979—. Pres. United Ch. Women East Jefferson (La.), 1958-59, LWV Jefferson Parish, La., 1961-64; pres. LWV La., 1967-71, bd. dirs., 1962-67; mem. probation services com. Community Services Council, Jefferson, 1966-73, v.p., 1970-72; mem. Library Devel. Com. La., 1967-71, Nat. Com. Support of Pub. Schs., 1967-72; mem. Goals Found. Council Met. New Orleans, 1969-75, sec., 1970, 72; mem. Goals La. Task Force State and Local Govt., 1969-70; pres. MMM Investment Club, 1969-72; bd. mem. New Orleans Area Health Planning Council, 1969-75; adv. council La. State Health Planning, 1971-75, La. Commn. Status of Women, 1971-72, La. Consumer Council, 1971-72; mem. La. Citizens Ednl. Found. Criminal Justice, 1973-76, Council Internat. Visitors, 1962—; title I adv. council La. State Dept. Edn., 1970-72; adv. bd. Muscular Dystrophy Assn. New Orleans, 1975-77; chmn. Jefferson Women's Polit. Caucus, 1979-80; bd. dirs. New Orleans Area/Bayou River Health Systems Agy., 1978—, pres., 1980; bd. dirs. La. Child Support Enforcement Assn., 1980—; mem. Task Force La. Talent Bank of Women. Recipient Outstanding Citizens award Rotary Club, Metairie, La., 1962; River Ridge award, 1976. Mem. New Orleans Panhellenic Assn. (pres. 1956-57), Women in Communications, Alpha Xi Delta. Presbyterian (elder). Home: 210 Stewart Ave River Ridge LA 70123

HUNTER, THOMAS ALEXANDER, III, state ofcl.; b. Galveston, Tex., Dec. 31, 1929; s. John Charles and Laura Mae (Kelso) H.; grad. N. Tex. State Coll., 1951; postgrad. St. Mary's Sem., 1971-73; Th.B., U. St. Thomas, 1973. Ordained deacon Roman Cath. Ch., 1972. Various assignments in acctg. dept. Tex. Transport & Terminal Co., Galveston, 1951-52; teller Hutchings-Sealy Nat. Bank, Galveston, 1952-58; 1st asst. assessor City of Galveston, 1958-79; assessor and collector of taxes Galveston County Mcpl. Utility Dist. 1, 1974—; tax cons. Village of Jamaica Beach, Tex., 1979—; tax assessor and collector Galveston County Drainage Dist. 4, 1979—, Havre Lafitte Property Owners Assn., Galveston, 1979—, City of La Marque (Tex.), 1979—. Pres. Young Adult Catholics of Galveston County, 1960-63. Recipient Apostolic Benediction of Pope John XXIII, 1960. Registered tax assessor. Mem. Internat. Assn. Assessing Officers, Tex. Assn. Assessing Officers, Nat. Council Young Adult Catholics, Holy Name Soc., Permanent Diaconate Assn., Gammadion Honor Soc., Chi Gamma Chi, Sigma Phi Nu. Democrat. Clubs: K.C., Sacred Heart Men's (moderator 1972-79). Home: 2410 Beluche Galveston TX 77550 Office: 322 Laurel St La Marque TX 77568

HUNTINGTON, ROBERT GRAHAM, air pollution control co. exec.; b. Mt. Holly, N.J., Mar. 12, 1934; s. Harold Graham and Mary Helen (Curtis) H.; B.M.E., Union Coll., Schenectady, 1956; M.S. in Engring., Harvard U., 1959, postgrad. mgmt. devel. program, 1968; m. Patricia Ann Pearsall, Jan. 28, 1956; children—Gracia Curtis, Anne Wolcott. With Carrier Corp., Syracuse, N.Y., 1959-60; with Am. Air Filter Co., Inc., Louisville, 1960—, v.p., 1972—, mgr. air pollution control div., 1972—. Served with AUS, 1956-58. AEC fellow, 1958-59. Mem. Pub. Health Soc. (hon.), Indsl. Gas Cleaning Inst. (dir.), Assn. Iron and Steel Engrs., Delta Omega. Presbyterian. Patentee gas cleaning systems, thermoelectric cooling and dehumidification apparatus. Home: 1724 Casselberry Rd Louisville KY 40205 Office: 215 Central Ave Louisville KY 40208

HUNTINGTON, STERLING HICKS, physician; b. Schenectady, 1922; s. Frank Allen and Marguerite Sanford (Hicks) H.; B.A., Union Coll., 1943; M.D., Albany Med. Coll., 1946; m. Laura Parmele Johnson, Sept. 24, 1945; children—Dixie Jeanne, Allen Parmele. Intern, Rochester (N.Y.) Gen. Hosp., 1946-47; pvt. practice gen. medicine, Burlington, N.C., 1947-57; resident VA Hosp., Coral Gables, Fla., 1957-58, resident in phys. medicine and rehab., 1958-60; pvt. practice phys. medicine and rehab., Coral Gables, 1960-77, Boca Raton, Fla., 1978—; active staff Boca Raton Community Hosp.; cons. Spain Rehab. Center, Birmingham, Ala., 1968—, USPHS, 1968-78, U. Miami Med. Sch., 1961-66; chmn. dept. rehab. medicine Bapt. Hosp., Miami, 1960-74. Diplomate Am. Acad. Phys. Medicine and Rehab. Fellow Am. Acad. Phys. Medicine and Rehab.; mem. Fla., So. med. assns., Fla. (past pres.), S.E. socs. phys. medicine and rehab., Am. Heart Assn., Am. Congress Rehab. Medicine, Palm Beach Med. Soc., Handicapped United. Congregationalist. Contbr. several papers in field; reviewer med. books. Home: 1040 SW 1st St Boca Raton FL 33432 Office: 900 NW 13th St Suite 106 Boca Raton FL 33432

HURD, ERIC RAY, physician; b. Columbus, Kans., July 5, 1936; s. Myron Alexander and Isobel (Moore) H.; B.S., U. Tulsa, 1958; M.D., U. Okla., 1962; m. Beverly Jean Button, June 14, 1962; children—Sherryl Lynn, Susan Rae, Brent Eric. Intern, St. John's Hosp., Tulsa, 1962-63, resident, 1963-65; fellow U. Tex. at Dallas, 1965-67, instr. internal medicine, 1967-68, asst. prof., 1968-73, asso. prof. internal medicine Grad. Sch. Faculty in Immunology, 1973—; cons. rheumatology, attending physician Parkland, Vets hosps.; cons. rheumatology, dir. John Peter Smith Hosp. Arthritis Clinic; clin. investigator VA Hosp., 1972-75, also mem. med. research merit rev. bd. immunology. Served to maj. AUS, 1963-74. Recipient clin. scholar award Arthritis Found., 1975-77, postdoctoral fellow, 1970-73. Mem. A.C.P., Am. Assn. Immunologists, Am. Fedn. Clin. Research, Am. (cooperating clinics com. 1968-74), Tex. (sec.-treas. 1976-79, 2d v.p. 1979-80) rheumatism assns., Tex., Dallas County med. socs., Phi Eta Sigma. Democrat. Methodist. Contbr. articles to profl. jours. Office: 5323 Harry Hines Blvd Dallas TX 75235

HURD, HARRY THOMAS, ednl. adminstr.; b. Roanoke, Va., May 26, 1938; s. Harry T. and Beulah B. (Price) H.; B.S. in Bus. Adminstrn., Va. Poly. Inst. and State U., 1968; postgrad. Radford U.; m. Jane Dowdy, Mar. 21, 1958. Asst. dir. contract and grant adminstrn. Va. Poly. Inst. and State U., Blacksburg, 1978—, mgr. contracts and grants, 1977-78; buyer Corning Glass Works, Blacksburg, 1968-69, indsl. engring. specialist, 1969-70, supr. planning Blacksburg plant, 1970-77. Mem. Blacksburg Planning Commn., 1973-75, Blacksburg Vol. Fire Dept., 1958—; pres., 1963—; mem. Gov.'s Hwy. Safety Council, Montgomery County, 1974—, chmn., 1976—. Served with U.S. Army, 1962-63. Mem. Nat. Council Univ. Research Adminstrs., Soc. Research Adminstrs. Methodist. Clubs: Masons, Shriners. Home: 320 Hearthstone Dr Blacksburg VA 24060 Office: 304 Burruss Hall Va Poly Inst Blacksburg VA 24061

HURD, WILLIAM BROMLEY, ret. govt. ofcl., transit cons.; b. Lynn, Mass., Aug. 27, 1915; s. William B. and Elizabeth Ellen (Rogers) H.; A.B., U. N.H., 1937; intern Nat. Inst. Pub. Affairs, 1937-38; postgrad. Am. U., Washington; m. Mariette Rae Bowles, Jan. 17, 1942 (dec. 1978); 1 son, William Bromley. With Interior Dept., Washington, 1938-42, 46-52, Indian Ser., 1938-42, with Bur. Reclamation, 1946-51, with Office Sec. Interior, 1951-52; with Office of Adminstr. HHFA, 1952-62, dep. asst. adminstr. transp., 1962-66; dep. dir. Urban Transp. Adminstrn., HUD, 1966-68; asso. adminstr. Office Program Ops., Urban Mass Transp. Adminstrn., Transp. Dept., 1968-72; ret., 1972; transit cons. City of Richmond (Va.), 1972—, Met. Atlanta Rapid Transit Authority, 1972-79, City of Lynchburg (Va.), 1974-75, 78—, City of Roanoke (Va.), 1974-75; transit cons., Washington, 1976—. Pres., Old Town Civic Assn., 1956-58, Alexandria (Va.) Assn., 1958-60; mem. Commn. on Orgn. Alexandria City Govt., 1954-55; mem. Community Devel. Com., Alexandria, 1957-58, City Planning Commn., 1958-64, No. Va. Regional Planning and Econ. Devel. Commn., 1960-64, Spl. Charter Com., 1967, 75—; chmn. Alexandria Civil War Centennial Com., 1959-69; mem. Alexandria Sch. Bd., 1969-74, chmn., 1972-74; mem. Alexandria Transp. Planning Bd., 1974-75. Served with C.E. AUS, 1942-46. Mem. Alexandria Hist. Soc. (pres. 1977-78).

HURLBERT, RAYMOND DONALD, ednl. television exec.; b. Pitts., Mar. 21, 1902; s. Ernest Sanford and Alice Lillian (Jenkins) H.; A.B., Birmingham So. Coll., 1924, M.A., 1936; m. Rachel Bell, Apr. 1, 1925 (dec. Mar. 10, 1939); m. 2d, Wynelle Una Reeves, Aug. 20, 1941; children—Raymond Donald, Marion Patricia, Ramona Wynelle. High sch. tchr., Birmingham, Ala., 1924-30; elementary sch. prin., Birmingham, 1930-55; gen. mgr. Ala. Ednl. TV Commn., Birmingham, 1953-73; cons. R.P.I. Cons. Services, 1973—. Pres. Birmingham area council Boy Scouts Am., 1948-49. Mem. Nat. Assn. Ednl. TV (pres. 1968), Nat. Assn. Ednl. Broadcasters TV (chmn. bd. 1962-63), Ala. Edn. Assn. (pres. 1948, trustee 1949), Ala. Battleship Commn. (exec. com. 1963-70), Ala. Ednl. TV Commn. (pres. 1953-55), Birmingham Area Crepe Myrtle Assn. (pres. 1960), Newcomen Soc., Kappa Phi Kappa, Alpha Tau Omega, Omicron Delta Kappa. Baptist. Rotarian (pres. club 1958, dist. gov. 1962). Club: The Club. Contbr. articles to profl. jours. Home: 1853 Southwood Rd Birmingham AL 35216

HURLBURT, HARLEY ERNEST, oceanographer; b. Bennington, Vt., Apr. 12, 1943; s. Paul Rhodes and Evelyn Arlene (Lockhart) H.; B.S. in Physics (scholar), Union Coll., Schenectady, 1965; M.S., Fla. State U., 1971, Ph.D. in Meteorology, 1974. NASA trainee Fla. State U., 1970-72; postdoctoral fellow advanced studies program Nat. Center Atmospheric Research, Boulder, Colo., 1974-75; staff scientist JAYCOR, Alexandria, Va., 1975-77; oceanographer Naval Ocean Research and Devel. Activity, Bay St. Louis, Miss., 1977—. Vice pres. Burgundy Citizens Assn., 1976-77. Office Naval Research grantee, 1975-77; Dept. Energy grantee, 1975-78; Tex. A&M U. grantee, 1976. Mem. Am. Meteorol. Soc., Sigma Xi, Sigma Tau, Chi Epsilon Pi. Methodist. Contbr. articles to sci. jours. Home: 274 Hermitage Ct Pearl River LA 70452 Office: Naval Ocean Research and Devel Activity Code 322 Bldg 1100 Nat Space Tech Lab Station MS 39529

HURLBURT, HARVEY ZEH, chem. engr.; b. Kellogg, Idaho, Sept. 2, 1921; s. Harvey Seymour and Vera (Zeh) H.; B.A., U. Tex., 1942, B.S., 1943, M.S., 1947; Sc.D., Mass. Inst. Tech., 1950; m. Gertrude Mildred Lepick, May 7, 1943; children—Geoffrey, Victoria (Mrs. Sidney H. Stevens), Veronica (Mrs. David Mayfield), Susan (Mrs. James R. Bruton, Jr.), Barbara, Claudia (Mrs. Tom Kendall), Tobias, Octavia. Process engr. U.S. Rubber Co., Institute, W.Va., 1943-47; research engr. Consol. Chem. Industries, 1950-55; mgr. Peiser Research Labs. Stauffer Chem. Co., Houston, 1955—. Registered profl. engr., Tex. Fellow Am. Inst. Chem. Engrs., Sigma Xi, Sigma Phi Epsilon, Omega Chi Epsilon. Republican. Catholic. Patentee processes for mfg. heavy inorganic chems. Home: 7814 Santa Elena Dr Houston TX 77061 Office: 8410 Manchester St Houston TX 77012

HURLBUT, FLOYD WAYNE, petroleum exploration co. exec.; b. Jennings, La., Sept. 21, 1939; s. Virgil Floyd and Nettie (Myers) H.; B.S. in Acctg., La. State U., 1970; M.B.A., So. Ill. U., 1974; m. Nancy Bernhardt, Sept. 4, 1965; children—Nicole, Steven Floyd. Region cost and budget analyst Internat. Paper Co., Georgetown, S.C., 1974-75, sr. fin. analyst, N.Y.C., 1975-76, corp. project mgmt. cons., 1976-77; asst. group controller internat. group Ethyl Corp., Baton Rouge, 1977-79; partner Franklin-Hurlbut, Lafayette, La., 1979—; instr. Internat. Paper Co. Bus. Mgmt. Sch. Served with USMC, 1961-67. Decorated Air medal with oak leaf cluster. Mem. Nat. Assn. Accts. (named Most Valuable Mem. Charleston, S.C. chpt. 1972), Jaycees (v.p. Georgetown chpt. 1974). Methodist. Home: PO Box 53811 Lafayette LA 70505 Office: Suite 106 Oil and Gas Bldg 3 1001 Pinhook Rd Lafayette LA 70503

HURLEY, FRANK THOMAS, JR., realtor; b. Washington, Oct. 18, 1924; s. Frank Thomas and Lucille (Trent) H.; A.A., St. Petersburg Jr. Coll., 1948; B.A., U. Fla., 1950. Reporter, St. Petersburg (Fla.) Evening Ind., 1948-53; editor Arcadia (Calif.) Tribune, 1956-57; reporter Los Angeles Herald Express, 1957; v.p. Frank T. Hurley Assos., Inc. Realtors, 1958-64, pres., 1964—; sec., dir. Beau Monde, Inc., 1977-79. Mem. St. Petersburg Beach Bd. Commrs., 1965-69; candidate Fla. Ho. of Reps., 1966; chmn. Pinellas County Traffic Safety Council, 1968-69; pres. Pass-A-Grille Community Assn., 1963, Gulf Beach Bd. Realtors, 1969; mem. St. Petersburg Mus. Fine Arts; mem. governing bd. Palms of Pasadena Hosp., 1979—. Served with USAAF, 1943-46. Mem. Fla. Assn. Realtors (dist. v.p. 1971), Vina del Mar Island Assn., Am. Legion, St. Petersburg Beach C. of C. (pres. 1975-76), Sigma Delta Chi, Sigma Tau Delta. Author: Surf, Sand and Post Card Sunsets, 1977. Home: 2808 Sunset Way Saint Petersburg Beach FL 33706 Office: 2506 Pass-A-Grille Way Saint Petersburg Beach FL 33706

HURLEY, JAMES LAURENCE, lawyer; b. N.Y.C., Nov. 29, 1920; s. James and Luqueer Laurence (Thom) H.; student Cornell U., 1939-40; B.A., U. Va., 1947, LL.B., 1950; m. Patricia Vale Norford, Aug. 6, 1950; 1 son, James Norford. Admitted to Fla. bar, 1959; asso. firm Kirlin, Campbell & Keating, N.Y.C., 1950-59; partner, mng. dir. firm Fowler, White, Burnett, Hurley, Banick & Knight, Miami, Fla., 1959—; dir. Royal Caribbean Cruise Line, Inc., Royal Caribbean Tours, Inc. Hon. consul of Norway. Served with USCG, 1942-46. Fellow Am. Coll. Trial Lawyers; mem. Am. Judicature Soc., Am., Fla. (chmn. admiralty com. 1977-78), Dade County bar assns., Propeller Club Miami, Maritime Law Assn. Clubs: Riviera Country, India House (N.Y.C.), Ocean Reef Country, Bankers. Home: 6275 S W 106th St Miami FL 33156 Office: 25 W Flagler St Miami FL 33130

HURST, LEONA PEARL BASS, housing authority ofcl.; b. Newberry, Fla., Nov. 10, 1933; d. David Irvin and Mary Pearl (Slaughter) Bass; ed. public schs.; m. David William Hurst, July 25, 1951; children—Constance Leona, Glenn Montgomery, David Randall, Barbara Lynne. Tenant acct. Eastman (Ga.) Housing Authority, 1954, exec. dir., 1954—, now exec. dir., acct. in Eastman and McRae, acct. in Abbeville and Rochelle. Sec., Eastman-Dodge County Planning Commn., 1961—; chmn. Eastman-Dodge County Council on Aging, 1969-79; sec.-treas. Nutrition Program, 5 counties, 1978—; leader Anchor Club, 1975—. Mem. Nat. Assn. Female Execs., Ga. Assn. Housing and Redevel. Ofcls., Nat. Assn. Housing and Redevel. Ofcls. Mem. C. of Christ. Club: Eastman Pilot (pres. 1967-68, 74-75, dir. 1978—). Home: 403 College St Eastman GA 31023 Office: 235 Reddock Center Eastman GA 31023

HURST, MARK SLUDER, educator; b. Charlotte, N.C., Dec. 3, 1951; s. Edwin Sluder and Maxine (Beckham) H.; B.S., Appalachian State U., 1974, M.A., 1975; m. Ellen Jackson Greear, Dec. 30, 1972; 1 son, Mark Edwin. Asso. dir. admissions Chowan Coll., 1975-76, co-dir. admissions, 1976-77; tchr. English, Houston County Sch. System, Perry, Ga., 1977—. Mem. Am., N.C. personnel and guidance assns., Am., N.C. coll. personnel assns., Am. Assn. Coll. Registrars and Admissions Offices, Carolinas Assn. Coll. Registrars and Admissions Offices. Episcopalian. Home: 1733 Greenwood Circle Perry GA 31069

HURST, OTIS RAY, hosp. assn. exec.; b. Randalett, Okla., Dec. 7, 1924; s. Edgar S. and Lucy (Moore) H.; B.B.A. with honors, Stephen F. Austin U., Nacogdoches, Tex., 1949; m. Eleanor E. Miles, Dec. 21, 1947; children—Raelynn, Miles Randall. Accounting supr. United Gas Corp., Beaumont, Tex., 1949-50; adminstrv. asst., bus. mgr. Baptist Hosp. of Southeast Tex., Beaumont, 1953-56; exec. dir. Tex. Hosp. Assn., Austin, 1956-69, exec. v.p., 1969-74, pres., 1974—; dir., mem. exec. com. Med. Info., Inc., Dallas, 1968-78; dir. Citizens Nat. Bank, Austin, Tex. Hosp. Assn. Credit Union, Austin, 1970-77; pres. Tex. Hosp. Edn. and Research Found., Austin, 1965—; pres. Tex. Hosp. Assn. Health Services Corp., Austin, 1973—; guest lectr. Baylor-Brooke Army Program in Health Care Adminstrn., Fort Sam Houston, Tex., 1960-75; adj. prof. Grad. Program in Health Care Adminstrn., Trinity U., San Antonio, Tex., 1965—. Mem. Tex. Com. on Aging, 1958-61; chmn. Tex. State Hosp. Adv. Council, 1959—; mem. adv. council or vocat. rehab. Tex. Edn. Agy., 1968-69; co-chmn. Financial Mgmt. Panel, Hosp. Productivity Study, Nat. Commn. on Productivity, 1973. Served with USNR, 1942-46, 50-53; PTO. Named health assn. Exec. of the Year, Hosp. Mgmt. Mag., 1970. Fellow Am. Acad. Med. Adminstrs. (hon.); mem. Am. Hosp. Assn., Am. (dir. 1974-77, v.p. 1977-78; Key Outstanding State Assn. Exec. award 1974, Mgmt. Achievement Grand award 1977, 1979), Tex. (dir. 1971-73, sec.-treas. 1977-78, v.p. 1978-79, pres. elect 1979-80) socs. assn. execs. Found. of Am. Soc. Assn. Execs. (dir. 1972-77), State Hosp. Assn. Execs. Forum (1st pres. 1965), Tex. Pub. Health Assn., Found. of Tex. Soc. Assn. Execs. (initial trustee 1975), Baylor-Brooke Army Program in Health Care Adminstrn. Alumni Assn. (hon.), C. of C. of U.S. (assn. com. of 100 1972-77). Baptist. Club: Lambs (Austin). Editor Tex. Hosps. Jour., 1956—. Home: 3607 Arrowhead St Austin TX 78731 Office: PO Box 15587 Austin TX 78761 also 6225 US Hwy 290 E Austin TX 78723

HURST, THOMAS CHARLES, III, transp. co. exec.; b. Norfolk, Va., June 17, 1920; s. Thomas Charles and Eliza (Toler) H.; B.E.E., U.S. Naval Acad., 1942; summer student Oxford U., 1964; Am. U., 1968-69; m. Nancy Gifford Owen, Dec. 25, 1947; children—Terry Lee Hurst Halston, Leigh Gifford. Commd. ensign U.S. Navy, 1942, advanced through grades to capt., 1962, submarine comdr., 1952-55, internat. relations, 1962-65, adviser U.S. State Dept. in Nuclear Warfare, 1966-69; ret., 1970; pres., dir. Norfolk Balt. & Carolina Lines, Norfolk, Va., 1970—; cons. engr. Active Boy Scouts Am.; trustee Averett Coll., Danville, Va., 1977—. Mem. Traffic Club. Club: Propeller. Home: 2704 Shepherds Quarter Virginia Beach VA 23452 Office: 937 Water St Norfolk VA 23510

HURT, ALLIE TEAGUE, real estate broker; b. Celina, Tex., 1923; s. Lucious T. and Mary Lee (Whitley) Teague; student El Centro Jr. Coll., 1967-68; B.S., Bishop Coll., 1973; postgrad. N. Tex. State U., 1973-74. Sec., Excelsior Life Ins., Dallas, 1953-56; ins. agt. Universal Life Ins., Dallas, 1957-58; mgr. Pruitt Ins. Agy., Dallas, 1960-65; soc. editor Dallas Express Newspaper, 1973-75; substitute tchr. Dallas Ind. Sch. Dist., 1967-71; real estate sales agt., 1967-72, 75—; owner, mgr., broker Allie T. Hurt Real Estate Co., 1978-79; pianist various chs., 1959-69; chatelaine, instr. Eta Phi Beta, Dallas, 1978-79. Recipient Cert. of Recognition award Eta Phi Beta, 1978; Cert. of Recognition, Iota Phi Lambda, 1979. Mem. Eta Phi Beta, NAACP. Baptist. Clubs: Rosicrucian Order, P.U.S.H. Home: 5324 Mystic Trail Dallas TX 75241

HURT, FRANK BENJAMIN, educator; b. Ferrum, Va., Oct. 22, 1899; s. John Kempleton and Lelia (Angle) H.; A.B., Washington and Lee U., 1923; M.A., U. Va., 1925; A.M., Princeton U., 1926; postgrad. Johns Hopkins, 1929-30, Harvard, summers 1938-40; m. Mary Ann Wescott, June 3, 1942. Teaching fellow U. N.C., 1926-27; instr. Ferrum Coll., 1927-29; asso. prof. polit. sci. Western Md. Coll., 1930-65, prof. emeritus, 1965—, head div. polit. sci., 1949; head div. social sci. Ferrum Jr. Coll., 1965—, prof. emeritus, 1970—; lectr. sch. spl. and continuation studies U. Md., 1950-65; instr. summers Hun Sch., Princeton, 1927-32. Dir. First Nat. Bank, Ferrum, v.p., 1977—. Trustee, Longwood Coll. Found., 1976—. Mem. Am. Polit. Sci. Assn., Am. Hist. Assn., Am. Acad. Polit. and Social Sci., Nat. Collegiate Fgn. Lang. Soc., Franklin County Hist. Soc. (pres. 1969-70), AAUP, Pi Gamma Mu, Phi Theta Kappa. Democrat. Methodist. Lion (pres. Ferrum 1968). Author History of Ferrum College, 1975. Address: Ferrum Coll Ferrum VA 24088

HUSE, MARTHA RUTH, coll. librarian; b. Weimar, Tex., Dec. 15, 1925; d. Chester Allen and Viola Rosina (Voitle) Grobe; A.A., Weatherford Jr. Coll., 1966; B.A., Tex. Woman's U., 1967, M.L.S., 1969; m. Louis D. Huse, June 2, 1944; 1 dau., Connie Sue. Sec., M.G. Feeds, Weimar, 1942-45; clerical positions Weatherford (Tex.) Jr. Coll. Library, 1962-66, asst. librarian, 1967-69, head librarian, 1969—. Mem. Bicentennial Commn. Weatherford. Mem. Bus. and Profl. Women's Club (rec. sec. 1970-72, treas. 1972-74, 2d v.p. 1974-75, pres. 1975-76), Tex. Library Assn., Tex. Jr. Coll. Tchrs. Assn., Delta Kappa Gamma. Lutheran. Home: Rural Route 6 Box 186 Weatherford TX 76086

HUSHEN, STANLEY CECIL, photog. co. exec.; b. Everett, Mass., Oct. 28, 1926; s. Stanley Cecil and Hilda May (Thomson) H.; student Boston Mus. Sch. Fine Arts, 1948-52; m. Shirley Curtis, May 31, 1953; Staff artist Livestock Weekly mag., 1952-54; founder, pres., owner Stan's Printing Service Inc., Bartlett, Tenn., 1970—; art dir. Armistead Advt. Agency, Memphis, 1959-61; pub.'s rep. R.L. White Co. Inc., Bartlett, 1966—; pub. Bartlett Express Newspaper, 1978—; pres., owner Prestige Printing; owner, mgr. office, mfg. bldg. Bartlett, 1976—; cons. in field. Served with U.S. Army, 1944-46; PTO. Mem. Memphis Bd. Realtors (affiliate, ofcl. photographer), Home Builders Assn. Memphis (asso.), Memphis Club Printing House Craftsmen (dir. 1974—), Navy League U.S. Mem. Disciples of Christ. Home: 6149 Ivanhoe St Bartlett TN 38134 Office: 2874 Shelby St Bartlett TN 38134

HUSKETH, ALMA ORMOND (MRS. EDWARD THOMAS HUSKETH, JR.), librarian; b. Dover, N.C., Aug. 17, 1918; d. William Henry and Ella Carrie (White) Ormond; B.A. in English, Woman's Coll. U. N.C., 1939; M.S. in L.S., U. N.C. at Chapel Hill, 1967; m. Edward Thomas Husketh, Jr., June 12, 1943; children—Edward Thomas III, William Ormond, Craig Moss. Tchr., Wilton (N.C.) High Sch., 1939-44, 46-51, 57-61; tchr. Lenoir County (N.C.) Schs., 1944-46; librarian South Granville High Sch., Creedmoor, N.C., 1962—. Cons. rev. panel N.C. Emergency Sch. Assistance Program, 1971, Emergency Sch. Aid Act, 1973, 74, 75, 76, 77, 78. Mem. scholarship com. U. N.C. at Greensboro, 1969-73; Granville county dir. N.C.P.T.A., 1970-72. Bd. dirs. Richard H. Thornton Pub. Library, Oxford, N.C. Mem. N.C. Edn. Assn. (sec. East Central dist. 1965, pres. dir. 1978-80), N.C. Classroom Tchrs. Assn. (pres. Granville County unit 1951-52, 77-78), N.C. High Sch. Library Assn. (dir. East Central dist. 1969—), Nat. Grange, Alpha Delta Kappa (pres. Rho chpt. 1972-74, v.p. Dist. IV 1976-78). Methodist (Sunday sch. tchr. 1940—; dir. youth activities 1962-73; active Women's Soc. Christian Service). Home: Box 198 Brassfield Rd

Creedmoor NC 27522 Office: PO Box 395 South Granville High School Creedmoor NC 27522

HUSKETH, EDWARD THOMAS, JR., ins. agt., farmer; b. Creedmoor, N.C., Sept. 28, 1914; s. Edward Thomas and Lillian Henderson (Moss) H.; student Elon Coll., 1931-33; m. Alma Ormond, June 12, 1943; children—Edward Thomas III, William Ormond, Craig Moss. Ins. agt. Farmer's Mut., Oxford, N.C., 1965—; farmer, Granville County, 1946—. Tchr. Sunday sch., chmn. adminstrv. bd. Banks United Meth. Ch., 1975-80, chmn. bd. trustees, 1972-80; com. chmn. Agrl. Stabilization and Conservation Service, 1960-80. Served with USAAF, 1942-46. Mem. Farm Bur. Democrat. Club: South Granville Country. Address: Box 198 Brassfield Rd Greedmoor NC 27522

HUSKINS, JOSEPH PATTERSON, editor, pub., former state legislator N.C.; b. Burnsville, N.C., June 23, 1908; s. Joseph Erwin and Mary Etta (Peterson) H.; A.B. in Journalism, U. of N.C., 1930; m. Mildred Amburn, Sept. 29, 1934; 1 dau., Amburn Huskins Power. Pres., gen. mgr. Statesville (N.C.) Daily Record, 1946-76; v.p., Chowan Hearal, Edenton, N.C., 1964-79; pres. Associated Dailies of N.C., 1965-66; mem. N.C. Ho. of Reps., 1971—. Bd. dirs. Statesville Zoning Bd., 1960-62; bd. dirs. N.C. Bd. of Higher Edn., 1966-71; bd. govs. U. of N.C., 1971-72; chmn. Mitchell Coll. Bd. of Trustees, 1968-73. Served to lt. USN, 1943-46. Mem. N.C. Assn. of Afternoon Dailies (pres. 1948-49), Statesville C. of C. (pres. 1965-66). Democrat. Methodist. Clubs: Statesville Country, Statesville City, Long Hope Fishing, Mason, Elks. Home: Our Dell Statesville NC 28677 Office: PO Box 1071 Statesville NC 28677

HUSTED, JOHN EDWIN, geologist; b. Lucasville, Ohio, Oct. 12, 1915; s. Edward Winthrop and Mary (Cary) H.; B.S., Hampden-Sydney Coll., 1939; student Va. Poly. Inst., summers 1938-40; M.A., U. Va., 1942; Ph.D., Fla. State U., 1970; m. Kathryn Fay Stewart, June 18, 1942; children—Stewart Winthrop, Mary Husted Hewett. Teacher sci. Crewe (Va.) High Sch., 1938-40; chemist, geologist U.S. Geol. Survey, Washington, 1942-45; plant chemist Consol. Feldspar Corp., Erwin, Tenn., 1945-46; instr. geology and chemistry Washington and Lee U., 1946-48; geologist Humble Oil & Refining Co., Midland, Tex., 1948-49; chmn. geology dept. Trinity U., 1949-51; resident geologist Va. Iron, Coal & Coke Co., Roanoke, 1951-55; prin. geologist Battelle Meml. Inst., 1955-57; research scientist Ga. Inst. Tech., 1958-63, head mineral engring. group, 1960-66, asso. prof. geology, 1963-67, head mineral engring. br., 1966-72, research prof. geology, 1967-71, prof. geology, 1971-74, prof. mineral engring. Sch. Chem. Engring., 1974—, chmn. multidisciplinary com. for mineral engring., 1977—, acting dir. Ga. Mining and Mineral Resource Inst. Coll. Engring., 1978-80, dir., 1980—; mem. Ad Hoc List of Visitors, Accreditation, Engring. Council for Profl. Devel., 1968—; dep. dir., designate Minerals Civil Def. Exec. Res. U.S. Dept. Interior, Emergency Minerals Adminstrn., Southeastern U.S., 1969-72, dir. designate Miscellaneous Non-Metals div., 1972—. NSF Sci. Faculty fellow, 1966-67. Fellow Geol. Soc. Am.; mem. Am. Assn. Petroleum Geologists, Am. Geophys. Union, Am. Inst. Mining, Metall. and Petroleum Engrs. (nat. council dels. 1966-67), Soc. Mining Engrs. (edn. com. 1965-68, 1970-77, accreditation com. bd. edn. 1977-79, 80—), Ga. Geol. Soc. (council 1961-62), Sigma Xi. Mem. editorial adv. bd., author indsl. minerals sect. Mining Engineering Handbook, 1973; mem. editorial bd. 4th edn. Industrial Minerals and Rocks. Home: 2255 Brianwood Ct Decatur GA 30033 Office: Sch Chem Engring Ga Inst Tech Atlanta GA 30332

HUSZTI, ALLEN WARREN, musician, educator; b. Lorain, O., Nov. 4, 1938; s. Joseph Menhert and Rose Priscilla (Farkas) H.; B.Mus., Oberlin Coll., 1961; M.Mus., New Eng. Conservatory Music, 1963; postgrad. Boston U., 1963-65; m. Sara Keep, Aug. 23, 1964; children—Douglas Allen, Hannah Elizabeth. Dir. music Ch. of the Covenant, Boston, 1965-72; instr. music Mount Ida Jr. Coll., Newton Centre, Mass., 1967-72; lectr. music, acting chmn. dept. Emerson Coll., Boston, 1971-72; asso. prof. music Sweet Briar Coll. (Va.), 1972—, conductor Concert Choir, 1975—. Organist/choir dir. Grace Meml. Episcopal Ch., Lynchburg, Va., 1973—, mem. vestry, 1976-78. New Eng. Conservatory fellow, 1962-63; Cabell grantee Sweet Briar Coll., 1973-75, 77-78; Smith-Richardson humanities grantee, 1976. Mem. Am. Choral Dirs. Assn., Nat. Assn. Tchrs. Singing, Coll. Music Soc. Protestant Episcopal. Home: House 5 Faculty Row Sweet Briar VA 24595 Office: Babcock Hall Rm 126 Sweet Briar Coll Sweet Briar VA 24595

HUTCHENS, EUGENE GARLINGTON, coll. adminstr.; b. Birmingham, Ala., Nov. 26, 1929; s. Wallace Luther and Reydonia (Corry) H.; B.A., Samford U., 1952; Th.M., New Orleans Baptist Theol. Sem., 1970; M.S. in Econs., U. Mo.-Columbia, 1972; m. Betty Frances Goode, Aug. 26, 1951; children—Dale Eugene, Wayne Goode, Dennis Wade. Ordained to ministry, Baptist Ch., 1952; minister N. Brewton Bapt. Ch., Brewton, Ala., 1952-56, 1st Bapt. Ch., Ashland, Ala., 1956-63, Highlands Bapt. Ch., Huntsville, Ala., 1963-67; tchr. public schs., Huntsville, 1967-71; instr. econs. N.W. Ala. State Jr. Coll., 1972-77, dir. Tenn. Valley Center of N.W. Ala. State Jr. Coll., Tuscumbia, 1977—; mem. Ala. Bapt. State Exec. Bd., 1961-63; v.p. Ala. Bapt. State Pastors Conf., 1966. NSF grantee, 1971-72. Mem. Ala. Edn. Assn., NEA, Ala. Council Sch. Adminstrn. and Supervision, Nat. Council Geog. Edn. Club: Kiwanis. Home: 402 N Dickson Tuscumbia AL 35674 Office: 1105 Hwy 72 W Tuscumbia AL 35674

HUTCHENS, (SIDNEY) GAIL RAKES, analytical lab. exec.; b. Bentonville, Ark., Aug. 22, 1938; d. Sidney Baxter and Mary Dena Maurine (Harral) Rakes; B.S., Ark. State Tchrs. Coll., 1958; m. Charles V. Hutchens, Mar. 4, 1967; children—Kimberly Gail, David Charles. With Galbraith Labs., Knoxville, Tenn., 1958—, v.p., 1960-67, exec. v.p., 1967—, also dir.; cons. U. Tenn. Mem. Am. Chem. Soc. (exec. com. small chem. bus. sect. 1979-80), Internat. Microchem. Soc., Bus. Women's Club, Alpha Chi. Baptist. Clubs: Ski, Garden (past pres.). Home: 9640 Briarwood Blvd Knoxville TN 37919 Office: 2323 Sycamore Dr Knoxville TN 37921

HUTCHERSON, DONNA DEAN CLARK, musician; b. Dallas, July 10, 1937; d. Lamar Schaffer and Lenora Fay (Newbern) Clark; student So. Methodist U., 1955-56; B.Mus. Edn., Sam Houston State U., 1957; Mus.M., Stephen F. Austin U., 1974; m. George Henry Hutcherson, Jan. 31, 1959; children—Lamar, Michael, Mark, Holly (dec. 1967), Shela. Tchr. elementary music, Carthage, Tex., 1958-59; tchr. elementary music, high sch. choir dir., Hallsville, Tex., 1969-77, intermediate music, 1977—; tympanist Marshall Symphony; pianist, organist Meth. and Presbyterian chs. Bd. dirs., treas. Hallsville Baseball Assn., 1972—; del. Methodist Conf., 1970-79; sec. Longview Dist. Meth. Ch. Council Ministries, 1971-77; mem. dist. nominating com., Meth. Conf. Commn. on Status and Role of Women, 1977-80. Tex. Tchrs. Assn. Region VII grantee, 1975-76, 78-80. Mem. Tex., Hallsville tchrs. assns., Tex. Music Educators Assn., Choristers Guild, Gamma Phi Beta, Tau Beta Sigma. Address: Route 2 Box 107C Hallsville TX 75650

HUTCHESON, EDWARD CHAPPELL, ret. lawyer; b. Houston, Mar. 11, 1920; s. William Palmer and Eleanor Lee (Thomson) H.; A.B., Princeton, 1942; LL.B., S. Tex. Coll. of Law, 1949; m. Beatrice Hale Chew, July 22, 1944; children—Edward Chappell, Beatrice (Mrs. Robert J. Seymour), Joseph C. II. Admitted to Tex. bar, 1949; partner Hutcheson, Taliaferro & Hutcheson, Houston, 1949-69; individual practice law, Houston, 1969-79. Pres., Julia C. Hester House, Houston, 1958-60; chmn. Houston chpt. World Neighbors, Inc., 1963; pres. Tex. Bill of Rights Found., 1964-65. Chmn. bd. dirs. Amigos de las Americas, 1973; trustee S. Tex. Coll. of Law, Houston; bd. dirs. Neighborhood Centers - Day Care Assn., Houston. Served to lt. USNR, 1942-45. Mem. State Bar Tex., Am., Houston bar assns., Am. Judicature Soc., Houston Philos. Soc., Phi Delta Phi. Episcopalian. Clubs: Princeton (N.Y.C.); Conanicut Yacht (Jamestown, R.I.). Author: The Freedom Tree, 1970; The Sound of Wings, 1974. Home: 2521 Stanmore Dr Houston TX 77019

HUTCHESON, GUY CARLTON, cons. radio engr.; b. Springtown, Tex., Mar. 14, 1911; s. James D. and Mattie Elizabeth (McCracken) H.; student N. Tex. State U., 1928-29; B.S. in Elec. Engring., Tex. A. and M. U., 1933; m. Mittie Ruth Beal, July 14, 1938; children—Elizabeth Beal Hutcheson Carroll, Mary Ann Hutcheson Hightower. Asst. recorder seismic crew Texaco, Houston, 1933; radio engr.-operator 2d Byrd Antarctic expdn. to Little America, 1933-35; radio engr., gen. engring. dept. CBS, N.Y.C., 1935-41, chief Latin Am. engr., 1941-42, engr. in charge internat. broadcasting, 1942-44, acting engr. in charge radio frequency div., 1944-45; pvt. practice radio engr. cons., Arlington, Tex., 1945—. Trustee Arlington Ind. Sch. Dist., 1950-69; mem. Arlington Recreation Bd., 1954-56. Decorated Spl. Congl. medal for duty with Byrd expdn. Registered profl. engr., Tex. Mem. IEEE (sr.), SAR, Tau Beta Pi, Eta Kappa Nu. Methodist. Clubs: Rotary, Masons, K.T. Home: 1100 W Abram St Arlington TX 76013 Office: PO Box 808 Arlington TX 76010

HUTCHESON, JAMES STERLING, physician; b. Richmond, Va., Apr. 17, 1936; s. James Preston and Daisy Clarke (Lorentz) H.; student Roanoke Coll., 1953-55; B.A., U. Va., 1957; M.D., Johns Hopkins U., 1961; m. Nancy Montgomery Sanders, May 20, 1961; children—Anne Farrar, Betsy Dulaney. Intern, U. Va. Hosp., Charlottesville, 1961-62, fellow in allergy, 1964-65; resident in internal medicine Med. Coll. Va., Richmond, 1962-64, asst. prof. medicine, chief adult allergy, 1967-68; staff Nalle Clinic, Charlotte, N.C., 1968—; practice medicine specializing in allergy Charlotte, 1968—. Served to capt. M.C., USAF, 1965-67. Diplomate Am. Bd. Allergy and Immunology. Fellow Am. Assn. Clin. Immunology and Allergy, Am. Acad. Allergy, Am. Assn. Certified Allergists; mem. Southeastern Allergy Assn., AMA, N.C. Med. Soc., Am. Soc. Internal Medicine, N.C. Soc. Allergy and Clin. Immunology. Lutheran. Club: Lake Norman Yacht. Home: 4200 Arbor Way Charlotte NC 28211 Office: 1350 S Kings Dr Charlotte NC 28207

HUTCHINGS, BRENDA TOWLES, life ins. rep.; b. Pasadena, Tex., May 3, 1940; d. Sam B. and Julia E. (Pitts) Towles: B.A. in Religion and English, Tex. Christian U., 1962, M.R.E., 1969; 1 dau., Judith Renee. Dir. Christian edn. Univ. Ch., Austin, Tex., 1962-64; asst. student activities dir. Tex. Christian U., Ft. Worth, 1964-65; social worker State of Mich., Detroit, 1966-67; asst. to dir. Harper Hosp. Sch. Nursing, Detroit, 1971-75; exec. dir. Houston council Camp Fire Girls, 1975-78; spl. rep. Jefferson Standard Life Ins. Co., Houston, 1978—. Mem. Nat. Assn. Life Underwriters, Tex. Assn. Life Underwriters, Houston Assn. Life Underwriters, Coastal Plains Area Christian Chs., Nat. Assn. Social Workers, Tex. Christian U. Alumni Assn. (Houston Area steering com.). Mem. Disciples of Christ Ch. Home: 2404 Muscadine Ln Pasadena TX 77502 Office: 8323 SW Freeway Suite 700 Houston TX 77074

HUTCHINS, JEROME ROBERT, homebuilding co. exec.; b. Tulsa, May 18, 1952; s. Jerome C. and Rose L. (Istriano) H.; B.B.A., U. Tex., 1975; m. Dale L. Wheeler, Oct. 2, 1976; children—Brent, Robert. Acct., Lennox Industries, Ft. Worth, Tex., 1973-75; div. pres. Gen. Homes, Houston, 1975-78; v.p. Gemcraft Homes, Houston, 1978—. Mem. Greater Houston Builders Assn., Nat. Assn. Home Builders, Tex. Assn. Builders, Phi Gamma Delta. Republican. Methodist. Home: 6714 Casa Del Monte Houston TX 77083 Office: 1304 Langham Creek Dr Suite 170 Houston TX 77084

HUTCHINS, MAX VERNON, educator; b. Asheville, N.C., Apr. 13, 1949; s. Willard V. H.; B.S., Appalachian State U., 1971, M.A., 1973; cert. advanced grad. studies Va. Poly. Inst. and State U., 1978. Mem. exec. mgmt. staff Garrett & Garrett, Comml. Developers, Greenville, S.C., 1973-77; instr., chmn. dept. office edn. Asheville Buncombe Tech. Coll., Asheville, 1973—; cons. small bus. mgmt. Mem. Am. Vocat. Assn., N.C. Vocat. Assn., Nat. Bus. Edn. Assn., N.C. Bus. Edn. Assn., N.C. Assn. Dept. Heads, Delta Pi Epsilon. Home: 709 Holly Ave Black Mountain NC 28711 Office: 340 Victoria Rd Asheville NC 28801

HUTCHINS, WAYNE FREDERICK, coll. adminstr.; b. Trenton, N.H., Sept. 25, 1954; s. Harry Stuart and Anne (Zenich) H.; B.A. (basketball scholarship 1975-77), DePauw U., Greencastle, Ind., 1977; M.A. in Student Personnel and Counseling (scholar), Bowling Green (Ohio) State U., 1978; m. Betty Ann Clifton, Nov. 18, 1978. Resident hall dir., admissions counselor, spl. programs asst. Ashland (Ohio) Coll., also prison counselor, 1976-77; resident hall counselor, coordinator jud. affairs U. Tampa (Fla.), 1978—, dir. univ. basketball club, 1979. Mem. Am. Personnel and Guidance Assn., Am. Coll. Personnel Assn., Nat. Assn. Student Personnel Adminstrs., Ohio Coll. Personnel Assn. Republican. Methodist. Home: Box 70F Univ Tampa Tampa FL 33606 Office: 401 W Kennedy St Tampa FL 33606

HUTCHINSON, J. EDWARD, congressman; b. Fennville, Mich., Oct. 13, 1914; s. Marc C. and Wilna (Leland) H.; A.B., U. Mich., 1936, J.D., 1938; m. Janice Eleanor Caton, Sept. 19, 1959. Admitted to Mich. bar, 1938; mem. Mich. Ho. of Reps., 1946-50, Mich. Senate, 1951-60; mem. 88th to 94th congresses from 4th Mich. Dist.; ranking Republican mem. Judiciary Com., 1965-77; mem. Standards of Ofcl. Conduct Com., 1969-77. Del., v.p. Mich. Constl. Conv., 1961-62. Served with AUS, 1941-46. Republican. Home: 2905 Gulf Shore Blvd N Naples FL 33940 Office: House Office Bldg Washington DC 20515

HUTCHINSON, LEONARD HUGH, educator; b. Richwood, W.Va., July 5, 1917; s. Leonard Anthony and Elverta (Groves) H.; B.S.M.E., Purdue U., 1939; Cert. Meteorology, U. Chgo., 1943; M.Ed., Ga. State U., 1971; J.D., Woodrow Wilson Coll. Law, 1978; m. Sophia Farbach, Mar. 14, 1942; 1 dau., Tevis. Commd. 2d lt., U.S. Air Force, 1941, advanced through grades to lt. col., 1968, staff meteorologist, 1943-68, comdr. 21st Weather Squadron, Torrejon Air Base, Spain, 1956-59, comdr. 32d Weather Squadron, Dobbins AFB, Ga., 1959-61, dir. Joint Typhoon Warning Center, Guam, 1961-63, staff weather officer USAF Command Post & Air Force One, 1963-65, staff weather officer Joint Task Force Eight, AEC, 1965-68, ret., 1968; tchr. sci. and math. College Park High Sch., Atlanta, 1968-70; asst. prof., asst. dean Coll. Urban Life, Ga. State U., 1970—. Mem. Am. Meteorol. Soc., Am. Geophys. Union, Am. Legion, Delta Tau Delta. Patentee control of tropical cyclone formation. Home: 7312 Cardigan Circle NW Atlanta GA 30328 Office: Coll Urban Life Ga State U University Plaza Atlanta GA 30303

HUTCHINSON, RICHARD CHARLES, maintenance and mgmt. cons.; b. Franklin, Mass., Dec. 9, 1916; s. Charles Bassett and Helen Adeline (MacCarthy) H.; B.S. in Bus. Engring. and Adminstrn., Mass. Inst. Tech., 1937; M.Engring. Adminstrn., U. South Fla., 1968; m. Mary Ellen Johnston, Oct. 19, 1940; 1 dau., Judith (Mrs. Joseph W. Hodges III). Various positions in diversified industries, 1937-53; chief indsl. engr. Celanese Corp., Narrows, Va., 1953-56; v.p., asst. gen. mgr. Hapman Dutton Co., Kalamazoo, 1956-58; sr. indsl. engr. Internat. Minerals & Chem. Corp., Bartow, Fla., 1958-70; mgr. indsl. engring. Systems Devel., Inc., Bartow, 1970-74; owner Richard C. Hutchinson, maintenance and mgmt. cons., 1974—; dir. Sayre (Pa.) Printing Co., 1951-77. Registered profl. engr., Fla. Named Outstanding Indsl. Engr. Southeastern U.S., Am. Inst. Indsl. Engrs., 1963-64. Mem. Nat. Soc. Profl. Engrs., Am. Inst. Indsl. Engrs. (chpt. pres. 1961-62, nat. dir. community services 1963-65, regional v.p. 1974-76), Fla. Engring. Soc. Mason (Shriner). Home: 716 Shady Ln Lakeland FL 33803 Office: PO Box 5019 Lakeland FL 33803

HUTCHINSON, WILLIAM SEELY, JR., chem. engr., former army officer; b. Washington, Oct. 30, 1914; s. William Seely and Susan Eleanora (Buckler) H.; B.S. in Chem. Engring., Lehigh U., 1936; S.M., Mass. Inst. Tech., 1949; student Nat. War Coll., 1960-61; m. Sara Elizabeth Stauffer, Nov. 24, 1937; children—William Seely III, Ann Darby. Salesman, Gen. Chem. Co., N.Y.C., 1936-39; product sales mgr. Mallinckrodt Chem. Works, St. Louis, 1939-41; commd. 1st lt. U.S. Army, 1941, advanced through grades to col., 1952; comdr. 83d Chem. Mortar Bn., North Africa, Sicily, Italy, 1943-44; chief declassification and publ. Manhattan Engr. Dist., 1945-47; armorer George Shot, 1st man-made thermonuclear explosion Los Alamos Sci. Lab., Eniwetok, 1951; chief staff 2d Inf. Div., Korea, 1954; co. comdr. 503d Airborne Inf. Regiment, Ky. and Munich, W. Ger., 1955-56; chief weapons effects test div. Def. Atomic Support Agy., 1957-60; dep. asst. chief staff orgn. and tng. Allied Forces So. Europe, NATO, 1961-63; chief staff and Army dep. comdg. officer Joint Task Force Eight (for nuclear testing), Washington, 1964-66; ret., 1966; chem. engr. Cornell Lab., Thailand, 1966-69, Buffalo, 1970-71; dep. dir. pub. works City of Jacksonville, Fla., 1971-75; program engr. Flood & Assos., Inc., Jacksonville, 1975—; ret., 1975; pvt. engring. practice, 1975—. Mem. Fla. Solid Waste Mgmt. Adv. Council, 1974-75. Republican candidate U.S. Congress 15th Dist. Pa., 1966. Decorated Silver Star, Legion Merit with oak leaf cluster, Purple Heart (U.S.); Italian Mil. Valor Cross. Registered profl. engr., D.C., Pa. Mem. Nat. Assn. Counties (solid waste task force, 1972-73), Am. Chem. Soc., SAR, English Speaking Union, Psi Upsilon. Republican. Episcopalian. Clubs: Royal Bangkok Sports; Ponte Vedra (Fla.); Army Navy Country (Arlington, Va.); Royal Varuna Yacht (Thailand); Fla. Yacht. Home: Jacksonville FL Office: 4635 Ortega Blvd Jacksonville FL 32210

HUTCHISON, WILLIAM FORREST, parasitologist; b. Lakeland, Fla., Oct. 7, 1925; s. Chester Boyer and Verna Louise (Warren) H.: B.A., Emory U., 1949, M.S., 1952; Ph.D., Tulane U., 1958; m. Nellie Niles Booth, June 5, 1951; children—Florence Niles, David Forrest, Martha Ellen, Rebecca Warren, Robert Chester. Instr. parasitology Tulane U. Sch. Medicine, New Orleans, 1954-55: asst. prof. preventive medicine and clin. lab. sci. U. Miss. Sch. Medicine, Jackson, 1955-59, asso. prof., 1959-71., prof., 1971—; cons. Jackson VA Hosp., 1955—; parasitologist U. Hosp., Jackson, 1955-72. Served with AUS. 1943-46. La. State U. Sch. Medicine fellow in tropical medicine, 1959. Mem. AAAS, Am. Soc. Parasitologists, Am. Soc. Tropical Medicine and Hygiene, Internat. Filariasis Assn., S.E. Assn. Parasitologists, Miss. Acad. Sci. (pres. 1972-73), Sigma Xi, Phi Sigma, Kappa Alpha. Club: Yacht (commordore 1973) (Jackson). Home: 1910 Bellewood Rd Jackson MS 39211

HUTMAN, BURTON SIMSON, psychiatrist, educator; b. N.Y.C., Feb. 6, 1932; s. Herman W. and Regina (Cohen) H.; B.A. with honors in Psychology, Johns Hopkins U., 1954; M.D., U. Pitts., 1960; certificate U. Pitts. Western Psychiat. Inst., 1964; m. Jacqueline C. Kalchman, Mar. 5, 1961; children—Wayne, Cherie, Bernard, Michael. Intern, Jewish Hosp., Cin., 1960-61; resident U. Pitts. Western Psychiat. Inst., 1961-64; sr. attending psychiatrist Washington Hosp. Center, 1966-70; vice chmn. psychiatry Cafritz Hosp., Washington, 1967-70; pvt. practice psychiatry, Washington, 1966-70; asst. prof. psychiatry U. Miami (Fla.), 1970-78, clin. asst. prof., 1978—; dir. psychiatry Crisis Intervention Emergency Service, Miami, 1970-76, chief pvt. psychiatry inpatient service, 1976—; mem. staff Jackson Meml. Hosp., Miami, Mt. Sinai Med. Center, Dodge Meml. Hosp., Cedars Med. Center; pvt. practice psychiatry, cons. community mental health and geriatric psychiatry. Active Cub Scouts Am., 1971-73; bd. govs. Hebrew Acad. Greater Miami, 1971—; mem. doctors adv. bd. Shaare Zedek Hosp., Jerusalem, Israel, 1973—. Served to lt. comdr. USNR, 1964-66. Mem. Am., South Fla. psychiat. assns., Fla., Dade County med. assns., Am., Fla. colls. emergency physicians, Assn. Orthodox Jewish Scientists (nat. bd. govs. 1974-77), Phi Delta Epsilon, Phi Sigma Delta. Office: PO Box 402085 Miami Beach FL 33140

HUTTENSTINE, MARIAN LOUISE, educator; b. Bloomsburg, Pa., Jan. 26, 1940; d. Ralph Benjamin and Marian Louise (Engler) H.; B.S., Bloomsburg State Coll., 1961, M.Ed., 1966; postgrad. (NDEA fellow, Newspaper Fund fellow), Rutgers U., 1962-63; Ph.D., U. N.C., 1978. High sch. English, journalism tchr., dept. chmn., 1961-66; asst. prof. Lock Haven (Pa.) State Coll., 1966-73, asso. prof. English, 1973-74; teaching asst., lectr. Sch. Journalism, U. N.C., Chapel Hill, 1974-76; cons., dir. Diener & Assos., Research Triangle Park, N.C., 1975-77; asst. prof. journalism Sch. Communication, U. Ala., Tuscaloosa, 1977—; cons. various publs., Ala., 1977—. Active Girl Scouts U.S.A., 1959—; adult leader, vol. worker Luth. Ch., 1962—. Mem. Assn. Edn. in Journalism, Soc. Profl. Journalists, Internat. Communication Assn., Am. Advt. Fedn., Am. Acad. Advt., AAUW, Kappa Tau Alpha, Sigma Delta Chi. Clubs: Tuscaloosa Advt., Ala. SPJ-SDX. Contbr. papers to profl. lit. Home: Apt 1224 4527 18th Ave E Tuscaloosa AL 35405 Office: Box 1482 Journalism Dept U Ala University AL 35486

HUTTO, EARL, Congressman; b. Midland City, Ala., May 12, 1926; s. Lemmie and Ellie (Mathis) H.; B.S., Troy State U., 1949; m. Nancy Myers, July 8, 1967; children—Lori, Amy. Tchr. Cottonwood (Ala.) High Sch., 1949-51; sports and program dir. Sta. WDIG, Dothan, Ala., 1951-54; sports dir. Sta. WEAR-TV, Pensacola, Fla., 1954-60; pres. Sta. WPEX-FM, Pensacola, 1960-65; sports dir. Sta. WSFA-TV, Montgomery, Ala., 1961-63; sports dir., new editor Sta. WJHG-TV, Panama City, Fla., 1963-74; mem. Fla. Ho. of Reps., 1972-78; mem. 96th Congress from 1st Dist. Fla. Served with USNR. Mem. Gideons Internat. (Panama City Camp). Baptist. Club: Civitan (dep. dist. gov. Ala-West Fla. dist. 1967-71). Office: 508 Cannon House Office Bldg Washington DC 20515

HUTTON, JERRY B., educator; b. Gorman, Tex., Apr. 28, 1938; s. Alvie C. and Dora Lucille (English) H.; B.A., Howard Payne Coll., 1960; M.S., N.Tex. State U., 1962; Ph.D., U. Houston, 1970; m. Sandra Jeane Brumlow, July 17, 1959; children—Cynthia, Jerry, Blake, Jeffrey, Jennifer. Clin. psychologist Child Devel. Clinic, Houston, 1964-67; clin. psychologist Richmond (Tex.) State Sch., 1967-69; asst. prof. psychology Dallas Bapt. Coll., 1969-70; instr. pediatrics U. Tex. Health Sci. Center, 1970-71; dir. Fairhill Sch.,

Dallas, 1971-72; asso. prof. spl. edn. E.Tex. State U., Dallas, 1972—. Cons. to Lancaster, DeSoto, Garland, Dallas Ind. Sch. Dists. Treas., Dallas Area Council for Exceptional Children, 1973-74, parliamentarian, 1974-75. Bd. dirs. Fairhill Sch., Dallas, 1972—, pres. chmn. bd., 1973-74. Mem. Am. Psychol. Assn., Nat. Assn. Sch. Psychologists, Council for Exceptional Children, Dallas Psychol. Assn., Dallas Assn. Children with Learning Disabilities (pres. 1974-75). Contbr. articles to profl. jours. Home: 727 Little Creek Duncanville TX 75116 Office: 11325 Pegasus Dallas TX 75238

HUYKE-LUIGI, ROBERTO, educator; b. Santurce, P.R., June 3, 1943; s. Roberto and Ana (Luigi) Huyke-Iglesias; student U. P.R., 1961-64; B.C.E., Worcester Poly. Inst., 1966; M.C.E., Cornell U., 1967, Ford Found. fellow, 1972—; m. Lois E. Nicole, July 29, 1968; children—Lois E., Roberto R., Gretchen. Mem. faculty civil engring. U. P.R., 1967—, asso. prof., 1970—; cons. Mem. Am. Concrete Inst., Prestress Concrete Inst., Colegio Ingenieros Arquitectos Agrimensores P.R., Phi Eta Mu, Chi Epsilon. Home: Road 351 983-B Villa Sonsire Mayaguez PR 00708

HUYSMAN, ARLENE WEISS, psychologist; b. Phila., June 14, 1929; d. Max and Anna (Pearlene) Weiss; B.A., Shaw U., 1973; M.A., Goddard Coll., 1974; Ph.D., Union Grad. Sch., 1980; children—Pamela Claire, James David. Actress, dir. Dramatic Workshop, N.Y.C., also various theaters in Fla., 1956-68; music and drama critic and columnist Orlando (Fla.) Sentinel Star, 1966-68; psychodramatist Volusia County Guidance Center, Daytona Beach, Fla., 1966-68; pres. C.S. Advt. Inc., Coral Gables, Fla., 1969-72; free-lance journalist, 1968-70; psychodramatist Psychiat. Inst., Jackson Meml. Hosp., Miami, 1972-77, acting dir. Adult Day Treatment Center, 1974-75, dir., 1975-77, dir. Lithium Clinic, 1976-77; psychodramatist S. Fla. State Hosp., Hollywood, 1971-72; adj. instr. U. Miami, 1976—. Mem. adv. panel Fine Arts Council Fla., 1976-77; mem. Fla. Gov.'s Task Force on Marriage and the Family Unit, 1976; vol. Rec. for Blind, 1974—. Recipient Best Dirs. award and Best Actress award Fla. Theatre Festival, 1967. Mem. Am. (asso.), Fla. (asso.) psychol. assns., Mental Health Assn. Dade County, Assn. Humanistic Psychology, Internat. Assn. Group Psychotherapy, Am. Assn. Group Psychotherapy and Psychodrama, Moreno Acad., Fedn. Partial Hospitalization Study Groups, Fla. Assn. Practicing Psychologists. Office: Group and Family Therapy Center 317 NE 24th St Miami FL 33137

HYDE, BARBARA LEVEARN, nurse, educator; b. Clinton, La., Nov. 8, 1946; d. Chester Arthur and Jauanita (McCoy) H.: B.S., Northwestern State U., 1968; M.S., U. Ala., Birmingham, 1971; postgrad. La. State U., 1976—. Staff nurse Earl K. Long Meml. Hosp., Baton Rouge, 1968-69, head nurse, 1969-71; instr. nursing Southeastern La. U., Baton Rouge, 1971-74, asst. prof., 1974—; instr. ARC. Served to maj. USAR, 1976—. Mem. Am. Nurses Assn., La. State Nurses Assn., Baton Rouge Dist. Nurses Assn., Res. Officers Assn., Nurses Assn. Am. Coll. Obstetricians and Gynecologists, Nat. Council Family Relations, U. Ala. Nursing Alumni Assn., Sigma Theta Tau, Phi Kappa Phi. Democrat. Baptist. Club: Woodmen of World. Home: 9620 Ashentree St Baton Rouge LA 70811 Office: Southeastern La U 3638 North Blvd Baton Rouge LA 70805

HYDE, CLARENCE BRODIE, II, oil producer; b. Fort Worth, Oct. 22, 1937; s. Clarence Edgar and Frances (Williams) H.; B.S., Tex. Wesleyan Coll., Ft. Worth, 1961; M.B.A., U. Tex., Austin, 1963; grad. So. Meth. U. Grad. Sch. Banking, 1973; m. Sylvia Flower, June 5, 1960; children—Clarence Brodie III, Brooke Allison, Brett Kinlock, Blair Elizabeth. Vice pres., asst. mgr. lending group, chmn. loan com. Ft. Worth Nat. Bank, 1963-76; ind. oil producer, Ft. Worth, 1976—; pres., chmn. bd. Hyde Oil & Gas Corp. Bd. dirs. Tarrant County chpt. Salvation Army, 1969—, chmn. bd., 1972-74; trustee Trinity Valley Sch., Ft. Worth, 1970; mgmt. com. Camp Amon Carter, Ft. Worth, 1970-76, adv. mem., 1976—; trustee Tex. Wesleyan Coll., 1971—; bd. dirs. Big Bros. Tarrant County, 1971; Radiation Center S.W., Ft. Worth, 1971—; bd. dirs., exec. com. Harris Hosp., Ft. Worth, 1971—; trustee, treas., exec. com. Tarrant County chpt. ARC, 1971-73; bd. dirs. Ft. Worth Opera Assn., 1971—, v.p., treas., 1972-74; bd. dirs., exec. com. Hurst-Euless-Bedford Hosp., Ft. Worth, 1973—. Mem. Ind. Petroleum Assn. Am., Tex. Hosp. Assn. Republican. Methodist. Clubs: Rivercrest Country, Shady Oaks Country, Ft. Worth, Steeplechase, Ridotto, Century II (Ft. Worth). Home: 8 Westover Rd Fort Worth TX 76107 Office: 1115 Ridglea Bank Bldg Fort Worth TX 76116

HYDE, JOSEPH R., III, business exec.; b. Memphis, 1942; A.B., U. N.C., 1965; married. With Malone & Hyde Inc., Memphis, 1965—, pres. Super D Drugs subs., 1966, v.p. parent co., 1967-68, exec. v.p., 1968-69, pres., chief exec. officer, 1969-72, chmn. bd., 1972—, also dir.; dir. 1st Tenn. Corp., Wal-Mart Stores, Inc., Fed. Express Corp., Browning Ferris Inc. Bd. dirs. Memphis U. Sch. Office: Malone & Hyde Inc 1991 Corporate Ave Memphis TN 38132

HYDE, LAWRENCE PERRY, allergist, immunologist; b. Buchanan, Va., Jan. 25, 1924; s. Frank Zimmerman and Emily (Redmond) H.; B.S. in Chemistry and Psychology Hampden-Sydney Coll., 1947; M.D., U. Va., 1951; m. Alda Muriel Hash Meredith, Feb. 24, 1963; children—Crystal Star, Autumn Lea, Laura Sherry, Lena Emily. Intern Sewickley Valley Hosp., Sewickley, Pa.; gen. practice medicine, Pulaski, Va., 1951-62, practice medicine specializing in allergies and immunology, 1962—; chief staff Pulaski Community Hosp., 1977—, dir. respiratory therapy, 1974—, dir. cardiac emergency med. treatment, 1977—; med. advisor Va. Assn. Vol. Rescue Squads. Bd. dirs. Western Va. EMS Council, Pulaski Community Hosp., Va. affiliate Am. Heart Assn.; mem. Va. Gov.'s Advisory Council Emergency Med. Ser. Served with USN, 1943-46. Fellow Am. Acad. Family Physicians; mem. AMA, Va. Med. Soc., Am. Thoracic Soc., Am. Acad. Allergy, Am. Assn. Allergy, Am. Assn. Clin. Allergy and Immunology. Contbr. articles to med. jours. Home: 1104 Prospect Ave Pulaski VA 24301 Office: PO Box 1529 Pulaski VA 24301

HYDER, MELVIN H., bank exec.; b. Asheville, N.C., Mar. 24, 1946; s. Andy S. and Juanita R. (West) H.; B.S. in Bus. Adminstrn., Western Carolina U., 1968, M.Ed., 1970, M.B.A., 1977; m. Sandy Hamrick Wood, Dec. 5, 1975. Corporate employee benefits rep. Aetna Life & Casualty Life Ins. Co., Charleston, W. Va., 1970-74; mgr. Hyder's Inc., Hendersonville, N.C., 1974-76; sr. credit officer Northwestern Bank, North Wilkesboro, N.C., 1977—. Nat. Tchrs. Corps fellow, 1968-70. Mem. Assn. M.B.A. Execs., Kappa Alpha, Phi Kappa Phi. Democrat. Home: 404 Mark Ln North Wilkesboro NC 28659 Office: Oakwoods Dr North Wilkesboro NC 28659

HYDRICK, BOB DURRETT, advt. agy. exec.; b. Sylacauga, Ala., Jan. 6, 1939; s. Julius Cannon and Esther (Durrett) H.; B.S., Mercer U., Auburn U., 1961; m. Ruth Stephens, Feb. 17, 1962; children—Robert, Stephen, John, Susan. With Royal Crown Cola Co., Columbus, Ga., 1961-73; mayor City of Columbus, 1973-74; v.p. Kinnett Dairies, Columbus, 1975-76; prin. Bob Hydrick, Inc., Columbus, 1976—. Recipient Am. Advt. Fedn. Silver medal, 1970. Mem. Advt. Club Columbus. Republican. Baptist. Club: Kiwanis (pres. elect 1979—). Office: Box 2651 Columbus GA 31902

HYMAN, ALBERT LEWIS, physician; b. New Orleans, Nov. 10, 1923; s. David and Mary (Newstadt) H.; B.S., La. State U., 1943; M.D., 1945; postgrad. U. Cin., U. Paris (France), U. London (Eng.); m. Neil Steiner, March 27, 1964; 1 son, Albert Arthur. Intern, Charity Hosp., 1945-46, resident, 1947-49, sr. vis. physician, 1959-63; resident Cin. Gen. Hosp., 1946-47; instr. medicine La. State U., 1950-56, asst. prof. medicine, 1956-57; asst. prof. medicine Tulane U., 1957-59, asso. prof., 1959-63; asso. prof. surgery Tulane Med. Sch., 1963-70, prof. research surgery in cardiology, 1970—, adj. prof. pharmacology, 1974—; dir. Cardiac Catheterization Lab., 1957—; sr. vis. physician Touro Hosp., Touro Infirmary, Hotel Dieu; chief cardiology Sara Mayo Hosp.; cons. in cardiology USPHS, New Orleans Crippled Children's Hosp., St. Tammany Parish Hosp., Covington, La. area VA, Hotel Dieu Hosp., Mercy Hosp., East Jefferson Gen. Hosp., St. Charles Gen. Hosp.; electrocardiographer Metairie Hosp., 1959-64, Sara Mayo Hosp., Touro Infirmary, St. Tammany Hosp.; cons. cardiovascular disease New Orleans VA Hosp.; cons. cardiology Baton Rouge Gen. Hosp., Barlow lectr. in medicine U. So. Calif., 1977. Diplomate Am. Bd. Internal Medicine. Fellow A.C.P., Am. Coll. Chest Physicians, Am. Coll. Cardiology, Am. Fedn. Clin. Research; mem. Am. (fellow and regional rep. council clin. cardiology), La. (v.p. 1974) heart assns., Am. Soc. Pharmacology and Exptl. Therapeutics, So. Soc. Clin. Investigation, So. Med. Soc., Am. Physiol. Soc., AAUP, N.Y. Acad. Scis. Contbr. articles to profl. jours. Research in cardiopulmonary circulation. Home: 5550 Jacquelyn Ct New Orleans LA 70124 Office: 3629 Prytania St New Orleans LA 70115

HYMAN, CAROLINE GRIGGS, occupational therapist; b. Waterbury, Conn., May 29, 1937; d. Robert Foote and Anne (Tranker) Griggs; student Simmons Coll., 1955-57; B.S., Tufts U.-Boston Sch. Occupational Therapy, 1960; M.S. in Spl. Edn., Syracuse U., 1963; m. Gerold Frederick Hyman, Oct. 24, 1965; children—William Morris, Alice Elizabeth. Occupational therapist Sunnyview Rehab. Center, Schenectady, 1960-62, United Cerebral Palsy Cin., 1963-66; occupational therapist children's unit New Haven Rehab. Center, 1966-67; occupational therapist Suffolk Rehab. Center, Commack, N.Y., 1973-77, Tulsa County Public Health Nursing Service, Inc., 1979—; occupational therapy cons. Berkshire Nursing Center, West Babylon, N.Y., 1974-77, Muscular Dystrophy Assn. Suffolk County, 1974-77. Office Vocat. Rehab. tuition grantee, 1962-63. Mem. Am., N.Y. State, L.I. Dist., Okla. occupational therapy assns. Home: 2605 E Dallas St Broken Arrow OK 74012 Office: 1637 S Yale St Tulsa OK 74112

HYMES, DEAN MICHEAL, coal co. ofcl.; b. Bluefield, W.Va., Mar. 5, 1949; s. Nelson Arlie and Ethel Florence (Spence) H.; A.S., Ferrum Jr. Coll., 1969; B.S. in Mgmt., Concord Coll., 1971; M.B.A., W.Va. Coll. Grad. Studies, 1978; m. Cecelia E. Glaviano, June 19, 1971; children—Martin Nelson, Aaron Spence. Personnel asst. Consol. Coal Co., So. Appalachia Region, Pocahontas, Va., 1972-75, supr. workmen's and unemployment compensation, 1975-76, mgr. indsl. relations, 1976-78, regional mgr. indsl. and employee relations, 1978—; adv. com. S.W. Va. Community Coll. Mining Curriculum. Mem. So. W.Va. Personnel Assn., So. W.Va./S.W. Va. Communicators Roundtable. Republican. Methodist. Club: Tazewell Jaycees. Office: Consol Coal Co Southern Appalachia Region Water St Pocahontas VA 24635

IACOBUCCI, GUILLERMO ARTURO, chemist; b. Buenos Aires, Argentina, May 11, 1927; s. Guillermo Cesar and Blanca Nieves (Brana) I.; M.Sc., U. Buenos Aires, 1949, Ph.D. in Organic Chemistry, 1952; m. Constantina Maria Gullich, Mar. 28, 1952; children—Eduardo Ernesto, William George. Came to U.S., 1962, naturalized, 1972. Research chemist E.R. Squibb Research Labs., Buenos Aires, 1952-57; research fellow in chemistry Harvard, Cambridge, Mass., 1958-59, prof. phytochemistry U. Buenos Aires, 1960-61; sr. research chemist Squibb Inst. Med. Research, New Brunswick, N.J., 1962-66; head bio-organic chemistry labs. Coca-Cola Co., Atlanta, 1967-74, asst. dir. corporate research and devel., 1974—. Adj. prof. chemistry Emory U., 1975—. John Simon Guggenheim Meml. Found. fellow, 1958. Mem. A.A.A.S., Assn. Harvard Chemists, Am. Chem. Soc., N.Y. Acad. Scis., Am. Soc. Pharmacognosy, Assn. Quimica Argentina. Contbr. articles on organic chemistry to sci. jours. Patentee in field. Home: 160 North Mill Rd NW Atlanta GA 30328 Office: Coca Cola Co PO Drawer 1734 Atlanta GA 30301

I'ANSON, LAWRENCE WARREN, state supreme ct. chief justice; b. Portsmouth, Va., Apr. 21, 1907; s. James Thornton and Emma (Warren) I'A.; A.B., Coll. William and Mary, 1928, LL.D., 1964; LL.B., U. Va., 1931; m. May Frances Tuttle, Aug. 5, 1933; children—Lawrence Warren, May F. Ramsey. Admitted to Va. bar, 1931; practiced in Portsmouth, 1931-41; commonwealth's atty., Portsmouth, 1938-41; judge Ct. of Hustings (now Circuit Ct.), 1941-58; justice Supreme Ct. of Va., 1958-74, chief justice, 1974—. Mem. Jud. Council, 1948—; chmn. com. that prepared Handbook for Jurors used in all courts of record in Va.; pres. Nat. Center State Cts., 1979-80; chmn. Conf. Chief Justices, 1979-80. Mem. Council Higher Edn. Va., 1956-59; pres. Beazley Found., Found. Boys Acad. Chmn. bd. trustees Frederick Mil. Acad. Recipient William and Mary Alumni medallion, U. Va. Sesquicentennial award, Lincoln Harley award Am. Judicature Soc., Distinguished Service award Va. Trial Lawyers. Mem. Va. State Bar Assn. (chmn. jud. sect. 1949), Phi Beta Kappa, Pi Kappa Alpha, Omicron Delta Kappa, Order of Coif, Phi Alpha Delta. Democrat. Home: 214 West Rd Portsmouth VA 23707 Office: Supreme Ct Va Richmond VA 23219 also Va Fed Bldg Portsmouth VA 23704

IBACH, DOUGLAS THEODORE, clergyman; b. Pottstown, Pa., July 23, 1925; s. Hiram Christian and Esther (Fry) I.; B.S. in Edn., Temple U., 1950, postgrad. Sch. Theology, 1950-52; M.Div., Louisville Presbyn. Theol. Sem., 1954; m. Marion Elizabeth Torok, Sept. 2, 1950; children—Susan Kay, Marilyn Lee, Douglas Theodore, Grace Louise. Ordained to ministry Presbyn. Ch., 1953; pastor, Pewee Valley, Ky., 1952-55, West Nottingham Presbyn. Ch., Colora, Md., 1955-61, Irwin, Pa., 1961-67, Knox Presbyn. Ch., Falls Church, Va., 1967-72, United Christian Parish Reston (Va.), 1972—. Youth Ministry cons. Nat. Capital Union Presbytery, 1967—; bd. dirs. Crossroads Program Fairfax County; adv. bd. Christmas Internat. House, Crossroads Drug Program, Fairfax County; mem. Fairfax County Litter Control Com. Served with USNR, 1943-44. Mem. Council Chs. Greater Washington (pres.), Piedmont Synod U.P. Ch. (dir. youth, camping), Acad. Parish Clergy (dir.), ACLU, Assn. Presbyn. Christian Educators, Fairfax County Council Chs. (pres.), Com. 100 Fairfax County. Club: American Field Service (Vienna, Va.). Home: 11709 Riders Ln Reston VA 22091 Office: 2222 Colts Neck Rd Reston VA 22091

IBACH, JOHN RAYMOND, JR., physician; b. Massena, N.Y., Aug. 22, 1933; s. John Raymond and Margaret Lucille (Rodger) I.; A.B., Hamilton Coll., 1955; M.D., U. Rochester, 1959; m. Catherine Henlin, Mar. 24, 1959; children—Karen, Michael, Kristin, John Rodger, David. Intern, resident in surgery Phila. Gen. Hosp., 1959-64; practice medicine specializing in gen. surgery, Phila., 1964-67; fellow in cardiovascular and thoracic surgery U Fla., 1969-71; practice medicine specializing in cardiovascular and thoracic surgery Cardiovascular & Thoracic Assos., Profl. Assn., Jacksonville, Fla., 1971—; mem. staff Bapt. Meml. Hosp., Meml. Hosp. Jacksonville, Jacksonville Children's Hosp. Mem. Fla. Council for Clean Air, 1974-77; trustee Riverside Presbyn. Day Sch., 1975-78. Served to maj. M.C., AUS, 1967-69; Vietnam. Diplomate Am. Bd. Surgery, Am. Bd. Thoracic Surgery. Fellow A.C.S.; mem. Soc. Thoracic Surgeons, Am. Coll. Cardiology, Am. Coll. Chest Physicians, So. Thoracic Surg. Assn., Northeast Fla. Lung Assn. (pres. 1977-79), Northeast Fla. Heart Assn. (pres. 1979-80), Alpha Delta Phi, Pi Delta Epsilon. Republican. Presbyterian. Home: 12362 Mandarin Rd Jacksonville FL 32223 Office: Laurette J Howard Doctors Bldg Suite 315 Jacksonville FL 32207

ICHINOSE, HERBERT, physician; b. Koloa, Kauai, Hawaii, July 25, 1931; s. Samuro and Katsue (Yamamoto) I.; student U. Hawaii, 1949-51; B.S., Tulane U., 1953, M.D., 1957; m. Elaine Okimoto, Dec. 19, 1955; children—Linda, Lorna, John, Eugene. Intern Charity Hosp. New Orleans, 1957-58, resident, 1958-62; practice medicine, specializing in pathology, New Orleans, 1958—; vis. pathologist Charity Hosp., 1964—; cons. pathologist Meth. Hosp., New Orleans, 1972—; mem. faculty dept. pathology Med. Sch., Tulane U., New Orleans, 1958—, asso. prof., 1967-71, prof., 1971-74, clin. prof., 1974—. Service Club scholar, 1949, USPHS grantee, 1954; recipient John Herr Musser Mem. award Tulane Med. Sch., 1957, Undergrad. Research award Border Co., 1957. Diplomate Am. Bd. Pathology. Mem. New Orleans Acad. Pathology (pres.), Thoracophilus Soc., Orleans Parish, La. med. socs., AMA, N.Y. Acad. Scis., Am. Soc. Clin. Pathologists. Contbr. articles to profl. jours. Home: 2813 Calhoun St New Orleans LA 70118 Office: 1430 Tulane St New Orleans LA 70112

IDDINS, MILDRED, librarian; b. Fountain City, Tenn., Sept. 14, 1915; d. Joseph Franklin and Lucy Ann (Chandler) Iddins; A.B., Carson-Newman Coll., 1935; B.S., Peabody Coll., 1941. Tchr., Bell House, Knoxville, Tenn., 1936-37; tchr.-librarian Roane County High Sch., Kingston, Tenn., 1937-41; librarian Dandridge (Tenn.) High Sch., 1941-43; army librarian Ft. Oglethorpe, Ga., 1943-44; librarian Carson-Newman Coll., Jefferson City, Tenn., 1944—. Mem. Am., Southeastern, Tenn. library assns. Clubs: Monday Lit., Modern Book. Home: 403 Russell St Jefferson City TN 37760 Office: Library Carson-Newman Coll Jefferson City TN 37760

IERARDO, DOMENICK, educator; b. Italy, Sept. 9, 1926; s. Salvatore and Maria (Valentino) I.; came to U.S., 1954, naturalized, 1956; B.A., State Tchrs. Coll., Vibo Valentia, Italy, 1945; M.A., U. Naples, 1954; M.A., N.Y.U., 1963, Ph.D., 1974; m. Anna Ferraro, May 17; children—Salvatore, Anthony, Dorothy. Tchr., Pontano Inst., Naples, 1949-51; instr. Romance and classical langs. U. Conn., Storrs, 1964-67; asst. prof. So. Conn. State Coll., New Haven, 1967-70; asst. prof. Italian, U. South Fla., Tampa, 1970—; founder, advisor Circolo Culturale Italiano; lectr. in field; dir. Italian lang. radio programs. Com. mem. Italian Anti-discrimination League, Sons of Itlay in Am., 1976. Served with U.S. Army, 1955-57. Decorated Order of Crown of Atavilla-Commendatore, Rome; Sovereign Order St. John of Jerusalem, Knights of Malta, Knight of Grace, Knight of Merit; recipient WUSF-AM Community Service award, 1976. Mem. Am. Assn. Tchrs. of Italian, N.Y. U. Alumni Assn., Modern Lang. Assn. Am., S. Atlantic Modern Lang. Assn. Democrat. Roman Catholic. Club: Masons. Author: Petrarca Critico; contbr. articles to profl. jours. Home: 10918 N 22d St Tampa FL 33612 Office: U South Florida Tampa FL 33620

IEYOUB, RICHARD PHILLIP, lawyer; b. Lake Charles, La., Aug. 11, 1944; s. Phillip Assad and Virginia Khoury I.; B.A., McNeese State U., 1968; J.D., La. State U., 1972; m. Sandra Claire Bates, Aug. 12, 1972; children—Amy Claire, Nicole Anne. Admitted to La. bar, 1972; spl. counsel to atty. gen. State of La., Baton Rouge, 1972-74; asso. firm Camp, Carmouche, Lake Charles, 1974-76; mem. firm Stockwell, Sievert, Lake Charles, 1976-78; mem. firm Baggett, McCall, Singleton, Ranier and Ieyoub, Lake Charles, 1978—; instr. criminal law McNeese State U.; lectr. criminal law La. Bar Assn. Mem. Am. Bar Assn., Am. Trial Lawyers, Nat. Assn. Criminal Def. Lawyers, La. State Bar Assn., S.W. La. Bar Assn. (exec. com. 1979). Democrat. Roman Catholic. Office: Baggett McCall Singleton Ranier and Ieyoub 1130 Pithon St Lake Charles LA 70601

IGBOKWE, EMMANUEL CHUKWUEMEKA, biologist; b. Enugwu-Ukwu, Nigeria, Jan. 18, 1941; came to U.S., 1965; s. Aaron and Edna I.; B.S. in Zoology, U. Nigeria, 1965; M.S. in Entomology, Mich. State U., 1967; Ph.D. in Biology, Queen's U., (Ont., Can.), 1971; M.D., U. Juarez, Chihuahua, Mexico, 1981; m. Gwendolyn Capers, Jan. 27, 1975. Postdoctoral research asso. U. Notre Dame (Ind.), 1970; prin. research investigator NIH research grant, project dir. NSF grant, 1975; resident research asso. Argonne (Ill.) Nat. Lab., 1972; prof. biology, head dept. Rust Coll., Holly Springs, Miss., 1971—. Mem. Am. Genetic Assn., Genetics Soc. Can., Entomol. Soc. Am., Entomol. Soc. Can., Am. Soc. Parasitologists, AAAS, Miss. Acad. Scis., Am. Soc. Zoologists. Contbr. articles to profl. jours.

IGBOKWE, GWENDOLYN MATTIE CAPERS, ednl. counselor; b. Jacksonville, Fla., Jan. 24, 1950; d. Eddie C. and Juliet (Capers) Williams; B.S. in Sociology, Tuskegee Inst., 1973, M.A. in Guidance and Counseling, 1976 m. Dr. Emmanuel Igbokwe, Dec. 27, 1975. Vol. mental health counselor VA Hosp., Tuskegee, Ala., 1970-74; asst. coordinator vets. program Wayne State U., Detroit, 1974-75; mental health counselor Mental Health Center, Tuskegee Inst., 1975-76; grad. student advisor Memphis State U., 1976-77; dir. spl. services and Upward Bound program Rust Coll., Holly Springs, Miss., 1977-79; coordinator counseling N.Mex. State U., Las Cruces, 1979—. Mem. Am. Personnel and Guidance Assn., Psychology Club, Behavioral Sci. Club, Tuskegee Guidance (pres. 1976), Phi Delta Kappa. Producer TV shows on African art and on poetry with Montevallo U. Broadcasting System, 1975. Home: 5925 Escondido El Paso TX 79912 Office: PO Box 4450 NMex State U Las Cruces NM 88003

IGLAR, ALBERT FRANCIS, educator; b. New Kensington, Pa., July 17, 1939; s. Albert Francis and Mary I.; B.S., Carnegie-Mellon U., 1961; M.P.H., U. Minn., 1966 Ph.D., 1970; m. Loretta Ruth Streich, Aug. 2, 1964; children—David Alan, Deborah Ruth. San. engr. Pa. Dept. Health, Meadville, 1961-62, Harrisburg, 1962-65; research asso./fellow U. Minn., Mpls., 1966-70; asst. prof. E. Tenn. State U., Johnson City, 1970-73, asso. prof., 1973—, faculty research participant Pitts. Energy Tech. Center; mem. Tenn. Air Pollution Control Bd.; chmn. NEHA Com. on Community Water Supplies and Sewage Disposal Systems. U.S. Dept. Energy grantee, 1978-80; Fisk Systems grantee, 1977-78; registered profl. engr., Minn., environmentalist. Mem. Nat. Environ. Health Assn., Tenn. Environ. Health Assn., Water Pollution Control Fedn., Ky.-Tenn. Water Pollution Control Assn., Tenn. Water and Wastewater Assn., Air Pollution Control Assn., NEA, Tenn. Edn. Assn., E. Tenn. Edn. Assn. Baptist. Club: Metro Johnson City Kiwanis. Contbg. editor Jour. Environ. Health; contbr. articles to publs. Home: 605 Pine Ridge Rd Johnson City TN 37601 Office: East Tenn State U PO Box 24449 Johnson City TN 37601

IGLESIAS, JOSE VICTOR, thoracic surgeon; b. Barranquilla, Colombia; s. Jose Vicente and Aurora Maria (Escorce) I.; came to U.S., 1966; M.D., U. Antioquia (Colombia), 1964; m. Sara E. Dib, Jan. 30, 1965; children—Jose Luis, Sarita, Betty. Intern, S. Balt. Gen. Hosp., 1966-67; resident in gen. surgery, 1967-71; resident in thoracic and cardiovascular surgery U. Md., 1972-73; mem. staff M.D. Anderson Hosp., Houston, 1973-74; practice medicine specializing in thoracic surgery, Houston, 1974—; mem. staff N.W. Med. Center Hosp., Houston, chmn. surgery, 1977—, pres. med. staff, 1979—; clin. instr. dept. surgery U. Tex.; mem. staff St. Joseph, Herman hosps., Meml. Hosp. System. Diplomate Am. Bd. Surgery, Am. Bd. Thoracic Surgery. Fellow A.C.S., Am. Coll. Angiology; mem. AMA, Tex., Harris County med. assns., Soc. Thoracic Surgeons, U. Md. Surg. Soc., Houston Surg. Soc. Office: 17200 Red Oak St Suite 204 Houston TX 77090

IGOU, VIRGINIA GOLDSTON, steel co. exec.; b. Oakdale, Tenn., July 23, 1927; d. Rebuin and Nell (McCartt) Goldston; grad. Chattanooga Public Schs.; m. Willard F. Igou, Dec. 28, 1945, (dec.); 1 dau., Deborah I. Igou Henderson. With Koblentz Dept. Store, Chattanooga, 1946-51; with Siskin Steel & Supply Co., Inc., Chattanooga, 1951—, controller, 1979—. Office: Siskin Steel Co PO Box 1191 Chattanooga TN 37401

ILAHI, ARIFA ASLAM, anesthesiologist; b. Lahore, Pakistan, July 26, 1942; d. Riyaz and Anwar (Begum) Qadeer; came to U.S., 1971; F.Sc., Lahore Coll. for Women, 1961; M.B.B.S., Fatima Jinnah Med. Coll., 1966; m. Mohammad Aslam Ilahi, May 9, 1963; children—Omer, Irum, Maryam, Shereen. Intern, Salem (Mass.) Hosp., 1968; pvt. practice medicine, Lahore, Pakistan, 1969-71; resident in anesthesiology Michael Reese Hosp., Chgo., 1971-73; practice medicine specializing in anesthesiology, Baytown, Tex., 1973—. Diplomate Am. Bd. Anesthesiology. Fellow Am. Coll. Anesthesiologists; mem. Am., Ill. socs. anesthesiologists. Office: 1610 Bowie Dr Baytown TX 77520

ILER, ARTHUR TRIPLETT, judge; b. Rockport, Ky., Mar. 3, 1900; s. William Perry and Nellie (Young) I.; student Western Ky. State Coll., 1917-19; LL.B., Columbus U., 1934; m. Kathryn Wallace, June 19, 1927; children—Richard W., William Perry II. With Washington Herald, Washington News, 1930-33; with FHA, D.C., Ky., 1934-40; admitted to Ky. bar, 1935; practiced in Louisville, 1940-41; asst. atty. gen. Ky., 1941-43; atty. Muhlenberg County, 1954-56; circuit judge 45th Jud. Dist. Ky., Greenville, 1956-76; farmer, horse raiser, 1950—. Pres., Muhlenberg County Fair Bd., 1948-58; mem. Ky. Horse Council. Bd. dirs. Travelers Protective Assn. Served with inf. U.S. Army, 1918. Named Man of Year, Central City C. of C., 1958. Mem. Am. Legion (post comdr.), 40 and 8, Ky. Thoroughbred Assn., Sigma Delta Kappa. Presbyn. (elder). Clubs: All States Society (past pres. Washington); Rotary (past pres. Central City, Ky.). Home: 1004 Broad St Central City KY 42330 Office: PO Box 268 Central City Ky 42330

ILOFF, PHILLIP MURRAY, JR., chemist; b. State College, Pa., Jan. 8, 1921; s. Phillip Murray and Ethel May (Rumburger) I.; B.S. in Chemistry, Stanford U., 1949, Ph.D., 1957; m. Edith Marie Griffin, Dec. 26, 1954; children—Glen Phillip, Helen Marie. Research chemist U. Calif., Berkeley, 1952-56, Callery Chem. Co. (Pa.), 1956-59, Aerojet Gen. Corp., Azusa, Calif., 1959-62; asst. prof. chemistry Whittier (Calif.) Coll., 1962-70; head dept. chemistry Piedmont Coll., Demorest, Ga., 1970—. Served with AUS, 1943-46. Shell Chem. Dept. fellow, 1950. Mem. Am. Chem. Soc., Am. Inst. Chemists, Sigma Xi. Congregationalist. Home: Box 446 Demorest GA 30535 Office: Chemistry Dept Piedmont Coll Demorest GA 30535

ILVENTO, BARBARA KAUTZ, sales exec.; b. Long Branch, N.J., Sept. 6, 1941; d. Charles Anthony and Palmy Maria (Tomaino) Kautz; A.A., Carnegie Coll., 1961; B.A., Fla. Internat. U., 1975; M.Ed., U. Miami, 1977; m. Charles Louis Ilvento, May 4, 1963; children—Charles Louis, Lauren Marie. Med. asst. to physicians, Red Bank, N.J., 1960-63, Hackensack, N.J., 1964, Elting Diagnostic Center, Teaneck, N.J., 1964; exec. sec. Beech-Nut Life Savers, Inc., N.Y.C., 1964-66, Leukemia Soc., Inc., N.Y.C., 1966-67, also mgr., 1966-67; exec. sec., mgr. Penta & Ilvento C.P.A.'s, Wanamassa, N.J., 1968-72; pres. Appleby's, Miami, Fla., 1977-79; asst. sales mgr. Bengis Assos., Inc., Miami, 1979—; v.p. Internat. Research Inst. Am., Miami, 1976. Asst. to chmn. Mental Health Task Force on Child Abuse, 1975; chairwoman N.J. Med. Asst. Assn. State Conv., 1964. Mem. Mental Health Assn., Am. Personnel and Guidance Assn., Psi Chi. Roman Catholic. Home: 16923 SW 87th Ave Miami FL 33157 Office: 7447 NW 48th St Miami FL 33166

IMBROGNO, EUGENE FRANCIS, real estate investment co. exec., restaurant chain exec.; b. Montgomery, W.Va., Oct. 26, 1922; s. Eugene and Marguerite (Gay) I.; B.S. in Bus. Adminstrn., W.Va. Inst. Tech., 1942; m. Alice Winkiewicz, Sept. 6, 1943; children—Catherine Imbrogno Jones, Eugene F., Ellen Imbrogno Spencer, Mark, Mary. Real estate investor, 1950—; real estate coordinator BBF Restaurants. Charleston, W.Va., 1962-69; pres. Realmark Develops., Inc. (formerly So. Realty Investments), Charleston, 1962—; real estate coordinator retail div. Borden, Inc., Columbus, Ohio, 1969-72; v.p. Montgomery Nat. Bank, 1971—; sec.-treas. Wendy's of W.Va., Inc., Sea Food of Ohio, Inc., Wendy's of So. Fla., Inc., Sea Food of Fla., Inc., Churchick, Inc., 1973-79, Rax of Tidewater, Gulfwest Foods, 1978; cons. various restaurant chains, real estate depts. Pres., Upper Kanawha Valley Devel. Assn., 1953-57, Montgomery C. of C., 1957-60; commr. Charleston Urban Renewal Authority, 1977—; bd. visitors Coll. Bus. W.Va. U., 1979. Served with USNR, 1942-56. Named Hon. Citizen Korea, 1962; Hon. Gov. Ohio, 1974. Mem. Internat. Council of Shopping Centers. Republican. Roman Catholic. Clubs: Berry Hills Country, Hawks Nest Country, Elks, Eagles, K.C. Home: 3 Dreamview Ln Charleston WV 25314 Office: Wendy Bldg Summers & Lee Sts Charleston WV 25301

IMPARATO, EDWARD THOMAS, securities co. exec.; b. Flushing, N.Y., Jan. 6, 1917; s. Charles and Romilda (DelliBovi) I.; B.S. in Bus., U. Tampa (Fla.), 1963; grad. Inst. Investment Banking, U. Pa., 1972; m. Jean Catherine deGarmo, Aug. 19, 1947; 1 son, Edward Thomas. Flying instr., comml. pilot, 1937-39; commd. 2d lt. USAAF, 1939, advanced through grades to col., 1944; test pilot, co. marshall; chief staff Carribean Air Command, 1958-61; ret., 1961; instr. course portfolio mgmt. St. Petersburg (Fla.) Jr. Coll., 1964; mem. bd., founding dir. Med. Sci. Internat. Corp., Clearwater, Fla., 1968-71, Vikintactin Instrument Co., Clearwater, 1968-71, Snibbe Publs., Inc., Clearwater, 1969-71; account exec. Goodbody & Co., 1963-69, mgr., 1969-71; with Merrill Lynch, Pierce, Fenner & Smith, Inc., Clearwater, 1971-74, v.p., 1973-74. Treas. Clearwater chpt. ARC, 1963; mem., pres. Morton F. Plant Hosp. Found., Clearwater, 1974—; mem. Com. 100 Pinellas County (Fla.), 1973—; trustee St. Petersburg Mus. Fine Arts, 1970-72; pres. Fla. Gulf Coast Art Center, 1967-69; bd. dirs. Clearwater Concert Assn., 1969—. Decorated Legion of Merit, D.F.C., Air medal with 2 oak leaf clusters, Berlin Airlift medal. Mem. Mil. Order World Wars, Ret. Officers Assn., Ret. Officers Assn., Am. Security Council, Internat. Platform Assn., Delta Sigma Phi. Episcopalian. Club: Sword and Shield (U. Tampa). Author: How to Manage Your Money, 4th edit., 1967. Home: 155 Bayview Dr Belleair FL 33516 Office: 323 Jeffords St Clearwater FL 33516

IMPRESCIA, STELIO ZARATUSTRA, pathologist; b. N.Y.C., Apr. 24, 1911; s. Gaetano and Domenica Mimi (Catalano) I.; student L.I. U., 1929-32; B.S., U. Louisville, 1933; M.D., U. Louisville, 1937; m. Zella Orr, Mar. 31, 1961; stepchildren—Pamela, Nona, Judy. Intern in medicine Kings County Hosp., 1937-38, in pathology, Kings L.I. Coll. Div., 1938-39, in surgery Bellevue Hosp., 1940; resident in gen. surgery Hosp. Spl. Surgery, 1940-41, in pathology, Harlan Miners Meml.-Appalachian Regional Hosp., Harlan, Ky., 1962-64; dir. Cancer Clinics in Ky., 1949-50; chief surgeon Evans Meml. Hosp. and Imprescia Clinic, Middlesboro, Ky., 1951-60; asst. pathologist Harlan Miners Meml. Hosp., 1960-61; dir. pathology Harlan Appalachian Regional Hosp., 1969-75, Middlesboro Appalachian and Pineville (Ky.) Community Hosps., 1975-79; chief pathology, dir. clin. lab. Pineville Community Hosp., 1979—; active staff in pathology Middlesboro Community Hosp., 1979—; cons. pathologist Harlan Appalachian Regional Hosp., 1975—, Whitesburg Appalachian Regional Hosp., 1965—. Diplomate Am. Bd. Pathology. Fellow Am. Coll. Pathologists, Am. Soc. Clin. Pathologists, Am. Coll. Chest Physicians, Internat. Coll. Surgeons; mem. Bell County Med. Soc. (pres. 1969). Contbr. articles in field to profl. jours. Home: 4310 Spurr Rd Lexington KY 40511 Office: Pineville Community Hosp Pineville KY 40977

INCAPRERA, FRANK PHILIP, internist, indsl. physician; b. New Orleans, Aug. 24, 1928; s. Charles and Mamie (Bellipanni) I.; B.S., Loyola U. of South, 1946; M.D., La. State U., 1950; m. Ruth Mary Duhon, Sept. 13, 1952; children—Charles, Cynthia, James, Christopher, Catherine. Intern, Charity Hosp., New Orleans, 1950-51, resident, 1951-52; resident VA Hosp., New Orleans, 1952-54; practice medicine specializing in internal medicine, New Orleans, 1957—; adminstrv. mgr. Internal Medicine Group, New Orleans, 1973—; med. dir. Owens-Ill. Glass Co., New Orleans, 1961—, Kaiser Aluminum Co., Chalmette, La., 1975—, Tenneco Oil Co., Chalmette, 1978—; co-founder Med. Center E. New Orleans, 1975; clin. asso. prof. medicine Tulane U. Sch. Medicine, 1971—; mem. New Orleans Bd. Health, 1966-70. Bd. dirs. Methodist Hosp., 1971—, Lutheran Home New Orleans, 1976—, Chateau de Notre Dame, 1977—; mem. New Orleans Human Relation Com., 1968-70; bd. dirs. Emergency Med. Services Council, 1977—, pres., La. southeastern region. Served to capt. USAF, 1955-57. Diplomate Am. Bd. Internal Medicine. Fellow A.C.P., Am. Occupational Medicine Assn., Am. Geriatrics Soc.: mem. La. (v.p. 1975-76, Orleans Parish (sec. 1972-74) med. socs., New Orleans Acad. Internal Medicine (pres. 1969), La. Occupational Medicine Assn. (pres. 1971-72), New Orleans East C. of C. (dir. 1979—), Blue Key, Delta Epsilon Sigma. Home: 2218 Lake Oaks Pkwy New Orleans LA 70122 Office: 5640 Read Blvd New Orleans LA 70127

INGE, MILTON THOMAS, educator; b. Newport News, Va., Mar. 18, 1936; s. Clyde Elmo and Bernice Lucille (Jackson) I.; B.A., Randolph-Macon Coll., 1959; M.A., Vanderbilt U., 1960, Ph.D., 1964; 1 son, Scott Thomas. Instr. English, Vanderbilt U., 1962-64, vis. prof. English, summer 1969; asst. prof., asso. prof. Am. thought and lang. Mich. State U., 1964-69; asso. prof. English, Va. Commonwealth U., Richmond, 1969-73, prof., 1973—, chmn. dept. English, 1974—; gen. editor Research Guides in English (St. Martin's Press), Am. Critical Tradition series (Burt Franklin Pub.), American Popular Culture: A Reference Series (Greenwood Press); editorial cons. several pubs.; reader English Composition Test, Coll. Entrance Exam. Bd., 1967, 69, 77; book reviewer Nashville Tenneseean, Richmond Times-Dispatch, Menomonee Falls Gazette. Bd. dirs. Friends of Richmond Pub. Library, San Francisco Acad. Comic Art. Fulbright-Hays grantee to teach Am. lit. Spain, 1967-68, Argentina, 1971, Soviet Union, 1979, research grantee Am. Philos. Soc., 1970, Mich. State U., 1965, 66, 68; Coll. Teaching Career fellow So. Fellowships Fund, 1959-62. Mem. MLA (del. assembly 1976-78, chmn. elections com. 1980), Am. Studies Assn., Popular Culture Assn., Am. Humor Studies Assn. (treas. 1975-77, pres. 1978), Soc. Study So. Lit. (exec. council 1971-73, 78—), Soc. Study Midwestern Lit., Melville Soc., Thoreau Fellowship, Ellen Glasgow Soc. (exec. council 1974—), Mus. Cartoon Art (nominating com. Hall of Fame 1975—), Am. Assn. Tchrs. Spanish and Portuguese, Phi Beta Kappa, Omicron Delta Kappa, Pi Delta Epsilon, Lambda Chi Alpha. Club: Va. Writers. Author: (with T.D. Young) Donald Davidson: Essay and Bibliography, 1965, Donald Davidson, 1971; editor: Sut Lovingood's Yarns, 1966; High Times and Hard Times, 1967; Agrarianism in American Literature, 1969; A.B. Longstreet, 1969; Faulkner: A Rose for Emily, 1970; Wm. Byrd of Westover, 1970; Studies in Light in August, 1971; Frontier Humorists: Critical Views, 1975; Ellen Glasgow: Centennial Essays, 1976; Black American Writers: Bibliographic Essays, 2 vols., 1978; Handbook of American Popular Culture, Vol. I, 1978, Vol. II, 1980; Bartleby the Inscrutable, 1979; also Resources for American Literary Study, 1971—; American Humor: An Interdisciplinary Newsletter, 1974-79. Office: Dept English Va Commonwealth U Richmond VA 23284

INGERICK, ELDYN LAYNE, accountant; b. Canton, Pa., Dec. 2, 1944; s. Elwyn Layne and Enid Henrietta (Morgan) I.; B.B.A., Stetson U., 1966; M.B.A., Ind. U., 1972; m. Marylin Mann, June 22, 1968; children—Teresa Jeannette, Renee Michelle, Robin Lee. Pvt. practice C.P.A., Pearsall, Tex., 1974-76; partner firm John Winn & Assos., Pearsall, 1976-77; pvt. practice, Pearsall, 1977—; v.p. Pearsall Devel. Co., 1976-77, pres., 1977—. Vice chmn. Pearsall Housing Authority. Served to capt. USAF, 1966-73. C.P.A., Tex. Mem. Am. Inst. C.P.A.'s, Tex. Soc. C.P.A.'s Republican. Roman Catholic. Club: Rotary (pres. 1979-80). Home: 1217 E Comal Pearsall TX 78061 Office: 111 N Ash Pearsall TX 78061

INGERTON, WILLIAM THOMAS, lawyer; b. Danville, Pa., June 30, 1924; s. Phillip Sheridan and Effie Denny (Rankin) I.; B.A., U. Ky., 1967, J.D., 1969; m. Helen Murray Roach, Oct. 16, 1948; children—Phyllis Ingerton Rapier, Helen Ingerton Schlubach, William Rhodes. Farmer, Midway, Ky., 1952—; sec. Goodwin Brothers Leasing, Lexington, Ky., 1972; admitted to Ky. bar, 1969; individual practice law, Lexington, 1970—. Mem. Am., Ky., Fayette County, Woodford County (v.p., 1973-74) bar assns., Assn. Trial Lawyers Am., Am. Soc. Law and Medicine, Ky. Civil War Round Table, Sigma Alpha Epsilon, Phi Alpha Phi. Clubs: Lafayette, Lexington (dir.). Home: Ingerton Farm Midway KY 40347 Office: 181 N Mill St Lexington KY 40507

INGRAM, ARBUTUS BOYD, mfg. co. exec.; b. Ferrum, Va., Mar. 29, 1930; d. Ted Lee and Gladys (Spencer) Boyd; student Ferrum Coll., 1947, Cornett Bus. Sch., 1947-48; m. Alexander Fountin Ingram, Jr., Nov. 16, 1948. Sec. to v.p. Clover Creamery Co.. Roanoke, Va., 1948-50; with Double Envelope Corp., Roanoke, 1950—, sec. to pres., 1954-75, v.p. and asst. to pres., 1975-76, asst. to chmn. bd. and chief exec. officer, 1977—. Sec., North Roanoke Civic League. Mem. Bus. and Profl. Women's Club, Nat. Secs. Assn. Democrat. Episcopalian. Clubs: Jefferson, Alpine Garden (past pres.). Home: 7823 Alpine Rd NW Roanoke VA 24019 Office: 7702 Plantation Rd NW Roanoke VA 24019

INGRAM, BENNY GALE, environ. designer, planner; b. Toccoa, Ga., Aug. 2, 1943; s. Colvin C. and Georgia Martha (McCollum) I.; Asso. Sci., Gainesville Jr. Coll., 1973; B. Landscape Architecture, U. Ga., 1976; M.City Planning, Ga. Inst. Tech., 1979; m. Tommie Nail Carpenter, Aug. 24, 1973; 1 stepson, Anthony Wayne Williams. Fireman, Hall County Fire Dept., 1968-73; tech. environmental planner Ga. Mountain Area Planning and Devel. Commn., 1976-78, regional planner, 1978-79, sr. planner, Gainesville, 1979—; adv. Alfa Com., 1977-78. Mem. adv. com. Boy Scouts Am., Oakwood, Ga., 1979; mem. Com. for Better Govt., Hall County, Ga., 1979; mem. Johnson Athletic Assn., 1977. Served with U.S. Army, 1964-68. Mem. Am. Planning Assn., Am. Forestry Assn., Am. Soc. Landscape Architects, Nat. Wildlife Fedn., Appalachian Trail Conf., Ga. Planning Assn., Bldg. Ofcls. Assn. Ga. Democrat. Baptist. Clubs: Kiwanis, Montgomery Meml. Brotherhood. Home: Route 11 Box 441 Gainesville GA 30501 Office: PO Box 1720 Gainesville GA 30501

INGRAM, DEBRA ANN, accountant; b. Columbus, Ga., July 29, 1952; d. Harry Eugene and Bobby Grace (Hicks) Ingram; B.S.Ed., Auburn U., 1974, B.S. in Bus. Adminstrn., 1976. Accountant, Weiss Moore Cubbedge & Howren, Marietta, Ga., 1976-77, Draffin & Tucker C.P.A.'s, Albany, Ga., 1977-79, Blazer & Co., Atlanta, 1979—. Mem. Am. Inst. C.P.A.'s, So. States Conf. C.P.A.'s, Ga. Soc. C.P.A.'s. Home: 4930 Roswell Rd Apt 15 Atlanta GA 30342 Office: Lenox Towers I 3390 Peachtree Rd NE Suite 1608 Atlanta GA 30326

INGRAM, GILBERT LEWIS, prison ofcl.; b. Laurel, Md., Nov. 16, 1940; s. James Howard and Erma C. (Rockenbaugh) I., Jr.; B.S., U. Md., 1962, M.A. (grad. teaching asst.), 1965, Ph.D., 1967; m. Ruth Ann White, Sept. 9, 1960; children—Charles Brock, Teresa Marie. Tech. writer Dept. Def., Washington, 1960-63; trainee in psychology VA, Washington, 1963-65; dir. research project Nat. Tng. Sch., Washington, 1965-68; chief psychologist Robert F. Kennedy Youth Center, Morgantown, W.Va., 1968-71; coordinator mental health Fed. Correctional Instn., Tallahassee, 1971-73, asso. warden, Englewood, Colo., 1973-75, warden, Miami, Fla., 1975-77, Butner, N.C., 1977—; lectr. U. N.C. at Chapel Hill, 1977—, Fla. State U., 1971-73, U. Miami, 1975-77, W.Va. U., 1968-71, U. Md., 1963-65; cons. Youth Devel. Center, Waycross, Ga., 1972-73; mem. Fed. Exec. Bd., Miami, 1975-77; participant program for sr. execs. on pub. issues Brookings Instn., 1975. Mem. combined fed. campaign United Givers Fund, Miami, 1975—. Mem. Am. Psychol. Assn., Am. Acad. Polit. and Social Sci., Am. Correctional Assn., Am. Assn. Wardens and Supts., Am. Assn. Correctional Psychologists, Md. Alumni Assn., Psi Chi. Presbyterian. Club: Masons. Contbr. articles to profl. jours, numerous govt. publs.; book reviewer Correctional Psychologist, 1971-73. Office: PO Box 1000 Old NC Hwy 75 Butner NC 27509

INGRAM, JAMES DUGGER, assn. exec., ret. naval officer; b. Giles County, Tenn., Oct. 7, 1921; s. George Marvin and Mary Annie (Dugger) I.; B.A., Stanford, 1962; M.S., U. Tenn., 1971, postgrad. (Univ. fellow), 1972; m. Dorothea Rogers Pursley, July 9, 1945; children—April Ann, Allison Dee. Commd. ensign USN, 1943, advanced through grades to capt., 1964; mem. faculty Naval War Coll., Newport, R.I., 1960-62; prof. naval sci. Vanderbilt U., Nashville, 1967-70; ret., 1970; dir. continuing med. edn. Tenn. Med. Assn., Nashville, 1972—. Decorated D.F.C. Mem. Ret. Officers' Assn., Phi Kappa Phi. Methodist (adminstrv. bd. 1973-75). Home: 6605 Sussex Circle Nashville TN 37205 Office: 112 Louise Ave Nashville TN 37203

INGRAM, JAMES LLOYD, union ofcl.; b. Birmingham, Ala., Oct. 21, 1927; s. Lark Denver and Thelma Irene (Swatzell) I.; student pub. schs., Ensley, Ala.; m. Vera Belle Perry; 1 dau., Barbara Gail. Usher, Ensley Theatre, 1941; dockhand Ry. Express Co., Birmingham, 1942; craneman Tenn. Coal, Iron & Land Co., Ensley, 1945; driver Nabisco, Inc., Birmingham, 1948—, union shop chmn., 1954—; sec.-treas. United Bakery Workers Union AFL-CIO, 1958—; exec. sec. Retail, Wholesale & Dept. Store Union Ala. Mid-S. Council, 1974—, rec. sec., 1961-74; sec.-treas. Birmingham Labor Council AFL-CIO, 1970-76. Treas., Ala. Labor Bicentennial Com., 1975-77. Served with U.S. Army, 1946-48. Democrat. Baptist. Editor, pub. Birmingham Labor Council News, 1975. Home: 1722 Decatur Ave Birmingham AL 35208 Office: 1901 10th Ave S Birmingham AL 35205

INGRAM, LUCILE WILLIAMS, educator; b. Natchitoches, La., Nov. 6, 1942; d. James Henry and Claudia Melle (Scarborough) Williams; B.S., La. State U., 1963; M.A. in Edn., Northwestern State U., Natchitoches, 1965, M.S. in Edn., 1978; m. Ralph C. Ingram, Jr., Aug. 24, 1963; children—Henry, Chris, Mary Lucile, Michelle, Cherry. Grad. asst. Northwestern State U., 1963-66, instr., 1966-74, asst. prof. English, 1975—. Mem. Natchitoches Service League, D.A.R. (sec. 1972-73), Assn. for Preservation Hist. Natchitoches. Roman Catholic. Home: Route 1 Box 215 Natchitoches LA 71457

INGRAM, MARY MEEKER, hosp. adminstr.; b. Greeley, Colo., Jan. 3, 1934; d. Paul Palmer and Mary (Hulburd) Meeker; student U. No. Colo., 1952-54, Meth. Hosp. Dallas, 1959; B.S. in Health Care Adminstrn., E. Tex. State U., 1978; 1 son, Stanley Paul. Instr. fundamentals of nursing Meth. Hosp., Dallas, 1959, staff nurse, 1960-61, emergency room staff nurse, 1969-71; staff nurse Caruth Rehab. Center, Dallas, 1961-62, dir. nursing, 1962-73; med. services coordinator Dallas Rehab. Inst., 1973-78, asst. adminstr. for med. services, 1978—. Mem. Tex. Soc. Hosp. Nursing Service Adminstrs., Am. Nurses Assn., Tex. Nurses Assn., Tex. Rehab. Assn., Methodist Hosp. Alumni. Home: 659 Bizerte Dallas TX 75224 Office: Dallas Rehab Inst 7850 Brookhollow Rd Dallas TX 75235

INGRAM, RILEY EDWARD, real estate broker; b. Halifax County, Va., Oct. 1, 1941; s. Sterling Thomas and Mary Helen (Moore) I.; grad. Realtors Inst., U. Va., 1975; m. Mary Ann Brinkley, Jan. 29, 1960; children—Tracy Eileen, Stacy Rileen, Riley Edward. With U.S. Post Office, Hopewell, Va., 1961-68; salesman Cuddihy Real Estate, Hopewell, 1968-74, v.p., 1972-74; partner Ingram & Houser Real Estate, Hopewell, 1975—. Commr., Hopewell Redevel. and Housing Authority, 1976—. Real estate broker, Va., 1972. Mem. Nat., Va., Hopewell assns. realtors, Nat. Inst. Real Estate Brokers, U.S., Hopewell jaycees. Mem. Ch. of Nazarene. Clubs: Moose, Jordan Point Country. Home: 714 Cedar Level Rd Hopewell VA 23860 Office: 3302 Oaklawn Blvd Hopewell VA 23860

INGRAM, ROBERT A., physician; b. Dallas, June 6, 1922; s. Henry Lee and Bernice (Benedict) I.; B.A., Rice Inst., 1947; M.D., U. Tex., 1951; m. Dorace McGill, Sept. 7, 1946; 1 dau., Ruth Elizabeth. Intern, Baptist Meml. Hosp., San Antonio, 1951-52; practice gen. medicine, Orange, Tex., 1952—; mem. staff Orange Meml. Hosp. Served with USNR, 1944-46. Diplomate Am. Bd. Family Practice. Fellow Am. Acad. Family Physicians; mem. Am., Tex. med. assns., Mensa. Home: 1906 Link Orange TX 77630 Office: 908 12th St Orange TX 77630

INGRAM, ROBERT BERNARD, city ofcl.; b. Miami, Fla., Aug. 5, 1936; s. Harold Atlaston and Arimentha Doretha (Womble) I.; A.A. with honors, Miami-Dade Coll., 1974; B.S., Fla. Internat. U., 1974, M.S., 1975; Ph.D., Union Experimenting Colls. and Univs., Cin., 1978; m. Delores Newsome, June 25, 1961; children—Tirzah Chezarena, Tamara Cheri. Officer, Miami (Fla.) Police Dept., 1959—; instr. Miami-Dade Community Coll., 1975—; adjunct prof. Nova U., Ft. Lauderdale, Fla., 1977—. Bd. dirs. Opa Locka Family Mental Health Center, Biscayne Coll., 1976-77, chmn., 1976—; bd. dirs. Children's Psychiatric Center, Inc. of Dade County, Fla., 1976-77, Mental Health Bd., Miami, 1977—. Served with U.S. Army, 1956-59.

Recipient officer of yr. award, Miami Police Dept., 1969, William D. Pawley award, Fraternal Order Police, 1969; named one of eleven outstanding police officers Nat. Internat. Assn. of Police Chiefs and Parade Magazine, 1970; police sci. award nominee, 1976. Mem. Community Police Benevolent Assn. (pres. 1967), Fraternal Order of Police, Internat. Assn. of Police Chiefs, Nat. Assn. Blacks in Criminal Justice (founder Fla. chpt., pres.), Fla. Police Assn., Criminal Justice Educators, Applied Social and Behavioral Scientists, Phi Theta Kappa, NAACP. Democrat. Baptist. Clubs: Elk, Knights Templar, Shriner. Contbr. poem, articles to profl. jours; active in documentary films; selected as 1st Black officer in all white area, to ride motorcycle patrol, and to supervise vice control, internal security, and police tng. unit. Home: 3800 NW 171 Terrace Miami FL 33054

INGRAM, RUPERT JOSEPH, JR., hosp. adminstr.; b. Winona, Miss., Sept. 5, 1945; s. Rupert Joseph and Wilma (Parish) I.; B.B.A., Delta State Coll., 1970; M.S., U. Ark., 1977; m. Carolyn Anne Simpson, July 25, 1965; children—Rupert Joseph, William Bradley, Mary Suzanne. Regional acct. Riverside Chem. Co., Blytheville, Ark., 1970-73; gen. acctg. supr. C-B div. Wayne Corp., Blytheville, 1973; controller Magnolia Hosp., Corinth, Miss., 1973-77; adminstr. Hillcrest Hosp., Calhoun City, Miss., 1977—; dir. Shared Hosp. Services of Miss., Inc.; instr. div. continuing edn. U. Miss., 1979. Served with USMC, 1963-67. Decorated Purple Heart (2). Mem. Hosp. Fin. Mgmt. Assn. Democrat. Baptist. Club: Rotary (dir.). Home: PO Box 168 Calhoun City MS 38916 Office: PO Box 770 Calhoun City MS 38916

INGRAM, SAM HARRIS, state edn. ofcl.; b. Acton, Tenn., Jan. 31, 1928; s. J. Quinn and Lois (Abernathy) I.; student Memphis State Coll., 1947; B.S. in Social Sci., Bethel Coll., McKenzie, Tenn., 1951; M.A., Memphis State Coll., 1953; Ed.D., U. Tenn., Knoxville, 1959; m. Betty White, July 14, 1950; children—Sam W., Glenn D. Prin. pub. elementary, high sch., McNairy County, Tenn., 1949-57; supr. curriculum Tenn. Dept. Edn., 1959-62; asst. prof. edn. Memphis State U., 1962; chmn. dept. edn. Middle Tenn. State U., 1962-67, dean Sch. Edn., 1967-69; pres. Motlow State Community Coll., 1969-75; commr. edn. State of Tenn., 1975—. Trustee Bethel Coll. Served with USMC, 1946-47. Mem. Nat., Tenn. edn. assns., Council Chief State Sch. Officers, Am. Assn. Higher Edn., Tenn. Profs. Edn. Adminstrn. (pres. 1964-65), Tenn. State Curriculum Com. (chmn. 1961-62), Edn. Commn. U.S., Tenn. Assn. Supervision and Curriculum Devel., Phi Delta Kappa. Office: 100 Cordell Hull Bldg Nashville TN 37219*

INGRAM, THOMAS BENJAMIN, constrn. co. exec.; b. Jacksonville, Fla., Feb. 9, 1937; s. Thomas Benjamin and Daisyana (Massey) I.; student Emory U., 1954-56; B.S. in B.A., U. Fla., 1961; children—Thomas Davidson, Michael Elmore. Staff acct. Hall & Fisher, C.P.A., Jacksonville, 1961-65; chief acct. Universal Marion Corp., Jacksonville, 1965-67; controller Unicapital Corp., Jacksonville, 1967-69; treas., dir. Daylight Industries, Jacksonville, 1969-71; sr. v.p., dir. Adcom Metals Co., Jacksonville, 1972-77; v.p. fin. The Haskell Co., Jacksonville, 1977—. Served with USMC, 1956-58. C.P.A., Fla. Mem. C. of C., Fla. Inst. C.P.A.'s. Clubs: The River, Ponte Vedra, Sawgrass. Home: 2415 Costa Verde Blvd Jacksonville Beach FL 32250 Office: The Haskell Co Haskell Bldg Jacksonville FL 32204

INGRAM, WALLACE HARRY, osteo. physician; b. El Paso, Tex., Jan. 10, 1935; s. Wallace Kelly and Leona (Brown) I.; B.S., U. Tex., El Paso, 1959; D.O., Kansas City Coll. Osteo. Medicine, 1963; m. Gretchen Teichgraeber, Nov. 24, 1960; children—Suzanne Allison, Wallace Harry III. Intern, East Town Osteo. Hosp., Dallas, 1963-64; practice osteo. medicine, Dallas, 1964—; asst. prof. family medicine Tex. Coll. Osteopathy and Surgery, 1971-73; staff mem. Garland Meml. Hosp., Garland Community Hosp., 1972—. Served with USAF, 1953-56. Diplomate Am. Coll. Gen. Practice, Am. Bd. Family Practice. Mem. Am. Osteo. Assn., Tex. Osteo. Med. Assn., Dist. V Osteo. Assn., Am. Acad. Family Physicians, Tex. Acad. Family Physicians (exec. com. bd. edn. 1979-83). Episcopalian. Office: 10346 Ferguson Rd Dallas TX 75228

INKS, JAMES MOSS, rancher; b. Llano, Tex., Nov. 9, 1921; s. Roy Banford and Myrtle Louise (Moss) I.; grad. N.Mex. Mil. Inst., 1941; student U. Tex., 1941-42; m. Marie Rushing, Feb. 19, 1966; children—Roy Banford, Suzanne. Commd. lt. comdr. USAF, 1942, advanced through grades to lt. col., 1962; combat pilot World War II, Korea; squad ops. officer, Japan, 1948-50, squad comdr., 1956-59; v.p. Skyknight, Inc., Dallas, 1962-65; owner, mgr. Inks Ranch, Llano, 1966—; owner Inks, Realtor, Llano, 1971-77, Jim Inks, Realtor, 1977—; pres. Legend and Lore Lodge, Inc., Llano, 1972—; owner Flamingo Motel, Lake Buchanan, Tex., 1974-75. Pres., Llano Area Indsl. Found., 1971-79; chmn. Llano County Democratic Del., 1972-73; bd. dirs. Eastern Hill Country Resource Conservation and Devel., 1970-72, Llano County Community Action, 1971-73. Decorated D.F.C., Air medal with seven oak leaf clusters, Purple Heart. Mem. Ind. Cattleman's Assn., Nat., Tex. assns. realtors, Farm Land Inst., Aviation and Space Writers Assn., Nat. Fedn. Ind. Bus., S.W., Tex. cattle raisers assns., Tex. Farm Bur., Hill Country Livestock Raisers Assn. (pres. 1970-71), Exotic Wildlife Assn. (dir. 1974—), Highland Lakes Bd. Realtors (v.p. 1977-79), Llano C. of C. (v.p. 1969-70), Highland Lakes Tourist Assn. (dir. 1975—), Ret. Officers Assn., Air Force Assn., Nat. Assn. Rod and Gun Clubs (pres. 1957-58), Llano Golf Assn. (pres. 1974-75), Highland Lakes Recreation Assn., Packsaddle Golf Assn., N.Mex. Mil. Inst. Alumni Assn. (life), Internat. Platform Assn., Phi Kappa Psi. Presbyterian. Clubs: Lions, Toastmasters (pres. 1958-59), Liberator, Horseshoe Bay Country, St. Anthony, Caterpillar, Tex. 13 (v.p. 1979—). Author: Eight Bailed Out, 1965. Contbr. articles to profl. jours. Home: Box 186 Llano TX 78643 Office: 103 E Main St Llano TX 78643

INTERDONATO, FRANK, synthetic oil co. exec.; b. Newark, Mar. 22, 1942; s. Angelo Frank and Mary Ann (San Giecomo) I.; grad. public schs. With Pathmark Supermarkets, Newark, 1955-67; with Bestline Corp., San Jose, Calif., 1971-73; owner, mgr. Southeastern Products Inc., Tamarac, Fla., 1973—. Served with U.S. Army, 1967-70. Roman Catholic. Address: 6636 NW 57th St 108 Tamarac FL 33319

INTINDOLA, RANDOLPH JOHN, govt. ofcl.; b. Miami, Dec. 16, 1950; s. Gerard and Santina Macaluso I.; student Washburn U., Topeka, 1970-73, Miami-Dade Community Coll., 1969-70, 73-74, Fla. Internat. U., 1973-74; B.A. in Polit. Sci., U. Ark., 1974; postgrad. Ky. State U., 1977-79; m. Nita J. Prescott, May 8, 1973; children—Andria, Randy. Asst. dir. employee relations City of Little Rock, 1975-76; pres. Randolph-Gerard Assos., Inc., 1977-80; dir. mgmt. ops. office Lexington (Ky.) Fayette Urban County Govt., 1980—; cons. Pres. Task Force to Reorganize U.S. Civil Service Commn., 1977. Mem. Internat. City Mgmt. Assn., Internat. Personnel Mgmt. Assn., Am. Soc. Public Adminstrn. (mem. exec. bd.), Nat. Computer Graphics Assn. (state pres.). Democrat. Roman Catholic. Club: K.C. Author: Parks Maintenance Program, 1979. Home: 3380 Boston Rd Lexington KY 40503 Office: 136 Walnut St Lexington KY 40507

IPSEN, KENT FORREST, artist, glassworker; b. Milw., Jan. 4, 1933; s. Victor August and Muriel (White) I.; B.S., U. Wis., 1961, M.S., 1964, M.F.A., 1965; m. Shyla Mae Fischer, Nov. 7, 1957; children—Vicki Lynn, Steven Jay, Lisa Ann, Laura Kay, Nina Beth. Exhibited in group shows Toledo Mus., Mus. Contemporary Crafts, N.Y.C., Smithsonian Instn., Washington, Chicago Art Inst., Scripp's Coll., Ball State U.; represented in permanent collections Milw. Art Center, Chrysler Mus., Norfolk, Va., Bergstrom (Wis.) Art Center, Kohler (Wis.) Art Center, Johnson Wax Co. Craft Collection, Western Mich. State U., Corning Glass Mus., Toledo Mus. Art, Chgo. Art Inst. Asst. prof. glassworking Mankato (Minn.) State Coll., 1965-68; asso. prof. glassworking Chgo. Art Inst., 1969-73; asso. prof. dept. crafts Va. Commonwealth U., Richmond, 1973—. Artist-in-residence Prairie Sch., Racine, Wis., 1971—, No. Ariz. U., 1972. Served with AUS, 1954-56. Nat. Endowment for Arts grantee, 1975. Mem. Am. Craftsmen's Council, Wis. Designer-Craftsmen, Ill. Craft Council (pres. 1970-72), Nat. Council for Edn. in Ceramic Arts, Phi Sigma Epsilon, Presbyn. Home: 11761 Bollingbrook Dr Richmond VA 23235 Office: Va Commonwealth U Richmond VA 23220

IRBY, BOBBY NEWELL, educator; b. Meridian, Miss., Mar. 17, 1932; s. William Ezra and Ada (Smith) I.; A.A., E. Miss. Jr. Coll., 1955; B.A., U. Wash., 1957; M.S., U. Miss., 1962, Ed.D. (NDEA fellow), 1967; m. Lois Pettit, Mar. 15, 1953; 1 dau., Karen Ruth. Tchr. sci. Chamberlain-Hunt Acad., Port Gibson, Miss., 1957-58; tchr., head dept. sci. pub. schs., Clarksdale, Miss., 1959-61, 63-64; instr. chemistry N.E. La. U., Monroe, 1964-65, asst. prof., 1967-69; prof., chmn. dept. sci. edn. U. So. Miss., Hattiesburg, 1969—; pres. Irby, Pettit, Gonnet, Inc. Served with USAF, 1950-53. Fellow Am. Inst. Chemists; mem. Am. Chem. Soc., Nat., Miss. sci. tchrs. assns., AAAS, Miss. Acad. Sci., Phi Delta Kappa. Author: Caves of Mississippi, 1974; Guide to Marine Resources of Mississippi, 1975; contbr. articles to profl. jours. Home: Route 13 Box 812 Lake Serene Hattiesburg MS 39401

IRELAND, ANDREW PAYSELL (ANDY), Congressman; b. Cin., Aug. 23, 1930; s. Ellsworth Frederick and Dorothy Marie (Poysell) I.; B.S. in Indsl. Adminstrn., Yale Sch. Engring. 1952; grad. La. State U. Sch. Banking of the S., 1959; m. Diana Elmes, June 13, 1953; children—Debbie, Mimi, Drew, Dutch. Former chmn. bd. Barnett Bank of Winter Haven, Cypress Gardens, Auburndale, Fla.; former trustee Fla. Bankers Assn. Ins. Trust, former treas. Fla. Bankers Assn.; former dir. Jacksonville (Fla.) br. Fed. Res. Bank Atlanta; program chmn. several Fla. Bankers Assn. Forums in field of edn.; former Fla. state v.p. Am. Bankers Assn.; mem. 95th-96th Congresses from 8th Fla. Dist. Former mem. admissions com. Sch. Banking of South, La. State U.; mem. Winter Haven City Commn., 1966-68; mem. Polk County Democratic Exec. Com. Mem. Winter Haven Area C. of C. (past pres.). Episcopalian. Clubs: Masons; Shriners; Jesters; Elks; Kiwanis; Moose; Florida; Orangebelt Touchdown; Winter Haven High Sch. Boosters. Office: 115 Longworth House Office Bldg Washington DC 20515*

IRELAND, EVELYN F., state ofcl.; b. Shattuck, Okla., Nov. 20, 1949; d. Carl A. and Eva B. (Chace) Meeks; B.F.A., Tex. Tech. U., 1972; M.P.A., U. Tex., 1976; 1 son, David Austin Hacker. Illustrator, Dept. Biology, Tex. Tech. U., Lubbock, 1969-72; adminstrv. asst. Tex. Ho. of Reps., Austin, 1972-74; legis. intern U.S. Senator Lloyd Bentsen, Washington, 1975; research asst. Mass. Gen. Ct., 1975; govt. liaison coordinator Tex. State Bd. Ins., Austin, 1976, asst. to dep. commr. for research and compliance, 1977-78, acting dir. research and compliance, 1979—; lectr. in field. Mem. Nat. Assn. Ins. Commrs. task force on A & H ins. discrimination, 1977-79; del. Dem. County Conv., 1976; precinct coordinator Bentsen in '76 campaign. Sears Roebuck Found. scholar, 1968-69; Harvard U. Tuition grantee, 1975; Lyndon B. Johnson Sch. Public Affairs fellow, 1974-76. Mem. Tex. Women's Polit. Caucus (membership chmn. 1978-79, chairperson 1979-80), Austin Women's Polit. Caucus (vice chmn. 1973-74, 78-79), Nat. Assn. Female Execs., LBJ Sch. Alumnae Assn., Smithsonian Asso., Nat. Women's Polit. Caucus (steering com. 1979-80), Women's Equity Action League, Phi Kappa Phi, Alpha Lambda Delta. Contbr. articles to profl. jours. Home: 5007 Westview Dr Austin TX 78731 Office: 1110 San Jacinto St Austin TX 78786

IRISH, WILFRED ERNEST, bank holding co. exec.; b. Niagara Falls, N.Y., Jan. 21, 1923; s. Wilfred Ernest and Mary Genevieve (Tyson) I.; B.S., Niagara U., 1949; M.S., Stetson U., 1961; A.M.P., Harvard U., 1973; m. Vera Katherine Schmitz, Nov. 9, 1947; children—Kathryn, Jennifer, Bud, Laura, Kurt. Enlisted in U.S. Army, 1943, advanced through grades to col., 1969; mem. grad. faculty Army Command and Gen. Staff Coll., 1962-65; v.p., dir. personnel Deposit Guaranty Nat. Bank, Jackson, Miss., 1976-78; v.p., acting chief operating officer Deposit Guaranty Services Co. subs. Deposit Guaranty Corp., Jackson, 1978—; chmn. mil. sci. dept. U. So. Miss., 1974-76. Mem. Republican Nat. Com., 1978-79; chmn. United Fund drive, 1977-78; troop sponsor Boy Scouts Am., 1969-71. Decorated Legion of Merit (2), Bronze Star (2), Purple Heart. Mem. Am. Soc. Personal Adminstrn., Nat. Adv. Bd. of Am. Security Council, Assn. U.S. Army. Republican. Presbyterian. Clubs: Optimist (chmn. fund raising com. 1978), Masons. Home: 4631 Hickory Ridge Rd Jackson MS 39211 Office: One Deposit Guaranty Plaza Jackson MS 39201

IRIZARRY, GUILLERMO, cons. pub. adminstrn. and estate planning, agronomist; b. Mayaguez, P.R., Apr. 12, 1916; s. Jose Irizarry-Cruz and Candida Rubio-Hernandez; B.S. in Agr., U. P.R., 1939; M.S. in Econs., La. State U., 1950; m. Carmen E. Ramirez, Oct. 14, 1942; children—Carmen E., Margarita R. Mem. research staff dept. agronomy Tobacco Inst. P.R., Rio Piedras, 1939-43; contact officer VA, San Juan, P.R., 1946-49; mktg. specialist P.R. Dept. Agr., 1950-53, budget technician, 1953-57, exec. sec., 1957-60; dir. P.R. Bur. of the Budget, 1960-66, sec. of state, 1966-69; acting gov. Commonwealth of P.R., 1967-69; spl. asst. to exec. dir. of P.R. Aqueduct and Sewage Authority, 1969-71; mem. Council on Higher Edn., U. P.R., Rio Piedras, 1973—, pres., 1973-75; cons. on pub. adminstrn.; dir. Mining Resources Devel. Corp., 1975—. Mem. Consulting Citizens Com., Planning Bd. of P.R., 1975-77; mem. governing bd. A.G. Mendez Found., 1972—, v.p. Served with inf., U.S. Army, 1943-46. Mem. Coll. of Agronomy of P.R., Phi Beta Kappa, Gamma Sigma Delta. Roman Catholic. Clubs: Lions (pres. 1973-74, dep. gov. 1976-77, dist. gov. 1979-80). Contbr. articles on agriculture and pub. adminstrn. to profl. publs. Home: 207 Rossy St Hato Rey PR 00918

IRLINGER, FRANK SERAPH, engr.; b. N.Y.C., Dec. 11, 1929; s. Franz and Josephine (Knott) I.; Asso. in Applied Sci., Pratt Inst., 1960; B.S. in Engring., Cooper Union Sch. Engring and Sci., 1967; M.B.A. magna cum laude, Middle Tenn. State U., 1972; J.D., Nashville YMCA Night Law sch., 1979; m. Elsie Munster, Dec. 28, 1951; children—Frank Ernest, Ronald Walter. Machine devel. engr. Automotive Products div. Scovill-Schrader, N.Y.C., 1957-67, machine devel. mgr., Dickson, Tenn., 1967-68, engring. mgr. research and devel., 1968—. Mem. adv. com. mech. engring. tech. Nashville State Tech. Inst. Served with AUS, 1951-53. Registered profl. engr., Tenn.; certified mfg. engr. Mem. Pi Tau Sigma, Delta Mu Delta, Soc. Automotive Engrs., Nat. Soc. Profl. Engrs., Am. Soc. M.E. (chmn. Nashville sect. 1972-73), Nat. Mgmt. Assn. (pres. Schrader chpt. 1972, Outstanding Service award 1972), Am. Alpine Club, Sierra Club. Contbr. articles to profl. jours. Home: 6805 Alto Vista Dr Nashville TN 37205 Office: PO Box 586 Dickson TN 37055

IRVINE, JACQUELINE JORDAN, educator; b. Ft. Benning, Ga., July 2, 1947; d. Eddie Walter and Sarah Louise (Harris) Jordan; B.A., Howard U., 1968, M.A., 1970; Ph.D., Ga. State U., 1979; m. Russell William Irvine, Nov. 29, 1969; 1 dau., Kelli Simone. Asst. to dean, asst. dir., counselor Cleve. State U., 1970-74; research asso. So. Regional Edn. Bd., Atlanta, 1974-76, Ga. State U., Atlanta, 1976-78, asst. prof., 1979; asst. prof. Div. Ednl. Studies, Emory U., Atlanta, 1979—; cons. Delta Sigma Theta, 1978-79, Office of Edn., 1976-77, GSA, 1977. Vice pres. Spring Valley Civic Assn., 1975-76; mem. S. DeKalb County Coalition, 1975—, Atlanta Urban League, 1978—. Howard U. fellow, 1968-70; Urban Life Center grantee, 1977-78; Women's Ednl. Equity grantee, 1976-78. Mem. Am. Personnel and Guidance Assn. (senator 1976-79), Am. Coll. Personnel Assn. (exec. council 1976-79), Am. Assn. Sch. Adminstrs., Phi Delta Kappa. Contbr. articles to profl. jours. Home: 3557 Springside Dr Decatur GA 30032 Office: Div Ednl Studies Emory Univ Atlanta GA 30322

IRVINE, JOEL REYNOLDS, sales exec.; b. Hartford, Conn., Mar. 8, 1946; s. Lawrence Lee and Virginia Pauline (Mascolo) I.; ed. Hartford State Inst. Tech., 1965, U. Conn., 1966-68; m. Eva Rozalia Daum, Nov. 18, 1971. Project engr. Henry So. Engring., Hartford, 1968-70; plant engr. Plasticrete Corp., Newington, Conn., 1970-71; with Solite Corp., Richmond, Va., 1971—, div. sales mgr., Hubers, Ky., 1978—; mem. exec. bd. Kentuckiana Masonry Council, 1981; instr. U. Ky. Certification Sch. Concrete Tech., 1978-80; chmn. New Eng. energy code com. New Eng. Concrete Masonry Assn., 1975-76. Mem. Am. Concrete Inst., Constrn. Specification Inst., Ohio Concrete Masonry Assn., Ind. Concrete Masonry, Ky. Ready Mix Concrete Assn. (dir.), Sigma Alpha Epsilon. Clubs: L & N Golf, Moose. Home: 2311 Old Mill Stream Ln Shepherdsville KY 40165 Office: PO Box 38 Brooks KY 40109

IRVINS, BOBBIE ANN, educator; b. Atlanta, Mar. 8, 1939; d. Horace Lewis and Lutcher Frances (Arnold) Irvins; B.A., Spelman Coll., 1960; M.S., N.Y. State U., 1968; Ed.D., U. Ky., 1973. Tchr., Atlanta Public Schs., 1960-66; counselor Wis. State U., Eau Claire, 1967-68, Prairie View (Tex.) U., 1968-69, Ark. A. M. & N., Pine Bluff, 1969-70; teaching asst. U. Ky., Lexington, 1970-73; dir. counseling and testing services/asso. prof. edn. U. Ark., Pine Bluff, 1973—; cons. Student Services Inst., Atlanta, 1972—; mem. Ark. Bd. Examiners in Counseling, 1979—. Recipient cert. of Appreciation, S.E. Ark. Area Agy. on Aging, 1978. Mem. Am. Personnel and Guidance Assn., Nat. Assn. Coll. and Univ. Counseling Center Dirs., Am. Coll. Personnel Assn., Assn. Black Psychologists. Office: PO Box 152 U of Ark Pine Bluff AR 71601

IRWIN, DAURICE JUNE, educator; b. Laneville, Tex., Aug. 4, 1925; B.S., Stephen F. Austin State U., 1946; M.A., Tex. Woman's U., 1949; D.P.Ed., Ind. U., 1958. Instr. phys. edn., Tenaha, Tex., 1944-45, Nacogdoches, Tex., 1945-46, Joinerville, Tex., 1946-47; instr. health and phys. edn. Stephen F. Austin Coll., Nacogdoches, Tex., 1947-54, asst. prof. health, phys. edn. and recreation, 1955-58, dean women, 1958, asso. prof. health, phys. edn. and recreation, 1958-67, prof., 1967-69, prof., head dept. health and phys. edn. for women, 1969-74, prof., head health and phys. edn. div. for women, 1975—; grad. asst. Ind. U., Bloomington, 1954-55. Bd. dirs. Nacogdoches County unit Am. Cancer Soc. Recipient Alumni Disting. Prof. award Stephen F. Austin U., 1974. Fellow AAHPER; mem. NEA, AAUW (pres. 1961-63), Nat. Assn. Phys. Edn. for Coll. Women, So. Assn. Health, Phys. Edn. and Recreation, Tex. Assn. Health, Phys. Edn. and Recreation (honor award 1970), So. Assn. Phys. Edn. Coll. Women, Tex. State Tchrs. Assn., Tex. Safety Assn. (pres. 1953), Tex. Assn. Coll. Tchrs., Stephen F. Austin U. Alumni Assn. (life), Phi Delta Kappa, Kappa Delta Pi, Delta Psi Kappa. Baptist. Home: 123 Lloyd St Nacogdoches TX 75961 Office: Box 3016 Nacogdoches TX 75962

IRWIN, JAMES CURTIS, utility co. engr.; b. Jacksonville, Tex., Jan. 19, 1949; s. James C. and Vivian Mary (Clements) I.; A.A., Tyler Jr. Coll., 1969; B.S. in Mech. Engring., U. Tex., Arlington, 1972; 1 dau., Lisa Vivian. Student engr. So. Union Gas Co., Dallas, 1970, transmission engr., 1973-74, dist. engr., 1974-77, sr. staff engr., 1977—; pvt. practice engring., Arlington, 1970-71. Campaign mgr. United Way, 1976; counselor Jr. Achievement. Mem. Nat. Assn. Corrosion Engrs. Republican. Baptist. Program com. co-chmn. measurement short course; contbr. article to profl. publ. Office: Southern Union Co First International Bldg Dallas TX 75270

IRWIN, PAT, chief justice Okla. Supreme Ct.; b. Leedey, Okla., June 12, 1921; s. Marvin J. and Ollie D. (Newton) I.; student Southwestern State Coll., 1939-41; LL.B., U. Okla., 1949; m. Margaret Boggs, Aug. 18, 1950; children—William, Margaret. Admitted to Okla. bar, 1949; county atty., Dewey County, 1949-50; pvt. practice law, 1950-58; sec. to commrs. land office State Sch. Land Commn., State Okla., 1955-58; justice State Supreme Ct. Okla., 1959—, chief justice, 1969-70. Mem. Okla. State Senate, 1950-54. Served as capt. USMC, 1942-46; PTO. Mem. Am. Legion, Delta Theta Phi. Democrat. Mason. Home: 1325 Andover Ct Oklahoma City OK 73120 Office: State Capitol Bldg Oklahoma City OK 73105

ISAAC, JOSEPH WILLIAM ALEXANDER, gynecologist; b. Antigua, W.I.; B.S., CUNY, 1967; M.D., Howard U., 1971. Intern, Howard U., Washington, 1971-72, resident in Ob-Gyn, 1972-76; practice Ob-Gyn, Norfolk and Portsmouth, Va., 1976—; family planning physician Norfolk Health Dept., 1976-77; mem. staff Portsmouth Gen. Hosp., Maryview Hosp., Portsmouth, Norfolk Community Hosp., Med. Center Hosp., Norfolk. Mem. med. adv. com. Tidewater March of Dimes. Served with AUS, 1959-62. Diplomate Am. Bd. Ob-Gyn. Fellow Am. Coll. Obstetricians and Gynecologists; mem. AMA, Va. Med. Soc., Norfolk Med. Soc., Norfolk Acad. Medicine, Portsmouth C. of C. Office: 549 E Brambleton Ave Norfolk VA 23510 also 2221 High St Portsmouth VA 23704

ISAAC, ROBERT EDWARD, mcht.; b. Appalachia, Va., Mar. 31, 1930; s. Dave Elias and Julia (Tamer) I.; student Va. Poly. Inst. and State U., 1950-54; m. Dorothy Ann Skorupa, June 18, 1958; children—Kimberly Marie, Robert Edward, Michael Kevin. Operator clothing store, Norton, Va., 1957-64; owner Dave's Dept. Store, Norton, 1964—; dir. Wise County Nat. Bank. Pres., Greater Norton, Inc., 1962; mem. fair com. Va. Ky. Dist. Fair, 1968—; vice chmn. Norton City Planning Commn., 1976—; mem. Norton Sch. Bd., 1977—; v.p. Wise County-City of Norton YMCA. Served with USAF, 1954-56. Mem. Wise County C. of C. (pres. 1969-70, dir.). Clubs: Lonesome Pine Country (dir.), Norton Kiwanis (dir., past pres.). Home and Office: PO Box 468 Norton VA 24273

ISAAC, WALTER, psychologist; b. Cleve., June 13, 1927; s. Walter Roy and Irene (Pillars) I.; B.S., Western Res. U., 1949; M.A., Ohio State U., 1950, Ph.D., 1953; m. Dorothy Jane Emerson, Oct. 14, 1949; children—Susan Irene, Walter Lon. Predoctoral fellow USAF, Sch. Aviation Medicine, Austin, Tex., 1953; research instr. Sch. Medicine, U. Wash., Seattle, 1954-56; asst. research psychologist Sch. Medicine, UCLA, 1956-57; asst. prof. psychology Emory U., Atlanta, 1957-60, asso. prof., 1960-65, prof., 1965-68; prof. psychology U. Ga., Athens, 1968—. Served with USNR, 1945-46. Fellow AAAS; mem. Psychonomic Soc., Am. Assn. Lab. Animal Sci., Nat. Acad. Neuropsychologists, Soc. Behavioral Medicine, Southeastern Psychol. Assn., So. Soc. Philosophy and Psychology. Home: 180 Chinquapin Way Athens GA 30605 Office: Dept Psychology U Ga Athens GA 30602

ISAACS, FREDERICK WILSON, JR., athletic goods co. exec.; b. Durham, N.C., Aug. 29, 1926; s. Fred Wilson and Catharine Inez (Watkins) I.; student Princeton U., 1943; B.S., Wake Forest U., 1950; M.A., Columbia U., 1952; m. Edith Cornelia Rawls, Jan. 28, 1950; children—Cornelia Rawls, Catharine Merritt, Josephine Rowlette, Marianna Watkins, Margaret Inez. Athletic dir., head football coach Virginia Beach (Va.) City Schs., 1950-57; pres. Coaches Sporting Goods, Virginia Beach, 1957-61; pres. All Sports, Inc., Norfolk, Va., 1961-66; pres. So. Athletic, Inc., Knoxville, Tenn., 1966-75, chmn. bd. dirs. Colgate-Palmolive Sports div., Knoxville, 1976-77; pres. Athletic Goods Assos., Inc., Cosby, Tenn., 1978—; dir. Wildwood Acres Devel. Corp., Holiday Ventures of Fla., Inc. Bd. dirs. United Way, Great Smoky Mountain council Boy Scouts Am., Knoxville Boys Club, Knoxville Tourist Bur., Travelers Aid Soc., Knoxville YMCA, Newport Rescue Squad, Va. All Star Football Found. Served with USNR, USMCR, 1943-46. Mem. Sporting Goods Mfrs. Assn., Nat. Sporting Goods Assn., Internat. Entrepreneurs Assn., Athletic Inst., Sports Found. Inc., Am. Football Found., SAR. Republican. Southern Baptist. Clubs: Smoky Mountain Country, Knights of the Garter, Plantagenet Soc., Order of Washington, Barons of Magna Charta, Masons, Shriners. Home: Old English Mountain Rd Cosby TN 37722 Office: PO Box 666 Cosby TN 37722

ISABEL, ROY JAMES, chemist; b. Memphis, Mar. 8, 1939; s. James Henry and Dorothy Marie (Robinson) I.; B.S., Tenn. A&I State U., 1964; Ph.D., Howard U., 1969; m. Frances Tomaseena Baxter, Aug. 14, 1965; children—Mark Jefferson, Lesley Anita. Grad. research asso. Howard U., 1964-69; postdoctoral research asso. Drexel U., Phila., 1969-71; mem. faculty S.C. State Coll., Orangeburg, 1971—, asso. prof. chemistry, 1978—, Percy Julian disting. prof., 1976—. Recipient DuPont Outstanding Teaching award Howard U., 1967-68. Mem. Am. Chem. Soc., Am. Inst. Chemists, Danforth Found. Assos., Jack and Jill (chpt. editor 1977—), Phi Delta Kappa, Omega Psi Phi. Methodist. Author papers in field. Home: PO Box 1974 SC State Coll Orangeburg SC 29117 Office: Dept Natural Scis SC State Coll Orangeburg SC 29117

ISADA, RODRIGO TUANTE, physician; b. Philippines, Apr. 8, 1938; came to U.S., 1965, naturalized, 1975; s. Luis E. and Dominga T. (Tuante) I.; M.D., U. Santo Tomas, Manila, 1964; m. Amelia V., June 6, 1965; children—Marie Louise, Karen Ann. Med. intern Paterson (N.J.) Gen. Hosp., 1965-66; surg. resident Newark City Hosp., Jersey City, 1966-69; surg. house staff Irvington (N.J.) Gen. Hosp., 1971; emergency room physician Clinch Valley Clinic Hosp., Richlands, Va., 1972-73; family practice medicine, Saltville, Va., 1974—, provider free clinic and medicine migrant workers; sec. med. staff T.K. McKee Hosp. Active spl. ministry St. John Roman Cath. Ch., Marion, Va. Diplomate Am. Bd. Family Practice. Fellow Am. Acad. Family Physicians; mem. Va. Acad. Family Physicians, Tazewell County Med. Soc., Sinyth County Med. Soc., Med. Soc. Va., S.W. Va. Assn. Philippine Physicians (pres.), Va. Assn. Philippine Physicians (regional v.p.), Saltville C. of C. Clubs: Saltville Rich Valley Lions (pres.). Address: PO Box 627 Saltville VA 24370

ISBELL, EUCLID ARNOLD, JR., physician; b. Gadsden, Ala., Feb. 29, 1936; s. Euclid Arnold and Wilma (Gipson) I.; B.A., Vanderbilt U., 1958; M.D., Tulane U., 1963. Intern, Charity Hosp., New Orleans, 1963-64; resident in gen. surgery So. Pacific Hosp., 1964-65; resident in otolaryngology U.S. Naval Hosp., Phila., 1965-68; practice medicine specializing in otolaryngology, Gadsden, Ala., 1971-78, Bessemer, Ala., 1979—; mem. staff Bessemer Carraway Hosp., Brookwood and Eye Found. hosps., Birmingham, Ala., Shelby Meml. Hosp., Alabaster, Ala.; cons. Noble Army Hosp., Ft. McClellan, Ala. Served to lt. comdr. USNR, 1965-71; Vietnam. Diplomate Am. Bd. Otolaryngology. Mem. Am. Acad. Ophthalmology and Otolaryngology, ACS, Internat. Coll. Surgeons, Am. Soc. Ophthalmologic and Otolaryngologic Allergy, Mensa. Republican. Baptist. Home: 2925 MacAlpine Birmingham AL 35243 Office: 800 Memorial Dr Bessemer AL 35020

ISBELL, JIMMY EUGENE, pediatrician; b. Cedartown, Ga., Oct. 29, 1947; s. Herman Eugene and Magdalene Elizabeth (Heath) I.; B.S., U. Ala., 1968, M.D., 1972; m. Patricia Ann Lewis, May 8, 1971; children—Deanna Carol, Virginia Elizabeth. Intern, Children's Hosp., Birmingham, Ala., 1972-73, resident, 1973-75; practice medicine specializing in pediatrics, Meridian, Miss., 1975—; mem. staff Rush Found. Hosp., Anderson's Hosp., Riley's Hosp.; pediatrician Rush Med. Group P.A., Meridian. Diplomate Am. Bd. Pediatrics. Fellow Am. Acad. Pediatrics; mem. AMA (Physicians Recognition award), Miss. Med. Assn., E. Miss. Med. Assn., Phi Beta Kappa, Phi Eta Sigma. Baptist. Home: 1024 S Hillview Dr Meridian MS 39301 Office: 1314 19th Ave Meridian MS 39301

ISBELL, LINDA JOAN, educator; b. Winchester, Tenn., Sept. 6, 1947; d. Joe Lawton and Maggie Lee (Holder) I.; B.S. in Elem. Edn., David Lipscomb Coll., Nashville, 1969; M.Ed. in Guidance and Counseling, Middle Tenn. State U., 1977. Tchr. schs. in Tex. and Tenn., 1969-78; tchr. 4th grade Madison Acad., Huntsville, Ala., 1979—; tchr. basic adult edn., Winchester, Tenn., 1977-78. Mem. Am. Personnel and Guidance Assn., Ala. Personnel and Guidance Assn. Mem. Ch. of Christ. Home: 1505 Sparkman Dr Apt 302 Huntsville AL 35806 Office: 301 Max Luther Dr Huntsville AL 35806

ISBELL, TERRY ROBERTS, furniture co. exec.; b. Hopkinsville, Ky., Jan. 1, 1946; s. Stanley Larmon and Rosa Merritt (Head) I.; B.S., Western Ky. U., 1968, M.B.A., 1977; J.D., Woodrow Wilson Coll. Law, Atlanta, 1979; m. Carol Ann Kozlowski, July 5, 1969; children—Kimberly Ann, Christopher Michael. Personnel mgr. prodn. scheduling mgr. Findlay Refractories div. Glasrock Products, Inc., Washington, Pa., 1971-73, mgr. adminstrv. services corp. office, Atlanta, 1973-74; dir. personnel Haverty Furniture Cos., Inc., Atlanta, 1974—; employee relations com. Am. Retail Fedn. Served with USN, 1968-69. Mem. Am. Soc. Personnel Adminstrn., Risk and Ins. Mgmt. Soc. Methodist. Home: 3786 Canvasback Ct Marietta GA 30062 Office: 866 W Peachtree St NW Atlanta GA 30308

ISHIKAWA, YOSHINORI, biochemist; b. Shari, Hokkaido, Japan, Feb. 28, 1928; came to U.S., 1966; s. Koji and Isa I.; B.S. in Agrl. Chemistry, Hokkaido U., 1951, Ph.D. in Biochemistry (Rockefeller Found. fellow), 1961; postgrad. Osaka (Japan) U., 1952-53; m. Toyoko Nakaya, Dec. 15, 1958; 1 son, Tomonori. Asst., Hokkaido U., 1954-64, lectr., 1964-66; research asso. U. Vt., 1966-76, instr., 1968-74; research asst. prof. chemistry U. S.C., 1976—; tech. cons. Nippon Yoshu Co. Ltd. Japan. NIH grantee, 1968—; Vt. Rheumatic Disease Found. grantee, 1976. Mem. Agrl. Chem. Soc. Japan, Japanese Biochem. Soc., Am. Chem. Soc., Am. Soc. Biol. Chemists, AAAS, N.Y. Acad. Sci., S.C. Acad. Sci., Sigma Xi. Buddhist. Contbr. numerous articles to profl. jours. Home: 312 Hearthstone Rd Columbia SC 29210 Office: Chemistry Dept U SC Columbia SC 29208

ISON, GERTRUDE SUTTON, educator; b. Vest, Ky., Apr. 21, 1913; d. Joseph David and Sarah (Coburn) Sutton; A.B., Morehead State U., 1943; M.S., U. Ky., 1965; m. Lovell Ison, Apr. 14, 1934; children—Virchel, Lowell, Evelyn (Mrs. Orville J. Doyle), Clinton. Tchr. Knott County Grade Sch., Hindman, Ky., 1932-44, Knott County High Sch., Hindman, 1944-58; mem. faculty Pikeville Coll., 1958—, chmn. math. dept., 1970-77, dir. workshops for modern math. Treas. Opportunity Workshop, 1971-72. Recipient Community Leader of Am. award, 1969. Mem. A.A.U.W. (treas. 1970-76, br. pres. 1976—), A.A.U.P. (treas. 1972-75, sec. 1975—), Pi Mu Epsilon, Delta Kappa Gamma. Democrat. Presbyn. Mem. Order Eastern Star. Author: Modern Elementary Math; Modern Mathematics for Elementary Teachers, 1976. Home: 116 Poplar St Pikeville KY 41501 Office: Pikeville Coll Pikeville KY 41501

ISRAILI, ZAFAR HASAN, medicinal chemist, clin. pharmacologist; b. Moradabad, July 2, 1934; s. Siddiq H. and Zahida I.; came to U.S., 1961, naturalized, 1977; B.Sc., Aligarh M. U. (India), 1951, M.Sc. (Merit scholar 1951-53), 1953; Ph.D., U. Kans., 1968; m. Sally Jean Smith, Oct. 24, 1970; children—Shahnaz Joy, Taj Hasan, Rana Shereen. Lectr. Aligarh M. U., 1953-54; sr. research scholar, 1954-57; research asst., jr. sci. officer AEC India, 1957-61; research asso. U. Kans., 1968-69; sr. research chemist Alza Corp., Lawrence, Kans., 1969-70; asst. prof. medicine (clin. pharmacology) and chemistry Emory U., Atlanta, 1970-75, asso. prof. medicine, 1975-80, prof., 1980 asso. prof. chemistry, 1974-78, prof., 1978—; mem. sci. staff Grady Hosp.; research pharmacologist Atlanta VA Med. Center, 1979—. Recipient Asian Found. award, 1962; Merck Co. grantee, 1977; NIH grantee, 1978-82; VA grantee, 1979-82. Mem. Am. Soc. Clin. Pharmacology and Therapeutics, Am. Soc. Pharmacology and Exptl. Therapeutics, Soc. Exptl. Biology and Medicine, Am. Assn. Cancer Research, Am. Chem. Soc., Chem. Soc. London, Am. Aging Assn., Sigma Xi, Phi Lambda Upsilon, Rho Chi. Moslem. Contbr. numerous articles to profl. jours. Asso. editor Drug Metabolism Revs., 1974—. Home: 3567 Cloudland Dr Stone Mountain GA 30083 Office: Med Research Atlanta VA Hosp 1670 Clairmont Rd Decatur GA 30303

IVANS, GALEN JOHN DAVID, plastics engr.; b. Urbana, Ind., Aug. 11, 1914; s. Fred and Ruth (Krom) I.; student Mass. Inst. Tech., 1955, U. Chgo., 1962; m. Ruth Mingonne Moon, May 8, 1937; children—Sally Susan, Crosby, John David. Tool and die apprentice Delta Electric Co., Marion, Ind., 1935-39; with Allison Engring., Indpls. 1939-41, Delta Electric Co., Marion, 1941-50, Hagen Mfg. Co., Fairmount, Ind., 1950-52; supt. Alloy Products Co., Marion, 1952-54; supt. Twigg Industries Brazil, Ind., 1953-56; with Tarzian Inc., Bloomington, Ind., 1956-68, engring. mgr., 1968; process mgr. Ocalla Precision Co., Dunnellon, Fla., 1968-69; design engring. coordinator Massie Tool & Mold Inc., St. Petersburg, Fla., 1969—. Bd. dirs. Girl Scouts U.S.A.; leader Boy Scouts Am.; mgr. Little League. Mem. Soc. Plastics Engrs. Republican. Clubs: Country, East Bay Country, Elks, Moose. Patentee in assembly, TV tuners and cartridge. Address: 2000 Main St 511 Dunedin FL 33528

IVER, WILLIAM HENRY, dentist; b. Port Chester, N.Y., June 22, 1917; s. Alex R. and Beulah (Levy) E.; student U. Wis., 1936-38; D.D.S. cum laude, Georgetown U., 1942; m. Shirley Kaplan, Nov. 13, 1977; children—Robert Drew, Randolph. Pvt. practice dentistry, Miami Beach, Fla., 1945—; dir. Lincoln Small Bus. Investment Corp., Ka-Line Mfg. div. Sun Engring. Corp. Served to lt. comdr. USNR, 1942-45. Mem. ADA, Fla., East Coast, Miami Beach dental assns. Clubs: Cricket, Jockey, Carriage. Home: Charter Club Miami FL Office: 605 Lincoln Rd Miami Beach FL 33139

IVES, JOHN ELWAY, hosp. adminstr.; b. Hartford, Conn., Oct. 21, 1929; s. Louis King and Marcella (Elway) I.; A.B., Dartmouth Coll., 1951; M.S., Yale U., 1956; m. Elizabeth Ann Poindexter, June 23, 1951; 1 son, Ralph. Asst. dir. Yale New Haven Hosp., 1955-65; asst. to dean Yale U. Sch. Medicine, New Haven, 1963-65; adminstr. Middlesex Meml. Hosp., Middletown, Conn., 1965-66; hosp. dir. U. Conn. Health Center, Farmington, 1966-77; exec. dir. Shands Teaching Hosp., U. Fla., Gainesville, 1977—, affiliate prof. health and hosp. adminstrn., 1977—. Served with U.S. Army, 1951-53. Mem. Soc. Health Service Adminstrs., Am. Hosp. Assn. Clubs: Gainesville Golf and Country, Hartford Golf. Home: 5723 SW 36th Way Gainesville FL 32601 Office: Box J-326 Gainesville FL 32610

IVESTER, JULIUS RAY, anesthesiologist; b. Walhalla, S.C., Aug. 12, 1924; s. John C. and Thelma M. (Smith) I.; B.S., Clemson U., 1949; M.D., Med. U. S.C., 1953; m. Mary Elizabeth Elrod, May 26, 1946; children—M. Susan, Julius Ray, Laurie, A.D. Sonde. Intern, Roper Hosp., Charleston, S.C., 1953-54; resident Med. Center Hosps., Charleston, 19S4-56; practice medicine specializing in anesthesiology, Charleston, 1956—; mem. staff Roper Hosp., 1956—, dir. and chmn. dept. anesthesiology, 1965—, also vice chmn. bd. commrs. mem. staff St. Francis Xavier Hosp; cons. in anesthesiology VA Hosp.; asso. clin. prof. anesthesiology Med. U. S.C., Charleston; pres. Anesthesia Assos., P.A. Served in U.S. Army, 1943-46. Diplomate Am. Bd. Anesthesiology. Fellow Am. Coll. Anesthesiologists; mem. AMA, Am. Soc. Anesthesiologists, S.C. Med. Assn., S.C. Soc. Anesthesiologists (past pres.), So. Med. Assn. Lutheran. Clubs: Sertoma (past pres.), Country (Charleston). Home: 19 Guerard Rd Charleston SC 29407 Office: 154 Wentworth St Charleston SC 29401

IVEY, EVA NEVELS, mfg. co. exec.; b. Erwinville, La., Dec. 26, 1939; d. Marlin Martin and Ruth Leona (Edwards) Nevels; student U. Ala., 1976; m. Richard L. Ivey, Apr. 1, 1959; children—Ronald S., Jodi Layne. Personnel sec., statistician Ga. Pacific Corp., Gloster, Miss., 1967-76, asst. personnel mgr., 1976-77, personnel mgr., 1977—. Mem. exec. com. Amite County Democratic party, 1976—. Mem. Am. Mgmt. Assn., Gloster C. of C. (sec. 1978-79). Club: Pine Hills Country. Home: 1150 West St Gloster MS 39638 Office: Georgia Pacific Corp Frank Schuh Dr Gloster MS 39638

IVEY, PARA LEE SMITH, nurse; b. Tallahassee, July 25, 1943; d. William M. and Pearlie F. Smith; asso. degree in nursing Miami Dade Community Coll., 1968; B.S. in Nursing, Fla. Internat. U., 1974; m. Lucious Ivey, Feb. 26, 1966; 1 son, Victor. Staff nurse Jackson Meml. Hosp., Miami, Fla., 1969, asso. head nurse, 1969-72, head nurse, 1972-74, instr. med./surg. nursing, 1974-77; dir. nursing Christian Hosp., Miami, 1977-78; nurse counselor Hialeah (Fla.) Hosp., 1978—. Registered nurse, Fla. Mem. Black Profl. Nurses Assn. Clubs: Suburbanites Social and Civic, Order of Eastern Star. Home: 2200 NW 107th St Miami FL 33167 Office: Hialeah Hosp 651 E 25th St Hialeah FL 33013

IVEY, SARA ANNE (LEE), editor, pub.; b. Atlanta, Mar. 20, 1936; d. Hubert Floyd and Margaret Emry (Morris) Lee; student public schs., Ga.; m. William F. Ivey, Dec. 14, 1968; children—Alecia Lee Cash, Tresia Anne Ivey. Sec., bookkeeper MKD Industries, Decatur, Ga., 1974-76; bookkeeper Decatur Clinic, 1976-77; sec. Morgan Equipment Co., Decatur, 1977-78; editor, pub. Dixie Bus. Mag., Decatur, 1978—. Pres., Midway Manor Community Orgn., Decatur, 1979—. Named hon. Ky. col. Presbyterian. Clubs: Atlanta Advt., Colony Sq. Bus. and Profl. Women's, Atlanta Press. Office: 4592 Covington Rd Decatur GA 30035

IVEY, TIM WILLARD, computer co. exec.; b. Wilmington, N.C., Sept. 18, 1942; s. Jason Woodrow and Estelle (Smith) I.; B.S., Fla. State U., 1969, M.B.A., 1970; m. Gretchen Bartlett Walter, June 16, 1962; 1 son, Robb Bartlett. Fin. statements analyst Gen. Electric Co., Daytona Beach, Fla., 1970-71; systems engr. Electronic Data Systems, Dallas, 1971-73; mgr. systems and programming Fed. Land Bank/Fed. Intermediate Credit Bank of Columbia (S.C.), 1973-79; pres. Computer Systems Architects, 1979—; cons. data processing. Scoutmaster Boy Scouts Am., 1973-77. Served with USMC, 1960-61. Mem. M.B.A. Assn. Republican. Home: 119 Chillingham St Irmo SC 29063 Office: 1136 Washington St Suite 40 Columbia SC 29201

IYENGAR, KRISHNA PRAKASH RANGANATHAN, nuclear engr.; b. Bombay, India, Aug. 31, 1946; s. Mysore Krishna Iyengar and Padma (Iyengar) Ranganathan; came to U.S., 1968; student S. Indian Edn. Soc. Coll. Arts and Sci., Bombay, 1961-63; B. Tech. with honors, Indian Inst. Tech., Bombay, 1968; M.S., Mont. Coll. Mineral Sci. and Tech., 1970; Ph.D., Kans. State U., Manhattan, 1973; m. Sheela Dass, Aug. 21, 1970; children—Nikhil Krishna, Savita. Grad. teaching asst. metall. engring. Mont. Coll. Mineral Sci. and Tech., Butte, 1968-70; grad. research asst. nuclear engring. Kans. State U., 1970-73; postdoctoral fellow math., chemistry U. Ottawa (Ont.), Can., 1973-74; sessional lectr. related scis. Algonquin Coll., Ottawa, 1974-75; sr. nuclear generic licensing engr. So. Co. Services Inc., Birmingham, Ala., 1975-79; nuclear licensing Specialist Middle South Sers., Inc., New Orleans, 1979—. Registered profl. engr., Ala. Mem. Am. Soc. Metals, Am. Nuclear Soc. Hindu. Home: 31 Normandy Dr Kenner LA 70062 Office: PO Box 61000 New Orleans LA 70161

IYENGAR, SITHARAMA, educator; b. Bangalore, India, Aug. 26, 1947; came to U.S., 1970, naturalized, 1976; s. S. N. Sundaraja and S. (Mahalakshmi) I.; B.S., Bangalore U., 1968; M.S., Indian Inst. Sci., 1970; Ph.D., Miss. State U., 1973; m. Manorama Rama, Aug. 30, 1974; children—Puneeth, Veneeth. Asst. prof. dept. computer sci. Jackson (Miss.) State U., 1973-77, asso. prof., 1977—; vis. prof. U. Bonn (Germany), 1977. Indian Inst. Sci. research scholar, 1968-70. Mem. Assn. Computing Machinery, Simulation Council. Hindu. Contbr. articles to profl. jours. Home: 504 Greenmont Dr Jackson MS 39212 Office: Dept Computer Sci La State Univ Baton Rouge LA 70803

IZQUIERDO, LUIS RAMOS, JR., real estate broker; b. Havana, Cuba, Oct. 20, 1934; s. Luis A. and Mirtha (Guerra) Ramos-Izquierdo; came to U.S., 1961, naturalized, 1965; LL.B., Villanova U., 1957; m. Helena Novoa, Aug. 31, 1958; children—Helena, Luis. Admitted to Cuban bar, 1957; pvt. practice law, Havana, Cuba, 1957-61; research co. exec., 1961-65; with real estate div. Trust Mortgage Corp., San Juan, P.R., 1965-71; pres. Luis Ramos-Izquierdo and Assos., San Juan, 1971—. Named Realtor of Year, P.R. Assn. Realtors, 1976. Mem. San Juan Bd. Realtors, Mortage Bankers Assn., Home Builders Assn., P.R. Assn. Realtors (dir. 1976—). Home: 29 Fresa St Milaville Guaynabo PR 00657 Office: Suite 1408 Housing Inv Bldg Hato Rey PR 00918

IZZO, PATRICIA MARIE, public relations adminstr.; b. N.Y.C., Oct. 25, 1949; d. Patrick I. and Louise Rose (Gammello) I.; B.A. in Eng. Lit., George Washington U., 1971; M.A. in Communications, U. Iowa, 1973. Editorial asst. Electronic Industries Assn., Washington, 1971; newscast editor, Iowa Ednl. Broadcasting Network, U. Iowa, 1971-72, Bklyn. Network News, 1972-73; researcher, adminstrv. asst. to gen. news editor AP, N.Y.C., 1972-74; reporter, polit. columnist Daytona Beach (Fla.) News Jour., 1974-77; asst. dir. community affairs Daytona Beach Community Coll., 1977—; cons. community relations to various colls., 1978—. Mem. Ormond Beach Cultural Affairs Commn., 1976—. Active Volusia County ARC. Mem. Am. Assn. Women in Community and Jr. Colls., Nat. Council for Community Relations, Fla. Assn. Community Colls. (chmn. profl. improvement program 1979—), AAUW (parliamentarian, historian, community liasion Ormond Beach 1974—), Nat. Assn. for Female Execs., Council for Advancement and Support Edn., Nat. Council Jewish Women, Smithsonian Instn., Met. Mus. Art, Nat. Trust for Historic Preservation in U.S. Office: PO Box 1111 Daytona Beach FL 32015

JABLONSKI, T. HENRY, ednl. adminstr.; b. Wilmington, Del., Jan. 9, 1915; s. Frank W. and Wladysawa (Wilchinska) J.; B.S., Trenton State Coll., 1938; L.H.D., Tusculum Coll., 1978; m. Laura Marian Depue, Nov. 7, 1936; children—Thaddeus Henry, Alice (Mrs. Thayer Smith), Frank, Alfred, Joh, Kathryn (Mrs. Richard Swayze), Laura (Mrs. Dennis Hamilton), Richard. Indsl. arts instr. Merchantville (N.J.) High Sch., 1939-43; Radnor High Sch., Pa., 1943-45; asst. exec. dir. Pa. Soc. for Crippled Children, 1945-52; pres. Washington Coll. Acad., Washington College, Tenn., 1952—. Pres., Washington County Soc. for Crippled Children, 1958-60. Active Boy Scouts Am. Presbyn. Mason, Rotarian. Home: Washington College TN 37681

JACHIMCZYK, JOSEPH ALEXANDER, physician, lawyer; b. Bridgeport, Conn., Sept. 15, 1923; s. Michael A. and Mary M. (Wozny) J.; M.D., U. Tenn., 1948; J.D., Boston Coll., 1958; m. Loretta T. Slomski, June 17, 1950; children—Jane, Michael, Peggy, Mary. Intern, Queen's Hosp., Honolulu, 1948-49; resident pathology Hamot Hosp., Erie, Pa., 1949, Norwalk (Conn.) Hosp., 1949-50, Cleve. City Hosp., 1950-53; practice medicine, specializing in pathology, Houston, 1957—; asst. med. examiner State of Md., Balt., 1953; teaching fellow dept. legal medicine Harvard U., Boston, 1954-57; forensic pathologist Harris County, Houston, 1957-60, chief med. examiner, 1960—; admitted to Tex. bar, 1959, Fed. bar So. Dist. Tex., 1960, U.S. Supreme Ct. bar, 1979; asso. clin. prof. pathology Baylor U. Med. Sch.; clin. prof. pathology U. Tex. Dental Sch., U. Tex. postgrad. Sch. Biomed. Scis.; instr. law enforcement La. State U., Baton Rouge; sr. cons. in pathology M.D. Anderson Tumor Inst., Houston. Served with AUS, 1943-45; to sr. surgeon USPHS, 1954-56. Diplomate Am. Bd. Pathology. Fellow Coll. Am. Pathologists, Am. Soc. Clin. Pathologists; mem. AMA, Am., Houston bar assns., State Bar Tex., Tex., Mid-S., So., Harris County med. assns., Soc. Nuclear Medicine, Nat. Med. and Dental Assn., Nat. Assn. Med. Examiners, Tex. Soc. Pathologists, Houston Soc. Clin. Pathologists, Nat. Advs. Soc., Law Sci. Acad. Am., Law Enforcement Officers Assn. Tex., Polish Inst. Arts and Scis., Phi Chi. Contbr. articles to med. jours. Home: 3403 Bradford Pl Houston TX 77025 Office: Room 700 914 Preston St Houston TX 77002

JACK, CARL WILLIAM, data processing co. exec.; b. Leechburg, Pa., Sept. 19, 1939; s. Eugene William and Francis Alice (Hagar) J.; M.B.A., Pepperdine U., 1979; m. Glenda Faye Murphy, Aug. 3, 1961; children—Renee Michele, Carla Jean, Jeffery Scott. Applications engr. Gen. Electric Co., Charlotte, N.C., 1962-65, sr. project mgr., Phoenix, Rome, N.Y., 1965-68; mgr. applications devel. Internat. Telecomputer Network Corp., Bethesda, Md., 1968-70; dir. engring. Bunker Ramo Corp., Rolling Meadows, Ill., 1970-74; nat. mgr. computer mktg. Tex. Instruments Inc., Austin, Tex., 1974-78; v.p. market strategy Datapoint Corp., San Antonio, 1978—. Mem. exec. com., bd. dirs. Capital Area United Way, Austin, 1977-78; exec. adv. Jr. Achievement, 1979-80; mem. Camino Real Health Systems Agy., Cardiac Care Work Planning Group, San Antonio. Home: 9219 Bent Elm Creek Ln San Antonio TX 78230 Office: 8400 Datapoint Dr San Antonio TX 78284

JACK, WILLIAM HARRY, lawyer; b. Kaufman, Tex., Dec. 13, 1899; s. William Harry and Kosci (Snow) J.; J.D., U. Tex., 1922, A.B., 1923; m. Marian Price, Nov. 27, 1928 (dec.); children—Robert W., Patricia Allen (Mrs. J.W. Porter, Jr.), Marian E. Jenkins; m. 2d, Josephine Hunley Dillon, Aug. 16, 1969. Admitted to Tex. bar, 1922; partner Jack & Jack, attorneys, Corsicana, Texas, 1923-26; mem. Saner, Jack, Sallinger & Nichols, Dallas, 1926—. Dir. Booth, Inc. Pres., dir. Blanche Mary Taxis Found.; dir. past pres. Child's Guidance Clinic; vice chmn. bd. trustees Southwestern Legal Found., 1970-75. Served as pvt. U.S. Army, 1918, maj. USAAF, 1942-44; lt. col. JAG Dept. U.S. Army Res. Fellow Am. Bar Found., Southwestern Legal Found, Am. Coll. Probate Counsel (pres. 1963-64); mem. State Bar Tex. (past dir., v.p.), Dallas (pres. 1951), Am. (ho. of dels.) bar assns., Phi Beta Kappa, Phi Delta Phi, Sigma Delta Chi. Democrat. Presbyn. (elder; bd. Christian edn. Presbyn. Ch. U.S.). Mason (Shriner, 33 deg., Scottish Rite). Clubs: National Exchange (past v.p.; pres.), Dallas Country, Dallas. Home: 4349 Potomac Ave Dallas TX 75205 Office: Republic Nat Bank Bldg Dallas TX 75201

JACKMAN, GEORGE TWYFORD, educator, contractor; b. Houston, May 19, 1929; s. Twyford George and Kathleen (Buser) J.; B.B.A., N.Mex. State U., 1952; M.B.A., U. Tex., Austin, 1960. Mem. faculty U. Tex., Arlington, 1974—; owner, mgr. Enchanted Homes, Dallas, 1972—. Registered profl. homebuilder; lic. Realtor, Tex. Mem. Nat. Assn. Home and Apt. Bldrs., Res. Officers Assn. Home: 6033 Melody Ln Dallas TX 75231 Office: Dept Bus Adminstrn U Tex Arlington TX 76019

JACKSON, B. GORDON, guidance counselor; b. St. Petersburg, Fla., Jan. 27, 1936; s. Perry Gordon and Delsie E'thell (Register) J.; student Chipola Jr. Coll., 1956-58; B.S., Troy State U., 1960; M.A., U. Ala., 1965; m. Barbara Ann Nelson, July 23, 1967. Tchr. pub. schs., Ft. Walton Beach, Fla., 1960-62; curriculum coordinator, testing specialist, Bay County, Fla., 1962-70; guidance counselor, Vernon, Fla., 1970—. Served with U.S. Army, 1953-56. Mem. Am. Personnel and Guidance Assn., NEA, Bay County Mental Health Assn., Phi Delta Kappa. Methodist. Clubs: Masons; Lions (v.p. Chipley, Fla. 1977). Home: Route 3 Box 111B Chipley FL 32428

JACKSON, BENJAMIN FRANKLIN, III, hosp. adminstr.; b. Montgomery, Ala., June 10, 1940; s. Benjamin Franklin and Kathleen Ann (Flanagan) J.; student Auburn U., 1958-61; cert. health services adminstrn. U. Ala., 1968-69; m. Carolyn Tatum, Nov. 23, 1963; children—Benjamin Franklin, Brent Tatum, Kathleen Elizabeth. With Jackson Hosp. & Clinic, Montgomery, 1962—, adminstr. asst., dir. purchasing materials, 1969—. Bd. dels. United Way Montgomery; mem. boys work com. YMCA of Montgomery. Served with N.G., 1962-68. Mem. Am. Hosp. Assn., Ala. Hosp. Assn., Nat. Purchasing Mgmt. Assn., Central Ala. Purchasing Mgmt. Assn., Nat. Jogging Assn. Roman Catholic. Club: Lions (Montgomery). Office: Jackson Hospital and Clinic 1235 Forest Ave Montgomery AL 36106

JACKSON, BETTY RUTH, nurse, educator; b. Maypearl, Tex., Oct. 12, 1930; d. William Roy and Mary Anne (Underwood) Hutchins; student Tex. Christian U., 1948-49; grad. Harris Coll. Nursing, 1951; B.S.N., W. Tex. State U., 1975; M.S. in Nursing, U. Tex. at Austin, 1977, postgrad., 1978—; m. James Robert Jackson, Jan. 27, 1952; children—Jamie Beth, Julie Anne, George Robert. Charge nurse Harris Hosp., Fort Worth, Tex., 1951-52; office nurse, Lubbock, Tex., 1953; staff nurse Deaconess Hosp., Oklahoma City, 1954-55; Midland Meml. Hosp., Midland, Tex., 1957-59; indsl. nurse Shell Oil Co., Midland, 1962; charge nurse, head nurse, nursing supr. Midland Meml. Hosp., 1962-74; asso. prof. nursing program Odessa (Tex.) Coll., 1974—. Mem. Am. Nurses Assn., Nat. League Nursing, Tex. Nurses Coalition Action Politically, AAUP, Council Nurse Practitioners in Nursing of Children, Tex. Jr. Coll. Tchrs. Assn., Sigma Theta Tau, Phi Kappa Phi. Lutheran. Home: 1907 Ward Midland TX 79701 Office: PO Box 3752 Odessa TX 79760

JACKSON, BLYDEN, educator; b. Paducah, Ky., Oct. 12, 1910; s. George Washington and Julia Estelle (Reid) J.; A.B., Wilberforce U., 1930; A.M., U. Mich., 1938, Ph.D. (Rosenwald fellow 1947-49), 1952; m. Roberta Bowles, Aug. 2, 1958. Tchr. English, Louisville pub. schs., 1934-45; asst., then asso. prof. English, Fisk U., 1945-54; prof. English, head dept. So. U., 1954-62, dean Grad. Sch., 1962-69; prof. English, U. N.C., Chapel Hill, 1969—, asso. dean Grad. Sch., 1973-76; spl. research criticism Negro lit. Mem. Coll. Lang. Assn. (pres. 1957-59), Modern Lang. Assn., Nat. Council Tchrs. English (Distinguished lectr. 1970-71, chmn. coll. sect. 1971—), Coll. English Assn., Speech Assn. Am., La. Edn. Assn., Alpha Phi Alpha. Contbr. articles to profl. jours.; asso. editor CLA Bull., 1959—; mem. editorial adv. bd. So. Lit. Jour. Home: 102 Laurel Hill Rd Chapel Hill NC 27514

JACKSON, BOBBY BRITTON, youth orgn. exec.; b. Buffalo Valley, Tenn., June 5, 1936; s. Claude Britton and Mary (McKinley) J.; B.B.A., Ga. State U., 1979; m. Judith Moore, June 8, 1957; children—Jacqueline, James, Jennifer. Asst. dir. Boys Club, Oak Ridge, Tenn., 1958-59, phys. dir., Knoxville, Tenn., 1959-60, health edn. dir., camp dir., Richmond, Va., 1960-63; exec. dir. Wayne County Boys Club, Goldsboro, N.C., 1963-72; exec. dir. Boys Club, Asheville, N.C., 1972-75; asso. exec. dir. Met. Atlanta Boys Club, 1975—. Mem. Nat. Soc. Fund Raisers, Boys Club Profl. Assn. Methodist. Home: 1585 Oak Creek Dr Atlanta GA 30066 Office: 100 Edgewood Ave NE Atlanta GA 30303

JACKSON, DELLA ROSETTA HAYDEN, civic worker, educator; b. Mill Spring, N.C., Mar. 2, 1905; d. Robert Twitty and Amanda (Petty) Hayden; B.A., Johnson C. Smith U., 1948; M.A., N.C. Coll., 1956; m. G. Franklin Davenport, Sept. 28, 1930 (dec. Jan. 1936); children—Evelyn Frances Davenport Petty, Amanda Elizabeth Davenport Gray, Robert Franklin; m. 2d, Clarence Eugene Jackson, Oct. 30, 1943 (dec. Mar. 1951); children—Mae Carolyn Jackson Williams, Clarence Stinson. Tchr., Stony Knoll Sch., Polk County, N.C., 1927-30, Tryon Sch., 1930-31, Pea Ridge Sch., 1932-39, Union Grove Sch., 1939-48, Edmund Embury Sch., 1949-51, Cobb Elementary Sch., Tryon, N.C., 1951-65; tchr. adult edn. Isothermal Community Coll., Mill Spring, N.C., 1971-77; organizer, librarian Stony Knoll Community Library, 1937—, pres., 1972—, also chmn. bd. trustees; spl. edn. tchr. Polk Central High Sch., Mill Spring, 1966-69. Mem. Central Highlands Health Council, 1968-70; 2d v.p. Polk County Homemakers Council; pres. Polk County Extension Homemakers, 1974-75; sec.-treas. Polk County Community Devel. Council; mem. Polk County Family Life Study Com., 1978-79; mem. Ancillary Manpower Planning Bd., Region C, 1972—, mem. exec. com., 1976—; leader 4-H Club; v.p. Polk County Child Devel. Council, 1971-75, Eastern Appalachian Children's Council, 1971-73; chmn. Polk County Child Care Com., 1971-73; mem. Polk County Emergency Med. Service Adv. Com., 1973-75, Polk County Commn. on Aging, 1974—, N.C. Child Care, N.C. Children's 100; bd. dirs. Isothermal Health Council, sec., 1972-76; bd. dirs. Polk County Mental Health Council, 1972-73, St. Luke Hosp. Aux., 1970-77, Regional Health Council Eastern Appalachia, 1970-77, Polk County unit Am. Cancer Soc., 1979—; bd. govs., mem. exec. com. Western N.C. Health System Agy., 1977—, mem. resource devel. com., 1978—; steering com. Gov.'s Regional Conf. on Leadership Devel. for Women, 1978-79; mem. Region C Employment and Tng. Adv. Com., 1978—, Polk County Interagy. Council, 1978—, Polk County Family Life Council, 1978. Named Mother of Year, Afro, 1948, Mother of Year, Homemakers Council Polk County and Western Dist. N.C., 1971; recipient cert. service N.C. Recreation Soc., 1962; cert. leadership for service Western N.C. Community Devel. Program Asheville Agrl. Devel. Council, 1962; award for outstanding leadership and service Western N.C. Devel. Assn., 1979, Woman of Year, 1979; cert. of award Polk County Hist. Assn., 1980. Mem. LWV (dir. 1970—), Stony Knoll Recreation Soc., Polk County Hist. Assn. Club: Stony Knoll Community (pres. 1959-62). Home: Box 95 Mill Spring NC 28756

JACKSON, DOROTHY LOUISA GREENLEE (MRS. FRED KNOX JACKSON), ct. reporter; b. Hamburg, Iowa, Feb. 19, 1911; d. Henry Oliver and Mattie (Landreth) Greenlee; student pub. schs.; m. Fred Knox Jackson, Oct. 3, 1944. Asst. county ct. reporter, Auburn, Nebr., 1927-29; sec. local atty., 1927-29; sec. Berksons, Kansas City, Mo., 1929-33; corr. A.A.A., Washington, 1933-36; sec. Intelligence Unit, Kansas City, St. Louis, 1936-40; free-lance ct., conv. reporter, St. Louis, 1940-44; free-lance ct. reporter, Prattville, Ala., 1948—; contract reporter Ala. Pub. Service Commn., Montgomery. Co-owner, operator Prattville Quick Freeze, 1948-63; owner Quiet Acre, Cottonwood, Ala., 1968-73. Chmn., Autauga County Operation Santa Claus, State Christmas Card, Bryce Mental Hosp., Tuscaloosa, Ala., 1963-70. Recipient award for 50 yrs. Outstanding service, Ala. Shorthand Writer's Assn., 1978. Mem. Nat. League Am. Pen Women (br. pres. 1964-68, 72-74, 76-78, state v.p. 1970-71, state pres. 1972-74), Ala. Writers Conclave, Montgomery Press and Authors Club (pres. 1971-72), Ala. Shorthand Reporters Assn., Montgomery Assn. Legal Secs., Nat. Shorthand Reporters Assn., Internat. Platform Assn., Ala. Poetry Soc. Club: Autauga County Bus. and Profl. Women's (named County Woman of Achievement 1971). Author: Fallen Leaves, 1968; Poody, Story of a Cat-Nothing But a Cat, 1970. Home: 856 Gillespie St Prattville AL 36067

JACKSON, GARY MANUEL, psychologist; b. Herrin, Ill., June 5, 1947; s. Manuel Lee and Linnie Mae (Purdie) J.; B.A. in Psychology, So. Ill. U., 1972, Ph.D. in Ednl. Psychology, 1976; M.A. in Psychology, Sangamon State U., 1973; m. Roseann Jackson, Nov. 3, 1976; 1 dau., Kary Colleen; stepchildren—Randy, John, King, Ginger. Psychologist III, Lincoln Devel. Center, Lincoln, Ill., 1974-76; dir. behavior therapy Sunland Center, Miami, Fla., 1976-78; asst. prof., dir. gerontology Residential Treatment Project, Fla. Mental Health Inst., Tampa, 1978—. Clin. fellow Behavior Therapy and Research Soc.; mem. Am. Psychol. Assn., Assn. Advancement Behavior Therapy, Am. Assn. Mental Deficiency. Contbr. articles to profl. publs.; editorial cons. Mental Retardation. Home: 217 Tampa Downs Blvd Lutz FL 33549 Office: 13301 N 30th St Tampa FL 33612

JACKSON, HARRY C., city ofcl.; married; 2 children. Mayor, Consol. Govt. of Columbus (Ga.), 1979—. Office: Govt Center PO Box 1340 Columbus GA 31902

JACKSON, HORACE FRANKLIN, state ofcl.; b. Dillon, S.C., Oct. 1, 1934; s. Redden Haney and Daisy Belle (Moody) J.; B.S., U. S.C., 1961, M.B.A., 1971; m. Margie Jan Phillips, June 1, 1955; children—Margie Jan, Horace Darrin. Staff acct. J.W. Hunt & C.P., C.P.A.'s, 1961-64; staff auditor State Auditor S.C., Columbia, 1964-68, sr. budget analyst, 1968-70; dir. fin. S.C. Dept. Social Services, Columbia, 1970-72, dep. commr. fin. mgmt., 1973-75, dep. commr. fiscal opns., 1975-78, exec. asst. for fin. mgmt., 1978—. Mem. Gov.'s Task force on Nursing Home Reimbursement, 1969, on Medicaid, 1970, Gov.'s Health Planning Com., 1973, HEW Task Force on Welfare Cost Allocation, 1979—. Served with AUS, 1957-61. Mem. Am. Public Welfare Assn., S.C. State Employees Assn. (dir. 1976-77), Assn. MBA Execs., Assn. State Welfare Fin. Officers (dir. 1973-74), U. S.C. Alumni Assn. Methodist. Office: PO Box 1520 Columbia SC 29202

JACKSON, JAMES WARREN, art conservator, restorer, artist; b. Charlottesville, Va., Jan. 4, 1941; s. Lewis Willie and Bessie Blanche (Jackson) J.; B.A., U. Va., Charlottesville, 1964; M.F.A., Chgo. Tech. Inst., 1965; art conservation, restoration internship with Eugene Okarma, Oliver Anderson, Victorius Art Collection, 1965-69; m. Ann Harris, Jan. 4, 1962; children—Bonita Maria, Jamie Therese. Dir. art conservation and restoration, staff artist and designer Paul B. Victorus Art Collection, Charlottesville, 1963-69; dir. art conservation, artist, designer J. Warren Jackson Studio, Charlottesville, 1969—; art conservator numerous maj. paintings in museums, also pvt. collections; cons. in field. Fellow Am. Inst. Conservation of Hist. Works; mem. Internat. Inst. Conservation of Hist. and Artistic Works, Albermarle Art Assn., Am. Tae-Wando Assn., Internat. Platform Assn. Club: Monticello Tae-Wando Group. Address: 114 Montpelier St Charlottesville VA 22903

JACKSON, JAMES WILLIAM, surgeon; b. Lawrenceville, Ga., Nov. 26, 1941; s. Jesse Clay and Sleetie Mae (Doss) J.; B.S., U. Ga., 1965; M.D., Med. Coll. Ga., 1969; m. Sandra L. Cole, June 26, 1965; children—Lissa, Jimmy. Intern, Memorial Med. Center and Med. Coll. of Ga., Savannah, 1969-70, resident in surgery, 1970-74; practice medicine and surgery, 1974—; with Surgery Assos. P.C., Savannah, 1974—; asst. prof. Med. Coll. Ga., 1976—; mem. staff Memorial Med. Center, St. Joseph's Hosp., Candler Gen. Hosp. (all Savannah). Served with USNR, 1959-62. Diplomate Am. Bd. Surgery. Mem. AMA, Am. Coll. Surgeons, Southeastern Surg. Congress, Med. Assn. Ga., Ga. Med. Soc. Office: 1 Medical Arts Center Savannah GA 31405

JACKSON, JERRLYNE ALLEN, educator; b. Sopchoppy, Fla., Feb. 14, 1942; B.S., Fla. A&M U., 1963, M.Ed., 1967; postgrad. Fla. State U., 1972—; m. Eddie Jackson, June 14, 1969; 1 dau., Allesa Paige. Sec., adminstrv. asst. Fla. A&M U., Tallahassee, 1963-68, asst. prof. bus. edn., 1968—. Active Girl Scouts U.S. Mem. Fla. Bus. Edn. Assn., So. Bus. Edn. Assn., Nat. Bus. Edn. Assn., Internat. Bus. Edn. Assn., Fla. Vocat. Assn., Am. Vocat. Assn., Am. Bus. Women's Assn., Kappa Delta Pi, Pi Omega Pi, Alpha Kappa Alpha, Phi Beta Lambda. Office: Fla A&M U Tallahassee FL 32307

JACKSON, JOE LOUIS, b. Crystal Springs, Miss., Sept. 14, 1937; s. John H. and Eula J.; B.S. in Social Scis., Jackson (Miss.) State Coll., 1959; M.Ed. in Sch. Adminstrn., U. Ark., Fayetteville, 1968; advanced M.Ed. in Supervision and Adminstrn., U. Miss., 1972; m. Nora M. Jackson; children—Willie, Joseph. Tchr., N. Panola High Sch., Como, Miss., 1961-64; prin. Green Hill Sch., Sardis, Miss., 1964-74; program supr. N. Panola Consol. Schs., Sardis, 1974—. Commr., Sardis Housing Authority, 1975—; treas. Sardis Community Center, 1970—. Certified in edn., supervision and adminstrn., Miss. Mem. Order Eastern Stars (state dir. edn.), Phi Beta Sigma, Phi Delta Kappa. Home: Davis Chapel Rd PO Box 291 Sardis MS 38666 Office: Hwy 51 N Sardis MS 38666

JACKSON, JOHN WINGFIELD, lawyer; b. Washington, Dec. 30, 1905; s. E. Hilton and Ann (Wingfield) J.; B.S. in Econs., U. Pa., 1928; J.D. with highest honors, George Washington U. Law Sch., 1932; m. Eleanor Murdoch Lind, Jan. 12, 1935; children—John Wingfield, Margaret M. (Mrs. Jerry R. Russom), Beverley Anne L. (Mrs. James J. Johnston, Jr.). Admitted to D.C. bar, 1931, Va. bar, 1941; individual practice law, Washington, 1933, 41-61, Va., 1961—; investigator Dept. Interior, PWA, 1933-36; asst. U.S. Atty., D.C., 1936-41; sometime spl. asst. to atty. gen. U.S., 1952-54. Cons., OSS, 1945; adj. prof. law George Washington U. Law Sch., 1948-79; substitute judge Juvenile and Domestic Relations Ct. Arlington County, Va., 1966—. Former mem. bd. dirs. Washington Criminal Justice Assn., Arlington chpt. A.R.C. Mem. No. Va. Estate Planning Council (pres. 1966-67), Nat. Assn. Estate Planning Councils (dir. 1966-70, 72-76), Order of Coif, Phi Delta Phi. Club: Metropolitan. Home: 4844 N Rock Spring Rd Arlington VA 22207 Office: 1515 N Courthouse Rd Arlington VA 22201

JACKSON, JUAQUITA ELAINE HARRIS, speech-lang. pathologist; b. Chgo., Sept. 10, 1948; d. Jeannette Eunice Harris; B.S. in Speech Pathology (scholar), Northwestern U., 1970; M.S. in Speech Pathology (Zeta Phi Eta fellow), U. Mich., 1971; m. Harold Jackson, Dec. 12, 1971; 1 son, Julian Harold. Grad. trainee in speech pathology U. Mich., Ann Arbor, 1970-71; speech therapist Chgo. Bd. Edn., 1971-72; speech pathologist Savannah (Ga.) Speech and Hearing Center 1972-74; speech specialist Met. Nashville Pub. Schs., 1974-75; speech-lang. pathologist Inst. for Study of Mental Retardation and Related Disabilities U. Mich., Ann Arbor, 1976-77; clin. instr., coordinator supr. speech pathology Speech, Hearing and Lang. Devel. Center, Tenn. State U., Nashville, 1977—, mem. faculty, 1979—. Mem. Am. Speech-Lang. and Hearing Assn. (certificate of clin. competence in speech pathology), Tenn. Speech and Hearing Assn., Council of Univ. Suprs. of Practicum in Speech Pathology and Audiology, Nat. Black Assn. for Speech, Lang. and Hearing, Nashville Assn. on Young Children, Zeta Phi Eta, Delta Sigma Theta. Baptist. Home: 1837 Willow Springs Dr Nashville TN 37216 Office: Dept Communication Area of Speech Pathology and Audiology Tenn State U 3500 Centennial Blvd Nashville TN 37203

JACKSON, KAREN ELIZABETH EASTWOOD, social worker; b. Hale Center, Tex., Nov. 4, 1951; d. Louis D. and Margaret A. (Bush) Eastwood; A.A., Northeastern A&M Jr. Coll., Okla., 1972; B.A., U. Okla., 1974, M.S.W., 1977; B.S. cum laude, Okla. Bapt. U., 1975; m. Johnny David Jackson, Aug. 26, 1978 (div.); 1 dau., Gretchen Leigh. Asst. adminstr. Eastwood Manor Nursing & Rehab. Center, Commerce, Okla., 1970-74; sec. Environ. Devel. Corp., Oklahoma City, 1974-75; social services dir. South Community Hosp., Oklahoma City, 1975-78; social worker Ottawa County Guidance Center, Miami, Okla., 1978-79; psychiat. social worker Eastern State Hosp., Tulsa, 1979—; mem. Okla. Vocat. Rehab. Services State Task Force, 1978; home health care cons. Ottawa, Craig and Delaware Health Depts., 1978—. Vice pres. Delaware County Young Democrats, 1978-79; sec Delaware County Democratic Women, 1978—; mem. Ladies Aux. to VFW, 1977-79. Mem. Nat. Assn. Social Workers (sec. Okla. northeastern chpt. 1978—), Am. Hosp. Assn. of Social Service Dirs., Okla. Soc. for Hosp. Social Work Dirs. (chmn. nominating com. 1977-78), Oklahoma City Council of Med. Social Services Dirs. (pres. 1977-78), Okla. Health and Welfare Assn., Okla. State Bd. Nursing Homes, Acad. Cert. Social Workers, Ottowa & Delaware County Mental Health Assn. (sec. 1979—). Roman Catholic. Home: 8019 S 79 East Ave Tulsa OK 74133 Office: 628 N Country Club Dr Tulsa OK 74127

JACKSON, LARRY ARTOPE, coll. pres.; b. Florence, S.C., Feb. 7, 1925; s. Arthur Edward and Rosa (Gilbert) J.; A.B., Wofford Coll., 1947, D.Litt. (hon.), 1976; B.D., Union Theol. Sem., N.Y.C., 1953; D.D. (hon.), U. of Pacific, 1961, M.A., 1972; m. Barbara Atwood, June 27, 1953; children—Elizabeth, Arthur Edward, Barbara Gilbert, Charles Rhett. Dir., Santiago (Chile) Coll., 1959-64; provost Callison Coll., U. Pacific, Stockton, Calif., 1964-70; v.p. adminstrn. U. Evansville (Ind.), 1970-73; pres. Lander Coll., Greenwood, S.C., 1973—; mem. Fulbright Commn. for Chile, 1961-64. Pres., United Way, Greenwood, 1978. Served to 1st lt. USAAF, 1943-45. Decorated Air medal with 2 oak leaf clusters. Mem. Am. Assn. Higher Edn., AAUP, Assn. State Colls. and Univs., Greenwood C. of C. (dir. 1976-78), ACLU, NAACP, Phi Delta Kappa, Pi Gamma Mu. Democrat. Quaker. Club: Rotary (Greenwood). Office: Lander Coll Stanley Ave Greenwood SC 29646

JACKSON, MAYNARD HOLBROOK, JR., lawyer, mayor Atlanta; b. Dallas, Mar. 23, 1938; s. Maynard H. and Irene (Dobbs) J.; B.A. (Ford Found. Early Admission scholar), Morehouse Coll., 1956; J.D., N.C. Central U., 1964; m. Valerie Richardson, Nov. 1977; children—Elizabeth, Brooke, Maynard Holbrook. Admitted to bar, 1965; atty. Emory Community Legal Services Center, 1967-69; founder, partner firm Jackson, Patterson, Parks & Franklin, Atlanta, 1970-74; vice mayor, pres. bd. aldermen Atlanta, 1970-74, mayor, 1974—. Address: 68 Mitchell St NW Atlanta GA 30303

JACKSON, MORRIS KENT, educator; b. Clifton, Tex., Nov. 2, 1945; s. George Emory and Evelyn Estrem (Orbeck) J.; B.S., Baylor U., 1968, M.S., 1971; Ph.D., Med. Coll. Ga., 1975; m. Sarah Nell Myers, July 27, 1974; 1 dau., Rebecka Nell. Research asst. biology dept. Baylor U., Waco, Tex., 1968, grad. teaching asst., 1968-71; grad. teaching asst. dept. anatomy Med. Coll. Ga., Augusta, 1971-75; instr. dept. anatomy La. State U. Med. Sch., Shreveport, 1975-77, asst. prof., 1977—. Served with Tex. Army Nat. Guard, 1969-71. Lutheran acad. scholar, 1964-68. Recipient D. Dwight Davis award, 1971. Mem. Am. Assn. Anatomists, So. Soc. Anatomists, AMA, Soc. Study Amphibians and Reptiles, Shreveport Coin Club (dir. 1977—), Sigma Xi, Beta Beta Beta, Omicron Delta Kappa. Contbr. articles to profl. jours. Home: 6126 Lovers Lane Shreveport LA 71105

JACKSON, NICK KING, data processing mgr.; b. San Angelo, Tex., Oct. 3, 1943; s. Garland R. and Iva Dean (Eades) J.; student McMurray Coll., 1962-64, Dallas Tabulating Inst., 1967; m. Judith Kay Bockes, July 21, 1978; children by previous marriage-Maridean, David. Computer operator Procter & Gamble, Dallas, 1967-68; computer operator, scheduler, ops. supr. Anderson, Clayton & Co., Dallas, 1968-78; ops. mgr. Chilton Corp., Dallas, 1978-79; tech. support mgr. J.C. Penney Ins. Cos., Great Am. Res., Dallas, 1979—. Mem. Dallas Virtual Systems Users Group, S.W. Computer Measurement Group, Data Processing Mgmt. Assn. Republican. Baptist. Office: 2020 Live Oak St Dallas TX 75221

JACKSON, PERRY CARR, ednl. adminstr.; b. Winona, Tex., Apr. 29, 1932; s. Clarence Guyton and Annie Laura (Carr) J.; B.S., U. Tex., Austin, 1952, M.S., 1958; m. Alicia Hodges Downes, June 6, 1968; children—Lawrence Jackson, Myles Downes. Tchr., Port Neches/Groves Ind. Sch. Dist., 1955-58; tchr. Austin (Tex.) Ind. Sch. Dist., 1958-61, counselor, 1961, asst. prin., 1962-67, prin., 1967-72, asst. dir. personnel, 1972-74, dir. personnel, 1974—. Served with inf. U.S. Army, 1952-54. Sch. adminstr. certificate Tex. Edn. Agy. Mem. Am. Assn. Sch. Personnel Adminstrs., Tex. Assn. Sch. Personnel Adminstrs., Assn. Tex. Educators, Tex. PTA (hon. life). Unitarian. Home: 7104 Sungate St Austin TX 78731 Office: 6100 Guadalupe St Austin TX 78752

JACKSON, RANDALL C(ALVIN), lawyer; b. Baird, Tex., Mar. 21, 1919; s. Rupert and Anna (Faust) J.; J.D., U. Tex., 1946; B.B.A., 1941; m. Betty S. Johnson, June 18, 1955; 1 son, Randall Calvin. Admitted to Tex. bar, 1946, practiced in Baird, 1946-62, Abilene, 1962—; sr. partner firm Jackson & Jackson, 1949—; v.p., dir. 1st Nat. Bank,

Baird; dir. T. S. Lankford & Sons Co.; dir., gen. counsel Bank of Commerce, Abilene; mem. Tex. Securities Bd., 1966-69; chmn. Abilene Spl. Housing Study Com. Former pres. bd. dirs. Boys Ranch, Abilene; former chmn. bd. regents Tex. Woman's U., 1961-66; mem. Tex. Dem. Exec. Com., 1960-64; former chmn. bd. trustees Sears Methodist Retirement Center. Enlisted USAC, 1942, disch. capt., 1946, assigned Exec. Office Statis. Control Unit, Guam. Fellow Am. Coll. Probate Counsel; mem. Southwestern Legal Found., Tex. Bar Found. (charter mem.), State Bar Tex. (vice chmn. legal bd. specialization), Am., Callahan-Taylor County (pres. 1979-80) bar assns., Am. Judicature Soc., Am., Tex. (dir.), West Tex. (pres.), Sweetwater (dir.) hereford assns., Abilene Livestock Show Assn. (pres. 1979-80), Am. Legion (past comdr.), Abilene C. of C. Methodist (chmn., dist. trustee). Clubs: Masons (32 deg.), Shriners; Headliners (Austin, Tex.); Abilene Country (Abilene). Home: Route 2 Box 703 Abilene TX 79601 Office: Bank of Commerce Bldg Abilene TX 79602

JACKSON, RONALD GENE, exec. dir. Tex. Youth Council; b. Kansas City, Mo., Sept. 28, 1940; s. Donald Wayne and Emily Alexander (Shurley) J.; B.A., U. Tex., 1964, M.S.S.W., 1970; m. Polly Ann Miller, Aug. 21, 1965; children—Donald Webb, Ann Robinson. Dir. Brownwood (Tex.) Diagnostic Reception Center, 1970; supr. Brownwood State Home and Sch., 1970-73; exec. dir. Tex. Youth Council, Austin, 1973—; mem. Gov. Tex. Task Force Youth Care and Rehab.; exec. com. Tex. Commn. Sers. to Children and Youth, Criminal Justice Council Standards and Goals. Served to capt. AUS, 1964-70. Mem. Nat. Assn. Social Workers, Am. Correctional Assn. (gov.), Nat. Assn. Juvenile Delinquency Program Adminstrs. (pres.), Tex. Corrections Assn., Nat. Council Crime and Delinquency. Episcopalian. Club: Rotary. Home: 8301 Silver Ridge Austin TX 78759 Office: 8900 Shoal Creek Austin TX 78758

JACKSON, RONALD LOUIS, ins. cons.; b. Richmond, Va., Apr. 26, 1948; s. Robert Louis and Margaret Bourne J.; B.A., Randolph Macon Coll., 1972; m. Tanya Maria Thomasian, Aug. 15, 1971; children—Jared Thomas, Christopher Robert. Agt., Provident Mut., Richmond, 1972-76, brokerage mgr., 1976-79; life ins. cons. Wheat First Securities, Richmond, 1979—. C.L.U. Mem. Nat. Assn. Life Underwriters, Am. Assn. C.L.U.'s, C.L.U. Soc. Republican. Lutheran. Clubs: Jaycees (dir. Richmond chpt. 1978—), Bon Air-Southampton Quarterback (coach). Home: 3316 Cheverly Rd Richmond VA 23225 Office: Wheat First Securities PO Box 3T Richmond VA 23207

JACKSON, STEPHEN THOMAS, soft drink co. exec.; b. Atlanta, June 10, 1952; s. Gordon Preston and Frances (Matthews) J.; B.B.A., U. Ga., 1975. Exec. asst. to pres. Ball-Stalker Co., Atlanta, 1976-78; dist. mgr. Atlanta/N. Ga., Coca-Cola U.S.A., Atlanta, 1979—. Mem. Atlanta Jaycees, Kappa Alpha Order. Presbyterian. Clubs: Press, Polo (Atlanta); Cherokee Town and Country. Home: PO Box 227 Graysou GA 30221 Office: PO Drawer 1734 Mail Code M6EI Atlanta GA 30301

JACKSON, TERRY WIGHTMAN, clergyman; b. Palestine, Tex., June 19, 1939; s. Chester Warren and Vera Anna (Wightman) J.; B.A., U. Kans., 1961; M.Div. (Seabury fellow), Seabury-Western Theol. Sem., 1964; M.S., Fla. Inst. Tech., 1972; D.Ministry (Episcopal Ch. Bd. Theol. Edn. grantee, 1979), Princeton Theol. Sem., 1980; m. Donna Ruth Knutson, Aug. 8, 1959; children—Kimberley Kay, Deborah Lynn, Michelle Ann, Jennifer Elizabeth. Ordained to ministry Episcopal Ch., 1964; asso. rector Holy Trinity Episcopal Ch., Melbourne, Fla., 1964-67; rector St. John's Episcopal Ch., Melbourne, 1968-73; rector St. James Episcopal Ch., Leesburg, Fla., 1973—; mem. governing bd. Diocese of Central Fla. Pres., Family Service Bur., Brevard County, 1969; pres. dist. III, Mental Health Bd., State of Fla. Mem. AAUP, Nat. Assn. Social Workers, Acad. Parish Clergy, Assn. Mental Health Clergy, Assn. of Couples for Marriage Enrichment, Leesburg Ministerial Assn. (pres. 1975). Author: Introduction to Philosophy, 1970; The World's Religions, 1970. Home: 201 N Orange St Leesburg FL 32748 Office: St James Episcopal Ch 204 N Lee St Leesburg FL 37248

JACKSON, TOMMY HUGH, life ins. co. exec.; b. Chattanooga, Aug. 2, 1944; s. Jay Hugh and Annie Irene (Groves) J.; B.S., U. Chattanooga, 1966; m. Sandra Joyce Sewell, Aug. 19, 1967; children—Jeffrey Hugh, Bradley Keith. With Provident Life & Accident Ins. Co., 1966—, sec. life dept., 1979—. Pres., Alpine Crest PTA, 1979; mem. Hixson Improvement League. Fellow, Life Office Mgmt.; C.L.U.; registered prin. Nat. Assn. Security Dealers. Mem. Am. Soc. C.L.U.'s, Nat. Assn. Life Underwriters. Baptist. Club: Highland Sertoma. Office: Provident Bldg Fountain Sq Chattanooga TN 37402

JACKSON, VIRGINIA LEA, hosp. exec.; b. Delaware, Okla., Feb. 27, 1935; d. William McKinley and Myrtle MaeBelle (Corbin) Lewis; grad. Bartlesville Bus. Coll., 1954; m. Ronald Joe Jackson, July 10, 1953; children—Rhonda Elaine, Michael Joe, Tammy Kay, Kenneth Don. Exec. sec. Phillips Petroleum Co., 1954-56; various office positions, also tchrs. aide, 1968-69; dir. vols. Jane Phillips Episcopal-Meml. Med. Center, Bartlesville, Okla., 1970—; v.p. Washington County chpt. Am. Cancer Soc., 1977, service chmn. Washington County, 1977. Mem. Am. Hosp. Assn., Okla. Hosp. Assn. (dir. 1972-76; Service award 1978), Okla. Soc. Dirs. Vols. Services (pres. 1978-79), Am. Bus. Women's Assn. (chpt. scholarship chmn. 1976, yearbook chmn. 1977, 78, 79). Club: Pilot (chpt. yearbook chmn.). Home: 3440 Silver Lake Rd Bartlesville OK 74003 Office: 3500 E Frank Phillips St Bartlesville OK 74003

JACKSON, WILLIAM FRED, newspaper publisher; b. Sarasota, Fla., June 24, 1938; s. Fred and Catherine (Morris) J.; student Bethune-Cookman Coll., Daytona Beach, Fla., 1957-61; m. Francell Juanita Beluin, Feb. 26, 1979; 1 dau. by previous marriage, Pamela Voncyna. Pub., The Bulletin, Sarasota, 1961—; lectr. in field. Chmn. membership Sarasota br. NAACP, 1977—. Mem. S.W. Black Pubs., Black Media, Newtown Bus. and Profl. Assn. Democrat. Mem. Ch. of Christ. Clubs: Top Ten Men (pres. 1970—), K.P., Elks. Home: 1422 16th St Sarasota FL 33577 Office: The Bulletin 2700 N Washington Blvd Sarasota FL 33578

JACKSON, WILLIAM HOWARD, pub. co. exec.; b. Nashville, Oct. 19, 1924; s. Norman Andrew and Martha Eunice (Holt) J.; grad. Art Students League of N.Y.C., 1949; B.S. in Design, U. Mich., 1953; m. Elva Ruth Davidson, Mar. 15, 1957. Mag. designer United Methodist Pub. House, Nashville, 1953-65, mag. design chief, 1965-75, mgr. art and production services, 1975—. Judge Outside N.Y. Art Dir. Show, 1975. Served with U.S. Army, 1943-48; ETO. Decorated Purple Heart; recipient gold award for mag. design Art Dir. Club, 1972, 1973, awards of excellence, 1965, 1967, certificates of merit, 1958, 61, 68, 71; purchase prize for art work Art Students League of N.Y.C., 1946. Mem. Art Dir. Club of Nashville (v.p. 1967), Am. Inst. Graphic Arts, Graphic Arts Tech. Found. Home: Route 5 Box 299 Nashville TN 37221 Office: 201 8th Ave S Nashville TN 37202

JACKSON, WILLIAM PAUL, mfg. co. exec.; b. Shreveport, La., Apr. 26, 1938; s. Newton Burgess and Elizabeth (Railsback) J.; B.A., La. State U., 1961; M.A., U. Houston, 1968; postgrad. Centenary Coll., summer 1957-60; m. Flavia Ann Leary, Apr. 26, 1962; children—Michelle, Christopher, Monica, Paul. Analyst coordinating and planning dept. Tex. Eastern Transmission Corp., Houston, 1961-66; dir. market research AMF Indsl. Products Group, Shreveport, La., 1966-69; asst. mktg. mgr. Ball Valve div. Cameron Iron Works, Houston, 1969-75; mgr. market devel. Hydril Co., Houston, 1975—; cons. in field. Mgr. indsl. div., United Fund, Shreveport, 1967; mem. regional export expansion council Dept. Commerce, 1968; active Little League, 1958-59, 75-78; study participant Nat. Petroleum Council, 1979. Mem. Nat. Assn. Bus. Economists, Am. Mktg. Assn. Presbyterian. Contbr. articles to profl. jours. Home: 12718 Pebblebrook St Houston TX 77024 Office: 3300 N Belt E Houston TX 77205

JACKSON, WILLIAM PAUL, JR., lawyer; b. Bexar, Ala., July 7, 1938; s. William Paul and Evelyn Mabel (Goggans) J.; B.S. in Physics, U. Ala., 1960, LL.B., 1963, J.D., 1969; m. Barbara Anne Seignious, Sept. 30, 1966; children—Jennifer Anne, Susan Barrett, William Paul III. Admitted to Ala. bar, 1963, D.C. bar, 1969, Va. bar, 1975; law clk. to Judge Aubrey M. Cates, Ala. Ct. Appeals, Montgomery, 1965; asso. firm Bishop and Carlton, Birmingham, Ala., 1965-68, Todd, Dillon and Sullivan, Washington, 1968-70; founding partner Jackson & Jessup, Washington and Arlington, Va., 1970-76; pres., sr. atty. Jackson, Jessup & Howard, P.C., 1976—; mem. adv. bd. Oren Harris chair of transp. U. Ark., 1974—. Vice pres. McLean (Va.) Hunt Homeowners' Assn., 1974, pres., 1975-76; bd. dirs. McLean Citizens' Assn., 1976-78; pres. McLean Legal Action Fund, Inc., 1977—. Served to lt. Signal Corps, U.S. Army, 1963-65. Recipient Pub. Service awards Am. Radio Relay League, 1958, Armed Forces Communications and Electronics Assn., 1963; Sigma Delta Kappa scholar, 1963. Mem. Birmingham (Ala.), Arlington (Va.), Fed., Fed. Communications, Am., Ala., Va., D.C. bar assns., Motor Carrier Lawyers Assn., Assn. ICC Practitioners, Am. Judicature Soc., So. Traffic League (exec. sec. 1970—), Eastern Indsl. Traffic League (exec. sec. 1978—), Bench and Bar Legal Honor Soc. (pres. 1963). Contbr. articles to legal jours. Home: 7807 Foxhound Rd McLean VA 22101 Office: 3426 N Washington Blvd Box 1240 Arlington VA 22210

JACOB, PAUL BERNARD, JR., elec. engr.; b. Columbus, Miss., June 9, 1922; s. Paul Bernard and Sarah Dorsey (Jamison) J.; B.S. in Elec. Engring., Miss. State U., 1944; M.S. in Elec. Engring., Northwestern U., 1948; m. Mildred Evelyn Hammack, Aug. 20, 1946; children—William Boswell, Paul Bernard, III. Jr. engr. Tenn. Eastman Corp., Oak Ridge, 1944-46; instr. in elec. engring. Miss. State U., 1946-48, asst. prof. elec. engring., 1948-51, asso. prof., 1951-56, prof., 1956—, asso. head dept. elec. engring., 1962—; consulting elec. engr.; dir. Miss. State U. High Voltage Lab. Mem. East Miss. Council; chmn. bd. deacons 1st Bapt. Ch., Starkville, Miss., 1962. Mem. IEEE (sr.), Am. Soc. Engring. Edn., Power Engring. Soc. (chmn. nat. com.), Tau Beta Pi, Eta Kappa Nu, Sigma Xi, Phi Kappa Phi, Omicron Delta Kappa, Sigma Alpha Epsilon (nat. pres. 1969-71, Nat. Distinguished Service award 1975). Research, publs. in high voltage phenomena relating to electric power systems. Home: PO Box 5252 Mississippi State MS 39762 Office: PO Drawer EE Mississippi State MS 39762*

JACOB, WALTER MATTHEW, hosp. exec.; b. Bronx, N.Y., Jan. 12, 1944; s. Matthew Charles and Hildegard Elizabeth (Boerner) J.; B.A., E. Carolina U., 1966; M.B.A. (NIH fellow 1967-68), Am. U., 1968; m. Diane Marie Komsie, Dec. 27, 1974. Personnel mgmt. specialist NIH, 1967-69; asst. dir. personnel Greater Southeast Community Hosp., Washington, 1969-71; dir. personnel Anne Arundel Gen. Hosp., Annapolis, Md., 1971-74; asso. Modern Mgmt. Methods, Inc., Chgo., 1974-75; asst. adminstr. personnel affairs Arlington (Va.) Hosp., 1975—; dir. Arlington Hosp. Employees Credit Union. Scoutmaster local Boy Scouts Am., 1978—. Mem. Am. Arbitration Assn. (arbitrator), Am. Soc. Hosp. Personnel Adminstrn., Am. Hosp. Assn., Va. Hosp. Personnel Adminstrn. Assn., Washington Personnel Assn., Hosp. Council Nat. Capital Area, S.P.E.B.S.Q.S.A., Phi Sigma Tau, Pi Kappa Phi. Lutheran. Home: 9824 Wolcott Ct Burke VA 22015 Office: 1710 George Mason Dr Arlington VA 22205

JACOBS, BARRY, physician; b. May 9, 1945; B.S., Lamar U., 1966; M.D., U. Tex., Galveston, 1970; m. Geri; 3 children. Intern, Hosp. Good Samaritan, Los Angeles, 1970-71; resident in Ob-Gyn, U. Tex., San Antonio, 1971, Baylor U. Coll. Medicine, Houston, 1973-76, fellow in gynecol. endocrinology, 1976-78; asst. prof. Ob-Gyn, U. Tex., Houston, 1978—; clin. asst. prof. Ob-Gyn, Baylor U. Coll. Medicine, Houston, 1978—; med. dir. Seven Acres Home for Aged, 1979—. Served to capt. USAF, 1971-73. Diplomate Am. Bd. Ob-Gyn. Fellow Am. Coll. Obstetricians and Gynecologists, Am. Fertility Soc.; mem. Houston Soc. Ob-Gyn, Harris County Med. Soc., Tex. Med. Assn., Phi Delta Epsilon. Author publs. in field. Address: 8902 Petersham Houston TX 77071

JACOBS, DANIEL MARTIN, engring. co. exec.; b. Tarboro, N.C., Sept. 16, 1940; s. Frank Lamar and Minnie Esther (Smith) J.; B.S., N.C. Wesleyan Coll., 1966; postgrad. Coll. William and Mary, 1974, Old Dominion U., 1970, George Washington U., 1975; m. Janet Marie Baker, Nov. 24, 1961; children—Deana Marie, Mercedes Lynne, Daniel Martin, Adam Christopher. Dist. rep. Phillips Petroleum Co., Richmond, Va., 1966-69; pres. Air Control, Inc., Hampton, Va., 1969-74; asst. to pres. Mech. Projects, Inc., Hampton, 1974-75; pres. Jacobs and Assos., Inc., Hampton, 1975—; gen. partner Contractors Assos. Active United Fund, 1973-76; bd. dirs., vestryman Grace Episcopal Ch., Yorktown, Va., 1973-76. Served to capt. USAR, 1966-76. Mem. Hampton Retail Mchts. (dir. 1972), C. of C., Am. Soc. Heating, Refrigeration and Air Conditioning Engrs., Nat. Contract Mgmt. Assn. (pres. chpt. 1979-80). Republican. Clubs: Lions (pres. Hampton 1976-77), Yacht, Elks, Masons. Home: 104 Three Point Ct Yorktown VA 23690 Office: 28 Research Dr Hampton VA 23666

JACOBS, EUGENE ROBERT, radiologist; b. N.Y.C., Sept. 22, 1929; s. Kalman Monroe and Sylvia (Hurwitz) J.; B.A. cum laude, Syracuse U., 1951; M.D., State U. N.Y. at Syracuse, 1955; m. Carol Ruth Levine, July 1, 1951; children—Lori Ellen, Susan Robin. Intern, Temple U. Hosp., 1955-56, resident radiology, 1956-59; chief radiology U.S. Army Hosp., Ft. Jay, N.Y., 1959-61; dir. radiology Nat. Orthopaedic and Rehab. Hosp., Arlington, Va., 1961—; mem. No. Va. Orthopaedic and Allied Spltys. Clinic, Alexandria, 1965—; asst. clin. prof. radiology George Washington U. Sch. Medicine and Health Scis., 1974-78, asso. clin. prof., 1978—. Mem. Alexandria Sanitation Authority, 1967—. Served to capt. AUS, 1959-61. Diplomate Am. Bd. Radiology. Mem. Alexandria Med. Soc. (treas., pres. 1978), Med. Soc. Va. (del. 1979, 80), Am., So. med. assns., Am. Geriatrics Soc. (founding fellow So. div.), Am. Coll. Radiology (pres. D.C. area chpt. 1979), A.C.P., Med. Council No. Va. (pres. 1979), Va. Water Pollution Control Assn., Phi Delta Epsilon. Home: 203 Yoakum Pkwy Alexandria VA 22304 Office: 2500 N Van Dorn St Alexandria VA 22302

JACOBS, FREDERIC WEIL, foundry exec.; b. Indpls., Oct. 25, 1917; s. Frederic Burnham and Mina (Price) J.; B.S., Case Inst. Tech., 1939; m. Honora Mary Masters, Jan. 17, 1942; children—Frederic C., Gary N., Philip J. Metallurgist, Lake City Malleable Co., Cleve., 1939-41, chief metallurgist, Ashtabula, Ohio, 1944-48, asst. plant mgr., 1948-50; prodn. mgr. Columbus Malleable Iron Co., 1941-44; chief metallurgist Tex. Foundries, Inc., Lufkin, 1950-57, tech. dir., 1957—; chmn. tech. com. Metals Research and Devel. Found., 1973, 78-79. Bd. dirs. Angelina County Tb Soc.; bd. dirs. Salvation Army, Lufkin, chmn. bd., 1972-73. Mem. Am. Foundrymen's Soc. (chmn. malleable div. 1960-61, exec. com. 1961-78, research bd. 1975-78), Malleable Founders Soc. (chmn. research and tech. com. 1968-70), Tex. Soc. Profl. Engrs. (state dir. 1962-65, chpt. chmn. 1961), Alpha Delta, Phi Kappa Tau. Methodist (chmn. commn. on edn. 1969-71, chmn. council on ministries 1971-73). Clubs: Kiwanis (dir. 1971-73, 1st v.p. 1973-74, pres. 1974-75, lt. gov. 1979-80), Exchange (v.p. 1968). Home: 1112 Wildbriar Dr Lufkin TX 75901 Office: PO Box 1608 Lufkin TX 75901

JACOBS, JESSIE FRED, city ofcl.; b. Corsicana, Tex., May 27, 1931; s. Arvel Lee and Myrtle Elizabeth (Jergins) J.; Asso. Sci., Eastfield Coll., 1974; m. Lourine Higginbotham, June 9, 1951; children—Wesly Earl, Freeda Jean, Lowell Wayde. Crane operator Oil City Iron Works, Corsicana, 1950-52; storage supr. Lone Star Ordinance, Texarkana, Tex., 1952-53; supr. Corsicana Water Dept., 1954-57; supt. Cleburne Water Dept., Tex., 1957-62, 64-67; supr. Richardson Water Dept., Tex., 1968; supt. Mesuite Water Dept., Tex., 1969-72, 76—; asst. gen. mgr. Southwest Water Services, Inc., Dallas, 1972-76; instr. part-time public service careers tng. Tex. A. and M. Extension Service, 1971-72. Chmn. mcpl. div. United Way, 1979. Served with U.S. Army, 1961-62. Recipient Meritorious Service award East Tex. Regional Short Sch., 1977. Mem. Am. Water Works Assn. (trustee Tex. sect. 1974-75), Water Pollution Control Fedn., Tex. Water Utilities Assn. (v.p. 1971-73, pres. 1980), Cedar Creek Utilities Assn. (Man of the Year 1978), Blacklands Water Utilities Assn., Apollo Water Utilities Assn., N. Tex. Council of Govts. (mem. task com. 1970-71), Mesquite Softball Ofcls. Assn. Baptist. Home: 1311 Richard St Mesquite TX 75149 Office: PO Box 137 Mesquite TX 75149

JACOBS, JOSEPH LESLIE, research engr.; b. Hartsville, S.C., June 1, 1937; s. W.S. and L.P. J.; student Ga. Inst. Tech., 1956-57; B.S. in Chem. Engring., U. S.C., 1959; children—Joseph Leslie, Rebecca, Mark, Eric. With Atlanta Paper Co., 1959-60, Hartsville (S.C.) Oil Processing, 1960, Sonoco Products Co. Research, Hartsville, 1960-79, sr. research engr. corp. research lab., 1976-79, product mgr.-cones, 1979—. Served with U.S. Army, 1960-61. Mem. S.C. Acad. Sci., Textured Yarn Assn. Am., Am. Inst. Chem. Engrs. Episcopalian. Clubs: S.C. Jaycees (state dir. 1958-59), Masons. Patentee slip sleeves for textile carrier processing, U.S. and Can.; contbr. article to Can. publs. Home: 709 Prestwood Dr Hartsville SC 29550 Office: Sonoco N 2nd St Hartsville SC 29550

JACOBS, KEITH WILLIAM, psychologist, educator; b. Ames, Iowa, Feb. 24, 1944; s. Cyril W. and Sylvia Jacobs; B.A., U. No. Iowa, 1968; M.A., Eastern Ill. U., 1972; Ph.D., U. So. Miss., 1975. Adj. instr. psychology Natchez br. U. So. Miss., 1974-75; asso. prof. psychology Loyola U., New Orleans, 1975—; lectr. psychology Our Lady of Holy Cross Coll., New Orleans, 1976—; aux. faculty William Carey Coll. Sch. Nursing, New Orleans, 1979—. Active Childbirth Edn. Assn. New Orleans, ACLU; exec. bd. Oak Harbor Homeowners Assn., 1979—. Served with U.S. Army, 1968-71. Mem. Am. Psychol. Assn., Am. Assn. Sex Educators, Counselors and Therapists (cert. sex educator and counselor), Am. Ednl. Research Assn., La. Acad. Scis., Southeastern Psychol. Assn., Sigma Xi. Contbr. articles to sci. publs. Home: PO Box 102 Pearlington MS 39572 Office: Dept Psychology Loyola U New Orleans LA 70118

JACOBS, KENNETH ROY, historian, educator; b. Franklin, N.C., July 9, 1933; s. Floyd Stevenson and Wilma Marie (Angel) J.; B.A. in History, Quincy Coll., 1967; postgrad. SW Tex. State U., summer 1968; M.A., Hardin-Simmons U., 1970; Ph.D. (O'Brien award), Tex. Tech. U., 1977; m. Marilyn Jean Page, Apr. 28, 1962. History tchr. Sweetwater (Tex.) High Sch., 1968-71; part time instr. history Tex. Tech. U., Lubbock, 1971-76; asst. prof. history Hardin-Simmons U., Abilene, Tex., 1977—; mem. Tex. com. of Nat. Coordinating Council for Promotion of History. Served with USAF, 1950-54. Mem. Am. Hist. Assn., Tex. State Hist. Assn., W.Tex. Hist. Assn. (contbr. yearbook, 1978, asso. editor yearbook, 1979), Permian Basin Hist. Assn., Phi Alpha Theta, Pi Gamma Mu. Baptist. Home: 2466 Simmons St Abilene TX 79601 Office: Hardin-Simmons U Box 1160 Abilene TX 79698

JACOBS, NORMAN FREDERICK, JR., physician; b. Mineola, N.Y., Oct. 18, 1946; s. Norman Frederick and Helen Danow J.; B.A. cum laude, U. Conn., 1967; M.D. with highest honors, Upstate Med. Center, Syracuse, N.Y., 1971; m. Kathleen Ann Burgess, Aug. 19, 1967; children—Douglass, Nicole. Intern, Strong Meml. Hosp., Rochester, N.Y., 1971-72, resident, 1972-73; med. research officer Center for Disease Control, Atlanta, 1973-75; resident, fellow in medicine Emory U. Sch. Medicine, 1975-77; attending physician Grady Meml. Hosp., 1977—, DeKalb Gen. Hosp., Decatur, Ga., 1977—; clin. asst. prof. medicine Emory U. Sch. Medicine, 1977—; vol. physician Scottdale Med. Clinic, 1977-78. Served with USPHS, 1973-75. NIH fellow, 1976-77. Mem. A.C.P., Am. Soc. Microbiology, Am. Fedn. Clin. Research, AMA, Med. Assn. Ga., DeKalb Med. Soc., Phi Beta Kappa, Alpha Omega Alpha. Contbr. chpts. to books; contbr. articles to med. jours. Office: 2712 N Decatur Rd Decatur GA 30033

JACOBSEN, JAMES ALVA, musician; b. Norwood, Colo., May 8, 1920; s. Arthur Chris and Kathryn Georgia (Zunich) J.; B.A., U. No. Colo., 1942; M.Mus.Ed., Tex. Christian U., 1952; D.Mus. (hon.), So. Coll. Fine Arts, 1955; m. Wyneth Louise Berry, Dec. 15, 1946; children—Carol Lynn Jacobsen Alexander, James Kent. Dir. bands, prof. music edn. Midwestern U., 1945-55; dir. bands, prof. music edn. Tex. Christian U., 1955—; guest condr.; band contest adjudicator; music cons.; band workshop lectr. Served with USAAF, 1943-45. Named One of 10 Outstanding Ednl. Music Dirs. Am., Sch. Musician, Dir. and Tchr. Mag., 1972. Mem. Am. Band Masters Assn., Coll. Band Dirs. Nat. Assn. (past dist. pres., past nat. dir.), Music Educators Nat. Conf., Tex. Music Educators Assn., Tex. Bandmasters Assn., SW Conf. Band Dirs. Assn. (pres.), Phi Mu Alpha Sinfonia, Kappa Kappa Psi (nat. pres. 1969-71), Phi Beta Mu, Blue Key. Democrat. Mem. Christian Ch. Clubs: Masons (32 deg.), Shriners. Home: 4300 Whitfield St Fort Worth TX 76109

JACOBSEN, RUTH JUNE, nurse; b. Remer, Minn., Sept. 16, 1934; d. John William and Josephine Agnes (Steiner) Budd; B.S., Walla Walla (Wash.) Coll., 1958, M.A., 1961; postgrad. Cath. U. Am., UCLA, U. Calif. (San Francisco); m. Donald Gene Jacobsen, Feb. 6, 1972; stepchildren—Jerry, Randy. Head nurse Walla Walla Gen. Hosp., 1959-61; clin. instr. Walla Walla Coll. at Portland (Oreg.) Sanitarium, 1961-64; clin. instr. Pacific Union Coll., Angwin, Calif., 1964-66; asso. dir. Sch. Nursing, Glendale (Calif.) Adventist Hosp., 1966-72; asst. dir. nursing service Kettering Med. Center, Ohio, 1972-74; asst. prof. nursing Columbia Union Coll., Md., 1974-79; asst. prof. nursing Andrews U., Berrien Springs, Mich., 1979—; participant workshops, convs. and confs. Named nurse of year Assn. Seventh-day Adventist Nurses, 1971. Mem. Marriage Encounter (with husband, nat. pastoral couple). Seventh-day Adventist. Author: Do It the Right Way, 1970; contbr. articles profl. jours. Home: 507 Stonemont Dr Stone Mountain GA 30087

JACOBSOHN, GUY, mathematician; b. Paris, Oct. 15, 1938; came to U.S., 1956, naturalized, 1972; s. Samuel Simon and Rachel Leone (Lefevre) J.; B.S. in Elec. Engring., Calif. State Coll., Long Beach, 1961, B.A. in Math., 1963, M.S. in Math., 1964; m. Nancy Creel Winborne, Apr. 4, 1969; 1 stepdau., Elizabeth Sullivan. Instr. math., chmn. dept. Marymount Coll., Palos Verdes Estates, Calif., 1964-66; engr.-scientist research div. McDonnel Douglas Aircraft Corp., 1966-67; asst. prof. math. Fayetteville (N.C.) State U., 1968-70, U. S.C., Spartanburg, 1970—. Mem. AAUP, Math. Assn. Am., Alliance Francaise (past pres. Piedmont chpt.), AAU (v.p. S.C. 1977—), Eastern Collegiate Judo Assn. (v.p. 1975—). Club: Alpin Français. Home: 143 Cornelius Rd Spartanburg SC 29301 Office: Univ SC Spartanburg SC 29303

JACOBSON, ALAN FRANK, psychologist; b. Portland, Maine, Sept. 19, 1947; s. Myer and Nellie (Levin) J.; A.B., U. Miami, 1969, M.S., 1971, Ph.D., 1973; m. Rose Frankel, June 14, 1970; children—Mark Howard, Brian Scott. Instr. dept. psychiatry Sch. Medicine, U. Miami (Fla.), 1973-76, asst. prof., 1976—; cons. psychologist Sunrise Sch. for Retarded. NSF grantee, 1974-75, NIH grantee, 1976, 77; lic. psychologist, Fla. Mem. Am. Psychol. Assn. (charter div. health psychology), Fla. Psychol. Assn. (cert. profl. psychologist), Dade County Psychol. Assn., Assn. for Advancement of Behavior Therapy, Biofeedback Soc. Am., S. Fla. Behaviorist Soc. (mem. at large), Biofeedback Soc. Fla. (dir.), Biofeedback Soc. S.E. Fla. (pres. 1979-80), Psi Chi. Home: 8122 SW 103d St Miami FL 33156 Office: U Miami Sch Medicine (D-29) Dept Psychiatry PO Box 016960 Miami FL 33101

JACOBSON, BERNARD, lawyer, investment co. exec.; b. Hartford, Conn., Feb. 27, 1930; s. Samuel Barnard and Lillian (Canter) J.; A.B., Amherst Coll., 1951; LL.B., Columbia U., 1954; m. Florence Ellen Greenberg, Oct. 7, 1956; children—Daniel, Alice, Nancy. Admitted to Conn. bar, 1955, Fla. bar, 1957; practiced in Miami, 1957—; mem. firm Fine, Jacobson, Block, Klein, Colan & Simon, Miami, 1968—; pres. Mortgage Investment Services, Inc., 1973—, dir., 1969—; trustee Republic Mortgage Investors, 1968—, sec., 1969—, pres., 1979—; dir. Dade Savs. and Loan Assn., Mfrs. Nat. Bank. Chmn. Dade County Citizens Adv. Com. on Community Improvement, 1969-70. Lectr. law U. Miami, 1965-66. Served with CIC, AUS, 1955-57. Mem. Am., Fla., Dade County bar assns., Phi Delta Phi. Office: 2401 Douglas Rd Miami FL 33145

JACOBSON, DAVID, rabbi; b. Cin., Dec. 2, 1909; s. Abraham and Rebecca (Sereinsky) J.; A.B., U. Cin., 1931; rabbi Hebrew Union Coll., 1934, D.D. (hon.), 1959; Ph.D., St. Catherine's Coll., U. Cambridge (Eng.), 1936; LL.D., Our Lady of Lake Coll., 1964; m. Helen Gugenheim, Nov. 6, 1938; children—Elizabeth Ann, Dorothy Jean Jacobson Miller. Instr., Hebrew Union Coll., 1933-34; rabbi W. Central Liberal Congregation, London, Eng., 1934-36, Indpls. Hebrew Congregation, 1936-38, Temple Beth-El, San Antonio, 1938-76, emeritus, 1976—; pres., exec. dir. Am. Inst. Character 1976-78; Edn., host show KSAT-TV; pres. Kallah of Tex. Rabbis, 1950-51, chancellor-historian, 1977—; pres. S.W. region Central Conf. Am. Rabbis, 1969-70, chmn. health com., 1967-73, chmn. nominating com., 1979-80; chmn. Rabbinical Placement Commn., 1973-78, Tex. Ethics Com., 1971, Tex. Task Force on Medicaid, 1977; mem. com. on welfare reform Tex. Senate, 1970; arbitrator San Antonio Typographical Union 172; founder U. Ind. Hillel Found., 1938. Pres. San Antonio Soc. Crippled Children and Adults, 1963-66; pres. Goodwill Industries San Antonio, 1956-60, also mem. bd.; mem. bd. Goodwill Industries Am., 1965-78; pres. Bexar County chpt. Nat. Tb Assn., 1955-57; founder Community Welfare Council San Antonio, 1944, pres., 1951-53; pres. Tex. Social Welfare Assn., 1967-69; bd. dirs. Bexar Metro chpt. Am. Cancer Soc., 1977—; life mem., exec. com. Tex. United Community Services, Inc., 1970—, USO Nat. Council, 1968—; commr. Housing Authority San Antonio, 1954-58; pres. Alamo chpt. Multiple Sclerosis Soc., 1974-77; bd. dirs. Our Lady of Lake Coll., 1966-75, Nat. Jewish Welfare Bd., 1964-72, Nat. Council Crime and Delinquency, 1971-; chmn. Bexar County Community Corrections Commn., 1979—, bd. govs. Hebrew Union Coll.-Jewish Inst. Religion, 1966-69, alumni bd. overseers, 1973—; bd. dirs. S.W. Texas Meth. Hosp., San Antonio Med. Found.; mem. exec. com., bd. dirs. Alamo council Boy Scouts Am.; bd. dirs. Children's Hosp. Found., Keystone Sch., San Antonio; pres. San Antonio Area Found., 1965-73; pres. San Antonio Manpower Devel. Council, 1968-73; pres. San Antonio br. Tex. Soc. to Prevent Blindness, 1980—. Served as chaplain USNR, 1944-46. Recipient Silver Beaver award Boy Scouts Am., 1958; Aristotle-Aquinas award Cath. Coll. Found. S.A., 1959; Golden Deeds award Exchange Club San Antonio, 1959; Keystone award Boys Clubs Am., 1962; Edgar J. Helms award Goodwill Industries Am., 1972; Humanitarian award Nat. B'nai B'rith, 1975; named Outstanding Jew, NCCJ, 1961; Outstanding Citizen of Year, Sembradores de Amistad, 1971. Mem. Tex. PTA (hon. life), Nat. Conf. Social Welfare (dir. 1967-69, 75—, pres. 1976-77), Am. Arbitration Assn. (labor arbitration panel 1977—), Sigma Alpha Mu, Pi Tau Pi. Clubs: Rotary, B'nai B'rith (hon. pres. chpt. 1973), Torch (past pres.), Argyle (San Antonio). Author: Social Background of the Old Testament, 1942; The Synagogue Through the Ages, 1958; also articles. Home: 207 Beechwood Ln San Antonio TX 78216 Office: 211 Belknap Pl San Antonio TX 78212

JACOBSON, HELEN G. (MRS. DAVID JACOBSON), civic worker; b. San Antonio; d. Jac Elton and Rosetta (Dreyfus) Gugenheim; B.A., Hollins Coll.; m. David Jacobson, Nov. 6, 1938; children—Elizabeth Ann, Dorothy Jean (Mrs. Sam Miller). News, spl. events staff NBC, N.Y.C., 1933-38. First v.p. San Antonio, Bexar County council Girl Scouts U.S.A., 1957-63; Tex. state rep. UNICEF, 1964-69, bd. dirs. U.S. Com. UNICEF; chmn. Mayor's Commn. on Status of Women, 1972-74; mem. Tex. coordinating com. Internat. Women's Year, 1977; mem. criminal justice planning com. Alamo Area Council Govts., chmn., 1975-77; pres. women's com. Ecumenical Center Religion and Health, 1975-77; bd. dirs. Nat. Fedn. Temple Sisterhoods, 1973-77, Temple Beth-El Sisterhood, mem. Commn. Social Action of Reform Judaism, 1973-77; bd. dirs. Community Guidance Center, chmn. bd., 1960-63; bd. dirs. Sunshine Cottage Sch. for Deaf Children, chmn. bd., 1952-54; pres. bd. trustees San Antonio Pub. Library, 1957-61; nat. trustee Nat. Council on Crime and Delinquency, 1964-70, now bd. mem. Tex. council; trustee San Antonio Mus. Assn., 1964-73; sec. Nat. Assembly Social Policy and Devel., 1969-73; pres. Community Welfare Council, 1968-70; bd. dirs. Tex. United Community Services; bd. dirs. Foster Grandparents Bexar County, pres., 1968-69, v.p., 1970-73; mem. gov.'s steering com., del. 1970 White House Conf. on Children and Youth; bd. govs., sec. Cancer Therapy and Research Found. South Tex., Am. Inst. for Character Edn.; pres. Central and S. Tex. Coalition Juvenile Justice, 1977-79; chmn. women's campaign Jewish Fedn. San Antonio; bd. dirs. San Antonio chpt. NCCJ, Youth Alternatives, Inc. Recipient Headliner award for civic work San Antonio chpt. Theta Sigma Phi, 1958, Nat. Humanitarian award B'nai B'rith, 1975; named Vol. Woman of Year, Express-News, 1959; Brotherhood award San Antonio chpt. NCCJ, 1970; Non-Govtl. Orgns. UNICEF Vol. of Year, 1977; honoree Jewish Nat. Hosp. and Research Center, 1978; Hannah G. Solomon award chpt. Nat. Council Jewish Women, 1979. Mem. San Antonio Women's Fedn., Tex. Fedn. Women's Clubs (past bd. mem. Alamo dist.), Nat. Council Jewish Women, Symphony Soc. (women's com.). Club: Argyle. Home: 207 Beechwood Ln San Antonio TX 78216

JACOBSON, LEO, clothing mfg. exec.; b. Buenos Aires, Argentina, Nov. 3, 1937; s. Samuel and Celia Irene J.; came to U.S., 1965, naturalized, 1971; student U. Derecho, Buenos Aires; m. Harriet Perry, May 16, 1960; children—Danisa Irina and Diego (twins). Garment cutter Amgus Knitting Co., Bronx, N.Y., 1965; foreman Gotthelf Knitting Co., Boonton, N.J., 1965-66; from foreman to v.p. Gibraltar Industries Inc., Bklyn., 1966-78; chmn. bd., chief exec. officer Amertex Enterprises Ltd., San Lorenzo, P.R., 1978—. Named Ky. col., 1973. Mem. P.R. Mfrs. Assn., Am. Apparel Mfrs. Assn. Inventor collapsible container. Office: PO Box P Route 183 Km 78 San Lorenzo PR 00754

JACOBSON, LEONARD I., educator, psychologist; b. Bklyn., Aug. 9, 1940; s. Harry L. and Violet (Natkin) J.; A.B. cum laude (N.Y. State Regents scholar), City U. N.Y., 1961; Ph.D., State U. N.Y., Buffalo, 1966. Research psychologist Children's Hosp., Buffalo, 1965-66; asst. prof. psychology U. Miami, Coral Gables, Fla., 1966-71, asso. prof. psychology, 1971-76, prof., 1976—; adj. asst. prof. Guidance Center, 1969-70; cons. Sunland Tng. Center at Miami, Opa-Locka, 1969-72; clin. psychology cons. Miami Mental Health Center, 1968-79; cons. Camarillo (Cal.) State Hosp., 1970; cons. clin. psychology Mailman Center for Child Devel., U. Miami Sch. Medicine, 1972-75; cons. psychologist Miami Lighthouse for the Blind, 1975—. USPHS clin. fellow, 1962-63, research grantee NSF, 1966-68, NIMH, 1967-68, NIH, 1968, Soc. Psychol. Study Social Issues, 1969, NASA, 1969-71. Mem. Am., Southeastern, Western, Fla. psychol. assns., AAAS, Assn. for Advancement of Behavior Therapy, Am. Assn. Workers for the Blind, Soc. for Research in Child Devel., Psychonomic Soc., Soc. for Psychotherapy Research, Sigma Xi, Psi Chi. Republican. Contbr. articles to profl. publs. Office: Dept Psychology U Miami Coral Gables FL 33124

JACOWAY, BRONSON COOPER, lawyer; b. Dardanelle, Ark., Mar. 26, 1909; s. Henderson Madison and Margaret Helena (Cooper) J.; student Hendrix Coll., 1925-27, U. Ark., 1927-29; LL.B., Harvard U., 1932; m. Daisy Tribble, Apr. 23, 1938; children—Bronson Cooper, Daisy Elizabeth, Madison Doak. Admitted to Ark. bar, 1932, U.S. Supreme Ct. bar, 1939; practice of law, Little Rock, 1932—; asst. state counsel Home Owners Loan Corp., 1933-37; city atty. City of Little Rock, 1940-46; counsel Hwy. Audit Commn., 1953-54; mem. firm Jacoway and Sherman, 1969—. Pres. bd. Ark. Children's Hosp., 1947-50; bd. dirs. YMCA; chmn. Little Rock Civil Service Commn., 1966-69; tchr. Sunday sch., mem. bd. stewards Methodist Ch. Mem. Am. Bar Assn., Ark. Bar Assn. (mem. ho. of dels. 1972), Pulaski County Bar Assn. (pres.). Democrat. Clubs: Little Rock Country, Little Rock, Sigma Chi Alumni, Masons, Shriners. Home: 1800 N Spruce St Little Rock AR 72207 Office: 504 Pyramid Bldg Little Rock AR 72201

JACQUES, RICHARD DOUGLAS, city ofcl.; b. Trenton, N.J., Dec. 7, 1949; s. Henry Pinkham and Dorothy Killion J.; B.A., Lynchburg Coll., 1971; M.S. in Pub. Adminstrn., George Washington U., 1978; m. Carolyn Wingfield, Feb. 9, 1974; children—Richard Douglas, Jaclyn Elizabeth. Asst. city planner City of Lynchburg, Va., 1971, intergovtl. relations coordinator, 1971-74, staff asst. to city mgr., 1974-76, mgmt. services adminstr., 1976-78, dir. dept. community planning and devel., 1978—; adj. faculty Averett Coll.; bd. treas. Greater Lynchburg Transit Co., Inc.; v.p. Central Va. Spl. Transportation Co., Inc. spl. liaison Va. Gen. Assembly, 1973. Ex-officio mem. Lynchburg Drug Abuse Task Force, 1972-74, Lynchburg Bicentennial Commn., 1972-76; bd. dirs. Central Va. Regional Health Planning Council, 1972-76; mem. bd. Va. Regional Med. Program, 1972-74; mem. adv. com. Lynchburg Overall Economic Devel. program, 1977—; sect. leader United Way, Lynchburg, 1977-78, div. leader, 1978—, bd. dirs., 1980—. Mem. Lynchburg Pub. Relations Assn., Greater Lynchburg Jaycees, Internat. City Mgmt. Assn., Nat. Council Urban Econ. Devel., Am. Planning Assn. Presbyterian. Home: 1374 Wakefield Rd Lynchburg VA 24503 Office: City Hall PO Box 60 Lynchburg VA 24505

JACQUES, WILFRED JAMES, JR., lawyer, financial cons. co. exec.; b. Chatham, Ont., Can., May 5, 1932; s. Wilfred James and Almeda (Buie) J.; student U. Ga., 1950-51; B.A., U. Western Ont., 1956; LL.B., U. Ga., 1956; LL.M., N.Y. U., 1964; student Advanced Mgmt. Program, Harvard U., 1970; m. Mary Aleece Strickland, Mar. 7, 1958; 1 son, Wilfred James. Admitted to Ga. bar, 1957; with Deen and Jacques attys. at law, Alma, Ga., 1957-63; with Straus Duparquet Inc., House Counsel, N.Y.C., 1964-65; with Harrell Internat. Inc. and subsidiaries, Jacksonville, Fla., 1965-71, sr. v.p., dir., until 1971; chmn. Jacques Co., Fin. Cons., 1971—; practice law, Waycross, Ga., 1973—; prof. mgmt. U. No. Colo., Greeley, 1977—. Home: PO Box 447 Waycross GA 31501 Office: 701 Carswell Ave Waycross GA 31501

JACYNA, GARRY MICHAEL, research scientist; b. Amsterdam, N.Y., Mar. 7, 1951; s. John Stephen and Lillian Ann (DeGroff) J.; B.S. in Physics, Rensselaer Poly. Inst., 1973, M.S. in Math., 1974, Ph.D. in Applied Math., 1977; m. Patricia Ann Essler, May 25, 1974. Sr. research scientist Planning Systems, Inc., McLean, Va., 1977—; adj. prof. elec. engring. Cath. U. Am.; tech. cons. acoustics and signal processing. Mem. Acoustical Soc. Am., Soc. Indsl. and Applied Math., IEEE, Pi Mu Epsilon. Roman Catholic. Club: TRS 80 Microcomputer. Reviewer, contbr. to Jour. Acoustical Soc. Am.; reviewer IEEE. Home: 8948 Sweetbriar St Manassas VA 22110 Office: 7900 Westpark Dr McLean VA 22101

JAEGER, RAYMOND ALPHONS, veterinarian; b. Pitts., June 28, 1928; s. Alphons Otto and Hedwig Marie (Wuermel) J.; student Villanova U., 1946-47, Keystone Coll., 1947-48, Lynchburg Coll., 1960-62, Va. Poly. Inst., 1961; D.V.M., U. Ga., 1966; m. Joah Marie Cellone, Jan. 27, 1950; children—A. Gregory, Robin A., Ivajoan M. Research technician Gulf Oil Corp., 1948-50; parts mgr. Bridgeville Sales Co., 1950-53; farmer, Lynchburg, Va., 1953-66; insp. U.S. Dept. Agr., Athens, Ga., 1966-67; disease control veterinarian Va. Dept. Agr., Lynchburg, 1967-68; practice veterinary medicine, Lynchburg, 1968—; pres. Diagnostic Aid Service Co. Inc., Street Zoo Inc. Mem. AVMA, Va. (dir.), Piedmont (pres.) veterinary med. assns., Va. Fedn. Dog Owners (dir.), Am. Radiol. Soc., Internat. Veterinary Acupuncture Soc. Roman Catholic. Home: 2533 Link Rd Lynchburg VA 24503 Office: 3709 Old Forest Rd Lynchburg VA 24501

JAFFE, DAVID BRUCE, steel co. exec.; b. Great Neck, N.Y., Dec. 23, 1941; s. Herman and Hannah Louise (Blum) J.; B.A., Lafayette Coll., Easton, Pa., 1963; postgrad. Fordham U. Sch. Law, 1963-65, Bernard Baruch Sch. Bus. Adminstrn., 1964-66; m. Georganne Klee Vogel, Dec. 14, 1969; children—Pamela Klee, David Bruce. Sr. mgmt. cons. Ernst & Ernst, N.Y.C., 1965-67, 69-70; project dir. Cadence Industries, Inc., N.Y.C., 1970-73; ind. cons., N.Y.C., 1973; exec. v.p., chief exec. officer and dir. Peerless Plastics, Inc. subs. Faber, Coe & Gregg, Inc., N.Y.C., 1974-76; pres., dir. Quinn Sheet Metal Crp., Ft. Worth and Jaffe-Klee Corp., Ft. Worth, 1977—; instr. U.S. Army Logistics Mgmt. Sch., Va., 1967-68. Served to capt. U.S. Army, 1967-69; Vietnam. Decorated Bronze Star. Mem. Assn. Corp. Growth (exec. v.p. 1979-80), Assn. Mgmt. Cons., Delta Kappa Epsilon. Clubs: Shady Oaks Country (Ft. Worth); Yale (N.Y.C.). Home: 4545 S Lindhurst Dallas TX 75229 also 19 E 88th St New York NY 10028 Office: 3313 May St Fort Worth TX 76110

JAFFE, HERMAN, accountant; b. N.Y.C., Jan. 24, 1903; s. Morris S. and Rose (Weiss) J.; B.S., N.Y. U., 1924; m. Hannah Louise Blum, Aug. 19, 1934; children—Richard R., David B., Kenneth P. C.P.A., N.Y. State, Tex. Individual practice, N.Y.C., 1928—; admitted to practice, Tax Ct. U.S., 1928—. Mem. Internat. Fiscal Assn., Am. Inst. C.P.A.'s, N.Y. State, Conn., Tex. socs. C.P.A.'s. Author, lectr., instr., cons. internat. tax law. Home: 7920 Royal Ln Dallas TX 75230 Office: 2200 LTV Tower Dallas TX 75201

JAHN, EDWARD LOUIS, tech. writer; b. Omaha, Mar. 11, 1915; s. James John and Antoinette Cecilia (Pliska) J.; student U.S. Mil. Acad. 1934-36; B.A., Wayne State U., 1971; M.S., East Tex. State U., 1976, Ph.D., 1980; m. Billie Jane Downing, Dec. 6, 1942; children—Antoinette, James T., Thomas L., Edward Louis, Janette E. Accountant, Firestone Tire and Rubber Co., 1947-49; gen. mgr. Leisure Mat Corp., 1950-58; office engr. Mich. Hwy. Dept., 1963-72; tech. writer, rancher, Mt. Vernon, Tex., 1973-78; research scientist Dos Cabezas, Inc., 1978, pres., 1979—. Served with U.S. Army, 1939-47; with USAF, 1959-62. Decorated Silver Star; Order of Suvorov; Croix de Guerre (France). Mem. AAAS, Am. Math. Assn., Am. Math. Soc., Soc. for Indsl. and Applied Math., Am. Geophys. Union, Am. Geol. Inst. Internat. Platform Assn., Kappa Delta Pi, Phi Delta Kappa. Democrat. Roman Catholic. Club: K.P. Co-author: Computer Usage in Education, 1976; co-author Psychopathology for Nursing Students, 1977; Community College Administration, 1978. Contbr. articles to profl jours. Home: PO Box 594 Mount Vernon TX 75457 Office: PO Box 340 Mount Vernon TX 75457

JAIN, RAJENDRA KUMAR, urologist; b. Damoh, India, July 13, 1940; s. Phundilal and Smt Kosha (Bai) J.; M.D., M.G.M. Med. Coll., Indore, India, 1966; came to U.S., 1968, naturalized, 1971; m. Shashi Jain, Dec. 8, 1966; children—Rajiv, Vivek, Preeti. Intern, Bergen Pines County Hosp., Paramus, N.J., 1968; resident in surgery Englewood (N.J.) Hosp., 1969-71; resident in anesthesia and urology Hahnemann Med. Coll., Phila., 1971-76; attending urologist W. Jersey Hosp., Camden 1976, A.R. Hosp., South Williamson, Ky., 1977, St. Marys Hosp., Huntington, W.Va., 1978—, Cabell Huntington Hosp., 1978—; clin. asso. prof. urology Marshall Med. Coll., Huntington. Diplomate Am. Bd. Urology. Mem. Cabell County Med. Soc., W.Va. Med. Soc Home: 114 Larkspur Dr Huntington WV 25705 Office: 1426 6th Ave Huntington WV 25701

JAIN, SURESH CHAND, indsl. engr.; b. India, July 1, 1941; s. Jyoti Swarup and Vimla Devi Jain; came to U.S., 1969, naturalized, 1976; M.S. in Indsl. Engring., Mont. State U., 1970; M.B.A., U. Dallas, 1976; m. Pramila Jain, Nov. 16, 1964; children—Shefali, Shiraz. Mech. engr. Heavy Engring. Corp., India, 1962-69; mfg. engr. Harris Corp., Dallas, 1972-75; sr. quality assurance engr. Docutel Corp., Dallas, 1975-76; sr. mfg. engr. Abbott Labs., Dallas, 1976—. Registered profl. engr., Tex. Mem. Am. Inst. Indsl. Engrs. (sr.), Sigma Iota Epsilon. Home: 3531 Appalachian Way Plano TX 75075 Office: 4757 Irving Blvd Dallas TX 75247

JAMES, ADVERGUS DELL, JR., coll. adminstr.; b. Garden City, Kans., Sept. 24, 1944; s. Advergus Dell and Helen Gertrude (Lee) J.; B.S., Langston (Okla.) U., 1966; M.S., Okla. State U., 1969; m. Anna Glenn, Dec. 25, 1971. Asst. registrar Langston U., 1966-68, instr. bus. dept., dir. admissions and records, 1969-70; grad. asst. Okla. State U., 1968-69; asst. prof. bus dept., dir. student financial aid Prairie View (Tex.) A. and M. U., 1970—. Regional instr. data mgmt. and systems for 2-year colls. Mem. Am., Okla. assns. collegiate registrars and admissions officers, Nat Bus. Edn. Assn., Am. Vocational Assn., Nat. Assn. for Financial Assistance to Minority Students, So. Coll. Personnel Assn., Higher Edn. Alumni Council, Langston U., Okla. State U. alumni assns., N.A.A.C.P., Nat., Southwestern assns. student financial aid adminstrs., Phi Beta Lambda, Alpha Phi, Phi Delta Kappa, Kappa Delta Pi Mason (32 deg.), Optomist (charter Prairie View chpt.); mem. Order Rising Star. Home: 4734 Geneva Dr Houston TX 77066 Office: Drawer C Prairie View TX 77445

JAMES, ANTHONY JOSEPH, JR., advt. agy. exec.; b. New Orleans, Feb. 19, 1943; s. Anthony Joseph and Catherine (Nesmith) J.; student McNeese State Coll.; m. Gladys L. Oqueli, June 13, 1972; 1 son, Arden Christopher. Exec. v.p. INFOads, Advt., Charleston, S.C., 1979—; pres. Unichem, Inc., Charleston, 1978—, also dir.; dir. Transmedia Entertainment, Cajam Film Prodn. Co. Chmn. pub. relations and program coms. Com. to Bring Miss USA Back to Charleston; mem. steering com. Charleston Miss USA. Recipient Pub. Service awards ARC, Cancer Soc., Heart Fund, Printing Industry of Carolinas Assn. Democrat. Roman Catholic. Club: Snee Farm Country. Home: 205 Columbia Dr Ladson SC 29456 Office: Suite 115 Fairfield Office Park Charleston SC 29401

JAMES, BARBARA ODOM, educator; b. Jasper, Tex., May 7, 1948; d. Elzie Delano and Ruby Odom; B.S., Incarnate Word Coll., 1969, postgrad., 1977—; children—Krystal Levonne, Amber Odonne. Mental health record coordinator Bexar County Community Mental Health Center, San Antonio, 1969-71; dir. med. record dept. Bexar County Hosp., San Antonio, 1971-72; sr. med. record adminstr. Bexar County Hosp. Dist., San Antonio, 1972-73; dir. med. record adminstrn. Incarnate Word Coll., San Antonio, 1977—, instr., 1973-77. Mem. Am. Med. Record Assn. (dist. III-A dir. 1973), Tex. Med. Record assn. (del. nat. conv. 1976), San Antonio Med. Record Assn. (pres. 1972). Democrat. Baptist. Home: 5100 NW Loop 410 Apt 2803 San Antonio TX 73229 Office: 4301 Broadway San Antonio TX 78209

JAMES, CALVIN ELLINGTON, SR., mfg. co. exec.; b. La Grange, Ga., Sept. 7, 1937; s. F. H. and Rebecca Francis (Ellington) J.; B.Indsl. Engring., Ga. Inst. Tech., 1961; m. Dora Kathryn Hanson, Mar. 19, 1961; children—Sidney Porter, Calvin Ellington, Kathryn-Aimee. Salesman, Ryder Truck Lines, Atlanta, 1963-64; with Diversified Products Corp., Opelika, Ala., 1964—, v.p. sales and mktg., 1965-73, exec. v.p., 1973-78, pres., chief exec. officer, 1978—, chmn. bd., 1978—; dir. Farmers Nat. Bank, First Fed. Savs. & Loan of Lee County. Bd. dirs. Ala. Safety Council, Lee County Ednl. Found. Served to capt. USAR, 1961-63. Mem. Nat. Sporting Goods Assn., Sporting Goods Mfrs. Assn. Methodist. Club: Elks. Office: 309 Williamson Ave Opelika AL 36801

JAMES, CALVIN REX, JR., aero. engr.; b. Elk Creek, Va., Apr. 20, 1928; s. Calvin Rex and Hallie (Collins) J.; B.S. in A.E., Va. Poly. Inst. and State U., 1949; m. Nancy Ellen Repass, July 29, 1950; children—Calvin, Marion, Jean, Matthew, Paul. With Chance Vought, Dallas, 1949—, sr. engr., tech. project mgr., 1975—; pres. Triple J Enterprises, 1977-79. Mem. Sch. Bd. Cedar Hill (Tex.), 1964-74, pres., 1964, 74; asst. scoutmaster Boy Scouts Am., 1964-66, instl. rep., 1967-79. Mem. AIAA. Methodist. Contbr. articles to profl. jours. Home: Route 1 Box 145 Cedar Hill TX 75104 Office: PO Box 225907 Dallas TX 75265

JAMES, CHARLES GRIFFIN, data processor; b. Chireno, Tex., June 4, 1933; s. Earnest Marlin and Edna Myrtle (Little) J.; B.S., Stephen F. Austin State U., 1952; M.R.E., Southwestern Bapt. Sem., 1958; m. Betty Jean Powell, Feb. 12, 1955; 1 dau., Ruth Ann. With City Pub. Service Bd., San Antonio, 1959-66; asst. v.p. Groos Nat. Bank, San Antonio, 1968-72, v.p. charge Computer Center, 1972-76; instr. data processing San Antonio Coll., 1966-76; data processor Milchem, Inc., Houston, 1977-79, Big Three Industries, Houston, 1979—. Mem. Bexar County Hist. Survey Com., 1973-76. Served with USAF, 1953-55. Certified data processor. Mem. Data Processing Mgmt. Assn. (past v.p., dir. San Antonio chpt.), Assn. Systems Mgmt., East Tex. Hist. Assn., Mensa, Sons Republic Tex. (past chpt. pres.), SCV, Order Stars and Bars, Stephen F. Austin State U. Alumni Assn., Tex. Bapt. Hist. Soc., SAR. Baptist. Home: 9326 Willowview Ln Houston TX 77080 Office: PO Box 3047 Houston TX 77001

JAMES, DAVID DWIGHT, investment co. exec.; b. Russellville, Ala., July 7, 1954; s. Hazel Norris and Doris Marie (Holden) J.; grad. high sch., Russellville; m. Tamra Lynne Gilley, June 2, 1974; children—Christopher Michael, David Brandon. With V.J. Elmores, Birmingham, Ala., 1973-75; mgr. P.N. Hirsch & Co., Savannah, Tenn., 1975-79; mgr. Kents, Inc., Red Bay, Ala., 1979—; pres. Diversified Investment Corp., Red Bay, 1978—; dir. Delta Internat. Corp., Savannah. Treas., Russellville chpt. Future Farmers Am., 1972-73, recipient Pub. Speaking award. Democrat. Baptist. Home: PO Box 597 Red Bay AL 35582 Office: 4th Ave S Red Bay AL 35582

JAMES, DONALD WILLIAM, elec. engr.; b. Champaign, Ill., July 5, 1939; s. Gerald Allen and Eva V. (Shull) J.; B.S., U. Ill, 1969; M.S.E.E., Okla. State U., 1972; D.Eng., U. Okla., 1980; postgrad. Ohio State U., 1971, U. Okla., 1970-71; m. Wilma Jo Meike, Oct. 1, 1961; children—Donald M., Kristofer J., Kimberly J. Test engr. Western Electric Co., Oklahoma City, 1970-72; logic engr. Honeywell Info. Systems, Oklahoma City, 1972-75; project engr. Magnetic Peripherals Inc., Oklahoma City, 1975-79, prin. system engr., 1980—; engring. cons.; tchr. Oklahoma City Southwestern Coll., 1976-77; adj. prof. elec. engring. U. Okla., 1980—. Registered profl. engr., Okla. Mem. IEEE (outstanding contbn. award Oklahoma City sect. 1977); IEEE Computer Soc., Nat., Okla. socs. profl. engrs. Mem. Ch. of Christ. Home: 7801 NW 20th St Bethany OK 73008 Office: PO Box 12313 Oklahoma City OK 73112

JAMES, EARL EUGENE, JR., aerospace engring. exec.; b. Oklahoma City, Feb. 8, 1923; s. Earl Eugene and Mary Frances (Godwin) J.; student Oklahoma City U., 1940-41; B.S., U. Okla., 1945; postgrad. Tex. Christian U., 1954-57; M.S., So. Methodist U., 1961; m. Barbara Jane Marshall, Dec. 15, 1945; children—Earl Eugene III, Jeffrey Allan. Asst. mgr. Rialto Theatre, 1939-42; with Consol. Vultee Aircraft Co., San Diego, 1946-49; with Convair, Fort Worth, 1949—, group engr., 1955-57, test group engr. supr. fluid dynamics lab., 1957—. Asst. dist. commr. Boy Scouts Am., 1958-59; adviser Jr. Achievement, 1962-63; mem. sch. bd. Castleberry (Tex.) Ind. Sch. Dist., 1969—; chmn. bd. N.W. Br. YMCA, 1971. Served to lt. USNR, 1942-46; PTO. Asso. fellow Am. Inst. Aeros and Astronautics; mem. Air Force Assn., Gen. Dynamics Mgmt. Assn., Nat. Mgmt. Assn., Okla. U. Alumni Assn. (life), Tex. Congress Parents and Tchrs. (hon. life), Pi Kappa Alpha, Alpha Chi Sigma, Tau Omega. Methodist. Democrat. Clubs: Squaw Creek Golf, Camera, Elks. Author, editor articles in field. Home: 5037 Glade St Fort Worth TX 76114 Office: Fluid Dynamics Lab Mail Zone 5850 Box 748 Fort Worth TX 76108

JAMES, FORREST HOOD, JR., gov. Ala.; b. Lanett, Ala., Sept. 15, 1934; B.S. in Civil Engring., Auburn U., 1955; m. Bobbie James; 3 children. Profl. football player, Can.; constrn. supr., Ala., 1958-62; founder Diversified Products, 1962; gov. State of Ala., Montgomery, 1979—. Democrat. Episcopalian. Office: Office of Governor State Capitol Bldg Montgomery AL 36130

JAMES, GARY MICHAEL, mortgage banker; b. Tulsa, Dec. 9, 1945; s. J.T. and Helen Marie (Housley) J.; student U. Tulsa, 1964-66; A.A., Okla. Sch. Accountancy, 1968, B.Comml. Sci., 1971; grad. Sch. Mortgage Banking Northwestern U., Chgo., 1972; children—Jody, Julie, Jeanne. Insp., N.Am. Aviation (now Rockwell Internat.), Tulsa, 1964-67; price and audit clk. Skelly Oil Co., Tulsa, 1967-68; tchr. Okla. Sch. Accountancy, 1977—; instr. Tulsa Jr. Coll.; v.p. Lomas & Nettleton Co., Tulsa, 1968—; pres., owner Mike James Properties, Walker Motel, Lucky Motel, James Apts. and Rental Houses, Maple Leaf Laundry and Dry Cleaners. Advisory com. Tulsa Jr. Coll., 1977-80. Mem. Tulsa Met. Bd. Realtors, Tulsa Met. Homebuilders Assn. (chmn. fin. com. 1975), Rogers County Homebuilders Assn., Okla. (dir. 1976—), Tulsa (pres. 1974) mortgage bankers assns., Tulsa Milti-list Service. Democrat. Christian. Home: 7230 S Richmond Tulsa OK 74136 Office: 3105 E Skelly Dr Tulsa OK 74105

JAMES, GORDON PRICE, biochemist; b. Logan, Utah, July 17, 1936; s. David Wilmer and Irva (Price) J.; B.S., Utah State U., 1964; Ph.D. (NIH fellow 1964-68), U. Hawaii, 1968; postgrad. (NIH fellow) U. Wash., 1968-70; m. Nancy Lynn Gisseman, July 30, 1964; children—Valerie, Andrew, Lisa, Laura. Dir. ops. Pathology Assos. Med. Labs., Honolulu, 1970-73, BioSci. Hosp. and Clin. Labs., Los Angeles, 1973-75; asst. prof. dept. pathology and asso. dir. clin. labs. dept. pathology U. Tex. Med. Br., Galveston, 1975—. Served with USN, 1955-59. NSF undergrad. summer research grantee, 1964. Mem. Am. Assn. Clin. Chemistry, Acad. Clin. Lab. Physicians and Scientists, Nat. Acad. Clin. Biochemistry, Am. Acad. Clin. Toxicology. Mormon. Contbr. articles in field to profl. jours. Home: 18302 Barbuda Ln Houston TX 77058 Office: Dept Pathology U Tex Med Br Galveston TX 77550

JAMES, H. RHETT, clergyman, educator; b. Balt., Dec. 1, 1928; s. Samuel Horace James and Tannie Etta (Judkins) J.; A.B. in Sociology, Va. Union U., 1950; M.Ed., Our Lady of the Lake Coll., 1951; M.Div., Va. Union U., 1957; Th.M., Tex. Christian U., 1961; postgrad. summer 1970, U. Paris, U. Tokyo, 1970, Harvard Inst. Mgmt., 1973, Columbia U., 1974; Ph.D., U. Tex. at Arlington, 1979. Instr., San Antonio Pub. Schs., 1950-55, St. Phillips Jr. Coll., 1954-55; instr. psychology, edn. Va. Union U., Richmond, 1955-58; ordained to ministry Baptist Ch., 1955; pastor New Hope Bapt. Ch., Dallas, 1958—; asst. prof. social sci. Bishop Coll., Dallas, 1962—, dir. Urban Affairs and Community Devel. Center, 1972—, also dir. continuing edn. Exchange prof. social sci. U. Tex. at Arlington, 1969-71; vis. prof. history Austin Coll., Sherman, Tex., summer 1971. Del. to White House Conf. on Equal Employment Opportunities; del. Pres.'s Com. on Equal Employment Opportunities, 1961-63; founder, pres. Dallas Frontiers Internat., 1969-73; bd. dirs. Original Goals for Dallas Commn., 1968—; mem. Fourteen Man Com. of Dallas Desegregation Team, 1962—; bd. dirs. N. Dallas Am. Cancer Soc., Dallas City Council Bd. Solicitation; founder Dallas Opportunities Industrialization Center; bd. dirs. Tex. Council Chs., Vis. Nurse Assn., Family Guidance Center, Community Action Com., Dallas County; bd. dirs., Lintz award selection com. Dallas United Way; bd. govs. Ursuline Prep. Acad. Recipient Big Bros. Community Service award, 1969, Goals for Dallas Community Service award, 1970. Mem. Day Care and Child Devel. Council Am., AAUP, Tex. Assn. of Developing Colls. (dir. 1968-70), Dallas Urban League (dir. 1968-75), Am. Mensa Soc., So. Hist. Assn., NAACP (pres. Dallas 1962), Assn. Governing Bds. of Univs. and Colls., Sigma Pi Phi, Kappa Alpha Psi. Club: Masons (33 deg.). Home: 4739 Mill Creek Rd Dallas TX 75234

JAMES, JAMES FRANCIS, architect; b. Sumter, S.C.; s. Jasper Thomas and Sallie Marie (Jenkins) J.; B.A. in Architecture, Clemson U., 1934; m. Helen DuPre Montague, June 17, 1939; children—Helen DuPre, J.F., Jr., Marie DuPre. Practice architecture, 1938—; cons. James, Durant, Mathens & Shelley A.I.A. Architects, Sumter; pres. Sumter Casket Co.; vice chmn. bd. B.L. Montague Co., Sumter; pres. James Realty Co., Sumter. Served to maj. C.E., U.S. Army, World War II. Decorated Bronze Star. Real estate broker, S.C. Mem. AIA. Clubs: Thalian, Cotillion, Assembly, Roads End, Millwood (Sumter, S.C.); Longwood (Berkley County); Rotary. Home: 500 Haynesworth St Sumter SC 29150 Office: 128 E Liberty St Sumter SC 29150

JAMES, JOHN V., corp. exec.; b. Plains Twp., Pa., July 24, 1918; s. Stanley S. and Catherine N. (Jones) J.; B.S. in Econs., U. Pa., 1941, certificate in mgmt., 1948; D.B.A. (hon.), Hillsdale Coll., 1976; D.C.S. (hon.), St. Bonaventure U.; m. Helen L. Brislin, June 25, 1949; 1 dau., Barbara Ann. Office mgr., controller Carr Consol. Biscuit Co., Wilkes Barre, Pa., 1941-42; div. controller Corning Glass Works, 1948-56, mgr. budgets and procs., 1956-57; asst. controller Dresser Industries, Inc., Dallas, 1957-58, v.p. finance subsidiary Clark Bros. Co., Olean, N.Y., 1958-60, controller parent co., 1960-65, v.p., 1962-65, group v.p. machinery, 1965-68, exec. v.p., 1968-69, pres., chief exec. officer, 1970—, chmn. bd., 1976—, also dir. Served to capt. AUS, 1943-46. Mem. Financial Execs. Inst., Nat. Assn. Accountants (dir. 1960-62), Beta Gamma Sigma. Conglist. Mason, Rotarian (pres. Corning 1957). Office: Dresser Bldg 1505 Elm St Dallas TX 75221*

JAMES, JOHN WILLIAM, theatre arts educator; b. Wayne, Mich., Nov. 18, 1935; s. Richard Wallace and Marion Edna (Waddell) J.; student U. Louisville, 1953-54, Western Ky. State U., 1955-56; B.A., Los Angeles State Coll., 1959, M.A., 1963; m. Joyce Branson, Aug. 4, 1956; children—Gregory, Laura, Jeffrey, Christopher. Stage technician, scenery designer Los Angeles State Coll., 1959-63; instr. speech, drama, also tech. dir. theater Kans. State Tchrs. Coll., Emporia, 1963-65; instr. speech and drama, also tech. dir. theater Western Ill. U., Macomb, 1965-67; prof. fine arts Manatee Jr. Coll., Bradenton, Fla., also dir. theater, 1967—. Vice pres., sec. Little League Bradenton, 1974-75, Babe Ruth League Bradenton, 1976-77. U. So. Calif. coll. program devel. grantee, 1970-71. Mem. AAUP (pres. chpt. 1967-69, 79—), Mem. Am. Theatre Assn., Fla. Assn. Jr. Colls., Fla. Theatre Conf. Republican. Home: 308 46th St W Bradenton FL 33505 Office: Dept Theater Arts Manatee Jr Coll 5840 26th St W Bradenton FL 33507

JAMES, JOSEPH B., educator; b. Clearwater, Fla., July 17, 1912; s. L. P. and Ilah J. (Miles) J.; B.A.E., U. Fla., 1934, M.A., 1935; Ph.D., U. Ill., 1939; m. Jacquelyn McWhite, June 8, 1937; children—Glenn Joseph, William Bruce. Instr. gen. extension div. U. Fla., 1935-36; asst. and fellow U. Ill., 1936-39; head dept. history and polit. sci. Williamsport Dickinson Jr. Coll., 1939-40; Union Coll., Ky., 1940-43; dean of faculty William Woods Coll., 1943-45; head dept. social studies Miss. State Coll. for Women, 1945-58; dean of coll. Wesleyan Coll., Macon, Ga., 1958-71, Callaway prof. polit. sci., 1971—; vis. prof. summer sessions U. Fla., U. Miss., Florence (Ala.) State Tchrs. Coll., Middle Tenn. State Coll. Mem. So., Ga. (exec. council) polit. sci. assns., Am. Acad. Polit. Sci., So. Hist. Assn., Assn. Coll. Honor Socs. (council), Phi Beta Kappa (past pres. Middle Ga. Grad. Assn.), Phi Kappa Phi (past pres. Wesleyan chpt.), Kappa Delta Pi, Kappa Phi Kappa, Pi Gamma Mu (nat. pres. emeritus, trustee). Methodist (adminstrv. bd.). Club: Rotary. Author: The Framing of the Fourteenth Amendment, 1956, rev. edit., 1965; contbr. to scholarly jours. and reference publs. Home: 3450 Osborne Pl Macon GA 31204

JAMES, MARY SHROPSHIRE, educator; b. Lancaster, S.C., July 7, 1936; d. Andrew and Maggie Lillian (Young) Shropshire; B.S., N.C. Coll., 1959; M.S., N.C. Central U., 1973; postgrad. U. S.C., 1967; m. Charles Herbert James, Dec. 22, 1963; children—Charles Herbert II, Marlon Chandler. Phys. edn. tchr. Upchurch High Sch., Raeford, N.C., 1961-62; sci. tchr. Wilson Jr. High Sch., Florence, S.C., 1962-67; dir. elementary phys. edn. Brockington & Cain Elementary Sch., Darlington, S.C., 1967-68; asst. prof. health and phys. edn. Paine Coll., Augusta, Ga., 1968—, chmn. intramural sports program, 1977; instr. Upward Bound, 1978-79. Choreographer, Augusta Adult Soc., 1974; chmn. bd. dirs. Augusta Mini Theatre, 1978-79; bd. dirs. Belle-Terrace Day Care. Mem. AAHPER, Augusta Arts Councils, Delta Sigma Theta. Home: 2353 Sumac Dr Augusta GA 30906 Office: Paine Coll 1235 15th St Augusta GA 30901

JAMES, MICHAEL LYNN, photographer; b. Kennett, Mo., Sept. 24, 1946; s. Jesse Ransom and Lona Mae (Reagan) J.; student U. Mo., 1964; B.S., Harding U., 1973; m. Elizabeth Jane Hogan, June 27, 1970; children—Jennifer Elizabeth, Jeremy Michael. Photographer Cine-Grafix, Inc., Omaha, 1971; owner James Photography, Searcy, Ark., 1971—; partner Varsity Photography, 1973-80; dir. photography Harding U. Public Relations, 1973—, instr. journalism dept., 1979—, photog. adv. Harding U. Yearbook. Sponsor Theta Tau Delta. Served as officer AUS. Mem. Profl. Photographers Am., Searcy C. of C., Alpha Phi Gamma. Mem. Ch. of Christ. Clubs: Searcy Golf, Optimist (Searcy). Home: 6 Julner St Searcy AR 72143 Office: Box 759 Sta A Searcy AR 72143

JAMES, PHILIP WAYNE, assn. exec.; b. Dallas, Sept. 11, 1934; s. Dalton L. and Minnie R. (Caldwell) J.; B.S., Tex. Tech U., 1957, M.S., 1964; m. Peggy J. Welling, May 31, 1971. Field sec. Tex. Tech. Ex-Students Assn., 1957-60, exec. dir., 1960-78; sec.-treas. Tex. Tech Loyalty Fund, 1960-78; pres. Tex. Tech Spltys., Inc., 1974-78; exec. dir. Southwestern Meat Packers Assn., 1978—; instr. mass communications dept. Tex. Tech U., 1971. Bd. dirs. Tex. Tech U. Found.; exec. v.p. Tex. Tech Ex-Students Assn. Endowment Trust Fund, 1974-78, trustee, 1978—. Recipient Regional and nat. awards in alumni activities Am. Alumni Council. Cert. assn. exec. Mem. Am. Alumni Council (dir. 1969-74), Pub. Relations Soc. Am., Am. Soc. Assn. Execs., Tex. Soc. Assn. Execs. (dir. 1979—), Council for Advancement and Support Edn., Sigma Delta Chi, Phi Delta Kappa, Alpha Phi Omega. Mason (Shriner), Rotarian. Clubs: Tex. Tech Century, Red Raider, Lubbock, University City (Lubbock); Dallas Press. Editor Tex. Techsan, 1960-78. Home: 2604 High Oak Dr Arlington TX 76012 Office: 2225 E Randol Mill Rd #215 Arlington TX 76011

JAMES, RONALD DAVID, dentist; b. Greeneville, Tenn., Feb. 22, 1951; s. John David and Ruby (Wills) J.; B.S., Tusculum Coll., 1972; D.D.S., U. Tenn., 1975; m. Rhonda Carleen Gass, July 2, 1970; children—John Rondon, Johnna Ronette, Christy Ronea. With Tenn. State Health Dept., Johnson City, 1975; dental surg. officer USPHS, Surgoinsville, Tenn., 1975-76; pvt. practice dentistry, Surgoinsville, 1976—. Recipient U. Tenn. Dentistry Acad. Certificate of Honor, 1975; Internat. Coll. of Dentists award, 1975; licensed dentist, Tenn. Mem. Acad. Gen. Dentistry, First Assembly, ADA, Tenn. Dental Assn., Kingsport Dental Soc. Clubs: Kiwanis (sec.-treas.) (Allandale); U. Tenn. Pres.'s. Home: 209 Scotland Rd Kingsport TN 37660 Office: Route 2 PO Box A73A Old Stage Rd Surgoinsville TN 37873

JAMES, TED LOWELL, veterinarian; b. Waynesville, N.C., Jan. 4, 1932; s. Norman Crawford and Nellie (Green) J.; B.S., N.C. State U., 1954; D.V.M., U. Ga., 1957; m. Joy Patricia Putnam, July 6, 1957; children—Keith, Bruce, Kerry, Joni. Asso. veterinarian Catawba Animal Clinic, Newton, N.C., 1957-59; veterinarian, owner, mgr. James Animal Clinic, Salisbury, N.C., 1959—. Treas., Inter-Civic Council of Salisbury, 1976-78. Mem. N.C. Veterinary Med. Assn. (pres. 1977-78), AVMA, Am. Animal Hosp. Assn., Am. Veterinary Radiology Soc., Am. Assn. Equine Practitioners, N.C. Assn. Professions, N.C. Veterinary Research Found., N.C. Acad. Small Animal Medicine, N.C. Cattlemens Assn., Farm Bur., N.C. Wildlife Fedn., Humane Soc., N.C. Holstein Assn., Salisbury-Rowan C. of C. (chmn. agrl. com. 1978-80). Democrat. So. Baptist. Clubs: Lions (pres. Salisbury 1976-77, dep. dist. gov. 1979-80), Keystone Investment. Home: 530 D Ave Salisbury NC 28144 Office: 3002 S Main St Ext Salisbury NC 28144

JAMES, WILLIAM WESLEY, JR., utility exec.; b. Gulfport, Miss., Feb. 24, 1936; s. William Wesley and Mamie (Swanner) J.; B.E.E., Miss. State U., 1958; m. Beverly Elaine Banderet, Oct. 28, 1952; children—William Wesley, Cheryl Elaine, Carl Byron, Troy Lee. With Fla. Power & Light Co., Miami, 1957-77, system ops. engr., 1969-72, supr. distbn., 1972-73, mgr. apprentice tng., 1973-77; vice gen. mgr. Big Rivers Electric Corp., Henderson, Ky., 1977—; faculty Manatee Jr. Coll., Bradenton, Fla., 1958-69, U. Miami, 1970-77, U. Evansville (Ind.), 1978—. Chmn. elec. tech. craft com. Manatee Vocat. & Tech. Center, Bradenton, Fla., 1959-69; coach basketball and football Boys' Club, Bradenton, 1961-64; football coach Pop Warner League, 1970-77; youth basketball coach, 1974-77; mem. gen. adv. bd. tech. edn. Manatee Jr. Coll., 1959-69, Manatee Profl. Guidance Bd., Pub. Schs., 1961-68, council Manatee County PTA, 1964-67; mem. adv. com. Henderson Community Coll., 1978—, U. Evansville Center Mgmt. Edn., 1979—. Named Ky. col.; registered profl. engr., Ky. Mem. Ky., Nat. socs. profl. engrs., IEEE, Ky. Engring. Soc. Methodist (mem. ofcl. bd.). Home: 930 Frontier Dr Henderson KY 42420 Office: PO Box 24 Henderson KY 42420

JAMESON, DONALD FENTON BOOTH, engring. co. exec., strategic analyst; b. Indpls., Feb. 23, 1925; s. Donald Ovid Butler and Margaret (Booth) J.; B.S., U.S. Naval Acad., 1945; cert. Russian Inst., Columbia U., 1949, M.A. in Internat. Relations and Law, 1949; m. Louise Rodman, 1969; children—Jeremy, Margaret Grace, Thomas H.B. With CIA, 1951-73; sr. scientist Tetra Tech. Systems Div., 1973-75; sec.-treas. Tetra Tech. Internat., Inc., Arlington, Va., 1975—; lectr. on Soviet affairs for Dept. of Def., CIA, pvt. orgns.; lectr. Soviet history U. Va., 1975. Served as ensign USN, 1945-47. Recipient medal CIA, 1973. Mem. Acad. Polit. Sci., Am. Assn. Advancement Slavic Studies. Republican. Episcopalian. Clubs: Cosmos, Army and Navy (Washington). Maj. contbr. to Securing the Seas: The Challenge of the Soviet Navy, 1978; contbr. articles to Atlantic Mag. Office: 1911 N Fort Myer Dr Arlington VA 22209

JAMESON, JOHN ROBERT, SR., historian; b. Annapolis, Md., May 30, 1945; s. Robert Olen and Martha Marie (Stinson) J.; B.A., Austin Coll., 1967; M.A., E. Tex. State U., 1970; Ph.D., U. Toledo, 1974; m. Marie Wakefield Dickinson, June 22, 1968; children—John Robert, Andrew Dickinson. Museum curator Sam Rayburn House, Bonham, Tex., 1974-77, mus. dir., 1977-78; cons. cultural resource mgmt., Bonham, 1974—; adj. instr. history Austin Coll. and Paris Jr. Coll. Sr. warden Holy Trinity Episcopal Ch., Bonham, 1975-77, vestry, 1975—; bd. dirs. Ft. Inglish Soc., 1975—. Served with USMCR, 1967-68. Grantee Nat. Endowment for Humanities, 1978, Inst. Mus. Services, 1978. Mem. Bonham C. of C. (dir. 1977-79), E. Tex. C. of C. (dir. tourism devel. 1977), Am. Hist. Assn., Tex. Hist. Assn., E. Tex. Hist. Assn., Red River Hist. Assn., Soc. for History Edn. Research editor Am. Indian Quar., 1975-77; asst. editor Assn. Living Farms and Agrl. Mus., ann. proceedings, 1978—.

JAMESON, PRESCILLA KAREN HOLMES, educator; b. Chgo., Sept. 4, 1925; d. Presley Dixon and Mildred Priscilla (Rufsvold) Holmes; A.B. in Speech, U. Mich., 1947, M.A. in Speech, 1953; postgrad. U. Va., James Madison U., George Washington U., George Mason U.; m. Dorence C. Jameson, Aug. 16, 1948; children—Scott Kelly, Terence Alan, Patrick Brian. Dir. drama, Mt. Morris, Mich., 1947; tchr. lang. arts, Albuquerque, 1950; pvt. practice speech pathology, 1959-63; tchr. pub. schs., Marietta, Ohio, 1966-67; speech pathologist, dept. human resources Child Growth and Devel. Center, Arlington, Va., 1967-68; dir. speech activities Washington Irving Intermediate Sch., Springfield, Va., 1969—, dir. gifted talented program, 1976-79; instr. Fairfax County Staff Devel. Mem. Polit. Action Com. for Edn., 1976-79; tchr. Sunday sch. class for exceptional children Grace Presbyterian Ch., 1970. Mem. United Teaching Professions, NEA, Va. Edn. Assn., Fairfax Edn. Assn. (sec., dir. 1977-78), Am. Speech and Hearing Assn., Council for Exceptional Children, AAUW (v.p. Springfield-Annandale br. 1961-63), Zeta Phi Eta, Alpha Delta Kappa. Republican. Home: 6024 Selwood Pl Springfield VA 22152 Office: 8100 Keene Mill Rd Springfield VA 22152

JAMIESON, ADDIE MAE, civic worker; b. Ripley, Miss., May 9, 1919; d. Jesse Darnel and Frances Ardena (Moore) J.; A.B., Blue Mountain Coll., 1943; M.A., Scarritt Coll., 1949; postgrad. Emory U., summers 1953, 58, New Coll., Edinburgh, Scotland, 1974. Tchr., Dry Creek Elementary Sch., Booneville, Miss., 1939-43, Slate Spring (Miss.) High Sch., 1944, Wilkinson County, 1945, Ripley High Sch., 1945-47; rural worker Fla. Conf., Tallahassee Dist., 1949-55; coordinator Ga. Coop. Rural Work, N. and S. Ga. Confs. Methodist Ch., Macon, 1955-60; dir. Christian edn. Mulberry St. Meth. Ch., Macon, 1960-65, coordinator Holston Meth. Conf., Johnson City, Tenn., 1965-72. County dir. Cancer Drive, Liberty County, Fla., 1951; charter mem. Ga. Meth. Federal Credit Union, 1961—, v.p. bd. dirs., 1963-65; mem. exec. com. N. Miss. Town and Country Commn., 1972—; chmn. N. Miss. Conf. Bd. Diaconal Ministry, 1976—. Bd. dirs. Wesley Found., Ga. So. Coll., Statesboro, 1963-64; v.p. Miss. Ch. and Community Leadership Inst., 1976, pres., 1977; mem. Town and Country Commn.; mem. S. Ga. Conf. Meth. Ch., exec. com. 1955-60, Holston conf., 1965-72, bd. edn., 1955-63, exec. com., 1960-63, pres. deaconess bd., 1957-59, interconf. com. Meth. student work 1960-64, fellowship Christian edn. com. 1962-63, community worker, 1972-80; exec. com. N. Miss. United Meth. Women, 1972-80. Mem. United Meth. Deaconess Home Missionary Service (nat. com. 1964-72, Juris rep., chmn. by-laws, 1964-72), Fellowship Christian Educators (v.p. N. Miss. chpt. 1974-75, treas. 1977-80), Louisville Bus. and Profl. Women's Club (corr. sec. 1974-75, pres. 1976, Woman of Achievement 1975), Red Hills Arts Assn. Home: PO Box 100 Ripley MS 38663

JAMIESON, FRANK MARTIN, loan analyst; b. Houston, Sept. 26, 1948; s. Frank and Mary Catherine (Martin) J.; B.B.A. in Mgmt., Tex. A&M U., 1970, B.B.A. in Fin., 1977, M.B.A. in Fin., 1978. Office mgr., regional acct. Universal Mobile Services Corp. subs. Wickes, Waco, Tex., 1973-74, acct., Houston, 1974-75, internal auditor, 1975, regional rep., Denver, 1976; mortgage loan analyst Am. Nat. Ins. Co., Galveston, Tex., 1979—; instr. real estate fin. Tex. A&M U. Bd. dirs. Galveston County unit Am. Cancer Soc. Served to 1st lt. U.S. Army, 1970-73. Mem. Tex. A&M U. Former Students Assn. Home: 8100

Seawall Blvd Galveston TX 77551 Office: Am Nat Ins Co One Moody Plaza Galveston TX 77550

JAMISON, JOHN AMBLER, judge; b. Florence, S.C., May 14, 1916; s. John Wilson and Elizabeth Ambler (Fleming) J.; LL.B., Cumberland U., 1941; postgrad. George Washington U., 1944-45; grad. Indsl. Coll. Armed Forces, 1962; J.D., Samford U., 1969; m. Mildred Holley, Sept. 22, 1945. Admitted to S.C. bar, 1941, Va. bar, 1942, U.S. Supreme Ct. bar, 1945; atty. Va. Div. Motor Vehicles, Richmond, 1947-54; practice law, Fredericksburg, 1954-72; asso. judge County Cts. Stafford and King George Counties (Va.), Municipal Ct., Fredericksburg, 1956-72; judge 15th Va. Jud. Circuit, 1972—, chief judge, 1976—; dir., counsel Nat. Bank Fredericksburg, 1968-73. Mem. adv. com. Gov.'s Hwy. Safety Commn., 1956-58; pres. Fredericksburg Rescue Squad, 1960-62, now hon. life mem.; hon. chmn. Fredericksburg Area Bicentennial Commn., 1975-77; chmn. bd. Fredericksburg Area Mental Hygiene Clinic, 1962-63; bd. dirs. Rappahannock Area Devel. Commn., 1960-66; mem. adv. bd. Cumberland Sch. Law. Served from ensign to comdr. USN, 1941-46; comdg. officer Richmond Naval Res. Div., 1948-56; naval aide to govs. of Va., 1954-72. Recipient award S.C. Confederate War Centennial Commn., 1965; Decorated Cross Mil. Service. Mem. Am., S.C., Va., 15th Va. Jud. Circuit (pres. 1959-60, 69-70) bar assns., Cumberland Law Sch. Alumni Assn. (nat. pres. 1978-79), Jud. Conf. Va., Am. Judicature Soc., Am. Law Inst., Cumberland Order Jurisprudence, Res. Officers Assn. U.S., Mil. Order World Wars, Thomas Jefferson Inst. Religious Freedom (founding), SAR, Jamestowne Soc., UDC, Am. Legion (post comdr. 1951-52), Blue Key, Sigma Delta Kappa. Episcopalian (past warden, vestryman, lay reader). Clubs: Masons (32 deg.), Shriners, Jesters, Kiwanis (past dir.). Address: PO Drawer 29 Fredericksburg VA 22401

JANDER, HARTWIG PETER, radiologist; b. Stettin, Germany, Dec. 23, 1939; s. Karl Heinrich and Inge Lieselotte (Muller) J.; came to U.S., 1967; B.S., Bismarckschule, Neusprachliches and Mathematisch Naturwissenschaftliches Gymnasium, 1960; M.D., U. Freiburg (Germany), 1967; Ph.D., U. Minn., 1973; m. Jesusa Castaneda Turqueza, Mar. 29, 1969; children—Markus Alexander, Jan Marlon. Intern, County Hosp., Tegernsee, Germany, 1966, St. Josef's Hosp., Koetzting, Germany, 1966-67, St. Mary's Hosp., Passaic, N.J., 1967-68; fellow in radiology Mayo Clinic and Mayo Grad Sch. Medicine, Rochester, Minn., 1968-73, fellow in immunology, 1969-70; asso. cons. diagnostic radiology dept. Mayo Clinic, Rochester, 1972-73; instr. diagnostic radiology dept. Sch. Medicine, U. Ala., Birmingham, 1973-74, asst. prof., 1974-76, asso. prof., 1976—, chief tumor imaging research, 1973—, chief peripheral angiography, 1974—. VA grantee, 1975. Diplomate Am. Bd. Radiology. Mem. AMA, Radiol. Soc. N.Am., Ala., Minn. radiol. socs., Undersea Med. Soc., Am. Roentgen Ray Soc., Am. Coll. Radiology, Med. Assn. Ala., Jefferson County Med. Soc., Ala. Acad. Radiology. Lutheran. Contbr. articles to profl. jours. Home: 3325 Springhill Rd Birmingham AL 35223 Office: 619 S 19th St Birmingham AL 35233

JANES, ROBERT HARRISON, JR., surgeon; b. Little Rock, Nov. 13, 1939; s. Robert Harrison and Fahy Helen (Mathers) J.; B.S., U. Ark., 1965, M.D., 1965; m. Patricia Mayes, June 30, 1962; children—Robert, Clayton, Matthew. Intern surgery U. Ark. Hosps., Little Rock, 1965-66, resident surgery, 1966-70; practice medicine, specializing in surgery Holt-Krock Clinic, Fort Smith, Ark., 1972—; mem. staff Sparks Regional Med. Center, chief surgery, 1977-78; mem. staff St. Edwards Mercy Med. Center; instr. surgery U. Ark., Little Rock, 1969-70, asst. clin. prof. surgery, 1976—. Pres. Sebastian County (Ark.) unit Am. Cancer Soc., 1975-76, bd. dirs. Ark. div., pres. Ark. div., 1978-79; bd. dirs. Ft. Smith Symphony, 1979—. Served to maj., M.C., USAF, 1970-72. Diplomate Am. Bd. Surgery. Fellow A.C.S., Southwestern Surg. Congress; mem. AMA, Ark. Med. Soc., Lambda Chi Alpha. Methodist (adminstrv. bd. 1974-77). Clubs: Hardscrabble Country, Fort Smith Racquet, Town of Fort Smith. Contbr. articles to profl. jours. Home: 3707 Old Oaks Ln Fort Smith AR 72903 Office: 1500 Dodson Ave Fort Smith AR 72901

JANN, WARREN WILLIAM, mgmt., health care cons.; b. Chgo., July 9, 1939; s. Edward W. and Mildred (Barton) J.; B.S., North Tex. State U., 1968, M.S., 1980. Adminstrv. planner Gen. Dynamics, Ft. Worth, 1969-71; developer, adminstr., drug and alcohol programs, Hennepin County, Minn., 1971-75; developer mktg. and fin. plan for health maintenance orgn. Portland (Oreg.) Met. Health, 1973; pvt. practice mgmt. and health care, Ft. Worth, 1977—. Recipient plaque Portland Metro Health, 1976. Mem. Am. Mgmt. Assn., Assn. Mental Health Adminstrs., Am. Public Health Assn., Gerontol. Soc., Am. Coll. Hosp. Adminstrs., Am. Coll. Long Term Care Adminstrs. Participant in devel. of health maintenance orgns. in Tex. Home and Office: 4371 Sandage Ave Fort Worth TX 76115

JANN, WILLIAM KENNETH, SR., ordnance engr.; b. Bklyn., Sept. 1, 1925; s. Gustav Albert and Mary Louise (Gerhart) J.; B.S. in Mech. Engring., U. Colo., 1949; grad. Command and Gen. Staff Coll., 1969; M.A. in Pub. Adminstrn., U. Okla., 1970; postgrad. Indsl. Coll. Armed Forces, 1968-71; m. Clara Louise Dellva, Apr. 23, 1949; children—William Kenneth, Donald Charles, Patricia Marie. Research engr. Bur. Mines Oil Shale Demonstration Plant Rifle, Colo., 1949-50, Bur. Reclamation, Denver, 1950-51; mech. engr. Stearns Rogers Engring. Co., Denver, 1951-52, U.S.N. Pub. Works and Utilities Office, Great Lakes, Ill., 1952-54; ordnance engr. U.S. Army Ordnance Ammunition Command, Joliet, Ill., 1954-56; various key engring. mgmt. positions, currently dep. project mgr. Pershing weapon system Army Ballistic Missile Agy. (name changed to U.S. Army Missile R&D Command), Redstone Arsenal, Ala., 1956—; dir. instrn. nat. security mgmt. course Indsl. Coll. Armed Forces, U.S. Army Reserve, Huntsville, Ala., 1971—; fellow intergovtl. affairs fellowship program gov.'s staff State of Tenn., 1974. Served to sgt. USAAF, 1944-45; col. U.S. Army Res. C.E. (ret.). Decorated Air medal with four oak leaf clusters, Meritorious Service medal, Meritorious Civilian Service medal (2). Registered profl. engr., Ala. Mem. Am. Ordnance Assn., Res. Officers Assn. U.S., Assn. U.S. Army, Delta Sigma Phi. Elk. Home: 1406 Elmwood Dr SE Huntsville AL 35801 Office: USAMICOM Redston Arsenal AL 35809

JANNA, WILLIAM SIED, mech. engr., educator; b. Toledo, Mar. 23, 1949; s. Sied William and Emily J.; B.S. in Mech. Engring., U. Toledo, 1971, M.S., 1973, Ph.D., 1976; m. Marla Rae Treichel, Apr. 26, 1975; 1 son, Sied William. Research asso. U. Toledo, 1976; asst. prof. mech. engring. U. New Orleans, 1976, chmn. mech. engring., 1979—; instr. adult and continuing edn. courses; cons. in field. Named outstanding mech. engring. tchr., 1976-77. Mem. Am. Soc. Engring. Edn., Sigma Xi, Pi Tau Sigma. Secured gifts, autos and auto engines, for univ. Author lab. manuals; contbr. reviews and articles to profl. publs. Office: Univ New Orleans Lakefront New Orleans LA 70122

JANNASCH, JAMES R., JR., personnel exec.; b. Galveston, Tex., Feb. 7, 1922; s. James R. and Florence Eugenia (Poplar) J.; B.A., U. Tex., Austin, 1949. Paymaster, Gray's Iron Works, Inc., Galveston, 1950-51; exec. dir. personnel ops. U. Tex. Med. Br., Galveston, 1951—. Served with Med. Adminstrv. Corps, U.S. Army, 1942-46. Decorated Bronze Star. Mem. Am. Soc. Hosp. Personnel Dirs., Tex. Soc. Hosp. Personnel Dirs., Houston Soc. Hosp. Personnel Adminstrn., Coll. and Univ. Personnel Assn., Personnel Adminstrs. Tex. Sr. Colls. and Univs. (pres.). Democrat. Roman Catholic. Club: K.C. (Galveston). Home: 2624 Ave O Galveston TX 77550 Office: U Tex Med Br 301 University Blvd Galveston TX 77550

JANOSIK, STEVEN MICHAEL, univ. ofcl.; b. Richmond, Va., May 18, 1951; s. James Philip and Mildred (Leonard) J.; B.S. in Bus. Adminstrn., Va. Poly. Inst. and State U., 1973; M.Ed. in Student Personnel and Counseling, U. Ga., 1975; m. Rhoda Ann Corbett, Aug. 25, 1973. Coordinator men's residence halls Wake Forest U., Winston Salem, N.C., 1975-76, dir. residence life, 1976-78, tchr. psychology, 1976-78; asst. dean student life Curry Coll., 1978-79; asso. dir. Univ. Housing Sers. Va. Poly. Inst. and State U., 1979—; cons. community colls., univs., 1973—. Adult leader Boy Scouts Am., 1977—. Certified instr. Effectiveness Tng., Inc. Mem. Am. Coll. Personnel Assn. (regional editor commn. III newsletter 1975—), Am. Personnel and Guidance Assn., Nat. Assn. Student Personnel Adminstrs., Assn. Specialists in Group Work. Home: 300-D Foxridge Apts Blacksburg VA 24060 Office: Patton Hall Va Poly Inst and State U Blacksburg VA 24601

JANSEN, CYNTHIA LEA, real estate broker; b. Ft. Worth, Oct. 21, 1947; d. Leon and Joyce Yvonne (Taylor) Sykes; B.A. in English, U. Houston, 1969; 1 son, John Stephen. Account exec. Starr Broadcasting, Inc., Houston, 1970-74, Sta. KENR, Houston, 1974-75, Sta. KRBE, Houston, 1975-77; real estate agt., income property sales Coldwell Banker Comml. Brokerage, Houston, 1977—. Mem. Am. Women in Radio and TV (past pres.), Houston Bd. Realtors. Office: Coldwell Banker Comml Brokerage 2500 W Loop S Houston TX 77027

JANSSEN, BEATRICE DARLEEN, psychologist; b. Crowley, La., Oct. 9, 1944; d. Harry and Beatrice Hebert (Breaux) Broussard; B.S., Houston Bapt. U., 1976; M.A., U. Houston, 1977; m. George Janssen, June 23, 1962; 1 dau., Corby. Instr. psychology Houston Bapt. U., 1977-78; tchr. spl. edn. Alief Ind. Sch. Dist., Houston, Tex., 1978-79; psychol. asso. Drs. Katz & Weinberger, Houston, 1977—; asso. psychologist Houston Ind. Sch. Dist., 1979—; teaching fellow doctoral program U. Houston, 1978-79. Mem. sch. bd., 1973-75; pres. P.T.A., 1970-72; bd. mem. Bloomingdale Athletic Assn., 1973-75. Mem. Am. Psychol. Assn., Am. Personnel and Guidance Assn., Tex. Psychol. Assn., Houston Psychol. Assn., Psi Chi. Roman Catholic. Home: 12730 Tennis Dr Houston TX 77099

JANSSEN, FELIX GERARD, bldg. materials co. exec.; b. Netherlands, Aug. 18, 1925; s. Hendrik and Anna Christina (Sanders) J.; came to U.S., 1961, naturalized 1966; B.S. in mining and mech. engring., Hoge Technische Sch.; m. Irma Wouters, Aug. 20, 1949; 1 son, Robert Henry. Pres., U.S. Acoustics Corp., 1957—; pres., dir. Internat. Perlite Products, Inc., 1973—; chmn. bd. Internat. Sludge Reduction Inc., 1977—; dir. U.S. Environ. Products Inc., 1978—; partner Gen. Consulting Services, S.A., 1973—; dir. Concorde Shipping Lines; cons. in acoustics. Served as capt. Royal Netherlands Air Force, 1944-56. Mem. Internat. Aeronautic Fedn. Republican. Roman Catholic. Club: U.S. Power Squadron. Patentee in acoustical products. Home: 6000 N Ocean Blvd Apt 16A Fort Lauderdale FL 33308 Office: AI duPont Bldg Suite 1629 169 E Flager St Miami FL 33131

JANTUNEN, KAUKO ILMARI, physician; b. Ruokolahti, Finland, Aug. 27, 1941; came to U.S., 1970, naturalized, 1978; s. Heimo and Helvi Sivia (Teppana) J.; M.D., U. Helsinki (Finland), 1967; m. Aila Ropo, June 1, 1963; children—Pertti Tapio, Timo Juhani. Gen. practice medicine, Kiihtelysvaara, Finland, 1967-69, Pajala, Sweden, 1969-70; intern St. Luke's Hosp., Fargo, N.D., 1970-71; practice family medicine, New York Mills, Minn., 1971-75, Lake Worth, Fla., 1975—; staff Drs. Hosp. Diplomate Am. Bd. Family Practice. Fellow Am. Acad. Family Physicians; mem. AMA. Finnish Pentecostal Ch. Address: 1622 S Dixie Hwy Lake Worth FL 33460

JAQUES, THOMAS FRANCIS, librarian; b. Crowley, La., Dec. 25, 1938; s. Robert Edward and Frances (Broussard) J.; B.B.A., U. Southwestern La., 1961; M.S., La. State U., 1969; m. Trudy Sue Seidel, May 16, 1964; children—Michael Thomas, Christopher Seidel. Asst. librarian Rapides Parish (La.) Library, 1969-73; asst. state librarian Miss. Library Commn., 1973-75; state librarian La. State Library, Baton Rouge, 1975—. Recipient La. Adminstrv. Librarian Exec. certificate, 1972. Mem. Am., Southwestern, La. library assns., Chief Officers of State Library Agys., Beta Phi Mu. Democrat. Episcopalian. Home: 12348 E Sheraton Ave Baton Rouge LA 70815 Office: 760 Riverside Mall PO Box 131 Baton Rouge LA 70821

JAQUES, WILLIAM EVERETT, physician, educator; b. Newbury, Mass., July 11, 1917; s. Arthur Wellington and Helen Alice (Colby) J.; student U. N.H., 1935-38; M.D., C.M., McGill U., 1942; m. Betty Charlene Mansfield, Mar. 30, 1968; children—William, Roberta Gail, Alice Penelope, Judith Anne, Pamela Jane, Arthur William, David Everett. Intern, Bridgeport (Conn.) Hosp., 1943-44, resident pathology, 1946-47; resident pathology Mass. Meml. Hosp., Boston, 1947-49; instr. Harvard Med. Sch., 1949-53; resident Children's Med. Center, Boston, 1949-50, asst. pathologist, 1950-51; asso. pathologist Peter Bent Brigham Hosp., Boston, 1951-53; asso. prof. pathology La. State U., 1953-57; prof., chmn. dept. pathology U. Okla. Med. Sch., 1957-65; mem. staff Univ. Hosp., Oklahoma City, 1957-65; vis. prof. Nat. Def. Med. Center, Taipei, Taiwan, 1965-66; prof., chmn. dept. pathology U. Ark. Med. Center, 1966-74; dir. pathology Nat. Center Toxicology Research, Jefferson, Ark., 1971-74; clin. prof. pathology U. Okla., Tulsa, 1974—. Mem. exec. com. Okla. div. Am. Cancer Soc., 1959-65. Served with armed forces, 1943-46. Mem. A.M.A., Am. Assn. Pathologists and Bacteriologists, Am. Soc. Exptl. Pathology, Am. Assn. Med. Colls., Internat. Acad. Pathology, Am. Coll. Angiology, Am. Soc. Coloposcopy, Am. Legion, Sigma Xi, Alpha Omega Alpha. Co-author: Introduction to Colposcopy, 1960. Contbr. articles to profl. jours. Home: 1556 E 37th St Tulsa OK 74105 Office: 1923 S Utica St Tulsa OK 74104

JARMAN, EDGAR RAY, educator, food cons.; b. Palmyra, Tenn., Apr. 22, 1922; s. I.W. and Kattie (Waynick) J.; B.S., U. Tenn., 1947, M.S., 1951; children—Katrina, Karla. With U. Tenn. Expt. Sta., 1950-51, U. Ga., 1951-54; asst. animal husbandtry Tex. Tech. U. and Tex. A & M U., 1955-60; head sci. dept. Coronado High Sch., Lubbock, Tex., 1965—; quality control cons. food and chem. industry; crop adjuster. Served with AUS, 1941-45. Decorated Bronze Star, Purple Heart with 2 oak leaf clusters; recipient 8 NSF grants. Mem. Am. Chem. Soc. (regional Tchr. of Year 1971), Am. Dairy Sci. Assn., Tex. Tchrs. Assn., NEA, South Plains Plant Soc. Baptist. Club: Men's Garden. Contbr. articles profl. jours. Home: 2522 62d St Lubbock TX 79413 Office: 3301 Vicksburg St Lubbock TX 79410

JARREAU, JOSEPH NIEL, counselor, clergyman; b. New Orleans, Sept. 10, 1926; s. Lucien Leon and Alice (Voorhies) J.; student St. Charles Coll., 1943-47; A.B., Spring Hill Coll., 1949; postgrad., 1949-50; B.S.T., St. Louis U., 1958. Joined S.J., 1943, ordained priest Roman Catholic Ch., 1956; tchr. high sch. Shreveport, La., 1950-53; dean men Jesuit House of Studies, Mobile, Ala., 1961-66; counselor Jesuit High Sch., Dallas, 1966-76, Tampa, 1976—; lectr., leader workshops and retreats. Mem. Am. Personnel and Guidance Assn., Fla. Personnel and Guidance Assn., Counselors Assn. Non-Public Schs. Democrat. Address: 4701 N Himes Ave Tampa FL 33614

JARRELL, GEORGE ROBERT, univ. dean; b. Tampa, Fla., Mar. 3, 1926; s. Larence Herman and Merle Locke (Futrell) J.; B.S., U. Fla., 1949, M.R.C., 1961; Ph.D., U.S.C., 1970; m. Nancy Lu Morgan, Apr. 17, 1965. Rehab. counselor Dept. Vocat. Rehab., Tallahassee, Fla., 1961-64, S.C. Mental Health Commn., Columbia, 1964-66; asst. dir., instr. edn. U. S.C., 1966-69; asso. prof. rehab. counseling Va. Commonwealth U., 1969-72; asst. dean Sch. Community Services, 1972-79; vocat. expert Bur. Hearings and Appeals, Social Security Adminstrn., HEW. Served with USAAF, 1944-46. HEW grantee, 1960. Mem. Nat. Rehab. Assn., Nat. Rehab. Counselors Assn., Am. Personnel and Guidance Assn., Am. Rehab. Counselors Assn. Methodist. Clubs: Masons, Shriners. Contbr. chpts. in books. Home: 5004 Evelyn Byrd Rd Richmond VA 23225 Office: 817 W Franklin St Richmond VA 23284

JARRELL, MARION LEE, surgeon; b. Alexandria, La., Dec. 17, 1921; s. Marion Fahy and Ethel (Lee) J.; B.S., Tulane U., 1945, M.D., 1945; m. Jane Ann Foote, May 15, 1948; children—Elizabeth Ray, Jane Ann, Salley Foote, Cornelia Fahy. Intern, Charity Hosp., New Orleans, 1945-46; resident Tulane U. Surg. Service, Charity Hosp., 1948-52; practice medicine, specializing in surgery, Alexandria, 1952—; mem. staff St. Frances Cabrini Hosp., Huey P. Long Charity Hosp., Pineville, Rapides Gen. Hosp., Alexandria; asso. prof. surgery Tulane U., 1962—; pres., dir. Lee Lumber Co. Ltd., 1965—, Beauregard Devel. Co., 1965—; dir. Rapides Bank & Trust Co., Alexandria. Served with USNR, 1946-48. Diplomate Am. Bd. Surgery. Mem. A.C.S., Southeastern Surg. Congress, La. Surg. Assn., Alton Ochsner Surg. Soc. (dir. 1970-73), Alexandria Pineville C. of C. (pres. 1974, dir. 1973-75), Rapides Parish, La. med. socs., AMA, Phi Kappa Sigma, Nu Sigma Nu. Methodist. Clubs: Lions, Coastal (dir.). Home: 3907 Pecan Dr Alexandria LA 71301 Office: 1470 McArthur Dr Alexandria LA 71301

JARRETT, MICHAEL DOUGLAS, banker; b. Bartlesville, Okla., Nov. 6, 1949; s. Donald Lee and Mary Izora (Holtzclaw) J.; B.B.A., U. Tex., Arlington, 1972; M.B.A., So. Meth. U., 1975; m. Teresa Margaret Lynch, Apr. 27, 1973. With Fed. Res. Bank Dallas, 1970-77, officer mgmt. trainee, 1972-73, supr. transfer of funds, 1974-75, resources adminstr., sr. expense analyst, 1975-77; mgr. credit dept., asst. v.p. Nat. Bank Commerce, Dallas, 1978, v.p. corr. banking, 1979—. Vol., Big Bros. Am. Mem. Phi Gamma Delta (Durrance award 1976, gen. officer). Republican. Roman Catholic. Home: 912 Tulane Dr Arlington TX 76012 Office: 1525 Elm St Dallas TX 75221

JARRETT, RANDALL FRANKLIN, pump mfg. co. exec.; b. Gainesville, Ga., Jan. 25, 1943; s. Marion F. and Sacile D. (Sailors) J.; B.S.A.E., U. Ga., 1965; m. Linda S. Barnett, Aug. 25, 1963; 1 dau., Sonja. Design engr. Roper Pump Co., Commerce, Ga., 1965-69, numerical control engr., 1969-71; chief engr. Dubie-Clark Co., Toccoa, Ga., 1971-74; nat. and internat. sales mgr. Patterson Pump Co., Toccoa, 1974—. Served with USAFR, 1966-72. Registered mech. engr., Ga. Mem. Ga. Soc. Profl. Engrs., Nat. Soc. Profl. Engrs., Gainesville Jaycees (past dir.). Baptist. Club: Toccoa Country. Home: 307 Lakeside Dr Cornelia GA 30531 Office: PO Box 790 Toccoa GA 30577

JARVINEN, SANDRA TORMALA, med. technologist; b. Detroit, Jan. 9, 1946; d. Aunert and Ellen E. Tormala; B.S. in Med. Tech., U. Detroit, 1967; grad. Providence Hosp. Sch. Med. Tech., Southfield, Mich., 1968. Med. technologist microbiology sect. Northland-Oakland Med. Labs., Southfield, 1968-71; supr. hematology Drs. Hosp. of Lake Worth (Fla.), 1972-74, supr. microbiology, 1974-76, chief technologist clin. lab., 1976—, also coordinator lab. in-service edn. programs, safety and quality control. Mem. Registry of Med. Technologists, Am. Soc. Med. Technologists, Am. Soc. Clin. Pathologists, Fla. Soc. Med. Technologists, Clin. Lab. Mgmt. Assn., Internat. Oceanographic Found., Oceanic Soc., Nat. Wildlife Found., Palm Beach County Shell Club, Sigma Sigma Sigma. Office: Doctors Hosp of Lake Worth 2829 10th Ave N Lake Worth FL 33462

JARVIS, EDMUND, educator, ret. air force officer; b. Semmes, Ala., Mar. 16, 1930; s. Henry Milton and Ida Jo (Lee) J.; B.S., Auburn U., 1952; M.B.A., U. Ga., 1969; m. Virginia Carol Sanford, May 24, 1953; children—Michael Edmund, Stephen Ellis. Commd. 2d lt. U.S. Air Force, 1952, advanced through grades to lt. col., 1968; mem. combat crews, 1952-66; asst. prof. aerospace sci. U. Ga., 1966-69; NATO airborne command post crew mem., Europe, 1969-72, wing exec. officer RAF base in Eng., 1969-72, ret., 1972; instr. aerospace edn., dept. head Mainland Sr. High Sch., Daytona Beach, Fla., 1972—. Decorated Air medal, Air Force Commendation medal, Nat. Def. Service medal, Vietnam Commendation medal. Mem. Mil. Order World Wars, Am. Security Council, Ret. Officers Assn., Air Force Assn., Fla. Real Estate Commn., Am. Soc. for Aerospace Edn. Clubs: Daytona Golf and Country, Shrine (past local pres.), Elks, Masons (32 deg.). Home: 1416 Suwanee Rd Daytona Beach FL 32019 Office: 125 S Clyde Morris Blvd Daytona Beach FL 32014

JARY, LLOYD WALKER, architect; b. Ft. Worth, Nov. 12, 1933; s. Lloyd Walker and Mary (Roderus) J.; B.Arch., U. Tex. at Austin, 1960; student Tex. A. and M. U., 1952-54; m. Mary V. Canales, Apr. 18, 1958; children—Lloyd Walker III, Elisa Ruth, Mary Bettina, Pamela Ann. With Bartlett Cocke & Assos., 1960-61, Reginal Roberts & Assos., 1961-62; pvt. archtl. practice, San Antonio, 1962—; prin. Jary-Sanchez & Assos., 1977—. Mem. bd. rev. San Antonio Hist. Dist., 1970-74, San Antonio River Walk, 1968-70; bd. dirs. San Antonio Urban Renewal, 1975-76; chmn. Madonna Neighborhood Center; chmn. Northeast YMCA, 1976-77; chmn. State Vols. Council Mental Health Mental Retardation, 1969-70; chmn. Vols. at San Antonio State Hosp., 1967-69. Bd. dirs., San Antonio Bldrs. Assn., 1974—, v.p., 1975. Recipient Lay Leadership award YMCA, 1975. Mem. AIA, Tex. Soc. Architects, Constrn. Specifications Inst. (pres. 1969-70, 77-78), San Antonio Jaycees (pres. 1964-65, outstanding young man award 1965). K.C. (pres. San Antonio chpt. 1966-67, 74-75). Home: 2900 Scattered Oaks San Antonio TX 78216 Office: 2426 Ceegee Suite 205 San Antonio TX 78217

JARY, ROLAND SAUNDERS, civil engr.; b. Ft. Worth, Jan. 26, 1936; s. Roland Edmund and Jane Elizabeth (Saunders) J.; B.A., Tex. Christian U., 1959, M.S., 1977; B.S., Tex. A&M U., 1965; postgrad. George Washington U., 1957-68, U. Hawaii, 1961-62; grad. Def. Lang. Inst., 1970, Command and Gen. Staff Coll., 1974; m. Linda Ann Gordanier, May 11, 1968; children—Janiece Lorraine, Matthew Saunders. Commd. 2d lt. U.S. Army, 1959, advanced through grades to maj., 1974; constrn. engr. C.E., Ft. Belvoir, Va., Honolulu, Saigon, and Korat, Thailand, 1959-67; topog. engr., Ft. Belvoir, 1968-70; project dir. Inter-Am. Geodetic Survey, Santiago, Chile and Quito, Ecuador, 1970-73; mem. coll. faculty Sch. of Americas, C.Z., 1970-71; hon. discharge, 1974; materials engr. constrn. Southwestern Labs., Ft. Worth, 1974—; mem. Ambassador's Country Team, Chile and Ecuador, 1971-73; cons. Carter-Stephens, Inc. Deacon Calvary Presbyterian Ch., 1975—; councilman Town of Pantego, Tex., 1979—; adv. com. civil and constrn. tech. program Tarrant County Jr.

Coll. Dist., 1979-80, mem. engring. tech. faculty, 1979. Decorated Bronze Star, Meritorious Service Medal, Army Commendation Medal (U.S.); Cross of Gallantry (Vietnam); registered profl. engr., Tex. Mem. Nat. Soc. Profl. Engrs., Tex. Soc. Profl. Engrs. (sec.-treas. Ft. Worth chpt.), Soc. Am. Mil. Engrs. (v.p. Ft. Worth chpt.), ASCE, (continuing edn. com. Tex. sect. 1979-80), Am. Water Works Assn. Club: Steeplechase (Ft. Worth). Contbr. articles to Civil Engr., Tech. Div. Engring. Jour., Mil. Engr. Home: 1600 Trail Glen Ct Arlington TX 76013 Office: PO Box 1379 Fort Worth TX 76101

JASIN, DAVID ALBIN, diversified real estate co. exec.; b. Pitts., June 19, 1942; s. Albin Anthony and Ann Marie Kelmeckis; B.S., Fla. State U., 1964; postgrad. U. Fla., 1965; U. W. Fla., 1976; m. Betty Church, June 26, 1965. Comml. mortgage officer, real estate appraiser, Travelers Ins. Co., Orlando, Fla., 1969-70, Atlanta, 1970-71; with Continental Mortgage Investors, Atlanta, 1971-73; sr. officer Gt. Am. Mortgage Investors, Atlanta, 1973-74; exec. v.p. Boykin Investments, Mobile, Ala., 1974-75; pvt. practice real estate consulting, Destin, Fla., 1975-77; exec. v.p., gen. mgr. Fairfield Harbour Community, New Bern, N.C., 1977-79; sr. v.p. U.S. Home Corp., Houston, 1979-80; v.p. prodn. Babcock Co. div. Weyerhaeuser Co., Fla., 1980—. Served to capt. USAF, 1965-69. Registered real estate salesman and mortgage broker, Fla. Mem. Am. Soc. Appraisers (sr.), Nat. Assn. Review Appraisers (certified review appraiser), Adminstrv. Mgmt. Soc. (cert. adminstrv. mgr.), Nat. Assn. Corp. Real Estate Execs. (founding mem.), Mortgage Bankers Assn. Am., Am. Econs. Assn., Urban Inst., Profl. Assn. Diving Instrs. (master instr.), Toastmasters Internat., Jr. C. of C., Sierra Club, Lambda Chi Alpha, Sigma Delta Pi. Contbr. articles to profl. jours. Home: 2998 Virginia St Coconut Beach FL 33133

JASPER, GENE WOODROW, water conditioning co. exec.; b. Somerville, Tex., Apr. 7, 1946; s. Thurman and Lois Faye Hill (McGregor) J.; A.A., Lee Coll., 1967; m. Julie K. Similie, June 24, 1966; children—Mick Chiron, Taft McClay. Sta. installer Western Electric Co., Houston, 1964-65; research technician Peninsular Chem. Research, Gainesville, Fla., 1967-68; with Continental Water Conditioning Co., Inc., 1969—, mgr. ops. for Fla. and Ala., Gainesville. Home: 119 SE 73d Terr Gainesville FL 32601 Office: 2305 NE 19th Dr Gainesville FL 32601

JASPER, MARTIN THEOPHILUS, educator; b. Hazlehurst, Miss., Mar. 19, 1934; s. Thomas Theophilus and Alice Maie (Norton) J.; B.S., Miss. State U., 1955, M.S., 1962; postgrad. Stevens Inst. Tech., 1963; Ph.D., U. Ala., 1967; m. Mary Altha Ledbetter, Nov. 2, 1963; children—Nellie Rebecca, Alice Hesta, Martin Theophilus, Mary Margaret, William Richard. Engr., Am. Cast Iron Pipe Co., Birmingham, Ala., 1955-56; plant metallurgist Vickers, Inc., Jackson, Miss., 1957-59; sr. design engr. missile div. Chrysler Corp., Huntsville, Ala., 1959-60; instr. mech. engring. Miss. State U., 1960-63, asst. prof., 1966-68, asso. prof., 1968-75, prof., 1975—. Served to 2d lt. M.S.C., AUS, 1956-57. NSF fellow, 1963; NASA fellow, 1963-66. Registered profl. engr., Miss. Mem. ASME (chmn. Miss. sect. 1971-72), Soc. Mfg. Engrs. (chpt. chmn. 1969-70, chmn. nat. research edn. grants com. 1974-75), Am. Soc. Engring. Edn., Miss. Acad. Sci., N.Y. Acad. Sci., Sigma Xi, Pi Mu Epsilon, Tau Beta Pi, Pi Tau Sigma. Democrat. Baptist. Mason (K.T., Shriner), Kiwanian. Contbr. articles to profl. jours. Research on fluid dynamics, combustion and incineration, systems design and analysis. Home: PO Box 155 Mississippi State MS 39762

JAVED, MUHAMMAD RAMZAN, cardiologist; b. Pakistan, July 15, 1946; came to U.S., 1973; s. Chiragh Din Javed; M.B., B.S., Punjab U., 1970; m. Bushra Ashiq, Oct. 24, 1971; children—Kamran, Adnan, Rakhshanda, Farkhanda. Intern, Bon Secours Hosp., Grosse Pointe, Mich., 1973-74; resident in internal medicine Misericordia Hosp. Med. Center, Bronx, N.Y., 1974-77; fellow in cardiology Bridgeport (Conn.) Hosp., 1977-79; practice medicine specializing in cardiology, Richlands, Va., 1979—; dir. spl. care units Clinch Valley Community Hosp., Richlands; cons. Tazewell (Va.) Community Hosp. Diplomate Am. Bd. Internal Medicine (cardiovascular disease). Fellow Am. Coll. Cardiology, Royal Coll. Physicians Can.; mem. A.C.P., AMA, Tazewell County Med. Soc. Home: Route 1 Box 556 Pounding Mill VA 24637 Office: 2943 W Front St Richlands VA 24641

JAVELLAS, INA JUNE, social worker; b. Pawhuska, Okla., June 15, 1934; d. Tom D. and Grace E. (Hyde) Javellas; B.A., U. Okla., 1956, M.S.W., 1958. Social work asst. Central State Griffin Meml. Hosp., Norman, Okla., 1957-58, psychiat. social worker, 1958-62; social work supr. Enid State Sch., 1962-63; social work supr. Eastern State Hosp., Vinita, Okla., 1963; psychiat. social worker Community Services Project, Tulsa, 1963-65; coordinator community mental health div. Dept. Mental Health, Oklahoma City, 1965-78, dep. dir. community mental health, 1978-79; pvt. mental health cons., 1979—; participant teaching program for student nurses Central State Griffin Meml. Hosp., Norman, Okla., 1960-62, psychiat. residency teaching program, 1961-62; cons. tng. headstart program trainees Okla. State U., 1966, Vista workers tng. program, 1966; mem. Gov.'s Adv. Com. for Planning Vocat. Rehab. Services and Sheltered Workshops and Facilities, chmn. task force on sheltered workshops and rehab. services, 1966-68; cons. tng. seminar Urban League, U.S. Dept. Labor, Neighborhood Program Trainees, 1968; mem. health edn. com. Interagy. Tech. Panel for Study of Health Edn. of Children and Youth in Okla., 1969-70; mem. Gov.'s Adv. Com. on Employment of Handicapped, 1969-70; participant Project Hope, Internat. Social Service Project, 1964-69; cons. NIMH, 1972—; cons. Region VI, Alcohol, Drug Abuse and Mental Health Adminstrn., USPHS, HEW, 1976—; mem. Okla. Bd. Registration Social Workers, 1961—. Bd. dirs. Okla. Health and Welfare Assn., 1972—. Grad. Counselor scholar Phi Mu, Atlanta, 1956-57. Recipient citation Tulsa County Mental Health Assn., 1966; named Outstanding Young Woman in Am., 1965. Mem. Nat. Assn. Social Workers (sec. ad hoc com. on grad. edn. Western Okla. chpt. 1969-71, named social worker of year 1970), Conf. Social Workers in State and Territorial Mental Health Programs (editor Newsletter 1967—, chmn. 1975-76, pres.-elect 1980-81), AAUW, Acad. Certified Social Workers, Phi Mu. Democrat. Episcopalian. Home: 3447 SE 44th St Apt 231 Del City OK 73135

JAY, EDWARD GEORGE, JR., research entomologist; b. Atlanta, Mar. 23, 1932; s. Edward George and Reba Allene (Davis) J.; B.S.A., U. Fla., 1958, M.S.A., 1961; Ph.D., U. Ga., 1970; m. Letitia Warren Little, June 10, 1955; children—Cheryl Diane, Douglas Edward. Entomologist, U.S. Dept. Agr., Orlando, Fla., 1959-61, Savannah, Ga., 1961-76, 77—; prin. research scientist Commonwealth Sci. and Indsl. Research Orgn., Canberra, Australia, 1976-77. Served with USN, 1951-55. Mem. Entomol. Soc. Am., Am. Assn. Mammalogists, British Ecol. Soc., Ga. Entomol. Soc., Am. Peanut Research and Edn. Assn., Sigma Xi. Clubs: Geechee Sailing (commodore 1978-79). Editor for Americas, Jour. Stored Product Research, 1979—. Contbr. articles on control of stored-product insects, modified atmospheres to sci. jours. Home: 404 Sharondale Rd Savannah GA 31406 Office: 3401 Edwin St PO Box 22909 Savannah GA 31403

JAY, JAMES ALBERT, ins. co. exec.; b. Superior, Wis., Aug. 24, 1916; s. Clarence William and Louie (Davies) J.; student pub. schs., Mpls.; m. Margie Hoffpauir, Dec. 23, 1941; 1 son, James A. Franchise with The Stauffer System of Calif., 1946-49; Ala. dist. mgr. Guaranty Savs. Life Ins. Co., Montgomery, Ala., 1949-51, state mgr. La., 1951—, dir., 1952—, La. gen. agent, 1964—; La. gen agt. Gen. United Life Ins. Co. of Des Moines, 1969—. Com. chmn. Attakapas council Boy Scouts Am., Alexandria, La., 1955, council commr., 1961-62, commr. Manchac dist., 1967—. Served as cpl. USMC, 1942-45, PTO. Decorated Purple Heart. Mem. Nat., Baton Rouge life underwriters assns., Gen. Agts. and Mgrs. Conf., C. of C., Internat. Platform Assn. Methodist. Elk. Home: 5919 Clematis Dr Baton Rouge LA 70808 Office: 3404 Convention St Baton Rouge LA 70806

JAYROE, AUBREY L., accountant, data processing exec.; b. Forrest City, Ark., July 23, 1952; s. Jerry Cecil and Mattie Ruth (Reynolds) J.; degree in acctg., Crowleys Ridge Vocat. Tech. Sch., Forrest City, 1971; cert. in computers, IBM Computer Sch., Memphis, 1976; m. Brenda Kaye Ruff, Aug. 19, 1971; 1 son, Trenton Alan. Clk., St. Francis County Farmers Assn., Forrest City, 1970; enrolled to practice before IRS, 1974; acct., gen. mgr. Thomas D. Seay & Co., P.A., also gen. mgr. Computer Consultants Co., Forrest City, 1971—. Mem. adv. staff bus. dept. Crowleys Ridge Vocat. Tech. Sch., 1976—, adv. staff coop. edn. East Ark. Community Coll., 1978—. Mem. Ark. Soc. Pub. Accts., Nat. Soc. Pub. Accts., Accts. Computer Users Tech. Exchange. Mem. United Pentecostal Ch. Home: 859 Inglewood Forrest City AR 72335 Office: 815 S Washington St Forrest City AR 72335

JEANE, ISAAC LYNN, hosp. adminstr.; b. Pitkin, La., June 17, 1943; s. Isaac Lafayette and Evelyn (Mathis) J.; B.S., Northwestern State U. La., 1966; M.B.A., Columbus (Ga.) Coll., 1979; m. Patricia Fitzpatrick, July 21, 1971; children—Christopher, Gretchen. Project specialist, dir. emergency services Baylor U. Med. Center, Dallas, 1969-71; dir. admissions Hotel Dieu Hosp., New Orleans, 1971-73; adminstrv. asst. materials and services Lanier Meml. Hosp., Langdale, Ala., 1973-79; asso. exec. dir. McFarland Hosp., Lebanon, Tenn., 1979—. Served with U.S. Army, 1966-69. Decorated Bronze Star. Mem. Am. Soc. Hosp. Materials Mgmt., Ala. Soc. Hosp. Materials Mgmt. (dir.), Hosp. Fin. Mgmt. Assn. Club: Kiwanis (v.p. Lanett, Ala. chpt. 1978-79). Office: 500 Park Ave Lebannon TN 37087

JEANES, SHIRLEY RUTH REILEY, speech and lang. pathologist; b. Beeville, Tex., Sept. 4, 1948; d. Marvin Adolf and Ruby Elizabeth (Pettit) Reiley; B.S., U. Tex., Austin, 1970, M.A., 1976; m. William Franklin Jeanes, Mar. 22, 1975; children—Heather Leigh, Derek William. Speech and lang. pathologist South San Antonio (Tex.) Ind. Sch. Dist., 1970; intern Austin Evaluation Center, 1972; speech and lang. pathologist Clear Creek (Tex.) Ind. Sch. Dist., 1972-75; pvt. practice speech and lang. pathology, Friendswood, Tex., 1979—; cons. Friendswood Community Edn., 1977—. Mem. Am. Speech-Lang.-Hearing Assn., Houston Area Assn. Children with Communication Disorders, U. Tex. Ex-Students Assn. (Outstanding Service award 1979). Methodist. Club: Friendswood Tennis (pres. 1978-80).

JEANSONNE, LOUIS OLIVER, III, pediatrician; b. Augusta, Ga., Dec. 22, 1945; s. Louis Oliver, II, and Gloria (Quin) J.; B.S., Tulane U., 1967, M.S., 1970, M.D., 1972; m. Rose Mary D'Agostino, Aug. 10, 1968; children—Louis Oliver IV, Bryan Grant. Intern, then resident in pediatrics Charity Hosp., New Orleans, 1972-75; practice medicine specializing in pediatrics, Baton Rouge, 1977—; asst. clin. prof. Tulane U. Served to maj. M.C., U.S. Army, 1975-77. Fellow Am. Acad. Pediatrics; mem. AMA, La. Med. Soc., East Baton Rouge Parish Med. Soc., Baton Rouge C. of C. Republican. Author: Practical Manual of Pediatrics, 1975. Office: 7946 Goodwood Blvd Baton Rouge LA 70806

JECKOVICH, DAVID MARIJAN, diversified co. exec.; b. Niagara Falls, N.Y., Dec. 2, 1956; s. John Joseph and Delphine Ann Jeckovich; student in bus. adminstrn. and real estate Niagara U., 1974-76; m. Joann Patterson, Jan. 21, 1975; children—David John, Thomas. Owner, mgr. Ambassador Services, Ormond Beach, Fla., 1977—. Mem. Nat. Assn. Realtors. Home: 1594 Sherris Ln Holly Hill FL 32017 Office: 595 N Nova Rd Suite 201 Ormond Beach FL 32074

JEDEL, PETER HAROLD, mfg. co. exec.; b. Bklyn., May 19, 1939; s. Joseph L. and Marjory (Zucker) J.; B.A., Cornell U., 1960; M.B.A., N.Y. U., 1962; m. Elaine T. Binder, July 1, 1962; children—Marc, Lynn. Credit analyst Chem. Bank, 1960-63; fin. analyst Gen. Foods Co., 1963-65; sr. fin. analyst Xerox Co., Rochester, N.Y., 1965-68; mgr. strategic planning TWA, N.Y.C., 1968-69; investment banker Alan-Maged, N.Y.C., 1969-70; chief economist Cities Service Co., Tulsa, 1970—; chmn. adv. com. Tulsa Sch. Econs. Mem. Northeastern Okla. Econs. Adv. Com.; mem. Mayor's Budget Rev. Served with U.S. Army, 1962-63. Mem. UN Assn., Nat. Assn. Bus. Economists (council), Tulsa Econs. Club (chmn., founder), Am. Econ. Assn. Republican. Jewish. Club: Tulsa So. Racquet. Home: 7308 E 68th Pl Tulsa OK 74133 Office: PO Box 300 Tulsa OK 74102

JEFFERDS, JOSEPH CROSBY, JR., indsl. machinery distbg. co. exec.; b. Charleston, W.Va., June 24, 1919; s. Joseph Crosby and Agnes Atkinson (Arbuckle) J.; B.S. in Mech. Engring., Mass. Inst. Tech., 1940; Sc.D. (hon.), W.Va. Inst. Tech., 1969; m. Olivia Polk Evans, May 15, 1943; children—Joseph C. III, Marion Jefferds Sinclair, Olivia Polk, Robert Grosvenor. Trainee, Bethlehem Steel Co. (Pa.), 1940; v.p., dir. Kanawha Drug Co., Charleston, 1946-47, Distbr.'s Corp., Charleston, 1970—; pres. Jefferds Corp., Charleston, 1947—, Mech. Equipment Service Co., Charleston, 1952—; dir. C & P Telephone Co. W.Va., Kanawha Banking & Trust Co. Mem. W.Va. Bd. Edn., 1957-65, pres., 1963; trustee W.Va. Inst. Tech. Found., Montgomery, Highland Hosp., Charleston, U. Charleston. Served from 2d lt. to lt. col. AUS, 1941-46. Mem. Charleston Area C. of C. (pres. 1972), ASME, Am. Ordnance Assn., Am. Inst. Indsl. Engrs. Republican. Episcopalian. Clubs: Charleston Rotary (past pres.); Edgewood Country (past pres.), Berry Hills Country. Author: A History of St. John's Episcopal Church, 1976. Home: 3 Scott Rd Charleston WV 25314 Office: PO Box 757 US Route 35 St Albans WV 25177

JEFFERS, FLORICE STRIPLING, writer; b. Bullard, Tex.; d. James Carl and Mary Evie (Shipp) Stripling; m. Frank Grover Jeffers (dec. Nov. 1976); children—Mary Allyne (Mrs. Wallace B. Landrum), Gordon Frank. With Jeffers Oil Co., Jeffers Drilling Co., Jeffers Pipe & Supply. Judge, critic, poetry contests; condr. programs on poetry, other lit.; contbr. to anthologies, poetry mags. Named poet laureate of Tex., 1976-77. Mem. Nat. Fedn. State Poetry Socs., Acad. Am. Poets (donor), Poetry Soc. Tex. (awards and prizes, mem. council), Wichita Falls Poetry Soc. (past pres.), Tex. Fedn. Women's Clubs (poet laureate 1960), Current Lit. Club (past pres.), Woman's Forum Wichita Falls (past pres. writers dept.). Baptist. Author: Walk a Tall Shadow, 1976. Home and office: 608 Meadow Dr PO Box 638 Burkburnett TX 76354

JEFFERS, JEROME LEW, architect; b. Terre Haute, Ind., Jan. 18, 1935; s. Alfred Glen and Irene Opal (Wilson) J.; B.S., Ind. State U., 1961; m. Marilyn M. Starrett, Jan. 16, 1953; children—Debra Dawn Jeffers Wright, Jerome Lew. Archtl. designer Miller & Miller Assos., Terre Haute, 1961-64, Delnoce Whitney Goubert, N.Y.C., 1964-66, Reynolds Smith & Hills, Merritt Island, Fla., 1966-71; architect, owner Jerome Jeffers & Assos., Cocoa Beach, Fla., 1971—; cons. Cottage Row Inner City Redevel. Group (Cocoa Beach). Served with USAR, 1953-59. Registered architect, Fla. Mem. Fla. Planning and Zoning Assn., Inc., AIA (past pres.). Republican. Methodist. Home: 1140 S Brevard Ave Cocoa Beach FL 32931 Office: Suite 30 1325 N Atlantic Ave Cocoa Beach FL 32931

JEFFERSON, FRANKLIN DAVID, educator; b. Canton, Miss., Jan. 25, 1941; s. Thomas and Elizabeth (Peale) J.; B.S., Jackson (Miss.) State Coll., 1964; M.A.T., Antioch-Putney U., Yellow Springs, Ohio, 1968; M.Ed., U. Wash., Seattle, 1973; Ph.D., U. S.C., Columbia, 1976; m. Celestine Lenora Russell, June 21, 1967; children—Vernessa Lenora, Elizabeth Joann, Dawatha Chikeda. Tchr. dept. social sci. edn. and geography Jackson (Miss.) State U., 1968—, asst. prof., 1977—; curriculum developer Govt. Tech. Coll., Ombe, West Cameroon, Africa, 1964-66. Sec., Madison County Union for Progress; bd. dirs. Madison-Yazoo-Leake County Health Centers. Recipient award Wall St. Jour., 1964; Tng. of Tchr. Trainers grantee, 1971. Mem. Nat. Council Social Studies, Assn. Study Negro Life and History, NAACP (chmn. polit. action, awards com. Madison-Ridgeland-Tougaloo br.), Phi Delta Kappa. Baptist. Home: Route 1 Box 33D Madison MS 39110 Office: 1325 Lynch St Jackson MS 39217

JEFFORDS, EDD ALAN, inst. exec.; b. Rector, Ark., Nov. 28, 1945; s. Roy Ezra and Sylvia Belle (Dickinson) J.; A.A., Victor Valley Coll., 1967; student U. Ark., 1974, Roger Williams Coll., 1976-77, U. Wis. Mgmt. Inst., 1977; B.A., U. Minn., 1978; m. Linda Smart, Apr. 15, 1963 (div. 1979); 1 son, Dana Alan. Editor, Auburn (Wash.) Globe-News, 1967; fine arts editor Tacoma News-Tribune, 1967-72; gen. mgr. OAC, Inc., Eureka Springs, Ark., 1973-76; exec. dir. Ozark Inst., Eureka Springs, 1976—; lectr., cons. arts mgmt., 1973—. Mem. Ark. State Task Force on Environ. Edn., 1976—, Govs. Conf. on Libraries, 1977—; bd. dirs. Ark. Solar Coaltion, 1978—; chmn. Eureka Springs Cultural Affairs Com., 1976; mem. Eureka Springs Centennial Commn., 1979; bd. dirs. Nat. Family Farm Coalition, 1979—. Served with USAF, 1963-67. Named Humanist of Yr. Ark. Endowment for Humanities, 1976. Mem. Newspaper Guild, Ozark Soc., Ark. Press Assn. Democrat. Editor: Uncertain Harvest, 1979. Office: Ozark Inst PO Box 549 99 Spring St Eureka Springs AR 72632

JEFFORDS, JEAN GARRETT, planning cons.; b. Waycross, Ga., Feb. 8, 1921; d. Quillian Lemuel and Glenn Antoinette (Allen) Garrett; A.B., U. Ga., 1942; M.A. in Polit. Sci. (Univ. fellow), 1944; m. William Quintillus Jeffords, Jr., Oct. 15, 1954 (dec.); 1 son, Lawrence Garrett. With fgn. service Dept. State, Guatemala, 1945-48; asst. to dean Coll. Spl. and Continuation Studies, U. Md., College Park, 1948-49; prin. planner Jacksonville (Fla.) Area Planning Bd., 1965-74; planning dir. Central Fla. Regional Planning Council, Bartow, 1974-79; planning cons., 1979—. Mem. Am. Planning Assn., Polk County Hist. Assn., Alpha Delta Pi. Democrat. Episcopalian. Author reports in field. Home: 1140 S Broadway Bartow FL 33830 Office: PO Box 1282 Bartow FL 33830

JEFFRIES, CHARLES RAY, assn. exec., educator; b. Cleburne, Tex., Nov. 13, 1938; s. Joe Norris and Lillie Mae (Foster) J.; B.F.A., Tex. Christian U., 1961; M.A., Trinity U., 1972; postgrad. Colo. State Coll. at Greeley, 1965; 1 son, Charles Brett. Tchr. high sch. drama, Hobbs, N.Mex., 1961-62, MacArthur High Sch., San Antonio, 1964-67, Highlands High Sch., San Antonio, 1968-74, John Jay High Sch., San Antonio, 1974—; state dir. Internat. Thespian Soc., 1969-70, regional dir., 1970-72, bd. dirs., 1972-78; founder, 1st pres. Youtheatre, Fort Worth, 1956-58; asst. adminstrv. staff Casa Manana Musicals, Fort Worth, 1958-59; artistic dir. Hobbs Community Theatre, 1961-63; actor Little Theatre of Rockies, Greeley, Colo., 1963; dir. entertainment Fort Sam Houston Theatre, U.S. Army, 1964; lighting designer Peninsula Playhouse, New Braunfels, Tex., 1965; asst. mgr. Hemisfair Theatre & Arena, San Antonio, 1967-68; bd. dirs. Billboard Theatre, San Antonio, 1966-70, pres., 1969-70; instr., tech. dir. Incarnate Word Coll., San Antonio, 1970-71; chmn. drama instrs. San Antonio Ind. Sch. Dist., 1970-74; guest drama dir. Trinity U., summer 1977, 78, Incarnate Word Coll., San Antonio, 1978; prodn. dir. Harliquin Dinner Theatre, San Antonio, spring 1978. Recipient Tex. Star award KBAT radio, 1970, Citizen of Day award KEEZ radio, 1971; winner Dist.-Area State One-Act Play Contest, 1972-77. Mem. Secondary Schs. Theater Assn. (regional dir. 1971-74, nat. bd. dirs. 1972-75, membership sec. 1973-74, editor newsletter 1973-74, pres. 1978-79), Tex. Secondary Sch. Theatre Assn. (bd. dirs. 1967-72), S.W. Theatre Assn. (chmn. secondary schs. div. 1969-73), Alpha Psi Omega. Home: 9427 Millbrook St San Antonio TX 78245 Office: 7611 Marbach Rd San Antonio TX 78227

JEFFRIES, TONI HARMON, speech pathologist, educator; b. Little Rock, Jan. 30, 1951; d. Robert Ferrell Harmon and Frances (Hibbs) Harmon Briney; B.A. in Speech Pathology, U. Ark., 1972, M.A., 1973; m. Charles Cole Jeffries, Jr., Aug. 11, 1973; 1 dau., Courtney Dawn. Tchr. aide Headstart, North Little Rock, Ark., 1969; asst. speech therapist C & Y Project, U. Ark. Med. Center, Little Rock, 1971; grad. asst. Speech and Hearing Clinic, Fayetteville, 1972-73; lang. devel. specialist Ark. Mental Retardation-Devel. Disabilities Services, Little Rock, 1973; speech pathologist Easter Seals Speech and Hearing Clinic, Virginia Beach, Va., 1974, Portsmouth (Va.) Public Schs., 1974-75, Accotink Acad., Springfield, Va., 1979—; pvt. practice speech pathologist, 1979—; asso. prof. aviation Los Angeles Community Coll. Overseas, Subic Bay, Philippines, 1976-77; FAA instrumental and comml. ground instr. ATC Flight Tng. Center, Springfield, 1978—. Lic. basic, instrument, comml. ground instr., pvt. pilot FAA. Mem. Am. Speech and Hearing Assn. (cert. clin. competence), Aircraft Owners and Pilots Assn., Stardusters, Alpha Chi Omega (v.p. No. Va. alumni assn.), Kappa Sigma. Clubs: Naval Officer Wives, Judge Adv. Gen. Corps Wives, Andrews-Bolling Air Force Flying, Quantico Flying. Home: 273 Richmond Hill West Helena AR 72390 Office: 9424 Goshen Ln Burke VA 22015

JEHLE, HERBERT, physicist; b. Stuttgart, Germany, Mar. 5, 1907; s. Julius V. and Maria (Gminder) J.; came to U.S., 1941; Dipl. Ing., Inst. Tech. Stuttgart, 1930; Dr. Ing., Inst. Tech., Berlin, 1933; postgrad. Cambridge (Eng.) U., 1933-34; m. Dietlinde von Kuenssberg, May 30, 1952; children—Eberhard, Dietrich. Editorial collaborator Jahrbuch Fortschritte d. Math., Berlin, 1935-36; research asst. U. Southhampton (Eng.), 1937; research asso. U. Brussels, 1938-40; instr. Harvard U., 1942-46; guest NRC seeing aid project Franklin Inst., 1946; mem. Inst. for Advanced Study, Princeton, N.J., 1947; asst. prof. physics U. Pa., 1947-49; asso. prof. U. Nebr., 1949-54, prof., 1954-59; prof. George Washington U., 1959-72, prof. physics emeritus, 1972—; research asso. Calif. Inst. Tech., 1956-57; cons. Nat. Cancer Inst., 1972-77; sr. fellow U. Md., 1972—; guest Max Planck Inst. fur Physik und Astrophysik, Munich, W.Ger., 1973-74, Uppsala (Sweden) U., 1975, 76, U. Amsterdam, 1975—; guest prof. U. Munich, 1977-83. NIH fellow, 1965-66. Fellow Am. Phys. Soc.; mem. Am. Astron. Soc., Biophys. Soc., Am. Math. Soc., Soc. Quantum Biology. Quaker. Author: Charge Fluctuation Forces, 1958; Nucleic Acid Replication, 1965; Bilateral Symmetry in Morphogensis, 1970; Statistical Hypotheses in Gravitational Systems, 1973; Intermolecular Forces and Biological Specificity, 1973; Flux Quantization and

Particle Physics, 1977. Home: 1208 Sherwood Rd Charlottesville VA 22901

JELENEVSKY, ALEX MICHAEL, lab. mgr.; b. Paris, France, Jan. 5, 1947; s. Michael and Lydia (Koresha) J.; came to U.S., 1947, naturalized, 1959; B.S., Syracuse U., 1969; B.S., State U. N.Y. Coll. Forestry, 1969; student Upstate Med. Center, 1969-70; m. Robin Hollway, Sept. 1, 1979; children—Peter, Michael, Paul. Research chemist Bristol Meyers, Syracuse, N.Y., 1969-74; asso. devel. chemist Ciba-Geigy, Greensboro, N.C., 1974-76; lab. mgr. Abbott Lab., Rocky Mount, N.C., 1976—; cons. tech. tng. program Ciba-Geigy. Recipient NSF grant, 1967, 68, 69. Mem. Am. Chem. Soc., Am. Forestry Assn., State U. N.Y. Environ. and Forestry Alumni Assn., Syracuse U. Alumni Assn. Patentee antiarrhythmic agts., cardiovascular drugs. Office: PO Box 2226 Rocky Mount NC 27801

JELKS, ALLEN NATHANIEL, SR., physician; b. Macon, Ga., Aug. 2, 1930; s. Howard Coates and Beulah Louise (Smith) J.; student Emory U., 1948-51; B.S. in Medicine, Duke, 1953, M.D., 1955; m. Mary Larson, June 16, 1957; children—Helen Irene, Allen Nathaniel, Howard Larson, Alice Coates. Intern pediatrics Johns Hopkins Hosp., 1955-56, resident pediatrics, 1958-59; instr. pediatrics U. Fla. Hosp., Gainesville, 1950-61; practice medicine, specializing in pediatrics, Sarasota, Fla., 1961—; mem. staff Sarasota Meml. Hosp. Pres. Sarasota County (Fla.) Heart Assn., 1963-64; mem. com. advance gifts United Appeal, Sarasota, 1965-72. Served with USNR, 1956-57. Diplomate Am. Bd. Pediatrics. Mem. Am., Fla. acads. pediatrics, Fla., Sarasota County pediatric socs., Sarasota County Med. Soc., Sarasota County C. of C., Phi Delta Theta, Alpha Omega Alpha. Rotarian. Home: 1930 Clematis St Sarasota FL 33579 Office: 1700 S Osprey Ave Sarasota FL 33579

JELKS, JAMES WILLIAM, food and alcohol processing co. exec.; b. Sand Springs, Okla., Nov. 22, 1920; s. Clarence Clay and Bess (Harris) J.; student U. Tulsa, 1938-39; student U. Ark., 1939-40, U. Kan., 1941, U. Cin., 1945; m. Mary Kathleen McVay, Oct. 2, 1943; children—Kathleen (Mrs. David Ward), Barbara (Mrs. David Chicherio). Project engr. Spartan Aircraft Co., Tulsa, Boeing Airplane Co., Wichita, Kan., Aeronca Aircraft, Middletown, Ohio, 1938-45; owner, operator Jelks Co., engrs., Middletown, 1945-59; sr. engr. N.Am. Aviation, Tulsa, 1959-65; operator food processing co., Sand Springs, 1965—. Registered profl. engr., Ohio, Okla. Episcopalian. Research, publs. on Froth Flotation De-inking and making animal feed from cellulose wastes. Patentee in field. Developer paper reclamation process, process to produce alcohol from cellulose wastes. Home: Route 4 Box 6 Sand Springs OK 74063 Office: PO Box 21 Sand Springs OK 74063

JELKS, JOSEPH WILLIAM, JR., textile co. exec.; b. Southport, N.C., Mar. 27, 1916; s. Joseph William and Josie (Garrett) J.; B.S. in Math. and Sci., Wake Forest U., 1936; m. Ann Elizabeth Ray, Aug. 15, 1936; children—Peggy Jelks Williamson, Joseph William III. Indsl. relations mgr. Winnsboro Mills, U.S. Rubber Co., 1939-51; personnel dir. Ware Shoals div. Riegel Textile Corp., 1951-57; v.p. J.P. Stevens & Co., Inc., 1957—; dir. 1st Nat. Bank of S.C. Tchr. personnel adminstrn. and indsl. safety U. S.C. Extension, 1947-50; tchr. indsl. engring. Methods Engring. Council Pitts., 1954-56. Dir. So. Indsl. Relations Conf., 1963—. Chmn. Fairfield County chpt. ARC, 1948, Fairfield County chpt. Nat. Found., 1950; dir.-at-large S.C. Tb Assn.; bd. dirs. Unemployment Benefit Advisors; mem. adv. bd. Liberty Mut. Ins. Co. Hon. life mem. So. Conf. Football Ofcls. Assn.; mem. Southeastern Personnel Assn. (dir., past chmn.), S.C. Textile Mfrs. Assn. (chmn. safety com., past chmn., dir. personnel div.), Wake Forest U. Alumni Council, Soc. Advancement Mgmt., Am. Textile Mfrs. Inst., S.C. Accident Prevention Conf., S.C. (v.p.), Greater Greenville chambers commerce, Am. Soc. Personnel Adminstrn. Episcopalian. Clubs: Greenville Country, City, Poinsett (Greenville). Home: 34 Sirrine Dr Greenville SC 29605 Office: Daniel Bldg Greenville SC 29602

JELKS, LOUIS ROLLWAGE, physician, surgeon; b. Memphis, Nov. 16, 1906; s. John Lemuel and Minnie (Rollwage) J.; M.D., U. Tenn., 1933; m. Ruth Goddard, May 4, 1929; children—Leigh (Mrs. Wade Hughes Threlkeld), Louis Rollwage Jr. Intern, Knoxville (Tenn.) Gen. Hosp., 1933-34; asso. with father, Dr. J.L. Jelks for postgrad. work in surgery, Memphis, 1934-35; practice medicine, specializing in surgery, Reidsville, Ga., 1935—; adminstr., owner Jelks Hosp., 1938—; examining physician SSS, 1940—, N.G., 1948— (both Tatt County). Mem. Tattnall County Sch. Bd. Dir. FHA, Reidsville, Ga., mem. Civil Def. Bd. Mem. Am., So. med. assns., Ga., S.E. Ga. (pres. 1969, 76, 78), 1st Dist. Ga. med. socs., Am. Soc. Abdominal Surgeons. Methodist. Club: Vidalia Country. Home: 416 Brazell St N Reidsville GA 30453 Office: Jelks Clinic PC 203-7 Main St Reidsville GA 30453

JELLINEK, HAROLD LESTER, physician; b. N.Y.C., June 2, 1915; s. Henry and Edna (Comings) J.; B.S., N.Y. U., 1934; M.D., N.Y. Med Coll., 1939; m. Lucille Doris Jacobs (dec.); children—Hollis Maura, Leslie Jellinek San; m. 2d, Jacqueline Margaret Rumley, Oct. 18, 1975. Intern, Morrisania City Hosp., N.Y.C., 1939-41, resident in internal medicine, 1946-47; practice medicine specializing in internal medicine, N.Y.C., 1941-42, 47-49; clin. asst. medicine Morrisania City Hosp., 1947-48, asst. vis. electrocardiographer, 1948-49; internist VA Center, Dayton, 1949-50; internist, cardiologist Golden Clinic and Meml. Gen. Hosp., Elkins, W.Va., 1950—. Served to maj. AUS, 1942-46. Diplomate Am. Bd. Internal Medicine. Fellow Am. Coll. Cardiology, Am. Coll. Chest Physicians, Am. Coll. Angiology; mem. AMA, So. Med. Assn., Am. Soc. Internal Medicine, AAAS, Am. Heart Assn. (council clin. cardiology), Meml. Gen. Hosp. Assn. (dir. 1958—, pres. bd. 1971-79, chmn. bd. 1979—). Clubs: Masons, Elks. Home: 30 Boyd St Elkins WV 26241 Office: Memorial General Hospital Golden Clinic Elkins WV 26241

JELSMA, EDWARD RICHARD, transp. cons.; b. Enid, Okla., Mar. 15, 1915; s. Edward Darwin and Orilla (Hackathorn) J.; B.S., Okla. State U., 1937, M.S., 1938; postgrad. Stanford U., 1939-40; m. Marjorie Marie Crain, Feb. 12, 1948; children—Schuyler, Richard, Lisa. Asst. to tax counsel Standard Oil Co. Calif., San Francisco, 1940-41; dep. fiscal dir. Bur. Ordnance, U.S. Navy Dept., Washington, 1946-48, asst. fiscal dir. dept., 1948-49; engaged in citrus industry, 1949—; profl. mem. Interstate and Fgn. Commerce Com., U.S. Senate, 1949-55; dir. bur. transport econs. and statistics ICC, 1955-58; pres. E.R. Jelsma & Assos., transp. cons., 1958—; grad. asst. Okla. State U., 1937-38; instr. Northwestern State Coll., 1938-39, Am. U., 1946-49; guest lectr. U. Louisville, 1942-43. Served from ensign to lt. comdr., USNR, 1941-46. Mason. Author: Minimum Wage Legislation, 1938. Office: 1811 Morningside Dr Mount Dora FL 32757

JEMISON, JAMES DAVID, coll. adminstr.; b. Fairfield, Ala., Jan. 21, 1920; s. Thomas and Ella Bell (Chambliss) J.; A.B., Miles Coll., 1942; M.B.A., Columbia U., 1956; postgrad. U. Omaha, 1957, Va. State Coll., Petersburg, 1953, 54; m. Evelyn Bradford Watkins, Dec. 16, 1946; children—Jan Karenina, Elania Sadella. Asst. bus. mgr. Storer Coll., Harpers Ferry, W.Va., 1947-50; budget officer Elizabeth City (N.C.) State Tchrs. Coll., 1950-51; acct., bus. mgr., asst. v.p. adminstrn. Va. State U., Petersburg, 1951—, asst. prof. fin., 1972—. Chmn., Petersburg Hosp. Authority, 1976; mem. Va. Hosp. Adv. Council, 1976; bd. dirs. Mary Carter Beacon House for Physically Handicapped, United Way Southside Va., Robert E. Lee council Boy Scouts Am.; trustee Zion Bapt. Ch., Thelma Olaker Youth Ballet Co. Recipient awards Boy Scouts Am., United Way. Mem. Nat. Assn. Coll. Aux. Services (pres.), Nat. Assn. Coll. and Univ. Bus. Officers. Club, Beaux Twenty. Home: 20600 Southlawn Ave Petersburg VA 23803 Office: Va State U Petersburg VA 23803

JENDREK, JOHN PAUL, JR., air force officer; b. Balt., Nov. 26, 1941; s. John Paul and Carolyn Janet (Eberenz) J.; B.A., Johns Hopkins U., 1963; Ph.D. (Gen. Foods fellow), Tulane U., 1967; grad. Air War Coll., 1979; m. Pamela Lee Hoshall, June 15, 1963; children—John Paul III, Scott Kenneth. Chem. engr. Celanese Corp., Charlotte, N.C., 1967; commd. 2d lt. U.S. Army, 1963; project scientist Army Ballistics Research Lab., Aberdeen Proving Grounds, Md., 1967-69; transferred to U.S. Air Force, 1969, advanced through grades to maj.; project scientist AF Rocket Propulsion Lab., Edwards AFB, Calif., 1969-71; asso. prof. chemistry Air Force Acad., Colo., 1971-76; chief explosives br. Air Force Armament Lab., Eglin AFB, Fla., 1976—; instr. Oskaloosa Walton Jr. Coll., Niceville, Fla. Commr., Little League Baseball; coach Youth Football. Named Outstanding Grad., Air War Coll. Mem. N.Y. Acad. Scis., Sigma Xi. Democrat. Roman Catholic. Research on high energy explosives and propellants. Home: 322 St Andrews Dr Niceville FL 32578 Office: AFATL DLDE Eglin Air Force Base FL 32542

JENKINS, CLARA BARNES, educator; b. Franklinton, N.C.; d. Walter and Stella (Griffin) Barnes; B.S., Winston-Salem State U., 1939; M.A., N.C. Central U., 1947; Ed.D., U. Pitts., 1965; postgrad. N.Y. U., 1947-48, U. N.C., Chapel Hill, N.C. Agrl. and Tech. State U.; m. Hugh Morris Jenkins, Dec. 24, 1949 (div. Feb. 1955). Faculty Fayetteville State U., 1945-53, Rust Coll., Holly Spring, Miss., 1953-58; asst. prof. Shaw U., 1958-64; now prof. edn. and psychology St. Paul's Coll., Lawrenceville, Va.; vis. prof. edn. Friendship Jr. Coll., Rock Hill, S.C., summer 1947, N.C. Agr. and Tech. State U., summers 1966-79. Bd. dirs. Winston-Salem State U. United Negro Coll. Fund Faculty fellow, 1963-64; grantee Am. Bapt. Conv., Valley Forge, Pa., 1963-64. Mem. AAUP, Nat. Soc. for Study Edn., NEA, AAUW, Am. Hist. Assn., Va. Edn. Assn., Am. Acad. Polit. and Social Sci., AAAS, Internat. Platform Assn., Doctoral Assn. Educators, Assn. Tchr. Educators, Marquis Biog. Library Soc., Am. Assn. for Higher Edn., Acad. Polit. Sci., Am. Psychol. Assn., History of Edn. Soc., Soc. for Research in Child Devel., Jean Piaget Soc., Phi Eta Kappa, Zeta Phi Beta. Episcopalian. Home: 920 Bridges St Henderson NC 27536 Office: St Pauls Coll Lawrenceville VA 23868

JENKINS, DARLENE, real estate mgr.; b. Winnie, Tex., Nov. 24, 1939; d. Charles Everett and Ruby Pfleider; B.Acctg., Stephen F. Austin U., 1961; student real estate, Lamar U., 1975-76; grad. Realtors Inst.; children—John, Stephen. Programmatic Flexowriter Systems specialist Gulf Supply Co., Inc., 1960-63; bookkeeper, sec. 1st United Meth. Ch. of Winnie-Stowell, Tex., 1971-75; agt. du Perier Real Estate, 1977-80; mgr. Maida Real Estate, Beaumont, Tex., 1978. Bd. dirs. ARC; La Petite chair Tex. Rice Festival. Mem. Nat. Assn. Realtors, Tex. Assn. Realtors, Women's Council of Real Estate, Beaumont Bd. Realtors, Beaumont C. of C., TIPS Club (pres.), Bus. and Profl. Men's Club. Republican. Methodist. Clubs: Altrusa Internat.; Internat. (Beaumont). Home: 9525 McLean St Beaumont TX 77707 Office: 3190 Liberty St Beaumont TX 77704

JENKINS, DAVID TERRELL, biologist, mycologist; b. Knoxville, Tenn., Apr. 2, 1947; s. Verlin Martell and June (Owens) J.; B.S., U. Tenn., Knoxville, 1969, Ph.D., 1974; m. Jeannie Bess Andes, Mar. 20, 1970; 1 dau., Tiffan Suzanne. Grad. teaching asst. U. Tenn., Knoxville, 1970-74; asst. prof. biology dept. U. Ala., Birmingham, 1974—. NSF grantee, Highlands Biol. Sta., 1970-71, 71-72, grad. trainee, 1971-74; research grantee, 1972-74, faculty research grantee U. Ala., 1974-79. Mem. Mycol. Soc. Am., So. Appalachian Botan. Club, Am. Inst. Biol. Scis., N.Am. Mycol. Assn., AAUP, Mycotaxon, Sigma Xi (research grantee, 1971), Phi Kappa Phi, Phi Sigma. Methodist. Club: Ala. Mycol. Soc. (pres.). Researcher Amanita genus of mushrooms; author, co-author articles, books, abstracts in field to publs. Home: 2448 Regent Ln Birmingham AL 35226 Office: Dept Biology Univ Alabama Birmingham AL 35294

JENKINS, DEANNA SUE DUNCAN, nurse, educator; b. Chattanooga, Tenn., Mar. 1, 1942; d. William Quentin and Mamie Dean (Rogers) Duncan; R.N., Johns Hopkins Hosp. Sch. of Nursing, Balt., 1963; student George Washington U., 1964-65; B.S. in Health Scis., Athens Coll., 1978; postgrad. Ala. A&M U., 1978—; m. Cecil D. Jenkins Jr., Dec. 18, 1965; children—Amanda Foree, Amelia Fine. Staff nurse Johns Hopkins Hosp., Balt., 1963, George Washington U. Hosp., Washington, 1964-65; evening supr. Colbert County Hosp., Sheffield, Ala., 1966-67; supr. Crestwood Hosp., Huntsville, Ala., 1967; charge nurse, instr. U.S. Army Hosp., Redstone, Ala., 1969-72; inservice coordinator Fifth Ave. Gen. Hosp., Huntsville, 1972-75; dir. div. of edn. Huntsville Hosp., 1975—; mem. faculty, continuing edn. U. Ala., Huntsville; affiliate faculty Ala. Heart Assn.; guest lectr. Huntsville Coop. Sch. Med. Tech.; dir. Ala. Con sortium for Progressive Edn., 1975—. CPR chmn. Madison County chpt. Am. Heart Assn., 1975-76; regional chmn. emergency cardiac care com. Ala. Heart Assn., 1976-78; hosp. co-chmn. Madison County United Givers Fund, 1977-79. Recipient certificate of merit Ala. Heart Assn., 1976, 77, 78, 79; registered nurse, Ala., Md. Mem. Am. Nurses Assn., Ala. Nurses Assn., Madison County Nurses Soc. (dir. 1977—, treas. 1979—), Ala. Soc. for Health Edn. Tng., Johns Hopkins U. Alumni Assn., Am. Diabetes Edn. Assn. Democrat. Episcopalian. Club: Altrusa (rec. sec. 1979-80). Office: Huntsville Hosp 101 Sivley Rd Huntsville AL 35801

JENKINS, ED (EDGAR) LANIER, congressman; b. Towns County, Ga., Jan. 4, 1933; s. Charlie Swinfield and Evia Mae (Souther) J.; A.A., Young Harris Coll., 1951; LL.B., U. Ga., 1959; m. Beni Jo Thomasson, Dec. 27, 1959; children—Jan, Amy. Admitted to Ga. bar, 1959; adminstrv. asst. to Rep. Phil M. Landrum, 1959-62; asst. U.S. atty. No. Dist. Ga., 1963-65; sr. partner firm Jenkins & Landrum, Jasper, Ga., 1965-76; mem. 95th-96th Congresses from 9th Ga. Dist., 1977—. Served with USCG, 1952-55. Mem. Ga., Am. bar assns., Farm Bur., VFW, Am. Legion. Democrat. Baptist. Club: Lions. Office: 217 Cannon House Office Bldg Washington DC 20515

JENKINS, EDWARD MATTHEWS, microbiologist; b. Neenah, Va., May 31, 1926; s. Eddie Matt and Bessie Tate J.; B.S., Va. State Coll., 1949; M.S., Cath. U., 1960; D.V.M., Tuskegee Inst., 1964; Ph.D., Colo. State U., 1972; m. Patsy Jane Johnson, June 15, 1964; children—Greta Lynn, Shawn Edward. Research asso. Tuskegee Inst., Tuskegee Institute, Ala., 1961-67, asst. prof. microbiology, 1967-68, asso. prof., 1972-78, prof., 1978—; mem. Task Force on Swine Research Needs in the So. Region, U.S. Dept. Agr.; adv. panel U.S. Army Med. Research and Devel. Command, 1979—. Ruling elder Westminster Presbyn. Ch., Tuskegee Inst., 1975. Recipient Faculty Achievement award Tuskegee Inst., 1978; NIH fellow, 1970-72; various govt. and pvt. grants. Mem. Am. Soc. for Microbiology, AVMA, Conf. of Research Workers in Animal Diseases, Am. Assn. Swine Practitioners, NAACP, Sigma Xi, Alpha Phi Alpha, Beta Beta Beta. Democrat. Club: Optimist. Contbr. articles in field to profl. jours. Home: 128 Marable Dr Tuskegee AL 36083 Office: Sch Vet Medicine Tuskegee Inst Tuskegee Institute AL 36088

JENKINS, JANE JOHNSON, educator; b. Lisle, Mo., Feb. 10, 1929; d. Huber Ernest and Golda May (Davis) Johnson; student Kans. State Coll. Pitts., 1946-49; B.S., U. Houston, 1973, M.Ed., 1979; m. Gene Mitchell Jenkins Jan. 30, 1949; 1 son, John Mitchell. Sec. to v.p., gen. mgr. Rounds & Porter Co., Wichita, 1949-57; sec. to v.p., cashier 4th Nat. Bank, Wichita, 1957-59; instr. office careers San Jacinto Coll., Pasadena, Tex., 1975—, instr. bus. adminstrn., 1979. Mem. nominating com. Parkview Estates Assn.; supt. ch. sch. 1st Christian Ch., Pasadena; block worker Heart Fund. Mem. Nat. Bus. Edn. Assn., Tex. Bus. Edn. Assn., Tex. Jr. Coll. Tchrs. Assn., Mortar Bd., Alpha Gamma Delta, Fi Omega Pi, Delta Pi Epsilon. Club: Order Eastern Star. Home: 2011 N Fisher Ct Pasadena TX 77502 Office: 13735 Beamer Rd Houston TX 77089

JENKINS, MELVIN HOWARD, furn. co. exec.; b. Lenoir, N.C., May 12, 1931; s. Melvin A. and Cora M. (Summerlin) J.; student Lenoir Rhyne Coll., 1950-54; m. Peggy Craig, Jan. 26, 1951; children—Rebecca Jean, David Howard. Asst. foreman, veneer dept. Hibritten Furniture, Lenoir, 1952-56; acctg. clk. Blowing Rock Furniture, Lenoir, 1956-63 data processing operation supr. Consol. Furniture Co., Lenoir, 1963-73; data processing mgr. Singer Furniture, Roanoke, Va., 1973—. Mem. bd. advisors for data processing Caldwell County Community Coll., 1966-72. Mem. Data Processing Mgmt. Assn. (chpt. dir. 1966-67). Democrat. Baptist. Home: 107 Briarwood Ln Lenoir NC 28645 Office: 3322 Read Rd NW Roanoke VA 24012

JENKINS, NOLIE ROSE, spl. services exec.; b. Rocky Mount, N.C., Oct. 1, 1947; d. Zeno Hardy and Nolie (Highsmith) Rose; A.A., Peace Coll., 1967; B.A., U. N.C., Wilmington, 1976; m. Joseph Thomas Jenkins, Feb. 24, 1978; children from previous marriage—Nolie Keel Parnell, Robert Hardy Parnell. Social worker New Hanover County Dept. Social Services, Wilmington, N.C., 1976-78, Wake County Dept. Social Services, Raleigh, N.C., 1978; dir. spl. services project Roanoke-Chowan Tech. Inst., Ahoskie, N.C., 1978—. Mem. Am. Personnel and Guidance Assn., N.C. Assn. Developmental Studies. Democrat. Episcopalian. Home: Rt 2 Box 17-P Ahoskie NC 27910 Office: Rt 2 Box 46-A Ahoskie NC 27910

JENKINS, ORVIE CONN, advt. agy. exec.; b. Slaton, Tex., Sept. 6, 1940; s. Ocie Clifton and Ireland Carlene (West) J.; student Lubbock Christian Coll., 1959-60, 61-62; B.A. in Advt. Art and Design, Tex. Tech. U., Lubbock, 1967; m. Karen Paulette Lang, Aug. 26, 1961; 1 son, Brent Wesley. Checker, Furr Foods, Lubbock, 1954-61; printer, salesman Field's & Co., Lubbock, 1961-67; artist Curtis Taulbee Advt., San Angelo, Tex., 1967-73; pres. Jenkins Advt. Agy., San Angelo, 1973—. Recipient Service award United Way, 1976, 3 Addy awards Am. Advt. Fedn., Abilene, Tex., 1978, 2 Silver awards, 1978. Mem. Tex. Pub. Relations Assn., San Angelo Advt. Fedn. (pres.), C. of C. Concho Cadre. Mem. Ch. of Christ. Clubs: San Angelo Press, S.W. Kiwanis (dir. 1978). Home: 3352 Clark St San Angelo TX 76901 Office: Suite 400 17 S Chadbourne St San Angelo TX 76903

JENKINS, RICHARD ELLIS, mech. engr.; b. Monroe, La., Jan. 25, 1935; s. Hubert Otto and LaEtta (Crane) J.; B.S. in Mech. Engring., U. Tex., Austin, 1959; m. Sherrell Sellers, Dec. 30, 1972. Project engr. U.S. Naval Ordnance Test Sta., China Lake, Calif., 1959-62; project engr. Rocketdyne Solid Rocket div. N.Am. Aviation, McGregor, Tex., 1962-66; propulsion project engr. missiles and space div. LTV Aerospace Corp., Grand Prairie, Tex., 1966-68; mgr. quality engring. Tracor, Inc., Austin, Tex., 1968-72, dir. quality and reliability assurance, 1974—; supr. mfg. engring. Tex. Instruments, Austin, 1972-73; quality engr. Atlantic Research Corp., Gainesville, Va., 1973-74. Served with USMC, 1953-55. Registered profl. engr., Tex. Mem. Am. Soc. Quality Control. Republican. Mem. Ch. of Christ. Home: 11103 Hidden Bluff Dr Austin TX 78754 Office: 6500 Tracor Ln Austin TX 78721

JENKINS, VERNON HENRI, social worker; b. Clarendon, Ark., Oct. 3, 1910; d. William Alphonso and Eva (Deloney) Henri; B.A., Morris Brown Coll., 1954; M.S.S.W. (Univ. grantee 1965-67), U. Tenn., 1967; m. Fitzgerald Huntington Jenkins, July 6, 1935; children—Eva D., M. Joyce, Fitzgerald Huntington, Margery L. Jenkins Smith, Beverly L. Tchr., Union Acad., Washington, 1931-37, Berean Acad., Atlanta, 1948-49, 50-53, 54-55; editorial sec. Message Mag., Nashville, 1955-59; sec., adminstrv. asst. Office of Devel., Meharry Med. Coll., Nashville, 1960-65, coordinator social services, 1974—, asst. dir. Ann Dickerson Child Devel. Center, 1977—, asst. prof. dept. pediatrics, 1971—; field work supr. U. Tenn. Sch. Social Work, 1971-78, adj. prof., 1977—. Bd. dirs. Davidson County Assn. Retarded Citizens, 1973-77, Outlook Nashville, 1973-75, 77—, Heads Up Child Devel. Center, 1975—; Child Care Center, 1977-78; mem. sch. bd. F.H. Jenkins Elem. Sch., 1967—, chmn., 1978—. Mem. Assn. Cert. Social Workers, Nat. Assn. Social Workers, Phi Alpha. Democrat. Seventh-day Adventist. Home: 2513 Gardner Ln Nashville TN 37207 Office: 1005 18th Ave N Nashville TN 37208

JENKINS, WAYNE LAMAR, mfg. co. exec.; b. Bessemer, Ala., Nov. 8, 1939; s. Arthur and Pearl E. Jenkins; B.S. in Chem. Engring., Auburn U., 1962; m. Frances Heaton, Oct. 2, 1965; children—Stephen, Lexie, Cynthia. Project engr. Tenneco Chems., Pensacola, Fla., 1962-70; design engr. Union Carbide Corp., Chickasaw, Ala., 1970-72, prodn. engr., 1972-73, maintenance supt., 1973-76, mfg. supt., 1976-78, mfg. mgr., 1978—. Indsl. vice chmn. United Fund, 1979; deacon Dauphin Way Baptist Ch. Mem. Am. Inst. Chem. Engrs. (past chmn. Pensacola sect.), Indsl. Mgmt. Club, Mobile Area C. of C. Club: Kiwanis (Mobile). Home: 812 Deerfield Ct Mobile AL 36608 Office: Linde Dr Chickasaw AL 36611

JENKS, SALLIE ANNE, med. technologist; b. Ashland, Ky., Nov. 13, 1935; d. Dan Hugh and Zoe Ellen (Lashbrook) Jenks; student U. Miami, 1953-55, Fla. Coll. Med. Tech., 1955-56. Research technician Nat. Children's Cardiac Hosp., Miami, Fla., 1956-60; research technician dept. preventive medicine U. Miami, 1960-62, research technologist div. oral biology, 1962-68; research asst. Cordis Labs., Miami, 1968—. Pres., Kirk Keys Orgn., 1966; active Wesley Minstrels, 1970-76, Young Republican Orgn.; adult co-coodinator First United Meth. Ch. Coral Gables, 1978-80. Licensed med. tech., Fla. Bd. Health. Mem Am. Soc. for Med. Tech., Am. Soc. for Microbiologists, AAAS, Fla. Soc. Med. Technologists, Beta Sigma Phi (chpt. sec. 1975). Contbr. articles to profl. jours. Home: 6140 SW 65th Ave S Miami FL 33143 Office: 2140 N Miami Ave Miami FL 33127

JENNE, FRANK ARTHUR, TV co. exec.; b. Waukegan, Ill., June 13, 1924; s. Clarence Arthur and Retta Marie (Wood) J.; m. Sally Mae Ridgeway, Sept. 2, 1949; children—Retta Jenne Turbeville, Ruth Jenne Dorriety. Staff engr. Sta. WWPG, Palm Beach, Fla., 1946-47; tech. dir. Sta. WJMX-WSTN, Florence, S.C., 1947-67; ETV sta. supr. Sta. WJPM-TV, S.C. ETV Commn., Florence, 1967—. Served with U.S. Mcht. Marine, 1944-46. Mem. Soc. Broadcast Engrs. Baptist. Club: Optimist. Home: 2113 W Fernleaf Ln Florence SC 29501 Office: Route 1 Box 532 Florence SC 29501

JENNINGS, FLOYD LEE, clin. psychologist; b. Seminole, Okla., Dec. 15, 1940; s. Floyd Isaac and Velma Lee (Pugh) J.; B.A. in Math., McMurry Coll., 1961; B.D., So. Meth. U., 1964, S.T.M., 1969; Ph.D. in Psychology, U. Tex. Southwestern Med. Sch., 1971; m. Shirley Ann Gardner, Mar. 27, 1976; children—Sherry, Glenn, LeAnne, Lynne. Intern clin. psychology U. Tex. Southwestern Med. Sch., 1968-71; instr. psychology Temple Jr. Coll. and Mary Hardin-Baylor Coll., Belton, Tex., 1972-73; clin. psychologist VA, Temple, Tex., 1971-77, also pvt. practice clin. psychology, Temple, 1974-77; dir. Washakie County Mental Health Services, Worland, Wyo., 1977-78; pvt. practice clin. psychology, Houston, 1978—; adj. faculty Baylor U., 1973-75, clin. faculty Sch. Medicine, 1978—; cons. CTG Child Abuse and Neglect Demonstration Orgn., 1976-77; chmn. internship tng. VA, Temple, 1976; mem. faculty Southwestern Group Psychotherapy Inst., 1973-76. Lic. psychologist, Tex., Wyo.; certified Nat. Register of Health Service Providers in Psychology. Mem. Am., Southwestern, Tex., Central Tex., Bell County (pres. 1975-77) psychol. assns., Am. Group Psychotherapy Assn., Southwestern Group Psychotherapy Soc. Methodist. Club: Masons. Contbr. articles to profl. jours. Home: 14307 Piping Rock Houston TX 77077 Office: Memorial City Profl Bldg 902 Frostwood #154 Houston TX 77024

JENNINGS, FRANK CLAY, author, publisher, printing co. exec.; b. Garrard County, Ky., June 30, 1913; s. Hamlet Manford and Jane (Reynolds) J.; student pub., pvt. schs. Ky.; m. Helen Maurine Music, Aug. 24, 1940. Area fin. officer Fed. Works Agy., Ky., 1935-41; chief wage adminstr. War Dept., Ft. Knox, 1942-46; free lance writer, 1947-49; asso. editor Thoroughbred Record, 1950-51, mng. editor, 1952-54, exec. dir. Thoroughbred Record, Inc., gen. mgr. Thoroughbred Press, Inc., 1955-78, treas., 1957—; dir. v.p., treas. Record Pub. Co., Inc., 1963—. Mem. Lexington Kennel Club, Throughbred Club Am., Thoroughbred Farm Mgrs., Blue Grass Sportsmens' League. Home: 1715 Courtney Ave Lexington KY 40502 Office: PO Box 580 Lexington KY 40586

JENNINGS, JERRY LEE, EDP tech. systems analyst; b. Memphis, Apr. 3, 1949; s. C.E. and Earlene Vivian J.; B.S. in Math., Memphis State U., 1971; m. Nancy Carol Little, Aug. 7, 1970; children—Julie Carol, Matthew Adam. Statis. programmer Memphis State U. Academic Computer Center, 1967-71; programmer analyst Memphis Speech & Hearing Center, 1971-74; sr. programmer analyst Union Planters Nat. Bank, Memphis, 1974-75; tech. systems analyst Dobbs-Life Savers, Memphis, 1975—. Recipient Appreciation certificate Am. Speech Hearing Assn., 1972; Spoke award Memphis Jaycees, 1975. Home: 3752 Stonehill Dr Memphis TN 38134 Office: 5100 Poplar St Memphis TN 38137

JENNINGS, JOHN JAMES, waste mgmt. and investment cons.; b. N.Y.C., May 26, 1947; s. Michael J. and Catherine M. (Dugan) J.; B.S., St. John's U., 1968, M.B.A., 1970; certificate in investment analysis N.Y. Inst. Fin., 1969; m. Wendy Christina Larson, June 7, 1975. Portfolio mgr., analyst G.A. Saxton & Co., Inc., N.Y.C., 1968-69; dir. mktg. Academe of Applied Motivation, 1970-72; exec. v.p. Entrepreneurial Devel. Corp., Inc., Amherst, N.Y., 1972-73, now dir.; pres. IWM, Inc., Orlando, Fla., 1973—; dir. Storybook Village, Inc., Indsl. Waste Mgmt., Inc., Jennings & Jennings Assos., Inc. Chmn. Citizens and Pvt. Bus. Awareness Com., 1977, 78, 79. Recipient Tablet Cath. Action award, 1967, Human Relations award C.A.U.S.E., 1968; Motivator of Year award, 1972. Hon. fellow Truman Library Inst. Mem. Assn. Investment Brokers, Soc. Advancement Mgmt., Solid Waste Mgmt. Assn., Bus. Adminstrn. Soc. Seminole City Bd. Realtors, Smithsonian Assos. Roman Catholic. Office: 504 29th St Orlando FL 32805

JENNINGS, JOHN MELVILLE, assn. exec.; b. Toano, Va., Oct. 22, 1918; s. John Melville and Grace Armistead (Davis) J.; B.A., Coll. William and Mary, 1938, LL.D., 1968; M.A., Am. U., 1948. Curator manuscripts and rare books Coll. William and Mary, 1939-43, 46-47; librarian Va. Hist. Soc., Richmond, 1948-51, dir., 1953-79, emeritus, 1979—. Mem. adv. bd. Assn. Preservation Va. Antiquities, The Papers of John Marshall, The Papers of James Madison; cons. Robert E. Lee Meml. Found.; mem. Va. State Hist. Records Bd. of Nat. Hist. Records and Publs. Commn. Served with USNR, 1944-46, 51-53. Fellow Soc. Am. Archivists; mem. Bibliog. Soc. Am., Mass. Hist. Soc., Am. Antiquarian Soc., Phi Beta Kappa (past pres. Alpha of Va. chpt.). Home: 204 N Granby St Richmond VA 23220 Office: PO Box 7311 Richmond VA 23221

JENNINGS, JOSEPH LESLIE, JR., textile mfg. co. exec.; b. LaGrange, Ga., Dec. 20, 1937; s. Joseph Leslie and Marie Lamar (Lanier) J.; B.S. in Bus. Adminstrn., U. Ala., 1961; m. Ann B. Martin, June 10, 1961; children—Joseph Leslie, III, John Martin, Clayton Lanier. Mgmt. trainee West Point (Ga.) Pepperell Inc., 1964-65, various mfg. positions, 1965-73; asst. v.p. Mt. Vernon Mills, Inc., Greenville, S.C., 1974-78, v.p. ops., 1978—, also dir.; dir. C&S Bank of West Ga. Mem. bd. advs. Greenville Tech. Coll., 1977—. Served to 1st lt. USMC, 1961-64. Mem. S.C. Textile Mfrs. Assn. (dir.), Inst. Textile Tech. (tech. adv. com.). Episcopalian. Clubs: Greenville Country, Met. Home: 24 Sirrine Dr Greenville SC 29605 Office: Daniel Bldg Greenville SC 29602

JENNINGS, RICHARD LOUIS, civil engr., educator; b. Newark, N.J., July 28, 1933; s. Louis Alpheus and Florence Eva (Warnecke) J.; student Marietta Coll., 1951-54; B.S. in Math., Ohio U., 1956, B.S. in Civil Engring., 1957; M.S. in Civil Engring., U. Ill., 1958, Ph.D., 1964; m. Jan Hayden Bush, Sept. 2, 1956; children—Sheryll, Gregory. Constrn. supt. Am. Tel. & Tel. Co., White Plains, N.Y., 1955-56; prof. civil engring. U. Va., Charlottesville, 1963—. Cons. in structural analysis and aerospace tech., nuclear reactor stress analysis; cons. earthquake analysis of nuclear reactor facilities; cons. to U.S. Army on mil. logistics. Pres. Charlottesville PTA Council, 1969-73; chmn. joint bd. Charlottesville-Albemarle Tech. Edn. Center, 1973-74. Bd. dirs. Planned Parenthood of Central Va., 1969-76; bd. mgrs. Va. Congress of Parents and Tchrs., 1970-72; citizen mem. Va. High Sch. League, 1979—; bd. dirs. Ednl. TV, Harrisonburg, Va., 1979—. Past NASA-ASEE fellow. Mem. Charlottesville City Sch. Bd., 1972—, vice chmn., 1974-76, chmn., 1976—. Mem. ASCE, Sigma Xi, Tau Beta Pi, Alpha Tau Omega. Democrat. Episcopalian. Clubs: Torch, Colonnade. Contbr. articles on deflections of radio telescopes, cable-suspended structures, overloaded hwy. pavements and earthquakes to profl. publs. Home: 1607 Jamestown Dr Charlottesville VA 22901

JENNINGS, ROBERT WENDELL, public relations exec.; b. Sulphur Springs, Tex., Mar. 13, 1932; s. Thelma Lee and Ida Vallerie (Mann) J.; student Los Angeles City Coll., 1956, Swift & Co. Merchandising Sch., Chgo., 1955. Acctg. and inventory clk. San Union and Tribune Newspaper, San Diego, 1954-55; talent scout, merchandising rep. Horace Heidt NBC-TV Show, 1955; adminstrv. asst. to ops. mgr. Samuel Goldwyn Studios, Hollywood, 1955-59; nat. sales v.p. Youth Entertainment Services, Inc., N.Y.C., 1959; public relations, advt., sales mgr. U.S. Oberammergau Passion Play, N.Y.C., 1959-61; sales and merchandising rep. nat. touring prodn. Broadway show Fiorello, 1961; publicity dir. Charlotte (N.C.) Summer Theatre, 1962-63; public relations dir. Lakewood Playhouse, Maine, 1962-63; public relations dir. Nat. Repertory Theatre, N.Y.C., 1963-68; advance press agt. nat. touring cos. Broadway shows Fiddler on the Roof, Cabaret, 1776, Promises, Promises, Company, The Clown Company, Applause, Grease, Lorelei, Give 'Em Hell Harry, Very Good Eddie, 1968-75; artist mgr., dir. public relations Peggy Taylor Talent, Inc., Dallas, 1976—. Served with USNR, 1952-54. Mem. Assn. Theatrical Press Agts. and Mgrs., Actors' Fund Am., Air line Passengers Assn. Episcopalian. Club: Mr. Wabbi. Office: 3616 Howell St Dallas TX 75204

JENNINGS, RUFUS EDWARD, ret. sch. prin.; b. Saluda, S.C., Jan. 8, 1909; s. John D. and Martha (Chapman) J.; B.A., Newberry Coll., 1933; M.Ed., U. S.C., 1948; m. Virginia Timmerman, Dec. 22, 1936. Jr. high sch. prin., athletic coach Edgefield (S.C.) High Sch., 1933-41; asst. prin., coach Tarpon Springs (Fla.) High Sch., 1941-44, prin., 1949-51; athletic dir., coach Plant City (Fla.) High Sch., 1945-49; supervising prin. Arcadia City (Fla.) Sch., 1951-57; asst. prin. Boone High Sch., Orlando, Fla., 1957-58; prin. Colonial High Sch., Orlando, 1958-71, Parker Elementary Sch., Edgefield, S.C., 1971-72, Wardlaw Acad., Johnston, S.C., 1972-73, now ret. Served with U.S. Mcht. Marine, 1944-45. Mem. Orange County Secondary Principals Organization (pres. 1963), Metro Conf. (pres. 1964-65), Fla. High Sch. (dist. dir. Dist. VII 1966-67) athletic assns., P.T.A. Fla. Clubs: Lions (pres. 1976-77), Kiwanis (dir. 1953). Home: Route 3 Box 105 Edgefield SC 29821

JENNINGS, WALTER STANLEY, physician; b. nr. Norfolk, Va., Apr. 22, 1926; s. Walter Edward and Edna (Davis) J.; A.A., Coll. William and Mary, Norfolk div., 1946; student U. Va., 1946-47; M.D., Med. Coll. Va., 1951; m. Emily Estelle Doughty, July 27, 1947; children—Stanley, Jennifer, Elizabeth Helon. Intern, Norfolk Gen. Hosp., 1951-52; practice medicine, Hickory, Va., 1952, South Norfolk, Chesapeake, 1952—; mem. staff Leigh Meml., Norfolk Gen., Kings Daus., Chesapeake Gen. hosps.; pres. Harstan Corp. Mem. Chesapeake Hosp. Authority. Served with USAAF, 1944-45. Mem. AMA, Va., Chesapeake, Norfolk County, So. med. socs., Am. Acad. Family Practice, Theta Kappa Psi. Home: 1160 Virginia Ave Chesapeake VA 22046 Office: 1446 Chesapeake Ave South Norfolk Chesapeake VA 22324

JENRETTE, JOHN WILSON, JR., congressman; b. Conway, S.C., May 19, 1936; s. John Wilson Jenrette and Mary Herring Jenrette Housand; A.B., Wofford Coll., 1958; LL.B., U. S.C., 1962; m. Rita Carpenter, 1976; children—Elizabeth, Harold. Admitted to S.C. bar; city judge, Ocean Dr. Beach, S.C., 1962-68, city atty., 1962-69; mem. S.C. Ho. of Reps., 1965-72; congressman from 6th S.C. Dist. Democratic candidate 93d-96th Congresses from 6th S.C. Dist.; dep. Majority Whip, 1975—. Served with U.S. Army, 1959; now maj. USAFR. Recipient Distinguished Service award S.C. Mcpl. Assn. Mem. S.C., Horry County, Am. bar assns., Farm Bur., C. of C. Democrat. Methodist. Clubs: Lions, Elks. Home: 160 North Carolina Ave SE Washington DC

JENSEN, BRUCE HOWARD, elec. engr.; b. Mesa, Ariz., May 29, 1948; s. Howard Warren and Audrey Naomi (Pearson) J.; B.S. in Elec. Engring. and Computer Sci., U. Colo., 1976; M.S. in Elec. Engring., U. Ky., 1979; m. June Gail Powell, Feb. 5, 1972; children—Michael David, Cheryl Leanne. Mem. logic and memory tech. group Office Products Div., IBM Corp., Lexington, Ky., 1977—. Served with USN, 1967-73. Mem. Tau Beta Pi, Eta Kappa Nu. Home: 263 Tangley Way Lexington KY 40503 Office: 740 New Circle Rd Lexington KY 40501

JENSEN, DAVID WILLIAM, neuroscientist; b. Lynn, Mass., Feb. 21, 1948; s. William Raymond and Patricia Margaret Edith (Curry) J.; B.S. with distinction in Zoology, U. Ill., 1969, M.S. in Physiology, 1970; Ph.D. in Neoroscis., U. Calif., San Diego, 1977. Research asst. U. Ill., Urbana, 1969-70, U. Calif., San Diego, 1971-76, postgrad. research neuroscientist, 1977-78; asst. prof. faculty neurosci. and dept. otorhinolaryngology, Baylor Coll. Medicine, Houston, 1978—; researcher, brain mechanisms of postural control. NIH physiology trainee, fellow, 1969-70, trainee fellow in neurosci., 1971-77; biomed. research support grantee, 1979. Mem. Assn. for Research in Otolaryngology, Soc. for Neurosci., Am. Physiol. Soc. Contbr. sci. articles to profl. publs. Office: Dept Otorhinolaryngology and Communicative Scis A-513 Baylor Coll Medicine 1200 Moursund Ave Houston TX 77030

JENSEN, ROBERT WILLIAM, engr.; b. Mpls., Feb. 28, 1943; s. Christian and Ellen Josephine (Landgren) J.; student Mankato State Coll., 1961-63; Engr. of Mines, Colo. Sch. Mines, 1967; m. Carol Jean Koepp, Sept. 3, 1964; children—Michael Steven, Kristin Leigh, Gregory Ian. Mining engr. Utah Internat., Inc., Queensland, Australia, 1969-73; sr. mining engr. Gulf Mineral Resources Co., Denver, 1973-75; staff dir. project engring. Phillips Coal Co., Dallas, 1975-79; v.p., mining engr. 1st Nat. Bank, Dallas, 1979-80; project mgr. Central and S.W. Fuels, Inc., Dallas, 1980—; mem. Nat. Coal Assn. and Am. Mining Congress joint com. on fed. surface mining regulations, 1978—. Served with USN, 1967-68. Registered profl. engr., Tex. Mem. AIME, Rocky Mountain Coal Mining Inst. Republican. Lutheran. Home: 3206 Bridle Path Ct Garland TX 75042 Office: 2700 One Main Pl Dallas TX 75250

JENSON, SHERMAN MILTON, ins. co. exec.; b. Berthold, N.D., Jan. 15, 1920; s. Canute t. and Emma (Rohne) J.; B.A., Luther Coll., 1941; diploma bus. adminstrn. LaSalle U., 1948; m. Mary G. Blaul, Oct. 14, 1948; 1 dau., Jennifer Ann. Chemist, Solvay Process Co., Hopewell, Va., 1941-43; pharm. salesman Lakeside Labs., St. Paul, 1946-47; regional group mgr. Minn. Mut. Life Ins. Co., Chgo., 1947-55; v.p. group Am. United Life Ins. Co., Indpls., 1955-69; gen. mgr. group div. Bankers Life & Casualty Co., Chgo., 1969-73; pres., chief exec. officer, chmn. exec. com. Nat. Investors Life Ins. Co., Little Rock, 1973—; pres., chmn. bd. NOR Securities Co.; v.p. Baldwin-United Corp., Cin.; mem. exec. com., dir. Midwest Nat. Life Ins. Co., Nashville, Nat. Investors Fire & Casualty Co., Little Rock; dir. Investors Equity Life Ins. Co. Hawaii, Nat. Equity Life Ins. Co. Hawaii. Served with USNR, 1943-46. Clubs: Little Rock, Pleasant Valley Country. Home: 11900 Fairway Dr Little Rock AR 72212 Office: 2d & Broadway Little Rock AR 72201

JENT, LAVOISE ROARK, editor; b. Scottsville, Ky., Nov. 18, 1920; d. William Harvey and Gay Nell (Swindle) Roark; ed. spl. courses Consol. Bus. Sch., Indpls., U. Tenn., Watkins Inst.; m. Roosevelt Jent, Nov. 28, 1940; children—Sharon Jent Barton, Sonja Lynn. Copywriter, Castner-Knott's Dept. Store, Nashville, 1948-50; promotion mgr. WLAC Radio, Nashville, 1950-51; asst. editor Nashville Elec. Service, 1952-68; editor employee publs., 1968—. Mem. Nashville Fedn. Bus. and Profl. Women's Club (pres. 1955-58, 74-75, named woman of achievement 1969), Internat., So. assns. bus. communicators, Middle Tenn. Bus. Press Club (pres. 1955). Home: 124 Rhine Dr Madison TN 37115 Office: 1214 Church St Nashville TN 37246

JENTZ, GAYLORD ADAIR, educator, author; b. Beloit, Wis., Aug 7, 1931; s. Merlyn Adair and Delva (Mullen) J.; B.A., U. Wis., 1953, J.D., 1957, M.B.A., 1958; m. JoAnn Mary Hornung, Aug. 6, 1955; children—Katherine Ann, Gary Adair, Loretta Ann, Rory Adair. Admitted to Wis. bar, 1957; pvt. practice law, Madison, 1957-58; from instr. to asso. prof. bus. law U. Okla., 1958-65; vis. instr. to vis. prof. U. Wis. Law Sch., summers 1957-65; asso. prof. to prof. U. Tex., 1965-68, prof., 1968—, chmn. gen. bus. dept., 1968-74. Served with AUS, 1953-55. Recipient Outstanding Tchr.'s award Tex. U. Coll. Bus., 1967, Jack G. Taylor Teaching Excellence award, 1971, Joe D. Beasley Teaching Excellence award, 1978; Outstanding Achievement in Edn. award Alpha Kappa Psi, 1979; award CBA Found., 1979. Mem. Am. Arbitration Assn. (nat. panel 1966—), Am. (pres. 1971-72), So. (pres. 1967) bus. law assns., Tex. Assn. Coll. Tchrs. (pres. Austin chpt. 1967-68, exec. com. 1969-70, state pres. 1971-72), SW Fedn. Adminstrv. Disciplines (v.p. 1979-80), Wis. Bar Assn., Alpha Kappa Phi, Phi Kappa Phi, Omicron Delta Kappa. Author: (with others) Business Law Text and Cases, 2d edit., 1968; Texas Uniform Commercial Code, 1967, rev. edit., 1975; (with others) Business Law Text and Cases, 1978; contbr. articles to profl. jours.; dep. editor Social Sci. Quar., 1966—; editorial staff Am. Bus. Law Jour., 1967-69, editor-in-chief, 1969-74, adv. editor, 1974—. Home: 4106 North Hills Dr Austin TX 78731

JERGER, RICHARD MITCHELL, ins. exec.; b. St. Petersburg, Fla., July 16, 1918; s. Louis H. and Clifford Pauline (Mitchell) J.; A.A., St. Petersburg Jr. Coll., 1938; student Pratt Inst., 1939-41; m. Evelyn May Wichelns, Feb. 4, 1944; children—Richard Mitchell, Thomas John, Dean Wichelns. Owner, Dick Jerger & Assos., Pinellas Park, Fla., 1950—; partner Jerger-Shepard Ins. Agy., St. Petersburg Beach, Fla., 1952—; founder Mortgage Mart Ins. Agy., 1959 (became Jerger & Sons, Inc. 1972), chmn. bd., 1969—; pres. White Towers, Inc., St. Petersburg, 1970—, Mobile Homeowners Ins. Agys., Inc., Pinellas Park, 1964—; owner Down Yonder Mobile Home Village, Largo, Fla., 1970—; dir. Fla. Mut. Funds, Citizens Nat. Bank, St. Petersburg, The Nat. Bank, St. Petersburg. Served from pvt. to maj. USAAF, 1941-45. Decorated D.F.C. with oak leaf cluster, Air medal with 4 oak leaf clusters,; Croix de Guerre (France). Mem. Independent Insurors Fla., Ind. Ins. Agts. Am. (dir. 1952-54, 56), Suncoasters. Lutheran. Clubs: Bucketeers (capt. fleet 1976-77), Lions (Lion of Year 1952). Home: 43 Dolphin Dr Treasure Island FL 33706 Office: 7785 66th St N PO Box 80 Pinellas Park FL 33565

JERMSTAD, GLEN LYNCH, business exec.; b. St. Louis, July 10, 1935; s. Robert J. and Lorene (Lynch) J.; B.S., U.S. Naval Acad., 1958; grad. U.S. Naval Sch. Justice, 1959, U. Naval Sch. Flight Tng., 1958; m. Merle Warner Katterjohn, June 8, 1957; children—Glen Lynch, George K., Curtis W. Commd. ensign U.S Navy, 1957, advanced to lt., 1960, ret., 1962; v.p. Katterjohn Concrete Products, Inc., North Little Rock, 1962-75, gen. mgr., 1962-67; secretarial rep. Southeastern region U.S. Dept. Transp., Atlanta, 1975-77; gen. mgr. ops. Tradco-Vulcan Ltd., Dhahran, Saudi Arabia, 1977—. Ark. dir. Office Econ. Opportunity, Little Rock, 1967-68; spl. cons. rural and urban affairs to gov. Ark., 1968-69, spl. asst. for fed. and state relations, 1969-71, chmn. So. Gov.'s Exec. Staff Adv. Com., 1970-71, spl. cons. bus. devel. in aviation field, 1971-72; exec. dir., sec. Coalition for Rural Am., Washington, 1972; sec. Rural Resources Inst., Washington and Little Rock, 1972—. Dir. Ark. Nixon/Agnew Campaign, 1968; mem. Pulaski County Election Commn., 1965-66; chmn., commr. North Little Rock Planning Commn., 1964-68. Bd. dirs., v.p. N. Little Rock Boys Club, 1964-67. Recipient Outstanding Young Man award N. Little Rock, 1965. Mem. Ark. Sales and Marketing Execs. Club (dir. 1967-68), North Little Rock C. of C. (dir. 1966-68). Episcopalian. Rotarian, Elk. Office: care Tradco-Vulcan PO Box 7497 Birmingham AL 35223

JERNER, R. CRAIG, metall. engr.; b. St. Louis, Oct. 12, 1938; s. Roland Axel and M. Marie (Hayes) J.; B.S. in Metall. Engring., Washington U., St. Louis, 1961, M.S., 1962; Ph.D., U. Denver, 1965; m. C. Elizabeth Johnson, June 7, 1958; children—Michael Craig, Elisabeth Gay, Stephen Andrew. Mem. faculty U. Okla., Norman, 1965-76, asso. prof. metall. engring., 1969-76, asst. dean Grad. Coll., 1971-72, adj. prof. metall. engring., 1976—; chmn. bd., partner, sr. profl. staff mem. S.W. Metall. Cons., Inc.; sr. profl. staff EMTEC Corp.; asso. staff Transp. Safety Inst., Dept. Transp. Recipient award for excellence in undergrad. instrn. Standard Oil Co., Inc., 1970; grantee NSF, NASA, USAF, Okla. Research Inst. Registered profl. engr., Okla. Mem. Nat. Assn. Profl. Engrs., ASTM, Soc. Mfg. Engrs., Am. Inst. Mining, Metall. and Petroleum Engrs. (chmn. Okla. 1970, 75), Am. Soc. Metals (chmn. Central Okla. 1970, 75), Am. Acad. Forensic Sci., Microbeam Soc., Tex. Soc. Electron Microscopy, Sigma Xi, Alpha Sigma Mu. Home: 5104 SE 53d St Oklahoma City OK 73135 Office: 3503 Charleston Rd Norman OK 73069

JERNIGAN, WARREN HAMILTON, former mem. staff U.S. Ho. of Reps.; b. Pensacola, Fla., Apr. 25, 1937; s. William and Edna (Jones) J.; student George Washington U., 1959, U. Md., 1964-67; m. Helen Demirtashev, Jan. 31, 1959; children—Warren Hamilton, Robert William. Doorman, U.S. Ho. of Reps., 1958-63, chief doorman, 1963-78; legis. asst. to Rep. Robert L.F. Sikes, 1967-77. Mem. adminstrv. bd., mem. com. on edn. Arlington (Va.) United Methodist Ch., 1977-78, pres. Meth. Men, 1977-78, adminstrv. bd. Ferry Pass Meth. Ch.; instl. rep. Boy Scouts Am., 1976-78, editor-in-chief Threshold, 1976-78, exec. com., advancement chmn., dist. com., 1979—; usher Presdl. Breakfast, 1971-72, 74-77; pres. Patrick Henry Elementary Sch. PTA, Arlington, 1977, mem. exec. com., 1976-77; adv. bd. W. Fla. Hosp., CETA; treas. Pensacola Employ Handicapped Council; pres. Pensacola Pen Wheels, Fla. Council Handicapped Orgns.; ofcl. rep. to mayor and city council Office of Handicap; vice chmn. Gulf Coast Com. for Disabled Artists; mem. Fla. Coordinating Council Transp. Disadvantaged, Fla. Transp. Policy Study Commn.; bd. dirs. Boys Clubs Escambia County, Epilepsy of N.W. Fla. Served with USAF, 1955-58. Mem. U.S. Ho. of Reps. Doormens Soc. (founder, pres. 1969-77, Exemplary Service award 1971, Meritorious Service award 1975), Assn. Worshipful Masters of D.C. (pres. 1977), Fla. State Soc., U.S. Capitol Hist. Soc., Nat. Jogging Assn. (Spirit of 76 Jog), Talhook Assn., N.C. State Soc., Pensacola C. of C. (chmn. transp. study com.), Ensley C. of C. (dir., chmn. handicapped affairs). Clubs: Masons (32 deg., master D.C. 1977); Toastmasters Internat.; Pensacola Press. Home: 8535 N Davis Hwy Pensacola FL 32504

JESSEL, JOSEPH BRAND, retail exec.; b. Houston, Dec. 26, 1922; s. Maurice K. and Esther (Brand) J.; student U. Tex.; m. Dorothy Marian Lieberman, Nov. 5, 1944; children—Barbara Jessel Lack, Susan Jessel Martin, Jack L. Stockboy, Battelsteins Co., Houston, 1937-39; with Liebermans, Robstown, Tex., 1946—, v.p., 1960-70, pres., 1970—; dir. State Nat. Bank, Robstown. Pres. Coastal Bend Youth City, 1968-69, life mem. bd. dirs., 1964—; bd. dirs. Driscoll Found. Children's Hosp., 1976—; v.p. S.W. region Union Am. Hebrew Congregations, 1973—. Served with USNR, 1942-46. Decorated Air medal. Named Outstanding Jewish citizen B'nai B'rith, 1974. Mem. Tex. Retailers Assn., Navy League. Club: Rotary. Office: PO Box 1106 Robstown TX 78380

JESSUP, JOE LEE, mgmt. cons.; b. Cordele, Ga., June 23, 1913; s. Horace Andrew and Elizabeth (Wilson) J.; B.S., U. Ala., 1936; M.B.A., Harvard U., 1941; LL.D., Chung-Ang U., Seoul, Korea, 1964; m. Genevieve Quirk Galloway, Aug. 29, 1946; 1 dau., Gail Elizabeth. Sales rep. Proctor & Gamble, 1937-40; liaison officer bur. pub. relations U.S. War Dept., 1941; spl. asst. and exec. asst. Far Eastern div. and office exports Bd. Econ. Welfare, 1942-43; exec. officer office deptl. adminstrn. Dept. State, 1946; exec. sec. adminstr.'s adv. council War Assets Adminstrn., 1946-48; v.p. sales Airkem Capitol & Service

Co., 1948-49; pres. Joe L. Jessup & Co., 1957—; exec. v.p., gen. mgr. Hunter Labs., Inc., Fairfax, Va., 1965-69, also dir., mem. exec. com. to 1969; asso. prof. bus. administrn. George Washington U., 1949, prof., 1952-57, prof. emeritus, 1977—, asst. dean Sch. Govt., 1951-60; dir. Giant Food, Inc., Washington, 1971-75, mem. audit com., 1974-75; dir. Internat. Careers Inst., Inc., Los Angeles, 1972-73; coordinator resources mgmt. program U.S. Air Force, 1951-60; regional chmn. Harvard Bus. Sch. Fund, 1960-61; del. 10th Internat. Mgmt. Conf., Sao Paulo, Brazil, 1954, 11th, Paris, 1957, 12th, Sydney and Melbourne, Australia, 1960, 13th, N.Y.C., 1963, 14th, Rotterdam, Holland, 1966, 15th, Tokyo, 1970, 16th, Munich, Germany, 1973; mem. Md. Econ. Devel. Adv. Commn., 1973, 75. Nat. adv. council Center for Study of Presidency, N.Y.C., 1974—; mem. Arlington County (Va.) CSC, 1952-54; trustee Tng. Within Industry Found., Summit, N.J., 1954-58. Served from 2d lt. to lt. col. AUS, 1941-46. Decorated Bronze Star; recipient certificate of appreciation Sec. Air Force, 1957. Mem. Acad. Mgmt. Clubs: Coral Ridge Yacht (Ft. Lauderdale); Harvard (N.Y.C.). Home: 2801 NE 57th St Fort Lauderdale FL 33308

JESURÚN, HAROLD MÉNDEZ, physician; b. San Juan, P.R., Dec. 24, 1915; s. Willy and Esterlinda (Méndez) J.; B.A., Columbia U., 1937; M.D., U. Mich., 1940; m. Dolores López y Piñero, May 17, 1947; children—Carlos Antonio, John Alberto, Maria Celeste, Richard James. Intern, Kings County (N.Y.) Hosp., Bklyn., 1940-41; commd. 1st lt., M.C., U.S. Army, 1941, advanced through grades to col., 1959; area med. dir. Brit. Guiana, 1942-43; malariologist, New Guinea, 1943-44; chief provincial health officer, Taegu, Korea, 1945-46; exec. officer, chief cholera control officer, Korea, 1946; asst. resident Fitzsimmons Gen. Hosp., Denver, 1947-48; resident to chief sr. resident Brooke Gen. Hosp., San Antonio, 1948-50, asst. chief obstetrics and gynecology service, 1952-55; chief obstetrics and gynecology William Beaumont Gen. Hosp., El Paso, Tex., 1950-51, Percy Jones Gen. Hosp., Battle Creek, Mich., 1951-52, U.S. Army Hosp., Ft. Ord, Calif., 1952, Rodriguez Army Hosp., San Juan, 1955-58; chief obstetrics and gynecology, chief instr. obstetrics and gynecology Letterman Gen. Hosp., San Francisco, 1958-62; chief obstetrics and gynecology service, dep. comdr. U.S. Army 97th Gen. Hosp., Frankfurt, Germany, 1962-66; chief obstetrics and gynecology service, asst. chief profl. service Madigan Gen. Hosp., Tacoma, 1966-67; ret., 1967; program director obstetrics and gynecology St. Michael Hosp., Newark, also asso. clin. prof. N.J. Coll. Medicine and Dentistry, 1967-69; clin. dir. obstetrics and gynecology R. E. Thomason Gen. Hosp., El Paso, 1969-73; project dir. Family Planning OEO, El Paso, 1970-73; clin. investigator Am. Women's Health Program, Temple U., 1972-73; prof. obstetrics and gynecology U. Tex. at Houston, 1973—; asst. prof. obstetrics Baylor Med. Sch., 1954-55; cons. U.S. Army Europe, 1962-66, 6th U.S. Army Area, San Francisco, 1958-62. Bd. dirs., pres. El Paso chpt. Am. Cancer Soc., 1971-72, bd. dirs. Houston chpt., 1975. Decorated Bronze Star, Army Commendation medal, Legion of Merit; recipient Physician's Recognition award AMA, 1969. Diplomate Am. Bd. Obstetrics and Gynecology. Fellow A.C.S., Am. Coll. Obstetricians and Gynecologists; mem. AAAS, Soc. Med. Cons. to Armed Forces, Houston Obstet. and Gynecol. Soc., Assn. Profs. Gynecology and Obstetrics, Tex. Assn. Obstetrics and Gynecology, Am. Assn. Tropical Medicine and Hygiene, Bishop Alonso Manso Soc. (v.p. 1957-58), Assn. Mil. Surgeons, Harris County (Tex.) Med. Soc., Am. Med. Soc. of Vienna (Austria) (life), Phi Rho Sigma (v.p. 1939-40). Contbr. numerous articles to profl. jours. Home: 2610 Glen Haven Houston TX 77025

JETER, KATHERINE LESLIE BRASH, lawyer; b. Gulfport, Miss., July 24, 1921; d. Ralph Edward and Rosa Meta (Jacobs) Brash; B.A., Tulane U., 1943, J.D., 1945; m. Robert McLean Jeter, Jr., May 11, 1946. Admitted to La. bar, 1945; asso. mem. Montgomery, Fenner & Brown, New Orleans, 1945-46, Tucker, Martin, Holder, Jeter & Jackson (and predecessor firms), Shreveport, La., 1947—. Pres., Little Theatre Shreveport, 1966-67, YWCA, 1963, LWV, 1950-51; treas. Am. Nat. Theatre and Acad., Shreveport, 1963; 1st v.p. Shreveport Art Guild, 1973-74, pres., 1974-75. Mem. Am., La., Shreveport bar assns., Nat. Assn. Women Lawyers, La. State Law Inst. (council), Jr. League Shreveport, Order of Coif, Phi Beta Kappa. Editor Tulane Law Rev., 1945. Home: 3959 Maryland Ave Shreveport LA 71106 Office: 1300 Beck Bldg 400 Travis St Shreveport LA 71101

JEWELL, ROBERT BURNETT, engring. exec.; b. Binghampton, N.Y., Mar. 20, 1906; s. Howard Clinton and Anne (Burnett) J.; B.S. in Civil Engring., Lehigh U., 1928; m. Helen Louise Pflug, May 18, 1935; children—Robert William, Linda Louise. Asst. engr. Friestedt Found. Co., N.Y., 1928-30; asst. engr. Port of N.Y. Authority, 1930-39; with Mason & Hanger Co., 1939-43, field engr. Rays Hill Tunnel, 1939-40; chief draftsman Radford Ordnance Works, 1940-41; asst. chief engr. design Badger Ordnance Works, 1942; resident engr. constrn. Bklyn.-Battery Tunnel, 1942-43; job mgr. hemp mill constrn., Polo, Ill., 1943; with Silas Mason Co., 1943-55; asst. prodn. supt. operation La. Ordnance Plant, 1943-46, chief engr. design of facilities U.S. AEC, Iowa Ordnance Plant, 1947-48; project mgr. constrn. Fort Randall Dam Outlet Works Tunnels, 1948-50, AEC Pantex Ordnance Plant, 1951-52; project mgr. engring. services AEC Nev. Test Site, 1951-53; chief engr., co. rep. Harvey Canal Tunnel, 1953-55; v.p. Mason & Hanger-Silas Mason Co., Inc., 1955—, v.p., chief engr., 1959-64, v.p. ops., 1964-75, exec. v.p., 1975-76, pres., 1976—, also dir.; chmn. bd. Mason Chamberlain Inc. Trustee, Lees Jr. Coll., Jackson, Ky. Registered profl. engr., N.Y., Ky. Fellow ASCE; mem. AIAA, Nat. Soc. Profl. Engrs., Am. Ordnance Assn., The Moles, The Beavers, Tau Beta Pi. Presbyn. Rotarian. Club: Lexington Country. Home: 1036 The Lane Lexington KY 40504 Office: 200 W Vine St Lexington KY 40507

JEWELL, WILLIAM HORACE, lawyer; b. Hope, Ark., Dec. 16, 1919; s. Albert Taliaferro and Eliza (Winn) J.; LL.B.. U. Ark., 1944; m. Irma Hearst Murphy, Sept. 18, 1944; children—Martha Anne Jewell Ederington, Judith Kay Jewell Freeman, Rebecca Jane Jewell Verble, Joseph Winn, John Mason. Admitted to Ark. bar, 1944; atty. firm House, Holmes & Jewell, Little Rock, 1944—; dir. Arlington Hotel, Henry Enterprises, Inc. Mem. Am., Ark., Pulaski County bar assns., Phi Alpha Delta. Home: 306 Fairfax St Little Rock AR 72205 Office: 1550 Tower Bldg Little Rock AR 72201

JIMENEZ, ANDRES LAUREANO, psychiatrist; b. Ciego de Avila, Cuba, July 4, 1943; s. Armando A. and Juanita J.; B.S., Colegio de Belen, 1960; B.S., John Carroll U., 1967; M.S., Case Western Res. U., 1969; M.D., U. Miami, 1973; m. Lucila Venet, Aug. 19, 1967; children—Andres Francisco, Javier Eduardo, Cristina Elena. Intern, Jackson Meml. Hosp., Miami, Fla., 1973-74, resident in psychiatry, 1974-76; dir. geropsychiatric unit Cedars of Lebanon Health Care Center, Miami, 1977-78; chief psychiatrist Miami Mental Health Center, 1978; staff psychiatrist Douglas Gardens Geriatric Mental Health Center, Coral Gables, 1977—; clin. instr. U. Miami Med. Sch., 1976—. Bd. dirs. Fellowship House, Miami, United Family and Childrens Services, Miami. Mem. Am. Psychiat. Assn., Dade County Med. Assn. Roman Catholic. Office: 470 Biltmore Way Coral Gables FL 33134

JIMENEZ, RAUL, food products co. exec.; b. Dallas, July 1, 1932; s. Felix and Alejandra (Munoz) J.; m. Maria Del Refugio Quiroga, 1953; children—Raul, Patricia. Owner, Jimenez Restaurant, Fort Worth, 1963—; pres., chmn. bd. Jimenez Food Products Inc., San Antonio and Fort Worth, 1953—; dir. Pamex Foods Inc., Fort Worth. Committeeman dist. 19, mem. fin. council Tex. Democratic Party, 1977—; mem. Tex. Bd. Human Resources, 1976—, Tex. Bd. Health Resources, 1975-76; named Ambassador Goodwill Tex., 1974—; del. Democratic Mini-Convention, 1974; trustee Our Lady of the Lake U., San Antonio; bd. dirs. NW Hosp., Ft. Worth; v.p. Mex. Am. Dems. in San Antonio; founder Raul Jiminez Ednl. Center, Advance Parent-Child Ednl. Program, San Antonio. Day named in his honor by Gov. Tex., 1976; named Humanitarian of Year, Fort Worth Press Club, 1975; named Outstanding Citizen of Year, Tarrant County Commrs. Ct., 1975, Community Builder of Year, City of San Antonio, 1974, one of Top Ten Mex. Am. Execs. in Tex., 1979; recipient Chamizal Settlement Medallion, 1967. Mem. Nat. Food Distbrs. Assn., Tex. Restaurant Assn., Tex. Pub. Health Assn., Mex.-Am. Bus. and Profl. Assn., San Antonio and Fort Worth C. of C.'s, San Antonio Mfrs. and Bus. Assn., Tex. Assn. Bus. Roman Catholic. Club: Rotary. Home: 618 Delaware St San Antonio TX 78210 Office: 616 Delaware St San Antonio TX 78210

JIMENEZ-TORRES, CARLOS FEDERICO, physician; b. Aquada, P.R., Oct. 19, 1921; s. Carlos and Pura (Torres) Jimenez; student U. P.R., 1936-39; M.D., George Washington U., 1943; postgrad. radiology U. Pa., 1948-49; m. Domitila Ferrer, June 18, 1949; children—Lorraine, Carlos Federico, Luis Javier, Pura Elaine, Janet Arlene. Intern, Fajardo Dist. Hosp., 1943-44; resident Presbyn. Hosp., Phila., 1949-51; physician VA Center and Hosp., San Juan, P.R., 1946-48; practice medicine specializing in radiology, Ponce, P.R., 1952—; instr. radiology U. Pa. Sch. Medicine, 1950-51; lectr. radiology U. P.R. Sch. Medicine, 1952—; asso. clin. prof. radiology Cath. U. P.R. Sch. Medicine, 1979—; cons. radiology Ponce Med. Center. Bd. dirs., past treas. Liceo Ponceno. Served with AUS, 1944-46. Diplomate Am. Bd. Radiology. Mem. Am., Pan Am., P.R. med. assns., Am. Coll. Radiology, P.R., Inter-Am. radiol. socs., Radiol. Soc. N.Am., Am. Legion, USCG Aux., U.S. Power Squadron. Roman Catholic. Clubs: K.C., Lions (past dist. zone chmn., past pres. Ponce), Ponce Yacht (past commodore). Home: 16 Universidad St Ponce PR 00731 Office: Lorraine Bldg Ponce PR 00731

JINDIA, JASWANT RAI, economist; b. Nabha, Punjab, India, Dec. 28, 1930; s. Roshan Lal and Kala (Wanti) J.; came to U.S., 1966, naturalized, 1977; M.A., Punjab U., 1960; diploma statistics Inst. Agrl. Research Stats. India, 1961; M.S., U. Ill., 1968, Ph.D., 1970; m. Satya Vati, Mar. 8, 1956; children—Sudha Rani, Sanjiv Kumar, Rajiv Kumar, Ajay Kumar. Asst. statistician Punjab Agrl. U., India, 1960-66; asst. prof. econs. So. U., Baton Rouge, 1970-73, asso. prof., 1973-79, prof., 1979—; mem. income study com. Gov.'s Conf. on Aging, 1976. Mgr., Vedic Cultural Soc. Baton Rouge, 1975. Mem. Am. Econs., Assn., Am. Agrl. Econs. Assn., So. Regional Sci. Assn., La. Acad. Sci., Acad. La. Economists. Hindu. Author: Economic Production Possibilities of Soybeans in Northern India, 1973. Home: 718 Bancroft Way Baton Rouge LA 70808 Office: Dept Econs So U Baton Rouge LA 70813

JINDRA, ROY I., petroleum exploration co. exec.; b. Omaha, Oct. 25, 1920; s. Joseph George and Ruth Marie (Kutscher) J.; B.S., U. Kans., 1948; m. Fern True Jindra, Sept. 22, 1978; 1 son, Michael Scott. Geologist Amerada Petroleum Corp., Tyler, Tex., 1948-50, San Antonio, 1950-51; chief geologist Kirkwood & Co., Alice, Tex., 1951-56; sr. v.p., geologist Harkins & Co., Alice, 1956—. Served with USMC, 1942-45. Certified profl. geologist Assn. Profl. Geol. Scientists. Mem. Am. Assn. Petroleum Geologists (certified petroleum geologist), Gulf Coast Assn. Geol. Socs., Miss., Corpus Christi geol. socs. Office: Box 1940 Alice TX 78332

JIVIDEN, RANDOLPH LANE, psychiat. social worker; b. Buffalo, W.Va., June 27, 1923; s. Oren L. and Belva D. Jividen; B.A., Drury Coll., 1951; M.S.W., U. Louisville, 1959. Psychiat. social worker W.Va. Dept. Welfare, 1955-60, Charleston (W.Va.) Guidance Clinic, 1960-79, Community Mental Health Center, Inc., Huntington, W.Va., 1979—; program supr. Mason County Mental Health Center, 1979-80; asst. adminstr., sr. social worker Charleston Guidance Clinic. Served with USAAF, 1943-46. Mem. Acad. Cert. Social Workers (cert.), Nat. Assn. Social Workers (grad. leadership tng. program). Home: PO Box 8074 South Charleston WV 25303

JOBE, WARREN YANCEY, electric utility co. exec.; b. Burlington, N.C., Nov. 12, 1940; s. Talmage Moton and Frances (Malone) J.; B.S.B.A. in Acctg., U. N.C., 1963; m. Sally Crumpler, June 6, 1964; children—Warren Yancey, Marshall C. Tax mgr. Arthur Andersen & Co., Charlotte, N.C., 1963, Atlanta, to 1971; asst. comptroller So. Co. Services, Inc., Atlanta, 1971-75; v.p., comptroller Ga. Power Co., Atlanta, 1975—. Mem. adv. bd. Ashford Dunwoody YMCA, Atlanta, 1979—. C.P.A., N.C., Ga. Mem. Am. Inst. C.P.A.'s, Ga. Soc. C.P.A.'s, Nat. Assn. Accts. Republican. Episcopalian. Office: 270 Peachtree St Atlanta GA 30302

JOE, ARTHUR F., airline exec.; b. Palestine, Tex., Oct. 16, 1925; s. Fred Roosevelt and Lee Tisha (Roberson) J.; A.A., U. San Francisco, 1965; A.A., Fed. City Coll., 1971; B.S., Paul Quinn Coll., 1952; m. Daisy Evella Coleman, Nov. 11, 1967; children—Barbara Denise, Cynthia R., Earnia A., Arthur F. With U.S. Postal Service, Waco, Tex., San Francisco and Dallas, 1953-71; with Braniff Airways, Inc., Dallas, 1973—, supr. facilities and grounds, 1976—. Mem. Dallas Planning Citizens Adv. Com., 1967-69; vol. Joint Action in Community Services, 1969-73; mem. Greater Dallas Community Relations Commn., 1970-74, Greater Dallas Housing Opportunity Center, 1970-75; bd. dirs. Dallas Legal Services Project, Inc., 1970-74; vice chmn. Doris Miller YMCA bd., Waco, 1960-64; pres. Local 2504, Internat. Assn. Machinist and Aerospace Workers Union, 1971-73; treas. Voter Registration Project, Inc., Dallas, 1969-70; sec. Citizens Complaint Center, Greater Dallas, 1969-72. Served with USN, 1943-46. Mem. NAACP (exec. sec. 1955-64), Nat. Alliance Postal and Fed. Employees (pres. 1957-61). Mem. AME Ch. Home: 9703 Carnegie Dr Dallas TX 75228 Office: PO Box 61747 Mail Sta 107 Dallas Fort Worth Airport TX 75261

JOE, YOUNG-CHOON CHARLES, physician, educator; b. Seoul, Korea, Jan. 23, 1936; s. Kyoung Hwan and Geel Hwa (Kim) J.; came to U.S., 1965, naturalized, 1973; M.D., Yonsei U., 1961; M.S., U. Wash., 1973; m. Hee Mee Yoo, May 29, 1965; children—Jeannie, John, Jeffrey. Intern, Scandinavian Nat. Med. Center, Seoul, 1961-62, resident in otolaryngology, 1962-64; intern Mt. St. Mary's Hosp., Lewiston, N.Y., 1965-66; resident in surgery Bismarck (N.D.) Hosp., 1966-67; resident in family practice St. Joseph Hosp., Flint, Mich., 1967-68; fellow in otolaryngology Johns Hopkins U., Balt., 1968-70; fellow in phys. medicine and rehab. U. Wash., Seattle, 1971-73; med. dir. Wash. State Pen. Hosp., Wash. Dept. Social and Health Services, 1973-75; asst. prof. family medicine Meharry Med. Coll., Nashville, 1975-76, asso. prof., 1976—; asso. prof. family practice Coll. Medicine, East Tenn. State U., Johnson City, 1976—. Adviser Korean Community Assn. Middle Tenn. Recipient Michael A. Gorman award for med. research, Flint, 1967; Physician's Recognition award AMA, 1969, 72, 75. Diplomate Am. Bd. Family Practice. Fellow Am. Acad. Family Physicians, Am. Soc. Abdominal Surgeons, Internat. Coll. Surgeons; mem. Am. Assn. Med. Colls., Soc. Tchrs. Family Medicine, Pan Am. Med. Assn., Am. Coll. Emergency Physicians. Methodist. Contbr. articles to med. jours. Home: 1113 Chickering Park Dr Nashville TN 37215 Office: Div Family Medicine Meharry Med Coll Nashville TN 37208 also 3517 Old Clarksville Pike Joelton TN 37080

JOHANNESSON, PAUL, advt. exec.; b. Dover, N.H., Aug. 12, 1951; s. Philip William and Norma Theresa (Couture) J.; B.S. Bus./Advt., B.S. Bus./Pub. Relations, Fla. State U., 1973. Copywriter, production mgr. WFSO Radio, Pinellas Park, Fla., 1973-74; account exec. Media Design Advt., Clearwater, Fla., 1975-76; promotion dir. Trizec Ltd., Clearwater, 1977-78; exec. v.p., chief exec. officer Johannesson, Reeser & Assos., Inc., Pinellas Park, 1978—; pres. LEO Promotions, Inc., St. Petersburg, Fla., 1979. Mem. Am. Advt. Fedn. (Addy awards). Office: 5444 Park Blvd Pinellas Park FL 33565

JOHN, DAVID RUSSELL, JR., financial cons.; b. N.Y.C., Sept. 8, 1937; s. David Russell and Elizabeth (Dumbris) J.; B.S. in Econs., U. Pa., 1959; m. Carolyn Beer, Nov. 24, 1962; children—Jennifer Lynn, David Russell, Jessica Elaine. Exec. trainee Mfrs. Trust Co., N.Y.C., 1959-60; v.p. Fla. Capital Corp., Palm Beach, 1960-68; v.p., fin., dir. Cinecom Corp., N.Y.C., 1968-69; chmn. bd. Indsl. Electronics Assos., Inc., Palm Beach, 1969-71; chmn. bd., pres. Beefy King Internat., Inc., 1970-71, also Southeastern Cons.'s, Inc., Palm Beach; owner, dir. Mcht. Police of Palm Beaches, Inc.; owner Sonitrol Security Systems of Palm Beaches, Sonitrol Systems of Martin County, Inc.; mem. State Fla. Private Security Adv. Council, 1978—. Mem. Fla. N.G., 1960-66. Mem. Sigma Nu. Home: 242 List Rd Palm Beach FL 33480 Office: P B Towers 44 Cocoanut Row Palm Beach FL 33480

JOHN, PATRICIA SPAULDING, harpist, composer; b. Canton, Ill., July 16, 1916; d. Alfred Morgan and Grace (Spaulding) John; student Mills Coll., Calif., 1935, Curtis Inst. Music, Phila., 1936; B.A., Rice U., 1941; m. Frank Geoffrey Keightley, Mar. 1, 1957; children—Patricia Keightley Bolding, Pamela Keightley Hughes. Prin. harpist Springfield (Ill.) Civic Symphony, 1947-48, Galveston (Tex.) Civic Symphony, 1952-55; asso. harpist Houston Symphony Orch., 1955-56; mem. faculty dept. music Houston Baptist U., 1976—; solo recitals at Clifton Hall, Trinidad, B.W.I., 1957, Eduard van Beinum Found., Queekhoven, Breukelen, Netherlands, 1973, Rice U., Houston, 1974, 76, U.K. Harpists Assn., Brit. Inst. Recorded Sound, London, 1975, Contemporary Arts Mus., Houston, 1975, Sta. KPFT, Houston, 1975, Music Guild, Houston, 1976, Ysgol Y Delyn, Wales, 1977, Internat. Harpcentrum Nederland, Rolduc, Kerkrade, Netherlands, 1977, U. Houston, Clear Lake, 1979, Rothko Chapel, Houston, 1979; dir., pub. Pantile Press. Mem. Am. Harp Soc. (life mem., pub. relations dir. N.Y.C. 1969, editor Harpists in New York 1969-70, founder Houston chpt. 1966, pres. San Jacinto chpt., Houston 1975, v.p. 1979), U.K. Harpists Assn., Welsh Harp Soc., L'Assn. Internat. des Harpists, Musicians Club N.Y.C., Nat. Assn. for Am. Composers and Condrs., Curtis Inst. Music Alumni Assn. (sec. region XIV-Tex. 1975), Galveston Mus. Club (pres. 1954). Composer: Sea Changes (suite), Fog off Pelican Spit, Summer Squall, Surf, 1968, Mnemosyne, Aprille, 1969; Tachystos, 1971; Henriette, 1974; Let's Play Series: Clown Dance, Arithmetic, Canoe, 1975; Americana (suite): Preamble, Time of Snow, Imago Ignato, 1978; contbr. articles to mus. publs. Home: 1414 Milford Ave Houston TX 77006

JOHN, PAUL ROBIN, architect, planner, artist; b. Brunswick, Ga., May 18, 1929; s. Paul Robert and Thelma Debo (Winget) J.; B.Arch., U. Fla., 1953; m. Carol Erskine, 1951; children—Linda, Paul Robert Iv, Jodi Kristen; m. 2d, Laura Calhoun, May 22, 1971. Pvt. practice architecture, Pompano Beach, Fla., 1956-69; prin. Abraben, Bennett & John architects, Fort Lauderdale, 1969-71; exec. v.p. Abraben, John Perkins & Will, 1971-72; owner Paul Robin John, Mount Dora, Fla., 1975—; pres. Robin John Inc., developers, 1972—, L'Atelier Studio and Gallery, Mt. Dora, Fla., 1975-77. Co-chmn. Oklawaha River Basin Charette, Ocala, Fla., 1971, Downtown Fort Lauderdale, 1974; mem. Planning Commn. Pompano Beach, 1967-69; mem. Nat. Com. on Design, 1974; mem. Mt. Dora Devel. Commn. Mem. AIA (various design awards, pres. Broward chpt. 1967-68). Presbyterian (deacon, elder). Clubs: Exchange, Hillhouse Bath and Tennis. Prin. works include Fort Lauderdale City Hall, 1969, Broward Community Coll. campus, 1971 (various art awards 1973-75), restoration John D. Rockefeller home, Ormond Beach, Fla., into cultural center, 1977. Home: 1806 Lakeshore Dr Mount Dora FL 32757 Office: 644 N Donnelly St Mount Dora FL 32757

JOHNS, DONALD LIGHTHALL, ins. exec.; b. Plainfield, N.J., May 12, 1925; s. Kenneth Major and Ina Julia (Lighthall) J.; student U. Ala., 1942-43; m. Shirley A. Figlow, July 26, 1972; children—Sandra L. Keith, Patricia A. Johns Fountain, David L., Robert A. Adjuster, Johns & Co., Sarasota and Miami, Fla., 1946, br. mgr., 1947-53, partner, 1954-66; pres. Johns & Co., Ins. Adjusters, Inc., Sarasota, 1966-70; pres. Johns Eastern Co., Inc., Sarasota, 1971—; chmn. bd. S.E. Bank of Siesta Key, Sarasota, 1976-78; dir. S.E. First Nat. Bank of Sarasota, 1979—. Mem. Sarasota County Bd. Pub. Instrn. for Sarasota County, 1954-58; founder, pres. Jefferson Center, Inc., Sarasota, 1962-70. Served to cpl., U.S. Army, 1943-46; ETO. Mem. Nat. Assn. Ind. Ins. Adjusters (sec.-treas. 1979-80), Internat. Inst. Loss Adjusters (regional v.p. 1975-77), Canadian Ind. Adjusters Conf., Atlanta Claims Assn., W. Coast Claims Assn., Pinellas County Claims Assn., Sarasota-Bradenton Claims Assn. Republican. Unitarian. Clubs: Field, Univ. Home: 501 Sandy Cove 4 4900 Ocean Blvd Sarasota FL 33581 Office: PO Box 4175 2238 Gulf Gate Dr Sarasota FL 33578

JOHNS, ELBERT BRUMFIELD, ret. orgn. exec.; b. Jessamine County, Ky., Apr. 5, 1911; s. Robert Lee and Inice (Brumfield) J.; A.B., Berea (Ky.) Coll., 1935; m. Myrtle Metcalf, Sept. 1937; children—Carolyn Johns French, Elbert Brumfield. With Vt. YMCA, 1935-37; ednl. adviser Civilian Conservation Corps, 1937-41; supr. Atlas Powder Co., 1941-45; with Boy Scouts Am., 1945-77, exec. Four Rivers Council, 1959-68, dir. of programs, Louisville, 1968-77, named fellow, 1955; pres. Louisville Prayer Breakfast Group; trustee Ky. Lions Eye Found. Mem. Am. Camping Assn., Berea Coll. Alumni Club (pres. 1973-74), Order of Arrow, Paducah C. of C. Methodist (mem. bd., lay speaker). Clubs: Lions (pres. chpt. 1953, v.p. 1975, pres. Downtown Louisville club 1978—), Filson. Author publs. in field. Home: 2232 Wynnewood Circle Louisville KY 40222 Office: PO Box 21068 Louisville KY 40221

JOHNS, FRED THOMAS, educator; b. Cameron, Tex., Jan. 16, 1932; s. William Henry and Ida Inez (Andrews) J.; A.A., Blinn Coll., 1952; B.S., A. and M. U., 1954; M.S. (NSF fellow), Okla. State U., 1959. Operator, Bilsing Orr Pest Control Co., Bryan, Tex., 1954-55; tchr. math and sci. Cameron (Tex.) Ind. Sch. Dist., 1955—. Pres., Walker's Creek Cemetery Assn., 1970-80, Walkers Creek Cemetery Found., 1974-80. Texaco fellow, 1956; NSF summer fellow, 1957, 58, 65, 69, 72, 73; Shell merit fellow Stanford U., 1963. Mem. Entomol. Soc. Am., Internat. Platform Assn., NEA (del. convs. 1976-78), Tex. Tchrs. Assn. (del. conv. 1979 (human relations award individual category 1980), Cameron Classroom Tchrs. Assn. (pres. 1976-77, treas. 1979-80), Milam County Tchrs. Assn. (sec.-treas., 1975-76, chmn. polit. action com. 1977-78), Milam County A. and M. Club (pres., 1968), Phi Delta Kappa. Clubs: Lions (pres. 1975-76), Evening.

Home: Route 1 Box 325 Cameron TX 76520 Office: Box 712 Cameron TX 76520

JOHNSEN, RUSSELL HAROLD, chemist, ednl. adminstr.; b. Chgo., Aug. 5, 1922; s. Harold Gunnar and Irene (Gaul) J.; B.S., U. Chgo., 1947; Ph.D., U. Wis., 1951; m. Dorothy Ruth Pehta, Jan. 20, 1948; children—Peter Berghsey, Margaret Andrea. Research chemist Ninol Labs., Chgo., 1946-48; asst. prof. chemistry Fla. State U., 1951-55, asso. prof., 1956-60, prof., 1961—, asso. dean grad. studies, 1976—. Served to 1st lt. USAAF, 1943-46. AEC grantee, 1955-75; ERDA grantee, 1975-77; Dept. Energy grantee, 1977—. Fellow AAAS; mem. Am. Chem. Soc., Am. Phys. Soc., Am. Soc. Mass Spectroscopists, Radiation Research Soc., Sigma Xi. Club: Appalachee Bay Yacht (rear commodore). Author: Atoms, Molecules and Chemical Change, 1971; Introductory Chemistry, 1972; contbr. numerous articles on fundamentals of radiation chemistry and mass spectroscopy to profl. jours. Office: Chemistry Dept Fla State U Tallahassee FL 32306

JOHNSON, ALCEE LABRANCHE, educator; b. Fernwood, Miss., July 22, 1905; s. Jonas Edward and Bertha (LaBranche) J.; student Alcorn Coll., 1925; A.B., Fisk U., 1927; M.A., Columbia, 1956; postgrad. U. So. Cal., 1962; D. Humanities (hon.), Miss. Bapt. Sem., 1972; m. Thelma M. Wethers, Dec. 25, 1931; children—Joyce (Mrs. James L. Bolden), Al Wethers. Instr. Prentiss (Miss.) Inst. Jr. Coll., 1927-30, dir. instrn., 1931-36, 37-71, pres., 1971—; Miss. state supr. Survey Vocational Edn. and Guidance, Office Edn., Dept. Interior, Washington, 1936-37; chmn. bd. dirs. State Mut. Fed. Savs. & Loan Assn.; inst. rep. Heifer Project, Inc. Mem. Miss. Regional Med. Program, Merit Commn. Miss. Econ. Council, Phelps-Stokes Fund Conf. Edn. Leaders. Former chmn. Western div. Boy Scouts Am., com. mem. JDC Mut. Fed. Credit Union, 1960—; del. White House Conf. on Aging, 1971; mem. Miss. Probation and Parole Bd., 1972—. Mem. Voters League, 1964—, now pres. Bd. dirs. So. Miss. Planning and Devel. Dist. So. Interracial Commn. grantee, 1930; recipient Silver Beaver award Boy Scouts Am., 1960. Mem. Am., Miss. (past pres.), 6th Dist. (past pres.) tchrs. assns., N.E.A. (life), N.A.A.C.P. (local coordinator), Jefferson Davis County, Miss. chambers commerce, Alpha Phi Alpha, Phi Delta Kappa. Mem. Ch. of Christ (trustee). Mason (33 deg.). Home: PO Box 112 Prentiss MS 39474 Office: Drawer C Prentiss MS 39474

JOHNSON, ALFRED MASSEY FISHER, hydrologist, engr.; b. Belding, Mich., Jan. 7, 1912; s. Charles and Marie (Belliss) J.; B.C.E., Mich. State U., 1935; m. Ruth Marian Arnold, June 8, 1938; children—Charles Ernest Arnold, William Alfred. Sr. engring. aide TVA, Chattanooga, 1935-36; jr. engr. Miss. River Commn., Vicksburg, 1937-41; hydraulic engr. U.S. Geol. Survey, Chattanooga, 1948-68, Atlanta, 1968-70, hydrologist, Atlanta, 1970-77. Served to lt. col. Arty., AUS, 1941-47. Decorated Bronze Star; recipient Silver Beaver award Boy Scouts Am., 1964; registered profl. engr., Tenn.; cert. profl. land surveyor. Mem. ASCE (v.p. 1967-68), Nat. Soc. Profl. Engrs. (v.p. 1967-68), Nat. Ry. Hist. Soc., Tenn. Valley R.R. Mus. Author: (with W.J. Randolph) Floods on Chattanooga Creek, 1962; (with George Wood) Characteristics of Tennessee Streams, 1962; (with John Wilson) Water Use in Tennessee, 1968-70; (with R. Fred Carter) Water Use in Georgia, 1974. Home: 116 Arnold Dr Chattanooga TN 37412 Office: 6481 Peachtree Industrial Blvd Suite B Doraville GA 30340

JOHNSON, ALLEN HUGGINS, physician, educator; b. Columbia, S.C., May 25, 1937; s. Allen H. and Mae Elizabeth (Burgess) J.; B.S., U. S.C., 1958; M.D., 1962; m. Kathryn Brooks, June 24, 1961; children—Allen Huggins, Kathryn Ann, Brooks Burgess. Intern Med. U. of S.C. Hosp., Charleston, 1962-63, asst. resident, 1965-67; USPHS fellow dept. of medicine, Emory U. Sch. of Medicine, Atlanta, 1967-69; practice medicine, specializing in internal medicine Charleston, 1973-77; asst- prof. medicine Med. U. of S.C., Charleston, 1969-72, asst. prof. microbiology, 1970-72, asso. prof. medicine and microbiology, 1972-77, prof., 1977—, acting chmn. dept. medicine, 1979-80; chief med. service Charleston County Hosp., 1972-73; chief univ. med. service St. Francis Xavier Hosp., Charleston, 1974—. Served to capt., M.C., AUS, 1963-65. Diplomate Am. Bd. Internal Medicine. Fellow A.C.P.; mem. Am. Soc. Microbiology, Am. Fedn. Clin. Research, Charleston County Med. Soc., Sigma Chi. Contbr. articles on microbiology and internal medicine to profl. jours. Home: 549 Coinbow Dr Mount Pleasant SC 29464 Office: 171 Ashley Ave Charleston SC 29403

JOHNSON, ARTHUR MARCELLUS, coll. pres.; b. Redwater, Tex., Feb. 22, 1923; s. Walter M. and Nadine (Spencer) J.; A.S., Texarkana Coll., 1947; B.S., East Tex. State U., 1948, M.S., 1949; m. Iva Nell McClurg, Nov. 14, 1944; 1 dau., Nedra Sue Johnson Cook. Tchr., Talco (Tex.) High Sch., 1949-50; instr., coach Panola Jr. Coll., 1950-64, registrar, 1964-66, dean, 1966-74, pres., 1974—. Pres., United Fund, Panola County, Tex., 1968; sec.-treas. Panola County Indsl. Found.; trustee 1st United Methodist Ch., Carthage. Served with USAAF, 1943-46. Named Citizen of Year, Panola County, 1974. Mem. Tex. State Tchrs. Assn. (life), Tex. Jr. Coll. Instrnl. Adminstrs., Tex. Public Community-Jr. Coll. Assn., East Tex. Council Higher Edn. (chmn. 1977—), Panola County C. of C. (pres. 1978), Kappa Delta Pi. Democrat. Club: Lions (dep. dist. gov. 1972, 74). Office: Panola Jr Coll Carthage TX 75633

JOHNSON, AUDREYE EARLE, social worker, educator; b. Memphis, Aug. 18, 1929; d. Lyncha Adolphus and Mary Elizabeth (Hairston) J.; B.A., Fisk U., 1950; M.A., U. Chgo., 1957; Ph.D., U. Denver, 1975. Clk., Universal Life Ins. Co., Memphis, 1950-51; caseworker Tenn. Dept. Public Welfare, Memphis, 1952-54, child welfare worker, Chattanooga, 1955-56; social worker Michael Reese Hosp., Chgo., 1957-67; dir. social service MLK Neighborhood Health Center, Mt. Sinai Hosp., Chgo., 1967-69; asst. clin. prof., dir. consultation and edn. dept. psychiatry Community Mental Health Center, Meharry Med. Coll., Nashville, 1969-73; asso. prof. Sch. Social Work, U. N.C., Chapel Hill, 1975—. Mem. human rights adv. com. Murdoch Center, 1976-78, 78—; bd. dirs. Mental Health Research and Devel. Center, Howard U., 1976; bd. dirs. Afro-Am. Family and Community Services, Chgo. Mem. Nat. Assn. Black Social Workers (v.p. 1978—, sec. 1974-78), Am. Public Health Assn. (program chairperson 1978-80), Nat. Conf. Social Welfare, N.C. State Assn. Black Social Workers (v.p., state conf. coordinator 1978-79), Triangle Assn. Black Social Workers, Acad. Cert. Social Workers, Council Social Work Edn., N.C. Conf. Social Services, N.C. Public Health Assn., Nat. Urban League, NAACP, N.C. Sr. Citizens Fedn. Roman Catholic. Contbr. articles to profl. jours. Home: 4100 Five Oaks Dr Apt 19 Durham NC 27707 Office: Sch Social Work U NC 223 E Franklin St Chapel Hill NC 27514

JOHNSON, BEN BUTLER, physician; b. Bklyn., May 23, 1920; s. Louis Collins and Jeanne Farrell (Payne) J.; grad. Choate Sch., 1937; A.B., Harvard U., 1942, M.D., 1944; m. Barbara Ann Maltby, Dec. 22, 1962; children—Louis Collins III, Charles Martin, Michael David, Mary Jeanne, Margaret Ann. Intern, N.Y. Hosp., 1944-45; resident N.Y. U. div. Bellevue Hosp., N.Y.C., 1947-49; research fellow medicine Bassett Hosp. and Stanford U., 1949-53; instr., asst. prof. medicine Stanford U., 1955-59; practice medicine specializing in internal medicine and nephrology, Jackson, Miss., 1959—; mem. staff Univ. Hosp.; chief renal and electrolyte div. dept. medicine U. Miss. Med. Center, 1959—, residency program dir. internal medicine, 1960—; asst. prof. U. Miss., 1959-62. asso. prof. medicine, 1962—; dir. Diabetes Clinic, Stanford Hosps., 1956-59. Mem. Miss. Nutrition Council, 1961—, chmn., 1962-64. Bd. dirs. Kidney Found. of Miss., 1964-71, sec.-treas., 1965-71, chmn. med. adv. bd., 1971-73; mem. nat. med. adv. council Nat. Kidney Found., 1970—, sec., 1971-73. Served to lt. (j.g.) M.C., USNR, 1945-46; served to lt. USNR, 1953-55. Diplomate Am. Bd. Internal Medicine and subsplty. in nephrology, Nat. Bd. Med. Examiners. Fellow A.C.P.; mem. Am., Internat. socs. nephrology, Endocrine Soc., Am. Diabetes Assn., Am. Soc. Internal Medicine, Am. Fedn. for Clin. Research, Western Soc. for Clin. Research, Assn. Program Dirs. in Internal Medicine, Am., Miss. heart assns., Soc. Mayflower Descs. (surgeon Miss. soc. 1971-74, gov. 1974—, surgeon gen. 1978—), AAUP (pres. Miss. conf. 1968-69), Sigma Xi. Contbr. articles to profl. jours. Home: 1540 Kimwood Circle Jackson MS 39211 Office: Univ of Miss Medical Center 2500 N State St Jackson MS 39216

JOHNSON, BESS VISE, guidance counselor; b. Heavener, Okla., Oct. 26, 1935; d. Haskell Lee and Dessie Elizabeth (Pierce) V.; B.S., Pittsburg State U., 1962, M.S., 1965; postgrad. La. Tech. U., 1972-78; m. Derrell Edward Johnson, Sept. 26, 1953; 1 son, Steven Edward. Tchr. public schs., Frontenac, Kans., 1962-63, Shreveport, La., 1963-68; sch. guidance counselor, Shreveport, 1968-79; guidance counselor Summer Grove Sch., Shreveport, 1979—. Named Outstanding Young Tchr. of Yr. for Caddo Parish, Jaycees, 1967. Mem. NEA, Am. Personnel and Guidance Assn., La. Personnel and Guidance Assn., La. Sch. Counselor Assn. (La. Outstanding Counselor of Yr. 1978), Caddo Sch. Counselor Assn., La. Assn. for Measurement in Guidance (sec.-treas. 1976-77), La. Vocat. and Guidance Assn. (sec.-treas. 1978), La. Counselor Assn. (v.p. 1974-76), Shreveport Counselor Assn. (pres. 1978-79), Alpha Delta Kappa (local pres. 1972-74, 75-76, regional pres. 1972-74). Democrat. Baptist. Club: West Shreveport Polit. Elem. editor Jour. of Counseling Services, La. State U., 1977—. Home: 1814 Hunter Circle Shreveport LA 71119 Office: Summer Grove Sch 2955 Reisor Rd Shreveport LA 71118

JOHNSON, BILLY JOE, engring. co. exec.; b. Wetumka, Okla., Sept. 22, 1929; s. Joe Willie and Lutie Elizabeth (Roberts) J.; B.S., Okla. A. and M. Coll., 1956; M.E., Okla. U., 1966; C.E., U. Houston, 1971; m. Mona Jean Hays, Apr. 1, 1951; children—Vicki Linn, Joe Kent. Asphalt chemist Kans. State Hwy. Commn., El Dorado, 1953-54; chemist Halliburton Co., 1956-60, sr. chemist, 1960-66, div. chemist, service sales engr., 1966-72, coordinator environ. services, 1968-72, dir. environ. affairs, 1972-74; pres. V. & J. Chem. and Engring. Services Inc., 1975—, chief exec. officer, 1980—; cons. engr. Served with USN, 1948-52; PTO. Registered profl. engr., Okla., Ark., La., Tex. Mem. Tex. Safety Assn., Nat. Safety Council, S.E. La. Safety Assn., Soc. Petroleum Engrs. of Am. Inst. Mining Engrs., Petroleum Equipment Suppliers Assn., Nat. Ocean Industries Assn., Tex. Mfg. Assn., Rubber Mfg. Assn., VFW (post comdr. 1979—, charter mem. Nat. Home for Vets.' Children and Widows). Patentee in field. Home: 2910 Fairway Dr Sugar Land TX 77478 Office: PO Box 1214 Bellaire TX 77401

JOHNSON, BRUCE ALAN, assn. exec.; b. Portland, Maine, July 26, 1930; s. John Henry and Berta Clarke (Langstroth) J.; B.A., U. Calif., Berkeley, 1953; B.S., U. Md., 1970, M.B.A., 1970; m. Shirley A. Knight, Feb. 23, 1953; children—Jacquelyn, Craig, Keith, Mark. Commd. 2d lt., U.S. Army, 1950, advanced through grades to col., 1968; ret., 1970; nat. sales mgr. Automated Bldg. Components, Miami, Fla., 1970-75; dir. mktg. Linen Supply Assn. Am., Hallandale, Fla., 1975—; vis. lectr. univs.; mem. Council Hotel, Restaurant and Instnl. Edn. Decorated Legion of Merit, Silver Star, 2 Bronze Stars, Meritorious Service Medal, Army Commendation Medal. Mem. Am., Fla. socs. assn. execs., Sales and Mktg. Execs. Internat., Am. Mktg. Assn., Ret. Officers Assn., DAV, Alpha Sigma Lambda. Clubs: Army-Navy Country, Pembroke Lakes Racquet. Contbr. articles to hospitality trade publs., profl. jours., Linen Supply News. Office: 1250 E Hallandale Beach Blvd Hallandale FL 33009

JOHNSON, BRUCE KING, physician, educator; b. Harriman, Tenn., Oct. 24, 1918; s. Samuel King and Laura Monro (Jones) J.; B.S., Birmingham-So. Coll., 1940; M.D., U. Tenn., 1944; m. Leila Newman Wright, Apr. 4, 1942 (dec. Nov. 1957); children—Bruce King, Samuel Paul, Thomas Sterling, Leila Anne; m. 2d, Iris Dudley Thomas, Mar. 14, 1959. Intern Hillman Hosp. and Norwood Hosp., Birmingham, Ala., 1944-45; resident N.C. Bapt. Hosp.-Bowman Gray Med. Sch., Winston-Salem, 1949-51; sr. resident U. Ala. Hosps., Birmingham, 1951; gen. practice medicine, Flat Creek, Ala., 1945-49, specializing in internal medicine, Birmingham, 1952—; med. dir. Birmingham Med. Group Clinic, 1959-68; mem. staff, bd. govs. Simon-Williamson Clinic; mem. active staff U. Ala. Hosps.; mem. active and teaching staff Bapt. Med. Center, Princeton; mem. courtesy staff Bapt. Med. Center, Montclair, St. Vincents Hosp., South Highlands Infirmary; clin. instr. U. Ala., 1952-63, clin. asst. prof. dept. internal medicine, 1963—. Bd. dirs. Vis. Nurse Assn., 1962-69, chmn. med. adv. bd., 1970-78. Fellow A.C.P.; mem. Birmingham Soc. Internists, Birmingham Acad. Medicine, Am., Ala. socs. internal medicine, Am. Heart Assn., So., Ala., Jefferson County med. assns., Lambda Chi Alpha, Omicron Delta Kappa (hon.), Alpha Kappa Kappa, Alpha Omega Alpha (hon.). Methodist (mem. adminstrv. bd.). Home: 3016 Warrington Rd Birmingham AL 35223 Office: 801 Princeton Ave SW Birmingham AL 35211

JOHNSON, BYRON T., JR., physician; b. Electra, Tex., May 17, 1922; s. Byron T. and Helen S. (Wheat) J.; A.A., So. State Coll., 1947; M.D., B.S.M., U. Ark., 1951; M.P.H., Johns Hopkins U., 1962; m. Helen I. Wilson, Nov. 28, 1944; children—Patricia S. (Mrs. George E. McCormic), Rebecca J., Michael R. Intern Ark. Baptist Hosp., Little Rock, 1951-52, practice medicine, Ark., 1952-59; commd. USAF, 1959; advanced through grades until 1968; physician aviation and occupational medicine Pan Am. World Airways, N.Y.C., 1968-72; med. dir. occupational medicine Atlantic Richfield Co., Houston, 1972—; mem. Medichem-Occupational Health in the Chem. Industry; cons. preventive medicine N.Y. State Workmen's Compensation Bd., 1969-75. Decorated 2 Bronze Star medals. Diplomate Am. Bd. Preventive Medicine. Fellow Am. Coll. Preventive Medicine; mem. Am., Tex. med. assns., Harris County Med. Soc., Aerospace Med. Assn., Am. Occupational Med. Assn., Am. Soc. Contemporary Medicine and Surgery, Airline Med. Dirs. Assn., So. Med. Assn. Home: 2911 Kevin Ln Houston TX 77043 Office: PO Box 2451 Houston TX 77001

JOHNSON, CARL PHILLIP, tobacco co. exec.; b. Centralia, Ill., June 13, 1948; s. David George and Naomi Ruth (Ward) J.; B.S. in Agr., U. Ill., 1970; m. Pamela Jean Williams, Aug. 30, 1969; children—Phillip, Matthew, Emily. Asst. editor Hampshire Herdsman, Peoria, Ill., 1970-71; editorial dir. Specialized Agrl. Publs. Inc., Raleigh, N.C., 1973-75; asso. editor S.E. Farm Press, Raleigh, 1975-77; mgr. agrl. relations and analysis Philip Morris U.S.A., Richmond, Va., 1977—. Served with AUS, 1971-73. Mem. Am. Agrl. Editor's Assn., N.C. Farm Writers and Broadcasters Assn. (dir. 1976), Plant Food Assn. N.C., Pesticide Assn. N.C., N.C. Farm Bur. Fedn., Nat. Agri-Mktg. Assn. (dir. Va.-Carolinas chpt. 1977—), Agrl. Relations Council, Capitol Grange. Home: 131 Arkwright Rd Richmond VA 23235 Office: PO Box 26603 Richmond VA 23261

JOHNSON, CARLOS EDWARD, accountant; b. Durma, Miss., May 6, 1941; s. Carlos N. Johnson and Oleta Mae (Walker) Marshall; B.S., East Central Okla. State U., 1964; M.S., Okla. State U., 1966, Ed.D., 1977; m. Karen Ann Johnson, Aug. 7, 1960; 1 dau., Terri. Staff asst. controller Okla. State U., Stillwater, 1964-66; chmn. dept. bus. adminstrn. East Central Oklahoma State U., Ada, 1966-73; partner Horne & Co., Ada, 1973-77; mgr. Peat, Marwick, Mitchell & Co., Oklahoma City, 1977—. Pres. Ada Community Chest, 1975—; active Arbuckle Area Council Boy Scouts Am. Served with AUS, 1959, 60-61. C.P.A., Okla. Mem. Ada C. of C. (dir. 1974—), Okla. Soc. C.P.A.'s (dir., pres. SE chpt.), Am. Inst. C.P.A.'s, Beta Gamma Sigma, Beta Alpha Psi, Delta Pi Epsilon. Methodist. Kiwanian. Home: 3013 Rock Ridge Oklahoma City OK 73120 Office: Suite 1200 E 1st Nat Center Oklahoma City OK 73102

JOHNSON, CARVER LISTER, data processing exec.; b. Willacoochee, Ga., July 30, 1949; s. Moses G. and Sarah Bell Gordon (Hugee) J.; B.S., D.C. Tchrs. Coll., 1971; M.S. in Sci. Teaching, Am. U., 1974; m. Algernon Veronica Daniels, Dec. 10, 1976; children—Eric, Okorie, Nadia. Tchr. math. and data processing D.C. pub. schs., 1971-72; mathematician, programmer Nat. Bur. Standards, Gaithersburg, Md., 1972-73; sr. programmer, analyst Navy Recruiting Command, Arlington, Va., 1973-75; systems and programming supr., project mgr. Dade County Schs.-MIS, Miami, Fla., 1975—; adj. prof. data processing Fla. Internat. U., 1976—. NSF fellow, 1972, 73, 74. Democrat. Mem. A.M.E. Zion Ch. Home: 1095 NW 83d St Miami FL 33150 Office: 13135 SW 26th St Miami FL 33175

JOHNSON, CHARLES FREDERIC, JR., lawyer; b. Sinton, Tex., July 13, 1923; s. Charles Frederick and Clara Aileen (Barnard) J.; student Tex. A. and I. U., 1939, John Tarlton Coll., 1939-42; J.D., U. Tex., 1950; m. Alice Eloise Fraser, Dec. 20, 1947; children—Mary Ann Johnson Hall, Charles Frederic. Admitted to Tex. bar, 1950; individual practice law, Sinton, 1950—; pres., dir. Chiltipin Devel. Co., Community Computers, Inc.; planning cons. Bd. dirs. Sinton Indsl. Found., 1965—; chmn. San Patricio County Hist. Survey Com., 1963; chmn. county com. Democratic Party, 1958-70, mem. Tex. Dem. Exec. Com., 1960-62. Served with USMC, 1942-46. Decorated Air medal. Mem. Am., Tex., San Patricio County bar assns., Nueces County Trial Lawyers Assn., Am. Inst. Planners, AAAS. Episcopalian. Home: 4 Northwood Rd Sinton TX 78387 Office: 111 N Odem Bldg Sinton TX 78387

JOHNSON, CHARLES JAMES, mgmt. analyst; b. Erieville, N.Y., Dec. 23, 1934; s. Herbert Cramer and Nina Nattie (Waters) J.; B.S., Fla. So. Coll., 1964; M.B.A., Tex. Christian U., 1970; postgrad. Tex. A&M U., 1975; m. Gloria M. Rhea, Apr. 20, 1956; children—Celeste Ann, Valerie Leah. Commd. 2d lt. U.S. Air Force, 1955, advanced through grades to lt. col.; now officer U.S. Air Force Res.; with Gen. Dynamics, Ft. Worth, 1967-70; with VA, 1971—, sr. mgmt. analyst VA Med. Center, Waco, Tex., 1973—; adj. prof. mgmt. devel. McLennan Community Coll., Waco, 1973—. Deacon, 1st Presbyn. Ch., Waco. Mem. Am. Hosp. Assn., Tex. Hosp. Assn., Nat. Mgmt. Assn., Tex. Assn. Adult and Continuing Edn. Democrat. Clubs: Lions, Masons. Home: 301 Brookwood Waco TX 76710 Office: Memorial Dr Waco TX 76703

JOHNSON, CHARLES OWEN, ret. lawyer; b. Monroe, La., Aug. 18, 1926; s. Clifford U. and Laura (Owen) J.; B.A., Tulane U., 1946, J.D., 1969; LL.B., Harvard, 1948; LL.M., Columbia, 1955. Admitted to La. bar, 1949, practiced in Monroe, 1949-50; mem. law editorial staff West Pub. Co., St. Paul, 1953; atty. Office of Chief Counsel, Internal Revenue Service, Washington, 1955-79, chief Ct. Appeals br. Tax Ct. Div., 1968-79. Served with AUS, 1950-52. Mem. Fed., La. bar assns., Nat. Lawyers Club, Soc. Colonial Wars (dep. gov. D.C. soc.), SAR, SR (pres.), (past nat. trustee, past pres. D.C. soc.), Soc. War of 1812 (past pres. D.C. soc.), S.C.V., Sons Union Vets., St. Andrew's Soc. Washington, Royal Soc. St. George, Sons and Daus. of Pilgrims, Huguenot Soc. S.C., Soc. Descs. Jersey Settlers, La. Colonials, Jamestowne Soc., Soc. Descs. Old Plymouth Colony, Order Ams. of Armorial Ancestry (pres.), Soc. Descs. Colonial Clergy, Hereditary Order Descs. Colonial Govs. (gov. gen.), Order Founders and Patriots of Am. (past gov.), Order First Families Miss. 1699-1817 (gov. gen. 1967-69), Mil. Order Stars and Bars (judge adv. gen.), Soc. Cin., Nat., Va. geneal. socs., Miss., Va. hist. socs., Phi Beta Kappa. Mason (Shriner, K.T., 32 deg.); mem. Order Eastern Star. Clubs: Pendennis of New Orleans (charter mem.); Arts, Army and Navy (Washington). Author: The Geneology of Several Allied Families, 1961. Home: 2111 Jefferson Davis Hwy Apt 109S Arlington VA 22202

JOHNSON, CHARLES WILLIAM, microbiologist, univ. dean; b. Ennis, Tex., Jan. 25, 1922; s. Charles Edward and Jason Elizabeth (McDaniel) J.; B.S., Prairie View State Coll.; M.S., U. So. Calif., 1947; M.D., Meharry Med. Coll., 1953; m. Mattie Shavers, Apr. 11, 1944; children—Charles William, Phillip Noel, Livette Suzanne. Postdoctoral fellow Rockefeller Inst. Med. Research, 1957-59; instr. bacteriology and parasitology Meharry Med. Coll., Nashville, asst. prof. dept. microbiology, successively asso. prof., chmn. dept., v.p. for research, dean Sch. Grad. Studies. Bd. govs. Cumberland Heights; bd. dirs. Mid-Cumberland Council on Drug and Alcohol Abuse, Nashville Urban Obs. Served with USCG, 1942-45. Rockefeller Found. fellow; NIH grantee; NSF grantee; Smith-Kline French Research grantee. Mem. Am. Soc. Pathologists, Am. Soc. Microbiologists, AAAS, Am. Acad. Allergy, Am. Fedn. Clin. Research, Alpha Phi Alpha. Presbyterian. Club: The Boule. Office: Meharry Med Coll 1005 18th Ave N Nashville TN 37208

JOHNSON, CHARLES WILLIAM, electric utility exec.; b. Knoxville, Tenn., Aug. 4, 1934; s. Lloyd David and Louise Margaret (Jenkins) J.; B.S. in Elec. Engring., U. Tenn., 1961; m. Margie Lee Finn, Oct. 25, 1952; children—Deborah Ann (Mrs. Bobby Gene Cherry), David, Dale, Lynda, Glenn. Engr., Fla. Power & Light Co., Cocoa, 1961-68; dir. electric utilities City of Washington, N.C., 1968-73; systems engr. Tideland Electric Membership Corp., Pantego, N.C., 1973-74; gen. mgr. Rockwood (Tenn.) Electric Utility, 1974—. Vice-chmn. Catoosa dist. Boy Scouts Am., 1974-76, cubmaster, Rockledge, Fla., 1965-68. Served with USAF, 1953-57. Registered profl. engr., Fla., N.C., Tenn. Mem. Am. Pub. Power Assn., Tenn. Valley Pub. Power, Roane County C. of C. (pres. 1976). Club: Civitan (Rockwood, Tenn.). Home: Route 2 Box 449 Rockwood TN 37854 Office: PO Box 108 Rockwood St Rockwood TN 37854

JOHNSON, CHERYL ANN, coll. ofcl.; b. Newark, June 27, 1949; d. Alvin Norwood and Lillian Marie (Jones) Kearney; B.S., U. Cin., 1971; M.Ed., Tex. So. U., 1977; m. Albert Alphonso Johnson, Jr., Dec. 29, 1973; 1 son, Albert Alphonso Johnson III. Bilingual fin. aid officer Essex County Coll., Newark, 1972-73; student fin. aid asst. Houston Community Coll., 1974—. Mem. planning com. Houston Conf., Nat. Scholarship Service and Fund for Negro Students, 1976. Mem. Am., Tex. personnel and guidance assns., Assn. Non-White Concerns, Tex. Assn. Non-White Concerns, Nat., Tex., S.W. assns. student fin. aid adminstrs., Tex. Assn. Coll. and Univ. Student Personnel Adminstrs., Jr. Coll. Student Personnel Assn. Tex., Alpha

Kappa Alpha. Home: 15107 Steeple Chase Missouri City TX 77459 Office: 320 Jackson Hill Houston TX 77007

JOHNSON, CHRISTINE CURRIN, educator; b. Memphis, Mar. 26, 1938; d. Jacob Russell and Florence Wardell (Simons) Currin; B.A., LeMoyne-Owen Coll., 1959; M.Ed., Memphis State U., 1969, postgrad., 1972-73; m. Carl Everett Johnson, June 5, 1959; children—Carl Everett, Cheryl Cerise. Tchr. dance Bethlehem Center, Memphis, Tenn., 1956-64; elementary tchr. Caldwell Sch., Memphis, 1959-61, Norris Sch., Memphis, 1961-71, Grant Sch., Memphis, 1971-73, Leath Elementary Sch., Memphis, 1973-74; curriculum tchr. Leath and Grant Schs., 1974-75; curriculum writer CABLECOM, Memphis, 1975-77; elementary sch. tchr. Orleans Sch., Memphis, 1977-79; acting prin. Levi Elem. Sch., 1980—; adminstrv. aid Westwood High Sch.; tchr. summer program for gifted Alcy Elementary Sch., Memphis, summer 1971. Leader, Brownie Troop, Memphis; ser. unit chmn. Met. Ch. unit Girl Scouts U.S.A.; active Overton High Sch. Band Boosters, Orleans Elementary Sch. PTA, Suzuki Talent Edn. Assn. of Memphis; dir. children's choir Met. Ch. Named Tchr. of the Yr., Norris Elementary Sch., 1968-69. Mem. Nat., Tenn., Memphis edn. assns., Assn. for Supervision and Curriculum Devel., Tenn (treas.), Memphis (v.p. S.W. area) assns. childhood edn., Assn. for Childhood Edn. Internat., Memphis Area Conf. of Black Educators, Internat. Black Writers Conf., NAACP, YMCA. Baptist.

JOHNSON, CLARICE WELLS, coll. adminstr.; b. Gaston County, N.C., Feb. 26, 1920; d. Christopher Sylvester and Lorena Dora (Nance) Wells; B.A., Presbyn. Coll., 1941; M.A., U. S.C., 1966, Ph.D., 1970; m. Robert Edgar Johnson, June 20, 1942; children—Janet Elizabeth, Robert Edgar, Thomas Gary. Tchr. secondary schs. S.C., 1941-59; sec., bookkeeper Laurens County Sch. Dist. 56, S.C., 1959-64; instr. guidance Presbyn. Coll., Clinton, 1964-65, asst. dir. career and personal counseling center, 1965-66, dir., 1967—. Mem. grants com. Bailey Found., Clinton, 1974—; mem. Ch. Employed Women's Com. Presbyn. Ch. U.S., 1974—; bd. dirs. S.C. Ct. Update, 1974—. Named woman of year Civic Clubs Clinton, 1966. Mem. Internat. Assn. Counseling Services (dir. 1972-76), Bus. and Profl. Women's Club (pres. Clinton 1966-68, 71-73, bd. dirs. ednl. found. S.C. 1972-76, sec.-treas. 1974-76), S.C. Mental Health Assn., Am. Coll. Personnel Assn. (pres. S.C. br. 1969-70), Nat. Vocat. Guidance Assn. (pres. S.C. br. 1977—), Assn. Measurement and Evaluation in Guidance (dir. S.C. br. 1976-77), S.C. Personnel and Guidance Assn. (dir. 1976—), Delta Kappa Gamma (pres. Epsilon chpt. 1977—). Home: 207 W Walnut St Clinton SC 29325

JOHNSON, CLARK ALEXANDER, physician; b. Denison, Tex., Jan. 10, 1925; s. Clark Alexander and Estelle (Ivie) J.; student U. Tex., Austin, 1944; M.D., U. Tex., Galveston, 1948; m. Dorothy Marie Webb, Mar. 3, 1953; children—Craig Alexander, Mary Elizabeth, Bruce Allen. Intern, Denver Gen. Hosp., Denver, 1949; resident in pediatric surgery, Children's Orthopedic Hosp., Seattle, 1951; pvt. practice, Sweetwater, Tex., 1951-76; asso. prof. family practice Tex. Tech. U. Med. Sch., Lubbock, 1976—, dir. family practice residency program, 1977—. Served to lt. M.C., USNR, 1949-50, 53-54. Diplomate Am. Bd. Family Practice. Mem. AMA, Am. Acad. Family Physicians, Soc. Tchrs. Family Medicine, Am. Soc. Abdominal Surgeons, Tex. Med. Assn., Tex. Pediatrics Soc. Mem. Christian Ch. (Disciples of Christ). Office: Family Practice Tex Tech Univ Med Sch Lubbock TX 79430

JOHNSON, CLIFTON HERMAN, historian-archivist; b. Griffin, Ga., Sept. 13, 1921; s. John and Pearl (Parrish) J.; student U. Conn., 1943-44; B.A., U. N.C., 1948, Ph.D. 1959; M.A. U. Chgo., 1949; postgrad. U. Wis., 1951; m. Rosemary Brunst, Aug. 2, 1960; children—Charles, Robert, Virginia. Tutor, LeMoyne Coll., Memphis, 1950-53, asst. prof., 1953-56, prof., 1960-61, 63-66; asst. prof. East Carolina Coll., 1958-59; asst. librarian and archivist Fisk U., 1961-63; dir. Amistad Research Center, New Orleans, 1966—. Dir., Nat. Com. Against Discrimination in Housing, 1967—. Served with AUS, 1940-45. Mem. So. Hist. Assn., Soc. Am. Archivists, Assn. for Study Negro Life and History, Orgn. Am. Historians, Nat. Assn. Human Rights Workers, Nat. Cath. Conf. for Inter-racial Justice. Author: (with Carroll Barber) The American Negro: A Selected and Annotated Bibliography for High Schools and Junior Colleges, 1968. Editor: God Struck Me Dead: Religious Conversions and Experiences and Autobiographies of Ex-Slaves, 1969. Home: 6910 Manchester St New Orleans LA 70126 Office: Dillard U New Orleans LA 70122

JOHNSON, CLINTON CHARLES, dentist; b. Hector, Minn., Aug. 15, 1927; s. Oscar Theodore and Mayme (Burris) J.; B.A. in Chemistry, Macalester Coll., 1953; B.S. in Dentistry, U. Minn., 1957, D.D.S., 1957, M.S. in Dentistry, 1965; m. Irene Julia Gross, July 19, 1952; children—Deborah, Kent, Constance, Cynthia, Mark. Staff dentist VA Hosp., Mpls., 1960-65; oral pathologist Armed Forces Inst. Pathology, Washington, 1965-67; chief dental service VA Hosp., Buffalo, 1967-72, VA Hosp., Dallas, 1972-74, VA Outpatient Clinic, Lubbock, Tex., 1974—. Instr., U. Minn. at Mpls., 1962-65; asso. prof. State U. N.Y. at Buffalo, 1967-72, Coll. Dentistry, Baylor U., Dallas, 1972-74, S.W. Med. Sch., Dallas, 1972-74; mil. cons. Surgeon Gen. USAF. Served with AUS and USAF, 1946-47, 50-51, 58-60. Diplomate Am. Bd. Oral Pathology. Fellow Am. Coll. Dentists, Am. Acad. Oral Pathology; mem. Am. Dental Assn. Contbr. profl. jours. Home: 4713 78th St Lubbock TX 79424 Office: VA Outpatient Clinic 1205 Texas Ave Lubbock TX 79401

JOHNSON, CONE, physician, educator; b. Eastland, Tex., Nov. 20, 1926; s. Earle Clay and Eloise (Trigg) J.; B.S., North Tex. State U., 1949; M.D., U. Tex., Galveston, 1954; m. Patricia Zeller, Oct. 20, 1956; children—Deborah Lynn, Cynthia Kay, Barbara Anne. Intern John Sealy Hosp., Galveston, 1954-55; resident medicine U. Tex. Med. Br. Hosps., 1955-58; commd. 1st lt. M.C., U.S. Air Force, 1956, advanced through grades to maj., 1962; ret., 1963; mem. sr. staff Scott-White Clinic, 1963-68; practice medicine specializing in respiratory therapy and environmental diseases, Abilene, Tex., 1968-69, 70; asso. Cardiopulmonary Inst., Meth. Hosp., Dallas, 1969-70; clin. asst. prof. medicine U. Tex. Southwestern Med. Sch., Dallas, 1969—; clin. asso. prof. medicine Tex. Tech U. Sch. Medicine, 1974—; med. dir. respiratory therapy service and pulmonary physiology labs. West Tex. Med. Center Hosp., Abilene, 1970—, Abilene State Sch., Tex. Dept. Mental Health and Retardation, 1971-73, Rolling Plains Meml. Hosp., Sweetwater, Tex., 1970—, Cox Meml. Hosp., Abilene, 1970-75, Med. Center Meml. Hosp., Big Spring, Tex., 1973-74, Root Meml. Hosp., Colorado City, Tex., 1970—, Shepperd Meml. Hosp., Burnet, Tex., 1976—; med. dir. West Tex. Community Sch. Respiratory Tech., 1971—; cons. in pulmonary physiology VA Hosp., Big Spring, 1968—. Dir. Respiratory Therapy Assos., Abilene. Bd. dirs. West Tex. Med. Center Research Found., 1968. Served with USNR, 1943-46. Diplomate Am. Bd. Internal Medicine with subsplty. pulmonary diseases. Fellow A.C.P., Am. Coll. Chest Physicians (pres. Tex. chpt.); mem. AAAS, Research Engring Soc. Am., Am. Coll. Sports Medicine, A.M.A., Am. Fedn. Clin. Research, Am. Thoracic Soc., Am. Heart Assn. (dir.), Aero Medics of Tex., Central Tex. Research Soc., N.Y. Acad. Scis., Mu Delta (award for outstanding intern 1955). Contbr. articles to profl. jours. Home: 770 Sayles Dr Abilene TX 79605 Office: 1026 N 21st St Abilene TX 79601

JOHNSON, CONSTANCE HOWIE, ednl. adminstr.; b. Winston-Salem, N.C., Oct. 29, 1939; d. Ulysses and Susie (Morrison) Howie; B.A., N.C. Central U., 1961; M.S., N.C. Agrl. and Tech. U., 1966; PH.D., So. Ill. U., 1973; m. Victor Johnson, Jr., June 9, 1962; 1 dau., La Tanja Kim. Dormitory counselor State Tng. Sch. Girls, Kinston, N.C., 1961; tchr. Winston-Salem/Forsyth County Schs.(N.C.), 1962-65, social worker, 1966-67; counselor Winston-Salem State U., 1967-71, dir. counseling services, 1973-78, dir. div. gen. studies, 1978—; asst. to dean undergrad. advisement edn. So. Ill. U., Carbondale, 1971-72, dir. residence halls, 1972-73; sch. psychologist North Wilksboro (N.C.) City Schs., 1974-75. Treas. Winston-Salem/Forsyth County Schs. PTA Council, 1975-79; dir. St. Paul United Methodist Ch. Vacation Bible Sch., 1975-76; bd. dirs. Bethlehem Center, Inc. Mem. Am., N.C. personnel and guidance assns., Assn. Non-White Concerns, Council Basic Edn., N.C. Assn. Developmental Studies, Assn. Black Psychologists (chmn. membership N.C. 1975—), So. Coll. Personnel Assn., Guys and Dolls, Alpha Kappa Alpha. Methodist. Club: Altrusa. Home: 2315 Manchester St Winston-Salem NC 27105

JOHNSON, DAVE TOBIN, ins. co. exec.; b. Pensacola, Fla., May 2, 1909; s. Joseph I. and Annie (Tobin) J.; grad. parochial schs.; m. Mary Catherine Comforter, Dec. 16, 1937; children—Mary Catherine (Mrs. James R. Thompson), Patricia Ann (Mrs. Gregory Deal), David Tobin Jr. With Fisher-Brown, Inc., Pensacola, 1923—, asst. sec., 1932-39, v.p., 1939-50, exec. v.p., 1950-55, pres., 1955-75, chmn. bd., 1975—; dir. Citizens & Peoples Nat. Bank. Mem. adv. bd. Bapt. Hosp. Served with USMCR, 1943-45. Named Boss of Year, Bus. Man of Year, 1963; recipient Kiwanis Cup for Outstanding Civic Achievement, 1963. Fellow U. West Fla.; mem. Pensacola Fire and Casualty Agts. (past pres.), Nat. (past chmn. nat. advt. com., fidelity, surety com., v.p., past mem. exec. com., past pres.), Fla. (past pres.) assns. ins. agts., So. Agts. Conf. (past chmn.). Democrat. Roman Catholic. Rotarian, Elk, K.C. (4 deg.). Clubs: Pensacola Country, Yacht, Executive. Home: 1517 N 19th Ave Pensacola FL 32503 Office: Box 711 Pensacola FL 32593

JOHNSON, DAVID HEYWOOD, engr., physicist; b. Coral Gables, Fla., Nov. 22, 1952; s. Loftin and Melvene (Young) J.; A.A., Fla. State U., 1972; B.S. with high honors, U. Fla., 1974; S.M., M.I.T., 1976, Sc.D., 1978. Teaching asst. dept. nuclear engring. M.I.T., 1974-76, research asst., 1977-78; grad. research asst., solid state sci. div. Argonne Nat. Lab., 1976; fellow Adv. Com. on Reactor Safeguards, Washington, 1979—. Gen. Electric Found. fellow, 1976-77. Mem. AAAS, Am. Phys. Soc., N.Y. Acad. Scis., Sigma Xi, Tau Beta Pi, Sigma Tau Sigma, Phi Kappa Phi, Phi Eta Sigma. Methodist. Contbr. articles to profl. jours. Home: 2111 Jefferson Davis Hwy 1207-S Arlington VA 22202

JOHNSON, DAVID HORACE, ednl. adminstr.; b. Crowley, La., Dec. 1, 1925; s. Joseph Andrew and Rosa (Bell) J.; B.A., Lane Coll., Jackson, Tenn., 1949; M.S., U. Wis., Madison, 1954; Ph.D. in Ednl. Adminstrn., Tex. A&M U., 1972; m. Gladys Mae Alluns, Dec. 16, 1960; children—Hortense, LaRose. Instr., Richwood High Sch., Monroe, La., 1949-50; prin. Swartz Elem. Sch., Monroe, 1950-54, Carver Elem.-Jr. High Sch., Monroe, 1954-61; asst. prof. edn. Tex. Coll., Tyler, 1961-64, dean of students, 1962-73, spl. adminstrv. asst. to pres., 1965, chmn. dept. edn., prof., 1969—, dir. coll. prep. clinics, 1966, 67, 70, 71, mem. vis. team Tex. Edn. Agy., 1974, dir. self studies, 1974, 78; cons. workshop for counselors Prairie View A&M Coll., 1972. Mem. Tyler Human Relations Council, 1970-72; bd. dirs. Campfire Girls, 1978—. Served with inf. U.S. Army, 1944-46; NATOUSA, ETO. Ford found. grantee, 1969-70; recipient award Lane Coll., 1973; cert. of appreciation City of Tyler, 1972. Mem. Am. Assn. Higher Edn., Am. Personnel and Guidance Assn., Nat. Assn. Student Personnel Adminstrs., Tex. Assn. Colls. Tchr. Edn., Tex. State Tchrs. Assn., Tex. Assn. Tchr. Educators, Phi Delta Kappa, Alpha Kappa Mu, Kappa Alpha Psi. Democrat. Methodist Episcopal. Home: 1429 Northridge Dr Tyler TX 75702 Office: 2404 N Grand Ave Tyler TX 75702

JOHNSON, DAVID L(IVINGSTONE), engring. ednl. adminstr.; b. Gustavus, Ohio, Feb. 17, 1915; s. David Charles and Margaret (Delaney) J.; A.B., Berea Coll., 1936; M.A., State U. Ia., 1938, B.S. in Elec. Engring., 1942; M.S., Okla. State U., 1950, Ph.D., 1957; m. Eugenia Gibson McQuarie, Jan. 23, 1954. Instr. U.S. Naval Tng. Sch., Okla. State U., 1942-44; field engr. Airborne Coordinating Group, 1944-45; instr. Spartan Sch. Aeros., Tulsa, 1945-48; asst. prof. Okla. State U., 1948-55; prof., head dept. elec. engring. La. Tech U., Ruston, 1955—. Cons. automatic controls. Registered profl. engr., La., Okla. Mem. AAAS, IEEE, Am. Soc. Engring. Edn., Assn. Computing Machinery, Nat. Soc. Profl. Engrs., Soc. Indsl. and Applied Math., AAUP, Am. Soc. Info. Sci., Instrument Soc. Am., Sigma Xi, Eta Kappa Nu, Phi Kappa Phi, Pi Mu Epsilon, Omicron Delta Kappa, Upsilon Pi Epsilon, Tau Beta Pi. Home: 1604 Valley Dr Ruston LA 71270

JOHNSON, DAVID MARK, internist; b. Springfield, Mo., Nov. 29, 1940; s. Ralph James and Hazel Maurine (Bryant) J.; student Ark. State Coll., 1958-59, U. Ark., 1960; M.D., U. Ark., 1965; m. Adonna Kaye New, Dec. 22, 1966; children—Adonna Daye. Intern, U. Hosp., Little Rock, 1965-66, resident in medicine, 1966-69; practice medicine specializing in internal medicine Searcy (Ark.) Med. Center, 1969—; exec. com. White County Hosp., Searcy, 1973-76, chief of staff, 1975; chest cons. Ark. Health Dept., 1973—; med. advisor Bd. Govs., SSS, 1973. Served to maj. Army N.G., 1971-73. Diplomate Am. Bd. Internal Medicine. Fellow A.C.P., Am. Coll. Chest Physicians, Am. Coll. Cardiology; mem. White County, Ark. med. socs., Ark. Thoracic Soc., Am., Ark. quarter horse assns., Am., Ark. hereford assns., Democrat. Mem. Ch. of Christ. Contbr. articles to med. jours. Home: Route 3 Hwy 36 W Searcy AR 72143 Office: 2900 Hawkins St Searcy AR 72143

JOHNSON, DAVID PITTMAN, educator; b. Nashville, July 29, 1936; s. Calvin Leonard and Charles Bernice (Cagle) J.; B.S., Huntingdon Coll., 1963; M.S.W., Tulane U., 1966, D.S.W., 1972; m. Edna Marie Wooten; 1 son, Michael David; m. 2d, Linda June Russell. Clin. social worker Montgomery Mental Health Center, Montgomery, Ala., 1966-69; dir. Christian Counseling Center, New Orleans, 1971-72; dir. outpatient services Montgomery (Ala.) Area Mental Health Authority, 1972-75; pvt. practice psychotherapy, Montgomery, 1974-75; asst. prof. social work U. Ala., 1975—. George Wheeler Meml. scholar, 1962-63, 64-66, 66, 69-72. Mem. Am. Coll. Heraldry (bd. govs 1972—), Heraldry Soc. (Eng.) Haraldry Soc. Scotland, Nat. Soc. SAR (nat. geneal. com.), St. Andrew's Soc. of Montgomery, Culedonian Soc. Ala., Clan Johnston-e of Am. Democrat. Mem. Ch. of Christ. Editor: Armiger's News. Home: 56 Brookhaven Tuscaloosa AL 35405 Office: PO Box 1935 University AL 35486

JOHNSON, DEWEY E(DWARD), dentist; b. Charleston, S.C., Mar. 19, 1935; s. Dewey Edward and Mabel (Momeier) J.; A.B. in Geology, U. N.C., 1957, D.D.S., 1961. Practice dentistry, Charleston, 1964—, asso. to Stanley H. Karesh, D.D.S., 1970-76. Served to lt. USNR, 1961-63. Mem. Royal Soc. Health, Charleston C. of C. (cruise ship com. 1969), ADA, Charleston Dental Soc., Hibernian Soc., Charleston Museum, Internat. Platform Assn., Phi Kappa Sigma, Sigma Gamma Epsilon, Psi Omega. Congregationalist. Club: Optimist. Home: 142 S Battery Charleston SC 29401 Office: Ashley House Suite 1-F Charleston SC 29401

JOHNSON, DORIS BETHEA, educator; b. Vernon, Fla., Feb. 19, 1930; d. Millard D. and Katie Virena (Roulhac) Bethea; B.S., Fla. A&M U., 1950, M.S., 1951; postgrad. Tuskegee Inst., Fla. State U.; m. Henry L. Johnson, Dec. 28, 1952; children—Valerie Diane, Leisa Virginia. Tchr. high schs. and jr. coll. in Fla., 1951-73; asst. prof. English, Gulf Coast Community Coll., Panama City, Fla., 1973—; cons. in field. Mem. Bay County Democratic Exec. Com., 1976—; pres. Bay Dem. Women, 1975-79; mem. Bay County Econ. Devel. Com., 1976—. Lewis scholar, 1946; grantee Internat. Paper Co., Rosenwald Jr. Coll.; recipient Outstanding Service award Bay County Dem. Women, 1979. Mem. Fla. Council Tchrs. English, Fla. Assn. Community Colls., Zeta Phi Beta. Democrat. Methodist. Club: Order Eastern Star. Home: 825 Bay Ave PO Box 453 Panama City FL 32401 Office: Gulf Coast Community Coll W Hwy 98 Panama City FL 32401

JOHNSON, DOUGLAS ELLIOTT, physician, educator; b. San Antonio, Sept. 28, 1934; s. Max Edward and Elizabeth M. (McGehee) J.; B.A., Princeton, 1956; M.D., U. Tex. Med. Br., 1960; m. Gayle Mahan, Dec. 30, 1959; children—Michael, Max, George. Intern Toronto (Ont., Can.) Gen. Hosp., 1961; fellow Mayo Clinic, Rochester, Minn., 1962; resident U. Ia. Hosp., Iowa City, 1962-66; practice medicine specializing in urology, Houston, 1968-79; head dept. urology U. Tex. System Cancer Center, M.D. Anderson Hosp. and Tumor Inst., Houston, 1968—, asst. prof., 1968-70, asso. prof., 1970-74, prof., 1974—. Served to capt., USAF, 1966-68. Diplomate Am. Bd. Urology. Mem. A.C.S., Am. Fertility Soc., Am. Geriatric Soc., Am., So., Tex. med. assns., Am. Radium Soc., Am., Houston urol. socs., Harris County (Tex.) Med. Soc., Soc. Air Force Clin. Surgeons, Soc. Univ. Urologists, Houston Surg. Soc., German Club. Mason (Shriner). Clubs: San Antonio Country, Conpus. Author: Testicular Tumors, 1972. Contbr. numerous articles to profl. jours. Home: 14210 Carolcrest St Houston TX 77024 Office: 6723 Bertner Ave Houston TX 77025

JOHNSON, EDD WILSON, hosp. adminstr.; b. New Middleton, Tenn., Sept. 23, 1911; s. James Frank and Lydia (Clark) J.; student Air U., 1946, LaSalle Law Sch., 1951; m. Ruby West, July 25, 1941; children—James David, Martha (Mrs. Martha Stephens), John Daniel. Commd. 2d lt., U.S. Air Force, 1930, advanced through grades to lt. col., 1953; personnel officer, 1945-50, air insp. mgmt. analysis, 1952-56; ret., 1959; adminstr. Miller County Hosp., Calquitt, Ga., 1967-69; adminstr. Worth County Hosp., Sylvester, Ga., 1969-73, Mitchell County Hosp., Camilla, Ga., 1973—. Chmn. bd. U.S. Civil Service Examiners in Northeast Air Procurement Dist., Boston, 1951. Licensed nursing home adminstr. Mem. Am. Legion, VFW. Clubs: Lions, Kiwanis. Home: Route 5 Colquitt GA 31737

JOHNSON, EDNA FAY HOGAN (MRS. LANDON CARTER JOHNSON, JR.), data processor; b. Tennyson, Tex., Aug. 23, 1923; d. Eddie H. and Mary Elizabeth (Hodges) Hogan; student San Angelo Coll., 1940-41; B.A., Howard Payne Coll., 1944; M.A., U. Tex., 1948; m. Landon Carter Johnson, Jr., Aug. 23, 1945; children—Robert Eugene, William Luke, John Michael. Prin., Tennyson Pub. Schs., 1942-43; instr. in math. Ranger (Tex.) Jr. Coll., 1943-44; tchr. math. Brownwood (Tex.) High Sch., 1944-45; asst. prof. math. Howard Payne Coll., Brownwood, 1945-54; data processing analyst Conoco, Inc., Ponca City, Okla., 1955-63, analyst ops. research, 1965-76, supervising analyst, 1976-78, asst. dir., 1978—; instr. data processing No. Okla. Coll., Tonkawa, 1963-65. Mem. SHARE, Inc. (math. programming mixed integer com. 1969-74). Pres. Mother's Club Ponca City Future Farmers of Am., 1968-69. Mem. Math. Assn. Am., AAUW, Assn. Computing Machinery, Alpha Chi. Democrat. Baptist. Home: 8 Woodlands Ponca City OK 74601 Office: Drawer 1267 Ponca City OK 74601

JOHNSON, EDWARD WILLIAM, mech. engr.; b. Chgo., May 3, 1909; s. Axel Edward and Hilda (Johansson) J.; B.S., Ill. Inst. Tech., 1934, B.S. in Mech. Engring., 1935; postgrad. Carnegie Inst. Tech., 1936-40, Mass. Inst. Tech., 1943, McGill U., 1950, George Washington, U., 1953-57; m. Irmgard Marie Zeisberg, Mar. 15, 1957; 1 son, Robert David. Jr. mech. engr. Internat. Harvester Co., Chgo., 1934-39; asst. insp. naval material U.S. Navy Dept., Pitts., 1939-40; asso. mech. engr. U.S. Army Ordnance, Balt., 1940-42; mech. engr., asst. chief vehicle devel. U.S. Army C.E., Ft. Belvoir, Va., 1946-47, chief engring. sect. climatic research, 1947-48; environmental engr. Bur. Yards and Docks, Washington, 1948-52, head research programming, 1953-57; mech. engr. U.S. Naval Weapons Lab., Dahlgren, Va. 1957-59; head engring. specifications U.S. Naval Weapons Plant, Washington, 1959-60; sr. engr., asst. chief procurement U.S. Bur. Pub. Rds., 1960-62; asst. chief postal lab., office research engring. U.S. Post Office Dept., Washington, 1962-71; v.p. Basic Testing Labs., Inc., Centreville, Va., 1971-72; program mgr. design and devel. Value Engring. Co., Alexandria, Va., 1972—; cons. mech. engr., 1971—. Served with USNR, 1943-46. Registered profl. engr., D.C. Mem. ASME, Am. Inst. Aeros. and Astronautics, Nat., D.C., Va. socs. profl. engrs., Soc. Automotive Engrs., Am. Ordnance Assn., Am. Polar Soc., Explorers Club, Swedish Hist. Soc. Mason (32 deg., Shriner). Contbr. articles to profl. jours. Home: 6944 Essex Ave Springfield VA 22150 Office: Springfield VA 22150

JOHNSON, ERRIC JASON, agrl. engr.; b. Cottonwood, Tex., Feb. 8, 1917; s. Leanerd J. and Leora Melinda (Earls) J.; B.S., Prairie View A&M Coll., 1947; postgrad. Tex. A&M U., 1960-61; M.S., Iowa State U., 1955; m. Thelma Lois Brown, Dec. 25, 1947. Tchr. vocat. agr., Omaha, Tex., 1947-52; instr. agr. Miss. Vocat. Coll., 1955-56; mem. faculty Prairie View A&M U. (Tex.), 1957—, now prof., head agrl. engring. Nat. adv. Baptist Student Movement. Served with U.S. Army Air Corps, 1942-46. Mem. Am. Soc. Agrl. Engrs. Democrat. Club: Optimist. Home: 105 Pine St Prairie View TX 77445 Office: Coll Agr Prairie View TX 77445

JOHNSON, EUGENE BAKER, ins. co. exec.; b. Greenville, N.C., June 2, 1947; s. Paul Eugene and Juanita (Brickhouse) J.; B.S. with honors, U. N.C., Charlotte, 1973; m. Vickie Lynn Crotts, June 7, 1969. Sr. acct. Haskins & Sells, Charlotte, N.C., 1973-76; controller The Shoe Show Inc., Kannapolis, N.C., 1976; treas. Johnson & Higgins Carolinas Inc., Charlotte, N.C., 1976—; lectr. in field. Vice-pres. U. N.C., Charlotte, Athletic Found., 1979-80; bd. dirs. Family and Childrens Service, Charlotte, 1979. Served to capt. U.S. Army, 1967-71. Decorated Army Commendation medal, Joint Services Commendation medal; C.P.A. Mem. U. N.C. Charlotte Alumni Assn. (pres. 1978-79), Charlotte C. of C. (chmn. task force on parks and recreation 1978-79), Am. Inst. C.P.A.'s, N.C. Assn. C.P.A.'s, Nat. Assn. Accts. Home: 920 Berkeley Ave Charlotte NC 28203 Office: Johnson & Higgins Carolinas Inc 1600 Southern Nat Center Charlotte NC 28202

JOHNSON, FIELDING HOLMES, chem. engr.; b. Baton Rouge, Dec. 15, 1934; s. Perry Mark and Oline Marie (Judice) J.; B.S. in Chem. Engring., La. State U., 1956; m. Mary Anna Jurgensen, July 19, 1958; children—Fielding, Stuart, Barton, Margaret Kelley. With plastics div. E.I. DuPont de Nemours & Co., Inc., Washington, W.Va.,

1956-61, Orange, Tex., 1961-66; production supt., constrn. mgr. Kaiser Aluminum & Chem. Corp., Gramercy, La., 1966-72; pres. Barber & Johnson, Inc., Cons. Engrs., Baton Rouge, 1972—. Served to capt. USAF, 1957-59. Registered profl. engr., La., Tex., Miss. Mem. Nat. Soc. Profl. Engrs., Am. Inst. Chem. Engrs. (former sec., exec. com. Baton Rouge sect. 1973-75), Cons. Engrs. Council La. (pres. 1979-80), La. Engring. Soc., Am. Cons. Engrs. Council, Delta Kappa Epsilon. Democrat. Roman Catholic. Clubs: Rotary (Baton Rouge), Aquatic (pres. 1971-72). Home: 961 Tifton Dr Baton Rouge LA 70815 Office: 2147 Government St Baton Rouge LA 70806

JOHNSON, FLOYD DRAYTON, supt. schs.; b. Polk County, N.C., Oct. 10, 1916; B.S. in Agr., Clemson (S.C.) Coll., 1939, M.S. in Agr., 1960; married; 2 children. Tchr. agr. York (S.C.) Sch. Dist I, 1939-65, vocat. dir., tchr. agr., 1966-75, supt., 1975—; agrl. cons. manpower dir. S.C. Com. for Tech. Edn., Columbia, 1965-66. Past mem. Pres. Kennedy's Panel Consultants for Vocat. Edn. Mem. S.C. Agrl. Tchrs. Assn. (past pres.), Nat. Vocat. Agrl. Tchrs. Assn. (life, past pres.), Am. Vocat. Assn. (life, past pres.), S.C. Vocat. Assn., York County Edn. Assn. (past pres.). Home: PO Box 277 York SC 29745 Office: PO Box 770 York SC 29745

JOHNSON, FRANK MINIS, JR., fed. judge; b. Winston County, Ala., Oct. 30, 1918; s. Frank Minis and Alabama (Long) J.; student Massey Bus. Coll., 1937; LL.B., U. Ala., 1943, LL.D. (hon.), 1977; LL.D. (hon.), U. Notre Dame, 1973, Princeton U., 1974, Boston U., 1979; J.D. (hon.), St. Michael's Coll., Winooski, Vt., 1975; m. Ruth Jenkins, Jan. 16, 1938; 1 son, James Curtis (dec.). Admitted to Ala. bar, 1943; mem. firm Curtis, Maddox & Johnson, Jasper, Ala., 1946-53; U.S. atty. No. Dist. Ala., Birmingham, 1953-55; judge U.S. Dist. Ct., Middle Dist. Ala., Montgomery, 1955-79; judge U.S. Ct. Appeals 5th Circuit, Montgomery, 1979—; mem. rev. com. Jud. Conf., 1969-78, jud. ethics com., 1978—, spl. com. habeas corpus, 1971-78. Served with AUS, 1943-46. Decorated Purple Heart with 1 oak leaf cluster, Bronze Star, Combat Infantryman's badge. Mem. Ala. Acad. Honor. Office: PO Box 35 Montgomery AL 36101

JOHNSON, FREDERICK DEAN, former food co. exec., cons.; b. Shreve, Ohio, Feb. 27, 1911; s. Harry H. and Grace Marcella (Cammarn) J.; A.B., Coll. Wooster (Ohio), 1935; m. Haulwen Elizabeth Richey, June 19, 1937; children—Frederick Dean II, Mary Haulwen, Grace Elizabeth. Dir. research Bama Co. (now Bama Products Borden Foods div. Borden Inc.), Birmingham, Ala., 1961-65, dir. research, Houston, 1965-76, dir. product devel. and tech. adviser, 1976-78, cons., 1978—. U.S. del. FAO/WHO Codex Alimentarius Commn. Processed Fruits and Vegetables, 1973, 74, 75. Bd. dirs. Afton Oaks Civic Club, 1967-70. Mem. Internat. Jelly and Preserve Assn. (chmn. quality control adv. com. 1969-73, chmn. standards com. 1973-76, citation and plaque 1974), Inst. Food Technologtists (charter), Am. Chem. Soc. (past sec., chmn. Wooster sect.), AAAS. Republican. Presbyterian (ruling elder). Home: 4546 Shetland Ln Houston TX 77027 Office: 5501 Clinton Dr Houston TX 77020

JOHNSON, GARY LYNN, environ. engr.; b. Durham, N.C., Aug. 18, 1947; s. Robert William and Grace Christine (Ellis) J.; B.S., N.C. State U., 1969, M.S., 1980; m. Phyllis Eva Strickland, July 28, 1973; 1 son, Griffin Lee. With Duke Power Co., Charlotte, N.C., 1969-70, project engr., 1970-74; project officer U.S. EPA, Indsl. Environ. Research Lab., Research Triangle Park, N.C., 1974—; EPA program mgr. Environ. Assessment Data Systems, 1978—; EPA rep. Nat. Fuel Cell Coordinating Group. Aubrey Lee Brooks scholar, 1965; recipient Fed. Womens Program Service award, 1976. Mem. Am. Nuclear Soc. (vice chmn. local sect. 1976-77, chmn. 1977-78), Mecklenburg Jaycees (v.p. 1972-74, dir. 1970-72). Republican. Baptist. Contbr. articles in field to profl. jours. Home: 1524 Cone Ave Apex NC 27502 Office: US EPA Mail Drop 63 Research Triangle Park NC 27711

JOHNSON, GARY RAY, computer systems co. exec.; b. Knoxville, Tenn., Oct. 1, 1949; s. Raymond Earl and Hazel Lee (McAfee) J.; B.S. in Chem. Engring., U. Tenn., 1970; postgrad. U. South Ala., 1971, U. Richmond, 1973; m. Judy Carol Lewis, Apr. 24, 1971; children—Samuel, Robin. Project engr. Internat. Paper Co., Mobile, Ala., 1970-73; process engr. Philip Morris Co., Richmond, Va., 1973-74; software/control engr. Measurex Systems, Atlanta, 1974-77, field tech. mgr., 1977, regional tech. mgr., 1977—. Mem. TAPPI (sec. quality control com.). Contbg. author process control sect. Pulp and Paper Manufacture Textbook, 3d edit. Office: 2965 Flowers Rd S Suite 135 Atlanta GA 30341

JOHNSON, GARY REID, business exec.; b. Ingram Branch, W.Va., Feb. 23, 1934; s. Ernest Reid and Sophrona Edyth (Tredway) J.; Mus.B., U. Mich., 1954, M.B.A., 1956, M.A., 1958. Sponsored research asst. bus. mgr. U. Mich., 1958-65; spl. asst. to dean U. Calif. at Davis, 1965-69; asst. to vice chancellor for health scis. U. Calif. at San Diego, 1969-74; dir. budget and finance Health Scis. Center, Tex. Tech U., 1974-76, exec. dir. bus. and finance, 1976-79; pres. SERGJCO, Inc., 1979—. Cons. Hawaii Legis. Coms. on Higher Edn., 1968-72. Fellow Am. Acad. Med. Adminstrs.; mem. Acad. Mgmt., Acad. Polit. Sci., Am. Acad. Polit. and Social Sci., Am. Soc. Public Adminstrn., Am. Assn. Sch. Adminstrs., Am. Hosp. Assn., Assn. Supervision and Curriculum Devel., Nat. Assn. Coll. and Univ. Bus. Officers, So. Assn. Coll. and Univ. Bus. Officers, Assn. Am. Med. Colls., S.A.R., Sons Confederate Vets., Soc. Colonial Wars, Internat. Soc. Philos. Enquiry, Intertel, Mensa, Tau Kappa Epsilon, Alpha Kappa Psi, Phi Mu Alpha, Kappa Kappa Psi. Contbr. articles to profl. jours. Home: PO Box 6545 Santa Barbara CA 93111 also PO Box 5430 Lubbock TX 79417

JOHNSON, GARY WAYNE, elec. engr.; b. Covington, Okla., Oct. 17, 1940; s. John D. and Geraldine Bernice (Johnson) J.; B.S. in Elec. Engring., Okla. State U., 1964; M.B.A., U. Houston at Clear Lake City, 1979; m. Coe Ann Swift, Aug. 24, 1963; children—Jeffrey Wayne, Gregory Scott, Krista Michelle. With NASA, Houston, 1964—, former group leader power control and lighting, head equipment and installation sect., space shuttle elec. power distbn. WBS mgr., subsystem mgr. Skylab Command and Service Modules, 1972, mem. Apollo-Soyuz test project working group, 1972-75, now dep. br. chief flight control div.; mem. test team USSR Baikonour Space Launch Complex, 1975—; mem. Apollo 204 fire investigation; leader Apollo 13 investigation elec. team; mem. lunar landing test accident bd.; mem. wire investigation team. Active Boy Scouts Am. Recipient Hamilton Watch award, 1964; Sustained Superior Performance award NASA, 1965, Superior Achievement award, 1970; certificate of commendation, 1971, NASA Exceptional Service medal, 1974, certificate of recognition, 1975. Mem. IEEE, Tex. Soc. Profl. Engrs., Eta Kappa Nu, Sigma Tau, Phi Kappa Phi, Lambda Chi Alpha. Lutheran (bd. stewardship 1970-71, chmn. stewards 1971-73, mem. ch. council 1971-73; chmn. bd. elders 1975, mem. 1974—). Contbr. reports, articles, revs. to profl. lit. Home: 16443 Havenpark Dr Houston TX 77059 Office: Nasa Rd 1 Houston TX 77058

JOHNSON, GEORGE, JR., physician; b. Wilmington, N.C., Apr. 6, 1926; s. George W. and Evelyn (Hill) J.; B.S., U. N.C., 1948, certificate medicine, 1950; M.D., Cornell U., 1952; m. Marian Patterson Ritchie, July 1, 1950; children—Sally Hope, George William, David Ritchie, Robert Hill. Intern, resident surgery N.Y. Hosp., 1952-59; pvt. surg. practice, 1959-62; asst. prof. to prof., chief div. vascular surgery U. N.C., Chapel Hill, 1962—, Roscoe B.G. Cowper distinguished professorship in surgery, 1973—, also vice chmn. dept. surgery, 1977—; chmn. adv. com. N.C. Emergency Med. Services; mem. stroke council Am. Heart Assn., 1977—. Served to 1st lt. inf., AUS, 1944-46. Mem. Univ. Assn. Emergency Med. Services (pres. 1974), A.C.S. (pres. N.C. chpt. 1975, mem. com. on trauma 1974, exec. com. 1977, chmn. N.C. com., 1972, 77), So. Assn. Vascular Surgery (exec. council 1978), Durham-Orange County Med. Soc. (pres. 1971), Am., So. surg. assns. Presbyterian. (deacon 1969-72). Club: Rotary (Chapel Hill). Contbr. articles to profl. jours., chpts. to books. Home: 410 Westwood Dr Chapel Hill NC 27514

JOHNSON, GEORGE EDWARD, ins. cons.; b. St. Joseph, Mo., Nov. 9, 1905; s. George E. and Minnie (Adams) J.; A.B., U. Nebr., 1928, LL.B. magna cum laude, 1929; m. Elizabeth Durisek, Jan. 3, 1930; children—George Edward, III, Robert Alan, Susan Elizabeth. Owner, operator sta. WLAF, Lincoln, Nebr., 1920-29; sec.-treas. Econ. Bridge Assn., Lincoln, 1924-29, Lincoln Sch. Aviation, 1926-29; admitted to N.Y. bar, 1930; asso. firm Root, Clark, Buckner, Howland & Ballantine, N.Y.C., 1929-35; from atty. to v.p., gen. counsel Tchrs. Ins. & Annuity Assn., N.Y.C., 1939-55; v.p., gen. counsel Coll. Retirement Equities Fund, N.Y.C., 1952-55; pres. Variable Annuity Life Ins. Co. Am., Washington, 1955-56; pres., chmn. Equity Annuity Life Ins. Co., Washington, 1956-59; trustee, mem. exec. com., chmn. ins. com., mem. long range planning com., v.p. Nat. Health and Welfare Retirement Assn., Inc., 1964-65, acting pres., 1965-66; trustee Health and Welfare Life Ins. Assn., Inc., 1966-72, acting pres., 1966; investment investment adv. com. TVA Retirement System, 1957; cons. variable annuities numerous ins. cos. including Met. Life Ins. Co., 1967-69, N.Y. Life Ins. Co., 1969-70. Bd. dirs. Nat. Commn. on Aging, 1950's; mem. 1st and 3d White House Confs. on Aging. C.L.U. Fellow Life Office Mgmt. Assn., Gerontol. Soc. (founding); mem. Order of Coif, Phi Delta Phi, Delta Sigma Rho, Phi Gamma Delta. Author: Variable Annuities, 1961; The Variable Annuity, 1967. Address: 448 Plumhollow Ln Maitland FL 32751

JOHNSON, GEORGE EDWIN, ret. otolaryngologist; b. Tennille, Ala., Mar. 30, 1914; s. Joseph Macon and Eunice Clyde (Hildreth) J.; A.B., U. Ala., 1935; M.D., U. Chgo., 1940; certificate N.Y. U. Postgrad. Med. Sch., 1948; m. Essie Melba Toney, May 24, 1941 (dec. Dec. 1965); children—Judith Ann, Sue Johnson Adkinson, Patricia Johnson Wolf; m. 2d, Agnes Hilda Burkett, June 18, 1966. Intern, Charity Hosp. of La., New Orleans, 1940-41; resident Univ. Hosp., Birmingham, Ala., 1948-50; gen. practice medicine, Auburn, Ala., 1945-47; practice medicine, specializing in otolaryngology, Dothan, Ala., 1950-76; mem. staff S.E. Ala. Gen. Hosp. Served to lt. col. M.C., AUS, 1941-45. Decorated Air medal. Diplomate Am. Bd. Otolaryngology. Fellow A.C.S., Am. Acad. Otolaryngology and Ophthalmology (inactive); mem. Med. Assn. State Ala., Houston County Med. Soc. (pres. 1954). Home: Route 7 Box 113 Dothan AL 36301

JOHNSON, GEORGE LEE, health ins. co. exec.; b. Sumter, S.C., Nov. 10, 1945; s. Robert Musco and Ila Lee (Dority) J.; B.A., Furman U., 1968; postgrad. U. S.C.; m. Anita Jane Grossman, 1979. Dir. pub. info. Furman U., Greenville, S.C., 1969-70; pub. relations mgr. Liberty Corp., Greenville, 1970-77; mgr. media/advt. Nancy Stevenson for lt. gov. State of S.C., Columbia, 1977-78; asst. v.p. communications Blue Cross and Blue Shield of S.C., Columbia, 1978—; cons. in field. Bd. dirs. Greenville Urban League, 1971-73; exec. council and exec. com. S.C. Democratic party, 1974-78; chmn. adv. council Greenville Hosp. System, 1975-76; chmn. bd. Vol. Greenville, 1976-77. Served with USAF, 1968. Mem. Pub. Relations Soc. Am., Advt. Fedn. Columbia, S.C. Press Assn., S.C. Broadcasters Assn. Home: 1825 Saint Julian Pl Columbia SC 29204 Office: Blue Cross and Blue Shield of SC Columbia SC 29219

JOHNSON, GERALD FREDERICK ROSS, indsl. engr.; b. Knoxville, Tenn., Jan. 30, 1930; s. Everett Enos and Katherine Cecelia (Long) J.; B.S. in Indsl. Engring., U. Tenn., 1956, M.S. in Indsl. Mgmt., 1963. With nuclear div. Union Carbide Corp., Oak Ridge Nat. Lab., 1956—, chief indsl. engr., 1963—; cons. in field. County squire Anderson (Tenn.) County, 1956-59. Served with USMCR, 1948-49, 50-52. Mem. Am. Inst. Indsl. Engrs., Soc. Advancement Mgmt., Am. Soc. Personnel Adminstrn. Democrat. Roman Catholic. Club: Elks. Home: 110 Dayton Rd Oak Ridge TN 37830 Office: PO Box X Oak Ridge TN 37820

JOHNSON, GERALD OLIVER, air force officer, EDP adminstr.; b. Trinity, Tex., July 20, 1932; s. Gerald Harrott and Pat (Bridges) J.; B.B.A., Baylor U., 1954; postgrad. St. Marys U., San Antonio, 1965; m. Oneta Fern Zavodsky, Sept. 17, 1952; 1 son, Steven Carl. Commd. col. USAF, 1974; instr. officers tng. sch., San Antonio, 1962-67; fund mgr., air staff Pentagon, Washington, 1973-74, EDP site mgr., MacDill AFB, Fla., 1974—. Decorated Silver Star, Meritorious Service medal, Air medal (U.S.); Gallantry Cross with palm (Vietnam). Home: 914 Homewood Dr Brandon FL 33511 Office: Box 6033 MacDill AFB FL 33608

JOHNSON, GILMER BROOKS, physician; b. Jackson, Miss., Sept. 12, 1916; s. Gilmer Brooks and Lena Leoti (Brown) J.; student Sul Ross State U., 1934-35, 46-47; B.S., Northwestern U., 1948, M.D., 1950; m. Avis Elizabeth Palmer, Oct. 9, 1942; children—Carolyn, Gilmer Brooks, David Wallace. Intern, Baylor U. Med. Center, Dallas, 1951; practice family medicine, Plainview, Tex., 1952—; chief staff Central Plains Gen. Hosp., E. O. Nichols Meml. Hosp., Plainview; asso. clin. prof. Tex. Tech U. Med. Sch., 1973—. Chmn. Med. com. Mex. Rural Work Program; v.p. Hale County chpt. Am. Heart Assn. Served with AUS, 1936-46. Decorated Bronze Star. Diplomate Am. Bd. Family Practice. Fellow Am. Acad. Family Physicians (pres. chpt. 1976); mem. AMA (Physician's Recognition award 1970, 73, 76), Hale-Briscoe-Floyd County Med. Soc. (pres. 1962-63). Baptist (deacon). Home: 205 Yucca Terr Plainview TX 79072 Office: 814 W 8th St Plainview TX 79072

JOHNSON, GLENDON E., lawyer; b. 1924; B.S., U. Utah, 1948; J.D., Harvard, 1952; m. Bobette Johnson; children—Glendon E., Tawny. Clk. to justice Utah Supreme Ct., 1952-54; adminstrv. asst. to Senator Wallace F. Bennett, 1954-58; mem. firm Ray, Rawlins, Jones & Henderson, 1958-59; v.p., gen. counsel Am. Life Conv., 1959-68; sr. exec. v.p., then pres., dir. Gt. So. Life Ins. Co., 1968-70; pres. Am. Nat. Ins. Co., Galveston, Tex., 1970-77, chief adminstrv. officer, 1970-71, chief exec. officer, 1971-77, chmn. bd., 1972-77, also dir.; also. firm Routier & Johnson, Washington. Pres. South Central region Boy Scouts Am., 1975—. Served with AUS, 1942-46. Office: 1725 K St NW Suite 1412 Washington DC 20006

JOHNSON, GORDON GUSTAV, mathematician; b. Chgo., June 23, 1936; s. Gustav Hjalmar and Selma Maria (Hultman) J.; B.S., Ill. Inst. Tech., 1958; Ph.D., U. Tenn., 1964; m. Nancy May Shupe, June 29, 1957; children—Cathy Lynn, Kim Marie, Carl Gustav, David Hjalmar. Asst. prof. math U. Ga., 1964-69; asso. prof. Va. Poly. Inst., 1969-71; asso. prof. math. U. Houston, 1971-73, prof., 1973—. Dir. Clear Creek Basin Authority, 1973-74, pres., 1974-75. Oak Ridge Inst. Nuclear Studies fellow 1963-64; NRC sr. research asso., 1978-80. Mem. Am., Swedish math. socs., Sigma Xi. Founding editor Houston Jour. Math. Home: 2010 Fairwind Houston TX 77062 Office: Cullen Blvd Houston TX 77004

JOHNSON, GUERRY WAYNE, constrn. co. exec.; b. Charleston, S.C., Nov. 8, 1947; s. Thaxton Charles and Mable (Ramsey) J.; A.S. in Civil Engring., Trident Tech. Coll., Charleston, 1971; m. Diane Lynn Parker, Oct. 22, 1976; 1 dau., Angela Yvonne. Project mgr. Palmetto Constrn. Co., Charleston, 1971-77; pres., treas. Johnson Bldg. Corp., Charleston, 1977—, also dir.; tchr. civil engring. Trident Tech. Coll., evenings 1971-73. Served with U.S. Army, 1966-68. Mem. Assn. Gen. Contractors, Trident C. of C., Amvets. Democrat. Office: Fairfield Office Park Suite 303 Charleston SC 29407

JOHNSON, HARLIE B., state ofcl.; b. Troy, Ala., Sept. 27, 1920; s. John Macon and Arkey Leola (Dyess) J.; A.A.B., San Antonio Community Coll., 1954; B.B.A., Tex. Technol. U., 1960; M.S.P.A., Fla. State U., Tallahassee, 1975; m. Anna Louise Emerson, Dec. 15, 1945; children—Harlien Marie, Lee Ann. Served as enlisted man U.S. Army, 1940-41, U.S. Army Air Corps, 1941-44; commd. 2d lt. U.S. Air Force, 1944, advanced through grades to maj., 1968; adminstrv. officer Lackland AFB, Tex., 1949-54, weapons controller, Alaska, 1955-56, tng. officer, Tex., 1957-60, commdr. and adv., Philippines, Vietnam, Thailand, 1960-62; comdr. Tatalina AFB, Alaska, 1964-65, tactical control sys. Shaw AFB, S.C., 1965-68, ret., 1968; tng. and human devel. dir. Fla. Dept. Transp., Tallahassee, 1969—. Mem. (Fla.) Gov.'s Planning Com. on Comprehensive Employment and Tng. Act, 1977-79. Mem. Am. Soc. Tng. and Devel. (pres. N. Fla. chpt. 1970-71), Dept. Transp. Central Office Golf Assn. (pres. 1976), Fla. Personnel Officers Assn., Tallahassee Ret. Officers Assn. Am. Legion. Democrat. Presbyterian. Clubs: Seminole Golf, Masons. Home: 2124 Cambridge Dr Tallahassee FL 32304 Office: Fla Dept Transp 605 Suwannee St Tallahassee FL 32301

JOHNSON, HAROLD BENJAMIN, JR., educator; b. Hastings, Nebr., Mar. 17, 1931; s. Harold Benjamin and Patricia (Armstrong) J.; B.A., Cambridge U., 1953, M.A., 1960; Ph.D., U. Chgo., 1963. Lectr. U. Chgo., 1961-63, Yale, 1965-67; asso. prof. history U. Va., Charlottesville, 1969—, dir. Latin Am. studies, 1971-73. Served with AUS, 1953-55. Social Sci. Research Council fellow, 1964; Ford Found. fellow, 1965-66; Fulbright Hayes fellow, 1968-69. Mem. Am. Hist. Assn., Conf. Latin Am. History, Phi Beta Kappa. Author: From Reconquest to Empire, 1970. Contbr. to profl. jours. Office: Randall Hall Univ Va Charlottesville VA 22903

JOHNSON, HARRY WALLACE, gynecologist; b. Weldon, N.C., Nov. 23, 1928; s. Harry Wallace and Virginia Lee (Inge) J.; A.B., Duke U., 1951, M.D., 1955; m. Jimmie Irene Matthews, June 11, 1955; children—Harry Wallace, Stanhope M., J. Craig, Jonathan I. Intern, U. Va. Hosp., Charlottesville, 1955-56; resident in obstetrics and gynecology Duke Med. Center, Durham, N.C., 1956-60; asst. prof. obstetrics and gynecology Duke Med. Sch., 1962-64; pvt. practice obstetrics and gynecology, Greensboro, N.C., 1964—; chief service Moses H. Cone Meml. Hosp., 1976—. Served to lt. comdr. USN, 1960-62. Diplomate Am. Bd. Obstetrics and Gynecology. Mem. AMA, N.C. Med. Soc., Guilford County Med. Soc., Greensboro Acad. Medicine, Am. Coll. Obstetrics and Gynecology, South Atlantic Assn. Obstetrics and Gynecology, N.C. Obstet. and Gynecol. Soc. Club: Rotary. Home: 2003 Carlisle Rd Greensboro NC 27408 Office: 104 W Northwood St Greensboro NC 27401

JOHNSON, HERBERT ALAN, legal historian; b. Jersey City, Jan. 10, 1934; s. Harry Oliver and Magdalena Gertrude (Diemer) J.; A.B., Columbia U., 1955, M.A., 1961, Ph.D., 1965; LL.B., N.Y. Law Sch., 1960; m. Barbara Arlene Balcerak, Sept. 24, 1955; children—Amanda Blair, Vanessa Paige. Research asst. Columbia U., 1961-63; lectr. history Hunter Coll., City U. N.Y., 1964-65, asst. prof., 1965-67; asso. editor Papers of John Marshall, Inst. Early Am. History and Culture, Williamsburg, Va., 1967-70, co-editor, 1970-71, editor, 1971-77; prof. history and law U. S.C., Columbia, 1977—; lectr. history Coll. William and Mary, 1967-77. Mem. City of Williamsburg Bd. Adjustments and Appeals, 1971-77. Served with USAF, 1955-57. Recipient Paul S. Kerr history prize N.Y. State Hist. Assn., 1970; Am. Council Learned Socs. fellow, 1974-75. Mem. Am. Hist. Assn. (chmn. Littleton-Griswold com. 1979-81), Assn. Am. Law Schs. (chmn. sect. legal history 1979), Am. Soc. Legal History (v.p. 1972-74, pres. 1974-75), Am. Law Inst., Selden Soc., Stair Soc., Internat. Assn. Study of History of Parliamentary Instns. Author: The Law Merchant and Negotiable Instruments in Colonial New York 1664-1730, 1963; John Jay, 1745-1829, 1970; Imported Eighteenth-Century Law Treatises in American Libraries, 1700-1799, 1978; editor: (with C. T. Cullen) The Papers of John Marshall, vols. 1, 2, 1974, 77. Home: 615 LaBruce Ln Columbia SC 29205 Office: Gambrell Hall Dept History U SC Columbia SC 29208

JOHNSON, HERMAN BLUITT, savs. and loan assn. exec.; b. Canton, Miss., July 28, 1925; s. Clark Albert and Gertrude (Shivers) J.; B.S. in Bus. Adminstrn., Anderson (Ind.) Coll., 1948; m. Harriett Lucille Joiner, July 5, 1948; children—Judy Diane (Mrs. John D. Worrel), Nancy Carol Shockey, Barbara Lynn. Owner, operator H&H Grocery and Market, Meridian, Miss., 1949-54; mgr. Godwin Radio and TV Co., Birmingham, Ala., 1954-58; pres., treas. First Fed. Savs. and Loan Assn., Sylacauga, Ala., 1958—, also dir.; dir. Investors Fidelity Life Ins. Co. Treas. Sylacauga Salvation Army, 1966-68; campaign chmn. Sylacauga United Givers Fund, 1969, pres., 1973. Bd. dirs., pres. Talladega Acad., 1970-73; trustee Warne So. Coll., Lake Wales, Fla., 1965-73; bd. dirs. local Boy Scouts Am., 1971—, Sylacauga Beautification Council, 1972—. Mem. Sylacauga C. of C. (dir. 1976—, v.p. 1970-73). Mem. Ch. of God (trustee 1952—, vice chmn. 1972—). Kiwanian (pres. Sylacauga 1963, lt. gov. 1965). Home: 2404 Lake Terr Sylacauga AL 35150 Office: Norton Ave Sylacauga AL 35150

JOHNSON, HERSCHEL ANTHONY, credit union exec.; b. Lincolnton, N.C., Apr. 22, 1929; s. Fred Garrison and Margaret (Anthony) J.; B.C.S., Benjamin Franklin U., 1956; m. Laureen Ferguson, June 26, 1954; children—Steven Anthony, Kelvin Matthew, Sharon Lee. With proof dept 1st Nat. Bank of Washington, 1951-52; teller Nat. Capital Bank of Washington, 1952-54; comptroller Pentagon Fed. Credit Union, Washington, 1954-57; treas., gen. mgr. Fort Belvoir Fed. Credit Union (Va.), 1957 1957-69, Fairfax Sch. Employees Fed. Credit Union (Va.), 1969—; founder, chmn. bd. Credit Union Mortgage Assn., 1978—. Pres., Mount Vernon Woods-Fairfield Citizens Assn., 1963; pres., chmn. bd. Mt. Vernon-Lee C. of C., 1969-70; treas. campaign state del. T.J. Rothrock, 1975-78. Mem. Met. Area Credit Union Mgmt. Assn. (charter), Credit Union Exec. Soc. (charter), Met. Area Mgrs. Assn. (founder). Democrat. Methodist. Club: Masons. Home: 12186 Queens Brigade Dr Fairfax VA 22030 Office: Fairfax Sch Employees Fed Credit Union PO Box 440 Fairfax VA 22030

JOHNSON, IMOGENE DANIELS, educator; b. Pikeville, Ky., Apr. 25, 1932; d. David and Lillian (Bevins) Daniels; B.A., Eastern Ky. U., 1953, M.A., 1974, postgrad., 1976; children—John Richard, Kerri. Tchr. pub. schs. in Ky., 1953-74; counselor Pikeville (Ky.) Coll., 1975, dean students, 1976-78; ednl. and counseling cons., 1978—. Bd. dirs. Pikeville Concert Assn., Jenny Wiley Amphitheatre. Named Tchr. of Year, Nat. Honor Soc., 1974-75, Educator of Year, Delta

Kappa Gamma, 1977. Mem. Am. Mental Health Assn., Am. Personnel and Guidance Assn., AAUW, Profl. Women's Club, Nat. Assn. Student Personnel Adminstrs., Ky. Assn. Women Deans, Adminstrs. and Counselors, Ky. Personnel and Guidance Assn., Delta Kappa Gamma. Address: Box 24 MSS Pikeville KY 40501

JOHNSON, JACK BARRY, social worker; b. Benton, Ky., May 17, 1943; s. Jack William and Mary Irene (Wolfe) J.; B.A., Lambuth Coll., 1965; M.S. in Social Work, U. Wis., Milw., 1967; m. Lynnette L. Manske, June 22, 1968; children—Jennifer, Judith. Vol., Peace Corps, India, 1965; community services cons. State of Wis., 1967-69; instr. dept. sociology and social work Lambuth Coll., 1970-71; asst. prof. social work Murray State U., 1971-76, coordinator Univ. Year for Action, 1976; clin. social worker Kelley Psychiat. Clinic, Paducah, Ky., 1980—. Served with U.S. Army, 1969-70. Decorated Bronze Star; recipient Outstanding Service award Jackson (Tenn.) Civic Action Council, 1971. Cert. social worker. Mem. Nat. Assn. Social Workers, Acad. Cert. Social Workers, Ky. Welfare Assn., Biofeedback Soc. Am., Internat. Concept Therapy Inst. Democrat. Methodist. Club: On The Beam Philosophy. Home: Route 12 Box 164 Paducah KY 42001 Office: Route 5 Box 325-A Paducah KY 42001

JOHNSON, JACQUELYN MCCLUNEY, computer exec.; b. Milledgeville, Ga., July 1, 1938; d. Joseph Franklin and Rhosland (Leaptrott) McCluney; B.A. in Psychology, Ga. State Coll. for Women, 1957; children—Bonny K., Mark E. Dist. mgr. applications engring. Gen. Electric Computer Dept., Dallas, 1959-65; large scale mgr. UNIVAC, Atlanta, 1965-68; pres. Computer Generation, Inc., Atlanta, 1968—; dir. Internat. Claims, Ltd., St. Mary's. Contbr. articles to periodicals. Home: 3240 Indian Valley Trail Atlanta GA 30341 Office: 3301 Buckeye Rd Atlanta GA 30341

JOHNSON, JAMES ANDREW, mfg. co. exec.; b. Kenedy, Tex., Dec. 4, 1924; s. James Walter and Ruth Addie (Byars) J.; student U. Tex., Austin, 1946-47, Bee County Coll., 1968—; m. Mildred Schultz, Aug. 22, 1947; children—James Allen, Trudy Lynn. Buyer, expeditor Flour Corp., 1948-50; office mgr. Danaho Refining Co., 1950-56; Toronto Pipe Line Co., Dallas, 1956-66; plant acct. Gen. Mill Inc., Kenedy, Tex., 1967-77; purchasing mgr. Henkel Corp., Kenedy, 1977—. Mgr., Little League, 1957-73, pres., 1974-79. Lay leader, Methodist Ch., 1972-78. Served with AUS, 1944-46. Mem. Kenedy C. of C. (dir.). Home: 406 Hackberry St Kenedy TX 78119 Office: Henkel Corp 1 Mill St Kenedy TX 78119

JOHNSON, JAMES GIBB, physician; b. Knoxville, Tenn., Nov. 2, 1937; s. James William Kelly and Katherine Elizabeth (Goodlett) J.; A.B., U. Tenn., 1959, M.D., 1963; m. Mackie Lou Stooksbury, June 20, 1961; children—Lee Anne and Leslie Lou (twins). Intern, City of Memphis Hosp., 1963, resident in internal medicine, 1964-66, chief resident in internal medicine, 1966-67, med. dir., 1975-79; intern Columbia div. Bellevue Hosp., N.Y.C., 1963-64; NIH fellow in nephrology U. Tenn., Memphis, 1967-68, NIH spl. fellow in nephrology, 1968-69, instr. medicine, 1966-69, asst. prof., 1969-72, asso. prof., 1972-75, prof., 1975—, asso. dean for hosp. affairs, 1975-79, asso. dean grad. med. edn., 1979—. Second v.p. Kidney Found. Western Tenn., 1976—; chmn. med. adv. com. Tenn./Venezuela Partners of Americas, mem. state bd. dirs. Diplomate Am. Bd. Internal Medicine with subsplty in nephrology. Fellow A.C.P.; mem. Am. Fedn. Clin. Research, Am. Heart Assn., AMA, Am., Internat. Socs. nephrology, Memphis Acad. Internal Medicine, So., Tenn. med. assns., Memphis and Shelby County Med. Soc., Tenn., Memphis heart assns., Am. Soc. Internal Medicine, Tenn. Soc. Internal Medicine, S.E. Dialysis and Transplantation Assn., Alpha Omega Alpha (sec.-treas. 1975-78). Contbr. articles to med. jours. Home: 2906 Iroquois St Memphis TN 38111 Office: 800 Madison Ave Memphis TN 38163

JOHNSON, JAMES HENRY, accountant; b. Columbus, Tex., Dec. 25, 1946; s. Issac B. and Grace Etta (Johnson) Kemp; student Tex. So. U., 1975—. Registrar, instr. Houston Bus. Coll., 1966-71; accounts payable mgr. Leopold, Price & Rolle, Houston, 1971—. Democrat. Baptist. Home: 3711 Southmore St Apt 508 Houston TX 77004 Office: 4701 Nett St Houston TX 77007

JOHNSON, JAMES KARL, engr., educator; b. Clinton, S.C., Feb. 5, 1928; s. James Karl and Ruby (Cunningham) J.; B.S., Clemson U., 1950, M.S., 1958; M.S., Ga. Inst. Tech., 1967; m. Josephine Wiles, Sept. 5, 1959; children—Jane Ann, James Karl III. Engr., Clinton Textiles Inc., 1950-55; from instr. to asso. prof. mech. engring. Clemson (S.C.) U., 1955—, dir. continuing edn., 1972—; engring. cons. Platt Saco-Lowell, Lockheed, Gen. Electric, Owens Corning, Lowenstein, Md. Casualty, others; mem. S.C. Cert. Bd. for Environ. Systems, 1972-74. Served with U.S. Army, 1945-47. Sci. Faculty fellow, 1963-64; registered profl. engr., S.C. Mem. ASME (v.p., mem. council, merit awards 1959-79), Nat. Soc. Profl. Engrs. (Engring. Educator of Yr. 1975), (state dir.), Am. Soc. for Engring. Edn. (sect. exec. com.), Soc. for Biomaterials (hon.), S.C. Soc. Engrs. Presbyterian. Contbr. articles to profl. jours.; editor several research procs. Home: 306 Augusta Rd Clemson SC 29631 Office: Clemson U Clemson SC 29631

JOHNSON, JAMES ROLAND, educator; b. Dallas, Sept. 18, 1921; s. Ward C. and Elsie Marilla (Lawhon) J.; B.S. in Bus. Adminstrn., N. Tex. State U., 1947, M.B.A., 1948, Ed.D., 1963; m. Wilma Virginia Barton, Aug. 24, 1946; children—Karyn Virginia, Janna Gaye, Roma Lynne. Instr. bus. edn. Ark. Poly. Coll., Russellville, 1948-49, N. Tex. State U., Denton, 1949-63; asst. prof. bus. edn. U. Denver, 1963-64; prof., head dept. bus. edn./office adminstrn. W. Tex. State U., Canyon, 1964—; lectr. No. Ariz. U.; cons. Panhandle Ednl. Services Orgn. Bd. deacons 1st Baptist Ch. of Canyon. Named Exec. of Year, Tierra Blanca chpt. Nat. Secs. Assn., 1979; recipient Cert. of Appreciation, Office Edn. Assn. of Tex., 1978. Mem. Adminstrv. Mgmt. Soc., Am. Records Mgmt. Assn., Am. Vocat. Assn., Tex. Vocat. Tchrs. Assn., Mountain-Plains Bus. Edn. Assn., Nat. Bus. Edn. Assn., Tex. Assn. Coll. Tchrs., Tex. Bus. Edn. Assn. (named Tex. Bus. Tchr. of 1978), Tex. Bus. Tchr. Edn. Council, Delta Pi Epsilon, Phi Delta Kappa. Democrat. Home: 1124 Hillcrest St Canyon TX 79015 Office: Sch Business W Tex State U Canyon TX 79016

JOHNSON, JANE GAULT, librarian; b. Union, S.C., Sept. 28, 1935; d. James William and Louise (Patterson) Gault; student Mary Washington Coll., 1953-54; A.B., Converse Coll., 1957; student U. S.C., 1954-56, 1962-63, 1965-67, 1968; student Wofford Coll. summers 1954, 55, Queens Coll. (NDEA fellow 1965), 1965; M.S. in L.S., La. State U., 1968; postgrad. Ga. State U., 1975-76; m. James Delane Johnson, Sept. 29, 1954 (div. Oct. 1975); children—James Delane II, William David. Instr. Spanish, Spartanburg (S.C.) High Sch., 1960-61; asst. librarian Greenville (S.C.) Sr. High Sch., 1961-62; librarian Spartanburg Day Sch., 1962-63; librarian Fremont Elementary Sch., Spartanburg, 1963-68; head librarian Spartanburg Regional Campus U. S.C., 1968-75; asst. head acquisitions dept. Ga. State U. Library, 1975-77; head acquisitions dept. Ga. So. Coll. Library, 1977—. Mem. Bulloch Meml. Hosp. Aux. Recipient Omicron Delta Kappa-Mortar Bd. Outstanding Sr. award La. State U., 1969. Mem. Ga. (membership com.), Am. (sec. ACRL/NDEA com. 1973-75), Southeastern, library assns., A.A.U.W. (br. rec. sec. 1964-66, br. treas. 1970-72; creativity topic chmn. S.C. div. 1974), AAUP (membership com.) Delta Kappa Gamma (chmn. research com). Episcopalian (sec. Mission Council, Altar Guild, v.p. Episcopal Ch. Women). Club: Faculty (sec. governing bd.). Home: PO Box 2482 Statesboro GA 30458 Office: Ga So Coll Library Statesboro GA 30458

JOHNSON, JAY LYNN, JR., restaurant owner, comml. leasing co. exec.; b. Houston, Sept. 7, 1938; s. Jay Lynn and Ida Louise (Briel) J.; student U. Tex., Austin, 1964-67; m. Sharon Street, Sept. 7, 1979; children—Julie Ann, Jan Laura, Jay Lynn III, James David. Partner, Canters Bar-B-Q, Austin, 1962-73; owner Jay Johnson Enterprises, Austin, 1962—, Jay's Bar-B-Q Hut, 1973—; dir. Austin Apt. Assn. Gen. chmn. 20th Ann. Cavalcade of Commerce, 1967; treas., chmn. Tex. Met. Conf., 1969-70; dir. Community Council, 1970; campaign chmn. Travis County March of Dimes, 1970, chmn. bd. dirs., 1971-73; del. Nat. Leadership Conf., 1969, 72; pacesetter chmn. United Fund, 1968. Councilman, Austin City Council, 1969, 71, mayor pro tem, 1971. Pres., East 6th St. Assn.; pres. bd. dirs. Austin Citizens League; bd. dirs. Peace Officers Found.; mem. adv. bd. for Community Decency, M.H. Darrel Royal Workshop. Mem. Austin Jr. C. of C. (dir. 1963-71, pres. 1969, orientation chmn. 1972-73). Home: 2910 Manchaca Rd Austin TX 78704 Office: 421 E 6th St Austin TX 78701

JOHNSON, JERRY DOUGLAS, educator; b. Salina, Kans., Sept. 1, 1947; s. Maynard Eugene and Norma Maude (Moss) J.; B.S. in Zoology, Ft. Hays (Kans.) State Coll., 1973; M.S. in Biology U. Tex., El Paso, 1975; m. Kathy A. Brodbeck, May 12, 1973; 1 son, George Walker. Instr. biology El Paso Community Coll., 1975—. Served with USMC, 1966-69. Mem. Am. Soc. Ichthyologists and Herpetologists, Soc. for Study Amphibians and Reptiles, Kans. Acad. Sci., Herpetologists League, Southwestern Assn. Naturalists, Sigma Xi, Beta Beta Beta, Sigma Tau Gamma. Republican. Lutheran. Asso. editor Southwestern Naturalist, 1977—. Contbr. articles to profl. jours. Home: 3815 Monroe St El Paso TX 79930 Office: Biology Dept El Paso Community College PO Box 20500 El Paso TX 79998

JOHNSON, JERRY WRIGHT, educator, mktg. cons.; b. Palestine, Tex., Sept. 4, 1939; s. Harry and Mabel (Wright) J.; B.B.A., Baylor U., 1964, M.B.A., 1965; Ph.D., U. Ark., 1974; m. Jane E. Barnett, May 30, 1970; 1 son, Marcus Elliott. Vice-pres. Marketing Assos., Fayetteville, Ark., 1968-70; asso. v.p. fiscal affairs U. Ark., 1970-74; dir. pub. affairs Hankamer Sch. Bus., Baylor U., 1974—; pres. Marketing Specialists, Waco, Tex., 1975—. Mem. Am. Mktg. Assn., Acad. Mktg. Scis., Lambda Chi Alpha. Baptist. Home: 2900 Sanger St Waco TX 76707 Office: Hankamer Sch Bus Baylor U Waco TX 76703

JOHNSON, JOEL FRANKLIN, physician; b. Denver, Apr. 2, 1941; s. Joel Franklin and Renzie Lee (Farr) J.; B.S., Centenary Coll., 1963; M.D., La. State U., 1967; m. Marian Francis Hodge, Dec. 31, 1973; children—James Nathanel, Jonathan David. Intern, Confederate Meml. Hosp., Shreveport, La., 1967-68, resident in surgery, 1968-72; practice medicine specializing in surgery, Crossville, Tenn., 1972-77, Sparta, Tenn., 1977—; mem. staff White County Community Hosp. Diplomate Am. Bd. Surgery. Fellow Internat. Coll. Surgeons, Southeastern Surg. Congress; mem. AMA, Tenn. Med. Assn., White County Med. Soc., Christian Med. Soc. Office: Sewell Rd Sparta TN 38583

JOHNSON, JOHN HENRY, JR., social worker; b. Carswell, W.Va., June 14, 1939; s. John Henry and Violet Marie (Herron) J.; B.S., Bluefield State Coll., 1967; M.S.W. (Commonwealth of Va. grantee 1968-70), W.Va. U., 1970; m. Barbara Jane Ross, May 5, 1962; children—Robbin Marie, John Henry, Michael Anthony. Dir. social services Appalachian Regional Hosp., Beckley, W.Va., 1970-74, dir. alcoholism and psychiat. program, 1974-76; psychiat. social worker Beckley Mental Health Orgn., 1976-77; psychiat. social worker, clinic mgr. Raleigh Psychiat. Services, Beckley, 1977—. Bd. dirs. Appalachian Regional Comprehensive Alcoholism Program, Beckley, 1976-79, Fellowship Home, Beckley, 1976—, Health Maintenance Orgn., Beckley, 1979—. Served with U.S. Army, 1962-65. Mem. Nat. Assn. Social Workers. Office: 24 Mallard St Beckley WV 25801

JOHNSON, JOHN LAMAR, bank exec.; b. Greeneville, Tenn., Sept. 8, 1945; s. Earl Lamar and Theodora Nolita (Rankin) J.; B.S.B.A., U. Tenn., 1967; M.S. in Indsl. Mgmt., U. N.D., 1971, M.S. in Acctg., 1972. Supervising sr. auditor Peat, Marwick, Mitchell & Co., Atlanta, 1972-75; sr. v.p. First Ga. Bank, Atlanta, 1975—; treas. First Ga. Bancshares, Inc., 1975—; dir. Gany Corp. Bd. dirs. Atlanta Jaycees, 1976-77, treas., 1977-78, pres., 1978-79; bd. dirs. Water Task Force, Atlanta, 1978-80; mem. regional devel. planning and adv. council Central Atlanta Progres, 1979—; transp. chmn. Hugh O'Brian Internat. Youth Seminar, Atlanta, 1979; mem. adv. bd. Atlanta Assn. Retarded Citizens, 1979-80; v.p. area council Atlanta C. of C. 1980; dist. bd. dirs. Ga. Jaycees, 1980. Served to capt. USAF, 1967-72. C.P.A., Ga. Mem. Nat. Assn. Accts. (dir. Atlanta Central chpt. 1979-80), Planning Execs. Inst., Ga. Soc. C.P.A.'s, Am. Inst. Banking (chmn. steering com. Atlanta chpt. 1978-79), Atlanta C. of C. (dir.). Republican. Presbyterian. Clubs: Atlanta Athletic, Benedicts of Atlanta, YMCA. Office: PO Box 1700 Atlanta GA 30301

JOHNSON, JOHN MEADE, physician; b. Paris, Tex., July 10, 1937; s. John Newton and Estes (Meade) J.; B.A., Rice Inst., 1959; M.S.H., U. Minn., 1963; M.D., U. Tex., Galveston, 1967; m. Betsy Borden, Nov. 3, 1974; children—Stacey Kathleen, John Christopher, Amy Elizabeth. Clin. research fellow Tex. Med. Br., Galveston, 1960-61; intern Good Samaritan Hosp., Dayton, Ohio, 1967-68; family physician Family Diagnostic Med. Center, Hillsboro, 1970—, corp. dir., 1978—; med. dir. Grant-Buie Hosp., Hillsboro, Tex., 1971—, chief staff, 1972, 80; city health officer, Hillsboro, Tex., 1977-78; county health officer, Hill County, Tex., 1978—; preceptor family practice program Southwestern Sch. Health Scis., Dallas, 1974—; team physician Hill Jr. Coll., 1971—; regional dir. emergency cardiac care Am. Heart Assn., 1973-75, bd. dirs. Tex. affiliate, 1976—. Instl. dir. Cub Scouts Am., Hillsboro, 1978—; regional bd. dirs. March of Dimes; mem. adminstrv. bd. First Methodist Ch. Served to lt. comdr. USPHS, 1968-70. Diplomate Am. Bd. Family Practice. Fellow Am. Acad. Family Physicians; mem. AMA (Physicians Recognition award 1979), Am. Heart Assn., Am. Public Health Assn., Tex. Med. Assn., Tex. Acad. Family Physicians, Hill County Heart Assn. (pres.), Hill County Med. Soc. (pres.), Hill County Cancer Soc., Hillsboro C. of C. (Public Service award 1976, chmn. public health com.), Phi Beta Pi. Clubs: Masons, Lions, Hill Junior Coll. Century, Rice University Presidents. Republican. Methodist. Home: 905 Park Dr Hillsboro TX 76645 Office: 101 Circle Dr Hillsboro TX 76645

JOHNSON, JOHN RILEY, JR., research engr., former air force officer; b. Providence, Ky., Mar. 22, 1922; s. John R. and Zita M. (Lucas) J.; B.S. in Indsl. Chemistry, U. Ky., 1949; M.S. in Nuclear Chemistry, Ohio State U., 1951; M.A., George Washington U., 1964; grad. USAF Air Command and Staff Coll., 1958; diploma Army War Coll., 1964; m. Lou Avah Pevlor, Sept. 22, 1945; children—Jenefer Lee, Cindy Lou, John Riley III. Commd. 2d lt. U.S. Army Air Corp, 1943, advanced through grades to col., 1963; combat pilot Troop Carrier Command, Europe, 1943-44; prisoner-of-war, Germany, 1944-45; design and devel. engr. Wright-Patterson AFB, Ohio, 1949-50; nuclear chemist McLellan AFB, Calif., 1951-55; comdr. tech. unit Yokota AFB, Japan, 1955-56; lab. chief McLellan AFB, 1958-60, dep. lab. dir., 1960-63, dep. dir. for reporting Fgn. Tech. Div., Wright-Patterson AFB, 1966-67; dir. tech. ops. Task Force Alpha, NKPRT AFB, Thailand, 1967-69; asst. dep. dir. Sci. and Tech. Intelligence, Def. Intelligence Agy., 1969-72, dep. dir., 1972-73, ret., 1973; head U.S. del. NATO Mil. Com. for Sci. and Tech. Intelligence, 1971-72; ex-officio mem. Def. Intelligence Agy., sci. adv. com., 1971-73; cons. Decision and Designs, Inc., McLean, Va., 1973-74; mem. tech. staff Gen. Research Corp., McLean, 1974—, sr. engr., 1974—. Chmn. ch. bd. Methodist Ch., North Highlands, Calif., 1962-63; bd. dirs. No. Va. Youth Symphony Assn., 1979—. Decorated Air Medal with oak leaf cluster, Legion of Merit with one oak leaf cluster. Mem. Officers Club, Sigma Xi, Alpha Chi Sigma. Democrat. Contbr. articles on def. related studies to profl. publs.; editor: Handbook of Radiochemical Procedures, 1962. Home: 2009 Kirby Rd McLean VA 22101 Office: General Research Corp Westgate Research Park McLean VA 22101

JOHNSON, JOHN ROBERT, petroleum co. exec.; b. Omaha, Apr. 17, 1936; s. Robert William and Hazel Marguerite (White) J.; B.S., Davidson Coll., 1958; m. Margaret Elizabeth Roberts, June 20, 1959; children—Robert Hance, Martha Elizabeth. With Johnson Oil Co., Morristown, Tenn., 1951—, pres., 1963—; dir. Lakeway Pubs., United So. Bank. Magistrate, Hamblen County Ct., 1968-78, chmn., 1971-72; elder 1st Presbyterian Ch., Morristown; pres. Hamblen County United Fund; pres. Great Smoky Mountain council Boy Scouts Am., 1977; mayor Morristown, 1977—. Served to lt. U.S. Army, 1958-61. Recipient Distinguished Service award Morristown Jr. C. of C., 1966. Mem. Morristown C. of C. (pres. 1976), Tenn. Oil Marketers Assn. (v.p. 1976-77). Democrat. Club: Rotary. Home: 505 Hale Ave Morristown TN 37814 Office: 1206 S Cumberland St Morristown TN 37814

JOHNSON, JOYCE DUNDALOW, nursing home adminstr.; b. Norfolk, Va., June 21, 1933; grad. Louise Obici Sch. Nursing, Suffolk, Va., 1954; m. James Marshall Johnson, Oct. 16, 1954; 1 son, John Nelson. Nurse, Raiford Meml. Hosp., Franklin, Va., 1955-57, 62-63, Virginia Beach (Va.) Gen. Hosp., 1963-66; owner, operator Johnson's Home for Adults, Inc., Suffolk, 1978—. Youth dir. Va. Winnebago Clubs, 1978-79; mem. Tidewater chpt. Home for Adults. Mem. Suffolk C. of C., Tenn. Walking Horse Assn. Clubs: Bus. and Profl. Women's, Va. Coasters Camping. Home: 3008 Catalina Ave Suffolk VA 23434

JOHNSON, KENNETH LEROY, ret. air force officer, program mgmt. co. exec.; b. Chgo., Jan. 24, 1922; s. Stanley C. and Nell L. (Lundberg) J.; student Kans. State Coll., 1940-42, U. So. Calif., 1956-57; B.S., U. Omaha, 1959; m. Tran Thi Phuong, July 3, 1946; children—Jeffery John, Candy Ann, James John; children by previous marriage—Kenneth LeRoy, Terri Ann, Jeff J. Commd. U.S. Air Force, 1942, advanced through grades to col., 1960; ret., 1969; contract mgr. Pacific Architects & Engrs. Co., Vietnam, 1970-74; program mgr. Bell Helicopter Internat., Tehran, Iran, 1977-79. Decorated D.F.C. with oak leaf cluster, Purple Heart, Bronze Star, Air medal with seven oak leaf clusters, numerous others. Mem. Nat. Assn. Security Dealers. Republican. Club: Masons. Home: PO Box 1076 Rogers AR 72756

JOHNSON, LARRY CECIL, sales exec.; b. Provo, Utah, Aug. 28, 1942; s. Grant Jennings and Leah P. (Pierce) J.; B.S. in Bus. Mgmt., Brigham Young U., 1969; m. Marna L. Schmidt, June 1, 1963; children—Scott David, Kevin Patrick, Eric Grant, Brian Edward. Economist, Caterpillar Tractor Co., Peoria, Ill., 1969-71; dist. mgr. AC Spark Plug div. Gen. Motors, Peoria and Springfield, Ill., 1971-74; pres. Auto Parts Hdqrs., Granger, Utah, 1974-76; regional mgr. Jacuzzi Whirlpool Bath, Chgo., 1977-79; v.p. sales and mktg. Gulf Pool Equipment Co., San Antonio, 1979—; lectr. San Antonio Coll., 1979—. Served with USAF, 1961-65. Mem. Sales and Mktg. Execs. of San Antonio. Republican. Mormon. Home: 305 Mecca San Antonio TX 78232 Office: 10430 Gulfdale San Antonio TX 78216

JOHNSON, LARRY WILSON, assn. exec.; b. Raleigh, N.C., Jan. 24, 1938; s. Lewis Marvin and Della (Wilson) J.; A.A., Campbell Coll., 1957; A.B., U. N.C., 1960, M.Ed., 1965; children—Elizabeth, Anne, John; m. 2d, Sondra Elizabeth Baker, Nov. 29, 1974; children—Robert, Patricia, Larry Jr., James. Tchr. indsl. edn. pub. schs., Cary, N.C., 1960-63; asst. state supr. State Bd. Edn., Raleigh, 1963-65; founder, nat. exec. dir. Vocational Indsl. Clubs of Am., Falls Church, Va., 1965—. Mem. Loudoun County Adv. Com. on Vocational Edn., Leesburg, Va., 1974—; U.S.A. del. Internat. Skill Olympics Organizing Council, Madrid, Spain, 1973—; chmn. Nat. Coordinating Council for Vocational Student Orgn., Washington, 1972, 77-78; chmn. bus. edn. adv. com. Fairfax County Bd. Edn., 1972, mem. adult edn. adv. com., 1972-73; mem. liaison com. for study vocat. Edn. Nat. Inst. Edn. Founder, 1st chmn. Loudoun County Pub. Nominating Fedn., 1970-71; mem. vestry St. Peter's Episcopal Ch., Purcellville, Va., sr. warden, 1977-79. Served with USMCR, 1957-63. Named Outstanding Vocat. Educator Ednl. Exhibitors Assn., 1979. Cert. assn. exec. Mem. Nat. Assn. for Trade and Indsl. Edn. dir. 1973—), Am. Vocat. Assn. (nat. adv. council trade and indsl. edn. 1974—, policy and planning com.), Nat. Assn. Industry Edn. Coop., Am. Soc. Assn. Execs., Vocational Indsl. Clubs of Am. (hon., life mem.) Editor-in-chief Vica Mag. Contbr. articles to profl. publs. Office: 105 N Virginia Ave Falls Church VA 22046

JOHNSON, LEANDER FLOYD, plant pathologist, educator; b. Lecompte, La., Aug. 3, 1926; s. Francis Menard and Margarete Mae (Hearn) J.; B.S., U. Southwestern La., 1948; M.S., La. State U., 1951, Ph.D., 1953; m. Jean Perry Cawood, May 24, 1978; children by previous marriage—Darryl L., James M. Tchr. sci. Urania (La.) High Sch., 1948-49; grad. research asst. dept. botany La. State U., Baton Rouge, 1949-53; instr. botany U. Tenn., Knoxville, 1953-54, asst. prof. plant pathology, 1954-57, asso. prof., 1957-70, prof., 1970—. Served with USN, 1944-45. Recipient Research award Gamma Sigma Delta, 1974. Mem. Am. Phytopathol. Soc., Am. Rose Soc., Oak Ridge Isochronous Observation Network, Tenn. Rose Soc., Knoxville Sci. Club, Sigma Xi, Gamma Sigma Delta, Sigma Pi. Contbr. articles to profl. jours. Author: Methods for Studying Soil Microflora - Plant Disease Relationships, 1959; Methods for Research on the Ecology of Soil Borne Plant Pathogens, 1972. Home: 8617 Fox-Lonas Rd Knoxville TN 37923 Office: Dept Agrl Biology U Tenn Knoxville TN 37901

JOHNSON, LEE, educator; b. Richmond, Va., May 11, 1931; d. Mildred Simms Wible; B.A., Pa. State U., 1950; postgrad. Trinity Coll., Hartford, Conn., Columbia U., New Sch., N.Y.C.; m. J. Jay Johnson, June 3, 1950. Pub., editor Kids' Stuff mag., 1960—; tchr. Malverne (N.Y.) Jr. High Sch., 1971-74, Jr. Acad., Bklyn., 1973; book critic Richmond Times-Dispatch, 1965-71; tchr. Roger Ludlow High Sch., Fairfield, Conn., 1962-65, Central High Sch., Bridgeport, Conn., 1963; founder, asst. librarian Calvary Jr. Library, Bridgeport, 1965-68; mgr. Treasure-trove, rare books and records, Avondale, Ga.; psychol. counselor Alpha Psi Omega. Sec., Fed. Grand Jury Assn., 1965-75. Mem. AAUW (ways and means chmn. 1963), Nat. League Am. Pen Women, DeKalb Hist. Soc. Episcopalian. Clubs: N.Y. Classical, Regal Cultural, Avondale Estates Woman's (archivist, publicity chmn. 1978—), Avondale Garden. Home: 7 Exeter Rd

Avondale Estates GA 30002 Office: Box 1 Avondale Estates GA 30002

JOHNSON, LEHMAN HOLSON, III, telecommunications co. ofcl.; b. Wilson, N.C., Aug. 16, 1942; s. Lehman Holson and Genevieve R. (Wooten) J.; B.S. in Elec. Engring., The Citadel, 1964; m. Susan Pamela Allender, Dec. 17, 1966; children—Michael, Nicole. Engr. research and devel. dept. ITT Telecommunications, Raleigh, N.C., 1966-69, sr. engr., 1969-72, project engr., 1972-75, mgr. digital terminal devel. group, 1976—. Active numerous community orgns. Served with U.S. Army, 1964-66. Recipient N.C. Longleaf Pine Public Service award, 1974. Methodist. Club: Exchange. Patentee in field. Home: 7006A Longstreet Dr Raleigh NC 27609 Office: 2912 Wake Forest Rd Raleigh NC 27611

JOHNSON, LESTER B., JR., engring. technologist; b. Savannah, Ga., Aug. 26, 1926; s. Lester B. and Lucille Baldwin (Spencer) J.; B.S. in Archtl. Engring., Hampton Inst., 1949; postgrad. S.C. State U., 1966; Ph.D. in Vocat. Edn., U. Mo., Columbia, 1973; m. Constance Mosley, Aug. 11, 1951; children—Joyce, Lester B., Lynt, Lisa, Leslie. Tchr. indsl. arts, head dept. A. E. Beach High Sch., Savannah, 1949-69; instr. Savannah State Coll., 1969-71; asso. prof. engring. tech., head dept. Savannah State Coll., 1973—; pvt. practice archtl. engring.; mem. Accreditation Bd. Engring. and Tech. Trustee, Greater Savannah Athletic Hall of Fame; mem. Revolutionary Battlepark Tech. Com., Savannah; bd. dirs. Savannah Area Minority Contractors Assn. Served with U.S. Army, 1945-46. Recipient Ednl. Profl. Devel. Leadership award, 1971; named Tchr. of Yr. Beach High Sch., 1961. Mem. Am. Soc. Engring. Edn. (sec. Southeastern sect.), Ga. Indsl. Arts Assn., S.E. Indsl. Arts Conf., Am. Vocat. Assn., Am. Inst. Design and Drafting, Nat. Assn. Indsl. and Tech. Tchr. Educators, AIAA, NAACP, Nat. Eagle Scout Assn., Epsilon Phi Tau, Alpha Phi Gamma, Phi Delta Kappa, Omega Psi Phi. Democrat. Roman Catholic. Clubs: Wolves Social, Holy Name Soc. Home: 1905 Fitzgerald St Savannah GA 31405 Office: Savannah State Coll Savannah GA 31404

JOHNSON, LLOYD HARLIN, aero. engr.; b. Granite, Okla., May 15, 1928; s. Olie (Pope) J.; B.S., U. Ala., 1952; M.S. in Tech. Mgmt., Am. U., 1975; m. Mary Frances Maddox, Dec. 27, 1959; children—Amanda, Julian, Wendell. Aerodynamics engr. Chance Vought Aircraft, Dallas, 1953-59; methods group chief Temco Electronics & Missiles Co., Dallas, 1959-61; chief aerodynamic heating and fluid dynamics U.S. Army Missile Command. Redstone Arsenal, Ala., 1961-65; phsy. scientist CIA, Washington, 1965-73; sr. aerospace engr. Computer Scis. Corp., Silver Spring, Md., 1973-75; engring. mgr. tech. staff Autonetics group Rockwell Internat., Arlington, Va., 1976—. Vice pres. Fairfax (Va.) Little League; commr. basketball Fairfax Police Youth Club. Served with USAF, 1952-53. Registered profl. engr., Tex. Fellow Am. Inst. Aeros. and Astronautics (Martin Schilling award Ala. sect. 1965) (asso.); mem. Am. Soc. Naval Engrs. Presbyterian. Contbr. articles to profl. publs. Home: 10223 Raider Ln Fairfax VA 22030

JOHNSON, LOUISE BRAZZEL, ins. co. exec.; b. Dubach, La., Oct. 6, 1924; d. Tom A. and Ethel (Holley) Brazzel; student Hartford Ins. Sch., 1971; B.A., magna cum laude, La. Tech. U., 1979; m. Sam Johnson, Dec. 19, 1942 (dec. Jan. 1978); 1 son, Samuel W. Owner, pres. Bernice (La.) Ins. Agy., 1964—; mem. La. Legis., 1972-76; pres. D'arbonne Water System, Bernice, 1976-79. Chmn., Union Parish Tourist Com., 1975-79; sec. Bernice Indsl. Devel. Corp., 1976-79, Vo.-Tech. Adv. Com., 1978-79, La. Tech. Sch. Nursing, 1979—; bd. dirs. Tri-Ward Hosp., 1976-79. Recipient Outstanding Agt. award Ins. Advt. Conf., 1967; Nat. Oscar, Ins. Advt. Conf., 1969. Mem. La. Assn. Ins. Agts., Nat. Assn. Inst. Agts., C. of C., N.W. Tourist Commn. Democrat. Baptist. Contbr. articles in field to profl. jours. Address: 407 S Cherry St Bernice LA 71222

JOHNSON, MARIAN RITCHIE, marriage and family therapist; b. Concord, N.C., Aug. 27, 1927; d. William Alexander and Margaret (Chason) Ritchie; B.A.. Converse Coll., Spartanburg, S.C., 1948; M.Ed. in Counseling and Guidance, U. N.C., 1973; m. George Johnson, Jr., July 1, 19S0; children—Sally Hope, George William, David Ritchie, Robert Hill. Asst. to Presbyn. campus minister, founder and dir. A Woman's Place, U. N.C., Chapel Hill, 1973-76; counselor in tng. Pastoral Care and Counseling Inst., Durham and Chapel Hill, Inc., 1975-77, staff counselor, 1979—; pvt. practice personal and family counseling, Chapel Hill and Durham, 1977—. Mem. Orange County Commn. for Women, 1976-78; mem. Citizens Adv. Com., 1968-70; chmn. P.T.A. Thrift Shop, 1967-69; ruling elder Presbyn. Ch., Chapel Hill, 1974-80; mem. council Orange Presbytery, 1976-79, Co-ordinating Council N.C. Presbyn. Ch. in U.S., 1977-80. Mem. Am. Assn. Marriage and Family Therapy, Am. Personnel and Guidance Assn., Am. Coll. Personnel Assn. Democrat. Home: 410 Westwood Dr Chapel Hill NC 27514 Office: 151 E Rosemary St Suite 106 Chapel Hill NC 27514

JOHNSON, MARTHA FLOWERS, banker; b. Coffee County, Ala., Nov. 1, 1943; d. John Freeman and Myrtie Bell (Scarbrough) Flowers; student public schs., Zion Chapel, Ala.; m. Kenneth M. Johnson, Feb. 8, 1963. Sec., Daniel Acctg. Agy., Elba, Ala., 1961-62; accounts receivable and payroll clk. Peacock Warren Mfg. Co., Enterprise, Ala., 1962-63; sec., asst. claims mgr. United Security Ins. Co., Birmingham, Ala., 1963-67; asst. mgr. loan servicing Birmingham Fed. Savs. & Loan Assn., 1967-70; mgr. loan servicing City Fed. Savs. & Loan, Montgomery, Ala., 1970-75; asst. cashier retail banking So. Bank N. Am., Montgomery, 1975—. Mem. Pinedale Civic Assn. Mem. Am. Inst. Banking (pres. Montgomery chpt.), Nat. Assn. Bank Women (past v.p. Central Ala. group), Am. Bus. Women's Assn. (woman of yr. com. Montala chpt.), Nat. Assn. Female Execs., Pineforest Homeowners Assn. Baptist. Clubs: Rolling Hills Golf and Racket, Fairmeadows Garden (past pres.) (Montgomery). Home: 3840 Pineforest Ave Montgomery AL 36116 Office: PO Box 869 Montgomery AL 36102

JOHNSON, MARVIN MERRILL, chemist; b. Salt Lake City, Mar. 21, 1928; s. John Ivan and Hildur Elizabeth J.; B.S.Ch.E., U. Utah, 1950, Ph.D.Ch.E., 1956; m. Marilyn White, May 8, 1951; children—Mark, Jennifer, Lorelie, Marianne. Sr. research engr. Phillips Petroleum Co., Bartlesville, Okla., 1956-65, mgr. hydrocarbon processes, 1965-68, research asso., 1968-74, sr. research asso., 1974-78, sr. scientist, 1978—. Named Engr. of Year, Okla. Soc. Profl. Engrs., 1979. Mem. Am. Chem. Soc., Am. Inst. Chem. Engrs., Am. Soc. Profl. Engrs., S.W. Catalyst Club, Sigma Xi. Republican. Mormon. Patentee in field. Home: 4413 Woodland Rd Bartlesville OK 74003 Office: 206 RB-6 Phillips Research Center Bartlesville OK 74004

JOHNSON, MICHAEL ROBERT, headmaster; b. Chgo., Mar. 28, 1938; s. Carl George Otto and Lyda Pearl (Leeper) J.; B.A. in English, Aurora (Ill.) Coll., 1960; M.A. in History, No. Ill. U., DeKalb, 1963; m. Carole LaVonne Grimes; children—Steven, Jennifer, William. Instr., No. Ill. U., 1963-65; asst. prof. Coll. Emporia (Kans.), 1965-67; chmn. dept. history Spartanburg (S.C.) Day Sch., 1967-69, 71—, headmaster, 1971—; instr. Prairie Sch., Racine, Wis., 1969-71. Trustee Routh Meml. Presbyn. Ch. Mem. So. Assn. Colls. and Schs. (chmn. central rev. com. for pvt. schs., mem. state secondary com.), So. Assn. Ind. Schs., Palmetto Athletic Assn. (pres.), Cum Laude Soc. Home: 244 E Park Dr Spartanburg SC 29302 Office: 1701 Skylyn Dr Spartanburg SC 29302

JOHNSON, NICHOLAS WAYNE, state ofcl.; b. Charleston, W.Va., Oct. 1, 1943; s. James Alexander and Edith Esther (Mamoran) J.; B.A., W.Va. Inst. Tech., 1965; J.D., U. Ky., 1968; m. Linda Sue Belcher, Apr. 5, 1969; children—Emily Beth, Ehren Ashley. Admitted to W.Va. bar, 1969, U.S. Supreme Ct. bar, 1973; contract adminstr. FMC Corp., 1968-69; exec. dir. W.Va. Indsl. Devel. Authority, 1969-70; asst. atty. gen. W.Va., Charleston, 1970-75, dep. atty. gen., 1976—. Vice pres. Young Democrats W.Va., 1965; trustee Ohio Valley Coll., Parkersburg, W.Va. Mem. Am. Judicature Soc., W.Va. State Bar, Phi Alpha Delta. Mem. Ch. of Christ (trustee). Club: Lions. Home: 4503 Chesterfield Ave Charleston WV 25304 Office: Office Dep Atty Gen Ground Floor Main Unit Charleston WV 25305

JOHNSON, PATRICIA ANN, editor; b. Springfield, Mo., Dec. 2, 1952; d. Elvis Eugene and Jean Alice (Cain) J.; B.S., U. Mo., Columbia, 1975. With Am. Nat. Ins. Co., Galveston, Tex., 1975—, pub. asst., 1975-77, editor The Tower, 1977—. Bd. govs. Upper Deck Theatre, 1976-80, chmn. governing bd., 1977-78, sec., 1978-80. bd. dirs. Galveston County unit Am. Cancer Soc., 1977-79, sec., 1978-79. Presbyterian. Clubs: Galveston Country, Galveston Yacht. Home: 25 Adler Circle Galveston TX 77550 Office: 1 Moody Plaza Galveston TX 77550

JOHNSON, PAUL ROBERT, lawyer; b. Shamrock, Fla., June 16, 1941; s. George Washington and Mary Bess (Williams) J.; student Fla. So. Coll., 1960-62, Jacksonville U., 1963; B.A., Fla. State U., 1964; J.D., N.C. Central U., 1971. Admitted to Fla. bar, 1972; practiced in Trenton, Mayo, Cross City, Monticello; pvt. practice law, Tallahassee, 1975-77. Active Girl Scouts U.S.A., Dialogue of Arts, Inc.; v.p. Internat. Christian Leadership Conf., 1975-77; patron Sch. of Theatre, Fla. State U. Served with A.G.C., U.S. Army, 1964-66. Mem. Am. Bar Assn., Fla. Bar, Phi Alpha Delta. Democrat. Episcopalian. Home: 6449 E Hwy 98 Panama City FL 32401

JOHNSON, PERRY ELLIOTT, real estate broker; b. Dover, Fla., Oct. 31, 1933; s. John A. and Beulah A. (Claville) J.; B.S.A., U. Fla., 1955; m. Jean Woodard, Dec. 21, 1952 (div. 1972); children—Deborah Jean, Gregory Elliott, Sean Dale. Vocat. agr. tchr. Fort Meade (Fla.) High Sch., 1955-57; real estate salesman and broker Perry E. Johnson, Realtor-Appraiser, Plant City, Fla., 1958—; pres. Perry Johnson Realty, Inc., Plant City, 1971—; adj. prof. U. Fla., Plant City, 1970-74; pres. Plant City Bd. Realtors, 1972-74. Mem. horseman's com. Fla. Downs, Tampa, 1973-74. Named Realtor of Year, Plant City Bd. Realtors, 1972. Mem. Nat. Assn. Ind. Fee Appraisers (sr.), Fla. Thoroughbred Breeders Assn. Club: Elks. Home: Rural Route 7 Box 3420 Plant City FL 33566 Office: PO Box 1411 Plant City FL 33566

JOHNSON, PETER MICHAEL, tech. co. exec.; b. Mpls., Oct. 21, 1945; s. Raymond Lawrence and Evelyn Harriet (McGowan) J.; B.S., U. Minn., 1967; m. Vivian Helen Langsdorf, Nov. 5, 1977. Mgr. quality control, Feinberg Reuben Meats, Mpls., 1973-74; dir. product devel. Stewart Sandwich Co., Mpls., 1974-77; plant mgr. Pasquale Food Co., Birmingham, Ala., 1977-79; dir. product analysis and devel. Del Taco Corp., Atlanta, 1979—; cons. in field. Pres. environ. commn., also mem. long-range planning commn. City of Crystal (Minn.), 1971-73. Served with U.S. Army, 1967-69. Mem. Inst. Food Technologists, Am. Assn. Cereal Chemists, Ry. and Locomotive Hist. Soc. Home: 814-H Tahoe Ridge Roswell GA 30075 Office: Del Taco Corp 1100 Spring St NW Atlanta GA 30309

JOHNSON, PHILIP LEWIS, research and ednl. assn. exec.; b. Oneonta, N.Y., May 26, 1931; s. Robert A. and Hazel S. (Shaffer) J.; B.S. in Agr., Purdue U., 1953, M.S. in Natural Resources, 1955; Ph.D. in Ecology, Duke U., 1961; m. Judy Rodgers, Nov. 17, 1973. Agrl. economist fruit and vegetable div., sect. program analysis U.S. Dept. Agr., Washington, 1955; James B. Duke fellow in botany Duke U., 1957-59; instr. botany U. Wyo., Laramie, 1959-61; botanist U.S. Forest Service, Laramie, 1961-62; ecologist U.S.-Cold Regions Research and Engring. Lab., Hanover, N.H., 1962-67; asst. prof. biology Dartmouth, 1963-67; asso. prof. botany, forestry U. Ga., Athens, 1967-70, exec. dir. Environ. Center, 1970; dir. program Ecosystem Analysis Program, NSF, Washington, 1968-69, dep. head Office Interdisciplinary Research, 1970-71, dir. div. Environ. Systems and Resources, 1971-74; exec. dir. Oak Ridge Asso. Univs., 1974—; research collaborator Brookhaven Nat. Lab., 1963-65; appt. to N.H. Pesticide Control Bd., 1965-67; mem. primary productivity com. Internat. Biol. Program, 1967-68, adv. com. tundra biome, 1968-70, deciduous forest biome coordinating com., 1968, 70; mem. environ. biology panel fgn. currency program Smithsonian Instn., 1969-70; mem. adv. council Pub. Broadcast Environment Center, Washington, 1970; vice chmn. interagy. com. ecol. research Fed. Council Sci. and Tech./Council Environ. Quality, 1972; mem. U.S. com. Man and Biosphere Program 1973-74; exec. com. East Tenn. Cancer Research Center, Knoxville, 1975-77; regional com. Southeastern Plant Environment Lab., 1975—; mem. fellowship adv. panel in environ. affairs Rockefeller Found., 1974—; trustee Inst. Ecology, 1976—. Served with AUS, 1955-57. Recipient Commendation award Cold Regions Research and Engring. Lab., 1964, 66, Meritorious Sci. Achievement award, 1966, Meritorious Service award NSF, 1973. Fellow Arctic Inst. N.Am.; mem. Ecol. Soc. Am., Brit. Ecol. Soc., N.Y. Acad. Scis., Am. Inst. Biol. Scis., AAAS, Sigma Xi, Phi Eta Sigma, Alpha Zeta, Kappa Delta Pi, Xi Sigma Pi. Club: Cosmos. Editorial bd. Ecol. Monographs, 1968-70, Jour. Remote Sensing of Environment, 1971-75. Home: 808 W Outer Dr Oak Ridge TN 37830

JOHNSON, PHILIP MARTIN, govt. ofcl.; b. Twin Falls, Idaho, Jan. 19, 1931; s. Ira Martin and Mae (Sheets) J.; B.A., Idaho State U., 1953; LL.B., Blackstone Sch. Law, 1964; postgrad. Ga. State U., 1966-67; M.B.A., U. N. Fla., 1975; m. Muriel Daye, Dec. 12, 1969; children—Mary Carla, Carl Denton, Robert Philip, Phyllis Susanne. Real estate broker, appraiser, Atlanta, 1956-61; appraiser FHA, Atlanta, 1961-63, asst. chief underwriter, 1963-65; chief rehab. loan br. HUD, Atlanta, 1965-71, dir. operations/chief underwriter, Jacksonville, Fla., 1972-75, dir. community planning and devel., 1975—. Instr. real estate and appraising Atlanta Bd. Edn., 1960-66, Am. Inst. Real Estate Appraisers, 1968-70, 78—, U. N. Fla., 1975—. Served with AUS, 1953-55. Mem. Soc. Real Estate Appraisers (chpt. pres. 1966-67, dir. 1964-68, 74-79), Am. Inst. Real Estate Appraisers (state chpt. dir. 1980-82, regional dir. edn. 1980, MAI prof. designation 1967—, prof. recognition 1979), Rho Epsilon, Alpha Psi Omega. Democrat. Presbyterian (ruling elder, trustee 1980-82) Mason (32 deg., Shriner), Lion. Contbr. articles to profl. jours. Editor The Atlanta Appraiser, 1963-66. Home: 3345 Eunice Rd Jacksonville Beach FL 32250 Office: 661 Riverside Ave Jacksonville FL 32204

JOHNSON, RALPH DONALD, cons. geologist; b. Shiawassee County, Mich., Jan. 5, 1921; s. Don W. and Hazel R. (Runyan) J.; B.S., Mich. State U., East Lansing, 1951; m. Henrietta L. Beach, Aug. 20, 1949; children—Edward L., Lenea F. Geologist, Chevron Oil Co., Tex. and N.Mex., 1951-71; cons. geologist, Midland, Tex., 1971—. Served with USMC, 1944-46. Decorated Purple Heart. Mem. Am. Assn. Petroleum Geologists (certified), Assn. Profl. Geol. Scientists (certified), W. Tex. Geol. Soc., Sigma Gamma Epsilon. Methodist. Club: Masons. Home: 3406 Shell St Midland TX 79703 Office: Box 2793 Midland TX 79702

JOHNSON, RALPH EMIL, physician; b. Chgo., Apr. 10, 1933; s. Carl Herman and Ethel Irene (Dahlstrom) J.; M.D., Northwestern U., 1958; children—Kathryn Ann, Carol Marie, Mary Ethel, Philip Ralph. Intern, U. Calif. Hosp., San Francisco, 1958-59; resident in therapeutic radiology Penrose Cancer Hosp., Colorado Springs, Colo., 1959-62; chief radiation oncology br. Nat. Cancer Inst., Bethesda, Md., 1964-77; prof. radiology, div. radiation therapy, Shands Teaching Hosp., U. Fla. Med. Coll., Gainesville, 1977-78; dir. Gulfcoast Oncology Center and dir. dept. radiation oncology Bayfront Med. Center, St. Petersburg, Fla., 1978—. Served with USPHS, 1962-64. Recipient Superior Service award HEW, 1974. Mem. Am. Assn. Cancer Research, Am. Soc. Therapeutic Radiologists, Am. Radium Soc., Beta Theta Pi, Nu Sigma Nu. Patentee compensating filters for mantle field radiation therapy. Contbr. articles to profl. jours. Home: 1935 Brightwaters Blvd NE Saint Petersburg FL 33704 Office: 701 6th St S Saint Petersburg FL 33701

JOHNSON, RAYMOND LEROY, office supply co. exec.; b. Long Beach, Calif., Jan. 27, 1931; s. Albin Carl and Vera Maxine (Leaf) J.; B.S. in Math., Centenary Coll., Shreveport, La., 1960; m. Myna June Westbrook, Oct. 20, 1950; 1 dau., Raynelle Denise Johnson Wilkinson. With M. L. Bath Co. Ltd., Shreveport, 1952—, mgr. printing dept., 1965-70, mgr. furniture dept., 1970-71, sales mgr., 1972-73, plant supt., 1973-74, v.p., sales mgr., 1975—, asst. corp. sec., dir., 1975—. Bd. dirs. Better Bus. Bur., 1978—, treas., 1980; vice chmn. United Way, 1977, 79. Served with U.S. Army, 1949-52. Mem. Sales and Mktg. Execs. (v.p. 1979-80), C. of C. (v.p. 1980). Republican. Episcopalian. Clubs: Red River Obedience Tng. (past pres.), Masons, Shriners, Am. Legion, Kiwanis (pres. 1978-79). Home: 6560 Quinn Church Rd Shreveport LA 71129 Office: PO Box 48 Shreveport LA 71161

JOHNSON, RICHARD ALVIN, mgmt. engr.; b. Edwardsville, Ill., July 8, 1934; s. William and Elma Marie (Blixen) J.; A.S., George Washington U., 1960; B.S.E.E., Mich. State U., 1963; m. Linda Covington, July 18, 1978; children—Richard Alan, Teresa Lynn, William Allen. Electronic field engr. Gen. Dynamics/Electronics, 1960-65; systems engr. ITT Fed. Labs., 1965-66; program analyst Gen. Elec. Co., 1966-71; dir. Miss. State U. Research Center, 1971-74; v.p. AMCO Constrn. Co. Inc., Bay St Louis, Miss., 1974-76; sr. partner Johnson & Assos., 1976-77; sr. mem. tech. staff Arabian Am. Oil Co., 1977—; dir. Miss. Environmental Protection Systems Co., Jackson, Miss. Lectr. mgmt. seminar Miss. State U.; adj. faculty U. So. Miss. Served with Signal Corps, AUS, 1955-58. Recipient tech. award in environmental sci. Am. Astronautical Soc., 1970. Mem. I.E.E.E., Am. Mgmt. Assn., Am. Inst. Cons. Engrs. Author: (with others) Operations Management, 1972. Contbr. tech. articles to profl. jours. Home: 17 Poplar Circle Gulfport MS 39501 Office: Box 5734 Dhahran Saudi Arabia

JOHNSON, RICHARD CARL, educator; b. Chgo., Sept. 2, 1933; s. Carl Helmer and Anne Katherine (Johnson) J.; B.A. in Liberal Arts, U. Chgo., 1954; postgrad. U. So. Cal., 1956-57; B.A. in Philosophy, U. Calif. at Los Angeles, 1958; M.A., U. Colo., 1962; m. Ann Elizabeth Faust, July 3, 1958; children—Eric Richard, Tawny Elizabeth. Asst. to acad. dean U. Colo., Boulder, 1963-65; dean students Tougaloo (Miss.) Coll., 1965-67, asst. prof. philosophy, 1967—, chmn. dept. philosophy and religion, 1969—. Cons. adult basic edn. research project Boston U., 1970. Pres., Jackson Area Council on Human Relations, 1969-71; treas. Am. Civil Liberties Union of Miss., 1971-76, pres., 1976-79, mem. exec. com., 1970—, mem. nat. bd., 1978—; founding bd. mem. Community Coalition for Pub. Schs., 1970-73. County and state del. Democratic party, 1963-64. Served with AUS, 1954-56. Mem. Am., Miss. (pres. 1972-73, 75-76) philos. assns., Southwestern Philos. Soc., Urban League, AAUP, Beta Theta Pi. Mem. Ecumenical Ch. Reconciliation. Home: 735 Lawrence Rd Jackson MS 39206 Office: Tougaloo Coll Tougaloo MS 39174

JOHNSON, RICHARD E., ins. co. exec.; b. Springfield, Mo., Dec. 24, 1926; s. Billy Bothwell and Nettie Gertrude (Gorsuch) J.; student Westminster Coll., Fulton, Mo., 1944-45, Western Mich. U., 1945, Northwestern U., 1945-46; B.A. in Econs., Drury Coll., Springfield, Mo., 1947; m. Mary Lou Pulliam, Nov. 25, 1952; 1 dau., Jeanne Karen. With Equitable Life Assurance Soc., 1947—, claims mgr., Fitts., 1958-60, Detroit, 1960-66, dir. health programs dept., Nashville, 1966-76, asst. v.p. health programs dept. N.Y.C., 1977-78, asst. v.p. group benefits So. Region, Atlanta, 1979—; cons. prof. U. Tenn., 1970-77. Served with U.S. Navy, 1944-46. Mem. Health Ins. Assn. Am. (Tenn. state council chmn. 1972-76). Office: Suite 2436 100 Peachtree St NW Atlanta GA 30303

JOHNSON, RICHARD J. V., newspaper pub. co. exec. Pres., Houston Chronicle Pub. Co., Houston. Office: Houston Chronicle Pub Co 801 Texas St Houston TX 77002

JOHNSON, ROBERT BRUCE, chemist; b. Birmingham, Ala., June 15, 1922; s. Walter Newhall and Sara (Hamilton) J.; B.S., Birmingham-So. Coll., 1946; postgrad. Ohio State U., 1949; M.S., U. Ala., 1953; m. Elizabeth Lay, Aug. 11, 1962. Research asso. biochem. Spies' Nutrition Clinic, Hillman Hosp., Birmingham, Havana, Cuba, 1944-46; research asso. Med. Coll. Ala., 1946-55; chemist dept. toxicology and criminal investigation State of Ala., 1955-58, toxicologist in charge Birmingham div., 1958-75; supr. sci. investigation Birmingham Police Dept., 1975—; instr. in forensic sci. Mem. Jefferson County Citizens Com. of the Study of Juvenile Delinquency, 1961-63; adv. bd. Jefferson State Jr. Coll., Birmingham, 1967-70. Fellow Am. Inst. Chemists; mem. Am. Chem. Soc., AAAS, Ala. Peace Officers Assn., Am. Soc. Crime Lab. Dirs., So. Assn. Forensic Sci. Ala. Acad. Sci., Sigma Xi. Presbyn. Mason (32 deg., Shriner). Home: 1508 S 13th St Birmingham AL 35205 Office: Birmingham Police Dept City Hall Birmingham AL 35203

JOHNSON, ROBERT CLIFFORD, petroleum co. exec.; b. Montgomery County, Miss., July 18, 1908; s. Nathan Harris and Margret Ethel (Caffey) J.; B.E.E., Miss. State U., 1929; m. Madeline Martin, Apr. 19, 1936. Mgr., dist. engr., dist. mgr. Miss. Power & Light Co., Grenada, 1929-45; with Grenada Hardware, 1945-48; part owner J.H. Oliver & Co., Grenada, 1948-54; area supr. Billups Petroleum Co., Rio Grande Valley, Tex., 1954-64, Economy Oil Co., Weslaco, Tex., 1968—; pres., owner Cliff Johnson Petroleum Co., Weslaco, 1954—. Mem. Weslaco Library Bd., 1969—, chmn., 1970-76; mem. Hidalgo County (Tex.) Library Bd., 1978—. Recipient Weslaco Outstanding Citizen award, 1977. Mem. Weslaco C. of C. (pres. 1963), Tex. Oil Jobbers. Baptist. Club: Rotary (pres. Weslaco 1961-62). Home: 906 W 9th St Weslaco TX 78596 Office: Cliff Johnson Petroleum Co 301 W Hwy 83 Weslaco TX 78596

JOHNSON, ROGER DALE, educator; b. Prestonburg, Ky., Oct. 8, 1950; s. Earl and Goldia (Meade) J.; Mus.B., Western Ky. U., 1972; M.A. in Edn., Morehead State U., 1978; m. Debra Sue Bates, Aug. 18, 1971. Tchr. music schs. in Ky., 1973—; dir. music, drill team sponsor, majorette sponsor Pike County Bd. Edn., Pikeville, Ky., 1977—.

Mem. Music Educators Nat. Conf., Am. Personnel and Guidance Assn., Ky. Music Tchrs. Assn., Eastern Ky. Music Educators Assn., Pike County Music Tchrs. Assn. Democrat. Baptist. Home: Indian Hills Apt 59 Prestonsburg KY 41653 Office: Mullins High Sch Pikeville KY 41501

JOHNSON, RONALD WAYNE, furniture store exec.; b. Le Compte, La., Nov. 2, 1942; s. Anderson Crawford and Gladys Mable (Walding) J.; student La. State U., Alexandria, Northwestern U.; m. Beverly Dawn Antilley, Sept. 5, 1965. Outsideman, Merit Fin. Co., Alexandria, 1963-64, mgr., 1964-67; mgr. Pico Fin. Co., Shreveport, La., 1967-68; mgr. A. Sencond Mgmt. Co., Shreveport, 1969; mgr. United Cos. Mortgage & Investment, Shreveport, 1969-72; owner, operator Smith Johnson Furniture Co., Ruston, La., 1976—. Bd. dirs. Ruston Family YMCA, 1977-78. Served with U.S. Army, 1964-65. Mem. Ruston Jaycees (v.p. 1977), La. Tech. Basketball Cager Treasure Club. Methodist. Office: Smith Johnson Furniture Co 202 N Vienna St Ruston VA 71270

JOHNSON, RUTH ALICE, hosp. exec.; b. Oklahoma City, Dec. 10, 1917; d. George H. and Effie C. (Outler) Romberger; student Central State Coll., 1935-36, Hills Bus. Coll., 1936-37; student Jacques Gourmet Cooking Sch., 1977-78; m. William A. Johnson, Sept. 11, 1938 (dec. 1968); children—Jan Johnson Smith, Jerry, Judie Johnson Duncan, Jill Johnson Pence. Columnist Nichols Hills News, 1945-47; sec. vol. services Children's Meml. Hosp., Oklahoma City, 1969-70; supr. vol. services Hosps. of U. Okla., Oklahoma City, 1971-73; coordinator of vols. U. Hosp., 1973-74, Bapt. Med. Center, Oklahoma City, Okla. 1974-76; dir. vols. Deaconess Hosp., Oklahoma City, 1976—. Girl scout leader Redland council Girl Scouts U.S., 1944-69; pres. Youth Study Club, Oklahoma City, 1947—; pres. West Nichols Hills PTA, 1960-61; pres. Christian Womens Fellowship Crown Heights Christian Ch., 1967-68, Sunday sch. tchr., 1954-56. Mem. Am. Hosp. Assn., Am. Soc. of Dirs. of Vols, Okla. Soc. for Dir. Vols. Compiler (girl scout guide) Our Treasure Chest, 1967. Home: 1708 Guilford Ln Oklahoma City OK 73120 Office: Deaconess Hosp 5501 N Portland Oklahoma City OK 73112

JOHNSON, SAM D., justice Supreme Ct. Tex.; b. Hubbard, Tex., Nov. 17, 1920; s. Sam D. and Flora (Brown) J.; B.B.A., Baylor U., Waco, Tex., 1946; LL.B., U. Tex., Austin, 1949; postgrad. N.Y. U. Coll. Law, 1968; m. June Page, June 1, 1946; children—Page Johnson Harris, Janet Johnson Clements, Sam J. Admitted to Tex. bar; county atty. Hill County, 1953-54, dist. atty., 1955-58, dist. judge, 1959-65; 1st dir. Houston Legal Found., 1965-67; asso. justice 14th Ct. Civil Appeals, Houston, 1967-72; justice Supreme Ct. Tex., 1973—. Elder, deacon Covenant Presbyn. Ch., Austin; trustee Presbyn. Children's Home and Service Agy., Itasca, Tex. Served with AUS, 1942-45; ETO. Decorated Combat Inf. badge, Purple Heart, Bronze Star. Recipient Disting. Alumnus award Baylor U., 1978. Fellow Am. Bar Found., Tex. Bar Found.; mem. Am. Bar Assn. (bd. govs., jud. mem.-at-large 1979-81, council jud. adminstrn. div. 1977—), Inst. Jud. Adminstrn., Nat. Legal Aid and Defender Assn. (dir., Arthur von Briesen award 1978), Am. Judicature Soc., State Bar Tex. (chmn. elec. jud. sect. 1978-79), Houston Bar Assn., Travis County Bar Assn., United Urban Council Austin, Baylor Ex-Students Assn. (pres. 1973-74), Order of Coif (hon.), Phi Delta Kappa (hon.). Democrat. Contbr. articles legal jours. Home: 1811 Exposition Blvd Austin TX 78703 Office: PO Box 12248 Capitol Station Supreme Ct Texas Austin TX 78711

JOHNSON, SAMUEL, educator; b. Waterloo, Ark., July 12, 1943; s. Robert and Winnie J.; B.A. in Sociology, Wilberforce U., 1968; M.S. in Edn., No. Ill. U., 1976; m. Rosemary Tipton, Aug. 17, 1968; children—Gregory Alexander, Nyasha Ganelle, Kinshasha Uzoma. Mental health caseworker Singer Zone Center, Mental Health Clinic, Rockford, Ill., 1968-69; project dir. Neighborhood Youth Corps, Rockford, 1969-72; dir. participant services Rockford CETA, 1974-76; recruiter/counselor Beloit (Wis.) Coll., 1972-74; asso. dir. coop. edn. office Central State U., Wilberforce, Ohio, 1976-77; asso. prof. edn., Head Start tng. officer Va. Commonwealth U., Richmond, 1977--. Pres. Black Big Bros. Orgn., Rockford, 1973-74; bd. dirs. Rockford Meml. Hosp., Nursing Sch., 1972-74; mem. Rockford City/County Planning Commn., 1975-76. Recipient Outstanding Citizen award Mark-V Corp., Rockford, 1975-76. Mem. Am. Personnel and Guidance Assn., Omega Psi Phi. Methodist. Home: 10902 London Dr Glen Allen VA 23060 Office: Head Start Office Virginia Commonwealth Univ Richmond VA 23284

JOHNSON, SAMUEL WARREN, lawyer; b. Hamilton, N.C., Sept. 9, 1947; s. Henry Samuel, Jr. and Irma Faye (House) J.; A.B., Duke U., 1969, J.D., 1972; m. Velma Gray Harrison, Aug. 30, 1970; children—Henry Samuel III, Katherine Harrison. Admitted to N.C. bar, 1972, since practiced in Rocky Mount; asso. firm Biggs, Meadows, Batts, Etheridge & Winberry, 1972-75, partner, 1976—. Bd. dirs. Historic Hamilton Commn., 1972—, pres., 1975—; trustee Thomas Hackney Braswell Meml. Library, 1974-80, chmn., 1976-78; mem. N.C. Hist. Commn., 1977—. Recipient Halifax Resolves award, 1979. Mem. Am. (antitrust sect.), N.C., Nash-Edgecombe bar assns., N.C. Lit. and Hist. Assn., N.C. Symphony Soc., Duke Alumni Assn. (pres. Nash-Edgecombe chpt. 1975-77). Democrat. Baptist. Clubs: Congregation Social, Benvenue Country. Home: 508 Glenn Ave Rocky Mount NC 27801 Office: PO Drawer 153 Rocky Mount NC 27801

JOHNSON, STANLEY STEVENS, geologist; b. Richmond, Va., Jan. 18, 1940; s. Milton and Zelda (Lawson) J.; B.A., U. Va., 1963; m. Shelby Jean Roberts, Jan. 21, 1961; children—Linda Gail, David Wendell. Geologist, Va. Div. Mineral Resources, Charlottesville, 1963—, geophys. investigation sect. chief, 1970—. Fellow Geol. Soc. Am.; mem. Soc. Exploration Geophysicists, Potomac Geophys. Soc. (sec. 1979-80), Am. Inst. Profl. Geologists (cert., sec.-treas. sect. 1979). Republican. Mem. Christian Ch. (Disciples of Christ). Contbr. articles on geophysics and geology of Va. to profl. jours. Home: 1016 Holmes Ave Charlottesville VA 22901 Office: McCormick Rd Charlottesville VA 22903

JOHNSON, TERRENCE LYNN, hosp. adminstr.; b. Detroit Lakes, Minn., June 1, 1942; s. Eugene Godfrey and Eleanor Beulah (Zurn) J.; B.S. in Mech. Engring., N.D. State U., 1964; M. in Health Adminstrn., Duke U., 1974; m. Marilyn Elaine Greer, June 3, 1967. With VA, 1965—, asst. dir. VA Med. Center, Memphis, 1976—. Served with Army N.G., 1964-65. Registered profl. engr., Ill., Ind. Mem. Am. Coll. Hosp. Adminstrs., U.S. Power Squadron. Episcopalian. Home: 2085 Woodcreek Dr Germantown TN 38138 Office: 1030 Jefferson Ave Memphis TN 38104

JOHNSON, TERRY DUANE, physician; b. Rockford, Ill., Oct. 7, 1948; s. Carl Gunnard and Norma Margaret Johnson; B.S. in Physiology, U. Ill., 1970; M.D., Loyola U., Chgo., 1974; m. Nancy Kay Johnson, Sept. 5, 1970; children—Chad Alexander, Travis Duane, Nathan Thomas. Resident in family practice Spartanburg (S.C.) Gen. Hosp., 1974-76; pvt. practice family medicine, Spartanburg, 1976—; asso. prof. Med. U. S.C.; vice chmn. dept. family practice Spartanburg Gen. Hosp. Diplomate Am. Bd. Family Practice. Mem. AMA, Am. Acad. Family Practice, S.C. Acad. Family Practice, S.C. Med. Assn., Spartanburg County Med. Assn. Baptist. Office: 125 Powell Mill Rd Spartanburg SC 29301

JOHNSON, THOMAS NELSON PAGE, JR., investment banker; b. Farmville, Va., Mar. 2, 1918; s. Thomas Page and Elizabeth Rebecca (Robertson) J.; B.A., U. Va., 1946; postgrad. bus. law U. Richmond; m. Helen Elizabeth Smith, July 7, 1942; children—Mary Parke, Thomas Nelson Page, Elizabeth Anne, Helen, James. Asst. supt. leaf dept. Export Leaf Tobacco, Richmond, Va., 1944-47; mgr. Eastern Bldg. Supply Co., Norfolk, Va., 1947-50; pres. North Linkhorn Devel. Corp., 1950-58; account exec. Anderson & Strudwick, Virginia Beach, Va., 1958-60; sales mgr. Scott and Stringfellow, Richmond, 1960-62; br. mgr. Anderson & Strudwick, Virginia Beach, 1962-63; v.p. Investment Corp. Va., Norfolk, 1963-76; sr. v.p. Davenport & Co. of Va., Richmond, 1976—, also dir.; former gen. partner Coriva Assos.; past dir. Va. Monetary Agts., Carmatic Systems Inc., Auto Motor Exchange; chmn. bd. Va. Ventures, Inc.; dir. Wythe Corp. Former trustee, mem. exec. com. Student Aid Found. U. Va.; steering com. Emergency Coronary Care Program; past chmn. athletic adv. com. U. Va. Served as pilot, 1st lt. USAAF, 1941-43. Mem. Raven Soc., Fin. Analyst Soc. (past mem. exec. com.), Soc. Descs. of Signers Declaration of Independence, JamesTowne Soc., Bond Club Va. (exec. com., pres., dir.), Virginia Beach C. of C. (past dir.), Phi Gamma Delta. Clubs: Princess Anne Country (Virginia Beach); Bull and Bear, Country of Va. (Richmond); Farmington Country (Charlottesville); Harbor, Va. (Norfolk). Home: 400 W 51st St Virginia Beach VA 23451 Office: Davenport & Co Va 311 Ross Bldg Richmond VA 23219

JOHNSON, TOM LYNN, jeweller, diamond invester; b. Durant, Okla., Aug. 21, 1951; s. Leonard R. and Tommie J. Johnson; student Southeastern Okla. State U., 1969-71; diploma diamond appraising Gemological Inst. Am., Los Angeles, 1976; m. Peggy Stanfield, Aug. 11, 1969; children—Christy, Cynthia, Robin. Owner francises Honda and Yamaha motorcycles, Durant, 1969-75; partner Durant Jewellers, 1975—, pres., 1979—; pres. TLS Mgmt. Inc., Durant, 1978—, Gem Jewelers of Holdenville (Okla.), Inc., 1979—, Kimberly Collection Inc., Durant, 1979—; cons. diamond appraising, employee motivation, time orgn. Bd. dirs. Durant United Way. Cert. diamond appraiser Diamond Council. Mem. Durant C. of C. (dir. 1975—), Durant Jaycees (dir. 1976--), Retail Jewelers Am., Okla. Retail Jewelers Assn., Jewelers Security Alliance, Jewelers Vigilance Com., Retail Mchts. Assn. Durant (dir.). Democrat. Club: Lions. Author: The Consumer's Guide to Diamonds, 1978. Office: Durant Jewelers Inc 217 W Main St Durant OK 74701

JOHNSON, WILLIAM R., univ. adminstr.; b. Houston, Jan. 12, 1933; s. Ernest H. and Rosabelle (Thompson) J.; B.S., U. Houston, 1958; M.A., U. Houston, 1959; Ph.D., U. Okla., 1963; m. Freida Marilyn Kennedy, June 26, 1954; children—William Scott, Alison Gaye. Asso. prof. history Tex. Tech. U., Lubbock, 1968-76, asso. dean arts and scis., 1972-73, interim v.p. acad. affairs, 1973-75, v.p. acad. affairs, 1975-76; pres. Stephen F. Austin State U., Nacogdoches, Tex., 1976—. Served with USAF, 1951-55. Recipient L.R. Bryan Jr. award Tex. Gulf Coast Hist. Assn., 1961. Mem. Tex. Sr. Colls. and Univs. (chmn. council of pres.'s 1979), Am. Hist. Assn., Orgn. Am. Historians. Methodist. Clubs: Rotary, Boosters. Author: A Short History of the Sugar Industry in Texas, 1961. Home: 505 E Starr Nacogdoches TX 75961 Office: Box 6078-SFA Station Nacogdoches TX 75962

JOHNSON, WILLIAM ROYSTER, architect; b. Raleigh, N.C., Aug. 18, 1901; s. Charles Cousins and Maude Eleanor (Harris) J.; student Hampden-Sydney Coll., 1918-21, U. Va., 1921-25, Art Students League, 1926-27; m. Elizabeth Terry Niedringhaus, Oct. 9, 1959; 1 son, William Royster. Designer, M.S. Wyeth, architect, 1925-26, chief designer, 1927; designer Wyeth & King, architects, 1926, partner, 1932; partner Wyeth, King & Johnson, architects, Palm Beach, Fla., 1944-73; individual practice William R. Johnson, Architect, Palm Beach, 1973—; mem. archtl. rev. commn. Town of Palm Beach, 1971—. Bd. dirs. Palm Beach Art League, 1948-55, pres., 1954-55. Recipient Hon. Mention, Archtl. League N.Y., 1938. Mem. AIA, Soc. Four Arts, Palm Beach Art League, Kappa Sigma. Democrat. Episcopalian. Clubs: Bath and Tennis, Garden (hon.) (Palm Beach); St. Louis Country. Prin. archtl. works include Vietor Residence, Palm Beach, Norton Gallery and Sch. of Art, West Palm Beach, Fla., Dining Hall, Mercersburg Acad., Gerard Lambert residence, Manalapan, Fla. Home: 214 Plantation Rd Palm Beach FL 33480 Office: 361 S County Rd Palm Beach FL 33480

JOHNSON, WINFRED VAN, educator; b. Norfolk, Va., Aug. 21, 1925; s. Molden and Gracie L. J.; B.D., Capitol Sem., 1958; B.A., Livingston Coll., 1949; m. Shirley Alfred Johnson, July 7, 1973. Youth sec. YMCA, Shreveport, La., 1949-52, Columbus, Ohio, 1952-55; dir. student YM-YWCA, instr. sociology Prairie View (Tex.) A&M U., 1958-70, dean of chapel, asso. prof. sociology, 1970—. Recipient Disting. Service award Prairie View A&M U., 1979; named Tex. Minister of Yr., Tex. Black Ministers Conf., 1974. Mem. Tex. Sociol. Soc., NAACP, Urban League. Democrat. Methodist. Home: 14743 Perthshire Rd Houston TX 77079 Office: PO Box 2073 Prairie View A&M U Prairie View TX 77445

JOHNSTON, ALAN CRAIG, chiropractor; b. Bklyn., Dec. 27, 1944; s. Alvin Clifford and Eva Mae (Pendergast) J.; A.A., St. Johns River Jr. Coll., 1966; D.Chiropractic with honors, Palmer Chiropractic Coll., 1970; m. Barbara Belle McGuire, June 29, 1968; children—Kim Michelle, Alan Craig. Chief of staff G.T. Owen Chiropractic Center, Jacksonville, Fla., 1972-73; chiropractic med. practice, Jacksonville, 1971—. Diplomate Nat. Chiropractic Bd., Bd. Roentgenologists. Mem. Internat., Am., Fla., N.E. Fla. chiropractic assns., Am. Council Chiropractic Orthopedics (certified). Home: 1829 Lindberg Dr Jacksonville FL 32205 Office: 1173 Cassat Ave Jacksonville FL 32205

JOHNSTON, BOBBY CONRAD, clergyman; b. Charlotte, N.C., Nov. 20, 1929; s. Gratt H. and Lucille V. (Cloninger) J.; B.A., Bob Jones U., 1952; B.D., Southeastern Bapt. Sem., 1955, D.Min., 1979; m. Cherry Brooks, May 29, 1952; children—Tina, Teresa, Gregory. Ordained to ministry Bapt. Ch., 1952; pastor Mambrino Ch., Gradbury, Tex., 1954, Eastland St. Ch., Fort Worth, 1954-57, Matoaca (Va.) Ch., 1958-61, First Ch., Edgefield, S.C., 1963-70; sr. minister Salem (Va.) Bapt. Ch., 1970—; preacher Home Mission Bd. in Panama, 1966; speaker for various state evangelistic confs. Pres., Edgefield PTA, 1965-67; organizer Edgefield County Human Relations Com., 1968; v.p. Broad St. Elem. PTA, 1973-74; mem. standards of quality for personnel com. Roanoke County (Va.) Sch., 1974-75; bd. dirs. Beckman Health Center, Greenwood, S.C., 1968-70; trustee Fork Union Mil. Acad., 1976-79. Named Man of Year, Edgefield, S.C., 1965. Edgefield Assn. (moderator 1965-67). Contbr. articles to religious publs. Home: 301 N Broad St Salem VA 24153 Office: 103 N Broad St Salem VA 24153

JOHNSTON, CHARLES ERNEST, optometrist; b. Winchester, Va., Mar. 29, 1928; s. Wilbur Russell and Vergie Pauline (Carpenter) J.; student Shepherd Coll., 1951-54; B.S., So. Coll. Optometry, 1959, O.D., 1959; m. Amelia Irene Rockwell, Nov. 11, 1950; children—Erica Lynn, Benjamin Luther. Technician, Bausch & Lomb, Winchester, 1945-47, Brondstater Opticians, Winchester, 1947-48; with Winchester P.O., 1949-50, 51-52; individual practice optometry, Winchester, 1959—. Organizer, Va. Optometric Polit. Action Com., 1974, pres., 1974-76; treas. Northwestern Mental Health Assn., 1967-69; chmn. troop com. Boy Scouts Am., 1969-74. Served with U.S. Army, 1948-49, 50-51. Named Va. Optometrist of Year, 1977. Fellow Am. Sch. Health Assn., Va. Acad. Optometry; mem. Am. Optometric Assn., So. Council Optometrists (trustee 1972-74), Va. (pres. 1973-74), Shenandoah Valley (pres. 1964-68) optometric socs., Coll. Optometrists in Vision Devel., Nat. Eye Research Found. (photokeratoscopy sect.), Izaak Walton League, Tau Kappa Epsilon, Phi Theta Upsilon. Methodist (steward 1969—, chmn. adminstrv. bd. 1978—). Home: 327 Ridge Ave Winchester VA 22601 Office: 27 W Boscawen St PO Box 2200 Winchester VA 22601

JOHNSTON, ERNESTINE BRIGHTON, nursing adminstr.; b. Memphis, Nov. 27, 1925; d. Ernest Leonard and Annie Lillian (Lunn) Green; R.N., Bapt. Meml. Hosp., Memphis, 1946; B.S. in Nursing, U. Tulsa, 1970, M.S., 1975; m. Robert Samuel Johnston, Jan. 6, 1973; children—Ira Emmett Brighton, Harry Lee Brighton, Val Lynn Brighton. Head nurse obstetrics St. John's Hosp., Tulsa, 1961-63; supr. pediatrics Mabee Children's Hosp., Hillcrest Med. Center, Tulsa, 1963-64, instr. Sch. Nursing, 1964-66, maternal-child health coordinator, 1966; dir. nursing services Hissom Meml. Center, Sand Springs, Okla., 1966—; active state-wide orientation in mental retardation to schs. of nursing; mem. Dirs. of Nursing Service and Nursing Edn. Group, Tulsa. Active Tulsa Area Health and Planning Council, 1970—. R.N., Okla., Tenn.; cert. in mgmt., U. Ala., Birmingham, 1973. Mem. Am. Nurses Assn., Okla. State Nurses Assn. (hosting com. for state conv. 1979, publicity chmn. 1979-80, bd. dirs. Tulsa dist. 1980—), Am. Assn. Mental Deficiency, Parent Guardian Assn.-Hissom Meml. Center, Theatre Tulsa, U. Okla. Alumnae. Democrat. Home: 2832 S Pittsburg St Tulsa OK 74114 Office: Hissom Memorial Center Route 2 Box 14 Sand Springs OK 74063

JOHNSTON, FREEMAN LEON, surgeon; b. Vandervoort, Ark., July 10, 1920; s. Nathornish Robert and Alice Ora (Nations) J.; B.S. with honors, U. Ark., 1941; M.D., Washington U., St. Louis, 1944; m. Margaret Alice Wilson, Mar. 9, 1945; children—Nancy, James, Joanne, Martha. Intern, St. Louis City Hosp., 1944-45; resident in pathology Charleston (W.Va.) Gen. Hosp., 1947-48, gen. surgery, 1948-52; with Stevens Clinic, Welch, W.Va., 1952—, chief surgery, 1964—; practice medicine specializing in gen. surgery Welch, 1952—. Bd. dirs. Bluefield Sanitarium, 1963—. Served from 1st. lt. to capt. U.S. Army, 1945-47. Diplomate Am. Bd. Surgery. Mem. McDowell County Med. Soc. (pres. 1957), W. Va., Am., So. med. assns., ACS, Phi Eta Sigma, Alpha Epsilon Delta, Omicron Delta Kappa, Phi Beta Kappa. Baptist. Kiwanian (pres. Welch 1960). Home: 1436 Stewart St Welch WV 24801 Office: Stevens Clinic Welch WV 24801

JOHNSTON, IRA JUDSON, accountant; b. Willard, Mo., Mar. 11, 1924; s. Jesse Walter and Martha (Crutcher) J.; student Bryant and Stratton Bus. Coll., Louisville, 1947; m. Ann Laura Allen, May 28, 1949; children—Mary Jane, Joel Allen. Insp., Retail Credit Co., Madisonville, Ky., 1947-55, Daytona Beach, Fla., 1955-56; jr. accountant J.W. Johnston Jr., Brinkley, Ark., 1956-60; accountant Ligon Specialized Hauler, Inc., Madisonville, 1960-64; partner Amick & Helm C.P.A.'s, Madisonville, 1964—; dir. North City Ford, Inc., Madisonville. Trustee, Ky. Lions Eye Found., Louisville. Served with AUS, 1943-45. Decorated Combat Infantryman's Badge. Mem. Internat. Platform Assn. Baptist (deacon). Lion (dist. gov. 1970-71). Home: 1707 Hillcrest St Madisonville KY 42431 Office: 173 W Lake St Madisonville KY 42431

JOHNSTON, J(OHN) BENNETT, U.S. senator; b. Shreveport, La., June 10, 1932; s. J. Bennett and Wilma (Lyon) J.; student Washington and Lee U., 1950-51, 52-53, U.S. Mil. Acad., 1951-52; LL.B., La. State U., 1956; m. Mary Gunn, 1956; children—J. Bennett III, Norman Hunter, Mary Lyon, Sarah Lee. Admitted to La. bar, 1956; U.S. senator from La., 1972—, mem. budget com., appropriations com., com. on energy and natural resources, chmn. subcom. energy and water devel., subcom. energy regulation; chmn. Democratic Senatorial Campaign Com., 1975-77. Mem. La. Ho. of Reps., 1964-68, La. Senate, 1968-72. Former bd. dirs. Goodwill Industries. Served with U.S. Army, 1956-59. Mem. Am., La. bar assns., Phi Delta Theta. Democrat. Baptist. Clubs: Masons, Shriners. Office: 421 Russell Office Bldg Washington DC 20510

JOHNSTON, JAMES ROBERT, elec. engr.; b. Cookeville, Tenn., Feb. 10, 1931; B.S., Tenn. Tech. U., 1954; m. Mattie F. Rodgers, Sept. 18, 1949 (dec. Oct. 1968); children—James E., Mark R.; m. 2d, Dorothy R. Miller, June 26, 1970; step-children—Lee O., Janey A., Peggy Sue Miller. Elec. maintenance dept. head Union Carbide Nuclear div. Oak Ridge Nat. Lab., 1954-66; supt. electric shop Dow Chem. Co., Freeport Tex., 1966-69, supt. magnesium prodn. plant, 1969-73, project mgr., 1973-75; project mgr. Dow Chem. Pacific Ltd., Seoul, Korea, 1975-78, Dow Chem. Tex. div., Freeport, 1978—. Registered profl. engr. Tenn., Tex. Mem. Nat., Tex. socs. profl. engrs., IEEE (sr. mem., sec. subcom. on measurements of dielectrics), ASTM. Home: 129 Red Bud St Lake Jackson TX 77566 Office: Dow Chem Co Tex Div PO Box 877 Clute TX 77531

JOHNSTON, JEFFREY SMITH, state senator; b. Seminole, Okla., Jan. 16, 1951; s. Charles Walter and Arlene (Smith) J.; B.A., U. Okla., 1973, J.D., 1977; m. Janet Elizabeth Smith, Mar. 19, 1977; children—Katherine Lynn. Mem. Okla. Ho. of Reps. from 28th Dist., 1974-78; admitted to Okla. bar, 1977, since practiced in Seminole as partner firm Gipson & Johnston; mem. Okla. Senate from 50th Dist., 1979—. Mem. Am. Bar Assn., Okla. Bar Assn., Seminole C. of C. (past dir.), Seminole Arts Council, Seminole Hist. Soc., Phi Beta Kappa, Phi Delta Theta. Democrat. Presbyterian. Bd. dirs. Okla. Law Rev., 1973-77. Home: 914 Hoover St Seminole OK 74868 Office: PO Box 1641 Seminole OK 74868

JOHNSTON, JERRY LYNN, oil field equipment exec.; b. Hampton, Ark., Apr. 26, 1933; s. Clarence and Zula (Blann) J.; B.S., Okla. U., 1955, M.S., 1956; m. Gayle Ann Toland, July 16, 1955; children—Karen L., Susan G., Robert Mark. Pres., Toland & Johnston, Inc.; partner Toland & Johnston. Registered profl. engr., Okla., La. Episcopalian. Home: PO Box 94336 Oklahoma City OK 73111 Office 3409 SE 75th St Oklahoma City OK 73109

JOHNSTON, JOHN WALLIS, educator; b. Dallas, Mar. 1, 1921; s. John A. and Adelia (Clifton) J.; student Draughon's Bus. Coll., 1938-39; B.B.A., U. Tex., 1949; postgrad. U. Fribourg, Switzerland, summer 1949, Loras Coll., summer 1951-52, Assumption Sem., 1952; M.A. in Econs., U. Notre Dame, 1954; postgrad. State U. Iowa, 1954-55; Ph.D. in Bus. Adminstrn., U. Tex., 1968. Adminstrv. asst. to dir. Foremanship Devel. Program, U. Notre Dame, 1953-54; grad. teaching asst. econs. State U. Iowa, 1954-55; asst. prof. econs. St. Francis Xavier U., Antigonish, N.S., Can., 1955-56; asst. prof. dept. bus. adminstrn. and econs. St. Ambrose Coll., Davenport, Iowa, 1957-60; lectr. dept. mktg. adminstrn. U. Tex., Austin, 1960-61; mem. faculty dept. commerce Rice U., Houston, Tex., 1961-67, chmn. dept. commerce, 1964-67; asso. prof. mgmt. Georgetown U., Washington, 1967-68; asso. prof. bus. adminstrn. U. Mo., Columbia, 1968-71; asso. prof. mgmt. U. Miss., University, 1971-79, Jackson (Miss.) State U.,

1979—. Served from pvt., inf. to 1st. lt., Q.M.C., U.S. Army, 1943-46; ETO. Mem. Am. Econ. Assn., Am. Mgmt. Assn., Acad. Mgmt. Roman Catholic. Author: The Department Store Buyer, 1969; contbr. articles in field to bus. jours.

JOHNSTON, JOSEPH EUGENE, physician; b. Oxford, Miss., June 25, 1928; B.A., U. Miss., 1950, M.S. in Pharmacology, 1951, med. certificate, 1953; M.D., Cornell U. Med. Coll., N.Y.C., 1955; m. JoAnn Meloan, 1951; children—Gene, Word, Clay. Rotating intern U. Tex. Med. Br. Hosp., Galveston, 1955-56; gen. practice medicine and surgery, Mt. Olive, Miss., 1956-77; mem. staff Covington County (Miss.) Hosp., Collins, 1956-77, chief of staff, 1964, 69, 73, 77; mem. staff Magee (Miss.) Gen. Hosp.; mem. Miss. Three-Man Gov's. Com. on Rural Health; mem. Miss. Profl. Rev. Com. Chmn. bd. Mt. Olive United Meth. Ch., 1973-76; active Boy Scouts Am.; chmn. Mt. Olive Sch. Bd., 1962-77; alderman, mayor pro-tem Town of Mt. Olive. Served to 1st lt. inf. AUS, 1951-53. Diplomate Am. Bd. Family Practice. Fellow Am. Acad. Family Practice (charter, chmn. cancer com.); mem. Am., Miss. State, So. Miss., Pan-Am. med. assns., South Miss. Med. Soc. (pres. 1973-74), Med. Diving Assn., Miss. Acad. Family Practice (pres. 1967-68), Scabbard and Blade, Beta Beta Beta, Alpha Epsilon Delta, Sigma Nu, Phi Chi. Office: PO Box 248 Mount Olive MS 39119

JOHNSTON, MARY BAGWELL, educator; b. Noble, Ky., Dec. 13, 1938; d. Clyde Edward and Matilda Hays Bagwell; A.A., Paducah Jr. Coll., 1967; B.Ed., Murray State U., 1969, M.Ed., 1970; m. James Vernon Johnston, Aug. 12, 1954; children—James Gregory, Melissa Gaye. Tchr., Paris (Tenn.) Spl. Schs., 1969-73; reading specialist Rocky Mount (N.C.) City Schs., 1973-74; asst. prof. edn. N.C. Wesleyan Coll., Rocky Mount, 1974-77; tchr. remedial English high sch. Clark County Schs., Winchester, Ky., 1977—; cons. in field. Chmn. Nash County Right to Read Council. Mem. Clark County Edn. Assn., Ky. Edn. Assn., NEA, Ky. Council Reading Tchrs., Phi Delta Kappa, Kappa Delta Phi, Democrat. Baptist. Clubs: Winchester Christian Womans, Lioness. Home: 113 Churchill Dr Winchester KY 40391 Office: 620 Boone Ave Winchester KY 40391

JOHNSTON, OTTO WILLIAM, educator; b. N.Y.C., Feb. 26, 1942; s. William P. and Emma M. (Horn) J.; student U. Heidelberg (West Germany), 1961-62, U. Vienna (Austria), 1963-64, U. Gottingen (West Germany), 1966-67; B.A., Wagner Coll., 1963; M.A., Columbia U., 1966; Ph.D., Princeton, 1969. Tchr. Berlitz Lang. Sch., Heidelberg, 1961-62; instr. English, Columbia, N.Y.C., 1965-66; prof. U. Fla., Gainesville, 1969—, dir. undergrad. studies dept. Germanic Langs., 1972—, dir. internat. exchange with U. Bonn, West Germany, 1975—, chmn. Germanic and Slavic langs., 1978—. Named Outstanding Tchr. Standard Oil Co., 1972, Outstanding Prof., Omicron Delta Kappa, 1973, Teacher of Year U. Fla., 1973. Alexander von Humboldt Found. fellow, 1973-74. Mem. Modern Lang. Assn., Am. Assn. Tchrs. German (pres. Fla. chpt. 1976), Fla. Fgn. Lang. Assn. (pres. 1979-80), Gainesville German-Am. Soc. (pres. 1975—), Gainesville German Soc. and Stammtish. Contbr. articles to profl. jours. Home: 3939 NW 46th Ave Gainesville FL 32603 Office: 139 ASB College Union Rd Dept Germanic Languages U Florida Gainesville FL 32611

JOHNSTON, RICHARD LEROY, strategic planning cons.; b. Clinton, Okla., June 6, 1947; s. Donald LeRoy and Pauline Temple (Branstetter) J.; B.S., USAF Acad., 1970; M.B.A., U. Wyo., 1977. Commd. 2d lt. U.S. Air Force, 1970, advanced through grades to capt., 1973; wing weather officer 3d Weather Wing, McConnell AFB, Kans., 1971-73; missile flight comdr. 320th Strategic Missile Squadron, F.E. Warren AFB, Wyo., 1973-74, exec. officer, a.d.c. 4th Air Div., 1974-77; chief planning and control Army and Air Force Exchange Service, Dallas, 1977-79; ret., 1979; strategic planning cons. Federated Dept. Stores, Inc., Cin., 1979—; lectr. mktg. U. Tex., Dallas, 1977-79. Decorated Air Force Commendation medal with 2 oak leaf clusters. Mem. Am. Mgmt. Assn. Republican. Baptist. Club: Cin. Athletic. Home: 18 Sterling Ave Fort Thomas KY 41075 Office: 7 W 7th St Cincinnati OH 45202

JOHNSTON, RUTH LE ROY, nosologist, med. record adminstr.; b. Elizabeth, N.J., June 19, 1915; d. James Archibald and Frances Ione Davis (Austin) Le Roy; B.A., Bob Jones U., Greenville, S.C., 1945; postgrad. in medicine Emory U.; m. Earl Benton Johnston, Aug. 19, 1944; 1 son, Jonathan Bruce (dec.). Various hosp. positions Atlanta, Asheville, N.C., 1948-55; chief med. record librarian VA Hosp., Richmond, Va., 1955-60, Wood, Wis., 1960, Hines, Ill., 1960-62; supervisory med. classification specialist, nosologist research and statistics, Social Security Adminstrn., HEW, Balt., 1962-68; med. record cons. health data service Md. Blue Cross-Blue Shield, Balt., 1970-71; chief med. record adminstr. Good Samaritan Hosp., West Palm Beach, Fla., 1971-74; med. record adminstr. Gorgas Hosp., U.S. Canal Zone, Panama, 1974-77; library asst. North Palm Beach Public Library; lectr. in field, cons. Mem. Save the Panama Canal Club; 1st vice-chmn. bd. dirs. Paradise Harbour Condominium, 1973. Registered med. record adminstr., nosologist, Fla. Mem. Va. (treas. 1957-58, pres. 1960), Md. (v.p. 1963), Fla., Am. med. record assns. Home: 100 Paradise Harbor Blvd North Palm Beach FL 33408

JOHNSTON, THOMAS GIBSON, allergist; b. Dardanelle, Ark., Nov. 24, 1922; s. Thomas Glynn and Pauline (Gibson) J.; B.S., U. Ark., 1943, M.D., 1945; m. Amy Holcombe Ball, Nov. 14, 1963; children—Thomas Glenn, Marcella. Intern, U. Ark. Hosp., Little Rock, 1945; resident in internal medicine Gorgas Hosp., Ancon, Canal Zone, 1948-50, U. Mich. Hosp., 1950-51; now allergist Allergy Assos., P.A., Little Rock, asso. clin. prof., U. Ark.; cons. St. Vincent Infirmary, Baptist Hosp., Children's Hosp. Served with U.S. Army, 1947-49. Recipient Bela Shick award, 1959; diplomate Am. Bd. Allergy and Immunology. Mem. Am. Coll. Allergists (v.p. 1966), Am. Acad. Allergists, Am. Assn. Allergy and Clin. Immunology, AMA, Ark. Med. Assn., So. Med. Assn. (past chmn. allergy sect.), U. Ark. Med. Alumni Assn. (past pres.). Presbyterian. Contbr. articles in field to profl. jours. Home: 5315 Scenic Dr Little Rock AR 72207 Office: 5326 W Markham St Drawer A Hillcrest Sta Little Rock AR 72205

JOHNSTONE, CHARLES ALBERT LESESNE, JR., lawyer; b. Mobile, Ala., Dec. 3, 1910; s. Charles Albert Lesesne and Virginia (Inge) J.; B.A., U. Ala., 1932, LL.B., 1934; m. Olivia Mayton, Oct. 12, 1940; 1 dau., Virginia Inge Johnstone Smith. Admitted to Supreme Ct. U.S. bar, Supreme Ct. Ala. bar, U.S. Ct. Claims bar, U.S. Ct. Appeals 5th Circuit bar; with NRA, 1934-35; individual practice law, 1935-36; with firm Stevens, McCorvey, McLeod, Goode & Turner (name now Johnstone, Adams, May, Howard & Hill), Mobile, 1937—, now sr. partner; dir. The Merchants Nat. Bank, Mobile. Served with U.S. Army, 1942-45. Mem. Am., Ala., Mobile (pres. 1956) bar assns., Mobile C. of C. Episcopalian. Clubs: Country (Mobile), Internat. Trade. Home: 201 Ridgewood Pl Mobile AL 36608 Office: Merchants Bank Bldg Annex Mobile AL 36601

JOHNSTONE, JAMES DECATUR, lawyer, educator; b. Georgetown, S.C., Mar. 5, 1923; s. James Decatur and Alice Amanda (Chandler) J.; student Washington and Lee U., 1940-42, U. N.C., 1955; LL.B., U. S.C., 1958, J.D., 1970; m. Ouilda McDaniel, May 6, 1944 (div. 1948); 1 dau., Jeanette Scott. Admitted to S.C. bar, 1958; gen. atty. SEC, 1958-61; co-developer pub. ltd. partnership as investment vehicle, 1961-65; vice chmn. Petroleum Acquisitions, Inc., Wilmington, Del., 1965-69; commodity trader, 1962—; tchr. U.S. and S.C. history Georgetown County pub. schs., 1966—. Served to maj. Gen. Staff, U.S. Army, 1942-54; ETO, Korea; communications adviser to Turkish Arty., 1949-52. Decorated Soldiers medal, Bronze Star with V device; Cross Mil. Service (UDC), 1949. Mem. SAR, Magna Charta Barons, Soc. Descs. Knights Most Noble Order Garter, Order Washington, Mil. Order World Wars, Mil. Order Fgn. Wars, Horry County, Bladen County hist. socs., Scottish-Am. Heritage, Phi Alpha Delta. Methodist Episcopalian. Compiler: The Johnstone Papers, 1976. Address: 1524 Front St Georgetown SC 29440

JOKL, ERNST F., clin. physiologist; b. Breslau, Ger., Aug. 8, 1907; came to U.S., 1950, naturalized, 1958; s. Hans and Rose (Oelsner) J.; M.D., Beslau U., 1931; M.B., B.Ch., Witwatersrand U., Johannesburg, S. Africa, 1936; m. Erica Lestmann, June 3, 1933; children—Marion Jokl Ball, Peter. Mem. faculty U. Ky. Coll. Allied Health Professions, Lexington, prof. physiology, 1952—, disting. prof., 1964—; pres. research com. Internat. Council Sport and Phys. Edn., UNESCO, 1960—. Decorated Grand Cross Merit (Fed. Republic Ger.); recipient Brit. Commonwealth Research medal Harveian Soc., 1950; research fellow Nat. Library Medicine, Bethesda, Md., 1977; hon. prof. univs. Berlin and Frankfurt/Main. Fellow Am. Coll. Cardiology; mem. AMA, Aerospace Med. Assn., N.Y. Acad. Medicine; hon. mem. Internat. Fedn. Sports Medicine. Club: Rotary. Author books, papers in field. Home: 340 Kingsway Dr Lexington KY 40502 Office: Coll Allied Health Professions Univ Ky Lexington KY 40506

JOLLY-FRITZ, ROLETTA OLGA (MRS. RALPH A. FRITZ), psychiat. cons.; b. Pleasantville, Iowa, Sept. 17, 1896; d. Francis M. and Ida E. (Smith) Jolly; B.S., U. Iowa, 1921, M.D., 1923; m. Ralph A. Fritz, July 9, 1925; children—Lolita Fritz Binford, Jolee, Marcia Fritz Hartman. Intern, Psychopathic Hosp., Iowa City, Iowa, 1923-24, psychiatrist, 1925-31; practice medicine specializing in psychiatry, Pittsburg, Kans., 1928-42, 43-45; sr. psychiatrist Central State Hosp., Nashville, 1942-43; psychiatrist in-unit for children Allentown (Pa.) State Hosp., instr. Sch. Affiliated Nurses, 1946-56; chief out-patient clinic Osawatomie (Kans.) State Hosp., 1956-59; dir. Central Nebr. Mental Hygiene Clinic, 1959-65; clin. psychiatrist Guilford County (N.C.) Mental Health Center, Greensboro, 1966—; psychiat. cons. Guilford County Children and Youth Clinic, 1973-76, Mandala Center, Winston-Salem, N.C., Guilford County Mental Health Center, 1975-76; lecturing prof. Vanderbilt Med. Sch., Meharry Med. Coll., Nashville, 1942-43. Recipient Distinguished Alumni Achievement award U. Iowa, 1976. Fellow Am. Psychiat. Assn. (life); mem. AMA, World Med. Assn., Midcontinent Psychiat. Assn., N.C., Guilford County med. socs., Am. Med. Women's Assn., World Fedn. Mental Health, N.C. Mental Health Assn., N.C. Psychiat. Soc. Methodist. Home: 708 Plummer Dr PO Box 8003 Greensboro NC 27410 Office: 300 N Edgeworth St Greensboro NC 27401

JONAS, GORDON KEITH, banker; b. Las Vegas, Nev., Feb. 2, 1946; s. Gordon Elester and Mary Elizabeth (McGown) J.; B.A., Bowdoin Coll., 1968; m. Shirley Ann Ostrander, Feb. 14, 1971; children—Gwendolyn Kimberly, Ann Randolph. Asst. cashier First & Mchts. Nat. Bank, Richmond, Va., 1970, asst. v.p., 1972, v.p., 1975; v.p., dir. corp. systems First & Mchts. Corp., Richmond, 1975—, sr. v.p., 1978—. Mem. bus. adv. com. Va. Rehab. Bd., 1975-76; deacon 2d Presbyterian Ch., Richmond, 1969—. Mem. Assn. Systems Mgmt., Am. Inst. Banking, Psi Upsilon.

JONAS, JOHN CHARLES, bus. cons.; b. Warsaw, Ind., Aug. 24, 1926; s. John Charles and Margarete Irene (Underwood) J.; B.E.E., Ill. Inst. Tech., 1952; m. Mary Elizabeth Rice, Nov. 5, 1948 (div. May 1970); children—Robert D., Nancy Lynn. Specialist electronic equipment, tech. writer Electronic Supply Office U.S. Navy, Great Lakes, 1947-52; head specifications dept., components engring. div. Raytheon TV & Radio Corp., Chgo., 1952; with Lear Siegler Inc., Grand Rapids, Mich., 1952-64, tech. writer, 1962-63, staff engr., 1963-64; freelance tech. writer, Grand Rapids, 1964-65; personnel mgr., sales engr. Techniques, Inc., Grand Rapids, 1965-68; personnel mgr. Advanced R & D Inc., engrs., Orlando, Fla., 1968-74; pres. Projects Unltd. Inc., Cons.'s, Winter Park, Fla., 1974—; v.p., dir. Am. Recovery Service, Inc., Orlando, 1975—. Served with USNR, World War II; PTO. Mem. IEEE, Comml. Law League Am. Home: 638-4 N Semoran Blvd Winter Park FL 32789

JONES, ALAN IVEY, real estate co. exec.; b. Shreveport, La., Oct. 20, 1938; s. Joseph Reid and Ruby (Ivey) J.; student Kilgore Jr. Coll., 1957-59; B.S., Tex. Christian U., 1962; postgrad. So. Meth. U., 1967-69; m. Camilla Ann Patrick, Nov. 22, 1972; children by previous marriage—Juliana, Kathleen Elizabeth. Owner, Alan I. Jones Ins., Dallas, 1962-66; asso. Henry S. Miller Co., Dallas, 1966-69; v.p. M.L. Godwin Investments, Inc., Dallas, 1968-71; chmn. Alan I. Jones Investments, Inc., Dallas, 1971—; chmn. Alan I. Jones Devel. Co., Resource Energy Corp.; owner 4J Cattle Co., 4J Beefmasters. Served with USNR, 1962, 68. Mem. Sales and Marketing Execs. Dallas (dir. 1975), Dallas C. of C., Dallas Better Bus. Bur., Internat. Platform Assn., Beefmaster Breeders Universal, Tex. and Southwest Cattle Raisers Assn., Tex. Farm Bur. Presbyn. (deacon 1967-68). Rotarian (pres. chpt. 1967-68, dist. sec. 1970-71). Home: PO Box 1556 Kilgore TX 75662 Office: Allied Citizens Bank Bldg Kilgore TX 75662

JONES, ALBERT CECIL, cons. engr.; b. Montevallo, Ala., July 29, 1938; s. Albert Cecil and Thelma Evelyn (Hearn) J.; B.C.E., Auburn U., 1959; 1 son, Albert Cecil; m. Juanita S. Summers, Jan. 21, 1978. Bridge and bldg. supr. So. Ry., 1962-65; process engr. So. Ry., Atlanta, 1965-69; sr. design engr. Rust Engring., Birmingham, Ala., 1969-72; mgr., Harland Bartholomew & Assos., Birmingham, 1972—, asso. partner, 1974—; mem. faculty U. Ala., Birmingham, 1971-72. Served to 1st lt. C.E. AUS, 1960-62. Registered profl. engr., Ala., Ark., Fla., Ky., Miss., Ga. Mem. ASCE, Nat. Soc. Profl. Engrs., Inst. Traffic Engrs. Clubs: Masons, Shriners; The Club, Relay House (Birmingham). Home: 1525 Hidden Lake Dr Birmingham AL 35235 Office: 1608 S 13th Ave Suite 221 Birmingham AL 35205

JONES, ALBERT FOXWELL PAUL, army officer; b. Georgetown, S.C., Apr. 27, 1929; s. Robert Owen and Maude (Ainsworth) J.; B.A. in Internat. Relations, U. Md., 1971; M.A., George Washington U., 1974; grad. Nat. Army Command and Gen. Staff Coll., 1966, Army War Coll., 1973, Nat. War Coll., 1974; m. Vivian Leslie Liles, Aug. 15, 1954; children—Vivian Catherine, Susan Elizabeth, Linda Michelle. Commd. U.S. Army, 1951, advanced through grades to col., 1980; service in W.Ger., Thailand and Vietnam; comdr. U.S. Army Intelligence and Threat Analysis Center, Arlington, Va., also dep. chief staff intelligence and threat analysis U.S. Army Intelligence and Security Command, 1977—. Chmn. edn. com. Prince of Peace Lutheran Ch.-Mo. Synod, Springfield, Va., 1971-73, 79, 80, pres. congregation, 1973-75, elder, 1978, chmn. sch. bd., 1978-79; soccer commr., Ft. Bragg, N.C., 1976-77; dir. soccer league, Springfield, 1978-79. Decorated Legion of Merit (3), Bronze Star, others. Mem. Assn. U.S. Army, Nat. Mil. Intelligence Assn., Acad. Polit. Sci., Assn. Army Spl. Security Group, Nat. Counter-Intelligence Corps Assn., U. Md. Alumni Assn., George Washington U. Alumni Assn. Republican. Home: 8507 Ivybridge Ct Springfield VA 22152 Office: INSCOM Arlington Hall Sta Arlington VA 22212

JONES, ALBERT PEARSON, lawyer; b. Dallas, Tex., July 19, 1907; s. Dr. Bush and Ethel (Hatton) J.; student So. Meth. U., 1924; A.B., U. Tex., 1927, A.M., 1927, LL.B., 1930; m. Annette Lewis, Oct. 3, 1936; children—Dan Pearson, Lewis Avery. Admitted to Tex. bar, 1930, to U.S. Dist. Ct. So. and Eastern Jud. Dists. Tex., U.S. Ct. Appeals 5th Circuit, U.S. Supreme Ct.; asso. Baker, Botts, Andrews & Wharton, Houston, 1930-43; mem. firm Helm & Jones, Houston 1943-62; prof. law U. Tex. at Austin, 1962-77, prof. emeritus, 1977—; 1st asst. to atty. gen. State of Tex., 1963-64 (on leave). Trustee St. Lukes Hosp., 1949-62, Lulu Bryan Rambaud Charitable Trust, 1947-62. Fellow Am. Coll. Trial Lawyers; mem. State Bar Tex. (pres. 1950-51, dir. 8th congl. dist. 1948-50), Houston, Am. bar assns., Am. Law Inst. (life) Order of Coif, Phi Beta Kappa, Phi Delta Phi. Episcopalian. Home: 3195 Del Monte Houston TX 77019

JONES, ALLEN HUGHES, JR., semiconductor co. exec.; b. Washington, May 6, 1946; s. Allen Hughes and Phyllis (Gray) J.; B.S., U. Miami, 1968; M.S., U. Colo., 1970; m. Ann Brown, July 23, 1966; children—Sandra Gray, Samantha Lynn. Research chemist Dow Chem. Co., Midland, Mich., 1970-72; mem. tech. staff Tex. Instruments, Dallas, 1972-74; prin. engr. Harris Semiconductor, Melbourne, Fla., 1974—; adj. prof. chemistry Fla. Inst. Tech., Melbourne, 1978—; dir. Am. Tackle Corp. Mem. Electrochem. Soc., Soc. Photo-Optical Instrumentation Engrs., Phi Lambda Upsilon. Republican. Episcopalian. Home: 605 Robert Way Satellite Beach FL 32937 Office: PO Box 883 Melbourne FL 32901

JONES, ALVIN THOMAS, govt. ofcl.; b. Johnstown, Pa., Aug. 18, 1938; s. Elbert O. and Lilly M. J.; B.S., Central State U. (Ohio), 1960; M.P.A., Okla. U., Norman, 1975; D.P.A., Nova U., Ft. Lauderdale, Fla., 1979; m. Barbara Ann Streety, Dec. 28, 1963; children—Alvin Thomas, Lena Marie. Asst. acct. N.Y.C. Housing Authority, 1960; commd. 2d lt. U.S. Army, 1961, advanced through grades to maj., 1968; personnel dir. Office Human Affairs, Newport News, Va., 1978; project mgr. U.S. Army Tng. Support Command, Ft. Eustis, Va., 1979—; vis. prof. St. Leo U., 1975-76. Pres. Luther Machen Elem. Sch. PTA, Hampton, Va., 1974-75; active Les Hummes Social and Civic Club, Hampton. Decorated D.F.C., Bronze Star medal, Meritorious Service medal, Air medal with 33 oak leaf clusters; recipient cert. of appreciation as dir. Talent Search Program, Hampton Inst., 1979. Mem. Am. Soc. Pub. Adminstrs., Internat. Personnel Mgmt. Assn., Am. Personnel and Guidance Assn., Army Res. Officers Assn., Omega Psi Phi. Home: 118 Sacramento Dr Hampton VA 23666 Office: Hdqrs US Army Tng Support Center Army Extension Tng Fort Eustis VA 23604

JONES, ANDREW MELVIN, educator; b. Attala County, Miss., Mar. 10, 1932; s. Clint and Opal Irene (Peeler) J.; B.A., Miss. Coll., 1952; M.A., U. So. Miss., 1954; Ed.D., U. Miss., 1969; m. Elizabeth Reid, Dec. 20, 1959; children—Amy Elizabeth, John R. Tchr., French Camp (Miss.) Acad., 1952-53, tchr., prin., 1955-57; tchr. math. Weir (Miss.) High Sch., 1958; instr. U. Miss., Oxford, 1958-59, Miss. U. for Women, Columbus, 1959-69; prof. Delta State U., Cleveland, Miss., 1969—. Served with U.S. Army, 1957. Dir. Miss. Youth Congress, 1961—. Recipient Service Key, Phi Delta Kappa, 1961. Mem. NEA, Miss. Assn. Educators, Miss. Speech Assn. (pres. 1960-61, exec. sec. 1964—), So. Speech Communication Assn., Miss. Sch. Adminstrs. Assn. Democrat. Baptist. Home: 809 Pecan St Cleveland MS 38732 Office: Drawer D-1 Delta State U Cleveland MS 38733

JONES, ANGELINE, hosp. exec.; b. Ben Hill County, Ga., Aug. 3, 1938; d. George and Mercy Dee (Walker) Gillis; student S. Ga. Coll., 1972-74; m. Herbert Lewis Jones, Aug. 24, 1958; children—Arnold, Jacquelin, Lethia, Herbert Lewis. Owner, PoJo's Snackhouse & Restaurant, Fitzgerald, Ga., 1972-74; supply clk. Dorminy Meml. Hosp., Fitzgerald, 1974-76, supr. supply dept., 1976-78, purchasing and material mgr., 1978—. Fin. sec. Willing Workers club Mt. Calvary Bapt. Ch., 1974—, mem. sr. choir, 1962—, v.p. Pastoral Aide club, 1967—; active Ben Hill County Civic League, 1970—, Ben Hill County Voters League, 1976—. Mem. Ga. Hosp. Assn., Ga. Soc. Hosp. Purchasing Material Mgrs. Democrat. Club: Elks. Office: Dorminy Meml Hosp PO Box 989 Perry House Rd Fitzgerald GA 31750

JONES, ANN OWINGS, vocational cons.; b. Ashland, Ky., July 6, 1927; d. Thomas Perry and Mabel Carlisle (Lanter) Owings; student U. Ky., 1945-46, 65-66; B.A., Marshall U., 1968, M.A., 1970; m. Edward Curtis Jones, Sept. 7, 1946; children—Judith, Patricia, Thomas. Prin. employment counselor Ky. State Employment Service, Ashland, 1968-76; ind. contractor-cons. in vocations, Ashland, 1976—. Mem. Am. Personnel and Guidance Assn., Am. Vocational Assn., Ky. Employment Counselors Assn., Ky. Personnel and Guidance Assn. Episcopalian. Address: 1508 Hilton Ave Ashland KY 41101

JONES, ANNA LOUISE WOOD, social worker; b. Corbin, Ky., Dec. 9, 1926; d. Edd D. and Nevada (Turner) Wood; student U. Tenn., Wayne State U., U. Ky., Cumberland Coll.; m. Thomas J. Jones, Mar. 4, 1945; children—Gary, Stephanie, Eddie Joe. Office mgr. London (Ky.) Motor Co., 1962-65; gen. office mgr. Wood Products Co., Corbin, Ky., 1965-66; sec. Ky. Dept. Human Resources, Barbourville, 1967—, eligibility worker, food stamps, 1973—, Knox County, 1967—. Vol. ARC; mem. Corbin City Advisory Com., sec., 1968-74; mem. Tri-County Democratic Woman's Club; substitute Sunday sch. tchr. Central Bapt. Ch., Ky. a-d-c. Ky. col. Mem. Am. Legion Aux., DAV Aux., Ky. Welfare Assn., Nat. Bus. and Profl. Womans Club, Tri-County Bus. and Profl. Womens Club (past pres.), Ky. Fedn. Bus. and Profl. Women (past mem. nominating com.), Internat. Platform Speakers Assn. Home: 800 4th St Corbin KY 40701 Office: Box 71 Barbourville KY 40906

JONES, B. CORINE, bank exec.; b. Statesboro, Ga., Jan. 28, 1925; d. Mallie C. and Maude (Gay) Jones; grad. high sch. Clk., Western Auto Supply Co., Savannah, Ga., 1943-46; teller Carolina Nat. Bank, Anderson, S.C., 1950-51; with Liberty Nat. Bank & Trust Co., Savannah, 1946-50, 59—, clk., 1959-69, asst. cashier, 1969-72, banking officer, 1972—. Active United Community Services, March of Dimes, Cancer Soc. Mem. Inter City Credit Council (Outstanding Credit Women 1965, 71, 76), Savannah Credit Women's Club (pres. 1959-60), Ga. Assn. Credit Women (pres. 1970-71), Credit Women Internat., Nat. Assn. Bank Women, Am. Inst. Banking, Soc. Certified Consumer Credit Execs., Internat. Consumer Credit Assn. (pres. dist. III 1979-80). Home: 3605 E Gate Dr Savannah GA 31404 Office: PO Box 8668 Savannah GA 31412

JONES, BILL FRANK, health care exec.; b. Eunice, N.Mex., Jan. 21, 1938; s. Harvey F. and A. Claudine (Fowler) J.; B.S., Abilene Christian U., 1960, B.B.A., 1960; M.S., Okla. State U., 1963; postgrad. U. Wis., 1968, M.I.T., 1973; m. Janis Beth Capps, July 4, 1958; children—Julie Beth, Jennifer Bliss, Jessica Blair, Bryan Frank. Asst. to pres., instr. dept. community medicine U. Tex. Health Sci. Center, Dallas, 1969-74; exec. dir. Kimbro Clinic, Cleburne, Tex., 1974-76; instr. U. Tex. Health Sci. Center, Dallas, part-time, 1976-78; mgmt. cons., Dallas, 1976-78; exec. dir., ltd. partner Valley Diagnostic Clinic, Harlingen, Tex., 1978—; spl. Health Maintenance Orgn. cons. to Tex. Inst. aide to John Connally, 1968. Lic. psychologist, Tex. Mem. Tex. Psychol. Assn., Tex. Hosp. Assn., Med. Group Mgmt.

Assn., Soc. for Advanced Med. Systems, Med. Adminstrs. of Tex. Republican. Ch. of Christ. Contbr. articles to profl. jours. Home: 3129 Clifford Dr Harlingen TX 78550 Office: 2121 Pease St Harlingen TX 78550

JONES, BILLY RUAL, physician; b. Amarillo, Tex., June 11, 1926; s. Rual and Bess (Crutchfield) J.; B.S., Tufts U., 1946; M.D., Columbia, 1950; m. Elizabeth Anne Corbey, May 3, 1952; children—Deborah Anne, Kevin Timothy, Sharon Elizabeth, Julia Marie, Anne Claire. Intern Roosevelt Hosp., N.Y.C., 1950-51, resident, 1951-53; resident VA Hosp., Nashville, 1956-57; practice medicine specializing in internal medicine, Amarillo, 1957—; past pres. staff High Plains Bapt. Hosp.; past chief staff N.W. Tex. Hosp.; past chief med. service Bapt. Hosp., N.W. Tex. Hosp., St. Anthony's Hosp.; asso. prof. medicine Tex. Tech U. Sch. Medicine. Pres. Potter-Randall County Heart Assn., 1959, 63. Bd. dirs. Potter-Randall County Blood Bank, 1962-66; trustee Dad's Assn., Tex. Tech U. Served with USNR, 1944-45, 54-56. Fellow ACP; mem. A.M.A., Am. Soc. Internal Medicine, Tex. Med. Assn., Tex. Acad. Internal Medicine, Tex. Soc. Internal Medicine, Potter-Randall County Med. Soc. Baptist. Rotarian. Clubs: Amarillo, Tascosa Country (Amarillo). Home: 2808 Teckla St Amarillo TX 79106 Office: 5211 W 9th St Amarillo TX 79106

JONES, BOBBY, educator; b. N.Y.C., Feb. 28, 1932; s. Willie and Nettie Mae (Holloway) J.; A.B., Morehouse Coll., Atlanta, Ga., 1953; M.A., Columbia U., 1957; Ed.S., U. Ga., 1970, Ed.D., 1973; m. Dolores T. Williams, Mar. 31, 1964; children—Lisa, Ivan. Mem. faculty Mercer U., Macon, Ga., 1972—, prof. edn., 1973—, chmn. dept., 1979—. Address: Dept Edn Mercer Univ Macon GA 31207

JONES, BUDDY CALVIN, museum curator; b. Gladewater, Tex., Oct. 31, 1938; s. James Lafayette and Wavie Estelle (Dorsett) J.; B.A., U. Okla., 1961, M.A., 1968; m. Patsy Ann Olive, Apr. 18, 1965. Established Caddo Indian Museum, Longview, Tex., 1958, dir., 1958-61, curator, 1961—; archaeologist Archives, History and Records Mgmt. div. Office of Sec. of State of Fla., Tallahasssee, 1968—. Dir. field activities East Tex. Archaeol. Soc., Tyler, Tex., 1956. Served with AUS, 1963. Mem. Am., Tex. archaeol. socs., Soc. for Hist. Archaeol. Soc., Fla. Anthrop. Soc. Home: 2912 Jim Lee Rd Tallahassee FL 32301 Office: Office Sec of State State Capitol Tallahassee FL 32304

JONES, CHARLES ALVIS, clergyman, librarian; b. Alexander City, Ala., Aug 7, 1926; s. Ulio I. and Bertha (Smith) J.; A.B., Samford U., 1951; B.D., Southwestern Bapt. Theol. Sem., 1964; M. in Librarianship, Emory U., 1965; Ed.D. in Tchr. Edn., U. Ga., 1977; postgrad. Troy (Ala.) State Coll., 1955, New Orleans Bapt. Theol. Sem., 1955, North Tex. State U., 1962; m. Hazel Smith, May 23, 1948; children—Margaret Elizabeth, Hazel Rebecca. Ordained to ministry Baptist Ch., 1950; pastor Bapt. chs. Covington County, Ala., 1950-52, 55-61, Conecuh County, Ala., 1952-55, 58-60, Sunny South, Ala., 1954-55, Cobb, Tex., 1961-62, Connerville, Okla., 1964, Tate, Ga., 1967-69, Hiawassee, Ga., 1971-72, Villa Rica, Ga., 1972-73, Commerce, Ga., 1974-77; prin. elementary sch. Covington County (Ala.), 1955-57, 58-59, tchr. jr. high sch., 1959-60; tchr. Hawaii Bapt. Acad., Honolulu, 1962-63; librarian, part-time instr. speech and Bible, Reinhardt Coll., Waleska., Ga., 1965-69; librarian Truett McConnell Coll., Cleveland, Ga., 1969-71; instr. div. librarianship Emory U., Atlanta, 1966: instr. library edn. extension center U. Ga., Canton, 1967; instr. library edn. U. Ga., summer 1969, full time, 1971-77; owner, operator Rome (Ga.) Bible Book Store, 1977—. Mem. Am., Southeastern, Ga. (chmn. coll. and univ. library sect. 1969-71) library assns., Ga. Edn. Assn., Trident, Beta Phi Mu, Phi Kappa Phi. Optimist. Home: 102 Azalea St Rome GA 30161

JONES, CHARLIE WALTER, trade assn. exec.; b. Macon, Miss., Sept. 2, 1916; s. Wyatt Moy and Annie Rix (Clary) J.; B.S. in Agrl. Econs. with spl. honors, Miss. State U., 1948; m. Patricia Marie Manning, Sept. 2, 1944; children—Catherine Jones Millichap, Annie Jones von Rosenberg, Dorothy O'Dea, Robert Charles. Asst. dir. prodn. and mktg. Nat. Cotton Council, Memphis, 1948-52, Washington rep., 1952-54; adminstrv. asst. to U.S. Senator Stennis, Washington, 1954-55, legis. asst., 1955-60; v.p. Am. Carpet Inst., Washington, 1960-67; asst. to v.p. Signal Co., Washington, 1967-70; pres. Man-made Fiber Products Assn., Washington, 1970—; pres., chmn. bd. Textile Economic Bur., N.Y.C., 1973—; dir. Mohasco Corp., N.Y.C.; mem. mgmt. labor textile advisory com. Dept. Commerce, Washington, 1972—. Pres. Men of Ch., Old Presbyterian Meeting House, Alexandria, Va., 1958-59, Miss. Soc. Washington, 1967-68, Assn. Ex-Senate Aids of Washington, 1969; bd. dirs. Miss. State U. Devel. Found., 1974—. Served to capt. USAAF, 1941-46. Mem. Washington Trade Assn. Execs., Golf Trade Assn. Democrat. Clubs: Belle Haven Country (dir.) (Alexandria); N.Y. Empire State, Union League (N.Y.C.); Univ., Nat. Press (Washington); King and Queen Rod and Gun (Tappahannock, Va.). Home: 2111 Belle Haven Rd Alexandria VA 22307

JONES, CONSTANCE JAUCHLER, mathematician; b. Jefferson City, Mo., Jan. 24, 1922; d. Thomas Griffith and Miriam Maude (Jauchler) Jones; B.A., Incarnate Word Coll., 1943; M.A., U. Tex., 1950; postgrad. Harvard, 1943-44, Mass. Inst. Tech., 1944, Clark U., summer 1959, Rutgers State U., summer 1960, U. Tex. at Austin, part time, 1962-68. Instr. sci. Incarnate Word Coll., San Antonio, 1946-47; analytical chemist Tex. Pharmacal Co., San Antonio, 1951-57; asst. prof. math. San Antonio Coll., 1957-62; teaching asst. U. Tex., Austin, 1962-66; asst. prof. math. Trinity U. San Antonio, 1966-69; cons. mathematician, San Antonio, 1969-71; mathematician Office Mgmt. Analysis, Lackland AFB, Tex., 1971-72; asst. prof. math. Incarnate Word Coll., 1972-73, N.E. Ind. Sch. Dist., 1973—. Judge Alamo Regional Sci. Fair, 1975, 76, 77, 78, 79, Alamo Dist. Sci. Fair, 1957-59, 67, 72, Navy award Internat. Sci. Fair, Dallas, 1966, Fort Worth, 1969. Served with USNR, 1943-46; comdr. Res. ret. Named Hon. adm. Tex. Navy. Mem. Am. Chem. Soc. (treas. 1960), Res. Officer Assn, AAAS, Tex. Acad. Sci., Math. Assn. Am., Am. Math. Soc., League Women Voters, San Antonio Conservation Soc., U.S. Naval Inst., Daus. Republic Tex. (v.p. 1957-59, 71-73), Incarnate Word Coll. Alumnae Assn. (pres. 1952-54), St. Monica's Guild Charitable Assn. (v.p. 1969-71), North East Tchrs. Assn. (dir. 1977-78, pres. elect 1979-80, pres. 1980—), Sigma Xi, Delta Kappa Gamma. Home: 148 E Elsmere St San Antonio TX 78212

JONES, DAVID MORGAN, JR., educator; b. Marshallville, Ga., Aug. 23, 1931; s. David Morgan and Ethel Myrtice (Smisson) J.; student Oxford Coll. of Emory U., 1948-50; B.A., Emory U., 1952; M.A., U. Ga., 1954; m. Mary Alice Lee, June 17, 1956; children—David Lee, Mary Elizabeth. Instr., U. Ga., 1956-60; tchr. Lovett Sch., Atlanta, 1960-66; asso. prof. English, Kennesaw Coll., Marietta, Ga., 1966—, asst. chmn. humanities div., 1979—. Bd. dirs. Cobb County Youth Mus., 1977—; mem. adminstrv. bd. First United Methodist Ch., Smyrna, Ga. Mem. Southeastern Modern Lang. Assn., Delta Tau Delta. Republican. Club: Robert Burns (dir. 1975)(Atlanta). Served with Mil. Police Corps, U.S. Army, 1954-56. Editor: Twenty-Five Georgia Historic Mothers, 1976; contbr. articles and poems to various newspapers and mags. Home: 1070 Canterbury Dr Smyrna GA 30080 Office: Kennesaw Coll Marietta GA 30061

JONES, DAVID ROBERT, real estate broker; b. Sumter, S.C., Oct. 27, 1953; s. Hugh Robinson and Mary Ann (Kerester) J.; Asso. in Bus. Mgmt. magna cum laude, No. Va. Community Coll., 1973. Salesman, Myers & Hill, Inc., Springfield, Va., 1973-75; salesman, broker Myers & Hill, Inc., Springfield, Va., 1975-78; salesman/broker John T. Bell Realty & Ins. Co., Goldsboro, N.C., 1977—; owner, pres., prin. broker Country and Suburban Properties, Inc., Fairfax, Va., 1978—. Licensed real estate broker, Va., N.C. Mem. Nat., N.C., Va. assns. realtors, No. Va. Bd. Realtors. Home: 5414 Rumsey Pl Fairfax VA 22032 Office: 9567 Braddock Rd Fairfax VA 22032

JONES, DONALD COLLINS, educator, coach; b. Carroll County, Ga., Sept. 6, 1938; s. James Clifford and Catherine Loraine (Brown-Baxter) J.; A.B., Wofford (S.C.) Coll., 1961; M.S., U. Tenn., 1967; postgrad., La. State U., 1971 summer; m. Patsy Diana Farmer, June 30, 1962; children—William Kyle, Bradley Clifford. Tchr., coach Liberty (S.C.) High Sch., 1963-64; tchr., athletic dir., coach Randolph-Henry High Sch., Charlotte Ct. House, Va., 1964-66; instr., coach Berry Coll., Mt. Berry, Ga., 1967-71, asst. prof., coach, 1971-73, asst. prof., head basketball coach, track coach, 1973-78, asst. prof., head basketball coach, track coach, asso. athletic dir., 1976-78; with ednl. adminstrn. and supervision dept. U. Tenn., Knoxville, 1978—; camp dir. Camp Kanuga, Hendersonville, N.C., summers 1975—. Served with U.S. Army, 1961-63. Named Cross-Country Coach of Year, Ga. Intercollegiate Athletic Conf., 1972-76, Track Coach of Year, 1972-77. Mem. Nat. Assn. Intercollegiate Athletics, Ga. Automobile Assn., Ga. Assn. Health, Phys. Edn. and Recreation. Democrat. Methodist. Clubs: Coosa Country; Lions (pres. 1976-77), Track (pres. 1969-73) (Rome). Home: 59 Springside Dr Hendersonville NC 28739 Office: 201 Henson Hall U Tenn Knoxville TN 37916

JONES, DONNIE HUE, JR., physician; b. Micro, N.C., Feb. 26, 1918; s. Donnie Hue and Odessa (Batten) J.; B.S., Wake Forest (N.C.) Coll., 1939; certificate in medicine, 1940; M.D., U. Va., 1942; m. Linnie Mabel Johnson, June 26, 1942; children—Donnie Hue III, Jennifer, Robert, Marianne, Nancy. Intern U. Va. Hosp., 1942-43, resident, 1943; practice medicine specializing in family practice, Princeton, N.C., 1946—; mem. staffs Johnston Meml. Hosp., Smithfield, N.C., Wayne County Meml. Hosp., Goldsboro, N.C. Mem. Johnston County (N.C.) Bd. Health, 1960; state mem. Johnston County Bd. Pub. Welfare, 1961-63; mem. Johnston County Area Mental Health Bd., 1973—; team physician Princeton High Sch. Dept. Athletics, 1946—. Mem. Johnston County Sch. Bd., 1963-69, chmn., 1967-68; pres. Princeton Little TarHeel League, 1960—. Mayor, Princeton, 1954-55. Bd. dirs. Johnston County Health Dept., 1960-61; trustee Johnston Tech. Inst., 1973—. Served to maj., M.C., USAAF, 1942-46; ETO. Mem. N.C. State, Johnston County (pres. 1950-51), Fourth Dist. (vice-counselor 1955-56) med. socs., A.M.A., Am. Acad. Gen. Practice (charter), A.A.A.S. Republican. Baptist (deacon). Home: Route 2 Box 378 Princeton NC 27569 Office: PO Box 158 Princeton NC 27569

JONES, EARL IRVEN, mfg. co. exec.; b. Vernon, Wilbarger, Tex., Aug. 16, 1928; s. Roy J. and Rockie (Oglesby) J.; B.B.A., So. Meth. U., 1956, M.B.A. (Univ. Trustee scholar), 1958; m. Avis June Koontz, Oct. 18, 1948 (div. June 1975); children—Lindy, Layne, Shelley, Lance; m. 2d, Jeanette Mallet Roberts, Nov. 22, 1975; stepchildren—Terri Roberts, Art Roberts. Sr. engr. Chance Vought Aircraft, Dallas, 1957-60; indsl. engr. mgr. Tyler Pipe Industries (Tex.), 1960-67; indsl. engr. mgr. Texstar Corp., Grand Prairie, Tex., 1967-68, v.p., 1969—; pres. Texstar Plastics, Grand Prairie, 1969—. Served with USAF and AUS, 1951-54; Korea. Decorated Am. Spirit Honor medal. Mem. Am. Inst. Indsl. Engrs. (pres. E. Tex. chpt. 1965-66), Tex. Safety Council (regional v.p. 1964-65), Am. Soc. Safety Engrs., Dallas Sales and Mktg. Execs., Sigma Iota Epsilon. Home: 2204 Adams Dr Arlington TX 76012 Office: PO Box 1530 Grand Prairie TX 75050

JONES, ED, congressman; b. Yorkville, Tenn., Apr. 20, 1912; s. Will Frank and Hortense (Pipkin) J.; B.S., U. Tenn., 1934; postgrad. U. Wis., U. Mo.; D.Litt., Bethel Coll.; m. Llewellyn Wyatt, June 9, 1938; children—Mary Liew Jones McGuire (dec.), Jennifer Kinnard. Insp., Tenn. Dept. Agr., 1934-36; supr. Tenn. Dairy Products Assn., 1936-41; agrl. agt. Ill. Central R.R., West Tenn., 1941-48, Yorkville, 1953-69; commr. agr. State Tenn., 1949-52; asso. farm dir. Radio Sta. WMC, Memphis, 1952-69; pres. bd. dirs. Yorkville (Tenn.) Telephone Coop., 1950—; elected to U.S. Ho. Reps. in spl. election 7th Dist. Tenn., 1969; mem. 92d to 96th Congresses from 7th Dist. Tenn. State chmn. Farmers for Kennedy-Johnson, 1961; pres. bd. trustees Bethel Coll., 1950-67. Named Man of Year, Progressive Farmer mag., 1952, also Memphis Agrl. Club. Mem. 4-H (state farmer). Presbyterian (elder 1940—). Clubs: Masons, Shriners, Moose, Elks. Office: 108 Cannon House Office Bldg Washington DC 20515

JONES, EDITH SHIPE, hosp. dietetic adminstr.; b. Knoxville, Tenn., Aug. 19, 1924; d. Ernest Lafayette and Mabel Susan (Davis) Shipe; B.S., U. Tenn., 1946; m. Lee Caswell Jones, Apr. 30, 1955; children—Emily, Katherine, Lee Caswell. Dietetic intern Peter Bent Brigham Hosp., Boston, 1946-47, relief dietitian, 1948; therapeutic dietitian Oak Ridge Hosp., 1947-48; therapeutic dietitian East Tenn. Bapt. Hosp., Knoxville, 1948-49, dir. dietetics, 1949—. Recipient award for superlative achievement in food service design Instns. Internat. Awards Program, 1970, Gold Menu award Nat. Restaurant Assn., 1972, cert. service for 30 yrs. East Tenn. Bapt. Hosp., 1979; named winner Instn. mag.'s Merchandising Miracles Contest, 1972. Mem. Am. Dietetic Assn., Tenn. Dietetic Assn. (sec.-treas. 1950-52, pres. 1954-55), Knoxville Area Dietetic Assn. (pres. 1953-54), Am. Soc. Hosp. Food Service Adminstrs. (pres. Greater Knoxville area chpt. 1978-79), Tenn. Hosp. Assn., Kappa Delta. Republican. Presbyterian. Home: 5211 Holston Hills Rd Knoxville TN 37914 Office: PO Box 1788 Knoxville TN 37901

JONES, ELIZABETH ELEANORE JONES (MRS. HERBERT LEA JONES, SR.), civic worker; b. Delaware. Ohio Sept. 28, 1916; d. Charles Aubrey and Ireta (Lowe) Jones; student Ohio State U., 1937; m. Herbert Lea Jones, Feb. 5, 1938; children—Nancy (Mrs. Thomas Pfahler, Jr.), Donald, Elizabeth Carr, Charles Allen, Herbert Lea. Sec. Bristol (Va.) C. of C., 1962-71. Active Appalachian council Girl Scouts U.S., 1939—, mem. orgn. com. Camp Sky-Wa-Mo, 1945-52; mem. exec. com., bd. dirs. Bristol United Fund, 1950-65; chmn. housing com. Southeastern Band Fest., 1950—, also asst. sec. bd. dirs.; sec., v.p. Bristol Meml. Hosp. Aux., 1963-64; rep. Va. High Sch. PTA to Bristol Sch. Bd., 1969-74; charter mem. Ch. at Bristol, 1972—, also elder, sec.; pres. Bristol Democratic Women, 1969-71; del. Bristol Dem. Central Com., 1972—. Bd. dirs. Bristol Boy's Club, 1953-68, Bristol Speech and Hearing Center, 1967-80, sec.-treas., 1977-78; bd. dirs. Salvation Army, Bristol, 1971—, sec., 1976—; bd. dirs. YWCA, 1974-80, treas., 1974-80. Recipient Man and Boy award Bristol Boys Club, 1963; Thanks award Girl Scouts, 1952. Mem. D.A.R. Club: Altrusa Bristol, (Va.-Tenn.). Home: 959 Long Crescent Rd Bristol VA 24201

JONES, ELIZABETH RIEKE (MRS. WAYNE VAN LEER JONES), club woman; b. Chgo., Oct. 15, 1903; d. Henry Edward and Vina Genevieve (Coulter) Rieke; A.B., Northwestern U., 1925; m. Wayne Van Leer Jones, Jan. 14, 1926; 1 son, Wayne Van Leer. Dir. Houston Grand Opera Assn. Mem. Nat. Assistance League (nat. fin. com. 1970-72), Univ. Women's Alliance (pres. 1951-53, scholarship chmn. 1963—), Houston Geol. Aux. (parliamentarian 1950-51, 60-61, 63-64), Kappa Kappa Gamma, Theta Sigma Phi. Republican. Presbyterian. Home: 5572 Longmont Dr Houston TX 77056

JONES, ELVA JOHNSON, computer scientist; b. Franklinton, N.C., Oct. 1, 1948; d. Sanford and Bettie Johnson; B.S., Winston Salem State U., 1970; M.S., U. N.C., Greensboro, 1974; m. Emory Eugene Jones, Apr. 5, 1969; 1 son, Emory Eugene II. Computer programmer Winston Salem (N.C.) State U., 1970-72, programmer, asst. data processing mgr., 1972-73, instr. computer sci., 1974—, dir. acad. computer center, 1974—; cons. faculty research analysis. Mem. NAACP, Data Processing Mgmt. Assn., Assn. Ednl. Data Systems, Nat. Bus. Edn. Assn., Delta Sigma Theta. Baptist. Office: PO Box 13302 Winston Salem NC 27102

JONES, ERNEST LEE, artist, religious educator; b. Norfolk, Va., Oct. 5, 1931; s. Lee and Mary (Austin) J.; student Oakatree Sch. Art, 1960; B.A., Johnson C. Smith U., 1970; student Nationwide Tech. Inst., 1973; m. Paulette, Sept. 28, 1970; children—Dawn, Mary, Mia. Community organizer, youth guidance art tchr., Norfolk, Va., 1966-72; recruiter Job Corps inter-city social problems, Norfolk, 1972-76; vol. United Christian Front for Brotherhood, Norfolk, 1979—; paintings include Praying Man, Pride of the First American, The Rage of Poe, Child of Innocence; participant Midcity Art Show, 1977; art tchr. for disturbed youth. Vol. Service to Am., 1971; co-founder Boys Club, 1965; active Church Outreach, 1979. Frederick Douglas speaker, 1979. Home: 1015 Elkin St Norfolk VA 23523

JONES, ERNEST LEWIS, data systems dir.; b. Winona, W.Va., June 18, 1927; s. Lewis P. and Neva (Goode) J.; student Ohio State U., 1944-45; B.A., Marshall U., 1952, M.A., 1952; m. Patricia Ann O'Connor, Nov. 18, 1950; children—Barbara Carole, Deborah Ann, Sandra Lee. Vets. coordinator, registrar's office Marshall U., 1953, asst. registrar, 1953-55; supr. data processing W.Va. U., Morgantown, 1955-63, asst. dir. Computer Center, 1963-66, dir., 1966-68; dir. Data Systems and Services Ind. U., 1968-79; mgr. univ. project GUIDE Internat.; dir. Office Computer and Mgmt. Services, Appalachian State U., Boone, N.C., 1979—; pres. State U. Data Processing Assn., 1970—; cons. Acad. Ednl. Devel.; v.p. Coll. and U. Systems Exchange, 1965, pres., 1966, program com., 1976; chmn. Coll. and U. Machine Records Conf., 1979, bd. dirs., 1977—, chmn. spl. projects com., 1979-80; guest speaker IBM Exec. Class, 1965-66; mem. survey team A study of Ednl. Statistics in W.Va., W.Va. Bd. Edn., 1960; mem. Faculty Coll. Bus. Mgrs. Inst., U. Ky., 1975. Bd. dirs. CAUSE, 1970-71, project mgr., 1972-73. Served with USAF, 1945-48. Mem. W.Va. Assn. Collegiate Registrars and Admissions Officers (pres.), Assn. Ednl. Data Systems (asso. editor jour.), Assn. Computing Machinery, Sigma Phi Epsilon. Democrat. Club: Morgantown Civitan (past sec.). Contbr. articles to profl. jours. and procs. Home: 408 Appalachian Dr Boone NC 28607 Office: Appalachian State U Boone NC 28608

JONES, FRANCES MARIAN FREELAND, govt. ofcl.; b. Plum Branch, S.C., Oct. 7, 1930; d. Hugh Manning and Lula Self Freeland; student Jr. Coll. Augusta, 1948-49, Sch. Nursing, Med. Coll. Ga., 1948-50; m. Clyde Willis Jones, July 8, 1953; 1 dau., Tamblyn Freeland. With U.S. Dept. Army, 1951—, adminstrv. officer Signal Center, Ft. Gordon, Ga., then Fed. Women's Program mgr., Ft. Gordon, 1978—. Mem. Fed. Mgrs. Assn., NOW, Federally Employed Women, Assn. Children with Learning Disabilities. Democrat. Baptist. Clubs: Augusta Civic Women's, Westlake Country, Sea Pines Inn & Beach. Home: 1024 River Ridge Dr Augusta GA 30909 Office: Fort Gordon GA 30905

JONES, FREIDA ANN, chemist, educator; b. Muskogee, Okla., Mar. 10, 1920; d. Hugh Julius and Lillie Ann (Peppers) J.; B.A. with honors, U. Ark., 1942, M.S., 1960; B.S. with honors, U. Tulsa, 1948; postgrad. Oak Ridge Inst. Nuclear Studies, 1965, Okla. State U., 1969-71, Argonne Nat. Lab., 1966, Rice U., 1968, Okla. U., 1971-73. Jr. chemist Lone Star Ordnance Plant, Texarkana, Tex., 1942-44; jr. research chemist Carter Oil Co., Tulsa, 1944-50; teaching, research asst. U. Ark., Fayetteville, Ark., 1960-63; head dept. chemistry Eastern Okla. State Coll., Wilburton, 1963—. Precinct chmn. Dem. party. Mem. NEA, Okla. Edn. Assn., AAAS, Am. Chem. Soc., AAUP, AAUW, Okla. Acad. Sci., C. of C., Sigma Xi, Delta Kappa Gamma, Kappa Delta Pi, Zeta Tau Alpha. Baptist. Club: Bus. and Profl. Women. Contbr. articles to profl. jour. Home: PO Box 1103 Eastern Okla State College Wilburton OK 74578 Office: Eastern Okla State Coll Wilburton OK 74578

JONES, GARLAND MATTHEW, real estate broker; b. Salisbury, N.C., Oct. 7, 1950; s. Robert and Ruby Crawford J.; B.S. in Acctg., N.C. Agrl. and Tech. U.; grad. N.C. Realtors Inst.; m. Dec. 16, 1975. Staff auditor div. Gen. Motors Corp., Indpls., 1972-74; real estate analysis mgr., fin. analysis reporter Mobil Oil Co. and Mobil Chem. Co., Richmond, Va., 1974-77; exec. v.p. Executive Realty Co., Inc., Winston-Salem, N.C., 1977—; pres. Quality Realty of Piedmont, Inc., Winston-Salem, 1979—. Trustee Shiloh Baptist Ch. Mem. Nat. Bd. Realtors, Winston-Salem Bd. Realtors, N.C. Assn. Realtors, Nat. Fedn. Ind. Businesses, Winston-Salem C. of C., N.C. Real Estate Exchangers, Winston-Salem Jr. C. of C., N.C. Agrl. and Tech. U. Alumni Assn. (treas. state chpt.). Author: The Life of an Athlete, 1969. Home: 214 Cheltenham Dr Winston-Salem NC 27103 Office: Executive Realty Co Inc 928 Burke St Winston-Salem NC 27101

JONES, GEORGE HERBERT, ophthalmologist; b. Baton Rouge, Mar. 7, 1922; s. George Herbert and Mary Weir (Tucker) J.; B.S., La. State U., 1942, M.D., 1953; postgrad. Tulane U., 1954-57; m. Klileen Leister, June 16, 1946. Cons. engr., La. and Mexico, 1946-49; intern Charity Hosp., New Orleans, 1953-54, resident in ophthalmology, 1954-57; practice medicine specializing in ophthalmology, Baton Rouge, 1957—; asst. prof. Tulane U. Sch. Medicine, New Orleans, 1965—; staff Baton Rouge Gen. Hosp., 1957—, Our Lady of the Lake Hosp., Baton Rouge, 1957—; eye surgeon Ill. Central R.R., 1959—. Bd. dirs. Baton Rouge Little Theater, 1962-65; bd. dirs. Baton Rouge Community Concert Assn., 1965—, pres. 1966-70; bd. dirs. Baton Rouge Symphony, 1970-73, Christian Social Concerns, Meth. Ch., 1968-72; bd. govs. Camelot Club, 1976—, La. State U. Union, 1973-75. Served to capt. AUS, 1942-46; ETO. Diplomate Am. Bd. Ophthalmology. Mem. Am. Acad. Ophthalmology, La. Ophthamol. Soc. (pres. 1963, 69, 74), La. Med. Soc., La.-Miss. Ophthalmology and Otolaryngology Soc. (councilor 1973-75), Internat. Brotherhood Magicians, Alpha Omega Alpha, Omicron Delta Kappa, Nu Sigma Nu, Sigma Chi (nat. v.p.). Democrat. Methodist. Clubs: Camelot, Allen Resident (pres. 1975—), Masons (Shriner). Home: 2727 E Lakeshore Dr Baton Rouge LA 70808 Office: 4550 North Blvd Baton Rouge LA 70806

JONES, GRANT, state senator; b. Abilene, Tex., Nov. 11, 1922; s. Morgan and Jessie (Wilder) J.; B.B.A., So. Methodist U., 1947; M.B.A., Wharton Sch. U. Pa., 1948; m. Anne Smith, Aug. 21, 1948; children—Morgan Andrew, Janet Elizabeth. Casualty underwriter Trezevant and Cochran, Dallas, 1950-54; ins. agt., Abilene, 1948-73; admitted to Tex. bar, 1974; pvt. practice law, also ind. ins. agt.,

1954—; mem. Tex. Ho. of Reps. from 62d Dist., 1965-72, Tex. Senate from 24th Dist., 1973—. Served as pilot USAAF, World War II. C.P.C.U. Mem. Nat. Assn. Ins. Agts. (dir. 1963), Tex. Assn. Ins. Agts. (past pres.), Soc. C.P.C.U. Democrat. Methodist. Home: 1509 Woodridge St Abilene TX 79605 Office: PO Box 5138 Abilene TX 79605

JONES, HENRY EARL, dermatologist; b. Detroit, Jan. 24, 1940; s. Henry Clay and Treva Jewel (Jones) J.; B.S., Murray State U., 1961; M.D., Tulane U., 1965; children by previous marriage—Gregory, Laronda, Tamara. Intern, Tripler Gen. Hosp., Honolulu, 1965-66; resident in dermatology Letterman Gen. Hosp. and U. Calif., San Francisco, 1966-69; chief resident in dermatology Letterman Gen. Hosp., 1968-69; asst. chief div. dermatology Letterman Army Inst. of Research, San Francisco, Calif., 1970-73, dir. cutaneous infection and immunology lab., 1970-73; asst. prof. dermatology U. Mich., 1973-76; prof. of dermatology Emory U., 1976—, chmn. dept., 1977—, dir. Emory affiliated Dermatology Tng. Program, 1976. Served to lt. col. U.S. Army, 1965-73. Decorated Bronze Star; recipient John Herr Musser Meml. award Tulane U., 1965, Outstanding Resident award Letterman Gen. Hosp., 1969; diplomate Am. Bd. Dermatology. Mem. Am. Acad. Dermatology Soc. Investigative Dermatology, Am. Dermatologic Soc. Allergy, Immunology, Dermatology Found., Am. Soc. Microbiology, Assn. Profs. Dermatology, Ga. Dermatology Soc., Atlanta Dermatol. Assn., Am. Assn. Immunology, Am. Dermatol. Assn., Alpha Omega Alpha. Home: 758 Wildwood Rd NE Atlanta GA 30324 Office: Emory U Sch Medicine 215 WMB Atlanta GA 30322

JONES, HENRY THOMAS, II, utility exec.; b. Maxton, N.C., Sept. 28, 1944; s. Henry Thomas and Nannie Ruth Jones; B.S. in Acctg., Pembroke State U., 1972; M.A. in Mgmt., Central Mich. U., 1979; m. Joyce McDougald, Dec. 30, 1965; 1 dau., Thomasia Elva. Office supr. trainee Carolina Power & Light Co., Raleigh, 1972-73, office supr., 1973, area acctg. supr., 1973-76, acctg. systems analyst, 1976, dir. equal employment opportunity programs, 1976-77, instr. acctg., 1977-79, adminstrv. asst. to chief exec. officer and chmn., 1979—. Served with USAF, 1963-67. Mem. Am. Soc. for Tng. and Devel., Am. Legion, Alpha Phi Alpha. Democrat. Methodist. Home: 725 Ravel St Raleigh NC 27606 Office: 411 Fayetteville St Raleigh NC 27602

JONES, HOWARD LEON, educator; b. Phoenixville, Pa., Oct. 20, 1940; s. Walter R. and Marie (McCann) J.; B.S., Millersville (Pa.) State Coll., 1962; M.A., U. Tex., 1964, Ph.D., 1966; m. Renda M. Nowell, Dec. 28, 1963; children—Stephen K., Kelly L. Project asso., research asso., instr. U. Tex., 1964-66; vis. prof. Okla. State U., summer 1965; asst. prof. sci. edn. Syracuse U., 1966-68; asso. prof. edn. U. Houston, 1968-73, prof. edn., 1973—, asso. dir. competency-based tchr. edn. program, 1971-73, dir., 1973-74, coordinator elementary edn., 1974-75, chmn. tchr. edn., 1976-78; program mgr. div. pre-coll. edn. in sci. NSF, 1975-76; sci. cons. Eastern Regional Inst. for Edn., 1967-69; cons. Exploratory Com. for Assessment of Edn. Progress, Ednl. Testing Service; mem. Tex. Bd. Examiners for Tchrs. Edn., 1974-76. Fellow AAAS. Author: (with G.E. Hall) Competency-Based Education: A Process for the Improvement of Education, 1976; contbr. articles to profl. jours. Home: 1503 Ashford Pwy Houston TX 77077

JONES, JACQUELYN ELAINE, counselor; b. Greensboor, N.C., Nov. 12, 1951; d. Leroy and Marye Willie (McCorkle) J.; B.A., Shaw U., 1973; M.S., N.C. A&T State U., 1975. Counselor, Livingstone Coll., Salisbury, N.C., 1975—, assisting dir. counseling and testing center, 1978—. Mem. NAACP, Nat. Assn. Personnel Workers, Am. Personnel and Guidance Assn., Am. Coll. Personnel Assn., Assn. Non-White Concerns in Personnel and Guidance, Alpha Kappa Alpha. Democrat. Methodist. Home: Salisbury NC 28144 Office: 701 W Monroe St Salisbury NC 28144

JONES, JAMES BURTON, engring. co. exec.; b. Biloxi, Miss., Dec. 13, 1931; s. George Edward and Genevive (Braun) J.; B.S., U. So. Miss., 1952; M.S., Fla. Inst. Tech., 1970; m. Ileana Antonia Rodriguez, Apr. 17, 1955; children—James Burton, Edward A., Gail M., Richard J., Thomas A., Teresa I. Design engr. Rockwell Internat., Columbus, Ohio, 1959-63, group engr., 1963-69; mgmt. cons., Cocoa Beach, Fla., 1969-70; dir. engring., then v.p. ops. Novatronics, Pompano Beach, Fla., 1970—. Mem. industry adv. com. Fla. Atlantic U., 1975—; mem. exec. com. Nova U. Served with USAF, 1952-59. Mem. Broward Mfrs. Assn., Novatronics Mgmt. Club (pres. 1971-72). Republican. Roman Catholic. Club: K.C. Patentee in field. Home: 2151 NE 44th Ct Lighthouse Point FL 33064 Office: PO Box 878 Pompano Beach FL 33064

JONES, JAMES CLIFTON, chem. co. exec.; b. Osceola, Ark., Jan. 17, 1950; s. Porter and Henrietta (Hill) J.; B.S. in Bus. Adminstrn., U. Ark., Pine Bluff, 1972; m. Sheryl Monroe, Mar. 1, 1975; 1 son, Stacy B. Accountant, Sun/DX Oil Co., Tulsa, 1974-75; accountant Agrico Chem. Co., Tulsa, 1975-77, buyer, 1977—; cons. Nat. Alliance Bus., 1979—, RCA Govt. Services Contracts, 1978—. Served with U.S. Army, 1972-74. Mem. Nat. Purchasing Mgmt. Assn., Tulsa Purchasing Mgmt. Assn., U. Ark. Alumni Assn. (pres. Tulsa chpt.). Home: 748 N Zenith Ave Tulsa OK 74127 Office: PO Box 3494 Tulsa OK 74101

JONES, JAMES HARDWICK, SR., real estate investor; b. Calhoun, Ga., Nov. 30, 1947; s. Henry Thomas and Helen Malet (Hardwick) J.; student South Ga. Jr. Coll., 1965-66; m. Beverly Joan King, June 15, 1968; children—James Hardwick, Jennifer Renee. Patrolman, Clearwater, Fla., 1970-71; pres. J. H. J. Enterprises Inc. doing bus. as The Rejuvenators, Clearwater, 1972-79; pres. adv. bd. Pro Hardware Stores for Fla., 1975-76. Served with USCG, 1966-70. Named Pro Hardware of Year, 1974. Mem. Tri-City Mchts. Assn. (pres. 1973-76). Democrat. Methodist. Home: 2918 Magnolia Trace Tarpon Springs FL 33589

JONES, JAMES HARVEY, radiologist; b. Columbia, Miss., Dec. 18, 1939; s. Malcom Otis and Willie Maude (Eaton) J.; B.S., U. Miss., 1961, M.D., 1965; m. Betty Gwynn, July 1, 1962; children—Gia Lori, James Harvey II, Jason Neal, Julie Alison. Resident in radiology, U. Tex., Houston, 1969-73; radiologist Space Center Meml. Hosp., Houston, 1973-74, Houston Northwest Med. Center, 1974-75, Parkway Meml. Hosp., Houston, 1975—. Served with AUS, 1966-68; Vietnam. Decorated D.S.M. Mem. Radiology Soc. Houston, Radiology Soc. Am., Radiology Soc. Tex., Harris County Med. Soc., Tex. Med. Soc. Republican. Baptist. Home: 5522 Theall St Houston TX 77066 Office: 150 W Parker St Houston TX 77067

JONES, JAMES HENRY, lumber co. exec.; b. Plainview, Tex., Nov. 13, 1915; s. Henry Floyd and Margaret Frances (Swann) J.; student W. Tex. State U., Amarillo, 1950-51, So. Meth. U., 1952; m. Sara Nell Rives, May 13, 1941; 1 son, James Henry. Mgr., Rockwell Bros. & Co., 1937-42, 46-50; estimator Amarillo Lumber Co. (Tex.), 1950-52; mgr. S.W. Moulding Co., Dallas, 1952-68; pres., owner J. H. Jones Lumber Co., Addison, Tex., 1968—. Served with USAAF, 1942-46. Republican. Baptist. Club: Aircraft Owner and Pilots Assn. Home: 533 Pittman St Richardson TX 75081 Office: 15304 Midway Rd Addison TX 75001

JONES, JAMES MERRILL, II, physician; b. Lewes, Del., Sept. 20, 1946; s. James Merrill and Lenore (King) J.; B.S., Shepherd Coll., 1968; M.D., Jefferson Med. Coll., 1975; m. Cynthia Sue Landis, Aug. 7, 1971; children—John Tyler, Reagan Anne. Intern, W.Va. U. Hosp., Morgantown, 1975-76, resident in internal medicine, 1976-78; fellow in clin. hematology Milton S. Hershey Med. Center, Hershey, Pa., 1978-79; practice medicine specializing in internal medicine, hematology, Martinsburg, W.Va., 1979—; mem. staff Kings Daus., City hosps., Martinsburg. Served with AUS, 1969-71. Diplomate Am. Bd. Internal Medicine. Mem. A.C.P., W.Va. Med. Assn., Eastern Panhandle Med. Soc. Episcopalian. Home: 114 N Tennessee Ave Martinsburg WV 25401 Office: 302 Rock Cliff Dr Martinsburg WV 25401

JONES, JAMES ODELL, univ. dean; b. Parsons, Tenn., Oct. 5, 1920; s. Johnnie J. and Gertrude (Frizzell) J.; B.S., U. Tenn., 1942; m. Lorene Johnson, Dec. 12, 1943; children—Michael J., Keith O., Nancy L., Karen G., Kenneth A. Coop. edn. student in engring. TVA, 1940-42; instr. U. Tenn., Martin, 1946, chmn. dept. engring. and math., 1949, dean coop. edn., 1974, dean coop. edn. and placement, 1976—; cons. in field; mem. adv. council Southeastern Center for Coop. Edn., U. South Fla., Tampa, 1975—; mem. Tenn. Gov.'s Coop. Edn. Adv. Com., 1976—, chmn. planning activities, 1976—; mem. Coop. Edn. Tng. Center Council, Auburn (Ala.) U., 1977-79. Mem. indsl. bd. City of Martin, 1971—, chmn., 1978—; bd. dirs., sec.-treas. Thompson Creek Watershed, 1964—. Served with USAAF, 1942-45; to lt. col. USAR. Registered profl. engr., Tenn. Mem. Tenn. Soc. Profl. Engrs. (chpt. pres. 1973-74, state dir. 1974-75), Am. Inst. Indsl. Engrs. (pres. 1964), Am. Soc. Engring. Edn. (sec. coop. edn. div. 1965-66), Tenn. Coll. Placement Assn. (dir. 1976-78, v.p. coll. relations 1979—), So. Coll. Placement Council, Am. Legion (comdr. 1978-79), Weakley County C. of C. (dir. 1974-75), Tau Beta Pi, Phi Kappa Phi. Baptist. Club: Lions (pres. 1950-51, dir.). Home: 115 Ryan Ave Martin TN 38237 Office: Univ of Tenn 260 University Center Martin TN 38238

JONES, JAMES R., congressman; b. Muskogee, Okla., May 5, 1939; A.B. in Journalism and Govt., U. Okla., 1961; LL.B., Georgetown U., 1964; m. Olivia Barclay, 1968; children—Geoffrey Gardner, Adam Winston. Admitted to Okla. bar, 1964; legislative asst. to Congressman Ed Edmondson, 1961-64; spl. asst. to Pres. Lyndon Johnson, 1965-69; mem. 93d-96th Congresses, 1st Dist. Okla. Served as capt. CIC, U.S. Army, 1964-65. Mem. Am., Okla., Tulsa bar assns., Am. Legion, Tulsa C. of C. Democrat. Rotarian. Home: Tulsa OK Office: 203 Cannon House Office Bldg Washington DC 20515

JONES, JAMES RICHARD, educator; b. Saginaw, Mich., May 25, 1940; s. George B. and F. Rena (Jerome) J.; B.A., Mich. State U., 1962, M.B.A., 1964; D.B.A., Ariz. State U., 1969. Staff asst. Mich. Pub. Service Commn., Lansing, 1962; systems analyst Allis Chalmers Mfg. Co., W. Allis, Wis., 1964-65; asst. prof. U. Houston, 1967-70; asso. prof. U. Ga., 1970-72; spl. asst. to asst. sec. for policy U.S. Dept. Transp., Washington, 1972-73, transp. economist, 1974-76; distinguished prof. transp. Memphis State U., 1976—; cons. in field; bd. examiners Am. Soc. Traffic and Transp. Keeshin fellow, 1963. Mem. Am., So., Southwestern mktg. assns., Am. Soc. Traffic and Transportation, Transp. Research Bd., Transp. Research Forum, World Trade of Memphis. Mem. editorial rev. bd. Jour. Business Logistics, 1977—. Contbr. articles in field to profl. jours. Home: 4037 Camelot Ln Memphis TN 38118 Office: College of Business Administration Memphis State University Memphis TN 38152

JONES, JARL HAMILTON, commodity brokerage exec.; b. Cin., Jan. 9, 1939; s. Henry Stewart and Sara (Roddis) J.; student Purdue U., 1956-58; B.B.A., U. Wis., 1961; J.D., U. Denver, 1964; m. Katherine Covert Soles, Aug. 8, 1964; children—Lance Stewart, Brett Hamilton, Stacey Elizabeth. Admitted to Colo. bar, 1964; sr. staff indsl. analyst Amoco Prodn. Co., New Orleans, 1964-75; pres. br. office PMC Corp., Arlington, Tex., 1976—. Republican precinct chmn., Arlington, 1977—; bd. dirs. Tulsa Multiple Sclerosis Soc., 1969-72. Mem. Theta Chi. Episcopalian. Clubs: Toastmasters, Kiwanis, Arlington Swim (bd. dirs. 1979—). Home: 4818 Ferncreek Ct Arlington TX 76017 Office: 2304 W Park Row Arlington TX 76013

JONES, JAY CARL, III, found. exec.; b. Kinston, N.C., Jan. 16, 1946; s. Jay Carl, Jr. and Helen May (Rouse) J.; student Def. Lang. Inst., Calif., 1968; B.S. in Bus., U. N.C., 1973, M.B.A., 1975; m. Mary Fletcher Parrott, May 11, 1968; children—William Arendall, Marian Fuller. Co-founder Carolina Traders, Inc., Chapel Hill, N.C., 1971-74; asso. dir. adminstrn. Health Edn. Found., Tarboro, N.C., 1975—; asso. dir. Community Medicine Found., Tarboro, 1978—; dir. N.C. Primary Health Care Assn. Bd. dirs. Tarboro-Edgecombe Acad. Served with USAF, 1967-71. Decorated Air medal with 2 oak leaf clusters. Mem. N.C. Primary Health Care Assn., M.B.A. Assn. Democrat. Methodist. Club: Chapel Hill Lions (past pres.). Home: 2013 Glissom St Tarboro NC 27886 Office: Health Edn Found PO Box 1319 Tarboro NC 27886

JONES, JENKIN LLOYD, JR., editor; b. Tulsa, June 24, 1936; s. Jenkin Lloyd and Juanita Rose (Carlson) J.; B.A. in Polit. Sci., U. Colo., 1958; m. Carol Beatrice Jaros, June 27, 1959; children—Janette Lloyd, Landon Lloyd. Sports writer Mpls. Tribune, 1959; reporter, news editor Anchorage Times, 1959-61; state capital corr. Tulsa Tribune, Oklahoma City, 1961-62, Washington corr., 1962-63, copy editor, Tulsa, 1963-64, chief copy desk, 1964-65, asst. city editor, 1965-66, asst. mng. editor, 1966-67, mng. editor, 1968-74, exec. editor, 1974—; v.p. Tulsa Tribune Co. Bd. dirs. Goodwill Industries Tulsa. Served with USAFR, 1958-64. Mem. AP Mng. Editors' Assn. (past dir.), U. Tulsa Hurricane Club, Am. Soc. Newspaper Editors, Internat. Press Inst. Republican. Unitarian. Club: So. Hills Country. Home: 6447 S Louisville St Tulsa OK 74136 Office: PO Box 1770 315 Boulder Ave Tulsa OK 74103

JONES, JIMMY WAYNE, editor; b. Bowie, Tex., May 20, 1935; s. John Roy and Nancy Vera (Kilcrease) J.; B.A., N. Tex. State U., 1957; M.A., Tex. Christian U., 1967. Reporter, feature writer, columnist Fort Worth Star Telegram, 1957-63, suburban editor Evening Star Telegram, 1963-75, met. editor, 1975-78, religion editor, 1978—; cons. pub. relations. Served with USAF, 1957-58. Recipient Tex. Bapt. Press award, 1963. Mem. Nat. Profl. Soc. Journalists, Fort Worth Press Club, Sigma Delta Chi, N. Tex. State U. Alumni Assn. (dir. 1968-71). Baptist. Democrat. Club: Fort Worth Tennis Assn. Home: 4761 E Lancaster St Apt 216 Fort Worth TX 76103 Office: 400 W 7th St Fort Worth TX 76101

JONES, JOHN ALVIS, III, indsl. engr.; b. Evansville, Ind. Jan. 21, 1943; s. John Alvis and Audrey Etta (Lee) J.; A.A., Hiwassee Coll., 1962; B.S., U. Tenn., 1964; m. Marty Floyd, Oct. 25, 1967; children—John, Shannon. Indsl. engr. Overhead Engring. br., Robins AFB, Ga., 1965-69; indsl. engr. Adminstrv. Contracting Office, Arnold Engring. Devel. Center, Tullahoma, Tenn., 1969-70; with Facilities and Equipment Engring. br. Warner Robins Air Logistics Center, Robins AFB, Ga., 1970-78, supervisory gen. engr. Facilities Engring. br. Directorate of Maintenance, 1979—. Coach youth soccer, basketball and baseball teams Warner Robins recreation program, 1977—. Mem. Robins AFB Better Mgmt. Assn., Tech. Mktg. Soc. Am., Nat. Suprs. Assn., Alpha Pi Mu. Baptist. Club: Masons. Home: 419 Kimberly Rd Warner Robins GA 31093 Office: Warner Robins ALC/MADE Robins AFB GA 31098

JONES, JOHN BELL, farm equipment co. exec.; b. Elihu, Ky., Mar. 31, 1916; s. Parker Lee and Bula (Nelson) J.; B.S., U. Ky., 1939; m. Nancy K. Nonn, Dec. 26, 1964; children—Linda Kay, Jean Karen. Tchr. high sch. agr., Ky., 1939-44; personnel trainee Ind. Farm Bur. Coop., Indpls., 1944-45; gen. mgr. Tenn. Farmers Coop., 1946-54, regional sales mgr., 1954-71; v.p. Four Star, Inc., College Grove, Tenn., 1958-71, pres., 1971—. Patentee bale handling equipment. Office: Four Star Inc Box 97 College Grove TN 37046

JONES, JOHN DONALD, ednl. adminstr.; b. Cobb County, Ga., Aug. 10, 1932; s. Jeff Young and Leola (Wilson) J.; B.A., Berry Coll., 1955; M.A., U. Tenn., 1962, postgrad., 1963-64. Instr. English, Berry Acad., Mt. Berry, Ga., 1955-57; instr., counselor Baylor Sch., Chattanooga, 1957-65; admissions officer Emory U., Atlanta, 1965-67, asst. dean of students, 1967-69, dean student activities, 1969—. Bd. dirs. Atlanta Humane Soc., ARC, Mental Health Assn. Mem. Am. Personnel and Guidance Assn., Nat. Assn. Student Personnel Adminstrs., So. Coll. Personnel Assn., Ga. Assn. Sch. Counselors, Atlanta Kennel Club (1st v.p.), German Shepherd Club Atlanta (pres.). Democrat. Episcopalian. Internat. dog show judge. Home: PO Box 23505 Emory Univ Atlanta GA 30322 Office: Drawer TT Emory Univ Atlanta GA 30322

JONES, JOHN HERBERT, lawyer; b. Miami, May 17, 1943; B.A., Emory U., 1965; M.B.A., Ga. State U., 1972; J.D., U. Fla., 1976, LL.M., 1976; m. Apr. 28, 1979. Admitted to Fla. bar, 1976, Ga. bar, 1976, D.C. bar, 1976; individual practice law, Gainesville, 1976-78; partner firm Reiman & Jones, Gainesville, 1978—. Mem. citizens' adv. com. N. Central Fla. Regional Planning Council; mem. citizens' adv. com. on community devel. City of Gainesville. Served with USNR, 1966-69. Mem. Am. Bar Assn., Lawyers Title Guaranty Fund, Gainesville C. of C., Am. Legion. Office: 35 N Main St Suite 30 Gainesville FL 32601

JONES, JOHN WALTER, JR., engr.; b. Miami, Fla., Nov. 23, 1913; s. John Walter and Elinor Burwell (Hickson) J.; student Colo. Sch. Mines, 1933-35; m. Mildred Vivian Puckett, July 20, 1940; children—Elinor Burwell Jones Pyles, Melanie Vivian Jones Brown, Ann Spotswood Jones Wood, Walter Martin, Pamela Sue. Office engr. Biscayne Engring. Co., Miami, 1935-41; asst. airport engr. Pan Am. Airways, 1941-50; propr. J. Walter Jones, Jr. and Assos., South Boston, Va., 1950—; pres. South Boston Devel. Corp., 1967—; mem. Va. Bd. Exam. and Certification Architects, Profl. Engrs. and Land Surveyors, 1964-74, pres., 1968. Fellow ASCE; mem. Am. Congress Surveying and Mapping, Danville Soc. Engring. and Sci. (pres. 1967), N.C. Soc. Surveyors, Va. Assn. Surveyors (pres. 1962), Kappa Sigma. Clubs: Masons, Lions. Home: 8 Maplewood Dr PO Box 773 South Boston VA 24592 Office: Security Bldg 554 N Main St South Boston VA 24592

JONES, JUANITA SAWYERS, librarian; b. Johnson County, Tex., Mar. 8, 1919; d. Lonnie Buford and Letha Jewel (King) S.; B.A., Sam Houston State U., Huntsville, Tex., 1962, M.A., 1964; M.L.S., N. Tex. State U., Denton, 1972; m. William David Jones, Mar. 15, 1946; children—David Buford, Charles Robert. Instr. English, Sam Houston State U., 1962-65; tchr. English, Richfield High Sch., Waco, Tex., 1965-66; instr. English, Temple (Tex.) Jr. Coll., 1966-69, asst. librarian, 1969-73; librarian U. Mary Hardin-Baylor, Belton, 1973—, head librarian, since 1975—. Teaching fellow Sam Houston State U., 1962-63. Mem. Tex. Library Assn., Alpha Sigma Lambda, Alpha Chi, Sigma Tau Delta. Methodist. Home: 3309 Chisholm Trail Temple TX 76501 Office: Townsend Meml Library U Mary Hardin-Baylor Belton TX 76513

JONES, JUDY FRANCES, counselor; b. Altus, Okla., Aug. 9, 1947; d. Austin Edward and Gladys (Loman) Marsh; student Altus Jr. Coll., 1966; B.S. in Edn., Southwestern State U., 1968; M.Ed., Central State U., 1972; m. Elbert Lewis Jones, May 5, 1972; 1 dau., Keisha Elbertine. Elem. tchr. public schs., Clinton, Okla., 1968-69; elem. tchr. public schs., Oklahoma City, 1969-71, Headstart presch. tchr., summer 1970 adult edn. tchr., 1970-72; reading specialist Kennedy Jr. High Sch., Oklahoma City, 1971-72; counselor Oklahoma City pub. schs., 1972—; sales asso. Alert Realty, Oklahoma City, 1973-74; owner, broker J.J.'s Realty, Oklahoma City, 1974—. Licensed real estate broker, Okla. Mem. Am. Personnel and Guidance Assn., Okla. Personnel and Guidance Assn., Oklahoma City Personnel and Guidance Assn., Kappa Delta Pi. Democrat. Ch. of Christ. Home: Route 1 PO Box 264A Oklahoma City OK 73111 Office: Office of Guidance and Counseling 900 N Klein St Oklahoma City OK 73102

JONES, LEON HERBERT (HERB), artist; b. Norfolk, Va., Mar. 25, 1923; s. Leon Herbert and Edna May (Curling J.; student William and Mary Coll., 1942-44; m. Barbara Dean, Sept. 14, 1947; children—Robert Clair, Louis Herbert. Marine structural draftsman and designer Norfolk (Va.) Shipbuilding & Dry Dock Co., 1944-46; freelance comml. artist, 1946-49; prin. Herb Jones Realty, Norfolk, 1949-58; owner, mgr. Herb Jones Art Studio, Norfolk, 1958—; one-man shows: Norfolk Mus., 1968, Potomac Gallery, Alexandria, Va., 1979, Salisbury Gallery, 1979, Walter C. Rawls Mus., Courtland, Va., 1967; group shows include: Chrysler Mus., Norfolk, 1973, 74, SUNY, Buffalo, 1966, Springfield (Mass.) Mus. Fine Arts, 1966, Mariners Mus., Newport News, Va., 1967-73, Va. Mus., Richmond, 1969, 71, Columbia (S.C.) Mus. Art, 1972, Winston-Salem (N.C.) Gallery Contemporary Art, 1970, 72, Norfolk Mus., 1963-69, Vladimir Arts, Winsbach, W. Ger., 1978, 79; represented in permanent collections; Chrysler Mus., wardroom USS Skipjack, USS John F. Kennedy, USS Dwight D. Eisenhower, U. Va., Charlottesville, U.S. Treasury Dept., also pvt. collections. Mem. Nat. Soc. Arts and Lit., Tidewater Artists Assn. Methodist. Home and Office: 238 Beck St Norfolk VA 23503

JONES, LEONARD LEE, accountant; b. Mulberry, Kans., Aug. 27, 1938; s. Lloyd Keith and Beulah Isadore (Hunsaker) J.; B.S., Pittsburg State (Kans.) U., 1960; postgrad. Emporia State Coll., Tex. Christian U., Kan. U., U. Tex. at Arlington; m. Marilyn Ann Gammaitoni, May 27, 1961; children—Kerri Lynnette, Brett Ashley. Bank examiner FDIC, Kansas City, Mo., 1961; cost accountant Didde-Glaser, Inc., Emporia, Kans., 1961-63; audit mgr. Arthur Young & Co., Ft. Worth, 1963-70; partner Larue, Lawrence, Wood & Kelley, Ft. Worth, 1970-72; controller, treas. Crest Container Corp., Ft. Worth, 1972-73; partner Lee Jones C.P.A., Fort Worth, 1973—; dir. Bondurant Corp., Profl. Pharm. Co.; fin. cons.; trustee First Nat. Bank, Cisco, Tex. Adviser, Jr. Achievement Tarrant County, 1965-67; del. Tarrant County Rep. Conv., 1968. C.P.A., Tex., Okla. Mem. Am. Inst. C.P.A.'s, Tex. Soc. C.P.A.'s, Internat. Assn. Fin. Planners, N.Am. Mensa, N. Tex. Mensa (v.p. 1968). Republican. Methodist. Clubs: Shady Oaks Country; Ft. Worth Cosmopolitan (judge adv. S.W. Fedn. 1972-73). Contbr. articles to profl. jours.; seminar instr. Home: 8932 Van Deman Dr Fort Worth TX 76116 Office: 3825 Hwy 377 S Fort Worth TX 76116

JONES, LOIS MONAHON, educator; b. Germantown, Ky., Apr. 28, 1933; d. Harry and Calma (Case) Monahon; B.A. magna cum laude, Georgetown Coll., 1955; M.A., George Peabody Coll. for Tchrs., 1958; m. Robert Hopkins Jones, Aug. 8, 1959. Project tchr. Malaga Sch. of the Wolfe County Sch. System, Campton, Ky., 1955-57; elem. tchr. Crieve Hall Sch. of Davidson County Sch. System, Nashville, 1958-63; supervising tchr. 3d grade Peabody Demonstration Sch., George Peabody Coll., Nashville, 1963-66, substitute tchr., 1966-70; instr. edn. Belmont Coll., Nashville, 1970-73, asst. prof., 1973—. Mem. Sunday sch. council First Bapt. Ch., Nashville, 1966—, mem. edn. adv. com., 1975-77, mem. spl. com. on renovation of ednl. facilities, 1976-79. Mem. NEA, Tenn. Edn. Assn., Assn. for Supervision and Curriculum Devel., Middle Tenn. Edn. Assn., Assn. for Childhood Edn., Assn. Tchr. Educators, Friends of Public Library of Nashville, Delta Kappa Gamma (rec. sec. 1968-70, pres. 1976-78), Sigma Alpha Iota, Kappa Delta Pi (counselor chpt. 1979—). Democrat. Club: Adelicia Acklen Woman's (pres. 1974-75, chmn. spl. projects com. 1978-79). Office: Belmont Coll Nashville TN 37203

JONES, MAX KESLER, univ. adminstr.; b. Hereford, Tex., May 9, 1938; s. Harold Kesler and Maudetha (Miller) J.; B.A., Tex. Christian U., 1960; M.Div., Yale U., 1964; m. Suzanne Smith, Sept. 8, 1962; children—Kinley Nan, Kyle Weldon, Lacey Suzanne. Ordained to ministry Christian Ch., 1964; pastor Christian Ch., Roswell, N.Mex., 1964-67; regional dir. Joint Action in Community Service, Austin, Tex., 1967-69; asst. dean Sch. Law, So. Meth. U., Dallas, 1969-71; dir. regional campaigns Tex. Christian U., Ft. Worth, 1971-74; pres. Ark. Council Ind. Colls. and Univs., Little Rock, 1974-78; pres. Tex. Ind. Coll. Fund, 1978—; cons. on resource devel. Mem. bd. higher edn. Christian Ch. Mem. Nat. Assn. Ind. Colls. and Univs., Ind. Coll. Funds Am., Ft. Worth C. of C. Democrat. Club: Rotary. Office: 2630 West Freeway Suite 224 Fort Worth TX 76102

JONES, MERRIAM ARTHUR, chemist; b. Hankinson, N.D., Jan. 4, 1913; s. Arthur Phineus and Abramina (Gunderson) J.; B.A., U. N.D., 1933; postgrad. U. Minn., 1933-36; Ph.D., George Washington U., 1950; m. Alvilda Grace Bangs, June 6, 1933; 1 dau., Marilyn Jones Feldkamp. With U.S. Treasury, 1936, Bur. Standards, 1936-37; cryptanalyst War Dept., 1937-39; chemist Fed. Expt. Sta., Mayaguez, P.R., 1939-46; chemist U.S. Dept. Agr., Washington, 1946-51; chemist, research mgmt. adviser AID, Guatemala, Haiti, Iraq, Iran, Lebanon and Turkey, 1951-68; asst. div. chmn. phys. scis., prof. chemistry No. Va. Community Coll., Annandale, 1968—. Served with AUS, 1935-36. Mem. Am. Chem. Soc., Sigma Xi, Alpha Chi Sigma. Contbr. to profl. jours. Home: 5936 N 3d St Arlington VA 22203 Office: Dept Chemistry No Va Community Coll Annandale VA 22003

JONES, MICHAEL DARWIN, engr.; b. Hope, Ark., Sept. 1, 1944; s. Charles Darwin and Effie Cordella (Lorance) J.; student So. State Coll., 1962-64; B.S.A.E., U. Ark., 1967, M.S.A.E., 1968; M.E.I.E., Tex. A&M U., 1970; M.B.A., Fla. Inst. Tech., 1980; m. Yvonne Eugenie Koenigseder, June 24, 1967; children—Glen Michael, Christopher. Engring. intern Red River (Tex.) Army Depot, 1968-70; engr. U.S. Army Mobility Equipment Command, St. Louis, 1970-73; test design and evaluation engr. U.S. Army Operational Test and Evaluation Agy., Washington, 1973-76; chief test and evaluation div. U.S. Army Logistics Center, Ft. Lee, Va., 1976-80; mgr. quality engring. Propulsion div. Atlantic Research Inc., Gainsville, Va., 1980—; mem. Domestic Action Council, Dept. Def., 1972-73; instr. Fla. Inst. Tech., 1979-80. Chmn. Cub Scout pack com. Robert E. Lee council Boy Scouts Am., 1977-79; chmn. bd. dirs. Chester Montessori Sch., Inc., 1978-80. Recipient Civilian Meritorious Service award Dept. Army, 1977. Mem. Soc. Logistics Engrs., Assn. U.S. Army, U.S. Coast Guard Aux., Float Fishermen of Va. Club: Chesdin Yacht. Contbr. articles to profl. jours. Home: care Lavery 14571 Leilani Dr Woodbridge VA 22193 Office: Propulsion Div Atlantic Research Corp PO Box 38 Gainsville VA 22065

JONES, MILDRED JOSEPHINE, realtor; b. Anniston, Ala., Jan. 29, 1927; d. Howard McFadden and Gladys Eulala (Carr) Jones; student Howard Coll., Birmingham, Ala., 1947. Retail and secretarial positions, 1948-65; area, then dist. mgr. in Montgomery, Ala. for Field Enterprises Ednl. Corp., 1965-71; engaged in real estate sales, 1971—; owner Southland Realty Co., Montgomery, 1974—. Mem. advisory bd. Am. Christian Coll. Mem. Nat. Assn. Realtors, Farm and Land Inst., Montgomery Bd. Realtors. Presbyterian. Club: Point Aquarius Country. Home: 3024 Biltmore Ave Montgomery AL 36109 Office: 2006 Mulberry Montgomery AL 36106

JONES, MIRIAM ESTHER, hosp. adminstr.; b. Logan County, Ohio, Nov. 10, 1923; d. Thomas Russell and Mary Olga (Ansley) Crisler; A.S. in Nursing, Polk Community Coll., 1974; certified enterostomal therapist Emory U., 1976. Operating room technician Winter Haven (Fla.) Hosp., 1961-72, dir. central service, 1972—, enterostomal therapist, 1976—; cons. in field. Mem. Internat. Assn. Hosp. Central Service Mgmt., Internat. Assn. Enterostomal Therapists. Democrat. Home: 136 Miller Dr SE Winter Haven FL 33880 Office: 200 Ave F NE Winter Haven FL 33880

JONES, MYRTIS IDELLE (MRS. C.W. JONES), library cons.; b. Prescott, Ark., May 16, 1908; d. Andrew Brice and Ethel (Hardwick) Barham; A.A., Little Rock Jr. Coll., 1952; B.E., Ark. State Tchrs. Coll., 1958; M.L.S., George Peabody Coll. Tchrs., 1965; m. B.H. Harrison, Oct. 31, 1925, (div. Mar. 1933); children—Jack Barham, Charles Ray, Mary Anna Harrison Scheie; m. 2d, J.W.E. Moore, Mar. 16, 1933 (dec. June 1950); children—William Robert, Jonathan Edward, Ethel Rachel Moore Hubka, Paul David; m. 3d, C.W. Jones, June 2, 1952 (dec. Jan. 1969). Library asst. Little Rock Jr. Coll., 1950-52; librarian Holly Grove (Ark.) High Sch., 1955, Vanndale (Ark.) High Sch., 1955-56, Stuttgart (Ark.) Sr. High Sch., 1956-59; supr. sch. libraries Stuttgart Pub. Schs., 1956-59; librarian Ark. Sch. for the Blind, Little Rock, 1959-74, library cons., 1974—; mem. library com. Commn. on Standards and Accreditation of Services of the Blind; mem. awards com. Joseph Campbell Citation. Mem. Ret. Sr. Vol. Program; coordinator activities Pulaski County Council Aging. Mem. Ark. Student Librarians Assn. (sponsor exec. councils 1957—), Assn. Am. Librarians, ALA, Library Service to the Blind, Ark. (v.p. 1966-67), S.W. library assns., Council Exceptional Children, Assn. Educators of Visually Handicapped (chmn. library sci. workshop 1964-68), Ark. Edn. Assn., Ark. Assn. Classroom Teachers, NEA, Internat. Platform Assn., Alpha Beta Alpha. Mem. Ch. of Nazarene. Club: Order Eastern Star. Home: 5608 Geyer Springs Rd Little Rock AR 72209

JONES, NONA MAE, nursing home adminstr.; b. Kissimmee, Fla., Nov. 27, 1919; d. Arthur Eugene and Nina Mae (Sharpe) Jones; nursing home adminstr. licensure St. Petersburg Jr. Coll., 1972; 1 adopted dau., Sandra Jane Jones Dempsey. Bookkeeper, sales clk. H.B. Allen Firestone Store, Kissimmee, 1945-53; bookkeeper, key punch operator Tupperware Home Parties, Orlando, Fla., 1953-60; bookkeeper, office mgr. Cinderella Internat., Orlando, 1960-62; NCR operator/key punch Corporate Group Services, Orlando, 1963-68; bookkeeper, asst. adminstr. John Milton Nursing Home, Inc., Kissimmee, 1967-78, adminstr., 1978—; bd. dirs. Osceola County Mental Health Dept. Mem. Fla. Health Care Assn. (treas. dist. 3), C. of C. Osceola County. Mem. Christian Ch. (Disciples of Christ). Democrat. Home: PO Box 2312 809 N Brack St Kissimmee FL 32741 Office: John Milton Nursing Home Inc 1120 W Donegan Ave Kissimmee FL 32741

JONES, NORWOOD ELTON, mcht., real estate broker; b. Jackson, Tenn., July 10, 1930; s. William Norwood and Bessie Mae (Scammerhorn) J.; student Lambuth Coll., 1948-51; B.S., Memphis State U., 1952; m. Joyce Ann Taylor, Aug. 17, 1951; children—William Randolph, Leigh Ann. Vice pres. Jasper Transfer & Storage, Memphis, 1951-65; pres. Brooks Shaw & Son Old Country Store, Jackson, 1965—; owner Old Country Store Land Office, Jackson, 1967—. Mem. exec. com. Tourism Assn. S.W. Tenn.; mem. Commn. on Aging; mem. Jackson Hist. Zoning Commn. Mem. Nat. Fedn. Ind. Bus. (com. mem.), Tenn. Assn. Realtors, Nat. Assn. Realtors, Jackson Area C. of C. Club: Optimist (pres. Jackson 1972). Home: 151 Montclair Dr Jackson TN 38301 Office: Casey Jones Village Jackson TN 38301

JONES, OLIVER, JR., city agy. adminstr.; b. Baton Rouge, Jan. 10, 1945; s. Oliver and Johnnie Mae (Albert) J.; B.A., So. U., 1966; M.A., George Washington U., 1973; m. Ethel M. Cole, Aug. 16, 1975; 1 son, Keith Raynaurd. Vol., Vista, 1969-70; tng. dir. A.L. Nellam & Assos., Chgo. and Ft. Wayne (Ind.), 1970-71; program officer Peace Corp, Jamaica, West Indies and St. Croix, V.I., 1971-73; chief employee devel. officer City of Baton Rouge, 1974-79; asst. dir. tng. East Baton Rouge Parish Assestment Center, 1979—. Mem. Am. Soc. Tng. and Devel., La. Equal Opportunity Assn., Scottandville Jaycees, Pi Gamma Mu. Democrat. Methodist. Office: PO Box 1471 Baton Rouge LA 70821

JONES, PATRICIA, computer analyst; b. Algood, Tenn., Mar. 5, 1939; d. Mayhew Pettus and Sara Josephine (Currin) J.; B.S., George Peabody Coll. Tchrs., 1960, M.A., 1971; Ed.D. (hon.) U.S. U. Am., 1974. Ednl. sec. First Bapt. Ch., Alexandria, Va., 1967-68; data processing supr. So. Bapt. Fgn. Mission Bd., Richmond, Va., 1968-70; asst. coordinator women's residence halls Western Carolina U., Cullowhee, N.C., 1971-72; asso. dean students, asst. prof. math. W.Va. Wesleyan Coll., Buckhannon, 1972-74; computer systems analyst and computer systems devel. supr., Va. State Police, Richmond, 1974-77; sr. computer systems analyst Systems Engring. Computer Co., Richmond, 1977—. Emergency med. technician West End Vol. Rescue Squad. Served as officer USNR, 1960-66. Mem. AAUW (exec. bd. 1972-74). Republican. Baptist. Home: 5907 Old Richmond Ave Richmond VA 23226 Office: Systems Engring Computer Co Richmond VA 23230

JONES, PATRICIA ANN INGRAM, counselor; b. Winnsboro, La., Oct. 19, 1951; d. Jackson Homer and Rose Elizabeth (Lee) Ingram; B.A., Northwestern State U., 1973; M.Ed., N.E. La. U., 1977; M.A. in Rehab. Counseling, Northwestern State U., 1980; m. Millard Joseph Jones, Sept. 14, 1974; 1 adopted son, Millard Ruebon. Dir. social services Franklin Guest Home, Winnsboro, 1974-76; vocat. rehab. counselor MAVTEC, Monroe, La., 1979—. Semi-finalist Miss Wheelchair La., 1978. Mem. Am. Personnel and Guidance Assn., Am. Rehab. Counseling Assn., Nat. Rehab. Assn., Physically Ltd. Assn for a Constructive Environment La. Coalition for Citizens with Disabilities, NE La. Found. Handicapped, Psi Chi. Democrat. Baptist. Club: Eastern Star. Served as wheelchair del. to La. Gov.'s Conf. on Handicapped Individuals, 1976. Home: Route 5 Box 126 Winnsboro LA 71295

JONES, PAUL RONALD, chemist, educator; b. York, Pa., Dec. 19, 1940; s. Robert Lewis and Lavona Yvonne (Dorish) J.; B.S., Pa. State U., 1962; Ph.D., Purdue U., 1966; m. Priscilla Anne Carney, Sept. 16, 1967; children—Kevin, Anne. Research asso. U. Wis., 1966-67, lectr., 1967; asst. prof. chemistry N. Tex. State U., 1968-73, asso. prof., 1973-79, prof., 1979—. Mem. Am. Chem. Soc., Sigma Xi, Alpha Chi Sigma, Phi Lambda Upsilon. Office: Dept Chemistry N Tex State Univ Denton TX 76203

JONES, PERRY THOMPSON, hosp. adminstr.; b. Atlanta, June 11, 1937; s. Perry and Marion (Thompson) J.; A.B., Duke U., 1959; M.S. in Hosp. Adminstrn., Northwestern U., 1961; children—Holly E., Christopher Perry. Asst. adminstr. Watts Hosp., Durham, N.C., 1962-63; evening adminstr. Weiss Hosp., Chgo., 1963-65; asst. dir. Moses Cone Hosp., Greensboro, N.C., 1965-67; pres. Community Gen. Hosp., Thomasville, N.C., 1967—. Bd. dirs. Davidson County Youth and Family Counselor Service. Served with U.S. Army, 1960-67, U.S. Navy, 1974-79. Fellow Am. Coll. Hosp. Adminstrs.; mem. N.C. Hosp. Assn. (trustee 1976-79), Thomasville Area C. of C. (dir.), Am. Hosp. Assn. Republican. Methodist. Club: Rotary. Office: Box 789 Thomasville NC 27360

JONES, PHILIPPA STOKES, counselor, guidance dir.; b. New Castle, Pa., July 31, 1910; d. James Wilbur and Caroline Bartle (Jenkins) Stokes; A.B., Geneva Coll., 1931; postgrad. U. Pitts., 1932-33; M.A., U. Fla., 1960; postgrad. Fla. Atlantic U.; m. William Stanley Jones, Apr. 29, 1933 (dec. Oct. 1966); 1 son, William Stanley. Tchr., Aliquippa, Pa., 1931-33; with U.S. Govt., Washington, 1937-42; tchr., Mobile, Ala., 1945-48, Raleigh, N.C., 1948-54, Hickory, N.C., 1954-56; tchr.-counselor, Ft. Pierce, Fla., 1956-59; dir. guidance St. Lucie (Fla.) County Jr. High Sch., 1959-70; counselor Lincoln Park Sch., Ft. Pierce, 1970-73; dir. guidance Ft. Pierce (Fla.) Central High Sch., 1973—; mem. steering com. Fla. State-wide 9th Grade Testing Program, 1965-69. Pres., Ft. Pierce-St. Lucie County Mental Health Assn., 1965-66. Mem. Indian River Area personnel and guidance assns., Nat. Vocat. Guidance Assn., Am. Sch. Counselors Assn., St. Lucie County Classroom Tchrs., U. Fla. Alumni Assn., AAUW, Alpha Delta Kappa, Kappa Delta Pi. Clubs: Soroptimist Internat. Home: 2403 Barbara Ave Ft Pierce FL 33450 Office: Ft Pierce Central High School Ft Pierce FL 33450

JONES, REBA BROUGHTON, psychologist; b. Lamesa, Tex., Oct. 29, 1917; d. James Thomas and Florence (Jordan) Broughton; B.A., Tex. Christian U., 1954, M.A., 1958; m. Ross Edward Jones, June 12, 1937. Self-employed comml. pilot, Albuquerque, 1943-45; psychologist Tex. Christian U. Testing Center, 1952-54; psychologist public schs., Fort Worth, 1954-66; head dept. psychol. services Fort Worth Ind. Sch. Dist., 1966—; project dir. Edn. in Living, 1974—, Local Growth Center Project, 1975—, SW Regional Growth Center Project, 1977—, Career Planning Acad., 1977—; counselor, vis. tchr. Tex. Edn. Agy., 1954—; cons. Hilton Shepherd Assos., 1960—; pvt. practice psychology, Ft. Worth, 1958—. Bd. dirs. Tarrant County Mental Health Assn., 1966—, pres., 1972; bd. dirs. Tex. Mental Health Assn.; mem. Mental Health Task Force, Tex. Area 5 Health Systems Agy., 1977—; mem. Tarrant County Health Planning Council, 1977—. Recipient Disting. Service award Tarrant County Mental Health Assn. Mem. Am. Psychol. Assn. (chmn. ethics com. 1978-81), NEA, Southwestern Psychol. Assn., Tex. Psychol. Assn., Tex. State Tchrs. Assn., Tarrant County Psychol. Assn., Fort Worth Ind. Sch. Dist. Adminstrs. Assn., Fort Worth-Tarrant County Adminstrv. Women's Assn., Delta Kappa Gamma. Cons. editor Jour. Sch. Psychology, 1978, reviewer books, 1974—. Home: 4617 Hildring Dr East Fort Worth TX 76109 Office: 3210 W Lancaster St Fort Worth TX 76107

JONES, RICHARD LLOYD, JR., newspaper exec.; b. Nyack, N.Y., Feb., 22, 1909; s. Richard Lloyd and Georgia (Hayden) J.; Ph.B., U. Wis., 1932; LL.D., Oral Roberts U.; m. Martha Meredeth Corder, Mar. 4, 1933; children—Richard, Dana. Apprentice mech. depts. Tulsa Tribune, 1933-34, with telegraph desk, 1935, display advt. dept., 1935-38, became v.p., bus. mgr., 1938, now pres.; v.p., bus. mgr. Newspaper Printing Corp., 1941-51, pres., 1951; v.p., treas. Hennepin Paper Co., Little Falls, Minn., 1953-56; dir. Brookside State Bank, Tulsa, McDonnell Douglas Corp.; mem. bd. dirs. AP, 1964-73, vice chmn., 1972-73. Chmn. Tulsa Airport Authority; dir. state fair, livestock expn., Tulsa. Served as lt. USNR, World War II, comdg. officer gun crew U.S.S. Sharon Victory, U.S.S. Dickinson Victory. Mem. Tulsa C. of C. (dir. 1954—, pres. 1960-61), So. Newspaper Pubs. Assn. (chmn. labor com. 1948-52, pres. 1953-54, chmn. bd. 1954-55), Am. Newspaper Pubs. Assn. (chmn. bd. bur. advt. 1956-58), Aviation Writers Assn., Phi Gamma Delta. Unitarian. Club: So. Hills Country (Tulsa). Home: 2422 E 72d St Tulsa OK 74136 also Shangri La Route 3 Afton OK 74331 Office: Tulsa Tribune 315 S Boulder St Tulsa OK 74102

JONES, RICHARD PALMER, JR., architect; b. Lakeland, Fla., June 2, 1921; s. Richard Palmer and Pauline (Overby) J.; B.Arch., U. Fla., 1950; m. Alice Ruth Adams, May 14, 1944; children—Ralph Lloyd, Margaret Jones Campbell, Richard Palmer. Asso. firm Thomas Y. Talley, architect, Lakeland, 1950-58; practice architecture, Lakeland, 1958-59, 65—; partner firm Jones & Renfroe, architects (named changed to Jones, Renfroe, Setliff, Architects 1963), Lakeland, 1959-65; dir. Acre Mor Corp., Mine & Mill Supply Co. Ind. (both Lakeland). Pres. Lakeland Little Theater, 1972; city commr. Lakeland, 1975-76. Served with USNR, 1942-45. Mem. AIA (treas. chpt. 1972-73). Methodist (chmn. ofcl. bd. 1966-68). Home: PO Box 486 Lakeland FL 33802 Office: 129 S Kentucky Ave Lakeland FL 33801

JONES, RIVES RANDOLPH, III, chem. engr.; b. Bluefield, W.Va., Jan. 2, 1933; s. Rives Randolph, Jr. and Mary Jane (Haynes) J.; B.S. in Chem. Engring., Ohio State U., 1956, M.B.A., 1957; m. Barbara Ann Jones, Mar. 16, 1956; children—Pamela, Linda, Rives Randolph, IV. Dist. mgr. Allied Chem. Co., 1957-65; area mgr. Houston Chem. Co., 1965-77; dir. mktg. Reliance Cons. Group Inc., 1977-78, group v.p., Tulsa, Okla., 1978—. dir. Petrogas, Inc., Rampart Systems. Rockefeller fellow, 1957. Mem. Am. Petroleum Inst., Nat. Petroleum Refiners Assn., Am. Chem. Soc., Acme. Republican. Methodist. Clubs: Tulsa Petroleum Oaks Country, Bellefonte Country. Address: 5330 S 77th East Ave Tulsa OK 74145

JONES, ROBERT BRINKLEY, historian; b. Richmond, Va., Mar. 29, 1942; s. Robert Brinkley and Mary Valerie (LeMasurier) J.; B.A. with distinction, U. Va., 1964; M.A., Vanderbilt U., 1968, Ph.D. (NDEA fellow), 1972; m. Roberta Clark Blevins, Feb. 26, 1966; 1 son, Robert Brinkley. Asst. prof. history Middle Tenn. State U., Murfreesboro, 1970-74, asso. prof., 1974—, asst. v.p. for acad. affairs, 1977—, pres. faculty senate, 1976-77. Mem. Rutherford County (Tenn.) Bicentennial Commn., 1976-77. Served with USN, 1964-66. Decorated D.S.M.; Am. Council Learned Socs. publ. grantee, 1975; Tenn. Hist. Commn. grantee, 1975; recipient Distinguished Service award Vanderbilt U., 1973. Mem. So. Hist. Assn., Tenn., Rutherford County (pres. 1976-77) hist. socs., Phi Alpha Theta, Pi Gamma Mu. Democrat. Roman Catholic. Club: Vanderbilt (pres. Murfreesboro club 1976—). Author: Tennessee at the Crossroads: The State Debt Controversy, 1870-1883, 1977. Home: 819 W Northfield Blvd Murfreesboro TN

JONES, ROBERT BRINKLEY, JR., elec. engr.; b. Richmond, Va., June 12, 1910; s. Robert Brinkley and Rose (Morris) J.; B.S. in Engring., U. Va., 1932, Elec. Engr., 1933; m. Valerie LeMasurier, June 22, 1940; children—Robert Brinkley, Rosemary Jones Serfilippi, Valerie Jones Rea, Michael Harrison (dec.). With Chesapeake & Potomac Telephone Co. Va., Richmond, 1935-75, engring. asst. 1941-46, engr., 1946-75. Asst. dist. commiteeman Robert E. Lee council Boy Scouts Am., 1967-68. Served to lt. comdr. USNR, 1942-54; Res. ret. Registered profl. engr., Va. Mem. IEEE (sr.), Nat. Soc. Profl. Engrs., Raven Soc., Delta Tau Delta, Tau Beta Pi. Episcopalian. Home: 3433 Grove Ave Richmond VA 23221

JONES, ROBERT MOORE, acct.; b. Winston-Salem, May 22, 1954; s. Harry Donald and Virginia (James) J.; student Wake Forest U., 1972-74; B.S. in B.A., Western Carolina U., 1977, postgrad.; m. Diane Phillips, Nov. 25, 1978; 1 dau., Catrina. Student operator Western Carolina U. Computer Center, Cullowhee, N.C., 1976-77, computer programmer 1977-78, systems acct. Bus. Office, 1979—; systems programmer Clemson (S.C.) U. Computer Center, 1978-79. Bus. mgr. Western Carolina U. Coll. Union, 1976. Methodist. Home: PO Box BN Cullowhee NC 28723 Office: Bus Office Western Carolina Univ Cullowhee NC 28723

JONES, ROBERT SIDNEY, scientist; b. Gatesville, Tex., Dec. 17, 1936; s. Dean B. and Rose F. Jones; B.A., U. Tex., 1959, M.A., 1963; Ph.D. (Bur. Comml. Fisheries fellow 1966-67), U. Hawaii, 1967; m. Sally Travis, Jan. 9, 1958; children—Robert Dean, Jeffrey Travis. Prof. marine sci., dir. U. Guam Marine Lab., 1967-74; fisheries biologist Johnson Sci. Lab., Harbor Branch Found., Inc., Fort Pierce, Fla., 1974-76, dir., 1976—; program mgr. U. Tex. Bur. Land Mgmt. outer-continental shelf program, 1976. Served to lt. (j.g.) USN, 1959-61. EPA grantee, 1972-73; Bur. of Land Mgmt. grantee 1976. Mem. Am. Soc. Ichthyologists and Herpetologists, Sigma Xi. Office: Rural Route 1 Box 196 Fort Pierce FL 33450

JONES, ROBERT STEPHEN, social worker; b. Springfield, Mo., Feb. 5, 1945; s. Robert Leavitt and Mildred Lorriane (Meier) J.; student SW Mo. State U., 1963-64; B.A., Drury Coll., 1968; M.S. in Social Work, U. Mo., 1971; m. Teresa Annette Kirkpatrick, Oct. 4, 1968; children—Brian Scott, Erik Donald. Psychiat. social worker Omaha VA Hosp., 1971-75, Muskogee (Okla.) VA Hosp., 1975-77, outpatient med. social worker, 1977-79; social work supr. Tulsa VA Outpatient Clinic, 1979—; asso. prof. dept. psychiatry U. Okla., 1975—, clin. asst. prof. dept. social work, 1979—. Master, Mid-Am. council Boy Scouts Am., Omaha, 1973-74. Mem. Acad. Cert. Social Workers, Nat. Assn. Social Workers. Office: 635 W 11th St Tulsa OK 74127

JONES, ROGER HODGES, educator; b. Quicksand, Ky., May 14, 1929; s. Roger Walter and Mattie M. (Hodges) J.; A.B., Georgetown Coll., 1951, M.A., U. Ky., 1959; Ed.D., Ind. U., 1973. Tchr. English, Estill County High Sch., 1951-52; tchr. art, journalism and Spanish, Breathitt County High Sch., 1953-65; prof. art edn. Morehead State U., 1965—, chmn. univ. senate; del. World Confedn. Orgns. of Teaching Profession, Addis Ababa, Ethiopia, 1965—. Ky. Col.; recipient Distinguished Alumni award Georgetown Coll., 1965. Mem. Upper Ky. Schoolmasters Club (pres.), Ky. (pres. 1964-65), Upper Ky. River (pres.), Ky. (pres. dept. classroom tchrs.), Morehead State U. (pres.) edn. assns., Nat. Assn. State Edn. Assn. Pres.'s (v.p.), Phi Delta Kappa (pres. Morehead chpt.), Kappa Delta Pi, Kappa Pi, Sigma Tau Delta. Home: 216 Bell Ct E Lexington KY 40508 Office: Morehead State U Morehead KY 40351

JONES, RONALD LEE, photographer; b. Sweetwater, Tex., May 29, 1946; s. Lee Willie and Lorena Maxine (McQuiston) J.; B.F.A., Fla. State U., 1976; m. Virginia Rebecca Jetton, Aug. 12, 1975; children—Jennifer Leigh, Djar Lacoda Horn, Ronald Lee. Project photographer Underwater Archeol. Research sect. Fla. State Archives, Tallahassee, 1974-75, supr. photography, 1976—; project photographer Tex. Antiquities Com., Padre Island, Austin, Tex., 1975; cons. U. N.C., Wilmington, 1978-79. Served with USMC, 1966-68; Vietnam. Decorated Purple Heart. Mem. Fla. Motion Picture and TV Assn. (dir. 1977-78). Fla. Profl. Photographers Assn., Southeastern Profl. Photographers Assn. Club: Masons. Office: Dept State Capitol Bldg Tallahassee FL 32301

JONES, RONALD LOUIS, sales exec.; b. Nacogdoches, Tex., Sept. 24, 1945; s. Louis Scott and Martha Elizabeth (Feazell) J.; B.S. in Math. and Physics, Northwestern State U., La., 1967, postgrad., 1967; m. Adele Suzanne Flash, June 29, 1968; children—Ronald Louis, Adele Rene. With Union Carbide, 1967—, chem. plant, Taft, La., 1967-73, maintenance supr., engr., Dallas, 1973-77, sales rep. new bus. devel., project leader, Houston, 1977-78; area sales mgr. chems. and plastics, Houston, 1978—. Recipient award Sales Mgmt. Council, 1977. Mem. ASME, Houston Chem. Club. Baptist. Clubs: Tennis Assn. Baton Rouge (v.p. 1976-77), Men's Golf and Tennis, Kingwood Country. Author, presenter paper to profl. conv. Home: 3307 Fawn Creek Dr Kingwood TX 77339 Office: 2 Greenway Plaza E Houston TX 77046

JONES, S. TODD, magazine exec.; b. Gainesville, Fla., Oct. 13, 1948; s. Sam L. and Frances Siddie (Hoepfner) J.; B.J., U. Tex., Austin, 1971; m. Donna Rae Billie, Aug. 5, 1978. Account exec. Adcraft Advt., Corpus Christi, Tex., 1972; continuity dir. Sta. KIII-TV, Corpus Christi, 1973; account exec. Ray Hall Advt., Austin, 1973-74; asst. dir. public relations Tex. Med. Assn., 1974-75; owner S. Todd Jones Advt. & Public Relations, Austin, 1975-76; advt. dir. Tex. Parade, Inc., Austin, 1977-79; dir. advt. sales SA—The Mag. of San Antonio, 1978—. Mem. San Antonio Advt. Fedn., San Antonio C. of C., N. San Antonio C. of C., U. Tex. Ex-Students Assn. Home: 611 Coronet San Antonio TX 78216

JONES, SHERMAN J., univ. adminstr.; b. Newport News, Va., Jan. 12, 1946; s. Sherman E. and Leola M. (Pryor) J.; B.A., Williams Coll., 1968; M.B.A., Harvard U., 1970, Ed.D., 1978; m. Jessica Janice Seales, Dec. 22, 1967; children—Kimberly, Sherman. Asst. dir. Office Coop. Acad. Planning, Inst. Services to Edn., Washington, 1971-72; Woodrow Wilson adminstrn. intern Central State U., 1970-71; cons. Cresap, McCormick & Paget, Inc., Washington, 1972-75; teaching fellow edn. Harvard Grad. Sch. Edn., 1976-77; sr. program officer mgmt. div. Acad. Ednl. Devel., Inc., Washington, 1975-77; v.p. adminstrn. Fisk U., Nashville, 1977—. Bd. dirs. Better Bus. Bur. of Nashville and Middle Tenn. Mem. Fin. Execs. Inst., Assn. M.B.A. Execs. Unitarian. Author: (with John Millett, Robert Sandin, Kurt Moses) Planning in Higher Education, 1976; (with E. Oscar Woolfolk) Academic Planning, 1972. Home: 929 18th Ave N Nashville TN 37208 Office: Fisk U 17th Ave N Nashville TN 37203

JONES, SIDNEY THEODORE, mfg. chem. engr.; b. Biloxi, Miss., Apr. 16, 1927; s. Carl Oscar and Faye Ethyl (Brodnax) J.; m. Polly Melba North, Aug. 23, 1950; children—Lucinda Jane Jones Hollier, Molly Ellen Jones. Operator, night supt., unit supr. Jefferson Chem. Co., Port Neches, Tex., 1947-76; gen. ops. foreman, ops. supr. Texaco Chem. Co., Port Arthur, Tex., 1976—. Served with U.S. Mcht. Marine, 1945-47. Mem. Am. Inst. Chem. Engrs. Democrat. Methodist. Clubs: Masons, Shriners. Patentee in field. Home: 1900 Stella Circle Port Neches TX 77651 Office: Box 712 Port Arthur TX 77640

JONES, TALOVA LANE, real estate exec.; b. Henryetta, Okla., Dec. 27, 1925; d. Everett Ray and Ruby Mae (Tarwater) Lane; student Muskogee Jr. Coll., 1943, Baldwin-Wallace Coll., 1956-58, Fairleigh Dickinson U., 1959-60; m. Vincent Carlyle Jones, Oct. 31, 1948; children—Karen Jones Nolan, Marta Jones Briscoe, Marygaye Prosper. Sec. various firms, 1955-68; sales asso. Boehmer Hedlund Realtors, Barrington, Ill., 1969-70, The Country Squire, Realtors, Barrington, 1970-72; sales mgr. Bob Turner Inc., Realtors, Edmond, Okla., 1972-75; sales mgr. Red Carpet Realtors, Edmond, 1975-76; broker, owner Talova Jones, Realtors, 1976-78; sales mgr. Abide, Inc., Realtors, 1978—; cons. in field. Active, Drug and Narcotics Com., Barrington, Ill., 1971-72, Environ. Affairs Com., Edmond, Okla., 1974. Elected to Million Dollar Club Ill. Assn. Realtors, 1971; cert. real estate brokerage mgr. Mem. Oklahoma City Met., Edmond (Realtor of Yr. 1975, pres. 1975, dir.) bds. realtors, Okla. Realtors Inst. (dean 1976—), Okla. Assn. Realtors (designated Graduate Realtors Inst. 1972 regional v.p. 1978, dir.), Women's Council Realtors, Realtors Nat. Mktg. Inst., Nat. Assn. Realtors, Edmond C. of C., Epsilon Sigma Alpha. Republican. Methodist. Clubs: Republican Women's, Order of Eastern Star. Contbr. articles in field to newspapers, profl. jours. Home: 2112 Tall Oaks Trail Edmond OK 73034 Office: 108 E 15th St Edmond OK 73034

JONES, THOMAS FERRIS, newspaper printing co. exec.; b. Nashville, Dec. 17, 1934; s. James Leslie and Harriett Ellen (Roberts) J.; student Belmont Coll., 1953-55, U. Tenn., Nashville, 1972-73; m. Betty McKinney, Oct. 7, 1956; children—Thomas Scott, Sandra Ellen. With Newspaper Printing Corp., Nashville, 1946—, Tenn. circulation mgr., 1972-74, asst. promotion mgr., 1975-78, asst. state circulation mgr., 1978-79, state circulation mgr., 1979—; asst. v.p. Tennessean Newspapers, Inc., Nashville, 1973—. Mem. Am. Mktg. Assn. (v.p. 1978-79), So. Circulation Mgrs. Assn., Internat. Circulation Mgrs. Assn. Home: 627 Galaxie Dr Nashville TN 37209 Office: 1100 Broad St Nashville TN 37202

JONES, THOMAS L., lawyer; b. Breckinridge County, Ky., Apr. 10, 1931; s. V.A. and Elizabeth (Lambirth) J.; B.S., U. Ky., 1959, LL.B., 1961; LL.M., U. Mich., 1965; m. Shelley Edwards, July 15, 1961. Asst. prof. law U. Ala., Tuscaloosa, 1962-65, asso. prof., 1965-68, prof., 1968—, acting dean Sch. Law, 1970-71; acting dir. Ala. Law Inst., 1972-75; vis. prof. U. Ky., Lexington, 1965, U. Ill. Coll. Law, 1971-72; Ala. commr. Nat. Conf. Commrs. on Uniform State Laws, 1967—, mem. exec. com., 1975-77, v.p., 1975-77. Served with USAF, 1951-55. Mem. Am. Law Inst., Assn. Am. Law Schs. (exec. com. 1975-77). Editor Ala. Will Manual Service, 1965—. Home: 907 Indian Hills Dr Tuscaloosa AL 35406

JONES, THOMAS LANE, accountant; b. Jayton, Tex., June 8, 1927; s. Thomas Lemarcus and Itha (Lane) J.; B.S., Tex. A&M U., 1950; B.B.A., Lamar State Coll., 1956; m. Katherine Olivia Harris, Aug. 6, 1978; children—Thomas Lemarcus, Richard Hamilton. Mgr. plant systems Eastex, Inc., Beaumont, Tex., 1960-67; chief accountant Star Engraving Co., Houston, 1966-67; mgr. plant systems Rockwell Internat. Corp., 1967-71; v.p., dept. mgr. Cameron-Brown Co., Raleigh, N.C., 1977—. Served with USN, 1945-47. C.P.A., N.C., 1962. Mem. Am. Inst. C.P.A.'s, Tex. Soc. C.P.A.'s. Democrat. Methodist. Home: 5866 N Hills Dr Raleigh NC 27609 Office: 4300 Six Forks Rd Raleigh NC 27609

JONES, THURSTON LIMAR, labor relations specialist; b. Alexandria, La., Aug. 12, 1946; s. Thurston Limar and Eola Mae Jones; B.S. in Zoology, So. U., Baton Rouge, 1968; postgrad. La. State U., 1971, N. Tex. State U., 1977—; m. Kelley L. Mayfield, Aug. 30, 1969; children—Shana Nicole, Joi Lynn. With Tactical Air Command, U.S. Air Force, various locations, 1970-74; asso. dir. Personnel Mgmt. Tng. Inst., Dallas Region Tng. Center, U.S. CSC, 1974-78; labor relations specialist Dallas Region Office of Labor Relations, U.S. Office of Personnel Mgmt., 1979—. Served with U.S. Army, 1968-70. Decorated Bronze Star; recipient Sustained Superior Performance awards, 1972, 77. Mem. Soc. Labor Relations Profls., Intergovtl. Tng. Assn., Human Resource Devel. Network, Fed. Exec. Bd.'s Labor Relations Officers Assn. Home: 2825 Emerwood Dr Garland TX 75043 Office: 1100 Commerce St Dallas TX 75242

JONES, WALTER, JR., hosp. engr.; b. Huntsville, Ala., Feb. 14, 1929; s. Walter and Claudia Ann (Parton) J.; student Blanton's Bus. Coll., 1947; m. Betty Jean Fritschy, Nov. 28, 1947; children—Linda Lee, Brenda Kay, Walter Michael. Served as enlisted man U.S. Air Force, 1947-57, advanced through grades to m/sgt., discharged, 1957; pres. Fritschy's Inc., Asheville, N.C., 1957-69; dir. plant ops. St. Joseph's Hosp., Asheville, N.C., 1969—. Mem. adv. bd. Caldwell Community Coll., 1978-79. Decorated Air Force Commendation medal; lic. hosp. maintenance cons., City of Asheville; certified hosp. engr. N.C. Hosp. Engrs. Assn. Mem. Internat. Assn. for Hosp. Security, Nat. Fire Protection Assn., Nat. Assn. Hosp. Engrs., Am. Soc. for Hosp. Engring., Southeastern Hosp. Engrs. Assn., N.C. Hosp. Engrs. Assn. Democrat. Baptist. Home: 311 Barnard Ave Asheville NC 28804 Office: St Josephs Hosp 428 Biltmore Ave Asheville NC 28801

JONES, WALTER BEAMAN, congressman; b. Fayetteville, N.C., Aug. 19, 1913; s. Walter George and Fannie (Anderson) J.; B.S., N.C. State U., 1934; m. Doris Long, Apr. 26, 1934; children—Dot Dee Moye, Walter Beaman II. Mem. N.C. Gen. Assembly, 1955-59; mem. N.C. Senate, 1965; mem. 89th-96th Congresses from 1st Dist. N.C. Dir. Security Savs. & Loan Assn., Farmville, N.C. Mayor, Farmville, 1949-53. Former trustee Campbell Coll., U. N.C. Recipient Watchdog of Treasury award Nat. Assn. Businessmen, 1966; named Farmville Man of Year, 1955. Democrat. Baptist (deacon). Mason (32 deg., Shriner), Elk, Rotarian, Moose. Home: May Blvd Farmville NC 27828 Office: 201 Cannon House Office Bldg Washington DC 20515

JONES, WAYNE VAN LEER, cons. geologist, pvt. investor; b. Chgo., June 18, 1902; s. Frank Edgar and Josephine Louella (Van Leer) J.; A.B., Northwestern U., 1923; m. Elizabeth Rieke, Jan. 14, 1926; 1 son, Wayne Van Leer. Accountant, then chief auditor Mission Oil Co., Kansas City, Mo., 1923-28; with F.E. Jones & Son, oil operators, Wichita, Kans., 1928-30; asst. mgr. Exchange Petroleum Co., Shreveport, La., 1930-34; geologist Midcontinent div. Tidewater Asso. Oil Co., Houston, 1934-41, chief geologist, 1941-53; v.p. charge exploration Union Texas Natural Gas Corp. (formerly Union Sulphur & Oil Corp., Union Oil & Gas Corp. of La., merger Allied Chem. Corp., 1962, name now Union Tex. Petroleum div. Allied Chem. Corp.), Houston, 1953-59, sr. v.p., 1959-63, also past v.p. dir. subs.' Union Petrolera Venezolana, C.A., Union Petrolera Boliviana, S.A. Unola de Argentina, Ltd., Uno-Tex Petroleum Corp.; cons. geologist, Houston, 1963-72; pvt. investor, 1972—; mem. Am. Commn. Stratigraphic Nomenclature, 1947-53. Alumni regent Northwestern U., 1965-75, life regent, 1975—. Mem. Am. Assn. Petroleum Geologists, geneal. socs. N.J., Md., Pa., N.Y. Geneal. and Biog. Soc., Soc. Genealogists (London), Houston Geol. Soc., Phi Beta Kappa, Sigma Xi, Sigma Alpha Epsilon. Clubs: Houston, Meml. Dr. Country (Houston). Author: Jacob Woodward Colladay and His Descendants, 1976; The Rieke Family of Bavenhausen and America, 1979. Address: 5672 Longmont Dr Houston TX 77056

JONES, WHIPPLE VAN NESS, JR., govt. ofcl.; b. St. Louis, Oct. 26, 1942; s. Whipple Van Ness and Mary Sue (McCulloch) J.; B. Ed., U. Miami (Fla.), 1965, M.Ed., 1969; m. Maryann Causseaux, Nov. 18, 1972; children—Bruce McCulloch, Vanessa Carroll, Kimberly Douglas, Whipple Van Ness III. Tchr., Dade County (Fla.) Schs., 1965-68; active campaign Richard Stone for Fla. Sec. of State, Tallahassee, 1970, for U.S. Senate, 1974; exec. asst. to Richard Stone, sec. of state State of Fla., Tallahassee, 1971-74, U.S. Senator, Tallahassee, 1975—. Pres. Tallahassee Family YMCA, 1978—, also bd. dirs. Mem. Nat. Council Tchrs. English (life), Am. Soc. Public Adminstrn. (sec., council N. Fla. chpt. 1976—), Fla. Econs. Club (dir. 1978—, sec. 1980—). Democrat. Clubs: Rotary, Tiger Bay (Miami), University (Miami); Capital Tiger Bay (Tallahassee). Home: 1590 Hickory Ave Tallahassee FL 32303 Office: Office of US Senator Richard Stone Suite 200B 2639 N Monroe St Tallahassee FL 32303

JONES, WILLIAM ROBERT, bus. exec.; b. Letcher County, Ky., June 15, 1935; s. William Robert and Mayme (Turner) J.; student U. Louisville, 1953-54; B.S., U.S. Naval Acad., 1958; M.S., George Washington U., 1967; m. Mary Sue Daniel, June 7, 1958; children—Lori Sue, Mark Turner, Anne Daniel, Elizabeth Sergent. Vice-pres., Stanwick Corp., Norfolk, Va., 1963-69; pres., QED Systems, Inc., Virginia Beach, Va., 1969—; dir. Virginia Beach area bd. Bank Va. Served as lt. USNR, 1958-63. Named hon. Ky. col., 1971. Mem. Am. Soc. Naval Engrs. (life), Am. Defense Preparedness Assn. (life), Am. Inst. Indsl. Engrs., U.S. Naval Acad., George Washington U. alumni assns. Methodist (vice-chmn. adminstrv. bd. 1973-74). Mason (Shriner). Home: 2213 Windward Shore Dr Virginia Beach VA 23451 Office: 4646 Witchduck Rd Virginia Beach VA 23455

JONES, WOODROW WILSON, fed. judge; b. Rutherfordton, N.C., Jan. 26, 1914; s. Bernard Bartlett and Karl Jane (Nanney) J.; student Mars Hill Coll., 1932-34; LL.B., Wake Forest U., 1937; m. Rachel Elizabeth Phelps, Nov. 22, 1936; children—Woodrow Wilson, Michael Anthony. Admitted to N.C. bar, 1937; practiced law, Rutherfordton, 1937-67; solicitor Rutherford County Recorders Ct., 1941-43; mem. N.C. Gen. Assembly, 1947-49, U.S. Ho. of Reps., 1950-56; judge U.S. Dist. Ct. for Western N.C., Rutherfordton, 1967—, chief judge, 1968—; dir. Union Trust Co., Shelby, N.C., Citizens Fed. Savs. & Loan Assn., Rutherfordton. Chmn., N.C. Democratic Exec. Com., 1958-60. Trustee Gardner-Webb Coll., Bolling Springs, N.C. Served to lt. (j.g.) USNR, 1943-45. Recipient spl. citation for outstanding service Gardner-Webb Coll., 1968. Mem. Am., N.C., Rutherford County bar assns., Am. Judicature Soc. Baptist (deacon). Club: Kiwanis. Office: PO Box 741 Rutherfordton NC 28139*

JONES Y DIEZ ARGUELLES, GASTON ROBERTO, educator; b. Cardenas, Cuba, Dec. 6, 1910; s. Guillermo Rafael Jones and Maria de los Angeles Diez Arguelles; came to U.S., 1963, naturalized, 1971; B.Letters and Scis., Matanzas Inst. Cuba, 1928; Dr. Law, U. Havana, Cuba, 1937; M.A., U. Ala., 1969; m. Dolores Carricarte, May 19, 1950. Practice law, Havana, 1937-60; municipal judge, Cuba, 1938-40; cons. atty. Cuban Treasury Dept., 1943-60; instr. dept. fgn. langs. Sacred Heart Coll., Cullman, Ala., 1965-70, St. Bernard Coll., Cullman, 1967-70; asst. prof. U. Ala., Birmingham, 1971—. Mem. Nat. Bicentennial Com. for celebration of Nat. Fgn. Lang. Discovery Week, 1975—. Mem. Am. Assn. Tchrs. Spanish and Portuguese (past pres. Ala. chpt., chmn. So. and mountain states regional pub. relations com. 1975-77, chmn. nat. pub. relations and publicity com. 1977—), Ala. Assn. Fgn. Lang. Tchrs. (past dir., chmn. com. for advancement fgn. langs. in Ala. 1973—), Birmingham-Cobán Ala.-Guatemala Partners of Americas (v.p.), Sociedad Nacional Hispanica, Am. Council Teaching Fgn. Langs., Modern Lang. Assn. Americas, S. Atlantic Modern Lang. Assn., AAUP, Resources in Edn., Cuban Bar Assn. in Exile, Sigma Delta Pi, Omicron Delta Kappa. Roman Catholic. Club: Cuban Rotary in Exile. Contbr. articles to profl. jours. Successfully promoting nat. campaign to make Americans aware of need for fgn. langs. in U.S. Home: 219 B Chastaine Circle Birmingham AL 35209 Office: Dept Fgn Langs U Ala Birmingham AL 35294

JONNALAGADDA, MURALI MOHAN RAO, psychiatrist; b. Nellore, India, June 29, 1941; came to U.S., 1975; s. Ramaniah and Venkata Subbamma (Vinjamuri) J.; M.B.B.S., Guntur Med. Coll., 1964; D.P.M., All India Inst. Mental Health, Bangalore, 1968; m. Venkata Thirumala-Devi Vutla, Aug. 6, 1965; children—Devi Penusila, Venkata Ramanamba. Lectr., head dept. psychiatry Rangaraya Med. Coll., Kakinada, India, 1968-71; sr. registrar Mental Handicap and Child Psychiatry, Bristol (Eng.) Clin. Area, 1971-74; cons. psychiatrist St. Davnet's Hosp., Monaghan, Ireland, 1974-75; staff psychiatrist Cherry Hosp., Goldsboro, N.C., 1975—; asst. clin. dir., 1978—; asst. clin. prof. dept. psychiatry E. Carolina U., 1978—. Mem. Royal Coll. Psychiatrists, Royal Soc. Medicine, Brit. Med. Assn., Irish Med. Assn., Soc. Clin. Psychiatrists, Am. Assn. Mental Deficiency, Am. Psychiat. Assn., AAAS, AMA, Fedn. Am. Scientists. Hindu. Home: 531 Parkwood Ln Goldsboro NC 27530 Office: Cherry Hosp Goldsboro NC 27530

JOORFETZ, (JOHN) COLTON, orgn. devel. cons.; b. Memphis, Mar. 24, 1948; s. John Frederick and Helen Margaret (Smith) J.; student in Architecture, La. State U., 1966-68; B.S. in Personnel Mgmt. and Prodn. Mgmt., Miss. State U., 1971; M.B.A., Miss. Coll., 1976; m. Clara Beall Watson, Aug. 13, 1977. With prodn. control final assembly plant Packard Electric div. Gen. Motors Corp., Clinton, Miss., 1973-74, component prodn. plant, 1974-75, indsl. engr., 1976-78, organizational devel. cons., 1978—, condr. careers in mgmt. program, pre-employment evaluation programs; part time instr. Sch. Bus. and Public Adminstrn., Miss. Coll. Vol., United Givers Fund, 1976; adv. Jr. Achievement, 1977; vol. Follies, St. Dominic Hosp., 1978-80. Served with USAF, 1969, with Air N.G., 1969-75. Presbyterian. Guest speaker profl. and ch. groups; author, editor, compiler various manuals for prodn., tng., orientation and devel. Home: 1632 Wilhurst Jackson MS 39211 Office: PO Box 260 Clinton MS 39056

JORDAN, ARCHIBALD CURRIE, educator; b. Caldwell, N.C.; s. Archibald Currie and Octavia Graham (Stroud) J.; A.B. Duke U., postgrad. Law Sch.; A.M., Columbia U.; m. Jane Myers, Sept. 2, 1941; children—Ann Myers, Patsy Jane, Sally Rida, Julie Anna. Gen. Edn. Bd. fellow Columbia U.; admitted to N.C. bar; adviser N.C. Textbook Commn.; asst. prof. English, Duke U.; past pres., chmn. research com. N.C. English Teachers Council; judge N.C. high sch. English ann. award creative writing; v.p. Coll. English Assn. N.C., Va. and W.Va. Deacon, First Presbyterian Ch. Mem. AAAS, So. Atlantic Modern Lang. Assn., AAUP, Am. Dialect Soc., N.C. English Tchrs. Assn., Am., N.C. (award appreciation) bar assns., Council Basic Edn., Phi Delta Kappa, Kappa Delta Pi. Democrat. Author: Essentials of English Composition; College English Tests (forms A and B); College Handbook of Composition; Fundamentals of College Composition; How to Write Correctly; Everyday Grammar; A Comprehensive Examination in the Fundamentals of Correct English Usage, 1960; The Writer's Manual, 1963, rev. edit., 1967; asst. to editors So. Jour. Orthopaedic Surgery; editorial cons. Duke U. Med. Center, Am. Assn. Orthopaedic Surgeons, others. Address: Box 6006 Duke U Durham NC 27708

JORDAN, BARBARA C., former congresswoman, educator; b. Houston, Feb. 21, 1936; d. Ben and Arlyne Jordan; B.A. in Polit. Sci. and History magna cum laude, Tex. So. U.; J.D., Boston U., 1959. Admitted to Mass. bar, 1959, Tex. bar, 1959; adminstrv. asst. to county judge, Harris County, Tex.; mem. Tex. Senate, 1966-72, pres. pro tem, chmn. labor and mgmt. relations com. and urban affairs study com.; mem. 93d-95th congresses from 18th Dist. Tex. com. on judiciary, com. on govt. ops., mem. spl. task force 94th congress, mem. steering and policy com. House Democratic Caucus; Lyndon B. Johnson prof. public affairs U. Tex., 1979—. Named One of 20 Women Who could be Pres., Redbook mag.; led poll of Women who could be Supreme Ct. Justice, 1979. Mem. Am., Tex., Mass., Houston bar assns., NAACP, Delta Sigma Theta. Baptist. Office: LBJ Sch Public Affairs U Tex Austin TX 78712

JORDAN, BROOXIE N., ch. orgn. ofcl.; b. Hollow Rock, Tenn., Aug. 20, 1938; d. Jesse Lee and Nolie Ann (Melton) Jordan; student Bethel Coll., McKenzie, Tenn., 1956-57. Pastor's sec. 1st Bapt. Ch., Huntingdon, Tenn., 1956-68; receptionist Hart, Freeland and Roberts, architects, Nashville, 1968-69; with Bapt. Sunday Sch. Bd., Nashville, 1969—, adminstrv. asst. Bible Teaching div., 1977—, leader confs., 1960—. Mem. Nat. Secs. Assn. Baptist. Home: 675 Harding Pl Nashville TN 37211 Office: 127 9th Ave N Nashville TN 37234

JORDAN, CHARLES EDWARD, III, physician; b. Columbus, Ohio, Jan. 16, 1940; s. Charles Edward and Alice Oleta (Smith) J.; B.S., U. Ohio, 1962; M.D., Ohio State U., 1966; m. Patricia Jane Price, June 19, 1966; children—Kelly Kristin, Jodi Anne. Intern, Tripler Army Hosp., Honolulu, 1966-67; resident in otolaryngology Ohio State U., Columbus, 1969-73; practice medicine specializing in otolaryngology and head and neck surgery, Cookeville, Tenn., 1973—; mem. med. staff Cookeville Gen. Hosp., 1973—, chief of staff, 1976-77; dir. Am. Bank & Trust Bank. Served with U.S. Army, 1966-69. Decorated Bronze Star, Combat Med. Badge. Diplomate Am. Bd. Ophthalmology and Otolaryngology. Fellow A.C.S., Am. Acad. Facial Plastic and Reconstructive Surgery; mem. Middle Tenn. (pres. 1976), Putnam County (pres. 1975) med. socs., AMA, Am. Acad. Ophthmology and Otolaryngology, Am. Council Otolaryngology, Nashville Acad. Ophthmology and Otolaryngology, Am. Soc. for Head and Neck Surgery, Putnam County C. of C. (dir., pres. 1979). Methodist. Club: Rotary. Home: 42 Buck Mountain Rd Cookeville TN 38501 Office: 220 Oak Ave Cookeville TN 38501

JORDAN, DAVID LEWIS, newspaper and communications exec.; b. Peoria, Ill., Nov. 2, 1937; s. Paul Howard and Marie Theresa J.; B.A., Duke U., 1959; M.B.A., U. Chgo., 1961; m. Susan Tuhy, Oct. 2, 1952; children—Jodi, Jonathan David. Corp. mgr. forward plans Ford Motor Co., Dearborn, Mich., 1962-65; asso. Booz, Allen and Hamilton, Detroit, 1965-69; v.p., treas. 1st Banc Group, Columbus, Ohio, 1969-73; dir. corp. fin. Xerox Corp., Stanford, Conn., 1973-75; v.p. fin. Media Gen., Richmond, Va., 1975—; cons. Ohio Public Utility Commn. Trustee Nat. Music Camp, Interlochen, Mich. Served with U.S. Army, 1961-62. Mem. Fin. Execs. Inst., Fin. Analysts Fedn. Presbyterian. Clubs: Scioto Country, Willow Oaks Country, Commonwealth (Richmond). Home: 4406 Custis Rd Richmond VA 23225 Office: 333 E Grace St Richmond VA 23219

JORDAN, DENNIS DEE, pharmacist; b. Coffeyville, Kans., Nov. 29, 1948; s. John Dee and Norma Katherine (Brunkhorst) J.; B.S. in Pharmacy, Southwestern Okla. State U., 1971; m. Darlene Ann Bertini, Oct. 3, 1969; children—Lisa Michelle and Dawn Marie (twins). Pharmacy intern Jane Phillips Meml. Med. Center, Bartlesville, Okla., 1971-72, staff pharmacist, 1972, asst. dir. pharmacy services, 1973-74, dir. pharmacy services, 1974—, materials mgr., 1978—; clin. instr. Sch. of Pharmacy, S.W. Okla. State U.; pharmacy cons., purchasing, linen cons. adv. com. Shared Service Orgn. Mem. Am. Soc. Hosp. Pharmacists (mem. nat. council organizational affairs 1977-80), Nat. Assn. Hosp. Purchasing Mgrs., Okla. Hosp. Purchasing Assn., Okla. Pharm. Assn., Okla. Soc. Hosp. Pharmacists (past pres., dist. chmn. 1974-78). Democrat. Lutheran. Club: Elks. Home: 4726 Melody Ln Bartlesville OK 74003 Office: Jane Phillips Meml Med Center 3500 E Frank Phillips St Bartlesville OK 74003

JORDAN, DUPREE, JR., publisher, pub. relations exec., educator, cons.; b. Decatur, Ga., May 14, 1929; s. DuPree and Roslyn (Moncrief) J.; A.B., Mercer U., 1947; postgrad. Crozer Theol. Sem., 1948; M.Ed., Emory U., 1954; LL.B., Atlanta Law Sch., 1951, LL.D., 1963; postgrad. Inst. Life-Long Learning, Harvard U., 1979, Inst. Ednl. Mgmt., 1980; m. Margaret Virginia Malone, Dec. 28, 1948; children—Margaret Jordan DeSear, DuPree III, Roslyn Jordan Whitworth, Terri Lee Chesser. Ordained to ministry Bapt. Ch., 1945; reporter Macon (Ga.) Telegraph, 1945-47, Chester (Pa.) Times, 1948-49; news dir. WVCH, Chester, 1948-49; asso. dir. Radio-TV Commn., So. Bapt. Conv., 1949-52, acting dir., 1952-53; tchr. Westminister Schs. and Atlanta div. U. Ga., 1953-55; pastor Duluth (Ga.) Bapt. Ch., 1953-54; editor, pub., owner West End Star, Atlanta Weekly newspaper, 1955-67; owner, pub. Piedmont Satellite, 1967-68, North DeKalb Record, Chamblee, 1956-64, Tri County Graphic, 1962-64; pres. Jordan & Jordan, advt. and pub. relations, 1954—, Jordan Enterprises, 1957—, Success Publs., Inc., 1969—; dir. Successful Selling Seminars; pres. Ga. Coll. for Leadership Devel., Success Leaders Speakers Service, 1973—; dir. numerous corps. Mem. Gov.'s Com. for a World's Fair in Atlanta; mem. Rapid Transit Com. of 100; dir. pub. affairs for S. States Office Econ. Opportunity, 1965-69, spl. asst. to regional dir., 1967-69, nat. religious liaison dir., 1968; exec. dir. Assn. Pvt. Colls. and Univs. in Ga., 1970—; mem. cons. staff Gov. Ga., 1962-66, 70-78; bd. dirs. Atlanta Girls Club, Boy Scouts Am., YMCA. Recipient numerous awards from various orgns., including Ga. Press Assn., Nat. Editorial Assn., Sigma Delta Chi, Jr. C. of C.; Distinguished Service award Office Econ. Opportunity, 1967; DuPree Jordan, Jr., Day proclaimed Dec. 18, 1973. Mem. Pub. Relations Soc. Am., Nat. Editorial Assn., Ga. Press Assn. (bd. mgrs.), Adminstrv. Mgmt. Soc. (dir. Atlanta chpt.), Am. Mgmt. Assn., Am. Soc. Pub. Adminstrn., Soc. Advancement Mgmt., Am. Soc. Tng. Dirs., Sales and Mktg. Execs. Internat., Sales and Mktg. Execs. Atlanta, Assn. Mgmt. Cons., Inc., Nat. Assn. Ind. Colls. and Univs., State Assn. Execs. Council, AIM, Internat. Mgmt. Council, Mgmt. Assn. Atlanta, Am. Mktg. Assn., Ga., Internat. assns. bus. communicators, West End (pres. 1962), Chamblee-Doraville (pres. 1963) businessmen's assns., Ga., DeKalb County, Atlanta chambers commerce, Am., Ga. socs. assn. execs., Soc. Assn. Mgrs., Christian Council Met. Atlanta (pres. 1973), Nat. Press Club, Sales Exec. Club N.Y., Nat. Speakers Assn., Meeting Planners Internat., So. Assn. Colls. and Schs. (chmn. state coll. execs.), Sigma Delta Chi (dir. Atlanta chpt. 1963). Home: 1204 Warren Hall Ln NE Atlanta GA 30319 Office: 3121 Maple Dr NE Suite 1 Atlanta GA 30305

JORDAN, EDWIN PRATT, physician; b. Chgo., Nov. 2, 1902; s. Edwin Oakes and Elsie Fay (Pratt) J.; student Harvard U., 1921-22; S.B., U. Chgo., 1923; M.D., Rush Med. Coll., Chgo., 1928; m. Marjorie Crichton, Sept. 18, 1930; children—Deborah Spiller, David C., Mary Jordan Baker. Intern, Presbyn. Hosp., Chgo., 1928-29; fellow McCormick Inst., 1929-30; instr. medicine U. Chgo., Rush Med. Coll., Northwestern U., 1930-40; asso. editor Jour. AMA, Chgo., 1937-47; dir. edn. Cleve. Clinic, 1947-50; exec. dir. Am. Assn. Med. Clinics, Charlottesville, Va., 1951-68; editor Group Practice, Charlottesville, 1952-68; cons. HEW; lectr. U. Va. Med. Sch. Recipient certificate Merit Nat. Soc. Med. Research, 1956. Mem. AAAS, AMA, Am. Rheumatism Assn. (charter mem., past v.p.). Club: Cosmos. Author: (with W.C. Shepard) Rx for Medical Writing, 1951; You and Your Health, 1954. Editor: Standard Nomenclature of Disease and Operations, 1936-47, The Physician and Group Practice, 1958, Modern Drug Encyclopedia, 1958. Address: Route 10 Box 35 Charlottesville VA 22901

JORDAN, GARY LEON, telephone co. ofcl.; b. Gadsden, Ala., July 29, 1948; s. Luther Leon and Willie Mae (Rains) J.; B.S. in Elec. Engring., U. Ala., 1971; M.B.A., Samford U., 1979; m. Clara Ann Neighbors, Aug. 15, 1970; children—Todd, Matt. Supr., S. Central Bell, Montgomery, Ala., 1971-72, industry relations rep., Birmingham, Ala., 1972—. Corp. exec. United Appeal; loaned exec. Jr. Achievement. Mem. IEEE, Ala.-Miss. Ind. Telephone Assn. Baptist. Club: Birmingham Jaycees. Home: 932 Mountain Branch Dr Birmingham AL 35226 Office: 1706 2d Ave N Birmingham AL 35203

JORDAN, GEORGE LYMAN, JR., surgeon; b. Kinston, N.C., July 10, 1921; s. George L. and Sally (Herndon) J.; B.S., U. N.C., 1942; M.D., U. Pa., 1944; M.S. in Surgery, Tulane U., 1949; m. Florence Fisher Henszey, June 23, 1945; children—Florence Elizabeth, Amy Henszey, Jacob Henszey. Intern Grady Meml. Hosp., Atlanta, Ga., 1944-45; fellow in surgery, Tulane U., New Orleans, La., 1947-49, Mayo Found., Rochester, Minn., 1949-52; practice medicine specializing in surgery Houston, 1952—; instr. in surgery Baylor U. Coll. of Medicine, Houston, 1952-54, asst. prof. surgery, 1954-57, asso. prof., 1958-64, prof., 1964—; dep. chief of surgery Ben Taub Gen. Hosp., Houston, 1961-68; chief of the med. staff Harris County (Tex.) Hosp. Dist., Houston, 1968—; med. adviser to HEW, Social Security Adminstrn., region IV, 1965—; sr. cons. in surgery Nat. Inst. of Gen. Med. Scis., 1966; mem. surg. research tng. grants com. NIH, 1968-70; adviser Houston chpt. Nat. Found. for Ileitis and Colitis, Inc., 1974—. Chmn. commn. on edn. St. Paul's Meth. Ch., 1967-69, mem. adminstrv. bd., 1963—, chmn., 1978—, chmn. pastor-parish relations com., 1977. Served to capt., M.C., U.S. Army, 1945-47. Diplomate Am. Bd. Surgery (vice-chmn. 1975-77). Fellow A.C.S. (pres. southeastern Tex. chpt. 1966-67, gov. 1976—, exec. com. 1977—, chmn. bd. govs. 1980—); mem. Am. (2d v.p. 1980), So., Western (dist. rep. on exec. com. 1976—), Pan-Pacific surg. assns., Tex. (council mem. 1975—), Houston (pres. elect 1979) surg. socs., Am. Assn. for Surgery of Trauma, Soc. for Surgery of the Alimentary Tract (pres. 1978), U. Assn. for Emergency Med. Services, Am. Assn. for Cancer Research (sec. southwestern sect. 1959-60), Tex., Pan Am. med. assns., AMA, Harris County Med. Soc., Harris County Unit, Am. Trauma Soc. (dir. 1974—), Am. Cancer Soc. (dir. Tex. div. 1966-68), Southwestern Surg. Congress, Transplantation Soc., Internat. Cardiovascular Soc., Soc. of U. Surgeons, Houston Gastroenterological Soc., Soc. for Exptl. Biology and Medicine, N.Y. Acad. Scis., Collegium Internat. Chirurgiae Digestivae, So. Soc. for Clin. Investigation, Pancreas Club, Am. Soc. for Exptl. Pathology, Assn. for the Advancement of Med. Instrumentation, Phi Beta Kappa, Alpha Omega Alpha. Methodist. Author: (with John M. Howard, M.D.) Surgical Diseases of the Pancreas, 1960; contbr. numerous articles in field of specialty to profl. jours.; editorial bd. Am. Jour. Surgery, 1968—, Advances in Surgery, 1971—. Home: 1748 North Blvd Houston TX 77098 Office: 1200 Moursund Ave Houston TX 77030

JORDAN, HENRY PRESTON, JR., mfrs. co. rep.; b. Roanoke, Va., Sept. 3, 1926; s. Henry Preston and Emily Lucile (Luck) J.; B.S. in Commerce, U. Va., 1950; m. June Farley Dyson, Sept. 4, 1948; children—Kathryn Jordan Streetman, Rebecca Leigh, June Preston. Supt. comml. and indsl. construction Richardson Wayland Elec. Corp., Roanoke, Va., 1952-56; sales engr. H.C. Gundlach Co., Richmond, Va., 1956-64; pres. Jordan Metal Co., Richmond, 1964-76, Jordan Mech. Sales Inc., Richmond, 1976—; chmn. lay adv. bd. sheet metal dept. Richmond Tech. Center. Sec., Jr. Achievement, Roanoke, 1961-62, v.p., Richmond, 1972-74; v.p. Big Bros. Richmond, 1971-73; pres. Beaumont Learning Center Aux., 1979—. Served with USAF, 1945-46. Recipient Achievement award, Big Bros. Richmond, 1969; Douglas S. Freeman 12th Man award, 1971. Mem. Am. Soc. Heating, Refrigerating and Air Conditioning Engrs., Inc., Beta Theta Pi, Theta Tau, Lamda Pi. Republican. Baptist. Club: West Richmond Rotary (pres. 1973-74). Home: 8810 Three Chopt Rd Richmond VA 23229 Office: PO Box 29785 Richmond VA 23229

JORDAN, JOHN RICHARD, JR., lawyer; b. Winton, N.C., Jan. 16, 1921; s. John R. and Ina Love (Mitchell) J.; student Chowan Coll., 1938; B.A., U. N.C., 1942, J.D., 1948; m. Patricia Exum Weaver, June 19, 1949; children—Ellen Meares, John Richard III. Admitted to N.C. bar, 1948; mem. staff Atty.-Gen. of N.C., 1948-51; mem. Law Offices John R. Jordan, 1951—; mem. N.C. Senate, 1959-65. Mem. N.C. Gov.'s Cancer Commn., 1962-64; pres. N.C. Arthritis Found., 1966-70; state chmn. ARC, 1966; pres. N.C. div. Am. Cancer Soc., 1960-61; chmn. Friends of the Library of N.C. State U., 1966-67; chmn. Commn. on Med. Aid for the Aged in N.C., 1962-63; N.C. rep. on Nat. Com. for Support of the Public Schs., 1962—; mem. Gov.'s Commn. on Edn. Beyond the High Sch., 1961-62, Gov.'s Coordinating Com. on Traffic Safety, 1961-62; vice chmn. N.C. Reapportionment Commn., 1955-56; del. Democratic Nat. Conv., 1956; candidate for lt. gov. N.C., 1964; chmn. State Dem. Conv., 1974; Am. observer Brit. Nat. Election of 1964; bd. govs. U. N.C., 1973—; bd. dirs. State Capitol Found., 1977—, N.C. Med. Found., 1977—; trustee Ravenscroft Found., 1971—, N.C. Cancer Inst., 1961-63. Recipient Disting. Service award N.C. Public Health Assn., 1964, gold medal Am. Cancer Soc., 1970. Mem. Am. Bar Assn., N.C. Bar Assn., Wake County Bar Assn. (chmn. exec. com. 1955-56), Am. Judicature Soc., Internat. Bar Assn., N.C. Acad. Trial Lawyers, N.C. State Bar, Phi Delta Phi, Pi Kappa Alpha, Exec. Club of Raleigh. Baptist. Clubs: Lions, Torch, City of Raleigh; Carolina Country; Sphinx. Contbr. articles on politics and govt. to mags. and newspapers; editorial bd. State Dept. of Archives and History, N.C., 1961-63, N.C. Law Rev., 1947-48; contbg. editor (N.C.) The Construction Lien and Claim Manual, 1969. Home: 809 Westwood Dr Raleigh NC 27607 Office: Suite 1414 Branch Banking & Trust Bldg Fayetteville Mall Raleigh NC 27602

JORDAN, JOHN WILLIAM, chemist; b. Pitts., Apr. 25, 1912; s. Frank Craig and Harriet Sophia (Caywood) J.; A.B., Marietta Coll., 1934, Sc.D., 1959; Ph.D. in Chemistry, Columbia U., 1938; m. Marian Emily Spies, June 1, 1936 (dec.); children—Emily Jordan Oaks, Frank, John, Edward, Andrew; m. 2d, Norine H. Granquist, Apr. 8, 1979; children—Elizabeth, Victor, Erik Granquist. Asst. food analysis and colloids Columbia U., 1935-38; with Mellon Inst., Pitts., 1938-39; plant chemist Pitts. Corning Corp., Port Allegany, Pa., 1939-41; sr. fellow Mellon Inst., 1941-51; tech. dir. Baroid div. NL Industries, Houston, 1951-75, cons., 1976—. Mem. Am. Chem. Soc., AAAS, Clay Minerals Soc. (pres. 1973-74), Horseless Carriage Club Am., Phi Beta Kappa, Sigma Xi. Contbr. articles to tech. jours. Patentee in field. Home: 1505 Butlercrest Houston TX 77080 Office: PO Box 1675 Houston TX 77001

JORDAN, JOSEPH LOREN, diver; b. Washington, Mar. 24, 1944; s. John Harris and Rosalie (Campbell) J.; grad. Def. Lang. Inst., Monterey, Calif., 1966; B.A. in Linguistics, U. Tex., Austin, 1969. Pvt. practice comml. diving, Houston, 1969—; owner, operator Blue Water Diving Sch., Houston, 1962—; cons. oil cos. Served with USN, 1964-69; Vietnam. Decorated Air medal. Mem. Underwater Learning Assn., Undersea Med. Soc. (asso.), Sierra Club, Cousteau Soc., Rolls Royce Owner's Club. Contbr. articles in field to tech. jours. Office: 910 Westheimer St Houston TX 77006

JORDAN, LUCIUS DONALD, JR., investor; b. Kosciusko, Miss., Sept. 12, 1929; s. Lucius Donald and Elva (Allen) J.; B.S., Miss. Coll., 1951; M.B.A., Harvard U., 1953; m. Marlene Drury, June 28, 1958; children—Cynthia, Jennifer, Lucius Donald III. Unit mgr. Procter & Gamble, Tex., Ga., 1955-59; dir. mktg. First Miss. Corp., Jackson, 1959-61; western regional mgr. Mead Johnson & Co., Tex. and Calif., 1961-68; v.p. nat. accounts Drackett Products Co., Cin., 1969; v.p. sales Internat. Distbrs. div. Plough Inc., Memphis, 1970-72; exec. v.p. Selective Mktg. Inc., Memphis, 1972-75; mng. partner Jor-Lo Co., Memphis, 1975—. Served with U.S. Army, 1953-55. Mem. SAR. Republican. Presbyterian. Clubs: Harvard Alumni, Racquet (Memphis). Home: 2276 Wickerwood Cove Memphis TN 38138

JORDAN, LYNDON KIRKMAN, JR., physician; b. Mount Olive, N.C., Jan. 6, 1935; s. Lyndon Kirkman and Rachael Loucille (Hazelton) J.; B.A., Duke U., 1957, M.D., 1961; m. Beverly Hayes Brooks, Aug. 19, 1961; children—Lyndon Kirkman, Christopher Page, Patrick Brooks. Intern, Watts Hosp., Durham, N.C., 1961-62; staff physician Dorothea Dix Hosp., Raleigh, N.C., 1962; practice gen. medicine, Smithfield, N.C., 1964—; mem. staff Johnston Meml. Hosp., Smithfield, chief staff, 1971, 80; asst. prof. community health scis. Duke Med. Sch., 1972—, dir. family practice residency, 1972-73. Sponsor, presenter Jordan Citizenship award Mt. Olive Coll., 1959-77; bd. dirs. Johnson County United Fund, 1966-69. Served with USAF, 1962-64. Named Rotarian of Year, 1969-70. Diplomate Am. Bd. Family Practice (charter). Mem. AMA (Physician Recognition award 1971, 77), 4th Dist. Med. Soc. N.C. (v.p. 1970, pres. 1971), N.C. (del. 1971, 77), Johnson County (sec. 1968, 77, pres. 1978) med. socs., Am., N.C. (pres. 1979—) acads. family physicians, Smithfield-Selma C. of C. (dir. 1971-72). Club: Rotary (pres. Smithfield 1971-72). Home: 410 Wellons St Smithfield NC 27577 Office: 415 N 7th St Smithfield NC 27577

JORDAN, ROBERT ATKIN, physician; b. Olean, Mo., July 15, 1917; s. Robert Lee and Laura Melsenia (Atkin) J.; B.S., Baker U., 1939; M.D., U. Kans., 1944; M.S. in Medicine, Mayo Clinic and Found., 1951; m. Gladys LeTresa Tyler, June 5, 1943; children—Michael Andrew, Susan Elaine, James Thomas, Linda Jean. Intern, U. Kans. Med. Center, Kansas City, 1944, student health physician, instr. physiology, 1947-48, instr., 1951-54, asst. prof. medicine, 1954-58; practice medicine specializing in internal medicine, Lawrence, 1951-54; partner Springer Clinic, Tulsa, 1958—; electrocardiographer St. Frances Hosp., Tulsa, bd. dirs., chief of staff. Served to capt. M.C. AUS, 1945-47. Diplomate Am. Bd. Internal Medicine. Fellow A.C.P.; mem. AMA, Tulsa County Med. Assn., Sigma Xi, Alpha Omega Alpha, Delta Tau Delta, Phi Beta Pi. Republican. Methodist. Clubs: Masons (Lawrence), Scottish Rite (Tulsa). Contbr. articles to profl. med. publs. Home: 3417 E 75th St Tulsa OK 74136 Office: 6160 S Yale Ave Tulsa OK 74136

JORDAN, STEPHEN MARION, physician; b. Sylvania, Ga., Jan. 29, 1942; s. Marion J. and Florine H. Jordan; B.S., U. Ga., 1965; M.D., Med. Coll. Ga., 1969; m. Cecelia Looney, Aug. 12, 1967; children—Alison, Stephen. Intern, Tampa (Fla.) Gen. Hosp., 1969-70; resident Mayo Grad. Sch. Medicine, Rochester, 1970-71, Med. Coll. Ga., 1971-73; practice medicine specializing in internal medicine, Statesboro, Ga., 1975—; mem. staff Bulloch Meml. Hosp., Statesboro, 1975—; cons. staff Screven County Hosp., Sylvania, Ga., 1976—; cons. staff Candler County Hosp., Metter, Ga., 1976—. Organizing mem. Ogeechee River Field Trial, 1976. Served to maj. MC U.S. Army, 1973-75. Diplomate Am. Bd. Internal Medicine. Mem. Ogeechee River Med. Soc., Med. Assn. Ga., A.M.A., Am. Coll. Physicians, Am. Soc. Internal Medicine, Am. Coll. Sports Medicine. Clubs: Forest Heights Country, Statesboro Rotary, Ducks Unltd. Home: 1 Honey Ln Statesboro GA 30458 Office: 356 Northside Dr E Statesboro GA 30458

JORDAN, WILLIAM DITMER, JR., utility co. engr.; b. Laurel, Miss., Aug. 10, 1948; s. William Ditmer and Carolyn (Carter) J.; B.M.E., U. Ala., 1973. Jr. engr. Ala. Power Co., Tuscaloosa, Ala., 1974, Alabaster, Ala., 1974-76, sr. II engr., 1976-77, Tuscaloosa, Ala., 1977—. Served with USNR, 1971-72. Mem. Am. Soc. Mech. Engrs., Nat. Mgmt. Assn., Capstone Engring. Soc., Kappa Alpha Order, Theta Tau, Pi Tau Sigma. Democrat. Home: 212 Cedar Crest Tuscaloosa AL 35401 Office: 915 Queen City Ave Tuscaloosa AL 35401

JORDAN, WILLIAM THOMAS, publisher; b. Everett, Mass., Oct. 13, 1923; s. William Thomas and Belle Macmaster (Graham) J.; B.B.A., Northeastern U., 1952, M.B.A., 1958; m. Beverly Ann Fraizer, Aug. 31, 1968. Sales promotion mgr. Farm and Ranch Publ. Co., Nashville, 1951-53; editor, advt. mgr. Nashville Record, 1953-54; prodn. mgr., copywriter Culbertson Advt., Nashville, 1954-56; advt. copy writer, editor B.F. Goodrich Co., Watertown, Mass., 1956-60; editor, publisher Jordan Publs., Inc., Spencer, Mass., 1960-67, editor, gen. mgr., 1967-70, mng. editor The Winchester (Mass.) Star, 1970-72; editor, publisher The Clifton (Tex.) Record, 1973—; lectr. journalism Baylor U., 1975-76. Mem. adv. com. Central Tex Fair Assn., 1975—; mem. Clifton Housing Authority, 1973—. Served with AUS, 1945-46. Episcopalian. Club: Rotary. Home: 314 North Ave T Clifton TX 76634 Office: 310 5th St W Clifton TX 76634

JORDAN, WILLIS POPE, JR., physician, educator; b. Rossville, Ga., Oct. 7, 1918; s. Willis Pope and Mary Sue (Cook) J.; B.S., Emory U., 1939, M.D., 1943; m. Jewelle Turner, June 26, 1952; children—Willis Pope III, Jennifer Sue, Julianne, Jerri Lucille; m. 2d, Bette Adams, Aug. 24, 1974. Intern Emory U. Hosp., Atlanta, 1943-44; resident Columbus Med. Center, Ga., 1944; chief resident, 1944-45; preceptorship in urology, Columbus, Ga., 1947-52; asst. resident in surgery, VA Hosp., Atlanta, 1952-53; asst. resident in urology VA Hosp., New Orleans, 1953-54, sr. resident, 1954-55; sect. chief in urology VA Hosp. Lake City, Fla., 1955-68; clin. asso. in surgery U. Fla. Coll. Medicine, Gainesville, 1964-65, asst. prof. surgery, 1965-68; sect. chief in urology VA Hosp., Memphis, 1968—; asso. prof. surgery, asso. prof. urology U. Tenn. Coll. Medicine, 1968-77, prof. urology, 1977—, dep. chmn. dept. urology, 1972—; chmn. Combined U. Tenn.-VA Urology Teaching Conf., 1968-73. Mem. hormone com. Urological Research Group, 1968; sec. Nat. Cyrosurgery Prostate Study Group, 1968; mem. Senate Faculty U. Tenn. Coll. Medicine, 1971—. Served to capt. M.C. AUS, 1945-47. Diplomate Am. Bd. Urology. Fellow A.C.S.; mem. Am. (mem. Southeastern sect. sci. awards com. 1959, reception com. 1962), VA (treas. 1964-66, exec. com. 1964, pres. 1968-69), Memphis (exec. com. 1977—) urological assns., AMA, So. Med. Assn., Assn. VA Urologists, N.Y. Acad. Sci., Soc. for Cyrobiology, Soc. for Cyrosurgery, Bowers Surg. Soc., Societe de Urologie Internale, Soc. Univ. Urologists, Assn. Am. Med. Schs., Soc. Govt. Service Urologists, Royal Soc. Medicine. Contbr. numerous articles to profl. publs. Home: 1663 Poplar Estates Pkwy Germantown TN 38138 Office: VA Hospital Jefferson Ave Memphis TN 38104

JORDRE, WILLIAM STARLING, ret. mech. engr.; b. Mantorville, Minn., June 1, 1906; s. John I. and Anna (Andrist) J.; student Antioch Coll., 1924-28; B.M.E., U. Minn., 1931; m. Hazel E. Olson, Nov. 21, 1931; children—Starling Ann Jordre Kephart, Sue H. Jordre James, Diane Jordre Meyerratken, J. William, JoAnn. Erector, Babcock & Wilcox Co., Barberton, Ohio, 1931-38, dist. erection supt. Cin. office, 1938-43, Chgo. office, 1943-45; exec. v.p., dir. Oberle-Jordre Co., Inc., 1945-74; ret., 1974; dir. Crestview Lands, Inc. Bd. dirs. Trinity-St. Philips Found. Mem. Engring. Soc. Cin. (life), Nat., Ohio, socs. profl. engrs., ASME. Episcopalian. Clubs: Masons (32 deg.), Bankers. Home: Rt 1 Harrodsburg KY 40330

JORGENSEN, CARL EDWARD, ednl. adminstr.; b. Mt. Kisco, N.Y., Aug. 30, 1936; s. Kingo J. and Hilda Christine (Johnson) J.; B.S., Richmond (Va.) Profl. Inst., 1957; M.S., Va. Commonwealth U., 1968; m. Phoebia Jean Phillips, Sept. 23, 1967. Bus. tchr. coordinator John Marshall High Sch., Richmond, 1957-65; asst. dir. Nat. Bus. Edn. Assn., Washington, 1965-66; asst. state supr. bus. edn. State Dept. Edn., Richmond, 1966-72, coordinator vocat. edn. research, 1972-73, state supr. bus. edn., 1973—. Named Outstanding Bus. Tchr., Nat. Office Mgmt. Assn., 1964 Mem. Nat. Bus. Edn. Assn. (sec. treas. 1978—), Va. Bus. Edn Assn. (cons. to exec. bd. 1972—, mem. exec. bd. 1970—), So. Bus. Edn. Assn. (chmn. secondary edn. div. 1960-61, Outstanding Bus. Educator award 1978), Am. Vocat. Assn. (mem. bus. and office edn. membership com. 1977—), Nat. Assn. State Suprs. Bus. and Office Edn. (pres. elect 1980—), Delta Pi Epsilon (v.p. 1978—). Contbr. articles on bus. edn. to profl. publs. Home: 2201 Kingsbrook Dr Richmond VA 23233 Office: PO Box 6Q Richmond VA 23216

JORGENSON, WALLACE JAMES, broadcasting co. exec.; b. Mpls., Oct. 31, 1923; s. Peter and Adelia (Bong) J.; student St. Olaf Coll., 1941-42, Gustavus Coll., 1943; A.B., Bowling Green State U., 1944; L.H.D., Lenoir-Rhyne Coll., 1971; m. Solveig Elizabeth Tvedt, Feb. 24, 1945; children—Kristin, Peter, Mark, Lisa, Philip. Staff announcer WCAL, Northfield, Minn., 1941-43; officer in charge Armed Forces Radio Network, Kyushu, Japan, 1945-46; mgr. KTRF, Thief River Falls, Minn., 1946-48; with Jefferson-Pilot Broadcasting Co., Charlotte, N.C., 1948—, v.p., 1966-68, exec. v.p., 1966-78, pres., 1978—; chmn. First Union Nat. Bank. Chpt. chmn. ARC, 1969-70, bd. dirs., 1970—, nat. bd. govs., 1977—, chmn. centennial com., vice chmn. resolutions com., 1974, mem. S.E. area adv. council, 1975-77; chmn. bd. dirs. Lenoir Rhyne Coll., 1971-77; bd. visitors Davidson Coll.; chmn. United Way Campaign, 1978; bd. dirs. Arts and Sci. Council. Served to 2d lt. USMCR, 1942-46. Recipient Distinguished Service award Lenoir Rhyne Coll., 1969; Silver Medal award Charlotte Advt. Club 1975; Communications award N.C. Council Chs., 1976. Mem. Charlotte C. of C. (2d vice chmn.), Nat. Assn. Broadcasters (TV Code Bd. 1973-78), Assn. Maximum Service Telecasters (1st vice chmn. 1977—). Clubs: Charlotte City, Quail Hollow Country (Charlotte). Home: 2742 Meade Ct Charlotte NC 28211 Office: 1 Julian Price Pl Charlotte NC 28208

JORY, STEPHEN GODFREY, lawyer; b. Washington, Aug. 4, 1944; s. John Godfrey and Ruth (Ekstrand) J.; A.B., Marietta Coll., 1966; J.D., W.Va. U., 1969; m. Jean A., June 15, 1968. Admitted to

W.Va. bar; law clk. to chief judge U.S. Dist. Ct. No. Dist. Va., 1969-70; asst. U.S. atty. No. Dist. W.Va., 1970-76, U.S. atty., 1977—. Dist. chmn. Boy Scouts Am., 1975-76; pres. bd. trustees Elkins (W.Va.) YMCA, 1976-78. Mem. W.Va. State Bar Assn., Am. Bar Assn. Christian Scientist. Club: Rotary. Office: PO Box 190 Elkins WV 26241

JOSEL, NATHAN, library adminstr.; b. New Orleans, Sept. 28, 1941; s. Nathan A. and Elise (Blummer) J.; B.A., Tulane U., 1963; M.S., La. State U., 1965; m. Jacqueline M. Nielsen, Dec. 15, 1979; children—Laura P., Nathan A. Various positions Enoch Pratt Free Library, 1965-69; head local history Memphis-Shelby County Public Library, 1969-71, head history and travel, 1971-74; asst. dir. Madison (Wis.) Public Library, 1974-80; dir. El Paso Public Library, 1980—; lectr. U. Wis. Library Sch. Commr., Shelby County Hist. Records Commn., 1972-74, Shelby County Hist. Commn., 1973-74. Mem. ALA, Tex. Library Assn., SW Library Assn., Border Regional Library Assn. Contbr. chpts. to reference books for small and medium libraries. Office: 501 N Oregon St El Paso TX 79901

JOSEPH, ELEANOR COHEN (MRS. PERCY T. JOSEPH), librarian; b. Waco, Tex., July 10, 1919; d. Lawrence B. and Sadie (Weinberger) Cohen; B.A., Newcomb Coll., 1940; B.L.S., La. State U., 1941; m. Percy T. Joseph, Jan. 6, 1944; children—Edward L. (dec.), David B. Librarian, New Orleans Pub. Library, 1941-43; sec. Howell, Soskin Pub. Co., N.Y.C., 1944; asst. librarian Rapides Parish Library, 1946-48; head reference dept. East Baton Rouge Parish Library, 1954-74, head reference services, 1974-78, coordinator library info. service, 1978—. Mem., pres. United Cerebral Palsy Assn. Greater Baton Rouge, 1954—. Recipient Baton Rouge Jr. C. of C. Outstanding Pub. Servant award, 1962. Mem. Baton Rouge Library Club (pres. 1962), La. Library Assn. (chmn. La. Lit. award com. 1963, chmn. Essae M. Culver award com. 1966, chmn. pub. library sect. 1965-66), ALA (reference and subscription books rev. com. 1971, info. and referral guidelines subcom. 1978—). Home: 1816 Chopin Dr Baton Rouge LA 70806 Office: 7711 Goodwood Blvd Baton Rouge LA 70806

JOSEPH, FRED IRVING, ins. agt.; b. Charlottesville, Va., Nov. 18, 1929; s. Irving Richard and Bedder E. J.; B.S. in Math., N.C. State U., 1956; m. Sydney Robinson, Dec. 14, 1957; children—Richard Scott, Robert David, Amy Lynne, Elizabeth Cecile. Mgr., Crown Petroleum Corp., 1957-58; with Shenandoah Life Ins. Co., 1958—, agy. mgr., Greensboro, N.C., 1979—; dir. Wall Furniture Co. Trustee Louisburg Coll.; pres. Greensboro Sports Council; v.p., bd. dirs. N.C. State Student Aid Assn.; co-chmn. Greensboro Coll. Athletic Fund; mem. athletic council N.C. State U. Served with U.S. Army, 1948-52. Mem. Greensboro Life Underwriters (pres.), Nat. Assn. Life Underwriters, Gen. Agts. and Mgrs. Assn., Chartered Life Underwriters, Phi Kappa Phi, Delta Sigma Phi. Democrat. Methodist. Home: 2005 Downing St Greensboro NC 27410 Office: PO Drawer Z-1 Greensboro NC 27402

JOSEPH, KENNETH EDWARD, educator; b. LaJunta, Colo., Aug. 17, 1927; s. John Henry and Veda Viola (Wilson) J.; B.A., Adams State Coll., 1951; M.S., Mich. State U., 1968, Ph.D., 1970; m. GeorgeAnna Morgan, Sept. 24, 1948; children—Kenneth G., Keith M. Investigator, FBI, 1951-70, supr. tng. div., Washington, 1970-72; head dept. edn. and communication arts FBI Acad., Quantico, Va., 1972-74, head dept. research and devel., 1974—, acad. dean, 1975-77, asst. dir., 1977-78, exec. asst. dir. law enforcement services, 1980—. Dir. Muskegon (Mich.) Jr. Hockey Assn., 1960-65, Greater Lansing (Mich.) Jr. Hockey Assn., 1965-70; pres. Western Mich. Dist. Golf Assn., 1963-65. Served with USNR, 1945-47. Recipient Outstanding Alumnus award Adams State Coll., 1977. Mem. Am. Assn. Higher Edn., Assn. Supervision and Curriculum Devel., Am. Assn. Community and Jr. Colls., Nat. Soc. Study of Edn., Internat. Assn. Chiefs Police (exec. com. 1978—), Am. Legion, Acad. Criminal Justice Scis. (co-chmn. accreditation and standards com. 1980-81), Phi Delta Kappa. Clubs: Masons, Elks. Office: FBI Acad Quantico VA 22135

JOSEPH, MILDRED DANIEL, counselor; b. Jackson, Ky., May 25, 1920; d. LaRue and Maude (Davis) Daniel; B.S. in Home Econs., U. Ky., 1948; M.Ed. in Counseling and Guidance, U. Louisville, 1969; m. Julius C. Joseph, Aug. 16, 1944; children—Julius Lynn, Marc Ward. Tchr., Breathitt County and Harlan County (Ky.) schs., 1940-44, 48, 52; employment counselor Ky. Employment Services, 1965-72; trainer r. Manpower Services, Ky. Dept. Human Resources, 1972-78, tng. officer, Frankfort, 1978—. Mem. Internat. Assn. Personnel in Econ. Security, Am. Personnel and Guidance Assn., Nat. Employment Counselors Assn., Ky. Personnel and Guidance Assn., Ky. Employment Counselors Assn. Democrat. Methodist. Club: Order Eastern Star. Office: DHR Bldg 275 E Main St Frankfort KY 40621

JOSEPHSON, JOHN EVERETT, hosp. adminstr.; b. Rochester, N.Y., July 24, 1945; s. John William and Margaret Bernice J.; B.S., Northwestern Coll., 1970; M.B.A., Northwestern U., 1971; m. Kathryn Diane Zeller, Jan. 18, 1969; children—Michelle, John Mark. Mgmt. trainee Heisner Bos., Rochester, N.Y., 1971; instr. mgmt. Northwestern State U., 1974; asst. adminstr. Doctor's Hosp., Shreveport, La., 1975; adminstr. Minden (La.) Med. Center, 1975—. Pres., Harper Elem. PTO, 1979-80. Served with USAF, 1963-67. Mem. La. Hosp. Assn. (trustee 1977-79, pres. N.W. dist. 1975-76), Minden C. of C. (dir.). Office: Number 1 Medical Plaza Minden LA 71055

JOST, GEORGE RICHARD, safety officer; b. Boston, July 22, 1917; s. George William and Evelyn Jessie (Reid) J.; asso. degree in bus. adminstrn. Oxford Coll., Cambridge, Mass., 1939; m. Evelyn Jane Whitefield, Oct. 1, 1944; children—Diane Evelyn, Deborah Whitfield. Served as enlisted man U.S. Army, 1941-42; commd. 2d lt. U.S. Army, advanced through grades to lt. col., 1962, ret., 1965; with Civil Service/Army Intelligence, Ft. Holabird, Md., 1967-72; police chief, safety officer VA Med. Center, Durham, N.C., 1972-75; safety dir. VA Med. Center, Fayetteville, N.C., 1975—; mem. exec. bd. Fed. Safety Adv. Council of Southeast. Decorated Silver Star, Bronze Star with 2 oak leaf clusters, Purple Heart. Mem. Nat. Safety Council, Nat. Fire Protection Assn. (cert. mem. indsl. fire protection sect.). Club: Masons (Ft. Thomas, Ky.). Office: VA Hosp 2300 Ramsey St Fayetteville NC 28301

JOYCE, EDWIN ANTHONY, JR., biologist; b. Hampton, Va., Feb. 23, 1937; s. Edwin Anthony and Leah Bell (Gates) J.; B.A. in Botany-Zoology, Butler U., 1959; M.S. in Marine Biology, U. Fla., 1961; postgrad. U. South Fla., 1966; m. Mary Dale Smith; children—Edwin Anthony, William Christopher Kathy Smith, Kim Smith, Beth Smith, Kelly Smith, Carson Smith. Marine biologist Fla. Bd. Conservation (now Fla. Dept. Natural Resources), 1961-67, sr. fisheries biologist, 1967-68, lab. supr., 1968-72, chief Bur. Marine Sci. and Tech., Tallahassee, 1972—, dir. div. marine resources; mem. bd. dirs. Gulf and Caribbean Fisheries Inst.; alt. mem. South Atlantic/Fed. Fisheries Mgmt. Bd.; mem. Coastal Plains Regional Commn.; mem. sci. adv. com. Atlantic States Marine Fisheries Commn.; mem. tech. coordinating com. Gulf States Marine Fisheries Commn.; mem. stats. and sci. com. Gulf of Mex. Fishery Mgmt. Council. Bd. dirs. Coastal Plains Center Marine Developmental Sers. Mem. Nat. Shellfisheries Assn., Am. Inst. Fishery Research Biologists, Audubon Soc., Sigma Xi, Lambda Chi Alpha. Democrat. Club: Kiwanis (v.p. 1972, chmn. conservation com.). Contbr. articles to profl. publs. Home: Route 1 Box 180-H Tallahassee FL 32303 Office: Fla Dept Natural Resources 202 Blount St 530 Crown Bldg Tallahassee FL 32304

JOYCE, JAMES LESLIE, coal co. exec.; b. Welch, W.Va., Nov. 9, 1940; s. Tom Herman and Ida Ora (Horn) J.; student Pa. State U., 1969-70, Va. Poly. Inst. and State U., 1968-69; m. Shelby Chambers, Apr. 16, 1960; 1 son, James Leslie. With Royalty Smokeless Coal Co., Premier, W.Va., 1959-77, supt., 1966-69, v.p., 1970-74, pres., 1974-77; div. pres., chief operating officer 7 coal cos. Wyomac Coal Co., Inc., Welch, 1977—. Mem. AIME. Club: Rotary. Home: Gen Delivery Premier WV 24878 Office: Wyomac Coal Co PO Drawer G Welch WV 24801

JOYCE, WILLIAM MARTIN, lawyer; b. Bklyn., May 13, 1927; s. John Patrick and Mary Kate (Flannery) J.; B.A., St. John's U., Bklyn., 1952, J.D., 1954; m. Mary Catherine Kunak, Oct. 17, 1959; children—John, William. Admitted to N.Y. State bar, 1955; claims adjuster U.S. Fidelity and Guaranty, N.Y.C., 1954-55, atty.-adviser Phila. Quartermaster Dist., 1955-56; atty. Glenn L. Martin Co., Balt., 1956-57, Orlando, Fla., 1957-58, mgr. contracts, 1958-60; counsel div. Martin Marietta Corp., Orlando, 1960—. Bd. dirs. Cath. Social Services, Orlando, 1962-73, 76—, pres., 1977; bd. dirs. Bishop Moore High Sch., Orlando, 1969-73, pres., 1971-72. Served as staff sgt. AUS, 1946-48. Mem. Am. Bar Assn. (vice-chmn. subcom. truth in negotiations sect. pub. contract law 1974-76), Serra Internat. (dist. gov. 1973-74), Fla. C. of C. (dir. 1970-76), Asso. Industries Fla. (sec., dir. 1966-72). Clubs: K.C., Elks. Home: 1241 Oxford Rd Maitland FL 32751 Office: PO Box 5837 Orlando FL 32805

JOYE, CHANNING STELL, newspaper and TV co. exec.; b. Pamplico, S.C., Dec. 6, 1942; s. Acue Stoll and Amy Roberta (Evans) J.; B.S.B.A. in Acctg. magna cum laude, U. S.C., 1965; m. Sylvia Elaine West, Jan. 21, 1965; children—Amy, Rodney, Ashley. Staff acct. Elliott, Davis & Co., Greenville, S.C., 1965-66; acct. J.W. Hunt & Co., Columbia, 1966-70, partner, 1971-76; v.p., treas. State-Record Co., Columbia, 1976—, also dir.; mem. adv. bd. First Nat. Bank S.C., Columbia. Bd. dirs. Columbia C. of C.; chmn. adminstrv. bd. Bethel United Methodist Ch., Columbia, 1976-78; treas. Dentsville Youth Football League, Columbia, 1977-79; dist. chmn. Wateree dist. Boy Scouts Am. C.P.A., S.C. Mem. Am. Inst. C.P.A.'s, S.C. Assn. C.P.A.'s, Nat. Assn. Accts., Inst. Newspaper Controllers and Fin. Officers, Phi Beta Kappa. Clubs: Wildwood Country, Summit. Office: PO Box 1333 Columbia SC 29202

JOYNER, DELORES W., educator; b. Brooklet, Ga., Sept. 16, 1936; d. John Paul and Mildred (Wilson) Williams; B.A. in Elementary Edn., Mercer U., Macon, Ga., postgrad. in Social Work; postgrad. in edn. Fort Valley (Ga.) State Coll., Ga. Coll., Milledgeville; m. James P. Joyner; children—Connie Joyner Hall, Robin. Tchr. 2d grade Crawford County Elementary Schs., Roberta, Ga., 1973-74; remedial reading tchr. North Elementary Complex I, Dry Branch, Ga., 1974—. Mem. NEA, Ga. Assn. Educators. Certified elementary tchr., Ga. Established music scholarship Macon Jr. Coll. Home: Route 2 Fort Valley GA 31030 Office: Crawford County Elem Sch Roberta GA

JU, WOO JUNG, educator; b. Buchun, Korea, Oct. 3, 1935; came to U.S., 1956; s. Kan Yup and Kye Soon (Lee) J.; B.A., E. Tex. State U., 1961; M.A., Miss. Coll., 1962; Ph.D., Miss. State U., 1967; m. Wook Ja Ju, Dec. 27, 1969; 1 dau., Su Sie. Asst. prof. Tex. Coll., Tyler, 1967-68, asso. prof., 1968-69; prof. history Elizabeth City (N.C.) State U., 1969—. Pres., Han Min Shin Bo, Arlington, Va., 1979—. Mem. AAUP. Author: The Rise and Fall of the Djakarta-Peking Axis, and the Origins of Johnson's War, 1976; The Sino-Indonesian Relations and the Johnson Doctrine in Asia, 1979. Home: 648 Rosaer Ln Virginia Beach VA 23464 Office: Elizabeth City State U Elizabeth City NC 27909

JUDD, DANIEL STEWART, financial and mgmt. cons.; b. West Asheville, N.C., Mar. 6, 1924; s. Oscar John and Mabel (Moyers) J.; student Berea (Ky.) Coll., 1941-43, U. Okla., 1943, U. N.C. at Asheville, 1946; m. Margaret Norvelle Shipman, Dec. 8, 1946; children—Daniel Stewart, Mary Margaret (Mrs. Douglas Guy Wood), Oscar Herbert. Partner Judd Furniture & Supply Co., West Asheville, 1949-54; owner Judd Supply Co., West Asheville, 1954-64; practicing accountant, West Asheville, 1962-68; accountant Columbia (S.C.) Coll., 1968-73; financial and mgmt. cons., Irmo, S.C., 1973—. Instr. extension div. Asheville-Buncombe Tech. Inst., 1966-67; dir. So. Bank & Trust Co., Irmo; mem. S.C. Tax Council. Pres., Buncombe County (N.C.) Republican Club, 1950; sec. Buncombe County Rep. Exec. Com., 1954-60; chmn. 12th Dist. N.C. Rep. Com., 1960-62; dist. dir. 1960 Census for 11th congressional dist. N.C.; charter pres. Buncombe County Young Reb. Club; mem. Buncombe County Bd. Elections, 1948-50, N.C. Bd. Elections, 1961-62. Served with armed forces, 1943-45. Decorated Bronze Star. Mem. Nat. Assn. Accountants, Nat., S.C. assns. pub. accountants, Berea Alumni Assn. (pres. Asheville chpt. 1957). Methodist (Sunday sch. tchr., adminstrv. bd., lay speaker, conf. del.). Lion (pres. West Asheville 1955-56, pres. Seven Oaks club Columbia 1970-71, editor bulls. 1964-67, 68—), Mason. Club: Mid-Carolina. Home: 612 Old Friars Rd Columbia SC 29210 Office: PO Box 68 7400 Woodrow Av Irmo SC 29063

JUDE, JAMES RODERICK, cardiac surgeon; b. Maple Lake, Minn., June 7, 1928; s. Bernard Benedict and Cecilia Mary (Leick) J.; B.S., Coll. St. Thomas, 1949; M.D., U. Minn., 1953; m. Sallye Garrigan, Aug. 4, 1951; children—Roderick, John, Cecilia, Victoria, Peter, Robert, Chris. Intern Johns Hopkins Hosp., 1953-54, resident in surgery, 1954-55, 58-61, fellow in cardiovascular research, 1955-56; instr. surgery Johns Hopkins U. and Med. Sch., 1961-62, asst. prof., 1962-64; prof. surgery, chief thoracic and cardiovascular surgery U. Miami Sch. Medicine, 1964-71, clin. prof., 1971—; practice medicine specializing in cardiovascular surgery, Miami and Ft. Lauderdale, Fla., 1971—; dir. cardiovascular center St. Francis Hosp., Miami Beach, Fla., 1973-78, chief surgery, 1973-78; chmn. N. Ridge Heart Found., Ft. Lauderdale, 1979—. Mem. Coral Gables (Fla.) Planning Bd., 1973-77. Served with USPHS, 1956-58. Fellow Am. Coll. Chest Physicians, Am. Coll. Cardiology, A.C.S.; mem. Am. Assn. Thoracic Surgery, So. Surg. Assn., Soc. Vascular Surgery, Soc. Thoracic Surgeons, Am. Heart Assn., Soc. Univ. Surgeons, Am. Surg. Assn., Soc. Internal Surgery. Democrat. Roman Catholic. Contbr. articles to med. jours. Home: 200 Edgewater Dr Coral Gables FL 33133 Office: 3661 S Miami Ave Miami FL 33133

JUDKINS, RODDIE REAGAN, chem. engr.; b. Sunbright, Tenn., Dec. 31, 1941; s. Ammon Eston and Hazel Louise (McAfee) J.; B.S., Tenn. Poly. Inst., 1963, M.S., 1965; Ph.D., Ga. Inst. Tech., 1970; m. Teressa Dean, June 27, 1964; children—Bridget Renee, Lisa Suzanne, Emily Robin. Instr. chemistry Ga. Inst. Tech., Atlanta, 1965-70, DuPont teaching asst. fellow, 1968; plant mgr., v.p. Nuclear Chems. and Metals Corp., Huntsville, Tenn., 1970-73; sr. tech. asso., v.p. Nuclear Audit & Testing Co. subs. E.R. Johnson Assos., Inc., Vienna, Va., 1973-77; devel. engr. metals and ceramics div. Oak Ridge Nat. Lab., 1977—. Registered profl. engr., Calif. Mem. Am. Chem. Soc., Sigma Xi. Republican. Methodist. Home: 9917 Rainbow Dr Knoxville TN 37922 Office: PO Box X Oak Ridge TN 37922

JUDSON, HOWARD WILLIAM, oil co. exec.; b. Flushing, N.Y., Oct. 8, 1921; s. Jack and Bess J.; B.S. in Mech. Engring., CCNY, 1943; M.S. in Mech. Engring., Columbia U., 1950; m. Christina H. Rust, Oct. 18, 1943; children—Ron A., Carole L. Judson Foxley, Jeanne M. Judson Fredericks. Test engr. Wright Aero. Corp., Woodbridge, N.J., 1943-44; with Shell Oil Co., 1946—, div. engr., New Orleans, 1953-56, supt. distbn., Detroit, 1956-58, div. engr., N.Y.C., 1958-61, ops. mgr. western div. Shell Can., 1961-63, sales supr. Sacramento, 1963-65, mgr. advt. and sales promotion, N.Y.C., 1965-69, ops. mgr. western region, 1969-70, head consultancy div. Shell Internat. Petroleum Co. Ltd., London, Eng., 1970-73, consumer relations and mktg. research mgr., Houston, 1973-75, consumer relations and advt. mgr., Houston, 1975—. Dir. religious edn. com. Unitarian Ch., Port Washington, 1950-52; v.p. PTA, Arkmonk, N.Y., 1960; chmn. nominating com. sch. bd., Arkmonk, 1961. Served to warrant Officer C.E. U.S. Army, 1944-45; served to 1st. lt. C.E. USAR, 1950-55. Profl. engr., N.Y. Mem. Nat. Advt. Review Bd., Soc. Consumers Affairs Profls. in Bus. (bd. dirs., treas.), Assn. Nat. Advertisers, Council of Better Bus. Burs. (Nat., consumer relations consultive com.), Better Bus. Bur. Houston (steering com. consumer relations, 1976—), Conf. Consumer Orgns., Nat. Consumers League. Developer Shell corp. advt. program Come to Shell for Answers. Home: 307 Rainier Dr Houston TX 77024 Office: 1 Shell Plaza PO Box 2463 Houston TX 77001

JUERGENSEN, ILSE DINA, poet; b. Frankfurt/Main, Ger.; d. Alfred and Martha T. Loebenberg; came to U.S., 1940, naturalized, 1945; diploma Frankfurt/Main High Sch., 1938; postgrad. U. So. Fla., Tampa; m. Hans Juergensen, Oct. 27, 1945; 1 dau., Claudia Jeanne Juergensen Noble. Poet-in-schs., Tampa, 1973—; author: The Second Time, 1972; I Don't Want a Thunderbird Anymore, 1977; represented in anthologies; editor: (anthology children's poems) From Feather to Feather, 1976; cons. editor Gryphon mag. Recipient award Fla. Poetry Rev. Mem. Nat. Fed. State Poetry Socs. (sec. 1968-70, 1st prize poems 1970, 71), Friends of Poetry, Poetry Soc. Am. Democrat. Jewish. Address: 7815 Pine Hill Dr Tampa FL 33617

JUKOFSKY, S. LAWRENCE, ophthalmologist; b. Hackensack, N.J., Mar. 13, 1925; s. I. and R. (Meltzer) J.; B.A., Columbia, 1944; M.D., N.Y. Med. Coll., 1948; m. Elizabeth A. Cushing, Dec. 26, 1947; children—Michael A., Diane. Intern, Hackensack Hosp., 1948-49; resident McMillan Hosp., St. Louis, 1949, St. Louis County (Mo.) Hosp., 1949-52; practice medicine specializing in ophthalmology, Westwood, N.J., 1954—, Hilton Head, S.C., 1978—; attending staff Hilton Head Hosp. Diplomate Nat. Bd. Med. Examiners, Am. Bd. Ophthalmology. Fellow Am. Acad. Ophthalmology and Otolaryngology, A.C.S.; mem. Soc. Eye Surgeons, Pan Am. Ophthalmol. Soc., Pan Pacific Surg. Congress, S.C. Med. Soc., So. Med. Assn. Served with USN, 1942-46, USMC, 1950-53. Republican. Club: Rotary. Home: 36 Angel Wing Dr Hilton Head Island SC 29928 Office: LaMotte Profl Bldg Hilton Head Hosp Hilton Head Island SC 29928

JULIAN, HAROLD EUGENE, foods co. exec.; b. Boonville, Ind., July 8, 1926; s. Harold and Katherine J.; student, Purdue U., 1958-59, Washington U., St. Louis, 1960-67, Columbia U., 1967-69; m. Lois Joel Thompson, Aug. 26, 1944; children—Danny Le, Deborah, Darlene, Donald. Partner supermarket chain, Evansville, Ind.; host TV program Julian's Food With Flair, Evansville, 1960-68; dir. tng. and corp. mgmt. devel. Wetterau Foods, St. Louis, 1968-70, dir. mktg. for 3 affiliated cos., 1971-73, dir. new mktg. devel. and regional mgmt., Winter Haven, Fla., 1973—; seminar specialist, dir. mktg. J. W. Allen Co.; cons. Served in USN, 1944-46; PTO, ETO. Recipient awards from Evansville Indsl. Found., Kiwanis, others. Mem. Food Mktg. Inst., Associated Retail Bakers Am., Am. Soc. Tng. and Devel., Retail Bakers Am. Clubs: Winter Haven (Fla.) Bass; United Bass Fishermen; Bass Angelers Soc.; Masons, Shriners. Author: Dairy Merchandising; Creative Grocery Merchandising; Public Relations Supermarket Management; Cash Control; others. Home and Office: 309 Suwanee Rd Winter Haven FL 33880

JULIFF, WALTER FAY, veterinarian; b. Granbury, Tex., Sept. 15, 1921; s. Walter Fay and Zuma Agra (Cogdell) J.; D.V.M., Tex. A. & M. U., 1946; m. Eva Nell Roper, Jan. 30, 1951; children—Walter David, Jennifer, Britt Lynn. Individual practice veterinary medicine, San Angelo, Tex., 1946-75; meat insp., pub. health cons. City of San Angelo, 1951-75; asso. prof. Coll. Veterinary Medicine, Tex. A. & M. U., 1975—; rep. Nat. Bd. Vet. Med. Examiners. Active United Fund, Boy Scouts Am. Named Layman of Year, San Angelo Jr. C. of C., 1954. Mem. Tex. Acad. Veterinary Practice, Am. Animal Assn., Tex. Pub. Health Assn., Am. (del.), Tex. (pres. 1959) vet. med. assns. Presbyterian (elder). Club: Rotary. Contbr. articles to profl. jours. Home: 10 Forest Dr College Station TX 77840 Office: Box JA College Station TX 77840

JUMP, WALTER STANDLY, II, TV sales exec.; b. Paris, Ill., Apr. 4, 1945; s. Walter Standly and Kathryn B. Jump; B.A., Fla. Tech. U., 1971; m. Theresa E. McAloon, Apr. 27, 1968; 1 son, John Standly. Studio cameraman Sta. WESH-TV, Orlando, Fla., 1969, projectionist, 1970, projectionist, switcher, 1970-71, salesman, 1972, local sales mgr., 1976-78, regional sales rep., 1979—; tchr. mktg. and advt. Organizer, Big Bros. of Orange County; active Seminole County Assn. Retarded Children, Children's Village of Seminole County. Served with USMC, 1964-68; Vietnam. Mem. Orlando Area Advt. Fedn. (past dir.). Methodist. Club: Winter Park West Rotary. Office: PO Box 7697 Orlando FL 32854

JUNG, RODNEY C., physician; b. New Orleans, Oct. 9, 1920; s. Frederick Charles and Clara (Cuevas) J.; B.S. in zoology with honors, Tulane U., 1941, M.D., 1945, M.S. in parasitology, 1950, Ph.D., 1953. Intern Charity Hosp. La., New Orleans 1945-46; dir. Hutchinson Meml. Clinic, 1948; asst. parasitology Tulane U., 1948-50, instr. tropical medicine, 1950-53, asst. prof., 1953-57, asso. prof. tropical medicine 1951-63, prof. tropical medicine, 1963—, clin. prof. internal medicine, 1975—, head div. tropical medicine, 1960-63; health dir. City of New Orleans, 1963-70, 79—; internist-in-charge Ill. Central Hosp., New Orleans, 1956-70; sr. vis. physician Charity Hosp., 1959—; sr. in internal medicine Touro Infirmary; John and Mary Markie Scholar in med. sci.; Served as lt. (j.g.) M.C., USNR, 1946-48. Diplomate Am. Bd. Internal Medicine. Fellow A.C.P.; mem. Internat. Society Tropical Dermatology, Am. Royal socs. tropical medicine and hygiene, Am. Soc. Parasitologists, La. State, Orleans Parish med. socs., Nat. Rifle Assn., La. Mosquito Control Assn., La. Pub. Health Assn., Am., La. socs. internal medicine, Am. Def. Preparedness Assn., Phi Beta Kappa, Sigma Xi, Alpha Omega Alpha. Presbyn. Office: 3600 Chestnut New Orleans LA 70115

JUNGMAN, YOUNG FRANK, real estate broker; b. Houston, Mar. 18, 1929; s. J. Frank and Thelma Katherine (Young) J.; B.B.A., U. Tex., 1948, J.D., 1950; postgrad. U. Houston, Wichita State U., U. Ga., So. Methodist U.; m. Marilyn Virginia Skipwith, June 7, 1952; children—Robert Frank, John Skipwith. Sec.-treas., dir. Paul E. Wise Co., Inc., and affiliated cos., 1954-61; real estate broker, appraiser, cons., Houston, 1961—. Admitted to Tex. bar, 1950, U.S. Supreme Ct.

bar, 1954; instr. real estate U. Houston, 1970-73. Mem. Harris County Flood Control Task Force, 1975-77; mem. Harris County Democratic Exec. Com., 1978—. Mem. Houston City Library Bd., 1965-76, v.p., 1973-76. Served to 1st lt. USAF, 1951-53. Mem. Nat., Tex., Houston assns. realtors, Tex., Houston bar assns., Pi Kappa Alpha, Phi Alpha Delta. Episcopalian. Mason (Shriner, 32 deg.). Home: 5325 Willers Way Houston TX 77056 Office: 1502 1st City Nat Bank Bldg Houston TX 77002

JUNGMEYER, DENNIS EDWIN, assn. exec.; b. California, Mo., Oct. 11, 1946; s. Edwin Otto and Norma June (Weaver) J.; B.S., Lincoln U., 1970; M.B.A., Ga. Coll., 1973; m. Gayla Sue Lynes, July 23, 1966; 1 son, Shawn Michael. Prodn. supt. Am. Hosp. Supply Corp., Milledgeville, Ga., 1971-73; dir. Motor Vehicle dept. Mo. Dept. Revenue, Jefferson City, Mo., 1973-76; dir. field services Mo. Automobile Dealers Assn., Jefferson City, Mo., 1976-78; exec. v.p. Ark. Automobile Dealers Assn., Little Rock, 1979—; adminstr. Am. Western Life Ins. Co.-Ark. Motor Vehicle Commn., 1979—. Scoutmaster Five Rivers council Boy Scouts Am., 1973-78. Mem. Am. Mgmt. Assn., Nat. Conf. Service Dirs. (chmn. Midwest field service dirs. 1977-78), Ark. Hwy. Users Fedn., Am. Soc. Assn. Execs., Ark. Soc. Assn. Execs., Little Rock C. of C., Nat. Automobile Dealers Assn., Automotive Trade Assn. Mgrs. Republican. Lutheran. Clubs: Jaycees, Rotary, Eagles, Elks, Toastmasters Guild. Office: 600 Chester St Little Rock AR 72201

JUNKIN, WILLIAM FRANCIS, III, physicist; b. Baguio, Philippines, Feb. 15, 1942 (parents Am. citizens); s. William F. and Jessie Woodrow (McElroy) J.; A.B., King Coll., 1963; Ph.D. in Physics (fellow), Mass. Inst. Tech., 1967; m. Margaret L. Gilkeson, Aug. 21, 1964; children—Anne, David, Margaret Ruth. Asst. prof. dept. physics U. Richmond (Va.), 1967-70, 73-74; asso. prof. Tunghai U., Taiwan, 1970-73; asso. prof. dept. physics Erskine Coll., Due West, S.C., 1974—, chmn. div. natural sci. and math., 1976—. Home: PO Box 184 Due West SC 29639 Office: Erskine Coll Due West SC 29639

JUNKINS, BOBBY MAC, librarian; b. Gadsden, Ala., Nov. 1, 1946; s. L.D. and Grace Coolidge (Tedder) J.; student Gadsden Jr. Coll., 1965-67; B.S., Jacksonville State U., 1969, M.S., 1972; postgrad. U. Ala., 1978-79; m. Barbara Lynn Woodall, June 12, 1966; children—Jason Clay, Annie Blair. With Gadsden Public Library, 1965-68; library technician Jacksonville Elemen. Library (Miss.), 1968-69, Cherokee County High Sch., Centre, Ala., 1969-73; dir. Gadsden-Etowah County Public Library, 1976—; tchr. Cherokee Adult Edn. Mem. State Democratic Exec. Com. Dist. 30, 1978—. Mem. Gadsden Metro C. of C. (v.p. human resources 1978-79, Key Man award 1978), ALA, Southeastern Library Assn., Ala. Library Assn., Ala. Hist. Assn. Methodist. Club: Kiwanis (v.p., dir.). Home: Route 3 Box 80-D Centre AL 35960 Office: 254 College St Gadsden AL 35901

JUNOD, PATRICIA LEE, real estate broker; b. Jay County, Ind., Jan. 23, 1929; d. Willard Arthur and Dorothy Jeanette (Glendening) White; student pub. schs., Northville, Mich., 1947; m. Aubrey Sidney Junod, Sept. 26, 1947 (div.); children—Suzanne Junod Hopper, Lorayne Junod Evans, Andrew Arthur, Elizabeth Lee. Saleswoman, Juno Beach Realty Inc. (Fla.), 1960-65; broker-saleswoman Ketter Realty Co., Lake Park, Fla., 1966-67, Kenneth P. Foster Inc., West Palm Beach, 1967-71; pres., broker PGA Realty Inc., Palm Beach Gardens, Fla., 1971-79; pres. Heritage PGA Inc., 1970—. Mem. N. Palm Beach (Fla.) Planning and Zoning Bd., 1966-70; pres. Pal-Mar-Water Mgmt. Dist., Martin and Palm Beach County, 1972-78, South Indian River Drainage Dist. Mem. Nat., Fla. assns. realtors, No. Palm Beach County Bd. Realtors, Nat. Fedn. Ind. Bus., Palm Beach County Mental Health Assn., No. Palm Beach C. of C. Republican. Home: 935 Turner Quay Jupiter FL 33458 Office: 2400 PGA Blvd Palm Beach Gardens FL 33410

JURGENS, WILLIAM KARL, JR., athletic dir.; b. Atlanta, Jan. 24, 1946; s. Armenda H. Jurgens; B.A. in Biology, Jacksonville (Fla.) U., 1968; M.S. in Edn., Fla. Inst. Tech., Melbourne, 1979; m. Audrey Susan Hudsbeth, Dec. 5, 1974; children—Scott, Amanda. Head crew coach Fla. Inst. Tech., 1969—, dir. athletics, 1975—; mem. U.S. Olympic Rowing Com.; mem. sports com. Melbourne Area C. of C. Mem. Nat. Assn. Amateur Oarsmen (dir.), Fla. Intercollegiate Rowing Assn. (pres.). Methodist. Home: 441 S Bluff Dr Melbourne FL 32901 Office: Fla Inst Tech Country Club Rd Melbourne FL 32901

JURTSHUK, PETER, JR., microbiologist; b. N.Y.C., July 28, 1929; s. Peter and Mary (Ferens) J.; A.B., N.Y. U., 1951, M.S., Creighton U., 1953; Ph.D., U. Md., 1957; postdoctoral fellow enzyme chemistry U. Wis., 1959-62; m. Rebecca J. Jones, Jan. 2, 1971; children—Peter, Larissa. Asst. prof. pharmacology L.I. U., Bklyn, Coll. Pharmacy, 1957-59; asst. prof. enzyme chemistry U. Wis., 1962-63; asst. prof. microbiology U. Tex. at Austin, 1963-69; asso. prof. biology U. Houston, 1970-76, prof., 1976—, chmn. undergrad. biology, 1977—; mem. vis. biologists program Am. Inst. Biol. Scis., 1969-72. NIH grantee, 1964-75. Fellow Am. Inst. Chemists, Am. Acad. Microbiology; mem. Am. Soc. Microbiology (pres. Tex. br.), Am. Soc. Biol. Chemists, Am. Soc. Cell Biology, N.Y. Acad. Scis., AAAS, AAUP, Am. Chem. Soc., Sigma Xi (pres. br. 1979-80). Contbr. articles to profl. jours. Home: 3107 Norris Dr Houston TX 77025

JUSTICE, BRUCE MORGAN, architect; b. Richmond, Va., Jan. 28, 1940; s. Charles Chappell and Mary Brodnax (Malone) J.; student U. Va., 1958-61, U. Richmond, 1962-63; B.Arch., U. Va., 1967; m. Linda Rae Hayes, Feb. 9, 1963; children—Brian Christopher, Todd Morgan. With Marcellus Wright & Son Architects, Richmond, 1962-63, Stainback & Scribner Architects, Charlottesville, Va., 1963-67, Ballou and Justice Architects & Engrs., Richmond, 1967-79, Jones and Strange-Boston Architects and Engrs., 1979—. Mem. Richmond Mayor's Com. on Handicapped, 1975-78; pres. Roslyn Hills Civic Assn., 1973; bd. dirs. Wilton L. Barnes Civitan Workshop for Mentally Retarded, Richmond, 1975, Chesapeake dist. Civitan Internat. Found. for Mentally Retarded and Handicapped, 1975—, Richmond area Mental Health Assn., 1979—; mem. subcom. on mental retardation Henrico County Chpt. 10 Bd. Mem. AIA (vice chmn. pub. edn. com. Va. chpt. 1971-73, vice chmn. design awards com. 1975—), U. Va. Alumni Assn. (life), Civitan (sec. Richmond 1970, dir. 1972, v.p. 1973-74, pres. elect 1974-75, pres. 1975-76). Home: 219 Melwood Ln Richmond VA 23229 Office: Ross Bldg 8th and Main Sts Richmond VA 23219

JUSTICE, CHARLES CHAPPELL, architect; b. Hartford, Conn., July 11, 1909; s. Edward and Blanche (Morgan) J.; B.Arch., Ohio State U., 1935; m. Mary Brodnax Malone, Dec. 31, 1938; children—Bruce Morgan, Irene Walker Justice Myers. Archtl. draftsman Lee, Smith & Van Dervoort, 1930-35; asso. Louis W. Ballou, Architect, 1935-42; chief draftsman Merrill C. Lee, Architect, 1942-45; partner Ballou & Justice Architects and Engrs., 1945— (all Richmond); archtl. lectr.; faculty dept. math. Va. Mechanics Inst., 1939-45; mem. Va. Bd. Examiners and Certification of Architects, Engrs. and Land Surveyors, 1958-68, pres., 1966. Bd. dirs. Richmond chpt. ARC, Central Richmond Assn., Westham Civic Assn. Mem. Nat. Council Archtl. Registration Bds. (chmn. regional conf. 1968), AIA (past dir., treas., sec., v.p., pres. Va. chpt.). Clubs: Bachelor, Commonwealth, Downtown. Prin. works include: City Hall, Richmond, Restoration of Va. State Capitol, St. Mary's Hosp., Richmond, Jamestown Festival Park, Yorktown Victory Center, Restoration of rotunda U. Va., State of Va. Twin Towers, Richmond. Home: 204 Sunset Dr Richmond VA 23229 Office: 530 E Main St Richmond VA 23219

JUSTICE, DAVID BLAIR, psychologist, author; b. Dallas, July 2, 1927; s. Sam Hugh and Lou-Reine (Hunter) J.; B.A., U. Tex. at Austin, 1948; M.S., Columbia U., 1949; M.A., Tex. Christian U., 1963; Ph.D., Rice U., 1966; m. Rita Norwood, July 26, 1972; children by previous marriage—Cynthia, David, Elizabeth. Reporter, Ft. Worth Star-Telegram, 1952-55; sci. writer N.Y. Daily News, 1955-56, Ft. Worth Star-Telegram, 1956-64; sci. editor, columnist Houston Post, 1964-73; exec. asst. to Mayor of Houston, 1966-72; prof. psychology Health Sci. Center, U. Tex. at Houston, 1968—; sr. social psychologist, group therapist Tex. Research Inst. Mental Scis.; community asso. Rice U., Lovett Coll.; cons. child abuse Tex. Dept. Pub. Welfare; film maker. Gen. chmn. Houston Job Fair, 1967-73; chmn. Houston Manpower Area Planning Council, 1972-74; mem. Tex. Urban Devel. Commn., 1970-72. Bd. dirs. Houston Housing Devel. Corp.; sec. bd. mgrs. Tarrant County Hosp. Dist., 1961-64; pres. Houston Area Council on Sudden Infant Death Syndrome, 1977—; mem. nat. adv. com. Marine Biomed. Inst., U. Tex. Med. Br., 1971—. Served with USNR, 1945-46. Recipient most outstanding book award Tex. Writers Roundup, 1970, award of recognition, City of Houston, 1973; named One of Five Outstanding Young Men of Tex., 1962; recipient numerous awards for sci. writing. Mem. Nat. Assn. Sci. Writers (exec. com. 1965-67), Houston Psychol. Assn. (pres. 1975), Phi Beta Kappa. Clubs: Houston Racquet, Tex. Gridiron (pres. 1963). Author: Violence in the City, 1969; Detection of Potential Community Violence, 1967; The Abusing Family, 1976; The Broken Taboo: Sex in the Family, 1979; Stress is in the Eye of the Beholder, 1980. Home: 6331 Brompton Rd Houston TX 77005 Office: 6901 Bertner St Houston TX 77030

JUSTICE, FRANKLIN PIERCE, JR., oil co. exec.; b. Wanego, W.Va., May 5, 1938; s. Franklin Pierce and Jeneta Ruth (Cooley) J.; B.S. in Bus. Adminstrn., W.Va. State Coll., 1967; M.B.A., Marshall U., 1977; postgrad. U. Louisville, 1971-72; m. Eva Mae Hartley, June 8, 1960; children—Kerry, Kelly, Kevin. Reporter, Dun & Bradstreet, Inc., Charleston, W.Va., 1960-63, reporting mgr., 1963-65, office mgr., Huntington, W.Va., 1966-68; domestic trade specialist U.S. Dept. Commerce, Charleston, 1968-70; pres., investment mgr. Equal Opportunity Fin., Inc., Ashland, Ky., 1970—, adminstrv. asst. to v.p. personnel, 1973-74, adminstrv. asst. to v.p. external affairs, 1974-75, mgr. spl. projects, 1975-76, dir. public affairs, 1976—; v.p. public relations Ashland (Ky.) Oil, Inc., 1979—. Cons., Ashland Tennis Commn., 1975-79; mem. Ashland Human Rights Commn., 1977-79; bd. dirs. Tri-State Fair & Regatta, 1978-79; v.p., bd. dirs. Ky. Council Econ. Edn., 1978-79; pres. Greater Ashland Found., 1979. Mem. Ashland Area C. of C. (1st v.p. 1978-79, pres. 1980, dir. 1978-80), Ky. C. of C. (dir. 1978-79). Republican. Home: 103 Arizona Dr Russell KY 41169 Office: PO Box 391 Ashland KY 41101

JUSTICE, WILLIAM MARION, JR., county ofcl.; b. Amesville, La., Apr. 11, 1910; s. William Marion and Clara (Wall) J.; B.S., La. State U., 1933, M.E., 1946. Tchr., coach Westwego (La.) High Sch., 1933-38; prin. L.H. Marrero (La.) High Sch., 1938-56; clk. 24th Jud. Dist. Ct. of Jefferson Parish, 1956—. Dir. Merc. Bank & Trust Co., Gretna, La. Served with USAAF, 1942-45. Mem. Nat. Assn. County Clks. and Recorders, Nat. Assn. County Ofcls., La. Clks. of Ct. Assn. (dir. 1971-72, chmn. ins. com., 1966—, legis. com., 1968—), Am. Legion (comdr. 1945-47, area D comdr. 1947-48), La. State U. Alumni Assn. (pres. 1965-66), Jefferson Parish, La. fire dept. assns., Amvets, Phi Delta Kappa. Mem. United Ch. Christ. Clubs: Jefferson Parish Quarterback, Lafitte Yacht. Home: 547 Barataria Blvd Marrero LA 70072 Office: Courthouse Bldg Gretna LA 70053

JUSTINE, CLAIRE, artist, poet; b. San Antonio, May 26, 1932; d. Leonard Mark and Mary Antoinette (Rodesney) Hess; B.A., Fontbonne Coll., St. Louis, 1954; student San Antonio Art Inst., 1961-62, Art League Houston, 1966-70, 13-10 Studio, Houston, 1968-71; pvt. study with artists including Harold Roney, Chester Snowden, Bud Biggs, Rex Brandt, Jack Burch, Henry Faulkner; m. Paul Richard Grabowski, Sept. 1, 1956 (div.); children—Jean Elizabeth, Paul Richard II, Jon Daniel. One woman shows Brooks AFB, 1964, Ring Library, Houston, 1969, Framemakers Shop, 1972, Cinima Gallery, Louisville, 1975, Hunter Gallery, Louisville, 1976; numerous gallery exhibits in San Antonio, Houston and Louisville, also Michaelangelo Art Club Gallery, Naples, Italy, 1977, LaScalle Gallery, Florence, Italy, 1977; also exhibited abroad at Ovar (Portugal) Mus., 1974, Lluc Mus., Barcelona, Spain, 1974, Zeyer, Paris, 1974, Joan Miro competition, Barcelona, 1974-77; represented in collections Ovar Mus., DaVinci Accademia, Rome, Moka Club, Paris, others, also numerous pvt. collections; lectr., poetry reader; condr. bus. Very Personal Greetings, hand painted cards. Mem. internat. com. Centro Studie Scambi Internat., Rome, 1971. Girl Scout art badge tchr. Recipient awards River Art Group competition, 1967, Nat. League Am. Pen Women, 1970-72; also awards poetry Poetry Soc. Tex. Fellow Internat. Poetry Soc.; mem. Artists Equity Assn., Lexington Art League, Centre Studie Scambi Internazionali, Acad. Internat. Leonardo da Vinci, Nat. League Am. Pen Women, Poetry Soc. Tex., Accedemia Leonardo da Vinci. Author: Thursday's Child; works included in anthologies. Home: PO Box 7101 Louisville KY 40207

JUSTINIANI, FEDERICO ROBERTO, physician; b. Havana, Cuba, Aug. 15, 1929; s. Federico Luis and Margarita (Longa) J.; came to U.S., 1964, naturalized, 1969; B.S., De La Salle Coll., Havana, 1947; M.D., Havana U., 1954; m. Maria Suarez, Nov. 29, 1955. Intern, resident in internal medicine Havana U. Hosp., 1955-61; practice medicine, Havana, 1961-64; intern St. Francis Hosp., Miami Beach, Fla., 1965; resident in internal medicine Mt. Sinai Hosp., Miami Beach, 1966-69, program coordinator residency in internal medicine, 1969-74; dir. med. edn. Mt. Sinai Med. Center, Miami Beach, 1974—; instr. medicine U. Miami, 1969-72, asst. prof., 1972—. Diplomate Am. Bd. Internal Medicine. Fellow A.C.P.; mem. AMA (Physicians' Recognition award 1969, 72, 76, 79), Fla., So., Dade County med. assns., Am. Soc. Internal Medicine, Am. Geriatrics Soc., Assn. Hosp. Med. Edn., Royal Soc. Medicine, Alliance for Continuing Med. Edn., Assn. Program Dirs. in Internal Medicine, Cuban Med. Assn. in Exile. Contbr. articles to profl. jours. Home: 9633 S W 11th Terr Miami FL 33174 Office: 4300 Alton Rd Miami Beach FL 33140

JUSTISS, WILL ALAN, psychologist; b. Ravenscroft, Tenn., Feb. 1, 1920; s. Srygley Claude and Thula Flossie (Dodson) J.; A.A., Jacksonville U., 1950; B.A., U. Fla., 1952, M.A., 1954, Ph.D., 1957; m. Joanne Beryl Cox, June 14, 1974; children by previous marriage—Charles Alan, Pamela Irene Justiss Cooper, Stephanie Lorraine Justiss Gilley, David Byron, Kathleen Anita. Dir., Moosehaven Research Lab., Orange Park, Fla., 1957-62; field supr. grad. sch. Washington U., St. Louis, 1962; research cons. Yerkes Lab. Primate Biology, Orange Park, 1956-65; cons. Center for Study of Aging, Duke U., Durham, N.C., 1964-68, Duval County Sch. Bd., Jacksonville, Fla., 1967-71, Cathedral Health and Rehab. Center, Jacksonville, 1971-75; pvt. practice clin. psychology 1954—; lectr. Jacksonville U., 1964-66. Served with USAAF, 1942-45. NIMH fellow, 1954-57. Mem. Duval Assn. Retarded Children (pres. 1967), Fla. Psychol. Assn. (exec. council 1965, pres. N.E. chpt. 1959-61, 75—). Club: Jacksonville Rudder (commodore 1966). Contbr. articles to profl. jours. Home: 2824 Corinthian Ave Jacksonville FL 32210 Office: 2819 Oak St Jacksonville FL 32205

KABALKA, GEORGE WALTER, chemist, educator; b. Wyandotte, Mich., Feb. 1, 1943; s. Walter George and Rose Marie K.; B.S., U. Mich., 1965; Ph.D., Purdue U., 1970; m. Beth Ann Swaim, Aug. 31, 1968; children—Stephen, Katherine. Asso. prof. chemistry U. Tenn., Knoxville, 1970—; cons. in field. Mem. Am. Chem. Soc., Sigma Xi, Phi Lambda Upsilon. Democrat. Contbr. articles to profl. publs. Office: Chemistry Dept U Tenn Knoxville TN 37919

KADAR, DAVID BARRY, bus. machines co. exec.; b. Wheeling, W.Va., June 19, 1952; s. Kenneth K. and Dorothy L. (Wagner) K.; B.S., West Liberty State Coll., 1974; M.B.A. (Scholar), L.I. U., 1975. Margin clk. Bayrock Advs., N.Y.C., 1975-76; account mgr. NCR Corp., Wheeling, W.Va., 1976-79. Named Outstanding Young Man of Am., U.S. Jr. C. of C., 1978. Home: 16 Leatherwood Ln Wheeling WV 26003 Office: NCR Corp 98 E Cove Ave Wheeling WV 26003

KADLECEK, EDWARD JOHN, JR., mech. engr.; b. Houston, July 31, 1934; s. Edward John and Louise (Jakubec) K.; B.S. in Mech. Engring., U. Houston, 1958, B.S. in Indsl. Engring., 1961; M.S. in Systems Mgmt., St. Mary's U., 1979; m. Marilyn Martha Holtman, Nov. 3, 1962; children—Edward John III, Karen Ann, Nancy Lynn. Chief engr. Fed. Steel Corp., Houston, 1964-65; chief maintenance indsl. engring. dept. Structural Metals, Inc., Sequin, Tex., 1965-67; chief programs devel. 12th C.E. squadron USAF, Randolph AFB, Tex., 1967—. Ambassador, Tex. Folklife Festival; chmn. Czechfest, New Braunfels; chmn. entertainment and spl. events New Braunfels Wurstfest, 1970—, sec., bd. dirs., 1978—; bd. dirs. Little League; committeeman Boy Scouts; mem. Tex. Gov.'s Com. Waste Water Mgmt. Recipient Sustained Superior Performance award Def. Dept., 1968, Outstanding Performance award, 1972, 75, 78; registered profl. engr., Tex. Mem. Nat., Tex. (dir.) socs. profl. engrs., Am. Inst. Indsl. Engrs., Wurst Assn. New Braunfels, Phi Kappa Theta. Clubs: Eagles, K.C. Home: 367 Oakcrest St New Braunfels TX 78130 Office: 12 CES Randolph AFB TX 78148

KADROVACH, DAN GEORGE, hosp. dir.; b. Mich., Aug. 22, 1920; s. Joseph and Victoria Francis (August) K.; B.S., U. Md., 1953; M.S.H.A., Northwestern U., 1955; postgrad. Cornell U. Sloan Inst., 1958; children by previous marriage—Cathy, Karen, Connie, Dan George; m. Nancy Gatlin, Jan. 3, 1975; stepchildren—Stephen, John, Cecil, Nancy. Served in U.S. Army Med. Service Corps, 1942-62, commd. 2d lt., 1943, advanced through grades to col., 1962; various med. services to field hosps. assignments, 1943-46; adminstrn. officer Far Eastern command, Tokyo, Japan, 1946-49; controller Walter Reed Med. Center, Washington, 1949-53; advanced mil. officer tng., Ft. Sam Houston, Tex., 1953-55; exec. officer Army Med. Center, Landstuhl, Germany, 1955-58; asso. prof. hosp. adminstrn. Baylor Army Program, Ft. Sam Houston, 1958-62; ret., 1962; asst. dir. Johns Hopkins Med. Inst., 1962-66; exec. dir. Hermann Hosp., Tex. Med. Center, Houston, 1966-75; dir. VA Med. Center, New Orleans, 1975-79, Southeastern region VA, North Little Rock, 1979—; bd. dirs. Health Services Agency, New Orleans; mem. La. Gov.'s Council on Physician Manpower for La.; mem. Health Edn. Authority of La.; mem. faculty Tulane U. Decorated Army Commendation medal with 2 oak leaf clusters; recipient Malcolm T. MacEachern award Northwestern U., 1955, Adminstr.'s award VA, Washington, 1979. Presdl. Cost Reduction Contbrs. award VA, 1978, Chief Med. Dir.'s Commendation, VA, 1978. Fellow Am. Coll. Hosp. Adminstrs.; mem. Am. Hosp. Assn., Council Teaching Hosps., La. Hosp. Assn., Am. Assn. Child Care in Hosps. (charter). Episcopalian. Office: Bldg 32 VA Med Center North Little Rock AR 72114

KAESER, CLIFFORD RICHARD, leisure products mfg. co. exec.; b. Boise, Idaho, Feb. 17, 1936; s. Clifford M. and Bertha (Minton) K.; B.A., Coll. Idaho, 1959; J.D., Yale U., 1962; m. Carol Lynn Roach, May 11, 1979; children—Richard Lynn, Cindy Marie, Kenneth Ray. Admitted to Calif. bar, 1962; asso. firm Lawler, Felix & Hall, Los Angeles, 1962; asst. div. counsel Lockheed Missile & Space Div., Sunnyvale, Calif., 1963; group counsel, then acquisition counsel Litton Industries, Beverly Hills, Calif., 1963-68; adminstrv. v.p., gen. counsel Hitco, Los Angeles, 1968-70; pres. Chaparral Industries, Inc., 1970-72; pres. Red Dale Coach Cos. subs.'s Armco Steel Corp., to 1972; v.p., gen. counsel Conroy, Inc., San Antonio, 1972-80; v.p., gen. counsel Dobbs Houses, Inc., 1980—. Mem. Am. Bar Assn., State Bar Calif., Am. Mgmt. Assn., Mchts. and Mfrs. Assn. Home: 3103 Eisenhaur M-29 San Antonio TX 78209 Office: Dobbs Houses Inc 5100 Poplar Ave Memphis TN 38137

KAESER, JOSEPH MICHAEL, mktg. exec.; b. Hamilton, Ohio, May 19, 1923; s. John and Hannah Ignatious (Cahalane) K.; student Coll. of Great Falls, 1951-52, U. Ala., 1943, U. Miss., 1952-53. Electronic design engr. Hayes Aircraft Corp., Birmingham, Ala., 1953-54; field project mgr. RCA, various locations, 1954-68; dir. field services in N. Am. and S. Am., Page Communications Engrs., Washington, 1968-70; program devel. mgr. Raytheon Corp., Burlington, Mass., 1970-75; with Sverdrup/ARO Corp., Washington, 1976-78; dir. internat. programs and market planning Computer Scis. Corp., Washington, 1978—; mgmt. cons. in field project bus. Served with USAF, 1943-53. Decorated Air medal with 2 oak leaf clusters; recipient Engr. of the Yr. award, Inst. Radio Engrs., 1959. Fellow AIAA (asso.); mem. IEEE (sr.), Soc. Flight Test Engrs., Electronic Industries Assn., Nat. Security Indsl. Assn., Nat. Council Tech. Service Industries. Roman Catholic. Home: 3003 Arlington Blvd Arlington VA 22201 Office: 6565 Arlington Blvd Falls Church VA 22046

KAGAN, ROBERT LLOYD, physician; b. N.Y.C., June 3, 1946; s. Aaron and Marcia (Rosen) K.; B.A., Bucknell U., 1968; M.D., Georgetown U., 1972; m. Marci Ann Mednick, June 3, 1972; children—Jarrett Brandon, Evan Scott. Intern, U. Calif., San Francisco, 1972-73; resident in clin. pathology NIH, 1973-75, resident in nuclear medicine, 1975-76, staff physician, 1976-77; dir. nuclear medicine, asso. pathologist Holy Cross Hosp., Ft. Lauderdale, Fla., 1977—; clin. asso. faculty Nuclear Medicine Inst., Mayfield Heights, Ohio. Served to lt. comdr. USPHS, 1973-77. Diplomate Nat. Bd. Med. Examiners, Am. Bd. Pathology, Am. Bd. Nuclear Medicine. Mem. Am. Soc. Clin. Pathologists (bd. registry nuclear medicine examination com. 1978—), Coll. Am. Pathology, Am. Soc. Microgiology, Assn. Clin. Scientists, Soc. Nuclear Medicine, Am. Assn. Clin. Chemistry, Clin. Radioassay Soc., Am. Cancer Soc. Jewish. Patentee detection device for automated bacteremia diagnosis, 1976. Contbr. articles to med. jours. Home: 700 Poinciana Dr Fort Lauderdale FL 33301 Office: 4725 N Federal Hwy Fort Lauderdale FL 33307

KAGGWA, LAWRENCE NYOMBI, journalist, educator; b. Kampala, Uganda, Oct. 10, 1938; came to U.S., 1963; s. Zoziwa and Alice (Nabinaka) Musoke; B.A., Rutgers U., New Brunswick, N.J., 1967; M.A., UCLA, 1968; Ph.D., So. Ill. U., 1972. Info. officer

Uganda Ministry of Info., 1958-63; reporter Ridgewood (N.J.) Herald News, summer 1964, Hartford (Conn.) Courant, summer 1965, Sta. WNJR, Newark, summer 1966, Los Angeles Times, 1968-69; prof., head dept. journalism Norfolk (Va.) State U., 1972—. Mem. E. Va. Health Edn. Consortium Publicity Com., 1978—; bd. dirs. Nat. Consortium for Minority Representation in Communication Media and Grad. Schs., 1978—; adv. bd. New Jour. and Guide, Norfolk, also John Q. Jordan Endowment; mem. Com. on Consumer Edn. Gov. Dalton State of Va., 1979—. African Students Program in Am. Univs. scholar, 1963-67, Inst. Internat. Edn. fellow, 1967-68, Phi Beta Kappa fellow, 1967-68, Spl. Doctoral fellow, 1969-72. Mem. Public Relations Soc. Am. (dir. 1978—), Internat. Assn. Bus. Communicators. Assn. Edn. for Journalism, Norfolk State Cluster Com., Soc. Profl. Journalists/Sigma Delta Chi. Democrat. Roman Catholic. Home: 3832 Charter Oak Rd Virginia Beach VA 23452 Office: Norfolk State Univ 2401 Corprew Ave Norfolk VA 23504

KAHAN, BARRY DONALD, surgeon; b. Cleve., July 25, 1939; s. Jacob Marvin and Pearl (Schultz) K.; B.S., U. Chgo., 1960, Ph.D., 1964, M.D., 1965; m. Rochelle Liebling, Sept. 5, 1962; 1 dau., Kara. Intern, Mass. Gen. Hosp., Boston, 1965-66, resident in surgery, 1968-72; staff asso. in immunology NIH, 1966-68; asst. prof. surgery and physiology Northwestern U. Sch. Medicine, Chgo., 1972-74, asso. prof., 1975-76; prof. surgery U. Tex. Med. Sch., Houston, 1977—, dir. program in immunology Grad. Sch. Biomed. Scis., 1978—, dir. divs. organ transplantation and immunology. Bd. dirs. Ill. Kidney Found., 1974-76. Mem. A.C.S., AAAS, Soc. Univ. Surgeons, Am. Soc. Clin. Investigation, Am. Soc. Transplant Surgeons, Internat. Transplantation Soc. (charter), Am. Assn. Immunologists, Am. Assn. Cancer Research. Home: 4 Rain Hollow St Houston TX 77024 Office: 6431 Fannin Ave Houston TX 77030

KAHAN, SUSAN ELLEN, educator; b. Middletown, Ohio, Sept. 10, 1948; d. Jack Edwin and Mary Amo (Beard) Peebles; B.S. (HEW fellow), George Washington U., 1970; M.A., Catholic U. Am., 1978, postgrad., 1978—; m. Jonathan Kahan, Aug. 1, 1970; 1 dau., Rachel. Tchr., George Mason Center, Arlington (Va.) Public Schs., 1970-75, Career Center, 1975-77, Jackson Elem. Sch., 1977-80, tchr. adminstr. spl. edn. programs and services, 1980—; instr. dept. edn. Cath. U. Am., 1979-80; cons. in field; condr. workshops on handicapped children. Mem. NEA, Council Exceptional Children (Jennie Brewer award 1975), PTA, Assn. Retarded Citizens, Am. Assn. Mental Deficiency. Author: Cooking Activities for Retarded Children, 1974; editor: Parents Handbook for Special Education, 1979. Home: 3153 N 21st St Arlington VA 22201 Office: 1426 N Quincy St Arlington VA 22205

KAHLE, GEORGE KENT, oil service co. exec.; b. St. Louis, Sept. 1, 1951; s. George Hermann and Gratia Underhill K.; grad. Deerfield Acad., 1970; A.B., Brown U., 1974; m. Cynthia Stewart Vietor, Oct. 8, 1977. Asst. mktg. mgr. Nabisco, Inc., N.Y.C., 1974; internat. cons. Wean United, Inc., Pitts., 1974-75; spl. asst. to sec. of interior and commerce, adminstrv. asst. to Rogers C.B. Morton, Pres. Ford's Adminstrn., Washington, 1975-77; mgr. investor services Geosource, Inc., Houston, 1977—. Mem. Nat. Investor Relations Inst. Republican. Episcopalian. Club: Met. Racquet. Home: 2110 Hazard St Houston TX 77019 Office: Suite 2000 2700 S Post Oak Rd Houston TX 77056

KAHLER, TAIBI, psychologist; b. Kewanna, Ind., June 30, 1943; s. George Junior and Madelyn Nellie (Malia) K.; B.A. in English Lit., Purdue U., 1968, M.S. in Child Devel., 1971, Ph.D. in Family Life, 1972; m. Sandra Louise Payne, June 16, 1977; 1 stepdau., Laura. Research and teaching asst. Purdue U., West Lafayette, Ind., 1969-72; asso. dir. Halcyon Inst., West Lafayette, 1972-74; dir. clin. tng. San Diego Inst. for Transactional Analysis, 1974-75; dir. Transactional Analysis Inst. for So. Calif., San Diego, 1975-76; co-dir. Human Devel. Assos., Little Rock, 1976—; cons. to various orgns. and agys. Lic. clin. psychologist, Ark.; lic. child, marriage and family counselor, Calif. Mem. Am. Psychol. Assn., Internat. Transactional Analysis Assn. (v.p., Eric Berne Sci. Meml. award 1977), Assn. Marriage and Family Therapists (clin.), Calif. Assn. Marriage and Family Counselors, Am. Group Psychotherapy Assn., Internat. Assn. Group Psychotherapists, Am. Assn. Marriage and Family Counselors, Triple Nine Soc., Internat. Soc. for Philos. Inquiry, Intertel, Mensa. Author: Notations, A Guide to Transactional Analysis Literature, 1977; Transactional Analysis Revisited, 1979; editor: Transactional Analysis Journal, 1975; contbr. articles to profl. jours. Office: Cantrell Place Bldg Suite 270 2311 Biscayne St Little Rock AR 72207

KAHN, ALBERT MICHAEL, artist, designer; b. Gorky, Russia, July 4, 1917; s. Samson and Bertha (Kashket) K.; came to U.S., 1929, naturalized, 1942; grad. Pratt Inst., 1937, Art Students League, 1938; student U. Mexico, 1946, U. Lima Bellas Artes, 1949; m. Rose Menacer, Dec. 21, 1947 (div. 1970); children—Sharon Beth, Brenda Jo. Art dir. McCann Erickson Advt., 1947; mural painter, Mexico, 1948-50; graphic designer, Washington, 1950, San Francisco, 1951-54, 60-65; instr. San Francisco Art Sch., 1961-65; painter in Central and S.Am., 1955-59, in Europe and Israel, 1966-68; graphic cons. Matson Navigation Co., San Francisco, 1969-70; world painting tour, 1971; painter in Spain, 1972-73; painter, graphic artist Miami, Fla., 1974—; represented in permanent collections in museums in U.S., pvt. collections in U.S., Europe, S.Am., C.Am. Served with C.E., AUS, 1940-45. Decorated C.E. Commendation medal, U.S. Army C.E. Surg. Gen. commendation in graphics; recipient Art Dir.'s medal Washington, 1950, Art Dir.'s awards San Francisco, 1962, 63. Mem. Artists Equity Assn., Internat. Soc. Artists, Art Dir.'s Club of San Francisco, Nat. Soc. Pub. Poets, Nat. Geog. Soc. Jewish. Author: Requiem, 1970; contbr. articles to profl. jours. Home: 35-F Venetian Way Miami Beach FL 33139

KAHN, CHARLES BADER, physician; b. Phila., Feb. 3, 1938; s. Leo and Clara (Bader) K.; B.S., Muhlenberg Coll., 1959; M.D., Jefferson Med. Coll., 1963; m. Elaine C. Marghilano, June 28, 1964; children—Samantha, Evan. Rotating intern Atlantic City Hosp., 1963-64; resident in internal medicine U. Miami (Fla.) Med. Sch., 1966-68; fellow in rheumatology U. Pa. Hosp., Phila., 1968-69; practice medicine specializing in internal medicine and rheumatology, Hollywood, Fla., 1969—; chief medicine Hollywood Med. Center, 1976-78, v.p. med. staff, 1976, chief of staff, 1979-80. vol. clinic dir. Arthritis Found. Clinic, Hollywood, 1971-75; chmn. med. adv. com. Broward County unit Arthritis Found., 1977-79; bd. dirs. Broward-Collier Profl. Standards Rev. Orgn., 1979—. Served as capt. USAF, 1964-66. Recipient Nat. Arthritis Found. Vol. of Year award, 1973. Diplomate Am. Bd. Internal Medicine with subsplty. in rheumatology. Fellow A.C.P.; mem. Fla. Arthritis Found. (chmn. med. adv. com., 1977—), Am., Fla. socs. internal medicine, AMA, Am. Rheumatism Assn., Fla., Broward County med. assns., Fla. Soc. Rheumatology (program chmn. 1979-80). Office: 4700 C Sheridan St Hollywood FL 33021

KAHN, ELLIS IRVIN, lawyer; b. Charleston, S.C., Jan. 18, 1936; s. Robert and Estelle (Kaminski) K.; A.B., The Citadel, 1958; J.D., U. S.C., 1961; postgrad. So. Meth. U., 1962-63; m. Janice Weinstein, Aug. 11, 1963; children—Justin, David, Cynthia Anne. Admitted to S.C. bar, 1961, D.C. bar, 1978; law clk. U.S. Dist. Judge Robert W. Hemphill, Columbia, 1964-66; with firm Solomon, Kahn, Roberts & Smith, Charleston, 1966—. Served to capt. USAF, 1961-64. Mem. Am. Bar Assn., S.C. State Bar, Am. (state committeeman 1970-74), S.C. (pres. 1976-77) trial lawyers assns., Phi Delta Phi (chpt. pres. 1960). Democrat. Jewish. Club: B'nai B'rith (pres. 1968-71). Editor The Brigadier, 1957-58. Home: 316 Confederate Circle Charleston SC 29407 Office: 39 Broad St Charleston SC 29402

KAIMAN, MARVIN, steel co. exec.; b. N.Y.C., Oct. 10, 1930; s. Sidney and Fay (Alpert) K.; m. Beverly Ruth Soclof, June 28, 1952; children—David, Jay. Asst. sec.-treas. Pensacola Scrap Processors (Fla.), 1955-57, pres., 1966—; sec.-treas., 1957-64; founder, pres. SFK Steel and Supply Co., Pensacola, 1959—; chief exec. officer Auto-Shred Industries, 1976—. Chmn. Pensacola-Escambia Devel. Commn., 1971-76; chmn. Fla. Regional Energy Adv. Council; bd. dirs. United Way, 1974—, U. W.Fla., 1973—, Sacred Heart Hosp., 1975—; vice chmn. U.S. Dept. Commerce Fla. Export Expansion Council, 1971—. Served with USAF, 1951-54. Named Maritime Man of Year; recipient Pres.'s award Pensacola Arts Council, 1972, Indsl. Leader of Year award Pensacola News Jour. and C. of C., 1978, various leadership awards. Mem. Assn. Steel Distbrs. (nat. v.p., Pres.'s award, 1977), Inst. Scrap Iron and Steel, Pansacola C. of C. (pres.). Club: Rotary. Office: PO Box 17009 Pensacola FL 32522

KAINRAD, ALAN, mfg. co. exec.; b. Ravenna, Ohio, Sept. 16, 1951; s. John and Else (Nussbaumer) K.; student Akron U., 1969-70; B.S., Ohio State U., 1979. Sales rep. Folger's Coffee, Milw., 1973-74; owner A-J Leathercraft, Milw., 1974-75; pres., controller Koleaco, Inc., Garland, Tex., 1975—. Mem. Nat. Fedn. Ind. Businesses, U.S. C. of C., Garland C. of C. Roman Catholic. Club: Rotary. Office: 203 N Kirby St Garland TX 75042

KAISER, GERARD ALAN, surgeon; b. Bklyn., Dec. 9, 1932; s. Harry and Lois (Friedman) K.; A.B., Princeton, 1954; M.D., Columbia, 1958; m. Joyce Ellen Kosh, June 5, 1955; children—Beth, Jordan, Charles. Intern, Presbyn. Hosp., N.Y.C., 1958-59, resident gen. surgery, 1964-65, cardiac surgery, 1967-68 ; practice medicine specializing in thoracic and cardiovascular surgery, N.Y.C., 1968-71, Miami, Fla., 1971—; asst. prof. surgery Mt. Sinai Sch. Medicine, 1968-69; asso. prof. Columbia Coll. Phys. and Surgs., N.Y.C., 1969-71; prof. U. Miami, 1971—, also chief thoracic and cardiovascular surgery Sch. Medicine and Jackson Meml. Hosp. Bd. dirs. Miami Heart Assn. Otto G. Storm investigator Am. Heart Assn., 1970. Served to lt. comdr. USPHS, 1962-64. Diplomate Am. Bd. Surgery, Bd. Thoracic Surgery. Mem. Am. Assn. Thoracic Surgery, Soc. U. Surgeons, Assn. Acad. Surgery, A.C.S., Soc. Thoracic Surgeons, Am. Coll. Cardiology. Office: Sch Medicine U Miami Miami FL 33152

KAISER, ROBERT LEE, engr.; b. Louisville, June 28, 1935; s. Harlan K. and LaVerne (Peterson) K.; student U. Louisville, 1953-54, U. Ky., 1958-61; m. Margaret Siler; children—Robin Lee, Robert Lee. Draftsman, deisgner E.R. Ronald & Assos., Louisville, 1953-54, Thompson-Kissell Co., 1954-56; estimator, engr. George Pridemore & Son, Lexington, Ky., 1956-58; designer, engr., supr. Frankel & Curtis, Lexington, 1958-61; engr. Hugh Dillehay & Assos., 1961-65; owner, engr., operator K-Service, Inc., 1965-74; cons. engr., 1974—; v.p. Webb-Dillehay Design Group, 1977—. Mem. charter commn. merger Lexington-Fayette County govts. Registered profl. engr., Ky. Mem. ASME, Nat., Ky. socs. profl. engrs., Lexington C. of C., Am. Soc. Heating, Ventilating and Air Conditioning Engrs. Episcopalian. Club: Lions (past pres. local club). Home: 236 Osage Circle Lexington KY 40509 Office: PO Box 419 Lexington KY 40585

KAJS, LEONARD RANDALL, social worker; b. Harlingen, Tex., Aug. 21, 1948; s. Laddie A. and Frances B. (Kubacak) K.; B.A. in Psychology, St. Mary's U., San Antonio, 1970; M.Div. and cert. pastoral counseling, Notre Dame Sem., New Orleans, 1974; M.S.W., Our Lady of the Lake U., San Antonio, 1977. Deacon, Catholic Diocese of Brownsville (Tex.), 1975-76; caseworker, therapist Austin-Travis County Mental Health and Mental Retardation, 1977-77; counseling specialist Travis County Correctional Center, Austin, 1977-79; dir. social services, program dir. hospice Holy Cross Hosp., Austin, 1979—; instr. Austin Community Coll. Bd. dirs. Tex. div. Am. Cancer Soc. Mem. Am. Assn. Marriage and Family Therapists, Nat. Assn. Social Workers. Home: 3312 Galesburg Dr Austin TX 78745 Office: 2600 E MLK Austin TX 78702

KALASINSKY, VICTOR FRANK, educator; b. Columbus, Ohio, Dec. 30, 1949; s. Frank and Waleria K.; B.S., Mass. Inst. Tech., 1972; Ph.D., U. S.C., 1975; m. Kathryn Elaine Schade, June 15, 1974. vis. asst. prof. dept. chemistry U. S.C., Columbia, 1975-76; asst. prof. dept. chemistry Furman U., 1976-77; asst. prof. dept. chemistry Miss. State U., 1977-80, asso. prof., 1980—. Mem. Am. Chem. Soc., Am. Phys. Soc., Soc. for Applied Spectroscopy, Coblentz Soc., Miss. Acad. Scis., Sigma Xi, Phi Lambda Upsilon. Mem. editorial bd. Jour. Raman Spectroscopy; contbr. sci. articles to profl. jours. Home: 505 Chestnut Dr Starkville MS 39759 Office: Dept Chemistry Miss State U Mississippi State MS 39762

KALBFLEISCH, JOHN MCDOWELL, physician; b. Lawton, Okla., Nov. 15, 1930; s. George B. and Etta Lillian (McDowell) K.; Asso. Sci., Cameron A&M Coll., 1950; B.S., U. Okla., 1952, M.D., 1957; m. Jolie Harper, Dec. 29, 1961. Intern, U. Okla. Med. Center, 1957-58, fellow, 1961-62, NIH trainee in cardiovascular disease, 1964-65; resident VA Hosp. and U. Okla. Hosp., Oklahoma City, 1958-61; chief resident U. W.Va. Med. Center, Morgantown, 1960-61; practice medicine specializing in cardiology, Tulsa, 1969—; instr. medicine U. Okla. Med. Center, 1964-66, asst. prof. medicine, 1966-69, clin. asst. prof. medicine Tulsa br., 1969-72, clin. asso. prof., 1972-78, clin. prof., 1978—; dir. cardiovascular services St. Francis Hosp., 1975—; mem. City of Tulsa Physician's Adv. Bd., 1979—. Served with USPHS, 1962-64. Diplomate Am. Bd. Internal Medicine. Fellow A.C.P., Am. Coll. Cardiology (gov. Okla. 1978-80), Assn. Am. Med. Colleagues, Council on Clin. Cardiology, Am. Heart Assn.; mem. Okla. Heart Assn. (v.p. 1975-76), Okla. Cardiac Soc. (pres. 1976), Tulsa County Heart Assn. (dir. 1975-79, pres. 1974), Am. Fedn. Clin. Research, Am. Inst. Nutrition, Tulsa County Med. Soc., AMA, AAAS, Tulsa Internists Soc. Republican. Presbyterian. Contbr. articles on cardiology to med. jours. Office: 6565 S Yale St Suite 310 Tulsa OK 74177

KALDERON, ALBERT ELI, pathologist; b. Istanbul, Turkey, July 27, 1933; came to U.S., 1961, naturalized, 1969; certificate of maturity (baccalaureate) in scis. Coll. St. Michel, Istanbul, 1952, Istanbul U. Faculty of Scis., 1953; M.D., Istanbul U. of Medicine, 1961; m. Janet Louise Seuferer, Apr. 2, 1963; children—Mark, Steven. Intern, Mercy Hosp., Des Moines, Iowa, 1961-62; resident in pathology, instr. Albert Einstein Coll. Medicine and Bronx Municipal Hosp. Center, N.Y.C., 1962-66; research fellow dept. anatomy Sch. Medicine, McGill U., Montreal, 1966-67; asst. pathologist R.I. Hosp.-Brown U., Providence, 1967-70; instr. Tufts Med. Sch., Boston, 1968-71; assoc. pathologist Roger Williams Gen. Hosp.-Brown U., Providence, 1970-71; asst. prof. medical scis., sect. pathology, div. biol. and med. scis. Brown U., Providence, 1971-75; prof. pathology U. Ark. for Med. Scis., 1975—; dir. anatomical pathology Univ. Hosp., Little Rock, 1975; prof. Grad. Sch., U. Ark. for Med. Schs., 1976—; cons. VA Hosp., Little Rock; pres. R.I. Soc. Pathologists, 1971-72. Recipient Golden Apple award U. Ark., 1978; Brown Hazen Fund grantee, 1971-73; R.I. Cancer Soc. grantee, 1969-70; NIH grantee, 1974-77. Diplomate Am. Bd. Pathology. Fellow Am. Coll. Pathology, Am. Soc. Clin. Pathologists; mem. AAAS, Am. Thyroid Assn., Internat. Acad. Pathology, Am. Assn. Pathologists, Arthur Purdy Stout Soc. of Surg. Pathologists, N.Y. Acad. Scis., Sigma Xi. Contbr. articles to profl. jours. Office: Dept Pathology U Ark for Med Scis 4301 W Markham St Little Rock AR 72201

KALEKO, GILBERT S., mfg. co. exec.; b. Newark, Jan. 13, 1931; s. Charles and Edith Kaleko; B.B.A., CCNY, 1952; postgrad. Seton Hall U., 1958-61; m. Carol Bernstein, June 22, 1956; children—Jed Martin, Tom Laurence, Jill Crystal. Diamond cutter Bawscher & Kaleko, N.Y.C., 1954-56; prodn. control supr. Maidenform Brassiere Co., Bayonne, N.J., 1956-61; prodn. control mgr. Perfect Brassiere Co., Jersey City, N.J., 1961-66; prodn. planning, inventory control mgr. Plus Mark, Inc., Greenville, Tenn., 1966—. Mem. Greenville Little Theatre; Woodbridge Circle Players; New Shrewsbury Fair Com. Served with U.S. Army, 1952-54. Home: 1251 Tanglewood Dr Greenville TN 37743 Office: Bohannon Ave Greenville TN 37743

KALIN, ROBERT, mathematician, educator; b. Everett, Mass., Dec. 11, 1921; s. Benjamin and Celia (Kraff) K.; student Northeastern U., 1940-43; B.S., U. Chgo., 1947; M.A., Harvard U., 1948; Ph.D., Fla. State U., 1961; m. Madelyn Pildish, Aug. 17, 1962; children—Susan Leslie, John Benjamin, Sandra Kim, Richard Dean. Tchr. mathematics Holten High Sch., Danvers, Mass., 1948-49, Beaumont High Sch. and Hadley Tech. Schs., St. Louis, 1949-52; ednl. statistician Naval Air Tech. Command, Norman, Okla., 1952-53; test specialist, asso. in research Ednl. Testing Service, Princeton, N.J., 1952-55; exec. asst. Commn. on Math., Coll. Entrance Examination Bd., 1955-56; instr. dept. math. edn. Fla. State U., Tallahassee, 1956-61, asst. prof., 1961-63, asso. prof., 1963-65, prof., 1965—, asso. dept. head, 1968-73, program leader, 1975-78. Served with U.S. Army, 1943-46. Mem. Nat. (chmn. external affairs com. 1972-73), Fla. councils tchrs. mathematics, Math. Assn. Am., Pi Mu Epsilon. Club: Capital Tiger Bay. Author: (with others) Elementary Mathematics: Patterns and Structure, 11 vols., 1966; (with G. Green) Modern Mathematics for the Elementary School Teacher, 1968; (with E.D. Nichols) Analytic Geometry, 1973; (with others) Holt School Mathematics, 9 vols., 1974, rev. edit., 1978. Home: 1120 Cherokee Dr Tallahassee FL 32301 Office: Coll Edn Fla State U Tallahassee FL 32306

KALINA, JOHN FRANK, service co. exec.; b. Cleve., Feb. 10, 1922; s. John Joseph and Agnes (Polusny) K.; student Case Inst. Tech., 1940-41; B.S., U.S. Naval Acad., 1944; M.S., M.I.T., 1950; m. Irene Smith, Jan. 5, 1946; children—John A., Richard B., Gail C., Thomas D., James E. Commd. ensign, U.S. Navy, 1944, advanced through grades to capt., 1965, ret., 1969; v.p. Stanwick Corp., Arlington, Va., 1970-78; exec. v.p., dir. Stanwick Internat., Inc., Arlington, 1972-78, Stanwick Corp., Arlington, 1978—; pres., dir. Metier Internat., Inc., Arlington, 1974—; dir. Bekaert Stanwick, Inc., Belgium. Decorated Legion of Merit. Mem. Soc. Naval Architects and Marine Engrs., Am. Soc. Naval Engrs., Sigma Xi. Roman Catholic. Club: Toastmasters. Author: System Analysis Case Problems, 1961. Home: 9714 St Andrews Dr Fairfax VA 22030 Office: 1401 Wilson Blvd Arlington VA 22209

KALKOFEN, ULRICH PAUL, parasitologist; b. Bingen am Rhein, Ger., May 17, 1934; immigrated to U.S., 1953, naturalized, 1954; B.A. in Zoology, U. Maine, Orono, 1963, M.S. in Zoology and Parasitology (Danforth scholar 1963-65), 1965; Ph.D. in Parasitology (NIH fellow 1965-69), Tulane U., 1969. Teaching asst. U. Maine, 1963-65; with Tulane U. Sch. Public Health and Tropical Medicine, 1965-69, NIH postdoctoral fellow, 1969-70; research asso. Coll. Vet. Medicine, U. Ga., Athens, 1970-79; consumer product research coordinator research labs. A.H. Robins Co., Richmond, Va., 1979—; investigator in field. Served with USAF, 1958. Mem. AAAS, Am. Assn. Vet. Parasitologists, Am. Heartworm Soc., Am. Soc. Parasitologists, Am. Soc. Tropical Medicine and Hygiene, Animal Disease Research Workers in So. States, Conf. Research Workers in Animal Disease, German Soc. Parasitology, Royal Soc. Tropical Medicine and Hygiene, Southeastern Soc. Parasitologists, Southwestern Assn. Parasitologists, Sigma Xi. Sigmu Mu Sigma. Author papers in field. Address: A H Robins Co 1211 Sherwood Ave Richmond VA 23220

KALLER, BRUCE EDWIN, mfr.; b. Milw., May 29, 1937; s. Charles and Dorothy (Schwartz) K.; B.S. in Accounting, U. Ariz., 1962; M.B.A. in Orgn. Analysis, Pepperdine U., 1969; m. Delores V. Smith, Jan. 2. 1978. Program controller Signal Cos. (Garrett), Torrence, Calif., 1964-66; supr. mgmt. services Northrop Corp., Los Angeles, 1966-71; dir. corp. internal audit Rockwell Internat., Dallas, 1971—; cons., lectr., speaker. Served with USNR, 1955-58. Certified internal auditor. Mem. Am. Mgmt. Assn., Inst. Internal Auditors. Home: 8225 Southwestern Dallas TX 75206 Office: 1200 N Alma Rd Richardson TX 75080

KALLESTAD, JAMES STUART, lab. exec.; b. Mpls., Jan. 21, 1941; s. Hursel O. and Helen (Dela) K.; A.A. in Psychology, U. Minn., 1965, Asso. Liberal Arts in Chemistry, 1967, certificate, 1971; certificate Advanced Mgmt. Research, Inc., 1969, 72, 73, Am. Mgmt. Assn., 1970. With Kallestad Labs., Inc., Mpls., 1968—, ops. controller, 1968-69, treas., 1969-70, mktg. mgr., 1970-72, dir. mktg., 1972-73, v.p. mktg., 1973-74, tech. salesman, 1975—; pres. Kallestad Properties, Inc., Miami, Kallestad Charters, Inc., Miami. Served with USMC, 1959-63. Mem. Am. Mktg. Assn., AAAS, Am. Mgmt. Assn., Nat. Contract Mgmt. Assn. Home: 6619 SW 116th Pl Miami FL 33173 Office: 1000 Lake Hazeltine Dr Chaska MN 55318

KALMANSON, NEIL BARRY, educator; b. Bklyn., Aug. 3, 1941; s. Charles I. and Grace (Katz) K.; B.F.A. with honors, Pratt Inst., 1964; M.F.A., U. Fla., 1971; m. Mary Fanchyon Ashworth, July 4, 1969; 1 dau., Leah Ellen. Tchr. art Patchogue (N.Y.) High Sch., 1967-68; lamp decorator Peerless Art Co., Bklyn., 1968-69; tchr. art Lake Shore Jr. High Sch., Belle Glade, Fla., 1971-73; asst. prof. art Emanuel County Jr. Coll., Swainsboro, Ga., 1972—; exhibited in one-man shows at Emanuel County Jr. Coll., Lauren's County Library, Dublin, Ga., 1979, U. Benito Juarez, Oaca, Mex., 1967. Chmn. arts and crafts Six County Fiesta Fair, Swainsboro, 1974-78; tchr. decoupage classes Emanuel County Nursing Home, 1974; tchr. mural classes Emanuel County Hosp., 1974; tchr. painting classes Swainsboro Nursing Home, 1978. Recipient 1st prize Decatur Art Guild, 1980; named Outstanding Young Man in Am., Jaycees, 1975. Jewish. Home: Route 2 Box 812 Old Nunez Rd Swainsboro GA 30401 Office: Thigpen Dr Swainsboro GA 30401

KALMBACH, MIRIAM KIESCHNICK, nursing adminstr.; b. Walburg, Tex., Mar. 4, 1932; d. Oscar Henry and Lena Doering Kieschnick; A.A., Temple Jr. Coll., 1952; diploma nursing Scott and White Hosp., Temple, Tex., 1952; student U. Tex., Austin, 1979—; m. Ardell Kalmbach, Sept. 28, 1952; children—Brock Robert, Susan Jan, Kari Kay. Public health nurse Williamson County Health Dept., Georgetown, Tex., 1954-55; head nurse obstetrics dept. Scott & White Hosp., Temple, Tex., 1957-58; staff nurse, dir. nursing, dir. vocational nurse sch., nurse cons. Georgetown (Tex.) Hosp., 1958-79, nursing service adminstr., 1979—; nursing cons. Wesleyan Homes, Inc.,

Georgetown, 1975; tchr. Georgetown Ind. Sch. Dist., 1975. Active Am. Cancer Soc. Mem. Nat. League Nursing, Am. Nurses Assn., Am. Soc. Nursing Service Adminstrs., Women's Polit. Caucus, Tex. League Nursing, Tex. Nurses Assn., Tex. Hosp. Assn., Tex. Soc. Nursing Service Adminstrs. Lutheran. Home: Route 2 Box 48A Georgetown TX 78626 Office: 2000 Scenic Dr Georgetown TX 78626

KALSON, EMILIA-MILA RADOMSKA, indsl. engr.; b. Kielce, Poland, June 30, 1943; came to U.S., 1961, naturalized, 1967; d. Wincenty J. and Maria Anna (Kempa) Radomski; B.S. in Arch., U. Warsaw, 1961; B.S. in Indsl. Engring., Fla. Internat. U., Miami, 1977; children—Maria, Michael, Norman. Indsl. engr. Cordis Corp., Miami, 1977-78; indsl. engr., dept. head Amphenol N. Am. div. Bunker Ramo Corp., Hollywood, Fla., 1979—. Registered profl. engr., Fla. Mem. Nat. Soc. Profl. Engrs., Am. Mgmt. Assn., Am. Inst. Indsl. Engrs. (sec. Miami chpt. 1968-69), Methods-Time Measurements Assn. Democrat. Roman Catholic. Home: 1195 NW 143d St North Miami FL 33168 Office: 6401 NW Sheridan St Hollywood FL 33024

KALTER, ZANE GARY, physician; b. Bklyn., July 21, 1945; s. Hyman Aaron and Janet (Blumenfeld) K.; B.A. magna cum laude, Harpur Coll., SUNY, Binghamton, 1966; M.D., N.Y. U., 1970; m. Linda Barbara Fishkin, July 27, 1969; children—Jeremy Lawrence, William Jacob, Sharon Renee. Intern, N.Y. U.-Bellevue Hosp., 1970-71, resident in pediatrics, 1971-72, 74-75, fellow in pediatric infectious disease, 1975-76; practice medicine, specializing in pediatrics, Orlando, Fla., 1976—. Served with M.C., U.S. Army, 1972-74. Mem. Am. Acad. Pediatrics, Fla. Med. Assn., Fla. Pediatric Soc., Central Fla. Pediatric Soc., Orange County Med. Soc. Jewish. Office: 22 W Lake Beauty Dr Orlando FL 32806

KAMAN, MARK JOSEPH, planning exec.; b. Memphis, Apr. 15, 1947; s. Julian Joseph and Katherine (McCullough) K.; B.B.A., Memphis State U., 1969, M.A., 1970; cert. in advanced mgmt. U. San Diego, 1978; m. Katherine Jane Pomeroy, Aug. 12, 1972; children—Brian, Paul, Emily. Market research analyst Nat. Cotton Council of Am., Memphis, 1971-72; chmn. div. bus. and commerce Shelby State Community Coll., Memphis, 1972-75; corp. economist Holiday Inns, Inc., Memphis, 1975-78, economist, 1978-79, dir. strategic planning, 1979—. Mem. Nat. Planning Execs. Inst., Nat. Assn. Bus. Economists. Presbyterian. Home: 8636 Pepper Bush Ln Germantown TN 38138 Office: 3796 Lamar Ave Memphis TN 38118

KAMAS, LEWIS MELVIN, state legislator; b. Knowles, Okla., Oct. 24, 1921; s. Frank Munsor and Mable Frances (Shalloup) K.; student Northwestern Okla. State, Okla. State U.; m. Mary Darlien Cohlima, Oct. 23, 1944; children—Leslie Allan, Carol Jeanne Kamas Rooney. Engaged in Ranching, 1946—; mem. Okla. Ho. of Reps., 1966—, sec. Republican caucus, 1969-70, minority whip, 1971-74, asst. minority leader, 1974-76. Served with USAAF, 1942-45; prisoner of war. Mem. Am. Legion, VFW. Clubs: Masons, Shriners, Elks. Home: Box 175 Freedom OK 73842 Office: State Capitol Bldg Oklahoma City OK 73105

KAMAT-MHAMAI, MANOHAR PANDURANG, engr., educator; b. Panjim, India, Feb. 20, 1940; came to U.S., 1966, naturalized, 1972; s. Pandurang K. Kamat-Mhamai and Laximbai P. Pai-Kuchelkar; B.C.E., U. Poona, India, 1961; M.S., Ga. Inst. Tech., 1969, Ph.D. in Engring. Mechanics, 1972; m. Evelyne Marianne Chaney, Apr. 8, 1967; children—Subhash Manohar, Nikhil Manohar. Aircraft structures engr. Lockheed-Ga. Co., Marietta, 1966-68, 69-71; asso. prof. dept. engring. sci. and mechanics Va. Poly. Inst. and State U., Blacksburg, 1972—. Mem. AIAA, Am. Soc. Engring. Edn., Sigma Xi. Contbr. articles on engring. mechanics to profl. jours.

KAMM, ROBERT B., educator, former univ. pres.; b. W. Union, Iowa, Jan. 22, 1919; s. Balthasar and Amelia (Etter) K.; B.A., U. No. Iowa, 1940; M.A., U. Minn., 1946, Ph.D., 1948; m. Maxine Moen, July 10, 1943; children—Susan, Steven. Tchr., Belle Plaine (Iowa) High Sch., 1940-42; research asst., counselor Gen. Coll., U. Minn., 1946-48; dean students Drake U., 1948-55; dean student personnel services, 1956-58; dean Coll. Arts and Scis., Okla. State U., 1958-65, v.p. acad. affairs, 1965-66, pres., 1966-77; dir. Helmerich & Payne, 1976—; mem. commn. coll. student Am. Council Edn., 1957-60; mem. commn. acad. affairs, 1976—; chmn. div. arts and scis. Assn. State Univs. and Land-Grant Colls., 1963-64, co-chmn home econs. commn., 1968-70, chmn. council of pres.'s 1974-75; chmn. Mid-Am. State Univs. Assn., 1968-69, mem. council on post secondary accreditation, 1977-78; mem. adv. panel USAF ROTC, 1967-69, Army ROTC, 1975-78; mem. nat. vocat. rehab. and edn. adv. com. VA, 1970-72; mem. Pres. Nixon's Commn. Observance 25th Anniversary UN, 1970-71; mem. So. regional adv. bd. Inst. Internat. Edn., 1974—, mem. nat. adv. bd., 1976-78; U.S. mem. exec. bd. UNESCO, 1976-77. Pres. Bi-State Mental Health Assn., 1967-69; v.p. Will Rogers council Boy Scouts Am., 1965-66, pres., 1977-80; chmn. Okla. com. Nat. Library Week, 1971; bd. visitors Air U., 1968-70; v.p. Frontiers Sci. Found. Okla., Inc., 1966-69; chmn. bd. dirs. Wesley Found., 1962-64; bd. dirs. Okla. Heritage Assn., 1970-77; chmn. bd. trustees World Neighbors, 1977-79; mem. Okla. State Fair Bd., 1974—, chmn. master plan commn., 1976-77. Civilian radio instr. USAAF, 1942-44, coordinator on staff, 1944; naval aviation radar technician, USNR, 1944-46. Recipient Air Force ROTC Outstanding Service award, 1970; Alumni Achievement award U. No. Iowa, 1970; Outstanding Achievement award U. Minn., 1971; Disting. Service award Okla. State U., 1977; named to Okla. Hall Fame, 1972; named Oklahoman of Year, 1976, Okla. Broadcasters Assn., 1977. Fellow Am. Psychol. Assn.; mem. Am. Coll. Personnel Assn. (exec. council 1954-56, pres. 1957-58, mem. past pres. adv. council 1977—), Am. Personnel and Guidance Assn., Assn Higher Edn., (com. on undergrad. edn. 1961-64), Nat. Vocat. Guidance Assn., NEA (div. higher edn.), Okla. Edn. Assn. (pres. Okla. State U. chpt. 1962-63), Assn. Gen. and Liberal Studies, C. of C. (dir., v.p. 1965, 66), Kappa Kappa Psi, Omicron Delta Kappa, (mem.-at-large gen. council 1970-77), Phi Delta Kappa, Psi Chi, Kappa Delta Pi, Theta Alpha Phi, Kappa Mu Epsilon, Alpha Phi Omega, Phi Mu Alpha Sinfonia (Orpheus award 1977), Phi Kappa Phi, (distinguished mem. 1977), Blue Key. Methodist. Rotarian (pres. 1962-63, Paul Harris fellow 1977). Author: It Helps to Laugh, 1980; contbr. articles on student personnel work and higher edn. profl. jours. Home: 1103 Springdale Dr Stillwater OK 74074

KAMMAN, WILLIAM, historian; b. Geneva, Ind., Mar. 23, 1930; s. Harry August and Ruth Lois (Shoemaker) K.; A.B., Ind. U., 1952, Ph.D., 1962; M.A. (H. Bulkley scholar), Yale U., 1958; m. Nancy Ellen Prichard, Apr. 19, 1957; children—Frederick William, Elizabeth Ellen, David Paul. Tchr. pub. schs., Bloomington, Ind., 1955-57, 58-59; asst. prof. history North Tex. State U., 1962-66, asso. prof., 1966-69, prof., 1969—, chmn. dept. history, 1977—. Mem. Denton (Tex.) Planning and Zoning Commn., 1976-79. Served with U.S. Army, 1952-54. Mem. Am. Hist. Assn., Orgn. Am. Historians, Soc. Historians Am. Fgn. Relations, Phi Alpha Theta. Methodist. Club: Kiwanis. Author: A Search for Stability: United States Diplomacy Toward Nicaragua, 1925-1933, 1968; contbg. author: Makers of American Diplomacy, 1974, Ency. American Foreign Policy, 1978. Home: 2225 Scripture St Denton TX 76201 Office: History Dept North Tex State U Denton TX 76203

KAMPSCHAEFER, GEORGE E(DWARD), JR., metallurgist; b. Chgo., June 2, 1929; s. George E. and Marion (Horne) K.; B.S. in Metall. Engring., Purdue U., 1951; m. Peggy Molloy, Oct. 25, 1952; children—George E., III, Scott J. With ARMCO, Houston, 1956—, product devel. engr., 1963-65, mgr. tech. services div. Western Steel, 1965—; mem. Marine Transp. Research Bd., 1970-76. Served with USN, 1952-56; Korea. Mem. Am. Soc. Metals (dir. Tex. chpt. 1971-72), Am. Welding Soc. (chmn. Houston chpt. 1975-76), Houston Engring. and Sci. Soc., Soc. Naval and Marine Engrs. Roman Catholic. Contbr. articles on high strength steels and welding to profl. jours.; patentee in field; co-inventor high strength alloy steels. Office: 1455 W Loop S Houston TX 77027

KANDA, JANICE HUMPHREY, interpreter for deaf; b. Amarillo, Tex., Apr. 3, 1947; d. C.J. and Ophelia (Hatton) Humphrey; Asso. in Sci., Dallas Bapt. Coll., 1970; B.A., W.Tex. State U., 1971; m. Ronald Alan Ricks, Dec. 23, 1966 (div. June 1977); children—Kimberly, Kristina; m. 2d, Masato Kanda, Nov. 18, 1978. Staff 1st Bapt. Ch., Amarillo, 1971-79, dir. spl. ministries, 1970-79; faculty Amarillo Coll. Sch. Continuing Edn., 1975-79; lead interpreter Tex. State Tech. Inst., Waco, 1979—; interpreter for the deaf. Mem. Tex. Soc. Interpreters for the Deaf, Registry of Interpreters of the Deaf, Profl. Rehab. Workers with Adult Deaf, Nat. Assn. of the Deaf, Internat. Assn. Parents of the Deaf. Baptist. Co-author: Miss Lilian, 1974. Home: Route 1 Box 139-B China Spring TX 76633 Office: Tex State Tech Inst Waco TX 76705

KANDIL, OSAMA ABD EL MOHSIN, educator; b. Cairo, Egypt, Oct. 25, 1944; came to U.S., 1971, naturalized, 1977; s. Abd El Mohsin and Attiat El-Sayed (El-Shazli) K.; B.S. in Mech. Engring., Cairo U., 1966; M.S. in Mech. Engring., Villanova U., 1972; Ph.D. in Engring. Mechanics, Va. Poly. Inst., 1974; m. Rawia Ahmed Fouad, Oct. 20, 1968; children—Dalya O., Tarek O. Instr. mech. engring. dept. Cairo U., 1966-70; grad. teaching asst. mech. engring. dept. Villanova (Pa.) U., 1971-72; grad. research asst. engring. sci. and mechanics dept. Va. Poly. Inst., Blacksburg, 1972-74, asst. prof. engring. sci. and mechanics dept., 1975-78; asso. prof. mech. engring. and mechanics dept. Old Dominion U., Norfolk, Va., 1978—. NASA grantee, 1975-80, U.S. Army Research Office grantee, 1975-78, NASA-Am. Soc. Engring. Edn. fellow, 1978-79. Mem. AIAA, AAUP, Am. Acad. Mechanics, Am. Soc. Engring. Edn., Soc. Engring. Scis., Va. Acad. Scis., Sigma Xi, Phi Kappa Phi. Moslem. Contbr. articles to profl. jours. Home: 7212 Midfield St Norfolk VA 23505 Office: Mech Engring and Mechanics Dept Old Dominion U Norfolk VA 23508

KANE, HOWARD L., chemist; b. Pitts., Dec. 11, 1911; s. Benjamin Hertz and Rose (Julius) K.; B.S., U. Pitts., 1932, Ph.D., 1936; m. Belle Friedman, Aug. 20, 1932; children—Benita Kane Jaro, Harriet Kane Lihs. Chief research chemist Nat. Starch Products, N.Y.C., 1936-46; v.p. Polymer Industries, Inc., Stamford, Conn., 1946-64; chmn. div. math. and sci. Edison Community Coll., Ft. Myers, Fla., 1964-76, instr., 1976—; instr. chemistry U. Conn., 1954-58. Dir. S.W. Fla. Opera Assn., 1972. Fellow AAAS; mem. Am. Chem. Soc., Fla. Assn. Community Colls., Sigma Xi, Pi Tau Phi, Phi Delta Kappa (Heritage award 1979). Club: Rotary (pres. Stamford 1964). Patentee adhesive compositions of matter. Home: 1495 Whiskey Creek Dr Fort Myers FL 33907

KANE, JEAN DUVAL, museum dir.; b. Oklahoma City, Apr. 29, 1933; s. Bernard Evan and Ruth (Wade) K.; B.S., U. Fla., 1957; m. Judith Anne Flatter, Oct. 5, 1957; children—Elisha Kent, Aletris Anne. Asst. preparator Fla. State Mus., 1958-61; sci., tech. cons. Ill. State Mus., 1961-63; dir. Mus. of Arts and Scis., Dayton, Fla., 1963-64; curator exhibits N.C. State Mus., 1964-67; asst. dir. Valentine Mus., Richmond, Va., 1967-72, dir., 1975—; dir. Tenn. State Mus., 1972-75; cons. in field. Mem. Southeastern Mus. Assn. (past pres.), Am. Assn. Museums (mem. council), Am. Assn. State and Local History, Nat. Wildlife Fedn., Audubon Soc., Fla. Audubon Soc. Republican. Mormon. Club: Rotary. Home: 3013 Brook Rd Richmond VA 23220 Office: 1015 E Clay St Richmond VA 23219

KANE, JERRY, meat co. exec.; b. Prague, Czechoslovakia, July 1, 1947; came to U.S., 1949, naturalized, 1954; s. Sam and Aranka K.; B.B.A. with honors, U. Tex., Austin, 1969; m. Glenda Lorraine Rubin, Aug. 20, 1967; children—David, Jeffrey. With Sam Kane Cos., Corpus Christi, Tex., 1969—, mgr. Sam Kane Beef Processors, Inc., 1973—, v.p., 1974—. Mem. Nueces County Democratic Com., 1974-78; mem. Tex. Natural Resources Commn., 1978—; mem. exec. bd. Combined Jewish Appeal, 1976-79, co-chmn. campaign, 1979; pres. Bnai Israel Synagogue, 1979—. Mem. Nat. Meat Assn. (dir. 1979—), Southwestern Meat Packers Assn. (dir. 1976-79), Nat. Ind. Meat Packers Assn. Clubs: B'nai B'rith, Leadership Corpus Christi Alumni, Corpus Christi Town (sec. 1976-79). Home: 1017 Sudan St Corpus Christi TX 78412 Office: 9001 Leopard St Corpus Christi TX 78409

KANE, JOHN EWING, economist, accountant; b. Quitman, Ark., Apr. 2, 1914; s. Robert Lee and Beulah (Jenkins) K.; B.S., U. Ark., 1936, M.S., 1939; postgrad. U. Minn., 1940; Ph.D., Am. U., 1950; m. Katherine Edna Miller, Sept. 10, 1939; children—Carolyn, Phyllis Anne. Accountant, Lion Oil Co., El Dorado, Ark., 1937-39; instr. U. Ark., Fayetteville, 1939-41, asst. prof., asso. prof., prof., 1946—, asso. dir. Bur. Bus. and Econ. Research, 1949-50, chmn. dept. gen. bus., 1950-55, chmn. dept. econs., 1966—, chmn. athletic council, 1966-73, acting v.p. finance, 1967-68; economist U.S. Dept. Commerce, 1942-43; exec. v.p. McIlroy Bank, Fayetteville, 1956-58, bus. and econ. cons., dir. Bd. dirs., faculty Southwestern Grad. Sch. Banking, Dallas; faculty Sch. Banking of South, Baton Rouge, faculty Nat. Assemblies for Bank Dirs. Sec.-treas. N.W. Ark. Regional Airport Authority. Served to lt. comdr. Supply Corps. USNR, 1943-46. Mem. Southwestern Social Sci. Assn. (past pres.), Am. Inst. C.P.A.'s, Ark. Soc. C.P.A.'s, Am. Econ. Assn., Am. Finance Assn., Am. Accounting Assn., So., Midwest econ. assns., Fayetteville C. of C. (past treas.), Alpha Kappa Psi. Methodist (bd. dirs.). Contbr. to Financial Accounting Theory, 1965, 73. Home: 1245 Columbus Blvd Fayetteville AR 72701

KANE, JOHN KENT, II, environ. cons.; b. Bryn Mawr, Pa., May 11, 1934; s. Frank Paul and Levina Sevier (Hammond) K.; A.B., Washington and Lee U., 1956; postgrad. Va. Poly Inst., 1959-61; m. Nancy Claire Baumes, Sept. 1, 1956; children—John Kent III, Robert Tenney, Evan Paul. Grad. instr. Va. Poly. Inst., 1959-61; Richmond Dist. geologist Va. Dept. Hwys., 1961-67, also partner Fielding & Kane, Cons. Geologists, Richmond, 1963-67; asst. mgr. geology sect. Roy F. Weston, Environ. Scientists and Engrs., West Chester, Pa., 1967-71; asst. mgr. environ. div. A.W. Martin Assos., Inc., King of Prussia, Pa., 1971-75; pres. Russnow-Kane & Assos., Inc., Environ. Cons.'s, Newport News, Va., 1975—; dir. Shamus McGregor Corp. Capt. CAP, 1964—, recipient 2 meritorious services award. Served with USMC, 1956-59. Registered profl. geologist, Calif., Maine, Del., Ga. Mem. Assn. Profl. Geol. Scientists (pres. Va. sect.), Assn. Internationale des Hydrogeologues, Am. Water Resources Assn., Am. Waterworks Assn., Geol. Soc. Am., Nat. Water Well Assn., Va. Water Pollution Control Assn., Marine Corps League (past comdt. Herbert G. Smith Jr. Detachment), Sigma Gamma Epsilon, St. Nicholas Soc. N.Y., St. Andrews Soc. Phila., Swedish Colonial Soc., Mil. Order Loyal Legion, Baronial Order of Magna Charta, Mil. Order of Crusades, Soc. S.R., Co. Mil. Historians, Hampton Roads Power Squadron (comdr. 1979-80). Clubs: Corinthian Yacht (Phila.); Engrs. (Hampton Roads, Va.); Warwick Yacht and Country; Kiwanis (past dist. pres.). Episcopalian. Home: 101 Sleepy Hollow Ln Yorktown VA 23692 Office: 11524 Jefferson Ave Newport News VA 23601

KANE, ROGER COLEMAN, coll. adminstr.; b. Cranford, N.J., June 26, 1934; s. Edward J. and Emma Katherine (Coleman) K.; A.A., Houston Community Coll., 1978; m. Carolyn Ray Peters, Dec. 21, 1959; children—Sandra, James, Larry, Edward Jay, Roger Coleman. Adminstr., Nat. Coll. Dist. Attys., Coll. Law, U. Houston, 1974—. Pres., Killeen-Fort Hood (Tex.) chpt. Parents of Retarded Children, 1965-68; active Boy Scouts Am. Served with U.S. Army, 1952-74. Decorated Bronze Star medal (2). Mem. Ret. Officers Assn., Am. Legion, VFW. Jewish. Home: 12407 Longbrook St Houston TX 77099 Office: Nat Coll Dist Attys Coll Law U Houston Houston TX 77004

KANE, SAM, meat co. exec.; b. Spisske Podhradie, Czechoslovakia, June 23, 1919; s. Leopold and Bertha (Narcisenfeld) Kannengiesser; grad. Rabbinical Coll. Galanta, 1939; m. Aranka Feldbrand, Jan. 15, 1946; children—Jerry, Harold Ira, Esther Barbara. Came to U.S., 1948, naturalized, 1953. Pres. Sam Kane Wholesale Meat, Inc., Corpus Christi, Tex., 1956—, Sam Kane Meat, Inc., Corpus Christi, 1956—, Sam Kane Packing Co., Corpus Christi, 1962—, Kane Enterprises, Inc. (merger Sam Kane Beef Processors Inc.), Corpus Christi, 1956—; dir. Guaranty Nat. Bank, Corpus Christi, Corpus Christi Bank & Trust. Pres., Jewish Welfare Appeal, 1962—; v.p. Combined Jewish Appeal, 1968, chmn. bd., 1962-64; mem. regional bd. Anti-Defamation League; nat. bd. dirs. United Jewish Appeal. Recipient award chmn. bd. edn. B'nai Israel Synagogue, 1965; Israel Service award, 1966. Mem. Assembly. Jewish (pres. synagogue 1964-65). Club: B'nai B'rith (named Outstanding Jewish Citizen 1966). Home: 27 Hewit Dr Corpus Christi TX 78404 Office: 9001 Leopard St Corpus Christi TX 78410

KANE, SETH MYLES, textile co. exec.; b. Providence, Oct. 30, 1948; s. Albert D. and Gloria T. Kane; B.S. in Econs., U. Pa., 1970. Mgmt. trainee N. Am. Mills, Gastonia, N.C., 1970-71, dept. head, 1971-72, sales mgr., 1972-75; pres. The Sero Carpet Co., Charlotte, N.C., 1975-78, Sero Industries, Inc., Serotex, Ltd., Charlotte, 1978—. Club: Mask and Wig (Phila.). Home: 932 Habersham Dr Charlotte NC 28209 Office: 4827 Park Rd Charlotte NC 28209

KANTER, ETTALEA ESTHER, educator; b. Hampton, Va., Mar. 17, 1937; B.S. in Distributive Edn., U. N.C., Greensboro, 1959; M.Ed. in Sch. Adminstrn. and Supervision, Coll. William and Mary, Williamsburg, 1968. Tchr., Newport News (Va.) Pub. Schs., 1959-65, supr. distributive edn., 1965-75, supr. distributive edn. and career edn., 1975—; mem. Va. Dist. Adv. Council SBA. Mem. Am. Vocat. Assn., Va., Nat. assns. distributive edn. tchrs., Delta Kappa Gamma. Home: 4026 Chesapeake Ave Hampton VA 23669 Office: 12465 Warwick Blvd Newport News VA 23606

KANTO, WILLIAM PETER, JR., pediatrician; b. Norton, Va., Sept. 10, 1940; s. William Peter and Lila Mae (Odom) K.; A.B., U. Va., 1962, M.D., 1966; m. Barbara Ann Newell, Aug. 15, 1964; children—Susan Meredith, Ann Katherine, William Peter III. Intern, U. N.C., 1966-67; resident in pediatrics U. Va. Hosp., 1967-69; neonatology fellow U. Mich., 1972-74, instr. pediatrics, 1973-74; asst. prof. pediatrics Med. Coll. Ga., 1974-77; asst. prof. Emory U., Atlanta, 1977-78, asso. prof., 1978—; mem. perinatal morbidity and mortality com. Eugene Talmadge Meml. Hosp., 1975-77. Served with M.C., U.S. Army, 1969-72. Diplomate Am. Bd. Pediatrics. Mem. Ga. Perinatal Assn. (pres. 1977), So. Perinatal Assn., Am. Acad. Pediatrics, So. Perinatal Soc., So. Soc. Pediatric Research, Med. Assn. Ga., AMA. Roman Catholic. Author: Primary Care of the Newborn, 1977. Home: 1449 Ragley Hall Rd Atlanta GA 30319 Office: 69 Butler St SE Atlanta GA 30303

KANTOR, DAVID, librarian; b. Atlanta, Nov. 2, 1915; s. Sam and Celia (Shafran) K.; B.S., U. Fla., 1938; Licentiate in microbiology Universite Libre de Bruxelles, 1939; B.L.S., Drexel U., 1941; m. Lee Finberg, Nov. 26, 1942. Cataloger U. Fla., 1941-42, chem.-pharmacy librarian, 1942-43; tech. librarian U. S. Army Signal Corps, Ft. Monmouth, N.J., 1943-44; librarian Wash. State Reformatory, 1944-46, 47-49; librarian Farragut Coll., 1946-47; librarian Calif. Dept. Corrections, Folsom Prison, 1949-62; dir. ext. Volusia County Pub. Libraries, Daytona Beach, Fla., 1962-63, dir. libraries Volusia County, 1964—; cons. instn. libraries Fla. State Library, State Bur. Blind Services, Fla.; bldg. cons. Fla. pub. libraries. Mem. Calif. (pres. Golden Empire dist. 1958, dir. 1958), Am. (regional membership com. 1955, hosp. and instns. com. 1956), Fla. (chmn. pub. library sect. 1970-71, v.p., pres. 1972-73) library assns. Author: Survey of Public Library Service in Volusia County, 1964; Survey of Libraries and Library Services in the State Institutions of Florida, 1967. Office: Volusia County Public Libraries City Island Daytona Beach FL 32014

KANTOR, NEIL MICHAEL, physician; b. Bklyn., July 4, 1940; s. Emanuel and Esther A. (Altsman) K.; B.A. in Biology and English, N.Y. U., 1961; D.O., Phila. Coll. Osteo. Medicine, 1965; m. Felice Zimmerman, June 20, 1955; children—Robert, Sheryl, Michelle, Adam. Rotating intern Doctors Hosp., Columbus, Ohio, 1965-66; resident in pediatrics Grandview Hosp., Dayton, Ohio, 1966-68; neonatology fellow U. Hosp. of Jacksonville (Fla.), 1975-78; practice osteo. pediatrics, Dayton, 1968-75, Jacksonville, 1975—; mem. staff Grandview Hosp., Dayton, 1968-75, chmn. dept. pediatrics, 1971-75; chmn. dept. pediatrics Jacksonville Gen. Hosp., 1975-78; clin. instr. Wright State Sch. Medicine, Dayton, 1975; mem. staff Barney's Children's Med. Center, Dayton, 1973-75; med. dir. div. spl. infant nurseries Meml. Hosp. Jacksonville, 1978-79; dir. neonatal intensive care Jacksonville Children's Hosp., 1979—; asso. dir. regional neonatal intensive care U. Hosp. of Jacksonville, 1979—; asst. prof. dept. pediatrics U. Fla., Jacksonville, 1978—; mem. profl. adv. bd. Vis. Nurse Assn. Montgomery County (Ohio), 1969-75; mem. med. adv. bd. Tay-Sachs Screening Program, Jacksonville, 1976-77. Bd. dirs. Hillel Acad., Dayton, 1972-73, Speech and Hearing Council Met. Dayton, 1971-75; bd. dirs. United Cerebral Palsy, Dayton, 1972-75; mem. adv. bd. United Cerebral Palsy, Jacksonville, 1980—. Diplomate Am. Bd. Osteo. Pediatrics, Am. Bd. Pediatrics. Named Outstanding Tchr., Grandview Hosp., 1972. Fellow Am. Acad. Pediatrics; mem. Am. Osteo. Assn., Fla. Osteo. Med. Assn., Northeast Fla. Pediatric Assn., So. Perinatal Assn., Fla. Perinatal Soc., Am. Coll. Osteo. Pediatricians. Jewish. Contbr. articles to profl. jours. Home: 3701 Montclair Dr Jacksonville FL 32217 Office: Univ Hosp Jacksonville 655 W 8th St Jacksonville FL 32209

KAPIL, BALVIR LAXMINARAYAN, surgeon; b. India, July 14, 1934; s. Laxminarayan S. and Sushila (Hosali) K.; B.Sc., St. Xavier's Coll., Bombay, India, 1949-53; M.D., Med. Coll. Nagpur (India), 1960; m. Usha Rani Rathore, Mar. 17, 1962; children—Vikram, Raksha, Kanishka, Nidhi. Intern, Youngstown (Ohio) Hosp., 1962-63, resident in surgery, 1963-64; resident in surgery Watts Hosp., Durham, N.C., 1965-66, Richmond (Va.) Meml. Hosp., 1966-68; sr. registrar in cardiothoracic surgery Leeds (Eng.) Gen. Infirmary, 1968-72; med. dir.'s asso. for surg. affairs Richmond Meml. Hosp., 1973-78; practice medicine specializing in gen. and vascular surgery,

Richmond, 1974—; mem. med. evaluation com. S. Central Va. PSRO, 1978—. Diplomate Am. Bd. Surgery. Mem. Med. Soc. Va., Richmond Acad. Medicine, Richmond Gen. Surg. Soc., Richmond Surg. and Gynecol. Soc. Office: 1400 Westwood Ave Suite 103 Richmond VA 23227

KAPILOFF, MARK CARL, clothing co. exec.; b. Belfast, Maine, July 6, 1935; s. Lawrence E. and Ethel (Maisel) K.; B.A., Bowdoin Coll., 1957; m. Lillian Rodgers, Dec. 30, 1958; children—Marsha, Paula, Susan, Richard. Cutting foreman Neobel, Inc., Atlanta, 1957-58; gen. mgr. KYM Co., Jackson, Ga., 1958-73, pres., 1974—. Mem. adv. staff Griffin-Spalding County Vocat.-Tech. Sch. Served with U.S. Army, 1958. Home: 840 Hillcrest Ave Griffin GA 30223 Office: 325 Alabama Blvd Jackson GA 30233

KAPLAN, BRUCE, veterinarian; b. Lexington, Ky., Feb. 26, 1939; s. Bernard and Dorothy (Cohen) K.; student U. Ky., 1957-59; D.V.M., Auburn U., 1963; LL.B., LaSalle Extension U., 1973; m. Sharon Lyn Kupp, July 26, 1964; children—Kevin Bernard, Kathy Lauren. USPHS officer N.J. State Health Dept., Trenton, 1963-65; pvt. practice small animal medicine and surgery with East End Animal Clinic, Louisville, 1965—; clin. investigator Bristol Labs., 1972-74; weekly radio human-animal pub. service announcements Sta. WKLO, 1975-78; mem. Ky. Bd. Health, 1972-74; chmn. Jefferson County Adv. Commn. on Ecol. Relationship between Humans and Animals, 1974-75. Mem. AVMA, Ky. (pub. relations dir.), Jefferson County (pub. relations dir.) veterinary med. assns., Ky. Humane Soc. (dir. veterinary med. and legis. affairs 1973-74), Am. Animal Hosp. Assn. (affiliate), U.S. Animal Health Assn. (practitioner mem. rabies com.), Louisville Zool. Soc. (dir. 1975—). Jewish. Democrat. Club: Masons. Columnist Louisville Courier-Jour., 1975-78; contbr. articles to profl. jours. Home: 9 Ridge Rd Louisville KY 40205 Office: 3812 Bardstown Rd Louisville KY 40218

KAPLAN, DONALD DAVID, meat packing and cattle feeding co. exec.; b. Weehawken, N.J., Dec. 23, 1930; s. Adolph and Celina Kaplan; B.Mus., U. Miami (Fla.), 1952; m. Jane Malkove, Sept. 8, 1957; children—John Steven, David Louis. Pres., chief exec. officer Kaplan Industries Inc., Bartow, Fla., 1952—; dir. Citrus & Chem. Bank of Bartow. Mem. Fla. Cattlemen's Assn., Agri-Bus. Inst., Nat. Ind., Fla. meat packers, Polk County Farm Bur. (dir.). Democrat. Jewish. Clubs: Lakeland Yacht and Country, Lone Palm Golf, Peace River Country. Home: 2724 Easton Terr Lakeland FL 33803 Office: PO Box 427 Bartow FL 33830

KAPLAN, EVELYN GERBER, market research corp. exec.; b. Bklyn., June 3, 1925; d. Paul and Ida (Silverman) Jacobs; student Columbia U., 1943-44; B.A. in Sociology, Adelphi Coll., 1947; m. Benson Kaplan, Dec. 11, 1948; children—Paul Stuart, Ivan. Interviewer, field supr., asst. to v.p. S.W. Research Inc., Dallas, 1963-67; field supr., asst. to v.p., nat. field dir. M/A/R/C, Dallas, 1967-68; founder, pres. Key Research Inc., Houston, 1978—; collector field data polit. polls and govt. agencies. Mem. Mktg. Research Assn., Am. Mktg. Assn. Jewish. Home: 5711 Sugar Hill 119 Houston TX 77027 Office: 3115 W Loop South Suite 32 Houston TX 77057

KAPLAN, MURIEL SHEERR, sculptor; b. Phila., Aug. 15, 1924; d. Maurice J. and Lillian J. (Jamison) Sheerr; B.A., Cornell U., 1946; postgrad. Sarah Lawrence Coll., 1958-60, U. Calif. at Oxford (Eng.), summer 1971, U. Florence (Italy), summer 1973, Art Student's League, N.Y.C., 1975-78, New Sch., 1974-78, m. Murray S. Kaplan, June 3, 1946; children—Janet Belsky, James S., Jerrold, Amy. Exhbns. at Women's Clubs in Westchester, 1954-60, Allied Artists Am., 1958-73, Nat. Assn. Women Artists, 1966-78, Bklyn. Museum, 1968, Sculptors Guild, 1972, Bergen County (N.J.) Mus., 1974; represented in permanent collections, Jerusalem, Israel, Columbia U., Brandeis U., U. Tex.; executed twin 30 foot cor-ten steel sculptures, Tarrytown, N.Y., 1972, 2 large rotating steel sculptures Art Park, Trans-Lux Corp., 1978; art cons., interior designer, 1971—; sec. commn. to establish art mus. in Westchester, 1956; chmn. Westchester Creative Arts Festival, 1956. Bd. dirs. Fedn. Jewish Philanthropies, 1965. Recipient prizes Nat. Assn. Women Artists, 1966, Westchester Women's Club, 1955, 56, Allied Artists Am., 1969. Mem. Nat. Assn. Women Artists, Artists and Engrs. in Tech. Democrat. Address: 339 Garden Rd Palm Beach FL 33480

KAPLUN, ROBERT MARIO, bus. cons.; b. Santiago, Chile, Sept. 30, 1946; came to U.S., 1972; s. Mitchell R. and Ethel K.; M.S. in Elec. Engring., Universidad Tecnica del Estado, Chile, 1972; M.B.A., U. Tex., El Paso, 1974; m. Doris Zeldis, Jan. 22, 1971; children—Jeannette, Edward. Prof. electric circuit analysis U. Tecnica Del Estado, Santiago, 1967-71; pres. RK Electronics Imports-Exports, El Paso, 1973—; instr. bus. stats., mktg., internat. mktg. U. Tex., El Paso, 1974-77; sr. partner Kaplun, Palmore, Roth & Assos., Bus. Cons., El Paso, 1974-77; ins. cons. Nat. Western Life Ins. Co., Austin, Tex., 1976—; researcher in internat. markets Bur. Bus. and Econ. Research, U. Tex., 1974-76. Named Hon. Citizen, El Paso. Mem. AAUP, Assn. M.B.A. Execs., Assn. Borderland Scholars. Jewish. Club: Condor No. 9 (Santiago). Author: Introduction to Electrical Circuit Analysis, 1971.

KAPP, JOHN PAUL, physician; b. Galax, Va., Feb. 22, 1938; s. Paul Homer and Jesse Katherine (Vass) K.; B.S., Duke U., 1966, M.D., 1963, Ph.D., 1967; m. Emily Lureese Evans, June 23, 1961; children—Paul Hardin, Emily Camille. Intern, Med. Coll. Va., Richmond, 1963; resident in surgery Duke U., Durham, N.C., 1964, resident in neurosurgery, 1964-69; attending neurosurgeon Bay Meml. Med. Center, Panama City, Fla., 1972—, Gulf Coast Community Hosp., 1977-80; asso. prof. neurosurgery U. Miss., 1980—; asso. prof. U. Tenn., 1971-72. Served to maj. M.C., AUS, 1969-71. USPHS fellow in neurosurgery, 1965-67. Diplomate Am. Bd. Neurol. Surgery. Mem. Bay County Med. Soc. (pres. 1978), Fla. Area I Found. for Profl. Standards Rev. (dir. 1977-80), AMA, Fla. Med. Assn., Congress Neurol. Surgeons, A.C.S., So. Neurosurg. Soc., Am. Assn. Neurol. Surgeons, Phi Beta Kappa, Alpha Omega Alpha. Democrat. Methodist. Contbr. articles to profl. jours. Home: 109 Whipporwill Rd Brandon MS 39042 Office: U Miss Med Center 2500 N State St Jackson MS 39216

KAPPELMAN, MARK DAVID, surgeon; b. Balt., Apr. 21, 1945; s. Melvin Daniel and Marian Leah K.; B.A., Western Md. Coll., 1965; M.D., U. Md., 1969; m. Susan Jane Kirchem, Nov. 24, 1978; 1 son, Paul Andrew. Intern, Charity Hosp. of New Orleans, 1969-70; resident in gen. surgery Tulane Med. Center, New Orleans, 1970-74, resident in cardiothoracic surgery, 1974-76; practice medicine specializing in thoracic and vascular surgery, New Orleans, 1976—; mem. staffs Jo Ellen Smith Meml. Hosp., F. Edward Hebert Hosp.; mem. staff, asst. clin. prof. surgery Tulane Med. Center. Am. Cancer Soc. fellow, 1974-75; diplomate Am. Bd. Surgery, Am. Bd. Thoracic Surgery, Nat. Bd. Med. Examiners. Fellow A.C.S.; mem. New Orleans Surg. Soc., Alton Ochsner Surg. Soc., La. Surg. Assn., So. Thoracic Assn., Am. Coll. Chest Physicians, Southeastern Surg. Congress. Democrat. Jewish. Office: 4400 General Meyer Ave New Orleans LA 70114

KAPPELMAN, RAYMOND VERNON, mech. engr.; b. Chgo., Dec. 20, 1920; s. Oswald E. and Loretta (Taylor) K.; grad. Wilson Jr. Coll., Chgo., 1939-41; B.S. in Mech. Engring., Ill. Inst. Tech., 1949; B.S. in Elec. Engring., U. Ariz.; m. Lynn A. Bauch, Oct. 27, 1960. Trainee Magnolia Petroleum Co., Dallas, Tex., 1950-52; lead engr. Chance-Vought Co., Dallas, 1952-60; elec. engr. Collins Radio Co., Richardson, Tex., 1960-68, Western Electric Co., Lisle, Ill., 1970-72, Stewart-Warner Co., Chgo., 1973-76; sr. engr. Electrospace Systems Inc, Richardson, Tex., 1976—. Served with USAAF, 1945-46. Registered profl. engr., Tex. Mem. ASME, Phi Kappa Phi, Pi Tau Sigma, Sigma Beta Pi. Democrat. Baptist. Home: 920 Melrose Dr Richardson TX 75080 Office: 1101 E Executive Dr Richardson TX 75081

KARASIEWICZ, WALTER RICHARD, cons. environ. engr.; b. Newark, Dec. 23, 1942; s. Walter John and Sally M. (Starzynski) K.; B.S.C.E., U. Miami, 1965; M.S. in Sanitary Engring. (USPHS fellow), Ga. Tech. Inst., 1966; m. Paula Gwen Steele, Aug. 7, 1976; children by previous marriage—Shannon Elizabeth, Courtney Brooke. Design engr. Poznak & Assoc., Asbury Park, N.J., 1965; project engr. Hensley Schmidt, Atlanta, 1966; sr. pub. health engr. N.J. State Dept. Health, Trenton, 1967-69; project mgr. Black, Crow & Eidsness, Atlanta, 1969-71; process engr. Brown & Root, Houston, 1971-72; v.p. LBC &W, Harwood Beebe Co., Columbia, S.C., 1974-77, dir., 1974-77, office mgr., 1972-77; partner McNair, Gordon, Johnson & Karasiewicz, Columbia, 1977—, v.p., sec., 1977—; dir., 1977—. Served with U.S. Army, 1966-67. Recipient Young Engr. of Yr. award S.C. Soc. Profl. Engrs., 1976; registered profl. engr., S.C., N.C., Va., Ga., Nebr.; licensed wastewater plant operator, S.C., Tex.; certified fallout shelter analyst, Def. Dept.; licensed arbitrator Am. Arbitration Assn. Mem. S.C. Water Pollution Control Assn. (chmn. program com., chmn. pub. relations com., 1976—), ASCE, Nat. Soc. Profl. Engrs., Water Pollution Control Fedn., Am. Water Works Assn., Ga. Water Pollution Control Assn. Roman Catholic. Contbr. designs for textile and mfg. plant, both of which received awards. Home: 2308 Quail Hollow Ln West Columbia SC 29169 Office: PO Box 84 Columbia SC 29202

KARAU, WILLIAM ALFRED AUGUST, oil co. exec.; b. Ridley Park, Pa., Nov. 23, 1934; s. Arno Wilhelm and Clara Suzanne (Mock) K.; B. Chem. Engring., U. Del., 1956; M.B.A., U. Pitts., 1965; m. R. Mazie Gerhart, Oct. 27, 1956; children—Lynn Anne, Lori Jane, Lisa Beth, William Howard, Leslie Diane. Jr. engr. Gulf Oil Co., Phila., 1956-60, engr. computer liasion research and devel., Harmarville, Pa., 1960-66, sr. fin. analyst, Pitts., 1966-68, syr. analyst capital projects, 1968-70, staff analyst long range studies, 1970-71, sr. staff analyst, 1971-72, mgr. corp. devel., Houston, 1972-74; mgr. mktg. Inexco Oil Co., Houston, 1974—, v.p., 1978—; dir. Greenwich Oil Corp., Hutchison Hayes Internat., Inc., 1973-74. Umpire Houston Little League, 1973; pres., trustee Hempfield (Pa.) Civic Assn., 1962-65; mem., incorporator Vol. Ambulance Corps., Irwin, Pa., 1967-69; sec. Hempfield Twp. (Pa.) Planning Commn., 1965-71; councilman Holy Trinity Lutheran Ch., Irwin, 1970-72; fin. sec. Lord of Life Luth. Ch., Houston, 1972-73; dir. building program Hosanna Luth. Ch., Houston, 1976—. Served with U.S. Army, 1957-58. Recipient Annual Award citation Systems Mag., 1964. Mem. Am. Inst. Chem. Engrs., Am. Chem. Soc., N.Am. Soc. Corporate Planning, Nat. Gas Men Houston, Houston Area Ret. Officers Assn. Republican. Contbr. article to chem. jour. Home: 17707 Butte Creek Rd Houston TX 77090 Office: Inexco Oil Co Suite 1900 1100 Milam Bldg Houston TX 77002

KARCH, ROBERT E., diversified co. exec.; b. Bklyn., May 30, 1933; s. Charles H. and Etta R. (Becker) K.; A.B., Syracuse U., 1953, M.B.A., 1957; m. Brenda Schechter, Sept. 7, 1958; children—Barry, Karen, Brian. Pres., prin. stockholder Karch Beauty Supply Co., Inc., Syracuse, N.Y., 1969—, v.p., 1974—; pres. Midstate Credit Corp., 1970-77; v.p. Peril Protectors Ins., 1971-75; v.p., prin. stockholder Masterguard Systems of El Paso, Tex., 1977—; v.p. sales, mktg. Helen Troy Corp., El Paso, 1974-79; partner BKB Properties, 1979—; v.p. Bormex Constrn. Inc., 1980—. Served with U.S. Army, 1953-56. Lic. real estate agt., Tex. Mem. Beauty and Barber Supply Inst., Direct Mktg. Mgmt. Assn. Club: El Paso Aviation Assn. Lic. instrument comml. pilot. Home: 6016 Torrey Pines El Paso TX 79912 Office: 11012 Pebble Hills Blvd El Paso TX 79936 also 2600 Erie Blvd E Syracuse NY 13224

KARGLEDER, CHARLES LEONARD, educator; b. Milbank, S.D., July 19, 1939; s. George Leonard and Ruby Theresa (Gulck) K.; A.B., U. S.D. at Vermillion, 1960; M.A. (NDEA fellow), U. Ala. at Tuscaloosa, 1962, Ph.D., 1968. Instr., Spring Hill Coll., Mobile, Ala., 1963-65, asso. prof. langs., 1967—, chmn. dept., 1971—. Mem. Am. Assn. Tchrs. Spanish and Portuguese, AAUP, Am. Translators Assn., Am. Council Teaching Fgn. Langs., Latin Am. Studies Assn., Southeastern Conf. Latin Am. Studies, South Atlantic Modern Lang. Assn. Roman Catholic. Author: A Selective Bibliography of Costa Rican Literature, 1978; translator: Adios (Jorge Guillen), 1964-65. Home: 9 Provident Ln Mobile AL 36608

KARLIK, CARLTON WILLIAM, indsl. engr.; b. Waco, Tex., Dec. 17, 1947; s. Albin Cyril and Ida Marie (Matustik) K.; B.S. in Indsl. Engring., Tex. A&M U., 1971; m. Mary Frances Janek, June 30, 1973. Tech. sales rep. Union Carbide Corp., Los Angeles, 1971-74; sr. project cost analyst Pullman Kellogg Co., Houston, 1974—. Registered profl. engr., Tex. Mem. Am. Assn. Cost Engrs., Nat. Soc. Profl. Engrs., Tex. Soc. Profl. Engrs. Republican. Roman Catholic. Home: 5602 Bent Bough Houston TX 77088 Office: 1300 Three Greenway Plaza E Houston TX 77046

KARNES, ROY EUGENE, steel fabricating co. exec.; b. Tupelo, Miss., Aug. 23, 1923; s. Charles Delno and Julia Elta (Sours) K.; student U. Ala., Birmingham, 1953-54, Centennary Coll., Shreveport, La., 1950-51; m. Miriam Constance Eley, Mar. 27, 1943; children—Roy Eugene, Charles Randy. Field cost clk. Ingalls Shipbldg. Corp., Pascagoula, Miss., 1943-49; estimator J.B. Beaird, Shreveport, 1949-51; time study engr. Ingalls Iron Works, Birmingham, 1951-55, indsl. engr., 1955-59, gen. supt., 1959-62: plant mgr. Ark. Steel Co., El Dorado, 1962-64, v.p., 1964-69; plant mgr. Internat. Steel Fabricators, Inc., Houston, 1969-71, v.p., 1971-74; pres. Trinity Steel Fabricators, Inc. (Tex.), 1976—, also dir. Served with USAF, 1943-45. Decorated Purple Heart, Air medal (5), D.F.C. Mem. Trinity C. of C. (dir.), Am. Legion, VFW. Republican. Methodist. Clubs: Masons, Shriners. Home: PO Box 447 Trinity TX 75862 Office: 200 Pine Valley Dr Trinity TX 75862

KAROW, ARMAND M(ONFORT), pharmacologist; b. New Orleans, Nov. 11, 1941; s. Armand M. and Eunice Louise (Durham) K.; B.A. in Zoology, Duke U., 1962; Ph.D. in Pharmacology, U. Miss. Med. Center, Jackson, 1968; m. Ramona Evelyn McClelland, Sept. 5, 1964; children—Christopher Armand, Jonathan Carter. Research instr. dept. surgery Med. Coll. Ga., 1968-71, research asst. prof., 1971-77, research asso. prof., 1977—, asst. prof. pharmacology, 1968-70, asso. prof. pharmacology, 1970-75, prof. pharmacology, 1975—, dir. grad. studies, dept. pharmacology, 1973—, dir. frozen sperm program, 1972—; ind. grant application reviewer NIH; cons. in field; founder, operating officer, pres. Xytex Corp., Augusta, Ga., 1975—, also dir.; lectr., chmn. various seminars, workshops; mem. vis. faculty Fla. Blood Bank Assn., 1974; guest lectr. Polish Acad. Scis., Warsaw, 1977, U. Odense (Denmark), 1978, Royal Free Hosp., London, 1978, Tissue Bank, Hradec Kralove, Czechoslavkia, 1977. Mem. adminstrv. bd. Aldersgate Methodist Ch., Augusta, Ga., 1970-74, 75—, mem. sch. bd., 1975-79; gen. chmn. Central Savannah River Sci. Fair, Augusta, 1973-74, bd. dirs., 1973—. Recipient Teaching award Summer Sci. Program, Med. Coll. Ga., 1977; lic. clin. lab. dir., Ga. Fellow AAAS, N.Y. Acad. Sci.; mem. Am. Heart Assn. (Bronze medal 1975, Silver medal 1978), Richmond County Heart Assn. (exec. com. 1974—), Ga. Heart Assn. (dir. 1978—), Am. Chem. Soc., Am. Soc. Clin. Pathology (asso.), Am. Soc. Pharmacology and Exptl. Therapeutics, Soc. Cryobiology (charter, guest referee Cryobiology 1974-76, editorial bd. Cryobiology 1976-79, sec. 1977-80), Transplantation Soc., Sigma Xi (pres. Med. Coll. Ga. chpt. 1972-73, 76-77). Author: Pharmacology of Cytotoxic Drugs, 1974; (with others) Handbook of Objectives in Oncology, 1976; contbr. numerous articles to profl. publs.; editor and contbg. author: (with others) Organ Preservation for Transplantation, 1974; research chems. and pharmacol. agts. which permit cells and organs to survive in frozen state; co-creator pharmacology grad. program at Med. Coll. Ga. Office: Med Coll Ga Dept Pharmacology Augusta GA 30912

KARP, BRIAN THOMAS, assn. exec.; b. Chgo., May 28, 1946; s. Robert Edward and Lorraine Muriel K.; student Carthage Coll., 1965; B.A., U. Ill., 1968; children by former marriage—Shannon, Matthew. Sales div. mgr. Chgo. Suburban Paddock Publs., Arlington Heights, Ill., 1971-72; nat. sales rep. U.S. Suburban Press Inc., Chgo., 1972-74, asso. dir. Midwest sales, 1974-76, dir. So. sales, Atlanta, 1976—. Served as inf. officer U.S. Army, 1968-71. Decorated Army Commendation Medal with oak leaf cluster. Clubs: Atlanta Advt. Club, Atlanta Lawn Tennis Assn., Terminus Internat. Racquet, Pinecrest at Indian Hills. Home: 4067 Audubon Dr Marietta GA 30067 Office: 6520 Powers Ferry Rd Atlanta GA 30339

KARRENBAUER, BEVERLY WOLFORD, educator; b. Marion Center, Pa., Aug. 5, 1938; d. Clarence Frederick and Thelma Pearl (MacArthur) Wolford; B.Ed., Ind. U. of Pa., 1959; M.Ed. (Frick Found. grantee, 1962), U. Pitts., 1963; m. Raymond Joseph Karrenbauer, Aug. 20, 1960; 1 son, Raymond Joseph, III. County resource tchr. Allegheny County, Pitts., 1961-63; dir. edn. Pa. Vision Inst., Pitts., 1963-64; supr. primary units Keystone Oaks Public Schs., Pitts., 1964-69; supr. early childhood edn. and basic skills Dade County Public Schs., Miami, Fla., 1969—; sr. cons. early childhood program Scholastic Mag., Inc. Mem. Gov.'s Commn. on Internat. Year of Child, 1979; chmn. NE Improvement Assn. of Miami. Recipient Service award Assn. Children with Learning Disabilities, 1970. Mem. Assn. Childhood Internat., Internat. Reading Assn., Delta Kappa Gamma. Home: 1040 NE 82d St Miami FL 33138 Office: 1410 NE 2d Ave Miami FL 33132

KARST, CHARLES EDWARD, lawyer; b. New Orleans, Sept. 18, 1931; s. Charles and Ethel Marie (Drouin) K.; B.A., Tulane U., 1952; J.D., Loyola U., 1965; m. Judith Ward Steinman, Dec. 27, 1965; children—Alexander Regard, Alicia Barrows, Jacqueline Ward. Indsl. engr. Boeing Co., New Orleans, 1963-66; admitted to La. bar, 1965; atty. Ward-Steinman & Karst, New Orleans, 1965-67, Alexandria, La., 1966—. Dir. Maderas Conglomeradas S.A. Mayor, City of Alexandria, La., 1969-73; v.p. Cenla Mayor's Council, 1971, pres., 1972. Bd. dirs. Rapides Parish Planning Commn.; co chmn. La. Arthritis Found. Victory Drive, 1977. Served with USAF, 1952-54. Mem. Am. Trial Lawyers Assn., Am., La., Alexandria bar assns., La. Municipal Assn. (v.p. 1972-73), Alexandria C. of C. (dir.), VFW, Am. Legion. Roman Catholic. Lion. Home: 2236 Jackson St Alexandria LA 71301 Office: 1130 9th St Alexandria LA 71301

KASDAN, MORTON LEE, reconstructive plastic surgeon, hand surgeon; b. Louisville, Mar. 21, 1936; s. K.M. and Sarah (Packman) K.; A.B., Bellermine Coll., 1959; M.D., U. Louisville, 1963; m. Ann Schmitt, Apr. 15, 1977. Intern, U. Louisville, 1963-64, resident, 1964-67; resident in plastic surgery Duke U., 1968-71; chief plastic surgery Wright Patterson AFB, Dayton, Ohio, 1971-73; asst. prof. plastic surgery U. Ky. Med. Center, Lexington, 1973—; cons. VA Hosp., Lexington, 1973—; individual practice medicine specializing in reconstructive plastic surgery and surgery of hand, Louisville, 1973—. Bd. overseers Bellermine Coll., Louisville, 1976-80, pres.'s soc., 1976-80. Served to lt. col. USAF, 1971-73. Diplomate Am. Bd. Plastic Surgery. Fellow A.C.S.; mem. Cleft Palate Assn., Am. Burn Assn., Ohio Valley, Am., Ky., Southeastern socs. plastic and reconstructive surgery, Am. Assn. Hand Surgery, Jefferson County Med. Soc., N.Y. Acad. Sci., Am. Soc. Regional Anesthesia. Office: Suite 7F Suburban Med Plaza 4001 Dutchman's Ln Louisville KY 40207

KASE, JUDITH BAKER, educator; b. Wilmington, Del., Dec. 13, 1932; d. Charles Robert and Elizabeth (Baker) Kase; A.B., U. Del., 1955; M.A., Case Western Res. U., 1956. Instr. theatre, designer technician Agnes Scott Coll., Decatur, Ga., 1956; instr. theatre and speech, dir. Carousel Children's Theatre, U. Tenn., Knoxville, 1957-58; coll. registrar Sembach AFB Edn. Center, instr. speech and rhetoric U. Md. Overseas, Germany, 1958-60; tchr. Kent Sch., Englewood, Colo., 1960-61; dir. children's theatre, Helen Bonfils Civic Theatre, Denver, 1960-61; membership dir. Speech Assn. Am., Bloomington, Ind., 1961-62; instr. theatre, U. N.H., Durham, 1963-69; project dir. theatre resources for youth Project TRY, Somersworth, N.H., 1966-69; asst. prof. theatre, U. South Fla., Tampa, 1969-75, asso. prof. edn., 1975—; cons. Performing Arts Project Title III, Wilmington, 1968; condr. workshops, N.Eng. and SE; sec. N.Eng. Theatre Conf., 1967; regional gov. Children's Theatre Assn. Am., 1965-67; adjudicator Nat. Arts Festival, Govt. of Bahamas, 1976-77, 79-80. Mem. theatre adv. panel Tampa Arts Council; arts adminstrn. panel Hillsborough schs. Recipient regional citation N.Eng. Theatre Conf., 1967. Mem. Am. Theatre Assn., Children's Theatre Assn. Am. (pres., 1977-79, chmn. Wingspread Conf. Theatre 1979, cert. of merit, 1970), Univ. and Coll. Theatre Assn., Secondary Schs. Theatre Assn., Southeastern Theatre Assn. (Sara Spencer Child Drama award 1980), Speech Communication Assn., Fla. Theatre Assn. (adv. panel), United Faculty of Fla., Tampa Bay Art Center, Fla. Alliance Arts Edn. (vice chmn. 1979) Assn. Internat. Theatre for Children and Youth. Club: Carrollwood Village. Author plays; contbr. writings to theatre books for youth, articles in theatrical jours. Home: Route 2 Box 1360E Lutz FL 33549 Office: Dept Social Sci and Letters Coll of Edn U South Florida Tampa FL 33620

KASH, ROSCOE CONKLING, physician, educator; b. Muskogee, Okla., Dec. 11, 1906; s. S. Perkins and Alice (Bowman) K.; A.B., U. Ky., 1925; M.D., Vanderbilt U., 1929; M.P.H. (Commonwealth Fund fellow), Johns Hopkins U., 1939; m. Ladye Ruth Stephens, Sept. 6, 1932; children—Graham Stephens, Lewis LeSueur. With hosp. div. USPHS, 1929-33; intern U.S. Marine Hosp., Ellis Island, N.Y., 1929-30; resident Marine hosps., New Orleans, Pitts.; 1930-33; dir. pub. health Tenn. Health Dept., 1933-44; pvt. practice medicine, Lebanon, Tenn., 1945—; med. examiner Wilson County (Tenn.). Mem. Ch. of Christ. Clubs: Masons, Odd Fellows. Author: Medical Essays, 1958. Home: 619 W Spring St Lebanon TN 37087 Office: 202 S College St Lebanon TN 37087

KASSIN, HAROLD HOWARD, lawyer; b. Bklyn., Dec. 2, 1927; s. Louis and Anna (Gorelick) K.; student Columbia U., 1948; J.D., U. Miami, 1951; m. Delores Jean Robey, Nov. 27, 1971; children—Kimberly Ann, Dawn Elizabeth. Admitted to Fla. bar, 1951, U.S. Supreme Ct. bar, 1955, also other U.S. bars; pvt. practice law, Miami, Fla.; sec. Kassin Investment Corp., Miami, Flagler-Ponce Realty Corp., Miami; partner Kensington Assos., Miami; instr. real estate North Campus, Miami-Dade Community Coll. Served with AUS, 1946-47. Registered real estate broker, Fla. Mem. Am., Fla., Dade County bar assns., Nu Beta Epsilon. Democrat. Home: 1921 NE 188th St Sky Lake North Miami Beach FL 33179

KASSNER, HERBERT ALAN, govt. ofcl.; b. Macon, Ga., June 9, 1927; s. Irving Edward and Rose Velma (Kessler) K.; student Davidson Coll., 1943-44; A.B., Mercer U., 1949; postgrad. U. Wis., 1967; m. Ruby G. Branch, Sept. 2, 1956; children—David, Christopher, Karen. News reporter, news dir. Stas. WMAZ and WMAZ-TV, Macon, 1947-57; in advt. sales, 1957-59; public info. officer IV U.S. Army Corps, Jacksonville, Fla., 1959-61; public info. officer, asst. chief public affairs, Fort Rucker, Ala., 1961-69; chief public affairs office U.S. Army Engr. div., Lower Mississippi Valley div., Mississippi River Commn., 1969—. Bd. dirs. Warren County (Miss.) Dept. Public Welfare, 1973—. Served with U.S. Army, 1945-46, 50-51; col. Res. Decorated Army Commendation medal. Mem. Public Relations Soc. Am., Public Relations Assn. Miss., Soc. Am. Mil. Engrs., Assn. U.S. Army. Methodist. Office: PO Box 80 Vicksburg MS 39180

KATIMS, MILTON, condr., violist; b. Bklyn.; s. Harry and Caroline K.; A.B., Columbia; Mus.D. (hon.), Whitworth Coll., 1959, Seattle U., 1974, Cornish Inst., 1975; m. Virginia Peterson; children—Peter Michael, Pamela Artura. Solo violist, asst. condr. WOR (MBS), 1935; mem. N.Y. Quartet, 1945-54; assisting artist with Budapest String Quartet, 1940-54; first desk violist under Arturo Toscanini, NBC Symphony, 1943-54; staff condr. NBC, 1944-54; mem. faculty Juilliard Sch. Music, 1946-54; guest condr. NBC Symphony, 1947-54, also Buffalo, Detroit, Houston, Montreal, Indpls., Chgo., Paris, Brussels, Barcelona, Israel, Hollywood Bowl, Dallas, Vancouver Festival; mus. dir., condr. Seattle Symphony, 1954-76; artistic dir. Sch. Music, U. Houston, 1976—; guest condr. Philharmonia Orch., London, also Cleve., Phila., Boston, N.Y. Philharmonic, and St. Louis orchs.; condr. Seattle World's Fair Festival, 1962; mus. dir. Menton Festival, 1963; guest condr. Japan Philharmonic, 1967, Bergen, Norway, 1973, Caracas, Venezuela, 1975, Oslo, 1975, Helsinki, Finland, 1975. Recipient Columbia U. medal, 1953, Alice M. Ditson Condr. award, 1963; named Seattle Man of Year, 1966. Editor-transcriber numerous viola works; contbg. editor N.W. Today. Contbr. articles to N.Y. Times, Saturday Rev. Lit., Music Pubs. Jour., Columbia Records and RCA., Victor Records, Vox Records. Office: Sch Music U Houston Houston TX 77004

KATRAGADDA, CHANDRA SEKHARARAO, radiologist; b. Vijayawada, India, June 2, 1948; came to U.S., 1973; s. Janardana Prasad and Akhilandeswari (Tummala) K.; M.B., B.S., Andhra U., 1971; m. Lata Pinnamaneni, June 4, 1971; 1 dau., Aparna. Intern, Luth. Med. Center, St. Louis, 1973-74; resident in radiology Norfolk (Va.) Gen. Hosp., 1974; resident in diagnostic radiology U. Tex., Houston, 1975-77, asst. prof., 1977-79; practice medicine specializing in radiology, Corpus Christi, Tex.; mem. staff M.D. Anderson Hosp. & Tumor Inst. Diplomate Am. Bd. Radiology. Mem. Am. Coll. Radiology, Radiol. Soc. N.Am., Tex. Radiol. Soc., Tex. Med. Assn., Harris County Med. Soc. Hindu. Office: 1415 3d St Corpus Christi TX 78404

KATTERJOHN, GEORGE WILLIAM, concrete products co. exec.; b. Paducah, Ky., Apr. 15, 1899; s. George William and Maude (Kelly) K.; student U. Ill., 1917-19; m. Merle Warner, Jan. 4, 1929; children—Ann Katterjohn Longshore, Merle Katterjohn Jermstad, Georgia N. Owner, mgr. Katterjohn Bldg. Co., Paducah, 1957—, Katterjohn Concrete Co., Owensboro, Ky., 1946—, Katterjohn Concrete Products, Little Rock, 1952—. Mem. Paducah-McCracken County Airport Commn., 1946-73; bd. dirs. U. Ill. Found. Served with Armed Forces, World War I. Mem. Beta Theta Pi. Clubs: Masons, Elks, Paducah Country. Home: 40th and Pines Rd Paducah KY 42001 Office: Katterjohn Bldg 1500 Broadway Paducah KY 42001

KATZ, ALLAN ROBERT, physician; b. N.Y.C., Apr. 1, 1942; s. Milton and Mildred (Pfeffer) K.; B.A., N.Y. U., 1963; M.D., Med. Coll. Va., 1967; m. Patti Jayne Ross, May 23, 1976. Intern, Maimonides Med. Center, Kings County Hosp., N.Y.C., 1968; resident Albert Einstein Coll. Medicine, N.Y.C., 1974; asst. prof. dept. obstetrics, gynecology U. Tex., Houston, 1975—, dir. genetics and endoscopy depts., 1976—. Served to capt. U.S. Army, 1968-70. Decorated Bronze Star, Air medal. Diplomate Am. Bd. Obstetricians and Gynecologists. Fellow Am. Coll. Obstetricians and Gynecology; mem. Alumni N.Y. U., Alumni Med. Coll. Va., Am. Fertility Soc., Am. Assn. Gynecol. Laparoscopists, Tex. Med. Assn., Am. Soc. Colposcopists and Colpomicroscopists, Harris County Med. Soc., Tex. Perinatal Assn., So. Perinatal Assn., Tex. Assn. Obstetricians and Gynecologists, Houston Gynecol. and Obstet. Soc., Assn. Profs. Gynecology and Obstetrics. Home: 9449 Briar Forest Houston TX 77063 Office: 6431 Fannin St Houston TX 77030

KATZ, ANDRES UNGAR, vascular surgeon; b. Caracas, Venezuela, Apr. 7, 1948; came to U.S., 1972, naturalized, 1980; s. Alesandro Ferenczi and Isabel Krasna-Piorova (Ungar) K.; M.D., U. Navarra (Spain), 1972; m. Patricia Moreno, May 5, 1973. Intern, St. Paul Hosp., Dallas, 1972-73, resident in gen. surgery, 1973-77; fellow in vascular surgery U. Man. (Can.), Winnipeg, 1977-78; practice medicine, specializing in vascular surgery, Dallas, 1978—; mem. staff Presbyn. Hosp., St. Paul Hosp. Diplomate Am. Bd. Surgery. Mem. AMA, Tex. Med. Assn., Dallas County Med. Soc. Office: 8210 Walnut Hill 802 Dallas TX 75231

KATZ, DORIS BARRY (MRS. MORRIS KATZ), educator; b. Wrens, Ga., Dec. 20, 1920; d. Dixie Gerald and Rosa Lee (Farr) Barry; A.A., Middle Ga. Coll., 1939; postgrad. Ga. State Coll. for Women, 1940, 51-52, Bklyn. Coll., 1951, U. Va., 1956-60, 64-65, Coll. William and Mary, 1960-61; B.A., Am. U., 1963; postgrad. George Washington U., 1967-68; M.Ed., James Madison U., Harrisonburg, Va., 1975; m. Sidney Magelof, June 27, 1943 (div. 1963); children—Susan Gail (Mrs. Randolph Macon Gilbert), Barbara Ruth (Mrs. Lawrence Richard Parlee); m. 2d, Morris Katz, July 10, 1966; stepchildren—June Diane (Mrs. Paul Marvin Levine), Stephen Gary, Mark Allen, Lisa Beth. Elementary tchr. Reedy Creek Sch., Ocilla, Ga., 1939-41; tchr. Irwinville, Ga., 1941-42; telephone operator So. Bell Tel. and Tel. Co., Augusta, Ga., 1942-43; clk. Am. Tel. & Tel. Co., N.Y.C., 1943-44; tchr. Wrens (Ga.) High Sch., 1952-53; service rep. Chesapeake & Potomac Telephone Co., Falls Church and Arlington, Va., 1954-59; tchr. Tuckahoe Jr. High Sch., Richmond, Va., 1960-61; tchr. Fairfax (Va.) County Pub. Schs., 1961—, Herndon High Sch., 1972—; learning disabilities resource tchr. Chantilly (Va.) Secondary Sch., 1975—. Tchr. word devel. Arlington County (Va.) Adult Edn. Program, 1962-66. Mem. Nat., Va. edn. assns., Fairfax County Ednl. Assn., Council for Exceptional Children, Assn. for Children with Learning Disabilities, Nat. Trust for Historic Preservation, Am. Hort. Soc. Jewish. Home: Route 2 Box 66A Stanley VA 22851 Office: Chantilly Secondary School 4201 Stringfellow Rd Chantilly VA 22021

KATZ, FRED NORMAN, physician; b. N.Y., Apr. 26, 1941; s. Samuel I. and Molly (Budman) K.; B.S., L.I. U., 1962; D.O., Coll. Osteopathic Medicine and Surgery, 1966; m. Doris Strauss, June 20, 1964; children—Barrie Gail, Michelle Stacey. Intern, Detroit Osteo. Hosp., 1966-67, resident, 1969-72; chief radiology Doctors Hosp., Tucker, Ga., 1972—; program chmn. Am. Osteo. Coll. Radiology, 1980—; vis. lectr. radiology W.Va. Coll. Osteo. Medicine. Vice-pres. Atlanta region Zionist Orgn. Am., 1979-80; bd. dirs. Atlanta Jewish Welfare Fedn., 1979-82; mem. nat. bd. Young Leadership Cabinet, United Jewish Appeal, 1978-82. Served to capt. AUS, 1967-69. Decorated Bronze Star medal. Mem. Ga. Osteo. Med. Assn. (past pres.), Am. Osteo. Assn., Ga. Soc. Nuclear Medicine, Am. Osteo. Coll. Radiology, Am. Coll. Nuclear Physicians, Am. Med. Joggers Assn., Am. Physicians Fellowship. Jewish. Club: Standard. Office: 2160 Idlewood Rd Tucker GA 30084

KATZ, HYMAN, real estate broker; b. Manhattan, N.Y., July 19, 1913; s. Gershon and Minnie K.; student public schs.; m. Bella Brown, Oct. 14, 1939; 1 dau., Barbara. Real estate salesman Security Real Estate, Miami, Fla., 1950-60; real estate broker Ruport Realty, Coral Gables, Fla., 1970-79. Mem. Homes Am. Properties, Inc. Served with AUS, 1943-45; ETO, USCG, 1945-73. Mem. Jewish War Vets. Democrat. Jewish. Home: 1210 Placetas Ave Coral Gables FL 33146 Office: 15090 Biscayne Blvd Miami FL 33181

KATZEFF, MICHAEL DAVID, chem. co. exec.; b. Bklyn., Sept. 20, 1945; s. Jacob and Ruth (Breiterman) K.; B.S. in Chem. Engring., Tulane U., 1966; M.B.A., UCLA, 1968; m. Harriet Cyrelle Rothkop, June 17, 1973; children—Howard Marcus, Shoshana Ruth. Fin. analyst Baytown chem. plant Exxon Chem. Co., Baytown, Tex., 1970-73, distbn. planner, Houston, 1973-74, bus. analyst, N.Y.C., 1974-75, analyst Houston chem. plant, 1976-78, adminstrv. services head Bayport high performance polymers, Pasadena, Tex., 1978—. Bd. dirs., v.p., past treas. Northfield Sec. I and II Civic Club. Served to 1st lt. U.S. Army, 1968-70. C.P.A., Tex. Mem. Am. Inst. C.P.A.'s, Tex. Soc. C.P.A.'s. Jewish. Home: 10730 Valley Hills Dr Houston TX 77071 Office: Exxon Chem Co 9701 Bayport Blvd Pasadena TX 77507

KATZIN, MORDICAI, optometrist; b. Winston-Salem, N.C., Dec. 22, 1923; s. Samuel Leazer and Hettie (Vosk) K.; D.Optometry, Pa. Coll. Optometry, 1944; m. June Rubenstein, Dec. 28, 1947; children—Marcy, David. Pvt. practice optometry, Winston-Salem, 1945-47, Jacksonville, N.C., 1948—. Lectr. So. Council Optometry, Middle Atlantic Optometric Conf., N.C. Optometric Soc.; mem. N.C. State Bd. Examiners in Optometry, 1978—. Mem. exec. council Jacksonville U.S.O., 1953—; pres. Onslow County Tb Assn., 1955-64; mem. profl. adv. com. State Commn. for Blind, 1969-70; mem. N.C. Commn. for Blind, 1970-75. Chmn. Jacksonville Planning and Zoning Bd., 1967; dir. Civil Def., Jacksonville and Onslow County, 1960-65. Diplomate contact lens sect. Am. Acad. Optometry. Mem. Am. Optometric Assn., So. Council Optometry, N.C. Optometric Soc. (pres. 1963-64), Beta Sigma Kappa. Kiwanian (pres. 1966); mem. B'nai B'rith. Research soft contact lenses. Home: 4 Park Pl Jacksonville NC 28540 Office: 200 Doctors Dr Suite K Jacksonville NC 28540

KAUFFMAN, DRAPER LAURENCE, ret. naval officer; b. San Diego, Aug. 4, 1911; s. James Laurence and Elizabeth Kelsey (Draper) K.; B.S., U.S. Naval Acad., 1933; postgrad. Naval War Coll., 1950-51; m. Margaret Cary Tuckerman, May 1, 1943; children—Margaret Cary, Draper Laurence, Edith Kelsey. Commd. lt. USNR, 1941, transferred to U.S. Navy as comdr., 1946, advanced through grades to rear adm., 1961; organizer, 1st comdg. officer Navy Bomb Disposal Sch., 1942; organizer Navy Underwater Demolition Teams, 1943; comdr. underwater demolition teams on Saipan, Tinian, Iwo Jima and Okinawa, World War II; comdr. U.S.S. Gearing, 1948-50, U.S.S. Bexar, 1957-58, U.S.S. Helena, 1960-61, Destroyer Div. 122, 1953-54, Cruiser Destroyer Flotilla 3, 1961-62; aide, exec. asst. to sec. navy Gates, 1955-57; chief strategic plans and policy div. Joint Staff, Joint Chiefs Staff, 1962-63; dir. Office Program Appraisal on staff sec. navy Nitze, 1963-65; supt. U.S. Naval Acad., 1965-68; comdr. U.S. Naval Forces, Philippines, 1968-70; comdt. 9th Naval Dist., comdr. U.S. Naval Base, Great Lakes, Ill., 1970-73; ret., 1973; pres. Marion (Ala.) Mil. Inst., 1974-76. Mem. adv. bd. Nat. Council Drug Abuse, 1972—. Decorated Navy Cross (2), D.S.M. (2), Legion of Merit, Navy Commendation medal (3); Croix de Guerre with star (France); Oak Leaf and Def. medal (England); Legion of Honor (Philippines). Mem. U.S. Naval Inst. (v.p. 1965-68). Club: N.Y. Yacht. Home: PO Box 1088 Ponte Vedra Beach FL 32082

KAUFFMAN, GLENN EDWARD, computer co. exec.; b. Lancaster, Pa., Dec. 14, 1944; s. Walter L. and Lillian J. (Geisler) K.; A.B. in Math. and Physics, Lycoming Coll., 1965; B.S.E.E., Bucknell U., 1967; M.S.E.E., Rochester Inst. Tech., 1972; m. Ann E. Robinson, Jan. 31, 1964; children—Brian C., Sherry L. Research and devel. engr., buyer Eastman Kodak Co., Rochester, N.Y., 1967-72; systems sales engr. Systems Instruments Research Co., Atlanta, 1972-73; sales engr. Data Gen. Co., Atlanta, 1973-75; mfr.'s rep. Gentry Assos., Atlanta, 1975-76; pres. Atlanta Minicomputer Assos., Inc., 1976—; speaker on minicomputers, 1974—. Vice chmn. social action com. Central Congl. Ch., 1974-77, chmn. pledge campaign, 1977; mem. sponsoring com. Button Gwinnett United Ch. of Christ, 1978-79; adult adv. Boy Scouts Am. Mem. Data Processing Mgmt. Assn. Club: Atlanta Area Microcomputer Hobbiest. Inventor computerized ultrasonic transducer mfg. system. Home: 3127 Sumac Dr Atlanta GA 30360 Office: 150 Technology Park Norcross GA 30092

KAUFFMAN, PETER WRIGHT, cons. engring. co. exec.; b. Erie, Pa., Dec. 24, 1944; s. Walter Lee and Elizabeth Kellar (Wright) K.; B.S., Pa. State U., 1970, M.A., 1971; postgrad. Johns Hopkins U., 1975; m. Margaret Helen Hatch, Sept. 2, 1968; children—Karen Christine, Anne Rogers, Charles Wright. Indsl. engr. Am. Meter Co., Erie, Pa., 1968-69; systems analyst Aerojet Gen., Frederick, Md., 1971-72; sr. cons. Mgmt. Services Co., Sacramento, 1972-74; v.p. J.J. Davis Assos., McLean, Va., 1974-75; pres., chmn. bd. Mgmt. Engrs., Inc., Reston, Va., 1975—. Served to 1st lt. U.S. Army, 1965-68. Mem. Am. Inst. Indsl. Engrs., AIME, Soc. Automotive Engrs. Home: 11712 Blue Smoke Trail Reston VA 22091 Office: Mgmt Engrs Inc 11800 Sunrise Valley Dr Reston VA 22091

KAUFMAN, HERBERT EDWARD, ophthalmologist; b. N.Y.C., Sept. 28, 1931; s. Benjamin and Claire (Krinsky) K.; A.B., Princeton U., 1952; M.D. magna cum laude, Harvard U., 1956; children—Stephen, Joshua, Claire; m. Maija H. Uotila, 1976. Intern, 1956-57; clin. asso. in clin. ophthalmology and research NIH, 1957-59; trainee Mass. Eye and Ear Infirmary, Boston, 1959-62, also head Uveitis Lab.; asso. prof., chief ophthalmology U. Fla., Gainesville, 1962-64, prof., chmn. dept. ophthalmology, prof. pharmacology, 1964-77, acting dean Coll. Medicine, 1972; chmn. dept. ophthalmology La. State U., New Orleans, 1978—. Named one the Ten Outstanding Young Men Am., Jaycees, 1968; recipient Humanitarian award Lions Internat., 1968. Mem. Assn. Research in Vision and Ophthalmology (trustee, pres. 1975; Proctor award 1978). Editor Jour. Investigative Ophthalmology, 1968-77; contbr. med. research papers to profl. jours. Office: La State U Eye Center 136 S Roman St New Orleans LA 70112

KAUFMAN, HOWARD HERSCHEL, neurosurgeon; b. Flint, Mich., Mar. 26, 1941; s. Lewis Dallas and Stella (Lande) K.; B.A. magna cum laude (Nat. Merit scholar), Yale U., 1962; postgrad. Harvard Med. Sch., summer 1964, Karolinska Inst., Stockholm, summer 1965; M.D., Columbia U., 1966; m. Romaine Hillary Marilyn, June 30, 1974; children—Ezekiel Ari, Zachary Daniel Coleman. Surg. intern U. Minn. Hosp., Mpls., 1966-67; fellow Nat. Hosp. for Nervous Diseases, London, 1967-68; clin. asso. in surg. neurology Nat. Inst. Neurol. Disease and Stroke, NIH, Bethesda, Md., 1968-70; resident in neurol. surgery Neurol. Inst. N.Y., Columbia Presbyn. Med. Center, N.Y.C., 1970-74; asst. prof. div. neurosurgery U. Ariz. Med. Sch., 1974-75; asst. prof. U. Tex. Med. Sch., Houston, 1975-78, asso. prof. div. neurosurgery, 1978—. Diplomate Am. Bd. Neurol. Surgery. Fellow Am. Heart Assn. Stroke Council; mem. Am. Assn. Neurol. Surgeons, Am. Assn. Tissue Banks, A.C.S., AMA, Am. Trauma Soc., Congress Neurol. Surgeons (Found. for Internat. Edn. in Neurol. Surgery), So. Neurosurg. Soc., Rocky Mountain Neurosurg. Soc., Soc. for Neuroscis., Inst. of Soc., Ethics and Life Scis., Tex. Assn. Neurol. Surgeons, Tex. Med. Assn., Harris County Med. Assn., Houston Neurol. Soc., Research Soc. Neurol. Surgeons. Jewish. Contbr. articles in field to profl. jours. Home: 10914 Braes Forest Dr Houston TX 77071 Office: Dept Neurosurgery U Tex Med Sch 6431 Fanin St Houston TX 77030

KAUFMAN, IRA SAUL, orthopedic surgeon; b. N.Y.C., Feb. 25, 1945; s. Oscar Lawrence and Miriam (Spiegel) K.; A.B., Colgate U., 1966; M.D., SUNY, Bklyn., 1970; m. Donna Wortheim, Dec. 25, 1967; children—Rebecca, Jonathan. Intern, Montefiore Hosp. & Med. Center, Bronx, N.Y., 1970-71, resident in gen. surgery, 1971-72, resident in orthopedic surgery, 1972-75; practice medicine specializing in orthopedic surgery, Humble, Tex., 1977—; attending physician N.E. Med. Center; staff N.W. Hosp., Houston, Baylor U. Med. Center, Houston. Served to maj. M.C., USAF, 1975-77. Diplomate Am. Bd. Orthopedic Surgeons. Fellow Am. Acad. Orthopedic Surgeons; mem. Houston Orthopedic Soc. Club: Exchange. Address: 18553 Memorial Blvd Humble TX 77338

KAUFMAN, JACK HAMMER, lawyer; b. San Antonio, Dec. 15, 1925; s. Leon Brown and Karleen Wilma (Hammer) K.; B.B.A., U. Tex., 1950, J.D., 1951; m. Estelle Lieberman, June 18, 1950; children—William Thomas, Karleen Pearl, Nancy Ann. Admitted to Tex. bar, 1951, U.S. Supreme Ct. bar, 1965; asst. dist. atty. Bexar County, San Antonio, 1951-55; practice law, San Antonio, 1955—. Dir., Northside Bank, San Antonio. Councilman, City of San Antonio, 1961-65. Bd. dirs. Nat. Conf. Christians and Jews, San Antonio, 1975—; trustee San Antonio Waterworks Bd., 1966-73, chmn., 1972-73; trustee Alamo Heights Sch. Found., 1972-75, pres., 1974-75. Served with USAAF, 1944-45. Mem. San Antonio, Tex., Am. bar assns., Zeta Beta Tau. Jewish (trustee temple 1955—, pres. 1967-69). Kiwanian. Home: 8104 Countryside Dr San Antonio TX 78209 Office: 900 Alamo National Bldg San Antonio TX 78205

KAUFMAN, RAYMOND HENRY, obstetrician, gynecologist; b. Bklyn., Nov. 24, 1925; s. Morris and Anne Markewich (Lipton) K.; student Coll. William and Mary, U. N.C., 1943-44; M.D., U. Md., 1948; m. Patricia Anne Katherine Judson, June 23, 1946; children—Susan Jo, Wendy Beth Murri Ellen, Elisabeth Anne. Prof. obstetrics and gynecology, chmn. dept. obstetrics and gynecology, prof. pathology Baylor U. Coll. Medicine, Houston, 1973—. Served with USN, World War II, USAF, Korean War. Mem. Central Assn. Obstetricians and Gynecologists, Am. Coll. Obstetricians and Gynecologists, A.C.S., Am. Soc. Cytology, Tex., Am. assns. obstetricians and gynecologists, Am. Gynecol. Soc., Houston Gynecol. and Obstet. Soc. Jewish. Author: (with H. O. Gardner) Benign Disease of the Vulva and Vagina, 1969; contbr. numerous articles to profl. jours. Home: 11002 Hunters Park Dr Houston TX 77024 Office: 1200 Moursund St Houston TX 77030

KAUFMANN, GODFREY FRENSZ, cons. geologist; b. Omaha, Mar. 26, 1895; s. Charles and Laura (Frensz) K.; student Syracuse U., 1914-17; E.M., Colo. Sch. Mines, 1921; m. Helon M. McDonald, Dec. 31, 1949; 1 dau., Jean Ann Kaufmann Guinn. Paymaster, Edison Chem. Works, Bloomfield, N.J., 1917; field geologist Cia. Mex. El Aquila, Shell Oil, 1921-25; chief geophysicist Standard Oil N.J. Affiliates, Mex., 1926-38, Venezuela, 1938-44; research geologist, geophysicist Standard Vacuum Oil Co., N.Y.C., 1944-45, 47, 49, 55-59, China, 1946, Japan, 1948, Indonesia, 1950-51, India, 1952-54, 56, cons., Thailand, 1960, Pakistan, 1967; cons. geologist and geophysicist, Yorktown Heights, N.Y., 1959-75), Jensen Beach, Fla., 1976—. Served to 2d lt. U.S. AC, 1918-19. Recipient merit certificate nat. resources sect. U.S. Occupational Forces, Japan, 1949. Fellow Geol. Soc. Am., Am. Geog. Soc., AAAS, N.Y. Acad. Scis.; mem. Am. Assn. Petroleum Geologists (asso. editor Far East 1956-62, pres. Eastern sect. 1961-62), Soc. Econ. Paleontologists and Mineralogists, Soc. Exploration Geophysicists, Am. Geophys. Union, European Geophys. Soc., Am. Inst. Mining Metall. and Petroleum Engrs., Japanese Paleontol. Soc., Tau Beta Pi, Sigma Beta, Beta Theta Pi. Contbr. articles to sci. bulls. and mags. in U.S. and fgn. countries. Home: 18 Netherby Ave Jensen Beach FL 33457 Office: PO Box 643 Jensen Beach FL 33457

KAUFMANN, HANS ALEX, ins. agy. owner; b. Hannover, Germany, Nov. 12, 1923; s. Julius and Irma (Levy) K.; came to U.S., 1938, naturalized, 1943; B.S., La. State U., 1948; m. Betty Jane Waldman, Sept. 5, 1948; children—Donald, Janet (Mrs. Douglas Black). Elec. engr. Stone & Webster Corp., Baton Rouge, 1948; salesman Knitgoods, Inc., High Point, N.C., 1948; agt. Franklin Life Ins. Co., Baton Rouge, 1948-53, gen. agt., 1953-58; v.p. La. Cos., Inc., Baton Rouge, 1958-63, gen. agt. Occidental Life Cal., Baton Rouge, 1963—. Chmn. Israel Bond Drive, 1970-71. Bd. dirs. Baton Rouge Jewish Welfare Fedn., 1973. Served with AUS, 1943-46. Decorated Purple Heart. Recipient Nat. Quality award, Nat. Sales Achievement award; named Underwriters Man of Year, 1978. Mem. Baton Rouge Assn. Life Underwriters (pres. 1970), Million Dollar Roundtable (life), Phi Epsilon Pi. Clubs: Am. Contract Bridge League (life master), City Baton Rouge, Sertoma. Home: 3720 S Lakeshore Dr Baton Rouge LA 70808 Office: 451 Florida St Baton Rouge LA 70801

KAVALEWITZ, MICHAEL JOHN, securities co. exec.; b. Bklyn., Feb. 18, 1946; s. Leonard Mafera and Mercedes (Keefe) K.; B.B.A., Bernard M. Baruch Coll., 1972; M.B.A., U. Houston, 1980; m. Velia Rita Capasso, Oct. 9, 1965; children—Michael Jason, Amy Jennifer, Jason Paul. Auditor, Central Savs. Bank, 1964-67; acct. A.G. Becker & Co., N.Y.C., 1967-68; asst. audit mgr. Lehman Bros., Inc., N.Y.C., 1968-75; dir. compliance, v.p. Rotan Mosle, Inc., Houston, 1975—. Cert. internal auditor. Mem. Securities Industry Assn., Inst. Internal Auditors, Am. Mgmt. Assn., Sigma Alpha Delta. Roman Catholic. Club: Kingwood Runners. Office: 1500 S Tower Pennzoil Pl Houston TX 77002

KAVANAGH, ROGER PIERCE, JR., constrn. co. exec.; b. Greenwich, Conn., Aug. 27, 1917; s. Roger Pierce and Eleanor (Geffem) K.; student Princeton U., 1936-38; m. Jeanette Rusovich,

June 5, 1943; children—Basil John, Roger Pierce. Mgr., N.Mex. Timber Co., 1938-40; salesman Am. Houses, Inc., N.Y.C., 1945-53; pres. Kavanagh, Smith & Co., Greensboro, N.C., 1953-66; pres. Westminster Co., Greensboro, 1967—; dir. N.C. Nat. Bank. Mem. N.C. Conservation and Devel. Bd., 1960-64, N.C. State Sediment Control Commn., 1974—; state chmn. Radio Free Europe, 1966. Served with Ordnance Dept., AUS, 1941-45. Decorated Bronze Star. Mem. Nat. Assn. Home Builders, Greensboro C. of C. (dir.). Home: 605 Sunset Dr Greensboro NC 27408 Office: 200 W Wendover St Greensboro NC 27405

KAVANAUGH, RAPHAEL RYAN, JR., educator; b. Springfield, Ohio, Dec. 16, 1945; s. Raphael Ryan and Harriet Elizabeth (Anderton) K.; B.A., Coe Coll., 1968; M.A., Ball State U., 1972; Ed.D., Temple U., 1977; m. Judy Ann Rechberger, Aug. 7, 1976. Curriculum devel. specialist Research for Better Schs., Phila., 1972-74; grad. asso. Temple U., Phila., 1974-76; asst. prof. counselor edn. U. Central Fla., Orlando, 1976—; pvt. practice orgn. devel. Center for Human Awareness, Orlando, 1976—. Bd. dirs. Orange County Additions, Spouse Abuse Inc. of Orange County. Served with USAF, 1968-72. USAF ROTC scholar, 1967-68. Mem. Am. Personnel and Guidance Assn., Fla. Personnel and Guidance Assn., Assn. Counselor Edn. and Supervision, Assn. Humanistic Edn. and Devel., Greater Orlando C. of C. Democrat. Roman Catholic. Clubs: United Health, Nautilus Fitness Center. Home: PO Box 731 Oviedo FL 32765 Office: Box 25000 Coll Edn U Central Fla Orlando FL 32816

KAVANAUGH, ROBERT LEE, mfg. co. exec.; b. Farmerville, La., May 11, 1945; s. Jimmy Lee and Audrey (Bearden) K.; B.A., Henderson State U., Arkadelphia, Ark., 1969; m. Toni Renee Miller, May 11, 1975; 1 son, Jason Miller. Tchr. Am. history, Pine Bluff, Ark., 1969-72; asst. mgr. Rosswood Country Club, Pine Bluff, 1972-73; indsl. sales rep. Motorola C & E, Inc., Monroe, La., 1973-76, indsl. dist. sales mgr., 1976-77, indsl. account exec., 1977, indsl. account exec. mgr., 1978—. Recipient Distinguished Service award Motorola, 1975, 76, 77, 78, Indsl. Inner Circle award, 1978. Mem. Sigma Tau Gamma. Democrat. Baptist. Home: Route 1 Box 521 Farmerville LA 71241 Office: 3320 Belt Line Dr Dallas TX 75234

KAWAGUCHI, HARRY HARUMITSU, psychologist; b. Watsonville, Calif., Oct. 14, 1928; s. Kikuzo and Kino (Tanaka) K.; B.A., U. Tex., 1953, M.A., 1957; m. Meredith Ferguson, Apr. 22, 1977; 1 dau., Emily Eastham. Clin. psychologist Austin (Tex.) State Hosp., 1961-73; pvt. practice clin. psychology, Austin, 1973—; cons. Tex. Vocat. Rehab. Assn., Tex. Com. on Alcoholism. Bd. dirs. Salvation Army Youth Center. Mem. Tex. Psychol. Assn., Assn. Advancement of Psychology, Council for Nat. Register for Health Service Providers in Psychology, Internat. Platform Assn. Democrat. Episcopalian. Home: 5009 Westview Dr Austin TX 78731 Office: 1600 W 38th St Suite 400-7 Austin TX 78731

KAWAHATA, HENRY HAJIME, farmer; b. Brownsville, Tex., Aug. 11, 1919; s. James Minoru and Toku (Kondo) K.; B.S. in Agrl. Adminstrn., Tex. A. and M. U., 1940; m. Elsie Sueyasu, Nov. 10, 1945; children—David, Joyce, Gail, Ann. Pres., Kawahata Farms, Hidalgo, Tex., since 1940; dir. Valco Oil Mill, Harlingen, Tex., 1950-57, 281 Cotton Gin, Pharr, Tex., 1950-57; pres. McAllen Farm Bur., 1951-52. Alderman, City of Hidalgo, 1960-64, 68-70, 72-73; bd. dirs. McAllen Internat. Museum, 1969-73, McAllen Bot. Gardens, 1970-72, Region One Edn. Ser. Center, 1979; councilor Tex. A. and M. Y. Research Found., 1976-82. Baptist. Address: PO Box 206 Hidalgo TX 78557

KAY, HERBERT JACK, redevel. agy. exec.; b. N.Y.C., Aug. 16, 1919; s. Harry and Rose (Wiener) K.; A.A., U. Fla., 1938, B.S., 1940; postgrad. Emory U., 1940-41, Manhattan Coll., 1941-42, N.Y. U., 1946-47; M.A., Ohio State U., 1959; postgrad. Boston U., 1969-70; m. Jeanne Sandra Young, Jan. 1, 1943; children—Carol (Mrs. Allen Monosoff), Robin (Mrs. Terry Covel), Dennis Michael. Engring. draftsman Gibbs & Hill, cons. engrs., N.Y.C., 1941-42, M.W. Kellog Co., N.Y.C., 1942, 46; mgr. H.J. Kay Gen. Contractor, Miami Beach, Fla., 1947-51; commd. 2d lt. U.S. Army, 1940, advanced through grades to col., 1967; chmn. rev. bd., dep. comdr. U.S. Army Phys. Disability Agy., Washington, 1967-68; chief ind. tng. div., dep. chief of staff, personnel Dept. Army, Pentagon, 1966-67; dir. research and oral communications Info. Sch., Dept. Def., Ft. Benjamin Harrison, Ind., 1964-66; comdr. 2d Arty. Bn., 2d F.A., Ft. Sill, Okla., 1963-64; ret., 1968; mgr. employment and employee devel. Quincy Shipbldg. div. Gen. Dynamics (Mass.), 1968-73, corp. mgr. Equal Opportunity Program, St. Louis, 1973-75; corp. mgr. Mgmt. Devel. and Communications, 1975-77; pres. Acupuncture Treatment Centers, Inc., Miami, Fla., 1977-78; mgmt. cons., 1978-79; exec. adminstr. Miami Beach Redevel. Agy., 1979—; instr. speech U. Md. at Heidelberg, Germany, 1961-63. Commr. Boy Scouts, Ft. Sill, Okla., 1963-64; commr. Ft. Sill Little League Football, 1963-64; mem. adv. bd. Positive Program for Boston, NAACP, 1969-73; mem. Gov.'s South Shore Adv. Bd. to Mass. Commn. Against Discrimination, 1971-73; bd. dirs. Work, Inc. sheltered workshop for handicapped, Quincy, 1971-73; mem. Amigos de Ser Jobs for Progress, 1973-75; mem. bd. St. Louis Am. Jewish Com., 1976-77. Served with AUS, 1942-46. Decorated Legion Merit, Bronze Star medal with oak leaf cluster, Joint Services Commendation medal; Army Occupation medal (Germany). Mem. Ohio State Alumni Club (chpt. treas. 1971-73), Am. Soc. Tng. and Devel., Am. Bus. Communications Assn., Internat. Platform Assn., Nat. Assn. Uniformed Services, Nat. Assn. Housing and Redevel. Ofcls., Assn. U.S. Army, Ret. Officers Assn., Speech Communications Assn., DAV, Phi Beta Delta. Home: 330 N Hibiscus Dr Miami Beach FL 33139 Office: 335 Alton Rd Miami Beach FL 33139

KAY, ROBERT KRAFT, clin. social worker; b. Pitts., July 20, 1943; s. Lewis Gallagher and Mary Perkins (Dauler) K.; B.A., Am. U., 1967; M.Ed., U. Md., 1971; M.S.W., Catholic U., 1975; m. Virginia Elizabeth Wells, Jan. 20, 1979. Sr. rehab. therapist, rehab. program coordinator Psychiat. Inst. Washington, 1972-74; family therapist Family Service Agy. Prince Georges County (Md.), 1974-75; psychiat. emergency therapist Woodburn Mental Health Center, Fairfax, Va., 1976-78; pvt. practice group and family psychotherapy, Alexandria, Va., 1978—; outpatient program dir. Prince William County Community Mental Health Center, Dumfries, Va., 1973—; lic. examiner Va. Bd. Behavioral Sci., 1978—. Served with USMCR, 1963-64. Harris scholar, 1966-67; HEW grantee, 1970-72. Mem. Am. Acad. Psychotherapists, Acad. Cert. Social Workers, Va. Assn. Mental Health Providers. Home: 2252 Mary Baldwin Dr Alexandria VA 22307 Office: 916 N Main St Dumfries VA 22026

KAYE, HAROLD STANLEY, microbiologist; b. New Britain, Conn., Feb. 1, 1920; s. Simon and Rose Sarah (Horwitz) Koplowitz; B.A., U. Conn., 1949; M.S., U. Mich., 1963; m. Annette Rudman, Dec. 23, 1949 (dec.); children—Marilyn Janice, Randi Sue; m. 2d, Miriam Davis, June 6, 1971. Sr. bacteriologist Conn. Dept. Health, Hartford, 1956-59; med. bacteriologist Nat. Communicable Disease Center, Atlanta, 1959-64, research microbiologist, 1964-68, supervisory research microbiologist, 1968—. Served with USAAF, 1939-45. Decorated Air medal. Mem. Am. Soc. for Microbiology, Am. Acad. Microbiology, U. Mich. Alumni Assn., U. Conn. Alumni Assn., Sigma Xi. Contbr. articles to profl. jours. Home: 1618 N Gatewood Rd NE Atlanta GA 30329 Office: National Communicable Disease Center 1600 Clifton Rd Atlanta GA 30333

KAYE, NEAL WALLACE, JR., beverage corp. exec.; b. Tampa, Fla., Mar. 31, 1949; s. Neal Wallace and Ruth Hammond (Drew) K.; B.S., Babson Inst., 1971; m. Pamela Fort Pipes, Oct. 19, 1974. Vice pres., gen. mgr. Neal W. Kaye, Inc., New Orleans, 1971—, also dir. Vice chmn. industry div. United Way, 1975. Served with USNR, 1971-77. Decorated Meritorious Service medal. Mem. Nat. La. beer wholesalers assn. Clubs: New Orleans Country, Sch. Design, Alpine, Internat. House, Big Game Fishing. Home: 1919 State St New Orleans LA 70118 Office: 201 Laitram Ln Harahan LA 70123

KAYE, SIDNEY, toxicologist, educator; b. Bklyn., Mar. 10, 1912; s. Isaac and Ida (Lefkowitz) Kozinsky; B.S., N.Y. U., 1935, M.S., 1939; Ph.D., Med. Coll. Va., 1956; m. Carmen Maria Jimenez Calzada, June 7, 1951; children—Cynthia Susan, Frederic Joseph. Toxicoldgist, St. Louis Police, 1946-47; instr. Washington U., St. Louis, 1946-47; state toxicologist State of Va., 1947-62; asso. prof. Med. Coll. Va., Richmond, 1947-62; state toxicologist, P.R., 1962—; asso. dir. Inst. Legal Medicine, prof. toxicology, pharmacology and legal medicine U. P.R., San Juan, 1962—; cons. to U.S. Army, VA; adj. prof. Caribe U.; coordinator Poison Control Center, Va., 1950-62, P.R., 1962—; lectr. in field. Served to col. Med. Service, U.S. Army, 1941-46. Decorated Army Commendation medal, Legion of Merit; recipient certificate of appreciation U.S. CD, P.R. CD, Indsl. Coll. Armed Forces; diplomate Am. Bd. Clin. Chemistry, Am. Bd. Toxicology. Mem. Nat. Safety Council, Am. Acad. Forensic Scis. (founding, recipient award of merit), Soc. Toxicolog (founding), Pan Am. Med. Assn. (Latin Am. v.p. taxicology), Soc. Mil. Surgeons (life), Sigma Xi (founding pres. P.R.). Contbr. chpts. on toxicology, to books, articles to profl. jours. Author: Emergency Toxicology, 4th edit., 1979. Home: 116 Lilas St Rio Piedras PR 00927 Office: GPO Box 5067 Sch Medicine U PR San Juan PR 00936

KAZEN, ABRAHAM, JR., congressman; b. Laredo, Tex., Jan. 17, 1919; student U. Tex., 1937-40, Cumberland Law Sch., Lebanon, Tenn., 1941; m. Consuelo Raymond; children—Abraham III, Mrs. E. C. Dillman, Jr., Christina (Mrs. Ronald K. Attal), Catherine, Jo-Betsy. Admitted to Tex. bar, 1942; mem. Tex. Ho. of Reps., 1947-52; mem. Tex. Senate, 1952-66, pres. pro tempore, 1959; acting gov. State of Tex., 1959; mem. 90th-96th congresses from 23d Dist. Tex. Served to capt. USAAF, World War II; NATOUSA; MTO; CBI. Mem. Tex., Laredo bar assns., Am. Legion, VFW, AFA, U. Tex. Ex-Students Assn. Democrat. K.C. Home: Laredo TX 78040 also 6216 Loch Raven Dr McLean VA 22101 Office: 2411 Rayburn House Office Bldg Washington DC 20515

KEADY, WILLIAM COLBERT, fed. judge; b. Greenville, Miss., Apr. 2, 1913; LL.B., Washington U., St. Louis, 1936; m. Dorothy Clark Thompson. Mem. Miss. Ho. of Reps., 1940-43, Miss. Senate, 1944-45, commr. Miss. State Bar for the 4th circuit, 1954-55; practiced law in Greenville; judge U.S. Dist. for No. Miss., 1968—, now chief judge. Mem. Am., Miss. bar assns. Democrat. Address: US Dist Ct PO Box 190 Greenville MS 38701

KEARLEY, F. FURMAN, educator; b. Snowdoun, Ala., Nov. 7, 1932; s. John Ausburn and Zelma S. (Suggs) K.; B.A., Ala. Christian Coll., 1954; M.A., Harding Coll., 1956, M.R.E. and Th.M., 1965; M.Ed., Auburn U., 1960; Ph.D., Hebrew Union Coll., 1971; m. Helen Joy Bowman, July 18, 1951; children—Janice Gail, Amelia Lynn Kearley Burks. Ordained to ministry, Ch. of Christ, 1951; prof. Bible, Ala. Christian Coll., Montgomery, 1956-69, chmn. dept. Bible, 1962-69, dean Sch. Religion, 1967-69; chmn. humanities div. and bibl. studies div. Lubbock (Tex.) Christian Coll., 1970-75; prof. Bible, Abilene (Tex.) Christian U., 1975—, dir. grad. studies in Bible, 1979—; staff writer World Evangelist, 1972—; minister Burkett (Tex.) Ch. of Christ, 1976—. Mem. Soc. Bibl. Lit., Nat. Assn. Hebrew Profs., Oriental Research Soc., Evang. Theol. Assn., Mod. Fgn. Lang. Assn., Phi Delta Kappa. Club: Rotary. Author: God's Indwelling Spirit, 1974; contbr. articles in field to profl. jours. Home: 726 Diamond Lake Dr Abilene TX 79601 Office: Abilene Christian U PO Box 8159 Abilene TX 79601

KEARNEY, KEVIN EMMETT, coll. adminstr.; b. Bogota, N.J., Jan. 19, 1929; s. Thomas F. and Dorothy C. (Dinnebeil) K.; B.S., U. Vt., 1954; M.A., U. Fla., 1955, Ph.D., 1960; m. June C. Tripp, Aug. 13, 1967; children—Katherine, Kevin. Instr. speech dept. Butler U., Indpls., 1958-60; asst. prof. speech U. Ala., Tuscaloosa, 1960-64; asst. prof. speech U. South Fla., Tampa, 1964-66, asso. prof., 1966—, dir. Bachelor Independent Studies, external degree program, 1968—; cons. for external study for So. Assn. Colls. and Schs., 1975—. Served with USN, 1946-48, USNR, 1950-52. Recipient Distinguished Service award So. Speech Assn., 1969; U. Fla. grad. sch. fellow, 1957; Eli Lilly faculty grantee Butler U., 1959. Mem. Nat. Univ. Extension Assn., So. Speech Communication Assn., Fla. Hist. Soc., Phi Kappa Phi, Tau Kappa Alpha. Democrat. Presbyn. Editor: Proceedings of a Nat. Conf. on Spl. Adult Degree Programs, 1970; author: Speaker's Bureau Training Manual, 1969. Home: 1905 E 114th Ave Tampa FL 33612 Office: BIS External Degree Program U South Fla Tampa FL 33620

KEATHLEY, ORMON MAYNARD, naval officer; b. Jacksonville, Fla., Apr. 25, 1940; s. Oscar Maynard and Elma Claudia (Skyes) K.; B.A., Pepperdine U., 1978; m. Betty Jean Bryant, June 12, 1979; children—Ormon Maynard, Sheila Janese, Robert LaVern. Enlisted in U.S. Navy, 1964, advanced through grades to sr. chief petty officer, 1977; supply support center supr. Naval Air Sta., Marietta, Ga., 1971-74; weapon system mgr., chief Naval Res., New Orleans, 1974-77; supply leading chief, contracting officer Naval Air Sta., Dallas, 1977-78, supply leading chief, planning officer, 1979—. Served with USAF, 1959-62. Mem. Fleet Res. Assn., Chief Petty Officer Assn., VFW, Am. Legion. Republican. Baptist. Clubs: Masons, Moose. Home: 1216 W Mitchell St Arlington TX 76013 Office: Code 601 Naval Air Station Dallas TX 75211

KEATING, FRANK, state senator; b. St. Louis, Feb. 10, 1944; s. Anthony F. and Anne M. (Martin) K.; A.B., Georgetown U., 1966; J.D., Okla. U., 1969; m. Catherine Heller, Nov. 17, 1972; children—Carrie, Kelly, Anthony F. III. Admitted to Okla. bar, 1969; spl. agt. FBI, 1969-71; asst. dist. atty. Tulsa County, 1971-72; practice in Tulsa, 1972—; partner firm Blackstack, Joyce, Pollard, Blackstock & Montgomery, 1978—; mem. Okla. Ho. of Reps. from 70th Dist., 1972-74, Okla. Senate from 38th Dist., 1974—; chmn. Met. Tulsa Transit Authority, 1979—. Mem. Arts and Humanities Council Bd. Tulsa. Republican. Roman Catholic. Home: 2423 E 31st St Tulsa OK 74105 Office: 515 South Main Mall Tulsa OK 74103

KEATING, JEAN CLARKE, ednl. adminstr.; b. Athens, Ga., Mar. 3, 1938; d. Zack H. and Katherine E. (Cason) Clarke; B.S. in Math. and Physics, U. Ga., 1958; M.S. in Info. Systems, George Washington U., 1978; m. Gerald Maurice Keating, July 9, 1960. Aerospace engr. NASA, Langley Research Center, Langley Field, Va., 1958-68; dir. spl. programs Coll. of William and Mary, Williamsburg, Va., 1971-73, asst. dir. instl. research, 1973-78; higher edn. coordinator State Council Higher Edn. for Va., 1979—. Spl. Service award NASA, 1968; named Va.'s Young Woman of 1970. Va. Assn. Ednl. Data Systems (dir. 1975—), Coll. and Univ. Machine Records Assn., Gen. Fedn. Women's Clubs, Hampton Assn. for Arts and Humanities (dir. 1969-72), Va. Lung Assn. (mem. state health edn. com. 1974-75). Clubs: Jr. Woman's (pres. 1968-69, 70-71), Girl's (dir. 1970-71) (Hampton); Woman's of Williamsburg (pres. 1974). Contbr. articles to profl. publs. Home: 209 Matoaka Ct Williamsburg VA 23185 Office: State Council Higher Edn Va 700 Fidelity Bldg Richmond VA 23219

KEAY, JAMES WILLIAM, banker; b. Manley, Iowa, Nov. 16, 1921; s. William J. and Valborg (Biorn) K.; B.A. in Econs., U. Colo., 1947; M.B.A., Northwestern U., 1948; grad. Rutgers U. Grad. Sch. Banking, 1956, Advanced Mgmt. Program, Harvard, 1964; m. Frances Lee Oglesby, Mar. 20, 1954; children—Martha Evelyn, James William, Stuart Enslie. With Republic Nat. Bank, Dallas, 1949—, asst. cashier, 1953, asst. v.p., 1953-56, v.p., 1956-61, sr. v.p., 1961-63, mem. exec. com., 1962—, exec. v.p. loans, 1963-65, exec. v.p. adminstrn., 1965, pres., dir., 1965-74, chmn. bd., chief exec. officer, 1974—; vice chmn. bd., dir. Republic of Tex. Corp., 1974—; dir. United Fidelity Life Ins. Co., Gen. Am. Oil Co. Tex., Gen. Automotive Parts Corp., Dallas Power & Light Co., Austin Industries. Bd. dirs. State Fair of Tex. Served with AUS, World War II; ETO, MTO. Mem. Assn. Res. City Bankers, Am. Bankers Assn., Pi Gamma Mu. Lutheran (elder). Clubs: Augusta Nat. Golf, Idlewild, Brook Hollow Golf, Dallas, Dallas Petroleum, Dallas Country, Terpsichorean, Preston Trail Golf (Dallas). Home: 4550 Westway Dallas TX 75205 Office: Republic Nat Bank PO Box 225961 Dallas TX 75265

KECK, ALFRED RAY, foam co. owner; b. Marlow, Okla., Oct. 7, 1936; s. Victor John and Violet Juanita (Rowe) K.; degree in bus. adminstrn., Gen. Motors accounting, Tyler Comml. Coll., 1956; m. Dorothy Faye Woodlief, June 29, 1956; children—Jimmy Ray, Robert Allen, John Charles. Clk., Santa Fe R.R., Ft. Worth, 1956-58, purchasing agent A. Brandt Furniture Co., Ft. Worth, 1958-62; mgr. Foam Products Co., San Antonio, 1962-64, owner, operator, 1964—; owner, operator San Antonio Upholstery Supply, Capitol City Upholstery Supply, Austin. Bd. dirs. Teen Challenge, San Antonio. Republican. Home: Route 1 Box 139-B Comfort TX 78013 Office: 1119 N Mesquite St San Antonio TX 78202

KECK, RAYMOND CHARLES, oil, minerals, chems. mfg. co. exec.; b. N.Y.C., May 31, 1919; s. Charles and Freida F. (Haab) K.; B.S., Pace Coll., 1940; postgrad. Coll. of Pacific, 1941, Columbia U., 1945-47, N.Y. U. Extension, 1947-49; m. Lillian Lenford, June 27, 1949; children—Robert Charles, Richard Charles. Trainee, Kelly Mason Advt. Agy., N.Y.C., 1937; copywriter advt. dept. Cities Service Co., N.Y.C., 1937-38, prodn. mgr. advt. dept., 1945-47, asst. advt. mgr., 1947-50, mgr. advt.-sales promotion dept. Cities Service Oil Co., N.Y.C., 1951-59, mgr. advt. dept. Cities Service Co., N.Y.C., 1959-62, Tulsa, 1962-76, mgr. corp. advt. and publs., 1976—; pres. C. S. Advt. Inc. Bd. dirs. Tulsa Better Bus. Bur., 1972-75. Served as meteorologist USAAF, 1941-45; CBI. Recipient Clio TV Comml. awards, 1969-71; Addy awards Am. Advt. Fedn., 1970, 72, 78; awards Printing Industries N.Y., 1973-75. Mem. Mktg. Communications Execs. Internat. (life, co-founder 1964, dir. 1964-69), Assn. Nat. Advertisers, Am. Advt. Fedn. Clubs: Tulsa Country (dir. since 1979—), Petroleum. Home: 7207 S Richmond St Tulsa OK 74136 Office: Cities Service Co Corp Advt and Publs 110 W 7th St Tulsa OK 74102

KEDER, VIRKO, systems engr.; b. Tartu, Estonia, Sept. 20, 1930; s. Jakob and Leida (Anton) K.; came to U.S., 1949, naturalized, 1955; B.S. in Elec. Engring., Purdue U., 1955, M.S., 1956; postgrad. N.Y. U., 1959-65; m. Ellen Dagmar Voll, Nov. 19, 1960; 1 dau., Tiina. Mem. tech. staff Bell Telephone Labs., Murray Hill, N.J., 1956-65, Computer Scis. Corp., Paramus, N.J., 1965-68, Mitre Corp., McLean, Va., 1968—. Bd. dirs. Estonian Students Fund in U.S.A., Inc., 1960—, pres., 1958-59. Mem. Assn. Estonian Am. Students in U.S.A. (pres. 1961-62), Estonian Am. Nat. Council (officer 1964-67), Washington Estonian Soc. (pres. 1973), IEEE (sr.), IEEE Computer Soc., Aerospace and Electronic Systems Soc., Armed Forces Communications and Electronics Assn., Sigma Xi, Tau Beta Pi, Eta Kappa Nu. Lutheran. Club: Rotalia, Inc. (pres. 1960, 1963). Contbr. articles to tech. jours. Home: 6548 Hitt Ave McLean VA 22101 Office: 1820 Dolley Madison Blvd McLean VA 22101

KEDIA, PRAHLAD RAY, lawyer; b. Lachhmangarh, Rajasthan, India, July 4, 1937; s. Kaluram Shrinarayan and Kanchandevi (Sureka) Kedia; came to U.S., 1971, naturalized, 1975; intermediate sci. degree U. Rajasthan, 1957; LL.B., U. Bombay, 1961, LL.M., 1965; m. Sushila Poddar, Mar. 7, 1962; children—Kavita, Sarita, Anita. Asst. mgr. Jaipur (India) Hotel, 1954-57; asst. accountant, then accountant Indora Malwa United Mills Ltd., Bombay, 1958-65; called to bar, 1965; practicing atty. High Ct., Bombay, 1965-71; asst. prof. law Grambling (La.) State U., 1971—, dir. criminal justice center, 1975-78, dir. criminal justice and law adminstn. center, head dept. criminal justice, 1979—, adv. bd. Criminal Justice and Paralegal programs, 1975—; leader seminars. Active Ruston (La.) Peach Festival, 1972-77. Grantee U.S. Dept. Justice, HEW. Mem. Acad. Criminal Justice Scis., Bombay Bar Assn., Am. Legal Studies Assn., Am. Bus. Law Assn., Am. Criminal Justice Assn., Lambda Alpha Epsilon. Author papers in field. Home: Route 2 Box 507 Hwy 80 Choudrant LA 71227 Office: PO Box 383 Grambling LA 71245

KEE, RUTH THOMPSON, nurse; b. Smithville, Miss., Apr. 29, 1929; d. Ira Denton and Betty (Ferguson) Thompson; grad. Columbus City Hosp. Sch. Nursing, 1952; m. Mar. 16, 1957; children—Ronald Denson, Donald Ferguson. Staff nurse operating room Columbus City Hosp., 1952-55, Newman (Ga.) City Hosp., 1955-70; asst. dir. nursing, dir. nursing and operating room supr. Gwinnett County Hosp. Authority, Buford, Ga., 1970-77; head nurse Winder (Ga.) Barrow Hosp., 1978—. Mem. Ga. Nursing Service Dirs. Assn., Assn. Operating Room Nurses. Republican. Baptist. Club: Ladies Auxillary of VFW. Home: PO Box 1046 Winder GA 30680

KEECH, CHARLES DEVHON, optical co. exec.; b. Anniston, Ala., Jan. 31, 1950; s. Jesse DeVhon and Agnes K.; student Gadsden Jr. Coll., 1969-70. Loan officer Cumberland Capital, Bessmer, Ala., 1969-70; foreman Cumberland Optical, Nashville, 1970-71; foreman Keech Optical Lab., Anniston, 1971-76, pres., 1976—; pres. Keech Hearing Aid Center, Anniston, 1973—, also chmn. Pres., Wak-Way Displays of Tenn., Chattanooga, 1978. Mem., Anniston Zoning Bd., 1979. Mem. Nat. Hearing Aid Soc., Ala. Hearing Aid Assn., Optical Assn. Am., Ala. Optical Assn. Club: Jaycees (dir. 1971-75). Office: 1804 Noble St Anniston AL 36201

KEEFE, JOHN RUSSELL, accountant; b. Poughkeepsie, N.Y., June 2, 1946; s. Robert Lincoln and Mildred Doris (Pullman) K.; B.B.A., Stetson U., 1968; m. Elizabeth Edith Haddock, July 27, 1967; children—Pierce Russell. Tchr., Nova Sr. High Sch., Ft. Lauderdale, Fla., 1968-70; staff accountant Ringle, Heeb & Co., C.P.A.'s, Ft. Lauderdale, 1970-72; mng. partner Keefe, McCullough & Co., C.P.A.'s, Margate, Fla., 1972—; pres. Top Floor, Inc., Margate, 1973-77; treas. Don Jon Enterprises, Inc., Margate, 1973-77, pres., 1978-80. Sponsor, Jr. Exchange Club of Nova High Sch., Ft. Lauderdale, 1968-70; dir. Margate summer baseball program, 1977-79; mem. com. Big League World Series, Ft. Lauderdale. Mem.

Margate Athletic Assn. (pres. 1974-75), Margate Khoury League (treas. 1972—, pres. 1978-80), Am. Inst. C.P.A.'s, Nat. Football Found., Fla. Inst. C.P.A.'s, Omicron Delta Kappa, Sigma Nu (comdr. 1967-68), Green Circle (pres. 1966-67). Clubs: Rotary, Optimist (pres. 1970-71), Stetson U. Hatter Booster. Home: 104 Palm Dr Margate FL 33063 Office: 400 N State Rd 7 Suite 340 Margate FL 33063

KEEFER, THOMAS ADRIAN, mech. engr.; b. Charleston, W.Va., Sept. 26, 1952; s. Charles and Mamie Arretta (Carpenter) K.; B.S. in Mech. Engring., W.Va. Inst. Tech., 1974; m. Rose Linda Lacy, Oct. 12, 1974; children—Christina Dawn, Charles Thomas. Design project engr. duPont Co., Belle, W.Va., 1974-75, plant safety engr., 1975-79, mech. area maintenance supr., 1979—. Democrat. Methodist. Home: 54 Riverdale Estates Winfield WV 25213 Office: 901 W Dupont Ave Belle WV 25015

KEEHNER, ELIZABETH KATARINE SCHARHAG, resort exec.; b. Mannheim, Germany, July 11, 1931; came to U.S., 1951, naturalized, 1959; s. Heinrich Joseph and Caty (Ickstadt) Scharhag; student U. Md., 1951; m. Ronald H. Keehner, Sept. 15, 1968; 1 dau., Suzanne. Hostess, Howard Johnson, 1956; trouble shooting mgr. Interstate Hosts, 1959-63; with Walker Enterprises, Balt., 1965-70; with Circle D Resort, Bastrop, Tex., 1971—, now gen. mgr. Mem. Nat. C. of C. Home and Office: Box 687 Bastrop TX 78602

KEEL, DONALD STEPHEN, univ. adminstr.; b. N.Y.C., June 10, 1946; s. Donald Knight and Katherine K.; B.A., U. N.C., Chapel Hill, 1968; m. Pamela Jane Mosier, Nov. 15, 1975. Unit dir. major corps. div. United Fund Greater N.Y., N.Y.C., 1968-69; cons. C.W. Shaver & Co., Inc., N.Y.C., 1969-73; dir. planning and devel. Nat. Recreation and Park Assn., Washington, 1973-74; v.p. for devel. services Taft Corp., Washington, 1974-76; dir. devel. Nat. Public Radio, Washington, 1976-77; sr. asso. McManis Assos., Washington, 1977-79; dir. corp. relations U. S.C., Columbia, 1979—; cons. Mem. Council for Advancement and Support of Edn. Club: N.Y. Athletic. Home: 4 Gibbes Ct Columbia SC 29201 Office: U SC 1716 College St Columbia SC 29208

KEEN, MARY LOIS, land mgmt. and devel. co. exec.; b. Colquitt, Ga., Jan. 8, 1937; d. Byron Roger and Mildred Louise (Oxenrider) Pope; student U. Tenn., 1977, 78, Tenn. State Tech. Sch., 1978; m. Hampton C. Keen, May 20, 1956; children—Michael, Mark. Gen. office worker Dr. W. C. Price and Dr. Fred Gachet, 1955-57; cashier Time Loan Co., 1956-57; clk. Coastal Gas Co., 1959-61; sec., receptionist Dr. E. H. Austin, Dr. Thomas Philpot, 1967-69; sec. First Presbyn. Ch., 1970-71; reexam. clk. Knoxville Community Devel. Corp. (Tenn.), 1971-77; sec., receptionist Bull Run Oil Co., Oak Ridge, 1976-77; mgr. M & M Properties, Knoxville, 1977—. Active March of Dimes. Mem. Exec. Women Assn., Am. Bus. Women Assn. (v.p. Cumberland Belles 1978-79), Knoxville C. of C., Knoxville Apt. Council, Beta Sigma Phi. Democrat. Baptist. Home: 4220 Cranbrook Dr Powell TN 37849 Office: PO Box 6179 Knoxville TN 37914

KEEN, PAUL, govt. ofcl.; b. Trammel, Ky., Sept. 27, 1900; s. Edward Jackson and Lou Etta (Holland) K.; A.A., Bethel Coll., 1921; A.B., Union U., 1922; J.D., U. Ky.; m. Sarah Anne Howell, June 12, 1933; children—Edward Shain, John Paul. Prin., Ozark (Ala.) City High Sch., 1922-23, Dale County High Sch., Ozark, 1923-24; admitted to Ky. bar, 1926, D.C. bar, 1932; with D.C. Govt., 1928-69, chief property insp., 1928-42, bus. mgr. Glenn Dale Sanatorium, 1942-50, dep. supt. Dist. Gen. Hosp., 1950-57, exec. asst. Dept. Pub. Health, 1957-64, regulations devel. officer, 1964-69, ret., 1969. Bd. dirs. Found. Mentally Retarded and Handicapped Children of Chesapeake dist. Civitan Internat., Inc., 1959-79, pres., 1976-78. Recipient Distinguished Service award U. Ky., 1971; Honor Key award Civitan Internat. Mem. D.C. (life), Fed. (chmn. admissions com. 1970-73) bar assns., D.C. Bar, Met. Washington Bd. Trade (life), Ky. Soc. Washington (past pres.), Phi Alpha Delta. Baptist. Clubs: Civitan, U. Ky. Alumni, Nat. Lawyers, Capitol Hill (life) (Washington). Home: 209 W Greenway Blvd Falls Church VA 20046

KEENAN, CHARLES WILLIAM, educator; b. Ft. Worth, Apr. 10, 1922; s. Charles and Catherine (Markey) K.; B.S., Centenary Coll. La., 1943; Ph.D., U. Tex., 1949; m. Elizabeth Alden Pabody, Feb. 3, 1945; children—John Markey. Faculty dept. chemistry U. Tenn., Knoxville, 1949—, prof., 1958—, asso. dean Liberal Arts, 1973-77. NSF fellow Cambridge (Eng.) U., 1957-58, 64-65. Served with USNR, 1945-46. Recipient Outstanding Tchr. award U. Tenn., 1972, Phi Eta Sigma teaching excellence award, 1979. Mem. Am. Chem. Soc., AAUP, Phi Beta Kappa, Sigma Xi, Phi Kappa Phi. Author: (with D.C. Kleinfelter and J.H. Wood) General College Chemistry, 1957, 61, 66, 71, 76, 80; (with W.E. Bull and J.H. Wood) Fundamentals of College Chemistry, 1963, 68, 72. Home: 4501 Appleby Ridge Knoxville TN 37920

KEENE, JAMES DENNIS, respiratory therapist; b. Houston, May 27, 1949; s. James Dixie and Mildred Lurlene (Pickens) K.; student San Jacinto Coll., 1967-68; A.A.S., Houston Community Coll., 1971; m. Susan LaDora Eason, July 25, 1970; children—Dixie Lee, Jennifer Robyn. Clin. instr. respiratory therapy program San Jacinto Coll., Pasadena, 1976, adv. bd., 1976; tech. dir. pulmonary medicine St. Joseph E. Hosp., Memphis, 1977-78; tech. dir. respiratory therapy, Pasadena Bayshore Hosp., 1978—. Mem. Christian Men's Bus. com., Pasadena, 1979. Pasadena Bayshore Hosp. scholar, 1970-71; registered respiratory therapist. Mem. Am. Assn. for Respiratory Therapy. Baptist. Office: 4000 Spencer St Pasadena TX 77504

KEENER, LARRY HUBERT, state senator; b. Gadsden, Ala., Jan. 1, 1944; s. Hubert James and Helen Louise (Payne) K.; student Jacksonville (Ala.) State U., 1964; LL.B., Cumberland Sch. Law, Samford U., 1967; m. Mary Thrasher Gibbs, Dec. 29, 1963; children—Larry Hubert, Sharon Diane. Admitted to Ala. bar, 1967, since practiced in Gadsden; partner firm Floyd, Keener & Cusimano, 1977—; dep. dist. atty. Etowah County, 1972-74; dir. Gadsden Water Works and Sewer Bd., 1976-78; mem. Ala. Senate from 10th Dist., 1978—. Pres., Boys' Clubs Etowah County, 1979. Named Outstanding Young Man in Gadsden, 1972. Mem. Am. bar Assn., Am. Trial Lawyers Assn., Ala. Bar Assn., Ala. Trial Lawyers Assn., Etowah County Bar Assn. (pres. 1977-78), Gadsden C. of C. Democrat. Clubs: Lions, Quarterback, Mountain Top (Gadsden). Home: 120 Argyle Ln Gadsden AL 35901 Office: 816 Chestnut St Gadsden AL 35901

KEENEY, ARTHUR JOSEPH, newspaper pub.; b. Akron, Ohio, Jan. 12, 1925; s. Arthur Joseph and Blanche Pearl K.; student Albion (Mich.) Coll., 1946-49; B.S. in Journalism, Northwestern U., 1951, M.S. in Journalism, 1951; m. Gioia M. Passarelli, Aug. 25, 1951; children—Arthur Louis, Kevin Charles, Megan Marie, Michael Joseph. Sales rep. Galesburg (Ill.) Register-Mail, 1951-52; promotion dir. Brush Moore Newspapers, Canton, Ohio, 1952-61, Houston Post, 1961-64; mktg. dir. Houston Sports Assn., 1964-66; exec. dir. Alley Theatre, Houston, 1966-71; pub. Corsicana (Tex.) Daily Sun, 1971—; pres. Southwest Group, Harte-Hanks Communications, v.p. parent co.; lectr. media planning and promotion. Served with inf., AUS, 1943-46. Decorated 2 Purple Hearts, 2 Bronze Stars; recipient media award Tex. Arts Council, 1978. Mem. Am. Newspaper Pubs. Assn., Internat. Newspaper Promotion Assn. (pres. So. and Midwest regions), So. Newspaper Pubs. Assn., Internat. Newspaper Controllers and Fin. Officers, Am. Mktg. Assn., Am. Mgmt. Assn., Sigma Delta Chi, Corsicana C. of C. (pres. 1977). Clubs: Cipango-21 (Dallas); Lubbock (Tex.) City. Home: 2208 Highland Circle Corsicana TX 75110 Office: 401 W Collin St Corsicana TX 75110

KEENEY, WILLIAM EDWIN, JR., space systems co. exec.; b. Clarinda, Iowa, Aug. 22, 1930; s. William Edwin and Dorothy LaVerne (Enerson) K.; B.B.A., U. Nebr., 1952, B.E.E., 1958; m. Doree Jeanne Canaday, Oct. 27, 1951; children—William Edwin, Brant Andrew, Daniel Paul. With AC Electronics div. Gen. Motors, Milw., 1959-67, successively as systems engr., engring. supr., systems engring. group head; with Perkin-Emler Corp., Wilton, Ct., 1967—, successively as spacecraft cabin analyzer program mgr., test equipment sect. mgr., systems integration sect. mgr., systems engring. dept. mgr., solid state sensor camera program mgr.; dir. govt. orbital payloads Harris Corp., Melbourne, Fla., 1977—; asst. prof. U. Notre Dame, South Bend, Ind., 1954-56. Mem. Danbury (Conn.) City Council, 1973-77; bd. dir. Assn. Religious Communities, Danbury; chmn. com. Conn. council Boy Scouts Am. Served to lt. USN, 1952-56. Mem. IEEE, Smithsonian Inst., Air Force Assn. Democrat. Presbyterian. Book reviewer Jour. Astronatical Scis., 1976—. Home: 305 Highway A1A Satellite Beach FL 32937 Office: PO Box 37 Melbourne FL 32901

KEEPLER, MANUEL, mathematician; b. Atlanta, Nov. 4, 1944; s. Gus Henry and Charssie Nobell (Prothro) K.; B.S., Morehouse Coll., 1965; M.A. (Woodrow Wilson fellow), Columbia U., 1967; Ph.D. (Presbyterian Grad. fellow, So. Funds Found. fellow), U. N.Mex., 1973; m. Dannie Lee Hornsby, June 17, 1966; 1 dau., Adriane Kapayl. Instr., Miles Coll., Birmingham, Ala., 1966-68; asst. prof. Va. State U., Petersburg, 1970-71; chmn., asso. prof. Langston (Okla.) U., 1971-72; chmn., asso. prof. S.C. State Coll., Orangeburg, 1973-76, asso. prof. math. and computer sci., 1976—. Mem. Am. Math. Soc., Am. Statis. Assn., Inst. Math. Stats., Math. Assn. Am., Nat. Assn. Mathematicians, NAACP, U.S. Chess Fedn., Esquire XIII Social Frat., Phi Beta Sigma. Baha'i. Home: Box 1656 SC State Coll Orangeburg SC 29117 Office: Nance Hall SC State Coll Orangeburg SC 29117

KEFAUVER, ELIZABETH MCGEE, educator; b. Dallas, Nov. 8, 1923; d. Morris George and Lois (McKee) McGee; B.F.A., U. Okla., Norman, 1945; M.E. in Supervision, Trinity U., San Antonio, 1965; m. John Moody Kefauver; children—Alexander Tedford Barclay III, Christopher Moris Barclay, Benner McKee Barclay. Tchr. art Fox Tech High Sch., San Antonio, 1959-67; art supr. San Antonio Ind. Sch. Dist., 1970—. Trustee S.W. Craft Center, 1970—. Bd. dirs. Opera Guild, San Antonio Symphony; v.p. Ruth Taylor Fine Arts Center, Trinity U. Mem. NEA, Tex. State Tchrs. Assn., Nat. (life), Tex. (life) art edn. assns., Ala. Area Assn. for Supervision and Curriculum Devel., San Antonio Area Sch. Arts Assn. Certified as profl. life supr., Tex., as tchr., Tex. Home: 216 Lilac Ln San Antonio TX 78209 Office: 141 Lavaca St San Antonio TX 78210

KEFFLER, WILLIAM ANTHONY, city adminstr.; b. Brownfield, Tex., Sept. 23, 1953; s. Joseph William and Ruth Ann (Koehler) K.; B.A., U. Notre Dame, 1975; M.P.A. (Clarence E. Ridley scholar 1976), Tex. Tech. U., 1977. Planning asst. Permian Basin Regional Planning Commn., Midland, Tex., 1974-75; legis. asst. to U.S. congressman, 1976; adminstrv. asst. City of Richardson (Tex.), 1977-79, asst. to city mgr., 1979—; teaching asst. Tex. Tech. U., 1975-77. Mem. Internat. City Mgmt. Assn., Urban Mgmt. Assts. N. Tex. (pres. 1979), Tex. City Mgmt. Assn. (dir. 1980—), N.Tex. City Mgmt. Assn. Home: 8755 Southwestern St Apt 1123 Dallas TX 75080 Office: 319 E Main St Richardson TX 75080

KEHL, JOSEPH JOHN, data processing co. exec.; b. Louisville, Jan. 20, 1922; s. Joseph Peter and Louise Victoria (Young) K.; m. Martha Jean Leachman, May 9, 1945; children—Michael Richard, Mary Constance, Denise Jean. Data entry operator L & N R.R., Louisville, 1941-55; unit record operator Am. Fire & Casualty Co., Orlando, Fla., 1955-58; with Martin Marietta Data Systems, Orlando, 1958—, sr. bus. systems analyst, 1971—. Served with USNR, 1942-45. Mem. Martin Marietta Mgmt. Club. Republican. Roman Catholic. Club: Elks. Home: 403 Parson Brown Way Longwood FL 32750 Office: Bldg 6000 Lake Elinore Dr Orlando FL 32801

KEHOE, CATHARINE ELLEN, pvt. sch. owner, educator; b. New Orleans, Feb. 3, 1929; d. Charles Vincent and Catharine Ann (Roth) Kehoe; B.A., Ursuline Coll., 1949; M.A. with honors, U. So. Miss., 1951. Head dept. health, phys. edn. Ursuline Coll., New Orleans, 1951-53; chmn. dept. health, phys. edn. St. Mary's Dominican Coll., New Orleans, 1953-64; pres. Kehoe Day Camp and Swimming Sch., New Orleans, 1957—; pres., prin., prof. Kehoe Acad., New Orleans, 1962—. Vol. water safety, first aid instr. ARC, 1945-70; chmn. New Orleans bd. Nat. Ofcls. Rating Com., 1957-58. Fellow AAHPER; mem. AAUP, Nat., La. assns. secondary sch. prins., Nat., So. assns. phys. edn. coll. women, Internat. Platform Assn., Phi Epsilon Kappa. Home: 265 Midway Dr New Orleans LA 70123 Office: Kehoe Acad 10931 Jefferson Hwy New Orleans LA 70123

KEHOE, ROBERT EMMET, publishing exec.; b. Scranton, Pa., June 23, 1943; s. Michael Francis and Eleanor Theresa K.; B.S., U. Fla., 1968; m. Mimi Buxbaum, Sept. 1, 1968; children—Kelly Sue, Kimberly Ann. Gen. mgr. Wilmar Inc., Charlotte, N.C., 1968-71; v.p. Synetics, Inc., Charlotte, N.C., 1971-74; v.p., gen. mgr. Trend Publs., Inc., Tampa, 1974-80, also dir.; pres. Key Energy Systems, Inc., Tampa, 1980—; cons. communications field. Served with AUS, 1964-66. Mem. Assn. Area Bus. Publs. (pres.), Club: Exchange. Lectr., speaker So. and sunbelt economy. Office: PO Box 2350 Tampa FL 33601

KEHRBERG, JOHN HERMAN, assn. exec.; b. Sheldon, Iowa, July 22, 1935; s. Richard Frank and Mary Elizabeth (Utz) K.; B.S., Missouri Valley Coll., 1957; postgrad. U. Wis., 1961-62; m. Shirley Mae Nordine, Apr. 25, 1964; children—Mary, Karl. Mem. staff Am. Hardware Mut. Ins. Co., Mpls., 1957-58, Boy Scouts Am., Lake Geneva, Wis., 1958-60, Rand McNally & Co., Chgo., 1960-61; with Vols. of Am., Mpls., 1963-67, Houston, 1968—, Tex. state officer, 1972—, trustee So. Regional Contingency Fund, 1977-78. Served with U.S. Army, 1957-58. Cert. fin. planner Coll. for Fin. Planning. Mem. Religious Public Relations Council (pres. Gulf Coast chpt. 1977-78), Nat. Soc. Fundraising Execs. (pres. Houston chpt. 1979), Public Relations Soc. Am. (accredited), Tex. Correctional Assn. (cert. correctional worker), Am. Correctional Assn., Am. Protestant Correctional Chaplains Assn., Inst. Cert. Fin. Planners, Internat. Assn. Fin. Planners, Nat. Rifle Assn., Tex. State Rifle Assn. Clubs: Houston Press, Houston Metro Racquet, Kiwanis (dir. Houston 1978-79). Home: 7703 Betty Jane Ln Houston TX 77055 Office: Vols of Am PO Box 1621 Houston TX 77001

KEIBER, HOLLAN FREDERICK, ophthalmologist; b. Stark, Fla., Feb. 9, 1946; s. Henry Frederick and Marie K.; B.S., U. Fla., 1968; M.D., U. Miami, 1972; m. Sharon Elizabeth Guldi, Feb. 24, 1979; children—Scott Frederick, Michael Lance, Eric Christian. Intern, Greater Balt. Med Hosp., resident in ophthalmology, 1972-75; practice medicine specializing in ophthalmology, Sebring, Fla.; mem. staffs Highland Hosp., Gen. Hosp., Walker Meml. Hosp. Med. dir. Fla. Brethren Homes, 1976-78; med. advisor Highlands County Schoolboard, 1978—. Diplomate Am. Bd. Ophthalmology. Fellow A.C.S.; mem. Fla. Soc. Ophthalmology, Fla. Med. Assn., Highlands County Med. Assn. (pres. 1979—). Republican. Lutheran. Clubs: Elks, Lions. Office: 112 Med Centgr Sebring FL 33870

KEIFER, HARRY KEITH, trucking co. exec.; b. Vine Prairie, Ark., Mar. 1, 1943; s. Claude Hunter and Freida May (Fisher) K.; A.A., Westark Community Coll., 1962; B.S.E., U. Ark., 1964; m. Gloria Jean Ernst, June 2, 1967; children—Harry Keith, Michael Keith. Tchr., Van Buren (Ark.) pub. schs., 1964-68; chief clk. Mo.-Pacific R.R. Co., Ft. Smith, Ark., 1968-69; dir. traffic and warehousing DeSoto, Inc., Ft. Smith, 1969-78; asst. to pres. David Beneux Produce & Trucking, Inc., Mulberry, Ark., 1978—; instr. transp. Westark Community Coll., Ft. Smith. Mem. Transp. Club of Ft. Smith, Delta Nu Alpha. Methodist. Home: 407 Azure Hills Dr Van Buren AR 72956 Office: David Beneux Produce & Trucking Inc Hwy 64W Mulberry AR 72947

KEIL, ERNEST WILLIAM, psychiatrist; b. Russell, Kans., Dec. 25, 1914; s. Victor Emanuel and Elizabeth (Pope) K.; B.A., Fort Hays State Coll., Hays, Kans., 1947; M.D., U. Kan. at Lawrence, 1951; m. Judith Morin, Feb. 11, 1944; children—Judith Elizabeth (Mrs. Henry Laurens), Katherine Regina (Mrs. Leo Tellier), Ernest William, Mary Maynard. Intern, Scott and White Meml. Hosp., Temple, Tex., 1951-52; practice medicine, specializing in family practice, Temple, 1952-61; resident psychiatry Austin (Tex.) State Hosp., 1961-64; chief psychiatry VA Center, Temple, 1964-69, 75, staff psychiatrist, 1971-75, chief psychiatry, 1975-80; chief staff VA Hosp., Bedford, Mass., 1969-71; mem. psychiat. staff Mass. Gen. Hosp., Boston, 1970-71. Clin. instr. psychiatry Harvard U., Boston, 1970-71; mem. adv. com. on mental health Commr. Health, State of Tex., 1956-64. Mem. Temple Indsl. Found., 1956-80; mem. Bell County (Tex.) Farm Bur., 1958-80. Bd. dirs. Harvest House, Temple, 1969, 71-73. Served with AC, USNR, 1941-45, comdr. Res., ret. Mem. Tex. Geriatric Soc. (charter, v.p. 1955), Tex. Soc. Aging (pres. 1957, dir. 1956-70), Tex. Med. Assn. (mem. com. on aging 1957-63, prize for therapy exhibit 1966), Am., Tex. psychiat. assns., Boston Soc. Geriatric Psychiatry, Phi Chi, Exchange Club (pres. chpt. 1968-69). Contbr. articles to profl. jours. Home: 107 E King St Temple TX 76501

KEILLER, JAMES BRUCE, coll. dean, clergyman; b. Racine, Wis., Nov. 21, 1938; s. James Allen and Grace (Modder) K.; diploma Beulah Heights Bible Coll., 1957; B.A., William Carter Coll., 1963, Ed.D. (hon.), 1973; LL.B., Blackstone Sch. Law, 1964; M.A., Evang. Theol. Sem., 1965, B.D., 1966, Th.D., 1968; M.A. in Ednl. Adminstrn., Atlanta U., 1977; Ph.D. cand., Ga. State U.; m. Darsel Lee Bundy, Feb. 8, 1959; 1 dau., Susanne Elizabeth. Ordained to ministry Internat. Pentecostal Assemblies, 1957; pastor Maranatha Temple, Boston, 1957-58, Midland (Mich.) Full Gospel Ch., 1958-64; dean Beulah Heights Bible Coll., Atlanta, 1964—, trustee, 1964—; nat. dir. youth and Sunday sch. dept. Internat. Pentecostal Assemblies, 1958-64, dir. world missions, Atlanta, 1964-76, youth commn., 1958-64, missions com., 1964-76, exec. bd., 1964-76, missionary editor Bridegroom's Messenger, 1964—; dir. global missions Internat. Pentecostal Ch. of Christ, 1976—, mem. exec. com., 1976—. Named Alumnus of Year, William Carter Coll., 1965. Mem. Woodmen of World, So. Accrediting Assn. Bible Insts. and Bible Colls. (exec. sec.), Soc. Pentecostal Studies, Ind. Order Foresters, Evang. Theol. Soc. Club: Kiwanis (pres. elect). Home: 892 Berne St SE Atlanta GA 30316 Office: 906 Berne St SE Atlanta GA 30316

KEIM, CHRISTOPHER PETER, ednl. cons.; b. Tecumseh, Nebr., Apr. 6, 1906; s. Jacob Henry and Mary (Pohlenz) K.; A.B., Nebr. Wesleyan U., 1927, D.Sc. (hon.), 1960; postgrad. U. Pitts., 1927-28; M.S., U. Nebr., 1932, Ph.D. (Samuel Avery fellow), 1940; m. Lucille Parli, June 25, 1929; children—Virginia Ann Keim Hayes, Robert Christopher. Equipment engr. Lincoln Telephone Co., 1928-31; hwy. engr. State of Nebr., 1932-33; head dept. phys. sci. York Coll., 1933-37; instr. chemistry U. Tulsa, 1940-41; research engr. Sylvania Electric Products Co., 1941-42; research fellow Mellon Inst. Indsl. Research, 1942-44; research physicist, supt. pilot plant for electromagnetic separation of uranium isotopes Tenn. Eastman Corp., 1944-47; dir. stable isotopes div., dir. tech. info. div. Oak Ridge Nat. Lab., 1947-71; cons. edn. and sci. info., 1971—; cons. Roane State Community Coll., 1971—; dir. Mgmt. Services, Inc., 1952-75, pres., gen. mgr., 1973-75; dir. Oak Ridge Utilities Dist., 1950-71. Mem. bd. higher edn. Holston conf. United Methodist Ch. Fellow AAAS; mem. Tenn. Acad. Sci. (pres. 1960), Aircraft Owners and Pilots Assn., Pilots Assn., Oak Ridge C. of C., Sigma Xi. Republican. Clubs: Rotary, Masons, Shriners. Contbr. articles to profl. jours.; patentee. Home: 102 Orchard Ln Oak Ridge TN 37830

KEIM, KENNETH BEADLEY, ins. co. exec.; b. Moline, Ill., Dec. 5, 1946; s. John Howard and Myrtle Carolyn (Gascon) K.; A.A., Lincoln Coll., 1967; B.B.A., Memphis State U., 1970; m. Kathleen Mary Arnold, Oct. 21, 1972; children—Andrew Lawrence, John Todd. With Northwestern Mut. Life Ins. Co., 1970—, field dir., 1976, dist. agt., Jackson, Tenn., 1978—; ednl. cons. Jackson Assn. Life Underwriters, 1979—; instr. local C.L.U. courses. Exec. bd. Jackson Arts Council, 1979—; bd. dirs. Jackson Symphony Assn., 1979—. Recipient Nat. Sales Achievement award, Northwestern Mutual Life Ins. Co., 1979, Nat. Quality award, 1979; C.L.U. Mem. Nat. Assn. Life Underwriters, Nat. Assn. Certified Life Underwriters. Republican. Presbyterian. Club: Million Dollar Round Table. Home: 37 Chickering St Jackson TN 38301 Office: 203 E Main St Jackson TN 38301

KEISER, EDMUND DAVIS, JR., biologist; b. Appalachia, Va., Feb. 18, 1934; s. Edmund Davis and Ora Elizabeth (Wade) K.; B.S. in Vertebrate Zoology, So. Ill. U., 1956, M.S. in Biol. Scis., 1961; Ph.D. in Zoology, La. State U., 1966; m. Patsy Ann Oswalt, Sept. 3, 1960; children—Mark Edmund, Julie Ann. Dist. sci. coordinator Sch. Dist. 70, Freeburg, Ill., 1958-62; instr. LaSalle-Peru-Oglesby Jr. Coll., 1962-64; instr. U. Southwestern La., 1966, successively asst. prof. biology, asso. prof., prof., to 1976; prof., chmn. dept. biology U. Miss., 1976—; dir. Lafayette Natural History Mus. and Planetarium, 1973; commr. Miss. Dept. Wildlife Conservation, 1978, 80—. Mem. Miss. Gov.'s Select Com. on Radioactivity and Radioactive Waste Depository, 1979, Miss. Natural Heritage Com., 1980—. Served with USMC, 1957. Recipient Disting. Prof. award U. Southwestern La. Found., 1973, Meritorious Service award Gov. Miss., 1979. Fellow Explorers Club N.Y.; mem. Am. Soc. Ichthyologists and Herpetologists, League Herpetologists, Soc. Study Amphibians and Reptiles, Soc. Systematic Zoology, Brit. Herpetological Soc., Herpetological Assn. Africa, Phila. Herpetological Soc., Associacion de Ictiologos e Herpetologos de Latino-Americana, La. Acad. Aci. (exec. council mem. and dir. sci. teaching 1972-74), Miss. Acad. Sci., Md. Herpetological Soc., Southwestern Assn. Naturalists, Caribbean Inst. Sci., Nat. Sci. Tchrs. Assn., Sigma Xi (pres. chpt. 1976, 79-80, pres.-elect chpt. 1978), Beta Beta Beta, Phi Eta Sigma, Phi Kappa Phi. Roman Catholic. Clubs: Civitan (club exec. council 1976) (Lafayette, La.); Exchange (Oxford, Miss.). Contbr. numerous articles to profl. publs. Office: Dept Biology U Miss University MS 38677

KEITH, CHARLES DAVID, educator; b. CaruthersVille, Mo., Feb. 1, 1949; s. Harry Langford and Helen (McTernan) K.; B.S., William Jewell Coll., 1971; M.M., Southwestern Bapt. Theol. Sem., 1974, postgrad., 1975—; m. Mary Eloise Clibourn, Dec. 21, 1969; 1 son, Benjamin Wesley Blake. Dir. choral activities Howard Payne U., Brownwood, Tex., 1975-79; minister of music First Bapt. Ch., Odessa, Mo., 1969-71, South Hills Bapt. Ch., Fort Worth, 1972-74; guest instr. conducting Southwestern Bapt. Theol. Sem., Ft. Worth, 1979—. Recipient Music award Genter Stephens, 1970. Mem. Am. Choral Dirs. Assn., So. Bapt. Ch. Music Conf., Tex. Music Educators Assn., Tex. Choral Dirs. Assn., Phi Mu Alpha Sinfonia, Choristers Guild. Democrat. Club: Lion. Author publs. in field. Home: 3721 Wilkie Way Fort Worth TX 76122 Office: Southwestern Theol Sem Fort Worth TX 76122

KEITH, DAVID BOX, diversified energy co. exec.; b. Brownwood, Tex., May 26, 1934; s. George Enid and LaVert (Box) K.; B.B.A., U. Houston, 1957; m. Suzann Prim, June 7, 1957; children—Lynda, Laurabeth. With Houston Natural Gas Corp., 1960—, advt. mgr., 1965-70, dir. advt. and public relations, 1970-75, v.p. corp. communication, 1975— guest lectr. U. Houston Sch. Communications. Chmn. public affairs com. ARC; mem. exec. com. Girl Scouts Am. Served with U.S. Army, 1958-60. Mem. Am. Advt. Fedn. (vice chmn., Silver medal 1980), Public Relations Soc. Am., Harris County Heritage Soc. (dir.). Methodist. Club: Nat. Press. Home: 11011 Sagemeadow Ln Houston TX 77089 Office: PO Box 1188 Houston TX 77001

KEITH, HOWARD BARTON, thoracic surgeon; b. Enid, Okla., Aug. 23, 1932; s. John Austin and Dorothy Olive (Murphy) K.; M.D., U. Okla., 1957; m. Joanne Norman Keith, Mar. 12, 1954; children—Preston J., Kimberly Ann, Shaun Howard, Spencer Norman. Intern surgery U. Okla. Med. Center, Oklahoma City, 1957-58, resident, 1958-63; practice medicine specializing in surgery, Oklahoma City, 1958-63, specializing in thoracic-cardiovascular and gen. surgery, Shattuck, Okla., 1963—; mem. staff Newman Med. Center, Newman Meml. Hosp.; mem. adv. com. Physicians Asso. Program, 1973—, Adv. Com. on Med. Care for Pub. Assistance Recipients, 1971—; cons. region 6 utilization and peer rev. HEW, 1973-77; med. adviser N.W. Okla., Okla. Tb Assn., 1964—. Mem. bd. edn. Shattuck Pub. Sch. System, 1964-71; bd. dirs. Convalescent Center Shattuck, 1964—; exec. bd. dirs. Great Salt Plains council Boy Scouts Am., 1969—, mem. fin. com., 1970—; bd. dirs. Western Rural Health Services Orgn., 1974—. Mem. Am., Okla. (chmn. state peer rev. com. 1965-77) med. assns., A.C.S. (council 1977, chmn. com. trauma 1978), Soc. Thoracic Surgeons, So. Thoracic Surg. Assn., Southwestern Surg. Congress, Okla. Surg. Assn. (pres. 1977), Okla. Thoracic Soc. Club: Lions (pres. 1967-68). Home: 822 E 8th St Shattuck OK 73858 Office: Newman Med Center Inc 905 S Main St Shattuck OK 73858

KEITH, JAMES MELVIN, clergyman; b. Jackson, Miss., June 22, 1943; s. Hardy Melvin and Mary Frances (Walton) K.; B.A., Miss. Coll., 1966; M.Div., Southwestern Bapt. Theol. Sem., 1969, Th.D., 1975; m. Saundra Elaine Gordon, Aug. 20, 1966; children—James Scott, Gordon Todd, Kristin Elaine. Ordained to ministry So. Baptist Conv., 1967; pastor Antelope Bapt. Ch. (Tex.), 1967-69, 1st Bapt. Ch., Blum, Tex., 1970-71, 1st Bapt. Ch., McGregor, Tex., 1971-72, 1st Bapt. Ch., San Marcos, Tex., 1972-74, 1st Bapt. Ch., Laurel, Miss., 1974-77, 1st Bapt. Ch., Gulfport, Miss., 1977—; grad. asst. dept. preaching Southwestern Bapt. Theol. Sem., 1970-72; adj. prof. Old Testament, William Carey Coll., 1977; adj. prof. homiletics William Carey Coll., 1978—; pres. Jones County Bapt. Pastor's Conf., 1975-76. Bd. trustees William Carey Coll., 1976-79, 79-82, N.P. bd. trustees, 1980. Mem. Miss. Bapt. Conv. (chmn. order of bus. com. 1978), Miss. Coll. Ministerial Alumni Assn. (pres. 1977-78, Southwestern Bapt. Theol. Sem. Alumni (pres. 1980). Home: 29 Bayou View Dr Gulfport MS 39501 Office: PO Drawer 70 Gulfport MS 39501

KEITH, RICHARD MILTON, agrl. engr.; b. Knoxville, Tenn., Dec. 2, 1939; s. Perry Lester and Marguerite Colan (Hawkersmith) K.; B.S. in Agrl. Engring., U. Tenn., 1962; m. Norma Jean Smith, June 14, 1960; children—Lesia Diane, Julie Ann, Pamela Sue. With Soil Conservation Service, U.S. Dept. Agr., 1959—, successively area engr., project engr., planning engr. design engr., Maryville, Tenn., Johnson City, Tenn., Somerville, Tenn., Celina Tenn., 1959-65, Dadeville, Ala., Evergreen, Ala., Auburn Ala., 1965-67, Ozark, Ala., 1967—. Recipient 5 certs. Merit Dept. Agr.; registered profl. engr., Ala. Mem. Am. Assn. Agrl. Engrs., Soil Conservation Soc. Am., Nat. Assn. Conservation Dist. Home: 602 Spring Ln Ozark AL 36360 Office: PO Box 190 Ozark AL 36360

KELLAM, LUCIUS JAMES, JR., oil distbg. co. exec.; b. Belle Haven, Va., Sept. 25, 1911; s. Lucius James and Carrie (Polk) K.; student Trinity Coll., Hartford, Conn., 1931-35, D.Sc. (hon.), 1972; m. Dorothy Douglass, Sept. 12, 1936; children—Dorothy Douglass Kellam Patterson, Lucius James. Treas., Sturgis Oil Co., Inc., Belle Haven, 1935-38, pres., 1938-46; pres., dir. Kellam Distbg. Co., Inc., Belle Haven, 1946-74, chmn. bd., 1974—; pres. Shore Savs. & Loan Corp., Accomac, Va., 1961-70, chmn. bd., 1970—; pres. Kellam Propane Gas Co., Inc., Belle Haven, 1956-74, chmn. bd., 1974—; dir. Va. Nat. Bank, Va. Indsl. & Devel. Corp., Peoples Trust Bank; dir. Smith-Douglass Co., Inc., 1954-65. Chmn., Chesapeake Bay Ferry Commn., 1954-60, Chesapeake Bay Bridge & Tunnel Commn., 1960—; mem. Va. Safety Council, Accomack County, 1951-76; mem. Delmarva Adv. Council, Salisbury, Md., 1964-70, pres., 1970—; mem. indsl. com. Coastal Plains Regional Commn., 1977—. mem. Accomack County Democratic Central Com., 1947-76, State Dem. Fin. Com., 1965; del. Dem. Nat. Conv., 1960; trustee Old Dominion Coll. Ednl. Found., Norfolk, Va., St. James Sch., Hagerstown, Md., Eastern Va. Med. Sch. Found., Broadwater Acad., 1966-73, Exmore, Va., Va. Mus. Fine Arts, 1966-76; trustee, exec. com. Northampton Accomack Meml. Hosp., 1968-76, treas. 1964—, pres., 1967, 68; bd. dirs. Tidewater Automobile Assn., 1941—, v.p., 1964-77, pres., 1977-79; bd. dirs. Internat. Bridge, Tunnel and Turnpike Assn., 1962-66, Tidewater Regional Health Planning Council, 1968-76; bd. dirs., v.p. Ocean Hwy. Assn., 1954—; bd. dirs., 1st v.p. Va. Travel Council, 1953-66; bd. dirs. Va. Travel Devel. Council, 1967—. Served to lt. USNR, 1943-46. Mem. Delta Psi. Episcopalian. Clubs: Rotary (pres. 1939); Eastern Shore Yacht and Country (Melfa, Va.); Princess Anne Country (Virginia Beach, Va.); Commonwealth, Downtown (Richmond, Va.); Harbor (Norfolk, Va.); St. Anthony (N.Y.C.). Home: Mount Pleasant Belle Haven VA 23306 Office: Kellam Distbg Co Belle Haven VA 23306

KELLAM, RICHARD B., fed. judge; b. 1909. Admitted to Va. bar, 1934; chief judge U.S. Dist. Ct. for Eastern Dist. Va. Office: US Courthouse Room 316 Norfolk VA 23510*

KELLEHER, DANIEL JOSEPH, mgmt. cons.; b. Newark, Apr. 29, 1935; s. Daniel Joseph and Marie Helen (Smith) K.; A.A., Monmouth Coll., 1962; B.L.S., U. Okla., 1974, M.L.S., 1976; m. Muriel Agnes Courduff, Feb. 22, 1963; children—John, Daniel. Electronics technician Bendix Corp., Eatontown, N.J., 1953-57; electronics instr. U.S. Army Signal Sch., Ft. Monmouth, N.J., 1957-63; field engr. Dept. Def., ETO, 1963-65, PTO, 1966-68, U.S., 1968-71; security assistance adviser Dept. Def., Washington, 1977—; cons. solar energy El-JaMeer Corp., Atlantic Highland, N.J., Dept. Def., Dept. Energy, Washington. Served in U.S. Army, 1954-57. Recipient Civilian Service medal U.S.A., 1967. Mem. Soc. Advancement Solar Energy (dir.), AAAS, Fedn. Am. Scientists, Solar Energy Industries Assn. Democrat. Roman Catholic. Clubs: Pentagon Officers Athletic (Washington); Elks (Red Bank, N.J.). Home: 12 S Van Dorn St Apt V608 Alexandria VA 22304

KELLEHER, HERBERT DAVID, lawyer; b. Camden, N.J., Mar. 12, 1931; s. Harry and Ruth (Moore) K.; B.A. with honors (Olin scholar), Wesleyan U., 1953; LL.B. with honors (Root Tilden scholar), N.Y. U., 1956; m. Joan Negley, Sept. 9, 1955; children—Julie, Michael, Ruth, David. Admitted to N.J. bar, 1957, Tex. bar, 1962; clk. N.J. Supreme Ct., 1956-59; asso. firm Lum, Biunno & Tompkins, Newark, 1959-61; partner firm Matthews, Nowlin, Macfarlane & Barrett, San Antonio, 1961-69; sr. partner Oppenheimer, Rosenberg, Kelleher & Wheatley, Inc., San Antonio, 1969—; founder, gen. counsel, dir. S.W. Airlines Co., Dallas, 1967—, chmn. bd., 1978—, Mem. bus. adv. council Trinity U., San Antonio, U. Tex. Grad. Sch. Bus. Found. Advisory Council; campaign coordinator Connally for Gov., 1961, 63, 65; Bexar County dir. Bentsen for Senator, 1970, state co-chmn., 1975-76; chmn. Senate Dist. 19 Democratic Com., 1968-70; del. Dem. Nat. Conv., 1964, 68; mem. state steering com. Bentsen for Pres., 1975-76; pres. Travelers Aid Soc. San Antonio; pres. bd. trustees St. Mary's Hall, San Antonio. Mem. Am., San Antonio, N.J. bar assns., State Bar Tex., San Antonio C. of C. (dir.), Order of Alamo, Tex. Cavaliers. Home: 144 Thelma Dr San Antonio TX 78212 Office: 711 Navarro St San Antonio TX 78205

KELLER, ALEXANDER PAUL, JR., physician; b. Athens, Ga., May 19, 1921; s. Alexander and Henriette (Douen) K.; B.S., U. Ga., 1941; M.D., Emory U., 1944; m. Saidee Hodgson, Sept. 6, 1942; children—Alexander Paul III, Susanne, Patricia, Dianne. Intern, Emory U. Hosp., 1944; resident in eye, ear, nose, throat, Lawson VA Hosp., Chamblee, Ga., 1946-50; practice medicine specializing in otology and ophthalmology, Athens, 1950—; mem. staff Athens Gen., St. Mary's hosps., Athens. Pres., KSM Corp., Athens. Chmn. Cherokee dist. Boy Scouts Am., 1956-58; bd. dirs. Community Chest, 1956-58; trustee St. James Methodist Ch. Served to capt. AUS, 1945-46, to maj. USAF Res., 1950-61. Diplomate Am. Bd. Otolaryngology, Am. Bd. Ophthalmology. Mem. Am. Acad. Otolaryngology and Ophthalmology (life), Triological Soc., Ga. Soc. Ophthalmology and Otolaryngology, Am. Council Otolaryngology, AMA, Med. Assn. Ga., Crawford Long Med. Soc., Tri State Otolaryng. Assembly, Nat. Rehab. Assn. (life). Phi Chi, Phi Beta Kappa, Phi Kappa Phi, Alpha Omega Alpha, Phi Eta Sigma. Clubs: Rotary, Athens Country, Classic City Tennis, Mens Garden. Contbr. articles to profl. jours. Home: 120 Witherspoon Dr Athens GA 30606 Office: 1010 Prince Ave Athens GA 30606

KELLER, DANIEL FLOYD, pathologist; b. Oklahoma City, May 15, 1933; s. Wilbur Floyd and Kathryn Margaret (Bruen) K.; B.S. with spl. distinction in Zoology, U. Okla., 1954; M.D., Washington U., St. Louis, 1958; m. Marilyn May Fuller, Aug. 21, 1954; children—Kathryn Margaret, Daniel William, Michael Dee, James Riley. Intern, Wesley (Presbyn.) Hosp., Oklahoma City, 1958-59, pathologist, dir. labs., 1964-68; fellow in clin. pathology Cleve. Clinic Ednl. Found., 1962-64; asst. clin. prof. dept. pathology U. Okla. Sch. Medicine; cons. pathologist hosps., Okla. Served to 2d lt., Med. Service Corps, U.S. Army, 1957-58, to capt. M.C., 1959-62. Diplomate Am. Bd. Pathology; mem. Phi Beta Kappa. Fellow Coll. Am. Pathologists, Am. Soc. Clin. Pathologists. Contbr. articles to med. jours. Home: 7309 Lancet Ln Oklahoma City OK 73120 Office: 254 Pasteur Bldg 1111 N Lee St Oklahoma City OK 73103

KELLER, JAMES HAWTHORNE, dir. computer programming, educator; b. Columbia, S.C., Sept. 6, 1934; s. Francis William and Dorothy (Reeves) K.; B.S., Furman U., 1956; M.A., U. Ala., Huntsville, 1967; m. Pearl McJunkin, June 15, 1957 (dec. 1977); children—Paul Furman, Bruce Gordon; m. 2d, Nancy Nicholson Ogden Rogers, Nov. 22, 1979. Computer programmer IBM, Poughkeepsie, N.Y., 1961-64, Huntsville, Ala., 1964-67; dir. computer programming, asst. prof. computer sci. Furman U., Greenville S.C., 1967—. Served with U.S. Army, 1960-61. Baptist. Home: 13 E Chaucer Rd Greenville SC 29609 Office: Computer Center Furman University Greenville SC 29613

KELLER, OSWALD LEWIN, JR., chemist; b. N.Y.C., May 24, 1930; s. Oswald Lewin and Katherine Doris (Leiding) K.; B.S., U. of South, 1951; Ph.D. (Rockefeller fellow, Visking Corp. fellow), Mass. Inst. Tech., 1959; m. Dona Claire Guild, Oct. 9, 1953; children—Christopher Guild, Claire, Elaine, Elizabeth. Chemist, Oak Ridge Nat. Lab., 1960-66, dir. transuranium research lab., 1966-74, dir. chemistry div., 1974—; mem. transplutonium program com. AEC, 1966-74, panel on nuclear physics Nat. Acad. Scis., 1971-73; mem. transuranium tech. group ERDA, 1974-77. Served with AUS, 1954-56. USPHS fellow, Mass. Inst. Tech., 1959-60. Mem. AAAS, Am. Chem. Soc., Phi Beta Kappa, Sigma Xi. Home: 101 Morgan Rd Oak Ridge TN 37830 Office: PO Box X Oak Ridge TN 37830

KELLER, ROBERT ALEXANDER, lawyer; b. Oklahoma City, Apr. 12, 1930; s. Robert Alexander and Martha Ezelle (Barrett) K.; B.B.A., U. Okla., 1951; J.D., Stanford U., 1958; m. Judith Ann Sample, Sept. 26, 1970; children—Susan L., Stephen B., Christopher D., Jennifer P. Admitted to Calif. bar, 1958; mem. firm Orrick, Herrington, Rowley and Sutcliff, San Francisco, 1958-65; asst. dean Stanford Law Sch., Palo Alto, Calif., 1965-70; mem. firm Munger, Tolles & Rickershauser, Los Angeles, 1971-72; atty. Coca-Cola Co., Atlanta, 1972-78, sr. v.p., gen. counsel, 1978—. Mem. Calif. Gov.'s Commn. on Adminstrv. Procedures, 1961; mem. Palo Alto Human Relations Counsel, 1967-68; bd. dirs. ACLU, San Francisco, 1966-68. Served to lt. USNR, 1951-55. Mem. Calif. Bar Assn., So. Center Internat. Studies, Am. Bar Assn. Democrat. Home: 2610 Woodward Way Atlanta GA 30305 Office: PO Drawer 1734 Atlanta GA 30301

KELLER, WILLIAM BRYAN, merchant; b. Westminster, S.C., Sept. 8, 1912; s. Isaac Leonard and Mayette (Brown) K.; B.S., Clemson U., 1933; m. Lila Vandiver, June 8, 1940; 1 son, Isaac Leonard. Asst. chemist S.C. Agrl. Exptl. Sta., Clemson U., 1934-38; agent Bur. Plant Industry, USDA, Clemson U., 1939-42; owner, operator Judge Keller's Store, Clemson, S.C., 1946—. Served with U.S. Army, 1942-46. Notary public S.C. Mem. Am. Def. Preparedness Assn., Am. Chem. Soc. Lutheran. Clubs: Masons, Clemson Fellowship, K.T. Home: 107 Poole Ln Clemson SC 29631 Office: 119 College Ave Clemson SC 29631

KELLERMAN, ROBERT EUGENE, petroleum co. exec.; b. Beggs, Okla., Dec. 20, 1927; s. John Austin and Mary (Bungard) K.; B.S. in Petroleum Engring., U. Tex., 1949; m. Shirley Pulley, Sept. 3, 1949; children—Robert Scott, Shelby Kay. Dist. engr. Republic Natural Gas Co., 1949-52; dist. engr., chief engr., gen. mgr. Tex. Crude Oil Co., Ft. Worth, 1952-71; pres. N.Am. Internat., Inc., 1965-71, Petroleum Leaseholds, Inc., 1965-71, Tex. Crude Oil Co., Inc., 1965-71; v.p. Pipeline Transp. Inc. 1965-71; pres. Oppenheimer Oil & Gas, Inc., Ft. Worth, 1971—, Opco Prodn. Co., 1978—, Opco Oil Devel., Inc., 1978—; dir. Gateway Nat. Bank. Central area chmn. Oil Info. Com., 1958-60, recipient silver certificate for service, 1958. Registered profl. engr. Mem. Tex. Mid-Continent Oil and Gas Assn., Am. Petroleum Inst., Am. Inst. Mining, Metall. and Petroleum Engrs., Tarrant County Tex. Ex-Students Assn. (pres. 1967), Friars, Ft. Worth Wildcatters, Tau Beta Pi, Sigma Gamma Epsilon. Democrat. Mem. Disciples of Christ (deacon, elder). Home: 1517 Hillcrest St Fort Worth TX 76107 Office: 3309 Winthrop St Suite 207 Fort Worth TX 76116

KELLETT, WILLIAM HIRAM, JR., architect, engr., educator; b. Bryan, Tex., Oct. 15, 1930; s. William Hiram and Elizabeth (Minsky) K.; A.A., Victoria Coll., 1954; B.Arch., Tex. A. and M. U., 1960, M.Arch., 1967; m. Christiana Maria Binsch, Feb. 2, 1962 (div.); children—Elizabeth Julia, Rene Janine, Kira Lorraine; m. 2d, Ann Robertson Wilkins, Dec. 11, 1971; children—Robert Lynn, Patricia Ann. Elec. technician W.E. Kutzschbach Co., Bryan, Tex., 1950-51; engring. technologist Johnston & Davis, Victoria, Tex., 1952-54; mech., elec. systems designer Hall Engring. Co., Bryan, 1955-62; mech. and elec. systems designer Environments, Inc., Bryan, 1962-74; pres. Mech & Elec Cons., Bryan, 1974-76; owner William H. Kellett, Cons. Engrs., Bryan, 1976—; prof. environ. design, architecture and bldg. constrn. Tex. A. and M. U., College Station, 1962—. Vice chmn. City Charter Com., Bryan, 1969; chmn. Bd. Equalization, 1969-70. Registered architect, engr. Mem. AIA, Illuminating Engr. Soc., AAUP, Am. Soc. Heating, Refrigeration and Air Conditioning Engrs., Refrigeration Engrs. and Tech. Assn., Nat., Tex. socs. profl. engrs., Phi Theta Kappa, Tau Beta Pi, Tau Sigma Delta. Home: 1000 Esther Blvd Bryan TX 77801 Office: Coll Architecture and Design Tex A and M U College Station TX 77840

KELLEY, DAVID LEE, petroleum engr.; b. San Antonio, Apr. 24, 1936; s. Buster Arnold and Magdeline Edna (Shepherd) K.; B.S. in Petroleum Engring., U. Tex. at Austin, 1959, M.S. in Petroleum Engring., 1966; m. Suzanne Elizabeth Simons, Nov. 26, 1960; children—Leah Elizabeth, Travis David. Jr. gas engr. Mobil Oil Corp., Edna, Tex., 1959-60; petroleum engr. Continental Oil Co., Sweetwater, Tex., 1960-64; research petroleum engr. Tex. Petroleum Research Com., Austin, 1964-66; petroleum engr. Monsanto Co., Houston, 1966-68; pres. McRae Consol. Oil & Gas Corp. & Subsidiaries, Houston, 1968—; dir. McRae Cons., McRae Oil, Petrofunds Inc., La. Gas Purchasing Corp., La. Gas Intrastate Inc., McRae Exploration Inc. Served with AUS, 1960. Mem. Am. Inst. Metall., Mining and Petroleum Engrs., Ind. Petroleum Assn. Am., Soc. Profl. Engrs., Sigma Gamma Epsilon, Pi Epsilon Tau. Republican. Methodist. Clubs: Champions Golf, Athletic of Houston. Home: 14114 Bonney Brier Houston TX 77069 Office: 800 Dresser Tower Houston TX 77002

KELLEY, DUANE NEIL, real estate devel. co. exec.; b. Cody, Wyo., Aug. 13, 1953; s. Billy Gene and Maxine Jane (Hill) K.; B.B.A., Morehead State U., 1977; m. Debra Lynne Keeton, May 10, 1975; 1 dau., Jalayna Lynne. Central office adminstr. Ky. Drilling and Operating Corp., Lexington, 1974-77; comptroller Correll Enterprises, Somerset, Ky., 1978—, also dir. Mem. Am. Mgmt. Assn., Nat. Fedn. Ind. Bus., Nat. C. of C., Ky. C. of C., Somerset-Pulaski C. of C. Democrat. Baptist. Home: 214 Walnut Ave Somerset KY 42501 Office: Suite 205 Correll Bldg Somerset KY 42501

KELLEY, JAMES MARVIN, JR., physician; b. Hartselle, Ala., Sept. 6, 1927; s. James Marvin and Marie (Hicks) K.; B.A., Rice U., 1950; M.D., Duke, 1954; m. Eva Gottschall, Mar. 20, 1954; children—James Marvin III, William F., Eva Marie. Intern, later resident Duke Hosp., 1954-60; asso. Harbin Clinic, Rome, Ga., 1960-75, Northwest Ga. Orthopedic Clinic, Rome, 1975—; cons. orthopedic surgery Northwest Ga. Regional Hosp.; trustee Floyd Hosp. Served with USNR, 1945-46. Mem. Ga. Orthopedic Soc. (pres. 1973-74). Clubs: Rome Rotary (pres. 1968-69), Coosa Country (pres. 1974). Home: 215 Greenview St Rome GA 30161 Office: 310 W 10th St Rome GA 30161

KELLEY, JUDY RAE, speech pathologist; b. Clarksburg, W.Va., Oct. 1, 1945; d. Orville and Ruby Charleen (Williams) K.; B.A., Salem Coll., 1967; M.S., W.Va. U., 1969. Speech lang. pathologist Monongalia County Schs., Morgantown, W.Va., 1969-75, head speech lang. pathologist, 1975—; instr. part-time W.Va. U., 1969—. Mem. Assn. Supervision and Curriculum Devel. (regional pres. 1978-79, local pres. 1976-77), Am. Speech and Hearing Assn., W.Va. Speech and Hearing Assn. Republican. Methodist. Home: 1411 Fairfield St Apt 6 Star City WV 26505 Office: 48 Edgewood St Annex 10 Morgantown WV 26505

KELLEY, LARRY HOWARD, ins. co. exec.; b. Harpersville, Ala., Sept. 14, 1949; s. Delma Eugene and Mildred (Evans) K.; B.S., Troy State U., 1977; m. Bettye Earl Morris, Apr. 3, 1971; children—Christopher Robin, Christy Lynn. Service order typist South Central Bell, Montgomery, Ala., 1974-77; sales rep. Met./So. United Life Ins. Co., Anniston and Columbiana, Ala., 1977-78; farmer nr., Childersburg, Ala., 1978; ins. adjuster Kemper Ins. Co., Birmingham, Ala., 1978--. Served with USN, 1969-73. Mem. Troy State U. Alumni Assn., Alpha Sigma Lambda, Gamma Beta Phi. Democrat. Baptist. Home: Route 1 Box 215 Childersburg AL 35044 Office: Kemper Ins Co Bldg 15 Suite 110 Office Park Circle Birmingham AL 35223

KELLEY, MARY ELIZABETH MCDOWELL, automotive supply co. exec.; b. Bonita, La., May 29, 1924; d. George Robert and Vinnie Mae (McLeod) McDowell; grad. Draughan's Coll. Bus., 1943; m. James Eugene Kelley, Mar. 16, 1947 (dec.). Exec. sec. to pres. Voss-Hutton-Barbee Co., Little Rock, 1944-46; sec. to pres. and gen. mgr. Motor Supply Co., Monroe, La., 1946-66; exec. sec. to pres. Motor Supply Warehouse, Inc., Monroe, 1966—. Mem. Am. Soc. for Personnel Adminstrn., D.A.R. Democrat. Baptist. Clubs: Quota Internat., Order of Eastern Star. Home: 2212 Redwood Dr Monroe LA 71201 Office: 2200 Booth St Monroe LA 71201

KELLEY, RUSSELL T., state ofcl.; b. Stamford, Tex., July 16, 1947; s. Roland R. and Rosa (Crockett) K.; student Tex. Technol. U., 1965-67; B.B.A., U. Tex., 1969; m. Janet Smith, July 7, 1973; 1 son, Russell T. Exec. asst. sgt. at arms Tex. Senate, Austin, 1971-73; chief sgt. at arms Tex. Ho. of Reps., Austin, 1973-76, exec. asst. to speaker of the house, 1979—; v.p. Tex. Savs. and Loan League, 1976-77. Mem. Nat. Conf. State Legislatures (mem. exec. com. 1979), Nat. Security Execs. Assn., Nat. Soc. Mgmt. Baptist. Home: 2133 Barton Hills Dr Austin TX 78704 Office: Tex Ho of Reps Box 2910 Austin TX 78704

KELLY, BECKY TRUXELL, banker; b. Sharon, Pa., Mar. 5, 1953; d. Robert Harvey and Mary (Luse) T.; B.A. cum laude, Longwood Coll., 1975; M.B.A., James Madison U., 1977; m. Patrick Joseph Kelly, May 28, 1977. Adminstrv. asst. trust dept. 1st and Mchts. Nat. Bank, Staunton, Va., 1978-79, asst. trust officer, 1979—. Mem. Am. Inst. Banking, Estate Planning Council, AAUW, Alpha Delta Pi. Home: 1609 Armstrong Ave Staunton VA 24401 Office: PO Box 390 Staunton VA 24401

KELLY, CECILIA MARY, artistic dir., choreographer; b. Beckenham, Eng., Mar. 22, 1922; d. James Robert and Emily Monica (Hewitt) Ellis; came to U.S., 1946, naturalized, 1949; student Ballet Sch., LaScala Theatre, Milan, Italy, 1931-36; m. Eugene Joseph Kelly, May 22, 1945; children—Eugene James, Chinta Monica (Mrs. Alvin Tucker). Mem. LaScala Co., Milan, 1936-38; concerts in Far East, Bombay, Cape Town, Penang, Singapore, 1938-41; mem. Sadler's Wells Ballet, England, 1941-46; guest chr., lectr. N.H., 1946-54; master classes, Taiwan, 1955-59; founder, dir. ballet, Ark. Arts Center, Little Rock, 1960-63; founder, dir. Shreveport (La.) Symphony Ballet, 1966-72, El Dorado Civic Ballet (Ark.), 1967-70; founder, dir. Twin City Civic Ballet, Monroe, La., 1970—; artist in residence Shreveport Symphony Ballet, 1974-75; guest artist So. Methodist U., Dallas, 1972. Chmn., Save the Whale Com. La.; benefit performances March of Dimes, 1954, 70. Recipient award Gov. Faubus. Mem. Nat. Soc. Arts and Letters (nat. dance chmn., 1970-72, 74-76, nat. career award chmn. 1977—). Roman Catholic. Home: PO Box 171 Greenwood LA 71033

KELLY, CLEO BELL, librarian; b. Clearwater, Nebr., Jan. 20, 1914; d. John L. and Anna Bell (Woodard) Kelly; B.A., Wayne (Nebr.) State Coll., 1946; postgrad. U. Nebr., summers 1951, 52; M.A. in L.S., U. Denver, 1953. Tchr. pub. schs. Neb., 1937-51; revisor, U. Denver Sch. Librarianship, summer 1953; asst. librarian Peru (Nebr.) State Coll., 1953-57; reference librarian S.D. State U., Brookings, 1957-60; cataloger Kans. State U., Manhattan, 1960-62; chmn. tech. processes dept. Kans. State Coll., Pittsburg, 1962-66; mem. staff Stephen F. Austin State U. Library, Nacogdoches, Tex., 1966—, asst. humanities librarian, 1973—; tchr. library sci. Peru State Coll., 1954-57, S.D. State U., 1958-59. Mem. Am., Mountain-Plains, Southwestern, Tex. (council 1971-72, chmn. dist. 8, 1972) library assns., Assn. Coll. and Research Libraries, AAUP, Tex. Assn. Coll. Tchrs., U. Denver Alumni Assn., Univ. Profl. Women, Pi Gamma Mu. Clubs: Univ. Women, Camillia Soc. (Nacogdoches). Home: 315 Blount St Nacogdoches TX 75961

KELLY, ELIZABETH PETERSON ALEXANDER, psychotherapist; b. Whiteville, N.C., May 23, 1942; d. John Dixon and Lillian Blue (Squires) Peterson; B.A., Meredith Coll., 1963; M.Ed., N.C. State U., 1968, Ed.D., 1975; m. Claiborne Merle Kelly, Nov. 19, 1971; children—Christopher Merle Kelly, Sean Andrew Kelly. Personnel asst. N.C. Dept. Social Services, Raleigh, 1964-66, research asst., 1966-67; manpower specialist N.C. Council on Mental Retardation, Raleigh, 1967-68; pub. relations cons. N.C. Dept. Mental Health, Raleigh, 1968-70; chmn. mental health dept. Sandhills Community Coll., Southern Pines, N.C., 1971-72; dir. psychotherapy Youth and Adult Counseling Center. Raleigh, 1972—; pvt. practice psychotherapy, Raleigh, 1972—. Founder Camp and Recreation Program for Handicapped Children in Raleigh and Wake County (N.C.), 1967. Named Raleigh's Young Career Woman, 1965, Outstanding Young Career Woman of Am., 1966, Outstanding Civic Leader of Am., 1967; N.C. Mental Health grantee, 1970. Mem. NC, Am. personnel and guidance assns., N.C., Wake County mental health assns., Raleigh Bus. and Profl. Woman's Club (pres. 1965), Raleigh Jr. Woman's Club, Raleigh Jacettes. Home: 3413 Fairhill Dr Raleigh NC 27612 Office: 220 N Boylan Ave Raleigh NC 27603

KELLY, FRANK ALLAN, lawyer; b. Kingsport, Tenn., Mar. 22, 1940; s. Frank H. and Lovie (Baker) K.; B.A. in History, Tenn. Technol. U., 1962; J.D. (Cooper D. Schmidt fellow), U. Va., 1965; m. Mary Alice Boyd, Aug. 3, 1963; children—Alice Jones, Tricia Ann. Admitted to N.Y. bar, 1965, Va. bar, 1965, Tenn. bar, 1966; asso. firm Everett, Johnson & Breckenridge, N.Y.C., 1965-66; partner firm Hunter, Smith, Davis, Norris & Treadway, Kingsport, Tenn., 1966—; pres., chief exec. officer Oakwood Markets Inc., Kingsport. Adviser Boys Club, Kingsport, 1967—; mem. Kingsport Citizens Adv. Com., 1966—, Tri-Cities Planning Council, 1967—, Kingsport Mental Health Assn., 1966—. Mgr. Sullivan County div. Baker for Senate U.S., 1972. Bd. dirs. Kingsport chpt. A.R.C. Mem. Kingsport (v.p.), Tenn., N.Y. State, Va. bar assns., Nat. Life Underwriters Assn. Elk, Moose. Clubs: Ridgefields Country, Kingsport Racquet Inc. Editor: Va. Jour. Internat. Law, 1964-65. Home: 621 Ridgefields Rd Kingsport TN 37660 Office: 1101 Eastman Rd Kingsport TN 37664

KELLY, FRANK JOSEPH, JR., mfg. ofcl.; b. Pitts., Feb. 27, 1944; s. Frank Joseph and Jane S. K.; B.S. in Bus. Adminstrn., Villanova U., 1968; m. Ruth Smith, Dec. 27, 1966; children—Tracey Ann, Kimberly Korin. Quality control engring. supr. PPG Industries, Inc., Cumberland, Md., 1968-70; salesman Eastern region Indsl. Rubber Product Co., Balt., 1970-72; asst. to v.p. and gen. mgr. Rubber Rolls, Inc., Meadowlands, Pa., 1972-74; plant mgr. Calgon Corp., Houston, 1974-76, regional mgr. Activated Carbon div., Houston, 1976—. Pres., bd. dirs. North Woodland Hills Community Assn., 1979; mem. security com. Kingwood Service Assn., 1979. Served with USAR, 1964-70. Mem. Am. Mgmt. Assn., Beaumont C. of C., Clearlake Sports Car Club, Sports Car Club Am. Roman Catholic. Club: Kingwood Country. Home: 2106 River Village Dr Kingwood TX 77339 Office: 4800 W 34th St Suite B8 Houston TX 77092

KELLY, JAMES FREDRICK, machinery mfg. co. exec.; b. Phoebus, Va., Dec. 18, 1922; s. James Floyd and Ray (Newsom) K.; B.S. in Civil Engring., N.C. State U., 1943; postgrad. U. N.C., 1955-56; m. Helen Francis Golson, Nov. 6, 1949; children—James Fredrick, David Palmer, Mark Charles. Architect, U.S. Naval Base, Charleston, S.C., 1943-46; with Aeroglide Corp., Raleigh, N.C., 1946—, v.p., 1949-56, pres., 1956—; pres. Aeroglide Ams. Inc., 1968—; pres. Am. Machinery Corp., Orlando, Fla., 1965—; dir. Peden Steel Co., Wachovia Bank and Trust Co., Raleigh. Bd. advisers N.C. Sci. and Tech. Utilization Bd.; mem. com. econs. edn. N.C. Pub. Schs., 1969-71; pres. N.C. Ednl. Council on Nat. Purposes, 1968—, N.C. World Trade Assn., 1976-77; nat. asso. Boys Club Am.; chmn. devel. council N.C. State U.; mem. N.C. Export Expansion Council; advisory bd. N.C. Internat. Trade Center. Named Outstanding Engring. Alumnus, N.C. State U., 1968. Registered profl. engr., N.C., Md. Mem. Raleigh Sales and Mktg. Execs. Club, Nat., N.C. (Outstanding Engring. Achievement 1979) socs. profl. engrs., N.C. Engrs. Soc., Am. Soc. Agrl. Engrs., Process Equipment Mfrs. Assn. (dir. 1979—), Raleigh C. of C. (dir.), Chief Execs. Forum, Young Presidents Orgn., Blue Key, Alpha Zeta, Phi Kappa Phi, Pi Kappa Alpha, Gamma Sigma Delta, Theta Tau. Methodist. Mason, Lion. Home: 3207 Darien Dr Raleigh NC 27607 Office: 7100 Hillsborough Rd Raleigh NC 27611

KELLY, JAMES JOSEPH, oil co. exec.; b. El Reno, Okla., Dec. 8, 1912; s. John P. and Helen (Weber) K.; student Cameron State Jr. Coll.; B.C.E., Okla. State U., 1936; m. Lue Elsie Daley, Oct. 29, 1938; children—Karen Batchelor, Thomas J. State engr. Nat. Youth Adminstrn., 1936-37; v.p. Allied Materials Corp., 1937-46; dir. Kerr-McGee Corp., Oklahoma City, Standard Testing Co., Oklahoma City, Fidelity Bank, Oklahoma City. Bd. dirs. St. Gregory's Coll.; bd. govs. Devel. Found., Okla. State U.; bd. dirs. Asphalt Inst., Am. Petroleum Inst.; trustee St Anthony Hosp., Oklahoma City; nat. advisory bd. Goodwill Industries Am., Inc. Mem. Am. Soc. Mil. Engrs., Twenty-Five Year Club Petroleum Industry, Newcomen Soc., Am. Assn. Cost Engrs., ASCE, Nat. Soc. Profl. Engrs., Soc. Chem. Industry, Conf. Bd., Higher Edn. Alumni Council Okla. Clubs: Beacon, Whitehall, Oklahoma City Golf and Country (Oklahoma City); Chgo. Oil Men's. Home: 6325 N Villa Unit 153 Oklahoma City OK 73112 Office: Kerr-McGee Bldg Oklahoma City OK 73102

KELLY, JOE LOUIE, mfg. co. exec.; b. Lawrenceburg, Tenn., Mar. 3, 1932; s. Woodrow Wilson and Maggie T. (Moore) K.; B.S., Miss. State U., Starkville, 1957; m. Dorothy Ann Errington, Dec. 4, 1952; children—Rebecca JoAnn, Dorothy Marie. Mgr. indsl. engring. ITT Telecommunications, Corinth, Miss., 1957-65, mgr. mfg., 1966-77, dir. mfg., 1977-78, v.p., plant mgr., 1978—; mgr. telephone mfg. ITT Can., Montreal, Que., 1965-66. Pres., Corinth Jr. C. of C., 1959-60. Served with U.S. Army, 1952-54. Mem. Soc. Mfg. Engrs. (chmn. No. Miss. 1962), Am. Soc. Indsl. Engrs. Baptist. Home: 139 College St Milan TN 38358

KELLY, JOHN SCHLAGLE, petroleum geologist; b. Mont Clare, Pa.; s. William Thomas and Emma Bertha (Schlagle) K.; grad. Wyo. Sem., 1923; student Lehigh U., 1923-24, Pa. State U., 1925-26; B.S., U. Houston, 1942, M.S., 1943; children—John J.H. and Constance Grace (twins). With Marathon Oil Co., Tulsa, Houston, and Midland, Tex., 1936-44; dist. geologist Am. Republics Corp., San Antonio and San Angelo, Tex., 1944-51; chief geologist Cosden Petroleum Corp., Big Spring, Tex., 1951-59; v.p. Crescendo Corp., Midland, 1965-67; cons. petroleum geologist, Midland, 1968-78. Certified petroleum geologist, Tex. Mem. Am. Assn. Petroleum Geologists (dist. rep. 1959-62), Am. Inst. Mining and Metall. Engring., W. Tex. Geol. Soc., Soc. Econ. Paleontologists and Mineralogists, Soc. Exploration Geophysicists. Episcopalian. Clubs: Lions, Toastmasters (chpt. pres.). Contbr. articles to World Oil, Oil and Gas Jour. Home: 603 Watson St Midland TX 79702 Office: PO Box 583 Midland TX 79702

KELLY, JONATHAN MCMULLEN, educator; b. Mansfield, La., Dec. 8, 1929; s. Frank Leon and Maud Allen (Nelson) K.; B.S., La. Coll., Pineville, 1951; M.Ed., La. State U., 1958, postgrad., 1958-62; m. Marion Ann Cates, June 9, 1975; 1 son, Jonathan Gene; stepchildren—Joseph Lumpkin, David Lumpkin, Mark Lumpkin, Dana Lumpkin. Sales rep. J.B. Beaird Co., Shreveport, La., 1953; tchr. bus. Logansport (La.) High Sch., 1954-57; asst. prof. bus. Nicholls State U., Thibodaux, La., 1957-63; asst. prof. bus. Ouachita Bapt. U., Arkadelphia, Ark., 1963—, chmn. dept. office adminstrn. Bd. dirs. La. Heart Assn., 1961-63, Ark. Heart Assn., 1964-66; mem. Republican County Com., Arkadelphia, 1966; founder Clean Up TV, Inc., 1977; Ark. rep. Nat. Fedn. Decency, 1978-79. Served with AUS, 1951-52. Mem. Ark. Coll. Tchrs. Econs. (pres. 1976-77), Ark. Bus. Edn. Assn., So. Bus. Edn. Assn., Nat. Bus. Edn. Assn., Am. Bus. Communications Assn., Nat. Wild Turkey Fedn., Nat. Rifle Assn. Mem. Ch. of Christ. Clubs: Lions (Lion of Yr. award 1971), Masons, Shriners. Home: 309 Hardin St Arkadelphia AR 71923 Office: Ouachita Bapt U Arkadelphia AR 71923

KELLY, JUDITH ANN FRENCH, educator, theatre dir.; b. Buffalo, Aug. 8, 1941; d. Edward Benedict and Ellen Bernadine (Makey) French; B.A. in English, U. Dallas, 1963; postgrad. English, U. Ark., 1963-64; M.A. in Drama, Marquette U., 1966; m. Patrick James Kelly, Dec. 28, 1968. Dir. Dallas High Sch. Summer Speech Inst., 1960-62; English instr. U. Ark., Fayetteville, 1963-64; theatre mgr. Teatro Maria, Marquette U., Milw., 1964-66; chmn., founder drama dept. U. Dallas, Irving, Tex., 1966—; planning and design cons. Margaret Jonsson Theater, Irving, 1972, dir., prodn. coordinator, 1972—; dir. Community Thanksgiving Presentations, 1968, 73. Mem. Am. Theatre Assn. (chmn. symposium recycled bldgs. for performance spaces 1976), Ann. Colloquium Directing Modern Theater, Nat. Theatre Arts Conf. (regional dir. 1962—), Tex. Arts Alliance, Tex. Ednl. Theatre Assn., SW Theater Conf. (charter), Theater Communications Group, Univ. and Coll. Theater Assn. Roman Catholic. Office: Drama Dept U Dallas Irving TX 75061

KELLY, KAREN JEAN, nurse, educator; b. Elizabeth, N.J., Dec. 14, 1949; d. Richard Carl and Mary Hasson Stuhler; diploma in Nursing, Holy Name Hosp., Teaneck, N.J., 1970; B.S. in Nursing, SUNY, Albany, 1979; m. Leo Charles Kelly, Sept. 25, 1971; 1 dau., Shannon Helene. Staff nurse emergency dept. St. Elizabeth Hosp., Elizabeth, N.J., 1970-71; staff nurse ophthalmology unit Washington Hosp. Center, Washington, 1972, head nurse, 1972-74; staff nurse emergency dept. Loudoun Meml. Hosp., Leesburg, Va., 1974-76, staff devel. coordinator, educator, 1976—; chmn. CPR task force Loudoun County unit Am. Heart Assn.; affiliate faculty Met. Washington Advanced Life Support project. Mem. No. Va. Council Health Care Educators (pres. 1978-79), Va. Nurses Coalition for Action in Politics, Am. Nurses Assn., Va. Soc. Health Manpower Educators and Trainers (district 8 Nurse of the Year 1978), Loudoun County Bus. and Profl. Womens Club (named Young Careerist, 1977). Roman Catholic. Home: 517 Fillmore Ave Sterling VA 22170 Office: 70 W Cornwall St Leesburg VA 22075

KELLY, MARGARET RICAUD (MRS. THOMAS W. KELLY), educator; b. Dillon, S.C., Mar. 22, 1910; d. Robert Barry and Lulu Mowry (Crosland) Ricaud; A.B., Winthrop Coll., 1931; postgrad. Duke, 1931, U. Miami, 1937, U. Fla., 1938, U. N.C., 1950, 52, 53, U. S.C., 1954, Coker Coll., 1954-55; m. John Quinton Maynard, Jan. 1, 1936; m. 2d, Thomas W. Kelly, Sept. 12, 1950. Tchr. high sch., Elizabethtown, N.C., 1931-32; prin. Ebenezer Sch., Bennettsville, S.C., 1932-35; tchr. pub. schs., Homestead, Fla., 1937-39; tchr. Fletcher Meml. Sch., McColl, S.C., 1940-46; 67-69; attendance tchr. Marlboro County Schs., Bennettsville, 1946-50; tchr. elementary sch., Tabor City, N.C., 1950-51; tchr. pub. schs., Cordova, N.C., 1951-56, Society Hills, S.C., 1956-67; tchr. spl. edn. Blenheim (S.C.) primary schs., 1970-73; individual tutor, Bennettsville, 1973-77. Mem. Nat., S.C. edn. assns., Marlboro County Tchrs. (past chmn. pub. relations), S.C., Marlborough hist. socs., Mental Health Assn. Marlboro County, Marlboro Arts Council, Nat. Geneal. Soc., South Carolinian Soc., Colonial Dames 17th Century, Magna Charta Dames, Most Noble Order of Garter, Geneal. Soc. London, S.C. Ret. Tchrs. Assn., Am. Assn. Ret. Persons, French Huguenot Soc., Colonial Order of Crown, Nat. Soc. Poetry, Pee Dee Queue. Author: Jack and the Flying Saucer, 1973; Poems by Margaret Ricaud Kelly, 1974; The Ricaud Family, a genealogical history, 1976; A Short History of Marlboro County 1600-1979, 1979. Contbr. poetry to anthologies, 1972—, articles to various local newspapers. Home: 402 Fayetteville Ave Bennettsville SC 29512

KELLY, MICHAEL GARCIN, food co. ofcl.; b. Montgomery, Ala., Dec. 13, 1946; s. John Richard and Elizabeth Marie (Garcin) K.; B.S. in Indsl. Mgmt., Fla. State U., 1969; m. Margaret Evelyn Orsini, Mar. 20, 1971; children—John Richard, Brittany Ann. Cost acct. Owens Corning Fiberglas Co., Aiken, S.C., 1969-70; traffic service supr. Southwestern Bell Telephone Co., Springfield, Mo., 1970, Houston, to 1973; methods engr. Savannah Foods & Industries (Ga.), 1973-79, corp. safety dir., 1979—. Liturgical chmn. St. Michaels Parish Council, Tybee Island, Ga.; track coach Benedictine High Sch., Savannah. Named to Athletic Hall of Fame, Fla. State U., 1979. Mem. Am. Soc. Safety Engrs., Internat. Mgmt. Council, Nat. Safety Council, Ga. Safety Council, Ga. Placement Council, Sigma Alpha Epsilon. Republican. Roman Catholic. Clubs: K.C., St. Michael's Men's, Atlanta Track. Home: PO Box 504 Tybee Island GA 31328 Office: PO Box 710 Savannah GA 31402

KELLY, PATRICIA KATE, banker; b. Dallas, Mar. 13, 1949; d. John Lory and Lillian (Dillahe) Heffernan; B.S.E., U. Ark., 1971, M.Ed., 1974; m. Arthur Lee Kelly, Aug. 9, 1970; children—Katherine Leeann, Thomas Arthur. Tchr., USAF Perry Sch., Philippines, 1971-72; head resident U. Ark. Residence Halls, 1972-74; equal employment opportunity specialist State of Ark., 1974-75, tng. and devel. specialist, 1975-76; asst. v.p., mgr. human resources devel. center 1st Nat. Bank, Little Rock, 1976—. Mem. Ark. Soc. Tng. and Devel. (regional conf. dir. 1978, mem. nat. prof. devel. com. 1977-78, named outstanding mem. of year 1978, state bd. dirs. 1979—), Nat. Assn. Bank Women (edn. com.), Am. Mgmt. Assn. Episcopalian. Office: PO Box 1471 Little Rock AR 72203

KELLY, RICHARD, congressman; b. Atlanta, July 31, 1924; A.B., Colo. State Coll. Edn., 1949; postgrad. Vanderbilt U. Coll. Law; J.D., U. Fla., 1952; cert. Coll. State Trial Judges, Reno, 1971; m. Judy Wilder. Admitted to Fla. bar, 1952, U.S. Supreme Ct. bar; former atty. City of Zephyrhills (Fla.); sr. asst. U.S. dist. atty. So. Dist. Fla., 1956-59; former atty. FEI; judge 6th Jud. Circuit Ct. Fla., 1960-74; mem. 94th-96th congresses from 5th Dist. Fla., mem. com. on banking, currency and housing, com. on agr. Commr. 111th Gen. Assembly, Presbyn. Ch. U.S.; mem. Jud. Commn., Synod of Fla., Presbyn. Ch. Served with USMCR, 1942-46. Mem. Am., Fed. bar assns., Fla. Bar, Am. Judicature Soc., Am. Legion, VFW (life). Republican. Presbyterian (past trustee, elder). Lion, Eagle (hon. life). Office: 307 Cannon Bldg Washington DC 20515

KELLY, ROBERT FRANK, biochemist; b. Fond du Lac, Wis., May 21, 1919; s. William and Marie Ida (Ruechel) K.; student Oshkosh (Wis.) State Tchrs. Coll. 1940-42; B.S., U. Wis., 1948, M.S., 1953, Ph.D., 1955; m. Olive Ann Bloedow, July 31, 1944; children—Paul R., Kathryn (Mrs. Allen Atkins), Patricia, Jean, Daniel, Michael. Farmer, 1938-43; tchr. vocational agr. Waukesha High Sch., 1948-51; prof. meat and animal sci. Va. Poly. Inst. and State U., Blacksburg, 1955—. Cons., Williams-Waterman Fund, N.Y.C., Ohio Dept. Agr., Pa. Dept. Agr.; judge Nat. Ham-Bacon-Sausage Show. Sec., Diocesan Council Catholic Men, 1972-73. Served with USAAF, 1944-46. Mem. A.A.A.S., Am. Meat Sci. Assn. (dir. 1967-68, recipient Distinguished Tchr. award 1973), Inst. Food Technologists, Am. Soc. Animal Sci., Res. Officers Assn. (pres. Montgomery chpt.), Meat Judging Coaches Assn. (pres.), Sigma Xi, Gamma Sigma Delta, Alpha Zeta. Contbr. articles to profl. jours. Home 2801 Shadow Lake Rd Blacksburg VA 24060

KELLY, THOMAS LAWRENCE, JR., utility exec.; b. Mobile, Ala., Nov 1, 1921; s. Thomas Lawrence and Alma (Zimlich) K.; grad. pub. high sch.; m. Margaret Ecc Leston, Jan. 20, 1946 (dec. Mar. 1969); children—Thomas L., Robert T., William T., Michael T., Daniel T.; m. 2d, Margaret Carol McCue, Dec. 4, 1971. With Mobile Gas Service Corp., 1940—, asst. storekeeper, 1953-60, purchasing agt., supr. stores, 1960—. Served with AUS, 1943-46. Mem. Nat. Assn. Purchasing Mgmt. (2d v.p.), Mobile Assn. Purchasing Mgmt. (pres. 1975-76). Address: PO Box 2248 Mobile AL 36601

KELSAW, JAMES WILLIAM, sociologist, educator; b. Gastonburg, Ala., Aug. 7, 1926; s. Thornton R. and Ethelyn (Anthony) K.; B.A. in English, Talladega Coll., 1951; M.A. in Sociology, Fisk U., 1955; Ph.D. in Sociology, Wash. State U., 1960; postgrad. (research fellow) U. Mich., 1965-66; m. Rosemary Smith, Jan. 26, 1967; children—Ethelyn Ericka, James William, Tanya Keley. Instr., Selma (Ala.) U., 1951-53; teaching asst. Wash. State U., Pullman, 1955-58, acting instr. dept. of sociology 1958-59; asst. prof. sociology So. U., Baton Rouge, 1959-61, asso. prof., 1961-62, prof., 1962-63; prof. sociology Ala. A. and M. Coll., Normal, 1963-64; prof. sociology So. U., New Orleans, 1964-65, head dept. sociology, 1964-65; asso. prof. sociology Tex. So. U., Houston, 1966-69, acting head dept. of sociology, 1969; Callaway prof. sociology Savannah (Ga.) State Coll., 1969-71; asso. prof. sociology U. Houston, 1971—. Lectr.-cons. Ga. Center for Continuing Edn. of U. Ga., 1970-71, Tng. Officers Workshop, Savannah, 1971; vice chmn. acad. com. on sociology and anthropology U. System Adv. Council of Ga., 1970-71. Mem. staff camp Cowles Inland Empire council Boy Scouts Am., Newport, Wash., 1958. Mem. Community Sch. Bd. St. Pius X Community Sch., Savannah, 1970-71. Served with AUS, World War II; ETO. Mem. Am., Southwestern social. assns., Assn. Social and Behavioral Scientists, Soc. for Study Social Problems, AAAS, Tex. Acad. Sci., Black Educators Council for Human Services, Caucus of Black Sociologists, Pi Gamma Mu, Psi Chi. Home: 3340 Charleston Houston TX 77021 Office: 3801 Cullen Blvd Houston TX 77004

KELSAY, GENE WILSON, educator; b. Bagnell, Mo., Feb. 2, 1930; s. Oris Emerson and Nellie Belle (Farriss) K.; B.A., Kansas City (Mo.) U., 1958; M.A. in Music Edn., U. Mo. at Kansas City, 1964, Ph.D. in Mus. Arts, 1969; m. Shirley Lee Frisbey, Mar. 4, 1958; children—Mark, Lindy, Leslie, Christopher, Lori. Grad. asst. U. Mo. at Kansas City, 1955-58; dir. choral activities William Christian High Sch., Independence, Mo., 1958-64; prof. music So. Ark. U., Magnolia, Ark., 1964—. Guest condr., clinician, adjudicator, soloist in recitals, oratorios, operas. Served with USN, 1951-55. Mem. Nat. Assn. Tchrs. Singing (lt. gov. 1968-72), Optimists Internat. (pres. chpt. 1974-75), Pi Kappa Lambda, Phi Mu Alpha. Home: 1420 Mockingbird St Magnolia AR 71753

KELSEY, CLYDE EASTMAN, JR., univ. adminstr.; b. Wadena, Minn., Mar. 30, 1924; s Clyde Eastman and Lorraine Lamb (Bagley) K.; B.A., U. Tex., El Paso, 1948; M.A., U. Tulsa, 1951; Ph.D., U. Denver, 1960; hon. degree, U. de Oriente, Venezuela, 1969; m. Betty Jean Williams, Apr. [illegible], 1949; children—Becky (Mrs. James C. Marcin), Nancy. Dir. counseling bur. U. Tex., El Paso, 1951-61, prof., head dept. philosophy, psychology, 1961-62, dean of students, dir. Inter-Am. Inst., 1962-66; program adviser Venezuela, Ford Found., 1966-69; vice chancellor pub. affairs U. Denver, 1969-72; v.p. devel. and univ. relations Tex. Tech. U., Lubbock, 1972—. Lectr., 4th Army U.S., 1961-65; cons. U.S. Dept. State, Peace Corps, 1961-66; dir. seminars U.S. Dept. State/Ministries Edn. Colombia, Mexico, Venezuela, 1961-66; vis. scientist NSF Program, 1962-66. Mem. adv. bd. Kans. Wesleyan Coll., 1969-71; v.p. Colo. Partners of Alliance, 1971-73. Bd. dirs. El Paso Mental Health Assn., 1951-58, pres., 1952-53; bd. dirs. El Paso Sch. for Retarded Children, 1952-57, pres., 1953-55; bd. dirs. Lubbock Goodwill Industries, 1972—, v.p., 1973-77, pres., 1978—. Served with USNR, 1942-45. Decorated Order San Carlos Republic of Colombia; recipient Distinguished Alumni Service award U. Denver, 1972; Fulbright scholar, Colombia, 1960-61. Fellow Tex. Acad. Sci.; mem. Am., S.W., Tex. psychol. assns., AAAS, Am. Ednl. Research Assn. Contbr. articles to profl. jours. Home: 3307-A 74th St Lubbock TX 79423 Office: PO Box 4650 Lubbock TX 79409

KELSO, EDWARD GREY, personnel ofcl.; b. Lynn Grove, Ky., Apr. 7, 1942; s. James Howard and Selena (Azzilee) K.; student San Antonio Coll., 1962-63, U. Okla., 1964-66; B.A., Ga. State U., 1972; m. Mary Ellen Cupit, Oct. 25, 1960; children—Sherri, Sheree, John. Electronic systems technician Lockheed Ga. Co., 1968-73; with Marconi Avionics, Atlanta, 1973—, personnel mgr., 1976—. Served with USAF, 1960-68. Mem. Am. Mgmt. Assn., Am. Soc. Personnel Adminstrs., Am. Helicopter Soc., Navy Helicopter Soc., Air Force

Assn. Republican. Baptist. Home: 2650 Bentley Rd 9B Marietta GA 30067 Office: 4500 N Shallowford Rd Atlanta GA 30338

KELTON, MAI HOGAN, organist; b. Dover, Tenn., Jan. 2, 1929; d. Alexander Rosson and Rosa Lee (Albright) Hogan; student Martin Coll., 1945-47; B.S., Middle Tenn. State Coll., 1948; M.A., George Peabody Coll. Tchrs., 1951; postgrad. Eastman Sch. Music, summer 1958; m. Allen Kelton, Sept. 26, 1959; children—Mary Katherine, John Allen. Instr. music Holcomb (Mo.) Consol. Schs., 1948-49, Trousdale County High Sch., Hartsville, Tenn., 1949-50; instr. voice, organ, piano, music lit. East Central Jr. Coll., Decatur, Miss., 1951-54; instr. voice, music edn., theory and organ Wartburg Coll., Waverly, Iowa, 1954-58; instr. music edn. and voice George Peabody Coll. and Demonstration Sch., Nashville, 1958-60; ch. musician, Presbyterian, Episcopal, Methodist and Christian chs., Nashville, 1958-68, Presbyn. chs., Tuscaloosa, Ala., 1970—. Mem. Am. Guild Organists, Nat. Assn. Tchrs. Singing, Presbyn. Assn. Musicians, Christers Guild, Tenn. Folklore Soc., Sigma Alpha Iota. Presbyterian. Clubs: Tuscaloosa Music, Univ. Ala. Women's. Home: 13-I Northwood Lake Northport AL 35476 Office: 113 Hargrove Rd Tuscaloosa AL 35401

KEMERY, FRED DAVIDSON, ins. co. exec.; b. Woodbury, N.J., May 23, 1936; s. Fred Berkibile and Josephine Madelaine (Davidson) K.; B.S. in Econs., Commerce and Fin., Bucknell U., 1958; m. Gail Christine Griffin, Jan. 15, 1960; children—David Alan, Douglas Craig. Asst. mgr. dept. premium accounts Acacia Mut. Life Ins. Co., Washington, 1960-65; dir. adminstrv. services Nat. Variable Annuity Co. of Fla., Jacksonville, 1965-68, 2d v.p., 1968-70; 2d v.p. Voyager Securities Inc., Jacksonville, 1969-71, v.p. adminstrn., treas., 1971—, also dir.; 2d v.p. Voyager Life Ins. Co., Jacksonville, 1970-71, v.p. adminstrn., 1971—; v.p. adminstrn. Eaglets' Nat. Life Ins. Co., Cin., 1971-72, dir., 1972—; v.p. adminstrn. Nat. Life of Fla. Corp., Jacksonville, 1971—; chmn. bd. mgrs. Voyager Variable Annuity Fund, 1972—; v.p. First Protection Life Ins. Co., 1975—; v.p. adminstrn. Voyager Property & Casualty Ins. Co., 1978—, Voyager Life Ins. Co. S.C., 1978—. Sec.-treas. Fla. Jr. Coll. Found. Served to capt. USAR, 1958-64. Mem. Am. Soc. Personnel Adminstrn., Am. Mgmt. Assn., Adminstrv. Mgmt. Soc., Jacksonville C. of C. (com. of 100). Republican. Congregationalist. Club: Sertoma. Home: 5377 Floral Ave Jacksonville FL 32211 Office: 2255 Phyllis St Jacksonville FL 32204

KEMMERER, ANDREW JOSEPH, govt. ofcl.; b. Bryan, Tex., Feb. 11, 1938; s. Arthur Russel and Dorothy Ann (Lindsey) K.; B.S. with honors, U. Ariz., 1960, M.S., 1965; Ph.D., Utah State U., 1970; m. Madeleine Diane Brown, Aug. 27, 1960; children—Scott Lee, Mark Arthur. Fisheries research biologist Ariz. Game and Fish Dept., Phoenix, 1965-67; ecologist Engring. Sci., Inc., Honolulu, Washington, 1970-71; program mgr. Nat. Marine Fisheries Service, Pascagoula, Miss., 1971-73, tech. coordinator, Washington, 1973-74, dir. tech. div., Bay St. Louis, Miss., 1974-77, dir. Nat. Fisheries Engring. Lab., 1977—; cons. Engring. Sci., Inc., 1971-72, Tetra Tech, Inc., Pasagoula, Miss., 1972; adj. asso. prof. Miss. State U., 1975—. Active Save Kaneohe Bay, 1971, Little League Football, 1974, Little League Baseball, 1974, Friends of Picayune Library, 1975. Served to capt. USAF, 1960-63. Recipient awards NOAA, 1974, 76, Dept. Commerce, 1979. Mem. Am. Fisheries Inst., Am. Soc. Limnology and Oceanography, Miss. Coast Assn. Fed. Adminstrs., Miss. Heart Assn., Scabbard and Blade, Delta Tau Delta. Democrat. Presbyn. Club: Picayune Millbrook Country. Contbr. articles to profl. jours. Home: 215 Boley Dr Picayune MS 39466 Office: Nat Marine Fisheries Service Nat Space Tech Labs Bay St Louis MS 39520

KEMMERLY, JAMES ROBERT, physician; b. Baton Rouge, Aug. 15, 1936; s. Carl Edward and Edith May (Wright) K.; B.S., La. State U., 1957, M.D., 1960; postgrad. Perkins Sch. Theology, So. Meth. U., 1957-59; m. Linda Sue Martin, June 12, 1960; children—David Lee, Kelly Rene. Intern, So. Bapt. Hosp., New Orleans, 1960-61, resident, 1963-66; practice medicine, specializing in obstetrics and gynecology, Minden, La., 1966—; clin. asst. prof. La. State U. Sch. Medicine, Shreveport, 1972-79; pres. med. staff Minden Med. Center, 1972, 76, 77; dir. Peoples Bank & Trust Co., Minden. Served as capt. USAF, 1962-63. Diplomate Am. Bd. Obstetrics and Gynecology. Fellow Am. Coll. Obstetricians and Gynecologists; mem. AMA, Webster Parish Med. Soc. (pres. 1972). Methodist (chmn. council on ministries 1975, mem. bd. ch. and society La. ann. conf. 1974—, chmn. adminstrv. bd. 1976-77, lay del. 1976 Gen. Conf.). Home: 1501 N Chrislo Dr Minden LA 71055 Office: 425 Homer Rd Minden 71055

KEMP, CYNTHIA JO BILLINGSLEY, med. social worker; b. Carroll County, Tenn., Nov. 21, 1934; d. Martin Eugene and Frances Ella (Thomas) Billingsley; B.S., Bethel Coll., McKenzie, Tenn., 1957; M.S.W., Tulane U., 1965; m. James Andrew Kemp, Oct. 22, 1978. With Tenn. Human Service Dept., 1958-68; psychiat. social worker W. Ky. Mental Health Center, Paducah area, 1968-74; med. social worker Henry County Hosp., Paris, Tenn., 1974—, dir. social service, 1974—; chmn. Henry County Interagency Council. Mem. Nat. Assn. Social Workers, Acad. Certified Social Workers. Democrat. Methodist. Clubs: Democratic Woman's, D.A.R. (chaplain), UDC, Quota Club (bd. dirs.), County Geneal. Soc. (program chmn.), Order Eastern Star (marshall Paducah, 1972-73, officer McKenzie, Tenn., 1975-76, Paris, Tenn., 1977-78). Home: Box 3554 Henry TN 38231 Office: Henry County Hosp Tyson Ave Paris TN 38242

KEMP, HARRIS ATTERIDGE, architect; b. Kewanee, Ill., July 3, 1912; s. John Edward and Pauline (King) K.; B.S., U. Ill., 1934, M.S., 1935; M.Arch., M.I.T., 1937, postgrad. (Francis J. Plym fellow), 1937-38; m. Carol Western, Sept. 18, 1937; children—David A., Peter A., Constance S. Architect, State of Wis., 1938-40; chief designer George L. Dahl-Architects & Engrs., Dallas, 1940-55; partner Harper & Kemp, Architects, Dallas, 1955-75, Harper, Kemp, Clutts & Parker, Architecture/Planning, Dallas, 1975—; mem. Dallas Zoning Revision Com., Dallas West Revitalization Commn., Urban Design Task Force, Central Dist. Plan Com.; mem. Public Adv. Panel, region 7 GSA. Trustee, Dallas Symphony Assn.; bd. dirs. Central Bus. Dist. Assn., Dallas. Fellow AIA (pres. Dallas chpt. 1957); mem. Tex. Soc. Architects (dir. 1964-68). Presbyterian. Clubs: Dallas Country, Kiwanis (Dallas). Maj. work: Dallas City Hall. Home: 5328 Waneta Dr Dallas TX 75209 Office: 1201 Elm St Suite 720 Dallas TX 75270

KEMP, HERBERT LEE, oil co. exec.; b. Ft. Worth, Apr. 11, 1939; s. James Clyde and Mary Jean (Johns) K.; B.B.A., U. Houston, 1966; m. Penny Darnell White, Mar. 19, 1962; 1 dau., Brandi Kay. Audit mgr. Arthur Young & Co., 1966-75; controller TransOcean Oil, Inc., Houston, 1975-76, v.p. fin., treas., 1976—; dir. Paloma Pipeline Co. Served with USAF, 1958-63. C.P.A. Mem. Am. Inst. C.P.A.'s, Tex. Soc. C.P.A.'s. Home: 3403 Redwood Lodge Ct Kingwood TX 77339 Office: 1700 First City East Bldg Houston TX 77002

KEMP, HERBERT LYLE, JR., accountant; b. Beaver Falls, Pa., May 8, 1930; s. Herbert Lyle and Clara Margaret (McNutt) K.; B.A., Robert Morris Coll., 1956; postgrad. Western Community Coll., 1966, U. Va., 1972; m. Mary Louise Atkins, Apr. 5, 1952; children—Douglas Lyle, Mark Allen. Auditor, Standard Coffee Co., New Orleans, 1952-54; chief accountant Skyline Lumber, Roanoke, Va., 1957-60; office mgr. Kane Furniture Co., Charlottesville, Va., 1960-64; auditor, Roanoke, Va., 1964-70, asst. city auditor, 1970-75; pres. Accounting & Tax Cons., Roanoke, Va., 1975—, treas., controller; pres. Blue Ridge Investigation Service, Inc., 1966—, Structural Detailing, Inc., 1970—, Perfection Muffler Service, 1973—, Kelley Advt. Art, 1970— (all Roanoke). Sr. counselor United Comml. Travelers, 1974-75; state chmn. Retarded Children's Fund, United Comml. Travelers Found., Roanoke, Va., 1966—; gt. ruler, fin. officer Ancient Mystic Order Bagman-United Comml. Travelers, Internat., 1972-77. Served with USNR, 1946-52. Recipient Civil Merit award State Va., 1970, Certificate of Credit, State Va., 1973. Mem. Nat. Assn. Accountants (pres. 1974—, dir. governing bd. 1974-75, recipient spl. awards). Baptist. Home: 172 Verndale Dr NE Roanoke VA 24019

KEMP, JAMES BRADLEY, JR., lawyer; b. New Orleans, Apr. 10, 1932; s. James Bradley and Honora Arlene (Pickren) K.; B.B.A., Tulane U., 1953, J.D., 1958; m. Marguerite Bradburn Freret, Sept. 6, 1952; children—James, Randolph, Ann, Robert. Admitted to La. bar, 1958, U.S. Supreme Ct., 1970, U.S. Customs Ct., 1969; internat. admiralty atty. Phelps, Dunbar, Marks, Claverie & Sims, New Orleans, 1958—, partner, 1964—; speaker Southeastern Admiralty Law Inst., 1975, bd. govs., 1977—; speaker U. New Orleans Maritime Seminar, 1977; mem. met. area com. Bur. Govtl. Research. Solicitor, United Fund, New Orleans, 1963-68, Heart Fund, New Orleans, 1975. Served to 1st lt. AUS, 1953-55. Mem. Maritime Law Assn. (mem. com. on mcht. marine programs 1973—, com. nav. and coast guard matters 1976—, com. marine fisheries 1979—, com. fisheries in U.S. 1979—), Fed., La. (com. bar admissions 1978—), New Orleans bar assns., Internat. Bar Assn., Marine Tech. Soc. (com. marine law and policy 1979—), Def. Research Inst., Propeller Club U.S., Internat. House, New Orleans, La. def. counsel assns., Average Adjusters Assn., Phi Delta Phi. Republican. Presbyn. (deacon, elder; chmn. bd. deacons 1969, chmn. planning and coordinating com. 1977-79). Clubs: So. Yacht, Plimsoll, Whitehall, Blenville, Mariners of the Port New Orleans, U.S. Yacht Racing Union. Bd. editors Tulane Law Rev., 1956-58. Home: 241 Bellaire Dr New Orleans LA 70124 Office: 1300 Hibernia Bank Bldg 313 Carondelet St New Orleans 70112

KEMP, MAURICE CLARENCE, microbiologist; b. Stettler, Alta., Can., Dec. 27, 1946; came to U.S., 1970, naturalized, 1981; s. Walter H. and Lillian Marjorie Kemp; B.S., U. Alta., Can., 1970; Ph.D. (fellow) in Virology, U. Miss., 1975; postgrad. U. Ala., 1975-80; m. Yvonne Van Driven, Aug. 30, 1969. Asso. scientist Diabetes Research and Tng. Center, U. Ala., Birmingham, 1977-80; vis. scientist CDC, Atlanta, 1980—. Nat. Cancer Inst. fellow, 1978-79; Anna Fuller Fund fellow, 1975-77; Juvenile Diabetes Found. fellow, 1977. Mem. Am. Soc. Microbiology, AAAS, Sigma Xi. Republican. Contbr. articles on virology and liquid chromatography to sci. jours. Office: CDC Bldg 7 Atlanta GA 30333

KEMP, RAMEY FLOYD, chiropractor, state legislator; b. High Point, N.C., Sept. 29, 1919; s. William T. and Etta G. (Dailey) K.; D. Chiropractic, Logan Chiropractic Coll., 1950; m. Emily L. Betts, Aug. 4, 1939; children—Ramey Floyd, Gregg D. Pvt. practice as chiropractor, Mocksville, N.C., 1950—; mem. N.C. Bd. Chiropractic Examiners. Mem. Davie County Bd. Elections, 1958-74; chmn., Davie County Democratic party, 1974—; mem. N.C. State Dem. Exec. Com., 1974—; mem. N.C. Ho. of Reps., 1978—. Served with AUS, 1944-46. Recipient Distinguished Service awards Jaycees, 1954, N.C. Chiropractic Assn., 1973, 74. Fellow Internat. Coll. Chiropractors; mem. Am. (del. 1976—), N.C. (pres. 1960-61) chiropractic assns. Mason, Moose, Rotarian. Home: 842 Halander St Mocksville NC 27028 Office: PO Box 361 600 Wilkesboro St Mocksville NC 27028

KEMP, ROBERT AITKEN, educator; b. Paulina, Iowa, Mar. 2, 1929; s. Bert F. and Ruth J. (Aitken) K.; student N.C. State U. and U. N.C., 1956-58; B.A. in Bus., George Washington U., 1964; B.S. in Mil. Sci., U. Md., 1966; M.B.A., Ariz. State U., 1969, D.B.A., 1979; m. Alice Arlene Mills, Dec. 23, 1950; children—Robert Randolph, Joyce Elizabeth. Served as enlisted man U.S. Army, 1950-52, commd. 2d lt., 1952, advanced through grades to lt. col., 1968, served C.E., engr. troop command and staff assignments, airborne troop comdr., served Germany, Japan, Korea, Turkey at Theater Army and Dept. Army levels, ret., 1973; Champlin prof. mktg. and mgmt., dir. Center Bus. and Communication, Phillips U., Enid, Okla., 1976—; cons., instr. SBA and Small Bus. in Okla.; pvt. cons. mgmt., mktg., internat. bus. Okla. del. White House Conf. on Small Bus., 1980; active Gt. Salt Plains council Boy Scouts Am., mem. nat. com. on tng. lit. Decorated Legion of Merit, Meritorious Service medal with oak leaf cluster. Recipient Silver Beaver award, Boy Scouts Am., 1971. Mem. Soc. Mil. Engrs., Nat. Assn. Purchasing Mgrs. (grantee 1977-79), Enid Assn. Personnel Mgrs. Republican. Mem. Christian Ch. (Disciples of Christ). Club: Kiwanis. Contbr. articles to mil. publs., paper to internat. bus. meeting, France, 1975. Office: Phillips U University Station Enid OK 73701

KEMPA, JOHN FRANCIS, plastic mfg. co. exec.; b. Krosno, Poland, Aug. 1, 1929; s. Rudolf and Maria (Medrek) K.; M.E., Lilford (Eng.) Tech., 1948; m. Masie Nolan, Mar. 2, 1952; children—Anthony J., Susan M., Kellie C. Devel. engr. Brit. Indsl. Plastics, 1949-51; tool engr. A.V. Roe Aircraft, Malton, Can., 1951-54; procedure engr. De Haviland Aircraft Co., Toronto, Ont., Can., 1954-60; tool engr. Chevrolet div. Gen. Motors Corp., Massena, N.Y., 1960-66; pres., chmn. bd. Kempa Industries Inc., Palm Bay, Fla., 1966—. Served with U.S. Navy, 1945-46. Mem. Brevard County Mfg. Assn. (treas. 1976, co-chmn. Expo 77), Brevard Mfg. Co. (dir.). Democrat. Roman Catholic. Club: Aztec. Office: Kempa Industries Inc PO Box 454 Palm Bay FL 32905

KEMPER, ROBERT MITCHELL, JR., cost estimating engr.; b. Hapeville, Ga., Mar. 20, 1926; s. Robert Mitchell and Joelma (Gibson) K.; student N.C. State Coll., 1943-44, Ohio State U., 1944-45; B.S. in Civil Engring., U. Tenn., 1949; m. Janette Jackson, June 5, 1948; children—Kathy Jo, Barbara Ann, Linda Susan. Design engr. nuclear div. Union Carbide Corp., Oak Ridge, 1953-55, constrn. engr., 1955-61, cost estimating engr., 1961—; partner R.M. Kemper & Son, Oak Ridge, 1954-60; instr. Tng. and Tech. Sch. Oak Ridge, 1960-64. Chmn. UN Com. Oak Ridge, 1957-58; campaign dir. Oak Ridge chpt. March of Dimes, 1958; pres. Savoyards, Light Opera Co., Oak Ridge, 1958-59; merit badge counselor Pellissippi dist. Smoky Mountain council Boy Scouts Am., 1959—; active Girl Scouts U.S., 1958-69. Served with S.C., AUS, 1943-46, C.E., 1950-51. Registered profl. engr., Tenn. Mem. Am. Assn. Cost Engrs., Dixie Round Dance Council (chmn. 1972-73, sec., newsletter editor 1970-71), Tenn. Soc. Profl. Engrs., Sons Confederate Vets., Legacy, Round alab; Order Star and Bars (aide to comdr.-in-chief), Germanna Found., Internat. Platform Assn., VFW, Am. Legion, Pellissippi Geneal. Soc., Tenn. Assn. Sq. and Round Dance Clubs (pres.). Square, round dance choreographer, instr.; exhbn. round dance at convs., meetings. Home: 102 Case Ln Oak Ridge TN 37830 Office: Nuclear Div Union Carbide Corp Oak Ridge TN 37830

KEMPTHORNE, RICHARD LEWIS, constrn. industry exec.; b. Orange, N.J., Jan. 7, 1927; s. James Lewis and Eleanor (McKelvey) K.; Asso. Bus. Adminstrn., Nichols Coll., 1949; B.S., Syracuse U., 1951; m. Alice Clair Prost, Feb. 26, 1949; children—James Lewis III, Ann. Vice pres. Sprayed Insulation Inc., Newark, 1951-53; head Columbia Acoustics & Fireproofing Co., Stanhope, N.J., 1954-56; chief exec., sec.-treas. Fla. Insulation & Fireproofing Co., Miami, 1957-65; pres., dir. Sprayed Fibers, Inc., Miami, 1963-71, Spraydon Overseas Corp., Miami, 1966-71; v.p. Tex. Fireproofing Co., Houston, 1960-63; pres., dir. Sprayon Research Corp., Ft. Lauderdale, Fla., 1964—; pres., dir. Midwest Sprayon Corp., Miami, 1966-71, Sprayon Internat. Inc., N.Y.C., 1971-73, Spraydon Corp., 1974—, Spraydon Corp. Ltd., 1974—; pres. Am. Energy Products Corp., 1977—; acoustical cons. Mem. bd. elections Young Republicans of Miami, 1958—. Pres. Miami Shores Prep. Sch., 1968-72. Served with USNR, 1944-46. Mem. Am. Soc. Testing Materials, Nat. Fireprotection Assn., Internat. Assn. Walls and Ceilings Contractors, Amateur Athletic Union. Clubs: Miami Shores Country (pres. swimming assn. 1964-67); Marine Bay. Patentee in field. Address: 5701 Bayview Dr Fort Lauderdale FL 33308

KENDALL, LLOYD DAVID, data processing corp. exec.; b. LeCenter, Minn., Nov. 28, 1936; s. Roy Victor and Dorothy Marie (Poehler) K.; B.S. in Fgn. Service, Georgetown U., 1965; div.; 1 son, Michael Henry. Editor, Nat. Inst. Municipal Law Officers, Washington, 1959-68; exec. v.p. Autocode, Inc., Washington, 1968-70, Autocomp, Inc., Bethesda, Md., 1970-75; dir. info. services Aspen Systems Corp. (subs. Am. Can Co.), Germantown, Md., 1975-76; v.p., gen. mgr. Informatics, Inc. (subs. Equitable Life Assurance Soc. of U.S.), Rockville, Md., 1976—; sr. staff Informatics, Inc., 1977—. Active PTA, Arlington, Va., Washington-Lee High Sch. Boosters, Arlington. Served with USAF, 1955-59. Mem. Am. Mgmt. Assn., Nat. Assn. Watch and Clock Collectors, Graphic Computer Communications Assn. Republican. Lutheran. Editor of Law and Computer Technology, 1968. Home: 1312 Deep Run Ln Reston VA 22090 Office: 6811 Kenilworth Ave Riverdale MD 20840

KENDALL, ROBERT LEON, educator; b. Smith County, Kans., Nov. 13, 1930; s. Bernard and Thelma (Swallow) K.; B.D., Christian Theol. Sem., 1961; M.A., Butler U., 1963; Ph.D., Ind. U., 1972; m. Judith Ann Borchelt, Nov. 24, 1972; children—Kristine Kendall Williamson, David. Ordained to ministry Christian Ch., 1953; lectr. Christian Theol. Sem., Indpls., 1960-64; writer/producer Insight, Sta. WFMB-TV, Indpls., 1960-64; teaching asso. Ind. U., Bloomington, 1964-67; asso. minister Bedford (Ind.) Christian Ch., 1964-67; asst. prof. mass communication Central Mo. State Coll., Warrensburg, 1967-74; asso. prof. pub. relations Coll. Journalism and Communications, U. Fla., Gainesville, 1972—; pub. relations cons. Planned Parenthood of North Central Fla., 1976—. Mem. Assn. for Edn. in Journalism, Pub. Relations Soc. Am. (accredited, nat. accreditation bd. 1979—, v.p. north Fla. chpt. 1977-78), Speech Communication Assn., Fla. Pub. Relations Assn., Humanist Soc. Gainesville, Eta Beta Rho. Democrat. Unitarian Universalist. Contbr. articles to profl. jours. Home: 625 NW 36th Ave Gainesville FL 32601 Office: 234 Stadium U Fla Gainesville FL 32611

KENDALL, SARAH ANN ANTROBUS, speech pathologist; b. Clarendon, Tex., Feb. 17, 1943; d. Barcus Coleman and Annie Beatrice (Williamson) Antrobus; B.A., W. Tex. State U., 1964; M.A., Tex. Technol. U., 1967; m. Sam A. Kendall, Jr., June 4, 1969; children—Becky Kay, Sam Coleman Robinson, Cliff Reagan. Speech pathologist Slaton (Tex.) Public Schs., 1964-65; teaching asst. speech Tex. Technol. U., Lubbock, 1965; speech pathologist Hereford (Tex.) Public Schs., 1966-67, Odessa (Tex.) Public Schs., 1967-69, Petersburg (Tex.) Public Schs., 1971-73, Plainview (Tex.) Public Schs., 1969-71, 73—; cons. Eleanor S. Griffin Tng. Center, 1969-71; cons. in field. Troop leader, organizer Girl Scouts U.S.; mem. Plainview Citizens Paper Recycling Com., 1975-79. Mem. Am. Speech-Lang.-Hearing Assn. (cert. clin. competence in speech pathology), AAUW, Tex. Tchrs. Assn., Tex. Classroom Tchrs. Assn. (1st v.p. 1979-80), Tex. Speech and Hearing Assn., NEA. Presbyterian (youth sponsor, children's Sunday Sch. tchr., mem. Christian edn., fellowship coms.). Clubs: Kappa Kappa Iota (pres. chpt. 1974—), Sigma Alpha Eta, Jaycettes. Home: 2907 Edgemere Dr Plainview TX 79072 Office: 2601 W 20th St Plainview TX 79072

KENDELL, NEVIN EUGENE, coll. adminstr.; b. Milledgeville, Ill., Nov. 27, 1920; s. Glen Wayland and Hazel Mary (Robinson) K.; B.S., U. Ill., 1942; Dipl., McCormick Theol. Sem., 1945; m. Rachel Agnes Martin, Dec. 31, 1949; children—Anita Carol, Jennifer Martin. Ordained to ministry, Presbyn. Ch., 1945; exec. for racial and cultural relations Presbyn. Bd. Christian Edn., Phila., 1945-47; dir. Presbyn. Settlement House, Pursglove, W.Va., 1947-50; editor youth curriculum Presbyn. Bd. Christian Edn., Phila., 1950-58; pastor North Presbyn. Ch., North Tonawanda, N.Y., 1958-65; capital campaign area dir. United Presbyn. Ch., N.Y.C., 1965-67; v.p. for devel. Davis and Elkins Coll., 1967—. Contbr. articles to religious jours. Office: Davis and Elkins Coll Elkins WV 26241

KENDERDINE, JOHN MARSHALL, mfg. co. exec.; b. Ft. Worth, Dec. 6, 1912; s. Robert Leonard and Caroline (Raab) K.; B.S. in Petroleum Engring., Tex. A. and M. Coll., 1934; grad. Army War Coll., 1953, Advanced Mgmt. Program, Harvard, 1959, Exec. Decision Inst., 1962; m. Su Anne Carroll, Feb. 26, 1937; children—James Marshall, Su Carroll Hain Petroleum engr. Gulf Oil Corp., 1934-37; br. mgr. Norvell-Wilder Supply Co., Midland, Tex., 1938-41; commd. 1st lt. U.S. Army, 1941, advanced through grades to brig. gen., 1962; mil. logistician in France, Germany and U.S., World War II; spl. asst. to adminstr. War Assets Adminstrn., 1946; mil. staff and command assignments, 1947-60; joint petroleum officer Europe, 1961; exec. dir. supply ops. Def. Supply Agy., 1962-65; comdr. Def. Indsl. Supply Center, Phila., 1965-66, Def. Personnel Support Center, Phila., 1966-67; ret., 1967; v.p. spl. tech. Scott Paper Co., Phila., 1967-70; pres. C.F. Adams, Inc., Fort Worth, 1970—. Decorated D.S.M., Legion of Merit, Joint Service Commendation medal, Commendation ribbon with 3 oak leaf clusters. Registered profl. engr., Tex. Mem. Soc. Logistics Engrs., Def. Supply Assn., Assn. U.S. Army, Airline Passengers Assn. (adv. bd.), Phila. C. of C. (dir. 1966), Am. Mgmt. Assn. Club: Petroleum. Contbr. articles on handling and safety of aviation fuels, especially turbine fuels to profl. jours. Home: 3212 Chapparal Ln Fort Worth TX 76109 Office: Box 253 Fort Worth TX 76101

KENDRICK, HERBERT SPENCER, JR., lawyer; b. Brownfield, Tex., Nov. 16, 1934; s. Herbert Spencer and Elsie (Woosley) K.; B.B.A., So. Methodist U., 1957, LL.B., 1960; LL.M., Harvard U., 1961; m. Carol Ann Puckett, Sept. 6, 1958; children—Herbert Spencer III, Kathryn Gene. Admitted to Tex. bar, 1960; trial atty. tax div. U.S. Justice Dept., Washington and Ft. Worth, 1961-65; practiced in Dallas, 1965—; partner Kendrick & Kendrick, 1965-69, Turner, Rodgers, Winn, Scurlock & Sailers, 1969-71, Kendrick, Kendrick & Bradley, 1971-76, Jenkens & Gilchrist, 1976—; dir. Capital Bank, Dallas; adj. prof. taxation Law Sch., So. Methodist U., Dallas, 1966—. Bd. dirs. Tex. Hist. Found., Austin. Mem. Am., Tex., Dallas bar assns., So. Meth. U. Law Alumni Assn. (council 1979—, dir. 1979—), Phi Alpha Delta, Sigma Alpha Epsilon. Presbyterian. Mason (32 deg., Shriner). Clubs: Dallas, Brook Hollow Golf. Author: (with John J. Kendrick, Jr.) Texas Transaction Guide, 12 vols., 1972, 73. Home: 4421 Larchmont Ave Dallas TX 75205 Office: First Nat Bank Bldg Dallas TX 75202

KENDRICK, PETER JOHN, telecommunications co. exec.; b. Staten Island, N.Y., July 7, 1954; s. Arthur Huey and Jean (Trowern) K.; B.S., Purdue U., 1976; M.B.A., George Washington U., 1980; m. Marian J. Messro, Aug. 28, 1977. Asst. editor Water Pollution Control Fedn., Washington, 1976-77; profl. services mgr. SCS Engrs., Washington, 1977-79; gen. mgr., sec. Capitol Telecomputing Corp., McLean, Va., 1979—. Mem. planning and zoning com. Reston Community Assn. Mem. Assn. M.B.A. Execs., Am. Mgmt. Assn., Soc. Advanced Mgmt. Contbr. articles to profl. jours. Home: 1434 Greenmont Ct Reston VA 22090 Office: 1616 Anderson Rd McLean VA 22102

KENEIPP, TIMOTHY WYN, architect; b. Antigo, Wis., Mar. 22, 1946; s. Mervin Dale and Leola Wynifred (Jordon) K.; B.Arch., Tex. A&M U., 1970, M.Arch., 1971; m. Rita Baker King, Dec. 23, 1971. Architect/planner, SW Planning Assos., Inc., Bryan, Tex., 1971-73; architect I, Dept. Facilities Planning & Construction, Tex. A&M U., College Station, 1973-76; prin. Keneipp & Assos.: Architects, College Station, 1976—; pres. Habitex Devel. Corp., 1979—. Mem. Building Code Bd. of Adjustment, City of College Station, 1977—. Dir. StageCenter, Inc., Bryan, 1975-77, Brazos Valley March of Dimes, Bryan-College Station, 1977-78. Mem. AIA (pres. Brazos chpt. 1978), Tex. Soc. Architects. Democrat. Christian Scientist. Club: College Station Morning Lions. Home: 203 Suffolk St College Station TX 77840 Office: PO Box 9281 College Station TX 77840

KENNARD-KUNKEL, SARA SUE, cable TV office adminstr.; b. Beggs, Okla., Feb. 22, 1924; d. Frank James and Bobbie Ethel (Landers) Kennard; student in comml. art (Univ. scholar) Oklahoma City U., 1942; B.S. in Sociology, East Carolina U., 1944, M.S. in Anthropology; postgrad. in indsl. research U. Ark., 1971-72; m. Peter H. Kunkel, 1966; children—Gene Mapes, Ambher Alexander, Margeurite Trickey, Raymond Robbins, Robin Robbins. Office mgr. Village CATV, Inc., Bentonville, Ark., 1973— Vol., OEO, Fayetteville, Ark. Served with WAC, 1942-44; PTO. Mem. Profl. Writers Am., Nat. Small Bus. Assn. Baptist. Author: Spout Springs, a Minority Community, 1972; research on slavery. Home: 2 Deben Circle Bella Vista AR 72712 Office: Vill Catv Inc Route 6 Box 80 Bentonville AR 72712

KENNEDY, HARVEY JOHN, JR., lawyer; b. Barnesville, Ga., Apr. 9, 1924; s. Harvey John and Marisu (Reeves) K.; grad. Gordon Mil. Coll., 1942; J.D., U. Ga., 1949; m. Jean McRitchie King, Apr. 8, 1950; children—Marisu, Jean Gay. Admitted to Ga. bar, 1948; county atty., Lamar County, 1950-52; city atty., Barnesville, Ga., 1953-65; atty. Lamar Elec. Membership Corp.; atty. Lamar County, 1958-60, 65-68; atty. Town of Milner (Ga.), 1963-68; govt. appeal agt. local bd. 89, 1958-76. Trustee Gordon Mil. Coll., 1953-63; mem. Indigent Def. Council Ga., 1979-83. Served as 2d lt. to capt., 86th Inf. Div., ETO, PTO, AUS, 1942-46; capt. U.S. Army Judge Adv. Gen. Corps. Res., 1949-52. Decorated Bronze Star medal. Mem. Am. Judicature Soc., Am., Ga. (bd. govs. 1957-58), Flint Circuit (pres. 1961, 64-65) bar assns., Am. Trial Lawyers Assn., Internat. Platform Assn., State Bar Ga., Peace Officers Assn. Ga. (asso.), Am. Acad. Polit. and Social Sci., Ga. Assn. Plaintiffs Trial Attys. (v.p. 1968-72), Ga. Trial Lawyers Assn. (v.p. 1972—), Am. Legion, VFW, Chi Phi, Delta Theta Phi. Democrat. Baptist. Mason (32 deg., Shriner), Moose, Rotarian (pres. 1959-60). Home: 392 Spencer St Barnesville GA 30204 Office: 217 Zebulon St Barnesville GA 30204

KENNEDY, JOHN ELMO, biol. chemist; b. Louisville, June 21, 1932; s. John E. and Anna L. (Smith) K.; B.S., U. Louisville, 1959, Ph.D. (NIH fellow), 1963; m. Carolyn M. Kaleher, Sept. 11, 1954 (div. June 1976); children—Kevin P., Eric B., John E. III, Brian B. With Ky. Color & Chem. Co., 1955-59; chemist dept. exptl. medicine U. Louisville, 1959-61; biol. chemist Brown & Williamson Tobacco Corp., Louisville, 1963—, scientist, 1970-76; instr. dept. chemistry U. Louisville, 1976-77; cons., 1977—. Mem. dist. exec. com., merit badge counselor, cubmaster, scoutmaster Boy Scouts Am. Served with AUS, 1953-55. Fellow Am. Inst. Chemists; mem. Am. Chem. Soc. (treas. 1972, chmn. 1975), AAAS, N.Y. Acad. Scis., Sigma Xi, Phi Lambda Upsilon. Contbr. papers on tobacco chemistry. Patentee in field. Home and Office: 3201 Leith Ln Apt 803 Louisville KY 40218

KENNEDY, ROBERT LOUIS, hosp. adminstr.; b. Metter, Ga., Sept. 21, 1940; s. Robert Louis and Leola (Elkins) K.; A.B., Duke U., 1963, M.H.A., 1966; m. Pamela Macnair, Nov. 29, 1969; children—Amy Leigh, Robin Rae, Justin James. Asst. adminstr. North Broward Hosp., Pompano Beach, Fla., 1968-72, adminstr., 1972—. Bd. dirs. Trinity United Methodist Ch. Served with USPHS, 1966-68. Fellow Am. Coll. Hosp. Adminstrs.; mem. Pompano Beach C. of C. (dir.), Deerfield Beach C. of C. (dir.). Clubs: Greater Pompano Beach Jaycees (past pres.), Rotary (pres. Deerfield Beach chpt. 1978-79). Home: 2910 NE 41st St Lighthouse Point FL 33064 Office: 201 E Sample Rd Pompano Beach FL 33064

KENNEDY, SUSAN ESTABROOK, historian; b. N.Y.C., June 8, 1942; d. Austin Lovell and Dorothy (Ogden) Estabrook; B.A. summa cum laude, Marymount Manhattan Coll., 1964; M.A., Columbia U., 1965, Ph.D., 1971; m. E. Craig Kennedy, Jr., Nov. 28, 1970. Lectr. in history Hunter Coll., City U. N.Y., 1966-67; instr. Temple U., 1967-72, asst. prof., 1972-73; asst. prof. history Va. Commonwealth U., 1973-76, asso. prof., 1976—; cons. oral history. John Simon Guggenheim Meml. Found. fellow, 1978-79. Mem. Richmond Oral History Assn. (sec. 1974-76, pres. 1976-77), Am. Hist. Assn., Orgn. Am. Historians, AAUP, Oral History Assn., Va. Oral History Assn. Author: The Banking Crisis of 1933, 1973; If All We Did Was to Weep at Home: A History of White Working Class Women in America, 1979. Contbr. articles to profl. jours. Home: 8200 Notre Dame Dr Richmond VA 23228 Office: Virginia Commonwealth U Richmond VA 23284

KENNEDY, THOMAS WILLIAM, JR., constrn. and design engr.; b. Charleston, S.C., June 24, 1942: s. Thomas William and Gertrude Lillith (Von Glahn) K.; B.S. in Civil Engring., The Citadel, 1964, M.B.A., 1979; M.S. in Civil Engring., W.Va. U., 1966; m. Lorena Jeanette Maher, June 18, 1966; children—Thomas William III, Tamara Leigh. Structural engr. U.S. Navy, 1964-66; soils and founds. engr. Law Engring. & Testing Co., Jacksonville, Fla., 1969-70; sales engr. Sloan Constrn Co. Inc., Columbia, S.C., 1970-72; project engr. Ballenger Corp., Republic of Panama, 1972-74; v.p., treas. Palmetto Engring. Co. Inc., Columbia, S.C., 1974-76; project engr. Epting Ballenger Corp., Charleston, S.C., 1976-78; cost and engring. scheduling engr. Ballenger Corp., Greenville, S.C., 1979-80; chief of design engring. S.C. State Ports Authority, Charleston, 1980—. Served in USAF, 1966-69. Decorated Air Force Commendation medal with oak leaf cluster. Registered profl. engr., S.C., Ga., N.C., Fla., C.Z.; registered land surveyor, S.C.; lic. gen. contractor, S.C. Mem. Nat. Soc. Profl. Engrs., Assn. Citadel Men (life), Res. Officers Assn. U.S. Roman Catholic. Clubs: Civil Engrs. (Charleston, S.C.); Century, Brigadier, Elks.

KENNEDY, WILLIAM CHARLES, educator; b. St. Paul, Sept. 7, 1935; s. Fred Clarence and Beatrice Evelyn (Munson) K.; B.S., U. Minn., 1962; M.F.A., U. Wis., 1967; m. Patricia Rae Ringer, July 21, 1962; children—William Charles, Derek Thomas. Tchr. art Beloit (Wis.) Pub. Schs., 1962-64, Madison (Wis.) Pub. Schs., 1965-66; research asst. U. Wis., 1966-67, teaching asst., 1967; freelance graphic designer, Madison, 1967-68; publs. designer Wis. State U. at Whitewater, 1968; asst. prof. art U. Tenn., 1968-75, adviser Coll. Liberal Arts, 1971-75, curriculum chmn. dept. art, 1972-75, asso. prof. art, 1975—, adminstrv. asst. art, 1977-78, asso. dept. head, 1978—; design cons. to industry; artist, works exhibited in one and two-man shows, pub. collections. Bd. dirs. Knoxville Montessori Assn., 1968-71, v.p., 1969-70. Served with USAF, 1955-58. Mem. AAUP, Coll. Art Assn., Southeastern Coll. Art Conf., Nat. Conf. Art Adminstrs. Home: 7018 Shady Land Dr Knoxville TN 37919

KENNEDY, WILLIAM MORRIS, advt. agy. exec.; b. Pitts., June 3, 1948; s. Morris Frame and Dorothy Ann K.; A.A. in Music, Miami-Dade Community Coll., 1969; B.S. in Advt., U. Fla., 1975. Copywriter, Canon Advt., Tallahassee, Fla., 1970-72; graphics coordinator Black, Crow & Eidsness, Gainesville, Fla., 1972-75; creative dir. Wolff/Orlando, Winter Park, Fla., 1975—; mem. U. Fla. Advt. Adv. Council. Recipient numerous Addy awards, Am. Advt. Fedn. Mem. Am. Mktg. Assn., Bus./Profl. Advt. Assn. Home: 5573-1307 N Semoran Blvd Winter Park FL 32792 Office: 199 S Knowles Ave Winter Park FL 32789

KENNEDY, WILLIAM ROSS, surgeon; b. Jackson, Miss., Feb. 27, 1940; s. Enoch Lyle and Edwin Catherine (Huggins) K.; M.D., Tulane U., 1964; m. Judy Marie James, Sept. 24, 1962. Intern, Mcleod Infirmary, Florence, S.C., 1964-65; resident gen. surgery Roosevelt Hosp., N.Y.C., 1967-68; resident orthopaedic surgery N.Y. Orthopaedic Hosp., N.Y.C., 1968-70, Annie C. Kane fellow in orthopaedic surgery, 1970-72, chief resident, 1971-72; practice medicine specializing in orthopaedic surgery, Sarasota, Fla., 1972—; clin. instr. orthopaedic surgery Coll. Physicians and Surgeons, Columbia U., 1971-72; mem. staff Doctors Hosp., Sarasota, 1972—; mem. staff Sarasota Meml. Hosp., chmn. phys. therapy dept., 1974-80, chief orthopaedic sect. surgery, 1976-77. Bd. dirs. Fla. Arthritis Found., 1975—. Served to lt. USN, 1965-67. Diplomate Am. Bd. Orthopaedic Surgery. Fellow A.C.S., Am. Acad. Orthopaedic Surgeons; mem. Fla. Med. Assn., Am. Rheumatism Assn., AMA, Sarasota County Med. Soc. Methodist. Club: Field (Sarasota). Contbr. articles to med. jours. Home: 1572 Harbor Dr Sarasota FL 33579 Office: 1818 Hawthorne St Sarasota FL 33579

KENNEMAN, PAUL EDWARD, mfg. co. exec.; b. Cleve., June 14, 1928; s. Edward J. and Marie Elizabeth (Turnau) K.; B.S. in Indsl. Mgmt., Syracuse U., 1969; cert. mfg. mgmt. Fenn Coll., 1962; m. Loretta Kenneman, Apr. 21, 1951; children—William, Denise, Paula, Steven. Vice pres. mfg. Oravisual Inc., St. Petersburg, Fla., 1976—; methods engr. Diamond Shamrock Corp., Painesville, Ohio, 1954-63; mgr. mfg. engring. Carrier Corp., Syracuse, 1963-76. Mem. adv. bd. St. Petersburg Vocat. Tech. Sch., 1977—. Served with USCG, 1946-49. Registered profl. engr., Calif.; cert. mfg. engr. Mem. Suncoast C. of C., Soc. Mfg. Engrs. (sr.). Republican. Clubs: St. Petersburg Softball Mgrs., Half Century. Home: 2027 59th St N Clearwater FL 33520 Office: 321 15th Ave S St Petersburg FL 33701

KENNER, CHARLES THOMAS, educator; b. Waxahachie, Tex., Oct. 20, 1910; s. Francis Buckner and Rozetta (Morse) K.; B.S. magna cum laude, Trinity U., Waxahachie, 1932; M.S. (teaching fellow), U. Tenn., 1935; Ph.D., U. Tex. at Austin, 1939; m. Bessie Will Harrison, Mar. 21, 1942; 1 dau., Elizabeth Anne (Mrs. Walter Ross Purkey). Instr. chemistry U. Tex. at Austin, 1935-38; asst. prof. The Citadel, Charleston, S.C., 1938-42; chief chemist Hurley div. Thor Corp., Chgo., 1946; dir. research Central Testing, Inc., Chgo., 1947; mem. faculty So. Meth. U., Dallas, 1948—, asso. prof. chemistry, 1951-54, prof., 1954-76, emeritus, 1976—. Owner, Kenner Labs., Dallas, 1955—; sci. adviser Dallas Dist. FDA, 1967-77; mem. advanced sci. cluster adv. com. Dallas Ind. Sch. Dist., 1971—. Bd. dirs. Dallas Regional Sci. Fair, 1963—. Served with AUS, 1942-46. Recipient Phi Eta Sigma Outstanding Tchr. award, 1960, Favorite Doctor award Meth. Hosp. Sch. Nursing, 1970. Mem. Am. Chem. Soc. (W.T. Doherty award 1976), Soc. Applied Spectroscopy, Dallas Soc. Analytical Chemists (Analyst of Year award 1968), Sigma Xi, Phi Lambda Upsilon. Author: Analytical Separations and Determinations, A Textbook in Quantitative Analysis, 1971; Laboratory Directions for Analytical Separation and Determinations, 1971; Instrumental and Separation Analysis, 1973; Quantitative Analysis, 1979. Contbr. articles to profl. jours. Home: 7210 Clemson Dr Dallas TX 75214

KENNER, PAUL ADRIAN, JR., mfg. co. exec.; b. Williamsport, Pa., Jan. 26, 1945; s. Paul Adrian and Anne Bell (Kline) K.; A.S.S., So. Ill. U., 1972; m. Rebecca Lee Ruppert, May 27, 1972; children—Michelle Lee, Cynthia Leeanne. Sales mgr., park operator High Orchard Mobile Homes, Inc., Peoria, Ill., 1972-75; mfrs. rep. Schuit Homes, Sarasota, Fla., 1977—. Served with AC, U.S. Army, 1967-70. Cert. fin. planner. Mem. Fla. Mobile Home and Recreational Vehicle Assn. Clubs: Internat. Dinner, Sarasota Coin, Sertoma. Office: PO Box 4038 Sarasota FL 33580

KENT, BARTIS MILTON, physician; b. Terrell, Tex., June 23, 1925; s. Bartis William and Annie (Smalley) K.; student So. Meth. U., 1942-44; M.D., Baylor U., 1948; m. Ann L. Kiel, July 6, 1954; children—Susan Ruth, Martha Lucille, Bartis Michael. Intern, Jefferson Davis Hosp., Houston, 1948-49; resident pathology Mass. Meml. Hosps., Boston, 1951; resident in internal medicine Baylor U., 1953-56; indsl. physician Humble Oil Co., Houston, 1949-51; instr. dept. medicine U. Iowa, 1956-58; staff physician Iowa City VA Hosp., 1956-58; practice medicine specializing in internal medicine, Muskogee, Okla., 1958—; dir. radioisotope service Muskogee Gen. Hosp.; cons. Muskogee VA Hosp.; clin. asst. prof. medicine U. Okla. Sch. Medicine, 1975—. Chmn., Muskogee County chpt. Am. Nat. Red Cross, 1963-65. Served with USAF, 1951-53. Decorated Air medal. Diplomate Am. Bd. Internal Medicine. Mem. A.C.P., Indsl. Med. Assn., Soc. Nuclear Medicine, Am. Fedn. Clin. Research, Am. Heart Assn., Aero. Med. Assn., Am., Okla. socs. internal medicine, Muskogee C. of C. Methodist. Mason (Shriner). Home: 800 N 45th St Muskogee OK 74401 Office: 211 S 36th St Muskogee OK 74401

KENT, JOHN BRADFORD, lawyer; b. Jacksonville, Fla., Sept. 5, 1939; s. Frederick Heber and Norma (Futch) K.; grad. Phillips Exeter Acad., 1957; B.A., Yale U., 1961; J.D., U. Fla., 1964; LL.M. in Taxation, N.Y. Grad. Sch. Law, 1965; m. Monett Powers, Dec. 18, 1969; children—Katherine Lane, Monett Bradford, Susan Whitfield Powers, Sally Marshall McLeod. Admitted to Fla. bar, 1964; asso. atty. firm Ulmer, Murchison, Kent, Ashby & Ball, Jacksonville, 1965-67; partner firm Kent, Watts, Durden, Kent & Mickler and predecessor firms, Jacksonville, 1967—; pres., dir. Kent Investments, Inc., Jacksonville, 1977—; pres. Kent Theatres, Inc., Jacksonville, 1967-70, v.p., gen. counsel, 1970—, also dir.; v.p., dir. Kent Enterprises, Inc., Kent Properties, Inc., Melbourne Theatres, Inc., Blanding Theatres, Inc., Kent Amusements, Inc. Treas., trustee St. Mark's Episcopal Day Sch., Jacksonville, 1971-74; bd. dirs., v.p. Children's Home Soc. Fla., 1976-77, dir., 1974—, asst. counselor, 1974—, asst. sec., 1977—, pres. NE div., 1976-77; bd. dirs. Jacksonville Legal Aid Soc., 1973-75; bd. govs. Fla. Jr. Coll. at Jacksonville Found., 1973—, pres., 1976-77. Mem. Am., Fla., Jacksonville bar assns., Am. Judicature Soc., Nat. Assn. Theatre Owners (dir. 1972), Nat. Assn. Theatre Owners Fla. (v.p. 1968-72, dir. 1973—), Delta Kappa Epsilon, Phi Delta Phi, Manuscript Sr. Hon. Soc. (Yale). Episcopalian (former vestryman). Clubs: Ponte Vedra, River, Friars, Ye Mystic Revellers, Timuquana, YMCA, Highlands (N.C.) Country, Mory's Assn. (New Haven), Rotary (treas. 1976-77). Home: 4948 Morven Rd Jacksonville FL 32210 Office: 850 Florida Nat Bank Bldg PO Box 4700 Jacksonville FL 32201

KENT, JOHN PATRICK, lawyer; b. Frederick, Okla., Jan. 27, 1950; s. John Wade and Betty Lee K.; B.S., Okla. State U., 1972; M.B.A., Okla. U., 1974, J.D., 1976; m. Duana June Laney, Aug. 10, 1971; 1 son, Brad Wesley. Admitted to Okla. bar, 1976; partner firm McBee, Benson & Kent, Frederick, Okla., 1976—; vis. prof. bus. law Vernon (Tex.) Jr. Coll., 1978-79; v.p., dir. K&T Farm & Ranch, Inc. Sunday Sch. tchr. Methodist Ch., 1976—, trustee, 1978—, mem. fin. com., 1978—, youth coordinator, 1979—; bd. dirs. United Fund, 1979. Mem. Am. Bar Assn., Okla Bar Assn., Tillman County Bar Assn. (pres. 1979—), S.W. Legal Inst. (pres. 1979-80), Frederick C. of C. (dir., pres. 1980). Democrat. Methodist. Clubs: Lions (sec.), Jaycees (v.p.). Home: 1515 N 14th St Frederick OK 73542 Office: 9th and Floral St Frederick OK 73542

KENTON, ODIS WILSON, mgmt. systems cons.; b. Camden, N.J., May 1, 1943; s. Edgar J. and Jessie E. (Smith) K.; A.B. in Bus. Adminstrn. and Acctg., Rutgers U., 1978; student Community Coll. of Air Force, 1962, 67-68; children—Odis Wilson, Darnela Renee, Celeste Sheree. Engring. asso. Westinghouse DECO, McLean, Va., 1969-70; radio communications systems field installations engr. Melpar Inc., Falls Church, Va., 1970; propr. ODO Enterprises, Camden, 1970, cons. to elec. contractors, 1974-75; sr. research and devel. lab. technician Applied Metro Tech. Inc., Barrington, N.J., 1970-71, chief technician, 1971-72, mgr. field service and customer relations depts., 1972-74; v.p. Village Sound Palace Inc., Willingboro, N.J., 1975-76; sr. electronics technician Port Authority Transit Corp., Camden, 1974-78; tech./adminstrn. cons. to Trident submarine program coordinator Naval Sea Systems Command, Washington, 1978-79; mgr. prefaulted module program coordination program ACC, 1979—, also sr. ILS engr. Trident tng. facility, TDL program mgr. Served in USAF, 1961-69; Vietnam. Mem. Am. Soc. Cert. Engring. Technicians, Instr. for Cert. Engring. Technicians, Am. Mgmt. Assn. Home: 4508 Commons Dr Apt 201 Annandale VA 22003 Office: 401 Wythe St Alexandria VA 22314

KENTON, WILLIAM HARVEY, mfg. co. exec.; b. Lexington, Ky., Nov. 18, 1929; s. Kemper Clay and Edith (Matthews) K.; B.S., U. Ky., 1953; grad. Gen. Electric Co. Bus. Tng. program, 1958; m. Doris Kell, Aug. 12, 1951; children—William Matthew, Kathryn Leigh, Patricia Jean. With Gen. Electric Co., Louisville, 1955-59; with Martin Marietta Corp., Orlando, Fla., 1959—, program controller maj. mil. communication program, 1977—; v.p. fin., dir. Vacations Motels, Inc., Orlando, 1969-75. Pres., PTA, Orlando, 1968-69, bd. dirs., 1975-78; chmn. various coms. Powers Dr. Baptist Ch., Orlando. Mem. Nat. Assn. Accts., Armed Forces Communication and Electronic Assn., Air Force Assn. Home: PO Box 861 Windermere FL 32786 Office: PO Box 5837 Orlando FL 32805

KENYON, ALBERT PRENTICE, cons., former govt. ofcl.; b. Westerly, R.I., Oct. 13, 1906; s. Albert Prentice and Mabel (Tuckerman) K.; A.B., Milton Coll., 1929; M.A., Columbia, 1936; m. Chloe H. Jenkins, June 4, 1931 (dec. Mar. 1975); m. 2d, Martha Louise Hoover, July 30, 1976. Tchr. high sch., Chadwick, Ill., 1929-37, Westerly 1937-42; with Bur. Naval Personnel, Washington, 1943-72, asst. dir. tng. mgmt. div., 1950-60, supervisory edn. and tng. planner, 1960-72; spl. asst. for policy to dir. edn. and tng. Office of Chief of Naval Ops., Washington, 1972-73; cons. Dept. Agr., 1973; pvt. firm, 1975; lectr. in physics George Washington U., 1946-59. Served with USNR, 1942-46, 47-48, capt. Res. ret. Mem. U.S. Naval Inst., Phi Delta Kappa. Methodist (trustee). Author: Reminscences of Naval Personnel, Naval Training, 1973. Home: 908 Allison St Alexandria VA 22302

KEOGH, FRANCES TROXLER, communications and mfg. exec.; b. Rockingham County, N.C., Jan. 28, 1926; d. James Harrison and Pearl Lee (Simpson) Troxler; bus. adminstrn. cert. Elon Coll., 1958; m. John Milton Keogh, Dec. 23, 1948; 1 son, James Robert. With Western Electric Co., 1951-66, 72—, profl. adminstrv. employee, methods devel., Greensboro, N.C., 1972-77, profl. adminstrv. employee, corp. benefits, 1977-80, chief corp. records sect., 1980—; sales service asst. So. Bell Telephone Co., Cocoa Beach, Fla., 1966-67. Adv. Secretarial Explorer Post, Nat Greene council Girl Scouts U.S.A.; sec. Greensboro Inter Club Council, 1974-75. Recipient PPP award Western Electric Co., 1975. Mem. Am. Bus. Women's Assn. (pres. local chpt. 1959, 73, 75, Woman of Yr. 1975), Am. Mgmt. Assn., Telephone Pioneers Am., Internat. Platform Assn. (hospitality com. 1979), Beta Sigma Phi (treas. 1972-73). Democrat. Methodist. Originator, pub. govt. systems secretarial manual. Home: 1 Hastings Circle Greensboro NC 27406 Office: I-85 Guilford Center Greensboro NC 27420

KEPHART, EARL LAWRENCE, nurse; b. Madera, Pa., Dec. 15, 1919; s. Lawrence and Cora (Lockett) K.; R.N., Pa. Hosp., 1943; B.S. in Edn., U. Pa., 1949; M.Ed., U. Va., 1959; m. Harriet Hosmer, Nov. 29, 1944; 1 son, Larry Herbert. Head nurse, then instr. Pa. Hosp., 1943-49; mem. nursing staff VA, 1949—; chief nursing service VA Med. Center, Shreveport, 1973—. Active local Boy Scouts Am. Served with AUS, 1944-45. Mem. Am. Soc. Hosp. Nursing Service Adminstrs., Assn. Mil. Surgeons U.S., Am. Radio Relay League, Sigma Theta Tau, Kappa Phi Kappa. Republican. Presbyterian. Author ednl. TV material. Home: 2106 Cynthia Ln Shreveport LA 71118 Office: 510 E Stoner Ave Shreveport LA 71130

KERBY, LESLIE GLEN, bank exec.; b. Sweetwater, Tex., May 10, 1938; s. Leslie George and Fannie Lorene (Price) K.; student Cisco Jr. Coll., 1956-60; B.B.A., Tex. Tech. Coll., 1962; postgrad. So. Meth. U., 1967-70; m. Ethel Lavonia Weldon, Oct. 5, 1956; children—Carie Lynn, Sandra Denise, Paul Glen, David Leslie. With 1st Nat. Bank, Baird, Tex., 1956-60; with First Nat. Bank, Lubbock, Tex., 1960-62; asst. nat. bank examiner U.S. Dept. Treasury, Dallas and Abilene, Tex., 1962-65, nat. bank examiner, 1965-67; examiner-in-charge of Abilene, Tex. sub-region, 1967-68; with Central Nat. Bank, San Angelo, Tex., 1968—, exec. v.p., dir., 1973-79, chmn. exec. com., exec. v.p., 1979—. Bd. dirs. Tom Green County Library, 1970-74, chmn., 1973-74; bd. dirs. W. Tex. Lighthouse for Blind, 1972-75, chmn., 1974; bd. dirs. San Angelo United Fund, 1972-78, treas. 1973—, chmn., 1975; bd. dirs. San Angelo Indsl. Fund, 1971-73; bd. dirs. Mental Health-Mental Retardation Center, San Angelo, 1971-75, chmn., 1973-74; bd. dirs. Salvation Army, 1972-78, W. Tex. Rehab. Center, 1979—. Mem. Am. Inst. Banking (San Angelo chpt. 1968-71), Robert Morris Assos. (bank rep. 1967-71), Phi Alpha Kappa. Methodist. Odd Fellow. Clubs: River (dir. 1971-78, sec.-treas. 1974), San Angelo Country (San Angelo), Bentwood Country (chmn. bd. 1979). Home: 2801 Palo Duro Dr San Angelo TX 76901 Office: 18 W Beauregard San Angelo TX 76901

KERCHER, JOHN WESLEY, III, accounting co. exec.; b. Dayton, Ohio, Mar. 23, 1941; s. John Wesley and F. Elizabeth (Blakeslee) K.; B.A., Ohio Wesleyan U., 1963; M.B.A. (Bus. Found. fellow), U. N.C., 1964; m. Diane M. Grotz, Sept. 7, 1963; children—Lee Elizabeth,

John Wesley, IV. With Price Waterhouse & Co., 1964—, mgr., Pitts., 1971-74, partner mgmt. adv. services, Tampa, Orlando and Jacksonville, Fla. offices, 1974—; speaker in field. Bd. dirs. Pitts. Symphony Soc., 1973-74; bd. dirs. Fla. Gulf Coast Symphony, 1974—, pres. elect, 1978-79, mem. exec. com., 1974-80, chmn. fund raising dr., 1976-78, pres., 1979-80. Bd. fellows U. Tampa; mem. Tampa Mayor's Performing Arts Hall Com. C.P.A., Fla., other states. Mem. Am. Inst. C.P.A.'s, Fla. C.P.A. Soc. (past chmn. state/local govt. relations, mgmt. sers. com.), Ohio Wesleyan Alumni Assn. (Tampa area chmn.), Tampa C. of C. Democrat. Episcopalian. Clubs: Tampa Yacht and Country, Tower of Tampa. Home: 5142 San Jose St Tampa FL 33609 Office: PO Box 2640 Tampa FL 33601

KERGOSIEN, GREGORY GAINES, pharm. co. exec.; b. Bay St. Louis, Miss., Jan. 23, 1928; s. Horace Leonard and Mathilde Elizabeth (Gaines) K.; student La. State U., 1944; B.S., U. Miss., 1949; m. Marian Lorene Whitaker, Aug. 20, 1950; children—Marian Elizabeth, Gregory Gaines, Patricia Jane. Pharm. salesman Upjohn Co., Memphis, 1949-50, Columbia, Tenn., 1950-55, Baton Rouge, 1955-60, Clearwater, Fla., 1960-61, mgr. dist. sales North Fla. Dist., Clearwater, 1961-65, mgr. regional merchandising, Chamblee, Ga., 1965-68, govt. adminstr., Chamblee, 1968—; lectr. in field; vis. lectr. Coll. Pharmacy U. Tenn., Memphis, 1969, 71, 75. Mem. adv. com. Ga. Regional Med. Program, 1973-75. Served with USNR, 1945-47, to 1st lt., AUS, 1951-52. Fellow Upjohn Sales Acad.; mem. Ga. Pharm. Assn., Pharm. Mfrs. Reps. Assn. Tex., Assn. Medicaid Pharmacy Adminstrs. (co-founder 1968), Miss. Acad. Sci., Kappa Sigma. Roman Catholic. Home: 1554 N Springs Dr Dunwoody GA 30338 Office: 5251 Peachtree Indsl Blvd Chamblee GA 30341

KERN, ANDREW ELLIOT, investment adviser; b. N.Y.C., Nov. 29, 1943; s. Max I. and Matilda (Patrick) K.; B.B.A., U. Miami, Coral Gables, Fla., 1965; M.B.A., L.I. U., 1966; m. Linda Carmella Kainz, Nov. 23, 1968. Account exec. Hayden Stone & Co., Bal Harbour, Fla., 1967-70, Francis I. duPont & Co., Miami Beach, 1970-72; account mgr. Blyth Eastman Dillon & Co., Miami, Fla., 1972-74; pres. First Biscayne Corp., Miami, 1974-77; v.p. Avatar Assos., Miami, Fla., 1977—; lectr. U. Miami. Served with USCGR, 1966-67. Mem. Nat. Assn. Security Dealers, Finance Soc. N.Y. Democrat. Jewish. Clubs: Bankers, Bond (Miami). Address: PO Box 530307 Miami FL 33153

KERN, BERNARD DONALD, physicist; b. New Castle, Ind., Oct. 31, 1919; s. William Bernard and Cecile (Hudson) K.; B.S., Ind. U., 1942, M.S., 1947, Ph.D., 1949; m. Nedda Wisler Burdsall, Aug. 20, 1946; children—Richard B., Jonathan K., Arthur R. Physicist, Signal Corps, Manhattan Project, Chgo., 1942-43; sr. physicist Oak Ridge Nat. Lab., 1949-50; mem. faculty U. Ky., Lexington, 1950—, prof. physics, 1958—, chmn. dept. physics and astronomy, 1967-69; physicist U.S. Naval Radiol. Def. Lab., 1957-58; Dept. State-U. Ky. vis. prof. Inst. Teknologi, Bandung, Indonesia, 1961-62; cons. in field, 1958—. Served to lt. (j.g.) USNR, 1943-46. Fellow Am. Phys. Soc.; mem. Am. Inst. Physics, Am. Assn. Physics Tchrs. Author articles on nuclear physics. Address: Dept Physics and Astronomy U Ky Lexington KY 40506

KERNS, ALLEN FRANKLIN, univ. ofcl.; b. Columbus, Ohio, Oct. 13, 1923; s. Clyde Allen and Mabel Della (Wells) K.; B.A., Eastern Nazarene Coll., 1949; M.Div., Boston U., 1952; M.S., Fla. State U., 1971; Ed.D., Nova U., 1979; m. Jean Ruby, Aug. 12, 1944; children—Mark Allen, Timothy Allen. Ordained to ministry Meth. Ch., 1953; pastor chs. Mass., Ohio, Mich., 1949-57; social worker Fla. Dept. Public Welfare, 1957-58; med. social counselor Fla. Council for Blind, 1958-60; vocat. rehab. counselor Calif. Dept. Rehab., Long Beach, Fresno, Sacramento, 1961-66, Fla. Dept. Edn., St. Petersburg, 1967-70; job devel. specialist Fla. Div. Vocat. Rehab., St. Petersburg, 1970-71; dir. Pinellas County Vocat. Tech. Inst. Vocat. Evaluation Center, Clearwater, Fla., 1971-74; asst. dir. vocat. edn. rehab. spl. needs program U. South Fla., Tampa, 1974—; cons. Seffner Juvenile Offender Program. Mem. Fla. Vocat. Evaluation and Work Adjustment Assn. (William M. Rabucha award 1977), Am. Vocat. Assn., Am. Personnel and Guidance Assn., Nat. Rehab. Assn., Council for Exceptional Children, Nat. Assn. Career Edn., Nat. Assn. Vocat. Edn. Spl. Needs Personnel, AAUP. Democrat. Author: Administrative and Instructional Management: Career Guidance and Counseling, 1975; contbr. articles to Guidance. Home: PO Box 16455 Temple Terrace FL 33617 Office: Univ South Fla Tampa FL 33620

KERNS, ROBERT LOUIS, educator; b. Cedar Rapids, Iowa, May 1, 1929; s. William Edward and Nellie (Sawyer) K.; B.A., U. Iowa, 1956; M.A., Syracuse U., 1970; m. Jean Adair Slater, May 20, 1961; children—William Patrick, Heather. Photographer, Davenport (Iowa) Democrat, 1956; photographer, pictorial editor Cedar Rapids (Iowa) Gazette, 1958-59; dir. public relations photography Goodyear Tire and Rubber Co., Akron, Ohio, 1960-64; prof. Syracuse (N.Y.) U., 1964-72; prof. U. South Fla., Tampa, 1972—. coordinator visual communications, dept. mass communications; dir. workshops, cons. in field. Trustee Carrollwood Recreation Dist. Served with USAF, 1951-56. Recipient Don Christianson Meml. Award for outstanding journalism in Iowa, 1950. Mem. Assn. for Edn. in Journalism, Internat. Assn. Bus. Communicators (pres. Suncoast chpt. 1977-78), World Futurists Soc., Sigma Delta Chi. Presbyterian. Club: Masons. Author: Photography With a Purpose, 1980; Creative News Photography, 1961; patentee Kerns camera strap; lectr. in field; recent photo shows: Marjorie Kinnan Rawlings in Retrospect, 1979, The Quiet Moments, 1978. Home: 10503 Orange Grove Dr Tampa FL 33618 Office: Mass Communications Dept Univ South Florida Tampa FL 33602

KERR, CHARLES MACDONALD, III, inst. exec.; b. New Orleans, July 3, 1912; s. Charles Macdonald, II and Helen M. (Coppee) K.; B.B.A., Tulane U., 1935; postgrad. seminars Bard Coll., Rhinebeck, N.Y., 1957-58; m. Eleanor Carol Morris, July 8, 1961; children—Charles M. IV, Theresa Helen. Cost accountant Nfld. (Can.) Constructors, Marquise, 1941-42; treas. Cuban Mining Co., El Cristo, Oriente, Cuba, 1943-44; supr. field accounting Pendleton Shipyards, New Orleans, 1944; mem. nat. staff A.R.C., cons. amputee rehab. to Surgeons Gen., U.S. Army, USN, Washington, 1944-47; co-organizer, dir. patient tng. Kessler Inst. Rehab., West Orange, N.J., 1948-50; dir. amputee tng. Hasbrouck Heights (N.J.) Hosp., 1950; office mng. North Atlantic Constructors, N.Y.C., 1951-52; dir. Nat. Inst. for Amputee Rehab., Montclair, N.J., 1952—; cons. phys. edn. dept. Tulane U., also mem. faculty athletic dept.; cons. rehab. Nat. Ins. Group; dir. Inst. Devel. Human Performance, 1972—; faculty Bard Coll., 1977; condr. rehab. clinics. Tchr. communication seminars, Phila., N.Y.C., West Orange, Montclair, 1958-63; lectr. Internat. Congress Surgeons, U. Madrid, USPHS, Inst. Gen. Semantics, Lakeville, Conn., N.Y. Soc. Gen. Semantics; past pres. Bell-Kerr Realty Co., Bell-Kerr Corp.; past chmn. bd. Dizzy Dean Corp., Jackson, Miss.; master clinician Lifetime Sports Found.; cons., lectr. George Washington U. Recipient War Dept. commendation for service to injured servicemen World War II, 1945; named Man of Year, Goodwill Industries New Orleans, 1959. Mem. Am. Badminton Assn. Clubs (past chmn. nat. rules com., chmn. Nat. Umpires Assn.). Club: Montclair Tennis (pres., dir.). Author: (with Dr. H. H. Kessler) Civilian Amputees in action, 1948; (with Signe Brunnstrom) The Leg Amputee: Pre-Prosthetic Training, 1951; Training of the Lower Extremity Amputee, 1956. Home: Box 4033 New Orleans LA 70178

KERR, DENNIS C., ednl. adminstr.; b. Charleston, Miss., Sept. 3, 1935; s. Chester H. and Agnes H. K.; B.S., La. State U., 1957; m. Diane Kerr, Dec. 29, 1969; children—Randy, Darryl, Lisha, Lawanna. Admissions rep., admissions dir. Massey Coll., Jacksonville, Fla., 1959-68; admissions dir. Memphis Sch. Commerce, 1968-76; gen. mgr. Delta Sch. Bus., Baton Rouge, 1976—. Served with USAF, 1957-59. Mem. Am. Vocat. Assn., So. Bus. Edn. Assn., La. Fin. Aid Assn., S.W. Fin. Aid Assn., Nat. Fin. Aid Assn. Republican. Baptist. Home: 3708 Woodland Ridge Baton Rouge LA 70816

KERR, JAMES RICHARD, acad. counselor; b. Portland, Oreg., Dec. 12, 1931; s. William Cornelius and Mildred Helen (Matney) K.; B.S., U. Ala., 1962, M.A., 1963, M.A., 1965; Ph.D., Fla. State U., 1980; m. Tempie Glawn Jones, Jan. 20, 1961; children—Karen, Robert, Jennifer, Sharon. With USAF, 1948-60; asso. prof. phys. edn. Stillman Coll., Tuscaloosa, Ala., 1962-65, asso. prof. edn., 1968-69; mgr. married students housing U. Ala., 1965-66; asst. dir. housing student family housing N.Mex. State U., 1966-68; asst. prof. psychology Valdosta (Ga.) State Coll., 1969-75; admissions counselor, acad. counselor Sch. Nursing, Fla. State U., Tallahassee, 1975—. Bd. dirs. Lowndes County A.R.C., 1970-74, Valdosta Girls Club, 1971-74. Served to lt. comdr. USNR Res. Mem. Nat. Assn. Student Personnel Adminstrs., Am. Personnel and Guidance Assn., Am. Coll. Personnel Assn., Fla. Coll. Personnel Assn., So. Coll. Personnel Assn., So. Assn. Coll. Registrars and Admissions Officers, Phi Delta Kappa. Republican. Episcopalian. Club: Mason. Home: 2061 Greenwood Dr Tallahassee FL 32303 Office: 103B Sch of Nursing Fla State U Tallahassee FL 32306

KERR, JOHN WARD, JR., acct.; b. Fort Monroe, Va., July 30, 1937; s. John Ward and Florence (Bricker) K.; B.B.A., Old Dominion U., 1960; J.D., George Washington U., 1965; m. Carole Anne Alexander, Jan. 18, 1958; children—Katherine Lynne, John Ward III, Elizabeth Carole. Appellate conferee and agt. IRS, Washington, 1960-65; tax mgr. Coopers & Lybrand, Richmond, 1965-69; tax mgr. Peat, Marwick, Mitchell & Co., Richmond, 1969-72; tax coordinator J.K. Lasser & Co., Jacksonville, Fla., 1972-73; partner Goodman & Co., Norfolk, Va., 1973—; prof. taxation Old Dominion U., Norfolk. C.P.A. Mem. Am. Inst. C.P.A.'s, Va. Soc. C.P.A.'s (tax com. chmn.), Am., Va. bar assns., Nat. Assn. Accountants, Fed. Govt. Accountants Assn., Alpha Kappa Psi, Pi Kappa Alpha, Phi Alpha Delta. Presbyterian. Kiwanian. Club: Harbor (Norfolk). Home: 1160 Revere Point Rd Virginia Beach VA 23455 Office: Bank of Virginia Bldg Norfolk VA 23455

KERR, TRUMAN CARROLL, clergyman; b. Norman, Okla., Oct. 27, 1929; s. Truman Lee and Ruby Dorothy (Clark) K.; B.A., Okla. Baptist U., 1951; B.D., Southwestern Bapt. Theol. Seminary, 1954, M.Div., 1973; m. Faye Shelburne, Sept. 1, 1950; children—Carol Faye, Jennifer Kaye, Thomas Lee. Ordained to ministry So. Bapt. Conv., 1950; pastor, Addington, Okla., 1951-55, Lindsay, Okla., 1955-57, Hennessey, Okla., 1957-58; minister edn. First Bapt. Ch., Minden, La., 1958-61; asso. pastor Broadmoor Bapt. Ch., Shreveport, La., 1961-78; exec. asst. to exec. dir. La. Bapt. Conv., Alexandria, 1978—. Mem. So. Bapt. Public Relations Assn., So. Bapt. Religious Edn. Assn., Southwestern Bapt. Religious Edn. Assn., Nat. Jogging Assn. Democrat. Home: 5236 Argonne St Alexandria LA 71301 Office: 1250 MacArthur St Alexandria LA 71301

KERRIGAN, ROBERT EMMETT, lawyer; b. New Iberia, La., Sept. 30, 1902; s. John Esmond and Alice (Fourcade) K.; A.B., Tulane U., 1923, LL.B., 1925; m. Catherine Wiggin Gomila, Sept. 21, 1939; children—Catherine Torrey, Robert Emmett. Admitted to La. bar, 1925, practiced New Orleans, 1925—, mem. firm Deutsch, Kerrigan & Stiles, 1926—. Past pres. Asso. Cath. Charities. Mem. Am. Law Inst., Am. Coll. Trial Attys., Internat. Acad. Trial Lawyers, Internat. Assn. Ins. Counsel, Fedn. Ins. Counsel, Am., La. bar assns., Am. Judicature Soc., Assn. of Commerce, Bur. Govtl. Research. Clubs: Louisiana, New Orleans Country (past pres.), Pickwick. Home: 2100 St Charles Ave New Orleans LA 70130 Office: Ohe Shell Sq New Orleans LA 70139

KERSHNER, KAREN, advt. agy. exec.; b. Port Arthur, Tex., Aug. 28, 1951; d. Hugh Cleveland and Eleanor Lucille (Beaty) K.; B.J., U. Tex., Austin, 1973; m. Jim Slack, Jr., May 12, 1979. Public relations dir. Lakeway Co., Austin, Tex., 1973-74; account coordinator, copywriter Point Communications, Inc., Houston, 1974-76; account exec. CRA, Inc. (name changed to Rochelle Marketing Co., Jan., 1979), Houston, 1976-78, v.p., 1978—; career cons. Houston Community Coll. Mem. company relations com. United Way; co-founder Austin Community TV, 1973. Mem. Internat. Assn. Bus. Communicators. Club: Internat. Divers. Home: 24 Pinedale Houston TX 77006 Office: Rochelle Marketing Co 11 Greenway Plaza Suite 620 Houston TX 77002

KERSKER, PETER WHEELER, lawyer, restaurateur; b. St. Petersburg, Fla., Dec. 27, 1942; s. Peter Benjamin and Marjorie (Wheeler) K.; B.S., Johns Hopkins U., 1965; J.D., Tulane U., 1968. Admitted to Fla. bar, 1969, since practiced in St. Petersburg; founder, 1973, since propr. Peter's Place, cafe internat., St. Petersburg; propr. Pegasus Properties, interior design, St. Petersburg, 1979—; asso., founding dir. Fantasy Adventures Travel, St. Petersburg, 1979; dir. O'Neill Pub. Co., Tampa, Fla., Pelar Corp., St. Petersburg. Bd. dirs. Fla. Gulf Coast Symphony, San Carlo Opera Co., St. Petersburg Opera Co. Mem. Fla. Bar, St. Petersburg Bar Assn. Clubs: St. Petersburg Yacht, Feather Sound Country. Home: Bayfront Tower 1 Beach Dr Saint Petersburg FL 33701 Office: 224 1st Ave N Saint Petersburg FL 33701

KERSTETTER, REX EUGENE, educator; b. Ashland, Kans., Nov. 22, 1938; s. Roy Everett and Blanche Elizabeth (Sailor) K.; B.S., Ft. Hays Kans. State Coll., 1960, M.S., 1963; Ph.D. (NASA traineeship), Fla. State U., 1967; m. Elizabeth Sue Edwards, June 5, 1960; children—Kelvin Tod, Derek Edward. Asso. prof. biology Furman U., Greenville, S.C., 1967—; Lilly vis. scholar Duke U., 1977. Pres., Greater Greenville Environmental Council, 1972-73. NSF summer research fellow, Purdue U., 1969. Mem. A.A.A.S., Bot. Soc. Am., Am. Soc. Plant Physiologists, Kans., S.C. acads. sci., Sigma Xi. Author: The Ecosphere: Organisms, Habitats and Disturbances, 1974. Home: 16 Zelma Dr Greenville SC 29609

KESELOWSKY, GEORGE ALAN, mech. engr.; b. Schenectady, Jan. 30, 1948; s. George and Doris M. (McKenzie) K.; B.S. in Mech. Engring., U. S. Fla., 1972; m. Jacquelyn Joy Tabbutt, June 26, 1970; children—Christine Marie, Benjamin George. Asst. to pres. Atlas Refrigeration Service, Tampa, Fla., 1968-72; applications engr. Tampa Electric Co., 1972-76, voltage engr. Tampa div., 1976-77, performance engr., 1977—. Adv. Jr. Achievement, Tampa, Fla., 1976; loaned exec. United Fund, 1975-76. Served with USAF, 1970. Recipient Adv. of Yr. award Jr. Achievement, 1976. Mem. ASME. Democrat. Methodist. Club: Optimist. Home: 1009 108th Ave Tampa FL 33612 Office: 111 N Dale Mabry Tampa FL 33609

KESSER, MICHAEL BARRON, realty co. exec.; b. Norfolk, Va., July 9, 1942; s. Lewis Kernal and Sylvia Harriet (Finkelstein) K.; A.A., U. Va., 1961, postgrad. appraisals, 1968-69; B.B.A., U. Ga., 1963; postgrad. in Appraisals Clemson (S.C.) U., 1970; m. Kay Harriet Zedd, Aug. 25, 1963; children—Bradley William, Wendy Shuman. Realty appraiser Keystone Realty Co., Norfolk, Va., 1959-70, owner, realty appraiser, cons., 1970—; dir. Multiple Listing Service of Tidewater. Advisor to bd. dirs. Bank of Commonwealth; instr. real estate Tidewater Community Coll., Virginia Beach, Va., 1973-75, Golden Gate U., Virginia Beach, 1973-75. Bd. dirs. adv. bd. Salvation Army. Mem. Va. Assn. Realtors (dir.), Norfolk/Chesapeake Bd. Realtors (dir., pres. 1973). Mason, Rotarian. Contbr. articles to profl. jours. Home: 6829 Gardner Dr Norfolk VA 23518 Office: 109 W City Hall Ave Norfolk VA 23510

KESSLER, VINCENT GARLAND, JR., cargo cons.; b. Queens, N.Y., Sept. 3, 1942; s. Vincent Garland and Eleanor Marie (Cohen) K.; student pub. schs., Jamaica, N.Y., Ellsworth, Maine; m. Stella Maria Russotti, June 6, 1964; children—Richard, Julie, Ronald. Sta. mgr. Air Express Internat., Miami, Fla., 1965-67, Circle Airfreight Corp., Miami, 1967-70; asst. v.p. Frontier Freight Forwarders, Miami, 1970-72; v.p. Airguide Freight Forwarders, Miami, 1972-75, Action Cargo Systems, Inc., Miami, 1975-76; pres. Land Sea Air Cargo Expediters, Inc., Miami, 1976-78; pres. Crossworld Sers. Unltd., Inc., Miami, 1978—; v.p. Airguide F.F., Miami, 1972-75; v.p., sec. Action Cargo, Miami, 1975-76, Maritime Cartage Co., Miami, 1974-75, Greater Miami Air Freight, 1972-75. Mem. Custom Brokers and Forwarders Assn. of Miami, Coral Gables Jr. C. of C., Delta Nu Alpha. Republican. Roman Catholic. Club: Miami Traffic. Home: 3021 SW 117 Ct Miami FL 33175 Office: 7100 NW 12th St Miami FL 33126 also PO Box 520305 Miami FL 33152

KEVORKIAN, RICHARD, artist; b. Dearborn, Mich., Aug. 24, 1937; s. Kay and Stana (Bedeian) K.; B.F.A., Richmond Profl. Inst., 1961; M.F.A. in Painting, Calif. Coll. Arts and Crafts, 1962; m. Karen Kay Kirland; children—Anna, Raffi, Soseh and Ellina (twins). Instr. drawing and painting Richard Bland Coll., Petersburg, Va., 1961-64; instr. dept. fine arts Va. Commonwealth U., Richmond, 1962-66, asst. prof. dept. painting and printmaking, 1967-69, asso. prof., 1969-77, prof., 1977—, chmn. dept., 1969—; exhbns. include: Birmingham (Ala.) Mus. Art, Greenville County (S.C.) Mus. Art (both 1977), Southeastern Center Contemporary Art, Winston-Salem, N.C., 1977, 78, Hunter Mus. Art, Chattanooga, 1978. Mem. selection bd. for visual arts Va. Center for Creative Arts, Sweet Briar. Served with N.G., 1955-63. NEA individual sr. artists grantee, 1972; Va. Commonwealth U. Sch. Arts faculty creative reserach grantee, 1974; Nat. Endowment for Arts/Southeastern Center Contemporary Arts grantee, 1976; Guggenheim fellow, 1978. Address: 325 N Harrison Richmond VA 23220

KEY, ROBERT MERTON, petroleum landman; b. Holdenville, Okla., May 15, 1929; s. Homer Denning and Althea Jessie (Lawler) K.; student So. Meth. U., 1946-47; B.B.A., U. Tex., 1951; m. Patricia Brown, Feb. 5, 1966; children—Robert Merton, Karen, Bryan, Annette. Production clk. Sun Oil Co., Colorado City, Tex., 1953-55; oil scout, regional staff asst. Phillips Petroleum Co., Bartlesville, Okla., 1955-61; land mgr. J. C. Trahan Drilling Contractor, Inc., Shreveport, La., 1961-69; v.p., land dept. Tex. Internat. Petroleum Corp., Shreveport, 1969-75, pres. Universal Hydrocarbons, Inc. subs. Tex. Internat. Petroleum Corp., Shreveport, 1975—. Area dir. and fin. chmn. La. Republican Party, 1964-65. Served with USNR, 1951-53. Mem. Arklatex Landmen's Assn. (pres. 1971, dr. 1972, 77), Am. Assn. Petroleum Landmen, Ind. Producers Assn. Am., La. Assn. Ind. Producers and Royalty Owners, Shreveport C. of C., La. Assn. Bus. & Industry, Ducks Unlimited, Sigma Alpha Epsilon. Republican. Presbyterian. Clubs: Cotillion, Ambassadors, Petroleum, East Ridge Country, Rotary (v.p. E. Shreveport 1973, 79), Jaycees. Home: 7370 Camelback Dr Shreveport LA 71105 Office: 916 Mid South Towers Shreveport LA 71101

KEY, WILLIAM KENNETH, investment banker; b. Columbus, Ga., Sept. 23, 1949; s. William B. and Vera Elanor (Cochran) K.; student Columbus Coll., 1967-69, Miami Inst. Fin., 1974, N.Y. Inst. Fin., 1975. Asst. to corp. credit mgr. Rhodes Inc., Atlanta, 1969-72; comptroller Nat. Can Corp., N.Y.C., 1972-73; investment banker Hibbard O'Connor & Weeks, Ft. Lauderdale, Fla., 1973-74; account exec. Thomson & McKinnon, Ft. Lauderdale, 1974-75; v.p. legal Ashcraft & Winston, Ft. Lauderdale, 1976; investment banker E.S.M. Group Inc., Ft. Lauderdale, 1977-79; pres. Spa Performance Inc., Ft. Lauderdale, 1979—, Spa Encounters Inc., Ft. Lauderdale, 1979—; sec.-treas. Spa Installation & Design Co., Ft. Lauderdale, 1979—. Clubs: Hundred of Broward County, Tower, Le Club Internat. Co-author: The New Challenge: Asset Management. Home: 2929 NE 40th St Fort Lauderdale FL 33308 Office: 4431 NE 11th Ave Fort Lauderdale FL 33334

KEY, WILLIAM PIKE, aerospace co. exec.; b. LaGrange, Ga., Jan. 20, 1924; s. William Crawford and Ruth Elizabeth (Pike) K.; B.B.A., Emory U., 1946, postgrad. Law Sch., 1950-51; M.B.A., Ga. State U., 1971; postgrad. Exec. Program in Bus. Adminstrn. Columbia U., 1976; m. Norma Jean Cobb, Aug. 12, 1961; children—William T., Catherine Elizabeth, Michael Scott, Christianne. Asst. personnel mgr. Sears, Roebuck & Co., Atlanta, 1946-48; personnel mgr. Economy Auto Stores, Atlanta, 1948-51; with Lockheed-Ga. Co., 1951—, asst. to dir. indsl. relations, Marietta, 1966-72, dir. indsl. relations, 1972—; mem. employment security agy. advisory council Ga. Dept. Labor, 1974—; bd. dirs. So. Indsl. Relations Conf., 1976—. Bd. dirs. Goodwill Industries of Atlanta, Inc., 1974—, vice chmn., 1976; mem. Ga. State U. Advisory Council Center Profl. Edn.; bd. advisers Morris Brown Coll. Served to 1st lt. USMC, 1943-46. Decorated Purple Heart; recipient 100% Right Club award Atlanta Daily World, 1975. Mem. Am., Nat. (Silver Knight of Mgmt. award 1975) mgmt. assns., Aerospace Industries Assn., Personnel Round Table of Atlanta, Midwest Indsl. Relations Council, Ga. Bus., Industry Assn. (gov. and com. chmn. 1975—), Atlanta C. of C., Peachtree-Dunwoody Hills Civic Assn. (pres. 1966-67), Alpha Kappa Psi, Sigma Iota Epsilon. Baptist. Home: 690 Starlight Dr Atlanta GA 30342 Office: 86 S Cobb Dr Marietta GA 30063

KHALIL, GHASSAN ABOU, surgeon; b. Tyr, Lebanon, May 6, 1934; s. Ibrahim Abou and Fahima (Wahid) K.; Baccalaurat, French Lycee of Lebanon, 1954; Sci. and Lit. Doctorate, French Faculty of Medicine, Lebanon, Ph.D., M.D., 1960; m. Genevieve Bourdis, July 15, 1963; children—Olivier, Yasmine, Natacha. Intern, Pasteur Hosp., Nice, France, 1960-61, Queen Gen. Hosp., N.Y.C., 1961-62; resident gen. surgery Maimonides Med. Center, N.Y.C., 1962-66, vascular research fellow, 1966-67; resident in plastic surgery Jackson Meml. Hosp., Miami, 1967-68; practice medicine specializing in surgery, Parkersburg, W.Va., 1968—; attending surgeon Camden Clark, St. Joseph hosps., Parkersburg; cons. surgeon Marietta (Ohio) Meml. Hosp. Diplomate Am. Bd. Surgery. Fellow A.C.S., Am. Coll. Angiology; mem. AMA, So., W.Va. med. assns., Am. Soc. Clin. Hypnosis, Internat. Acad. Cosmetic Surgery. Contbr. articles to profl. jours. Home: 22 Lynnwood Height St Vienna WV 25105 Office: 1122 Market St Parkersburg WV 25101

KHAN, AMANULLAH, physician; b. Jullundhar, India, Mar. 2, 1940; s. Ahmad Ali and Qamar (Nisa) K.; licentiate state med. faculty West Pakistan Med. Sch., 1959; M.B.B.S., King Edward Med. Coll., Lahore, 1963; Ph.D., Baylor U., 1968; m. Fran Elise Austin, Dec. 9, 1972; children—Roxanna, Sabrina. Rotating intern Samaritan Hosp.,

Troy, N.Y., 1965-66; fellow in hematology and oncology Wadley Insts. of Molecular Medicine, Dallas, 1966-69, chief research fellow, 1969-70, chmn. dept. immunotherapy, 1970—; adj. prof. Tex. Womans U., 1975—, N.Tex. State U., 1975—; mem. staff Morton Cancer & Research Hosp., Dallas, Brookhaven Hosp., Dallas, Doctor's Hosp., Dallas. Diplomate Am. Bd. Allergy and Immunology. Fellow Am. Coll. Physicians, Am. Coll. Allergists; mem. Am. Assn. Immunologists, Am. Soc. Clin. Oncology, Am. Soc. Hematology, AMA, Dallas County Med. Soc., Tex. Med. Assn., King Edward Med. Coll. Alumni Assn. (pres. 1975-71, 78-79). Author: Immune Regulators in Transfer Factor, 1979; Interferon: Properties and Clinical Uses, 1980; editor: Jour. of Clinical Hematology and Oncology, 1971—; mem. editorial bd. Exptl. Hematology, 1973-75; contbr. articles to sci. jours. Home: 4328 Briar Creek Ln Dallas TX 75214 Office: 9000 Harry Hines Dallas TX 75235

KHAN, SEKENDER ALI, biologist, ednl. adminstr.; b. Chandanbaisa, Bogra, Bangladesh, Feb. 1, 1933; s. Dianat Ullah and Masiran Nesa (Ashraf) K.; came to U.S., 1957; B.Agr., Dacca (Bangladesh) U., 1953, M.Agr., 1954; Ph.D., La. State U., 1959; m. Mumtaz Bano Naqvi, May 25, 1963; children—Nurjehan Ali, Shahjehan Ali. Tech. asst. East Pakistan Indsl. Devel. Corp., Rangpur, 1955-57; asst. cane devel. officer Carew & Co., Darsana, East Pakistan, 1957; prof. biology Tex. Coll., Tyler, 1959-60; chmn. div. natural scis. and math., 1960-63; chmn. dept. biology Elizabeth City (N.C.) State U., 1964-78, prof. biology, 1966—, dir. Research Improvement and Devel. Program, 1974-79. Research Initiation for Minority Inst. Improvement grantee, 1975-76. Mem. AAAS, Bot. Soc. Am., Sci. Am., Bangladesh Bot. Soc. Author lab. manuals: General Botany, 1963, Biological Science, 1965, Microbiology, 1965, General Zoology, 1966; author books of poems: Snake Venom, 1967, Bee Sting, 1970. Office: Elizabeth City State U Box 132 Elizabeth City NC 27909

KHASNAVIS, PRATYUSH KUMAR, educator; b. Varanasi, India, June 15, 1942; came to U.S., 1965, naturalized, 1979; s. N.C. and Smt. Sanatani (Devi) K.; B.A., Banaras Hindu U., 1960, M.A., 1962, B.Ed., 1963, M.Ed., 1964; postgrad. U. Oreg., 1965-66; Ed.D., Baylor U., 1969; m. Concepción Guadalupe Harper-Tinajero. Instr., K.B. Degree Coll., Mirzapur, India, 1964-65; instr. Peace Corps Tng. Center, U. Mo., Columbia, 1966; grad. asst. Baylor U., 1967-68; asst. prof. edn. Bishop Coll., Dallas, 1969—. Mem. Am. Assn. Colls. for Tchr. Edn., Nat. Council for Social Studies, Tex. Council for Social Studies, Tex. Assn. Tchr. Educators, Tex. Soc. Coll. Tchrs. of Edn. Contbr. articles in field to profl. jours. Office: Bishop Coll 3837 Simpson-Stuart Rd Dallas TX 75241

KHATRI, ABDULLAH AHMED, educator; b. Mandvi-Kutch, India, Aug. 3, 1924; s. Ahmed Ismail and Aminabai Suleman (Khatri) K.; came to U.S., 1970; B.A., Bombay U., 1946, LL.B., 1948, M.A., 1949; M.Sc., U. London (Eng.), 1956, Ph.D., 1970; m. Manju Dedhia, Aug. 25, 1967; children—Parinda, Snehal. Lectr., Samaldas Coll., Bhavanagar, India, 1949-50; asst. vocat. guidance officer Govt. of Bombay Guidance Bur., 1950-51; sr. psychologist B.M. Inst., Ahmedabad, India, 1957-65, chief psychologist, 1967-70; asst. prof. Jacksonville U., 1965-67; asst. prof. U. Ala., 1970-78, asso. prof., 1978—; expert mem. Bds. Indian Univs. viz Bombay, Nagpur, Baroda, Gujarat, 1960-70. Recipient grants Indian, Am. govt. agys.; Fulbright sr. scholar, 1965-67. Mem. Internat., Am. sociol. assns., Indian Sociol. Soc., Am. Psychol. Assn., Nat. Council on Family Relations, So. Sociol. Soc. Contbr. numerous articles to profl. jours. Home: 806 16th St S Birmingham AL 35205 Office: Sch Social Sci Univ Sta Birmingham AL 35294

KIBLER, LOUIS CHARLES, energy services co. ofcl.; b. Toledo, May 17, 1941; s. Edwin Wilson and Judy F. (Patthey) K.; A.A., Jackson Community Coll., 1965; B.G.S., U. Dayton, 1977; m. Janet J. Haehnle, Aug. 25, 1962; children—Steven, Robert, David, Nancy, Anne. Corp. purchasing coordinator Hayes-Albion Co., Jackson, Mich., 1962-74; mgr. corp. purchasing NCR Corp., Dayton, Ohio, 1974-77; mgr. materials systems and devel. J. Ray McDermott & Co., Inc., New Orleans, 1977—. Mem. adv. council Sinclair Coll. Mem. Nat. Assn. Purchasing Mgmt., Assn. Children with Learning Disabilities. Republican. Roman Catholic. Contbr. articles to profl. jours., also other publs. Home: 803 Jefferson Ct Slidell LA 70458 Office: 1010 Common St New Orleans LA 70160

KIBLER, WILLIAM BENJAMIN, orthopedic surgeon; b. Kingsport, Tenn., Sept. 29, 1946; s. Jacob B. and Della Louise (McPherson) K.; B.A. magna cum laude, Vanderbilt U., 1968, M.D., 1972; m. Elizabeth Fay Mugler, June 20, 1970; children—Chase, David. Intern, Parkland Hosp., Dallas, 1972-73; resident Vanderbilt Hosp., Nashville, 1973-77; practice medicine, specializing in orthopedic surgery, Lexington (Ky.) Clinic, 1977—. Diplomate Am. Bd. Orthopedic Surgery. Mem. Ky. Med. Assn., Phi Beta Kappa. Democrat. Methodist. Home: 613 Edgewater Dr Lexington KY 40502 Office: 1221 S Broadway Lexington KY 40504

KIDD, VIRGINIA STEADMAN, advt. agy. exec.; b. Carlton, Ga., June 21, 1931; d. Alexander Hamilton and Martha Ruth (Amason) Steadman; student Elberton Comml. Coll., 1948-49; m. Jan. 15, 1950; children—Laura Joy Kidd Patterson, Martha Gay. With Univ. Chevrolet Co., Athens, Ga., 1950-56; with Ga. Outdoor Advt., Inc., Athens, 1962—, v.p. fin., office mgr., 1979—. Sunday sch. dir. 1st and 2d grades Prince Ave Baptist Ch., Athens. Mem. Adminstrv. Mgmt. Soc. (sec. Athens chpt.), LWV. Office: Ga Outdoor Advt Inc PO Box 5875 Athens GA 30604

KIDRON, ARYEH, physicist; b. Izmir, Turkey, Feb. 15, 1929; came to U.S., 1969, naturalized, 1974; s. Solomon and Kaden (Saul) K.; M.Sc. in Physics, Hebrew U., Jerusalem, 1959; D.Sc. in Physics, Technion, Haifa, Israel, 1961; children—Eyal, Sarah. Research asso. Columbia U., 1962-64; asst. prof. physics Technion, 1964-69; vis. scientist U. Ky., 1969-71; sr. research asso. Northwestern U., 1971-72; sr. sci. specialist Hayes Internat. Corp., Huntsville, Ala., 1972-74; asso. research prof. U. Ala., Huntsville, 1974—; cons. to govt. agys. NASA fellow, summers, 1976, 77. Mem. Am. Crystallography Assn., Am. Soc. Metals. Contbr. articles to profl. jours.; patentee in field. Home: 420 Curtis Dr Huntsville AL 35803 Office: Physics Dept U Ala Huntsville AL 35807

KIDWELL, LYNN PETE, librarian; b. Morgan City, La., Dec. 11, 1946; d. Guy Anthony and Ruby Rita (Landry) Pete; B.A., Tex. Woman's U., 1969, M.L.S., 1979; children—Shawn Anthony, Cynthia Leigh, Jacquelyn Helene, Jeralyn Hope. Tchr. 5th grade Martin Elem. Sch., Brownsville, Tex., 1969-70; adult librarian Pan Am. Br. Library, San Antonio, Tex., 1971-72; asst. librarian Tex. Southmost Coll. Library, Brownsville, 1972-74, dir. Learning Resource Center, 1974—. Trustee, Cameron County Commn. on Status of Women, 1977-78. Mem. ALA, Tex. Library Assn. (sec. 1976-77, sec.-treas. dist. 1975-76), Southwest Library Assn., Valley Library Assn. (treas. 1978-80), Bus. and Profl. Women's Club. Democrat. Roman Catholic. Home: 264 W Park Dr Brownsville TX 78520 Office: 1825 May St Brownsville TX 78520

KIEFER, MICHAEL PETER, biol. research co. exec.; b. San Antonio, Jan. 12, 1946; s. George V. and June M. (Fleming) K.; student San Antonio Coll., 1964-66, La. State U., 1966; B.S., W. Tex. State U., 1971, M.S., 1972; Ph.D., Stanton U., 1974; m. Felice Ingram, Mar. 31, 1974; 1 son, Andrew. Pres., M.P.K. Omega Co., Amarillo, Tex., 1972—, Alpha Co., biol. research cons., Amarillo, 1977-80. Served with USAF, 1966-69; Vietnam. Mem. Internat. Authors Biol. Assn., Nat. Biol. Soc. (Award of Excellence), Amarillo Biol. Assn. (pres.). Republican. Hindu. Author: Abyss to Omega Point, Vol. I, 1973, Vol. II, 1977. Office: M P K Omega Co 3615 Carson St Amarillo TX 79109

KIELL, HILARY KRAM, research co. exec.; b. N.Y.C., May 15, 1953; d. Martin and Janet Kram; B.A., Lake Forest Coll., 1974; M.B.A., Wash. State U., 1977; m. Jonathan Kiell, May 30, 1974. Configuration and data mgmt. specialist Martin Marietta Aerospace Co., Orlando, Fla., 1978-79; market research fin. analyst Fla. Solar Energy Center, Cape Canaveral, Fla., 1979—; dir. Tony Coppola Assos., Inc., Orlando. Mem. Assn. M.B.A. Execs. Author: Turning on the Sun: A Comprehensive Guide to Solar Energy, 1980. Office: 300 State Rd 401 Cape Canaveral FL 32920

KIENAST, BETTIE STEWART, social worker; b. Richmond, Va., Aug. 31, 1940; d. Marion H. and Loreighn (Cummings) Stewart; B.A., Mary Washington Coll., 1962; M.S.W., Va. Commonwealth U., 1973; m. Joseph King Kienast, June 26, 1965. Child welfare worker Richmond Social Services Bur., 1962-65; caseworker Louisa County Dept. Social Services, Louisa, Va., 1965-66; ct. social worker Albemarle County Dept. Social Services, Charlottesville, Va., 1966-69; sr. probation officer 16th Dist. Juvenile and Domestic Relations Ct., Charlottesville, 1969-71; social work supr., adminstrv. asst., Charlottesville Dept. Social Services, 1973-77, asst. dir., 1977—; field instr. Va. Commonwealth U. Sch. Social Work, 1977-79. Mem. Region X Mental Health/Mental Retardation Services Bd., 1973-79, chmn., 1976-78; bd. dirs. Region X Info. and Referral, 1979-80; bd. dirs. Adventure Bound, chmn., 1979-80; mem. alumni bd. Va. Commonwealth U. Sch. Social Work, 1978; mem. profl. adv. com. Charlottesville-Albemarle Shelter for Abused Women, 1979-80. Mem. Acad. Cert. Social Workers, Nat. Assn. Social Workers, Am. Soc. Public Adminstrn., Am. Public Welfare Assn., Va. League Social Service Execs. Presbyterian. Home: PO Box 126 Troy VA 22974 Office: 4912 W Marshall St Richmond VA

KIENE, PAUL CARL, hosp. health care cons.; b. Shreveport, La., Mar. 30, 1927; s. Errol A. and Beatrice (McFarlane) K.; B.S. in Bus. Adminstrn., La. Tech. U., 1951; m. Elaine Gray, Nov. 15, 1950; children—Michael, Mark, Debra, Jennifer, Martha, Matthew. Hosp. adminstr., various locations, 1953-70; owner Paul C. Kiene and Assos., Hosp. Health Care Consultants, Baton Rouge, 1970—. Served with USN, 1945-46. Named Outstanding Young Man, Ruston Jaycees, 1961. Fellow Am. Assn. Hosp. Consultants (dir. 1976-79); mem. Am. Hosp. Assn., La. Hosp. Assn., Cath. Hosp. Assn., Pioneer Am. Soc., Nat. Assn. Watch and Clock Collectors. Contbg. editor Pioneer America. Home: 1600 Stanford Ave Baton Rouge LA 70808 Office: 5551 Corporate Blvd Suite 3L Baton Rouge LA 70808

KIENHOLZ, RICHARD LESLIE, dentist, educator; b. Spokane, Wash., Aug. 27, 1922; s. Leslie Joseph and Annabel (Bowns) K.; student Walla Walla Coll., 1941-43; D.M.D., U. Oreg., 1946; m. Louise Seever, Sept. 28, 1968. Instr. operative dentistry U. Oreg. Dental Sch., 1946; served to capt. AUS, 1946-48; pvt. practice dentistry, Grants Pass, Oreg., 1948-53; capt. assigned USAF, 1953, advanced through grades to lt. col. Dental Corps, 1970; ret., 1970; asst. prof. Baylor Coll. Dentistry, Dallas, 1970-75, dir. dental materials sci., 1970—, asso. prof. dental materials sci. and operative dentistry, 1975—. Fellow Internat. Coll. Dentists, Acad. Gen. Dentistry; mem. ADA, Tex. Dental Assn., Dallas County Dental Soc., AAAS, Am. Assn. Dental Schs., Am. Soc. Forensic Scis., Am. Soc. Mil. Surgeons, Internat. Assn. Dental Research (dental materials group), Am. Assn. Dental Research, Acad. Operative Dentistry, Fedn. Dentaire Internat., Nat. Rifle Assn. (life), Am. Acad. History of Dentistry, Ret. Officers Assn. (life), Air Force Assn., Sigma Xi, Psi Omega, Omicron Kappa Upsilon. Republican. Presbyn. Club: Petroleum, Woodhaven Country (Ft. Worth). Author: Dental Materials Lecture and Laboratory Manuals. Research in dental materials. Home: 6920 Tumbling Trail Fort Worth TX 76116 Office: Baylor Coll Dentistry 3302 Gaston Ave Dallas TX 75246

KIERE, JACQUES ISIDORE, govt. ofcl.; b. Big Timber, Mont., Sept. 4, 1933; s. Raymond and Jeanne (Kennis) K.; student mining U. Ariz., 1955; m. Maria C. Battaglia, Sept. 1, 1956; children—Simone, Micheline, Michael, Mimi. With Drug Enforcement Adminstrn., various locations, 1961—, chief European intelligence sect., Washington, 1972-74, dir. El Paso (Tex.) Intelligence Center, 1974-76, regional dir., Mexico City, 1976-79, chief planning and evaluation, Dallas, 1979—. Served with U.S. Army, 1952-55. Mem. Internat. Assn. Chiefs of Police, Tex. Narcotic Enforcement Officers Assn. Republican. Roman Catholic. Home: 2904 Preston Trail Rockwall TX 75087 Office: 1880 Regal Row Dallas TX

KIERNAN, RICHARD DANIEL, JR., mfg. co. exec.; b. N.Y.C., July 21, 1943; s. Richard Daniel and Anna Deloras (Cappiello) K.; A.A.S., Rockland Community Coll., 1963; B.S., Fairleigh Dickinson U., 1967; postgrad. E. Carolina U., 1977—; m. Yvonne Marie Brenner, Oct. 12, 1968; children—Richard Daniel, Kelly Ann, Kevin Joseph. Quality assurance, devel. chemist Am. Cyanamid, Pearl River, N.Y., 1963-69; quality assurance lab. supr. Burroughs Wellcome Co., Greenville, N.C., 1969-72, adminstrv. staff specialist, 1972-75, supr. quality control, 1975-77, quality assurance adminstrv. sect. head, 1977-78, adminstrv. dept. head, 1978-79, tech. ops. mgr. drug regulatory affairs, Research Triangle Park, N.C., 1979—. Vice pres., organizer Greenville Bicentennial Celebration, 1974; chmn. bus. sect. Pitt County United Fund, 1974; local capt. Pitt County Republican Party, 1971-72; bd. dirs. Pitt County Boys Club, 1972-75. Recipient N.C. Jaycees Keyman award, 1971, Speak-up award, 1972. Mem. Am. Chem. Soc., Parenteral Drug Assn., Pharm. Mfrs. Assn., Greenville Jr. C. of C. (v.p. 1974). Republican. Roman Catholic. Office: 3030 Cornwalis Rd Research Triangle Park NC 27709

KIESS, EDWARD MARION, educator; b. Washington, Mar. 10, 1933; s. Carl C. and Harriet (Knudsen) K.; B.S., Mass. Inst. Tech., 1955; M.S., Pa. State U., 1962, Ph.D., 1965; m. Ruth Stromberg, June 27, 1959; children—Raymond Brian, Thomas Edward, Sandra Marie. Physicist, HRB-Singer, Inc., State College, Pa., 1960-64; asst. prof. Lycoming Coll., Williamsport, Pa., 1966, Batelle Meml. Inst., Columbus, Ohio, 1967-68; asso. prof. physics Hampden-Sydney (Va.) Coll., 1968—. Served with U.S. Army, 1956-60. Research corp. grantee, 1971. Mem. Optical Soc. Am. Home and office: Box 175 Hampden-Sydney VA 23943

KIHLE, DONALD ARTHUR, lawyer; b. Noonan, N.D., Apr. 4, 1934; s. John Arthur and Linnie Wilhelmena (Ljunggren) K.; B.S. in Indsl. Engring., U. N.D. at Grand Forks, 1957; J.D., U. Okla. at Norman, 1967; m. Judith Ann Hudson, July 18, 1965; children—Kevin, Kirsten, Kathryn, Kurte. Engr. trainee Continental Pipe Line Co., Ponca City, Okla., 1957, staff engr., 1960-61, 63-64, sr. staff engr., 1964-65; project engr. Oasis Oil Co., Libya, Inc., Tripoli, Libya, 1961-62, sr. project engr., 1962-63; admitted to Okla. bar, 1967; asso. firm Huffman, Arrington, Scheurich & Kincaid, Tulsa, 1967-71; mem. firm Huffman, Arrington, Scheurich & Kihle, Tulsa, 1971—. Trustee Undercroft Montessori Sch., Inc., Tulsa, 1973-79. Served to 1st lt. AUS, 1957-59. Mem. Am., Okla., Tulsa County bar assns., Order of Coif, Sigma Tau, Sigma Chi, Phi Delta Phi. Clubs: Tulsa, So. Hills Country. Bd. editors Okla. Law Rev., 1965-67. Home: 4717 S Lewis Ct Tulsa OK 74105 Office: 510 Oklahoma Natural Bldg 624 S Boston Ave Tulsa OK 74119

KIKER, JOHN EWING, JR., civil engr.; b. Americus, Ga., Apr. 26, 1906; s. John Ewing and Emma Estelle (Argo) K.; student Ga. Inst. Tech., 1922-25, N.Y. U., 1929-30; B.S. in Gen. Engring., Mass. Inst. Tech., 1930; M.C.E., N.Y. U., 1941; m. Mary Mildred Hayes, Dec. 16, 1935 (dec. Oct. 1968); children—Joan (Mrs. Ronald J. Kruse), Carol (Mrs. Richard W. Townsend); m. 2d, Florence Fort Collins, Apr. 17, 1972. Chem. engr. H.C. Nutting Co., Tampa, Fla., Newark, 1925-30; san. engr. Internat. Water Co., Saigon, Indo-China, 1930-35; dist. engr. N.Y. State Dept. Health, Poughkeepsie, 1936-47; asso. prof., prof., chmn. dept. environ. engring. U. Fla., Gainesville, 1947-69, prof. emeritus civil engring., 1969—; spl. cons. USPHS, 1954-68; nat. cons. to surgeon gen. USAF, 1962-68. Served from 1st lt. to maj., AUS, 1942-46. Recipient Distinguished Faculty award Fla. Blue Key, 1964. Mem. ASCE (Engr. of Year award Fla. sect. 1967), Am. Pub. Health Assn., Water Pollution Control Fedn. (dir. 1953-56, A.S. Bedell award 1956), Nat. (dir. 1955-57), Fla. (pres. 1955-57) socs. profl. engrs., Am. Water Works Assn., Am. Soc. Engring. Edn. (pres. Fla. br. 1952-54), Fla. Engring. Soc. (Outstanding Service award 1958), Fla. Pollution Control Fedn. (pres. 1952-53), others. Clubs: Mason, Shriner, Rotary, Americus Country. Author: Subsurface Sewage Disposal, 1948. Contbr. numerous articles to engring. jours. Home and office: Lake Shore Dr Route 1 Americus GA 31709

KIKTA, ANNETTE JOYCE, chem. engr.; b. Dayton, Ohio, Aug. 19, 1951; d. William Anthony and Mary Jane (Mestemaker) Topp; B.S. in Applied Sci. (Pulp and Paper Found. grantee), Miami U., Oxford, Ohio, 1973; m. Frank James Kikta, July 7, 1973; 1 son, Keith James. Technologist, Champion Papers, Pasadena, Tex., 1973-75, sr. technologist, 1975-76; process engr. Soltex Polymer Corp., Deer Park, Tex., 1976-78, tech. supr. Textar div., 1980—. Mem. TAPPI, Am. Inst. Chem. Engrs. Home: 11430 Sageking St Houston TX 77089 Office: PO Box 1000 Deer Park TX 77536

KILBORNE, ROBERT STEWART, ret. bus. exec.; b. N.Y.C., Aug. 1, 1905; s. Robert Stewart and Katharine (Skinner) K.; grad. Groton (Mass.) Sch., 1923; student Yale, 1923-25; m. Barbara Briggs, Nov. 28, 1925 (dec. 1968); children—Belle (Mrs. Richard S. Taylor), Robert Stewart III (dec.) George Briggs; m. 2d, Jane Lowes, May 2, 1969. Joined William Skinner & Sons (Mass. Common Law Trust), N.Y.C., 1925, pres. Truhu Fabrics Corp. (a subsidiary), 1933, v.p. William Skinner & Sons, 1941, trustee, 1945-61, pres., 1947-61; dir. The Equitable Life Assurance Soc. U.S., 1946-77. Commr. of conservation N.Y. State Conservation Dept., 1966-70; spl. asst. to the Gov. on conservation affairs, 1970-72; mem. Industry adv. com. OPA, Washington, 1943-46, OPS, 1951-53; mem. adv. com. Research & Devel. br. Mil. Planning Div. Office Q.M. Gen., Washington 1943-49. Synthetic br. Broad Woven Fabrics div. Quartermaster Assn., Washington, 1951-61; chmn. Saratoga Springs Commn., 1966-70; alt. to gov. N.Y. State for Delaware River Basin Commn., 1966-71; bd. dirs. Saratoga Performing Arts Center, 1966-72, Gt. Lakes Commn., 1966-77, Hudson River Valley Commn., 1966-77, Interstate Oil Compact Commn., 1966-70, State Air Pollution Control Bd., 1966-70, commr. N.Y. State Taconic Park Commn., 1963-76; trustee Arthur W. Butler Meml. Sanctuary, 1967-77; bd. dirs. Union Theol. Sem., 1950-66, Humane Soc. Glynn County (Ga.); bd. dirs. Sea Island Property Owners Assn., 1979—, v.p., 1980; elder Presbyterian Ch. Mem. Am. Cotton Mfrs. Inst., Inc. (dir. 1958-62), Nat. Fedn. Textiles, Inc. (dir. 1949-58, pres. 1954-55), Am. Arbitration Assn., Am. Textile Mfrs. Inst. (hon. dir. 1962—), Soc. Mayflower Descs. (bd. assts. 1968-72), Bedford Hist. Soc. (dir. 1971-78), New Eng. Soc. of N.Y., Nat. Aero. Assn., Coastal Ga. Hist. Soc., Delta Kappa Epsilon. Republican. Clubs: Sea Island Golf, Yale, Wings (N.Y.C.). Home: 137 W Cherokee Rd Sea Island GA 31561

KILBRIDE, WADE ROBERT, coll. adminstr., air force officer; b. Chgo., Aug. 13, 1928; s. Mathias Joseph and Anna (Wade) K.; B.S., Regis Coll., 1950; M.A., U. Tex. at Austin, 1957, postgrad., 1967—; m. Ruth Dickinson, June 17, 1961; children—Marc, Lynn. Commd. 2d lt. USAF, 1952, advanced through grades to lt. col., 1968; fighter pilot, 1952-57; instr. USAF Acad., Colo., 1961-64, asso. prof. econs., 1967-73, head dept. econs., 1968-72; chief profl. relations div. Community Coll. Air Force, Lackland AFB, Tex., 1973-78; asst. dean Coll. Bus. Adminstrn. U. Central Fla., Orlando, 1978—; instr. econs. San Antonio Coll., 1973-75, U. Tex. at San Antonio, 1975-78. Decorated D.F.C. with four bronze oak leaf clusters, Air medal with silver oak leaf cluster and four bronze oak leaf clusters. Mem. Am., Midwest econ. assns., Am. Assn. Higher Edn., Rocky Mountain Social Sci. Assn., Omicron Delta Epsilon, Sigma Iota Epsilon, Phi Delta Kappa. Home: 3210 Bravura Ct #A Orlando FL 32807 Office: Coll Bus Adminstrn U Central FL 32816

KILBURN, MARY BROWN, psychologist; b. Conway, Ark., Feb. 2, 1934; B.S. cum laude, Memphis State Coll., 1956; M.S. in Psychology, N.C. State U., Raleigh, 1969, Ph.D. in Clin./Community Psychology, 1977; married; 2 children. Asst. dir., office mgr. Girls' Club Memphis, 1955-56; gen. agt. Trans-Continental Life Ins. Co., Little Rock, Ark., 1956-57; adminstrv. sec. div. med. psychology dept. psychiatry Duke U. Med. Center, Durham, N.C., 1957-58; pvt. practice psychology, Raleigh, N.C., 1965— research asst. cognitive tng. project N.C. State U., Raleigh, 1965-66, teaching asst. dept. psychology, 1966-67; mem. faculty Peace Coll., Raleigh, 1969-70; psychologist N.C. Div. Social Services, Raleigh, 1970-73; clin. psychologist Mental Health Center, N.C. Dept. Corrections, Raleigh, 1973; asst. dir., chief clin. services Developmental Evaluation Center, Raleigh, 1973-77; head psychol. services br. Div. Social Services, N.C. Dept. Human Resources, Raleigh, 1977—, div. rep. State Advisory Council on Wilderness Camping for Emotionally Disturbed Children. Chmn. steering com. N.C. Consumer's Council, 1966-68. Certified sch. psychologist, licensed psychologist N.C. Mem. Am. (mem. div. mental retardation, div. community psychology, sect. clin. child psychology), N.C. (asso.) psychol. assn., N.C. Group Behavior Soc., Phi Kappa Phi, Psi Chi, Tau Kappa Alpha. Author research papers. Office: 1300 St Mary's St Raleigh NC 27605

KILGO, JOHN LEE, JR., ins. co. exec.; b. Macon, Ga., July 15, 1944; s. John Lee and Virginia Crews K.; B.S. in Bus. Adminstrn., U. Fla., 1966; m. Alice Patricia Hennessey, Apr. 19, 1967; 1 son, John Patrick. Owner, operator Hillis Music Studios, Gainesville, Fla., 1971-72; acct. U. Fla., Gainesville, 1972-73; account rep. Variable Annuity Life Ins. Co., Gainesville, 1973-76; v.p., dir. Pub. Employees Services Co., Tallahassee, 1976—; dir. Pub. Employees Equities Services Co. Served to capt. USAF, 1967-71. Decorated Air Force Commendation medal. Mem. Am. Mgmt. Assn. Home: 4440 Widgeon Way Tallahassee FL 32303 Office: Pub Employees Services Co 449 W Georgia St Tallahassee FL 32301

KILGORE, ANNABELLE THOMPSON, guidance counselor; b. Helena, Ark., May 3, 1924; d. Willie P. and Callie L. (Lacey) Thompson; B.A., Roosevelt U., 1959, M.Ed., 1965, M.A. in Counseling and Guidance, 1973; m. Shirley Franklin Kilgore, Aug. 22, 1948; 1 dau., Joyce Evelyn. Personnel dept. Boeing Aircraft Co., Seattle, 1943-46; elementary sch. tchr. City Schs. Gary (Ind.), 1960-72; guidance counselor Emerson High Sch., Gary, 1972—, also basic skills coordinator, test coordinator, career edn. chmn. Recipient Outstanding Alumni award Tuskegee Inst., 1971, award USAF, 1977; named hon. admission counselor U.S. Naval Acad., 1975-76. Mem. Am. Fedn. Tchrs. (merit award 1971, 74, 75), Am. Personnel and Guidance Assn., Ind. Personnel and Guidance Assn., AAUW, Nat. Assn. Study Negro Life and History, NAACP, Tuskegee Alumni Assn. (regional dir. N. Central region, Outstanding Service award 1979, nat. Robert Russa Moton award 1979), Phi Delta Kappa (pres. Beta Mu chpt.). Democrat. Lutheran. Contbr. articles to profl. publs. Home: 6565 Kimberly Mill Rd College Park GA 30349

KILGORE, CHARLES NICKELS, banker; b. Richlands, Va., Apr. 18, 1947; s. Charles Taft and Evelyn Irene (Nickels) K.; A.A.S. in Acctg., S.W. Va. Community Coll., 1971; grad. Am. Inst. Banking, 1969; m. Merry Tillou Henderson, July 9, 1972. Sr. auditor Dominion Bankshares Corp., Richlands, 1971-73; ops. officer 1st Nat. Exchange, Richlands, 1973-76; v.p. Sentinel Savs. & Loan Assn., Richlands, 1977; sr. v.p. Cumberland Bank, Grundy, Va., 1977—; chmn. S.W. study group Am. Inst. Banking; mem. bus. adv. com. S.W. Va. Community Coll. Mem. Am. Inst. Banking, Va. Bankers Assn., Richlands Jaycees. Episcopalian. Home: 205 Shale Dr Richlands VA 24641 Office: Box 709 Grundy VA 24614

KILGORE, DONALD GIBSON, JR., pathologist; b. Dallas, Nov. 21, 1927; s. Donald Gibson and Gladys (Watson) K.; student So. Methodist U., 1943-45; M.D., Southwestern Med. Coll., U. Tex., 1949; m. Jean Upchurch Augur, Aug. 23, 1952; children—Michael Augur, Stephen Bassett, Phillip Arthur, Geoffrey Scott, Sharon Louise. Intern, Parkland Meml. Hosp., Dallas, 1949-50; resident pathology Charity Hosp. La., New Orleans, also Tulane, 1950-54; asst. pathologist Charity Hosp., 1952-54; pathologist Greenville (S.C.) Hosp. System, 1956—, dir. labs. Greenville Meml. Hosp., 1972—; cons. pathologist St. Francis, Shriners hosps., Greenville, Easley Baptist Hosp.; vis. lectr. Clemson U., 1963—; asst. prof. pathology Med. U. S.C., 1968—. Bd. dirs. Greenville County United Fund, 1966-74, Greenville Community Council, 1968-71, Friends of Greenville County Library, 1966-74; trustee Sch. Dist. Greenville County, 1970—; bd. govs. S.C. Patient Compensation Fund, 1977—; patron Greenville Mus. Art, Greenville Little Theatre, 1956—. Served to capt. USAF, 1954-56. Recipient Distinguished Service award S.C. Hosp. Assn., 1976. Diplomate Am. Bd. Pathology. Fellow Coll. Am. Pathologists (assemblyman for S.C. 1968-71), Am. Soc. Clin. Pathologists (councilor S.C. 1959-62); mem. Am. Assn. Blood Banks (adv. council 1962-67, insp. committeeman Southeast dist. 1965—), AMA, So. Med. Assn., S.C. Med. Assn. (exec. council 1969-76, pres. 1974-75), Am. Soc. Cytology, Am. Coll. Nuclear Medicine, S.C. Inst. Med. Edn. and Research (pres. 1974—), S.C. Soc. Pathologists (pres. 1969-72), Richard III Soc. (co-chmn. Am. br, 1966-75), Soc. Ancient Numismatics (charter), Am. Numis. Soc., Am. (life), Blue Ridge (life) numis. assns. Royal Numis. Soc. (life), Mensa, S.C. Congress Parents and Tchrs. (life), Greenville County Dental Soc. (hon. life), Greater Greenville C. of C. (ednl. task force 1962-70, chmn. 1965-70), U.S. Power Squadron, Les Amis du Vin (hon. life mem., v.p. Greenville chpt. 1971—), St. Andrews Soc. Upper S.C., Phi Eta Sigma, Phi Chi. Democrat. Presbyn. (ruling elder 1969—). Rotarian (sr. active mem., dir. 1970-72). Clubs: Poinsett, Greenville Country, Thirty-Nine (sec.-treas. 1979—). Home: 129 Rockingham Rd Greenville SC 29607 Office: 11 Sumner St Greenville SC 29601

KILGORE, GEORGE WALTER, mfg. co. exec.; b. Sewanee, Tenn., Sept. 26, 1929; s. Clarence E. and Theona A. (Haynes) K.; student U. South La., 1969-70; m. Irmgard I. Kreuzer, Dec. 17, 1959; children—Wynn, Alan, Gary, Connie. Prodn. foreman E.I. duPont, Chattanooga, 1951-57; supr. mfg. Albritton Engring. Co., Bryan, Tex., 1957-59, plant supt., 1959-64, employment mgr., asst. personnel mgr., 1964-65, safety dir., 1965-67; area safety mgr. Cabot Corp., Lafayette, La., 1967-72, western regional safety mgr., Pampa, Tex., 1972-73, corporate dir. safety, 1973—. Mem. Carbon Black Industry Com. for Environ. Health, 1972—; bd. dirs. United Fund, 1966-68; bd. dirs. Gray County Assn. Retarded Children, 1974—, pres., 1976-77. Certified hazard control mgr. Mem. Am. Soc. Safety Engrs., Nat. Safety Mgmt. Assn., . Am. Soc. Indsl. Security, Tex. Safety Assn. (bd. dirs.), Tex. Chem. Occupational Safety Com. Club: Masons. Home: 1900 Holly Ln Pampa TX 79065 Office: PO Box 1101 Pampa TX 79065

KILGORE, JAMES ELBERT, marriage and family counselor; b. Douglasville, Ga., July 25, 1936; s. Woodard Elbert and Mary Louise (Smith) K.; B.A., Calif. Baptist Theol. Coll., 1958; M.R.E., Am. Bapt. Sem. of West, 1963; Religion D., Sch. Theology at Claremont, 1967; post-doctoral certificate U. Minn., 1969; m. Ruth Marie Buerge, Aug. 2, 1957; children—James C., Joy Marie, Jeffrey Mark. Ordained to ministry Bapt. Ch., 1954; pastor People's Bapt. Ch., Atlanta, 1954-56, First Bapt. Ch., Claremont, Calif., 1960-67; marriage counselor Domestic Relations Ct., Sacramento, 1968; pvt. practice marriage and family counseling, Atlanta, 1969—; pres. Northside Counseling Center, Atlanta, 1972—; lectr., Clayton Jr. Coll., 1972-74; chmn. Ga. Marriage and Family Counselor Licensing Bd.; pres. Internat. Family Found., 1976—. Fellow Am. Assn. Marriage and Family Therapy (treas. 1978-79); mem. Am. Psychol. Assn., Am. Assn. Sex Educators, Counselors and Therapists (charter, certified), Ga. Assn. Marriage and Family Counselors (legis. rep., founding chmn.). Author: Pastoral Care of the Hospitalized Child, 1968; Billy Graham the Preacher, 1968; Being a Man in a Woman's World, 1975; Getting More Family Out of Your Dollar, 1976; Being Up in a Down World, 1977; Letters on Life and Love, 1978; Try Marriage Before Divorce, 1978. Home: 665 Glenairy Dr Atlanta GA 30328 Office: 204 Northside Med Center 275 Carpenter Dr NE Atlanta GA 30328

KILLEBREW, FLAVIUS CHARLES, herpetologist; b. Canadian, Tex., Apr. 2, 1949; s. Wilbur Newton and Nellie May (Davidson) K.; B.S., W. Tex. State U., 1971, M.S., 1972; Ph.D., U. Ark., 1976; m. Mary Jaynet Johnson, Sept. 10, 1969; 1 child, Arian Jaye. Teaching asst. W. Tex. State U., Canyon, 1969-72, research asst., 1972, asst. prof. dept. biology, 1976—; instr. U. Ark., Fayetteville, 1972-76; mus. asst. U. Ark. Mus. Fayetteville, 1976; cons. to state and fed. govt. agys. Sigma Xi grantee, 1972; W. Tex. State U. grantee, 1976-79; C.E. grantee, 1978; Dept. Interior grantee, 1978-79. Mem. AAUP, Am. Soc. Ichthyologists and Herpetologists, Herpetologists League, Tex. Acad. Sci., Southwestern Assn. Naturalists, Soc. for Study of Amphibians and Reptiles, W. Tex. State U. Soc. Naturalists, Sigma Xi, Sigma Nu, Alpha Chi, Beta Beta Beta. Club: Masons. Contbr. articles in field to biol. jours. Home: 1204 12th St Canyon TX 79015 Office: W Tex State U Dept Biology Canyon TX 79016

KILLEBREW, JAMES ROBERT, architect, engr.; b. Okmulgee, Okla., Dec. 10, 1918; s. Robert Herman and Edith (Tyler) K.; B.S. in Archtl. Engring., U. Tex., 1949; m. Prebel Lee Thompson, Nov. 14, 1966; children—Debra Lee, Tod Nenian, Linda Gayle; 1 dau. by previous marriage, Laura Janice. Chmn. bd. Killebrew-Rucker and Assos., Inc., architects and engrs., Wichita Falls, Tex., 1954—, works include elementary schs., one selected by Tex. Edn. Agy., as one of 25 outstanding since 1950, Bethania Hosp., Parker Sq. State Bank, Texas Hwy. Dept. Bldgs., 1st State Bank, Archer City Hosp., Muenster Meml. Hosp., Gen. Hosp., Plainview, Tex., Vernon (Tex.) Hosp., Vernon Geriatrics Psychiat. Hosp., Wichita Gen. Hosp., Gen. Hosp., Nocona, Tex., addition to Crippled Childrens Hosp., Wichita Falls, Tex., Sci. Bldg., Phys. Edn. Bldg. and Fine Arts Bldg. of Midwestern U., Teenage Drug Addiction Center, Vernon, Tex., hosps. at Eastland, Tex., Post Office, Denton, Tex., other pub. bldgs., AC Spark Plug div. Gen. Motors Corp. Ceramic Complex, Wichita Falls, Tex., other indsl. plants; asst. instr. Midwestern State U., 1970. Served from ensign to lt. comdr. USNR, 1940-45, PTO, capt. Res. Licensed archtl. engr. Fellow AIA (pres. Wichita Falls chpt. 1966-67); mem. Nat., Tex. (pres. North Central Tex. chpt. 1960-61, sec.-treas. 1958-59) socs. profl. engrs., Am. Soc. Archtl. Engrs. (charter mem.), Am. Soc. Heating, Ventilating and Air Conditioning Engrs., C. of C. (chmn. beautification com. 1958-59, bldg. code com. 1955-56, aviation com. 1958-59; dir.), Navy League U.S. (pres. 1967-68), Fine Art Soc. Tex. (bd. dirs., pres. 1970, chmn. bd. 1973—), Tex. Ret. Officers Assn. Mem. Christian Ch. (elder). Home: 1559 Hanover St Wichita Falls TX 76302 Office: 600 Petroleum Bldg Wichita Falls TX 76301

KILLEBREW, MACK LEON, veterinarian; b. Carroll County, Miss., Apr. 25, 1939; s. John Arthur and Gladys (Rodgers) K.; B.S., Miss. State U., 1961; D.V.M., Auburn U., 1965; m. Anita Dolores Bigner, Apr. 16, 1960; children—Melissa Leigh, Laura Lynn, Sacha Margaret. Owner, veterinarian Holmes County (Miss.) Animal Clinic, Lexington, 1965—. Cons. to ranches. Recipient Veterinarian award Auburn U., 1965. Mem. Am., Miss. vet. med. assns., Delta Council, Sigma Phi Epsilon, Alpha Psi. Baptist. Mason, Lion. Club: Holmes County Country. Contbr. articles to profl. jours., newspapers. Home: 102 Chestnut St Lexington MS 39095 Office: Hwy 12 E Lexington MS 39095

KILLEBREW, STEVE LEE, acct.; b. Richmond, Va., Jan. 19, 1926; s. O. Steve and Elizabeth H. (Wagner) K.; B.B.A., U. Tex., 1951; m. Gloria M. Mire, May 4, 1947; children—Stephanie (Mrs. L. Wesley Crippen), Kathryne (Mrs. Kathryne L. Girouard), Kent M., Beth Ann. Staff accountant O. Steve Killebrew & Co., 1951-59, office mgr., 1959-66, gen. partner, 1966-78; pvt. practice acctg., 1978—; pres. Live Oak Cemetery, 1972—; treas. B.C.D., Inc., C.K.D., Inc.; dir. 1st Bank & Trust of Groves (Tex.). Treas., Assn. of Retarded, 1969—. Served with USMCR, 1944-47; PTO. Decorated Purple Heart. C.P.A., Tex., La. Mem. Am. Inst. C.P.A.'s, Sertoma Internat. (past pres. Port Arthur, dist. gov. E. Tex. 1971-73, state dir. 1973-74). Home: 2042 Ray Ave Groves TX 77619 Office: 2348 Procter St Port Arthur TX 77640

KILLEFFER, FREDRICK AYRES, surgeon; b. Harriman, Tenn., Aug. 20, 1934; s. Louis A. and Julia Helena (Dunlap) K.; M.D., U. Tenn., 1958; m. Raisa Edwards, Dec. 22, 1957; children—Julia Elizabeth, James Alexander, Stephen Eugene. Intern, Queen's Hosp., Honolulu, 1958-59; resident in gen. surgery Manhattan VA Hosp., N.Y.C., 1960-62; resident in neurol. surgery U. Calif. Med. Center, Los Angeles, 1964-69, resident in neurosurgery, 1965-66, chief resident in neurosurgery, 1967; chief resident in neurosurgery Wadsworth VA Hosp., Los Angeles, 1968; practice medicine specializing in neurosurgery Los Angeles, 1969-72, Knoxville, Tenn., 1972—; physician Miners Meml. Hosp., Hazard, Ky., 1959-60; chief of neurosurgery VA Center, Los Angeles, 1969-72, Wadsworth Gen. Hosp., Los Angeles, 1969-72; asst. prof. neurosurgery Med. Center, U. Calif., Los Angeles, 1969-72; asso. prof. clin. neurol. surgery U. Tenn. Meml. Research Center and Hosp., Knoxville, 1972—; mem. Med. Advisory Bd., March of Dimes, 1976-80. Served to capt. M.C., U.S. Army, 1962-64. Diplomate Am. Bd. Neurol. Surgery. Fellow A.C.S.; mem. So. Neurol. Soc., Am. Assn. Neurol. Surgeons, Tenn. Med. Assn., Congress of Neurol. Surgery, Tenn. Med. Assn., AMA, Fedn. of Western Socs. of the Neurol. Scis., E. Tenn. Wine Soc. (dir. 1979-80). Republican. Episcopalian. Club: Cherokee Country. Contbr. articles on neurol. pathology and diagnosis to profl. jours. Home: 4763 Calumet Dr Knoxville TN 37919 Office: Physicians Office Bldg 1928 Alcoa Hwy Knoxville TN 37920

KILLGORE, CHARLES ALDEN, chem. engr., corp. exec.; b. Lisbon, La., Aug. 19, 1934; s. Millard B. and Alice D. (Monk) K.; B.S., La. Tech. U., 1956, M.S., 1963; postgrad. Iowa State U., summer 1961, Kans. State U., summer 1965, Okla. State U., 1968-71; m. Patti Jean Nicholas, June 1, 1954; children—Michael D., Byron Neill, Chris Alan. Instr. chem. engring. La. Tech. U., Ruston, 1959-62, asst. prof. chem. engring., 1962-69, also dir. nuclear center, asso. prof., 1969-73, also dir. nuclear center, asso. dean engring., also dir. Engring. Research, 1973-75; pres. Kilgore's, Inc., Ruston, 1975—; cons. mgmt., engring. and radiation. Sec. Lincoln Parish Coordinating Com. Bd. dirs. Cedar Creek Sch., chmn., 1972—; bd. dirs. Wesley Found., pres., 1974-76. Served to capt., USAF, 1956-59. Recipient Silver Beaver award Boy Scouts Am., 1969. Registered profl. engr., La. NSF fellow, 1968, 69, 71. Mem. Am. Inst. Chem. Engrs., La. Engring. Soc., Health Physics Soc., Am. Soc. Engring. Edn. (named outstanding faculty mem. 1970), Am. Nuclear Soc., Tau Beta Pi, Omicron Delta Kappa. Methodist. Lion (pres. 1972-73). Author: Evaluation of Potential Uses for Radiation Processing in Louisiana Industries, 1966; Lecture Notes on CPM, 1964. Address: 506 Hundred Oaks Dr Ruston LA 72170

KILPATRICK, DONALD WAYNE, state senator; b. Sayre, Okla., Sept. 2, 1939; s. Wayne and Mary Evelyn (Gesell) K.; LL.B., Oklahoma City U., 1963; m. Barbara Jean Cowan, Sept. 1, 1973; 1 son, Kent. Admitted to Okla. bar, 1963; atty. firm Berry & Berry, Oklahoma City, 1963-64, State Farm Ins. Co., Washington, 1965-68; pvt. practice, Oklahoma City, 1968—; partner firm Kilpatrick & Jordan, 1975—; mem. Okla. Ho. of Reps. from 93d Dist., 1970-76, Senate from 43d Dist., 1976—. Bd. dirs. Okla. League Blind, 1979. Mem. Am. Bar Assn., Okla. Bar Assn., Okla. County Bar Assn., Oklahoma City C. of C. Democrat. Mem. Christian Ch. (Disciples of Christ). Clubs: Masons, Lions. Home: 9917 Trafalgar St Oklahoma City OK 73139 Office: 3900 SE 29th St Del City OK 73115

KILPATRICK, EARL BUDDY, biologist, educator; b. Burkburnett, Tex., June 21, 1920; s. Earl Kennedy and Margaret May (Chitwood) K.; B.S., U. Okla., 1942, M.S., 1949, Ph.D. (NSF fellow), 1959; m. Jack Ann Nichols, Apr. 20, 1956; children—Cheryl, Janet (Mrs. John Thomas), Toni (Mrs. Charles Stiefer), John, Alan, Rebecca. Asst. prof. biology Southeastern State Coll., Durant, Okla., 1949-60, asso. prof., 1960-62, prof., 1962—, also head dept. biology, 1961—. Mgr., treas. Southeastern Tchrs. Credit Union, 1973—. State chmn. Long Range Planning Com., 1971-72. Bd. dirs. Okla. Lions Eye Bank, 1969—, treas., 1973, v.p., 1974, pres., 1975. Served to capt. AUS, 1942-46; ETO; col. Res. Fellow Okla. Acad. Sci. (cons. speakers bur. 1966—); mem. AAAS, Southwestern Assn. Naturalists, Res. Officers Assn., Gideon's, Sigma Xi, Sigma Tau Gamma (faculty adv. 1956—). Lion (zone chmn. 1968-69, dist. gov. 1969-70, pres. 1970-71). Home: 1223 N 5th St Durant OK 74701

KILPATRICK, JAMES RAY, ch. adminstr.; b. Kilgore, Tex., Mar. 12, 1932; s. LeRoy and Sarah (Browning) K.; student Bapt. Bible Coll., 1951; fellow in ch. bus. adminstrn. U. Cin., 1962; B.B.A., Miller Coll., 1963; m. Lucille Hasty, Mar. 28, 1953; children—Connie, James Richard. Teller, 1st Nat. Bank, Cin., 1951-52; bus. adminstr. Landmark Baptist Temple, Cin., 1952-67; auditor, bus. adminstr. Dade Christian Schs. Inc., Miami, Fla., 1967-70; comptroller Dudley M. Hughes Funeral Homes Inc., 1970-76; bus. adminstr. Jupiter Road Bapt. Ch., Garland, Tex., 1976—. Registrar clk. Dallas County; lic. pilot. Mem. Nat. Assn. Ch. Bus. Adminstrs., Aircraft Owners and Pilots Assn., Nat. Guild Organists, Nat. Assn. Theatre Organists, Interpublications, Inc., Broadcast Music Inc., Am. Mgmt. Assn. Clubs: Rotary, Top of the Cliff, Eastern Hills Country. Contbr. articles to religious newspapers and mags.; composer, pub. mus. works. Home: 2106 Lansdowne St Garland TX 75040 Office: Jupiter Road Baptist Ch 2422 N Jupiter Rd Garland TX 75040

KILROY, JAMES FRANCIS, educator; b. Chgo., Sept. 7, 1935; s. John Patrick and Nora (Joyce) K.; B.A., DePaul U., 1957; M.A., U. Iowa, 1961; Ph.D., U. Wis., 1965; m. Mary Elizabeth Carroll, July 1, 1961; children—Maurya, James Dennis, Mark Justin. Tchr., Pub. High Schs., Chgo., 1957-61; asst. prof., Vanderbilt U., 1965-69, asso. prof., 1969-77, prof., 1977—, chmn. dept. English, asso. dean Grad. Sch., 1973-76. Am. Council Learned Socs. fellow, 1967-68; Nat. Endowment Humanities fellow, 1968. Mem. Modern Language Assn., Soc. for Values in Higher Edn. Roman Catholic. Author James Clarence Mangan, 1970; The Playboy Riots, 1971; The Modern Irish Drama (3 vols.), 1975, 75, 78; The Playboy as Poet, 1969; co-editor: Lost Plays of the Irish Renaissance, 1970; mem. editorial bd. Jour. of Irish Literature, Soundings. Home: 113 Carnavon Parkway Nashville TN 37205 Office: Dept of English Vanderbilt U Nashville TN 37235

KIM, HO-KYUN, pediatrician; b. Seoul, Korea, Mar. 5, 1938; s. Soong Moon and Botan Kim; came to U.S., 1965, naturalized, 1977; M.D., Seoul Nat. U., 1962; m. Gilja Park, May 23, 1965; children—Jenny Miyon, Linda Misun, David Hyunchul. Intern, Good Samaritan Hosp., Cin., 1965-66; resident in pediatrics Children's Hosp., Louisville, Ky., 1966-68; fellow in pediatric infectious disease, dept. pediatrics U. Louisville, 1968-70, St. Jude Children's Research Hosp., Memphis, 1970-72; individual practice medicine specializing in pediatrics, Tullahoma, Tenn., 1972—. Served with the Army of the Republic of Korea, 1962-65. Diplomate Am. Bd. Pediatrics. Mem. AMA, Tenn. Med. Assn., Tenn. Thoracic Soc., Am. Soc. Microbiology. Contbr. research papers in field of infectious disease. Home: 223 Lakewood Dr Tullahoma TN 37388 Office: 606 N Jackson St Tullahoma TN 37388

KIM, JIN BAI, educator; b. Sangju, Korea, June 23, 1921; s. Chill Bok and Jumni (Moon) K.; B.S., Yonsei U., Korea, 1950; M.S., U. Chgo., 1956; Ph.D., Va. Poly. Inst., 1965; m. Gunja Lee, July 7, 1945; 1 dau., Theresa Kyong. Asst. prof. Yonsei U., Seoul, Korea, 1948-61, chmn. dept., 1955-61; asst. prof. Mich. State U., East Lansing, 1965-67; from asst. prof. to prof. math. W.Va. U., Morgantown, 1967—; cons. in algebra George Washington U., 1969-71. Fulbright grantee, 1955-56; W.Va. U. Found. assos. awardee, 1973-74; W.Va. U. Senate research grantee, 1977. Mem. Am. Math. Soc., Tensor Soc., American Go Assn., Sigma Xi. Presbyterian. Club: Go (W.Va. U.). Contbr. articles to profl. jours.; reviewer Math. Revs., 1967—. Home: 332 Kenmore St Morgantown WV 26505 Office: Dept Math WVa U Morgantown WV 26505

KIM, JUNG HWAN, pathologist; b. Pusan, Korea, May 7, 1939; s. Kim Dong Ik and Kim Yang Soo; came to U.S., 1967, naturalized, 1977; M.D., Pusan Nat. U., 1964; m. Sung Heh Cho, May 2, 1970; 1 dau., Jeannette. Intern, DePaul Hosp., Norfolk, Va., 1967-68; resident in pediatrics Kings County Med. Center, Bklyn., 1968-69; resident in pathology Albert Einstein Coll. Medicine, Bronx, N.Y., 1969-73; fellow in pathology Yale U. Sch. Medicine, New Haven, 1973-76; asst. chief pathology USPHS Hosp., New Orleans, 1976-79, chief of pathology, New Orleans, 1979—; med. dir. Sch. Med. Tech., USPHS Hosp., New Orleans; lectr. pathology Tulane U. NIH grantee, 1974-75; diplomate Am. Bd. Pathology. Fellow Coll. Am. Pathologists; mem. Assn. Mil. Surgeons U.S. Contbr. med. articles to profl. jours. Home: 812 Oaklawn Dr Metairie LA 70005 Office: USPHS Hosp 210 State St New Orleans LA 70118

KIM, SEONG-SOO STEVEN, surgeon; b. Seo-Wha-Ri, Kangwon-Do, Korea, Sept. 9, 1940; s. Heon and Kap-soon (Lee) K.; M.D., Seoul Nat. U., 1965; m. Ok-Jin Ko, Nov. 11, 1972; children—Jane Soon-Mee, Lawrence Jee-Tae. Rotating intern Good Samaritan Hosp., Cin., 1965-66; gen. surg. resident St. Joseph Infirmary, Louisville, 1966-70; thoracic surg. resident U. Louisville Hosps., 1970-72; resident instr. U. Louisville, dept. surgery, 1970-72; practice medicine specializing in gen., thoracic and cardiovascular surgery, Henderson, Ky., 1972—; mem. active staff Community Meth. Hosp., Henderson, 1972—; owner Green River Internat., Henderson, 1977—. Diplomate Am. Bd. Surgery, Am. Bd. Thoracic Surgery. Fellow A.C.S.; mem. Ky. Med. Assn., Ky. Surg. Soc. Home: 103 Villa Dr Henderson KY 42420 Office: Suite 203 1413 N Elm St Henderson KY 42420

KIM, SUK KI, physician; b. Seoul, Korea, Dec. 25, 1942; came to U.S., 1970, naturalized, 1978; s. See Hee and Sun Shim (Pai) K.; M.D., U. Korea, 1967; m. Kuiza Lee, Dec. 7, 1967; children—Susan, Joseph, Jane. Intern, Trumbull Hosp., Warren, Ohio, 1971-72; resident U. Louisville, 1972-74; anesthetist VA Hosp., Louisville, 1976-79, Children's Hosp., Louisville, 1974—, Norton Hosp., Louisville, 1976—, Louisville Gen. Hosp., 1974-79; instr. dept. anesthesiology U. Louisville Med. Sch., 1975-77, asst. prof., 1977-78; practice medicine, specializing in anesthesiology, Owensboro, Ky., 1979—. Served to capt. Korean Army, 1967-70. Diplomate Am. Bd. Anesthesiology. Mem. AMA, Ky. Med. Assn., Jefferson County Med. Soc., Ky. Soc. Anesthesiologists, Am. Soc. Anesthesiologists. Seventh-day Adventist. Home: 3506 Aristides Dr Owensboro KY 42301 Office: 301 Leitchfield Rd Owensboro KY 42301

KIMBALL, AUBREY PIERCE, educator; b. Lufkin, Tex., Oct. 20, 1926; s. Aubrey Joseph and Eula Bernice (Pixley) K.; B.S., U. Houston, 1958, Ph.D., 1961; postdoctoral Stanford Research Inst., 1961-62; m. Kay Tabor, Mar. 29, 1975; children by previous marriage—Kathleen, Erin, Lisa. Research biochemist Stanford Research Inst., 1962-67; asso. prof. biochemistry U. Houston, 1967-72, prof., 1972—, planning dir. central campus cancer program, 1976—, chmn. dept. biophys. scis., 1977-78. Served with USNR, 1944-46, 50-52. Roche fellow, 1952-54. Grantee Robert A. Welch, 1968-82, NIH, 1969-80. Fellow Am. Inst. Chemists, N.Y. Acad. Scis.; mem. Am. Chem. Soc., Am. Assn. Cancer Research, Soc. Exptl. Biology and Medicine, Am. Soc. Biol. Chemists, S.W. Sci. Forum (dir., v.p., pres.-elect), AAAS, Sigma Xi (v.p., pres.-elect U. Houston chpt.). Editor: (with J. Oro') Prebiotic and Biochemical Evolution, 1972. Contbr. articles to sci. jours. Home: 1501 Bonnie Brae Houston TX 77006

KIMBALL, VERA F., editor, writer; b. Seward, Alaska, Feb. 8, 1903; d. Irving L. and Della (Carpenter) Kimball; A.B., Columbia, 1929; m. William T. Castles, Jr., Dec. 2, 1942. On clerical staff Legis. of Ter. of Alaska, 1923; with Alaska R.R., Anchorage, 1923-24, N.A.

Newspaper Alliance, Met. Mus. Art, Gen. Foods Corp., Todd-Robertson & Todd (all N.Y.C.), part time 1924-29; asst. to sec. Am. Inst. Chemists, 1929-35; editor The Chemist, N.Y.C., 1935-68, asso. editor, 1968-70. Mem. N.Y. Acad. Scis., Am. Inst. Chemists (hon. life, sec. S.C. chpt.), AAAS, Cook Inlet Hist. Soc., Alaska (charter mem.), Chester County (S.C.) hist. socs. Club: Barnard College (N.Y. City). Author: (with W.T. Castles) Firearms and Their Use, 1942; (with M.R. Bhagwat) Your Future in Chemistry, 1943; contbg. author The Ives Papers, 1979. Contbr. to World Scope Ency., The Ency. of Chemistry, Am. Chemists and Chem. Engrs., year books, profl. and popular mags. Home: Magnolia Apts B-4 Chester SC 29706 Office: Route 2 Box 491 Chester SC 29706

KIMBALL, WILLARD CHILD, III, petroleum landman; b. Washington, Feb. 21, 1916; s. Harry Cady and Maude Elizabeth (Irey) K.; student Tex. Coll. Mines and Metallurgy, 1935-37; m. Nell Beal, Apr. 23, 1938; children—Patricia (Mrs. Bobby Elliott), Karen (Mrs. Jeffrey Edwards), Robert Cady. Oil scout, prodn. clk. El Paso Natural Gas Co., Jal, N.Mex., 1937-43; scout, landman Phillips Petroleum Co., Midland, Tex., 1943-50; owner, operator Midland Directory Service, 1951—, Midland Enterprises, 1955—; land mgr. Husky Oil Co., Denver, 1956-63; ind. landman Midland, 1950-56, 63—; lectr. Permian Basin Grad. Sch., Midland. Democratic del. Midland County conv., 1950. Charter mem. Midland Meml. Hosp. Trust; chmn. landmen and scouts com., charter mem. Permian Basin Mus. Library and Hall of Fame; troop com. chmn. Boy Scouts Am. Mem. Permian Basin Landmen's Assn. (charter, dir. 1964-65), Permian Basin Pioneer Oil Scouts (pres.), N.Mex. (pres. 1942) oil scouts assns., Am. Assn. Petroleum Landmen (charter, Distinguished Service award 1956), Alpha Phi Omega. Mem. Christian Ch. (deacon, ch. bd. sec.). Elk (past exalted ruler), Lion. Clubs: Midland Country; Rolling Hills Country (Golden, Colo.); Ponderosa Country; Cloudcroft (N.Mex.). Pub. Midland Landmen, 1951—. Home: 2513 Neely Ave Midland TX 79701 Office: PO Box 1424 219 West Bldg 401 N Colorado St Midland TX 79701

KIMBELL, ANNIE MAE, ret. educator; b. Lyerly, Ga., Nov. 3, 1911; d. Edward L. and Lena (Grogan) Bishop; B.A. in Elementary Edn., shorter Coll., Rome, Ga., 1957; M. in Elementary Edn., U. Chattanooga, 1966; postgrad. in Learning Disabilities, W. Ga. Coll., Carrolton, 1975; m. Robert F. Kimbell; 1 son, Joe Frank. Tchr. Chattooga County (Ga.) Bd. Edn., Summerville, 1957-71, tchr. reading, 1971-74, resource tchr. learning disabilities, 1975-78. Mem. NEA, Chattooga Edn. Assn., Ga. Assn. Educators, Council Exceptional Children, Kappa Kappa Iota (state nominating com., past local pres.). Certified in specific learning disabilities, Ga. Home: PO Box 206 Alpine St Lyerly GA 30730

KIMBERLY, MARION JOSEPHINE, mgmt. and career cons.; b. N.Y.C., Jan. 20, 1938; d. Jonathan Hutcheson and Anna Livingston (Hanan) Conrow; B.A., Mt. Holyoke Coll., 1959; M.A., U. Tex., Perian, 1975; m. June 13, 1959; children—Karen, John, David. Regional dir. Perian Basin Sr. Citizens Project, Midland, Tex., 1970-72; exec. dir. Midland Community Action Agy., 1972-75; mgmt. and career cons., Midland, 1975—. Bd. dirs. Laos House Ednl. Center, Austin, Tex. Named Woman of Yr., Dist. 8, Tex. Fedn. Bus. and Profl. Women, 1978. Mem. Am. Personnel and Guidance Assn., Tex. Personnel and Guidance Assn., Am. Soc. for Tng. and Devel., LWV. Home: 3101 Shell St Midland TX 79701 Office: PO Box 7921 Midland TX 79703

KIMBLE, GLADYS AUGUSTA LEE, nurse, civic worker; b. Niagara Falls, Can., June 28, 1906; d. William and Florence Augusta Baker (Buckton) Lee; R.N., Christ Hosp., Jersey City, 1929; B.S., Columbia U. Tchrs. Coll., 1938, M.A., 1948; m. George Edmond Kimble, Jan. 5, 1952. Nurse, Willard Parker Hosp., N.Y.C., 1931; asst. and supervisory relief nurse Margaret Hague Maternity Hosp., Jersey City, 1931-37; staff nurse, relief supr. Manhattan Eye, Ear and Throat Hosp., 1937-38; sr. staff, asst. nurse supr. Vis. Nurse Service, N.Y.C., 1938-41; sr. public health nurse USPHS, Little Rock, 1941-43; public health supr. Providence Dist. Nursing Assn., 1943-46; edn. dir. Jersey City Public Health Nursing Service, 1946-49, also instr. Seton Hall U., 1947-48; public health nurse cons. U.S. Inst. Inter-Am. Affairs, Brazil, 1949-51; dir. public health dept. Englewood (N.J.) Hosp., 1951-53; nurse coordinator exchange visitor nurse program Overlook Hosp., Summit, N.J., 1964-71; mem. Ladies Oriental Shrine of N.Am., 1978—. Recipient woman of year award Essex County Bus. and Profl. Women, 1968. Fellow Am. Public Health Assn.; mem. Sarasota Geneal. Soc. (charter mem.), AAUW. Episcopalian. Home: 1111 N Gulf Stream Ave Apt 13D Sarasota FL 33577

KIMBREL, MONROE, banker; b. Miller County, Ga., Aug. 4, 1916; s. Charlie C. and Effie (Folds) K.; B.S., U. Ga., 1936; grad. Stonier Grad. Sch. Banking, Rutgers U., 1949; m. Nita Matlock, Apr. 17, 1941; children—Jenny Wood (Mrs. James Bunn III), Charles Daniel. With Farm Credit Adminstrn., Columbia, S.C., 1936-46; with First Nat. Bank. Thomson, Ga., 1946-65, chmn. bd., 1961-65; chmn. Bank Ft. Valley, Ga., 1963-65; dir. Fed. Res. Bank Atlanta, 1960-65, sr. v.p., 1965, 1st v.p., 1965-68, pres., 1968-80. Mem. Am. (pres. 1962-63), Ga. (pres. 1956-57) bankers assns., U. Ga. Alumni Assn. (pres. 1970-71, 72-73). Rotarian (past dist. gov.). Home: 620 Peachtree St Atlanta GA 30308 Office: Fed Res Bank of Atlanta 104 Marietta St NW Atlanta GA 30303

KIMBREL, WALTER REID, JR., plastics distbg. co. exec.; b. Dallas, Dec. 6, 1930; s. Walter Reid and Mabel C. (Knight) K.; student public schs., El Paso, Tex.; m. Lydia M. Wichterich, Apr. 16, 1966; children—Joel, Alvin, Toni. Converting mgr. Container Service, Arlington, Tex., 1959-64; asst. plant mgr. Donald Palmer, Inc., New Orleans, 1964-66; v.p., converting mgr. Poly Converters, Inc., New Orleans, 1966-67; area supr. converting Paramont Packaging Corp., Murfreesboro, Tenn., 1967-68; plant mgr. Poly Flex-M Co., Summit, Miss., 1968-72; plant mgr. So. Packaging Materials, New Orleans, 1972-75; converting mgr. Jackson Plastic Films, Clinton, Miss., 1975-76; gen. mgr. Plastics Distbrs. Co., Metairie, La.. 1976—. Served with U.S. Army, 1951-53. Mem. Modern Plastics Mgmt. Adv. Panel. Office: 1251 S Front St New Orleans LA 70130

KIMBRELL, ODELL CULP, JR., physician; b. Spartanburg, S.C., May 2, 1927; s. Odell Culp and Leona (Nicholas) K.; A.B., Duke U., 1947; M.D., U. Pa., 1951; m. Annabel Hickey, Aug. 19, 1952; children—Odell Culp III, Cynthia Anne. Intern, Med. Coll. Va., Richmond, 1951-52, resident in internal medicine, 1954-56; resident in internal medicine VA Hosp., Phila., 1956-57; practice medicine specializing in internal medicine and endocrinology, Gallipolis, Ohio, 1957-60, Raleigh, N.C., 1960—; med. dir. Occidental Life Ins. Co. N.C., Raleigh, 1967—; clin. prof. medicine U. N.C. Med. Sch., 1970—. Trustee Wake County Hosp. System, Inc., Raleigh, 1971—, sec., 1973-74, pres., 1974-76; bd. dirs. Wake Health Facilities and Services, Inc., 1975—, pres., 1975-76; deacon Hudson Meml. Presbyn. Ch., Raleigh, 1971-73. Served with USAF, 1952-54. Diplomate Am. Bd. Internal Medicine, Bd. Life Ins. Medicine. Fellow ACP; mem. AMA, N.C., Wake County med. socs., Am., N.C. socs. internal medicine, Raleigh Acad. Medicine, Assn. Life Ins. Med. Dirs. Am., Mid-Atlantic Med. Dirs. Club (pres. 1979-80). Democrat. Club: Lions. Contbr. articles to med. jours. Home: 4917 Hermitage Dr Raleigh NC 27612 Office: 232 Bryan Bldg Raleigh NC 27605

KIMBRO, GEORGE THOMAS, ins. agt.; b. Burleson, Tex., Dec. 11, 1930; s. Welborn Jordan and Mary (Sharp) K.; B.S., N. Tex. State U., 1952; M.B.A., Tex. Tech U., 1974; m. Manon Muncy, Sept. 15, 1962; children—Camille, Paul Michael, Suzanne. Tchr., Ft. Worth Public Schs., 1955-58; commd. 2d. lt., U.S. Army, 1952, ret., 1955, rejoined service, 1958, advanced through grades to full col., 1977 comdr. COA 326 Engr. Bn., 101st Airborne, 1965-66; exec. officer 307th Engr. Bn., 82d Airborne Div., 1970-72; full prof. mil. sci. Tex. Tech U., Lubbock, 1974-78, ret., 1978; agt. Mass. Mut. Life Ins. Co., San Antonio, 1979—. Treas., St. Paul's Ch., Lubbock, 1976-77. Decorated Legion of Merit, Bronze Star with cluster, Army Commendation Medal with 2 clusters, Combat Infantryman's Badge; Gallantry Cross with palm (Vietnam) Mem. Lubbock C. of C., San Antonio C. of C., Nat. Assn. Life Underwriters, Soc. Am. Mil. Engrs. (Itschner award 1965). Republican. Episcopalian. Clubs: Am. Legion, Kiwanis (dir. Lubbock 1976-77). Contbr. article to Military Engr. Mag. Home: 15619 Trail Bluff San Antonio TX 78247 Office: Mass Mut Life Ins Co Suite 600 GPM S Tower 800 LP 410 San Antonio TX 78216

KIMBROUGH, EDWARD ERNEST, III, orthopedic surgeon; b. Gainesville, Ga., Sept. 29, 1929; s. Edward Ernest and Theodora Alberta (Ham) K.; B.A., Vanderbilt U., 1950, M.D., 1953; m. Jeanette O. Ludgate, Nov. 20, 1954; children—Catherine, Nancy, Carolyn, Edward Ernest. Intern, U. Minn., 1953-54, resident in surgery, 1953-55; practice medicine, specializing in orthopedic surgery, Moore Clinic, Columbia, S.C., 1963—, pres., 1974-76; asst. clin. prof. orthopedic surgery Med. U. S.C., 1974—; asso. clin. prof. U. S.C., Charleston, 1978—; chief of surgery Richland Meml. Hosp., 1977-78. Mem. Bd. Sch. Commrs. Richland County (S.C.), 1972-76, chmn. bd., 1972-73; head profl. div. United Way of Midlands, 1979. Served with U.S. Army, 1955-63. Diplomate Am. Bd. Orthopedic Surgery; recipient Certificate of Appreciation, Republic of S. Vietnam, 1967. Mem. Columbia Med. Soc. (pres. 1977-78), Royal Soc. Health (Eng.), S.C. Med. Assn., AMA, S.C. Orthopedic Assn. (sec.-treas. 1979), Am. Acad. Orthopedic Surgeons. Republican. Presbyterian. Club: Kiwanis. Editor Jour. S.C. Med. Assn., 1973—; contbr. articles in field to med. jours. Home: 1470 Greenhill Rd Columbia SC 29206 Office: 3321 Medical Park Rd Columbia SC 29203

KIMBROUGH, JAMES MILTON, real estate mktg. cons.; b. Lufkin, Tex., Mar. 11, 1948; s. John Milton and Beatrice K.; student Murray State Coll., 1966-68; A.Paralegal, Oscar Rose Jr. Coll., 1976. Asst. food mgr. Holiday Inn, 1967-68; prodn. control civilian Tinker AFB, Oklahoma City, 1970-76; state mktg. cons. Century 21 Real Estate of N. Tex., Okla. & Ark., Inc., Oklahoma City, 1976—; pres. J.M. Kimbrough Enterprises, Inc.; v.p. Wilshire Investment Co., Student Tours, Inc. Served with USMC, 1968-70. Recipient Mktg. Cons. Spl. Achievement award Century 21, 1978, 79. Baptist. Inventor emergency early warning system for emergency vehicles, 1978. Office: 4334 NW Expressway Suite 263 Oklahoma City OK 73116

KIME, CHARLES EDWIN, surgeon; b. Jackson, Mich., Feb. 5, 1919; s. Erwin N. and Lelah (Burns) K.; B.S., Ind. U., 1940, M.D., 1942; m. Rosemary Canary, July 24, 1943; children—Robert, Kathleen, Mary, Paul, William. Intern, Ind. U. Med. Center, 1943 and after, resident in otolaryngology and bronchoesophagology, to 1947; practice medicine specializing in surgery, Richmond, Ind., 1947-67, Houston, 1967—; mem. staff Baylor U. Hosp., Westbury Hosp., Twelve Oaks Hosp., Rosewood Hosp.; asst. clin. prof. otolaryngology Baylor Sch. Medicine. Served in M.C., U.S. Army, 1953-55. Fellow Am. Acad. Ophthalmology and Otolaryngology (sr.), A.C.S., Am. Acad. Facial Plastic and Reconstructive Surgery. Roman Catholic. Clubs: K.C., Rotary. Contbr. articles to profl. jours. Home: 12819 Memorial Dr Houston TX 77024 Office: 9100 Westheimer St Suite 23 Houston TX 77063

KIME, JOHN CHARLES, civil engr.; b. Huntington, W.Va., Apr. 30, 1940; s. Edward Blaine and Dorothy Flo (Smith) K.; student Marshall U., 1958-60, Davis and Elkins Coll., 1960-61; m. Patricia Ann Mann, Feb. 1, 1964; children—Karen Flo, John Charles. Designer, U.S. Army Corp Engrs., Huntington, W.Va., 1960-70; asst. supr. airports Connell Assos. Inc., Miami, 1970-73; project engr. airport and hwy. design Brevard Engring. Co., Miami, 1973-77; dir. dept. transp. Connell, Metcalf & Eddy, Miami, 1978-79; asst. chief civil div. H. J. Ross Assos., Miami, 1979—. Chmn. bd. deacons Presbyterian Ch., 1978-79. Served with U.S. Army, 1962-68. Recipient Sustained Superior Performance award U.S. Army, 1969. Mem. Am. Soc. Certified Engring. Technicians, Soc. Am. Mil. Engrs., Inst. Certification Engring. Technicians. Home: 3240 126th Ave SW Miami FL 33175 Office: 2660 Brickell Ave Miami FL 33129

KIMERER, NEIL BANARD, SR., psychiatrist, educator; b. Wauseon, Ohio, Jan. 13, 1918; s. William and Ruby (Upp) K.; B.S., U. Toledo, 1941; M.D., U. Chgo., 1944; postgrad. (fellow) Menninger Sch., 1947-50; m. Ellen Jane Scott, May 23, 1943; children—Susan Leigh, Neil Banard, Brian Scott, Sandra Lynn. Intern, Emanuel Hosp., Portland, Oreg., 1944; resident psychiatry Winter VA Hosp., Topeka, 1947-50; asst. physician Central State Hosp., Norman, Okla., 1950, cons., 1955—; chief out-patient psychiat. clinic U. Okla. Sch. Medicine, Oklahoma City, 1951-53, instr. dept. psychiatry, 1951-52, asso. prof., 1952-53, asst. prof. dept. psychiatry, neurology and behavioral scis., 1955-61, asso. prof., 1961-69, clin. prof., 1969—; practice medicine specializing in psychiatry, Oklahoma City, 1953—; med. dir. Oklahoma City Mental Health Clinic, 1953-68; cons., spl. lectr. dept. psychology U. Okla., Norman, 1951-58. Mem. Comprehensive Health Survey Com., Oklahoma City, 1961—; mem. exec. com. Okla. Family Life Assn., 1958-60; bd. dirs. Oklahoma City Jr. Symphony Soc., 1959. Served as pfc, ASTP, 1943-44; to capt. M.C., AUS, 1945-47, Diplomate Am. Bd. Psychiatry. Fellow Am. Psychiat. Assn.; mem. Am., Okla. State med. assns., Oklahoma County Med. Soc., Oklahoma City Clin. Soc., Mid-Continent Psychiat. Soc., AAAS, Alpha Kappa Kappa (pres. Nu chpt. 1943). Rotarian. Author: To Get and Beget, 1971. Contbr. article in field to profl. jour. Home: 2800 NW 25th St Oklahoma City OK 73107 Office: 2600 NW Hwy Oklahoma City OK 73112

KIMMEL, JERRY E., wholesale distbr.; b. Marshall, Mich., June 23, 1937; s. Gerald Enos and Edna M. (Whipple) K.; student Western Mich. U.; m. Carmen Jean Rendall, Mar. 29, 1957; children—Christine Sue, Amy L., Gregory Gerald. Office mgr. Pak-R-Board Corp., Marshall, 1957-63; sales mgr. S.H. Leggitt Co., Marshall, 1963-64; owner, partner, pres. Kevco, Inc., Ft. Worth, 1965—; pres. Aqua Technics Inc., Ft. Worth, 1976—; dir. Aero Flow Dynamics Co., N.Y.C., 1969-74; founder, dir. Nat. Bank Marshall, 1971-75. Sr. warden Trinity Episcopal Ch., Marshall, 1966; chmn. spl. gifts United Fund, 1969-72. Mem. Manufactured Housing Inst. (dir. 1977-78, bd. govs. suppliers div. 1976-78). Republican. Clubs: Ft. Worth Petroleum, Ft. Worth. Home: 8945 Random Rd Fort Worth TX 76179 Office: 301 Loop 820 NE Hurst TX 76053

KINARD, HARGETT YINGLING, fin. cons.; b. York, Pa., May 29, 1912; s. Henry and Edith (Yingling) K.; student Drexel Inst., Phila., 1928-29; grad. Rider Coll., 1933; m. Pearl E. Greenhill, Aug. 20, 1932; children—Joan S. (Mrs. Edward J. Mercado), Lois E. (Mrs. Jerry Branch), Gail E. (Mrs. Joseph R. Eastburn). With Lybrand, Ross Bros. & Montgomery, Phila., 1933-51; with Electric Storage Battery Co., Phila., 1951-55, comptroller, 1952-55; v.p., treas. Maule Industries, Inc., 1955-58, v.p. fin., 1958-59; financial cons. to various internat. firms, 1959-60; v.p., comptroller First Union Nat. Bank of N.C., 1960-71, exec. v.p., comptroller, until 1971; sr. v.p., treas. First Union Nat. Bancorp, Inc.; now financial cons.; asst. commr. motor vehicles State of N.C., 1974; asst. sec. N.C. Dept. Transp., 1974-77. Trustee N.C. State Tchrs. and Employees Retirement Fund, 1974-77. C.P.A., Pa. Mem. Am., Pa. insts. C.P.A.'s, N.C. Assn. C.P.A.'s, Fin. Execs. Inst. Greater Clearwater (Fla.) C. of C. Presbyn. Clubs: Kiwanis, Carmel Country, Charlotte Executives, Goodfellows. Home: 5825 Lansing Dr Lansdowne Charlotte NC 28211 also 2079 Broadway Clearwater FL 33515 Office: 5825 Lansing Dr Charlotte NC 28211

KINARD, IRENE HURLEY, hosp. central supply adminstr.; b. Saratoga Springs, N.Y., May 31, 1919; d. Fred William and Lena-Belle (Henry) Hurley; B.S. in Nursing, Med. Coll. Ga., 1979; m. Furman Devilus Kinard, Sept. 6, 1948; children—Joyce M., Furman Devilus, III (dec.), Gary Patrick, Linda Grace. Head nurse Underwood Typewriter Corp., Hartford, Conn., 1940-45; staff nurse Aetna Fire Ins. Co., Hartford, 1947-48; supr. emergency room Univ. Hosp., Augusta, Ga., 1948-50; supr. central supply Med. Coll. of Ga. Talmadge Hosp., 1955—; ann. lectr. on sterilizing Physician Asst. Jr. Class, Med. Coll. Ga., 1978; chmn. children's com. Cerebral Palsy Telethon, Augusta, 1959-60. Served to 1st lt. Nurse Corps, U.S. Army, 1945-47; PTO Mem. Am. Soc. Hosp. Central Supply Personnel, ARC, Sigma Theta Tau. Episcopalian. Club: Amvets Aux. Home: 2418 Forest Park Dr Augusta GA 30904 Office: 1120 15th St Augusta GA 30901

KINCAID, JOHN PETER, educator, psychologist; b. Pitts., Sept. 16, 1942; s. John Frank in and Nancy (Ange) K.; B.A., Oberlin Coll., 1964; M.A., Roosevelt U., 1966; Ph.D. in Exptl. Psychology, Ohio State U., 1970; m. Calliope Deliyanni, Jan. 29, 1966; 1 son, John Franklin II. Research psychologist USAF, Wright-Patterson AFB, Ohio, 1966-69; asso. prof. psychology Ga. So. Coll., Statesboro, 1970-77; human factors psychologist Martin-Marietta Corp., Orlando, Fla., 1977-78 psychologist, project mgr. U.S. Navy Tng. Analysis and Evaluation Group, Orlando, 1978—; adj. instr. U. Central Fla., 1977—; cons. McDonnell Douglas Corp., 1974-75; research contract with USN, 1974. HEW grantee, 1971. Mem. Human Factors Soc., Southeastern Psychol. Assn., Sigma Xi. Contbr. articles and tech. reports to profl. jours. Home: 1345 Sawgrass Ct Winter Park FL 32792 Office: US Naval Tng Center Orlando FL 32813

KINCHLOW, HARVEY BEN, broadcasting exec.; b. Uvalde, Tex., Dec. 27, 1936; s. Harvey and Jewel (Gafford) K.; grad. S.W. Tex. Jr. Coll., 1971; m. Vivian Carolyn Jordan, Jan. 16, 1959; children—Nigel, Levi, Sean. Mgr., His Place, Uvalde, 1968-70; dir. Christian Farms, Killeen, Tex., 1972-75, area dir. Christian Broadcasting Network, Inc., Dallas, 1974-75, co-host "700 Club", dir. corr. ministry, 1977—. Served with USAF, 1955-68. Office: Christian Broadcasting Network Virginia Beach VA 23463

KINDER, EUGENE HARRILL, counselor; b. Kincaid, W.Va., Apr. 5, 1943; s. William Harrill and Gustava Marjorie (Kincaid) K.; B.S., W.Va. U., Morgantown, 1967, M.A., 1971, postgrad., 1977-79; m. Patricia Ann Massullo, June 5, 1966; children—Eric Eugene, Raymond Harrill. Tchr. Mingo Junction High Sch., Indian Creek Sch. Dist., Wintersville, Ohio, 1967-69; tchr. Sabraton Jr. High Sch., Monongalia County Bd. Edn., Morgantown, W.Va., 1969-70; counselor Harper's Ferry, Charles Town and Jefferson high schs., Jefferson County Bd. Edn., Charles Town, W.Va., 1970-78; counselor youth employment and tng. Hedgesville High Sch., Berkeley County Bd. Edn., Martinsburg, W.Va., 1978—; summer counselor James Rumsey Vocat. Tech. Sch., Martinsburg, 1975-78; counselor life planning seminars Davis and Elkins Coll., Elkins, W.Va., 1976-77; state trainer for Basic Ednl. Opportunity Grant, 1976-77. Chmn. Eastern Panhandle chpt. Nat. Found. March of Dimes, 1975-77, treas., 1978—; active Town Meeting '76, Berkley County (W.Va.) community forum. Cert. tchr., W.Va. Mem. NEA, W.Va., Edn. Assn., Berkeley County Edn. Assn., Am. Personnel and Guidance Assn., W.Va. Personnel and Guidance Assn. (regional v.p. 1974-77), Am. Sch. Counselor Assn., W.Va. Sch. Counselor Assn. Club: Civitan (sec. chpt. 1973-74, chmn. youth activities 1977—, treas. 1979—). Contbg. author Career Education: A Structured Intervention Curriculum for Appalachian Youth, 1974. Home: 2002 York Rd Martinsburg WV 25401 Office: Hedgesville High Sch Route 1 Box 89 Hedgesville WV 25427

KINDER, JACK, JR., mgmt. cons.; b. Pekin, Ill., Mar. 5, 1928; s. Jack and Edythe (Lauterbach) K.; B.S., Ill. Wesleyan U., 1950; m. Mary Sue Weers, Oct. 5, 1955; 1 dau., Jayne. Athletic coach, Chgo., 1952-53; ins. salesman Equitable Life Ins. Co., Pekin, Ill., 1953-62, Louisville, 1962-67, mgr., Detroit, 1967-68, regional v.p., Chgo. office, 1968-69, v.p., chief staff Home office, N.Y.C., 1970-71; dir., chief mktg. Southland Life Ins. Co., Dallas, 1972-74; partner Kinder Bros. & Associates, Dallas, 1975—, sales and mgmt. cons., 1975—; instr. Mgmt. Sch., Purdue U., 1970-79. Bd. dirs. Goodwill Industries, 1978-79, Am. League Baseball Chapel, 1970-79. Named Young Mgr. of Yr., Equitable Life Ins. Co., 1965. Mem. Gen. Agts. and Mgrs. Assn. (nat. trustee 1961-68), C.L.U.'s Assn., Nat. Assn. Life Underwriters. Republican. Baptist. Clubs: Bent Tree Country, Masons. Author: Kinders on Agency Management, 1970; The Selling Heart, 1974; (With Bill Glass and William Arthur Ward) Positive Power for Successful Salesmen, 1972; (with Garry D. Kinder) Upward Bound, 1979. Home: 7232 Winterwood St Dallas TX 75243 Office: 10400 N Central Dallas TX 75231

KINDRED, ELIZABETH MATHENY, educator; b. Sarasota, Fla., Jan. 31, 1916; d. Charles Woodburn and Virginia (Yates) Matheny; A.B. in Edn., Fla. State U., 1937; postgrad. U. Fla., 1939; M.Ed. in Counseling, U. Va., 1967; postgrad. George Mason U., 1970, Gallaudet Coll., 1971-72; M.Ed. in Deaf Edn., Western Md. Coll., 1974; postgrad. Boston U., 1975, U. Wyo., 1978, Radford Coll., 1979; m. Worth L. Kindred, Mar. 5, 1949; children—Tari K., Julia E. Tchr. secondary sch. Sarasota, Fla., 1937-44, clk. book dept. U.S. Arty. Sch., 1944-48; English tchr. intermediate sch., Herndon, Va., 1967-68, counselor, 1967-69; substitute tchr. public schs., Fairfax County, Va., 1969-70; coordinator, tchr. hearing impaired secondary sch. program, Arlington, Va., 1971-79, tchr. learning disabilities program, 1979—; Va. Fed. and Local Action Group coordinator A.G. Bell Assn., 1977-78, mem., 1979—. Active PTA. Mem. NEA, Va. Edn. Assn., Arlington Edn. Assn., Council for Exceptional Children (pres. chpt. 174 1977-78, Jennie Brewer award 1978), Speech and Hearing Assn. Va., Internat. Reading Assn., Va. Reading Assn., Greater Washington Reading Council, A.G. Bell Assn., Conv. Am. Instrs. of the Deaf, Am. Deafness and Rehab. Assn., Assn. for Edn. of Hearing Impaired Children (v.p.), Nat. Assn. of Deaf, Internat. Assn. Parents of Deaf, Am. Orgn. for Edn. of Hearing Impaired (Tchr. of Yr. 1979), Va. Assn. for Children with Learning Disabilities, Arlington Assn. for Children with Learning Disabilities, Am. Personnel and Guidance Assn., Va. Personnel and Guidance Assn., No. Va. Personnel and Guidance Assn., DAR, Phi Delta Kappa, Phi Delta Gamma. Episcopalian. Clubs: Gen. Fedn. Women's Clubs. Contbr. articles to publs. Home: 6213 N 12th St Arlington VA 22205 Office: Yorktown High School 5201 N 28th St Arlington VA 22207

KING, BILLY JOE, govt. ofcl.; b. Canadian, Tex., Feb. 6, 1930; s. St. Elmo Murray and Callie Vandora (Hodges) K.; student Amarillo Coll., 1956-58; B.B.A., W. Tex. State U., 1965, M.B.A., 1970; m. Irene Kirschenamann, Feb. 25, 1951; children—Jonita Ione, Rockwell Lee, Monte Joe, Ron Allen, Brady James. With various local cos., Canadian, Tex., also Petty Geog. Co., San Antonio, 1949-51; farmer, Regent, N.D., 1953-54; with Borden Co., Amarillo, Tex., 1954-56; with Burlington Lines, Amarillo, 1955-56; with Bur. of Mines, 1956—, computer systems adminstr., 1968-76, chief br. adminstrn., Amarillo, 1976—; asso. prof. W. Tex. State U., 1966-71. Served with U.S. Army, 1951-53. Mem. Data Processing Mgmt. Assn. (exec. v.p. 1969). Home: 5019 John St Amarillo TX 79110 Office: 317 E 3d St Amarillo TX 79101

KING, CARLENE, hosp. adminstr.; b. Carnegie, Okla., Nov. 11, 1916; d. James Stvus and Lena (Selvey) Wheeler; student U. Tex., Austin, S. Plains Coll., N. Tex. State U.; m. Jack Warren King, Oct. 25, 1936; children—Kerry Wheeler, Keith Lynn, Jack Warren, Carol Anne. With Agrl. Conservation Service, 1934-37, W.S. Wagley Realty Co., 1942-43, French Tool Supply Co., 1944-46; with Med. Arts Hosp., Littlefield, Tex., 1954-56, 59—, hosp. adminstr., 1964—; sec. IT & L Corp., Littlefield, 1978—. Mem. adv. bd. S. Plains Coll.; chmn. Easter Seals, 1976—. Lic. nursing home adminstr. Mem. Tex. Hosp. Assn. Mem. Ch. of Christ. Home: 504 E 5th St Littlefield TX 79339 Office: 500 LFDDr Littlefield TX 79339

KING, CHARLES OSSIE, air conditioning contractor; b. nr. Franklin, Ind., Nov. 17, 1919; s. Ossie Lloyd and Lily Mae (Ervin) K.; grad. high sch.; m. Ruth Isabel LePage, July 12, 1944; children—Charles E., Carolyn R., Michael J. Mech. supt. Gen. Am. Transp. Corp., Orlando, Fla., 1946-51; salesman Boys Roofing & S/M Works, Inc., West Palm Beach, Fla., 1951-58; pres. Air Conditioning Designers, Inc., West Palm Beach, 1958—. Served with USN, 1937-45. Mem. Am. Soc. Heating, Refrigerating and Air Conditioning Engrs. (past pres. Gold Coast chpt.), Palm Beach County Roofing and Sheet Metal Contractors Assn. (past pres.), Palm Beach Country Air Conditioning Contractors Assn. (past pres.), Am. Subcontractors Assn. (past pres. Gold Coast chpt.), Sheet Metal and Air Conditioning Contractors Nat. Assn., Air Conditioning Contractors Am. (past pres.), Fla. Roofing, Sheet Metal and Air Conditioning Contractors Assn. (past pres.), Am. Mensa Ltd. Rotarian (past pres.). Contbr. articles to jours. Home: 17 Harbor Dr Lake Worth FL 33460 Office: 1601 N Military Trail West Palm Beach FL 33409

KING, CHARLES R., community coll. adminstr.; b. Fort Pierce, Fla., Mar. 22, 1934; s. Hiram C. and Ida Mae (Chandler) K.; B.S., U. Fla., 1957, M.S., 1963, Ed.S., 1964, Ed.D., 1964; m. Mary Louise Lloyd, Jan. 26, 1957; children—Charles, Cheryl, Chandler, Chadwick. Tchr., St. Lucie County Jr. High Sch., Fort Pierce, 1957-59, Dan McCarty High Sch., Fort Pierce, 1959-62; dean instruction Southeastern Community Coll., Whiteville, N.C., 1965-67; pres. SW Va. Community Coll., Richlands, Va., 1967—. Mem. Cumberland Plateau Planning Dist. adv. com. SW Va. Health Services Adv. Bd. Mem. Am. Assn. Higher Edn., Am. Assn. Sch. Adminstrs., Am. Assn. Community and Jr. Colls., Am. Mgmt. Assn., Assn. Supervision and Curriculum Devel., Am. Tech. Edn. Assn., Nat. Assn. Mgmt. Educators, Assn. Va. Colls., Tazewell County Sch. Div. Planning Council. Home: Route 4 Glory Rd Blountville TN 37617 Office: PO Box SVCC Richlands VA 24641

KING, CLYDE RICHARD, educator, writer; b. Gorman, Tex., Jan. 14, 1924; s. Clyde Stewart and Mary Alice (Neill) K.; A.S., John Tarleton State Coll., 1943; B.A., U. Okla., 1948, M.A., 1949; Ph.D., Baylor U., 1962. Dir. news service, instr. journalism Mary Hardin-Baylor Coll., Belton, Tex., 1950; asst. prof. English, Tarleton State Coll., Stephenville, Tex., 1951; dir. news service, instr. journalism East Tex. State Coll., Commerce, 1952-56; asst. prof., asso. prof. U. Tex., Austin, 1956-62, prof. journalism, 1965—, mem. faculty adv. com. U. Tex. Press, 1977-80; free-lance writer, 1948—. Mem. Winedale Adv. Com., 1969-71; pres. bd. Stephenville Hist. House Mus., 1976-79. Served with AUS, 1943-45; ETO. Research grantee U. Tex., 1960. Mem. Tex., West Tex. hist. assns., Sigma Delta Chi, Sigma Phi Epsilon. Methodist. Mason. Author: Ghost Towns of Texas, 1953; Wagons East, 1965; Mañana with Memories, 1964; Watchmen of the Walls, 1967; Susanna Dickinson: Messenger of the Alamo, 1976. Editor: Letters from Fort Sill, 1886-1887, 1971; Victorian Lady on the Texas Frontier, 1971, Brit. edit., 1972. Home: 830 Alexander Rd Stephenville TX 76401

KING, CURTIS L., accountant; b. Jefferson County, Tenn., Nov. 26, 1928; s. Charles and Alverta (Whaley) K.; B.S., U. Tenn., 1954; m. Barbara Anne Lee, July 1, 1955; children—Kathy Anne, Laura Lee. Sec.-treas. Hwy. Transport, Inc., Knoxville, Tenn., 1957-63; sec.-treas. E. Tenn. Machinery, Inc., Knoxville, 1963-68; sec.-treas. Princess Supply, Inc., Knoxville, 1968-74; office, credit, sales mgr. Westburne Supply, Inc. (formerly Crane Supply Co.), Knoxville, 1974—. Mem. Nat. Assn. Credit Mgmt., Full Gospel Bus. Men's Fellowship Internat. Home: 420 Abner Cruze Rd Knoxville TN 37920 Office: PO Box 18 1417 Branner Ave Knoxville TN 37901

KING, DELUTHA HAROLD, JR., urologist; b. Weir, Kans., Jan. 17, 1924; s. Delutha Harold and Julia (Banks) K.; B.S., Western Res. U., 1952; M.D., Howard U., 1956; m. Lois Weaver, Sept. 3, 1960; children—Michael, Ronald. Intern, Freedmen's Hosp., Washington, D.C., 1956-57, resident in urology, 1957-61; practice medicine specializing in urology, Atlanta, 1965—; mem. staff Hughes Spalding Pavilion, SW Community Hosp., Ga. Baptist Hosp., Crawford W. Long Meml. Hosp., Physician and Surgeons Hosp., St. Joseph's Infirmary, Atlanta W. Hosp. Pres. Atlanta Health Care Found., Inc., 1973—; chmn. bd. Metropolitan Atlanta Health Plan, Inc.; sec., co-founder, chmn. bd. Sickle Cell Found. Ga., Inc.; bd. dirs. Cancer Network for Ga. State Com., Met. Atlanta Counsel on Alcohol and Drug Abuse; chmn. physicians com. Ga. Partners, 1976; participant Gov. Task Force for Health Systems Agencies Devel., 1975; v.p. N. Central Ga. Health Systems Agency. Served to technician 4th grade U.S. Army, 1943-45; ETO. Diplomate Am. Bd. Urology. Fellow A.C.S.; mem. Am. Urol. Assn., Atlanta Urol. Soc., Nat. (rep., regional chmn. Region 3), Ga. State (1st v.p.), Am., Atlanta (pres. 1974-75) med. assns., Med. Assn. Ga., Nat. Assn. Sickle Cell Disease (2d v.p.), Am. Cancer Soc., Howard U. Alumni Assn. (S.E. regional chmn. 1977, nat. pres. 1978—), Atlanta Club of Howard U. Alumni Assn. (past pres.), Alpha Omega Alpha, Kappa Alpha Psi. Contbr. articles in field to Jour. Med. Assn. Ga., Jour. Nat. Med. Assn. Home: 1895 Loch Lomond Trail SW Atlanta GA 30331 Office: 2600 Martin Luther King Dr SW Atlanta GA 30311

KING, DENNIS GERARD, lawyer; b. Erie, Pa., Mar. 28, 1938; s. John McCarthy and Eleanor Ann (Niebauer) K.; A.B. with distinction, U. Mich., 1960; LL.B., Harvard U., 1966. Admitted to Fla. bar, 1966, U.S. Supreme Ct. bar, 1970, D.C. bar, 1975; practiced in Miami, 1966—; mem. firm Patton, Kanner, Segal, Zeller, LaPorte & King. Pres., Tigertail Assn., 1975, Elephant Forum, 1975. County exec. committeeman Republican Com., 1968—. Served with USMCR, 1960-63; capt. Res. Mem. Am., Dade County, Fed. bar assns., D.C. Bar, Fla. Bar (lectr. continuing legal edn. program). Roman Catholic. Clubs: Bankers, University. Home: 2915 Emathla St Coconut Grove Miami FL 33133 Office: 150 SE 2d Ave Miami FL 33131

KING, DENNIS RAY, psychologist; b. Cin., July 22, 1947; s. Granville P. and Loretta K.; B.A., U. Cin., 1969; M.S., Calif. State U., San Diego, 1973. Psychol. examiner Cleveland (Tenn.) Cleveland-Bradley Counties Regional Mental Health Center, 1973-75; psychol. examiner, coordinator adult, gen. services Hiwassee Mental Health Center, Cleveland, 1975-77, dir. program planning, resource devel. and evaluation, 1977—, acting exec. dir., 1978-79, exec. dir., 1979-80; bio-med. dir. Health Mgmt. Services, Cleveland, 1980—; pvt. practice psychol. examining, Cleveland, 1974—; instr. psychology Cleveland State Community Coll., 1975—; bd. dirs. Child Shelter Inc., Cleveland, 1974—, sec., 1974-75, pres., 1975-76, v.p., 1976-77; bd. dirs. Tenn. Assn. Mental Health Centers, 1978-80, Bradley-Cleveland Community Sers. Agy., 1979-80. Recipient 1st Pl. award Jaycee Week Project of Yr., 1975; named Project Chmn. of Yr., Cleveland Jaycees, 1975; lic. psychol. examiner, Tenn.; cert. community coll. instr. and counselor, Calif.; cert. sex therapist. Mem. Am. (asso.), Tenn., Chattanooga Area (charter) psychol. assns., biofeedback socs. Am., Tenn. Contbr. article to profl. jour. Home: 750 Beech Circle NW Cleveland TN 37311 Office: Cherokee Park Med Center Cleveland TN 37311

KING, DONALD ALTON, mfg. co. exec.; b. Quitman, Ga., June 10, 1943; s. Alton William and Lillian Evelyn (McKinnon) K.; B.S. in Civil Engring., U. Fla., 1966, M.Environ. Engring., 1967; m. Lillie Faye Fletcher, June 13, 1965; children—Bryant Alton, Julie Anne. Chief incineration research USPHS, Cin., 1968-70; research and devel. engr. Davco-Defiance Co., Thomasville, Ga., 1970-72, research and devel. supr., 1972-74, engring. mgr., 1974-76, 78-79, div. mgr. Indsl. Waste Systems, 1976-77. Registered profl. engr., Ga., Fla., N.C., S.C., Ala., Tenn., Miss. Mem. ASCE, Fla. Pollution Control Assn., Water Pollution Control Fedn. Baptist. Patentee large sewage treatment plant of circular design. Home: 1009 Joree St Thomasville GA 31792 Office: PO Box 1448 Thomasville GA 31792

KING, DWADE ROBERT, ednl. adminstr.; b. Anson, Tex., Oct. 8, 1931; s. James Robert and Clara Louise (McCaleb) K.; B.S., Abilene Christian Coll., 1952, M.Ed., 1959; Ed.D., Tex. Tech. U., 1975; m. Barbara Elston, Sept. 6, 1952; children—Dan, Don, Chris. Asst. prof. edn. Abilene Christian U., 1964-66; asst. dir. regional edn. service center Edinburg, Tex., 1966-67; ednl. media coordinator U. Tex., Austin, 1967-68; asst. supt. McAllen (Tex.) Ind. Sch. Dist., 1968—. Bd. dirs. McAllen Citizens League; mem. schs. and colls. com. Tex. div. Am. Cancer Soc.; mem. City Traffic Commn. Served to 1st lt. USAF, 1952-57, to lt. col. USAFR, 1979—. Mem. McAllen C. of C., Am. Assn. Sch. Adminstrs., Tex. Assn. Sch. Adminstrs., Phi Delta Kappa, Kappa Delta Pi, Phi Kappa Phi. Club: Kiwanis. Home: 1501 Redbud St McAllen TX 78501 Office: 2000 N 23d St McAllen TX 78501

KING, EUNICE M., health adminstr.; b. Venus, N.Mex., Mar. 15, 1921; d. William Oscar and Clara May (Martin) Bassett; R.N., N.W. Tex. Hosp. Sch. Nursing, 1942; B.S., W. Tex. State U., 1963, M.Ed., 1966; postgrad. U. Tex., 1976—; m. Turner King, Nov. 15, 1941; children—Janet Paterson, Kathy Farber. Charge nurse St. Mary's Hosp., Roswell, N.Mex., 1942-43; chief nurse Outpatient Clinic, U.S. Air Force, Roswell, 1944; supr. St. Joseph's Hosp., N. Hollywood, Calif., 1945; head nurse N.W. Tex. Hosp./Amarillo Hosp. Dist., 1944-46, supr., 1947-48, asst. dir., 1948-49, dir. nursing service, 1950-59, dir. Sch. Nursing, 1959-72, adminstr. patient services, 1972-74, adminstr. div. mental health services and edn., 1974—; developer various nursing programs local schs. U. Tex. System, 1967-76; pres. Tex. Bd. Nurse Examiners, 1970-72, 75-76, mem. 1965-77, chmn. Region V, 1956-64. Bd. dirs. Amarillo Multiservice for Aging, 1977—. Established Eunice King scholarship Fund of Susanna Wesley Class, Polk St. Meth. Ch., 1965; Eunice King Lyceum Trust Fund for Continuing Edn. in Nursing, 1974. Mem. Amarillo C. of C. (dir. women's div. 1978—), Tex. League for Nursing (pres. 1965-68), Nat. League for Nursing (bd. review dept. diploma programs 1967-71), Am. Nurses Assn., Am. Acad. Nursing, Tex. Nurses Assn. (dir. 1977—), Am. Hosp. Assn. Soc. Nursing Service Adminstrs., Nursing Project Council of Tex. Coll. and Univ. System Coordinating Bd., Alpha Chi, Kappa Delta Delta, Delta Kappa Gamma. Methodist. Author: (with others) Illustrated Manual of Nursing Techniques, 1977; author: 10 lessons Curriculum Development, Nebr. TV Council, 1967-70. Home: 6202 W 39 St Amarillo TX 79109 Office: PO Box 1110 Amarillo TX 79175

KING, GARY DON, trailer-truck equipment co. exec.; b. Amarillo, Tex., Mar. 20, 1948; s. R.B. and Virginia Ann (Petty) K.; student W. Tex. State U., 1967-68; m. Carolyn Jean Teague, Jan. 26, 1965; children—Lorri Kim, Jimmy Clay. Salesman, Levitz Furniture Co., Dallas, 1969; service mgr. King Trailer and Equipment Co., Amarillo, 1973-74, salesman, 1975, v.p., 1975-76, pres., 1977—, also dir.; mem. advisory bd. Truck Driving Sch. of Tex. State Tech. Inst. Bd. dirs., S.W. Amarillo Kiwanis, 1976-77, St. Paul United Meth. Ch., 1975-76. Named Dealer of the Yr., Timpte Inc., 1975. Mem. Tex. Motor Transp. Assn. (Pres. club 1976), Truck Body and Equipment Assn., Distributors Assn. Home: 6410 Oakhurst St Amarillo TX 79109 Office: 5823 Canyon Dr Amarillo TX 79110

KING, GERALD LAMAR, investment co. exec.; b. Anniston, Ala., Apr. 12, 1922; s. Thomas Cobb and Sadie (Cox) K.; B.A., U. Ala., 1943, postgrad. in law, 1941-43; m. Martha Morrow Patton, July 29, 1943; children—Gerald Lamar, Thomas Patton, Martha Cox. With T.C. King Pipe & Foundry Co., Anniston, 1946-61, v.p., 1946-61, sec., 1946-61; partner T.C. King Co., Anniston, 1945-61; plant mgr. Anniston Soil Pipe div. U.S. Pipe & Foundry Co., 1961-74; pres. King Factors, Inc., Anniston, 1961—; dir. Anniston Nat. Bank. Commr. Anniston Airport Bd., 1955—; chmn., trustee Stringfellow Meml. Hosp., Anniston. Served to capt. AUS, 1943-46; PTO. Mem. Nat. Planning Council, Alpha Tau Omega. Club: Anniston Country. Home: 8 Sunset Dr Anniston AL 36201 Office: Box 1148 Anniston AL 36201

KING, GILBERT LEONARD, JR., beer distbr.; b. N.Y.C., July 31, 1936; s. Gilbert Leonard and Agnes Eleanor K.; B.S., Salem Coll., 1962; m. Barbara Anderson, Sept. 9, 1964; children—Dawn, Scott, Lesley. Sales trainee Am. Can Co., N.Y.C., 1962-64, asst. commodity mgr., 1964-65, sales rep., Atlanta, 1965-67, account mgr., New Orleans, 1967-69; product mgr. Quickick Internat., Houston, 1969, nat. sales mgr., 1970; dist. sales mgr. Pearl Brewing Co., Houston, 1970-73; sales mgr. Houston Distbg. Co., 1973, v.p., 1974, exec. v.p., gen. mgr., 1975—. Pres., Gulf Coast chpt. Leukemia Soc. Am., 1979—, trustee, 1978-79; committeeman Houston Livestock Show and Rodeo, 1975-79; tournament chmn. Dan Pastorini Celebrity Golf Tournament. Recipient certs. Advt. Club N.Y., Am. Mgmt. Assn. Sales and Mktg., Wharton Sch. of U. Pa., Leukemia Soc. Mem. Wholesale Beer Distbrs. Tex., 100 Club of Houston, Allied Food Dealers of Houston, Retail Grocers Assn., Tex. Restaurant Assn. Republican. Roman Catholic. Home: 6515 Elmgrove Rd Spring TX 77379 Office: 2121 Edwards St Houston TX 77007

KING, HARRY ROBERTSON, savs. and loan exec.; b. Louisville, Apr. 13, 1922; s. Harry Robertson and Grace Elizabeth (Ruter) K.; student Hanover Coll., 1942; certificate in credit mgmt. U. Louisville, 1953; m. Frances Lawton, Feb. 12, 1947; children—Harry Robertson III, Joseph L. Sec., Colonial Fed. Savs. & Loan Assn., Louisville, 1948-55, exec. v.p., 1955-57, pres., 1957-68, pres., chmn. bd., 1968—; dir. Dean Tire & Rubber Co. Campaign treas. Louisville and Jefferson County Republican Party, 1964-66. Pres., Louisville Theatrical Assn., 1964-65; v.p. Better Bus. Bur., 1958-60; bd. dirs. Ky. chpt. Arthritis Found., 1963-68; mem. pres.'s civic council Bellarmine Coll., 1970—. Served with USAAF, 1942-45; ETO. Mem. Ky. Savs. and Loan League (pres. 1965), Louisville Urban League, English Speaking Union, Louisville Com. Fgn. Relations (chmn. 1978—). Episcopalian. Clubs: Louisville Boat, Pendennis. Home: 431 Country Ln Louisville KY 40207 Office: 3808 Lexington Rd Louisville KY 40207

KING, HERBERT I-TURN, hosp. exec.; b. Shanghai, China, May 27, 1936; s. Yu-I and Shee-Cheng (Chen) K.; B.A., Nat. Taiwan U., 1957; B.C.S., Seattle U., 1964; M.B.A., U. Wash., 1966; m. Peggy Young, July 4, 1964; children—Henry C., Patricia C. Came to U.S., 1959, naturalized, 1973. Accountant, Quinn & Calahan, Moses Lake, Wash., 1966-68; mgmt. systems programmer Lockheed Electronic Corp., Houston, 1968; mng. accountant Ernst & Ernst, Houston, 1968-69; asst. v.p., dir. budget and analysis Sch. Health Care Systems, 15 hosps., Houston, 1969—. Bd. dirs. Bay Area Hosp. Authority. C.P.A., Tex. Fellow Hosp. Fin. Mgmt. Assn. (dir. 1973-74); mem. Am. Inst. C.P.A.'s, Tex. Soc. C.P.A.'s, Am. Mgmt. Assn. Club: Newport Country. Home: 18646 Martinique St Houston TX 77058 Office: 6400 Lawndale St Houston TX 77023

KING, HUGH ALY, JR., psychiatrist; b. Lake Providence, La., June 18, 1936; s. Hugh Aly and Ercell (Weems) K.; B.S., La. Tech. U., 1958; M.D., La. State U., 1961; m. Dianne Cecilia Rance, May 8, 1965; children—Susan Elizabeth, Gail Lilian, Linda Dianne. Intern, Charity Hosp., New Orleans, 1961-62; resident in psychiatry La. State U. Med. Sch., New Orleans, 1965-68; staff psychiatrist Central La. State Hosp., Pineville, 1968-70, 74-76, clin. dir., 1976—; practice medicine specializing in psychiatry, New Orleans, 1970-74; cons. VA Hosp. and La. Tng. Inst. for Girls. Bd. dirs. People for People, 1979. Served as lt. M.C., USN, 1963-65. Diplomate Am. Bd. Psychiatry and Neurology. Mem. Am. Psychiat. Assn., La. Psychiat. Assn., Am. Med. Soc. on Alcoholism. Democrat. Roman Catholic. Home: PO Box 488 Pineville LA 71360 Office: PO Box 31 Pineville LA 71360

KING, JEAN DOSTER, public relations exec.; b. Monroe, Ga., Nov. 1, 1937; d. Jake Monroe and Flora Jean Doster; student U. Ala., Tuscaloosa, 1955-58; children—Jean Christiana King, Donna Carole King. Editor, writer Mobile Press Register, 1963-69; dir. public affairs Delchamps, Inc., Mobile, 1969-77; pres., owner Jean King & Assos. Public Relations/Advt., Mobile, 1977—; mem. consumers affairs com. Food Mktg. Inst., 1970-77; chmn. Mobile County Nutrition Council, 1974-76. Publicity dir. Mobile County chpt. Nat. Found.-March of Dimes, 1964-68, also sec. bd. dirs.; mem., chmn. com. Mobile Bicentennial Community Com., 1975-76; bd. dirs. Sr. Citizens Services Mobile County, 1976-79; sec. bd. dirs. Mobile Public Parks and Recreation Bd., 1977-79; mem. curriculum study com. Mobile County Public Sch. System, 1976; nat. civic chmn. U.S. Singletons, 1971-73, nat. mem.-at-large, 1971-73. Mem. Public Relations Soc. Am. (dir. Ala. chpt. 1979—), Am. Advt. Fedn., Public Relations Council Ala. (pres. 1973-74), So. Public Relations Fedn. (charter mem., dir. 1972-76), Better Bus. Bur. S. Ala./N.W. Fla. (dir. 1973-77). Baptist. Home: 2316 E High Point Dr N Mobile AL 36609 Office: One Office Park Suite 417 Mobile AL 36609

KING, JEROME STOVALL, neurosurgeon; b. Denver, Dec. 17, 1937; B.A., U. Va., 1959; M.D., George Washington U., 1963. Intern, U.S. Naval Hosp., Camp Pendleton, Calif., 1963-64; resident in surgery U. Ky., Lexington, 1967-68; resident in neurosurgery U. Calif., San Francisco, 1968-73; practice medicine specializing in neurosurgery, Florence, S.C., 1979—; mem. staffs McLeod Regional Med. Center, Bruce's Hosp.; asst. prof. neurosurgery U. Calif., San Francisco, 1973-74, U. N.C., Chapel Hill, 1976-79. Served to lt. M.C., USN, 1962-67. Diplomate Am. Bd. Neurol. Surgery. Mem. AMA, Am. Assn. Neurol. Surgeons, Florence County Med. Soc., Womack Surg. Soc., Congress of Neurol. Surgeons. Republican. Clubs: Chevy Chase; Met. (Washington). Contbr. articles in field to profl. jours. Office: 314 S McQueen St Florence SC 29501

KING, JOHN EUGENE, educator; b. Birmingham, Ala., Jan. 8, 1940; s. Richard Eugene and Mary Catherine (Enright) K.; B.A., St. Mary's Coll., 1961; M.S.W., Tulane U., 1971; m. Lynne C. George, June 13, 1970; children—Michael, David. Ordained priest Roman Cath. Ch., 1965; asst. pastor Diocese of Birmingham (Ala.), 1965-70; drug and alcohol counselor Ft. Rucker, Ala., 1972; asso. prof., chmn. Dept. Social Welfare, U. Ark., Fayetteville, 1972—. Chmn. bd. dirs. Youth Bridge, Inc., Fayetteville, 1977-80. Recipient Liberty Bell award, Washington County Bar Assn., 1976. Mem. Nat. Assn. Social Workers, Council on Social Work Edn., Acad. Certified Social Workers. Democrat. Club: Exchange (v.p. 1979—). Home: 423 Hawthorn Fayetteville AR 72701 Office: OH236 Univ of Ark Fayetteville AR 72701

KING, JON JOE, fossil fuel treatment mfg. co. exec., mech. engr.; b. Canton, N.C., May 15, 1938; s. John J. and May (Harbin) K.; B. Mech. Engring., Ga. Tech. U., 1962; postgrad. U. Fla., 1962-64; m. Donna Rae Hartman, Apr. 17, 1965; 1 dau., Amanda Elizabeth. Engr., Pratt & Whitney Aircraft Co., Fla. Research Center, West Palm Beach, 1962-67; staff engr. TRW Systems, Redondo Beach, Calif., 1967-73; Fla. tech. mgr. of KVB, Inc., Jacksonville, 1973-75; v.p. so. region The Rolfite Co., Jacksonville, Fla., 1975—. Mem. ASME. Address: 1239 Montevideo Rd Jacksonville FL 32216

KING, KEITH LYNN, historian; b. Graham, Tex., Feb. 22, 1944; s. Jack Warren and Carlene (Wheeler) K.; B.A., Abilene Christian Coll., 1965, M.A., 1970; postgrad. U. Ill., 1975-78, U. Tex., 1965-66. Internal auditor Tex. State Bd. Mental Health and Mental Retardation, Austin, 1966-67; tchr. Floydada (Tex.) High Sch., 1969-70; instr. history San Jacinto Coll., Pasadena, Tex., 1970-75, San Jacinto Coll.-North, Houston, 1978—. Del., Democratic State Conv., 1972, 74. Mem. Tex. Jr. Coll. Tchrs. Assn., Orgn. Am. Historians, So. Hist. Assn., Tex. State Hist. Assn., Walter P. Webb Hist. Soc. (mem. state adv. com. 1973-75), Alpha Psi Omega, Phi Alpha Theta. Mem. Ch. of Christ. Editor: S.E. Tex. Hist. Jour., 1978-79. Home: 12955 Woodforest Blvd #E-42 Houston TX 77015 Office: 5800 Uvalde Houston TX 77049

KING, KENNETH LEE, lawyer, photographer; b. Des Moines, Aug. 19, 1940; s. Oliver Kenneth and Sarah Aileen (Sandy) K.; B.S., Iowa State U., 1962; J.D., Georgetown U., 1967; m. Jean Adams Christie, Aug. 7, 1965 (dec. Sept. 1977); children—Kenneth Michael, Robert Shane. Admitted to D.C. bar, U.S. Supreme Ct. bar; partner, litigation counsel firm Pollock, Vande Sande & Priddy (formerly Moore & Hall), Washington, 1965-79; pres. Bauman Bible Telecasts, Arlington, Va., 1970-80, also trustee; freelance photographer, cinematographer, 1980—; past sec., dir. Electro Gen., Inc., Dallas; past chmn. bd. Crossfield Investment Corp.; sec., dir. Nikki Smith, Inc. Trustee Center for Support of Family; bd. dirs. Concern Group; past trustee, adminstrv. bd. Foundry United Methodist Ch., Washington. Recipient Bronze medal N.Y. Film Festival; Silver medallion Screen Producers Guild; Eastman Kodak awards; others. Mem. D.C. Bar

Assn., Am. Patent Law Assn., Am. Soc. Mag. Photographers, Delta Theta Phi. Contbr. photographers to mags. and books. Home: 3629 Vacation Ln Arlington VA 22207 Office: 3436 Lee Hwy Arlington VA 22207

KING, LEWIS TAYLOR, printing co. exec.; b. Henderson, Ky., Nov. 30, 1938; s. Arthur Paxson and Elizabeth Caroline (Taylor) K.; student Ill. Inst. Tech., 1956-58; B.S., U. Ky., 1961; m. Linda Marie Wieffenbach, Nov. 21, 1964; children—William Taylor, Caroline Nemoyer., Sales rep. R.R. Donnelley & Sons, Inc., Chgo., 1961-68; dist. mgr. Western Pub. Co., Racine, Wis., 1969-76, Ohio, 1970-72, regional mgr. S.E., 1972-76; nat. sales mgr. W.R. Bean & Son, Inc., Atlanta, 1972-76, v.p. sales, 1977-79; v.p. sales W.A. Krueger Co., Inc., 1979—. Precinct capt. Republican Party, Dayton, Ohio, 1972; pres. Woodsong Assn., 1976. Mem. Printing Assn. Ga. (dir.), Graphic Arts Computer Assn., Printing Industries Am., Delta Tau Delta. Mem. Disciples of Christ Ch. Clubs: Airplane (v.p.), Dunwoody Country. Home: 5523 Woodsong Trail Dunwoody GA 30338 Office: 1760 Century Circle Atlanta GA 30345

KING, MARCENE JARRETT, counselor; b. Davenport, Iowa, Oct. 8, 1925; d. Nathaniel Higgon and Gladys Inez (Sweeney) Jarrett; B.S., U. Tampa, 1961; M.A., Appalachian State U., 1969; Ed.S., Fla. State U., 1978; m. Russell Sage King, Feb. 2, 1958; children—Gladiene Bean Keaveny, Roy K., John William Pugh. Tchr. exceptional children LaVoy Sch., Tampa, 1961-65, Sligh Jr. High Sch., Tampa, 1965-67, English, Dowdell Jr. High, 1967-70, guidance counselor, dept. chmn., Dowdell Jr. High, 1970-79, Monroe Jr. High Sch., 1979—. Mem. N.Am. Soc. Adlerian Psychology, Internat. Transactional Analysis Assn., Am. Personnel and Guidance Assn., Fla. Personnel and Guidance Assn., Hillsborough County Personnel and Guidance Assn. (treas.), Jr. High Counselors Hillsborough County (chairperson adv. council), Phi Delta Kappa. Democrat. Methodist. Cons., author, lectr. in field. Home: 3820 Obispo St Tampa FL 33609 Office: 1208 Wishing Well Way Tampa FL 33619

KING, MARJORIE SOMMERLYN, med. photographer; b. Conway, S.C., June 22, 1925; s. Bernard St. Lawrence and Mary Essie (Lupo) Sommerlyn; student Coker Coll., 1943-45; m. John L. King, Jan. 11, 1945; children—John Bernard, William Lawrence, Mary Elizabeth. Photopprinter for editor bus. pages Miami Daily News, 1954; owner, operator King's Portrait Studio, Conway, S.C., 1956-58; clk. bacteriol. lab. Jackson Meml. Hosp., Miami, 1963-65; photo lab. technician biomed. communications dept. U. Miami Med. Sch., 1965-67, photo lab. technician II, 1967-70, photographer III trainee, 1970-72, photographer III, 1973-76, photographer III supr., 1977-80. Den mother Boy Scouts Am. Recipient Golden Key award Boy Scouts Am., 1957. Mem. Biol. Photog. Assn., D.A.R., United Daus. of Confederacy. Democrat. Episcopalian. Clubs: Miami Yacht, Coconut Grove Sailing (C gull pres.), West End Pool Aquatic (pres.). Home: 8035 SW 17th St Miami FL 33155 Office: PO Box 520875 Miami FL 33152

KING, MARY KATHERINE, mathematician; b. Miraj, India, Sept. 8, 1940; d. Richard Edgar and Anne Clyde (Price) Strain; came to U.S., 1942; B.A., Vanderbilt U., 1961; diploma edn. Inst. Edn., Makerere Coll., Kampala, Uganda, 1962; M.S., Tex. A. and M. U., 1969; m. Anthony Laurence King, Jan. 11, 1964; 1 dau., Anita Katherine. Math. mistress, Kenya, 1962-64, Western Australia, 1964-66; instr. math. Tex. A. and M. U., 1969-76; head dept. math. Allen Acad., 1976-77; instr. math. Auburn (Ala.) U., 1977—; founder Internat. Ednl. Cons., London, Perth, Western Australia, and Auburn, 1979—; lectr. tropical studies program Tex. A. and M. U., 1973-76. AID Overseas fellow, 1961-62; Tex. A. and M. Research grad. fellow, 1968-69. Mem. Tex. Assn. Coll. Tchrs. (past chpt. sec.), Math. Assn. Am., Am. Women in Math., Phi Kappa Phi, Pi Mu Epsilon, Phi Delta Gamma. Episcopalian. Contbr. to textbook. Home: 425 Kimberly Dr Auburn AL 36830

KING, MARY NINA, ch. adminstr.; b. Franklin, Pa., Feb. 1, 1921; d. Lucian and Florence (Keeley) Leta; student Franklin Bus. Coll., 1939-40, Tarrant Jr. Coll., 1940-43; m. Paul A. King, Oct. 31, 1941; children—John Michael, Timothy Mark. With Printz Co., Franklin, 1939-41; sec., St. Andrew's Cath. Ch., Ft. Worth, 1956-76, bus. mgr., 1976—; diocesan ins. agt. Cath. Diocese Ft. Worth, 1976—. Pres., Civic League Franklin, 1954-56. Named Woman of Yr., St. Andrews Parish, 1977. Mem. Nat. Secs. Assn. Clubs: St. Andrew's Garden, Edgecliff Garden, St. Andrews Circle 12, St. Bartholomew's Circle 10. Home: 51 Chelsea Dr Fort Worth TX 76134 Office: 3717 Stadium Dr Fort Worth TX 76109

KING, MILTON STANFORD, educator; b. Aransas Pass, Tex., Apr. 4, 1929; s. Lynn Durward and Marcheva (Amason) K.; B.B.A., Tex. A&I U., 1959, M.S. in Bus. and Econs., 1964; D.B.A., Miss. State U., 1973; m. Billie Jo Barrows, Dec. 22, 1961; children—Kelly Lynn, Kevin Wayne. Inventory clk. Harley Sales Co., Houston, 1946-48; personnel asst. Standard Oil of Tex., Houston, 1959-61; field mktg. rep. Continental Oil Co., Houston, 1961-63; cons., program leader Am. Inst. U. of Wholesale Distbn., Washington, 1965-74; dir. Mgmt. Devel. and Studies Inst., prof. mgmt. Eastern Ky. U., Richmond, 1975—; mgmt. cons., 1965—; dir. Lynn King and Assos., 1979—. Served with USMC, 1948-56; Korea. Mem. Acad. of Mgmt., Soc. for Advancement of Mgmt., Am. Soc. Tng. Dirs., Small Bus. Inst. Dirs. Assn., Delta Sigma Pi, Beta Gamma Sigma, Sigma Tau Alpha, Alpha Chi. Democrat. Methodist. Clubs: Order Eastern Star, Masons, Scottish Rite, Shriners. Office: Combs 215 Eastern Ky U Richmond KY 40475

KING, PHILLIP EDWARD, state legislator; b. Covington, Ky., Feb. 23, 1929; s. Mortimore Jack and Martha Edith (Richardson) K.; student Georgetown (Ky.) Coll., 1948-50, U. Ky., 1959; LL.B., U. Cin., 1959; m. Zelma Evelyn Roberts, May 12, 1951; children—Sandra King Hammons, Phillip Edward, James Christopher, Teresa Jean. Admitted to Ky. bar, 1960, Ohio bar, 1960; practice in Covington, 1959—; mem. Ky. Ho. of Reps. from 64th Dist., 1965—, vice chmn. judiciary com., 1968-76, vice chmn. banking and ins. com., 1968; mem. Gov. Ky. Com. Edn., 1966. Served with AUS, World War II. Mem. Ohio, Ky., Kenton County bar assns., Taylor Mill Boosters Baseball Assn. Democrat. Baptist. Home: Route 1 Box 212 Senour Rd Fort Mitchell KY 41017 Office: 15 W Southern Ave Covington KY 41015

KING, ROBERT AUGUSTIN, engring. co. exec.; b. Marion, Ind., Sept. 3, 1910; s. Roy Melvin and Estella Bernice (Sheron) K.; B.S. in Chem. Engring., U. Okla., 1935; m. Johanna A. Akkerman, July 19, 1975; children—Robert Alexander, Sharon Johanna; children by previous marriage—Hugh Melbourne, Mary Elizabeth. Chief chemist Phillips Petroleum Co., Borger, Tex., 1935-43; sr. process engr. E.B. Badger & Sons, N.Y.C., London, 1944-53; dist. mgr. Stone & Webster, N.Y.C., 1954-56; mng. dir. Badger Co., The Hague, Netherlands, 1957-64; pres. King-Wilkinson, Inc., Houston, 1965—, also dir. Mem. Am. Inst. Chem. Engrs., Am. Chem. Soc., Inst. of Petroleum (London). Democrat. Episcopalian. Clubs: Petroleum (Houston); Univ. (Wash.); Chemists (N.Y.C.). Home: 3259 Las Palmas Houston TX 77027 Office: 3000 Richmond Ave Houston TX 77098

KING, ROBERT DANIEL, microbiologist; b. Tulsa, Feb. 5, 1944; s. Hatler Borden and Katherine Belle (Hubbard) K.; B.S., Okla. State U., 1967, Ph.D., 1971; m. Mary Josephine Daniel, Aug. 18, 1967. Commd. lt. U.S. Army, 1967, advanced through grades to capt.; chief microbiology sect., pathology dept. Letterman Army Med. Center, San Francisco, 1971-73; research microbiologist dermatology div. Letterman Army Inst. Research, 1973-76; ret., 1976; cons. Dept. Army, Brooke Army Med. Center, San Antonio, 1976—; asst. prof. microbiology U. Tex. Health Sci. Center, San Antonio, 1976—; pres. Diversified Technology, Inc., San Antonio, 1978—, also dir. Recipient grants NIH, 1976—. Mem. Am. Soc. Microbiology, Am. Fedn. Clin. Research, AAAS, Sigma Xi. Club: Fair Oaks Ranch Golf and Country. Contbr. articles to profl. jours.; patentee in field. Home: 12710 Kings Forest San Antonio TX 78230

KING, ROLLIN WHITE, investment exec.; b. Cleve., Apr. 10, 1931; s. Warren Griffin and Elizabeth (White) K.; student Choate Sch., 1946-48; student Cornell U., Ithaca, N.Y., 1950-54; B.A., Western Res. U., 1955; M.B.A., Harvard, 1962; m. Mary Ella Ownby Dewar, July 5, 1976; children—Rollin White, Edward Prescott. Mem. mgmt. staff NSA, Washington, 1955-60; v.p. King, Pitman Co., investment counsel, San Antonio, 1962-63; pres. Southwest Airlines, Inc., San Antonio, 1963-68; founder, 1st pres., dir. Southwest Airlines Co., Dallas, 1967—; partner King Investments Co., Dallas, 1977—; chmn. bd., pres. Seafood Ser. Systems, Inc., Dallas, 1978—; cons. air transp. Dept. Communication Royal Thai Govt., Bangkok, 1969. Trustee S.W. Outward Bound Sch. Served with AUS, 1956-58. Clubs: Harvard Business Sch. (Dallas-Ft. Worth); Brook Hollow Golf; Dallas; Harvard (N.Y.C.). Address: Two Turtle Creek Village Dallas TX 75219

KING, SEMMES WALMSLEY, trade and devel. co. exec.; b. New Orleans, Nov. 6, 1943; s. Frederick Jenks and Augusta (Walmsley) K.; A.B., Francisco Coll., 1967, LL.B., 1971; m. Elizabeth Hanna Hood, Jan. 31, 1970. Pres., King Petroleum Co., Bains, La., 1971-79; pres. Semmes, Inc., Bains, 1979—. Home: Cedars Plantation Bains LA 70713 Office: PO Box 2 Bains LA 70713

KING, SPENCER BIDWELL, III, cardiologist; b. Charleston, S.C., May 12, 1937; s. Spencer Bidwell and Caroline Janet (Paul) K.; A.B., Mercer U., 1959; M.D., Med. Coll. Ga., 1963; m. Judith Gail Hayes, Aug. 17, 1963; children—Spencer Bidwell IV, Susan Gail. Intern, Walter Reed Hosp., Washington, 1963-64; resident in internal medicine Emory U., Atlanta, 1966-68, in cardiology, 1968-70, asst. prof. 1972-76, asso. prof. medicine and radiology, 1976—, dir. cardiovascular lab. univ. hosp., 1972—; co-dir. cardiovascular lab. St. Luke's Hosp., Denver, 1970-72; individual practice medicine specializing in cardiology Atlanta, 1972—; cons. in field. Trustee Mercer U., 1975—; bd. dirs. Ga. Heart Assn., 1976—; co-pres. Arts Council Druid Hills, 1977—. Served with M.C., U.S. Army, 1963-66. Decorated Bronze Star, Combat Med. Badge. Diplomate Am. Bd. Internal Medicine, Am. Bd. Cardiovascular Diseases. Fellow Council Clin. Cardiology of Am. Heart Assn., A.C.P., Am. Coll. Cardiology (gov. 1979-82); mem. AMA, Ga. Med. Assn., S. Atlantic Cardiovascular Soc. (treas. 1975—), Atlanta Clin. Soc., Med. Assn. Atlanta (trustee 1979-82). Democrat. Methodist. Club: Druid Hills Golf. Contbr. articles to profl. publs. co-developer single catheter percutaneous technique for coronary arterography. Office: 1365 Clifton Rd Atlanta GA 30322

KING, STEPHEN, pediatrician; b. N.Y.C.; s. Harry and Grace (Fruchter) K.; B.A., N.Y. U., 1965; M.D., State U. N.Y., Bklyn., 1969; m. Joan Eden, Sept. 3, 1966; children—Traci, Lisa. Intern. U. Hosps. Cleve., 1969-70, resident in pediatrics, 1970-71; resident in pediatrics Yale-New Haven Hosp., 1971-72; chief of pediatrics Dover AFB, Del., 1972-74; pvt. practice specializing in pediatrics, Atlanta, 1974—; instr. Emory U.; asso. prof. Ga. State U.; chmn. newborn nurseries and premature intensive care Northside Hosp.; asst. chmn. pediatrics Scottish Rite Hosp. for Children. Adv. bd. Cesarians Concerned; bd. dirs. Jewish Community Center, Jewish Family and Children's Services; pres. Congregation Etz Chaim, 1975-78. Served with USAF, 1972-74. Decorated D.S.M. Diplomate Am. Bd. Pediatrics. Mem. AMA, Atlanta, Ga. med. assns., Am. Acad. Pediatrics, Alpha Omega Alpha. Contbr. articles to med. jours. Home: 970 Riverside Trail Atlanta GA 30328 Office: 6667 Vernon Woods Dr Atlanta GA 30328

KING, TERRY DEBBS, mech. contractor; b. Goose Creek, Tex., Dec. 19, 1928; s. Jesse Lee and Virginia Agnes (Young) K.; B.B.A., U. Tex., 1952; m. Vera Louise Buck, Oct. 8, 1955; children—Kathleen Buck, Terry Debbs. Sales engr. to sales supr. Mpls.-Honeywell Co., 1955-64; mfr.'s rep., mech. equipment, Barber Colman Co., H.D. Grant Co., Houston, 1964-66; sales engr. Atlas Air Conditioning Co., 1966-71, sales mgr., 1971-76, gen. mgr., 1976-79; founder King Envirco, Inc., 1979—. Regent Autry House, Tex. Med. Center, 1971—; exec. bd. Episcopal Diocese Tex., 1970-73, chmn. planning and strategy, 1966-68, chmn. dept. stewardship, 1967-70. Served from ensign to lt., USNR, 1952-55. Mem. ASHRAE, Assn. Energy Engrs., Am. Subcontractors Assn., Constrn. Specifications Inst. Republican. Sigma Phi Epsilon, Alumni Assn. U. Tex. Researcher engring. design energy savs. air conditioning systems. Home: 10031 Valley Forge St Houston TX 77042 Office: PO Box 42999/177 Houston TX 77042

KING, VORIS, wholesale grocery co. exec.; b. Lake Charles, La., Jan. 20, 1917; s. Alvin Olin and Willie Lee (Voris) K.; student U. South, 1934-36; m. Frances Thompson, Dec. 19, 1935; children—Charles Stirling, Virginia Lee (Mrs. Sanford Ayres), William Voris, Alvin Bardine. Dir., King Corp., Lake Charles; v.p. Little Lake Misere Corp., Lake Charles, 1958—; pres., gen. mgr. Kelly, Weber & Co., Inc., Lake Charles, 1961—; pres. Lake Charles Grain & Grocer Co., Inc., 1961—; dir. Am. Bank Commerce. Chmn. 7th dist. La. USO, 1953—, nat. dir., 1969—; pres. Calcasieu-Cameron chpt. ARC, 1957, Calcasieu Area Safety Council, 1960; pres. Orange Grove-Graceland Cemetery Assn., 1968—; mem. adv. bd. Salvation Army, 1964-70; adv. council area 3 CD, 1953-74, Lake Charles Sr. Civilian Adv. Council, 1953-75; bd. dirs. S.W. dist. Fat Stock Show and Rodeo, Inc., Lake Charles Civic Symphony, Calcasieu Area council Boy Scouts Am., Lake Charles chpt. NCCJ, La. Heart Assn., Calcasieu Parish Heart Fund Assn., McNeese State U. Found.; trustee emeritus Centenary Coll. La. Served with USNR, 1943-45. Recipient Outstanding Citizen award Lake Charles Salvation Army, 1964, Brotherhood award NCCJ, 1972. Mem. U.S. (v.p. 1962), La. (pres. 1952) wholesale grocers assns., Lake Charles C. of C. (civic ser. award 1960, pres. 1964), Better Bus. Bur. (pres. 1958), La. Tourist Assn., Blue Key. Methodist (chmn. bd. trustees 1965—). Mason (33 deg., Shriner), Odd Fellow, Rotarian, Elk (past exalted ruler), Moose. Clubs: Lake Charles Golf and Country; Pioneer, Contraband Citizens' Band (pres. 1962), Coastal (dir.). Home: PO Box 28 Lake Charles LA 70602 Office: Box 1120 Lake Charles LA 70601

KING, WILLIAM C., acct.; b. Stockdale, Tex., Oct. 9, 1911; s. William H. and Neppie (Ware) K.; B.B.A., Baylor U., 1936; postgrad. St. Mary's Law Sch., 1938-39; m. Mayme Johnson, Sept. 15, 1945; children—Kathleen (Mrs. Ronald Koehler), William E. Office mgr. A.B. Frank Co., 1936-42; supr. Ernst & Ernst, San Antonio, 1945-51; pvt. practice pub. accounting, San Antonio, 1951—. Served with USNR, 1942-45; ETO. C.P.A., Tex. Mem. Am. Inst. C.P.A.'s, Tex. Soc. C.P.A.'s. Presbyterian (elder, trustee). Odd Fellow (noble grand 1954, trustee 1971). Home: 443 Oak Glen Dr San Antonio TX 78209 Office: 1802 NE Loop 410 San Antonio TX 78217

KING, WILLIAM HAMPTON, accountant, state ofcl.; b. Heidelberg, Miss., Oct. 1, 1909; s. William E. and Sarah E. (Covington) K.; student Hinds Jr. Coll., 1925-28; B.A., U. Miss., 1930; postgrad. YMCA Grad. Sch., Nashville, 1930-33; m. Eldridge Douglas Banks, July 6, 1934; children—Carolyn Douglas (Mrs. E.J. Andrew), Sarah Kathryn. Social worker Tenn. Transient Bur. and Resettlement Adminstrn., Nashville, Crossville, 1934-35; cannery mgr. Homesteads Co-op Assn., Crossville, 1935-39; instr. social studies Clarke Jr. Coll. Newton, Miss., 1940; transp. supr. U.S. War Dept., Flora, Miss., 1941-44; accountant Woods Bldg. Supply Co., Jackson, Miss., 1945-47, Scott Bldg. Supply & Allied Corps., Cleveland, Miss., 1947-53; staff auditor Miss. Dept. Audit, Jackson, 1953-55, asst. dir., 1956-61, dir., 1962-63; auditor pub. accounts State of Miss., Jackson, 1964—. C.P.A., Miss. Mem. Am. Inst. C.P.A.'s, Miss. Soc. C.P.A.'s (pres. Jackson chpt. 1959), Nat. Assn. State Auditors, Controllers and Treasurers (treas. 1969, pres. 1973), Municipal Finance Officers Assn., Southeastern Intergovtl. Audit Forum, Nat. Intergovtl. Audit Forum, New Stage, Jackson Music Assn., Jackson Symphony League. Democrat. Methodist. Mason. Clubs: University, Knife and Fork (dir. 1969-72), Optimist (pres. 1969-70, lt. gov. 1970-71) (Jackson, Miss.). Home: 404 Colonial Circle Jackson MS 39211 Office: PO Box 1060 Sillers State Office Bldg Jackson MS 39205

KINGDON, DOUGLAS ERNEST, educator; b. Toronto, Ont., Can.; s. Ivor Carson and Bertha Louise (Redman) K.; B.A., Houghton Coll., 1957; M.S., State Coll. Tchrs., Buffalo, 1959; Ed.D., SUNY, Buffalo, 1971; m. Mary Lee Nichols, Sept. 8, 1956; children—Dwight Douglas, Kim Allison. Tchr., Iroquois Central Sch., Elma, N.Y., 1957-60; dir., tchr. elem. edn. dept. Houghton (N.Y.) Coll., 1960-63; tchr. Amherst (N.Y.) Central Sch., 1963-68; co dir., supr. ghetto program elem. edn. SUNY, Buffalo, 1968-69; faculty East Aurora Middle Sch., 1969-7_; instr. U.S. Office Edn. Reading Insts., Savannah (Ga.) State Coll., 1971-72; prof., coordinator reading program U. Tenn., Chattanooga, 1972—. Mem. devel. staff Boys Clubs. Mem. Internat. Reading Assn., Nat. Reading Conf., Nat. Council Tchrs. English, Reading World, Reading Horizons, Reading Improvement, Phi Delta Kappa. Presbyterian. Contbr. articles to profl. jours. Home: 570 Leafwood Dr Chattanooga TN 37443

KINGSLAND, FRANK, mgmt. cons.; b. Passaic, N.J., June 25, 1943; s. Louis and Anna K.; B.S., Newark Coll. Engring., 1965; M.B.A., Ga. State U., 1973; m. Faye Doss, May 30, 1968; children—Drenda, Shelley, Kelly, Jason. Prodn. control analyst Lockheed Ga. Aircraft Co., Marietta, Ga., 1969-72; indsl. engring. supr. United Parcel Service, Atlanta, 1972-74; asst. prof. Ga. Inst. Tech., 1975-77; owner, mgr. 1-Stop Business Clinic, Ltd., Smyrna, Ga., 1976—. Mgr., Milford Community Little League, 1978-79; pres. Osborne High Sch. PTA, 1977-78. Served with USNR, 1965-67. Mem. S.E. Assn. Minority Mfrs. (dir.), Nat. Mgmt. Assn., Am. Inst. Indsl. Engrs. Baptist. Home: 429 White Oak Dr SW Marietta GA 30060 Office: 2945 Stone Hogan Connector Suite 160 Atlanta GA 30331

KINNA, MEREDITH LEE, assn. exec.; b. Middletown, Md., Apr. 5, 1938; s. Glenn William and Lola Grace (Gladhill) K.; student Frederick Community Coll., 1966-68; m. Peggy Irene Rhodes, July 11, 1957; children—Todd Meredith, Lori Ann. Br. dir. trainee Goodwill Industries Inc., Frederick, Md., 1966-69, exec. dir., Johnstown, Pa., 1969-72, Savannah, Ga., 1972-78, Greensboro, N.C., 1978—, sec.-treas. Northeastern Assn. Goodwill Industries, 1971-72, chmn. Southeastern Assn., 1973-75. Mem. Gen. Greene council Boy Scouts Am., 1977-79; trustee Ga. Infirmary Non-Profit Housing, Inc., 1977-79. Served with AUS, 1956-57, 61-62. Mem. Nat. Rehab. Assn., N.C. Rehab. Assn. (sec.-treas. 1977), Jaycees (v.p. 1966-69, outstanding jaycee award 1968), Assn. United Way Execs. Democrat. Clubs: Rotary, Lions (dir. Johnstown 1970-71). Home: 636 Parkview St Asheboro NC 27203 Office: 1235 S Eugene St Greensboro NC 27406

KINNAN, ROY FRANK, sales exec.; b. Tulsa, Nov. 9, 1915; s. Ralph P. and Dessie J. (Wilson) K.; student U. Tex., 1935-37; m. Mary Emma Paternostro, Mar. 8, 1938; children—Ann Carol (Mrs. John R. Helton), Pamela Kay. Engr., salesman Oil Well Supply Co., Dallas, 1938-41; sales engr. Gates Rubber Co., Tulsa, 1941-55, sales mgr., Okla. and Ark., 1956-61, southwest sales mgr., Dallas, 1962-75, field sales mgr., 1976-78; sales mgr. Indsl. Products div. Regal Internat. Inc., 1980—. Mem. Ark. Racing Commn., N.M. Racing Commn., Mich. Racing Commn. Named Outstanding Nat. Dist. Mgr., 1966. Mem. Dallas C. of C., Tex. Thoroughbred Breeders Assn., Am. Brahman Breeders Assn. Methodist. Mason (32 deg.), Toastmaster (award 1963), Royal Oaks Country. Home: 4718 Forest Bend Rd Dallas TX 75234 Office: PO Box 1237 Corsicana TX

KINNARD, ARTHUR HENRY, JR., educator; b. Franklin, Tenn., Apr. 15, 1933; s. Arthur Henry and Era Elizabeth (Smith) K.; B.A., Tenn. State U., 1955, M.S., 1965; Ph.D., Kans. State U., 1976; m. Ouida C. Clemons, May 17, 1959; children—Arthur Henry, Keven, Carl, Carla. Tchr. social studies Hinds County Agrl. High Sch., Utica, Miss., 1956-61; tchr. social sci. Utica Jr. Coll., 1961-62, dean instrn., supr. adult basic edn., 1962-71, acting pres., 1971-74; asst. prin. Manhattan (Kans.) High Sch., 1974-76; asso. prof. history Mississippi Valley State U., Itta Bena, 1974—. Mem. Miss. State Com. on Community Service and Continuing Edn.; bd. dirs. Opera South. Mem. Am. Hist. Assn., Assn. Study of Negro Life and History, NEA, Negro in Miss. Hist. Soc., Phi Delta Kappa, Gamma Theta Upsilon, Sigma Rho Sigma. Democrat. Baptist. Home: PO Box 141 MVSU Itta Bena MS 38941 Office: PO Box 123 MVSU Itta Bena MS 28941

KINNE, HAROLD CLARENCE, former army officer, data systems exec.; b. Providence, Dec. 28, 1924; s. Harold C. and Mildred Elaine (Cutler) K.; B.S. in Chemistry, Brown U., 1949; M.S. in Physics, U.S. Navy Postgrad. Sch., 1957; M.B.A., George Washington U., 1963; Ph.D. in Mgmt. Sci., U. Tex., Dallas, 1979; grad. with honors U.S. Air Force Command and Staff Coll., 1963; grad. U.S. Army War Coll., 1967; m. Sarah Ellen Gunby, Aug. 10, 1946; children—Anne, Thomas. Served with Chem. Corps, U.S. Army; advanced through grades to col., 1968; various assignments, Germany, 1945-62; instr. math. U. Md. in Germany, 1959-62; supr. research and devel. ops., Pentagon, Washington, 1964-66; staff adv. planning div. U.S. Army, Pacific, 1967-68; sr. chem. staff adv. to Chief of Mil. Assistance Command, Vietnam, 1968-69; chief sci. sec. Pacific staff, 1970; sr. adv. to Joint Chiefs of Staff, Pentagon, 1970-72, dir. Advanced Research Projects Agy. office, Middle East, 1972-75; ret., 1975; v.p. PRW & Assos., investment banking, Iran, 1975-76; mem. faculty bus. dept. U. Tex., Dallas, 1976-79; tech. dir. Electronic Data Systems Corp., Dallas, 1979—. Vol. instr. CPR, Am. Heart Assn., 1976-80. Decorated Bronze Star, Air medal (3), Legion of Merit (2), Meritorious Service medal, others. Mem. IEEE, Assn. Computing Machinery, Ret. Officers Assn., Assn. Army of U.S., Sigma Xi, Sigma Nu. Club: Masons. Home: 2514 Custer Pkwy Richardson TX 75080 Office: 14580 Midway Rd Dallas TX 75234

KINNEBREW, JACKSON ALLENDER, pub. acct.; b. Pauls Valley, Okla., Aug. 14, 1915; s. Jackson Alvin and Dorella (Allender) K.; A.B., U. Okla., 1935; m. Mary Lucille Metcalfe, Feb. 27, 1940; children—Jackson Metcalfe, James Alvin, Mary Louise. Vice pres. Kinnebrew Motor Co., Oklahoma City, 1935-41, Denison Motor Co., 1946-51; farmer, Pauls Valley, 1951-64; pub. acct. Jack Kinnebrew, 1961-72; partner Kinnebrew & Readnour, Pauls Valley, 1972-78, firm Kinnebrew, Readnour & Hunt, 1978—. Served with AUS, 1941-46. Mem. Am. Inst. C.P.A.'s, Okla. Soc. C.P.A.'s, C. of C. (dir., treas. 1963—), Phi Beta Kappa, Beta Theta Pi. Presbyterian. Mason (32 deg., Shriner), Elk. Home: 200 Rennie Rd PO Box 269 Pauls Valley OK 73075 Office: 110 W Paul St Pauls Valley OK 73075

KINNEY, ABBOTT FORD, radio broadcasting exec.; b. Los Angeles, Nov. 11, 1909; s. Gilbert Earl and Mabel (Ford) K.; student Ark. Coll., 1923, 26, 27; m. Dorothy Lucille Jeffers, Sept. 19, 1943; children—Colleen, Joyce, Rosemary. Editor Dermott News, 1934-39; partner Delta Drug Co., 1940-49; pres., gen. mgr. S.E. Ark. Broadcasters, Inc., Dermott and McGhee, 1951—; corr. Comml. Appeal, Memphis, Ark. Gazette, Little Rock, 1935-53; research early aeronautics Inst. Aero. Scis., 1941, castor bean prodn., 1941-42; mem. bd. McGhee-Dermott Indsl. Devel. Corp. Mem. Ark. Geol. and Conservation Commn., 1959-63, Ark. State Planning Commn. 1963—; mem. Miss. River Parkway Commn.; exec. bd. DeSoto Area Council Boy Scouts Am.; past pres. Hosp. Adv. Bd.; mem. Chicot Fair Assn. Bd., Park Commn.; chmn. Chicot County Library Bd. Recipient Silver Beaver award Boy Scouts Am.; State Community Leader Ark. C. of C., 1968, Man of Year, 1978. Mem. Nat. Assn. Radio and TV Broadcasters, Ark. Broadcasters Assn. Ark. (charter mem. Ark. Econ. Council), S.E. Ark. (charter) chambers commerce, Ark. Hist. Assn. (charter), Am. Numis. Assn., AIM, Chicot County Hist. Soc. (charter). Rotarian (past pres., sec.). Adv. editorial bd. Internat. Broadcasters Soc. Home: Dermott AR 71738 Office: Dermott AR 71738 also McGhee AR 71654

KINNEY, BURTON CHESTER, motor carrier exec.; b. Worcester, Mass., Sept. 15, 1917; s. Alfred R. and Edith (Creamer) K.; student Biltmore Jr. Coll., 1937; LaSalle Extension U., 1944; m. Mary Elizabeth Jennings, Sept. 3, 1948; children—Caroline (Mrs. William Michael McConochie), Betty (Mrs. Robert Dempsey), Anita Jeanne (Mrs. Dan Thornton). With Ga. Hwy. Express, Inc., Atlanta, 1943-58, successively rate clk., chief rate clk., overcharge claim agt., asst. traffic mgr., 1948-53, gen. traffic mgr., 1953-58; gen. traffic mgr. Terminal Transport Co., Inc., Atlanta, 1958, v.p. traffic, 1958-76; dir. research and devel. Am. Motor Carrier Directory, Atlanta, 1977-78, gen. mgr., 1978—. Mem. Central and So. Motor Freight Tariff Assn. (dir. 1965-76), Transp. Club Atlanta (pres. 1955), Nat. Classification Com., I.C.C. Practitioners Assn. (chpt. chmn. 1956), Traffic Clubs Internat. (dir. 1957-66, regional v.p. 1966-70), Am. Soc. Traffic and Transp. (pres. Atlanta chpt. 1973, certified), Fla. Trucking Assn., So. Shipper and Motor Carrier Council (pres. 1969-70), Nat. Assn. Shipper-Motor Carrier Confs. (pres. 1974-75), Delta Nu Alpha (chpt. pres. 1955, regional nat. v.p. 1957-61). Home: 406 Homestead Rd Rex GA 30273 Office: 6291 Barfield Rd NE Atlanta GA 30328

KINNEY, GORDON JAMES, musicologist, musician; b. Rochester, N.Y., Apr. 10, 1905; s. Clarence Edward and Hettie Linsey K.; B.M., Eastman Sch., 1930; M.M., U. S.D., 1941; Ph.D., Fla. State U., 1962; m. Katherine Mary Kaull, Aug. 8, 1932; 1 dau., Morvyth. Instr. music Morningside Coll., 1937-41, Ohio U., 1941-45, U. Colo., 1945-48; mem. faculty dept. music U. Ky., Lexington, 1948—, prof., to 1974, prof. emeritus, 1974—; cellist Lexington Philharmonic Orch., 1965—; performed numerous cello recitals, 1930-66. Mem. Am. Musicol. Soc., Viola da Gamba Soc., Dolmetsch Found., Am. String Tchrs. Assn., Am. Recorder Soc. Democrat. Pub. edits. old music. Home: 149 Rosemont Garden Lexington KY 40503

KINNEY, PATRICK EDMUND, acct.; b. Trenton, Mich., June 12, 1949; s. Leo Michael and June (Packard) K.; student Ind. State U., 1967-70; B.B.A., U. Houston, 1975; m. Patricia Catherine Dimond, Aug. 11, 1972. Technician air pollution control City of Houston, 1971-76; acct. Hudson Engring., Houston, 1976-77; internal auditor, corporate acct. Bawden Drilling, Houston, 1977—. Mem. Delta Sigma Pi. Roman Catholic. Clubs: Ducks Unlimited, Bayou Rifle. Home: 10722 Archmont St Houston TX 77070 Office: 4544 Post Oak Pl Dr Houston TX 77027

KINNEY, THOMAS EDWARD, JR., human factor specialist; b. Jersey City, June 19, 1936; s. Thomas Edward and Lucille (Mitchell) K.; student U. Rochester, 1954-56, U. Okla., 1967, U. Del., 1974; m. Donna Anne Dromerick, July 26, 1975; 1 son, Dirk Edward. Commd. 2d lt. U.S. Army, 1957, advanced through grades to maj., 1967; instr., adviser, gen. staff officer, and battery, battalion and group comdr. in field arty., Europe, S.E. Asia, U.S., 1956-76; ret., 1976; human factor specialist U.S. Army Human Engring. Lab., Aberdeen Proving Ground, Md., 1976—. Decorated Bronze Star, Meritorious Service medal, Army Commendation medal. Mem. Am. Def. Preparedness Assn. Roman Catholic. Contbr. articles to profl. jours.; researcher in artillery.

KINNEY, WILLIAM LIGHT, JR., newspaper editor, publisher; b. Bennettsville, S.C., Oct. 26, 1933; s. William Light and Annie Laurie (Mayer) K.; B.S., Wofford Coll., 1954; B.A. in Journalism, U. S.C. Coll. Journalism, 1977; m. Margaret René Pegues, Mar. 21, 1964; children—Elisabeth Mayer, William Light III. Copy editor The State, newspaper, Columbia, S.C., 1955-58; reporter Marlboro Herald-Advocate, Bennettsville, 1958-59, advt. mgr., 1959-60, bus. mgr., 1960-65, mng. editor, 1965-70, editor, pub., 1970—; dir., sec. Marlboro Savs. & Loan Assn., Bennettsville, 1970—, First Nat. Bank of S.C., Bennettsville, 1973—; pres., dir. Greater Pee Dee Press, Inc., 1972—; v.p. Hamlet (N.C.) News, Inc., 1973—; pres. Bennettsville Parking and Devel. Co., 1964. Pres. United Fund, Bennettsville, 1963-64; chmn. Marlboro County Com. for S.C. Tricentennial, 1970, for U.S. Bicentennial, 1974—. Councilman, City of Bennettsville, 1967-69, mayor pro-tem, 1967-69. Bd. dirs. The Kinney Found., 1971—, chmn., 1975—; bd. dirs. Indian Mus. of Carolinas, 1972—; trustee Whipple Found., 1979—, S.C. Press Found., 1978—; trustee Neil Monroe Trust Fund, 1965—, chmn., 1977—; adv. bd. SBA, 1962-64. Served with AUS, 1956-58. Named Bennettsville and S.C. Young Man of the Year, 1961. Mem. S.C. Press Assn. (pres. 1972-73), Marlboro County (S.C.) Devel. Bd., Marlboro County Hist. Preservation Commn., S.C. State (dir. 1964-68, 75-78), Bennettsville (dir. 1964-67, 75-78) chambers commerce, Bennettsville Jaycees (pres. 1962), Marlborough Hist. Soc. (dir. 1967—, pres. 1975-79), U.S. Caroliniana Soc. (dir. 1972—, vice chmn. 1977—), Wofford Coll. Alumni Assn. (dir. 1968-72), S.C. Confedn. Hist. Socs. (dir., treas. 1975-78, v.p. 1978—), Phi Beta Kappa, Sigma Alpha Epsilon, Sigma Delta Chi. Methodist (lay leader 1971-73, trustee S.C. Methodist Advocate 1968-76). Club: Marlboro Country. Rotarian. Editor and pub. Sherman's March-A Review, 1961. Home: Magnolia 508 E Main St Bennettsville SC 29512 Office: 201 McColl St Bennettsville SC 29512

KINZBACH, ROBERT BENTON, mech. engring. cons.; b. Houston, Mar. 8, 1908; s. Frank and Anna (McGuire) K.; student U. Tex., 1926-31; m. Mary Chandler Lyman, Aug. 25, 1931; children—Mary Ellen (Mrs. Richard O. Wilson), Harriett Ann (Mrs. J. DeWitt Morrow, Jr.). Vice pres. Kinzbach Tool Co., Inc., 1931-60; pres. Kinzbach Engring. Co., Houston, 1961-69. gen. mgr., 1969-70; engring. cons., Houston, 1970-76; project engr. Weatherford/DMC, 1976-78, chief project engr., 1978—. Mem. ASME (sect. chmn.), Soc. Mfg. Engrs., Am. Soc. Metals, Am. Def. Preparedness Assn., Am, Petroleum Inst., Nomads, Houston Engring. and Sci. Soc. (past pres.), Sigma Phi Epsilon, Tau Beta Pi. Presbyterian (elder). Clubs: Houston, Masons, Kiwanis. Patentee in field. Home: 6203 Valley Forge Dr Houston TX 77057 Office: PO Box 19007 Houston TX 77024

KINZE, PAUL MARSHALL, fin. exec.; b. Seattle, May 22, 1931; s. Paul William and Ada Ethyl (Marshall) K.; B.B.A., U. Houston, 1966; m. Frances Margo Vines, Mar. 12, 1962; children—Conrad Nick, Joseph Dudley, Blanche Lynnette, Paul William. Acct., Am. Oil Co., Texas City, Tex., 1950-58; office mgr. Amoco Chem. Corp., Texas City, 1958-67; cost acctg. mgr. Chemplex Co., Rolling Meadows, Ill., 1967-70; treas., chief fin. officer Oxirane Corp., Houston, 1970—. First aid instr. ARC, 1956-59; dir. fire and rescue CD North Galveston County, 1958-59; treas. Boy Scouts Am., 1972-74. Mem. Nat. Assn. Accts. (past v.p. adminstrn., past v.p. membership), Risk and Ins. Mgmt. Soc., Houston Assn. Credit Mgmt., Houston Computer Users Group, Tax Research Assn. Republican. Episcopalian. Home: 426 Cedar Ln Seabrook TX 77586 Office: 4550 Post Oak Pl Dr Houston TX 77027

KIPE, AUDREY CLINE, hosp. ofcl.; b. Smithsburg, Md., Mar. 4, 1928; d. William Harry and Anna Beatrice Cline; Asso. Sci., Polk Community Coll., 1975; m. Samuel E. Kipe II, Jan. 15, 1949; children—Jeffery L., Samuel E. III, Yvonne M. Typist scheduling dept. Fairchild Aircraft Co., Hagerstown, Md., 1946-50; library aide Lake Wales (Fla.) High Sch., 1966-69; cataloger media dept. Polk Community Coll., Winter Haven, Fla., 1969-72, Webber Coll., Babson Park, Fla., 1972-74; dir. social services Lake Wales Hosp. Assn., Inc., 1975--. Adv. bd. Community Mental Health; mem. Lake Wales Community Nursing Council bd.; alt. bd. dirs. Vis. Nurse Assn. Polk County; 1st. v.p. Quota, 1978; Sunday Sch. tchr., sec. bd. edn. Burns Ave. Ch. of God, Lake Wales. Mem. Fla. chpt. Soc. Hosp. Social Work Dirs. of Am. Hosp. Assn., Women of Ch. of God (chmn. spiritual life Lake Wales 1977—), Phi Theta Kappa. Home: 2500 Martha Dr Lake Wales FL 33853 Office: Lake Wales Hosp Assn Inc 410 S 11th St Lake Wales FL 33853

KIPER, (RAN) RALPH ORIAN, II, architect; b. Shreveport, La., Sept. 17, 1947; s. Ralph O. and Kittye Leah (Buford) K.; B. Arch., La. State U., 1972; m. Patricia Ann Thatcher, Sept. 25, 1976. Supr. sch. and coll. plants La. Dept. Edn., Baton Rouge, 1972-73; asst. to dir. Facility Planning and Control Dept., Office of Gov., State of La., Baton Rouge, 1973-74; architect Cimini & Merk & Assos., New Orleans, 1975; dir. polit. campaign P.J. Mills for Sec. of State of La., 1975; partner Ralph Kiper Architect, Shreveport, 1976—; sec.-treas. Dee's Photo Supply Inc., Shreveport, 1978—. Sec.-treas. Downtown Devel. Authority Shreveport, 1979—; bd. dirs. Historic Preservation of Shreveport. Mem. AIA (treas. Shreveport chpt. 1978—), Shreveport C. of C. Democrat. Office: Ralph Kiper Architect 1008 Petroleum Tower Shreveport LA 71101

KIRBY, GEORGE FRANCIS, petroleum co. exec.; b. Cheneyville, La., Dec. 7, 1916; s. George Francis and Vesta (Mason) K.; A.B., La. Coll., 1936; M.S., La. State U., 1938, Ph.D., 1940; postgrad. Harvard, 1952; m. Nannette Dutsch, Dec. 12, 1941; children—Michael E., John M. With Ethyl Corp., N.Y.C., 1940-69, v.p. research and devel., 1955-62, exec. v.p., 1963-64, pres., 1964-69, also dir.; dir., mem. exec. com. Tex. Eastern Corp., Houston, 1969—, exec. v.p., 1970-71, pres., 1971—, chief exec. officer, 1973—, also chmn.; dir. La. Nat. Bank, 1st City Nat. Bank, Houston. Bd. dirs. La. State U. Found. Mem. Am. Chem. Soc., Am. Inst. Chem. Engrs., AAAS, Am. Petroleum Inst. (dir.), Gulf Research Inst. (trustee), Soc. Automotive Engrs., Gulf Univs. Research Consortium (trustee). Clubs: Chemists, Pinnacle (N.Y.C.), Baton Rouge Country, Camelot (Baton Rouge); Houston, Petroleum, Ramada (Houston). Office: 1221 McKinney St McKinney TX 77002 also 277 Park Ave New York NY 10017

KIRCHHOFF, ALBERT ELWOOD, computer service co. exec.; b. Olton, Tex., June 13, 1951; s. Robert Elwood and Shirley Ruth (Gravelle) K.; B.S. in Chemistry, Wayland Bapt. Coll., 1976; m. Barbara Hollingsworth, Apr. 1, 1972; 1 dau., Juli Marissa. Paper processor Meisel Photochrome, Dallas, 1972-73; quality supr. Ga.-Pacific Corp., Quanah, Tex., 1976-78; owner, pres. KMK Enterprises, Plainview, Tex., 1978—. Pres., Young Republicans of Hale County, 1969-70. Mem. Digital Equipment Computer Users Soc. Presbyterian. Home: Route 2 Hale Center TX 79041 Office: KMK Enterprises 3109 Olton Rd Plainview TX 79072

KIRCHNER, JOHN CHRISTOPHER, constrn. co. exec.; b. Washington, June 17, 1949; s. Theodore Edmond and Mary Joan (Holt) K.; B.A., Tulane U., 1971; M.B.A., James Madison U., 1978. Legis. asst. to Congressman Bill D. Burlison, U.S. Ho. of Reps., Washington, 1973-76; asst. controller Miller & Smith, Inc., McLean, Va., 1978—. Mem. Va. Rugby Union (dir. at large 1977-78), Potomac Rugby Union (dir. 1975-76). Club: Old Red Rugby (capt. 1st XV)(Washington). Home: 3107 Covington St Fairfax VA 22031 Office: Miller & Smith Inc 1301 Beverly Rd McLean VA 22101

KIRK, DONALD WILLIAM, architect, engr.; b. W. Concord, Minn., Feb. 6, 1921; s. Donald William and Manila (Nordman) K.; B.S. in Archtl. Engring., U. Tex. at Austin, 1943; m. Barbara Furr Barclay, July 1, 1978; children—Kathy, Don, Mike, Andrew. Structural engr. Gen. Dynamics Corp., 1943-45, Wyatt C. Hedrick, architect, Ft. Worth, 1946, Preston M. Geren, architect, Ft. Worth, 1947-56; propr. Don W. Kirk, architect-engr., Ft. Worth, 1956-65; partner architecture and engring. firm Kirk, Voich & Gist, Ft. Worth, 1965—; dir. Kibah Corp., Ft. Worth; prin. works include erection tower for Moscow Dome, 1959, Leonard's M&O Subway, Ft. Worth, 1962-63, skywalk between Continental Nat. Bank and garage, Ft. Worth, 1972, Bell Helicopter plant, Ft. Worth, 1957-74. Chmn. Ft. Worth Bldg. Code Rev. Com., 1968-70; mem. Ft. Worth Plan Commn., 1976—, vice-chmn., 1979; mem. Ft. Worth Econ. Devel. Policy Bd., 1979, Ft. Worth Public Transp. Adv. Com., 1979. Mem. AIA (v.p. chpt. 1979), Nat. Council Archtl. Registration Bds., Cons. Engrs. Council (pres. Tex. 1958), ASCE (mem. task com. for Bibliography on Bolted and Riveted Joints 1959). Mason, Rotarian. Clubs: Colonial Country, River Crest Country, Ft. Worth, Ridotto, Steeplechase (Ft. Worth). Contbr. articles to profl. publs. Office: PO Box 572 Fort Worth TX 76101

KIRK, IVAN WAYNE, agrl. engr.; b. Lark, Tex., Jan. 25, 1937; s. Percy Lee and Annie B. (Wilson) K.; student Abilene Christian U., 1954-56; B.S., Tex. Technol. U., 1959; M.S., Clemson U., 1960; Ph.D., Auburn U., 1967; m. Latrelle Venable, June 3, 1960; children—Kimberly, Kendal, Wayne. Research agrl. engr. Cotton Mechanization Research, Agrl. Research Service, U.S. Dept. Agr., Lubbock, Tex., 1960-71, dir. SW Cotton Ginning Research Lab., Mesilla Park, N.Mex., 1971-77; asst. dir. So. Regional Research Center, New Orleans, 1977—; vis. asst. prof. Tex. Technol. U., 1963-65. Asst. dist. commr. Boy Scouts Am., 1970-71; mem. devel. commn. Children's Home of Lubbock, 1969-71. Nat. Cotton Council fellow, 1959. Recipient Arthur S. Flemming award Washington Jaycees, 1975; Alumnus Citation award Abilene Christian U., 1978. Mem. Am. Soc. Agrl. Engrs. Mem. Ch. of Christ. Club: Lions. Contbr. articles to profl. jours. Home: 336 Eden Isles Dr Slidell LA 70458 Office: PO Box 19687 New Orleans LA 70179

KIRK, JOHN MICHAEL, landscape architect; b. El Paso, Tex., Oct. 12, 1942; s. Robert Pugh and Francis Newberry (McClure) K.; A.A., N.Mex. Mil. Inst., 1963; B. Landscape Architecture, U. Ga., 1967; m. Joyce Elizabeth Pruet, Oct. 29, 1964 (div. Feb. 1972); 1 dau., Joyce Michelle; m. C. Jane Jerrell, July 1975 (div. Feb. 1978). Pvt. practice as landscape architect, Birmingham, Ala., 1965; landscape architect, contractor Landscape Services, Birmingham, 1966-67, 69-72; landscape architect, pres. Environ. Design Collaborative, Birmingham, 1972—; cons. to various archtl. offices; cons. Beautification Bd., City of Homewood, Ala., 1971—. Served to 1st lt. C.E., AUS, 1967-69. Recipient awards for Birmingham Green, Dept. Transp., 1975, Am. Assn. Nurserymen, 1975. Mem. Am. Soc. Landscape Architects (sec., treas. Ala. sect. 1969-72, chpt. chmn. pub. relations 1974-76, pres. 1976-78). Republican. Presbyn. Home: 5208 Scenic View Dr Birmingham AL 35210 Office: 1100 27 St S Birmingham AL 35205

KIRK, PRESTON FLOYD, public relations exec.; b. Corpus Christi, Feb. 1, 1945; s. Albert Monroe and Robbie Lorraine (Porterfield) K.; B.A. in Journalism, Baylor U., Waco, Tex., 1968; m. Ronda Dale Massey, Aug. 17, 1968. Reporter, Galveston (Tex.) Daily News, 1967; reporter, asst. bur. mgr. UPI, Houston, 1968-71; founding asso. editor Houston Bus. Jour., 1971-74; account exec., corp. sec. Churchill Group, Inc., fin. public relations, Houston, 1974-76; founding editor-in-chief Tex. Bus. mag., Dallas, 1976-77; corp. mgr. media relations E-Systems, Inc., Dallas, 1977—; bd. dirs. Freedom of Info. Found. N. Tex. Sec. Water Control and Improvement Dist. 93, 1973-75. Served as pvt. USAR, 1963. Baylor U. journalism scholar; recipient Reporting award SBA, 1973, award excellence corp. newspapers Dallas Press Club, 1979. Mem. Soc. Profl. Journalists, Public Relations Soc. Am., Internat. Assn. Bus. Communicators, Aviation-Space Writers Assn., Tex. Solar Energy Soc., Poetry Soc. Tex., Acad. Am. Poets. Baptist. Club: Dallas Rotary. Co-author: Big Town, Big Money, The Business of Houston, 1973. Home: 1511 Jennifer St Richardson TX 75081

KIRK, VICTOR CLARK, univ. adminstr.; b. Monroe, La., Aug. 13, 1949; s. Rogers and Alberta (Williams) K.; B.S., Southern U., 1971, M.A., 1978; postgrad. Loyola U., New Orleans, 1977—, U. Mich., 1979; cert. of tng. in law enforcement, La. State U., 1977; m. Eva Baylock, Aug. 31, 1970; 1 dau., Melanie Rene. Sr. counselor, alcoholism program Community Advancement, Inc., Baton Rouge, 1971-72; police-community relations specialist La. Commn. on Human Relations, Rights and Responsibilities, Baton Rouge, 1972-74; field coordinator La. Bur. Human Relations, Baton Rouge, 1974-75; exec. asst. to the interim dir. Charity Hosp., New Orleans, 1976-77; exec. asst. to the undersec. for mgmt. and fin. Dept. Health and Human Resources, Baton Rouge, 1975-78; dir. Bur. for Civil Rights, Baton Rouge, 1978; mgmt. analyst, spl. asst. to the dep. commr. adminstrn. Office of Gov., Baton Rouge, 1978-79; dir. planning and research Grambling (La.) State U., 1979-80; exec. dir. La. Legis. Black Caucus, 1980—; mem. La. Planning Council for Devel. Disabilities, 1977—, La. Adv. Com. for Family Planning, 1978—. Vice pres. La. Assn. Sickle Cell Anemia, 1978—; trustee Gulf South Research Inst., 1979. Mem. Am. Soc. for Tng. and Devel., Omega Psi Phi. Democrat. Baptist. Home: 802 S 27th St Monroe LA 71201 Office: PO Box 2901 Baton Rouge LA 70821

KIRK, VIRGINIA, clin. psychologist; b. Kirksville, Mo., Dec. 22, 1895; d. Sherman and Harriet Rose (White) Kirk; A.B., Drake U., 1917; B. Nursing, Yale, 1927, M.S., 1930; Ph.D., U. Chgo., 1949. Research asst. Yale Psycho-Clinic, 1930-31; dir. nursing Emma Pendleton Bradley Home, Riverside, R.I., 1931-35; research asso. Williamson County Child Guidance Study, Franklin, Tenn., 1935-42; instr. clin. psychology sch. medicine Vanderbilt U., 1943-47, asst. prof., 1947-53, asso. prof., 1953-60, asso. clin. prof., 1960-61, emerita, 1961—; pvt. practice cons. clin. psychologist, 1961—; cons. clin psychologist Family and Children's Service, 1953-73, SCOR, Vanderbilt U. Hosp., 1963-74; lectr. U. Tenn. Sch. Social Work, 1951-60. Recipient Distinguished Service award Drake U., Drake U. Nat. Alumni Assn., 1965. Diplomate in clin. psychology Am. Bd. Profl. Psychology. Fellow Am. Psychol. Assn.; mem. AAAS, Tenn. Acad. Sci., Southeastern, Midwestern, Tenn. (Honors award 1976) psychol. assns., Am. Assn. Mental Deficiency, Am. Soc. Psychologists in Pvt. Practice, N.Y. Acad. Scis. Author articles in field. Home: 666 Timber Ln Regency Park Nashville TN 37215

KIRKENDALL, JAMES VERNON, retail exec.; b. Kokomo, Ind., Apr. 20, 1939; s. E. Howard and Martha Elizabeth (Unger) K.; B.A., Mich. State U., 1961; m. Linda Rae Brethen, Dec. 17, 1960; children—Brent Scott, Todd Mitchell, Jamie Chambers. Mgmt. trainee Jewel Cos., Chgo., 1965-66; pres. Village Pantry div. Marsh Supermarkets, 1966-70; gen. mgr. Marsh Supermarkets, Yorktown, Ind., 1971-72; mktg. cons., Yorktown and Sarasota, Fla., 1972-77; sr. v.p. UtoteM Stores div. Fairmont Foods, Houston, 1977—. Commiteeman Houston Livestock Show and Rodeo, 1978-79; bd. dirs. Kidney Found. of Houston. Mem. Aircraft Owners and Pilots Assn., Nat. Assn. Convenience Stores (dir. 1968-71), Mich. State U. Alumni Assn. Methodist. Home: 12807 Carvel Ln Houston TX 77072 Office: 5200 W Loop S Houston TX 77027

KIRKENDALL, WALTER MURRAY, physician, educator; b. Louisville, Mar. 31, 1917; s. Charles Allen and Margaret C. (Caplinger) K.; M.D., U. Louisville, 1941; m. Margaret Jane Allen, Mar. 31, 1948; children—William Charles, James Allen, Matthew John, Thomas Murray, David Edwin, Nancy Jane, Mary Margaret, Kathryn Ann, Joseph Howard, Michael Bruce. Intern, Univ. Hosps., Iowa City, 1941-42, resident internal medicine, 1946-49; jr. asst. resident internal medicine Gen. Hosp., Louisville, 1945-46; research asst. anatomy U. Louisville Coll. Medicine, 1938-39; staff mem. State U. Iowa Hosps., 1949-72; asst. dept. internal medicine U. Iowa Coll. Medicine, 1949-50, asso., 1950-51, asst. prof., 1951-52, clin. asso. prof., 1952-58, asso. prof., 1958-59, prof., 1959-72, dir. cardiovascular research labs., 1958-70, dir. renal-hypertension-electrolyte div., 1970-72; chief med. service VA Hosp., Iowa City, 1952-58, cons. in medicine, 1958-72; prof. medicine U. Tex. Med. Sch., Houston, 1972—, chmn. dept. internal medicine, 1972-76; dir. med. service Hermann Hosp., 1972-76, dir. hypertension div., 1976—; cons. VA Nat. Programs for Research in Therapy of Hypertension, 1958-73, USPHS Coop. Study on Treatment Hypertension, 1967—; mem. med. adv. bd. Council High Blood Pressure Research, Am. Heart Assn.; mem. exec. com. Undergrad. Cardiology Tng. Programs, Nat. Heart Inst., 1969-72. Served from 1st lt. to maj., M.C., AUS, 1942-46. Decorated Army Commendation medal; recipient Bierring award Iowa Tb. and Health Assn., 1966; named Internist of Year, Iowa Soc. Internal Medicine, 1971; Louis Mark lectr. Am. Coll. Chest Physicians, 1963. Diplomate Am. Bd. Internal Medicine. Fellow A.C.P., Am. Coll. Cardiology; mem. AMA, AAUP, AAAS, Central Clin. Research Club, Am. Fedn. Clin. Research (counselor Midwestern sect. 1955-57), Central Soc. Clin. Research, Am. Coll. Chest Physicians (gov. Iowa 1964), Internat., Am. socs. nephrology, Internat. Soc. Cardiology, Am. Clin. and Climatol. Assn., Soc. Exptl.

Biology and Medicine, So. Soc. Clin. Investigation, N.Y. Acad. Scis., Assn. Profs. Medicine, Am., Houston socs. internal medicine, Nat. Kidney Found., Am. Coll. Pharmacology and Chemotherapy, Am. Thoracic Soc., Am. Soc. Pharmacology and Exptl. Therapeutics, Tex. Med. Assn., Harris County Med. Soc., Sigma Xi, Alpha Omega Alpha, Phi Chi. Contbr. articles to profl. jours. Home: 5203 Del Monte Houston TX 77056 Office: Box 20708 Houston TX 77025

KIRKLAND, DONALD FRANK, mfg. co. exec.; b. Oklahoma City, Sept. 29, 1940; s. Ernest D. and Blanche M. (Forester) K.; B.S. in B.A., Okla. State U., 1962; postgrad. U. Tulsa, 1965, 66; m. Mary E. Garcia, Feb. 28, 1964; children—Justin D., Matthew Scott. Indsl. engr. Rockwell Mfg., Tulsa, 1962-64; chief indsl. engr. Sperry Rand-Vickers, Tulsa, 1964-67, prodn. control mgr., 1967-70; dir. mgmt. services Arthur Young & Co., Tulsa, 1970-79; pres., chmn. exec. com., chief operating officer Leland Equip. Co., Tulsa, 1979—; cons. in field. Mem. Mayor's Council on Alcoholism, Tulsa, 1977-78. Mem. Am. Mgmt. Assn. Republican. Clubs: Tulsa, Cedar Ridge Country. Author: Cost Systems: Handbook of Business Problem Solving, 1979. Office: PO Box 45128 Tulsa OK 74145

KIRKLAND, VIRGINIA DREADEN, pub. relations exec.; b. Grayville, Ill., June 3, 1944; d. William McLean and Virginia Mae (Hancock) Dreaden; B.A., Auburn U., 1966; m. Robert E. Kirkland, Oct. 31, 1970; 1 son, Christopher Nelson. Personnel dir. Computer Applications, Inc., Cape Kennedy Space Center, Fla., 1966; continuity dir., copywriter Sta. WMAK, Nashville, 1967; news editor Ga. Inst. Tech., Atlanta, 1968-70, fine arts dir. Student Center, 1970-72; v.p. Dreaden, Inc., Atlanta, 1972-76; sales asso. Clover Realty, Atlanta, 1977—. Active League Women Voters, Mt. Paran Civic Assn.; bd. dirs. Pro-Mozart Soc., Atlanta Playhouse Theatre, Atlanta Opera Theatre, Atlanta Lyric Opera, Roswell Hist. Soc. Recipient Atlanta Artist Club award, 1973, W.S. Beaver award for community service, 1972. Mem. Am. Collegiate Pub. Relations Assn., Am. Colls. and Univs. Union Mgrs., Atlanta Bd. Realtors, Atlanta Council for Arts, Delta Zeta. Republican. Author: Georgia Girl, 1976; editor: Campus, 1968-69; asst. editor Alumnus mag., 1968-69; contbr. articles to Accent mag., 1972. Home: 4724 Dudley Ln NW Atlanta GA 30327 Office: 3131 Peachtree St NE Atlanta GA 30305

KIRKLAND, WALLACE TALMAGE, real estate appraiser, cons.; b. Guntersville, Ala., July 15, 1931; s. Grover and Ona (McClendon) K.; B.S., Auburn U., 1953; postgrad, U. Fla., 1955-56; m. Martha Alma Cotter, June 2, 1962; children—Lorraine Phyllis, Dawn Ellen. Pres., Kirkland Builders, Guntersville, 1958-59; asso. regional appraiser Gen. Services Adminstrn., Atlanta, 1959-65; pres. Kirkland & Co., Atlanta, 1965—. Served with USAF, 1953-55. Mem. Am. Inst. Real Estate Appraisers, Soc. Real Estate Appraisers, Inst. Real Estate Mgmt., Pi Kappa Phi, Delta Sigma Pi. Home: 1656 Merton Rd NE Atlanta GA 30306 Office: 400 Colony Square Tower Atlanta GA 30361

KIRKMAN, WILLIAM ERNEST, photo co. exec.; b. May 2, 1936; s. Roscoe and Irene (Cummins) K.; B.S. in Bus., Butler U., Indpls., 1958; spl. courses U. Ill., 1964, So. Meth. U., 1975; m. Janice Sheritt, Mar. 29, 1958; children—Kevin, Kelly, Kent, Keith. Dist. mgr. Dynacolor Corp. div. 3M Co., Rochester, N.Y., 1958-62; owner Bill Kirkman Photo Centers, Indpls., 1962-67; successively regional mgr., nat. field sales mgr., v.p. dealer sales, sr. v.p. mktg., pres. dealer div. Fox-Stanley Photo Products, Inc., San Antonio, 1967—. Bd. trustees Christian Ch. Pension Fund; pres. Bluebonnet area Christian Ch., also mem. Gen. Bd. Served with Army N.G., 1958-64. Mem. Photo Mktg. Assn. (workshop speaker), Am. Mktg. Assn. (v.p. San Antonio chpt.). Home: 426 Wood Shasow St San Antonio TX 78216 Office: 8750 Tesoro Dr San Antonio TX 78286

KIRKPATRICK, DORCAS CHRISTINE GILBERT, counselor; b. Cordova, Ala., Mar. 2, 1927; d. Carroll Jackson and Hattie (Minor) Gilbert; student Walker Jr. Coll., 1945; B.S., U. Ala., 1964, M.A., 1966, Ed.S., 1970; m. Charles Melvin Kirkpatrick, Jan. 26, 1945; 1 dau., Melba Belinda Kirkpatrick. Tchr., Walker County Sch. System, Jasper, Ala., 1948-49, 61-65; work-study placement counselor U. Ala., Tuscaloosa, 1965, acad. counselor for women, 1965-66; registrar U. Ala., Birmingham, 1966-68; counselor Jefferson County Sch. System, Birmingham, 1968—; sec. Bd. Family Counseling, 1972-73. Mem. NEA, Ala. Edn. Assn., Am. Personnel and Guidance Assn., AAUW, Ala. Personnel and Guidance Assn. (v.p. 1974-75, pres. dist. IV 1975-76, editor newsletter 1974-75, pres.'s award for outstanding service and outstanding counselor 1976), Jefferson County Counselors Assn., Jefferson County Edn. Assn., 78 West Bus. and Profl. Women (v.p. 1977-78, named Woman of Yr. 1977), Beta, Alpha Lambda Delta. Democrat. Baptist. Club: Adamsville Lioness (pres. 1978-79). Contbr. articles to profl. publs. Home: Route 1 Box 516C Gail Dr Midway Estates Adamsville AL 35005 Office: Jefferson County Sch System 400 Hillcrest Rd Adamsville AL 35005

KIRKPATRICK, FORREST HUNTER, mgmt. cons.; b. Gallon Ohio, Sept. 4, 1905; s. Arch. M. and Mildred (Hunter) K.; student U. Dijon, 1926; A.B., Bethany (W.Va.) Coll., 1927, LL.D., 1949; A.M., Columbia, 1931, profl. diploma, 1934, 36; postgrad. U. Pitts., U. London, U. Pa., U. Cambridge; LL.D., Coll. of Steubenville, 1958, Drury Coll., 1968. Dean, prof. Bethany Coll., 1927-40, 46-52, adj. prof., 1970—; gen. mgr. personnel adminstrn. RCA, 1941-46, ednl. cons., 1946-53; prof., vis. prof. N.Y. U., Columbia, U. Akron, U. Pitts., U. Wis., 1946-53, W.Va. U., 1970-80; asst. to pres. and chmn. Wheeling-Pitts. Steel Corp., v.p., 1964-70, also past dir.; dir. Sharon Tube Co., Banner Fiberboard Co., W.Va. Hosp. Service, Inc.; cons. Am. Council on Edn., 1938-45, War Manpower Commn., 1942-44, Dept. State, 1944, Ednl. Testing Ser., 1946-52, U.S. Civil Service, 1945, Post Office Dept., 1953; mem. mission to Sweden Dept. Labor, 1962; mem. manpower advisory com. Dept. Labor, 1963-68; mem. W.Va. Commn. on Higher Edn., 1964-70, Edn. Commn. of States, 1973-78, W.Va. Water Resources Bd., 1975—, W.Va. Commn. for Humanities and Pub. Policy, 1972-77, White House Conf. on Edn., 1955. Bd. govs. W.Va. U., 1957-69, pres. bd. 1961-62; trustee Ohio Valley Med. Center, Inc., Wheeling, 1954—; bd. dirs. Wheeling Symphony Soc., 1950— Wheeling Coll., 1972—, Wheeling Country Day Sch., 1953-64, 70-73, No. Manhandle Mental Health Center, 1974—. Mem. Acad. Polit. Sci. (life), Am. Personnel and Guidance Assn. (life), Nat. Alliance Businessmen (metro chmn. 1971-72), NEA (life), Am. Mgmt. Assn., Nat. Vocat. Guidance Assn. (profl. mem.), Indsl. Relations Research Assn. (life), AAUP (emeritus), Am. Econ. Assn., NAM (dir. 1967-70), Beta Gamma Sigma, Phi Delta Kappa, Beta Theta Pi, Alpha Kappa Psi, Kappa Delta Pi. Clubs: Wheeling Country, Ft. Henry (Wheeling); University, Duquesne (Pitts.); University (N.Y.C.); Lakeview Country (Morgantown, W.Va.); Soc. Friends of St. George (Windsor). Contbr. articles on mgmt. and labor econs. to profl. jours. Home: Tally-Ho Apts 931 National Rd Wheeling WV 26003 Office: PO Box 268 Wheeling WV 26003

KIRKPATRICK, JAMES FRANCIS, JR., surgeon; b. Decatur, Ga., Nov. 11, 1929; s. James Francis and Ruth Elios (Kehrer) K.; B.S., U. Ga., 1950; M.D., Med. Coll. Ga., 1954; m. Joan Harriet Breitlow, June 11, 1966; children—James Francis, III, Stephen Robert, Jane Grace, Andrea Michelle, Melissa Ruth, Heather Lynn. Intern, Ga. Bapt. Hosp., 1954-55; resident in surgery Bowman-Gray Sch. Medicine, Winston-Salem, N.C., 1957-58, Atlanta VA Hosp., 1958-60; chief resident in surgery Emory U. Hosp., Atlanta, 1960-61; instr. in surgery Emory U., 1961-62, asso. in surgery, 1962-64; practice medicine specializing in gen. and vascular surgrey, Tifton, Ga., 1964—; mem. staff Tift Gen. Hosp., 1964—, chief staff, 1972-73; pres. Tifton Surg. Clinic; dir., mem. exec. com. S.W. Ga. chpt. Health Systems Agy., 1975—; dir. Heritage Fed. Savs. & Loan, Tifton, 1976—. Mem. exec. bd. 1st Meth. Ch., Tifton, 1972-76. Served with M.C. U.S. Army, 1955-57. Diplomate Am. Bd. Surgery. Fellow A.C.S. (liaison fellow commn. on cancer); mem. Am. Coll. Angiology, Soc. Clin. Vascular Surgery, Ga. Surg. Soc., Med. Assn. Ga., So. Med. Assn., AMA, Assn. So. R.R. Physicians, Internat. Platform Assn. Republican. Club: Elks. Home: 2606 Murray Ave Tifton GA 31794 Office: 1493 Kennedy Rd Tifton GA 31794

KIRKPATRICK, JERALD LEE, clergyman; b. McAllen, Tex., Dec. 28, 1944; s. Joseph Rayner and Elnora Marian (Anderson) K.; B.A. summa cum laude, Tex. Christian U., 1967; B.D., Yale U., 1970; m. Brenda Leo Lokey, May 7, 1977; 1 son, Andrew Barton. Dir. ch. sch. Church of Christ, Yale U., New Haven, Conn., 1969-70; ordained to ministry Christian Ch., 1970; asso. minister First Christian Ch., El Paso, 1970-73; minister of edn. First Christian Ch., Amarillo, Tex., 1973-77; asso. minister Bethany Christian Ch., Houston, 1977—. Mem. gen. bd. Christian Ch. (Disciples of Christ) in U.S. and Can., 1969-71, mem. program and arrangements com. of gen. assembly, 1969-71; chmn. div. Christian edn. Hi-Plains Area Christian Chs., 1975-77; mem. regional assembly program com. Christian Ch. in S.W., 1977-78; chmn. leadership devel. dept. Coastal Plains Area Christian Chs., 1980—. Mem. S.W. Assn. of Christian Ch. Educators (pres. 1972-73). Home: 11118 Cedarhurst Dr Houston TX 77096 Office: 3223 Westheimer Rd Houston TX 77098

KIRKPATRICK, JOYCE COLLINS, ednl. adminstr.; b. New Orleans, Sept. 16, 1941; d. Emmett and Henrietta Thompson Collins; B.A., Bennett Coll., 1963; M.A., Fla. A&M U., 1970; Ed.D. (fellow), U. Fla., 1980; m. Edison Avon Kirkpatrick, June 3, 1963; 1 dau., Danita Arlene. Tchr., New Orleans Public Schs., 1963-65, Duval Public Schs., Jacksonville, Fla., 1965-70; tchr. Atlanta Public Schs., 1970-73, public relations liaison/community relations liaison, 1973-75, exec. high sch. interhships liaison, 1975—. Mem. Assn. Curriculum and Supervision Devel., Alpha Kappa Alpha, Phi Delta Pi, Phi Delta Kappa. Methodist. Home: 5735 Vandiver Rd SW Atlanta GA 30331 Office: Atlanta Pub Schs 224 Central Ave Atlanta GA 30303

KIRSCH, KERRY JOHN, counselor; b. Lafayette, La., July 28, 1948; s. Harry John and Alice Maire (Lemoyne) K.; B.A., Nicholls State U., 1970; M.S. (vocat. rehab. tng. grantee), U. Southwestern La., 1973. Tchr., St. Mary Parish Schs., Morgan City, La., 1970-71, vocat. rehab. counselor, 1973-76; childrens counselor, asst. psychologist Dept. Health and Human Resources, Patterson, La., 1977—. Bd. dirs. Family Focus; mem. Mayor's Com. on Employment of Handicapped. Vocat. rehab. tng. grantee Tex. Health and Sci. Center, Dallas, 1974. Mem. La. Rehab. Assn., Nat. Rehab. Assn., Am. Mental Health Center Counseling Assn., Am. Personnel and Guidance Assn. Democrat. Roman Catholic. Home: 122 Becky Dr Patterson LA 70390 Office: PO Box 790 Patterson LA 70390

KIRVEN, LEO EDWIN, JR., psychiatrist, state ofcl.; b. Summerton, S.C., July 18, 1923; s. Leo Edwin and Theo (Cain) K.; B.S., Clemson U., 1949; M.D., Med. Coll. S.C., 1954; children—Leo Edwin III. Intern, Columbia (S.C.) Hosp., 1954-55; resident in psychiatry Eastern State Hosp., Williamsburg, Va., 1961-63, Central State Hosp., Petersburg, Va., also Med. Coll. Va. Hosp., Richmond, 1963-64; asst. clin. dir. Central State Hosp., 1965-71, dir., 1971-75; asst. commr. mental health Va. Dept. Mental Health and Mental Retardation, Richmond, 1975-76, acting commr., 1976-78, commr., 1978—; psychiat. cons. Va. State Penitentiary, Richmond, Petersburg Psychiat. Inst.; chmn. com. mental health and human services So. Regional Edn. Bd., 1979; mem. steering com. Va. Council Health and Med. Care; ex-officio mem. Gov.'s Adv. Council on Medicaid-Medicare; adv. com. Va. Center on Aging. Served as pilot USAF, 1942-45. Mem. Neuropsychiat. Soc. Va. (exec. com.), Am. Psychiat. Assn., 4th Dist. Med. Soc., Med. Soc. Va., AMA, So. Med. Assn., Nat. Assn. Mental Health Supts., Nat. Assn. State Mental Health Program Dirs., Assn. Mental Health Adminstrs. Author articles in field. Office: PO Box 1797 Richmond VA 23214

KISER, CHARLES BYRON, architect; b. Trion, Ga., May 18, 1937; s. Grover G. and Annie Mae (Bagwell) K.; B.S. in Bldg. Constrn., Ga. Inst. Tech., 1960; m. Joyce Elaine Lassitter, June 23, 1956; children—Lisa Elaine, Lené Michelle, Sharon Monique. From draftsman to architect, several offices, Atlanta, 1956-69; prin. own firm, 1969—; pres., founder Money, Inc., real estate devel. and mgmt. co., Atlanta, 1972—, Take-a-turkey, Inc., used car rental, 1977—; pres. Hails Design Assos., Inc.; v.p., devel. coordinator Hails Cos.; pres. The Orange Group, Inc. Chmn., Good Govt. of Ga., 1976-77, ABC-PAC, 1976-80. Served with USAF, 1961-62. Registered architect, Ga., Fla., Ala., N.C., S.C. Mem. Asso. Builders and Contractors of Ga. (chmn. 1976-77, chmn. legis. com.), Ga. Taxpayers League, So. Center Internat. Studies, Nat. Right to Work Com. Republican. Patentee, author in field. Home: PO Box 76329 Atlanta GA 30328 Office: PO Box 76329 Atlanta GA 30328

KISER, LAWRENCE STEPHEN, architect; b. Indpls., Nov. 8, 1946; s. Eugene W. and Mary Frances (Arnold) K.; B. Arch., U. Tex., 1972; m. Kathryn Dell Wilhelm, Aug. 21, 1971; 1 dau., Lauren Dell. Project mgr. Dallas Market Center Devel. Co., 1976-79; v.p. design and devel. Crow Hotel Devel. Co., Dallas, 1979-80; dir. design and engring. Innkeepers Supply Co. div. Holiday Inn, Memphis, 1980—. Served with USMCR, 1966-67. Registered architect, Tex. Mem. AIA, Tex. Soc. Architects, Lambda Chi Alpha. Methodist. Home: 6621 Tulip Ln Dallas TX 75230 Office: PO Box 18127 Holiday City Station Memphis TN 38118

KISER, PHILLIP WAYNE, landscape architect; b. Hazard, Ky., Nov. 23, 1939; s. Walter Ellis and Erna Marian (Francis) K.; B.Landscape Arch., U. Fla., 1963; m. Marguerite Grimball Gayle, Aug. 11, 1962; children—Gayle Ann, Alisa Lynette. Asso., Milo Smith & Assos., Tampa, Fla., 1968-69; head landscape architecture dept. Reynolds, Smith & Hills, Jacksonville, Fla., 1969-73; v.p. Edward D. Stone, Jr. & Assos., Ft. Lauderdale, Fla., 1973—. Served to capt. USAF, 1964-68. Decorated Commendation medal. Mem. Am. Soc. Landscape Architects (pres. Fla. 1978), Am. Inst. Planners. Presbyterian. Home: 2541 NE 26th Ave Ft Lauderdale FL 33305 Office: 2400 E Oakland Park Blvd Ft Lauderdale FL 33306

KISER, SAMUEL CURTIS, lawyer, state legislator; b. Oskaloosa, Iowa, June 17, 1944; s. Ira Manley and Emma Jean (Raley) K.; B.A. in Polit. Sci., U. Iowa, 1967; J.D., Fla. State U., 1970; m. Sara Margaret Hess, Aug. 27, 1966; children—Jennifer Lynn, Kevin Curtis. Admitted to Fla. bar, 1970; research asst. Office Gov. Fla., 1968-69; asst. legal counsel to gov., 1970; mem. adv. council Fla. Dept. Community Affairs, 1971-72; mem. Fla. Ho. of Reps. from 54th Dist., 1972—, minority leader, 1979-80; chmn. Pinellas County Legis. Del., 1976-77. Mem. Greater Pinellas County Young Republican Com. Named One of Five Outstanding Freshman Legislators, Jacksonville Times Union, 1973. Mem. Am., Fla., Clearwater bar assns., Dunedin C. of C (Outstanding Young Man of 1972), Dunedin Jaycees. Home: 14 Petersor Ln Palm Harbor FL 33563 Office: 535 S Fort Harrison Clearwater FL 33516

KISER, WILLIAM ROGER, banker; b. Lebanon, Va., Nov. 23, 1946; s. W.A. and Hope E. (Horne) K.; student Carson Newman Coll., 1965-66; B.S. in Bus. Adminstrn., U. Tenn., 1968; m. Lou King, Aug. 31, 1968; 1 son, Scot. Various positions Citizens and So. Nat. Bank, Atlanta, 1969-73; v.p. Hamilton Bancshares, Chattanooga, 1973-76; sr. v.p. United Am. Bank, Johnson City, Tenn., 1976—; guest lectr. Sch. Continuing Edn., E. Tenn. State U. Vice chmn. fin. div. United Way, 1978, chmn., 1979. Mem. Nat. Assn. Rev. Appraisers, Bank Adminstrn. Inst., Johnson City/Washington County C. of C. Club: Johnson City Lions. Home: 2808 Steven Dr Johnson City TN 37601 Office: United Am Bank 208 Sunset Dr PO Box 1998 Johnson City TN 37601

KISER, WILLIAM RUSSELL, lawyer; b. Wise, Va., Apr. 16, 1921; s. Henry Jefferson and Vivian Russell (McLemore) K.; A.B., Washington and Lee U., 1942, LL.B., 1943; m. Keta Virginia Still, Oct. 11, 1939; children—Jennifer (Mrs. David R. Khaliel), Billie (Mrs. Gregory A. Pickesimer). Admitted to Va. bar, 1943; partner Kiser & Kiser, Wise, 1943—. Commr. accounts Circuit Ct. Wise County, 1970—. Named Ky. col. Mem. Va. State Bar, Wise County Bar Assn. (pres. 1956-57), Pi Kappa Alpha, Phi Delta Phi. Republican. Baptist. Kiwanian. Home: Spring St Box 1247 Wise VA 24293 Office: Main St Wise VA 24293

KISPERT, WAYNE EARL, constrn. co. exec.; b. Clinton, Ind., Sept. 26, 1925; s. Ortie Curtis and Euphemia Broatch (Thorburn) K.; student Ind. State Tchrs. Coll., 1943-44; B.S. in C.E., Purdue U., 1950; m. Patricia Mason, June 20, 1948; children—Kenneth Allen, Philip Neil, David Wayne. Hydraulic engr. U.S. Geol. Survey, Indpls., 1948-51; control engr. constrn. E.I. duPont DeNemours, Wilmington, Del., 1951-55; gen. supt. Anning Johnson Co., Indpls., 1955-60, v.p. constrn., Melrose Park, Ill., 1960-71, sr. v.p., Orlando, Fla., 1971—, v.p. Anning Johnson Supply & Mfg. Co., Orlando, 1972—, also dir., v.p. Anning Johnson Internat. Ltd., 1977—. Pres., Medinah (Ill.) Civic Assn., 1964-65, bd. dirs., 1965-68. Exec. bd. DuPage Area council Boy Scouts Am., 1968-70; bd. dirs. Spring Valley Lake Assn., Medinah, Ill., 1963-65. Served with USNR, 1943-45. Mem. ASCE, ASTM, Nat. Acoustical Contractors Assn. (com. chmn. 1965-67, 75-77), Cellular Concrete Assn. (pres. 1973-74, dir. 1975), Am. Legion. Presbyterian. Mason. Clubs: Bay Hill, Executive, Wally Byam Caravan Internat. (pres unit 1979-80). Home: 6118 Cheshire Ln Bay Hill Orlando FL 32811 Office: Sun Bank Bldg Suite 425 Lake Buena Vista FL 32830

KISSLING, FRED RALPH, JR., ins. agy. exec.; b. Nashville, Feb. 10, 1930; s. Fred Ralph and Sarah Elizabeth (FitzGerald) K.; B.A., Vanderbilt U., 1952, M.A., 1958; m. Ruth M. Kissling; children—Sarah FitzGerald, Jane Kirkpatrick. Spl. agt. Northwestern Mut. Life Ins. Co., Nashville, 1953-62, gen. agt., Lexington, Ky., 1962—; pres. Employee Benefit Cons., Inc., Lexington, 1961—; partner Kennington Assos., 1967—; pub. Leader's Mag., 1972—; dir. Bank of Lexington. Adv. bd. Salvation Army, Lexington, 1971—; campaign chmn. United Way Blue Grass, 1975; bd. dirs. United Way, 1975-77, 80—, Lexington Humane Soc., 1976—; chmn. bd. trustees Lexington Children's Theatre, 1979—. Mem. Am. Soc. Chartered Life Underwriters (chpt. pres. 1969-70, regional v.p. 1972-73), Ky. Gen. Agts. and Mgrs. Assn. (pres. 1965-66), Nat. Assn. Life Underwriters (life mem. Million Dollar Round Table 1960—, v.p. program 1976), Am. Soc. Pension Actuaries (dir. 1971-76, pres. 1974), Assn. Advanced Life Underwriters (sec.-treas. 1979), Sigma Chi. Mason (Shriner). Clubs: Nashville City; Lexington, Lexington Polo; Lafayette. Author: Sell and Grow Rich, 1966. Editor: Questionaire in Pension Planning, 1971, Questionnaire in Estate Planning, 1971. Home: 2091 Norborne Lexington KY 40502 Office: 98 Dennis Dr Lexington KY 40503

KISSNER, JACOB, mfg. co. exec.; b. Frankfurt on Main, Germany; s. Josef and Lina (Sann) K.; ed. business coll.; m. Johanna Ditt, Aug. 27, 1931 (dec.); 1 dau., Olivia; m. 2d, Henrietta Lusby, June 27, 1975. Founder, owner Folbot Works, London, 1932-35; founder, 1935, since pres. Folbot Corp., L.I.; developer Folbot paddle and cruising excursions, White Water Sport, 1937; lectr. Mem. Am. Canoe Assn., Jamaica Estates Assn., Pack and Paddle Soc. Roman Catholic. Clubs: Kiwanis (pres.), Touring Kayak. Author: Foldboat Holidays, 1941; Fabulous Folbot Holidays, 1972; contbr. articles, picture stores to profl., sport publs. Holder Nat. White Water championship, 1941—. Office: Stark Indsl Park Charleston SC 29405

KISTLER, ERNEST LOSSON, mech. and ocean engr.; b. San Antonio, Oct. 30, 1931; s. Ernest Losson and Angie Mae (Smith) K.; B.S. in Aero. Engring., U. Tex., Austin, 1955, M.S. in Aero. Engring., 1957; Ph.D. in M.E., Rice U., 1969; m. Dorothy Palmer, June 22, 1952; children—Ernest Losson III, Linda, Steven. Research scientist mil. physics lab. U. Tex., Austin, 1955-56; sr. engr. Gen. Dynamics-Convair, Ft Worth, 1956-60; chief tech. design Stanley Aviation, Denver, 1960-61; project mgr. Martin Marietta, Denver, 1961-67; mgr. systems engring. Lockheed Electronics Co., Houston, 1967-72; asso. prof. marine sci., civil engring. and ocean engring. and head systems engring. program Tex. A. and M. U., Galveston, 1972-76; chief engr. R.J. Brown & Assos. of Am., Houston, 1976-78; owner, pres. Ernest L. Kistler & Assos., Inc., Houston, 1978—. Scoutmaster, Explorer advisor Sam Houston Area council Boy Scouts Am., 1966-73, awarded Brotherhood Order of Arrow; mem. Le Tourneau Coll. Council. Served with C.E., AUS, 1957. Recipient Apollo achievement award NASA, 1970. Asso. fellow Am. Inst. Aeros. and Astronautics (past chmn. Houston sect.); mem. Marine Tech. Soc. (past chmn. Houston sect.), Engrs. Council Houston (past pres.), Soc. Petroleum Engrs. Soc. Naval Architects and Marine Engrs., Houston C. of C. (sci. tech. com.), Phi Gamma Delta. Tech. editor: Jour. Petroleum Tech./SPE Jour., 1979-80. Home: 1515 Haven Lock Houston TX 77077

KITAY, DEANNA SOLOMON, neurophysiologist; b. N.Y.C., Feb. 7, 1939; d. Melven and Ausney (Avner) S.; Ph.D., U. Mo., 1973; m. Julian I. Kitay, June 24, 1973. Research asst. Albert Einstein Coll. Medicine, Bronx, N.Y., 1958-63; instr. C.W. Post Coll., L.I., N.Y., 1963-67; research asso. Neuropsychol. Lab. of N.Y., 1967-68; research technician U. Miss. Space Research Center, 1968-69; Alfred P. Sloan fellow in neuropharmacology U. Va. Sch. Medicine, Charlottesville, 1973-77, research asst. prof. physiology, 1977-78; asst. prof. neurosurgery, exec. adminstr. Center for Study of Central Nervous System Injury, U. Tex. Med. Br., Galveston, 1979—; co-founder, pres. Neurosci. Tech. Internat., Ltd., Tarzana, Calif., 1978—. Mem. Aerospace Med. Assn. Home: 3126 Beluche Dr Galveston TX 77551 Office: U Tex Med Br Dept Surgery/Neurosurgery Div Neurosurgery Galveston TX 77550

KITCHEN, JAMES LEE, air force officer; b. Akron, Ohio, Dec. 19, 1946; s. Willard Clair and Luiza Belle K.; B.S. Agrl. Econs., Miss. State U., 1968; m. Martha Diane Rider, June 23, 1973; children—Kathryn Luann, Adam Lee. Commd. 2d lt. USAF, 1968, advanced through grades to maj., 1980; aircraft comdr. Korat RTAFB, Thailand, 1972-73; instr. undergrad. pilot tng., Webb AFB, Big Spring,

Tex., 1974-77; instr., Dyess AFB, Tex., 1977—; squadron standardization/evaluation pilot, 1978—. Decorated Air medal with oak leaf cluster. Mem. Air Force Assn. Methodist. Home: 3274 Primrose Dr Abilene TX 79606 Office: 773 TAS Dyess AFB TX 79607

KITCHIN, MALINDA LOUISE, mfg. co. exec.; b. Norfolk, Va., Sept. 28, 1943; d. Jack Frank and Wilma Iona (Hales) Kitchin; student Old Dominion U., 1960-64; 1 son, James Hunter Cantwell. Bookkeeper, Hillcrest Farms, Virginia Beach, Va., 1963-74; owner, sec.-treas. Hillcrest Farms South, Inc., Southern Pines, N.C., 1970-75; area mgr., sales agt. Larasan Realty Corp., Virginia Beach, 1973-75; br. mgr., v.p. Kitchin Equipment Co., Inc., Chesapeake, Richmond and Salem, Va., 1975—; pres., treas. Salem Machinery Co., Inc., 1977—. Mem. Va. Road Builders Assn. (mem. legis. com. 1977), Salem C. of C. (bd. dirs. 1976—), Am. Road and Transp. Builders Assn. (bd. dirs. 1976—), Aircraft Owners and Pilots Assn. Republican. Episcopalian. Clubs: Fox Hunt, Moore County Hounds. Address: 1340 Roanoke Blvd PO Box 1364 Salem VA 24153

KITCHING, JENNIE CECILE, home economist; b. Sherman, Tex., Aug. 15, 1941; d. Stanley Lee and Marion Cecile (Davis) Kitching; B.S., E. Tex. State U., 1963; M.S., U. Tenn., 1967; Ph.D., Fla. State U., 1972. County extension agt. Liberty County, Tex., 1963-64, Jefferson County, Tex., 1965-66; teaching asst. U. Tenn., 1966-67; extension family life edn. specialist, 1967-70; teaching asst. Fla. State U., 1971-72; extension family life edn. specialist, 1972-75; asst. dir. home econs. Tex. Agrl. Extension Service, 1975—. Omicron Nu research fellow, 1971-72; Farm Found. Fellow, 1971-72. Mem. Am. (chmn. extension sect., adv. bd. Center for the Family), Tex. (pres. 1976-77) home econs. assns., Nat., Tex. councils family relations, Nat. Assn. Edn. Young Children, Assn. Adminstrs. Home Econs., Adult Edn. Assn. U.S.A., Nat. Assn. State Univs. and Land-Grant Colls. (home econs. commn.). Methodist. Home: 1522 Wolf Run College Station TX 77840 Office: 102 System Administration Bldg Texas A and M University College Station TX 77843

KITT, DONALD JOHN, automotive holding co. exec.; b. Beaverdale, Pa., Oct. 19, 1934; s. John and Esther Marie K.; B.S. in Edn. (Scholar), Auburn U., 1961; masters degree Ga. So. Coll., 1968; m. Bette Harvard, June 27, 1964; children—Amanda, John, Allyson, Joseph. Tchr., football coach, athletic dir. Chatham County Bd. Edn., Savannah, Ga., 1961-67; counselor Columbus Vocat. Sch., Columbus, Ga., 1968-69; personnel dir. Chatham County Dept. Family and Children's Services, Savannah, 1969-72; with Key Royal Automotive Co., Birmingham, Ala., 1972—, now v.p. Served with USAF, 1953-57. Mem. Am. Mgmt. Assn., Kappa Delta Pi. Presbyterian. Office: Key Royal Automotive 813 Shades Creek Pkwy Birmingham AL 35226

KITTLITZ, RUDOLF GOTTLIEB, JR., chem. engr.; b. Waco, Tex., Apr. 19, 1935; s. Rudolf Gottlieb and Lena Hulda (Landgraf) K.; B.S. in Chem. Engring., U. Miss., 1957; m. Linda Ann Watkins, Nov. 24, 1966; children—Lenell, Theresa, Liesel, Rolf. Engr., polychems. research E.I. du Pont de Nemours & Co., Wilmington, Del., 1957-60, engr., textile fibers dept., Seaford, Del., 1960-62, sr. engr., textile fibers dept., Seaford, 1962-67, sr. engr., textile fibers dept., Chattanooga, Tenn., 1967-68, sr. research engr., Chattanooga, 1968—; lectr. in field. Vice chmn. Community Action Com., Seaford, Del., 1966. Mem. Am. Soc. Quality Control (certified quality engr., chmn. Chattanooga sect. 1975-76, councilor region 11 chem. div. 1975—), Am. Statis. Assn. Democrat. Baptist. Club: Lakeshore. Home: 5373 Sky Valley Dr Chattanooga TN 37443 Office: 4501 Access Rd Chattanooga TN 37415

KLAPPER, STANFORD, mktg. cons. co. exec.; b. N.Y.C., Aug. 4, 1934; s. Howard G. and Lillian K.; A.B., Dartmouth Coll., 1956; M.B.A., Amos Tuck Sch. Bus. Adminstrn., 1957. Market mgr. Merrell Nat. Overseas Labs., N.Y.C., 1957-61; gen. mgr. Caribe Stores, Inc., Aguirre, P.R., 1961-65; owner, pres. Stanford Klapper Assos., Inc., San Juan, P.R., 1965—. Bd. govs., mem. exec. com. United Fund P.R. Recipient Top Mgmt. award Sales and Mktg. Execs. Assn. San Juan, 1978. Mem. Am. Marketing Assn. Club: Rotary. Home: 2 Taft St San Juan PR 00911 Office: Stanford Klapper Assos Inc 117 Eleanor Roosevelt St Hato Rey PR 00918

KLASS, JOEL VICTOR, psychiatrist; b. Miami, Oct. 5, 1942; s. Morris A. and Erna (Katz) K.; B.S., Tulane U., 1964; M.D., U. Miami, 1969; m. Maryse J. Israel, Mar. 18, 1973; children—Joanna Lauren, Jeremy David. Intern, U. Kans. Med. Center, 1970; resident in psychiatry Bellevue Hosp., N.Y.C., 1972-74; resident in child psychiatry N.Y. U. Med. Center, 1974-76; practice medicine specializing in child psychiatry, Hollywood, Fla., 1976—. Served with USAR, 1970-76. Mem. AMA, Am. Psychiat. Assn., Am. Acad. Psychoanalysis, Internat. Dermatoglyphic Soc., Soc. Med. Psychoanalysts, Am. Acad. Child Psychiatry. Contbr. articles to profl. jours. Home: 3370 N 41st Ct Hollywood FL 33021 Office: 3700 Washington St Hollywood FL 33021

KLEDARAS, CONSTANTINE GEORGE, social worker, educator; b. Raleigh, N.C., July 22, 1934; s. George Harold and Mary (Masouras) K.; B.A., Duke U., 1956; M.S.W. (NIMH grantee), U. N.C., 1960; D.S.W. (NIMH grantee), Catholic U. Am., 1971. Dir. outpatient services, supr. social service dept. Dorothea Dix Hosp., Raleigh, 1960-67; prof. dept. social work and correctional services Sch. Allied Health and Social Professions, E. Carolina U., Greenville, N.C., 1971—; cons. Caswell Center, Kinston, N.C., 1979—. Served with U.S. Army, 1957-58. Mem. Council on Social Work Edn., N.C. Council on Social Work Edn., Nat. Assn. Social Workers, Acad. Cert. Social Workers, N.C. Soc. for Clin. Social Work, Registry Clin. Social Workers, Otto Rank Soc., Am. Hellenic Ednl. Progressive Assn. Greek Orthodox. Clubs: Mason, Shriners. Home: PO Box 25581 1415 Hillsborough St Raleigh NC 27611 Office: Dept Social Work and Correction Services Sch Allied Health and Social Professions East Carolina U Greenville NC 27834

KLEE, LUCILLE HOLLJES (MRS. JAMES BUTT KLEE), educator; b. Balt., Dec. 8, 1924; s. Henry Diedrich and Elizabeth Carin (Kennedy) Holljes; B.A., Bryn Mawr Coll., 1946, M.A., 1947, Ph.D., 1951; m. James Butt Klee, Sept. 20, 1959; children—Margaret Ann, Kathren Elizabeth. Chemist, Sloan-Kettering Found., N.Y.C., 1946; instr. chemistry Barnard Coll., Columbia U., N.Y.C., 1950-54, class adviser, 1954-56; research chemist Toni Co. div. Gillette Co., Chgo., 1956-57; lectr., research asso. Brandeis U., Waltham, Mass., 1957-67; asso. prof. chemistry Lowell (Mass.) State Coll., 1967-71; asso. prof. sci. edn. and environ. studies W. Ga. Coll., Carrollton, 1971-76, asso. prof. sci. edn., 1976-79, prof. edn., 1979—. Faculty mem. Sarah Lawrence Coll., Bronxville, N.Y., 1950-52; sci. supr. Douglas County Bd. Edn., Douglasville, Ga., 1969-70; dir. Merrimac Valley Elementary Sci. Project, Lowell, Mass., 1970-71; cons. Dracut (Mass.) Sch. System, 1971, Carroll County Early Childhood Devel. Center, 1974-75. Pres. Carrollton Jr. High Sch. PTA, 1974-76. Mem. Am. Chem. Soc., AAAS, Nat. Sci. Tchrs. Assn., D.A.R., League Women Voters, Ga. Conservancy. Author: Laboratory Text in General Chemistry, 1957, rev. edit., 1959, Editor: Merrimac Valley Elementary Sci. Newsletter, 1970-71, W. Ga. Energy Tech. Newsletter, 1977-78.

KLEEMAN, FRANCIS SIDNEY, cons. environmental and chem. engr.; b. Springfield, Mo., Jan. 17, 1916; s. Walter E. and Louise S. (Thieme) K.; B.S., Washington U., 1937; M.S., U. Mich., 1940; postgrad. U. Pitts., 1940-43, U. Miami, 1969-70; m. Virginia Ellen Frisinger, Sept. 6, 1941; children—David F., Robert E., Janice E. (Mrs. Gerald E. Kardas). Partner New Castle Foundry Co. (Pa.), 1947-49; pres. Kleeman Alloy & Chem. Co., Havertown, Pa., 1960-67; v.p. engring. Applied Research Labs, Hialeah, Fla., 1968-69; pres. Kleeman Engring., Inc., Ft. Lauderdale, Fla., also v.p. engring. Nalews, Inc., Ft. Lauderdale, 1973—; environmental seminar cons. Broward Community Coll. Civic rep. Mainlands sect., Tamarac, Fla., 1968-69. Fellow Am. Inst. Chemists; mem. Nat. Soc. Profl. Engrs., Fla. Engring. Soc., Am. Soc. Metals, Water Pollution Control Fedn., Air Pollution Control Assn., Am. Foundrymens Soc., Iota Alpha. Contbr. articles profl. jours. Patentee in field. Home: 4300 NW 44th St Fort Lauderdale FL 33319 Office: 404 N Andrews Ave Fort Lauderdale FL 33301

KLEIMAN, LOUIS ALVIN, systems engring. cons.; b. Richmond, Va., Mar. 1, 1945; s. Louis and Lila Arlene (Hilton) K.; S.B., MIT, 1965, S.M., 1966, Sc.D., 1975; 1 son, Louis Chandler. Technician in math. Gen. Electric Co., Syracuse, N.Y., 1963; computer programmer MIT Exptl. Astronomy and Instrumentation Labs., Cambridge, 1963-65; aerospace engr. NASA, Manned Spacecraft Center, Houston, 1964-65, aerospace engr. Electronics Research Center, Cambridge, 1965-70; chief Office of Beacon Systems Programs, U.S. Dept. Transp., Transp. Systems Center, Cambridge, 1970-75; dir. S. Ross & Co., Washington, 1975-77; tech. dir. H.H. Aerospace Design Co., Inc., Washington, 1977—; teaching asst. MIT Dept. Aeronautics and Astronautics, 1968-72; cons. in fields of air traffic control and computer simulation. MIT scholar, 1962-65; Rosamond Gifford Community scholar, 1962-65; recipient Apollo Achievement award, NASA, 1970. Mem. IEEE, AIAA, Sigma Xi. Editor, Project Icarus, 1968; contbr. articles in field to profl. jours. Home: 9620 Cinnamon Creek Dr Vienna VA 22180

KLEIN, BERNARD, publisher, author; b. N.Y.C., Sept. 20, 1921; s. Joseph J. and Anna (Wolfe) K.; B.A., Coll. City N.Y., 1942; m. Betty Stecher, Feb. 17, 1946; children—Cheryl Rona, Barry Todd, Cindy Ann. Founder, pres. U.S. List Co., N.Y.C., 1946—; founder, pres., chief editor B. Klein Publs., Coral Springs, Fla., 1953—. Cons. on direct mail advt. and reference book pub. to pubs. and industry, 1950—. Served with AUS, 1942-45; ETO. Mem. Direct Mail Advt. Assn. Mason. Author: Guide to American Directories, Guide to American Educational Directories, Mail Order Business Directory, Directory of College Media, Directory of Coll. Stores, Ency. of Am. Indian, all pub. biennially, 1954—. Home: 7309 Corkwood Terr Tamarac FL 33321 Office: PO Box 8503 Coral Springs FL 33065

KLEIN, EDWARD LAWRENCE, govt. ofcl.; b. Roscoe, Pa., Feb. 17, 1936; s. Julius Herman and Grace Regina (Carroll) K.; B.S., Pa. State U., 1958, M.S., 1961; M.B.A., Baylor U., 1963; Ph.D., La. State U., 1968; m. Linda Anne Copeland, Aug. 24, 1963; children—Paul, John, Erin, Stephanie. Asst. dist. forester Md. Dept. Forests and Parks, Oakland, 1958-60; teaching and research aide Pa. State U., 1960-61; instr. forestry La. State U., 1963-68; market analyst Northeastern Forest Expt. Sta., U.S. Forest Service, Princeton, W.Va., 1968-69; supr. econs. and mktg. sect., div. forestry, fisheries and wildlife TVA, Norris, Tenn., 1969-73, staff asst. to dir., 1975-77, projects mgr.-wood for energy research, forestry div., 1977—; dir. mfg. Indsl. Wood & Pallet Co., Cleve., 1973-75; cons.; producer TV program on La. plywood industry, 1965. Mem. Soc. Am. Foresters, Forest Products Research Soc. (nat. div. chmn. 1971-72), Xi Sigma Pi. Roman Catholic. Club: K.C. Home: 8528 Andersonville Pike Knoxville TN 37918 Office: TVA Forestry Bldg Norris TN 37828

KLEIN, ELIAS, chemist, sci. research adminstr.; b. Leipzig, Germany, 1924; B.S. in Chemistry, Tulane U., 1951, M.S., 1952, Ph.D. (Am. Cyanamid fellow), 1954. Research chemist So. Regional Research Lab., U.S. Dept. Agr., New Orleans, 1954-58; sr. chemist research dept. Courtaulds N. Am., Inc., Mobile, Ala., 1958-60, sect. head phys. chemistry, 1960-62, mgr. research dept., 1962-64, dir. research and devel., 1964-66; sci. dir. phys. and engring. scis. Lake Pontchartrain Labs., Gulf South Research Inst., New Orleans, 1967-79, v.p. sci., 1980—; adj. prof. chemistry Loyola U., New Orleans, 1972; adj. prof. chem. engring. Tulane U. Mem. Am. Chem. Soc., Am. Assn. Textile Chemists and Colorists, Am. Inst. Chemists, N.Y. Acad. Scis., Am. Soc. Artificial Internal Organs, Sigma Xi, Phi Beta Kappa. Contbr. articles on textiles and indsl. chemistry to profl. jours. Office: PO Box 26518 Gulf South Research Inst New Orleans LA 70186

KLEIN, GARNER FRANKLIN, cardiologist; b. San Pedro, Calif., June 21, 1933; s. John William and Anna Louise (Trietsch) K.; B.A., N. Tex. State U., 1953; M.A., U. Tex., 1956, M.D., 1958; children—Kevin W., Samuel K., Lisa K., Garner Franklin. Intern, U.S. Naval Hosp., Camp Pendleton, Calif., 1958-59; resident, VA Hosp., Dallas and Southwestern Med. Sch., 1962-66; practice medicine specializing in cardiology, Harlingen, Tex., 1966—; cardiologist Valley Diagnostic Clinic, Harlingen, 1966—; dir. coronary care unit Valley Bapt. Hosp., Harlingen, 1967—; dir. cardiac catheterization lab. Valley Bapt. Hosp., 1977—. Served with USN, 1958-62. Diplomate Am. Bd. Internal Medicine. Fellow ACP, Am. Coll. Cardiology; mem. Am. Heart Assn. (pres. elect Tex. 1979—), Tex. Med. Assn., AMA, Am. Fedn. for Clin. Research, Tex. Soc. Internal Medicine, Am. Soc. Internal Medicine, Cameron-Willacy County Med. Soc. (pres. 1978), Sigma Xi, Alpha Omega Alpha. Home: PO Box 2306 Harlingen TX 78550 Office: 2121 Pease St Harlingen TX 78550

KLEIN, GEORGE CHARLES, microbiologist; b. Westfield, N.J., Feb. 17, 1922; s. Charles Henry and Guenne (Tinsley) K.; student So. Meth. U., 1939; B.A., U. Tex., Austin, 1943; M.S., U. Tex., Austin, 1957; m. Dorothy Patricia Jones, Sept. 1, 1973; children—Kimberly Anne, Steven Gray. Bacteriologist, Tex. State Dept. Health, Austin, 1943-48, Communicable Disease Center, Atlanta, 1948-55; instr. dept. biology Southwestern U., Georgetown, Tex., 1956-57; bacteriologist VA Hosp., McKinney, Tex., 1958-60; research biologist VA Hosp., Oklahoma City, 1960-62; microbiologist Center Disease Control, Atlanta, 1962-66; research microbiologist, 1966-75; chief immunodiagnostic lab. Center Disease Control, Atlanta, 1975—. Served with USPHS, 1949-55. Mem. Am. Soc. Microbiology, Sigma Xi, Ga. Herpetological Soc. Episcopalian. Contbr. articles to profl. jours. Home: 4567 Westhampton Dr Tucker GA 30084 Office: Center for Disease Control Atlanta GA 30333

KLEIN, LOUIS SAMUEL, accountant; b. Chgo., Sept. 13, 1908; s. Joseph and Lena (Groveman) K.; C.P.A., U. N.Y., 1946; m. Syd Bass, June 2, 1934; children—Letty Sandra, Adele Phyllis, Walter Jay. Acct., auditor Federated Purchaser, Inc., N.Y.C., 1932-35; comptroller, acct. Ala. Braid & Ribbon Co., C. M. Offray & Son, Gadsden, 1935-37; practicing C.P.A., 1937—; partner Bloomberg, Max, Louis S. Klein & Co., Gadsden, Klein, Harwood & Lambert, now partner Cherry, Bekaert & Holland; pres., dir. Comml. & Financial Corp.; pres. Klein & Assos.; mng. gen. partner Comml. & Financial Co. Ltd. Auditor, Gadsden Concert Assn., 1961-72, 77—; mem. Jewish Welfare Bd. Etowah County. Mem. C. of C., N.Y., Ala. (past v.p., chmn. Gadsden-Anniston chpt., past mem. state council) socs. C.P.A.'s, Am. Inst. C.P.A.'s, Am., So. insts. mgmt., Am. Accounting Assn., B'nai B'rith, Coosa Lodge (past pres.). Mem. Beth Israel Temple (past pres.). Club: Civitan Internat. (past pres., lt. gov.). Home: 102 Cleveland Ct Gadsden AL 35901 Office: 228 S 6th St Gadsden AL 35902

KLEIN, PAUL ANTHONY, mfg. co. exec.; b. San Antonio, Tex., Apr. 11, 1945; s. James Hooks and Francis Lucille (Wildenthal) K.; student Lee Coll., 1963-65; m. Barbara Lee Lotz, Feb. 28, 1964; children—Donna Francene, Deborah Lee, Paul Anthony. With Southwest Chem. & Plastic Co., Seabrook, Tex., 1966—, unit mgr., 1976-79, prodn. mgr. New Crockett, 1979—. Mem. parish council steering com., fin. com., bldg. com. St. Johns Roman Catholic Ch., Baytown, Tex., also youth minister and dir. Cath. Youth Orgn. Clubs: Optimist, K.C. Home: Martin Lake Grapeland TX 75844 Office: PO Box 331 Crockett TX 75835

KLEIN, RICHARD PAUL, businessman, rancher; b. Amarillo, Tex., May 4, 1943; s. Eugene H. and Ruth Margret (Lefforge) K.; student Tex. Tech. U., 1961-63, U. Tex., 1963-64; m. Frances Whittenburg, Dec. 26, 1963; children—Gladys Kimberley, Paul Coble. Rancher, Amarillo, 1964—; partner oil drilling bus., Amarillo, 1976—; pres. State Chem. Co., Amarillo, also dir.; chmn. bd. Stirrup Corp. Mem. Tex., Southwestern cattle raisers assns., Panhandle Livestock Assn. (past pres.) Amarillo C. of C. (chmn. aviation com.), Tri-State Fair Bd. Presbyterian. Home: 1702 N Julian Amarillo TX 79105 Office: Box 2411 Amarillo TX 79105

KLEIN, ROBERT EDWARD, physician; b. Huntington, W.Va., Nov. 19, 1923; s. Harvey S. and Hannah (Yingling) K.; B.S., Marshall Coll., 1947; M.D., Wake Forest Coll., 1951; m. Ruth Maxine Knight, Sept. 9, 1949; children—Sandra Elaine, Stephen Robert. Intern in surgery Vanderbilt U. Hosp., Nashville, 1951-52; asst. resident N.C. Baptist Hosp., Winston-Salem, N.C., 1953-54, fellow in pathology, 1954-55, resident in pathology, 1955-56; pathologist Alachua Gen. Hosp., Gainesville, Fla., 1959-77, dir. labs, 1959-77; individual practice medicine specializing in pathology, Concord, N.C., 1957-58, Gainesville, 1958-77; dir. New Orleans Blood Bank, 1977-79; dir. Blood Center SE La., 1979—, staff Coll. Medicine, U. Fla., Gainesville, 1958-60; instr. pathology Bowman Gray Sch. Med., Winston-Salem, 1956-57, U. Fla., 1958-61, clin. prof., 1971-77; bd. dirs. Fla. Assn. Blood Banks, pres., 1961; bd. dirs. Am. Assn. Blood Banks, 1962-64, pres., 1964-65; ann. lectr. S. Central Assn. Blood Banks, 1979. Served with AUS, 1943-46. Decorated Purple Heart; recipient John Elliot Meml. award Am. Assn. Blood Banks, 1977. Fellow Am. Soc. Clin. Pathologists, Coll. Am. Pathologists. Baptist. Contbr. articles to profl. jours. Home: 212 E Gatehouse Dr Metairie LA 70001 Office: 312 S Galvez St New Orleans LA 70119

KLEIN, RONALD DEAN, educator; b. Plainfield, Ind., Aug. 28, 1931; s. Herbert Albert and Vesta May (Hise) K.; M.B.A., Ga. State U., 1972, postgrad., 1975-80; m. Edith Elaine Lipstraw, Oct. 29, 1955; children—Eileen Cheryl, William Lawrence, Rebecca Ann. Data analyst and programmer Inst. for Systems Analysis, U. Mich., Ann Arbor, 1955-60; project scientist Stanford Research Inst., Menlo Park, Calif., 1960-67; mgr. applied tech. Mellonics div. Litton Industries, Sunnyvale, Calif., 1967-72; v.p. for eastern ops. Ops. Research Assos., Palo Alto, Calif., 1972-74; asst. prof. mgmt. Columbus Coll., U. Ga. System, 1974—; adj. prof. Am. U., Ft. Benning Campus, 1968-70; cons. to various corps. Mem. Inst. for Mgmt. Sci., Ops. Research Soc. Am., Mil. Ops. Research Soc., Am. Inst. for Decision Scis., Assn. for Bus. Simulation and Experiential Learning, Assn. U.S. Army. Lutheran. Contbr. articles to profl. jours. Home: 3437 Tomahawk Dr Columbus GA 31907 Office: Columbus Coll Columbus GA 31907

KLEIN, RONALD LLOYD, elec. engr., educator; b. Bloomington, Ill., Apr. 26, 1939; s. Frank Samuel and Lila Mabel (Sharp) K.; B.S., U. Ill., 1962, M.S., 1963; Ph.D. in E.E., U. Iowa, 1969; m. Nancy Ann Jones, Aug. 20, 1961; children—Laura, Karla. Mem. tech. staff Bell Tel. Labs., North Andover, Mass., 1963-67; elec. engr. Ill. Bell Tel. Co., Chgo., 1967; asst. prof. U. Kans., 1969-74, asso. prof., 1974-78, prof. elec. engring., 1978-79; prof. elec. engring., chmn. dept. W.Va. U., Morgantown, 1979—. U.S. Air Force Research grantee, 1975-77; NSF Research grantee, 1973-75. Mem. IEEE. Author: Modern Linear Systems, 1979. Contbr. articles to tech. jours. Home: 124 Poplar Dr Baker's Ridge Morgantown WV 26505 Office: Room 825 Engring Scis West Virginia Univ Morgantown WV 26506

KLEINE, GLEN ALBERT WILLIAM, educator; b. St. Louis, Sept. 12, 1936; s. Erwin G. and Veneta Della (Gebhardt) K.; B.S., U. Mo., 1957, M.A., 1959; Ed.S., Eastern Ky. U., 1973; m. Joan Kay Johnson, Aug. 29, 1960; children—Kevin Dale, Keith Dee, Kris David. Tchr. journalism Mehlville Schs., St. Louis, 1959-65; ednl. cons. St. Louis Post-Dispatch, 1965-66; exec. dir. Met. Service Assn., St. Louis, 1966-67; asst. prof. dept. mass communications Eastern Ky. U., Richmond, 1967—; asst. dir. Taft Seminar, 1977—; cons. Ky. Dept. Transp., 1974, SE U.S. Solar Project. Chmn. pub. relations and manpower Kit Carson dist. Boy Scouts Am., 1976-77; mem. photography com. Ky. 4-H, 1976-77; mem. cultural facilities subcom. St. Louis Bond Issue Screening Com., 1966; del. Mo. Republican Conv., 1964. Served with U.S. Army, 1955-61. Am. Newspaper Pubs. Assn. grantee, 1964; Wall St. Jour. scholar, 1960; recipient Excellence in Teaching award Eastern Ky. U., 1974; Presdl. citation Nat. Council Coll. Publs. Advisers, 1973, others. Mem. Ky. Council Edn. Journalism, Nat. Council Coll. Publs. Advisers, NEA, Phi Delta Kappa. Episcopalian. Editor Coll. Press Rev., 1970-72; contbg. editor Photolith Mag., 1969—. Home: 64 Frankie Dr Deacon Hills Richmond KY 40475 Office: Box 500 Eastern Ky Univ Richmond KY 40475

KLEINER, JANELLYN PICKERING, librarian; b. Harrisburg, Ill., Dec. 9, 1936; d. Herschel Laurence and Hester Perle (Rutherford) Pickering; B.A., La. State U., 1958; M.S.L.S., 1965, M.A., 1974; m. Arthur Anthony Kleiner, Aug. 22, 1959 (div. 1972); 1 son, Mark Laurence. Police reporter, criminal cts. reporter Baton Rouge Morning Advocate, 1958-60; copywriter James E. Hundemer Assos., Baton Rouge, 1960, 62-63; asst. circulation librarian La. State U., 1965, chief circulation librarian, 1966-67, asst. documents librarian, 1967-68, info. desk librarian, 1968, head interlibrary loan dept., 1968-78, central reference librarian, 1978—; faculty senator La. State U., 1977—, exec. bd., 1978—. Publs. dir. Baton Rouge Arts and Humanities Council, 1975. Mem. ALA, Nat. Assn. Coop. Library Orgns., Southwestern (past editor), La. library assns., La. Real Estate Assn., Phi Kappa Phi, Theta Sigma Phi, Beta Phi Mu, Delta Gamma Alumnae Assn. Democrat. Methodist. Club: Baton Rouge Press. Home: 5357 Bennington Ave Baton Rouge LA 70808 Office: La State U Library Baton Rouge LA 70803

KLEINHANS, ROBERT BURTON, ret. educator, painter; b. Reynoldsville, Pa., Nov. 22, 1907; s. Louis D. and Mary Jane (Copping) K.; A.B., Western Res. U., 1931, M.A., 1933, postgrad., 1933-34; student Rutgers U., 1957-59, U. Fla., 1946, Pratt Inst., 1960, St. Peter's Coll., 1963-66; m. May B. Hummer, July 30, 1937; children—Theda Mae Kleinhans Reichman, Roberta Rae Kleinhans Bryan, Beverly Jane Kleinhans Dollner, Ellen Claire Kleinhans Buck. Asst. in biology Western Res. U., Cleve., 1931-34; instr. biology

Athens Coll. (Greece), 1934-36, head description dept. Am. Gas Assn., Cleve., 1937-41; exec. sec. Allied Mission Observing Greek Elections, Island of Crete, 1946; asst. prof. biology Rollins Coll., Winter Park, Fla. and dir. Thomas R. Baker Mus., 1946-48; prof. biology Xavier U., Cin., 1948-52; head sci. dept. N. Plainfield (N.J.) High Sch., 1957-58; research chemist Internat. Nickel Ltd., Bayonne, N.J., summer 1958; instr. chemistry and biology Union County (N.J.) regional high schs., 1958-74; one-man shows of paintings (under name of Petitjean) include: Wilshire Fed. Gallery, Los Angeles, 1967, Penny-Owsley Salon, Los Angeles, 1969; group shows include: Carter Gallery, Aiea, Hawaii, Makai Art Village, Lihue, Hawaii, Skyline Gallery, Killeen, Tex., Mall Gallery, London; represented in permanent collections U.S., Europe including: Deutscher Klub, Clark, N.J., Athens Coll., also pvt. collections; instr. pastel painting L'ecole Petitjean, Clermont, Fla., 1974—. Served as lt. comdr. USNR, 1940-46. Recipient numerous awards including Blue Ribbon award Leavenworth Plaza Art Show, 1970, Fla. Fedn. Art, 1976. Mem. So. Lake Art League, Fla. Fedn. Art, Clermont, Philosophy Club, Ret. Officers Assn. Club: Kiwanis. Contbg. editor to Gallery mag., 1975-76. Address: 1723 Disston Ave Clermont FL 32711

KLEMEK, GARY MICHAEL, shopping center adminstr.; b. Paterson, N.J., May 10, 1946; s. Michael Walter and Bertha Helen (Babin) K.; B.S., Widener Coll., 1968, B.A., 1968; grad. Naval Officers Candidate Sch., 1968, Navy Mess Mgmt. Sch., 1970; postgrad. Internat. Council Shopping Centers Mgmt. Sch., 1973, 74; m. Joan Ellen Briggs, July 13, 1968; children—Christopher Briggs, Courtney Briggs. Food service dir. Loyola U., New Orleans, 1969-70; gen. mgr. Laffaits Restaurant, Alpert Corp., Jacksonville, Fla., 1970-71, gen. mgr. Forum 303, Ltd., Shopping Center, Arlington, Tex., 1971—; v.p. Alpert Investment Corp., 1975—; pres. Forum Fair Inc., Arlington, 1978—. Mem. adv. bd. distributive edn. Sam Houston High Sch., Arlington, 1973-74; cons. in ice rink constrn., mgmt. Mem. consumer ethics com. Arlington YMCA, 1972—. Served to lt. USNR, 1968-77. Mem. Hotel Sales Mgmt. Assn., Internat. Council of Shopping Centers, Ice Skating Inst. Am., Arlington C. of C., Theta Chi. Club: Young Men of Arlington. Home: 2811 Marquis Circle E Arlington TX 76016 Office: 2900 E Pioneer Pkwy Arlington TX 76010

KLEPPEL, JERRY WAYNE, social worker; b. Hickory, N.C., Jan. 28, 1940; s. Herman Hugo and Martha Sue (Ivey) K.; B.A. in Bus. Adminstrn. and Psychology, Pfeiffer Coll., 1962; M.S.W., U. N.C., Chapel Hill, 1967; m. Emily Claire Blackwell, June 2, 1967; 1 son, Eric Michael. Supr., Dept. Social Services, Concord, N.C., 1967-69; family therapist Family and Children Services, Charlotte, N.C., 1969-72; social work services dir. Winthrop Coll. Family Edn. Program, Rock Hill, S.C., 1972-73; services coordinator Catawba Center Mental Health, Rock Hill, 1973—; instr. Winthrop Coll. Bd. dirs. St. John's Methodist Ch., Girls Home, 1974-79, chmn. program com., 1975-76; active Mental Health Assn., 1973-79, Child Abuse Council, 1975. Served with Air NG, 1963-69. Mem. Nat. Assn. Social Workers (chmn. local unit), Council Family Relations (past treas.), Acad. Cert. Social Workers (cert.). Democrat. Clubs: Optimist, Masons. Home: 420 Barksdale Ct Rock Hill SC 29730 Office: 166 Dotson St Rock Hill SC 29730

KLEVANOSKY, CLYDE STANLEY, systems cons.; b. Rockville Center, N.Y., Apr. 10, 1953; s. Stanley William and Helen K.; A.A.S. in Data Processing, Nassau Community Coll., 1973; B.S. in Computer Sci. and Acctg., Hofstra U., 1975; m. Paula A. Bartlewitz, June 14, 1975. Account exec. Parity Systems Corp., Huntington, N.Y., 1971-75; product line mgr. Electronic Data Systems Corp., Dallas, 1975-79; exec. systems cons. Nat. CSS, Inc., Dallas, 1979—. Mem. Am. Mgmt. Assn. Roman Catholic. Office: 4835 LBJ Freeway Dallas TX 75234

KLEY, JOHN ARTHUR, ret. banker; b. Jericho, N.Y., Oct. 24, 1921; s. John and Annie (Upton) K.; grad. Stonier Sch. Banking, Rutgers U., 1952; B.P.S., Pace U., 1974; m. Florence Elizabeth Cannon, Sept. 1, 1945; 1 dau., Martha Anne. With Washington Irving Trust Co. and successor County Trust Co., White Plains, N.Y., 1937-76, asst. treas., asst. v.p., v.p., 1951-57, exec. v.p., 1957-60, pres., 1960-72, chmn. bd., 1972-76, also dir.; vice-chmn., dir. Bank of N.Y. Co., N.Y.C., 1969-76, also dir.; chmn. bd. County Trust region Bank of N.Y., 1976-77; vice chmn. bd. Bank of N.Y., 1976-77. Trustee emeritus Westchester Community Coll., chmn., 1968-71; past chmn. bd. regents Stonier Grad. Sch. Banking. Served from pvt. to lt. col. AC, U.S. Army, 1942-46. Recipient Leffingwell medal, 1960. Mem. Nat. Office Mgmt. Assn. (life hon.). Episcopalian. Clubs: Imperial Golf (Naples, Fla.); Whippoorwill. Home: Apt 102 1900 Gulf Shore Blvd N Naples FL 33940

KLIEWER, WILLIAM PHILIP, ins. and real estate agy. exec.; b. Weatherford, Okla., Feb. 13, 1950; s. William Gerald and Ollie Fern (De Cou) K.; B.S. in Econ., Nicholls State U., 1972; M.S. in Mgmt., Am. Tech. U., 1979; m. Mary Helen Bigham, Dec. 23, 1976. Partner, Bigham Ins. and Real Estate Agy., Killeen, Tex., 1978—. Pres., Killeen Downtown, Inc., 1979. Served with U.S. Army, 1972-77. Mem. Assn. U.S. Army (chpt. v.p. 1979—), Greater Killeen C. of C. (com. chmn. 1979—), Ind. Ins. Agts. Am., Ind. Ins. Agts. Tex., Greater Killeen Life Underwriters Assn., Nat. Assn. Realtors, Tex. Assn. Realtors, Ft. Hood Area Bd. Realtors, Ind. Ins. Agts. of Central Tex. (pres. 1980). Democrat. Christian Ch. Club: Cen-Texan Kiwanis (dir. 1978-80). Home: 1005 Mary Jane Ct Killeen TX 76541 Office: PO Box 996 807 N 8 St Killeen TX 76541

KLINE, DAVID GELLINGER, educator; b. Phila., Oct. 13, 1934; s. David Francis and Lois Ann (Gellinger) K.; A.B. in Chemistry, U. Pa., 1956, M.D., 1960. Intern, U. Mich., Ann Arbor, 1960-61, resident in gen. surgery, 1961-62, teaching asso. in neurosurgery, 1964-67; research investigator Walter Reed Army Inst. Research and Walter Reed Gen. Hosp., 1962-64; instr. La. State U. Med. Sch., New Orleans, 1967-68, asst. prof., 1968-70, asso. prof., 1970-73, chmn. neurosurgery, 1971—, prof., 1973—, chmn. dept., 1976—. Cons., USPHS Health Center Hosp., New Orleans VA Hosp., Keesler Air Force Base Hosp.; vis. investigator Delta Regional Primate Center, Covington, La. Bd. mem. Dana G. How Social Service Fund. Served with M.C. U.S. Army, 1962-64. Recipient Frederick Coller Surg. prize, 1967; numerous grants. Diplomate Am. Bd. Neurologic Surgery (sec.-treas.). Mem. Am. Acad. Neurol. Surgery, Soc. Neurol. Surgeons, Am. Assn. Neurol. Surgeons, Soc. U. Neurosurgeons, Assn. Acad. Surgery, Soc. Univ. Surgeons, A.C.S., Phi Beta Kappa, Kappa Sigma, Phi Chi, others. Episcopalian (lay reader, vestryman). Contbr. articles to sci. jours., chpts. to med. books, also on editorial bds. surg. jours. Home: 46 Thrasher St New Orleans LA 70124

KLINE, DONALD CRAIG, JR., hosp. adminstr.; b. Detroit, June 10, 1929; s. Donald Craig and Martha (Baggott) K.; student U. Miami (Fla.), 1952-53, U. Mich., 1953-54; m. Raynelle Crocker, Oct. 8, 1950; children—Donald Craig, Mark Gregory, Todd Elliot, Susan Lynne. Asst. tab operator Citizens Mut. Auto Ins. Co., Howell, Mich., 1955-57; asst. supr. IBM dept. King-Seeley Corp., Ann Arbor, Mich., 1957-59; data processing mgr. Buhr Machine Tool Co., Ann Arbor, 1959-61; data processing supr. Jackson Hosp. and Clinic, Montgomery, Ala., 1962-66, controller, 1966-74, personnel dir., 1969—; sec.-treas. Small World, Inc., Montgomery, 1972—. Served with USAF, 1948-52. Mem. Hosp. Fin. Mgmt. Assn. (advanced), Am. Soc. for Personnel Adminstrn., Montgomery Area Personnel Assn., Ala. Soc. Hosp. Personnel Adminstrs. Presbyterian. Home: 4612 Fox Hollow Circle Montgomery AL 36109 Office: 1235 Forest Ave Montgomery AL 36106

KLINE, EUGENE ARDEN, chemist; b. Troy, N.Y., Aug. 15, 1940; s. Maurice Montgomery and Hazel Elouise (Campbell) K.; B.A., Allegheny Coll., 1962; M.S., U. No. Iowa, 1969; Ph.D., Iowa State U., 1973; m. Ruth Ann Kerr, Aug. 17, 1962; 1 dau., Natalie Joan. Tchr. chemistry Phillipsburg (N.J.) High Sch., 1962-67; teaching asst. Iowa State U., 1968-73; asso. prof. chemistry Tenn. Tech. U., 1973—; participant NSF Acad. Yr. Inst., U. No. Iowa, 1967; Asso. Western Univs. faculty participant Grand Forks Energy Tech. Center Lignite Coal Research, 1978, 79. Recipient Outstanding Tchr. award Iowa State U., 1973. Mem. NEA, Tenn. Edn. Assn., Am. Chem. Soc., Tenn. Acad. Sci. (chmn. sect. chemistry 1978-79), Wesley Found. (v.p. bd. 1978, pres. bd. 1979). Methodist. Clubs: Masons; Lions (Cookeville). Home: 1491 Hillsdale Dr Cookeville TN 38501 Office: Foster Hall 222 Dept Chemistry Tenn Tech U Cookeville TN 38501

KLINE, HARRY BYRD, pub. speaker agy. exec.; b. Nevada, Mo.; s. George W. and Bonnie M. (Garrett) K.; B.A., Phillips U., 1920, B.S. in Speech, 1922; m. Marian K. Shimeall, Aug. 15, 1923 (dec. Feb. 1968); children—Jerome W., Madelyn K.; m. 2d, Dorothy Champlin May, Nov. 26, 1968. Tchr. high sch., Enid, Okla., 1922-23; Minister First Christian Ch., Hobart, Okla., 1924-25, Port Arthur, Tex., 1926-29; dir. Little Theatre, Port Arthur, Tex., 1926-29; owner, dir. So. Sch. Assemblies, Dallas, 1930-57, Harry Byrd Kline Celebrity Service, Dallas, 1957—; developer Flamingo Bay retirement village, Pine Island, Fla., 1960-68. Pres. Laymen's League of Tex. Christian Chs., 1948-51. Mem. Internat. Platform Assn. (life, pres. 1951-52, Outstanding Service award 1958, 70), Greater Pine Island C. of C. (pres. 1962, 64, 66), SAR, Tex. Farm Bur. Mem. Christian Ch. Home: 5516 Williamstown Rd Dallas TX 75230

KLINE, IRVING BERTHOLD, automobile sales exec.; b. Balt., May 20, 1894; s. Jacob D. and Amelia (Schoolherr) K.; ed. Friends Quaker Sch., Balt. City Coll.; m. Isabelle Hofflin, Oct. 8, 1925; children—Richard Hofflin, James Martin. Owner, propr. Kline Motor Co., Ford dealer, Balt., 1916-17, Kline Chevrolet Sales Corp., Chesapeake, Va., 1925—; dir. Hewett Chevrolet, Myrtle Beach, S.C., 1971—; past pres. Consolvo Tent Co. Mem. Gen. Motors Dealer Planning Com. Mem. OPA Bd., 1941-45; capt. Norfolk Aux. Fire Dept., 1941-45; founder, past pres. Norfolk Safety Council, Norfolk Traffic Ct., Tidewater Better Bus. Bur., Norfolk Citizens Emergency Com.; mem. Nat. Safety Council, Pres.' Hwy Safety Com., Va. Traffic Safety Study Commn., Gov.'s Hwy. Safety Com. Bd. dirs. DePaul Hosp., Easter Seal Soc., Am. Humane Soc.; pres. Soc. for Prevention Cruelty to Animals; bd. dirs. Tidewater Multiple Sclerosis Assn. Served with USNR, 1918-20. Recipient Time Mag. Quality Dealer award, 1971; Distinguished Service citation Nat. Auto Dealers, 1966. Mem. Tidewater Automobile Assn. (1st pres., dir.), Va., Norfolk Retail Mchts. Assn. (dir.), Norfolk-Portsmouth Auto Dealers Assn. (past pres.), Va. Dealers Assn. Friends of Myer House, Chrysler Mus., Am. Legion, Fraternal Order Police Assn. (Outstanding Citizen award 1953), Norfolk Dog Tng. Club, Saints and Sinners (past pres.). Mason, Kiwanian (camp dir.). Clubs: Greenbrier Saddle (founder, past pres.) (Chesapeake, Va.); Commodore Country (Virginia Beach, Va.). Home: 1440 Kline Dr Virginia Beach VA 23452 Office: 1495 S Military Hwy Chesapeake VA 23320

KLINE, JACOB, educator; b. Boston, Aug. 3, 1917; s. Joseph and Jennie (Goldman) K.; B.S., Mass. Inst. Tech., 1942, M.S., 1951; Ph.D. (NSF fellow), Iowa State U., 1962; m. Barbara Fine, Dec. 22, 1957; children—David, Jonathan, Pamela. Electronics engr. ITT, Newark, 1942-46; chief viedeo sect., optical research lab. Boston U., 1946-48; research asst. Mass. Inst. Tech., Cambridge, 1948-51, research engr., 1951-52; mem. faculty U. R.I., Kingston, 1952-66, asso. prof. engring. elec., 1956-60, dir. biomed. engring. program, 1962-66; prof., dir. biomed. engring. program U. Miami, Coral Gables, Fla., 1966—; cons. Boston Psychiat. Hosp., Tufts Coll. Dental Sch., Boston, Mass. Mental Health Center, Boston, Cable Electric Corp., Providence, South Miami Hosp., Venice (Fla.) Hosp., St. Francis Hosp., Miami Beach, Leviton Mfg. Co., Bklyn., others. NASA/Am. Soc. Engring. Edn. fellow, summers 1965, 66. Mem. IEEE (dir. 1943—), Am. Soc. Artificial Organs, Am. Assn. Advancement Med. Instrumentation. Contbr. to profl. jours. Patentee myocardial prosthetic device. Home: 1445 Trillo Ave Coral Gables FL 33146 Office: Dept Biomedical Engineering Univ Miami Coral Gables FL 33124

KLINE, JAMES MARTIN, physicist; b. Dayton, Ohio, Mar. 4, 1926; s. Wilbur Martin and Wilhelmina Agnes (Boedigheimer) K.; B.S.M.E., U. Cin., 1949, M.S., 1951; Ph.D., U. Ky., 1964; m. Helen Godat, Aug. 25, 1956; children—Tricia Lynn, Martin Godat. Asst. prof. physics U. Miss., 1955-58; research asst., instr. U. Ky., 1958-61; asso. prof. physics and astronomy Murray (Ky.) State U., 1964-65, prof., 1965-79, chmn. dept. physics and astronomy, 1970-75; supr. design Tideland Signal Corp., Houston, 1980—; asso. dir. NSF Sci. Insts., 1970-72; mem. grant rev. panel NSF, 1977. Bd. dirs. Murray Civic Music Assn., 1965-79; elder 1st Presbyterian Ch., Murray. Served with USNR, 1944-46, 51-53; PTO, CBI. Am. Cancer Soc. fellow, 1950—; Danforth asso., 1970—. Mem. Am. Phys. Soc., N.Y. Acad. Sci., Sigma Xi, Omicron Delta Kappa, Alpha Chi, Sigma Pi Sigma, Alpha Lambda Delta, Phi Mu Alpha. Contbr. articles to profl. jours. Office: 4310 Directors Row Houston TX 77052

KLINE, JOHN ALVIN, communications cons., educator; b. Marshalltown, Iowa, July 24, 1939; B.S. in English and Speech Edn., Iowa State U., 1967; M.A. (NDEA fellow) in Speech Communication, U. Iowa, 1968, Ph.D. (NDEA fellow), 1970; m. Ann Louise Henry, Dec. 14, 1975; 1 dau., Teri. Asst. prof. speech communication U. N.Mex., Albuquerque, 1970-71; asso. prof. U. Mo., 1971-75, dir. grad. studies in speech, theatre and broadcasting, 1971-75; adv. to comdt., acad. instr. Fgn. Officer Sch., Air U., Maxwell AFB, Ala., 1975—, lectr. and dir. workshops in communication and curriculum Air Command and Staff Coll., Squadron Officer Sch., Air U., 1975—; adj. prof. speech communication Auburn U., Montgomery, Ala., 1977—; guest lectr., condr. workshops various profl. assns., colls. and mil. schs., 1975—. Mem. Internat. Communication Assn., So. Speech Communcation Assn., Speech Communication Assn., Ala. Speech Communication Assn., Phi Delta Kappa, Phi Kappa Phi. Baptist. Author: (with Bill Eadie) Orientations to Interpersonal Communication, 1976; contbr. articles on speech communication to profl. jours. Home: 3415 N Water Mill Rd Montgomery AL 36116 Office: AIFOS/CAK Maxwell AFB AL 36112

KLINGBIEL, PAUL HERMAN, cons.; b. Watertown, Wis., Nov. 3, 1919; s. Herman Carl and Elsa Helen (Zilisch) K.; Ph.B., U. Chgo., 1948, B.S., 1950; M.A., Am. U., 1966; m. Mildred Louise Wells, Nov. 30, 1968; stepchildren—Alice J. Lawson, Jo Ann Lawson. Abstractor, Armed Services Tech. Info. Agy., DOD, Washington, 1953-58, editor Tech. Abstract Bull., 1958-60, dir. Office of Lexicography, 1960-66; phys. sci. adminstr., linguistics research Def. Documentation Center, 1966-79; sr. cons. Aspen Systems Corp., 1979—; lectr. Am. U., Washington, 1966-69. Cons. div. med. scis. Nat. Acad. Scis., 1969-70. Served with AUS, 1943-46. Recipient Meritorious Civilian Service award, 1974, Disting. Career award, 1979. Mem. Linguistic Soc. Am., Assn. Computational Linguistics, Am. Soc. Info. Sci. Lutheran. Contbr. articles to profl. jours. Research in field of computers. Home: 7480 Jayhawk St Annandale VA 22003 Office: 1600 Research Blvd Rockville MD 20850

KLINGER, ARTHUR RUSSELL, engr.; b. Chgo., June 3, 1937; s. John Bernard and Edith Marie (Ives) K.; B.S. with honors, Clemson U., 1959; postgrad. U. Wis., 1959-60; M.S. cum laude, Fla. Technol. U., 1973; Asso. Applied Sci., Community Coll. of Air Force, 1977; m. Cynthia Elizabeth Martin, July 10, 1962; children—Alicia E., John R., David M. Asst. physics lab. instr. Clemson U., 1957-58; commd. 2d lt. USAF, 1959, advanced through grades to maj., 1970; weather forecaster Donaldson AFB, Greenville, S.C., Kindley AFB, Bermuda, 1959-63; staff weather officer Shaw AFB, Sumter, S.C., 1963-65; instr., squadron tng. officer USAF Officer Tng. Sch., San Antonio, 1965-69; detachment comdr., staff weather officer McCoy AFB, Orlando, Fla., 1970-74; biomed. equipment technician Med. Equipment Repair Center, Sheppard AFB, Wichita Falls, Tex., 1974-77, chmn. new equipment br., 1978-79; chief biomed. equipment maintenance br., detachment 119, Izmir, Turkey, 1977-78; pres. Klinger Electrodynamics, 1974-79; supt. process engring. Cryovac div. W.R. Grace, Iowa Park, Tex., 1979—; freelance tech. writer, cons., 1970—. Mem. Soc. Biomed. Equipment Technicians, Tau Beta Pi, Alpha Zeta. Democrat. Episcopalian. Contbr. articles on electronics and safety to profl. jours. Home: 4659 Balboa Dr Wichita Falls TX 76310

KLINTWORTH, GORDON KENNETH, pathologist, educator; b. Fort Victoria, Rhodesia, Aug. 4, 1932; s. John George and Iveagh Irene (Gordon) K.; came to U.S., 1962, naturalized, 1967; B.Sc., U. Witwatersrand, South Africa, 1954, M.B., B.Ch., 1957, B.Sc. with honors, 1961, Ph.D., 1966; m. Felicity Helen Tait, Dec. 14, 1957; children—Susan, John, Sandra. Intern, resident Johannesburg (S. Africa) Gen. Hosp.; faculty Duke, 1964—, prof. pathology, 1973—. Vis. prof. U. London Inst. Ophthalmology, 1970. Victor Kark scholar, 1961-62; USPHS fellow, 1962-64; Louis B. Mayer scholar, 1972-73. Recipient Research Career Devel. award Nat. Eye Inst., 1971-76. Diplomate Am. Bd. Pathology. Mem. Am. Soc. Exptl. Pathology, Am. Assn. Pathologists and Bacteriologists, Internat. Soc. Neuropathologists, N.Y. Acad. Sci., Internat. Acad. Pathology, Am. Assn. Neuropathologists, AAAS, Am. Acad. Neurology, Assn. for Research in Vision and Ophthalmology, Eastern Ophthalmic Pathology Soc., Nat. Geog. Soc., Sigma Xi. Author: (with B.F. Fetter, W.S. Hendry) Mycoses of the Central Nervous System, 1967; (with M.B. Landers, III) The Eye: Structure and Function in Disease. Contbr. articles to med. jours. Home: 2718 Spencer St Durham NC 27706

KLOCK, JOSEPH PETER, JR., lawyer; b. Phila., Mar. 14, 1949; s. Joseph Peter and Mary Dorothy (Fornace) K.; B.A., LaSalle Coll., 1970; J.D., U. Miami (Fla.), 1973; m. Susan Marie Girsch, Mar. 17, 1979. Admitted to Fla. bar, 1973, since practiced in Miami; partner firm Steel, Hector & Davis, 1977—; adj. prof. U. Miami Law Sch., 1974—. Bd. dirs. YMCA Camp Fla., 1974-79. Mem. Am. Bar Assn., Fla. Bar (chmn. civil procedure rules com. 1979—), Pa. Bar Assn., D.C. Bar Assn., Dade County Bar Assn., Iron Arrow Soc., Phi Kappa Phi, Omicron Delta Kappa. Democrat. Roman Catholic. Home: 6600 Maynada St Coral Gables FL 33146 Office: 1400 First Nat Bank Bldg Miami FL 33131

KLOEK, GERRIT PAUL, educator; b. Mpls., Sept. 16, 1940; s. LaDell Arthur and Meriel Helen K.; Ph.D., So. Ill. U., Carbondale, 1972; m. Darlene Susann Wilson, Aug. 14, 1964; children—Andrew, Daniel. Instr. biology So. Ill. U., 1971-72; asst. prof. Ky. State U., Frankfort, 1972-76, asso. prof., 1977—; adv. council environ. edn. Ky. Dept. Edn. NASA grantee, 1974—. Mem. Am. Ornithologists Union, Ky. Acad. Sci. (sec. zoology and entomology sect. 1979, chmn. 1980), Ky. Environ. Edn. Assn., Aerospace Med. Assn., Antique Automobile Assn. Am., Early Ford V-8 Club Am., Sigma Xi. Contbr. articles to profl. jours. Home: 666 Montclair Rd Frankfort KY 40601 Office: Ky State U Dept Biology Frankfort KY 40601

KLOESS, LAWRENCE HERMAN, JR., lawyer; b. Mamaroneck, N.Y., Jan. 30, 1927; s. Lawrence Herman and Harriette Adelia (Holly) K.; A.B., U. Ala., 1954, J.D., 1956; grad. Air Command and Staff Coll., 1974, Air War Coll., 1976, Indsl. Coll. Armed Forces, 1977; m. Eugenia Underwood, Sept. 27, 1952; children—Lawrence H., Price Mentzel, Branch Donelson, David Holly. Served to lt. col. Judge Adv. Gen. Corps U.S. Air Force Res., Maxwell (Ala.) AFB, 1954—; admitted to Ala. bar, 1956, U.S. Dist. Ct. bar, 1956, U.S. Ct. Appeals bar, 1957, U.S. Supreme Ct. bar, 1971, U.S. Ct. Mil. Appeals bar, 1971; individual practice law, Birmingham, Ala., 1956-60, 62-66; corporate counsel Bankers Fire and Marine Ins. Co., Birmingham, 1960-62; dist. counsel U.S. VA, Montgomery, Ala., 1966—. Exec. com. Citizens' Conf. Ala. Cts., Inc., 1973—; mem. Ala. Election Law Commn., 1979-80; vestryman Episcopal Ch. Holy Comforter, Montgomery, 1971-74, del. diocesan conv., 1973; mem. del. assembly United Appeal, 1972-77; adv. bd. Salvation Army, 1980—. Recipient Certificate of Merit Montgomery Area C. of C., 1972, 78; Spl. Achievement award VA, 1973; Outstanding Meritorius Service award Res. Officers Assn. U.S., 1975, named to Brigade of Vols., 1976; Outstanding Alumni award Theta Chi, 1976; Air Force Commendation award, 1973; U.S. Meritorious Ser. award, 1978. Mem. Am., Ala., Montgomery Fed. (pres. 1973), Montgomery County (chmn. bd. dirs. 1977), Birmingham bar assns., Ala. (judge adv. 1977), Montgomery (pres. 1977) res. officers assns., Farrah Law Soc., Sigma Delta Kappa (pres. 1956). Clubs: Montgomery Country, Capital City, Maxwell-Gunter Officers, Rotary (pres. 1979). Contbr. articles to legal jours.; mem. editorial adv. bd. The Ala. Lawyer, 1972—, chmn., 1975-79; editor Montgomery County Bar Jour., 1979. Home: 3174 Highfield Dr Montgomery AL 36111 Office: 234 Aronov Bldg 474 S Court St Montgomery AL 36104

KLONTZ, MARY PAYSINGER (MRS. HAROLD E. KLONTZ), educator, librarian; b. Rock Hill, S.C., Apr. 4, 1918; d. John Benjamin and Annie (Caldwell) Paysinger; B.A., Columbia Coll., 1938; B.S. in L.S., U. N.C., 1943, M.S. in L.S., 1970; M.Ed., Auburn U., 1968; m. Harold Emerson Klontz, June 10, 1944; 1 dau., Florence Anne. Librarian, tchr. pub. schs. of S.C., 1938-44; librarian instr. Sch. Library Sci., U. N.C., 1944-46; librarian Auburn (Ala.) Pub. Library, 1947-49, Horseshoe Bend Regional Library, Dadeville, Ala., 1957-63; library supr. Auburn City Schs., 1963-68; with Learning Resources Center, Sch. Edn., Auburn (Ala.) U., 1969-70, asst. prof. Sch. Edn., 1970-74, also instr., summers 1965-68; coordinator media services Phenix City (Ala.) Pub. Schs., 1974-80. Cons. Khartoum, Sudan, Jan.-Mar. 1962. Trustee Auburn Pub. Library, 1956-63; mem. bd. zoning adjustment, Auburn, 1956-62. Mem. Am., Ala., Southeastern library assns., Am. Assn. U. Women (local pres. 1950-53), Fedn. Women's Clubs (nominating del. 5th dist. 1956-58). Woman's Soc. Christian Service, League Women Voters (chmn. local organizing com. 1956-57, pres. 1959-61), Delta Kappa Gamma (pres. 1974-76), Phi Delta Kappa. Home: 839 Moore's Mill Rd Auburn AL 36830

KLOPMAN, WILLIAM A., mfg. co. exec.; b. 1921; student Williams Coll.; married. With Burlington Industries Inc., 1946—, pres. Klopman Mills div., 1963-71, group v.p. parent co., Greensboro, N.C., 1971-72, exec. v.p., 1972-74, pres., mem. exec. fin. com. and mgmt.

policy com., 1974-76, chmn. bd., pres., chief exec. officer, 1976—, also dir. Served with USN, 1942-45. Office: Burlington Industries Inc 3330 W Friendly Ave Greensboro NC 27410

KLORFEIN, FRUEMA ANNETTE, salesman real estate; b. Boston, Mar. 7, 1931; d. Harry and Thelma (Aborn) Nannis; B.S., Simmons Coll., 1952; postgrad. Tulane U., 1953-55, Harvard U., 1953; m. Elliot H. Klorfein, Aug. 16, 1953; children—Stephen Richard, Tamara Joy, Jonathan Scott. Jr. exec. William Filene & Sons, Boston, 1952-53; tchr., Gretna, La., 1953-54, New Orleans, 1954-55, Miami, 1955-56, Ft. Meade, Md., 1956, Armed Forces Sch., Kitzingen, W.Ger., 1957-58, Miami, 1958-59; salesman real estate Robert E. List Co., North Palm Beach, Fla., 1970—. Vice-pres. Palm Beach County chpt. Hadassah, 1963-67, pres., 1967-69, mem. regional exec. bd., 1967-71, regional bd. dirs., 1966-71; v.p. B'nai B'rith Palm Beach, 1963-64; bd. dirs. League Women Voters Palm Beach County, 1971, Women's Aux. Palm Beach County Med. Soc., 1964-65, 66-67. Recipient award of merit United Jewish Appeal, 1975, Service award Hadassah, 1966, Presdl. award Hadassah, 1969. Mem. Palm Beach Bd. Realtors. Home: 254 N Woods Rd Palm Beach FL 33480

KLOS, WILLIAM ANTON, elec. engr., educator; b. Houston, Aug. 14, 1936; s. Andrew Anton and Ruth Irene (Walters) K.; B.S. in Mech. Engring. cum laude, U. Houston, 1963, Ph.D. in Elec. Engring. (NASA fellow), 1969; m. Rose Lee O'Bryan, Feb. 3, 1962; 1 son, Vaughn Bryan. Grad. research asst. U. Houston, 1966-69; prin. engr. Lockheed Electronic Co., Houston, 1969-70; asso. prof. elec. engring. U. Southwestern La., Lafayette, 1970-75, prof., 1975—, head dept., 1970—. Pres., PTA, Broussard, La., 1971-72. Served with USAF, 1954-58. Registered profl. engr., La., Tex. Mem. IEEE (sec.-treas. Lafayette sect. 1972-73), La. Engring. Soc. (sec. Lafayette chpt. 1972-73, 1st v.p. Lafayette chpt. 1973-74, pres. 1974-75), Sigma Xi (sec. U. Southwestern La. club 1971-73), Eta Kappa Nu (nat. dir. 1971-73, v.p. 1973-74, pres. 1974-75), Tau Beta Pi, Phi Kappa Phi. Home: Route 3 Box 357 Arnaudville LA 70512 Office: U Southwestern Louisiana Box 4-3890 Lafayette LA 70504

KLOTTER, JAMES CHRISTOPHER, editor; b. Lexington, Ky., Jan. 17, 1947; s. John Charles and Marjorie Virginia (Gibson) K.; B.A., U. Ky., 1968, M.A., 1969, Ph.D., 1975; m. Freda Campbell, Dec. 28, 1966; children—Karen, Christopher, Katherine. Research analyst Ky. Hist. Soc., Frankfort, 1973-75, asst. dir. publs., 1975-78, mng. editor, 1978—. Mem. adv. bd. Ky. Oral History Commn. Served with Signal Corps, U.S. Army, 1970-71. Nat. Endowment for Humanities fellow, 1979. Mem. Orgn. Am. Historians, So. Hist. Soc., Ky. Hist. Soc., Ky. Council Archives, Ky. Assn. Tchrs. History, Ky. Civil War Roundtable. Club: Filson. Contbr. articles in field to profl. jours. Home: 1048 Pinebloom Dr Lexington KY 40504 Office: Kentucky Historical Society PO Box H Frankfort KY 40602

KLOTZ, HERBERT WERNER, corp. exec.; b. Berlin, Germany, Feb. 24, 1917; s. Herbert and Gertrude (Koppel) K.; B.A., Zuoz (Switzerland) Coll., 1935; student U. Zurich (Switzerland), 1935-36; m. Patricia Radford Hopkins, Apr. 3, 1954; children—Radford Werner, Leslie Ritchie, James Taylor. Came to U.S., 1937, naturalized, 1944. With Smith, Barney & Co., and predecessor, N.Y.C., 1937-42, W.E. Hutton & Co., N.Y.C., 1946-48; engaged in mgmt. personal investments, 1949-52; with Winslow, Douglas & McEvoy, N.Y.C., 1953-54; pres., treas. Tex. Securities Corp., N.Y.C., 1957; with Alex Brown & Sons, Washington, 1957-60; spl. asst. to sec. commerce, 1961, dep. to sec. commerce, 1961-62, asst. sec. commerce for adminstrn., 1962-65; exec. v.p. Am. Growth Investment Co., 1966-67; dir. Govt. Systems Center, Kurt Salmon Assos., Inc.; mgmt. cons., 1968-69; pres. Quest Research Corp., McLean, Va., 1970—; chmn. bd. Dynamic Engring., Inc., Newport News, Va., 1976; chmn. bd. Donovan, Hamester & Rattien, Inc., Washington, 1978—. Bd. dirs. Washington Internat. Horse Show, Inc., 1970—; asso. dir. Nat. Com. Bus. and Profl. Men and Women for Kennedy-Johnson, 1960. Served to 1st lt. AUS, 1942-45; maj. Res. ret. Democrat. Episcopalian. Clubs: 1925 F Street, Metropolitan, Federal City (Washington); Warrenton Hunt, Fauquier (Warrenton, Va.). Home: 1401 Langley Pl McLean VA 22101 Office: 6845 Elm St McLean VA 22101

KLUSKA, B. HARRIET, retailing exec.; b. Florence, S.C., Oct. 28, 1947; d. Harry Presley and Margaret Ernestine (Jones) McMillan; B.S. in Bus. Adminstrn., Oral Roberts U., 1970; postgrad. in psychology U. Tulsa, 1971-73; m. Dale Francis Kluska, June 16, 1973. Personnel mgr. Lit Bros., Reading Pa., 1974-75, Belk Simpson Co., Greenville, S.C., 1976-77; group tng. and communications mgr. Belk Hudson Co., Spartanburg, S.C., 1977-78, sales, basic inventory control mgr., 1978-79, group personnel dir. and ops. mgr., 1979—; speaker in field Tri-County Jr. Coll., 1976; mem. Vocat. Tech. Assn., 1975, Merchant Assn., 1975, Greenville Area Personnel Assn., 1977. Adv. com. on community services Spartanburg Tech. Coll.; judge Miss Reading Fair contest, 1975; pres. bd. dirs. Westgate Mall, 1980; mem. retail adv. com. Spartanburg Methodist Coll., 1980. Republican. Contbr. article to orgn. publ. Home: 1212 Farragut Dr Spartanburg SC 29302 Office: PO Box 5787 Westgate Mall Spartanburg SC 29301

KNAPE, CLIFFORD STANLEY, psychologist; b. Austin, Tex., Dec. 7, 1916; s. Carl Johann and Edla (Widerstrom) K.; B.A., U. Tex., 1941, M.A., 1941; M.A., Baylor U., 1951; Ph.D., U. Tex., 1958; m. Anne Sabra Ramsey, May 30, 1942; children—Mildred Anne, Sabra Jane, Carl Guinn. Clk-psychometrist Rehab. div. Tex. Dept. Edn., Austin, 1934-41; psychologist U.S. VA, Waco, Tex., 1945-51, 53—, now chief psychology service; adj. prof. Baylor U., 1953—. Trustee Waco Ind. Sch. Dist., 1964-76, pres., 1969-70, 75-76; bd. mem. Tex. Rehab. Commn., 1969-78. Served with USAAF, 1941-45, to maj. USAF, 1951-53. Certified rehab. counselor. Mem. Am., Tex. psychol. assns., Nat., Tex. (pres. 1962-63) rehab. assns., McLennan Mental Health Assn. (pres. 1962-63), Tex. Assn. for Mental Health (v.p. for program 1964), Tex. Congress Parents and Tchrs. (state mental health chmn. 1962-65), Phi Beta Kappa. Democrat. Presbyterian. Home: 4319 Cedar Mountain Dr Waco TX 76708 Office: VA Hosp Waco TX 76703

KNAPP, DENNIS RAYMOND, fed. judge; b. Buffalo, W.Va., May 13, 1912; s. Amon Lee and Ora Alice (Forbes) K.; A.B., W.Va. Tech., 1932, LL.D., 1972; A.M., W.Va. U., 1934, LL.B., 1940; m. Helen Ewers Jordan, June 1, 1935; children—Mary F., Margaret Ann, Dennis Raymond. High sch. tchr. Putnam County, W.Va., 1932-35, supt. schs., 1935-37; admitted to W.Va. bar, 1940, practiced in Nitro, W.Va., 1940-56; judge Ct. Common Pleas, Kanawha County, W.Va., 1957-70; U.S. dist. judge So. Dist. W.Va., Charleston, 1970—; v.p., dir. Bank of Nitro, 1949-70; v.p. Hygeia, Inc., 1968-70. Adv. bd. Marshall U., Huntington, W.Va. Served with AUS, 1944-46. Named W.Va. Tech. Alumnus of Year, 1967. Mem. Am., W.Va. bar assns., W.Va. Jud. Assn., W.Va. Tech. Alumni Assn. (pres. 1968). Republican. Methodist. Home: 2109 21st St Nitro WV 25143 Office: 500 Quarrier St Charleston WV 25329

KNAPP, RICHARD BRUCE, anesthesiologist; b. N.Y.C., Oct. 17, 1933; s. John J. and Hilda K. (Appel) K.; A.B., Columbia U., 1955; M.D., N.Y. Med. Coll., 1959; m. Harriett Hollister Boynton, June 1, 1953; children—Laurie (dec.), Carolym, Pamela, Richard Benjamin. Intern, C.V. Meml. Hosp., Johnstown, Pa., 1959-60; resident in anesthesiology N.Y. Hosp., Cornell Med. Centerm 1960-62, chief resident, 1962; anesthesiologist Robert Packer Hosp. Guthrie Clinic, Sayre, Pa., 1964-66, chmn. sect. anesthesiology, 1965-66; anesthesiologist Greenwich (Conn.) Hosp., 1966-74; prof., chmn. dept. anesthesiology W.Va. U. Med. Center, Morgantown, 1974—; clin. instr. Cornell Med. Coll., 1960-62; asst. clin. prof. N.Y. Med. Coll., 1968-72, asso. clin. prof., 1972-74. Served to lt., M.C., USNR, 1962-64. USPHS fellow, 1959-60. Diplomate Am. Bd. Anesthesiology. Mem. Am. Coll. Anesthestists, Am. Coll. Chest Physicians, AMA, N.Y. Acad. Scis. Club: Lakeview Country. Home: Box 15 Harewood Morgantown WV 26505 Office: W Va U Med Center Morgantown WV 26506

KNAPPENBERGER, PAUL H., JR., astronomer, mus. adminstr.; b. Reading, Pa., Sept. 5, 1942; s. Paul H. and Kathryn (Medrick) K.; A.B., Franklin and Marshall Coll., 1964; M.A., U. Va., 1966, Ph.D., 1968; m. Peggy Ann Witmyer, Aug. 31, 1963; children—Paul Charles, Timothy Alan. Obs. dir. Fernbank Sci. Center, Atlanta, 1968-72; asso. prof. Va. Commonwealth U., Richmond, 1973—; dir. Sci. Mus. Va., Richmond, 1973—; adj. asso. prof. U. Richmond, 1973—. Pres., Windsor Forest Community Assn., 1978. NASA fellow, 1965-68. Mem. Assn. Sci.-Tech. Centers (dir.), Am. Astron. Soc. (chmn. task group edn.), AAAS, Internat. Planetarium Soc., Va. Acad. Sci., Richmond Astron. Soc. Home: 11760 Heathmere Crescent Midlothian VA 23113 Office: 2500 W Broad St Richmond VA 23220

KNARR, CATHERINE ANN KEITH, nurse, educator; b. Jackson, Miss., Dec. 12, 1940; d. William Jerry and Nellah Catherine (Smith) Keith; B.S.N., Columbia Union Coll., 1963; student U. Tenn., 1978-80; m. Ronald Charles Knarr, May 2, 1965; children—Jody, Cheryl, Jill. Team leader, asst. recovery room supr., Washington Adventist Hosp., Washington, 1963-65; supr. OB, Buchanan Community Hosp., Buchanan, Mich., 1965-66; nursing supr. Putnam Meml. Hosp., Palatka, Fla., 1970-73; staff nurse Fla. Gov.'s Migrant Project, 1973; instr. nursing So. Missionary Coll., Collegedale, Tenn., 1974—. Mem. Assn. Seventh-day Adventist Nurses. Home: 4441 Surhie Dr Collegedale TN 37315 Office: Mazie Herrin Hall So Missionary Coll Collegedale TN 37315

KNAUB, DONALD EDWARD, museum dir.; b. York, Pa., Dec. 18, 1936; s. Harry N. and Mary C. (Keeney) K.; A.B. in Liberal Arts, Elizabethtown (Pa.) Coll., 1959; M.F.A., Boston U., 1962; cert. arts adminstrn. Harvard U., 1965; m. Karen E. Palmer, June 21, 1970; children—Zackary Daniel, Andrea Rachel. Info. asst. Library/Mus. Performing Arts, Lincoln Center, N.Y.C., 1964-68; arts coordinator City of Davis (Calif.), 1972-77; exec. dir. Muchenthaler Cultural Center, Fullerton, Calif., 1977-79; dir. Huntsville (Ala.) Mus. Art, 1979—; bd. dirs., exec. com. Alliance Calif. Arts Council, 1975-79; mem. leisure services policy com. League Calif. Cities, 1978-79; chmn. fine arts com. Orange County Spl. Mus. Task Force, 1978-79. Mem. Am. Assn. Museums, So. Arts Fedn., Western Assn. Art Museums. Home: 902 Kennamer Dr Huntsville AL 35801 Office: 700 Monroe St Von Braun Civic Center Huntsville AL 35801

KNAUR, JOHN SHERMAN, JR., aero. engr.; b. Dallas, Mar. 7, 1924; s. John Sherman and Lillian (Sommer) K.; student N. Tex. Agrl. Coll., 1941, So. Meth. U., 1947; B.S. in Aero. Engring., U. Colo., 1949, postgrad., 1949-50; m. Jean Davey, Sept. 13, 1947; children—John D., James A., Sandra Lee, Nancy Jean. Aero. structures design upper atmosphere research U. Colo., Boulder, 1948-50; preliminary design engr. Gen. Dynamics, Fort Worth, 1950-60; research specialist Boeing Co., Wichita, Kans., 1960-63, sr. group engr., Huntsville, Ala., 1963-70; mgr. corp. engring. Brougham Industries Inc., Sanger, Tex., 1970-77; service engr. Bell Helicopter Co., 1977—; mgr. Apollo landing system rev. and certification NASA, 1967-68. Block capt. Republican party, 1966-68, phone com. capt., 1967-68. Served with USAAF, 1942-45; ETO. Decorated Air medal with clusters, Bronze Star. Recipient New Tech. award NASA, 1969. Registered profl. engr., Tex., Ala. Fellow Am. Inst. Aeros. and Astronautics (tech. chmn. local sect. 1954-63). Mason (Shriner). Home: 7211 Briley Dr Fort Worth TX 76188 Office: BHT PO Box 76102 Ft Worth TX

KNEE, RUTH IRELAN (MRS. JUNIOR K. KNEE), health care cons.; b. Sapulpa, Okla., Mar. 21, 1920; d. Oren M. and Daisy (Daubin) Irelan; B.A., U. Okla., 1941, certificate social work, 1942; M.A., U. Chgo., 1945; m. Junior K. Knee, May 29, 1943. Psychiat. social worker, asst. supr. Ill. Psychiat. Inst., U. Ill. at Chgo., 1943-44; psychiat. social worker USPHS Employee Health Unit, Washington, 1944-46, chief psychiat. social worker, 1946-49; psychiat. social work asso. Army Med. Center, Walter Reed Army Hosp., Washington, 1949-54; psychiat. social work cons. HEW, Region III, Washington, 1955-56; with NIMH, Chevy Chase, Md., 1956-73, chief spl. grants support sect., 1966-67, chief mental health care adminstrn. br., 1967-72, asso. dep. adminstr. Health Services and Mental Health Adminstrn., 1972-73; dep. dir. Office Nursing Home Affairs, HEW, 1973-74; cons. in field, 1974—; mem. com. illness and elderly HEW, 1976-77; mem. Task Force Legal and Ethical Issues Pres.'s Commn. Mental Health, 1977-78; chmn. Forum Long Term Care, 1977-79; mem. nat. adv. mental health council NIMH, 1977—. Bd. dirs. Hillhaven Found., 1975. Fellow Am. Pub. Health Assn. (sec. mental health sect. 1968-70, chmn. 1971-72), Am. Orthopsychiat. Assn. (life); mem. Am. Assn. Psychiat. Social Workers (pres. 1951-53), Nat. Conf. Social Welfare (nat. bd. 1968-71, 2d v.p. 1973-74), Council on Social Work Edn., Nat. Assn. Social Workers (sec., nat. bd. 1955-57, chmn. competence study com., practice and knowledge com. 1963-71), Am. Gerontol. Soc., Am. Pub. Welfare Assn., D.A.R., Phi Beta Kappa, Psi Chi. Mem. editorial com. Health and Social Work, 1979—. Home: 8809 Arlington Blvd Fairfax VA 22031

KNEEDLER, WILLIAM HARDING, physician; b. Phila., Aug. 13, 1900; s. Henry Martyn and Alice (Harding) K.; A.B., Princeton, 1922; M.D., U. Pa., 1926; postgrad. London Sch. Tropical Medicine and Hygiene, 1929-30; m. Christina Butler Harris, Apr. 30, 1930; children—Alice Harding (Mrs. Charles A. Savage), Cornelia Harris (Mrs. I.B. Hudson Jr.), William Howard. Intern, Pa. Hosp., 1927-29; Presbyn. med. missionary, Thailand, 1930-41, 49-51; cons. tropical medicine Jefferson Hosp., Phila., 1942-47; practice internal medicine, Concord, N.C., 1951—; mem. staff Cabarrus Meml. Hosp., Concord, 1951—; asso. in medicine Jefferson Med. Sch., 1942-47. Diplomate Am. Bd. Internal. Medicine. Fellow A.C.P.; mem. AMA, Am. Soc. Internal Medicine. Home: 234 Scenic Dr NE Concord NC 28025 Office: 865 N Church St Concord NC 28025

KNEESE, VICTOR SCOTT, lawyer; b. Dallas, Nov. 7, 1939; s. Victor Carl and Katherine (Dunne) K.; B.B.A., U. Tex., 1961, LL.B., 1964; m. Carolyn Beatrice Calvin, Dec. 27, 1962; children—Kyle Calvin, Regan Scott. Admitted to Tex. bar, 1964, U.S. Dist. Ct. Eastern Dist. Tex. bar, 1971, No. Dist. Tex. bar, 1964, So. Dist. Tex. bar, 1968, U.S. Ct. Appeals 5th Circuit bar, 1967, U.S. Supreme Ct. bar, 1972; practiced in Dallas, 1964-67, Houston, 1967—; asso. firm Cervin and Stanford, 1964-67; mem. firm Childs, Fortenbach, Beck and Guyton, 1967-77; partner firm Bracewell & Patterson, 1977—. Mem. State Bar Tex. (chmn. com. on coordination with other groups 1971-75), State Jr. Bar Tex., Am. (mem. com. on practice and procedure under Nat. Labor Relations Act, chmn. subcom. on pending legislation), Houston, Houston Jr. bar assns., Alpha Tau Omega. Clubs: Houston Athletic, Briar, Houstonian, Plaza. Contbg. editor The Developing Labor Law. Home: 3109 Avalon Pl Houston TX 77019 Office: 2900 South Tower Pennzoil Pl Houston TX 77002

KNEISEL, RICHARD SAMUEL, ednl. adminstr.; b. Louisville, May 31, 1919; s. Robert Richard and Lena Lydia (Tschopp) K.; A.B., U. Louisville, 1941; M.S. in Edn., Ind. U., 1951, postgrad., 1967-68; D.H.L., Boston U., 1979; m. Marjorie Walker, Feb. 25, 1943; children—R. Craig, Kent W., Constance G. Tchr., Louisville Secondary Sch., 1942-43; tchr. Southern Jr. High, Louisville, 1946-47, guidance counselor, dean students, 1949-51, 51-57; chief chemist dept. indsl. hygiene State of Ky., 1947-49; edn. advisor U.S. Army Chem. Sch., Ft. McClellan, Ala., 1957-68; edn. advisor U.S. Army Infantry Sch., Ft. Benning, Ga., 1968-73, spl. asst. to asst. commandant, 1979—; dir. edn. U.S. Army Europe, 1973-79; v.p. Johnson & Kneisel, Inc., Consulting Chemists, 1946-51. Served with U.S. Army, 1942-46, 51-52. Decorated Bronze Star; recipient Dept. Army Meritorious Civilian medal, 1975; Sec. Army Exceptional Civilian Service medal, 1979. Lic. counselor, Ky. Mem. Am. Personnel and Guidance Assn., Nat. Vocat. Guidance Assn., Am. Soc. Curriculum Devel., Assn. U.S. Army, Am. Soc. Tng. Devel., Phi Delta Kappa, Theta Chi Delta. Presbyterian. Club: Windsor Park. Contbr. articles in field to profl. jours. Home: 5908 Canterbury Dr Columbus GA 31904 Office: US Army Inf Sch Fort Benning GA 31905

KNERR, ROBERT JAMES, physician; b. Parma, Ohio, Apr. 28, 1935; s. Elmer Ellsworth and Margaret Jeanette (Miller) K.; student Johns Hopkins U., 1953-56; M.D., Ohio State U., 1956-60; m. Linda Ann Foote, June 14, 1958; children—Michael, Laura, Jeffrey. Intern Akron City Hosp., 1960-61; resident in pediatrics Columbus (Ohio) Children's Hosp., 1961-63; individual practice medicine, specializing in pediatrics, Vienna, Va., 1965—; instr. pediatrics Georgetown U., 1965—. Served with U.S. Army, 1963-65. Diplomate Am. Bd. Pediatrics. Mem. AMA, Va. Med. Soc., Am. Acad. Pediatrics, Va., No. Va. pediatric socs. Republican. Presbyterian. Home: 10609 Vickers Dr Vienna VA 22180 Office: 410 W Maple Ave Vienna VA 22180

KNIGHT, ALPHONSO WILBERT, ednl. adminstr.; b. Henderson, N.C., Dec. 12, 1925; s. Julius L. and Mary F. (Lawrence) K.; B.S., Hampton Inst., 1947; M.A., Webster Coll., 1970; postgrad. St. Louis U., Harris Tchrs. Coll.; m. Lottie E. Saunders, Jan. 2, 1948; children—Alphonso Wilbert, Jacquelyn E., Curtis E. Supt. bldgs. and grounds Fessenden Acad., Martin, Fla., 1947-48, tchr., tech. sch. dir., 1947-48; supt. bldgs. and grounds Va. Union U., Richmond, 1948-53; tchr. St. Louis Bd. Edn., 1953-72; instr. Fed. Manpower Tng. Program, St. Louis, 1962-67; instr. Forest Park Community Coll., St. Louis, 1968-72; practice architecture, St. Louis, 1957-72; dir. alumni affairs Hampton (Va.) Inst., 1972—. James Hardy Dillard Meml. scholar, 1943-45; NSF fellow, 1966-67. Mem. Council for Advancement and Support of Edn., Nat. Hampton Alumni Assn., NAACP, Omega Psi Phi. Presbyterian. Home: 32 Kings Point Dr Hampton VA 23669 Office: Tyler and Queen Sts Hampton VA 23668

KNIGHT, DONALD GARDNER, investment co. exec.; b. Holyoke, Mass., Jan. 27, 1918; s. Harold Wilson and Ethel (Gardner) K.; B.A., Dartmouth Coll., 1941; postgrad. U. Maine, 1941; M.B.A., Columbia U., 1942; m. Sara Marie Woolley, June 5, 1948; children—Melinda, John. Vice pres. Bulkley Dunton Pulp Co., Inc., N.Y.C., 1946-62, exec. v.p., 1962-67; pres. Bulkley Dunton & Co., Inc., 1967-76; pres. Vaughan Knight, Inc., N.Y.C., 1975—; dir. Swedish Forest Products Co., Kalamazoo Paper & Box Corp., Bulkley Dunton & Co., Bulkley Dunton Pulp Co., Vaughan Knight, Inc. Served to lt. USNR, 1942-46. Republican. Presbyterian. Clubs: Sawgrass; Ponte Vedra (Fla.). Home: 403 San Juan Dr Ponte Vedra Beach FL 32082 Office: 140 Broadway New York City NY 10005

KNIGHT, GARY DALE, govt. photographer; b. Indpls., Aug. 2, 1954; s. Guy Dale and Nancy Lou (Bundy) K.; Asso. Applied Sci., Randolph Tech. Inst., 1974; m. JoAnne Hodgens, Aug. 29, 1976; 1 son from previous marriage, Bryan Dean. Photographer, Goldsboro (N.C.) News-Argus, 1973; free-lance photographer, Goldsboro, 1974-75; forensic photographer N.C. State Bur. Investigation, Raleigh, 1975-77, City-County Bur. Identification, Raleigh, 1978—. Mem. Internat. Council of Evidence Photographers, Internat. Assn. Identification. Home: 225 Clarendon Crescent Raleigh NC 27610 Office: PO Box 550 Wake County Courthouse Raleigh NC 27602

KNIGHT, JAMES ARLIE, JR., ins. exec., publisher; b. Texarkana, Tex., Jan. 2, 1931; s. James Arlie and Carrie Carnice (Stinson) K.; B.B.A., Texarkana Coll. Central Baptist, 1953; m. Vanita Jo Cummings, June 18, 1950; children—James Arlie, Judy, Jane. With pub. relations, Tex. Hwy. Dept., 1950-51; ins. investigator, with jr. mgmt. Retail Credit Co., Texarkana, 1951-58; ins. agt. N.Y. Life Ins. Co., Texarkana, 1958-66; adminstrv. asst. Day and Zimmerman, Inc., Texarkana, 1966-70; gen. agt. Hartford Ins. Group, Texarkana, 1970—; founder, exec. dir. Am. Assn. Civil Service Employees, Texarkana, 1976—; pub. The News Digest, Texarkana, 1977—. Pres. local chpt. Am. Cancer Soc., 1956-57. Served with USMC, 1948-50. Mem. Nat. Life Underwriters (Million Dollar Round Table), Texarkana C. of C. Clubs: Northridge Country, Bass Anglers Sportsmen Soc., Am. Bass Assn., Masons, Shriners. Contbg. editor Tex. Girl, Houston, 1979. Home: 4700 Walnut St Texarkana TX 75503 Office: 1902 Wood St Texarkana TX 75501

KNIGHT, JAMES PERRY, JR., wholesale and retail chain store exec.; b. Columbus, Miss., Dec. 19, 1929; s. James Perry and Eloise (Copeland) K.; student Miss. State U., 1947-49; m. Janice Dell Jackson, Aug. 23, 1953; children—Geoffrey, Jay, James Perry. With White Stores, Fort Worth, 1949-59, store mgr., 1951, dist. mgr., 1955-59; chmn. bd. dirs. Babcock's Auto Stores, Arlington, Tex., 1969—; with Hercules Western Tire Co., Arlington, 1964—, also Maverick Tire Centers, J.P. Knight, Investments, Hercules Aviation Corp., J-K Ranches, K-C Investments, K-D Investments; chmn. bd., pres. Knight Oil Co., Dallas; dir. Metroplex Nat. Bank. Served with USAF, 1946-47. Club: Rotary (pres. Ft. Worth chpt. 1969-70). Home: 1201 Greenbriar Ln Arlington TX 76013 Office: 1506 Pioneer Pkwy W Suite 206 Arlington TX 76013

KNIGHT, MICHAEL EDGAR, bakery exec.; b. Hot Springs, Ark., July 27, 1939; s. Edgar Thaddeus and Mary Katherine (Hampel) K.; B.S., U. Ark., 1963; m. Linda Margaret Pharris, Sept. 16, 1979; children—Michael Sean, Gregory Patrick, Brian Christopher, Nicole Elise. Office mgr. Meyer's Bakery, Little Rock, 1963, plant controller, 1963-65, corporate controller, 1965-74, sec., treas., dir., 1974—; dir. Multiplex, Inc. Mem. Nat. Assn. Accts. Roman Catholic. Club: Pleasant Valley Country. Office: PO Box 1038 Hope AR 71801

KNIGHT, ROBERT LEE, cons.; b. Kansas City, Kans., Sept. 11, 1928; s. Walter Carl and Carrie Elizabeth (Groves) K.; B.A., U. Kansas City, 1954; m. Susan Barbara Kutscheid, Aug. 12, 1967; 1 dau., Monica Maureen. Dist. mgr. mktg. Frontier Airlines, Denver, 1956-65; regional interline mgr. Ozark Airlines, 1965-67; v.p. Brit. West Indian Airways, N.Y.C., 1967-70; cons. Continental Airlines, Aloha Airlines, Hawaii Visitors Bur., Caribbean Tourist Assn., Denver, 1970-75; cons. tourism City of El Paso (Tex.), 1975—; liaison cons. Tex. Tourism Dept., U.S. Dept. Commerce, U.S. Travel Service; cons. Western Internat. Hotels, Mexico; spl. adv. aviation Gov. Colo.,

1965-67; spl. adv. tourism Gov. Hawaii, 1972-74. Mem. Forward Met. Denver Program, N.M. Amigos. Served with USMC, 1946-49. Recipient certs. of appreciation U.S. Dept. Commerce, 1978, U.S. Council Mayors, 1977. Home: 10720 La Subida St El Paso TX 79935 Office: 5 Civic Center Plaza El Paso TX 79901

KNIGHT, ROBERT VERNON, JR., fin. co. exec.; b. Edgecombe County, N.C., Oct. 27, 1928; s. Robert V. and Ruth S. (Dedmon) K.; B.S., Davidson Coll., 1949; m. Betsy Rue Knott, May 9, 1952; children—John Ruffin, Ruth Sydnor. Exec. trainee Wachovia Bank & Trust Co., Winston-Salem, N.C., 1953-55, asst. to regional v.p., Raleigh, N.C., 1955-58; mgr. Eastern N.C. ops. Home Fin. Group, Inc., Durham, 1958-60, dir. advt. dept., Charlotte, 1960-65; v.p. Am. Credit Corp., Charlotte, 1965-75, dir. adminstrv. div., sr. v.p., Charlotte, 1975-79; dir. adminstrv. div., sr. v.p. Barclays Am. Corp., Charlotte, 1979—; dir. Consumer Fin. Assn., 1967. Campaign chmn. Arts and Sci. Council, Inc., 1969, pres., 1971-72; mem. Mecklenburg County council Boy Scouts Am., 1965-67; trustee, treas. Charlotte Latin Sch., 1969-76; campaign chmn. capital funds drive Jr. Achievement, 1978. Served to capt. USAF, 1951-53. Mem. Charlotte Mchts. Assn. (dir. 1976-80), Phi Delta Theta. Presbyterian. Clubs: Charlotte Country, Charlotte City. Home: 326 Colville Rd Charlotte NC 28207 Office: PO Box 31488 201 S Tryon St Charlotte NC 28231

KNIGHT, VICTOR MARION, broadcasting exec.; b. St. Petersburg, Fla., Aug. 14, 1928; s. Texas Hampton and Iris (Johnson) K.; B.S. in Communications and Radio, Butler U., 1950; asso. degree in music Jordan Conservatory of Music, Indpls., 1950; m. Patricia Jeanne Miller, Aug. 21, 1948; children—Theodore Hampton, Beth Ann, Joanne Louise. Founder, pres. Vic Knight Entertainment Agy., Indpls., 1946-66; with WXIW, Indpls., 1950-65; owner, operator Vic Knight Orchestras, midwest, 1955-68; founder, pres., chmn. bd. Quality Broadcasting Corp. of Fla., Delray, 1965—; pres., chmn. WDBF Radio, Delray Beach, Fla., 1965—; pres., producer Seven Decades of Sounds, syndicated radio program, 1968-80; condr. WDBF Orch., 1978—; lectr. to various colls.; cons. to radio stas. Recipient Spl. Presdl. citation C. of C., 1970-71; Nat. Abe Lincoln Merit award S. Bapt. Radio/TV Commn., 1979; nat. award for network programming and promotion CBS Network, 1970-71. Mem. Nat. Radio Broadcasters Assn., Hist. Soc. Fla. Pioneers, Am. Fedn. Musicians, Delray C. of C., Boca C. of C., Boynton C. of C., Sigma Chi. Episcopalian. Clubs: Rotary, Ad. Office: WDBF Radio Box 1420 Delray Beach FL 33444

KNIGHT, WILLIAM LEWIS, real estate broker; b. Binghamton, N.Y., Sept. 12, 1938; s. Alonzo Taft and Alta Lillah Weir K.; B.S. in Bus. Adminstrn., Babson Coll., 1959; m. Nancy Gordon Winslow, Sept. 5, 1959; children—Tammie Sue, William Lewis, Vicki Lea, James Winslow, Tricia Ann. Real estate salesman M.N. Weir, Pompano, Fla., 1959, broker, 1960; v.p. Fla. Sites Inc., Boca Raton, 1961-63, pres., chmn., 1963—; pres., chmn. Caiman Inc., Centro Inc., Payara Inc., Tigre Inc., Knight Properties Inc., Priority Properties Inc. (all Boca Raton); chmn. Computer Food Stores Inc., Boca Raton, 1968—; pres. Selected Sites, Inc., 1974—, Knight Devel., Inc.; gen. partner B.D.M. Devel. Ltd., 1975—, Camino Real Investment Ltd., 1974—, Camino Real Centre Ltd., 1977—, Old Harbor Assos., 1979—, Old Harbor Plaza Assos., Fairways Profl. Plaza Assos.; chmn. bd., chief exec. officer Knight Enterprises, Inc. Recipient Nat. Environ. award, 1970. Presbyterian. Home: 819 Orchid Dr Boca Raton FL 33432 Office: 7000 W Camino Real Boca Raton FL 33433

KNIGHTON, GEORGE WILLIAM, nuclear engr.; b. Wilmington, Del., July 9, 1926; s. Isaac L. and Isabel D. (Dobson) K.; B.M.E., U. Del., 1951; m. Ingrid Helene Schneider, Apr. 25, 1953; children—Denise, Donna, Karen, Brian, Janine. Chief condenser design and proposal sect. Foster Wheeler Corp., N.Y.C., 1951-55; sr. mech. engr. Alco Products, Inc., Schenectady, N.Y., 1956-57, project mgr., 1957-60; chief mech. engring. br. U.S. Corps Engrs., Ft. Belvoir, Va., 1960-66, dep. chief engring. div., 1966-69; chmn. Army Reactor Health and Safety Commn., Dept. Army, Washington, 1969-70; project mgr. U.S. AEC, 1971-72; chief environ. projects br. NRC, Bethesda, Md., 1972-78, chief environ. evaluation, 1978—. Chmn. bd. edn. Lutheran Weekday Sch., Alexandria, Va., 1966-70; pres. local PTA, 1963-64, sec., 1970-71; pres. Citizens Assn., New Alexandria, Va., 1968-69. Served with AUS, 1944-46. Mem. ASME (vice chmn. nuclear and spl. cycles com. 1974-75), ASTM (sec. E10.02 1972-73, chmn. task group reactor vessel inplace annealing 1970-74). Lutheran (mem. council 1970-71). Home: 6417 10th St Alexandria VA 22307 Office: 7920 Norfolk Ave Bethesda MD 20114

KNIPFING, VINCENT PHILIP, coll. adminstr.; b. Rockville Centre, N.Y., May 26, 1942; s. Joseph V. and Helen J. K.; B.S. in Edn., U. Dayton, 1964; M.A., Ohio U., 1966. Dean men Wheeling (W.Va.) Coll., 1968-70, dean student affairs, 1969-72; dean student affairs Loyola U., New Orleans, 1972-74, v.p. student affairs, 1974—; cons. Athletics and Intramural sports St. Louis U. Bd. dirs. New Orleans E. Mental Health Assn., 1976. Served with USAR, 1966-68. Mem. Nat. Assn. Student Personnel Adminstrs., Conf. Jesuit Student Personnel Adminstrs. (past pres.), Am. Coll. Personnel Assn., Am. Personnel and Guidance Assn., La. Assn. Coll. and Univ. Student Personnel Adminstrs. (exec. com.), So. Coll. Personnel Assn. Roman Catholic. Office: Loyola U New Orleans LA 70118

KNOEBEL, DANIEL MCCLELLAN, manufactured housing co. exec.; b. Sunbury, Pa., Jan. 16, 1928; s. Edward Lott and Mary Susan (James) K.; student pub. schs., Northumberland, Pa.; m. Dorothy Wilson, July 9, 1948; children—Norwood B., Sandra M., Steven M., Deborah. Propr., D.M. Knoebel, Builder and Developer, Vero Beach, Fla., 1950-61, D.M. Knoebel, distbrs. U.S. Steel Homes, Vero Beach and Winter Park, Fla., 1962-65; pres., treas., chmn. bd. D.M. Knoebel Corp., Orlando, Fla., 1965-74, Nobel Homes Corp., Orlando, 1975—. Mem. Am. Arbitration Assn. (panel arbitrators 1979). Author: Applied Theory of Prerequisites of Manufactured Housing, 1972; Code Compliance Manual, 1972-77. Home: 911 Osceola Ave Winter Park FL 32789 Office: 3748 Bengert St Orlando FL 32808

KNOLL, FRANK STEPHEN, separations co. exec.; b. N.J., Sept. 30, 1942; s. Frank J. and Helene C. (Kerekes) K.; B.S., Iowa State U., 1964; M.Sc. in Engring., Royal Sch. Mines, Eng., 1971; m. Alicia Vernon, Nov. 8, 1969; children—Felix, Garrett. Geologist, Peace Corps, Dept. State, India, 1965-67; insp., geologist Dept. Navy, 1967-69; research engr. Carpco, Inc., Jacksonville, Fla., 1969-71, mgr. process devel., 1972-74, v.p. mktg., 1975, pres., 1976—, also dir. Recipient Value Engring. award Dept. Navy, 1969. Mem. Inst. Mining and Metallurgy, Am. Inst. Mining Engrs. Patentee in field elec. separation devices. Office: 4120 Haines St Jacksonville FL 32206

KNOLLE, MARY ANNE, human resources co. ofcl.; b. Kilgore, Tex., Jan. 7, 1941; d. Evert Eric and Frances Leone (Scott) Ericson; B.A., North Tex. State U., 1962; M.A., U. Tex., Austin, 1968; postgrad. UCLA, 1964-66, U. Houston, 1974-76; children—Clayton Eric, Sonja Alexis. Editor co. publs. Gt. S.W. Life Ins. Co., 1962; prof. U. Balt., 1968, Miami (Fla.) Dade Coll., 1968, Savannah (Ga.) State Coll., 1969, U. Houston, 1972-76; dir. public relations Alvin (Tex.) Coll., 1970-72; founder, pres. Panorama Programs, Houston, 1972-76; mgmt. devel. tng. coordinator Brown & Root, Inc., Houston, 1970-79; div. founder, mgr. mgmt. and organizational devel. systems Diversified Human Resources Group, Inc., Houston, 1979—; founder, pres. Panorama Mgmt. Inst., Houston, 1979—; cons. moot ct. U. Tex. Law Sch., 1965—. Regional speech contest judge Houston Jaycees. Recipient Blockbuster award United Way, 1979. Mem. Am. Soc. Tng. and Devel., Houston C. of C. (chmn. edn. com.), Alpha Delta Pi (pres. alumnae). Presbyterian. Club: Houston Indoor Tennis. Office: 12307 Broken Arrow Houston TX 77024

KNORI, BETTY JOYCE (B. J.), recreational cons.; b. Claremore, Okla., Oct. 30, 1944; d. Otto and Lettie Lou (Castleberry) Penner; A.S., San Jacinto Coll., 1970; m. Gerald W. Knori, Sept. 7, 1962. Asst. designer Wilson Office Furnishings, Houston, 1970-71; archtl. designer, drafter Kentron Hawaii, LTV Corp., Houston, 1971-72; asst. dist. mgr. U.S. C. of C., Washington, 1976-77; owner Knori Assos., Friendswood, Tex., 1972—. Mem. Nat. Recreation and Park Assn., Tex. Recreation and Park Soc., Phi Theta Kappa. Lutheran. Clubs: Bay Area Divers, Clear Lake Ski. Address: 2305 Airline Dr Friendswood TX 77546

KNORR, JOHN EDWARD, baseball coach; b. Peoria, Ill., Sept. 18, 1949; s. John Andrew and Julia Elizabeth (Donohue) K.; B.B.A. in Fin., U. Notre Dame, 1971; M.Ed. in Phys. Edn., S.W. Tex. State U., 1976; m. Mary Christine Morrison, June 4, 1971. Asst. baseball coach St. Edward's U., Austin, Tex., 1972-73, instr. phys. edn., baseball coach, athletic dir., 1977—; secondary sch. tchr., baseball and football coach, Del Valle, Tex., 1973-76, Gatesville, Tex., 1976-77. Mem. Am. Assn. Coll. Baseball Coaches, Tex. High Sch. Coaches Assn., Tex. High Sch. Baseball Coaches Assn., AAHPER, Fellowship Christian Athletes. Democrat. Roman Catholic. Contbr. articles profl. jours. Office: 3001 S Congress St Austin TX 78704

KNOTTS, GLENN R(ICHARD), editor, educator; b. East Chicago, Ind., May 16, 1934; s. V. Raymond and Opal Ione (Alexander) K.; B.S., Purdue U., 1956, M.S., 1960, Ph.D., 1968; M.S., Ind. U., 1964; Dr. Med. Sci. (hon.) Union Coll., 1975; Sc.D. (hon.), Ricker Coll., 1975. Mem. profl. staff Bapt. Meml. Hosp., San Antonio, 1957-60; instr. chemistry San Antonio (Tex.) Coll., 1958-60; adminstrv. asst. AMA, Chgo., 1960-61, research asso., 1961-62, dir. advt. evaluation, div. sci. activities, 1963-69; exec. dir. Am. Sch. Health Assn., Kent, Ohio, 1969-72; vis. disting. prof. health sci. Kent State U., 1969-72, prof., mem. grad. faculty dept. allied health scis., 1972-75, coordinator grad. studies and research, 1975; editor-in-chief, prof. med. journalism U. Tex. System Cancer Center M.D. Anderson Hosp. and Tumor Inst., Houston, 1975-79, head dept. med. info. and publs., 1975-79, dir. div. ednl. resources, 1979—, asst. to pres., 1979—; vis. prof. health edn. Madison (Va.) Coll., summer, 1965, Union (Ky.) Coll., summers, 1965, 66, 69, Utah State U., 1965; vis. lectr. Ind. U., 1965-66; vis. lectr. pharmacology Purdue U., 1968-69; vis. prof. Pahlavi U. Med. Sch., Iran, summer, 1970; adj. prof. dept. allied health scis. Kent State U., 1975—; prof. dept. biomed. communications U. Tex. Sch. Allied Health Scis., Houston, 1976—; prof. health edn. U. Tex. Sch. Public Health, 1977—; cons. health scis. communications, 1969—; pres. Health Scis. Inst., 1973—; mem. exec. com. Internat. Union Sch. and Univ. Health and Medicine, Paris, 1969—. Bd. dirs. Med. Arts Pub. Found., Houston, 1977—; mem. adv. bd. World Meetings Inc., 1971—. Served with U.S. Army, 1956-58. Recipient Gold medal award French-Am. Allergy Soc., 1973. Fellow Am. Public Health Assn., Am. Sch. Health Assn. (mem. exec. com. 1968-72, editor Jour. 1975-76, Disting. Service award 1973), Am. Inst. Chemists, Royal Soc. Health; mem. Internat. Union Health Edn., AAHPER, Am. Acad. Pharm. Scis., Am. Med. Writers Assn., Am. Pharm. Assn., AAUP, Am. Chem. Soc., AAAS, AMA, Purdue U. Alumni Assn., Ind. U. Alumni Assn., Union Coll. Alumni Assn., Ricker Coll. Alumni Assn., Sigma Xi, Rho Chi, Sigma Delta Chi, Eta Sigma Gamma, Phi Delta Kappa, Kappa Psi. Republican. Presbyterian. Clubs: Merines Meml. (San Francisco); Akron (Ohio) City; Purdue Chemists; Century, President's (Kent); Purdue, Press, Internat. Triangle, Whitehall (Chgo.); Univ. Faculty, Doctor's (Houston). Co-author of various texts and filmstrips on health sci.; contbr. numerous articles in field to profl. jours.; editor Jour. Sch. Health, 1975-76; cons. editor Clin. Pediatrics, 1971—; contbg. editor Annals of Allergy, 1972—; exec. editor Cancer Bulletin, 1976—; mem. numerous editorial bds. Home: 2600 Bellefontaine Houston TX 77025 also 363 Barrello Ln Cocoa Beach FL 32931 also 1726 Broadway Galveston TX 77550 Office: Office of Pres U Tex System Cancer Center Tex Med Center Houston TX 77030

KNOTTS, JO ANN, artist, builder, developer; b. Oklahoma City, Jan. 26, 1951; d. Ivan Ray and Lois K.; student Northeastern A&M Coll., Miami, Okla., 1969, So. State Coll. Mo., 1970, U. Ark., 1971, So. Meth. U., 1971; B.A., Tulsa U., 1972; m. Douglous Kann, 1972 (div. 1974); 1 dau., Angela L. Freelance artist, banks, museums, businesses; one woman show Lynn Kottler Gallery, N.Y.C., 1979; owner, mgr. Fountain East Addition, Miami, 1978—, East Gate Builders, Miami, 1979—, East Gate Interiors, Miami, 1979—. Bd. dirs. March of Dimes. Mem. Midwest Profl. Artists (v.p.), Bus. and Profl. Women, Tulsa Metro Builders, Nat. Assn. Home Builders. Methodist. Address: Route 1 Box 2490 Miami OK 74354

KNOWLES, CHARLES ULMER, elec. engr.; b. Lynn, Mass., Jan. 8, 1927; s. Lester Douglas and Janet (Tripp) K.; B.S., Northeastern U., 1955; m. Jean Margaret Mondor, Sept. 1, 1951; children—Paul Douglas, Stephen Edward. With Western Electric Co., Inc., 1955—, sr. engr. Arlington, Va., 1964—; cons. telephone cos., D.C., Md., Va., W.Va., 1964—. Bd. dirs. Franconia (Va.) Vol. Fire Dept., 1973—, asst. chief, 1979—; active Boy Scouts Am., 1966-78. Served with USNR, 1944-46. Recipient ARC Service award, 1973, 75. Mem. IEEE (sr.). Home: 5942 Thomas Dr Springfield VA 22150 Office: 1201 S Hayes St Arlington VA 22202

KNOWLES, MALCOLM SHEPHERD, educator; b. Livingston, Mont., Aug. 24, 1913; s. Albert Dixon and Marian (Straton) K.; A.B., Harvard U., 1934; M.A., U. Chgo., 1949, Ph.D., 1960; m. Hulda Elisabet Fornell, Aug. 20, 1935; children—Eric Stuart, Barbara Elisabeth Knowles Harti. Dep. adminstr. Nat. Youth Adminstrn. Mass., Boston, 1935-40; dir. adult edn. YMCA, Boston, 1940-43, dir. USO, Detroit, 1943-44, exec. sec., Chgo., 1946-51; exec. dir. Adult Edn. Assn. U.S., Chgo., 1951-59; prof. edn. Boston U., 1959-74, N.C. State U., 1974-79; mem. Task Force on Lifelong Edn., UNESCO Inst. Edn., 1972—; dir. Leadership Resources, Inc., 1962-67, Project Assos., Washington, 1967-78; cons. on tng. Democratic Nat. Com., 1956-60; cons. Office Consumer Affairs, Office of Pres., 1972-73, IBM, Polaroid, Steel Co. Can., United Airlines, Mass. Dept. Mental Health, NIMH, Overseas Edn. Fund, Nat. Council Chs., Girl Scouts U.S.A., U.S. depts. Labor, Justice, Post Office, HEW, Urban League, various schs. and univs., others. Mem. adv. council Franklin Pierce Coll., Rindge, N.H., 1969—. Served with USNR, 1944-46. Recipient Delbert Clark award W. Ga. Coll., Carrollton, 1967; Nat. Tng. Labs. Inst. for Applied Behavioral Sci. fellow, 1969—. Mem. Adult Edn. Assn. U.S., AAUP, Authors Guild. Club: Harvard of Boston. Author: Informal Adult Education, 1950; (with Hulda Knowles) How to Develop Better Leaders, 1955, Introduction to Group Dynamics, 1959; The Adult Education Movement in the U.S., 1962; Higher Adult Education in the U.S., 1969; The Modern Practice of Adult Education: Andragogy vs. Pedagogy, 1980; The Adult Learner: A Neglected Species, 1978; Self-Directed Learning: A Guide for Learners and Teachers, 1975; A History of Adult Education in the U.S., 1977; contbr. articles to profl. jours. Host TV series The Dynamics of Leadership, NET, 1962; And Now We Are People, Group W Network, 1969. Home: 1506 Delmont Dr Raleigh NC 27606

KNOWLES, PORTER-CARROLL, geol. engr., hydrologist; b. Georgetown, Ky.; s. Carroll Wilson and Ruth (Sheldon) K.; student Yale U., 1958-61; profl. engring. degree Colo. Sch. Mines, 1965; m. Mary Ann Phelps, June 10, 1965; children—Christopher-Carroll, Victoria Leilani. Civil engr. Los Angeles Flood Control Dist., 1965-68; geologist Dames & Moore, cons. engrs., Honolulu, 1968-71, geologist, engr., Atlanta, 1971-74, asso., Boca Raton, Fla., 1974-77, partner, 1977—. Bd. dirs. YMCA of Boca Raton, 1978—. Registered profl. engr., Ga., Ala., Fla.; registered profl. geologist, Ga. Mem. Fla. Engring. Soc., ASCE, Assn. Engring. Geologists, Nat. Water Well Assn., Nat. Soc. Profl. Engrs. Contbr. articles to profl. jours. Home: 22111 Serenata Circle W Boca Raton FL 33432 Office: 301 W Camino Gardens Blvd Boca Raton FL 33432

KNOWLES, THOMAS GEORGE, architect; b. Ft. Worth, Feb. 17, 1928; s. George Lucian and Mary Inez (Eddins) K.; student Tex. A. and M. U., 1945-46, 48-49 U. Houston, 1949-50; grad. Internat. Corr. Schs., 1954; m. Dorothy Genell Peacock, Dec. 22, 1951; children—Mark, Warren Steven Lloyd, Glenn Russell. Asso. architect B.M. Smith, G. Marble, S. Brown, Roper, Vance, Harper and Kemp, architects, Dallas, 1952-60; prin. T.G. Knowles, architect, Dallas, 1960-65; asso. architect Simons, Tyler, Tex., 1965-73; prin. T.G. Knowles, architect, Tyler, 1973—. Active Boy Scouts Am., 1967—. Bd. dirs. Tyler Civic Choral, treas. Served with USNR, 1946-48. Mem. AIA (dir. N.E. chpt. 1973), Tex. Soc. Architects, Constrn. Specifications Inst., Tyler C. of C. Republican. Baptist. Kiwanian. Prin. works: Salem Ch., Dallas, 1962; Garland (Tex.) Bible Coll. Dormitory, 1963; Big Town Nursing Home, Mesquite, 1964; Med. Center Hosp., Tyler, 1968; Jr. Coll. Library, Tyler, 1967. Home: 2407 Hunter St Tyler TX 75701 Office: 530 S Beckham St Tyler TX 75701

KNOWLES, WILLIAM THOMAS, engr.; b. Charleston, S.C., June 13, 1945; s. Thomas Earl and Frances Ruth (Hatch) K.; B.S. in Civil Engring., Clemson U., 1967, M.S. in Environ. Systems Engring., 1973; m. Velma Ann Hallman, Feb. 17, 1968; children—Mary Ruth, Kristin Elizabeth. Cons. engr. Davis & Floyd Engrs., Greenwood, S.C., 1973-75; cons. engr. Harwood Beebe Co., Columbia, S.C., 1975-76; cons. engr. Johnny T. Johnson & Assos., Columbia, 1976-80, exec. v.p., 1978-80, also dir.; dir. Letts, Inc., Columbia. Served with USAF, 1968-72. EPA fellow, 1972-73. Registered profl. engr., Ga., S.C., N.C. Mem. Water Pollution Control Fedn., ASCE, Nat. Soc. Profl. Engrs., Water and Pollution Control Assn. S.C., S.C. Soc. Civil Engrs., Chi Epsilon. Presbyterian. Home: 112 Sonning Rd Irmo SC 29063 Office: PO Box 21066 Columbia SC 29221

KNOWLTON, BETTYE MAURINE JAMES, accountant, retail store exec.; b. Hugo, Okla., July 22, 1923; d. Raymond D. and Ruth Jane (High) James; student pub. schs., Antlers, Okla.; m. E.M. Knowlton, Feb. 15, 1974; children by previous marriage—Pamela, James, Delbert, Marlis. Bookkeeper, Denison Motor Co. and Clark Motor Co., Plymouth, 1947-58; partner firm D & B Gen. Contractors, 1958-62; accountant comptroller Dunn Buick, Inc., 1962-71, James-Childers, Architects & Assos., Inc., Ada, Okla., 1971—; owner Mr. J's, Ada, 1972—; partner Ada Travel Service (Okla.), 1974—; treas. James-Childers & Assos. Inc.-Mini Enterprises, Inc., Environ. Specialists Inc.-Devel Services, Inc.; partner Knowlton & Knowlton Investments, 1975—; owner B. Dean Bookkeeping Service, 1961—. Mem. Ada Arts and Humanities Council, 1971-79, pres. 1972, treas., 1973-75; bd. dirs. Ada Community Concerts, 1973-79; mem. adminstrv. bd. First United Meth. Ch., 1972—, mem. fin. com., 1973-75, 77, trustee, 1978-80. Named Woman of Year, Am. Bus. Women's Assn., 1971 Mem. Ada C. of C. Democrat. Club: Oak Hills Golf and Country. Home: 1612 Northcrest Dr Ada OK 74820 Office: 117 N Broadway Ada OK 74820 also 114 W Main St Ada OK 74820

KNOX, BEVERLY LOU BROOKOVER, physician; b. Newark, Ohio, Aug. 15, 1938; d. Lawrence William and Rosie (Rey) Brookover; B.S., Ohio State U., 1959, M.D., 1963; m. Grover Knox; children—Marla Michele, William Brookover, Wesley Voris, Latour Rey. Intern Grant Hosp., Columbus, Ohio, 1963-64; practice medicine, West Union, Ohio, 1964-75, Sun City Center, Fla., 1975-79, Brandon, Fla., 1979—; mem. staff Adams County Hosp., v.p., 1971-72, chief of staff, 1973-75; mem. staff Brandon Community Hosp., 1977—. Mem. AMA, Fla., Hillsborough County med. assns., Am. Acad. Family Physicians, Fla. Acad. Family Physicians, Am. Med. Women's Assn., Alpha Lambda Delta, Alpha Epsilon Iota, Alpha Epsilon Delta (sec. 1958-59). Mem. Order Eastern Star. Home: 3913 John Moore Rd Brandon FL 33511 Office: 305 S Bryan Rd Brandon FL 33511

KNOX, DAVID JAMES, wholesale distbg. co. exec.; b. Dallas, Jan. 29, 1950; s. Samuel Earl and Martha (Dyer) K.; student Tulane U., 1968-73; m. Cynthia Ann Janes, Oct. 18, 1975; 1 son, Clayton David. With Knox Supply, 1973—, v.p. in charge ops., 1975—. Bd. dirs. Camp Grady Spruce YMCA. Mem. Nat. Assn. Home Bldrs., Wholesale Distbg. Assn. Tex., Dallas Exec. Assn. Republican. Office: 11232 Indian Trail Dallas TX 75229

KNOX, HAROLD TODD, educator; b. Poplar Bluff, Mo., Jan. 1, 1942; s. Harold Benton and Mary Kathryn (Todd) K.; B.A. (Honor award in French 1965), Centenary Coll. La., 1965; M.A. (grad. asst. 1966-68), U. Ark., 1968; m. Shirley Paul Coward, Mar. 12, 1968. Instr. French, Centenary Coll., 1968; dir. lang. lab. U. Southwestern La., Lafayette, 1971—; cons. New Iberia (La.) Parish Sch. Bd. Served with USNR, 1968-71. Decorated Navy Commendation medal. Mem. Am. Assn. Tchrs. French, AAUP, La. Assn. Educators, Nat. Fgn. Student Assn. Democrat. Baptist. Club: Rotary. Home: 500 Monteigne Dr Lafayette LA 70506 Office: Dept Fgn Langs Univ Southwestern La Lafayette LA 70501

KNOX, JANE WEATHERLY M., oil co. exec.; b. Scott County, Va., Mar. 8, 1911; d. Joseph Preston and Ida Weatherly; student Clinch Valley Coll., Wise, Va; m. Samuel A. Knox, Mar. 1, 1945; children—Samuel A., Joseph Morton, Jimmy Morton (dec.). Mgr., Sears Roebuck Co., Bristol, Tenn., 1940-50; pres. Knox & Sons Oil Co., Wise, 1960—, chmn. bd., 1979—. Mem. Va. Jobbers Assn. (state dir.), DAR (state chmn.), Bus. and Profl. Womens Club (pres.). Presbyterian. Office: PO Box 397 Wise VA 24293

KNOX, LUCY MAE nursery exec.; b. Clearwater, Fla., Jan. 31, 1921; d. Charley C. and Cynthia Eunice (Irey) Knox; student Bus. U. Tampa, 1947, Peter O. Knight Aviation Engring. Sch., 1947. Metalsmith, Pasco Packing Co., Dade City, Fla., 1939-42; with Tampa (Fla.) Ship Yard, 1942-43; accounts receivable clk. Lykes Pasco Packing Co., Dade City, 1956-71, credit supr., 1971-76, fruit acct., 1977-78, records retention and microfilm mgr., 1978—; also partner Lucy Mae Nursery, Zephyrhills, Fla. Served with USN, 1943-45, 50-52; PTO. Named Tampa Bay Credit Woman of Year, 1971; lic. pvt. pilot. Mem. Tampa Bay Credit Women (charter pres. 1970), Am. Legion (post comdr. 1951, 60, 68, dist. comdr. 1967, state vice comdr. 1973, state chaplain 1974, 75, 77), Honor Soc. of Women

Legionnaires (nat. dir. 1968, nat. judge adv. 1977-80), Fla. Nursery and Growers Assn., Fla. W. Coast Orchid Soc., W. Pasco Orchid Soc., Fla. Am. Legion Press Assn., Nat. Am. Legion Press Assn. Democrat. Baptist. Home: 740 W Hwy 54 Zephyrhills FL 33599 Office: PO Box 97 Dade City FL 33525

KNUDSON, HELON RUTH, nurse, hosp. ofcl.; b. Cranfills Gap, Tex., Aug. 28, 1936; d. Ernst Walter and Caroline H. (Rachuig) Viertel; R.N., Providence Hosp. Sch. Nursing, Waco, Tex., 1957; m. Trent H. Knudson, Sept. 28, 1957; 1 dau., Ruth Jane. Instr., Lic. Vocat. Nursing Sch., supr. operating room, dir. nursing Holt Hosp., Meridian, Tex., 1957-59; clinic nurse S.L. Witcher, physician, Clifton, Tex., 1960-72; surgery staff nurse Goodall-Witcher Clinic, Clifton, 1960-72, operating room, central supply, 1972—, supr. Goodall-Witcher Hosp. Found., Clifton, 1960. Sec. Cranfills Gap Lions Booster Club, 1970—; sec. St. Olaf Luth. Ch., Clifton, 1977—. Mem. Central Tex Assn. Operating Room Nurses (sec. 1980-81), Tex. Assn. Operating Room Nurses, Assn. Operating Room Nurses. Address: Goodall-Witcher Hosp Found Box 549 Clifton TX 76634

KNUTSON, JOYCE ANGUS, nurse; b. Lawler, Iowa, July 2, 1936; d. Stanley John and Druzilla Rebecca (Braun) Angus; R.N., Silver Cross Sch. Nursing, Joliet, Ill., 1956; m. Donald R. Knutson, Aug. 27, 1965; children—Deborah, John, Ralph. Staff nurse to charge nurse Silver Cross Hosp., Joliet, 1956-65; staff nurse to operating room supr. Kennestone Hosp., Marietta, Ga., 1965-70; operating room supr. Apollo Med. Center, St. Petersburg, Fla., 1970-73; dir. operating room and recovery room Meml. Hosp., Sarasota, Fla., 1973—. Mem. Assn. Operating Room Nurses (dir. 1977—, sec., 1979—). Republican. Presbyterian. Clubs: Moose, Jobs Daus. Home: 1125 Idlewild Ct Sarasota FL 33580 Office: Memorial Hosp 1901 Arlington St Sarasota FL 33579

KOBAYASHI, HERBERT SHIN, indsl. engr.; b. Webster, Tex., Feb. 6, 1929; s. Mitsu Toro and Moto (Shita) K.; B.S. in E.E., U. Houston, 1951; M.S. in E.E., U. Mich., 1959, M.S. in Indsl. Engring., 1960; m. Haruko Orita, June 1, 1965; children—June, Naomi, Ken. Jr. engr. Southwestern Indsl. Electronic Co., Houston, 1960; engr. Boeing Co., Huntsville, Ala., and New Orleans, 1962-64; engr. Lockheed Electronics Co., Houston, 1964; aero space technologist NASA, Houston, 1964—. Served with U.S. Army, 1954-56. Mem. IEEE, Am. Inst. Aeros., Astronautics. Home: 1428 FM 528 W Webster TX 77598 Office: NASA JSC 1 Houston TX 77058

KOBB, ALEX, dentist; b. N.Y.C., May 28, 1938; s. Louis and Gladys (Landsman) Kobrinetz; B.A., Harpur Coll., 1959; D.D.S., Temple U., 1964; m. Marcia Lynn Goldberg, June 9, 1962 (div. 1976); children—Amy Jo, Wendy Lee. Leukemia research asst. Downstate Med. Center, Bklyn., 1959-60; practice dentistry, Hollywood, Fla., 1966—; mem. staff Hollywood (Fla.) Meml. Hosp., Hollywood Med. Center. Mem. Dade County Dental Research Inst., Miami, 1969-75; sec. Broward County Dental Research Clinic, 1975-76, v.p., 1976-77, pres. elect 1977-79, pres., 1979-80. Campaign worker Jewish Welfare Fedn., Hollywood, Fla., 1967-71; v.p. Young Leaders Council, 1971-72. Bd. dirs. Fla. region Anti-Defamation League. Served with USNR, 1964-66. Recipient Alumni award Temple U. Sch. Dentistry, 1964. Fellow Acad. Gen. Dentistry. Mem. Am. Dental Assn., Acad. Gen. Dentistry, East Coast Dist. Dental Soc. (profl. relations com., chmn. exhibitors com. ann. meeting), Fla. Dental Assn., Am., Fla. (dir. 1974-75, sec. 1975-76) socs. preventive dentistry, Greater Hollywood Dental Soc. (treas. 1972-73, sec. 1973-74, pres. 1975-76), Jewish War Vets. Jewish religion. Home: 3500 Washington St Apt 116 A Hollywood FL 33021 Office: 650 S Federal Hwy Hollywood FL 33021 also 10450 Taft St Pembroke Pines FL 33026

KOBERT, NORMAN, mgmt. cons.; b. N.Y.C., Apr. 15, 1929; s. Murray Hyman and Rose (Winger) K.; B. Indsl. Engring., N.Y. U., 1949; M.B.A., Marquette U., 1959; D.C.S. (hon.), Cambridge (Eng.) U., 1973; m. Natalie Toby Tanhauser, Nov. 23, 1955; children—Robyn Beth, Roy Scott, Jay Stuart, Lisa Ellen. Chief indsl. engr. N.J. Consol. Laundries, Newark, 1949-51; chief mgmt. engring. services, Picatinny Arsenal, N.J., 1951-53; mgr. mgmt. services U.S. Army Ordnance Corps., Washington, 1953-57; asst. dir. Mgmt. Center, Marquette U., Milw., 1957-59; exec. v.p. Bayer, Kobert & McElrath, Detroit, 1959-65; v.p. Stevenson, Jordan & Harrison, N.Y.C., 1965-72; prin. N. Kobert & Assos., Ft. Lauderdale, Fla., 1972—; guest lectr. Rutgers U., N.C. State U., Clemson U.; cons. time mgmt., inventory control, productivity. Named to Euril Vanes chair Cambridge U., 1969-70; mem. Panel of Experts for Productivity for Boardroom Reports. Mem. Am. Inst. Indsl. Engrs., Soc. Advancement Mgmt., ASME, British Technion Soc. Clubs: Crockfords and Claremont (London); Lago Mar, Harbor Beach Surf (U.S.). Author: Inventory Strategies, 1979; The Aggressive Management Style, 1980; Managing Executive Time, 1980; Practical Applications of Short Interval Scheduling, 1977; Inventory Control for Purchasing Personnel, 1975; Improving the Secretary's Management of Time, 1970. Contbr. articles to profl. jours. Home: 1611 S Ocean Dr Fort Lauderdale FL 33316 Office: PO Drawer 21396 Fort Lauderdale FL 33335

KOBOS, JOSEPH CASIMER, clin. psychologist; b. Chgo., Nov. 23, 1942; s. Casimer and Josephine K.; B.A., St. Benedict's Coll., 1964; M.S., Ohio U., 1967, Ph.D., 1970; m. Carolyn June Fetko, Aug. 28, 1965; children—Philip, Paul, Adam. Psychology resident U. Ill. Med. Center, Chgo., 1968-70; clin. psychologist U. Tex. Health Sci. Center, San Antonio, 1970—, dir. counseling service, 1976—; adj. asst. prof. Trinity U., San Antonio, 1970—; cons. San Antonio State Hosp., 1974—. Mem. Am., Tex. (pres. 1979), Bexar County (pres. 1975, 78) psychol. assns., Am. Group Psychotherapy Assn. Home: 6621 Countess Adria St San Antonio TX 78238 Office: U Tex Health Science Center 7703 Floyd Curl Dr San Antonio TX 78294

KOCH, FRANCES ANN, nurse; b. Spur, Tex., Apr. 13, 1939; d. T.J. and Mary Frances (Van Meter) Taylor; R.N., B.S., Tex. Christian U., 1961; postgrad. Tex. Tech. U., summer 1958, nights 1967-68; M.S. in Nursing (USPHS grantee), U. Ariz., 1971; m. Stuart Alan Koch, Mar. 20, 1970; children—Lesleigh, Brett, Todd. Operating room supr. W.Tex. Hosp., Lubbock, 1961-69; operating room supr., instr. nursing Coll. Medicine, U. Ariz., Tucson, 1970-73; sch. nurse Torrejon AFB, Madrid, Spain, 1974-75; dir. operating room Seton Med. Center, Austin, Tex., 1975-79; dir. surg. services Scott & White Meml. Hosp., Temple, Tex., 1979—; adv. com. operating room tech. program Pima County Jr. Coll., Austin Community Coll.; Nursing cons. Am. Cancer Soc., Lubbock, 1968, profl. edn. com., Ariz., 1972. Mem. Assn. Operating Room Nurses, Am. Nurses Assn., Sigma Theta Tau. Republican. Methodist. Instr. continuing edn. for operating room nurses, U. Ariz., 1972, speaker on subject nat. congress Assn. Operating Room Nurses, 1974. Home: Route 1 Box 62C Troy TX 76579 Office: 2400 S 31st St Temple TX 76501

KOCH, RICHARD LEE, accountant; b. St. Louis, Apr. 18, 1943; s. Russell M. and Helen E. K.; B.S. in Acctg., Okla. State U., 1965. Asst. to controller Guy H. James Industries, Midwest City, Okla., 1965-67; budget dir. Taylor Pub. Co., Dallas, 1967-69; staff acct. Price Waterhouse & Co., Dallas, 1969-71; adminstrv. partner Ervin, Prater, Pickens, Snodgrass & Koch, Arlington, Tex., 1971—. Sec.-treas. Young Men for Arlington. C.P.A., Tex. Mem. Am. Inst. C.P.A.'s, Tex. Soc. C.P.A.'s, Mid-Cities Assn. C.P.A.'s (dir.). Republican. Club: Greater Arlington Lions (treas., Lion of Yr. 1977-78). Home: 3710 Lynnwood St Arlington TX 76013 Office: 300 Arlington Bank and Trust Bldg Arlington TX 76010

KOCHER, ERIC GLENN, lawyer; b. Brussels, Feb. 29, 1948; s. Eric and Margaret (Helburn) K.; B.A. in Polit. Sci., Am. U., 1969; J.D., Boston Coll., 1972. Mem. staff U.S. Senator Edward M. Kennedy, Washington, 1966-69; mem. staff press sect. Presdl. Campaign of Robert F. Kennedy, Washington, 1968; admitted to Ga. bar, 1972; mng. atty. Brunswick (Ga.) Legal Aid Soc., 1972-73; atty. Glynn County Pub. Defenders Office, Brunswick, 1973-75; pvt. practice law, Brunswick, 1975-77; pub. defender Brunswick Jud. Circuit, 1976-78; mng. atty. Ga. Legal Services Program, Gainsville Regional Office, 1978—. First v.p. St. Simons (Ga.) Concerned Citizens Assn., 1974-75, pres., 1975-76; mem. Mental Health Adv. Council for six county area, Ga., 1974-76, chmn., 1975-76; mem. profl. adv. bd. Patterns Drug Counseling Center, Brunswick, 1973-74; bd. dirs. Ga. Clearinghouse on Prisons and Jails, 1973-75. Mem. ACLU, Nat. Assn. Criminal Def. Lawyers, Nat. Legal Aid and Defender Assn., Am., Brunswick (dir. 1975-76, pres. young lawyers sect. 1974-75) bar assns., State Bar Ga. (exec. council young lawyers sect. 1974-76), Glynn County Civic Assn., Coastal Ga. Audubon Soc. (dir. 1975-76), St. Simons Island Players. Advisory bd. Nat. Clearinghouse Rev., 1979—. Home: PO Box 231 Gainsville GA 30501 Office: PO Box 1337 Gainsville GA 30501

KOEHLER, HERMAN RICHARD, JR., musician, univ. adminstr.; b. Olympia, Wash. Sept. 26, 1933; s. Herman Richard and Frances Suzanna (Schwartz) K.; student Whitman Coll., 1951-54, 56-57; B.Music, U. Puget Sound, 1959, M.Music, 1967; Ph.D., U. Oreg., 1974; m. Loretta Marie Mason, Nov. 23, 1956. Tchr. jr. and sr. high sch., Aberdeen, Wash., 1959-62; tchr. vocal music high sch., Seattle, 1962-71; asst. to dean U. Oreg. Sch. Music, 1974-76; asst. to dean Shepherd Sch. Music, Rice U., Houston, 1976—. Musical dir. (U.S.A.) Strathclyde Internat. Youth Choral Festival. Served with U.S. Army, 1954-56. Mem. Wash. Music Educators Assn., Tex. Music Educators Assn., NEA, Nat. Assn. Partners of the Americas, Am. Fedn. Tchrs., Oreg. Music Educators Assn., Pi Kappa Lambda, Phi Mu Alpha Sinfonia. Club: Rotary. Home: 9926 Cliffwood Dr Houston TX 77096 Office: PO Box 1892 Houston TX 77001

KOEHLER, WANDA MAE, educator; b. Hennepin, Okla., July 9, 1933; d. Jame Clifford and Ila Mae (Lowe) McGaw; B.A., East Central U., Ada, Okla., 1956; M.A. in Elem. Edn., No. Ariz. U., 1974, M.A. in Jr. Coll. Teaching, 1975, M.A. in Social Sci., 1976; postgrad. Okla. U., 1976—; children by previous marriage—Sandra, Valorie, Wesley Cannon. Tchr. English, Jenks (Okla.) Public Schs., 1956-57; tchr. kindergarten Durfee Sch., El Rancho Sch. Dist., Pico Rivera, Calif., 1968-72; instr. Central Ariz. Community Coll., 1972-76; chmn. interdisciplinary unit Pauls Valley (Okla.) State Sch., sch. for retarded, 1976—; cons. Navajo Reservation, 1973-76. Mem. Nat. Assn. Social Workers, Okla. Health and Welfare Assn., Am. Assn. Mental Deficiency, Okla. Solar Energy Assn., Common Cause. Democrat. Baptist. Home: 318 W Joy St Pauls Valley OK 73075 Office: PO Box 609 Pauls Valley OK 73075

KOEN, BILLY VAUGHN, nuclear engr.; b. Graham, Tex., May 2, 1938; s. Ottis Vaughn and Margaret May (Branch) K.; B.A. in Chemistry, U. Tex., 1960, B.S. in Chem. Engring., 1961; S.M. in Nuclear Engring., Mass. Inst. Tech., 1962, Sc.D., 1968; diplome d'ingenieur in Génie Atomique (Rotary Internat. fellow), l'Institut Nat. des Scis. et Techniques Nucléaires, Saclay, France, 1963; m. Deanne Rollins, June 3, 1967; children—Kent Vaughn, Douglas Branch. Research asst. Los Alamos Sci. Lab., summers 1961, 65, Cadarache, French AEC Lab., summer 1963, Argonne (Ill.) Nat. Lab., summer 1964, Mass. Inst. Tech., Cambridge, 1963-66; asst. prof. U. Tex. at Austin, 1968-71, asso. prof. nuclear engring., 1971—, dir. Bur. Engring. Teaching; vis. cons. Los Alamos Sci. Lab., 1969; cons. French AEC, Saclay, 1971-72, lectr. on engring. edn. and self-paced instruction, profl. meetings; council rep. Oak Ridge Associated Univs., 1973-75, bd. dirs., 1975-76. Recipient Outstanding Teaching award Standard Oil Ind. Found., 1969, Distinguished Adviser award Coll. Engring., U. Tex. at Austin, 1970; Engring. Found. Faculty award, 1973, 74; Oak Ridge nat. fellow, 1961-63; NSF grantee, 1969-70; Fulbright travel grantee, France, 1971; Univ. Research Inst. grantee, 1971; registered profl. engr., Tex. Mem. Am. Nuclear Soc., Am. Soc. Engring. Edn. (chmn. ednl. research and methods div.), N.Y. Acad. Scis., AAAS, Assn. des Ingenieurs en Génie Atomique, Sigma Xi, Phi Beta Kappa, Tau Beta Pi, Alpha Chi Sigma, Pi Lambda Upsilon, Omega Chi Epsilon, Phi Eta Sigma, Pi Tau Sigma. Contbr. articles on engring. edn. and tech. articles to sci. jours. U.S. and France. Home: 7303 Woodhollow Apt 492 Austin TX 78731 Office: Dept Mech Engring U Tex Austin TX 78712

KOEN, OTTIS VAUGHN, writer, photographer, educator; b. Mills County, Tex., Nov. 15, 1906; s. Clairborne and Rose (Qualls) K.; B.S., Tex. Technol. U., 1929; M.A., Columbia U., 1932; postgrad. U. Tex., 1935-37; m. Margaret Branch, Jan. 30, 1937; children—Billy Vaughn, Beverly Koen La Grone. Free-lance writer, 1925—; tchr. gen. sci. Lubbock (Tex.) public schs., 1929-30; tchr., prin. Ft. Davis (Tex.) public schs., 1933-34; tchr., adminstr. Graham (Tex.) public schs., 1937-42; tchr., head English dept. Mt. Pleasant (Tex.) public schs., 1935-36; owner, operator photographic bus., Austin, Tex., 1945-68; tchr. Austin public schs., 1979-80; free-lance photographer. Past chmn. bd. deacons Univ. Presbyterian Ch., Austin. Served with USN, 1944-45. Mem. Austin Photographers Assn. (past pres.). Club: Rotary (past pres. Graham, Tex., past sec. Austin, past gov. dist. 587). Author: The Glory Trail, 1975; contbr. articles to newspapers and mags. including: Tex. Outlook, Rotarian, Profl. Photographer.

KOEPKE, JOHN ARTHUR, lab. dir.; b. Milw., Mar. 25, 1929; s. Elmer Paul and Meta Clara (Jennrich) K.; B.A., Valparaiso U., 1951; M.D., U. Wis., 1956; M.S., Marquette U., 1964; m. Evelyn Mae Lovekamp, June 18, 1955; children—Mary E., John F., Mark D., James R. Intern, Milw. Hosp., 1956-57, resident clin. pathology, 1957-60; mem. faculty U. Ky. Med. Sch., Lexington, 1960-71, asso. prof. pathology, 1965-70; clin. asso. prof. Coll. Allied Health, 1970-71; prof. pathology, vice chmn. dept. Coll. Medicine U. Iowa, 1972-79; vis. scientist Karolinska Inst., Stockholm, 1967-68; vis. scientist Royal Postgrad. Med. Sch., London, 1978; med. dir. Central Ky. Blood Center, 1969-71; med. dir. transfusion service U. Ia., 1972-79; chief pathologist VA Hosp., Iowa City, 1972-78; prof. pathology Duke U., Durham, N.C., 1978—, dir. Transfusion Services and Hematology, Med. Center, 1978—. Recipient President's award Valparaiso U., 1951. Diplomate Am. Bd. Pathology. Fellow Am. Soc. Clin. Pathologists, Coll. Am. Pathologists (chmn. hematology resource com. 1968-78); mem. AMA, Am. Fedn. Clin. Research, Acad. Clin. Lab. Physicians and Scientists, Am. Assn. Blood Banks, Central Soc. for Clin. Research, Am. Soc. Hematology, Soc. Exptl. Biology and Medicine, Sigma Xi. Lutheran. Author 2 books, numerous articles in field. Home: 3924 St Mark's Rd Durham NC 27707 Office: Duke U Med Center PO Box 3712 Durham NC 27710

KOESTER, FREDERICK HENRY, JR., elec. engr.; b. Mt. Vernon, N.Y., Aug. 28, 1932; s. Frederick Henry and Frances Anna (Moore) K.; student Drexel Inst. Tech., 1950-51; B.S., U.S. Naval Acad., 1955; B.S. in Elec. Engring., U.S. Naval Postgrad. Sch., 1962; M.S. in Adminstrn., George Washington U., 1972; m. Eileen Rose Bobb, Dec. 30, 1961; children—Robert, John, Thomas. Commd. ensign U.S. Navy, 1955, advanced through grades to lt. comdr., 1964; gunnery officer, navigator U.S.S. Arnold J. Isbell, 1955-58; exec. officer U.S.S. Pierre, 1958; comdg. officer U.S.S. Lamar, 1959-60; exec. officer U.S.S. Shields, 1968-69; weapons officer U.S.S. Luce, 1963-65; inspector Bd. Inspection Survey, Washington, 1974-75; sci. and tech. intelligence officer Naval Ordnance Systems Command, 1972-75; ret., 1975; engr./cons. in naval warfare planning, research and devel. Booz-Allen Applied Research, Bethesda, Md., 1975-79; engr. auto test equipment Man Tech Internat., 1979—; cons. program appraisal techniques, future forecasting. Athletic coach Annandale (Va.) Boys Club, 1971-79. Mem. Am. Def. Preparedness Assn., Jacques Costeau Soc., Mensa, Internat. Naval Research Orgn., Ret. Officer Assn. Republican. Roman Catholic. Editor: Proc. of Digital Systems Symposium, 1966. Home: 7601 Gaylord Dr Annandale VA 22003 Office: Man Tech Internat Suite 930 Century Bldg Jefferson Hwy Arlington VA

KOGUT, LAWRENCE LEROY, educator; b. Chgo., June 26, 1931; s. Joseph Francis and Antoinette Fabus (Sipka) K.; B.S., Northwestern U., 1957, M.B.A., 1958; D.B.A., Ind. No. U., 1970; Owner accounting practice, Kokomo, Ind., 1960-70; prof. Tampa Coll., St. Petersburg, Fla., 1970-73; prof. accounting, chmn. bus. adminstrn. Hillsborough Community Coll., Tampa, 1973—, mem. pres.'s council, 1974—. Bd. dirs. Howard County Retarded Children's Assn., 1965-68, Salvation Army, Kokomo, 1964-67. Served with USMCR, 1950-53. Named Kiwanian of Year, Kokomo, 1970. Mem. Am. Acctg. Assn., Nat. Soc. Pub. Accts., Nat. Assn. Accts. (dir.). Author: How to Read and Understand Financial Statements, 1973; co-author: Accounting Principles for Midmanagement, 1979; also numerous articles in profl. jours. Home: 4460 32d Ave N Saint Petersburg FL 33713 Office: PO Box 22127 Tampa FL 33622

KOHL, CHARLES WILLIAM, printing co. exec.; b. Topeka, Kans., May 6, 1916; s. Charles W. and Emma (Pierce) K.; student U. Kans., 1938-40; m. Dora Marie Dierks, Feb. 27, 1944; 1 son, Charles Johann. Publisher, Hull (Tex.) Daisetta News, 1948-50; printer Trinity Pub. Co., Liberty, Tex., 1950-55, Galveston (Tex.) News Pub. Co., 1955-60; printing exec. Oak Creek Press, Houston, Tex., 1960-67; propr., dir. Black Gold Press, Liberty, Tex., 1967—; founder, propr. Texas-La Envelope Co., Liberty, Tex., 1967—. Scoutmaster Jayhawk council Boy Scouts Am., 1934-38. Served with Signal Corps, U.S. Army, 1940-45; PTO. Decorated 2 Bronze Stars. Mem. Nat. Assn. of Printers and Lithographers, Southwest Litho Club. Democrat. Presbyterian. Home: 2001 Magnolia St Liberty TX 77575 Office: 1406 Browning St Liberty TX 77575

KOHL, DORA DIERKS (MRS. CHARLES WILLIAM KOHL, JR.), savs. and loan exec.; b. Sugar Land, Tex., Aug. 7, 1922; d. Hans Fritz and Elizabeth Amelia (Pilz) Dierks; student pub. schs.; m. Charles William Kohl, Jr., Feb. 27, 1944; 1 son, Charles Johann. With Marshall Canning Co., Sugar Land, 1939-45, Montgomery Ward, Denver, 1945-46; with Liberty County Fed. Savs. & Loan Assn., Liberty, Tex., 1951—, treas., controller, 1972-77, v.p. personnel, 1977-79, v.p., adminstrv. asst., 1979—. Sec., Liberty chpt. Am. Cancer Soc. Mem. Am. Savs. and Loan Inst. (pres. Beaumont chpt.), Nat. Soc. Controllers and Financial Officers. Home: 2001 Magnolia St Liberty TX 77575 Office: 400 Main St Liberty TX 77575

KOHLAND, WILLIAM FRANCIS, geologist; b. Chester, Pa., May 13, 1925; s. Francis William and Martha Marie (Pittman) K.; A.A., Rutgers U., 1949; A.B., Bucknell U., 1951; M.S., Ph.D., U. Tenn., 1969; postdoctoral Western Mich. U., 1971; m. Sylvia R. Hurlock, Jan. 5, 1957; 1 son, Louis. Deck officer marine div. United Fruit Co., 1946-48; ops. agt. United Air Lines, 1954-59; asst. prof. Edinboro State Coll., 1959-67; prof. Middle Tenn. State U., Murfreesboro, 1967—. Served with USNR, 1943-46. Danforth grantee, 1961-62. Mem. Nat. Assn. Geology Tchrs., Geol. Soc. Am., Soil Sci. Soc. Am., Am. Soc. Agronomy, Internat. Soil Sci. Soc., Delta Sigma Phi, Theta Alpha Phi. Republican. Methodist. Author: Guide to Mineral Identification. Home: Route 3 Murfreesboro TN 37130

KOHLER, ANNE TRIMBLE, state ofcl.; b. Ft. Worth, Sept. 4, 1925; d. Terrill Marshall and Elizabeth (Llewellyn) Trimble; B.S., U. Tex., 1948, M.A., 1952; m. William R. Kohler, Aug. 10, 1950 (dec. Feb. 1961); children—Robert Daniel, Raymond Llewellyn. Dir., Pease Elementary Child Care Center, Austin, Tex., 1948-55; psychiat. social worker Austin State Hosp., 1959-61, vocat. rehab. counselor for mentally ill, 1961-69; research utilization specialist Tex. Rehab. Commn. and Region VI, HEW, Austin, 1969-72; program adminstr. research utilization project Tex. Gov.'s Com. Aging, Austin, 1972-76; program dir., research utilization project Tex. Dept. Human Resources, Austin, 1976-78, program specialist aged, blind and disabled, 1978—. Mem. Am., Tex. personnel and guidance assns., Austin Social Welfare Assn. (pres. 1969), Tex. United Community Services, Nat., Tex. rehab. counseling assns., Tex. Psychol. Assn., Mental Health Assn. Austin-Travis County, Austin Personnel Assn., Nat. Gerontol. Soc., Internat. Soc. Rehab. of Disabled, Nat. Council on Aging. Contbr. articles to profl. jours. Home: 3902 Idlewild St Austin TX 78731 Office: Reagan Bldg Dept Human Resources Austin TX 78711

KOHLER, DEBORAH ALICIA, public relations exec., educator; b. New Orleans, Nov. 27, 1950; d. Irvin Joseph and Doris Mae (Gantenbein) Kohler; B.A., Loyola U. of South, 1972; M.A., U. New Orleans, 1974. Grad. asst. dept. drama/communications, U. New Orleans, 1973-74; film editor WGNO-TV, Channel 26, New Orleans, 1975; communications specialist public relations Delgado Community Coll., New Orleans, 1976—, instr., 1976—. Mem. Assn. Continuing Higher Edn. Democrat. Roman Catholic. Home: 625 Rosa Ave Metairie LA 70005 Office: 615 City Park Ave New Orleans LA 70119

KOHLER, JERRY ALLEN, SR., savs. and loan exec.; b. Houston, Nov. 21, 1937; s. Allen Delman and Doris Lee K.; student Howard County Jr. Coll., 1957-60; student architecture Tex. A&M U., 1960-63; m. Nov. 26, 1957; children—Jerry Allen, Jeannine, Jeffrey, Kathy, Kristin. Real estate mgmt. officer Dept. Air Force, Big Spring, Tex., 1966-71; constrn. analyst VA, Dallas, 1971-73; chief appraiser, loan officer Cleburne (Tex.) Savs. & Loan, 1973-76; sr. v.p., secondary market mgr. Continental Savs., Freeport, Tex., 1976—; dir., treas. Continental-First Service Corp., Houston, 1978—. Served with USAF, 1956-60. Mem. Brazosport C. of C., Soc. Real Estate Appraisers (asso.), Tex. Savs. and Loan League, U.S. Savs. and Loan League. Methodist. Clubs: Lions, K.P. Office: PO Box 2078 Freeport TX 77541

KOHLER, KARL EUGENE, architect; b. Washington, Oct. 26, 1932; s. Frederick Leslie and Nora (Gibson) K.; B.S. in Bldg. Design, Va. Poly. Inst., 1954, M.S. in Architecture, 1957; m. Betty Sampson, June 13, 1954; children—Mark Allen, Eric Leslie, Janis Lynn, James Robert. Asst. instr. architecture Va. Poly. Inst., Blacksburg, 1956-57; architect in tng. William N. Denton, Jr., architects, Washington, 1957-60, architect in charge, 1960-61; architect with Beery and Rio, architects, Annandale, Va., 1961-63; prin. Kohler-Daniels, Daniels architects, Vienna, Va., 1963-68; prin. Kohler-Daniels Associates,

Vienna, 1968-77; pres., treas. Kohler-Daniels-Harrelle Associates, Ltd., Vienna, 1977—; exec. v.p. Windmill Point Marine Resorts, Inc., White Stone, Va., 1977—; maj. archtl. works include: Hilton Hotel, Williamsburg, Va., 1968, 307 Office Bldg., Vienna, 1975, 301 Office Complex, Vienna, 1979. Treas., Mill Creek Park Civic Assn., 1962, pres., 1963-64; deacon Calvary Hill Baptist Ch., 1966-68; bd. dirs. Fairfax County Jr. Achievement, 1975-77. Served to 1st. lt., C.E., U.S. Army, 1954-56. Recipient Honor award Am. Soc. Landscape Architects, 1979, 1st Ann. Bldg. Beautification award Fairfax County, 1969; cert. architect Va., Md., Washington, N.Y. Mem. AIA, No. Va. Builders Assn. (Bldg. awards 1969-75), Tau Sigma Delta. Baptist. Clubs: Windmill Point Yacht; Lodge Creek Yacht (commodore 1975-76). Home: 8205 Woodland Ave Annandale VA 22003 Office: 301 Maple Ave West Vienna VA 22180

KOHLER, LINDA LEE, plastics co. exec.; b. Allentown, Pa., Sept. 16, 1947; d. Ernest Elwood and Anna Alinda K.; student U. Fla., 1965-66, S. Fla. Jr. Coll., 1966-67, Polk Jr. Coll., 1967-68; 1 son, David Wayne. Vice pres. Fla. Containers, Inc., Sebring, 1969-75, pres., 1975—; mem. County Indsl. Devel. Bd.; pres. Sebring Air Terminal Operators; mem. Fla. Small Bus. Adv. Council, White House Conf. on Small Bus. Women's Task Force. Named Fla. Small Business Person of Yr., Small Bus. Adminstrn., 1979. Mem. Soc. Plastics Engrs., Single Service Inst., C. of C. Democrat. Home: 2026 Beach Dr Sebring FL 33870 Office: Fla Containers Inc PO Box 1149 Sebring FL 33870

KOHLER, PETER OGDEN, med. educator; b. Bklyn., July 18, 1938; s. Dayton McCue and Jean Stewart (Ogden) K.; B.A., U. Va., 1959; M.D., Duke U., 1963; m. Judy Lynn Baker, Dec. 26, 1959; children—Brooke Terrill, Stephen Edwin, Todd Randolph, Adam Stewart. Intern, fellow Duke Hosp., Durham, N.C., 1963-65; clin. asso., sr. investigator Nat. Cancer Inst. and Nat. Inst. Child Health and Human Devel., NIH, Bethesda, Md., 1965-72, head endocrinology service, 1972-73; resident in medicine Georgetown U., Washington, 1969-70; chief endocrinology div., prof. medicine and cell biology Baylor Coll. Medicine, Houston, 1973-77; prof., chmn. dept. medicine U. Ark., Little Rock, 1977—; cons. St. Luke's and Houston VA hosps., 1973-77, Little Rock VA Hosp., 1977—; attending physician Methodist and Ben Taub hosps., 1973-77. Recipient Quality awards NIH, 1969, 71. Diplomate Am. Bd. Internal Medicine. Fellow A.C.P.; mem. Am. Fed. Clin. Research (pres. So. sect. 1976, nat. council 1977-78), Am., So. socs. clin. investigation, Endocrine Soc., Am. Soc. Cell Biology, Am. Diabetes Assn., Phi Beta Kappa, Omicron Delta Kappa, Alpha Omega Alpha. Editor: (with G.T. Ross) Diagnosis and Treatment of Pituitary Tumors, 1973. Contbr. articles to med. jours. Home: 13280 Rivercrest Little Rock AR 72212 Office: Dept Medicine U Ark 4301 W Markham St Little Rock AR 72205

KOHLHAAS, ROBERT FRANK, lawyer; b. Algona, Iowa, Dec. 12, 1923; s. Philip Joseph and Adelaide (Harig) K.; student Loras Coll., 1940-42; B.A., Iowa U., 1947, LL.B., 1950; m. Charlotte Maxine Zirkle, June 14, 1956; children—Kim Michell, Kathy Ann, Gregory Michael, Christopher Mark. Admitted to Va. bar, 1956; practiced in Arlington, 1956-70, Falls Church, 1970-75; asso. firm Adams, Porter & Radigan, Arlington, Va., 1952-56; mem. firm Tramonte, Kohlhaas & Garnier, Falls Church, Va., 1956-75, Kohlhaas & Garnier, Fairfax City, Va., 1975—. Pres., Poplar Heights Recreation Assn., 1971. Served with USNR, 1942-46. Mem. Iowa, Va., Am. bar assns., Phi Kappa Theta, Delta Theta Phi. Democrat. Roman Catholic. Club: Internat. Town and Country. Home: 7501 Venice Court Falls Church VA 22043 Office: Kohlhaas & Garnier Fairfax City VA

KOHN, ERWIN, phys. scientist, educator; b. Vienna, Austria, Aug. 23, 1923; s. Julius G. and Laura (Deutsch) K.; came to U.S., 1939, naturalized, 1943; B.S., U. Ill., 1948; M.S., U. Notre Dame, 1950; Ph.D., U. Tex., 1956; m. Henrietta Lucille Klapman, Nov. 12, 1949; children—Joseph, Michael, Daniel, Benjamin, Samuel, Susan. Research specialist Monsanto Chem. Co., Texas City, Tex., 1955-66; asso. prof. chemistry Southwestern Okla. State U., 1966-68; asso. prof. polymers and coatings N.D. State U., 1968-72; project scientist Mason & Hanger, Burlington, Ia., 1972-74, sr. project scientist, Amarillo, Tex., 1974—. Dir. NSF Colloquium for 2-Yr. Coll. Chemistry Tchrs., 1971-72. Served with AUS, 1943-46. Sigma Xi grantee, 1967; NSF Instnl. grantee, 1969; Humble Oil fellow, 1951-55; U. Notre Dame fellow, 1948-50; U. Tex. Teaching fellow, 1953-55. Fellow Am. Inst. Chemists; mem. Am. Chem. Soc. (councilor, chmn. Panhandle Plains sect.), Am. Phys. Soc., Soc. Plastics Engrs., League Women Voters, Electron Microscopy Soc. Am., Microbeam Soc., Sigma Xi, Alpha Chi Sigma. Mem. editorial bd. Jour. Liquid Chromatography, 1978—. Contbr. articles to sci. jours. Home: 3613 Nebraska Amarillo TX 79109 Office: Mason & Hanger PO Box 30020 Amarillo TX 79177

KOHN, VERA GROSS, physician; b. Kimberley, S.Africa, June 7, 1906; d. Frank and Lilian (Jacobs) Gross; B.A., Grey Coll., S.Africa, 1923; M.B., Ch.B., U. Witwatersrand (S.Africa), 1941; m. Stanley Victor Emanuel, Apr. 14, 1927 (div.); children—Fleur Strand, Frank Victor Emanuel; m. 2d, Anthony Kohn, Mar. 6, 1956. Came to U.S., 1949, naturalized, 1955. Pvt. practice, Johannesburg, S.Africa, until 1949; cons. cerebral palsy N.Y. State Health Dept., 1949-50; pvt. practice, L.I., 1950-72; past mem. med. staff Southside Hosp., Bay Shore, Good Samaritan Hosp., West Islip; attending pediatrician Suffolk Psychiat. Hosp.; cons. pediatrician Central Islip State Hosp.; clin. cons. pediatrics N.Y. Dept. Health. Diplomate child health Royal Coll. Physicians and Surgeons, Eng.; mem. Royal Coll. Physicians Edinburgh, 1946; diplomate Am. Bd. Pediatrics. Fellow Am. Acad. Pediatrics; mem. Suffolk County Med. Soc., Am. Women's, Brit. med. assns., AAUW, Alumni Assn. Babies Hosp. Columbia-Presbyn. Med. Center, Women's Med. Soc. N.Y. State, Miami Mineral. and Lapidary Guild, Fla. Audubon Soc., Fla. Craftsmen, Fla. Marine Aquarium Soc. Home: 1111 Crandon Blvd Apt A 301 Key Biscayne FL 33149

KOHNE, HAROLD JEROME, geneticist; b. Washington, Mo., Oct. 28, 1945; s. Herman Edward and Hilda Louise (Altemeyer) K.; B.S. in Poultry Sci., U. Mo., 1967, M.S. in Turkey Prodn. and Mgmt., 1969; Ph.D. in Physiology of Reprodn., Clemson U., 1975; m. Mary Frances Halley, Mar. 11, 1967; children—Kimberly Annette, Christina Louise. Geneticist, Arbor Acres Farms, Inc., Rose Hill, N.C., 1974-76; geneticist research and devel. Nash Johnson and Sons Farms, Inc., Rose Hill, 1976—. Served with U.S. Army, 1969-71. Mem. Poultry Sci. Assn., Soc. Study Reprodn., Sigma Xi, Gamma Sigma Delta. Mem. United Churches of Christ. Contbr. articles to profl. jours. Home: 507 Forest Ln Wallace NC 28466

KOK, LOKE-TUCK, entomologist; b. Ipoh Perak, Malaysia, Nov. 10, 1939; s. Fook-Chong and Lai-Fong (Tang) K.; B.Agr.Sc. with honors (Harrisons & Crosfield Agrl. Group scholar), U. Malaya (Malaysia), 1963, M.Agr. Sc. in Entomology, 1965; Ph.D. in Entomology, U. Wis.-Madison, 1971; m. Victoria Tsuk-Yin Lim, Feb. 19, 1966. Tutor, U. Malaya, 1963-65, asst. lectr., 1965-68, lectr., 1968-71; research asst. U. Wis., 1968-71, postdoctoral research asso., 1971; asst. prof. entomology Va. Poly. Inst. and State U., 1972-77, asso. prof., 1978—. Internat. Rice Research Inst. Research scholar, 1964. Mem. Entomol. Soc. Am., Weed Sci. Soc. Am., Internat. Orgn. Biol. Control, Ga. Entomol. Soc., Va. Acad. Sci., Sigma Xi, Gamma Sigma Delta. Contbg. author: The Careless Technology: Ecology and International Development. Mem. spl. adv. com. for pesticide series in Environment, 1969. Contbr. articles to profl. jours. Home: 10 Azalea Dr Blacksburg VA 24060 Office: Dept Entomology Va Poly Inst and State U Blacksburg VA 24061

KOKENZIE, HENRY FAYETTE, county ofcl.; b. Gray's Landing, Pa., July 13, 1918; s. John and Antonia (Philimonova) K.; B.A., U. Denver, 1948; m. Irene Mildred Owens, May 24, 1941; children—Henry Fayette, Antoinette I., John R., Nicholas A. Bus. mgr. athletics U. Denver, 1948-49; dep. clk. Mcpl. Ct. Savannah (Ga.), 1952-58; mgr. truck sales Key West Ford, Inc. (Fla.), 1961-72; dir. vets. affairs Monroe County, Key West, 1972—; exec. sec. Vets. Council Monroe County, 1972—. Mem. Monroe County Democratic Exec. Com., 1960-69. Served to capt. U.S. Army, 1939-46. Recipient Thomas H. Gigniallat award, Savannah, 1958. Mem. Fla. Pub. Relations Assn. (pres. Fla. Keys/Conch chpt. 1977-78), County Vets. Service Officers Assn. Fla. (pres. 1977-79), Navy League U.S. (life), DAV (life), Ret. Officers Assn., Noncommd. Officers Assn. (life), Nat. Assn. Civilian Conservation Corps Alumni, Am. Legion, Key West C. of C., Mil. Order World Wars, Phi Beta Kappa, Omicron Delta Kappa, Pi Gamma Mu. Roman Catholic. Club: Elks, Moose (Key West). Home: 3413 Riviera Dr Key West FL 33040 Office: Pub Service Bldg Stock Island Key West FL 33040

KOLANSKY, S. KALMAN, psychiatrist; b. Carbondale, Pa., Dec. 27, 1937; s. Abe and Miriam (Raker) K.; A.B., Temple U., 1959, postgrad. in cellular physiology, 1959-61; M.D., Georgetown U., 1965; m. Ellen Judith Saltz, Sept. 5, 1965; children—Joshua Andrew, Jennifer Anne. Intern, D.C. Gen. Hosp. on George Washington Med. Service, 1965-66; resident in psychiatry Downstate Med. Center Kings County Hosp., Bklyn., 1966-68; resident, then chief resident child psychiatry Hahnemann Med. Center, Phila., 1968-70; chief child psychiatry tng. Overholser div. tng., psychiatry residency tng. program St. Elizabeth's Hosp., D.C., 1972—; practice medicine specializing in psychiatry and psychoanalysis, Alexandria, Va., 1972—; asst. clin. prof. psychiatry George Washington U. Med. Sch., 1973-78, Georgetown U. Med. Sch., 1978—. Served as maj. U.S. Army, 1970-72. Decorated Meritorious Service medal; diplomate Am. Bd. Psychiatry, Child Psychiatry. Mem. AMA (Physician's Recognition award 1971, 75, 78), Am. Psychiat. Assn., Washington Council Child Psychiatry (chmn. com. on continuing edn. 1976-, exec. council 1978—), Alexandria, Va. med. socs., AAAS, Washington Psychiat. Soc. Office: 110 N St Asaph St Alexandria VA 22314

KOLB, MICHAEL JOSEPH, mfg. co. exec.; b. Balt., Mar. 26, 1938; s. Edward Michael and Miriam (Coffee) K.; B.B.A. in Bus., U. Miami, 1967; postgrad. U. Mich., 1979; m. Marilyn Ann Fairbanks, Nov. 19, 1967; 1 dau., Carolyn Ann. Mem. sales staff Swift & Co., 1963-72; mem. sales staff Proturf div. O. M. Scott & Sons, ITT, 1972-76, so. regional mgr., 1976—. Served with USMCR. Mem. Fla. Turf Grass Assn., Tex. Turf Grass Assn. Republican. Roman Catholic. Home: 3423 Oleander Way Gulf Stream FL 33444 Office: O M Scott Sons ITT 333 Maple St Marysville OH 43040

KOLB, ROBERT FRANK, II, state ofcl.; b. Abbeville, S.C., May 25, 1946; s. Hugh Marshall and Bleka Anita (Cherry) K.; B.A. in Econs., Clemson U., 1968, M.Ed. in Personnel, 1978. Asst. mgr. S.C. Employment Security Commn., Liberty, 1968—; instr. bus. and econs. Tri County Tech. Coll., Pendleton, S.C., 1972—. Bd. dirs., treas. Pickens County (S.C.) Humane Soc., 1974—; bd. dirs. Easley Pickens County YMCA, 1972—; chmn. Pickens County Republican Party, 1976—; dir. Sunday sch. Liberty (S.C.) 1st Baptist Ch., 1979—. Recipient State of S.C. Service award, 1978. Mem. Am. Mgmt. Assn., Liberty C. of C., Internat. Assn. Personnel in Employment Security, S.C. State Employees Assn., Pickens Area Personnel Assn., U.S. Chess Fedn., S.C. Chess Assn., Liberty Jaycees (internal v.p. 1976-78, pres. 1978-79, chmn. bd. 1979—). Home: PO Box 146 Norris Rd Liberty SC 29657

KOLB, WILLIAM PAYTON, psychiatrist; b. Hope, Ark., Oct. 16, 1919; s. Allie Carl and Amanda Rachael (Payton) K.; A.B., Baylor U., 1941; M.D., U. Louisville, 1944; m. Margaret Lucile Sparks, Mar. 9, 1946; children—John Dudley and William Ernest (twins; dec.), Carl Spurgeon (dec.), Sarah Louise. Intern, Louisville Gen. Hosp., 1944-45; gen. practice medicine, Searcy, Ark., 1947-48; resident VA Hosp., North Little Rock, Ark., 1948-50, asst. chief acute treatment service, asst. chief profl. edn., 1950-53; dir. research and edn. Ark. State Hosp., Little Rock, 1954-56; practice medicine specializing in psychiatry, Little Rock, 1956—; cons. Ark. Enterprises for Blind, 1954—; clin. prof. psychiatry U. Ark., Little Rock, 1949—; mem. adv. council State Mental Health Plan; sec. Ark. Bd. Correction, 1968-70. Bd. dirs., mem. exec. com. Central Ark. Health Systems Agy.; bd. dirs. Ark. Found. Med. Care. Served with U.S. Army, 1943-47, 53-54. Diplomate Am. Bd. Psychiatry and Neurology. Fellow Am. Psychiat. Assn. (chmn. com. constn. and bylaws 1977-79); mem. Am., Ark. (past pres.), Pulaski County (past pres.) med. socs., Mid-continent Psychiat. Assn. (past pres.), Ark. Psychiat. Soc. (Meritorious Service award 1979), Am. Assn. Workers for Blind, Little Rock C. of C., Phi Mu Alpha. Democrat. Baptist. Contbr. chpts. to med. texts. Home: 224 Colonial Ct Little Rock AR 72205 Office: 230 Medical Towers Little Rock AR 72205

KOLESZAR, GEORGE EDMUND, air force officer; b. Newark, Nov. 22, 1941; s. George Emil and Alice Angela (Nugent) K.; B.S., N.J. Inst. Tech., 1963; M.S., U. Mo., 1969; Ph.D., Ohio State U., 1975; m. Irene Marie Hauck, July 13, 1963; children—Loretta Marie, John Edmund, Jean Margaret, Mary Ellen. Commd. 2d lt. U.S. Air Force, 1963, advanced through grades to lt. col., 1979; elec. engr., research and devel. ops. NSA, Ft. George G. Meade, Md., 1963-68; chief signal analysis br. European Def. Analysis Center, Wiesbaden, W. Ger., 1969-73; instr. supr., telecommunications systems staff officer course, coordinator, telecommunications mgmt. program, adj. faculty U. So. Miss., Biloxi, 1975-78; chief System Integration Office, Def. Communications Agy., Washington, 1978—. Judge, Fairfax County (Va.) Regional Sci. Fairs, 1979—. Mem. IEEE, Armed Forces Communications Electronics Assn., Sigma Xi, Air Force Assn. Home: 2500 Bristol Circle Woodbridge VA 22192 Office: DCA/WSE Washington DC 20305

KOLI, ANDREW KAITAN, educator; b. Bombay, India, Aug. 1, 1925; came to U.S., 1968, naturalized, 1973; s. Kaitan A. and Maria K.; B.S., Bombay U., 1955; M.S., Howard U., 1964, Ph.D., 1968; m. May 12, 1964; children—Vijay A., Sangita A. Teaching fellow, grad. research asst. Howard U., Washington, 1961-66, research asso., 1966-67, instr. dept. pharmacy, 1967-68; prof. chemistry S.C. State Coll., Orangeburg, 1968—. Recipient award for disting. achievement in research, 1977; U.S. Dept. Agr. grantee, 1973-77, 77—. Mem. Am. Chem. Soc., Indian Chem. Soc., Smithsonian Instn., Sigma Xi. Roman Catholic. Clubs: Internat., Columbian, K.C. Contbr. articles to sci. publs. Home: 1548 Northside NE Orangeburg SC 29115 Office: SC State Coll Orangeburg SC 29117

KOLIN, IRVING SEYMOUR, psychiatrist; b. Bklyn., Feb. 15, 1940; s. Leo and Jean (Dreier) K.; B.A. cum laude, U. Buffalo, 1961; M.D., State U. N.Y. Sch. Medicine at Buffalo, 1965; m. Rochelle Tinkelman, Sept. 4, 1966; children—Lawrence, Marc. Intern in pediatrics Med. Coll., Cornell U., N.Y.C., 1965-66, resident in psychiatry Payne Whitney Clinic, 1966-69, resident in child psychiatry, 1968-69; psychiat. cons. Brevard County Comprehensive Mental Health Center, Rockledge, Fla., 1969-71; psychiat. cons. Orange Meml. Hosp. Comprehensive Mental Health Center, Orlando, Fla., 1971-72, med. dir., 1972—; practice medicine specializing in psychiatry, Orlando, 1971—; teaching fellow psychiatry Cornell U. Med. Coll., 1967-69; asst. clin. prof., vis. faculty psychiatry Coll. Medicine, U. Fla., Gainesville, 1971-72, 72—; clin. prof. psychology, vis. faculty Fla. Technol. U., Orlando, 1973—. Served to lt. comdr. M.C., UNSR, 1969-71. Diplomate Am. Bd. Psychiatry and Neurology (examiner 1979). Mem. AMA, Fla. Med. Assn., Am., Fla., Central Fla. (pres. 1979) psychiat. socs., Am. Orthopsychiat. Assn., Am. Acad. Child Psychiatry, Phi Beta Kappa. Contbr. articles to profl. jours. Office: 1315 S Orange Ave Suite 3G Orlando FL 32806

KOLLAR, MICHAEL ANTHONY, counselor; b. Quantico, Va., Feb. 1, 1951; s. Frank Paul and Patricia Maureen (O'Boyle) K.; B.S., Western Carolina U., 1973, M.A. in Edn., 1974; Counselor, Job Corps, Franklin, N.C., 1973, Coll. of Charleston, S.C., 1974-77; grad. asst. Western Carolina U., Cullowhee, N.C., 1973-74, U. of Tenn., Knoxville, 1977—; mem. staff Am. Coll. Obstetricians Gynecologists, Med. U. S.C., 1977; pvt. practice counseling, Charleston, S.C., 1976-77. Mem. Am. Personnel and Guidance Assn., Assn. for Specialists in Group Work, Am. Assn. Sex Educators, Counselors, and Therapists, Am. Assn. Marriage and Family Counselors, Assn. of Sex Therapists and Counselors, Psi Chi. Office: Box 1 1701 Andy Holt Ave Melrose Hall Knoxville TN 37916

KOLLIKER, WILLIAM AUGUSTIN, art agy. exec., artist; b. Bern, Switzerland, Oct. 12, 1905; s. Augustin and Agnes (Lechner) K.; came to U.S., 1922, naturalized, 1935; student Nat. Acad. Art, 1922-23, Md. Inst., 1924-25; children—Doris Joanne, Frances Elizabeth; m. 2d, Helen M. Magruder-O'Brennan, Oct. 10, 1953; 1 dau., Katherin Kevin. Art dir., editor Am. Weekly, N.Y.C., 1930-52; art dir. Cunningham & Walsh Advt. Agy., N.Y.C., 1952-53, White & Shuford Art Agy., El Paso, Tex., 1954-65; painter, etcher, El Paso, 1965—; one-man shows: Dept. Interior, Washington, El Paso Mus. Art, Public Library Alamogordo (N.Mex.), Art Center Las Cruces (N.Mex.), Pub. Library Midland (Tex.), Santa Fe Art Mus., U. N.Mex., Museo de Arte e Historia, Ciudad Juarez, Mex., others; group shows include: Barry Stevens Gallery, N.Y.C., El Paso Art Mus., Dallas Art Mus., U. Tex. at Austin, Jinx Gallery, El Paso, numerous others; represented in permanent collections: U. Tex. at El Paso, El Paso Nat. Bank, El Paso Art Mus.; instr. art U. Tex., El Paso., 1955-58. Mem. Rio Bravo Watercolor Soc., El Paso Art Assn. Republican. Clubs: Art Dirs. (N.Y.C.); Rotary, Coronado Country. Home: 3812 Hillcrest Dr El Paso TX 79902 Office: 4100 Rio Bravo El Paso TX 79902

KOLODGY, JOHN STEPHEN, emergency med. technician; b. Miami, Fla., Mar. 13, 1940; s. Charles Stephen and Dora Maebelle (Chandler) K.; E.M.T., Miami-Dade Community Coll., 1972. Staff mem., estimator Giffen Industries, Inc., Coral Gables, Fla., 1959-62; shift comdr., asst. chief ops. Randle Eastern Ambulance Service, Inc., Miami, 1963-78; salesman Kaufman & Roberts, Pompano Beach, Fla., 1979; founder Emergency Med. Services Consultation Service, Interlachen, Fla., 1979—. Served with U.S. Army, 1958. Recipient Key to City of Miami Beach (Fla.), 1978. Mem. Nat. Assn. Emergency Med. Technicians (founding), EMT and Paramedic Soc. Fla. (founding), Fla. Assn. Emergency Med. Technicians (pres. 1974-75, 77-78). Democrat. Roman Catholic. Home: 7441 SW 1st St Margate FL 33063 Office: Route 3 Box 67 Interlachen FL 32048

KOLTER, WILLIAM HENRY, JR., surgeon; b. Houston, Nov. 15, 1927; s. William Henry and Jennie Katharine (Kerr) K.; A.B., Baylor U., 1950, B.S., 1952, M.D., 1955; m. Mary Neil McClellen, June 19, 1953; children—Kenneth Andrew, Elaine Katherine. Intern, Hermann Hosp., Houston, 1955-56, resident in surgery, 1956-60, now mem. staff; practice medicine specializing in surgery, Houston, 1960—; mem. staff Meml. Hosp. System, 1960—, chief surgery, 1965, 77; mem. staff Rosewood Gen. Hosp., 1964—, dir. div. surgery, 1972-74; mem. staff Meml. City, Methodist hosps. Past pres. Frostwood Elementary Sch. PTA; mem. ambulance adv. bd. City of Houston; deacon South Main Baptist Ch.; bd. dirs. Homes of St. Mark, Houston; trustee Meml. Hosp. System, Houston, 1974—. Served in Armored Inf., U.S. Army, 1946-47. Recipient Recognition award City of Houston, 1971. Diplomate Am. Bd. Surgery. Fellow A.C.S.; mem. AMA, Tex., Houston surg. socs., Tex. Med. Assn., Harris County Med. Soc. (recognition award 1970). Clubs: Doctors (Houston); Masons. Home: 12506 Mossycup St Houston TX 77024 Office: 616 Meml Profl Bldg 7777 Southwest Freeway Houston TX 77074

KOLTUN, STANLEY PHELPS, research chem. engr.; b. Bogalusa, La., Mar. 5, 1925; s. Sam and Ida Slipakoff; student John McNeese Jr. Coll., 1941-43, Tulane U., 1943-44, U. N.C., 1944-45; B.S. in Chem. Engring., La. State U., 1948; m. Janice Goldstein, July31, 1955; children—Karen Sue, Ellen Kay, Patricia Lyn. Chem. engr. gen. chem. div. Allied Chem. & Dye Corp., Baton Rouge, 1948-49; constrn. engr. U.S. C.E., New Orleans, 1951-54; chem. engr. So. Regional Research Center, U.S. Dept. Agr., New Orleans, 1956-59, cost engr., 1959-63, project leader, 1963-70, research chem. engr., 1970-76, acting research leader engring. and devel. lab., 1976—. Vice pres. Lynn Park Civic Assn., Metairie, La., 1957. Served with USNR, 1943-45. Recipient Dept. Agr. Superior Service award, 1976, Disting. Service award Fed. Bus. Assn., 1979; registered profl. engr., La. Mem. Am. Inst. Chem. Engrs., Nat. Soc. Profl. Engrs., La. Engring. Soc., Am. Oil Chemists Soc. (aflatoxins com.), Assn. Ofcl. Analytical Chemists, Am. Legion, Naval Res. Officers Assn., Mil. Order World Wars, Sigma Xi, Phi Epsilon Pi. Democrat. Clubs: German Shepherd Dog La., Greater New Orleans German Shepherd Dog Obedience Tng., Masons (32 deg.), Shrine (Arabians unit Jerusalem Temple), Past Masters Club. Contbr. sci. articles to profl. jours.; patentee. Home: 5601 Avron Blvd Metairie LA 70003 Office: 1100 Robert E Lee Blvd New Orleans LA 70179

KOMORN, ROBERT MELVIN, head and neck surgeon; b. Detroit, June 24, 1939; s. William and Gertrude (Katzman) K.; M.D., U. Mich., 1964; m. Judith Gail Katz, Aug. 21, 1961; children—Sherri Lynne, Deborah Susan, Janet Elizabeth. Intern, Sinai Hosp., Detroit, 1964-65; resident in otolaryngology U. Mich. Hosp., Ann Arbor, 1966-70; chief otolaryngology sect. VA Hosp., Houston, 1970-74; practice medicine specializing in otolaryngology, Houston; mem. staff Methodist, St. Joseph, St. Luke's, Tex. Children's hosps.; chief otolaryngology, dir. audio-vestibular lab. St. Joseph Hosp.; asst. prof. otolaryngology Baylor U. Coll. Medicine, 1970-74, clin. asst. prof., 1974—. Diplomate Am. Bd. Ophthalmology and Otolaryngology. Fellow A.C.S., Am. Acad. Otolaryngology, Soc. Univ. Otolaryngologists, Am. Soc. Head and Neck Surgery, Am. Acad. Facial Plastic and Reconstructive Surgery; mem. AMA, Tex. Med. Assn., Harris County Med. Soc., Tex. Otolaryn. Assn., Houston Otolaryn. Soc. (pres. 1976-77), Alpha Omega Alpha, Phi Kappa Phi. Contbr. chpts. to books, articles to med. jours. Home: 5219 Loch Lomond St Houston TX 77096 Office: 2000 Crawford Suite 1010 Houston TX 77002

KOMOSA, ADAM ANTHONY, educator; b. Pitts., Aug. 24, 1913; s. Simon and Kathrine K.; diploma Advanced Inf. Officers Sch., 1947; certificate The Army Signal Sch., 1952; diploma Air Groun Ops. Sch., 1952; A.A., U. Fla., 1960; B.A., Fla. State U., 1962, M.A., 1963, Ph.D., Inter-American U., 1967; m. Naomi Evlyn Beard, Feb. 11, 1949; children—Katherine Louise, Adam Anthony. Commd. as pvt. U.S. Army, 1932, advanced through grades to lt. col., 1951; radio operator, China, 1935-38; parachute inf. co. comdr, plans and tng officer, World War II, 1942-46; sr. regimental adviser Korean Mil. Advisory Group, 1950-52; gen. staff officer plans and ops., 1956-58; camp dir. nat. rifle and pistol matches, Camp Perry, Ohio, 1957. ret., 1958; prof. history No. Mich. U., 1968-78, prof. emeritus, 1978—; adv. Am. Security Council. Decorated Silver Star, Bronze Star with Oak Leaf Cluster, Purple Heart and others. Recipient certificate of appreciation U.S. Army Chief of Staff, 1957; Presidential commendation, Sygman Rhee, Pres. of Republic of Korea, 1951; certificate of Merit, Korean Army, 1951; certificate of Recognition, Polish Guard, 1955. Mem. Polish-Am. Congress, Am. Assn. Advancement of Slavic Studies, Polish Am. Hist. Assn., The Kosciuszko Found., Soc. Wireless Pioneers, Phi Kappa Phi, Phi Alpha Theta, Alpha Kappa Psi. Clubs: Campbellsville Golf and Country, Rotary Internat., Elks. Author: Third Flank Over Sicily, 1963; La Batalla de la Angostura, 1967. Home: Circle K Acres Columbia KY 42728

KONANTZ, RONALD J., petroleum engr.; b. Ft. Leavenworth, Kans., Dec. 22, 1946; s. Harold J. and Gwendolyn (Streeter) K.; student Lake Sumter Jr. Coll., 1967; A.A., U. Fla., 1967, B.E.E., 1970; m. Martha Sue Jones, Apr. 2, 1968; children—Pamela Kristine, Leslie Jean. Aerospace technologist NASA, Cape Kennedy, 1970; elec. design engr. Dept. Def., Patrick AFB, Fla., 1970-71; sales engr. Schlumberger, New Orleans, 1971—. Mem. IEEE, Soc. Petroleum Engrs., Nat. Pilots Assn., Am. Mgmt. Assn., Aircraft Owners and Pilots Assn., Soc. Profl. Well Log Analysts. Club: Univ. Fla. Century. Home: 106 Hemphill Houma LA 70360 Office: 1428 Elk Pl Med Plaza New Orleans LA 70112

KONDONASSIS, ALEXANDER JOHN, economist; b. Kozani, Greece, Feb. 8, 1928; s. John I. and Eve (Hatzistylianou) K.; came to U.S., 1948, naturalized, 1960; A.B. (Edward Rector scholar), DePauw U., 1952; M.A., Ind. U., 1953, Ph.D., 1961; m. Patricia Mundorf, Feb. 2, 1956; children—John, Yolanda. Lectr., Ind. U., Ft. Wayne, 1956-58; faculty dept. econs. U. Okla., Norman, 1958—, asso. prof., 1962-64, prof., 1964—, chmn. dept., 1961-71, David Ross Boyd prof., 1970—, dir. advanced program in econs., 1971—, dir. div. economics, 1979—; Fulbright prof. Athens (Greece) Sch. Econs. and Bus. Sci., 1965-66; vis. scholar vis. scientist program Am. Econ. Assn., 1971—; guest lectr. various groups, 1963—; mem. Gov.'s Adv. Council on Export Expansion, 1964-65, adv. council Inst. Mediterranean Affairs, N.Y.C., 1967. Bd. dirs. Okla. Council Econ. Edn., Am. Friends Wilton Park, N.Y.C. Recipient Okla. U. Regent award for superior teaching, 1964; Teaching award Merrick Found., 1977; Alumni Rector Scholar Silver Anniversary award DePauw U., 1977. Mem. Am., So., S.W. econ. assns., AAUP (chpt. pres.), Phi Beta Kappa, Beta Gamma Sigma, Omicron Delta Epsilon. Author articles, monographs, books; chmn. editorial policies com. SW Social Sci. Quar., 1974-77. Home: 512 Manor Dr Norman OK 73069

KONES, RICHARD JOSEPH, physician; b. N.Y.C., Apr. 8, 1941; s. Joseph I. and Ruth Murphy (Winkler) K.; B.S. in Chem. Engring. (N.Y. State Regents scholar 1958-60, Eshborn scholar 1960), N.Y. U. Heights, 1960; M.D. (Arthritis and Rheumatism Found. scholar, Physiology Honors Program scholar), N.Y. U., 1964; m. Sandra Lee Morrissey, Dec. 28, 1969; children—Kimberly Susan, Robin Melissa (dec.), Melanie Ann, Sabrina Lee. Fellow in physiology N.Y. U., 1961-62, in surgery, 1963; intern in medicine Kings County Hosp., Bklyn., 1964-65; resident in surgery Albert Einstein Coll. Medicine/Bronx Municipal Hosp., 1965-66; resident in medicine Lenox Hill Hosp., N.Y.C., 1966-68; teaching fellow in cardiology, physician-in-charge intensive care unit Knickerbocker and Logan Meml. hosps., N.Y.C., 1968-69; fellow in cardiology, acting chief resident VA Hosp., New Orleans, 1969-70; instr. internal medicine Tulane U., 1969-71, USPHS-Nat. Heart, Lung and Blood Inst. fellow in cardiology, 1970-71, vis. physician sect. cardiology, 1972—; asst. prof. clin. cardiology N.Y. Med. Coll., 1971-77; dir. med. edn., coordinator and dir. noninvasive ECG lab. No. Westchester Hosp.-Cornell Med. Center, N.Y., 1972-75; practice medicine specializing in cardiology, N.Y.C., 1971—, Bridgeport, Conn., 1976—; mem. staff Cabrini Health Care Center-Columbus/Italian Hosp., Park East, Park West hosps., N.Y. U. Med. Center-Midtown Hosp., Logan Meml. Hosp., Albert Einstein Coll. Medicine, Madison Ave., Community, Parkchester Gen., Flatbush Gen., Westchester Sq., Lefferts Gen., Mt. Eden Gen. hosps. (all N.Y.C.), Park City Hosp., Bridgeport; cons. cardiologist ot hosps. and numerous ins. cos.; cons. N.Y. and Conn. burs. disability determinations Social Security Adminstrn., HEW; medicolegal cons. Tech. Adv. Service for Attys., Phoenix; lectr. in field. Recipient Freshman Chemistry Achievement award N.Y. U. Dept. Chemistry, 1958, Continuing Edn. awards AMA, 1969, 71, 76, 78. Diplomate Am. Bd. Internal Medicine. Fellow Am. Acad. Law and Sci., Am. Coll. Chest Physicians, Am. Coll. Cardiology, Am. Coll. Legal Medicine, Am. Coll. Clin. Pharmacology, Royal Soc. Health (London), Royal Soc. Medicine, Am. Coll. Angiology, Am. Geriatrics Soc. (founding mem.), Am. Soc. Bariatric Physicians, Soc. Advanced Med. Systems, Internat. Coll. Angiology, N.Y. Cardiol. Soc., Am. Coll. Emergency Physicians (charter); mem. A.C.P., Am. Physiol. Soc. (asso., charter mem.), Soc. Gen. Physiologists, Am. Fedn. Clin. Research, Am. Soc. Exptl. Biology, Am. Acad. Clin. Toxicology, Am. Soc. Internal Medicine, Am. Cancer Soc., Am. (councils on basic sci., cardiopulmonary diseases, circulation, thrombosis, clin. cardiology), N.Y., La., Conn., Westchester heart assns., Am. Toxicology Soc., Am. Chem. Soc. (award in chemistry achievement), Am. Soc. Clin. Pharmacology and Exptl. Therapeutics, Am. Med. Writers Assn., French Soc. Advancement of Sci., AAAS, Am. Diabetes Assn., Am., La. thoracic socs., Am. Zool. Soc. (charter mem. comparative physiology group), Am. Acad. Social and Polit. Sci., Am. Statis. Assn., Am. Inst. Biol. Scis., Am. Pub. Health Assn., Am. Math. Soc., Am. Lung Assn., Laennec Soc., Biophys. Soc., Biomed. Engring. Soc., Engring. in Biology and Medicine Group, Audio Engring. Soc., Am. Assn. Advancement Med. Instrumentation, Belgian Soc. Cardiology, Soc. Critical Care Medicine Med. Electronics and Data Soc., Internat. Study Group Research Cardiac Metabolism, Microcirculatory Soc., IEEE, Internat. Soc. Thrombosis Haemostatsis, World Fedn. Nuclear Medicine and Biology, Internat. Soc. Internal Medicine, Internat. Soc. Cardiology, Internat. Soc. Heart Research, Internat. Diabetes Fedn., Internat. Union Physiol. Scis., Internat. Union Pure and Applied Biophysics, U.S. Bioenergetics Group, Société Française de Cardiologie, So. Med. Assn., N.Y. Acad. Scis., N.Y. Trudeau Soc., N.Y. Allergy Soc., N.Y. State Soc. Internal Medicine, Musser-Burch Soc., Am. Med. Tennis Assn., N.Y. U. Sch. Medicine Alumni Found., U.S. Lawn Tennis Assn., Am. Mus. Natural History, East African Wildlife Soc. (Kenya), Nat. Geog. Soc., Nat. Wildlife Fedn., Tulane U., Albert Einstein med. alumni assns. Author: The Molecular and Ionic Basis for Altered Myocardial Contractility, 1973; Cardiogenic Shock, 1974; Glucose, Insulin, Potassium And the Heart, 1975; Shock Cardiogenico (in Spanish), 1977; Coronary Care Unit Handbook, 1979; (with J. H. Phillips) Inherited Diseases and the Heart, 1979, Advanced Electrocardiology, 1979; editor: Controversies in Cardiology, vols. 1-3, 1979—; contbr. numerous articles to profl. publs.; editor: (with J. H. Phillips) Basic and Clinical Pharmacology of the Heart, 1979; contbg. editor: Chest, Am. Hosp. Formulary Service, Current Prescribing; cons. editor Futura Pub. Co. Home: 356 Horseshoe Hill Rd Pound Ridge NY 10576 Office: 133 E 73 St New York City NY 10021 also PO Box 1919 Bridgeport CT 06601 also 305 Baronne St Suite 901 New Orleans LA 70112

KONICOFF, DONALD STEPHEN, ophthalmologist; b. N.Y.C., July 6, 1934; s. Thomas and Esther (Jacobson) K.; student Rutgers U., 1952-55; M.D., N.Y. Med. Coll., 1958; m. Doris Ellen Solomon, Aug. 5, 1956; children—Larry, Craig, Tammy. Intern, Phila. Gen. Hosp., 1958-59; resident ophthalmology Washington U., St. Louis, 1959-62; practice medicine specializing in ophthalmology, Boca Raton, Fla., 1964—; pres. med. staff Boca Raton (Fla.) Community Hosp., 1974-76. Mem. mgmt. adv. council Fla. Ocean Scis. Inst., 1974-75. Served to capt. USAF, 1962-64. Diplomate Am. Bd. Ophthalmology. Fellow A.C.S., Am. Acad. Ophthalmology and Otolaryngology; mem. Soc. Eye Surgeons, Fla. Med. Assn., Miami, Fla. ophthalmol. socs., Broward County, Palm Beach County eye socs., Phi Beta Kappa, Alpha Omega Alpha. Office: 120 W Palmetto Park Rd Boca Raton FL 33432

KONIDITSIOTIS, CORNELIA YAVIS, speech pathologist; b. Memphis, Apr. 21, 1945; d. Harry David and Sophie (Pappas) Yavis; B.A., U. Ala., 1966, M.A., 1968; Ph.D., U. New Orleans, 1979; m. John Elias Koniditsiotis, July 19, 1970; children—Elias, Harry. Lang. cons. Dept. Interior, 1964; speech and lang. therapist YMCA, Athens, Greece, summer 1968; instr., dir. presch. program hearing impaired, dept. speech pathology and audiology Memphis State U., 1968-70; instr., cons. La. State U., New Orleans, 1970-73; cons. Ochsner Med. Found., New Orleans, 1972-73; pvt. practice speech pathology. Mem. Am. Speech, Lang. and Hearing Assn., La. Speech and Hearing Assn., New Orleans Assn. Parents Deaf Children (founder), Greek Community PTA (pres. 1978-80), Daughters of Penelope (bd. govs. 1979-80), Am. Hellenic Ednl. Progressive Assn., Kappa Delta Pi, Phi Delta Kappa, Phi Kappa Phi. Mem. Greek Orthodox Ch. Author papers in field. Address: 1055 Homestead Ave Metairie LA 70005

KONKEL, RICHARD JOSEPH, quality control engr.; b. Manitowoc, Wis., Nov. 4, 1943; s. Edward Anthony and Helen (Glowienka) K.; ed. pub. schs. in Wis. Quality control engr. Paragon Electric Co., Two Rivers, Wis., 1965-72; quality assurance mgr. Aluminum Splty. Co., Manitowoc, 1973-77; quality control engr. Aero Cast Co., Miami, Fla., 1978—. Served with U.S. Army, 1962-65. Mem. Am. Soc. Quality Control, Am. Soc. Nondestructive Testing. Democrat. Home: 4719-A Madison Circle Homestead FL 33030

KONO, TETSURO, physiologist; b. Tokyo, May 17, 1925; s. Ichiro and Hiroko (Sasaki) K.; came to U.S., 1963; Ph.D., U. Tokyo, 1958; m. Seiko, Dec. 18, 1962; children—Michiko, Masahiro, Kenji. Instr., U. Tokyo, 1960-63; asst. prof. physiology Vanderbilt U. Med. Sch., 1963-69, asso. prof., 1969-74, prof., 1974—. NIH grantee, 1962—. Mem. Japanese Biochem. Soc., Am. Soc. Biol. Chemists. Buddhist. Contbr. numerous articles to profl. jours. Home: 2009 Stonehurst Dr Nashville TN 37215 Office: Dept Physiology Vanderbilt U Med Sch 21st Ave S Nashville TN 37232

KONRAD, HERMANN, cons. pollution control engr.; b. Berlin, Dec. 6, 1926; s. Erich and Ida (Frank) K.; C.E., U. Cauca, Popayan, Colombia, 1955; postgrad. in hydraulics U. Andes, Mérida, Venezuela, 1957; m. Stella Delgado, 1953; children—Marianela, Ann Astrid. Came to U.S., 1966, naturalized, 1972. Railrd. constrn. work in Colombia, Madigan-Hyland Cons. Engrs., N.Y.C., 1955-57; asst. prof. hydraulics U. Andes, Merida, 1958-62, head hydraulics lab., 1960; cons. engr. irrigation projects in Colombia, Bogotá, 1962-66; with environ. dept. Gilbert Assos., Reading, Pa., 1966-68; prin. asso., sr. engr. for water and pollution control facilities Post, Buckley, Schuh & Jernigan, Inc., Miami, Fla., 1968—. Registered profl. engr., Fla. Mem. ASCE, Fla. Engring. Soc., Nat. Soc. Profl. Engrs. Home: 1420 S Bayshore Dr Apt 205 Miami FL 33131 Office: PO Box 660 764 Miami Springs FL 33166

KOO, ROBERT CHUNG JEN, horticulturist; b. Shanghai, China, Mar. 20, 1921; s. Tse Zung and Ge Tsung (Tse) K.; came to U.S., 1940, naturalized, 1961; B.S., Cornell U., 1944; M.S., U. Fla., 1950, Ph.D., 1953; m. Margaret Wei Shan Chung, Mar. 19, 1949; children—Robert, Kenneth, Dennis. Lang. specialist civil service U.S. Dept. Navy, 1945-47; faculty horticulture U. Fla., Lake Alfred, 1953—, prof., 1969—; cons. horticulture to citrus growers, various cos. U.S. Dept. Interior Water Resources research grantee, 1970-73. Mem. Am. Soc. Hort. Sci., Fla. Hort. Soc. (Presdl. gold medal award 1965, hon. mem.), Sprinkler Irrigation Soc., Am. Agronomy Soc., Crop and Soil Sci. Soc. Fla., Fla. Fruit and Vegetable Assn. (research award 1975). Episcopalian. Club: Rotary (sec. 1972-73, v.p. 1973-74, pres. 1974-75). Author: (with others) The Role of Potassium in Agriculture, 1968. Home: 2223 12th St NW Winter Haven FL 33880 Office: PO Box 1088 Lake Alfred FL 33850

KOONS, RUSSELL EUGENE, chemist; b. Montpelier, Ind., July 25, 1918; s. James Porter and Blanche (Henderson) K.; B.Chemistry, U. Tulsa, 1941; m. Geraldine Elizabeth Moore, July 3, 1942; children—Harriet, Beverly, Blanche. Chemist, Am. Smelting & Refining Corp., Sand Springs, Okla., 1941-42; mem. compounding dept. Gates Rubber Co., Denver, 1942-43; plant foreman, rubber plant CoPolymer Corp., Baton Rouge, 1943-46, research chemist, 1946-48; research chemist Lion Oil Co., El Dorado, 1948-61, Monsanto Chem. Co., St. Louis, 1961-73; research group leader Lion Oil div. Tosco Corp., El Dorado, 1973—. Mem. Am. Chem. Soc., ASTM. Patentee in petrochem. and asphalt fields. Home: 1254 W Oak St El Dorado AR 71730 Office: Tosco Corp El Dorado AR 71730

KOONTS, JONES CALVIN, educator; b. Lexington, N.C., Sept. 19, 1924; s. Harvey Hill and Elsie (Tussey) K.; A.B. in English and History magna cum laude, Catawba Coll., Salisbury, N.C., 1945; M.A. in Sociology, George Peabody Coll., Nashville, 1949, Ph.D. in Edn., 1958; m. Cortlandt Morper, Sept. 6, 1953; children—Carlisle Woodson, Camille Walton. Tchr. English and social studies Boyden High Sch., Salisbury, 1945-48; dir.-asst. student teaching George Peabody Coll., 1951-52; mem. faculty Erskine Coll., Due West, S.C., 1949—, prof. edn., chmn. dept., 1949—, chmn. div. tchr. edn., 1975—; tchr. adult edn. Abbeville (S.C.) County Community Center, 1955; tchr. grad. courses U. S.C., also Clemson U., 1956—; rep. S.C. Bd. Edn., 1966-71; bd. commnrs. Piedmont Tech. Coll., 1972-75; alumni bd. dirs. Catawba Coll., 1966. Jesse H. Jones scholar, 1951; Algernon Sydney Sullivan scholar, 1951; fellow Council So. Univs., 1957-58; Peabody-Harvard scholar, 1960; Fulbright grantee, 1964; recipient Distinguished Service key Phi Delta Kappa. Mem. N.C. Edn. Assn. (chpt. sec.-treas. 1946-47), S.C. Assn. Student Teaching (founder, 1st pres. 1955-56), S.C. Council Tchr. Edn., S. Atlantic Philosophy Edn. Soc., Poetry Soc. S.C. (dir.), Nat. Assn. Tchr. Educators (del S.C.), Am. Assn. Colls. Tchr. Edn., S.C. Assn. Colls. Tchr. Edn. (pres. 1979-80, William Gimore Simms Poetry prize 1973, Unicorn Poetry prize 1974, Lyric Poetry prize 1975, Elizabeth B. Coker Poetry award 1977, Acad. Am. Poets. Presbyterian. Author: (poetry) Since Promontory, 1967, Straws in the Wind, 1968, Under the Umbrella, 1971; editor Green Leaves in January, 1972; A Slice of the Sun, 1976. Home: PO Box 163 Due West SC 29639 Office: Dept Edn Erskine Coll Due West SC 29639

KOONTS, ROBERT HENRY, lawyer, ins. co. exec.; b. Greensboro, N.C., May 8, 1927; s. Henry Valentine and Margaret (Andrew) K.; B.S. in Commerce, U. N.C., 1949, LL.B., 1952; grad. exec. program, 1967; m. Edna Mildred Matthes, Mar. 8, 1952; children—Linda Suzanne, Barbara Jane. Admitted to N.C. bar, 1952; gen. practice, High Point, N.C., 1952-57; now v.p., asso. gen. counsel Jefferson Standard Life Ins. Co., Greensboro; v.p., asso. gen. counsel Jefferson Pilot Corp., Greensboro; sec., dir. Jefferson-Pilot Publs., Inc., Greensboro; sec., dir. Beamont Newspapers, Inc. (Tex.), Clearwater Newspapers, Inc. (Fla.), Laredo Newspapers, Inc. (Tex.), Texas City Newspapers, Inc. (Tex.), Altus Newspapers, Inc. (Okla.), Plant City Newspapers Inc. (Fla.). Served with USNR, 1945-46. Mem. Assn. Life Ins. Counsel, Am., N.C., Greensboro bar assns. Phi Delta Theta, Phi Delta Phi. Presbyterian. Clubs: Greensboro Country, Greensboro City. Home: 3600 Starmount Dr Greensboro NC 27403 Office: Jefferson Standard Life Ins Co Greensboro NC 27420

KOONTZ, JOSEPH PATRICK, system software specialist; b. San Angelo, Tex., Oct. 27, 1948; s. Patrick Henry and Dorres (Stavinoha) K.; B.S. in Physics, Angelo State U., 1970; M.S. in Computer Sci., Tex. A. and M. U., 1972; m. Gladys Anne Duggan, July 15, 1978. Systems programmer Angelo State U., San Angelo, 1969-71; student mgr. minicomputer facilities Tex. A. and M. U., College Station, 1971-72, dir. digital data lab., physics dept., 1973-74; system software specialist Agy. Records Control Inc., Bryan, Tex., 1974-78; staff cons. Systems Application Engring. Inc., Houston, 1978—. Mem. staff, mentally retarded children's day camp, San Angelo. William C. Wilson Jr. scholar, 1967-69. Registered emergency med. technician, Tex. Mem. Am. Inst. Physics, Soc. Physics Students, Am. Assn. Physics Tchrs., Assn. Computer Machinery, Data Processing Mgmt. Assn., Tex. Assn. Emergency Med. Technicians, Nat. Assn. Emergency Med. Technicians. Roman Catholic. Home: 10031 Cedar Creek Houston TX 77042 Office: Systems Application Engring Inc 6250 Westpark Suite 270 Houston TX 77053

KOP, TIMOTHY M., psychologist; b. Aug. 3, 1946; s. Michael and Antoinette Wanda K.; B.A., U. Hawaii, 1972; M.A., U. N.C., 1975; M.A., Mich. State U., 1976; postgrad. Calif. Grad. Inst., 1977-78, U.S. Internat. U., 1978—; m. Yoshino Fujita, Aug. 9, 1975; 1 dau., Maile K. Guidance counselor U.S. Army, Hawaii, 1974-75, dep. chief Directorate of Personnel and Community Activity, Japan, 1975-77; chief profl. devel. U.S. Army Computer Systems Command, Falls Church, Va., 1978—; cons. in ednl. psychology, Tokyo Lang. Sch., 1976. Served with U.S. Army, 1965-68, 77-78. Mem. Am. Personnel and Guidance Assn., Am. Rehab. Counseling Assn., Am. Sch. Counseling Assn., Assn. of Asian-Am. Psychologists, Am. Soc. for Aerospace Edn., Hawaii Career Guidance Assn., Disabled Am. Vets., Nat. Psychiatric Assn., Air Force Assn., Assn. Mil. Surgeons of U.S., Canadian Psychol. Assn., Res. Officers Assn., Am. Psychol. Assn., Am. Orthopsychiatric Assn. Home: PO Box 2294 Falls Church VA 22042 Office: 7700 Arlington Blvd Falls Church VA 22042

KOPECKO, NORBERT ROBERT, JR., accountant; b. Richmond, VA., Mar. 23, 1944; s. Norbert Robert and Dorothy (Ellener) K.; B.S., Va. Poly. Inst. and State U., 1967; postgrad. in bus. adminstrn., 1967; m. Helen Margaret Keith, Aug. 20, 1966; children—Thomas Keith, Stephen Christopher. Staff acct. Ernst & Ernst, Richmond, Va., 1967, advanced staff, 1968, sr. acct., 1969, supr., 1969-72, mgr., 1972-77; mgr. in charge Ernst & Whinney, Roanoke, Va., 1977, partner in charge, 1977—. Group chmn. United Way Richmond, 1970-72; treas., dir. Richmond Area Assn. Retarded Citizens, 1971-74; mem. fin. com. St. Marys Catholic Ch., 1973; chmn. profl. div. United Way Roanoke, 1979; bd. dirs. St. Vincents Home, 1979. Mem. Nat. Assn. Accts. (treas., dir. Richmond), Va. Soc. C.P.A.'s Clubs: Shenandoah, Hunting Hills Country, Chatmoss Country. Home: 5139 Remington Rd Roanoke VA 24014 Office: 825 Colonial Plaza Bldg Roanoke VA 24011

KOPEL, KENNETH FRED, clin. psychologist; b. Austin, Tex., July 29, 1947; s. James and Helen (Eshman) K. K.; B.A. in Psychology with spl. honors, U. Tex., Austin, 1968, Ph.D. in Clin. Psychology, 1972; m. Sandra Marks, Aug. 25, 1968; children—Gregory Brian, Andrew Charles, Deborah Leigh. Intern in clin. psychology VA Hosp., also Children's Mental Health Service, Houston, 1971-72; psychol. cons. med. services VA Hosp., Houston, 1972—; clin. asst. prof. psychology Baylor Coll. Medicine, Houston, 1973—, U. Houston, 1973—; clin. psychologist Cons. Psychol. Services, Houston, 1973—; instr. Inst. Creative Living, U. St. Thomas, Houston; lectr. Tex. Women's U. Sch. Nursing. Bd. dirs. Kidney Found. Houston and Greater Gulf Coast. Fellow USPHS, 1968-69, VA, 1969-72. Mem. Am., Tex., Houston psychol. assns., Am., Houston group psychotherapy assns., Am. Soc. Adlerian Psychology, Soc. Psychol. Study Social Issues. Jewish. Author articles in field. Home: 7622 Rollingbrook Dr Houston TX 77071 Office: 6065 Hillcroft St Suite 311 Houston TX 77036

KOPP, STEVEN HOWELL, state govt. ofcl.; b. Phila., Sept. 28, 1945; B.A. in Geography, Wittenberg U., Springfield, Ohio, 1968; J.D., Nashville YMCA Night Law Sch., 1978. Applications engr. Deutsch Co., Dayton, Ohio, 1972-74; personnel mgmt. analyst Tenn. Dept. Personnel, Nashville, 1974-77; with Tenn. Energy Authority, Nashville, 1977—, state allocation officer, 1978, chief resource mgmt., 1978—; admitted to Tenn. bar, 1978. Mem. Am. Bar Assn., Am. Soc. Public Adminstrn. Home: 3710 Auburn Ln Nashville TN 37215 Office: Tenn Energy Authority Capitol Blvd Bldg Suite 707 Nashville TN 37219

KORBEL, ALLEN ROBERT, fin. planner; b. Milw., Apr. 16, 1931; s. Alfred and Ruth Murial (Knoernschild) K.; B.B.A., U. Wis., 1957; m. Grace Marie Barteck, Sept. 15, 1956; children—Mary Grace, Janice Lynn. Pres., dir. Lake Shore Stores, Inc., Madison, Wis., 1955-56; spl. agt. Central Life Assurance Co., Des Moines, 1957-66; pres., dir. Korbel Corp., Milw., 1966-78; owner, operator Am. Mortgage Assn. Co., McAllen, Tex., 1979—, Korbel Co., 1978—. Served with USAF, 1950-54. Mem. bd. dirs. Family Hosp., 1964-74, treas., 1971-72. Mem. Milw. Assn. Life Underwriters (pres. 1964-65, dir. 1959-66), Universal Shelter Corp. (dir. 1970-74, v.p. 1972-74), Million Dollar Round Table, Alpha Kappa Psi. Contbr. articles to trade publs. McAllen TX 78501

KORDOMENOS, VANGALIA LUKES, educator; b. Mobile, Ala., Mar. 25, 1933; d. George Nick and Maria (Xenakes) Lukes; B.S., Auburn U., 1954; M.A., U. Ala., 1958; cert. in edenl. leadership, U. South Ala., 1978; postgrad. U. Ala., 1974—; m. Nick John Kordomenos, June 2, 1963; children—John, James. Tchr., Mobile (Ala.) County Public Schs., 1954-66, curriculum writer, 1966-68; asst. prof. edn. Mobile Coll., 1968—; with Sterling Assos., Krikos, Inc., Cons., 1979—. Shell grantee, 1978. Mem. Assn. Suprs. and Curriculum Dirs., Assn. Tchr. Educators, Internat. Reading Assn., Alpha Delta Kappa. Greek Orthodox. Club: Daus. of Penelope. Office: PO Box 13220 Mobile AL 36613

KORENBLIT, JACK IZAAK, realtor; b. Lublin, Poland, June 7, 1916; s. Samuel Mayer and Bella (Wekstein) K.; came to U.S., 1946, naturalized, 1952; student U. Reims (France), 1934-35; chemist degree U. Caen, Calvados, France, 1938, Engr. Chemistry, 1939; m. Paula Geliebter, Oct. 17, 1937; 1 dau., Gloria Fay Korenblit Steckler. Owner, chemist Velvet Cosmetics, Manila, 1939-41; prisoner of war, Santo Thomas, Manila, 1942-45; self-employed in export bus., 1946-55; owner Allsun Realty, Miami Beach, 1958—; pres. Trend Realty, Inc., Cocoa Beach, 1964—; pres. Multiple Listing Service Cape Kennedy Area Bd. Realtors, 1968-69. Chmn. realtors and developers div. United Way, 1973, chmn. Brevard County, 1977; chmn. Bonds of Israel Dr. for Brevard County, 1978, 79. Named Fla. Realtor of Year, 1975. Mem. Fla. Assn. Realtors (Creative Bus. Ability in Real Estate award 1971, v.p. 1971, life dir., treas. 1977, Churchwell edn. award 1974), Cape Kennedy Area Bd. Realtors (Realtor of Year 1969, 71, 74, 75; pres. 1973), Cape Kennedy Area C. of C. (Citizen of Year 1971, pres. 1972, life dir.), Melbourne Area Bd. Realtors (hon. life). Democrat. Jewish. Clubs: Rotary, K.P. Home: 133 Bimini Rd Cocoa Beach FL 32931 Office: 1733 N Atlantic Ave Cocoa Beach FL 32931

KORGEN, BENJAMIN JEFFRY, oceanography cons.; b. Duluth, Minn., Jan. 6, 1931; s. Benne Hanson and Helen Louise (Slattum) K.; B.S., U. Minn., 1956; M.A., U. Mich., 1958; Ph.D., Oreg. State U., 1969; m. Judith Kay Waggoner, Aug. 15, 1959; children—Susan Kay, Jeffry David, James Matthew. Phys. oceanographer U. N.C., Chapel Hill, 1969-74, asst. prof., 1969-74; cons. in oceanography, Sandwich, Mass., 1974—; cons. Harper & Row Pubs., 1972-74, Thermonetics Corp., San Diego, 1972-74; textbook writer Allyn & Bacon, Boston, 1974— oceanographer U.S. Naval Oceanographic Office; adj. asso. prof. Tulane U.; adv. com. Miss.-Ala. Sea Grant Consortium. Served with USN, 1951-54. U. Mich. grad. fellow, 1957-58; NSF grantee, 1965; Office Naval Research fellow, 1966-69; Office Naval Research-NSF grantee, 1968-69; NSF grantee, 1969-70; U. N.C. Research Council grantee, 1969-72; N.C. Bd. Sci. and Tech. grantee, 1971-72; Naval Oceanographic Office contractee, 1971-73. Mem. Am. Soc. Limnology and Oceanography, Internat. Oceanographic Found., Am. Geophys. Union, AAAS, Geol. Soc. Am., Woods Holl Assos. Contbr. articles in field to profl. jours. Home: 219 Loop Dr Slidell LA 70458

KORNBERG, ELLIOT HAROLD, surgeon; b. Queens, N.Y., June 14, 1942; s. William and Goldie (Suslak) K.; A.B., Columbia U., 1964; M.D., SUNY, Bklyn., 1968; m. Patti Phillips, Sept. 4, 1965; children—Bonnie, Joel. Intern in surgery Beth Israel Hosp., Boston, 1968-69, jr. resident, 1969-71; teaching fellow in surgery Harvard Med. Sch., 1970-71; sr. and chief resident in surgery R.I. Hosp., Providence, 1971-73; teaching fellow Brown U., Providence, 1972-73; practice medicine specializing in gen., vascular and thoracic surgery, Cocoa Beach, Fla., 1975—; mem. staff Cape Canaveral Hosp. Pres. Temple Beth Shalom, 1977—. Served with USAF, 1973-75. Diplomate Am. Bd. Surgery. Fellow A.C.S.; mem. Fla. Med. Soc., Brevard County Med. Soc. Club: Cocoa Beach Men's. Home: 650 N Atlantic Ave Penthouse 5 Cocoa Beach FL 32931 Office: 475 Minutemen Causeway Cocoa Beach FL 32931

KORNEGAY, HOBERT, dentist; b. Meridian, Miss., Aug. 28, 1923; s. Hobert and Mary Louise (Gaines) K.; B.S., Morehouse Coll., 1945; D.D.S., Meharry Med. Coll., 1948; postgrad. Med. Field Service Sch., 1953, Walter Reed Inst. Dental Research, 1968-71; m. Ernestine Price, June 10, 1948; children—Carmen Kateena, Patricia Louise, James Price, Donna Michele. Individual practice dentistry, Meridian, 1948-53, 1955—; mem. staffs Riley's Hosp., Meridian, Matty Hersee Hosp., Meridian. Cons. preventive dentistry Miss. Head Start, U. P.R. Dental Sch., 1970-71; cons. Miss V.I. Program, 1970-71, USPHS, 1971-72; clinician Jackson Comprehensive Health Clinic, Utica, Miss., 1970-72; dental surgeon Volt Tech. Corp., Atlanta, 1971-72, Westinghouse Learning Corp., Washington and Silver Spring, Md., 1971-72. Mem. Govs. com. Health Needs Children Miss., 1971-72; mem. task force Miss. Council Child Devel., 1971; chmn. Chetaw Area council Boy Scouts Am., 1955-65; chmn. Lauderdale Econ. Opportunity Program, 1971-72; dir. Meridian Redevel. Authority Urban Renewal, 1971-72; councilman, vice mayor Meridian, 1977—; bd. dirs. St. Francis Homes, 1971—. Served as capt. AUS, 1953-55. Mem. Acad. Gen. Dentistry, Nat., Am. dental assns., Am. Pub. Health Assn., Pierre Fauchard Acad., NAACP (life), Meridian C. of C., Omega Psi Phi (dir.). Republican. Baptist (trustee 1950, treas., 1970). Mason (Shriner), Elk, PGER, Toastmaster (pres. 1969-72). Contbr. articles to newspaper. Home: 1420 39th Ave Meridian MS 39301 Office: 2416 5th St Meridian MS 39301

KORNREICH, DAVID VICTOR, lawyer; b. Parkchester, N.Y., Jan. 22, 1943; s. Anton and Sadie (Muhlrad) K.; B.A., U. Miami, 1963; J.D., N.Y. U., 1966; postgrad. George Washington U., 1966-67; m. Joan Ruth Bregman, Aug. 25, 1965; children—Kevin Scott, Craig Stephen. Fed. mgmt. intern, also asst. to dir. fed. employee-mgmt. relations U.S. Dept. Labor, Washington, 1966-67; admitted to Fla. bar, 1966; trial atty. NLRB, Labor Relations Miami and Tampa, Fla., 1967-69; partner, treas. law firm Muller, Mintz, Kornreich, Caldwell & Casey, Miami, 1969—; guest lectr. labor relations in edn. Grad. Sch. Edn., U. Miami, 1969-72, on labor law Sch. Law, 1970-74; lectr. pub. employee labor relations Broward (Fla.) Community Coll., 1975; witness before U.S. Senate Subcom. on Housing and Urban Affairs to promote utilization of improved tech. in federally assisted housing, 1972; speaker trade assn. confs. Fellow Fla. Acad. Labor-Mgmt. Attys.; mem. Am., Fla. (labor relations law com. 1967—) bar assns., City-County Attys. Assn., Dade County (Fla.) League of Cities, Internat. Found. Employee Benefit Plans. Republican. Club: Kings Bay Country (Miami). Home: 6500 SW 133 Dr Miami FL 33156 Office: One S Biscayne Blvd Miami FL 33132

KOSAR, JOHN JOSEPH, JR., accountant; b. Butler, Pa., Mar. 3, 1946; s. John Joseph and Alfred Elizabeth (Marini) K.; student Robert Morris Coll., 1965-67; A.A.S. cum laude, No. Va. Community Coll., 1975. Acct., Kramer & Assos., Fairborn, Ohio, 1967-69, Capital City Fed. Savs. & Loan, Washington, 1973-74; controller Am. Press Inst., Reston, Va., 1974-78; acct. Nat. Bus. Edn. Assn., Reston, 1974—; acctg. coordinator PRC Realty Systems, McLean, Va., 1978-79; controller PRC Tech. Applications, Inc., McLean, 1979—. Served with USAF, 1969-73. Mem. Nat. Bus. Edn. Assn. Home: 2002 Colts Neck Rd #22A Reston VA 22091 Office: 7600 Old Springhouse Rd McLean VA 22102

KOSCHNY, WILLIAM SIMON, chem. engr., ret. govt. ofcl.; b. Newport, R.I., Aug. 21, 1921; s. William and Theresa Marie (Czforeck) K.; B.S., Northeastern U., 1949; M.S., McKinley-Roosevelt, Inc., 1952; M.E.A., George Washington U., 1958; postgrad. Am. U., 1958-66, U. South Africa, 1968-72; student So. Bapt. Sem., 1980—; m. Bertha Margaret Clarkin, Jan. 1953 (div. Apr. 1958); children—Theresa Mary and Laura Louise (twins); m. 2d, Mae Margarette McVay Leader, June 20, 1962. Asst. to gen. supt. Lewiston Gas Light Co. (Me.), 1949-50; cadet chem. engr. Lynn Gas & Electric Co. (Mass.), 1950-51; ordnance engr. Bur. Ordnance, USN, Newport, 1951-53, Washington, 1953-54, mech. engr., Bur., Aeros., 1954-56, aero. research engr., 1956-58; mil. intelligence specialist, chief staff intelligence U.S. Army, Washington, 1958-62; supervisory gen. engr. U.S. P.O. Dept., 1962-69, head planning and systems analysis research div., bur. research and engring., Washington, 1962-66, chief design assurance and value engring. div., bur. research and engring., Bethesda, Md., 1966-67, personal staff asst. to asst. dir. engring., Washington, temporary detail as tech. adviser to U.S. Postal Service Inst., Bethesda, Md., 1967-69; tech. adviser/gen. engr. tech. proposal evaluation staff, Bur. Research and Engring., Washington, 1969-71, gen. engr., program mgr. Area Mail Systems div. Bulk Mail Dept. Operations Group, U.S. Postal Service, Washington, 1971-74, program mgr., facilities planning br. Bldgs. and Analysis div. Real Estate and Bldgs. Dept., 1974-76, program planning mgr. Program Planning div., 1976-78. Served with USAAC, 1943. Registered profl. engr., D.C., R.I. Mem. Am. Chem. Soc. (sr. mem.), Am. Inst. Indsl. Engrs. (sr. mem., rec. sec. 1964-65), Fed. Profl. Assn. Washington (sr.), Soc. Am. Value Engrs., R.I. Honor Soc., Pi Sigma Alpha. Contbr. articles to various publs. Home: 3341 Tournament Blvd Sarasota FL 33580

KOSH, RONALD WALTER, bus. exec., mgmt. cons.; b. Pottsville, Pa., May 17, 1945; s. V. Walter and Helen (Marham) K.; B.A. in Fgn. Service and Internat. Politics, Pa. State U., 1970; J.D., Internat. Sch. Law, 1978; m. JoAnne P. Droege, July 3, 1976; 1 dau., Nicole M. Field supr. approved accommodations Am. Automobile Assn., Inc., Falls Church, Va., 1970-73, mgr. ops. nat. travel dept., 1973-77, mgr. club standards and accreditation, 1977-78, dir. field ops. mgmt. services dept., 1978—; sec., dir. Top Notch Industries, Inc., Wildwood Interiors Corp., 1979—. Vice pres., dir. Washington Jaycees, 1974-75. Served with USAF, 1962-67; Vietnam. Decorated Air Medal, AF Commendation Medal. Mem. Am. Mgmt. Assn., Adminstrv. Mgmt. Soc., Penn State Alumni Assn. (pres., dir. 1978-79), Alpha Phi Omega, Xi Gamma Iota. Republican. Byzantine Catholic. Club: Nittany Lions. Contbr. articles profl. jours. Home: 10305 Galpin Ct Great Falls VA 22066 Office: 8111 Gatehouse Rd Falls Church VA 22047

KOSHUBA, WALTER JOSEPH, engring. exec.; b. St. Paul, Aug. 22, 1917; s. John and Pauline (Rychley) K.; B.Metall. Engring., U. Minn., 1940; m. Renella J. Waaland, Sept. 8, 1945; children—Walter Joseph, Mykola J. Supt. research engring. Allis Chalmers Mfg. Co., Milw., 1940-46; gen. supt. Solar Aircraft Co., Des Moines, 1946-47; head materials sect. NEPA div. Fairchild Engine & Airplane Corp., Oak Ridge, 1947-51; head metall., ceramic engring. aircraft nuclear propulsion div. Gen. Electric Co., Cin., 1951-56, mgr. tech. prodn., 1956-61; mgr. Nuclear div. Beryllium Corp. (name now Kawecki-Berylco Industries, Inc.), Hazleton, Pa., 1961-64, gen. mgr. div., 1964-65, mgr. alloy div., 1965-71, mgr. mfg. tech., 1971-72; mgr. facilities and equipment engring. United Nuclear Corp. Naval Reactors div., 1972-74; v.p. engring. and constrn. Uranium Recovery Corp., Mulberry, Fla., 1974-79, v.p. spl. projects, 1979—. Mem. Hazleton Indsl. Council. Fellow Am. Inst. Chemists; mem. Pa. Mfrs. Assn., Am. Soc. Metals (chmn. Cin.), Am. Inst. Mining, Metall. and Petroleum Engrs., Am. Ceramic Soc., Am. Powder Metallurgy Inst., Inst. Ceramic Engrs., Am. Nuclear Soc. Home: 3621 Dan Unie Ln Lakeland FL 33803 Office: Uranium Recovery Corp Box 765 Mulberry FL 33860

KOSKA, ROBERT FRANCIS, computer engr.; b. Kansas City, Kans., Sept. 27, 1952; s. Anthony Paul and Gladys Elizabeth (Skiers) K.; B.S.E.E., So. Meth. U., 1975. Sesimic field engr. Mobil Oil Co., Dallas, 1975-77; computer engr. Mobil E & P Services Inc., Dallas, 1977—. Mem. IEEE. Roman Catholic. Clubs: N. Central Tex. Alumni Assn. of Alpha Phi Omega (treas.), Cath. Alumni of Dallas. Home: 3227 Northaven Dallas TX 75229 Office: 1930 Empire Central St #130 Dallas TX 75235

KOSSMANN, CHARLES EDWARD, cardiologist; b. Bklyn., Apr. 20, 1909; s. Edward and Anna (Seidel) K.; B.S., N.Y. U., 1928, M.D., 1931, Med. Sc.D., 1938; postgrad. U. Mich., 1934; m. Margaret Musgrave, Dec. 28, 1946; children—Michael Musgrave, Margaret Olive. Intern, Bellevue Hosp., N.Y.C., 1931, house physician, 1932-33, mem. staff, 1934-67, chief adult cardiac clinic, 1940-56, cons., 1968—; asst. in medicine U. Mich. Med. Sch., 1934; practice medicine, N.Y.C., 1935-67; instr. N.Y. U. Sch. Medicine, 1938-42, asst. prof., 1942-49, asso. prof., 1949-64, prof. medicine, 1964-67; prof. medicine U. Tenn. Coll. Medicine, Memphis, 1967-76, prof. emeritus, 1976—, chmn. div. circulatory diseases, 1967-74; mem. staff Lenox Hill Hosp., N.Y.C., 1937-64, chief adult cardiac clinic, 1949-56, cons. cardiologist, 1964-67; mem. staff Univ. Hosp., N.Y.C., 1949-67, City of Memphis Hosp., 1968—; cons. physician Norwalk (Conn.) Hosp., 1962-67, N.Y. VA Hosp., 1964-67, Memphis VA Hosp., Bapt. Meml. Hosp., Memphis; mem. com. aviation medicine NRC, 1947-50; cons. to surgeon gen. USAF, 1948-53, George Washington U. Computer Facility, 1966; chief cons. in cardiology Central Office, VA, 1951-56; mem. sci. adv. bd. to chief of staff USAF, 1952-56; med. insp. N.Y.C. Bd. Edn., 1958-67; mem. med. bd. Irvington House, 1954-67; chmn. tng. grants and awards com. Nat. Heart Inst., 1960-64; cons. div. regional med. programs USPHS, 1966-73; mem. central com. Memphis Regional Med. Program, 1968-73. Served with M.C., USAF, 1941-45; col. Res. (ret.). Decorated Legion of Merit. Diplomate Am. Bd. Internal Medicine (exam. bd. cardiovascular disease 1950-55). Fellow AAAS, A.C.P., N.Y. Acad. Scis., N.Y. Acad. Medicine; mem. Am. (chmn. So. regional research rev. and adv. com. 1968-70), N.Y. (pres. 1961-63), Tenn. (research com. 1968-71), Memphis (dir. 1968-74) heart assns., N.Y. U. Sch. Medicine Alumni Assn. (pres. 1961-62), Am., Tenn., Memphis, Shelby County med. socs., Harvey Soc., Soc. Alumni Bellevue Hosp., Am. Soc. Clin. Investigation (emeritus), Sociedad Mexicana de Cardiologia, Soc. Exptl. Biology and Medicine, Assn. Am. Physicians (emeritus), Assn. Univ. Cardiologists (emeritus), Memphis Acad. Internal Medicine, Memphis Med. Seminar (pres. 1971-72), Sigma Xi, Alpha Omega Alpha. Clubs: Univ. (N.Y.C.); Windyke Country (Memphis); San Antonio Country. Editor: Advances in Electrocardiography, 1958; Diseases of the Heart and Blood Vessels, Nomenclature and Criteria for Diagnosis, 6th edit., 1964; asso. editor Advances in Internal Medicine, 1969—; mem. editorial bd. Am. Heart Jour., 1948-49, Circulation, 1950-51, 58-63, 64-68; Cardiologia, 1949-70, Circulation Research, 1952-57, Am. Jour. Cardiology, 1972-77; mem. editorial bd. Bull. N.Y. Acad. Medicine, 1959-68, chmn., 1962-68; contbr. articles on circulation and electrophysiology to med. jours. Home: 6365 Wood Bridge Rd Memphis TN 38138 Office: 800 Madison Ave Memphis TN 38163

KOTAS, ROBERT VINCENT, research physician; b. Buffalo, Nov. 26, 1938; s. Vincent John and Regina Agnes (Hadynka) K.; B.S., Canisius Coll., 1959; M.D., U. Buffalo, 1963; m. Ilona Rae Fielding, Mar. 2, 1968; children—Nicole, Timothy, Robert, Rebecca. Research asso. McGill U., 1969-70; intern Buffalo Childrens Hosp., 1963-64; resident in pediatrics Johns Hopkins Hosp., Balt., 1964-66; asst. prof. pediatrics U. Okla. Med. Sch., 1970-72, dir. newborn services, 1970-72; dir., div. devel. physiology; career investigator W.K. Warren Med. Research Center, Tulsa, 1972-76, sci. dir., 1976—; clin. prof. pediatrics U. Okla. Med. Sch., Tulsa, 1977—; guest scientist Nat. Inst. Child Health and Human devel., Bethesda, Md., 1975-77. Served as capt. USAF, 1966-68. Mosby scholar, 1963; recipient grants NIH, 1969-70, 75-77, USPHS, 1968-69; diplomate Am. Acad. Pediatrics. Fellow Am. Coll. Obstetricians and Gynecologists (asso.); mem. Johns Hopkins Med. and Surg. Assn., Southern Soc. Pediatric Research, Am. Thoracic Soc., Soc. Pediatric Research, Am. Physiol. Soc., Soc. Exptl. Biology and Medicine, Soc. Gynecol. Investigation. Contbr. articles to profl. jours. and books. Office: 6465 Yale St S Tulsa OK 74177

KOTSALIS, PAUL NICK, bus. services co. exec.; b. Johnstown, Pa., Apr. 20, 1925; s. Nick P. and Alice N. K.; ed. high sch., Johnstown; m. Ann Vagias, June 11, 1950; children—Helene, Nicholas. Gen. mgr. New Style Co., Johnstown, 1945-50; co-owner United Co., constrn. cons.'s, Johnstown, 1950-62; pres. United Co., Cape Coral, Fla., 1963—, chmn. bd., 1964—. Co-founder New Annunciation of the Virgin Mary Greek Orthodox Ch., Ft. Myers, Fla., 1974, pres., 1979. Served with Airborne Corps, U.S. Army, 1943-45; ETO. Decorated Purple Heart. Clubs: Rotary (pres. Cape Coral 1977-78), Amvets (life), Cape Coral Country, Am. Legion, Moose. Home: 5948 SW 1st Ave Cape Coral FL 33904 Office: United Co 619 Cape Coral Pkwy PO Box 832 Cape Coral FL 33904

KOTT, GARY LYNN, oil drilling co. exec.; b. Houston, Feb. 25, 1942; s. R. K. and Jean K.; B.S.Ch.Eng., U. Tex., 1965; M.B.A. in Fin., U. Pa., Wharton Sch., 1969; m. Barbara Gibbs; children—R. Charles, J. Reagan. Project control supr. Eastex, Inc., Silsbee, Tex., 1965-68; teaching fellow U. Pa., Wharton Sch., 1968-69; sr. cons. Arthur Andersen & Co., Houston, 1969-71; v.p. ops. Western Oceanic, Inc., Houston, 1971-78; v.p. engring. Global Marine Drilling Co., Houston, 1978, then sr. v.p. ops., pres. C.P.A., Tex. Mem. Nat. Acad. Scis. (marine bd.), Com. Offshore Regulations, Internat. Assn. Drilling Contractors, Am. Inst. C.P.A.'s. Methodist. Club: Univ., Pine Forest Country.

KOTTER, JAMES IVY, mech. engr.; b. Asheville, N.C., Sept. 29, 1925; s. John James and Inez Doretta (Koper) K.; B.S. in Mech. Engring., Southwestern La. Inst., 1951; m. Johanna Frances Maloney, Jan. 31, 1949; children—JoAnn, James Ivy, Don Christopher, Kenneth Coburn, Barbara Lynn. Mech. engr. U.S. Army C.E., New Orleans, 1951-53; shipbldg. insp. U.S. Navy and Naval Inspection of Ordnance 8th Naval Dist., 1953-54; research mech. engr. So. Regional Research Center, U.S. Dept. Agr., New Orleans, 1954-79, supervisory mech. engr. advanced systems, cotton textile processing lab., 1968-79; tech. adv. and cons. mech. and textile engring. Served with USAAF, 1944-45. Recipient Outstanding Performance award Dept. Agr., 1967, Superior Service award, 1978; 3d award Internat. Prize Paper Competition, 1968; lic. profl. mech. engr., La. Mem. ASME, Fiber Soc., Sigma Xi. Contbr. numerous articles to profl. publs.; patentee in field. Home: 1911 Lakeshore Dr Mandeville LA 70448

KOTZEBUE, ROBERT WILLIAM, SR., air conditioning co. exec.; b. Moulton, Tex., Mar. 28, 1909; s. George William and Adelia (Helmcamp) K.; ed. high sch.; m. Mary Lou Wanek, May 18, 1929; children—Robert William, Kenneth Lee. Mgr. air conditioning dept. Straus-Frank Co., San Antonio, 1934-41; partner Bell-Kotzebue Co., San Antonio, 1945-60; owner, operator Kotzebue Distbg. Co., San Antonio, 1960—, chmn. bd., 1968—. Served to capt., C.E., U.S. Army, 1941-45. Registered profl. engr. Tex. Mem. San Antonio C. of C., San Antonio Power Squadron (comdr. 1971-72), Am. Soc. Heating, Refrigeration Air Conditioning Engrs. (life). Republican. Lutheran. Clubs: Oak Hills Country, St. Anthony, Turtle Creek Country. Home: 149 Lou-Jon Circle San Antonio TX 78213 Office: 1031 NE IH 410 PO Box 17369 San Antonio TX 78217

KOUBEK, KENNETH GENE, chemist; b. Hackensack, N.J., Dec. 20, 1944; s. John Frank and Mildred Ann (Sefcik) K.; B.A. in Chemistry, Montclair State Coll., 1972; M.A. in Bus. Mgmt., Central Mich. U., 1978; m. Beverly Jean Baker, Nov. 20, 1971; children—Kristine Denise, Kenneth Michael. Quality control chemist Azoplate div. Am. Hoechst Co., Murray Hill, N.J., 1972-73; lab. supr., quality control dept., plastics div. ICI-Am. Inc., Bayonne, N.J., 1973-75, residue chemist residue lab., agrl. chems. div., Goldsboro, N.C., 1975—. Served in U.S. Army, 1966-68. Decorated Army Commendation medal. NSF grantee, 1971. Mem. Am. Chem. Soc., Alpha Sigma Mu, Sigma Iota Epsilon. Roman Catholic. Home: 215 Ashby Ln Goldsboro NC 27530 Office: PO Box 208 Goldsboro NC 27530

KOUCHOUKOS, NICHOLAS THOMAS, surgeon; b. Grand Rapids, Mich., Dec. 26, 1936; s. Thomas Paul and Antoinette (Karver) K.; student (James B. Angell scholar) U. Mich., 1954-57; M.D. cum laude, Washington U., 1961; m. Judith Buell, Aug. 24, 1966; children—Nicholas Thomas, Robert Buell, Thomas Paul. Intern, Barnes Hosp., Washington U. Med. Center, St. Louis, 1961-62, asst. resident in surgery, 1962-65, chief adminstrv. resident, 1965-66, sr. clin. trainee in surgery (USPHS), 1966-67, asst. in surgery Sch. Medicine Washington U., 1961-65, instr. surgery, 1965-67; research fellow surgery Sch. Medicine, U. Ala., Birmingham, 1967-68, instr. surgery, 1967-69, advanced trainee thoracic, cardiovascular surgery, 1968-70, asst. prof. surgery, 1969-71, asso. prof., 1971-74, prof., vice-dir. div. thoracic and cardiovascular surgery, 1974—; mem. cardiovascular research study com. Am. Heart Assn., 1977—; surgery study sect. USPHS, Bethesda, Md., 1977—; ad hoc cons. Specialized Centers in Research Arteriosclerosis, Nat. Heart and Lung Inst., Bethesda, 1971-72, mem. ad hoc rev. com. for collaborative studies on coronary artery surgery, 1973—, surgery A study sect., 1976-77; mem. merit rev. bd. in cardiovascular studies VA, Washington, 1976—. Fellow Southeastern Surg. Congress, Am. Coll. Cardiology (finalist Young Investigators award 1962), A.C.S.; mem. Am. Assn. Thoracic Surgery, AAUP, AMA, Am. Surg. Assn., Assn. Academic Surgery, Jefferson County, Ala. med. socs., John Kirklin Soc., Soc. Thoracic Surgeons, Soc. Univ. Surgeons, Soc. Vascular Surgery, Internat. Cardiovascular Soc., Phi Beta Kappa, Alpha Omega Alpha. Home: 3148 Guilford Rd Birmingham AL 35223 Office: Dept Surgery U Ala Med Center Univ Sta Birmingham AL 35294

KOUSKY, LINDA KAY (RUBAC), educator; b. Temple, Tex., Aug. 25, 1953; d. Emil Martin and Albina (Kratochvil) Rubac; student Temple Jr. Coll., 1971-73; B.S. in Elementary Edn., Tex. A. and M. U., 1975, M.S. in Edn. Psychology, 1976; m. Bruce Francis Kousky, Sept. 1, 1973; 1 dau., Jennifer Michelle. Receiving clk. Sears Roebuck & Co., Bryan, Tex., 1974-77; research asst. Tex. A. and M. U., 1976-77; tchr. Lamar Elementary Sch., Bryan, 1977-78, Corrigan-Camden Intermediate Sch., 1978—. Mem. Am., Tex. personnel and guidance assns., Nat. Sci. Tchrs. Assn., Tex. State Tchrs. Assn. Roman Catholic. Club: Forestry and Range Wives Aux. (pres. 1977-78). Home: 2605 S 1st St Apt 116 Lufkin TX 75901

KOUTRAS, PHOEBUS, thoracic and cardiovascular surgeon; b. Athens, Greece, Aug 31, 1932; s. Demetrius and Helen (Kongos) K.; came to U.S., 1965, naturalized, 1977; M.D., U. Athens, 1958; m. Helen Nicolacopoulos, Sept. 4, 1960; children—Elena, Jim, Charles. Intern, Trumbull Meml. Hosp., Warren, Ohio, 1965-66; resident in thoracic and cardiovascular surgery Southwestern Med. Sch., 1967-69; fellow in cardiovascular surgery Baylor Hosp., Dallas, 1971-72; practice medicine, specializing in thoracic and cardiovascular surgery, Midland, Tex., 1973-74, Garland, Tex., 1974—; mem. staffs Meml. Hosp., Garland Community Hosp., Med. City Dallas Hosp., Richardson Gen. Hosp., Plano Gen. Hosp., Baylor U. Med. Center. Diplomate Am. Bd. Surgery, Am. Bd. Thoracic Surgery. Fellow A.C.S., Mem. Am., Tex. med. assns., Dallas County

Med. Soc., Am. Coll. Angiology, Am. Coll. Cardiology, Soc. Clin. Vascular Surgery. Contbr. articles to med. jours. Office: 315 N Shiloh St Garland TX 75042

KOVSKI, JOHN JOSEPH, elec. engr.; b. Erie, Pa., May 21, 1916; s. John Jacob and Esther Emma (Schauble) K.; B.S. in Elec. Engring., Bucknell U., 1940; m. Jacquelyne June Coffey, Feb. 27, 1946; children—John Jeffrey, Alan Duane. Marine service engr. Sperry Gyroscope Co., Inc., Cleve., 1940-41; Signal Corps insp. War Dept., U.S. Govt., Washington, 1941, radio engr., 1941-45, electronic scientist, Wright Field, Ohio, 1945-51; research electronics engr. Glenn L. Martin Co., Balt., 1951-52, electronics design specialist, 1952-55; staff engr. Lockheed Missiles Systems Div., Van Nuys, Calif., 1955-56; staff to chief engr., mgr. reconnaissance system dept., mgr. tech. services Melpar, Inc., Falls Church, Va., 1956-60; staff engr. Republic Aviation Corp., Farmingdale, N.Y., 1960-62, v.p. engring. staff, 1962-64; sr. tech. specialist, supr. ops. analysis N.Am. Aviation Corp. div. Rockwell Internat., Columbus, Ohio, 1965-68; sr. systems engr. Hazeltine Corp., Plainview, N.Y., 1968-70; systems mgr. Cardion Electronics Co., Woodbury, N.Y., 1971-73; engring. design draftsman CARPCO Research and Engring. Co., Jacksonville, Fla., 1974-75; engr. power engring. div. Jacksonville Elec. Authority, 1976—. Mem. IEEE (sr.), Assn. Old Crows, Am. Def. Preparedness Assn. (life), U.S. Air Force Assn., Phi Lambda Theta. Patentee in electronics field. Home: 913 Le Brun Dr Jacksonville FL 32205 Office: 233 W Duval St Jacksonville FL 32202

KOWERT, ARTHUR HERMAN, newspaper editor; b. Staunton, Ill., July 4, 1911; s. Herman George Theodore and Mathilde Anne (Schuricht) K.; B.B.A., U. Tex. at Austin, 1934; m. Elise Weber, Nov. 11, 1937; children—Bruce A., Nancy L. Kowert Dreher. Advt. mgr. Fredericksburg Pub. Co., Inc. (Tex.), 1934-41, mng. editor, 1941—, pres., 1980—; pres. Hill County Community Press Inc., Fredericksburg, 1969—. Mem. Bd. Edn., Fredericksburg Ind. Sch. Dist., 1951-63; Bethany Lutheran Ch., Fredericksburg, 1948-52; precinct chmn. Gillespie County (Tex.) Democratic Com.; active Hill Country Council Boy Scouts Am., 1937-78. Recipient Boss of Yr. award Fredericksburg Jaycees, 1959; Silver Beaver award, Lamb award Boy Scouts Am., 1954-59. Mem. Tex. (pres. 1953-54), S.Tex. (pres. 1944-45) press assns., Fredericksburg C. of C. (pres. 1945-46), Sigma Delta Chi. Democrat. Lutheran. Lion (pres. 1944-45). Photographer for book: Old Homes and Buildings of Fredericksburg, 1976; editorial contest winner Railroads of Tex., 1962. Home: 107 E Schubert St Fredericksburg TX 78624 Office: 108 E Main St Fredericksburg TX 78624

KOWITZ, GERALD THOMAS, educator; b. Port Huron, Mich., Mar. 30, 1928; s. William C. and Martha M. (von Hochlietner) K.; B.A. in Psychology, Mich. State U., 1948, M.A. in Psychology, 1950, Ph.D. in Edn., 1954; m. Norma M. Giess, Nov. 25, 1952; children—G. Kristine, M. Louise, L. Marlane. Tchr., Lansing, Mich., 1953-54; sch. psychologist, Dearborn, Mich., 1954-55; asso. prof. U. Ark., Little Rock, 1955-57; research asso. in psychometrics dept. edn. SUNY, Albany, 1957-60; coordinator exptl. programs N.Y. State Edn. Dept., Albany, 1960-63; asso. prof. U. Houston, 1963-64; dir. Bur. Ednl. Research, 1964-66; prof. edn. U. Okla., Norman, 1966-67, chmn. ednl. psychology and guidance, 1967-70, asst. dean budgets and spl. projects, 1970-73, prof. human devel., 1973—. Mem. NEA, Am. Psychol. Assn., Am. Ednl. Research Assn., Phi Delta Kappa, Psi Chi. Served with USNR, 1945-47, USAR, 1949-54. Author: Guidance in the Elementary Classroom, 1959; Operating Guidance Services in the Modern School, 1968; An Introduction to School Guidance, 1971. Office: 820 Van Vleet Oval Norman OK 73019

KOZEK, JOHN ROBERT, psychiatrist; b. Des Moines, Oct. 16, 1943; s. Oscar Kenneth and Jeanette (Hamilton) K.; B.A., Drake U., 1967; D.O., Coll. Osteo. Medicine, 1968; m. Maria Vidalis, June 5, 1971. Intern, Portland Osteo. Hosp., 1969-70; resident psychiatry Cherokee (Iowa) Mental Health Inst., 1972-74; gen. practice medicine, Portland, 1971; practice medicine specializing in psychiatry, Dunedin, Fla., 1975—; staff West Pasco Hosp., New Port Richey, Fla., now chief dept. internal medicine; staff Suncoast Osteo. Hosp., Largo, Fla., Met. Hosp., Pinellas Park, Fla., Community Hosp., New Port Richey; clin. instr. Coll. Osteo. Medicine, Des Moines, 1969; U.S. rep. 6th Ann. European Behavior Conf., 1976; cons. Fla. Dept. Health and Rehab. Services; chief psychiatrist Upper Pinellas Assn. Retarded Children; pres. M & J Accounting & Investing Agy. Served to capt., M.C., AUS, 1969-71. Decorated Bronze Star medal, Purple Heart. Diplomate Am. Bd. Psychiatry and Neurology. Recipient Rockwell Physician of the Year award, 1971. Mem. Cherokee Mental Health Inst. Residents Assn. (pres. 1972-73), World, Am., Fla., Iowa psychiat. assns., Am. Coll. Neuropsychiatrist, Isaac Walton League, VFW. Clubs: K.C., Commondore Internat. Yacht (dir.). Contbr. articles to profl. jours. Address: 3150 Las Olas Dr Dunedin FL 33528

KOZLOWSKI, RONALD STEPHAN, library adminstr.; b. Chgo., Oct. 18, 1937; s. Stephan James and Helen Marie (Tancula) K.; student Wright Jr. Coll., 1958-59; B.S., Ill. State U., 1961; M.L.S., Rosary Coll., 1968; m. Barbara Hartlein, Aug. 8, 1964; children—Ann, Keith, Ellen, Brent. Audiovisual librarian Triton Jr. Coll., River Grove, Ill., 1968-69; br. librarian Evansville Pub. Library (Ind.), 1969-70; head reference and acquistions Ind. State U., Evansville, 1970-71; asst. dir. Evansville Pub. Library, 1971-74; dir. West Fla. Regional Library, Pensacola, 1974-77; dir. Louisville Free Pub. Library, 1977—. Served with USN, 1955-58. Mem. ALA, Southeastern, Ky. library assns., Greater Louisville C. of C. Roman Catholic. Home: 412 Trinity Hills Ln Louisville KY 40207 Office: Louisville Free Pub Library 4th and York Sts Louisville KY 40203

KOZMA, MINERA THERESA, hosp. adminstr., nurse; b. Georgetown, S.C., Feb. 11, 1924; d. Joseph and Wadia Masad K.; diploma St. Francis Sch. Nursing, Clarleston, S.C., 1949; student Coll. Charleston, 1958-62; B.S.N., U. Fla., 1967, M.S.N., 1972. With Roper Hosp., Charleston, 1949-65, asst. dir. nursing, 1960-62, acting dir. nursing, 1962-65; head nurse VA Hosp., Gainesville, Fla., 1967-72; dir. nursing No. Fla. Regional Hosp., Gainesville, 1972-77; v.p. patient services Alachua Gen. Hosp., Inc., Gainesville, 1977—; mem. adv. com. to asso. degree nursing Santa Fe Community Coll.; mem. adj. faculty U. Fla. Coll. Nursing; mem. adv. com. Emergency Med. Tech. Tng. Program. Mem. Fla. Soc. Nursing Services Adminstrs., Am. Hosp. Soc. Nursing Services Adminstrn., Fla. League Nursing, Nat. League Nursing, Phi Kappa Phi, Sigma Theta Tau. Democrat. Roman Catholic. Home: 4421 NW 18th Pl Gainesville FL 32605 Office: 801 SW Second Ave Gainesville FL 32602

KOZMETSKY, GREGORY ALLEN, investment co. exec.; b. Boston, Apr. 4, 1946; s. George and Ronya (Keosiff) K.; student St. Edward's U., 1969-70; B.B.A., U. Tex., 1972; m. Cynthia Jane Hendrick, Sept. 7, 1968; children—Aaron Wood, Daniel Allen, Sarah Katherine. Trust adminstrv. officer Laredo Nat. Bank (Tex.), 1973; v.p., asst. to chmn. bd. Federated Devel. Co., Houston, 1974-76; gen. partner GAK, Ltd., 1976—; pres. KMS Ventures, Inc., Austin, Tex., 1977—, chmn. bd., 1977—; chmn. bd. Arrowsmith Tool and Mfg. Co., 1978—; dir. Pertron Controls Corp., Napp, Inc., Tex. State Bank, Md. Realty Trust, Quad Mud Logging, Inc. Mem. adv. com. Muscular Dystrophy Assn., central Tex. chpt., 1977—; mem. council ministries Tarrytown Meth. Ch., 1979—, mem. adminstrv. bd., 1979—; trustee RGK Found., 1972—, v.p., 1978—. Served with U.S. Army, 1964-69. Mem. Aircraft Owners and Pilots Assn. Home: 4802 Ridge Oak Dr Austin TX 78731 Office: 902 Vaughn Bldg Austin TX 78701

KRACKE, ROBERT RUSSELL, lawyer; b. Decatur, Ga., Feb. 27, 1938; s. Roy Rachford and Virginia Carolyn (Minter) K.; student Birmingham So. Coll.; B.A., Samford U., 1962; J.D., Cumberland Sch. Law, 1965; m. Barbara Anne Pilgrim, Dec. 18, 1965; children—Shannon Ruth, Robert Russell, Rebecca Anne, Susan Lynn. Admitted to Ala. bar, 1965; individual practice law Birmingham, Ala., 1965—. Vice-chmn. Jefferson County Dem. exec. com., 1972—; deacon Ind. Presbyn. Ch., Birmingham, 1973-76, pres. adult choir, 1968—. Served with USNR, 1955-57. Mem. Birmingham (chmn. law library, law day 1976), Ala., Am. (award merit law day 1976) bar assns., Am. Judicature Soc., Phi Alpha Delta (pres. chpt. 1964-65), Sigma Alpha Epsilon. Democrat. Clubs: Civitan (pres. Birmingham Breakfast 1975-76, lt. gov. Ala. Dist. 1976—), Downtown. Editor Birmingham Bar Bull., 1974—. Contbr. articles to profl. publs. Home: 4410 Briarglen Dr Birmingham AL 35243 also Deerwood Lake Harpersville AL 35078 Office: 2220 Highland Ave Birmingham AL 35205

KRAFT, BEVERLY JOYCE TERRY, real estate developer; b. Long Beach, Calif., Dec. 19, 1952; d. Jack Howard and Ruby Mae Terry. B.S. in Real Estate cum laude (scholar), Ariz. State U., 1974; m. Robert Lawrence Kraft, May 25, 1974. Fin. clk. Valley Nat. Bank, Dealer Fin. div., Phoenix, 1970-74; sr. planner Columbus-Bartholomew Planning Dept., Columbus, Ind., 1974-77; closing mgr., asst. project mgr. Am. Design & Devel. Corp., Miami, Fla., 1977-79, v.p. closings, 1979—. Named Miss. Ariz. Industry, 1973-74. Mem. Bus. and Profl. Women's Orgn., Ariz. State U. Alumni Assn., Phi Chi Theta. Office: 1915 Brickell Ave Miami FL 33055

KRAFT, LELAND MILO, JR., geotech. engr.; b. Gloversville, N.Y., Feb. 27, 1942; s. Leland Milo and Doris E. (Snyder) K.; B.C.E., Ohio State U., 1965, M.S., 1965, Ph.D., 1968; m. Rita Anne Lawyer, Sept. 2, 1967; children—Lisa Anne, Michelle Leigh. With Ohio State U., 1964-68, research asso. civil engring. dept., 1967-68; soil engr. Columbus (Ohio) Testing Lab., 1968-69; asst. prof. civil engring. Auburn U., 1969-72; cons. Scott Constrn. Co., Opelika, Ala., 1971-72, City of Auburn, 1971-72, Harman, White and Assos., Inc., Opelika, 1970-72; project engr. McClelland Engr., Inc., Houston, 1972-74, mgr. spl. projects group, 1974—. Mem. ASCE (chmn. soil mechanics found. div. tech. activities com. Ala. sect. 1970-72, com. on reliability and probabilities concepts geotech. engring. div. 1973—, com. on publs. 1975—, com. offshore structure reliability 1975—; State-of-the-Art award 1979), Internat. Soc. Soil Mechanics, Fedn. Internationale de la Precontrainte (com. 1977), Offshore Tech. Conf., Coastal Soc., Transp. Research Bd., U.S. Metric Assn., Marine Tech. Soc. (panel seafloor engring. 1979), Sigma Xi, Chi Epsilon, Tau Beta Pi. Contbr. articles to tech. jours. Home: 2020 Briargreen Dr Houston TX 77077 Office: McClelland Engr Inc 6100 Hillcroft Houston TX 77081

KRAIKITPANITCH, SOMPONG, physician; b. Thailand, Oct. 4, 1942; came to U.S., 1968; s. Kraikit and Tieng Kaou; M.D., Chiengmai U., 1967; m. Suwanee Wongsaisuwan, May 7, 1972; children—Tom, Wanda. Intern, Chiengmai Hosp., 1967-68; intern in surgery Beverly (Mass.) Hosp., 1968-69; resident Med. U. S.C., Charleston, 1969-72; clin. fellow in nephrology U. Colo. Med. Center, 1972-73; practice medicine specializing in nephrology and hypertension, Florence, S.C., 1973-74; study physician VA Mild Hypertensive Study, NIH, 1974-75; asst. prof. medicine U. Okla., Health Sci. Center, 1974-76, asso. dir. renal failure care unit, 1975-76; research fellow in nephrology U. Okla. Med. Center, 1976—; med. dir. Honorage Nursing Center and Faith Health Care Facility, 1976—; med. dir. Florence (S.C.) Dialysis Center, 1976—; mem. med. adv. bd. Kidney Found. of Okla., 1975-76. Bd. dirs. Kidney Found. of S.C., 1972—. Diplomate Am. Bd. Internal Medicine. Fellow A.C.P.; mem. Am. Soc. Nephrology, Internat. Soc. Nephrology, Am. Fedn. Clin. Research, Sigma Xi. Buddhist. Contbr. numerous articles on nephrology to med. jours. Home: 1120 Donvegan St Florence SC 29501 Office: 255 S Warley St Florence SC 29501

KRAMER, EDWARD FRANCIS, JR., physician; b. LeCompte, La., Dec. 21, 1929; s. Edward Francis and Viola Maye (Shows) K.; B.S., La. State U., 1952, M.D., 1963; M.P.H., U. Calif., Berkeley, 1966; m. Georgia Jene Lester, Mar. 30, 1961; children—Edward Francis, Rebecca Susan. Intern, Malcolm Grow USAF Hosp., Andrews AFB, Md., 1963-64; resident, USAF Sch. Aerospace Medicine, San Antonio, 1966-68; commd. capt. U.S. Air Force, 1963, advanced through grades to col., 1975; dir. aerospace medicine Edwards AFB, Calif., 1967-68, dir. life support, 1971-73; dir. aerospace medicine Beale AFB, Calif., 1968-71; chief flight medicine Royal Australian Air Force, Canberra, Australia, 1973-75; dep. dir. research and devel. Aerospace Med. div. Brooks AFB, Tex., 1975-77; ret., 1977; pvt practice family and aviation medicine, San Antonio, 1977—. Served with USAF, 1952-77. Decorated Legion of Merit, Air medal, Meritorious Service medal with oak leaf cluster. Diplomate Am. Bd. Preventive Medicine, Am. Bd. Family Practice. Fellow Am. Coll. Preventive Medicine, Aerospace Med. Assn. (asso.); mem. Am. Coll. Family Physicians, AMA, Tex. Med. Assn., Bexar County Med. Soc., Assn. Mil. Surgeons U.S. Republican. World record endurance flight for jet fighter aircraft, USAF Operation Will-Travel, 1964. Home: 11502 Whisper Dew San Antonio TX 78230 Office: 7342 Oak Manor Dr San Antonio TX 78229

KRAMER, GERARD MARTIN, security service co. exec.; b. Heidelberg, Germany, July 9, 1927; came to U.S., 1938, naturalized, 1944; s. Hermann and Mathilde (Blaeser) K.; m. Praxeda A. LaPhan, Mar. 8, 1966; children—Allison, Karin, Robin, Joanna. Vice pres. ops. Dale System, Inc., N.Y.C., 1954-56; pres. Gray Security Services, Miami, 1956-59; pres. Hallmark Corp., Miami, 1959-73; pres. Marriott Security Systems, Inc. div. Marriott Corp., Miami, 1973-76; pres. Graymark Security Group, Inc., Miami, 1976—; cons. Fla. Restaurant Assn.; chmn. polygraph com. Fla. Pvt. Security Adv. Council, 1979—. Served with AUS, 1945-47. Mem. Am. Mgmt. Assn., Am. Polygraph Assn., Am. Soc. Indsl. Security, Council Polygraph Examiners (chmn. polygraph com. 1964—), Fla. Polygraph Assn. Democrat. Lutheran. Club: Key Biscayne Yacht. Home: 111 Cape Florida Dr Key Biscayne FL 33149 Office: 8515 Biscayne Blvd Miami FL 33138

KRAMER, GREGORY KENT, univ. adminstr.; b. Boston, Mar. 8, 1952; d. George William and Dorothy M. (Flynn) K.; B.Ed., U. Miami (Fla.), 1975, M.Ed. (grad. asst. 1975-77), 1977; m. Gina Gayle Gardner, Mar. 4, 1978. Asst. mgr. Univ. Rathskeller Inc., U. Miami, 1975-77, mgr., 1977—; mem. Alcohol Awareness Task Force. Mem. Am. Personnel and Guidance Assn., Am. Coll. Personnel Assn., Assn. Coll. Unions Internat., Nat. Assn. Student Personnel Adminstrs., Order of Omega, Phi Epsilon Kappa, Tau Kappa Epsilon (chpt. adv., dir.). Roman Catholic. Home: 8000 SW 81st Dr Apt 406 Miami FL 33156 Office: 1330 Miller Dr Coral Gables FL 33146

KRAMMER, ARNOLD PAUL, educator; b. Chgo., Aug. 15, 1941; s. David and Eva Julia (Vas) K.; B.S., U. Wis., Madison, 1963, M.S., cert. of Russian area studies, 1965, Ph.D., 1970; diploma U. Vienna (Austria), 1964; m. Rhoda Miriam Nudelman, June 19, 1968 (div. 1980); 1 son, Adam. Faculty preceptor Parsons Coll., 1965-68; instr. Soviet fgn. policy U. Wis., Madison, 1968-70; asst. prof. modern Europe, German and Soviet history Rockford (Ill.) Coll., 1970-74; asso. prof. modern German history Tex. A&M U., College Station, 1974-79, prof., 1979—, prin. investigator Center for Energy and Mineral Resources, 1976-79. Am. Council Learned Socs. grantee, 1973-76; Am. Philos. Soc. grantee, 1972, 76; Nat. Endowment for Humanities grantee, 1975. Mem. Historians of Second World War, Soc. Historians of Am. Fgn. Relations, Am. Assn. for Advancement of Slavic Studies, Western Assn. German Studies, Am. Hist. Assn. Jewish. Author books including: Nazi Prisoners of War in America, 1979; contbr. articles to profl. jours. Office: Dept History Tex A&M U College Station TX 77843

KRANCER, ANTHONY EDWARD, geologist; b. Bogota, Colombia, Dec. 28, 1952 (parents Am. citizens); s. Herbert and Elizabeth Krancer; B.S., U. Miami, 1973; M.S., U. Okla., 1975; m. Roxane June Bartel, June 4, 1973. Micropaleontologist, Exxon Co. U.S.A., Houston, 1976-78, prodn. geologist, Andrews, Tex., 1978-79; exploration geologist SOHIO Petroleum, Houston, 1979—. Mem. Am. Assn. Petroleum Geologists, Geol. Soc. Am., Houston Geol. Soc., Andrews Geol. Soc. (pres. 1979), Paleontol. Inst., Gulf Coast Assn. Geol. Scis., Sigma Xi, Sigma Gamma Epsilon. Contbr. articles to profl. jours. Home: 2639 Highlands Dr Sugarland TX 77478 Office: 8303 Southwest Freeway Suite 600 Houston TX 77074

KRANNICHFELD, JON MICHAEL, emergency physician; b. Pine Bluff, Ark., Jan. 16, 1950; s. James Henry and Patricia Elizabeth (Van Dover) K.; B.A. in Chemistry and Zoology, U. Ark., Fayetteville, 1971; M.D., U. Ark., Little Rock, 1975; m. Sherry Ann Short, June 13, 1970; children—James Brian, Michelle Lee. Intern U. Ark. Med. Scis., Little Rock, 1975, resident in family practice, 1976-78, chief resident, 1977-78, med. dir. regional toxicology center, 1979, med. dir. dept. emergency med. scis., 1979, chief emergency medicine service Univ. Hosp., 1979—; med. dir. stadium emergency services War Meml. Stadium, Little Rock, 1978—; affiliate faculty mem. Am. Heart Assn., 1979. Diplomate Am. Bd. Family Practice. Mem. Am. Coll. Emergency Physicians, Univ. Assn. Emergency Medicine. Home: 615 W Allen Ave Springdale AR 72764 Office: Springdale Meml Hosp Emergency Room 609 W Maple St Springdale AR 72764

KRAUS, ANNA JOSEPHINE, educator; b. Brookville, Pa., Apr. 11, 1927; d. Alexander Bernard and Bernadine Mary (Lyle) K.; B.A., Avila Coll., 1958; M.S., SUNY, Buffalo, 1973; postgrad. Pasadena City Coll., 1967-69; M.P.H., UCLA, 1972. Dir., cons. various med. record depts. in hosps. in Calif., Pa., W.Va., 1960-72; part-time nurse various hosps., Calif., 1968-72; dir. and asst. dir. med. record dept. St. Joseph Med. Center, Burbank, Calif., 1969-72; asst. dir., instr. med. record adminstrn. program, York (Pa.) Coll./Hosp., 1974-75; dir. med. record adminstrn. program Alderson-Broaddus Coll., Philippi, W.Va., 1976—; cons. in field; short-term med. record cons. Pan Am. Health Orgn., Princess Margaret Hosp., Nassau, Bahamas. Mem. Barbour County Citizens Coordinating Council, 1979—. Recipient Leadership and Service award Student Nurses Assn., 1969; SUNY grantee, 1972-73. Mem. W.Va. Med. Record Assn. (pres. 1980—), AAUW (sec. 1977—), W.Va. Nurses Assn., Am. Med. Record Assn., Am. Nurses Assn., AAUP, Am. Hosp. Assn., W.Va. Health Systems Agy., Am. Pub. Health Assn., W.Va. Pub. Health Assn. Democrat. Roman Catholic. Club: Faculty. Newsletter editor Calif. Med. Record Assn., 1967-68; editorial bd. Jour. Clin. Computing, 1973—. Home: 107 Cross St Philippi WV 26416 Office: PO Box 306 Philippi WV 25416

KRAUSE, CHARLES DONALD, ret. obstetrician, gynecologist; b. Chgo., Feb. 11, 1912; s. Charles Ewald and Jenny (Morrison) K.; student U. Ill., Champaign, 1930-32; B.S., Chgo., 1937, M.D., 1937; m. Mildred Flora Schaus, Oct. 10, 1938; children—Sharlene Krause Teubner, Judith Krause Wick, Charles Donald. Intern, resident in obstetrics and gynecology Research and Edn. Hosp., U. Ill., Chgo., 1938-41; practice medicine specializing in obstetrics and gynecology, Chgo. and Oak Lawn, Ill., 1945-73; asst. clin. prof. obstetrics and gynecology U. Ill. and Rush Med. Sch., Chgo., 1947-73; chief obstetrics and gynecology Evang. Hosp., Chgo., 1952-58, chief staff, 1958-59; chief obstetrics and gynecology Christ Hosp., Oak Lawn, 1960-66, v.p. staff, 1971-72. Served to lt. col., M.C., USAAF, 1941-45. Diplomate Am. Bd. Obstetrics and Gynecology. Fellow A.C.S. (sr.), Am. Coll. Obstetrics and Gynecology (founding); mem. Chgo. Gynecology Soc. Clubs: Minocqua Country (Wis.); Boca Raton Hotel (Fla.). Address: 2000 S Ocean Blvd Apt 14J Boca Raton FL 33432

KRAUSE, KENNETH EDWARD, air force officer; b. Sturgis, Mich., Oct. 18, 1943; s. Richard Julius and Wahnetta Mildred (Balyeat) K.; B.S., U.S. Air Force Acad., 1965; M.A., Golden Gate U., 1976; m. Carol Ann Wagner, Dec. 27, 1965; children—Danisha Lynn, Kenneth Edward. Commd. 2d lt. U.S. Air Force, 1965, advanced through grades to maj., 1976; served as F-4 pilot, 1966-76, combat missions Vietnam, 1967-68; instr. pilot, 1973-76; student Air Command and Staff Coll., 1976-77; chief programs and publs. div. Office of Safety, Hdqrs. Tactical Air Command, Hampton, Va., 1977—; staff officer U.S. Coast Guard Aux. Flotilla, 1978-79. Decorated D.F.C. with 3 oak leaf clusters, Air medal with 13 oak leaf clusters. Address: 70 Apollo Dr Hampton VA 23669

KRAUSE, MANFRED OTTO, physicist; b. Stuttgart, Germany, Mar. 11, 1931; s. Friedrich Bernhard and Fridel Ernstine (Mann) K.; B.S., Technische Universität Stuttgart, 1954, diploma in physics, 1957, Ph.D., 1960; m. Josephine Winifred Cammer, Dec. 26, 1963. Came to U.S., 1960, naturalized, 1970. Sr. physicist Wm. H. Johnston Labs., Inc., Balt., 1960-63; sr. scientist Oak Ridge Nat. Lab., 1963—; prof. d'échange U. Paris, 1975; Alexander-von-Humboldt awardee, 1975-76. Fellow Am. Phys. Soc.; mem. AAAS, Smithsonian Instn., Natural History Soc., Audubon Soc., Internat. Platform Assn. Contbr. articles on electron-, charge-, and x-ray spectrometry to sci. publs., chpts. to books. Discoverer X-ray spectrometry based on photoelectric effect, 1971. Home: 125 Baltimore Dr Oak Ridge TN 37830 Office: Oak Ridge Nat Lab PO Box X Oak Ridge TN 37830

KRAUSZ, MARJORIE VEGO, marriage and family therapist; b. Pasadena, Calif., Apr. 30, 1949; d. Hyman and Mariam (Goodstein) Vego; B.A. in Dance Therapy, UCLA, 1971; M.A. in Marriage, Family and Child Clin. Services (scholarship child devel. 1972), U. Calif., San Diego, U.S. Internat. U., San Diego, 1976; Ed.D. in Guidance and Counseling, U. Houston, 1979; m. Howard I. Krausz, Dec. 29, 1973. Vol. dance therapist VA Hosp., La Jolla, Calif., 1972; dance therapist, part-time recreation therapist Mesa Vista Psychiat. Hosp., San Diego, 1972-74; recreation supr., marriage and family therapist San Diego County Mental Health Hosp., 1974-76; client program coordinator Gulf Coast Regional Mental Health-Mental Retardation Center, Galveston, Tex., 1976-77; asst. to program dir., therapist Galveston County Jail, 1977-79; pvt. practice marriage and family therapy, Coral Gables, Fla., 1979—; instr. Miami-Dade Community Coll., 1979—. Lic. marriage and family counselor, Calif.

Mem. Am. Assn. Marriage and Family Therapists, Am. Personnel and Guidance Assn., Am. Dance Therapy Assn., Orthopsychiatric Assn. Democrat. Jewish. Home: 9864 N Kendall Dr Miami FL 33176 Office: 63 Merrick Way Coral Gables FL 33134

KREAGER, DAVID JAY, JR., lawyer; b. Tulsa, Apr. 28, 1929; s. David Jay and Ethel Mae (Martin) K.; B.A. with honors, Tex. A. and M. U., 1950; J.D. with honors, U. Tex., 1953; m. Ann Fleetwood, Mar. 22, 1949; children—David, Michael, Cameron, Heather, Gretchen, Paige. Admitted to Tex. bar, 1953, since practiced in Beaumont; partner firm Orgain, Bell and Tucker. Cert. civil trial and personal injury trial Tex. Bd. Legal Specialization. Mem. Beaumont Civil Service Commn., 1961-70. Mem. Tex. Bar Found. (chmn. bd. trustees 1977-79), State Bar Tex. (dir. 1973-76), Am., Jefferson County (pres. 1960-61) bar assns., Tex. Assn. Def. Counsel (dir. 1977-80), Am. Judicature Soc., Fedn. Ins. Counsel, Internat. Assn. Ins. Counsel, Order of Coif. Presbyterian. Club: Rotary. Home: 1245 Nottingham Ln Beaumont TX 77706 Office: PO Box 1751 Beaumont TX 77704

KREBS, PETER JOACHIM, pharm. co. exec.; b. Gleiwitz, Germany, Dec. 15, 1925; s. Willi and Edith Marlene (Pindus) K.; Abitur, Schlesische Friedrich's Wilhelm Universitët, Breslau, 1944; J.D. magna cum laude, Woodrow Wilson Coll. Law, 1973, LL.M., 1974; B.B.A. cum laude, Mercer U., 1976; m. Rose Maria Guerrero Vasquez Godoy, Feb. 12, 1965; children—Allison Grace, Patricia-Johanna, Glenda. Came to U.S., 1947, naturalized, 1952. Div. mgr. E.S. Miller Labs., Los Angeles, 1950-55; with Medics Pharm. Corp., Decatur, Ga., 1955—, pres., chmn. bd., 1959—; dir. U.S. Chem. Corp., Decatur, U.S. Chem. Drug Products Div., Inc. Mem. State Bar Ga., Am., Atlanta, Decatur-DeKalb bar assns., Nat. Ethical Pharm. Assn., Ga., Am. trial lawyers assns., Internat. Union of Advocates, Am. Soc. Legal History, Parenteral Drug Mfg. Assn., Alpha Tau, Sigma Delta Kappa. Home: 3643 Winbrooke Ln Tucker GA 30084 Office: 203 Rio Circle Decatur GA 30030

KREJS, GUENTER JOSEF, internist; b. Waidhofen an der Ybbs, Austria, Mar. 14, 1945; s. Philipp and Margarita (Wobora) K.; student U. Vienna, 1963-66, 67-69, M.D., 1969; student Med. Sch. U. Zurich, 1966-67; m. Gertrud Josefa Strauss, May 22, 1968; children—Bibiana, Patrick, Oliver. Resident, City Hosp. Krems, Austria, St. Anna Childrens Hosp., Vienna, 1969-71; resident in internal medicine Triemli City Hosp., Zurich, 1971-73, fellow in gastroenterology, 1973-75; instr. medicine U. Tex., Dallas, 1975-76, asst. prof., 1976-79, asso. prof., 1979—; sr. attending gastroenterologist Parkland Meml. Hosp., Dallas, Dallas VA Med. Center. Diplomate Am. Bd. Internal Medicine. Mem. Am. Fedn. Clin. Research, Am. Gastroenterol. Assn., Am. Soc. Gastrointestinal Endoscopy. Roman Catholic. Contbr. articles on gastroenterology to profl. jours. and books. Research in intestinal physiology and pathophysiology. Home: 3444 Mockingbird Ln Dallas TX 75205 Office: 5323 Harry Hines Blvd Dallas TX 75235

KREMENTZ, EDWARD THOMAS, surgeon; b. Newark, Apr. 30, 1917; s. Albert Martin and Agnes Templeton (Aiguier) K.; A.B., Wesleyan U., 1939; M.D., U. Rochester, 1943; m. Carolyn Butler, Oct. 5, 1946; children—Edward T., Anne Butler, Krementz, Cynthia Aiguier Krementz Geoghegan, David George, Elizabeth Avery. Asst. in surgery Yale U., 1943-48, Jane Coffin Childs Meml. Fund fellow, 1948-49, instr. surgery, 1948-50; instr. surgery Tulane U., 1950-53, asst. prof., 1953-57, asso. prof., 1957-61, prof., 1961—, acting chmn. dept., 1967-68, 76-77, cancer teaching coordinator, 1953—, dir. Tulane Cancer Clin. Research Center, Charity Hosp., 1961-75, Am. Cancer Soc. prof. clin. oncology, 1977—, sr. vis. surgeon Charity Hosp.; sr. asso. Touro Infirmary, New Orleans, 1963—; mem. staff Hotel Dieu, New Orleans, 1959—; surg. cons. 6 hosps.; chmn. bd. dirs. La. Tumor Registry, 1973—) Charity Hosp. La., 1955—. Recipient Research Career award Nat. Cancer Inst., NIH, 1962-67. Mem. AAAS, Am. Assn. Cancer Edn., Am. Assn. Cancer Research, Am. Cancer Soc., A.C.S., AMA (co-recipient Hektoen Gold medal 1959) Am. Soc. Clin. Oncology, Soc. Surg. Oncology, Am. Surg. Assn., La., Orleans Parish med. socs., New Orleans, So. (Shipley Gold medal 1964) surg. socs., Soc. Exptl. Biology and Medicine, Société Internationale de Chirurgie, Soc. Univ. Surgeons, Southeastern Surg. Congress, Southeastern Cancer Research Assn., So. Med. Assn., Surg. Assn. La., WHO Internat. Group Clin. Study Melanoma, Sigma Xi, Alpha Omega Alpha. Clubs: New Orleans Country; Pendennis. Home: 500 Walnut St New Orleans LA 70118 Office: 1430 Tulane Ave New Orleans LA 70112

KREMSER, FRANK JOSEPH, JR., radiator mfg. co. exec.; b. Birmingham, Ala., June 8, 1923; s. Frank Joseph and Marie Weston (Rowland) K.; B.S., U.S. Mil. Acad., 1947; M.S. in Civil Engring., Purdue U., 1955; m. Pauline M. Holjes, June 3, 1947; children—Stephanie, Frank J. III, Thomas, Annette, Geffory, Frederick. Commd. 2d lt. U.S. Air Force, 1947, advanced through grades to capt., 1951, resigned, 1957; developer, builder, Stuart, Fla., 1957-60; v.p. Kremser Radiator Co., Miami, Fla., 1960-72; v.p. Industria Puertorriqueña de Radiadores, Inc., Catano, P.R., 1972-78; gen. mgr. Perfex Catanò and Co., 1978-79; pres. Internat. Muffler Corp., 1980—. Served with U.S. Army, 1942-44. Republican. Roman Catholic. Home: 22 Mimosa Santa Maria Rio Piedras PR 00927 Office: PO Box 235 Catano PR 00632

KRENEK, RICHARD FRANK, indsl. engr.; b. Cleve., Oct. 7, 1940; s. Frank John and Helen Marie (Aron) K.; B.Engring. Sci., Cleve. State U., 1966; M.S., Ohio State U., 1967, Ph.D., 1970; m. Geraldine Ann Ulicky, July 6, 1963; children—Richard, Robert. Devel. engr. Lewis Research Center, NASA, Cleve., 1966; research asso. Systems Research Group, Ohio State U., 1966-70; asst. prof. Sch. Indsl. Engring., U. Okla., 1970-72; v.p. OMEC, Inc., Norman, Okla., 1972-73, pres., 1973-78; asso. prof. U. Okla., 1979—; Bd. dirs. Cleveland County chpt. ARC, 1976—, chmn. bldg. fund drive, 1976, 1st vice chmn. chpt., 1977-78, chpt. chmn., 1979—; mem. Okla. region blood services, Tulsa county chpt. ARC, bd. dirs., 1979—, mem. exec. com., 1979—; chmn. Norman chmn. Norman Parking Authority Com., 1975-76, Norman Polit. Action Com., 1977. Served with AUS, 1958-61. Registered profl. engr., Okla. Mem. Transp. Research Bd., Nat. Soc. Profl. Engrs., Okla. Soc. Profl. Engrs. (v.p. Canadian Valley chpt. 1979-80, pres. 1980—), Am. Inst. Indsl. Engrs., Human Factors Soc., Norman C. of C. (dir. 1975-77), Sigma Xi, Tau Beta Pi, Alpha Pi Mu, Pi Mu Epsilon. Republican. Roman Catholic. Clubs: Norman Rotary (dir. 1975-79, chmn. funds com. 1975-78, pres. 1978-79), Univ. Home: 4209 Oxford Way Norman OK 73069 Office: 202 W Boyd Norman OK 73019

KRESHON, MARTIN JOHN, ophthalmologist; b. East Liverpool, Ohio, Nov. 11, 1929; s. James I. and Elizabeth (Augustine) K.; B.S. cum laude, Geneva Coll., 1950; M.D., Marquette U., 1954; m. Yolanda Mae Jerome, Aug. 31, 1952; children—Kathleen, Susan, Karol, Marty, Amy, Michael, Beth, John. Intern, Hamot Hosp., Erie, Pa., 1954-55; resident Duke U. Hosps., 1957-60, instr., 1960-69, clin. asst. prof. ophthalmology, 1969-7S, clin. asso. prof., 1976—; practice medicine specializing in ophthalmology, Charlotte, N.C., 1961—; mem. staff Charlotte Eye Ear Nose and Throat, Presbyn., Meml., Mercy hosps. Bd. dirs. N.C. Cancer Soc., Piedmont Science Fair, Mecklenburg Assn. for the Blind, 1961-70, Piedmont Eye Clinic, 1969-77, N.C. Eye Bank, 1961—. Served with U.S. Army, 1955-57. Mem. Am. Acad. Ophthalmology, So. Med. Soc., Charlotte Ophthalmol. Soc., N.C. (pres. 1978), S.C. ophthalmology and otolaryngology socs., Eastern Lions. Republican. Roman Catholic. Home: 260 Cherokee Rd Charlotte NC 28207 Office: 1600 E 3d St Charlotte NC 28204

KRETCHMAR, RUTH GOLDMAN, artist; b. Little Rock, Apr. 18, 1918; d. Abraham Joseph and Augusta (Finger) Goldman; B.S., U. Ill., 1939; B.A., U. Ark., 1968; m. Lee Kretchmar, 1940 (dec. July 5, 1976); 1 son, Kent. Art cons. Main Galleries, Little Rock, 1969-70; exhibited one-man shows: Ark. Arts Center, 1972, 73, 74, 75, 76, Little Rock Arts and Crafts Design Fair, 1973-74, 1st Nat. Bank of Little Rock, 1976; exhibited group shows: Spar Nat. Art Exhbn., Shreveport, La., 1973, S.E. Ark. Arts and Scis. Center, Pine Bluff, 1973, U. Little Rock, 1974-75, Columbus (Ga.) Mus. Arts and Scis., 1978, Ark. Arts Center Traveling exhibit, 1978, represented in permanent collections: 1st Nat. Bank of Little Rock, 1st Am. Bank of North Little Rock. Mem. budget com. United Fund, 1954; mem. State White House Conf. Children and Youth, 1960; mem. nat. bd. women's com. Brandeis U., 1969-71. Mem. Mid-So. Water Colorists (dir.), So. Watercolor Soc., AAUW (work rep. mag. cover 1979). Home and Studio: 2 Beverly Pl Little Rock AR 72207

KRETZER, HAROLD LLOYD, JR., govt. ofcl.; b. Grayson, Ky., Oct. 27, 1947; s. Harold Lloyd and Mary Jo (Justice) K.; B.S., Va. Poly. Inst., 1970; m. Kathy Kay Kester, June 29, 1974; 1 dau., Sara Elizabeth. With Va. Employment Commn., Richmond, 1970—, employment security program mgr., 1974—. Mem. Internat. Assn. Personnel Employment Security (chpt. pres. 1977-78), Va. Govtl. Employees Assn., Va. Poly. Inst. Alumni Assn., Mid-Atlantic Manpower Profls. Assn., Richmond Jaycees, Va. Tech. Student Aid Assn., Richmond Choral Soc. Republican. Baptist. Home: 1502 W 41st St Richmond VA 23225

KREUTZ, OSCAR R., savs. and loan assn. exec.; b. Sioux City, Iowa; s. John and Jennie (Pehrson) K.; student schs., Sioux City, Cambridge, Mass.; m. Marion Benton, 1926 (dec. Apr. 1972); m. 2d, Virginia F. Skelton, Oct. 20, 1973; children—Mary Ann Kreutz Dodson, Barbara Jane Kreutz Barrett. Organizer, First Fed. Savs. & Loan Assn., Sioux City, 1923, mgr. officer, 1923-33; sec. Iowa Bldg. and Loan League, 1925-33; v.p. Fed. Home Loan Bank Chgo., 1934; chmn. rev. com. Fed. Home Loan Bank Bd., 1934-41; gen. mgr. Fed. Savs. and Loan Ins. Corp., Washington, 1941-44; exec. mgr. Nat. League Insured Savs. Assn., Washington, 1944-53, exec. cons., 1953-54, mem. exec. com., 1953-54; exec. v.p. Fla. Fed. Savs. and Loan Assn. (formerly First Fed. Savs. and Loan Assn.), St. Petersburg, 1953-54, pres., chmn. bd., 1954-68, chmn. bd., 1968-75, chmn. emeritus and cons., 1975—; hon. v.p. Internat. Union Bldg. Socs. and Savs. Assn. Pres. bd. dirs. United Fund, St. Petersburg, 1956-57; pres. Com. 100, St. Petersburg, 1958-59; pres. St. Petersburg Improvement Found., 1961-62; mem. adv. bd. Abilities Inc. Fla.; hon. bd. dirs. Sci. Center, St. Petersburg, St. Petersburg Symphony Soc.; trustee Eckerd Coll. Named Mr. Sun, Producers of Sunshine Festival of States, 1962. Mem. Fla. Savs. and Loan League (pres. 1961), Nat. Savs. and Loan League (pres. 1960), Suncoasters of St. Petersburg, Inc. (pres.), Navy League U.S., Am. Legion. Clubs: Masons, Rotary, St. Petersburg Yacht, Golden Triangle Civic. Presbyterian. Author: The Way It Happened, 1972. Office: Fla Fed Bldg Suite 902 Saint Petersburg FL 33701

KRIEG, RICHARD JOSEPH, JR., anatomist; b. Stockton, Calif., Mar. 26, 1944; s. Richard Joseph and Harriet Beatrice (Barone) K.; B.S., U. San Francisco, 1967; M.S. (Calif. State fellow), U. Calif., Davis, 1969; Ph.D. (Eli Lilly fellow), UCLA, 1975; m. Ana Yec, Dec. 24, 1977. Asst. prof. anatomy Med. Coll. Va., Richmond, 1975—. Served as 1st lt., arty., U.S. Army, 1969-70. Mem. AAAS, Am. Assn. Anatomists, Soc. Exptl. Biology and Medicine, Soc. for Neurosci., Va. Acad. Sci. Contbr. articles to profl. jours. Office: Dept Anatomy Med Coll VA MCV Station Box 709 Richmond VA 23298

KRIEG, WILLIAM LLOYD, electronics mfg. co. exec.; b. St. Louis, Jan. 28, 1946; s. Lester P. and Maxine J. Krieg; B.S. in Elec. Engring., U. Mo., 1968; postgrad. N. Tex. State U., 1970; m. Phyllis Carol Adams, Jan. 25, 1969; children—Kristen Lea, William Jason. Asst. engr. Chevrolet div. Gen. Motors Corp., St. Louis, 1965-68; process engr. mfg. Tex. Instruments, Inc., Dallas, 1969-70; diode div. operation mgr. Transitron Electronics Corp., Laredo, Tex., 1970-72; exec. v.p. Meridian Industries, Inc., Laredo, 1973—, also dir.; v.p., dir. Industrias Ensambladoras S.A. de C.V., Nuevo Laredo, Mex. 1973—; dir. Chill Air, Inc. Named Small Bus. Person of Yr., State of Tex., 1979. Home: 311 Belair Dr Laredo TX 78041 Office: 4602 Modern Ln Laredo TX 78041

KRIEGER, DAVID, embroidery mfg. firm exec.; b. Kolno, Poland, Dec. 8, 1924; s. Morris and Baila (Burak) K.; came to U.S., naturalized, 1938; m. Page Miller, Sept. 24, 1972; children—Karen, Kenneth, Robert. Founder, pres., chief exec. officer Emb-Tex Corp., Travelers Rest and Liberty (both S.C.), 1964—. Served with AUS, 1943-45; ETO. Patentee in field. Home: 101 Hathaway Circle Greenville SC 29609 Office: Emb-Tex Corp Hwy 25 PO Box 398 Travelers Rest SC 29690

KRIEGLER, ARNOLD MATTHEW, electronics mfg. co. exec.; b. Omaha, July 29, 1932; s. Matthew and Mildred Elsie (Svoboda) K.; B.Sc. in Engring. and Bus. Adminstrn., U. Omaha, 1955; postgrad. U. Iowa, 1957-58; m. Joan Virginia Godsey, Nov. 24, 1954; children—Kurt, Karen. Chief draftsman The Ballantyne Co., Omaha, 1948-55; various mfg. mgmt. positions Collins Radio Co. div. Rockwell Internat., Cedar Rapids, Iowa, 1957-76, dir. prodn. ops. Collins Transmission Systems div., Dallas, 1976—; mem. com. on computer-aided mfg. Nat. Acad. Sci.-NRC, 1978—. Loaned exec. United Way Campaign, Cedar Rapids, 1973. Served with USAF, 1955-57. Mem. Am. Inst. Indsl. Engrs. (sr. mem., chpt. pres. 1973-74), Nat. Mgmt. Assn. (dir. Dallas chpt. 1978-79), Theta Chi. Republican. Presbyterian. Home: 3605 Seltzer Dr Plano TX 75023 Office: PO Box 10462 Dallas TX 75007

KRISE, EDWARD FISHER, charter yacht owner; b. Detroit, June 28, 1924; s. W. Gomer and Dorothy (Fisher) K.; A.B., Brown U., 1949; M.A., U. Chgo., 1950, Ph.D., 1958; m. Elizabeth Ann Bradt, Aug. 5, 1948; children—Patricia Lynn Krise Kane, Thomas Warren. Chief social work service Walter Reed Gen. Hosp., 1964-65; chief personnel services div. Hdqrs. USCONARC, 1965-69; dir. Race Relations Inst., Dept. Def., 1970-72; owner, master sailing yacht on charter in W.I., 1975—; asso. prof. U. Md., 1973-75; research asso. Island Resources Found., St. Thomas, V.I., 1979—. Served with U.S. Army, 1942-73; col. Res. (ret.). Decorated Silver Star, Legion of Merit with oak leaf cluster, Meritorious Service medal, Bronze Star, Purple Heart. Mem. Nat. Assn. Social Workers, Acad. Cert Social Workers, Ret. Officers Assn., U.S. Power Squadron. Democrat. Presbyterian. Clubs: Annapolis Yacht, Old Point Comfort Yacht, Dockside Dem. (v.p. 1978-80). Office: Sandia IV Homeport Saint Thomas VI 00801

KRISTOFFERSON, KARL ERIC, writer; b. Jacksonville, Fla., Mar. 3, 1929; s. Gustave Edward and Oma Nancy (Reynolds) K.; A.A., Jacksonville U., 1961; B.S. with honors in Journalism, U. Fla., 1963; m. Barbara Elaine Dalton, Jan. 22, 1954; children—Karol, Paul, Scott. Motion picture film booker Paramount Pictures, Warner Bros. Pictures and United Artists, 1954-59; engring. writer Pratt & Whitney Aircraft Co., West Palm Beach, Fla., 1963; publs. supr. Ling-Temco-Vought Ops., Kennedy Space Center, Fla., 1964-72; chief public affairs IRS Dist. Hdqrs., Greensboro, N.C., 1972-74; chief writer/editor NASA Public Affairs, Kennedy Space Center, 1974—; free-lance writer for TV, motion pictures and maj. nat. mags. and publs., 1960—; regular assignment writer Reader's Digest. Served with USAF, 1950-53; Korea. Decorated Air medal; recipient Apollo Achievement award NASA, 1969; Aviation Space Writers Assn. award for articles writing, 1974. Mem. Sigma Delta Chi, Phi Kappa Phi, Kappa Tau Alpha Democrat. Lutheran. Home: 3500 Melrose Ave Titusville FL 32780 Office: PA-PIB Kennedy Space Center FL 32899

KRIVOY, WILLIAM AARON, pharmacologist; b. Newark, Jan. 2, 1928; s. Samuel and Rose (Hirschenhorn) K.; B.S., Georgetown U., 1948; M.S., George Washington U., 1949, Ph.D., 1953. Pharmacologist, Chem. Corps Med. Labs., Army Chem. Center, Md., 1950-54; postdoctoral research fellow U. Pa., 1954-55, dept. pharmacology U. Edinburgh (Scotland), 1955-57; instr. dept. pharmacology Tulane U., 1957-59; asst. prof. dept. pharmacology Baylor U., 1959-63, asso. prof., 1963-68; with Addiction Research Center, Nat. Inst. Drug Abuse, Lexington, Ky., 1968—, now pharmacologist. Mem. Am. Soc. Pharmacology and Exptl. Therapeutics, Brit. Pharm. Soc., Soc. Exptl. Biology and Medicine, N.Y. Acad. Scis., Am. Coll. Neuropsychopharmacology, Biophys. Soc., Tex. Acad. Sci., Western Pharmacology Soc., Sociedade Brasileira de Farmacologia e de Terapeutica Experimental, Sigma Xi. Contbr. numerous articles to profl. jours. Home: 3100 Kirklevington Dr Lexington KY 40502 Office: Nat Inst Drug Abuse Addiction Research Center Lexington KY 40583

KROCH, KENNETH CARL, mgmt. cons.; b. Blair, Nebr., May 27, 1927; s. Harvey U. and Birdie Irene (Merhans) K.; B.S., U. Nebr., 1950; M.S., Purdue U., 1955; m. Judith Anne Smith, Nov. 26, 1952; children—Kathleen Carla, Deborah, Stephen. With Kaiser Aluminum Co., 1956-58, Sandia Corp., 1958-63, Argonne (Ill.) Nat. Lab., 1963-67, Peat, Marwick, Mitchell & Co., 1967-72; partner Jenkins-Krogh Internat., Inc., Dallas, 1972—. Pres. sch. bd., 1971-74. Served with USNR, 1945-46. Mem. Am. Mgmt. Assn., Am. Soc. Tng. and Devel. Baptist. Office: PO Drawer 38165 Dallas TX 75238

KROEGER, CARROLL VINCENT, mgmt. cons., educator; b. Trenton, Mo., Jan. 3, 1926; s. August Carl and Sarabel (Newman) K.; student Rice U., 1945-46; B.A., Vanderbilt U., 1949, M.B.A., 1973; m. Grace Lee Bolton, Oct. 20, 1946; children—Carroll V., Sheryl Lynn. Engr., Blackstone Valley Gas Electric Co., 1949-50, Central Ind. Gas Co., 1952-56, Washington Natural Gas Co., 1956-59; cons. Stone & Webster Mgmt Cons., N.Y.C., 1959-64; sr. advisor Standard Oil Co., The Hague, Netherlands, 1964-66; advisor Esso Europe, London, 1966-69; pres., founder Kroeger & Smith S.A., Switzerland, 1969-71; project cons. Vanderbilt U., 1973-74; dir. Tenn. Energy Office, 1974-75; prof. Belmont Coll. Bus. Sch., 1978—; pvt. practice mgmt. cons., Nashville, 1975—. Served with USNR, 1943-46, 50-52. Fellow Inst. Energy, Inst. Dirs., Inst. Gas Engrs. (Gt. Britain); mem. Assn. Technique L'Industrie Gas France, ASME, Am. Gas Assn. Episcopalian. Internat. editor Gas mag., 1970-72, Energy mag., 1973-74. Contbr. articles to profl. jours. Office: 1617 17th Ave S Nashville TN 37212

KROGH, KENNETH CARL, mgmt. cons.; b. Blair, Neb., May 27, 1927; s. Harvey U. and Birdie Irene (Merhans) K.; B.S., U. Neb., 1950; M.S., Purdue U., 1955; m. Judith Anne Smith, Nov. 20, 1952; children—Kathleen Carla, Deborah Anne, Stephen John. Ind. tng. mgr. Panama Canal Co., 1950-53; asso. prof. Purdue U., Lafayette, Ind., 1954-56; supt. indsl. relations Kaiser Aluminum Co., 1956-58; supr. mgmt. tng. Sandia Corp., 1958-63; mgr. employee devel. Argonne (Ill.) Nat. Lab., 1963-67; mgr. human resources Peat, Marwick, Mitchell & Co., 1967-72; pres. Jenkins-Krogh Internat., Inc., Dallas, 1972—; vis. prof. U. South Africa, Pretoria, 1976-77. Pres. sch. bd., Dallas, 1971-74. Served with USNR, 1945-46. Mem. Am. Mgmt. Assn., Am. Soc. Training and Devel. Baptist. Club: Rotary. Home: 9705 Trailhill Dr Dallas TX 75238 Office: PO Drawer 38165 Dallas TX 75238

KROL, JOSEPH, engr., educator; b. Warsaw, Poland, Jan. 14, 1911; s. Kazimierz and Feliksa (Tokarzewski) K.; M.S., Warsaw (Poland) Inst. Tech., 1937; Ph.D. U. London (Eng.), 1947; m. Evelyn Swingland, Apr. 15, 1952. Came, to U.S., 1956, naturalized, 1962. Tech. officer with directorate ammunition prodn. Brit. Ministry of Supply, London, Eng., 1941-45; research scientist U. London, 1946-47; cons. engr., Montreal, Que., Can., 1948-51; asso. prof. mech. engring. U. Manitoba (Can.), 1951-56; prof. indsl. engring. Ga. Inst. Tech., 1956—. Recipient George Stephenson prize, 1951. Registered profl. engr., Ga. Fellow Instn. Mech. Engrs.; mem. Am. Inst. Indsl. Engrs., Engring. Inst. Can., Corp. Profl. Engrs. Que., Am. Econ. Assn., ASME, Instrument Soc., Am., AAAS, Am. Statis. Assn., Econometric Soc., Inst., Mgmt. Scis., Sigma Xi. Author articles on engring. and mgmt. subjects. Home: 710 Peachtree St NE Atlanta GA 30308

KROLAK, PATRICK DENNIS, educator; b. LaSalle, Ill., June 1, 1940; s. Stanley Anthony and Sarah Bridget (Brady) K.; B.S., U. Chgo., 1962; M.S., Washington U., St. Louis, 1964, D.Sc., 1968; m. Rita Ann Moffat, Sept. 4, 1965; children—Patrick Michael, Karen Susan, Michael Sean. With Monsanto Co., St. Louis, 1964-68, So. Ill. U., Edwardsville, 1967-68; prof. computer sci. Vanderbilt U., Nashville, 1968—; partner Decision Graphics, 1975—; cons. NSF, USAF, Battelle Meml. Labs., U.S. Army. Ill. State scholar, 1968-62; AEC fellow. Mem. Assn. Computing Machinery (nat. lectr.), Ops. Research Soc. Am., Math. Programming Soc., Am. Inst. Decision Scis., Simulation Councils. Sigma Xi. Asso. editor Simulation; research in transp. sci., integer programming, computer graphics. Home: 504 Colice Jeanne Rd Nashville TN 37221 Office: Box 1717B Vanderbilt U Nashville TN 37235

KROLL, JAMES CLARENCE, biologist; b. Waco, Tex., Nov. 5, 1946; s. C.P. and Doris K.; B.S., Baylor U., 1969, M.S., 1970; Ph.D., Tex. A&M U., 1973; m. Susan Masters, June 4, 1978; 1 son, James Cody. Asst. prof. biology Salem (Va.) Coll., 1972-73; asst. prof. forest wildlife Stephen F. Austin State U., Nacogdoches, 1973-78, asso. prof., 1978—. NSF trainee, 1970-71; grantee U.S. Forest Service, U.S. Fish and Wildlife Service. Mem. Wildlife Soc., Southeast Deer Study Group, Tex. Forestry Assn., Wilson Soc., Sigma Xi, Beta Beta Beta, Xi Sigma Pi, Phi Sigma. Republican. Lutheran. Contbr. articles to profl. jours.; author: Woodpeckers and the Southern Pine Beetle, 1979; staff editor Tex. Hunting Mag., 1978-79. Home: 1116 Virginia St Nacogdoches TX 75961 Office: Box 6109 Stephen F Austin St Nacogdoches TX 75962

KROLL, WOODROW MICHAEL, minister, educator; b. Ellwood City, Pa., Oct. 21, 1944; s. Frank Michael and Marvel Betty (Corbin) K.; B.A., Barrington Coll., 1967; M.Div., Gordon-Conwell Theol. Sem., 1970; Th.M., Geneva Theol. Sem., 1971, Th.D., 1973; doctoral candidate U. Va., 1977—; m. Linda Kay Piper, June 27, 1965; children—Tracy, Timothy, Tina, Tiffany. Ordained to ministry Baptist Ch., 1969; pastor 1st Bapt. Ch., Middleboro, Mass., 1968-70;

asso. dir. Christian Jew Found., San Antonio, 1973-75; chmn. Bible dept. Practical Bible Tng. Sch., Binghamton, N.Y., 1970-73; chmn. div. religion, prof. Liberty Bapt. Coll., Lynchburg, Va., 1975—. Named to Va. Cultural Laureate, 1976. Mem. Soc. Bibl. Lit., Evang. Theol. Soc., Evang. Philos. Soc., Assn. Bapt. Profs. Religion. Author: It Will Be Worth It All, 1977; The Liberty Commentary on the New Testament, 1978; gen. editor Prescription for Preaching, 1980; The Liberty Commentary on the Old Testament, 1980. Home: Route 3 Sunnymeade Acres 93 Rustburg VA 24588 Office: Liberty Bapt Coll Lynchburg VA 24506

KRONICK, DAVID ABRAHAM, librarian; b. Connelsville, Pa., Oct. 5, 1917; s. Barnet L. and Rose L. (Miller) K.; B.A., Western Res. U., 1940, B.L.S., 1941; Ph.D., U. Chgo., 1956; m. Marilyn Abramson, Oct. 25, 1959; children—Steven Leonard, Beryl Leah. Librarian, Western Res. U. Sch. Medicine, Cleve., 1946-49, U. Mich. Med. Sch., Ann Arbor, 1955-59; dir. Cleve. Med. Library, 1959-64; chief reference div. Nat. Library Medicine, Washington, 1964-65; librarian U. Tex. Med. Sch., San Antonio, 1965—. Pres. Friends San Antonio Pub. Library, 1967-68, Tex. Council Health Scis. Libraries, 1969. Served to capt. M.C., AUS, 1941-46. Council Library Resources fellow, 1971. Mem. Med. Library Assn., Am. Assn. History Medicine, Am. Soc. Info. Sci. Club: B'nai B'rith. Contbr. articles to profl. jours. Home: 1223 Mount Riga Dr San Antonio TX 78213 Office: U Tex Health Sci Center 7703 Floyd Curl Dr San Antonio TX 78284

KROUSKOP, THOMAS ALAN, rehab. engr.; b. Washington, July 11, 1945; s. Ned Carter and Constance Asenath (Barrows) K.; B.S., Carnegie Inst. Tech., 1967; M.S., Carnegie-Mellon U., 1969, Ph.D., 1971; m. Arlene A. Swatsworth, Jan. 20, 1968; children—Peter, Barbara, Mark. Design engr. Gen. Analytics Co., Pitts., 1969; design engr. E. D'Appolonia Engrs., Pitts., 1970-71; faculty Tex. A&M U., College Station, 1971—; asso. prof. Baylor Coll. Medicine, Houston, 1972-79, adj. asst. prof., asst. prof. bioengring., 1979—; dir. Rehab. Engring. Center, Houston, 1978—; dir. Meiller Co. Bd. dirs. Shrine Hosp. Gait Lab., Houston, 1977—; active Boy Scouts Am., 1978—. Served with USMCR, 1968. Mem. ASTM, Nat. Soc. Profl. Engrs., Am. Congress Rehab. Medicine, Tex. Soc. Profl. Engrs. (named young engr. of year Sam Houston chpt. 1975), Sigma Xi. Mem. Ch. Jesus Christ of Latter-Day Saints. Developer pressure evaluation pad system, 1977. Home: 11915 Meadowtrail Ln Stafford TX 77477 Office: Rehab Engring Center Inst Rehab Research 133 Moursund Ave Houston TX 77030

KRUEGER, DAVID WAYNE, physician; b. San Angelo, Tex., July 16, 1947; s. Leslie Adolph and Avis Floy (Loudamy) K.; B.A., U. Tex., Austin, 1969; M.D., La. State U., 1973; m. Vicki Millsap, Aug. 9, 1969; children—Ryan Jason, Lauren Nicole. Splty. tng. in psychiatry U. Colo. Med. Sch., 1973-76; asso. dir. Baylor Psychiatry Clinic, Baylor Coll. Medicine, Houston, 1976-78; dir. Baylor Psychiatry Clinic, 1978—; cons. Tex. Instn. Rehab. and Research, Tex. Rehab. Commn., So. Meth. U.; v.p. Millsap Enterprises, Inc., 1976—. NIMH fellow, 1970-72. Diplomate Am. Bd. Psychiatry and Neurology. Mem. Am. Psychiat. Assn., Am. Psychoanalytic Assn., Houston Galveston Psychoanalytic Inst. and Soc., Assn. Advancement Psychotherapy, So. Psychiat. Assn. Contbr. articles to profl. jours. Home: 11110 Holly Springs St Houston TX 77042 Office: 1200 Moursund St Houston TX 77030

KRUEGER, GEORGE EDWARD, dentist, prosthodontist; b. Chgo., Mar. 10, 1921; s. Alonzo and Elizabeth Olive (Matthews) K.; D.D.S., Northwestern U., 1943; M.S. in Clin. Dentistry, Prosthodontics, Marquette U., 1967; m. Joan Eileen Fellows, Aug. 6, 1949; children—Leila Krueger Zschau and George (twins), Leslie, Lydia and Laura (twins), Gerard, Gregory, Gordon. Asst. clin. prof. Marquette U., Milw., 1967-72, asso. clin. prof., 1972; prosthetic cons. U.S. Navy Hosp., Great Lakes, Ill., 1968-72. Served with USNR, 1943-46, ret. Res., 1956. Diplomate Am. Bd. Prosthodontics. Fellow Am. Coll. Prosthodontists, Am. Coll. Dentists; mem. ADA, Fla. Dental Assn., Am. Prosthodontic Soc., Fla. Prosthodontic Assn. (pres. 1977-78), Am. Equilibration Soc., West Coast Dist. Dental Soc., Pierre Fauchard Acad., Fedn. Dentaire Internationale. Roman Catholic. Clubs: K.C. (4 deg.), Serra (dist. gov. 1979-80). Home: 8269 33d Ave N Saint Petersburg FL 33710 Office: 6533 Central Ave St Petersburg FL 33710

KRUGER, RUDOLF, music condr.; b. Berlin, Germany; s. Eduard and Julie Eva (Herz) K.; came to U.S., 1939, naturalized, 1944; diploma Staatsadademie fuer Musik und Darstellende Kunst, Vienna, Austria, 1938; m. Ruth Elizabeth Scallan, Aug. 25, 1951; children—Karen Elizabeth, Philip Edward. Asst. condr. So. Symphony Orch., Columbia (S.C.) Choral Soc., 1939-42; asst. condr. New Orleans Symphony Orch., 1942-45, condr. young people's concerts, 1942-45; asst. condr. New Orleans Opera House Assn., 1942-45, condr. light opera div., 1943; guest condr. Mid-Western tour Chgo. Light Opera Co., 1946-47; music dir. Jackson (Miss.) Opera Guild, 1948-51, Mobile (Ala.) Opera Guild, 1949-55, New Orleans Light Opera Co., 1949-50; 1st. condr. Crescent City Concerts Assn., New Orleans, 1954-55; dir. opera workshop Tex. Christian U., 1955-58; music dir., condr. Ft. Worth (Tex.) Opera Assn., 1955-58, gen. mgr. and music dir., 1958—; resident music dir. Ft. Worth Symphony Assn., 1963-65; music dir., condr. Ft. Worth Ballet Assn., 1965-66; guest condr. Shreveport (La.) Civic Opera, 1962-63, 75-79, Cin. Summer Opera, 1969, Dallas (Tex.) Civic Ballet Assn., 1971, P.R. Opera, 1972, State Opera Hannover, Germany, 1974, Teheran (Iran) Opera, 1976, Conn. Grand Opera, 1979. Served with U.S. Army, 1945-46. Recipient Tex. Fedn. of Music Clubs award, 1967. Mem. Am. Fedn. Musicians. Episcopalian. Club: Rotary. Home: 5732 Wessex Fort Worth TX 76133 Office: 3505 W Lancaster Fort Worth TX 76107

KRULL, DAVID JOHN, physician; b. Kendallville, Ind., May 15, 1944; s. Gerhard John and Eilleen K.; A.B., Ind. U., 1966, M.D., 1970; m. Sandra Bye, June 22, 1968; children—Lisa, Linda, Lori. Intern, Miami Valley Hosp., Dayton, Ohio, 1970-71, resident, 1971-73; family practice medicine, Palmetto, Fla.; mem. staff Manatee Meml. Hosp. Served with N.G., 1970-76. Mem. AMA, Fla. Med. Assn., Manatee County Med. Soc., Am. Acad. Family Practice, Fla. Acad. Family Practice, Manatee C. of C. Club: Bradenton Yacht. Office: 606 4th Ave W Palmetto FL 33561

KRUMM, KENT MEARS, speech and lang. pathologist; b. Detroit, Mar. 2, 1937; s. Kenneth T. and Marion Virginia (Condon) K.; B.A., Tex. Tech. U., 1969; postgrad. U. Ky., 1973; m. Francoise Charlotte Schaguene, Nov. 16, 1957; children—Patricia Florence, Mark Mears, David Charles. Speech therapist Upper Ky. River Comp Care, 1971-73, speech therapist cons. Lee and Owsley County schs., 1974; speech therapist Letcher County Schs., Whitesburg, Ky., 1973-74; dir. speech services Upper Ky. Mental Health and Mental Retardation Care Center, Hazard, Ky., 1974-76; pvt. practice speech pathology, Hazard, 1976-77; dir., trustee Speech Clinic, Hazard, 1977—. Pres., Walkertown PTA, Hazard, 1975-76. Served with USAF, 1956-64. Mem. Am. Speech and Hearing Assn., Ky. Speech and Hearing Assn., Ky. Health Systems, Fellowship Christian Speech Pathologists and Audiologists, Internat. Assn. Laryngectomies, DAV. Baptist. Clubs: Eastern Ky. Lost Chord, Masons, Order Eastern Star. Home: 200 Couch St Hazard KY 41701 Office: 542 Main St Hazard KY 41701

KRUMME, GEORGE WILLIAM, oil co. exec.; b. Okemah, Okla., Dec. 15, 1922; s. Roy A. and Ruth (Bryan) K.; student Okla. A. and M. Coll., 1939-41; B.A., Pomona Coll., 1947; M.S., U. Tulsa, 1965, Ph.D., 1975; m. Edwynne Rollestone Freeland, Dec. 14, 1941; children—David William, Robert Bryan. Vice pres., sec. Ill. Refining Co., Bristow, Okla., 1961—; partner Krumme Oil Co., Bristow, 1947—; dir. Community Bank of Bristow (Okla.) Del., Dem. Nat. Conv., Miami, 1972; mem. Dem. Nat. Com. from Okla., 1976-80; chmn. UN Day, Okla., 1977; mem. exec. com. bd. dirs. Tulsa Opera, 1979-80. Served with U.S. Army, 1942-46. Decorated Silver Star. Mem. Am. Assn. Petroleum Geologists (pres. midcontinent sect. 1977-79), Soc. Petroleum Engrs. Okla. Ind. Petroleum Assn., Ind. Petroleum Assn. Am., Tulsa Geol. Soc. (pres. 1978-79). Democrat. Unitarian. Club: Rotary (pres. Bristow 1956). Contbr. articles to profl. jours. Home: 3470 S Florence Pl Tulsa OK 74105 Office: 210 E 9th St Bristow OK 74010

KRUSE, PAUL ROBERT, ret. librarian, educator; b. What Cheer, Iowa, Feb. 26, 1912; s. Carl Fred and Phoebe (Mumby) K.; A.B., John Fletcher Coll., 1933; B.S. in L.S., U. Ill., 1940; Ph.D., U. Chgo., 1958; m. Esther Moe, June 3, 1939 (div.); 1 son, Robert Leroy. Librarian, John Fletcher Coll., University Park, Iowa, 1932-33; librarian Bolles Sch., Jacksonville, Fla., 1934-38; reference librarian Jacksonville Pub. Library, 1938-42; reference asst. in charge reference collections Library of Congress, Washington, 1942-45; established library for UN Conf., San Francisco, 1945; instr. library sch. Cath. U., Washington 1943-48; bibliographer Ency. Brit., 1946-47; editor A. N. Marquis Co., 1949; vis. asst. prof. library sch. U. So. Calif. 1950, George Peabody Coll., 1950-51; reorganized library for Rollins Coll., Winter Park, Fla., 1951-52; vis. asso. prof. library sch. U. Ill., 1952-53; asso. prof. library sch. U. Denver, 1954-55; librarian Golden Gate Coll., San Francisco, 1955-65; asso. prof. sch. Library and Information Scis. North Tex. State U., Denton, 1965-77, ret., 1977. Fulbright lectr., library adviser U. Tehran, 1962-64, U. Ceylon, 1964-65. Library cons. U.S. AID, U. Santa Maria la Antigua, Panama, 1968. Active Community and profl. theatre groups. Mem. Am., Tex. library assns., Spl. Libraries Assn. (conf. chmn. 1961). Republican. Methodist. Mason (32 deg., Shriner). Author: The Story of the Encyclopaedia Britannica, 1763-1943. Editor Index for Lend Lease Weapon for Victory, 1944; bibliographies for Ten Eventful Years, 1947; Profiles of Special Libraries, 2d edit., 1980; cons. Pergamon Press, 1978-79. Contbr. articles to profl. jours. Home: 2207 Jacqueline St Denton TX 76201

KRUSE, RICHARD HARRY, microbiologist; b. Gilman, Vt., June 3, 1927; s. Harry John and Carla Methyne (Hansen) K.; student Duke U., 1944-45; B.S., U. Richmond, 1952; m. Eloise Christenberry, Oct. 31, 1948; 1 dau., Cynthia Jo. Microbiologist indsl. health and safety div., Fort Detrick, Md., 1953-63, chief research sect., 1963-72; dir. mycology lab. State Mycology Center, Paris, Ky., 1973-77; pres. MEDI, Inc., North Middleton, Ky., 1977—. Served with U.S. Army, 1946-49. Mem. Am. Soc. Microbiology, Internat. Soc. Human and Animal Mycology, S.C. Assn. Clin. Microbiology, Southeastern Assn. Clin. Microbiology, Med. Mycological Soc. Am., Sigma Xi. Baptist. Contbr. articles to profl. jours. Home: Bourbon Arabians North Middletown KY 40357 Office: Box 145 North Middletown KY 40357

KUBALA, MARK JEROME, neurol. surgeon; b. East Bernard, Tex., Oct. 24, 1933; s. Jerome David and Frances (Poessel) K.; B.A., U. Tex., 1955, M.D., U. Tex. Med. Br., Galveston, 1958; m. Betty Jean Fertitta, Feb. 15, 1958; children—Thomas Jerome, Mark Jerome, Daniel Jerome, Anne Marie. Intern, Hermann Hosp., Houston, 1958-59; resident in neurol. surgery Baylor U., 1959-66, clin. instr. neurol. surgery, 1966—; fellow in neurology Mayo Clinic, Rochester, Minn., 1963; practice medicine specializing in neurol. surgery, Beaumont, Tex., 1966—; mem. staff St. Elizabeth, S.E. Tex. Bapt., Beaumont Med. and Surg. hosps. Mem. adv. bd. Beaumont Civic Opera, 1972—; mem. Kelly High Sch. Bd., Beaumont, 1975—, Beaumont Diocesan Sch. Bd., 1976. Served with USAF, 1961-62. Diplomate Am. Bd. Neurol. Surgery. Mem. Tex. (del.), Am. med. assns., Royal Soc. Medicine, Congress Neurol. Surgeons, Am. Assn. Neurol. Surgeons, So., Rocky Mountain, Houston neurol. socs., Neurol. Surgery Soc., A.C.S., Beaumont Acad. Medicine, Phi Beta Kappa, Alpha Omega Alpha, Alpha Epsilon Delta, Mu Delta. Roman Catholic. Office: 3260 Fannin St Beaumont TX 77701

KUBE, ADOLPH MARTIN LUDWIG, oil co. exec. b. Lexington, Tex., Nov. 12, 1916; s. William and Mary (Helms) K.; B.S. in Indsl. Engring., Tex. Tech. U., 1942; m. Aliene Laverne May, Aug. 22, 1942; children—Laverne, Mary, Kenneth. With Phillips Petroleum Co., Borger, Tex., 1942—, dist. engr., 1956-59, asst. regional mgr., 1959-61, region mgr., 1961—. Mem. indsl. adv. bd. Tex. Tech. U., placement bd. West Tex. U., Found. Bd. Tex. Tech. U. Pres., Phillips (Tex.) Sch. Bd., 1960-66; v.p. Adobe Walls council Boy Scouts Am.; chmn. United Way. Recipient Distinguished Engr. award Tex. Tech. U., 1973, Silver Beaver award Boy Scouts Am., 1974. Mem. Am. Petroleum Inst., Borger C. of C. Lutheran. Home: 1411 Primrose St Borger TX 79007 Office: Box 358 Borger TX 79007

KUCHMAK, MYRON, chemist; b. Jaworiv, Ukraine, Mar. 26, 1915; s. Paul and Catherine (Fedun) K.; M.S., Lwiv Poly. Inst., 1939; Ph.D., Mich. State U., 1961; m. Luba Golenko, Nov. 1, 1943; 1 son, George. Came to U.S., 1950, naturalized, 1961. Instr. Lwiv Poly. Inst., Ukraine, 1939-41; research asst. Lwiv Chamber of Agr., 1941-44; lab., technician Mich. State U., East Lansing, 1956-58, research asst., 1958-61, NIH fellow, 1961-63; supervisory research chemist Center for Disease Control, Atlanta, 1963-70, chief Lipid Standardization Lab., 1970—; sci. dir. Internat. Reference Center for Lipid Determination in Cardiovascular Research, WHO, 1970—. Recipient Superior Service award HEW, 1965. Mem. Am. Chem. Soc., Am. Oil Chem. Soc., Am. Plant Physiol. Soc., AAAS. Contbr. articles in field to profl. jours. Home: 3288 Raymond Dr Doraville GA 30340 Office: 1600 Clifton Rd Atlanta GA 30333

KUCINSKAS, DENNIS PAUL, geophysicist; b. Athol, Mass., Nov. 22, 1951; s. Alfred John and Rejina Joan (Landry) K.; B.S., Bowling Green State U., 1973; M.S., Boston Coll., 1975. Asst. dir. Bowling Green Seismol. Obs., Bowling Green Ohio, 1971-73; asst. to instr. Bowling Green Geology Field Camps, Socorro, N.Mex., 1972, Durango, Colo., 1973; research asst. Weston Obs., Boston Coll., 1974-75; geophysicist Exxon Co., U.S.A., Houston, 1975-77; petroleum geophysicist Conoco, Houston, 1977-79; geophysicist Tex. Oil and Gas, Dallas, 1979—. Mem. Soc. Exploration Geophysicists, Houston Geophys. Soc. Home: 5619 Southwestern Blvd Dallas TX 75209 Office: Tex Oil and Gas Fidelity Union Tower Dallas TX

KUCSERA, ABBIE KENT, author; b. Detroit, Mar. 14, 1916; d. Walter Green and Marion Ella (Szekrak-Miller) Kent; student Detroit Inst. Technology, 1954; m. Carl Coleman Kucsera, Oct. 17, 1936; children—Lorraine Joan, Carl Walter. Journalist, editor Pontiac (Mich.) Press, 1947-57; mng. editor Inter-Lake News, Walled Lake (Mich.) Bur., 1959-61; promotion, publicity writer City of Sunrise (Fla.), 1961-62; writer-editor On-the-Go mag., Fort Lauderdale, Fla., 1963; copywriter Fla. Advt. Inc., Fort Lauderdale, 1963; author: Prize Winning Watercolors, North America, 1964; Best of Show, Flower Arrangements, America, 1964; editor (as Jan Malcolm) Hell Turned Wrong Side Out, 1965-66. Recipient Appreciation certificate Palm Beach County Bar Assn., 1975; poet laureate Southeast Fla. Dairy Inst., 1965. Mem. Forest History Soc. Baptist. Home: 45 Seminole Trail Whispering Pines FL 32039 Office: PO Box 209 Georgetown FL 32039

KUDIESY, NORMA MARTHA, librarian; b. Burlington, Vt., Nov. 21, 1931; d. Jacob J. and Margaret M. (Alafat) Kudiesy; B.S., U. Vt., 1954; M.L.S., Tex. Woman's U., 1969. Br. librarian Spl. Services Libraries, Ft. Bliss, Tex., 1967-69, reference librarian, 1969-74; pub. services librarian USAADS Library, 1974—. Mem. Cath. Daus. Am. (fin. sec. 1973-77, regent 1977-79), Tex. (sec.-treas. dist. 1972-73), Border Regional (exec. bd. 1971-72, rec. sec. 1971-72, 2d v.p. 1974-75) library assns., ALA, Am. Legion Aux. (sec. 1953-55, 75-76, 76-77, historian 1975-76, pres. 1979-80), Ninety Nines (treas. 1973-74, news reporter 1974-75, membership chmn. 1975-76), Altar Soc. (v.p. 1976-77), Nat. Women's Polit. Caucus, Fed. Employed Women. Roman Catholic. Home: 5401 Raymond Telles El Paso TX 79924 Office: USAADS Library Fort Bliss TX 79916

KUEHL, HOWARD WILLIAM, JR., accountant; b. Richmond, Va., Jan. 28, 1940; s. Howard William and Anne Baldwin (Caswell) K.; diploma Smithdeal-Massey Bus. Coll., 1961; B.Commerce, U. Richmond, 1973; children—Deborah Anne, Nancy Emaline. Sr. accountant Arthur Young & Co., Richmond, Va., 1963-69; mgr. Lybrand, Ross Bros. & Montgomery, Richmond, 1969-71; adj. faculty Smithdeal Massey Bus. Coll., Richmond, 1971-73, U. Richmond, 1976-79; proprietor H. William Kuehl, Jr., C.P.A., Richmond, 1971-73; adj. faculty Am. Coll. C.L.U.'s, Bryn Mawr, Pa., 1975-76; owner Wm. Kuehl, C.P.A., Richmond, Va., 1973—. Acting state treas. Republican Party of Va., 1975-76, mem. state central com., exec. com., state budget dir., 1972-76; served as treas. statewide and nat. Rep. political campaigns; treas. 3d Dist. Rep. Com., 1976-79; mgr., trustee Smithdeal Massey Bus. Coll., 1975-76; apptd. State Bd. Accountancy by Gov. Va. Recipient Certificate of outstanding service for Community and Professions, Va. Assn. Professions, 1976; Disting. service award 3rd Dist. Rep. Com. Mem. Am. Inst. C.P.A.'s, Va. Soc. C.P.A.'s (awarded most outstanding mem. 1978), Va. Assn. Professions (pres. 1978-79), Nat. Assn. State Bds. Accountancy (mem. practice enforcement com.), Va. Jaycees (life, Key Man award of Richmond 1975, Outstanding Jaycee of Va. Region III 1975, v.p. 1975, state dir. Richmond 1974). Clubs: Richmond First, Willow Oaks Country, Downtown. Editor: Jour. of the Professions. Home: 2315 Crowncrest Dr Richmond VA 23229 Office: 1001 E Main St Richmond VA 23219

KUEHNEGGER, WALTER, med. engring. exec., educator; b. Graz, Austria, Aug. 8, 1928; s. Vincent and Vilma Ludmilla (Riegler) K.; came to U.S., 1955, naturalized, 1961; Ph.D. in Mech. Engring., U. Graz, 1948; A.M.I.E.T. in Aero. Engring., Brit. Inst. Engring. Tech., London, 1951; postgrad. courses aerospace medicine; certificate in orthotics Northwestern U., 1973; m. Susy Margarita Zarth, Aug. 23, 1961; 1 adopted dau., Elvira Susy. Head bioengring. lab. Northrop Space Labs., Hawthorne, Calif., 1962-66; dir. Kaman Work Scis. Lab., Bethesda, Md., 1966-68; dir. bioengring. lab. Litton Washington Research Center, Bethesda, 1968-69; dir. Camp Orthotic Research Clinic, Jackson, Mich., 1969-73; v.p. Orthodyne Inc., Great Falls, Va., 1973—; asso. prof. dept. orthopedic surgery Howard U. Med. Sch., Washington; mem. vis. faculty Northwestern U. Med. Sch., 1972—; cons. VA, N.Y.-Prosthetic Center. Diplomate Am. Bd. Orthotics and Prosthetics. Mem. Aerospace Med. Assn., Am. Coll. Sports Medicine, Am. Acad. Orthotistic Prosthetists (charter), Am. Assn. Orthotists and Prosthetists, Internat. Soc. Prosthetics and Orthotics, ASTM, Soaring Soc. Am. Editorial staff Medical Orthopaedie-Technik, 1975—. Patentee in field. Introduced orthometry, a subdiscipline for measurement techniques in orthopedics. Address: 9416 Brian Jac Ln Great Falls VA 22066

KUFFEL, LAWRENCE, retail pharms. co. exec.; b. Chgo., May 16, 1949; s. Louis Gaylord and Dolores Marie (Wycklendt) K.; B.B.A., U. Wis., Whitewater, 1971. With Walgreen Co., 1971—, food mgr., Glendale, Wis., 1973-74, Milw., 1974-77, dist. mgr. trainee, Chgo., 1977, dist. restaurant mgr., Orlando, Fla., 1977—. Recipient cert. achievement Nat. Restaurant Assn., 1978. Mem. Fla. Restaurant Assn. Roman Catholic. Home: 1713 Canterbury Circle Casselberry FL 32707 Office: Walgreen Co Suite 204 616 E Semoran Blvd Altamonte Springs FL 32701

KUGLEN, CRAIG CHARLES, ophthalmologist; b. Rutherford, N.J., Oct. 14, 1935; s. Harold Francis and Dorothy Bailey (Craig) K.; B.A., Colgate U., 1957; M.D., U. Ala., 1962; m. Margaret Ann Melick, Dec. 26, 1959; children—Julia A., Meredith S., Craig Charles, Jeffrey S. Intern, U. Tex. Med. Br., Galveston, 1962-63, resident in ophthalmology, 1963-66; practice medicine specializing in ophthalmology, Harlingen, Tex.; mem. staffs Valley Bapt. Med. Center, Dolly Vinsant Meml. Hosp., Harlingen State Chest Hosp. Served in U.S. Army, 1968-70. Diplomate Am. Bd. Ophthalmology. Fellow A.C.S., Am. Acad. Ophthalmology and Otolaryngology, Tex. Med. Assn., Tex. Ophthal. Assn., Cameron-Willacy County Med. Soc., Am. Intra-ocular Implant Soc. Inventor intra-ocular lens manipulator. Home: 509 Lake Dr Harlingen TX 78550 Office: 2001 E Carey Dr Harlingen TX 78550

KUHLER, RENALDO GILLET, museum ofcl.; b. Teaneck, N.J., Nov. 21, 1931; s. Otto August and Simonne L. (Gillet) K.; B.A., U. Colo., 1961. Curator of history Eastern Wash. State Hist. Soc. Mus., Spokane, 1962-67; museum artist-illustrator N.C. State Mus. Natural History, Raleigh, 1969—; designer, executor of art work for sci. illustrations, awards, brochures, pamphlets and periodicals Dept. Agr., N.C., 1972-74; designer, executor of emblem N.C. Student Acad. Sci., 1973. Mem. Nat. Trust Historic Preservation, N.C. Student Acad. Sci. (hon.). Democrat. Office: Box 27647 Raleigh NC 27611

KUHN, ANNE NAOMI WICKER (MRS. HAROLD B. KUHN), educator; b. Lynchburg, Va.; d. George Barney and Annie (Hicks) Wicker; diploma Malone Coll., 1933, Trinity Coll. Music, London, 1937; A.B., John Fletcher Coll., 1939; M.A., Boston U., 1942; postgrad. (fellow) Harvard, 1942-44, Boston U.; m. Harold B. Kuhn. Instr., Emmanuel Bible Coll., Birkenhead, Eng., 1936-37; asst. in history John Fletcher Coll., University Park, Ia., 1938-39; librarian Harvard, 1939-44; tchr. adult edn. program U.S. Armed Forces, Fuerstenfeldbruck Air Base, Germany, 1951-52; prof. Union Bibl. Sem., Yeotmal, India, 1957-58; lectr. Armenian Bible Inst., Beirut, Lebanon, 1958; prof. German, Asbury Coll., Wilmore, Ky., 1962—. Co-dir. ednl. tour to East and West Germany, 1976, 77, 79; lectr. in field, Korea, Taiwan, Hong Kong. Del. Youth for Christ World Conf., 1948, 50, London Yearly Meeting of Friends, Edinburgh, Scotland, 1948, World Council Chs., Amsterdam, 1948, World Friends Conf., Oxford, Eng., 1952, World Methodist Conf., Oslo, Norway, 1961, Deutscher Kirchentag, Dortmund, Germany, 1963, Internat. Conf. World Evangelization Lausanne, Switzerland, 1974. Recipient German Consular award, Boston, 1965, Thomas Mann award Boston U., 1967. Fellow Goethe-Institut fur Germanisten, Munich, 1966-68, 70-71. Mem. AAUW, Am. Assn. Tchrs. German (del. conf. Bonn 1974), NEA, Ky. Ednl. Assn., Lincoln Lit. Soc., Delta Phi Alpha (award 1963, 65). Mem. Soc. of Friends. Club: Cosmopolitan (Wilmore). Author: (pamphlet) The Impact of the Transition to

Modern Education Upon Religious Education, 1950; The Influence of Paul Gerhardt upon Wesleyan Hymnody, 1960. Home: 406 Kenyon Av Wilmore KY 40390

KUHN, CHARLES, indsl. exec.; b. Cin., Nov. 29, 1919; s. Leo and Vivian (Van Hallenger) K.; student Purdue U., 1938-39; m. Elma Jane Smith, Nov. 17, 1944 (div. 1975); children—James Roland, Karen Jo Ann; m. 2d, Patricia L. McVicar, Nov. 27, 1976 (div. 1980). Vice pres. Fansteel Metall. Corp., 1945-55, Hills McCanna Co., 1955-58; v.p. Dresser Mfg. div. Dresser Industries, Inc., 1958-60, pres., 1960-64, group v.p., dir. parent co., 1964-65; exec. v.p., 1965-68, pres., 1968-69, also chief ops. officer, dir. subs. cos., 1970-72; pres., chief exec. officer, dir. Wylain, Inc., Dallas, now chmn. bd., chief exec. officer; dir. Gen. Portland Corp., Dallas, Valley View State Bank, Dallas, Falcon Products Inc., St. Louis, Equitable Bank, Dallas. Pres. Dallas Arthritis Found., 1970. Served with USNR, 1940-42. Mem. Am. Gas Assn., Newcomen Soc. N.Am., Tex. Christian U. Mgmt. Alumni Assn., Am. Water Works Assn., Pa. Soc., Canadian Gas Assn., Tex. Mid-Continent Oil and Gas Assn., Dallas Citizens Council, Dallas Symphony Assn., City Leaders Econ. Devel. Council. Clubs: Belfry-New Century (London); Chemists (N.Y.C.); Congressional Country (Washington); La Quinta (Calif.) Country; Dallas, Cipango, Preston Trail Golf, Northwood, Dallas Petroleum, Bent Tree Country, 2001 (Dallas). Home: 10820 Netherland Dr Dallas TX 75229 Office: 17250 Dallas Pkwy Dallas TX 75231

KUHN, GUS DAVID, JR., discount store exec.; b. Nashville, Dec. 14, 1922; s. Gus David and Caroline Rose (Weil) M.; B.A., Vanderbilt U., 1943; m. Barbara Jacobs, June 26, 1946; children—William I., Gus D., Irwin J. With Kuhn's Big K Stores Corp., Nashville, 1943—, v.p., 1948-77, pres., chief operating officer, 1977—, also dir. Mem. Davidson County Democratic exec. com., 1972-74, 76—, del. Dem. conv., 1974; bd. dirs. Meharry Med. Sch., 1975, NCCJ, 1970—; adv. bd. Aquinas Coll., 1974—; vice chmn. Union Am. Hebrew Congregations, 1971-75, exec. com., 1971—. Mem. Mass Retailers Inst., Assn. Gen. Mdse. Cos., Nashville C. of C. (dir. 1979—). Democrat. Jewish (pres. temple 1966-68). Clubs: Masons (33 deg.), Rotary, B'nai B'rith, Woodmont Country, University. Home: 1214 Chickering Rd Nashville TN 37215 Office: 245 Great Circle Rd Nashville TN 37228

KUHN, HAROLD BARNES, clergyman, educator; b. Belleville, Kans., Aug. 21, 1911; s. John William and Ida Alice (Morey) K.; diploma Malone Coll., 1934; A.B. magna cum laude, John Fletcher Coll., 1939; S.T.B., Harvard U., 1942, S.T.M., 1943; Ph.D. (Hopkins fellow), 1944, postgrad., 1965-67, 70; postgrad. U. Munich (Germany), 1951-52; D.D., Houghton Coll., 1970; m. Anne Naomi Wicker, June 11, 1934. Ordained to ministry Soc. of Friends, 1935; pastor Rescue (Va.) Friends Ch., 1934-36, Dartmouth (Mass.) Friends Ch., 1939-41, Waldo Congregational Ch., Brockton, Mass., 1941-44; lectr. theology Emmanuel Bible Coll., Birkenhead, Eng., 1936-37; asst. dept. history Harvard U., 1942-44; research fellow in philosophy U. Ky., 1944-45; prof. philosophy of religion Asbury Theol. Sem., Wilmore, Ky., 1944—, chmn. div. theology and philosophy of religion, 1959—; interim minister West Medway (Mass.) Congl. Ch., 1966-67; research scholar univs. Mainz, Erlangen, London, Free U. Berlin, 1960; lectr. World Congress Evangelism, Berlin, 1966: vis. prof. philosophy of religion Eastern Nazarene Coll., 1965-67; observer World Council Chs., Amsterdam, 1948; fellow Goethe Inst., Munich, summer 1967; lectr., retreat leader Ft. Campbell, Ky., U.S. Army, 1968; retreatmaster U.S. Army and Air Force, Europe, summers 1957, 60, 65, 68, 69-75, Chaplain div. Fort Polk, 1974, Fort Knox, 1975-76; del. World Conf. Methodism, Oslo, 1961, Evangelischer Kirchentag, Munich, 1961, Dortmund, Germany, 1963; chaplains supply missioner AUS, USAF, Europe, 1953-77; dir., lectr. Flying Seminar to Bible Lands, 1954; ednl. cons. USAF, Europe, 1951-52; prof. Union Theol. Sem., Yeotmal, India, 1957; lectr. U.S. Army War Coll., 1962; travel-ministry to W. Ger., Czechoslovakia, Hungary, summer 1972, Poland, summer 1973, E. Ger. and W. Ger., 1976-79; lectr., Warsaw, Poland, 1973, 78, Hong Kong Bapt. Coll. and Sem., 1978-79; co-dir. tour E. Ger. and W. Ger., 1976, 77, Inst. Social Change, Norman, Okla., 1965, 190th Anniversary U.S. Chaplains Corps, Berlin, 1965; Protestant del. Notre Dame Conf. on Vatican II, 1966; lectr. Nat. Conf. Adult Christian Edn., Notre Dame, 1972; participant Internat. Congress World Evangelization, Lausanne, Switzerland, 1974; Staley lectr. Wheaton (Ill.) Coll., 1976. First aid instr. ARC, 1942; active refugee relief and rehab., Germany, 1945—; trustee Malone Coll., Canton, O.; bd. dirs. Christian Freedom Found. Named Alumnus of Year, Malone Coll., 1968, Alumnus of Year in Edn., Vennard Coll., 1975. Mem. Soc. Bibl. Lit., AAUP, Evang. Theol. Soc., Acad. Polit. Sci., Am. Assn. Christian Social Ethics, Am. Philos. Assn., Delta Phi Alpha, Theta Phi. Club: Harvard Faculty. Author: Colossians and Philemon (Aldersgate Bibl. series); An Examination of Liberal Theology, 1943; editor Asbury Seminarian, 1946—; cons. editor Zondervan Pub. Co. 1964—; editorial bd. Christianity Today, 1956—, contbr., editor-at-large, 1970—; contbr. articles to religious jours. and books. Home: 406 Kenyon Ave Wilmore KY 40390

KUHN, JAMES CLIFFORD, JR., ins. co. exec.; b. Ft. Worth, Tex., Oct. 10, 1941; s. James Clifford and Hazel Blanche (Holcomb) K.; B.S., U.S. Air Force Acad., 1963; B.Internat. Mgmt. with honors, Thunderbird Grad. Sch., 1970; M.A. in Public Adminstrn., U. Okla., 1970; m. Charlie Ann Faver, June 24, 1965; children—Matthew Christian, Pilar Noelle. Project mgr. Lockheed Aircraft Internat. Los Angeles, 1970-71; dist. sales mgr. Softens div. Bausch & Lomb, New Orleans, 1971-72; nat. sales mgr. Replacement Lens Inc., Peoria, Ill., 1973-75; rep. Omega Optical Co., Peoria, 1975-78; pres., dir. Omega Contact Lens Ins. Co., Dallas, 1978—; adminstrv. bd., fin. teaching staff First United Meth. Ch., Carrollton, Tex., 1978—; exec. bd. Dallas Assn. for Parent Edn., 1978—. Served with to capt. USAF, 1963-69. Recipient Outstanding Achievement award Bausch & Lomb, Inc., 1971; cert. flight instr., 1976—. Fellow Nat. Acad. Opticianry; mem. Aircraft Owners and Pilots Assn. Methodist. Home: 1310 Lincoln Dr Carrollton TX 75006 Office: 13515 N Stemmons Freeway Dallas TX 75234

KUHNS, HOWARD HILL, JR., hosp. adminstr.; b. Edgewood, Pa., Oct. 29, 1924; s. Howard Hill and Alma Lenhart (Cale) K.; B.S. in Bus. Adminstrn., U. Pitts., 1948; postgrad. U. Pitts. and U. Tenn., 1950-62; m. Barbara Jenn Beard, Dec. 27, 1947; children—James Howard, Ronald David, Timothy Richard. Ordained to ministry Ch. of God, 1962; acct. Arthur Young & Co., Pitts., 1948-49; sr. acct. Cale Co. Accts. and Auditors, Uniontown, Pa., 1950-54; fin. mgr. White Wing Pub. House and Press, Cleveland, Tenn., 1955-57; asst. adminstr., controller Bradley Meml. Hosp., Cleveland, 1958-76, asso. adminstr., 1977—; lectr. Jewish history and customs Kent Coll.; instr. Cleveland State Community Coll.; chmn. systems com. Tenn. Hosp. Computer Center. Mem. Com. Alcohol and Drug Abuse. Served with USAAF, 1943-46; CBI. Mem. Hosp. Fin. Mgmt. Assn. (advanced mem., William G. Follmer merit award), Tenn. Hosp. Fin. Mgmt. Assn. (dir.), Am. Coll. Hosp. Adminstrs., Tenn. Hosp. Assn., Chattanooga Area Hosp. Council (sec.). Clubs: Exchange, Optimist, Kiwanis. Home: 2036 Brentwood Rd Cleveland TN 37311 Office: Bradley Meml Hosp PO Box 45 Cleveland TN 37311

KUHRE, CALVIN JEREMY, chem. engr.; b. Salt Lake City, Feb. 6, 1922; s. Newell John and Ruth Marie (Jeremy) K.; B.Chem. Engring. (John McMullen scholar 1940-43), Cornell U., 1948; Chem. E., U. Calif., Berkeley, 1956; m. LaRoma L. Chem. Engrs., Am. Chem. Soc., Alpha Phi Omega. Mormon. Clubs: Algonquin of Cornell U. (pres. 1947). Contbr. writings to handbooks, encys., publs.; patentee in field of process engring. Home: 13703 Barryknoll Ln Houston TX 77079 Office: Box 3105 Houston TX 77001

KUHRT, HARRY LUGENE, chemist; b. Denver, June 29, 1929; s. Harry William and Dorsie Anna (Hubbard) K.; B.A. in Psychology, U. Denver, 1950, B.S. in Chemistry, 1951; M.S. in Chemistry, U. Colo., 1953; m. JoAnn Hubbard, Dec. 27, 1950; children—Melinda Lou, Stephen Delbert, Bethany Ann, Morris Gene. Pharmacist, Walgreen Drug Co., Denver, 1950-52; chief chemist O.M. Franklin Veterinarian Supplies, Denver, 1952-53; research and devel. staff Phillips Petroleum Co., Bartlesville, Okla., 1953-58, chief chemist, lab. mgr., quality control mgr., Borger, Tex., 1958—; dir. lab. analysis of drugs and controlled substances. Mem. Phillips (Tex.) Sch. bd., 1963-72. Mem. Internat. Inst. Synthetic Rubber (dir. toxicology div.), Am. Chem. Soc., Rubber Mfg. Assn., AAAS, Am. Soc. for Quality Control, Water Pollution Control Fedn. Baptist. Clubs: Lions, Rotary, Masons, Shriners. Contbr. articles to tech. jours.; patentee in field of rubber and polymer chemistry. Home: #6 Smoot St Phillips TX 79071 Office: PO Box 1231 Borger TX 79007

KULBERG, LESLIE ERVIN, electronic engr.; b. Bisbee, N.D., Feb. 17, 1909; s. Ole O. and Anna Julia (Uhren) K.; B.S. in Elec. Engring., Pa. State U., 1933; postgrad. George Washington U., 1956; m. Margaret Anna Stubbs, Feb. 14, 1934; 1 dau., Judith Beatrice Kulberg Bracewell. Jr. radio engr. Westinghouse Electric Corp., Chicopee Falls, Mass., 1936-38; radio inspector and engr. FCC, N.Y.C., 1940-41, Washington, 1945-51; radio/electronic engr. Dept. Def., Washington, 1941-45, 51-56; supr. guided missile engr. Hawk Missile project Army Missile Huntsville, Ala., 1956-61; devel. engr., specialist and lead engr. Lockheed Ga. Co., Marietta, 1962-66; research specialist Apollo program Boeing Co., Hunstville, 1966-69, mem. Boeing AWACS team Seattle, 1969; Skylab program Martin Marietta Corp., Huntsville, 1972-74; chief engr. Precision Electronics Labs., Fayetteville, Tenn., 1974—. Recipient certificates of appreciation from all Skylab astronauts; registered profl. engr. D.C. Mem. IEEE (life). Home: Route 2 Fayetteville TN 37334

KULICK, PAUL ABRAHAM, social worker; b. Wheeling, W.Va., Aug. 30, 1911; s. Julius Louis and Hinde Miriam (Rosenson) K.; A.B., U. Pitts., 1932; cert. Grad. Sch. Jewish Social Work, 1934; postgrad. N.Y. Sch. Social Work, 1937-38; m. Sarah Buff, Aug. 6, 1939; children—Gilbert David, Frances Elizabeth Kulick Travis. Exec. dir. Jewish Community Center, Schenectady, 1934-39, Houston, 1939-41, Stamford, Conn., 1941-45, Jewish Ednl. Alliance, Savannah, Ga., 1945-50, Savannah Jewish Council, 1945-58, Jewish Fedn., San Antonio, 1958-72, Jewish Community Council, Sarasota, Fla., 1972-73, community services cons. Savannah Jewish Council, 1973—; founding editor Savannah Jewish News, 1949—. Bd. dirs. Ga. Assn. Mental Health, 1952-58, Tex. Assn. Mental Health, 1960-68; pres. Chatham-Savannah Mental Health Assn., 1956-58. Mem. Nat. Assn. Social Workers (chmn. S. Tex. chpt. 1964-66, del. nat. assembly 1964, 73), Nat. Assn. Jewish Center Workers, Conf. Jewish Communal Service (dir.), Assn. Jewish Community Orgn. Personnel, Sigma Delta Chi. B'nai B'rith. Home: 10611 Abercorn Expressway Apt 172 Savannah GA 31406 Office: 5111 Abercorn St Savannah GA 21405

KULKARNI, DATTATREYA VITHAL RAO, educator; b. Chass, Nasik, India, Mar. 25, 1911; s. Vithalrao Anandrao and Rukmini (Joshi) K.; came to U.S., 1965; B.A., Nagpur U., 1933, M.A., 1935; M.S., Columbia U., 1947; Ph.D., Brandeis U., 1969; m. Kamala Badave, Dec. 1, 1944; children—Chandrashekmar, Sandhyarani, Swaroop Kumari. With Soc. Protection Children in Western India, 1938-41; supt. Govt. Maharashtra, 1941-59, 63-65; dir. social welfare Delhi Adminstrn., 1959-63; chief insp. cert. schs. and instns., reclamation officer Maharashtra State, 1947-59; prof. social work U. Ala., University, 1969—. Sec., Indian Leprosy Assn., Delhi, 1960-63. Willard Straight fellow, 1945-47; Wein fellow, 1965-69; King Edward Meml. scholar, 1929-35. Mem. Nat. Assn. Social Workers, Council Social Work Edn., Acad. Cert. Social Workers. Contbr. articles to profl. jours. Home: 2216 2d Ave Apt 1 Broadmoor Tuscaloosa AL 35401

KULLMAN, J. WAYNE, bus. exec.; b. Phila., June 29, 1940; s. Charles H. and Catherine R. (Jordan) K.; B.S., LaSalle Coll., 1962; m. Peggy Bonenberger, Apr. 4, 1964; children—Suzanne, Lynn, J. Wayne, Sean. Account mgr. Price Waterhouse & Co., N.Y., 1962-72; v.p. Rouse Constrn. Internat., Atlanta, 1972-78; exec. v.p. Arthur Rubloff & Co., Atlanta, 1978—; dir. various corps. Mem. Florham Park Jaycees, v.p., 1961-62. Recipient Outstanding Young Man of Am. award, 1972; C.P.A., N.Y. Mem. Am. Inst. C.P.A.'s, N.Y. State Soc. C.P.A.'s, Am. Mgmt. Assn. Republican. Roman Catholic. Club: Hampton Farms. Home: 5069 Riverhill Rd Marietta GA 30067 Office: 134 Peachtree Rd NW Atlanta GA 30303

KULP, SAMUEL LESTER, computer systems analyst; b. Mishawaka, Ind., Nov. 23, 1942; s. Lester Charles and Frances Bernice (Chamness) K.; B.S., Purdue U., 1970; m. Constance Lenora White, June 26, 1965. Systems programmer Purdue U. adminstrv. data processing center, West Lafayette, Ind., 1969-70; info. analyst Eli Lilly and Co., Indpls., 1970-73; sr. programmer analyst Am. United Life Ins. Co., Indpls., 1973-78, EDP tng. coordinator, 1978-79; data systems analyst So. Bell Telephone Co., Atlanta, 1979—. Scoutmaster, leadership devel. chmn., dist. commr. Boy Scouts Am. (recipient Eagle award, Scouters Key, Dist. Award of Merit, mem. Order of Arrow). Mem. Assn. Computing Machinery (past treas. Central Ind. chpt.), Am. Soc. Tng. and Devel., Nat. Eagle Scout Assn., Cousteau Soc. Baptist. Home: 160 Leeward Ln Roswell GA 30076

KUMAR, GANESH NAGABHUSHAN, educator; b. Mysore, India, May 3, 1946; came to U.S., 1973; s. Krishnappa Nagabhushanam and Gowramma Venkat; B.S., Bangalore (India) U., 1966; M.S., Indian Inst. Tech., 1968; M.B.A., St. Joseph's Coll., 1972; Ph.D. in Mech. Engring., Auburn U., 1978; m. Anita Kagal, Dec. 16, 1976; 1 son, Vinay. Lectr. mech. engring. Bangalore U., 1968-73; instr. Auburn (Ga.) U., 1973-78; asst. prof. mech. engring. Sch. Engring., Tuskegee (Ala.) Inst., 1978-79, asso. prof., 1979—. Mem. ASME, Nat. Soc. Profl. Engrs., Instn. Engrs. (India), Sigma Xi. Hindu. Home: PO Box 1027 Auburn AL 36830 Office: Sch of Engring Tuskegee Inst Tuskegee AL 36088

KUMAR, MADHURENDU BHUSHAN, geologist; b. Khagaria, India, Jan. 4, 1942; came to U.S., 1969, naturalized, 1971; s. Sita Ram Prabhas and Bhavani Devi Kumar; A.I.S.M., Indian Sch. Mines, Dhanbad, India, 1962; M.Sc., Ranchi U., Ranchi, Bihar, India, 1962; Ph.D., La. State U., 1972; m. Sharda Swarnkar, July 7, 1965; children—Madhuresh, Vinita. Instr., Indian Sch. Mines, 1962-63; sci. office Dept. Atomic Energy, New Delhi, India, 1963; geologist Oil India Ltd., 1963-69; grad. teaching and research asst. dept. geology La. State U., 1969-72, research asso. Inst. Environ. Studies, summers 1975, 77, 76, research asso. Inst. Environ. Studies, 1978—; sr. investigator geohydrology, salt dome project Dept. Energy, 1978—; cons. and exploration geologist, 1972-74; mem. faculty dept. geology and geography Hunter Coll., City U. N.Y., 1974-77; mem. faculty dept. geology La. State U., 1977-78, U. Southwestern La., spring 1979, dept. civil engring. So. U., Baton Rouge, 1978—; cons. in field. Recipient Sir Henry Hayden medal Mining, Metall. and Geol. Inst. India, 1962, Disting. Alumni award Indian Sch. Mines, 1978. Mem. Geol. Soc. Am., Am. Assn. Petroleum Geologists (cert. petroleum geologist), Am. Inst. Profl. Geologists (cert. profl. geol. scientist), Soc. Petroleum Engrs., Sigma Xi. Research, publs. on subsurface petroleum geology, computerized mapping, geopressured reservoirs, geothermal and geopressure patterns, salt dome tectonics, geohydrology of salt mines. Home: 7744 Wimbledon Ave Baton Rouge LA 70810 Office: Inst Environ Studies La State U 42 Atkinson Hall Baton Rouge LA 70803

KUMIN, IVRI MATTHEW, psychiatrist, psychoanalyst; b. San Francisco, Sept. 7, 1946; s. Emanuel Max and Mollie (Rosen) K.; student Tulane U., 1964-67, M.D., 1971, postgrad. div. psychoanalytic medicine, 1971-76; m. Linda Sue Waltman, June 30, 1968; children—Avi Lev, Esther Rael. Intern, Tulane U., 1971-72, resident in psychiatry, 1971-74; practice psychiatry and psychoanalysis, New Orleans, 1974—; clin. asst. prof. psychiatry Tulane U., 1975—, supervising and tng. analyst Tulane Div. Psychoanalytic Medicine, 1977—; cons. Jewish Family and Children's Service. Diplomate Am. Bd. Psychiatry. Fellow Am. Acad. Psychoanalysis; mem. Am. Psychiat. Assn., La. Psychiat. Assn., New Orleans Psychiat. Assn. Book reviewer Jour. Am. Acad. Psychoanalysis, 1979. Office: 2731 Napoleon Ave New Orleans LA 70115

KUMMER, FREDERIC ARNOLD, ret. advt. agy. exec.; b. Catonsville, Md., Mar. 27, 1913; s. Frederic Arnold and Marion Jane (McLean) K.; grad. Boy's Latin Sch., Balt., 1931; m. Harriet Jean Rowland, May 31, 1964; children—Jane K. Kummer Hardee, John Frederic. Clerical worker N.Y. Life Ins. Co., 1931-35; free lance writer stories and articles pub. U.S. and abroad, 1935-41; copy chief VanSant-Dugdale Advt. Agy., Balt., 1941-52; copy dir. Ross Roy, Inc., advt., Detroit, 1952-58; creative v.p. Houck & Co., Roanoke, Va., 1959-77; instr. advt. U. Balt., evenings 1947; advt. cons. Recipient numerous awards for outstanding ads. Republican. Episcopalian. Club: Roanoke Country. Home: 2439 Robin Hood Rd Roanoke VA 24014

KUMPE, ROY FRANKLIN, orgn. dir.; b. Little Rock, Jan. 18, 1910; s. David Franklin and Mary E. (Prichard) K.; student Little Rock Jr. Coll., 1929-30; LL.B., Ark. Law Sch., 1938; LL.D., U. Ark., 1972; m. Berenice Gray, Nov. 30 1939; children—Roy Chadwick, Peter Gray. Salesman, S.W. Pubg. Co., Nashville, 1930-36; admitted to Ark. bar, 1938; practice law, Little Rock, 1938-40; dir. rehab. of blind Dept. Pub. Welfare, Little Rock, 1939-44; supr. services for blind, vocat. rehab. Dept. Edn., Little Rock, 1944-46; exec. dir., founder Ark. Enterprises for Blind, Little Rock, 1946—. Pres., Ark. Canteen Service, Inc., Little Rock, 1948-67. Chmn., Gov.'s Com. on Employment Handicapped, 1947-48; mem. Pres.'s Com. on Employment Handicapped, 1949—. Alderman, Little Rock City Council, 1943-48; mem. Little Rock Planning Commn., 1945-57. Exec. v.p. Internat. Services for Blind, Inc., 1971—. Recipient Merit citation Nat. Rehab. Assn., 1962, award Ark. Assn. Vending Stand Operators, 1964, Migel medal Am. Found. for Blind, 1970. Regional award Am. Assn. Workers for Blind, 1972, IRS award, 1972, Roy Kumpe award Am. Assn. Workers for Blind, 1972. Mem. Am. Assn. Workers for Blind (pres. 1951-53, Ambrose Shotwell medal 1975), Nat. Council State Agys. Serving Blind (a founder, pres. 1944-46), Internat. Services for Blind (organizer, exec. v.p. 1971), Nat. Council Rehab. Centers for Blind (charter pres. 1972). Mem. Christian Ch. (elder, chmn. bd., tchr.). Lion (various citations; dist. gov. 1967-68), Mason (32 deg.). Contbr. articles to profl. jours. Home: 7610 Choctaw Little Rock AR 72205 Office: 2811 Fair Park Blvd Little Rock AR 72204

KUNKEL, ROY DELBERT, oil co. exec.; b. Mandan, N.D., Mar. 12, 1919; s. James Oliver and Elsie Marie (Houge) K.; m. Betty Jean Hesrick, Jan. 24, 1943; children—Ethelyn Kay, Rodger Dean. Machinist, Gen. Motors Corp., Defiance, Ohio, 1960-73; ter. supr. Cities Service Oil Co., Naples, Fla., 1975—. Served with U.S. Army, 1942-45. Decorated Bronze Star with five clusters. Club: Moose. Home: 625 93d Ave Naples FL 33940 Office: 3300 9th St N Naples FL 33940

KUNTZ, HAL GOGGAN, petroleum exploration co. exec.; b. San Antonio, Tex., Dec. 29, 1937; s. Peter A. and Jean M. (Goggan) K.; B.S.E., Princeton U., 1960; M.B.A., Oklahoma City U., 1972; m. Nannie A. Berendson, May 23, 1969; children—Hal Goggan II, Peter V, Michael B. Line and staff positions Mobil Oil Corp., Dallas, Oklahoma City and New Orleans, 1963-74; co-founder CLK Corp., New Orleans and Houston, 1974, pres., chief exec. officer, dir., 1974—; pres. IPEX Co., CLK High Seas Peru; gen. partner Gulf Coast Exploration Co. Served with U.S. Army, 1960-63. Winner amateur golf tournaments, 1955, 56, 63. Mem. Am. Mgmt. Assn., Nat. Small Bus. Assn., Inter-Am. Soc., Soc. Exploration Geophysicists, Aircraft Owners and Pilots Assn., Houston Mus. Fine Arts, Houston Opera Soc. Republican. Roman Catholic. Clubs: Presidents, Univ., Order of Alamo. Office: 510 5373 W Alabama Houston TX 77056

KUNZ, FREDERICK GEORGE, II, mech. engr.; b. Cin., Apr. 21, 1924; s. Fred George and Ruth Louise (Forder) K.; Mech. Engr., U. Cin., 1950; children—Frederick Charles, Daniel Amor, Russel Stewart. Chief engr. Stedfast and Roulston, Boston, 1950-64; v.p. charge engring. and sales Leu Machinery Co., Hialeah, Fla., 1964-71; chief machine design engr. Connell/Metcalf & Eddy, archtl./engring. co., Coral Gables, Fla., 1971—; pres., owner Leef Engring. Co., cons. engrs., Miami, 1965—, Leef Nursery, Miami, 1972—; cons. in field. Served with AUS, 1942-45; PTO. Decorated Bronze Star; Engring. scholar Pi Tau Sigma, 1949; recipient Eagle award Boy Scouts Am., 1939; registered profl. engr., Fla., Ohio. Mem. Internat., Ala. solar energy socs., Nat. Soc. Profl. Engrs., Am. Welding Soc., Fairchild Gardens, S. Fla. Fern Soc., Fla. Engring. Soc., Smithsonian Assos. Club: Masons. Home: 5330 SW 101st Ave Miami FL 33165 Office: 1320 S Dixie Hwy Coral Gables FL 33146

KUNZE, KENNETH RICHARD, chemist; b. N.Y.C., Apr. 11, 1952; s. Richard and Alice (Holler) K.; B.A., Queens Coll., City U. N.Y., 1974; M.A., Rice U., 1977, Ph.D., 1978; m. Aug. 11, 1974. With Exxon Prodn. Research Co., Houston, 1977—, sr. research chemist, 1978—. N.Y. State Regents scholar, 1970; Robert A. Welch pre-doctoral fellow, 1974-77. Mem. Soc. Petroleum Engrs., Phi Beta Kappa, Sigma Xi. Office: Exxon Prodn Research Co 3120 Buffalo Speedway Houston TX 77001

KUONEN, ERNEST ANTHONY, aerospace exec.; b. White Plains, N.Y., Feb. 10, 1943; s. Ernest and Josefine (Gassman Von Tuken) K.; B.S.M.E., Fla. Atlantic U., 1968; M.S.M.E., U. R.I., 1969; Ph.D., Duke U., 1972; m. Ingrid Gerda Menz, Sept. 6, 1969; children—Christopher David, Chara Dawn. Research asso. mech. engring. dept. Duke U., Durham, N.C., 1971-72; project engr. Lasers, Pratt & Whitney Aircraft, United Technologies Corp., West Palm

Beach, Fla., 1973-76; pres. Erning Corp., Jupiter, Fla., 1968—; program mgr. Lasers, Optics and Applied Tech. Lab., United Technologies Corp., West Palm Beach, 1977—. Mem. Dist. 5 Mental Health, Drug Abuse and Alcoholism Bd., State of Fla., 1978—. Served with USNR, 1960-64. NASA grantee, 1970-71. Registered profl. engr., Fla. Mem. ASME, AAUP, ASHRAE, Am. Mgmt. Assn., Sigma Xi, Phi Theta Kappa, Sigma Epsilon Mu. Clubs: Racquet (Jupiter), K.C. Contbr. articles to profl. jours. Home: 105 Elsa Rd Jupiter FL 33458 Office: PO Box 2691 West Palm Beach FL 33402

KURIE, ANDREW EDMUNDS, mining geologist; b. Dallas, May 30, 1932; s. Charles Winfred and Katherine Doyle (Edmunds) K.; B.S. in Geology, Sul Ross State Coll., Alpine, Tex., 1954; M.A. in Geology, U. Tex. at Austin, 1956; m. Judith Ann Hankins, Feb. 14, 1970; children—Andrea, Mary Kay, Michael, Thomas, Teresa. Petroleum geologist Pure Oil Co., Fort Worth, 1956-63; geologist Utah State Dept. Hwys., Salt Lake City, 1964-67; mining geologist LaDomincia S.A. de C.V., Marathon, Tex., 1968—, exploration supt., 1972-76, mgr. mines and exploration, 1977—. Certified profl. geologist. Fellow AAAS; mem. Geol. Soc. Am., Am. Assn. Petroleum Geologists, Assn. Profl. Geol. Scientists, Explorer's Club. Editor: West Tex. Geol. Soc. Membership Directory, 1962; contbr. articles to profl. jours. Home: 200 N Ave D Marathon TX 79842 Office: PO Drawer 457 Marathon TX 79842

KURIGER, RICHARD CHARLES, III, ins. broker; b. Bronxville, N.Y., July 10, 1942; s. Richard Charles and Frances May (Arena) K.; B.A., Principia Coll., 1964; C.L.U., Am. Coll., 1970, M.S. in Fin. Services, 1979; m. Lynn Elliott Smith, July 25, 1964; children—Richard Charles IV, Melinda Mitchell. Agt., Conn. Mut. Life Ins. Co., Houston, 1964—, asst. gen. agt., 1975—; partner Woodcreek Resort Inc., Wimberly, Tex., 1966—; owner, operator Kuriger & Assos., ins. brokers, Houston, 1970—; dir. Woodcreek Devel. Co., Houston Aeros Hockey Club, So. Living and Leasure Inc., Smithland Co. Served with USAF, 1966-68. Cert. ins. counselor. Mem. Million Dollar Round Table (life, qualifying), Am. Soc. Pension Actuaries (asso.), Houston Estate and Financial Forum, Houston Bus. and Estate Planning Council, Advanced Assn. Life Underwriters, Am. Soc. C.L.U.'s, Tex. Leaders Round Table (dir.), Houston Assn. Life Underwriters (dir.). Republican. Clubs: Principia Alumni, Woodcreek Country, Rotary. Home: 11620 Blalock Forest Houston TX 77024 Office: 520 S Post Oak Rd Suite 100 Houston TX 77027

KURLAND, GERALD, historian; b. Bklyn., July 24, 1942; s. Carl and Sophia Gertrude (Spar) K.; B.A., L.I. U., 1963; M.A., Bklyn. Coll., 1964; Ph.D. CUNY, 1968. Research asst. CUNY, 1965-67; lectr. Kingsborough Coll., 1968-69; lectr. history Bklyn. Coll., 1966-75; free lance writer, 1975—. Mem. Am. Hist. Assn., Orgn. Am. Historians. Republican. Author: Seth Low, 1971; American History I, Western Civilization I & II, 1971. Editor: The United States in Vietnam, 1975; The Origins of the Cold War, 1975. Address: 6990 SW 30th St Miramar FL 33023

KUROSKY, ALEXANDER, biochemist, educator; b. Windsor, Ont., Can., Sept. 12, 1938; came to U.S., 1972; s. Peter and Stella (Gemper) K.; B.Sc., U. B.C., 1965; M.Sc., U. Toronto, 1969, Ph.D., 1972; m. Anna Kinik, May 18, 1963; children—Lisa Kathryn, Tanya Kristine, Stephanie Ann. Research technician Can. Dept. Agr., Harrow, Ont., and Vancouver, B.C., 1959-64; chemist research and devel. Can. Breweries Ltd., Toronto, Ont., 1965-67; faculty Med. Br., U. Tex., Galveston, 1973—, asso. prof., 1978—. Province of Ont. grad. fellow, 1968-71; grantee Burkitt Found., NIH, Nat. Cancer Inst. Mem. Am. Soc. Biol. Chemists, Am. Chem. Soc., AAAS, Can. Biochem. Soc., Am. Soc. Human Genetics, Sigma Xi. Contbr. articles to sci. publs. Home: 6605 Golfcrest Dr Galveston TX 77551

KURTZ, LAWRENCE WILLARD, fin. exec.; b. St. Louis, Dec. 19, 1950; s. Willard Lawrence and Violet Olive (Schoenberg) K.; student U.S. Mil. Acad., 1968-69; A.B. in Econs., Princeton U., 1972; M.A. in Journalism, Mo. U., 1975; m. Melissa Adams Leeds, May 12, 1979. Overseas credit analyst Chase Bank, N.Y.C. and Frankfurt, Germany, 1973-74; account exec. Burson-Marsteller, N.Y.C., 1975-77, sr. account exec., Chgo., 1977-78; treas., dir. corporate communications Southwestern Group Fin., Inc., Houston, 1978-80; account supr. Burson-Marsteller, Houston, 1980—. Mem. Nat. Investor Relations Inst., Public Relations Soc. Am. Club: Sunrisers. Home: 2555 Bering St Apt 9 Houston TX 77057 Office: 6363 Richmond St Suite 300 Houston TX 77057

KURTZ, ROBERT LEE, research and devel. co. exec.; b. Rustburg, Va., May 21, 1933; s. Thomas Edward and Vernie (Bryant) K.; B.S., Lynchburg Coll., 1960; M.S. in Physics, Va. Poly. Inst., 1968, Ph.D. in Physics, 1971; m. Dec. 26, 1954; children—Lee Ann, Nancy. Physicist, Army Ballistic Missile Agy., Huntsville, Ala., 1960-61; with Naval Research lab., Washington, 1961-63; br. chief Space Scis. Lab., NASA, Marshall Space Flight Center, Huntsville, Ala., 1963-77; pres. T A I Corp., Huntsville, 1977—. Served with U.S. Army, 1953-55. NSF scholar, 1966-71. Mem. Soc. Photo-optical Instrumentation Engrs., Optical Soc. Am., Phi Beta Phi, Phi Kappa Phi, Sigma Xi, Sigma Pi Sigma. Patentee. Office: T A I Corp 12010 S Memorial Pkwy Huntsville AL 35803

KURZEN, RENEE, behavioral specialist; b. Canton, Ohio, July 22, 1953; d. Robert Ressler and Rosemary Eileen K.; B.S., Fla. State U., 1975; M.S. in Spl. Edn. (Bur. Edn. for Handicapped scholar), George Peabody Coll., Nashville, 1976. Tchr. public schs., Nashville, 1976-77; research asst. George Peabody Coll., 1977, curriculum specialist, 1978, coordinator Project Change, 1977-78; behavioral specialist Upper Pinellas Assn. for Retarded Citizens, Clearwater, Fla., 1978-79, supr. Dept. Edn. Profoundly Mentally Retarded Program, Pinellas County Public Schs., 1979—; cons. in field; mem. Fla. Health & Rehab. Services Level III Com. on Behavior Mgmt. in Community Facilities. Mem. Am. Assn. Edn. Severely/Profoundly Handicapped, Am. Assn. Mental Deficiency, Council Exceptional Children, Nat. Sierra Wilderness Club, Am. Soc. Tng. and Devel., AAUP. Republican. Lutheran. Home: F-12 551 N Saturn Ave Clearwater FL 33515

KURZWEG, ULRICH HERMANN, physicist; b. Jena, Germany, Sept. 16, 1936; came to U.S., 1947, naturalized, 1952; s. Hermann Herbert and Erna Herta (Michaelis) K.; B.S., U. Md., 1958; M.A. (Woodrow Wilson fellow), Princeton U., 1959, Ph.D. in Physics, 1961; m. Sophia Speth, Dec. 21, 1963; 1 dau., Tina. Sr. theoretical physicist United Tech. Research Labs., East Hartford, Conn., 1962-68; prof. engring. scis. U. Fla., Gainesville, 1968—; adj. asst. prof. Rensselaer Poly. Inst. Hartford Grad. Center, 1964-67, adj. asso. prof., 1967-68. Fulbright grantee, 1961-62; recipient Sigma Tau-Beta Pi award for excellence in undergrad. engring. teaching, 1970, 73. Mem. Am. Phys. Soc., N.Y. Acad. Scis., AAAS, Sigma Xi, Sigma Tau. Contbr. articles to sci. jours. and revs. Home: 8407 NW 4th Pl Gainesville FL 32601

KUSCH, POLYKARP, physicist; b. Blankenburg, Germany, Jan. 26, 1911; s. John Matthias and Henrietta (van der Haas) K.; came to U.S., 1912, naturalized, 1922; B.S., Case Inst. Tech., 1931; D.Sc. 1956; M.S. U. Ill., 1933; Ph.D. 1936; D.Sc., 1961; D.Sc., Ohio State U., 1959; D.Sc., Colby Coll., 1961, Gustavus Adolphus Coll., St. Peter, Minn., 1963, Yeshiva U., 1976; m. Edith Starr McRoberts, Aug. 12, 1935 (dec. 1959); children—Kathryn, Judith, Sara; m. 2d, Betty Jane Pezzoni, 1960; children—Diana, Maria. Engaged as asst. U. Ill. 1931-36; asst. U. Minn., 1936-37; instr. Columbia U., 1937-41, asso. prof. physics, 1946-49, prof., 1949-72, chmn. dept. physics, 1949-52, 60-63, acad. v.p. and provost, 1969-72; engr. Westinghouse, 1941-42; research asso. Columbia U., 1942-44; mem. tech. staff Bell Telephone Labs., 1944-46; prof. physics U. Tex. at Dallas, 1972—, Eugene McDermott prof., 1974—. Recipient Nobel prize in physics, 1955; fellow Center for Advanced Study in Behavioral Sciences, 1964-65; Illini achievement award U. Ill., 1975. Fellow Am. Phys. Soc., AAAS; mem. Am. Acad. Arts. and Scis., Am. Philos. Soc., Nat. Acad. Scis. Democrat. Research in atomic molecular and nuclear physics. Office: Dept Physics U Tex PO Box 688 Richardson TX 75080

KUSHNER, FREDERICK GARY, cardiologist; b. N.Y.C., May 20, 1948; s. Jack and Gloria K.; B.A., Columbia U., 1970, M.D., 1974; m. Ivy Erica Sommerstein, May 8, 1977. Intern, Beth Israel Hosp. Harvard Med. Sch., Boston, 1974, resident in internal medicine, 1974-76; fellow in cardiology U. Pa., 1976-78, Mass. Gen. Hosp., Boston, 1978-79; research and clin. fellow in medicine Harvard Med. Sch., 1978-79; practice medicine specializing in cardiology Marrero, La., 1979—; mem. staff W. Jefferson Gen. Hosp., Marrero. Diplomate Am. Bd. Internal Medicine; cert. in isotopes New Eng. Roentgen Ray Soc., 1979; S.E. Pa. Heart Assn. grantee, 1977. Fellow Am. Coll. Cardiology; mem. Jefferson Parish Med. Soc., La. Med. Soc., AMA, A.C.P., Am. Fedn. Clin. Research, New Orleans Acad. Internal Medicine, Paul Dudley White Soc., Alpha Omega Alpha. Contbr. articles to profl. jours. Office: 4500 11th St Marrero LA 70072

KUSUMI, YOSHI-TARO, physician, psychiatrist, acupuncture specialist; b. Tokyo, Dec. 10, 1935; s. Hiyoshi and Toshi (Isozaki) K.; came to U.S., 1969; B.A., Nihon U., 1957, M.D., 1961; m. Mariko Ouchi, Jan. 23, 1966; children—Kenro, Arisa. Intern, Ome Gen. Hosp., Tokyo, 1961-62; resident psychiatry Tokyo U., 1962-65, U. N.C. Sch. Medicine, Chapel Hill, 1970-72; dir. clin. research Cherry State Hosp., 1969-71; clin. asst. prof., dept. psychiatry U. N.C., 1973—; dir. mental health center, Kinston, 1973-75; psychiat. cons. Lenoir Meml. Hosp., 1972-75; staff psychiatrist Rex Hosp., Wake Med. Center, Raleigh and dir. Pain Control Clinic, 1976—. NIMH research grantee, 1970. Mem. Am. Psychiat. Assn., Neuropsychiat. Assn. Japan, Am. Inst. Hypnosis, Japanese Acad. Acupuncture and Chinese Medicine. Research and publs. on lithium carbonate, X-chromosome disorders and affective psychosis, psychiat. application of acupuncture. Home: 8721 Ft Macon Ct Raleigh NC 27614 Office: 1004 Dresser Ct Raleigh NC 27609 also Kusumi Pain Clinic Dressor Ct Raleigh NC 27609

KUTCH, JOHN MICHAEL, JR., govt. ofcl., health care adminstr.; b. Perth Amboy, N.J., Feb. 9, 1943; s. John Michael and Theresa Catherine (Shaker) K.; B.Ed. in English, U. Miami, 1965; M.B.A., Xavier U., Cin., 1970; m. Phyllis Jane GolbEski, Jan. 25, 1970; children—John Michael, Aaron A., Nhu-Anne A. Commd. officer USPHS, advanced through grades to comdr.; asst. adminstr. Alaska Native Med. Center, Anchorage, 1971-74; adminstr. Winslow (Ariz.) Indian Hosp., 1974-76; dir. Colo. Rivers Service Unit, Parker, Ariz., 1976-78; med. care adminstr., med. program U.S. Bur. Prisons, Washington, 1978—; participant U.S.-Romanian Health Exchange, 1976. Served to capt. U.S. Army, 1965-71. Recipient award for position paper Navajo Nation, 1975, Commendation medal USPHS, 1976. Fellow Royal Soc. Health; mem. Am. Coll. Hosp. Adminstrs., Commd. Officers Assn. USPHS, Assn. Mil. Surgeons U.S., Scabbard and Blade. Roman Catholic. Author papers.

KUTKA, NICHOLAS, nuclear physician; b. Czechoslovakia, Dec. 17, 1926; came to U.S., 1970, naturalized, 1977; s. Vladimir and Agatha (Flenko) K.; M.D., Comenius U., Bratislava, Czechoslovakia, 1951; Ph.D., Slovak Acad. Scis., Bratislava, 1962; m. Anna Cizmar, Aug. 14, 1965; children—Andrew, Gregory. Asst. prof. Inst. Physiology, Comenius U., 1951; intern, resident in internal medicine Mil. Hosp., Bratislava, 1952-55; chief dept. Inst. Endocrinology, Slovak Acad. Scis., 1956-69; technician asst. Internat. Atomic Energy Agy., Bogota, Colombia, 1969-70; resident in nuclear medicine Duke U., 1971-73; asst. prof. radiology Baylor Coll. Medicine, Houston, 1973—; dir. nuclear medicine service Ben Taub Gen. Hosp., Houston, 1978—; mem. med. staff univ. affiliated hosps.; mem. faculty Sch. Nuclear Medicine Technologists; fellow Internat. Atomic Energy Agy, Rome, 1962-63. Served with Health Service Czechoslovak Army, 1952-54. Recipient prize in nuclear medicine Med. Soc. J.E. Purkyne, Prague, Czechoslovakia, 1965; diplomate internal medicine, Inst. Postgrad. Edn. of Physicians, Bratislava, 1955; diplomate Am. Bd. Nuclear Medicine, 1973. Mem. Harris County Med. Soc., Tex. Med. Assn., Soc. Nuclear Medicine, Am. Coll. Nuclear Physicians. Contbr. numerous articles to profl. jours.; editorial bd. Endocrinologia Experimentalis, 1964-70. Office: Baylor Coll Medicine Dept Radiology 1200 Moursund St Houston TX 77030

KUTNER, RICHARD ALLAN, fin. cons.; b. N.Y.C., Aug. 6, 1928; s. Irving Milton and Diana (Mohr) K.; B.S. in Economics and Finance, N.Y. U., 1949; m. Daina Hildreth Gerson, Dec. 26, 1954; children—Kathy Lyn, Richard Allan, Charlotte Rene. With R.G. Rankin & Co., N.Y.C., 1949-50; S.D. Leidsedorf & Co., N.Y.C., 1953-54; owner, operator retail businesses, Monroe, La., 1954-69; buyer mdse. mgr. Oshman's Sporting Goods, Inc., Houston, Tex., 1969-72; fin. cons., investor, Houston, 1972—; dir. Carpet World, Inc., Houston; partner Andres, Schildhauer, Kutner, 1975—; instr. bus. ins., estate planning and fed. income taxes in continuing edn. dept. U. Houston. Bd. trustees mem. Temple Emanuel, Houston. Served with U.S. Army, 1950-52. Chartered life underwriter. Mem. New Eng. Life Leaders Assn., Nat., Houston assns. life underwriters, Nat. Assn. Securities Dealers, Tex. Real Estate Commn. Jewish. Presenter estate tax and fin. planning seminars for corp. and individual investors, 1973-77. Home: 4970 Valkeith St Houston TX 77096 Office: Suite 300 550 S Post Rd Houston TX 77056

KUTTLER, CARL MARTIN, JR., coll. adminstr.; b. Daytona Beach, Fla., Jan. 31, 1940; s. Carl M. and Winona Ellis K.; A.A., St. Petersburg Jr. Coll., 1960; B.S., Fla. State U., 1962; J.D., Stetson Coll. Law, 1965; m. Evelyn Flathmann, June 29, 1963; children—Cindy, Carl, Erika. Admitted to Fla. bar, 1965, U.S. Dist. Ct. bar, 1969; instr. St. Petersburg (Fla.) Jr. Coll., 1965-77, asst. to v.p. for adminstrn., 1967-68, dean adminstrv. affairs, 1968-78, pres., 1978—; counsel Pinellas County Legis. Del., 1974. Chmn., Fla. Student Fin. Aid Commn.; bd. overseers Stetson U. Coll. Law. Mem. Pinellas County Secondary Sch. Adminstrs. Assn., Nat. Assn. Coll. and Univ. Attys., Fla. Assn. Community Colls., Fla. Bar Assn., St. Petersburg Bar Assn., Nat. Orgn. Legal Problems in Edn., NAACP, Gulf Beach-Seminole Bd. Realtors. Republican. Methodist. Home: 8336 40th Ave N St Petersburg FL 33709 Office: PO Box 13489 St Petersburg FL 33733

KUYKENDALL, JAMES RAY, pharmacist; b. Ft. Payne, Ala., Dec. 9, 1927; s. Leonard Lankford and Ola Mae (Downs) K.; B.S. in Pharmacy, Auburn U., 1949; m. Allie Ruth Kirby, Nov. 28, 1954; children—Leonard Kirby, Lucia Ruth. Pharmacist, Palace Drug, Anniston, Ala., 1949-50, Central Drug, Fayette, Ala., 1954-55, pharmacies Ft. Payne, Ala., 1956—, pharmacist, store mgr. Harco Super Drug of Tuscaloosa, Ala., Ft. Payne, 1973—. Pres., DeKalb County Tourist Assn., 1965-66; co-founder Landmarks of DeKalb County, Inc., 1969, pres., 1969-71, 77-78; ordained deacon First Bapt. Ch. Ft. Payne. Served with USN, 1951-54. Decorated Bronze Star; recipient citation Ala. Sesquicentennial Commn., 1969, Disting. Service award Ala. Hist. Commn., 1978. Mem. Ala. Pharm. Assn. (trustee, service award 1975, researcher, chmn. com. award winning book Profiles of Alabama Pharmacy 1974), DeKalb County Pharm. Assn. (co-founder, pres.), Am. Inst. History of Pharmacy (cert. of commendation, 1975), Ft. Payne C. of C. (dir. 1974-77), Ala. Hist. Assn. (exec. com.), Nat. Trust for Hist. Preservation, Am. Assn. for State and Local History, Jaycees (pres. Ft. Payne 1963-64), Masons, Am. Legion, VFW. Club: Ft. Payne Rotary. Editor: Landmarks News, 1975-80; gen. mgr. DeKalb Legend, 6 vols., 1972-80. Home: 706 Alabama Ave NW Fort Payne AL 35967 Office: Harco Super Drug DeKalb Plaza Fort Payne AL 35967

KUZILIK, MARTHA SUE, nurse; b. Barnsdall, Okla., Jan. 9, 1936; d. Andrew William and Minnie Kathryn (Smith) K.; R.N. (scholar), St. John's Hosp., Tulsa, 1957; B.S.N. with honors, U. Tulsa, 1971, postgrad., 1977—. Staff nurse operating room St.John's Hosp., 1957-58, 59-69, head nurse operating room, 1969-70, operating room supr., 1970-72, asst. dir. nursing service, 1972-73, dir. nursing service, 1974-77, dir. nursing support services, 1977—, dir. operating room, 1979—; office nurse Dr. J.D. Shipp, Tulsa, 1958-59. Republican. Mem. Disciples of Christ. Home: 1754 S Utica St Tulsa OK 74104 Office: 1923 S Utica St Tulsa OK 74104

KVINTA, CHARLES JAMES, lawyer; b. Hallettsville, Tex., Feb. 16, 1932; s. John F. and Emily P. (Strauss) K.; B.A., U. Tex., 1954, LL.B., 1959; m. Margie N. Brenek, Oct. 9, 1954; children—Charles James, Sherri A., Kenneth E., Chris E. Admitted to Tex. bar, 1959; pvt. practice, Yoakum, 1960—; city atty., Yoakum, 1977—; cons. to industry. Founder Bluebonnet Youth Ranch, 1968, pres., 1968-75; mem. St. Joseph's Cath. Sch. Bd., 1970; chmn. fund raising campaign Boy Scouts Am.; pres. Yoakum Ind. Sch. Dist., 1975-80; dir., mgr. Yoakum Little League, Yoakum Teenage League. Served as 1st lt. AUS, 1954-55. Mem. State Bar Tex., Yoakum C. of C. (dir.), Am. Legion. Democrat. Club: K.C. Home: 713 Coke St Yoakum TX 77995 Office: 413 W Grand St Yoakum TX 77995

KWIECINSKI, CHESTER MARTIN, artist, museum ofcl.; b. Youngstown, Ohio, July 7, 1924; s. Martin and Angeline (Babcznska) K.; B.F.A., Kansas City Art Inst., 1949, M.F.A., 1951; m. Marianne Williamson, June 4, 1970. Artist, designer Design, Inc., Youngstown, 1951-54; tchr. Warren (Ohio) City Schs., 1954-66; prof. art Coll. of Artesia (N.Mex.), 1967-71; dir. Abilene (Tex.) Fine Arts Mus., 1973—; exhibited at Mo. State Fair (1st prize in watercolor); represented in permanent collections at Butler Inst. Am. Art, Youngstown; chmn. graphic arts Western Res. High Sch., Warren; art chmn. Internat. Cowboy Cookoff. Served with AUS, 1943-46; CBI. Mem. Nat. Assn. Am. Museums. Author: Elementary Teachers Art Handbook, 1976. Pioneer new watercolor medium, 1971. Home: 4010 Potomac St Abilene TX 79605 Office: Box 1858 Abilene TX 79604

KWON, TAI HYUNG, physicist; b. Yechon, Korea, Sept. 15, 1932; came to U.S., 1960; s. Myung Jin and Ki Young Kwon; B.S., U. Ga., 1963, M.S., 1965, Ph.D., 1967; m. Young Ju Choi, July 25, 1969; 1 son, Wade. Postdoctoral research fellow Ga. Inst. Tech., Atlanta, 1967-69; asst. prof. physics U. Montevallo (Ala.), 1969-75, asso. prof., 1975—. Served to capt. arty. Republic Korea Army, 1953-60. Recipient Wheatley Physics award, 1963; Frederick Gardner Cottreel grantee, 1971. Mem. Am. Phys. Soc., Am. Assn. Physics Tchrs., Phi Beta Kappa, Sigma Xi, Phi Kappa Phi. Contbr. articles to sci. jours. Home: 1877 Tall Timbers Dr Birmingham AL 35226 Office: Dept Physics U Montevallo Montevallo AL 35115

KYLE, ANDREW CROCKETT, III, biomed. electronics co. exec.; b. Eagle Mountain Lake, Tex., Nov. 3, 1945; s. Andrew Crockett and Betty (Magdaleno) K.; B.S. with honors, U. Tex. at Austin, 1968; m. Regina Anne Walker, Apr. 26, 1975; children—Andrew Crockett, Tricia Anne. Design engr. Paragon System Co., Houston, 1969; engr. biomed. electronics Baylor Coll. Medicine, Houston, 1969-74; chief engr. Life-Tech Instruments, Inc., Houston, 1974-77, v.p., 1977—. H.A. Lott scholar, 1964-68; Engring. fellow, 1964-68. Mem. Tau Beta Pi, Eta Kappa Nu, Phi Eta Sigma. Democrat. Author: A Hierarchical Minicomputer System for Continuous Post-Surgical Monitoring, 1975. Office: PO Box 36221 Houston TX 77036

KYLE, DONALD DEAN, chain saw co. exec.; b. North Platte, Nebr., Sept. 7, 1937; s. William Wallace and Carie Lenore (Pro) K.; student Iowa State Tchrs. Coll., 1955-56, U. Ill., 1959-60; m. Marilyn Joan Henzler, June 28, 1959; children—Kathleen, Kristeen, Kimberly, Donald David. Prodn. clk. Northrup King & Co., Mpls., 1960-62; salesman Heritage House div. Diamond Alkali, Cleve., 1962-66; dist. mgr. Vistron div. Standard Oil Ohio, Lima, 1966-70; dist. mgr. J.I. Case Co., Mpls., 1970-72; gen. sales mgr. L & G div. AMF, Des Moines, 1972-76; dir. sales Stihl Inc., Virginia Beach, Va., 1976-77, v.p. sales, 1977-78, exec. v.p., 1978—. Served with USN, 1957-60. Episcopalian. Office: 36 Viking Dr Virginia Beach VA 23452

KYLES, LOUISA BELLE, govt. ofcl.; b. Jasper County, Tex., Feb. 27; d. McRay and Lallie B. (Adams) Shankle; Sec. Sci. degree, Prairie View (Tex.) A&M U., 1967; diploma Christian edn., tchrs. cert., C.H. Mason Bible Coll., Beaumont, Tex., 1978; m. Rufus Kyles, Jr., Oct. 8, 1966; children—LaJuan, Ysidra Minyon. Various secretarial positions, 1964-72; substitute tchr. Jasper Ind. Sch. Dist., 1972-73; with Deep E. Tex. Council Govts., Jasper, 1973—, personnel officer EEO, affirmative action coordinator, public info. officer, 1977—; tchr., sec. C.H. Masons System Bible Colls., 1977—. Bd. dirs. Home Health Care, Jasper. Recipient various certs. appreciation. Mem. Internat. Personnel Mgmt. Assn., Am. Mgmt. Assn., E. Tex. Human Services Tng. Consortium, Jasper C. of C. Mem. Ch. of God in Christ. Home: PO Box 656 Kirbyville TX 75956 Office: PO Drawer 1170 Jasper TX 75751

LABARBERA, FRANK THOMAS, auto leasing rep.; b. Lakeland, Fla., Mar. 13, 1944; s. Frank Thomas and Florence (Patrinostro) LaB.; A.A., St. Leo Coll., 1962, B.A., 1964; m. Joyce Marie Chenel, Aug. 8, 1964; children—Frank Thomas III, Paul Andrew, Michelle. Displayman, Sears, Roebuck & Co., Lakeland, 1964-69; display mgr. Montgomery Ward & Co., Lakeland, 1969-75; interior designer, sales rep. Badcock Furniture Corp., Lakeland, 1975—; from 1975; now fleet and leasing rep. Lakeland Ford Co. pres. Success Technologies Ltd. Mem. Polk County Bicentennial Steering Com., 1972-76; work with prisoners, Fla. prisons, 1965—; active Lakeland Juvenile Diabetes Assn. Named Outstanding Jaycee of Yr., Plant City Jaycees, 1967, 69. Mem. Fla. (state v.p. 1973-74, regional dir. 1974-75, external v.p. 1976-77), Plant City (pres. 1972-73) Jaycees, C. of C. Clubs: Lions (3d v.p. 1976-77) (Mulberry, Fla.); Italian-American, Seminole Gun; Sertoma. Home: PO Box 1395 Plant City FL 33566 Office: 1420 W Memorial Blvd Lakeland FL 33566

LA BELLE, DONALD JOSEPH, city ofcl.; b. Kansas City, Mo., Sept. 8, 1942; s. James and Grace Hilland (Smith) LaB.; B.A. in Personnel Adminstrn., U. Kans., 1966, M.Pub. Adminstrn., 1973; m. Sharon Kay Popp, Sept. 5, 1965; children—Todd Alan, Renee Kathleen. Summer intern Kansas City (Mo.) Police Dept., 1960-65;

sr. budget analyst, research and budget dept. City of Fort Worth, 1972-73, asst. dir. pub. works, 1973—; adj. prof. pub. adminstrn. Tex. Christian U., Fort Worth, 1976—. Chmn., Service to Those In Need Com., First Presbyn. Ch. Fort Worth, 1976, chmn. budget and fin. com., 1977, ruling elder, chmn. ops. com., 1979—. Served to capt. USAF, 1966-71. Mem. Internat. City Mgmt. Assn., Am. Pub. Works Assn. Contbr. articles to profl. jours. Home: 151 Cotillion Rd Fort Worth TX 76134 Office: 1000 Throckmorton St Fort Worth TX 76102

LABORDE, MARY PURCELL (MRS. JOSEPH GASTON LABORDE), club woman, ret. educator; b. Pelican, La., May 19, 1905; d. George Dowell and Ela Lee (Browne) Purcell; Christian culture diploma M.E. Ch. S., 1922; licensed instr. Mansfield (L.I.) Female Coll., 1923; postgrad. La. State U., 1924, 45, Centenary, 1925-26; certificate N.Y. Sch. Interior Decorating, 1931; B.A., Nicholls State Coll.; m. Joseph Gaston LaBorde, Apr. 24, 1926; 1 son, Joseph Newton. Tchr. Caldwell Parish, La., 1923-25; tchr. S. Highlands Sch., Shreveport, La., 1925-26; tchr. Lady of Mercy Sch., Baton Rouge, 1958-60, St. Theresa's Sch., Shreveport, 1960-61, Trinity Elementary Sch., Baton Rouge, 1969-70; active in glee club, ch. and club music. Recipient awards (2) Nat. Soc. So. Dames Am., 1966, 2d v.p. U.D.C., Henry W. Allen chpt., Baton Rouge, 1960-61, 3d v.p. Martha Ried chpt., 1954-57; bd. dirs. Children of Confederacy, Emma Gayle McFadden chpt., Jacksonville, Fla., 1955-57, dir. John McGrath chpt., Baton Rouge, 1958-60, organizing dir. G.B. Saucier chpt., 1974-76; mem. and del. Katherine Livingston chpt. D.A.R., Jacksonville, 1949-52, del. nat. congress, 1950-63, treas., Kan Yuk Sa, 1955-57, del. state conf., 1964; chmn. music La. 6th dist. La. Fedn. Women's Clubs, 1974-76; organized Jr. Nat. Soc. Sons and Daus. of Pilgrims; acitve Gray Ladies ARC; mem. Confederate Mus., Richmond, Va., 1971-72; hostess Found. for Hist. La., 1965-71. Mem. Descs. Knights of Garter, Plantagenet Soc., Ams. Royal Descent, Nat. Trust Historic Preservation, Magna Charta Dames (v.p. La. Soc. 1967-69, rec. sec. 1974—), Nat. Soc. Sons. and Daus. of Pilgrims (gov. La. br. 1962-64, nat. rec. sec. 1965-66, del. nat. congress 1963, del. Gen. Ct., state registrar 1968-70), Nat. Soc. So. Dames, Am. (award 1966, charter; La. eye bank chmn. 1964-65, v.p. La. 1964-65, award of merit 1967), UDC (nat. com. preservation hist. sites and records 1967-68, nat. and state geneal. records, 1967-69, rec. sec. H.W. Allen chpt. 1966-67, chmn. music 1967-68), W.S.C.S., Tchrs. Assn., La. Parliamentarins, Nat. Assn. Parliamentarians, Huguenot Soc. La. (compiled handbook; state registrar 1975-77), Marquis Biog. Library Soc. (adv.), Washington Family Descs., Tex. Geneal. Soc., Epsilon Sigma Omicron (chpt. book reviewer 1974-77). Methodist (youth dir.). Clubs: Music, Baton Rouge Women's, Baton Rouge Music, Order of Crown, High Heritage. Home: 11645 Archery Dr Baton Rouge LA 70815

LABRADOR, DANIEL PULIDO, JR., surgeon; b. Cabangan, Zambales, Philippines, Apr. 15, 1940; s. Daniel Rosario and Ambrosia Lago (Pulido) L.; cane to U.S., 1965; M.D., U. Philippines, 1965; m. Irene Joven, July 25, 1965; children—Allan Wayne, Daniel Pulido III. Intern, Wayne County (Mich.) Gen. Hosp., Eloise, 1965-66; resident Fairview Park Hosp., Cleve., 1966-67; resident in gen. surgery Baroness Erlanger Hosp., Chattanooga, 1967-71, resident in plastic surgery, 1971-73; practice medicine specializing in plastic and reconstructive surgery, Chattanooga, 1973—. Bd. dirs. The Debbie Fox Found., Chattanooga, 1978—. Diplomate Am. Bd. Plastic Surgery. Mem. Greater Chattanooga C. of C., Chattanooga and Hamilton County Med. Soc., Tenn. Med. Assn., AMA, Am. Soc. Plastic and Reconstructive Surgeons, Tenn. Soc. Plastic and Reconstructive Surgeons, Southeastern Soc. Plastic and Reconstructive Surgeons. Roman Catholic. Clubs: Chattanooga Radio Control, Racquet. Home: 9035 N Hickory Valley Rd Chattanooga TN 37416 Office: 721 Glenwood Dr Suite 561 Chattanooga TN 37404

LACEY, (JENNIFER) KAREN BEVAN, state ofcl.; b. Chattanooga, Oct. 24, 1948; d. Charles Vernon and Mary Catherine (Brown) Bevan; B.S., U. Ala., 1970; M.Public Adminstrn., 1972; postgrad. Ala. A&M U., 1973, Auburn U., 1976-77; m. Bert Lee Lacey, July 9, 1977. Civil archivist Ala. Dept. Archives and History, Montgomery, 1973-75; personnel analyst Ala. State Dept. Personnel, Montgomery, 1975-77; classification and wage technician La. Dept. Health and Human Resources, Baton Rouge, 1977-78; tax analyst La. Dept. Commerce, Baton Rouge, 1978-79; personnel officer La. Dept. Revenue and Taxation, Baton Rouge, 1979—. Project cons. State of La. Gov.'s Task Force on Child Protection, 1977—; alt. mem. State of La. Gov.'s Task Force on Talent Bank of Women, 1979—. Cert. tchr., Ala. Mem. Internat. Personnel Mgmt. Assn. (assessment council), Women in Mgmt. (charter, pres.). Episcopalian. Office: La Dept Revenue and Taxation PO Box 201 Baton Rouge LA 70821

LACHMAN, ROY, psychologist, educator; b. N.Y.C., Nov. 26, 1927; s. Morris and Lillian (Ladina) L.; B.S., Coll. City N.Y., Bklyn., 1955; Ph.D., N.Y. U., 1960; m. Janet L. Miner, Sept. 1, 1971; children—Dane Claire Barrett, Asst. prof. U. Hawaii, 1959; dir. research med. psychology Johns Hopkins U. Med. Sch., Balt., 1960; asst. prof. Hollins Coll., Roanoke, Va., 1961-63; from asso. to full prof. State U. N.Y., Buffalo, 1963-71; prof. U. Kans., Lawrence, 1971-74; prof. psychology U. Houston, 1974—; cons. in field. Served with U.S. Army, 1950-52. Author: Cognitive Psychology and Information Processing, 1979. Home: 3310 Merrick St Houston TX 77025 Office: Dept Psychology U Houston Houston TX 77004

LACHS, JOHN, educator; b. Budapest, Hungary, July 17, 1934; s. Julius and Magda (Brod) L.; came to U.S., 1957, naturalized, 1967; B.A. in Philosophy with 1st class honors, McGill U., 1956, M.A. in Philosophy, 1957; Ph.D. in Philosophy, Yale U., 1961; m. Shirley Marie Mellow, June 3, 1967; children—Sheila Marie, James Richard. Asst. prof. Philosophy Coll. William and Mary, Williamsburg, Va., 1959-62, asso. prof., 1962-66, prof., 1966-67; prof. philosophy Vanderbilt U., Nashville, 1967—; fellow in humanities Duke U.-U. N.C., 1965-66; lectr. in field. Mem. organizing com. Bicentennial Symposium of Philosophy; mem. panel pub. programs Nat. Endowment for Humanities, dir. Nashville human rights project Pub. Programs Div., 1973-74, dir. seminar for med. practitioners, summer, 1977, 78, 79; chmn. Tenn. Com. for Humanities, 1977-78; co-dir. project for creative humanities programming on TV, WDCN-TV, 1976-78. Recipient Phi Beta Kappa Faculty award for advancement scholarship, 1962; E. Harris Harbison award for distinguished teaching, Danforth Found., 1967; Chancellor's Cup, Vanderbilt U., 1969, Madison Sarratt prize for excellence in undergrad. teaching, 1972; Can. Council grantee, 1958; Coll. William and Mary faculty grantee, 1961-64; Titmus Found. grantee, 1962, 63, 66, 67; Am. Philos. Soc. grantee, 1965, 66, 72; Vanderbilt U. Research Council grantee, 1967, summer grantee, 1968, 69, 76; Nat. Endowment for Humanities research grantee, 1972-73; Tenn. Com. for Humanities pub. programs grantee, 1974-77. Mem. Am., Canadian, Va., Tenn. philos. assns., Metaphys. Soc. Am., Aristotelian Soc., Mind Assn., Royal Inst. Philosophy, Soc. Advancement Am. Philosophy (past pres.), So. Soc. Philosophy and Psychology (chmn. program com.), S. Atlantic Modern Lang. Assn. (sec. humanities circle), Am. Philosophy Group (chmn. program com.). Mem. bd. advisory editors So. Jour. of Philosophy, Internat. Jour. for Philosophy of Religion, Trans. of C.S. Pierce Soc., Forum on Medicine; contbr. numerous articles to profl. jours. Address: Vanderbilt Univ Dept Philosophy Nashville TN 37235

LACKEY, JAMES QUINN, III, chem. co. exec.; b. Huntington, W.Va., July 27, 1928; s. James Quinn and Ellen McClure (Hughes) L.; B.S. in Metall. Engring., U. Ky., 1951; m. Martha Ann Gauntt, June 26, 1951; children—James Q. IV, Martha Ellen, Rebecca Ann. Metall. engr. E.I. duPont de Nemours & Co., Wilmington, Del., 1951, Dana, Ind., 1951-52, asso. metall. engr., Wilmington, 1952-56, area engr., Antioch, Calif., 1956-57, service engr., Wilmington, 1957-58, spl. engr., Nashville, 1958-61, sr. engr., Wilmington, 1961-66, cons., 1966-72, sr. cons. materials engring., Camden, S.C., 1972—. Treas., PTA, 1969-72, pres., 1972-73, regional dir., 1970-72; mem. Kershaw County Vocat. Edn. Council, 1974—. Registered profl. engr., Del., Ky., S.C. Mem. Am. Soc. Metals (local dir.), Nat. Assn. Corrosion Engrs. (chmn. nat. com. corrosion prevention). Episcopalian. Club: Masons. Home: 2319 Moultrie Rd Camden SC 29020 Office: Box A Camden SC 29020

LACKEY, LARRY ALTON, lawyer; b. Galax, Va., Aug. 24, 1940; s. Alton and Reba Mae (Phipps) L.; B.S. in Accountancy, Southeastern U., 1962, postgrad. in Bus. Adminstrn., 1962; LL.D., (hon.), Midwestern U., 1963; diploma in advanced accountancy La Salle U., Chgo., 1965, LL.B., 1965; Ph.D. in Bus. Adminstrn., Calif. Pacific U., 1977; m. Irene Jane Minhinnett, June 7, 1963; children—Larry Alton, Teresa Ann, Lisa Marie. Asst. proof dept. Riggs Nat. Bank, Washington, 1958-59, bookkeeper corp. accounts, also comml. accounts teller, 1959, asst. head teller, 1959-60; asst. head teller, then head teller and head note teller, also br. asst. Old Dominion Bank, Arlington, Va., 1960-61; pub. accountant, bus. mgmt. analyst, Washington, 1961-68; dir. accounting, treas. W.W. Chambers Co. Inc., undertaking, Washington, 1968-69; exec. v.p., gen. mgr. Old Dominion Casket Co. Inc., Washington, 1969-70; sr. ops. analyst Macke Corp., vending and food service, Washington, 1970-71, asst. dir. corp. taxes, 1970-71; bd. dirs. Hamilton Bank & Trust Co., 1973-75; pub. accountant, tax analyst, bus. mgmt. counselor, efficiency analyst firm Mervin G. Hall Co., Oakton, Va., 1971, founder Bus. Mgmt. Services div., fin. analysis, 1971; chmn. bd. dirs. Internat. Moving & Storage Co. Inc.; pres., chmn. bd. dirs. Key Investment Corp.; sec., dir., founder, ALA Corp., nat. automotive system chain, 1975. Instr. Boyd Sch. of Bus., 1969-71, also trustee; spl. lectr. pub. high schs., Arlington County, Va., 1970-72; spl. cons. Commonwealth Doctors Hosp., Fairfax, Va., 1973—; founder, pres. Bus. Mgmt. Inst., 1978—. Treas., v.p. Camp Springs (Md.) Civic Assn., 1971-73; sec.-treas. Camp Springs Boys Club, 1971-73; baseball asst. Little League, Annandale, Va., 1974-76; trustee Calif. Pacific U., 1977—. Mem. Annandale Jaycees. Republican. Roman Catholic. Author: How To Start A Small Business, 1971.

LACKEY, MARILYN LOUISE, coll. adminstr.; b. Welch, W.Va., Aug. 1, 1935; d. Earle and Helen Louise (Roberts) Wood; B.S., Concord Coll., Athens, W.Va., 1959; M.S. (teaching fellow), Va. Poly. Inst. and State U., 1963; children—William Lawrence, Michael David. Tchr. home econs. Mercer County (W.Va.) Sch., 1959-62; prof. home econs. Concord Coll., 1963-76, dir. coll. relations, 1976—; sec. Concord Coll. Found.; exec. dir. Concord Coll. Alumni Assn. Named Alumnus of Yr., Concord Coll., 1976; recipient Outstanding FHA award for W.Va., 1969. Mem. Am. Home Econs. Assn., W.Va. Home Econs. Assn., Home Economists in Action, Kappa Omicron Phi. Republican. Presbyterian. Chief editor, contbr. to Concord Coll. Alumni News, 1976—. Home: 206 Weaver St Athens WV 24712 Office: College Center Bldg Concord College Athens WV 24712

LA COTTS, RALPH S., acct., computer and software co. exec.; b. De Witt, Ark., Mar. 19, 1941; s. Clarence Elmer and Esther Leona La C.; B.A. in Psychology, U. Ark., 1964; m. Patricia Hope Jones, Dec. 12, 1967; children—Dikina Daun, Lauren Monique, Kelli Kristelle, Ralph S., Jon Barton, Summer Nicole. Pvt. practice acctg., DeWitt, Ark., 1966—, Realtor, 1968—, ins. agt., 1971—; pres. Digital Systems Inc., 1975—. Chmn. bd. dirs. De Witt City Nursing Home, 1975-76. Mem. Ark. Soc. Public Accts., Nat. Soc. Public Accts., Nat. Assn. Enrolled Agts., Nat. Assn. Realtors, Ark. Realtors Assn. Address: Route 2 De Witt AR 72042

LADD, EDWARD JOHNSON, civil engr., cons. firm exec.; b. Boston, Nov. 24, 1906; s. Frederick Elisha and Atlanta Gertrude (Johnson) L.; B.S., Ga. Inst. Tech., 1930; m. Willie Lee Gilbreath, Sept. 5, 1931; 1 dau., Margaret Dale (Mrs. Gene Franklin Gainer). Engr., So. Refractories Co., Ft. Payne, Ala., 1930-36; cons. engr., Ft. Payne, 1936-41; pres. Ladd Engring. Assos. Ft. Payne, 1941—. Mem. Ft. Payne Indsl. Bd., 1970-74. Mem. Assn. Communication Engrs., Cons. Engrs. Council, ASCE. Clubs: Masons, De Soto County. Author: Gone to Alabama, 1973; Outline History of Southeastern States, 1974. Home: 503 Gault Ave Fort Payne AL 35967 Office: Box 29 3d and Clark Sts SE Fort Payne AL 35967 Died Nov. 16, 1978

LADD, JACK DEVERE, lawyer; b. Big Spring, Tex., Dec. 25, 1949; s. Walter DeVere and Tiny Ida (Smith) L.; B.B.A., U. Tex., 1973, J.D., 1976; m. Constance Susan Fradenburg, Aug. 16, 1975. Mgmt. cons. Nat. Leadership Methods, Inc., Austin, Tex., 1968-72, v.p., 1970-73; dir. Tex. Youth Conf. and Tex. Youth Leadership Inst., 1970-73; admitted to Tex. bar, 1976, also U.S. Dist. Ct. bar Western Dist. Tex.; asso. firm Stubbeman, McRae, Sealy, Laughlin & Browder, Midland, Tex., 1976—; tchr. Midland Coll. Mem. Nat., Midland County bar assns., State Bar Tex. Methodist. Author: For Parents Only, 1970. Home: 2509A Haynes St Midland TX 79701 Office: PO Box 1540 Midland TX 79702

LADER, WILLIAM JOSEPH, rental service exec.; b. N.Y.C., Aug. 9, 1941; s. Harry R. and Rose (Geller) L.; B.S., Fla. State U., 1963; m. Sunnie Taylor, Mar. 1, 1972; children—Gary, Darren, Michael. Exec. v.p. Mechanics Uniform Service, Miami, Fla., 1963-72; pres. Sno White Dust Control Service, Hollywood, Fla., 1972—. Pres. Hillel Found., Fla. State U.; treas., v.p. Hollywood Jaycees, 1963-70, dist. Speakup champion, 1968. Mem. Ft. Lauderdale Sales and Mkt. Club, Inst. Indsl. Launderers. Club: Toastmasters (pres. Hollywood club, 1969). Home: 8280 NW 14th St Coral Springs FL 33065 Office: 2015 Johnson St Hollywood FL 33021

LADIN, EUGENE, communications co. exec.; b. N.Y.C., Oct. 26, 1927; s. Nat and Mary (Cohen) L.; student in mil. scis. U. Md., Wiesbaden, Germany, 1954-56; B.B.A., Pace U., 1956; M.B.A., Air U.-Air Force Inst. Tech., 1959; postgrad. St. Louis U., 1959, George Washington U. Grad. Sch. Bus., 1966-69; m. Millicent D. Frankel, June 27, 1948; children—Leslie H., Stephanie J. Commd. 2d lt. U.S. Air Force, 1951, advanced through grades to capt., 1955; various mil. contract assignments, service in Europe; resigned commn., 1960; cost engr. Rand Corp., Santa Monica, Calif., 1960-62; mgr. cost and econ. analysis Northrop Corp., Hawthorne, Calif., 1962-66; dir. fin. planning Satellite Communication Corp., Washington, 1966-70; treas., chief fin. officer Landis & Gyr, Inc., Elmsford, N.Y., 1970-76; v.p., treas., comptroller P.R. Telephone Co., San Juan, 1976-77; v.p. fin. Comtech Telecommunications Corp., Smithtown, N.Y. and acting pres. subs. Comtech Antenna Corp., St. Cloud, Fla., 1977—; former asst. prof. So. Ill. U., George Washington U., U. Md.; vis. lectr. Pace U. Decorated Air Force Commendation medal. Home: 170 Spring Lake Hills Dr Maitland FL 32751 Office: 3100 Communications Rd Saint Cloud FL 32769

LADWIG, MICHAEL WILLIAM, counselor: b. Madison, Wis., June 26, 1944: s. Clifford and Lola Ione (Alderman) L.; B.A., U. Wis., Madison, 1969; M.A., Coll. of St. Thomas, 1977: postgrad. U. Fla., 1978—. Youth and camp dir. YMCA, also world service work Athens, Greece, 1969-72; mktg. specialist health maintenance orgns., also adminstrv. asst. Hennepin County (Minn.) pilot city health center, 1973-77; sr. counselor, dir. outpatients Volusia County Drug Council, Daytona Beach, Fla., 1977— Served with Med. Service Corps, U.S. Army, 1962-65. Mem. Am. Personnel and Guidance Assn., Fla. Personnel and Guidance Assn. Democrat. Methodist. Home: 1572 Primrose Ln Holly Hill FL 32017 Office: Volusia County Drug Council 554 N Oleander St Daytona Beach FL 32018

LAERM, JOSHUA, museum dir.; b. Waynesboro, Pa., Sept. 27, 1942; s. Rolf and Idella Virginia (Benchoff) L.; B.A., Pa. State U., 1965; M.S., U. Ill., 1972, Ph.D., 1976. Oceanographer, U.S. Naval Oceanographic Office, 1966-69; asst. prof. zoology, dir. univ. museum natural history U. Ga., Athens, 1976—. Smithsonian Instn. predoctoral fellow, 1973. Mem. AAAS, Am. Soc. Mammalogists, Am. Soc. Zoologists, Biol. Soc. Washington, Soc. Study Evolution, Soc. Vertebrate Paleontologists. Author papers in field. Home: Nowhere Rd Rural Route 1 Athens GA 30601 Office: Museum Natural History Univ Ga Athens GA 30602

LAFARGUE, AUBREY ALOYSIUS, JR., city ofcl.; b. Mobile, Ala., Feb. 20, 1937; s. Aubrey Aloysius and Lillian Pearl (Golemon) LaF.; B.S., U. Houston, 1959, postgrad., 1961-62, 62-64; m. Judy E. Fowler, July 24, 1961; children—Julie E., Lisa A., Aubra A., Aubrey A. III. Chemist, San Jacinto Water System, Houston, 1960-68, asst. mgr., 1975-79; chief chemist City of Houston, 1968-75, asst. mgr. public works, 1979—. Conf. chmn. Nat. Pollution Control Conf. and Exposition, 1969, gen. chmn , 1970-72; bd. dirs. Fullfillment Found., 1976-77, v.p., 1977. Served with U.S. Army, 1961-63. Mem. Water and Wastewater Analysts Assn. (charter pres. 1976, dir.-at-large 1977), S.E. Water Utilities Assn. (pres. 1977), Tex. Water Utilities Assn. (v.p. 1977), Am. Water Works Assn., Sam Houston Water Utilities Assn. Methodist. Contbr. articles to profl. jours.; founding editor Water Analyst, 1976. Home: 5213 Maple St Bellaire TX 77401 Office: 12555 Clinton Dr Houston TX 77015

LA FERNEY, DON HAROLD, contractor; b. Rector, Ark., Dec. 12, 1932; s. Louis Monroe and Fannie (Senco) LaF.; student Friend U.; m. Esther Jean Crockett, May 1, 1953; children—Donna Jean, Carol Sue, David Neal, Don Harold. Exec. supr. Wichita Eagle Beacon, 1953-65; circulation mgr. Pharos Tribune and Press, Logansport, Ind., 1965-67; circulation dir. Times—News, Kingsport, Tenn., 1967-75; v.p., circulation dir. Post, Kingsport, 1975-76; pres. LaFerney, Inc., Kingsport, 1976—. Republican. Mem. Ch. of God. Civitan. Office: 2352 Inglewood Dr Kingsport TN 37664

LAFFERE, LESLIE HARRY, farmer; b. Milam County, Tex., Feb. 12, 1920; s. Charles Fritz and Olga (Meeck) L.; student Durham Bus. Coll., 1938-40; m. Mattie Lee Traxler, Aug. 28, 1948; children—Delanie Jo, Charles Douglas, Donald Grady. Mgr. mortgage loan dept. Alexander Glass Investment Co., Corpus Christi, Tex., 1946-49; owner, operator 2000 acre farm, Uvalde, Tex., 1949—; chmn. bd. Uvalde Production Credit Assn.; past pres. Nueces River Auth.; pres. S. Tex. Onion Com.; dir. Winter Garden Coop Gin Co. Past pres. Uvalde Ind. Sch. Dist., 1960-63; past dir. C. of C. Served with USAAF, 1942-46; CBL Recipient Outstanding Man of Yr. in Agr. award Uvalde C. of C., 1968; Outstanding Conservationist award, Ft. Worth Press, 1969. Methodist. Club: Uvalde Rotary (past pres.). Home: 310 Louise Dr Uvalde TX 78801 Office: PO Box 1504 Uvalde TX 78801

LAFFEY, JAMES LAWRENCE, educator; b. Pitts., Dec. 4, 1934; s. Francis Michael and Dorothy Helen (Markey) L.; B.S. in Elementary Edn., Duquesne U., 1960; M.S. in Edn., U. Pitts., 1962, Ph.D., 1967; m. Julie Ellen Eckler, Dec. 27, 1958; children—Juliann, Dorothy, Patricia, James W., Michael D., John W. Elementary sch. tchr. Pitts. Public Schs., 1959-63; reading tchr. jr. and sr. high sch. student Allegheny County Schs. 1963-64; coll. developmental reading tchr. U. Pitts., 1963-66; asso. dir. Eric Clearinghouse on Reading (ERIC) Ind. U., Bloomington, 1966-69, dir., 1969-72; asso. prof. edn., 1968-72, dir. Measurement and Evaluation Center, 1972-73; prof. edn. James Madison U., Harrisonburg, Va., 1973—; cons. State Dept. Edn., 1978-79. Served with USAF, 1954-57. James Madison U. research grantee, 1975. Mem. Internat. Reading Assn. (Outstanding Dissertation award 1968), Nat. Council Tchrs. English, Nat. Reading Conf., Nat. Conf. Research in English, Va. State Reading Assn. Office: Reading Center James Madison U Harrisonburg VA 22807

LAFLEUR, KENNETH CHARLES, ophthalmologist; b. Lawtell, La., Aug. 22, 1941; s. Abram George and Mary Irene (Olivier) L.; B.S., U. Southwestern La., 1963; M.D., Tulane U., 1966; postgrad. U. Pa., 1967; m. Patricia Ione McNamara, Aug. 3, 1963; children—James Matthew, Suzanne Annette, Caroline Marie. Intern, Hermann Hosp., Houston, 1966-67, resident in ophthalmology, 1967-70; ophthalmologist Merrick J. Wyble, Ltd., Opelousas, La., 1972—. Parish council pres. St. Landry Roman Catholic Ch., 1977-78. Served to maj. M.C., U.S. Army, 1970-72. Diplomate Am. Bd. Ophthalmology. Mem. Am. Acad. Ophthalmology, Am., Pan Am. assns. ophthalmology, La. Ophthal. Assn., Contact Lens Assn. Ophthalmology, So. Med. Assn. Democrat. Clubs: Opelousas Tennis and Swim (pres. 1976-77), Belmont Acad. (pres. 1977-78), Elks. Home: 1240 E Prudhomme Ln Opelousas LA 70570 Office: 526 E Prudhomme Ln Opelousas LA 70570

LA FORGE, RAYMOND BERNARD, JR., mktg. cons.; b. Jersey City, Mar. 22, 1933; s. Raymond Bernard and Irene Veronica (Koeffler) LaF.; B.S. in Bus. Adminstrn., Monmouth Coll., West Long Branch, N.J., 1959; m. Sheridan J. Willie, Mar. 2, 1968; children—Raymond Bernard III, Ashley Alexandra. Salesman to sales mgr. West Side Fgn. Cars, Asbury Park, N.J., 1957-59; with Dun & Bradstreet, Inc., 1960—, credit analyst, N.Y.C., 1960-61, salesman Salesman Credit Service, 1961-67, sr. mktg. cons. Duns Mktg. Services, 1967—, mem pres.'s adv. council, 1979. Former mem. Miami Jaycees, recipient cert. of appreciation. Recipient cert. of appreciation Lindsey Hopkins Export Sch., 1960, Elliott Blood Bank, 1977. Mem. Am. Mktg Assn. S. Fla. (dir., former v.p. and treas.). Republican. Clubs: Country of Coral Gables, Racquet, Shriners, Masons. Home: 3275 Riviera Dr Coral Gables FL 33134 Office: 2050 Coral Way Miami FL 33145

LA FORTE, ROBERT SHERMAN, historian, archivist; b. Frontenac, Kans., Sept. 8, 1933; s. Modest Nathaniel and Josephine Anne (Slapschach) La F.; B.S., Kans. State Coll., 1959, M.S., 1959; M.L.S., U. Tex. at Austin, 1968; Ph.D., U. Kans., 1966; m. Frances Ann Crain, Dec. 19, 1959; children—Mark Francis, Geoffrey Louis, Russell Andre. Accountant, Internat. Harvester Corp., Kansas City, Mo., 1951-52; instr., asst. prof. history E. Tex. State U., Commerce, 1964-67; asst. prof. history N. Tex. State U., Denton, 1968-73, asso. prof., 1973-77, prof., 1977—, archivist, 1975—. Vice-chmn. Denton County and City Library, 1975-77; mem. San. Landfill Site Selection

Com. Denton County and City, 1977-79; mem. Denton Land Use Com., 1980; vice chmn. Denton 80's: Directions and Decisions; mem. bd. mgmt. Denton YMCA, 1974—; mem. Denton Planning and Zoning Commn., 1979—. Served with U.S. Army, 1955-57. NDEA fellow, 1967-68; Danforth Found. asso., 1979—. Mem. Orgn. Am. Historians, Soc. Am. Archivists, Soc. S.W. Archivists, S.W. Social Sci. Assn., Tex. Assn. Coll. Tchrs., Am. Legion. Episcopal. Author: Leaders of Reform, Progressive Republicans in Kansas, 1974. Home: 1401 Sherman Dr Denton TX 76201 Office: Room 438 A M Willis Library N Tex State U Denton TX 76203

LA FORTUNE, ROBERT, mayor Tulsa. Office: Civic Center Tulsa OK 74003*

LAGRONE, WILLIAM TAYLOR, lawyer; b. Browndell, Tex., Jan. 19, 1914; s. William Taylor and Lena Enola Westmorland LaG.; B.A., U. Tex., 1936, LL.B., 1939, J.D., 1971; m. Alta Mae Atteberry, Oct. 12, 1940; children—Linda Lee, Alta Eloise, Suzanne. Admitted to Tex. bar, 1939; practiced in Houston, 1939-52, Dallas, 1952—; v.p., gen. counsel Jake L. Hamon, Oil and Gas Operator, Dallas, 1952—. Atty. Dallas Crime Commn., 1953-56. Served to col., AUS, 1940-46. Mem. Am., Tex., Dallas bar assns., Tex. Mid-Continent Oil and Gas Assn., Dallas Petroleum Landmen Assn. (pres. 1955-56), Ind. Producers Assn. Am., Am. Assn. Petroleum Landmen, Ind. Producers Assn. Am. Methodist. Clubs: Northwood, Petroleum (Dallas). Home: 11535 W Ricks Circle Dallas TX 75230 Office: 3900 Republic Nat Bank Tower Dallas TX 75221

LAHIRI, SUBRATA, educator, artist; b. Calcutta, India, Feb. 28, 1932; s. Kiron Lal and Annapurna (Bhaduri) L.; came to U.S., 1959, naturalized, 1962; B.F.A., Calcutta U. 1953; M.F.A., Mich. State U., 1965; m. Betty Ann Schempp; children—Sabrina Ann, Kiron Lal. Dir. of illustration Human Resources Corp., East Lansing, Mich., 1965-66; project engr. design and development Allay Metal Casting Co., Lansing, Mich., 1970-72; prof. art U. Ark., Fayetteville 1972—; one-man shows in New Delhi and Calcutta, London, Paris, N.Y.C., Detroit, Lansing, East Lansing; group shows in Delhi and Calcutta, Paris, Dallas, Detroit, Fla., Ark.; represented in permanent collections: India, Japan, Indonesia, Germany, Eng., Italy, Greece and U.S., also numerous pvt. collections: works include Metamorphosis series on display Tokyo U., Mich. State U. and U. of Ark. UNESCO fellow. Mem. Internat. Sculpture Soc., Fine Art Acad. of India, AAUP, Art Tchrs. Assn. Hindu. Home: 530 Lakeridge Dr Fayetteville AR 72701 Office: Univ Arkansas FA116 Fayetteville AR 72701

LAHMEYER, JOHN D., indsl. maintenance exec.; b. Bellvue, Iowa, June 22, 1915; s. Harold Henry and Mary A. (Campbell) L.; grad. in indsl. maintenance mgmt. Air Force Inst. Tech., 1974; m. Marguerite B. Baker, Aug. 1, 1940; 1 son, John Detrick. Geophys. work Phillips Petroleum, 1937-38; geophysicist Frost Gravity Survey, Inc., Tulsa, 1938-42; with prodn. control dept. Douglas Aircraft Corp., Tulsa, 1942-45; research technician Well Surveys, Inc., Tulsa, 1945-48; owner Lahmeyer Geophys. Lab., Tulsa, 1948-56; cons. geologist, petroleum engr. Corpus Christi, 1956-68; chief maintenance trades sect. and value engring. Corpus Christi Army Depot, 1966—; pres. Lahmeyer Geophys. Lab., also cons. geologist, petroleum engring. value engr. Recipient numerous cost savs. awards U.S. Army. Mem. Soc. Mfg. Engrs., Army Aviation Assn., Boat Owners Assn. Democrat. Clubs: Ingleside Beach, Petroleum. Inventor radioactive detection device. Home: Box 182 Route 1 Ingleside TX 78362 Office: CCAD NAS Corpus Christi TX 78419

LAHSER, CONRAD BERNHARDT, JR., scouting exec.; b. Morvin, N.C., July 17, 1918; s. Conrad Bernhardt and Ethyl Maria (Barber) L.; M.E., N.C. State Coll., 1938; D. Profl. Scouting (Univ. fellow), Schiff U., 1962; Ph.D., Atlantic Northeastern U., 1962; m. Lee King, July 24, 1941; children—Conrad Bernhardt, III, Christine Lahser Daniel. Tchr. def. tng., 1942-44, pub. high sch., 1943-44; with NACA, 1944-45, dist. mgr., 1947-51; with Boy Scouts Am., 1945-47, 51—, scout exec., Olean, N.Y., until 1972, Virginia Beach, Va., 1972—. Clubs: Rotary (sec. local club 1949-50, 70-71), Kiwanis (chmn. pub. and bus. affairs local club 1948-55), Hampton Yacht; Starmount Country (Greensboro, N.C.). Author: It Never Rains at Philmont, 1954; Developing Scouting in Highly Densely Populated Low Income Areas, 1961. Developed programs, techniques for Boy Scouts Am., including fund-raising techniques, profl. work scheduling technique. Home and Office: 1075 General Booth Blvd Virginia Beach VA 23451

LAIR, HARRY REDMON, lawyer; b. Cynthiana, Ky., Apr. 28, 1910; s. Redmon Eugene and Bessie Clay (Dedman) L.; student Ga. Mil. Acad., 1927-29; B.S., U. Ky., 1933; LL.B., Jefferson Sch. Law, 1936; LL.B., U. Louisville, 1951; m. Margaret Jabine Newsom, Dec. 21, 1940; children—Jennie Scott, Harry Redmon. Admitted to Ky. bar, 1936; master commr. Harrison Circuit Ct., 1937—; gen. counsel Harrison Rural Electric Coop. Corp., 1939—; city atty. Cynthiana, 1942-54, 58-66; spl. circuit judge Harrison Circuit Ct., 1951, 53, 55; atty. Farmers Nat. Bank, 1957—. Mem. Am., Ky., Harrison County (past pres.) bar assns., Phi Delta Theta, Omicron Delta Kappa, Delta Sigma Phi. Presbyn. Home: 550 E Pike Cynthiana KY 41031 Office: 11 E Pike St Cynthiana KY 41031

LAIRD, ANGUS MCKENZIE, author, journalist; b. Opp, Ala., Oct. 9, 1903; s. John Henry and Ada (Zorn) L.; A.B., U. Fla., 1927, M.A., 1928; postgrad. Syracuse U., 1928-29, U. Chgo., 1930-31; m. Myra Adelia Doyle, June 8, 1938; children—Victoria Mell (Mrs. Henry Ackerman), Nan McKenzie. Teaching fellow Syracuse U., 1928-29; prof. history and polit. sci. U. Fla., Gainesville, 1929-30, 37-46, U. Denver, 1931-37; dir. Fla. Merit System, Tallahassee, 1946-60; dir. Municipal Code Corp., Inc.; v.p. Old St. Augustine Road Estates, Inc.; pres. Huesack Enterprises, Inc.; editor Wakulla News, 1967-71; dir. Pixie Internat., Inc., Elemental Analysis Corp. Pres., Fla. Heritage Found., 1973-76; coordinator Fla. Press Club award program, 1977; trustee Le Moyne Art Found., St. Andrews Soc.; bd. dirs. Monticello Opera. Recipient citation Fla. Cabinet, 1961. Mem. Fla. Pub. Health Assn. (pres. 1955), Fla. Pub. Personnel Assn. (pres. 1953), Pub. Personnel Assn. U.S. and Can. (hon., exec. council 1958-60), Fla. Heritage Found. (pres. 1973-76), Friends of Library of Fla. State U. (pres. 1974—). Author: City Manager Government in Florida, 1929; (with Wilson K. Doyle) Government and Administration in Florida, 1955; Centennial History of Kappa Sigma, 1969; My Brothers: Wallace and Ray, 1977. Home: 507 Plantation Rd Tallahassee FL 32303

LAIRD, THOMAS LEE, economist; b. Richmond, Ind., Aug. 13, 1944; s. Herman Thomas and Alma Kathleen L.; B.S. in Econs. and Bus., Manchester Coll., 1966; M.B.A. in Fin., U. Miami, 1968, M.A. in Econs., 1976, D.A. in Econs. (Carnegie Corp. fellow 1975-76), 1977; m. Sharon Kay Reed, Aug. 14, 1966; children—Kathleen Diana, Melanie Christine. Teaching asst. in fin. U. Miami, 1966-68; chmn. dept. bus. adminstrn. Miami-Dade Community Coll., 1969-74; asst. prof. fin. and real estate, coordinator real estate dept. Fla. Atlantic U., 1974—; cons. real estate; indsl. real estate developer, South Fla. Named Outstanding Young Man of Am., U.S. Jaycees, 1979; recipient award in fin. Wall St. Jour., 1967; Pratt-Whitney grantee, 1977. Mem. Fin. Analysts South Fla., Fla. Assn. Real Estate Educators (sec.), Econ. Soc. South Fla., Boca Raton Bd. Realtors, Nat. Assn. Realtors, Alpha Kappa Psi, Omicron Delta Epsilon, Riviera Civic Assn. Republican. Methodist. Home: 799 NE Boca Raton Rd Boca Raton FL 33432 Office: Fla Atlantic U Boca Raton FL 33431

LAIRSEN, MICHAEL GEORGE, retail clothing exec.; b. Dallas, Jan. 2, 1948; s. John M. and Marge L.; student El Centro Coll., 1967-69, Tyler Jr. Coll., 1966-67, Northwood Inst., 1969-70. With L & L Mfg. Co., Dallas, 1968-70, Merek Ltd., Hong Kong, 1970-71; with Margo's La Mode, Dallas, 1971—, v.p., gen. merchandiser of ready-to-wear, 1979—; pres. Contemporary Assos. Served with USCGR, 1966. Home: 7001 Fair Oaks St Apt 102 Dallas TX 75230 Office: Margo's La Mode 3909 Live Oak St Dallas TX 75207

LAKE, ALLEN LEONARD, biologist, educator; b. Jamestown, N.Y., Sept. 17, 1924; s. Carl Leonard and Alma Elenor (Seastrom) L.; B.S., Edinboro (Pa.) State Coll., 1949; Ed.M., U. Buffalo, 1950; postgrad. U. Ky., 1962-68; m. Betty Allie Phillips, May 29, 1948; children—Ann Lea, Aleson Leonard, Allen Lee, Mary Beth, Alma Lou. Head sci. dept. Lees Jr. Coll., Jackson, Ky., 1950-57; faculty Morehead (Ky.) State U., 1957—, asso. prof., 1965—. Chmn. Rowan County ARC, 1963; bd. dirs. Frontier Housing. Served with U.S. Army, 1943-45; ETO, MTO. Recipient Disting. Prof. award, 1970. Mem. Ky. Soc. Natural History (dir., v.p. photography 1977—), AAAS, Ky. Acad. Sci., Ky. Conservation Council. Presbyterian. Author: Scientific Etymology, 1968, rev., 1973; Lake Polychromatic Discs, 1973. Illustrator Payne and Falls' Modern Physical Science, 1974, 2d edit., 1979. Home: 910 Willow Dr Morehead KY 40351 Office: Dept Biol Scis Morehead State U Univ Box 782 Morehead KY 40351

LAKE, JOHN BYRON, newspaper publ. co. exec.; b. Follansbee, W. Va., Nov. 30, 1920; s. William Henry and Helen Alberta (Sanders) L.; student Ohio State U., 1938-40, U. Ala., 1940-41, Notre Dame U., 1943-44; m. Katharine Ann Kerr, June 28, 1947; children—Charlotte, Cynthia Lake Katzenberger, Diane. Salesman advt. dept. Eagle-Gazette Newspaper, Lancaster, Ohio, 1947-56; dir. advt. Elizabeth (N.J.) Daily Journal, 1956-60; with St. Petersburg (Fla.) Times & Evening Independdent, 1960—, exec. v.p., 1968—, publisher, 1971—; v.p., dir. Times Pub. Co., 1966—, Congressional Quarterly, Inc., Washington, 1966—; pres., dir. Semit Corp., St. Petersburg, 1971—; pres., dir. Modern Graphic Arts, St. Petersburg, 1976—; pres. Fla. Trend Mag. Bd. dirs. Fla. Council of 100, 1974—; trustee Poynter Fund, St. Petersburg, Modern Media Inst., St. Petersburg. Served with USNR, 1941-45, USAF, 1951-53. Mem. Fla. C. of C., Fla. Press Assn. (past pres.), Am. Newspaper Pubs. Assn. (bd. dirs.). Clubs: St. Petersburg Yacht, Bardmoor Country, Feather Sound Country. Office: PO Box 1121 Saint Petersburg FL 33731

LAKE, LARRY WAYNE, petroleum engr.; b. Del Norte, Colo., Jan. 31, 1946; s. Ralph Wayne and Ina Belle (Card) L.; B.S., Ariz. State U., 1967; Ph.D., Rice U., 1973; m. Carole Sue Holmes, Mar. 22, 1975; children—Leslie Sue, Jeffrey Wayne. Prodn. engr. Motorola Co., Phoenix, 1968-70; sr. research engr. Shell Devel. Co., Houston, 1973-78; asst. prof. petroleum engring. U. Tex., Austin, 1978—; cons. enhanced oil recovery INTERCOMP Resources & Engring., Gary Operating Co., Core Labs. Registered profl. engr., Tex. Mem. Soc. Petroleum Engrs., Sigma Xi, Tau Beta Pi, Pi Epsilon Tau. Baptist. Home: 11117 Alhambra Dr Austin TX 78759 Office: PEB 211 U Tex Austin TX 78712

LAKE, MICHAEL KENNEDY, aerospace engr.; b. Whittier, Calif., Oct. 17, 1925; s. Francis Wilbur and Geraldine Kennedy (Mack) L.; B.S., U.S. Naval Acad., 1949; B.S. in Aero. Engring., U. Tex., Austin, 1958. Engr., Convair, Fort Worth, 1958-59, AEDC, Tullahoma, Tenn., 1959-62, FAA, Oklahoma City, 1962-64, NASA, Houston, 1964—. Comml. pilot. Active YMCA, Houston, 1964—, Big Bros., Houston, 1976—. Served with USN, 1943-55. Decorated Air medal with oak leaf cluster; recipient Sustained Superior Performance award NASA, 1965, Superior Performance award, 1978; registered profl. engr., Okla. Home: PO Box 58264 Houston TX 77058 Office: NASA JSC Houston TX 77058

LAKERNICK, PHILIP STEPHEN, hosp. adminstr.; b. New Haven, Conn., Jan. 24, 1943; s. Benjamin and Elizabeth (Shalett) LaK.; A.S., U. New Haven, 1964, B.S., 1966; M.S. in Hosp. Adminstrn., Med. Coll. Va., 1968; m. Frances Paulette Ward, Aug. 20, 1967; 1 dau., Alecia Lynn. Adminstrv. resident Gen. Hosp. Virginia Beach (Va.), 1967; adminstrv. resident Kings Daus. Childrens Hosp., Norfolk, Va., 1968; asst. adminstr. Meml. Gen. Hosp., Golden Clinic and Med. Center, Elkins, W.Va., 1968-71, asso. adminstr., 1971-77; adminstr. Good Hope Hosp., Inc., Erwin, N.C., 1977; instr. hosp. mgmt. Salem Coll., 1968-70, Davis and Elkins Coll., 1973-77. Pres., Health Planning Authority, Region IV and VII, W.Va., 1969-76; dir. transp. Randolph County, W.Va., 1975-77; pres. Area Health Edn. Center Consortium of W.Va., 1973-75; preceptor Med. Coll. Va., 1974-77; mem. Appalachian Emergency Med. Sers. Council, 1975-77; mem. Tri-State Emergency Med. Service Council, 1975-77; mem. United Fund of Randolph County, 1969-77, pres., 1973, campaign chmn., 1972; pres. Randolph County Emergency Squad, 1969-77. Mem. Am. Coll. Hosp. Adminstrs., Am. Hosp. Assn., Hosp. Fin. Mgmt. Assn., Med. Coll. Va. Alumni Assn. (continuing edn. chmn. 1975-77), U. New Haven Alumni Assn. Elk. Home: 601 E Denim Dr Erwin NC 28339 Office: Good Hope Hosp Inc East H St Erwin NC 28339

LAKINS, ROBERT GENE, archtl. co. exec.; b. Rutledge, Tenn., Apr. 9, 1942; s. Daniel and Ora L.; B.S., U. Tenn., 1966; student Ga. State U., 1968, Vanderbilt U., 1976, 79; m. Laura Jane Nickless, Dec. 27, 1971. Regional sales mgr. E. F. Hauserman Co., Cleve., 1967-69; v.p., sales mgr. Interior Space Management, Charlotte, N.C., 1969-73; pres., chief exec. officer Yearwood & Johnson Architects, Inc., Nashville, 1973—; lectr. colls., univs. Mem. Soc. Mktg. Profl. Services (pres. 1976-77), Am. Mktg. Assn., Profl. Services Bus. Mgmt. Assn. Clubs: Northeast Racquet, Nashville Snow Ski. Office: 55 Music Square W Nashville TN 37203

LAM, AARON TAI-BOON, city govt. ofcl.; b. Hong Kong, Dec. 17, 1947; came to U.S., 1970, naturalized, 1976; s. King-Sing and Wai-Ying (Chik) L.; B.Sc., U. Alta., Edmonton, Can., 1970; M.Urban Planning, Tex. A&M U., 1974; postgrad. U. Wash., Seattle; m. Jane Wai-Lin Wong, Dec. 28, 1972; 1 child, Ranger Ho-Kee. Predoctoral research asso. U. Wash., 1974-75; planning coordinator, then asst. dir. dept. community devel. City of Edinburg (Tex.), 1975-78, dir. dept., 1979—; mem. adj. faculty Pan Am. U.; prin. Planning/Mgmt. Cons. Urban Extension fellow, 1973-74. Mem. Am. Planning Assn., World Future Soc., Urban Land Inst., Nat. Assn. Housing and Rehab. Ofcl., Nat. Community Devel. Assn., Am. Mgmt. Assn., Edinburgh C. of C. Club: Edinburg Rotary. Author papers, reports in field. Home: 1619 Norma St Edinburg TX 78539 Office: Box 1229 Edinburg TX 78539

LAM, CHI-KWONG, chem. engr.; b. Swatow, China, Oct. 23, 1940; s. Tai-Hoi and Kar-Lan (Chan) L.; came to U.S., 1960, naturalized, 1975; M.S., La. State U., 1969; m. Feng-Tuan Tang, Apr. 14, 1968; children—Victor, Lily. Sr. chem. process engr. C.E. Lummus Co., Houston, 1969-77; supervising process engr. Davy Powergas Co., Houston, 1977—. Registered profl. engr., Tex. Mem. Am. Inst. Chem. Engrs., Tau Beta Pi, Phi Lambda Upsilon. Home: 16206 Seattle St Houston TX 77040 Office: 6161 Savoy Dr PO Box 36444 Houston TX 77036

LAMAR, EWELL AYARS, instrument co. exec.; b. Galveston, Tex., Sept. 27, 1911; s. John H. and Emma (Ayars) L.; student U. Miss., 1928-29, La. State U., 1930-31, Ind. U., 1933-34; m. Nell Scanlon Mixon, Feb. 5, 1935; children—John A., Diane, Robert C. Leader orch., hotels, clubs, various cities, 1934-49; owner, operator So. Mansion Restaurant and Club, Indpls., 1941-49; sales mgr. Ind., Baldwin Piano Co., Indpls., 1949-50; pres. Automatic Detection and Alarm Co., Louisville, 1950-63, Protection Instrument Co., Louisville, 1963—; chmn. bd. AyrKing Corp., Louisville, 1974-77. Mem. Am. Fedn. Musicians (life). Presbyterian. Clubs: Wildwood Country, Bonnycastle. Composer: My Castle of Love, 1930. Home: 4217 Churchill Rd Louisville KY 40207 Office: PO Box 32323 Louisville KY 40232

LAMB, BETH HOWLEY, educator; b. Omaha, June 8, 1920; d. William Joseph and Camille Salerno (Saitta) Howley; B.A., U. Nebr., 1941; M.A., U. Okla., 1944; Ed.D., U. Tulsa, 1969; m. Walter Gray Lamb, Jr., Dec. 9, 1944; children—William, Walter, Philip. Tchr. kindergarten Tulsa Pub. Schs., 1959-66, supr. kindergarten edn., 1966-74; head primary sch. Holland Hall, Tulsa, 1974—; nat. lecture staff Gesell Inst. Child Devel., New Haven; cons. in field. Pres. Jr. Bd. for Tulsa Boys Home, 1958. Recipient Schoolman medal Valley Forge Freedoms Found., 1974. Mem. Tulsa (pres. 1962), Okla. (pres. 1966) kindergarten tchrs. assns., Okla. Assn. Children Under Six (pres. 1971), Assn. Supervision and Curriculum Devel., Phi Delta Kappa, Pi Beta Phi. Unitarian. Co-author: Kindergarten: An Intuitive Approach, 1968; author: Kindergarten Education. Office: 5666 E 81st Tulsa OK 74136

LAMB, FRANK MICHAEL, mfg. co. exec.; b. Langdale, Ala., July 5, 1938; s. Frank Wilson and Milbra (Grayce) L.; B.S. in Indsl. Mgmt., U. Ala., 1960, M.B.A., 1967. Quality control mgr. Tracor Inc., Austin, Tex., 1968-73; ops. mgr. Cerro Corp., Anniston, Ala., 1973-76; quality control mgr. Am. Sterilizer Co., Montgomery, Ala., 1976-78; dir. quality assurance Martin Industries Co., Florence, Ala., 1978—; dir. View All Inc. Served with USAR, 1960-63. Mem. Am. Soc. Quality Control, Am. Mgmt. Assn. Democrat. Baptist. Clubs: Valley Hill Country, Florence Country. Home: 426 N Cypress St Florence AL 35630 Office: 301 E Tennessee St Florence AL 35630

LAMB, JOHN P., JR., univ. dean; b. Washington County, Tenn., Dec. 4, 1916; s. John P. and Elsie (Hickman) L.; B.S., E. Tenn. State U., 1937; C.P.H., Vanderbilt U., 1938, M.P.H., 1949; m. Virginia Beatrice Yelton, Apr. 14, 1938. With Tenn. Dept. Public Health, 1938-49; prof., dean Coll. Health, E. Tenn. State U., Johnson City, 1949-78, prof., dean Sch. Public and Allied Health, 1978—; pres. Tenn. Bd. Examiners for Registered Profl. Environmentalists; regional adv. com. USPHS, 1968-69. Chmn., Carter County unit Am. Cancer Soc., v.p. Tenn. div.; active Sequoyah council Boy Scouts Am. Served with USPHS; aide de camp on gov.'s staff Tenn., 1963-64. Recipient numerous awards, including: R.H. Hutcheson award Tenn. Public Health Assn., 1976, Gov.'s Outstanding Tennessean award, 1978; John P. Lamb, Jr. Hall named in his honor, E. Tenn. State U., 1977. Fellow Am. Public Health Assn., Internat. Union Health Edn. of Public, Royal Soc. Health, Am. Sch. Health Assn., Soc. Public Health Educators; mem. Tenn. Acad. Health Edn. (pres. 1976-78, award established in his honor 1979), Tenn. Dental Assn. (asso.), Johnson City Area C. of C. (dir. 1973-75, exec. com. 1974-75, chmn. council on health services 1974-75). Episcopalian. Club: Elizabethton Kiwanis (pres., dir., lt. gov. Ky.-Tenn. dist. 1947-48). Co-author: Health Teaching: A Guide for Grades 1 Through 12, 1952. Home: 1512 Ashewood Dr Johnson City TN 37601 Office: PO Box 21 190A East Tenn State U Johnson City TN 37601

LAMB, JONES WELDON, surgeon; b. Paragould, Ark., Aug. 26, 1915; s. Jones Houston and Nora Lee (Tyner) L.; student Washington U., St. Louis, 1931-33; M.D., Tulane U., 1938; m. Alma Elizabeth Rittenhouse, Jan. 3, 1939; children—Judith, Jones Weldon, Jr., Susan. Intern Kansas City (Mo.) Gen. Hosp., 1938-39, resident contagious diseases, 1939-40; pvt. practice medicine and surgery, Paragould, Ark., 1940-42; Wynne, Ark., 1946-50; fellow surgery Luth. Hosp., Vicksburg Clinic, Vicksburg, Miss., 1950-54; pvt. practice surgery, Lexington, Miss., 1954-55, Greenwood, Miss., 1955—; mem. staff Leflore County (Miss.) Hosp.; asst. vis. surgeon Charity Hosp., New Orleans, 1950-51; asst. surgery dept. Tulane U., 1950-51. Served to capt. USAF, 1942-46. Decorated Air medal. Diplomate Am. Bd. Surgery. Fellow Pan Am. Med. Assn., Am. Coll. Surgeons; mem. AMA, Miss. Med. Assn., So. Med. Assn., Delta Med. Soc. (bd. govs., past pres.), C. of C., VFW. Episcopalian. Home: 125 Riverside Dr Greenwood MS 38930 Office: 405 River Rd Greenwood MS 38930

LAMB, MARY KAY, rehab. counselor; b. Morganfield, Ky., Apr. 22, 1953; d. Charles and Martha Lewis (Pride) Pryor; B.S., Murray State U., 1975, postgrad., 1977—; m. Donald W. Lamb, Aug. 7, 1976; 1 son, Chad Pryor. Counselor, Breckinridge Job Corp Center, Morganfield, Ky., 1975-78; program coordinator, asst. adminstr. Higgins Learning Center, Morganfield, 1978—. Mem. Nat. Rehab. Assn., Am. Assn. Mental Deficiencies, Ky. Rehab. Assn. Baptist. Home: 124 E 4th St Sturgis KY 42459 Office: Rural Route 4 Higgins Learning Center Morganfield KY 42437

LAMB, PAUL HOWARD, III, civil engr.; b. Petersburg, Va., Mar. 14, 1933; s. Paul Howard and Wilma Grace (Welch) L.; B.S. in C.E., Va. Mil. Inst., 1954; postgrad. Northwestern U., 1955, U. Richmond, 1959-60; m. Nancy Comer Williamson, July 7, 1979; children by previous marriage—Paul Howard, Sarah Katherine. Asst. engr. Allied chem. Corp., Hopewell, Va., 1956-58; with Brown & Williamson Tobacco, Petersburg, Va., 1958—, project engr., 1965-69, chief project engr., 1969-70, asst. br. engr., 1970-71, br. engr.-mgr., 1971—. Trustee, Petersburg Hosp. Authority, 1972—, vice chmn., 1978—; bd. dirs. Petersburg Hosp., 1972—, v.p., 1978—; mem. Contractors Bd. Appeals, Crater Planning Dist., Petersburg, 1978—. Served to 1st lt., USAF, 1954-56. Cert. plant engr., Va. Mem. Petersburg C. of C. (dir. 1975-77 recipient Citation for Community Service 1977), Am. Inst. Plant Engrs., Va. C. of C. Republican. Episcopalian. Club: Country (dir. 1964—, pres. 1980—). Home: 1739 Westover Ave Petersburg VA 23803 Office: 325 Brown St Petersburg VA 23803

LAMBA, RAM SARUP, chemist, univ. ofcl.; b. Calcutta, India, Dec. 29, 1941; came to U.S., 1966; s. Ram R. and Lajwanti Lamba; B.Sc. with honors in Chemistry, Delhi (India), U., 1962, M.S. in Organic Chemistry, 1964; Ph.D., East Tex. State U., 1973; m. Edda Aixa Nieves, Dec. 27, 1969; children—Nalini, Deepak. Research asso. Council of Sci. and Indsl. Research Labs., Dehradun, India, 1964-65; research fellow Lac Research Inst., Delhi U., 1965-66; asso. prof. chemistry Inter Am. U. of P.R., Hato Rey, 1973-76, chmn. dept. natural scis., 1976-77, acting dean acad. affairs, San Juan campus, 1977, dean acad. affairs, Met. campus, 1978—, prof. chemistry, 1980—; participant at various profl. confs. and symposia, 1972—. Mem. Am. Chem. Soc. (chmn. edn. com. P.R. chpt. 1975-76), Coll. of Chemists, Royal Inst. of Chemistry, AAAS. Contbr. articles to profl. jours. Home: 146 Gardenia St Round Hill Trujillo Alto PR 00760 Office: Inter American Univ PO Box 1293 Hato Rey PR 00919

LAMBERT, CAROL ANN, audiologist; b. Easton, Pa., June 15, 1947; d. Harry and Clara (Miller) L.; B.A., U. Tulsa, 1972, M.A., 1977; m. Michael Read Minshall, Mar. 19, 1973. Audiologist, Tulsa Otolaryngology, Inc., and U. Tulsa, 1977-78; speech reading instr. Tulsa Speech and Hearing Assn., 1977-78; audiologist Ear, Nose and Throat Consultants, Inc., Tulsa, 1978—; cons. Okla. State Dept. Health, Tulsa Scottish Rite Center for Childhood Aphasia, At Risk Parent-Child Program, Springer Clinic. Active hist. preservation project Jr. League of Tulsa. Mem. Am. Speech and Hearing Assn. (cert. in audiology), Acad. Dispensing Audiologists, Okla. Speech and Hearing Assn., Okla. Council for the Hearing Impaired, Acad. of Audiology, Tulsa Assn. Speech Pathologists and Audiologists (pres.), Tulsa Speech and Hearing Assn. Office: 2325 S Harvard Tulsa OK 74114

LAMBERT, DOUGLAS WARREN, environmentalist; b. Princeton, W.Va., Nov. 27, 1946; s. Errett Jay and Marjorie Murr (Mooney) L.; B.S. in Landscape Architecture, U. Ky., 1969; M. Public Affairs, Ky. State U., 1977; m. Beatrice Elaine Cain, Dec. 27, 1967; children—Douglas Warren, Jason Carey. Landscape architect Ky. Dept. Transp., Frankfort, 1969-70, asst. dir. div. environ. analysis, 1972—; coordinator Environ. Action Plan Task Force, 1976-79. Mem. Gov.'s Design Adv. Council, 1978—. Served with U.S. Army, 1970-72. Mem. Nat. Assn. Environ. Profls. (cert., mem. ednl. guidance com.), Am. Inst. Landscape Architects, Am. Soc. Public Adminstrn., Natural Resources Defense Council, U. Ky. Alumni Assn., Theta Chi. Methodist. Home: 1929 Pershing Dr Lexington KY 40504 Office: 419 Ann St Frankfort KY 40622

LAMBERT, KENNETH CHARLES, county exec.; b. Atmore, Ala., Jan. 11, 1934; s. George Howard and Cordelia Rebecca L.; B.S. in Indsl. Mgmt., U. Ala., 1960; M.B.A. in Mgmt., U. So. Miss., 1973; m. Ann Carolyn Galloway, Nov. 27, 1954; children—Kenneth Charles, Karen Lynn. Cost statistician Pan Atlantic S.S. Corp., Mobile, Ala., 1952-58; adminstrv. asst. Scott Paper Co., Mobile, 1960-61; purchasing agt. Bd. Sch. Commrs. Mobile County (Ala.), 1961-71, dir. purchasing and bus., 1971-75, treas.-comptroller, 1975—; instr. in mgmt. Troy U., U. South Ala. Bd. stewards Pleasant Valley Methodist Ch., Mobile, 1969-72. Served with USAR. Mem. Ala. Assn. Sch. Bus. Ofcls. (pres. 1969-79, dir. 1969-70, 78-80), Ala. Sch. Office Personnel (dir. 1979-81), Ala. Assn. Sch. Adminstrs., Ala. Council Sch. Adminstrn. and Supervision, Assn. Sch. Bus., Phi Delta Kappa. Club: Optimists (dir. club 1977) (Mobile). Office: 504 Government St Mobile AL 36601

LAMBERT, LAURA ANNE, univ. adminstr.; b. Geneva, Ala., June 30, 1938; d. Lamar and Abbie (Harris) Beck; student Judson Coll. for Women, 1956-57; B.S., Auburn U., 1960; postgrad. U. Hawaii, 1964-65, Calif. State U., 1973; M.Ed., U. South Ala., 1979; m. Isaac Noah Lambert, Aug. 11, 1959 (dec.); children—Margaret Elizabeth, Daniel Nyles. Tchr., Taylors, S.C., 1961-62; tchr. high sch., Honolulu, 1965-66; vol. coordinator Pan-Am. World Airways, also ground hostess San Francisco Internat. Airport, 1971-73; program coordinator U. South Ala., Mobile, 1977—. Mem. Assn. Continuing Higher Edn., Ala. Assn. Continuing Edn., Am. Personnel and Guidance Assn., Ala. Personnel and Guidance Assn., Internat. Mgmt. Council (head edn. com. 1978—). Presbyterian. Home: 1200 Marseille Dr Mobile AL 36609 Office: 280 Adminstrn Bldg U South Ala Mobile AL 36688

LAMBERT, LINDA RICE, bank exec.; b. Tacoma, Wash., May 14, 1940; d. Joseph G. and Bernice F. (Birchfield) R.; B.A., Fla. State U., 1962; postgrad. U. Mich., 1969-72, Fla. Internat. U., 1973-74; m. Hugh N. Lambert, Sept. 13, 1975; 1 dau., Susan B. Social worker State of Fla., 1963-66; system mgr. reservations and ticket office tng. Nat. Airlines, Inc., 1967-75; dir. human resources devel. Chase Fed. Savings & Loan, Miami, 1975—. Mem. Greater Miami C. of C., Am. Soc. Tng. and Devel., Internat. Assn. Bus. Communications, Inst. Fin. Edn., Am. Mgmt. Assn. Clubs: Am. Hibiscus Soc., Tropical Fern Soc. Office: 7300 N Kendall Dr Miami FL 33156

LAMBERT, MARGARET LARINE, phys. therapist; b. McAllen, Tex., Oct. 22, 1947; d. Lee Nolan and Gertrude (Rigler) Gorman; B.S. in Phys. Therapy, U. Md., 1972; M.S., U. S. Fla., 1977; m. David Arthur Lambert, Dec. 22, 1968. Staff phys. therapist VA Hosp., Fort Howard, Md., 1972, St. Joseph's Hosp., Albuquerque, 1972-73; staff phys. therapist James Haley VA Hosp., Tampa, 1973-74, supervisory phys. therapist, 1975—; lectr. in field. Lic. phys. therapist, Fla., Md. Mem. Am. Phys. Therapy Assn. (v.p. Fla. chpt. 1978—, chmn. program chmn. 1977—), Fla. Phys. Therapy. Republican. Methodist. Home: 210 Hickory Ln Lutz FL 33549 Office: 13000 N 30th St Tampa FL 33612

LAMBERT, MARTIN LEE, JR., pharmacist, educator; b. Pensacola, Fla., July 3, 1937; s. Martin Lee and Maude (Land) L.; B.S. in Pharmacy, Samford U., 1958; M.P.H., U. Tenn., 1976, Ph.D., 1978; m. Apr. 5, 1975; 4 children. Owner, pres. Lambert's Pharmacy I, Inc., Knoxville, Tenn., 1966—, Lambert's Pharmacy II, Inc., Knoxville, 1979—, Medicare Equipment Services of E. Tenn., Inc., Knoxville, 1976—, Health Care Mgmt. Services; asso. prof. pharmacy adminstrn. Samford U., Birmingham, Ala., 1979—. Mem. contbns. bd. Tenn. Pharmpac, 1979—; guest lectr. in field; participant Pharmacy-Industry com. on Nat. Health Ins., 1978-79, Joint Commn. of Pharmacy Practitioners, 1977-79, Sr. Citizens of Knox County Drug program, 1979; patient edn. research Hypertension Mgmt. Clinic, 1976, Knoxville Neighborhood Health Services, 1977-78; first aid instr. ARC; bd. mgmt. YMCA, Knoxville, 1975-77, 78—; mem. St. Mary's Med. Center, Devel. Council ann. support com., 1979—; bd. dirs. N.E. Area Residents Community Orgn., 1976-77; adv. com. E. Tenn. Kidney Found., 1975; bd. dirs. E. Tenn. Substance Abuse Council, 1979, others. Cert. ostomy appliance technician and fitter; cert. home health care cons.; cert. surg. appliance fitter; cert. surg. appliance technician; diplomate Am. Bd. Diplomates in Pharmacy. Fellow Am. Coll. Apothecaries (regional dir. and mem. bd. dirs. 1975-76, pres. pro tem, 1978, pres. 1978-79, chmn. bd. dirs. 1979-80), Am. Pharm. Assn.; mem. Acad. Pharmacy Practice, Nat. Assn. Retail Druggists, Am. Assn. Colls. Pharmacy, Am. Inst. History of Pharmacy, Am. Pub. Health Assn., Soc. for Pub. Health Edn., United Ostomy Assn., Assn. of Ind. Med. Equipment Suppliers, Tenn. Pharm. Assn., Knoxville Pharm. Assn. (pres. 1975-76, dir. 1978-79), Soc. for Pub. Health Edn., Tenn. Acad. Health Edn., Knoxville Ostomy Assn., Greater Knoxville C. of C., Mortar and Pestle, Phi Kappa Phi, Phi Delta Chi, Delta Sigma Phi. Clubs: F.O.P., Gideons Internat., Ark. Traveler, Ky. Col. Contbr. articles to profl. jours. Home: 1401 Grainger Ave Knoxville TN 37917 Office: PO Box 421 Knoxville TN 37901

LAMBERT, NORMAN ANDREW, educator; b. Fall River, Mass., Feb. 3, 1925; s. Arthur Adelard and Leda Mary (St. Armand) L.; student public schs.; m. Evelyn Provida DeCosta, Oct. 19, 1950; children—Debra, Steve. Served as non-commissioned officer C.E., U.S. Army, 1943-70; battle service in World War II, Korea, Vietnam; ret., 1970; instr. Edison High Sch., Alexandria, Va., 1970—; program cons. adult classes. Vice pres. Windsor Civic Homeowners Assn. Decorated Bronze Star; master lic. in refrigeration. Roman Catholic. Home: 6585 Windham St Alexandria VA 22310 Office: 5801 Franconia St Alexandria VA 22310

LAMBERTH, LEON ROBISON, fund raiser; b. Alexander City, Ala., Dec. 25, 1946; s. Edwin Joshua and Emma Enslen (Robison) L.; student Auburn U., 1965-68, B.S. in B.A., 1973; m. Martha Nell McGhee, Mar. 21, 1970; 1 dau., Enslen Elizabeth. Exec. asst. Multiple Assn. Mgmt. Service, Birmingham, Ala., 1973-74; asst. exec. v.p. Ala. Assn. Realtors, Montgomery, 1974-76; exec. dir. Diabetes Trust Fund, Inc., Birmingham, 1976—. Unit commr. Boy Scouts Am., Montgomery, 1975-76; adminstrv. bd. Christ Ch. United Meth. Ch., 1977-79, stewardship chmn., 1978-79, mem. Council of Ministries, 1977-79. Served with U.S. Army, 1969-72. Decorated Air medal with 19 oak leaf clusters, Air medal with V device; recipient Montgomery Jr. C. of C. Presdl. award, 1976; Ala. Jr. C. of C. Spoke award, 1976. Mem. Ala. Soc. Fund Raisers, Montgomery Jr. C. of C., Nat. Assn. Hosp. Developers. Clubs: The Club, Kiwanis. Home: 3832 Williamsburg Circle Birmingham AL 35243 Office: 1808 7th Ave S Birmingham AL 35294

LAMBERT-PILETTE, MARTHA JO, mental health counselor; b. Philippi, W.Va., May 2, 1943; d. William Lee and Martha Lee Lambert; B.A. in Psychology cum laude, Alderson Broaddus Coll., Philippi, 1976; M.A. in Counseling, Marshall U., Huntington, W.Va., 1979; children—Wendy, Alison. Day care specialist W.Va. Dept. Welfare, Grafton, 1976-77; dir. acad. adv. center Marshall U., 1978-79; substance abuse counselor Lansdowne Mental Health Center, Ashland, Ky., 1979—. Vice pres. Rome (N.Y.) Community Theatre, 1971-73; treas. Rome Choral Soc., 1971-73. Mem. Am. Mental Health Counselors Assn., Chi Beta Phi. Democrat. Unitarian.

LAMBETH, JAMES ERWIN, furniture co. exec.; b. Thomasville, N.C., Feb. 2, 1916; s. James Erwin and Mary Helen (McAulay) L.; A.B., Duke U., 1937; postgrad. Harvard Bus. Sch., 1937-38; m. Katharine Evermond Covington, Aug. 27, 1938; children—James Erwin III, Richard Covington, Mary Katharine Lambeth Cullens, William Roderick. Gen. supt. Standard Chair Co., 1938-46, sec.-treas., 1946-56; treas., chmn. bd. Erwin-Lambeth, Inc., Thomasville, 1946—; dir. Home Bldg. and Loan Assn., N.C. Nat. Bank. Pres., Piedmont Assn. Industries, 1963-64, bd. dirs., 1964-77; pres. Thomasville United Fund, 1964-65; mem. Nat. Citizens Adv. Council on Status of Women, 1967; pres. Uwharrie council Boy Scouts Am., 1967-68, council commr., 1970-71. Mayor pro tem, mem. Thomasville City Council, 1963-67; mem. N.C. Ho. of Reps., 1977-78, 79-80. Bd. dirs. Goodwill Industries, Thomasville, 1971-72; trustee Thomasville Community Found., 1963-64, Coll. Found., Inc., 1971-78. Recipient Silver Beaver award Boy Scouts Am., 1961. Mem. Thomasville C. of C. (pres. 1961-63), Davidson County (chmn. bd. dirs. 1971-72), Thomasville (pres. 1969-71) hist. socs., Newcomen Soc. N.Am., Phi Delta Theta. Methodist (chmn. stewardship and fin. com. 1964-65, past steward). Clubs: Masons, Rotary (pres. Thomasville 1960-61, gov. dist. 769, 1966-67, internat. dir. 1972-74, trustee Found.), High Point (N.C.) Executives (pres. 1962-63, dir. 1964—), North State Game (sec. 1971-72). Home: 214 Lake Dr E Thomasville NC 27360 Office: PO Box 308 Thomasville NC 27360

LAMBIRD, MONA SALYER, lawyer; b. Oklahoma City, July 19, 1938; d. B.M., Jr. and Pauline A. Salyer; B.A., Wellesley Coll., 1960; LL.B., U. Md., 1963; m. Perry A. Lambird, July 30, 1960; children—Allison Thayer, Jennifer Salyer, Elizabeth Gard, Susannah Johnson. Admitted to Okla. bar, 1968, also admitted to practice before Ct. Appeals Md., Supreme Ct. Okla., U.S. Dist. Ct., U.S. Supreme Ct.; atty. civil div. Dept. Justice, Washington, 1963-65; individual practice law, Balt. and Oklahoma City, 1965-71; mem. firm Andrews Davis Legg Bixler Milsten & Murrah, Inc., and predecessor firm, Oklahoma City, 1971—; cons. World Orgn. of China Painters; legal adv. Oklahoma City Media Council. Profl. liaison com. City of Oklahoma City, 1974—; mem. Hist. Preservation of Oklahoma City, Inc., 1970—; del. Oklahoma County and Okla. State Republican Party Conv., 1971—; women's com. Okla. Symphony Orch., legal advisor, 1973—, bd. dirs., 1973—; incorporator, bd. dirs. R.S.V.P. of Oklahoma County, Congregate Housing for Elderly, 1978—. Mem. Am., Md., Okla., Okla. County bar assns., Jr. League Oklahoma City (dir. 1973-76, legal adv.), Okla. County and State Med. Assn. Aux. (dir.). Methodist (adminstrv. bd.). Club: Seven Colls. (pres. 1972-76). Editor Briefcase of the Okla. County Bar Assn., 1976. Home: 419 NW 14th St Oklahoma City OK 73103 Office: 1600 Midland Center Oklahoma City OK 73102

LAMBIRD, PERRY ALBERT, pathologist; b. Reno, Feb. 7, 1939; s. Clifford D. and Florence T. (Knowlton) L.; B.A. with great distinction, Stanford U., 1958; M.D., Johns Hopkins U., 1962; M.B.A. with high honors, Oklahoma City U., 1973; m. Mona Sue Salyer, July 30, 1960; children—Allison Thayer, Jennifer Salyer, Elizabeth Gard, Susannah Johnson. Intern, Johns Hopkins Hosp., Balt., 1962-63, jr. asst. resident in pathology, 1965-66, asst. resident in pathology, 1966-68, chief resident pathologist, 1968-69; practice medicine specializing in pathology, Oklahoma City, 1969—; asso. pathologist Med. Arts Lab., 1969-70, pathologist, 1970—; cons. pathologist, dep. med. examiner Office State Med. Examiner Okla., 1969—; mem. staff Hosp. U. Okla., Presbyn. Hosp., Children's Meml. Hosp., St. Anthony Hosp., South Community Hosp., Mercy Health Center; cons. pathologist Okla. Breast Cancer Control Network, Okla. Med. Research Found., 1975—; spl. cons. Rees Assos., Oklahoma City, 1975—; clin. asso. prof. pathology U. Okla., 1970—, clin. asso. prof. orthopedic surgery, 1970—; asst. prof. Sch. of Mgmt. and Bus. Scis., Oklahoma City U., 1973—; reviewer So. Med. Jour., 1974—; propr. Lambird Mgmt. Cons. Services, Oklahoma City, 1974—. Chmn. Okla. County Citizens for Reagan, 1976; exec. com. Republican Party Okla. County, 1973-79; del. Rep. Nat. Conv., 1976; bd. dirs. Oklahoma City chpt. ARC, 1976—, Hist. Preservation, Inc., 1970—, Okla. Found. Peer Rev., 1979—; bd. Okla. Symphony Orch., pres. 1974-75, chmn. bd., 1975-77, chmn. adv. com., 1977-79; trustee Ballet Okla., pres., 1978-79; trustee Westminister Day Sch. Served with USPHS, 1963-65. Recipient Exec. Leadership award Oklahoma City U., 1976; named Outstanding Young Man, Oklahoma City Jaycees, 1972, Outstanding Young Oklahomans award (3), 1973; Outstanding Young Am. award U.S. Jaycees, 1974. Diplomate Am. Bd. Pathology. Fellow Coll. Am. Pathologists, Am. Soc. Clin. Pathologists; mem. Internat. Acad. Pathology, Okla. Assn. Pathologists (sec. 1973-74), So. Med. Assn., Am. Assn. Pathologists, Okla. Med. Assn. (chmn. council on govt. activities 1976—, mem. ho. dels. 1973—, trustee 1974—) AMA, (award 1969, 72, 74, 77), Oklahoma City Clin. Soc., Oklahoma County Med. Soc. (dir. 1976-78, 80—, v.p. 1977-78), Johns Hopkins Med. and Surg. Assn., Am. Soc. of Cytology, Osler Soc. Oklahoma City, Okla. Soc. Cytopathology, Fedn. Am. Socs. Exptl. Biology, N.Y. Acad. Scis., Phi Beta Kappa, Alpha Omega Alpha. Methodist. Contbr. articles on pathology to profl. jours. Home: 419 Northwest 14th St Oklahoma City OK 73103 Office: 254 Pasteur Bldg 1111 N Lee St Oklahoma City OK 73103

LAMEY, AUDREY ANNETTE, devel. commn. exec.; b. Biloxi, Miss., Sept. 9, 1936; d. Robert Wesley and Audrey Wilda (Manuel) Murray; certificate Am. Savings and Loan Inst., 1971; m. Robert H. Lamey, Aug. 15, 1954; children—Charles Robert, Mark Alan. Bookkeeper, Biloxi Seperate Sch. System (Miss.), 1958-61; acct. First Fed. Savs. & Loan, Biloxi, 1972-73, Biloxi Housing Authority-Urban Renewal, 1973-74; exec. dir. Biloxi Devel. Commn., 1974—. Mem. Nat. Community Devel. Assn., S.E. Regional Council Housing and Redevel. Ofcls., Miss. Assn. Housing and Redevel. Ofcls. (mem. community devel. com. 1977-80), Biloxi C. of C. (mem. bus. and industry com. 1979). Methodist. Clubs: Quota (v.p. Miss. Gulf Coast 1977-78), Elks. Home: 304 N Shore Dr Biloxi MS 39532 Office: 214 Lameuse St Biloxi MS 39530

LAMEY, STEVEN CHARLES, research chemist; b. Rebersburg, Pa., Mar. 5, 1944; s. Howard Z. and Elizabeth A. (Page) L.; B.A., Lock Haven State Coll., 1968; M.S., W.Va. U., 1973, Ph.D. (NSF trainee), 1975; m. Charlotte Irene Orndorf, Jan. 24, 1970. Research chemist Am. Aniline Corp., Lock Haven, Pa., 1968-70, Morgantown (W.Va.) Energy Tech. Center, Dept. Energy, 1975—. W.Va. U. Senate Research grantee, 1975. Mem. Am. Chem. Soc., W.Va. Acad. Sci., AAAS, Coblentz Soc., Sigma Xi, Phi Lambda Upsilon. Contbr. articles in field to profl. jours. Home: 821 Idlewood Dr Morgantown WV 26505 Office: Box 880 Collins Ferry Rd Morgantown WV 26505

LAMM, DANIEL ALLEN, indsl. engr.; b. San Antonio, June 24, 1949; s. Allen Gerald and Emily Catherine (Emig) L.; B.S. in Engring., St. Mary's U., 1972; M.B.A., Trinity U., 1977; m. Barbara Ann Grothues, Nov. 30, 1974; 1 son, Ryan Daniel. Engring. asst. dept. structural research S.W. Research Inst., San Antonio, 1969-72, asst. research engr. dept. spl. engring. services, 1972-73, research engr. Quality Assurance and Systems Engring. div., 1973-76, lead group engr. access engring. sect., 1976-77, asst. mgr. access engring. sect., 1977—. Served with U.S. Army, 1970. Mem. Am. Soc. Nondestructive Testing. Democrat. Roman Catholic. Author: Graphical Evaluation Review Technique: Applications towards Simulation, 1972; also papers on nuclear power plant inspection and design. Home: 7223 Horse Whip Ln San Antonio TX 78240 Office: 6220 Culebra Rd San Antonio TX 78284

LAMMERDING, JOHN JUDE, fin. and mgmt. advisor; b. Elizabeth, N.J., July 3, 1929; s. John Charles and Mary Margaret (Elmiger) L.; B.S. in Bus. Adminstrn., U. Ala., 1969; postgrad. N.Y. Inst. Fin., 1970, Inst. for Fin. Planning, 1972; m. Jane Annette Haglund, Jan. 15, 1950; children—Mark John, Amy Annette, Eric Richard. With Bur. Bus. Research, U. Ala., 1968-69; account exec. Walston & Co., 1969-73; bus. cons. fin., mgmt., Park Ridge, Ill., 1973-74; sr. fin. analyst Blue Cross and Blue Shield of Fla., Inc., Jacksonville, 1974—; banking and electronic funds transfer J.J. Lammerding & Assos., Inc., 1978—; mem. mgmt., mktg. dept. Jones Coll., Jacksonville, 1972. Dist. Chmn. Fla. Columbian Squires, 1975. Served with USAF, 1956-66. Mem. Aircraft Owners and Pilots Assn., Internat. Platform Assn. U. Ala. Alumni Assn. Democrat. Roman Catholic. Clubs: Captain's (Jacksonville Beach, dir. 1977—, treas. 1977-79); K.C. Home: Unit 1502 9252 San Jose Blvd Jacksonville FL 32217 Office: 1045 Riverside Ave Suite 235 Jacksonville FL 32204

LAMMERS, LOWELL architect, civil engr.; b. Chgo., Oct. 29, 1908; s. Herman C. and Antoinette (Belitz) L.; student Mass. Inst. Tech., 1930-33; B.S. in Architecture, Armour Inst. Tech., 1936; m. Jean C. Wegener, Oct. 17, 1936; children—John William, Carol Lee, Leslie Jean. Archtl. draftsman E.W. Bridges, 1931-34, Holsman & Holsman, 1934-39; chief draftsman J.C. Christensen, 1939-41; constrn. engr., archtl. practice, Baytown, Tex., 1941—; pres., dir. 201 Corp., 1960—; pres. Tex State Bldg. Co.; owner Real Estate Co. of Tex. Commr., City of Baytown Adv. Bd., 1958-62; mem. Tex. Water Commn., 1962; CD disaster engr., 1960-70; mem. disaster relief com. A.R.C., 1961; chmn. Baytown Civic Forum, 1955-57. Bd. dirs. Health Bd. Recipient citation Am. Assn. Sch. Adminstrs. for sch. design and constrn., 1957, citation for hosp. and clinic design Am. Hosp. Assn., 1959. Registered profl. engr., Ill.; registered architect, Ill., Tex., Ariz., Tenn.; cert. Nat. Council Archtl. Registration Bds. Mem. Constrn. Specifications Inst. (Houston chpt.), A.I.A., Tex. Soc. Architects, Am. Soc. Profl. Engrs., Soc. Am. Mil. Engrs., Baytown C. of C. (dir.), Houston Engring. Club. Rotarian (pres.). Clubs: Knife and Ford (dir.); Goose Creek Country, Newport Country. Writer, producer, actor radio program Your Home, 1948-60; moderator TV program Architecturally Speaking, 1962-64. Home: 4815 St Andrews St Baytown TX 77521 Office: Box 600 Baytown TX 77520

LAMON, HARRY VINCENT, JR., lawyer; b. Macon, Ga., Sept. 29, 1932; s. Harry Vincent and Helen (Bewley) L.; B.S. cum laude, Davidson Coll., 1954; LL.B. magna cum laude, Emory U., 1958; m. Ada Healey Morris, June 17, 1954; children—Hollis Morris, Helen Kathryn. Admitted to Ga. bar, 1958, D.C. bar, 1965; practiced in Atlanta, 1958—; mem. firm Hansell, Post, Brandon, Dorsey, 1958-73, Henkel & Lamon, 1973—. Adj. prof. Emory U., 1960—; pres. So. Fed. Tax Inst., Inc., 1967-68, So. Pension Conf., 1972-73; cons. Office Mgmt. and Budget, Washington. Mem. adv. council on employee welfare and pension benefit plans Dept. Labor, 1975-79. Chmn. adv. bd. Met. Atlanta Salvation Army, 1974-79, mem. nat. adv. council, 1976—; bd. dirs. Met. Atlanta Boys Clubs, Inc., 1964—; mem. exec. com. Atlanta Area Council Boy Scouts Am., 1974—. Served to 1st lt. AUS, 1954-56. Fellow Am. Coll. Probate Counsel, Atlanta Estate Planning Council, Atlanta Tax Forum, Am. Law Inst.; mem. Am., Ga., D.C., Atlanta, Fed. bar assns., Lawyers Club Atlanta, Internat. Acad. Estate and Trust Law, Nat. Emory U. Law Sch. Alumni Assn. (past pres.), Phi Beta Kappa, Omicron Delta Kappa, Phi Delta Phi, Phi Delta Theta (province pres. 1964-68). Episcopalian (sec. chpt.). Mason (Shriner), Kiwanian (pres. Downtown Atlanta 1973-74). Clubs: Breakfast, Commerce, Capital City, Cherokee Town and Country. Author: Fiduciary Responsibilities under Pension Reform Act, 1975. Home: 3375 Valley Rd NW Atlanta GA 30305 Office: 2500 Peachtree Center Cain Tower 229 Peachtree St NE Atlanta GA 30303 also 702 Longfellow Bldg 1201 Connecticut Ave NW Washington DC 20036

LA MONTAGNE, ARMAND M., artist; b. Pawtucket, R.I., Feb. 3, 1938; s. Raymond and Jeanne (Ferland) LaM.; student Boston Coll.; m. Lorraine A. Robitaille, Sept. 28, 1963; 1 dau., Lisa Anne. Artist and sculptor in wood; works include: bust of Gerald Ford, Ford Presdl. Library, Ann Arbor, Mich.; life size sculpture Abraham Lincoln; series of Indian and Western bronzes; bust of Walter Brennan, Nat. Cowboy Hall of Fame, Okla.; furniture maker, created Great Brewster Chair, erroneously authenticated by Henry Ford Mus. as being made in year 1620; lectr. Served with U.S. Army, 1960. Russell Grinnell Found. grantee, Florence, Italy, 1964. Address: PO Box 250 Oldsmar FL 33557

LAMOUREUX, WILLIAM A., poet; b. Montreal, Que., Can., Aug. 15, 1938; s. William C. and Beatrice (Benoit) L.; B.A., Tufts U., 1964; postgrad. Boston U., 1964-65, U. Hawaii, 1974; came to U.S., 1938, naturalized, 1953. Partner, Lamoureux Funeral Home, Gardner, Mass., 1949-76; founder, propr. Librairie Francaise, Santurce, P.R., 1970-73; broker-salesman J.M. Urner Inc., Realtors, Honolulu, 1974-76; broker, salesman Portner & Portner, Inc., Realtors, Hollywood, Fla., 1978—; right-of-way agent Fla. Dept. Transp., 1978—; works include: (poetry) La lumiere se retire du bord de la terrasse....., 1960; Comme je traversais le pays des licornes, 1961 Un oranger, supreme emeraude, 1962. Republican. Roman Catholic. Home: 923 Lincoln St Hollywood FL 33019 Office: 1317 NE 4th Ave Fort Lauderdale FL 33304

LAMPKIN, WILLIAM MCCAIN, mech. and metall. engr.; b. Tuscaloosa, Ala., Aug. 11, 1941; s. Charles Barnett and Julia White (McCain) L.; B.S. in Metal. Engring., U. Ala., 1964, M.S., 1965; M.A.

in Mgmt. and Bus. Adminstrn., Webster Coll., 1976; B.S. in Mech. Engring., Tex. A. & I., 1979; m. Beverly Ann Maynard, Mar. 19, 1968; 1 dau., Elizabeth Maynard. Research metallurgist U.S. Bur. Mines, Tuscaloosa, Ala., 1964-66; metallurgist Army Aero. Depot Maintenance Center, Corpus Christi, Tex., 1968-69, materials engr., 1969-74; materials structural engr. Army Aviation Systems Command, Corpus Christi, St. Louis, 1974-76; indsl. engr. bearing reclamation and BlackHawk integrated logistics support program mgr. Corpus Christi Army Depot, 1976—; instr. engring. Tex. A & I U., 1978—. Served with U.S. Army, 1966-68. Registered profl. engr., Tex.; recipient certificate of achievement U.S. Govt., 1970, 75; grad. fellowship, Nat's Wheelabrator, 1964-65; Aluminum Co. Am. scholarship, 1962-64; Foundry Ednl. Found. scholarship, 1963-64; U.S. Bur. Mines grad. fellowship, 1964-65. Mem. Am. Soc. for Metals, Am. Welding Soc., ASME, Tex. Soc. of Profl. Engrs., Nat. Soc. of Profl. Engrs., Am. Defense Preparedness Assn., Am. Security Council, Sigma Xi, Tau Beta Pi (past pres.), Theta Tau, Alpha Sigma Mu, Pi Mu Epsilon, Sigma Pi Sigma. Baptist. Clubs: Masons, Gideons Internat., Am. Legion, Magna Carta Barons, Order of the Stars and Bars, Order of Washington. Holder of patent in field. Home: 6206 Leprechaun Dr Corpus Christi TX 78413

LAMPLEY, WILLIAM ROBERT, JR., public accountant; b. Memphis, Sept. 23, 1924; s. William Robert and Audrey Miller (Hoy) L.; grad. accounting, Memphis Sch. of Commerce, 1947; m. Marjorie Christine Achord, Aug. 31, 1943; children—Mary Rebecca (Mrs. James Logan Fortner II), William Robert III, Deborah Sue, Chris Jolene. Partner firm Lampley & Lampley, Memphis, 1950—. Mem. adminstrv. com. Tenn. Bd. Accountancy, 1966-69, vice chmn., 1968-69; chmn. Council for Profl. Devel. in Accountancy, 1978-79; mem. Accreditation Council for Accountancy, sec.-treas., 1973-74. Vice pres. Memphis Youth Symphony, 1972-73; treas. Indsl. Devel. Pollution Control Bd., Memphis, 1973—; active Explorers Chickasaw Council Boy Scouts Am., 1961-73. Served with AC, AUS, 1943-46. Named Outstanding Public Acct. in Tenn., 1965-66. Mem. Nat. Soc. Pub. Accountants (pres. 1976-77), Tenn. Assn. Pub. Accountants (pres. 1968-69). Mem. Pentecostal Ch. (sec. bd. deacons 1958-72). Optimist (pres. 1971-72). Home: 3594 Forrest Av Memphis TN 38122 Office: 3590 Forrest Av Memphis TN 38122

LAMY, MARY REBECCA, govt. ofcl.; b. Ft. Bragg, N.C., Nov. 21, 1929; d. Charles Joseph and Sarah Esther (Koonce) L.; B.A., U. N.C., Greensboro, 1952. Procurement analyst Air Force MIPR Mgmt. Office, Washington, 1958-60, procurement and fiscal officer, 1960-68; budget analyst Naval Air Systems Command, Washington, 1968-69, indsl. specialist, 1969-71; indsl. specialist A.D.T.C., Eglin AFB, Fla., 1971-74, Def. Logistics Agy., Alexandria, Va., 1974—. Recipient Outstanding Performance awards U.S. Air Force, 1956, 65, 72, 73, 79; Quality award Def. Logistics Agy., 1979, Outstanding Performance award, 1978, 79; others. Mem. U. N.C. at Greensboro. Alumni Assn. Office: Def Logistics Agy Cameron Sta Alexandria VA 22314

LAMZA, BILL GUS, JR., metals co. exec.; b. Floresville, Tex., Dec. 21, 1942: s. Gus Raymond and Willie Mae (Kelley) L.; student U. Houston, 1961-63, McMurray Coll., 1963, U. Md., 1964; m. Mary Catherine Chismar, Sept. 20, 1975; 1 son, Marc Kelley. With Standard Metals div. Azcon Co., Houston, 1971—, sales rep., 1972-74, asso. products mgr., 1974-77, products mgr., 1977-79; v.p. spl. products div. Engring. Metals, Houston, 1979—. Served with USAF, 1963-67. Mem. Am. Prodn. and Inventory Control Soc., Purchasing Mgmt. Assn. Houston, Steel Buyers Group. Baptist. Club: Inside Running Joggin. Home: 2010 Quail Valley E Dr Missouri City TX 77459 Office: Engring Metals Spl Products 16337 Park Row Houston TX 77084

LANASA, JOSEPH ALOYSIUS, JR., physician; b. New Orleans, Nov. 5, 1942; s. Joseph Aloysiusand Leola (Dalton) LaN.; B.S., U. Notre Dame, 1964; M.D., La. State U., 1968; m. Wanda Anne Garcia, June 15, 1968; children—Joseph Aloysius III, Connie Lee, Jonathan. Intern, Charity Hosp., New Orleans, 1968-69, resident in urology, 1971-75; fellow in infertility UCLA, others, 1975; mem. faculty La. State U. Med. Center, New Orleans, 1975—, asso. prof. urology, 1979—, acting head dept. urology, dir. fertility lab. and semen bank, 1979—. Served with AUS, 1969-71. Diplomate Am. Bd. Urology. Mem. Am. Urol. Assn., La. Urol. Assn. (pres. 1976-77), Am. Fertility Soc., La. State U. Urology Alumni Assn. (pres. 1977—), So. Med. Assn., Am. Soc. Andrology, Notre Dame Club New Orleans. Democrat. Roman Catholic. Home: 6220 Perlita Dr New Orleans LA 70122 Office: 2025 Gravier St New Orleans LA 70112

LANATA, GASTON ANTHONY, wholesale distbg. co. exec.; b. New Orleans, July 24, 1940; s. Gaston Anthony and Verna (Taylor) L.; student Spring Hill Coll., Mobile, Ala., Syracuse U.; m. Royce Elizabeth Payne, Dec. 19, 1960. Ops. mgr. Uniroyal stores Uniroyal Merchandising Co., Houston, 1970-75; gen. mgr. Capital Equipment Co., Little Rock, 1975-77; v.p. sales Stihl Southwest, Inc., Malvern, Ark., 1977—, The Power-Edge Corp., Malvern, 1977—. Served with USN, 1960-64. Republican. Roman Catholic. Office: Stihl Southwest Inc Hwy 270 W PO Box 518 Malvern AR 72104

LANCASTER, CARROLL TOWNES, JR., assn. exec.; b. Waco, Tex., Mar. 14, 1929; s. Carroll T. and Beatrice (Hollaman) L.; student U. Tex., 1948-51, 52-53; m. Catherine Virginia Frommel, May 29, 1954; children—Loren Thomas, Barbara, Beverly, John Tracy. Sales coordinator Union Tank div. Butler Mfg. Co., Houston, 1954-56, sales rep., New Orleans, 1956-57, br. mgr., 1957-60; asst. to exec. v.p. Maloney-Crawford Mfg. Co., Tulsa, 1960-62; marketing cons., sr. asso. Market/Product Facts, Tulsa, 1962-63; market devel. asst. Norriseal Controls div. Dover Corp., Houston, 1963-66; area dir. Arthritis Found., Houston, 1966-69, dir. S.W. div., 1969-70; exec. dir. United Cerebral Palsy Tex. Gulf Coast, 1971-74; exec. dir. Leukemia Soc. Am., Gulf Coast, 1974-76, Lancaster & Assos., 1976—. Christian edn. tchr., 1966-70, supr., 1971, asst. youth football coach, Bellaire, 1967-68, 70-71. Mem. Houston-Galveston Area Health Commn. Study Group, 1972-76; dir., essayist Tex. Low Vision Council, 1976-79, sec.-treas., 1978—; del. Houston Interfaith Sponsoring Com., 1979—. Bd. dirs. Council Chs. of Greater Houston, 1966-68, v.p., 1968. Served with USNR, 1946-48, 51-52. Recipient award for securing free blood for indigent Harris County Hosp. Dist., 1968. Mem. Am. Mktg. Assn., Huguenot Soc., Delta Sigma Phi. Episcopalian (vestryman 1975-78). Home: 4901 Holly St Bellaire TX 77401 Office: PO Box 745 Bellaire TX 77401

LANCASTER, JAMES WILLIAM, physician; b. Sunflower, Miss., Dec. 29, 1918; s. John Thomas and Elizabeth Wilson (Butler) L.; B.S., Millsaps Coll., 1940; M.D., Tulane U., 1950; m. Claudia Mary Sneed, Jan. 29, 1945; children—James William, Thomas Brooks, Jane Sneed. Intern, Yale U., 1950-51, resident in pediatrics, 1951-53; pvt. practice medicine, specializing in pediatrics, Coral Gables, Fla., 1953-72, Stuart, Fla., 1972—; mem. staff Martin Meml. Hosp., Ft. Pierce Meml. Hosp. Served with USNR, 1942-46. Diplomate Am. Bd. Pediatrics. Fellow Am. Acad. Pediatrics. Democrat. Episcopalian. Mem. editorial bd. Pediatrics, 1964-70. Home: 8 Middle Rd High Point Jensen Beach FL 33457 Office: 308 Hospital Ave Stuart FL 33494

LANCASTER, JOANNE RUSSELL, legal assistance orgn. ofcl.; b. Raleigh, N.C., Mar. 31, 1938; d. Robert Milton and Lillian Russell (Stuart) Clements; student Trident Tech. Sch., 1975-77, Baptist Coll., Charleston, S.C., 1978—; m. Rondel Alexander Lancaster, Dec. 20, 1975; children by previous marriage—Debra Ann Kerce Jones, Spencer Tracy Kerce, Jr. Sec., 1st. Baptist Ch., Johns Island, S.C., 1963-65, tchr. kindergarten, 1966-67; legal sec. Office of John C. Conway, Charleston, S.C., 1974; clk.-typist Profl. Staff Office, Med U. S.C., Charleston, 1974-75; clk. County of Charleston, 1967-73, ct. reporter, sec. to master in equity County of Charleston, 1975-76; adminstrv. sec. Neighborhood Legal Assistance Program, Inc., Charleston, 1976-79, program adminstrv. sec., 1977-79, adminstrv. sec., Summerville, S.C., 1979—. Mem. Charleston County Legal Secs. Assn. (sec. 1978-79). Baptist. Clubs: Ladies Aux. Am. Legion, Lakewood Ranches Ladies Aux. Home: Route 4 Lot 2 Lakewood Ranches Moncks Corner SC 29461 Office: Neighborhood Legal Assistance Program 905 N Main St Summerville SC

LANCASTER, LARRY EUGENE, nursing educator; b. Cadiz, Ky., July 22, 1946; s. Otis H. and Ruby R. (Ezell) L.; A.A., Henderson Community Coll., 1967; B.S. in Nursing, U. Evansville, 1970; M.S. in Nursing, Vanderbilt U., 1971. Head nurse surg. unit Jennie Stuart Meml. Hosp., Hopkinsville, Ky., 1967-68; staff nurse Welborn Meml. Bapt. Hosp., Evansville, Ind., 1968-70; instr. Hopkinsville Community Coll., 1971-72; dir. nursing services Muhlenberg Community Hosp., Greenville, Ky., 1972-73; clin. dir. nursing St. Thomas Hosp., Nashville, 1973-74; instr. (part-time) med.-surg. nursing Vanderbilt U. Sch. Nursing, Nashville, 1973-74, instr., 1974-76, asst. prof. med.-surg. nursing, 1976-79, asso. prof., 1979—; clin. specialist dialysis Vanderbilt U. Hosp., Nashville, 1974-77, nursing coordinator of continuing edn., 1977-78, clin. specialist nephrology, 1978—; cons. and lectr. renal disease U. Tenn., Nashville, 1976—. Bd. dirs. Middle Tenn. Kidney Found., 1975-79, med. adv. com., 1975-76, co-chairperson profl. edn. com., 1976-77. Mem. Am. Nurses Assn., Am. Assn. Nephrology Nurses and Technicians (exec. council 1977-78), Sigma Theta Tau. Episcopalian. Author: (with others) The Patient with End Stage Renal Disease, 1979; editorial bd. Nephrology Nurse, 1978—. Home: 925 Todd Preis Dr Nashville TN 37221 Office: Vanderbilt U Sch Nursing Nashville TN 37240

LANCE, HAROLD VAN NESS, folding carton co. exec.; b. Holmsburg, Pa., Mar. 15, 1944; s. Joseph and Mabel (Malone) L.; B.S. in Acctg. (Coll. scholar), LaSalle Coll., 1966; M.B.A. (U.S. Army grantee), Tex. A&I U., 1973; m. F. Mae Willis, May 28, 1966; children—Harold Van Ness, II, Adrianne, Derrick, Jonathan. Commd. 2d lt. U.S. Army, 1966, advanced through grades to capt., 1968; comdr. F.A. unit, Vietnam, 1968-69; ret., 1976; with Container Corp. Am., Arlington, Tex., 1976—, field sales mgr., 1978-79, sales mgr. folding carton, 1979—; pres. Internat. Product Devel. Co.; mgmt. cons.; guest lectr. mgmt. U. Tex., Arlington. Decorated Bronze Star with V device, Air medal with 2 oak leaf clusters, Army Commendation medal, Purple Heart; named Dir. of Yr. and Dist. Speak Up Champ Jaycees, 1975, Instr. of Yr. Regional ROTC, 1976. Mem. Mgmt. Inst. Am., Res. Officers Assn., Kappa Alpha Psi (life). Republican. Roman Catholic. Office: 925 Ave H E Arlington TX 76010

LANCIANO, CLAUDE OLWEN, JR., author; b. Phila., June 12, 1922; s. Claude Olwen and Cathryn (Conte) L.; student U.S. Naval Acad., 1940-43; B.S. in Social Sci. with distinction, Am. U., 1949; postgrad. Case Inst., 1961, Coll. William and Mary, 1961-62, U.S. Army Mgmt. Sch., 1969; m. Arline Scheibel, June 8, 1943; children—Claude Olwen III, Sheran, Scott, Darwin. Nautical scientist U.S. Naval Hydrographic Office, Suitland, Md., 1945-49; intelligence analyst Office Naval Intelligence, Washington, 1949-50; transp. research engr. Dept. Army, Ft. Eustis, Va., 1951-59, ops. research analyst, 1959-70; author: Manual of Ice Seamanship, 1948; Legends of Lands End, 1971; Capt. John Sinclair of Virginia, 1973, Rosewell, Garland of Virginia, 1978; cons. cargo handling, transp. systems. Mem. Gloucester (Va.) Hist. Bicentennial Publs. Com., 1975. Served with USN, 1940-43, to lt. comdr. U.S. Maritime Ser., 1943-45; ETO, Middle East. Recipient Distinguished Service award Chief of Transp. Dept. Army, 1960. Mem. Nat. Def. Transp. Assn. Club: Ruritan. Editor: Radio Navigational Aids, 1947, inventor trapped air life preserver, 1957, telescopic hose, 1958, paddle thrust propellor, 1959. Home and Office: PO Box 370 Gloucester VA 23061

LAND, JANE MOODY, musician, educator; b. Richmond, Va., Dec. 7, 1923; d. Earle C. and Carrie M. (Franck) Moody; B.S. in Music Edn., Madison Coll., 1946; postgrad. U. Va., 1958, Va. Commonwealth U., 1968-69; m. Weldon Bell Land, Apr. 27, 1951; children—Carolyn Johnson, Susan. Dir. music Highland Springs Schs., Henrico County, Va., 1944-45; tchr. Richmond Bus. Sch., 1946-47; dir. music Chesterfield County (Va.) Public Schs., 1947-49, Manchester High Sch., 1950-51; dir. music Clarke County (Va.) Public Schs., 1950-51; social worker youth service Dept. Welfare and Instns., Richmond, Va., 1951-53; dir. music Spotsylvania County (Va.), 1958-61; pvt. tchr. piano, organ, voice, Richmond, 1946-50, St. Simons Island, Ga., 1956-58, Fredericksburg, Va., 1958-71, Richmond, 1976—; tchr., adminstr. Land Sch. Music, Richmond, 1971—; organist Madison Coll., 1941-45; organist, choir dir. Christ Episcopal Ch., Richmond, 1940-41; organist Scottish Rite, Christmas season, 1942-56; organist Christ Episcopal Ch., St. Simons Island, Ga., 1956-58. Treas., Duntreath Civic Assn., 1979-80. Mem. Am. Guild Organists, Nat. Guild Piano Tchrs. (area chmn.), AAUW. Lutheran. Home: 906 Regester Pkwy Richmond VA 23226

LAND, NORVIS GLENDON, mortgage banker; b. Richland Springs, Tex., June 9, 1931; s. R. V. and Lois Elizabeth L.; B.S. in Animal Husbandry, Tex. A&M U., 1954; m. Beverly Smith, Sept. 11, 1951; children—Leigh Ann, Linda Kay. Asst. sec. El Campo (Tex.) Prodn. Credit Assn., 1956-60; asst. v.p. Fed. Intermediate Credit Bank Houston, 1960-67, sr. v.p., New Orleans, 1970—; exec. v.p., gen. mgr. Agrl. Livestock Fin. Corp., Houston, 1968-70. Served to 1st lt. USAF, 1954-56. Baptist. Club: Rotary. Home: 4001 S Post Oak Ave New Orleans LA 70114 Office: 860 St Charles Ave New Orleans LA 70130

LANDAU, SOL, clergyman, educator; b. Berlin, Germany, June 21, 1920; s. Ezekiel and Helene (Grynberg) L.; B.A., Bklyn. Coll., 1949; M.Hebrew Lit., Rabbi, Jewish Theol. Sem., 1951, D.D., 1977; M.A., N.Y. U., 1958; Ph.D., Fla. State U., 1977; m. Gabriela Mayer, Jan. 14, 1951; children—Ezra M., Tamara A. Rabbi, 1951; rabbi Whitestone (N.Y.) Hebrew Center, 1952-56; co-rabbi Park Synagogue, Cleve., 1956-60, 63-65; rabbi Beth Hillel Congregation, Wilmette, Ill., 1960-63, Beth David Congregation, Miami, Fla., 1965—. Chaplain Homestead Air Force Base, 1974-77; adj. prof. psychology U. Miami, 1979—. Pres., Dade County Mental Health Assn., 1973—; pres. Dade County Youth Adv. Bd. Served with AUS, 1942-45. Recipient Jerusalem award, citation City Miami, award Dade County Mental Health Assn.; Rabbinic Community award Fedn. Welfare Council, 1976. Mem. Rabbinical Assembly (pres. S.E. Region), Rabbinical Assn. Greater Miami (pres. 1977-78), AAUP, Am. Personnel and Guidance Assn., Adult Edn. Assn., Jewish War Vets., Am. Jewish Com. Author: Christian-Jewish Relations; Length of Our Days; Bridging Two Worlds. Home: 13050 SW 71st Ave Miami FL 33156 Office: 2625 SW 3d Ave Miami FL 33129

LANDER, JOEL RICHARD, oil co. exec.; b. Dallas, Dec. 19, 1923; s. Joel Samuel and Dorothy Paralee (Utley) L.; B.S., Tex. A&M U., 1948; m. Francie Maurice Shannon, June 17, 1950; children—Pamela Anne, Shannon Renee, Joel Klein. Tech. service engr., supr. process ops., head process dept. Exxon U.S.A., Baytown, Tex., 1960-63, head. mech. dept., 1963-71, head lab. dept., 1971—. Commr. Sam Houston dist. Boy Scouts Am., 1967-70; pres. East Harris County (Tex.) Community Chest, 1969-70; mem. Baytown City Council, 1971-79, mayor pro tem, 1973-79. Served with Airborne Inf., U.S. Army, 1943-46. Decorated Bronze Star; registered profl. engr., Tex. Mem. Am. Inst. Chem. Engrs. Episcopalian. Club: Kiwanis. Home: 102 Woodside St Baytown TX 77520 Office: Exxon USA PO Box 3950 Baytown TX 77520

LANDERS, RONALD WAYNE, fin. co. exec.; b. Altus, Okla., Mar. 4, 1946; s. Ernest Cecil and Lola Christine (Hickey) L.; student Paris Jr. Coll., 1964-66; B.B.A., E. Tex. State U., 1969, postgrad. 1976—; m. Milly Gale Igo, Mar. 29, 1969; children—Mara Kristia, Christian Dane. With Vought Corp., Dallas, 1969—, pricing acct., 1971-74, sr. contracts adminstr., 1974—. Pres., Area VI Assn. Future Farmers Am., 1963; pres. Paris Dist., Future Farmers Am., 1962. Recipient Santa Fe R.R. Ednl. award, 1963; Sears Roebuck Found. award, 1963. Mem. Nat. Contract Mgmt. Assn., Beta Gamma Sigma. Baptist. Home: 5723 Overridge Ct Arlington TX 76017 Office: PO Box 225907 Dallas TX 75265

LANDGRAF, NANCY KAREN, environ. planning adminstr.; b. Boston, Nov. 17, 1942; d. Grosvenor Wardwell and Lillian Reta (Orechia) Fish; B.S. in Math., U. Mass., 1964; postgrad. U. Ala., 1970, U. Louisville, 1969, U. Detroit, 1964. Tchr. math. Baker High Sch., Columbus, Ga., 1964; instr. math. U.S. Army Edn. Center, Mainz, Germany, 1965-66, asst. adminstr., examiner, 1966-67; planning analyst City of Sarasota, Fla., 1967-68; asst. planner Louisville and Jefferson County Planning Commn., 1968-69; prin. planner West Ala. Planning and Devel. Council, Tuscaloosa, 1969-74, dir. spl. planning, 1975—. Mem. planning commn. Girls Ranch, Ala., 1971-72. Named Young Distinguished Woman of Tuscaloosa, Jaycettes, 1972. Mem. Am. Planning Assn., Nat. Assn. Regional Councils, League Women Voters, Humane Soc., Chi Omega. Episcopalian. Clubs: Tuscaloosa Kennel, Soroptimist Internat., Bus. and Profl. Women. Home: 92 Cherokee Shores Northport AL 35476 Office: West Ala Planning and Devel Council Mcpl Airport Terminal 2d Floor Northport AL 35476

LANDMAN, GEORGINA BARBARA, lawyer, educator; b. Miami Beach, Fla., Feb. 16, 1938; d. August Swarz; certificate Sorbonne, U. Paris, France, 1966; B.A., Trinity U., 1967; J.D., U. Denver, 1970; M.A., St. Louis U., 1972; LL.M. (fellow), U. Mo., 1973; certificate U. Montreal, Que., Can., 1967; 1 son by previous marriage, Nathaniel Martin. Admitted to Okla. bar, 1975; law clk. to chief judge of 8th Circuit U.S. Ct. of Appeals, 1970-71; mem. legal staff HUD, St. Louis area office, 1971-72; spl. asst. regional adminstr. U.S. Dept. Justice, Kansas City, Kans., 1972-73; mem. firm Rogers & Bell, Tulsa, 1976-78; partner firm Williams, Landman & Savage, 1978—; asst. prof. law U. Tulsa, 1973-74, asso. prof., 1974-78, asst. dean, 1974-76; cons. Dept. of Community Affairs, State of Mo., 1972-73; cons. on housing Tulsa area Met. Area Planning Commn., 1973-75; cons. on flood-plain zoning, Davenport, Iowa, 1975—; speaker Internat. Congress Environment, Paris, 1976. Mem. exec. bd. Tulsa Citizens Crime Commn., 1977—. U. Tulsa faculty research grantee, 1973—. Mem. Am., Okla., Tulsa bar assns., Am. Assn. of Law Schs., Tulsa Met. C. of C. Contbr. articles on law to profl. jours.; editor Urban Lawyer, 1972-73. Home: 3241 S Troost St Tulsa OK 74105 Office: 324 Main Mall Suite 600 Tulsa OK 74103

LANDRENEAU, RODNEY EDMUND, JR., physician; b. Mamou, La., Jan. 17, 1929; s. Rodney Edmund and Blanche (Savoy) L.; M.D., La. State U., 1951; m. Colleen Fraser, June 4, 1952; children—Rodney Jerome, Michael Douglas, Denise Margaret, Melany Patricia, Fraser Edmund, Edythe Blanche. Intern, Charity Hosp., New Orleans, 1951-52, resident, 1952-54, 56-58; practice medicine specializing in surgery, Eunice, La., 1958—; pres., dir. Eunice Med. Center, Inc., 1960—; mem. staff Moosa Meml. Hosp. Eunice, 1958—, chief med. staff; vis. staff Opelousas Gen. Hosp., 1958—; asso. faculty La. State U.-Eunice; cons., staff Lafayette (La.) Charity Hosp. cons. staff surgery Savoy Meml. Hosp., Mamon, La.; pres. Eunice Med. Center Inc.; dir. Acadiana Bank & Trust Co. Mem. La. State Hosp. Bd., 1972—; mem. Evangeline council Boy Scouts Am. Served M.C., AUS, 1954-56. Recipient Physician's Recognition award AMA, 1978. Diplomate Am. Bd. Surgery. Fellow Internat. Coll. Surgeons, A.C.S., (local chmn. com. trauma), Southeastern Surg. Congress, Pan Pacific Surg. Congress; mem. Am. Bd. Abdominal Surgeons, Am. Geriatrics Soc., St. Edmunds Athletic Assn., St. Landry Hist. Soc. (v.p. chpt.), St. Landry Parish Med. Soc. (pres. 1969-71), Am. Legion, S.C.V., S.A.R., Alpha Omega Alpha. Democrat. Roman Catholic. Home: 1113 Williams St Eunice LA 70535 Office: 301 N Duson St Eunice LA 70535

LANDRESS, HARVEY J., social agy. exec.; b. N.Y.C., Dec. 6, 1946; s. Jack and Anne L.; B.A., SUNY, Binghamton, 1968, cert. in S.W. Asian, N. African studies, 1968, M.A. (U. teaching fellow), 1973; postgrad. (Fulbright-Hayes fellow), Gujarat U., India, 1971; M.S.W., U. Louisville, 1975; m. Susan Rae Sanges, Dec. 28, 1974. U.S. Peace Corps vol., Kangavar, Iran, 1968-70; adj. instr. polit. sci. U. Ky., Ft. Knox, 1973-76; juvenile counselor State Ky. Dept. for Human Resources, Hodgenville, 1973-74, social worker, Elizabethtown, 1975-76; social worker dept. neuropsychiatry Ireland Army Hosp., Ft. Knox, 1975; asst. prof. social work St. Leo (Fla.) Coll., 1976-79; adj. instr. criminal justice U. S. Fla., Tampa and St. Petersburg, 1979—; dir. program planning and devel. PAR Comprehensive Drug Abuse Programs, St. Petersburg, 1979—; cons. Pasco-Pinellas Public Defenders Office, 1978, Fla. Dept. Health and Rehabilitative Services, 1977—; group leader Expt. in Internat. Living, Sweden, 1978. Chmn., Fla. Coalition on Migrant Action, 1978-79. Recipient Outstanding Faculty Mem. award St. Leo Coll., 1979; Humanitarian award Dade City (Fla.) Community Action Agy., 1979; cert. social worker, Ky. Mem. Acad. Cert. Social Workers, Nat. Assn. Social Workers (sec. Fla. chpt. 1979—, editor local newsletter 1977-79), United Faculty of Fla.-AFL/CIO (1st v.p. St. Leo chpt. 1977-79), AAUP (chmn. St. Leo chpt. 1978-79), Common Cause (chmn. 5th Congressional Dist. Ky. 1973-75), Fla. Assn. Drug Abuse Treatment and Edn. Programs, Fla. Council for Community Mental Health, Pinellas Mental Health Assn. Democrat. Jewish. Editor Image: Jour. Creative Photography, 1968. Home: PO Box 2354 Saint Leo FL 33574 Office: PAR Comprehensive Drug Abuse Program 2620 5th Ave N Saint Petersburg FL 33713

LANDRETH, JACKIE, furniture retail co. exec.; b. Greensboro, N.C., Aug. 7, 1943; d. James Robert and Georgia Bessie Snyder; grad. high sch., 1961; 1 dau., Linda Carol Roberson. Founder Colfax Furniture, Greensboro, N.C., 1964, pres., 1964—, stores in Greensboro and Kernersville, N.C. Mem. Greensboro C. of C., Better Bus. Bur., Mchts. Assn. Club: Greensbo Woman's Forum. Office: 3501 McCuiston Ct Greensboro NC 27407

LANDRIEU, MOON, former mayor; b. New Orleans, July 23, 1930; s. Joseph and Loretta L.; B.B.A., Loyola U., 1952, LL.B., 1954; m. Verna Satterlee, Sept. 25, 1954; children—Mary, Mark, Melanie, Michelle, Mitchell, Madeleine, Martin, Melinda, Maurice. Atty. firm

Landrieu, Calogero & Kronlage, 1957-70; mayor City of New Orleans, 1970-77; pres. Joseph C. Canizaro, New Orleans, 1977-79; sec. HUD, 1979—. Mem. La. Ho. of Reps., 1960-66; councilman, New Orleans, 1966-70. Served with AUS, 1954-57. Democrat. Roman Catholic.

LANDRON, JOSÉ MANUEL, personnel exec.; b. Santurce, P.R., Feb. 4, 1936; s. José M. and Blanca R. (Villamil) L.; B.S., Clemson U., 1963; m. Judith A. Baralt, Oct. 5, 1974; children—Lindy Aurora, Bianca Alexandra. Engring. trainee Ralston Purina Co., Oklahoma City, 1963; regional dir. Economic Devel. Adminstr., Arecibo, P.R., 1964-68; personnel mgr. Blue Bell of P.R., Inc., Mayaguez, 1968; regional dir. Cooperative Devel. Adminstrn., Arecibo, P.R., 1969-71; personnel mgr., pub. relations dir. Caribe Motors Rio Piedras, P.R., 1971-73; dir. adminstrn. ITT Aetna Corp., Hato Rey, P.R., 1973-74; dir. indsl. relations Gulf and Western Caguas, P.R., 1974; personnel mgr., asst. dir. Personnel Div., Matsushita Electric of P.R., Rio Piedras, P.R., 1975—; instr. govt. employee program P.R. Office Labor Relations, 1979—; mem. evaluation com. P.R. Pvt. Industry Council, 1979—; mem. P.R. Vocat. Tng. Council, 1979—. Active various charitable orgns.; vice chmn. Pvt. Industry Council, Nat. Alliance Businessmen; advisor, Jr. Achievement, 1971-72. Recipient United Funds Award of Merit, 1972; citation, Jr. Achievement of P.R., 1970-71; named Employer's Rep. for the Year, Sec. of Edn. of P.R., 1972. Mem. Am. Soc. Personnel Adminstrn., Profl. Soc. for Accident Prevention of P.R., Engrs. Soc. for Accident Prevention. Roman Catholic. Club: Rotary. Author: Manual for Personnel Procedures, 1972; Responsibilites of Good Supervisors, 1972; contbr. articles in field to profl. jours. Home: 44 St 707 Fairview Rio Piedras PR 00926 Office: PO Box 184 Caguas PR 00625

LANDRUM, CARROL FRAZIER, physician; b. nr. Taylorsville, Miss., Apr. 3, 1926; s. Joseph David and Emma Elizabeth (Meadows) L.; student Perkinston Jr. Coll., 1946-47; B.S., Millsaps Coll., 1948; M.D., Tulane U., 1952; postgrad. in pediatrics Harvard, 1969-75, 76—; grad. Billy Graham Sch. Evangelism. Intern, Brooke Gen. Hosp., Ft. Sam Houston, Tex., 1952-53; practice medicine, Biloxi, Miss., 1954-58, Smith County, Miss., 1958-59, Edwards, Miss., 1959—. Served to capt. USAF, 1952-54. Mem. Internat. Platform Assn., Nat. Soc. Lit and Arts. Baptist. Mason (Shriner), Rotarian. Research in causes of malignant diseases. Home: PO Box 198 Edwards MS 39066

LANDRUM, SAMUEL EDWARD, surgeon; b. Martin, Tenn., Jan. 16, 1935; s. Lester Hawkins and Grace Newman (Killgore) L.; M.D., U. Tenn., 1956; m. Sara Annette Vaughn, July 5, 1955; children—Leslie, John, Janet, Emily. Intern, Druid City Hosp., Tuscaloosa, Ala., 1956-57; resident in surgery Henry Ford Hosp., Detroit, 1957-61; staff surgeon Sparks Hosp., St. Edward Mercy Hosp., Ft. Smith, Ark., 1963—; cons. Ark. Vocat. Rehab. Service; chmn. Ark. Emergency Med. Services Council, 1975—; expert lectr. emergency med. services. Served with M.C., U.S. Army, 1961-63. Fellow A.C.S. (trauma achievement award 1976); mem. S.W. Surg. Congress, Ark. Med. Soc., Am. Burn Assn. Methodist. Club: Town, Ft. Smith. Home: 11 Riverlyn Dr Fort Smith AR 72903 Office: 522 S 16th St Fort Smith AR 72901

LANDRY, ANDRE MYRTON, JR., educator; b. Opelousas, La., Sept. 12, 1945; s. Andre Myrton and Marie Beah (Andrepont) L.; student U.S. Naval Acad., 1964-66; B.S., Tulane U., 1968; Ph.D., Tex. A. and M. U., 1977, M.S., 1971; m. Lee Ann Day, July 9, 1966; children—Andre Myrton III, Honor Baylissa, Peter Day, Jacques Yves. Grad. research asst. Tex. A. and M. U., College Station, 1968-73, instr., 1975-77, asst. prof. dept. marine biology, 1977—; environ. cons. NUS Corp., Houston, 1973-75; Player agt. Little League Baseball, LaMarque, Tex., 1979; athletic dir. Tex. Youth Football, LaMarque, 1979. Served with USN, 1964-67. Named Tchr. of Yr., Galveston Island Rotary Club, 1979. Mem. AAAS, Am. Fisheries Soc., Am. Inst. Fisher' Research Biologists, Am. Soc. Ichthyologists and Herpetologists, Soc. Limnology and Oceanography, Tex. Acad. Sci., Sigma Xi, Phi Kappa Phi, Phi Sigma. Democrat. Roman Catholic. Contbr. articles to profl. jours.; researcher in fisheries scis. Home: 1304 Red Bud Ln LaMarque TX 77568 Office: Dept Marine Biology Tex A and M Univ PO Box 1675 Galveston TX 77550

LANDRY, TOM, profl. football coach; b. Mission, Tex., Sept. 11, 1924; grad. U. Tex.; degree indsl. engring. U. Houston, 1952; m. Alicia Landry; children—Tom, Kitty, Lisa. Player, N.Y. Yankees All-Am. Football Conf., 1949; player N.Y. Giants, 1950-53, player-coach, 1954-55, defensive coach, 1956-59; head coach Dallas Cowboys, 1960—. First v.p. Nat. Fellowship Christian Athletes, chmn. bd. Dallas chpt.; bd. govs. Dallas Town North YMCA. Served with USAAF, World War II. Named to All-Pro team, 1954. Methodist. Office: care Dallas Cowboys 6116 North Central Expy Dallas TX 75206*

LANDY, BURTON AARON, lawyer; b. Chgo., Aug. 16, 1929; s. Louis J. and Clara (Ernstein) L.; B.S., Northwestern U., 1950; J.D., U. Miami, 1952; student Nat. U. Mexico, 1948; scholar U. Havana, 1951; fellow Inter-Am. Acad. Comparative Law, Havana, Cuba, 1955-56; m. Eleonora M. Simmel, Aug. 4, 1957; children—Michael Simmel, Alisa Anne. Admitted to Fla. bar, 1952; gen. practice law in internat. field, Miami, 1955—; partner law firm Ammerman & Landy, 1957-63, Paul, Landy & Beiley and predecessor firm, 1964—; lectr. Latin Am. bus. law U. Miami Sch. Law, 1972-75, also Internat. Law Confs. Mem. Nat. Conf. on Fgn. Aspects of U.S. Nat. Security, Washington, 1958; mem. organizing com. Miami regional conf. Com. for Internat. Econ. Growth, 1958; mem. U.S. Dept. Commerce Regional Export Expansion Council, 1969-74, mem. Dist. Council, 1978—; mem. Fla. Council Internat. Devel., 1977—; mem. exec. com. U. Miami Citizens Bd., 1977—; chmn. Fla.-S.E. U.S.-Japan Assn.; mem. adv. com. 1st Miami Trade Fair of Ams., 1978; dir., sec. Greater Miami Fgn. Trade Zone, Inc. Mem. organizing com., lectr. 4 Inter-Am. Aviation Law Confs. Dir. Inter-Am. Bar Legal Found. Participant Aquaculture Symposium Sci. and Man of the Ams., Mexico City, Fla. Gov.'s Econ. Mission to Japan and Hong Kong, 1978; mem. bd. exec. adviser, internat. adv. bd. U. Miami Sch. Bus.; mem. internat. fin. council Office Comptroller U. Fla. Served with USAF Judge Adv. Gen. Dept., 1952-54, in Korea, 1953-54; maj. USAF Res. Hon. mem. Bar of Republic of South Korea, 1954. Mem. Inter-Am. (asst. sec.-gen. 1957-59, treas. 11th conf. 1959, co-chmn. jr. bar sect. 1963-65, mem. council 1969—, exec. com. 1975—), Am. (chmn. com. arrangements internat. and comparative law sect. 1964-65), Spanish-Am., Fla. (vice chmn. administrv. law com. 1965, vice chmn. internat. and comparative law com. 1967-68, chmn. aero. law com. 1968-69), Dade County (chmn. fgn. laws and langs. com. 1964-65) bar assns., Internat. Center, World Peace Through Law Center (pres.-elect), Miami Com. on Fgn. Relations, Instituto Ibero Americano de Derecho Aeronautico, Am. Soc. Internat. Law, Asociacion Latino Americana de Derecho Aeronautico, Reencuentro Cubano, Council Internat. Visitors, Am. Fgn. Law Assn. (pres. Miami 1958), Greater Miami C. of C., Phi Alpha Delta. Contbg. editor Economic Developments Lawyer of the Americas, 1969-74. Contbr. articles to legal jours. Home: 6255 Old Cutler Rd Miami FL 33156 Office: Penthouse Peninsula Fed Bldg Miami FL 33131

LANE, DANIEL MCNEEL, physician; b. Ft. Sam Houston, Tex., Jan. 25, 1936; s. Samuel Hartman and Mary Maverick (McNeel) L.; student U. Tex., 1953-57; M.D., Southwestern Med. Sch., Dallas, 1961; M.S., U. Tenn., 1967; Ph.D., U. Okla., 1973; m. Carolyn Ann Spruiell, Nov. 28, 1958; children—Linda Ann, Daniel McNeel, Maury Spruiell, Oleta Katherine. Intern, Children's Med. Center, Dallas, 1961-62, resident pediatrics, 1962-63; chief pediatric resident U. Miss., Jackson, 1962-64; fellow hematology U. Tenn., Memphis, 1964-66; asst. prof. pediatrics U. Okla., Oklahoma City, 1966-72; asso. prof. pediatrics Tulane Med. Sch., New Orleans, 1972-73; head hematology-oncology dept., mem. pediatrics dept. Oklahoma City Clinic, 1973-79; dir. clin. investigation Presbyn. Hosp., Oklahoma City, 1975-77; pvt. practice medicine specializing in hematology-oncology, Oklahoma City, 1979—; chmn. bd. Poplar Pike, Inc., Realtors, Memphis, 1972—. Nat. trustee Nat. Hemophilia Found., 1966-68, Okla. pres., 1966-67. USPHS fellow pediatric hematology, 1965-66; Nat. Heart and Lung Inst. spl. research fellow, 1969-72. Diplomate Am. Bd. Pediatrics with sub-splty. Bd. Pediatric Oncology-Hematology. Fellow Am. Acad. Pediatrics; mem. Am., Okla. med. assns., Oklahoma County Med. Soc., Am. Soc. Clin. Oncology, Am. Fedn. Clin. Research, So. Soc. Pediatric Research, Am. Assn. Cancer Edn., Am. Soc. Hematology. Club: Oklahoma City Tennis (pres. 1969-72). Contbr. articles to profl. jours. Home: 1504 Guilford Lane Oklahoma City OK 73120 Office: 711 Stanton Young Blvd Suite 604 Oklahoma City OK 73104

LANE, DONALD GERALD, athletic dir.; b. Versailles, Ky., Apr. 12, 1943; s. Raymond Bedford and Mildred (Carr) L.; B.S., Union Coll., 1965; M.A., U. Ky., 1968, Ed.S., 1971; m. Monna Williams, Aug. 6, 1966; children—Brian, Joy. Tchr., basketball coach Mt. Sterling (Ky.) schs., 1965-68, 69-70; asst. basketball coach Union U., 1968-69; tchr., athletic dir., basketball coach Woodford County High Sch., 1970-72; athletic dir., prof. phys. edn., basketball coach Ind. S.E. U., 1975-76; athletic dir., basketball coach Transylvania U., Lexington, Ky., 1972-75, 76—, also dir. basketball camp; dir. dirs. for Ky., Partners for Americas Sports Exchanges. Recipient Outstanding Service award Partners of Americas, 1978, Community award VA Hosp., Lexington, 1979. Mem. Nat. Basketball Coaches Assn., Coll. Athletic Dirs. Assn., Omicron Delta Kappa. Baptist. Office: 300 N Broadway Lexington KY 40508

LANE, EDWARD WOOD, JR., banker; b. Jacksonville, Fla., Apr. 4, 1911; s. Edward Wood and Anna Virginia (Tallaferro) L.; A.B., Princeton, 1933; LL.B., Harvard, 1936; m. Helen Spratt Murchison, Oct. 16, 1948; children—Edward Wood III, Helen Palmer, Anna Tallaferro, Charles Murchison. Admitted to Fla. bar, 1936; partner firm McCarthy, Lane & Adams, and predecessors, Jacksonville, 1941-60; vice-chmn., dir. Atlantic Nat. Bank, Jacksonville; chmn., dir. Atlantic Bancorp, Fla. Pub. Co. Trustee Cummer Museum Found. Served to lt. comdr. USNR, World War II. Mem. Jacksonville Area C. of C. (com. 100), Phi Beta Kappa. Clubs: Florida Yacht, Timuquana Country, River, Univ. (Jacksonville); Sawgrass, Ponte Vedra (Fla.). Home: 3790 Ortega Blvd Jacksonville FL 32210 Office: Atlantic Bancorp Gen Mail Center Jacksonville FL 32231

LANE, FAYE ROGAN, modeling sch. ofcl.; b. Tallulah, La., Jan. 12, 1935; d. George Wheeles and Lettie Elizabeth (Petty) Rogan; student Baton Rouge Bus. Coll., 1954; diploma John Robert Power Modeling Sch., 1955, Patricia Stevens Finishing Sch., 1956; m. Gerald Ray Lane, Mar. 8, 1958; children—Saundra Suzanne, Eric Rogan. Sec. law offices H. Alva Brumfield, Baton Rouge, 1954-58; Internat. Oil Queen (Queen Lagcoe), 1955-56; instr. modeling John Robert Powers Modeling Sch., Baton Rouge, 1956—. Inst., Our Lady of Lake Hosp. Aux., Baton Rouge, 1962-64. Mem. La. State Soc., Magnolia Garden Guild. Republican. Episcopalian. Clubs: Pascagoula Country, Longfellow House, Pascagoula Woman's, Magnolia Garden Guild (sec.). Home: 3204 E Washington Ave Pascagoula MS 39567

LANE, GERALD THOMAS, lumber co. exec.; b. Chester, Pa., July 16, 1950; s. John Dudley and Anna Alberta (Hopkins) L.; B.S. in Bus. Adminstrn., East Carolina U., 1972. Controller, corporate sec. Waterfront Lumber Co. Inc., Waterfront Ship Service Corp., both Newport News, Va., 1972—, also dir. Mem. Inst. Internal Auditors (treas.), U.S. Propeller Club. Republican. Baptist. Club: Hoo Hoo (pres.). Home: 209 Tipton Rd Newport News VA 23606 Office: PO Box 292 Newport News VA 23607

LANE, JAMES MONROE, anesthesiologist; b. Gaffney, S.C., Jan. 17, 1929; s. Bernie Monroe and Virginia Estelle (Gregory) L.; B.S., Davidson Coll., 1950; M.D., Med. U. S.C., 1953; m. Sarah Diane Goodwin, May 10, 1975; children—James Richard, Stuart Paul, Stephen Fuller. Intern, Greenville (S.C.) Gen. Hosp., 1953-54; gen. practice medicine, Kings Mountain, N.C., 1954-55; resident Duke U. Med. Center, Durham, N.C., 1957-59; anesthesiologist Greenville Hosp. System, 1959—. Served to maj. USAF, 1955-57. Diplomate Am. Bd. Anesthesiology. Fellow Am. Coll. Anesthesiology; mem. AMA, Am. Soc. Anesthesiologists, S.C., Greenville County med. assns. Presbyterian. Home: 7 Cunningham Circle Taylors SC 29687 Office: 5 Medical Ct Greenville SC 29601

LANE, JAMES WILLIAM, elec. engr.; b. Sumner, Miss., Sept. 2, 1938; s. Fred Conn and Essie Lee (Tierce) L.; A.A., Miss. Delta Jr. Coll., 1958-60; B.S. in Elec. Engring., Miss. State U., 1965; M.B.A., Miss. Coll., 1978; m. Joyce Ann Rains, May 27, 1959; children—Jim, Jeffrey Alan. Engr. North, Beasley and Swayze, cons. engrs., Jackson, 1966-71; design engr. Leigh Watkins III & Assos., cons. engrs., Jackson, 1971-74; prin. James W. Lane Cons. Engr., 1974—. Active Boy Scouts Am. Recipient Eagle Scout and Silver Explorer award Boy Scouts Am., 1954, God and Country award Sumner (Miss.) Bapt. Ch., 1953. Registered profl. engr., Ala., Miss., Tex., La.; N.C. E.E. Mem. Nat. Soc. Profl. Engrs., Miss. Engring. Soc., Cons. Engring. Council Miss. Baptist. Home: 939 Autumn Dr Jackson MS 39212 Office: 836 Medical Plaza Jackson MS 39204

LANE, JOHN EDWARD, architect, artist, interior designer; b. Chgo., July 29, 1938; s. John Alfred and Leora (Smith) L; B.Arch., U. Ill., Urbana, 1961; m. Margaret Lynn Wilkinson, Dec. 22, 1962; children—Kelly Ann, John Howard (Jay), Tracy Elizabeth. Project architect Leo A. Daly Co., Omaha, 1965-68; evening instr. architecture Tech. Inst., U. Omaha, 1966-67; architect Peckham Guyton Inc., Architects, St. Louis, 1969-71; architect, interior designer L K H & G, Architects, Ft. Smith, Ark., 1972-77; architect Drimmel/McDaniel Assos., Architects, Ft. Smith, 1977-78; partner Lane & Riggs, Architects, Ft. Smith, 1978-79; architect, artist, interior designer Lane & Assos., Architects, Ft. Smith, 1979—; cons. in field. Mem. Nebr. Mgmt. Analysis Study Com., 1966. Served with USNR, 1961-65. Recipient numerous art competition awards for watercolors; cert. Nat. Council Archtl. Registrations Bds.; registered architect Ark., Mo., Nebr., Okla. Mem. AIA (corp., chmn. Ft. Smith sect. 1980), Am. Soc. Interior Designers (profl.). Designer Bicentennial Tower, Greenwood, Ark., 1976. Created bicentennial coin for City of Ft. Smith, 1975. Home: 3900 Fresno St Fort Smith AR 72903 Office: Lane & Assos Architects 1318 N B St PO Box 3929 Fort Smith AR 72913

LANE, JOHN THOMAS, retail exec.; b. Mt. Sterling, Ky., Mar. 7, 1948; s. Douglas Laughlin and Carol (Wolstenholme) L.; B.A. in Acctg., Bellarmine Coll., 1970; m. Michele Shaw, June 7, 1969; children—John Thomas, Brian D., Joel D., Todd S. Staff acct. Henry M. Kaelin, Jr., C.P.A., Louisville, 1968-70; staff acct. W. Frank Allen, C.P.A., Mt. Sterling, 1970-74, partner, 1974-78; controller, treas. Maloney Enterprises, Inc., Mt. Sterling, 1978—. Head coach minor league baseball team; county chmn. blood donor program, 1978—; chmn. Planning and Zoning Adjustment Bd., 1977—; mem. parish council St. Patrick Catholic Ch. Ky. col.; C.P.A., Ky. Mem. Am. Inst. C.P.A.'s, Ky. Soc. C.P.A.'s, Bellarmine Coll. Alumni. Democrat. Club: Kiwanis (v.p. Mt. Sterling 1979—; Kiwanian of Year award 1972). Home: Rural Route 1 Bent Brook Subdiv Mount Sterling KY 40353 Office: Maloney Enterprises Inc Calk Rd Mount Sterling KY 40353

LANE, KEITH ANTON, pharm. co. exec.; b. Borger, Tex., Mar. 23, 1933; s. Keith Anton and Loyce Catherine (Landis) L.; A.A., Frank Phillips Coll., 1953; B.B.A., N. Tex. State U., 1955; postgrad. Mgmt. Devel. Program, Harvard U. Grad. Sch. Bus., 1978—, Imede Sch. Bus. U. Lausanne (Switzerland), 1978; m. Ila Lenore Tollefsen, Oct. 13, 1974; children—Kent, Kimberly, Keith III. Sales rep. Alcon Labs., Inc., Fort Worth, 1959-63, dist. mgr., 1963-68, field sales mgr., 1968-70, nat. sales mgr. splty. div., 1970-71, dir. mktg. Owen div., 1971-73, gen. mgr. Owen div., 1973-7S, corporate v.p. parent co., 1975—, exec. v.p. Owen, Mahdeen, and Cosmetic divs., 1975—; lectr. Tex. Christian U. Grad. Sch. Bus. Named High Sch. All Am. in basketball, 1951. Mem. Am. Mgmt. Assn. (course dir. in sales mgmt.), Phi Kappa Sigma. Baptist. Home: 3013 Overton Park Dr E Fort Worth TX 76109 Office: Alcon Labs Inc PO Box 1959 Fort Worth TX 76101

LANE, KENNETH EUGENE, guidance counselor; b. Shelbyville, Ind., Oct. 15, 1947; s. Hoyt Jesse and Mary Dorena (Hadley) L.; B.S., Ind. State U., 1969; M.Ed., U. Mo., 1973; m. Maury Vi Reardon, June 30, 1973. Tchr., counselor pub. schs., St. Louis, 1969-75; counselor Plano (Tex.) Ind. Sch. Dist., 1975-79, asst. prin., 1979—. Dir. Plano YMCA Day Camp, 1976, Dallas YMCA Camp Grady Spruce, 1977. Mem. NEA, Tex. State Tchrs. Assn., Am., Tex. personnel and guidance assns., Assn. Secondary Counselors Am., Fellowship Christian Athletes (chpt. pres.). Mem. Christian Ch. (Disciples of Christ). Club: Kiwanis of Plano (Tex.). Home: 3505 Marwick St Plano TX 75075 Office: 523 Spring Creek Pkwy Plano TX 75075

LANE, MALCOLM GRAHAM, computer scientist, educator; b. Kew Gardens, N.Y., Nov. 5, 1943; s. Willis DeForest and Anna Helen (Kuhlman) L.; B.S., Davidson Coll., 1965; M.A., Duke, 1968, Ph.D., 1971; m. Maureen Moran, June 25, 1966; children—Melanie Anne, Maura Louise. Staff computer dept. Gen. Electric Co., Charlotte, N.C., 1965, computation center Duke, 1966-67, IBM, Raleigh, N.C., 1968-70; asst. prof. computer sci. W.Va. U., Morgantown, 1971-75, asso. prof., 1975-79, prof., 1979—, asso. chmn., 1977—; cons. in field; pres. Software Systems Inc., Morgantown, 1975—, chmn. bd., 1975—. Served to capt. U.S. Army Res., 1965—. Named outstanding tchr. W.Va. U., 1974; NSF trainee, 1965-70; IBM fellow 1970-71. Mem. Assn. Computing Machinery (nat. lectr. 1973-76, chmn. lectureship com. 1977—), No. W.Va. chpt. Assn. Computing Machinery (founder, chmn. 1975-76), Sigma Xi. Baptist. Contbr. articles to profl. jours. Home: 1280 Colonial Dr Morgantown WV 26505 Office: Dept Statistics and Computer Sci 403 Hodges Hall WVa U Morgantown WV 26506

LANE, MARY CHARLOTTE, coll. dean; b. Corning, N.Y., Nov. 11, 1915; d. Raymond Thomas and Mary Elizabeth (Cole) L.; A.B., Mt. Holyoke Coll., 1937; postgrad. U. Chgo., 1937-41: M.S. in Edn., U. So. Calif., 1970, Ed.D. 1974; D.D. (hon.), Piedmont Coll., 1977. Commd. 2d lt. Women's Army Corps, 1943, advanced through grades to col., 1970, ret., 1971; prof. edn. Piedmont Coll., Demorest, Ga., 1974-78, prof. edn. and religion, 1974—, dean of coll., 1978—; ordained to ministry Congregational Ch., 1977. Decorated Legion of Merit with 2 oak leaf clusters, Army Commendation medal. Mem. Nat. Assn. Women Deans, Adminstrs. and Counselors, Am. Assn. for Higher Edn., Ret. Officers Assn. Author: The Melbo Years: History of the School of Education, University of Southern California, 1953-1973, 1973. Home: Box 606 Demorest GA 30535 Office: Piedmont Coll Demorest GA 30535

LANE, RICHARD NEWTON, physicist, research and devel. co. exec.; b. Eagle Pass, Tex., Feb. 6, 1919; s. William Bartlett and Virginia (Gardner) L.; B.A. U. Tex., Austin, 1940, M.A., 1941; m. Estelle Speed, Apr. 5, 1942; children—William B., Martha, Richard N., Laura. Acoustical engr. RCA, 1941, project engr. sonar sect., 1942-46; research asso. underwater sound lab. Harvard U., 1941-42; project physicist Def. Research Lab., U. Tex., Austin, 1946-48, asst. dir. lab., in charge div. Acoustics, 1950-57; mgr. sect. airborne magnetic surveys Edgar Tobin Aerial Surveys, San Antonio, 1948-49; cons. acoustics, 1950; pres. Tracor. Inc., Austin, 1955-70, chmn. bd. 1955-72; chmn. bd. TCC, Inc., Austin, 1972; pres. Lamac Environs., Inc., Austin, 1972-74; tech. dir. measurements and analysis long range acoustic propagation program Office Naval Research, Arlington, Va., 1974-76; pres. Gruy Fed., Inc., Houston, Arlington, Pitts., Bartlesville, Okla., 1976—; dir. Data Disc, Inc., Am. First Corp.; vis. prof. architecture and planning U. Tex., Austin, 1959-64. Fellow Acoustical Soc. Am.; mem. IEEE, Am. Mgmt. Assn., Phi Beta Kappa, Sigma Xi, Beta Gamma Sigma. Office: 2500 Tanglewilde Suite 150 Houston TX 77063

LANE, ROBERT EDGAR, mfg. co. exec.; b. Kaukauna, Wis., Mar. 29, 1931; s. Herbert John and Mabel T. (Tullis) L.; B.B.A., U. Wis., 1954, M.B.A., 1957; m. Cathy Jo Talarico, Dec. 31, 1962; 1 dau., Deborah Marie. With Johnson Controls, Inc., Georgetown, Ky., 1954—, mgr. ops. research, 1966-68, indsl. engring. group mgr., 1968-73, material control mgr., 1973-77, ops. mgr., Georgetown facilities, 1977—; instr. Milw. Tech. Coll., 1971-72; lectr. in field. Adv. council on curriculum Milw. Area Tech. Coll., 1972-77, Milw. Sch. Engring., 1974-77, Waukesha (Wis.) Area Tech. Coll., 1975-77. Mem. Am. Inst. Indsl. Engrs. (chpt. pres 1976-77), Milw. Prodn. and Methods Engrs. (pres. 1958-59), Georgetown Coll. Assos., Soc. Prodn. and Methods Engrs., Inst. Mgmt. Sci., Am. Soc. Inventory and Prodn. Control. Republican. Author: Administering and Controlling Plant Operations, 1979; contbr. articles in field to profl. jours. Home: 1628 Linstead Dr Lexington KY 40504 Office: Route 4 Georgetown KY 40324

LANE, WALTER RONALD, JR., advt. and mktg. exec.; b. Wilmington, N.C., Sept. 2, 1940; s. Walter Ronald and Dorothy Holmes) L.; A.B., U. Ga., 1963, M.A. (univ. fellow), 1964; m. Judy Carol Smith, Nov. 14, 1963; 1 dau., Sheri Lynn. Store mgr., promotion dir. Market St. Pharmacy, Bklyn., 1958; promotion mgr. Lane Labs., also Mentho-Mulsion Co., drug marketers, Wilmington, N.C., 1961-62; account exec. Am. Lithograph/Case-Hoyt Co., Atlanta, 1966-67; asso. prof. advt. U. Ga., 1973—; v.p. client services SLRS Communications, Inc., Athens, Ga., 1968-73, pres., 1973—; dir. Jour. Advt., 1973-79, nat. advt mgr., 1974-78; mem. screening com. George Foster Peabody awards, 1978; judge agrl. advt. competitions. Creative fellow Advt. Age mag., 1970; named Outstanding Prof., U. Ga., 1973; recipient Disting. Service award Alpha Delta Sigma, 1968. Mem. Am. Advt. Fedr. (acad. adv. com. 1978), Am. Acad. Advt.,

Atlanta Advt. Club, Greater Augusta Advt. Club, Athens Advt. Club. Democrat. Presbyterian. Author: Advertising Media Problems Solving, 1968, 70; also articles. Home: 155 Landor Dr Athens GA 30606 Office: PO Box 5488 Athens GA 30604

LANEY, JAMES EARL, state legislator; b. Hale Center, Tex., Mar. 20, 1943; s. Wilber G. and Frances L. (Wilson) L.; B.S., Tex. Technol. U., 1965; m. Nelda McQuien, Aug. 10, 1963; children—KaLyn, Jamey Kay, J Pete. Farmer, cattleman, Hale Center, 1965—; dir. Hale County Soil and Water Conservation Dist., 1968-72; v.p. Hale County Water Assn., 1969-71; mem. Urban Transp. Bd., 1973-74; sec. South Plains Soil and Water Assn., 1971-72; past pres. Hale County Farmers Union, Com. Tex. Water Plan; mem. Tex. Ho. of Reps., 1973—, chmn. house adminstrn. com., 1976-77, mem. com. on ways and means, 1976-77; del. Tex. Constl. Conv., 1974. Trustee High Plains Research Found.; mem. energy adv. com. Interstate Oil Compact Commn., 1974—; governing bd. Council State Govts.; chmn. Tex. Aircraft Pooling Bd. Mem. Tex. Flying Farmers (treas. 1976-77), Hale Center C. of C. (dir. 1971). Mason (Shriner, 32 deg.). Home: Route 2 Hale Center TX 79041 Office: 304 Skaggs Bldg Plainview TX 79072

LANG, ERICH KARL, physician, radiologist; b. Vienna, Austria, Dec. 7, 1929; s. Johann Hanns and Caecilia C. (Felkel) L.; came to U.S., 1950; naturalized, 1960; Arbitur, Realgymnasium, 1947; M.S., Columbia U., 1951; M.D., U. Vienna, 1953; m. Nicoli J. Miller, Apr. 21, 1956; children—Erich Christopher, Cortney Alexander Johann. Intern, U. Iowa Hosps., Iowa City, 1954-55, resident in internal medicine, 1955-56; resident in radiology Johns Hopkins U. Hosp., Balt., 1956-59, radiologist, 1956-61; instr. radiology Johns Hopkins U., 1956-61; radiologist, acting dir. radiology Methodist Hosp., Indpls., 1961-67; prof., chmn. dept. radiology La. State U. Med. Center, Shreveport, 1967-76, New Orleans, 1976—; chmn. dept. radiology La. State U., Tulane U. schs. of medicine, 1976—; dir. radiology Charity Hosp., New Orleans, 1976—. Served as maj. M.C., U.S. Army, 1961-65. Fellow ACP, Soc. Vascular Surgeons, Am. Coll. Radiology, Billroth Med. Soc.; mem. Radiol. Soc. N. Am., Am. Roentgen Ray Soc., Soc. Nuclear Medicine, Soc. Acad. Chmn. Radiology, Soc. U. Radiologists, La., New Orleans med. socs., Crescent City Radiol. Soc. Contbr. numerous articles in field. Office: 1542 Tulane Ave New Orleans LA 70112

LANG, JEAN MCKINNEY, editor, educator; b. Cherokee, Iowa, Nov. 6, 1921; d. Roy Clarence and Verna Harvey (Smith) McKinney; B.S., Iowa State U., 1945; M.A., Ohio State U., 1969; postgrad. U. South Fla., 1972; 1 dau., Barbara Jean (Mrs. Michael L. Wilcox). Merchandiser, jewelry buyer Rike-Kumler Co., Dayton, Ohio, 1952-59, Met. Co., Dayton, 1959-64; tchr. DeVilbiss High Sch., Toledo, 1966-67; chmn. dept. retailing Webber Coll., Babson Park, Fla., 1967-72; asso. editor Wet Set Illustrated, 1972-75; exec. editor Pleasure Boating, Largo, Fla., 1975—; tchr. bus. adminstrn. St. Petersburg (Fla.) Jr. Coll., 1974—. Presdl. appointee Nat. Boating Safety Adv. Council. Recipient recognition Nat. Retail Mchts. Assn., 1971, certificates of appreciation U.S. Power Squadron, 1976, Webber Coll., 1972. Mem. Greater Tampa C. of C., AAUW, Tampa Aux. Power Squadron, U.S. Coast Guard Aux., Sales and Mktg. Execs. of Tampa (pres.'s award 1973), Fla. Outdoor Writers Assn., Am. Mktg. Assn., Gulf Coast Symphony, Internat. Platform Assn., Fla. Council Yacht Clubs, Chi Omega. Republican. Presbyterian. Clubs: Toledo Yacht (hon.), Tampa Yacht and Country First woman to cruise solo from Fla. to Lake Erie in single-engine inboard, 1969, to be accepted into Fla. Council Yacht Clubs; yachting accomplishments published in The Ensign, Lakeland Boating, Yachting, Boote mags. Office: PO Box 402 Largo FL 33540

LANG, KURT, cartographer; b. Brasov, Rumania, Feb. 15, 1922; s. Rudolf and Martha Ida (Gruenanger) L.; came to U.S., 1950, naturalized, 1956; Engineur der Kartentechniken, Meister Schule der Reichshauptstadt, 1945; m. Hedy M. Bodenhausen, June 26, 1946; children—Thomas R., Ralph L. Cartographer, Dennoyer-Geppert Map Publs., Chgo., 1950-51; with U.S. Steel Co., Fairfield, Ala., 1951—, head comml. artist, 1956-65; owner, cartographer Kurt Lang Carto-Craft Map Co., Birmingham, Ala., 1975—. Mem. Am. Congress on Surveying and Mapping, Soc. Profl. Land Surveyors Ala. Republican. Lutheran. Club: Lion. Home: 2201 Lester Lane Birmingham AL 35226 Office: 701 Wenonah Rd Bessemer AL 35020

LANG, LARRY GEORGE, water treatment equipment co. exec.; b. Frederick, Wis., Oct. 4, 1939; s. George K. and Hilda S. Lang; B.S., U. Wis., 1964; postgrad. London Sch. Econs., 1965; m. Melba Sanchez, Sept. 16, 1966; 1 dau., Johanna G. Account exec. Ethyl Corp., Houston, 1966-69; sales engr. Betz Labs., Houston, 1969-74; regional sales mgr. Houdry div. Air Products Chems. Co., Houston, 1974-75; owner, v.p. Trans-Technology, Inc., Houston, 1975-77, pres., owner, 1977—; mem. dist. export council Dept. Commerce, 1979—. Mem. Entrepreneur Inst., Am. Inst. Chem. Engrs., World Trade Assn., Houston C. of C. (internat. bus. com.), Engring. Soc. Western Pa. Episcopalian. Home: 14019 Woodthorpe St Houston TX 77079 Office: 505 N Hutcheson St Houston TX 77003

LANG, ROGER MARK, chem. engr.; b. Redwood City, Calif., Sept. 19, 1953; s. Josh Mark and Margo June (Terzian) L.; B.S. in Chem. Engring., Ariz. State U., 1975; postgrad. bus. adminstrn. Tex. A. & I. U., 1976—. Stock clk. Newberry's Dept. Store, Phoenix, 1972-75, mgr. stockroom, 1973-75; chem. engr. dept. process engring., Celanese Co., Bishop, Tex., 1975—. Mem. Am. Inst. Chem. Engrs. Clubs: Chemcel, Kingsville Tennis. Home: 1100 W Corral Ave Apt 211 Kingsville TX 78363 Office: Box 428 Bishop TX 78343

LANGBERG, LESLIE SCOTT, food service co. exec.; b. Bklyn., July 22, 1953; s. Sol and Florence (Goodman) L.; B.S. cum laude, Boston U., 1975; m. Aug. 19, 1979. Asst. to exec. dir. Cooley's Anemia Found., Garden City, N.Y., 1975; supr. mktg. and community relations Met. Bus Authority, N.Y.C., 1976; dir. advt. and public relations Benihana of Tokyo, Miami, 1976—; lectr. in field. Mem. Am. Mktg. Assn., Public Relations Soc., Am. Club: B'nai B'rith. Home: 6604 SW 114th Pl Miami FL 33173 Office: Benihana of Tokyo 8685 NW 53d Ter Miami FL 33166

LANGDALE, NOAH NOEL, JR., coll. pres.; b. Valdosta, Ga., Mar. 29, 1920; s. Noah Noel and Jessie Katharine (Catledge) L.; A.B., U. Ala., 1941, LL.D., 1959; LL.B., Harvard, 1948, M.B.A., 1950; m. Alice Elizabeth Cabaniss, Jan. 8, 1944; 1 son, Noah Michael. Asst. football coach U. Ala., 1942; admitted to Ga. bar, 1951, and practiced in Valdosta, 1951-57; instr., then asst. prof. econs. and social studies, chmn. dept. accounting, econs., secretarial sci., bus. adminstrn. Valdosta State Coll., 1954-57; pres. Ga. State U., Atlanta, 1957—. Dir. Guardian Life Ins. Co. Am. Past mem. U.S. Adv. Commn. Ednl. Exchange. Served to lt. (s.g.) USNR, 1942-46. Recipient 1st Georgian of Year award Ga. Assn. Broadcasters, 1962; Silver Anniversary All-Am. award Sports Illustrated, 1966; Mrytle Wreath award Hadassah, 1970; Salesman of Yr. award Sales and Marketing Execs. of Atlanta, 1975; Silver Knight of Mgmt. award Lockheed-Ga. chpt. Nat. Mgmt. Assn., 1978. Mem. Am., Ga. bar assns., Ga. Assn. Colls. (pres. 1962-63), SAR (past v.p. Ga.), Gridiron Soc., Phi Beta Kappa, Omicron Delta Kappa, Delta Chi, Phi Kappa Phi. Methodist. Rotarian. Club: Capital City (Atlanta). Home: 3807 Tuxedo Rd NW Atlanta GA 30305 Office: Ga State Univ University Plaza Atlanta GA 30303

LANGDELL, ROBERT DANA, pathologist, educator; b. Pomona, Calif., Mar. 14, 1924; s. Walter Irving and Florence Delsa (Reichenbach) L.; student Pomona Coll., 1941-43; M.D., George Washington U., 1948; m. Alice Evelyn Pritt, June 3, 1948; children—Robert D., Sara Ellen. Intern, Henry Ford Hosp., 1948-49; fellow in pathology U. N.C., 1949-51, instr., 1951-55, asst. prof., 1956-58, asso. prof., 1959-61, prof. pathology, 1961—; mem. hematology study sect. NIH-USPHS. Served to capt. M.C., U.S. Army, 1944, 55-56. USPHS grantee, 1956-61, 61-66. Mem. Am. Assn. Blood Banks (pres. 1972-73), Am. Soc. Clin. Pathologists, AMA, Am. Assn. Pathologists, Coll. Am. Pathologists (gov. 1977—). Episcopalian. Home: 707 William Circle Chapel Hill NC 27514 Office: Dept Pathology Sch Medicine U NC Chapel Hill NC 27514

LANGE, EDIE LOUISE, personnel agy. exec.; b. Corpus Christi, Tex., Nov. 9, 1948; s. Edmund F. and Ima Belle (Nelson) L.; B.B.A., Tex. A&I U., 1969. Secretarial position Tenneco Chems., Houston, 1970; customer service rep. Agy. Records Control Co., Houston, 1970-72; land sec. Wesley West, oil operator, 1972-74; geology and land sec., leases coordinator, office mgr. Banner Petroleum Co., Houston, 1974-75; asst. to pres. Harry Lucas, ind. oil operator, 1975; petroleum cons., mgr. oil and gas, legal, and data processing divs. Burnett Personnel Cons.'s, Houston, 1975—. Baptist. Office: Burnett Personnel Consultants 3300 S Gessner St Suite 250 Houston TX 77063

LANGER, MARSHALL J., lawyer; b. N.Y.C., May 30, 1928; s. Samuel and Edna (Klein) L.; B.S. in Econs., U. Pa., 1948; J.D. summa cum laude, U. Miami, 1951; m. Sally Blass, Apr. 3, 1955 (div. 1967); children—Andrew H., Jeffrey S.; m. 2d, Barbara Slatko, Feb. 15, 1970. Admitted to Fla. bar, 1951, since practiced in Miami; mem. firm Shutts & Bowen, 1975—; lectr., acting dir. Inter-Am. law program U. Miami Sch. Law, 1955-56, adj. prof., 1965—; exchange prof. law U. Havana, Cuba, 1956; also lectr. tax insts. in U.S., Europe, Japan. Chmn. programs on doing bus. in Caribbean, also fgn. tax planning Practising Law Inst., 1972—. Mem. The Fla. Bar, Am., Inter-Am. (asst. sec. gen. 1956-61), Dade County bar assns., Internat. Fiscal Assn. (v.p. U.S. br. 1978—), Am. Fgn. Law Assn. (cht. pres. 1955), Greater Miami Tax Inst. (pres. 1967), Iron Arrow, Zeta Beta Tau (nat. historian, 1959-60), Omicron Delta Kappa, Phi Kappa Phi. Author: Practical International Tax Planning, 1979; (with others) Income Taxation of Foreign Related Transactions, 1980; contbr. chpts. to books, articles to profl. jours. Home: 444 Ave Rovino Coral Gables FL 33156 Office: 10th Floor SE First Nat Bank Bldg Miami FL 33131

LANGFORD, PAUL PEDEN, human relations co. exec.; b. Tampa, Fla., Jan. 6, 1929; s. Cecil Clifford and Eula Loice (Peden) L.; B.Gen.Edn., U. Omaha, 1965; m. Irene Walenkiewicz, Mar. 26, 1955; children—Keith Eugene, Eva Marie, Kay Jean, Pamela Ann. Commd. 2d lt., U.S. Army, 1949, advanced through grades to lt. col.; ret., 1976; pres. Dynamic Leadership, Dallas, 1976—. Decorated Legion of Merit (3), Bronze Star medal. Mem. Assn. U.S. Army, Retired Officers Assn., Nat. Mil. Intelligence Assn. Republican. Clubs: Salesman With a Purpose, Civitan. Home: 415 Provincetown Richardson TX 75080 Office: Citizens Bank Suite 500 Richardson TX 75080

LANGLAIS, GARY PAUL, architect; b. Queens County, N.Y., June 20, 1948; s. Arthur David and Dolores Barbra (Schmidt) L.; student N.Y. Inst. Tech., 1966-67, 69-70, L.I. Inst. Tech., 1967-69; B.Arch., U. Houston, 1973; m. Donna Marie Newton, June 14, 1975; 1 son, Shawn William. With Silberstein Asso., N.Y.C., 1967-70; staff architect Boone Amyx Architect, Houston, 1970; v.p. Cavitt McKnight Weymouth, Inc., Houston, 1971—. Dir. at large Bayou Rifles, Inc., 1974-75: trustee Our Savior Luth. Ch., Houston, 1975-79. Registered architect, Tex. Mem. AIA, Tex. Soc. Architects, Nat. Council of Archtl. Registration Bds., Constrn. Specifications Inst. Lutheran. Clubs: Ind. Order Foresters, Ancient and Benificent Order of Red Red Rose, Bayou Rifles Competitive Shooting. Office: 4600 Post Oak Pl Suite 110 Houston TX 77027

LANGLEY, JOHN JEFFERSON, supermarket exec.; b. Greenville, N.C., Oct. 27, 1932; s. Walter Raleigh and Betty (Gray) L.; grad. Pactolus (N.C.) High Sch., 1951; m. Doris Gray, July 14, 1951; children—Dawn Michele, John Barry. Mgr., J.P. Davenport & Son, Gen. Merchandise, Pactolus, 1951-57; salesman Ormond Wholesale Co., Inc., Greenville, 1957-74; sales mgr., div. mgr. Foodland-Clover Farm Group ops., Greenville, 1962-74; pres., gen. mgr. Shop-Eze Food Stores, Washington, N.C., 1966—. Dir. Rural Fire Dept., Pactolus, 1978-79. Recipient Cert. of Appreciation Pitt County (N.C.) Sch. Bd., 1976; Civic award Foodland Internat., 1974. Mem. N.C. Food Dealers Assn. (dir. 1974-79, 3d v.p. 1979), Nat. Assn. Retail Grocers, Greenville C. of C., Washington C. of C., Belhaven (N.C.) C. of C. Democrat. Baptist. Clubs: Pactolus Ruritan (v.p. 1975-76, pres. 1976-77), Moose. Home: Route 5 Box 311 Greenville NC 27834 Office: Shop-Eze Food Stores 300 Brown St Washington NC 27889

LANGLEY, WELBORN JAMES, physician; b. Westbrook, Tex., Sept. 12, 1926; s. Floyd Alford and Frances Willie (Cunningham) L.; B.A., Baylor U., 1953; M.D., Southwestern U., 1957; m. Dorothy Jean Lee; children—Beverly Jo (Mrs. Jack Mcdowell), Debbie Jean, Roger James, Brenda Diane, Rebecca Jane. Intern Baylor U. Hosp., 1958; resident surgery Harris Hosp., 1959; family practice physician, Dallas, 1969—. Served with AUS, 1944-50. Mem. AMA, Tex., Dallas County med. assns. Independent. Mem. Ch. of Christ. Office: 7777 Forest Ln Dallas TX 75230

LANGLOTZ, CAROLYN WEST DOROUGH, sch. counselor, psychol. asso.; b. Bellevue, Tex., Mar. 30, 1933; d. William Montgomery and Roxie Ibera (Wallace) Dorough; student Bethany Nazarene Coll., 1950-53; B.S., N. Tex. State U., 1963, M.Ed., 1973; postgrad. So. Meth. U., 1970; m. Wilburn Barry Langlotz, Aug. 27, 1954; children—Kimberly Ann Langlotz Chancey, Katherine Sue, Richard Edward. Tchr. Richardson (Tex.) Ind. Sch. Dist., 1963-73, secondary counselor, 1973—; cons. in field. Active Girl Scouts U.S. Mem. Tex. Psychol. Assn., Tex., Dallas psychol. assos., Am., Tex. personnel and guidance assns., Richardson Edn. Assn. Methodist. Club: Brookhaven Country. Researcher cross-cultural communication as regards perception of personality structure. Home: 1239 Navaho Trail Richardson TX 75080 Office: 13630 Coit Rd Dallas TX 75240

LANGRELL, LAWANDA JANE, retail exec.; b. England, Ark., Apr. 22, 1926; d. Troy Bricen and Flaura Jane (Ward) L.; grad. England pub. schs.; 1 son, Sigmund Wade Pemberton. Bookkeeper, Wallace Johnson Fairgrounds Homes, Pine Bluff, Ark., 1952-54; bookkeeper Brown Motor Co., Pine Bluff, 1954-62, bus. mgr., 1962—. Recipient Bus. Mgmt. award Lincoln-Mercury div. Ford Motor Co.; named Beta Sigma Phi State Girl of Yr., 1976; Citizen of Day, Pine Bluff, 1979. Mem. Pine Bluff C. of C., Beta Sigma Phi (pres. Xi Tau chpt. 1977-78). Democrat. Baptist. Home: 4603 Fir St Pine Bluff AR 71603 Office: 2101 W 6 St Pine Bluff AR 71601

LANGSDON, JOHN KINNARD, JR., mfg. co. exec.; b. Columbia, Tenn., Feb. 6, 1934; s. John Kinnard and Ree (Coleman) L.; B.Engring., Vanderbilt U., 1955; postgrad. U. Wash., 1955-56, U. Tenn., 1958; m. Bonnie Jean Strong, Sept. 3, 1955; children—Valerie Langsdon Wilson, John Kinnard, Rosemarie, James David, Joseph William. With Columbia Machine Works, Columbia, 1946-53, chief engr., 1958-59, plant mgr., 1959-69, pres., chmn. bd., 1969—; chemist DuPont Co., Columbia, 1954; research asst. Monsanto Co., Columbia, 1954; chem. engr. Union Carbide Nuclear Co., Oak Ridge, 1955; tchr. Central High, Columbia, 1956. Dist. commr. Boy Scouts Am., 1966-79, exec. bd. Middle Tenn. council, 1977—; bd. dirs. Jr. Achievement, 1972-79, Moury County United Givers Fund, 1975-79. Recipient Silver Beaver award Boy Scouts Am., 1976; named Outstanding Rotarian, 1976; Paul Harris fellow, 1979. Mem. Moury County C. of C. (sec.-treas. 1974-75), ASME, Am. Inst. Chem. Engrs. Republican. Ch. of Christ. Club: Rotary (dir. 1964-66). Home: 307 N Hardin Dr Columbia TN 38401 Office: PO Box 1018 Columbia TN 38401

LANGSTON, ELIZABETH RICKS, psychologist; b. Brady, Tex., June 22, 1946; d. Glenn Hall and Alice Glenn (Young) Ricks; B.S. in Speech Pathology, Southwest Tex. State U., 1968; M.Ed. in Ednl. Psychology, U. Tex., 1969; m. Jerry Lee Langston, June 13, 1975; 1 son, Larson Jerome. Head psychol. testing lab. Southwestern Med. Sch., U. Tex., Dallas, 1969-70; clin. and ednl. psychologist Callier Hearing and Speech Center, Dallas, 1970-73; instr. Richland Community Coll., Dallas, 1972-73; counselor and ednl. psychologist Los Alamos (N.Mex.) High Sch., 1973-74; sch. psychologist Santa Fe Pub. Schs., 1974-76; asso. psychologist Dewitt-Lavaca Spl. Edn. Coop., Cuero, Tex., 1976-78; staff psychologist Gulf Bend Center, Victoria, Tex., 1978-80. Cons. deaf blind project Regional Center, Dallas, 1971-73; cons. Children's House of Learning, El Dorado, Ark., 1971-76; cons. Indian Health Services, 1974-76; discussion leader Family Guidance, Dallas, 1973; mem. admissions com. Bluebonnet Youth Ranch, 1976-79; cons. psychologist to speech clinic Porter Meml. Hosp., Denver, 1975-79. Bd. dirs. Family Center, Inc., Dallas, 1972-74; bd. dirs. Victoria Youth Home, 1978-80; mental health cons. Indian Health Service, Taos, N.Mex., 1980—; co-owner Shop of the Blue-Eyed Man, 1980—. Mem. Am. Psychol. Assn., Council of Exceptional Children, Mental Health Assn. Dallas, Common Cause, Abortion Edn. Council of Dallas, Women's League of Voters, Tex. Astrological Assn., Internat. Transactional Analysis Assn., Kappa Delta Pi, Psi Chi, Chi Omega, Alpha Chi. Democrat. Episcopalian. Mem. Order Eastern Star. Club: Jaquar. Home: Route 5 Box 12 Pojoaque NM 87501 Office: Santa Fe Indian Hosp Cerrillios Rd Santa Fe NM 87501

LANHAM, HAROLD DAMRON, city ofcl.; b. Odessa, Tex., July 1, 1947; s. Frank Harold and Doris Marie (Damron) L.; B.A. in Gen. Bus., Tex. Tech. U., 1970; m. Kathy Ann Hardy, Sept. 19, 1979. Laborer, City of Midland (Tex.), 1966, truck driver, 1967, spl. employee, 1968, asst. st. supt., 1968-69; adminstrv. asst. to dir. public works City of Lubbock (Tex.), 1970-72, adminstrv. asst. to city mgr., 1972-73; asst. city mgr. City of Benbrook (Tex.), 1973-74, city mgr., 1974-76; pres. HDL Constrn., Ft. Worth, 1976-77; city mgr. City of Center (Tex.), 1977—. Bd. dirs. Deep East Tex. Workers Compensation Ins. Fund, 1977-80, Center C. of C., 1977-80; tournament chmn. Center Invitational, 1980; pres. Center Indsl. Devel. Authority. Served with USAR, 1970-74. Mem. East Tex. City Mgrs. Assn., Tex. City Mgrs. Assn., Internat. City Mgrs. Assn. Methodist. Clubs: Lions, Center Country (dir. and sec. 1978-80). Office: City Hall PO Box 311 Center TX 75935

LANIER, BOBBY GENE, physician; b. Collins, Ga., Apr. 29, 1938; s. Clinnie B. and Kinia (Powell) L.; grad. Emory U., 1958; M.D., Med. Coll. Ga., 1962; m. Alice Wolfe, July 2, 1961; children—Jeffrey Hunter, Kinia Lynn, Eleanor Jane. Intern, USPHS Hosp., New Orleans, 1962-63; resident internal medicine Mayo Grad. Sch., Rochester, Minn., resident clin. rheumatology, 1968-69; practice medicine specializing in internal medicine; mem. staff West Paces Ferry Hosp., St. Joseph's Infirmary, Northside Hosp. Served with USPHS, 1963-65. Diplomate Am. Bd. Internal Medicine. Mem. Am. Soc. Internal Medicine, Ga. Soc. Internal Medicine, Med. Assn. Ga., Med. Assn. Atlanta, So. Med. Assn., AMA, Atlanta Clin. Soc., Ga. Heart Assn., Am. Heart Assn., Am. Rheumatism Assn., Ga. Rheumatism Soc. (pres. 1974-75). Contbr. articles on internal medicine to profl. publs. Home: 1045 Mt Creek Trail NW Atlanta GA 30328 Office: West Paces Ferry Med Clinic 3250 Howell Mill Rd NW Atlanta GA 30327

LANIER, JAMES OLANDA, lawyer, banker, state legislator; b. Newbern, Tenn., Sept. 8, 1931; s. James Parker and Robbye (Sullivan) L.; student U. Tenn., 1949, U. Tenn. Jr. Coll., 1950-51; B.S., Memphis State Coll., 1955; J.D., Memphis State U., 1969; m. Carolyn Holland, June 1, 1950; children—James Elton, Donna Kay, Robbye Ann (dec.), Amy Claire. Indsl. engr. Milan (Tenn.) Arsenal, 1953-54; social worker Dept. Pub. Welfare, Memphis, 1955-57, sr. social worker, appeals examiner, 1957-58; dir. surplus Commodities, Dyer County, Tenn., 1958; pres., gen. mgr. Main Sporting Goods, Inc., Dyersburg, 1959-62; tech. engr. Milan Ordnance Plant, 1961-63; spl. investigator Tenn. Dept. Pub. Welfare, Nashville, 1963-67; ins. adjuster U.S. Fidelity & Guaranty Co., 1967-69; pvt. practice law, Dyersburg, 1969—; county atty. Dyer County, 1972—; admitted to U.S. Supreme Ct. bar, 1975; pres. Lanier Enterprises, Inc., Dyersburg, West Tenn, Inc., Dyersburg, Dukedom Bank (Tenn.), 1979—. Mem. Tenn. Ho. of Reps., 1959-62, 71—, chmn. com. on agr., 1961-62, chmn. com. on state and local govt., 1973-77, chmn. W. Tenn. Democratic House Caucus, 1975—, chmn. com. on calendar and rules, 1977—; chmn. Tenn. Tollway Authority, 1975—; state campaign coordinator Lamar Alexander for Gov., 1978; dir. Dyer County Levee and Drainage Dist., Obion-Forked Deer Basin Authority, 1979—. Pres. Dyer County chpt. Muscular Dystrophy Assns. Am., 1958-60. Mem. Jr. C. of C. (past treas.; hon.), Tenn. Law Enforcement Officers Assn., Am., Dyersburg-Dyer County (sec.-treas.) bar assns., Bar Assn. Tenn., Am., Tenn. trial lawyers assns., Am. Judicature Soc., Dyer County C. of C., Memphis State U. Alumni Assn. (nat. dir. 1976—), Sigma Delta Kappa (pres. 1967-68), Kappa Sigma. Democrat (W. Tenn. pres. Young Democrats of Tenn. 1957-63). Mem. Ch. of Christ. Moose (jr. gov. 1959-60, gov. 1960-62, chmn. com. civic affairs, recipient fellowship degree and gov.'s award of merit 1963), Elk. Clubs: Dyersburg Kiwanis, Dyersburg Country. Home: Route 4 Nauvoo Dyersburg TN 38024 Office: Lanier Bldg 208 N Mill St Dyersburg TN 38024 also Dukedom Bank Dukedom TN 38226 also 109 War Meml Bldg Nashville TN 37219

LANIER, SIDNEY EDWARD, mfg. co. exec.; b. Knox City, Tex., Aug. 1, 1945; s. S. E. and Ella (Wilson) L.; B.S. in Aerospace Engring., U. Tex., 1968, postgrad, 1969—; m. Bonnie Joy Root, July 31, 1971. Mng. partner L & L Investment Co., 1973—, pres., 1976—; Project test engr., sect. head, project engr., program mgr., dir. Chaff Products, Tracor, Inc.. 1968-75, v.p., gen. mgr., pres. Tracor Radcon, Inc., Austin, Tex., 1975—; pres. AIM Enterprises Unltd., 1976—; instr. math. U. Tex., 1970-73. Chmn., counselor, advisor Tex. Atty. Gen. Youth Conf., 1963-65; precinct chmn. Republican. Party, Austin, 1970-73; pres. bd. trustees I Am School, Inc., 1976—. Mem. Tex. Soc. Profl. Engrs., Aircraft Owners and Pilots Assn., Assn. Am.

Prepardness, Assn. Old Crows. Home: 5510 Shoalwood Ave Austin TX 78756 Office: 6500 Tracor Ln Austin TX 78721

LANKFORD, PAULETTE GLAZENER, educator; b. Brevard, N.C., Feb. 8; d. Paul Lindsey and Montaree Verona (Galloway) Glazener; student Maryville (Tenn.) Coll., 1954-56 B.S., Duke U., 1958; Ph.D., Vanderbilt U., 1973; m. Troy Wayne Lankford, May 15, 1960; children—Laura Elise, Keith Tyler. Research technologist Duke U. Med. Center, 1958-59, E. Tenn. Tb Hosp., 1959-60, Union Carbide Nuclear Co., 1960-61; instr. med. technology Hillcrest Hosp., Waco, Tex., 1961-62; ednl. coordinator med. technology program VA Hosp., Nashville, 1963-72, tech. and ednl. coordinator, 1972-74; instr. dept. pathology Vanderbilt U., 1970-76, asst. prof., 1976—, asst. dean div. allied health, 1973-77, asso. dean., 1977-79, dir. div. allied health professions, 1977—; cons. in field. Mem. Health Careers of Tenn. Adv. Bd., Nashville, 1974—; chmn. central allied health adv. com. Vol. State/Community Coll., Gallatin, Tenn., 1976—. O.A. Brines Meml. fellow, 1965. Mem. Am. Soc. Clin. Pathologists, Tenn. Assn. Blood Banks (dir. 1975-76, sec. 1976-77), Am. Soc. Med. Assts. (ednl. dir. 1976-77), Am. Soc. Allied Health Professions, Acad. Clin. Lab. Physicians and Scientists, Sigma Xi. Baptist. Home: Route 1 Box 465 Pegram TN 37143 Office: Vanderbilt University Medical Center Nashville TN 37232

LANKFORD, ROBERT J., ins. co. exec.; b. Edwardsville, Ill., Apr. 18, 1929; s. James M. and Wilma I. L.; student U. Ill., 1948; B.B.A., So. Meth. U., 1950; certificate in Estate Planning, Am. Coll. Life Underwriters, 1966, postgrad. certificate in accounting and bus. evaluation, 1977, cert. in advanced pension planning, 1978, cert. in bus. tax planning, 1979, postgrad. cert. in exec. benefit planning, 1980; m. LaVern Olney, Dec. 29, 1959; children—Bruce, Craig, Leigh, Stuart. Sales rep., Haughton Pub. Co., Dallas, 1950; agent New Eng. Mut. Life Ins. Co., Dallas, 1950; instr. personal fin. Bishop Coll., Dallas, 1970-71; mem. spl. task force com. investigating problems in sale of ins. in Tex., 1976-77; owner Bus. & Estate Analysts; bd. govs. Dallas Estate Planning Council, 1979—; mem. policyholder's service com. New Eng. Life Leaders Assn. Bd. dirs. So. Meth. U., YMCA, 1956-66, Downtown Br. YMCA, 1958-60; chmn. Dallas County Blood Security Program, 1968. Recipient Vanguard award New Eng. Life, 1975; C.L.U. Mem. Nat. Assn. Life Underwriters and C.L.U.'s, Dallas Assn. Life Underwriters (dir. 1968-76) Dallas Estate Planning Council (gov. 1966-68), Million Dollar Round Table (life and qualifying), New Eng. Life's Leaders Assn. (compensation com.), New Eng. Life's Hall of Fame. Republican. Presbyterian. Club: Willow Bend Polo and Hunt. Contbr. articles in field to The Pilots Log, Flitcraft Mag., 1966. Home: 4228 Caruth Blvd Dallas TX 75225 Office: Suite 1015 Turtle Creek Tower 3131 Turtle Creek Blvd Dallas TX 75219

LANNEN, MERRILL LAWRENCE, govt. adminstr.; b. Chgo., Nov. 21, 1932; s. Merrill Lawrence and Florence (Stokes) L.; B.A. in Bus. Adminstrn., Chgo. City Coll., 1957; m. Margaret Ann Young, Dec. 22, 1963; children—Merrill Lawrence, Andrew C. Right of way appraiser, right of way agt. Prince Georges County (Md.), 1967-70; cons. and appraiser in real estate, Silver Spring, Md., 1963-67, 70-75; real estate property mgr. in Md., Va., D.C., 1963—; real estate officer U.S. Postal Service, Fla., Ga. and S.C., Tampa, Fla., 1975—; cons., appraiser in real estate, Tampa, 1976—. Served with U.S. Army, 1950-54, 63-64. Mem. Am. Assn. Cert. Appraisers (sr. appraiser), Nat. Assn. Housing and Redevel. Ofcls., Am. Soc. Appraisers, Am. Acad. Consultants, Chautauqua Property Owners Assn., Rho Chi. Presbyterian. Home: 7904 Spring Valley Dr Tampa FL 33615 Office: PO Box 22725 Tampa FL 33622

LANTZ, JOHN MARTIN, nursing adminstr.; b. Johnstown, Pa., May 3, 1942; s. John David and Virginia Mae (Warsing) L.; diploma Western Pa. Hosp. Sch. Nursing, 1963; B.S.N., Duquesne U., 1969, M.Ed., 1970; M.P.H., U. Pitts., 1975; postgrad. Tex. A. and M. U. Owner, Crestvue Cottage Nursing Home, Butler, Pa., 1967-72; nurse educator Western Pa. Sch. Nursing, Pitts., 1968-72, U. Pitts., 1970-72, Duquesne U. Sch. Nursing, Pitts., 1972-75; nurse educator/adminstr. Incarnate Word Coll., San Antonio, 1975-78; nurse educator/adminstr., head dept. nursing Angelo State U., San Angelo, Tex., 1978—; cons. Tex. Hosp. Assn., 1976-78. Bd. dirs. Am. Heart Assn., San Angelo, 1978-79, Planned Parenthood Center, San Angelo, 1978-79; program chmn. Am. Heart Assn., San Angelo, 1978-79. Mem. Am. Nurses Assn. (cert. 1975-79), Adult Educators Assn., Tex. Nurses Assn. Home: PO Box 8846 Midland TX 79703 Office: Angelo State U Dept Nursing San Angelo TX 76901

LANZILLOTTI, ROBERT FRANKLIN, economist, educator; b. Washington, June 19, 1921; B.A., Am. U., 1946, M.A., 1947; Ph.D., U. Calif., Berkeley, 1953; m. Patricia Joy Jackson, Oct. 27, 1945; children—Robert J., Donna J. Teaching fellow econs. U. Calif., Berkeley, 1947-49; faculty Wash. State U., Pullman, 1949-61, prof. econs., 1959-61; research asso. Brookings Instn., Washington, 1956-57, 74-75; asso. prof. econs., chmn. dept. econs. Mich. State U., East Lansing, 1961-69; prof. econs., dean Coll. Bus. Adminstrn., U. Fla., Gainesville, 1970—; dir. First City Bank, Jim Walter Corp. Mem. U.S. Price Commn., 1971-72; mem. educator adv. com. U.S. Comptroller Gen., 1979—; mem. Econ. Adv. Bd. to Gov. Fla., 1973-78. Served to lt. (j.g.), USNR, 1943-45. Decorated Bronze Star with cluster. NATO fellow, 1964. Mem. Am. Econs. Assn., So. Econs. Assn. (1st v.p. 1962-63), Fla. Council of 100 (hon.), Phi Beta Kappa (hon.), Beta Gamma Sigma, Omicron Delta Kappa. Author: Hard-Surface Floor Covering Industry, 1955; Pricing, Production and Marketing Policies of Small Manufacturers, 1964; Banking Structure in Michigan, 1945-63, 1966; (with others) Pricing in Big Business, 1959; Phase II in Review: The Price Commission Experience, 1975; Editor: Economic Effects of Government-Mandated Costs, 1979. Editorial adv. bd. Indsl. Orgn. Rev., 1974-78. Home: 2135 NW 28th St Gainesville FL 32605 Office: 224 Matherly U Fla Gainesville FL 32611

LAPOINTE, ALLEN CARL, ednl. adminstr.; b. Menominee, Mich., May 1, 1951; s. Carl W. and Ruth A. (Schauer) LaP.; B.S. in Natural Scis., U. Mich., 1973; student U. Minn., 1971, Gallaudet Coll., Washington, 1975; m. Deborah Ann Schmittler, Apr. 13, 1975. With FBI Lab., Washington, 1973-78; instr. Lockmasters Sch., Satellite Beach, Fla., 1978—, dir., 1978—. Asst. scoutmaster Central Fla. council Boy Scouts Am., Indialantic, 1979—. Lic. comml. and instrument pilot; cert. flight instr. FAA. Mem. Associated Locksmiths of Am. (cert. bonded locksmith). Roman Catholic. Office: 476 AIA Satellite Beach FL 32937

LAPP, ROGER JAMES, pharmacist; b. Buffalo, Jan. 29, 1933; s. Roger Vincent and Georgia James (Saemenes) L.; student Mich. State U., 1952-53: B.S. in Pharmacy, U. Buffalo, 1957; m. Judith Bure, Mar. 30, 1956; children—Eric Roger, Mark Frederick. Pharmacist intern Nobb Hill Pharmacy, Buffalo, 1956-57; pharm. intern Buffalo Gen. Hosp., 1957, pharm. resident, 1958; pharmacy mgr. Morton Plant Hosp., Clearwater, Fla., 1960—; cons. pharmacy; preceptor Sch. Pharmacy U. Fla., Fla. A&M U.; tchr. profl. seminars. Chmn. Human Rights Advocacy Com. for Pinellas and Pasco Counties (Fla.), 1973—; pres. Pinellas Assn. for Mental Retardation Assns., 1970-72; pres. Am. Cancer Soc., Pinellas County, 1979-81, bd. dirs., 1971-80; pres. Pinellas Epilepsy Found., 1978-79; v.p. Fla. Assn. Retarded, 1971-75. Served with U.S. Army, 1958-60. Named Man of Yr., Upper Pinellas Assn. Retarded, 1970; recipient Bowl of Hygeia, Fla. Pharm. Assn. and A.H. Robins Co., 1975, Smith award Kiwanis Club, Clearwater Beach, 1978, cert. of merit for public edn. Am. Cancer Soc., 1978. Mem. Am. Soc. Hosp. Pharmacists, Fla. Soc. Hosp. Pharmacists (pres. 1972-73, chmn. bd. 1973-74, Hosp. Pharmacist of Yr. 1975), Fla. Pham. Assn., Pinellas Soc. Pharmacists, S.W. Fla. Soc. Hosp. Pharmacists, Am. Epilepsy Found., Fla. Assn. Retarded Citizens (v.p. 1971-75, Brother hood award 1975, Pres.'s award 1978, sr. v.p. 1979-80), Upper Pinellas Assn. Retarded Citizens, Pinellas Epilepsy Found., Gideons Internat. Republican. Baptist. Author: Antibiotics, 1974, 3d rev. edit., 1977; contbr. articles to pharmacy jours. Home: 1998 Temple Terr Clearwater FL 33516 Office: 323 Jeffords St Clearwater FL 33516

LARAMEY, THOMAS AVRIETT, JR., lawyer, state agy. exec.; b. Temple, Tex., Sept. 16, 1945; s. Thomas Avriett and Ruth El L.; B.B.A. in Accounting, Tex. A. and M. U., 1967; J.D., U. Tex., 1971; m. Charlene Elizabeth Weiss, June 7, 1969. Admitted to Tex. bar, 1971; head sect. spl. projects Tex. Office Econ. Opportunity, Austin, 1972, legal counsel, 1972-73; cons. Tex. Edn. Agy., Austin, 1973-74; gen. counsel Tex. Dept. Community Affairs, Austin, 1974-80, dep. exec. dir., 1980—; adviser to Tex. Ho. of Reps. Interim Com. on Poverty, 1972, Spl. Interagy. Task Force, 1972; seminar lectr. S.W. Tex. State U., 1976. Recipient Service award Tex. Assn. Community Action Agys., 1973, certificate of commendation State Bar Tex., 1975. Mem. Am. (chmn. com. on social services sect. local govt. law 1977), Tex., Travis County, Austin Jr. bar assns., Tex. Pub. Employees Assn., Hill Country Neighborhood Assn., Austin Soc. Pub. Adminstrn., ACLU. Author: (with Mary Ann Harvey) Poverty in Texas, 1973. Home: 1208-A Yaupon Valley Rd Austin TX 78746 Office: 210 Barton Springs Rd Austin TX 78746

LARASON, LARRY DEAN, library adminstr., artist; b. Shattuck, Okla., Nov. 7, 1935; s. Ernest A. and Doris L. (Massey) L.; B.A., U. Okla., 1959, M.L.S., 1961, Ph.D., 1975; m. Katherine Louise Shaeffer, May 9, 1961; children—Karen Lucinda, Christopher Malon. Asst. reference librarian U. Nebr., Lincoln, 1961-63, order librarian, 1963-65; head serials service Ariz. State U., Tempe, 1965-68, systems coordinator, 1968-71; library systems analyst U. Okla., Norman, 1973-74; coordinator tech. services N.E. La. U., Monroe, 1974-77, library dir., 1977—; project dir. Intermountain Union List of Serials, 1970-71; one-man shows of prints or collages include: Angelina Coll., Lufkin, Tex., 1977, N.E. La. U., Monroe, 1977; group shows include: Masur Mus., Monroe, 1976-79, Monroe Art Assn. Shows, 1975-79; represented in permanent collections: West Monroe City Hall, Casell Gallery, New Orleans, Haynes Gallery, West Monroe, White Crane Studio, Taos, N.Mex., others. Mem. ALA, La. Library Assn., SW Library Assn., Monroe Art Assn., Monroe Art Acad. Democrat. Home: 2221 Mallory Pl Monroe LA 71201 Office: Sandel Library Northeast La U Monroe LA 71209

LARESEN, RALPH IRVING, environ. research engr.; b. Corvallis, Oreg., Nov. 26, 1928; s. Walter Winfred and Nellie Lyle (Gellatly) L.; B.S. in Civil Engring., Oreg. State U., 1950; M.S., Harvard U., 1955, Ph.D. in Air Pollution and Indsl. Hygiene, 1957; m. Betty Lois Garner, Oct. 14, 1950; children—Karen Laresen Cleeton, Eric, Kristine Laresen Burns, Jan Alan. San. engr. div. water pollution control USPHS, Washington, 1950-54; chief tech. service state and community service sect. Nat. Air Pollution Control Adminstrn., Cin., 1957-61; with EPA and Nat. Air Pollution Control Adminstrn., 1961—, environ. research engr., environ. ops. br., meteorology and assessment div., Research Triangle Park, N.C., 1971—; adj. lectr. Inst. Air Pollution Tng., 1969—; Falls of Neuse community rep. City of Raleigh (N.C.), 1974—. Recipient Commendation medal USPHS, 1979. Mem. Air Pollution Control Assn. (editorial bd. jour.), Research Soc. Am., Conf. Fed. Environ. Engrs. Republican. Mem. Christian and Missionary Alliance Ch. Contbr. numerous articles to profl. jours. Home: 4012 Colby Dr Raleigh NC 27609 Office: MD-80 EPA Research Triangle Park NC 27711

LARIMORE, LEON, clergyman; b. Horse Cave, Ky., July 22, 1911; s. William C. and Myrtie D. (Isenberg) L.; grad. Campbellsville Coll., 1946, D.D., 1962; student Georgetown Coll., 1946; A.B., Western Ky. U., 1949; B.D., So. Bapt. Theol. Sem., 1952; m. Blanche Lile, July 13, 1929; 1 dau., Majorie Bell (Mrs. Levy Ray Broady). Ordained to ministry, Baptist Ch., 1937; pastor Bapt. Chs., Hart, Edmonson, Metcalfe, Green and Monroe Counties, Ky., 1937-57, 3d Ave. Bapt. Ch., Louisville, 1957—; field supr. Boyce Bible Sch., So. Theol. Sem., 1976—. Mem. State Mission Bd., 1972—; vice chmn. adminstrv. com. Ky. Bapt. Conv., chmn. assembly and camps, 1972—. Dir. South Central Rural Telephone Coop. Mem. Econ. Security Welfare Commn., 1951-57; chmn. Hart County unit Am. Cancer Soc., 1952-56. Trustee Campbellsville Coll., 1953-70, chmn., 1967-68; trustee Wigginton Bapt. Home for Men, 1962-77; bd. dirs. Bapt. Homes for Elderly, 1962-77. Named Ky. Col., Ky. Adm. Mem. Liberty Assn. So. Bapts. (moderator 1942-49, 52-57), Ky. Bapt. Conv. (v.p. 1965), Long Run Assn. So. Bapts. (moderator 1971-72; pres. exec. bd. 1971-72). Clubs: Masons, Shriners, Rotary (pres. club 1956). Home: 1041 Eastern Pkwy Louisville KY 40217 Office: 1726 S 3d St Louisville KY 40208

LARKAM, BEVERLEY MCCOSHAM, psychotherapist; b. Vancouver, Can., Mar. 3, 1928; d. William Howard and Marjorie Isabel (Jerome) McCosham; came to U.S., 1951; asso. Royal Conservatory of Mus. of Toronto, U. Toronto, 1948; B.A., U. British Columbia, 1949, B.S.W., 1950, M.S.W., 1951; children—Elizabeth, Charles, Daphne, Peter, John. Psychiatric social worker Brackenridge Hosp., 1952-54; chmn. dept. sr. high sch. Univ. Presbyn. Ch., Austin, Tex., 1952-55, mem. christian edn. com., 1961-67, mem. community orgn. to establish classes for mentally retarded children, 1966-68, bd. dirs. developing and organizing nursery sch., 1967-70; social worker Counseling-Psychol. Services Center U. Tex., 1971-72; psychiatric social worker, chief supr. adult mental health, children's mental health Human Devel. Center-South, Austin, 1972-79; pvt. practice marriage and family counseling, sex therapy and individual and group psychotherapy, Austin, 1975—; field supr. Sch. Social Work U. Tex.; cons. in field. Mem. City of Austin Commn. on Status of Women, 1978—. Licensed social psychotherapist, Tex. Mem. Am. Assn. Marriage and Family Therapy (approved supr.), Am. Assn. Sex Educators, Counselors and Therapists (cert. sex therapist), Am., Southwestern group psychotherapy socs., Acad. Certified Social Workers, Nat. Assn. Social Workers, Nat. Council on Family Relations, Am. Orthopsychiat. Assn., Soc. for Sci. Study of Sex, PEO. Presbyterian. Home and Office: 2102 Raleigh Ave Austin TX 78703

LARKIN, JOSEPH DENNIS, transit, auto parts co. exec.; b. Martinsburg W.Va., Aug. 23, 1944; s. James Franklin and Mazie Myra (Camby) L.; student Hagerstown Jr. Coll., 1964-65; Tchr. schs., colls., Chgo. 1963; staff drafting Acme Grand Union Beach Assn., Washington, 1963-65, Vepco, Arlington, Va., 1965-66; asst. mgr. Nichols Store, Martinsburg, 1967-71, dist. supr., 1971-74; pres. Orndorff Taxi Inc., Martinsburg, 1974—, Jefferson Transit Co., Inc., Martinsburg, 1975—, Larkin Bros. Co., Martinsburg, 1975—; owner, operator I-81 Auto Parts Co., Martinsburg, 1977—; cons. other taxi cos. Mem. Martinsburg C. of C., Internat. Taxicab Assn., Santa Gertrious Internat. Roman Catholic. Clubs: Moose, Elks. Home: PO Box 931 Martinsburg WV 25401 also Route 30 Inwood WV Office: Orndorff Taxi Inc 110 N College St Martinsburg WV 25401

LARKINS, JOHN DAVIS, JR., judge; b. Morristown, Tenn., June 8, 1909; s. C.H. and Mamie (Dorset) L.; adopted s. John D. and Emma (Cooper) L.; B.A., Wake Forest U., 1929, law student, 1930, LL.D. (hon.), 1977; LL.D., Belin U., 1957; m. Pauline Murrill, Mar. 15, 1930; children—Emma Sue (Mrs. D.H. Loftin), Polly (Mrs. J.H. Bearden). Admitted to N.C. bar, 1930, gen. practice in Trenton, 1930-61; U.S. conciliation commr., Jones County, N.C., 1934-36; U.S. dist. judge Eastern Dist. N.C., 1961—, chief judge, 1975-79, sr. judge, 1979—. Sec. Larkins Stores, Inc.; dir. Life Ins. Co. N.C. Nat. bd. dirs., vice chmn. Am. Cancer Soc. Del.-at-large Democratic Nat. Conv., 1940, 44, 48, 56, 60; sec. N.C. Dem. Exec. Com., 1952-54, chmn., 1954-58; mem. Dem. Nat. Com., 1958-60; mem. N.C. Senate 7th dist., 1936-44, 48-54, pres. pro tem, 1941-42. Chmn. gov.'s adv. budget commn., 1951-53; gov.'s liaison officer and legislative counsel, 1955. Trustee U. N.C., Bapt. Hosp., Wake Forest U. Served as pvt. AUS, 1945. Recipient distinguished service award Am. Cancer Soc.; Outstanding Alumni Service award Wake Forest U. Sch. Law, 1968. Mem. Am., N.C. bar assns., N.C. Bar, Inc. Baptist (chmn. bd. deacons 1930-70). Home: Trenton NC 28585 Office: US Post Office and Federal Bldg Trenton NC 28585

LA ROSE, ROBERT LEE, data communication co. exec.; b. Hudson Falls, N.Y., Jan. 13, 1937; s. Kenneth Lee and Stella (Kokosa) LaR.; student N.Y. State Tchrs. Coll., 1956-58; B.A. in Math. and Physics, Tex. A. and M. U., 1961; D.Computer Sci. (hon.), Marlowe U., 1968; certificate in mgmt. So. Meth. U., 1976; m. Janis Elaine Mahaffey, May 27, 1956; children—Robin Lee, Diana Dawn, Robert Lee Jr. Sr. sales rep. Honeywell EDP Co., Dallas, 1964-67, dist. mgr. information services operations div. Honeywell Corp., Dallas, 1969-71; v.p. marketing Associometrics, Inc., Dallas, 1967-69; mgr. Dallas dist. MSI Data Corp., 1971-75; dir. marketing C-Five, Inc., 1975-76; Southwest regional sales mgr. RCA Service Corp. div. RCA, 1976-79; dist. mgr. Data Access Systems, Inc., Irving, Tex., 1979—; chmn. bd. Software Technologies Inc., Dallas; Dale Carnegie instr. Served with USAF, 1954-53. Mem. Augustan Soc., Conn. Soc. Genealogists, Mayflower Soc. SAR, Nat. Rifle Assn., Nat. Assn. Fed. Licensed Gun Dealer. Episcopalian (vestryman). Contbr. to profl. jours., geneal. publs. Home: 1206 Northgate Dr Irving TX 75062 Office: 1717 Walnut Hill Irving TX 75062

LAROWE, GEORGIA ANN, educator; b. Kokomo, Ind., Oct. 22, 1923; d. Hershel H. and Mary E. Jennings; B.Ed. magna cum laude, U. Miami, 1964; M.S., Fla. State U., 1965; m. Donald P. LaRowe, Mar. 25, 1944 (dec.). Cashier, Grain Dealers Mut. Ins. Co., Indpls., 1947-58, treas. Grain Dealers Mut. Credit Union, 1954-58; bookkeeper Oakridge Elementary Sch., Hollywood, Fla., 1958-62; tchr. Leonard Wesson Sch., Tallahassee, 1965-66, Westwood Heights Elementary Sch., Fort Lauderdale, 1966-70, Parkway Middle Sch., 1970-74, Richards Middle Sch., 1974—. Mem. NEA, Fla. Teaching Profession, Classroom Tchrs. Assn., Kappa Delta Pi. Presbyterian. Home: 2755 28th St NE Apt C-4 Lighthouse Point FL 33064 Office: 6000 9th Ave NE Fort Lauderdale FL 33334

LARSEN, DONALD JEFFREY, cons. firm exec.; b. Berlin, Ger., Jan. 19, 1951; s. Dagfinn Thor and Elizabeth Madeline (Koch) L.; B.S. in Bus. Mgmt., George Washington U., 1971; m. Celia Mary Towsey, Sept. 1, 1979; 1 son, David Matthew. Asst. mgr. Comml. Fin. Bank of Am. Springfield, Va., 1971-73; v.p. ops. Munroe, Williams & Assos., Inc. Falls Church, Va., 1973-75; pres. Larsen & Assos., Fairfax, Va., 1975—. Mem. ASME, ASPA, Am. Public Works Assn., IPA, Water Pollution Control Fedn., Am. Mgmt. Assn. Baptist. Contbr. articles to profl. jours. Research in field. Home: 311 Prince St Alexandria VA 22134 Office: 9411 Lee Highway Fairfax VA 22031

LARSON, DAVID WILBUR, physician; b. Seattle, Feb. 24, 1940; s. Wilbur Edwin and Lillian Clara May (Nelson) L.; B.A., Kalamazoo Coll., 1961; M.D., U. Chgo., 1967; m. Susan Jane Schroeder, Mar. 28, 1967; children—Jennifer Ellen, Samuel David. Intern, U. Ill., Chgo., 1967-68; USPHS resident-trainee in pathology U. Chgo., 1968-70; resident in internal medicine, U. N.Mex. Hosps., Albuquerque, 1970-72; fellow in hematology/oncology, 1972-73; practice medicine specializing in internal medicine, Spruce Pine, N.C., 1973—; mem. staff Spruce Pine Hosp., 1973—; bd. dirs. Piedmont Oncology Assn., N.C. Baptist Hosp., Winston Salem. Served with U.S. Army, 1961-63. Diplomate Am. Bd. Internal Medicine. Mem. A.C.P., Am. Soc. Internal Medicine, Mitchell-Yancey County Med. Soc., Phi Beta Kappa. Democrat. Mem. Soc. Friends. Address: 408 Altapass Rd Spruce Pine NC 28777

LARSON, DONALD KNUTE, hosp. adminstr.; b. Rockford, Ill., Jan. 6, 1926; s. David Emanuel and Alma Sophia (Olson) L.; B.S. with honors in Mgmt., U. Ill., 1950; M.S. in Hosp. Adminstrn., Northwestern U., 1961; m. Joyce Aldyce Erickson, Oct. 6, 1961; children—Curtis, Steven, Valerie, Keith. Personnel dir. Nat. Lock Co., Rockford, 1950-57; personnel relations mgr. Passavant Meml. Hosp., Chgo., 1957-61; adminstrv. asst. Rockford Meml. Hosp., 1961-63; v.p. adminstrn. Meth. Med. Center Ill., Peoria, 1963-75; pres. Loudoun Meml. Hosp., Leesburg, Va., 1975—; pres. Health Found. Central Ill., 1967-69; bd. dirs. Galena (Ill.) Park Home, 1973-75. Bd. dirs. Heart of Ill. United Fund, 1969-72. Served with C.E., U.S. Army, 1944-46, ETO. Mem. Am. Coll. Hosp. Adminstrs., Am. Hosp. Assn., Va. Hosp. Assn., Loudoun County C. of C., Am. Legion (post comdr.), Chi Gamma Iota, Sigma Iota Epsilon. Republican. Office: 70 W Cornwall St Leesburg VA 22075

LARSON, LINDA JEAN, speech pathologist; b. Hawthorne, Calif., Aug. 29, 1946; d. Carl Herbert and Ruth Anne (Ulmer) L.; B.A., U. Ark., 1968; M.A., Tex. Christian U., 1970. Dir. speech pathology Easter Seal Soc. Adults and Children, Ft. Worth, 1970-74; dir. speech pathology Long Beach (Calif.) Meml. Hosp., 1974-76, Meml. Hosp. System, Houston, 1978—; instr. Grad. Sch. U. Houston, 1978—. Tex. Christian U. fellow, 1968-70. Mem. Am. Speech and Hearing Assn., Tex. Speech and Hearing Assn., Am. Heart Assn. (chmn. stroke com.).

LARSON, STANLEY EARL, aircraft parts sales co. exec.; b. Americus, Kans., Sept. 17, 1931; s. Walter Hilding and Velma Mildred (Getchell) L.; B.A., U. Wichita, 1957; m. Nancy Ann Felker, July 14, 1955; children—Larry Dean, Donald Everett, Deborah Nanette. Sheet metal assembler Boeing Airplane Co., Wichita, Kans., 1952-53; with Cessna Aircraft Co., Wichita, 1956-74, inventory systems and control mgr., 1964-74, data processing coordinator, 1974; mgr. spares and logistics support Mitsubishi Aircraft Internat., Inc., San Angelo, Tex., 1974—. Served with USN, 1948-52; Korea. Mem. Internat. Materials Mgmt. Soc. Clubs: Confederate Air Force, Masons, Optimists (dir. local chpt. 1975-77, 77-78). Author: Inventory Systems and Control Handbook, 1976. Office: PO Box 3848 San Angelo TX 76901

LARSON, VERNON DALE, audiologist; b. Sioux Falls, S.D., May 10, 1941; s. Leonard Gehard and Agnes Eleanor (Schjodt) L.; B.A. (Nat. Def. fellow), Augustana Coll. (S.D.), 1965; M.S. (Vocat. Rehab. fellow), Colo. State U., 1966; Ph.D., Okla. U. Med. Center, 1973; m. Janice Corinne Haugen, Aug. 25, 1962; children—Tamara Lyn,

Kristen Eve. Counselor S.D. Sch. for the Deaf, Sioux Falls, 1961-65, audiologist, 1966-68; coordinator Edn. of the Deaf, Augustana Coll., Sioux Falls, 1968-69; asst. prof. Kans State U., Manhattan, 1973-74; audiologist Model Secondary Sch. for the Deaf, Gaullaudet Coll., Washington, 1974-75; asso. prof., dir. hearing impaired program Central Mich. U., Mt. Pleasant, 1975-76; asso. prof. U. Wyo., Laramie, 1976-77; audiologist VA Med. Center, Oklahoma City, 1977—; adj. prof. dept. communication disorders Okla. U., Oklahoma City, 1977—; cons. in field. Mem. S.D. Gov's. Bd. for Licensure of Hearing Aid Dispensers, 1968-69; legis. com. Mich. Speech and Hearing Assn., 1976-77; chmn. Okla. Audiology Forum, 1978-79; mem. minority concerns com. U. Wyo., 1976-78. Served with U.S. Army, 1958-61. Recipient faculty research award Kans. State U., 1974; Creative Endeavors award Central Mich. U., 1976. Mem. Am. Speech and Hearing Assn. (joint com. audiology and edn. of the deaf, 1976-78), Acad. of Audiology. Republican. Lutheran. Co-editor: Trends in Hearing Prosthetics Research, 1979; contbr. chpts. to books, articles to profl. jours., papers to confs. Home: 5832 NW 88th St Oklahoma City OK 73132 Office: VA Medical Center A126 921 NW 13th St Oklahoma City OK 73104

LARSSON, DONALD ERIC, constrn. materials co. exec.; b. Jacksonville, Fla., July 27, 1941; s. Eric Joseph and Della (Palmer) L.; B.A., U. Fla., 1963; m. Irene Frances Boczar, June 17, 1978; children—Douglas Eric, Linda Frances. Ter. mgr. Litton Industries Inc., Jacksonville, Fla., 1971-72; v.p. New Markets, Inc., Jacksonville, 1972-75; mktg. mgr. Automated Bldg. Components, Inc., Miami, Fla., 1975-79; dir. sales Gory Asso. Industries, Inc., Miami, 1979—; nat. mktg. contracts cons. Gen. chmn. Jacksonville Public TV Auction, 1972. Served with USN, 1963-66. Mem. Consultative Council of Nat. Inst. Bldg. Scis. (charter), Nat. Assn. Homebuilders, Fla. Homebuilders Assn., U. Fla. Alumni Assn. (dir.), Gator Bowl Assn. Republican. Episcopalian. Home: 3046 NW 119th Ln Coral Springs FL 33065 Office: 1773 NE 205th St North Miami FL 33179

LASHMAN, FRANK A., answering service co. exec.; b. Washington, Aug. 28, 1920; s. Morris and Betty Lashman; ed. U. Miami (Fla.); 1 son, Michael A. Successively owner cosmetic co., dir. promotion and publicity for Janes Mansfield, ind. photographer; now owner Toll Free Am. Inc., nat. answering service, Ft. Lauderdale, Fla. Active local Boy Scouts Am.; bd. dirs. Broward Dolphin Booster Club. Served with U.S. Army, 1944-46. Mem. Associated Telephone Answering Exchanges, Ft. Lauderdale C. of C. Democrat. Clubs: Moose, Elks. Address: 5460 N State Rd Suite 215 Fort Lauderdale FL 33319

LASKY, SUZANNE TERRY (SCHLESINGER) (SUSAN), television personality/producer, public service mgr.; b. N.Y.C.; d. Alexander and Rosalyn Jeanette (Greenfield) Schlesinger; B.A., Hunter Coll.; M.S., Queens Coll.; m. Arnold Lasky. Tchr., Pub. Sch. No. 169, Bayside, N.Y.; documentary writer, reporter WTVJ-CBS, Miami, Fla.; pub. relations dir. WPBT Auction, Miami; pub. service mgr., talk show host, on air personality, writer, producer WCKT-NBC, Miami, 1971—; v.p. adv. council Center for Continuing Edn. of Women, Miami-Dade Community Coll., 1979—; mem. adv. council Inst. for Women, Fla. Internat. U., Miami, 1977—. Bd. dirs. Greater Miami Youth Symphony, Fellowship House, Miami; mem. info. com. Am. Cancer Soc., Miami. Recipient awards Fla. Dept. Alcoholic Rehab., Fla. Vets. Assn., Nat. Children's Cardiac Hosp., Dade County Assn. Retarded Children, U.S. Army 3d Recruiting Dist., U.S. Navy Recruiting Dist. S.Fla. and Caribbean, Fla. Internat. U. Inst. for Women, Mizrachi Women, Am. Jewish Congress, Dade Bus. and Profl. Women's Club, Jewish Nat. Fund Miami, Project New Born, Mus. of Sci. Recipient award Sisterhood of Temple Emanuel, Miami Beach; Suzanne Lasky Day proclaimed Met. Dade County, 1979. Mem. Am. Women in Radio and TV (v.p. Goldcoast chpt.), Women in Communications, NOW, Zool. Soc. Fla. Home: 7441 Wayne Ave Miami Beach FL 33141 Office: 1401 79th St Causeway Miami FL 33141

LASLETT, WILLIAM LENOX, architect; b. Albany, N.Y., Oct. 5, 1937; s. Basil George Frederick and Persis Louise (Lenox) L.; B.A., Colgate U., 1959; M.Arch., Yale U., 1963; M.P.H., U. N.C., 1980; children—William Lenox Bradford, Aliso Corning. Partner, Basil G. F. and Willim L. Laslett, Architects/Planners, Fayetteville, N.C., 1963—; vis. lectr. Sch. Design, Raleigh, N.C., 1974, Fayetteville Tech. Inst., 1971. Recipient Progressive Architecture citation for Wallace O'Neal Day Sch. Charrette, 1974; Honor award N.C. chpt. AIA, 1975, award of merit, 1975; HEW grantee, 1977; N.C. Dept. Archives and History grantee, 1979; Nat. Endowment for Arts grantee, 1979. Mem. AIA (dir. N.C. chpt. 1970, sec. 1971-72, v.p. 1973, dir. 1976; dir. S. Atlantic region 1973-74; pres. Eastern sect. N.C. 1970, 76; nat. com. arts and recreation 1977-80). Democrat. Presbyterian. Clubs: Yale (N.Y.C.); Kiwanis (Fayetteville). Prin. works include: U.S. Post Office, Fayetteville, 1965; Pope Elem. Sch., Ft. Bragg, N.C., 1965; Sci. Bldg., Fayetteville State U., 1967; Salvation Army Hdqrs., Fayetteville, 1969; Cape Fear High Sch., Vander, N.C., 1971; George Lee Butler Learning Center, Fayetteville State U., 1976; Dept. Public Health, Cumberland County, N.C., 1980; Sci. Complex, Fayetteville State U., 1980. Home: 314 W Park Dr Fayetteville NC 28305 Office: PO Box 53961 209 Fairway Dr Fayetteville NC 28305

LASLEY, CHARLES HADEN, cardiovascular surgeon; b. Lewisburg, Ky., Dec. 16, 1921; s. Marion Grinter and Helen Mae (Murray) L.; M.D., Harvard U., 1947; m. Janet Elizabeth Evans, Jan. 28, 1967; children—Mary Ann, Charles Haden, Robert Murray, David, Tiffany, Phillip. Intern in surgery Grady Hosp., Altanta, 1947-48, asst. resident in surgery, 1948-49; resident in surgery, Gorgas Hosp., Ancon, C.Z., 1950, sr. resident in surgery, 1951; resident in thoracic and cardiac surgery City of Hope Med. Center, Los Angeles, 1954-55; resident in thoracic and cardiovascular surgery VA Hosp., Asheville, N.C., 1955-56; practice medicine specializing in thoracic and cardiovascular surgery, Clearwater, Fla., 1956—; med. dir. Longevity Clinic, Inc., Largo, Fla.; mem. staff Morton F. Plant Hosp., Clearwater, Clearwater Community Hosp. Served with M.C., U.S. Army, 1949-54. Diplomate Am. Bd. Surgery, Am. Bd. Thoracic Surgery. Fellow A.C.S., Internat. Coll. Surgeons, Am. Coll. Chest Physicians (pres. Fla. chpt. 1969-70), Southeastern Surg. Congress; mem. Am. Assn. Thoracic Surgery, Soc. Thoracic Surgeons (founding), Fla. Soc. Thoracic and Cardiovascular Surgeons (pres. 1971-72), Am. Thoracic Soc., So. Thoracic Surgery Assn., Pinellas County Med. Soc. (chmn. com. health ins. rev. 1963-64), Fla. Med. Assn. (del. 1965-70). Republican. Mem. Christian Ch. Club: Ponte Vedra. Home: 461 Ponce de Leon Blvd Belleair FL 33516 Office: VA Hosp Bay Pines FL

LASSEN, RAYMOND VIGGO, JR., obstetrician, gynecologist; b. Kalamazoo, Aug. 25, 1935; s. Raymond Viggo and Rosa Edith (Helton) L.; B.S., U. Miss., 1959, M.D., 1963; m. Paula Sue McGraw, Aug. 18, 1956; children—Raymond Viggo, Kevin Derrick, Kimberley Sue, Kirsten Ilene. Intern, Brooke Gen. Hosp., San Antonio, 1963-64; resident in obstetrics and gynecology U. Miss., Jackson, 1964-67; individual practice medicine specializing in obstetrics-gynecology, Amory, Miss., 1967-73, Greenville, S.C., 1973—; chief obstetrics-gynecology Gilmore Meml. Hosp., Amory, 1968-72; attending staff Greenville Gen. Hosp., 1973—; attending staff St. Francis Community Hosp., Greenville, 1973—, chief obstetics-gynecology, 1976—, exec. committeeman, 1976—. Mem. Amory C. of C., 1968-73; warden St. John's Episcopal Ch., Aberdeen, Miss., rep. to diocesan council, Tombigbee council, Miss. Served with USAF, 1954-58, with U.S. Army, 1963-64. Diplomate Am. Bd. Obstetrics and Gynecology. Fellow Am. Coll. Obstetrics and Gynecology; mem. Miss. Gynesic Soc., Miss. State Med. Soc., AMA. Episcopalian. Office: 607 Arlington Ave Greenville SC 29601

LASSETER, PHILOMENA CARMEL NOVELLE, ednl. psychologist; b. N.Y.C., Sept. 26, 1922; d. Francis Paul and Maria Giovanna (Galluzzo) Novelle; B.A., Hunter Coll., 1944; M.A., U. Ala., 1969, Ph.D., 1979; m. Edward Lynn Lasseter, Sr., July 6, 1945; children—Edward Lynn, Jenny, William, Emily, Joseph, Paul, Teresa, Mary, Timothy. Elementary tchr. Etowah County Bd. Edn., Gadsden, Ala., 1966-68, tchr. high sch. chemistry and physics, 1968-70, psychometrist, 1971-73; part-time inst. U. Ala. Gadsden Center, 1970-73, 74-75; dir.-owner Reading Clinic & Learning Center, Gadsden, 1970-74, Oneonta Counseling Center and Ednl. Therapy Clinic, 1979—; psychometrist Tuscaloosa (Ala.) City Schs., 1977-79; sch. psychologist Oneonta (Ala.) City Schs., 1979—; tutor children with reading and math. learning problems, Gadsden, 1953-65. Dir. sch. religion St. James Roman Cath. Ch., Gadsden, 1960-65. Served with WAC, 1944-45. Grad. fellow U. Ala., 1969-70. Mem. Am. Psychol. Assn., Am. Personnel and Guidance Assn., Internat. Reading Assn., NEA, Ala. Edn. Assn., AAUW, Assn. Retarded Citizens, Assn. Children with Learning Disabilities, Council Exceptional Students, Etowah County Mental Health Assn., Delta Kappa Gamma, Kappa Delta Pi (chpt. sec. 1973-74, pres. 1974-75). Democrat. Club: Bus. and Profl. Women's. Home: Route 3 Box 96-A Altoona AL 35952 Office: Highway 75S PO Box 160 Oneonta AL 35121

LASSITER, JOE FRANK, JR., lawyer; b. Montgomery, Ala., May 1, 1943; s. Joe F. and Rose (Tatum) L.; B.S., U. Ala., 1965; J.D., Cumberland Sch. Law, 1968; m. Clare Cleere, June 6, 1966; children—Christine, Joe Frank. Admitted to S.C. bar, 1973, Ala. bar, 1968, U.S. Supreme Ct., 1972; asso. firm Miller & Hoffmann, Montgomery, 1970-73; asst. gen. counsel Daniel Internat. Corp., Greenville, S.C., 1973-74; v.p. purchasing Daniel Constrn. Co., 1974-79, v.p. mktg., counsel, 1979; v.p., sec., dir. SEIGE Corp., 1979—. Served with AUS, 1969-70; Vietnam. Decorated Bronze Star with cluster. Presbyterian. Home: 186 Chapman Rd Greenville SC 29607 Office: Daniel Bldg Co Greenville SC 29605

LASTRA, JESUS L., dentist; b. La Salud, Havana, Cuba, Jan. 5, 1928 (came to U.S., 1961, naturalized, 1968); s. Patricio and Antonia (Martinez) L.; B.S., Inst. of Havana, 1947; D.D.S., Havana U., 1952; D.M.D., U. Ala., 1966; m. Silvia M. Lopez, Aug. 6, 1950; children—Idalia, Teresa. Practice dentistry, Havana, 1952-61; instr. crown and bridge U. Havana, 1952-59, prof., 1959-61, prof. Summer Sch., 1956; instr., research asso. U. Ala., 1966-68; practice dentistry, Miami, Fla., 1968—; v.p. Dade County Dental Research Clinic. Fellow Acad. Gen. Dentistry, Internat. Coll. Dentists; mem. Am., Mexican, Cuban (past v.p., sec. sci. com.), Havana dental assns., Internat. Assn. for Dental Research, Am. Prosthodontic Soc., Latin Am. Dental Study Club (pres. 1973-74), SE Fla. Acad. Gen. Dentistry (pres. 1978-79), Greater Miami Dental Soc. (treas.), Delta Sigma Delta. Lion (pres. 1972-73). Club: Cuban Sertoma (pres. 1979-80). Contbr. articles to profl. jours. Home: 2100 SW 21st Terr Miami FL 33145 Office: 2150 SW 21st Ave Miami FL 33145

LATHAM, ALICE FRANCES PATTERSON (MRS. WILLIAM JOSEPH LATHAM), pub. health nurse; b. Macon, Ga., Dec. 18, 1916; d. Frank Waters and Ruby (Dews) Patterson; R.N., Charity Hosp. Sch. Nursing, New Orleans, 1937; student George Peabody Coll. Tchrs., 1938-39; B.S. in Pub. Health Nursing, U. N.C., 1954; M.P.H., Johns Hopkins U., 1966; m. William Joseph Latham, July 21, 1940; children—Jo Alice Latham Solomon, Marynette Latham Webb, Lauruby Cathleen. Staff pub. health nurse assigned spl. venereal disease study USPHS, Darien, Ga., 1939-40; county pub. health nurse Bacon County, Alma, 1940-41; USPHS spl. venereal disease project, Glynn County, Brunswick, 1943-47; county pub. health nurse Glyn County, 1949-51, Ware County, Waycross, 1951-52; pub. health nurse supr. Wayne-Long-Brantley-Liberty Counties, Jesup, 1954-56; dir. pub. health nursing Wayne-Long-Appling Bacon-Pierce Counties, Jesup 1956—, now dist. chief of nursing S.E. health dist., exec. dir. health dept. home care services (16 counties). Bd. dirs. Wayne County Mental Health Assn., 1959, 60, 61, Wayne County Tb Assn., 1958-62; a non-alcoholic organizer Jesup group Alcoholics Anonymous, 1962-63; mem. Ga. Community Health Task Force, 1974-76; adv. council Ware Meml. Hosp. Sch. Practical Nursing, Waycross, Ga., 1958; bd. dirs. S.E. Ga. Health Systems Agy. Inc., 1975—, mem. exec. com., 1975-76, 78—. Recipient recognition Gen. Service Bd., Alcoholics Anonymous, Inc. Fellow Am. Pub. Health Assn.; mem. Am., 8th Dist. (pres. 1954-58, dir. 1960-62, 1st v.p. 1962), Ga. (exec. bd. 1954-58) nurses assns., Ga. Pub. Health Assn. (chmn. nursing sect. 1956-57), Ga. Assn. for Dist. Chiefs of Nursing (pres. 1975-77). Contbr. to state nursing manuals. Home: 115 Harper St Jesup GA 31545 Office: Southeast Health District Office 1101 Church St Waycross GA 31501

LATHAM, FRANK WINFORD, JR., retail store exec.; b. Fort Worth, Jan. 30, 1945; s. Frank Winford and Mary Lucylle (Cox) L.; ed. Baylor U.; m. Jeannie Brown, Feb. 5, 1966; children—Frank, Robert Emery, John Harwell. With R.E. Cox Co., Waco, Tex., 1970—, merchandise mgr., 1972-76, v.p., 1976—, also dir. Chmn. bus. adv. com. Retail Inst. McLennan Community Coll.; bd. dirs. Historic Waco Found., 1978-79; pres. Heart of Tex. Goodwill Industries, 1979—; mem. adminstrv. bd. Austin Ave. United Meth. Ch., 1977—; bd. trustees Scottish Rite Found. of Tex., 1979—; advisory bd. Tex. Ranger Found., 1979; bd. dirs. Am. Soc. Prevention Cruelty to Children, 1980. Served with USAF, 1963-67. Recipient Silver Good Citizenship medal S.A.R., 1978, DeMolay Legion of Honor, 1979, Order of Red Cross of Constantine, 1980. Mem. Am. Soc. Indsl. Security, Assn. Former Intelligence Officers, Tex. Assn. Bus., Nat. Retail Mchts. Assn., Tex. State Hist. Assn. Clubs: S.A.R. (v.p. chpt.), Masons, Shriners, S.C.V. Office: 501 Westview Village Waco TX 76710

LATHAM, JAMES PARKER, geographer; b. Collingdale, Pa., June 2, 1918; s. William Harry and Martha (Curry) L.; B.S., U. Pa., 1949, M.S., 1950, M.A. in Econs., 1951, Ph.D., 1959; m. Eloise McDaniel, Mar. 7, 1945. Lectr. geography and industry Wharton Sch., U. Pa., 1951-59; asst. prof. geography Bowling Green (Ohio) State U., 1959-61, asso. prof., 1961-64; prof., chmn. dept. geography Fla. Atlantic U., Boca Raton, 1964-70, prof., dir. Remote Sensing Lab., 1970—; prin. investigator Office Naval Research project, 1965-74, U.S. Geol. Survey project, 1967-70, 78-80. Mem. com. remote sensing NRC, 1973-78. Mem. Bowling Green City Planning Commn., 1963-64, Beach Park Devel. Com., Boca Raton, 1967. Served with USAAF, 1942-46; maj. M.I., U.S. Army Res., 1947-71. Mem. Assn. Am. Geographers, Fla. Soc. Geographers (pres. 1966-67), AAAS, Am. Planning Assn., Am. Soc. Photogrammetry (pres. Fla. region 1969-70, nat. dir., mem. exec. com. 1971-74), Phi Kappa Phi. Methodist. Kiwanian. Contbr. articles to profl. jours. Home: 830 NE 69th St Boca Raton FL 33431

LATHAM, WILLIAM IGNATIOUS, JR., air force officer; b. El Paso, Tex., June 17, 1948; s. William I. and Martha Jane (Stark) L.; B.A., U. Tex., El Paso, 1970; postgrad. Utah State U., 1974-75; m. Tricia Lildella Caraway, July 5, 1969; children—William Ignatious III, Joshua Luke. Commd. 2d lt. U.S. Air Force, 1970, advanced through grades to capt., 1974; helicopter rescue pilot Da Nang Airfield, 1972-73; instr. pilot Combat Crew Tng. Sch., Hill AFB, 1973-76; instr. pilot for German Air Force fighter pilots, Sheppard AFB, Tex., 1976-78, wing chief flight ops. br. 80th Flying Tng. Wing, 1978—. Music dir., edn. dir. Calvary Baptist Ch., Odgen, Utah, 1977-79; young adult tchr. First Bapt. Ch., Wichita Falls, Tex., 1977-79; active Democratic election campaign, 1969. Decorated Air medals (7), Air Force Commendation medals (2). Named Outstanding Office of the Yr., 1550th Flying Tng. Squadron, Hill AFB, Utah, 1974. Mem. Air Force Assn., Internat. Brotherhood Magicians, Tex. Assn. Magicians, Wizards of Wichita Falls, Order of Daedalians, Pi Sigma Alpha. Democrat. Baptist. Club: Sheppard AFB Officers Open Mess. Home: 4803 Lovers Ln Wichita Falls TX 76310 Office: 80 FTW/DOOF Stop 100 Sheppard AFB TX 76311

LATHAN, SAMUEL ROBERT, internist; b. Charlotte, Apr. 28, 1938; s. Samuel Robert and Callie Mims (Purvis) L.; B.S., Davidson Coll., 1959; M.D., Johns Hopkins, 1963; m. Mary Amelia Hudson, Mar. 19, 1966; children—Caroline, Stewart, Robert. Intern, Duke Hosp., Durham, N.C., 1963-64; resident Grady Hosp., Atlanta, 1964-67; practice medicine specializing in internal medicine Lowance Clinic, Altanta, 1969-73, Colony Med. Group, Atlanta, 1973—; pres. 5th Cypress Corp., Atlanta, 1971-76; pres., dir. Colony Med. Group, 1976—; faculty Emory U., Atlanta, 1969—, Grady Hosp., 1969—. Chmn. Atlanta physicians group campaign United Way, 1974; vol. Hippie Clinic, 1969-72. Served with USAF, 1967-69. Diplomate Am. Bd. Internal Medicine. Fellow A.C.P., Am. Coll. Chest Physicians; mem. Med. Assn. Atlanta (trustee 1971), Ga. Med. Assn., AMA (physicians recognition awards 1969, 72, 76), Am. Soc. Internal Medicine, Ga. Heart Assn., Ga. Thoracic Soc., Am. Thoracic Soc., Atlanta Clin. Soc. (v.p. 1977—), Kappa Alpha. Episcopalian. Club: Capital City. Editor Atlanta Medicine, 1975—. Contbr. articles to profl. jours. Home: 1175 W Brookhaven Dr Atlanta GA 30319 Office: 400 Colony Sq Suite 1605 Atlanta GA 30361

LATHEM, JAMES ERNEST, surgeon; b. Easley, S.C., Jan. 24, 1934; s. James Garrison and Ernestine Chiles L.; student U. S.C., 1952-55; M.D., Med. U. S.C., 1959; m. Betty Ruth Lewis, June 13, 1959; children—Jim, Anne. Intern, resident urology Bowman Gray Sch. Medicine, Winston-Salem, N.C., 1960-65; asst. prof. urology Ohio State U., Columbus, 1965-66; practice medicine specializing in urology Greenville, S.C., 1966—; pres., chmn. bd. Willow Practice, Greenville, 1968—. Chmn. bd. Community Bank, Greenville, 1973—; dir. Engineered Custom Plastics, Greenville, AGS Food System Inc. Sec. S.C. Bd. Med. Examiners, 1978—. Mem. S.C. Med. Assn. (treas. 1974-78), AMA, A.C.S., Am. Urol. Assn. (T. Leon Howard award Southeastern sect. 1964), Soc. Pediatric Urology. Methodist. Club: Poinsett. Author, producer sci. med. exhibits, med. motion picture. Contbr. articles to profl. publs. Home: Route 2 Greenville SC 29607 Office: 24 Vardry St Greenville SC 29601

LATHROP, GERTRUDE ADAMS, chemist; b. Norwich, Conn., Apr. 28, 1921; d. William Barrows and Lena (Adams) Lathrop; B.S., U. Conn., 1944; M.A., Tex. Woman's U., 1953, Ph.D., 1955. Devel. chemist textiles Alexander Smith & Sons Carpet Co., Yonkers, N.Y., 1944-52; research asso. textiles Tex. Women's U., 1952-56; chief chemist Glasgo Finishing Plant div. United Mchts. & Mfrs., Inc. (Conn.), 1956-57, chief chemist Old Fort Finishing Plant div. (N.C.), 1957-63; research chemist U.M.R.C., 1963-64; lab. and warranty mgr. automotive div. Collins & Aikman Corp., Albemarle, N.C., 1964-78; chief chemist, lab. dir. Old Fort Finishing Plant United Mchts., 1979—. Mem. Am. Chem. Soc., Am. Assn. Textile Chemists and Colorists (sect. treas., vice chmn. 1963-64, research chmn. 1962; Charles H. Stone scholarship com., chmn. 1975-79), ASTM (chmn. transp. fabrics on flammability com. 1973-75), Bus. and Profl. Women's Club (pres. chpt. 1974-76, Career Woman of Year award 1979, 80), Iota Sigma Pi. Home: 301 Mountain St Black Mountain NC 28711 Office: Old Fort Finishing Plant Old Fort NC 28762

LATIMER, JAMES K., JR., oil field mfg. and sers. co. exec.; b. Rayne, La., July 20, 1938; s. James K. and Rose Lee (Stein) L.; B.S., Tex. A&M U., 1961, B.A. in Math, 1963, M.S. in Petroleum Engring., 1963; m. Shirley Darleen Gentry; children—Deborah Lynn, Cynthia Lea. Reservoir engr. Sun Oil Co., 1963-65; mgr. data processing IBM, Houston, 1965-74; programming cons., Houston, 1974-79; mgr. data processing Galveston Houston Co., Houston, 1979—. Served with AUS, 1961-62. Mem. Am. Prodn. and Inventory Control Soc. Home: 803 Forrest View St Friendswood TX 77546 Office: 5005 Riverway Houston TX 77056

LATIMER, THOMAS GOWER, ednl. adminstr.; b. Vidalia, Ga., Dec. 27, 1936; s. Gower and Reba (Thomas) L.; B.S. in Edn., Ga. So. Coll., Statesboro, 1960, M.Ed., 1966; D.Ed., N.C. State U., Raleigh, 1974; m. Carolyn Neill Cripps, July 23, 1967; children—David Gower, Laura Lynn. Tchr. indsl. arts Cairo (Ga.) High Sch., 1961-64, LaGrange (Ga.) High Sch., 1964-67; asst. prof. indsl. arts edn. E. Carolina U., Greenville, N.C., 1967-69; asst. prof., dept. chmn. indsl. arts edn. W.Va. Inst. Tech., Montgomery, 1969-74; adv. tech. tng. program Ch. World Service, Managua, Nicaragua, C. Am., 1974-75; tchr. indsl. arts Wilkinson High Sch., Irwington, Ga., 1975-76; dir./supr. vocat. edn. Worth County Bd. Edn., Worth County High Sch., Sylvester, Ga., 1976—. Served with USAR, 1960. Named Outstanding Tchr. of Yr. for Ga., Am. Indsl. Arts Assn., 1966-67; recipient cert. of service Evang. Com. for Assistance and Devel., 1975. Mem. Am. Indsl. Arts Assn. (life), Am. Council Indsl. Arts Tchr. Educators (life), Am. Vocat. Assn., NEA, Ga. Vocat. Assn., Ga. Assn. Educators, Epsilon Pi Tau, Phi Delta Kappa, Iota Lambda Sigma, Ga. Indsl. Arts Assn. (pres. 1966-67), Home: PO Box 582 Sylvester GA 31791 Office: N Monroe St Sylvester GA 31791

LATIN, DONALD EDWARD, investment banker; b. Oak Park, Ill., Oct. 28, 1930; s. Louis H. and Lillian H. (Himmelblau) L.; B.S. in Bus. Adminstrn., Northwestern U., 1952, M.B.A. with distinction, 1953; m. Mary H. Buttler, Apr. 27, 1957; children—Lynne, Richard. Analyst, Cruttenden, Podesta & Miller, Chgo., 1956-62; v.p. Walston & Co., Inc., Chgo., 1963-73; sr. asso. Bacon, Whipple & Co., Chgo., 1973-76; v.p., mgr. corporate fin. dept. Rauscher Pierce Refsnes Inc., Dallas, 1976-80, sr. v.p., 1980—, dir. IFS Industries, Inc., San Diego. Chmn. Commuter Bus Com., Northbrook, Ill., 1975-76. Served with U.S. Army, 1954-56. Mem. Inst. Chartered Fin. Analysts, Dallas Assn. Investment Analysts, Beta Gamma Sigma, Beta Alpha Psi. Presbyterian. Home: 14957 Lacehaven Dr Dallas TX 75248 Office: 900 Mercantile Dallas Bldg Dallas TX 75201

LATORRE, LUZ HELENA, govt. ofcl.; b. Colombia, Apr. 23, 1945; came to U.S., 1959, naturalized, 1977; d. Carlos and Mariela (Tobon) L.; grad. high sch.; children—Luz Helena Delgado, Melissa Delgado. Staff, Eastern Airlines, N.Y.C., 1964-66, Braniff Airways, N.Y.C., 1969; mgr. public relations and sales Pamtours, N.Y.C., 1972; sales Aerocondor Airlines, N.Y.C., 1973; sales mgr. Shelborne Hotel, Miami, 1973-75; dir. travel industry div. Miami Beach (Fla.) Tourist Devel. Authority, 1975-78; mgr. internat. sales Fontainebleu Hilton

Hotel, Miami Beach, 1978-79; sales dir. Latin Am. dept. Bahamas Govt. Tourist Office, Miami, 1979—. Adv. bds. tourism. Mem. Am. Mktg. Assn. (v.p. S. Fla. 1976-77), Hotel Sales Mgmt. Assn., Latin C. of C., Latin Am. Tour Operators Assn. Office: Latin Am Dept Bahamas Govt Tourist Office 255 Alhambra Circle Coral Gables FL 33134

LATORTUE, GERARD RENE, economist, educator; b. Haiti, June 19, 1934; s. Rene A. and Francoise A. (Dupuy) L.; LL.B., U. Haiti, 1955, LL.M., 1956; Degree in Econ. Devel., U. Paris (France), 1960; m. Marlene Zephirin, Sept. 3, 1966; children—Gaielle, Stephanie, Alexia. Economist, Labor Dept., Port-au-Prince, Haiti, 1960-62; prof. econs. U. Haiti, Port-au-Prince, 1961-63; prof. econs. Inter-Am. U. P.R., San German, 1963—, chmn. dept. econs. and bus. adminstrn., 1968-72; project mgr. assistance to small-scale industries in Togo, UN Indsl. Devel. Orgn., 1972-74, chief adviser, Togo, 1974-77, Ivory Coast, 1977—; owner Caribbean Research Assos. Decorated officer Nat. Labor Order (Haiti). Mem. Am. Econ. Assn., Soc. Internat. Devel., Am. Mktg. Assn., Nat. Planning Assn. Lion. Contbr. chpts. to books. Home: B-10 Urb San Ramon San German PR 00753 Office: 01 PO Box 1318 Abidjan Ivory Coast also 01 PO Box 1747 Abidjan Ivory Coast

LATTA, DIANA LENNOX, interior designer; b. Lahaina, Maui, Hawaii, Aug. 5, 1936; d. D. Stewart S. and Jean Marjorie (Anderson) Lennox; grad. The Bishop's Sch., La Jolla, Calif., 1954; student U. Wash., 1954-56; m. Arthur McKee Latta, Jan. 26, 1957; children—Mary-Stewart, Marion McKee. Dir., Vero Beach (Fla.) br. of Wellington Hall, Ltd., Thomasville, N.C., 1970-72; asst. to chief designer Rablen-West Interiors, Vero Beach, 1972-75; design and adminstrv. asst. to pres. Design Studio Archtl. & Interior Design Concepts, Inc., Vero Beach, 1975—. Mem. Indian River Meml. Hosp. Women's Aux., Vero Beach, 1957-70, chmn. Charity Ball, 1960, v.p., 1962-64; leading actress in Vero Beach Theatre Guild prodns.: The Laughmaker, 1964, Oklahoma, 1966; model for Holly Fashion Show, Vero Beach, 1962-69; mem. adv. bd. Indian River County 4-H Horsemaster Club, 1973-76; bd. dirs. Vero Beach Mut. Concert Assn., 1973-76, chmn. hospitality com. 1974; bd. dirs. Vero Beach Theatre Guild, 1964. Mem. Kappa Kappa Gamma. Republican. Episcopalian. Club: Riomar Bay Yacht (club tennis champion 1964, 66, chmn. tennis com. 1964-66). Home: 6885 1st St SW Vero Beach FL 32960 Office: 927 Azalea Ln Vero Beach FL 32960

LATTA, WILLIAM HARVEY, mfg. co. exec.; b. Harnett County, N.C., Jan. 21, 1945; s. Erastus B. and Nancy (Veasey) L.; B.S., Campbell Coll., 1966; m. Joyce Stephens, Jan. 18, 1968; children—Reginald Scott, Stephanie Elizabeth. Cost acct. Sylvania Electric Products Co., Smithfield, N.C., 1968-70; plant controller Beaunit Corp., Research Triangle Park, N.C., 1970-72; fin. dir. Brown Wooten Mills Co., Burlington, N.C., 1972-74; controller, dir. data processing Stanly Knitting Mills, Inc., Oakboro, N.C., 1974—; part-time instr. acctg. Stanly Tech. Inst., 1974-75. Mem. System III Users Group. Republican. Presbyterian. Club: Stanly County Country. Home: 379 Park Rd Albemarle NC 28001 Office: PO Box 479 Oakboro NC 28129

LATTIMORE, JOY RENEE, coll. adminstr.; b. Goldsboro, N.C., Jan. 18, 1954; d. Albert and Zudora (Baldwin) Powell; B.S. in Edn., Barber-Scotia Coll., Concord, N.C., 1976; M.A. in Childhood Edn. (fellow), Ohio State U., 1977; m. Dec. 16, 1978. Office staff Barber-Scotia Coll., 1975-76, dir. career placement/alumni affairs, 1977-78, dir. alumni affairs, 1978-79, also supr. student tchrs., tutor in English. Vice pres. Young Democratic Com. Wayne County (N.C.), named Miss Zeta Phi Beta, 1973-74, Ms. Archonian, Barber-Scotia Coll., 1973-74. Greater Dillard Alumni scholar, 1972. Mem. Nat. Alumni Assn., Smithsonian Assos., Phi Delta Kappa, Alpha Kappa Mu, Zeta Phi Beta. Methodist. Home: 43 Fenix Dr SW Concord NC 28025 Office: 145 Cabarus Ave W Concord NC 28025

LATTING, PATIENCE SEWELL (MRS. TRIMBLE B. LATTING), mayor, civic worker; b. Texhoma, Okla., Aug. 27, 1918; d. Frank Asa and Leila (Yates) Sewell; A.B. magna cum laude, U. Okla., 1938; M.A., Columbia U., 1939; m. Trimble B. Latting, Aug. 23, 1941; children—Francelia Latting Wilson, Nancy Sewell Latting Spelman, James Trimble, Cynthia Longley Latting Weimar. Asst. to research librarian Chase Nat. Bank, N.Y.C., 1938-39. Mem. Oklahoma City Council, 1967-71, mayor, 1971—; legis. chmn. Okla. Congress Parents and Tchrs., 1960-67, bd. mgrs., 1959-67, mem. exec. com., 1963-67; mem. exec. com. Oklahoma City Council PTA's, 1960-62; pres. Edgemore PTA, Oklahoma City, 1963-64; mem. Okla. Gov.'s Reapportionment Com., 1960, Gov.'s Advisory Com. on Edn., 1964, Oklahoma City Citizen's Emergency Fin. Com., 1965; mem. bd. trustees U.S. Conf. Mayors; apptd. officer of the ct. to aid in reapportionment Okla. Legislature, 1964; Named Outstanding Sr. Woman, Theta Sigma Phi, U. Okla., 1938; recipient Amy B. Onken award to outstanding undergrad. mem. Pi Beta Phi, 1938, Phi Beta Kappa award to Outstanding Oklahoman, 1976; named Woman of Yr. in Civic Work, Oklahoma City chpt. Theta Sigma Phi, 1961, Outstanding Woman award, 1968; named Outstanding Woman of Okla., Soroptimist, 1969; named hon. col. State of Okla., 1960. Mem. League Women Voters (mem. Oklahoma City bd. 1958-59), Oklahoma City Tennis Assn. (mem. bd. 1965—), Mortar Bd., Huguenot Soc. Founders of Manakin in the Colony Va., Phi Beta Kappa (v.p. Oklahoma City alumni 1965—), Alpha Lambda Delta, Sigma Alpha Iota, Chi Delta Phi, Pi Mu Epsilon, Pi Beta Phi (pres. Oklahoma City alumni 197-48), Delta Kappa Gamma (hon.). Clubs: 20th Century (sec. 1961-62), Oklahoma City Golf and Country, Altrusa (hon.). Home: 3600 Harvey Pkwy Oklahoma City OK 73118 Office: City Hall 200 N Walker St Oklahoma City OK 73102

LATTMANN, STEPHEN EDMUND, archtl. designer, gen. contractor; b. Bklyn., Nov. 10, 1946; s. Robert Theodore and Margaret Julia L.; B.S. in Architecture, N.Y. Inst. Tech., 1969; m. Mary Candace Moore, Oct. 15, 1977. Job capt., office mgr. Davis & Sands, Architects, N.Y.C., 1966-72; job capt. Twitchell & Allen, Architects, Sarasota, Fla., 1972-73; sr. v.p. Ramar Group Cos., developers, Sarasota, 1973—; prof. tech. dept. Manatee Jr. Coll., Bradenton, Fla., part time 1972-75. Served with USAR, 1969-75. Mem. AIA, Nat. Home Builders Assn., Fla. Planning and Zoning Assn. Home: 3219 Beneva Rd Sarasota FL 33582 Office: PO Box 1845 Venice FL 33595

LAU, RAY DENNIS, educator; b. Clinton, Okla., Aug. 10, 1946; s. Alvin and Viola Eleanora (Steigman) L.; B.A. in Edn. magna cum laude, Southwestern Okla. State U., 1967, M.Ed., 1973; M.L.S., Emporia Kans. State U., 1971; postgrad. Northwestern Okla. State U., 1977-80; m. Cherie Ann Garriott, May 25, 1968; children—Marc Garriott, Justin Ray. Tchr. English, chmn. dept. lang. arts Anadarko (Okla.) public schs., 1967-70; tchr., librarian Drummond (Okla.) public schs., 1970-71; cataloger, instr. library sci. Southwestern Okla. State U., Weatherford, 1971-74; dir. libraries, chmn. dept. library sci. Northwestern Okla. State U., Alva, 1974—; mem. Sequoyah Children's Book award com., 1974-77, chmn., 1975-76; cons., dir. numerous workshops in Okla., Kans. Mem. Okla. Curriculum Guide Com. for Teaching Library Skills, 1974-75: adv. council U. Okla. Sch. Library Sci., 1976-79; evaluation team mem. for various accreditation evaluations N. Central Assn. Colls. and Secondary Schs., 1975-76; ofcl. del. Okla. Gov.'s Conf. on Libraries and Info. Services, 1978. Served with U.S. Army, 1968. Recipient Community Leaders and Noteworthy Ams. award, 1977. Mem. Okla. Library Assn. (sec. Library Edn. div. 1976-77), Am. Hist. Soc. of Germans from Russia, Concordia Hist. Inst., German from Russian Heritage Soc., Higher Edn. Alumni Council of Okla., Wheatland Evangelistic Assn., Emporia Kan. State U. Alumni Assn., Alpha Phi Sigma. Christian Ch. Co-author: Curriculum Guide for Teaching Media Skills, K-12, 1975; contbr. articles in field to profl. jours. Home: 1801 Cherry St Alva OK 73717 Office: Univ Library Northwestern Okla State Univ Alva OK 73717

LAUBACH, HAROLD EDWARD, microbiologist, educator; b. Okeene, Okla., Sept. 13, 1946; s. Herbert Edward and Ruby Marie Laubach; student Northwestern Okla. State U., 1964-66; B.S., Southwestern Okla. State U., 1968; postgrad. U. Iowa, 1968, U. Okla., 1972-73; M.S., Okla. State U., 1975, Ph.D., 1977; m. Janet Lynn Hollander, July 26, 1966; children—Timothy Edward, Amy Lynn. Microbiologist dept. parasitology and microbiology Okla. State U., Stillwater, 1973-76, research asso., 1976-77; NIH postdoctoral research fellow in immunology dept. microbiology U. Ala., Birmingham, 1977-78; chmn., asst. prof. dept. microbiology W.Va. Sch. Osteo. Medicine, Lewisburg, 1978—; researcher in field. Served with U.S. Army, 1969-72. Decorated Bronze Star; NSF Molecular Biology Inst. Grantee, 1969; Am. Cancer Soc. grantee, 1979-80; Smith, Kline and French research grantee, 1979-80. Mem. Am. Soc. Parasitology, Sigma Xi. Democrat. Club: Kiwanis (v.p. Lewisburg). Contbr. articles to profl. publs. Home: 9 Greenbriar Ave White Sulphur Springs WV 24986 Office: 400 N Lee St Lewisburg WV 24901

LAUBER, EVELYN GREMLI, real estate broker; b. Sarasota, Fla., July 8, 1917; d. Erwin and Mamie (Rewiss) Gremli; student Juilliard Sch. Music, 1940-42; grad. Realtor Inst.; m. Merritt Russell Lauber, July 28, 1940; children—Merritt Erwin, Douglas Ross. Owner, Erwin Gremli Real Estate, Inc., Sarasota, 1970—. Mem. Adelphi Opera Workshops. Certified residential specialist, residential broker. Mem. Sarasota Bd. Realtors, Women's Council Realtors (pres. 1976; Realtor of Year 1977), Multiple Listing Service Sarasota (sec.-treas.), Realtors Nat. Mktg. Inst., Fla. Assn. Realtors, Sarasota C. of C., 100 Club (charter). Presbyterian. Club: Order Eastern Star. Home: 230 Scott St Sarasota FL 33580 Office: 1535 2d St Sarasota FL 33577

LAUDERDALE, MICHAEL LYNN, social psychologist, educator; b. Hobart, Okla., Dec. 9, 1941; s. Tommie Lee and Almeta Carolyn (Cantrall) L.; B.A., U. Okla., 1963, M.S., 1964, Ph.D., 1967; m. Camille Teresa Contreras, Dec. 28, 1966; children—Gregory, Lynn Marisa Lauren. Lectr. psychology U. Okla., Norman, 1966-67; asst. prof. psychology N.Mex. State U., Las Cruces, 1967-69; asst. prof. social work U. Tex., Austin, 1970-74, asso. prof., 1974—, dir. continuing edn. Sch. Social Work, 1970; cons. in field. NIMH predoctoral fellow, 1964-67. Bd. dirs. S.W. Center Child Abuse and Neglect, 1975—. Research grants aging. Mem. Am. Psychol. Assn., Council Social Work Edn., Am. Sociol. Assn. Methodist. Author: (with others), Community Development, 1970, Planning for Change, 1970, Service Delivery Systems, 1970. Editor: Social Service Improvement Series, 10 vols., 1970-71. Home: 4510 Spanish Oak Trail Austin TX 78731 Office: 2206 University Ave U Tex Austin TX 78712

LAUFER, PETER, social worker; b. Vienna, Austria, July 13, 1933; s. Edward D. and Fritzi (Winter) L.; B.A., Ohio State U., 1956; M.A., U. Chgo., 1961; m. Elisabeth J. Beerman, June 12, 1960; children—Erik Marc, David Andrew, Caryn Ruthe, Matthew Scott. Social worker Inst. for Juvenile Research, Rockford, Ill., 1961-66; adminstrv. dir. adolescent unit H. Douglas Singer Zone Center, Rockford, 1966-70; individual practice psychiat. social work, Coral Gables, Fla., 1965—; cons. Occidental Ins. Co., Narconon; mem. faculty Med. Sch. U. Miami, 1972—. Served with U.S. Army, 1956-58. Mem. Southeastern Group Psychotherapy Assn., Am. Group Psychotherapy Assn., Fla. Soc. Clin. Social Workers, Nat. Assn. Social Workers, Am. Orthopsychiat. Assn. Club: Arvida Soccer (v.p.). Office: 1320 S Dixie Hwy Suite 221 Coral Gables FL 33146

LAUFFER, CAROLYN GIBSON, educator; b. Georgetown, S.C., Dec. 9, 1930; d. Robert James and Lydia (Ray) Gibson; A.B., U. N.C., Greensboro, 1954; M.A., Glassboro State Coll., 1968; Ph.D., Duke U., 1977; m. Richard A. Lauffer, Apr. 9, 1955; children—Daniel, Lisa, Laura. Tchr., Camp Lejeune (N.C.) High Sch., 1954-55; Lumberton (N.C.) pub. schs., 1958-60; substitute tchr. Pembroke (N.C.) State U., 1962; tchr. Glassboro, N.J., pub. schs., 1964-68; asst. prof. English, Campbell Coll., Buies Creek, N.C., 1968-76; chmn. dept. English and gen. studies Wilson County (N.C.) Tech. Inst., 1976-79; instr. English, Pitt Community Coll., 1979—. Z. Smith Reynolds grantee, 1971. Mem. S. Atlantic Modern Lang. Assn., Nat. Council Tchrs. English, Southeastern Conf. on Teaching English in the Two-Year Coll. Democrat. Presbyterian. Home: 220 York Rd Greenville NC 27834 Office: PO Drawer 7007 Greenville NC 27834

LAUGHBAUM, ANNA BELLE, educator; b. Galion, Ohio, Mar. 14, 1915; d. Edwin Howard and Julia (Johnson) L.; A.B., Greenville Coll., 1943; A.M., U. Ill., 1944, Ph.D., 1948; postdoctoral, U. Birmingham (Eng.), 1953. Asst. prof. Greek, N.T. and English, Bethany (Okla.) Nazarene Coll., 1946-50, prof. English, 1955—; asso. prof. English, Seattle Pacific Coll., 1950-55. Mem. Nat. Council Tchrs. English, AAUW (state coordinator corp. reps.), Conf. Christianity and Lit., Okla. Council Tchrs. English, S. Central MLA, Phi Delta Lambda. Republican. Mem. Ch. of Nazarene. Contbr. articles and poetry to religious pubs. Home: 5337 NW 44th St Oklahoma City OK 73122 Office: Bethany Nazarene Coll Bethany OK 73008

LAUGHLIN, MYRON PENN, profl. engr.; b. Lowell, Mass., May 7, 1893; s. George and Ella A. (Penn) L.; m. Julia A. Esposito, Apr. 27, 1946. Admitted to Ga. bar. Registered profl. engr., Ga. Mem. Order of Lafayette. Episcopalian. Mason. Author: Money from Ideas, 1950. Patentee elec. precipitation, boilder combustion devices, ship steering telemotors, mech. marine stoker, grass mowers, mechanochem. plant control devices, others. Research on ecology of fertilizers. Pres., creator M. Penn L. research and summation awards for law and engrng. students at Emory, Vanderbilt univs., Tex. Inst. Tech., other schs. Inventor lift fulcrum invalid walker assigned to Fla. Lions aid to the blind.

LAUHOFF, HERMAN EDWARD, state legislator; b. St. Joe, Tex., Aug. 8, 1933; s. Edward Philip and Patricia Aleen (Jennings) L.; student S. Tex. Jr. Coll., 1956-58, U. Houston, 1960; m. Carol Ann Colby, July 27, 1957; children—Kurt Edward, Jill Ellen. Draftsman, Tenneco Co., Houston, 1958-59, Tex. Hwy. Dept., Houston, 1960; personnel adminstr. Tex. Gulf, Inc., Houston, 1965-76; mem. Tex. Ho. of Reps., 1974—. Pres., Greater Houston Civil Council, 1972-74, Parkway Civic Club, 1970-74. Served with U.S. Army, 1953-55. Recipient Tex. Consumer Assn. award 1975. Democrat. Roman Catholic. Home: 5430 Winding Way Houston TX 77091 Office: State Capitol Austin TX 78767

LAUR, WILLIAM EDWARD, dermatologist; b. Saginaw, Mich., Nov. 17, 1919; s. Vertner L. and Ruth Gae (Eyre) L.; B.S., Mercer U., 1940; M.D., U. Mich., 1943; M.S., Wayne U., 1949; m. Mary Elizabeth Kirby, Dec. 31, 1943; children—Eric William, Edward Vertner, John Kirby, James Michael. Intern, John Sealy Hosp., Galveston, Tex., 1943; resident, fellow in dermatology Wayne State U., Detroit, 1946-49; practice medicine specializing in dermatology, Amarillo, 1949—; pres. High Plains Dermatology Center, Amarillo, 1975—; asso. clin. prof. Tex. Tech. Med. Sch., 1974—; cons. Santa Fe Ry., Amarillo VA Hosp. 1960—; mem. staff N.W. Tex. Hosp., High Plains Bapt. Hosp., St. Anthony's Hosp. Served with M.C., AUS, 1944-46; ETO. Diplomate Am. Bd. Dermatology. Mem. Potter Randall County Med. Soc. (pres. 1965), AMA, Tex. med. Assn., So. Med. Assn., Tex. Dermatology Soc., Am. Acad. Dermatology, Noah Worcester Dermatology Soc., Southwest Dermatology Soc., Alpha Tau Omega. Republican. Episcopalian. Clubs: Lions, Toastmasters. Contbr. articles to profl. jours. Home: 1607 Fannin St Amarillo TX 79102 Office: 3101 S Georgia St Amarillo TX 79109

LAUREANO-GERENA, LUCAS, hosp. food service dir.; b. Loiza, P.R., July 25, 1940; s. Lucas Laureano Torres and Angelina Gerena Arroya; B.B.A., World U., 1978; m. Felicita Fuentes de Laureano, Apr. 20, 1968; children—Gloria M. Laureano, Gilbran Laureano. Food service dir. A.R.A. at Auxilio Mutuo Hosp., San Juan, P.R., 1966-73, Saga Food Service Corp., 1973-78; pres. Hosp. Food Service, 1978—. Served with U.S. Army, 1964-66; Vietnam. Mem. Am. Soc. Hosp. Food Service Adminstrn., P.R. Chef Assn., Lewis Alumni Assn. Democrat. Roman Catholic. Clubs: P.R. Readers, Club Tanamá (Canóvanas, P.R.). Home: 4 EN 8 Via Fabiana Carolina PR 00630 Office: Hospital Auxilio Mutuo Ave Ponce de Leon Hato Rey PR 00919

LAURENT, SHERRY JANELL, real estate and ins. co. exec.; b. Port Arthur, Tex., June 26, 1936; d. Euclid Newton and Lodecia Elbertice (McDaniel) McLeod; student U. Tex., 1954-55, Lamar U., 1955, 69, 70; m. Marvin Alvin Laurent, Dec. 23, 1954; children—Sheryl Lynn, Kimberly Leigh, Scott Alvin. Supr., IRS and Regional Service Center, Austin, Tex., 1958-67; saleslady Duperier Real Estate, Beaumont, Tex., 1969-73; owner, Sherry Laurent Real Estate & Ins. Co., Beaumont, 1973—. Mem. Nat. Assn. Realtors, Tex. Assn. Realtors (dir. 1977-80), Beaumont Bd. Realtors (dir. 1974-77), Beaumont Multiple Listing Service Ind. Ins. Agents Tex., Beaumont C. of C. Club: Sales and Mktg. Execs. Office: Sherry Laurent Real Estate & Insurance Co 4110 Calder Ave Beaumont TX 77706

LAURIE, RAYMOND FRANCIS, county ofcl.; b. Chgo., Sept. 28, 1944; s. Frank James and Marie A. Laurie; A.A., Pierce Coll., 1967; B.A. in History, U. Calif., Northridge, 1971; M.Ed. in Correctional Counseling, Ga. State U., 1977. Asst. mgr. Monte's for Men, Canoga Park, Calif., 1965-66; mgr. Pacific Savs. & Loan Assn., Canoga Park, 1967-68; social worker Cook County Dept. Social Services, Chgo., 1971-72; adult probation officer Fulton County, Atlanta, 1972—. Served with U.S. Army, 1968-70. Mem. Fulton County Employees Assn. (pres. 1976—), Probation and Parole Assn. Ga., Atlanta Services Coop. (pres. 1974), Sigma Chi Theta. Roman Catholic. Office: 160 Pryor St 300 Atlanta GA 30303

LAUS, MICHAEL DANIEL, ednl. adminstr.; b. Pitts., Oct. 27, 1943; s. Daniel Joseph and Antonette Marie (Dileo) L.; B.S., California (Pa.) State Coll., 1967; M.Ed., U. Pitts., 1971, Ph.D., 1978; m. Janet Renschigai, May 28, 1966; children—Kristin, Michael. Orientation and mobility specialist Greater Pitts. Guild for the Blind, 1968-71; tchr. visually impaired Pitts. Public Schs., 1971-72, orientation and mobility specialist, 1972-77; mgmt. tng. specialist U. Ala., Birmingham, 1977—; cons. in field. Mem. Council Exceptional Children, Am. Assn. Mental Deficiency, Nat. Assn. Devel. Disabilities Mgrs. Club: Penn Hills Bocce. Author: Travel Instruction for the Handicapped, 1977. Home: 3332 Pembrooke Ln Birmingham AL 35226 Office: PO Box 313 Univ of Ala Birmingham AL 35294

LAUTH, LAURENCE VINCENT, coll. adminstr.; b. St. Paul, July 31, 1931; s. Harold Vincent and Kerrie M. (Denevan) L.; A.B., Fordham U., 1959, M.A in Edn., 1960; Ph.D., Mich. State U., 1969; m. Mary Elyn Gregory, Aug. 5, 1967; children—Amy Elizabeth, Laurence Vincent, Laura Elyn. Instr., St. Joseph's Coll. Prep. Sch., Phila., 1959-62; asst. dir. student union, dir. student activities U. Md., College Park, 1963-67; instr. Mich. State U., 1968-69; dean student services, asso. prof. No. Va. Community Coll., Annandale, 1969-70, coordinator student services, 1970-72; pres. Wytheville (Va.) Community Coll., 1972—; bd. dirs. Wythe Community Hosp. Bd. dirs. Wythe County United Fund; pres. St. Mary's Parish Council; bd. dirs. Child Care Center, No. Va. Community Coll. Mem. Am. Assn. Community and Jr. Colls., Am. Assn. Higher Edn., Am. Council Edn., Pres.'s Adv. Council of Va. Community Coll. System, State Council of Higher Edn. Continuing Edn. Adv. Com., Phi Delta Kappa. Roman Catholic. Club: Rotary. Office: 1000 E Main St Wytheville VA 24382

LAVELLE, JOHN BROH, ednl. adminstr.; b. Chgo., Dec. 24, 1925; B.S. in Bus. Adminstrn., Western Ill. U., Macomb, 1952, M.S. in Sch. Adminstrn., 1957; m. Mary Sue Turner; children—Christine, Andrea, Marc. Supt. media elem. sch., 1953-58; supt. Neponset (Ill.) High Sch., 1958-62; prin. Amboy (Ill.) Community Unit, 1962-66; prin. Clinton (Ill.) Community Unit, 1966-67; supt. Henry (Ill.) Senachwine High Sch., 1967-79; dean instrn. Ala. Inst. Bus., Northport, 1979—. Bd. dirs BMP Spl. Edn. Coop. Mem. Ill. Assn. Sch. Adminstrs., Ill. Prins. Assn., Nat. Assn. Secondary Sch. Prins., Ill. High Sch. Assn. (legis. com., dir.), Phi Delta Kappa. Home: 24 Hagler Mill Northport AL 35476 Office: Ala Inst Bus PO Box 1813 Tuscaloosa AL 35403

LAVENDER, WILLIAM THOMAS, JR., lawyer; b. Sumter, S.C., Sept. 14, 1951; s. William Thomas and Anne (Gibson) L.; B.S. in Mech. Engring., Clemson (S.C.) U., 1973; J.D., U. S.C., 1976; m. Cynthia Daniel Robertson, Oct. 13, 1979. Admitted to S.C. bar, 1976; environ. engr. S.C. Dept. Health and Environ. Control, 1976-77, staff counsel, 1977—. Del., S.C. Dem. Conv., 1976. Mem. Am. Bar Assn., S.C. Bar Assn., Richland County Bar Assn. Methodist. Club: Masons. Home: 501 S Ott Rd Columbia SC 29205 Office: 2600 Bull St Columbia SC 29201

LAVERY, WILLIAM EDWARD, univ. pres.; b. Genesco, N.Y., Nov. 20, 1930; s. John Raymond and Mary Irene (O'Brien) L.; B.S., Mich. State U., 1953; M.A., George Washington U., 1959; Ph.D., U. Wis., 1962; m. Peggy J. Johnson, Apr. 7, 1956; children—Debra, Kevin, Lori, Mary. Tchr. Clarence (N.Y.) Central High Sch., 1953-54; asst. to adminstr. Fed. Extension Service Dept. Agr., Washington, 1956-66; dir. adminstrn.-extension div. Va. Polytech. Inst. and State U., Blacksburg, 1966-68, v.p. finance, 1968-73, exec. v.p., 1973-75, pres., 1975—; AID cons. to El Salvador, 1969; dir. Dominion Bankshores Corp., Shenandoah Life Ins. Co. Mem. United Fund-Community Fedn., 1968-72; bd. dirs. Montgomery County Hosp. Served with AUS, 1954-56. Recipient Brotherhood award NCCJ, 1979. Kellogg Found. fellow, 1960-62. Club: Rotary (Blacksburg). Home: 604 Rainbow Ridge Blacksburg VA 24060

LAVEZZOLI, CHARLES EDWARD, ins. co. exec.; b. Hartford, Conn., Mar. 24, 1942; s. Charles Louis and Theresa (Noble) L.; B.A., St. Michael's Coll., 1964; J.D., Boston U., 1967; m. Jane Harriet Cairns, Jan. 29, 1971; children—Brian Edward, Grant Douglas. With Met. Life Ins. Co., 1969—, asso. European mgr., Frankfurt, Ger.,

1971-72, resident mgr., London, 1972-74, dist. sales mgr. Skyway dist., Flushing, N.Y., 1973-76, v.p. Southeastern terr., Tampa, Fla., 1976—. Served with U.S. Army, 1968-69. Mem. Am. Soc. Chartered Life Underwriters, Am. Coll. Life Underwriters (C.L.U.), Nat., Tampa assns. life underwriters, Gen. Agts. and Mgrs. Conf., Gen. Agts. and Mgrs. Assn. Roman Catholic. Home: 4905 New Providence Ave Tampa FL 33609 Office: Met Life Ins Co Southeastern Head Office Metropolitan Plaza Tampa FL 33607

LAVIN, JOHN THOMAS, food co. exec., entertainer; b. Gurdon, Ark., Apr. 5, 1916; s. John T. and Ruby Leah (Black) L.; Mus.B., Ouachita Bapt. U., 1937; Mus.M., So. Coll. Fine Arts, 1952; m. Dorothy M. Carroll, Apr. 28, 1968; 1 dau. by previous marriage, Carolyn Lavin Calvert. Instr. music in various pub. schs., colls., 1938-50; mfr.'s rep., entertainer, 1951-53; exec. sec. Natural Food Assos., Atlanta, Tex., 1954-75, exec. dir., 1975—. Active as an after dinner entertainer, 1948—. Pres., Tex. Forest Festival, Atlanta, 1969-72; chmn. Centennial Celebration, Atlanta, Tex., 1972. Mem. Internat. Platform Assn. Mason (Shriner, 32 deg.), Lion (pres. 1949-50). Author: A Concept of Laughter, 1961; Laughing All the Way, 1964; Holiday for Fun, 1973. Home: 702 Florence Atlanta TX 75551 Office: Hwy 59 W Atlanta TX 75551

LAVINE, BARBARA ESTHER, hosp. exec.; b. Detroit, July 9, 1949; d. Patrick Joseph and Ruth Marion (Pentelnik) Mullin; B.A. in Social Sci., Mich. State U., 1971; cert. in health services mgmt. U. Va., 1976; postgrad. George Washington U., 1978-80; m. Robert A. Lavine, Apr. 23, 1977. Personnel coordinator Medox subs. Drake Internat. Corp., Washington, 1973-74; employment mgr. Providence Hosp., Washington, 1974-76; personnel dir. Nat. Orthopedic and Rehab. Hosp., Arlington, Va., 1976—. Mem. Met. Washington Hosp. Personnel Council (dirs. div.), Va. Assn. Personnel Adminstrs. (co-chairperson No. Va. personnel dirs. div.). Home: 2830 S Buchanan St Arlington VA 22206 Office: 2455 Army Navy Dr Arlington VA 22206

LAVINGHOUSEZ, WILLIAM E., Realtor, TV broadcaster; b. Mobile, Ala., Apr. 12, 1921; s. John Edward Brooks and Minnie Lee (McCurdy) L.; ed. pub. schs., Mobile; m. Geraldine Elaine Morrison, Apr. 12, 1947; children—William E., Gilbert Brooks (dec.), Gerry Anne. With Ballard & Ballard Co. (merged with Pillsbury Co. 1951), Mobile, Ala., 1938-42, 46-65, office mgr., 1940-42, br. mgr., 1950, mgr. feed div. S. Ala. and N. Fla., 1951-59, plant mgr., Tampa, Fla., 1959-65; mgmt. cons. Internat. Milling Co., 1965; bus. mgmt. cons. Internat. Bus. Info. Bur., 1965; broadcaster sta. WFTV, Orlando, Fla., 1965—; adjudicator Poultry Princes Contest, Miss Southland Contest; Realtor Lavinghousez Realty, Orlando, 1965—; tchr. of small bus. mgmt. for adult evening classes at Lake-Sumpter Jr. Coll., Fla., 1965—. Served with USN, 1942-45. Recipient numerous awards including Nat. Forestry Service award, 1976, Future Farmers of Am. award, 1975, U.S. Dept. Agr. award, 1977. Mem. Nat. Assn. of Farm Broadcasters, Orlando Area C. of C. (chmn. hospitality forum O.J. Forum 1980—), Am. Soc. of Personnel Adminstrs., Nat., Fla. assns. realtors, Orlando-Winter Park Bd. of Realtors (chmn. welfare and bloodbank com.). Democrat. Roman Catholic. Clubs: K.C., St. Charles Men's. Home: 636 W Yale St Orlando FL 32804

LAW, JOSEPH GILLESPIE, JR., criminologist; b. Mobile, Ala., Feb. 8, 1947; s. Joseph Gillespie and Elma Idonia (Antoine) L.; B.S., Spring Hill Coll., 1969; M.S., U. South Ala., 1976; postgrad. Auburn U., 1977—; m. Pamela Leona McFerrin, Dec. 5, 1975; children—Joseph Gillespie III, Jonathon Roberts. Pres., gen. mgr. Southeastern Security Systems, Mobile, 1974-75; pvt. practice security cons., polygraph examiner, Opelika, Ala., 1975—. Served with U.S. Army, 1969-73. Decorated Bronze Star, Air medal. Mem. Nat. Honor Soc. in Psychology, Am. Polygraph Assn., Ala. Assn. Polygraph Examiners, Ala. Psychol. Assn., Am. Personnel and Guidance Assn., Am. Mental Health Counselors Assn., Scabbard and Blade. Methodist. Club: Exchange. Contbr. articles in field to profl. jours. Home: 839 Tullahoma St Auburn AL 36830

LAW, PHILIP AUSTIN, acct., bus. exec.; b. Wetumpka, Ala., Mar. 4, 1941; s. Max Austin and Vivian Inez (McGlamery) L.; student U. Houston, 1964-69; B.B.A., Sam Houston State U., 1970, M.B.A., 1971; m. Elizabeth Jane Zschiesche, May 31, 1974. Acct., corp. sec.-treas. Pizza Mgmt., Inc., Del Rio, Tex.; speaker EDP. Office: 2114B Avenue F Del Rio TX 78840

LAW, RALPH AREGOOD, chemist; b. Little Rock, Nov. 20, 1927; s. Ralph Aregood and Frances Louise (Weber) L.; B.A. in Chemistry, U. Ark., 1950; m. Frances Carolyn Adair, Aug. 4, 1973; children by previous marriage—David, Leslie, Brian. Chemist, Coca-Cola Co., Atlanta, 1955-60, Pennsalt Chem. Corp., Indsl. Mfg., Dallas, 1960-64; chief chemist Core Labs, Inc., Indsl. Water Tech., Dallas, 1964-71, Ecology Audits, Inc., subs. Core Labs., Inc., after 1974; div. mgr., chief chemist Water Sers. Ecology Audits, Inc.; chem. engring. supr. Herman Blum, Cons. Engrs., Dallas, 1971-74; cons. in field. Served with USN, 1946-48. Mem. Am. Chem. Soc., Water Pollution Control Fedn., Nat., Tex. rifle assns. Republican. Episcopalian. Home: 1934 Rambling Ridge Ln Carrollton TX 75007 Office: 11061 Shady Trail Dallas TX 75229

LAW, WALTER CHARLES, mgmt. info. specialist; b. Houston, Mar. 26, 1951; s. Wilkie Gilhart and Eloise Margaret (Wilson) L.; B.A., Tex. So. U., 1974, M.A., 1976. Ordained minister Ch. of God in Christ, 1974; statis. coordinator Ch. of God in Christ, Tex. S. Central, Houston, 1972—; dean of Insts. state sunday sch., youth and missions depts., Tex. So. U., Houston, 1974-76; grad. asst. in statistics, exptl. and intro. psychology Tex. So. U., 1974-75, mgmt. info. specialist, 1975—, tchr. statistics and research, 1975-77; cons. mgmt. and organizational systems. Chmn. The Houston Com., Inc. 1976—; minister of music Law Meml. Ch. of God in Christ, Houston, 1970—. Recipient Career Achievement award Future Soc. of Atlanta, 1975, Houston Com., 1976, 1977, merit award Eagle Scouts, Boy Scouts Am., 1977; Career Achievement award, 1978; Community Ser. and Profl. Achievement award, Houston, 1979. Mem. Assn. Black Psychologists, State Ministers Alliance, Assn. Instl. Research, So. Assn. Instl. Info. System, Kappa Delta Pi, Phi Mu Alpha Sinfonia. Author: The Quintessence of Higher Edn., 1975; Mgmt. Info. Systems and the University, 1977; Academic Creativity: New Innovations in Higher Edn., 1977; What Affects Intelligence: Genetics or Culture?, 1977; The Urban University: Finding a New Commitment, 1977; Relationship of Transaction Information Systems to the Institutional Information System: A Conceptual Approach; Instructional Evaluation and Institutional Responsibility; Institutional Research and Institutional Management: A Connubial Relationship; A College Education: Redefining the Curriculum, the Degree or Both?, 1979. Home: 4801 Wipprecht St Houston TX 77026 Office: 3201 Wheeler St Box 18 Houston TX 77004

LAWALL, DAVID BARNARD, museum curator; b. Detroit, Aug. 27, 1935; s. Russell Maurice and Edith Roe (Mabie) L.; B.A., Oberlin (Ohio) Coll., 1956; M.F.A., Princeton U., 1959, Ph.D., 1966; m. Willa Kay Samors, June 7, 1963; children—Julia Laetitia, Mark Lewis. Instr. art history U. Mo., 1959-61, Ohio State U., 1961-64; acting asst. prof. U. Va., Charlottesville, 1964-66, asso. prof. art history 1969—, curator univ. mus., 1971—; designer, supr. renovation Bayly Mus. Bldg., 1971-74. Fellow Nat. Endowment Humanities, spring 1969. Mem. AAUP, Archaeol. Inst. Am. Author: Durand: Art and Art Theory, 1977; Durand: Catalogue of Paintings, 1978; also exhbn. catalogues. Home: 108 Bollingwood Rd Charlottesville VA 22903 Office: Bayly Museum Rugby Rd Charlottesville VA 22903

LAWHORN, JESS SHERMAN, finance co. exec.; b. Cin., Jan. 20, 1933; s. Jess Sherman and Dorothy E. (Riggs) L.; B.B.A. in Marketing and Econs., U. Miami, 1953; postgrad. Sch. Mortgage Banking Northwestern U., 1960-63, Mich. State U., 1969-70; m. Hilda D. Foxworth, Oct. 12, 1957; 1 son, Jess S. Officer, dir. Shaw Bros. Shipping Co., Miami, Fla., 1964-68, Shaw Marine Co., 1964-68; officer Lon Worth Crow Co., Miami, 1958-64, 69-71; Lon Worth Crow Realty Co., Miami, 1970-71; officer, dir. Southeast Mortgage Co., Miami, 1971—; pres. Semco Services, Inc., 1974—. Lectr. mortgage banking U. Ga., 1973—, So. Meth. U., 1973—, Mich. State U., 1973—. Chmn. United Fund Div. Served to 1st lt. USAF, 1954-56. Mem. Econ. Soc. South Fla., Fla. Bankers Assn. (com. chmn. 1974-75, div. chmn. 1975-76), Fla. Mortgage Bankers Assn. (dir. 1975-76, pres. 1978-79), C. of C., SAR, Soc. Real Estate Appraisers (pres. Greater Miami chpt. 1966), Marine Council Greater Miami (pres. 1968-69). Order Founders and Patriots Am., Sigma Alpha Epsilon. Rotarian. Clubs: Riviera Country, University, Miami. Home: 500 Perugia Ave Coral Gables FL 33146 Office: 1390 Brickell Ave Miami FL 33131

LAWHORNE, LARRY WAYNE, physician; b. Charlottesville, Va., Apr. 16, 1947; s. George and Irene Helen (Rhoten) L.; B.A., U. Va., 1969, M.D., 1973; m. Anne Elizabeth L. Runninger, June 15, 1968; children—Clinton, Stephen, Elizabeth. Intern, U. Iowa Hosps. and Clinics, 1973, resident in family practice, 1973-76; practice medicine specializing in family practice, Lone Tree, Iowa, 1976-78; clin. asst. prof. U. Iowa Med. Sch., 1976-78; dir. med. edn. Mercy Hosp., Iowa City, 1977-78; attending physician Shenandoah Geriatric Treatment Center Western State Hosp., Staunton, Va., 1978—. Sec. Johnson County (Iowa) Bd. Health, 1978; adv. bd. Johnson County Vis. Nurses Assn., 1976-78. Recipient Mead Johnson award family practice residents, 1974. Diplomate Am. Bd. Family Practice. Mem. Am. Acad. Family Practice, Am. Geriatrics Soc., Geront. Soc., Va. Acad. Family Practice, Va. Med. Soc., Augusta County Med. Soc. Unitarian-Universalist. Asso. editor: Yearbook Family Practice, 1977-79. Office: Western State Hosp Staunton VA 24401

LAWING, EUGENE MORRIS, mail order specialist; b. Charlotte, N.C., Sept. 13, 1937; s. Eugene Augustus and Hazel Morris (Ritch) L.; Asso. Bus. Adminstrn., Charlotte Coll., 1957; A.B. in History, U. N.C., Chapel Hill, 1959. Vice pres. H.V. Caton Co., Charlotte, 1959-61; propr. Collias-Lawing & Co., Charlotte, 1961—; judge Small Claims Ct., 1964-68. Precinct capt. Democratic Party. Mem. Nat. Rifle Assn. (life), Am. Orndance Assn. (life), Ohio (life), N.C. (life, bd. dirs. 1968-70, pres. 1971-75) gun collectors assns., S.C. Arms Collectors (charter). Presbyterian. Home: 1300 Reece Rd Apt 506 Charlotte NC 28209 Office: 1020 Central Ave Charlotte NC 28204

LAWLER, EDWARD J., lawyer; b. Chgo., Sept. 15, 1908; s. Edward James and Sarah (Gahan) L.; Ph.B., U. Chgo., 1926-30; LL.B., Harvard, 1933; m. Elizabeth Falls Dunscomb, Dec. 16, 1939. Admitted to Ill. bar, 1933, Tenn. bar, 1941; atty., auditor income tax sect. Office Collector Internal Revenue, Chgo., 1933-34; spl. atty. Bur. Internal Revenue, 1935-36; practice law, 1937-38; atty. SEC, 1939-40; practiced in Memphis, 1941—; dir. Chromasco Ltd. Can.; mem. State Dept. Adv. Panel on Internat. Law, 1967-76. Served as lt. comdr. USNR, 1942-45. Decorated Bronze Star medal. Fellow Am. Bar Found.; mem. Am., Tenn., Memphis Shelby County bar assns., Phi Beta Kappa. Home: 644 S Belvedere Blvd Memphis TN 38104 Office: 1st Nat Bank Bldg Memphis TN 38103

LAWLER, ROBERT CLAIR, real estate developer; b. Richmond, Ind., May 9, 1902; s. William F. and Mary M. (McManus) L.; student pub. schs.; m. Elizabeth Francis, Apr. 28, 1931; children—Mary Louise, Betty Ann, Nancy C. Owner Lawler's, Inc., Richmond, New Castle and Muncie, Ind,. 1932-52; real estate developer, builder shopping centers and apts., Clearwater, Fla., 1952—; dir. Indian Rocks Bank; mem. adv. bd. dirs. S.E. First Bank of Largo (Fla.); pres. Lawlers, Inc. Elk, Kiwanian. Home and office: 817 Osceola Rd Belleair Clearwater FL 33516

LAWRENCE, CARL CONN, univ. adminstr.; b. Jayess, Miss., Dec. 22, 1933; s. Carl E. and Florine B. L.; B.S., U. So. Miss., 1961, postgrad., 1961-62; m. Sue Gunn, Apr. 14, 1962. Cost acct. phys. plant U. So. Miss., Hattiesburg, then payroll acct., fin. secs. office, dir. placement and student employment, pres. bd. Credit Union, 1967, treas., 1970—. Mem. Gov's. Com. on Employment of Handicapped, 1978-79. Served with USAF, 1953-57. Mem. Coll. Placement Council, Inc., Assn. Sch., Coll. and Univ. Staffing, So. Coll. Placement Assn., S.W. Coll. Placement Assn., Miss. Coll. Placement Assn. (pres. 1976-77), Miss. Credit Union League (dir. 1976—, v.p. 1979-80), U. So. Miss. Alumni Assn. (life, Forrest County Outstanding Mem. award 1969-70), Alpha Epsilon Alpha. Baptist. Clubs: University Civitan (projects dir. 1972-73, sec.-treas. Miss. Magnolia dist. 1978-79), Hattiesburg Inter-Civic (dir. council 1969-70), Century, Big Gold (treas. 1969-70), Hardwood. Home: 1216 Windsor Dr Hattiesburg MS 39401 Office: So Sta Box 5014 Hattiesburg MS 39401

LAWRENCE, GEORGE CALVIN, physician; b. Greene County, Ga., Apr. 11, 1919; s. Noel and Lozie Ann (Favors) L.; B.S., Morehouse Coll., 1941; M.D., Meharry Med. Coll., 1944; m. Pauline Blackstreet, July 8, 1944; children—Brenda, Montrois, George Calvin. Intern, Homer G. Phillips Hosp., St. Louis, 1945-46, resident, 1965-68; faculty Emory U., Atlanta, 1968-73; chief obstetrics and gynecology Atlanta Southside Clinic, 1968-78; pvt. practice specializing in obstetrics and gynecology, Atlanta, 1968—; staff, Crawford W. Long Meml. Hosp., 1968—. Bd. dirs. George Washington Carver Boys' Club. Served to comdr. M.C., USNR, 1953-56. Recipient award for 25 yrs. service Morehouse Coll., award for disting. service Meharry Med. Coll. Fellow Am. Coll. Obstetricians and Gynecologists; mem. Atlanta Med. Assn. (pres. 1963, award for 25 yrs. service), Ga. Med. Assn. (sec. 1962-65), AMA (Physician's Recognition award 1979), Nat. Med. Assn., Atlanta Guardsmen, Omega Psi Phi. Baptist. Club: Masons (32 deg.). Address: 75 Piedmont Ave NE Suite 516 Atlanta GA 30303

LAWRENCE, HARDING LUTHER, airlines exec.; b. Perkins, Okla., July 15, 1920; s. Muncey Luther and Helen Beatrice Lawrence; B.B.A., U. Tex., 1942; LL.B., S. Tex. Coll. Law, Houston, 1949, J.D. (hon.), 1972; LL.D., U. Portland (Oreg.), 1968; m. Mary Wells, Nov. 25, 1967; children—James B., Deborah M., State R., Pamela, Katy. From asst. v.p. ops. to v.p. traffic and sales Pioneer Air Lines, Houston, 1946-55; from v.p. traffic and sales to exec. v.p. Continental Airlines, 1955-65; pres. Braniff Airways, Inc., Dallas, 1965-70, chmn. bd., 1968—, chief exec. officer, 1970—, also dir.; dir. First Internat. Bancshares, Inc. Bd. dirs. Dallas Council World Affairs. Served with USAAF, World War II. Decorated Order Sun (Peru), Order Balboa (Panama), comdr. Order O'Higgins (Chile); named Man of Yr., Americas Found., 1978. Address: Braniff Airways Braniff Blvd Dallas-Fort Worth Airport TX 75261

LAWRENCE, RAYMOND EUGENE, clergyman, coll. adminstr.; b. Grant County, Ky., Nov. 14, 1921; s. Ray and Mary (Sams) L.; A.B., Georgetown Coll., 1949; M.Div., So. Bapt. Sem., Louisville, 1955; m. Eula Whiteker, Sept. 8, 1948; children—Deborah, Dora. Ordained to ministry Bapt. Ch., 1946; pastor 1st Bapt. Ch., Mt. Vernon, Ky., 1953-57, 1st Bapt. Ch., Neosho, Mo., 1951-53, 1st Bapt. Ch., Shelbyville, Ky., 1957-62, Central Bapt. Ch., Corbin, Ky., 1962-72; asst. to pres., prof. religion Cumberland Coll., Williamsburg, Ky., 1972—. Treas., bd. dirs. Southeastern Ky. Bapt. Hosp.; dir. Ky. Hosp. Commn. Served to staff sgt., AUS, 1942-45. Decorated Bronze Star. Mem. Ky. Geneal. Soc. Republican. Author: Don't Give Up the Ship, 1974; History of Ten Mile Association of Baptist, 1954. Home: 1502 Forest Circle Corbin KY 40701 Office: Box 195 College Station Williamsburg KY 40769

LAWRENCE, STEVEN RAY, religious assn. exec.; b. Murfreesboro, Tenn., Aug. 6, 1943; s. Lonnie and Catherine B. (Brown) L.; B.S., Middle Tenn. State U., 1967, M.A., 1970; m. Marjory L. Bolton, Aug. 24, 1963; 1 dau., Amy Elizabeth. Sales engr. Chromalox, Inc., Murfreesboro, 1962-68; job and salary analyst So. Baptist Sunday Sch. Bd., Nashville, 1968—, mgr. adminstrv. services dept., 1971-80, mgr. personnel dept., 1980—; instr. bus. and econs. Vol. State Community Coll., Nashville, 1973—. Mem. Adminstrv. Mgmt. Soc. Democrat. Baptist. Club: Kiwanis. Home: 741 Goodpasture Terr Nashville TN 37221 Office: Baptist Sunday School Board 127 9th Ave N Nashville TN 37234

LAWRENCE, TELETÉ ZORAYDA (MRS. ERNEST LAWRENCE), speech and voice pathologist, educator; b. Worcester, Mass., Aug. 5, 1910; d. James Newton and Cora Valeria (Hester) Lester; A.B. cum laude, U. Calif., Berkeley, 1932; M.A., Tex. Christian U., 1963; pvt. study voice with Edgar Schofield, N.Y.C., 1936-41, drama with Enrica Clay Dillon, N.Y.C., 1937-40; m. Ernest Lawrence, Oct. 9, 1939; children—James Lester, Valerie Alma. Mem. Am. Lyric Theatre, 1939—; instr. speech Sch. Fine Arts, Tex. Christian U., Ft. Worth, 1959-66, asst. prof., 1966-71, asso. prof., 1971-75, prof., 1975-76, emeritus prof., 1976—; specialist disorders of voice and related therapeutic procedures; pvt. practice speech and voice therapy, 1960—; cons. voice disorders. Participant, contbr. numerous internat. congresses, 1965—, including Congress Internat. Assn. Sci. Study of Mental Deficiency, Montpellier, France, 1967, Semmelweis Anniversary Week Acad. Scis., Budapest, Hungary, 1968, Internat. Congress Logopedies and Phoniatrics, Sch. Medicine, U. Buenos Aires (Argentina), 1971, Lucerne, Switzerland, 1974, Copenhagen, 1977, Internat. Congress Phonetic Scis., Charles U., Prague, Czechoslovakia, 1967, McGill U., Montreal, Que., Can., 1971, U. Leeds (Eng.), 1975, Third World Congress of Phoneticans, Tokyo, 1976. Bd. dirs. Sunshine Haven, home for retarded children, 1957-59; gen. chmn. Ft. Worth and Tarrant County, Nat. Retarded Children's Week, 1954; mem. family and child welfare div. Community Council of Ft. Worth and Tarrant County, 1955-57; mem. health and hosp. div., 1959-60; mem. women's com. Ft. Worth chpt. NCCJ, 1956-59; exec. v.p. Fine Arts Found. Guild of Tex. Christian U., 1955-56, exec. sec., 1956-58, financial sec., 1958-59. Tex. Christian U. faculty research grantee, 1961, on leave to Gt. Britain, Western Europe, Hungary, 1968. Mem. Nat. Council Chs. (bd. dirs. joint com. missionary edn. Pacific Coast area, 1952-55), United Ch. Women of Ft. Worth (chmn. Christian world missions dept. 1955-57, pres., 1957-59), Ft. Worth Area Council Chs. (v.p. 1955-57, exec. com. 1957-59, dir. 1959-60), U. Calif. Alumni Assn. (life), Am. Speech, Lang. and Hearing Assn. (life; cert.), Tex. Speech and Hearing Assn., Ft. Worth Council for Retarded Children, Speech Communication Assn. Am. (sec. speech and hearing disorders interest group 1962, 63), American Dialect Soc., A.A.U.P., Phoenetic Soc. Japan, Internat. Assn. Logopedics and Phoniatrics, Internat. Soc. Phonetic Scis., Tex. Speech Assn., Phi Beta Kappa (pres. Delta of Tex. chpt. 1973-74), Delta Zeta, Psi Chi, Sigma Alpha Eta. Republican. Mem. Christian Ch. Clubs: Woman's of Fort Worth; Women of Rotary. Author: Handbook for Instructors of Voice and Diction, 1968. Contbr. articles to profl. publs. Home: 3860 South Hills Circle Fort Worth TX 76109

LAWRENCE, WALTER WILLIAM, JR., chem. engr.; b. New Brunswick, N.J., May 8, 1929; s. Walter William and Mildred Irene (Wright) L.; B.S., Rutgers U., 1951; Ph.D., Ia. State U., 1959; m. Hazel Marilyn Hermanson, June 15, 1957; children—Brian, Andrea, Carin. Research chemist Barrett div. Allied Chem. Co., 1951-54; research chemist Ethyl Corp., Baton Rouge, 1959-73, process devel. engr., 1973-75, sr. process devel. engr., 1975—. Active Boy Scouts Am. Mem. Am. Chem. Soc. (edn. chmn. Baton Rouge sect. 1971), Am. Inst. Chem. Engrs., Conn. Soc. Genealogists, Wickland Terrace Citizens Assn. (pres. 1962-63), Phi Lambda Upsilon. Republican. Methodist (mem. ofcl. bd. 1969-70). Contbr. to Chem. and Process Tech. Ency., 1974, Van Nostrand's Sci. Ency., 5th and 6th edits. Home: 12288 Armstrong Dr Baton Rouge LA 70816 Office: PO Box 341 Baton Rouge LA 70821

LAWRENCE-BERREY, ROBERT EDMOND, pathologist; b. Calgary, Alta., Can., Oct. 8, 1934; s. Jack Edmond and Ruth Evelyn (Eiseman) L.-B.; came to U.S., 1946, naturalized, 1958; B.A. in Chemistry, Whitman Coll., 1956; M.D., U. Wash., 1962; m. Shirley Anne Davis, Feb. 23, 1962; children—Ruth Elizabeth, Robert Edmond, Julia Anne. Intern in pathology Good Samaritan Hosp. and Med. Center, Portland, Oreg., 1962-63, resident in anat. and clin. pathology, 1963-66, staff pathologist, 1968-71; practice medicine specializing in pathology, Portland, 1968-72, Parkersburg, W.Va., 1972—; staff pathologist Salem (Oreg.) Meml. Hosp., 1971, Providence Hosp., Portland, 1971-72; pathologist, dir. Gen. Consultants Med. Labs., Inc., Parkersburg, 1972—; pres. L.-B. & J. Investments, Inc., 1972—, Gen. Cons. Inc., 1976—; clin. instr. clin. pathology U. Oreg. Med. Sch., Portland, 1970-72; clin. instr. Sch. Med. Tech., Parkersburg Community Coll., 1972—; cons. pathologist, dir. labs. Guernsey Meml. Hosp., Cambridge, Ohio, 1972—, Barnesville (Ohio) Hosp. Assn., 1972—, Selby Gen. Hosp., Marietta, Ohio, 1972—, Calhoun Gen. Hosp., Grantsville, W.Va., 1972—; cons.-adviser Sch. Med. Tech., Jefferson County (Ohio) Tech. Inst., 1974—; Bishop of La. Council, Polk Meml. Episcopal Mission, 1967-68; mem. fin. com. St. Bartholomew's Episc. Ch., Beaverton, Oreg., 1971-72; trustee Parkersburg Community Coll. Found., 1975—, pres., 1979-80. Served with M.C., U.S. Army, 1966-68. Diplomate Am. Bd. Pathology. Fellow Am. Soc. Clin. Pathologists, Coll. Am. Pathologists; mem. Am. Soc. Nuclear Medicine, Parkersburg Acad. Medicine, Am. Soc. Cytology, Oreg. Pathologists Assns., W.Va. Med. Assn., AMA, Alpha Kappa Kappa, Phi Delta Theta. Club: Rotary (Parkersburg). Home: 30 Oakwood Estate Parkersburg WV 26101 Office: PO Box 1229 1217 Ann St Parkersburg WV 26101

LAWSON, BRENDA MICKLOW, fin. planner; b. Birmingham, Ala., Feb. 19, 1954; d. Andrew William and Geraldine (Cooley) Micklow; B.S., Jacksonville State U., 1976, M.S., 1977; m. James Ronald Lawson, July 24, 1976. With Underwood Fin. Planning, Inc., Birmingham, 1979—. Named 1st runner up Miss Ala. U.S.A., 1974. Mem. Internat. Assn. Fin. Planners, Am. Personnel and Guidance Assn., Am. Mktg. Assn., Phi Mu. Democrat. Author: The Cashless Society, 1976; Religion and Value Issues in Behavioral Counseling, 1978. Composer: When, 1978. Home: 3165A Old Columbiana Rd

Birmingham AL 35226 Office: 400 Century Park S Suite 208 Birmingham AL 35226

LAWSON, DAVID WILLIAM, JR., architect; b. Pensacola, Fla., Sept. 4, 1939; s. David William and Kathryn Inita (Lewis) L.; B.Arch., U. Fla., 1968; m. Lise M. Dagneau, Mar. 4, 1962; children—Jacques D., Christine E., Carolyn M. Designer, C.R. Wedding and Assos., 1968-69, RMBR Architects, 1969-71; prin. David W. Lawson and Assos., 1971-73; sr. partner Lawson/Wedding Architects, Planners AIA, P.A., Tampa, Fla., 1973—; lectr. constrn. tech. Hillsborough Community Coll. Mem. adv. com. human relations program Hillsborough County Pub. Schs., Nat. Endowment Arts architect in residence program, 1979-80, dist. emergency sch. aid act, 1979-80. Served to 1st lt. USAF, 1959-63. Cert. gen. contractor, Fla.; cert. Nat. Council Archtl. Registration Bds. Mem. AIA (pres. Tampa, Merit awards for service to chpt.), Am. Soc. Planning Ofcls., Constrn. Specifications Inst., C. of C. Com. 100, Fla. Ocean Racing Assn., St. Petersburg Sailing Assn. Democrat. Roman Catholic. Club: Aero Flying. Office: Larson/Wedding Architects Planners AIA PA 4112 Cypress St Tampa FL 33609

LAWSON, EUGENE MCKINLEY, JR., constrn. and devel. co. exec.; b. Richmond, Va., Mar. 11, 1947; s. Eugene McKinley and Irline Marie (Jenkins) L.; B.E.E., Va. Poly. Inst. and State U., 1969. Tech. dir. Va. Tech. Choral Music Orgns., Blacksburg, 1966-71; pres. Audio-Tronics, Inc., Blacksburg, 1971-73; pres. Design Research Corp., Blacksburg, 1975-77; gen. mgr. Commonwealth Homes Va., Inc., Blacksburg, 1977—; sec., gen. mgr. Forest Hills Devel. Corp., Blacksburg, 1976—; mng. partner Lawson, Sterl Properties, Blacksburg, 1973, LBS Partnership, Blacksburg, 1976—. Pres., Downtown Blacksburg, Inc., 1972, v.p., 1971; fin. chmn. Montgomery County Republican Com., 1970-72. Mem. Nat. Assn. Home Bldrs., Blacksburg C. of C., Am. Radio League, Nat. Rifle Assn. Republican. Christian Scientist. Home: 710 Cedarview Dr Blacksburg VA 24060 Office: 126 Jackson St NW Blacksburg VA 24060

LAWSON, FRED RAULSTON, banker; b. Sevierville, Tenn., Mar. 26, 1936; s. Arville Raulston and Ila Mary (Lowe) L.; student U. Tenn. at Knoxville, 1953-59, La. State U., 1965-68, Harvard, 1968; children—Terry Lee, Laura Ann. With Blount Nat. Bank, Maryville, Tenn., 1958—, pres., 1968—, pres., dir. Tenn. Nat. Bancshares, Inc., 1971—; dir. Bank of Pensacola (Fla.), Bank of Cannon County, Woodbury, Tenn., Mchts. & Farmers Bank, Greenback, Tenn., Citizens Nat. Bank, McMinnville, Tenn., Blount Nat. Bank, Southeastern Life Ins. Co., Tipton Investments, Chilhowee, Inc., E.M. Todd. Vice chmn. Tenn. Banking Bd., 1973—; mem. select fin. com. Maryville Coll., 1970-71, mem. community advisory com.; mem. chancellors assos. U. Tenn. at Knoxville, 1972—; mem. Tenn. Indsl. Devel. Authority, 1972—. Pres., former Bd. dirs. Blunt County Indsl. Bd., 1969—; bd. dirs. Tenn. Bapt. Childrens Home, 1972—, pres., 1978—; bd. dirs. United Fund, 1973—. Served with USNR, 1956-57. Recipient Tenn. Indsl. Devel. Vol. award, 1977. Mem. Tenn. (chmn. fed. legis. com., 1973—), Am. (govt. relations com.), bankers assns., C. of C., Assn. Registered Bank Holding Cos. Republican. Baptist. Mason (32 deg.). Home: PO Box 333 Maryville TN 37801 Office: PO Box 608 Maryville TN 37801

LAWSON, JOSEPH WEAVER, motivation cons.; b. Atlanta, July 16, 1928; s. Joseph and Annis Elizabeth Lawson; student Spring Hill Coll., 1946-49; m. Mary Louise Bawcum, June 16, 1962; children—Joseph Weaver, Dan F., Teresa, Tracy, Jon. With Rhodes, Inc., Atlanta, 1949-57, Central Chevrolet Inc., Atlanta, 1957-64, McMillan Co., Atlanta, 1964-72; pres. Jomar Investments, Inc., Joe Lawson & Assos., Roswell, Ga., 1972—. Served with USMCR, 1949-51. Roman Catholic. Club: Toastmasters. Address: Joe Lawson & Assos 1160 Martin Ridge Rd Roswell GA 30076

LAWSON, KENNETH RAY, educator; b. Oneida, Tenn., July 7, 1945; s. Virgil and Freela Wanda (King) L.; A.B., Eastern Ky. U., 1968; M.A., U. Dayton (Ohio), 1971; Ed.D. (Va. fellow 1975-76, grad. teaching asst. 1974-76), Va. Poly. Inst. and State U., 1976. Tchr. social studies Northeastern Local Schs., Clark County, Ohio, 1968-74, Citrus County (Fla.) schs., 1979—; editor A New Concept, Springfield, Ohio, 1976-79; instr. Central Fla. Community Coll., 1979—. Mem. Am. Acad. Polit. and Social Scis., Am. Psychol. Assn., Am. Hist. Assn., Am. Ednl. Research Assn., Assn. Supervision and Curriculum Devel., Nat. Council Social Studies, Fla. Council Social Studies, Fla. Assn. Supervision and Curriculum Devel., U.S. Tennis Assn., Fla. Tennis Assn., Phi Delta Kappa, Phi Kappa Phi, Kappa Delta Pi, Phi Alpha Theta, Pi Kappa Alpha. Democrat. Roman Catholic. Club: Plantation Tennis. Author papers in field. Home: 773 NE 9th St Apt 6 Crystal River FL 32629 Office: 1205 NE 8th Ave Crystal River FL 32629

LAWSON, RICHARD HENRY, educator; b. San Francisco, Jan. 11, 1919; s. Henry Porter and Alice (Hanchett) L.; student Multnomah Coll., 1937-39; B.A., U. Oreg., 1941, M.A., 1948; Ph.D., U. Calif. at Los Angeles, 1956; m. Eldene Laura Balcom, Aug. 26, 1950. Instr. Wash. State U., 1953-57; asst. prof. San Diego State U., 1957-62, asso. prof. German, 1962-66, prof. German, 1966-76, chmn. dept. German and Russian, 1965-68, chmn. div. humanities, 1968-69, asst. dean grad. studies, 1970-72, 73-74, acting asso. dean grad. studies, 1972-73, prof. U. N.C., Chapel Hill, 1976—, chmn. dept. Germanic langs., 1976-79. Cons. Webster's New Internat. Dictionary, 1956-58. Served from pvt. to 1st lt. USAAF, 1941-46; maj. Res. Decorated Air medal. Mem. AAUP, Modern Lang. Assn. Am., Am. Assn. Tchrs. German, Am. Comparative Lit. Assn., Internat. Arthur Schnitzler Research Assn., Internationale Vereinigung fuer germanische Sprach-und Literaturwissenschaft. Author: Edith Wharton and German Literature, 1974; Edith Wharton, 1977. Contbr. articles to profl. jours.; bibliog. editor 20th Century Lit., 1967—. Research in Germanic linguistics, modern German lit. and comparative lit. Home: 904 The Oaks Apts Chapel Hill NC 27514

LAWSON, SAMUEL ROBBINS, stockbroker; b. Houston, Aug. 12, 1942; s. Frank Allyn and Virginia (Cronin) L.; student (fellow), U. Vienna, 1966-67, U. Austria, 1966-67; B.A., U. Tex., 1968; m. Donna Ruth Sunday, May 7, 1977; 1 dau., Jennifer Robbins. Program dir. for police cadet tng. Planned Assos. Ltd., Beaumont, Tex., 1972-73; dir. planning and research City of Beaumont, 1973-75; account exec., options specialist E.F. Hutton & Co., Beaumont, 1975—; v.p. Hajdik Constrn. Co., Rosenberg, Tex., 1975—. Deacon, Praise Christian Center, Beaumont, 1978—. Served with M.I., U.S. Army, 1968-72. Decorated Bronze Star, Army Commendation medal. Mem. Nat. Assn. Security Dealers, N.Y. Stock Exchange (asso.), Tex. Bd. Ins., Phi Kappa Psi. Club: Lions. Home: 2298 Central Dr Beaumont TX 77706 Office: EF Hutton & Co 588 Park St Beaumont TX 77701

LAWSON, VERNA REBECCA, plant physiologist; b. Crossville, Tenn., Apr. 7, 1943; d. Horace Freeman and Zera Erline (Currie) Lawson; B.S., Tenn. Tech. U., 1966, M.S., 1968; Ph.D., George Washington U., 1973; student Goethe Inst., Lüneberg, Ger., 1964. Mem. faculty Alcorn State U., Lorman, Miss., 1973-77, asso. prof. plant physiology, 1973-77, chmn. div. sci. and math. Bethune-Cookman Coll., Daytona Beach, Fla., 1977—; on leave to Extramural Assos. Program, NIH, 1980. Smithsonian Instn. predoctoral fellow, 1972; Dept. Agr. grantee, 1973. Mem. Am. Inst. Biol. Sci., Am. Soc. Plant Physiology, AAUP, Am. Soc. Hort. Sci., AAAS, Fedn. Am. Scientists, Miss. Acad. Scis., Smithsonian Assos., Sigma Xi, Beta Beta Beta, Phi Beta Sigma. Baptist. Address. Div Sci and Math Bethune-Cookman Coll 640 2d Ave Daytona Beach FL 32015

LAWSON, WILFRID NOEL, ednl. adminstr.; b. Dallas, Dec. 25, 1930; married, 1 child. B.S. in Edn. and Econs., N. Tex. State U., Denton, 1951, M.Ed. in Sch. Adminstrn., 1961. Dir. cafeterias Birdville Ind. Sch. Dist., Fort Worth, 1959-63, dir. spl. services, 1963-73, adminstrv. asst. for planning, research, and evaluation, 1974—; adj. prof. Tex. Christian U., Fort Worth, 1972—. Mem. Am. Ednl. Research Assn., Nat. Council on Measurement in Edn., Tex. Assn. for Planning, Evaluation, and Research, Phi Delta Kappa. Certified in elementary and secondary edn., sch. adminstrn. and supervision, spl. edn., Tex. Home: 1524 Bob Dr Fort Worth TX 76118 Office: 6125 E Belknap St Fort Worth TX 76117

LAWTON, THOMAS OREGON, JR., lawyer; b. Barton, S.C., Nov. 10, 1924; s. Thomas Oregon and Alexania (Easterling) L.; student Wofford Coll., 1941-43; A.B., Duke, 1947, J.D., 1950; m. Bess White Macaulay, July 12, 1952; children—Thomas Oregon, III, Margaret Macaulay, Angus Macaulay. Admitted to S.C. bar, 1950; practiced in Georgetown, 1950-51, Allendale, 1951—; mem. firm McNair and Lawton, 1951-65, Lawton and Myrick, 1965-79; city atty., Allendale, 1951—; county atty., Allendale County, S.C., 1951—; treas. Allendale County Recreation Assn., 1958-59, Hampton-Allendale County Community Concert Assn., 1961-65; vice chmn. Allendale County Devel. Bd., 1956-70, chmn., 1970—; vice chmn. Savannah River Basin Devel. Commn., 1966—; chmn. S.C. Tricentennial Commn., 1966-71, Allendale-Hampton Indls. Devel. Commn., 1972—; past curator, v.p. S.C. Hist. Soc.; mem. S.C. Dept. Archives and History Commn., 1968—. Chmn., Allendale County Democratic Com., 1968-78. Served with AUS, 1943-45. Decorated Bronze Star medal, Purple Heart. Mem. Am., S.C. (v.p. 14th jud. circuit, past v.p., past mem. grievance com.), Allendale County (pres. 1965-73) bar assns., S.C. City Atty. Assn. (pres. 1967-68), U. S.C. Soc. (dir.), Am. Trial Lawyers Assn., S.C. C. of C. (chmn. tourist and travel council 1960-62), Savannah English Speaking Union, Huguenot Soc. for S.C., Soc. of The Cincinnati (N.C.), St. Andrew's Soc. of Columbia, Sons Colonial Wars, Sigma Alpha Epsilon, Phi Delta Phi. Democrat. Episcopalian (sr. warden 1968-70). Clubs: Fairdale Country (past pres.); Sea Pines (Hilton Head Island); Summit (Columbia). Home: Hampton Grove Allendale SC 29810 Office: Memorial Ave Allendale SC 29810

LAY, KENNETH LEE, energy exec.; b. Tyrone, Mo., Apr. 15, 1942; s. Omer and Ruth (Reese) L.; B.A., U. Mo., 1964, M.A., 1965; Ph.D., U. Houston, 1970; m. Judith Diane Ayers, June 10, 1966; children—Mark Kenneth, Elizabeth Ayers. Corp. economist Exxon, Houston, 1965-68; tech. asst. to commr. Fed. Power Commn., 1971-72; dep. undersec. for energy Dept. Interior, Washington, 1972-74; v.p. corp. devel. Fla. Gas Co., 1974-76; pres. Fla. Gas Transmission Co., Winter Park, Fla., 1976-79; exec. v.p. to pres. Continental Resources Co. (formerly Fla. Gas Co.), 1979—, corp. v.p. The Continental Group, Inc., parent co.; asso. prof., lectr. econs. George Washington U., 1969-73. Dir., John Young Mus., Orlando, Fla., 1974-76; dir. Winter Park Library, 1977-78. Served with USNR, 1968-71. Mem. So. Gas Assn. (dir.), Gas Research Inst. (dir.), Slurry Transport Assn. (chmn. bd. dirs. 1979—), Am. Econ. Assn., Am. Gas Assn. (dir.), Interstate Natural Gas Assn. (dir.), Young Presidents Assn. Republican. Methodist. Club: Winter Park Racquet, Citrus. Home: 641 Via Lugano Winter Park FL 32789 Office: PO Box 44 Winter Park FL 32790

LAY, RODNEY KINTORE, energy cons.; b. Southsea, U.K., Oct. 27, 1938; came to U.S., 1967, naturalized, 1977; s. Horatio Alick Kintore and Aileen Eva Dalrymple (Nash) L.; B.Sc. with honors, Queen Mary Coll., U. London, 1960; Ph.D., U. Aston, 1967; m. Marguerite Anne Green, June 3, 1961; children—Richard, James, Catherine. Apprentice, Met. Vickers Ltd., Manchester, U.K., 1956-61; design engr. elec. machines AEI Ltd., Birmingham, U.K., 1961-64; research fellow U. Aston, Birmingham, 1964-67; generator advance design engr. Gen. Electric Corp., Schenectady, 1967-69; dept. head fossil energy planning and analysis MITRE Corp., McLean, Va., 1969—. Chartered engr., U.K. Council Engring. Instns. Mem. IEEE, Instn. Elec. Engrs. Contbr. reports to profl. jours., confs. Office: MITRE Corp 1820 Dolley Madison Blvd McLean VA 22102

LAYDEN, WILLIAM EDWARD, opthalmologist; b. Rutland, Vt., Oct. 26, 1937; s. William Henry and Mildred Mary (Batchelder) L.; B.S., U. Vt., 1960, M.D., 1963; m. Nancy L. Waldman, Aug. 13, 1976; children—Tracey Kathleen, William H. Intern, Hartford (Conn.) Hosp., 1963-64; resident in ophthalmology U. Louisville Hosps., 1967-72, U. Calif., San Francisco, 1972-73; practice medicine specializing in ophthalmology, Tampa, Fla., 1973—; asso. prof. ophthalmology U. South Fla., Tampa, 1975-80, prof., 1980—, chmn. dept., 1980—; mem. nat. adv. bd. Prevention of Blindness in Glaucoma, 1975—. Served with M.C., USAF, 1964-67. Heed Found. fellow, 1972-73; NIH research fellow, 1972-73. Fellow A.C.S.; mem. AMA, Nat. Assn. Residents and Interns, Fla. Soc. Ophthalmology, Fla. Med. Assn., Am. Acad. Ophthalmology. Republican. Mem. editorial bd. Perspectives in Ophthalmology, 1976—; contbr. articles to profl. jours. Home: 4144 Northmeadow Circle Tampa FL 33624 Office: Dept Ophthalmology U South Fla Tampa FL 33612

LAYMAN, DAVID LOUIS, clothing mfg. co. exec.; b. Harrisonburg, Va., Mar. 15, 1949; s. Melvin Hubert and Helen Virginia (Painter) L.; A.A.S. in Acctg., Blue Ridge Community Coll., Weyers Cave, Va., 1969; student acctg. James Madison U.; m. Beverley Sue Durrett, Sept. 10, 1970; children—Christopher David, Shaun Casey. With Metro Pants div. Mellville Corp., Bridgewater, Va., 1970, 72—, resident indsl. engr., then product devel. mgr., 1977-78, product devel. and quality control mgr., 1976—. Served with U.S. Army, 1970-72. Decorated Army Commendation medal. Presbyterian. Address: Metro Pants Div Melville Co Dry River Rd Bridgewater VA 22812

LAYMAN, RICHARD L., editor; b. Louisville, Sept. 7, 1947; s. Lewis L. and Mary A. (Smith) L.; student Ind. U., 1965-68; B.A., U. Louisville, 1971, M.A., 1972; Ph.D., U. S.C., 1975; m. Nancy Staats, May 12, 1973; 1 son, Abraham Richard. Asst. dir. Center for Editions Am. Authors, Columbia, S.C., 1975-76; teaching asso. U. S.C., 1976-77; mng. editor Bruccoli Clark Pubs., Columbia, S.C., 1977—. Home: 6519 Olde Knight Pkwy Columbia SC 29209 Office: 1210 Pendleton St Columbia SC 29201

LAYNE, ROBERT G., systems, computers and fin. cons.; b. Ann Arbor, Mich., Apr. 1, 1928; s. Gustave and Frances Dicks; B.S., Wayne State U., 1951; m. Verna C. Olson. Salesman, sales mgr. Grosse Pointe Packard Co. (Mich.), 1951-52; dist. mgr. Packard Motor Car Co., Cin., 1952-53; owner RonDel Distbrs. Co., Dearborn, Mich., 1954-59; account exec. Gen. Motors Corp. account Burroughs Corp., Detroit, 1959-67; salesman, zone mgr., dist. mgr., regional mgr. Litton ABS, Atlanta, Phila., 1967-77; systems, computers and fin. cons. to health care and mfg. cos., Atlanta, 1977—. Christian Scientist. Designer semi-automated acctg. and statis. system for community mental health centers. Home: 2575 Peachtree Rd NE Atlanta GA 30305 Office: Suite 22-H The Plaza Tower S Atlanta GA 30305

LAYTON, CAROLYN DIANE, speech pathologist; b. Natalbany, La., Jan. 27, 1943; d. James Hersery and Doris Audrey (Tate) Durbin; student Milsaps Coll., Jackson, Miss., 1960-61, Southeastern La. Coll., 1961-62; B.S., U. So. Miss., 1964, M.S., 1976; m. John Allan Layton, Nov. 4, 1964; children—Gregory Allan, Shellye Diane. Speech pathologist Sch. for Exceptional Children, Pascagoula, Miss., summer 1964, Gulfport (Miss.) Mcpl. Separate Sch. Dist., 1964-65, New Hope Cerebral Palsy Sch., Harrison County, Miss., 1965-67, Harrison County Sch. for Exceptional Children, 1972; head speech pathologist Harrison County Sch. Dist., Gulfport, 1972—; mem. Miss. State Field Testing Team, 1978. Supt. edn. County of Harrison, 1976, 79. Licensed speech pathologist, Miss. Mem. Am. Speech and Hearing Assn. (cert. clin. competence), Miss. Speech and Hearing Assn. (local publicity chmn. state conv. 1976), Gulfport Jaycettes (v.p. 1972; most outstanding Jaycette 1974), Gulf Coast Speech and Hearing Soc. (pres. 1977), Epsilon Sigma Alpha. Methodist. Clubs: Northwood Hills Garden, Kenwood Garden (treas. 1978-79). Home: 115 Kencrest Dr Gulfport MS 39503

LAZAR, MARTIN LEWIS, neurol. surgeon; b. Montreal, Que., Can., Feb. 6, 1941; came to U.S., 1968; s. Harry and Evelyn (Greenspoon) L.; B.Sc., McGill U., 1962; M.D., U. Ottawa, 1966; m. Marilyn Frances Rittenberg, Feb. 3, 1963; children—Jodi, Andrea, Nancy. Rotating intern Jewish Gen. Hosp., Montreal, 1966-67, surg. resident, 1967-68; fellow in neurol. surgery U. Tex. Southwestern Med. Sch., Dallas, 1968-73; postgrad. fellow U. London Nat. Hosp. Nervous Diseases, 1970; neurol. surgeon, asso. Tex. Neurol. Inst., Dallas, 1974—; clin. instr. neurosurgery U. Tex. Health Sci. Center, Dallas, 1973—. Diplomate Am. Bd. Neurol. Surgery. Fellow A.C.S., Internat. Coll. Surgeons, Am. Heart Assn.; mem. Am. Assn. Neurol. Surgeons, AMA, Assn. Advancement Med. Instrumentation, Congress Neurol. Surgeons. Inventor Biotome surg. device, 1977; contbr. articles to med. jours. Office: Tex Neurol Inst at Dallas 7777 Forest Ln Suite 2420 Dallas TX 75230

LAZARE, JOHN NICHOLAS, printing co. exec.; b. Chgo., May 24, 1925; s. Nicholas J. and Elizabeth M. (Stapf) L.; ed. Printing Industry Sch. Estimating, Chgo., 1948-49; m. Martha Helfrich, Jan. 8, 1946; 1 son, John Nicholas. Apprentice pressman McCord Printing Co., Chgo., 1946-48, pressman, 1948-52, foreman, 1952-64; partner John Lazare Printing Co., Chgo., 1964-75, owner, 1975—. Mem. MidAm. Commodity Exchange, Chgo. Served with USNR, 1943-46; PTO. Mem. Lincoln Park C. of C., VFW, Printing Industry Ill. Inc., North Side Printers Guild Chgo. (dir. 1975-76), Royal Arcanum. Club: Board of Trade Fellowship (dir. 1963-69, 75-82, v.p. 1970-71, pres. 1972-74). Home: 15332 Harbor Dr Madeira Beach FL 33708 Office: 709 W Wrightwood Ave Chicago IL 60614

LAZARUS, JOHN DANIEL, realtor; b. Long Branch, N.J., May 31, 1909; s. Joshua Yates and Madeline Viola (Meyer) L.; m. Mary Gray Kiefer, Feb. 15, 1953; children—Jack D., Donald E. Kiefer. Pres. David S. Meyer, Inc., Long Branch, 1929-34; pres. Meyer's Agency, Asbury Park, N.J., 1954-55; pres. Realty Interests, Inc., Asbury Park, 1958-75; pres. John D. Lazarus, Inc., Asbury Park, 1964—, chmn. bd. Appraisal Assos., 1977—; instr. real estate appraisal Brookdale Coll., Lincroft, N.J., 1973-77; v.p. Ocean Twp. Indsl. Commn., 1958-59. Trustee Temple Beth Miriam, Elberon, N.J., 1938-79, Monmouth County Orgn. Social Services, 1973—. Licensed real estate broker, N.J., N.Y., Pa. Mem. Nat., N.J., Monmouth County (bd. dirs.) real estate bds., Nat. Ind. Fee Appraisers (sr. mem., counselor, pres. 1968-69), Nat. Assn. Review Appraisers, Am. Assn. Certified Appraisers, Am. Right of Way Assn., Am. Soc. Real Estate Counselors, Nat. Inst. Real Estate Brokers, Real Estate Bd. N.Y., Inc., Internat. Traders Club, Nat. Assn. Real Estate Appraisers, Regional Plan Assn. Home: 1277 Bellflower St Sarasota FL 33582 Office: 1025 Hwy 35 Asbury Park NJ 07712

LEACH, CHARLES SELLERS, merchant, farmer; b. Jackson, Tenn., Jan. 17, 1926; s. Wendall Clifford and Ruth Maybell (Evans) L.; B.A., U. Mich., 1947; student Milligan Coll., 1944-45, Central Mich. Coll., 1945-46; m. Mary Sophia May, July 23, 1949; children—Jim, John, Robert, Charlie. Owner, operator Leach's Music & TV, Paris, Tenn., 1950—; leader orch., Paris, Tenn., 1951-68; farmer, Paris, 1968—. Served to lt. comdr., USNR, 1944-68. Mem. Paris-Henry County C. of C., Downtown Businessman Assn. Paris, Jackson Symphony Orch., Tennessee Valley, Am. polled hereford assns., Am. Quarter Horse Assn., Ret. Officers Assn. Roman Catholic. Clubs: Rotary (v.p. Paris 1971-72), Paris Elks, Henry County Saddle (pres. 1977). Home: Route 4 Paris TN 38242 Office: 122 E Washington St Paris TN 38242

LEACH, CLAUDE, JR., Congressman; b. Leesville, La., Mar. 30, 1934; m. Laura Alexander; children—Mary O'Dell, Lucille Ann, Claude Alexander. Admitted to bar; former mem. firm Cabra, Leach and Tilley; former mem. La. Ho. of Reps.; mem. 96th Congress from 4th Congl. Dist. La. Served with U.S. Army. Democrat. Episcopalian. Office: Room 1229 Longworth House Office Bldg Washington DC 20515*

LEACH, CRAIG PATRICK, forester; b. Bunkie, La., Nov. 21, 1949; s. Russell Richard and Janet Elizabeth (Callegari) L.; B.S. in Forestry, La. State U., 1971, M.S., 1973; postgrad. Northwestern State U., La., 1976-78; m. Janice Jane Gauthier, Feb. 23, 1974; 1 son, Bryan Patrick. Staff forester Ga. Pacific Co., Gloster, Miss., 1973-74; staff forester Bodcaw Co., Pineville, La., 1974-76, sr. staff forester, 1976-77, area mgr., 1977—. Mem. Nat. Rifle Assn., Soc. Am. Foresters, La. State U. Alumni Assn., Alpha Zeta, Phi Sigma Pi. Democrat. Roman Catholic. Home: 507 Holiday Circle Pineville LA 71360 Office: Bodcaw Co PO Box 870 Williams Lake Rd Pineville LA 71360

LEACH, JAMES MOORE, chemist; b. Warren County, N.C., Nov. 29, 1924; s. John Pelorides and Sally Miles (Johnson) L.; B.S. in Chemistry, High Point (N.C.) Coll., 1945; m. Helen Elizabeth Wilson, June 27, 1953; children—Deborah Johnston, Kathryn Marie, Susan Elizabeth. Cons., George C. Brown Co., Greensboro, N.C., 1954-56; research asst. Morton Chem. Co., Greensboro, 1945-46, research chemist, 1946-49; chief chemist Morton-Withers Chem. Co., Greensboro, 1949-57; product devel. mgr. Pfizer, Inc., Greensboro, 1957-71; research dir. Piedmont Chem. Industries, Inc., High Point, 1971—. Mem. Am. Chem. Soc., Am. Assn. Textile Chemists and Colorists, Am. Oil Chemists Soc., N.C. Zool. Soc. Democrat. Clubs: Elks, Sportsman Wildlife (sec. 1963-64, bd. dirs. 1963-67). Patentee in field. Home: 603 Florham Dr High Point NC 27260 Office: PO Box 2728 High Point NC 27261

LEADBETTER, BRUCE C., investment co. exec.; b. Hugo, Colo., Sept. 4, 1938; s. Merton King and Edith (Cline) L.; student U. Ariz., 1956-57, Mexico City Coll., 1957, No. Ariz. U., 1958-60; divorced; children—Reagan Jessica, Tiffany Amber. Pres., dir. Post Co., Dallas, 1968—; chmn. Exec. Investment Corp., 1966-69; pres. Summit Properties, Inc., 1966—, Kona-Post Corp., 1969—, Aspen-Post Corp., 1969—, The Post Corp., 1969—; dir. Tres Vidas En La Playa Inc., Levitz Furniture Co.; chmn. dir. Stores Trading Group, 1978—. Bd. dirs. Salvation Army, 1971-74. Mem. Am. Assn. Small Bus., N. Ariz.

Bd. Realtors (pres. 1961-65), Nat. Assn. Ind. Businessmen, Practising Law Inst. Named Outstanding Businessman of Ariz., 1972; hon. citizen Tex., 1966; nominee for Man of Year, Dallas, 1965. Republican. Episcopalian. Clubs: Phoenix Country, Tres Vidas Country. Address: 8755 C Meadow Park Dallas TX 75234

LEADER, (MARY) SUSANNA, automotive equipment co. exec.; b. South Bend, Ind., Mar. 25, 1925; d. Stephen E. and Leta B. (Lenon) Metzger; student public schs.; m. John J. Leader, June 28, 1943; children—Mary Pamela, Kim Ann, Beth Jean, Robert John, Kelli Sue. Sec., Security Loan Co., South Bend, 1942-43, South Bend Supply Co., 1943-63; sec., office mgr. Indsl. Metal Fab Inc., South Bend, 1965-67; exec. sec. Bendix Automotive Aftermarket, South Bend, 1967-77, sr. sales adminstr., Jackson, Tenn., 1977—. Clubs: Bus. and Profl. Women's, Bendix Mgmt., (Jackson); Humboldt (Tenn.) Golf and Country. Home: 29 Comanche Trail Jackson TN 38301 Office: Bendix Automotive Aftermarket 1094 Bendix Dr Jackson TN 38301

LEAHY, ROBERT EMMETT, dentist; b. N.Y.C., July 1, 1936; s. Richard Sloan and Dorothy Catherine (Gunn) L.; B.S., Manhattan Coll., 1958; D.D.S., U. Pa., 1962; m. Rita Louise Branca, Oct. 1, 1977. Served with U.S. Army, 1962—; chief operative dentistry and diagnosis, Ft. Bliss, Tex., 1962-67; dental surgeon 18th Surg. Hosp., Viet Nam, 1967-68; brigade dental surgeon 3d Brigade, 82d Airborne Div., Viet Nam, 1968; chief oral diagnosis and operative dentistry 87th Med. Detachment, Neurnberg, Germany, 1969-72; gen. dentistry resident Ft. Ord, Calif., 1972-74; chief oral diagnosis and operative dentistry U.S. Army Dental Detachment, Okinawa, 1974-75; chief clinician Edgewood Dental Clinic, Aberdeen Proving Ground, Md., 1975-79; col. Dental Corps, chief clinician Oliver Dental Clinic, Ft. Jackson, S.C., 1979—. Recipient Fellowship award Acad. Gen. Dentistry, 1977, Mastership award, 1979; decorated Bronze Star medal, Army Commendation medal with oak leaf cluster, Combat Med. Badge; diplomate Armed Forces Bd. Gen. Dentistry. Mem. ADA, Acad. Gen. Dentistry, Assn. Mil. Surgeons. Roman Catholic. Office: US Army Dental Activity (DENTAC) Fort Jackson SC 29207

LEAKE, PRESTON HILDEBRAND, chemist, tobacco mfg. co. exec.; b. Proffit, Va., Aug. 8, 1929; s. Perry H. and Lydia V. (Cox) L.; B.S., U. Va., 1950; M.A. (fellow), Duke U., 1953, Ph.D., 1954; m. Elizabeth Ann Kelly, Dec. 5, 1954; children—Luther Hildebrand, Lawrence Albert. Research supr. organic chemistry Allied Chem. Corp. Hopewell, Va., 1954-60; asst. research dir. Albemarle Paper Mfg. Co., Richmond, Va., 1960-65; asst. to mng. dir. research and devel. dept. Am. Tobacco Co., Hopewell, 1965-68, asst. mng. dir., 1968-70, asst. research and devel. dir., 1970—; adj. prof. organic chemistry Va. Commonwealth U., 1963-64. Mem. Chesterfield County (Va.) Sch. Adv. Com., 1969-70; chmn. PTA, Providence Jr. High Sch., 1968-70, Clover Hill Sr. High Sch., 1971-72; chmn. bd. trustees Chesterfield Co ty Public Libraries, 1974-77. Mem. Am. Chem. Soc. (Disting. Service award Va. sect. 1976, councilor 1976—, chmn. publs. bd. Va. sect. 1965-67), Am. Inst. Chemists (chmn. Va. chpt. 1962-63), TAPPI (program chmn. Va.-N.C. chpt. 1964-65), Sigma Xi, Phi Lambda Upsilon. Clubs: James River Catfish, Ruritan. Contbr. articles on organic chemistry to sci. jours.; patentee in field. Home: 5400 Tomahawk Dr Midlothian VA 23113 Office: PO Box 899 Hopewell VA 23860

LEAL, ALMA GLORIA, coll. adminstr.; b. Brownsville, Tex., May 4, 1953; d. Leonel Melchor and Margarita (Cantu) L.; B.S., Pan Am. U., Edinburg, Tex., 1973, M.Ed., 1974. Tchr., Longoria Elementary Sch., Brownsville, 1973-76; asst. planner advanced instl. devel. program Tex. Southmost Coll., Brownsville, 1976-77, job placement coordinator, 1977—; publs. editor Fedn. Bilingual Tng. Resource Center, Denton, Tex., 1978-79; project asst. psychology E. Tex. State U., Commerce, 1979; doctoral asst. Dean's Office, Coll. Edn., East Tex. State U., Commerce, 1979-80; migrant tutor, Brownsville, 1974-75; tutor La Esperanza Home Boys, Brownsville, 1975-76. Instr. religious program Cath. Christian Doctrine, Roman Cath. Ch., Brownsville, 1977-78, Commerce, Tex., 1979-80. Mem. Am. Personnel and Guidance Assn., Am. Coll. Personnel Assn., Tex. Assn. Coll. and Univ. Student Personnel Adminstrs., N.E. Tex. Counselors Assn., Southmost Bus. and Profl. Women's Club (charter), Tex. Southmost Coll. Alumni Assn. (sec. 1976-77), E. Tex. State U. Forum (sec. 1978-79), E. Tex. State U. Guidance Club (v.p. 1979), Phi Delta Kappa, Psi Chi. Democrat. Home: 1444 E Tyler St Brownsville TX 78520

LEARY, MARY JO, mfg. co. ofcl.; b. Springfield, Mass., Aug. 17, 1953; d. Joseph Cornelius and Rita May (Manning) Leary; B.A. in Sociology, Emmanuel Coll., Boston, 1975. Consumer relations rep. Amtrak, Washington, 1975-78, task force leader for public opinion poll, 1977; dir. customer service John H. Harland Co., Atlanta, 1978—. Mem. Am. Mgmt. Assn., Soc. Consumer Affairs Profls. Clubs: Raquetball, Photography. Office: 2939 Miller Rd Decatur GA 30035

LEARY, PRIEUR JAMES, JR., lawyer, marine service co. exec.; b. New Orleans, Oct. 4, 1943; s. Prieur James and Miriam Cecile Hartson L.; LL.B., Tulane U., 1967; LL.M. in Taxation, N.Y. U., 1968; m. Mathilde Thomas Stone, July 29, 1967; children—Prieur James III, Mathilde, Ashley. Admitted to La. bar, 1967, since practiced New Orleans; asso. firm Jones, Walker, Waechter, Poitevent, Carrere & Denegre, New Orleans, 1968-71, Liskow & Lewis, New Orleans, 1971-74; sec.-treas. Acadian Marine Service Inc., New Orleans, 1971-73, pres., chmn. bd., 1974—; dir. Continental Underwriters Ltd.; bd. dirs. Internat. Trade Mart, New Orleans, 1980—. Mem. New Orleans Met. Area Com. Bd. dirs., pres., chmn. Jr. Achievement, New Orleans; sec. bd. dirs. Met. Crime Commn., New Orleans; trustee Trinity Sch., New Orleans. Mem. La., Am. bar assns., Am. Soc. Internat. Law (sec.), Young Pres.'s Orgn. Roman Catholic. Clubs: Pickwick, Stratford, New Orleans Lawn Tennis, Internat. House (New Orleans); D.K.E. (N.Y.). Author: Journal of Taxation, 1968. Home: 1542 Calhoun St New Orleans LA 70118 Office: Acadian House 419 Decatur St New Orleans LA 70130

LEASE, SHARON ALBERT, educator; b. Oklahoma City, Sept. 1, 1943; d. Ronald James and Anita Grace (George) Albert; B.A., Oklahoma City U., 1965; M.Ed., Millersville State Coll., 1970; M.Ed., U. Guam, Mangilao, 1975; m. Kenneth Trevor Lease, Sept. 1, 1967; children—Stephanie Renee, Elizabeth Gail. Vol., U.S. Peace Corps, Sarikei, Sanawak, Malaysia, 1965-67; tchr., Phila., 1968, Terre Hill, Pa., 1969; grad. asst. Millersville (Pa.) State Coll., 1970; guidance counselor Garden Spot High Sch., New Holland, Pa., 1971; elem. guidance cons., asst. prin. Govt. Guam, Agana, 1972-75; guidance counselor Passargad Internat. Sch., Ahwas, Iran, 1976-78; reading coordinator Am. Sch., Rio de Janeiro, Brazil, 1979-80; asst. coordinator dropouts program Central Innovative High Sch., Oklahoma City, 1980—; co-dir. jrs. tennis programs The Courts, Oklahoma City, 1980—. Mem. Am. Personnel and Guidance Assn., Nat. Vocat. Assn., Am. Sch. Counselor Assn., U.S. Profl. Tennis Assn. (cert. mem.), Council Exceptional Children (past sec.), Govs. Council Gifted, Phi Delta Kappa (past chpt. treas.), Pi Lambda Theta. Democrat. Baptist. Home: 6002 NW Expressway Oklahoma City OK 73132 Office: Central Innovative High Sch 900 N Klein St Oklahoma City OK

LEATH, JAMES MARVIN, Congressman; b. Henderson, Tex., May 6, 1931; student Kilgore Jr. Coll.; B.B.A., U. Tex., 1954; m. Alta Ruth Neill, 1954; children—Thomas, Jim (dec.). Freshman line coach U. Tex., Austin, 1953-54; football and track coach Henderson High Sch., 1957-59; salesman, 1959-62; banker, from 1962; officer, dir. 5 Tex. banks, 2 mfg. cos.; spl. asst. to Rep. W.R. Poage, 1972-74; mem. 96th Congress from 11th Dist. Tex. Active in community and indsl. devel. in central Tex. Served with U.S. Army, 1954-56. Democrat. Presbyterian (elder). Office: Room 1331 Longworth House Office Bldg Washington DC 20515

LEATHER, RAYMOND FREEMAN, oil co. exec.; b. Saugus, Mass., Oct. 28, 1951; s. Percy Raymond and Phyllis Jean (Knights) L.; student Salem State Coll., 1972; B.S. in Civil Engring., Merrimack Coll., 1973; M.S. in Energy Mgmt., and Power, U. Pa., 1974; postgrad. Villanova U., 1974, U. Houston, 1979-80; m. Jane Marie Halloran, June 26, 1976. Research fellow U. Pa., 1973-74; with Gulf Oil Co.-U.S., 1975-77, 78, project mgr. new ventures devel., Houston, 1975-77, engring. adv., 1978; bus. mgr. Stage II Vapor Recovery Systems, comml. devel. and mktg. div. Gulf Research & Devel. Co., Pitts., 1977-78; dir. govt. inquiries and planning Gulf Oil Corp., Houston, 1979—. Mem. exec. com. Houston Ind. Sch. Dist. Follow Through Program, 1976-77. NSF fellow, 1973-74; registered profl. engr. in tng., Mass. Mem. ASCE, Nat. Fire Protection Assn., Am. Soc. Petroleum Ops. Engrs. (nat. pres. 1978-79, dir. 1979-80), Mu Chi Epsilon. Republican. Episcopalian. Home: 3206 Big Spruce Dr Kingwood TX 77339 Office: PO Box 2001 Houston TX 77001

LEATHERMAN, HUGH KENNETH, SR., corporate exec.; b. Lincoln County, N.C., Apr. 14, 1931; s. John Bingham and Ada Annis (Gantt) L.; B.S. in Civil Engring., N.C. State U., Raleigh, 1953; m. Jean Helms, Nov. 11, 1978; children—Sheila Dianne, Hugh Kenneth, Karen Ann, Joyce Lynn. Engr., then sec. Florence Concrete Products Inc. (S.C.), 1955-72, pres., 1972—; pres. Ebb Tide Inc., Myrtle Beach, S.C., 1972—, Atlantic Investments Inc., Myrtle Beach, 1970—, Leisure Inns Inc., Charleston, S.C., 1975—, Pee Dee Block Inc., Marion, S.C., 1975—, Mid-Lands Broadcasting Corp., 1979—; sec. Hugh-Stan Inc., Myrtle Beach, 1974—. Commr. S.C. Dept. Consumer Affairs. Baptist. Home: Timberlane Dr Country Club of SC Florence SC 29501 Office: PO Box 5506 Florence SC 29502

LEATHERMAN, RICHARD WILLIAM, mgmt. cons.; b. Norfolk, Va., Dec. 8, 1938; s. Richard Wismer and Ida May (Brunk) L.; B.S., Va. Commonwealth U., 1979; m. Nancy Ann Powell; children—Laurie, Richard, Matthew, Leanne. Mgr. edn. and tng. 3M Co., St. Paul, 1963-74; pres. Indsl. Tng. Cons., Inc., Richmond, Va., 1974—; asso. prof. Va. Commonwealth U. Mgmt. Center, 1975—. Pres. Central Minn. Area PTA Council, 1974. Served with USAF, 1961. Mem. Am. Soc. Tng. and Devel., Am. Soc. Bus. and Mgmt. Cons., Sales and Mktg. Execs., Am. Soc. Personnel Adminstrn. Author books in field. Office: PO Box 3213 Richmond VA 23235

LEATHERS, MARY ELIZABETH, oilfield equipment co. exec.; b. Houma, La., Jan. 20, 1941; d. William Dana and Jeanne Elizabeth (Somme) L.; student La. State U., 1959-60, Gulf Park Coll., 1960-62, U. Miss., 1962-63. Acct., Delta Iron Works (now Chromalloy Natural Resources Co.), Houma, 1964-68, adminstrv. asst. fin., 1968—. Campaign worker United Way, Houma. Mem. Profl. Women in Bus. Orgn. Democrat. Roman Catholic. Home: #4 Dallas Dr Houma LA 70360 Office: Industrial Blvd Houma LA 70360

LEAVITT, AUDREY FAYE COX, TV sta. exec.; b. Old Hickory, Tenn., June 1, 1932; d. James Aubrey and Bernice (Hudnall) Cox; student David Lipscomb Secondary Sch. and Coll., 1947, Tenn. Sch. Broadcasting, 1949-50, Vanderbilt U., 1948-50; children—Jack, Teresa. Woman commentator, continuity chief radio sta. WGNS, Murfreesboro, Tenn., 1949-50; announcer, continuity chief, traffic dir. Sta. KDWT, Stamford, Tex., 1950-51; sales account exec. Sta. KMAC, San Antonio, 1952; continuity chief, announcer Sta. KEYL-TV, San Antonio, 1952-54, also firm dir.; film buyer, mgr. Sta. WOAI-TV, San Antonio, 1954-68, ops. mgr. film, video-tape traffic, continuity, 1968-71; film and videotape operations mgr., film buyer Sta. KENS-TV, San Antonio, 1972-79; exec. producer The Lone Star Sportsman Show, 1979—; writer, exec. producer and dir. TV series Weather or Not; writer, producer gourmet cooking show For Men Only. Republican. Home: 6900 N Vandiver Apt A-208 San Antonio TX 78209 Office: PO Box 1178 San Antonio TX 78294

LEAVITT, MARY JANICE DEIMEL (MRS. ROBERT WALKER LEAVITT), educator; b. Washington, Aug. 21, 1924; d. Henry L. and Ruth (Grady) Deimel; B.A., Am. U., Washington, 1946; postgrad. U. Md., 1963-65, U. Va., 1965-67, George Washington U., 1966-67; m. Robert Walker Leavitt, Mar. 30, 1945; children—Michael Deimel, Robert Walker, Caroline Ann. Tchr., Rothery Sch., Arlington, Va., 1947; dir. Sunnyside, Children's House, Washington, 1949; asst. dir. Coop. Sch. for Handicapped Children, Arlington, 1962, dir., Arlington, Springfield, Va., 1963-66; tchr. mentally retarded children Fairfax (Va.) County Pub. Schs., 1966-68; asst. dir. Burgundy Farm Country Day Sch., Alexandria, Va., 1968-69; tchr. specific learning problem children Accotink Acad., Springfield, Va., 1970—, now substitute tchr.; also substitute tchr. Children's Achievement Center, McLean, Va., Psychiat. Inst., Washington, 1976—; tchr. Home-bound Tchrs. program Fairfax County (Va.) Schs., 1979—; asst. research specialist Ednl. Research Service, Inc., Rosslyn, Va., 1974-76. Den mother Nat. Capital Area Cub Scouts, Boy Scouts Am., 1962; troop fund raising chmn. Nat. Capitol council Girl Scouts U.S.A., 1968-69; capt. amblyopia team No. Va. chpt. Delta Gamma Alumnae, 1969, mem. edn. subcom. Va. Commn. Children and Youth, 1973-74. Recipient award Nat. Assn. for Retarded Children, 1975. Mem. AAUW (co-chmn. met. area mass media com. 1973-75, v.p. Alexandria br. 1974-76, fellowship chmn. 1979), Delta Gamma (treas. 1974-76, pres. alumnae chpt. 1977-79, found. chmn. 1979). Roman Catholic. Club: Arlington Hall Officer's Wives. Home: 7129 Rolling Forest Ave Springfield VA 22152

LE-BA, JOHN KONG (LE BA KONG), publisher; b. Hong Kong, June 2, 1925; s. Thoan Duc Le and Lan Thi Tran; came to U.S., 1975; B.A. in English Lit., Hong Kong U., 1947; postgrad. Hanoi U., 1951; m. Mary Thi-Ngoan Vu, May 7, 1949; children—John Hung, Anthony Tam. Contbg. editor to Thoi Su (Time) Daily, Hanoi, Vietnam, 1948-52, Dan Quyen mag., Hanoi, 1952-54; mng. editor Thanh Hoa Mag., Saigon, Vietnam, 1961-64; prin. Zien Hong Lang. Sch., Hanoi, 1950-54, Saigon, 1960-75; academic dir. Dung Lac Catholic High Sch., Hanoi, 1949-54; head of Confidential Secretariat, Ministry of Defense, Republic of VietNam, 1955-60; mng. dir., propr. Zien-Hong Publishing Co., Saigon, 1960-75; sr. v.p. Phuong Hai Sea Products Co., 1974-75; mgr., propr. Zieleks Pub. Co., Houston, 1975—; mng. dir. Le-Ba Co., Houston, 1975—; pres. N.B.D.-Astro Homes, Inc., 1979—; v.p. Viet-Nam High Sch. Tchrs. Union, 1950-54. Recipient First Class medals for Distinguished Social Services, Republic of Viet-Nam, 1967, for Outstanding Cultural and Ednl. Services, 1972. Mem. Vietnam Free Tchrs. Assn. (pres. 1970-75), Internat. Polit. Sci. Assn., Vietnamese Cath. Community in Galveston-Houston (pres. 1977—). Roman Catholic. Clubs: Lions (pres. Saigon sect. 1973-74), Jaycees (pres. Vietnam chpt. 1966-67). Author: English-Vietnamese Vietnamese-English Dictionary, 1951; English Grammar for Vietnamese Learners, 1953; Modern English, 4 vols., 1972-75; numerous texts in English and Vietnamese; translator various English and Am. works. Address: 11215 Sageland Dr Houston TX 77089

LEBLANC, DENNIS, mgmt. cons., engr.; b. Danbury, Conn., Feb. 7, 1930; s. Joseph H. and Marie Rose (Lessard) LeB.; student in mech. engring., Ind. Tech. Coll., 1949-50, Fairleigh Dickenson U., 1950-51; B.S. in Indsl. Engring., U. Md., 1957; m. Bernadette M. Melanson, 1955 (dec. 1973); children—Suzanne M., Thomas A., Rose Marie, Dennis N., Louise A., John H.; m. 2d, Katherine M. Moore, Dec. 24, 1975. Indsl. engr. Neptune Meter Co., N.Y.C., 1957-62; chief indsl. engr. Standard Packaging Corp., Clifton, N.J., 1962-64; mfg. cons., Wyckoff, N.J., 1964-66; div. indsl. and plant engr. Indian Head Inc., N.Y.C., 1966-69; corp. indsl. engr. Export Leaf Tobacco Co., Richmond, Va., 1969-72; mgmt. and indsl. engring. cons. Wiley & Wilson, Lynchburg, Va., 1972-75; pres. White & Assos., Inc., Lynchburg, 1975—; founder, inventor Chiropractic Equipment Co., Lynchburg, 1977—, also dir., treas.; instr. labor econs. Central Va. Community Coll. Served with U.S. Army, 1951-53. Mem. Am. Inst. Indsl. Engrs., Am. Inst. Plant Engrs., Soc. for Advancement of Mgmt., Soc. Am. Value Engrs., Nat. Assn. Fin. Consultants. Roman Catholic. Club: Chi Sigma Phi. Inventor new chiropractic adjustment table, 1978. Home and Office: 1031 Dandridge Dr Lynchburg VA 24501

LE BLANC, EDMOND PATRICK, JR., ins. co. exec.; b. Breaux Bridge, La., Dec. 7, 1927; s. Edmond J. and Octavia T. (Therjot) Le B.; student U. Southwestern La., 1944-47; m. Maria Loretta Pastor, Sept. 4, 1950; children—Edmond P., Milton L., Marc A., Anne M. Agt., Life Ins. Co. of Ga., Lafayette, La., 1948, staff mgr., 1950, dist. mgr., 1955—; tchr. Life Underwriters Tng. Council, 1962-69, ednl. chmn., 1955-79. Chmn., Am. Cancer Soc., Lafayette, 1959. Served with La. N.G., 1948-63. Named Salesman of Yr., Life Ins. Co. Ga., 1978, 79. Mem. Nat. Assn. Life Underwriters (Nat. Quality award 1970, 79), Acadiana Assn. Life Underwriters (Man of Yr. 1979), Gen. Agts. and Mgrs. Republican. Roman Catholic. Clubs: Exchange (pres. 1962, 76), Krewe of Zeus. Home: 1401 E Bayou Pkwy Lafayette LA 70508 Office: 2402 W Congress St Lafayette LA 70505

LE BLANC, KEITH EDWARD, accountant; b. Charenton, La., Aug. 29, 1937; s. Abel Edward and Jeanne Marie (Fuselier) LeB.; B.S. in Commerce, U. Southwestern La., 1962; m. Patricia Gayle Bacala, Jan. 31, 1959; children—Jeanne, Keith Edward, Joni, Jennifer, Kenneth. With Price Waterhouse & Co., New Orleans, 1962-67, Ernst & Ernst, New Orleans, 1967-68; sec.-treas., dir. Plantation Fried Chicken, New Orleans, 1968-69; controller Sutton Industries, New Iberia, La., 1969-70; partner Matt, Sonnier & Co., C.P.A., Lafayette, La., 1970-73; pvt. practice accounting, Franklin, La., 1973—. Bd. dirs. St. Mary Parish Sch. Employee Fed. Credit Union, 1976—; bd. dirs. West End Acad. Pvt. Sch., Franklin, La., 1974-75; sec., treas. St. Mary Parish Waterworks Dist. 6, 1970—; bd. dirs. North Bend Fed. Credit Union, 1977—. C.P.A., La. Mem. Am. Inst. C.P.A.'s, La. Soc. C.P.A.'s, C. of C. Clubs: Optimist, Lions, K.C. (fin. sec. 1979—). Home: PO Box 297 Charenton LA 70523 Office: No 26 Gulf Central Plaza Franklin LA 70538

LE BLANC, LEONA LACY, mental health center ofcl.; b. Scott, La., July 15, 1935; d. Percy and Rena Marie (Breaux) L.; student S.W. La. Vocat. Sch., Port Arthur Coll., U. Southwestern La., La. State U.; m. Thomas Clayton LeBlanc, Feb. 19, 1955; children—Thomas, Michael, Holly. Various secretarial and office positions, 1956-60; staff mem. Acadiana Mental Health Center, Lafayette, La., 1960—, adminstrv. asst., 1973-75, exec. asst., 1976—. Active local PTA, Roman Catholic Ch. Mem. La. Personnel Council, La. Hosp. Assn. Soc. Personnel Dirs., La. Assn. Retarded Citizens (dir., membership chmn. Lafayette chpt. 1979-81), Acadiana Personnel Assn., Nat. Secs. Assn. (pres. Azalea chpt. 1976-77). Democrat. Home: 101 Breaux Dr Scott LA 70583 Office: 400 St Julien St Lafayette LA 70506

LEBOVITZ, JOYCE LESLIE, bus. exec.; b. St. Paul, Mar. 12, 1942; d. Oscar and Vivian (Anton) Guberman; B.A. in Sociology, UCLA, 1966, M.A. in Counseling, 1973; postgrad. New Sch. for Social Research, 1969-70; m. Robert Lebovitz, Apr. 17, 1964; children—Mark, Richard, Joel. Research asst. in psychology UCLA, 1963, 68-69; dir. Washington Sq. Village, N.Y.C., 1974; social worker Methodist Hosp., Dallas, 1974, supr. social services, 1975; dir. social sers. Meth. Hosps. of Dallas, 1976-80; pres. Community Introductions, Inc., Dallas, 1980—; coordinator Scope of Alcoholism symposium, 1977; mem. exec. bd. Substance Abuse Network of Dallas, 1978; mem. med. adv. bd. Ostomy Assn.; lectr. in field. Mem. exec. bd. Assemblage, Dallas, 1979; mem. hospitality com. Chamber Music Soc., Dallas. Mem. Nat. Assn. Social Workers, Nat. Rehab. Assn., Nat. Rehab. Counseling Assn., Am. Hosp. Assn. Social Work Dirs., Tex. Hosp. Assn. Social Work Dirs. Democrat. Jewish. Club: Southwestern Med. Sch. Faculty Wives. Home: 10054 Inwood Rd Dallas TX 75229 Office: PO Box 5728 LBJ Freeway Suite 400 Dallas TX 75240

LEBRON, AMARYLLIS VELILLA (MRS. RAMON CLEMENTE LEBRON), statistician; b. San Juan, P.R., July 24, 1937; d. Rafael and Dolores Urrutia (Vega) Velilla; B.B.A., U. P.R., 1958; postgrad. P.R. Inst. Statistics, 1958-65, P.R. Sch. Pub. Health, 1967-69; M.P.A., P.R. Grad. Sch. Pub. Adminstrn., 1975; m. Ramon Clemente Lebron, Dec. 15, 1962; children—Vanessa, Amaryllis, Ramon Clemente. Statistician II, Bur. Labor Statistics, Dept. Labor, 1958-60, statistician III, 1960-62; statistician, Caribbean Orgn., 1962-64; statistician IV Office Sci. Research, Dept. Health, 1965-67, statistician V, statistics and econs. studies sect., Planning Research and Evaluation Office, 1967-72; program analyst I, Bur. Budget, Office Gov., San Juan, P.R., 1972-73, program analyst II, 1973, program analyst III, 1974-79, program analyst IV, chief sect. D social devel. area, budget analysis div., 1975-79; dir. budget, stats., systems and procedures P.R. Dept. Housing, Rio Piedras, 1979—. Pres. pub. relations com. Comprehensive Health Planning Week, 1971; coordinator pharmacy com. State Bd. Health, 1969-71, asst. of exec. dir., 1969-71. Active PTA, Al-Anon. Recipient Scholarship, Govt. P.R., 1954; Manuel A. Pórez award for outstanding service Govt. of P.R., 1979. Mem. Am. Statis. Assn. (chpt. sec. P.R. chpt. 1971-75), P.R. Statis. Soc. (sec. 1970-71). Home: 1 L-19 Nogal Ave Royal Palms Bayamon PR 00619 Office: 606 Barbosa Ave PO Box W Rio Piedras PR

LEBRON, BARBARA ANN WILLIAMS, guidance counselor; b. Charlottesville, Va., Jan. 8, 1939; d. Roscoe and Netta (Jackson) Williams; B.S. in Edn., D.C. Tchrs. Coll., 1961; M.A. in Secondary Edn., George Washington U., 1963; m. Angel Luis LeBron, Mar. 25, 1961; children—Ramona, Monica, Kysha. Tchr. bus. edn. public schs. in Washington and V.I., 1962-70; guidance counselor Govt. V.I., St. Thomas, 1970—. Mem. Am. Personnel and Guidance Assn., Am. Fedn. Tchrs., St. Thomas/St. John Personnel and Guidance Assn., AAUW, Alpha Kappa Alpha. Roman Catholic. Home: Est Misgunst 7J PO Box 7214 St Thomas VI 00801 Office: Charlotte Amalie High Sch PO Box 630 St Thomas VI 00801

LECKY, WILLIAM RALSTON, III, elec. engr.; b. Richmond, Va., July 8, 1940; s. William Ralston and Allene (Pace) L.; B.S. in Elec. Engring., Va. Poly. Inst., 1963; m. Susan Evans Hearn, June 6, 1964; children—Jennifer Jill, Kathryn Pace, Susan Arrington. Asso. engr., plant engring. Mobile (Ala.) Mill, Internat. Paper Co., 1963-64, project engr., 1966-68, sr. project engr., central design engring., 1968-74, design engr., 1974-76, sr. design engr., 1976-78, supr. engring. sers. Natchez (Miss.) Mill, 1978—. Adviser, Jr. Achievement, 1967-68; active United Fund Canvass, 1971-72; v.p. Mobile Soap Box Derby, Inc., 1972-73. Bd. dirs. Greater Gulf State Fair, Inc., 1972-77, chmn. bd., 1977, chief engr., mgr. constrn. new fair grounds, 1973-74, pres. Greater Gulf State Fair, 1975. Served to 1st lt. AUS, 1964-66. Registered profl. engr., Miss., Ala. Mem. IEEE (sr. mem., sect. treas. 1971-72, sec. 1972-73, chmn. 1974-75), Va. Tech. Alumni Assn., Mobile Jr. C. of C. (sec. 1971-72, bd. dirs. 1974, 75, 77), Omicron Delta Kappa. Mem. Christian Ch. Clubs: Bellwood Country, Delta Yacht. Home: #1 Village Pl Natchez MS 39120 Office: PO Box 311 Natchez MS 39120

LECOUR, PAUL LOUIS, auto. parts co. exec.; b. Houston, Jan. 26, 1944; s. John J. and Frances Margaret (Ivey) LeC.; student U. Southwestern La., 1965, E. Jefferson Tech. and Vocat. Sch., 1966; m. Marie Elise Horrell, July 26, 1969; children—Lauren Elise, Frances Clare, Paul Louis. Gen. mgr. LeCour Corp., New Orleans, 1965-69; factory rep. trouble shooter and instr. Rayloc div. Genuine Parts, Atlanta, 1971-76, product engr., 1976—; cons. parts return program Dept. Transp., 1971-75; Vol. automotive instr. E. Jefferson Tech. Sch., 1971-76; mem. recreation com. Home Owners Assn., Marietta, Ga., 1978-79. Served with U.S. Army, 1969-71. Recipient various certs. Nat. Inst. for Automotive Service Excellence, 1976. Mem. Automotive Parts Rebuilders Assn. (chmn. elec. inst. 1978-79). Democrat. Roman Catholic. Home: 3102 Sycamore Ln NE Marietta GA 30066 Office: 600 Rayloc Dr SW Atlanta GA 30336

LEDBETTER, CHARLES AUSTIN, orthopedic surgeon; b. Benton, Ark., June 14, 1941; s. Austin Andrew and Birdie Mary (Baber) L.; B.S., U. Ark., 1963, M.D., 1967; m. Suzanne Lane, Aug. 16, 1963; children—Lane, Brynn, Greer, Blair. Intern, U.S. Naval Hosp., Jacksonville, Fla., 1967-68; resident in orthopedic surgery U. Ark. Med. Center, Fayetteville, 1970-74; sec. med. staff Boone County Hosp., Harrison, Ark., 1976, attending orthopedist, 1974—, vice chief staff, 1977, chief staff, 1978-79; clin. instr. orthopedic surgery U. Ark. Med. Sch., Little Rock, 1979—; cons. Baxter Gen. Hosp., Mountain Home, Ark., 1974—; mem. Ozark Orthopedic Assos., Ltd., Harrison, 1974—. Served to lt. comdr. M.C., USN, 1967-70. Diplomate Am. Bd. Orthopedic Surgery. Mem. AMA (Physicians Recognition award 1979), Ark. Orthopedic Soc., So. Med. Assn., Boone County Med. Soc., Ark. Med. Soc. Presbyterian. Home: 1211 Floyd Ave Harrison AR 72601 Office: Ozark Orthopedics 224 W Erie St Harrison AR 72601

LEDBETTER, DIXIE ACTON, speech pathologist; b. Beaver, Okla., Feb. 18, 1952; d. Dudley Durham and Ruth Marie (Gustafson) Acton; B.S. in Speech Pathology cum laude, Tex. Christian U., 1974; M.S. in Speech Pathology, U. Okla., 1976; m. Albert Jay Ledbetter, Aug. 7, 1976. Lang. devel. specialist Children's Convalescent Center, Bethany, Okla., 1976-78; speech pathologist Southwest Guidance Center, Oklahoma City, 1978-79; speech-lang. pathologist Baptist Med. Center of Okla., Oklahoma City, 1979—. Mem. Am. Speech and Hearing Assn. (cert. clin. competence), Tex. Christian U. Alumni Assn., Okla. Speech and Hearing Assn. Republican. Mem. Disciples of Christ. Home: 5801 NW 31st Terr Oklahoma City OK 73122 Office: 3300 Northwest Expressway Oklahoma City OK 73112

LEDBETTER, JAMES PAUL, JR., automotive co. exec.; b. Randleman, N.C., Dec. 28, 1920; s. James Paul and Allie Steed (Hinshaw) L.; Asso. Sci., Bentley Coll., 1950; B.B.A., Northeastern U., 1950-52; M.B.A., U. N.C., 1967-68; m. Eleanor Travers Jones, Aug. 21, 1943; children—Jane Ledbetter Elias, Ann, William J. Office mgr. Arrow Automotive Industries, Boston, 1947-52, gen. mgr., Spartanburg, S.C., 1952-61, v.p., 1961-68, exec. v.p., chief operating officer, 1968—; dir. First Citizens Bank & Trust Co. Chmn., Spartanburg Tech. Coll. Bd., 1962-79. Served with USN, 1940-46. Mem. Automotive Parts Rebuilders Assn. (dir. 1970-73), Automotive Service Industries Assn. (dir. 1975-78), So. Automotive Show (dir. 1960-63). Presbyterian. Clubs: Optimist, Rotary. Home: 326 Lanham Circle Spartanburg SC 29302 Office: Arrow Automotive Industries PO Box 1748 Spartanburg SC 29304

LEDBETTER, LEE ROY, hosp. adminstr.; b. Live Oak, Fla., Feb. 24, 1926; s. Fred Cleveland and Bammer Lou Bertha (Garrison) L.; student U. Miami, 1944; B.S., Tulane U., 1946; postgrad. U.S. Naval Postgrad. Sch.; m. Georgia Louise Wolfe, June 9, 1946; children—Lee Roy, Holy Lea, Editha Lorena, Greta Loraine. Commd. in U.S. Navy, advanced through grades to lt. comdr.; ret., 1966; controller, dir. fin. Meml. Hosp., Jacksonville, Fla., 1969-74; exec. dir. Greater Orange Park (Fla.) Community Hosp., 1974—; v.p. Fla. Health Data Corp.; bd. dirs. Health Systems Agy. N.E. Fla. Chmn., Clay County Health Adv. Com.; bd. dirs. Jacksonville chpt. ARC; chmn. Fla. Com. on Cost of Med. Care; mem. Bishop's Commn. on Ministry, 1972-75; vestryman Grace Episcopal Ch., 1972-75. Paul Harris fellow Rotary Found. Fellow Hosp. Fin. Assn.; mem. Am. Coll. Hosp. Adminstrs., Fla. Hosp. Assn. (dir.), Fla. League Hosps. (pres. 1977-78), Fedn. Am. Hosps. (dir.), Am. Hosp. Assn. Republican. Clubs: Timuquana Country, Univ. (Jacksonville); Continental (Orange Park). Home: 2334 Birdwood Dr Orange Park FL 32073 Office: 2001 Kingsley Ave Orange Park FL 32043

LEDBETTER, PEGGY JEAN, coll. dean; b. New Hope, Ala., Jan. 3, 1939; d. Smith Edward and Elizabeth (Jordan) L.; B.S., Samford U., 1961; B.S.N., U. Ala., 1962, M.S.N., 1964, Ed.D., 1968. Staff nurse Baptist Hosp., Birmingham, Ala., 1960-61; nurse cons. Ala. Health Dept., 1962-63; asst. prof. nursing U. Miss. Med. Center, 1964-66, U. Ala., 1966-68; dean Coll. Nursing, Northwestern State U. of La., 1968—; nurse mem. adv. bd. La. Dept. Health and Human Resources; mem. state planning com. Am. Council on Edn.'s Task Force on Women; mem. exec. com. So. Regional Edn. Bd. Collegiate Council on Nursing; coordinator Nat. Endowment for Humanities Grant to Northwestern State U. of La. for Liberal Arts and Nursing; nurse cons. Surgeon Gen. USAF; mem. def. adv. com. on women in services Dept. Def. Mem. Shreveport (La.) C. of C. Legis. Affairs Task Force. Mem. Assn. for Preservation Hist. Natchitoches. Democrat. Baptist. Office: 1427 Kings Hwy Shreveport LA 71103

LEDFORD, WILLIAM LESTER, elec. engr.; b. Cleveland, Tenn., Sept. 12, 1935; s. Canary Bascom and Anna Pauline (Harrison) L.; B.S., U. Tenn., 1959; postgrad. U. Utah, 1961-62; m. Martha Sue Cunningham, Nov. 12, 1960; children—John William, Benjamin James. Elec. engr. trainee TVA, Nashville, 1959-60, Chattanooga, 1962-63, elec. engr., Bowling Green, Ky., 1964-65, Paradise, Ky., 1966-69, Muscle Shoals, Ala., 1970—. Served with Chem. Corps, AUS, 1960-62. Mem. I.E.E.E., Engrs. Assn., Nat., Ala. socs. profl. engrs. Baptist (treas. 1962, tchr. 1960-69, 73-77). Home: 1841 W Tannehill Dr Florence AL 35630

LEDINGTON, JOE DAVID, real estate broker, developer, contractor; b. Barbourville, Ky., Feb. 16, 1940; s. Clarence Lee and Alta Lee (Yeager) L.; student Knoxville (Tenn.) Bus. Coll., U. Tenn., 1973; m. Luella Sue Borden, June 4, 1963; 1 son, Joe David. Self-employed barber, 1961-63; owner, mgr. Modern Barber Shop, Knoxville, 1964—; owner, mgr. Modern Home Improvement Co., Knoxville, 1967—; owner, mgr. Joe Ledington Realtors, Knoxville, 1974—. Served with AUS, 1963-65. Mem. Knoxville Bd. Realtors, Tenn. Assn. Realtors, Knoxville C. of C., Better Bus. Bur., Nat. Assn. Realtors. Home: Route 2 Box 260 Maynardville TN 37807 Office: 3905 Fountain Valley Knoxville TN 37918

LEDOCK, ARTHUR H., JR., physician's asst.; b. Jacksonville, Fla., Feb. 15, 1922; s. Arthur H. and Lydia LeD.; B.S., U. S.C., 1941; m. Gertrude Walker, June 4, 1961; children—Lynda, Elizabeth, James, Cynthia. Physician's asst. VA, Augusta, Ga., 1953-61, Dept. Justice, Montgomery, Ala., 1969-72; physician's asst. State of Miss., Meridian, 1972-79; cons. East Miss. State Hosp., Meridian, 1972—. Served with USNR, 1941-46. Decorated Silver Star, Purple Heart medal. Democrat. Methodist. Address: PO Box 48 Quitman MS 39355

LEDOUX, JACK, author, ret. race track exec.; b. Orlando, Fla., Oct. 4, 1928; s. Leonard K. and Louise (Downs) L.; B.S. in Journalism, U. Fla., 1950; m. Geraldine C. Collins, Sept. 12, 1949; children—Michele, Lance, Stephen, Lola. Sportswriter, columnist Orlando Sentinel-Star, 1948-53; pub. relations dir. Sarasota, Daytona Beach (Fla.) Kennel Clubs, 1953-55; gen. mgr., corp. sec. Sanford-Orlando Kennel Club, 1955-72; gen. mgr., exec. v.p. Black Hills Kennel Club, Rapid City, S.D., 1964-71; pres., co-owner Exec. Travel, Winter Park, Fla., 1977—, Triex Enterprises, Inc., Winter Park, 1977—; ind. editorial columnist, free-lance writer, 1972—; dir. Combank Casselberry Bank, Tropicana Pools, Inc. Mem. Fla. Golf Assn. (chmn. adv. com. 1964-65, dir., pres.), Am. Greyhound Track Operators Assn. (publ. and supervisory com. Am. Greyhound Racing Ency., pub. 1963; nat. pres.), World Racing Fedn. (chmn.), World Greyhound Racing Fedn. (pres.), Internat. Platform Assn., U. Fla. Alumni Assn. (past pres. Sarasota County chpt.), Sigma Delta Chi, Theta Chi. Democrat. Clubs: Univ., Country, Touchdown (Orlando); Winter Park (Fla.) Racquet. Home: 501 Village Ln Winter Park FL 32792

LEDUC, ALBERT L., educator; b. Vincennes, Ind., June 18, 1911; s. David and Helen (Fish) L.; A.B., Ind. U., 1931, M.A., 1935; Ph.D., U. Wis., 1952; m. Rachel Wineinger, Sept. 1, 1933; children—Albert, Louise (Mrs. Arthur Zierzow), Theodore. Faculty mem. Earlham Coll., 1931-33, Ind. U., 1933-36, Huntingdon Coll., 1936-40, U.S. Mil. Acad., 1942-47; asst. prof. modern langs. Fla. State U., 1947-53, asso. prof., 1953-62; prof. modern langs. Hampden-Sydney (Va.) Coll., 1962-72, prof. emeritus, 1972—. Vis. prof. S.F. Austin State U., summer 1961, Appalachian State U., summers 1965, 68. Served as col. USAAF, World War II. Mem. South Atlantic Modern Lang. Assn. (officer 1948-49, 59-61), Am. Assn. Tchrs. French (state pres. 1950-53, 65-67, 68-70), Ind. U. Alumni Club Tallahassee (pres. 1976-78), Phi Beta Kappa (pres. Alpha Fla. chpt. 1955-56), Pi Delta Phi, Sigma Delta Pi. Methodist. Rotarian (pres. 1967-68). Editor: (with James A. Preu) The Selected Speeches of Robert M. Strozier. Contbr. to French Rev., Am. Travelers Companion, other profl. publs. Home: 2035 Doomar Dr Tallahassee FL 32308

LE DUC, ALBERT LOUIS, JR., coll. adminstr.; b. Montgomery, Ala., Feb. 1, 1937; s. Albert Louis and Rachel Nancy (Wineinger) LeD.; student Duke U., 1954-55; B.A., Fla. State U., 1958, M.S., 1960; m. Ellen Heath, June 18, 1960; children—Albert Louis III, Charles Andrew. Civilian mathematician Army Rocket Guided Missile Agy., Huntsville, Ala., 1958, 59; mathematician analyst RCA Service Co., Patrick AFB, Fla., 1960-63, programming leader, 1963-67, project mgr., Eglin AFB, Fla., 1967-69, mktg. adminstr., Cherry Hill, N.J., 1969-71; tech. dir. Ind. U., Bloomington, 1971-77; dir. analysis programming Miami-Dade Community Coll., Miami, Fla., 1977—; part-time instr. Fla. State U., 1958-60, Brevard Engring. Coll., 1961-62, Ind. U., 1972-77. Bd. dirs. Coll. and Univ. Machine Records Conf., 1979—. Mem. Assn. Computing Machinery (Best Paper award 1973). Author: The Computer for Managers, 1972. Home: 10321 SW 107th St Miami FL 33176 Office: 11011 SW 104th St Miami FL 33176

LEDWELL, JO STARNES, clin. psychologist; b. Monroe, N.C., Feb. 8, 1934; d. Thomas Howard and Ruby Lee (Stewart) Starnes; B.A. cum laude, Bridgewater Coll., 1968; M.S., Ohio U., 1971, Ph.D., 1973; m. John David Ledwell, Sept. 1, 1956. Staff psychologist Kennedy Youth Center, Morgantown, W.Va., 1973-74, coordinator mental health, 1974-76; pvt. practice psychology, Morgantown, 1976—; asst. prof. dept. behavioral medicine and psychiatry W.Va. U., 1973—, also dept. rehab. counseling 1975-76; mem. staff Monongalia Gen. Hosp. Mem. Am., W.Va. psychol. assns., Lambda Soc., Phi Kappa Phi, Psi Chi. Democrat. Lutheran. Home: Route 1 Box 274 Independence WV 26374 Office: 75 University Ave Morgantown WV 26505

LEE, BARBARA DERENNE, nurse; b. Florence County, S.C., May 25, 1937; d. James Matthew Lee and Pearl (Stephens) Lee Truluck; R.N. diploma Presbyn. Hosp. Sch. of Nursing, 1958; B.S., Queens Coll., 1961; M.Ed., U. N.C., Charlotte, 1976. Staff nurse Presbyn. Hosp., Charlotte, N.C., 1958-59, head nurse, 1959, instr. nursing, 1968-78; head nurse gynecology Mt. Zion Hosp. and Med. Center, San Francisco, 1959-60; pub. health nurse Duval County Pub. Health Dept., Jacksonville, Fla., 1960-61; dir. nursing, Richard Baker Hosp., Hickory, N.C., 1961-68; dir. operating room and recovery room Catawba Meml. Hosp., Hickory, N.C., 1978—. Registered nurse, N.C., Fla., Calif. Mem. Am. Nurses Assn., Assn. Operating Room Nurses. Republican. Baptist. Home: Route 3 Box 191 Statesville NC 28677 Office: Catawba Meml Hosp Fairgrove Church Rd Hickory NC 28601

LEE, C. E., math. physicist; b. San Jose, Calif., Aug. 18, 1931; s. Jack and Bertha Jean (Stüssy) L.; B.A., U. Calif., 1953; M.A., Cornell U., 1962; Ph.D., U. Colo., 1973; m. Martha Owings, Feb. 29, 1976; children—Christopher, Katherine, David; stepchildren—Marcene, Marcella, Marietta, Margo. Mem. staff Los Alamos Sci. Lab., 1953-78, cons., 1978—; cons. Los Alamos Tech. Assos., 1977; prof. dept. nuclear engring. Tex. A. and M. U., College Station, 1978—; vis. guest scientist Kernforschungsanlage, Jülich, 1977. AEC fellow, 1955-56. Mem. Am. Phys. Soc., Am. Nuclear Soc., AAAS, Sigma Xi. Author papers in field. Home: 3005 Normand Dr College Station TX 77840 Office: Dept Nuclear Engineering Texas A and M U College Station TX 77843

LEE, CARMEL D(IO), hosp. ofcl.; b. Putnam County, Tenn., Sept. 22, 1940; s. Charlie Benjamin and Nellie Mae (Davis) L.; m. Linda Pierce, June 1, 1969; children—Ginger Jacquelene, Jason Pierce. Staff, Jere Whitson Hardware, elec. appliance service, Cookeville, Tenn., 1962-64; installer, switchman Gen. Telephone Co., Cookeville, 1967-70; maintenance supr. Plateau Mental Health Center, Cookeville, 1970-76; maintenance staff Cookeville Gen. Hosp., 1964-67, dir. environ. services, 1976—. Mem. Tenn. Hosp. Engrs. Assn., Tenn. Biomed. instrumentation Assn. Baptist. Developer hosp. preventive maintenance program, 1973. Home: Box 295 Route 1 Cookeville TN 38501 Office: Cookeville Gen Hosp Box 340 142 W 5th St Cookeville TN 38501

LEE, CHARLES RICHARD, risk mgmt. cons.; b. McCallsburg, Iowa, Mar. 15, 1949; s. Franklin Sanford and Selma D. (Stensland) L.; B.B.A., State U. Iowa, 1971; m. Donna Rae Eggers, June 6, 1970; 1 dau., Jessica Lynn. Underwriter, Kemper Ins. Group, Chgo., 1971-72, Dallas, 1972-74; account exec. Ben C. Doherty & Co. Ins. Agy., Dallas, 1974-75; prin., sr. cons. Rimco Risk Mgmt., Inc., Dallas, 1975—; lectr. in field. C.P.C.U.; asso. in risk mgmt. Mem. Soc. C.P.C.U.'s. Republican. Lutheran. Contbr. articles in field to profl. jours. Home: 1913 Palo Alto Circle Plano TX 75074 Office: 10300 N Central Expressway Suite 350 Dallas TX 75231

LEE, CHING YUNG, pathologist; b. Taiwan, China, Sept. 22, 1935; s. Muh Yuen and Jane Chen L.; M.D., Nat. Taiwan U., 1961; Ph.D., U. Mich., 1970; m. Sabrina Lin, Dec. 27, 1966; children—Steven, Scott, Julia. Intern, St. John's Episcopal Hosp., N.Y.C., 1963-64; resident in pathology U. Minn. Hosp., Mpls., 1976-78; asst. prof., cons. Mayo Clinic and Mayo Med. Sch., Rochester, Minn., 1974-75; asst. prof. dept. lab. medicine and pathology U. Minn., 1977-79; asso. prof. dept. pathology and lab. medicine U. Tex. Med. Sch., Houston, 1979—. NIH grantee. Mem. AAAS, Tissue Culture Assn., Endocrine Soc. Contbr. articles to med. jours. Home: 11803 Braesridge Houston TX 77071 Office: Dept Pathology and Lab Medicine Univ Tex Med Sch Houston TX 77025

LEE, CHOO HYUNG, internist, hematologist; b. Heungnam City, Korea, Mar. 24, 1925; s. Lee Chung Soo and Moon Mo Jong; came to U.S., 1971, naturalized, 1978; M.D., Yonsei U., 1948, D.M.Sc., 1964; m. Hae Sook Kim, Apr. 3, 1948; children—Yoon Sup, Insup, Joon Sup. Intern, Severance Hosp., Seoul, Korea, 1948-49; resident Lincoln Hosp., N.Y.C., 1956-57, Charles S. Wilson Meml. Hosp., Johnson City, N.Y., 1957-58, Montefiore Hosp., Pitts., 1958-59; research asso. VA Cancer Chemotherapy Study Group, VA Hosp., Pitts., 1959-60; asst. prof. medicine Yonsei U., Seoul, 1963-65, asso. prof., 1965-69, prof., 1969-71; dir. alcoholic unit Broughton Hosp., Morganton, N.C., 1971-78, internist, hematologist, 1971—; mem. staff Grace Hosp., Morganton. Served with Korean Army, 1961-62. Diplomate Am. Bd. Internal Medicine. Mem. A.C.P., Korean Soc. Internal Medicine, Korean Soc. Hematology, Am. Soc. Internal Medicine, AMA. Methodist. Club: Mimosa Hills Golf and Country (Morganton). Home: 247 Camelot Dr Morganton NC 28655 Office: Broughton Hosp Morganton NC 28655

LEE, DAN MCKINNON, judge; b. Petal, Miss., Apr. 19, 1926; s. B.A. and Pherbia Anna (Camp) L.; student U. So. Miss., 1946-47; LL.B., J.D., Jackson (Miss.) Sch. Law, 1949; diploma Nat. Coll. Stata Judiciary, 1972; m. Peggy Daniel, Nov. 27, 1948 (dec. May 1952); m. 2d, Mary Alice Gray, Sept. 30, 1956; children—Sheron D. Lee Anderson, Dan McKinnon. Admitted to Miss. bar, 1948; individual practice, Jackson, 1948-71; partner firm Lee, Moore & Countiss, 1954-71; mem. Miss. Oil and Gas Bd., 1968-71; circuit judge Hinds County, Jackson, 1971—. Served with A.C., USNR, 1944-46. Mem. Am. Bar Assn., Miss. Bar Assn., Hinds County Bar Assn., VFW, Am. Legion. Democrat. Baptist. Club: Masons. Home: 2278 E Manor Dr Jackson MS 39211 Office: PO Box 327 Jackson MS 39201

LEE, DAVID KEITH, physician; b. Deadwood, S.D., Jan. 12, 1947; s. Kenneth M. and Rebecca Jane (Furze) L.; B.A., Johns Hopkins U., 1969; M.D., Harvard U., 1973; m. Joan Marie Cowan, Aug. 7, 1970; children—Mark David, Matthew Charles. Intern, Southwestern Med. Sch. Affiliated Hosps., 1973-74, resident in internal medicine, 1974-76; asst. dir. ambulatory care div. U. Tex. Hosps., Dallas, 1976-78, asso. chief of staff for ambulatory care, 1978—, asst. prof. medicine, 1976—. Mem. A.C.P., Tex. Med. Assn., Dallas County Med. Soc., Soc. for Research and Edn. in Primary Care Internal Medicine, Phi Beta Kappa. Episcopalian. Office: Ambulatory Care Div U Tex Hosps 4500 S Lancaster St Dallas TX 75216

LEE, DONALD EDWIN, energy co. exec.; b. San Antonio, Sept. 22, 1930; s. Lonnie and Eva (Gates) L.; B.A., U. Tex., 1951; postgrad. in mktg. N.Y. U., 1963; m. Janice Kniker, Sept. 8, 1951; children—Lisa, Jennifer. With Exxon or Exxon affiliates, 1954—, various positions, including advt. staff, mktg. rep., sales promotion mgr., advt. mgr., merchandising coordinator, dist. mgr., regional public affairs mgr., media relations mgr., Houston, 1972-74, public affairs mgr. Exxon Coal USA, Inc., Houston, 1974—; edn. com. Am. Petroleum Inst., 1967. Mem. New Orleans Campfire Girls Commn., 1970; mem. adv. bd. Sch. Communications, Tex. Technol. U. Served to capt. USMC, 1951-53. Named Hon. Citizen, Dallas, 1958, New Orleans, 1969. Mem. Nat. Coal Assn. (govt. relations com., public relations com.), Houston Advt. Forum (chmn. 1966). Presbyterian. Clubs: Houston Advt. (dir. 1965-67), Houston Spartanaire (pres. 1976-77), Order Ky. Cols. Home: 818 Thornbranch Dr Houston TX 77079 Office: 1230 Dresser Tower 601 Jefferson Houston TX 77001

LEE, DORIAN LATHAM, speech pathologist; b. Norfolk, Va., Nov. 3, 1954; d. Warren Walter and Walter-Lee Simmons L.; B.S., Hampton Inst., 1977; M.S., Indiana U. Pa., 1978. Speech pathologist Albermarle Regional Center for Communication Disorders, Edenton, N.C., 1978—. Hampton Inst. Pre-Coll. scholar, 1973. Mem. Am. Speech and Hearing Assn., Nat. Black Speech, Lang. and Hearing Assn., Zeta Phi Beta. Home: 121 E Church St Edenton NC 27932 Office: Edenton-Chowan Schs PO Box 206 Edenton NC 27932

LEE, FREEMAN GORDON, govt. ofcl., engr.; b. Washington, Dec. 31, 1929; s. Freeman Gaylord and Odessa (Wardlaw) L.; degree U. Md., 1955; high speed aerodynamics degree U. Calif. at Los Angeles, 1957; grad. Def. Systems Mgmt. Coll., Indsl. Coll. Armed Forces; m. Mildred Marie Potter, July 19, 1952; children—Lucile Jean, Melodie Susan, Celeste Ann, Montgomery Delta. Controls engr. Vanguard project Glenn L. Martin Co., Balt., 1955-56; flight test analysis engr. Lockheed-MSD, Van Nuys, Calif., 1956-57; analysis engr. aero-space systems Marquardt Aircraft Co., Van Nuys, 1957-58; sr. systems analysis engr. Pershing project The Martin Co., Orlando, Fla., 1958-59; tech. staff, asst. to chief engr. aerospace systems Melpar, Inc., Falls Church, Va., 1959-60; sr. physicist ASW research Aerojet-Gen. Corp., Frederick, Md., 1960-61; sr. systems analysis engr. aero-space projects Naval Air Engring. Center, Phila., 1962-64; electronics project engr., tech. expert land combat systems U.S. Army Missile Command, Redstone Arsenal, Ala., 1964-73; gen. engr. Office of Chief of Staff, U.S. Army, 1973—. Committeeman, Explorer Post 280, Boy Scouts Am., Absecond, N.J., N.J., 1962-64, roundtable commr. Tennessee Valley council Arrowhead Dist., 1970-73; asst. dist. commr. Nat. Capitol Area council, 1973-75, chmn. orgn. and extension dist. com., 1975-76. Served with 88th Blue Devil Div., 1945-49, Italy; with 1092d Combat Engrs., 1950-51, Korea. Recipient Navy commendation for personal contbns. to space effort, 1963; Meritorious award and Medal of Merit, Boy Scouts Am., 1972; Patriotic Civilian Service award Dept. Army, 1971; Humanitarian award HEW, 1972. Registered profl. engr., Calif. Fellow Brit. Interplanetary Soc. (br. chmn. D.C. 1959-61); mem. Am. Rocket Soc. (sect. v.p. 1958), Soc. Am. Mil. Engrs. (nat. award of merit 1966, 76, pres. Ft. Belvoir post 1976, nat. officer 1977—), Assn. U.S. Army, Am. Astronautical Soc., Am. Legion, Sons Confederate Vets., Order Stars and Bars (vice comdr.-in-chief 1963-64). Conducted controls analysis on all vanguard rockets and post flight analyses of Vikings; designed fuel flow and shock positioning system for BOMARC Missile; system analysis and reentry studies of Pershing Missile; developed airborne radiation analyzer, air def. command and control system, automatic multi-system test equipment for land combat missile systems and support equipment, operational testing of major mil. systems; certified fallout shelter analyst, radiol. officer. Home: 7303 Old Keene Mill Rd Springfield VA 22150 Office: US Army Operational Test and Evaluation Agy Fort Belvoir VA 22060

LEE, HANK SUNG, surgeon; b. Korea, Dec. 11, 1941; came to U.S., 1966, naturalized, 1972; s. Hwa C. and Bok J. (Park) L.; M.D., Cath. Med. Coll. (Korea), 1966; m. Mar. 23, 1968; 1 dau., Millie S. Kim. Rotating intern L.I. Coll. Hosp., 1966-67, resident in surgery, 1967-68; gen. surgery resident Wilmington (Del.) Med. Center, 1968-69; chief resident Med. Coll. of Ohio, Toledo, 1969-72; practice medicine specializing in surgery, Haleyville, Ala., 1977—; mem. staff Burdick-West Meml. Hosp. Diplomate Am. Bd. Surgery. Mem. AMA, Pan-Pacific Surg. Assn. Home: Route 4 Box 368X-1 Haleyville AL 35565 Office: Profl Bldg Downtown Mall Haleyville AL 35565

LEE, JIMMY CHE-YUNG, city planner; b. Canton, China, May 29, 1946; s. Chi Dui and Fong-Yee (Leung) L.; came to U.S., 1969; grad. Sir Robert Black Coll. Edn., Hong Kong; B.A., U. Tex., 1973, M.A., 1975; m. Annie On-lin Chan, Nov. 29, 1970. Tchr. English and Chinese, Asbury Meth. Primary Sch., Hong Kong, 1966-69; asst. mgr. Trader Vic's Restaurant, Dallas Hilton Inn, 1971-75; planner Dallas County Community Action Agy., 1975, dir. projects and resource devel. div., 1975—; pres. U-Asia Corp., Hong Kong; owner CAP Security Systems of Tex., Inc. Mem. Am. Inst. Planners (asso.), Tex. Assn. Community Action Agys., Hong Kong Registered Tchrs. Assn., Oakcliff C. of C. Baptist. Home: 2955 Flowerdale Dallas TX 75229 Office: 2208 Main St Dallas TX 75201

LEE, JOE R., food co. exec.; b. Blackshear, Ga., Dec. 18, 1940; s. John Pope and Audice L. L.; student U.S. Air Force Acad., 1960-62, Valdosta State Coll., 1966-67; m. Carolyn Dale Lee, Sept. 5, 1961; children—Michael Frederick, Keena Rene. Farmer, Blackshear, Ga., 1963-66; restaurant mgr. Ramada Inn., Valdosta, Ga., 1966-67; restaurant mgr. Darden Enterprises, Waycross, Ga., 1967-68; with Red Lobster, Orlando, Fla., 1968-79, v.p. ops., 1972-75, pres., 1975-79; v.p. Gen. Mills, Orlando, 1975, group v.p. Gen. Mills Restaurant group, 1979—; dir. Sun 1st Nat. Bank of Orlando; mem. marine and fisheries adv. com. NOAA, U.S. Dept. Commerce. Bd. dirs. John Young Mus. and Planetarium. Served with USAF, 1959-63. Mem. Nat. Restaurant Assn. (dir.), Orlando C. of C. (dir.). Republican. Baptist. Club: Citrus. Home: PO Box 38 Gotha FL 32734 Office: PO Box 1431 Orlando FL 32802

LEE, JOHN EDWARD, hosp. adminstr.; b. Montgomery, Ala., Oct. 29, 1936; s. Charles Robert and Annabel (Fuqua) L.; B.S., Auburn U., 1961; M.A. in Hosp. Adminstrn., U. Iowa, 1963; m. Harriet Ann Marsh, Sept. 2, 1961; children—John Edward, Virginia M., Cynthia A. Adminstrv. asst. U. Ala. Hosps. and Clinics, Birmingham, 1963-65; asst. adminstr. Huntsville (Ala.) Hosp., 1965-71; adminstr., exec. v.p. Andalusia (Ala.) Hosp., Inc., 1971—; asst. prof. bus. Lurleen B. Wallace State Jr. Coll.; mem. adv. com. Ala. Regional Med. Program; mem. adv. bd. Regional Neonatal Center. Served with U.S. Army, 1958-60. Mem. Ala. Hosp. Assn. (trustee), S.E. Ala. Hosp. Council, Andalusia Area C. of C. (dir. 1976-78). Methodist. Club: Rotary. Home: Route 4 Box 450A Andalusia AL 36420 Office: PO Box 760 Andalusia AL 36420

LEE, MARTHA ANNE, educator, nurse; b. Mobile, Ala., Jan. 21, 1935; d. Ronald Earl and Ann (Fitch) Fussell; B.S., U. Ala., 1957; M.N., U. Ala., 1964; m. Joe David Lee, Mar. 30, 1957. Instr. nursing Birmingham (Ala.) Baptist Sch. Nursing, 1958-65; instr. Jefferson State Jr. Coll., Birmingham, 1965-69; asst. dir. nursing Ala. Regional Med. Program, Birmingham, 1970-73; asst. prof. coordinator nursing course, team leader nursing program Samford U., Birmingham, 1973—. Tchr. adult Sunday sch. class Huffman Baptist Ch.; past mem. nursing service com. local ARC. Named Outstanding Tchr. Samford U. Sch. Nursing, 1976. Mem. Am., Ala. (mem. by-laws com., dist. dir.) nurses assns., Nat., Ala., N. Ala. (past pres.) leagues nursing, Sigma Theta Tau, Phi Theta Kappa. Home: 908 Sharp Dr Birmingham AL 35235 Office: Samford U Sch Nursing 800 Lakeshore Dr Birmingham AL 35209

LEE, MARYAT (MARY ATTAWAY LEE), playwright, producer, dir., painter; b. Covington, Ky., May 26, 1926; d. DeWitt Collins and Grace Barbee (Dyer) Lee; student Northwestern U., 1940-41; B.A., Wellesley Coll., 1945; student Middlebury Coll., summer 1944; postgrad. Union Theol. Sem., 1949-50, Columbia, 1949-51, M.A., 1955; m. David Phillips Foulkes Taylor, July 4, 1957 (dec. Sept. 1966). Engaged in film editing, 1946-48; instr. Wesleyan Coll., Macon, Ga., 1948-49; asst. to Margaret Mead, 1952-53; writer, dir. DOPE!, a street play, 1951 (pub. in Best Short Plays of 1952-53); producer, founder, playwright Soul and Latin Theater, 1968-70, trustee, pres., 1969-70; founder, dir. EcoTheatre. Mem. faculty New Sch. for Social Research, 1965-70, adj. faculty W.Va. Coll. Grad. Studies, 1978—; fellow Va. Center for Creative Arts, Sweet Briar, 1979. Co-dir. drama and writing workshops Fed. Reformatory for Women, 1972-75; mem. adv. panel Expansion Arts program Nat. Endowment Arts, 1973-75. Grantee N.Y. State Council on Arts, 1971, Rockefeller Found., 1973, DJB Found., 1974. Mem. Dramatists Guild, Council on So. Mountains, Amateur Chamber Music Soc. Author (plays): Kairos, 1954; Clytemnestra, 1957; Love In 57th Street Gallery, 1960; Four Men & A Monster, 1967, 80; The Tightrope Walker, 1963-67; Meat Hansom, 1962; FUSE, 1971, 80; (street plays) DOPE!, Day to Day, After the Fashion Show, The Classroom, Luba. Participating playwright Office for Advanced Drama Research, 1967—; contbr. articles to Theatre 4, Theatre Quar., others. Developed 1st modern street theater, painting shows Sci. and Cultural Center, Charleston, Bluefield Coll., 1978. Home Powley's Creek Route 1 Box 189 Hinton WV 25951 also Montreat NC 28711

LEE, NORMAN RAY, utility exec.; b. Grayson, La., Oct. 24, 1924; s. John Wesley and Lillie Ellen (Bozone) L.; B.S., Calif. Inst. Tech., Pasadena, 1947; grad. Advanced Mgmt. Program, Harvard U., 1967; m. Nell Ray, Jan. 15, 1950; children—Norman Ray, Rebecca Nell. Engr., Standard Oil Co. Calif., 1946-47, Allis-Chalmers Co., Milw., 1947-48; with Gulf States Utilities Co., 1949—, sr. v.p., then exec. v.p., 1970-73, pres., Beaumont, Tex., 1973—, also dir.; dir. Am. Nat. Bank, Beaumont. Campaign chmn. United Way Beaumont, 1978, 1st v.p., 1979. Served with USNR, 1943-46, 51-52. Registered profl. engr., Tex. Mem. Beaumont C. of C. (pres. 1979). Methodist. Club: Beaumont Rotary (past dir.). Home: 1220 Wilchester Circle Beaumont TX 77706 Office: PO Box 2951 Beaumont TX 77704

LEE, RICHARD GEORGE, clergyman; b. Toccoa, Ga., July 1, 1946; s. William Bryan and Ongie Lee (Hitt) L.; B.A. magna cum laude, Mercer U., 1976; M.Div., Luther Rice Sem., 1978, D.Min., 1980. m. Judith Elaine Starr, Sept. 4, 1964; children—Christopher Jason, Tonya Elizabeth. Youth evangelist So. Bapt. Conv., 1958-64, ordained to ministry, 1966, evangelist, Atlanta, 1965-74; minister New Hope Bapt. Ch., Atlanta, 1974-78, Rehoboth Bapt. Ch., Tucker, Ga., 1979—; founder, pres. Richard G. Lee Evangel. Assos. Inc., 1977—; host minister Miracle Hour TV program, 1976—. Mem. Ga. Bapt. Conv., Conf. So. Bapt. Evangelists. Columnist, Parson's Point, Fayette News Syndicate, 1974. Home: 3458 Canadian Way Tucker GA 30084 Office: 2997 Lawrenceville Hwy Tucker GA 30084

LEE, RONALD JAMES, interior design contractor; b. Red Bank, N.J., Aug. 9, 1945; s. Leonard Robert and Alvena Ursula (Vittitoe) L.; student public schs. Hollywood, Fla.; m. Suzanne Kay Miller, Apr. 20, 1979; children by previous marriage—Bonnie Jean, Stephanie Jean, Jessica Rene. With All State Carpet Service, 1960-63, Flacks Carpet Service, 1963-66; founder, pres. Duffy & Lee Co., Miami, 1966—; pres. Carpet Plaza, Inc., 1978—; sec. South East Interiors, 1976—; dir. all cos. Mem. Nat. Home Fashion League, Retail Flooring Inst., S. Fla. Floor Covering Assn. (exec. dir.). Clubs: Winchester Fort Lauderdale Gun, Pembroke Lakes Racquet. Home: 1611 W Fairway Rd Pembroke Pines FL 33026 Office: 2349 NW 147th St Miami FL 33054

LEE, THOMAS ALAN, med. adminstr.; b. Chippewa Falls, Wis., Sept. 6, 1939; s. Oscar A. and Ruby May (Bailkey) L.; B.S., U. Wis., Eau Claire, 1961; Ph.D., U. Ariz., 1967; M.B.A., U. N.C., 1978; m. Felicia Webster, Oct. 19, 1968; 1 dau. Heidi Louisa. Research asso. Goddard Inst. for Space Studies, NASA, N.Y.C., 1968-69; asst. prof. U. Ariz., Tucson, 1969-75; project data coordinator Midrex Corp., Charlotte, N.C., 1975-76; adminstrv. dir. Family Practice Residency Program, Charlotte Meml. Hosp. and Med. Center, 1977—. Bd. dirs., treas. Four Seasons Homeowners Assn., 1979. NDEA fellow, 1961-64; NASA grantee, 1971-73. Mem. Am. Med. Group Mgmt. Assn., Soc. Tchrs. Family Medicine, N.C. Med. Group Mgmt. Assn., Am. Soc. Tng. and Devel. Home: 6138 Bent Tree Charlotte NC 28212 Office: PO Box 32861 Charlotte NC 28232

LEE, THOMAS ELDRED, III, ins. exec.; b. Fredericksburg, Va., May 1, 1949; s. Thomas Eldred and Nannie Harding (Curtis) L.; B.S. in Math., U. Richmond (Va.), 1971; m. Susan Jean Frederick, Dec. 20, 1975; 1 dau., Kathrina Lecil. Engaged in ins. bus., 1971—; exec. v.p., part owner Lee-Curtis Ins. Service, Inc., Fredericksburg, since 1977. First v.p. Rappahannock United Way, 1976, city drive chmn., 1976, mem. bd. Va., 1973-77; chmn. budget rev. com. Va. Assn. Mental Health, 1977-77; chmn. Fredericksburg Cablevision Commn., 1973-75; chmn. advancement Rappahannock dist. Boy Scouts Am., 1974, mem. at large dist., 1973-78. Served as 2d lt. AUS, 1971; capt. USAR. Mem. Nat., Fredericksburg (past pres., nat. committeeman) assns. life underwriters, Prof. Ins. Agts. Assn., Fredericksburg Ins. Agts. Assn. (pres. 1978), Am. Legion (past post comdr.), Jaycees. Baptist. Clubs: Kiwanis. Home: 3 Browns Ln Fredericksburg VA 22401 Office: PO Box 847 Fredericksburg VA 22401

LEE, WALTER C., supt. schs.; b. Florien, La., Oct. 5, 1934; s. Robert E. and Eloice (Pruitt) L.; B.S., Northwestern State Coll., Natchitoches, La., 1958; M.B.A., La. Poly. Inst., 1967; m. Connie Terral Lee, Feb 18, 1960; 1 son, Mark. Sch. auditor Caddo Parish Sch. Bd., Shreveport, La., 1958-60, dir. fin., 1962-77, supt., 1977—; public auditor Peat, Marwick, Mitchell & Co., 1960-62. Mem. La. Democratic State Central Com., 1975—, Caddo Parish Dem. Exec. Com., 1975—; bd. dirs. Shreveport chpt. ARC, Shreveport Jr. Achievement. Served with AUS, 1953-55. Mem. Assn. Sch. Bus. Ofcls. U.S. and Can., La. Assn. Sch. Bus. Ofcls. (past pres.), La. 4th Dist. Supts. Assn. (chmn. 1979), Adminstrs. Club Caddo Parish Sch. System, Phi Delta Kappa. Baptist. Club: Rotary. Home: 2007 Urban Dale Shreveport LA 71118 Office: PO Box 37000 Shreveport LA 71130

LEE, WENDELL BARRY, pharmacist; b. Danville, Va., Dec. 20, 1947; s. Asa B. and Dorothy M. (Hammond) L.; B.S. in Pharmacy, U. S.C., 1971; M.B.A., U. Tampa, 1979; m. Linda Leigh Poston, Mar. 10, 1973; 1 son, Hunter Poston. Clin. pharmacist VA Hosp., Tampa, Fla., 1974-77, inpatient supr., 1977-79; chief pharmacy service VA Med Center, Beckley, W.Va., 1979—. Served with U.S. Army, 1971-74. Mem. Am. Soc. Hosp. Pharmacists, W.Va. Hosp. Pharmacists, Phi Eta Sigma, Kappa Psi. Home: 225 Granville Ave Beckley WV 25801 Office: Pharmacy Service VA Med Center Beckley WV 25801

LEE, WILLIAM MALCOLM, bldg. materials co. exec.; b. Atlanta, Sept. 25, 1941; s. Clarence Gordon and Florabel (McGoogan) L.; B.A., Emory U., 1963; postgrad. Ga. State U., 1963-64; m. Lynn Gayle McKinley, June 8, 1963; children—William Malcolm, Elizabeth Shannon. Dist. counselor Atlanta Newspapers, Inc., Atlanta, 1963-65; sales rep., sales mgr. GAF Corp., N.Y.C., 1965-69; corp. v.p. Builder Marts of Am., Inc., Greenville, S.C., 1969—. Lay reader, vestry mem. Episcopal Ch. of the Redeemer. Mem. Nat. Lumber and Bldg. Material Dealers Assn., Greenville C. of C. Democrat. Episcopalian. Home: 440 Henderson Rd Greenville SC 29607 Office: 728 Pleasantburg Dr Greenville SC 29607

LEE, WILLIAM STATES, utility co. exec.; b. Charlotte, N.C., June 23, 1929; s. William States and Sarah (Everett) L.; B.S. in Engring. magna cum laude, Princeton, 1951; m. Janet Fleming Rumberger, Nov. 24, 1951; children—Lisa, States, Helen. With Duke Power Co., Charlotte, 1955—, engring. mgr., 1962-65, v.p. engring., 1965-71, sr. v.p. engring. and constrn., 1971-75, exec. v.p., 1976-78, pres., chief operating officer, 1978—, dir., 1968—, mem. exec. com., 1971—, fin. com., 1978—. Mem. U.S. Com. on Large Dams, 1963—; mem. N.C. Energy Policy Council; bd. dirs. United Community Services; bd. advisors Engring. Sch. U. N.C. at Charlotte; trustee Queens Coll. Served with C.E., USNR, 1951-54. Registered profl. engr., N.C., S.C. Fellow ASME (George Westinghouse Gold medal 1972), ASCE; mem. Nat. Acad. Engring., Inst. Nuclear Power Ops. (chmn. 1979—), Nat. Soc. Profl. Engrs., Am. Nuclear Soc., Charlotte C. of C. (chmn. 1979), Phi Beta Kappa, Tau Beta Pi. Presbyterian (ruling elder). Home: 1632 Beverly Dr Charlotte NC 28207 Office: 422 S Church St Charlotte NC 28242

LEE, WILTON AMBROSE, social worker; b. Ponchatoula, La., July 31, 1931; s. Ambrose and Ima Adelia (Pritchard) L.; B.A., Southeastern La. Coll., 1958; M.S.W., Tulane U., 1959; postgrad., 1968-75; postgrad. Smith Coll., 1961; m. Marilyn M. Miller, June 24, 1971; children—Kurt, Niki, Warren. Social worker Southeast La. Hosp., 1959-61, Chattanooga Psychiat. Clinic, 1961-76; pvt. practice social work, Chattanooga, 1962—; mem. part time faculty U. Tenn., 1962-72, So. Missionary Coll., 1968-72; cons. Juvenile Ct. Bd. dirs. St. Peters Kindergarten, 1974—. Served with USAF, 1951-58. Mem. Nat. Assn. Social Workers (state council), Acad. Cert. Social Workers, Tenn. Soc. Clin. Social Workers, Tenn. Health Care Assn., Social Work Vocat. Bur., Am. Orthopsychiat. Assn., Nat. Registry Health Care Providers in S.W. Methodist. Home: 525 Briar Park Ln Hixson TN 37343 Office: 514 Uptain Bldg Chattanooga TN 37411

LEE, YOON YOUNG, chem. engr.; b. Seoul, Korea, July 19, 1941; came to U.S., 1967, naturalized, 1977; s. Byong Lin and Kyong Suhk (Choi) L.; B.S., Seoul Nat. U., 1964; M.S., U. S.C., 1969; Ph.D., Iowa State U., 1972; m. Young Wha Mok, Sept. 2, 1971; children—Grace-Soyon, Janet-Sojong. Process engr. Korea Oil Corp., Seoul, 1966-67; vis. asst. prof. chem. engring. Iowa State U., Ames, 1972-74; asst. prof. Auburn (Ala.) U., 1974-78, asso. prof., 1978—. Served with Korean Army, 1964-66. Mem. Am. Chem. Soc., Am. Inst. Chem. Engring., Sigma Xi, Phi Kappa Phi, Omega Chi Epsilon, Phi Lambda Upsilon. Contbr. articles to profl. jours. Home: 304 Tullahoma St Auburn AL 36830 Office: Dept Chem Engring Auburn U Auburn AL 36830

LEECH, WILLIAM MCMILLAN, JR., atty. gen. Tenn.; b. Charlotte, Tenn., Nov. 5, 1935; B.S., Tenn. Technol. U., 1958; J.D., U. Tenn., 1966; married; 3 children. Admitted to Tenn. bar; practiced law, 1967-78; former mcpl. judge; former asst. dist. atty. gen.; atty. gen. Tenn., Nashville, 1978—. Bd. dirs. Tenn. Performing Arts Found.; former chmn. alumni adv. com. U. Tenn. Coll. Law. Fellow Am. Bar Found.; mem. Am. Bar Assn., Tenn. Bar Assn., Maury County Bar Assn., Tenn. Def. Lawyers Assn., Nat. Assn. Criminal Def. Lawyers, Maury County C. of C., Nat. Assn. Attys. Gen. Democrat. Office: Office of Atty Gen 450 James Robertson Pkwy Nashville TN 37219*

LEEK, JAMES MICHAEL, elec. contractor; b. Bowling Green, Ky., Nov. 1, 1949; s. James F. and Doris Jean (Meeks) L.; A.A., U. Fla., 1969; B.S., Western Ky. U., 1971; postgrad. Law Sch. U. Denver, 1979, Masters Inst., Williamsburg, Va., 1979; m. Penelope Susan Corey, Aug. 26, 1972; children—Tamra Chantel, Natasha Nicole, Troy J., Dawn M. Gen. mgr. Village Electric Inc., Pompano, Fla., 1971-72; gen. mgr. Delta Elec. and Mech. Contractors, Inc., Orlando, Fla., 1973-75; v.p. Broyles & Broyles, Inc., Lawrence, Kans., from 1975; now v.p. Industrotech Constructors, Inc., Atlanta. Mem. Am. Mgmt. Assn., Elec. Council, Am. Soc. Profl. Estimators. Republican. Roman Catholic. Club: Cosmopolitan. Home: 412 Ambrose Dr Clarksville TN 37040 Office: PO Box 175 Fort Campbell KY 42223

LEEPER, JOHN PALMER, museum exec.; b. Denison, Tex., Feb. 4, 1921; s. John Palmer and Maryanne (Platter) L.; B.Journalism, So. Methodist U., 1942; M.A. in Art History, Harvard, 1947; m. Blanche Wheeler Magurn, Sept. 18, 1948; 1 dau., Maryanne M. Keeper W.A. Clark Collection, Corcoran Gallery Art, Washington, 1948, asst. dir. gallery, 1949-50; dir. Pasadena (Cal.) Art Inst., 1950-53; dir. Marion Koogler McNay Art Inst., San Antonio, 1954—. Instr. Dexter Sch., Boston, 1947-48; lectr. Pasadena Sch. Fine Arts, 1952-53, U. So. Cal., Los Angeles, 1952, Trinity U., San Antonio, 1957-59. Pres. San Antonio Little Theatre. Trustee San Antonio Art Inst. Served with USAAF, 1942-45. Mem. Am. Assn. Museums, Assn. Art Mus. Dirs., Tex. Soc. Arts and Letters (hon.). Club: Harvard (San Antonio). Address: 6000 New Braunfels San Antonio TX 78209*

LEER, STEVEN FORREST, coal mine co. exec.; b. Vermillion, S.D., July 9, 1952; s. Bruce M. and Mary Lou (McLaughlin) L.; B.S. in Elec. Engring., U. Pacific, 1975; M.B.A., Washington U., 1977. Fin. analyst Ashland Coal Inc (Ky.), 1977-78, adminstr. asst., mining adminstr., 1978, mine supt. Addington Bros. Mining Inc. subs. Ashland Coal, Paintsville, Ky., 1978—. Mem. Am. Mgmt. Assn. Republican. Home: PO Box 681 Ashland KY 41101 Office: PO Box 391 Ashland KY 41101

LEES, WILLIAM RHODES, educator; b. Plainview, Tex., May 12, 1938; s. Will R. and Mary Burton (Wayland) L.; B.S., Tex. Tech. U., 1967, M.S., 1969; m. Mary Fullingim, Nov. 14, 1969; 1 dau., Kathryn Carla. Instr. in geology Tex. Tech. U., Lubbock, 1971-73, instr. in field geology, 1976-77; instr. in field geology W. Tex. State U., Canyon, 1975; secondary tchr. math. and sci. Lubbock Public Schs., 1973—, chmn. math. and sci. depts. Carroll Thompson Jr. High Sch. Active orgn. and extension com. South Plains Council Boy Scouts Am., 1969. Served with USN, 1958-62. Welch Found. fellow, 1970-71; NASA fellow, 1969-70; guest investigator Geophys. Lab. Carnegie Instn. Washington, 1969. Mem. Geol. Soc. Am., AAAS, NEA, Tex. Tchrs. Assn., Tex. Classroom Tchrs. Assn., Sigma Xi, Phi Kappa Phi, Sigma Gamma Epsilon. Roman Catholic. Clubs: Elks (Salida, Colo.), Kappa Sigma. Co-author articles in profl. jours., paper presented conf. profl. assn. Home: 3424 68th Dr Lubbock TX 79413 Office: 2000 14th St Lubbock TX 79401

LEETZOW, LEONARD ERMOND, JR., investment co. exec.; b. Elgin, Ill., Mar. 29, 1938; s. Leonard Herman and Alvina Elizabeth (Meinke) L.; B.S., U.S. Naval Acad., 1962; grad. N.Y. Inst. Fin., 1965; student Coll. Cert. Fin. Planning, 1977; m. Cherie Lee Cuthbart, Nov. 27, 1959; children—Joni Lynn, Michael Leonard, Mark Winston. Design engr. Electro-Mech. Research Inc., Sarasota, Fla., 1959-64; sr. v.p. Shearson Loeb Rhoades Inc., Sarasota, 1964—, mem. mgmt. adv. council, 1966-73, mem. pres.'s council, 1974-80. Bd. deacons Presbyterian Ch. of the Palms, Sarasota, 1965-68, trustee, 1968-71, mem. bd. elders, 1972-75; bd. dirs. Girls Club of Sarasota County, 1975—, treas., 1977-79; bd. dirs. Sarasota County 4-H Found., 1975—; bd. dirs., youth adviser Sarasota County chpt. Am. Cancer Soc. Served with USN, 1956-59. Mem. Sarasota County C. of C. (dir. 1976-80). Clubs: Field, Gator Creek Golf, Masons, Shriners; Kiwanis (founder club 1970, pres. 1972-73, dir. 1971-76) (Sarasota). Home: 7007 Clark Rd Sarasota FL 33583 Office: 2045 Siesta Dr Sarasota FL 33579

LEFEBER, EDWARD JAMES, physician; b. Wauwatosa, Wis., June 1, 1911; s. Cornelius George and May (McCord) L.; B.S., U. Wis., 1934, M.D., 1936; m. Ellie Hancock Weisiger, June 4, 1938; children—Edward James, Robert Randolph, John Courtney, Ann Elizabeth, Donald Louis, Nancy Ellen. Intern, resident in medicine Med. Coll. Va. Hosps., Richmond, 1936-40; mem. faculty Med. Br., U. Tex., Galveston, 1940—, clin. asso. prof. medicine, 1951—, dir. Student Health Service, 1943-46; practice medicine, specializing in internal medicine with Internal Medicine Assos., Galveston, 1948—; chief out-patient service Galveston office Houston Regional Office, VA, 1946-48; cons. gastroenterology USPHS Hosp., Galveston, 1952-53; pres. staff St. Mary's Infirmary, Galveston, 1961. Mem. adv. com. on nursing home affairs Tex. Dept. Health, 1976—. Bd. dirs. Galveston chpt. A.R.C., 1958-78; mem. Galveston Civic Orch., 1957-60; mem. Tex. Bd. Licensure for Nursing Home Adminstrs., 1979—. Bd. dirs. Moody House, 1964-65, 67-71, med. dir. Diplomate Am. Bd. Internal Medicine. Fellow A.C.P.; mem. Galveston County Med. Soc. (pres. 1954, sec.-treas. 1948-53), AMA, Tex., So. med. assns., Am., Tex. (pres. 1977) socs. internal medicine, Am. Soc. Gastro-Intestinal Endoscopy, Tex. Club Internists, Phi Chi. Episcopalian (vestryman). Mason. Home: 2927 Ave P Galveston TX 77550 Office: Sealy Smith Profl Bldg 200 University Blvd Galveston TX 77550

LEFKOFF, CHARLES B., patent agt., invention mktg. and acquisition co. exec.; b. Atlanta, Feb. 16, 1945; s. Louis R. and Hessie (Hirsch) L.; B.S., Ga. State U., 1968. Mktg. positions Sperry Univac Co., Atlanta, 1968-71, Compucorp, Atlanta, 1971-74; mgr. software devel. and mktg. CLM Sales Inc., Atlanta, 1976-77; patent agt., invention mktg. and acquisition agt., Atlanta, 1978—; lectr. Emory U. Registered patent agt. U.S. Patent Office. Mem. Inventor Assos. Ga. (pres. 1978—). Pub. Invention Protection, Acquisition and Marketing Newsletter, 1980—, Directory Patent Searchers, 1980—; patentee in field. Office: 1132 W Peachtree St Suite 115 Atlanta GA 30309

LEFLER, CHARLES DEEMS, physician; b. Durham, N.C., Jan. 8, 1944; s. Hugh Talmage and Ida Eley (Pinner) L.; A.B., U. N.C., Chapel Hill, 1966, M.D., 1970; m. Susan Bartee McIntyre, June 11, 1966; children—Nathan, Jason, Page, Miriam. Intern, Univ. Hosp., Lexington, Ky., 1970-71; resident in internal medicine U. Ky., Lexington, 1971-72, 74-75; cons. VA Hosp., Lexington, 1975-76; practice medicine specializing in internal medicine, Lexington, 1976—; mem. staff Transylvania Community Hosp., Brevard, N.C. Bd. dirs. PSRO of Western N.C., 1977-78. Served to lt. cmdr. M.C.,

USNR, 1972-74. Mem. N.C. Soc. Internal Medicine, Am. Soc. Internal Medicine, Phi Beta Kappa. Episcopalian. Home: 202 S Caldwell St Brevard NC 28712

LEFLER, WADE HAMPTON, JR., ophthalmologist; b. Statesville, N.C., Feb. 27, 1937; s. Wade Hampton and Eunice Trudye (Chilcoat) L.; A.B., U. N.C., Chapel Hill, 1959; M.D., Bowman Gray Sch. Medicine, 1963; m. Katherine Webb Davis, Apr. 1, 1961; children—Elizabeth Ashley, Rosemary Kirsten. Med. intern N.Y. Hosp., Cornell Med. Center, 1963-64; resident in ophthalmology Duke U. Med. Center, 1966-69; practice medicine specializing in ophthalmology, Hickory, N.C., 1969—; partner Graystone Eye, Ear, Nose, Throat Center, Hickory, 1974—; clin. asso. prof. ophthalmology Duke Med. Center, 1969—; mem. staff Catawba Meml. Hosp., Hickory, Glenn R. Frye Meml. Hosp., Hickory, Western Carolina Center, Morganton, Duke Eye Center, Durham, N.C., Broughton Hosp., Morganton, N.C., Oteen VA Hosp., Asheville, N.C. Served to capt. M.C., U.S. Army, 1964-66. Duke U. Med. Center grantee, 1968-70; diplomate Am. Acad. Ophthalmology. Mem. AMA, N.C. Med. Soc., Catawba County Med. Soc., Phi Beta Kappa, Alpha Omega Alpha. Presbyterian. Club: Lake Hickory Country. Home: 614 2d Ave NW Hickory NC 28601 Office: PO Box 2588 Hickory NC 28601

LEFTWICH, MAXINE ELLEN, academic counselor; b. Enid, Okla., Aug. 17, 1920; d. Vincent Earnest and Maud Irene (Luther) Dieterich; B.A., Southwestern Coll., 1942; M.A., U. Chgo., 1944; student Instituto Norteamericano-Chileno, Santiago, Chile, 1962-63; m. Richard Henry Leftwich, Mar. 11, 1945; children—Judith Elaine, Gregory Vincent, Bradley Rush. Caseworker, Ill. Childrens Home and Aid Soc., Chgo., 1944-45; probation officer Juvenile Ct., Washington, summer 1945; caseworker Chgo. Child Care Soc., 1946-48; counselor Coll. Arts and Scis., Okla. State U., 1966—, chmn. premed. adv. com., coordinator allied health professions advisement, 1966—. Trustee, Southwestern Coll., 1974—; mem. exec. com. United Fund, 1972-74, chmn. budget com., 1973; newsletter editor Stillwater Arts and Humanities Council, 1975-77. Leila Houghteling fellow, 1943-44. Mem. Am. Personnel and Guidance Assn., Am. Coll. Personnel Assn., So. Assn. Advisers for the Health Professions, Okla. Writers Fedn., Ninety-Nines, Alpha Epsilon Delta. Democrat. Home: 818 W Knapp St Stillwater OK 74074 Office: Arts & Scis Office Student Services Okla State U Stillwater OK 74074

LEFTWICH, ROBERT VERNON, educator; b. Columbus, Ga., June 21, 1940; s. John Vernon and Jonie Amanda (Funderburk) L.; B.S., Troy State U., 1961; M.A., Western Carolina U., 1969; postgrad. U. Ga., 1974—; m. Ann Louise Davis, Dec. 27, 1963; children—Karen Annette, Kevin Vernon. Tchr., Richard Russell Elementary Sch., Smyrna, Ga., 1961-63, Cherokee County (Ga.) Schs., 1967-68; grad. teaching asst. edn. Western Carolina U., Culowhee, N.C., 1968-69; guidance counselor Kings Mountain (N.C.) High Sch., 1969-73, Dent Jr. High Sch., Columbia, S.C., 1973-74; men's advisor Oxford (Ga.) Coll. of Emory U., 1974-76; asst. prof. edn. Asbury Coll., Wilmore, Ky., 1977—. Coach Little League, Kings Mountain, 1971-72; v.p. Cleveland County (N.C.) Mental Health Assn., 1973; chmn. edn. funds Walton County chpt. Am. Cancer Soc., 1977. Served with USAF, 1963-67. Mem. Kings Mountain Jaycees (pres. 1971, state dir. 1972; Spoke award 1970), Am., Ky., So. personnel and guidance assns., Gideons Internat. (treas. chpt. 1975, 78-80), Am. Coll. Personnel Assn., N.C. Assn. Educators, S.C., Nat. edn. assns., Ky. Assn. Tchr. Educators, So. Coll. Personnel Assn., Kappa Delta Pi, Phi Delta Kappa. Methodist. Clubs: Wilmore-Nicholasville Optimist, Rotary (dir. Kings Mountain 1972-73). Home: 501 Corbitt Dr Wilmore KY 40390

LEFURGEY, EDORIS ANN, biologist; b. Rock Hill, S.C., Aug. 20, 1945; d. Edward Earl and Doris (Brannon) LeF.; B.S., Maryville Coll., 1967; M.S., U. N.C., 1972, Ph.D., 1976. Research asst. Research Triangle Inst., Research Triangle Park, N.C., 1968-70; grad. research fellow marine sci. U. N.C., 1970-74; research asso. dept. entomology N.C. State U., Raleigh, 1974-75; research asso. dept. pathology Duke U. Med. Center, Durham, N.C., 1978—, postdoctoral research fellow 1976-79. Mem. AAAS, Electron Microscopy Soc. Am. Office: Box 3014 Duke Univ Med Center Durham NC 27710

LEGG, WILLIAM EDWARD, savs. and loan assn. exec.; b. Honolulu, Nov. 10, 1947; s. Oliver Morton and Mary Ann (Francis) L.; B.S. in Econs., Northwestern Okla. State U., 1969; M.B.A., Okla. State U., 1971; m. Mary Nell Puckett, Aug. 24, 1968; 1 son, Jason Roy. Sr. public relations rep. Walt Disney World Co., Orlando, Fla., 1971-74; dir. hosp. relations Orange Meml. Hosp., Orlando, 1974-76; dir. civic affairs Orlando Area C. of C., 1976-78; asst. v.p. Winter Park Fed. Savs. and Loan Assn. (Fla.), 1978—; adj. faculty mem. Valencia Community Coll., Orlando, 1974—; pres. Orlando Central Bus. Dist., 1979—; chmn. x-ray sch. adv. com. Orlando Regional Med. Center, 1980—. Bd. dirs. John Young Mus. and Planetarium, 1978-81, dir. devel., 1978-80, treas., 1979-80; 2d v.p., bd. dirs. Pine Castle Center of the Arts, 1979—; mem. City of Orlando Appeals Rev. Bd., 1978—. Served to capt., U.S. Army, 1971—. Mem. Orlando Area C. of C. Republican. Baptist. Club: Rotary. Home: 2410 Lyndell Dr Kissimmee FL 32741 Office: PO Box 1060 Winter Park FL 32790

LEGGETT, NOLA MCKEE, speech pathologist; b. Greenville, Miss., July 26, 1945; d. George and Olivia (White) McK.; student Jackson State U., 1963-66; B.A. in Spl. Edn., U. Miss., 1968, M.C.D. (HEW trainee), 1974. Speech and lang. pathologist Greenville Pub. Schs., 1968-73, Clarksdale Separate Schs., 1974-76, Mississippi Valley State U., 1976-77, Friends of Children of Miss., 1977-78; speech, hearing and lang. specialist Leland (Miss.) Consol. Schs., 1978—. Pres., Nat. Council Negro Women, 1976-77, 79-80. Mem. Miss. Speech and Hearing Assn., Nat. Black Assn. Speech, Lang. and Hearing (pres. elect Miss. affiliate 1980-82), Nat. Council Negro Women (state coordinator internat. div. 1980-81), N.W. Miss. Speech and Hearing Assn., Delta Sigma Theta (sgt. at arms Greenville Alumnae chpt.). Democrat. Roman Catholic. Author: Psycholinguistic Abilities of Black and White Grade One Children, 1974. Home: 526 E Walker St Greenville MS 38701 Office: 404 E 3d St Leland MS 38756

LEGRAND, CHARLES HEYWARD, bank holding co. exec.; b. Jacksonville, Fla., Jan. 9, 1949; s. Walter Heyward and Evelyn Hazel (Thomas) LeG.; B.S., Auburn U., 1972; m. Sharon Elaine Lee, Mar. 9, 1969; children—Valerie Abbi, Christen Elaine. Programmer, analyst Prudential Ins. Co., Jacksonville, Fla., 1972-74; lectr. Jacksonville U., 1973-76; sr. electronic data processing auditor Blue-Cross-Blue Shield of Fla., Jacksonville, 1974-76; sr. EDP auditor Blue-Cross/Blue Shield of Colo., Denver, 1976, mgr. EDP audit, 1976-77, mgr. internal audit, 1977; EDP auditing officer Barnett Banks of Fla., Inc., Jacksonville, 1978—. Cert. internal auditor; cert. in data processing; cert. info. systems auditor. Mem. Inst. Internal Auditors, Data Processing Mgmt. Assn., Electronic Data Processing Auditors Assn. Home: 7503 Ponce Ct Jacksonville FL 32217 Office: 4800 Spring Park Rd Jacksonville FL 32207

LEGRAND, HARRY ELWOOD, geologist; b. Concord, N.C., May 19, 1917; s. William Pleasant and Nancy Elizabeth (White) LeG.; B.S., U. N.C., 1938; m. Undine Nye, Dec. 23, 1945; children—Harry, Jr., Edmund. With U.S. Geol. Survey, 1946-74, dist. geologist water resources div., Raleigh, N.C., 1949-57, chief radiohydrology sect., Washington, 1960-62, research geologist, Raleigh, 1962-74; cons. geologist, Raleigh, 1974—. Served with AUS, 1941-46. Decorated Bronze star. Fellow Geol. Soc. Am.; mem. Am. Water Resources, Internat. Assn. Hydrogeologists (chmn. nat. com. 1972), Am. Geophys. Union, Soc. Econ. Geologists, Am. Assn. Petroleum Geologists, Am. Inst. Mining Engrs., Nat. Water Well Assn. (dir.). Author 2 books; contbr. articles to profl. jours. Address: 331 Yadkin Dr Raleigh NC 27609

LEHMAN, DAVID HERSHEY, geologist; b. Lancaster, Pa., Nov. 24, 1946; s. Roy Jacob and Esther Elizabeth (Hershey) L.; A.B., Franklin and Marshall Coll., 1968; Ph.D., U. Tex., Austin, 1974; married, 1 child. Research geologist Exxon Prodn. Research Co., Houston, 1974-77; exploration geologist Exxon Co. U.S.A., New Orleans, 1977—. Served with U.S. Army, 1968-70. NSF trainee, 1976. Mem. Am. Assn. Petroleum Geologists, Geol. Soc. Am. Home: 7527 Willow St New Orleans LA 70118 Office: Exploration Dept PO Box 61812 New Orleans LA 70161

LEHMAN, WILLIAM, congressman; b. Selma, Ala., Oct. 5, 1913; s. Maurice M. and Corinne L. (Leva) L.; m. Joan Feibelman, 1939; children—William, Kathy Lehman Weiner (dec.), Tom. Owner car sales and finance bus., Miami, 1936-41, 46-66; owner William Lehman Buick, North Miami Beach, 1966-72; tchr. Dade County Public Schs., Miami-Dade County Community Coll., 1963-66; mem. 93d-96th Congresses from 13th Dist. Fla., mem. com. on appropriations. Mem. Dade County Sch. Bd., Miami, 1966-72, chmn., 1971-72. Named Humanitarian of Year, Am. Jewish Com., 1972. Democrat. Office: 2440 Rayburn House Office Bldg Washington DC 20515

LEHMANN, FREDERICK OTTO, JR., accountant; b. Dallas, Apr. 14, 1942; s. Frederick O. and Virginia Jane (Gates) L.; B.S., Austin Coll., 1964. Partner, Jones, Lehmann & Hess, C.P.A.'s, Sherman, Tex., 1980—; instr. Grayson County Jr. Coll., Denison, Tex., 1973-79. Served with USN, 1966-69. C.P.A., Tex. Mem. Am. Inst. C.P.A.'s, Tex. Soc. C.P.A.'s (dir. Dallas chpt. 1979—; state membership com. 1974-77, map coordinating com. 1976-79), Sherman C. of C. (mem. govtl. affairs com. 1977—, mem. urban devel. com. 1975—). Presbyn. Home: 1200 N Leslie Sherman TX 75090 Office: Boardwalk Bldg 2d Floor Sherman TX 75090

LEHTONEN, ALFRED JOHN, lawyer, community devel. co. exec.; b. Englewood, N.J., Oct. 10, 1930; s. John E. and Eva (Raitanen) L.; B.A., Rutgers U., New Brunswick, N.J., 1952; LL.B., U. Tex., Austin, 1959, J.D., 1972; m. Lucille Elotta Fisher, June 26, 1954; children—Alfred John, Alice Lucille. Dist. mgr. Phillips Petroleum Co., Houston, 1954-56; admitted to Tex. bar, 1959, D.C. bar, 1977; asso. firm Redwine & Lehtonen, Austin, Tex., 1959-62, mem. firm, 1962-69; adminstr. Office of Interstate Land Sales Registration, HUD, Washington, 1969-71; v.p., gen. counsel Horizon Corp., Tucson, 1971-79, exec. v.p., 1979—; dir. Can. Cablevision Co., Tucson Adv. com. to N.Y. State Sec. of State, 1971-72; pres., bd. dirs. Nat. Land Council, 1971-72; pres. Tierra Grande Improvement Assn., Tucson, 1973—, also bd. dirs.; Served with USAF, 1952-54. Mem. D.C. Bar Assn., Fed. Bar Assn., Tex. Bar Assn., Delta Theta Phi. Republican. Lutheran. Clubs: Tucson Nat. Country, Masons (32 deg.), Shriners. Home: Waterwood Box 52 Huntsville TX 77340 Office: Waterford Box 1 Huntsville TX 77340

LEIDIG, RAYMOND H., refrigeration engr., cons.; b. Lake Charles, La., Jan. 10, 1910; s. E.G. and Anna (Liechty) L.; grad. Himphill Diesel Elec. Engring. Schs., 1930; m. Myrtice E. Reynolds, Dec. 24, 1934; 1 son, Raymond H., Jr. Mgr. Diesel Elec. Engring. Co., Los Angeles, 1928-34, 34-64; with Automatic Transp. Corp., Chgo., 1941-42, Def. Plat Corp., 1942-44; cons., designer, builder Pure Ice Cold Storage Properties Ice Plants, La., Tex., Miss. and Ark., 1967-78; refrigeration engr., Lake Charles, 1964—; cons. in field U.S., Mexico, S.Am. Sec., v.p. Lake Charles Rotary, 1945-55, Lake Charles YMCA, 1942-78; active vol. United Appeal, Salvation Army fund drs., 1946-77, Lake Charles C. of C., 1934-72. Served with La. State N.G., 1944-47. Recipient certificate for civilian def. capt. Lake Charles Civil Def. Mem. United Inventors, Scientists and Refrigeration Engrs. Democrat. Presbyterian. Holder 4 patents for belt ice, rim power hydraulic motors, all-wheel hydraulic dr. tractor, roto-sod seeder. Home: Route 14 Box 6 Lake Charles LA 70605

LEIFERMAN, IRWIN HAMILTON, indsl. and investment exec.; b. Chgo., Jan. 8, 1907; s. Beril and Ida (Rosenbaum) L.; student Crane Jr. Coll., 1923, Northwestern U., 1924-29; m. Silvia Weiner, Apr. 20, 1947. Purchasing agt. Hamilton-Ross Corp., Chgo., 1924-30; pres. Hamilton Industries Co., Chgo. and Miami Beach, Fla., 1931-64, chmn. bd., 1964—; past pres. Leiferman Investment Co., now cons.; v.p. Comet Prodns. Inc., TV, 1965—. Mem. com. industry U.S. Dept. Labor, 1940. Asso. Cancer Research Found. U. Chgo., 1958; mem. adv. com. Brandeis U., 1961-62, life dir.; mem. Mt. Sinai Hosp. Chgo.; charter mem. WPBT, Channel 2, Miami, Fla.; co-founder, pres. Silvia and Irwin H. Leiferman Found.; pres Bonds for Israel; founder Mt. Sinai Hosp., Miami Beach, 1969, Miami Med. Center, Greater Technion Israel Inst. Tech., 1972; mem. hon. com. Lowe's Gala, 1972; patron Royal Ballet Soc. Miami, Lowe's Museum Miami, Greater Art Center Miami, Philharmonic Soc. Miami; patron Greater Miami Cultural Art Center, hon. gala com., 1972. Trustee, life mem. Nathan Goldblatt Soc. Cancer Research. Recipient spl. awards War Bond Program Sec. Treasury, U.S. Dept. Labor, Spl. award Mt. Sinai Hosp., Miami Beach, 1972. Mem. Chgo. Assn. Commerce and Industry, Ill. Mfrs. Assn., Ill. C. of C., Friends Lowes Mus., Am. Contract Bridge League, Jewish Home for Aged Men's Club, Bayshore Service Club. Jewish (dir. temple). Clubs: B'nai B'rith; Brandeis U. (life), Executives, Standard, Bryn Mawr Country (Chgo.); Runaway Beach, Jockey, Brickell Bay, Westview Country (Miami). Home: 10155 Collins Ave Bal Harbour FL 33154 also Standard Club 320 S Plymouth Ct Chicago IL 60604

LEIFERMAN, SILVIA WEINER (MRS. IRWIN HAMILTON LEIFERMAN), artist, civic worker, bus. exec., philanthropist; b. Chgo.; d. Morris M. and Anna (Caplan) Weiner; student U. Chgo., 1960-61; studied design and painting, Chgo., Mexico, Rome, Madrid, Provincetown, Mass.; m. Irwin Hamilton Leiferman, Apr. 20, 1947. One woman shows include: D'Arcy Galleries, N.Y.C., 1964, Stevens Annex Bldg., Chgo., 1965, Hollywood (Fla.) Mus. Art, Schram Galleries, Ft. Lauderdale, Fla., 1966, 67, Miami Mus. Modern Art, 1966, 72, Contemporary Gallery, Palm Beach, Fla., 1966, Westview Country Club, 1968, Gallery 99, Miami Beach, Fla., 1969, Hall Gallery, Miami Beach; group shows include: Bryn Mawr Country Club, 1961, 62, Riccardo Restaurant Gallery, Chgo., 1961, 62, Covenant Club, 1963, D'Arcy Galleries, N.Y.C., 1965, 66, 67, Miami Mus. Modern Art, 1967, Baccardi Gallery, Miami, 1967, Internat. Platform Assn., 1967, Barry Coll., 1968, Gallery 99, Miami Beach, 1968, Hollywood Mus. Art, 1968, Lowe Art Mus., Beau Art Gallery Lowe Mus. at U. Miami; work represented in numerous pvt. collections; v.p., sec. Leiferman Investment Co., 1969-78, chmn. bd., 1968—; pres. Active Accessories by Silvia, v.p., sec. Silvia and Irwin H. Leiferman Found. Founder, Mt. Sinai Hosp., Miami Beach, 1969, Greater Technion Israel Inst. Tech.; organizer, met. chmn., charter mem. women's div. Hebrew U., Chgo., 1947; originator, met. Chgo. chmn. Ambassador's Ball, State of Israel, 1956, Presentation Ball, 1963, 64, 65; organizer women's div. Edgewater Hosp., 1954; chmn. salute to med. research met. campaign City of Hope, 1959; met. Chgo. chmn. Dior Israel Fashion Show, 1962; originator, chmn. presentation co. Ambassador's Ball, Bonds for Israel, 1963, 64, 65; originator, met. chmn. Paris in the Spring fashion show Nat. Council Jewish Women, also Alice in Fashion Land; originator met. chmn. Hawaii Holiday, Nathan Goldblatt Soc. Cancer Research; chmn. spl. sales and events Greater Chgo. Com. for State of Israel; met. chmn. opening gala luncheon, mem. bd. North Shore women's aux. Mary Lawrence Jewish Children's Bur.; internat. chmn. Bal Masque, Miami Ballet Soc., 1971, 72; patron Royal Ballet Soc. Miami, Lowe's Mus. Art, Greater Art Center Miami, Philharmonic Soc. Miami, Greater Miami Opera Guild; patron Greater Miami Cultural Arts Center, mem. hon. com. for gala, 1972; trustee, life mem. Nathan Goldblatt Soc. Cancer Research; trustee Jewish Fedn. Greater Miami; mem. bd. North Shore aux. Jewish Fedn. Chgo., Mary Lawrence chpt. Jewish Children's Bur., Nat. Council Jewish Women, Fox River Sanitorium, Temple Sholom, Edgewater Hosp., Orgn. Rehab. and Tng., women's guild Greater Miami Philharmonic Soc., numerous others; mem. nat. bd. govs. Bonds for Israel; donor Michael Reese Hosp., Chgo., 1978, St. Joseph Hosp., Chgo., 1978, Mt. Sinai Med. Center Greater Miami, 1978, Miami Heart Inst., 1979; hon. chmn. Miami Art Center. Named Woman of Valor, State of Israel, 1963; recipient Achievement award State of Israel, 1963; keys to all 5 met. dists. Miami and surrounding counties, 1972; Pro Mundo Beneficio gold medal and diploma Brazilian Acad. Humanities, 1976; Donor award Miami Heart Inst., 1976; numerous plaques and citations. Fellow Royal Soc. Arts and Scis. (life); mem. Internat. Platform Assn. (The Club), Internat. Council Museums, Am. Fedn. Arts, Miami Beach Opera Guild, Artists Equity assns., Miami Art Center, Greater Miami Cultural Art Center, Sculptors of Fla., Inc., Lowe Art Mus. (life), Friends of Lowe's Mus., Am. Contract Bridge League, Am. Friends of Hebrew Univ., Ft. Lauderdale Mus. Arts, Miami Mus. Modern Art (life), Art Inst. Chgo. (life), numerous others. Clubs: Internat., Whitehall, Key, Covenant, Standard, Bryn Mawr Country (Chgo.); Westview Country, Brickell (Miami); Greenacres Country (Northbrook, Ill.); Runaway, Jockey (Miami Beach). Address: Bal Harbor 101 10155 Collins Ave Bal Harbour FL 33154 also Standard Club 320 S Plymouth Ct Chicago IL 60604

LEIGH, CHARLES MICHAEL, mortgage co. exec.; b. Albany, Ga., Apr. 3, 1949; s. James Tillman and Angela (Nistal) L.; B.A., U. Tampa, 1970; m. Laurel Connolly, July 6, 1979; children—Marcie, James Michael, Katherine Michelle, Jennifer. Vice pres. Golden Eagle Antiques, Tampa, 1974-76, Domesticare, Tampa, 1976-77; v.p., chief exec. Certified Mortgage Co., Tampa, 1977—; dir. Combined Am. Services Inc., Golden Eagle Antiques, Inc., Tom Wolfe Corp., Cain Brothers, Inc., Heirloom Antiques Ltd., Inc. Served with U.S. Army, 1970-73. Republican. Roman Catholic. Office: 4005 S Dale Mabry Hwy Tampa FL 33611

LEIGH, THOMAS WATKINS, lawyer; b. Winnsboro, La., Apr. 8, 1903; s. Benjamin Watkins and Olive (Buckingham) L.; LL.B., La. State U., 1924; m. Louise Grisham, July 7, 1942. Admitted to La. bar, 1924; pvt. practice, 1924-29; mem. firm Theus, Grisham, Davis & Leigh, Monroe, La., 1929—. Dir. 1st Nat. Bank of West Monroe. Mem. Gov.'s Spl. Commn. to Study Needs of Higher Edn. in La., 1954-56; mem. Gov.'s Spl. Tidelands Adv. Com., 1964-72; mem. exec. com. Pub. Affairs Research Council La., bd. dirs. Council for Better La.; chmn. La. Mineral Bd., 1966-72; del. La. Constl. Conv., 1973. Bd. suprs. La. State U., 1940-60, chmn., 1948-50. Served as lt. comdr. USNR, 1942-45. Mem. Am. (ho. of dels. 1958—, bd. govs. 1975-78), La. (pres. 1954-55, gov.) bar assns., Am. Coll. Probate Attys., Am. Coll. Trial Lawyers, Am., La. (council, v.p.) law insts., Order of Coif, Gamma Eta Gamma, Theta Xi. Episcopalian (vestryman). Clubs: Army and Navy (Washington); Boston, Pickwick (New Orleans). Home: 1401 S Grand St Monroe LA 71202 Office: 1303 Bancroft Circle Monroe LA 71203

LEINWEBER, DONALD MCCLOUD, project engr.; b. Urich, Mo., Sept. 7, 1924; s. Alfred H. and Anna Lou (Thomas) L.; B.S. in Engring., Calif. Inst. Tech., 1945; m. Ada Louise Bruington, June 24, 1950; children—Mark, Paul, Bruce, Louise. Field engr. The Fluor Corp., Ltd., Los Angeles, 1946-51, project engr., 1951-56, project mgr., 1957: project mgr. C.W. Nofsinger Co., Kansas City, Mo., 1957-63; sr. project engr. Kaiser Aluminum & Chem. Corp., Baton Rouge, 1963-72, chief engr., 1972—, constrn. contract adminstr., 1964-65. Mem. Bd. of Zoning, City of Lee's Summit, Mo., 1961-63, East Baton Rouge Parish Sch. Bd. Bldg. Com., 1969-71. Served with USN, 1943-46, 52-53. Registered profl. engr., La. Mem. La. Engring. Soc Republican. Mem. Christian Ch. Club: Masons. Home: 11087 Mollylea Dr Baton Rouge LA 70815 Office: Kaiser Aluminum & Chemical Corp 9864 Professional Blvd Baton Rouge LA 70809

LEIPZIG, BRUCE, physician; b. Syracuse, N.Y., Apr. 5, 1947; s. Bill and Ellen (Gordon) L.; B.S. in Biology, Columbia U., 1969; B.H.L., Jewish Theol. Sem., 1969; M.D., SUNY, Syracuse, 1973; children—Benjamin Gordon, Deborah Elise. Intern in surgery Med. Coll. Va., Richmond, 1973-74; resident in surgery SUNY, 1974-75; resident in otolaryngology SUNY, Syracuse, 1975-78; fellow in head and neck oncology U. Tex. Med. Br., Galveston, 1978-79; practice medicine specializing in otolaryngology, Galveston, 1978—; instr. dept. otolaryngology U. Tex. Med. Br., 1978-79, asst. prof., 1979—, chief div. head and neck oncology, 1979—; cons. USPHS Hosp., 1978—; mem. staff Sealy Hosp., U. Tex. Med. Br., St. Mary's Hosp. Trustee Congregation Beth Jacob, 1979—, chmn. bd. edn., 1978-81. Recipient Leadership Citation of Merit, Nat. Fedn. Jewish Men's Clubs, 1976; diplomate Am. Bd. Otolaryngology. Mem. A.C.S., Am. Acad. Otolaryngology (continuing edn. com.), Soc. Univ. Otolaryngologists, Am. Council Otolaryngology, Am. Cancer Soc. (dir. 1979—, chmn. rehab. com. 1979—), Tex. Med. Assn., Galveston County Med. Soc., Am. Acad. Facial Plastic and Reconstructive Surgery, AMA (Physicians Recognition award 1977, 80), Southwest Oncology Group (head and neck com.). Contbr. articles on otolaryngology and oncology to med. jours. Home: 2505 Beluche Dr Galveston TX 77551 Office: Dept of Otolaryngology Univ Texas Galveston TX 77550

LEISCHUCK, GERALD STEVE, univ. adminstr.; b. Ramah, Colo., Dec. 14, 1935; s. Steve G. and Nellie (Yarish) L.; A.B., U. No. Colo. 1959, M.A., 1961; Ed.D., Auburn U., 1964; m. Emily Mitchell Reaves, Aug. 1, 1966. Tchr., prin. Kiowa (Colo.) Public Schs., 1957-60, Stockton (Calif.) Public Schs., 1961-62; research asst. Auburn (Ala.) U., 1962-64, research asso., 1964-65, asst. dir. instl. analysis, 1965-66, dir. instl. analysis, 1966—; cons. Ala. Commn. Higher Edn., 1970—. Mem. Auburn City Bd. Edn., 1978—; bd. dirs. Auburn U. Fed. Credit Union, 1977—, v.p., 1975-76. Mem. Assn. Study of Higher Edn., Assn. Instl. Research, Phi Delta Kappa (internat. pres. 1977-79; bd. govs. Ednl. Found. 1976-79), Phi Kappa Phi. Methodist. Club: Kiwanis (pres. 1973-74, div. lt. gov. 1975-76, dist. lt. gov. 1976). Disting. Club pres. 1973). Contbr. articles on higher edn. to profl. pubs. Home: 232 Kimberly Dr Auburn AL 36830 Office: Auburn Univ Auburn AL 36830

LEISK, JAMES CLARK, petroleum cons.; b. Waldo, Ark., May 3, 1929; s. William Charles and Julia Evelyn (Fincher) L.; B.S. in Petroleum Engring., La. State U., 1951; m. Anna Glen Gute, June 25,

1955; children—Julia Ann, Catherine Glen. With Union Producing Co., 1953-67, field drilling and prodn. supt., Tinsley, Miss., 1963-67; dist. petroleum engr., then sr. engr. Pennzoil Producing Co., 1967-72; cons. T.W. McGuire & Assos., Inc., Shreveport, 1972-78, Caddo Oil Co., Inc., 1978—. Served as 2d lt. C.E., AUS, 1951-52. Mem. Soc. Petroleum Engrs., Am. Petroleum Inst. (com. on standardization of prodn. equipment), U.S. Power Squadrons, Delta Kappa Epsilon. Republican. Baptist. Club: Shreveport Yacht. Home: 4026 Gilbert Shreveport LA 71106 Office: PO Box 800 Shreveport LA 71162

LEITNER, PAUL R., lawyer; b. Winnsboro, S.C., Nov. 11, 1928; s. W. Walker and Irene (Lewis) L.; A.B., Duke, 1950; LL.B., McKenzie Coll., 1954; m. Sandra Strickland, Dec. 29, 1972; children by previous marriage—David, Douglas, Gregory, Reid, Cheryl. Admitted to Tenn. bar, 1954; practiced in Chattanooga, 1954; asso. firm Leitner, Warner, Owens, Moffitt, Williams & Dooley, and predecessors, 1952-57, partner, 1957—; state chmn. Def. Research Inst., Inc., 1978—. Bd. dirs. Family Service Agy., 1957-63; mem. Chattanooga-Hamilton County Community Action Bd.; mem. Juvenile Ct. Commn., Hamilton County, 1955-61, chmn., 1958-59; chmn. Citizens Com. for Better Sch.; mem. Met. Govt. Charter Commn.; bd. dirs. U. Chattanooga Meth. Student Center, Camp Ocoee, YMCA. Served with AUS, 1946-47. Recipient Young Man of Year award, Chattanooga area, 1957. Mem. Jr. C. of C. (pres. 1956-57), Am., Chattanooga, Tenn. bar assns., Am. Judicature Soc., Fedn. Ins. Counsel, Internat. Assn. Ins. Counsel, Trial Attys. Am., Tenn. Def. Lawyers Assn. (pres. 1975-76). Methodist (chmn. ofcl. bd., lay leader, dist. bd. lay activities). Home: Augusta Dr Lookout Mountain TN 37350 Office: 3d Floor Pioneer Bldg Chattanooga TN 37402

LEJEUNE, FRANCIS ERNEST, JR., otolaryngologist; b. New Orleans, Jan. 3, 1929; s. Francis Ernest and Anna Lynne (Dodds) LeJ.; B.S., Tulane U., 1950, M.D., 1953; m. Ena Kay Hudson, Dec. 21, 1963; children—Francis III, Baltzer, Katherine, Ann. Intern Charity Hosp. La., New Orleans, 1953-54; resident U. Ia. Hosps., Iowa City, 1954-57; mem. staff dept. otolaryngology Ochsner Clinic, New Orleans, 1959—, chmn. dept., 1965—; clin. prof. dept. otolaryngology Tulane U. Sch. Medicine, New Orleans, 1977—. Served with USAF, 1957-59. Mem. A.C.S., Am. Laryngol., Rhinol. and Otol. Soc., Am. Broncho-Esophagological Soc., Am. Laryngol. Assn. Clubs: So. Yacht, Boston, Pendennis (New Orleans). Home: 334 Garden Rd New Orleans LA 70123 Office: 1514 Jefferson Hwy Jefferson LA 70121

LE JEUNE, ROBERT LEE, state ofcl.; b. Iota, La., Sept. 5, 1938; s. Christoval and Ruby (Fruge) LeJ.; B.A., Maryknoll Coll., 1960; M.Ed. Northwestern La. U., 1967; m. Doris Marie LeBlanc, Sept. 2, 1962; children—Simone Therese, Suzanne Marie, Paul Andre, Marcel Rene, Yvette Louise. Dir. mens and married housing U. Southwestern La., 1965-66; dir. student activities, asst. dir. univ. center U. Houston, 1967-69; dir. student center Lamar U., Beaumont, Tex., 1970-71; dir. Christian Life Center, Catholic Diocese Beaumont, 1971-74; regional edn. dir. Tex. Dept. Human Resources, Beaumont, 1974-79, regional bus. officer, 1979—. State dir. Texas Right to Life; state pres. family Life Dirs.; chmn. bd. Boys Club Am., 1976-77; v.p. Land Manor Halfway Houses, 1976; pres. St. Anthony Home and Sch. Assn., 1979; pres. sch. bd. Served to lt. comdr. USN, 1961-65: Vietnam. Mem. Tex. Pub. Employees Assn. (pres.), Am. Personnel and Guidance Assn., Am. Coll. Personnel Assn., Am. Soc. Tng. and Devel., Adminstrv. Mgmt. Soc., Am. Pub. Welfare Assn., Nat. Humane Soc., UN Assn., Phi Delta Kappa. Democrat. Roman Catholic. Clubs: Optimist, K.C., Serra (pres. 1979). Home: 1645 Orange St Beaumont TX 77701 Office: 1310 Penn St Beaumont TX 77701

LELAND, MICKEY, congressman; b. Lubbock, Tex., Nov. 27, 1944; George Thomas Leland and Alice (Lewis) Leland Rains; B.S. in Pharmacy, Tex. So. U., 1970. Instr. clin. pharmacy Tex. So. U., 1971; mem. Tex. Ho. of Reps. from 88th Dist., 1972-78; mem. 96th Congress from 18th Dist. Tex., freshman whip, 1979. Co-chmn. Nat. Black-Hispanic Coalition; mem. Democratic Nat. Com.; mem. Congl. Black Caucus. Democrat. Roman Catholic. Address: 1207 Longworth House Office Bldg Washington DC 20515

LE MAISTRE, CHARLES AUBREY, univ. pres., physician; b. Lockhart, Ala., Feb. 10, 1924; s. John Wesley and Edith (McLeod) LeM.; B.A., U. Ala., 1944; M.D., Cornell U., 1947; LL.D. (hon.), Austin Coll., 1970, U. Ala., 1971; D.Sc. (hon.), U. Dallas, 1978; m. Joyce Trapp, June 3, 1952; children—Charles Frederick, William Sidney, Joyce Anne, Helen Jean. Intern, then resident medicine N.Y. Hosp., 1947-49; research fellow infectious diseases Cornell U. Med. Coll., 1949-51, mem. faculty, 1951-54, asst. prof. medicine, 1953-54; mem. faculty Emory U. Sch. Medicine, 1954-59, prof. preventive medicine, chmn. dept., 1957-59; prof. medicine U. Tex. Southwestern Med. Sch., 1959-66, asso. dean, 1965-66; vice chancellor health affairs U. Tex. System, Austin, 1966-68, exec. vice chancellor, 1968-69, dep. chancellor, 1969-70, chancellor, 1971-78, pres. U. Tex. System Cancer Center, 1978; cons. epidemiology Communicable Disease Center, USPHS, 1953—; cons. medicine VA, Tuskegee, Ala., 1954-59, area med. cons. Atlanta area, 1958-59; vis. staff physician Grady Meml. Hosp., Atlanta, 1954-59, Emory U. Hosp., 1954-59, Parkland Meml. Hosp., Dallas, 1959-66; med. dir. Woodlawn Hosp., Dallas, 1959-65. Mem. Surgeon Gen. Adv. Com. Smoking and Health, 1963-64; mem. AMA-Edn. Research Found. com. research tobacco and health, 1964-66; chmn. Gov. Tex. Com. Tb Eradication, 1963-64; cons. internal medicine Baylor U. Med. Center, Dallas, 1962—, St. Paul Hosp., Dallas, 1966—; cons. div. hosp. and med. facilities USPHS, 1966—; mem. N.Y.C. Task Force on Tb, 1967-68; cons. Bur. Health and Manpower, Dept. Health, Edn. and Welfare, 1967-74; mem. Tex. Legislature Dept. Health, Edn. and Welfare, 1967—; mem. Tex. Legislature Com. on Organ Transplantation, 1968—, Carnegie Commn. Non-Traditional Study, 1971-73; mem. com. fed. health programs Assn. Am. Med. Colls., 1967—; mem. Pres.'s Commn. White House Fellows, 1971; mem. Am. Cancer Soc. Nat. Commn. Smoking and Pub. Policy, 1977—, med. dir. at large, 1978—, also Tex. div., 1979—; nat. panelist identification program for advancement women in higher edn. adminstrn. Am. Council Edn., 1977—. Chmn. steering com. Presbyn. Physicians for Fgn. Missions, 1960-62; mem. Ministers Cons. Clinic, Dallas, 1960-62; mem. bd. commrs. Nat. Commn. on Accrediting, 1973—; mem. adv. council Austin Symphony Orch., 1973—; mem. joint task force on continuing competence in pharmacy Am. Pharm. Assn.-Am. Assn. Colls. in Pharmacy, 1973-74. Bd. dirs. Ga. Tb Assn., 1955-59; trustee Biol. Humanics Found., Dallas; bd. dirs. Damon Runyon-Walter Winchell Cancer Fund, 1976—, chmn. exec. com., v.p., 1978-79, pres., 1979—; bd. trustees Austin Coll., 1979—, Stillman Coll., 1978—. Recipient Alumni award of distinction Cornell U., 1978. Mem. Am. (v.p. 1964-65), So. (pres. 1963-64) thoracic socs., Nat. Tb Assn., Am., Tex., Ga. med. assns., Central Soc. Clin. Research, Dallas Clin. Soc., Houston C. of C. (chmn. health com., dir. 1980—), Alpha Omega Alpha. Presbyterian. (deacon). Contbr. med. jours. Contbg. author: A Textbook of Medicine, 10 and 11th edits., 1963; Pharmacology in Medicine, 1958. Translating author: The Tubercle Bacillus, 1955. Editorial bd. Am. Rev. Respiratory Diseases, 1955-58. Home: 7000 Staffordshire Houston TX 77030 Office: University of Texas System Cancer Center Tex Med Center 6723 Bertner Ave Houston TX 77030

LE MASTER, HAROLD EUGENE, acct.; b. Union, S.C., Nov. 21, 1951; s. Roy Lee and Lillie Mae (Sinclair) LeM.; B.S., U. S.C., 1973; m. Patti Melinda Puckett, May 19, 1972; children—Barbara Sinclair, Greta Nicole. Staff acct. C.C. McGregor & Co., Columbia, S.C., 1974-75, T.C. Conrad, Jr., Spartanburg, S.C., 1975; owner, operator acctg. co., Union, 1975—; instr. acctg. U. S.C., Union, 1977—. C.P.A. Mem. Am. Inst. C.P.A.'s, S.C. Assn. C.P.A.'s. Baptist. Clubs: Fairwood Country, Sertoma (v.p. 1977-78), Civitan. Home: Woodhaven Estates Union SC 29379 Office: Harold E LeMaster W Main St Union SC 29379

LEMATTY, RODGER S., apparel co. exec.; b. 1907; grad. U. Ill., 1930; married. Office mgr. Globe Superior Corp., to 1936; with Blue Bell Inc., Greensboro, N.C., 1936—, treas., from 1943, v.p., 1948-62, exec. v.p., 1962-66, pres., mem. exec. com., 1966—, vice chmn. bd., 1973—, also dir. Office: 335 Church Ct Greensboro NC 27401*

LEMIEUX, DONALD JILE, archivist, historian; b. Lewiston, Maine, Sept. 14, 1936; s. Pierre Gerard and Clarisse (Letourneau) L.; B.A., U. N.Mex., 1962; M.A., Xavier U., Cin., 1963; Ph.D., La. State U., 1972; postgrad. Archives Nationale, Paris, 1971; m. Lurline Didier, Jan. 7, 1972; children—Garrett Lesley, John Geoffrey, Micheline Clarisse, Niquelle Elizabeth. Asst. prof. Latin Am. history La. Tech. U., 1965-69; fellow in Latin Am. History La. State U., 1969-72; records mgmt. officer State Archives and Records Service, Baton Rouge, 1973-74, state archivist and dir., 1974—; mem. La. Constl. Conv. Records Commn., 1975—, Nat. Hist. Pub., Records Commn., 1976—, State Com. Survey Colonial Documents, 1976—, State Com. to Study Ct. Record Retention, Storage, 1977; state coordinator La. Hist. Records Advisory Commn., 1976—; asso. Nat. Archives, 1977—. Mem. Nat. Assn. State Archives, Records Adminstrs., Am. Records Mgmt. Assn., socs. S.W., Am. archivists, La. Hist. Assn. (sec.-treas. 1978—), La. Hist. Soc. Democrat. Roman Catholic. Contbr. articles to profl. jours. Address: 4054 Palm St Baton Rouge LA 70808

LEMLEY, GEORGE WILSON, social worker, state ofcl.; b. Hector, Ark., Nov. 12, 1931; s. Henry Harmon and Euna Elma (Laffoon) L.; student Ark. Tech. U., 1955-56; B.S., Lamar State U., 1967; M.S.W. (Tex. Dept. Public Welfare grantee), La. State U., 1970; m. Mary Margaret Johnson, June 3, 1960; children—Cathy Gail, James Roy. Welfare worker I, Tex. Dept. Public Welfare, Paris, 1963-65, supr. fin. services 1965-68, supr. social services, 1970-72, program cons., 1972-75, social services program dir., 1975-76, welfare program cons., 1976-77, social work cons., 1977—; cons. to continuing edn. staff Paris Jr. Coll., 1976—. Councilman, City of Blossom (Tex.), 1975-78. Served with USN, 1951-55. Mem. Acad. Cert. Social Workers, Nat. Assn. Social Workers, Tex. Public Employees Assn. Baptist. Club: Lions (pres. 1979—). Home: Route 1 Blossom TX 75416 Office: 610 Clarksville St Paris TX 75460

LEMLEY, K(ENT) CHRISTOPHER, advt. agy. exec.; b. Ft. Myers, Fla., Oct. 10, 1946; s. Kermit Roosevelt and Maelee (Hollandsworth) L.; B.A., Furman U., 1968; M.B.A., Ga. State U., 1973. Media trainee Tucker Wayne & Co., Atlanta, 1968-69; sr. speechwriter, aide to gov. State of Ga., Atlanta, 1969; account exec. Stein Printing Co., Atlanta, 1970-73, Liller, Neal, Battle & Lindsey, Atlanta, 1973-77; sr. account exec. Cargill, Wilson & Acree, Atlanta, 1977-79, account supr., 1979—. Chief of staff CAP, 1970-74; mem. Atlanta Symphony Orch. League, 1978—. Recipient several awards for copywriting and mktg. Mem. Am. Mktg. Assn. (dir. chpt. 1977-79), Am. Advt. Fedn., Am. Film Inst., Aircraft Owners and Pilots Assn., Savs. and Loan Mktg. Assn., Atlanta Broadcast Execs. Episcopalian. Club: Variety Internat. Home: 210 Cedar Trace Roswell GA 30075 Office: Cargill Wilson & Acree Suite 1150 Tower Pl 3340 Peachtree Rd NE Atlanta GA 30326

LEMOINE, PERCY ANTHONY, state ofcl. La.; b. Mansura, La., Dec. 25, 1909; s. Thelis and Bertha (Chatelain) L.; B.S. in Agrl. Scis., La. State U., 1932, postgrad. 1932-40; m. Flossie E. Chatelain, July 1, 1934; 1 son, Percy Anthony. Vocational agr. tchr. Effie and Mansura, La., 1932-36; county agrl. agt. La. State U., Marksville, 1936-40; district supr. USDA, Baton Rouge, 1940-68; program dir. La. Economic Opportunity, Baton Rouge, 1968-73; dir. La. Dept. Vets. Affairs, Baton Rouge, 1973—. Agrl. specialist Fgn. Econ. Adminstrn., Washington, 1943; with AID program State Dept., Tananarive, Madagascar, 1966; land appraiser, loan cons. Bd. dirs. Baton Rouge Mental Health Assn.; La. del. White House Conf. on Children and Youth, 1960; mem. adv. com. East Baton Rouge Family Ct.; mem. Baton Rouge Mayor's Bi-Racial Com., Gov.'s 100-Man Com. on Ednl. Needs for La.; mem. juvenile delinquency com. La. Gov.'s Commn. on Law Enforcement and Criminal Justice; mem. community life bd. dirs. Diocese of Baton Rouge; active ch. orgns. and community affairs. Served with USNR, 1943-47. Mem. Nat. Assn. State Dirs. Vets. Affairs (v.p.), Army, Navy Airforce Vets. in Can. and U.S., Am. Legion (state comdr. 1962-63, past nat. chmn. child welfare, La. State U. Alumni Fedn. (pres. 1956), AMVETS, DAV, VFW, 40 and 8, Alpha Zeta, Alpha Tau Alpha. Clubs: Postmortem, K.C. (4 deg., grand knight 1968-69). Home: 7186 Richards Dr Baton Rouge LA 70809 Office: Dept Vet Affairs 4th Floor Old State Capitol Baton Rouge LA 70801

LENART, RAYMOND STUART, psychol. counselor; b. Houston, July 7, 1943; s. Alphonse Raymond and Jessie Nell (Dabney) L.; B.B.A., U. Houston, 1970, M.A. in Psychology, 1973; m. Barbara Lynn Scamman, Apr. 15, 1964; 1 son, Raymond Shalom. Sheet metal worker Straus-Frank Co., Houston, 1962-64; psychol. counselor U. Houston, 1973—; cons. Tex. Inst. Rehab. and Research, 1970—. Treas. Ind. Life Styles, Inc., 1972-73, asst. treas., 1973—; bd. dirs. Coalition for Barrier Free Living, 1975-76. Grantee NIMH, 1971-72, Tex. Inst. Rehab. and Research, 1972. Mem. Am. Personnel and Guidance Assn., Am. Coll. Personnel Assn. (presenter papers), Am. (asso.), Tex., Southwestern psychol. assns. Roman Catholic. Office: 4800 Calhoun St Houston TX 77004

LENFESTEY, FREDERICK THOMAS, coll. adminstr.; b. Tampa, Fla., Dec. 31, 1920; s. Harold Blondell and Iva Idella (Albaugh) L.; B.S., U. Tampa, 1947; M.A., U. Fla., 1949, Ed.D., 1956; m. Dorothy L. James, Sept. 3, 1949; children—Harold James, Robert Edward, Eva. Vocat. rehab. counselor, Tampa, 1947-48; asso. prof. Ga. So. Coll., Statesboro, 1952-55; v.p. Pensacola (Fla.) Jr. Coll., 1955-64; pres. Polk Community Coll., Winter Haven, Fla., 1964—; v.p. Profl. Assos., Inc. Chmn. Am. Cancer Soc.; v.p. United Way, Winter Haven. Served to capt. U.S. Army, 1943-46, 50-52. Mem. So. Assn. Jr. Colls. (pres.), Assn. Higher Edn., State of Fla. Pres.' Council. Democrat. Presbyterian. Clubs: Rotary, Winter Haven Flying (pres.). Home: 1300 Lake Mirror Dr Winter Haven FL 33880 Office: Polk Community Coll Winter Haven FL 33880

LENGEL, CLIFFORD JOHN, bldg. supply co. exec.; b. Cleve., July 20, 1943; s. John Steven and Frances L.; B.B.A., Cleve. State U., 1966; m. Roberta Janet Koenig, Sept. 7, 1976; children—Patricia, Mark. Supr., Ernst & Ernst, Cleve., 1966-73; mgr. internal audit FIrst Mortgage Investors, Miami Beach, Fla., 1973-74, controller, 1975-76; controller Context Bldg. Supply Co., Coral Gables, Fla., 1977—. C.P.A., Ohio. Mem. Nat. Assn. Accountants (v.p. Ft. Lauderdale chpt. 1980—), Am. Inst. C.P.A.'s, Ohio Soc. C.P.A.'s. Republican. Roman Catholic. Home: 2506 NE 14th St Fort Lauderdale FL 33304 Office: 200 San Lorenzo St Coral Gables FL 33146

LENNEY, JILL RUTH, social worker; b. N.Y.C., Sept. 22, 1948; d. Harry H. and Molly W. Lenney; B.A. summa cum laude, Hofstra U., 1971; M.S.W., Adelphi U., 1973. Clin. social worker S. Fla. State Hosp., Hollywood, 1973-74; clin. social worker Jackson Meml. Hosp., Miami, Fla., 1974-77, asst. adminstr., chief clin. social worker, 1977—; mem. Interagy. Task Force, Coordinating Council on Family Stress. Mem. Nat. Assn. Social Workers, Acad. Cert. Social Workers, Am. Hosp. Assn., Soc. for Hosp. Social Work Dirs. Democrat. Home: 3401 N Country Club Dr Miami FL 33180 Office: Jackson Meml Hosp 1611 NW 12th Ave Miami FL 33136

LENNON, CHARLES WOODBURY, II, trade assn. exec.; b. Washington, N.C., Oct. 16, 1934; s. Charles Downing and Helen Louise (Wilkinson) L.; student Va. Mil. Inst., 1952-53; grad. Inst. for Orgn. Mgmt., U. Notre Dame, 1977; m. Shirley Anne Clore, Mar. 27, 1971; 1 son, Sean Patrick. With Dun & Bradstreet, Richmond, Va., 1957-59; self-employed in pub. relations and sales, candy industry, Richmond, 1959-66; exec. mgr. Va. Assn. Plumbing-Heating-Cooling Contractors, Richmond, 1966-69; exec. officer Hydro Mech. Contractors Assn., Fort Lauderdale, Fla., 1969-75; exec. dir. Air Conditioning Contractors Assn. and Mech. Contractors Assn. So. Fla., Miami, 1975—. Mem. Broward County Charter Commn., 1974-78, vice chmn., 1975-76, chmn., 1976; mem. Progress for Broward County, chmn., 1973-74; mem. Broward County Personnel Rev. Bd., Ft. Lauderdale Com. Performing Arts. Bd. dirs. Broward County United Way Family Service Agy., 1972-78, pres., 1975—; bd. dirs. Fork Union Mil. Acad. Served with U.S. Army, 1953-57; Korea. Named Man of Year, W.Va. Wholesalers Assn., 1965, 66, Nat. Candy Wholesalers Assn., 1966. Mem. Am. (designated certified assn. exec. 1976), Fla. socs. assn. execs., Constrn. Industry Mgmt. Council Broward County, Constrn. Industry Advisory Council So. Fla., Am. Arbitration Assn. (panel of arbitrators 1976—), U. Notre Dame Alumni Assn. Club: Notre Dame of Greater Miami (sec. 1978). Contbr. articles to profl. jours. Home: 2406 NE 13th Ct Fort Lauderdale FL 33304 Office: 99 NW 183d St Suite 238 Miami FL 33169

LENNON, EDWARD JAMES, editor; b. Portland, Maine, June 25, 1914; s. Edward James and Mary Elizabeth (Dostie) L.; A.B., Anderson (Ind.) Coll., 1949; M.S., U. Wis., 1950, Ph.D., 1952; m. Helen Margaret McDermott, Dec. 26, 1947; children—Keith, Charla. State editor Portland Evening News, 1935-38; asso. editor Internat. Digest, N.Y.C., 1945-46; chmn. dept. communication disorders U. Montreal, 1961-66; editor-in-chief Acta Symbolica, Memphis, 1969-72; editorial cons. Found. Sci. Relaxation, Chgo., 1972—. Served with AUS, 1942-45. Mem. Am. Assn. Advancement Tension Control, Am. Speech-Lang.-Hearing Assn. Republican. Christian Scientist. Club: Shriners. Author: Le Bégaiement, 1962; also short stories, articles. Home: 1302 George St Brunswick GA 31520 Office: 55 E Washington St Suite 311 Chicago IL 60602

LENNOX, EDWARD NEWMAN, pub. affairs exec.; b. New Orleans, July 27, 1925; s. Joseph Andrew and May Alice (Newman) L.; B.B.A., Tulane U., 1949; m. Joan Marie Landry, Sept. 3, 1949; children—Katherine Sarah, Anne Victoria, Mary Elizabeth, Laura Joan. Marketing service clk. Shell Oil Co., New Orleans, 1949; with W.M. Chambers Truck Line, Inc., 1950-60, exec. v.p., 1954-60; v.p. Radcliff Materials, Inc., New Orleans, 1961-71, So. Industries Corp., New Orleans, 1971—; dir. Home Savs. & Loan Assn. Mem. La. Bd. Hwys., 1965-67; chmn. New Orleans Aviation Bd., 1960-67; bd. mem. Travelers Aid Soc., 1966-68; pres. Met. New Orleans Safety Council, 1969-70. Pres. bd. Levee Commrs. of Orleans Levee Dist., 1969-72; bd. dirs. Constrn. Industry Legislative Council, 1968—, Miss. Valley Assn., 1969-72; mem. Ala. Gov.'s Adv. Council on Econs., 1971-72, La. Gov.'s Adv. Com. on River Area Transp. and Planning Study, 1971-72; del. La. Constnl. Conv., 1973; bus. and fin. adviser Congregation Sisters of Immaculate Conception, New Orleans. Bd. dirs., mem. exec. com. Methodist Hosp., 1963—; bd. govs. La. Civil Service League, pres., 1977-78; adv. bd. Morality in Media of La., Inc., 1975-77; bd. dirs. New Orleans, Boys' Clubs Greater New Orleans, Inc., 1973—, Americanism Forum, Inc., 1975—; bd. dirs., exec. bd. Goodwill Industries New Orleans; mem. career advisement com. Tulane Grad. Sch. Bus. Adminstrn., 1972; bd. dirs. Tragedy Fund, Inc., La. Polit. Action Council. Served to capt. AUS, 1943-46. Recipient Industry Service award Asso. Gen. Contractors Am., 1967; New Orleans Jr. C. of C. award, 1960; certificate of merit. City New Orleans, 1964, 67; certificate Constrn. Industry Assn. New Orleans, 1972; Monte M. Lemann award La. Civil Service League, 1976; named hon. citizen, Jacksonville, Fla. Mem. La. Tank Truck Carriers (pres. 1954-55), La. Motor Transport Assn. (pres. 1963-64), La. Good Roads Assn. (exec. com. 1972-74), Am. (v.p. 1956-62), Ala. (v.p. 1956-60) trucking assns., So. Concrete Masonry Assn. (pres. 1963-68), Greater New Orleans Ready Mixed Concrete Assn. (pres. 1966-68), Pub. Affairs Research Council La. (area v.p. 1972-73, trustee 1970—), La. Shell Producers Assn. (pres. 1966-68), C. of C. New Orleans Area (pres. elect 1973, area v.p. external affairs 1969-72), Lakeshore Property Owners Assn. (bd. dirs. 1974—, pres. 1977, 79), Internat. House (bd. dirs. 1977-79), Tulane Alumni Assn. Clubs: Metairie Country (bd. govs. 1976—, v.p. 1979), Traffic (New Orleans). Home: 862 Topaz St New Orleans LA 70124 Office: 1010 Common St Suite 1710 New Orleans LA 70112

LENTZ, DAVID BRUCE, ins. co. exec.; b. Woburn, Mass., May 9, 1950; s. David Joel and Phyllis Lorraine (Hetzel) L.; B.A., Bates Coll., 1972; m. Carol Lee Thistle, Sept. 24, 1977. Editor, Prudential Ins. Co., Boston, 1974-76; specialist advt., sales promotion New Eng. Life Ins. Co., Boston, 1976-78; mgr. advt. and sales promotion U.S. Mktg. Pan-Am. Life Ins. Co., New Orleans, 1978—; cons. in field. Mem. New Orleans C. of C., Life Advertisers Assn. (advt. research com., 1st pl. award of Excellence coop. advt. 1978, other awards), Greater New Orleans Advt. Club, New Orleans Track Club, New Orleans Bus. Communicators, Coll. Club Bates Coll. Home: 423 Hillary St New Orleans LA 70119 Office: Pan-Am Life Ins Co 2400 Canal St New Orleans LA 70119

LENZ, RICHARD JOSEPH, pharm. co. exec.; b. Altoona, Pa., Jan. 18, 1928; s. Raymond Martin and Aimee Marie (Gillen) L.; B.S. Ed., St. Francis Coll., 1953; M.Ed., Pa. State U., 1956; m. Margaret T. Weinzierl, Dec. 27, 1954; children—Mark, Paula, Raymond, Joseph, David, Paul. Tchr., Atwater (Ohio) High Sch., 1953-54, Cresson (Pa.) Joint High Sch., 1954-60; with Pfizer Labs., various locations, 1960—, acting dir. manpower tng. and devel., N.Y.C., 1972-73, dir. manpower tng. and devel., 1973-75, regional mgr. Southwest region, Dallas, 1975—; mem. adv. bd. Cert. Med. Reps., Richmond, 1974-75. Chmn. crusade Am. Cancer Soc., Clearfield County, Pa., 1961; chmn. Heart Fund, 1962; pres. Human Growth, Inc., Pitts., 1969-70; mem. Montvale Schs. Bd. Edn., 1974-75. Served with AUS, 1947-48. Mem. Sales and Mktg. Execs. Dallas, Am. Mgmt. Assn., Am. Legion. Republican. Roman Catholic. Clubs: K.C., Elks. Home: 1502 Millbrook Dr Arlington TX 76012 Office: PO Box 222249 Dallas TX 75222

LEO, JIN-SHONE, physician; b. Taiwan, Mar. 6, 1943; came to U.S., 1970; s. Chia-Shian and Foon (Ho) L.; M.D., Nat. Taiwan U., 1969; m. Yii-Tzu Lin, Sept. 15, 1970; children—Eileen, Elaine. Resident in diagnostic radiology Albany (N.Y.) Med. Center, 1973-76; fellow in neuroradiology N.Y. U. Med. Center, N.Y.C., 1976-78, clin. asst. prof. radiology, 1978; chief div. neuroradiology Tex. Tech. U. Health Scis. Center, Lubbock, 1978—, asst. prof., 1978—. Mem. Am. Soc. Neuroradiology (sr.). Office: PO Box 4569 Lubbock TX 79409

LEONARD, GUY MEYERS, JR., audio visual prodn. co. exec.; b. Bluefield, W.Va., Sept. 22, 1926; s. Guy Meyers and Mabel (Bonham) L.; A.B., Morris Harvey Coll., 1949; B.Div., Southwestern Bapt. Sem., 1952; S.T.M., Harvard U., 1957; m. Pat Kirby, June 28, 1949; children—Calvin David, Dinah Lynn. Commd. ensign U.S. Navy, 1952, advanced through grades to capt., 1968, ret., 1972; dir. research and devel. Ency. Britannica Ednl. Corp., Chgo., 1972-76; pres. Communication Programming Services, Inc., Charleston, S.C., 1976—; cons. Ency. Britannica, Home Mission Bd. and Brotherhood Commn. So. Bapt. Conv. Sec., U.S. Power Squadron, Charleston, 1969; chmn. Spl. Commn. on Drug Abuse for Armed Forces, 1970-72; active Conn. council Boy Scouts Am., 1959-62. Served with USN, 1943-46. Decorated Legion of Merit, Meritorious Service medal, Navy Commendation medal; recipient Disting. Service award City of Louisville, 1963. Mem. Harvard Club S.C., C. of C., Trident Chamber (Charleston), Navy League U.S., Ret. Officers Assn. Baptist. Club: Kiwanis (spl. projects chmn., 1964-65). Designer, produced with Harvard U. and sta. WGBH, Boston, mediated coll. curriculum leading to B.S. degree for use by naval personel. Office: Suite 115 1064 Gardner Rd Charleston SC 29407

LEONARD, MARY EILEEN, med. technologist, educator; Charleston, S.C., Jan. 9, 1925; d. Edward Andrew and Honora Elizabeth (Price) L.; student Barry Coll., 1941-43: B.S., Coll. Charleston, 1945. Med. technologist Med. U. S.C., Charleston, 1946—, supr. immunology, 1950-79, asst. prof. med. technology, 1967-79, instr. Coll. Medicine, 1962-76, asso. Coll. Medicine, 1976-79. Recipient S.C. Med. Technologist of Year award, 1961. Mem. Med. U. S.C. Alumni Assn. (pres. 1976), S.C. Soc. Med. Technology (pres. 1955-56, 61-62), Coll. Charleston Alumni Assn., S.C. State Employees Assn., Am. Soc. Med. Technology, S.C. Acad. Sci. Roman Catholic. Club: K.C. Womens Bowling League (pres. 1975-76). Contbr. articles to profl. jours. Home: 1538 Dunnes Ln Charleston SC 29407

LEONARD, NANCY STEWART, counseling psychologist; b. Duncan, Okla., Feb. 1, 1938; d. Raymond Joseph and Nola Owens Stewart; B.S. in Edn., U. Okla., 1960, M. Counseling Psychology, 1979; m. Phillip H. Leonard, July 1, 1960; children—Phillip Stewart, Melissa Lee. Tchr., Traub Sch., Midwest City, Okla., 1960-64; tchr., dir. Nancy Leonard's Preschool, Duncan, Okla., 1967-76; counselor elementary sch., Duncan, 1979—. Mem. Am. Personnel and Guidance Assn., NEA, Okla. Edn. Assn., Am. Psychol. Assn., Okla. Psychol. Assn., PEO. Home: 2202 Twin Dr Duncan OK 73533 Office: 211 Beech St Duncan OK 73533

LEONARD, RICHARD VAUGHN, JR., comml. art designer; b. Troy, Ohio, Mar. 4, 1947; s. Richard Vaughn and Martha May (Oxley) L.; grad. Harris Sch. Art, Nashville, 1970; m. Donna Wright, Sept. 26, 1970; children—Neil Eugene, Justin Emerson. Staff artist Paramount Advt., Tampa, Fla., 1970, Perew Studios, St. Petersburg, Fla., 1971; prodn. dir. Brown, Dowling & Kitten, St. Petersburg, 1971-74; owner, artist Leonard Graphics, St. Petersburg, 1974-75, Corp. Communications and Mktg., Tampa, 1975; pres., owner Leonard Graphics, Inc., St. Petersburg, 1975—. Mem. adv. com. Tomlison Art Center, 1978; design cons. S.E. Sailing. Recipient merit award Fin. World, 1978, awards in packaging, bus., print and sales promotion. Mem. Am. Advt. Fedn. Democrat. Home: 2913 Villa Rosa Park Tampa FL 33611 Office: 9500 Koger Blvd Suite 109 Saint Petersburg FL 33702

LEONARD, SAMUEL ANDERSON, physician; b. Pensacola, Fla., Mar. 23, 1933; s. William Alexander and Ethel Margaret (Schneider) L.; B.S., Tulane U., 1957; M.S., 1960. M.D., 1960; m. Ethel Marie Karst, June 8, 1957; children—Gregory Thomas, Stephanie Ann. Intern, Touro Infirmary, New Orleans, 1960-61; resident Tulane U., 1961-65; pvt. practice medicine specializing in urology, New Orleans, 1965—; pres. med. staff East Jefferson Gen. Hosp., Metairie, La., 1974; mem. staff Lakeside Hosp., Metairie, VA Hosp., New Orleans, Charity Hosp., New Orleans; asst. prof. urology Tulane U., 1974—. Diplomate Am. Bd. Urology. Fellow A.C.S., Internat. Coll. Surgeons; mem. Royal Med. Soc., Jefferson Parish Med. Soc. (pres. 1977), La. State Med. Soc. (del. 1976—), Southeastern sect. Am. Urol. Assn., Am. Assn. Clin. Urologists. Democrat. Home: 9 Park Island New Orleans LA 70122 Office: 3700 Houma Blvd Metairie LA 70002

LEONARD, STEPHEN MICHEAL, radio sta. exec.; b. Ponca City, Okla., Nov. 17, 1951; s. Jess William and Patsy Sue (Sierman) L.; A.S. in Speech, No. Okla. Coll., 1972; postgrad. Okla. U., 1972-73; B.A., Okla. State U., 1976; m. Dorothy Annette Horton, June 8, 1973; 1 son, Bradley Marion. Announcer, newsman, salesman Sta. KLOR-FM, Ponca City, Okla., 1971-75, announcer, newsman, dir. public affairs, 1975—, dir. traffic, ops. mgr., 1976—. Recipient 1st. pl. documentary award UPI, 1978, 2d. pl. award for public affairs, Okla. region, 1978. Republican. Baptist. Home: 1923 N 6th St Ponca City OK 74601 Office: Sta KLOR-FM Suite 414 Community Bldg Ponca City OK 74601

LEON-SOTOMAYOR, LUIS ANGEL, physician; b. Ponce, P.R., Aug. 2, 1931; s. Jose Luis Leon-Parra and Olga Sotomayor-Falcon; B.S. cum laude, U. P.R., 1954, Med. Tech. summa cum laude, 1954, M.D. with highest honors, 1958; m. Rosita Fonfria, June 17, 1955; children—Olga Vanessa, Rose Valerie, Louis Angel, Wanda Lisette, Sharon, David. Extern surgery with highest honors Columbia Presbyn. Hosp., N.Y.C., 1957; intern with highest honors Charity Hosp. of La., New Orleans, 1958-59, resident internal medicine Tulane div., 1959-62; fellow in medicine, cardiology Johns Hopkins U., Balt., 1962-63; instr. medicine Tulane U., dir. Alcoholic Research div. Charity Hosp., New Orleans, 1961-62; instr. Med. Coll. Ga., Augusta, 1963-65, U. Tex. Med. Br., Galveston, 1965—; practice medicine, specializing in internal medicine and cardiology, Galveston, 1965—; chmn. dept. medicine Galveston County Hosp., Texas City, 1965-68; mem. staffs John Sealy Hosp., Galveston, St. Mary's Hosp., Galveston, Galveston County Meml. Hosp., Danforth Hosp., Texas City, Clear Lake and Space Center Meml. Hosp., Webster, Tex.; sec. Drs. Clinic, Galveston, 1970—; lectr. in field. Mem. Galveston Bd. Health, 1966-70; nat. advisory bd. Am. Security Council, 1976—. Served to capt. M.C., AUS, 1963-65. Recipient grant Tex. Heart Assn., 1969, Bay Area Heart Assn. Diplomate Am. Bd. Internal Medicine, Nat. Bd. Med. Examiners. Fellow A.C.P., Am. Coll. Cardiology, Am. Coll. Angiology, Am. Coll. Chest Physicians, Royal Soc. Medicine (U.K.), Royal Soc. Health; mem. Am. Heart Assn. (council clin. cardiology), Bay Area Heart Assn. (v.p. 1972—), AMA, Am. Law Enforcement Office Assn., AAUP, Sigma Xi, Alpha Omega Alpha. Clubs: Galveston Artillery, Galveston Country, Galveston Boat. Author: Myxedema Coma, 1964; Cirrhosis of Liver and Hepatoma, 1966; Epidemic Diencephalomyelytis, 1969. Contbr. articles to profl. jours. Developer cardiac pacemaker catheter with atrial pressure recorder; co-developer heated ultrasound nebulization machine. Home: 4402 Caduceous St Galveston TX 77550 Office: Drs Clinic 1501 Broadway Galveston TX 77550

LEOPOLD, LOUIS, aerospace electronics engr.; b. Boston, Mar. 8, 1918; s. Nathan and Mary (Meyers) L.; B.S., U. Mich., 1941, Ill. Inst. Tech., 1958; postgrad. U. Chgo., 1949-51; m. Wilma Erika Miron, Dec. 27, 1947; children—Robert Louis, Laurence Scott. Electronics devel. engr. Magnecord, Inc., Chgo., 1952-53; sr. electronics project engr., group leader Motorola, Inc., 1953-59; electronics aero. research engr. communications system Project Mercury, NASA, Langley Field, Va., 1950-60, head antennas and microwave systems Project Apollo, Manned Spacecraft Center, Houston, 1961-67; NASA rep. for Project Mercury, McDonnell Aircraft Corp., St. Louis, 1960-61; mgr. NASA office, Apollo High Gain and LEM Steerable High Gain Antennas, Dalmo Victor Co., Belmont, Cal., 1968-69; expt. mgr. NASA Apollo Lunar Orbital Missions, S-band Transponder and Bistatic Radar Expts., 1969-73, mgr. antenna and microwave systems study Space Solar Power Satellite and Space Base Station, Johnson Space Center, Houston, 1973—. Cons. AMA, Chgo., 1957-59, Motorola, Inc., Thompson Ramo Wooldridge, Inc., 1956-59. Served to capt. USAAF, 1942-46. Recipient NASA Achievement awards, 1963-75. Mem. Am. Inst. Aeros. and Astronautics, IEEE (chmn. aerospace group 1964-65), AAAS, Ill. Acad. Sci., U. Mich. Union, St. Louis Engrs. Club, U. Mich. Alumni Assn. (dir. Houston 1967-68). Home: 7751 El Rancho St Houston TX 77087 Office: NASA Johnson Space Center Houston TX 77058

LEPLEY, RENEE BROOKE, counselor; b. Charleston, W.Va., Nov. 13, 1945; d. Charles William and Addie Josephine (Childress) Snyder; A.B., Morris Harvey Coll., 1967; M.A., W.Va. U., 1973; m. Benjamin Franklin Lepley, May 27, 1967; children—Benjamin Todd, Monica Jo. Tchr., Charleston (W.Va.) Job Corps Center, 1967-68; tchr. English, Elkview (W.Va.) Jr. High Sch., 1969-73; counselor Thomas Jefferson Jr. High Sch., Charleston, 1973-77, John Adams Jr. High Sch., 1977—; tchr. needlework adult edn. program. Mem. Am. Personnel and Guidance Assn., Kanawah County Personnel and Guidance Assn., Am. Sch. Counselor Assn., Alpha Xi Delta. Democrat. Baptist. Club: Clendenin Womens (1st v.p. 1976-78, pres. 1978-80). Home: Box 155 Clendenin WV 25045 Office: 2002 Presidential Dr Charleston WV 25314

LEPPLA, JOAN E(LLEN), personnel exec.; b. St. Louis, Mar. 8, 1933; d. George Fred and Alice Marie (Lamm) Nolte; student Fla. Internat. U., 1978-79; m. Rudolph H. Leppla, Mar. 19, 1976; children—Mark Jones, Lee Jones, Julie Jones. Bus. devel. coordinator Century Banks, Ft. Lauderdale, Fla., 1973-76; dir. vol. services Bethesda Meml. Hosp., Boynton Beach, Fla., from 1976—; now dir. personnel Tropical Shipping Lines, Port of Palm Beach (Fla.). Named Citizen of Day, Radio Sta. WDXB, Boynton Beach, 1978. Mem. Am. Hosp. Dirs. Vol. Sers., South Fla. Council Dirs. Hosp. Vol. Services (corr. sec.), Fla. Hosp. Dirs. Vol. Services (rec. sec.). Republican. Home: 505 SE 5th Circle 12-B Los Mangos Boynton Beach FL 33435 Office: Tropical Shipping Lines Port of Palm Beach FL 33404

LEROY, THOMAS COY, mfg. co. exec.; b. Laurens, S.C., June 30, 1948; s. Coy Edward and Margaret (Schofield) L.; grad. Blanton's Bus. and Transp. Coll., 1966-68; diploma, Davidson County Community Coll., 1980. Rate clk., trainee Roadway Express, Inc., Kernersville, N.C., 1968-77; traffic analyst Hanes Hosiery, Inc., Winston-Salem, N.C., 1977—. Served with U.S. Army, 1969-70. Decorated Bronze Star. Home: 4009 Marie Dr Winston-Salem NC 27107 Office: Hanes Hosiery Inc PO Box 1413 Winston-Salem NC 27102

LESLIE, HENRY ARTHUR, banker; b. Troy, Ala., Oct. 15, 1921; s. James B. and Alice (Minchener) L.; B.S., U. Ala., 1942, J.D., 1948; J.S.D., Yale, 1959; grad. Sch. Banking, Rutgers U., 1964; m. Anita Doyle, Apr. 5, 1943; children—Anita Lucinda (Mrs. David Miller), Henry Arthur. Admitted to Ala. bar, 1948; asst. prof. bus. law U. Ala., 1948-50, 52-54, prof. law, asst. dean Sch. Law, 1954-59; v.p., trust officer Birmingham Trust Nat. Bank (Ala.), 1959-64; sr. v.p., sr. trust officer Union Bank & Trust Co., Montgomery, Ala., 1964-74, sr. v.p., dir., 1974-76, exec. v.p., 1976-78, pres., chief exec. officer, 1978—. Mem. Ala. State Bd. Bar Examiners. Chmn. bd. trustees St. John's Endowment Fund. Served to capt. AUS, 1942-46. Decorated Bronze Star medal. Mem. Am., Ala. Montgomery bar assns., Am., Ala. (trust div. pres. 1963-65) bankers assns., Farrah Order Jurisprudence (past pres.), Newcomen Soc. N.Am., Delta Sigma Pi, Phi Delta Phi, Omicron Delta Kappa, Pi Kappa Phi. Episcopalian (sr. warden). Kiwanian. Clubs: Maxwell Officers; Montgomery Country, Capital City. Contbr. articles to profl. jours. Home: 3332 Boxwood Dr Montgomery AL 36111 Office: Union Bank & Trust Co Montgomery AL 36104

LESLIE, THOMAS HERNDON, data processing and video products service exec.; b. Brookfield, Mo., Mar. 4, 1943; s. Kenneth Herndon and Bessie Gertrude (Woodward) L.; A.S., Calhoun Community Coll., Decatur, Ala., 1973; B.S. in Tech. Mgmt., Athens (Ala.) Coll., 1975; m. Mary Carolyn Bailey, Aug. 30, 1963; children—Kenneth Robert, Eric Todd. With Mosler Safe Co., 1970-76, ops. mgr., Cin., 1975-76; nat. service mgr. Infodetics Corp., Huntsville, Ala., 1976—. Served with USN, 1961-70. Mem. Nat. Micrographic Assn., Huntsville C. of C. Mem. Christian Ch. (Disciples of Christ). Office: 4825 Commercial Dr Huntsville AL 35805

LESNEVICH, KATHLEEN ROSE, hosp. adminstr.; b. Providence, Dec. 15, 1942; d. Richard Lee and Ethel (Maztel) Sprague; R.N., Roger Williams Gen. Hosp., Providence, 1963; B.S. in Nursing, Med. Coll. Ga., Augusta, 1973, M.Sc. in Nursing, 1974; M.B.A., Augusta Coll., 1979; children—Robert Warner, Carolyn Frances. Head nurse in psychiatry Ga. Regional Hosp., Augusta, 1969-71; dir. nursing Jennings Manor, Augusta, 1971-73; nursing adminstrv. supr. Univ. Hosp., Augusta, 1974-76, acting dir. nursing, 1976-77, adminstr. Extended Care Facility, 1977—; mem. hospice community relations com. St. Joseph's Hosp.; mem. nursing home task force East Central Ga. Health Systems Agy., Inc. Cert. nursing home adminstr., Ga. Mem. Ga. Hosp. Assn., Nat. Assn. County Health Facility Adminstrs., Nat. League Nursing, Nat. Hospice Assn., LWV. Republican. Roman Catholic. Club: Women's Growth Center. Home: 3037 Angela St Augusta GA 30907 Office: 1355 Nelson St Augusta GA 30901

LESSARD, RAYMOND W., bishop, Roman Catholic Ch. Ordained priest, 1956, consecrated bishop, 1973; bishop diocese of Savannah, Ga., 1973—. Office: 225 Abercorn St Savannah GA 31412*

LESSLIE, MARY STEWART, psychologist; b. Woodruff, S.C., June 23, 1932; d. William Tinsley and Mabel Percy (Moore) Stewart; B.A., U. N.C., Chapel Hill, 1954; M.A., U. S.C., 1974, Ph.D. in Psychology, 1977; m. Gordon Fleming Lesslie, Feb. 1, 1954; children—Katherine Moore, Linda Jacqueline, Judith Mary. Partner, Stewart Furniture Co., Woodruff, S.C., 1960-69; pres. CODAR, Inc., Columbia, S.C., 1975—; teaching asso. U. S.C., 1973-74. Mem. S.C. Psychol. Assn., S.C. Mensa (exec. sec. 1973-75). Presbyterian. Office: 1563 Brennen Rd Columbia SC 29206

LESTER, DARRELL REAKS, constrn. co. exec.; b. Temple, Tex., Mar. 5, 1943; s. Darrell George and Dorothy (Reaks) L.; B.B.A., Tex. Christian U., 1966, M.B.A., 1968; m. Marion Frances Wilkinson, June 26, 1966; children—Darrell Reaks, Jennifer Joy, Bryan Wilkinson. Programmer, systems analyst, corp. auditor Gen. Dynamics, Ft. Worth, 1966-69; corp. auditor Bonanza Internat. Inc., Dallas, 1969-70; mgmt. cons. Arthur Young & Co., Ft. Worth, 1970-73; v.p., dir. Haws & Garrett Gen. Contractors Inc., Ft. Worth, 1973—; treas., dir. Haws, Garrett & Kamrath Gen. Contractors Inc., 1975—; sec.-treas., dir. Am. Automatic Sprinkler, Inc., 1974—. Fin. cons. Treas., Miss. Tex. Scholarship Pageant Corp., 1970-72; active fund raising Tex. Christian U., 1966—, now also trustee; elder First Presbyn. Ch. of Fort Worth; budget dir. Colonial Nat. Invitational Golf Tournament, 1973—; bd. dirs. Trinity Valley Sch. Mem. Am. Inst. C.P.A.'s, Tex. State Soc. C.P.A.'s, Data Processing Mgmt. Assn., Inst. Internal Auditors, Nat. Mgmt. Assn., Tex. Christian U. Lettermans Assn. (dir.), Tex. Christian U. Alumni Assn. (pres. 1979—), Phi Kappa Sigma. Club: Colonial Country (chmn. finance com. 1974—). Home: 3721 Echo Trail Fort Worth TX 76109 Office: PO Box 1080 Fort Worth TX 76101

LESTER, DON LEE, educator; b. Bartow, Fla., Mar. 26, 1937; s. James Frank and Mary Lynn (Blair) L.; B.A. in Music Edn., Erskine Coll., Due West, S.C., 1959; Mus. M. in Voice, Cath. U. Am., 1962, postgrad. in Mus. Arts, 1965-69; m. Olga Dolores Dozier, June 21, 1959; children—Kimberly Elair, Lori Elliott, Don Lee. Tchr. music Dunedin (Fla.) High Sch., 1962-65; head dept. music Columbia (Mo.) Coll., 1969-74; asst. prof. voice Erskine Coll., 1974—. Clinician for high sch. choir programs. Served with AUS, 1959-62, 65-69. Mem. Fla. Vocal Assn. (chmn. dist. 1963-65), AAUP. Home: PO Box 475 Due West SC 29639

LESTER, EDGEL C., psychologist, mental health adminstr.; b. Middletown, Ohio, Aug 2, 1950; s. Edgel C. and Norma E. L.; B.A., Vanderbilt U., 1972; student Tenn. State U., 1973-74, U. Ky., 1974-75; M.A., Middle Tenn. State U., 1975; postgrad. U. Ala., Birmingham, 1976-77; m. Deborah Moore, Mar. 18, 1978; 1 dau., Whitney Dawn. Social worker Central State Psychiat. Hosp., Nashville, 1972-73; psychologist, area supr. Cumberland River Comprehensive Care, Corbin, Ky., 1973-76; clin. team leader N.W. Ala. Mental Health Center, Jasper, Ala., 1976-77; dir., adminstrn. and devel. N.W. Ala. Mental Health Center, Jasper, Ala., 1977—. Asst. dist. commr. Boy Scouts Am., 1978-79. Mem. Christian Ch. (Disciples of Christ). Office: 13 Hwy 78 W Jasper AL 35501

LESTER, EVERARD M., ret. mfg. exec.; b. Norwich, Conn., July 31, 1906; s. Walter Fitch and Rose Eva (Kasche) L.; B.S. in Mech. Engring., Mass. Inst. Tech., 1928, Hayden fellow bus. adminstrn., 1933; m. Helen Louise Jerome, July 19, 1930; children—Jerome Mason, Patricia (Mrs. R.F. Miller). Became asso. with Pratt & Whitney Aircraft, 1929; with Fairchild Engine div. Fairchild Engine and Airplane Corp., 1941-59, asst. gen. mgr., 1950-58, gen. mgr., 1958-59; became dir. mfg. govt. products group Am. Machine & Foundry Co., 1959, asst. group exec. comml. devel., advanced products group, AMF, York, Pa., until 1965; cons., pres. Tri-County Engring. Corp., Harrisburg, Pa., 1965-67; cons. Foster Wheeler Corp., Livingston, N.J., 1966-69, v.p., 1969-71; ret., 1971; past dir. Foster Wheeler John Brown Boilers, Ltd., London. Mem. Inst. Aero. Scis., Quiet Birdmen. Club: Middle Plantation. Contbr. report field. Airplane pilot, Air Corps Advance Tng. Sch., 1929. Address: 190 The Maine First Colony Williamsburg VA 23185

LESTER, JAMES ADAMS, editor, clergyman; b. Edison, Ga., Dec. 18, 1928; s. Paul Edwin and Myrtice (Peters) L.; grad. Norman Jr. Coll., Norman Park, Ga., 1946; B.A., Mercer U., Macon, Ga., 1949; B.D., New Orleans Bapt. Theol. Sem., 1953, Th.M., 1955; m. Lynne Owen; children—James Earl, Edwin Oliver, Jenna Leigh, Brian Everett. Ordained to ministry Baptist Ch., 1949; tchr. pub. schs., Mitchell County, Ga., 1947, Brooks County, Ga., 1950; dir. News Bur., Mercer U., 1949; mem. staff Times Picayune, New Orleans, 1951-57, copy desk, state news editor, 1955-57; dir. promotion and pub. relations, asso. to exec. sec.-treas. Ga. Bapt. Conv., Atlanta, 1957-68; editor Bapt. and Reflector news jour. Tenn. Bapt. Conv., Brentwood, 1968-74; dir. pub. relations Ga. Bapt. Conv., 1973—, also mgr. Bapt. Center. pastor Bapt. Chs., La., Miss., Ga. Mem. Pub. Relations Soc. Am., So. Bapt. Press Assn., Bapt. Pub. Relations Assn. Author: A History of the Christian Index, 1822-1953, 1955; A History of the Georgia Baptist Convention, 1822-1972, 1972; Who Said Quit!, 1978. Contbr. articles to profl. jours. Home: 1425 S Hairston Rd Stone Mountain GA 30088 Office: Ga Bapt Conv 2930 Flowers Rd S Atlanta GA 30341

LESTER, JAMES LUTHER, state senator; b. Augusta, Ga., Jan. 12, 1932; s. William McMorris and Elizabeth (Miles) L.; A.B., The Citadel, 1952; LL.B., U. Ga., 1957; m. Gwendolyn Gleason, Jan. 18, 1958; children—James Luther, Frank G. Admitted to Ga. bar; practiced in Augusta; mem. Ga. Senate, 1970—, chmn. banking, fin. and ins. com., 1979-80; chmn. Ga. Tax Reform Commn., 1978-79; mem. Ga. Com. Constl. Revision-Taxation Article, 1979. Bd. dirs. Augusta Met. Bd. YMCA, 1976-80; mem. Gov. Ga. Council Mental Health and Mental Retardation, 1976-80; adv. com. Ga.-Carolina dist. Boy Scouts Am., 1978-80; chmn. Richmond County Democratic Exec. Com., 1966-70. Served with AUS, 1952-54. Recipient various service awards. Mem. Am. Bar Assn., Ga. Bar Assn., Am. Legion. Methodist. Club: Augusta Kiwanis. Home: 770 Camellia Rd Augusta GA 30909 Office: 985 Broad St Augusta GA 30902

LESTER, ROBERT, orthodontist; b. Mt. Vernon, N.Y., Jan. 11, 1932; s. Herman and Eva (Kaplan) L.; A.B., Columbia Coll., 1953; D.D.S., Columbia U., 1957; certificate in orthodontics N.Y. U., 1970; m. Janice Sheila Wechter, June 8, 1957; children—Nina Beth, Jonathan. Gen. practice dentistry, Eastchester and Dobbs Ferry, N.Y., 1959-70, practice limited to orthodontics, Plantation, Fla., 1970—. Chmn., advancement chmn., membership mgmt. chmn. New River Dist. South Fla. council Boy Scouts Am., 1971-74. Served with USNR, 1957-59; mem. Res. Mem. Am., Fla., Broward County dental assns., Am. Assn. Orthodontists, Plantation Dental Study Group, U.S. Trotting Assn. Club: Civitan (treas. 1971-73, pres. 1976-77) (Plantation, Fla.). Home: 1039 E Tropical Way Plantation FL 33317 Office: 7500 NW 5th St Plantation FL 33313

LESTER, W(ILLIAM) BERNARD, state exec., agrl. economist; b. Havana, Fla., Jan. 9, 1939; s. William Duncan and Edith (Blackburn) L.; B.S.A., U. Fla., 1961, M.S.A., 1962; Ph.D., Tex. A&M U., 1965; m. Elaine Purnell, Mar. 30, 1961; 1 son, Mark Alan. Research asst. Tex. A&M U., 1962-65, agrl. economist, 1965-67; research economist dept. econ. research Fla. Citrus Commn. at U. Fla., 1967; econ. research dir. Fla. Dept. Citrus, Gainesville, 1968-76, dep. exec. dir. dept., Lakeland, Fla., 1976-78, exec. dir., 1979—; ex-officio mem. Growers and Shippers League of Fla., Orlando. Served with U.S. Army, 1956. Mem. Am. Mktg. Assn., Am. Agrl. Econs. Assn., So. Agrl. Econs. Assn. Democrat. Methodist. Author numerous research reports on econs. of various agrl. products, primarily citrus. Office: Fla Dept Citrus PO Box 148 1115 Memorial Blvd Lakeland FL 33802

LESTER, WILLIAM DALE, architect, engring. co. exec.; b. Mayfield, Ky., Oct. 29, 1922; s. Paul and Lottie Pearl (Hawes) L.; student Allegheny Coll., 1943-44, Murray State U., 1946-47; B.S. in Civil Engring., U. Ky., 1949; m. Carolyn Ray, Mar. 16, 1948; children—Dale, Paul. Supr. constrn. Ky. Dept. Hwys., Paducah, 1949-51; area engr. F. H. McGraw & Co., Paducah, 1951-53; structural supr. Giffels & Valet, Portsmouth, Ohio, 1953-55; structural designer Rust Engrs., Birmingham, Ala., 1955-56; v.p. prodn., mgr. Watson & Co., Tampa, Fla., 1956-76, pres., 1976—, vice chmn. bd., 1978—. Cub scout master Gulf Ridge council Boy Scouts Am., 1959; maj. United Fund, Tampa, 1961. Served with USAAF, 1943-45. Fellow Fla. Engring. Soc.; mem. Nat. Soc. Profl. Engrs., ASCE, Soc. Civil Engrs. Baptist. Clubs: Rotary, Palma Ceia Golf and Country. Office: 3010 Azeele St Tampa FL 33609

LESUEUR, ALEXANDER ARMAND, musician, educator; b. Holdenville, Okla., July 28, 1923; s. Trigg and Jette Emma Roberts L.; student Tulsa U., 1942, 46-47; B. Music, N. Tex. State U., 1949, M. Music, 1951; M. Music, U. Mich., 1963, D. Mus. Arts, 1967; m. Joan Clay Kavanaugh, Sept. 7, 1960; 1 son, Alexander Armand. Flutist, Atlanta Symphony Orch., 1949-53; band dir. Alpharetta (Ga.) Pub. Sch., 1949-50; Durant (Okla.) Pub. Schs., 1953-54, Itasca (Tex.) Pub. Schs., 1954-56, Forney (Tex.) Pub. Sch., 1956-58; asst. prof. music Morehead (Ky.) State U., 1959-65; asst. prof. music Fla. State U., Tallahassee, 1965-68; prof. music Western Carolina U., Cullowhee, N.C., 1968—; prin. flutist Asheville (N.C.) Symphony Orch., 1968-76; flute soloist, recitalist, clinician, adjudicator. Nat. bd. dirs. Am. Youth Symphony and Chorus, 1971—. Served with A.C., AUS, 1942-46. Mem. Music Educators Nat. Conf., N.C. Music Educators Conf., Nat. Flute Assn., Nat. Cathedral Assn. (co-chmn. Western N.C. 1975-79), Phi Mu Alpha, Pi Kappa Lambda. Episcopalian (warden, vestryman). Lion (sec. Cullowhee 1971). Contbr. articles to profl. publs. Home: Drawer AC Cullowhee NC 28723 Office: Music Dept Western Carolina U Cullowhee NC 28723

LETTS, THOMAS CLINTON, farmer, rancher, ret. educator; b. El Campo, Tex., Mar. 15, 1911; s. Henry Frank and Clara (Spencer) L.; student U. Houston, 1935-36, 47-48; B.S., Sam Houston State U., 1937; M.S., Tex. A. and M. U., 1945, postgrad., 1948-52; m. Margaret Evelyn McDaniel, Oct. 27, 1934; 1 dau., Margaret Sue (Mrs. Rufus Denman Hopper, Jr.). Tchr., prin., supt. pub. schs., Tex., 1929-42; clk. War Dept., 1942; work unit conservationist U.S. Dept. Agr., 1943-46; asso. prof. Sam Houston State U., 1946-58; agriculturist FOA, Tel Aviv, Israel, 1953-54; educationist ICA, Taipei, Taiwan, 1955-57, elementary edn. adviser, Asuncion, Paraguay, 1958-60; tchr. ednl. adviser USOM, Tegucigalpa, Honduras, 1960-62; elementary edn. adviser AID, Recife, Brazil, 1963-65; area devel. officer USOM, Dinh Turong Province, Vietnam, 1965, agrl. edn. officer AID, Saigon, Vietnam, 1966-71; farmer, rancher Walker and Williamson Counties, Tex., 1971—. Exec. com. Wharton County Inter-Scholastic League, 1935-37; v.p. Tex. joint legis. com. Nat. Ret. Tchrs. Assn./Am. Assn. Ret. Persons, 1978—. Mem. Tex. Tchrs. Assn. (pres. dist. VI ret. tchrs. sect.), Tex. Ret. Tchrs. (parliamentarian), Huntsville-Walker County Assn. (pres. 1977), Walker County C. of C. (dir. 1946-49), Kappa Delta Pi. Rotarian. (past pres.). Club: Vocational Agriculture (past pres.). Home: Route 5 Box 88 Huntsville TX 77340

LE VAN, DANIEL HAYDEN, business exec.; b. Savannah, Ga., Mar. 29, 1924; s. Daniel Hayden and Ruth (Harner) LeV.; grad. Middlesex Sch., 1943; B.A., Harvard, 1950; student Babson Inst., 1950-51. With underwriter's dept. Zurich Ins. Co., N.Y.C., 1951-52; liquified petroleum sales and engring. Gas, Inc., Lowell, Mass., 1952-54; customer relations Lowell Gas Co., 1954-56, in charge LP gas sales and promotion, 1956-58; trustee Colonial Gas Energy System; dir. Lowell Gas Co., Cape Cod Gas Co., Lowell Factors, Mass. Assos., Gas Appliances, Overseas Properties Ltd., N.Y.C. Served with AUS, 1943-46. Clubs: Harvard (N.Y.C.), Harvard (Boston). Home: Box 158 DeLeon Springs FL 32028

LEVEN, STEPHEN ALOYSIUS, clergyman; b. Blackwell, Okla., Apr. 30, 1905; s. Joseph J. and Gertrude (Conrady) L.; student St. Benedict's Coll., Atchison, Kans., 1920-21, St. Mary's Sem., LaPorte, Tex., 1921-22; student philosophy and theology Catholic U. Louvain (Belgium), 1922-28; Ph.D., Institut Superieur de Philosophie, Louvain, 1938; LL.D., St. Edward's U., Austin, Tex., 1957. Ordained priest Roman Catholic Ch., 1928; asst. pastor St. Joseph's Old Cathedral, Oklahoma City, Okla., 1928-32; pastor St. Joseph's Ch., Bristow, Okla., 1932-35; vice rector Am. Coll., Louvain, 1935-38; pastor St. Joseph's Ch., Tonkawa, Okla., 1938-48, St. Francis Xavier Ch., Enid, Okla., 1948-56; aux. bishop of San Antonio (Tex.), 1956-69; bishop of San Angelo (Tex.), 1969—. Office: 116 S Oaks St San Angelo TX 76901*

LEVER, OSCAR WILLIAM, JR., chemist; b. Greenville, S.C., Sept. 11, 1944; s. Oscar W. and Dorothy (Smith) L.; B.S., U. S.C., 1967, M.S., 1969; postgrad. U. London King's Coll., 1972; Ph.D., Mass. Inst. Tech., 1974. Sr. organic chemist Burroughs Wellcome Co., Research Triangle Park, N.C., 1974—. Recipient Am. Inst. Chemists medal U. S.C., 1967. Mem. Am. Chem. Soc., Sigma Xi, Pi Mu Epsilon. Methodist. Home: 317 Ashebrook Dr Raleigh NC 27609 Office: Organic Chemistry Dept Burroughs Wellcome Co Research Triangle Park NC 27709

LEVERETT, LYNN ARLIN, fast food exec.; b. Duke, Okla., Jan. 5, 1938; s. Amos Lilden and Annie Jewell L.; B.A., S.W. Okla. U., 1961; m. Paula Brock, Aug. 26, 1958; children—Jay Todd, Lisa Ann, Christopher William. Rep., tng. instr. Mobil Oil Co., 1961-67 resale area mgr. Mobil Oil Co., Houston, 1968-69; pres., owner U-Anchor Advt. Co., Amarillo, Tex., 1969-73; v.p. Church Fin. Co., Amarillo, 1974-78; owner, operator Mr. Burgers of Lubbock (Tex.), 1975—. Served with Army NG, 1954-60. Mem. Internat. Mr. Burger Franchise Holders Assn. (dir.). Democrat. Mem. Ch. of Christ.

LEVERETTE, SARAH ELIZABETH, lawyer; b. Iva, S.C., Dec. 28, 1919; d. Stephen Ernest and Allie E. (McGee) L.; A.A., Anderson Coll., 1938; A.B., U. S.C., 1940, LL.B., 1943; postgrad. Columbia U., summer 1947. Admitted to S.C. bar, 1943; legal research S.C. Labor Dept., Columbia, 1945-47; with Law Sch. U. S.C., Columbia, 1947-72, law librarian, 1947-72; commr. S.C. Indsl. Commn., 1972-78, chmn., 1976-77; legal cons., 1978—; mem. com. to Study Constn. S.C. Mem. Am. Assn. Law Librarians (Carolinas pres. 1948-50, chmn. scholarship com. 1959-71, coms. on membership, exchange and duplicates 1963-64, pres. Southeastern chpt. 1968-70; life), S.C. Bar Assn., S.C. Trial Lawyers Assn., Am. Judicature Soc., S.C. State Employees Assn. (dir. 1958-60), League Women Voters (pres. Columbia 1958-61, past 2d v.p. S.C.), Columbia Library Assn. (pres. 1951-52), Phi Beta Kappa, Zeta Tau Alpha. Episcopalian. Club: Pilot (past pres.) (Columbia). Co-compiler: Checklist of S.C. Session Laws, 1963. Home: Quail Run Apt 1182 Columbia SC 29206

LEVETAN, STEVEN LAWRENCE, scrap metal co. exec.; b. Atlanta, Oct. 26, 1950; s. Abraham Irving and Gertrude (Kuker) L.; B.S. in Indsl. Mgmt., Ga. Inst. Tech., 1972; m. Janice Stone, Mar. 18, 1973; 1 son, Joshua Benjamin. Gen. mgr. Dixie Iron & Metal Co., Atlanta, 1969—; treas. Joseph B. Levetan & Sons, Inc., 1972—. Vol. worker United Way Corporate Giving Program, DeKalb Beautiful, Atlanta Clean City Commn., Atlanta 2000; co-convenor Environ. Task Force; host Listening Post; active various local, state and nat. polit. campaigns. Recipient cert. of merit Atlanta Clean City Commn., 1979, 80. Mem. Inst. Scrap Iron and Steel (mem. exec. bd. Southeastern chpt. 1979—, chmn. legis. and environ. com. 1979—), Ga. Assn. Scrap Processors (pres. 1979—), Ga. Bus. and Industry Assn., Ga. Tech Alumnae Assn. Jewish. Club: B'nai Brith (trustee Kehillah lodge 1978-79, sec. 1979—). Home: 1801 Homestead Ave NE Atlanta GA 30306 Office: Dixie Iron & Metal Co 80 Milton Ave SE Atlanta GA 30315

LEVEY, DAVID VOE, explosive co. exec.; b. Ft. Worth, Oct. 27, 1939; s. Fred W. and Willie Macie (Tye) L.; B.A., Tex. Christian U., 1962; m. Judy M. Montgomery, June 3, 1977; children—Kelli, David, Kathy, Timmy, Tommy, Wesley. Test site mgr. The Western Co., Roanoke, Tex., 1964-67; sr. design engr. Gen. Dynamics, Ft. Worth, 1967-69; plant mgr. Gearhart-Owen Industries, Inc., Cleburne, Tex., 1969-76; pres. Goex, Inc., Cleburne, 1976—. Mem. Nat. Defense Preparedness Assn., Nat. Soc. Explosive Engrs. Baptist. Club: Mountain Valley Country. Home: 14 Roaring Springs Dr Joshua TX 76058 Office: Route 3 Box 423 Cleburne TX 76031

LEVIN, DAVID HAROLD, lawyer; b. Pensacola, Fla., Nov. 19, 1928; s. Abe Irvin and Rose (Lefkowitz) L.; A.B., Duke, 1949; J.D., U. Fla., 1952; m. Mona Joyce Lindy, Feb. 16, 1958; 1 dau., Lisa Ann. Admitted to Fla. bar, 1952, since practiced in Pensacola; asst. county solicitor, 1952; asso. Robinson, Roark & Hopkins, 1954-55; sr. partner Levin, Warfield, Middlebrooks, Mabie, Rosenbloom & Magie, 1955—. Pres., dir. Gator Boosters, Inc. Crusade chmn. Pensacola chpt. Am. Cancer Soc., 1964-65, pres., 1966-67; bd. dirs. Pensacola chpt. Am. Heart Assn., 1966-69; chmn. Pensacola United Jewish Appeal, 1967-68; chmn. Fla. Pollution Control Bd., 1971-74. Bd. dirs. U. Fla. Found., Inc. Served to capt. USAF, 1952-54. Fellow Fla. Trial Lawyers Assn.; mem. Am., Fla. (chmn. elect family law sect.) bar assns., Am. Judicature Soc., Am. Trial Lawyers Assn., Am. Acad. Matrimonial Lawyers (sec.-treas., bd. mgr.), Am. Legion, Pensacola U. Fla. Alumni Assn. (pres. 1960). Mason (32 deg., Shriner). Home: 3632 Menendez St Pensacola FL 32503 Office: 9th Floor Seville Tower Pensacola FL 32501

LEVIN, HERMAN, hotel exec.; b. Phila., Dec. 4, 1917; s. Samuel and Esther L.; student public schs.; m. Isabel Lavin, Oct. 29, 1939; children—Stephen, Lynda Levin Rybinski, David. Businessman, Phila., 1938-53; pres. Springlake Ranch, Ritz Lodge, Manatee River Hotel, New Fla. Hotel, Palm Beach Hotel, Sunset Hotel and Ritz Hotel, Lakeland, Fla., 1962—. Served with USNR, 1941-46. Recipient Outstanding Achievement recognition Pres. Roosevelt, 1945. Jewish. Office: 130 S Massachusetts Ave Lakeland FL 33801

LEVIN, SIDNEY HERBERT, state ofcl.; b. Balt., May 5, 1935; s. Jack and Ida (Kasoff) L.; B.A., Am. U., 1957; m. Sally Rubin, Feb. 2, 1957; children—Almee, Ira. Announcer radio sta. WITH-FM, Balt., 1952-53, program dir., 1953-55; sales mgr. WGMS, Washington, 1955-57; asst. mgr. WKAT, Miami, Fla., 1957-62, exec. v.p., gen. mgr., 1962-79; now sec. commerce State of Fla.; founding dir. Third Century Corp.; guest lectr. U. Miami, 1966-78. Past pres. Dade County Citizens Safety Council; commr. Met. Dade County, 1975-77; past pres. Greater Miami Inc. Mem. Miami Assn. Food Trades (past pres., dir.), Greater Miami Radio Broadcasters Assn. (founder, past pres.), Greater Miami C. of C. (dir., past pres.), Alpha Epsilon Rho. Jewish. Clubs: Miami, Miami Touchdown (past pres.). Home: 5084 Tallow Point Rd Tallahassee FL 32308 Office: Collins Bldg Tallahassee FL 32301

LEVIN, WILLIAM COHN, physician, univ. pres.; b. Waco, Tex., Mar. 2, 1917; s. Samuel P. and Jeanette (Cohn) L.; B.A., U. Tex., 1938, M.D., 1941; m. Edna Seinsheimer, June 23, 1941; children—Gerry Lee (Mrs. Eugene Hornstein), Carol Lynn. Intern Michael Reese Hosp., Chgo., 1941-42; resident John Sealy Hosp., Galveston, Tex., 1942-44; mem. staff U. Tex. Med. Br. Hosps., Galveston, 1944—, asso. prof. internal medicine, 1948-65, prof., 1965—, now also Warmoth prof. hematology; pres. U. Tex. at Galveston, 1974—. Past mem. cancer clin. investigation rev. com. Nat. Cancer Inst.; trustee Menil Found., 1976—, Houston-Galveston Psychoanalytic Found., 1975—. Served to lt. col. M.C., U.S. Army. Recipient Nicholas and Katherine Leone award for adminstrv. excellence, 1977. Diplomate Am. Bd. Internal Medicine. Fellow A.C.P., Internat. Soc. Hematology; mem. Tex. Club Internists (hon. 1977), Phi Beta Kappa, Sigma Xi, Alpha Omega Alpha. Home: 1301 Harbor View Dr Galveston TX 77550 Office: Office Pres U Tex Galveston TX 77550

LEVINE, HAROLD, lawyer; b. Newark, Apr. 30, 1931; s. Rubin and Gussie (Lifshitz) L.; B.S., Purdue U., 1954; J.D. with distinction, George Washington U., 1958; children—Linda Ellen, Brenda Sue, Jill Anne, Louise Abby. Marine engr., naval architect Navy Dept., Washington, 1954-55; patent examiner U.S. Patent Office, Washington, 1955-58; admitted to Va. bar, 1958, D.C. bar, 1959, Mass. bar, 1959, Tex. bar, 1972; with Tex. Instruments, Inc., 1959-77, asst. v.p., gen. patent counsel, Dallas, 1972-77; partner firm Sigalos & Levine, Dallas, 1977—; chmn. bd. Vanguard Security Inc., 1977—, Tex. Am. Realty Corp. Mem. Nat. Assn. Mfrs., Am. Mfrs. Assn., Am. Patent Law Assn., Am. Bar Assn., Tex. Bar Assn., Dallas-Ft. Worth Patent Law Assn., Dallas Bar Assn., Pacific Indsl. Property Assn. (pres. 1975-77), Electronic Industries Assn., U.S. C. of C., Alpha Epsilon Pi, Phi Alpha Delta. Club: Kiwanis. Home: 441 Salem St Richardson TX 75080 Office: Sigalos & Levine 1300 Republic National Bank Tower Dallas TX 75201

LEVINE, JANE SHEILA, nurse, hosp. exec.; b. Bklyn., Jan. 2, 1946; d. Irving Richard and Ann (Odell) Levine; grad. Bellevue Sch. Nursing, 1966; student Am. U., 1966-67, Marymont Manhattan Coll., 1967, Fla. Internat. U., 1976-78. Staff nurse Washington Hosp. Center, 1966; nurse N.Y. Office, Paramount Pictures, 1967-68; operating room nurse Beth Israel Hosp., N.Y.C., 1968-70; public health nurse Bellevue Hosp., N.Y.C., 1970-74; regional rep. N.Y. State Nurses Assn., 1974-75; asst. dir. nursing Parkway Gen. Hosp., Miami, Fla., 1975-77; dir. Staff Builders, Miami, 1977-78; v.p. for nursing Westchester Gen. Hosp., Miami, 1978—. Mem. Am. Nurses Assn., Fla. Nurses Assn., South Fla. Hosp. Assn. (council dirs. nursing service), Fla. Soc. for Hosp. Nursing Service Adminstrs. Home: 671 NE 195th St North Miami Beach FL 33179 Office: 2500 SW 74th St Miami FL 33155

LEVINE, JEROME EDWARD, physician; b. Pitts., Mar. 23, 1923; s. Harry Robert and Marian (Finesilver) LeV.; student U. Pitts., 1940-42, 44; M.D., Hahnemann Med. Sch., 1949; postgrad. opthalmology U. Pa., 1951-52; m. Marilyn Toby Hiedovitz, Apr. 14, 1957; children—Loren Robert, Beau Jay, Janice Lyn. Intern St. Francis Hosp., Pitts., 1949-50; resident opthalmologist Jefferson Med. Sch. and Hosp., Phila., 1952-54; opthamologist Leech Farm VA Hosp., 1955-59; chief eye dept. Stanocola Clinic, Baton Rouge, 1959-64; practice medicine specializing in ophthalmology, Baton Rouge, 1964—. Cons. La. State U. Infirmary, Villa Feliciana Geriatric Hosp., 1965-78, Women's Hosp., Dixon Meml. Hosp., Lane Meml. Hosp.; mem. staff Baton Rouge Gen. Hosp., Our Lady of Lake Hosp.; coding cons. div. blind La. State Dept. Pub. Welfare, disability determinations Social Security Adminstrn. instr. spl. edn. U. Southeastern La., 1971. Served with M.C., AUS, 1942-44. Fellow Am. Geriatric Soc., Royal Soc. Health; mem. La. Eye, Ear Nose and Throat Soc., New Orleans Acad. Ophthalmology, Inst. Glaucoma Research, AMA, So., Internat., Indsl., So. med. assns., La., East Baton Rouge Parish med. socs., Pi Lambda Phi, Phi Delta Epsilon. Home: 5876 Glenwood Dr Baton Rouge LA 70806 Office: 4560 North Blvd Baton Rouge LA 70806

LEVINE, JON HOWARD, endocrinologist; b. Toronto, Ont., Can., July 13, 1941; s. Sidney and Goldi Nessa (Wolfman) L.; M.D., U. Toronto, 1965, M.Sc., 1969; m. Elaine Krassov, May 31, 1964; children—Linda Ann, Julia Louise, Joshua Gregory. Intern, Toronto Gen. Hosp., 1965-66; resident in internal medicine Toronto Western Hosp., 1969-71; instr. medicine U. Toronto, 1966-69, Vanderbilt U., 1971-73; asst. prof. medicine Med. U. S.C., Charleston, 1973-78, asso. prof., 1978—, dir. student edn. dept. medicine, 1977—; attending physician Med. U. Hosp.; med. researcher. NIH research grantee, 1978—; recipient award Med. Research Fellowship of Can., 1966-69; diplomate Am. Bd. Internal Medicine. Fellow Royal Coll. Physicians and Surgeons of Can.; mem. Endocrine Soc., Am. Fedn. Clin. Research, So. Soc. Clin. Investigation, Can. Soc. Endocrinol. Metabolism Am. Diabetes Assn. Reviewer for endocrine jours.; contbr. articles profl. jours. Home: 1156 Deleisseline Blvd Mount Pleasant SC 29464 Office: Medical University of South Carolina 171 Ashley Ave Charleston SC 29403

LEVINE, RICHARD, architect, interior designer; b. Miami, 1936; s. Max and Mae (Mannis) L.; B.Arch., U. Fla., 1955. Partner firm Bleemer, Levine & Assos., Architects and Designers, Miami Beach, Fla. Founding dir. Am. Found. for Arts; dir. Mus. of Am. Found. for Arts; charter founder Fla. Internat. U. Served with USNR. Mem. AIA, Am. Assn. Museums (trustee), U. Fla. Alumni Assn., Fla. Planning and Zoning Assn., Design and Decorators Guild, Nat. Trust for Historic Preservation, Soc. Archtl. Historians, Victorian Soc. Clubs: Jockey, Menage, Scaramouche, Munity, Regines. Home: Grove Isle Dr Miami FL 33133 Office: 3814 NE Miami Ct Miami FL 33137

LEVINE, SAM, concrete mfr.; b. Savannah, Ga., Aug. 13, 1919; s. Jacob Herman and Ida (Hershman) L.; student N.Y.U., 1938-39; m. Marilyn Budovsky Grossman, Dec. 24, 1955; children—Jack Jeffrey, Randi Sue, Michael Edward, Nanci Gale, Robert James, Judi Lynn. Partner, Mursam Block Co., 1946-47, Samson Block Co., 1947—; pres. Samson Concrete Industries, Inc., 1955-68, Samson Block Co., Inc. of Miami, 1957-68; sec., treas. Samson Block Co., Inc. of Homestead, 1957-68; treas., chmn. bd. Builders Finance & Mortgage Co. (name now Samson Realty & Devel. Corp.), 1958—; v.p. Coral Aggregate Corp., 1961-65; pres. Perrine Devel. Co., 1960—. Served as lt. (j.g.) U.S. Maritime Service, 1943-45. Mem. Fla. Home Builders Assn., Engring. Contractors Assn., South Fla. Masonry Assn., C. of C., Zionist Orgn. Am. (pres. Miami Gables dist. 1957-59). Mason (Shriner), Kiwanian; mem. B'nai B'rith. Home: 13575 SW 68th Ct Miami FL 33156 Office: 420 S Dixie Hwy Suite 3-H Coral Gables FL 33146

LEVINGSTON, ERNEST LEE, engring. co. exec.; b. Pineville, La., Nov. 7, 1921; s. Vernon Lee and Adele (Miller) L.; B.S. in Mech. Engring., La. State U., 1960; m. Kathleen Bernice Bordelon, June 23, 1944; children—David Lewis, Jeanne Evelyn (Mrs. James Woltz), James Lee. Gen. foreman T. Miller & Sons, Lake Charles, La., 1939-42; sr. engr., sect. head Cities Service Refining Corp., Lake Charles, 1946-57; group leader Bovay Engrs., Baton Rouge, 1957-59; chief engr. Augenstein Constrn. Co., Lake Charles, 1959-60; pres. Levingston Engrs., Inc., Lake Charles, 1961—. Mem. Lake Charles Planning and Zoning Commn., 1965-70; mem. adv. bd. Sowela Tech. Inst., 1969—; mem. Regional Export Expansion Council, 1969-70, chmn. code com. 1966—; chmn. coordinating and adv. com. for Ward 1, Calcasieu Parish, La., 1976-77; bd. dirs. Lake Charles Meml. Hosp.; mem. La. Commerce and Industry Bd., 1979—. Served with USNR, 1942-46. Named Jaycee Boss of Year, 1972. Registered profl. engr., La., Tex., Miss., Ark., Tenn., Pa., Md., Del., N.J., D.C., Okla. Mem. La. Engring. Soc. (pres. 1967-68, state dir. 1967-68), Lake Charles C. of C. (dir. 1969-73), Inst. Cert. Engring. Technicians (exam. com.). Baptist (deacon 1955—). Clubs: Lake Charles Quarter Horse (pres. 1966—), Rotary. Home: Levinwood Rd Lake Charles LA Office: PO Box 1865 Lake Charles LA 70602

LEVINSON, DONALD EARL, investment, real estate broker; b. Galesburg, Ill., Nov. 19, 1923; s. Erland Leonard and Esther (Clausen) M.; A.A., North Park Coll., 1948; postgrad. Northwestern U., 1948; m. Lorraine Jeanette Rydstedt, July 15, 1947; children—James, John, Lynn J. Folgate. Sales trainee Hornblower & Weeks, Chgo., 1948-49, registered rep., 1949-53; resident mgr. Hornblower & Weeks-Hemphill, Noyes, Rockford, Ill., 1953-69, v.p., regional cons., 1969-72; pres. Levinson's, Inc., Boca Raton, Fla., 1972—; dir. Hook 'n Horn Ltd., Nestor Falls, Ont., Can. Pres., Friends of North Park Coll., Chgo., 1966-67. Exec. bd. Rockford Coll., 1964-67, counselor, 1958-72. Served with USNR, 1943-46. Mem. Evang. Ch. (chmn. pension fund 1966-67). Rotarian. Club: Mid-Day (pres. Rockford 1965). Address: PO Box 2455 Boca Raton FL 33432

LEVIT, JAY JOSEPH, lawyer; b. Phila., Feb. 20, 1934; s. Albert Jacob and Mary (Cohen) L.; A.B., Case Western Res. U., 1955; J.D., U. Richmond, 1958; LL.M., Harvard U., 1959; m. Heloise Bertman, July 20, 1962; children—Richard Bertman, Robert Edward, Darcy Francine. Admitted to Va. bar, 1958; with firm Williams, Williams, Williams and Williams, Richmond, Va., 1959-60; trial atty. Dept. of Justice, Washington, 1960-64; sr. atty. Electronics div. Gen. Dynamics Corp., Rochester, N.Y., 1965-67; partner firm Stallard & Levit, Richmond, 1967-77, Levit & Mann, 1978—; instr. law U. Mich., 1964-65; adj. asso. prof. law U. Richmond, 1974-77; lectr. labor relations. Served with U.S. Army, 1959-60. Recipient plaque Dept. of Justice, 1964. Mem. Am., Fed., Va. bar assns., Phi Alpha Delta. Democrat. Jewish. Home: 1608 Harborough Rd Richmond VA 23233

LEVITAS, ELLIOTT HARRIS, congressman; b. Atlanta, Dec. 26, 1930; s. Louis J. and Ida (Goldstein) L.; A.B., Emory U., 1952, J.D., 1956; B.A. (Rhodes scholar), Oxford U., 1954, M.A., 1958; postgrad. U. Mich., 1954-55; m. Barbara Hillman, June 8, 1955; children—Karen, Susan, Kevin. Admitted to Ga. bar, 1955; practiced in Atlanta, 1955-75; mem. firm Arnall, Golden, Gregory, 1955-75; mem. Ga. Ho. of Reps., 1965-75; mem. 94th-96th Congresses, 4th Dist. Ga.; mem. com. public works and transp., chmn. subcom. public bldgs. and grounds, mem. subcoms. aviation, oversight and rev.; mem. com. govt. ops., subcoms. commerce, consumer and monetary affairs, subcom. legislation and nat. security; lectr. Emory U., 1959-60, 68-70. Bd. dirs. Atlanta Jewish Community Center, Atlanta Jewish Welfare Fedn. Served to lt. USAF, 1956-58. Mem. Am., Ga., Atlanta, Decatur-DeKalb bar assns. Democrat. Home: 829 Castle Falls Dr NE Atlanta GA 30329 Office: House Office Bldg Washington DC 20515

LEVITCH, HARRY HERMAN, jeweler; b. Memphis, Dec. 24, 1916; s. Samuel and Lena (Feingold) L.; LL.B. cum laude, So. Law U., 1941; LL.B., Memphis State U., 1967; grad. Gemological Inst. Am., 1965; m. Frances Wagner, May 31, 1936; 1 son, Ronald Wagner. Jeweler, diamond specialist, jewelry designer, Memphis, 1936—. Gen. chmn. United Jewish Appeal Southwest Mo. and No. Ark., 1948-50;

del. conf. Am.'s problems, Washington, 1967-69, regional conf. U.S. fgn. policy, Louisville, 1969; mem. Memphis Community Relations Council. Mem. Shelby County exec. bd. Memphis area March of Dimes, 1966—; mem. exec. com. Memphis and Shelby County Music Commn.; mem. adminstrv. com., v.p. Leo N. Levi Nat. Arthritis Hosp., Hot Springs Nat. Park, Ark.; mem. exec. bd. B'nai B'rith Home and Hosp. for Aged. Served with USAAF, World War II. Recipient B award Diamonds Internat., 1969, City of Memphis Award of Merit, 1975. Mem. Memphis area C. of C. (welcoming com. 1965—), Jewelry Industry Council, Retail Jewelers Am., Moose former trustee), Mason (32 deg., Shriner); mem. B'nai B'rith (pres. dist. 7, 1974-75, internat. bd. govs. supreme lodge, 1976—, Vol. of Year 1966-67, del. leadership conf. Israel 1970, chmn. com. dist. pres.'s and immediate past pres.'s, internat. bd. govs.). Clubs: Petroleum, Ridgeway Country, Rotary. Home: 4972 Peg Ln Memphis TN 38117 Office: 400 Perkins Extended Memphis TN 38817

LEVITT, EDWARD HURLEY, real estate exec.; b. Budapest, Hungary, June 8, 1916; s. Louis and Rosza (Pascovits) L.; came to U.S., 1916; naturalized, 1926; student W. Va. U., 1925-26; LL.B. cum laude N.J. Sch. Law, 1929; m. Edna Mae Lankin, May 17, 1959; children—Rita E. (Mrs. Robert Zeleny), Lois (Mrs. John Monaco), Albert M. Pres. Sub-Div. Sales Corp., New Orleans, 1955-60; mng. dir. Crown Indsl. Co. Ltd., British Colony Hong Kong, 1960-71; community mgr. Raldon Housing Corp., Lewisville, Tex., 1972-75; v.p. marketing and sales Goldsmith Devel. Corp., Canyon Creek Ridge, Richardson, Tex., 1975; pres. Town Gate, Inc., Dallas, 1975—; exec. dir. The Landing devel. Columbia Communities, Inc., Houston; dir. sales and mktg. for Waterfall Crossing Condominiums, Dondi Homes. Served with USNR, World War II. Mem. Lewisville C. of C. Mason (32 deg., Shriner), Optimist. Clubs: Royal, Hong Kong Jockey. Contbr. articles to profl. jours. Home: 10732 Sandpiper Ln Dallas TX 75230 Office: 7995 LBJ Freeway Suite 118 Dallas TX 75251

LEVVIS, ROBERT WALTER, printing co. exec.; b. Washington, Sept. 27, 1940; s. Walter E. and Nelle H. (Hudgens) L.; B.A., Drake U., 1962; m. Lynn Barnes, Jan. 19, 1961; children—Tamara Lynn, Todd Jerome. With R.R. Donnelley & Sons Co., Chgo. and Washington, 1966-74; with Arcata Corp., Falls Church, Va., 1974—, regional sales mgr. Central and S.E. regions, 1975—. Coach, Youth Club Soccer, Fairfax, Va., 1971-77; Stroke and Turn judge/starter AAU, 1975-79. Served with USAF, 1962-66. Republican. Episcopalian. Home: 5354 Guinea Rd Fairfax VA 22032 Office: 6400 Arlington Blvd Falls Church VA 22042

LEVY, BETHOE GESSNER (MRS. GUS DANIEL LEVY), graphic arts co. exec.; b. Centralia, Ill., June 14, 1926; d. George Bagur and Ruby Lee (Wilson) Gessner; student Sophie Newcomb Coll., 1943-44; B.A., La. State U., 1947; m. Gus Daniel Levy, Nov. 25, 1948; children—Joel Gessner, Robert George, Gwynneth Alice. Advt. mgr. Home Gardening mag., New Orleans, 1948; script writer WDSU-TV, New Orleans, 1953-55; editor house organ Joseph Katz Co., New Orleans, 1957-58; account exec. Hal Ross Assos., advt. agy., 1958-61; v.p., treas., dir. Creative Services, Inc., New Orleans, 1961—; columnist Clarion Herald, New Orleans, 1963-70. Leader S.E. La. council Girl Scouts Am., 1955-57; various offices PTA, New Orleans, 1959-69; mem. adv. bd. Repertory Theatre of New Orleans, 1971-72. Mem. Women in Communications, Am. Needlepoint Guild (charter mem., officer Greater New Orleans unit 1975—), Alpha Delta Pi. Episcopalian. Home: 3429 Metairie Ct Metairie LA 70002 Office: 535 Gravier St New Orleans LA 70130

LEVY, GORDON HERMAN, family counselor; b. N.Y.C., Sept. 18, 1942; s. Eli Louis and Rose Levy; B.S., Wagner Coll., Staten Island, 1966; M.Ed., Iona Coll., New Rochelle, N.Y., 1971; m. Daphne Grad, June 30, 1968; 1 son, Rory Kirk. Tchr., counselor, 1966—; founder, since dir. Family Resource Center, W. Palm Beach, Fla., 1978—; cons. in field. Mem. Am. Personnel and Guidance Assn. Democrat. Jewish. Home: 1844 Evergreen Dr Lake Clarke Shores FL 33406 Office: 2611 Old Okeechobee Rd West Palm Beach FL 33409

LEVY, JULIUS LAZARD, II, surgeon; b. Clarksdale, Miss., Nov. 13, 1933; s. Julius Lazard and Jeannette (Sack) L.; B.S., Tulane U., 1954, M.D., 1957; m. Donna Ruth Berke, June 11, 1961; children—Laurie Ann, Richard Simon, Andrew Scott. Intern, Charity Hosp., New Orleans, 1957-58, resident surgery, 1958-62; pvt. practice medicine specializing in surgery, New Orleans, 1965—; asso. prof. surgery Tulane U. Sch. Medicine; past pres. Meml. Clinics, Inc. Bd. dirs. Council Jewish Fedns., Jewish Community Center, New Orleans Bd. Health; v.p. Jewish Fedn. New Orleans, past chmn. Jewish Welfare Fund. Served to lt. comdr. USNR, 1963-65. Diplomate Am. Bd. Surgery. Fellow A.C.S., Am. Coll. Gastroenterology; mem. So. Med. Assn., La., Orleans Parish med. socs., Southeastern Surg. Congress, Surg. Assn. La., New Orleans, Alton Ochsner, Oscar Creech surg. socs. Democrat. Jewish (past pres. temple brotherhood). Mason (32 deg., Shriner). Contbr. articles to profl. jours. Home: 4923 St Charles Ave New Orleans LA 70115 Office: 3715 Prytania St New Orleans LA 70115

LEVY, ROBERT ALAN, govt. ofcl.; b. Roxbury, Mass., May 23, 1946; s. Abraham and Florence (Shuman) L.; B.A., Boston U., 1964; M.S., Fla. State U., 1968; postgrad. U. Me., 1964, Auburn U., 1972. With Air Force Exchange Service, Ernest Harmon AFB, Stephenville, Nfld., 1964; researcher Inst. for Govtl. Research, Fla. State U., 1964-65, asst. dean men, 1965-66, counselor, instr., 1966-68; asst. prof. govt., asst. dean students Elmhurst Coll., 1968-69; asst. prof., dir. student activities Miami Dade Community Coll., 1969-72; model cities specialist, community devel. specialist Fla. Dept. Community Affairs, 1972-74; dep. dir. Greater Jacksonville (Fla.) Econ. Opportunity, 1974-76; evaluation analyst Broward Manpower Council, Ft. Lauderdale, Fla., 1976—. Mem. Nat. Council on Aging; nat. advisory council Boston U. Mem. Palm Beach County Community Action Council, S.E. Fla. Assn. Housing Authority Dirs. Mem. Fla. Assn. Community Action Agencies, Fla. State U. Alumni Assn., Nat. Assn. Housing and Redevel. Ofcls. Home: 8513 NW 9th Pl Plantation FL 33317 Office: 330 N Andrews Ave Fort Lauderdale FL 33311

LEWELLYN, JESS WILLIAM, mfg. co. exec.; b. Cedar Hill, Tex., Sept. 1, 1933; s. J.R. and Earlene (Burns) L.; B.S. in Mech. Engring., U. Tex. at Austin, 1960; student Arlington State Coll., 1958, Tex. Wesleyan Coll., 1953; m. Ann Truitt, Aug. 5, 1955; children—Debbie Jane, Jess William. Project engr. Texas Instruments, Dallas, 1959-64; mgr. mfg. Beta Corp. subsidiary Koppers, Dallas, 1964-67; dir. mfg. Gulf Aerospace Corp., Houston, 1967-69; dir. mfg. Volkswagen Products Corp., Fort Worth, Tex., 1969-76; gen. mgr. Royal Mfg. Co., Grand Prairie, Tex., 1976-77; chmn. bd., pres. Glass Center of Hurst, Inc. (Tex.), Metroplex Glass Center, Inc., Arlington, Tex., Metroplex Metal Products, Inc., Hurst, 1977—. Fund raiser, Abilene Christian Coll., 1967-68. Served with AUS, 1953-55. Mem. Tex. Soc. Profl. Engrs., ASME. Republican. Mem. Ch. of Christ (elder). Club: Lions. Home: 1608 Northridge Dr Arlington TX 76012

LEWENHAUPT, ERIC CLAES (COUNT OF SWEDEN), pub. relations exec.; b. Teheran, Iran, June 14, 1912; s. Eric and Marie (Weiss von Hamers) L.; came to U.S., 1962; B.A., U. Stockholm, 1933, B.S., 1937; postgrad. Royal Beskow Sch., Royal Swedish Naval Coll.; m. Countess Eugenia; 1 dau., Countess Alexandra Marie. Diplomat for Royal Swedish Fgn. Office in Moscow, Paris, Rome, and Madrid, 1935-39; admiralty posts, World War II; owner, operator travel burs. in Sweden and Switzerland, 1945-52; pub. relations dir. Royal Swedish Rys., 1953-58; dir. Swedish Clipper Line, 1959-62; exec. dir. Shine Hotels Corp., 1962-64; dir. Carillon Hotel, Miami Beach, Fla., 1965-68; v.p. Gibraltar Life Ins. Corp., 1969-71, Barcelona Hotel and Yacht Club, Miami Beach, 1971-73; internat. dir. GAC Corp., 1973-75. Chmn. City of Miami People to People Com., 1963-68; spl. ambassador for State of Fla., 1967. Served as lt. comdr., Royal Swedish Navy, 1939-45. Decorated knight Grand Cross and Prior of Fla. of Sovereign Order of St. John of Jerusalem, Knight of Malta, Imperial Iranian Order of Sun and Lion, Knight Grand Cross and Prior of Mil. Order of St. Agata, Chevalier de l'Order des Coteaux de Champagne; recipient civic service awards, Mayors of Miami, Miami Beach, Manatee and Dade County, golden plaque award, Am. Cancer Soc. Mem. House of Nobles (Sweden). Lutheran. Clubs: Royal Swedish Yacht; Cape Eleuthera Yacht and Country. Author: Archaeological and Anthropological Research Theses, 1952, 67; The Shardanas-Pharaos Bodyguards-18th Dynasty, 1958; The Vikings, Barbarians or Culturebearers, 1969. Contbr. articles newspapers and sci. mags. Home: Villa Royal Sweden 4531 Prairie Ave Miami Beach FL 33140

LEWIS, ALBERT, hosp. ofcl.; b. Cindy, Ky., May 31, 1932; s. Sherman and Mazie Fern (Sandlin) L.; cert. exec. housekeeper Somerset Community Coll., 1979; m. Anna Lee Dehart, May 24, 1958; children—Danny, Paul, Lesia, Rita, Larry. Coal miner, Hyden, Ky., 1950-64; motor operator Southeastern Ky. Bapt. Hosp., Corbin, 1966-67, exec. housekeeper, 1968—; laborer Peterson Furniture Mfg. Co., Chgo., 1967-68. Served with U.S. Army, 1953-55. Mem. Nat. Exec. Housekeepers Assn. (cert. mem., v.p. Bluegrass chpt. 1976-79). Baptist. Home: Route 6 Box 561 Corbin KY 40701 Office: Southeastern Ky Bapt Hosp 110 Mitchell St Corbin KY 40701

LEWIS, ANNA ELIZABETH, writer; b. Salisbury, N.C., Oct. 24, 1946; d. Samuel Clee and Ruth Geraldine (Weaver) Laster, Sr.; A.A., Stratford Coll., 1966; postgrad. Wake Forest U., 1966-67; m. Jesse Ray Lewis, Jr., Mar. 14, 1970; children—Mary Elizabeth, Laura Ellen. Reporter, advt. saleswoman, photographer Myrtle Beach (S.C.) Sun News, 1967-70, spl. feature writer, 1972-76; pub. relations staff Presdl. Yacht, U.S.S. Sequoia, North Myrtle Beach, S.C., 1978; free-lance writer; free lance advt. sales. Organizer, bd. dirs. Grand Strand Humane Soc., Myrtle Beach, 1969-70. Mem. New Hanover County Humane Soc., Beta Sigma Phi. Democrat. Episcopalian. Home: 410 Antoinette Dr Wilmington NC 28403

LEWIS, ARDEN ISAIAH, gerontologist; b. Stephenville, Tex., Aug. 17, 1914; s. Andrew Isaiah and Anna Marie (Wadley) L.; B.A., Our Lady of Lake U., San Antonio, 1966, M.S.W., 1968; m. Marian Lucile Donaho, Mar. 17, 1934; children—Marilyn (Mrs. Edward G. Wulfekuehler), Phillip Arden, Cynthia Anne, Judith Diane. Commd. 2d lt. U.S. Army, 1935, advanced through grades to col., 1957; ret., 1963; dir. Marshall St. Sr. Center, San Antonio, 1968-71; social service adviser, pvt. cons., 1969-71; adminstr. Office on Aging, San-Antonio-Bexar County, Tex., 1971-77; adv. com. Ret. Sr. Vol. Program, San Antonio, 1974-77; Tex. del. White House Conf. Aging, 1971. Pres. armed forces sect. Am. Recreation Soc.-Cal. Park and Recreation Soc., 1961-62. Decorated Legion of Merit, Army Commendation medal. Mem. Nat. Council Aging, Am. Gerontol. Soc., Ret. Officers Assn., Am. Assn. Ret. Persons, Pi Gamma Mu. Presbyn. (elder). Home: 919 Vanderhoeven Dr San Antonio TX 78209

LEWIS, BARBARA NANCY, correctional inst. counselor; b. Pitts., Jan. 16, 1953; d. Charles William and Dorothy Ann (Kallman) L.; B.A., Antioch Coll., 1972; M.Ed., Ed.S., U. Fla., 1975, Ph.D., 1979. Counselor, N. Central Fla. Community Mental Health Center, 1974-76; counselor drug abuse Fla. Correctional Inst., Lowell, Fla., 1976—. Mem. Am. Personnel and Guidance Assn., Assn. Specialists in Group Work, Phi Kappa Phi, Kappa Delta Pi, Pi Lambda Theta. Home: 3504-31C SW 30 Terr Gainesville FL 32608

LEWIS, CEYLON SMITH, JR., physician; b. Muskogee, Okla., July 19, 1920; s. Ceylon Smith and Glenn (Ellis) L.; A.B., Washington U., St. Louis, 1942, M.D., 1945; m. Marguerite Dearmont, Dec. 20, 1943; children—Sarah Lee Lewis Lorenz, Ceylon Smith, Carol D. Lewis Kast. Intern Salt Lake Gen. Hosp., 1945-46; resident in internal medicine Salt Lake VA Hosp., Salt Lake County Hosp., 1948-51; practice internal medicine and cardiology, Tulsa, 1951—; clin. prof. medicine U. Okla. Tulsa Med. Coll., 1971—; cons. internal medicine USPHS Indian Hosp.; mem. bd. commrs. Joint Commn. Accreditation of Hosps. Trustee, Coll. Ozarks, 1964-72; v.p. Am. Heart Assn., 1973-74; pres. Med. Mission Fund, 1972. Bd. dirs. Tulsa United Way, 1973—. Served to capt. M.C., AUS, 1946-48. Diplomate Am. Bd. Internal Medicine (bd. govs. 1976—). Fellow A.C.P. (gov. Okla. 1974-79); mem. Okla. Med. Assn. (pres. 1977—), Tulsa County Med. Soc. (pres. 1971), Okla. Soc. Internal Medicine (pres. 1971-72). Presbyn. Contbr. articles to profl. jours. Home: 3747 S Wheeling Tulsa OK 74105 Office: 1705 E 19th St Tulsa OK 74104

LEWIS, CHARLTON SCOTT, forest service ofcl. Dept. Agr.; b. Hazlehurst, Ga., Dec. 22, 1948; s. Earnest and Nancy Ann (Todd) L.; B.C.E., Ga. Inst. Tech., 1971; M.S. in Engring., U. Calif., Berkeley, 1976; m. Paulette Gupton, Mar. 29, 1970; children—Stephanie Lynne, Lorinda Ruth, Anna Maria. Civil engr. U.S. Forest Service, Dept. Agr., Asheville, N.C., 1971-75, Berkeley, 1975-77, Roanoke, Va., 1977—; instr. Asheville-Buncombe Tech. Inst., summer 1972. Mem. ASCE (asso.), Nat. Assn. Ch. Musicians in Church of God Mem. Church of God. Composer songs. Home: 1501 Ruritan Rd NE Roanoke VA 24012 Office: 210 Franklin Rd SW Caller Service 2900 Roanoke VA 24001

LEWIS, DANIEL CURTIS, JR., paper co. exec.; b. Suffolk, Va., Aug. 26, 1918; s. Daniel Curtis and Frances (Rawls) L.; A.B. cum laude, Washington and Lee U., 1942; M.B.A. with distinction, Harvard, 1948, D.C.S., 1954; m. Elizabeth Shirley Baer, June 5, 1948; children—Lawrence S., Clifford R., Robert D. Jr. staff accountant Lybrand Ross Bros. & Montgomery, Boston, 1948-49; asst. prof. commerce Washington and Lee U., 1949-52; research asso. bus. adminstrn. Harvard Grad. Sch. Bus. Adminstrn., 1952-54; asst. to pres. Lynchburg Foundry Co. (Va.), 1954-56, controller, 1956-60, sec., asst. treas., 1960-63; asst. sec. Woodward Iron Co. Birmingham, Lynchburg, 1961-63; asst. to pres. The Chesapeake Corp. Va., West Point, 1963-66, v.p. adminstrn., 1966—, also dir.; sec. Greenlife Products Co., 1969—, also dir.; pres. Chesapeake Bay Plywood Corp., 1967—, also dir.; dir. York River Oyster Research Corp., Cands Lumber Co. Chmn. West Point Sch. Bd., 1964-76; mem. Va. Commn. on Higher Edn., 1964-65, Va. Commn. on State and Local Revenues, Expenditures and Related Matters, 1962-63; chmn. Lynchburg Citizens Sch. Study Commn., 1960-61; treas. Va. Found. for Ind. Colls., 1957-63; mem. Va. State Bd. for Community Colls., 1966-76, vice chmn., 1970-71, chmn., 1971-76; mem. Va. Pub. Telecommunications Council, 1972-76. Pres., bd. dirs. Edn!. Found. for Community Colls. Va., 1968-76; mem. West Point Bi-racial Com., 1968—. Bd. dirs. United Fund Lynchburg, 1959-61, v.p., 1960-61; bd. dirs. Lynchburg Guidance Center, 1956-59, pres., 1958-59; bd. dirs. Lynchburg chpt. A.R.C., 1956-59, West Point Improvement Assn., 1964-67; trustee Va. Episcopal Sch., 1960-66, Va. Found. Ind. Colls., 1966-73, Williamsburg Community Hosp., 1967-70; bd. dirs. bus. sch. sponsors Coll. William and Mary. Served with USNR, 1942-46. Mem. Financial Execs. Inst., Newcomen Soc. N.Am., So. Forest Inst. (pres. 1971). Episcopalian (vestryman). Clubs: Harvard of Va., West Point Country (dir.), Ware River Yacht. Home: Tanager Ct West Point VA 23181 Office: The Chesapeake Corp Va West Point VA 23181

LEWIS, DAVID HOWE, physician; b. Rochester, N.Y., Nov. 1, 1935; s. Robert Francis and Emily Ann (Engle) L.; B.S., Denison U., 1957; M.D., U. Rochester Sch. of Medicine, 1962; m. Dorothy Epperly Goodman, Aug 9, 1958; children—Nancy Downing, David Andrew. Intern, U.S. Naval Hosp., St. Albans, N.Y., 1962-63, resident in urology, 1964-65, resident in gen. surgery, Portsmouth, Va., 1965-68; practice medicine specializing in gen. surgery, Martinsville, Va., 1971—. Bd. dirs. Am. Cancer Soc., United Fund, Am. Red Cross, YMCA. Served with USN, 1963-71. Decorated Navy Cross, Bronze Star. Diplomate Am. Bd. Surgery. Mem. Am. Coll. of Surgeons, Va. Surgical Soc., AMA, So. Med. Assn. Republican. Baptist. Club: Rotary. Home: 1245 Sam Lions Trail Martinsville VA 24112 Office: Medical Center Suite 206 Martinsville VA 24112

LEWIS, DON, textile mill exec.; b. Sapulpa, Okla., Aug. 25, 1935; s. Don and Alma M. (Frakes) L.; B.S. in Mech. Engring., Tenn. Tech., 1957; M.B.A., Winthrop Coll., 1975; m. Anne Wright Massey, 1956; children—Lee Anne, Elaine Lynda, Don T. Liaison engr. Chrysler Corp., Detroit, 1957-59 pres. Karting Ways Inc., Gallatin, Tenn., 1959-60; field engr. E.I. Du Pont de Nemours & Co., Wilmington, Del., 1960-67; maintenance engr. Atlas Chem. Industries, Chattanooga, 1967-69; plant engr., apparel div. Springs Mills Inc., Fort Mill, S.C., 1969—. Served with Ordnance Corps, U.S. Army, 1958—. Registered profl. engr., Del. Mem. ASME, Am. Inst. Plant Engrs. (Engr. of Yr. 1974), Instrument Soc. Am. Club: Toastmasters. Home: 1730 Colony Rd Rock Hill SC 29730 Office: Springs Mills Inc Ft Mill SC 29715

LEWIS, DOUGLAS EAZSINSKY, lawyer, hosp. adminstr.; b. Vicksburg, Miss., Aug. 10, 1941; s. Nathan B. and Olga Douglas Lewis; B.A., U. Miss., 1964, J.D., 1966; M.H.A., Va. Commonwealth U., 1973; m. Wanda Jane Wetherington, Dec. 9, 1969; children—Bryan Douglas, Michael Scott. Admitted to Miss. bar, 1966; adminstrv. resident Hamilton Meml. Hosp., Dalton, Ga., 1972-73; adminstrv. asst. Park View Hosp., Nashville, 1973; mem. mgmt. team Caldwell (Idaho) Meml. Hosp., 1974; adminstr. Putnam Meml. Hosp., Palatka, Fla., 1974, Putnam Community Hosp., Palatka, 1974-77; dir. domestic devel. Hosp. Corp. Am., Nashville, 1977—. Served from lt. to capt., U.S. Army, 1966-71; Vietnam. Decorated Bronze Star. Mem. Am. Bar Assn., Miss. Bar Assn., Am. Coll. Hosp. Adminstrs., Am. Soc. Hosp. Adminstrs. Republican. Jewish. Clubs: Rotary (sec. 1974-78), Masons, Shriners. Home: 8102 Dozier Pl Brentwood TN 37027 Office: Hosp Corp Am One Park Pl Nashville TN 37203

LEWIS, EARL CALVIN, clergyman; b. St. Joseph, Mo., Dec. 9, 1901; s. General Washington and Letha (Ramey) L.; B.A., Culver-Stockton Coll., 1930; M.Ed., La. State U., 1950; m. Nina Ruby Quidor, July 13, 1950; children—Alice Letha (Mrs. Dorman K. Gunter), Roberta (Mrs. Charles Davis), John Paul. Ordained to ministry Christian Ch., 1932 minister Bucklin (Mo.) Christian Ch., 1937-40, Baton Rouge Christian Ch., 1949-58, West Side Christian Ch., New Orleans, 1958-61, Harahen Christian Ch., New Orleans, 1962-66, Gould (Ark.) Christian Ch., 1966-67, First Christian Ch., North Little Rock, Ark., 1967-69, Carlisle (Ark.) Christian Ch., 1969—. Tchr., Central High Sch., Baton Rouge, 1956-57, Chalmette (La.) High Sch., 1957-66. Pres., Bayou Metro Civic and Recreation Assn., 1969—, Camp Galilee Campsite Assn., 1979—. Bd. dirs. La. Civic and Moral Found., 1943-58. Served with AUS, 1940-45; ETO. Mason (K.T.); mem. Order Eastern Star. Address: Route 2 Box 299 Jacksonville AR 72076

LEWIS, EVELYN ELDRED, nurse, ednl. adminstr.; b. Sulphur Springs, Ark., Jan. 7, 1935; d. Ben M. and Martha Elizabeth (McArtor) Eldred; diploma Sparks Hosp. Sch. Nursing, Ark., 1955; student West Ark Community Coll., 1955-56, Harding Coll., 1956-57; B.S. in Pub. Health Nursing, George Peabody Coll. for Tchrs., 1960; M.S. in Nursing, U. Colo., 1970; postgrad. U. No. Colo., 1973-74; children by previous marriage—James W. Taylor, Patterson W. Taylor. Staff nurse, Sparks Meml. Hosp., Fort Smith, Ark., 1955-56; office nurse, Fort Smith, 1956; clinic nurse Harding Coll. Health Service, Searcy, Ark., 1956-57; staff nurse Rodgers Hosp. Searcy, 1957; pub. health nurse Sumner County (Tenn.) Health Dept., 1958-59, 60; instr. St. Thomas Hosp. Sch. Nursing, Nashville, 1960-66, Northwestern State U. La., Shreveport, 1966-69; asst. prof. U. No. Colo., Greeley, 1970-74; asso. prof. nursing U. Ark., Fayetteville, 1975—; chmn. asso. degree nursing program curriculum com. U. Ark., 1976—; adv. bd. Home Health Services Ark., Inc., 1977-80; mem. edn. com. advisory bd. Ark. League Nursing; bd. dirs. N.W. Ark. Vis. Nurse Service, 1980—. Mem. Nat. League Nursing. Bus. and Profl. Women's Orgn., Sigma Theta Tau, Beta Sigma Phi. Republican. Episcopalian. Home: PO Box 10-A-6 Route 1 Lowell AR 72745 Office: 218-B Ozark Hall Univ of Arkansas Fayetteville AR 72701

LEWIS, FLOYD WALLACE, electric utility exec.; b. Lincoln County, Miss., Sept. 23, 1925; s. Thomas Cassidy and Lizzie (Lofton) L.; B.B.A., Tulane U., 1945, LL.B., 1949; m. Jimmie Etoile Slawson, Dec. 27, 1949; children—Floyd Wallace, Gail, Julie, Ann, Carol, Michael Paul. Admitted to La. bar, 1949; with New Orleans Public Service, Inc., 1949-62, v.p., chief fin. officer, 1960-62; v.p. Ark. Power & Light Co., Little Rock, 1962-63, sr. v.p., 1963-67; exec. v.p., dir. La. Power & Light Co., New Orleans, 1967-68, pres., 1968-70, chief exec. officer, 1968-71, chmn. bd., 1970-72; pres. Middle South Utilities, Inc., 1970-79, also dir., chief exec. officer, 1972—, chmn., 1979—; pres., dir. Middle South Services, Inc., New Orleans, 1970-75, chmn., chief exec. officer, 1975—; pres., dir. Middle South Energy, Inc., 1974—; chmn. bd. System Fuels, Inc., 1972—; dir. New Orleans br. Fed. Res. Bank, 1974-75, chmn., 1975; dir. Fed. Res. Bank Atlanta, Breeder Reactor Corp., New Orleans Pub. Service, Inc., Ark. Power & Light Co., Ark.-Mo. Power Co., La. Power & Light Co., Miss. Power & Light Co.; mem. adv. com. Elec. Cos. Advt. Program, 1969-72, chmn., 1970-71; mem. electric utility adv. com. to Fed. Energy Adminstrn., 1973-77; chmn. Edison Electric Inst., 1976-77, exec. com., 1974-78, chmn. policy com. on nuclear power, 1974-75; chmn. Electric Power Research Inst., 1979—; mem. exec. com. Assn. Edison Illuminating Cos., 1975—; mem. coal adv. com. Dept. Interior, 1976-78. Deacon, Baptist Ch., 1950—; commr., mem. exec. com. Quapaw Area council Boy Scouts Am., 1964-66, v.p. Quapaw Area council, chmn. Pioneer dist., 1967, mem. exec. bd. New Orleans Area council, 1967—, v.p., 1970-74, pres., 1975-76, mem. bd. South Central region, 1976—; vice chmn. campaign United Fund, New Orleans, 1970, chmn., 1971; bd. dirs. New Orleans Symphony Soc., 1974, Pub. Affairs Research Council of La.; trustee New Orleans Bapt. Sem. Found., 1969—, pres., 1974-76; trustee New Orleans Bapt. Theol. Sem., 1954-62, 63-76, v.p., 1970-75; trustee Com. Econ. Devel., 1973—; bd. adminstrs. Tulane U., 1973—, bd. visitors, 1968-71, gov. Med. Center, 1969-73, vice chmn., 1969-71, chmn.

alumni adv. council Grad. Sch. Bus., 1970-73; v.p. Internat. House, 1970; trustee Gulf South Research Inst.; trustee Com. Better La., 1975-76, sr. v.p., 1976-77, pres., 1977-78. Served to ensign USNR, 1945-46. Recipient Outstanding Alumni award Tulane U., 1970; Silver Beaver, Silver Antelope awards Boy Scouts Am. Mem. Am., La. bar assns., Tulane Alumni Assn. (exec. com., treas. 1970), New Orleans Area C. of C. (v.p. 1970, dir. 1970-73), Nat. Petroleum Council, Order of Coif, Beta Gamma Sigma, Omicron Delta Kappa, Beta Theta Pi, Phi Delta Phi. Home: 5557 Berkley Dr New Orleans LA 70114 Office: 225 Baronne St New Orleans LA 70161

LEWIS, GEORGE MCKOY, banker; b. Valley Mills, Tex., Aug. 3, 1902; s. Samuel Knight and Mary Rebecca (Barrett) L.; B.S., Tex. A. and M. U., 1924; M.B.A., Harvard, 1927; postgrad. U. Chgo., 1929-30; m. Mary Gregory Bunting, Feb. 10, 1940. Mem. staff U.S. Dept. Agr., 1924-25; staff Bur. Bus. Research, U. Tex., 1927-29; Inst. Meat Packing fellow U. Chgo., 1929-30; dir. marketing Am. Meat Inst., Chgo., 1939-57, v.p., 1950-63; vice chmn. bd., economist Jefferson State Bank, San Antonio, 1963—. Vice pres., dir. Am. Meat Inst. Found., 1957-63. Mem. S.A.R., Sons Tex. Republic. Mason (Shriner). Clubs: Quadrangle, Union League, University of Chicago, South Shore Country (Chgo.); Argyle (San Antonio). Home: 715 Wiltshire Ave San Antonio TX 78209 Office: Jefferson State Bank San Antonio TX 78284

LEWIS, GLADYS SHERMAN, nurse, educator; b. Wynnewood, Okla., Mar. 20, 1933; d. Andrew and Minnie Elva (Halsey) Sherman; R.N., St. Anthony's Sch. Nursing, 1953; student Okla. Baptist U., 1953-55; A.B., Tex. Christian U., 1956; postgrad. Southwestern Bapt. Theol. Sem., 1959-60, Escuela de Idiomas, San Jose, Costa Rica, 1960-61; m. Wilbur Curtis Lewis, Jan. 28, 1955; children—Karen, David, Leanne, Cristen. Mem. nursing staff various facilities, Okla., Tex., 1953-57; instr. nursing, med. missionary Baptist Hosp., Asuncion, Paraguay, 1961-70, missionary nurse So. Bapt. Fgn. Mission Bd. Mobile Clinic, 1968-70, mem. staff, 1972-73; vice-chmn. edn. commn. Paraguay Bapt. Conv., 1962-65; sec. bd. trustees Bapt. Hosp., Paraguay, 1962-65; chmn. personnel com., handbook and policy book officer Bapt. Mission in Paraguay, 1967-70; trustee Southwestern Bapt. Theol. Sem., Ft. Worth, Tex., 1974—, chmn. student affairs com., 1976-78, vice-chmn. bd., 1977-79; partner Las Amigas Tours; writer, conference leader, campus lectr., 1959—. Active Democratic party; leader Girl Scouts U.S.A., 1965-75; Okla. co-chmn. Nat. Religious Com. for Equal Rights Amendment, 1977—; tour host Meier Internat. Study League. Recognized for disaster relief work in Honduras, Fgn. Mission Bd., So. Bapt. Conv., 1975; named Woman of Yr., Midwest City, 1979. Mem. Nat. Women's Polit. Caucus, Okla. Women's Polit. Caucus, AAUW, Evang. Women's Caucus, Am. Nurses Assn., Internat., Am. colls. surgeons women's auxiliaries, Okla. State, Okla. County med. auxiliaries. Author religious instructional texts in English and Spanish; contbr. articles to So. Bapt. and secular periodicals; columnist Royal Service, Christian Med. Soc. News and Reports; editor Sooner Physician's Heartbeat. Home: 3620 Ridgehaven Dr Midwest City OK 73110 Office: Suite 10 2828 Park Lawn Plaza Midwest City OK 73110

LEWIS, HENRY FIELDING, JR., pub., investments ofcl.; b. Patterson, La., Nov. 2, 1930; s. Henry Fielding and Margaret Elizabeth (Peterman) L.; student U. So. La., 1948, Southeastern U., 1949; m. Gladys Louise Darby, Feb. 11, 1949; 1 dau., Paula Elizabeth Lewis Slaw. Lumber inspector May Bros. Cypress Co., Franklin, La., 1949-51; with Columbian Carbon Co., Franklin, 1953-56; pres. Franklin Bldg. Materials, Inc., 1958-71; pub. Franklin Post, 1971—, editorial writer; free lance writer; dir. La. Landowners Assn., First Nat. Bank, Riggs Land Co., Inc., Kyle-Peterman Group, Inc., Cour-Win Corp. Mem. West St. Mary Parish Port Commn., Gov.'s Commn. on Atchafalaya Basin; mem. St. Mary Parish Dem. Com. Served with USAF, 1948-49. Episcopalian. Clubs: Jackson Bayou Wildlife Protectors, Duck Hunters. Contbr. articles on land use and floodway to publs., articles to mags. Office: 810 Iberia St Franklin LA 70538

LEWIS, HERBERT D., elec. engr.; b. Cameron, Mo., May 25, 1927; s. Clyde A. and Tina (Dunham) L.; B.S. in Elec. Engring., U. Kans., 1950; m. Marion M. Schulz, Aug. 23, 1952; children—Laureen, Lynn, Leslie. With Wagner Electric Corp., St. Louis, 1950-75; v.p. sales mktg., engring. and customer service Van Tran Electric Corp., Waco, Tex., 1975-77; dist. sales mgr. Kuhlman Electric Co., Jackson, Miss., 1977—. Served with USN, 1945-46, USNR, 1947-59. Mem. Am. Nat. Standards Inst. (chmn. C57 sect. com. 1967-76), IEEE (sr.). Mem. United Ch. of Christ. Clubs: Masons. Home: 1224 Cliffdale Ln Clinton MS 39056 Office: 9 Lakeview Circle Suite B Jackson MS 39216

LEWIS, HOWARD EDWIN, educator; b. Columbus, Ohio, Nov. 14, 1926; s. William and Bessie Belle (Parks) L.; B.S., Ohio State U., 1949, M.A., 1954; Ed.D., Pa. State U., 1966; m. Margaret Williams, May 15, 1959. Mechanic, N. Am. Aviation, Columbus, 1952-53; instr., asst. prof. art, dir. art gallery Fla. A&M U., Tallahassee, 1954-58, asst. prof., asso. prof. art, head dept. art, 1958-62, asso. prof., prof. art, chmn. dept. art, 1964-65, 66-73, prof. art, dir. div. humanities and fine arts, 1973—; artist, research asst., depts. instructional services and art edn. Pa. State U., 1962-64. Mem. adv. council Fla. Alliance for Art Edn.; mem. youth art adv. com. Fla. State Fair; mem. adv. com. Leon County Sch. Dist. Project CARE; trustee Hist. Tallahassee Preservation Bd.; mem. Architecture Rev. Bd. Tallahassee, Tallahassee Arts Council. Served with U.S. Army, 1950-52. Decorated Bronze Star; recipient cert. of award Tallahassee Drifters, Inc., 1979; Exxon research fellow, 1972-74. Mem. Nat. Art Edn. Assn., Fla. Art Edn. Assn., AAUP, Nat. Conf. Artists, World Futurist Soc., Center Study of Democratic Instns., NAACP, Phi Delta Kappa, Alpha Phi Alpha. Democrat. Presbyterian. Home: 1805 Skyland Dr Tallahassee FL 32303 Office: 413 Tucker Hall Fla A & M U Tallahassee FL 32307

LEWIS, JAMES WOODROW, chief state supreme ct. justice; b. Darlington County, S.C., Mar. 8, 1912; s. W. J. and Mary Aletha (Bryant) L.; A.B., U. S.C., 1932; m. Alice Lee, Dec. 26, 1936; 1 dau., Barbara (Mrs. Olin D. Haynes). Admitted to S.C. bar 1935; mem. S.C. Hwy. Commn., 1936-40; mem. S.C. Ho. of Reps. from Darlington County, 1935-36, 43-45; judge 4th Jud. Circuit S.C., 1945-61; asso. justice Supreme Ct. S.C., Columbia, 1961-75, chief justice, 1975—. Office: PO Box 53 Darlington SC 29532

LEWIS, JESSE CORNELIUS, educator; b. Vaughan, Miss., June 26, 1929; s. Jefferson and Elizabeth (Hollins) L.; B.S., Tougaloo Coll., 1949; M.A., U. Ill., 1959, M.S., 1955; Ph.D., Syracuse U., 1966; m. Emma Goldman, May 5, 1973; 1 dau., Valerie. Instr. math. So. U., Baton Rouge, 1955-57, Prairie View (Tex.) Coll., 1957-58; research asst. computer center Syracuse (N.Y.) U., 1963-66; prof. math. Jackson (Miss.) State U., 1966—, dir. computer center, 1966—; sec., dir. State Mut. Savs. & Loan, Jackson, 1969-75. Cons., lectr. Am. Math. Assn., 1971—; chmn. faculty senate Jackson State Coll., 1970-73; project dir. NSF Computing Network, 1973—. NSF Sci. Faculty fellow, 1958, 61. Mem. Math. Assn. Am., Assn. Computing Machinery, Am. Math. Soc., Alpha Phi Alpha. Home: 1566 Schoolview Dr Jackson MS 39213

LEWIS, JOHN MILTON, cable TV co. exec.; b. nr. Slocomb, Ala., Mar. 29, 1931; s. Phil Truman and Vermell Beatrice (Avery) L.; grad. high sch.; m. Mary Lee Robledo, June 9, 1951; children—Janet Lee, Lee Michael. With Gulf Power Co., Panama City, Fla., 1949-56; self employed vehicle service co., Panama City, 1956-58; v.p., dir. Burnup & Sims, Inc., West Palm Beach, Fla., 1958-70; mgr. Cable Antenna TV div. Wometco Enterprises, Inc., Miami, Fla., 1970—, pres. Wometco Communications, Inc.; pres., dir. Middlesex Cablevision, East Brunswick, N.J., 1971—, Allstate Cablevision, Plainfield, N.J., 1971—, Plainfield Cablevision, 1971—, LaFourche-Communications, Inc., Thibodaux, La., 1972—, St. Landry Cable TV, Inc., Opelousas, La., 1973—, Ausable Communications, Inc., Plattsburg, N.Y., 1972—, Alert Cable TV Okla., Paior, Alert Cable TV, Inc., Fort Benning, Ga., Alert Cable TV N.C., Garner; pres. Wometco Home Theatre, Inc., N.Y.C.; cons. in field. Democrat. Mason. Home: 8385 SW 143d St Miami FL 33158 Office: 316 N Miami Ave Miami FL 33128

LEWIS, JOSEPH RAYMOND, advt. exec.; b. Salisbury, N.C., Aug. 20, 1944; s. Joseph Raymond and Marguerite Lewis; B.S., U. Tenn., 1966; m. Wanda Bailey, Mar. 16, 1966; children—Jennifer, Nicole. With Monsanto Co., 1968-72, mktg. mgr., St. Louis, 1970-72; br. mgr. Maritz, Inc., Nashville, 1972-75; account supr. Keller Crescent Advt., Nashville, 1975-77; v.p., gen. mgr. Lawler Ballard Little Advt., Atlanta, 1978—. Participant, Sch. Without Walls, Atlanta city schs. Served with USMCR, 1966-68. Mem. Am. Mktg. Assn., Am. Advt. Fedn., Bus. Profl. Advt. Assn., Atlanta Advt. Club, Atlanta C. of C. Home: 1363 Wesleyan Ct Marietta GA 30067 Office: 550 Pharr Rd NE Suite 300 Atlanta GA 30305

LEWIS, LAWRENCE GLENDON, advt. co. exec.; b. nr. Tuscaloosa, Ala., June 5, 1918; s. Monroe Jordan, Anna (Gardner) L.; student pub. schs.; m. Carrie Mae Hayes, Nov. 7, 1940; children—Robert Jordan, Harriet Anna. Agt., Life & Casualty Ins. Co. Tenn., Nashville, 1939-42, staff mgr. Mobile, 1942-48, tng. supr., 1948, dist. mgr., Jackson, Miss., 1948-56; v.p. Standard Life Ins. Co. of South, Jackson, 1956-65; sales and marketing dir. Mut. Savs. Life Ins. Co., Decatur, Ala., 1965-68; spl. accounts exec., v.p. ins. div. Francis & Lusky Co., Inc., Nashville, 1968—. Served with AUS, 1943-46. Decorated Purple Heart. Past pres. Miss. Assn. Life Underwriters. Baptist. Mason (32 deg., Shriner); mem. Order of Eastern Star (past worthy patron). Home: 127 Twin Bay Dr Hendersonville TN 37075 Office: 1450 Elm Hill Rd Nashville TN 37210

LEWIS, LLOYD JONES, mktg. co. exec.; b. Pangburn, Ark., Dec. 26, 1919; s. Festus C. and Ida (Jones) L.; student pub. schs., Pangburn; m. Anna Ruth Campbell, May 23, 1942; children—Karen, Barry, Anna Mary, Jonathan. Prin., Lewis & Assos., Little Rock, 1949-54; editor, pub. Architect & Builder Mag., New Orleans, 1955-61; sales and mktg. exec. Cornelius Co., Mpls., 1962-73, Rio de Janeiro, Brazil, 1972-73, Atlanta, 1970-73; pres. Refresco Internat. Corp., Atlanta, 1973—; pres. Modular Engring. Corp., Atlanta. Ark. State Commr. Athletics, 1951-53; chmn. Gov. Com. to Employ Physically Handicapped, 1953-54. Served with USN, 1941-45. Recipient Outstanding Archtl. Journalism award AIA, 1960. Mem. Am. Mgmt. Assn. Republican. Clubs: Broadwater Golf and Country, Miami Racquet. Home: 131 Keller Ave Bay Saint Louis MS 39520 Office: 2951 Flowers Rd S Atlanta GA 30341

LEWIS, MARIAN LOUISE MOORE, biochemist, microbiologist; b. Decatur, Ga., Mar. 5, 1937; d. James Marion and Josephen Waldrop (Hightower) Moore; B.A., Ga. State Coll. for Women, 1959; M.S., U. Ariz., 1968; Ph.D. in Biochemistry, U. Houston, 1979; m. Robert Eugene Lewis, Oct. 4, 1968; 1 son, Michael Moore. Technician, virologist Nat. Center for Disease Control, USPHS, Atlanta and Phoenix, 1959-64; virologist Baylor U. Coll. Medicine, Houston, 1964-66, M.D. Anderson Hosp. and Tumor Inst., Houston, 1968-71, Northrop Services Inc., NASA Johnson Space Center, Houston, 1971-73, bacteriologist, summer 1975; sr. research scientist, project leader Technology Inc., Houston, 1979—; microbiologist tissue culture, virology U. Ariz., Tucson, 1966-68. U.S. Dept. Interior grantee, 1966-68; Robert A. Welch predoctoral fellow, 1976. Mem. Am. Soc. Microbiology, Nat. Audubon Soc., Nat. Wildlife Fedn., N.Y. Acad. Scis., AAAS, Nature Conservancy, Sierra Club, Am. Horse Shows Assn., LWV, AAUW, Sigma Xi. Democrat. Methodist. Contbr. articles to sci. jours. Home: 1619 Bowline Rd Houston TX 77062 Office: Technology Inc NASA-JSC-SD-3 Houston TX 77058

LEWIS, MARY GENEVIEVE, librarian; b. Vincennes, Ind., Aug. 28, 1911; d. Claudius Ervin and Isa (Hollister) Lewis; B.A., Northwestern U., 1933, M.A., 1935; B.S., Columbia, 1938. Reference asst., reference librarian Oak Park (Ill.) Pub. Library, 1935-37, 38-43, head reference dept., 1938-43, 45-50; instr. English, head dept. Warren Wilson Coll., Swannanoa, N.C., 1950-61; reference librarian Stetson U., DeLand, Fla., 1961-73; book reviewer. Served to capt. WAC, 1943-45; ETO. Democrat. Presbyterian. Home: Winter Park Towers Room 312 1111 S Lakemont Ave Winter Park FL 32792

LEWIS, MARY GREEN, mgmt. cons., indsl. engr.; b. Dallas, Jan. 22, 1951; d. John A. and Magdalene May (Bucknell) Green; student Tex. Tech. U., 1969-71; B.S. in Indsl. Engring., U. Tex., Arlington, 1973; grad. student U. Tex., Dallas, 1973-74; m. Samuel E. Lewis, May 4, 1973. Research asst. U. Tex., Health Sci. Center, Dallas, 1973-74; sr. cons. Lifson, Wilson, Ferguson & Winick, Inc., Dallas, 1974-77; mgr. Arthur Young & Co., Dallas, 1977—. Mem. Am. Inst. Indsl. Engrs. (dir.). Club: Altrusa of Am. Home: 23 Highland Pl Richardson TX 75081 Office: 2900 Republic Nat Bank Bldg Dallas TX 75201

LEWIS, MICHAEL JUSTIN, physician; b. Point Pleasant, N.J., Apr. 10, 1943; s. Jacob Seyfried and Rebecca June (Cantley) L.; B.S., W.Va. Inst. Tech., 1965; M.S., Va. Poly. Inst., 1967, Ph.D., 1969; M.D., W.Va. U., 1974; m. Deanna Dare Bailey, Apr. 10, 1964; children—Beth Renee, Tana Michelle. Research engr., Union Carbode Corp., Charleston, W.Va., 1968-71; resident in family medicine W.Va. U. Hosp., Morgantown, 1974-75; practice family medicine, St. Marys, W.Va., 1975—; mem. staff St. Joseph's Hosp., Parkersburg, W.Va.; clin. asst. prof. W.Va. Med. Sch.; physician adv. Pleasants County Vol. Emergency Squad; adv. Am. Cancer Soc. Diplomate Am. Bd. Family Practice. Mem. AMA, W.Va. Med. Assn., Am. Acad. Family Physicians. Home: 514 Diamond St Belmont WV 26134 Office: 212 2d St Marys WV 26170

LEWIS, MITCHELL IVES, advt. exec.; b. New Rochelle, N.Y., May 21, 1927; s. Reuben Alexander and Sarah Stewart (Briggs) L.; B.A. cum laude, Washington and Lee U., 1950, Cert. Journalism (M.A.), 1950; m. Marie DuVergne Robert, Sept. 3, 1949 (div.); children—Hallie Cavett, Mitchell Ives, William Robert. Advt. sales staff Dallas Morning News, 1950-53; account exec. Bloom Advt., Dallas, 1954-56; gen. mgr. Couchman Advt. Agy., Dallas, 1956-59; nat. advt. and public affairs dir. McLendon Corp., Dallas, 1959-70; pres. Mitchell I. Lewis & Assos., Inc., Dallas, 1970—. Campaign dir. Noe for Gov. La., 1960, Hartke for U.S. Senate from Ind., 1964, McLendon for U.S. Senate from Tex., 1964. Mem. Sigma Chi, Sigma Delta Chi, Alpha Delta Sigma. Episcopalian. Clubs: Variety, Tent 12, Dallas Press. Home: 5940 Arapaho Rd #295 Dallas TX 75248 Office: 16250 Dallas Pky #201 Dallas TX 75248

LEWIS, ORVAL LEROY, mech. engr.; b. Higgins, Tex., July 27, 1916; s. Roy Henry and Annabee (Ray) L.; B.S. in Mech. Engring., Tex. Tech U., Lubbock, 1939; M.B.A., U. So. Calif., 1954; m. Debbie C. Crouch, May 30, 1939; children—James, Robert, Stephen. Engr., Jones & Laughlin Co., Tulsa, 1940-50; engring. and constrn. mgr. C.F. Braun & Co., Alhambra, Calif., 1950-67; mgr. engring. and constrn. div. Houston Research Inst., 1967-69; v.p., gen. mgr. Zapata Engrs., Inc., Houston, 1969-70; mgr. Fluor Engrs. & Constrn. Co., Houston, 1970-74; dir. bus. devel. Davy Inc., Houston, 1974—; pres. Engring., Sci. and Tech. Service Co., Houston, 1972—. Del. dist. and state Republican Convs., 1974; mem. Mus. Fine Arts. Recipient Outstanding Soil Conservation award Kans. Bankers Assn., 1972; Distinguished Engrs. award Tex. Tech. U., 1977. Fellow ASME (v.p. industry 1974-78, pres. 1978-79); mem. Am. Ordnance Soc. Methodist. Club: Summit (Houston). Contbr. to profl. jours. Office: PO Box 3644 Houston TX 77036

LEWIS, RICHARD KNOX, city ofcl.; b. Auburn, N.Y., June 25, 1946; s. Harry C. and Jean E. (Knox) L.; A.A., Auburn Community Coll., 1968; B.P.A., U. Miss., 1970, M.Urban and Regional Planning, 1972; m. Barbara Ann Blauvelt, Dec. 28, 1968; children—Wendy Michelle, Richard Adam. Project planner Mo. Dept. Community Affairs, Jefferson City, 1971-73; planning dir. City of Ocala, Fla., 1973-79, asst. city mgr., 1979—; chmn. Marion County Tech. Adv. Com.; bd. dirs. Fla. Downtown Devel. Mem. Fla. Planning and Zoning Assn. (pres. springs chpt.), Assn. Am. Inst. Cert. Planners, Assn. Urban Planning, Ocala/Marion C. of C. Republican. Episcopalian. Club: Ocala Silver Springs Rotary (dir.). Home: 3708 SE 4th St Ocala FL 32670 Office: Box 1270 Ocala FL 32670

LEWIS, ROBERT EDWIN, JR., immunologist; b. Meridian, Miss., Mar. 11, 1947; s. Robert E. and Cecille (Ryan) L.; B.A. in Chemistry, U. Miss., 1969; M.S. in Microbiology, 1973; Ph.D. in Pathology (Pathology scholar) U. Miss Med. Center, 1976. Instr. anesthesiology and pathology U. Miss. Med. Center, Jackson, 1976-77, asst. prof. anesthesiology and pathology, 1977—, asst. dir. clin. immunopathology, 1978—. Recipient Robert A. Mahaffey, Jr. Meml. award, 1977. Grantee Am. Cancer Soc., NIH at U. Miss. Med. Center. Mem. N.Y. Acad. Scis., Am. Soc. Anesthesiologists (grantee), Miss. Soc. Anesthesiologists, Can. Soc. for Immunology, Am. Soc. Microbiology, Reticuloendothelial Soc., Miss. Acad. Sci., Royal Soc. Health, Sigma Xi, AAAS, Beta Theta Pi. Baptist. Author: Immunity, Anesthesia and Surgery, 1980; contbr. articles on immunology to sci. jours. Home: 770 Lakeland Dr Jackson MS 39216 Office: Dept of Anesthesiology Univ of Mississippi Medical Center Jackson MS 39216

LEWIS, ROBERT EUGENE, aerospace engr., lawyer; b. Geary, Okla., Oct. 26, 1932; s. Arthur Ready and Mary Kathryn (Hoffman) L.; B.S., U. Tulsa, 1954; postgrad. in electronics So. Methodist U., 1957-60; J.D., U. Houston, 1977, postgrad. in bus. mgmt., 1977-79; m. Marian Louise Moore, Oct. 4, 1968; children—Robert Eugene II, Lisa Gayle (Mrs. Jack Hinkle), Johanna Carol, Michael Moore. Jr. research engr. Stanolind Oil and Gas Co., Tulsa, 1952-54; project engr. Tex. Instruments Inc., Dallas, 1956-63; subsystem mgr. lunar module primary guidance navigation and control system NASA, Johnson Space Center, Houston, 1963-69, avionics mgr. space shuttle studies, 1969-72, systems engring. and avionics mgmt. space shuttle, 1973—. Leader, Sierra Club, 1977—. Served to lt. USNR, 1954-56. Recipient numerous awards NASA. Mem. Tex. Soc. Profl. Engrs., AIAA (chmn. legis. affairs com. Houston chpt. 1978), Am., Houston, Tex. bar assns., Nature Conservancy, Sierra Club (leader 1977—), Tex. Am. Saddle Horse Assn., Order DeMolay (sr.). Contbr. articles to profl. jours. Home: 1619 Bowline St Houston TX 77062 Office: NASA/Johnson Space Center Houston TX 77058

LEWIS, ROSS EARL, Realtor; b. Tex., July 29, 1919; s. Ross Earl and Mattie Ester (Rand) L.; B.A., Tex. Coll., 1941; postgrad. U. So. Calif., 1946-47; m. Travis T. Howard, Nov. 27, 1942; 1 son, Ross Earl. With Civil Service, 1949-72; substitute tchr. Dallas Pub. Schs., 1951-73; salesman Gt. Western United, 1970-73; with Red Carpet Realtors, Dallas, 1974-77; Realtor, owner franchise Realty World, Dallas, 1977—. Served with U.S. Army, 1942-45; ETO. Recipient citation for service Boy Scouts, 1962, Big Bros. Am., 1965. Mem. Nat. Assn. Realtors Bds., Tex. Assn. Realtors, Greater Dallas Bd. Realtors, Urban League. Democrat. Methodist. Clubs: Regular Fellows, K.P. Home: 2807 E Kiest St Dallas TX 75216 Office: 2410 S Hampton Rd Dallas TX 75224

LEWIS, THOMAS EDWARD, comml. real estate devel. co. exec.; b. St. Louis, Aug. 12, 1945; s. Claude Edward and Marian Ann (Wright) L.; B.A., So. Meth. U., 1967; J.D., Emory U., 1970; div.; children—Frances W., Thomas Edward. Admitted to Ga. bar, 1970; mem. firm Stack, O'Brien & Neeley, Atlanta, 1970-72; project devel. mgr. John Portman & Assos., Atlanta, 1972-74; pres., chief exec. Trizec So., Ltd., Atlanta, 1974-78, So. Realty Group, Inc., 1978-79; partner First So. Holdings, 1978-79; pres. Tom Lewis & Assos., Palm Beach, Fla., 1974—; guest lectr. Practising Law Inst., 1975. Served with USAR, 1968-72. Mem. Am., Ga. bar assns. Democrat. Episcopalian. Club: Piedmont Driving. Home: 1200 S Flagler Dr West Palm Beach FL 33401 Office: 139 N County Rd Palm Beach FL 33480

LEWIS, WILBUR CURTIS, surgeon; b. Okmulgee, Okla., Sept. 10, 1930; s. Charles D. and Eula Alice (Cole) L.; B.S., Okla. Baptist U., 1952; M.D., Okla. U., 1955; m. Gladys Sherman, Jan. 28, 1955; children—Karen Kay, Mark David, Leanne Gwynneth, Cristen Sue. Intern, Harris Hosp., Ft. Worth, 1955-56; resident in surgery VA Hosp., Dallas, 1956-57, Univ. Hosp., Oklahoma City, 1965-67; med. missionary So. Bapt. Conv., Costa Rica and Paraguay, 1959-70; practice medicine specializing in surgery, Midwest City, Okla., 1970—; ordained to ministry So. Bapt. Conv., 1953; pastor chs., Okla., Paraguay; leader med. disaster relief team, Honduras, 1975, Guatemala, 1976, Dominican Republic, 1977; mem. staff Midwest City, Bapt., Deaconess, Mercy, St. Anthony hosps., Oklahoma City, Moore (Okla.) Hosp. Served as capt. USAF, 1957-59. Diplomate Am. Bd. Family Practice. Fellow A.C.S., Internat. Coll. Surgeons, Am. Soc. Abdominal Surgeons; mem. AMA, Christian Med. Soc., Oklahoma City Surg. Soc., Oklahoma City Clin. Soc., Midwest City C. of C. (pres.). Democrat. Home: 3620 Ridgehaven Dr Midwest City OK 73110 Office: 2828 Parklawn Dr Midwest City OK 73110 also 3141 NW Expy Oklahoma City OK 73112

LEWIS, WILLIAM CHARLES, television exec.; b. Longview, Tex., Jan. 12, 1947; s. Harry Leigh and Elaine (Bridges) L.; A.A., Kilgore Jr. Coll., 1967; B.S., U. Tex., 1971; m. Carolyn Showalter, Mar. 16, 1969; children—Frances Alison, Elizabeth Ashley. With prodn. dept. KTBC-TV, Austin, Tex., 1969-71; dir. various programming KVUE-TV, Austin, 1971-77; prodn. mgr. KBMT-TV, Beaumont, Tex., 1977-78; dir. KTBC-TV, Austin, 1978—; founder Video-Image Group (teleproduction facility), Austin; cons. Austin Ind. Sch. System, 1976-77.

LEWIS, WILLIAM HEADLEY, JR., mfg. co. ofcl.; b. Washington, Sept. 29, 1934; s. William Headley and Lois Maude (Bradshaw) L.; B.S. in Metall. Engring., Va. Poly. Inst., 1956; postgrad. Grad. Sch. Bus. Adminstrn., Emory U., 1978; m. Carol Elizabeth Cheek, Apr. 22,

1967; children—Teresa Lynne, Bret Cameron, Charles William, Kevin Marcus. Research engr. Lockheed-Ga. Co., Marietta, 1956-57, sr. research engr., 1960-63, research group engr., 1963-72, research and devel. program mgr., 1972-79, mgr. engring. tech. services, 1979—; dir. Applied Tech. Services, Inc., SafeTran Corp.; lectr. grad. studies and continuing edn. Union Coll., Schenectady, 1977—. Served to 1st lt. USAF, 1957-60. Registered profl. engr., Calif. Fellow Am. Soc. for Non-destructive Testing (cert.; nat. dir. 1976-78, chmn. nat. tech. council 1977-78, aerospace com. 1972-74); mem. Am. Soc. for Metals, Nat. Mgmt. Assn. Editor: Prevention of Structural Failures: The Role of Fracture Mechanics, Failure Analysis, and NDT, 1978; patentee detection apparatus for structural failure in aircraft. Home: 1205 W Nancy Creek Dr Atlanta GA 30319 Office: 86 S Cobb Dr Marietta GA 30063

LEWIS, WILLIAM HOMER, wood preserving co. exec.; b. Eufaula, Ala., Apr. 6, 1948; s. Jessie O'ree and Bernice Inez (Stanton) L.; A.A., George C. Wallace Jr. Coll., 1972; B.S. magna cum laude in Bus., Troy State U., 1973, B.S. in Acctg., 1978; m. Winnie Ruth Watford, July 19, 1968; children—William Chadwick, Jon Brett. Acct., G. C. Hartzog, C.P.A., Eufaula, 1974-76, Coats & Mc Cullar, Eufaula, 1976-77; v.p. Great So. Wood Preserving Co., Inc., Abbeville, Ala., 1977—. Served with USAF, 1968-69. Named Outstanding Jaycee, 1978; public acct., Ala. Mem. Abbeville Jr. C. of C. (v.p. 1979—), DAV, Phi Kappa Phi, Gamma Beta Phi. Methodist. Address: PO Box 134 Abbeville AL 36310

LEWIS, WILLIAM JOSEPH, travel cons.; b. Baton Rouge, Apr. 6, 1931; s. Joe F. and Mary Grace (Bonifay) L.; B.S., La. State U., 1952; diploma Nichols State Coll., 1950; m. Mercedes Bouteric, June 3, 1952; children—Catherine, Susan, William Joseph, Richard, Michael, Nancy, David, Anne, Mary, John Paul, Christopher. Shift supr. Delta Airlines, 1952-56; traffic supr. Ethyl Corp., Baton Rouge, 1956—. Mem. Cath. Diocese Sch. Bd., 1964-72. Mem. Nat. Passenger Traffic Assn., La. Motor Transport Assn. Democrat. Roman Catholic. Club: Baton Rouge Kiwanis (dir. 1960-62). Office: Ethyl Corp PO Box 341 Baton Rouge LA 70821

LEYENDECKER, IDA RAY, computer co. exec.; b. San Antonio, Aug. 30, 1941; d. Lloyd G. and Eddith R. (Oden) Williams; m. Arthur J. Leyendecker, Apr. 8, 1966; children—Patrick C., Bridget E. Legal sec. Gibbon & Gibbon, Attys., Harlingen, Tex., 1975; asst. comptroller Sea Breeze, Inc., Brownsville, Tex., 1975-77; exec. asst. to pres. Control Systems, Brownsville, 1977—. Office: 44 W Jefferson St Brownsville TX 78520

L'HERISSON, LAWRENCE EDWARD, psychiatrist; b. Minden, La., May 9, 1925; s. Charles Edward and Nellie Mai (Hehir) L'H.; B.S., La. State U., Baton Rouge 1945, M.D., New Orleans, 1947; m. Mary Vallie Sloan, Mar. 17, 1947; children—Laura Ann, Lawrence Edward, Sandra Sloan. Intern, Shreveport Charity Hosp., 1947-48; resident Huey B. Long Charity Hosp., Pineville, La., 1948-49; gen. practice medicine, Coushatta, La., 1949-72; resident in psychiatry Confederate Meml. Med. Center, Shreveport, 1973-75; practice psychiatry, Shreveport, 1975—; asst. prof. psychiatry La. State U. Med. Sch., Shreveport, 1976—; owner, mgr. L'Herrison Hanna Clinic and Hosp., Coushatta, 1952-72; dir. Am. Bank & Trust, Coushatta. Coroner, Red River Parish, 1961-72; dep. coroner Caddo Parish, 1976-78. Served with U.S. Army, 1944-45. Diplomate Am. Bd. Family Physicians, Am. Bd. Psychiatry and Neurology. Fellow Am. Acad. Family Physicians; mem. Caddo Parish, La. med. socs., AMA, La., Am. acads. gen. practice, La., Am. psychiat. assns., Am. Legion. Baptist. Clubs: Mason, Shriners. Home: 104 Chelsea Dr Shreveport LA 71105 Office: 827 Margaret Pl Shreveport LA 71101

LI, KU-YEN, chem. engr.; b. Taiwan, Aug. 4, 1945; came to U.S., 1972; s. Chia-Chou and Yeah-Lee (Tsai) L.; B.S., Cheng Kung U., Taiwan, 1968, M.S., 1970; Ph.D., Miss. State U., 1977; m. Sherry Tsong-Dsu Chang, May 25, 1973; 1 son, Joy Frank. Prodn. engr. Miss. Chem. Corp., Pascagoula, Miss., 1975-78; asst. prof. chem. engring. Lamar U., Beaumont, Tex., 1978—; prin. investigator Project of Silicon Material Task of Low-Cost Solar Array, U.S. Dept. Energy, 1978—. Registered profl. engr., Miss. Mem. Am. Inst. Chem. Engrs. (affiliate), Am. Chem. Soc., Sigma Xi, Phi Tau Phi. Contbr. articles to profl. jours. Home: 177 Briggs St Beaumont TX 77707 Office: Box 10053 Lamar University Beaumont TX 77710

LI, SHENG SAN, elec. engr.; b. Taiwan, Dec. 10, 1938; s. Swei Suen and Kou Shey (Ku) L.; B.S.E.E., Taiwan Cheng Kung U., 1962; M.S., Rice U., 1966, Ph.D., 1968; m. Bih-Jean Chen, Apr. 19, 1964; children—Jim, Grace, Jeanette. Electronics engr. Taiwan Electric Mfg. Co., Taipei, 1963-64; reseach asst. Rice U., Houston, 1964-67; electronics engr. Nat. Bur. Standards, Washington, 1975-76; prof. elec. engring. U. Fla., Gainesville, 1968—. Mem. IEEE, Am. Phys. Soc., Electrochem. Soc., ASTM, Sigma Xi. Contbr. articles in field to profl. jours. Home: 3531 NW 35th Pl Gainesville FL 32605 Office: 227 Benton Hall U of Fla Gainesville FL 32611

LIANG, SHU-JAN, educator; b. Canton, China, Apr. 21, 1934; s. We-Nan and Kao-Hsiun (Chen) L.; came to U.S., 1965; B.A., Nat. Taiwan U., 1958; M.A., U. Cal. at Los Angeles, 1967; Ph.D., U. Okla., 1970; m. Jane Lee, Mar. 24, 1962; children—Paul, Perry, Frank. Research asst. U. Okla., 1968-70; asst. prof. econs. Loyola U., New Orleans, 1970-73, asso. prof., 1973—. Gen. Electric Found. grantee, 1973. Mem. Am. Econ. Assn. Author: Progress Report On Oklahoma Economy, 1959-68, 1969; Progress of Louisiana Economy: 1960-1970, 1973; Manufacturing in Louisiana, 1975; Impact of the Government Sector on the Louisiana Economy, 1976; The Trade Sector of Louisiana Economy, 1977; The Agricultural Sector of the Louisiana Economy, 1979; The Mining Sector of Louisiana Economy, 1980. Home: 4100 Medoc Dr Kenner LA 70062 Office: Loyola U New Orleans LA 70118

LIBBEY, JAMES KEITH, coll. dean; b. Holden, Mass., May 16, 1942; s. Russell J. and Narcissa (Gleason) L.; B.A., Miami U., Ohio, 1964; B.S. Edn., 1967; M.A., Eastern Ky. U., 1971; Ph.D. (dissertation yr. fellow), U. Ky., 1976; m. Joyce M. Holmes, Dec. 28, 1963. Tchr., St. Michael Sch., Brookville, Ind., 1964-67; instr. U. Ky., Lexington, 1973-74; asst. prof. Eastern Ky. U., Richmond, 1974-78, asso. prof., 1978, asso. dean Coll. Arts and Humanities, 1979—; cons. So. W.Va. Community Coll., Logan, 1977. Mem. Richmond Food Bank Com., 1975—. Served with AUS, 1967-69. Recipient Book award Phi Alpha Theta, 1976. Mem. Am. Assn. Advancement Humanities, Am. Assn. Advancement Slavic Studies, Assn. Gen. and Liberal Studies, Ky. Hist. Soc., Orgn. Am. Historians, Soc. Historians Am. Fgn. Relations, Phi Alpha Theta, Phi Delta Kappa. Democrat. Roman Catholic. Author: Alexander Gumberg and Soviet-American Relations, 1977; Dear Alben: Mr. Barkley of Kentucky, 1979. Home: 937 Vickers Village Richmond KY 40475 Office: Eastern Ky U Richmond KY 40475

LICHTER, WOLF, microbiologist, researcher, educator; b. Liegnitz, Poland, July 17, 1930; came to U.S., 1957, naturalized, 1963; s. Josef Elijahu and Eva (Kaufmann) L.; B.S.C., U. Miami, 1965, M.S., 1974, Ph.D., 1977; m. Alice Kibrit, June 14, 1959; children—Leon, Eva, Janet, Josef. Project supr. Connaught Med. Lab., U. Toronto (Ont., Can.), 1955-57; sr. project supr. dept. microbiology U. Miami Sch. Medicine, 1957-70, research asst., 1970-72, research asso., 1972-78, research asst. prof., 1978—. Bd. dirs. South Dade Hebrew Acad., 1972-74; v.p. Torah Acad., 1975-77. Mem. Reticuloendothelial Soc., Tissue Culture Assn., Am. Soc. for Microbiology, Am. Assn. Immunologists, N.Y. Acad. Scis., Sigma Xi. Democrat. Jewish. Contbr. articles to profl. jours. and books. Home: 1235 NE 172d St Miami FL 33162 Office: U Miami Sch Medicine Dept Microbiology R91 PO Box 016960 1660 NW 10th Ave Miami FL 33101

LICKER, DANIEL, fabric book mfg. exec.; b. N.Y.C., Oct. 9, 1921; s. Jacob A. and Ann L.; student CCNY, 1941, Bklyn. Poly. Inst., 1943; m. Apr. 21, 1974; children—Sharyn Yesner, Joan Carsten, Guy Davis, Lee Davis. Tool engr. Brewster Aero. Corp., N.Y.C., 1942-45; supr. planning and estimating L.B. Smith Aircraft Corp., Miami, Fla., 1956-64; dir. planning and purchasing Aerosmith Products Co., Miami, 1964-70, pres., gen. mgr. Hea-Tar, Inc., Miami, 1971—. Fin. v.p. Temple Or Olom, Miami, 1976—. Served with AC, U.S. Army, 1945-46. Democrat. Office: Hea-Tar Inc 4763 E 11th Ave Hialeah FL 33012

LIDDELL, LILLIE FRANCES PAYNE, educator; b. Columbia, La., Nov. 5, 1944; d. Ollie and Olivia (Williams) Payne; B.S., Grambling (La.) State U., 1967; M.Ed., N.E. La. U., 1971; Ed.S., Miss. State U., 1976, Ed.D., 1979; m. Lewis Liddell, Nov. 3, 1967; children—Lewis, Ollie Eugene, Jeremiah Duane, Frances Olivia. High sch. tchr., 1967-71; asst. prof. bus. edn. Jackson (Miss.) State U., 1971—, also supr. bus. edn. student tchrs. Active Miss. Kidney Assn. Grantee Jackson State U., 1975-76; Kellogg fellow, 1975-76. Mem. Nat., So., Miss. bus. edn. assns., Am. Vocat. Assn., AAUW, Phi Delta Kappa, Phi Gamma Nu (co-sponsor Iota chpt.). Democrat. Baptist. Home: 568 Woodson Ct Jackson MS 39206 Office: Box 7075 Station C JR Lynch Jackson MS 39217

LIDDLE, WILLIAM DYER, JR., pediatrician; b. Welch, W.Va., Mar. 8, 1927; s. William Dyer and Esther (Jarrett) L.; B.A., U. Va., 1950, M.D., 1954; m. Betty Sebrell, Aug. 24, 1952; children—William D. III, Spencer S., Margaret E. Intern, resident in pediatrics U. Va. Med. Sch., 1954-57; practice medicine specializing in pediatrics, Fredericksburg, Va., 1957—; chief staff Mary Washington Hosp., 1963; chmn. bd. Blue Shield Va., 1977-78; dir. Rappahannock Savs. & Loan Assn. Served with AUS, 1946-47. Fellow Am. Acad. Pediatrics; mem. AMA, So. Med. Assn., Va. Med. Soc. Republican. Clubs: Potomac River Yacht, Fredericksburg Country, Farmington Country. Contbr. articles to med. jours. Home: 918 Mortimer Ave Fredericksburg VA 22401 Office: 2301 Fall Hill Ave Fredericksburg VA 22401

LIEBER, ARNOLD LOU, psychiatrist; b. Phila., Oct. 6, 1937; s. Marshall Max and Henrietta F. (Becket) L.; B.A., Trinity Coll. (Conn.), 1959; M.D., U. Miami, 1964; m. Linda Schlereth, June 12, 1961; children—Allison, Cynthia, Marshall. Intern, Malcom Grow USAF Hosp., Andrews AFB, Md., 1964-65; resident U. Miami (Fla.) Med. Sch., 1969-72; instr. psychiatry U. Miami Med. Sch., 1972, asst. prof., 1973, clin. asso. prof., 1979; chmn. dept. psychiatry St. Francis Hosp., Miami Beach, Fla., 1980—. Psychiat. cons. City of Miami Police Dept., 1972-75. Served to capt., M.C., USAF, 1964-68. Decorated USAF Commendation medal; recipient SAMA award in neuropsychiatry Roche Labs., 1972. Diplomate Nat. Bd. Med. Examiners, Am. Bd. Psychiatry and Neurology. Mem. Internat. Soc. Biometeorology, Am. Psychiat. Assn., South Fla. Psychiat. Soc. (legis. rep.), AMA. Author: The Lunar Effect, 1978. Contbr. articles to profl. jours., poetry to lit. and profl. jours. Home: 5934 Pine Tree Dr Miami Beach FL 33140 Office: 317 NE 24 St Miami FL 33137

LIEBERMAN, BARNARD LEON, physician; b. Chernigov, Russia, Dec. 13, 1902; s. Israil and Pearl (Jarnofsky) L.; B.S., Wayne State U., 1925, M.B., 1925, M.D., 1926; Sc.D., London Inst. Applied Research, 1973; m. Mary McKinney, Nov. 22, 1944; 1 son, Douglas Lionel. Came to U.S., 1906, naturalized, 1920. Intern Providence Hosp., Detroit, 1925-26; resident Herman Kiefer Receiving Hosp., 1926-28; instr. obstetrics Wayne State U., 1926-28; practice medicine specializing in obstetrics and gynecology, Detroit, 1928-69; attending obstetrician Evang. Deaconess Hosp., Detroit, 1928-43; chief staff North Detroit Gen. Hosp., 1944-65, now mem. staff emeritus. Cons. North Detroit Gen. Hosp., 1965-69. Bd. trustees North Detroit Gen. Hosp., 1944-65. Recipient Brotherhood Week award Armenian Ch. of North Am., 1962; Citation for Distinguished Leadership in Am. Reform Judaism, 1962; Religious Leadership award U. Am. Hebrew Congregations, 1969. Mem. A.M.A. (life), Phi Lambda Kappa (v.p. 1939). Jewish religion (pres. Temple Emanu El 1958-60). Mason (Shriner); mem. B'nai B'rith. Author: Vaccination in Pregnant Women and New Born Children. Contbr. articles to profl. jours. Address: 668 El Centro Longboat Key FL 33548

LIEBERMAN, DAVID MARTIN, educator; b. Jersey City, July 30, 1918: s. Joseph and Jennie (Jaffe) L.; B.A., U. N.C., Chapel Hill, 1939; J.D., St. John's U., Jamaica, N.Y., 1943; M.B.A., Adelphi U., Garden City, N.Y., 1971; m. Marion Hersh, Apr. 2, 1944; 1 son, Philip Alden. Admitted to N.Y. State bar, 1943; individual practice, 1943-73; mem. faculty Western Piedmont Community Coll., Morganton, N.C., 1973—, chmn. dept. bus., 1976—. Mem. Am. Bus. Law Assn., So. Risk and Ins. Assn. Jewish. Club: Rotary. Author: Your Introduction to Real Estate, 1979. Composer various works. Address: Route 10 Box 230 Morganton NC 28655

LIEBMANN, SEYMOUR W., constrn. co. exec.; b. N.Y.C., Nov 1, 1928; s. Isidor W. and Etta (Waltzer) L.; B.S. in Mech. Engring., Clarkson Coll. Tech., 1948; grad. Indsl. Coll. Armed Forces, 1963, Command and Gen. Staff Coll., 1966, Army War Coll., 1971; m. Hinda Adam, Sept. 20, 1959; children—Peter Adam, David W. Area engr. constrn. div. E.I. DuPont de Nemours & Co., Inc., 1952-54; constrn. planner Lummus Co., 1954-56; prin. mech. engr. Perini Corp., 1956-62; v.p. Boston Based Contractors, 1962-66; v.p. A.R. Abrams, Inc., Atlanta, 1967-74, pres., 1974-78, also dir.; founder Liebmann Assos., Inc., constrn. cons., Atlanta, 1979—; dir. Abrams Industries; mem. nat. adv. bd. Am. Security Council. Mem. USO Council, Atlanta, 1968—, v.p., 1978, mem. exec. com., 1975-79; mem. Nat. UN Day Com., 1975. Served to 1st lt. C.E., AUS, 1948-52; col. Res. ret. Recipient U.S. Army Res. medal, 1975; decorated Legion of Merit, Meritorious Service medal; elected to Old Guard of Gate City Guard, Atlanta, 1979. Registered profl. engr., N.Y., Mass., Ga. Fellow Soc. Am. Mil. Engrs.; mem. Soc. First U.S. Inf., Res. Officers Assn. U.S., Nat., Ga. socs. profl. engrs., Engrs. Club Boston, Assn. U.S. Army, Def. Preparedness Assn., Mil. Order World Wars. Mason (32 deg., Shriner), Elk. Clubs: Civitan (Atlanta); Ft. McPherson Officers. Author: Military Engineer Field Notes, 1953; Prestressing Miter Gate Diagonals, 1960. Contbr. articles to publs. Home: 3260 Rilman Dr NW Atlanta GA 30327 Office: 6520 Powers Ferry Rd Suite 200 Atlanta GA 30339

LIEBSCHER, ANTON IGNAZ, shoe mfg. equipment co. exec.; b. Czechoslovakia, Dec. 26, 1909; s. Anton and Marie (Schubert) L.; came to U.S., 1952, naturalized, 1958; B.S. in Chem. Engring., Tech. U., Dresden, Ger., 1933; B.A. in Bus. Adminstrn., U. Leipzig (Ger.), 1934; m. Gertrude Leitz, Aug. 21, 1937; children—Gerry, Ilse Liebscher Avery. From engr. to mng. dir. Deutsche Asbestos Co., Berlin, 1934-44; plant mgr., chief engr. Dicknow Machine Co., Goerlitz, Ger., 1944-46, Rhein Chemie Co., Mannheim, Ger., 1946-51; chief chemist WELLCO Shoe Corp., Waynesville, N.C., 1952-58; mng. dir. WELLCO Jamaica Ltd., Kingston, 1958-61; chief chemist, purchasing agt. WELLCO Ro-Search, Inc., Waynesville, 1961-65, dir., 1966—; v.p., tech. dir. WELLCO Enterprises, Waynesville, 1965—, also dir.; dir. Hi-Pals, Inc. Mem. Instn. Rubber Industries, Am. Def. Preparedness Assn. Patentee in field. Home: PO Box 224 Hazelwood NC 28738 Office: PO Box 188 Waynesville NC 28786

LIEF, THOMAS PARRISH, sociologist, educator; b. N.Y.C., Oct. 4, 1931; s. Alfred and Zola Nina (Vogel) L.; B.A., U. N.Mex., 1955, M.A., 1961; Ph.D., Tulane U., 1971; m. Dona Lee Keith, May 20, 1961; children—Aram Parrish, Shane Taylor. Tech. asst. dept. sociology Tulane U., 1951-64; instr., asst. prof., chmn. dept. sociology Loyola U., New Orleans, 1964-68, lectr. Inter-Am. Center, 1964-69; asso. prof., prof. sociology So. U., New Orleans, 1968—. Cons., AFL-CIO Am. Inst. Free Labor Social Devel., Loyola U., Tuskegee Inst.'s Social Work Drug Abuse Program; mem. teaching staff Tulane U. Tchr. Desegregation Program, Loyola U. Inter-Am. Center; research dir., bd. dirs. Drug Abuse Research Team; bd. advisors trainer/cons. Desire Narcotics Rehab. Center; dir. So. U. Tng. Program for Control Drug Abuse; mem. adv. bd. Tng. Corp. Am.; pres. adv. bd. Odyssey House La., 1972-73; bd. dirs., mem. exec. bd. Community Service Center; mem. La. Statewide Health Coordinating Council, New Orleans Assn. Drug Abuse Program Dirs., La. Conf. for Juvenile Correctional Workers; chmn. bd. cert. exam. La. Assn. Substance Abuse Counselors and Trainers; pres. bd. dirs. Discover, Inc., Delinquency-Drug Abuse Prevention Center, 1974—; pres. bd. dirs. Rehab. Services, Inc. Tech. adviser Mayor's Action Com. on Drug Abuse, 1971-73; mem. Mayor's Com. to Create Human Relations, 1968; mem. ad hoc drug task force New Orleans Criminal Justice Coordinating Council, 1971, ad hoc com. Mayor's Com. for New Orleans Odyssey House, 1972; mem. La. Drug Adv. Council, 1973—. Mem. adv. bd. La. Narcotics Rehab. Commn., New Orleans Bur. Drug Affairs. Served to capt. USAF, 1955-58. Recipient Merit award Inter-Am. Center, 1967, certificate of merit Mayor of New Orleans, 1973. NSF summer fellow, 1963. Fellow Soc. Applied Anthropology; mem. Am., So. sociol. assns., Am. Acad. Polit. and Social Scientists, Nat. Assn. Concerned Drug Abuse Workers, Soc. for Study Social Problems. Contbr. chpt. to Man and Race, 1965. Home: 1521 Hillary St New Orleans LA 70118 Office: 6400 Press Dr New Orleans LA 70126

LIEK, JAMES EUGENE, realtor; b. Cedar Rapids, Iowa, Apr. 26, 1926; s. James Clyde and June Marie (Cummins) L.; B.A., U. Iowa, 1950, M.A., 1952; m. Ellen Lucille Johnson, July 13, 1970; children—Robert, Barbara Ritter, Thomas Kolt, David Baker, Craig Baker. Vice pres. Mortgage Assos., Inc., Milw., 1962-65, First Wis. Nat. Bank, Milw., 1965-74; exec. v.p. Instl. Investors Trust Co., N.Y.C., 1974-77; pres. I.I.T. Fla. Corp., Boynton Beach, Fla., 1977—. Served with USNR, 1944-46. Mem. Soc. Real Estate Appraisers (past chpt. pres.). Home: 911 Gardenia Dr Apt 550 Delray Beach FL 33444 Office: 10236 Cedar Point Blvd Boynton Beach FL 33437

LIGHT, HERMAN OLVIE, JR., mfg. co. exec.; b. Norwood, Mo., Nov. 19, 1927; s. Herman Olvie and Verna Mae (Scott) L.; A.A., San Diego City Coll., 1967; m. Mary Elizabeth Dennis, Apr. 26, 1946; children—James Herman, Rebecca Ann, Mark Alan. Inspector, Rohr Industries, Chula Vista, Calif., 1956-61, quality assurance engr., 1961-69, mgr. quality assurance, 1970-73, mgr. quality assurance Rail div., Winder, Ga., 1973-76; mgr. quality assurance Blue Bird Body Co., Ft. Valley, Ga., 1976—. Served with USN, 1946-48. Democrat. Baptist. Club: Lions. Office: PO Box 937 Fort Valley GA 31030

LIGHT, LEE RAYMOND, physician; b. Chgo., Sept. 27, 1946; s. Theodore and Sylvia L.; B.A., U. Ill., 1968, M.D., 1972; m. Eugenia Scor, Aug. 23, 1970; children—Eric Harold, Gabrielle Elizabeth. Intern, U. South Fla., Tampa, 1972, resident in internal medicine, 1973-75; practice medicine, Naples, Fla., 1975—; chmn. dept. medicine Naples Community Hosp., 1978—. Diplomate Am. Bd. Internal Medicine. Mem. A.C.P., Am. Soc. Internal Medicine, AMA, Fla. Med. Assn. Office: 850 Central Ave Naples FL 33940

LIGHTSEY, SARA NELL, educator; b. Centreville, Ala., Feb. 28, 1928; d. David Henley and Martha Ardelle (McCrary) L.; B.S., U. Montevallo, 1950; M.A. in Home Econs. Edn., U. Ala., 1957. Home econs. tchr. Shelby County High Sch., Columbiana, Ala., 1950-54, Montevallo (Ala.) High Sch., 1954-57; tchr. home econs. U. Montevallo, 1957—, asso. prof., 1966-67; dir. Home Mgmt. House, 1957—. Mem. AAUW, Am. Home Econs. Assn., Ala. Home Econs. Assn., NEA, Ala. Edn. Assn., Kappa Delta Pi. Baptist. Office: Dept Home Econs U Montevallo Montevallo AL 35115

LIGON, HELEN HAILEY, educator; b. Lott, Tex., Feb. 7, 1921; d. Rolla Will and Bobbye A. (Ruble) Hailey; B.S., Tex. Women's U., Denton, 1942, M.A., 1945; Ph.D., Tex. A & M U., 1976; m. William Grady Ligon, Jr., July 26, 1941; 1 son, William Grady III. Instr., Tex. Women's U., 1942-45; secondary tchr. Lott Pub. Schs., 1947-52, Marlin (Tex.) Pub. Schs., 1952-55; asst. to contracting officer Phillips Petroleum Co., McGregor, Tex., 1955-56; sec. to factory mgr. Gen. Tire Co., Waco, Tex., 1956-58; instr. Hankamer Sch. Bus., Baylor U., Waco, 1958-60, asst. prof., 1960-62, asso. prof., 1962-77, prof. statistics and mgmt. info. systems, 1977—, dir. Casey Computer Center, 1962—. Named Most Popular Bus. Prof., Baylor U., 1962, 67, 78, Outstanding Baylor Faculty Woman, 1967, Outstanding Faculty Mem., 1979. Mem. Data Processing Mgmt. Assn., Assn. Computing Machinery, Soc. Mgmt. Info. Systems, Am. Statis. Assn., Beta Gamma Sigma, Delta Kappa Gamma (local pres. 1967-68, mem. state com. for research 1977-78), Sigma Iota Epsilon. Democrat. Presbyterian. Home: Box 388 Lott TX 76656 Office: Box 6278 Waco TX 76706

LIGON, JOHN JETER, state ofcl.; b. Pamplin, Va., Jan. 1, 1924; s. Thomas Jeter and Logan (Gilliam) L.; B.S., Va. Poly. Inst. and State U., 1949; m. Mary Eagleman, May 20, 1950; children—Wallace R., Arthur J., Jane G., Keith B. With Va. Dept. Agr., Richmond, 1950—, internat. trade specialist, 1966-68, internat. trade dir., 1968—; mem. trade mission to Peking, 1979. Vice pres., bd. dirs. McGuire Civic Assn.; chmn. bd. deacons Westover Bapt. Ch. Served with U.S. Army, 1942-46. Recipient Appreciation award People to People, 1973; Distinguished Service to Agr. award Va. Farm Bur., 1977. Mem. Atlantic Internat. Mktg. Assn. (1st pres.), So. U.S. Trade Assn., Richmond Export/Import Club. Author: (with Sidney Miller) International Marketing Handbook, 1977. Home: 7521 Dell Dr Richmond VA 23235 Office: 203 Governor St Richmond VA 23219

LIKES, DAVID HENRY, educator, ret. air force officer; b. N.Y.C., Aug. 4, 1914; s. Slyvan Henry and Mamie (Leopold) L.; B.A., Johns Hopkins, 1936; postgrad. Harvard U., 1938-39; M.A. (Univ. fellow), Georgetown U., 1948, Ph.D., 1949; m. Grace Ann McWilliams, Feb. 28, 1948 (dec. Dec. 1971); children—David McWilliams, Lawrence Andrew; m. 2d, Adeline Lee Stuckey, July 15, 1972; stepchildren—Elizabeth Stuckey Hagan, Lauren Stuckey Glass. Commd. 2d lt. USAF, 1941, advanced through grades to col., 1945; mem. U.S. Mil. North African Mission, Cairo, 1942; assigned desert air task force, component USAF Middle East 9th Air Force, USAF

Middle East, Egypt, 1942-43; mem. overlord planning staff, London, Eng., 1943-44; assigned 1st Airborne Army, 1944-45; mem. mil. del. Potsdam (East Germany) Conf., 1945; assigned War Plan div. USAF, 1948-51; mem. standing group NATO, Washington, 1951-52, U.S. Naval War Coll., 1952-53; mem. U.S. Mission to NATO, Paris, 1953-56; mil. air staff planner War Plans Div. Air Staff, Washington, 1956-58; dep. dir. NSC Affairs, Office Sec. Def., 1958-59; mem. faculty Nat. War Coll., 1959-61; mem. Aero. Space Studies Inst., Maxwell AFB, Ala., 1961-63; ret., 1963; prof., chmn. dept. internat. studies Southwestern at Memphis, 1963—. Cons. Inst. Internat. Studies U. S.C., Islamic and Arabian Devel. Studies Duke U., Durham, N.C.; Ford Found. postdoctoral research fellow Duke U., 1967-68; research fellow Center Middle Eastern Studies Harvard, 1975-76. Bd. govs. Internat. Group, English Speaking Union. Decorated Legion of Merit, Bronze medal with oak leaf cluster. Mem. Polit. Sci. Assn., Assn. Asian Studies, Middle East Studies Assn., Inst. Naval Procs., Am. Acad. Polit. Sci., Air Force Assn., Ret. Officers Assn., Gold Key Soc., Omicron Delta Kappa, Pi Sigma Alpha. Clubs: Tennessee (Memphis); Willowbrook Country (Tyler, Tex.). Author: Guerilla Warfare World War II, 1963; Organization of Defense Department, 1963. Home: 248 N McLean St Memphis TN 38112 also 118 W Dobbs St Tyler TX 75701

LILES, DANIEL EDWARD, educator; b. Birmingham, Ala., Nov. 18, 1943; s. George Phillip and Margaret S.L.; B.S., Ala. Coll., 1965; M.A. in Teaching, U. Montevallo, 1971, M. Bus. Edn., 1975; doctoral candidate Nova U. Tchr. bus. and history Marion County and Shelby County Sch. System, Ala., 1965-74; instr., chmn. dept. bus. adminstrn. Marion (Ala.) Mil. Inst., 1974—, mgr. bookstore, 1977—. Organist, Good Hope United Methodist Ch., Columbiana, Ala., 1977—, lay leader, 1978-80; rol. restoration pipe organ Ala. Theatre, organist summer children's shows, 1976, 78. Mem. Nat. Bus. Edn. Assn., Am. Bus. Communication Assn., Am. Soc. Public Adminstrn., Am. Theatre Organ Soc., Ala. Hist. Assn., Shelby County Hist. Soc. Home: Box 142-D Columbiana AL 35051 Office: Marion Military Institute Marion AL 36756

LILES, DONALD MELVIN, personnel mgr.; b. Pisgah, Ala., Apr. 30, 1941; s. James Robert Stell and Alice Luvada (Aikens) L.; A.S. in Sociology, N.E. State Jr. Coll., 1972; B.S. in Sociology, U. N.Ala., 1975. Personnel mgr. Hayes Internat. Corp., Huntsville, Ala., 1966-69, SCI Electronics Inc., Huntsville, 1969-71; employment interviewer Avco Electronics Inc., Huntsville, 1972-73; personnel mgr. John Blue Co., Huntsville, 1973-76; employment officer TVA, Nashville, 1976—. Served with USAF, 1962-66. Mem. Am. Soc. Personnel Adminstrs. Democrat. Methodist. Home: 2428 Kimberly Dr Nashville TN 37214 Office: 730 Lebanon Rd Nashville TN 37205

LILES, MAEFRED STEARNS, educator; b. Belvidere, Ill., June 26, 1926; d. Sumner Jason Stearns and Della Claire B. Stearns Crawford; A.B. in Social Studies cum laude, Carson-Newman Coll., 1948; postgrad. New Orleans Baptist Theol. Sem., 1961-63, U. Ala., 1948, U. Nev., 1955, U. Ark., 1971, U. N.C., Chapel Hill, 1963-65, N.C. State U., 1977; m. Vasser Glenwood Liles, Mar. 12, 1976; stepchildren—Rebecca L. Maye, Vasser Glenwood Liles, Jr. Tchr. pub. schs., N.C. and Nev., 1948-58, Winston Elementary Sch., Lakeland, Fla., 1958-61, Lakeside Sch., Metairie, La., 1962-63; head resource tchr. educable mentally retarded program, audiovisual coordinator Wake Forest (N.C.) Elementary Sch., 1963-76, resource tchr. Wake Forest Rolesville Middle Sch., 1976—; evaluator instructional materials Devel. Center, Winston-Salem, N.C. Tchr. sr. adults Sunday sch. Tabernacle Baptist Ch., 1974-79, Creedmoor Rd. Bapt. Ch., 1979—. Mem. NEA, N.C. Assn. Educators, Assn. Classroom Teachers Wake County. Home: PO Box 18152 Raleigh NC 27619 Office: Franklin St Wake Forest NC 27587

LILES, MIKE JAMES, heating and cooling contractor; b. Wilmington, N.C., Sept. 19, 1945; s. James Ervin and Mozelle D. L.; B.S., Middle Tenn. State U., 1973; m. Kathryn R. Rabon, Aug. 16, 1969; children—Jay Michael, Robert Andrew. Pres., dir. Central Heat & Air, Inc., Murfreesboro, Tenn., 1973—. Served with USN, 1964-68. Mem. Rutherford County Home Bldrs. Assn. (sec.-treas., dir.). Club: Rutherford County Optimists (pres.). Office: PO Box 1537 Murfreesboro TN 37130

LILES, WAYNE CONRAD, surgeon; b. Alexander City, Ala., Oct. 27, 1934; s. Willie Conrad and Ethel (Solley) L.; B.S., U. Ala., 1955, M.D., 1958; m. Janet Glunt, children—Wayne Conrad, Richard Martin. Intern Jefferson Davis Hosp., Houston, 1958-59; resident in surgery Univ. Hosp., Birmingham, Ala., 1961-64, Forsyth Meml. Hosp., Winston-Salem, N.C., 1964-66; practice medicine specializing in gen. surgery, Henderson, Ky., 1966—; pres., chmn. bd. Wayne C. Liles, Chartered; chief of surgery Community Meth. Hosp. Served with USAF, 1959-61. Diplomate Am. Bd. Surgery. Fellow A.C.S.; mem. A.M.A., Ky., So. med. assns., Southeastern Surg. Congress, Am. Soc. Abdominal Surgeons, Ky. Surg. Soc. Democrat. Home: 2160 Locust Dr Henderson KY 42420 Office: 110 3d St Henderson KY 42420

LILLIOTT, EDUARD LEVERETT, SR., analytical chemist; b. Perry, Fla., Apr. 1, 1945; s. Robert William and Martha Zelda (Leverett) L.; A.A., North Fla. Jr. Coll., 1965; B.S. in Chemistry, Valdosta State Coll., 1969; m. Wanda Jane Kemp, July 18, 1970; children—Jesika Jane, Eduard Leverett. With Olin Corp., St. Marks, Fla., 1969—, tech. supr. mfg., 1975-76, supr. analytical research and control, 1976—; cons. in analytical chemistry Fla. Dept. Archives; mem. Joint Army, Navy, NASA, Air Force Propellant Characterization Working Group. Communication specialist U.S. Coast Guard Aux., 1977—. Mem. Am. Chem. Soc. (certified in advanced gas and liquid chromatography), Soc. Applied Spectroscopy, ASTM, Am. Inst. Chemists. Democrat. Episcopalian. Club: St. Marks Men's. Developed rapid gas and liquid chromatographic techniques for organic compounds in propellant, rapid gas chromatograph technique for moisture content in propellant. Home: PO Box 5 Saint Marks FL 32355 Office: PO Box 222 Saint Marks FL 32355

LILLY, ROBERT EDMUND, research and devel. engr.; b. Lake Charles, La., Dec. 11, 1950; s. Edmund Deberry and Patricia Lilly; B.S.M.E., U. Tex., 1973; m. Kay Lynn Hutchings, Oct. 14, 1978. Sr. field engr. Schlumberger Overseas, Paris, Pescara, Italy, Groningen, Netherlands, Tripoli, Libya, and Tehran, Iran, 1973-76; ops. engr. Houston Oil & Minerals, Austin, Tex., 1977—. Mem. Soc. Petroleum Engrs. Home: 220 Reinerman St Houston TX 77007 Office: 1212 Main St Houston TX 77002

LIN, CHIANG C., polit. scientist; b. Chishan, Taiwan, Mar. 28, 1936; came to U.S., 1969; s. Kai Y. and Mei (Lou) L.; B.A., Taiwan U., 1960, M.A., 1964; Ph.D., U. Paris, 1969; m. Chi H. Wu, Sept. 19, 1963; 1 dau., Susan Y. Dir. acctg. dept. Kuofeng Textile Mill, Taiwan, 1961-62; asst. prof. polit. sci. Grambling (La.) State U., 1970-74, asso. prof., 1974—. Served with Chinese Air Force, 1960-61. Mem. Am. Polit. Sci. Assn., S.W. Conf. Asian Studies, La. Acad. Scis., La. Polit. Sci. Assn. Lutheran. Office: PO Box 960 Grambling LA 71245

LIN, EYIH, clin. chemist; b. Taipei, Taiwan, Jan. 8, 1941; s. Ai-Lai and Seh (Huang) L.; came to U.S., 1967, naturalized, 1975; Ph.D., U. Mo., 1972; m. Susan Tu, Sept. 7, 1968. Asst. dir. clin. labs. Helen Keller Meml. Hosp., Sheffield, Ala., 1972—; clin. instr. U. Ala. Mem. Am. Assn. Clin. Chemistry, Am. Chem. Soc., Soc. Applied Spectroscopy, AAAS. Contbr. articles to profl. jours. Home: 1903 Beechwood Ct Florence AL 35630 Office: Keller Meml Hospital Sheffield AL 35660

LIN, PING-HUANG, analytical chemist; b. Taichung, Taiwan, Sept. 2, 1943; s. Wu-Chang and Chen-Tsai L.; came to U.S., 1969; B.S., Nat. Cheng-Kung U., Taiwan, 1966; M.S., U. Nebr., 1971, Ph.D., 1973; m. Shiow-Jean Shyr, June 5, 1971; children—Alice, Grace. Research fellow U. Toronto, Canada, 1973-74; research asso. Mass. Inst. Tech., 1974-75; sr. chemist, mass spectrometrist Radian Corp., Austin, Tex., 1975—. Served to 2d lt. Chinese Air Force, 1966-67. NSF Grad. Summer fellow, 1970; 3M Corp. Grad. fellow, 1971-72; named Hon. Nebr. Citizen, 1973. Mem. Am. Chem. Soc., Am. Soc. Mass Spectrometry, Phi Lambda Upsilon. Contbr. articles to profl. jours. Home: 11314 Santa Cruz Dr Austin TX 78759 Office: Radian Corp 8500 Shoal Creek Blvd PO Box 9948 Austin TX 78766

LINCOLN, ALBERT WALLACE, counselor; b. Cass County, Tex., Mar. 12, 1919; s. William and Valreen Lincoln; B.S., Prairie View A&M U., 1948, M.S., 1955; cert. counseling Tex. Tech. U., 1967; m. Rose Marie Davis, Nov. 11, 1949; children—Alberta Marie, Lillian Erline, Sheila V. Tchr. vocat. agr. Leon County Vocat. Sch., Centerville, Tex., 1948-49, Luling (Tex.) Found. Farm, 1949-50; instr. agr. Lubbock (Tex.) Ind. Sch. Dist., 1950-63, counselor, 1963—; mem. state adv. com. Am. Coll. Testing Program, 1978—. Bd. dirs. YMCA, Lubbock Mental Health-Mental Retardation; bd. dirs. United Way. Served with AUS, 1942-45; PTO. Mem. NEA, Tex. Tchrs. Assn., Lubbock Educators Assn., Am. Personnel and Guidance Assn., Tex. Personnel and Guidance Assn. (bus. mgr. state conv. 1978-79), W. Tex. Personnel and Guidance Assn. (pres. 1978-79, bus. mgr. 1979-80), Tex. Classroom Tchrs. Assn., Lubbock Classroom Tchrs. Assn., Tex. Sch. Counselors Assn., Am. Legion, Phi Delta Kappa, Omega Phi Psi. Democrat. Methodist. Home: 1829 Manhattan Dr Lubbock TX 79404 Office: 3211 47th St Lubbock TX 79413

LIND, ALBERT WILLIAM, investment banker; b. Boston, Sept. 7, 1907; s. Albert John and Inez Aspegren (Anderson) L.; B.A., Harvard U., 1929, M.B.A., 1931; m. Mary Helen Clark, May 29, 1941; children—Albert Clark, Hoxie Robert, Mary Louise, Jon Aspegren, Mignon Inez, Thomas Martin. Various positions 1st Nat. Bank N.Y., N.Y.C., 1931-38; various positions Sterling, Grace & Co., N.Y.C., 1939-42, gen. partner, 1942-52, ltd. partner, 1952-71; partner Bass Rocks Devel. Co., Gloucester, Mass., 1971—; dir. Seaboard Assos. Inc., Welde Investors, Inc., Stuart (Fla.) Nat. Bank, Port Salerno (Fla.) Nat. Bank. Clubs: Jupiter Island, Hobe Sound Yacht (Hobe Sound, Fla.); Bass Rocks Golf, Bass Rocks Beach (Gloucester, Mass.); Le Mirador Country (Mont Pelerin, Switzerland), Masons (32 deg.), Shriners. Home: South Beach Rd Hobe Sound FL 33455

LIND, JAMES PETER, computer sci. cons.; b. Chgo., June 8, 1932; s. James and Mabel Antoinette (Nelson) L.; B.A. (Nat. Def. Transp. scholar), U. Minn., 1954, M.A.P.A., 1965. Mgmt. analyst Bur. Employment Security, Dept. Labor, Washington, 1965-66; dean of men U. Bridgeport (Conn.), 1966-68; sr. budget analyst Montgomery County (Md.), Rockville, 1968-72; dir. planning Office of Gov. S.C., Columbia, 1972-73; sr. cons. Northrop Services, Arlington, Va., 1973-75; v.p.-fin. Ability Devel. Services, Washington, 1975-76, dir., 1975—; sr. program analyst Social Rehab. Services, HEW, Washington, 1976-77; dept. mgr. Computer Scis. Corp., Falls Church, Va., 1977—; dir. Mid-Atlantic Capital Corp. Ward officer Democratic Farmer Labor Party, Mpls., 1959-65. Served to 1st lt. U.S. Army, 1955-58. Mem. Am. Soc. Pub. Adminstrs., Internat. City Mgmt. Assn., Internat. Platform Assn., World Future Soc., Am. Inst. Planners. Democrat. Presbyterian. Contbr. articles to adminstrn. jours. Home: Apt 1416 5375 Duke St Alexandria VA 22304 Office: 6565 Arlington Blvd Falls Church VA 22046

LINDAHL, RONALD GUNNAR, biologist; b. Detroit, Aug. 11, 1948; s. Gunnar Herman and Ruth Marie (Pierson) L.; student Central Mich. U., 1966-67; B.A., Wayne State U., 1970, Ph.D. (NSF trainee, U. assistantship), 1973; m. Diane Elizabeth Leja, June 12, 1970; 1 son, Jared Ronald. Staff mem. div. biol. and med. research Argonne (Ill.) Nat. Lab., 1974-75; asst. prof. U. Ala., University, 1975-79, asso. prof. biology, 1979—. Mem. Northport (Ala.) Zoning Bd. Adjustment, 1978—. U. Ala. research grantee, 1976, research fellow, 1977; Nat. Cancer Inst. grantee, 1979—. Mem. Am. Assn. for Cancer Research, AAAS, Genetics Soc. Am., Assn. Southeastern Biologists, Phi Beta Kappa, Sigma Xi. Contbr. articles to profl. jours. Office: Dept Biology U Ala University AL 35486

LINDBERG, DAVID SEAMAN, ednl. adminstr.; b. Merrill, Wis., July 17, 1929; s. Clifford Harvey and Dorothy Jo Lindberg; B.S. in Med. Tech., Wis. State U., Stevens Point, 1958; M.Ed., U. Fla., 1969, Ed.D., 1970; m. Frances Eleanor Cortelyou, Dec. 27, 1951; children—David Seaman, John Edward, Martha Joan. Med. technologist Marshfield (Wis.) Clinic, 1958-66; research asst. U. Fla. Teaching Hosp., Gainesville, 1966; supervisory med. technologist VA Hosp., Gainesville, 1967-68; asst. prof. health related professions and med. tech. U. Fla., Gainesville, 1971-74; asst. dean Sch. Allied Health Professions, La. State U. Med. Center, New Orleans, 1974-77, asso. dean, 1977—; cons. med. lab. continuing edn. and accreditation. Chmn. adminstrv. bd. Fitzgerald United Meth. Ch., Covington, La., 1977-80; mem. Naval Res. Med. Policy Bd., 1977-78; founder, pres. Fla. Tech-ucation Found., 1969-72; del. Fla. Health Planning Council, 1969-73; treas., bd. trustees Med. Lab. Tech. Polit. Action Com., 1976-77. Served with USN, 1950-54. Lic. lab. dir., Fla. Mem. Am. Soc. for Med. Tech. (Profl. Achievement award in edn. 1974, Outstanding Service award 1974, 75, 76, Silver award 1973, pres. Fla. div. 1973-74), Am. Soc. Allied Health Professions, Am. Soc. Clin. Pathologists, Assn. Mil. Surgeons U.S., Naval Res. Assn., Marine Corps Res. Officers Assn., Res. Officers Assn. Author: (with M.R. Williams) Introduction to the Profession of Medical Technology, 3d edit., 1979; mem. editorial bd. Am. Jour. Med. Tech., 1977—; contbr. articles to profl. jours. Home: Rural Route 4 Box 203XL Covington LA 70433 Office: 100 S Derbigny St New Orleans LA 70112

LINDBERG, WILMA JEAN, educator; b. Canton, Ohio, Dec. 8, 1924; d. Carl Estley and Bertha Cecilia (Franklin) Lindberg; A.B., Hanover Coll., 1946; certificate in occupational therapy Wayne State U., 1951, M.Ed., 1963; certificate U. Ala., 1974. Commd. 2d lt. U.S. Air Force, 1952, advanced through grades to capt., 1957, ret., 1961; asst. prof. occupational therapy U. Fla., Gainesville, 1961-67; asso. prof. occupational therapy U. Ala., Birmingham, 1967—, chmn. dept. occupational therapy, 1967-73, ednl. specialist Center for Research and Devel., 1974-76. Cons. Bur. Nursing Home Licensure, State of Ala. Mem. med.-profl. adv. bd. United Cerebral Palsy of Ala. Mem. Am. (council on edn.), Ala.-Miss. (treas., v.p.) occupational therapy assns., A.A.U.P., Ret. Officers Assn., Ala. Ornithol. Soc., Nat. Audubon Soc., Sierra Club, Eta Rho Pi, Alpha Rho Gamma, Kappa Delta Pi, Phi Delta Kappa, Alpha Eta. Club: Altrusa (Birmingham). Home: 2712 Millbrook Rd Birmingham AL 35243

LINDEMAN, JON BURTON, city ofcl.; b. Swampscott, Mass., Dec. 2, 1938; s. Warren Burton and Edna May (Hill) L.; B.A. in Econs., Bethany (W.Va.) Coll., 1962; M.S. in Adminstrn., George Washington U., 1973; m. Ellen Noel Sullivan, June 20, 1962; children—Jon Burton, Scott Edward. Served with U.S. Navy, Res., 1957-72, now comdr. Res.; asst. dir. resource mgmt. system City of Jacksonville, Fla., 1972-73; sr. mgmt. analyst City of Miami, Fla., 1973-76, chief mgmt. analysis, 1976-78, asst. dir. dept. mgmt. and budget, 1978—; instr. mgmt. fields Jones Coll., 1973. Div. leader fund raising campaign, Century Club mem. YMCA. Mem. Am. Inst. Indsl. Engrs., Am. Soc. Public Adminstrn. (chpt. bd. dirs.), Internat. City Mgmt. Assn., Naval Res. Assn. (Sidney Fields-Sunshine chpt. pres., v.p. budget and fin. Sixth Naval Dist., mem. nat. adv. council), Res. Officers Assn. (v.p. chpt.), Navy League. Democrat. Lutheran. Clubs: Army and Navy (Coral Gables); Miami Tiger Bay, Kiwanis (asst. sec.). Editor Sou'easter, Sixth Naval Dist., Naval Res. Assn. Home: 8480 SW 66th St Miami FL 33143 Office: Suite 506 174 E Flagler St Miami FL 33131

LINDEMAN, ROBERT PAUL, educator; b. Sublette, Kans., Oct. 24, 1926; s. Paul Elmer and Agnes Louetta (Wardlaw) L.; A.B., Midwest Christian Coll., 1957; postgrad. Lincoln Christian Coll., 1957-58, U. Ind. Christian Theol. Sem., 1959, Panhandle State Coll., 1965; M.S., Ft. Hays State Coll., 1966; Ed.D., Okla. State U., 1970; m. Wilma Grace Strobel, Dec. 4, 1945; children—Marda (Mrs. Steven Riley), David. Ordained to ministry Christian Ch., 1955; minister, Okla., Ill. and Ind., 1954-68; mem. faculty Midwest Christian Coll., Okla. State U., Milligan Coll., Emmanuel Sch. Religion, U. Va., E. Tenn. State U., 1970-75, also psychologist Watauga Area Mental Health Center, 1973-75; asso. prof. psychiatry, dir. behavioral scis. for family practice residency program East Tenn. State U., 1975—; cons. Johnson City and Washington County schs. Licensed psychologist, Tenn. Mem. Am. Soc. Clin. Hypnosis, Am., Tenn., Intermountain psychol. assns., Am. Assn. Marriage and Family Counselors (clin.), Soc. Tchrs. Family Medicine, Am. Assn. Sex Educators and Counselors (cert.), Phi Delta Kappa. Home: Rt 2 Box 240 Johnson City TN 37601 Office: East Tennessee State University Johnson City TN 37601

LINDENMEYER, CARL RAY, educator; b. Peru, Ill., Mar. 31, 1937; s. Ray S. and Ada L. (Knudson) L.; B.S. in Indsl. Engring., Northwestern U., 1961; M.S. in Tech., Western Mich. U., 1970; postgrad. Mich. State U., 1970-75; m. Karen Lauer, June 30, 1961; children—Victor and Vincent (twins), Brian. Asst. prof. mech. engring., U. Nebr., Lincoln, 1961-63; dir., tech. instr. Ferris State Coll., Big Rapids, Mich., 1963-69; asso. prof. indsl. engring. Western Mich. U., Kalamazoo, 1969-77; asso. prof. engring. tech., coordinator indsl. engring. tech. specialty, project adminstr. health care systems improvement program Clemson (S.C.) U., 1977—; pres., prin. cons. C.R. Lindenmeyer & Assos., Clemson, 1970—; productivity and mgmt. cons. to various cos. Walter P. Murphy scholar, 1955-60, fellow, 1960-61, Kellogg Found. fellow, 1974-75. Mem. Am. Inst. Indsl. Engrs. (sr. mem., pres. Greenville-Spartanburg chpt.), Am. Soc. Engring. Edn., Sigma Xi, Iota Lambda Sigma, Alpha Pi Mu, Tau Alpha Pi, Lambda Chi Alpha. Contbr. articles to profl. pubis. in field, reports to profl. meetings. Home: 400 Kings Way Clemson SC 29631 Office: Freeman Hall Clemson University Clemson SC 29631

LINDER, AUBRY LUDWEL, printer; b. Livingston Parish, La., Mar. 15, 1932; s. Willie and Ada Viola (Keen) L.; student La. State U.; m. Diane Ball, Mar. 7, 1970; children—Sheila Annette, Angela Gail, Norman Brent, Rhonda Lynn. Apprentice printer Livingston Parish Printing Co. (La.), 1950-53, 54-56; printer Capital City Press, Baton Rouge, 1956-73, supt. composing room, 1973—. Served with U.S. Army, 1953-54. Mem. So. Newspapers Pubs. Assn. (del.). Democrat. Baptist. Home: Route 1 Box 192 Denham Springs LA 70726 Office: 525 Lafayette Ave Baton Rouge LA 70802

LINDLER, BILL FRANKLIN, equipment handling co. exec.; b. Columbia, S.C., Apr. 14, 1947; s. Howard Franklin and Betty Whiteside (Boyle) L.; B.C.E., Ga. Inst. Tech., 1976; m. Elizabeth Brooks, Oct. 7, 1978; children—Bill Franklin, Joey French. Vice pres. House of Designs, West Columbia, S.C., 1964-67; project engr., dept. supr. Law Engring. Testing Co., Atlanta, 1967-76; with EVI Equipment Inc., East Point, Ga., 1976—, pres., dir., 1977—. Mem. ASCE, Internat. Material Mgmt. Soc. (v.p. Atlanta chpt. 1980—), Jonesboro Jaycees (pres. 1973-74, state dir. 1975-76, Jonesboro Jaycee of Yr. 1972-73), 16th Region Jaycees (v.p. 1974-75). Club: Kiwanis (Atlanta). Home: 5271 W Fayetteville Rd Apt G-2 College Park GA 30349 Office: EVI Equipment Inc 1014A Sampler Way East Point GA 30344

LINDLEY, JOHN ELLIS, physician; b. Macon, Miss., Apr. 23, 1926; s. Ancil Levinson and Brancie Ann (Stuart) L.; student Miss. State U., 1943-44, student U. Miss., 1950; B.S., Harvard, 1952; M.D., Baylor U., 1953; m. Helen Marie Puffenbarger, Aug. 21, 1954; children—Mary Lisa, John Ellis II, Mark Andrew. Intern Jefferson Davis Hosp., Houston, 1952-53, resident, 1953-56; practice medicine specializing in obstetrics, gynecology, Houston, 1956-57; staff obstetrician and gynecologist Jeff Anderson Meml., former chief staff; mem. staff St. Joseph, Riley hosps., Meridian, Miss.; asst. instr. obstetrics, gynecology Baylor U., 1953-57, instr., 1956-57; asst. prof. obstetrics, gynecology U. Miss., 1957-58; pres. Lindley-Jones Clinic Women. Pres. Lindley Enterprises, Inc., Diamond L Beef House, Inc.; owner Lindley Ranch, Lindley's Flowers' & Gift Castle. Mem. exec. staff Gov. of Miss., 1960-72; mayor of Marion, Miss. Bd. dirs. Am. Cancer Soc., Lauderdale County, Miss., 1960-63; pres., bd. dirs. Jefferson Davis Acad.; mem. Miss. State Jr. Coll. Commn. Served with USNR, 1944-46. Diplomate Am. Bd. Obstetrics and Gynecology. Fellow A.C.S., Am. Coll. Obstetrics and Gynecology, Central Assn. Obstetricians and Gynecologists; mem. Miss. Obstet. and Gynecol. Soc. (pres.-elect 1965), Am., Miss., So. med. assns., S.W. Postgrad., East Miss. (pres. 1963), Lauderdale County (pres. 1963) med. socs., Miss. Cattlemen's Assn., Miss. Farm Bur., Am. Quarter Horse Assn., S.C.V., S.A.R., V.F.W., Am. Legion, Nat. Hist. Soc., Meridian Little Theatre, Meridian Art Assn., Civil Round Table, Sigma Chi. Democrat. Baptist. Mason (Shriner). Contbr. articles to profl. jours.; inventor of Lindley Newborn Resuscitator. Home: Route 8 PO Box 30 Lindley Rd Meridian MS 39301 Office: 1410 20th Ave Meridian MS 39301

LINDLY, HORACE BISHOP, ret. piping mfg. co. exec.; b. Hill County, Tex., Sept. 12, 1914; s. George Calvin and Mary Ellen (Hicks) L.; student McMurry Coll., Abilene, Tex., 1934-36; m. Christine Amanda Owens, Aug. 21, 1935 (dec. July 25, 1942); m. 2d, Bess S. Churchwell, Dec. 24, 1943; children—Hershel Randal, Clarence Bishop, Ross Noble. Stock room clk. Lubbock Machine, Inc. (Tex.), 1937-40, welder's helper, 1940-41; operator West Point Farm, Tahoka, Tex., 1941-55; welder Gifford Hill, Inc., Lubbock, 1955-58, foreman, 1958-69, plant supt. Colby (Kans.) plant, 1970-71, machinery specialist, 1972-75, ret., 1975; tchr. welding Lynn County Vets. Sch., Tahoka, 1949. Mem. Fluid Power Soc., So. Plains Astronomy Club, So. Plains Geneal. Soc. Methodist. Author: Lindlys and Allied Families, 1971. Patentee in field. Home: 5323 31st St Lubbock TX 79407

445 WHO'S WHO IN THE SOUTH AND SOUTHWEST

LINDOW, LESTER WILLIAM, former telecasters orgn. exec.; b. Milw., Apr. 11, 1913; B.A. in Journalism, U. Wis., 1934; m. Andree de Verdor, Dec. 7, 1946; 1 dau., Suzanne Helene Lindow Gordon. Asso. editor Advt. Almanac, Hearst Newspapers, N.Y.C., 1934-35; with comml. dept. sta. WCAE, Pitts., 1935-36, nat. sales mgr., 1936-38, comml. mgr., asst. to gen. mgr., 1938-40; sec., gen. mgr. WFBM, Inc., Indpls., 1940-42; gen. mgr. stas. WRNY and WRNY-FM, Rochester, N.Y., 1946-47; sec., gen. mgr. Trebit Corp. operators sta. WFDF, Flint, 1947-60, sec., dir. 1948-60, v.p., 1954-60; sec.-treas. Landsmore Corp., 1952-57, v.p., 1954-57; mem. exec. com. NBC Radio Affiliates, 1955-57, chmn. exec. com., 1956-57; exec. dir. Assn. Maximum Service Telecasters, Inc., 1957-77, pres., 1977-78, also dir., asst. sec.-treas.; v.p., dir. Grelin Broadcasting Inc., sta. WWRI, West Warwick, R.I., 1957-69, Radio Buffalo, Inc., sta. WWOL and WWOL-FM, Buffalo, 1959-62. Treas., dir. A.R.C., 1953-56, nat. fund vice chmn. for Mich., 1956-57; bd. dirs., mem. exec. com., chmn. budget and fiscal com. Radio Free Europe/Radio Liberty, Inc., Washington. Served from 1st lt. to lt. col. U.S. Army, 1942-46; apptd. to Gen. Staff Corps, War Dept., 1946-47; col. Res. ret. Mem. Mich. Assn. Broadcasters, Mich. A.P. Broadcasters' Assn. (dir.), Res. Officers Assn., Nat. Assn. Radio and TV Broadcasters (dir. AM radio com.), Radio Advt. Bur. (Mich. chmn.), A.P. Radio Programming Com. N.Y.C., Assn. Profl. Broadcasting Edn. (dir.), A.P. Radio and TV Assn. (v.p., dir.), TV Allocations Study Orgn. (alternate dir.). Union U. Wis. Alumni Assn., Nat. Broadcasters Club of Washington (pres. 1964-65, gov. 1959-61, chmn. bd. 1965-66), Internat. Radio and TV Soc., Radio-TV Pioneers, Palm Beach Civic Assn., Ret. Officers Assn., Alpha Chi Rho, Scabbard and Blade, Iron Cross, White Spades, Sigma Delta Chi. Elk, Rotarian (pres.). Clubs: Flint Golf; Radio Executives (N.Y.C.); Nat. Broadcasters, Congressional Country, Internat. (Washington); Beach (Palm Beach, Fla.). Home: La Bonne Vie 3475 S Ocean Blvd Palm Beach FL 33480

LINDQUIST, DONALD AUGUST, lawyer; b. New Orleans, Sept. 28, 1924; s. Owen Henry and Anne Clair (Grimes) L.; B.S., U.S. Mcht. Marine Acad., 1945; LL.B., J.D., Loyola U. of New Orleans, 1951; m. Frances C. Gorton, June 6, 1953; children—Christine Lindquist Hickey, Catherine Anne, Donald C., Mary Frances. Admitted to La. bar, 1951; partner Chaffe, McCall, Phillips, Toler & Sarpy, New Orleans, 1953—; tchr., cons.; teaching lectr. Naval Res. Research and Devel., 1960-71. Served as ensign, USNR, 1945-46, as lt., 1951-53; comdr. Res. ret.; PTO. Recipient medal, Am. Legion, certificate of merit, City of New Orleans, 1971. Mem. Am., La., New Orleans, N.Y.C. bar assns., Maritime Law Assn. U.S., Internat. House. Democrat. Roman Catholic. Clubs: Metairie Country, Pickwick, Plimsoll, Semreh, Propellor. Home: 5511 Cherlyn St New Orleans LA 70124 Office: 210 Baronne St New Orleans LA 70112

LINDQUIST, JOHN HILLMANN, newspaper exec.; b. N.Y.C., May 9, 1942; s. John Wilbert and Marian (Hillmann) L.; grad. Broward Bus. Coll., 1961; A.A., Broward Community Coll., 1962; B.A., Fort Lauderdale U., 1964; m. Pamela Cullen, Feb. 9, 1962; children—Marian, Jessica, Kris. Ind. news dealer Gore Newspapers, Fort Lauderdale, Fla., 1959-72, dist. mgr., 1972, sales crew mgr., 1972-75, asst. promotion mgr., 1975-79, promotion mgr., 1979—. Pres., McNab Elem. Sch. PTA; v.p. Pompano Middle Sch. PTA, 1976-80, advt. chmn., 1976-80; publications chmn. Broward County PTA, 1978-79; chmn. dist. adv. com. Broward County Sch. Bd., 1978-79. Mem. Am. Acctg. Assn. Club: Marina Bay Yacht and Tennis. Home: 259 Algiers Ave Fort Lauderdale FL 33308 Office: 101 N New River Dr E Fort Lauderdale FL 33302

LINDSAY, DAVID BREED, JR., newspaper editor and pub.; b. Fayetteville, N.C., Dec. 25, 1922; s. David Breed and Helen Carter (Dodson) L.; B.S., PUrdue U., 1947; m. Elizabeth Hotchkiss Girvin, June 19, 1944; children—David G. B., Robert A., Ann C., Edward H. Reporter/photographer, Marion (Ind.) Chronicle, 1947-48; gen. mgr. Sarasota (Fla.) Herald-Tribune, 1948-55, pres., editor, 1955—; pres. Cavalier Aircraft Corp., 1955-70; cons. Piper Aircraft Corp. Founder, trustee New Coll., Sarasota, 1950-75. Served with U.S. Army, 1943-46; PTO. Decorated Army Commendation medal. Mem. Am. Newspaper Pubs. Assn. (dir.; pres. Found.), Inter Am. Press Assn. (dir.), Soc. Exptl. Test Pilots. Episcopalian. Clubs; Met. (Washington); Old Capital (Monterey, Calif.); Univ. (Sarasota). Inventor various aircraft systems, including Enforcer Aircraft. Office: PO Box 1719 Sarasota FL 33578

LINDSAY, EDWARD WILLIAMS, vacuum system co. exec.; b. Boyce, Va., Aug. 24, 1921; s. Winston Southgate and Marjorie (Harris) L.; student U. Tex., 1939-40; B.S. in Elec. Engring., Ala. Poly. Inst. (now Auburn U.), 1943, postgrad., 1946-47; postgrad. U. Pitts., 1951-52; m. Margaret Ruth Upton, June 24, 1948; children—Edward Williams, Winston, Margaret. Research engr. Westinghouse Electric Corp., Pitts., 1943-50, sr. design engr., 1950-56, sr. engr., 1957-63; chief research, devel. So. States Equipment Corp., Hampton, Ga., 1956; pres. Vacu-Maid, Inc., Ponca City, Okla., 1963—. Mem. Penn Hills (Pa.) Com. Republican party, 1958-61. Trustee Lindsay Trust. Named Boss of Year, Ponca City Jr. C. of C., 1973. Registered profl. engr., Pa. Mem. I.E.E.E. (Best Paper award Pitts. chpt. 1956), Built-In Cleaning Systems Inst., Antique Wireless Assn., Antique Radio Club Am., Eta Kappa Nu, Sigma Pi. Kiwanian. Clubs: Cotillion (Wilkinsburg, Pa.), Sylvan Canoe (Verona, Pa.). Home: 21 Hillcrest Rd Ponca City OK 74601 Office: PO Drawer 1708 Ponca City OK 74601

LINDSAY, FREDA THERESA SCHIMPF (MRS. GORDON JAMES LINDSAY), religious orgn. exec.; b. Burstall, Sask., Can., Apr. 18, 1914; d. Gottfred and Kaity (Saklofsky) Schimpf; student Life Bible Coll., Portland, Oreg., 1933-35, B.A., Los Angeles, 1938, D.D., 1977; m. Gordon James Lindsay, Nov. 14, 1937 (dec.); children—Carole Ann, Gilbert Livingston, Dennis Gordon. Came to U.S., 1919, naturalized, 1940. With Christ for the Nations, Dallas, 1948—, sec., 1960—, pres., 1973—; pres. Christ for the Nations Inst., Dallas; internat. dir., v.p. Full Gospel Fellowship Chs. and Ministers Internat., 1976. Author: My Diary Secrets, 1976. Editor Gordon Lindsays books including: Prayer That Moves Mountains, 1959; One Year to Live, 1972; One in Every Other Family, 1973; How to Be Enriched by Giving, 1974. Pub., editor Christ for Nation mag. Home: 441 Fawn Ridge Dr Dallas TX 75224 Office: Box 24910 Dallas TX 75224

LINDSEY, EDWARD STORMONT, educator, surgeon; b. West Palm Beach, Fla., June 3, 1930; s. Edward Austin and Jane (Stormont) L.; B.S., Tulane U., 1951, M.D., 1958, M.Med.Sci., 1968; m. Margaret Ann Turfitt, Oct. 20, 1953; children—Ann Stormont, Myron Turfitt. Intern Tulane U. Service, Charity Hosp. La., New Orleans, 1958-59, resident, 1959-64; asst. prof. surgery Tulane U., 1966-69, asso. prof., 1969-75, clin. asso. prof., 1975—; Nat. Heart Inst. fellow U. Edinburgh (Scotland), 1964-65; mem. staff So. Bapt. Hosp., Children's Hosp., Touro Infirmary. Trustee, Med. Benevolence Found. Served with USNR, 1952-55. Fellow A.C.S.; mem. So. Surg. Assn., Am. Assn. Thoracic Surgery, Transplantation Soc., So. Thoracic Surg. Assn., Société Internationale de Chirurgie, Oscar Creech Surg. Soc. (pres.), Kappa Sigma. Presbyterian. Club: Essex (New Orleans). Contbr. articles to profl. jours. Home: 4 Rosa Park New Orleans LA 70115 Office: Suite 410 4440 Magnolia St New Orleans LA 70115

LINDSEY, EVELYN G., govt. ofcl.; b. Dayton, Tenn., Oct. 2, 1934; d. Charles Lee and Beulah Elizabeth (Swafford) Gentry; B.S., Tenn. Tech. U., 1968; postgrad. U. Tenn., 1970-72; Middle Tenn. State U., 1969-75; m. William A. Lindsey, July 15, 1972; children by previous marriage—Thomas Lee Henderson (dec.), Yvonne Elizabeth. Legal sec. U.S. Atty. for Eastern Dist. Tenn., Dept. Justice, Chattanooga, 1963-66; with TVA, 1966-69, 75—, staff records officer, Chattanooga, 1975—; mktg. and mgmt. dept. head Walker County Tech. Sch., Lafayette, Ga., 1969-70; office occupations instr. State Area Vo-Tech. Sch., Chattanooga, 1970-72; instr. Edmondson Coll., Chattanooga, 1972-74; workshop instr. Chattanooga Area Literacy Movement Tchrs., 1978—; co-owner North County Carpet Cleaning, Inc.; cons. in field; notary pub., State of Tenn., 1962—. Sec., Fed. Employed Women, 1976; vol. First Offender program, Chattanooga, 1972-74. Mem. Assn. of Records Mgrs. and Adminstrs. (chpt. pres. 1979-80), Nat. Micrographics Assn. (dir. Tenn. Valley chpt. 1979-80), Chattanooga Paralegal Assn., Chattanooga Engrs. Club (pub. dir. for regional sci. and engring. fair 1976-79), Freedoms Found. Am. Democrat. Baptist. Clubs: Atlanta Skylarks Flying, Daisy Jr. Women's (pres. 1959-60). Home: 9022 Daisy Dallas Rd PO Box 215 Hixson TN 37343 Office: 205 Krystal Bldg Chattanooga TN 37401

LINDSEY, H. EDWARD, JR., oil well service co. exec.; b. Atlanta, Dec. 17, 1926; s. Hiram Edward D. and Carolyn (Spraggins) L.; B.S., Ga. Inst. Tech., 1948; m. Vangie Theis, Aug. 14, 1954; children—Kristin, Stephen C. Sales engr. Kobe, Inc., Huntington Park, Calif., 1948-50, Internat. Harvester Co., Chgo., 1950-52; pres., owner MWL Tool & Supply Co., Midland, Tex., 1952—; pres. Diamond Oil Well Drilling Co., Midland, 1961-72, Helco Fishing Tools, Inc., 1969-74, Bond-Coat, Inc., 1969-74. Served with USNR, 1943-46. Mem. Soc. Petroleum Engrs., Aircraft Owners and Pilots Assn., Am. Petroleum Inst. Baptist. Mason (Shriner), Rotarian. Clubs: Midland Petroleum, Midland Country. Home: 1611 Gulf St Midland TX 79701 Office: PO Drawer 631 Midland TX 79701

LINDSEY, JAMES LESLIE, mining engr.; b. Hopkinsville, Ky., May 16, 1910; s. James Leslie and Mamie (Stone) L.; student pub. schs., Hopkinsville; m. Imogene Dunning, Nov. 18, 1934; children—Arkie Hank, James Philip. Mine supt. Nashville & W.Ky. Coal Cos., 1950-57; gen. supt. Chem. Coke Co., Dawson Springs, Ky., 1957-60; supt. Rialto Coal Co., Inc., Madisonville, Ky., 1963-69, receiver, 1970; cons. engr. Big Rivers Electric Corp., Henderson, Ky., 1973—. Mem. Nortonville City Council, 1963-69; mem. Hopkins County Joint Planning Commn., 1967—. Mem. Ky. Mining Inst., Nat., Ky. (past treas.) socs. profl. engrs., Am. Congress on Surveying and Mapping. Mem. Disciples of Christ Ch. Mason (Shriner). Home: 2001 Lakeview Dr Madisonville KY 42431

LINDSEY, SARA ANN, sociologist, educator; b. Huntington, W.Va., Feb. 20, 1925; d. Alexis Brenier and Iris Neville (Smith) McMullen; A.B., Sweet Briar Coll., 1947; M.A., George Washington U., 1965; m. Douglas Griffith Lindsey, June 15, 1948; children—Douglas McMullen, Bruce McRee, Ann Griffith, Robert Warfield. Caseworker Va. Dept. Pub. Welfare, Alexandria, 1947-49; journalist Alexandria Gazette, 1951-54; instr. sociology U. Va. Sch. Continuing Edn., 1965—; cons. in field. Chmn. No. Va. Dist. Va. Conf. Social Work, 1953-54; mem. No. Va. planning com. Girl Scouts U.S., 1953—; founding mem. Fairfax County Health and Welfare Council, 1954-55; commr., vice-chmn. No. Va. Juvenile Detention Home, 1957-63; alumnae bd. Sweet Briar Coll., 1969-71; past pres. Alexandria Library Co., Alexandria Hosp. Corp.; v.p. met. area Homemaker Health Aide Service, 1966-75; bd. dirs. Alexandria Community Health Center; vice chmn. Region IV Episcopal Diocese Va., 1972-74, vestryman St. Paul's Ch., 1971-74. Mem. Va. Fedn. Women's Clubs (dist. chmn. health and welfare com. 1952-53), No. Va. Jr. Service League (v.p. 1957-59), Riverport (pres. 1957-56), Hunting Creek (pres. 1969-71) garden clubs, Garden Club Va. (bd. govs. 1969-71), D.C., Am. sociol. assns., Population Assn. Am., Am. Hort. Assn., Nat. Trust for Hist. Preservation, Democrat. Episcopalian. Club: Belle Haven Country. Home: 6104 Woodmont Rd Alexandria VA 22307

LINDSTROM, ERIC EVERETT, ophthalmologist; b. Helena, Mont., Nov. 28, 1936; s. Everett Harry and Nan Augusta (Johnson) L.; B.S., Wheaton Coll., 1958; M.D., U. Md., 1963; M.P.H., Harvard U., 1966; m. Nancy Jo Alexander, July 24, 1960; children—Laura Ann, Eric Everett. Intern, Madigan Army Med. Center, Tacoma, Wash., 1963-64; resident in aerospace medicine Sch. Aerospace Medicine, Brooks AFB, Tex., 1966-68, resident in ophthalmology Brooke Army Med. Center, Ft. Sam Houston, Tex., 1972-75; surgeon 12th combat aviation group U.S. Army, Vietnam, 1968-69, chief profl. services and aviation medicine Beach Army Hosp., Ft. Wolters, Tex., 1969-72; asst. chief ophthalmology clinic Madigan Army Med. Center, Tacoma, 1975-76; now with Laurel (Miss.) Eye Center; med. dir. Palo Pinto County (Tex.) Mental Health Clinic., 1970-72; cons. Tex. State Rehab. Com., 1971-72; flight surgeon Miss. Air N.G. Deacon, First Bapt. Ch., Laurel, 1978—. Decorated Bronze Star, Air medal with 2 oak leaf clusters, Meritorious Service medal. Diplomate Am. Bd. Preventive Medicine, Am. Bd. Ophthalmology. Fellow Am. Coll. Preventive Medicine, Aerospace Med. Assn. (asso.), Am. Acad. Ophthalmology and Otolaryngology; mem. AMA, Miss. Med. Assn., Am. Assn Ophthalmology, Flying Physicians Assn., Soc. Mil. Ophthalmologists, Aircraft Owners and Pilots Assn., Kiwanis, Nu Sigma Nu. Home: 809 Cherry Ln Laurel MS 39440 Office: Laurel Eye Center PO Box 2907 Laurel MS 39440

LINDSTROM, FRANK ELWOOD, JR., civil engr.; b. Washington, Mar. 28, 1945; s. Frank Elwood and Woodie (Ryan) L.; B.C.E., Auburn U., 1969; m. Shelley Shook Gearhart, Feb. 26, 1972; children—Frank Elwood III, Kristen, Kara, Thomas. Project engr. Sullivan, Long & Hagerty, Birmingham, Ala., 1969-71; sales engr. Taulman Co., Atlanta, 1971-73; project mgr. Black, Crow & Eidsness, Birmingham, 1973-76; co-owner, v.p. Engring. Service Assos., Birmingham, 1976—. Named Outstanding Civil Engring. Grad., Auburn U., 1969. Mem. ASCE (mem. polit. action com.), Am. Cons. Engrs. Council (mem. public relations com. and polit. action com.), ASME, Am. Water Works Assn., Water Pollution Control Fedn., Soc. Mktg. Profl. Services, Birmingham Area C. of C. (co-founder environ. econs. com.). Presbyterian. Clubs: Downtown, Mt. Brook, Atlanta City. Office: 2704 20th St S Birmingham AL 35209

LINDSTROM, ROBERT LEE, counselor; b. Tucson, Apr. 3, 1940; s. Olaf Reginald and Eleanor Rose (Moore) L.; A.S. magna cum laude, Blue Ridge Community Coll., 1974: B.A., James Madison U., 1975, M.Ed., 1976. Heavy equipment operator R.G. Foster & Co., Wadley, Ga., 1963-67; sales rep. IBM, Waynesboro, Va., 1967-70; partner Lindstrom & Co., New Market, Va., 1970-72; counselor Operation PAR, Clearwater, Fla., 1977-79; time-out room specialist PASS Project, Pinellas County (Fla.) Sch. Bd., 1979; pvt. practice counseling, Indian Rocks Beach, Fla., 1979—. Served with AUS, 1958-61. Cert. tchr., guidance counselor, Fla. Mem. Am. Personnel and Guidance Assn., Am. Mental Health Counselors Assn., Cousteau Soc., Profl. Assn. Diving Instrs., Phi Theta Kappa. Office: PO Box 151 Indian Rocks Beach FL 33535

LINEBAUGH, NATHANIEL LEE, JR., adminstrv. law judge HEW; b. Oklahoma City, Mar. 17, 1911; s. Nathaniel Lee and Lucy McKinney (Sims) L.; B.A., So. Methodist U., 1935, LL.B., 1937; m. Kathlyn Elizabeth Woolverton, Nov. 7, 1937; 1 son, Daniel Hollis. Admitted to Tex. bar, 1937, U.S. Supreme Ct. bar, also U.S. Dist. Cts.; practiced in Dallas, 1949-68; from claims mgr. to sr. claims supr. and chmn. home office claims com. Trinity Universal Ins. Co., Dallas, 1943-68; adminstrv. law judge Bur. Hearings & Appeals, HEW, Dallas, 1968—. Mem. Am. Bar Assn., State Bar of Tex., S.W. Legal Found., Fed. Trial Examiners Conf., Assn. Adminstrv. Law Judges in HEW. Methodist. Mason. Author: The Adjuster's Compilation, 1963; Manual of Claims Procedure, 1965; Volenti Non Fit Injuria-The Texas Application, 1967 Contbr. articles to profl. jours. Home: 11007 Aladdin Dr Dallas TX 75229 Office: 10830 North Central Expressway Dallas TX 75231

LINER, OLGA LEIGNADIER, dietitian; b. Colon, Republic of Panama, May 13, 1932; d. Humberto and Olga (Arcia) Leignadier; came to U.S., 1951, naturalized, 1959; B.S., St. Mary of the Woods Coll., 1955; m. Cornelius Ewell Liner, Aug. 23, 1956; children—Stephen Ewell, Constance Ann. Dietetic intern N.Y. Hosp., Cornell Med. Center, 1955-56; dietitian Panama Canal Co., Fed. Canal Zone, 1956-58, recreational specialist, 1965-66; chief dietitian Dale County (Ala.) Hosp., 1958-59, Geneva County (Ala.) Hosp., 1960; instr. dept. instl. mgmt. Kans. State U. Sch. Home Econs., Manhattan, 1969-71, asst. mgr. resident hall food service, 1970—; lang. instr. U.S. Army, Fort Clayton, Canal Zone, 1972; therapeutic dietitian U. Hosp., Augusta, Ga., 1973-76; chief dietitian patient service Aiken (S.C.) Community Hosp., 1976-77; dir. dietary services Gracewood (Ga.) State Sch. and Hosp., 1977—; cons. dietitian various area nursing homes, 1976-79; instr., preceptor food service course, extension div. U. Fla., Gainesville, Fla., 1976-79. Mem. Am. Dietetic Assn., Am. Soc. for Hosp. Food Service Adminstrs., Augusta Dist. Dietetic Assn. (pres. elect 1979—), Augusta Home Econs. Club (pres. 1978-79), Gracewood Employees Assn., Ga. Heart Assn., AAUW (chmn. food com. 1976). Democrat. Roman Catholic. Clubs: Westlake Country, Cranford Flower (v.p. 1976-78). Author diet manual, 1976. Home: 438 Sheffield Circle Augusta GA 30909 Office: Gracewood State School and Hospital Gracewood GA 30812

LINES, WILLIAM FREDRICK, real estate co. exec.; b. Miami, Nov. 2, 1938; s. Fredrick William and Evelyn Grace (Libby) L.; B.S., Mont. State U., 1967; postgrad. U. Conn., 1968, U. Hartford, 1971; children—Matthew M., Carter W. Archtl. draftsman William L. Pereira & Assos., Corona del Mar, Calif., 1963-65; archtl. designer O. Berg & Assos., Bozeman, Mont., 1965-67; dir. archtl. prodn. Asso. Architects, Farmington, Conn., 1967-71; mktg. and sales archtl. wood products Modern Woodcrafts, Farmington, 1971-72; constrn. mgmt. Longardner & Assos., Orlando, Fla., 1972-73; constrn. mgmt. T.D. Constrn. Mgmt., Orlando, 1973-75; corporate real estate planner Continental Mortgage Investors, Miami, 1975—; cons. in field. Cert. rev. appraiser. Mem. Nat. Assn. Rev. Appraisers, Mont. State U. Alumni Assn. Republican. Methodist. Home: 8054 SW 80th Ave Miami FL 33143 Office 5915 Ponce de Leon Blvd Coral Gables FL 33146

LINGAMNENI, JAGANMOHAN RAO, criminologist, sociologist; b. Dondapadu, A.P., India, Mar. 15, 1942; s. Satyanarayana and Satyavathi Settipalli L.; came to U.S., 1967, naturalized, 1974; B.S., A.P. Agrl. Coll., 1962; M.S., A.P. Agrl. U., 1965; Ph.D., Mich. State U., 1972; M.S. in Criminal Justice, U. Ala., Birmingham, 1979; m. Uma Uppaluri, Feb. 26, 1967; children—Santhisri, Pragathisri. Research asst. A.P. State Dept. Agr., 1964-65; instr. A.P. Agrl. U., 1965-66; research asst MSU/NICD Diffusion Project, 1966-67; teaching asst., grad. research asst., diffusion research fellow Mich. State U., 1967-70; lectr. Mich. State U./U.S. AID Communication Workshops, 1969-75; asst. prof. sociology W. Ga. Coll., 1970-75, dir. grad. program, 1973-75, 76—, vice-chmn. dept., 1973-74, asst. to chmn. dept., 1971-73, asso. prof., 1975—; adj. faculty mem. Emory U. Grad. Sch., 1976—. Pres., Carrollton Elementary PTA, 1977-78, v.p., 1976-77; mem. exec. bd. Carroll County Area PTA Council, 1976-78. Diffusion research fellow Mich. State U., 1967, 68. Mem. Am. Soc. Criminology (life; mem. adv. internat. liasion com. 1978—), Acad. Criminal Justice Scis. (mem. com. on internat. criminology and criminal justice 1978—, chmn. student affairs com. 1979-80), Internat. Communication Assn., Am. Sociol. Assn., So. Sociol. Soc. (mem. racial and ethnic minorities com. 1978—), So. Assn. Criminal Justice Educators (mem. awards com. 1977-78, chmn. awards com. 1978-79, sec.-treas. 1979-80), Ga. Sociol. Assn., Ga. Assn. Criminal Justice Educators, Alpha Kappa Delta, Lambda Alpha Epsilon. Hindu. Author: Status Inconsistency, Communication Behavior and Modernization, 1972; asso. editor So. Jour. Criminal Justice, 1977—; contbr. articles in field to profl. jours. Home: 115 W Allison Circle Carrollton GA 30117 Office: Social Sci Bldg W Ga Coll Carrollton GA 30118

LINGLE, KENDALL IDE, urban generalist, cons.; b. Chgo., June 30, 1910; s. Bowman Church and Bertha (Kendall) L.; B.S., Princeton U., 1933; m. Mary Bruce, Jan. 4, 1936; 1 son, Bowman Church, II. Exec. dir. various civic orgns. in Ill., 1935-40; chief personnel and tng. Ill. Dept. Pub. Health, 1940-41; field staff cons. Pub. Adminstrn. Service, 1941-45; active in civic and charitable affairs in Chgo. and nationally, 1945—; mem. Mayor's Adv. Com. on Youth Welfare, Chgo., 1948-59, exec. com., 1953-59; chmn. bd. mgrs., bd. dirs. Old Peoples Home of Chgo., 1948-58; mem. com. on aging and pub. affairs com. Met. Welfare Council of Chgo., 1948-65; mem. first nat. com. on aging Nat. Social Welfare Assembly, 1948-50; mem. Chgo. Commn. Youth Welfare, 1959-69; mem. adv. com. Chgo. Dept. Human Resources, 1969-74. Trustee New Coll., Sarasota, Fla., 1970-79; trustee Fund for Advancement of Camping, 1970—, nat. chmn., 1974—; trustee, bd. dirs. Am. Camping Assn., 1974—; project dir. Internat. Consortium on Alternatives for Youth-at-Risk, 1979—. Mem. Nat. Soc. Internships and Experiential Edn., Internat. Personnel Mgmt. Assn., Internat. City Mgmt. Assn., Am. Soc. Pub. Adminstrn., Govtl. Research Assn., Internat. Union of Local Authorities, Am. Polit. Sci. Assn., Nat. Municipal League, Adult Edn. Assn. U.S., Am. Acad. Polit. and Social Sci. Presbyterian. Clubs: Saddle and Cycle, Casino, Econ., Monroe, Rotary, Chgo. Yacht, Univ. (Chgo.); Princeton (N.Y.C., Sarasota); Elm (Princeton U.); Venice (Fla.) Yacht; Mission Valley Golf and Country, Field. Home: 316 N Casey Key Osprey FL 33559 Office: PO Box 3006 4502 N Tamiami Trail Sarasota FL 33578 also Suite 1024 19 S LaSalle St Chicago IL 60603

LINGO, KENNETH HARRY, univ. adminstr.; b. Wilmington, Del., June 12, 1950; s. Harry and Ann (Keller) L.; B.S., Duke U., 1972; M.B.A., Wharton Sch., U. Pa., 1977. Mem. adminstrv. staff U. Pa. Hosp., 1975-77; dir. ambulatory services Vanderbilt U. Hosp., 1977-78, asso. adminstr. med. services, 1978-79; chief transition officer Vanderbilt U. Med. Center, 1979-80, dir. med. center planning, 1979—; instr. med. adminstrn. Vanderbilt U. Med. Sch.; bd. dirs. Vanderbilt U. Credit Union. Mem. Am. Coll. Hosp. Adminstrs., Am. Soc. Hosp. Planners, Tenn. Hosp. Assn. Home: 2610 Sunset Pl Nashville TN 37212 Office: 1161 21st Ave S Nashville TN 37232

LINK, JAMES EARL, univ. adminstr.; b. Strong City, Kans., Dec. 9, 1942; s. Morville Earl and Irene Hannah (Thompson) L.; B.S. in Bus. Adminstrn., Kans. State Tchrs. Coll., 1972; M.B.A., Tex. Christian U., 1980; m. Karin Jean Dawson, June 3, 1962; children—James Earl, Jay Edward. Ranch foreman Evans Ranch,

Cedar Point, Kans., 1966-68; with Diddee-Glasser Inc., Emporia, Kans., 1968-71; trust adminstr., farm and ranch El Paso Nat. Bank (Tex.), 1972-73; asst. v.p., mgr. ranch mgmt. dept. Oppenheimer Industries, Inc., Kansas City, Mo., 1973-76; asst. dir., instr. ranch mgmt. program Tex. Christian U., Ft. Worth, 1976—; cons. in field. Active Boy Scouts Am., El Paso, 1972-73, Shawnee Mission, Kans., 1973-76. King scholar, 1971-72; recipient Outstanding Farmer award Top Farmer, 1973. Mem. Soc. Range Mgmt., Aircraft Owners and Pilots Assn., Nat. Rifle Assn. Methodist. Club: Masons. Home: Route 1 Box 34R Crowley TX 76036 Office: PO Box 30774 Fort Worth TX 76129

LINK, MAE MILLS (MRS. S. GORDDEN LINK), historian; b. Corbin, Ky., May 14, 1915; d. William Speed and Florence (Estes) Mills; B.S., Vanderbilt U., 1936; M.A., 1937; Ph.D., Am. U., 1951; grad. Air War Coll., 1965; m. S. Gordden Link, Jan. 11, 1936. Instr. social sci. Oglethorpe U., 1938-39; instr. English, Drury Coll., 1940-41; asso. dir. edn. Ga. Warm Springs Found., 1941-42; mil. historian Hdqrs. Army Air Forces, 1943-45, Office Mil. History, Dept. Army, 1945-51; spl. asst. to surgeon gen. and sr. med. historian USAF, Washington, 1951-62; cons. documentation and space medicine historian NASA, Washington, 1962-64, coordinator documentation and life scis. historian, 1964-70; research asso. Ohio State U. Found., 1970-72; trustee, dir. history fellows Amos R. Koontz Meml. Found., Riverton, Va., 1972—; cons. aerospace med. history, 1972—. Recipient Meritorious Service award USAF, 1955, Outstanding Performance awards, 1956, 62; Friday Nighters cup, 1960. Fellow Am. Med. Writers Assn. (past dir. Middle Atlantic region); mem. Aerospace Med. Assn. (standing com. sci. communication in bioastronautics and space medicine), Am. Inst. Aeros. and Astronautics (hist. adv. com.), Air Force Hist. Found. (charter), Am. Assn. Med. History, Internat. Congress History Medicine, Societe International d'Histoire de la Medicine. Episcopalian. Club: Garden of Va.; Nat. Space. Author: Medical Support of the Army Air Forces in World War II, 1955; Annual Reports of the U.S. Air Force Medical Service, 1949-62; Space Medicine in Project Mercury, 1965; co-author US/USSR Joint Publ. Foundations of Space Biology and Medicine, 1975. Editor: U.S. Air Force Med. Service Digest, 1957-62. Contbr. to Ency. Brit., Collier's Ency., Funk and Wagnalls Standard Reference Ency., New Ency., profl. jours. Home: Dellbrook Riverton VA 22651 Office: Koontz Center Advanced Studies Riverton VA 22651

LINKE, LAWRENCE JOSEPH, photo reprodn. co. exec.; b. N.Y.C., Oct. 14, 1938; s. Arthur Sterling and Winifred (Berger) L.; student Newark Coll. Engring., 1960, Contra Costa Coll., 1961; B.S., Syracuse U., 1966; m. Angelina May Nasti, Oct. 23, 1960 (div. Sept. 1977); children—Mark Joseph, Tracey Ann; m. 2d, Gail Swift Geralds, July 7, 1979. Tech. aide Bell Telephone Labs., Whippany, N.J., 1960-61; electronics technician Beckman Instruments Co., Berkeley, Calif., 1961; engring. asst. Gen. Electric Co., Syracuse, N.Y., 1962-66; tech. rep. E.I. duPont de Nemours & Co., Detroit and Wilmington, Del., 1966-72; v.p. Engring. Reprographics Assos., Inc., Greenville, S.C., 1972—, also dir. Served with USMC, 1956-59. Mem. Internat. Reprographic Assn., Southeastern Blueprinters Assn. Unitarian. Home: 61 Topsail Ct Greenville SC 29611 Office: Route 5 Donkle Dr Greenville SC 29609

LINKENHOKER, PATRICIA LILLY, ednl. adminstr.; b. Athens, W.Va., Mar. 22, 1929; d. Paris I and Tessie (Ross) Lilly; B.S. in Music Edn., Concord Coll., Athens, 1949; M.A. in Supervision, Marshall U., 1973; m. George William Linkenhoker, Jr.; 1 dau., Ruth Linkenhoker Boyles. Tchr. music resource Mercer County (W.Va.) Bd. Edn., Princeton, 1949-71, gen. elementary supr., 1971—. Dir. handbell and celestial choirs 1st United Meth. Ch., 1964—, chmn. council on ministries, mem. adult choir, mem Wesleyanna Sharing Group. Mem. Nat. (life), W.Va., edn. assns., Mercer County Edn. Assn., Mercer County Reading Council, Am., W.Va. assns. supervision, curriculum devel., W.Va. Soc. Supervision, Curriculum, Elementary Prins. Assn., W.Va. Reading Council, PTA (life), Phi Delta Kappa, Delta Kappa Gamma, Sigma Sigma Sigma. Named Tchr. of Year Mercer County, 1969-70. Certification: Gen. Supr. grades 1-12, 1973. Home: 1307 N Walker St Princeton WV 24740 Office: Mercer County Bd Edn 1420 Honaker Ave Princeton WV 24740

LINKOVICH, WILLIAM, civic engr.; b. Winsted, Conn., Oct. 7, 1943; s. Michael and Elizabeth Ruth (Houser) L.; student Stetson U., 1962-64; B.S., U. Fla., 1966; children—Theresa, Tiffany. Dist. drainage engr. Fla. Dept. Transp., Lake City, 1971—. Registered profl. engr., Fla. Mem. Fla. Engring. Soc., Nat. Soc. Profl. Engrs. Elk. Home: Route 9 Box 136 Lake City FL 32055 Office: PO Box 1089 Lake City FL 32055

LINN, (MARION) JOANNE LOVELL (MRS. ROBERT JOSEPH LINN), anesthesiologist, educator; b. Centerville, Tenn., Mar. 24, 1926; d. Joe William and Annie Louise (Stephenson) Lovell; A.B., Tusculum Coll., 1946; M.D., Vanderbilt U., 1950; m. Robert Joseph Linn, Aug. 30, 1949; children—Mary Louise (Mrs. Scott Peyton Fitzhugh), Joseph Lovell, Margaret Ruth, David Robert. Intern, Balt. City Hosps., 1950-51; resident anesthesiology Vanderbilt U. Hosps., Nashville, 1951-53, George Washington U. Hosp., Washington, 1953; instr. anesthesiology Vanderbilt U., 1955-58, asst. prof., 1958-72, asso. prof., 1972—; cons. anesthesiologist VA Hosp., 1955-63, 73—, St. Thomas Hosp., 1968—, Parkview Hosp., 1972— (all Nashville). Bd. dirs. Autistic Children Tenn., 1978-79; bd. dirs., pres. pro tem Nashville Center Autistic Children, 1979—. Mem. AMA, So., Tenn., Pan Am. med. assns., Internat. Anesthesiology Research Soc., Am. Soc. Anesthesiology, Tenn. Soc. Anesthesiologists (sec.-treas. 1971-78, pres. 1978—), So., Nashville (pres. 1956, 66, 70-71) anesthesiology socs., Am., Tenn., Middle Tenn. (exec. bd. 1970, 78-79, 79-80, sec. chmn. pub. edn. com. 1973-75) heart assns., Am. Med. Women's Assn. (charter, co-founder, 1st pres. Middle Tenn. br. 1967, 77, nat. chmn. lecturship com. 1971-72, internat. relations com. 1973, sec. 1974, com. for liaison with other orgns. 1975-76, 2d v.p. 1977-79, pres.-elect 1979, pres. 1980), Davidson County and Nashville Acad. Medicine, N.Y. Acad. Scis., AAUP, AAUW (Vanderbilt corp. rep. 1978-80), Am. Profl. Practice Assn., Nashville Area C. of C., Nat. Aero. Assn., Nat. Audubon Soc., Nat. Council on Alcoholism and Drug Abuse, Am. Mus. Natural History, numerous other orgns., Delta Kappa Gamma, Alpha Epsilon Delta. Presbyn. Clubs: Univ., Vanderbilt Woman's (Nashville), Davidson County Bus. and Profl. Womens. Home: 6532 Jocelyn Hollow Rd Nashville TN 37205 Office: Vanderbilt U Med Center Nashville TN 37232

LINSLEY, JERALD NETHERTON, chem. engr.; b. Jones County, Tex., Aug. 31, 1938; s. Elliott Netherton and Vera Lilly (Hunt) L.; B.S. in Chem. Engring., Tex. Tech. U., 1960; Ph.D. in Chem. Engring., Rice U., 1970. Chem. engr. Dow-Badische Chem. Co., Freeport, Tex., 1960-61; asso. research engr. Tidewater Oil Co., 1965-66; sr. systems analyst Univac, France, 1966-68; process and systems analysis cons. Intercon, Inc., 1970-72; process systems engr. Applied Automation, Inc., 1972-73; sr. petrochem. cons. Digital Resources Corp., 1974; equipment engr. Tellepsen Constrn. Co., 1974-75; asst. prof. McNeese State U., Lake Charles, La., 1975-77; sr. engr. Brown & Root Inc., Houston, 1977—; cons. in field. NSF fellow; NASA fellow, registered profl. engr., Tex. Mem. Tex. Soc. Prof. Engrs., Am. Inst. Chem. Engrs. Club: European (Houston). Contbr. articles to profl. jours. Patentee in field. Home: 206 Marshall St Houston TX 77006 Office: PO Box 3 Houston TX 77001

LINTHURST, RICK ALAN, ecologist; b. York, Pa., Aug. 3, 1950; s. Herman Albright and G. Loretta (Himmelright) L.; B.S., Lebanon Valley Coll., 1972; M.S., N.C. State U., 1977, Ph.D. in Botany, 1979; m. Susan Allyson Swalm, Aug. 11, 1973. Research technician Marine Inst., U. Ga., Sapelo Island, 1972-75; research asst. dept. botany N.C. State U., Raleigh, 1975-79, vis. asst. prof., 1979—, also coordinator EPA research program; mng. partner Coastal Cons., Raleigh, 1975—. Mem. Am. Soc. Agronomy, AAAS, Am. Inst. Biol. Scis., Estuarine Research Fedn., Ecol. Soc. Am., Brit. Ecol. Soc., Bot. Soc. Am., N.C. Acad. Sci., Soil Sci. Soc. Am., Sigma Xi, Phi Kappa Phi, Beta Beta Beta. Home: 3512 Horton St Raleigh NC 27607 Office: North Carolina State U PO Box 5186 Raleigh NC 27650

LINTON, CYNTHIA FURR, mezzo-soprano, educator; b. Dallas, May 10, 1936; d. Parks A. and Verna A. (Wiley) Yeats; student Westminster Choir Coll., N.J., 1954-57; Mus.B., U. Miss., 1967, Mus.M., 1969; student of Miklos Bencze, Oxford, Miss., 1967-69; m. William Hal Furr, July 25, 1955 (dec. 1974); children—Virginia L., Susannah L., Elizabeth; m. 2d, A. Royce Linton, May 2, 1976. Contralto soloist with Westminster Choir Coll., 1955-56; debut in opera as Mother in Amahland the Night Vistiors, Phila. Oratorio Choir, 1965; appeared as Dorabella in Cosi fan Tutti, 1967, Mrs. Page in Merry Wives of Windsor, 1966, mother in The Consul, 1968, Madam Flora in The Medium, 1975; numerous solo appearances with Jackson (Miss.) Choral Soc., 1973-79; soloist with Oklahoma City Symphony, 1966, Kingsport (Tenn.) Symphony, 1968, Virginia Symphony, 1961; guest soloist with Tupelo (Miss.) Symphony, 1973; soloist in various churches and synagogues, Phila., 1961-65; touring voice recitals in Jackson, Miss., Raleigh, N.C., and Wichita, Kans., 1974; mem. voice faculty U. Miss., University, 1969—, mem. U. Chamber Choir, 1974-75, mem. Collegium Musicum, since 1973—; recording artist Columbia Records. Mem. Nat. Assn. Tchrs. of Singing (Singer of Yr. award 1967), Miss. Music Tchrs. Assn., Am. Guild of Mus. Artists. Home: Northgate Apts Bldg E-1 Oxford MS 38655 Office: Box 133 Univ of Miss University MS 38677

LIOU, TANG-JYI, civil engr.; b. Chia-Yi, Taiwan, Mar. 15, 1939; s. Shen-Ming and Liu (Chen) L.; came to U.S., 1969, naturalized, 1976; B.S. in Hydraulic Engring., Cheng Kung U., Tainan, Taiwan, 1962; M.S. in Civil Engring., La. State U., Baton Rouge, 1971; m. Mei-Li Sun, Nov. 21, 1965; children—Wen-Huai, Wen-Hsian, Doris Wen. Asst. engr. Chia-Nan Irrigation Assn., Tainan, 1963-68; chief rd. engring. sect. Bur. Pub. Works, Taipei, Taiwan, 1968-69; draftsman, designer Singstad, Kehart, November & Hurka, N.Y.C., 1970; soil lab. asst., div. engring. research La. State U., 1969-70, 70-71; civil engr. Aillet, Fenner, Jolly & McClelland, Inc., Shreveport, 1971—. Served to 2d lt. Chinese Army, 1962-63. Registered profl. engr., La., Republic China. Home: 518 Yale Pl Bossier City LA 71111 Office: 1055 Louisiana Ave Shreveport LA 71101

LIPKE, WALTER HAYWARD, electronics engr.; b. Wichita, Kans., Sept. 10, 1942; s. Hayward Eugene and Imogene (Unruh) L.; B.S. in Physics Engring., U. Tulsa, 1964; M.S. in Physics, Okla. State U., 1968; postgrad. Def. Systems Mgmt. Coll.; m. Peggy Rose Kobs, June 3, 1967; children—Jennifer Susan, Tara Jean. Electronic engr. trainee Oklahoma City Air Material Area, Tinker AFB, Okla., 1964-65, jr. electronic engr., 1968-74, project chief, Air Logistics Center, 1975-77, sect. chief, 1977—; grad. teaching asst. Okla. State U., 1965-67, grad. research asst., 1967-68; sr. electronic engr. So. Communication Area, Oklahoma City, 1974-75. Chmn. playground com. McFarlin Methodist Ch., Norman, Okla., 1974-77. Am. Chem. Soc. fellow, 1968; NSF traineeship, 1967; registered profl. engr., Okla. Mem. Tinker AFB Soc. Profl. Engrs., Internat., Okla. racquetball assns., Phi Kappa Phi, Sigma Pi Sigma. Republican. Home: 2127 W Dakota St Norman OK 73069 Office: Oklahoma City ALC/MATTM Tinker AFB OK 73145

LIPMAN, BERNARD SYLVESTER, physician; b. St. Joseph, Mo., June 14, 1920; s. Harry and Sarah (Kross) L.; B.A., Washington U., 1941, M.D., 1944; m. Leslie Joy Garber, Apr. 23, 1949; children—Lawrence A., Robert B., Bradford C., William L. Intern Barnes Hosp., St. Louis, 1943-44, resident in medicine, 1944-45, 47-48; resident in medicine Yale U., 1948-49; asst. in medicine, teaching fellow cardiology Washington U. Sch. Medicine, St. Louis, 1949-50; instr. medicine Emory U., Atlanta, 1950-56, asso. in medcine, 1956-61, asst. prof. medicine, 1961-65, asso. prof. medicine, 1965-73, prof. medicine and cardiology, 1973—; guest lectr. cardiology U. Tenn., 1958, U. Minn., 1959, 73; dir. heart sta. St. Joseph Hosp., Atlanta, 1965—; co-dir. Giddings Heart Clinic, Atlanta, 1970-75. Co-trustee Albert Steiner Meml. Fund. Served to capt., M.C., AUS 1945-47. Nat. Heart Inst. grantee, 1949. Diplomate Am. Bd. Internal Medicine. Fellow A.C.P., Am. Coll. Cardiology; mem. Council Clin. Cardiology, Am. Heart Assn., Am. Fedn. Clin. Research, Altanta Med. Assn., Am. Soc. Internal Medicine, N.Y. Acad. Sci., Phi Beta Kappa, Sigma Xi, Alpha Omega Alpha. Author: Clinical Scalar Electrocardiography, 6th edit., 1974. Contbr. articles to profl. jours. Home: 2652 Brookdale Dr NW Atlanta GA 30305 Office: 1285 Peachtree St NE Atlanta GA 30309

LIPMAN, IRA ACKERMAN, security service co. exec.; b. Little Rock, Nov. 15, 1940; s. Mark and Belle (Ackerman) L.; student Ohio Wesleyan U., 1958-60; LL.D., John Marshall U., 1970; m. Barbara Ellen Kelly Couch, July 5, 1970; children—Gustave K., Joshua S., M. Benjamin. Salesman and exec. Mark Lipman Service, Inc., Memphis, 1960-63; pres. Guardsmark, Inc., Memphis, 1963—, chief exec. officer, 1966—, chmn. bd., 1968—. Mem. young leadership cabinet United Jewish Appeal, 1973-78, Pres.'s Council, Memphis State U., 1975—; nat. trustee NCCJ, 1980—; mem. exec. com. Nat. Council on Crime and Delinquency, 1976, chmn. fin. com., treas., 1978-79; met. chmn. Nat. Alliance Businessmen, 1970-71; bd. dirs. Nat. Council Crime and Delinquency, 1975; mem. environ. security com., pvt. security adv. council Law Enforcement Assistance Adminstrn., 1975-76; bd. dirs. Tenn. Ind. Colls. Fund, 1977-79, mem. exec. com., 1978-79; trustee Memphis Acad. Arts, 1977—; mem. Future Memphis, 1979—, bd. dirs., 1980—; mem. exec. bd. Chickasaw council Boy Scouts Am., 1978—; Shelby County chmn. U.S. Savs. Bonds, 1976. Mem. Internat. Assn. Chiefs Police, Am. Soc. Criminology, Internat. Soc. Criminology, Am. Soc. Indsl. Security (cert. protection profl.). Republican. Clubs: B'nai B'rith; Economic, Racquet, Summit, Delta, Petroleum, Ridgeway Country (Memphis); Internat. (Washington). Author: How to Protect Yourself from Crime; contbr. articles to jours. and newspapers. Home: 4490 Park Ave Memphis TN 38117 also 58 W 58th St New York NY 10019 also Gilberts Path Amagansett NY 11930 Office: 260 Madison Ave New York NY 10016 also 22 S 2d St Memphis TN 38103

LIPNER, HARRY, physiologist; b. N.Y.C., Aug. 26, 1922; s. Samuel and Sarah (Linkoff) L.; B.S., L.I. U., 1942; M.S., U. Chgo., 1947; Ph.D., U. Iowa, 1952; m. Ethel Lapis, Sept. 11, 1949; children—Laura Jean, Sandra Lea, William Fredrick, Michael Allen. Instr. clin. pathology Chgo. Med. Sch., 1955; mem. faculty Fla. State U., Tallahassee, 1955—, prof. physiology, 1965—; vis. prof. Harvard U. Med. Sch., 1969-70. Fulbright-Hays fellow, 1974-75; fellow Baxter Labs., 1951; fellow NIH, 1953, spl. fellow, 1969-70; mem. Am. Physiol. Soc., Endocrine Soc., Soc. Study Reprodn., AAAS, Sigma Xi. Co-author: Biochemical Endocrinology of the Vertebrates, 1971. Home: PO Box 212 Greensboro FL 32330 Office: Dept Biol Scis Fla State U Tallahassee FL 32396

LIPOVICH, GEORGE JAY, computer industry mgr.; b. Columbus, Ohio, June 8, 1948; s. George Jay and Ruth Lee (Fish) L.; B.S. in Computer and Info. Sci., Ohio State U., 1971. Account exec. Copac, Inc., Columbus, 1969-71; programmer Univac, Blue Bell, Pa., 1971-72; pres. Offax Services, Inc., Columbus, 1972-73; dir. products markets Tesdata Systems Corp., McLean, Va., 1973—; dir. Offax Services, Inc.; hon. mem. faculty Dept. Def. Computer Inst.; mem. adv. com. dept. computer sci. Ohio State U. Commr., Boy Scouts Am., 1969-71. Certified data processing educator. Mem. Am. Mgmt. Assn., Computer Mgmt. Group. Designer remote measurement device, performance monitoring network. Home: 107 Gold Thorn Way Sterling VA 22170 Office: 7921 Jones Branch Dr McLean VA 22101

LIPPERT, LUDWIG EDWARD, JR., lawyer; b. Brackenridge, Pa., Apr. 9, 1931; s. Ludwig Edward and Amelia F. (Neal) L.; B.A. (Outstanding Sr. Grad. 1953), U. Pitts., 1953, J.D., 1956; M.A., Creighton U., Omaha, 1965; m. Ruth I. Maeder, Aug. 25, 1956; children—Susan K., Jennifer E. Admitted to D.C. bar, 1956; commd. 2d lt. U.S. Air Force, 1956, advanced through grades to col., 1973; legal adv., legis. asst. to chmn. Joint Chiefs Staff, 1975-77; ret., 1977; mgr. Washington office Kentron Internat., Inc., 1978—; professorial lectr. mgmt. George Washington U., 1969—. Decorated Legion of Merit, Joint Services Commendation medal, Meritorious Service medal (2), Air Force Commendation medal (3). Mem. Am. Bar Assn., Fed. Bar Assn., D.C. Bar Assn. Club: Internat. (Washington). Home: 8422 Blakiston Ln Alexandria VA 22308 Office: 1745 Jefferson Davis Hwy Suite 612 Arlington VA 22202

LIPPITT, ALAN BRUCE, orthopedic surgeon; b. Norwich, Conn., June 22, 1941; s. Harold and Ruth (Sakowitz) L.; B.S., Trinity Coll. (Conn.), 1963; M.D., N.Y. Med. Coll., 1969; m. Linda Hovitz Nathanson, Aug. 1, 1975; children—Karen, Elizabeth, Daniel, Jennifer; stepchildren—Melanie, Scott. Intern, Hosp. for Joint Diseases, N.Y.C., 1969-70, resident in orthopedic surgery, 1970-74; practice medicine specializing in orthopedic surgery, Atlanta, 1976—; orthopedic surgeon Ga. Baptist Hosp., St. Joseph's Hosp., 1976—; cons. Ga. Regional Hosp. Served to maj. M.C., U.S. Army, 1974-76. Diplomate Am. Bd. Orthopedic Surgery. Mem. Am. Acad. Cerebral Palsy. Home: 1081 Ragley Hall Rd Atlanta GA 30319 Office: 315 Boulevard NE Suite 336 Atlanta GA 30312

LIPPMAN, ALFRED, aluminum corp. exec.; b. New Orleans, Mar. 13, 1908; s. Alfred and Belle (Levy) L.; B.Engring., Tulane U., 1929; m. Alyse M. Crum, Oct. 4, 1969; children by previous marriage—Alfred S., Tanya (Mrs. R.E. Murray), Darryl R. Successively asst. supt., research chemist, chief chemist, mgr. Bay Chem. Co., Weeks, La., 1929-31, 34-51; gen. mgr. Commonwealth Engring. Co. of Ohio, Dayton, 1951-53; plant mgr. Godchaux Sugars, Inc., Reserve, La., 1953-56; gen. dir. Alumina Research div. Reynolds Metals Co., Bauxite, Ark., 1956-71; sr. v.p., dir. research and devel. Toth Aluminum Corp., New Orleans, 1971—, also vice chmn. bd. Mem. finance com. Evangeline Area council Boy Scouts Am., 1949-51; mem. adv. bd. La. Indsl. Devel. Commn., 1949-51. Registered profl. chem. engr. Fellow Am. Ceramic Soc.; mem. Nat. Soc. Profl. Engrs., La. Engring. Soc., Am. Inst. Chem. Engrs., Am. Inst. Mining, Metall. and Petroleum Engrs., Am. Chem. Soc., Tau Beta Pi. Republican. Jewish religion. Lion, Rotarian. Contbr. articles profl. jours. Patentee in field. Home: 4613 Purdue Dr Metairie LA 70003 Office: PO Box 8080 New Orleans LA 70182

LIPSCOMB, GUY FLEMING, chemist, painter; b. Clemson, S.C., Apr. 11, 1917; s. Guy Fleming and Adelin L.; B.S., U. S.C., 1938; postgrad. U. Akron, 1944-45; m. Margaret Marshall Faut, June 20, 1942; children—Margaret, Louise, Georgia, Elizabeth. Mfg. mgr. E.I. duPont, 1942-45, Goodyear Tire & Rubber Co., 1945-47; with Continental Chem. Co., Columbia, S.C., 1938-42, 47—, chmn. bd., 1975-78; dir. 1st Fed. Savs. & Loan Assn. of Columbia; painter, works exhibited 20 one-man shows; works rep. Nat. Acad. (N.Y.C.). Chmn. Columbia Airport Commn., Richland Indsl. Devel. Com., Midland Indsl. Council (chmn.), S.C. Mus. Commn. Mem. Am. Chem. Soc., Columbia C. of C. (dir.). Presbyterian. Club: Rotary (past pres.). Home: 1717 W Buchanan St Columbia SC 29206 Office: 2000 S Belt Line Columbia SC 29250

LIPSHY, BEN ALLEN, mfg. co. exec.; b. Ft. Worth, Oct. 3, 1910; s. Julius and Sarah Ethel (Korman) L.; grad. pub. schs., Tex.; m. Udys Weinstein, Sept. 7, 1931; children—Joy Lipshy Burk, Barbara Lipshy Marcus, Bruce Arlen. With Zale Corp., Dallas, 1926—, supr., 1937, treas., 1947, pres., 1957—, chmn. bd., 1971—; dir. Republic of Tex. Corp., Dallas. Mem. Dallas Citizens Council, Jewish Welfare Fedn. Dallas, Dallas Alliance, Greater Dallas Crime Commn.; bd. dirs. Southwestern Med. Found., 1975—, World Trade Center, Nat. Jewish Hosp. Found., 1973—, Callier Center, Dallas County Community Coll. Dist. Found., St. Paul Profl. Bd., 1966—, State Fair of Tex. Mem. Tex. Retail Fedn. (dir.), Dallas Better Bus. Bur. Jewish. Clubs: Columbian, Masons, Shriners.

LIPSON, GOLDIE, artist, lectr., author; b. N.Y.C., Nov. 18, 1905; d. Herman and Tillie (Schroff) Goldman; studied with Carl Nelson; studied fresco mural painting, Mexico, 1951; m. Moe Lipson, July 24, 1924 (dec. July 1975); children—Adylin (Mrs. Murray Rosenblatt), Stanley. One-man shows Uptown Gallery, N.Y.C., 1942, Charles Barzansky Gallery, N.Y.C., 1946, 47, 49, 53, 58, 64, 67, Lake Wales Pub. Library, 1965, Ridge Art Assn., 1975; retrospective exhbn. County Center, White Plains, N.Y., 1953, Barzansky Gallery, 1967 Ridge Art Cultural Art Center, Winter Haven, Fla., 1970; demonstrations Nat. Acad. Art, 1945, 46, 47, 48, 62; dir., tchr. Goldie Lipson Studio Workshop, 1947-64; instr. Arnold Coll., Milford, Conn., 1951, 52; dir. art YM-YWHA, Mt. Vernon, 1951-55; dir. art classes YMCA, Bronx, N.Y., 1940-41; exhibits in traveling shows through U.S. and Can.; exhibited Aquarelles Gallery, Paris, 1949, nat. juried shows of Am. Water-Color Soc., Audubon Soc., Allied Artists Am., Nat. Acad. Art, Cosmopolitan Artists at Riverside Mus., 1951, 52, 54, N.Y. Coliseum Art, 1959, Artists Equity, 1959, Clarksville Art Center, Mamaroneck Beach and Y Club, 1966-68; agt. Barzansky Gallery, N.Y.C., from 1945; executed fresco murals, San Maguel Alanda, Mexico, 1951; mural in oil executed for Samuel Carson Collection, Purchase, N.Y., 1960, murals in tile, cement and oil, Orchid Spring, Winter Haven and Lake of the Hills, Fla., 1968—; represented in pvt. collections. Writer weekly column Our Guru Says, Daily Highlander, Lake Wales, 1971-72; tchr., lectr. Yoga. Recipient 1st prize oil Mt. Vernon Art Assn., 1947, 49, 54, 1st prize water color, 1948, 51; 1st prize New Rochelle Art Assn., 1948-50; top prize in oil Westchester County Center, 1949, prize for colored print, 1957. Mem. Fla. Fedn. Art (publicity chmn. 1970-72), Fla. Artists Equity (dir. 1956-65), Mamaroneck Artist Guild, Mt. Vernon, New Rochelle, Ridge, Lake Wales, Westchester art assns, Ridge Art Assn. Winter Haven, Lake Wales Arts Council, Fla. Artists Group, Fla. Bus. and Profl. Womens Group. Club: Lake Wales Garden. Author: Moods and Nudes, 1960. Author and illustrator; Rejuvenation, 1963; We, 1965; Beyond Yoga, 1970, 77; author: Rejuvenation through Yoga, 1965,

78, illustrator Yoga, Youth and Reincarnations, 1965. Subject of booklet Many Faces of Golda. Home: Lake of the Hills PO Box 1261 Lake Wales FL 33853

LIPSON, LEONARD BERGER, petroleum co. exec.; b. Chelsea, Mass., Mar. 2, 1922; s. Edward and Sara (Berger) L.; student Colo. Sch. Mines, 1940-41; B.A., U. Tex., 1942, M.A., 1946, Ph.D. in Physics and Math. (teaching fellow), 1953; m. Betty Cecile Hymans, Dec. 9, 1942; children—Lucienne Cecile, Nicole Gay. Sr. research physicist Mobil Oil Co., Dallas, 1948-54; asso. prof. engring. U. Houston, 1954-60; v.p. Mgmt. Decisions Inc., Houston, 1962-64; staff scientist Lockheed Corp., Houston, 1964-65, Atlanta, 1965-69; v.p. staff cons. Guernsey Petroleum Corp., Atlanta, 1969-72, New Orleans, 1972-79; v.p. planning and devel. ConVest Energy Corp., Houston, 1979—; instr. Ga. State U., Atlanta, part-time 1971; asso. prof. U. New Orleans, part-time 1973-79; professorial lectr. Loyola U., 1975—; adj. prof. Tulane U. Grad. Sch. Engring., 1979. Mem. Soc. Petroleum Engrs., Am. Inst. Decision Scis., Internat. Assn. Math. Geology, Am. Inst. Profl. Geologists, Planning Execs. Inst., Sigma Xi, Sigma Pi Sigma, Alpha Iota Delta. Club: Petroleum (New Orleans). Patentee in field. Contbr. articles to profl. jours. Home: 1836 Augusta Dr #6 Houston TX 77057 Office: 1700 W Loop S Suite 1000 Houston TX 77027

LIPSTATE, EUGENE JACOB, oil co. exec.; b. Tyler, Tex., Dec. 6, 1927; s. Philip H. and Gertrude (Faber) L.; B.S., U. Tex., 1949; m. JoAnne Davis, Feb. 26, 1950; children—James Mitchell, Betsy Ann. With Petroleum Service Co., San Antonio, 1949-50; Tex. dist. engr. Caran Bros. Engring. Co., San Antonio and Tyler, 1950-51; geologist Ryan Consol. Petroleum Corp., Dallas, 1951-52, Tex. dist. geologist, Abilene, 1953-54; geologist Midstates Oil Corp., San Antonio, 1955-58; Tenneco Oil Co., Houston, 1958-62; v.p. exploration Northwest Oil Co., Dallas and Lafayette La., 1962—; partner Tri-Ltd., Lafayette, 1977—; dir. Lipstate Creative Services, Inc., Lafayette, 1975—; pres. Eugene J. Lipstate, Inc., Lafayette, 1978—. Served to lt. USAF, 1952-53. Mem. Assn. Petroleum Geologists, Lafayette Geol. Soc., Gulf Coast Assn. Geol. Socs., U. Tex. Ex-Students Assn. Republican. Clubs: Lafayette Petroleum, Lafayette City, Lafayette Longhorn, Oakbourne Country. Home: 401 Shelly Dr Lafayette LA 70503 Office: PO Box 52421 Lafayette LA 70505

LIS, ANTHONY STANLEY, educator; b. Easthampton, Mass., Aug. 11, 1918; s. Antoni and Anna Barbara (Karczmarczyk) L.; B.S., Mass. State Coll. at Salem, 1950; M.S., Okla. State U., 1950-51; Ph.D., U. Minn., 1961; m. Jane Ann Mikus, June 25, 1951 (dec.); children—Anthony Stanley, Judith Ann, Sandra Jane. Instr. to asst. prof. bus. edn. Okla. State U., 1950-54; asst. prof. to asso. prof. bus. communication U. Tulsa, 1956-62; asso. prof. to prof. bus. adminstrn. U. Okla., 1962—; cons. to bus., govtl. agencies. Participant, 2d Congress Scholars of Polish Descent, Warsaw and Cracow, 1979. Served with U.S. Army, 1937-40, to lt. col. AUS, 1942-56. Decorated Bronze Star; Faculty fellow Joint Econ. Found., 1954. Mem. Adminstrv. Mgmt. Soc., Am. Bus. Communication Assn. (nat. dir.), Southwestern Social Sci. Assn. (gen. program chmn. 1963-76), Am. Assn. Advancement Slavic Studies, Polish Am. Hist. Assn. Roman Catholic. Lion. Home: 1827 Peter Pan St Norman OK 73069

LISANKE, ROBERT JOHN, chemist; b. N.Y.C., June 7, 1932; s. Clement Joseph and Anne Mary (Campbell) Liszanckie; B.S., Fordham U., 1954; M.S., U. Notre Dame, 1956; postgrad. Fairleigh Dickinson U., 1962-63, Pa. State U., 1969, Syracuse U., 1972-73, U. Calif., 1977; m. Patricia Ann Traum, Nov. 16, 1957; children—Robert John, Joseph, Michael, Jeanne. Teaching fellow U. Notre Dame, 1954, research asst., 1954-56; research chemist, silicones div. Union Carbide Corp., Sistersville, W.Va., 1956-59, Hooker Chem. Corp., Niagara Falls, N.Y., 1959-60, fuels devel. group Mobil Oil Corp., Paulsboro, N.J., 1960-66; process chemist video display equipment operation Gen. Electric Co., Syracuse, N.Y., 1966-73; sr. chemist Pratt & Whitney Aircraft div. United Technologies Corp., West Palm Beach, Fla., 1974—. Regional dir. Bayberry Community Assn., 1972-74; mem. nat. adv. bd. Am. Security Council, 1975—. Mem. Am. Chem. Soc., Am. Inst. Chem. Engrs., ASME, Soc. Advancement of Material and Process Engring., Am. Soc. Metals, IEEE. Republican. Roman Catholic. Club: U.S. Chess Fedn. Patentee in field. Home: PO Box 9101 Riviera Beach FL 33404 Office: PO Box 2691 West Palm Beach FL 33402

LISEMBY, DORIS MITCHELL, speech pathologist; b. Kingsland, Ark., June 19, 1918; d. Wallace E. and Jewell Graves Mitchell; B.S.E., Henderson State U., 1950; M.A., Tex. Women's U., 1960; postgrad. U. Houston, 1960; m. Doris M. Mitchell, Mar. 5, 1938; adopted children—Carole Loyd, Doug Lisemby, Greg Lisemby. Tchr., Deer Park (Tex.) Ind. Sch. Dist., 1959—, speech pathologist, 1980—. Mem. Am. Speech and Hearing Assn., NEA, Assn. Retired Persons, Tex. State Tchrs. Assn., Deer Park Tchrs. Assn. Baptist. Club: San Jacinto Faculty. Home: 2717 Huckleberry Ln Pasadena TX 77502

LISTON, WILLIAM HARRY, lawyer; b. Natchez, Miss., Mar. 13, 1931; s. William and Hester (Jordan) L.; student Miss. State U., 1950-51, U. Md. Extension (Europe), 1951-52; LL.B., U. Miss., 1958; m. Brenda Henson; children—William, III, Lori Layne. Admitted to Miss. bar, 1958; investigator Miss. Dept. Ins., Jackson, 1958; practiced in Winona, Miss., 1958—; former mem. firm Liston & Sumner; mem. firm William Liston, profl. assn. Served with USAF, 1951-54. Mem. Am., Miss. State, Montgomery County bar assns., Am. Trial Lawyers Assn., Miss. Trial Lawyers Assn., Pi Kappa Alpha, Phi Alpha Delta. Methodist. Home: 418 Johns St Winona MS 38967 Office: 128 N Quitman St Winona MS 38967 also 206 Dunn St Europa MS 39747

LITCHER, JOHN HANNIBAL, educator; b. Winona, Minn., Feb. 4, 1939; s. Hannibal John and Helen Katherine L.; B.S., Winona State U., 1964; M.A., U. Minn., 1967, Ph.D., 1970; m. Ramona Ann Olstad, June 4, 1960; children—Jade John, Jeffrey Claire, Danta Ann. Lab. technician Fiberite Corp., Winona, 1961-64; tchr. public shcs., Rochester, Minn., 1964-65; asst. prof. edn. U. Fla., 1970-73; asso. prof. Wake Forest U., Winston Salem, N.C., 1973—, dir. tchr. edn., 1973—; nat. cons. Head Start/Followthrough. Bd. dirs. Early Child Devel. Assn. Served with USN, 1958-61. Grantee HEW, NSF; cert. in naval law U.S. Sch. Mil. Justice. Mem. Internat. Reading Assn. (pres. Winston Salem chpt.), NEA, Nat. Council Social Studies, Nat. Assn. Supervision and Curriculum Devel., Phi Delta Kappa. Lutheran. Author: Social Studies: The Humanizing Process, 1973; contbr. articles to profl. jours. Home: 185 Tullyries Ln Lewisville NC 27023 Office: Sch Edn Wake Forest U Winston Salem NC 27109

LITHERLAND, JAMES GEORGE, JR., petroleum reservior engr.; b. Shreveport, La., Feb. 19, 1922; s. James George and Madeline Melissa (Worley) L.; B.S., La. State U., 1948; m. Evelyn Dunnam, May 7, 1945; children—James George III, Steven Richard. With Magnolia Petroleum Co., Morgan City, La., Falfurrias, Tex., Midland, Tex., Dallas, 1948-54, petroleum engr., 1948-52, staff engr., 1952-54; with DeGolyer and Mac Naughton, Dallas, 1954—, petroleum engr., 1954-61, v.p., 1961—, treas., 1969—. Precinct chmn. Republican Party, 1956-64, area chmn., 1958-64. Served with USAAF, 1942-46. Mem. Soc. Petroleum Engrs. (dir. 1974-76; Engr. of Year award Dallas sect. 1971), Am. Inst. M.E. (chmn. Dallas sect. Soc. Petroleum Engrs. br. 1970), Petroleum Engrs. Club of Dallas (pres. 1967). Clubs: Toastmasters (pres. 1958), Brookhaven Country. Home: 7827 Northaven Rd Dallas TX 75230 Office: One Energy Sq Dallas TX 75206

LITKENHAUS, RAYMOND ARTHUR, mining engr.; b. Limerick, Sask., Can., Jan. 26, 1920; s. Arthur Bernard and Elsie Kathyrn (Schaffer) L.; came to U.S., 1949, naturalized, 1956; B.Sc. Mining-Engring., U. Alta. (Can.), Edmonton, 1941; m. Cornelia Virginia Bumgarner, Nov. 25, 1954; 1 dau., Jaime Delphine. Partner Geosurveys Ltd., cons. engrs., Toronto, Ont., Can., 1947-49; engr. Elliot Co., Pitts., 1950-52; pres. R. A. Litkenhaus & Assos., Inc., Jacksonville, Fla., 1953—; v.p. Pan Arabian Co.; real estate broker. Served as lt. comdr. Canadian Navy, 1941-46. Mem. Am. Water Works Assn., Fla. Pollution Control Assn., Assn. Profl. Engrs., Geologists and Geophysicists of Alta., Jacksonville C. of C. (chmn. internat. finance seminar), Lambda Chi Alpha. Democrat. Presbyterian. Clubs: River, Deerwood, Ponte Vedra, Masons, Shriners, Kiwanis (sec. North Jacksonville club). Office: 7825 Baymeadows Way Suite 106B Jacksonville FL 32216

LITTLE, CARLTON GARRETT, utility exec.; b. Knoxville, Tenn., June 5, 1932; d. Hillborn Carlton and Mariam Boyd (Eaton) Garrett; student Knoxville Bus. Coll., 1949-50; m. Hugh H. Little, June 7, 1974. With Knoxville Utilities Bd., 1951—, adminstrv. asst. to gen. mgr., 1971-79, employee relations mgr., 1979—; mem. Knox County bd. advisers to Office Vocat. Edn. Bd. dirs. E. Tenn. Substance Abuse Council, 1979-80. Mem. Soc. Advancement Mgmt. (v.p. membership), Am. Public Power Assn., Am. Compensation Assn., Am. Soc. Tng. Dirs., Am. Soc. Personnel Adminstrs., Adminstrv. Mgmt. Soc., Tenn. Indsl. Personnel Conf. (area dir. 1980), Tenn. Valley Public Power Assn. (vice chmn. personnel sect. 1980), Tenn. Valley Personnel Assn. (past pres.), Knoxville Council Career Women (past pres.). Baptist. Home: 4120 Galbraith Rd Knoxville TN 37920 Office: 626 Gay St Knoxville TN 37901

LITTLE, DOYLE EDGAR, mfg. co. exec.; b. Henderson, Tex., Feb. 12, 1936; s. Walden Aderson and Eva Jo (Strickland) L.; B.A., Rice U., 1958, M.S., 1960; S.M. (Sloan fellow), Mass. Inst. Tech., 1969; m. Patricia Ann Kolb, Sept. 4, 1955; children—Sharon, Janet, Susan. Asst. to pres. Eastman Kodak Co., Longview, Tex., 1969-73; v.p. The Western Co. of N. Am., Fort Worth, 1973-77; pres. OPI Inc., Odessa, Tex., 1977—, also dir.; dir. OPI, Ltd., Edmonton, Alta., Can. Del. Democratic State Conv. Mem. Am. Inst. Mech. Engrs., Am. Inst. Chem. Engrs., Am. Chem. Soc., Am. Petroleum Inst. Clubs: Petroleum, Ridglea Country. Home: 2507 Stutz St Midland TX 78701 Office: 905 S Grandview St Odessa TX 79760

LITTLE, FREED SEBASTIAN, petroleum equipment mfg. co. exec.; b. Ft. Smith, Ark., May 4, 1926; s. Jess Edward and Floy Kimbrough (Witt) L.; B.A., U. Ark., 1950; m. Jana V. Jones, Dec. 9, 1951 (div.); 1 son, Mark McKenna. With Gilbarco Inc., Houston, 1964—, central area mgr., Chgo., 1969-73, Western regional mgr., Houston, 1974—. Served with USAAF, 1945-46. Mem. Am. Petroleum Inst., Petroleum Equipment Inst., Am. Mgmt. Assn., Sigma Alpha Epsilon. Presbyterian. Clubs: Houston City, Memorial Dr. Country. Home: 10121 Valley Forge Houston TX 77042 Office: 6400 Westpark Dr Suite 290 Houston TX 77057

LITTLE, HARRY WILSON, engineer; b. Weimar, Tex., Apr. 22, 1923; s. Homer Melton and Theresa (Shimek) L.; B.E.E., Ga. Inst. Tech., 1946, M.S. in Indsl. Engring., 1951; m. Thelma Phyllis Lewis, Sept. 9, 1950; children—Melton Harry, Catherine Melanie. Engr.-missionary Methodist Ch., Congo, 1950-61; outside plant engr. Gen. Telephone and Electronics, Tampa, Fla., 1961-64; engr. Marshall Space Flight Center, Huntsville, Ala., 1964-73, U.S. Postal Service, 1973-76, Tropicana Products, Inc., Bradenton, Fla., 1976—. Served with USN, 1941-45. NASA doctoral fellow, 1968-71; registered profl. engr. Mem. Am. Inst. Indsl. Engrs. (sr.), IEEE, Alpha Pi Mu. Republican. Methodist. Club: Kiwanis. Home: 2915 Bayshore Gardens Pkwy Bradenton FL 33507 Office: Tropicana Products Inc Box 338 Bradenton FL 33505

LITTLE, JOHN PATTERSON, JR., leasing co. exec.; b. New Orleans, Oct. 27, 1941; s. John Patterson and Claire (Dolph) L.; B.B.A., U. Miss., 1964; m. Carole Lee Andrews, Aug. 20, 1963; children—John III, Robert, Gregory. Pres., Telephone Equipment Co., Inc., Oxford, Miss., 1963-67; exec. v.p., gen. mgr. Miss. Transmission Co., Inc., Oxford, 1967-70; pres. Tounsley Communications, Inc., Lake Park, Fla., 1970-73, So. Leasing Services, Inc., North Palm Beach, Fla., 1974—, So. Factoring, Inc., North Palm Beach, 1977—, Comml. Factors, Inc., North Palm Beach, 1978—; dir. Nat. Comml. Fin. Conf., Inc., N.Y.C., 1978—. Served with USAFR, 1962. Mem. Exchange Club No. Palm Beaches. Democrat. Episcopalian. Home: 10858 Magnolia St Palm Beach FL 33410 Office: 618 US Hwy 1 North Palm Beach FL 33408

LITTLE, TED DAVID, state senator; b. Andalusia, Ala., June 21, 1942; s. Grover Henry and Hesta (Brogden) L.; B.S., U. Ala, 1964, J.D., 1967; m. Jonnie Dee Riley, Dec. 26, 1968; children—Mollie Dora, Terre Su. Admitted to Ala. bar, 1967; asst. prof. bus. Auburn (Ala.) U., 1968-74, adj. prof., 1974—; practice in Auburn, 1974—; mem. Ala. Senate from 21st Dist., 1974—. Mem. Lee County Democratic Exec. Com., 1972—. Mem. Am. Bar Assn., Ala. Bar Assn., Ala. Farm Bur., Omicron Delta Kappa, Pi Kappa Alpha, Phi Eta Sigma. Baptist. Club: Kiwanis (past pres. Greater Auburn). Office: 403-B E Magnolia St Auburn AL 36830

LITTLE, WALDEN PASKEL, ins. co. exec.; b. nr. Groesbeck, Tex., Mar. 14, 1920; s. Wilmer Preston and Georgia (Cates) L.; A.A., Westminister Coll., 1940; m. Billye Jean Bostick, June 9, 1965; children—Gregory, Regina. With Combined Underwriters Life Ins. Co., Tyler, Tex., 1949—, pres., 1956—. City commr. Tyler, 1966—, mayor, 1968—. Bd. dirs. YMCA. Mem. Tyler Sales Execs. Club. Mem. Christian Ch. Mason (Shriner). Home: 3326 Pollard St Tyler TX 75701 Office: 307 N Glenwood St Tyler TX 75701

LITTLE, WILLIAM D., JR., newspaper exec.; b. Ada, Okla., May 22, 1921; s. William Dee and Willie (Faust) L.; grad. McCallie Sch., 1938; A.B., East Central State Coll., Ada, 1942; m. Mary Louise Osborne, Sept. 13, 1942; children—Helen Jane Little Poston, Linda Brooks Little Steiner, William D. III. With News Publ. and Printing Co., Ada, 1942—, advt. solicitor, asst. to pub., 1946, v.p., bus. mgr., 1947-66, pres., 1966-78; pub. and gen. mgr. Ada Evening News, 1966—; dir. Home Fed. Savs. & Loan Assn., Ada, Ada Indsl. Devel. Corp., Okla. Gas & Electric Co. Trustee, Valley View Hosp., Ada, 1958-78, chmn., 1963—; mem. Okla. Econ. Adv. Council, 1963-66, Gov.'s Capital Expenditures Adv. Council, 1967; pres. E. Central Okla. Bldg. Authority, 1965—; mem. Okla. Health Council, 1968-72; v.p. Okla. Health Scis. Found., 1965-77; treas. Okla. Soc. Crippled Children; mem., former chmn. adv. council Salvation Army. Bd. dirs. Scis. and Natural Resources Found. Okla.; bd. govs. Okla. Natural Heritage Program; trustee, v.p. Okla. Newspaper Found.; trustee East Central State Coll. Found., Inc.; dir. Okla. Heritage Assn. 1975, 77—, mem. exec. com. Mem. Am., So. (dir. 1969-72) newspaper pubs. assns., Okla. A.P. Mng. Editors Assn. (pres. 1958), Okla. Press Assn., Ada (pres. 1954, dir.), Okla. (dir. 1971—, pres. 1975) chambers commerce, C. of C. of U.S., East Central Coll. Alumni Assn. (pres. 1949, Disting. Alumnus award 1979), Newcomen Soc. N.Am. Episcopalian. Home: South-on-Jack Fork PO Box 596 Ada OK 74820 Office: 116 N Broadway Ada OK 74820

LITTLE, WILLIS ANDREW, JR., broadcasting exec.; b. Hampton, Va., Mar. 7, 1940; s. Willis Andrew and Agnes (Simpson) L.; B.S. in Math. and Physics, Lynchburg (Va.) Coll., 1962; m. Betty Rhea Campbell, Aug. 2, 1960; children—Christie Renee, Willis Andrew III, Lisa Dawn. With Sta. WSET-TV, and predecessor, Lynchburg, 1959—, chief engr., 1976—. Bd. dirs. Lynchburg Baptist Royal Ambassadors, 1972-79. Mem. Soc. Motion Picture and TV Engrs., Lynchburg Soc. Engrs. Sci (dir. 1977-79, pres. 1980). Club: Civitan (1st v.p. Lynchburg 1979-80). Home: 111 Victor Dr Lynchburg VA 24501 Office: 2320 Langhorne Rd PO Box 11588 Lynchburg VA 24506

LITTLEFIELD, RICHARD WELLS, JR., lawyer; b. Jacksonville, Fla., Sept. 17, 1948; s. Richard Wells and Hazel Florence (Harper) L.; B.A. in Polit. Sci., Emory U., Atlanta, 1970; J.D., U. Ga., 1973; children—Stephanie Ann, Richard Wells. Admitted to Ga. bar; practice law, Brunswick, Ga.; partner firm Littlefield, Ossick & Rivers; asst. dist. atty. Brunswick Circuit; part-time instr. Coastal Ga. Police Acad. Mem. Am. Bar Assn., Am. Trial Lawyers Assn., Ga. Bar Assn., Ga. Trial Lawyers Assn., Ga. Assn. Criminal Def. Lawyers, Brunswick Jaycees. Democrat. Presbyterian. Club: Kiwanis. Home: 1308 Oak St St Simons Island GA 31522 Office: 777 Gloucester St Suite 404 Brunswick GA 31520

LITTLEJOHN, JAMES DEWITT, bus. exec., educator, journalist; b. El Paso, Tex., June 21, 1931; s. James Franklin and Mary Kathleen (Badgett) L.; B.A., Tex. Christian U., 1954; m. Sunny Gail Wright, May 25, 1968; children—James Hartwell, Kathleen Marie, Linda Louise. Tchr. pub. schs., San Angelo, Odessa, Tex., 1954-60; pres., Marlo Products Co., Odessa, 1960-61; asst. mgr. Greater Florence (S.C.) C. of C., 1961-63; sports editor, bur. chief Florence Morning News, Savannah (Ga.) Morning News, 1963-69; exec. dir. Hilton Head (S.C.) C. of C., 1969-74; editor Islander Mag., 1969-74; pres. Littlejohn Co., pub. relations, 1974—; asso. editor Island Events mag., 1979—. Mem. NEA, S.C. Ednl. Assn., Beaufort County Classroom Tchrs. Assn. Home: 53 Follyfield Rd Hilton Head Island SC 29928 Office: PO Box 1325 Hilton Head Island SC 29928

LITTLEJOHN, WALTER LEE, univ. adminstr.; b. Pine Bluff, Ark., Mar. 5, 1932; s. Ed and Beatrice M. Littlejohn; B.S., AM&N Coll., 1954; M.Ed., U. Ark., 1957, Ed.D., 1966; m. Virginia Lowery, June 12, 1955. Tchr. public schs., Magnolia, Ark., 1954-55, prin. high sch., 1956-57, supt. schs., 1957-64; asso. prof. edn. U. Ark., Pine Bluff, 1966-68, prof., 1968-74, chmn. secondary edn., 1974-75, dean div. tchr. edn., 1975—. Mem. NEA (life), Ark. Edn. Assn., AAUP, Am. Assn. Colls. for Tchr. Edn., Assn. Tchr. Educators, Pine Bluff C. of C. Baptist. Club: Kiwanis. Author: (with Clara Jennings) Good Programs for Young Children: A Guide for Care-Givers, 1979. Office: Div Tchr Edn U Ark Pine Bluff AR 71601

LITTON, LARRY BLAKE, mortgage banker; b. Doylestown, Ohio, Aug. 31, 1940; s. Ormal Blake and Cloa Myrtle (Burgess) L.; student Lee Coll., U. Houston Extension; m. Ruth Catherine Schultz, Feb. 14, 1964; children—Larry Blake, Darla, James, Tara. With Gulf Coast Investment Corp., Houston, 1963-75; 1st v.p., exec. com. N. Am. Mortgage Co., Houston, 1975—; vice chmn. bd., dir. Houston Bd. Realtors Fed. Credit Union. Apptd. to dist. com., Admissions Bd. of Law Examiners Bd. dirs., officer Northshore Booster Club, Northshore Pony/Colt Baseball League; mem. fin. com., past mem. adminstrv. bd. Holy Trinity United Meth. Ch. Recipient numerous awards for public service. Mem. Houston Mortgage Bankers Assn., Tex. Mortgage Bankers Assn. (moderator/panelist 1975-79). Office: 3000 Weslayan Houston TX 77027

LIU, PETER HAN-SHAN, polit. scientist; b. Calcutta, India, May 31, 1937; s. Kuo-Chen and Shu-Ying (Chen) L.; B.A., Nat. Chengchi U., Taiwan, 1963; M.A., So. Ill. U., 1969, Ph.D., 1972; m. Angela M. Chiang, Sept. 20, 1971; children—Alfred, Daniel. Tchr., Chung Shan High Sch., Indonesia, 1958-59; asst. editor U.S. Ednl. Found., Taipei, 1962-64; reporter China Post, Taipei, 1963-64; prof. polit. sci. Miss. Valley State U., Itta Bena 1971—. Mem. Am. Polit. Sci. Assn., So. Polit. Sci. Assn. Roman Catholic. Home: 111 Canary Cove Greenwood MS 38930 Office: Social Sci Dept Miss Valley State Univ Itta Bena MS 38941

LIUZZO, JOSEPH ANTHONY, educator; b. Tampa, Fla., Dec. 16, 1926; s. Joseph and Annie (Minardi) L.; student U. Fla., 1944-45, B.S., 1950, M.S., 1955; postgrad. U. So. Calif., 1952-53; Ph.D., Mich. State U., 1958; m. Elaine Grammer, Nov. 30, 1951; children—Paul Arthur, Patricia Joyce, Jolaine Marie. Microbiologist Stokely-Van Camp, Tampa, 1950; research asst. in nutrition U. Fla., Gainesville, 1950-51; head div. microbiology research Nutrilite Products, Inc., Buena Park, Calif., 1951-54; asst. prof. biochemistry La. State U., Baton Rouge, 1958-62, asso. prof. food sci., 1962-69, prof. food sci., 1969—, faculty chmn. of athletics; cons. food industry. Troop com. mem. Istrouma council Boy Scouts Am. Served with U.S. Army, 1945-46. Fellow AAAS, Am. Inst. Chemists; mem. Inst. Food Technologists, Am. Inst. Nutrition, Am. Legion (chmn. jr. baseball com.), Sigma Xi, Phi Tau Sigma, Gamma Sigma Delta. Democrat. Mem. Church of Christ. Contbr. sci. articles to profl. jours. Home: 620 Burgin Ave Baton Rouge LA 70808 Office: Dept Food Science Louisiana State U Baton Rouge LA 70803

LIVELY, BESSIE PINKOSON, ret. dietitian; b. Gainesville, Fla., Feb. 7, 1914; d. Charles and Lula O. (Perry) Pinkoson; B.S. in Home Econs., Fla. State Coll. for Women, 1934; M.S., Tex. Women's U., 1960; m. William McCain, Jan. 13, 1938; children—Susie Lively Ferguson, William McCain, Richard. Staff dietitian Cin. Gen. Hosp., 1935-36; asst. adminstrv. dietitian Jackson Meml. Hosp., Miami, Fla., 1936-38; cons. therapeutic diets for Dr. Lively, 1938-57; food production dietitian Parkland Meml. Hosp., Dallas, 1957-58, asst. chief dietitian, 1959-60; dir. dietetic services Dallas County (Tex.) Hosp. Dist., 1960-79, ret. 1979; mem. adv. com. for food service El Centro Coll., Dallas, 1975-79; dietary cons. to workshops Tex. State Dept. Health, 1975—. Named Disting. Health Care Food Ser. Adminstr. Mem. Am. Dietetic Assn., Tex. Dietetic Assn. (pres. 1967-68), Dallas Dietetic Assn. (sec. 1964-65), Am. Soc. for Hosp. Food Service Adminstrs. (pres. N.Central chpt. 1973). Republican. Methodist. Clubs: Order Eastern Star, Oak Cliff Country.

LIVELY, LLOYD LESTER, JR., missile system program mgr.; b. Phila., Sept. 14, 1927; s. Lloyd Lester and Olive (Stoner) L.; B.S., Auburn U., 1949; m. Phyllis Barnes, Sept. 3, 1949; children—Lloyd Lester III, Elizabeth Ann. Quality control engr. Mock, Judson, Voehringer Co., Greensboro, N.C., 1949-51, personnel mgr., 1951-52; supr. dyeing operation Gayley Mills, Marietta, S.C., 1952-53; weapon system engr. U.S. Army Rocket and Guided Missile Agy., Redstone Arsenal, Huntsville, Ala., 1953-57, dep. weapon systems project mgr., 1957-60, dep. chief functional div. indsl. operations, 1960-62, anti-tank, field artillery weapon systems project mgr., 1962-63, nuclear programs mgr., 1963-74, chief missile tech. ARPA Support Office, 1974-77, dep. project mgr. ATE mgmt. office, 1977-78, chief quality engring. div., 1978-80, dep. dir., product assurance dir., 1980—, high energy laser program mgr., 1967-69; mem. Dept. Army Standardization Task Group, 1955-56, panelist Armed Forces Communication and Electronics Assn. Fellowship Awards Bd., 1965, mem. U.S. Army Missile Comd. Laser Adv. Com., 1967-69; mem. Def. Atomic Support Agy. Dept. Def. Electromagnetic Pulse Test and Evaluation Com., 1968-74; mem. U.S. Army Integrated Effects (Nuclear) Com., 1968-74; exec. sec. U.S. Army Missile Research and Devel. Command Sci. Adv. Group, 1963—. Vice-pres. Rocket City Swimming Assn., 1969; bd. dirs. United Way of Madison County, 1976—. Mem. Nat. Soc. Profl. Engrs., Ala. Acad. Sci., Phi Psi, Sigma Alpha Epsilon. Presbyn. (trustee 1962-64, deacon 1958-62). Clubs: Lions, Kiwanis (bd. dirs. 1977—). Home: 1402 Dale Circle Huntsville AL 35801 Office: US Army Missile Command Attn DRSMI-QE Redstone Arsenal AL 35809

LIVELY, NOEL DALE, logging contractor; b. Okemah, Okla., Sept. 23, 1926; s. Shelton L. and Grace (McClanahan) L.; grad. high sch.; m. Eddie Arletta Nash, Sept. 16, 1945; children—Nancy Catherine, Larry Dale, Ted Bruce. With Crown Zellerbach and Van Vleet Logging Co., Seaside, Ore., 1948-61; partner L D & L Logging Co., Seaside, 1961-63, Craig, Colo., 1963-69; owner Lively Logging Corp., Saratoga, Wyo., 1969-74, Cromwell, Okla., 1974—, Quasada Ranch, Cromwell, 1978—. Served with Mcht. Marines, 1944. Democrat. Home: Cromwell OK 74837 Office: Route 2 Box 185 Okemah OK 74859

LIVESAY, THOMAS ANDREW, museum dir.; b. San Francisco, Feb. 1, 1945; s. Melvin Ewing-Clay and Madge Almeda (Hall) L.; B.F.A., U. Tex., Austin, 1968, M.F.A., 1972; diploma arts adminstrn., Harvard U., 1978; divorced; 1 dau., Heather Marie. Designer, U. Tex. Art Mus., 1965-72; curator Ney Mus., Austin, 1971-73; dir. Longview (Tex.) Mus. and Art Center, 1973-75; curator Amarillo (Tex.) Art Center, 1975-77, dir., 1977—. Served with AUS, 1969-71. Decorated Air medal, Army Commendation medal, Bronze Star. Mem. Am. Assn. Museums, Tex. Assn. Museums. Author exhbn. catalogues. Office: Box 447 Amarillo TX 79178

LIVINGSTON, MICHAEL KEITH, law enforcement officer; b. Tacoma, Jan. 26, 1948; s. Norman Noel and Maudine Clara (Templeton) L.; B.A., St. Edwards U., 1975; M.P.A., S.W. Tex. State U., 1977; grad. U.S. Dept. Justice, FBI Nat. Acad., 1979; m. Dianne Casey, Dec. 19, 1970; 1 son, Sloan Michael. With Austin (Tex.) Police Dept., 1969-73, pub. info. officer Community Relations Sect., 1973-75, patrol sgt. uniform div., 1975-78, sr. patrol sgt., 1978, chief Brackenridge Hosp. police, 1978—. Recipient letter of commendation J. Edgar Hoover, 1972. Mem. Tex. Crime Prevention Assn., Tex. Police Assn., Tex. Mcpl. Police Assn., Austin Police Assn., Capital Area Law Enforcement Assn., Internat. Assn. for Hosp. Security. Clubs: Masons, Elks. Home: 606 Arroyo Vista Manchaca TX 78652 Office: E 15 and East Ave Austin TX 78701

LIVINGSTON, PHILIP HENRY, physician; b. Columbus, Ga., Sept. 14, 1905; s. Sol and Zelda (Smullian) L.; B.S., Emory U., 1926, M.D. with honors, 1929; m. Jean Doris Wicksman, May 24, 1942; children—Richard, Ann, Dean. Intern, Jewish Hosp., St. Louis, 1929-30, 1931-33; resident Michael Reese Hosp., Chgo., 1930-31; practice medicine specializing in cardiology, Chattanooga, 1933—; attending physician Erlanger Hosp., Chattanooga, Tenn., 1934—, cardiologist, 1951—, chief med. services, 1952-53; attending physician Meml. Hosp., Chattanooga, 1951—. Bd. dirs. Allied Arts Council, Chattanooga; elected squire Quar. Ct., 1966, 72. Served to lt. col. M.C., AUS, 1942-45. Diplomate Am. Bd. Internal Medicine. Fellow A.C.P., Am. Coll. Cardiology, Am. Coll. Angiology, Am. Coll. Clin. Cardiology; mem. AMA, Am. Diabetes Assn., Am. Acad. Medicine, Vienna, N.Y. acads. sci. Democrat. Unitarian. Clubs: Kiwanis, Torch. Home: 1718 Minnekahda Rd Chattanooga TN 37405 Office: 111 Provident Bldg Chattanooga TN 37402

LIVINGSTON, ROBERT L., JR., congressman; b. Colorado Springs, Colo., Apr. 30, 1943; s. Robert L. and Dorothy (Godwin) L.; B.A., Tulane U., 1967, J.D., 1968; m. Bonnie Robichaux, 1965; children—Robert L. III, Richard, David. Admitted to La. bar, 1968; asst. U.S. atty., New Orleans, 1970-73; asst. dist. atty. Orleans Parish, 1974-75; asst. atty. gen. La., 1975-76; mem. firm Livingston & Powers, New Orleans, 1976—; mem. 95th-96th congresses from 1st Dist. La. Vice chmn. Orleans Parish Republican Exec. Com., 1974—. Served with USN, 1961-63. Named Outstanding Asst. U.S. Atty., 1973. Mem. Am., La. (ho. of dels. 1977), New Orleans bar assns., La. Trial Lawyers Assn. Episcopalian. Clubs: Masons, Young Men's Bus. Office: 130 Cannon House Office Bldg Washington DC 20515

LIVINGSTON, WALTER HENRY, physicist; b. Plainville, Conn., Oct. 21, 1920; s. Walter W. and Monica Irene (Simpson) L.; B.S. magna cum laude, Yale U., 1957, M.S., 1958; m. Elizabeth Jane Jeffries, Nov. 7, 1970. Design engr. New Departure div. Gen. Motors, Bristol, Conn., 1943-53, Heavy Ion Accelerator, Yale U., New Haven, 1958-61; sr. physicist Fafnir Bearing Co., New Britain, Conn., 1961-63; physicist David W. Taylor Naval Ship Research and Devel. Center, U.S. Navy, Washington, 1963—; formerly profl. pianist. Served with USAAF, 1943-46. Recipient spl. prize Anthony D. Stanley awards for excellence in pure and applied math. Pres. and Fellows of Yale U., 1954. Mem. Sigma Xi. Club: Yale (Washington). Contbr. articles in field for classified reports. Home: 9811 Fosbak Dr Vienna VA 22180 Office: David W Taylor Naval Ship Research and Devel Center Washington DC 20084

LLANES, CARLOS GILBERTO, physician; b. Havana Cuba, Mar. 31, 1919; s. Carlos G. and Mirtha (Fernandez) L.; B.S. and B.A., Instituto de la Habana, 1938; M.D., Sch. Medicine U. Havana, 1945; m. Martha Maria Borg, Sept. 18, 1948; children—Carlos Gilberto III, Patricia Ann, Mirtha Maria, Diana Lynn. Came to U.S., 1945, naturalized, 1950. Rotating intern St. Joseph's Hosp., Yonkers, N.Y., 1945-46; resident chest diseases Lakeland Chest Diseases Hosp., Blackwood, N.J., 1946-50; resident radiology Roosevelt Hosp., N.Y.C., 1950-53; spl. course radioactive isotopes Oak Ridge Inst. Nuclear Studies, Tenn., 1953; asso. radiologist Doctors' Hosp., Coral Gables, Fla., 1953-55; chief radiologist Murphy Army Hosp., Waltham, Mass., 1955-56; asso. radiologist Gorgas Hosp., Panama Canal Zone, 1956-57; radiologist, chief cobalt div. Mercy Hosp., Miami, Fla., 1957-59; pvt. practice radiology, Coral Gables, 1959-67, Miami, 1964—; dir. dept. radiology Palm Springs Gen. Hosp., Hialeah, Fla., 1965-67; chief depts. radiology and nuclear medicine Pan Am. Hosp., Miami. Past pres. League Against Cancer; bd. dirs. Dade-Monroe PSRO. Served from capt. to maj., AUS, 1955-57. Diplomate Am. Bd. Radiology, Am. Bd. Nuclear Medicine. Mem. Am., Fla., Dade County med. assns., Radiol. Soc. N.Am., Greater Miami Radiol. Soc., Fla. Radiol. Soc., Soc. Nuclear Medicine, Am. Coll. Radiology, Heart Assn. Greater Miami, Am. Coll. Nuclear Medicine. Lutheran (past pres. congregation). Home: 11225 SW 58th Ct Miami FL 33156 Office: 434 SW 12th Ave Miami FL 33130

LLERENA, MARIO RAFAEL, editor; b. Placetas, Cuba, Mar. 5, 1913; s. Rafael and Maria (Rodriguez) L.; Ph.D., U. Havana, 1940; B.Th., Princeton U., 1947; m. Laura Hernandez, Dec. 21, 1946; children—Mario A., Stella E. Llerena Portada. Instr. Spanish, Duke U., Durham, N.C., 1948-52; editor Mecánica Popular, Miami, Fla., 1965-67; editor U. Miami Press, 1967-72; sr. editor Logoi, Inc., Miami, 1972—. Mem. Princeton U. Alumni Assn. Republican. Presbyterian. Author: The Unsuspected Revolution, 1978; A Manual of Style for the Spanish Language, 1980; contbr. articles on Spanish lit. to profl. jours. Office: 4100 W Flagler St Miami FL 33134

LLEWELLYN, CHARLES ELROY, JR., physician; b. Richmond, Va., Jan. 16, 1922; s. Charles Elroy and Pearl Ann (Shield) L.; B.S., Hampden-Sydney Coll., 1943; M.D., Med. Coll. Va., 1946; M.S. (Psychiat.), U. Colo. Postgrad. Med. Sch., 1953; m. Sara Grace Eldridge, Sept. 25, 1948; children—Charles Elroy III, George Eldridge (dec. July 1970), Richard Shield. Intern, Bellevue, N.Y., 1947-48; resident in psychiatry Colo. Psychopathic Hosp., Denver, 1950-53; asso. in psychiatry, asst. chief adult psychiat. outpatient clinic, dept. psychiatry Duke Med. Center, 1955-56, asst. prof. psychiatry, 1956-63, asso. prof. psychiatry, 1963—, head psychiat. outpatient div., 1956-76, acting head div. community and social psychiatry, 1976-78, head div. community and social psychiatry, 1978—; dir. student mental health service, 1959-69, dir. Duke study group Inter-Univ. Forum for Educators in Community Psychiatry, 1967-71, dir. Duke Drug Abuse Rehab. Service, 1972-74; cons. drug rehab. program, 1972-79; med. dir. Durham Drug Counseling and Evaluation Service, 1979—; mem. N.C. Drug Abuse Worker Profl. Cert. Bd., 1978—; psychiat. cons. N.C. Medicaid Program, 1971-79; mem. norms of care com. N.C. Med. Peer Rev. Found., 1973-79; mem. vis. faculty, seminars Lab. Community Psychiatry, Harvard Med. Sch., 1964-67; practice gen. psychiatry, part time 1955—. Sr. psychiat. cons. N.C. Dept. Social Services, 1955-79; cons. Family Counseling Service Durham, 1966—, bd. dirs., 1971-77, pres., 1975-77; mem. N.C. Mental Health Council, chmn., 1965-69; mem. Forum for Improvement Quality of Life, 1974—; bd. dirs. N.C. United Health Services, 1974—. Cubmaster, Occoneechee council Boy Scouts Am., 1960-66 (named Cubmaster of Year Shawnee dist. 1962). Served to capt. M.C., AUS, 1953-55. Diplomate Am. Bd. Psychiatry and Neurology. Fellow Am., So. psychiat. assns., Am. Orthopsychiat. Assn., Pan Am. Med. Assn.; mem. A.M.A., Am. Group Psychotherapy Assn., Southeastern Group Psychotherapy Soc. (pres. 1965-66), Carolinas Group Psychotherapy Soc., Am. Acad. Religion and Mental Health, N.C. Neuropsychiat. Assn. (pres. 1971-73), N.C. Group Behavior Soc., N.C., Durham (chmn. med. adv. com. 1957-61) mental health assns. Methodist (pres. Sunday sch. 1957-58; mem. ofcl. bd. 1957-68; chmn. commn. social concerns 1963-68; trustee 1958-59). Office: Duke Univ Medical Center Durham NC 27710 Home: 3550 Hamstead Ct Durham NC 27707

LLOYD, WILLIAM BURTON, JR., mfg. co. exec.; b. Fostoria, Ohio, Oct. 21, 1938; s. William Burton and Elizabeth (Brightwell) L.; A.B., Dartmouth Coll., 1960; M.B.A., Central Mich. U., 1969; m. Roselyn Alice Karlovetz, June 18, 1960; children—Rebecca Anne, Michael Burton. Engr., Dow Chem. Co., Midland, Mich., 1964-70; group market mgr. Amspec, Inc., Columbus, Ohio, 1971-76; v.p. Southeastern Foam Products Inc., Conyers, Ga., 1976-77; pres. Am. Isowall Corp., Florence, Ky., 1977—, also chmn. bd. Served with USN, 1960-64. Club: Summit Hills Country. Office: 8055 Production Ave Florence KY 41042

LLOYD, WILLIAM NELSON, lawyer; b. Lewisburg, Tenn., July 24, 1920; s. William Houston and Rhoda (Hastings) L.; student Cumberland U., 1939-40, U. of South, 1941, U. Tenn., 1946; LL.B., Vanderbilt U., 1948, J.D., 1969; m. LaDelle Estes, Sept. 15, 1949; children—William Hastings, Robert Estes. Admitted to Tenn. bar, 1948, since practiced in Lewisburg; county atty., 1963—; dir. First Nat. Bank of Lewisburg, WSML, Inc. Judge, Ct. of Gen. Sessions, 1950-58; mem. Constl. Conv. Tenn., 1965; del. Democratic Nat. Conv., 1964. Served with USNR, 1942-46. Decorated Silver Star medal, D.F.C. with two oak leaf clusters, others. Recipient Long Rifle citation Boy Scouts Am., 1960. Mem. Am. Bar Assn., Am., Tenn. (bd. govs.) trial lawyers assns., Am. Judicature Soc., Am. Soc. Law and Sci. Presbyn. (elder). Home: 435 Manor Circle Lewisburg TN 37091 Office: 220 W Church St Lewisburg TN 37091

LO, CHING FANG, mech. and aeronautical engr.; b. Peking, China, Dec. 15, 1937; s. Yin and Yun Tze (Sun) L.; came to U.S., 1961; naturalized, 1972; B.S., Nat. Taiwan U., 1959; M.S. in Aeronautical Engring., Cornell U., 1964, Ph.D. in Theoretical and Applied Mechanics, 1967; m. Mary Mei-Lei Shih, Mar. 28, 1964; children—Joseph Kong, Thomas Hsin. Staff scientist Therm Advanced Research, Inc., Ithaca, N.Y., 1964-65; research engr. ARO, Inc., Arnold Air Force Sta., Tenn., 1967-74, supr., 1974—; prof. aero. engring. Space Inst., U. Tenn., Tullahoma, 1969—. Mem. Am. Inst. Aeros. and Astronautics (Gen. H.H. Arnold award 1971, mem. missile system tech. com.), Sigma Xi. Contbr. articles to profl. jours. Home: 305 Twelve Oaks St Tullahoma TN 37388 Office: Sverdup/ARO Inc Arnold Air Force Station TN 37389

LO, CHING-TSAN, systems analyst; b. Tainan, Taiwan, July 20, 1941; s. Chang and Tzu (Chung) L.; M.S. (fellow), U. Rochester, 1967; Ph.D. (fellow), Purdue U., 1970; m. Yeh-Sheng Chien, July 24, 1968; children—Julie Yu-Pu, Grace Hsiao-Wei, Eleanor Yu-Chen. Computer applications engr. El Paso Products Co., Odessa, Tex., 1970-73, sr. process improvements engr., 1973-76; process and systems analyst Am. Cyanamid Co., Westwego, La., 1976-78; sr. research engr. Shell Devel. Co., Houston, 1978—. Registered profl. engr., Tex. Mem. Am. Inst. Chem. Engrs. Patentee in field. Contbr. articles to profl. jours. Home: 18010 Oakworth Dr Houston TX 77084 Office: PO Box 1380 Houston TX 77001

LOAR, WARREN NELSON, III, hosp. adminstr.; b. Okmulgee, Okla., Nov. 29, 1927; s. Warren Nelson and Frederica Inez (Morton) L.; B.S., U.S. Naval Acad., 1950; M.B.A., U. So. Calif., 1966; M.H.A., Ga. State U., 1973; m. Betty Ann Propp, June 10, 1950 (dec.); m. 2d, Barbara Schuster Cox, July 10, 1968; children—Warren Nelson IV, Michael G., Andrew S., Frederica L.; stepchildren—Conde T. Cox, Prentiss E. Cox. Commd. 2d lt. USAF, 1950, advanced through grades to lt. col., 1966; pilot and aircraft comdr. SAC, 1950-67, chief propulsion br., Offutt AFB, Nebr., 1967-70; tactical airlift liaison officer Mil. Region III, Vietnam, 1970-71; ret., 1971; asst. adminstr. St. Mary's Hosp., Athens, Ga., 1973-76; adminstr. U. Ga. Health Services, Athens, 1976—. Decorated Bronze Star, Air medal with 2 oak leaf clusters. Mem. Air Force Assn., Am. Coll. Hosp. Adminstrs. Am. Mgmt. Assn., Ga. Hosp. Assn. Office: Health Service Herty Dr Athens GA 30602

LOBENSTERN, STANLEY LOUIS, ins. exec.; b. Bronx, May 20, 1933; s. Leopold and Elsa Henrietta (Halle) L.; student public schs. Mt. Vernon, Va.; m. Sandra Pozesky, Nov. 30, 1952; 1 dau., Iris G. Lobenstern Welch. Dist. mgr. Conger Life Ins. Co., Fla., 1955-61; mgr. Seewes Retail Stores, Los Angeles, 1961-68; Sales mgr. O.K. Furniture, Ft. Lauderdale, Fla., 1968-71; asst. cruise dir. Eastern S.S. Lines, Miami, Fla., 1971-72; owner, dir. Am. Health Services Co., Casselberry, Fla., 1973—. Bd. dirs. March of Dimes. Served with USN, 1950-51. Mem. Nat. Assn. Life Underwriters, Internat. Brotherhood Magicians (past pres.), Soc. Am. Magicians (past pres., internat. dep.), Acad. Magical Arts and Scis. Democrat. Jewish. Author: A Baker's Dozen, 1968; Stan's Sorcery, 1969; Just Notes, 1974. Home and Office: 1017 Crystal Bowl Circle Casselberry FL 32707

LOCHRIDGE, STANLEY KEITH, cardiovascular and thoracic surgeon; b. Tupelo, Miss., Jan. 24, 1947; s. Oscar Wendell and Willie Lou (Stidham) L.; B.S., U. Ala., Tuscaloosa, 1968; M.D., U. Ala., Birmingham, 1972; m. Jane Kay Weston, Aug. 2, 1968. Intern, Carraway Meth. Med. Center, Birmingham, Ala., 1972, resident in gen. surgery 1972-76; fellow in cardiovascular and thoracic surgery U. Iowa Hosps. and Clinics, Iowa City, 1976-78; practice medicine specializing in cardiovascular and thoracic surgery, Birmingham, 1978—; mem. teaching staff Bapt. Med. Center; mem. surg. staff Brookwood Med. Center, South Highlands, St. Vincent's, Lloyd Noland Found. hosps. Diplomate Am. Bd. Surgery, Am. Bd. Thoracic Surgery. Fellow A.C.S., Southeastern Surg. Congress; mem. AMA, Am. Coll. Cardiology, Am. Coll. Chest Physicians, Ala. Med. Soc., Jefferson County Med. Soc., Colo. Trudeau Soc., Am. Heart Assn., Ala. Heart Assn., Birmingham Acad. Medicine, Birmingham Chest Club, Birmingham Cardiovascular Soc., Alpha Omega Alpha, Alpha Epsilon Delta. Office: 1318 S 19th St Birmingham AL 35205

LOCHRIDGE, WILLARD FISKE, IV, electronics co. exec.; b. Evanston, Ill., Dec. 14, 1942; s. Willard Fiske and Patricia Marie (Daugherty) L.; B.S., Western Carolina U., 1965; m. Vija Mezulis, May 5, 1968; children—Whitney K., Brenton S. Sales rep. Control Data Corp., Rockville, Md., 1968-69; dir. mktg. U.S. Time Sharing Inc., Reston, Va., 1969-70; sr. staff engr. TRW Systems, McLean, Va., 1970-71; mgr. mktg. Planning Research Corp., McLean, 1971-74; sr. mktg. rep./spl. asst. Grumman Data Systems Co., Arlington, Va., 1974-75; v.p. fed. mktg. ops. Informatics Inc., McLean, 1975—. Served with USMC, 1965-68. Decorated Silver Star, Bronze Star with combat V (2), Purple Heart; Vietnamese Medal of Honor, Vietnamese Cross of Galantry. Mem. Assn. Data Processing Service Orgns., Time Sharing Users, Assn., Internat. Game Fish Assn., Western Carolina Univ. Alumni Assn., Theta Xi Alumni Assn. Presbyterian. Clubs: St. Augustine Yacht, Camp Fire of Am. Inventor in field. Home: 2613 Steeplechase Dr Reston VA 22091 Office: 7926 Jones Branch Dr McLean VA 22102

LOCKARD, JAMES ERNEST, stockbroker; b. Akron, Ohio, June 9, 1936; s. Myron Eugene and Clara Olive (Rusk) L.; student Ohio State U., 1954-55, Akron U., 1955-60, Kent State U., 1956-58, N.Mex. A&M U., 1956-57, Tampa Coll., 1973-76; m. Jane Ann Devereux, June 14, 1958 (dec.); children—Timothy J., Cheri L., Kristy D.: m. 2d, Darlene Jane Peeler, Jan. 1, 1979. Mfrs. rep. Ames Co., div. Miles Lab., Akron, 1959-65, Merrill Lynch Inc., Honolulu and Akron, 1965-70; asso. v.p. Dean Witter Reynolds, Inc., Tampa, Fla., 1975—. Chmn. Ohio State Camp Out Nat. Campers and Hikers Assn., 1967, conservation dir., 1964-68; precinct chmn., dist. chmn. Republican Com. Hawaii, floor leader state conv., 1971. Served with AUS, 1955-57. Mem. Stock and Bond Club St. Petersburg, Stow Jaycees (charter), Stow Aways Campers (charter). Club: Toastmasters (past area gov., pres.). Home: 1307 Ranchwood Dr E Dunedin FL 33528 Office: 1311 N Westshore Blvd Tampa FL 33607

LOCKARD, WILLIAM HARVEY, JR., veterinarian, cons.; b. Larkinsville, Ala., Nov. 22, 1926; s. William Harvey and Verma (Shelton) L.; student N. Ga. Coll., 1944; D.V.M., Auburn U., 1952; m. Barbara Jean Skinner, Sept. 5, 1948; children—Deborah Sue Slaton, Doris Pamela, William Douglas, Robert Dirk, David Ewell. Veterinarian, Zachary, La., 1952-63; pres. Gulf Coast Labs., Zachary, 1958-63; nat. sales mgr. Diamond Labs., Des Moines, 1963-66; pres., chmn. bd. Hart-Delta, Inc., Baton Rouge, 1966-75; pres. Lockard Assos., Inc., Fort Worth, 1975—; cons. in field. Mem. East Baton Rouge (La.) Parish Bd. Health, 1959-63. Served with AUS 1944-47. Named Boss of Year, Bus. Women Am., 1964, Vet. of Year, La. Vet. Med. Assn., 1968. Mem. La. (pres. 1960), Miss., Am. vet. med. assns., Indsl. Vets. Assn., Am. Vet. Exhibitors Assn., Internat. Platform Assn., Omega Tau Sigma. Presbyterian. Editor Auburn Veterinarian, 1951; Auburn Handbook, 1951; La. Veterinarian, 1958. Home: 6305 Greencastle Ct Fort Worth TX 76118

LOCKE, JOHN PHILLIP, ins. exec.; b. San Juan, P.R., Oct. 7, 1950; s. Patrick Roger and Esther Maurine (Holtsclaw) L.; student Northwestern State U. Nachitoches, La., 1968-72; m. Cynthia Gail Teekell, Jan. 17, 1974; children—Regan Lindsay, Ryan Kelly. Dist. mgr. United Companies Life, Baton Rouge, 1972; agency dir. Nat. Found. Life, Oklahoma City, 1972—; pres., Topco Mktg. & Devel. Inc., Louisville, 1975—; pres., chief exec. officer Topco Products Inc., Louisville, 1977—. Past chmn. Jr. Achievement, Louisville; bd. dirs. Jr. Achievement of Kentuckiana. Mem. Louisville C. of C., Better Bus. Bur., Sales and Mktg. Execs. Louisville, Phi Sigma Epsilon. Republican. Episcopalian. Home: 14009 Harbour Pl Prospect KY 40059 Office: 9200 Shelbyville Rd Louisville KY 40222

LOCKE, PAUL CLAYBROOK, data processing exec.; b. Nashville, Dec. 2, 1932; s. Sam Claybrook and Allie Eudora (Walker) L.; B.S., Peabody Coll. of Vanderbilt U., 1957, M.A., 1958; m. Evelyn Holley, Nov. 29, 1957; children—Holly Ann, Paula, Julia Dawn. Tech. specialist in data processing Avco Corp., Nashville, 1975-77, asst. dir. info. services, 1977-78, mgr. computer services, 1978—; dir. Sci. Mgmt. Services, Inc., Nashville. Mem. County Rep. Primary Bd., 1969—, chmn., 1973-77; co-chmn. Rep. Exec. Com., 1965-69; chmn. fin. com. Ch. of Christ, Nashville, 1974-79, deacon, 1978-79; elder Harpeth Mills Ch. of Christ, 1980—. Served with US Army, 1953-55. C.P.A., Tenn.; cert. data processor. Mem. Nat. Mgmt. Assn., Data Processing Mgmt. Assn., Tenn. Soc. C.P.A.'s, Am. Inst. C.P.A.'s. Republican. Ch. of Christ. Clubs: Avco Mgmt., Toastmasters (pres. 1976-77, Avco Toastmaster of Yr. 1978), Franklin High Boosters. Home: Route 2 Manley Ln Brentwood TN 37027 Office: PO Box 210 Nashville TN 37202

LOCKETT, ALLAN NEIL, educator; b. Stamford, Tex., Aug. 30, 1950; s. Tom and Lenora Marie L.; B.A., Prairie View A. and M. U., 1972; M.Ed., Abilene Christian U., 1975. Tchr., human relations coordinator Fannin Jr. High Sch., Amarillo, Tex., 1972-76; counselor Madison Jr. High Sch., Abilene, Tex., 1976-78, Abilene High Sch., 1978—. Cert. tchr., Tex.; cert. counselor, Tex. Mem. Am., Tex., Big Country (pres.-elect) personnel and guidance assns., NEA, Tex., Taylor County tchrs. assns., Tex., Abilene classroom tchrs. assns. Democrat. Baptist. Office: 2800 N 6 St Abilene TX 79603

LOCKETT, CORNELIUS RANDOLPH, JR., community coll. adminstr.; b. West Tocoi, Fla., Aug. 18, 1930; s. Cornelius Roosevelt and Salome (Freeman) L.; B.S., Fla. A&M U., 1959, M.Ed., 1968; postgrad. Auburn U., 1973. Instr., Duval County Public Schs., Jacksonville, Fla., 1959-69; announcer Sta. WRHC, Jacksonville, 1963-68; personnel adminstr. Corning Glass Works (N.Y.), 1969-70; dir. devel. edn. Fla. Jr. Coll., Jacksonville, 1970—; founder Century Nat. Bank, Jacksonville, 1976; cons., mem. staff Nat. Task Force on Disadvantaged and Post-Secondary Edn., Office of Edn., Washington, 1974. Bus. mgr. Fla. Jax, Inc., 1970-73; bd. dirs. N.W. Council, Jacksonville C. of C. Served with AUS, 1950-53. Ford fellow, 1973-74: Nat. Teaching fellow, 1974. Mem. Fla. Adult Edn. Assn., Internat. Reading Assn., Fla. Devel. Edn. Assn., Omega Psi Phi (Omega Man of Year 1966). Democrat. Presbyterian. Research on articulation between secondary schs. and community colls. Home: 5505 Trout River Blvd Jacksonville FL 32208 Office: 101 W State St Jacksonville FL 32202

LOCKETT, RAYMOND JACOB, historian; b. Franklin, La., Nov. 8, 1935; s. Jacob and Velma (Marks) L.; B.A., So. U., 1956, M.Ed., 1964, M.A. (Black Studies fellow), 1971; Ed.S. (Urban Sch. Adminstrn. fellow), U. Colo., 1972, Ed.D., 1973; m. Alene Banks, June 8, 1962; children—Sonya, Tammy. Prin., St. Mary Parish Sch. System, 1956, tchr. social studies, chmn. dept., coach, 1958-70; prof. history So. U., 1973—, dir. humanities program, 1974-79; vis. prof. Kans. State U., 1973; mem. West African Ethnic Heritage Summer Seminar, 1976. Pres. St. Mary Parish Community Action Agy., 1966-71; exec. bd. Evangeline Econ. Devel. Dist.; bd. dirs. St. Mary Parish Human Relations Bd., St. Mary Parish Credit Union, St. Mary Parish NAACP. Participant Caribbean Scholar Exchange, 1976. Mem. Assn. Study of Afro-Am. Life and History, Am. Hist. Assn., Assn. Social and Behavior Scis., La. Hist. Assn., Assn. Black Polit. Scientists, Assn. Black Social Workers. Democrat. Roman Catholic. Author: History of Black Leadership and Politics in St. Mary Parish, 1950-70, 1971; Social Political and Economic Profile of Louisiana Black School Board Members, 1973; Interdisciplinary Curriculum Guide and Materials, 1978; The City and Its Minorities. Home: 13607 Cadiz St Baker LA 70714 Office: PO Box 9241 Southern University Baton Rouge LA 70813

LOCKHART, VERDREE, edn. program cons.; b. Louisville, Ga., Oct. 21, 1924; s. Fred Douglas and Minnie Bell (Roberson) L.; B.S., Tuskegee Inst., 1949; M.A., Atlanta U., 1957; student George Peabody Coll., 1960; Ph.D., Atlanta U., 1975; m. Louise Howard, Aug. 5, 1950; children—Verdree, Vera Louise, Fernandez, Abigail. Teacher, Jefferson County Tng. Sch., Louisville, Ga., 1949-50, 51-58; sch. counselor Jefferson County High Sch., Louisville, Ga., 1958-63; edn. program cons. Ga. Dept. Edn., Atlanta, 1963-74, edn. program advisor, 1974-79, cons., 1979—; adj. prof. Valdosta State Coll., 1976—. Treas., Northwest Council Community Clubs of Atlanta, 1965—. Asst. council commr., bd. dirs. Atlanta Area council Boy Scouts Am.; treas. Atlanta br. NAACP, 1971—; trustee Atlanta U. Served with AUS, 1943-46, 50-51. Decorated Bronze Star medal. Recipient Silver Beaver award, Atlanta Area council Boy Scouts Am., 1969, Ga. Faithful Service award, 1973; Distinguished Service award, Atlanta U. Alumni assn., 1971. Mem. Am. Personnel and Guidance Assn., NEA, Am. Vocat. Assn., Atlanta U. (dir.), Tuskegee Inst. (dir.) nat. alumni assns.; Am. Sch. Counselor Assn., Assn. Counselor Edn. and Supervision, Nat. Vocat. Guidance Assn., Alpha Phi Alpha (award of Merit 1977). Democrat. Baptist. Home: 2964 Peek Rd NW Atlanta GA 30318 Office: 258 State Office Bldg Atlanta GA 30334

LOCKLEAR, JAMES B., oil co. exec.; b. Pembroke, N.C., Aug. 4, 1923; s. R.D. and Rocky Jane (Cummings) L.; A.B., Pembroke State Coll., 1951; m. Emma Jane Jacobs, Feb. 4, 1972; children—Dexter, James B., Hilda Angelina, R.D., II, Vera, Evangeline. Tchr., asst. prin. Waccaman High Sch., Bolton, N.C. and Pembroke Jr. High Sch., 1953-73; pres., Tourist Oil Co., Lumberon, N.C., 1968—; pres., sec. L.&.O. Corp., Lumberon, 1972—; sec. Ed Locklear Corp., 1965—; pres., owner Pembroke Meml. Works, 1973—. Active local Boy Scouts Am., A.R.C., Democratic Party. Served with AUS, 1944-46. Decorated Combat Inf. badge. Mem. NEA, N.C. Edn. Assn., Robeson County Edn. Assn., VFW. Baptist. Club: Lions. Home: Route 4 Box 266 Lumberton NC 28358 Office: Route 1 Box 315 Pembroke NC 28372

LOCKLEAR, JANET HOYLMAN, nurse, home care adminstr.; b. Augusta County, Va., May 22, 1934; d. James Marion and Mae Lillian (Heintzleman) Hoylman; student King Coll., 1951-53; B.S. in Nursing, Med. Coll. Va., 1956; m. Earl Locklear, June 25, 1960; children—Maurice Kent, Mark Edward, Valerie Lynn. Staff nurse King's Daus.' Hosp., Staunton, Va., 1956-57, dir. nursing service, 1961-79, dir. home care, 1979—; nurse Staunton-Augusta County Health Dept., 1957-58; tchr. practical nursing Wilson Meml. High Sch., Fishersville, Va., 1958-60; instr. U. Va. Sch. Nursing, 1960-61. Founder, Westside Swim Club, Staunton, 1969, pres., 1979—; pres. Staunton-West Augusta Heart Assn., 1977-79; vol. Republican Party. Named Outstanding Alumni, Med. Coll. Va. Sch. Nursing, 1977. Mem. Am. Nurses Assn., Med. Coll. Va. Alumni Assn. Presbyterian. Club: Quota (pres. local club 1977-79) (Staunton). Home: 503 Robin St Staunton VA 24401 Office: King's Daus' Hosp N Augusta St Staunton VA 24401

LOCKLEY, JEANETTE ELAINE (MRS. ARNOLD H. LOCKLEY), educator; b. Dallas; d. Robert Lee and Morita Foresta (Williams) Prince; B.S., Wiley Coll., 1953; M.S., Tex. So. U., 1954; M.S. in Statistics, Stanford, 1968, Ph.D. in Edn., 1970; m. Arnold Herbert Lockley, Aug. 5, 1952 (dec. Dec. 1973); 1 son, Geoffrey Lynn. Instr. math. Tex. So. U., Houston, 1954-57; prof. math. Merritt Coll., Oakland, Calif., 1958—; asst. prof. math. and edn., research asso. Macalester Coll., St. Paul, 1969-70; div. chmn. mathematics and tech. Mountain View Coll., Dallas; also cons., ednl. statistician; pres., exec. dir. Inst. Ednl. Research and Devel., Inc. John Hay Whitney fellow, 1958; NSF fellow, 1962. Mem. Am. Ednl. Research Assn., Am. Statis. Assn., Am. Math. Soc., Alpha Kappa Alpha (local pres. 1966-67), Pi Lambda Theta, Pi Mu Epsilon, Beta Kappa Chi. Club: San Francisco Links. Home: Dallas TX Office: Mountain View Coll 4849 Illinois Ave Dallas TX 75211

LOCKMAN, BARBARA BORNEMAN, pub. relations specialist; b. Havre de Grace, Md., Sept. 15, 1946; d. Thomas Earl and Elizabeth (Turner) Borneman; B.A. cum laude, Lynchburg Coll., 1968; m. James Charles Lockman, Apr. 15, 1979. Pub. relations officer Lynchburg (Va.) Gen. Hosp., 1968-69; pub. info. specialist City of Charlotte (N.C.) Model Cities Dept., 1970-72, adminstrv. asst. Charlotte Pub. Ser. and Info. Dept., 1972-74; dir. pub. relations Mercy Hosp., Charlotte, 1975-79; public relations specialist Click Communications, 1980—. Mem. edn. com. Resurrection Christian Sch., Charlotte, 1978. Mem. Lynchburg Coll. Alumni Assn. (dir. 1974-79, v.p. fin. affairs, 1977-78), Am. Soc. Hosp. Pub. Relations, Carolinas Hosp. Pub. Relations Soc. (dir. 1978—), Charlotte Pub. Relations Soc. (dir. 1977—), Greater Charlotte Hosp. Pub. Relations Council (chmn. 1978-79), Internat. Assn. Bus. Communicators. Home: 6201 Candlewood Dr Charlotte NC 28210 Office: 101 Circle Ave Charlotte NC 28207

LOCKWOOD, LAWRENCE BRUCE, JR., psychiat. facility adminstr.; b. Kansas City, Mo., Mar. 18, 1940; s. Lawrence Bruce and Virginia Lee (McCollum) L.; B.S. in Biology, U. Mo., Kansas City, 1963, M.A., in Counseling and Guidance, 1975; children—Richard Scott, Tania Michelle, Heather Christine. Inspector, FDA, Kansas City, Mo., 1963-66; criminal investigator, U.S. Bur. Drug Abuse Control, Los Angeles, 1966-68; acting spl. agt. in charge, U.S. Bur. Narcotics and Dangerous Drugs, Salt Lake City, 1968-70; law enforcement specialist, Law Enforcement Planning Agency, Salt Lake City, 1970-71; high sch. tchr., Lydia Patterson Inst., El Paso, Tex., 1971-73; dir. psychol. services, Harry S. Truman Children's Neurol. Center, Kansas City, Mo., 1973-75; psychologist, Child Guidance Center, El Paso, 1976; pvt. practice psychology, El Paso, 1975-76; adminstr., Southwestern Children's Home, Inc., El Paso, 1976-78; founder Northeast Counseling Services, 1978—. Bd. dirs. Planned Parenthood Assn., El Paso, 1976-77; committeeman W. Tex. Council Govts., El Paso, 1976-79; mem. penal code revision com. Utah State Senate, 1970; officer PTA, 1976. Dow Jones and Co. journalism fellow, 1972; recipient award of merit, commr. U.S. Bur. Narcotics and Dangerous Drugs, 1967; lic. Tex. Dept. Human Resources. Mem. Tex., Mo. assns. learning disabilities, Am. Personnel and Guidance Assn., El Paso County Mental Health Assn., Profl. Counselors Assn. Methodist. Office: 8888 Dyer St El Paso TX 79904

LODEN, KAREN CLARK, nurse; b. Perth Amboy, N.J., Aug. 23, 1946; d. Francis Anthony and Mary (Cupsie) Clark; B.S. in Nursing, Loretto Heights Coll., Denver, 1968; m. Michael Loden, May 1, 1969; 1 son, Jonathan. Staff nurse St. Anthony Hosp., Denver, 1968; charge nurse prince William Hosp., Manassas, Va., 1969; staff nurse, charge nurse ICU-CCU Meml. Gen. Hosp., Las Cruces, N.Mex., 1970-71; staff nurse, charge nurse ICU-CCU Lee County Hosp., Opelika, Ala., 1972-73; charge nurse, acting head nurse pediatrics Jackson County Schneck Hosp., Seymour, Ind., 1974-75; head nurse med.-surg. Drs. Meml. Hosp., Baton Rouge, 1975-77, inservice dir., 1977-79, asst. dir. nursing service, 1979—; CPR instr., trainer Am. Heart Assn. Vol. ARC, Baton Rouge. Mem. Am. Assn. Critical Care Nurses, Am. Soc. Nursing Service Adminstrs., Council Assos., Am. Heart Assn., Baton Rouge Soc. Gifted and Talented. Roman Catholic. Home: 204 Hearthstone Dr Baton Rouge LA 70806 Office: 2414 Bunker Hill Dr Baton Rouge LA 70808

LODGE, EDITH BENNETT (MRS. GEORGE TOWNSEND LODGE), poet; b. N.Y.C., Nov. 17, 1908; d. William Mason and Mary Evans (Umstead) Bennett; B.A., Oberlin Coll., 1929; M.A., Old Dominion U., 1970; m. George Townsend Lodge, June 18, 1929; children—Ann, David Townsend. Asst., Tchr.'s Coll. Library, Columbia, N.Y.C., 1944-45; asst. Duke Library, Durham, N.C., 1955-58; lectr. English, Old Dominion U., Norfolk, Va., 1970-72; poems and prose segments pub. in Saturday Rev., N.Y. Times, Kaleidograph, Lantern, Arrows in the Air, Christian Century, Presbyn. Survey, Pulpit, Oregonian Verse, The Lyric, Imprints Quar., other mags. and newspapers; poems included in Golden Year, 1960, Diamond Anthologies of Poetry Soc. Am., 1971, Golden Anthology of Poetry Soc. Va., 1974, Sandwich Isles, U.S.A., Anthology of Hawaii Writers Club, 1973. Recipient 1st prize for sonnet Irene Leache Meml. Contest, 1964, 1st prize for lyric, 1965. Mem. Poetry Soc. Am., Acad. Am. Poets, Poetry Soc. Va., AAUW. Presbyterian. Author: Song of the Hill, Selected Poems of Edith Lodge, 1964; Journey Through Noon (poems), 1974. Home: 1329 Oak Park Ave Norfolk VA 23503

LODGE, GEORGE TOWNSEND, clin. psychologist; b. Kent, Ohio, Nov. 2, 1907; s. Edward Ballard and Martha (Townsend) L.; B.A., Oberlin Coll., 1929; M.A., Ohio State U., 1932; Ph.D., Case-Western Reserve U., 1940; m. Edith Pardee Bennett, June 18, 1929; children—Ann, David Townsend. Chief clin. psychology tng. unit VA, San Francisco, 1946-48; chief psychologist Letterman Army Hosp., San Francisco, 1948-51; chief clin. psychologist VA Hosp., Lebanon, Pa., 1951-53, Durham, N.C., 1953-57; staff psychologist Tuskegee, Ala., 1957, Roanoke, Va., 1957-60; head human factors div. USN Aviation Safety Center, Norfolk, Va., 1960-67; prof. psychology, dir. student clin. psychol. center, Old Dominion U., Norfolk, 1967-74; prof. psychology Eastern Va. Med. Sch., 1975—; mem. state mental health and mental retardation profl. adv. bd., 1970—. Served with USN, 1941-46. Diplomate Am. Bd. Profl. Psychology. Fellow Am. Psychol. Assn., AAAS; mem. Internat. Assn. Applied Psychol., Va. Acad. Clin. Psychologists, Va., Southeastern psychol. assns., Sigma Xi. Contbr. articles to profl. jours. Home: 1329 Oak Park Ave Norfolk VA 23503

LODOWSKI, RUTH ELLEN, tech. co. exec.; b. Dallas, Feb. 15, 1951; s. Charles Harry and Genevieve (Gowaty) L.; B.S., U. Tex., Austin, 1972; M.B.A., N. Tex. State U., Denton, 1976. Resident asst. Castilian Dormitory, Austin, Tex., 1971-72, head resident, 1972-73; singer self-employed band Austin, 1972-74; bank teller Greenville Ave. Bank, Dallas, 1974-75; employment interviewer Tex. Employment Commn., Grand Prairie, 1975-76; personnel intern U.S. Dept. Justice, Seagoville, Tex., 1976-77; personnel asst. Army and Air Force Exchange Service, San Antonio, 1977-78; staffing adminstr. personnel adminstrn. dept. Tex. Instruments Inc., Dallas, 1978—. Active YWCA, ARC, Dallas Women for Change; bd. dirs. Children, Inc., for mentally retarded. Recipient Top 10 Medal of Honor, Kiwanis Internat., 1969. Mem. Am. Soc. Personnel Adminstrn., Dallas Personnel Assn., Sigma Alpha Eta. Clubs: Tex. Exes, S.W. Assn. Oriental Dancers. Home: 715 Green Hill Rd Dallas TX 75232

LOEBL, BURTON B., lawyer; b. Bklyn., Apr. 19, 1925; s. Richard and Blanche (Broudy) L.; J.D., U. Miami, 1949; m. Jocelyn Helene Planick, July 8, 1951 (div. 1977); 1 dau., Lauren Wynne. Admitted to Fla. bar, 1949, practiced in Miami Beach, 1949-60, North Miami Beach, 1960-69, 74—; city atty. North Miami Beach, 1969-74, 78; pub. utilities counsel North Miami Beach, 1969-74, 78—, Lauderdale Lakes (Fla.), 1974—; asso. municipal judge North Miami Beach, 1975; town atty. Surfside (Fla.), 1975-76; spl. counsel Pembroke Pines (Fla.), 1976—. Served with AUS 1943-45. Mem. N. Dade (pres. 1979), Dade County, Fla., Am. bar assns., North Miami Beach C. of C. (dir. 1974—). Democrat. Jewish. Clubs: Masons, Shriners, Rotary. Contbr. articles to profl. jours., also Miami Rev. Home: PO Drawer L North Miami Beach FL 33160 Office: 2020 NE 163 St North Miami Beach FL 33162

LOEFFLER, SHARON VARIAN, research engr.; b. Denver, July 13, 1943; d. Robert Albers and Thelma (Saling) Varian; B.Chem. Engring., U. Colo., 1966. With Dow Chem. Co. U.S.A., Freeport, Tex., 1966—, research specialist, 1978—. Mem. Nat. (asso.), Tex. socs. profl. engrs., Soc. Women Engrs. (chmn. Tex. sect. 1975-76, mem. nat. exec. com. 1975-80, chmn. career guidance com. 1975-76, nat. treas. 1977-78, chmn. student activities com. 1976-77, nat. 2d v.p. 1978-79, nat. 1st v.p. 1979-80), Am. Inst. Chem. Engrs. Republican. Methodist. Office: Dow Chem Co B-4101 Bldg Freeport TX 77541

LOEFFLER, THOMAS G., Congressman; b. Fredericksburg, Tex., Aug. 1, 1946; s. Gilbert and Marie Loeffler; B.B.A., U. Tex., 1968, J.D., 1971; m. Kathy Crawford; 1 son, Lance. Admitted to Tex. bar, 1971; legal counsel U.S. Dept. Commerce, 1971-72; chief legis. counsel to U.S. Senator John Tower of Tex., 1972-74; dep. for congressional affairs FEA, 1974-75; spl. asst. for legis. affairs to Pres. Gerald Ford, 1975-77; Washington counsel Tenneco Inc., 1977; pvt. practice law, 1977-78; mem. 96th Congress from 21st Dist. Tex. Mem. Am. Bar Assn., Tex. Bar Assn., D.C. Bar Assn. Republican. Lutheran. Office: Room 1213 Longworth House Office Bldg Washington DC 20515

LOEWENSTEIN, WERNER RANDOLPH, physiologist, biophysicist; b. Spangenberg, Germany, Feb. 14, 1926; came to U.S., 1957, naturalized, 1965; s. Siegfried and Adele (Muller) von Loewenstein; B.S., U. Chile, Santiago, 1945, Ph.D., 1950; m. Birgit Rose, Oct. 7, 1971; children—Claudia, Patricia, Harriett, Stewart. Instr. physiology U. Chile, 1951-53, asso. prof. physiology, 1955-57; fellow in residence Wilmer Inst., Johns Hopkins U., Balt., 1953-54; research zoologist UCLA, 1954-55; asst. prof. physiology Columbia U. Coll. Physicians and Surgeons, 1957-59, asso. prof., 1959-66, prof., 1966-71, also dir. cell physics lab.; prof. physiology and biophysics, chmn. dept. physiology and biophysics U. Miami (Fla.) Sch. Medicine, 1971—; Block lectr. U. Chgo., 1960; lectr. Royal Swedish Acad. Sci., 1966, Max Planck Inst., 1967, USSR Acad. Sci., Leningrad, 1975; Fulbright Disting. prof., 1970; mem. biochemistry, molecular genetics and cell biology cluster U.S. Pres.'s Biomed. Research Adv. Panel, 1975-77; corp. mem. Marine Biol. Lab., Woods Hole, Mass. Kellog Internat. fellow, 1953-55; Commonwealth Fund internat. fellow, 1967; NSF grantee, 1958-76; NIH grantee, 1958—. Fellow N.Y. Acad. Scis.; mem. Am. Physiol. Soc., Biophys. Soc., Harvey Soc. Clubs: Woods Hole Yacht, Coconut Grove Sailing, Royal Key Biscayne Tennis and Racquet. Contbr. numerous articles to profl. jours.; editor: Handbook of Sensory Physiology, 9 vols., 1971-77; editor Biochimica et Biophysica Acta, 1967-74; editor-in-chief Jour. Membrane Biology, 1969—; research in membrane biophysics, physiology of intercellular communication, neurophysiology. Office: Dept Physiology and Biophysics U Miami Sch Medicine PO Box 016430 Miami FL 33101

LOEWENTHAL, MAURICE ROBERT, radio sta. exec.; b. N.Y.C., May 8, 1922; s. Milton and Rae L.; B.S., N.Y. U., 1955, M.A., 1956; postgrad. Upsala U., Hunter Coll.; m. Barbara Kenny, Dec. 8, 1973; children by previous marriage—Phyllis, Robert. Real estate broker Sandean Constrn. Co., Princeton, N.J., 1955-65; real estate broker, mortgage broker J.I. Kislak Mortgage Co., Miami, 1965-70; mortgage broker Friedman-Drew, N.Y.C., 1970-71; v.p., gen. mgr. Sta. WTMIFM, Miami, 1971—. Bd. dirs. Fla. Philharm., 1975-78. Served with AC, U.S. Army, 1943-46. Mem. S. Fla. Radio Broadcasters Assn., Concert Music Broadcasters (v.p. 1979—). Clubs: Rotary. Publisher: The Fugue Mag., 1974—. Office: 2951 S Bayshore Dr Miami FL 33133

LOEWER, ERICH GEORGE, JR., accountant; b. Eunice, La., Oct. 23, 1942; s. Eric George and Hattie (Bieber) L.; B.A., U. Southwestern La., 1966; m. Jane Gilchriest, July 17, 1965; children—Laura K., Erich George. Accountant, Price Waterhouse & Co., Houston, 1966-69; partner Loewer Sikes & Co., Eunice, La., 1969-79; pres., dir. Reich Enterprises, Inc., Eunice, 1973—, LeCarre, Inc., 1973-79, Streifen, Inc., 1974—; pres., dir. Hallmad Co., Eunice, 1973-76, Plan Corp., 1973—, L & L Storage, Inc., Rayne, La., 1966—, Acadiana Bldg. Corp., 1970—; pres. Acadian Acres, 1973—; dir. Aachen Constrn., Inc., Acadiana Bank, Planters Securities Inc., Maverick Properties, Inc., Oilfield Testers and Equipment Co., 1975-79; partner Loewer Bieber Farms, 1976—, Kirk Farm, Cometa Farms, Richard Oil Co., Inc.; various farming and ranching activities. Mem. Am. Inst. C.P.A.'s, La., Tex. socs. C.P.A.'s, La. Cattlemen's Assn., La. Assn. Ind. Producers and Royalty Owners. Baptist. Home: 40 Rue Dauphine PO Drawer 1048 Eunice LA 70535 Office: 1231 E Laurel St Eunice LA 70535

LOFGREN, JOHN CARL, metals co. exec.; b. N.Y.C., Oct. 2, 1938; s. Carl Mulger and Ingrid Meria (Runn) L.; student Ohio State U., 1958-59; B.B.S. in Accts., U. Wis., Milw., 1969; m. Chiquita Dawn Long, Sept. 17, 1960; children—Sean, Brian. With Interstate Drop Forge Co., Milw., 1959-67, data processing mgr., dir. info. services; controller Interstate Southwest Forge Co., Navasota, Tex., 1976—. Served with U.S. Army, 1960-62. Fellow Data Processing Mgmt. Assn., NCR User Group (past dir.), Forging Industry Assn. (past dir.). Office: Interstate Southwest Forge Co PO Box 1030 Navasota TX 77868

LOFTIN, ROBERT IRA, assn. exec.; b. Monroe, Ga., Apr. 18, 1946; s. Robert T. and Vera Still L.; B.S. in Indsl. Mgmt., Ga. Inst. Tech., 1969; M.S. in Govtl. Adminstrn., Ga. State U., 1977; m. Judy Lee Hill, Aug. 16, 1968; 1 son, William T. Mgmt. analyst State of Ga., Atlanta, 1974-75; div. adminstr. TAPPI, Inc., Atlanta, 1976-78, prodn. and mktg. mgr. TAPPI PRESS, 1978-79, mgr., 1979—. Active Atlanta Zool. Soc., Atlanta Bot. Soc., Atlanta Humane Soc., DeKalb County Humane Soc., Atlanta Assn. Retarded Citizens. Served with USAF, 1970-74. Decorated D.F.C. (2), Air medal (10). Mem. Ga. Soc. Assn. Execs., Red River Valley Fighter Pilots Assn., Ga. Adoptive Parents Assn., Ga. Tech. Nat. Alumni Assn. Methodist. Clubs: Yellow Jacket, Civitan (pres. 1979-80), Greater Atlanta Ga. Tech. Office: TAPPI PRESS One Dunwoody Park Atlanta GA 30338

LOFTON, JEROME, JR., devel. engr.; b. Goldsboro, N.C., Dec. 2, 1954; s. Jerome and Essie Lucille (Johnson) L.; B.S.E.E., N.C. State U., 1976. Engr., Research Triangle Inst., Research Triangle Park, N.C., 1975; devel. engr. Communications div. Motorola Inc., Plantation, Fla., 1976—. Mem. IEEE, Nat. Soc. Profl. Engrs., Alpha Phi Alpha. Home: 1530 NW 7th Ave Plantation FL 33060 Office: 8000 W Sunrise Blvd Plantation FL 33322

LOGAN, CATHERINE ROSE, educator; b. Asheville, N.C., Apr. 2, 1939; d. Harry Rollins and Flora Virginia (McPhail) Logan; student Mars Hill Coll., 1957-59; B.A. in Music, Furman U., 1961; B.Ch. Music, So. Sem., 1964, M.Ch. Music, 1965; postgrad. Fla. State U., 1969-71. Instr., Union U., Jackson, Tenn., 1965-67, S.W. Bapt. Coll., Bolivar, Mo., 1967-69; prof. voice and music history Truett-McConnell Coll., Cleveland, Ga., 1971—; recitalist, adjudicator for profl., religious and civic orgns. in S.E., 1965—; choir dir. Bethlehem Bapt. Ch., Clarkesville, Ga., 1972—. Regional dir., v.p. music conf. Ga. Bapt. Conv., 1976—. Mem. Nat. Assn. Tchrs. Singing, Sigma Alpha Iota. Home: Route 2 Cleveland GA 30528 Office: Truett-McConnell College Cleveland GA 30528

LOGAN, ROBERT ALLEN, systems analyst; b. Houston, Nov. 17, 1934; s. Louis James and Iris (Allen) L.; B.S., Baylor U., 1956; M.B.A., U. Tex., Austin, 1968; m. Mary Lou Smith, Nov. 21, 1958; children—Robin Ann, Laura Marie. Geologist, Pure Oil Co., Houston, 1956-60; geologist, New Orleans, 1963-65; computer programmer VA, Austin, 1968-72; computer systems analyst U.S. Treasury Dept., Austin, 1972-78; computer programmer VA, Austin, 1978—. Treas., S. Austin Neighborhood E., 1977-78. Served to lt. (j.g.), USNR, 1960-63. Mem. Data Processing Mgmt. Assn. Baptist. Home: 3301 Catalina Dr Austin TX 78741 Office: 1615 E Woodward Austin TX 78772

LOGAN, WILLIAM BOYD, coll. pres.; b. Asheville, N.C., June 29, 1910; s. William Erwin and Rose Addie (Deaver) L.; student Mars Hill Coll., 1927-29; B.A., Furman U., 1939; M.S., U. N.C., 1944; Ph.D., Ohio State U., 1952; m. Annie Lou Bell, May 29, 1937; children—Susan Carole, William Boyd. Tchr., Lee H. Edwards High Sch., Asheville, 1935-40, coordinator distbv. edn., 1940-44; tchr. Biltmore Coll., Asheville, 1942-44; part-time tchr. Mars Hill Coll., 1944; acting supr. distbv. edn. N.C. Dept. Edn., 1944-46; asso. prof. edn. Woman's Coll., U. N.C., 1946-48; successively instr., asst. prof., asso. prof., prof. edn. Ohio State U., 1948-67, dir. distbv. edn. mgmt. insts., 1955-67; pres. Webber Coll., Babson Park, Fla., 1967—; vis. prof. summers Colo. A. and M. Coll., 1947, La. State U., 1952, U. N.C., 1955, George Peabody Coll., 1956, U. Mich., 1956, U. Ala., 1957, Ind. U., 1959, Colo. State Coll., 1960, Wayne State U., 1961, U. Wash., 1963, U. Calif. at Berkeley, 1965; edn. cons. Nat. Retail Hardware Assn.; lectr. mgmt. and sales tng.; chmn. Nat. Tchr. Tng. Conf. Distbn., 1957; instr. first Nat. Adult Distbv. Edn. Conf., 1958; mem. vocat. edn. survey team Oreg. Dept. Edn., 1958; worked with groups fgn. vocat. educators Ohio State U., 1955, 56; mem. Pres. Kennedy's Panel Cons. Vocat. Edn. to Sec. HEW, 1961-62; nat. panel cons. Vocat. Edn. Personnel Devel., Dept. HEW, Washington. Served on civic coms.; trustee Highlands Sch., Avon Park, Fla. Mem. Am. (chmn. nominating com. 1952, awards com. 1957-60, pres. 1961, editor various publs.), N.C. (sect. v.p. 1943), Ohio (membership sec. 1952-58) vocat. assns., NEA, Associated Orgns. Tchr. Edn. (chmn. 1967), Fla. Assn. Colls. and Univs. (pres. 1974), Lake Wales C. of C. (dir.), Delta Pi Epsilon (nat. historian 1944, nat. v.p. 1946), Phi Delta Kappa, Pi Omega Pi. Clubs: Masons (32 deg.), Shriners. Author: (with Beckley) The Retail Salesperson at Work, 1948; (with Robinson and Blackler) Store Salesmanship, 6th edit., 1966; (with others) Vocational Education in Rural America (yearbook), 1959; (with others) National Business Teachers Association Yearbook, 1947; (with Helen Moon) Facts About Merchandise, 1962, 2d edit., 1967; co-author: Merchandising Mathematics, 1970; Mathematics in Marketing, 2d edit., 1978; contbr. articles to profl. jours. Home: Presidents Home Webber Coll Babson Park FL 33827

LOGAN, WILLIAM DEWEY, JR., surgeon; b. Ecru, Miss., Mar. 20, 1927; s. William D. and Gladys (Huskison) L.; B.S., Miss. State U., 1948; M.D., Emory U., 1952; m. Beatrice Brisbane, Aug. 21, 1949; children—Melissa Logan Daubert, Rebecca, John. Intern, Grady Meml. Hosp., Emory U. Sch. Medicine, Atlanta, 1952-53, asst. resident, 1954-56, resident, 1956-57; asst. resident Duke U. Hosp., 1953-54; registrar in thoracic surgery Guys Hosp., London, 1957-58; resident in thoracic surgery Emory U. Hosp., 1958-59; practice medicine specializing in thoracic surgery, Atlanta, 1959—; mem. courtesy staff Piedmont Hosp., Doctors Meml. Hosp., Crawford W. Long Hosp., Henrietta Egleston Hosp., Northside Hosp.; mem. active staff Dekalb Gen. Hosp.; mem. active staff Scottish Rite Hosp., chief of cardiovascular surgery, 1972-78; pres. and dir. Atlanta Heart and Lung Clinic, 1971—; mem. active staff Georgia Bapt. Med. Center, chief cardiovascular surgery, 1972—, pres. med. staff, 1979, chief of staff, 1980—; asst. prof. thoracic surgery Emory U., Atlanta, 1962-66, asso. prof., 1966-71, clin. asso. prof. thoracic surgery, 1971—; adj. clin. prof. respiratory therapy Ga. State U., 1973—; mem. Ga. Regional Med. Adv. Group, 1973-75. Mem. health facilities task force Atlanta Regional Commn., 1971-75; bd. dirs. Atlanta Ballet, chmn., 1975-77; bd. dirs. Atlanta Health Evaluation Center. Served with USN, 1945-46. Diplomate Am. Bd. Surgery, Am. Bd. Thoracic Surgery. Fellow A.C.S., Am. Coll. Chest Physicians (bd. govs. 1977—), Am. Coll. Cardiology, Am. Coll. Angiology, Southeastern Surg. Congress; mem. Am. Assn. Thoracic Surgeons, So. Thoracic Surg. Assn. (v.p. 1979), Am. Thoracic Soc., Ga. Thoracic Soc., Soc. Thoracic Surgeons, Internat. Cardiovascular Soc., Atlanta Lung Assn. (pres. 1972-74, dir. 1968—), Ga. Lung Assn. (dir. 1973—, chmn. profl. edn. com. 1977—), Soc. Vascular Surgeons, Med. Assn. of Ga. (sec. 1978—, trustee 1975—), Med. Assn. of Atlanta (pres. 1975, chmn. public relations com. 1968-74), So. Med. Assn. (asso. councilor 1975—), AMA, Pan Am. Med. Assn., Am. Geriatrics Soc., Am. Fedn. Clin. Research, Ga. Heart Assn. (mem. ednl. com. 1960-61), Royal Soc. Health, Atlanta C. of C. Methodist. Contbr. numerous articles on cardiology and thoracic surgery to profl. jours. Home: 770 W Paces Ferry Rd NW Atlanta GA 30327 Office: 272 Boulevard NE Atlanta GA 30312

LOGAN, WILLIAM THOMAS, dentist; b. Dublin, Tex., Dec. 10, 1925; s. James Marvin and Eula (Kiker) L.; B.A., Hardin-Simmons U., 1948; D.D.S., U. Tex., 1952; m. Margaret Elaine Dobbins, May 31, 1947; children—Richard Alan, Diana Lynn. Practice dentistry, Borger, Tex., 1952—. Served with USNR, 1944-46; PTO. Fellow Acad. Gen. Dentistry; mem. Am., Tex. dental assns., Borger (pres. 1959), Panhandle Dist. (pres. 1966-67) dental socs., Am. Acad. Gold Foil Operators, Am. Inst. Oral Biology, Tex. Acad. Gen. Dentistry, Palo Duro (pres. 1960), Clyde Schuyler dental study groups, Tex. Jr. C. of C. (dir. 1954), Psi Omega. Methodist. Mason (Shriner, 32 deg.), Elk. Clubs: North Plains Knife and Fork (dir. 1962-64). Home: 1400 Bluebonnet Lane Borger TX 79007 Office: 706 S McGee St Borger TX 79007

LOGUE, ALAN KEITH, lawyer, state govt. adminstr.; b. Albany, Ga., May 17, 1950; s. Emmett Julian and Mable Lucille (Barnett) L.; A.A., Albany Jr. Coll., 1970; B.S., Auburn U., 1972; J.D., Atlanta Law Sch., 1976; m. Shannon Margaret Cowles, Aug. 28, 1976. Spl. agt. Ga. Dept. Revenue, Atlanta, 1972-73, criminal investigator, 1973-74, spl. agt./adminstrv. asst., 1974-76, chief of licensing, alcohol and tobacco tax, 1976; spl. asst. to exec. dir./hearing officer/legal advisor Ga. Peace Officer Standards and Tng. Council, Decatur, 1976-79; dir. N. Central Ga. Law Enforcement Acad., Marietta, 1979—; cons. law enforcement; fin. cons.; legis. liaison. Lt. col., aide de camp gov's. staff. Mem. Ga. Assn. Criminal Justice Educators, Nat. Assn. Securities Dealers, State Bar Ga., Am. Bar Assn., Ga. Acad. Dirs. Assn. (v.p.), Ga. Trial Laywers Assn., Ga. Mcpl. Assn. (public safety com.), Lambda Alpha Epsilon, Alpha Tau Omega. Lic. pvt. pilot; cert. police instr. Home: 3660 Chestnut Ridge Ct Marietta GA 30062 Office: 4301 Memorial Dr Suite I Decatur GA 30032

LOGUE, RICK LYNN, data processing systems analyst; b. Corpus Christi, Sept. 12, 1950; s. Floyd Franklin and Bernelle Elisabeth (Albrecht) L.; A.A.S., Del Mar Coll., 1977; B.B.A. cum laude, Tex. A&I U., 1977; m. Mary Jo Porter, July 30, 1977. Programmer, Corpus Christi Bank and Trust, 1972-76; programmer, analyst Swiff Train Co., Corpus Christi, 1976-78; mgr. data processing King Ranch, Inc., Kingsville, Tex., 1978—. Republican. Lutheran. Home: 819 S 19th St Kingsville TX 78363 Office: PO Box 1418 Kingsville TX 78363

LOHR, JACOB ANDREW, physician; b. Lexington, N.C., Aug. 15, 1940; s. Dermot and Blanche (Grimes) L.; A.B., U. N.C., 1962, M.D., 1967; children—Jason Merrill, Jonathan Waite. Intern, U. Va., Charlottesville, 1967, resident in pediatrics, 1968-70; instr. pediatrics Jefferson Med. Sch., Phila., 1970-72; asst. prof. U. Va., Charlottesville, 1972-76, asso. prof., 1976—, vice chmn. ambulatory pediatrics, 1974—, acting chmn. dept. pediatrics, 1980-81, med. dir., primary care center, 1977-78; v.p., bd. dirs. U. Va. Health Services Fedn., 1979—. Mem. adv. bd. Charlottesville Community Action Program. Served with USN, 1970-72. Recipient McLemore Birdsong Outstanding Tchr. award, 1976; diplomate Am. Bd. Pediatrics. Mem. Albemarle County Med. Soc., Va. Med. Soc., Am. Acad. Pediatrics, Ambulatory Pediatric Assn., Soc. Microbiology, So. Soc. Pediatric Research, Phi Chi, Pi Kappa Alpha. Lutheran. Club: Rotary (dir.). Contbr. articles to profl. jours. Research in nurse practitioner tng., health care delivery and pediatric infectious diseases. Home: 1319 Pin Oak Ct Charlottesville VA 22901 Office: Box 386 Dept Pediatrics Univ VA Hospital Charlottesville VA 22903

LOKEY, GEORGE HARRISON, oil co. exec.; b. Amarillo, Tex., Mar. 25, 1935; s. Ted Henry and Stella Alice (Yeatts) L.; B.A. in Bus. Adminstrn., U. Okla., 1957; m. Sheri Darlynn Mims, Nov. 2, 1968; 1 son, Alexander David. With Ted Lokey Oil Co., Amarillo, 1960—, v.p., gen. mgr., 1962-63, pres., chief exec. officer, 1963—; v.p. Ted Lokey Tire Co., Amarillo, 1963—; dir. Tascosa Broadcasting Co., 1974—. Chmn. Amarillo Bicentennial Commn., Amarillo Bd. Conv. and Visitors Activities; pres. Amarillo Zool. Soc., Panhandle Heritage Found.; bd. dirs. Discover Tex. Assn., Tex. Tourist Council, Greater S.W. Music Festival; bd. dirs. Tex. Panhandle council Boy Scouts Am. Served as 1st lt. USMCR, 1957-60. Named Outstanding Young Texan, Garland A. Smith Assos., 1976. Mem. Nat. Oil Jobbers Council, Tex. Oil Marketers Assn. (pres. 1978-79), W. Tex. C. of C., C. of C. (dir.), Les Amis du Vin (regional dir.), Confrerie des Vignerons de Saint Vincent de Macon, Confrerie de la Chaine des Rotisseurs (Bailli de Amarillo), Sigma Alpha Epsilon. Presbyterian. Clubs: Amarillo, Amarillo Country, T Bar M Racquet, Taos Ski and Cricket, Angle Fire Country, Amarillo Am. Bus. (past pres., past gov.). Home: 2801 S Hughes St Amarillo TX 79109 Office: 314 W 8th St PO Box 2627 Amarillo TX 79105

LOKKEN, ROY NORMAN, historian; b. Fargo, N.D., Oct. 28, 1917; s. Olaf Kornelius and Olga Emilia (Hendricksen) L.; B.A., U. Puget Sound, 1941; M.A., U. Wash., 1951, Ph.D. in History, 1955; m. Ruth Hayes, Oct. 15, 1966. Asst. archivist State Hist. Soc. Wis., Madison, 1955-58; research asso. Wis. Legis. Council, Madison, 1958-62; instr. U. Tex. at Arlington, 1962-64, asst. prof. history, 1964-67; asso. prof. East Carolina U., 1967-74, prof., 1974—. Served with AUS, 1942-45; PTO. Recipient Louis Pelzer award in history Mississippi Valley Hist. Assn., 1953, Nat. Soc. Colonial Dames Am. award, 1953, Nat. Endowment for Humanities Summer stipend, 1974; Am. Philos. Soc. grantee-in-aid, 1973. Mem. AAUP, Am., So. hist. assns., Orgn. Am. Historians, Société Française d'Étude du XVIII Siecle, N.C. Lit. and Hist. Assn., Phi Alpha Theta. Democrat. Baptist. Author: David Lloyd, Colonial Lawmaker, 1959; The Scientific Papers of James Logan, 1972; contbg. author: The Historian as Detective: Essays on Evidence, 1969; Dimensions of Change: Problems and Issues of Colonial History, 1972; Politics and Society in Colonial America: Democracy or Deference?, 1973; contbr. numerous articles to profl. jours. Home: 418 W 5th St Apt 2 C Greenville NC 27834 Office: Dept History East Carolina U Greenville NC 27834

LOLLAR, MARGARET MARY, retail co. exec.; b. Lytton Springs, Tex., Dec. 22, 1935; d. Salomon and Antonia (Rodriguez) Espinoza; student Eastfield Coll., 1977-80; m. Charles Sloan Lollar, July 8, 1954; children—Diane, Bruce, Susan. With Sanger Harris, Dallas, 1968—, corporate payroll mgr., 1978—. Mem. Am. Mgmt. Assn. Roman Catholic. Home: 3546 Demaret Dr Mesquite TX 75150 Office: 303 N Akard Dallas TX 75201

LOMASK, MILTON NACHMAN, author; b. Fairmont, W.Va., June 26, 1909; s. Samuel Josiah and Clara Regina (Reinheimer) L.; B.A., U. Iowa, 1930; M.A., Northwestern U., 1941. Sunday mag. editor Des Moines Register, 1930-37; copy editor N.Y. Jour.-Am., 1937-40; advt. mgr. Nedicks, Inc., N.Y.C., 1945-50; free lance writer, 1950—; lectr. Washington Sq. Writing Center, N.Y. U., 1950-60; lectr. on writing, adult div. Catholic U. Am., 1964—; editorial cons. NSF, 1971-72; hist. cons. NPACT-BBC TV prodn. The Impeachment Trial of Andrew Johnson, 1974; staff mem. Wesleyan-Suffield (Conn.) Writer-Reader Conf., 1974-76. Served with CWS, AUS, 1942-45. Mem. Am. Hist. Assn., Authors Guild. Author: The Man in the Iron Lung, 1956; Odd Destiny: A Life of Alexander Hamilton, 1958; Andrew Johnson: President on Trial, 1960; Seed Money: The Guggenheim Story, 1964; This Slender Reed: A Life of James K. Polk, 1966; (with Constance McL. Green) Vanguard: A History (AIAA History award), 1970; The First American Revolution (Horn Book Honors List, ALA Notable Book), 1974; A Minor Miracle: An Informal History of the National Science Foundation, 1976; Aaron Burr: The Years from Princeton to Vice President, 1979; The Spirit of 1787: The Making of Our Constitution, 1980; contbr. to Dictionary Am. Biography, 3d supplement, Ency. Americana, 1974; contbr. articles to popular mags. Office: 6758 Towne Lane Rd McLean VA 22101

LOMASNEY, THOMAS LAWRENCE, physician; b. Central Falls, R.I., May 29, 1920; s. Thomas Cornelius and Mary (Parks) L.; A.B., Brown U., 1941; M.D., Boston U., 1944; m. Kate Stewart Rutherford, Dec. 17, 1955 (div. 1978, remarried 1979); children—Robert Rutherford, William Stewart, Sarah Wright. Intern, Mass. Meml. Hosps., Boston, 1944-45; resident Boston City Hosp., 1946, VA Deans' Com. Hosp., Rutland Heights, Mass., 1947-49, Providence, 1950-52, Dartmouth Med. Group, Hanover, N.H., 1950; practice medicine specializing in thoracic and cardiac surgery, Knoxville, Tenn., 1952—, Middlesboro, Ky., 1952—; attending thoracic surgeon St. Mary's Hosp., Knoxville, 1952—, Ft. Sanders Presbyn. Hosp., Knoxville, 1952—. Served from lt. (j.g.) to lt., M.C., USNR, 1945-46, 53-54. Diplomate Am. Bd. Surgery, Am. Bd. Thoracic Surgery. Mem. AMA, Am. Thoracic Soc., So. Thoracic Surg. Assn., Pan Am. Med. Assn. (diplomate mem., sect. on thoracic surgery), Knoxville Surg. Soc., Soc. Thoracic Surgeons. Contbr. articles to med. jours. Home: 1431 Cherokee Trail Knoxville TN 37920 Office: 6311 Kingston Pike Suite 10W Knoxville TN 37916

LOMBARD, CHERYL RUTH, guidance counselor; b. Arlington, Mass., Mar. 17, 1949; d. Leon Ernest and Shirley Elizabeth (Johnson) Lombard; B.A., Gordon Coll., Wenham, Mass., 1970; M.Ed., Fla. Atlantic U., 1974. Service rep. New Eng. Telephone Co., 1971-72; guidance counselor Boca Raton Acad., 1974—. Mem. Am. Personnel and Guidance Assn., Fla., Southeastern psychol. assns., Fla. Assn. Sch. Psychologists. Republican. Office: 2700 St Andrews Blvd Boca Raton FL 33431

LOMBARD, LOUIS FELIX, economist; b. Elizabeth, N.J., Aug. 19, 1935; s. Felix Edward and Charlotte Jordan (Morris) L.; B.S. cum laude, Mt. St. Mary's Coll., Emmitsburg, Md., 1958; M.A., Fordham U., 1963; LL.B., LaSalle Extension U., 1970; m. Adrienne Jeanette Wire, Dec. 27, 1958; children—Kathleen Ann, Louis Felix. Asst. trust officer, estate planning Peoples Trust City Bank, Reading, Pa., 1962-65; fin. cons., Reading, Pa., 1965; project adminstr. AMF Corp., York, Pa., 1965-66; prin. economist Va. Water Control Bd., Richmond, 1966—, state coordinator flood ins. and flood plain studies, 1973-75; adj. faculty Va. Commonwealth U., Richmond, 1969-72. Mem. Chesterfield County Democratic Com., 1976—, del. state Dem. conv., 1976; pres. Wagstaff Circle Vol. Fire Dept., 1977, dir., 1979. Served with AUS, 1958-60. Mem. Am. Econ. Assn., Va. Assn. Economists. Author: Regional Analysis and Forecasting for Regional Areas, 1971. Contbr. articles to publs. Home: 11145 Northborough Ln Richmond VA 23235 Office: 2111 N Hamilton St Richmond VA 23230

LONDOS, THEODORE (SKIP), JR., bus. exec.; b. Oak Park, Ill., Oct. 26, 1948; s. Theodore and Mabel Junet (Strand) L.; B.A., Baylor U., 1970, M.A., 1974, doctoral student, 1978; postgrad. Evang. Theol. Sem., 1971; m. Sandra Lee Butler, Mar. 21, 1977; 1 dau., Mary Christina. Social worker Methodist Children's Home, Waco, Tex., 1972-73, dir. advanced edn., 1973-77, dir. coke div., 1977-79; dir. mktg. research Toys 'N Things, Waco, 1979—; instr. sociology McLennan Community Coll., Waco, 1974-75. Vol., Mexia State Sch., 1968-69, Lake Shore Bapt. Ch., 1975—. Nat. leader pro-sidewalk campaign. Recipient award Meth. Children's Home, 1973. Mem. Am. Mktg. Assn., World Future Soc., Am. Hypnotherapy Assn. (dir., dir. publs.), Inst. Gen. Semantics, Am. Personnel and Guidance Assn., Nat. Vocat. Guidance Assn., Mensa, Alpha Kappa Delta. Founder, dir. Motivation Research, 1976—. Home: 7033 Edmond Dr Waco TX 76710 Office: 4201 Lake Shore Dr Waco TX 76710

LONG, ALFRED B., oil co. exec.; b. Galveston, Tex., Aug. 4, 1909; s. Jessie A. and Ada (Beckwith) L.; student S. Park Jr. Coll., 1928-29, Lamar U., 1947-56, U. Tex., 1941; m. Sylvia V. Thomas, Oct. 29, 1932; 1 dau., Kathleen Sylvia Long Pearson. With Sun Oil Co., Beaumont, Tex., 1931—, driller geophys. dept., surveyor engring. dept., engr. operating dept., engr. prodn. lab., 1931-59, regional supr., 1960-69, now ret.; ind. oil cons., Beaumont, 1969—; mem. tech. adv. group Oil and Gas Drilling Inst., Lamar U. Mem. Jefferson County Program Planning Com., 1964. Mem. Soc. Petroleum Engrs., Am. Assn. Petroleum Geologists, IEEE, Houston, Beaumont geol. socs., Gulf Coast Engring. and Sci. Soc. (treas. 1962-75), Am. Petroleum Inst., Soc. Wireless Pioneers, U.S. Power Squadron. Inventor various oil well devices. Address: PO Box 7266 Beaumont TX 77706

LONG, BILLYE ANNE, mfg. co. exec.; b. Borger, Tex., Dec. 5, 1933; d. William Dewey and Anna Lee (McMahon) Ferrell; student Amarillo Coll., 1979; m. Noel Levi Long, July 27, 1976; children—Sharon Mangum, Dayle Bickerstaff, Kay Justice. With Bell Helicopter Textron, Amarillo, Tex., 1969—, supr. facilities, 1979—. Democrat. Baptist. Home: Route 2 Box 900 Lot 17 Amarillo TX 79101 Office: PO Box 31100 Amarillo TX 79120

LONG, CAMERON EUGENE, engr.; b. Danville, Pa., Aug. 23, 1927; s. Edward A. and Blanche E. L.; A.S., Williamsport Tech. Inst., 1950; B.S.M.E., Bucknell U., 1951; m. Lois N. Long, Apr. 21, 1950 (dec.); children—Thomas E., Cynthia C., Christopher C., Kimber M., Rebecca D. With Armour & Co., 1953-72, area engr. Southeastern dist., 1970-72; adminstrv. engr. Hosp. Affiliates, Nashville, 1972-76; dir. engring. Muir Hosp., Walnut Creek, Calif., 1976-78; dir. engring. Univ. Hosp., Augusta, Ga., 1978—. Served with USN, 1943-47, 51-52; Korea. Decorated Purple Heart; registered profl. engr., Colo., Oreg., Calif. Mem. Am. Soc. Hosp. Engrs., Nat. Fire Protection Assn. Republican. Baptist. Clubs: Elks. Home: 3749 Old Petersburg Rd Augusta GA 30907 Office: 1350 Walton Way Augusta GA 30902

LONG, CHARLES FARRELL, ins. co. exec.; b. Charlottesville, Va., Nov. 19, 1933; s. Cicel Early and Ruth Elizabeth (Shifflett) L.; C.L.U., The Am. Coll., 1972; m. Ann Tilley, May 28, 1960; children—C. Farrell, Linda. Founder, pres. Casualty Underwriters Inc., Charlottesville, 1959-72; founder, pres. Group Underwriters Inc., Charlottesville, 1959—; trustee P.A.I. Ins. Trust. Mem. Assay Commn. of U.S., 1975. Bd. dirs. Heart Assn. Served with U.S. Navy, 1954-58. Mem. Central Va. Estate Planning Council, Am. Soc. C.L.U.'s, Central Va. C.L.U.'s Assn. (dir.), Va. Press Assn., Va. Assn. Life Underwriters. Creator Queen's medal for Queen Elizabeth, 1976. Home: 1400 W Leigh Dr Charlottesville VA 22901 Office: Ivy Sq Ivy Rd Charlottesville VA 22901

LONG, DELWIN JAMES, coll. adminstr.; b. Houston, Sept. 9, 1947; s. James Douglas and Charlotte Rose (Threeton) L.; B.S., Sam Houston State U., 1970, M.Ed., 1973; A.A., San Jacinto Coll., 1970; postgrad. U. Houston, 1977—; m. Linda Marie Garrett, Mar. 27, 1969; children—Delwin James, William Garrett. Tchr. govt., econ., math. LaPorte (Tex.) Ind. Sch. Dist., 1970-74; instr. econ., polit. sci., history San Jacinto Coll., Pasadena, Tex., 1975-79, dir. weekend coll., 1979—; dir. First Bank Deer Park (Tex.). Mem. Tex. Commn. on Services to Children and Youth, 1978, vice chmn., mem. exec. com., 1979-80; mem. Community Devel. bd., Deer Park, 1975, bd. adjustments, 1976, alt. mem. planning and zoning comm., 1977; pres. Gulf Coast Am. Heritage Group, 1976-77; chmn. pub. com. Deer Park Bond Proposal election, 1974; adv. council Houston area Rapid Transit Authority, 1973; asst. precinct judge, Precinct 352, 1971-73; del. to senatorial 13 conv., 1972, 74; del. 1974 Tex. Dem. Conv.; campaign mgr. Deer Park City Council race, 1977. Mem. Assn. for Study of Higher Edn., Tex. Jr. Coll. Tchrs. Assn., Deer Park Parent Tchr. Orgn., Sam Houston State U. Alumni Assn., Deer Park C. of C., Alpha Chi, Omicron Delta Epsilon, Phi Delta Kappa. Clubs: Masons, Rotary (sgt.-at-arms 1978-79). Home: 1301 New Orleans St Deer Park TX 77536 Office: 8060 Spencer St Pasadena TX 77505

LONG, DONALD EUGENE, hosp. adminstr.; b. Shawnee, Okla., Jan. 4, 1944; s. Frank Eugene and Nina Frances (Campbell) L.; B.B.A. in Mgmt., Central State U., 1972; m. Wilma Louise Thornburgh, May 26, 1973; children—Elizabeth Mignon, Kristi Brooke. Evening officer mgr. Hillcrest Baptist Hosp., Waco, Tex., 1973-74, utilization rev. dir., 1974-75, acting dir. med. records, 1975-77; adminstr. Ranger (Tex.) Gen. Hosp., 1977—; cons. med. secretarial program McLennan Community Coll. Chmn., Ranger United Fund., 1978-79, pres., 1979-80. Served with U.S. Navy, 1965-69. Mem. Tex. Hosp. Assn. Republican. Baptist. Club: Lions (Ranger). Home: 216 Lula St Ranger TX 76470 Office: 102 College Circle Ranger TX 76470

LONG, GARY, civil engr.; b. Berwyn, Ill., Jan. 9, 1943; s. Don A. and Reta (Staff) L.; B.S.C.E., Bradley U., 1967; M.S., Tex. A&M U., 1968, Ph.D., 1973; postdoctoral work U. Notre Dame Law Sch., 1976-77; m. Jane Shaffer, Sept. 22, 1973. Engr. Trainee, jr. engr. DeLeuw, Cather & Co., Cons. Engrs., Chgo., 1961-65; engring. research asso. Tex. Transp. Inst., 1966-71; prin. engr., planner Wilbur Smith & Assos., Cons. Engrs. and Planners, Houston, 1971-75; prof. civil engring. U. Notre Dame, 1975-77, U. Fla., Gainesville, 1977—; cons. to research agencies and law firms; expert witness. Registered profl. engr., Ill., Fla.; cert. data process. Mem. Inst. Transp. Engrs. (Past Pres. award 1972, Tech. Council award 1977), Transp. Research Bd., Transp. Research Forum, Ops. Research Soc. Am., Regional Sci. Assn., Met. Assn. Urban Designers and Environ. Planners, Sigma Xi. Contbr. articles tech. jours. Home: 101 NW 28th St Gainesville FL 32607 Office: Dept of Civil Engineering University of Florida Gainesville FL 32607

LONG, GEORGE LORENZO, JR., hosp. adminstr.; b. Greenville, S.C., July 9, 1938; s. George Lorenzo and Mary Emily (Charping) L.; B.S., U. S.C., 1960; m. Sandra Lou Croxton, Jan. 5, 1973; children—Mary Kathryn, George Robert, James Emmett, Jennifer Cooke. Supr. employment S.C. Dept. Mental Health, Columbia, 1964-64; personnel mgr., asst. cashier S.C. Nat. Bank, Columbia, 1964-69; corp. dir. personnel Wilbur Smith & Assos., Columbia, 1969-73; exec. v.p. Am. Bus. Cons.'s, Inc., Columbia, 1973-76; dir. personnel Providence Hosp., Columbia, 1976—. Vice-pres., S.C. Lung Assn., 1976, 77, bd. dirs. 1963—, pres., bd. dirs. Central br.; pres. Richland (S.C.) Tb Assn., 1973, 74, bd. dirs., 1967—; bd. dirs. Columbia chpt. ARC. Decorated Order of Palmetto award Gov. S.C., 1971. Mem. Am. Soc. Personnel Adminstrn. (region V v.p. 1973, 74), Columbia Personnel Assn. (pres. 1971), Am. Hosp. Assn., Am. Soc. Hosp. Personnel Adminstrn., S.C. Hosp. Assn. Democrat. Methodist. Home: 2805 Wales Rd Columbia SC 29206 Office: Providence Hosp 2435 Forest Dr Columbia SC 29204

LONG, GEORGE ROBERT, assn. exec.; b. Roachdale, Ind., Feb. 23, 1917; s. George Batman and Stella (Sutherlin) L.; A.B., Wabash Coll., 1939; M.A., Ind. U., 1949; postgrad. U. Va., 1949-53; m. Mary Henley Spencer, Dec. 7, 1968. Instr. govt. Ind. U., Bloomington, 1949-53; research fellow Bur. Pub. Adminstrn., U. Va., Charlottesville, 1946-49; planning adminstr. Henrico County (Va.), Richmond, 1953-54; field rep. Va. Div. Planning and Econ. Devel., Abingdon, 1954-57; acting commr. Div. Planning and Econ. Devel., 1957-58; exec. dir. Wilson (N.C.) Indsl. Council, 1958-60; mng. partner Robinson, Long & McDonald, Cons., Charlottesville, 1960-62; field cons. League of Va. Counties, Charlottesville, 1962-64; exec. dir. Va. Assn. Counties, Charlottesville, 1964—; mem. State Rural Area Devel. Com., 1963, Mental Health Study Commn., 1964-66, Met. Areas Study Commn., 1966-68, Commn. Rights Pub. Employees, 1972-74. Gov.'s Com. on State and Local Cooperation, 1969-74; cons. Commn. Property Tax Reform, 1972-74, Commn. City-County Relations, 1973-76; mem. Va. Land Use Adv. Council, 1976-77, Va.

Local Govt. Adv. Council, 1977, Va. Supplementary Retirement System Study Commn., 1978—; lectr. on Va. county govt. U. Va., Fed. Exec. Inst., Christopher Newport Coll., George Mason Coll., U. No. Colo. Served with AUS, 1941-45. Mem. Nat. Assn. Counties (dir. 1969-70), Nat. Council County Assn. Execs. (pres. 1969-70), Lambda Chi Alpha. Democrat. Presbyterian (elder). Club: Masons. Home: 2310 Tarleton Dr Charlottesville VA 22901 Office: 2309 Commonwealth Dr PO Box 6306 Charlottesville VA 22906

LONG, GILLIS WILLIAM, lawyer, congressman, soybean farmer, investment banker; b. Winnfield, La., May 4, 1923; s. Floyd H. and Birdie (Shumake) L.; B.A., La. State U., 1949, J.D., 1951; m. Mary Catherine Small, June 21, 1947; children—George Harrison, Janis Catherine. Admitted to La. bar, 1951; legal counsel select com. small bus. U.S. Senate, 1951-53; chief legal counsel spl. com. campaign expenditures (elections) U.S. Ho. of Reps., 1952, 56, 58, 60; mem. 88th, 93d-96th congresses 8th Dist. La., mem. rules com., 1973—, joint econ. com., 1975—, chmn. subcom. on legis. process, 1977, co-chmn. subcom. on internat. econs., 1976, co-founder Congl. rural caucus, 1973, mem. exec. bd., 1973—; asst. dir. Office Econ. Opportunity, Exec. Office of Pres., 1964-65; dir. Mainstream, Inc.; legis. counsel Spl. Com. Historic Preservation, Spl. Com. Urban Growth Policy. Chmn. La. Suporport Task Force, pres., 1972; pres. La. Superport Authority, 1973, Lower Mississippi Flood Control Assn., 1973-74. Del. Democrat Nat. Conv., 1964; vice chmn. United Dems. of Congress, 1973-74, chmn., 1975—. Served to capt., inf., U.S. Army, World War II; ETO. Decorated Bronze Star, Purple Heart. Mem. Am., La., Alexandria bar assns., V.F.W., Am. Legion, Omicron Delta Kappa, Delta Kappa Epsilon. Baptist. Lion. Home: Alexandria LA Office: 2445 Rayburn House Office Bldg Washington DC 20515

LONG, HENRY ADDISON, JR., banker; b. Ft. Deposit, Ala., Jan. 8, 1936; s. Henry Addison and Frances N. Long; B.S. in Agrl. Sci., Auburn (Ala.) U., 1958; postgrad. schs. of Am. Inst. Real Estate Appraisers, 1966-73; m. Shannon Hope Anderson, June 8, 1963; children—Henry Addison, Mark A., Shannon Hope. Farmer, 1961-63; with appraisal dept. Fed. Land Bank, New Orleans, 1963-67; sr. v.p., trust officer First Nat. Bank, Birmingham, Ala., 1967—. Pres., Bluff Park Community Sch. PTA, 1974-75, treas., 1977-78; pres. Ira F. Simmons Jr. High Sch. PTA, 1979-80; treas. Shades Mountain Community Park, 1974-79. Served to 1st lt. USAF, 1958-61. Mem. Am. Inst. Real Estate Appraisers, Ala. Forestry Assn. (dir.), Am., Ala. socs. farm mgrs. and rural appraisers, Ala. Bankers Assn. (past chmn. agr. com.), Birmingham Bd. Realtors (dir. 1978-79), Birmingham C. of C. (chmn. rural affairs com.). Baptist. Home: 2281 S Sherrlyn Dr Birmingham AL 35226 Office: PO Box 11007 Birmingham AL 35288

LONG, HENRY ARLINGTON, real estate exec.; b. Arlington, Va., May 18, 1937; s. William Armstead and Emily Pearl (Garland) L.; B.S., Va. Poly. Inst., 1959; m. Betty Mae Horner, Dec. 28, 1963; children—Andrea Denise, Elissa Michell, Elizabeth Kristen, Henry Arlington. Ind. comml. real estate sales, Va. and Washington, 1965-68; co-owner Long & Foster, Inc., Fairfax, Va., 1968-79; owner/pres. The Henry A. Long Co., Fairfax, 1979—; mng. gen. partner Manassas Forum Assos. (Va.), 1973—, Snowden Village Assos., 1972—, Eskridge Indsl. Assos., 1974—, Reston Racquet Club Assos., 1976—; dir. No. Va. Bd. Realtors, 1973, 74. Trustee, The Potomac Sch., 1979—. Served as pilot SAC, USAF, 1959-65, USAFR, 1966-70. Recipient award for Mil. Merit, Chgo. Tribune, 1959; Distinguished Service award No. Va. Bd. Realtors, 1972, 73. Mem. Nat. Assn. Realtors, Nat. Assn. Homebuilders, Realtors Nat. Mktg. Inst., Real Estate Securities and Syndication Inst., Pi Delta Epsilon. Episcopalian. Clubs: Jaycees, Kiwanis (dir. Fairfax chpt. 1970-71). Producer, dir. TV film Moulders of Men, 1960. Home: 11214 Country Pl Oakton VA 22124 Office: 4085 University Dr Fairfax VA 22030

LONG, HERBERT ELWOOD, hosp. adminstr.; b. Cambridge, Ohio, Aug. 9, 1918; s. Lucian E. and Della Marie (Morrow) L.; B.S. in Bus. Adminstrn., Miami U., Ohio, 1942; m. Elizabeth Ann Pettis, May 15, 1943; children—Pamela, Linda, Matthew. Sr. acctg. clk. dept. cost acctg. Gen. Motors Corp., Flint, Mich., 1942-44; supr. accounts payable dept. Curtiss Wright Corp., Columbus, Ohio, 1944-48, credit mgr., 1948-51; chief acct. McLaren Gen. Hosp., Flint, 1951-53, asst. bus. mgr., 1953-59; comptroller Cleve. Met. Gen. Hosp., 1959-63; asso. controller Henry Ford Hosp., Detroit, 1963-66, controller, 1966-69; dir. fiscal services Mercy Hosp., Inc., Miami, Fla., 1969-70, asst. exec. dir., 1970-75, asso. exec. dir., 1975-76, exec. dir., 1976—. Fellow Hosp. Fin. Mgmt. Assn.; mem. Am. Hosp. Assn., Cath. Hosp. Assn., Fla. Hosp. Assn., S. Fla. Hosp. Assn. (dir.), Am. Coll. Hosp. Adminstrs., Nat. Council Community Hosps. Office: 3663 S Miami Ave Miami FL 33133

LONG, JAMES ALBERT, TV mfg. co. exec.; b. Pitts., June 14, 1927; s. Lloyd C. and Asa (Chestnut) L.; A.A. in Electronics, Milw. Sch. Engring., 1951; m. Donna Jeane Delores Amberg, Dec. 20, 1953; children—Nanette M., Gregory P., Cynthia A. Electronic technician to sr. design engr. Magnavox Co., Ft. Wayne, Ind. and Greenville, Tenn., 1951-66; mgr. radio engring. Arvin Industries, Columbus, Ind., 1966-72; v.p., dir. reliability, quality assurance, service and consumer relations Curtis Mathes Mfg. Co., Athens, Tex., 1973—. Served with USN, 1945-46. Registered profl. engr., Calif. Mem. IEEE, Am. Soc. Quality Control, ASTM, Am. Mgmt. Assn. Methodist. Contbr. articles to Popular Mechanics Mag., Times Mirror mag., patentee in field. Home: 900 Clifford St Athens TX 75751 Office: 1 Curtis Mathes Pkwy Athens TX 75751

LONG, JAMES STEPHEN, pharmacist; b. Lexington, Ky., Dec. 20, 1949; s. James Daniel and Iris Christine (Shurling) L.; student U. Ky., 1968-69, W. Ky. U., 1969-70; B.S. in Pharmacy, Mercer U., 1973; m. Barbara Carol Cheatham, July 16, 1969; 1 dau., Tracy Jeannette. Chief pharmacist Cave City Drugs (Ky.), 1973-77, owner, 1977—; cons. pharmacist Monroe County War Meml. Hosp., 1975; lectr. on drug abuse. Mem. Happy Valley Elementary Sch. PTA, 1975—. Recipient Rexall award for Outstanding Achievement in Pharmacy Edn., 1973. Mem. Glasgow-Barren County Jaycees, Am., Ky. pharm. assns., Kappa Psi. Home: 101 Sherry Dr Glasgow KY 42141 Office: 198 Broadway Cave City KY 42127

LONG, JERRY CARL, educator; b. Nowata, Okla., Mar. 18, 1941; s. Roy Orlando and Bernice (Cowdery) L.; B.S. in History and Edn., Northeastern State U., Tahlequah, Okla., 1966; M.S. in Secondary Edn., Okla. State U., 1968, Ed.D., 1972; m. Vida Davis, July 31, 1966; 1 dau., Kendra Beth. Instr., Okla. State U., 1967-68, 70-72; tchr. Winfield (Kans.) public schs., 1968-69; mem. faculty Ark. State U., 1972—, asso. prof. history, 1977—, dir. NSF summer insts., 1974-75. Served with USAF, 1960-64. Mem. Nat. Council Social Studies, NEA, Social Studies Suprs. Assn., Ark. Council Social Studies (pres. 1978-79), Ark. Edn. Assn., Ark. Assn. Coll. History Tchrs. Editor: Ark. Social Studies Tchrs., 1974-80, Teaching Social Studies Skills, 1977. Home: PO Box 33 State University AR 72467

LONG, JOHN MALOY, univ. dean; b. Guntersville, Ala., Dec. 28, 1925; s. Sam James and Lilian (Letson) L.; B.S., Jacksonville State U., 1949, LL.D., 1971; M.A., U. Ala., 1964; m. Mary Lynn Adams, July 7, 1950; children—John Maloy, Deborra Lynn. Dir. bands Oneonta (Ala.) High Sch., 1949-50, Ft. Payne (Ala.) High Sch., 1950-55, Robert E. Lee High Sch., Montgomery, Ala., 1955-65; dir. bands Troy (Ala.) State U., 1965—, chmn. music dept., 1969, dean Sch. Fine Arts, 1971, dean Coll. Arts and Scis., 1972—, new music bldg. at univ. named in his honor, 1975. Mem. Ala. Hist. Commn., 1974—; mem. Troy City Bd. Edn., 1972—, chmn., 1976—. Served with AUS, 1944-46. Recipient citation of excellence Nat. Band Assn., 1972, Distinguished Citizens Service award, Montgomery, 1964—, certificate of appreciation, State of Ala., 1964; named one of 10 top band dirs. in U.S., Sch. Musician Mag., 1969. Mem. Am. Bandmaster Assn., Am. Sch. Band Dirs. Assn. (state pres. 1968-72), Coll. Band Dirs. Nat. Assn. (state pres.), Omicron Delta Kappa, Phi Mu Alpha, Phi Beta Mu, Phi Delta Kappa, Kappa Kappa Psi, Delta Chi. Democrat. Methodist. Clubs: Masons, Rotary. Contbr. articles to mags. Home: 326 Homewood St Troy AL 36081

LONG, MARY COLE, educator; b. Dallas, Oct. 1, 1922; d. Ernest E. and Sadie Flynn (Boone) Farrow; B.A., Baylor U., 1944; M.A., 1965; m. William Bowman Long, June 3, 1944; children—William Farrow, Daryl Elizabeth, Robert John, Linda Sue. Instr. English, Mary Hardin-Baylor U., Belton, Tex., 1965-72, asst. prof. English, 1972—. Pres., Leon Heights PTA, 1956, City Council PTA, 1957. Mem. Central Tex. Poetry Soc. (pres. 1972-77), Poetry Soc. Tex. Democrat. Baptist. Home: 415 Downing St Belton TX 76513 Office: PO Box 359 Mary Hardin-Baylor Sta Belton TX 76513

LONG, PATRICK CAHILL, assn. exec.; b. Austin, Tex., Mar. 16, 1946; s. Thomas Brevard and Caroline Patricia (Charles) L.; B.B.A., U. Tex., 1968; J.D., 1970. Statis. analyst Tex. Parks and Wildlife, Austin, 1969; auditor R.R. Commn. Tex., Austin and Houston, 1972-73; admitted to Tex. bar, 1971; house counsel Lundberg-Pool & Co., Inc., Dallas, 1973-75; individual practice law Houston, 1975-79; exec. dir. Tex. Tank Carriers Assn., Austin, 1979—; ins. agt. Group II, So. County Mut. Ins. Co., Austin, 1975. Tournament dir. Parker Bros., Houston, 1977; advanced tournament dir. U.S. Chess Fedn., 1979. Mem. Houston Bar Assn., Travis County Bar Assn. Home: 6910 Hart Ln Austin TX 78731 Office: Tex Tank Carriers Assn 700 E 11th St Austin TX 78701

LONG, PAUL JUNIOR, scientist, artist; b. Tellico Plains, Tenn., May 27, 1927; s. Charles Ody and Maggie Lane (Rogers) L.; B.S., Tenn. Tech. U., 1950; M.S., U. Tenn., 1970; m. Willa Mae Williams, Nov. 16, 1952; children—David Paul, Susan Gayle, Gregory Lessel. Asst. to erector Combustion Engring., Newnan, Ga., 1950; foreman radiographic lab. Union Carbide Corp., Oak Ridge, 1951-53, supr. spl. pilot plant operations, 1953-55, supr. ultra-sonic and spl. nondestructive testing group, 1955-63, physicist in charge metall. services lab., 1963-69, head engring. test systems dept., 1969—. Exhibited in local group shows and art galleries, Knoxville, Tenn. Committeeman, Boy Scouts Am., Oak Ridge, 1969-71; vocational edn. chmn. Jefferson Jr. High Sch. P.T.A., Oak Ridge, 1971-72. Served with USAAF, 1945-46. Registered profl. engr., Tenn. Fellow Am. Soc. Nondestructive Testing (charter mem. Oak Ridge, chpt. dir.), S.A.R. Baptist (deacon). Author: Our Hill Country Heritage, Vol. I, Williams and Related Families, 1970; Our Hill Country Heritage, Vol. II, Longs and Related Families, 1972. Contbr. articles to profl. jours. Home: Route 2 Box 73 Hines Valley Rd Lenoir City TN 37771 Office: Union Carbide Y 12 Plant Oak Ridge TN 37830

LONG, REBECCA JANE, chem. mfg. co. exec.; b. Pittsboro, Miss., May 18, 1935; d. Thomas J. and Minnie A. (Keenum) L.; B.S. in Microbiology and Chemistry, Miss. State U., 1963; M.S., Memphis State U., 1969. Staff technologist dept. chemistry, lab. supr. Bapt. Meml. Hosp., Memphis, 1962-68; teaching supr. Hamilton Meml. Hosp., Dalton, Ga., 1968-69; tech. specialist Hycel, Inc., Houston, 1969-70; dir. med. lab. technician program Dalton Jr. Coll., 1970-72; lab. examiner Center for Disease Control, Atlanta, 1972-75; tech. specialist Searle Analytic, Inc., Atlanta, 1975-76; tech. specialist E.I. duPont de Nemours & Co., Claremont, Calif., 1976-77, product release chemist, Glasgow, Del., 1977-78, southeastern region tech. rep., Doraville, Ga., 1978—. Mem. Am. Soc. Med. Technologists, Am. Public Health Assn., Am. Soc. Clin. Pathology, Sigma Xi. Presbyterian. Home: 6612 Point Comfort Ln Pineville NC 28134 Office: 4280 Northeast Expressway Doraville GA 30362

LONG, RICHARD LOUIS, JR., research engr.; b. Kansas City, Mo., June 5, 1947; s. Richard Louis and Alta Marie (Giddens) L.; B.A., Rice U., 1969, Ph.D., 1973; m. Sharon Ann Snyder, Feb. 17, 1973; 1 dau., Christine Heather. Engr., Continental Oil Co., Ponca City, Okla., summers 1968, 69, 70; research engr. E.I. DuPont de Nemours Co., Orange, Tex., 1973-78, cons., 1978—; prof. dept. chem. engring. Lamar U., Beaumont, Tex., 1978—; cons. Time, Inc. Registered profl. engr., Tex. Mem. Nat., Tex. socs. profl. engrs., Am. Chem. Soc., Am. Inst. Chem. Engrs. Methodist. Clubs: Lions, Toastmasters. Home: 8408 Yorkshire Dr Orange TX 77630

LONG, RUSSELL B(ILLIU), U.S. senator; b. Shreveport, La., Nov. 3, 1918; s. Huey Pierce and Rose (McConnell) L.; B.A., La. State U., 1941, LL.B., 1942; m. Carolyn Bason, Dec. 23, 1969; children by previous marriage—Katherine (Mrs. Dean Mosely), Pamela Rust (Mrs. Prescott McCardell). Admitted to La. bar, 1942; practiced law, Baton Rouge, 1946-47; exec. counsel to gov. La., May-June, 1948; elected to U.S. Senate from La., for unexpired term ending 1950, reelected 1950—, asst. majority leader, 1965-68, chmn. fin. com., alt. chmn. joint com. on internal revenue, chmn. surface transp. subcom. of commerce com.; mem. Democratic steering com. Del. Dem. nat. conv., 1952. Served to lt. USNR, 1942-45; MTO, NATO. Mem. Am. Legion, Order of Coif, Delta Kappa Epsilon, Pi Delta Phi, Tau Kappa Alpha, Omicron Delta Kappa. Elk, Lion. Home: Baton Rouge LA Office: Senate Office Bldg Washington DC 20510

LONG, SHIRLEY DOBBINS, contractor; b. Guilford County, N.C., Feb. 5, 1943; d. Matt and Louiva (Davis) Dobbins; B.S. in Math., U. N.C., 1964; postgrad. U. Mich. 1966-69, 75-76; m. Bruce E. Long, Dec. 1967 (dec. Jan. 1969). Head steel purchasing dept. Struthers Wells Co., Greensboro, N.C., 1964-65; pres., owner Shirley D. Long Builders Inc., Greensboro and Jamestown, N.C., 1960—, Designs by Shirley, 1960—. Mem. N.C. Real Estate Bd., N.C. Gen. Contracting Bd., Profl. Builders N.C., Smithsonian Instn. Methodist. Author: The Pen Robbers. Home and Office: PO Box 19123 Guilford Coll Greensboro NC 27410

LONG, THAD GLADDEN, lawyer; b. Dothan, Ala., Mar. 9, 1938; s. Lindon Alexander and Della Gladys (Pilcher) L.; A.B., Columbia U., 1960; J.D., U. Va., 1963; m. Carolyn Frances Wilson, Aug. 13, 1966; children—Louisa Frances, Wilson Alexander. Admitted to Ala. bar, 1963; mem. firm Bradley, Arant, Rose & White, Birmingham, Ala., 1963-71, partner, 1971—; lectr. U. Ala. Law Sch., 1968-70. Bd. dirs. Birmingham Assn. Retarded Children, 1968-73; pres. Greater Birmingham Arts Alliance, 1977-79, chmn., 1979—; legal com. Ala. Assn. Retarded Citizens, 1974—. Recipient Distinguished Service award Ala. Assn. Retarded Children, 1972; Appreciation award Birmingham Council Exceptional Children, 1972. Mem. Am., Ala. State (chmn. sect. antitrust law 1973-74), Birmingham (chmn. grievance com.) bar assns., Phi Delta Phi. Methodist. Clubs: Birmingham Country, Relay House (Birmingham). Comments and projects editor Va. Law Rev., 1962-63; contbr. articles to profl. jours. Home: 3409 S Brookwood Rd Birmingham AL 35223 Office: 1500 Brown-Marx Bldg Birmingham AL 35203

LONG, WILLIAM BOWMAN, physician; b. Eddy, Tex., June 19, 1921; s. Roderick John and Ester Margueriete (Bowman) L.; D.D.S., Baylor U., 1945, M.D., 1951; m. Mary Cole Farrow, June 3, 1944; children—William F., Daryl E., Robert J., Linda S. Intern Jefferson Davis Hosp., Houston, 1951-52; practice medicine specializing in family practice, Belton, Tex., 1952—; mem. staffs Sewell-Long Hosp., Belton, Tex.; physician Mary Hardin Baylor Coll., 1969—; cons. Crestview Manor, 1970—; pres. Longkamp, Inc. Trustee, Belton Ind. Sch. Dist., v.p. 1966-72, pres., 1972-74. Served with AUS, 1943-44, USNR, 1945-47. Mem. Am. Acad. Gen. Practice, Am., Tex., Bell County med. assns., Belton C. of C. (pres. 1958, Belton Athletic Assn. (pres. 1955-56). Lion (pres. 1959-60). Home: 415 Downing St Belton TX 76513 Office: 402 N Main St Belton TX 76513

LONG, WILLIAM DAVID, food co. exec.; b. Crisfield, Md., Sept. 20, 1929; s. Thomas Berry and Etta (Luettinger) L.; student Va. Poly. Inst., 1947-50; m. Barbara Russell, July 15, 1959; children—Lisa Bea, William David, Beauregard Thomas. Pres., Long Farms, Inc., Apopka, Fla., 1961—, Long & Scott Farms, Inc., Apopka, 1964—, Apopka Properties, Inc., 1967—; pres. Apopka Devel. Co., 1970—; sec. Lust & Long Precooler Inc., Apopka, 1960—, Lust & Long Carrot Co., Apopka, 1969—; dir. State Bank Apopka, State Bank of Forest City; chmn. bd. Fla. Fed. Savs. & Loan, 1979—. Vice pres. Orange County Farm Bur., 1967-74, pres., 1974—; v.p., dir. Zellwood Drainage and Water Control Dist., 1962—; mem. Orange County Air and Water Pollution Control, 1970—; mem. Gov.'s Migratory Labor Com., 1967—; bd. dirs. NW Orange County Little League, 1979-80. Named Outstanding Young Farmer Orange County, Orlando Jr. C. of C., 1964, 65, Outstanding Young Farmer Fla. Jr. C. of C., 1965, 1964, 65, one of four outstanding young farmers in U.S., Nat. Jr. C. of C. and Nat. L.P. Gas Assn., 1966, Ford Found. award in vegetable crop mgmt., 1968; recipient Spl. Resolution 2782 for being selected one of four outstanding young farmers in U.S., Fla. Ho. of Reps., 1965. Mem. Fla. Fruit and Vegetable Growers Assn. (dir., conv. chmn. 1980), C. of C. (agr. com.). Presbyterian (elder 1974—). Clubs: Masons (32 deg.), Shriners, Jesters Elks, Zellwood (Fla.) Country (pres.). Home: 2860 E Green Acre Rd Apopka FL 32703 Office: PO Drawer 729 Apopka FL 32703

LONGACRE, CALVIN PAUL, advt. exec.; b. Reading, Pa., Aug. 1, 1930; s. Charles Calvin and Ruth Mary (Adams) L.; B.S., U. Md., 1960; postgrad. U. Mo., 1974; m. Betty Jo Webb, June 21, 1958; children—Christy Joy Steven Charles, Brian Paul. Promotion mgr. Burdine's Ft. Lauderdale Store, 1960-62, First br. advt. coordinator, 1962-68; traffic/prodn. mgr. Bailey Campbell Advt. Agy., Ft. Lauderdale, 1968-69; advt. asst. First Fed. of Broward, Ft. Lauderdale, 1969-73, asst. v.p. advt., 1973, v.p. advt., 1973-79; mktg. dir. Sun Banks of Broward County, 1979—; instr. human behavior and mktg. courses Inst. Fin. Edn., Ft. Lauderdale, 1971-79. Sunday sch. tchr. Coral Ridge Presbyn. Ch., 1969, deacon, 1970-74, elder, 1974-78, chmn. Christian edn. com., 1974-78, supt. jr. dept. Sunday sch., 1970-78, gen. Sunday sch. supt., 1979; bus. adv. Jr. Achievement, 1962, 68; vice chmn. communications United Way, 1977, mem. gifts and bequests com., 1979; chmn. Broward County Outdoor Sign Com., 1977; chmn. bd. dirs Free Enterprise Center. Served with USN, 1952-56. Recipient Community Service award Radio sta. WGMA, 1978; named Employer of Year, Coop. Bus. Edn., 1971-72. Mem. Am. Advt. Fedn. (Silver medal 1977, Pres. of Year Fla. 1978, Gov.'s Recognition award Fla. 1979, treas. Fla., nat. awards com.), Greater Ft. Lauderdale Advt. Fedn. (past pres.), Savs. and Loan Mktg. Soc. S.Fla. (past pres.), Inst. Fin. Edn. (past edn. chmn.), Ft. Lauderdale C. of C. (vice chmn. program task force 1978—). Democrat. Clubs: Masons (32 deg.); DeMolay (adv. 1961-65, gov. 1965-68, Cross of Honor 1965, Hon. Legion of Honor 1966); Friendly First Toastmasters. Home: 4820 NW 10th Terr Fort Lauderdale FL 33309 Office: 1501 NE 26th St Fort Lauderdale FL 33305

LONGENECKER, GESINA LOUISE LIZANA, pharmacologist; b. New Orleans, June 25, 1945; d. Florian Joseph and Shirley Louise (White) L.; B.S. with honors in Chemistry, Tulane U., 1965; Ph.D. in Pharmacology, Cornell U. Grad. Sch. Med. Scis., 1971; m. Herbert Eugene Longenecker, Jr., June 12, 1965; children—Lani Louise, Herbert Eugene III. Postdoctoral fellow in pharmacology Cornell Med. Coll., 1971-72; postdoctoral fellow in biochemistry Coll. Medicine, U. South Ala., 1972-74, instr. pharmacology, 1974-75, asst. prof., 1975—. Am. Lung Assn. grantee, 1979—. Mem. Neurosci. Soc., AAAS, N.Y. Acad. Scis., Bromeliad Soc. U.S., Bromeliad Soc. Greater Mobile, Sigma Xi. Editor: Jour. of Electrophysiol. Techniques, 1974—. Home: 3728 Claridge Road S Mobile AL 36608 Office: Dept Pharmacology Coll Medicine U South Ala Mobile AL 36688

LONGENECKER, HERBERT EUGENE, JR., biomed. scientist; b. Pitts., May 17, 1943; s. Herbert Eugene and Marjory Jane (Segar) L.; B.S., Tulane U., 1970; Ph.D., Rockefeller U., 1970; m. Gesina Louise Lizana, June 12, 1965; children—Lani Louise, Herbert Eugene. Fellow, Cornell U. Med. Coll., N.Y.C., 1969-72; asst. prof. neurosci. U. S. Ala. Coll. Medicine, 1972-74, asst. prof. physiology, 1975, asst. prof. pharmacology, 1976—, dir. interactive computer lab., 1976—; dir. Frederick Haer & Co., Brunswick, Maine, 1974—, chmn. bd., chmn. exec. com., 1980—; cons. small system installation and biomed. instrument design. NIH grantee, 1976-79. Mem. Neurosci. Soc., Computer Soc., Biomed. Engring. Soc., IEEE, Sigma Xi. Editor, Jour. Electrophysiol. Techniques, 1979, trustee, 1980—; contbr. numerous sci. and tech. articles to profl. jours. Home: 3728 Claridge Rd S Mobile AL 36608 Office: Interactive Computer Lab MSB 3086 U of South Ala Mobile AL 36688

LONGMIRE, MARSHALL LEE, educator; b. Conehatta, Miss., Feb. 7, 1935; s. Malcolm and Maggie (McFarland) L.; B.S., Alcorn State U., 1957; M.Ed., Tuskegee Inst., 1965; postgrad. Iowa State U., 1960-61, U. Ill., 1963; Ed.D. (fellow), Rutgers U., 1973; m. Barbara Sue Horton, Sept. 4, 1965; 1 dau., Tamera Diahn. Tchr. sci., math E.T. Hawkins High Sch., Forest, Miss., 1957-70; tchr. chemistry and physics Forest High Sch., 1970-71; asso. prof. sci. edn. Jackson (Miss.) State U. Supr., Community Recreation, Forest, 1973-79. Mason scholar, 1952; Elks scholar, 1953; NSF fellow, 1960-65; named Tchr. of Yr., 1979. Mem. Miss. Sci. Tchrs. Assn., Nat. Sci. Tchrs. Assn., AAAS, NEA, Alcorn State U. Alumni Assn., Jackson State U. Alumni Assn., Jackson Hinds County Mental Health Assn. Democrat. Baptist. Clubs: 100 Sports, Masons. Home: 1660 Lynch St Apt 22 Jackson MS 39203 Office: Dept Gen Scis Jackson State U Jackson MS 39217

LONGO, SALVADOR EUGENE, cons. biomed. and radiation physicist; b. New Orleans, Dec. 7, 1940; s. Joseph C. and Ruth (Cenas) L.; B.S. in Elec. Engring., La. State U., 1963, M.S. in Elec. Engring., 1966; Ph.D. in Physics (NSF fellow, NIH Cancer Research fellow), Tulane U., 1971; m. Pamela Marie Martina, Aug. 18, 1962; children—Sherri Anne, Debbie Marie, Michele Theresa, Salvador Eugene. Research engr. Boeing Co., New Orleans, 1963-67; instr. biomed. engring., dir. McCool Lab. for Laser Research Tulane U. Sch. Medicine, New Orleans, 1967-70; biomed. engr., med. physicist Ochsner Found. Hosp., New Orleans, 1970-71; pres., prin. Salvador

E. Longo & Assos., Inc., Cons. Biomed. and Radiation Physicists, Metairie, La., 1971—; mem. La. Engrs. Selection Bd.; cons. in field to various hosps. and med. schs. Chief of Communications Jefferson Parish (La.) Civil Def. Orgn., 1963-66. Registered profl. engr., La. Mem. IEEE, Nat. Soc. Profl. Engrs., Am. Phys. Soc., Am. Radio Relay League, Train Collectors Assn., Lionel Collectors Club Am., Sigma Pi Sigma. Roman Catholic. Club: Italian-Am. Marching. Contbr. articles in biomed. engring., med. physics, quantum physics, solid state physics, electromagnetic theory, and plasma physics to profl. jours. Home: 4728 Alphonse Dr Metairie LA 70002

LONGORIA, RAUL L., state senator; b. La Grulla, Tex., Feb. 22, 1921; s. Andres and Enriqueta L.; B.B.A., U. Tex., Austin, also LL.B.; m. Earlene Moorman, Sept. 9, 1947; children—Samuel Glenn, Janiece Maxene, Roy Alan, Martha Elaine and Cecilia Joyce (twins). Admitted to Tex. bar; asst. dist. atty. Hidalgo County, 1954-56; practice in Edinburg; individual practice, 1964—; mem. Tex. Ho. of Reps., 1961-73, Tex. Senate, 1973—. Served with USAAF, 1942-46. Recipient Reverance for Law award Fraternal Order Eagles, 1976, Friend of Edn. award Tex. Classroom Tchrs. Assn., 1979. Mem. Am. Bar Assn., State Bar Tex., Tex. Trial Lawyers Assn., Tex. Criminal Def. Lawyers Assn., Hidalgo County Bar Assn., Am. Legion, Rio Grande Valley C. of C., Edinburg C. of C. Democrat. Roman Catholic. Clubs: Lions, Eagles (Pharr). Office: PO Box 182 Edinburgh TX 78539

LONGSTRETH, HOWARD PAUL, physician; b. Pitts., June 30, 1920; s. Willis Lester and Ethel Ortman (Aid) L.; M.D., SUNY, Buffalo, 1945; m. Nancy Ferguson, June 23, 1945; children—Paul Scott, Allen Lee. Intern, Allegheny Gen. Hosp., Pitts., 1945-46; resident in pathology and internal medicine E.J. Meyer Meml. Hosp., Buffalo, 1946-50; practice medicine specializing in internal medicine and chest diseases, Buffalo, 1950-78; internal med. and chest specialist Student Health Service, U. Ga., Athens, 1978-80; asst. clin. prof. medicine SUNY, Buffalo, 1957-71, clin. asso. prof. medicine, 1971-78, asst. dean, 1957-59; cons. internal medicine and pulmonary diseases Athens Gen. Hosp., St. Mary's Hosp., 1978—. Served to maj. M.C., AUS, 1954-56. Diplomate Am. Bd. Internal Medicine. Fellow A.C.P., Am. Coll. Chest Physicians; mem. Am. Thoracic Soc., Royal Soc. Medicine (London affiliate), U. Buffalo Sch. Medicine Alumni Assn. (pres.), Buffalo Acad. Medicine (pres.). Clubs: Masons, Scottish Rite (Buffalo). Contbr. articles to med. jours. Home and Office: 140 Lost Tree Trail Athens GA 30605

LONGWITH, JEAN MARGUERITE, radio sta. mgr.; b. San Antonio, Mar. 15, 1918; d. Harold Eugene and Anna Frances (Marshall) L.; B.A. cum laude, U. Tex., 1937, M.Ed. cum laude, 1945; M.F.A. cum laude (fellow), U. Iowa, 1950. Tchr. sr. high sch., San Antonio, 1938-45; dir. Community Players, San Antonio, 1942-46, San Antonio Little Theatre, 1947-49; instr. communications TV Hour, U. Iowa, Iowa City, 1949-50; dir. WOC-TV, Davenport, Iowa, 1949-51; chmn. drama dept. Jefferson High Sch., San Antonio, 1952-64; gen. mgr. radio sta. KSYM-FM, San Antonio, 1966—; prof. radio, TV, film San Antonio Coll., 1964—, chmn. dept., 1978—; lectr. Our Lady of Lake Coll., San Antonio, 1956-59. Dir. Summer Dance Festival, San Antonio Recreation Dept., 1952-69; mem. San Antonio Bicentennial Com., San Antonio Fine Arts Com., 1976—, San Antonio Cable-TV Adv. Com., 1979. Named an Outstanding Woman of San Antonio, 1979. Mem. AAUW (pres. 1980), Zeta Phi Eta, Pi Lambda Theta, Phi Theta Kappa, Delta Kappa Gamma (pres. chpt. 1966-68; pres. coordinating council 1968-70). Episcopalian. Club: Zonta. Author: Adaptation of Three Short Stories for Television, 1950; The Community That Cares (play), 1960; Poetry for Interpretation, 1955; Ten Syllabi for Courses in Broadcasting, 1969. Home: 210 Quentin Dr San Antonio TX 78201 Office: 1300 San Pedro Ave San Antonio TX 78284

LOOFF, KARL MICHAEL, geologist; b. Ft. Madison, Iowa, July 23, 1939; s. Carl and Freta Fern (Sweezer) L.; student U. Iowa, 1958-60; B.S., U. Mo., 1963, M.A., 1968; m. Barbara Kay Nice, Feb. 20, 1960; children—Kurt, Kristeen, Kevin. Geologist, Chevron Oil Co., New Orleans, 1965-73; exploration geologist LaTerre Petroleum Corp., Houma, La., 1973-75; geol. supr. Gulf Coast div. Tenneco Oil Co., Houston, 1975, div. geologist, 1975-78, chief geologist, 1978—. Served with U.S. Army, 1957. Mem. Am. Assn. Petroleum Geologists, Houston Geol. Soc., Sigma Xi. Home: 907 Woodfield Ln Houston TX 77073 Office: Tenneco Oil Co PO Box 2511 Houston TX 77001

LOOMIS, GUY ALFRED, JR., realtor, ret. army officer; b. Malden, Mass., May 30, 1907; s. Guy A. and Julia (Miller) L.; B.S., Widener Coll., 1926; m. Dorothy L. Trumbull, June 7, 1935. Pres. Loomis & Ross Inc., investment counselors, N.Y.C., 1931-34; mem. staff Mfrs. Trust Co., N.Y.C., 1934-40; pres. Loomis Motor Corp., also Kaiser-Frazer Distributorship, Albany, N.Y., 1946-50; 1st Nat. Bank Miami, 1952-54, asst. v.p. 1st Nat. Bank Ft. Lauderdale, affiliate, 1954-60; v.p. Dania Bank (Fla.), 1960; realtor Ft. Lauderdale, Fla., 1958—. Chmn. Broward County drive ARC, 1956; chmn. publicity Broward County council Boy Scouts Am., 1957. Served to col. U.S. Army, 1942-46, 50-52. Decorated Silver Star, Bronze Star. Mem. Ft. Lauderdale Bd. Realtors, Am. Inst. Banking, Loomis Family Assn., N.Y. Athletic Club (life), S.A.R. Republican. Clubs: Tower, Ft. Lauderdale Country, Masons, Shriners. Home: 2100 S Ocean Ln Fort Lauderdale FL 33316 Office: 1023 E Las Olas Blvd Fort Lauderdale FL 33301

LOONEY, WILTON D., business exec.; b. 1919; married. With Genuine Parts Co., 1938—, br. mgr. Monroe, N.C., 1945-46, purchasing agt., 1946, mgr. wholesale ops., New Orleans, 1946-47, pres. Vanderbilt Parts Inc. subs., 1947-54, in charge wholesale ops. parent co., N.Y.C., 1954-55, pres., Atlanta, 1955-73, chief exec. officer, 1964-73, chmn. bd., chief exec. officer, 1973—, also dir. Served to maj. U.S. Army, World War II. Office: 299 Piedmont Ave NE PO Box 6006 Station H Atlanta GA 30308*

LOOP, CHARLES ARNOLD, aerial photography co. exec.; b. Oak Park, Ill., Nov. 14, 1938; s. Wilbur C. and Hazel M. (Arnold) L.; B.A., U. Ariz., 1961; m. Margaret Ann Humphrey, June 6, 1960; 1 son, Robert. News editor KVOA-TV, Tucson, 1961-63; supr. zone operations Jr. Achievement, Los Angeles, 1963-66; supr. reservations sales Am. Airlines, Los Angeles, 1966-69; sales rep. John H. Harland Co., Chgo., 1969-74; dir. mktg. Bank Cons. Am., Chgo., 1974-77, v.p. mktg., Denver, 1977-79; v.p. fin. services Mgmt. Planning Systems, Inc., Tulsa, 1979-80; v.p. mktg. MPSI Maps Inc., Dallas, 1980—. Bd. deacons Rivera First Bapt. Ch., Pico Rivera, Calif., 1968; bd. dirs. Salvation Army of Tucson, 1962, Center Grove Little League, Greenwood, Ind., 1970. Mem. Univ. Journalists, U. Ariz. Alumni Assn., Am. Mgmt. Assn., Airline Passengers Assn., Delta Tau Delta. Republican. Clubs: United Airlines Red Carpet, Court, Order of DeMolay. Office: 4310 Wiley Post Rd Addison TX 75001

LOOS, JOHN THOMPSON, JR., real estate investment exec.; b. Palm Beach, Fla., Mar. 3, 1947; s. John Thompson and Margaret (Browning) L.; A.A., U. Fla., 1967, B.S. in Bus. Adminstrn., 1970; m. Sharon E. Buckley, Apr. 3, 1971; children—Amy Lynn, John Thompson III. Exec. v.p. Am. Mktg. & Mgmt. Inc., Ft. Lauderdale, Fla., 1970—; founder, v.p. Westlawn Meml. Gardens, Ft. Lauderdale, 1970-78; dir. A M & M Investments, Ltd., Silver Oaks Mobile Home Village, Inc., Forest Lawn Meml. Gardens, Lauderdale Meml. Gardens, Quality Mobile Home Center, Inc., Broward Meml. Park. Mem. exec. council Nova U., 1977—; mem. fin. council Broward County (Fla.) Republican Party, 1978; bd. dirs. The Chord. Mem. Sigma Chi (pres. Broward County 1975). Republican. Episcopalian. Club: Lauderdale Yacht. Home: 1700 SE 9th St Fort Lauderdale FL 33316 Office: Am Mktg & Mgmt Inc 918 E Las Olas Blvd Fort Lauderdale FL 33301

LOPEZ, ANTONIO VINCENT, educator; b. Montgomery, Ala., Apr. 24, 1938; s. Joseph Charles and Eva Mae (Hall) Maschi; B.S., Auburn U., 1959, M.S., 1961; Ph.D., U. Miss., 1966. Asst. prof., chmn. dept. biol. scis. So. Sch. Pharmacy of Mercer U., 1967, asso. prof., chmn. dept. pharm. chemistry, 1969-74, prof., chmn. div. natural scis., 1974—, asst. dean, 1978-80, asso. dean, 1980—. Mem. Gov.'s Council Alcohol and Drug Abuse, 1978; a.d.c. Tenn. State Senate. Recipient Disting. Pharmacist award Phi Delta Chi, 1969, Drug Abuse Edn. award, 1972, 73, Lederle faculty research award, 1967, 72, Outstanding Prof. award Mercer U., yearly 1974-77. Fellow Am. Coll. Apothecaries; mem. Am., Ga. pharm. assns., AAAS, Kappa Psi (Tchr. of Year 1976, 77, 78), Rho Chi, Phi Lambda Sigma. Roman Catholic. Contbr. chpts. in books. Home: 1000 Montreal Rd Apt 1-H Clarkston GA 30021 Office: 345 Boulevard St NE Atlanta GA 30312

LOPEZ, ARNALDO VICTOR, orthopaedic surgeon; b. Havana, Cuba, May 19, 1936; s. Victor and Ana C. (Galarraga) L.; B.S., Instituto de la Habana, 1953; M.D., U. Habana, 1962; m. Emma De Albear, Nov. 25, 1962; children—Carlos, Marie La, Michelle. Intern, Calixto Garcia Hosp., Cuba, 1961; orthopaedic surgeon Colon Hosp., Cuba, 1962-63, Pinar del Rio Hosp., 1963-67, Camaguey Hosp., 1967-70; resident Mt. Sinai Hosp., Miami Beach, Fla., 1971-75; practice medicine specializing in orthopaedic surgery, Miami, Fla., 1975—; chief dept. orthopaedics Coral Gables Hosp. Diplomate Am. Bd. Orthopaedic Surgery. Fellow A.C.S.; mem. AMA, Fla. Med. Assn., Dade County Med. Assn., Cuban Med. Assn. in Exile, Am. Fracture Assn. Republican. Roman Catholic. Contbr. articles to med. jours. Home: 2812 Prairie Ave Miami Beach FL 33140 Office: 1545 SW 1st Miami FL 33140

LOPEZ, BETH BAILEY, speech pathologist; b. Houston, Dec. 30, 1950; d. Hubert Greer and Marguerite Fern (Magee) Bailey; B.A., Sam Houston State U., 1972; M.A., U. Houston, 1975; m. Santos Gregorio Lopez, Jan. 8, 1971; 1 dau., Erin Elizabeth. Speech pathologist Aldine Ind. Sch. Dist., Houston, 1971-77; grad. supr. U. Houston Speech Clinic, 1977-79; speech pathologist Asso. Speech & Lang. Sers., Houston, 1979—. Mem. Internat. Assn. Logopedics and Phoniatrics, Am. Speech and Hearing Assn., Tex. Speech and Hearing Assn., Houston Assn. Communication Disorders. Baptist. Home: 5034 Park Plaza Houston TX 77018

LOPEZ, ENCARNACION, chemist; b. Havana, Cuba, Nov. 7, 1946; d. Jose Rafael and Delia (Perez) Lopez; came to U.S., 1962, naturalized, 1970; B.S. magna cum laude, Cath. U. P.R., 1968; Ph.D. in Phys. Chemistry, U. Miami, 1973; m. Guillermo Fresco deJongh, Feb. 10, 1973 (dec.); 1 dau., Delia Anne Fresco. Research and teaching asst. U. Miami, 1968-73; asst. prof. chemistry and math. New World Center Campus, Miami-Dade Community Coll., 1974-79, asso. prof., 1979—; with research labs. Eastman Kodak Co., Rochester, N.Y.; review panelist NSF Sci. Faculty Profl. Devel. Program, 1977. Mem. Am. Chem. Soc. (award for paper Fla. sect. 1972), Soc. Coll. Sci. Tchrs., Delta Epsilon Sigma. Roman Catholic. Contbr. articles to profl. jours. Home: PO Box 341236 Coral Gables FL 33134 Office: 300 NE 2d Ave Miami FL 33132

LÓPEZ, WILMA IDA, temporary employment agency exec.; b. Santurce, P.R., June 9, 1938; d. Angel Luis and Verania (Morales) Lopez; B.A. in Psychology, U. P.R., 1959; children—Rene Luis Aviles, Angel Luis Aviles. Sales mgr. Empresas Diaz, Rio Piedras, P.R., 1964-67; real estate broker Mackle Bros., Daytona, Fla., 1967-70; record mgr. San Juan (P.R.) City Hall, 1970-73; mgr. for P.R. Kelly Services, Inc., Hato Rey, 1973—. Mem. Am. Soc. for Personnel Adminstrs., P.R. C of C., P.R. Mfrs. Assn., Sales and Mktg. Execs. Assn., Am. Bus. Women Assn., Zonta Internat. Republican. Roman Catholic. Office: Kelly Services Inc Pan-Am Bldg Suite 309 255 Ponce de Leon Ave Hato Rey PR 00917

LOPEZ PORTILLO, JOSE, pres. Mexico; b. Mexico City, July 16, 1920; s. Jose Lopez Portillo y Weber; LL.B., U. Mex., 1946; postgrad. in polit. sci. U. Chile; m. Carmen Romano; children—Jose Ramon, Carmen, Paulina. Practiced law; prof. gen. theory on state Nat. U. Mex., 1954, asso. prof. polit. sci., 1956-58; founder, prof. adminstrv. scis. doctorate Comml. Sch., Nat. Poly. Inst., 1961; mem. Nat. Revolutionary Party, 1959-64; tech. asso. head office Ministry Nat. Patrimony, 1960; coordinator Border Urban Devel. Com., 1962; dir. gen. legal affairs and legis. Ministry Presidency, 1965; mem. Intersecretarian Commn. for Nat. Affairs, 1966; undersec. Ministry Nat. Patrimony, 1970; dir. Fed. Electricity Commn., 1972; sec. for fin. and public credit, 1973; gov. for Mex., IMF; pres. Mexico, 1976—. Mem. Partido Revolucionario Institucional. Author: Valcracion de la Estatal, 1946; Genesis y Tecria del Estado Moderno, 1958; Quetzalcoatl, 1965; Don Q, 1976. Address: Palacio de Gobierno Mexico DF Mexico*

LOPEZ-ROIG, LUCY ENID, clin., indsl. psychologist; b. Rio Piedras, P.R., Nov. 23, 1936; d. Jose Antonio and Victoria Luisa (Roig) Lopez-Puig; B.A., Seton Hill Coll., 1958; M.S., Caribbean Center for Advanced Studies, 1969; Ph.D., Purdue U., 1972. Dir. tng., psychol. services P.R. Med. Center, Rio Piedras, 1966-67; chief psychol. services P.R. Police Dept., Hato Rey, 1961-66; chief psychol. services, chief selection program P.R. Water Resources Authority, Santurce, 1967-69, chief office of motivation, 1972-74, chief div. personnel, 1974-75, asst. exec. dir. for human relations, 1975-78; cons. to pres. Interam. U., Hato Rey, P.R., 1978—; pvt. practice clin. psychology, Hato Rey, 1972—; pres. Lucy Lopez-Roig & Assos., Hato Rey, 1978—; prof. dept. psychology U. P.R., Rio Piedras, 1972-76, Caribbean Center for Advanced Studies, Santurce, 1975—, dir., 1975-76, dir. internship program, 1977—; cons. Puerto Rican Dept. Edn., 1967-68, Colegio Puertorriqueno de Ninas, Puerto Rican Assn. Pvt. Schs., 1974—; bd. dirs. Instituto Psicologico de P.R., 1975-76. Leader workshop Family Life in a Religious Contest Evang. Crusade of P.R., 1974. Recipient award for contbr. in human relations P.R. Water Resources Authority, 1976; award for contbns. in edn. Puerto Rican Assn. Pvt. Schs., 1974; named Outstanding Woman of Year in Public Adminstrn., Blue Cross of P.R., 1975. Mem. Am. Psychol. Assn., Asociacion de Personal Publico, Sigma Xi. Author: An Approach to the Empathic Process, 1972; A Critical Review and Research Proposal for the Selection and Training of Paraprofessionals, 1971; Development of a Locus of Control Scale for Managers, 1972; (with R.D. Pritchard) Helping Supervisors to Cope, 1977. Home: 70 Kings Ct Santurce PR 00911

LOPEZ-SOLANO, JUDITH LOUISE, data processing cons.; b. C.Z., May 14, 1948; s. Fernando and Louise Tobias (Moyer) Lopez; B.S., Pa. State U., 1970; M.S., Fla. State U., 1971, Ph.D., 1975. Asst. counselor Fla. State U., 1970-71, teaching fellow, 1973-74; dir. student devel. No. Mich. U., 1971-73; staff asst. State U. System of Fla., Tallahassee, 1974-75, instl. data adminstrn. coordinator, 1975-79; cons. Info. Systems of Fla., Inc., Jacksonville, Fla., 1979—; guest lectr. Fla. State U. Mem. Am. Assn. Higher Edn., Phi Kappa Phi. Clubs: K-9 Dog Obedience (Jacksonville); Tallahassee Dog Obedience. Home: 9833 Cunningham Rd Jacksonville FL 32216 Office: PO Box 16101 Jacksonville FL 32216

LORBACH, HARRY MARTIN, engring. cons.; b. Circleville, Ohio, June 22, 1900; s. Henry Philip and Arista Mary (Dreisbach) L.; student Ohio State U.; m. Vista Helen Cranfield, Apr. 22, 1933; children—Barbara Ann, Jonathan Philip, Margaret Elizabeth. Home builder, West Palm Beach, Fla., 1924-48; refrigeration engr. with various corps., N.Y.C., 1924-36; refrigeration engr. Paul & Beekman, Phila., 1929-36, Mayer Body Co., Pitts., 1929-36; cons. engr. Research Assos. of Ft. Lauderdale (Fla.), 1936-43; v.p. George E. Merrick of Coral Gables, Palm Beach, Fla., 1938-42; pres. Fla. Quick Freeze, 1943-49, Master Freezers, Miami, Fla., 1943-49; v.p. Central Fla. Refrigerated Warehouse, 1949-51; cons. engr. refrigerating plants, 1950-54; owner-developer Lake Maitland Shores, 1951-54; in real estate bus., Boca Raton, Fla., 1960-62; pvt. practice mech. engring. cons., Atlanta, 1954—. Mem. Friends of Fernbank, Met. Museum Art, Smithsonian Assos. Republican. Clubs: Rotary, Masons, Elks. Home and Office: 620 Peachtree St NE Atlanta GA 30308

LORD, CATHARINE F., rehab. facility exec.; b. Cheyenne, Wyo., Aug. 31, 1952; d. Robert J. and Phyllis F.; A.A., Macon Jr. Coll., 1974; A.B. cum laude, U. Ga., 1975, M. Ed., 1977. Asst. dir. admissions Mercer U., Macon, Ga., 1977-78; dir. rehab. Goodwill Industries of Middle Ga. Inc., Macon, 1978-79, exec. dir., 1979—. Ad hoc com. End Stage Renal Disease Health Systems Agy.; bd. dirs. Bibb County (Ga.) Sr. Citizens Inc. Mem. Am. Personnel and Guidance Assn., Nat. Rehab. Assn., Phi Kappa Phi. Baptist. Home: 2638 Riverview Rd Macon GA 31204 Office: Goodwill Industries of Middle Ga Inc PO Box 955 Macon GA 31202

LORD, COLUMBUS ELLIS, architect, engr.; b. Abbot, Maine, Apr. 30, 1897; s. Alvah Brown and Addie Winifred (Colson) L.; student U. Maine, 1914-16; B.S. in Arch., Mass. Inst. Tech., 1924; m. Vera Dale Bolan, Feb. 18, 1928; children—Nancy Claire (Mrs. Philip Edwin Graves), Charles Ellis Bolan (dec.). Architect, various firms, Boston, 1924-31; civil engr. City Boston, 1931-34; architect, procurement div. Treasury Dept., Washington, 1934-37; with firm Clarence Wunder, Phila., 1937-38; Quartermaster, U.S. Army, Washington, 1938-41; engr. Corps Engrs. U.S. Army, Washington, 1941-47; chief engr. air facilities Def. Dept., Washington, 1947-67; cons. architect, engr., Arlington, Va., 1967—. Mem. pack council Cub Scouts, Washington, 1953-55; mem. PTA, Arlington, Va., 1955-63. Served with Signal Corps, U.S. Army, 1917-19. Registered profl. engr., Va., D.C., Mass., Vt.; registered architect, Va. Mem. Va. Soc. AIA (emeritus), ASCE, Nat. Soc. Profl. Engrs. (D.C. and Va. chpts.), Transp. Research Bd. of Nat. Acad. Scis., Nat. Aero. Assn., Va. Acad. Sci., AAAS, Nat. Pilots Assn., Aircraft Owners and Pilots Assn., Soc. Am. Mil. Engrs., Maine League Hist. Socs. and Museums, Maine Hist. Soc., Eastham Hist. Soc., Thomas Rogers Soc., Soc. Mayflower Descs., Nat. Trust Hist. Preservation in U.S., Soc. Preservation New Eng. Antiquities, Am. Assn. State and Local History, Smithsonian Assos., Woodrow Wilson Internat. Center for Scholars, Assos. Nat. Archives, Nat. Geog. Soc., New Eng. Hist. Geneal. Soc., Nat. Geneal. Soc., Alumni Assn. M.I.T. Clubs: Masons; Order Eastern Star; Aero of Washington, M.I.T. (Washington). Home and Office: 2000 N Adams St No 329 Arlington VA 22201

LORD, EVELYN MARLIN, legal adminstr.; b. Melrose, Mass., Dec. 8, 1926; d. John Joseph and Mary Janette (Nourse) Marlin; B.A. in Romance Langs., Boston U., 1948; M.A. in Polit. Sci., U. Del., 1957; J.D., U. Louisville, 1969; m. Samuel Smith Lord, Jr., Feb. 28, 1948; children—Steven A., Jonathan P., Nathaniel E., Victoria M., William K Dir., Pvt. Urban Renewal Corp., Wilmington, Del., 1956-62; mem. Del. Senate, 1962-64; admitted to Ky. bar, 1969, U.S. Supreme Ct. bar, 1973; exec. dir. Community Improvement Dist., Louisville, 1969-70; adminstr. asst. county judge Commr.'s Ct., Jefferson County, Ky., 1970-71; columnist News Jour. Co., Wilmington, 1972-75; office adminstr. firm Orgain, Bell & Tucker, Beaumont, Tex., 1978—; mem. Beaumont City Council, 1980—. Local pres. LWV, Wilmington, 1957-59, state pres. Del., 1960-62; pres. Kentuckiana council Girl Scouts U.S.A., 1968-69; Tex. chmn. Kennedy Center for Performing Arts; v.p. Three Rivers council Boy Scouts Am.; vice chmn. Lamar U. Excellence Com.; mem. budget com. United Way of Beaumont; chmn. Leadership Beaumont, 1979. Recipient Silver Beaver award Boy Scouts Am., 1979; named Outstanding Woman, U. Louisville Sch. Law. Mem. Ky. Bar Assn., Assn. Legal Adminstrs., Beaumont Symphony Women's League, Beaumont Art Gallery Guild, Heritage Soc., AAUW, Phi Kappa Phi. Republican. Presbyterian. Club: S.E. Tex. Press. Editor: Jour. Family Law, U. Louisville, 1968-69. Office: Orgain Bell & Tucker 400 Beaumont Savs Bldg Beaumont TX 77701

LORD, FONCHEN USHER (MRS. WILLIAM WALCOTT LORD), artist; b. St. Louis; d. Roland Green and Florence (Richardson) Usher; A.B., Radcliffe Coll., Harvard, 1933; M.A., Washington U., St. Louis, 1935; m. William Walcott Lord, June 12, 1935; children—Fonya (Mrs. James DeLong), William Pepperell, Carter Usher, Elizabeth Usher (Mrs. John Hawkins). Exhibited invitational one-man shows Stetson U., Deland, Fla., 1969, W.Va. Wesleyan Coll., 1970, Avanti Galleries, N.Y.C., 1970, Miami Mus. Modern Art, 1970, Broward Community Coll., Ft. Lauderdale, 1971, Polk Pub. Mus., 1972, 78, Trend House Gallery, 1972, Fla. So. Coll., 1974, Lakeland Civic Center Complex, Theatre Gallery, 1974—, Miller-King Gallery, Miami, 1975, 76, Artists Gallery, Madeira Beach, Fla., 1978, Russell B. Hicken Fine Arts Ltd., 1979; exhibited in group shows at Columbia Mus. Art, Columbus Mus. Arts and Crafts, Birmingham Mus. Art, Atlanta High Mus., Norton Gallery, Dulin Gallery Art, Ringling Mus. Art, Butler Inst. Am. Art, Jacksonville Art Mus., many others; represented in permanent collections: Fla. Ho. of Reps., City of Lakeland Civic Center, Miami Mus. Modern Art, W.Va. Wesleyan Coll., Lowe Mus., Fla. So. Coll., Polk Pub. Mus., New Coll., Sarasota, Fla. Pres., Palm Island Corp., Bartow, Fla., 1954-64, Braden River Ranchettes, Bartow, 1964-71; asst. treas. Paris Tanning Co., South Paris, Maine, 1944-48; artist-in-residence Fusion Dance Co., Miami, 1976—. Recipient Merit award Fla. State Fair, 1964; Clearwater Art Seminar award, 1961, 63; Sunshine Art Festival award, 1962; Ridge Art ann. competition awards 1963, 65, 66, 67, 70, 73; Chautauqua Nat. award, 1968; award Festival of States Ann., 1965; Sarasota Art Assn. juried awards, 1971, 73, 74; Cape Coral Nat. award, 1973. Fellow Royal Soc. Arts (London); mem. Fla. Artists Group (award 1978, 79), Nat. League Am. Pen Women, Zeta Tau Alpha. Episcopalian. Home: 4305 Oakglen Rd Lakeland FL 33803

LORD, MARIAN GORDIN, editor; b. Jacksonville, Fla., Apr. 19, 1944; d. Robert Kennington and Barbara Lewis (Pitt) Gordin; B.A., Mary Baldwin Coll., 1965; m. Gerald Douglas Lord, Aug. 17, 1968. Editorial asst. U. Press Va., Charlottesville, 1965-66; reporter news staff, spl. sects. Clarion-Ledger, Jackson, Miss., 1966-67; fed. ct. reporter Knoxville (Tenn.) Jour., 1967-68; asso. editor U. Tenn Publs. Service Bur. and Press, Knoxville, 1968-69; counselor Edn. Center, U.S. Army Security Agy. Field Sta., Bad Aibling, W.Ger., 1970-72; editor So. Assn. Colls. and Schs., Atlanta, 1972—; free lance editor.

Mem. Jr. League Atlanta. Methodist. Mem. Ednl. Press Assn. Am., Am. Soc. Assn. Execs., Internat. Assn. Bus. Communicators, Phi Alpha Theta. Home: 1288 Lenox Circle NE Atlanta GA 30306 Office: 795 Peachtree St NE Atlanta GA 30308

LORD, WILLIAM JACKSON, JR., educator; b. Milam, Tex., May 10, 1926; s. William Jackson and Ida Clara (Neal) L.; B.B.A., U. Tex., 1950, M.B.A., 1953; Ph.D. (Authors League grantee, Gulf Oil Co. grantee), U. Ill., 1961; m. Shirley Ruth Loveless, June 12, 1948; children—Michal Anne, William David, Mark Gregory. Instr., W. Tex. State U., 1951-54; instr. to asso. prof. U. Ill., 1954-64; prof., chmn. dept. gen. bus. U. Tex. at Austin, 1964—; John R. Emens Disting. prof. Ball State U., Muncie, Ind., spring 1978; cons. communications Franklin Life Ins. Co., Springfield, Ill., 1958-64, Austin Nat. Bank, 1971-74. Served with AUS, 1944-46. Decorated Bronze Star (3). Fellow Am. Bus. Communication Assn.; mem. S.W. Fedn. Adminstrv. Disciplines, Council Communication Socs., Delta Sigma Pi, Phi Kappa Phi, Pi Kappa Alpha. Recipient teaching excellence awards Student Assn., 1965, 66, 70. Baptist. Author: Functional Business Communication, 1968, 2d edit., 1974, Spanish edit., 1973; How Authors Make a Living, 1962; editorial asso. Social Sci. Quar., 1965-78, Jour. Bus. Communication, 1965-78. Home: 3500 Hillbrook Dr Austin TX 78731

LORDON, ROBERT EDWARD, physician; b. Pitts., Apr. 13, 1936; s. Francis Joseph and El Reno Ethyl (Ackerman) L.; B.S., Tufts U., 1958; M.D., Georgetown U., 1962; children—Robert E., Kimberly Ann. Commd. 2d lt. U.S. Air Force, 1961, advanced through grades to col., 1977; intern Wilford Hall USAF Med. Center, Lackland AFB, Tex., 1962-63, resident in internal medicine, 1963-66, fellow in renal disease, 1966-67, dir. histocompatibility lab., 1969—, ednl. coordinator dept. medicine, 1972-76, chief renal service, 1976—. Diplomate Am. Bd. Internal Medicine, Am. Bd. Nephrology. Fellow Am. Coll. Physicians; mem. Am., Internat. socs. nephrology, Am. Fedn. Clin. Research, Am. Assn. Clin. Histocompatibility Testing, Am. Assn. Tissue Banks, Kidney Found. of S. Tex. (dir. 1972—, pres. 1974-76), Nat. Kidney Found. (v.p. 1976). Contbr. articles to med., sci. jours. Home: 3413 Turtle Village San Antonio TX 78230 Office: Renal Service Wilford Hall USAF Med Center Lackland AFB TX 78236

LORENZ, HANS ERNEST, photographer; b. Karlsbad, Czechoslovakia, Sept. 11, 1940; s. Hugo and Maria (Gareis) L.; came to U.S., 1950, naturalized, 1954; B.A., Okla. Baptist U., 1962; m. Pamela Marie Carswell, May 27, 1978. Tchr. pub. schs., Prince George County, Va., 1964-65; mus. photographer Colonial Williamsburg Found., Williamsburg, Va., 1965—. Served with USN, 1962-64. Mem. Profl. Photographers Am., Am. Numismatic Assn. Baptist. Photographs contbr. to numerous books in field of 18th century antiques. Home: PO Box 336 Williamsburg VA 23185 Office: Audio Visual Dept Colonial Williamsburg Found Williamsburg VA 23185

LORENZO, FRANCISCO A., airline exec.; b. N.Y.C., May 19, 1940; s. Olegario and Ana (Mateos) L.; B.A., Columbia U., 1961; M.B.A., Harvard U., 1963; m. Sharon Neill Murray, Oct. 14, 1972. Fin. analyst TWA, 1963-65; mgr. fin. analysis Eastern Airlines, 1965-66; founder, chmn. bd. Lorenzo, Carney & Co., fin. advisers, N.Y.C., 1966—; chmn. bd. Jet Capital Corp., fin. advisers, Houston, 1969—; pres., chief exec. officer Tex. Internat. Airlines, Inc., Houston, 1972-79, chmn., chief exec. officer, 1979—. Served with AUS, 1963. Home: 11115 Wickway Houston TX 77024 Office: PO Box 12788 Houston TX 77017

LOREY, WILL(IS) EDWARD, II, mgmt. cons.; b. St. Clair Shores, Mich., Apr. 14, 1926; s. Willis Edward and Myrle Agnus (Bollenbacker) L.; B.S. in Edn., S.E. Mo. State U., 1950; M.S. in Edn., Columbia U., 1979; m. Nell Marie Conway, Nov. 22, 1975; children—Sandra, Sara, Marcia, Melissa. Served as enlisted man U.S. Marine Corps, 1943-46; commd. 2d lt. U.S. Air Force, 1950, advanced through grades to col., 1967, ret., 1970; mgr. tng. dept. Blue Cross/Blue Shield, Washington, 1970-76; dir. human resources The Drawing Board, Dallas, 1976-78; mgr. human resources Bell Ops. Corp. div. Bell Helicopter Co., Euless, Tex., 1978-79; pres. Lorey Assos., mgmt. cons., Smithfield, Tex., 1979—; course leader Am. Mgmt. Assns., 1979—; adj. prof. Richland Coll., N. Lake Coll., Dallas. Co. chmn. U.S. Savs. Bonds, 1978-79, United Way, 1978-79. Decorated Bronze Star with oak leaf cluster, Joint Services Commendation medal, Air Force Commendation medal with oak leaf cluster, Army Commendation medal. Mem. Am. Soc. Tng. and Devel. (dir., pres. elect Dallas chpt), Soc. for Humanistic Mgmt. (past pres.), Dallas Personnel Assn., Ret. Officers Assn. Republican. Methodist. Club: Alpine Ski. Contbr. articles in field to profl. jours. Home and Office: 740 Bandit Trail Smithfield TX 76180

LORIA, PHILIP RONALD, dermatologist; b. New Orleans, Jan. 17, 1928; s. Frank Leo and Pauline (Quaglino) L.; B.S., Tulane U., 1950, M.D., 1953; m. Margaret Carolyn Ott, Dec. 21, 1951; children—Philip Ronald, Carolyn Ott, Diane Ellen. Intern, Charity Hosp., New Orleans, 1953-54, resident, 1954-57; practice medicine specializing in dermatology, New Orleans, 1958—; mem. staff New Orleans Charity Hosp.; clin. asso. prof. medicine Tulane U. Sch. Medicine. Chmn. Citizen's R.R. Relocation Com. Served with USN, 1946-48. Fellow A.C.P.; mem. Orleans Parish, La. State med. socs., So. Am. med. assns., Assn. Am. Physicians and Surgeons, Am. Acad. Dermatology, Royal Coll. Physicians (affiliate mem.). Office: 921 Canal St New Orleans LA 70112

LOSAK, JOHN, coll. adminstr.; b. Marcus Hook, Pa., Nov. 4, 1933; s. Barney J. and Mabel M. (Harris) L.; B.A., U. Fla., 1957, M.A., 1959; Ph.D. (Kellogg fellow), Fla. State U., 1969; m. Patricia Ann Jahnke, Feb. 19, 1970; children—Sheri, Jay, Bonnie, Douglas, June. Sch. psychologist Dade County Bd. Pub. Instrn., Fla., 1960-63; instr. psychology, edn. Miami-Dade Community Coll., N.Campus, 1963-64, asst. prof., coordinator testing, 1964-66, asso. prof., 1966-69, chmn. counseling and testing dept., 1968-69, prof., div. dir. counseling, testing and research, 1969-75, dir. instl. research Dist. Office, Miami, 1975-77, dean instl. research and mgmt. info. systems, 1977—; cons. in field. Mem. Am. Psychol. Assn., Am. Ednl. Research Assn., Southeastern Assn. Community Coll. Researchers, Assn. Instl. Research. Contbr. articles to profl. publs. academically underprepared student, acceleration through proficiency exams. Home: 10585 SW 100th St Miami FL 33176 Office: 11011 SW 104th St Miami FL 33176

LOTHMAN, VICTOR OLIVER, cons. prodn. and inventory control; b. Akron, Ohio, Aug. 26, 1902; s. Edwin Oliver and Meta Hermina (Fruechtenicht) L.; student Concordia Coll., Fort Wayne, Ind., 1917-19; m. Mary Frances Chiles, Sept. 21, 1929; children—Mary Vic Lothman Mullins, Meta Ann. Accountant, Louisville and Chgo., 1920-35; asst. controller, mdse. controller Butler Bros., wholesalers, Chgo., 1936-49; inventory control mgr. Ford Motor Co., Dearborn, Mich., 1950-67; cons. prodn. and inventory control Vt. Am. Corp., Louisville, 1968—; cons. WPB, 1942. Ky. col.; C.P.A., Ind., Ill., Ky. Mem. Am. Contract Bridge League (life master). Republican. Lutheran. Home: 1048 Cherokee Rd Louisville KY 40204 Office: 100 E Liberty St Louisville KY 40202

LOTT, TRENT, congressman; b. Grenada, Miss., Oct. 9, 1941; s. Chester P. and Iona (Watson) L.; B.P.A., U. Miss., 1963, J.D., 1967; m. Patricia E. Thompson, Dec. 27, 1964; children—Chester T., Jr., Tyler Elizabeth. Admitted to Miss. bar, 1967; asso. firm Bryan & Gordon, Pascagoula, 1967; adminstrv. asst. to Congressman William M. Colmer, 1968-72; mem. 93d-96th Congresses from 5th dist. Miss.; chmn. Ho. Republican Research Com.; vice chmn. Republican Nat. Platform Com.; mem. Select Com. Outer-Continental Shelf. Field rep. for U. Miss., 1963-65; acting alumni sec. Ole Miss Alumni Assn., 1966-67. Mem. Am., Jackson County bar assns., Sigma Nu, Phi Alpha Delta. Republican. Baptist. Mason. Office: 2400 Rayburn House Office Bldg Washington DC 20515

LOTTERHOS, JULIUS LIEB, JR., lawyer; b. Crystal Springs, Miss., Dec. 8, 1918; s. Julius Lieb and Bessie (East) L.; student Copiah-Lincoln Jr. Coll., 1937-38, U. Miss., 1938-39; LL.B., Jackson Sch. Law, 1949; m. Ruth Norrell Hollingsworth, Aug. 27, 1939; children—Julius Lieb, Joseph Edward. Chief office dep. sheriff and tax collector Copiah County (Miss.), 1939-40; office mgr. Hammond Box Co. (La.), 1940-44; supr. bus. enterprises, div. rehab. blind Miss. Dept. Pub. Welfare, Jackson, 1947-51; admitted to Miss. bar, 1949; partner firm Henley, Lotterhos and Henley, Hazlehurst and Jackson, Miss., 1951—; spl. judge 14th Circuit Ct. Dist. Miss., 1967, 71-73; atty. Copiah County, 1952—, City of Crystal Springs, 1957-69. Del., Miss. Democratic Conv., 1952, 56, 60, 64, 68, 72; trustee Crystal Springs Sch., 1956-68; trustee Belhaven Coll., 1966—, chmn., 1970-72. Served with USNR, 1944-46. Mem. Copiah County (pres. 1967), Miss. (commr. 1964-65), Am. bar assns., Am. Judicature Soc., Comml. Law League Am. (chmn. 5th region 1971-72), Am., Miss. trial lawyers assns., Miss. Oil and Gas Lawyers Assn., Mid-Continent Oil and Gas Assn., Am. Soc. Hosp. Attys., Am. Soc. Law and Medicine, Nat. Assn. Civil County Attys., Miss. Bd. Suprs. Attys. Assn. (pres. 1975-76), C. of C., Miss. Econ. Council, Am. Legion, Sigma Delta Kappa. Presbyterian. Clubs: Lions, Univ., Rolling Hills, Masons (32 deg.), Shriners. Home: 435 Mathis Rd Crystal Springs MS 39059 Office: 141 S Caldwell Dr Hazlehurst MS 39083

LOUDEN, LESTER RICHARD, geochemist; b. Monroe, Wash., July 8, 1933; s. Lester A. and Mimi M. (Arnoldt) L.; came to U.S., 1963, naturalized, 1966; Ph.D., U. Würzburg (Germany), 1963; m. Edit Margit Toro, Apr. 14, 1963. Prof. geology U. Houston, 1963-64; geologist Magcobar, Houston, 1964-65, mgr. x-ray labs., 1965-68, mgr. analytical sect. Dresser Magcobar, 1969-70, tech. adviser research, 1970-72, devel. mgr. Dresser pollution, 1972-73, product mgr. pollution control and equipment, 1973-75; internat. product mgr. Dresser-SWACO, 1975-76; v.p. research The Analysts, Houston, 1976—. Mem. adv. bd. Foundry Research Assn., 1965-75. Served with AUS, 1957-58. NASA grantee, 1963-64. Mem. Marine Tech. Soc., Malasian Geol. Soc., German Geol. Soc., Clay Mineral Soc. Club: Nomads. Contbr. articles to tech. lit. Home: 8011 Highmeadow Houston TX 77063 Office: 4120 D Directors Row Houston TX 77092

LOUDERMILK, LOIS ADELINE WOOD (MRS. HAYDEN C. LOUDERMILK), civic worker; b. Bigelow, Ark., Aug. 25, 1911; d. William Edgar and Mary (May) Wood; B.S., U. Central Ark., 1948; M.L.S., Peabody Coll., 1965; m. Hayden C. Loudermilk, June 25, 1932; children—Billy Hayden, James Edwin. Tchr., librarian Perryville (Ark.) High Sch., 1942-62; librarian Joe T. Robinson High Sch., Little Rock, 1962-71; feature writer Ark. Gazette, 1945-46, Ark. Democrat, 1946-47. Historian, Perryville Extension Homemakers, 1973-75. Mem. Am. Assn. Ret. Persons, Nat. Ret. Tchrs. Assn., United Meth. Women, Alpha Delta Kappa. Clubs: Order Eastern Star, Garden (charter). Home: 301 Cedar St PO Box 38 Perryville AR 72126

LOUGHMILLER, GROVER CAMPBELL, psychologist; b. Dallas, July 5, 1937; s. George Campbell and Opal Lynn (Nicolaides) L.; B.A., N. Tex. State U., 1961; M.A., U. Oreg., 1966; Ph.D., U. Utah, 1970; postdoctoral George Peabody Coll., 1970; m. Carol Kay Beckstead, 1963; children—Trelesa, Lark, Kishl, Marlette, Velora. Counselor for handicapped children Camp Riley, Indpls., summer 1955-56; group counselor Salesmanship Club Boys Camp, Hawkins, Tex., 1959-60; tchr. secondary pub. schs. Andrews, Tex., 1960-61, Murray, Utah, 1963-64; counselor U. Oreg. Family Counseling Center, 1965-66; testing clk. U. Utah Counseling and Testing Center, Salt Lake City, 1967, research asst. in psychology research, 1967-69; asst. prof. psychology George Peabody Coll., Nashville, 1970-72, acting dir. counseling psychology program, 1971-72; mem. faculty dept. psychology (part-time) U. Tex., Tyler, 1975—; pvt. practice counseling psychology, 1972—. Instnl. rep. East Tex. Area council Boy Scouts Am., 1977—; exec. bd. Tyler Council Campfire Girls. Served with USMC, 1958-59. Certified psychologist and sch. psychologist, Tenn., Tex.; lic. social psychotherapist, Tex. Mem. Am. Assn. Marriage and Family Therapists (clin. mem., supr.), Am. Group Psychotherapy Assn. (clin. mem.), Am. Soc. Bus. and Mgmt. Cons.'s and Trainers, Am., Tex., Southwestern psychol. assns., Internat. Transactional Analysis Assn., Assn. Mormon Counselors and Psychotherapists. Republican. Mem. Ch. Jesus Christ of Latter-day Saints. Author: Study Guide and Topical Index to Major Source Materials in Transactional Analysis, 1974; Measurement and Predictors of Physician Performance, 1971; contbr. articles on physician performance to profl. publs. Home: Route 10 Box 566F Tyler TX 75707 Office: 305 S Broadway Tyler TX 75702

LOUGHRAN, WILLIAM RAYMOND, real estate exec.; b. Kingston, N.Y., Jan. 13, 1953; s. William Robert and Agnes Marie Loughran; student SUNY, Stone Ridge Campus, 1971-72, Ga. Inst. Real Estate, 1977. Mgr., Hotel Torenzicht, Amsterdam, Holland, 1973-74; helmsman sailing expdn. S.S. Zorsch, Bahama Islands, 1976-77; asso. realtor, fin. adviser, exec. sales rep. Jack Morris Realty Co., Atlanta, 1977—; chief exec. officer Am. Fin. Group, Atlanta, 1977—, pres., 1980—. Mem. Ga. Assn. Realtors, Dekalb Bd. Realtors (civic affairs com. 1979), Dekalb Council Young Realtors (vice chmn. 1979), Nat. Assn. Realtors. Democrat. Roman Catholic. Author: Home Buyer Manual for the Beginner, 1979. Home: PO Box 49212 Atlanta GA 30329

LOVE, BENTON F., banker; b. 1924; B.B.A., U. Tex., 1947; married. Founder Gift-Wraps, Inc., 1948-62, pres. Gift-Wraps Inc. div. Gibson Greeting Card Co., 1962-65; pres. River Oaks Bank & Trust Co., Houston, 1965-67; sr. v.p. Tex. Commerce Bank Nat. Assn., 1967-68, exec. v.p., dir., 1968-69, pres., dir., 1969-72, chmn. bd., chief exec. officer, 1972-77, sr. chmn., chief exec. officer, 1977—; pres. Tex. Commerce Bancshares, Inc., 1971-72, chmn. bd., chief exec. officer, 1972—; dir. Proler Internat. Corp., Hughes Tool Co., Cox Broadcasting Corp., A.P.S., Inc., El Paso Co., Capital Nat. Bank, Austin, Tex. Office: 712 Main St Houston TX 77001

LOVE, FRANKLIN SADLER, trade assn. exec.; b. Rock Hill, S.C., Nov. 9, 1915; s. Franklin Sadler and Edna (Hull) L.; A.B., Presbyn. Coll., Clinton, S.C., 1937; m. Jessie Huggins, Apr. 10, 1943; children—Judith Love Freeman, Beverly Love Highfill, Franklin Sadler III, Glenn. Sec., Cotton Mfrs. Assn. S.C., Clinton, 1937-42, Am. Cotton Mfrs. Assn., Charlotte, N.C., 1946-49; sec.-treas. Am. Textile Mfrs. Inst., Charlotte, 1949-79, v.p., 1979—. Mem. Charlotte adv. bd. Salvation Army; bd. dirs. Charlotte Council on Alcoholism. Served to capt. Ordnance Dept., AUS, 1942-46. Recipient alumni citation for outstanding achievement Presbyn. Coll., 1955, certificate of merit Ala. Textile Mfrs. Assn., 1972. Mem. Charlotte C. of C., Def. Supply Assn. (pres. Carolina chpt. 1950), Am. Trade Assn. Execs., Phi Psi. Presbyn. Rotarian (pres. Charlotte 1961-62, internat. del. 1961). Clubs: City, Westport Country, Goodfellows (Charlotte). Home: 139 Island View Ct Denver NC 28037 Office: Denver Profl Bldg Denver NC 28037

LOVE, IAN LESLIE, diagnostic radiologist; b. Chgo., Dec. 5, 1947; s. Hyman and Claire Felicia (Turkel) L.; B.A., Case Western Res. U., 1969; M.D., Chgo. Med. Sch., 1973; m. Lynn Elizabeth Posey, Dec. 29, 1979 Intern, Los Angeles County, U. So. Calif. Med. Center, 1973-74; resident diagnostic radiology Yale-New Haven Med. Center, 1974-77; fellow diagnostic ultrasound Parkland Meml. Hosp., Dallas, 1977-78; staff radiologist NIH, Bethesda, Md., 1978-79; asst. prof. diagnostic radiology Tulane U. Med. Center, New Orleans, 1980—. Served with USPHS, 1978-80. Recipient Grand Prize award Am. Urol. Assn., 74th Annual Conv., 1979. Mem. Am. Inst. Ultrasound in Medicine, Radiol. Soc. N.Am. Jewish.

LOVE, ISADORE, accountant; b. St. Joseph, La., Sept. 2, 1904; s. Joseph and Bertha (Meyer) L.; grad. Lake Comml. Sch., 1920-21; student Miss. State Coll., 1922-23; m. Ruby Rainey, Sept. 15, 1926; children—David J., Ann Rainey Love Suttle. Mgr., Rogers Candy Co., Meridian, Miss., 1935-41; chief accountant, office mgr. Ft. Barrancas Post Exchange, Pensacola, Fla., 1941-47; accountant Gabel & Reynolds Plastering Co. and Gabel & Reynolds Hdwe Co., Pensacola, Fla., 1947-62; owner, mgr. Love Bookkeeping Service, Pensacola, 1962—. Vice chmn. Greater Pensacola Civic Round Table, 1951; mem. Christian Bus. Men's com., 1964, sec.-treas., 1970-79; lt. gov. Ala.-W. Fla. dist. Civitan Internat., 1954-55, pres., 1951-52; bd. dirs., chmn. 90 & 9 Boys Ranch, 1962, Water Front Mission, 1962-64, sec., 1972—. Recipient Civitan of the Year award, Pensacola Civitan Club, 1975-76, Ala. W. Fla. dist. Civitan Internat., 1976-77, Honor Key award, 1977. Club: Masons (Shriner), Odd Fellow. Address: 101 Rue Max Pensacola FL 32507

LOVE, JAMES SANFORD, III, broadcasting co. exec.; b. Jackson, Miss., Aug. 4, 1944; s. James Sanford and Jo Ellis (Buie) L.; B.B.A., U. Miss., 1966; M.B.A., U Va., 1968; m. Barbara Ann Harris, June 11, 1966; children—James Sanford, IV, Caroline Elizabeth, Gillian Meredith. Account exec. J. Walter Thompson Co., 1968-70; asst. v.p., securities analyst Dean Witter & Co., N.Y.C., 1970-73; securities analyst Baker Weeks & Co., N.Y.C., 1973-75; pres., dir. Lakewood Meml. Park, Jackson, 1972—; chmn. bd., dir. WLOX Broadcasting Co., Biloxi, Miss., 1972—; v.p. research Paine, Webber, Jackson & Curtis, N.Y.C., 1975-77; investment research cons. Reinheimer Nordberg Inc., N.Y.C. 1979—. Recipient Instl. Investor mag. award, 1974, 75. Mem. N.Y. Soc. Security Analysts, Machinery Analysts N.Y.C. Episcopalian. Clubs: Downtown Athletic (N.Y.C.); Country of Jackson. Home: 1040 Carlisle St Jackson MS 39202 Office: PO Box 22685 Jackson MS 39205

LOVE, JOSEPH WILLIAM, JR., oil co. exec.; b. Tulsa, Mar. 31, 1928; s. Joseph William and Eva Elizabeth (Henderson) L.; B.S. in Bus. Adminstrn., U. Tulsa, 1949; postgrad. U. Houston, 1957-60. Sales rep. Tex. Gas Corp. Houston, 1956-60, credit mgr., 1960-61, mgr. credit and personnel, 1961-63; with Union Tex. Petroleum div. Allied Chem. Corp., Houston, 1963—, credit mgr., 1963-65, mgr. mfg. adminstrn., 1966-68, mgr. mktg. ops. analysis, 1968-73, mgr. mktg. services, 1973-77, mgr. mktg. planning and devel., 1977-79, mgr. hydrocarbon mktg. and ops. planning, 1979—; asso. mem. Tex. Bd. Realtors. Served to capt. USAF, 1951-55, Decorated Air medal; lic. real estate broker, Tex. Mem. Nat. Assn. Bus. Economists, N.Am. Soc. Corp. Planning, Nat. LP-Gas Assn. (mem. statis. com.), Gas Processors Assn. (mem. statis. com.), Adminstrv. Mgmt. Soc. (v.p. Houston chpt., recipient distinguished service certificate 1972), Sigma Phi Epsilon. Methodist. Home: 34 Lana Ln Houston TX 77027 Office: PO Box 2120 Houston TX 77001

LOVE, MARSHA LYNN, univ. adminstr.; b. West Palm Beach, Fla., Nov. 14, 1944; d. James Luther and Blanche Louise (Morrison) Love; B.A., Fla. State U., 1966; M.A., U. N.C., 1970. Tchr. English and journalism Forest Hill High Sch., West Palm Beach, 1967-68; counselor, office of dean of women Fla. Atlantic U., Boca Raton, 1971; asst. dean for student affairs, 1971—, asst. dean student affairs, dir. academic aid center, 1978—. Publicity chmn. Delray Affair, sidewalk art show, 1969; mem cast Delray Beach Playhouse, 1967-68; mem. Delray Beach Bicentennial Com. Bd. govs. Delray Beach Hist. Soc. Grad. counselor scholar Kappa Kappa Gamma, 1966-67; edn. chmn. Jr. Service League of Boca Raton, 1980—; chmn. exbhn. com., chmn. Am. folk art exhibit Singing Pines Mus., 1980—. Named Radio Sta. WDBF Citizen-of-the-Day. Mem. Nat. Assn. Women Deans, Adminstrs. and Counselors, Nat. Council Tchrs. English, AAUW, Fla. State U. Alumni Assn., Mortar Bd., Kappa Kappa Gamma, Phi Theta Kappa (hon.). Methodist (mem. adminstrv. bd. 1970-73). Clubs: Women's Executive (sec.), Women's Republican (parliamentarian). Contbr. articles to profl. jours. Home: 2000 S Ocean Blvd Delray Beach FL 33444 Office: 231 Student Services Bldg Fla Atlantic U Boca Raton FL 33431

LOVE, NORMAN DON, educator; b. Childress, Tex., May 15, 1946; s. Norman A. and Clydie L. (Glover) L.; B.A. in History, Midwestern State U., 1973, M.A., 1978; postgrad. doctoral program U. Ky., 1977—; m. Truma Glanel Webb, Aug. 20, 1977; 1 son Jason Marc. Teaching asst. Am. history Midwestern State U., Wichita Falls, 1975-77; intern Wichita Falls Mus. and Art Center, 1976-77, curator history exhibit, 1976-77: teaching asst. Am. history U. Ky., Lexington, 1977-79, instr., 1979—. curator World War I poster art collection King Library, 1978. Served with USAF, 1969-73. Phi Alpha Theta scholar, 1976-77. Mem. Am. Hist. Assn., Orgn. Am. Historians, So. Bapt. Hist. Soc., Ky. Hist. Soc. (cons. 1978), Phi Alpha Theta. Home: 2504 Larkin Rd Lexington KY 40503 Office: Dept History Univ of Kentucky Lexington KY 40506

LOVE, RICHARD ARTHUR, aerospace design engr.; b. San Diego, May 8, 1930; s. Arthur and Lora Elizabeth (Dieffenbach) L.; A.A., Boise State U., 1951 B.M.E., U. Wash., Seattle, 1956; m. Mary Verna Eberle, Sept. 30, 1952; children—William Duncan, Robert Douglas. With Boeing Co., Seattle, 1951-63, sr. preliminary design engr., 1961-63; project engr. Brown Engring. Co., Huntsville, Ala., 1963-64; sr. engr. Marshall Space Flight Center, NASA, Huntsville, 1964—. Served with USNR, 1951-53. Registered profl. engr., Ala. Mem. Marshall Engrs. and Scientists Assn. (v.p. 1970—), Am. Aviation Hist. Soc., Mensa, Sigma Xi. Home: 2002 Giles Dr Huntsville AL 35811 Office: PD 23 MSFC Huntsville AL 35812

LOVE, ROBERT MITCHELL, indsl. developer, assn. exec.; b. Chgo., Aug. 7, 1928 s. Quill Horace and Jemma (Mitchell) L.; student Monterey Peninsula Jr. Coll., 1960-61; grad. Inst. Orgn. Mgmt., U. Houston, 1968, Advanced Mgmt. Studies, Tex. Christian U., 1971; m. Shari Lee Cook, Dec. 12, 1964; children—Mark, Gregory, Wendi. Customer service agt. Am. Airlines, Memphis, 1951-55, customer service mgr., Washington, 1955-59, mgr. mil. traffic office, San Francisco, 1959-63; mgr. customer service and ops. Mohawk Airlines, N.Y.C., 1963-65; mgr. conv. and visitors bur. Little Rock C. of C., 1965-67; exec. v.p., also gen. mgr. Jonesboro (Ark.) C. of C., 1967-71;

dir. indsl. services Knoxville (Tenn.) C. of C., 1971-72; exec. dir. Melton Hill Regional Indsl. Devel. Assn., 1972-73; exec. v.p. Scott County (Tenn.) Indsl. Devel. Bd., Oneida, 1974-76; pres. Cumberland Wood Products, Inc., Oneida, 1976—. Served with AUS, USAF, 1946-51. Decorated Bronze Star, Purple Heart. Cert. indsl. developer. Mem. Am. Soc. Assn. Execs., Am., So., Tenn., Eastern Tenn. indsl. devel. councils. Methodist. Club: Masons. Home: Oneida TN 37841 Office: PO Box 423 Oneida TN 37841

LOVE, ROSALIE STOCKS (MRS. FRED EMERY LOVE), writer, ret. educator; b. Norphlet, Ark., Oct. 31, 1913; d. Carl Lee and Ora May (Hayes) Stocks; student Magnolia A. and M. Coll., El Dorado Jr. Coll., 1931-32; Henderson State Tchrs. Coll., 1932-33; B.S., So. State Coll., 1959; m. Fred Emery Love, June 29, 1934; children—David Edward (dec.), Gerry Beth Love Morris, Joe Fred. Piano tchr., Norphlet, Ark., 1930-52; state worker Ark. Baptist Tng. Union Dept., Little Rock, 1952-57; kindergarten tchr. First Baptist Ch., El Dorado, Ark., 1953-59; tchr. Union Sch., El Dorado, 1959-67, Norphlet Pub. Schs., 1967-75. Mem. Nat. League of Am. Pen Women (pres. 1978-80), Nat., Ark., Union County (pres. 1970-71), Norphlet (pres. 1972—) tchrs. assns., Poets' Roundtable of Ark., Delta Kappa Gamma. Contbg. author: Kindergarten Resource Book, 1965. Contbr. articles to profl. jours., curriculum materials to religious mags. Home: PO Box 430 Norphlet AR 71759

LOVEJOY, DALLAS LANDON, surveyor; b. Palermo, W.Va., July 29, 1936; s. Aaron and Thelma May (Spurlock) L.; student Internat. Corr. Schs., 1968, LaSalle Extension U., 1972; m. Elizabeth Ann Windsor, Nov. 8, 1959. With U.S. Geol. Survey, Huntington, W.Va., 1955, Michael Baker Cons. Engrs., 1956-63; resident engr. Chessie System R.R., Huntington, 1963—; land surveyor; cons. Certified land surveyor, W.Va., Ky. Mem. W.Va. Assn. Land Surveyors. Clubs: Ranch Lake Estates, Masons, Shriners. Home: 1245 1/2 Pike St Milton WV 25541 Office: C and O Depot 10th St Huntington WV 25701

LOVELACE, JOHN RUPERT, SR., surgeon; b. Indianola, Miss., Aug. 23, 1922; s. Dewitt Samuel, Sr., and Erma (Hogin) L.; B.S., Miss. State U., 1943; postgrad. U. Miss., 1946-48; M.D., Harvard U., 1950; m. Sarah Nickle, Dec. 22, 1946; children—Rebecca, Michael, John. Intern, Henry Ford Hosp., Detroit, 1950-51; family practice medicine, Batesville, Miss., 1951-52; surg. resident U. Tenn., Memphis, 1952-58; practice medicine specializing in gen. surgery, Batesville, 1958—; chief of surgery S. Panola Community Hosp., Batesville; mem. Miss. Bd. Health; chmn. med. com. Miss. Bd. Instns. of Higher Learning. Elder, First Presbyn. Ch., Batesville; mem. S. Panola Sch. Bd., 1963-68. Served with USAF, 1942-46. Diplomate Am. Bd. Surgery. Fellow A.C.S. (pres. Miss. chpt. 1977-78); mem. Miss. Med. Assn. (trustee), N. Miss. Med. Soc., Panola County C. of C. (dir. 1963-66). Democrat. Clubs: Univ. (Memphis); Univ., Capitol City (Jackson). Contbr. articles to profl. publs. Home: Route 3 Box 5 Batesville MS 38606 Office: 107 Eureka Batesville MS 38606

LOVELACE, (BYRON) KEITH, tech. ser. co. exec.; b. Vernon, Tex., Feb. 15, 1935; s. Joseph Edward and Hattie Pearl (Brians) L.; B.S. in Chem. Engring., U. Tex., Austin, 1958, M.S., 1961, Ph.D., 1973; J.D., S. Tex. Coll. Law, 1978; m. Sandra Alene Daniel, June 17, 1961; children—Kirk Daniel, Bethany Alene, Amy Kathleen. Research and devel. engr. Core Labs., Dallas, 1960-61; with Tex. Instruments, Inc., Dallas and Houston, 1961-78, mgr. process control for advanced tech., 1969-70, reliability mgr. metal oxide semicondr. (MOS) div., 1971-75, MOS reliability dir., 1975-78; pres. P-V-T Inc., Houston, 1978—; admitted to Tex. bar. Served with U.S. Army, 1953. Tex. Instruments fellow, 1965-68; FMC Corp. fellow, 1958-60; Eastern States Petroleum and Chem. scholar, 1957-58; Ethyl Corp. scholar, 1956-57. Mem. Am. Chem. Soc. (award 1958), Am. Inst. Chem. Engrs., Soc. Petroleum Engrs. (vice chmn. reservoir group 1979-80), Am. Bar Assn., State Bar Tex., Trial Lawyers Am., Tau Beta Pi (chpt. v.p. 1958-59), Omega Chi Epsilon. Contbr. articles to profl. jours. Patentee in field. Home: 11580 S Kirkwood Rd Houston TX 77477 Office: PO Box 37175 Houston TX 77036

LOVELACE, NOEL CRAWFORD, musician; b. Raleigh, N.C., Sept. 7, 1948; s. Marc Hoyle and Mary Louise (Gibson) L.; Mus.B., Stetson U., 1971; M.Mus., Ind. U., 1972, postgrad., 1973—; diploma Internationale Zomeracademie voor Organisten, Holland, 1969; m. Marion Anne Williams, June 6, 1970; 1 son, Marc Crawford. Asst. prof. music N.C. Wesleyan Coll., Rocky Mount, 1973—; music dir. St. Andrews Episcopal Ch., Rocky Mount, 1976—; co founder, dir. Rocky Mount Civic Chorus, 1976—. Mem. Am. Choral Dirs. Assn., Choristers Guild, Coll. Music Soc., Fellowship United Methodist Musicians, Hymn Soc. Am., Music Tchrs. Nat. Assn., Nat. Assn. Tchrs. Singing, Presbyn. Assn. Musicians. Democrat. Episcopalian. Club: Rotary. Composer: N.C. Wesleyan Coll. Alma Mater, 1977, also ch. anthems. Home: 3500 Sheffield Dr Rocky Mount NC 27801 Office: Box 265 College Station Rocky Mount NC 27801

LOVELL, JAN ADAIR, public relations exec.; b. Chickasha, Okla., Sept. 23, 1934; s. Darrel Adair and Helen Genevieve (Whitfill) L.; B.A., Okla. U., 1958; m. Katherine Belle Calland, May 9, 1970. Staff announcer Sta. KVSO, Ardmore, Okla., 1949-56; news/weatherman KPLC-TV, Lake Charles, La., 1957-58, KTBS-TV, Shreveport, La., 1958-63; announcer, pub. affairs program producer Sta. KWTV, Oklahoma City, 1963-70; news anchorman, producer-host, assignment editor, editorial dir. WIS-TV, Columbia, S.C., 1970-74; asso. editor Resolution mag., 1974-75; dir. devel. and public relations Providence Hosp., Columbia, 1975—; bd. dirs., exec. dir. Providence Hosp. Found.; mem. adj. faculty Goddard Coll. Mem. adv. bd. dirs. Central S.C. Lung Assn.; del S.C. Democratic Conv.; mem. South Carolinian of the Yr. Selection Com.; mem. indsl. adv. bd. S.C. Dept. Corrections. Recipient various civic and public service awards. Mem. Carolinas Hosps. Pub. Relations Soc. (dir.), Nat. Assn. for Hosp. Devel., U.S.C. Alumni Assn., Sigma Delta Chi. Home: 2913 Heyward St Columbia SC 29205 Office: Providence Hosp 2435 Forest Dr Columbia SC 29204

LOVELL, OTHEL EUGENE, JR., educator; b. Shreveport, La., Oct. 7, 1928; s. Othel E. and Paralee (Parrott) L.; B.A., Northwestern State U., 1949; M.Ed., La. State U., 1956, Ph.D., 1961; m. Rosemary Fleming, June 1963; 1 dau., Alicia Rosmonde. Asst. prof. edn. La. State U., New Orleans, 1959-62; dean Div. Edn., Nicholls State U., Thibodaux, La., 1963-66, dir. student teaching, 1962-63, prof. edn., 1963-66, dean grad. sch., 1966-71, dean acad. affairs, 1971, v.p. acad. affairs, 1971—; cons. to sch. dists. Recipient Disting. Service award Nicholls State U., 1978. Mem. Nat. Orgn. Legal Problems in Edn., Phi Delta Kappa, Phi Alpha Theta, Kappa Delta Pi, Kappa Phi Kappa. Democrat. Episcopalian. Club: Rotary (pres. 1976-77). Home: 211 E Plater Dr Thibodaux LA 70301 Office: PO Box 2002 University Sta Thibodaux LA 70301

LOVELL, SAVAGE MARKETTE (S. MARK LOVELL), investor; b. Brookhaven, Miss., Apr. 26, 1935; s. George Carroll and Bessie Maude (Marr) L.; B.A., Baylor U., 1958; LL.B., So. Meth. U., 1966; m. Sarah Ann Quinn, Apr. 6, 1958; children—Kimberly Ann, Jennifer Ellen, Betty Allison, Jeffery Markette. Engr., Pierce Enterprises, Dallas, 1958-59; engr., dir. quality control, contracts adminstr., legal counsel, div. mgr. Baifield Industries, 1959-67; real estate investor, Shreveport, La., 1967—; chmn. bd. Temtex Industries, 1971, Tex. Clay Industries, 1970; chmn. bd., pres. Quinn-L Corp., 1972—; pres. Q-L Corp., 1977—; cons. Former bd. dirs. Shreveport A.R.C., Shreveport Jr. Achievement; past pres., bd. dirs. Shreveport Civic Opera. Mem. Am., Dallas, Tex. bar assns., Shreveport C. of C. (past dir.). Democrat. Baptist. Home: 3851 Betty Virginia Circle Shreveport LA 71106 Office: 3003 Knight St Shreveport LA 71106

LOVESY, (THOMAS) CRAIG, SR., mag. subscription dir.; b. Alexandria, La., Dec. 2, 1921; s. Charles Lewis and Mae Odel (Jameson) L.; student Ark. Poly. Coll., Russellville, 1939-42; m. Doris Jean Sublett, Sept. 6, 1941: children—Jean Anne, Thomas Craig, Mary Lou. Owner, Craig Lovesy Photog. Service, Russellville, 1945-49; editor, mgr. Tribune and Advertiser newspapers, Russellville, 1949-55, Daily and Weekly Courier Dem. newspapers, Russellville, 1955-57; dir. mail subscription promotion mgr. Cowles Communications, Look Mag., Des Moines, 1957-72; asst. dir. Creative Services div. Nat. Wildlife Fedn., Washington, 1972-75; subscription dir. The Mother Earth News, Hendersonville, N.C., 1976—; judge nat. dir. mail promotion contest Direct Mail Mktg. Assn., 1970, conv. panel speaker, 1975. Served with USAAF, 1942-45. Recipient George Washington medal Freedoms Found., 1953. Mem. Direct Mail Mktg. Assn. Home: 1407 Kensington Ct Unit A8 Hendersonville NC 28739 Office: 105 Stoney Mountain Rd Hendersonville NC 28739

LOVETT, WILLIAM ERVIN, JR., agri-bus. co. exec.; b. Douglas, Ga., Oct. 12, 1945; s. William Ervin and Janelle (Griffin) L.; A. Agr., Abraham Baldwin Agr. Coll., 1965; B.A., Ga. State Coll., 1966; B.S. in Bus. Adminstrn., U. Ga., 1977, also postgrad.; m. Sandra Kay Hall, 1965; children—William Ervin III, Tiffany Anne. Owner, mgr. So. Peanut & Storage Co., 1973-76; pres. Lovett Mgmt. Corp., Dublin, Ga., 1973—; v.p. Lovett & Tharpe Hardware Co., Dublin, 1973—; partner Lovett & East Dublin Inc., 1973-77, W.H. Lovett & Son, 1976—; pres., founder W. Herschel Lovett Found., 1977—; dir. Heart of Ga. Area Planning and Training Council, 1977-78. Chmn. Laurens County (Ga.) Bd. Commrs., 1977-81; mem. Econ. Council Ga., 1977—; bd. dirs. Pine Forest Methodist Ch., 1977-78; chmn. speakers bur. Ga. Easter Seal Soc., 1977-78; active Carter presdl. campaign; mem. Ga. Public Service Commn., 1979—. Mem. So. Peanut Warehousemen's Assn. (dir.), Kappa Sigma. Club: Kiwanis. Home: 811 Bellevue Ave Dublin GA 31021

LOVEWELL, HUBART STONEX, JR., exec. recruiter; b. Mpls., Nov. 26, 1936; s. Hubart Stonex and Mable Isabel (Stengel) L.; B.A. in Journalism, U. Minn., 1960; m. Marjorie Ann Klingensmith, Aug. 6, 1960. Advt. sales rep. Mpls. Star & Tribune Co., 1958-63; advt. mgr. Snyders Drug Stores, St. Paul, 1963-66; account exec. Batten, Barton, Durstine & Osborne, Mpls., 1966-69, Henderson Advt., Atlanta, 1969-73; account supr., dir. new bus. Lawler Ballard Little Advt., Atlanta, 1973-75; pres. Jerry Fields/South, Inc., Atlanta, 1975—. Exec. com. DeKalb County Republican Party, 1971-72. Served with Army N.G., 1958-64. Mem. Atlanta Advt. Club, Am. Advt. Fedn., Am. Mktg. Assn. Republican. Episcopalian. Contbg. columnist to So. Advt. and Markets, 1975—. Home: 96 The Prado NE Atlanta GA 30309 Office: 100 Colony Sq Atlanta GA 30361

LOVIE, PETER MARSHALL, engring. exec.; b. Glasgow, Scotland, Nov. 21, 1940; s. Peter and Elizabeth Harrower (Marshall) L.; came to U.S., 1967; B.Sc., U. Glasgow, 1962; M. Applied Mechanics, U. Va., 1964; m. Ann Monroe, Apr. 9, 1971; 1 son, Peter Marshall. With Stewarts & Lloyds, Liverpool, Eng., 1964-67, Cameron Iron Works, Houston, 1967-68, Offshore Co., Houston, 1968, Acad. Computing Corp., Houston, 1968-70; founder, pres. Engring. Tech. Analysts, Inc., Houston, 1970-75, Lovie & Co., Houston, 1975—. Named Outstanding Young Texan, 1975; Fulbright scholar, 1962-64; E.S.U. Joint fellow, 1962-64; chartered engr., chartered naval architect, U.K.; registered profl. engr., Tex. Contbr. articles to tech. jours. Patentee in field. Office: PO Box 19733 Houston TX 77024

LOVVORN, ROBERT HENRY, ins. co. exec.; b. Cedartown, Ga., Mar. 9, 1916; s. William Barnes and Helen Louise (Cannon) L.; student pub. schs., Columbia, S.C.; C.L.U., 1952; m. Ellen Seabrook, June 11, 1938; children—Robert Henry, Mary Lovvorn Robinson. With Vol. State Life Ins. Co., 1941-44, 46-48, Atlantic Life Ins. Co., 1948-54; pres. Calhoun Life Ins. Co., also Calhoun Fire & Casualty Ins. Co., Columbia, 1954-73; v.p., dir. Appalachian Nat. Life Ins. Co., Knoxville, Tenn., 1970—; dir. Guardian Fidelity Corp., So. Bank & Trust Co., Appalachian Nat. Corp. Bd. dirs. Carolinas United Services; campaign chmn. S.C. Mental Health Assn.; commr. S.C. Dept. Mental Retardation, 1968—; trustee S.C. Mental Retardation Found., 1968—; sr. warden, chmn. Christian edn. com. Trinity Episcopal Ch., Columbia. Served with USNR, 1943-45. Recipient Heubner award, 1964, Service award S.C. Mental Health Assn. Mem. S.C. and Columbia Gen. Agts. and Mgrs. Assn. (past pres.), S.C. (past pres.), Columbia (past pres.) life underwriters assns., Nat. Assn. Life Underwriters (speakers bur.), Assn. S.C. Life Ins. Cos. (past pres., dir.), Am. Soc. C.L.U.'s, Nat., S.C., Columbia (past dir.) chambers commerce, Sales and Mktg. Execs. Internat., Columbia Sales Execs., S.C. Credit Ins. Assn. (trustee), S.C. Assn. for Retarded Children. Club (past pres.). Clubs: Forest Lake Country, Tarantella, Palmetto, Columbia Ball, Cotillion, Quadrille. Home: 4120 Linwood Rd Columbia SC 29205 Office: 5219 Trenholm Rd Columbia SC 29206

LOWE, BETTY ANN, pediatrician; b. Grapevine, Tex., Mar. 23, 1934; d. John W. and Winnie (Mercer) Lowe; B.S. cum laude, U. Ark., 1954, M.D. cum laude, 1956. Intern, Univ. Hosp., VA, Little Rock, 1956-57; resident in pediatrics Children's Med. Center, Boston, 1957-59; instr. pediatrics Med. Sch., Harvard U., Boston, 1959; chief resident in pediatrics Med. Sch., U. Ark., Little Rock, 1960-61, prof. pediatrics, 1975—; practice medicine specializing in pediatrics, Texarkana, Ark., 1961-75; med. dir. Ark. Children's Hosp., Little Rock, 1975—. Mem. Gov.'s Com. on Early Childhood, 1975. Lic. physician, Ark., Tex. Diplomate Am. Bd. Pediatrics. Mem. Am. Acad. Pediatrics (state chmn. 1974-77), So. Pediatric Research Soc., Ark., Pulaski County med. socs., Jr. League. Methodist. Home: 11 Hayfield Dr Little Rock AR 72207 Office: Ark Children's Hosp Little Rock AR 72201

LOWE, JAMES EUGENE, med. center adminstr.; b. Charleston, W.Va., June 26, 1944; s. James Elmer and Jolene Vera (Lussky) L.; B.B.A., W.Va. State Coll., 1972; m. Mary Julia McClure, Aug. 21, 1970; children—James Eric, Michael Aaron. Dir. surg. services Charleston Area Med. Center, 1972-75, adminstrv. asst. gen. div., 1975-76, staff asst. to adminstr., v.p., 1975-76, corp. dir. materiels mgmt., 1976—. Served with USNR, 1967-69. Mem. Am., W.Va., Capitol Dist. hosp. assns., Am. Mgmt. Assn., Tri State Purchasing Assn. Democrat. Baptist. Home: 436 Forest Circle South Charleston WV 25303 Office: 3000 MacCorkle Ave SE Charleston WV 25304

LOWE, JAMES TRAPIER, educator; b. Spartanburg, S.C., May 22, 1910; s. James Hudson and Nancy Alice (Henderson) L.; B.S. in Fgn. Service, Georgetown U., 1932, M.S., 1933, Ph.D., 1935; postgrad. U. Mich., 1933; m. Mary Jane McGee, Oct. 21, 1942; children—James Madison, William Richard. Prof., Georgetown U., 1935-42; with U.S. Dept. Def., 1945-53; with CIA, 1953-67, adj. prof. internat. relations U. Miami (Fla.), 1969—. Served to col. USAF. Decorated Legion of Merit; recipient Vicennial medal Georgetown U., 1956; Carnegie Found. fellow, 1934-35. Methodist. Home: 1114 Aduana Ave Coral Gables FL 33146

LOWE, JEAN HOLMES, educator; b. Highland Park, Ill., Jan. 1, 1941; d. John Russell and Clara Jean (Bullard) Holmes; B.A. in Anthropology, U. Calif. at Berkeley, 1963; m. Pardee Lowe, Jr., Jan. 26, 1963; children—Alice Bailey, Andrew Russell, Edward Dickinson, Carol Brainerd. Social worker County of Contra Costa, Calif., 1963-65; research asst. depts. consumer econs., transp., and oral history Cornell U., Ithaca, N.Y., 1966-74; dir. adult edn. Fairfax County Adult Detention Center, Fairfax, Va., 1975-79; coordinator adult basic edn. Fairfax County, 1979—; vol. dir. edn. Woodbridge Correctional Unit, State of Va. Bd. dirs. Tompkins County (N.Y.) Co-op. Extension, 1969-74, Tompkins County League Women Voters, 1968-74, ACLU of Va., 1978—; counselor Offender Aid and Restoration of Fairfax, 1974—; founder, chmn. Support Group for Va. Prisoners; treas., bd. dirs. Mental Health Assn. No. Va. Mem. Literacy Council No. Va., Va. Assn. Children with Learning Disabilities. Founder state orgn. to aid parolees. Home: 7810 Antopi St Annandale VA 22003 Office: 6131 Willston Dr Falls Church VA 22044

LOWE, PHILLIP HAROLD, educator, band dir.; b. Marion, Ind., May 15, 1949; s. David Harold and Evelyn Marie (Burkholder) L.; B.Mus., Hardin-Simmons U., 1972, M.Mus., 1973; postgrad. N.Tex. State U., 1974-75; m. Carol Ann Rentschler, Dec. 22, 1972; 1 son, John David. Band dir. Roby (Tex.) High Sch., 1972-73; asst. dir. bands Hardin-Simmons U., Abilene, Tex., 1972-74; grad. asst. N. Tex. State U., Denton, 1974-75; dir. bands, instr. music Hill Jr. Coll., Hillsboro, Tex., 1975—; third horn Abilene Philharm., 1969-74; Named Tchr. of Yr., Hill Jr. Coll., 1977-78. Mem. Music Educators Nat. Conf., Tex. Music Educators Assn., Internat. Horn Soc., Tex. Jr. Coll. Tchrs. Assn., Phi Mu Alpha Sinfonia (Andy J. Patterson award, 1971, Spears award, 1972), Alpha Chi. Republican. Baptist. Club: Hillsboro Lions. Composer two works for band, various smaller works. Home: 1406 Park Dr Hillsboro TX 76645 Office: Hill Junior College Hillsboro TX 76645

LOWE, RALPH STEPHEN, physician; b. El Paso, Jan. 19, 1947; s. Ralph Leroy and Martha Ann (Satterwhite) L.; B.S., U. Tex., El Paso, 1968; M.D., U. Tex., San Antonio, 1973; m. Helen Mellado, Dec. 22, 1969; children—Stephanie, Elizabeth, Sarah. Commd. lt. U.S. Air Force, 1972, advanced through grades to maj., 1980; resident in internal medicine Wilford Hall USAF Med. Center, San Antonio, 1973-76, fellow in allergy and clin. immunology, 1976-78, instr. alin. allergy physicians tng. course, 1976-78; staff allergist Keesler USAF Med. Center, Biloxi, Miss., 1978-80. Diplomate Am. Bd. Internal Medicine, Am. Bd. Allergy and Immunology. Mem. AMA, Assn. Mil. Allergists, A.C.P., Am. Acad. Allergy, Am. Coll. Allergists. Roman Catholic. Contbr. articles to profl. jours. Home: 721 River Elms Ct El Paso TX 79922 Office: 9398 Viscount Blvd Suite 4A El Paso TX 79925

LOWE, WILLIAM ERIC PENRHYN, telecommunications engr.; b. Karachi, Pakistan, Sept. 20, 1936; s. William Eric and Helen Georgina (Ball) L.; student Cable and Wireless Engring. Coll., Cornwall, Eng., 1952-55; m. Nilda Aurora Colorado, Mar. 9, 1960; children—William, Phillip, Robert, Dorothy, Richard, Rodney. Communications technician Cable and Wireless Ltd., Barbados, 1955-57, San Juan, P.R., 1957-59, supr. communications, 1961-64, project engr., 1964-68, mgr. engring., 1968-74; mgr. telecommunications P.R.-Latin Am., Westinghouse Electric Co., Hato Rey, P.R., 1974—. Served with Royal Corps of Signals, 1959-61. Mem. Armed Forces Communications and Electronics Assn. Roman Catholic. Club: Lion. Home: V-14 Los Angeles Carolina PR 00630 Office: PO Box 41254 San Juan PR 00940

LOWELL, ANTHONY M., statistician; b. Koniuchy, Ukraine, July 22, 1908; s. Anthony and Johanna Lotowycz; brought to U.S., 1912, naturalized, 1921; B.S., Alfred U., 1932; postgrad. U. Rochester, 1932-34; M.P.H., Mass. Inst. Tech., 1935, C.P.H., 1935; postgrad. Yale U., 1944. Supr. indsl. morbidity studies Mass. area USPHS, 1935-36; statistician Phila. Health Council, 1937-39; dir. statis. div. N.Y. Tb and Health Assn., N.Y.C., 1939-62; chief statistics and analysis Tb Control div. Nat. Center Disease Control, Atlanta, 1962-78; asso. mem. Henry Phipps Inst., Phila., 1937—; free-lance med. writer, 1978—; cons. in field. Served with AUS, 1943-45. Fellow Am. Public Health Assn.; mem. Am. Statis. Assn., Soc. Epidemiol. Research, Internat. Health Soc. U.S., Am. Med. Writers Assn., Internat. Union Against Tb. Author: Tb in New York City, ann. 1953-62; Advances in Tb Research, 1966; Tb in the United States, 1969; Tb in the World, 1976; contbr. to profl. jours. Home: 3645 Peachtree Rd NE Atlanta GA 30319

LOWENSTEIN, CHARLES DOUGLAS, ednl. services co. exec.; b. Bayonne, N.J., Apr. 22, 1942; s. Irving Eric and Barbara (Goldenberg) L.; B.S. in Commerce and Econs., U. Vt., 1963; m. Leslie Ann Diamond, Sept. 5, 1965; children—Lee Jay, Andrea Michelle, Evan Mitchell and Jaron David (twins). Supt. Lowenstein Metals Inc., Newark, 1964-67; registered prin. Penn Securities Co., East Orange, N.J., 1967-68; asst. dir. Nelson Sch. Securities, Mountainside, N.J., 1968-69; v.p. sales Ga. Internat. Securities Co., Atlanta, 1969-70; pres. Investment Tng. Inst., Inc., Atlanta, 1969—; tng. cons. Wiesenberger Services, Inc., N.Y.C., 1971-76. Mem. task force to design new industry tng. standards Nat. Assn. Securities Dealers, 1971; bd. regents Coll. for Financial Planning, Denver, 1972-73; pres. Atlanta dist. Zionist Orgn. Am.; mem. cabinet Atlanta, Israel Bonds; mem. Sabra Soc.; bd. dirs. Atlanta Jewish Community Center, 1977-80; bd. dirs. Yeshiva High Sch. of Atlanta, 1977-78, fin. sec., 1978-79, v.p., 1979-80; bd. dirs. Atlanta Jewish Fedn., Atlanta Men's ORT, Atlanta Chabad-Lubavitch, Atlanta Bur. Jewish Edn., 1977-80. Served with AUS, 1963. Mem. Internat. Assn. Fin. Planners (dir. 1973-74), Jr. C. of C., Nat. Assn. Securities Schs. (pres. 1974-76), Ga. Security Dealers Assn., Nat. R.R. Hist. Soc., Tau Epsilon Phi. Jewish (past trustee, past v.p. congregation). Home: 2974 Cravey Dr Atlanta GA 30345 Office: PO Box 29526 Atlanta GA 30359

LOWENSTEIN, GEORGE WOLFGANG, physician, UN cons.; b. Germany, Apr. 18, 1890; s. Julius Max and Augusta Victoria (Klettschoff) L.; student Royal William Coll., Germany, 1909, Friedrich William U., Germany, 1919, London (Eng.) Sch. Tropical Hygiene and Medicine, 1939; m. Johanna Sabath, Nov. 27, 1923; children—Peter F. Lansing (dec.) and Ruth Edith Lowenstein Gallagher (twins). Dir. pub. health Berlin Neubabelsberg, 1920-22; dir. pub. health and welfare Berlin, 1923-33; pvt. practice medicine, Berlin, 1933-38, Chgo., 1940-46, Chebeague and Dark Harbor, Maine, 1947-58; instr. Berlin Acad. for Prevention of Infant Mortality, Postgrad. Acad. for Physicians; permanent cons. Internat. Abolitionists Fedn. at ECOSOC, UN, 1947—; lectr. Morton Plant Hosp., Clearwater, also Clearwater campus St. Petersburg Jr. Coll. Served with German Army, 1914-18. Decorated Cross Merit I Class, Germany, 1965; recipient Commendation awards Pres. U.S., 1945, 70; 55 Year Gold Service Pin, AMA and ARC, 1970; Service to Mankind award Sertoma, 1972, 73, Sport award Pres. Carter, 1977, others. Fellow Am. Acad. Family Physicians (charter, life), AAAS, Am. Coll. Sport Medicine (emeritus, charter, life), Am. Pub. Health Assn. (life); mem. Brit. Med. Soc., German Assn. History of Medicine (life), Acad. on Mental Retardation (charter life), Am. Health Assn. (life), Fla. Health Assn. (life), Fla. Health Assn. (life), Brit. Public Health Assn. (life), AMA (hon.), Am. Assn. Mil. Surgeons (life), Steuben Soc., Richey Symphony Soc. (musicologist, charter), World Peace Through World Law Center. Clubs: City (Chgo. chmn. hygiene sect. 1944-46), Rotary, Masons, Shriners (comdr., 32 deg.). Contbr. articles to med. jours. Home: 880 Mandalay Ave #522 Clearwater Beach FL 33515

LOWENTHAL, LAWRENCE MARK (LARRY), advt. exec.; b. Chgo., Feb. 3, 1942; s. Daniel and Rose (Slaw) L.; B.A., U. Chgo., 1964; m. Janice Kathleen Johnson, Dec. 31, 1969; 1 son, Noah Todd. Asst. br. advt. mgr. Carson Pirie Scott & Co., Chgo., also freelance copywriter, 1965-68; staff writer Leo Burnett Co., 1969-70; freelance copywriter, Hollywood, Fla., 1970-72; pres. Lowenthal & Gemmi, Ft. Lauderdale, Fla., 1972—; v.p. Charles H. Greenthal of Fla., Inc., Lauderhill; former mem. community faculty Nova U., Coral Springs, Fla. Chmn., Cooper City Beautification and Appearance Bd. Recipient Addy awards Am. Advt. Fedn., pub. TV awards. Mem. Am. Advt. Fedn., Am. Mktg. Assn., Ft. Lauderdale Advt. Fedn. (1st v.p.). Author: Snowflakes, 1972. Home: 5221 SW 87th Ave Cooper City FL 33328 Office: 941 NE 19th Ave Fort Lauderdale FL 33304

LOWER, FRANK JOHN, educator; b. Watseka, Ill., Jan. 3, 1942; s. Frederick Youri and Nellie Martha (Woudenberg) L.; B.A., Adams State Coll., 1963, M.A., 1964; Ph.D., Fla. State U., 1974; m. Jacquelyn Dean, Feb. 3, 1967; children—Laura Dean, Malcolm Frederick. Instr. English, Metro. State Coll., Denver, 1965-66; tchr. English, journalism Warner Robins High Sch., Warner Robins, Ga., 1966-67; instr. speech and theater Ga. State U., Atlanta, 1967-72; grad. asst. Fla. State U., Tallahassee, 1972-73; instr. speech Fla. A. and M. U., Tallahassee, 1973-74; asso. prof. communication La. State U., Shreveport, 1974—. Local arrangements chmn. N.W. La. Foster Parents Assn., 1976—; bd. dirs. Theater of Performing Arts, Shreveport, 1975-78; parliamentarian La. PTA conv., 1978; moderator 4th Dist. Congressional Debate, 1978. Nat. Endowment for Humanities summer seminar, 1979. Mem. Speech Communication Assn., Internat. Communication Assn., Am. Forensic Assn., So. Speech Communication Assn., Phi Kappa Phi, Pi Kappa Delta, Delta Sigma Rho, Tau Kappa Alpha. Republican. Methodist. Clubs: Shreveport Bonsai, Bonsai Internat., Masons. Contbr. articles in field to profl. jours. Home: 217 Brenda Dr Shreveport LA 71115 Office: 8515 Youree Dr Shreveport LA 71115

LOWERY, CHARLES LEE, clin. psychologist; b. San Antonio, Jan. 16, 1946; s. Lucas Daugherty and Mary Lillian (Hammet) L.; B.S., S.W. Tex. State U., 1968; Ed.D., E. Tex. State U., 1974; M.A., St. Mary's U., 1971; m. Rita Claire Smith, Feb. 28, 1968; 1 dau., Laura Lee. Tchr., Rayburn Jr. High Sch., Northside Ind. Sch. Dist., San Antonio, 1968-70, Lowell Jr. High Sch., San Antonio Ind. Sch. Dist., 1972; exec. dir. Big Bros. Greenville (Tex.) Inc., 1973-74; asst. prof. psychology, counseling La. Tech. U., Ruston, 1974-77; pvt. practice clin. psychology San Antonio, 1977—. cons., lectr. in field. Bd. dirs. behavioral standards com. La. Tech. U., 1974-77; mem. adv. bd. Community Alcoholism Program, Ruston, 1976-77. Certified tchr., profl. counselor, psychologist, health service provider. Mem. Am., Tex. psychol. assns., Phi Delta Kappa, Psi Chi, Lambda Chi Alpha. Methodist. Home: Fair Oaks Route 4 Box 4856 Boerne TX 78006 Office: Oak Hills Med Bldg Suite 406 7711 Louis Pasteur Dr San Antonio TX 78229

LOWERY, JOHN STEWART, ins. exec.; b. Charlotte, N.C., Apr. 28, 1953; s. Jimmy Lee and Shirley Ann (Williams) L.; student Gaston Coll., 1971-72, various others; m. Kathy Maxine Lynn, Aug. 15, 1971; 1 dau., Jennifer Lynn. Photographer Barkley Studio, Lincolnton, N.C., 1970-71; owner, pres. John Lowery's Photography, Inc., Lincolnton, 1971-74; photographer WBTV News, Jefferson Pilot Broadcasting Co., Charlotte, 1974-77; instr. Lincoln Center of Gaston Coll., Lincolnton, 1972-74; agt. Gastonia Agy., Jefferson Standard Life Ins. Co. Pres. Lincoln County Heart Assn., Lincolnton, 1974, 75, bd. dirs. 1976—; chmn. steering com. for local referendum Lincoln County, 1977; dist. dir. N.C. Jaycees exec. com., 1978-79, regional dir., 1979—, also mem. exec. com.; bd. dirs., blood chmn. Lincoln County chpt. Red Cross, 1978—; mem. advisory council Lincoln County unit N.C. Dept. Corrections, 1978—. Recipient Founders' award N.C. Heart Assn., 1974, Pres. award, 1974-75; Distinguished Service award Lincoln County, 1977; Charles Hutchins Meml. award N.C. Jaycees, 1977-78, Seth L. Crapps Meml. award, 1977-78, Presdl. award of Honor, 1977-78; Presdl. award of Honor U.S. Jaycees, 1977-78, Golden Spikedriver award, 1977-78; fast start award and award of excellence Jefferson Standard Life Ins. Co., also leading new agt. award, 1979; named spokesmen of yr. Lincolnton Jaycees, 1974-75, Sparkplug of Yr., 1976-77, One of Top 10 Jaycees in State, 1976-77, One of Top 5 at Mid-yr., 1977-78, Young Man of Yr., 1977, Most Outstanding Jaycee in N.C., 1977-78; elected to Pres. club N.C. Jaycees, 1977-78, no. 1 Jaycee pres. in U.S., 1977-78, in N.C., 1977-78, Pres. Award of Honor, 1978-79, W.E. Sam Early Meml. award, 1978-79; other Jaycee awards; recipient Order of Long Leaf Pine, Gov. N.C., 1979. Mem. Nat. Assn. Life Underwriters, Lincoln County Life Underwriters Assn., Lincolnton Jaycees (internal. v.p. 1975-76, external v.p. 1976-77, pres. 1977-78), Lincoln County C. of C. (bd. dirs. 1977—). Democrat. Lutheran. Contbr. many news, sports stories to WBTV. Address: PO Box 433 Lincolnton NC 28092

LOWERY, LEE LEON, JR., educator; b. Corpus Christi, Tex., Dec. 26, 1938; s. Lee Leon and Blance (Deitrich) L.; B.S. in C.E., Tex. A. and M. U., 1960, M.S., 1961, Ph.D., 1965; m. Evelyn F. Lindsey, Sept. 6, 1960; children—Kelli Lane, Christianne Lindsey. Prof., research engr. Tex. A. and M. U., College Station, 1960—; pres. Tex. Measurements, Inc., College Station, 1968—, Pile Dynamics Found. Engring., Bryan, Tex., 1962—, Interface Engring. Asso., College Station, 1969—; ind. engring. cons., 1960—; dir. Braver Corp., 1973-79, Deep Found. Inst., 1977-79. Recipient Faculty Disting. Achievement award Tex. A. and M. U., 1979, Outstanding Prof. award, 1979; NDEA fellow, 1960-63. Mem. ASCE, Tex. Soc. Profl. Engrs., Am. Soc. Profl. Engrs., Am. Soc. Stress Analysis, Soc. for Marine Tech., Am. Soc. Engring. Edn., Prestressed Concrete Inst., Sigma Xi, Phi Kappa Phi, Tau Beta Pi. Baptist. Patentee in field; author chpt. in Numerical Methods in Geotechnical Engineering, 1977. Home: 1818 Shadowwood College Station TX 77840 Office: Dept Civil Engring Tex A and M U College Station TX 77843

LOWERY, SUE KING, credit union exec.; b. Allentown, Fla., June 7, 1936; d. M. Luther and O. Laylor (Smith) K.; student public schs.; children—Pamela R. Domulot, Randall Keith, Rodger Keane. Sec., bookkeeper Paul S. Amos Variety Store, Milton, Fla., 1950-55; reporter Credit Bur. Panama City (Fla.), 1956-57; bookkeeper Santa Rosa (Fla.) County Tax Assn., 1957-58; mgr. Cyanamid Employees Credit Union, Milton, 1966-79, Escambia County Employees Credit Union, Pensacola, Fla., 1979—; v.p. Fla. Credit Union Guaranty Corp., 1974—; sec. Escambia Credit Union, 1978-80. Mem. Santa Rosa County Democratic Com., 1978—. Scholar, Fla. Credit Union Mgmt. Inst., 1973. Mem. Fla. chpt. President's Assn. (past pres. Fla. chpt.), Credit Union Execs. Soc. (council Fla.), Nat. Credit Union Execs. Soc., Credit Union Founders Club, Pensacola Mgmt. Assn., Fla. Credit Union Mgmt. Inst. Alumni Assn., Beta Sigma Phi. Methodist. Club: Order Eastern Star. Editor newsletters. Home: PO Box 701 Milton FL 32570 Office: Suite 220 Plaza Bldg Pensacola FL

LOWMAN, KARL THOMPSON, ins. co. exec.; b. Ballentine, S.C., Nov. 8, 1930; s. Karl Stack and Lougenia (Thompson) L.; A.B., U. S.C., 1951; m. Arlene May Neatock, Apr. 7, 1955; 1 son, Joseph Christopher. Adminstrv. asst. Dept. Gen. Studies, U. S.C., 1955-57; acctg. machine sales Nat. Cash Register Co., Columbia, S.C., 1957-62; sales rep. Blue Cross & Blue Shield of S.C., Columbia, 1962-65, asst. to enrollment dir., 1965-68, Charleston-Columbia dist. mgr., 1968-70, gen. sales mgr. primary firms, 1970-74, dir. manpower devel. and tng., 1974-78, asst. v.p. mktg. adminstrn., 1978—. Served with USAF, 1951-55. Mem. U.S. Power Squadron. Lutheran. Club: Irmo Sertoma. Home: PO Box 22 Ballentine SC 29002 Office: Blue Cross and Blue Shield of SC 1-20 Alpine Rd Columbia SC 29219

LOWRY, LEO ELMO, petroleum exec.; b. Utopia, Kans., Dec. 4, 1916; s. Nim Roderick and Marticia (Veach) L.; B.A., Okla. A. and M. Coll., 1937; m. Elizabeth Watson, Sept. 5, 1940; children—Richard Clark, John Christopher, Janet Kaye. With Creole Petroleum Corp., Caracas, Venezuela, 1937-71, exec. v.p., 1961-64, pres., 1964-71; pres. Esso Inter-Am., Inc., Coral Gables, Fla., 1971-77.

LOWRY, WILLIAM HILLIS, ednl. adminstr.; b. Tehuacana, Tex., Aug. 28, 1941; s. Floyd Ada and Nora Nadine Lowry; B.A., Tex. A&M U., 1964, M.Ed., 1968, Ph.D., 1972; m. Cynthia Ann Hancock, Aug. 6, 1966; children—Timothy Bret, Donald Bart, John Chance, Robert Dale. Secondary sch. tchr., then asst. prin. public schs. in Tex., 1964-67; from research asso. to asso. dir. CATE project Tex. A&M U., 1969-69, dir. edn. media center, 1970-71; asst. dir. staff devel. dept. Mexia State Sch., Coolidge, Tex., 1971-73, supt., 1976—; asst. dept. commnr. Tex. Dept. Mental Health and Mental Retardation, 1973-76; cons. in field. City councilman, Coolidge, 1973. Mem. Am. Assn. Mental Deficiency, Nat. Assn. Supts. Public Residentail Facilities for Mentally Retarded, Tex. Assn. Mental Deficiency (chmn. 1977-78), Tex. Public Employees Assn., Phi Delta Kappa. Baptist. Club: Mexia Rotary. Author papers in field. Home: Box 455 Coolidge TX 76635 Office: Box 1132 Mexia TX 76667

LOWRY, WILLIAM KETCHIN, JR., accountant; b. Columbia, S.C., Oct. 4, 1951; s. William Ketchin and Beverly Hubbard (Frazee) L.; B.S. in Bus. Adminstrn., U. S.C., 1972, M. Accountancy, 1973; m. Ellen Marlene Morrow, May 12, 1973. Mem. audit staff Ernst & Whinney, Columbia, S.C., 1973—, audit supr., 1978—; instr. Midlands Tech. Coll., 1974-76. Co-chmn. adv. com. for acctg. curriculum Midlands Tech. Coll., 1975—; bd. dirs. Groves Homes Assn., 1976-77, pres., 1977. C.P.A., S.C.; C.L.U. Fellow Life Mgmt. Inst.; mem. Am. Inst. C.P.A.'s, Nat. Assn. Accts., Am. Acctg. Assn., S.C. Assn. C.P.A.'s, Am. Soc. C.L.U.'s, Omicron Delta Kappa, Beta Gamma Sigma, Beta Alpha Psi, Omicron Delta Epsilon, Sigma Phi Epsilon. Presbyterian. Clubs: Forest Lake, Met. Business. Home: 1341 Cactus Ave Columbia SC 29210 Office: Suite 500 C & S Bank Bldg Columbia SC 29202

LOYD, LOYE CARROLL, glass co. exec.; b. Yantis, Tex., May 19, 1926; s. Edward M. and Ava (Gilbreath) L.; student So. Meth. U., 1948-51; m. Barbara Ray, Feb. 16, 1952; children—Stanley Alan, Terry Ray. Mgr., Mid-West Glass Co., Midland, Tex., 1955-62; owner Glasco Glass Co., Midland, 1962—, dir., v.p., Casper, Wyo.; pres. Temple Glass & Mirror Co., Inc. (Tex.), 1969—, Bell Glass & Mirror Co., Killeen, Tex., 1970—, El Paso Glass & Mirror Co., Inc. (Tex.), 1970—, Killeen Glass & Mirror Co., 1974—; sec.-treas. Barber Glass & Mirror Co., Inc., Big Spring, Tex., 1968—; dir. Tex. Glass Distbrs., Inc., Ft. Worth, Glass Shack, Inc., Midland; sec.-treas., dir. Odessa Glass & Mirror Co., Inc. (Tex.); dir. El Paso Glass & Mirror Co., Inc., Eastex Glass Co. Inc., Nacogdoches, Tex., Western Glass & Mirror Co., El Paso, Glass Wholesalers, Inc., Houston, Weatherford Glass & Mirror Co., Inc. (Tex.), Stockton Glass & Mirror Co., Inc., Ft. Stockton, Tex., A-1 Glass Co., Coppras Cove, Tex., Ave. Glass Co., Inc., Temple, Tex., City Glass & Mirror Co., Hobbs, N.Mex., Quality Glass & Mirror Co., Big Spring, Tex., Tyler Mirror & Glass Co. (Tex.). Served with USNR, 1943-46. Mem. Assembly of God Ch. Club: Rotary (sec. 1965-66). Home: 2503 Dartmouth St Midland TX 79701 Office: 24 W Industrial Loop Midland TX 79701

LOYD, THELMA SPESSARD, clubwoman; b. Fayette County, W.Va., Oct. 8, 1899; d. Jacob Woods and Lucille Mildred (Richardson) Spessard; student W.Va. Bus. Coll.; m. A.C. Holcomb; children—Archer Clarence, Jr., Joseph Reid; m. 2d, Alfred Tracy Loyd, Dec. 31, 1942. Scout leader Girl Scouts U.S.A., 1937-45, pres. Girl Scout Leaders Club, 1943-45, pres. Roanoke council, 1948-50, 55-57, treas., 1958-62, 66-70, parliamentarian, 1969-75; state historian, chmn. edn. and bylaws Va. State Assn. Parliamentarians, 1960-70, chmn. bylaws, 1976—; pres. Thursday Morning Music Club, 1957-59, parliamentarian, 1959-67, 81—, dir. bd. govs., 1967-71; state chaplain Va. Fedn. Music Clubs, 1962-66, parliamentarian, 1966-75, pres., 1975—; pres. Windsor Hills Garden Club, 1949-50, 61-63, parliamentarian, 1955-56, 63-64, 80—; chmn. Flower Show, S.W. Dist. Garden Club, 1950-52, pres., 1952-54, dir., 1954-56; pres. Blue Ridge Dist., 1963-65, parliamentarian, 1965-67, 75-77; bd. dirs. Va. Fedn. Garden Clubs, bird chmn., 1959-61, corr. sec., 1961-62, 2d v.p., 1962-63, 67-69, rec. sec., 1965-67, 1st v.p., editor Yearbook, 1968-71, pres., mem. nat. bd., 1971-73, parliamentarian, chmn. adv. bd., 1973-75; com. chmn. S.Atlantic Region Garden Clubs, 1960-80; life mem. Nat. Fedn. Garden Clubs, Nat. Fedn. Music Clubs; treas. bd. trustees Nature Camp, 1955-60, trustee rep. Blue Ridge dist., 1960-76, pres., 1971-73, parliamentarian, 1973-75, trustee-at-large, 1973-81; mem. Blue Ridge Dist. Flower Show Judges and Va. Council Accredited Flower Show Judges, Va. Landscape Design Critics Council, UDC, DAR (chpt. regent 1980-83), Am. Rose Soc. Presbyterian. Recipient Environ. Action citation U.S. Army C.E., 1977; named Roanoke Mother of Year for Arts and Scis., 1977; nat. registered profl. parliamentarian; lectr. conservation. Home: Dios Mirar 2131 Deyerle Rd SW Roanoke VA 24018

LOYOLA, ANDREA ANGEL, public relations exec.; b. New Orleans, July 28, 1952; d. Angel Mina and Carmelite (Richter) L.; B.A. in Drama and Communications, U. New Orleans, 1973. Public relations/recreational adv. St. Vincent De Paul Center, New Orleans, 1970-72; stringer radio Sta.-WGSO, New Orleans, 1972-73; sales adv., reporter for New Orleans area Fox Photo Co., New Orleans, 1973; public relations asst. Hotel Dieu Hosp., New Orleans, 1973-74; weekend newscaster Sta.-WGNO-TV, New Orleans, 1974-76; dir. public relations and devel. Mercy Hosp. New Orleans, 1974-79, liaison to hosp. bd. devel., 1974-79, editor The Shield, hosp. quar., 1974-79; asso. Chachere Advt. Assos., 1979-80; dir. community relations DePaul Hosp., 1980—. Named one of 13 Outstanding Young Women of Am., 1975. Mem. Am. Assn. Hosp. Public Relations, Nat. Assn. Hosp. Devel., Internat. Assn. Bus. Communicators (award of excellence in spl. communications 1976), So. Assn. Bus. Communicators Women in Communication (profl.), Quill and Scroll, Media Arts Orgn. of U. New Orleans, New Orleans Assn. Health Care Communicators. Club: Press of New Orleans (2d Pl. award of excellence for publ. 1977). Home: 3500 Houma Blvd Apt 208 Metairie LA 70002

LOZZIO, BISMARCK BERTO, med. researcher, hematologist, oncologist; b. Patagones, Buenos Aires, Argentina, Jan. 27, 1931; s. Bartolo and Haydee Angela (Piucill) L.; B.S., Bernardino Rivadavia Coll., Buenos Aires, 1949; Physician, U. Buenos Aires, 1955, M.D., 1957; m. Carmen Irene Bertucci, Mar. 10, 1955; 1 dau., Graciela Irene. Came to U.S., 1965, naturalized, 1974. Asso. gastroenterologist, instr. internal medicine Tornú Hosp., U. Buenos Aires, 1955-58; asso. hematologist NIH, Buenos Aires, 1958-65; research asso. U. Tenn. Dept. Med. Biology/Meml. Research Center, Knoxville, 1965-67, asst. prof. research, 1968-71, asso. prof., 1971-75, prof., 1975—; lectr. U. Tenn. dept. microbiology, 1971—, Inst. Radiation Biology, 1978—. Served with Argentine Marine Corps, 1952-53. Nat. Council for Sci. and Tech. Research fellow, 1958-60; Career award, 1961-65; NSF grantee, 1966, Am. Heart Assn. grantee, 1966, 74-76, NIH grantee, 1968—, Am. Cancer Soc. grantee, 1970—, Nat. Found. Neuromuscular Disease grantee, 1969. Mem. Reticuloendothelial Soc., Internat. Soc. Hematology, Am. Soc. Hematology, Am. Soc. Lab. Animal Sci., AAAS, Soc. Exptl. Biology and Medicine, Am. Fedn. Clin. Research, Internat. Soc. Exptl. Hematology, N.Y. Acad. Scis., Am. Assn. Immunologists, Am. Assn. Cancer Research, Southeastern Cancer Research Assn., Asociación Médica Argentina, Sociedad Argentina de Biología, Sociedad Argentina de Immunología, Sociedad Argentina de Investigación Clínica, Sociedad Argentina de Hematología y Hemoterapia, Sigma Xi. Home: 9709 Tunbridge Ln Concord TN 37922 Office: U Tenn Dept Med Biology/Meml Research Center Center Health Scis 1924 Alcoa Hwy Knoxville TN 37920

LUARK, ERWIN EDWARD, psychiat. social worker; b. Fentress, Tex., Aug. 9, 1930; s. Ernest J. and Mary Elizabeth (Nixon) L.; A.A., Schreimer Coll., 1951; student U. Tex., 1950-51; B.S.W., Our Lady of the Lake U. of San Antonio, 1975, M.S.W., 1976; Ph.D., Walden U., 1978; m. Evva Smith, Sept. 28, 1951. Vice pres. Richmond Chem. Co. (Tex.), 1962-73; chief adminstrv. officer State Probation Dist., Jourdanton, Tex., 1976-77; psychotherapist in pvt. practice, San Antonio, 1977—; mgr. Community Alcoholic Treatment Program, San Antonio, 1978-79; cons. in field; vis. lectr. Our Lady of the Lake U. of San Antonio, 1977—; critic/reviewer AAAS, 1978—; mem. regional alcoholism adv. com., Alamo Area Council Govts., San Antonio, 1974-79. Served with USAF, 1951-58. Mem. Nat. Assn. Social Workers, Tex. Assn. Alcoholism Counselors, Nat. Psychiat. Assn., DAV, Pi Gamma Mu, Phi Theta Kappa. Contbr. articles to profl. jours. Address: 1008 SW 37 St San Antonio TX 78237

LUBBE, CATHERINE CASE (MRS. JOHN A. LUBBE), author; b. Villa Park, Ill., Sept. 24, 1898; d. John Joseph and Frances A. (Darmstadt) Case; student No. Ill. State Normal Coll., 1917; grad. Columbia Conservatory, 1923; L.H.D., l'Université Libre (Asie), 1970; m. John Andrew Lubbe, 1929; children—John Andrew, Kaye Don. Tchr. pub. and pvt. schs., Ill., 1916-25; author poems pub. in numerous mags., newspapers, anthologies, including Poets Am., Book of Year, Poetry Soc. Tex., Child Welfare, Dallas Morning News, Colo. Springs Gazette and Telegraph, Kaleidograph, Elmhurst Press, South and West, Encore, Hawk & Whippoorwill Recalled, others; dramatic reader poetry on various radio and TV programs, 1922-57; adminstr. Whitney and Vaida Stewart Montgomery lit. estate, 1972—. Active ARC. Recipient World Fair Gold medal Poetry Day award, 1940; Nyogen Senzaki Meml. Haiku award, 1966, 71; UN day Leadership award, 1967; Gold medal award United Poets Laureate Internat., 1968 Leadership in Poetry award Internat. Acad. Leadership, Philippines, 1970; Honor award 3d World Congress of Poets, 1976. Mem. Poetry Soc. Tex. (hon. life mem., corr. sec. 1952-56, dir. 1957—, librarian, poetry critic, mem. poetry day com. editorial com.; Old South award 197., Edsel Ford Meml. award 1971), Nat. Fedn. State Poetry Socs. Inc. (2d v.p. 1972-73, 1st v.p. 1973—, pres. 1974-76, awards chmn. 1972-73), Poetry Soc. Am., La. Poetry Soc., St. Edward's Altar Soc., Eugene Field Soc. (hon.), United Poets Laureate Internat. Roman Catholic. Clubs: Lakewood Garden, Compatriots. Home: 419 Clermont Ave Dallas TX 75223

LUBIN, SAMUEL, govt. ofcl.; b. Washington, Sept. 16, 1914; s. Israel H. and Annie (Cohen) L.; B.S., Wilson Tchrs. Coll., 1936; M.S.W., Nat. Cath. Sch. Social Work, 1947; m. Frances C. Reichman, Nov. 5, 1945; children—Michael Evan, Amy Ilene. Dir. UNRRA operations, U.S. Zone Germany, 1945-47; adminstr. Jewish Social Service Agys., 1949-53; regional dir. Am. Jewish Com., 1956-58; regional dir. Council Jewish Fedns. for S.E. States, 1958-63; manpower adminstrn. rep., regional youth and program cons., dir. tng. S.E. region U.S. Dept. Labor, Atlanta, 1963—. Served with AUS, 1942-45. Mem. Acad. Cert. Social Workers, Nat. Assn. Social Workers, Nat. Assn. Jewish Communal Workers, Sigma Tau Delta. Jewish. Home: 1602 Adelia Pl NE Atlanta GA 30329 Office: US Dept Labor 1371 Peachtree St NE Atlanta GA 30306

LUBKE, GEORGE WILLIAM, JR., mortgage banker; b. Yonkers, N.Y., Dec. 10, 1919 s. George William and Valeska (Kostka) L.; student N.Y.U., Columbia, N.Y. Tech. Inst., Newark U., 1938-42, Stetson U., 1946-47, Northwestern U., 1953-56; LL.D., Fla. Research Inst., 1970; m. Alice Myra Painter, Jan. 26, 1944; children—Robin Alice, George William III. Salesman, Mut. Benefit Life Ins. Co., Daytona Beach, Fla., 1945-49; dir. mortgages Realty World, Atlanta. Chmn., Tax Study Com. Volusia County, 1954; commr. on aging, State of Fla., 1962-67, chmn. exec. com., 1963-68. Vice pres. Young Democratic Clubs Fla., 1953-55. Chmn. bd. Daytona Beach Housing Authority, 1958-69. Served with N.Y. State N.G., 1941-42; with AUS, 1942-46. Named Man of Year, Daytona Beach Jr. C. of C., 1949. Mem. Am., Fla. mortgage bankers assns., Nat. Housing Conf. (dir., vice chmn. bd.), Nat. Housing Research Council (dir.), Nat., Fla. (past pres.) assns. housing and redevel. ofcls., D.A.V. (past treas. Fla.). Home: PO Box 341 Avondale Estates GA 30002 Office: 1800 Century Blvd Suite 600 Atlanta GA 30345

LUBLANEZKI, NANCY CARLAN, educator; b. Gastonia, N.C., Nov. 24, 1947; s. George and Verta Lee (Short) L.; student Drake U., 1965-67; B.S. in Pharmacy, U. Miss., 1970. Instr. pharmaceuticals U. Miss., University, 1972—; pharmacist Hogue Drugs, Inc., Greenwood, Miss., 1972—; presentor workshops and seminars to various pharmacy groups. Recipient Am. Pharm. Assn. Certificate of Commendation, 1970; registered pharmacist, Miss. Mem. Miss. Pharm. Assn., Kappa Epsilon, Rho Chi. Roman Catholic. Author, (with Paul Skierkowski) chpt. in Handbook of Non-Prescription Drugs, 5th and 6th edits., 1975, 76. Home: 220 Elm St Oxford MS 38655 Office: Faser Hall Univ of Miss University MS 38677

LUBRITZ, RONALD RAPHAEL, dermatologist; b. New Orleans, Aug. 3, 1934; s. Ephraim and Bella (Ball) L.; B.S., Tulane U., 1955; M.D., La. State U. 1959; m. Rachel Ann Holt, May 28, 1969; children—Geary, David Leslie, Paige, Jody. Intern, Touro Hosp., New Orleans, 1959-60; resident in dermatology Charity Hosp. La., New Orleans, 1960-63; practice medicine specializing in dermatology, Hattiesburg, Miss., 1963—; mem. part-time faculty Sch. Medicine, Tulane U., 1963—, clin. asso. prof. dermatology, 1974—; dermatology dir. Rudolph Ellender Med. Found., 1972—; Hattiesburg area chmn. United Jewish Appeal, 1969-70; pres. elect B'nai Israel Synagogue, Hattiesburg; mem. dist. bd. dirs. Anti-defamation League, 1973—; pres. Hattiesburg B'nai B'rith, 1973. Served to maj. Army N.G., 1963-74. Diplomate Am. Bd. Dermatology. Fellow A.C.P., Am.

Acad. Dermatology; mem. AMA, Miss., S. Miss. med. socs., La., Miss. (pres. 1977), Noah Worcester dermatol. socs., Miss. Found. Med. Care, Am. Soc. Dermatol. Surgery, Am. Coll. Cryosurgery (founding mem., v.p. 1977), Internat. Soc. Tropical Dermatology, N.Y. Acad. Scis., Hattiesburg Area Hist. Soc., Omicron Delta Kappa, Phi Delta Epsilon. Author: Cutaneous Cryosurgery, Treatment of Non-malignant Lesions, 1976. Editor: Manual of Dermatologic Cryosurgery, 1975, 76. Contbr. chpt. to book, articles to profl. jours. Home: 302 4th Ave Hattiesburg MS 39401 Office: 6 Medical Blvd Hattiesburg MS 39401

LUBY, GEORGE DAVID, JR., assn. exec.; b. Dallas, Feb. 4, 1953; s. George David and Barbara (Brubaker) L.; B.S. in Bus. Adminstrn., U. Ark., 1975. Night mgr. Southland Corp., Dallas, 1975-76; salesman ServiceMaster Inc., Dallas, 1976-77; loan officer Credit Union City of Dallas, 1977-78; asso. dist. exec. Circle Ten-Western Star dist. Boy Scouts Am., Irving, Tex., 1978—. Mem. Nat. Eagle Scout Assn., Boy Scouts Am., Profl. Alliance Assn., Sigma Pi. Office: 1922 Anson St Dallas TX 75235

LUCAS, AUBREY KEITH, univ. pres.; b. State Line, Miss., July 12, 1934; s. Keith Caldwell and Audelle Margaret (Robertson) L.; B.S., U. So. Miss., 1955, M.A., 1956; Ph.D., Fla. State U., 1966; m. Ella Frances Ginn, Dec. 19, 1955; children—Margaret Frances, Keith Godbold (dec.), Martha Carol, Alan Douglas, Mark Christopher. Asst. dir. reading clinic U. So. Miss., 1955-56, dir. admissions, 1957-61, registrar, 1963-69, dean Grad. Sch., 1970-71; instr. Hinds Jr. Coll., Raymond, Miss., 1956-57; pres. Delta State Coll., Cleveland, Miss., 1971-75, U. So. Miss., Hattiesburg, 1975—; past state rep. Am. Assn. State Colls. and Univs.; mem. Miss. Gov.'s Com. on Libraries; Miss. rep. So. Regional Edn. Bd. Bd. dirs. United Way, chmn. Forrest-Lamar; bd. dirs. Pine Burr area Boy Scouts Am.; mem. Miss. Arts Commn., Miss. Com. for Humanities; past Miss. crusade chmn. Am. Cancer Soc. Mem. Newcomen Soc. N.Am., PTA, Hattiesburg C. of C. (dir.), Miss. Assn. Colls. (pres.), Miss. Forestry Assn., Omicron Delta Kappa, Phi Kappa Phi, Pi Gamma Mu, Pi Tau Chi, Kappa Delta Pi, Phi Delta Kappa, Kappa Pi, Sigma Phi Epsilon. Clubs: Red Red Rose, Hub City Kiwanis. Author: The Mississippi Legislature and Mississippi Public Higher Education, 1890-1960; contbg. author: A History of Mississippi, 1973. Address: Box 5001 So Sta U So Miss Hattiesburg MS 39401

LUCAS, EDGAR ARTHUR, anatomist; b. Franklin, Ind., Oct. 28, 1933; s. Isaac Sampson and Catherine Geneva (Helms) L.; B.A., Ball State U., Muncie, Ind., 1961, M.S., 1965; Ph.D., U. Calif., Los Angeles, 1972; m. Margaret Barbara Culkosky, Dec. 17, 1960; children—Barbara Carol, Marilyn Denise. Tchr., Griffith (Ind.) city schs., 1961-62; with N. Am. Rockwell Co., 1962-66; asso. prof. anatomy, co-dir. Sleep Clinic, U. Ark. for Med. Scis. Med. Sch., Little Rock, 1972—. Served with AUS, 1955-57. Pres. elders quorum Mormon Ch., Little Rock, 1972-75, high councilman, 1976. Home: 7101 Kingwood Rd Little Rock AR 72207 Office: Univ Ark Med Scis 4301 W Markham St Little Rock AR 72201

LUCAS, PAULINE KIRKLEY, nurse, hosp. ofcl.; b. Nacogodoches County, Tex., Dec. 13, 1924; d. Jesse A. and Ruby (Bailey) Kirkley; student Lamar Coll., 1965-66; m. Wilbern Lucas, Dec. 11, 1943; children—James Edward, Carroll Dean, Paula Dian. Staff lab. B.F. Goodrich Co., Port Neches, Tex., 1943-44; charge nurse medication Mid-Jefferson County Hosp., Nederland, Tex., 1965-72; staff Meml. Hosp., Lufkin, Tex., 1972—, supr. central supply, 1976—. Mem. Angelina County (Tex.) Nurse League (pres. 1977—, nurse of yr. 1978-79), Am. Heart Assn., Am. Cancer Assn. Democrat. Baptist. Address: Meml Hosp Box 1447 Lufkin TX 75901

LUCAS, RICHARD ALBERT, psychologist; b. Sioux City, Iowa, May 27, 1939; s. Albert Henry and Lillian Grace (Anderson) L.; student Dakota Wesleyan U., 1957-59; B.S., U. Minn., 1964; Ph.D., U. N.C. at Chapel Hill, 1972; m. Carol Lee Nogle, Feb. 26, 1961; children—Wendy Lee, Sean Richard. Staff psychologist Durham (N.C.) VA Hosp., 1972—; part-time vis. asst. prof. dept. psychology U. N.C. at Chapel Hill, 1972—; asst. clin. prof. div. med. psychology, dept. psychiatry Duke U. Med. Center, 1975; part-time pvt. practice, Chapel Hill, 1972—. Served with U.S. Army, 1959-62. Recipient Outstanding Young Educator award Tucson Jr. C. of C., 1967, Martin S. Wallach award U. N.C., 1971. Mem. Am., N.C. psychol. assns., Assn. Advancement Psychology, Assn. Humanistic Psychology, Phi Beta Kappa, Pi Kappa Delta. Contbr. articles to profl. jours. Home: 2421 Sedgefield Dr Chapel Hill NC 27514 Office: VA Hosp Fulton St and Erwin Rd Durham NC 27705

LUCCASEN, RAPHEAL ANDREW, JR., health center exec.; b. Baton Rouge, Feb. 22, 1948; s. Rapheal Andrew and Sarah Ernestine (Piper) L.; B.S., La. State U., 1970, M.S.W., 1972; m. Linda Mary Charlet, Mar. 14, 1970; children—Rapheal Andrew, Racheal Anne, Russell Abraham. Psychiat. social worker Hill Crest Hosp., Birmingham, Ala., 1972, dir. therapeutic program, 1972-73; asso. Psychiatry Assos., Birmingham, 1973-77; v.p. Birmingham Psychiat. Med. Service, 1977-79; dir. human services St. Vincent's Hosp., Birmingham, 1979—. NIMH fellow, 1970-72. Mem. Nat. Assn. Social Workers (planning com. Ala. chpt. 1972), Am. Acad. Psychotherapists, Acad. Cert. Social Workers, Ala. Soc. for Clin. Social Workers (dir. 1975-76), Southeastern Group Psychotherapy Soc. (state chmn. 1976-80), Nat. Register Clin. Social Workers, Nat. Registry Health Care Providers in Clin. Social Work, Am. Group Psychotherapy Assn., Internat. Assn. Group Psychotherapy, Am. Orthopsychiat. Assn., Internat. Karate Assn., U.S. Kyokushin Karate Assn., Dixie Youth Baseball Assn. Roman Catholic. Contbr. articles to profl. jours. Home: 531 Cliff Pl Homewood AL 35209 Office: St Vincent's Hosp 2701 9th Ct S Birmingham AL 35201

LUCIAN, JUSTIN, educator, counselor; b. Mpls., Jan. 20, 1925; s. Joseph Paul and Rose Anna (Pelletier) Belanger; B.S., St. Mary's Coll., Minn., 1947; M.A., DePaul U., Chgo., 1952; D. Humanities, St. Paul Coll., Philippines, 1974. Chmn. grad. dept. guidance counseling for counselor tng. De La Salle U., Manila, Philippines, 1958-74; prof. human devel. and learning Christian Bros. Coll., Memphis, also dir. counseling dept. student affairs, 1974—; mem., speaker Internat. Round Table for Advancement Counseling, Paris, 1972, U. Oslo, 1978. Grantee NSF, 1975-76, NSF-AAAS, 1977—. Mem. Philippine Guidance and Personnel Assn. (life) (founder), Am. Personnel and Guidance Assn., Am. Coll. Personnel Assn., Commn. Internat. Dimensions for Student Personnel Work. Joined Bros. Christian Schs., 1943. Author: School Counseling: Philippine Cases and Techniques, 1974; Systematic Desensitization: A Self-Guided Program for the Reduction of Test Anxiety, 1976; columnist Lakeland Boating. Address: 650 E Pkwy S Memphis TN 38104

LUCIER, JAMES ALFRED, advt. exec.; b. Grand Forks, N.D., Feb. 5, 1920; s. Alfred Joseph and Mildred Perry (Fahar) L.; B.A., U. Minn., 1946; postgrad. So. Meth. U., 1965; m. Catherine Belle Stiles, June 11, 1961; children—John, Jane, James Alfred. Sales exec. Ft. Smith (Ark.) Times, 1946-47; sales mgr. Sta. KRKN, Ft. Smith, 1947-48; dir. advt. Fayetteville (Ark.) Times, 1948-51; sales exec. San Antonio Express, 1952-53; mgr. Sunday mag. Dallas Times, 1953-65; dir. advt. and pub. relations Home Furniture Co., Dallas, 1965—; owner Lucier Assos. Advt., Dallas, 1965—. Unit chmn. United Way, 1965—; precinct chmn. Democratic Party, 1974—; mem. bd. Dem. Com. of Rep. Govt., 1974—; pres., bd. dirs. Dallas council USO. Served with inf., AUS, 1942-44, USAAF, 1944-45, USAF, 1951-52. Decorated Air medal with 2 oak leaf clusters. Mem. Retail Furniture Assn. Greater Dallas (pres. 1971-72, dir.), Retail Furniture Assn. S.W. (dir. 1977—), Dallas Advt. League (edn. com.), Dallas C. of C., Sigma Delta Chi, Theta Chi. Episcopalian (vestry 1976-79). Clubs: Exchange (pres. E.Dallas 1967, pres. Tex. dist. 1969-70, nat. dir. 1970-72, chmn. nat. edn. com. 1974-76, nat. fin. com. 1977-79), U. Minn. Alumni (past pres.), Vagabond, Dallas Magic (past pres.). Home: 6942 Meadow Lake Dallas TX 75214 Office: 3725 Blackburn St Dallas TX 75219

LUCIUS, HAROLD WADDINGTON, educator; b. Guyana, S. Am., Aug. 3, 1937; came to U.S., 1969, naturalized, 1976; s. Wycliffe Theophilus and Louisa Henrietta (France) L.; B.A., InterAm. U. of P.R., 1966, M.B.A., 1967; Ph.D., U. Wash., 1972; m. Elaine Thomas, Dec. 19, 1965; 1 son, Harcourt Waddington. Asst. prof. mktg. U. P.R., Mayaguez, 1972-74, U. W. Fla., Pensacola, 1974-77; asso. prof., chmn. dept. mktg., MBA program dir. Jackson (Miss.) State U., 1977—; cons. African Tng. Center, Morocco, 1976—. Bd. dirs. Thriftco Consumers Corp., Jackson, 1978—, Al-Akhbar Inst. of Sci. and Tech., Fla., 1975—. Edna Benson dissertation fellow U. Wash., 1972. Mem. Am. Mktg. Assn., So. Mktg. Assn., Caribbean Studies Assn., Pensacola Area C. of C., Phi Kappa Phi, Delta Sigma Pi. Episcopalian. Clubs: Masons, Ind. Order of Mechanics. Contbr. articles in field to profl. jours. Home: 6127 Woodhaven Dr Jackson MS 39206 Office: Jackson State Univ Dept Mktg Jackson MS 39217

LUCKEY, DIANE VIRGINIA MCKENNEY, accountant; b. Meriden, Conn., July 16, 1946; d. Warren Harold and Adriance Imogene (Coosey) McKenney; ed. public schs., various seminars; m. Richard Anthony Luckey, Feb. 10, 1977; stepchildren—Tina Marie, Therasa Michell, Tonya Marcel. Stenographer, U.S. Govt., 1964-65, claims devel. clk., 1965-67; asst. bookkeeper Guaranty Loan & Real Estate Co., West Memphis, Ark., 1967-71; computer specialist, supr. Kandell Constrn. Co., Tequesta, Fla., 1971-75; bookkeeper, office mgr. Universal Coach, Hollywood, Fla., 1975-76; office and fin. acctg. mgr. Hillsboro News Co., Tampa, Fla., 1977—. Notary public, Fla., 1974—. Mem. Am. Mgmt. Assn., Women in Constrn. Orgn., Women in Mgmt. Assn., Nat. Def. Transp. Assn. (sec. br. 1964-65), Am. Quarter Horse Assn., Am. Horse Show Assn., Fla. Quarterhorse Assn., Palomino Horse Breeders Am. Republican. Baptist. Clubs: Fla. Comancheros, Eastern Star. Home: 11713 1/2 N 14th St Tampa FL 33612 Office: 2102 N Sterling Tampa FL 33607

LUCKEY, GEORGE PAUL, ret. bus. exec., physicist; b. Ontario, Calif., Apr. 4, 1891; s. George W. A. and Bertha (Musson) L.; A.B., U. Nebr., 1910, M.A., 1912, D.Eng. (hon.), 1952; postgrad. U. Goettingen (Germany), 1912-14; m. Olive Lehmer, July 12, 1922; children—George William, Helen L. Staff, Mt. Wilson Solar Obs., Pasadena, Calif., 1915; Charles E. Brush fellow Nela Research Lab., Cleve., 1916; physicist Westinghouse Research Lab., East Pittsburgh, Pa., 1917-19-20; physicist, instrument and equipment sect. McCook Field, Dayton, Ohio, 1920-26, asst. chief equipment sect., 1926-27; with Hamilton Watch Co., Lancaster, Pa., 1927-54, head tachometer div., 1927-30, dir. research, asst. gen. supt., 1930-33, factory mgr., 1933-40, v.p. charge mfg., 1940-52, pres., chmn. bd., 1952-54, dir., 1947-54, ret., 1954; dir. Nuclear Research Chems., Orlando, Fla., 1960-67. Mem. adv. bd. Phila. Ordnance Dist., 1950-54. Served with AC, U.S. Army, 1918. Recipient certificate of Appreciation, Joint Chiefs of Staff, 1951. Mem. AAAS, Am. Ordnance Assn., Horological Inst. Am. (hon.), Am. Phys. Soc., Winter Park C. of C., Sigma Xi. Clubs: Orlando Country; Univ. (Winter Park, Fla.). Patentee in field. Home: 461 Virginia Dr Winter Park FL 32789

LUDDEN, LINDA SUE, therapist; b. Dallas, Aug. 17, 1950; d. Keene Fred and Inez Oleta (Baker) Ludden; B.S., E. Tex. State U., 1972, M.S., 1973, Ed.D., 1979. Asst. to dir. student devel. E. Tex. State U., Commerce, 1972-73; asst. dir. for testing orientation, sch. relations, 1973-74; tchr. guided studies Irving Ind. Sch. Dist., Tex., 1974-75; rep. wholesale apparel V.M. Internat., Dallas, 1975-77; clin. supervision Dallas Pastoral Counseling, 1976—; tchr. human devel. Dallas County Community Coll. Dist., 1978-79; sales rep. Upjohn Pharm. Co., 1979—; therapist Baker and Ludden Med. Clinic, Dallas, 1980—; asso. Kessler Hosp., Dallas, 1980—; adv. bd. prevention prescription drug abuse for women Charlton Meth. Hosp., Dallas, 1980—; asst. dir. Galaxy Center, Garland, Tex., 1980—. Mem. Dallas Baptist Coll. Operating Fund com., 1977. Active Girl Scouts Am., 1957-68. Pub. edn. grantee, 1977. Mem. Am., Tex. assns. marriage and family therapists, Am., Tex. personnel, guidance assns., Nat. Council in Family Relations, Am. Assn. Sex Educators, Counselors and Therapists (cert.), Alpha Phi, Gamma Sigma Sigma, Phi Delta Kappa, Kappa Delta Pi. Methodist. Clubs: E. Tex. State Guidance. Contbr. pamphlets, articles in field. Home: 1347 Michigan St Dallas TX 75216

LUDLUM, BOBBY RAY, electronic engr.; b. Whiteville, N.C., Mar. 9, 1942; s. John Lency and Ora Blanch (Reeves) L.; B.S. in Elec. Engring. with honors, N.C. State U., 1964; M.E.E., U. Fla., 1978; m. Sharlet Joy Young, July 26, 1969; children—Holly Denise, Robyn Maria. Electronic engr. Naval Coastal Systems Center, Panama City, Fla., 1964—. Recipient Sustained Superior Performance award Navy Dept., 1966, Outstanding Performance award, 1973, Navy award of merit for group achievement, 1975; registered profl. engr., Fla. Mem. IEEE, Aircraft Owners and Pilots Assn., Internat. Mooney Soc., Eta Kappa Nu, Phi Kappa Phi. Baptist (deacon). Patentee in field. Research and devel. high resolution sonar systems and mine counter measures systems. Home: 226 Pine Ridge Dr Panama City FL 32405 Office: Code 721 NCSL Panama City FL 32401

LUDOVICI, ELAINE MARIE, educator; b. New Castle, Pa., Dec. 30, 1951; d. Joseph Anthony and Anntoinetta (Mangini) L.; B.A., Clarion State Coll., 1972, M.A., 1974; postgrad. U. Miami, 1979, Fla. Internat. U., 1979. English/reading coordinator Clarion (Pa.) State Coll., 1973, instr. English, 1973-74; instr. English, Miami-Dade Community Coll., Miami, 1974-75, asst. prof. English, dir. writing lab. North Campus, 1975—; basic skills rep. Coll. Entrance Exam. Bd. and Ednl. Testing Service, 1978; grad. teaching asst. Clarion State Coll., 1973-74; mem. essential acad. skills project Fla. State Dept. Edn. Mem. Nat. Assn. Remedial/Devel. Studies in Post-Secondary Edn., Fla. Assn. Community Colls., Fla. Devel. Edn. Assn. (exec. bd. 1980-82). Home: 777 NW 155th Ln Miami FL 33169 Office: 11380 NW 27th Ave Miami FL 33167

LUDWIG, ALLEN CLARENCE, chem. engr.; b. San Antonio, Nov. 3, 1938; s. Frederick and Eleanora Johanna (Wolff) L.; B.S. in Chem. Engring., Tex. A. and M. U., 1960; m. Mary Jo Grothues, Nov. 26, 1960; children—Amy, Allen Clarence, Theresa, Elizabeth. Chem. engr. Monsanto Chem. Co., Texas City, Tex., 1960; with Southwest Research Inst., San Antonio, 1963—, sr. research engr., 1967—; cons. UN, AID. Adviser parish youth club Roman Catholic Ch., 1963-65, sec. men's club, 1965, chmn. credit com., 1970-77, mem. sch. bd., 1973-76, pres. parish council, 1977-80. Served with USAF, 19606-3. Registered profl. engr., Tex. Mem. Am. Def. Preparedness Assn., Tau Beta Pi, Phi Kappa Phi, Phi Eta Sigma, Phi Lambda Upsilon. Roman Catholic. Contbr. articles in field to profl. publs. Patentee. Home: 5914 Brenda St San Antonio TX 78240 Office: 8500 Culebra Rd San Antonio TX 78284

LUDWIG, ERNEST EARL, chem. engr.; b. Austin, Tex., Mar. 6, 1920; s. Ernest and Agnes (Doehler) L.; B.S. in Chem. Engring., U. Tex., 1941, M.S. in Chem. Engring., 1942; m. Sue Belle Williams, Dec. 3, 1944; children—Dennis Earl, William Ernest. Instr. in chemistry U. Tex., Austin, 1940-42; process engr. Dow Chem. Co., Freeport, Tex., 1942-45, asst. engring. mgr., 1946-52, process engring. mgr., 1952-60; gen. works mgr., project mgr. chem. div. Dart Industries, Los Angeles, 1960-61, Odessa, Tex., 1961-67; v.p. Copolymer Rubber & Chem. Corp., Baton Rouge, 1967-69; pres. Ludwig Cons. Engrs., Inc., Baton Rouge, 1969—; mem. Tex. Chem. Council, 1964-66; mem. advisory com. U. Tex. Coll. Engring., 1964-66. Bd. dirs. Broadway Theater League, Odessa, 1962-63, Odessa United Fund, 1962-66. Recipient Citizenship award Am. Legion, Austin, 1932; registered profl. engr., La., Tex., Okla., Ark., Miss., N.Mex., Calif.; certified cost engr. Fellow Am. Inst. Chem. Engrs. (chmn. Baton Rouge sect., dir. petrochem. div.); mem. Am. Chem. Soc., ASME, Soc. Plastics Engrs., Am. Assn. Cost Engrs., Am. Mgmt. Assn., Baton Rouge C. of C. Lutheran. Clubs: Rotary, Lions. Author: Applied Process Design for Chemical and Petrochemical Plants, 3 vols., 1964, rev. edits., 1977; Applied Project Management for Process Industries, 1974; contbr. articles to profl. jours. Home: 12495 E Millburn Ave Baton Rouge LA 70815 Office: 11741 Market Place Ave Baton Rouge LA 70816

LUDWIG, RAY W., educator; b. Rio, W.Va., June 10, 1941. A.B. in Secondary Edn., Shepherd Coll., Shepherdstown, W.Va., 1964; A.M. in Secondary Adminstrn., W.Va. U., Morgantown, 1966, M.A. in Guidance and Counseling, 1972. Tchr. math. Ohio County Schs., Wheeling, W.Va., 1964-67; tchr. math., asst. prin. Berkeley Springs (W.Va.) High Sch., 1967-68; math. specialist Region II Curriculum Improvement Center, Shepherdstown, 1968-69; dir. spl. projects, coordinator secondary edn. Hardy County Schs., Moorefield, W.Va., 1969-76, English tchr., 1976—. Mem. Nat. W.Va., Hardy County (pres. 1977-78) edn. assns., Assn. for Supervision and Curriculum Devel., Hardy County Tchrs. Assn. (v.p. 1977-78). Certified in secondary edn., secondary adminstrn., counseling and guidance, W.Va. Home: PO Box 550 Moorefield WV 26836 Office: Moorefield High Sch Moorefield WV 26836

LUDWIG, VERNON ADAM, indsl. engr.; b. Lowell, Ohio, Apr. 30, 1918; s. George and Madie Susanna (Wagner) L.; B.S. in Indsl. Engring., Ohio U., Athens, 1939; m. Juanita Faa Abicht, June 29, 1940; 1 son, Timothy V. Plant engr. Champion Internat., Inc., Orangeburg, S.C., 1956-57; gen. supt. Chesapeake Bay Bridge & Tunnel Dist., Norfolk, Va., 1957-64; owner-operator Vernon A. Ludwig Co., engring. contracting, Norfolk, 1964-65; spl. project engr. Champion Internat., Inc., S. Boston, Va., 1965-67; program mgr. Logistic Support Systems, U.S. Navy, Williamsburg, Va., 1967-69, project engr. design nuclear class surface ships, Newport News, Va., 1969-71, prof. engr. cons. constrn. program, Norfolk, 1971-75; cons. engr. mech. systems, material mgmt., material handling, Norfolk and Orlando, Fla., 1975—. Recipient Letter of Commendation, Navy Dept., 1968; registered profl. engr., Va., Fla., S.C. Mem. ASME, Soc. Naval Architects and Marine Engrs.; affiliate Nat. Soc. Profl. Engrs., Va., Fla. engring. socs., Fraternal Order Police. Lutheran. Club: Commodore Country. Home: 1122 Edwards Ln Orlando FL 32804 also 6220 Wailes Ave Norfolk VA 23502 Office: PO Box 7964 Orlando FL 32804 also PO Box 12001 Norfolk VA 23502

LUECKE, FRANK MARTIN GEORGE, JR., journalist; b. Mountain Grove, Mo., July 17, 1931; s. Frank Martin George and Mabel Clare (Bedingfield) L.; B.J., U. Mo., 1953; children—Leslie Ruth, Martin Wright. News editor, adman Purcell (Okla.) Register, 1955-56; pub. Grand Prairie (Tex.) Banner, 1956-57; owner, editor, pub. Cameron (Tex.) Herald, 1957—. Pres., Cameron Pub. Library Bd., 1966-67. Bd. dirs. Central Tex. Symphony Assn., 1965-67, pres., 1968-69; bd. dirs. Cultural Activities Center, Temple, Tex., Cameron Indsl. Found., St. Edward Hosp. Devel. Fund. Served to 1st lt. AUS, 1953-55. Recipient 1st prize editorials Okla. Press Assn., 1955, hon. mention editorials, 1956; Golden Pencil award 1970; Golden Dozen editorialist award Internat. Conf. Weekly Newspaper Editors, 1970. Mem. Cameron C. of C. (dir. bd.), Cameron Jr. C. of C. (dir. 1958-59), Nat. Newspaper Assn. (com. chmn. 1969-72, 77, 79-80, state chmn. Tex. 1974-80), Tex. Press Assn. (prizes 1958, 62, dir. 1964-65, 72-73, 75-78, sec., treas. 1968-69, co-chmn. legis. com. chmn. legis. com.), Dallas Press Club, Rotarian (pres. 1966-67). Clubs: Cameron Country; Woodland Country (Houston). Contbr. articles to mags. Home: 106 E 1st St Cameron TX 76520 Office: 108 E 1st St Cameron TX 76520

LUEDECKE, WILLIAM HENRY, engring. co. exec.; b. Pittsburg, Tex., Apr. 5, 1918; s. Henry Herman and Lula May (Abernathy) L.; B.S., U. Tex., 1940; m. Mary Anne Copeland, June 3, 1939; children—William Henry, John Copeland. Mech. engr. Columbian Gasoline Corp., Monroe, La., 1940-41; supr. ship bldg., mech. engr. USN, Orange, Tex., 1941-42; gen. supr. factory mgrs. N.Am. Aviation Co., Dallas, 1942-44; air conditoning engr. Westinghouse Elec. Corp., Dallas, 1944-46; mech. engr., charge Chrysler Airtemp. div. Chrysler Corp., Los Angeles, 1946-50; owner Luedecke Engring. Co., Austin, Tex., 1950—, also Luedecke Investment Co.; dir. City Nat. Bank, Austin, 1st Tex. Fin. Corp., Dallas; chmn. bd. Mut. Savs. Instn., Austin. Bd. dirs. Travis County Heart Fund, Austin YMCA. Named Man of Year, Tex. Barbed Wire Collectors Assn.; registered profl. engr., Tex. Mem. Am. Soc. Heating, Refrigerating and Air Conditioning Engrs. (dir., pres. Austin chpt.), Tex., Nat. socs. profl. engrs., C. of C., Econ. Devel. Council, Better Bus. Bur., Nat. Fedn. Ind. Bus. (nat. adv. council). Lutheran. Clubs: Westwood Country (treas., dir.), Rotary. Home: 3403 Foothills Pkwy Austin TX 78731 Office: 1007 W 34th St Austin TX 78705

LUEDEMAN, GERALD WARREN, radiologist; b. Kansas City, Mo., Jan. 17, 1941; s. Clarence Henry and Hazel (McClure) L.; A.B., Harvard U., 1962; M.D., George Washington U., 1966. Intern, Grady Meml. Hosp., Atlanta, 1966-67; resident in radiology Med. Coll. Va. Hosp., Richmond, 1970-73; radiologist Ventura County Gen. Hosp., Ventura, Calif., 1973-75; diagnostic radiologist Dr. Burns & Assos., P.A., Winter Haven, Fla., 1975—. Served to capt. M.C., AUS, 1967-69. Diplomate Am. Bd. Radiology, Am. Bd. Nuclear Medicine, Mem. Am. Coll. Radiology, Soc. Nuclear Medicine, Fla. Radiol. Soc., Am. Inst. Ultrasound in Medicine, Fla. Med. Assn., Polk County Med. Assn. Republican. Episcopalian. Clubs: Harvard of W. Coast of Fla., Masons. Home: 212 Lake Link Rd Winter Haven FL 33880 Office: Dr Burns & Assos P A 200 Ave F N E Winter Haven FL 33880

LUEDEMAN, JOEL KERRY, fin. systems co. exec.; b. Ft. Wayne, Ind., Sept. 19, 1946; s. Oscar H. and Hillis E. (Friedrich) L.; B.S., Ind. Inst. Tech., 1968; m. Elizabeth Ann Gandy, Dec. 28, 1974. Systems engr. Ind. & Mich. Electric Co., Ft. Wayne, 1968; programmer/analyst TRW Systems, Houston, 1969-75; instr. EDP, South Tex. Jr. Coll., Houston, 1970-75; prin., founder CDS Inc., Houston, 1972—, also dir.; mgr. EDP, Gulf Coast Waste Disposal Authority, 1975—. Pres. Middlebrook Community Assn. Republican. Lutheran. Home: 16430 Brookford St Houston TX 77059

LUEKEN, PATTY WATSON, dietitian; b. Fayetteville, Ark., Oct. 20, 1953; d. Lavon Verdon and Evelyn Lucille (Bates) Watson, B.S., U. Ark., 1975; postgrad. U. Ark., 1977—; m. Thomas Whitten Lueken, Jan. 27, 1979. Adminstrv. dietitian VA Hosp., North Little Rock, 1976-77; dir. dietetics Central Bapt. Hosp., Little Rock, 1977—. Mem. Central Ark. Health Systems Agy., Am. Legion Aux., Am. Dietetic Assn., Ark. Interagy. on Nutrition, Am. Soc. for Hosp. Food Service Adminstrs., Ark. Dietetic Assn. (treas. 1978—), Alpha Delta Pi. Baptist. Office: 12th and Marshall Sts Little Rock AR 72201

LUGAR, RICHARD GREEN, U.S. senator; b. Indpls., Apr. 4, 1932; s. Marvin Leroy and Bertha (Green) L.; B.A., Denison U., 1954; B.A. (Rhodes scholar), Oxford (Eng.) U., 1956, M.A., 1956; m. Charlene Smeltzer, Sept. 8, 1956; children—Mark, Robert, John, David. Vice pres., treas. Thomas L. Green & Co., Inc., Indpls., 1960-67; treas. Lugar Stock Farm, Inc., Indpls., 1960; mayor Indpls., 1968-75; vis. prof. polit. sci. Ind. Central U., 1975-76; U.S. senator from Ind., 1977—. Mem. Adv. Commn. Intergovtl. Relations, 1969-75, vice chmn., 1970-75. Mem. Indpls. Sch. Bd., 1964-67, v.p., 1965-66; trustee Ind. Central U., 1965-75, Indpls., Denison U. Mem. adv. com. Marion County Republican Com., 1966—; del., mem. resolutions com. Rep. Nat. Conv., 1968, 72. Served to lt. (j.g.) USNR, 1957-60. Mem. Nat. League Cities (pres. 1970-71), Blue Key, Phi Beta Kappa, Omicron Delta Kappa, Pi Delta Epsilon, Pi Sigma Alpha, Beta Theta Pi. Methodist. Rotarian (v.p. Indpls. 1967-68). Home: 7841 Old Dominion Dr McLean VA 22102 Office: US Senate Washington DC 20510

LUGINBYHL, ROBERT IVAN, elec. engr.; b. Stinnett, Tex., June 3, 1925; s. Oliver Wesley and Cleora Zell (Ingram) L.; B.E.E., Tex. Tech U., 1950; m. Irene Johnson, Sept. 9, 1950; children—Joyce Marie, Glynna Ruth, Kathie Sue, James Wesley. Distbn. engr. Southwestern Pub. Service Co., Borger, Tex., 1950-55; elec. engr. J. M. Huber Corp., Borger, 1955-60; design engr. Profl. Engring. Services, Inc., Amarillo, Tex., 1963-66; elec. engr. City of Amarillo, 1966-77, Bennett-Carder & Assos., Inc., Borger, 1977-78; project engr. Mason & Hanger-Silas Mason Co., Inc.; tchr. Amarillo Coll., 1960-63; owner, operator L Bar Ranch, Hutchinson County, Tex., 1955—. Served with USNR, 1943-46, to 2d lt. Signal Corps, AUS, 1949-53. Registered profl. engr., Tex. Mem. IEEE (sr. mem.), Tex. Soc. Profl. Engrs. (pres. Panhandle chpt. 1959). Baptist. Clubs: Kiwanis (pres. North Amarillo 1974-75), Toastmasters (Borger). Home: PO Box 779 Stinnett TX 79083 Office: PO 30020 Amarillo TX 79177

LUIGS, A. MELVIN, JR., rubber co. exec.; b. Paducah, Ky., Feb. 2, 1953; s. A. Melvin and Mae O. (Marrs) L.; B.S., Murray State U., 1976, M.B.A., 1979; m. Linda Kay Griffin, Aug. 30, 1975. Credit mgr. Plumley Rubber Co., Paris, Tenn., 1976, profit plan mgr., 1977, asst. to pres., 1978-79, treas., 1979—, sec. dir. subs. Advisor, Jr. Achievement, Paris, 1977-78, treas., 1979-80. Mem. Assn. M.B.A. Execs. Republican. Roman Catholic. Clubs: Elks, K.C. (sec. 1979). Address: 1188 N Market St Paris TN 38424

LUIGS, CHARLES RUSSELL, bus. exec.; b. Evansville, Ind., Apr. 4, 1933; s. Charles Anthony and Agnes (Russell) L.; student St. Edwards U., 1951-52; B.S., U. Tex., 1957; m. Mary M. McClaine, Sept. 7, 1957; children—Charles Edwin, James Russell, Carol Lynn, Susan Nadine, Michael Alan. With U.S. Industries, various locations, 1957-76, v.p., 1969, exec. v.p., 1971-74, pres., 1974-76, dir., 1971-76; pres., chief exec. officer, dir. Global Marine, Inc., 1977—. Mem. Nat. Soc. Profl. Engrs., Am. Inst. Mining Metall. and Petroleum Engrs., Internat. Assn. Drilling Contractors (dir. 1978). Home: 31 Willowron St Houston TX 77024 Office: 811 W 7th St Los Angeles CA 90017 also 7500 San Felipe Suite 1000 Houston TX 77063

LUIKART, WILLIAM MCCOLLAM, physician; b. Baton Rouge, Aug. 20, 1921; s. Carl Bryan and Helene Carmelite (Coons) L.; B.S., La. State U., 1943, M.D., 1945; m. Nancy Irene Bird, June 22, 1946; children—William M., Carl S., Nancy B., Helen I. Resident in internal medicine La. State U., 1948-51; practice medicine La. State U., 1954—; bd. dirs. Am. Heart Assn.; nat. adv. bd. Vols. Am.; mem. state adv. council La. High Blood Pressure Control Program. Served to lt. (j.g.) M.C., USNR. Diplomate Am. Bd. Internal Medicine. Fellow Am. Coll. Cardiology, Council Clin. Cardiology of Am. Heart Assn., Royal Soc. Health; mem. Am. Diabetes Assn., So. Med. Assn., La. Med. Soc. (chmn. com. hypertension), Cath. Physicians Guild, Sigma Chi. Republican. Roman Catholic. Contbr. articles to med. jours. Address: 4730 North Blvd Baton Rouge LA 70806

LUING, GARY ALAN, coll. dean; b. Collins, Iowa, Apr. 24, 1937; s. Dwight Orn and Marjorie Mae (Clemons) L.; B.S. cum laude, Stetson U., 1960; M.A., U. Ill., 1961; m. Sherry Lea Gates, Dec. 19, 1954. Auditor, Arthur Andersen & Co., Chgo., 1963; prof. Fla. Atlantic U., Boca Raton, 1965-70, dean Sch. Bus., 1970—; cons. U.S. Treasury; dir. Fla. Liquid Assets. Chmn. Palm Beach County Transp. Com., 1972-75. Served to 1st lt. U.S. Army, 1961-63. Recipient Distinguished Service award Fla. Accountants Assn., 1971. Mem. Am. Accounting Assn., Accounting Research Assn., Am. Inst. C.P.A.'s. Baptist. Editor Fla. C.P.A., 1974; contbr. articles to profl. jours. Home: 9550 NW 42 Ct Coral Springs FL 33065

LUIS, JUAN FRANCISCO, gov. V.I.; b. Viegues, P.R., July 10, 1940; ed. U. P.R.; m. Luz Maria Luis. Formerly tchr. public schs.; indsl. relations mgr. Litwin Corp.; acct. Burns Internat.; personnel mgr., controller Estate Carlton Hotel; adminstr. personnel office V.I. Dept. Health; V.I. Dist. Senator, 1972-74; lt. gov. V.I., 1975-78, gov., 1978—. Served in U.S. Army. Mem. Ind. Movement. Office: Office Gov Govt House Charlotte Amalie VI 00801*

LUKAS, GAZE ELMER, accountant; b. Austria, Hungary, Nov. 9, 1907; s. Victor and Theresa (Dinzenberger) L.; came to U.S., 1909, naturalized, 1920; B.S. in Accountancy, U. Ill., 1930, M.S., 1933, J.D., 1956; m. Frances Adelaide Lyman, Nov. 25, 1932; 1 son, Victor Thomas. Instr. U. Ill., Urbana, 1930-35, asst. prof., 1954-55, asso. prof., 1955-56, prof., 1956-69, prof. emeritus, 1969—; dir. fin. U.S. Farm Security Adminstrn., Washington, 1935-42; chief accountant UNRRA, Washington, 1945-46; chief of renegotiation Quartermaster Gen.'s Office, Fgn. Service, State Dept., Rome, New Delhi, 1947-54; partner Paul M. Green & Assos., Bus. Edn. Cons., Champaign, Ill., 1955-68; Elmer Fox vis. prof. accounting Wichita (Kans.) State U., 1970-71; vis. prof. accounting Fla. Tech. U., Orlando, 1968-70, Fla. Atlantic U., Boca Raton, 1971-72; comptroller Palm Beach Atlantic Coll., West Palm Beach, Fla., 1979—. Mem. County Audit Adv. Bd. of Ill., 1962-68, chmn., 1964-66, recipient pub. service award, 1968. Served to maj. AUS, 1942-45; ETO. Decorated Bronze Star. Recipient Meritorious Civilian Service award Q.M. Gen., 1947; C.P.A., Ill. Mem. Am. Inst. C.P.A.'s, Ill. C.P.A. Soc., Appraisers Assn. Am., Order of Coif, Beta Gamma Sigma, Beta Alpha Psi, Pi Kappa Phi, Phi Eta Sigma, Sigma Alpha Epsilon, Phi Delta Phi, Alpha Kappa Psi. Contbr. articles to profl. jours. Address: 719 Lori Dr #19-210 Palm Springs FL 33461

LUKAS, RICHARD CONRAD, educator; b. Lynn, Mass., Aug. 29, 1937; s. Frank John and Elizabeth (Pelagia) L.; B.A., Fla. State U., 1957, M.A., 1960, Ph.D., 1963; m. Marita Louise Rokicki, Aug. 7, 1966; children—Jennifer, Renee. Research cons. lineage book project U.S. Air Force, 1957-58; asst. prof. history Tenn. Tech. U., Cookeville, 1963-66, asso. prof., 1966-69, prof., 1969—. Served with U.S. Army, 1960-66. Recipient Outstanding Faculty award Tenn. Tech. U., 1974-75, 78-79; History Book award AIAA, 1970; grantee Eleanor Roosevelt Inst., Nat. Endowment for Humanities, Am. Philos. Soc., Kosciuszko Found. Mem. Am. Hist. Assn., Soc. Historians Am. Fgn. Relations, So. Conf. Slavic Studies, So. Hist. Assn., Polish Am. Hist. Assn., Polish Inst. Arts and Scis. Democrat. Roman Catholic. Author: Eagles East: The Army Air Forces and the Soviet Union, 1941-45, 1970; From Metternich to the Beatles, 1973; The Strange Allies: The United States and Poland, 1941-45, 1978. Home: Rt 3 Box 278 Cookeville TN 38501 Office: Dept History Tenn Tech Univ Cookeville TN 38501

LUKOWSKY, ROBERT OWEN, justice Supreme Ct. Ky.; b. Covington, Ky., Aug. 23, 1927; s. Robert Owen and Esther Agnes (Cole) L.; J.D., U. Cin., 1949; LL.D., Salmon P. Chase Coll. Law, No. Ky. U., 1978; m. Rosemary Domaschko, Dec. 30, 1969. Admitted to Ky. bar, 1949, practice in Covington, 1949-52, 55-62; judge pro tem Kenton County Ct., 1952-55; judge 3d div. 16th Jud. Circuit Ct. Ky., Covington, 1962-74; judge Ct. of Appeals of Ky., Frankfort, 1975; justice Supreme Ct. Ky., Frankfort, 1976—; adj. prof. law Salmon P. Chase Coll. Law, No. Ky. U., 1973—; mem. faculty Nat. Jud. Coll., 1970—; mem. Ky. Crime Commn., 1967-75, Joint Com. Revision Substantive Criminal Law Ky., 1969-73. Bd. dirs. Ky. Assn. Mental Health, 1962-65, No. Ky. Mental Health Assn., 1959-62, Boys Club Kenton County, 1965-68. Served with USAAF, 1946; lt. col. Res. Mem. Am., Fed. (pres. Cin. 1976—), Ky., Kenton County (v.p. 1962) bar assns., Judge Advocates Assn., Appellate Judges Conf., Alpha Psi Omega, Sigma Delta Psi, Phi Alpha Delta. Contbr. articles to publs. in field. Home: 228 W Orchard Rd Fort Mitchell KY 41011 Office: Capitol Bldg Frankfort KY 40601

LUMME, VANCE HAROLD, chem. co. exec.; b. Plymouth, Wis., July 18, 1952; s. Roman Julius and Inez Ruth L.; B.S. in Chem. Engring., Case-Western Reserve U., 1974; m. Dolores Montemayor, Aug. 27, 1977; 1 dau., Bridgett Anne. Process engr. Diamond Shamrock, Deer Park, Tex., 1974-76; dist. rep. Nalco Chem. Co., Houston, 1976—. Arts Council Jazz Music fellow, 1973. Mem. Am. Inst. Chem. Engrs., Internat. Trombone Assn. Republican. Roman Catholic. Club: Toastmasters of Beaumont. Home: 309 Bull Run League City TX 77573 Office: Box 87 Sugarland TX 77478

LUMSDEN, (MARY) ISABEL, educator; b. Nacoochee, Ga., May 6, 1915; d. Walter B. and Minnie (Turk) Lumsden; student Piedmont Coll., 1932-35; B.S., U. Ga., 1936, M.S. in Edn., 1941, postgrad., 1961-64; postgrad. Duke U., 1938; m. Clarence E. Couch, Mar. 8, 1975. With Habersham County Schs., Clarkesville, Ga., 1958-69, curriculum dir. schs., 1958-69; asso. prof. edn. North Ga. Coll., Dahlonga, 1969-72; part-time tchr. U. Ga., 1972-78; cons., 1972—. Mem. White County Bd. Edn., 1979—. Mem. Habersham County Bus. and Profl. Women's Club (charter, pres. 1968-69), Nat., Ga. edn. assns., Delta Kappa Gamma, Kappa Delta Pi. Presbyterian (elder 1971—). Home: Sautee GA 30571

LUNA, MARLENE EUFEMIA, nurse, educator; b. Simonton, Tex., Aug. 29, 1938; d. Jose M. and Petra (Morales) Saenz; student U. Houston, 1969-72, U. Tex., 1957; B.S., Tex. Woman's U., 1973, M.S. in Nursing, 1979; m. Richard Luna, Dec. 13, 1959; children—Randy Alan, Cindi Ann. Staff nurse Houston Meth. Hosp., 1962-63, Diagnostic Clinic of Houston, 1963-66; staff nurse Diagnostic Center Hosp., Houston, 1966-67, head nurse, 1970-72, supr. recovery rooms, 1972-75; instr. dept. nursing San Jacinto Coll., Pasadena, Tex., 1975—. Vol. Am. Heart Found., ARC. Mem. Assn. Operating Room Nurses, Assn. Critical Care Nurses, Tex. Jr. Coll. Tchrs. Assn. Roman Catholic. Clubs: Woman's of the Church, Altar Soc. Home: Route 1 Box 647 Rosharon TX 77583 Office: 332 8060 Spencer Hwy Pasadena TX 77505

LUNA, SAMUEL E., JR., architect; b. San Antonio, Nov. 27, 1940; s. Samuel E. and Pauline (Buentello) L.; diploma architecture Columbia Tech. Inst., Arlington, Va., 1965; B.Arch., U. Tex., Austin, 1977; m. Mary Kathryn Low, Apr. 16, 1962; children—Samuel E. III, James, Stephanie, Gregory. Archtl. designer Woodward & Lothrop Dept. Stores, Washington, 1965-66, William Metcalf & Assos., Washington, 1966-67; sr. archtl. designer Robert V. Buck & Assos., San Antonio, 1967; sr. research architect S.W. Research Inst., San Antonio, 1967—. Active Citizens Orgn. for Public Service, Northside Sch. Dist. PTA, Columbia Little League Assn. Served with USAF, 1959-64. Mem. AIA, Am. Inst. Engring. Technicians, Am. Soc. Engring. Technicians, Am. Inst. Bldg. Design, Tex. Soc. Architects, Producer's Council, Tex. Inst. Bldg. Design. Democrat. Roman Catholic. Club: K.C. Home: 407 Bertetti St San Antonio TX 78227 Office: 6220 Culebra Rd San Antonio TX 78284

LUND, EUGENE HAROLD, air force officer; b. Mpls., July 7, 1940; s. Harold A. and Esther (Ryberg) L.; B.A. in Econs., St. Olaf Coll., 1965; M.B.A., U. Utah, 1974; postgrad. in bus. adminstrn. George Washington U., 1974-76; student Squadron Officers Sch., 1972, Armed Forces Staff Coll., 1978-79; m. Flory Ann Reed, Dec. 19, 1970. Commd. 2d lt. U.S. Air Force, 1965, advanced through grades to maj., 1976; officer-in-charge Telecommunications Ops., 91st Bombardment Wing, Glasgow AFB, Mont., 1966-67, chief communications-electronics ops., 1967, chief tactical communications, 1967-68; chief communications-electronics div. 4257th Air Base Squadron, Glasgow AFB, 1968; asst. chief communications-electronics sect. 4220th Air Refueling Squadron, Ching Chuan Kang Air Base, Taiwan, 1969, chief communications electronics maintenance, 1969-70, chief communications electronics sect., 1970; chief of maintenance 2143rd communications Squadron, Zweibrucken Air Base, Germany, 1971-74; radio frequency engr. U.S. Air Force Frequency Mgmt. Office, Washington, 1975-78; asst. dir. Joint Interoperability Communications, comdr.-in-chief Atlantic Command, Norfolk, Va., 1979—; wing rep. Jr. Officers Council, 1966-68, unit rep., 1969-70; project officer newspaper awards program Am. Heritage Found., 1967; mil. project officer Valley County (Mont.) Devel. Council, 1968; escort Public Land Law Rev. Commn., 1968; mil. aide to Vice Pres. Mondale, Presdl. Inauguration, 1977; accident prevention counselor FAA, 1977-79; escort officer, command briefing officer for comdr.-in-chief Atlantic Command, 1979. Committeeman Mont. council Boy Scouts Am., 1967-68; scout master Taiwan dist., 1969-70; bd. dirs. Tidewater council 1979—; comdr. Group II, Mont. Wing, CAP, 1967-68, safety officer Nat. Capital Wing, 1976-77, chief of staff Nat. Capital Wing, 1977-78, acting wing comdr., 1977; participant actual and simulated rescue missions for ARC. Decorated Air medal; Vietnam Gallantry Cross with palm; named Outstanding Safety Officer of Year, CAP, 1976, 77, recipient Paul W. Turner safety award, 1976, Grover Loening award for meritorious performance, 1978, Paul E. Garber award Gil Robb Wilson award for disting. service, 1978. Mem. Air Force Assn., Am. Mgmt. Assn., Aircraft Owners and Pilots Assn., Gideons Internat., Norfolk Navy Flying Club, Nat. Assn. Flight Instrs., Armed Forces Communications Electronics Assn., Norfolk C. of C. (econ. affairs com. 1979—). Lutheran. Columnist, Glasgow (Mont.) Courier, 1968; contbr. to AFB newspapers. Home: 427 Powhatan St Naval Station Norfolk VA 23511 Office: Hdqrs Atlantic Command/JO55 Norfolk VA 23511

LUND, FREDERICK HENRY, aerospace engr.; b. Seattle, June 2, 1929; s. Henry George and Minnie (Wilbern) L.; B.S. in Elec. Engring., U. Wash., 1951; postgrad. U. Calif., Los Angeles, 1954-56, 57-59; M.S. in Aeros. and Astronautics (USN Bur. Aeros. Armament Engring. scholar), Mass. Inst. Tech., 1957; m. Joyce Pauline Mon Pleasure, Sept. 8, 1950; children—Frederick Bradley, Christopher Michael, Peter Andrew, Andrea Leslie. With Naval Missile Center, Point Mugu, Calif., 1951-65; with Stanford Research Inst., Menlo Park, Calif., 1965-69; aerospace engr. Martin Marietta Aerospace Co., Orlando, Fla., 1969—. Com. chmn. Ventura (Calif.) Area council Boy Scouts Am., from 1960, asst. dist. commr. Stanford (Calif.) Area councils, until 1969, instnl. rep. Central Fla. council, 1972-74. Served to 1st lt. C.E., AUS, 1951-53; Germany. Registered profl. engr., Fla. Mem. IEEE (sect. chmn. 1962), Aerospace, Electronic Systems Soc. (chpt. chmn. 1972), Mil. Ops. Research Soc. (dir. 1962-66), Assn. Old Crowe (club sec. 1973), Adelphi (sub-chpt. pres. 1948-51), Sigma Xi. Clubs: Kiwanis, Wesley. Contbr. articles to profl. publs. Home: 610 S Lake Sybelia Dr Maitland FL 32751 Office: PO Box 5837 Orlando FL 32805

LUNDBERG, GUSTAVE HAROLD, mathematician, educator; b. Fremont, Nebr., Sept. 5 1901; s. Gustave Emil and Clara (Lindquist) L.; B.S., Midland Coll., 1924; M.A., Colo. State Coll., 1937, Vanderbilt U., 1942; Ph.D. George Peabody Coll., 1951; m. Hazel Alice Glenny, Oct. 30 1939. Faculty, Dana Coll., 1924-28; tchr. Consol. High Sch., Crowley, Colo., 1929-37, Allen Acad., Bryan, Tex., 1938-40; instr. Vanderbilt U., Nashville, 1942-45, asst. prof., 1945-53, asso. prof., 1953-56, prof. applied math., 1956-67, prof. emeritus, 1967—; prof. math. Austin Peay State U., 1967-72; faculty participant Boeing Airplane Co., summers 1955-56; research participant Oak Ridge Nat. Lab., summer 1957; faculty George Peabody Coll., summers 1961-62. Mem. Am. Math. Assn., Am. Math. Soc., AAAS, Engring. Assn. Nashville, Am. Soc. Engring. Edn., Tenn. Acad. Sci. (pres. 1969), Sigma Xi, Phi Delta Kappa. Editor Jour. Tenn. Acad. Sci., 1963-66; contbr. articles to profl. jours. Home: 2001 21st Av S Nashville TN 37212

LUNDBLADE, HOBERT PHILIP, dentist; b. Sandstone, Minn., Oct. 12, 1929; s. Joseph M. and Hilda C. (Nordgren) L.; B.S., U. Minn., 1952, D.D.S., 1954, M.S. in Dentistry, 1955; m. Evelyn Eleanore Parvey, Sept. 12, 1953; children—Deborah Diane, Gregory Scott. Practice dentistry, St. Paul, 1954-55; teaching asst., clin. instr. U. Minn., Mpls., 1954-55; practice endodontics, San Antonio, 1958—; instr. dental assisting San Antonio Coll., 1961-68; sec., dir. Beverage Cons.'s Am. Inc. Alderman, mayor City of Castle Hills (Tex.), 1961—; chmn. Joint Cities Land Reclamation and Beautification Bd.; mem. emergency med. service adv. com. San Antonio, 1977—. Served to capt. Dental Corps, AUS, 1955-58. Fellow Internat., Am. colls. dentists; mem. ADA, Tex., San Antonio Dist. (dir. 1967-75, pres. 1973-74) dental socs., Am. Assn. Endodontists, S.W. Soc. Endodontists, Bexar County Council Mayors, Alamo Area Council Govts., Omicron Kappa Upsilon. Club: Rotary. Research with isotopes on root canal sealers. Home: 503 Squires Row San Antonio TX 78213 Office: 1019 Shook Ave San Antonio TX 78212

LUNDE, ALFRED N , aerospace engr.; b. Bergen, Norway, Nov. 19, 1942; s. Nils L. and Borghild (Servoll) L.; came to U.S., 1957, naturalized, 1965; B.S. in Aerospace Engring., U. Tex., 1966; m. Anne de Mesquita, June 4, 1966. Aerospace engr. Johnson Space Center, NASA, Houston, 1966— Recipient Superior Achievement award NASA, 1970; Presdl. medal of Freedom for Apollo 13, 1970. Mem. Am. Inst. Aeros. and Astronautics, Aviation/Space Writers Assn., Nat. Space Inst., Os Aeroklubb, Norwegian-Am. C. of C. Author: Fottrinn Paa Maanen, 1974; contbg. author: Apollo-Soyuz Test Project, Summary Science Report, Vol. I: Astronomy, Earth Atmosphere and Gravity Field, Life Sciences and Materials Processing, 1977; also space column in Bergens Tidende, other newspapers in Norway. Home: 15807 Heatherdale Dr Houston TX 77059 Office: Johnson Space Center Houston TX 77058

LUNDSTROM, DAVID BLOM, indsl. engr.; b. Detroit, Apr. 26, 1928; s. Arthur John and Esther Catherine (Blom) L.; A.A., Lee Coll., 1948; m. Katherine Louise Sweezy, Feb. 24, 1951; children—Kent Laverne, Catherine Suzanne. Plant indsl. engr. J.P. Stevens Co., Seneca, S.C., 1952-65; chief indsl. engr. Riegel Textile Corp., LaFrance, S.C., 1965-57; asst. mgr. indsl. engring. Kendall Co., Pelzer, S.C., 1967-73, mgr. indsl engring., 1973-75, divisional indsl. engr., Charlotte, N.C., 1975-78. mgr. indsl. engring. Pelzer, S.C., 1978—; vice-chmn. Tri-City Med. Services, Pelzer, S.C., 1972-73; mem. presidents adv. council Lee Coll., Cleveland, Tenn., 1974—. Served with USN, 1948-52. Mem. Am. Inst. of Indsl. Engrs. (Named Indsl. Engr. of Year 1972, dir. 1971-72, chpt. pres. 1970-71). Mem. Ch. of God. Club: Lions (pres. 1972-73). Home: Route 1 Box 311 Greer SC 29651 Office: Kendall Co PO Box 396 Pelzer SC 29669

LUNDY, RAY OLVA, physician; b. Rosharon, Tex., Jan. 21, 1941; s. Seria Leon and Hallie (Keys) L.; B.S., Morehouse Coll., 1963; M.D., Meharry Med. Coll., 1967; m. Emma Jean Thibodeaux, May 24, 1976. Intern, Pontiac Gen. Hosp., Pontiac, Mich., 1967-68, med. resident, 1968-71; fellow in hematology U. of Mich., Ann Arbor, 1971-73; commd. maj., U.S. Army, 1973, advanced through grades to lt. col., 1976; staff hematologist 97th Gen. Hosp., Frankfurt, W. Ger., 1973-75; chief hematology-oncology Tripler Army Med. Center, Honolulu, 1976-79; asst. chief hematology Brooke Army Med. Center, Ft. Sam Houston, Tex., 1979—; adj. med. staff Queen's Med. Center, Honolulu, 1976-79. Hosp. cancer coordinator Am. Cancer Soc., Honolulu, 1976-79. Diplomate Am. Bd. Internal Medicine, Am. Bd. Hematology. Mem. ACP, Am. Soc. Internal Medicine, Am. Cancer Soc., Alpha Omega Alpha, Alpha Phi Alpha. Club: Masons. Office: PO Box 565 Brook Army Med Center Fort Sam Houston TX 78234

LUNN, WALLACE EDWARD, JR., boiler supply co. exec.; b. Nashville, Nov. 12, 1949; s. Wallace Edward and Gladys Elizabeth (Hunter) L.; B.A. in Music, Baylor U., 1972; m. Saralu Thompson, Dec. 29, 1970; children—Leigh Marie, Wallace Edward III. Corp. sec. Boiler Supply Co., Inc., Nashville, 1971-78, pres., 1978—. Bd. dirs. Tenn. chpt. Cystic Fibrosis, 1976—, v.p. Nashville branch, 1976-78; v.p. Nashville Booster Club; dir. Phi Mu Alpha Sinfonia, 1969-72; deacon Belmont Heights Bapt. Ch. Mem. ASHRAE (v.p. Nashville chpt.), Nashville Area C. of C., Tenn. Bus. Men's Assn. Democrat. Baptist. Clubs: Nashville City, Kiwanis (bd. dirs. Nashville club 1976-78, 1st v.p. 1980-81). Contbg. composer Good News, 1968; co-composer Happening Now, 1970. Home: 518 Shenandoah Dr Brentwood TN 37027 Office: 490 Craighead St Nashville TN 37204

LUNNEY, GERALD HUGH, educator; b. St. Paul, May 28, 1935; s. Edward Damien and Edna Marguerite (Pepin) L.; B.A., Coll. St. Thomas, St. Paul, 1957, M.Ed., 1960; Ph.D., U. Minn., 1968; m. Carol Ann Muckenhirn, Aug. 19, 1966; children—Michael, Colleen, Peter. Pub. sch. tchr., Minn., 1958-62; mem. faculty, U. Minn., 1962-66, U. Mass., 1966-68, C.W. Post Center of L.I. U., 1969-72; dir. instl. research Centre Coll., Danville, Ky., 1972-74; dir. research Council of Ind. Ky. Colls. and Univs., 1975—; mem. adj. faculty Coll. Edn. U. Ky., 1978—; research asso. Ednl. Research Council Am., Cleve., 1968-69. Mem. St. Peter and Paul Parish Council, Danville, 1978.

Served with AUS, 1957. Mem. Am. Ednl. Research Assn., Nat. Council Measurement in Edn., Am. Psychol. Assn., Assn. Instl. Research, Am. Assn. Higher Edn., Nat. Assn. Ind. Colls. and Univs. (research adv. council 1977—, state-nat. info. network adv. com. 1978—), Kappa Delta Pi, Phi Delta Kappa. Contbr. articles to profl. jours. Home: 2036 Old Lexington Rd Danville KY 40422 Office: Box 668 Danville KY 40422

LUNNON, BETTY SHEEHAN (MRS. JAMES LUNNON), librarian; b. Montgomery, Ala., May 29, 1908; d. Merrill Ashurst and Martha (Guice) Sheehan; student U. Ala., 1928, 30, 32-34; A.B., George Washington U., 1938; M.A., Appalachian State Tchrs. Coll., 1959; m. David White, Nov. 27, 1927 (div. 1936); m. 2d, James Lunnon, May 13, 1939 (dec. Nov. 1954); 1 dau., Penelope Anne Lunnon Fleeger. Tchr., librarian Hayneville (Ala.) Pub. Sch., 1927-29, Seale (Ala.) Pub. Sch., 1929-31, Dadeville (Ala.) Pub. Sch., 1931-32; case worker Ala. Dept. Pub. Welfare, Fed. Emergency Relief Adminstrn., 1933-35; statis. cataloger U.S. Govt., 1937-38; librarian Miami Edison Sr. High Sch., 1938-42, Fairlawn Elementary Sch., 1952-54; supr. Dade County Sch. Libraries, Miami, 1954-68; supr. libraries Dept. Edn., Pago Pago, Am. Samoa, 1968-73; librarian Cushman Sch., Miami, Fla., 1974—; asst. prof. U. Miami, summer 1960, evening sch., 1961, 63-66; prof. summer workshop Drexel Inst., 1965; library com. cons. Field Enterprises Ednl. Corp. Gray lady ARC, 1949-52; bd. dirs. Fla. Hearing and Speech Center, 1962-63. Mem. AAUW (br. v.p. 1950-51), DAR, Nat., Fla. edn. assns., Am. (nat. chmn. sch. library suprs. 1966-67), Fla. (pres. 1961-62) library assns., Dade County Sch. Library Assn. (pres. 1953), Am. (dir. southeastern states 1962-64, chmn. suprs. sect. 1966-67, dir. 1962-64), Fla. (pres. 1956) assns. sch. librarians, Kappa Delta Pi, Delta Kappa Gamma. Club: Quota (lt. gov. 27th dist.). Author: Jacarezinho Vadico, 1946; Two Shoes, 1951; contbr. articles to profl. jours. Home: 1002 Granada Blvd Coral Gables FL 33134

LUNSFORD, DAMON WAYNE, mcpl. ofcl.; b. Columbus, Ga., Dec. 4, 1942; s. William Damon and Ouida Mae (Copeland) L.; B.S. in Bus. Adminstrn., U. Ala., 1966; m. Vera Patkovic, Nov. 16, 1979. Indsl. engr. Burlington Industries, Charlotte, N.C., 1970-72; dir. mgmt. engring. South Miami Hosp., 1972-73; cons. Arthur Young & Co., Jacksonville, Fla., 1973-75; sr. mgmt. analyst City of Miami, 1975-77, asst. budget dir., 1977-79; asst. dir. Miami Beach (Fla.) Conv. Center, 1979—; contract cons. City of Miami Beach, 1977. Served to capt., USAF, 1966-70. Decorated AF Commendation medal. Sr. mem. Am. Inst. Indsl. Engrs. Democrat. Baptist. Home: 2965 N Bay Rd Miami Beach FL 33140 Office: 1901 Convention Center Dr Miami Beach FL 33139

LUPIN, E. RALPH, physician; b. New Orleans, Apr. 1, 1931; s. Albert and Yetta (Linnick) L.; B.S., Loyola of S., 1952; M.D., La. State U., 1956; m. Freda Merlin, Mar. 19, 1951; 1 son, Jay. Intern, Tulane U.; resident in obstetrics-gynecology Touro Infirmary, New Orleans, 1957-58, 60-62; individual practice medicine, specializing in obstetrics-gynecology, Gretna, La., 1962—; med. dir. Home Health Service, New Orleans, 1966; pres., chmn. bd. Unihealth Services Corp., Gretna, 1972—. Bd. dirs. New Orleans chpt. ARC, 1967—; chief dep. coroner City of New Orleans, 1974—; trustee La. State Mus., 1977—; bd. dirs. French Market Corp., 1976. Served with USAF, 1958-60. Mem. AMA, Am. Coll. Obstetrics-Gynecology, Nat. League Nursing. Democrat. Jewish. Clubs: Masons, Rotary. Home: 1021 Chartres St New Orleans LA 70116 Office: 515 Westbank St Gretna LA 70053

LUPINE, ELMER ALAN ROY, civil engr.; b. Pasadena, Calif., Nov. 19, 1908; s. Joseph Edward and Philipa Anne (Caracaus) L.; B.S., U. Ala., 1931; C.E., Roosevelt Grad. Coll., Chgo., 1944; postgrad. Columbia U., 1936-38; m. Mary Mac Smith, Aug. 2, 1955. Civil engr. Ala. State Hwy. Dept., Tuscaloosa, 1931-32, Carl B. Call, Architect, N.Y.C., 1933-34, Office of the Borough Engr., N.Y.C., 1934-39, mem. staff of Dept. Engr., San Juan, P.R., 1939-40; civil engr. design div. Dept. Navy, Atlantic Div. Naval Facilities Engring. Command, 1940-60, facilities mgmt., 1961-69, facilities planning, 1969-72; prin. E. A. Lupine & Assos., cons. engrs., Norfolk, Va., 1972—. Registered profl. engr., Va. Fellow ASCE (various coms.). Club: Norfolk Boat. Home: 212 86th St Virginia Beach VA 23451 Office: 218 W Bute St Norfolk VA 23510

LUPO, ROBERT MAXCY, JR., indsl. engr.; b. Hendersonville, N.C., Nov. 17, 1928; s. Robert Maxcy and Dessie (Dixon) L.; B. Indsl. Engring., Ga. Inst. Tech., 1949; m. Elizabeth G. Minnich, Jan. 30, 1970; children by previous marriage—Douglas Robert, Carol Lynne; stepchildren—John L. Kaufmann, Paul M. Kaufmann, Elizabeth K. Kaufmann. Engr., So. Bell Tel. & Tel. Co., Atlanta, 1949-63; with Cable and Spl. Power, Facility Engring. Directorate, NASA, Kennedy Space Center, Fla., 1963—. Served with USNR, 1952-54. Registered profl. engr., Ga., Ala., Fla., S.C. Mem. Fla. Engring. Soc., John Young Mus. and Planetarium, Titusville Rifle and Pistol Club, Nat. Rifle Assn., Nat. Police and Fire Fighters Assn., Nat. Wildlife Fedn., Audubon Founders Club, Nat. Eagle Scout Assn., Am. Inst. Indsl. Engrs., Air Force Communication Electronics Assn., Am. Security Council, Am. Fedn. Govt. Employees, Ga. Tech. Nat. Alumni Assn., Sigma Chi. Republican. Methodist. Clubs: Cape Kennedy Ga. Tech., Masons, Yellow Jacket. Home: PO Box 731 Titusville FL 32780 Office: Kennedy Space Center FL 32899

LUPTON, FREDERICK WILLIAM, II, elec. and mech. engr.; b. Chattanooga, July 29, 1932; s. Thomas Allen and Louise (Bass) L.; B.S. in Elec. Engring., Mass. Inst. Tech., 1955, B.S. in Mech. Engring., 1956; M.Div., Columbia U., 1959; m. Jane Adair Nicholson, Sept. 28, 1963; children—Frederick William III, Laura Louise. Asst. mech. engr. Pioneer Service & Engring. Co., Chgo., 1959-63; asst. co. engr. Dixie Yarn, Inc., Chattanooga, 1963-69; v.p., chief elec. engr. George S. Campbell & Assos., Chattanooga, 1969-75; v.p., co-owner Bell & Lupton Engring., Chattonooga, 1976-77; pres. Lupton Engring. Assos., Inc., Chattanooga, 1977—; v.p. Stone Ft. Land Co.; mem. faculty U. Tenn. eve. sch., 1965, 66; ordained to ministry United Presbyn. Ch. U.S., 1959; asst. pastor First Presbyn. Ch., Chattanooga, 1959-74, Central Presbyn. Ch., Chattanooga, 1974—. Pres. Senior Neighbors, Chattanooga, 1965; pres. bd. YMCA Ocoee Camp, 1974; mem. bd. CONTACT Ministry; mem. Hamilton County Rescue Squad; bd. dirs. Chattanooga United Fund. Rockefeller scholar, 1956. Mem. IEEE, Illuminating Engring. Soc., Soc. Am. Value Engrs., Nat. Fire Protection Assn., Am. Soc. Plumbing Engrs. Clubs: Chattanooga Engrs. (pres. 1978), Civitan. Home: 2562 Crestwood Dr Chattanooga TN 37405 Office: 607 N Market St Chattanooga TN 37405

LUPTON, MARY HOSMER (MRS. THOMAS GEORGE LUPTON), owner rare book search service; b. Olympia, Wash., Jan. 2, 1914; d. Kenneth Winthrop and Mary Louise (Wheeler) Hosmer; student Gunston Hall Jr. Coll., 1932-33; B.S. in Edn., U. Va., 1940; m. Keith Brahe Wiley, Oct. 12, 1940 (dec. Apr. 1955); children—Sarah Hosmer Wiley Guise, Victoria Brahe Wiley; m. 2d, Thomas George Lupton, Nov. 27, 1965; 1 stepson, Andrew Henshaw. Partner Wakefield Press, Earlysville, Va., 1940-55; owner, operator Wakefield Forest Bookshop, Earlysville, 1955-65, Forest Bookshop, Charlottesville, 1965—, Wakefield Forest Tree Farm, 1955—. Corr. sec. Charlottesville-Albemarle Civic League, 1963-64; sec. Instructive Vis. Nurses Assn., Charlottesville, 1961-62; chmn. pub. info. Charlottesville chpt. Va. Mus. Fine Arts, 1970-77; mem. writers' adv. panel Va. Center for Creative Arts, 1973-75, chmn. pub. info., 1976-77; asst. state historian Va., 1979—; mem. Albemarle County Forestry Com., 1961-62. Mem. AAUW, DAR, New Eng. Hist. Geneal. Soc., Va., Albemarle County hist. socs., LWV, Soc. Mayflower Descs., Am. Soc. Psychical Research, Brit. Soc. Psychical Research, So. Regional Council, Word Guild, Chi Omega. Mem. Soc. of Friends. Address: PO Box 5206 Charlottesville VA 22905

LUQUIRE, WILSON, librarian; b. Greenwood, S.C., July 28, 1942; B.A. in Ch. Music, Furman U., 1963, B.Mus. in Organ, 1963; M.Mus., Ind. U., 1968, M.L.S., 1970, D.Mus., 1973, Ph.D. in Library and Info. Sci., 1976. Organist, dir. music programs Tabernacle Presbyn. Ch., Indpls., 1967-77; librarian Ind. U. Libraries, 1969-77; acad. library mgmt. intern Council on Library Resources, Vanderbilt U. Library, Nashville, 1976-77; asso. dir. library services Joyner Library, asso. prof. E. Carolina U., Greenville, 1977—. Served with U.S. Army, 1963-65. Mem. ALA, N.C. Library Assn., Am. Assn. Univ. Adminstrs., Southeastern Library Assn., Ind. U. Library Assn., Ohio Group Tech. Services Librarians, Midwest Acad. Librarians Conf., Tenn. Library Assn., Am. Guild Organists, Fine Arts Soc. Indpls. Office: Joyner Library East Carolina U Greenville NC 27834

LUSK, GLENNA RAE KNIGHT (MRS. EDWIN BRUCE LUSK), librarian; b. Franklinton, La., Aug. 16, 1935; d. Otis Harvey and Lou Zelle (Bahm) Knight; B.S., La. State U., 1956, M.S., 1963; m. John Earle Uhler, Jr., May 26, 1956; children—Anne Knight, Camille Allana; m. 2d, Edwin Bruce Lusk, Nov. 28, 1970. Asst. librarian Iberville Parish Library, Plaquemine, La., 1956-57, 1962-68; tchr. Iberville Parish Pub. Schs., Plaquemine, 1957-59, Plaquemines Parish Pub. Schs., Buras, La., 1959-61; dir. Iberville Parish Library, Carriage House Mus., Plaquemine, 1969—; mem. La. State Bd. Library Examiners, 1979—. Mem. Iberville Parish Econ. Devel. Council, Plaquemine, 1970-71; sec. Iberville Parish Bicentennial Commn., 1973—; mem. La. Bicentennial Commn., 1974. Named Outstanding Young Woman Plaquemine, La. Jr. C. of C., 1970. Mem. La. (sect. chmn. 1967-68), Riverland (sec. 1973-74) libraries assns., Capital Area Libraries (chmn. com. 1972-74). Democrat. Episcopalian. Author: (with John E. Uhler, Jr.) Cajun Country Cookin', 1966; Rochester Clarke Bibliography of Louisiana Cookery, 1966; Royal Recipes from the Cajun Country, 1969; Iberville Parish, 1970. Home: 206 Pecan Tree Ln Plaquemine LA 70764 Office: 712 Eden St Plaquemine LA 70764

LUSKY, MALVERN DAVID, accountant, mgmt./fin. cons.; b. San Antonio, Oct. 27, 1947; s. Herman A. and Louise Adelle (Pincus) L.; B.J., U. Tex., Austin, 1970; postgrad. U. Houston, 1973-74; m. Judy Kaplan, Dec. 21, 1969; 1 dau., Lauren Jennifer. Internal auditor Sakowitz, Inc., Houston, 1975-76. ops. mgr. nat. mail order div., 1976-77; founder, owner Lusky Assos., Houston, 1976—; auditor United Fund of Houston and Harris County, Houston, 1977-78; audit supr. Am. Savs. & Loan Assn., Houston, 1978-79; mgmt. cons. to many bus., profl. orgns., 1976—; treas. A & W Delivery Service, Inc., Jalsco Corp. Del., 13th Senatorial Dist. Democratic Conv., 1974, 76, State Dem. Conv., 1976; treas. Harris County Dems., 1976-78, mem. Harris County Dem. Exec. Com., 1976—, active mem. election coms. several polit. candidates, 1974—; bd. dirs. Northbrook Homeowners Assn., 1975-77; mem. City of Houston Transp. Adv. Group, 1977—. C.P.A. Mem. Inst. Internal Auditors, Am. Inst. C.P.A.'s, Tex. State Soc. C.P.A.'s. Jewish. Home: 6107 Hummingbird St Houston TX 77096 Office: Malvern D Lusky CPA Suite 508 3100 Richmond Ave Houston TX 77098

LUSSKY, WARREN ALFRED, librarian; b. Chgo., Apr. 16, 1919; s. Arthur W. and Alma (Proegler) L.; B.A., U. Colo., 1946; M.A., U. Denver, 1948; student U. Ill., 1941-42;; m. Mildred Joann Island, June 12, 1948. Asst. librarian Pacific Luth. Coll., Parkland, Wash., 1948-49; librarian Hopkins Transp. Library, Stanford, 1950, Rocky Mountain Coll., Billings, Mont., 1950-55; head librarian Nebr. Wesleyan U., Lincoln, 1955-56; dir. library, asso. prof. Tex. Luth. Coll., Sequin, 1956—; mem. accrediting team Tex. Edn. Agy., U. Corpus Christi (Tex.), 1961. Mem. Am., Tex. (dist. vice chmn. 1965, chmn. 1966), S.W. library assns., Council Research and Acad. Libraries (dir. 1968—, pres. 1976-78), prin. contbr. to design new Tex. Luth. Coll. Library; research and publs. on design and functions coll. library bldgs. Home: 357 Irvington Dr San Antonio TX 78209 Office: Tex Luth Coll Library Seguin TX 78155

LUSTECK, JOSEPH ANTON, JR., real estate exec.; b. Bath., N.Y., Aug. 5, 1942; s. Joseph A. and Mary Frances (Smart) L.; B.S., U. Ariz., 1964, M.S., 1966, M. Pub. Adminstrn., 1967; m. Lloyd-Elizabeth Deddens, June 5, 1965; children—Jay, Robbie, Christy. Prin. planner Pima County (Ariz.) Planning Dept., Tucson, 1965-67; asst. planning dir. Jackson (Miss.) City Planning Bd., 1967-72; v.p. Wortman & Mann, Inc., Jackson, 1972-75, exec. v.p., 1975-77, pres., 1977-80, also dir.; pres. Joseph A. Lusteck & Assos., Inc., 198—. Mem. Am. Inst. Cert. Planners (pres. Gulf S.E. chpt. 1970), Am. Planning Assn., Am. Soc. Cons. Planners, Am. Soc. Real Estate Counselors, Jackson C. of C. Republican. Roman Catholic. Clubs: Country (Jackson); Univ., Optimists (pres. Capitol club 1976-77). Contbr. articles in field to profl. jours. Home: 125 Hillcroft Pl Jackson MS 39211 Office: 656 N State St Jackson MS 39205

LUSTER, RONNIE LEE, mfr.'s rep. co. exec.; b. Kingsport, Tenn., Nov. 19, 1947; s. Lee George and Hazel L.; B.S., East Tenn. State U., 1973; With Young's Supply Co., Boone & Lamont, Johnson City, Tenn., 1976-77; bus. mgr., controller Lancaster Assos., Johnson City, 1977—. Served with USMCR, 1966-69. Mem. Adminstrv. Mgmt. Soc., Japan Karate Orgn. Methodist. Clubs: Moose, Elks. Home: Fairway Apts Apt 13 Johnson City TN 37601 Office: 74 Wilson Ave Box 1100 Johnson City TN 37601

LUTEY, JOHN KENT, govt. ofcl.; b. Butte, Mont., Sept. 19, 1902; s. William John and Martha Louise (Williams) L.; student Wharton Sch., U. Pa., 1920-24; m. Agnes Theresa Sakal, Sept. 28, 1949; children—Iona Theresa, Vanessa Louise. With Henningsen Produce Co., Fed. Inc., U.S.A., Shanghai, China, 1925-40; founder, pres., dir. Kibon S.A., Sao Paulo and Rio de Janeiro, Brazil, 1940-62; dir. div. industry AID, Brazil, 1964-66; spl. ambassador of Iceland for inaguration Pres. Kubitschek of Brazil, 1956. Bd. dirs. Inst.-Brazil U.S., 1956-58; pres. Strangers Hosp., Rio de Janeiro, 1950-51; hon. consul of Iceland in Brazil, 1949-56, hon. consul gen., 1956-62. Decorated knight comdr. Order Falcon, 1953; grand knight Order Falcon, 1956 (Iceland). Mem. Am. C. of C. for Brazil (pres. 1951, permanent dir. 1952—), Am. Soc. Rio de Janeiro (pres. 1948). Methodist. Home: 400 Seasage Dr Delray Beach FL 33444

LUTHER, ROLAND CORNELIUS, coal mgmt. cons.; b. Pottsville, Pa., Mar. 31, 1913; s. Edwin Cornelius and Anna Atkins (Henning) L.; A.B., Princeton U., 1935; postgrad. Babson Coll., 1936; m. Sarah Katheryn Thompson, Feb. 11, 1939; children—Roland Cornelius, Edwin Cornelius, Ann Thompson. Sales rep. Peerless Coal & Coke Co., Vivian, W.Va., 1936-37, asst. to gen. mgr., 1938-39, v.p., 1939-48, exec. v.p., 1948-56, pres., 1956-59; pres., dir. Peerless Darby Coal Co., Ind., Harlan, Ky., 1942-47, Nassau Coal Co., Bluefield, W.Va., subs. Peerless Coal & Coke Co., 1947-55; v.p. Pocahontas Fuel Co. (Va.), 1957-61; pres., dir., chief exec. officer United Pocahontas Coal Co., Algoma, W.Va., 1962-72; pres., dir. Royal Coal Co. subs. United Pocahontas Coal Co., Mount Hope, W.Va., 1970-72; coal cons., Bluefield, 1972—; dir. McDowell County Nat. Bank, Welch, W.Va., 1941-76; dir. Flat Top Nat. Bank, Bluefield, 1947—, vice-chmn. exec. com., 1952-72, chmn. exec. com., 1973—; dir. Citizens Ins. Agy., Bluefield, 1948—, exec. com., 1973—; dir., mem. exec. com. Bluefield Hardware Co., 1963—, chmn. exec. com., 1968—; mem. solid fuels unit, exec. res. Dept. Interior, 1969-76; owner, operator Fincastle Farm, Bluefield, 1948—; pres., dir. Roland C. Luther, Inc., Bluefield, 1976—. Bd. dirs. Property Owners' Com., Washington, 1948-57; bd. dirs., mem. exec. com. Coal Producers Com. for Smoke Abatement, 1969; mem. Va. Adv. Legis. Com., 1959-61, 68-69; gen. campaign chmn. Bluefield Area Devel. Corp., 1954, pres., 1954-55, bd. dirs., 1954-75; vestryman Christ Episcopal Ch., Bluefield, 1947-70, sr. warden, 1954, chmn. bldg. fund com., 1957-58; vestryman St. Mary's Episc. Ch., Bluefield, 1977—. Mem. Pocahontas Operators Assn. (exec. com. 1945-57, 59-61), W.Va. (dir. 1955-56), Va. (dir. 1958-61) chambers commerce, Bluefield C. of C. (v.p. and dir. 1948-49, 54, pres. 1955-56), W.Va. Coal Mining Inst. (v.p. 1949-54, pres. 1955, exec. bd. 1955-60), So. Coal Producers Assn. (dir., mem. exec. com. 1959-61, dir. 1962-72), So. Va. Coal Assn. (dir. 1959-61, 62-67, exec. com. 1959-61, 62-72, treas. 1962-72), W.Va. Coal Assn. (dir., mem. exec. com. 1959-61, 62-72), Nat. Coal Assn. (land and water use com. 1959, edn. com. 1947-61, chmn. edn. com. 1958-61), Bituminous Coal Operators Assn. (dir. 1968-72), Tazwell Area Cattleman's Assn. (dir. 1973-76). Clubs: Rotary, Fincastle Country; Princeton (N.Y.C.). Home: Fincastle Farm Bluefield VA 24605 Office: PO Box 191 Bluefield VA 24605

LUTHER, STEPHEN WINSLOW, truck mfg. co. exec.; b. Boston, Aug. 25, 1943; s. Duane David and Marjorie M. (Mitchell) L.; B.A., Ga. Mil. Acad. (name now Woodward Acad.), 1962; B.S. in Fin., Fla. State U., 1965, B.A. in Econs., 1965; m. Elizabeth Clark Hanger, Sept. 21, 1943; children—Christina Clark, Stephen Hart, Elizabeth Wright. With Texaco Inc., 1962-70, v.p. mktg., in charge handing Texaco nationalization, Venezuela, 1970; gen. mgr. Blue Bird Bus Mfg. & Mktg. Co., C.Am., 1970-76; pres. Lyncoach & Body Co., Troy, Ala., 1976-78; pres., co-owner Semcor Truck Remfg. Co., Evergreen, Ala., 1978—; dir., part owner Polco Helicopter Co., Miami, Fla.; dir. Dowling Textile Mfg. Co., McDonough, Ga., J.E. Hanger Artificial Limb Co., St. Louis. Mem. adv. and cons. com. for Congressman Bill Dickinson. Mem. Am. Mgmt. Assn., Soc. Mayflower Descs., Bunker Hill Descs. Soc. Republican. Presbyterian. Clubs: Rotary, Troy Country, Lions.

LUTTRULL, RONALD RAY, electronics mfg. co. exec.; b. Ramona, Okla., Aug. 9, 1936; s. Loyd Jacob and Bessie Madelene (Barker) L.; B.S., Okla. State U., 1959; M.B.A., So. Meth. U., 1971; m. Jo Ann Ollar, Dec. 4, 1965; children—Lisa Renee, Jeffrey Todd. Mfg. indsl. engr. Collins Radio Co., Richardson, Tex., 1961-63, mgr. data control, 1964-67, mgr. data services, 1968-72; mgr. data services-engring. adminstrn. Rockwell Internat., Richardson, Tex., 1973—; dir. Comfco Corp. Adviser Jr. Achievement, 1976-77. Served with U.S. Army, 1959-61. Certified profl. mgr. Mem. Nat. Mgmt. Assn. Democrat. Baptist. Author: Energy Saving Guide, 1977. Home: 2724 Aspen Plano TX 75075 Office: 1200 N Alma Rd Richardson TX 75080

LUTZ, CLIFFORD LEWIS, civil engr.; b. Ceresco, Mich., Jan. 1, 1924; s. Arthur Willard and Ruth Mariah (Arnold) L.; B.S. in Civil Engring., La. Poly. Inst., 1952; m. Dencie Mae Partridge, Apr. 22, 1972; children by previous marriage—Norman V., Vicki (Mrs. Don Pitzer). Civil engr. La. Ordnance Plant, Minden, 1952-55; cons. engr., Minden, 1955-58; civil engr. FAA, Ft. Worth, 1958-65, chief civil and archtl. sect., 1966-75; owner Asso. Cons. Engrs., Ft. Worth, 1965-66; owner Lutz Internat. Engring., Cons.; cons. engr. for domestic and fgn. firms specializing in airport control tower design, airport planning studies and terminal navigational aids, Ft. Worth, 1975-76; v.p. engring. Metroplex Indsl. Constructors, Inc., 1976-77; v.p. engring. and constrn. air navigation facilities Lutz Internat. Engring. Cons., Inc., 1977—. designer Texarkana (Tex.), Lubbock (Tex.) and Houston-Hobby (Tex.) control towers; preliminary design layouts for Dallas/Ft. Worth Airport control tower. Served with USNR, 1943-46. Recipient Outstanding Performance award FAA, 1972, Spl. Achievement award, 1970. Registered profl. engr., Tex., La., Okla., Miss.; registered surveyor, La. Mem. Nat., Tex. socs. profl. engrs., Tau Beta Pi (life). Address: PO Box 18668 E Fort Worth TX 76118

LUTZ, THERESA PENCE (MRS. C. RALPH LUTZ), ret. ednl. adminstr.; b. nr. Greensboro, N.C.; d. Claude S. Stroud and Lelia (Powell) Pence; B.A., Mary Washington Coll., 1947; M.Ed., U.Va., 1956, postgrad., 1956-57; postgrad. George Washington U., summer 1961, 61-62, Am. U., 1963, Coll. William and Mary, 1964-71, Ph.D. (hon.), 1973; m. C. Ralph Lutz, May 30, 1931; children—Patricia Lutz Plummer, Philip (dec.). Tchr., New Market (Va.) Elementary Sch., 1944-46, New Market High Sch., 1946-47, Wilson Meml. High Sch., Fishesville, Va., 1947-57; tchr., counselor Mt. Vernon High Sch., Alexandria, Va., 1957-58; dir. guidance Lee High Sch., Springfield, Va., 1958-67; counselor, instr. grad. edn. No. Va. Center, U. Va., counselor West Springfield High Sch., 1967-75. Trustee, Marion Coll. Mem. NEA (life), Va. (chmn. tchr. and profl. standards com. 1966—), Fairfax edn. assns., Am., Va., No. Va. personnel and guidance assns., Nat. Vocat. Guidance Assn., Va. Guidance Assn., Delta Kappa Gamma (chpt. pres. 1972-74). Lutheran (counselor Luther League 1961-63). Author: (with Lillian W. Eisenberg) Central Evangelical Lutheran Church and Christ Evangelical Lutheran Church, 1953. Home: 1128 NE Abscott St Port Charlotte FL 33952

LUX, GEORGE RICHARD, elec. engr., educator; b. Chgo., June 17, 1937; s. Alfred M. and Grace C. (Lange) L.; B.S. in Elec. Engring., Valparaiso U., 1958; M.S. in Engring. Graphics, Ill. Inst. Tech., 1970; m. Myra Lee Bakalyar, July 17, 1976; children—Brian, Jason. Lab. asst. Valparaiso (Ind.) U., 1955-58, asso. prof., 1965-76; field engr. Schulman Electric Co., Chgo., 1958-59; engr. ITT-Kellogg, Chgo., 1959-63; systems engr. U.S. Air Force, 1963-66; asso. prof. Grove City (Pa.) Coll., 1976-77; asso. prof. engring. Va. Polytechnic Inst., 1977—; owner Lux Engring. Co., Valparaiso, 1970-76. NSF grantee 1972; recipient NSF awards 1966, 73. Lic. profl. engr., Ill., Ind., Pa., Va. Mem. ASME, Am. Soc. Engring. Edn., Soc. Am. Mil. Engrs., Armed Forces Communications and Electronics Assn., Nat. Wildlife Fedn., Tau Beta Pi. Club: Kiwanis. Home: 1503 Greendale Dr Blacksburg VA 24060 Office: Virginia Polytechnic Institute Blacksburg VA 24061

LUXENBERG, MALCOLM NEUWAHL, ophthalmologist; b. Philipsburg, Pa., July 29, 1935; s. Maurice and Henrietta (Neuwahl) L.; student Tulane U., 1953-56; M.D., U. Miami (Fla.), 1960; m. Sandra Diane Rosen, June 16, 1957; children—Steven Neuwahl, Cathy Ann. Intern, Cin. Gen. Hosp., 1960-61; resident in neurology U. Vt. Affiliated Hosps., Burlington, 1961-63; resident in ophthalmology Bascom Palmer Eye Inst., U. Miami-Jackson Meml. Hosp., Miami, Fla., 1963-66; asst. prof. ophthalmology Coll. Medicine, U. Iowa, Iowa City, 1968-70; chief ophthalmology service VA Hosp., Iowa City, 1968-70; practice medicine specializing in ophthalmology, West Palm Beach, Fla., 1970-72; prof., chmn. dept. ophthalmology Med. Coll. Ga., Augusta, 1972—; clin. asst. prof. ophthalmology Bascom Palmer Eye Inst., Sch. Medicine, U. Miami, 1971-72; cons. ophthalmology VA Hosp., Augusta, 1972—. Sr.

surgeon USPHS, 1966-68. Diplomate Am. Bd. Ophthalmology. Mem. AMA, Am. Acad. Ophthalmology, Am. Ophthal. Soc., Assn. for Research in Vision and Ophthalmology, Assn. Univ. Profs. in Ophthalmology, Ga. Soc. Ophthalmology, Med. Assn. Ga., Richmond County Med. Soc. Home: 512 Scotts Way Augusta GA 30909 Office: Dept Ophthalmology Med Coll Georgia Augusta GA 30912

LUZA, RADOMIR VACLAV, historian; b. Prague, Czechoslovakia, Oct. 17, 1922; s. Vojtech V. and Milada (Vecera) Luza; came to U.S., 1953; naturalized, 1959; Ju.Dr., Masaryk U., Brno, Czechoslovakia, 1948; M.A., N.Y. U., 1958, Ph.D., 1959; m. Libuse Podhrazska, Feb. 5, 1949; children—Radomir V., Sabrina. Asso. prof. modern European history La. State U., New Orleans, 1966-67; prof. Tulane U., 1967—; vis. prof. U. Hamburg, W. Ger., 1969-70. Mem. presidium Council Free Czechoslovakia, 1960—. Served with Czechoslovak Resistance Army, 1939-45. Recipient prize Theodor Koerner Found., Vienna, 1965; grantee Social Research Council, 1969, Am. Philos. Soc., 1971, 75, Council Learned Socs., 1972, 77, Fulbright Com., 1969-70. Mem. Am., So. hist. assns., Conf. Group German Politics, Central European, Czechoslovak (vice chmn. 1978) hist. confs., Am. Com. on History of Second World War, Assn. for Advancement Slavic Studies. Author: The Transfer of the Sudeten Germans, 1964; History of the International Socialist Youth Movement, 1970; A History of the Czechoslovak Republic, 1918-48, 1973; Austro-German Relations in the Anschluss Era, 1975; Österreich in der NS-Zeit, 1977. Home: 839 Roseland Pkwy New Orleans LA 70123 Office: Dept History Tulane U New Orleans LA 70118

LUZZI, LOUIS ANTHONY, pharm. scientist; b. Westerly, R.I., June 17, 1932; s. Patsy Louis and Mary E. Luzzi; B.S. in Pharmacy, U. R.I., 1959, M.S. in Phys. Pharmacy, 1963, Ph.D. in Phys. Pharmacy, 1966; m. Joyce B. Kaye, 1953; children—Glenda Elise, Patrissa Lou. Research pharmacist Abbott Labs., 1959-61; grad. asst. U. R.I., 1961-65, instr., 1965-66; asst. prof. U. Ga., 1966-69, asso. prof., 1969-73, prof., 1973-74, dir. FDA insp. tng. course, 1968-73; prof. phys. pharmacy, dean Sch. Pharmacy, U. W.Va., Morgantown 1974—; cons. various cos. Served with USCG, 1951-53. Fellow Acad. Pharm. Sci., Am. Acad. Sci.; mem. Am. Pharm. Assn., AAAS, Am. Assn. Colls. Pharmacy, Rho Chi. Office: Sch Pharmacy U WVa Med Center Morgantown WV 26506

LYALL, MARIANNE JOYCE, hosp. adminstr.; b. Denoya, Okla., May 14, 1923; d. Travis Lee and Mignon Grace (Harmon) Thomas; B.S., U. So. Miss., 1959; M.Ed., Miss. Coll., 1965; m. Jack Lawrence Lyall, Feb. 15, 1941; children—Larry, Jerry, Barry, Harry, Suzanne, Tammy. Dietetic intern Miss. Baptist Med. Center, Jackson, 1959-62, asst. dir. food services, 1962-63; dietitian psychiatry, pediatrics and food prodn. U. Med. Center, Jackson, Miss., 1963-65; dir. dietetics Hinds Gen. Hosp., Jackson, 1965—. Named Outstanding Dietitian State of Miss., 1974. Mem. Am. Dietetic Assn., Soc. Nutrition Edn., Am. Hosp. Soc. for Food Service Adminstrs., Miss. Found. Med. Care, Miss. Dietetic Assn. (pres. 1969-70), Kappa Delta Pi, Kappa Omicron Phi, Delta Omicron. Baptist. Home: 1200 Tanglewood Dr Clinton MS 39056 Office: 1800 Chadwick Dr Jackson MS 39209

LYDICK, LARRY STUART, oil and gas exploration co. exec.; b. Ft. Worth, Tex., July 23, 1936; s. John Stuart and Stella Bess (Stokes) L.; student UCLA, 1956, Tex. Christian U., 1955, 57, 58, U. Wis., 1960, 61; m. Margaret Ann Fuller, Nov. 14, 1975; children—Drew, Todd, Tracy, Janie, Kelly. Vice pres., dir. Union Bank of Ft. Worth 1961-62; v.p. Continental Nat. Bank, Ft. Worth, 1962-65; pres. Viking Exploration, Inc., Ft. Worth, 1965—, Inca Oil & Gas, Inc., Ft. Worth, 1967—; mng. gen. partner Century Petroleum, Ltd., Ft. Worth, 1970—. Active United Fund, Ft. Worth, 1965, YMCA, Ft. Worth, 1966. Served with USMC, 1959. Mem. Tex. Ind. Producers and Royalty Owners Assn., Ind. Producers Assn. of Am., Mid-Continent Oil and Gas Assn., Ft. Worth Wildcatters Assn. Republican. Methodist. Clubs: Brown Palace (Denver) Rivercrest Country, Petroleum, Century II, Ft. Worth, Steplechase (pres. 1960), Ft. Worth Horseshoe, Ft. Worth Boat. Home: 57 Westover Terr Fort Worth TX 76107 Office: 1404 Fort Worth Nat Bank Bldg Fort Worth TX 76102

LYERLY, ELAINE MYRICK, public relations counselor, designer; b. Charlotte, N.C., Nov. 26, 1951; d. J.M. and Annie Mary (Myrick) L.; A.S., Central Piedmont Community Coll., 1972. Free-lance illustrator fashion industry, Gastonia, N.C., 1971-72; designer, art staff WBT-WBTV, Jefferson Prodns., Charlotte, 1971-72; public relations counselor, graphics designer, photographer Monte J. Curry Mktg. & Communications Services div. Group C. Inc., Charlotte, 1972-77, exec. v.p. Group C. Inc., 1973-77; pres. Repro-Graphics, Charlotte, 1973-77; owner, operator Eve Communications Services, Charlotte, 1977—; adj. instr. public relations Queens Coll. Former public relations chmn. Greater Carolinas chpt. ARC, Charlotte; graphics designer, counselor Greater Mecklenburg Better Bus. Bur., Charlotte, 1976—; vol. Girl Scouts of Am., Charlotte; membership com. Little Theatre of Charlotte. Recipient Linweave creative award Brown Co., Holyoke, Mass., 1972, Recognition award Greater Mecklenburg Better Bus. Bur., Charlotte, 1976, Award of Excellence, Champion Paper Co., Strathmore Paper Co.; awards of excellence 8th Annual Internat. Tech. Publs. Competition, 1977; 1st pl. award for logo design Carolina chpt. Soc. Tech. Communication. Mem. Public Relations Soc. Am., Charlotte Soc. Communicating Arts (pres. 1979-80), Women in Communications, Inc. (program chmn.), Women Execs., Greater Charlotte C. of C. (polit. action com.). Designer, editor, producer Charlotte Sts. Booklet, 1976; designer several logos featured The Book of Am. Trademarks, 1976, 77, 78. Home: 500 Queens Rd Charlotte NC 28207 Office: One Charlottetown Center Suite 133 Charlotte NC 28204

LYKINS, JAY ARNOLD, assn. exec.; b. Shattuck, Okla., Feb. 13, 1947; s. George Eldridge and Lucy Lee (Croom) L.; student West Ga. Coll., 1965-66; El Centro Jr. Coll., 1970-71, U. Tenn., 1972; B.A., Covenant Coll., 1973; m. Mary Lynn Turner, Jan. 3, 1970; children—Mary Lee and Amy Lynn (twins), Jason Turner. Head resident Covenant Coll., Lookout Mountain, Tenn., 1972-73, conf. dir., student work dir. 1973-74; credit/fin. specialist Gen. Electricl Supply Co., Nashville, 1974-75; owner, mgr. Environment Control, Nashville, 1975-78; bus. adminstr. Youth for Christ, Atlanta, 1978—. Served with USN, 1966-68. Club: Nob Hill Country (pres. 1980). Home: 2076 Tanglewood Dr Snellville GA 30278 Office: Youth for Christ 215 Church St Suite 203 Decatur GA 30030

LYKINS, NOEL RAY, coll. adminstr.; b. Mt. Sterling, Ky., Aug. 23, 1932; s. Estill Curtis and Alta Delilah (McGuire) L.; B.A. (NROTC scholar), U. Louisville, 1954; B.D., Southeastern Baptist Theol. Sem., 1960, Th.M., 1961; Ed.D., N.C. State U., 1974; m. Juanita Clemons, June 12, 1954; children—David Dudley, Sarah Frances, Charles Montgomery. Minister edn. Mars Hill (N.C.) Bapt. Ch., 1961-62, First Bapt. Ch., DeLand, Fla., 1962-65, Emerywood Bapt. Ch., High Point, N.C., 1965-67; v.p. for student services Cleveland Tech. Coll., Shelby, N.C., 1967—; intern N.C. State U. Community Coll., 1970. Pres., Cleveland County Rose Soc., 1977-78. Served with USN, 1954-57. Mem. Nat. Council on Student Devel., AAUP, N.C. State Employees Assn., Am., N.C. personnel and guidance assns., Am., N.C. coll. personnel assns., N.C. Adult Edn. Assn., Carolinas Assn. Collegiate Registrars and Admissions Officers, N.C. Community Coll. Student Services Personnel Assn. (pres. 1977), Omicron Delta Kappa (Outstanding Student award U. Louisville Graduating Class 1954). Democrat. Home: Route 10 Box 3-A Shelby NC 28150 Office: 137 S Post Rd Shelby NC 28150

LYLE, JAMES RHEA, eye clinic exec.; b. Madison, Tenn., Oct. 12, 1948; s. G.C. and Betty Louise (Champion) L.; student U. S.C., 1966-67; A.A. in Acctg., Phillips Bus. Coll., 1977; m. Avis Ann Rollins, Feb. 11, 1979; 1 son, Paul Rhea. Br. office mgr. Am. Fin. and Tax System, Aiken and Anderson, S.C., Macon and Marietta, Ga., 1967-72; office mgr. Augusta Mill Supply (Ga.), 1973-74; bus. mgr. So. Eye Clinic, P.C., Augusta, 1974—; exec. sec. Richmond County Med. Soc. Coach, Little League Baseball. Recipient Outstanding Young Man in Am. award U.S. Jaycees, 1979. Mem. Greater Augusta C. of C. Club: Martinez-Evans Rotary (pres. 1979-80, past sec.). Home: 302 Habersham Rd Martinez GA 30907 Office: 1514 Anthony Rd Augusta GA 30904

LYLE, SAMUEL PATTERSON, ret. agrl. engr.; b. Memphis, Mo., Feb. 12, 1892; s. Edward Gerard and Jeanetta Wilson (Patterson) L.; B.S., Kans. State U., 1921; M.S., Iowa State U., 1922; m. Besse Maude MacQueen, Dec. 26, 1921 (dec.); children—Samuel Patterson (dec.), Marion Elizabeth Lyle Fowler, Alice Louise Lyle Cockrill. Head agrl. engring. dept. Ark. A. and M. Coll., 1922-24, U. Ga., 1924-30; sr. engr. Fed. Extension Service, Dept. Agr., Washington, 1930-40, prin. scientist charge specialists, 1941-58, dir. agrl. programs div., 1958-62; ret. Served as pursuit pilot USAAF, 1917-19. Fellow Am. Soc. Agrl. Engrs. (life, pres. 1938-39, John Deere Gold medal), AAAS (life); mem. Am. Soc. Engring. Edn., Engrs. Joint Council, Nat. Safety Council (hon. life), Nat. Inst. Farm Safety (hon. life), Orgn. Profl. Employees Dept. Agr., Soil Conservation Soc. Am., Nat. Assn. Ret. Fed. Employees, Vets. W.W. I, Am. Legion, VFW, Sigma Xi, Gamma Sigma Delta, Phi Kappa Phi, Epsilon Sigma Phi. Methodist. Contbr. articles to profl. jours. Home: 218 Spring St Huntingdon TN 38344

LYLES, JERRY LEE, psychologist; b. Vernon, Tex., Nov. 30, 1936; s. Curtis and Pairlee (Jones) L.; B.A., Midwestern U., 1967; M.A., Tex. Technol. U., 1969; Ed.D., Ind. U., 1976; 1 dau., Kimberly Rene. Psychiat. nurse technician Wichita Falls (Tex.) State Hosp., 1960-67; instr. Brescia Coll., Ownesboro, Ky., 1970-73, Webster Coll., Altus, Okla., 1975-78; psychologist Vernon (Tex.) Project for Drug Dependent Youth, 1974—. Served with U.S. Army, 1956-58. Mem. Am., Southwestern, Tex. psychol. assns., Am. Assn. Marriage and Family Counselors. Home: Route 1 Box 104 Vernon TX 76384 Office: Vernon Center South Vernon TX 76384

LYMAN, RUTH ANN, health services center exec.; b. Nashville, Ark., Feb. 2, 1948; d. Oren Ernest and Frances Emeline (Urban) Frerking; B.S., U. Ala., Tuscaloosa, 1969, M.A. (Ala. Dept. Mental Health fellow), 1972, Ph.D., 1974. Counselor, Camp Ponderosa, summer program for emotionally disturbed children, Mentone, Ala., summers 1969, 70; staff psychologist Montgomery (Ala.) Area Mental Health Authority, summer 1971; cons. Lowndes County (Ala.) Sch. System, 1971; tng. group leader Tuscaloosa Community Crisis Center, 1972; instr. in psychology Psychol. Clinic, dept. psychology U. Ala., Tuscaloosa, 1971-72, psychometrist, summer 1972, clin. psychologist Univ. Health Service, Coll. Community Health Scis., 1973-75, now adj. asst. prof. dept. psychology; instr. div. spl. studies U. Ala., Birmingham, 1977—, adj. asst. prof. psychology, 1978—; instr., clin. psychology intern U. N.C., Chapel Hill, 1973; asso. Resource Design and Devel. Corp., University, Ala., also N.Y.C., 1973-78; profl. dir. Tuscaloosa Pregnancy Counseling Center and Rape Relief Service, Tuscaloosa, 1973-75, chmn. bd. dirs., 1974-75; cons. NW Ala. Mental Health Center, Hamilton, 1974-75; mem. exec. com. Southeastern Assn. Crisis Intervention Centers, 1974-77; dir. Western Mental Health Center, Jefferson County Dept. Health, Birmingham, 1975—; mem. group home adv. com. Jefferson-Blount-St. Clair Mental Health/Mental Retardation Authority, Birmingham, 1976—; community rep. Head Start Policy Council, Jefferson County Com. Econ. Opportunity, 1976-79; bd. dirs., sec., mem. exec. com. Alcoholism Recovery Center, Birmingham, 1977—; chmn. mental health com. Birmingham Regional Health Systems Agency, 1978. Recipient Martin S. Wallach award, dept. psychiatry U. N.C. Sch. Medicine, 1973, Outstanding Young Career Woman award Tuscaloosa Bus. and Profl. Women's Club, 1975; licensed psychologist, Ala. Mem. Am., Southeastern, Ala. psychol. assns., Nat. Register Health Service Providers, Ala. Council Mental Health/Mental Retardation Dirs., Ala. Acad. Neurology and Psychiatry, Am., Ala. pub. health assns., Assn. Advancement Psychology, Assn. Licensed Psychologists Ala., Chestnut Hill Assn., Highland Neighborhood Assn. Methodist. Club: Zonta Internat. Contbr. articles to profl. publs. Home: 3228 Highland Dr Birmingham AL 35205 Office: 1701 Ave D Ensley Birmingham AL 35218

LYMANGROVER, JOHN ROBERT, physiologist; b. Ft. Wayne, Ind., July 24, 1944; s. Robert Donald and Mary Rose (Farley) L.; B.S., Xavier U., Cin., 1966; M.S. (grad. fellow), U. Ky., 1960; Ph.D. (grad. fellow), U. Cin., 1972. Postdoctoral fellow Med. Coll. Ohio, 1972-74; research asso. physiology U. Cin., 1974-74; asst. prof. physiology Tulane U., New Orleans, 1975—. Ednl. Found. grantee, 1977-79; Am. Heart Assn. grantee, 1979—. Mem. Assn. South Eastern Biologists, AAAS, N.Y. Acad. Scis., Sigma Xi. Roman Catholic. Research and publs. on control of adrenal cortical trophic hormone and adrenal cortical steroid secretion, role of cell membrane in control of cellular function. Home: 916 1/2 Governor Nicholls St New Orleans LA 70116 Office: Tulane University Medical School 1430 Tulane Ave New Orleans LA 70112

LYNCH, EDWARD S., contracting co. exec.; b. Tallahassee, Nov. 16, 1939; s. Pierce Jones and Lydia Mary (Smith) L.; B.S. in Elec. Engring., U. Fla., 1962, M.S. in Elec. Engring., 1964; m. Laura Jane Corwin, Oct. 16, 1966; children—Patricia Susan, Virginia Ann, Michael Kenneth. Engr., South Fla. Electric Co., Miami, 1966-68; project leader Computer Assos., St. Petersburg, Fla., 1968-70; team leader Magruder Electric Mfg. Co., Daytona Beach, Fla., 1970-73; owner, pres., chief exec. officer Lynch Contracting Co., Inc., Tallahassee, 1973—, Chgo., 1978—. Served with U.S. Army, 1964-66. Registered profl. engr., Fla., Ill. Mem. IEEE, Illuminating Engrs. Soc., Nat. Soc. Profl. Engrs., Tau Beta Pi, Sigma Nu. Republican. Baptist. Clubs: Engineers (Tallahassee); Masons. Home: 1649 79th St Tallahassee FL 33605 Office: First Federal Bank Bldg Tallahassee FL 33601 also 4035-F N Keystone St Chicago IL 60641

LYNCH, FRANK JOSEPH, plastic co. exec.; b. Teaneck, N.J., Dec. 27, 1946; s. Frank and Kathleen M. L.; m. Deborah Jill Portlock, May 4, 1974; 1 son, Michael. Prodn. mgr. Mooney Bros., Little Falls, N.J., 1967-71; prodn. mgr., ops. mgr. Precision Polymers, Rockaway, N.J., 1971-73, dir. corporate purchasing, Mountainside N.J., 1973-74; v.p., gen. mgr. Derbi Plastics, Inc., Temple, Tex., 1974-80; plastics cons., rancher, 1980—; mem. Modern Plastics Adv. Panel; cons. Internat. Rural Water Resources Devel. Precinct chmn. Republican Party. Mem. Soc. Plastics Industry (treas.), Tex. Water Conservation Assn., Tex. Assn. of Bus., Soc. Plastics Engrs., Soc. Mfg. Engrs. Roman Catholic. Home: Lazy Triangle Ranch Troy TX 76579

LYNCH, JOHN BROWN, surgeon; b. Akron, Ohio, Feb. 5, 1929; s. John A. and Eloise (Brown) L.; student Vanderbilt U., 1946-49; M.D., U. Tenn., 1952; m. Jean Crane, July 2, 1950; children—John Brown, Margaret Frances. Intern, John Gaston Hosp., Memphis, 1953-54; resident in gen. surgery U. Tex. Med. Br., Galveston, 1956-59, resident in plastic surgery, 1959-62; practice medicine specializing in plastic surgery, Galveston, 1962-73, Nashville, 1973—; instr. surgery U. Tex. Med. Br., Galveston, 1962, asst. prof. surgery, 1962-67, asso. prof., 1967-72, prof. surgery, 1972-73; prof., chmn. dept. plastic surgery Vanderbilt U. Med. Center, Nashville, 1973—; cons. USPHS, Galveston, 1967-72, Tex. State Dept. Health, Crippled Children's Div., 1963-72, USAF, Lackland AFB, Tex., 1968-72, St. Mary's Infirmary, Galveston, 1962-72; cons. plastic surgery to surgeon gen. USAF, 1974—. Served to capt., USAF, 1954-56. Diplomate Am. Bd. Surgery, Am. Bd. Plastic Surgery. Fellow A.C.S.; mem. Southeastern, Nashville, So. surg. socs., Am. Assn. Plastic Surgeons (dir. 1974-77), Am. Soc. Plastic and Reconstructive Surgeons (dir. 1974-77), Tenn., Southeastern socs. plastic surgeons, Am. Soc. Maxillofacial Surgeons, Am. Cancer Soc. (pres. Galveston County chpt. 1968), Soc. Head and Neck Surgeons, Am. Cleft Palate Assn., Plastic Surgery Research Council, Tenn., Pan Am., So. (chmn. plastic surgery sect. 1972-73), med. assns., AMA, Internat. Burn Soc., Sigma Xi. Contbr. articles on burns and reconstructive surgery to profl jours. Home: 2312 Valley Brook Rd Nashville TN 37215 Office: Vanderbilt Hospital Nashville TN 37232

LYNCH, JOHN ELLSWORTH, hosp. dir.; b. Fargo, N.D., June 8, 1935; s. John Joseph and Mary Louise (Paulson) L.; B.S. in Bus. Adminstrn., U. N.D., 1959 M.B.A., U. Mo., 1969; m. Beth Margaret Pallas, July 14, 1956; children—John Ellsworth, Michael, Kevin. Fin. mgr. U.S. Steel Corp., Chgo., 1959-63; controller Decatur and Macon County Hosp., Decatur, Ill., 1963-65; asst. exec. dir. Research Hosp. and Med. Center, Kansas City, Mo., 1965-70; chief exec. officer N.C. Baptist Hosps., Inc., Winston-Salem, 1970—; trustee N.C. Blue Cross/Blue Shield; dir. Winston-Salem Savs. and Loan Assn. Mem.-at-large Statewide Health Coordinating Council; trustee Forsyth County Red Cross. mem. Bd. Health Forsyth County. Served with U.S. Army, 1954-57. Mem. Am. Coll. Hosp. Adminstrs., N.C. Hosp. Assn. (trustee), Beta Gamma Sigma, Beta Alpha Psi. Republican. Baptist. Club: Rotary. Home: 430 Staffordshire St Winston-Salem NC 27104 Office: 300 S Hawthorne Rd Winston-Salem NC 27103

LYNCH, MICHAEL KEVIN, hosp. food service dir.; b. Stamford, Conn., Feb. 2, 1949; s. William F. and Mary P. (Sniffen) L.; A.A. in Food Service Mgmt., Miami-Dade Community Coll., 1974; B.S. in Restaurant and Food Service Mgmt., Fla. Internat. U., 1978; m. Kathleen Ann Flanigan, Mar. 19, 1971; children—Maureen, Brian, Kevin. Cooking apprentice Rolling Hills Country Club, Norwalk, Conn., 1964-67; kitchen supr. South Miami Hosp., 1970-71; food mgr. Hope Sch., Miami, 1971-72; food services dir. Variety Children's Hosp., Miami, 1972-75, Cedars of Lebanon Health Center, Miami, 1975-79, Boca Raton (Fla.) Community Hosp., 1979—; instr. dietetic students Fla. Internat. U., Miami-Dade Community Coll., Lindsey Hopkins Edn. Center. Served with AUS, 1968-70. Mem. Am. Soc. Hosp. Food Service Adminstrs. (Pres.' nat. nominating com.), South Fla. Hosp. Assn. Roman Catholic. Contbr. articles profl. jours. Office: 800 Meadows Rd Boca Raton FL 33432

LYNCH, WILLIAM CHARLES, theater chain exec.; b. Halifax County, Va., Aug. 5, 1922; s. John Henry and Annie Lee (Gilliland) L.; m. Beulah Boyd, Nov. 17, 1945; children—Larry Allen, Libby Carol Lynch Heskett. With Martinsville Theater Mgmt. Corp. (Va.), 1947—, gen. mgr., 1951-73, v.p., gen. mgr., 1973—. Bd. dirs. NATO of Va., 1963—. Served with AUS, 1942-45. Mem. United Comml. Travelers, Travelers Protective Assn., Am. Legion. Presbyterian. Clubs: Elks, K.P. Home: 1204 Spruce St Martinsville VA 24112 Office: 215 E Church St Martinsville VA 24112

LYNCH, WILLIAM WRIGHT, JR., real estate developer; b. Dallas, Aug. 26, 1936; s. William W. and Martha (Hirsch) L.; B.S. in E.E., Ariz. U., 1959; M.B.A., Stanford U., 1962; m. Sandra McVay, June 11, 1960; children—Mary Margaret, Katherine. Pres., Ins. Bldg. Corp., Dallas, 1965—, also sec., dir. Cimarron Properties Corp., 1972—; dir. Llano, Inc., Broadmoor Properties, Inc., N.Mex. Elec. Service Co., Hobbs Gas Co., Ins. Bldg. Corp. Bd. dirs. Dallas Civic Music, 1970-77, Ednl. Opportunities, Inc., 1973—, Dallas Symphony Orch., 1966-74. Served with AUS, 1959-60. Mem. Blue Key, Tau Beta Pi, Pi Mu Epsilon. Republican. Episcopalian. Club: Brook Hollow Golf. Home: 3604 Haynie Ave Dallas TX 75205 Office: 8333 Douglas St Suite 550 Dallas TX 75225

LYND, JAMES PAUL, social worker; b. Ironton, Ohio, Jan. 16, 1928; s. Ben H. and Frances (Schmitt) L.; student Rio Grande Coll., 1948-49, Cedarville Coll., 1949-51, Miami U., Oxford, Ohio, 1952; B.I.S., U. Mid-Fla., 1971, M.S., 1973, M.S. in Behavorial Scis., 1974; D.Christian Edn., Freedom U., 1978. Supr., Cal. Youth Authority, Norwalk, 1954-55; field counselor Ohio Juvenile Placement Bur., Dayton, 1955-59; supt. Butler County Juvenile Center, Hamilton, Ohio, 1959-63, Orange County Juvenile-Parental Homes, Orlando, Fla., 1963-74; exec. dir., pres. Seminole Youth Ranches, 1974—. Bd. dirs. Edgewood Boys Ranch, Drug Abuse Treatment Center. Served with USNR, 1945-46. Named Layman of Year Kiwanis; recipient Zeus award Epsilon Sigma Alpha. Mem. Fla. (chpt. pres. 1965-66), Nat. councils on crime and delinquency, Nat. Juvenile Detention Assn. (sec.-treas. 1971-72), Orlando Area C. of C. (Disting. Ser. award 1969) D.A.V. Lutheran. Mason (32 deg., Shriner). Club: Sertoma (dir. 1966-68, pres. 1979-80, Service to Mankind award 1975). Address: PO Box 31 Gotha FL 32734

LYNE, JAMES ANTHONY, JR., civil engr.; b. Nashville, Dec. 29, 1928; s. James Anthony and Anne Briggs (Evans) L.; student (Ky. Regional scholar) Mass. Inst. Tech., 1947-49; B.C.E. (Ky. Assn. Ins. Agts. scholar), U. Ky., 1952; m. Mary Rae Tucker, Oct. 27, 1950; 1 son, James Evans. Draftsman, Howard K. Bell, Lexington, Ky., 1949-52; v.p., dir. in charge civil engring. projects Howard, Nielsen, Lyne, Thomas, Aldred, Henry & O'Brien, Inc., engrs., architects, Nashville, 1952-73; v.p., sec., dir. Morton-Lyne & Assos., Inc., Nashville, 1973—. Chmn., Franklin Rd. Area fund dr. Boy Scouts Am., 1968-73. Mem. Nat. Soc. Profl. Engrs., Nashville Engrs. Assn., Water Pollution Control Fedn., Am. Water Works Assn., Phi Kappa Sigma, Tau Beta Pi Democrat. Methodist (adminstrv. bd. 1974-76, 78—). Club: Wildwood Swim and Tennis. Home: 730 Elysian Fields Rd Nashville TN 37204 Office: 217 24th Ave N Nashville TN 37203

LYNN, DANIEL REID, JR., dist. govt. ofcl.; b. Farmville, Va., Feb. 26, 1947; s. Daniel Reid and Frances (Barksdale) L.; B.A. in Polit. Sci., Washington and Lee U., 1969; M.A. in Public Adminstrn., U. Md., 1976; m. Jane Warwick Pritt, Jan. 31, 1969; children—Allison Lovelace, Carter Gatewood, Amy Reid. Budget analyst Budget Office, Montgomery County, Rockville, Md., 1973-76, asst. to dir. dept. community and econ. devel., 1976-77; exec. dir. Piedmont Planning Dist. Commn., Farmville, 1977—; chmn. Human Resources Roundtable, 1978—. Mem. Area Manpower Planning Council, also various area indsl. devel. groups. Served to capt. U.S. Army, 1969-73; Vietnam. Decorated Joint Forces Commendation medal, MD. Commendation medal. Mem. Am. Planning Assn. (charter Va. chpt.),

Internat. Assn. City Mgmt., So. Indsl. Devel. Council, Southeastern Community Devel. Assn., Va. Army N.G. Republican. Presbyterian. Club: Farmville Lions. Home: 414 4th Ave Farmville VA 23901 Office: 102 1/2 High St Farmville VA 23901

LYNN, PHILLIP WAYNE, cons. engr.; b. Woodbury, Tenn., Sept. 23, 1942; s. Luther Britton and R.A. (Burks) L.; student Middle Tenn. State U., 1960-62; B.S. in Civil Engring., U. Tenn., 1966, M.S., 1967; m. Mary Evelyn Harris, Nov. 4, 1967; children—Britton Earle, Tara Elaine. Research asst. U. Tenn. Water Resources Research Center, Knoxville, 1966-67; engr. Shell Oil Co., Norco, La., 1967-70; chief engr. Frank Foster and Assos., Inc., Kenner, La., 1970-72; dir. waste water control system City of Knoxville, 1972-76; pres. Plus Engring., Knoxville, 1976—. Chmn., Knoxville Tech. Soc. Environ. Resources Subcom. for Water, 1973-74, Pub. Tech. Inc. Water/Wastewater mgmt. user requirements com. Registered profl. engr. Mem. Am. Soc. C.E., Water Pollution Control Fedn., Nat., Tenn. (Young Engr. of Year 1975) socs. profl. engrs., La. Engring. Soc., Ky.-Tenn. Operators Assn., Chi Epsilon, Tau Beta Pi. Mem. Ch. of Christ. Republican. Home: Rt 1 Lynnwood Ln Rockford TN 37853 Office: 5410 Homberg Dr Suite 25 Knoxville TN 37919

LYNN, ROBERT DEWESE, former headmaster; b. Brighton, Tenn., Oct. 20, 1913; s. Lucius Ross and Edith Lenora (DeWese) L.; A.B., Presbyn. Coll., 1934; M.S.W., Coll. William and Mary, 1935; M.A., Memphis State U., 1961, Ed.D., 1968; m. Evelyn McDowell, June 28, 1941; children—Sara Frances, Robert DeWese, Elizabeth Jane. Athletic dir. Dublin (Ga.) High Sch., 1935-36; engaged in business, Clinton, S.C., 1937-38; asst. to pres. Thornwell Orphanage, Clinton, 1938-40; auto salesman, Laurens, S.C., 1941-43; instr. econs. Presbyn. Coll., Clinton, 1943-45; field sec. Pi Kappa Alpha frat., Atlanta, 1945-46, exec. sec., Memphis, 1946-59; headmaster The Hutchison Sch., Memphis, 1959-79. Adminstr. Nat. chpt. House Loan Fund; exec. v.p. Pi Kappa Alpha Meml. Found., 1948-59, chmn. scholarship com., 1960—. Mem. Coll. Frat. Secs. Assn. (pres.), Coll. Frat. Editors Assn. (pres.), Memphis Assn. Ind. Schs. (pres.), Nat. Assn. Prins. Schs. for Girls, Nat. Interfrat. Conf. (exec. com. 1962—, pres. 1970—), So. (exec. com. 1963—, pres. 1965-66), Mid-South (pres. 1969-70, exec. com. 1965—) Tenn. (pres. 1975-76) assns. ind. schs., Am. Assn. Sch. Adminstrs., Newcomen Soc. N.Am., English Speaking Union, Blue Key. Presbyterian (elder; lectr. men's Bible class). Clubs: Univ., Exec. Editor Shield and Diamond mag., 1949-70. Home: 4620 Wieuca Rd #12 Atlanta GA 30342

LYNN, WILLIARD EARL, fire log and charcoal co. exec.; b. Memphis, Oct. 13, 1943; s. Williard Earnest and Helen Marie (Maybee) L.; student Western Res. U., 1962-64, Baldwin Wallace Coll., 1966-69; m. Carolyn Jean Sickles, Dec. 10, 1966. With Clorox Corp., 1967-78, adminstrv. mfg. mgr., Oakland, Calif., 1978; ops. mgr. sub. Duraflame Co., Oakland, 1978-79, Louisville, 1979—, also adminstrv. mfg. mgr. Kingsford Charcoal Co., 1979—. Mem. Am. Mgmt. Assn., Bay Village Jaycees. Club: Oakland Athletic. Home: 8901 Denington Dr Louisville KY 40222 Office: Commonwealth Bldg PO Box 1033 Louisville KY 40201

LYON, GEORGE COOK, clergyman, psychotherapist; b. Lynn, Mass., Oct. 5, 1904; s. Clarence Albert and Sadie E. (Hall) L.; B.S., U. Mo., 1930; postgrad. Sch. Bus., Boston U., 1936-37; D.O., Osteo. Med. Sch., London, 1956; M.D., U. Mo., 1959, Ph.D., 1964; Ph.D., U.I., Saltillo, Mex., 1965; Ph.D., South African Med. Sch., 1967; D.D. (hon.), Thomas A. Edison Coll., 1970, LL.D. (hon.), 1971, others; m. Mabel L. Clough, June 18, 1937; children—Gail, Sandra. Intern, Gracie Inst., N.Y., 1964-69; resident South African Med. Coll., 1969; practice medicine specializing in psychiatry, Balt., 1957-63, N.Y.C., 1963-69, Palm Beach, Fla., 1969-79; dir. Palm Beach Psychotherapy Tng. Center, 1969—; ordained to ministry Episcopal Ch., 1970; pastor Bethesda-by-the-Sea, Palm Beach, 1969-74, St. Andrew's, Lake Worth, Fla., 1974-76; presiding bishop Holy Episcopal Ch., West Palm Beach, 1975—. Fellow South African Coll. Homeopathic Medicine, Am. Inst. Group Psychotherapy, Am. Coll. Clin. Hypnosis, Internat. Coll. Assos. Medicine and Surgery, Am. Coll. Clin. Adminstrs., Am. Acad. Behavioral Sci. (pres. 1969-79), Fla. Psychoanalytic Inst., Am. Bd. Examiners in Psychotherapy, Am. Assn. Criminology, Order St. John of Jerusalem. Republican. Clubs: Knights of Malta, Masons, Rotary. Author: Comprehensive Clinical Psychotherapy, 1971. Home: 5200 N Dixie Hwy PH6 West Palm Beach FL 33407 Office: 707 Chillingworth Dr West Palm Beach FL 33409

LYON, HARRY BENJAMIN, petroleum ops. engr.; b. Kansas City, Mo., Aug. 16, 1932; s. John Robert (stepfather) and Mary Frances (Benjamin) L.; student public schs., Mo., Kans., Va.; student pvt. schs., Okla., Conn.; m. Joan Paff Gibbs McNab, Oct. 22, 1959. Employed with various firms, 1951-56; owner, operator Harry B. Lyon Co., mfrs. agt. petroleum equipment, Alexandria, Va., 1956—. Mem. Am. Soc. Petroleum Ops. Engrs. (nat. pres. 1976-77, dir. 1977-78), Petroleum Equipment Inst., Am. Petroleum Inst., Nat. Fire Protection Assn., ASTM (D-2 com.), Bldg. Ofcls. and Code Adminstrs., Ind. Oil and Gas Assn. W.Va., Va. Oil and Gas Assn., Internat. Presbyterian. Clubs: Masons (past master); K.T. Home and Office: 7722 Northdown Rd Alexandria VA 22308

LYON, JOYCE GLASCOCK, educator; b. Virgilina, Va., Jan. 5, 1932; d. Allie Peyton and Ophelia (Vaughan) Glascock; B.A. in Music, Mary Washington Coll., U. Va., 1953; M.S., James Madison U., 1974; m. John Thomas Lyon, Jr., June 12, 1955; children—Thomas Peyton, James Pember, David John, Catherine Joyce. Music tchr. elementary schs., Danville, Va., 1952-55, LaCrosse, Va., 1955-58; grad. asst. dept. edn. James Madison U., Harrisonburg, Va., 1973-74; reading specialist Verona (Va.) Elementary Schs., 1974-76; reading specialist, resource person Hugh Cassell Elementary Sch., Waynesboro, Va., 1976—. Mem. AAUW (chpt. v.p. 1973-74), NEA, Va., Augusta County edn. assns., Shenandoah Valley Reading Assn. (sec.), Internat. Reading Assn., Delta Kappa Gamma. Republican. Persbyterian. Club: James Madison U. Women's. Research and articles in field. Home: 620 Circle Dr Harrisonburg VA 22801 Office: Hugh Cassell Elementary Sch Waynesboro VA 22980

LYON, ROBERT RANDOLPH, SR., ins. exec.; b. Atlanta, Aug. 2, 1922; s. Roland George and Ellen Sawtell L.; B.S. Bus., Rollins Coll., 1978; m. Lucy Carolyn Womack, June 19, 1948; children—Robert Randolph, Thornton W., Anthony L. Underwriter, Underwriters Employers Liability Assurance Corp., 1953-55; casualty supr. Underwriters Fireman's Fund, 1955-57; asst. br. mgr. Chubb & Son, Atlanta, 1957-64; treas. B. D. Cole, Inc., West Palm Beach, Fla., 1964-68; excess and surplus lines mgr. Continental Nat. Am., Orlando, Fla., 1968-71; v.p. Hall Bros. Agy., Orlando, Fla., 1971-74; v.p., dir. Dana Roehrig & Assos., Inc., Orlando, 1975—; adj. prof. Rollins Coll., Winter Park, Fla., 1978-80. Served with U.S. Army, 1951-53. Mem. Soc. Chartered Property and Casualty Underwriters, Nat. Security Agy., Fla. Surplus Lines Assn., Ins. Club Dallas. Republican. Episcopalian. Home: 2756 Lion Heart Rd Winter Park FL 32792 Office: 3319 McGuire Blvd Orlando FL 32803

LYONS, HARRY STEVEN, gas co. exec.; b. Atlanta, Apr. 9, 1948; s. John B. and Louise Blanche (McKnight) L.; student West Ga. Coll., 1966-69; m. Carol Jean Leiker, Nov. 1, 1969; children—S. Rhett, Tiffany Lorraine. Vice pres., sec.-treas. Greens Fuel Co. of Ga., Inc., Lawrenceville, 1969—, also dir.; dir. Lyons Heating & Air Conditioning, Inc. Com. chmn. Hi-Hope Celebrity Invitational Golf Tournament, 1975-77; baseball mgr. Greater Lawrenceville Athletic Assn.; del. Am. Bowling Congress, 1977. Served with USMCR, 1969-74. Mem. Nat. (dir.), Ga. (pres. 1975-76, past dir.) LP gas assns., Gwinnett County C. of C., Golf and Tennis Assn., Atlanta Lawn Tennis Assn. Democrat. Methodist. Club: Pine Ridge Country. Home: 2228 Walker Dr Lawrenceville GA 30245 Office: PO Box 73 321 E Pike St Lawrenceville GA 30246

LYONS, MARY HARDING DILLIN, educator; b. Ft. Worth; d. Jefferson Davis and Mabel (Harding) Dillin; B.S., Kans. State U.; M.A., Midwestern U., 1966; Ph.D., U. Tex., 1974; postgrad. Tex. Christian U., N. Tex. State U., Eastern Wash. State U.; children—Linda H., David B., Kathryn L. Lyons Dillard. English tchr. Burleson (Tex.) High Sch., 1961-63, Wichita Falls (Tex.) High Sch., 1963-68; faculty Tarrant County Jr. Coll., Ft. Worth, 1968—, prof. English and communications, chmn. dept. basic studies, 1969—; cons. devel. edn. Mem. Nat. Assn. for Remedial and Devel. Students, Tex. Jr. Coll. Tchrs. Assn., Phi Delta Kappa, Kappa Kappa Gamma, Mu Phi Epsilon, Phi Mu Alpha. Episcopalian. Club: Fort Worth Singles Sq. Dance. Home: 1529 Terbet Ln Fort Worth TX 76112 Office: Tarrant County Junior College Dept Basic Studies 5301 Campus Dr Fort Worth TX 76119

LYONS, PHILLIP MICHAEL, SR., ins. exec., acct., ins. cons., real estate broker; b. Gueydan, La., Nov. 22, 1941; s. Joseph Bosman and Elder (Richard) L.; student McNeese State Coll., 1959-62, Alvin Jr. Coll., 1964, Coll. of Mainland, 1974; B.B.A., U. Houston, 1977, postgrad., 1978—; m. Wynona Faye Meyers, Apr. 28, 1962; children—Phillip M., Wilton J. Adminstrv. trainee Am. Nat. Ins. Co., Galveston, Tex., 1965, asst. mgr., acting mgr. policy issue dept., 1966-67, mgr., 1967-68, mgr. pre-issue dept., 1968-71, systems analyst, 1971-72, div. mgr., policyholders service div., 1972-76, dir. ordinary policyholder's service, 1976-77, dir. combination policy records, 1977-79; supervising acct. materials acctg. comptroller's dept. Aramco Services Co., Houston, 1977-79, ins. adviser treas.' dept., 1979—; partner Lyons Real Estate, Sulphur, La., 1966—; bd. dirs. Studio B, Inc., Houston. Solicitor, United Fund, 1966-69. Fellow Life Office Mgmt. Assn.; mem. Risk and Ins. Mgmt. Soc., Jr. C. of C. (dir. 1972, state dir. 1972—, Sparkplug of Year 1972-73, Roadrunner of Year 1972-73), Beta Alpha Psi. Clubs: Neuman, Elks. Home: 223 W Sherwood Dr Alvin TX 77511 also 1012 S Stanford St Sulphur LA 70663 Office: 1100 Milam St Houston TX 77002 also 1339 Cypress St Sulphur LA 70663

LYONS, ROBERT RONDELL, fin. exec.; b. Bremerton, Wash., July 15, 1944; s. Rocky R. and Shirley E. (Poynter) L.; B.S. magna cum laude, U. Colo., 1971; M.B.A., U. Tex., 1980; m. Joan G. Curreri, Apr. 1, 1967; children—Krista D., Wendy J., Suzanne N. Mgmt. cons. Peat Marwick Mitchell & Co., Denver, 1972-73; corporate auditor Xerox Corp., Rochester, N.Y., 1973-75; v.p. adminstrn. Church's Fried Chicken Inc., San Antonio, 1975-80; controller/chief fin. officer Monier Resources, Inc. and Monier Holdings, Inc., San Antonio, 1980—. Served to capt. USMC, 1961-69. Decorated Purple Heart, D.F.C.; C.P.A., Colo., Tex. Mem. Am. Mgmt. Assn., Am. Mktg. Assn., Inst. Internal Auditors, Tex. Soc. C.P.A.'s, Assn. M.B.A. Execs., U. Colo. Alumni Assn. Club: Woodlake Country. Home: 10310 Severn St San Antonio TX 78217 Office: 11100 Osgood San Antonio TX 78233

LYTLE, TERRILL WILSON, mission exec.; b. Lansing, Mich., Oct. 1, 1927; s. Leon Wilson and Gladys Ellen L.; student Moody Bible Inst., 1945-47; m. Olive Ione Vander Linden, Mar. 27, 1948; children—Lyndella Dawne, Dennis Harrison, Kay Ann. Ordained to ministry Baptist Ch., 1948; pastor West Rome Bapt. Ch., Manitou Community Ch., Manitou Beach, Mich., 1950-58; founder Drive-In Ministries, Devils Lake, Mich., 1951-64, St. Petersburg, Fla., 1964—. Mem. Nat. Home Missions Fellowship (chmn.), Exptl. Aircraft Assn., Internat. Brotherhood Magicians, Fellowship Christian Magicians. Republican. Home: 6035 113th Ave N Pinellas Park FL 33565 Office: PO Box 12345 St Petersburg FL 33733

MA, MICHAEL DEN-CHAU, microbiologist; b. Shenyang, China, Sept. 22, 1938; came to U.S., 1964, naturalized, 1974; s. An-lan and Ling-ching (Ho) M.; B.S., Nat. Taiwan U., 1963; M.S., Purdue U., 1967; m. Stella Hsing Hung, Aug. 24, 1968; children—Joseph, David. Research asst. dept. botany and plant pathology Purdue U., 1965-67; research asst. biology dept. U. Chgo., 1968-74; research scientist Armour Pharm. Co., KanKakee, Ill., 1974-78; research scientist Frito-Lay, Inc., Dallas, 1978—. Served with Taiwan Army, 1963-64. Mem. Am. Soc. Microbiology, Sigma Xi. Contbr. articles to profl. jours.; patentee in field. Home: 3525 Pinehurst Dr Plano TX 75075 Office: 900 Loop 12 Irving TX 75060

MAA, PETER SHENG-SHYONG, chem. engr.; b. Taipei, Taiwan, Apr. 25, 1942; s. Kuen-chen and Tsai-fong (Chen) M.; came to U.S., 1965, naturalized, 1977; B.S., Nat. Taiwan U., 1964; M.S., Kans. State U., 1968; Ph.D., W.Va. U., 1971; m. Carol Yen, May 9, 1970; children—Edward F.T., Victor F.J. Research engr. W.Va. U., Morgantown, 1971-72; research asso. Inst. Mining Minerals Research U. Ky., Lexington, 1972-74; sr. staff engr. Exxon Research & Engring. Co., Baytown, Tex., 1974—; mem. Gordon Research Conf. on Fuel Sci., 1978, 79. Mem. Am. Chem. Soc., Am. Inst. Chem. Engrs. Club: Houston Formosan. Patentee. Home: 3708 Autumn Ln Baytown TX 77521 Office: PO Box 4255 Baytown TX 77520

MABE, DAVID LINWOOD, elec. technician; b. Stanleytown, Va., Mar. 22, 1941; s. Robert Homer and Nellie EuJean (Collins) M.; Danville Tech. Inst., 1962; student Central Va. Coll., 1972; m. Erika Gaertig, Sept. 1, 1974; children—Thomas Linwood, Michael David. Test technician Titan II Missile Communication Systems, Gen. Elec. Co., Lynchburg, Va., 1962-64, test and evaluation dept. Mobile Radio Dept., 1964-68, lead technician Calibration & Construction Lab., 1968-72, tech. specialist, foreman Mastr II Assembly, 1972-74, 1974-76, digital equipment specialist, 1976—. Mem. local Republican Campaign Com., 1964—; base comdr. Va. Community Alert Patrol, Lynchburg, 1976—; active in aid to handicapped and elderly; Sunday sch. tchr. Hyland Hgts. Bapt. Ch. Recipient 10 and 15 yr. service awards. Gen. Elec., 1972, 1977, award in microwave design, 1965, in transistors, 1964, transistor design, 1966, integrated circuits, 1975, computer BASIC, 1976, calculator and programming, 1976, quality control, 1973. Mem. Aircraft Owners and Pilot Assn., NRA, Nat. Geographic Soc., Smithsonian Asso. Republican. Baptist Club: Word of Life (leader). Applied for patents in improved pilot light assembly, for solar heater differential regulator. Home: Route 2 Box 68-B Lynchburg VA 24501 Office: Mt View Rd RM-4G-27 Lynchburg VA 24502

MABIRE, KENNETH EARL, ins. co. exec.; b. Pensacola, Fla., Jan. 8, 1946; s. Daniel Edward and Lora Lee (Hollingsworth) M.; B.S., U. West Fla., 1968; M.S., Rollins Coll., 1977; m. Erica Jane Frazier, Aug. 24, 1968. Vice pres. Flagship Banks, Inc., Orlando, Fla., 1974-77, v.p. subs. Seaforth, Inc., 1976-78, dir. Flagship Bank of West Orlando, 1976-77, v.p., Jacksonville, Fla., 1977-78; pres., dir. Investor Life of Fla., Winter Park, Fla., 1978—. Mem. Am. Soc. Personnel Adminstrn., Fla. Bankers Assn., Bank Adminstrn. Inst., Jacksonville, Orlando chambers commerce. Democrat. Methodist. Club: Rotary. Home: 814 Laurel Ave Orlando FL 32803 Office: 400 N New York Ave Suite 105 Winter Park FL 32789

MABRY, EDWARD BLOXTON, obstetrician-gynecologist; b. New Hanover County, N.C., Mar. 8, 1927; s. Carl Edward and Virginia (Bloxton) M.; B.S., Duke U., 1951, M.D., 1953; children—Edward Bloxton, Catherine Bryan, Mary Virginia, Rhett Nicholson, Carl Edward, Sarah Elizabeth; m. 2d, Martha Gray Preston, Nov. 1977. Intern, U.Va., Charlottesville, 1953-54; asst. resident in obstetrics and gynecology Duke U., Durham, N.C., 1954-55, asst. resident, 1957-59, resident, instr., 1959-60; practice medicine, specializing in obstetrics and gynecology, Burlington, N.C., 1960-61, Greensboro, N.C., 1961—; chief obstetrical and gynecological service Wesley Long Hosp., Greensboro, 1976—, pres. med. bd., 1980—. Served with USN, 1945-46, to capt., USAF, 1955-56. Diplomate Am. Bd. Obstetrics and Gynecology. Fellow Am. Coll. Obstetricians and Gynecologists; mem. Guilford County Med. Soc., N.C. Med. Soc., Am. Med. Assn., S. Atlantic Assn. Obstetrics and Gynecology, Am. Fertility Soc., N.C. Obstetrical and Gynecologic Soc., Bayard Carter Soc. Obstetricians and Gynecologists, Internat. Corres. Soc. of Obstetricians and Gynecologists. Methodist. Clubs: Iron Dukes, Civitan. Contbr. articles in field to med. jours. Home: 4706 Lake Jeannette Rd Greensboro NC 27405 Office: 1305 W Wendover Ave Greensboro NC 27408

MABRY, NELLOISE JOHNSON, educator; b. Valdosta, Ga., Sept. 8, 1921; d. Hansford Duncan and Maudelle (Williams) Johnson; student Bethel Woman's Coll., 1938-39, Wesleyan Conservatory, 1941; A.B., Mercer U., 1943, M.Ed., 1949; m. William Herbert Mabry, Mar. 5, 1942 (div. Nov. 1947); 1 son, William Herbert. Tchr., Cynthia H. Weir Elementary Sch., Macon, Ga., 1950—. Mem. Nat., Ga., Bibb edn. assns., Ga. Assn. for Childhood Edn. (state pres. 1964-66), Delta Kappa Gamma (chpt. scrapbook chmn. 1966-68, chpt. program chmn. 1974-76), A.A.U.W., Alpha Delta Pi, Alpha Psi Omega. Democrat. Baptist. Home: 1575 Adams St Macon GA 31204

MACAULAY, ANGUS HAMILTON, lawyer; b. Spartanburg, S.C., Apr. 1, 1928; s. Angus H. and Margaret (White) M.; A.B., The Citadel, 1950; LL.B., Yale, 1955; m. Amanda C. Tevepaugh, May 12, 1962; children—Angus H., Alexander M., Katherine. Admitted to S.C. bar, 1955, Va. bar, 1956, since practiced in Richmond, Va.; mem. firm Mays, Valentine, Davenport & Moore, 1961—. Dir. Colonial Life & Accident Ins. Co., Columbia, S.C. Mem. Richmond Air Pollution Control Bd., 1965-79; pres. Richmond Community Action Program, 1969-70, Richmond Jaycees, 1963-64; mem. Richmond Democratic Com., chmn., 1973-75; chmn. 3d Dist. Dem. com., 1975—; mem. Va. State Central Dem. Com., 1968—; mem. exec. bd. Robert E. Lee council Boy Scouts Am., 1978—; trustee Richmond Forward, 1965-79; bd. dirs. United Givers Fund, 1969-72; pres. Maymont Found, 1978—. Served with AUS, 1946-47, to 1st lt., 1951-53. Recipient Gold Feather award for outstanding community service, 1972. Mem. Am. (exec. council jr. bar conf. 1960-62), Va. (chmn. young lawyers sect. 1959-60, chmn. joint com. pub. info. 1966-68), Richmond bar assns. Presbyn. Kiwanian (dir. 1975-77). Clubs: Country of Va.; Downtown (Richmond). Home: 502 Henri Rd Richmond VA 23226 Office: F & M Center PO Box 1122 Richmond VA 23208

MAC BRIDE, DEXTER DUPONT, assn. exec.; b. Elizabeth, N.J., Aug. 18, 1917; s. Charles Munnerlyn and Flora T. (Jerome) MacB.; student William & Mary Coll., 1936-37; LL.B., Cumberland U., 1938; J.D., Samford U., 1970; M.A. in Valuation Scis., Hofstra U., 1979; m. Grace Anderson, Dec. 23, 1963; 1 son, Charles Dexter. Admitted to Va. bar, 1939; practiced in Norfolk, 1939-41; sr. right of way agt. City of Los Angeles, 1946-47; supervising right of way agt. State of Cal., Sacramento, 1948-63, asst. chief right of way agt., 1963-70; exec. v.p. Am. Soc. Appraisers, Washington, 1970—. Dir. Nat. Valutape Program ASA. Fellow Am. Soc. Appraisers, Inc. Soc. Valuers and Auctioneers (London); mem. Am. Right of Way Assn. (nat. sec.; exec. com., sr. mem.), Am. Arbitration Assn. (nat. panel arbitrators), Audubon Soc., Am. Soc. Assn. Execs. (certified), Lambda Alpha. Author: Power and Process. Editor: Valuation Quar.; The Bibliography of Appraisal Literature, 1974. Home: 11457 Washington Plaza W Reston VA 22070 Office: Dulles Internat Airport PO Box 17265 Washington DC 20041

MAC CAMMOND, MICKIE SHEFFIELD, speech pathologist; b. Evansville, Ind., Feb. 10, 1953; d. Corbett T. and Alice M. Sheffield; B.A., La. Tech. U., 1975, M.A., 1976; m. James A. F. MacCammond III, Aug. 6, 1977. Grad. asst. public speaking La. Tech. U., Ruston, La., 1975-76; tchr. of deaf parent-pupil edn. program La. State Sch. for Deaf, Baton Rouge, 1976-77; speech therapist Jackson Parish Sch. System, Jonesboro, La., 1977-78; office mgr., biofeedback technician Stress, Tension and Anxiety Tng. Clinics Inc., Arlington, Tex., 1978: speech pathologist Audio Communications Therapy Clinic Inc., Bedford, Tex., 1978—; cons. in field. Mem. Am. Speech-Lang.-Hearing Assn. cert. speech pathology, Am. Bus. Women's Assn. (rec. sec. 1979-80). Home: 6900 Briardale Dr Fort Worth TX 76180 Office: Audio Communications Therapy Clinic Inc 1305-J Brown Trail Bedford TX 76021

MACDONALD, JOHN MITCHELL, physician; b. Pitts., Jan. 7, 1937; s. Robert R. and Ruth (Johnson) M.; B.S., U. Notre Dame, 1958; M.D., U. Pa., 1962; m. Karen Day, Sept. 12, 1962; children—John, Christopher, Patrick, Ian. Intern, U. Miami-Jackson Meml. Hosp., 1962-63; resident in gen. and thoracic surgery U. Pitts.-Presbyn. U., 1965-70; sr. registrar in thoracic surgery St. Bartholomew's Hosp., Lonson, 1970-71; practice medicine specializing in gen., cardiovascular and thoracic surgery, Fort Lauderdale, Fla., 1971—. Served to capt. USAF, 1963-65. Diplomate Am. Bd. Surgery, Am. Bd. Thoracic Surgery. Mem. AMA, Fla. Med. Assn., Broward County Med. Assn., A.C.S., Fla. Soc. Thoracic and Cardiovascular Surgeons, Broward County Heart Assn. (past pres.), Ft. Lauderdale Thoracic Surg. Soc., Ft. Lauderdale Surg. Soc., Am. Coll. Chest Physicians, So. Thoracic Surg. Assn. Roman Catholic. Clubs: Coral Ridge Country, Caducean Soc. Greater Ft. Lauderdale. Contbr. articles to med. jours. Office: 1930 NE 47th St Fort Lauderdale FL 33308

MACDONALD, RALPH FABIAN, JR., tobacco co. exec.; b. Chgo., Jan. 27, 1930; s. Ralph Fabian and Catherine (Bacigalupo) MacD.; B.A., U. Va., 1950; m. Jeanne Marie Burckell, Dec. 26, 1952; children—Ralph Fabian, Mary Michele. With The American Tobacco Co., 1952—, asst. supt. Va. and Reidsville brs., 1952-64, asst. coordinator new products div. research and devel., Hopewell, Va., 1965-66, budget and staff coordinator dept. manufacture, N.Y.C., 1966-70, coordinator community relations, safety, equal employment opportunity, Richmond, Va., 1970—. Bus. curriculum advisor J. Sargent Reynolds Community Coll. Midlothian Dist. Republican chmn., 1962-64; mem. Richmond employer adv. com. Va. Employment Commn. Served with USMC, 1950-52. Mem. Am. Soc. Personnel Adminstrn., Va. State C. of C., Co. Mil. Historians.

Republican. Roman Catholic. Home: 2410 Wadebridge Rd Midlothian VA 23113 Office: Va br Am Tobacco Co PO Box 27531 Richmond VA 23261

MACDONALD, ROBERT RIGG, hist. museum dir.; b. Pitts., May 11, 1942; s. Robert R. and Ruth Anne (Johnson) M.; B.A., U. Notre Dame, 1964, M.A. (Univ. scholar 1965), 1965; M.A., U. Pa., 1970; m. Catherine R. Ronan, Nov. 27, 1965; children—Matthew, Robert, Catherine. Asst. curator Smithsonian Instn., Washington, 1965-66; dir. Mercer Mus., Doylestown, Pa., 1966-69, New Haven Colony Hist. Soc., 1970-74, La. State Mus., New Orleans, 1974—; asso. fellow Berkeley Coll., Yale U., 1974-80; mem. New Haven Bicentennial Commn., 1972-74; asst. sec. La. Dept. Culture, Recreation and Tourism, 1974-79. Named Outstanding Citizen, Inst. Human Understanding, 1979. Mem. Am. Assn. Museums (council), Am. Assn. State and Local History (council), La. Assn. Museums (pres. 1979). Roman Catholic. Editor: New Haven Colony Furniture, 1974; Louisiana's Black Heritage, 1979. Home: 8008 Jeannette Pl New Orleans LA 70118 Office: 751 Chartre St New Orleans LA 70116

MAC DONALD, RUSSELL WHITNEY, educator; b. Boston, Oct. 2, 1923; s. Raymond Henry and Florence Marion (Tesson) MacD.; B.S. in B.A., Fla. So. Coll., 1949; M.B.A., Stetson U., 1970; postgrad. Rollins Coll., 1968, U. Central Fla., 1969-70, U. N.C., 1972-73; m. Juanita A. Ergle, May 25, 1947; children—Russell W., Kyle Alan. Lead propulsion engr. Titan program Martin-Marietta Corp., Cape Canaveral, Fla., 1953-63; mem. tech. staff Aerospace Corp., Kennedy Space Center, 1963-65; environ. control systems engr. N. Am. Rockwell, Cape Kennedy, Fla., 1965-70; prof. bus. Wingate (N.C.) Coll., 1971—; with SAC, Vandenberg AFB, Calif., 1959-60. Served with USAAF, 1942-45. Decorated D.F.C., Air Medal, Purple Heart. Recipient Apollo Achievement award NASA, 1969. Mem. Am. Acctg. Assn., Acad. Mgmt., Am. Mktg. Assn., Missile Pioneers. Democrat. Baptist. Clubs: Elks, Moose. Home: 211 Elm St Wingate NC 28174 Office: Wingate Coll PO Box 572 Wingate NC 28174

MAC DONALD, RUTH LANE (MRS. ERNEST R. MACDONALD), librarian; b. Buffalo; d. Fred W. and Elizabeth G. (Thynge) Lane; B.A., State U. N.Y. at Buffalo, 1934, B.L.S., 1937, M.Ed., 1957; postgrad. Temple U., 1959, U. Del., 1960, Syracuse U., 1963, 64; m. 2d, Ernest R. MacDonald, Nov. 23, 1957; 1 dau. by previous marriage, Nancy J. Librarian, Gowanda (N.Y.) High Sch., 1934-37; supr. libraries Vestal (N.Y.) Central Sch. System, 1937-42; librarian Buffalo and Erie County Pub. Library, 1942-44; head librarian Amherst Central High Sch., Snyder, N.Y., 1945-47; dir. Learning Resources Centers, Erie Community Coll., Buffalo, 1947-76; lectr. Library Sch., State U. N.Y. at Buffalo, 1972, instr. adult reading courses Div. Continuing Edn., 1963-78; instr. Downtown Campus, Broward Community Coll., Ft. Lauderdale, Fla., 1977—. Active ARC; mem. Com. Woman, Buffalo, 1959-62; exec. bd. Niagara Frontier Reading Council. Mem. Spl. Libraries Assn. (nat. chmn. metals div. 1968, pres. Upstate N.Y. chpt. 1960), Coll. Reading Assn., N.Y. Library Assn. (coll. and univ. sect. treas. 1967-71, exec. bd. 1972-73), Bus. and Profl. Women's Assn., Sch. Info. and Library Sci. Alumni Assn., Internat. Reading Assn., U. Buffalo Alumni Assn., Sigma Kappa, Pi Lambda Theta (treas.). Contbr. articles to profl. jours. Home: 411 SE 2d Ave Pompano Beach FL 33060 Office: Broward Community Coll 225 E Las Olas Blvd Fort Lauderdale FL 33301

MACDONALD, THOMAS COOK, JR., lawyer; b. Atlanta, Oct. 11, 1929; s. Thomas Cook and Mary (Morgan) MacD.; B.S. with high honors, U. Fla., 1951, LL.B. with high honors, 1953; m. Gay Anne Everiss, June 30, 1956; children—Margaret Anne, Thomas William. Admitted to Fla. bar, 1953; practiced in Tampa, 1953—; mem. firm Shackleford, Farrior, Stallings & Evans, 1953—; dir. Royal Trust Bank, Tampa, Jim Walter Corp.; legis. counsel Gov. of Fla., 1963; del. 5th Circuit Jud. Conf., 1969—; mem. Supreme Ct. Com. on Jud. Ethics, 1976. Mem. Fla. Student Scholarship and Loan Commn., 1963-67, Hillsborough County Pub. Edn. Study Commn., 1965. Bd. dirs. Univ. Community Hosp., 1968-78. Served to 1st lt. Judge Adv. Gen. Corp., USAF, 1953-55. Recipient Disting. Alumnus award U. Fla., 1976. Fellow Am. Bar Found., Am. Coll. Trial Lawyers; mem. Am. Law Inst., Am. Bar Assn. (com. on ethics and profl. responsibility 1970-76), Fla. Bar (mem. com. on profl. ethics 1964-72, chmn. 1966-70, bd. govs. 1970-74), Fla. W. Coast Sports Assn. (sec. 1965—), U. Fla. Nat. Alumni Assn. (pres. 1973), Phi Kappa Phi, Phi Delta Phi, Fla. Blue Key, Kappa Alpha. Episcopalian. Home: 1904 Holly Ln Tampa FL 33609 Office: PO Box 3324 Tampa FL 33601

MAC DOUGALL, ROBERT DOUGLAS, geologist; b. McVille, N.D., Jan. 2, 1922; s. Rollo Dixon and Nettie Corinne (Syvertson) MacD.; student N.D. State Sch. Sci., 1939-41, U. N.D., 1946-47; B.A., U. Mont., 1949; M.S., U. Minn., 1952; m. Ingrid Margarete Heemann, Sept. 30, 1961; children—Jerome W., James F. Surface geologist Arabian Am. Oil Co., Saudi Arabia, 1952-56, subsurface geologist, 1956-59; cons. geologist, N.D. and Mont., 1959-62; geologist U.S. Geol. Survey, Washington, 1962-70, Metairie, La., 1970—. Served with USNR, 1942-46. Fellow Royal Geog. Soc.; mem. Am. Assn. Petroleum Geologists, New Orleans Geol. Soc. Home: 646 Oak St Mandeville LA 70448 Office: US Geol Survey Gulf of Mexico Region 3301 N Causeway Blvd PO Box 7944 Metairie LA 70011

MAC FADYEN, BRUCE VISCHER, JR., physician and surgeon; b. Phila., Nov. 4, 1942; s. Bruce V. and Renee S. (Smith) MacF.; B.S., Wheaton Coll., 1964; M.D., Hahnemann Med. Coll., 1968; m. Rosemary Mortensen, June 18, 1965; children—Sharon Ruth, Deborah Renee, Bruce Vischer III. Intern, Hosp. of U. Pa., 1968-69, asst. resident gen. surgery, 1969-72, Hermann Hosp., Houston, 1972-73, chief resident surgery, 1973-74; research fellow Harrison dept. surg. research U. Pa. Sch. Medicine, Phila., 1971-72; practice medicine specializing in surgery, Phila., 1968-72, Houston, 1972—; asst. instr. surgery U. Pa., Phila., 1969-72; instr. surgery U. Tex. Med. Sch., Houston, 1973-74, asst. prof. surgery, 1974-77, asso. prof. surgery, 1977—; mem. staff Hermann, Meml. S.W., Diagnostic, Park Plaza hosps., Houston. Diplomate Am. Bd. Surgery. Fellow A.C.S.; mem. Assn. Acad. Surgery, Am. Soc. for Parenteral and Engeral Nutrition, Soc. for Surgery of Alimentary Tract, Internat. Soc. Parenteral Nutrition, Soc. Surg. Oncology, Am. Cancer Soc. (dir. 1976-80), Harris County Med. Soc., AMA, Tex. Med. Assn., Tex. Surg. Soc., Ravdin-Rhoads Surg. Soc., Collegium Internat. Chirurgiae, AAAS. Baptist. Contbr. numerous articles on surgery and oncology to med. jours. Home: 10319 Holly Springs Houston TX 77042 Office: 6431 Fannin St Houston TX 77030

MAC GIBBON, HUGH CARLYSLE, appraiser; b. Birmingham, June 29, 1916; s. Hugh Carlysle and Ella (Holly) MacG.; student pvt. sch.; m. Kathryne Andrews, Jan. 31, 1942; children—Holly, Hugh, Heather. Instrument engr. Procter & Gamble Co., Memphis, 1940-41; owner ABC Diaper Service, Berkeley, Calif., 1946-47; owner Self-Serv Laundry, Punta Gorda, Fla., 1947-52; postmaster, Punta Gorda, 1952-72; owner Ind. Appraisal Service, Punta Gorda, 1966—; dir. 1st Fed. Savs. and Loan Assn., Charlotte County. Mem. City Council, Punta Gorda, 1949-50; mem. nat. advisory bd. Am. Security Council; pres. Charlotte Hosp. Assn., 1950; mem. 2 Charter Rev. Bds., Punta Gorda. Served with USN, 1935-39, with USAAF, 1942-45. Decorated D.F.C., Air medal with 4 oak leaf clusters, Purple Heart. Mem. Res. Officers Assn. (pres. S.W. Fla. chpt., 1956), Nat. Sojourners (founding pres. S.W. Fla. chpt.). Republican. Clubs: Masons, Kiwanis (pres. 1961), Gun (pres. 1953) (Punta Gorda). Home: Route 2 Box 1092 Punta Gorda FL 33950 Office: PO Box 1748 Punta Gorda FL 33950

MACHA, BARBARA JEAN, acct.; b. Sugar Land, Tex., Dec. 11, 1945; d. Raymond Joseph and Hattie Frances (Edar) Anhaiser; student Wharton County Jr. Coll., 1964-65, 74-75, U. Tex., 1965-67, Houston Community Coll., 1976-77; m. Gerald Charles Macha, May 2, 1970; 1 dau., Jennifer Jo. With Sperry-Sun, Inc., Houston, 1967—, acct., 1975-76, supr. acctg. control, 1976-77, sr. acct., 1977-79, supr. acctg., 1979—. Home: 1308 Miles St Rosenberg TX 77471 Office: Sperry-Sun Inc PO Box 36363 Houston TX 77036

MACHEMEHL, JERRY LEE, civil engr., educator; b. Bryan, Tex., Jan. 8, 1938; s. Louis Arnold and Martha Lillian (Anderson) M.; B.S. in Archtl. Constrn., Tex. A&M U., 1970, B.S. in Civil Engring., 1962, M.S. in Hydraulic Engring., 1968, Ph.D. in Civil Engring., 1970; diploma U.S. Army Command and Gen. Staff Coll., 1977; m. Pat Curry, Dec. 26, 1959; children—Terri, David, Traci. Civil engr. U.S. Army Engr. Dist., Little Rock, Ark., 1964, hydraulic engr., 1965; engring. research asso. coastal and ocean engring. div. dept. civil engring. Tex. A&M U., College Station, 1967-68, instr., 1969-70; research engr. Wilson Industries, Houston, Tex., 1969-70; asst. prof. civil engring. N.C. State U., Raleigh, 1970-76, asso. prof. civil engring., 1976-78, asso. prof. marine sci. and engring., 1978—; cons. in ocean and coastal engring., 1970—. Served with USAR, 1962—. U.S. Army Corps Engrs. fellow, 1968-69; W.G. Mills Meml. fellow, 1969; registered profl. engr., Tex., N.C. Mem. ASCE (mem. exec. com. pipeline div. 1978-83), Tau Beta Pi, Chi Epsilon, Sigma Xi, Phi Delta Kappa, Tau Sigma Delta, Phi Kappa Phi. Mem. Assembly of God Ch. Contbr. numerous articles on coastal and marine engring. to profl. jours.; research in hydrodynamics and coastal processes. Home: 6812 Electra Dr Raleigh NC 27607 Office: Dept Marine Science and Engineering North Carolina State Univ Raleigh NC 27650

MACHOVEC, MARVIN ANTHONY, petroleum cons.; b. Wahoo, Nebr., Oct. 17, 1933; s. Frank Anthony and Barbara Ann (Fisher) M.; B.S., U. Nebr., 1961, M.S., 1963; m. Barbara June Davis, Oct. 8, 1967; children—Kenneth Anthony, Kimberly Ann, Mark Allen. Geologist, Mobil Oil Corp., Houston, Victoria, Corpus Christi, Tex., 1963-68, wellsite supr., Mobil Producing, Nigeria, Fernado Po, Rep. Equatorial Guinea and Lagos, Nigeria, 1968-72; v.p. ops., Pexcon Inc., Dallas, 1972-74; v.p. and exploration mgr., Basin Exploration Corp., Houston, 1974-76, exploration cons., Houston, 1976—; dir. Pexcon, Inc. Served with U.S. Army, 1954-57. Registered profl. geologist, Calif. Mem. Am. Assn. Petroleum Geologists, Soc. Exploration Geophysicists. Republican. Roman Catholic. Home: 1914 Crystal Springs St Kingwood TX 77339 Office: 719 C and I Life Bldg 1006 Main St Houston TX 77002

MACIAS-RENDON, FERNANDO, univ. pres.; b. Los Angeles, Nov. 13, 1927; s. Miguel Angel Macias and Ana Maria Rendon; Chem. Engr., ITESM, Monterrey, Mex., 1950; M. Engring., Va. Poly. Inst., 1952; Litt.D.(hon.), William Woods Coll., 1977; LL.D. (hon.), U. Far East, 1979; m. Maria del Carmen Garza y Garza, Apr. 4, 1956; children—Fernando, Claudia. Prof. chem. engring. and math. ITESM, 1952-61; pres. Centro de Ensenanza Tecnica y Superior de Mexicali, 1961-67; asst. dir. finances and devel. ITESM, 1967-69; dir. Indsl. Dynamics Co., Mexico City, 1969-75; pres. U. Americas, St. Catarina Martir (Pue.), Mex., 1975—. Adv. bd. Puebla chpt. ARC. Mem. Internat. Assn. Univ. Presidents (vice chmn. N.Am. council), Assn. Free Enterprise Edn. (dir.). Clubs: Empresarios (adv. bd.), Golf (Puebla). Address: Apdo 100 Santa Catarina Martir (Pue) Mexico

MACK, DONALD JOSEPH, social worker; b. Port Arthur, Tex., June 1, 1937; s. Howard and Dorothy M.; B.S., Lamar State U., 1961; M.S.W., U. Tex., 1977; m. Gussie Lee Vinson, Dec. 29, 1963; 1 son, Todd. Dir., Neighborhood Action, Fort Worth, 1967-72, Community Action, Fort Worth, 1972-75, Fort Worth Center for Ex-Offenders, 1975—; instr. criminal justice U. Tex., 1978—. Trustee Fort Worth Country Day Sch., 1976—. Served with USN, 1955-59. Home: 3304 Lawndale St Fort Worth TX 76133 Office: Fort Worth Center for Ex-Offenders 2016 Evans St Fort Worth TX 76104

MACK, GARNETT LLOYD, educator; b. Chase City, Va., Apr. 26, 1931; s. Garnet and Susanna (Gayle) M.; B.A., Storer Coll., Harpers Ferry, W.Va., 1954; postgrad. Ohio State U., 1955; M.A., George Washington U., 1966, M.Philosophy, 1969, Ph.D. (So. Fellowships fellow), 1972; postgrad. Rydal Mt. Summer Sch., Eng., 1972, Emory U., summer 1975; m. Janice Deros McManus, June 1, 1963; children—Luis Garnett, Lloyd Joseph. Instr. English, Va. State U., Petersburg, 1964-67, asst. prof., 1967-71, asso. prof., 1971-73, prof., 1973—, coordinator grad. studies English, 1972—, editor Scip Anglia, dept. English newsletter, 1973—; lectr. English and Am. civilization George Washington U., summers 1968-70; ednl. specialist U.S. Dept. Agr. Research Center, Beltsville, Md., summer 1971; exec. dir. Mack's Secretarial Services; notary public. Tutor, vol. worker Childrens Home of Va. Baptists, Inc., Petersburg, 1972—, editor New Horizons newsletter; active Bapt. Home Improvement Assn., Big Bros. founder, pres. James Alexander Gayle Meml. Fellowship Fund, Inc., 1976—. Served with AUS, 1956-58; mem. Res. (ret.). Mem. MLA, Am. Studies Assn. (nat. Am. studies faculty), Wordsworth-Coleridge Assn., Am. Lit. Assn., South Atlantic Modern Lang. Assn., Coll. Lang. Assn., Comparative Lit. Assn., African Lit. Assn., Shakespeare Assn., Internat. Shakespeare Congress. Democrat. Presbyn. Home: 6900 Hickory Rd Petersburg VA 23803 Office: Va State U Box 376 Petersburg VA 23803

MACK, GARRY, city ofcl.; b. Atlanta, Sept. 6, 1945; s. Dennis and Jewel (Hillman) M.; B.S., Morris Brown Coll., 1967; postgrad. Ga. State U., 1970-76. Programmer analyst City of Atlanta, 1970-76, computer ops. asst. mgr., 1976—. Served with U.S. Army, 1967-69. Mem. Math. Assn. Am., Phi Beta Sigma. Baptist. Home: 1257 Weston Dr Decatur GA 30032 Office: City of Atlanta 68 Mitchell St SW Atlanta GA 30303

MACK, JAMES WALTON, educator; b. Darlington County, S.C., Dec. 26, 1927; s. John W. and Eva P. (Parott) M.; A.S., Florence-Darlington Tech. Coll., 1973; B.A., Clemson U., 1975; m. Lurlean B. Bess, May 6, 1946; children—James W., Loris C., Lerlita, Gabriella, Thaddeus A. Pitcher, Pitts. Pirates Orgn., 1958-62; tchr., Butler High Sch., Hartsville, S.C., 1962-67; with Union Carbide Corp., Florence, S.C., 1967-73; machine shop instr. Florence Darlington Tech. Coll., 1973—. Mem. Darlington Task for Progress, 1976, Commn. on Alcohol and Drug Abuse, Darlington County, 1977; pres. task force for progress Butler High Sch., 1978-79. Mem. ASME. Methodist. Club: Boys. Home: 240 Route 1 Lamar SC 29069 Office: PO Drawer F8000 Florence SC 29501

MACK, JAY ORD, JR., metallurgist; b. Wilkinsburg, Pa., May 2, 1922; s. Jay Ord and June (Shupe) M.; B.S. in Metall. Engring., Carnegie Inst. Tech., 1942, M.S. in Metall. Engring., 1950; postgrad. Pa. State U., 1945-47, U. Pitts., 1950-51; m. Nyla McCrory, May 22, 1943; children—Nyla Jane, Debra Lee. Metall. laborer, observer Edgar Thomson works U.S. Steel Corp., Braddock, Pa., 1941-42, supervising technologist applied research labs., Monroeville, Pa., 1947-51, chief control and devel. metallurgist Fairless works, Fairless Hills, Pa., 1951-59, chief steel prodn. metallurgist, 1959-64, asst. chief metallurgist, insp., 1964-71, chief metallurgist, 1971-77, mgr. process metallurgy, Pitts., 1977-80, mgr. tech. services Tex. works, Baytown, 1980—; welding engr. Naval Research Lab., Washington, 1943-45; research asst. Pa. State U., 1945-47. Mem. Am. Soc. Metals (John A. Roebling award lectr. 1976), AIME, Am. Iron and Steel Engrs. Contbr. articles to profl. jours. Office: US Steel Corp PO Box 29 Baytown TX 77520

MACK, THEODORE, lawyer; b. Ft. Worth, Mar. 5, 1936; s. Henry and Norma (Harris) M.; A.B. cum laude, Harvard, 1958, J.D., 1961; m. Ellen Feinknopf, June 19, 1960; children—Katherine Norma, Elizabeth Ellen, Alexandra. Admitted to Tex. bar, 1961, U.S. Supreme Ct. bar, 1971; asso. firm Mack & Mack, Fort Worth, 1961-62, partner, 1963-70; partner Wynn, Brown, Mack, Renfro & Thompson, and predecessor firms, 1970—; dir. So. Plow Co., Dallas, 1966—, v.p., 1968—, sec., 1976—. Bd. dirs. Jewish Fedn. Fort Worth, 1965-72, sec., 1967-68, 3d v.p., 1968-69; bd. dirs. Suicide Prevention of Tarrant County, Tex. 1963-64, Tarrant County Sr. Citizens Center, Inc., 1969—; trustee Ft. Worth Country Day Sch., 1976—; participant Leadership Ft. Worth, 1973-74; trustee several pvt. trusts. Mem. Am., Fort Worth Tarrant County bar assns., State Bar Tex. (chmn. dist. grievance com. 1973), Harvard Alumni Assn., Harvard Law Sch. Assn. (v.p. 1977), Harvard Law Sch. Fund (class agt. 1973—), Harvard Law Sch. Assn. Tex. (dir. 1970-73, treas. 1973-74, sec. 1974-75, v.p. 1975-76, pres. 1976-77). Democrat. Jewish (dir. congregation 1964-73, sec 1968-69, 72-73, pres. 1975-77). Club: Rotary (Ft. Worth). Editor: Bar News of Fort Worth Tarrant County Bar Assn., 1963-64. Home: 2817 Harlanwood Dr Fort Worth TX 76109 Office: Oil and Gas Bldg Fort Worth TX 76102

MACK, WILBUR OLLIO, univ. adminstr.; b. Seward, Okla., Aug. 11, 1919; s. Collister Milton and Addie Lee (Lowe) M.; B.S. Langston U., 1947; M.S.A.E., Okla. State U., Stillwater, 1954; m. Julia Mae Hobbs, May 19, 1945 (dec.); children—Ronald W., Mettonia G. Thomas, Waymond O., Larry W., Denise W.; m. 2d, Martha M. Griffin, Aug. 11, 1970. Tchr. public schs., Seminole, Okla., 1949-51; with dept. agrl. engring. Prairie View (Tex.) A. and M. U., 1953-57; head dept. agrl. engring So. U., Baton Rouge, La., 1957-62; head dept. hort. and soil sci. Fla. A. and M. U., Tallahassee, 1962—. Pres., Lee Manor Improvement Assn., 1963-67; leader Boy Scouts Am., 1962-68. Served with U.S. Army, 1941-45. Registered profl. engr., Tex., La. Mem. Am. Soc. Agrl. Engrs., Am. Soc. Soil Conservationists, Am. Soc. Crop Sci., Community Devel. Soc., Kappa Alpha Psi. Democrat. Baptist. Clubs: Chess, Bridge, Goodwill. Home: 710 Stafford St Tallahassee FL 32304 Office: Fla A and M U Tallahassee FL 32307

MAC KECHNIE, HORACE KNIGHT, elec. engr.; b. Somerville, Mass., Jan. 26, 1909; s. Arthur North and Marion Ardelle (Knight) MacK.; B.S., Mass. Inst. Tech., 1933; postgrad., Harvard, 1943, N.Y. U., 1942; m. Prudence Smith, Oct. 10, 1931; children—Margaret (Mrs. Richard Skillman), Joan North. Research asso. Harvard Radio Research Lab., 1942-46; lab. chief Air Materiel Command, Cambridge (Mass.) Field Sta., 1946-47, sr. engr. Mass. Inst. Tech., 1947; cons., mgr. various indsl. electronics cos., 1947-58; project mgr. Sylvania Elec. Products, Inc., Buffalo, N.Y., 1958-62; design rev. mgr. RCA, Camden, N.J., 1962-64; program mgr. Product Engring. Services Office, Dept. Def., Alexandria, Va., 1964-79; ret., 1979; engring. cons., 1979—. Mem. Town Meeting, Lexington, Mass., 1956-57. Served with AUS Res., 1933-40. Registered profl. engr., Mass., Ohio, Calif. Mem. IEEE (sr.), Nat. Soc. Profl. Engrs., Soc. Am. Valve Engrs., Mason. Club: Mass. Institute of Technology (Washington). Patentee elec. blanket control, high current switch. Home and office: 8315 Bound Brook Ln Alexandria VA 22309

MAC KENZIE, DUANE EDWIN, elec. designer; b. Hollywood, Calif., Aug. 25, 1924; s. Colin Archibald and Dorothy Helen (Williams) MacK.; student Los Angeles City Coll., 1946-47, Northrop Aero. Inst., 1947-49, N.C. State U., 1965; m. Lois Welborn, Apr. 29, 1966; children—Marilyn MacKenzie Weatherman, Colin. Elect. designer J.N. Pease, Assos., Architects and Engrs., Charlotte, N.C., 1962-63; owner Cons. Engring. Service, Inc., Winston-Salem, N.C., 1965-74; elec. cons., 1974-76; pres. Lighting Concepts, Inc., Vero Beach, Fla., 1976-78; illuminating engr. Reynolds, Smith & Hills, Jacksonville, Fla., 1978-79, elec. design cons., 1980—. Active Republican party. Served with USNR, 1942-46. Mem. Illuminating Engring. Soc. (regional v.p. 1971-73, nat. dir. 1973-74, pres. N.E. Fla. sect. 1979-80), U.S. Coast Guard Aux. Address: 7416 Holiday Rd S Jacksonville FL 32216

MAC KENZIE, JAMES DONALD, clergyman; b. Detroit, Nov. 17, 1924; s. James and Ida (Conklin) M.; student Moody Bible Inst., 1946-49, Union Theol. Sem., 1952; m. Elsie Joan Kerr, May 7, 1960; children—Janet Eileen, Kayly Kathleen, Christy Carol, Kenneth Kerr. Ordained to ministry Presbyn. Ch., 1953; pastor Calvary Ch., Swan Quarter, N.C., 1952-60, Kirkwood Ch., Kannapolis, N.C., 1960-64, Barbecue and Olivia Ch., Olivia, N.C., 1964-71, Elise Ch., Robbins, N.C., 1971—. Historian, Fayetteville Presbytery, 1975—, moderator, 1978. Founder, Conf. on Celtic Studies, Campbell Coll., Buies Creek, N.C., 1972—; councilor Conf. on Scottish Studies (Can.), 1968-75. Served with AUS, 1943-45; ETO. Decorated Purple Heart, Bronze Star. Mem. N.C. Presbyn. Hist. Soc. (pres. 1972-74, Author's award 1970, 75), Harnett Hist. Soc. (pres. 1968-71, Distinguished Service award 1970), Irish Uilleann Pipers Soc., Gaelic Soc. of Inverness, An Comunn Gaidhelach (life). Author: Colorful Heritage, 1970. Editor: The Uilleann Piper, 1974—. Contbr. articles to profl. jours. Home: PO Box 867 Robbins NC 27325

MAC KENZIE, MELISSA TAYLOR, musician, music tchr.; b. Brownsville, Tenn., Sept. 23, 1925; d. Lee Bond and Rose Eleanor (Harwood) Taylor; B.A., Peabody Coll., 1946, postgrad., 1946; postgrad. Memphis State U., summers 69-70; div.; 1 dau., Donna Reid. Soprano, Memphis Open Air Theatre, summer 1948; soprano Episcopal Actors' Guild of N.Y., 1949-51, Am. Theatre Wing, N.Y.C., 1949-51; concert singer, 1948—; pvt. tchr. piano, voice and organ, 1953—; tchr. music edn. Haywood County Bd. Edn., Brownsville, 1953—; soprano soloist, dir. music Temple Adas Israel, Brownsville, 1952—; dir. music Gay Valley Camp, Brevard, N.C., summers 1959-62; chmn.-elect Grace Moore Opera Scholarship, 1966—; mem. Tenn. Bicentennial Com., 1976. Mem. Nat. Fedn. Music Clubs, Tenn. Fedn. Music Clubs (parliamentarian, v.p.), Nat. Guild Piano Tchrs. (faculty, accredited music tchr.), Am. Coll. Musicians (Hall of Fame 1969), Tenn. Music Tchrs. Assn. (v.p., program chmn. West Tenn. div.), DAR (chmn. Am. music, regent David Craig chpt.). Wednesday Morning Musicale Brownsville (pres.), Rehearsal Club Alumnae Assn. N.Y., UDC, Haywood County Hist. Soc., Alpha Delta Kappa (pres.-elect Iota chpt.). Home: 647 W Main St Brownsville TN 38012

MAC KENZIE, ROLAND REDUS, realty exec.; b. Washington, Mar. 13, 1907; s. Albert Redus and Mary J. (Hummer) MacK.; grad. Brown U., 1929; m. Louise Parker Fownes, May 11, 1940; children—Clark Fownes, Margot Fownes. Rep. U.S. Walker Cup Golf Team, 1926, 28-30; with Dupont Laundry, Washington, 1930-32; pres., dir. Shamrock Properties, Inc., Balt., 1938—, pres. Shamrock

Realty Co., Greentree Realty Co., Towson, Md., Scottish Devel. Corp. Presbyn. Clubs: Country of N.C., Foxfire Golf and Country, Pinehurst Country (Pinehurst, N.C.); Gulf Stream Golf (Del Ray Beach); Elkridge-Greenspring (Balt.). Home: 3210 Polo Dr Gulfstream FL 33444 also McCaskill Rd Pinehurst NC 28374 also 111 Hamlet Rd Village of Cross Keys Baltimore MD 21210 Office: Lutherville MD 21093 also MacKenzie Bldg Southern Pines NC 28387

MACKIE, SHIRLEY MARIE, composer; b. Rockdale, Tex., Oct. 25, 1929; d. John Ransom and Marie (McLean) Mackie; Mus.B., La. State U., 1949, Mus.M., 1950, postgrad., 1951-53; postgrad. Aspen Inst., 1953, Conservatoire de Musique, Fontainebleau, France, 1959, 68. Profl. clarinetist, 1950-78; pvt. tchr. clarinet, piano, 1950-76; band dir. Forney (Tex.) High Sch., 1953-54; asst. prof. music U. Mary Hardin-Baylor, Belton, Tex., 1954-57; coordinator of music McLennan County Schs., Waco, Tex., 1959-70; band dir. Riesel High Sch., McLennan County, Tex., 1970-78. Admitted to Tex. Composers Hall of Fame. Fellow Intercontinental Biog. Assn.; mem. Tex. Composers Guild, Music Tchrs. Nat. Assn., Tex. Music Tchrs. Assn., Tex., Waco music tchrs. assn., Tex. Tchrs. Assn., Sigma Alpha Iota, Phi Kappa Phi. Mem. Order Eastern Star. Composer in media of orch., chorus, opera, ballet, band, vocal and instrumental solos, chamber music. Home: Route 1 Box 1449N 100 Wilderness Rd Waco TX 76710

MAC KINNON, CYRUS LELAND, newspaper exec.; b. Eldorado, Kans., Aug. 16, 1916; s. Frederick Benjamin and Cecil Prescott (Leland) MacK.; B.A., Dartmouth, 1938; m. Helen Wigglesworth, Feb. 25, 1939; children—Stephen, Peter, Cecil, Anne. Gen. trainee Automatic Electric Co., Chgo., 1938-41; personnel dir. Sherwin-Williams Co., Chgo., 1941-46; gen. mgr. Franklin Assn., Chgo., 1946-55; mng. dir. Inst. Newspaper Ops. (name later changed to Am. Newspaper Pubs. Assn. Research Inst.), Chgo., 1955-59; sales mgr., adminstr. R.R. Donnelley & Sons, Chgo., 1959-65; exec. v.p. Courier-Jour. & Louisville Times Co., 1965-75, pres., 1975—; WHAS, Inc., 1965-75, v.p., 1975—; exec. v.p. Standard Gravure Corp., Louisville, 1965—; dir. Bowne & Co., N.Y.C., 1977—, Nat. Public Radio. Met. chmn. Nat. Alliance Businessmen, 1968—; industry mem. Regional Wage Stablzn. Bd., Chgo., 1951-62. Chmn. bd. Action Now, Inc.; bd. dirs. Housing Now, Inc. Trustee Nat. Found. March of Dimes, 1977—. Mem. Indsl. Relations Assn. Chgo. (pres. 1946), So. Newspaper Pubs. Assn. (dir.), English Speaking Union, Casque and Gauntlet Soc., Psi Upsilon. Rotarian. Clubs: Helium, Jefferson, Louisville Country, River Valley (Louisville). Home: 5803 Orion Rd Glenview KY 40025 Office: 525 W Broadway Louisville KY 40202

MACLEAN, BRUCE MILLER, hygiologist; b. San Francisco, Sept. 8, 1937; s. Donald and Marie (Miller) M.; B.B.A., U. Houston, 1966, postgrad. 1972-77; M.A., Sam Houston U., 1977. Supt./counselor various civic, state agencies, 1972-78; dir. Employers Screening & Referral Service, Houston, 1978-80; pres. Teleos, Inc., Houston, 1976—; lectr. U. Houston, 1972-77. Adv. bd. mem. U. Cons. Program and City of Houston pub. inebriate and divergence project, 1978—; mem. Houston-Galveston Area Council (chmn. abuse subcom., 1977—). Served with U.S. Army, 1955-57. Tex. Commn. on Alcoholism grantee, 1977-80. Mem. Tex. Assn. Alcoholism Counselors. Republican. Eqiscopalian. Contbr. chpts.; Alcoholism Counseling, vol. II and vol. III, 1973. Home: 1922 Hawthorne St Houston TX 77098 Office: 2128B Welch St Houston TX 77019

MAC MILLAN, JUDITH RUTH, educator; b. Washington, Feb. 21, 1943; d. Walton Lovejoy and Gertrude Winston (Payne) MacMillan; B.S. in Music Edn., Carson-Newman Coll., 1965; Mus.M. in Music Edn., Ga. State U., 1974. Choral dir., gen. music tchr. Powder Springs (Ga.) Elem. Sch., 1965-66, E. Cobb Jr. High Sch., lMarietta, Ga., 1966-67, Mae Smythe Elem. Sch., Parks Elem. Sch., Pasadena, Tex., 1968-70, Beverly Hills Intermediate Sch., Pasadena, 1970-72; asst. prof., chmn. dept. music, choral dir. Reinhardt Coll., Waleska, Ga., 1974—; staff pianist, condr. musicals Ga. and N.C. summer camps; performer, condr. numerous civic and youth groups. Mem. Am. Choral Dirs. Assn., Music Educators Nat. Conf., AAUP. Democrat. Baptist. Composer, arranger sacred music. Home: 1422 Shiloh Trail E NW Kennesaw GA 30144

MACNABB, GEORGE MALCOLM, internist; b. Newnan, Ga., May 8, 1941; s. George Malcolm and Ella Gay (Parks) MacN.; B.A., Emory U., 1962, M.D., 1966; m. Mary Kathryn O'Callaghan, Aug. 7, 1965; children—Mary Lisa, Amy St. Clair, Benjamin Howell. Intern, Emory U., Atlanta, 1966-67, resident in internal medicine, 1970-72, fellow, 1972-73; practice medicine, specializing in internal medicine, Newnan, Ga., 1973—; staff Papp Clinic, Newnan, Ga., 1973—; chief internal medicine Newnan Hosp., 1976-77, Coweta Gen. Hosp., Newnan, 1977—. Served to lt. comdr., USN, 1967-70. Diplomate Am. Bd. Internal Medicine. Mem. Med. Assn. Ga., AMA, Am. Heart Assn., Am. Diabetic Assn., Assn. Mil. Surgions of U.S. Home: 29 Brookside Dr Newnan GA 30263 Office: 15 Cavender St Newnan GA 30263

MAC NAUGHTON, DONALD SINCLAIR, hosp. supply co. exec.; b. Schenectady, July 14, 1917; s. William and Marion (Colquhoun) MacN.; A.B., Syracuse U., 1939, LL.B., 1948; m. Winifred Thomas, Apr. 10, 1941; children—Donald, David. Tchr. history Pulaski (N.Y.) Acad. and Central Sch., 1939-42; admitted to N.Y. bar, 1948; pvt. practice, Pulaski, 1948-54; dep. supt. ins. N.Y. State, 1954-55; with Prudential Ins. Co. Am., 1955—, sr. v.p., spl. asst. to pres., 1961-65, exec. v.p., 1965-69, pres., chief exec. officer, 1969-70, chmn. bd., chief exec. officer, 1970-78; chmn., chief exec. officer Hosp. Corp. Am., Nashville, 1978—; dir. Exxon Corp., AT&T, Prudential Ins. Co. Am., Third Nat. Corp., Johnson & Johnson. Trustee, Syracuse U., Conf. Bd.; mem. bd. trust Vanderbilt U.; bd. overseers Wharton Sch. Served to 1st lt. USAAF, 1942-46. Mem. Am. Bar Assn., Bus. Council. Clubs: Eastward Ho, Links. Home: 109 Lynwood Terr Nashville TN 37205 Office: 1 Park Pl Nashville TN 37203

MACRAE, BRUCE FARQUHAR, food mfg. co. exec.; b. Detroit, Nov. 28, 1923; s. Keith William and Geraldine (Starr) M.; student Wayne U., 1942-43; B.S., U. Md., 1951; m. Laura Belle Wyatt, Sept. 6, 1952; 1 son, Stuart Wyatt. Asst. chief tariff compilations Am. Trucking Assn., Washington, 1951-53; asst. terminal mgr. Davidson Transfer and Storage, Washington, 1953-55; traffic analyst Ryder Truck Lines, Jacksonville, Fla., 1955-57; inco alloy salesmgr. J.M. Tull Metal and Supply Co., Jacksonville, 1957-60; traffic and distbn. mgr. Food Fair Stores, Inc., Jacksonville, 1960-78; asst. corp. dir. traffic Savannah Foods & Industries (Ga.), 1979—; instr. transp. Fla. Jr. Coll., Jacksonville, 1968—; lectr. transp. U. North Fla., Jacksonville, 1972-79. Treas., Opera Co. Jacksonville, Inc. Served with USNR, 1943-46, Naval Air Res., 1946—. Recipient Transp. Man of Yr. award Traffic Club, Jacksonville, 1972. Mem. Traffic Clubs Internat., Traffic Club Jacksonville, Navy League U.S. (v.p. Jacksonville council 1974-79, dir. 6th naval dist. Naval Sea Cadet Corps), Nat. Rifle Assn. (life), Nat. Def. Transp. Assn. (1st v.p. 1970-72), Delta Nu Alpha (nat. regional v.p. 1964-66), Sigma Pi, Delta Sigma Pi. Clubs: Lions (Savannah); Univ. (Jacksonville). Home: 306 Surrey Rd Savannah GA 31410

MACRAE, JOHN SUMTER, III, architect; b. Charlotte, Aug. 3, 1937; s. John Sumter and Agnes (Thorne) MacR.; B.Arch., N.C. State U., 1961; m. Eugenia Hickerson, June 13, 1959; children—John Douglas, Robert Thorne. Archtl. designer J. Hyott Hammond Assos., Architects, Asheboro, N.C., 1964-66; architect William F. Freeman Inc., High Point, N.C., 1966-67; v.p. Woodroof and MacRae Architects, Greensboro, N.C., 1967-68; pres. John MacRae Assos. Architects P.A., Greensboro, 1968—; tchr. archtl. design, interior design U. N.C., Greensboro. Pres. bd. dirs. Child Care Ministry, Greensboro, 1976-77. Served with U.S. Army, 1962-64. Registered architect N.C., S.C., Va. Mem. AIA, Guild Religious Architecture, Greensboro C. of C. Presbyterian. Clubs: Kiwanis, N.C. Citizens Assn. Home: 2107 Medford Ln Greensboro NC 27408 Office: 3608 W Friendly Ave Greensboro NC 27410

MAC RAE, ROBERT ALEXANDER, physicist, educator; b. Charlotte, N.C., Dec. 8, 1935; s. Rae Alexander and Nellie Susan (Haynes) MacR.; B.S., Davidson Coll., 1958; M.S. (AEC fellow), Vanderbilt U., 1960; m. Virginia Braden, Mar. 13, 1971; 1 stepson, Carey Neal. Instr. physics Davidson (N.C.) Coll., 1960-62; faculty research participant health physics div. Oak Ridge Nat. Lab., 1961-63, cons., 1963-77; asst. prof. U. N.C., Charlotte, 1962-65; prof. Central Piedmont Community Coll., Charlotte, 1965-67; asst. prof. Jacksonville (Ala.) State U., 1967—; pres. Air Brake Consultants. Mem. Am. Phys. Soc., Optical Soc. Am., Am. Assn. Physics Tchrs., Am. Soc. Aerospace Edn., Air Brake Assn., Sigma Xi, Sigma Pi Sigma. Republican. Presbyn. (elder). Club: Exchange (Jacksonville). Contbr. articles to profl. jours. Home: PO Box 359 624 7th Ave Jacksonville AL 36265 Office: Dept Physics Jacksonville State U Jacksonville AL 36265

MACUCH, EDWIN ROGER, steel co. exec.; b. Bridgeport, Conn., May 17, 1924; s. John and Julia (Hubak) M.; student Vanderbilt U., 1942-43; B.C.E., Ga. Inst. Tech., 1947; m. Elizabeth Lane, Jan. 13, 1945; children—A. Lee, Rodger Alan, William Louis. Vice pres., treas. Macuch Steel Products Inc., Augusta, Ga., 1954-70, pres., 1970—; v.p., treas. Augusta Doctors Med. Center, Inc., 1971—. Pres., Augusta Opera Assn., 1974; treas. Augusta Arts Council, 1970-71; treas., bd. dirs. Augusta Symphony, 1969-72; trustee Presbyterian Coll., 1968-70; ruling elder Greene St. Presbyn. W. Ch., 1975—; moderator Augusta-Macon Presbytery, 1976. Served to lt. comdr. USN, 1943-46. Club: Augusta Country.

MACY, ARTHUR WARREN, lawyer; b. Phila., July 1, 1919; s. Arthur Warren and Marietta (Nyland) M.; student U. Colo., 1939-41, 45-48; J.D., La. State U., 1952; m. Frances Walts, Sept. 7, 1948 (div. 1973); children—Patricia Ann, Susan Lyn, Mary Jane, Barbara Warren. Research asst. history dept. U. Colo., 1947-48; tchr. San Carlos (Ariz.) Apache Reservations, 1948-49; research asst. legal biography La. State U., 1949-50; admitted to La. bar, 1952; practiced in Hammond, La., 1952—; mem. firm Reid & Reid, 1952-54, Reid & Macy, 1955-68, Macy, Kemp and Newton, 1969-71, Macy, Kemp & McIntyre, 1971—; law clk. 1st Circuit Ct. of Appeal, State of La., 1962—. Served with USNR, 1941-45. Mem. Am., La., 21st Jud. Dist. La. (pres. 1965-67), bar assns., Order of Coif, Phi Kappa Phi, Phi Delta Phi, Pi Gamma Mu, Phi Kappa Psi. Democrat. Episcopalian. Mason (K.T.), Rotarian, Lion, Kiwanian. Asso. editor: La. Law Rev., 1951-52. Home: Route 2 Box 171M Hammond LA 70401 Office: 220 W Thomas St Hammond LA 70401

MADDEN, EDWARD BINGHAM, cons.; b. Newton, Miss., Dec. 11, 1912; s. Oscar Edwards and Carrie Lee (Bingham) M.; student La. Coll., 1929-30; B.S., Ga. Sch. Tech., 1934; postgrad., State U. Ia., 1941, U. Ark., 1952, 59, 60; m. Margaret Hughes Witherspoon, May 7, 1937; children—Margaret Donna (Mrs. Gerald Zolton Jacobi), Edward Bingham. Engring. aide to jr. engr. TVA, Murphy, N.C., 1934-39; with U.S. Army C.E., Little Rock, Ark., 1939-60, Dallas, 1960-71, chief sect. hydraulic design, 1967-71; pvt. cons. on hydraulic, river engring. and sediment transport studies in the U.S., Argentina, Bangladesh and Philippines, 1971—. Recipient Superior Performance award U.S. Army C.E., 1960; named to Gallery Distinguished Employees Southwestern div. C.E., 1973. Registered profl. engr., Ark., Tex. Mem. Internat. Assn. for Hydraulic Research, U.S. Com. on Large Dams, Nat. Soc. Profl. Engrs., Permanent Internat. Assn. Nav. Congresses, ASCE, Soc. Am. Mil. Engrs., Tau Beta Pi. Presbyn. Home: 10109 McCree Rd Dallas TX 75238

MADDEN, JOHN TIMOTHY, JR., health care adminstr.; b. Denver, May 7, 1933; s. John Timothy and Vera Marie (Vautrain) M.; B.A., U. Denver, 1955; M.A., 1961; M.H.A., Baylor U., 1969; m. Mary Lou Bauder, Aug. 14, 1954; children—Mark Patrick, Kevin Michael, Sean Brian. Commd. 2d. lt. M.C., U.S. Army, 1959, advanced through grades to col., 1978; adminstrv. resident Valley Forge (Pa.) Gen. Hosp., 1968-69, exec. officer, 29th. Evacuation Hosp., Vietnam, 1969-70, asst. prof. health care adminstrn. U.S. Army-Baylor grad. program Munson Army Hosp. and Moncrief Army Hosp., 1970-74; exec. officer Munson Army Hosp., Ft. Leavenworth, Kans., 1974-77; exec. officer med. dept. activities, Ft. Jackson, S.C., 1977-80; ret., 1980; v.p. legis. and adminstrv. services S.C. Hosp. Assn., 1980—; cons., lectr. in field. Bd. dirs. S.C. Emergency Services Com., 1977—. Decorated Bronze Star, Meritorious Service Medal with oak leaf cluster; Vietnam Cross of Gallantry with palm. Fellow Am. Coll. Hosp. Adminstrs.; mem. U.S. Army-Baylor U. Alumni Assn. (pres. 1976-77), Am. Hosp. Assn., Tex. Hosp. Assn., S.C. Hosp. Assn., Assn. Mil. Surgeons of U.S. Author: Study to Reduce Hospital Turnover, 1969. Editor several personnel mgmt. studies, 1972-73, in case studies health care adminstrn., 1978-79. Address: SC Hosp Assn PO Box 1236 101 Med Center West Columbia SC 29169

MADDOX, ALVA HUGH, asso. justice Ala. Supreme Ct.; b. Andalusia, Ala., Apr. 17, 1930; s. Christopher Columbus and Audie Lodella (Freeman) M.; A.B. in Journalism, U. Ala., 1952, LL.B., 1957; m. Virginia Ann Roberts, June 14, 1958; children—Robert Hugh, Patricia Jane. With Florala (Ala.) News, 1947-48, Treasurer's Office, U. Ala., 1949-52, 54-56; admitted to Ala. bar, 1957; law clk. Ct. Appeals of Ala., 1957; atty. field examiner VA, Montgomery, Ala., 1958; law clk. U.S. Dist. Ct., Montgomery, 1959-60; practiced in Montgomery, 1961-64; circuit judge 15th Jud. Circuit, Montgomery, 1963, asst. dist. atty., 1964; legal adviser to Gov. George Wallace of Ala., 1965-67, to Gov. Lurleen B. Wallace of Ala., 1967-68, to Gov. Albert P. Brewer of Ala., 1968-69; asso. justice Supreme Ct. Ala., Montgomery, 1969—; mem. Jud. Planning Commn. Permanent Study Commn. on the Judiciary. Active Youth Legislature, Montgomery Baptist Hosp. Found. Bd. dirs. YMCA, Montgomery, Tukabatchee council Boy Scouts Am. Served with USAF, 1952-54. Mem. Am., Ala. bar assns., Ala. Law Inst., Farrah Law Soc., Arnold Air Soc., Pershing Rifles, Jasons, Quadrangle, Omicron Delta Kappa, Phi Alpha Delta, Sigma Delta Chi. Democrat. Baptist (deacon). Kiwanian. Club: Maxwell AFB Open Mess. Home: 3137 Hathaway Pl Montgomery AL 36111 Office: PO Box 218 Montgomery AL 36101

MADDOX, CHARLES RICHARD, lawyer; b. San Antonio, Oct. 25, 1950; s. Robert Duke and Grace Frances (Holloway) M.; B.B.A., U. Tex., Austin, 1972; J.D., St. Mary's U., 1975; m. Sylvia Hernandez, Apr. 6, 1979; children—Sylvia Yvette Oakes, Maricella Semilla Oakes. Admitted to Tex. bar, 1975; with Bexar County Dist. Atty.'s Office, San Antonio, 1974—; individual practice law, San Antonio, 1975—; adminstrv. asst. to Tex. state rep., 1975-77; prof. family law and real estate law San Antonio Jr. Coll. Mem. Tex. Democratic Electoral Coll., 1976; exec. com. Bexar County Dem. Party; Dem. nat. del. to mini-conv., 1978. Mem. Tex. Trial Lawyers Assn., Tex. Criminal Def. Lawyers Assn. Methodist. Home: 13665 Toepperwein St San Antonio TX 78233 Office: 222 Main Plaza San Antonio TX 78205

MADDOX, DAN WAITE, credit corp. exec.; b. Easonville, Ala., June 9, 1909; s. William Notley and Minnie (Waite) M.; student Ga. Sch. Tech., 1925-29; m. Margaret Huffman, June 21, 1969; children—Judith E. (Mrs. Frank Isbel Nebhut), Ellen King (Mrs. Norman Christianson), James Notley. With Universal C.I.T. Corp., N.Y.C., 1930-41; founder, chmn. Assos. Capital Corp., Nashville, 1943-74; chmn. bd., chief exec. officer Assos. Corp. N.Am., Dallas, 1975-79; chmn. Assos. First Capital Corp., Dallas, 1979—; dir. Capitol Life Ins. Co., Denver, Colo., Shoney's Inc., Nashville, Commerce Union Bank, Nashville, Tenn. Valley Bankshares, Nashville. Mem. Economic Devel. Com., State of Tenn., 1971—, Tenn. Agrl. and Indsl. Commn., 1972—. Trustee, Montgomery Bell Acad.; trustee Cumberland Mus. Sci. Center, Nashville, v.p., 1971-74. Recipient Weatherby award Shikar Safari Internat., 1967. Mem. East African Profl. Hunters Assn. Clubs: Mill Reef (Antigua, West Indies); Explorers, Boone and Crockett (N.Y.C.); Belle Meade Country, Cumberland, City (Nashville); Council Internat. de la Chasse (Paris). Home: 1228 Chickering Rd Nashville TN 37215 Office: 601 Broadway Nashville TN 37203

MADDOX, JAMES FREEMAN, photographer, paving contractor; b. Atlanta, Jan. 22, 1926; s. Andrew R. and Ethel Mae M.; B.S., Ga. Inst. Tech., 1954; m. Ruby E. Willmore, Sept. 20, 1952; children—Larry F., Pamela J., Richard. With Patterson Sargent Co., 1954-57, Minn. Paints, 1957-60; owner, operator Jim Maddox Photography and Jim Maddox & Assos., Tucker, Ga., 1960—; paving contractor. Served with USAAF, 1944-48. Mem. Ga. Profl. Photographers, Southeastern Photographers Assn. Mem. Wesleyan Ch. Home: 5331 Hugh Howell Rd Tucker GA 30084 Office: PO Box 528 Tucker GA 30084

MADDOX, W. CEDRIC, city ofcl.; b. Atlanta, Mar. 3, 1937; s. Willie J. and Thelma (Harper) M.; B.S., Tuskegee Inst., 1958; m. Julia Cox, Nov. 25, 1962; 1 son, Julian. Mgr., Hunter St. Garage, 1958-60, Dozier Maddox Shell Service Sta., Atlanta, 1963-65; quality control engr. Ford Motor Co., Hapeville, Ga., 1965-74; dir. Bur. Gen. Services, City of Atlanta, 1974-77, dir. Bur. Motor Transport Services, 1977-79, dir. Bur. San. Services, 1979—. Mem. adv. com. Atlanta Area Tech. Sch., Atlanta Urban League program PREP. Served with U.S. Army, 1960-62. Deacon, West Hunter St. Bapt. Ch. Mem. Am. Public Works Assn., Soc. Automotive Engrs. Home: 3706 Garrison Dr SW Atlanta GA 30331 Office: 1540 Northside Dr NW Atlanta GA 30318

MADDUX, THOMAS JOE, electronics co. exec.; b. Garner, Tex., Sept. 12, 1942; s. Joncie Crawford and Reba Rebecca (Deakins) M.; A.A., Weatherford Coll., 1962; B.B.A., North Tex. State U., 1964; m. Scherry Jean Sanders, Apr. 27, 1968; children—Amy Elizabeth, Suzanne Elise. Data documentation analyst L.T.V. Corp., Dallas, 1967-68; project coordinator F-16 flight simulator Gen. Dynamics Corp., Ft. Worth, 1968—; partner Maddux Land and Cattle Co. Mem. Ft. Worth and Tarrant County Arts Council, Streams and Valley Commn. of Ft. Worth. Served with U.S. Army, 1965-67; Vietnam. Mem. Nat. Mgmt. Assn. Republican. Baptist. Club: Nat. Beta. Home: 6420 Curzon St Fort Worth TX 76116 Office: PO Box 748 Mail Zone 1242 Fort Worth TX 76101

MADEIRA, HARRY, sales exec.; b. Bristol, R.I., Sept. 30, 1940; s. Manuel and Angelina E. (Souza) M.; ed. U. Conn. Sales rep., New Eng., 1962-76; dir. mktg. Comatic Labs., Houston, 1976-80; cons. sales and mktg., 1980—; pres. Nat. Security Systems-Houston, Inc., 1980—; dir., treas. Three Realty, Inc. Mem. Inst. Cert. Bus. Counselors. Home: 9200 Bissonnet Houston TX 77074 Office: 6827 S Gessner Houston TX 77036

MADEY, DOREN LOUISE, research analyst; b. Oakland, Calif., July 29, 1952; d. Richard and Mary Louise (Kirch) M.; B.S. summa cum laude, Duke U., 1974, M.Ed. (EPDA fellow), 1975, Ph.D. in Law and Edn. (James B. Duke fellow), 1979. Intern to pres. DeKalb Community Coll., Atlanta, 1974; spl. asst. to dir. undergrad. admissions Duke U., 1974-75, intern to legal counsel, 1975-76; legis. analyst Interstate Project on Dissemination, Nat. Inst. Edn., 1975-76; edn. cons. NTS Research Corp., Durham, N.C., 1976, research analyst, 1976—; asst. project dir. evaluation of state dissemination grants program Nat. Inst. Edn., 1976-77, project co-dir., 1977-79, project dir., 1979—; cons. tech. assistance base U.S. Office Edn. Nat. Diffusion Network, 1979, Nat. Center Research in Vocat. Edn., Columbus, Ohio, 1978, Bibliog. Retrieval Services, Inc., Schenectady, 1977, Nat. Inst. Edn., 1980. Mem. Am. Ednl. Research Assn. (co-program chmn. spl. interest group/research utilization 1980-81), AAAS, Assn. Public Policy, Duke U. Alumni Assn. (exec. v.p. 1979-83), Phi Beta Kappa, Kappa Delta Pi. Club: Durham Women's City Tennis League. Home: 3086-E Colony Rd Durham NC 27705 Office: 2634 Chapel Hill Blvd Durham NC 27707

MADREN, JEAN COVERSTON, sch. ofcl.; b. Elkton, Va., Nov. 15, 1929; d. Metford W. and Clarice V. (Shipp) Coverston; B.S., Madison Coll., 1951, M.A., 1968; postgrad. Va. Poly. Inst. and State U., 1974 U. Va., 1976; m. William R. Madren, May 16, 1953. Lab. asst. Merck & Co., Inc., Elkton, Va., 1951-53, shift supr., 1953-56; tchr. Harrisonburg (Va.) Schs., 1956-58; tchr. Rockingham County Public Schs., Penn Laird, Va., 1958-60; guidance counselor Montevideo High Sch., Penn Laird, 1960-64, dir. guidance, 1964-80; dir. guidance Spotswood Sr. High Sch., Penn Laird, 1980—. Lic. counselor, Va. Mem. Nat. Vocat. Guidance Assn., NEA, Am. Personnel and Guidance Assn., Am. Sch. Counselor Assn., Va. Guidance Assn., Rockingham County Guidance Assn., Va. Edn. Assn., Rockingham County Edn. Assn., Delta Kappa Gamma. Club: Order Eastern Star. Home: 201 N Stuart Ave Elkton VA 22827 Office: Spotswood Sr High School Penn Laird VA 22846

MADUZIA, EDWARD S., lawyer; b. Chgo., Apr. 5, 1941; s. Wells H. and Dorothy (Voss) S.; B.S., Northwestern U., 1963; J.D., U. Chgo., 1966; m. Sandra J. Brantley, May 23, 1970; children—Amber Monite, Donald Kenrick. Admitted to Ill. bar, 1966, U.S. Supreme Ct. bar, 1970; asso. firm Thomas, Blass, Simpson & Tyler, Chgo., 1966-70, mem. firm, 1970-76; individual practice law, Chgo., 1976—; lectr. Loyola U., 1974—. Active Chgo. chpt. ARC, 1969—; mem. Library Renovation Com., 1977—. Recipient Outstanding Alumnus award Northwestern U., 1977. Mem. Am., Ill. bar assns., Am. Judicature Soc. Democrat. Clubs: Rotary, Elks, Masons. Home: 4505 N Manor Chicago IL 60625

MAGARIAN, ROBERT ARMEN, pharmacist, educator; b. East St. Louis, Ill., July 27, 1930; s. Leon and Pauline (Struel) M.; student Washington U., St. Louis, 1951-52; A.B., U. Miss., 1956, B.S. in Pharmacy with honors, 1960, Ph.D. in Medieval Chemistry (Am. Found. Pharm. Edn. fellow), 1966; m. Charmaine V. Kugler, June 24,

1950; children—Paula, Cindy, Leslie, Robert D. NIH postdoctoral fellow U. Kan. Coll. Pharmacy, 1966-67; asst. prof. med. chemistry St. Louis Coll. Pharmacy, 1967-70; asso. prof. med. chemistry Coll. Pharmacy, U. Okla., Oklahoma City, 1970-78, prof., 1978—. Served with AUS, 1952-54; Korea. Mead Johnson research grantee, 1968-69, NSF grantee, 1969-70; Man of Year award St. Louis Coll. Pharmacy, 1970; Outstanding Tchr. award U. Okla. Coll. Pharmacy, 1974, 76; Baldwin Teaching award U. Okla., 1978. Mem. Am. Chem. Soc. (organic, medicinal and nuclear chemistry divs.), Am. Assn. Colls. Pharmacy (chmn. grad. affairs com.), Sigma Xi, Rho Chi, Kappa Psi (exec. dir. 1980—). Home: 311 N Mercedes Dr Norman OK 73069 Office: Univ Oklahoma Coll Pharmacy Health Sciences Center 644 NE 14th St Oklahoma City OK 73190

MAGEE, JOHN MELVIN, clergyman; b. Mize, Miss., Sept. 24, 1915; s. John Grenald and Emma Catherine (Carr) M.; B.A., Maryville Coll., 1941; B.D., Columbia Theol. Sem., 1944, postgrad., 1948-50, M.Div., 1971; m. Margaret Christine Sisk, May 20, 1943; children—Connie Louise, Mary Rebecca, Nancy Christine. Ordained to ministry Presbyterian Ch., 1944; pastor, Nettleton, Saltillo, Plantersville, Tupelo, Bucy Garden chs. (all Miss.), 1944-48, Wee Kirk and Panthersville Presbyn. chs., Decatur, Ga., 1948-51, Union City, Tenn., 1951-55, Norris Memphis Ch., Memphis, 1955-62; asst. minister Covenant Ch., Memphis, 1962; pastor 1st Presbyn. Ch., Hammond, La., 1962-65, Concord (Tenn.) Presbyn. Ch., 1965-69; stated supply Chota Presbyn. Ch., Concord, 1965-69; pastor 1st Presbyn. Ch., Union City, Tenn., 1969-75; pastor erata Sandersville, New Liberty and McFarland Presbyn. Chs. (Miss.), also supply pastor Pisgah Presbyn. Chs., 1975—; past moderator Memphis Presbytery, Knoxville Presbytery; chmn. com. evangelism, mem. interch. relations com. Synod Tenn.; chmn. interch. relations com. Memphis Presbytery; chmn. com. TV, radio and vis. synod of Appalachia; past chmn. Women's work Presbytery of Knoxville; mem. women's work com. South Miss. Presbytery, moderator, 1978—; mem. com. on Christianity and health New Orleans Presbytery. Chmn. advancement com. Chickasaw council SW dist. Boy Scouts Am. Served with USMC, 1933-37; lt. col., dep. wing chaplain Tenn. Wing, CAP, 1969, wing chaplain Miss. Wing, 1977—, recipient Outstanding Sr. Mem. of Year award SE region, 1974, Exceptional Service award Tenn. Wing, 1975. Mem. Memphis, Union City (past pres.), Tangepahoa Parish (v.p.), Obion County (treas. 1970) ministerial assns., Knoxville Presbyn. Ministers Assn. (sec.-treas. 1967). Clubs: Masons (K.T., illustrious grand chaplain), Kiwanis (chmn. citizenship services com. Laurel, Miss.). Address: PO Box 500 Sandersville MS 39477

MAGEE, KIMBALL PRATT, sales co. exec.; b. Omaha, Sept. 28, 1927; s. Wayland Wells and Harriett Stella (Gage) M.; student U. Nebr., 1945-46; U. Omaha, 1949-50; B.S. in Elec. Engring., Iowa State Coll., 1953; m. Betty Mae Hawkins, Sept. 10, 1949; children—Kimball, Marshall, Michael. Engineer Magnavox Co., Fort Wayne, Ind., 1953-55; pres. Hollingsworth & Still, Inc., Atlanta, 1955—. Served with USN, 1946-48. Mem. Elec. Reps. Assn. (pres. Sunshine chpt., pres. Dixie chpt.), Dixie Elec. Reps. Inc., Riverbend Gun Club, VFW. Republican. Presbyterian. Home: 2388 Ledgewood Dr Altanta GA 30338 Office: 1611 Perimeter Center E Atlanta GA 30346

MAGINN, THOMAS RAYMOND, pub. co. exec.; b. Rochester, N.Y., Nov. 9, 1948; s. Raymond Joseph and Honora M.; B.B.A., St. John Fisher Coll., 1971; m. Margaret VanDame, Apr. 17, 1971; children—Amy Marie, Alan Thomas. Acct., Ernst & Ernst, Rochester, 1971-74; staff acct. Gannett Co., Inc., Rochester, 1974-75, internal auditor, 1975-76; controller, asst. sec. News Press Publ. Co., Fort Myers, Fla., 1976—. Treas., Lend-A-Hand Fund, Inc. Served with USNG, 1971. Mem. Fort Myers C. of C., Inst. Controllers and Fin. Officers. Home: 5589 Amoroso Dr Fort Myers FL 33907 Office: PO Box 10 Fort Myers FL 33902

MAGNAN, CHARLES GRAHAM, JR., plastic surgeon; b. Fairfield, Ala., Aug. 20, 1926; s. Charles Graham and Ann Marie (Venable) M.; student North Ga. Coll., 1943-44; B.S., U. Ga., 1948; M.D., Med. Coll. Ga., 1952; m. Barbara Beddingfield, June 2, 1956; children—Cathy, Patti. Intern Spartanburg (S.C.) Gen. Hosp., 1952-53; resident Med. Coll., 1956-57, Kansas City (Mo.) Gen. Hosp., 1959-61; practice medicine and surgery, Kingston, Tenn., 1956-57; practice medicine specializing in plastic and reconstructive surgery, Macon, Ga., 1961—. Served with USNR, 1954-56. Diplomate Am. Bd. Plastic Surgery. Mem. A.M.A., Med. Assn. Ga., So. Med. Assn., Bibb County Med. Soc. (pres. 1980), A.C.S., Southeastern Soc. Plastic and Reconstructive Surgeons, Am. Soc. Plastic and Reconstructive Surgeons, Greater Macon C. of C. Elk. Baptist. Clubs: Idle Hour Golf and Country, Civitan (bd. dirs., pres. 1971-72). Home: 429 Northminster Dr Macon GA 31204 Office: 380 Hospital Dr Macon GA 31201

MAGNANT, KENNETH KARL, mech. engr.; b. Rhinelander, Wis., Aug. 2, 1937; s. Earl Hamilton and Elsie (Segerlund) M.; B.M.E., U. Fla., 1960; student U. Ala., 1968-71; m. Catherine Anne Slater, Dec. 22, 1962; children—Lance Kenneth, Mark Raymond. Mech. engr. Brookley AFB, Mobile, Ala., 1960; mech. engr., aerospace technologist NASA, Huntsville, Ala., 1961-64; mech. engr. U.S. Army Missile Command, Redstone Arsenal, Ala., 1964—; exec. sec. Incom Inc., Huntsville, 1978—. Registered profl. engr., Ala. Patentee air bourne missile launcher, missile launch and guidance shoe, ultrasonic tube measuring device. Home: 8016 Tea Garden Rd Huntsville AL 35805 Office: US Army Missile Comd Redstone Arsenal AL 35809

MAGNUSON, CHARLES EMIL, physicist, educator; b. Rushville, Nebr., Dec. 19, 1939; s. Ivan Nathaniel and Lena (Ray) M.; B.A. in Physics, Nebr. Wesleyan U., 1962; postgrad. Nebr. State Coll., Chadron, 1961-63; M.A. in Physics, State U. of N.Y. at Buffalo, 1965; Ph.D., Tex. A&M U., 1974; m. Denise T. Maynard, Aug. 20, 1971; children—Ivan Gerard, Curt Emil, Todd Maynard. Grad. tchg. asst. physics State U. N.Y. at Buffalo, 1962-66; asst. prof. Carson-Newman Coll., Jefferson City, Tenn., 1966-70; researcher NSF program coll. tchrs. Tex. A&M U., College Station, 1968; participant extension program Carson-Newman Coll., 1968, chmn. sci. div., 1969-70; grad. tchg. asst. Tex. A&M U., 1970-74, lectr., research asso., 1975, research scientist biosystems div. indsl. engring., 1975—. Mem. exec. com. Brazos County (Tex.) Republican Com., College Station, 1974—, del to state convention, 1974, precinct chmn., 1974-75, 78—; scoutmaster Boy Scouts Am., 1967-70, mem. dist. com., 1967-68. Recipient God and Country award, Boys Scouts Am., 1956, grad. fellowship Tex. A&M U., 1971, grants AEC, Carson-Newman Coll., Jefferson City, 1969, NSF, Carson-Newman Coll., 1968, Tex. Agrl. Extension Service, 1978—. Mem. AAAS, Am. Phys. Soc. Am. Assn. Physics Tchrs., Tenn. Acad. Sci., AAUP (Tex. Sect.), Tex. Acad. Sci., Am. Physical Soc. (SE Section), Am. Assn. Physics Tchrs. (Tex. Section), Zeta Psi, Sigma Xi, Sigma Pi Sigma. Republican. Presbyterian. Clubs: Nat. Thespian Soc., Blue Key. Presenter various nat. conferences; contbr. articles to profl. jours. Home: Box 1955 College Station TX 77840 Office: Biosytems Div Dept Indsl Engring Tex A&M U College Station TX 77843

MAGOFFIN, RALPH MANNING, state govt. ofcl.; b. Balt., Nov. 1, 1921; s. Ralph VanDeman and Kate Hampton (Manning) M.; B.A. in Chemistry, N.Y. U., 1942; m. Sarah Lillian Love, Aug. 26, 1961; children—Kate Love, Ann Manning. Chemist dept. agrl., State of S.C., Columbia, 1942-68, petroleum chemist, 1942-46, food chemist, 1946-54, dir. bur. inspection, 1954-60, chief chemist, 1960-66, dir. lab., 1966-68, dep. commr., 1968—; mem. S.C. Water Resources Commn., 1968—; mem. S.C. Migrant Farm Workers Commn., chmn., 1972-79; mem. Pesticides Adv. Comm., 1975-79; mem. S.C. Agrl. Council, 1968—, sec., 1975. Recipient Honor award in adminstrn. Nat. Assn. State Depts. Agr., 1977; Superior Service award U.S. Dept. Agr., 1978. Mem. Assn. Food and Drugs of So. States (past pres., past sec.), Am. Soc. for Testing and Materials, Am. Chem. Soc., So. Weights and Measures Assn., Nat. Conf. Weights and Measures (past chaplain), Am. Metric Assn., Columbia Jaycees (pres. 1950-51; editor SC Jaycees Action Mag., 1954-55; mem. state bd. 1952-56), Columbia Sertoma Club (editor newletter 1953-60; dist. sec. 1954-55). Democrat. Episcopalian. Club: Masons (33 deg.). Contbr. articles in field to tech. jour. Home: 1211 Dearborn Rd Columbia SC 29204 Office: PO Box 11280 Columbia SC 29211

MAGRATH, LAWRENCE KAY, biologist; b. Garnett, Kans., Mar. 28, 1943; s. Charles Jerome and Ruth (Richardson) M.; B.S.E., Kans. State Tchrs. Coll., 1967, M.S., 1969; Ph.D., U. Kans., 1973. Asst. instr. biology U. Kans., Lawrence, 1970-72; instr. botany, acting curator of herbarium Okla. State U., Stillwater, 1972; asst. prof. biology, curator biology, curator of herbarium U. of Sci. and Arts of Okla., Chickasha, 1972—. Mem. AAUP, Am. Soc. Plant Taxonomists, Internat. Assn. Plant Taxonomists, Am. Inst. Biol. Scis., AAAS, Okla. (endangered species com.), Kans. acads. scis., Sigma Xi, Kappa Delta Pi, Beta Beta Beta, Sierra Club. Home: 1426 C Frisco Ave Chickasha OK 73018 Office: Box 3368 Univ of Sci and Arts of Oklahoma Chickasha OK 73018

MAGRUDER, HELEN ELAINE HAKALA (MRS. EUGENE ROSS MAGRUDER), ret. govt. ofcl.; b. Republic, Mich., Dec. 31, 1918; d. Jacob and Mary Louise (Lahenpera) Hakala; student Badger-Green Bay Bus. Coll., 1937-38, U. Dayton, 1956-59, U. Md., 1960-62; m. Harold Eugene Canada, May 14, 1948 (dec. Dec. 31, 1951); m. 2d, Eugene Ross Magruder, July 15, 1955; stepchildren—Lee Ann (Mrs. Richard Lee Naragon), Lawrence Ross, Kevin Michael. Claims adjuster Internal Revenue Service, Milw., 1943-49; adminstrv. asst. to sr. officer Displaced Persons Commn., Camp Grohn, Germany, 1949-50; chief custodial services br. Dept. Army, Nurnberg, Germany, 1950-51, chief real estate br., 1951; sec. psychol. warfare Hdqrs. U.S. Army, Washington, 1951-55; position classification specialist Air Force Logistics Command, USAF, Wright-Patterson AFB, Dayton, O., 1955-59; sec. counterintelligence div. Office Spl. Investigations USAF, Misawa Air Base, Japan, 1959-60, chief classification and wage adminstrn. br., 39th air div., 1960-62; position classification specialist aerospace med. div. USAF, Brooks AFB, San Antonio, 1962-64, chief classification and wage adminstrn. br., 1964-65; personnel mgmt. specialist Hdqrs., USAF, Washington, 1965-67, program devel. officer, 1967-71; chief operations br. div. personnel Office Mgmt. Services, Dept. Agr., Washington, 1971-72; dir. exec. assignment program Hdqrs. USAF, 1972-75. Grad. instr. advanced flower arranging Ikenobo Sch. Japanese Flower Arrangements, Tokyo, Japan, 1962. Hostess, U.S.O., 1943-45; sr. troop leader Girl Scouts U.S.A., 1947-48; Wis. state rep. Army Emergency Relief Soc., 1948-49; mem. Gray Ladies A.R.C., 1952-54. Recipient Scholastic Achievement medallion U. Md., 1961, Superior Performance awards USAF, Misawa, 1960, 62, Brooks AFB, 1965, Achievement awards Hdqrs. USAF, Washington, 1966, 68. Mem. Soc. Personnel Adminstrn. (program coordinator Dayton chpt. 1957-59), Classification and Compensation Soc. Mem. Order Eastern Star. Home: 1370 S Ocean Blvd Pompano Beach FL 33062

MAGRUDER, RICHARD ALLEN, author, photographer; b. Starkville, Miss., Apr. 1, 1924; s. Robert Henry and Helen Mildred (Porter) M.; student U. Tex., 1946-48, N. Tex. State U., 1948-49, Instituito Allende, Mexico, 1952-53; m. Mary Charles Price, May 13, 1972; children—Michael Lawrence, Robert Walter, Allen Patrick. Staff reporter, feature writer, artist, photographer, critic Beaumont (Tex.) Enterprise, 1950-51; news dir. Sta. KFDM, Beaumont, 1951-52; photog., creative writing instr. Instituto Allende, 1953-54; staff writer, Galveston (Tex.) Tribune, 1955-56; news editor, broadcaster, NBC string corr. Sta. WFAA, Dallas, 1957-61; pres. Allison-Drake Advt. Inc., Dallas, 1961-63, also dir.; pres. Allen Richards Advt. Inc., Dallas, 1964-65, also dir.; pres. Dallas N. Galleries, 1965-66; dir. promotion and Internat. Mag. editor Braniff Airways, Inc., 1966-69; editor Internat. Atlanta Mag., 1972-73; free lance writer and photographer, Atlanta, 1972—. Author: Mexico... Moods and Images, 1962; Mexico Revisited, 1965; A Snob's Guide To Mexico City, 1966; Tourguide To South America, 1967; A Brief History of American Literature, 1968. Contbr. articles, photos and illustrations to numerous mags. including Ford Times, Odyssey, Discovery, Cavalier. Contbr. to newspapers including N.Y. Daily News, Los Angeles Times. Served with USAAF, 1942-45. Recipient 1st prize award Recreation Vehicle Industry Assn., 1977, La Pluma de Plata Mexicana, Mex., 1979. Mem. League of Latin Am. Corrs., Soc. Am. Travel Writers, Am. Soc. Mag. Photographers, Outdoor Writers Assn. Am. Democrat. Home and Office: 2156 Snapfinger Rd Decatur GA 30035

MAGUIRE, CARY MCILWAINE, oil co. exec.; b. Ardmore, Pa., May 30, 1928; s. John Russell and Luna Neal (Ambler) M.; B.S., U. Pa., 1950; m. Ann Thompson, Feb. 27, 1960; children—Cary McIlwaine, Melinda Ambler, Ann Blaine. Mgr. Russell Maguire Oil Operations, Wichita Falls, also Dallas, Tex., 1955-67; chmn. bd., pres. Maguire Oil Co., Dallas, 1968—; pres. Camm Realty Co., St. Louis, 1967-71, Columbia Producing Co., N.Y.C., 1967-70; v.p. Alco Controls, St. Louis, 1956-69, Weber Dental Mfg. Co., Canton, Ohio, 1956-69; chmn. bd. Components Corp. Am., Dallas, 1976—, pres., 1977—; chmn. bd. Staco, Inc., Costa Mesa, Calif.; dir., mem. trust com. 1st Nat. Bank in Dallas, 1976—. Founder Maguire Oil & Gas Inst., 1975—. Mem. Nat. Rep. Finance Com., 1971—; chmn. Dallas County Rep. Finance Com., 1969-70. Mem. exec. bd. Internat. Trade Conf. S.W., 1975—; trustee Hockaday Sch., 1975—, vice chmn., 1979—, chmn. fin. com., mem. exec. com., 1976—; trustee St. Mark's Sch. Tex., 1974—, chmn. devel. com., mem. exec. com., 1977—; trustee So. Meth. U., 1976—. Mem. Nat. Petroleum Council, Ind. Petroleum Producers Assn. Am. (dir. 1956—, mem. tax com. 1974—), Tex. Ind. Producers and Royalty Owners Assn. (v.p. 1969-71), Dallas Wildcat Assn. (mem. exec. com. 1969-71), Tex. Mid-Continent Oil and Gas Assn. Clubs: Brook Hollow Golf, Dallas Petroleum, Idlewild, Terpsichorean, Calyx (Dallas). Home: 5146 Kelsey St Dallas TX 75229 Office: 4200 First Nat Bank Bldg Dallas TX 75202

MAGUIRE, CHARLOTTE EDWARDS, physician; b. Richmond, Ind., Sept. 1, 1918; d. Joe Blaine and Lydia (Betscher) Edwards; student Stetson U., 1936-38, U. Wichita, 1938-39; B.S., Memphis Tchrs. Coll., 1940; M.D., U. Ark., 1944; m. Raymer Francis Maguire, Sept. 1, 1948 (dec.); children—Barbara, Thomas Clair II. Intern, Orange Meml. Hosp., Orlando, Fla., 1944-46; resident Bellevue Hosp. and Med. Center, N.Y.U., N.Y.C., 1955; instr. nurses Orange Meml. Hosp., 1947-67, staff mem., 1946-68; staff mem. Fla. Sanatarium and Hosp., Orlando, 1946-60, Holiday House and Hosp., Orlando, 1950-68; mem. courtesy and cons. staff West Orange Meml. Hosp., Winter Garden, Fla., 1952-68; active staff, chief dept. pediatrics Mercy Hosp., Orlando, 1965-67; chief of staff physicians and dentists Central Fla. div. Children's Home Soc. Fla., 1947-56; dir. Orlando Child Health Clinic, 1949-58; practice medicine, Orlando, 1946-68; asst. regional dir. Region IV, HEW, 1970-72; med. services coordinator Fla. Dept. Health and Rehab. Services, 1975—; pediatric cons. Fla. Crippled Children's Commn., 1952-68, dir., 1968-70; asst. sec. for health Dept. Health and Rehab. Services, 1969-70. Mem. Fla. Adv. Coouncil for Mentally Retarded, 1965-69. Mem. Profl. adv. com. Fla. Center for Clin. Services at U. Fla., 1952-60; del. to Mid-century White House Conf. on Children and Youth, 1950; U.S. del. from Nat. Soc. for Crippled Children to World Congress for Welfare of Cripples, Inc., London, 1957; pres. corp. Eccleston-Callahan Hosp. for Colored Crippled Children, 1956-58; sec. Fla. chpt. Nat. Doctors' Com. for Improved Med. Services, 1951-52; med. adv. com. Gateway Sch. for Mentally Retarded, 1959—; bd. dirs. Forest Park Sch. for Spl. Edn. Crippled Children, 1949-54, mem. med. adv. com., 1955—, chmn. 1957—; dir. central Fla. poison control Orange Meml. Hosp.; mem. orgn. com., chmn. com. for admission and selection policies Camp Challenge. Mem. Nat. Rehab. Assn., Am. Congress Phys. Medicine and Rehab., Fla. Soc. Crippled Children and Adults, Central Fla. Soc. Crippled Children and Adults (dir. 1949-53, pres. 1956-57), Am. Assn. Cleft Palate, Fla. Soc. Crippled Children trustee 1951-57, v.p. 1956-57, prof. adv. com. 1957—), Am. Public Health Assn., Fla. Public Health Assn., Mental Health Assn. Orange County (charter mem.; pres. 1949-50, dir. 1947-52, chmn. exec. com. 1950-52, dir. 1963-65), Fla. Heart Assn., Orange County Heart Assn., AMA, Am. Med. Women's Assn., Fla. Med. Assn., So. Fla. Med. Assn. (chmn. com. on mental retardation), Orange County Med. Assn., Fla. Pediatric Soc., Orlando Pediatric Soc., Fla. Cleft Palte Assn. (counselor-at-large, sec.), Fed. Exec. Inst., Fed. Exec. Inst. Alumni Assn. (exec. officer 1974). Home: 2013 E Randolph Circle Tallahassee FL 32312 Office: 1323 Winewood Blvd Tallahassee FL 32301

MAGUIRE, JACK RUSSELL, inst. adminstr.; b. Denison, Tex., Apr. 10, 1920; s. Jeff Edward and Elizabeth (Russell) M.; student N. Tex. State Coll., 1940-41; B.J., U. Tex. at Austin, 1944; m. Patsy Jean Horton, Aug. 11, 1946; children—Jack Russell, Kevin Maguire. Reporter AP, Austin, 1943-44; pub. relations rep. M.-K.-T. R.R., St. Louis, 1945-50, T.P. & P. Ry., Dallas, 1950-51; dir. pub. relations Tex. Ins. Adv. Assn., Austin, 1950-56; exec. dir. U. Tex. Ex-Students' Assn., 1956-76; exec. dir. U. Tex. Inst. Texan Cultures, San Antonio, 1976—; pvt. practice as pub. relations cons., Austin, 1950-76; dir. Tex. Commerce Bank, San Antonio. Trustee Ednl. Projects for Edn., Inc., Washington, S.W. Research Inst.; mem. Tex. Sesquicentennial Commn. Recipient Master Publicist award San Antonio Advt. Fedn., 1979. Mem. Am. Ry. Mag. Editors Assn., Pub. Relations Soc. Am., Am. Soc. Assn. Execs., Philos. Soc. Tex., Sigma Delta Chi. Presbyn. Clubs: Rotary, Torch, St. Anthony, Headliner, University, Argyle. Author: Talk of Texas, 1973; Texas: Amazing, but True, 1980; editor: A President's Country. Columnist: Talk of Texas. Contbr. articles to profl. jours. Address: PO Box 1226 San Antonio TX 78294

MAGUIRE, PAT HORTON (MRS. JACK RUSSELL MAGUIRE), editor; b. Houston, Apr. 23, 1926; d. Pat Arthur and Hilde (West) Horton; B.A., U. Tex., 1946; m. Jack Russell Maguire, Aug. 11, 1946; children—Jack, Kevin. Free lance writer, researcher St. Louis, Dallas, Austin, 1946-56; dir. pub. relations Austin Presbyn. Theol. Sem., 1956-61; acting mng. editor U. Tex. Alumni Mag., ALCALDE, 1961, mng. editor, 1961-76, dir. alumni publs., 1964-76; dir. communications Ex-Students' Assn. U. Tex., 1971-76; publs. adviser Inst. Texan Cultures, U. Tex. at San Antonio, 1976-77, dir. publs., program coordinator, 1977—. Mem. Alpha Phi. Address: PO Box 1226 San Antonio TX 78294

MAGUIRE, THOMAS LOUIS, JR., personnel recruiting co. exec.; b. Balt., Md., May 2, 1941; s. Thomas L. and Elsie K. M.; B.E.E., U. Md., 1963; m. Charnell C. Maguire; 1 dau. Katherine Mary. Engr. def. group ITT, N.Y.C., 1962-66, mktg. mgr., 1967-68; v.p. McMugo Contracting Co., Inc. Mpls., 1968-69; owner, operator Availability Inc., Tampa, Fla., 1969—. Mem. select com. Greater Tampa C. of C.; mem. Select Tampa Indsl. Com. of 100 Served in USAF, 1958-62. Recipient commendation for forming ethics com. Personnel Cons. profession, Fla. Sec. of State, 1974, president's award Nat. Personnel Assos., 1976-77; certified personnel cons. Natl. Employment Assn.; certified Nat. Assn. Underwater Diving Instrs. Mem. Data Processing Mgmt. Assn., Nat., Fla. assns. personnel cons., Nat. Pilots Assn., Air Safety Found., Aircraft Owners and Pilots Assn., Nat. Personnel Assn. Republican. Episcopalian. Club: Rotary. Home: 285 Bayside Dr Clearwater Beach FL 33515 Office: 285 Lincoln Center Tampa FL 33609

MAHAN, QUILLAN ROBERT, realtor; b. Appalachia, Va., Mar. 28, 1907; s. Franklin Asbury and Sally Lee (Bishop) M.; grad. high sch.; m. Hazel Marie Sweet, Sept. 7, 1932; children—Darryl R., Delta L. (Mrs. James L. Garnett). Realtor, ins. agt. Mahan Realty, Pontiac, Mich., 1937-57; pres. Mahan Realty & Exchange, Inc., Clearwater, Fla., 1958—. Mem. Clearwater Indsl. Park Bd., 1959-61; mem. Bd. Adjustment and Appeals on Zoning, 1965—, chmn., 1969—; mem. Sr. Citizens Com., 1968—; mem. Clearwater Bicentennial Com., 1975—. Recipient award and citation, city of Clearwater, 1971, 75; named Outstanding Floridian, 1971. Mem. Nat. Soc. Exchange Counselors (bd. govs.), Nat. Real Estate Bd. (chmn. court ethics com. 1966-68), Clearwater-Largo-Dunedin Bd. Realtors (dir. 1972-73). Democrat. Baptist. Clubs: Masons (32 deg.), Shriners, Elks. Address: 100 S Aurora Ave Clearwater FL 33515

MAHAR, MARY VAUGHAN, automobile agy. exec.; b. Weatherford, Tex., Nov. 24, 1921; d. William Francis and Goldie Estell Vaughan; B.A., Tex. Christian U., 1954; postgrad. LaSalle Extension U., 1956-57; lic. vocat. nurse Campbell Sch. of Nursing, 1960; m. Douglas Atchison, Mar. 17, 1939 to Feb. 1976; children—Charles, Jimmy Lee, May Ann, Douglas, Lee, Roy, Ouida, Daniel; m. 2d, Walter Frank Mahar, May 13, 1978. With Convier Aircraft Co., Ft. Worth, 1942-45, Bliss Mortgate Investment Co., Ft. Worth, 1945-59; chief acct., Weatherford, Tex., 1959-63; vocat. nurse Keeland Nursing Home, Weatherford, 1965-69, Cox Convalescent Center, Weatherford, 1969-74; bus. mgr. Bill Duncan Toyota, Inc., Weatherford, 1975—. Mother adviser Order of Rainbow for Girls, Weatherford, 1972-76; spl. non-commd. dep. sheriff Parker County (Tex.). Recipient City of Weatherford Sec. of yr. award, 1977; services awards from local youth orgns. Mem. Bus. and Profl. Women's Club. Democrat. Mem. Ch. of Christ. Club: Order of Eastern Star. Home: 1005 Bridge St Weatherford TX 76086 Office: 504 Palo Pinto St Weatherford TX 76086

MAHER, BRIDGET, hosp. adminstr.; b. County Tipperary, Ireland, Dec. 7, 1918; d. Michael and Bridget (Ryan) M.; came to U.S., 1934, naturalized, 1944; student Incarnate Word Coll., San Antonio, Tex., 1938-39; B.S. in Pharmacy, Loyola U., New Orleans, 1944. Joined Sisters of Charity, 1936; dir. pharmacy Santa Rosa Med. Center, San Antonio, Tex., 1944-57; dir. pharmacy St. Joseph Hosp., Ft. Worth, 1957-59; dir. pharmacy and central supply Santa Rosa Med. Center, 1959-65; dir. pharmacy and central supply St. Anthonys Hosp., Amarillo, Tex., 1955-68; asst. adminstr. Santa Rosa Med. Center,

1968-70; dir. pharmacy Spohn Hosp., Corpus Christi, Tex., 1970—. Mem. Am. Soc. Hosp. Pharmacists, Am. Pharm. Assn., Tex. Soc. Hosp. Pharmacists, Tex. Pharm Assn. Home and Office: 1436 3d St Corpus Christi TX 78404

MAHESH, VIRENDRA BUSHAN, endocrinologist; b. India, Apr. 25, 1932; s. Narinjan Prasad and Sobhagyawati; came to U.S., 1958, naturalized, 1968; B.Sc. with honors, Patna U., India, 1951; M.Sc. in Chemistry, Delhi U., India, 1953, Ph.D., 1955; D.Phil. in Biol. Sci., Oxford U., 1958; m. Sushila Kumari Aggarwal, June 29, 1955; children—Anita Rani, Vinit Kumar. James Hudson Brown Meml. fellow Yale U., 1958-59; asst. research prof. endocrinology Med. Coll. of Ga., Augusta, 1959-63, asso. research prof., 1963-66, prof., 1966-70, Regents prof., 1970— Robert B. Greenblatt prof. endocrinology, 1979—, chmn. endocrinology, 1972—; dir. Center for Population Studies, 1971—; mem. reproductive biology study sect. NIH, 1977-81. Recipient Rubin award Am. Soc. for Study of Sterility, 1963; Billings Silver medal, 1965; NIH research grantee, 1960—. Mem. Chem. Soc. (England), Biochem. Soc. (England), Endocrine Soc., Soc. Biol. Chemists, Soc. for Gynecologic Investigation, Internat. Soc. Neuroendocrinology, Soc. for Study Reproduction, Am. Physiologic Soc., Am. Assn. for Lab. Animal Scis., AAUP, Am. Fertility Soc., Soc. for Exptl. Biology and Medicine, Internat. Soc. for Reproductive Medicine (pres. 1980—), N.Y. Acad. Scis., Sigma Xi. Mem. editorial bd. Steroids, 1963—, Jour. of Clin. Endocrinologic Metabolism, 1976-80; mem. adv. bd. Maturitas, 1977—; contbr. articles to profl. jours. and chpts. to books. Office: Dept Endocrinology Medical College of Georgia Augusta GA 30912

MAHMOOD, ARSHUD, civil engr.; b. Pakistan, Aug. 17, 1941; s. Mohammad Abdur and Sughra (Khalida) Rehman; came to U.S., 1969, naturalized, 1979; B.Sc., U. of the Punjab, 1961; B.Engring., U. Karachi, 1965; M. in Engring., Asian Inst. Tech., Thailand, 1968; M.S., U. Calif., Berkeley, 1972, Ph.D., 1973; m. Maliha Tanilon Mendoza, Sept. 20, 1971; children—Omar, Alia. Project engr. Woodward-Clyde Consultants, Orange, Calif., 1973-76; v.p. geotech. programs Bolt, Beranek and Newman Geomarine Services Co., Oxnard, Calif., 1976-77: sr. project engr. McClelland Engrs., Inc., Ventura, Calif., 1977-78, sr. geotech. engr., Houston, 1978-80, project mgr., 1980—; prof. (part-time) Calif. State U., Los Angeles, 1976-77; cons. on offshore projects in Chile and Venezuela, S.Am., 1977-79. NASA grantee, 1971; registered engr., Tex., Calif. Mem. ASCE, Internat. Soc. of Soil Mechanics and Found. Engring., Earthquake Engring. Research Inst., Sci. Research Soc. N. Am., Southeast Asian Soc. Soil Engring., Sigma Xi. Muslim. Contbr. articles on lunar soil and found. engring. to profl. jours. Home: 14402 Magic River Dr Cypress TX 77429 Office: 6100 Hillcroft Ave Houston TX 77081

MAHOOD, DAVID, banker; b. 1910; married. With 1st Nat. Bank, Raymondville, Tex., 1933-37; with 1st City Nat. Bank, Houston, 1937—, v.p., 1948-56, sr. v.p., 1956-68, exec. v.p. Comml. Banking div., 1968—; vice chmn. 1st City Bancorp. Tex., Inc., also dir. Address: 1001 Main St Box 2557 Houston TX 77001*

MAHRER, DAVID LEE, counseling psychologist; b. Edgeley, N.D., Dec. 29, 1943; s. Lorenz Dennis and Verna (Martinson) M.; B.S., U. N.D., 1968, M.S., 1969; Ph.D., U. Ariz., 1974. Asst. to dean records and placement Northland Coll., Ashland, Wis., 1968-71; counseling intern U. Ariz. Counseling Service, 1972-74; grad. teaching asso., dept. counseling and guidance, 1971-74; coordinator career devel. and new student services U. S.C., 1974-76, asso. dir. career planning and placement, 1976-78, coordinator grad. regional studies, asst. prof. counselor edn., 1978—; asso. dir. Gen. Electric Inst.; vis. faculty Daniel Mgmt. Center, Coll. Bus. U. S.C. Lic. psychologist, S.C. Mem. S.C. Personnel and Guidance Assn. (pres.), Am. Personnel and Guidance Assn., Nat. Vocat. Guidance Assn., S.C. Vocat. Guidance Assn., South Atlantic Yacht Racing Assn. Roman Catholic. Club: Columbia Sailing. Author: Lifestyle: What It Is and How to Do It, 1978; contbr. articles to profl. jours. Home: 229 3d Ave SW Aiken SC 29801 Office: 171 University Pkwy Aiken SC 29801

MAHRLE, BENJAMIN CARL, acct.; b. Clinton, Mich., May 19, 1942; s. Benjamin Oceola and Bernice Helen (Walker) M.; B.A. in Accounting, Mich. State U., 1964; m. Mary Ann Wuerth, June 14, 1964; 1 son, Matthew. With Young, Skutt & Brietenwischer, C.P.A.'s, Jackson, Cheboygan, Mich., 1964-66; tax and small bus. supr. Ernst & Ernst. C.P.A.'s, Tampa, Fla., 1970-74; prin. Benjamin C. Mahrle, C.P.A., Largo, Tampa, Fla., 1974-77, partner Mahrle & Schatzberg, C.P.A.'s, 1977—; lectr. and cons. in field. Pres., Town'n Country Civic Assn., Tampa. 1972; dir. Conservative Caucus, Inc., 5th congressional dist. Fla., 1976-77; trustee Fla. Suncoast Coll., 1978-79. C.P.A., Fla. Mem. Am., Fla. insts. C.P.A.'s, Nat. (Pres.'s Manuscript award 1972), W. Central Fla. (pres. 1977-78) assns. accountants, Estate Planning Council Pinellas County, Oldsmar, Largo, Tampa chambers commerce. Club: Kiwanis. Home: 736 Shore Dr E Oldsmar FL 33557 Office: 2450 W Bay Dr Largo FL 33540 also 5020 W Cypress Suite 211 Tampa FL 33607

MAIA, PHILIP PAUL, communications systems engr.; b. Brockton, Mass., Aug. 28, 1935; s. Antonio Oliverida and Nellie Viola (Drew) M.; B.S.E.E., U. Md., 1962; children by previous marriage—Paul, David, Linda, Sharee, Kimberly; m. Camille Loretta Nulta, July 10, 1972. Cons. elec. engr., 1962-70; mgr. communications systems-engring. Litton Data Systems, Pascagoula, Miss., 1970—. Instr., lectr. communications and electronics USAF, U.S. Armed Forces Inst., 1954-69. Pres. Biloxi (Miss.) Boys Club, 1964-68. Bd. dirs. USO, 1964-68. Served with USAF, 1953-58. Comml. pilot's license; 1st class licence FCC. Mem. I.E.E.E., Inst. Certification Engring. Technicians (life sr.), Nat. Soc. Profl. Engrs., Am. Naval Engrs., Litton Data Systems Mgmt. Club. Republican. Roman Catholic. Contbr. numerous articles to profl. jours. Designer naval communication systems for USN and fgn. govts. Home: 2604 Fernwood St Pascagoula MS 39567 Office: PO Box 1618 Pascagoula MS 39567

MAILANDT, PETER, mgmt. cons.; b. Berlin, June 2, 1941; s. Hanspeter and Erika Magarethe (Schuthe) M.; came to U.S., 1965; B.S., U. Berlin, 1963; M.S. (Academic exchange scholarship Berlin-Minn. 1965-66), U. Minn., 1967, M.B.A., 1970, Ph.D. in Physics, 1972; m. Sandra E. Powell, Sept. 27, 1973; children—Tonia, Cary. Research asso. in nuclear physics U. Minn., Mpls., 1966-72; strategic analyst Tex. Instruments, Inc., Dallas, 1972-73, control adminstr., 1973-75; sr. asso. mgmt. cons. McKinsey & Co., Dallas, 1975—. Contbr. articles in nuclear physics and bus. mgmt. to profl. jours. Home: 4031 Candlenut Ln Dallas TX 75234 Office: 5944 Luther Ln #600 Dallas TX 75225

MAIN, T(OM) TALMAGE, JR., bank exec., geologist; b. Hamilton, Tex., Jan. 9, 1922; s. Tom Talmage and Doris (Williams) M.; A.A., Tyler Tex. Jr. Coll., 1941; B.B.A., U. Tex. at Austin, 1947; M.Sc., Tex. Tech. U., 1950; postgrad. in law Jackson Miss. Sch. Law, 1955-59; m. (Virginia) Sue Pingree, Feb. 26, 1955; children—Deborah Sue, Steven Talmage. Field rep. Bur. Bus. Research U. Tex. at Austin, 1947; asst. to dist. traffic mgr. Phillips Petroleum Co., Houston, 1947-49; geologist Sun Oil Co., Dallas, 1952-59; geologist, asst. v.p., trust officer Mercantile Nat. Bank at Dallas, 1959—; dir. Dorchester Petroleum Co., King Ranch Oil & Lignite Co. Mem. Circle Ten Council Boy Scouts Am. Served to col., AUS, 1942-46, 50-52; ETO; Korea. Decorated Legion of Merit, Bronze Star medal, Meritorious Service medal; Medaille de Liberee (France). Mem. U.S. Res. Officers Assn. (life mem.; dept. pres. 1976-77, nat. councilman 1977-78, nat. treas. 1978—), Assn. U.S. Army (life, pres. chpt. 1970—), Mil. Order of World Wars (perpetual, comdr. chpt. 1973-74), Highland Park (Tex.) Community League (exec. com. 1966—, treas. 1975—), Knight Order of San Jacinto, Sons of Republic of Tex. (life, pres. 1973-75), Am. Inst. Banking, Dallas, Am. assns. petroleum landmen, Dallas Geol. Soc., Am. Assn. Petroleum Geologists, Dallas Mil. Ball Corp. (founder, sec.-treas. 1965—), United Service Orgn. (council 1970-73), Dallas Cares, Dallas C. of C., Nat. Mil. Intelligence Assn. (charter dir. 1974-76), Sigma Gamma Epsilon, Sigma Delta Kappa. Club: Dervish (Dallas). Presbyn. (elder, asst. clk. session 1970-76, 78—). Home: 4564 Arcady St Dallas TX 75205 Office: Mercantile Nat Bank 1704 Main St Dallas TX 75201

MAISEL, ELLIOT BENJAMIN, investment co. exec.; b. Mobile, Ala., Dec. 6, 1954; s. Herman Martin and Freida Gutlow M.; degree, U. Ala., 1976. Vice pres., sec.-treas. Herman Maisel Co., Mobile, Ala., 1976—. Mgr. congressional campaign, 1978. Mem. Mobile C. of C., Jr. C. of C., Sales and Mktg. Execs., Bldg. and Office Mgmt. Assn. Jewish. Club: Kiwanis. Home: 4218 Packingham St Mobile AL 36609 Office: PO Box 160247 Mobile AL 36616

MAJESTRO, TONY COLERIO, physician; b. Kimball, W.Va., Aug. 17, 1940; s. Antonio and Mary (Martella) M.; A.B., W.Va. U., 1962, M.D., 1966; m. Prudence Gaziano, Aug. 10, 1963; children—Anthony, Philip, Maria. Intern, Charleston (W.Va.) Meml. Hosp., 1966-67, resident surgery, 1967-68; resident orthopedic surgery Henry Ford Hosp., Detroit, 1968-71; staff orthopedist Charleston Area Med. Center, Charleston, W.Va., 1973—; vice-chmn. dept. orthopedics, asst. clin. prof. orthopedics W.Va. U. Med. Sch., 1976—. Served with AUS, 1971-73. Mem. Kanawha County, W.Va. State med. socs., A.M.A., Am. Bd. Orthopedic Surgery, Am. Acad. Orthopedic Surgeons, Eastern Orthopedic Assn. Roman Catholic. Club: Great Kanawha River Navy. Home: 620 Burkewood St Charleston WV 25314 Office: Suite 303 210 Brooks St Charleston WV 25301

MAJOR, JENAN SHIVERS, acct.; b. Randolph County, Ga., Oct. 5, 1949; d. William Idus and Elizabeth (Farr) Shivers; A.S., Andrew Coll., 1969; B.B.A. in acctg., U. Ga., 1971; m. Kenneth Boswell Major, Nov. 20, 1971. Acct., Learning Founds. Internat., Athens, Ga., 1969-71; budget analyst St. Mary's Hosp., Athens, 1972-79; acct. Shelton's Welding & Sheet Metal Co., Hull, Ga., 1979—; mem. adv. bd. for acctg. Athens Tech. Sch. Sec., rec. Cherokee Corner United Methodist Ch., 1978, 79. Mem. Hosp. Fin. Mgrs. Assn. Home: PO Box 53 Arnoldsville GA 30619 Office: Shelton's Welding & Sheet Metal Co PO Box 183 Hull GA 30646

MAJORS, DON YANCEY, office products mfg. co. exec.; b. Memphis, Aug. 29, 1940; s. Don Speer and Margaret Lee (Yancey) M.; B.S., U. Ark., 1962; m. Betty A. Kinley, Aug. 20, 1961; children—Don Yancey, Gregory Steven. Sales rep. Hallmark Cards, Kansas City, Mo., 1962-65; sales rep. IBM Corp., Memphis, 1965-68, mktg. mgr., 1968-71, br. mgr., Wichita, Kans., 1972, program mgr., Little Rock, 1973-75, br. mgr. corp. office products div., Tallahassee, Fla., 1976—. Recipient 4 Excellence in Mktg. awards, Golden Circle award; named Br. Mgr. of Yr., 1977. Office: 660 Apalachee Pkwy Tallahassee FL 32301

MAKANSI, MUNZER, chem. co. exec.; b. Aleppo, Syria, Dec. 23, 1923; s. Ismail and Amina (Khudari) M.; B.Sc. with honors, Fouad-I U., Cairo, Egypt, 1947; M.A., Columbia, 1950, M.S., 1951, D. Engring. Sci., 1957; m. Nellie M. Kotsakis, Jan. 2, 1951; children—Delal, Antar, Jason, Tarek. Tchr. Alma-Amoun High Sch., Aleppo, 1947-49; with DuPont Co., 1954—, Wilmington, Del., 1954-66, supr. research and devel., Chattanooga, 1966-76, research asso., 1976—. Mem. N.Y. Acad. Scis., Sigma Xi, Phi Lambda Upsilon. Author: Periodic Classification of Chemical Elements, 1949. Patentee in field. Home: 106 Stratford Rd Signal Mountain TN 37377 Office: Chattanooga DuPont Textile Fibers Plant Access Rd Chattanooga TN 37343

MAKAR, FAWZY AZIZ, mech. engr.; b. Cairo, Sept. 18, 1946; came to U.S., 1970, naturalized, 1976; s. Aziz M. and Sania (Pastaoras) M.; student N.Y. U., 1970-71; B.S. in Mech. Engring., U. Louisville, 1973, M.S., 1976; postgrad. Miss. State U., 1976—; m. Margaret Wagner, Jan. 14, 1977. Asst. to project engr. Louisville and Jefferson County Met. Sewer Dist., Louisville, 1972; asst. plant engr. Paramount Foods, Inc., Louisville, 1973-74; asst. plant engr. Lorillard Co., Louisville, 1974-76; instr. (part-time) graphics dept. engring. U. Louisville, 1974-76; instr. (part-time) math. and graphics dept. engring. tech. Jefferson Community Coll., Louisville, 1976; plant engr. Babcock & Wilcox Co., West Point, Miss., 1976-77, sr. plant engr., 1977—, mgr. plant engring., 1980—. Mem. ASME, Am. Soc. Mfg. Engring., Am. Soc. Profl. Engrs. Mem. Christian Ch. Home: 24 Colony Dr West Point MS 39773 Office: E Half Mile St West Point MS 39773

MAKIELSKI, STANISLAW JOHN, JR., polit. scientist; b. Charlottesville, Va., Feb. 8, 1935; s. Stanislaw John and Alice Lee (Patton) M.; B.S., U. Va., 1960; Ph.D., Columbia U., 1964; m. Sally Putnam Kimball, June 14, 1963. Asst. prof. govt. U. Va., 1964-68, asso. prof., 1968-71; prof. polit. sci. Loyola U. New Orleans, 1971—, chmn. dept., 1975—; research asso. Inst. Govt. U. Va., 1964-71. Served with U.S. Army, 1955-57. Mem. Am., So. polit. sci. assns., Southwestern Social Sci. Assn. Author: The Politics of Zoning, 1965; City County Consolidation, 1970; Beleaguered Minorities, 1973. Home: 4314 Annunciation St New Orleans LA 70115 Office: 6363 St Charles Ave New Orleans LA 70118

MALANIK, SHIRLEY ALICE, guidance counselor; b. Des Plaines, Ill., July 1, 1948; d. Charles, Jr., and Pearl M.; B.A., Judson Coll., 1970; M.A., U. South Fla., 1974. Spl. edn. tchr. Hillsborough County Public Schs., Brandon, Fla., 1970-73, guidance counselor Chamberlain High Sch., Tampa, Fla., 1974—. Vol. Dr. Martin Luther King Civic Center. Cert. tchr. guidance, jr. coll., history, sociology, social studies, mental retardation, Fla. Mem. Am. Personnel and Guidance Assn., Hillsborough County Personnel and Guidance Assn. Democrat. Baptist. Home: 13583 Orange Sunset Dr Tampa FL 33618 Office: 9401 North Blvd Tampa FL 33612

MALATAK, JOHN MICHAEL, assn. exec.; b. Pitts., Nov. 8, 1948; s. Michael and Anne (Wright) M.; A.S., S. Ga. Coll., 1968; B.S. in Ed., Ga. So. Coll., 1970; m. Ruth Weinmann, Apr. 15, 1972; 1 dau., Julia Michelle. Dir. safety ARC, Ft. Lauderdale, Fla., 1970-72, safety rep. Tenn. div., Nashville, 1972-74, European area, Stuttgart, W. Ger., 1974-77, dir. safety services, Knoxville, 1977-80, dir. safety services State of Tenn., Nashville, 1980—; scuba instr., 1967—. Bd. dirs. Vol. Rescue Squad, Mayor's Adv. Safety Com.; bd. dirs., affiliate faculty Am. Heart Assn. Recipient cert. of merit in lifesaving Pres. U.S., 1978. Mem. Am. Assn. Trauma Specialists, Nat. Assn. Trauma Specialists, Nat. Assn. EMT, Profl. Assn. Diving Instrs., Nat. Interscholastic Swim Coaches Assn., Am. Canoeing Assn., Nat. Assn. Scuba Instrs. (S.E. area commr.), Commodore Longfellow Soc. (S.E. membership chmn.). Democrat. Roman Catholic. Clubs: Sertoma, Optimists, K.C. Contbg. author: Programming Fun in Aquatics, 1978; Lifeguarding and Aquatic Management, 1979; Swimming and Water Safety, 1979; Methods of Teaching, 1979; tech. adv. film Teaching Johnny to Swim, 1974. Home: 1805 Sedgewick Dr Knoxville TN 37922 Office: 321 22d Ave N Nashville TN 37203

MALEK, RIAD GEORGE, engring. exec.; b. Tripoli, Lebanon, Dec. 11, 1943; came to U.S., 1963, naturalized, 1974; s. George Antoine and Yvonne (Abboud) M.; B.S.M.E., La. State U., 1966; M.S.M.E., La. State U., 1968, Ph.D. M.E., 1971; m. Danna L. Jones, May 26, 1968; 1 dau., Kristine Elizabeth. Mgr. thermal design Barnard & Burk, Inc., Baton Rouge, 1968-73; mgr. heat transfer engring. Richmond Engring. Co. (Va.), 1973-75; mgr. engring. and quality assurance Geosource, Inc., Corpus Christi, Tex., 1975—. Mem. Tubular Exchanger Mfg. Assn., Am. Mgmt. Assn., Tau Beta Pi, Pi Tau Sigma. Republican. Greek Orthodox. Home: 5526 Kenith Circle Corpus Christi TX 78413 Office: PO Box 4658 300 McBride Ln Corpus Christi TX 78408

MALETTA, ROSE HELEN (MRS. VINCENT S. CONTI), physician; b. N.Y.C., Apr. 25, 1916; d. Frank and Carmel (Ponterio) Maletta; student Hunter Coll., 1933-36; M.D., U. Naples, 1941; m. Vincent S. Conti, Mar. 4, 1943; children—Vincent R., Gloria Conti Griffin. Intern, Met. Hosp. Center, N.Y.C., 1941-42; resident Met. Hosp., Flower-Fifth Av. Hosp., N.Y.C., 1942-44; practice medicine, specializing in anesthesiology, N.Y.C., 1944-71, Ft. Lauderdale, Fla., 1971—; dir. anesthesia St. John's Hosp., Queens, N.Y.C., 1945-50; dir. anesthesia Lutheran Hosp., Bklyn., 1950-56, cons. anesthesiology, 1956-71; asst. prof. anesthesiology N.Y. Med. Coll., 1967-71; asst. attending anesthesiology Met. Hosp. Center, N.Y.C., 1967-71; anesthesiologist Broward Gen. Med. Center, Ft. Lauderdale, 1971—, Holy Cross Hosp., Imperial Point Hosps. Mem. AMA, Fla., Broward County med. socs., Am., Fla. socs. anesthesiologists, Am. Coll. Chest Physicians, Ft. Lauderdale Surg. Soc. Club: Coral Ridge Country. Home: 3550 Galt Ocean Dr Fort Lauderdale FL 33308 Office: 4001 N Ocean Dr Fort Lauderdale FL 33308

MALEY, EDWIN, Judo instr.; b. Bklyn., Dec. 29, 1931; s. Irving and Hannah M.; student U. Tampa, 1961-62; LL.D. (hon.), Nat. Police Acad., 1967; m. Toby Shebroe, Aug. 29, 1953; 1 son, Keith. Pres., Fla. Sch. of Judo, Inc., Tampa, 1963—. Served with USAF, 1951-63. Recipient diplomas and certificates in Swedish massage, numerous laurels from nat. and internat. Judo competition, including many coach and sportsmanship awards. Fla. State Overall Judo champion, 1959-65, Overall New Eng. and East Coast champion, 1959, Overall 8th Air Force champion, 1955-57; 2d degree Black Jujitsu; 2d degree Black Karate; 6th Red and White Judo; registered massage therapist; selected to make goodwill trip to Japan, 1955; Ed Maley's Fla. Sch. of Judo Week proclaimed by City of Tampa, Sept. 1979. Jewish. Home: 702 Forest Hills Dr Brandon FL 33511 Office: 530 S MacDill Ave Tampa FL 33619

MALIN, THOMAS ROBINSON, III, printing co. exec.; b. Dallas, July 20, 1942; s. Thomas Robinson and Elizabeth Hill M.; student E. Tex. State U., 1960-64, So. Meth. U., 1965; m. Lois Ann Brockles, Feb. 14, 1976; children—Thomas Edwin, Stephen Christopher, Angela Renee. Ins. salesman Prudential Life Ins. Co. Am., 1963, 65; with Clarke Checks, Mesquite, Tex., 1965—, area sales mgr. N. Tex.-La.-Ark.-Dallas div., 1974—; cons. to banks. Mem. Bank Mktg. Assn. (1st v.p. N. Tex. chpt. 1979-80), Corvette Club Tex. (past pres.). Methodist. Club: Masons. Home: 605 Trailwood Ct Garland TX 75043 Office: Clarke Checks 3535 Executive Blvd Mesquite TX 75149

MALLAMO, REGINALD ALFRED, business exec.; b. San Francisco, Feb. 20, 1943; s. Angelo Rocco and Palmira (Accari) M.; B.S.C., U. Santa Clara, 1965; m. Carlene P. Ferrell, June 19, 1965; children—Regina Grace, Paul Henry, Daniel James. With Trans World Airlines, San Francisco, 1965-72, account exec., 1971-72; dist. sales mgr. Foremost Ins., Missoula, Mont., 1973-74; dist. sales mgr. Holiday Inns, Memphis, 1974-75, regional sales and market mgr., 1975-77, v.p. sales devel., 1977-79; pres., chief exec. officer Holiday Clubs, Internat., 1979—. Recipient Award of Excellence, Trans World Airlines, 1971, Salesman of Yr., 1966, 67; Outstanding Achievement award Foremost Ins., 1974. Mem. Am. Soc. Assn. Execs., Am. Soc. Travel Agts., Am. Soc. for Tng. and Devel., Am. Bus. Assn., Nat. Indsl. Recreation Assn., Sales and Mktg. Execs. Memphis, Tourism Industry Assn. Am., U.S. Tour Operators Assn., Discover Am. Travel Orgns. Republican. Roman Catholic. Club: Germantown Soccer (coach 1976-79).

MALLARD, BOBBY JOE, coal, oil, gas co. exec.; b. Nacogdoches, Tex., Dec. 16, 1931; s. Albert Knight and Grace Elanor (Skeeters) M.; B.S., La. Tech. U., 1957; M.B.A., Pepperdine U., 1977; m. Sue Ellen Sparman, July 4, 1958; children—Sheri Lynn, Roger Scott. Mgr. gen. accounting Collins Radio Co., Dallas, 1957-68; controller Tracor Inc., Austin, Tex., 1968-70; sec.-treas. Q-Dot Corp., Dallas, 1970-72; treas. Petro Grande, Inc., Dallas, 1972-74; v.p., controller Gen. Exploration Co., Dallas, 1974—. Served with U.S. Army, 1954-56. Mem. Am. Mgmt. Assn., Nat. Assn. Accountants, Fin. Execs. Inst. Republican. Methodist. Home: 10647 Chesterton Dr Dallas TX 75238 Office: 4219 Sigma Rd Dallas TX 75234

MALLARD, LEO SESSIONS, newspaper and printing co. exec.; b. Albany, Ga., Dec. 28, 1937; s. Leo and Mary (Sessions) M.; student Mercer U., 1956; A.B. in Journalism, U. Ga., 1959; m. Barbara Gilbert, June 29, 1963; children—Leo Sessions, Lisa Dianne, Judson Dean, Clayton Todd. News and sports editor Times Free Press and Carroll County Georgian, Carrollton, Ga., 1960-61; asst. to pub., editor Covington (Ga.) News, Inc., 1961-78, pres., 1975—. Mem. Covington City Council, 1971-74; mem. exec. bd. Atlanta Area council Boy Scouts Am., 1973-79, active Cubmaster Pack 58, 1972-78, scoutmaster troop 222, 1978-80; chmn. Newton County (Ga.) Bicentennial, 1975-76; trustee Piedmont Acad., 1978-80; chmn. N.E. dist. bd. YMCA, 1977—, mem. Ga. bd., 1977—. Named Boss of Yr., Newton County Jaycees, 1976, Dist. award of merit Boy Scouts Am., 1976, Silver Beaver award, 1977. Mem. Ga. Press Assn., Nat. Newspaper Assn., Outdoor Writers Am. (asso.), Newton County C. of C. (pres. 1977-78), Eagle Scout Assn., Order of Arrow, Sigma Delta Chi. Republican. Baptist. Clubs: Kiwanis (pres. local club 1972-73), Elks (Covington); Jackson Lake Bass. Home: Box 226 3163 Monticello St Covington GA 30209 Office: Box 1278 Hwy 278W Covington GA 30209

MALLEN, SAUL TWOM, textile mfg. exec.; b. Boston, Dec. 18, 1914; s. Joseph and Ida (Seltzer) M.; LL.B., Northeastern U., 1937, J.D., 1972; m. Muriel S. Goldberg, June 10, 1939; children—Ted A., Steven L. (dec.), Peter J. Admitted to Mass. bar, 1938; with Sport-Wear Hosiery Mills, Inc. (co. name changed to Sport Wear Mills, Inc., 1968), Phila., 1938—, exec. mgr., Etowah, Tenn., exec. v.p., sec. treas., dir., chmn. 1942—; officer, chmn. bd. Windsor Hosiery Mills, Inc., Etowah; co-founder, exec. v.p., treas., chmn. Internat. Yarn Corp., San Juan, P.R., 1963, Cleveland, Tenn., 1967—; co-founder, dir., chmn. Knitco, Inc., N.Y.C., 1966-69, Amtex, Inc., Cleveland, 1972—. Pioneer drive to establish first blood bank in McMinn County, Tenn.; mem. Jewish Community Center; active Ochs Meml. Temple, Chattanooga, 1941—, dir. 1965-67; patron

Bright Sch., Chattanooga, 1946—; charter mem., dir. Cleveland Regional Speech and Hearing Center, 1971—. Bd. dirs. McCallie Sch., 1953-61, patron, 1953—. Mem. Nat. Assn. Am. Hosiery Mfrs., Am. Sci. Yarn Mfrs. Clubs: Masons (32 deg.), Shriners, Elks, B'nai B'rith, Valleybrook Golf and Country. Home: 3408 Harcourt Dr Chattanooga TN 37411 Office: Amtex Inc 20th St and Michigan Ave Cleveland TN 37311

MALLERY, WILLIAM HENRY, III, business exec., public adminstrn. cons.; b. McComb, Miss., Dec. 15, 1935; s. William Henry and Tot (McManus) M.; B.Pub. Adminstrn., U. Miss., 1958; postgrad. So. Meth. U.; m. Cecil Nolan, July 12, 1958; children—David, Mark, Kathy, Hank, John Paul, Beth. Asst. to city mgr., Farmers Branch, Tex., 1958-59; mgr. C. of C., Farmers Branch, 1959; self-employed as pub. relations counsellor, 1960; dir. pub. relations, asst. sales mgr. Magnolia Mobile Homes Sales Corp., 1961; purchasing agt., Vicksburg, Miss., 1962; program officer Program of Advances for Pub. Works Planning, U.S. Dept. Housing and Urban Devel., 1963-66; city mgr., Punta Gorda, Fla., Belle Glade, Fla., 1966-75; fed. programs coordinator Cities of West Point, Aberdeen, New Albany, Houston, and Grenada (Miss.), 1975-77; mgr. Aberdeen C. of C., 1975—; pres. William H. Mallery & Assos., public adminstrn. consultants, Aberdeen, 1977—. Chmn. PBJC Glades area steering com., 1972—. Mem. Internat., Fla., Palm Beach County (past pres.) city mgrs. assns. Unitarian. Home: 213 Meadowlane Aberdeen MS 39730 Office: 109 N Meridian St PO Box 887 Aberdeen MS 39730

MALLETTE, LILA MOHLER (SRI LILANANDA), assn. exec.; b. Fort Lauderdale, Fla., June 7, 1931; d. Marvin Francis and Silvia Ione (Kenney) Mohler; student U. N.Mex., 1963-65; children—Michael F., Polly A. Mallette McPeak, Jefferson A. Founder, dir. Council for World Community, Arlington, Va., 1975—. Mem. NOW, World Future Soc., Assn. for Humanistic Psychology, Planetary Citizens. Club: Mensa.

MALLETTE, REESE EWELL, JR., cons. geol. engr.; b. Atlanta, Oct. 29, 1931; s. Reese Ewell and Nell Matilda (Burdick) M.; B.S., U. Ala., 1954; M.A., Harvard, 1960; m. Jean Reid Shannon, Dec. 28, 1957; children—Reese Ewell III, Pope Shannon, Lee Hurley, Greer Burdick. Instr. U. Ala., 1956-57; engr. Ala. By-Products Corp., 1957-58, 62-66, Perini Corp., Boston, 1959, Gates Engring. Co., Beckley, W.Va., 1960-62; cons. geologist, engr. Reese E. Mallette Assos., Birmingham, Ala., 1966—; v.p. Dy-Met, Inc. Served to 1st lt. C.E., AUS, 1954-56. Mem. Am. Inst. Mining Engrs., Soc. Econ. Geologists, Geol. Soc. Am., Am. Inst. Profl. Geologists, Ala. Geol. Soc., Ala. Acad. Sci., Ala. Soc. Farm Mgrs. and Rural Appraisers, Kappa Alpha, Tau Beta Pi, Sigma Gamma Epsilon. Presbyn. Home: 3830 S Cove Dr Birmingham AL 35213 Office: 2610 3d Ave South Birmingham AL 35233

MALLIN, JAY, journalist; b. N.Y.C., Dec. 10, 1927; s. Albert Milton and Cecelia (Jaffe) M.; A.B., Fla. So. Coll., 1949; m. Caroll Sue Driftmeyer, Jan. 31, 1959; children—Jay, Linda Anne. News editor Havana (Cuba) Herald, 1951-53; stringer corr. Time and Life, 1956—; columnist Copley News Service, 1972-74; editor The Net, 1974—. Research scientist Center for Advanced Internat. Studies, Miami, 1967-69; cons. various corps., 1970—. Author: Fortress Cuba, 1965; Caribbean Crisis, 1965; Terror in Viet Nam, 1966; Che Guevara on Revolution, 1969; Strategy for Conquest, 1970; Terror and Urban Guerrillas, 1971; co-author: Merc: American Soldiers of Fortune, 1979; contbr. to Terrorism: Interdisciplinary Perspectives, 1977, also to gen., acad. and mil. jours. Home: 406 Savona Ave Coral Gables FL 33146

MALLINSON, JAMES ARTHUR, JR., counselor; b. Lancaster, Pa., Aug. 19, 1952; s. James Arthur and Barbara Mae (Musselman) M.; B.A., Catawba Coll., Salisbury, N.C., 1973; M.A. in Edn., Western Carolina U., 1975; m. Carla Ann Hoffmann, Aug. 24, 1973; 1 dau., Christine Louise. Alcoholism counselor Tri-County Mental Health Complex, Salisbury, N.C., 1976—; 1st pres. Crisis Council Salisbury-Rowan, 1977—; bd. dirs. Dial Help; cons., tchr. in field. Cert. alcoholism counselor. Mem. Am. Personnel and Guidance Assn., Alcoholism Profls. N.C. Democrat. Lutheran. Home: Route 1 Box 446-B Salisbury NC 28144 Office: 165 Mahaley Ave Salisbury NC 28144

MALONE, AVON LEE, educator; b. Dallas, Dec. 9, 1931; s. Joseph Colby and Glendelle Vay (Myers) M.; B.A., Abilene Christian U., 1954, M.A., 1974; m. Mary Ann Hart, Feb. 2, 1954; children—Glenda, Lavon, Nathan. Preacher chs., Waukegan, Ill., 1954-58, Aurora, Colo., 1958-60, Fort Worth, 1960-64, Denton, Tex., 1964-67, Denver, 1967-70, Abilene, Tex., 1971-74; asst. prof. Bible Harding U., Searcy, Ark., 1974-80. Bd. dirs. West Tex. Sch. Evangelism, Abilene, 1971-74. Home: 2 Foxboro St Searcy AR 72143 Office: Dept Religion Harding U Searcy AR 72143

MALONE, JAMES LEONARD, elec. contractor; b. McDavid, Fla., Nov. 6, 1918; s. Mannie A. and Seola (Roach) M.; student Coyne Elec. Sch., 1939; Asso. Elec. Engring., Bliss Elec. Sch., 1947; m. Kathryn Brock, June 15, 1940; children—Gloria (Mrs. J.D. McNeil), Carolyn Malone Williams, Faye (Mrs. Larry E. Carlton), Richard Glenn. Electrician, White Elec. Constrn. Co., Columbus, Ga., 1942-46, mgr. motor repair and sales, 1946-50; founder Ga. Elec. Co., Albany, 1950, pres., gen. mgr., 1950-69; founder J.L. Malone and Assos., Inc., Albany, 1969, pres., mgr., 1969—. Sec., S.W. Ga. Constrn. Tng. Council, Inc., Albany, 1973-74; mem. City Albany Elec. Examining Bd., 1964—, pres., 1972-73; mem. City Albany Water, Gas and Light Commn. Served with AUS, 1944-46. Registered profl. engr., Ga. Mem. IEEE, Nat. Elec. Contractors Assn., Ga. Soc. Profl. Engrs. Baptist. Home: 1724 Pineknoll Ln Albany GA 31707 Office: PO Box 3367 Albany GA 31706

MALONE, JOHN IRVIN, physician, educator; b. Altoona, Pa., Oct. 10, 1941; s. William Paul and Olive (Romine) M.; B.S., Pa. State U., 1963; M.D., U. Pa., 1967; m. Gloria Joyce Cromer, Sept. 5, 1964; children—John Irvin, Michael Albert, Jennifer Amy. Intern Children's Hosp. Phila., 1967-68, resident pediatrics, 1968-69, research fellow div. biochem. devel. and molecular diseases, 1969-71, chief resident pediatrics, 1971-72; instr. pediatrics U. Pa., Phila., 1969-72; asst. prof. pediatrics U. South Fla., Tampa, 1972-76, asso. prof., 1976—; co-dir. Fla.'s Camp for Children and Youth with Diabetes, 1973—; mem. staff Tampa Gen. Hosp., 1972—, All Children's Hosp., St. Petersburg, Fla., 1973—; med. dir. Juvenile Diabetes Assn.; mem. med. adv. bd. Children's Diabetes Found., Denver. Recipient Baldwin Lucke Meml. prize for med. student research, 1967. Diplomate Am. Bd. Pediatrics. Fellow Am. Acad. Pediatrics; mem. A.A.A.S., Am. Fedn. Clin. Research, Soc. Pediatric Research, So. Soc. Pediatric Research, Lawson Wilkins Pediatric Endocrine Soc., Am. Diabetes Assn. (dir. Fla. affiliate). Presbyn. Contbr. articles to profl. jours. Office: Dept Pediatrics Box 15 U South Fla Coll Medicine Tampa FL 33612

MALONE, PERRILLAH (PAT) ATKINSON, state ofcl.; b. Montgomery, Ala., Mar. 17, 1922; d. Odolph Edgar and Myrtle (Fondren) Atkinson; B.S., Oglethorpe U., 1956; M.A.T., Emory U., 1962. Asst. editor-acting editor Emory U., 1958-64; asst. project officer Ga. Dept. Pub. Health, Atlanta, 1965-68; asst. project dir. Ga. Ednl. Improvement Council, 1968-69; asso. dir. Ga. Edn. Improvement Council, 1970-71; dir. career services State Scholarship Commn., Atlanta, 1971-74; rev. coordinator Div. Phys. Health, Ga. Dept. Human Resources, Atlanta, 1974-79; asst. project dir. So. Regional Edn., Bd., Atlanta, 1979—; mem. Gov.'s Commn. on Nursing Edn. and Nursing Practice, 1972-75; book reviewer Atlanta Jour.-Constn., 1962-79. Recipient Recognition award Ga. Nursing Assn., 1976, Alumni Honor award Emory U., 1964. Mem. Nat. Ga. (pres.-elect 1979—, Korsell award 1974) leagues for nursing, Am., Ga. pub. health assns., Am. Acad. Polit. and Social Scis. Methodist. Club: Atlanta Press. Home: 1146 Oxford Rd NE Atlanta GA 30306 Office: 130 6th St NW Atlanta GA 30313

MALONE, ROBERT WILLIAM, med. mfg. co. exec.; b. Dunsmuir, Calif., May 31, 1934; s. George Ceral and Juanita Amelia (Green) M.; A.A., Hartnell Coll., 1960; B.A., San Jose State U., 1962; m. Loretta Platt, Feb. 21, 1975; children—Gregory Matthew, Patrick Colin, Abigail Platt. Chief technology, microbiologist VA Hosp., Palo Alto, Calif., 1963-66; tech. rep., dist. mgr., product mgr. BioQuest div. Becton-Dickinson Co., Cockeysville, Md., 1966-73; product mgr. Hycel div. Boehringer Mannheim Co., Houston, 1973-75, dir. reagent mktg., 1975-76, dir. mktg. ops., 1976—; bd. dir. KVM Engring. Co. Served with USAF, 1953-57. Mem. Am. Soc. Med. Technologists, Calif. Assn. Med. and Lab. Technologists. Home: 7819 Creekbend St Houston TX 77071 Office: 7920 Westpark St Houston TX 77063

MALONEY, JOHN PHILIP, banker; b. San Antonio, 1918; grad. Millsaps Coll., 1940, U. Miss. Law Sch., 1946. Chmn., chief exec. officer Deposit Guaranty Nat. Bank, Jackson, Miss.; pres. Deposit Guaranty Corp., Jackson; dir. Jackson Packing Co. Vice chmn. Miss. Oil and Gas Bd. Office: One Deposit Guaranty Plaza Jackson MS 39201*

MALONEY, LAWRENCE MICHAEL, govt. ofcl.; b. Seminole, Okla., Apr. 20, 1946; s. Maurice Anthony, Sr. and Effie Agnes (Sherrell) M.; B.S., Okla. State U., 1968, M.S., 1975; m. Marilee Jean Inselman, June 6, 1976. Writer, photographer Central Rural News, Stillwater, Okla., 1972-74; mng. editor Perkins (Okla.) Jour., 1973; photog. editor The Daily O'Collegian, 1972-74; editor Holdenville (Okla.) Daily News, 1975-76; chief photographer Athens (Tex.) Daily Review, 1976; photographer Daily Oklahoman and Oklahoma City Times, 1977; photojournalist, info. specialist Okla. Dept. Transp., Oklahoma City, 1977—; cons. small daily newspapers; tchr. propaganda analysis and techniques U.S. Army Inst. Mil. Assistance, summers 1975, 77; photog. works exhibited two-man show Okla. State U., 1975. Served to capt. AUS, 1968-71. Decorated Bronze Star; recipient 1st place awards Nat. Sigma Delta Chi photo contest, 1968, Regional photo contest, 1974, 2d place award Regional photo contest, 1974, Western Fairs contest, 3d place award E. Tex. photo contest, 1975, commendation for journalistic service to Hughes County, Okla. Ho. of Reps., 1976. Mem. Okla. Press Assn., Okla. Fedn. Writers (1st pl. award 1980), Pershing Rifles, Sigma Delta Chi, Alpha Phi Omega. Democrat. Roman Catholic. Club: Rotary. Home: 3041 W Park Pl Oklahoma City OK 73107 Office: Oklahoma Dept of Transportation 200 NE 21st St Oklahoma City OK 73105

MALOOF, JOYCE MORGAN, automobile agy. exec.; b. Coleman, Ga., May 28, 1928; d. Wheeler Austin and Catherine (Geeslin) Morgan; student Ga. State U., 1945, Piedmont Sch. Nursing, 1945; m. Harold M. Maloof (dec. Apr. 1974); 1 son, Harold M. Nurse, Piedmont Hosp. Sch. Nursing, Atlanta, 1945, Patterson Hosp., Cuthbert, Ga., 1947; with Maloof Motor Co., Inc., Columbus, Ga., 1955—, owner, pres. 1965—; ins. agt. moore Ins. Co., Atlanta, 1975—; del. to Am. Import Dealers Assn. Automotive Congress, 1976, Am. Import Congress, Washington, 1980; mem. S.E. Toyota Dealer Council, 1974, 79-80. Named one of 10 outstanding bus. women in Chattahoochee Valley, Chattahoochee Valley Bus. and Profl. Women's Club, 1972. Mem. bldg. com. Hilton Ter. Bapt. Ch., 1977. Mem. C. of C., Better Bus. Bur., Used Car Dealers Assn., New Car Dealers Assn., Nat. Bus. Mgmt. Club, Nat. Automboile Dealers Assn., Ga. Ind. Automobile Dealers Assn., Am. Bus. Women's Assn., Bus. Women's Club. Democrat. Baptist. Club: Big Eddy, Green Island Country. Pub., Temp mag., 1976—. Home: 5715 Green Island Dr Columbia GA 31904 Office: 1801 Box Rd Columbus GA 31907

MALOOLY, DONALD ALBERT, physician; b. El Paso, Tex., May 9, 1930; s. Elias A. and Mamie (Coury) M.; student Rice U., 1947-49; B.A., Tex. Western Coll., 1950; M.D., U. So. Calif., 1954; m. Mary Hill, July 9, 1955; children—Donald Ellis, Mary Elizabeth, Mark Hill. Intern, William Beaumont Army Hosp., Ft. Bliss, Tex., 1954-55; resident Scott and White Clinic, Temple, Tex., 1957-59, Long Beach (Calif.) VA Hosp., 1959-60; fellow Mayo Clinic, Rochester, Minn., 1960-61; practice medicine, specializing in cardiology, El Paso, 1962-78; chief cardiology sect. VA Med. Center, Amarillo, Tex., 1978—; asso. clin. prof. Tex. Tech. Sch. Medicine; mem. staff Providence Meml., St. Joseph's, Sun Towers hosps., Hotel Dieu, 1962-78. Served to capt. M.C., AUS, 1954-57. Diplomate Am. Bd. Internal Medicine, also cardiovascular bd. Fellow Am. Coll. Chest Physicians, Am. Coll. Cardiology, Royal Soc. Promotion Health; mem. AMA, Am. Heart Assn. (fellow, mem. council clin. cardiology), Tex. Acad. Internal Medicine, Tex. Med. Assn., Alpha Omega Alpha, Phi Rho Sigma, Phi Kappa Phi, Tau Kappa Epsilon. Episcopalian. Contbr. articles to profl. jours. Home: 6201 I40 W Tiffany II #229 Amarillo TX 79106 Office: VA Med Center Amarillo TX 79106

MALOOLY, MARY HILL, writer, civic worker; b. Austin, Tex., Feb. 10, 1928; d. Daniel Lafayette and Florence Chalfont (Peak) Hill; student U. Tex., El Paso, 1945-48; B.A., U. Ala., 1949, M.A., 1951; m. Donald A. Malooly, July 9, 1955; children—Donald Ellis, Mary Elizabeth, Mark Hill. Radio continuity writer Sta. KEPO, El Paso, 1949-50; editor U. Ala. Alumni News, Tuscaloosa, 1950; script TV writer Sta. KTSM-TV, El Paso, 1951-55; freelance writer, El Paso, 1951—; vol. tutor in field; dir. Potter-Randall Co. Bd. dirs. Vols. Pub. Schs., 1975-78; mem. Art Mus. Guild. Mem. El Paso County Hist. Soc., C. of C., U. Tex.-El Paso Women's Aux., El Paso County Med. Soc. Aux. (pres. 1977-78, dir.), DAR, Amarillo Art Assn. (dir.), Symphony Guild (dir.), Nat. Soc. Arts and Letters (v.p. 1953-55), AAUW (v.p. 1954-55), Delta Gamma (El Paso alumni pres. 1953-55, 75-77), Theta Sigma Phi, Alpha Chi, Delta Sigma Phi. Roman Catholic. Author: TV scripts, newspaper articles in field. Research in med. history. Home: 6201 I-40 W Tiffany II 229 Amarillo TX 79106

MALSON, WILLIAM ROSS, petroleum engr.; b. Oklahoma City, Aug. 15, 1927; s. Hunter Garnet and Ruth Ann (Blake) M.; B.S., U. Okla., 1950; m. Eula Ailene Childs, Jan. 10, 1970; children—Hunter Lee, Charles William, Samuel Ross, Lynn Ellis, Robert Keith, Paul Edwin. Drilling engr., Baroid, Tex., Venezuela, 1950-59; dist. supt. Lone Star Mud Service, Tex., 1959-62; product devel. engr. Gt. Western Drilling Co., Midland, Tex., 1962-63; drilling engr. Loffland Bros. Co., Odessa, Tex., 1963-66, div. engr., 1966-70; div. supt., 1970-77, mgr. So. div., New Iberia, La., 1977-79; v.p., gen. mgr. Butler Drilling Corp. subs. Mitchell Energy & Devel. Corp., Houston, 1979—. Mem. Soc. Petroleum Engrs., Am. Petroleum Inst. Methodist. Club: Woodlands Country. Office: PO Box 14291 Houston TX 77021

MALT, HAROLD LEWIS, urban designer, urban planner, author, educator; b. Pitts., Apr. 11, 1918; s. Isadore and Florence (Horance) M.; B. Indsl. Design, Carnegie-Mellon U., 1940; M.Environ. Design, Syracuse U., 1964; children—Bruce Elliott, Ilene Susan. Mem. faculty design dept. State U. N.Y., Buffalo, 1947-51; pres. Malt & Ness, Inc., designers and engrs., Buffalo, 1951-63; pres. Harold Lewis Malt Assos., Inc., environ. planners and designers, Washington and Miami, 1964—; dir. Center for Design Planning, Washington and Miami, 1974—; prof., chmn. dept. architecture and planning U. Miami, Coral Gables, Fla., 1972—. Served as fighter pilot USAF, 1942-45. Mem. Am. Inst. Cert. Planners, Indsl. Designers Soc. Am., Am. Soc. Landscape Architects. Author: Furnishing the City, 1970; Streetscape Equipment Sourcebook, 1979. Home: 3695 Saint Gaudens Rd Miami FL 33133

MAMO, GEORGE WILLIAM, assn. exec.; b. Phila., May 22, 1955; s. Bartholomew G. and Beatrice M. (Hills) M.; B.A., Rutgers U., Camden, N.J., 1976; postgrad. in public adminstrn. Am. U., 1976-78. Asst. to pres. Laurel (Md.) Area C. of C., 1976-77; adminstrv. asst. to dir. public works City of Bowie (Md.), 1977-78; asst. exec. sec. Tau Epsilon Phi Frat., Inc., Atlanta, 1978-79, exec. dir. and editor, 1979—. Recipient Faculty award for disting. service in advancement edn. Rutgers U., Camden, 1976; named Outstanding Young Man Am., U.S. Jaycees, 1977. Mem. Frat. Execs. Assn., Am. Soc. Assn. Execs. Author: (with others) Travel Patterns in the Baltimore-Washington Corridor: An Economic Assessment, 1977; founding editor Camden Mag., 1975—. Office: 3272 Peachtree Rd NE Atlanta GA 30305

MAN, EUGENE HERBERT, educator; b. Scranton, Pa., Dec. 14, 1923; s. E. Lester and Celia (Cohen) M.; A.B., Oberlin Coll., 1948; Ph.D. (Office Naval Research fellow, E.I. duPont fellow), Duke, 1952; m. Priscilla R. Perry, Sept. 15, 1976; children—Elizabeth Sue (Mrs. Carl B. Eichenberger), Barbara Ruth, Linda Jeanne, Bruce Jonathan. Research chemist E.I. duPont de Nemours & Co., Inc., Wilmington, Del., 1952-60, supr. tech. sect., Chattanooga, 1960-61, sr. supr., 1961-62; coordinator research U. Miami, Coral Gables, Fla., 1962-66, dean research coordination, 1966-77, dean research and sponsored programs, 1977-79, prof. chemistry and marine and atmospheric chemistry, 1979—; vis. investigator Scripps Instn. Oceanography, 1971-72; mem. acad. adv. com. South Fla. Water Mgmt. Dist., 1976-77. Bd. dirs. Health Planning Council, Dade County, Fla., 1970-71; mem. Mental Health Consortium, Dade County, pres., 1970-71; dir., chmn. Gulf Univs. Research Consortium, 1969-71; trustee, v.p. Community Mental Health Services, Dade County, 1968-72; trustee United Fund Dade County, 1967-69; council mem. Oak Ridge (Tenn.) Asso. Univs., 1973-79. Served to 1st lt. AUS, 1943-46. Recipient Harry N. Holmes award in chemistry, Oberlin Coll., 1948. Fellow Am. Inst. Chemists; mem. Am. Chem. Soc., A.A.A.S., Nat. Council Univ. Research Adminstrs. (exec. com. 1967-72), Sigma Xi, Phi Beta Kappa, Phi Lambda Upsilon. Contbr. articles to profl. jours. Patentee in field. Home: 5740 SW 64th Pl Miami FL 33143 Office: Dept Chemistry U Miami Coral Gables FL 33124

MANAHAN, HELEN MARIE, ret. educator; b. Piqua, Ohio, Nov. 14, 1906; d. George W. and Mary Caroline (Dunker) Manahan; B.S. in Edn., Ohio State U., 1929, M.S. in Physiology, 1930; M.S., Columbia, N.Y. Sch. Social work, 1947; postgrad. U. Mich., 1939-41, Smith Coll., 1954, Tulane Sch. Social Work, 1957-58. Instr. health, phys. edn. Iowa State Tchrs. Coll., Cedar Falls, 1930-32; caseworker Montgomery County, Hamilton County Welfare Depts., Ohio, 1933-37; psychiat. social worker Newberry (Mich.) State Hosp., 1939-40, Pontiac (Mich.) State Hosp., 1940-42, St. Elizabeth's Hosp., Washington, 1942-45; psychiat. caseworker cons., N.Y. chpt. A.R.C., 1946-48; asst. prof. Tulane Sch. Social Work, New Orleans, 1949-59; asst. prof. dept. social work Fla. State U. Sch. Social Welfare, Tallahassee, 1959-69; free-lance writer; inventory mgr. Capital Circle Vet. Hosp., Tallahassee, 1972-76. Mem. Senate, Tulane U., 1954-56, Fla. State U., 1963-65; participant Pilot Demonstration Workshop for Nurses, Tallahassee, 1963, 6th Ann. Fla. Nursing Home Short Course, Gainesville, Fla., 1964; del., Internat. Congress on Mental Health, London, Eng., 1948; condr seminars Little Rock, 1959, Jacksonville, Fla., 1960, St. Petersburg, Fla., 1960, Montgomery, Ala., 1963, Tampa, Fla., 1964, Clearwater, Fla., 1966. Mem. Nat. Assn. Ret. Tchrs., AAUP. Home: 1922 Sunset Ln Tallahassee FL 32303

MANAHAN, RICHARD ALLAN, univ. ofcl.; b. Bloomington, Ill., Apr. 26, 1939; s. John Verlin and Martha Edith Manahan; B.S. in Bus. Edn., Ill. State U., 1965, M.S. in Bus. Adminstrn., 1971, Ed.D., 1975; m. Lois Ann Smith, Jan. 3, 1961; children—Jennifer DeAnn, Eric Richard. Auditing asst. Springfield (Ill.) Marine Bank, 1965-66; staff auditor Alexander Grant & Co., Bloomington, Ill., 1966-68; dir. internal auditing Ill. State U., Normal, 1968-75; bd. of regents system auditor Ill. Bd. Regents, Springfield, 1975-76; v.p. bus. affairs Radford (Va.) U., 1976—; mem adv. bd. First & Mchts. Nat. Bank of Radford, 1977—. Chmn. fin. com. Blue Ridge Mountain council Boy Scouts Am., 1977-78; mem. econ. revitalization com. Radford City Council, 1978—; bd. dirs. Radford U. Found., 1976—, treas., 1976—. Served with U.S. Army, 1958-60. C.P.A. Mem. Am. Acctg. Assn., Am. Inst. C.P.A.'s, Inst. Internal Auditors, Va. Soc. C.P.A.'s, Ill. Soc. C.P.A.'s, Nat. Assn Coll. and U. Bus. Officers, Southern Assn. of Coll. and U. Bus. Officers, Am. Assn. Higher Edn., Assn. of Instl. Research, Southern Assn. for Instl. Research, Assn. of Phys. Plant Adminstrs. of Univs. and Colls., Ill. State U. Alumni Assn. (dir. 1975—), Kappa Delta Pi, Phi Delta Kappa. Clubs: Masons, Shriners. Contbg. author: School District Feasibility Study, 1971; contbr. articles on bus. edn. to profl. publs. Home: 105 Hidden Valley Dr Radford VA 24141 Office: PO Box 5550 Radford Univ Radford VA 24142

MANCHEE, KATHERYN HAIT (MRS. ARTHUR LEAVENS MANCHEE), historian, lectr.; b. Bklyn., Sept. 21, 1904; d. James Merritt and Belle (Silvey) Hait; ed. Parsons Sch. Art, 1923, Newark Sch. Art, 1924; student Western Res. U., 1941-43; m. William F. Dorflinger, Apr. 1927 (dec. 1944); 1 dau., June Dorflinger Hardy; m. 2d, Arthur Leavens Manchee, Sept. 21, 1957; step-children—Mrs. R.W. Bachelder, Mrs. James McD. Clark, Mrs. Harry Wortman. Instr., lectr. Cleve. Mus. Art, 1941-44; lectr., historian Steuben Glass, N.Y.C., 1946-48; dir. advt. and public relations Midhurst Importing Corp., N.Y.C., 1952-54; dir. pub. relations and product promotion Fostoria Glass Co., N.Y.C., 1954-58. Mem. Jr. League Morristown, N.J., 1930-39, 45-54, Cleve., 1939-44; vice chmn. jr. council Cleve. Mus. Art, 1943-44; vol. Cleve. Orch. Woman's Com., 1942-44, A.R.C. drives, Cleve., 1939-44; leader Girl Scouts U.S.A., Cleve., 1934-35. Life fellow Met. Mus. Art. Mem. Nat. Soc. Colonial Dames, Soc. Women Geographers, Asia Soc., English Speaking Union, China Inst. Am., Fgn. Policy Assn., Am. Pottery and Glass Assn., Nat. Home Fashions League, Am. Women in Radio and TV. Presbyterian. Clubs: Colony, Princeton, National Arts (N.Y.C.); Garden of Oranges; Nassau (Princeton). Contbr. articles to profl. publs. Home: Diplomat Club 1919 Gulf Shore Blvd North Naples FL 33940

MANCHIN, A. JAMES, state ofcl.; b. Farmington, W.Va., Apr. 7, 1927; s. Joseph and Kathleen (Roscoe) M.; B.A. in Polit. Sci. and Sociology, W.Va. U., 1951; M.Ed., 1962; Tchr.'s certificate, Fairmont State Coll., 1953; m. Stephanie Machel, June 9, 1951; children—Patricia Lee, Mark Anthony, Rosanna Stache. Tchr., W.Va. Sch. System; state dir. Farmers Home Adminstrn., Charleston, W.Va.,

1961-70, spl. asst. to nat. adminstr., 1970-73; sec. state W.Va., 1976—. Mem. W.Va. Ho. of Dels., 1949-51. Recipient Outstanding Service award Dept. Agr., 1968, Freedom Found. award of Valley Forge, 1969, Law and Order award Fairmont Police Dept., 1973; named Mr. W.Va., Salem Coll., 1974. Democrat. Roman Catholic. Home: Farmington WV Office: State Capitol Charleston WV 25305

MANCI, ORLANDO JOSEPH, JR., aerospace co. exec.; b. Bay Minette, Ala., Oct. 31, 1927; s. Orlando Joseph and Maude Seay (Lowrey) M.; B.S., U.S. Naval Acad., 1950; M.S. in Aero. Engring., U. Mich., 1957, Ph.D., 1960; m. Doris Eastland Smith, Mar. 23, 1951; children—Franklin Lee, Susan Camille, Sarah Denise. Commd. 2d lt. U.S. Air Force, 1950, advanced through ranks to col., 1968; exec. sec. U.S. Air Force Sci. Adv. Bd., Washington 1968-70, ret., 1970; mgr. analog and hybrid computer products Reliance Electric Co., Ann Arbor, Mich., 1970-72; dir. tech. devel. Vought Systems div. LTV Aerospace Corp., Dallas, 1972-73; asst. dean engring., prof. aerospace engring. Sch. Engring., Auburn (Ala.) U., 1973-75; dir. data processing Vought Corp. (formerly LTV Aerospace Corp.), Dallas, 1975-77, dir. advanced tech., 1977—. Decorated Legion of Merit. Registered profl. engr., Ala. Mem. Am. Inst. Aeros. and Astronautics, Soc. for Computer Simulation (treas. 1966-75), Nat. Soc. Profl. Engrs. Methodist. Clubs: Racquet, Shady Valley Golf (Arlington, Tex.). Home: 2209 River Ridge Rd Arlington TX 76017 Office: Vought Corp PO Box 5907 Dallas TX 75222

MANCILL, JAMES THORNTON, sch. adminstr.; b. Big Spring, Tex., Dec. 9, 1929; married, 1 child. B.S. in Health and Phys. Edn., Sul Ross State U., Alpine Coll., 1951; M.Ed. in Adminstrv. Edn., Tex. Wesleyan Coll., Fort Worth, 1959; Ed.D. in Adminstrv. Edn., Tex. Tech. U., Lubbock, 1974. Elementary prin. Shallowater (Tex.) Ind. Sch. Dist., 1961-65; elementary prin. Alpine pub. schs., 1965-66, adminstrv. asst., 1966-67; dir. adminstr. Region XIX Ednl. Service Center, El Paso, 1967—; prof. ednl. adminstrn. U. Tex., El Paso. Mem. NEA, Tex. State Tchrs. Assn., Assn. for Ednl. Communications and Tech., Trans-Pecos Tchrs. Assn., Tex. Assn. for Ednl. Tech., Am. Assn. Sch. Adminstrs., Assn. for Supervision and Curriculum Devel., Phi Delta Kappa. Specialist in health edn., social scis., elementary edn., instructional media, gen. adminstrn. Home: 9112 Lait St El Paso TX 79925 Office: PO Box 10716 El Paso TX 79997

MANDELKER, LESTER, veterinarian; b. Memphis, July 31, 1945; s. Maurice and Alice (Herman) M.; B.S., Mich. State U., 1967, D.V.M., 1968. Veterinarian Yarborough Animal Hosp., Miami, Fla., 1969-70; veterinarian Gulf Bay Animal Hosp., Clearwater, Fla., 1970-72; dir., owner, veterinarian Community Vet. Hosp., Largo, Fla., 1972—; owner, dir. Community Pet Mall. Recipient Citizenship award Sunrise chpt. B'nai B'rith, N.Y., 1963, Outstanding Athlete award, Brentwood, N.Y., 1963, Civic Pride award, Largo, 1973, 77; also numerous local tennis championships. Mem. Fla., Pinellas County, Am., vet. med. assns., Am. Animal Hosp. Assn. Clubs: Clearwater Tennis, Largo Tennis, Class, Inc. (founder, past pres.), Clearwater Men's (pres. 1973-75). Contbr. articles to profl. jours. Office: 1631 W Bay Dr Largo FL 33540

MANDELKERN, MOISES, architect; b. Havana, Cuba, Oct. 27, 1936; s. Julio and Margulisa (Fiszbaum) M.; B.Arch., Havana U., 1962; B.A. Arch., Columbia U., 1969; m. Herlinda Lee, May 13, 1962; 1 son, Glenn Alexander. Archtl. and interior designer, owner Contempor S.A., Havana, Cuba, 1956-62; project mgr. Bond Stores, Inc., N.Y.C., 1962-66; project mgr., archtl. designer C.N.I. Internat., N.Y.C., 1966-71; architect, M. Mandelkern & Assos., N.Y., 1971—; asst. dir. store planning and constrn. Bond Stores, Inc., N.Y.C., 1971-74; architect II, Metro-Dade County, Miami, 1976-78; constrn. coordinator, project mgr. Ferendino/Grafton/Spillis/Candela, Coral Gables, Fla., 1978—; archtl. cons. Third Century, U.S.A., 1976, Biltmore Renovation, 1978. Recipient Archtl. Design award Havana U., 1961; William Kinney Meml. traveling fellow, 1969-70. Mem. AIA, Nat. Bd. Archtl. Registration, Columbia U. Alumni Assn. Democrat. Jewish. Prin. archtl. works include Havana Hilton Hotel, Guama Resort Center, Smithtown Shopping Center, Macy's Dept. Store, Miami Free Zone, James Knight Internat. Center, Sacks 5th Ave., Bloomingdale Store, N.Y.C. Home: 3163 Sheridan Ave Miami Beach FL 33140 Office: 800 Douglas Entrance Coral Gables FL 33134

MANDELL, LOUISE RUEHLMANN, psychologist; b. Cin., Dec. 13, 1929; s. John F. and Henrietta (Mehrckens) Ruehlmann; student Cin. Conservatory Music, 1947-50; Mus.B., U. Cin., 1971; M.Ed., 1971, Ed.D., 1974; postgrad Xavier U., 1971; m. Maurice Stephen Mandell, Oct. 5, 1950; children—Melinda, Jocelyn, M. Stephen, Christopher (dec.), Christiane, Theodore. Coordinator, Adult Learning Center, Newport, Ky., 1971-72; guest lectr. U. Cin., 1972-73, 75, 76, 77; intern sch. psychologist Hamilton County Schs., Cin., 1973-74; staff psychologist Student Devel. Diagnostic Center, Cin. Pub. Schs., 1974—; pvt. practice psychology, Cin., 1975—, Erlanger, 1977—. Chmn. Pastoral Counseling Center advisory bd. Christ Ch. Episcopal, Cin., 1977-79; chmn. Bette Carter Morgan Meml. Amphitheater Fund, 1970—; chmn. Citizens Study Com. Erlanger-Elsmere Sch. Dist., 1968-72. U. Cin. fellow, 1972-73. Mem. Am. Psychol. Assn., Phi Delta Kappa, Kappa Delta Pi, Sigma Alpha Iota, Kappa Kappa Gamma. Democrat. Episcopalian. Clubs: Yoke Fellows Internat., Cin. McDowall Soc., Community Cross of Nails Internat. Author: The Effects of Three Types of Music on Group Test Performances, 1974. Home: 3812 Hope Ln Erlanger KY 41018 Office: 421 E 4th St Cincinnati OH 45202

MANDRELL, REGINA ANGELA MORENO, genealogist; b. Mobile, Ala., Mar. 10, 1906; d. Cameron Anderson and Seana Barkley (Crary) Moreno; A.B., Birmingham-So. Coll., 1926, postgrad., 1960; postgrad. U. Ky., 1964, Smith Coll., Northampton, Mass., 1965; m. George F. Kirchoff, Oct. 4, 1930 (dec.); children—George F., Margaret A. Kirchoff Handler; m. 2d, William F. Mandrell, Oct. 20, 1971 (dec.). Tchr., attendance supr. Birmingham (Ala.) Public Schs., 1926-71; adminstrv. asst. Jefferson County Mental Health Assn., Birmingham, 1956-59; mem. Ala. Devel. Bd. for Health Survey, 1930; writing and geneal. research compiling family history, 1932—. Recipient George Washington medal Freedom Found., 1961. Mem. Ala. Hist. Soc., Baldwin County (Ala.) Hist. Soc. (officer), Writers Group, Baldwin County Writers Club, Pensacola (Fla.) Hist. Soc., Alpha Chi Omega, Pi Gamma Mu, Chi Delta Phi. Methodist. Contbr. articles to profl. jours. Home: PO Drawer AM Fairhope AL 36532

MANDRY, GEORGE GILBERT, water conditioning co. exec.; b. San Antonio, Mar. 29, 1926; s. George Peter and Clarice Johannaa (Heubaum) M.; student Wartburg Coll., 1956, Internat. Corr. Schs., 1943-51; m. Edith Lenor Hamby, Sept. 23, 1962; children—Terry Ann, Sandra Kay, Vicki Marie, George Gilbert, Cindi Ann. Installer, Southwestern Bell Telephone Co., 1946, Western Electric Co., 1947; civil service employee, 1948-52; field engr., site mgr. RCA, 1952-60; electronics engr. Southwest Research Inst., San Antonio, 1960-65; owner, mgr. Oasis Liquor & Sporting Goods, Leon Valley, Tex., 1961-73. Mandry Gen. Hardware & Supply, Leon Valley, 1965-73; partner, mgr. Continental Water Conditioning Co., San Antonio, 1975—; pres. Mandry Enterprises, Inc., Coastline Developers Inc. Served with USAAF, 1944-46. Mem. Tex. Water Conditiong Assn. (pres.), San Antonio C. of C. Lutheran. Club: Elks. Home: Joleta Ranch Bandera TX 78003 Office: Continental Water Conditioning Co 6405 El Verde Rd San Antonio TX 78238

MANESS, GARRY AVALON, hosp. personnel adminstr.; b. Henderson, Tenn., Jan. 30, 1947; s. Millard E. and Wilma L. (Patterson) M.; student Freed-Hardeman Coll., 1965-66; B.B.A., Memphis State U., 1973, M.P.A. in Health Care Adminstrn., 1977; m. Jane Wilcoxson, June 21, 1968; 1 son, Cameron Jess. Employment interviewer Bapt. Meml. Hosp., Memphis, 1974-76, asst. personnel dir., 1976-79, mgr. employee relations, 1979; personnel adminstr. Le Bonheur Children's Med. Center, Memphis, 1979—; health careers counselor Memphis Bd. Edn. Bd. deacons. Sycamore View Ch. of Christ, also supr. teenage Bible dept. and active various coms.; active United Way, West Tenn. AGAPE. Served with U.S. Army, 1970-72. Mem. West Tenn. Soc. Personnel Adminstrs., Tenn. Soc. Hosp. Personnel Adminstrs., Am. Soc. Hosp. Personnel Adminstrs., Blue Ridge Park Assn., Lambda Chi Alph. Democrat. Home: 2051 Pennington Gap Memphis TN 38134 Office: 848 Adams Ave Memphis TN 38103

MANFRE, CHRISTOPHER FRANCIS, ins. exec.; b. Kansas City, Mo., Jan. 19, 1928; s. Chris and Frances Ann (Genova) M.; student U. Fla., 1949-50; m. Sandra Louise Urness, June 5, 1970; 1 dau., Gina Louise. Ins. agt. French, Postol & Manfre, Miami Beach, Fla., 1950-57; with Consol. Ins. Group, N.Y.C., 1957-69, v.p. mktg. dept., 1957-59; account exec. Titan Group, Chgo., also Miami, Fla., 1969-75; exec. v.p., gen. mgr. Savage-Manfre & Assos., Inc. North Miami Beach, Fla., 1975—; risk cons. County Nat. Bank, others. Served with USN, 1945-49. Mem. Profl. Ins. Agts. Fla., Ind. Ins. Agts. Fla., Ind. Ins. Agts. Dade County. Republican. Episcopalian. Clubs: Crickett (North Miami, Fla.), Calif. (Miami). Home: 1761 SW 53d Ave Plantation FL 33317 Office: 801 NE 167th St Suite 308 N Miami Beach FL 33162

MANGELS, JOHN, JR., cigar mfg. co. exec.; b. Jacksonville, Fla., Apr. 30, 1925; s. John and Ann E. (Ricker) M.; B.S. in Mech. Engring., Auburn U., 1949; m. Ann M. Lyon, June 5, 1949; children—Ann Reed, John Edward, Charles Robert. Plant engr. Jno. H. Swisher & Son, Inc., Jacksonville, 1949-57, chief engr. all plants, 1957-63, asst. to v.p. prodn., 1963-73, mgr. engring. and maintenance, 1973-76, v.p. engring., 1976—. Mem. vocat. tech. adv. com. Sch. Bd. of Duval County; mem. parish council Most Holy Redeemer Roman Catholic Ch. Served with Constrn. Bn., USNR, 1943-46. Mem. ASME, Jacksonville Area C. of C., Pi Tau Sigma. Democrat. Home: 1210 Crown Dr Jacksonville FL 32205 Office: PO Box 2230 Jacksonville FL 32203

MANGELSDORFF, ARTHUR DAVID, psychologist; b. N.Y.C., Sept. 11, 1945; s. Arthur Fred and Maesie (Rowland) M.; B.A., Dartmouth, 1967; M.A., U. Del., 1972, Ph.D. (NASA fellow), 1972. Instr. U. Del., 1968-72; staff cons. psychologist Crittenden Rehab. Center, Wilmington, Del., 1972; psychologist behavioral sci. div. Acad. Health Scis., Ft. Sam Houston, Tex., 1972-73, health care studies div., 1973-74, social sci. analyst, 1974—. Instr. San Antonio Coll., 1974—; counselor Free Clinic San Antonio, 1976-78. Served with USAR, 1972-74. Certified Tex. State Bd. Examiners Psychologists, Nat. Register Health Service Providers in Psychology. Fellow Am Psychol. Assn.; mem. Southwestern Psychol. Assn., Am. Public Health Assn., AAAS, Assn. for Advancement Psychology, Psychophysiology, Soc. Mil. Surgeons, Sigma Xi, Psi Chi. Presbyn. Contbr. articles to profl. jours. Home: 3425 Turtle Village Dr San Antonio TX 78230 Office: Health Care Studies Div Acad Health Sci Ft Sam Houston TX 78234

MANGER, WALTER LEROY, geologist; b. Balt., Sept. 24, 1944; s. Walter Casmir and Cordelia Lucelle (Scherry) M.; B.A., Coll. Wooster, 1966; M.S., U. Iowa, 1969, Ph.D., 1971; m. Margaret Helen McKee, Sept. 9, 1967; 1 dau., Julie Ann. Asst. prof. geology Northeastern U., 1971-72; asst. prof. U. Ark., Fayetteville, 1972-77, asso. prof., 1977—, curator of geology Univ. Mus., 1972—; cons. McClinton Bros. Corp., Fayetteville. NSF grantee, 1975-77, 77-79; Dames & Moore grantee, 1976-77. Mem. Soc. Econ. Paleontologists, Mineralogists, Paleontol. Soc., Palaeontol Assn., Internat. Paleontol. Union, Sigma Xi. Presbyterian. Club: Elks. Contbr. articles to profl. jours. Home: 1949 Austin Dr Fayetteville AR 72701 Office: Dept Geology U Ark Fayetteville AR 72701

MANGOLD, DAVID EUGENE, physician; b. Great Lakes, Ill., Sept. 26, 1948; s. Donald Eugene and Janice (Junker) M.; B.A., U. S.D., 1970, B.S., 1972; M.D., Tex. Tech. U., 1974; m. Theresa Russell, Dec. 3, 1977. Resident in surgery Baylor Coll. Medicine, Houston, 1974-78; practice medicine specializing in gen. and vascular surgery, Lubbock, Tex., 1978—; asst. clin. prof. surgery Tex. Tech. U. Med. Sch., Lubbock, 1979—; mem. staff Highland Hosp., Methodist Hosp., St. Mary's Health Sci. Center Hosp. Mem. Am. Coll. Emergency Physicians, Michael E. DeBakey Internat. Cardiovascular Soc. Roman Catholic Home: 4605 88th St Lubbock TX 79424 Office: 4809 University Ave Lubbock TX 79413

MANGOLD, LANA CAROLE PARAMORE, educator; b. San Antonio, Tex., July 30, 1943; d. Curtis E. and Bennie J. (Dockery) Paramore; A.S., Kilgore Jr. Coll., 1963; B.S., Tex. Woman's U., 1965; M.A., U. Tex., Austin, 1972, Ph.D., 1973; m. James L. Clark, Nov. 17, 1978. Teaching asst. home econs. dept. U. Tex., Austin, 1970; curriculum specialist Inst. for Study Health and Soc., Washington, 1970; tchr. home econs. Marsh Jr. High Sch., Dallas Ind. Sch. Dist., 1965-66; substitute tchr. Austin Ind. Sch. Dist., 1966, vocat. home econs. tchr. John H. Reagan High Sch., 1967-69; supr. ednl. adminstrn. Brazosport Ind. Sch. Dist., Freeport, Tex., 1971; teaching asso. dept. curriculum and instrn. U. Tex., Austin, 1971-72, research asso., 1972-73; field coordinator Comal and Eanes Ind. Sch. Dists., Austin, 1973; div. dir. vocat. edn. in home econs. Sch. Home Econs., Coll. Edn., N. Tex. State U., Denton, 1974—; cons./group leader Center for Public Sch. Ethnic Studies Group Technique/Culture Awareness Seminars and Workshops, Austin, Tex., 1972—. Mem. Am. Home Econs. Assn., NEA, Assn. Supervision and Curriculum Devel., Home Econs. Edn. Assn., Am. Vocat. Assn., Tex. Home Econs. Assn. (state chmn. public affairs 1977-80), Tex. Assn. Coll. Tchrs., Phi Theta Kappa, Omicron Nu, Phi Lambda Theta, Kappa Delta Pi, Phi Delta Kappa, Delta Kappa Gamma. Author, editor: Great Ideas-Teaching Homemaking through Bulletin Boards, 1979. Office: N Tex State U Sch Home Econs Denton TX 76203

MANGOLD, WILLIAM JOHNSON, JR., physician, lawyer; b. Columbus, Ohio, Mar. 21, 1943; s. William Johnson and Martha Lucille (Powell) M.; B.A., U. Tex., Austin, 1967, J.D., 1969; M.D., U. Tex., San Antonio, 1973. Admitted to Tex. bar, 1969; intern Bexar County Hosp., San Antonio, 1973-74; practice medicine, Lockney, Tex., 1974-75; resident surgery Eastern Va. Med. Sch. and Affiliated Hosps., Norfolk, Va., 1975-77; resident in plastic and reconstructive surgery U. Tex. Health Sci. Center, San Antonio, 1977-79, asst. prof. div. plastic surgery, 1979—; cons. med. malpractice, San Antonio, Lockney, 1970-75, Norfolk, 1975-77, San Antonio, 1977—; staff plastic surgeon Audie Murphy VA Hosp., San Antonio, 1979—; clin. asst. prof. dept. forensic medicine Tex. Tech. Med. Sch., Lubbock, 1972—. Mem. health issues adv. panel HEW Sec.'s Commn. on Med. Malpractice, 1971. Fellow Am. Coll. Legal Medicine; mem. Am. Bar Assn. (mem. com. law and medicine 1973—), A.M.A. (mem. exec. com. council on legis. 1974-99, vice chmn. 1977-79), Tex. Med. Assn., Am. Med. Polit. Action Com. (sustaining mem.), Am. Assn. Medico-Legal Consultants, Tex. Inst. for Med. Assessment Delta Theta Phi, Phi Chi. Editorial bd. Jour. Family Practice, 1974—. Contbr. articles to med. jours. Home: 2626 Babcock #805 San Antonio TX 75229 Office: 7703 Floyd Curl Dr San Antonio TX 78284

MANGRUM, ROBERT GLEN, historian; b. Abilene, Tex., May 6, 1948; s. Robert Elee and Glenna Josephine (Harber) M.; B.A., Hardin-Simmons U., 1970; M.A., N. Tex. State U., 1975, Ph.D., 1978. Instr. history N. Tex. State U., 1975-78, Tarrant County Jr. Coll., 1978; asst. prof., chmn. div. social sci. and bus. Clarke Coll., Newton, Miss., 1978—. Served with U.S. Army, 1970-73, served to capt. USAR. Mem. Orgn. Am. Historians, Am. Hist. Assn., So. Hist. Assn., Tex. State Hist. Assn., Am. Military Inst., Oral History Assn., Civil War Round Table Assos., So. Polit. Sci. Assn., Southwestern Social Sci. Assn., Assn. U.S. Army, U.S. Air Force Assn., U.S. Naval Inst., Res. Officers Assn., Phi Alpha Theta, Pi Gamma Mu, Pi Sigma Alpha, Alpha Chi. Baptist. Home: 2300 Magnolia Apt 31 Brownwood TX 76801

MANI, VENK, pathologist; b. Kumbakonam, India, Mar. 4, 1946; s. Karumanasseri Chidambaran Krishna and Pudukode Narayanan (Rajalakshmi) Iyer; came to U.S., 1969, naturalized, 1979; M.B.B.S., Jawaharlal Inst. Postgrad. Med. Edn. and Research, Pondicherry, India, 1967; m. Usha Ramaswamy, Sept. 7, 1975. Intern, resident in pathology Upstate Med. Center, Syracuse, N.Y., 1970-72, Med. Coll. Va, Richmond, Va., 1972-74; pathologist, nuclear medicine physician Meml. Hosp., Chattanooga, 1974—, asso. lab. dir., 1974—. Diplomate Am. Bd. Pathology, Am. Bd. Nuclear Medicine. Mem. AMA, Coll. Am. Pathologists, Am. Soc. Clin. Pathologists. Hindu. Office: 2500 Citico Ave Meml Hosp Chattanooga TN 37404

MANKA, WALTER RALPH, III, printing co. exec.; b. Jeffersonville, Ind., May 22, 1941; s. Walter Ralph and Mildred Louise (Maloney) M.; ed. high sch., Jeffersonville, 1953-57; m. Glendia Rae Ellis, Dec. 15, 1972. Laborer, Emco Container Corp., Jeffersonville, 1966-67; lead man Olin Matheson Chem. Co., Charleston, Ind., 1967-68; v.p. H.S. Albert Galleries Inc., Louisville, 1967-70; co-partner Small Accounting Service Co., Clayton, Ga., 1970-72; co-pub., prodn. mgr. A Guide to So. Highlands Mag., Lakemont, Ga., 1972-75; planning dir., CSA Printing & Bindery, Lakemont, 1973-79; pres. Macon Graphics, Inc., Franklin, N.C., 1979—. Served with U.S. Army, 1963-65. Home: Route 2 Hwy 76W Clayton GA 30525 Office: Macon Graphics Inc 244 Palmer St Franklin NC 28734

MANKINS, JAMES EARL, state legislator; trucking co. exec.; b. Electra, Tex., Feb. 9, 1926; s. Alma Earl and Thelma Inez (Cooper) M.; student Kilgore Coll., 1946-48; B.B.A., N. Tex. U., 1950; m. Virginia Lucille Henley, Jan. 25, 1948; children—Cherryl Jane (Mrs. Jeff Mercer), James Earl, Virginia Inez, Elizabeth Jan. Truck helper Eagle Trucking Co., Kilgore, Tex., 1946-48, truck driver, 1948-50, truck pusher, 1950-58, partner, asst. mgr., 1958-67, mgr.-partner, 1967-72, pres., 1972—; dir. First Savs. Assn., Kilgore, Copeland Ins. Agy., Longview, Tex. City commr., Kilgore, 1965-71; mem. Tex. Ho. of Reps., 1975—. Served with USAAF, 1944-46. Recipient Zeus award Epsilon Sigma Alpha, 1970, Albert Gallatin award, 1975. Mem. Oilfield Haulers Assn. (pres. 1969-70), Tex. Motor Transp. Assn. (dir. 1969-70), Am. Assn. Oilwell Drilling Contractors. Presbyn. Mason (Shriner), Rotarian. Home: 2211 Green Hills St Kilgore TX 75662 Office: Box 471 Kilgore TX 75662

MANKINS, SANDRA LEE, psychologist; b. Lake Lynn, Pa., Aug. 9, 1945; d. Ralph Patterson and Pauline Caroline (Rosnick) M.; B.S., Frostburg State Coll., 1967; M.A., Bowling Green State U., 1970, Ph.D. (fellow), 1973. Tchr., Braddock Jr. High Sch., Cumberland, Md., 1967-68; asst. prof. psychology Western Carolina U., Cullowhee, N.C., 1973—. Emergency med. technician, N.C., 1976—; instr. CPR, Am. Heart Assn., 1978—; park vol. Gt. Smoky Mountains Nat. Park, 1974-77, seasonal ranger, 1976. Western Carolina U. grantee, 1974. Mem. N.C. Acad. Sci., Sigma Xi. Home: PO Box 2186 Cullowhee NC 28723 Office: Dept Psychology Western Carolina U Cullowhee NC 28723

MANLEY, EDWARD HARRY, JR., hosp. food service dir., navy officer; b. S.I., N.Y., Sept. 12, 1941; s. Edward H. and Dorothy I.; B.S., Cornell U., 1975; M.S., Rollins Coll., 1978; m. Geri G. Manley; children—Deborah, Michael E. Joined U.S. Navy, 1959; commd. ensign, 1970, advanced through grades to lt. comdr., 1979—; food service dir. Naval Hosp., Annapolis, Md., 1972-73; asst. food service dir. Nat. Naval Med. Center, Bethesda, Md., 1971-72; food service dir. Naval Regional Med. Center, Orlando, Fla., 1975—; mem. adv. bd. Mid-Fla. Tech. Food Service Program, 1978-80. Mem. Internat. Food Service Execs. Assn. (pres. Orlando br. 1979-80, named mem. of year Orlando br. 1978), Cornell Soc. Hotelmen (pres. Central Fla. chpt. 1976-80), Fla. Restaurant Assn. (bd. dirs. 1980), Toastmasters Internat., Ret. Officers Assn., Mil. Order World Wars, Assn. Mil. Surgeons of U.S. Clubs: Cornell of Central Fla. (v.p. 1980), Naval Tng. Center Officer's (pres. 1978—). Home: 701 St Lucie Ln Orlando FL 32807 Office: Food Mgmt Service Naval Regional Med Center Orlando FL 32813

MANLEY, FRANK A., educator; b. Scranton, Pa., Nov. 13, 1930; s. Aloysius F. and Kathryn L. (Needham) M.; B.A., Emory U., 1952, M.A., 1953; Ph.D., Johns Hopkins U., 1959; m. Carolyn Holliday, Mar. 14, 1952; children—Evelyn, Mary. Instr. English, Yale U., 1959-61, asst. prof. English, 1961-64; asso. prof. Emory U., 1964-67, prof., 1967—, chmn. dept. English, 1968-70; cons. Am. Council Learned Socs. Served with U.S. Army, 1953-55; Morse fellow, 1963-64; Guggenheim fellow, 1966-67, 78-79. Mem. MLA, AAUP. Roman Catholic. Editor: Anniversaries (John Donne), 1963; A Dialogue of Comfort, vol. 12 of Yale Edition of the Complete Works of St. Thomas More, 1977. Home: Box 228 Route 5 Ellijay GA 30540 Office: Emory U Dept English Atlanta GA 30332

MANLEY, RICHARD SHANNON, lawyer, state legislator; b. Birmingham, Ala., June 23, 1932; s. Richard Sabine and Alice (Hughes) M.; B.S., U. Ala., 1953, LL.B., 1958; m. Lillian Grace Cardwell, Aug. 23, 1953 (div. Aug. 1975); children—Richard Shannon, Alyce Hughes; m. 2d, Rosemary Rankin Moseley, May 18, 1977. Admitted to Ala. bar, 1958, U.S. Dist. Ct. So. Dist. Ala., U.S. 5th Circuit Ct. of Appeals, U.S. Supreme Ct., U.S. Ct. Mil. Appeals; practiced in Demopolis, 1958—; mem. Ala. Ho. of Reps., 1967—; speaker pro tem, 1979—; dir. New Southland Nat. Ins. Co.; v.p. Demopolis Cable TV Co., Inc. Pres. Bd. Edn., Demopolis, 1969-70, Demopolis Jr. C. of C., 1961-62; v.p. Ala. Jr. C. of C., 1960-61; dir. U.S. Jr. C. of C., 1962-63. Bd. dirs. Marengo County Hist. Soc., Marengo County Mental Health Assn.; bd. advisers Ala. Hist. Commn., Gen. Holland M. Smith Meml. Served with USMCR, 1953-56; col. Res. Mem. Am., Ala. (mem. bd. of bar commrs. 1972—), 17th Judicial Circuit (past pres.) bar assns., Am. Trial Lawyers Assn., Comml. Law League Am., Am. Judicature Soc., Demopolis C. of C. (dir., past pres.), Marine Corps Res. Officers Assn., U. Ala. Nat. Alumni Assn. (v.p. 1967-68), Farrah Law Soc., Phi Delta Phi, Delta Chi. Methodist (trustee). Rotarian. Clubs: Demopolis Country (past pres., dir.), Demopolis Athletic, U. Ala. Alumni (pres. Marengo County 1965-66); Indian Hills Country (Tuscaloosa, Ala.); The Club (Birmingham, Ala.). Home: 1501 Country Club Dr SW PO Drawer U Demopolis AL 36732 Office: 105 S Walnut Ave Demopolis AL 36732

MANN, CHERYLE LYNNE, elec. contractor; b. Jackson, Tenn., Mar. 2, 1947; d. Robert Whitfield and Virginia Elizabeth (Stone) Bates; student Memphis public schs.; m. Victor Hayden Mann, May 5, 1970; children—Lisa Ann, Victor Hayden. Apprentice electrician, 1973, journeyman electrician, 1977; pres., chmn. bd. Mann Elec. Co., Inc., Memphis, 1975-79. Mem. adv. bd. Women Going Into Bus., Shelby State Community Coll. and SBA; hon. dep. sheriff Shelby County Sheriff's Dept., recipient Outstanding Achievement award, 1977. Mem. Asso. Builders and Contractors, Asso. Ind. Elec. Contractors, Asso. Gen. Contractors (asso.). Republican. Clubs: Memphis Bus. and Profl. Women's (pres.), Quota. Home: 3461 Holeman Pl Memphis TN 38118 Office: 3457 Holeman Pl Memphis TN 38118

MANN, FAROLYN SHAW, bank exec.; b. Houston, July 7, 1939; d. Farrell Hudson and Ivey (Renfro) Shaw; student U. Houston, 1957-59, Am. Inst. Banking, 1968-78; A.A., Houston Community Coll., 1979; student Dale Carnegie Courses, 1971; m. Manning Alden Mann, Mar. 22, 1975; 1 son, Charles Oliver Rice. Actuarial clk. Prudential Ins. Co., Houston, 1957-60; real estate agt. Oppermann and Assos., Houston, 1967-68; v.p. Merc. Bank of Houston, 1968—; regional market dir. Allied Bancshares, Inc.; instr. Houston Community Coll., 1974, mem. banking adv. com., 1978-79; bd. dirs. distributive edn. div. Houston Ind. Sch. Dist., 1975-77; counselor, instr. displaced homemaker's project Continuing Edn. Center, U. Houston; instr. counselor Continuing Edn. Center, U. Houston and SBA of Houston. Mem. adv. bd. Ind. Lifestyles, Inc., Houston, 1973—, Parents Without Partners, Houston, 1978-79; chmn. steering com. Braeswood Civic Assn., Houston. Mem. Nat. Assn. Bank Women Officers, Bank Women of Houston, Am. Inst. Banking (gov. 1972-74), Tex. Real Estate Commn., Houston C. of C. Republican. Methodist. Editor distributive edn. fin. and credit curriculum, 1976. Office: 4010 S Braeswood Houston TX 77025

MANN, HELENE DAVIS POWNER (MRS. CECIL W. MANN), psychologist; b. Greensburg, Ind., June 30, 1899; d. Charles Tracy and Olive (Davis) Powner; student U. Ariz., 1917-19; A.B., U. Calif., Berkeley, 1922; M.A., U. So. Calif., 1927; postgrad. U. So. Calif., Sorbonne, Paris, U. Madrid, 1927; pvt. study France, U.S.A.; m. Cecil William Mann, Oct. 16, 1937; 1 dau., Jennifer Olive. Psychologist, tchr. gifted children Pasadena (Calif) city schs., 1926-29; chief psychol. examiner Los Angeles County Juvenile Hall Clinic, 1929-39; spl. lectr. U. Denver, 1939-41; psychologist Bur. Testing and Guidance, also Specialized Tng. and Reassignment Unit, U.S. Army, La. State U., 1943-45; dir. Tulane U. reading improvement program, 1953-57; editor Charles T. Powner Corp., Regan Pub. Co., Chgo., 1922-60; pvt. practice psychology, New Orleans, 1945-61; pvt. practice, research, Jackson County, N.C., 1961-74; psychol. cons. Western N.C. U. Mental Health Center, 1969-70, Dept. Interior Bur. Indian Affairs, Cherokee, N.C., 1962-70; pvt. practice psychology, Henderson County, 1974-80; ret., 1980. Mem. AAUW, League Women Voters, Am., Southeastern, N.C. psychol. assns., Pi Beta Phi. Club: Book. Contbr. articles to profl. jours.; also children's stories. Address: 11 Quail Trail Hendersonville NC 28739

MANN, JACK ANDREW, banker; b. Palestine, Tex., Sept. 10, 1937; s. James Arnold and Ethel (Strickland) M.; B.B.A., U. Houston, 1963; m. Suzie Der Mott, Apr.; children—Mitchell A., Matthew A., Marcus A. Dist. mgr. Allied Concord Fin. Corp., Houston, 1959-67; asst. v.p. Tex. Commerce Bank, Houston, 1968; pres., chief exec. officer Port City State Bank, Houston, 1968-69, Fidelity Bank & Trust, Houston, 1969-71, Meyerland Bank, Houston, 1971—. Chmn., Met. Houston March of Dimes, 1977-78, treas., 1978—. Mem. dean's adv. bd. U. Houston Coll. of Bus., 1975—; bd. dirs. St. Paul's United Meth. Ch., 1967-76, St. Paul's Found., 1973-77, U. Houston Coll. of Bus. Alumni Ednl. Found., 1975—, Sam Houston council Boy Scouts Am., 1975-76. Served with USN, 1961-62. Recipient Disting. Alumnus award U. Houston Coll. Bus., 1976. Mem. Grey's Order, U. Houston Alumni Orgn. (exec. com. 1974-77), Pi Kappa Alpha. Club: Braeburn County. Home: 7655 S Braeswood #56 Houston TX 77071 Office: Meyerland Bank PO Box 35068 Houston TX 77035

MANN, JAMES ALAN, physician; b. Neoga, Ill., June 15, 1941; s. Laurence H. and Della C. Mann; M.D., U. Ill., 1967; m. Carol Gates, Nov. 29, 1962; children—Mitzi, Heather, Justin. Intern and resident in medicine City of Memphis U. Tenn. hosps., 1968-70, chief resident in medicine, 1970-71; fellow in gastroenterology, U. Tenn., 1972-74; practice medicine specializing in gastroenterology, Memphis, 1978—; mem. staff St. Joseph Hosp., chief dept. medicine, 1978—, dir. endoscopy lab., 1976—, mem. exec. com., 1977—, sec. med. staff, 1978-79; clin. asst. prof. medicine La. State U., Shreveport, 1971-73; asst. prof. medicine U. Tenn. Center for Health Scis., 1973-75, dir. Gastrointestinal Endoscopy Lab., 1975—, asso. prof. medicine, 1978—; cons. St. Jude's Children's Research Hosp., Memphis, 1979—. Served to maj. M.C., USAF, 1971-73. Diplomate Am. Bd. Internal Medicine. Mem. Am. Soc. for Gastrointestinal Endoscopy, A.C.P., Am. Gastroent. Assn., Am. Fedn. Clin. Research, Memphis-Shelby County Med. Soc., Tenn. Med. Assn., AMA. Episcopalian. Contbr. articles on gastroenterology to med. jours. Home: 267 S Belvedere St Memphis TN 38104 Office: 951 Court Ave Memphis TN 38163

MANN, JAMES ROBERT, lawyer; b. Greenville, S.C., Apr. 27, 1920; s. Alfred Cleo and Nina (Griffin) M.; B.A., The Citadel, 1941, LL.D. (hon.), 1978; LL.B. magna cum laude, U. S.C., 1947; m. Virginia Thomason Brunson, Jan. 15, 1945; children—James Robert, David Brunson, William Walker, Virginia Brunson. Admitted to S.C. bar, 1947; practice in Greenville, 1947-69, 79—; del. S.C. Ho. of Reps. from Greenville County, 1949-52; solicitor 13th Jud. Circuit, 1953-63; mem. 91st-95th Congresses from 4th Dist. S.C. Sec., Greenville County Planning Commn., 1963-67; chmn. Greenville County Heart Assn., 1952; mem. bd. devel. New Orleans Bapt. Theol. Sem. Bd. dirs. Family Service Agy., 1952; trustee Greenville Hosp. System, 1965-68; mem. at large Nat. council Boy Scouts Am. Served to lt. col. AUS, 1941-46; col. Res. (ret.). Mem. Am., S.C. bar assns., Am. Judicature Soc., Greater Greenville C. of C. (pres. 1965), VFW (dep. comdr. 1951-52), Am. Legion, Phi Beta Kappa, Omicron Delta Kappa. Democrat. Baptist. Mason (Shriner), Kiwanian, Elk; mem. Woodmen of the World. Home: 118 W Mountain View Ave Greenville SC 29609 Office: 812 E North St Greenville SC 29601

MANNEL, WILLIAM MORGAN, govt. ofcl.; b. Balt., Feb. 13, 1932; s. William Francis and Lillian (Gerhold) M.; B.S. in Elec. Engring., Carnegie Mellon U., 1953; M.S. in Elec. Engring., Pa. State U., 1957; M.S.N.E., Stevens Inst. Tech., 1958; m. Leah Jane Patterson, Nov. 24, 1956; children—Barbara Jeanne, William David. Staff engr. corp. hdqrs. ITT, 1958-61; div. dir. Philco Ford Corp., 1961-65; dir. research and devel. for strategic communications U.S. Army Communications Systems Agy., Ft. Monmouth, N.J., 1968-71; tech. dir. communications and electronics agy. U.S. Army Combat Devels. Command, Ft. Monmouth, 1971-73; sci. adv., tech. dir. for combat devels. U.S. Army Signal Center, Ft. Gordon, Ga., 1973—. Cons., Augusta Indsl. Devel. Com. Served with Signal Corps, U.S. Army, 1956-58. Decorated Commendation medal; recipient Outstanding Achievement award U.S. Air War Coll., 1979; comml. pilot; cert. flight instr. Mem. Armed Forces Communications Electronics Assn. (chpt. pres., asso. dir.), Nat. Assn. Flight Instrs., IEEE (sr.), Augusta C. of C. (visitors and conv. com., vice chmn. transp. com.). Presbyterian. Clubs: Kiwanis (chmn. major emphasis com. 1978) (Augusta); Ft. Gordon Army Flying (dir.). Contbr. articles to profl. jours. Home: 3622 Jamaica Dr Augusta GA 30909 Office: US Army Signal Center Fort Gordon GA 30905

MANNING, ALTHA FLOWERS, ednl. adminstr.; b. Bradenton, Fla., Aug. 23, 1939; d. William Doby and Aldonia Valeria (Hadley) Flowers; B.A., Fla. A. and M. U., 1961; M.S., Ill. Inst. Tech., 1971; m. George Russell Manning, June 24, 1967; 1 son, George Russell II. Tchr. Howard High Sch., Ocala, Fla., 1961-66, Miami (Fla.) Sr. High Sch., 1966-67; tchr. social studies Merrick-Moore High Sch., Durham; N.C., 1967-68; program asso. Learning Inst. N.C., Durham, 1968-70; tchr. High Point (N.C.) Central High Sch., 1971-72; regional coordinator Early Childhood Edn., Greensboro, N.C., 1972-75, N.C. dept. public instr.; instr. Child Devel. Daytona Beach (Fla.) Community Coll., 1976-78; coordinator spl. services, 1978—. Mem. Nat. Assn. for Edn. Young Children, Am. Personnel and Guidance Assn., Am. Assn. Jr. Colls., AAUW, Assn. for Childhood Edn. Internat., So. Assn. Equal Opportunity Program Personnel, Fla. Assn. Equal Opportunity Program Personnel, Fla. Assn. Community Colls., Fla. Assn. on Children Under Six, So. Assn. for Children Under Six. Democrat. Episcopalian. Home: 1405 Suwanee Rd Daytona Beach FL 32019 Office: Daytona Beach Community Coll PO Box 1111 Daytona Beach FL 32015

MANNING, ALTON WAYNE, electronics co. exec.; b. Jacksonville, Fla., Dec. 26, 1938; s. Alton and Helen (Goldberg) M.; m. Rosa Carol Dunn, Nov. 15, 1958; 1 son, David Wayne. Pres., Master Craft Builders and Bldg. Supply, Atlanta, 1961-67; fin. contract adminstr. Southeastern area Motorola Communications & Electronics, Decatur, Ga., 1967-75, collection mgr., 1967-75, Southeastern area spl. markets mgr., 1975—. Pres., Milford Home Owners Assn., 1970-74; rep. of religious community Community Adv. Council, 1979—. Served with U.S. Army, 1958-61. Republican. Baptist. Home: 969 Milford Church Rd Marietta GA 30060 Office: 5096 Panola Indsl Blvd Decatur GA 30032

MANNING, DOUGLAS HERMIT, leather co. exec.; b. nr. Yoakum, Tex., June 13, 1912; s. Martin Hermit and Janie Amanda (Ridgway) M.; grad. high sch.; m. Mary Edna Manning, Apr. 18, 1936; children—Norman Leland, Ronald Bryan, Gordon Lester, Melva Don (Mrs. Donald Ray Brown). With Tex Tan Western Leather Co., Yoakum, Tex., 1932-70, v.p. charge sales, 1945-70, dir., 1955-70; v.p. Tandy Corp., Ft. Worth, 1970-75; pres., chmn. bd. Tandy Brands Inc., Ft. Worth; chmn. bd. J.M. Bucheimer Co., Frederick, Md., Tex Tan Western Leather Co., Yoakum, Tex., Tex Tan Welhausen Co., Yoakum, Hickok Mfg. Co., Arlington, Tex., Western Sales Co., Arlington. Clubs: Lakeside Country (Yoakum); Shady Oaks Country, Petroleum, Ridglea Country (Ft. Worth). Home: 2921 Overton Park E Fort Worth TX 76109 Office: 1900 One Tandy Center Fort Worth TX 76102

MANNING, FRANCES TULLY, counselor; b. Birmingham, Ala., Dec. 11, 1944; d. Phillip Shelby and Earline (Hutcheson) T.; B.S., Auburn U., 1967; M.S., Jacksonville State U., 1975; m. James O. Manning, Apr. 12, 1969. Tchr. remedial reading Birmingham Bd. Edn., 1967-68; tchr. Mountain Brook Bd. Edn., Mountain Brook, Ala., 1969-74; counselor Gadsden (Ala.) State Jr. Coll., 1975; counselor elementary sch. Birmingham (Ala.) Bd. Edn., 1975—; cons. Birmingham So. Coll.; Anchor-Vol. Referral Agency, 1974-75; Birmingham Council of Christian Edn. Leadership Camp, 1979. Sears Found. fellow, 1972-73. Mem. NEA, Ala. Edn. Assn., Birmingham Edn. Assn., Am. Personnel and Guidance Assn., Am. Sch. Counselor Assn., Ala. Personnel and Guidance Assn. (dist. IV pres.), Ala. Sch. Counselor Assn., Delta Kappa Gamma. Methodist. Club: Ala. Warrior Ski (sec.-treas. 1968-72). Editor, developer Project G.R.I.N. cassette tape series, 1976-78, Project to the Fifth Power, 5th grade guidance program, 1978-79. Office: PO Drawer 10007 Guidance Dept Birmingham AL 35202

MANNING, ROBERT LEROY, indsl. engr.; b. Jacksonville, Fla., Feb. 6, 1932; s. Joshua Francis and Lillian Beatrice (Stewart) M.; B.S., Fla. A&M U., 1955; M.S., Ariz. State U., 1968; Logistics Exec. Devel., 1974; m. Marjoria A. Jenkins, Sept. 10, 1961; children—Terry Howard, Toni Elaine, Deidre Marie, Pamela Yvonne, Michelle Elizabeth. Commd. 2d lt. U.S. Army, 1955, advanced through grades to lt. col., 1969; served as comdr. and engr. various constrn. units, U.S., Europe and Asia, 1955-74; mgr. Army Constrn. Equipment Office, Warren, Mich., 1975-76; ret., 1976; sr. indsl. engr. Offshore Power Systems, subs. Westinghouse Corp., Jacksonville, Fla., 1976-78, mgr. environ. control, 1978—, mgr. facility planning, 1979—. Decorated Legion of Merit, 3 Bronze Stars, Purple Heart. Mem. Am. Mgmt. Assn., Kappa Alpha Psi. Mem. African Methodist Episcopal Ch. Home: 6405 Waltho Dr Jacksonville FL 32211 Office: 8000 Arlington Expressway Jacksonville FL 32211

MANNING, WALTER SCOTT, educator; b. nr. Yoakum, Tex.; B.B.A., Tex. Coll. Arts and Industries, 1932; M.B.A., U. Tex., 1940; m. Eleanor Mary Jones, Aug. 27, 1937; children—Sharon Frances, Walter Scott, Robert Kenneth. Asst. to bus. mgr. Tex. Coll. Arts and Industries, Kingsville, 1932; tchr., Sinton (Tex.) High Sch., 1933-37, Robstown (Tex.) High Sch., 1937-41; prof. Tex. A&M Coll., College Station, 1941-77. Cons. C.P.A. C.P.A., Tex. Mem. AAUP, Am. Accounting Assn., Am. Inst. C.P.A.'s, Tex. Soc. C.P.A.'s, College Station C. of C. (past pres.), Tex. Assn. U. Instrs. in Accounting (pres. 1963-64), Knights York Cross of Honor, Alpha Chi, Beta Gamma Sigma, Beta Alpha Psi. Democrat. Presbyn. (elder). Mason (32 deg., Shriner, K.T.), Kiwanian. Home: 405 Walton Dr E College Station TX 77840

MANNING, WILLIAM LINCOLN, JR., sch. adminstr.; b. Palestine, Tex., Nov. 25, 1917; s. William Lincoln and Annie (Jones) M.; B.S., Wiley Coll., 1939; M.S., Tex. So. U., 1948; m. Ernestine S. Powell, Apr. 22, 1944. Science teacher, asst. prin. Turner High Sch., Carthage, Tex., 1939-42; prin. Washington Elementary Sch., Palestine, 1946-49, 65-69, Lincoln High Sch., Palestine, 1949-65; prin.-at-large Palestine Ind. Sch. Dist., 1969-73; prin. Reagan Elementary Sch., Palestine, 1973-75, Southside Elementary Sch., Palestine, 1975—. Pres. Anderson County Civic League, 1974-77; mem. Parks and Recreation Bd., Palestine, 1977; bd. dirs. Palestine Day Care Center. Served with U.S. Army, 1942-46. Recipient Silver Beaver award Boy Scouts Am., 1961. Mem. Tex. State Tchrs. Assn., NEA, PTA (hon. life), Tex. Elementary Prin. Assn. and Suprs. Methodist. Clubs: Palestine Wiley (pres. 1967-77), Masons. Home: PO Box 526 Palestine TX 75801 Office: Route 5 Box 337A Palestine TX 75801

MANNONI, RAYMOND, univ. adminstr.; b. Pittsburg, Kans., July 11, 1921; s. Espartero U. and Mary Katherine (Scalet) M.; B.S., Kans. State U., 1944; M.Ed., U. Mich., 1946; postgrad. Northwestern U., 1947-48; D.Mus. Edn., Chgo. Mus. Coll., 1956; m. Karen Whittet, June 2, 1956; 1 dau., Barbara Gwen. Dir. bands U. Tulsa, 1946-48; 1st hornist Tulsa Symphony Orch., 1946-48; dir. bands, instr. music Kans. State Tchrs. Coll., Emporia, 1949-50; prof. music U. So. Miss., Hattiesburg, 1960—, dean Coll. Fine Arts, 1960-77; cons. music edn. dept. Lyon & Healy, Chgo., 1949-50; mem. LeBlanc Music Educators Nat. Adv. Bd., 1958-68. Served with USN, World War II; Res. ret. Recipient Alumni Certificate of award U. So. Miss., 1954-55, Award of Merit, Nat. Fedn. Music Clubs, 1962. Mem. Music Educators Nat. Conf. (life), Phi Kappa Phi, Phi Delta Kappa, Kappa Kappa Psi, Alpha Psi Omega, Phi Mu Alpha Sinfonia, Phi Kappa Lambda. Mason (Shriner), Elk. Club: Exchange (Hattiesburg). Co-author: Music Theory for Beginners, 1956. Home: 45 Fairlake Dr Country Club Estates Hattiesburg MS 39401

MANOLIU, VASILE VASILE, historian, physician; b. Ghermanesti, Rumania, Apr. 25, 1925; s. Vasile T. and Elena (Badulet) M.; M.D., Med Sch. Cluj (Rumania), 1950; M.A. in History, 1950; m. Elena Barbu, Nov. 15, 1953; children—Vasile-Mircea, Mihai-Dan. Instr. history of medicine Med. Sch. Cluj, Rumania, 1949-53; researcher history of medicine Center for Health Orgn. and History of Medicine, Bucharest, Rumania, 1953-60; asst. prof. history of medicine Med. Sch., Bucharest, 1958-61; prin. researcher history of medicine Inst. for Hygiene and Public Health, Bucharest, 1960-71; gen. practice medicine, Cluj, Bucharest, 1951-71, Vienna, Austria, 1972; sec. gen. Rumanian Soc. for History of medicine 1962-71; sec. gen. XXII Internat. Congress for History of Medicine, Bucharest-Constanta, Rumania, 1970; Mem. Am. Hist. Assn., Ga. Assn. Historians, Am. Assn. History of Medicine, Société d'Histoire de la Pharmacie, Société Internationale d'Histoire de la Mèdecine. Co-author: History of Medicine, Studies and Researches, 1957; From the Past of Rumanian Medicine, Iconography, 1957; The Communication of the Society of the Medical Sciences-History of Medicine-Abstracts of Papers Between 1956-61, 1961; From the History of Medicine in Rumanian and the World, 1961. contbr. articles to profl. jours. Home: 4510 Abercorn St Savannah GA 31405

MANOS, CHARLES GEORGE, chemist; b. Miami, Fla., Dec. 8, 1951; s. Charles George and Tula (Panos) M.; B.S. in Chemistry with honors, U. Fla., 1974, M.S.T. in Math., 1978; postgrad. dept. crop and soil scis. Mich. State U., 1979—. Grad. asst. instr. dept. chemistry U. Fla., 1974-75; bench chemist, coordinator soil chemistry research, soil characterization lab. Inst. Food and Agrl. Scis., Gainesville, Fla. 1976-78; quality assurance supr. Environ. Sci. and Engring., Inc., Gainesville, 1978-79; cons. to local environ. cons. firms. NSF research grantee. Mem. Am. Chem. Soc., Am. Soc. Quality Control, Phi Kappa Phi, Sigma Pi Sigma. Author quality assurance documents for EPA, 1979. Home: 713 NW 10th Ave Gainesville FL 32601

MANOS, PETER NICHOLAS, architect; b. Dallas, Sept. 23, 1932; s. Nicholas Peter and Angela M.; B.Arch., Tex. A&M U., 1954; student Columbia U., 1956-57; M.Arch., U. Pa., 1958; m. Libby Soutos, June 14, 1959 children—Angela Christine, Nicholas P., Holly. Designer, architect Alkon & Vanderwerff, Phila., 1958; architect-designer Roscoe DeWitt, Architect, Dallas, 1959-64; chmn. bd. Inter Systems Corp., Dallas, 1964—. Mem. Dallas City Transp. Bd., 1965-66. Served with USAF, 1954-56. Mem. AIA, Nat. Assn. Home Bldrs. Republican. Greek Orthodox (trustee). Home: 9766 Maple Hill Dr Dallas TX 75238 Office: 3000 Carlisle Plaza Dallas TX 75204

MANRIQUE, JORGE ALBERTO, art historian; b. Mexico City, July 17, 1936; s. Luis Esteban and Teodosia (Castaneda) M.; licenciado en historia, U. Nacional Autonoma de Mex., 1959, D.History Art, 1968; postgrad. U. Paris, U. Rome; m. Monica Mansour, Oct. 25, 1969; children—Lorenza, Martin, Julian. Prof. art history U. Veracruzana, 1959-61, dir. humanities dept., 1961-62; prof. El Colegio de Mex., 1964-69; researcher U. Nacional Autonoma, 1969—, dir. Inst. Investigaciones Esteticas, 1979—; dir. Historica Mexicana, revista, 1965-68, Revista de la Universidad, 1969-72. Recipient Premio critica joven, Mex., 1959; Rockefeller fellow, 1962-64. Mem. Acad. Mex Historia, Com. Mexicano Historia del Arte (sec. 1974—), Assn Latin Am. Art (v.p. contemporary art 1968), Soc. Mexicana Arquitectos Restauradores (hon.), Internat. Council Monuments and Sites, Asociación Internacional de Criticos de Arte. Co-author: El geometrismo mexicano, 1977; contbr. articles profl. publs. Home: 59-B A Zamora Mexico City DF 21 Mexico Office: Torre 1 de Humanidades 5 ceg piso Ciudad Universitaria Mexico 20 DF Mexico

MANRY, JOHN H., JR., banker; b. Miami, Fla., 1921. Chmn., pres., chief exec. officer Fla. Nat. Banks of Fla. Inc., Jacksonville; chmn. Fla. 1st Nat. Bank of Jacksonville; dir. Fla. Nat. Bank & Trust Co., Miami, Fla. Nat. Bank, Arlington. Office: Fla Nat Banks of Fla Inc Fla 1st Nat Bank Bldg Jacksonville FL 32202*

MANRY, WILLARD EDGAR, JR., physician; b. Montgomery, Ala., Dec. 9, 1916; s. Willard Edgar and Gladys Marie (Hunter) M.; student Auburn U., 1934-36; M.D., Tulane U., 1950; m. Katherine Ann Sands, Apr. 25, 1942; children—Ann Elizabeth, Katherine Ellen, John Willard. Intern, Duval Med. Center, Jacksonville, Fla., 1950-51, resident in surgery, 1951-52; practice family medicine, Lake Wales, Fla., 1952—; mem. staff Lake Wales Hosp., 1952—, pres. med. staff, 1959, 66. Pres., Heartland div. Am. Heart Assn. Served with U.S. Army, 1940-46. Decorated Bronze Star; diplomate Am. Bd. Family Practice. Fellow Am. Acad. Family Physicians; mem. AMA, Fla. Med. Assn. (asst. editor jour. 1968-74), Polk County Med. Assn. (pres. 1974, editor bull. 1960-65), Am. Acad. Family Practice, Fla. Acad. Family Physicians (pres. 1960, editor jour. 1964-65) Lake Wales C. of C. (pres. 1967). Republican. Club: Rotary (pres. 1958) (Lake Wales). Office: PO Box 1140 417 S 11th St Lake Wales FL 33853

MANSELL, PETER WILLIAM ANSON, physician; b. London, Eng., Sept. 19, 1936; came to U.S., 1972; s. Reginald A. and Gladys Mary (Ellison) M.; B.A., Cambridge (Eng.) U., 1958, M.A., 1962, M.B., B. Chir., 1962; m. Joanne Lucas, July 14, 1972. Intern St. Bartholomew's Hosp., London, 1962-64; practice medicine specializing in oncology, New Orleans, Montreal, Miami, Fla.; house surgeon and house physician St. Bartholomew's Hosp., London, Eng., 1962-63; house physician St. ANdrew's Hosp., London, 1963-64; demonstrator anatomy Royal Coll. Surgeons of Eng., 1964; demonstrator in pathology U. Bristol, Eng., 1965-66; sr. surg. house officer Bristol Royal Infirmary, 1966-67; research registrar dept. medicine U. Bristol, 1967-69, clin. asst. dept. plastic surgery, 1967-69, research asso. dept. pathology, 1969-72; served with dept. ear, nose and throat surgery Kenyatta Nat. Hosp., Nairobi, Kenya, 1969; research asso. clin. oncology dept. surgery Tulane U. Sch. Medicine, New Orleans, 1972-74, instr. surgery and clin. oncology, 1974; dir. div. oncology Royal Victoria Hosp., Montreal, Que., 1974-77; asst. surgeon Montreal Gen. Hosp., 1974-77; cons. oncology Montreal Chest Hosp., 1974-77; asso. prof. surgery McGill U., Montreal, 1974-77, asso. prof. exptl. medicine, 1974-77, asso. prof. therapeutic radiology, 1974-77; asso. prof. dept. med. oncology U. Miami (Fla.) Sch. Medicine, 1977—, adj. asso. prof. dept. biology, 1977—; chief div. edn. and tng. Comprehensive Cancer Center, State of Fla., 1977—. Fellow Med. Soc. London; mem. Am. Soc. Clin. Oncology,

Soc. for Surg. Oncology, Reticuloendothelial Soc., Am. Assn. for Cancer Research, Internat. Assn. for Study of Lung Cancer, Am. Cancer Soc. (dir. Dade county chpt. 1979—), Can. Soc. for Oncology, Brit. Assn. of Surg. Oncology, Internat. Registry of Immunotherapy, Sigma Xi. Contbr. numerous articles on oncology and immunotherapy to profl. jours. Home: 3618 Palmetto Ave Miami FL 33133 Office: Comprehensive Cancer Centre for the State of Florida PO Box 016960 Miami FL 33101

MANSEN, STEVEN ROBERT, automobile co. exec.; b. Chgo., Nov. 26, 1955; s. Robert Lee and Dorothy Nora (Nichols) M.; B.Indsl. Adminstrn., Gen. Motors Inst., 1978. Data processing system analyst in traffic Gen. Motors Corp., Oklahoma City, 1979—. Office: Gen Motors Corp PO Box 26527 Oklahoma City OK 73126

MANSFIELD, DANIEL JOSEPH, data processing co. exec.; b. Pascagoula, Miss., Nov. 21, 1931; s. Dan and Modeste Frances (Becht) M.; grad. parochial schs., Mobile, Ala.; m. Yvonne Broadus, May 25, 1957; children—Daniel Joseph, Catherine M., Susan A., Teresa A., Scott Jay. Automation technique specialist Brockley AFB, Mobile, 1951-64; systems analyst Data Processing, Inc., Mobile, 1964-66; pres. The Mansfield Corp., Mobile, 1966—. Served with USNG, 1951-54. Mem. Data Processing Mgmt. Assn. (certificate in data processing). Roman Catholic. Home: 1408 Blacklawn St Mobile AL 36604 Office: 1061 Dauphin St Mobile AL 36604

MANSFIELD, PHILIP DOUGLAS, veterinarian, educator; b. Glasgow, Ky., Mar. 30, 1941; s. William Arnold and Zada Mae (Proffitt) M.; student Eastern Ky. State U., 1960-63; D.V.M., Auburn U., 1967; m. Sheila Lynn Poynter, Aug. 26, 1970; children—Tamra Lynn, Kimberly Brooke. Veterinarian, Glasgow Animal Clinic, Glasgow, Ky., 1967-72; owner Mansfield Animal Hosp., Hopkinsville, Ky., 1972-78; asst. prof. small animal medicine and surgery Sch. Vet. Med., Auburn (Ala.) U., 1978—. Mem. Am., Ky., Western Central Ky. vet. med. assns., Am. Animal Hosp. Assn. (faculty affiliate mem.), Jr. C. of C. (dir. 1969, v.p., 1970). Democrat. Mem. Ch. of Christ. Home: 340 Deer Run Rd Auburn AL 36830 Office: Small Animal Clinic Auburn U Auburn AL 36830

MANSHIP, CHARLES PHELPS, JR., newspaper exec.; b. Baton Rouge, Aug. 13, 1908; s. Charles Phelps and Leora (Douthit) M.; student La. State U., 1926-27; B.J., U. Mo., 1930; M.B.A., U. Harvard, 1932; m. Paula Blanche Garvey, Sept. 27, 1938. Reporter, State Times-Morning Advocate Capital City Press, Baton Rouge, 1926-27, gen. mgr., 1938-42, pub., 1947-70, pres., 1970—, also dir.; mem. advt. dept. Times Picayune and New Orleans States, 1932-34; sect., treas., dir. B.R. Broadcasting Corp., sec. dir. La. TV Broadcasting; sec., dir. Mobile Video Tapes; dir. La. Nat. Bank of Baton Rouge, Capital Savs. Assn. Past chmn. East Baton Rouge chpt. ARC; mem. vestry St James Episcopal Ch., Baton Rouge; mem. adv. bd. Out Lady of the Lake Hosp., Baton Rouge. Served with U.S. Navy, 1942-45. Recipient SAR Good Citizenship award, 1976. Mem. So. Newspaper Pubs. Assn. (pres. 1959), Am. Newspaper Pubs. Assn., Soc. Profl. Journalists, Kappa Alpha. Clubs: Rotary, Baton Rouge Country, Baton Rouge City, Boson of New Orleans, Internat. House. Office: 525 Lafayette St Baton Rouge LA 70802

MANSHIP, DOUGLAS LEWIS, newspaper publisher; b. Baton Rouge, Nov. 3, 1918; s. Charles Phelps and Leora (Douthit) M.; student La. State U., Harvard U., Colo. U., Heidelberg (Germany) U.; m. Jane French, Jan. 31, 1942; children—Douglas L., Richard French, David Charles, Dina. Reporter, State-Times, 1947; pres. Baton Rouge Broadcasting Co., 1953; pres. Sta. WBRZ-TV, Sta. KRGV-TV and Radio, Weslaco, Tex., 1970; pub. State-Times, Morning Adv. and Sunday Advocate, Baton Rouge. Served with USAF. Recipient Brotherhood award, Baton Rouge chpt. NCCJ, 1973; Maggie Dixon Freedom of Info. award, 1974; La. Assn. Broadcasters Golden Mike award, 1978. Mem. Am. Newspaper Publishers Assn., C. of C., Nat. Assn. Broadcasters, Sigma Delta Chi. Episcopalian. Clubs: Baton Rouge Country; City, Boston, Plimsoll (New Orleans); Club de Caza Y pesca Las Cruces (Baja Calif., Mexico). Office: 525 Lafayette St Baton Rouge LA 70821

MANSKE, LEO J., artist, educator; b. N.Y.C., Oct. 3, 1949; s. Robert H. and Flavia M. Manske; student Tyler Sch. Art, Rome, 1969-70; B.F.A. in Printmaking, Temple U., 1971, M.F.A., 1974; student Positano Art Workshop, Italy, summer 1967; m. Cecilia B. Cerasoli, June 14, 1974; 1 dau., Fiavia Marla. Tchr. art Camp Wawokiye, N.Y.C., 1968-72; tech. asst. Tyler Sch. Art, Temple U., Phila., 1973, teaching asst., 1973, instr. in printmaking, summer 1973, 74-75, vis. asst. prof., summer 1977, guest lectr., 1976; asst. prof. fine arts dept. Coll. Charleston (S.C.), 1975—; adv. S.C. Arts Commn. Purchasing Com., 1978-79, S.C. Arts Commn. Ann. Show, 1975, Guild S.C. Artists, 1974-75; one-man shows of prints include: Phila. Art Alliance, 1973, Temple U., Phila., 1973, Mari Gallery, Mamaroneck, N.Y., 1974, Coll. Charleston, 1975, 76, 77, Gibbes Art Gallery, Charleston, 1976, Clemson U., Clemson, S.C., 1976, Presbyn. Coll., Clinton, S.C., 1977, Exhibitors Gallery, Charleston, 1978, 79, Glassboro (N.J.) State Coll., 1978; group shows include: S.I. Mus., N.Y., 1966, 67, 68, Tyler Sch. Art, Rome, 1969, Mari Gallery, Mamaroneck, 1971, 72, 73, 74, Great Hills Civic Center, N.Y.C., 1972, Dulin (Tenn.) Gallery Art, 1972, 76, Nat. Gallery Art, Washington, 1973, U. N.D., 1973, Cheltenham (Pa.) Art Center, 1973, U. Pa., Phila., 1974, River Gallery, Irvington, N.Y., 1974-75, U. Wis., Madison, 1975, Bradley U., Peoria, Ill., 1974, 76, Print Club, Phila., 1973, 74, 75, 76, Okla. Art Center, Oklahoma City, 1975, Mus. Art, Pa. State U., University Park, 1974, U. Hawaii, Honolulu, 1974, Nat. Collection Fine Arts, Washington, 1974, Newcomb Coll., New Orleans, 1975, Southeastern Graphics Council, 1975, Guild S.C. Artists, Charleston, 1975, U. Dallas, 1976, Galeria Spoleto, Charleston, 1977, Newhouse Community Gallery, N.Y.C., 1978, Coll. Charleston, 1978, Gibbes Art Gallery, Charleston, 1976, 78. Recipient numerous prize awards including Prize in etching Bradley Print Show, 1974, 76; S.C. Arts Commn. fellow, 1976-77; Faculty research grantee, 1978. Mem. Coll. Art Assn. Am., Southeastern Graphics Council, Print Club, Guild S.C. Artists (pres.-elect 1979—). Home: 154 Wentworth St Charleston SC 29401 Office: College of Charleston 66 George St Charleston SC 29401

MANSO, GILBERT, physician; b. Havana, Cuba, Dec. 16, 1942; s. Gilberto F. and Gricelda (Jimenez) M.; came to U.S., 1959, naturalized, 1968; B.A., U. Tex., Austin, 1965; M.D., U. Tex. Med. Br., Galveston, 1969; student U.S. Air Force Sch. Aerospace Medicine, 1970; m. Deborah L. Fowles, June 27, 1970; children—Wayne, Tammy. Rotating intern Meml. Bapt. Hosp., Houston, 1969-70; chief of staff Cochran Meml. Hosp., Morton, Tex., 1974-76; health officer Cochran County, Tex., 1974-76; chmn. med. care evaluation com. Tidelands Hosp., Channelview, Tex., 1976-77, vice-chief of staff, 1977-78, chief of staff, 1978—; pres. G. Manso, M.D., P.A., Channelview, Tex., 1976—. Pres., Manso Airmotive. Served to maj. MC USAF, 1970-75. Decorated Air medal. Diplomate Am. Bd. Family Practice. Mem. A.M.A., Tex. Med. Assn., Harris County Med. Soc., Houston Acad. Family Practice, Am. Coll. Emergency Physicians. Republican. Roman Catholic. Editor, pub.: The Houston Wine Scene, 1979—. Office: 15101 E Freeway Channelview TX 77530

MANSON, FREDERICK L., SR., counselor; b. Lignite, Va., Mar. 2, 1917; s. Saunders L. and Laura M.; B.S., So. U., 1947; M. Adminstrn. and Supervision, Tex. So. U., 1969, postgrad. 1969—; m. Evelyn Briggs, Jan. 25, 1948; children—Cheryl LaVerne Manson Thompson, Frederick Lee. Tchr. English, guidance counselor Iberville High Sch., Plaquemine, La., 1953-69; guidance counselor Plaquemine Sr. High Sch., 1969—; dir. Ednl. Talent Search, Plaquemine, La., 1965—. Served with AUS, 1942-45; ETO. Mem. Nat. Vocat. Guidance Assn., La. Edn. Assn., Am. Personnel and Guidance Assn., NAACP. Democrat. Baptist. Home: 1175 Savanna View Dr Baton Rouge LA 70810 Office: Plaquemine Sr High Sch Plaquemine LA 70764

MANUEL, CARROLL GENE, county adminstr.; b. Rileyville, Va., Aug. 24, 1930; s. L. Elmer and Ollie M.; B.S., Bridgewater Coll., 1959; M.A., Va. State U., 1978; children—Carroll G., Susan Rene. Adminstrv. asst. Titmus Optical Co., Petersburg, Va., 1960-63; dir. gen. services County of Chesterfield, Va., 1963-72, asst. county adminstr., 1972—. Robert E. Lee Boy Scouts Am., Richmond, Va., 1967-69. Served with U.S. Army, 1952-54. Mem. Am. Purchasing Soc., Nat. Assn. Govtl. Purchasing, Nat. Assn. County Adminstrs., Am. Soc. Public Adminstrs., Va. Assn. County Adminstrs. Methodist. Clubs: Civitan, Am. Legion. Home: PO Box 1011 Chester VA 23831 Office: PO Box 40 Chesterfield VA 23832

MANUEL, LETITIA VIEL, sch. food service adminstr.; b. Staunton, Va., Aug. 24, 1931; d. Charles Frederick and Clara (Argenbright) Viel; B.S. in Home Econs. and Instl. Foods Mgmt., Va. Poly. Inst. and State U., 1957; certificate Instrs. Inst., U. Okla., 1973; divorced; children—Carroll G. II, Susan Rene. Mgr.-dietitian trainee Va. Poly. Inst. and State U., Blacksburg, 1955-56; mgr. Richmond (Va.) Pub. Schs., 1957; dietitian Tuckers Hosp., Richmond, 1957; supr. sch. food service programs Petersburg (Va.) Pub. Schs., 1957—. Mem. adv. bd. for food service Va. Community Coll.; mem. certification com. Va. Dept. Edn. Mem. Am., Va. (pres. 1973-74) sch. food service assns., Va. Assn. Sch. Bus. Ofcls., Richmond Alumni Chpt. Va. Poly. Inst. Club: Women's of Chester. Home: 4840 Vestry Rd Richmond VA 23234 Office: 29 S Union St Petersburg VA 23803

MANUS, PATSY SUE, ednl. adminstr.; b. Joplin, Mo., June 17, 1940; d. William Earl and Mimi Lou (Woodruff) McCormick; student Henderson State U., 1976-79, U. Central Ark., 1977-79; m. Phillip Larry Manus, Dec. 27, 1958; children—Robin Gay, Belinda Sue, Lori Lyn, Phillip Cody. Receptionist/sec. Manus Clinic, Hope, Ark., 1967-73; dir. Sch. of Hope (Ark.), 1969—; mem. Gov. Ark. Developmental Disabilities Planning Council, 1979-84; mem. Gov. Ark. Council Handicapped Individuals, 1977-81; mem. govtl. relations com. Ark. Council Exceptional Children, 1977-78. Pres., Hempstead County Task Force for Child Protection, 1977-78; bd. mem. Hempstead County Suspected Child Abuse and Neglect, 1979-80; mem. Hope Community Edn. Adv. Council, 1976-78; mem. Adv. Council for Sr. Citizens Programs in Hempstead County, 1977-78; chmn. ednl. div. United Way Hempstead County, 1974-80. Recipient Service awards United Way Hempstead County, 1974, 75, 76, 77, Spl. Service award Hope-Hempstead County C. of C., 1978, elected mem. Ark. del. White House Conf. on Handicapped Individuals, 1977. Mem. Am. Assn. Mental Deficiency, Human Service Providers Assn., Parenting Assn., Ark. Assn. Spl. Edn. Adminstrs., Ark. Assn. Adminstrn. Community Programs for Developmentally Disabled, Hempstead County Assn. Retarded Citizens, Gamma Beta Phi, Delta Kappa Gamma, Alpha Chi. Democrat. Methodist. Home: Springhill Rd Route 1 Box 56M Hope AR 71801 Office: 819 S Laurel St Hope AR 71801

MARABLE, JAMES ROSE, JR., civil engr.; b. Atlanta, Oct. 5, 1924; s. James Rose and Mary Spotswood (Glinn) M.; B.C.E., Ga. Inst. Tech., 1949; M.S., La. State U., 1950; m. Dawn Io Key, Dec. 24, 1946; children—Nancy Marable Glenn, Jane, Anne Marable Leppek, James Stephen. Hydraulic engr. U.S. C.E., Vicksburg Waterways Expt. Sta., 1950-51; sr. designer Ga. Power Co., Atlanta, 1951-54; structural engr. Kuhlke & Wade, architects, Augusta, Ga., 1954-56; structural engr. W.Va. Pulp & Paper Co., Charleston, S.C., 1956-57; asst. chief structural sect. Union Bag-Camp Corp., Savannah, Ga., 1957-60; sr. structural engr. Robert & Co., Assos., architects and engrs., Atlanta, 1960-66; chief engr. br. office Simons-Eastern Co., cons.'s and engrs., Atlanta and Greenville, S.C., 1967-72; project mgr. Simons Eastern Co., 1972-75; v.p. Archtl. Corp. Atlanta, 1975-77; mgr. civil engring. div. Simons Eastern Co., engrs., Decatur, Ga., 1977—; instr. La. State U., 1949-50. Pres., Columbia Valley Civic Assn., Decatur, 1965-66; scoutmaster Boy Scouts Am., 1952-54. Served with AUS, 1943-46; ETO. Named Engr. of Year in Pvt. Practice Met. Atlanta, Engrs. Greater Atlanta, 1974, Engr. of Year in Pvt. Practice Ga., Ga. Soc. Profl. Engrs., 1974. Registered profl. engr., Ga., Ala., Tex., Okla., Fla., S.C., N.C., Tenn., Pa., Va. Fellow ASCE; mem. Ga. Engring. Found. (v.p. 1978, pres.-elect 1979, pres. 1980), Am. Legion (comdr. 1949), Chi Epsilon. Presbyn. (deacon 1965-67, 76-79, elder 1980—). Mason. Home: 3675 Tree Bark Trail Decatur GA 30034 Office: 1 W Court Sq Decatur GA 30030

MARAIST, LOUIS FRANCIS, III, acct.; b. St. Martinville, La., Mar. 18, 1944; s. Louis Francis and Gertrude Marie (Melancon) M.; B.S., U. Southwestern La., 1967, postgrad., 1967-69; postgrad. U. Houston, 1969-70; m. Marsha Lynn Thomas, Oct. 3, 1970; children—Michael Paul, David Matthew, Julie Catherine. Systems analyst First Nat. Bank, Lake Charles, La., 1971-73; staff acct. J.K. Lasser & Co., C.P.A.'s, Morgan City, La., 1973-74; acct. Arthur Levy, Inc., Morgan City, 1974-76; pres. Maraist Acctg., Morgan City, 1976—; dir. Barmar, Inc., Mamar Inc., Betmar Inc., Majestic Developments, Inc. Mem. Paul Hardy Election Com., 1969. Cert. data processor Inst. for Cert. Computer Profls. cert. data processing auditor EDP Auditors Assn. Mem. EDP Auditors Assn., Data Processing Mgmt. Assn., Cert. Data Processing Spl. Interest Group, U.S. Tennis Assn., Atchafalya Runners, Bayou Tennis Assn., Sigma Nu Alumni. Club: Petroleum (Morgan City). Home: 1006 Federal Ave Morgan City LA 70380 Office: Maraist Acctg 1316 1/2 Federal Ave Morgan City LA 70380

MARBLE, ROLAND DUDLEY, lawyer; b. Greenville, Miss., May 12, 1920; s. Frisby Griffing and Lucy Stovall (Turner) M.; B.A., Miss. Coll., 1946; J.D., U. Miss., 1948; m. Virginia Cowart McDonald, July 9, 1944; children—Lucy (Mrs. Henry W. Tucker), Roland Dudley. Admitted to Miss. bar, 1948; practiced in Tylertown, Miss., 1948-51; asso. firm Wells, Thomas & Wells, Jackson, Miss., 1951-54, partner, 1954-68; founding partner firm Wells, Wells, Marble & Hurst, Jackson, 1968—; dir. Miss. Drug Co. Inc., Instnl. Food Distbrs. Instr. banking classes Am. Inst. Banking, Jackson, 1954-65. Trustee Miss. Regional Blood Bank. Served to capt. AUS, 1940-45. Mem. Am. Legion (nat. vice comdr. 1969), Civitan Club (internat. v.p. 1972-74). Baptist. Mason (Shriner). Editor Miss. Law Jour., 1948. Home: 4065 Eastwood Dr Jackson MS 39211 Office: PO Box 131 Jackson MS 39205

MARBURY, LARRY ALONZA, pharmacist; b. Alexander City, Ala., Nov. 13, 1948; s. James and Lula Mae (Andrews) M.; asso. degree sci. Alexander City State Jr. Coll., 1969; B.S. in Pharmacy, Auburn U., 1973; 1 child, Jumanne. Intern in pharmacy Univ. Hosp., Birmingham, Ala., 1972-73; pharmacist Citizen's Drugs, Birmingham, 1974-75, Holloway and Humphry Pharmacy, Birmingham, 1975-76; owner, mgr. Marbury's Discount Pharmacy, Birmingham, 1976—; owner Marbury's Variety & Gift Shop, Birmingham, 1979—. Mem. Asso. Druggists. Mem. African Methodist Episcopal Ch. Club: Mason. Home: 228-3A Robert Jemison Rd Birmingham AL 35209 Office: 143 6th Ave SW Birmingham AL 35211

MARCHANT, TRELAWNEY ESTON, lawyer; b. Columbia, S.C., Dec. 9, 1921; s. Trelawney Eston and Lila (Cave) M.; B.S., U. S.C., 1942, LL.B., 1947; m. Caroline Melton Bristow, Nov. 10, 1951; children—Trelawney Eston III, Walter Bristow, Caroline Melton, Nancy Lila. Admitted to S.C. bar, 1947; practiced in Columbia, 1948—; mem. firm Marchant, Bates, Todd & Barber, 1952—; judge Municipal Ct., Columbia, 1956-61. Dir., 1st Palmetto Bank & Trust Co. Chmn., Richland County chpt. Nat. Found., 1954-55. Chmn., Richland County Democratic Party, 1963-68. Bd. dirs., v.p. U. S.C. Ednl. Found.; trustee U. S.C., 1965-70, chmn. bd. trustees, 1970-78. Served to capt. USMCR, 1942-46, now maj. gen. S.C. Nat. Guard; adj. gen. State of S.C., 1978—. Mem. Am., S.C., Richland County (pres. 1970-71) bar assns., Am. Judicature Soc., Acad. Polit. Sci., U.S. 4th Circuit Jud. Conf., U. S.C. Alumni Assn. (past pres.), N.G. Assn. S.C. (past pres.), Am. Legion, Mil. Order of World Wars (past pres.), Omicron Delta Kappa, Sigma Nu. Episcopalian. Clubs: Kiwanis (dir.); Summit; Forest Lake Country; Cotillion, Columbia Ball, Torch. Home: 5046 Courtney Rd Columbia SC 29201 Office: 1225 Bluff Rd Columbia SC 20201

MARCHETTI, JEAN WOOLLEY, educator; b. Homestead, Fla., Dec. 19, 1938; d. Charles Jackson and Margurite Elizabeth (Hinson) Woolley; B.S., Rollins Coll., 1973; M.A. in Guidance, Counseling, 1978; m. Alfred Marchetti, June 22, 1973; children by previous marriage—John, Mary, Teresa. Tchr. head start New Smyrna Beach, Fla., 1969-70, Sacred Heart Sch., New Smyrna, 1966-68, St. Teresa Sch., Titusville, Fla., 1970-71, St. John Vianney, Orlando, Fla., 1971-73, Thacker Ave. Elementary Sch. Kissimmee, Fla., 1972—; mem. P.T.O. Orgn. Mem. Osceola Classroom Tchrs. Assn., Fla., United teaching profs., N.E.A., Notary Pub. Assn., Am. Personnel, Guidance Assn., Smithsonian Insts. (mat. mem.). Democrat. Roman Catholic. Home: 1210 Plato Ave Orlando FL 32809

MARCHFIELD, RUDOLPH L., author; b. Chgo., May 29, 1907; s. Ignatius and Sali (Fleischer) M.; grad. pub. high sch.; m. Gloria Adams, June 22, 1937 (div. Feb. 1941), remarried Oct. 27, 1963. Author, mfr., poet, musician, lyricist, free-lance reporter. Mem. ASCAP, Voltaire Soc. (pres. emeritus), Internat. Platform Assn. Patentee kitchen and recreational products field. author: How To Stay Alive & Healthy with Diabetes, And How To Avoid Getting It, 1979. Home: 1837 N Azalea St Basswood Okeechobee FL 33472

MARCHISELLO, HERMAN SAMUEL, mfg. co. exec.; b. Decatur, Ill., Aug. 22, 1919; s. Benjamin I. and Philomena C. M.; B.S.M.E., U. Ill., 1949; P.G., U. Mich., 1953; m. Dorothy Helen Putnam, Feb. 14, 1946; children—James Lee, Nancy Jo. Mgr. motor ops. Haydon div. Gen. Time, Torrington, Conn., 1970-72; mgr. mfg. indsl. control div. Talley Industries, Thomaston, Conn., 1972-77; gen. mgr. Spartus Corp. subs. Walter Kidde, Louisville, Miss., 1977-78, v.p. mfg., 1978—. Chmn., Econ. Devel. Com., 1968-70; bd. dirs. YMCA, 1967-70; chmn. Spartus Found., 1977. Served with USAAF, 1942-45. Decorated D.F.C., Air medal with three bronze oak leaf clusters. Mem. Louisville C. of C., Delta Sigma Phi. Roman Catholic. Clubs: Louisville Country, Starkville Country. Home: 46 S Williamsburg Circle Starkville MS 39759 Office: PO Box 187 Louisville MS 39339

MARCIE, FRANK JOSEPH, chemist; b. LaGrange, Tex., Oct. 30, 1927; s. Frank Joseph and Olga Martha (Nesrsta) Marecic; B.S., St. Marys U., 1949, M.S., 1967; m. Virginia Small; children—Barbara, Frank Joseph, Patrick. Chemist, D.W. Heering Co. Inc., San Antonio, 1953-60, USAF Occupational and Environ. Health Lab., Brooks AFB, Tex., 1960—. Served with USAF, 1950-53. Mem. Am. Chem. Soc., Soc. Applied Spectroscopy, Am. Inst. Chemists, Am. Indsl. Hygiene Assn., Am. Conf. Govt. Indsl. Hygienists. Roman Catholic. Clubs: Moose, Order Sons of Hermann. Home: 4406 Irene Dr San Antonio TX 78222 Office: Bldg 140 Brooks AFB TX 78235

MARCUM, DEBRA LYNN, speech and lang. therapist; b. Campbellsville, Ky., Mar. 10, 1953; d. Huston Hays and Geneva (Wilcoxson) M.; B.A. cum laude, Western Ky. U., 1975, M.A., 1976. Speech and lang. therapist Barren River Comprehensive Care Center, Glasgow, Ky., 1976-77, Oakwood Tng. Facility, Somerset, Ky., 1978-79, Lake Cumberland Home Health Service, Somerset, 1979—. Mem. Am. Speech and Hearing Assn., Ky. Speech and Hearing Assn. Home: 304 Industrial Rd Greensburg KY 42743 Office: Convenient Bldg Langdon St Somerset KY

MARCUM, JAMES WALTON, educator; b. Crystal City, Tex., June 8, 1940; s. Clarence Edwin and Frances Caroline (Kooncе) M.; B.A., Tex. A & I Coll., 1960, M.A., 1961; Ph.D., U. N.C., 1970; M.P.A., U. Okla., 1978; m. Judith Paulyne Higginbotham, June 23, 1963; children—Virginia Ann, Jessica. Tchr., Donna (Tex.) High Sch., 1961-62; reporter, photographer Taylor (Tex.) Daily Press, 1962-63; instr. history Pfeiffer Coll., Misenheimer, N.C., 1963-65; instr. U. N.C., Chapel Hill, 1967, 69-70; prof. history Okla. Bapt. U., Shawnee, 1967—; vis. prof. history U. Okla., 1976-77. Chmn. 4th dist. Democratic Party Okla., 1975-77, mem. exec. com.; mem. Okla. Hist. Records Adv. bd., 1976-79. Mem. Am. Assn. Advancement Slavic Studies, AAUP (Okla. conf. pres. 1972-73), Am. Hist. Assn., Am. Soc. Public Adminstrn., Okla. Assn. Coll. History Profs. (pres. 1974-75), Southwestern Assn. Slavic Studies (pres. 1977-78), Southwestern Social Scis. Assn., Western Social Scis. Assn. Democrat. Methodist. Contbr. articles to profl. jours. Office: Dept History Okla Baptist U Shawnee OK 74801

MARCUS, LAWRENCE I., psychiatrist; b. Newark, Dec. 3, 1937; s. Samuel L. and Irene (Posner) M.; A.B. in Biology, Lafayette Coll., 1958; M.D., U. Louvain (Belgium), 1967; m. Andrea Candace Sills, Aug. 9, 1974; children—David E., Anthony M., Rebecca L. Intern, Jewish Gen. Hosp., Montreal, Que., Can., 1966-67; resident in psychiatry Albert Einstein Coll. Medicine, N.Y.C., 1967-69; resident in psychiatry Silver Hill Found., New Canaan, Conn., 1971-72, dir. alcohol rehab. program, sr. staff psychiatrist, 1972-76; clin. dir. Banyan Psychiat. Inst., Lake Worth, Fla., 1976-78; practice medicine specializing in psychiatry, Boca Raton, Fla., 1978—; clin. instr. U. Miami, 1977—; attending physician Boca Raton Community Hosp. Served to maj. M.C., USAF, 1969-71. Diplomate Am. Bd. Psychiatry and Neurology. Mem. AMA, Am. Psychiat. Assn., Fla. Psychiat. Soc., Palm Beach County Psychiat. Soc., Palm Beach County Med. Soc., Fla. Med. Assn. Contbr. articles to profl. jours. Office: 399 W Camino Gardens Blvd Boca Raton FL 33432

MARCUS, TERRY LEE, concrete mfg. co. exec.; b. Charles Town, W.Va., Dec. 9, 1946; s. Charles Calvin and Vivian Wenonah (McKee) M.; B.S. in Bus. Adminstrn. and Accounting, W.Va. U., 1970; m. Glenda Felyce Behar, Sept. 5, 1971 (dec. 1975); 1 son, Heath Lance. Staff accountant Dan Harmon & Assos., Martinsburg, W.Va., 1970-71; pres. Turf Enterprises, Inc., Charles Town, 1971—; sec., dir. So. Courts, Inc., 1970—, Panhandle Devel. Corp., 1973—; sec., dir. Sales Devel. Corp., 1974—; pres., dir. Fox Glen Utilities, Inc., 1976—; partner Panhandle Investment Assos., 1973—. Mem. Jefferson

County Economic Devel. Corp., 1977—. Mem. Charles Town Jaycees (treas., dir. 1971-73), Nat. Ready-Mix Concrete Assn., Nat. Home Builders Assn., Builders Supply Assn. W.Va., Jefferson County C. of C. Democrat. Episcopalian. Home: 536 E Washington St Charles Town WV 25414 Office: 608 E Washington St Charles Town WV 25414

MARET, ELIZABETH GARDNER, sociologist; b. Phila., Nov. 9, 1943; d. Raymond and Elizabeth (Clark) M.; B.A., U. Tex., 1967, M.A., 1971, Ph.D., 1973; m. V.S. House, 1977; 1 son, David Stanley. Asst. prof. sociology Huston-Tillotson Coll., Austin, Tex., 1972-73, Tex. Tech. U., Lubbock, 1973-76; asso. prof. Tex. A&M U., College Station, 1976—. Named Outstanding Educator, Tex. Tech. U., 1974; NIH postdoctoral fellow, 1975; U.S. Dept. Labor grantee, 1976-77. Mem. AAAS, AAUP, Am. Sociol. Assn., Rural Sociol. Soc., Southwestern Social Sci. Assn. Contbr. 15 articles to profl. jours. Home: Route 3 Box 240J Bryan TX 77801 Office: Dept Sociology Tex A&M U College Station TX 77843

MARGAN, IGOR, entertainment co. exec.; b. Rijeka, Yugoslavia, Sept. 15, 1947; s. Ernisio and Elena (Marich) M.; came to U.S., 1956, naturalized, 1967; m. Halina Ring, July 26, 1977. Salesman, Harold Life Ins. Co., New Orleans, 1970-73; engr. Margan Constrn. Co., New Orleans, 1973-75; v.p. V.&A. Constrn. Co. Inc., New Orleans, 1975-76; pres. Igor's Inc., lounges and entertainment centers, New Orleans, 1974—; pres., chief exec. officer Igor's Inc., real estate devel. and sales. Served with AUS, 1966-68; Vietnam. Decorated Bronze Star. Democrat. Roman Catholic. Address: 2133 St Charles Ave New Orleans LA 70130

MARGOLIS, GWEN LIEDMAN (MRS. ALLAN B. MARGOLIS), state legislator Fla.; b. Phila., Oct. 4, 1934; d. Joseph and Rose (Weiss) Liedman; student Temple U., 1951-54; spl. course U. Tampa; m. Allan Block Margolis, Sept. 12, 1953; children—Edward, Ira, Karen, Robin. Owner, broker Gwen Margolis Real Estate, North Miami Beach, Fla., 1965—; partner 16990 Corp.; mem. Fla. Ho. of Reps. Mem. human relations bd., vice chmn. bd. adjustments City of North Miami Beach. Bd. dirs. Keystone Point Homeowners Assn.; adv. bd. Big Sisters Dade County. Recipient Humanitarian of Year award City of Hope, Dade County bd. Girl Scouts U.S.A. Mem. Miami Bd. Realtors, Nat. Assn. Real Estate Bds., North Miami Beach C. of C. (dir.), Fla. Women's Polit. Caucus, League Women Voters, Anti-Defamation League (dir.). Home: 13105 Biscayne Bay Dr North Miami FL 33161 Office: 1451 NE 162d St North Miami Beach FL 33162

MARGULIES, STANLEY IRA, radiologist; b. Balt., Jan. 6, 1935; s. Oscar and Anne (Hendin) M.; A.B., Johns Hopkins, 1956, M.A., 1956, M.D., 1960; m. Karen Ann Mintz, Feb. 11, 1962; 1 dau., Robin. Intern, U. Hosps. of Cleve., 1960-61, asst. resident in gen. surgery, 1961-62; asst. resident and fellow in radiology Johns Hopkins Hosp. and Univ., Balt., 1964-67, fellow in acad. radiology, 1966-67; fellow in acad. radiology Nat. Inst. Gen. Med. Scis., HEW, 1966-68; instr. radiology Johns Hopkins, U. Balt., 1967-68, radiologist, 1967-72; vis. investigator Carnegie Inst. of Washington, 1967-71; asst. prof. radiology John Hopkins, Balt., 1968-70, dir. Cardiovascular Diagnostic Lab., 1969-70, asso. prof. radiology, 1970-72; clin. asso. prof. radiology U. Miami (Fla.), 1972-74; radiologist, chief radiology Meml. Hosp., Hollywood, Fla., 1972—; radiologist Hollywood Med. Center, 1974—, Pembroke Pines Gen. Hosp., 1975—; cons. Bur. Radiology Health, 1969-72; sec., dir. Am. Israel Investors, 1978—. Vice pres., gen. campaign chmn. Jewish Fedn. of South Broward, 1976-78, bd. dirs. 1974—; nat. campaign cabinet United Jewish Appeal, 1976-78; bd. dirs., mem. nat. exec. com. Am. Assos. of Ben Gurion U. of Negev, Israel, 1979—; campaign chmn. profl. divs. South County area United Way Broward County, 1978—; bd. dirs. Miami Jewish Homes and Hosp. for Aged, 1979—. Served with USNR, 1962-64. Recipient Young Leadership award, Jewish Fedn. of S. Broward, 1975; NIH training grantee, 1966-67. Diplomate Am. Bd. Nuclear Medicine, Am. Bd. Radiology. Mem. Am. Coll. Radiology, Radiol. Soc. N. Am., Radiol. Alumni Assn. of Johns Hopkins Med. and Surg. Alumni Assn., Am., Fla. med. assns. Jewish. Contbr. articles in field to med. jours. Home: 4350 Player St Hollywood FL 33021 Office: 3700 Washington St Hollywood FL 33021

MARICH, PETER, architect; b. Zargreb, Yugoslavia, July 27, 1935; came to U.S., 1939, naturalized, 1953; s. Milan Peter and Kathrine M.; ed. Art Inst. Chgo., 1951, U. Ill., 1957; m. Margery Newhall, Mar. 6, 1964; children—Michael, Christopher, Wendy. Designer, Leggett, Architect, Tampa, Fla., 1959, Reynolds, Smith & Hills, Architects, Tampa, 1960-65; draftsman Haddox, Architect, Clearwater, Fla., 1965-70; architect S.E. Engring., Clearwater, 1970; pres. Peter Marich Architect and Planners, Clearwater, 1970—; dir. Scope Groupe, Developers, T. & M. Enterprises, Land Developers. Mem. Downtown Devel. Bd., Largo, Fla., Bldg. Code Bd. Largo; bd. dirs. Assn. Retarded Citizens; commr. Crews Lake Rd. and Bridge Dist. Served with USMC, 1952-54. Mem. AIA (past pres. Clearwater sect.), Nat. Council Archtl. Registration Bds. Republican. Clubs: Clearwater Yacht, East Bay Country, Harborview, Touchdown (Clearwater). Prin. archtl. works include Med. Center Hosp., Largo, Morton Plant Hosp., Clearwater, Citrus Meml. Hosp., Inverness, Fla., Diagnostic Clinic, Largo. Home: 1584 Oak Ln Clearwater FL 33516 Office: 410 Pegasus St Clearwater FL 33515

MARIN, JAMES SCOTT, elec. engr.; b. Puyallup, Wash., Feb. 20, 1951; s. LeRoy C. and Adeline L. M.; B.S., S.D. Sch. Mines and Tech., 1973, M.S. in Elec. Engring., 1978; postgrad. So. Meth. U., 1979—. Research asst. S.D. Sch. Mines and Tech., Rapid City, 1972-73, 77; instr. amateur radio Austin Peay State U., Clarksville, Tenn., 1975; electronic design engr., signal processing lab., equipment group Tex. Instruments, Inc., Dallas, 1978—. Chmn. Com. to Organize Ednl. Radio Sta. KTEQ, Rapid City, 1972. Served with Signal Corps, U.S. Army, 1973-76. Mem. IEEE, Sigma Xi, Eta Kappa Nu, Central States VHF Soc. Clubs: Texins Rifle, Texins Archery. Home: 4702 Fordham Dr Garland TX 75042 Office: Tex Instruments Inc Box 225012 M/S 88 Dallas TX 75222

MARIN, VICTOR, state ofcl.; b. El Paso, Tex., Aug. 1, 1949; s. Jose E. and Maria Delores (Orozco) M.; B.S., U. Tex., El Paso, 1972, M.Ed., 1978; m. Brenda J. Phillips, Oct. 11, 1975. Public welfare worker Tex. Dept. Human Resources, El Paso, 1972-73, public welfare supr., 1973-74, adminstrv. asst. to regional dir. fin. services, 1974—. Disaster relief coordinator Disaster Emergency Services, 1974—, coordinator refugee repatriation program, 1975—. 20/30 Mens Club scholar, 1968. Mem. Am. Public Welfare Assn., Tex. Public Employees Assn., Am. Personnel and Guidance Assn., Trans Pecos Pesonnel and Guidance Assn., Am. Rehab. Counseling Assn. Democrat. Roman Catholic. Club: Border Chorders. Home: 10332 Bayo Ave El Paso TX 79925 Office: 5150 El Paso Dr El Paso TX 79905 also PO Box 10276 El Paso TX 79994

MARINO, ANGELO FRANCIS, epidemiologist; b. North Adams, Mass., Feb. 5, 1912; s. Gregory John and Helen (Downs) M.; grad. pub. schs.; m. Mary Elizabeth Harrell, Feb. 9, 1944; children—Ramon, Helen (Mrs. Robert Stamps), Ronald, Gregory. With Norfolk (Va.) Health Dept., 1938—, epidemiologist, 1940—. Guest lectr. Old Dominion U. Served with USNR, 1929-33, 42-45. Mem. Am., Va. pub. health assns., Am. Venereal Disease Assn. (exec. sec. 1970, treas. 1972—; Thomas Parran award 1976), Tidewater Rose Soc. (treas. 1970-71). Roman Catholic. Home: 1135 Georgetown Rd Norfolk VA 23502 Office: 401 Colley Ave Norfolk VA 23507

MARK, JONATHAN GREENFIELD, broadcasting co. exec.; b. N.Y.C., Dec. 22, 1948; s. Sidney Carl and Patricia (Greenfield) M.; B.A., U. Tex., Austin, 1971; M.A., U. Pa., 1976; postgrad. U. Okla., 1978-79. Vice-pres., Stas. KAKC-KBEZ, Tulsa, 1976—; vis. lectr. polit sci. U. Tulsa, 1977; vis. lectr. mass communications USAF Acad., 1977. Served with USAF, 1971-75, USAFR, 1975-79. Mem. Res. Officers U.S., Air Force Assn. Home: 6766 S Columbia Ave Tulsa OK 74136 Office: PO Box 970 Tulsa OK 74101

MARK, SIDNEY CARL, broadcasting exec.; b. N.Y., Feb. 27, 1914; s. Henry and Sarah (Berkowitz) M.; B.A., Coll. City N.Y., 1934; M.A. in English, U. Tulsa, 1974; m. Patricia Greenfield, Jan. 18, 1946; children—Priscilla, Jonathan Greenfield, Mary Alice, Sarah Edna, Henry Greenfield. Announcer, producer radio sta. WHN, N.Y., 1935; spl. events prodn. mgr., radio sta. WHK-WCLE, Cleve., 1937-43; radio-TV dir. Al Paul Lefton Co., 1943-48; pres., gen. mgr., radio sta. WTTM, Trenton, N.J., 1948-53; pres. Swern & Co. (Lit Brothers), Trenton, 1954-62; chmn., pres. Mark/way, Inc. (radio sta. KAKC and KBEZ AM-FM, Tulsa, KFUN AM-FM, KLVF-AM-FM, Las Vegas, N.M.); dir. Bankers Bond & Mortgage Co. Am. Dir. Bonwit Teller Co. Phila., 1957-62, Broad St. Nat. Bank, Trenton, 1957-63. Instr. radio-TV announcing and prodn. Western Res. U., Cleve., also Coll. City N.Y., 1937-53. Chmn. Trenton Planning Bd., 1955-59; v.p. Trenton Philharmonic Soc., 1953-63; v.p. Del. Valley United Fund, 1954-56; bd. dirs. Greater Phila.-S. Jersey Council, 1949-53; trustee Greater Trenton Council, 1956-62; bd. dirs. Arts and Humanities Council Tulsa, Tulsa chpt. A.R.C., Tulsa Philharmonic Soc., Tulsa Recreation Center for Physically Ltd., Downtown Tulsa-Unlimited, Tulsa Better Bus. Bur.; bd. dirs., pres. Tulsa Civic Ballet; v.p. Jr. Achievement of Tulsa, Inc.; pres. Concertime, Inc. of Tulsa; chmn. Tulsa Met. YMCA; finance chmn. Boy Scouts; treas. adv. council Salvation Army, Tulsa; chmn. bd. trustees, Fenster Gallery of Judaica; mem. Jewish Community Council, Tulsa; trustee Tulsa Performing Arts Center Trust. Pres. N.J. Broadcasters Assn., 1951-52. Mem. Mensa (chmn. Tulsa 1967-68). Clubs: Tulsa, Tulsa Petroleum, Tulsa Tennis, Tulsa Rotary. Home: 6766 S Columbia Ave Tulsa OK 74136 Office: KAKC Bldg 51st and S Peoria Box 970 Tulsa OK 74101

MARKHAM, ANNIE CATHERINE PARRISH (MRS. OSCAR C. MARKHAM), librarian; b. McNeill, Miss., Sept. 23, 1905; d. Robert Alexander and Daisy (Terry) Parrish; B.A., Belhaven Coll., 1925; M.A., Tulane U., 1928; postgrad. Peabody Coll., 1939, U. London, 1942; Ed.M. (Sch. Edn. scholar), Harvard U., 1944; postgrad. U. Edinburgh, 1962, Hellenic Inst., Athens, Greece, 1966; m. Oscar C. Markham, Feb. 15, 1957. Tchr., Arlington (Ky.) High Sch., 1925-28; faculty Bethel Woman's Coll., Hopkinsville, 1929-42, 46-55, dean faculty, 1946-47; faculty various schs., colls., 1942-45, 55-58; exchange tchr. Avery Hill Coll., Eltham, Eng., 1953-54; faculty Murray (Ky.) State U., 1958-68, asso. prof. English, 1967-68; librarian Mid-Continent Baptist Bible Coll., Mayfield, Ky., 1968-78, librarian emeritus, 1978—. Del. Bapt. World Alliance, Tokyo, 1970. Active Am. Cancer Soc. drives, Mayfield, 1962-67. Mem. ALA, Nat. Council Tchrs. English, Christian Librarians' Fellowship, Am. Theol. Library Assn. AAUW (life), Nat. Ret. Tchrs. Assn., Ky. Hist. Assn., Bus. and Profl. Women's Club, Chi Delta Phi (nat. sec. 1941-42, 67-70). Baptist (pres. Woman's Missionary Union 1966-67, ch. librarian 1961—). Club: Homemakers (pres. 1977—). Home: 101 Wilson Ave Mayfield KY 42066 Office: Route 2 Mid-Continent Baptist Bible College Mayfield KY 42066

MARKLE, LILLIE KAY MITCHELL, corrections ofcl.; b. Memphis, Oct. 25, 1948; d. Charles Leroy and Vera Kate (Barnard) Mitchell; B.S., U. Tenn., 1970; M.Ed., Memphis State U., 1971, postgrad., 1978—; postgrad. George Peabody/Vanderbilt U., 1979; m. Albert F. Markle, Jr., July 29, 1978; 1 son, Albert Franklin. Resident advisor, asst. dir. Allen & O'Hara, Inc. residence halls, Memphis, 1970-71; examiner test monitor testing div. Memphis State U., 1971; supr. counseling services John S. Wilder Youth Devel. Center, Tenn. Dept. Correction, Somerville, 1971—; hon. faculty social work suprs. program Lambuth Coll., 1973-74. Troop leader local council Girl Scouts U.S.A., 1968-72, sr. planning bd. advisor, 1972—; water safety and first aid instr. ARC. Recipient cert. of merit dept. sociology and anthropology U. Tenn., Martin, 1976, cert. Public Service Mgmt. Inst., 1977, Southeastern Correctional Mgmt. Tng. Council, 1975. Mem. Am. Correctional Assn., Tenn. Correctional Assn., Am. Personnel and Guidance Assn., Public Offender Counselor Assn., Delta Region Assn. for Problem Children (dir.), Kappa Delta Pi, Kappa Kappa Gamma Alumnae, Pickwick Sailing Assn. Methodist. Co-author mag. article. Home: PO Box 333 Somerville TN 38068 Office: PO Drawer A Somerville TN 38068

MARKLEY, ANNE MARIE, pub. co. exec.; b. Greenwich, Conn., June 16, 1946; d. Michael John and May (DeCarlo) Guerrieri; A.A., Mitchell Coll., 1967; student Emerson Coll., 1967-68; B.A., U. Denver, 1969, M.A., 1971; m. Jonathan Louis Markley, June 9, 1971. Speech/lang. pathologist Project Headstart, Denver, 1970; chief speech pathology and audiology Spalding Rehab. Center, Denver, 1971-72; speech pathologist Brown Schs. for Exceptional Children, Austin, Tex., 1972—; speech/lang. pathologist Austin Ind. Sch. Dist., Early Childhood Project, 1973-75; early childhood cons. Region XIII, Edn. Service Center, Austin, 1975-76; editor Learning Concepts Inc., Austin, 1976-77; acquisitions mgr. in Austin for Teaching Resources Corp., Boston, 1978—; cons. ednl. agys. Women's Library Assn. fellow, 1969, Rehab. Services Adminstrn. fellow, 1970-71; cert. clin. competence, cert. tchr. Colo., Tex. Mem. Am. Speech-Lang. Hearing Assn., Tex. Speech and Hearing Assn., Am. Assn. on Mental Deficiency, Assn. for Severely Handicapped, Council for Exceptional Children. Editor: Universal Articulation Program, 1978; The Token Test for Children, 1979; Birth to Three Developmental Learning and the Handicapped Child, 1979; Birth to Three Developmental Scale, 1979.

MARKS, ALLEN PHILLIP, health planner, hosp. adminstr.; b. Indpls., Sept. 9, 1946; s. Harold Lewis and Shirley M.; B.A., Ind. U., 1969; M.H.A., U. Mich., 1971; M.S. in Systems Mgmt., U. So. Calif., 1975; m. Debra Nan Bletterman, Aug. 17, 1969; 1 dau., Erin Jennifer. Secondary/Tertiary planner N. Central Ga. Health Systems Agy., Atlanta, 1978—; guest lectr. health systems Ga. Inst. Tech., 1978—. Mem. program organizing com. Atlanta Spl. Olympics; co-chmn. track meet State of Ga. Spl. Olympics. Served with Med. Service Corps. U.S. Army, 1971-78. Decorated Army Commendation medal. Mem. Am. Coll. Hosp. Adminstr., Am. Hosp. Assn., Assn. Mil. Surgeons, Hosp. Mgmt. Systems Soc., Royal Soc. Health, Ga. Hosp. Assn., Am. Inst. for Decision Scis., Ops. Research Soc. Am., B'nai B'rith. Jewish. Home: 1280 Moores Mill Rd Atlanta GA 30327 Office: N Central Ga Health Systems Agy 1447 Peachtree St Atlanta GA 30309

MARKS, BILLY GUINN, lawyer; b. Nashville, June 3, 1941; s. J.B. and Hautense (Fisher) M.; B.S., U. Tenn., 1964, LL.B., 1967; m. Marion Connie Mullican, Dec. 18, 1965; children—Thomas Randall, Michael Akers, Emily Diane. Admitted to Tenn. bar, 1967; asso. firm Morton, Lewis & King, Knoxville, Tenn., 1967-70; individual practice law, McMinnville, Tenn., 1970—; asst. dist. atty., McMinnville, 1971-73; coprorate dir. Pedigo Devel. Co. Troop leader Boy Scouts Am., McMinnville, 1975-76; bd. dirs. Warren County (Tenn.) Cerebral Palsy Soc., 1976-77. Mem. Am., Tenn. (ho. of dels. 1973-76) bar assns., Nat. Dist. Attys. Assn., Comml. Law League Am., Am. Trial Lawyers Assn., U. Tenn. Alumni Assn. (pres. Warren County chpt. 1974), Omicron Delta Kappa, Phi Delta Phi (sec. 1965). Mem. Chs. of Christ. Clubs Lions (sec. 1972), Jaycees (Knoxville and McMinnville chpts.). Home: 704 Sunset Dr McMinnville TN 37110 Office: 114 N College St McMinnville TN 37110

MARKS, CHARLES, surgeon, educator; b. nr. Kiev, Ukraine, USSR, Jan. 28, 1922; s. Abe and Sonia (Beck) M.; came to U.S., 1963; naturalized, 1968; M.D., U. Cape Town Med. Sch., 1945; M.S., Marquette U., Milw., 1956; Ph.D., Tulane U., 1973; m. Joyce Wernick, Dec. 11, 1949; children—Malcolm, Peter, Ian, Anthony. Intern, Groote Schuur Hosp., Cape Town, S.Africa, 1946, resident, 1947-49; resident Royal Coll. Surgeons affiliated hosps., Guys Hosp., London, 1950-53; cons. surgeon, Salisbury, Rhodesia, 1953-63; asso. prof. surgery Marquette U. Med. Sch., Milw., 1963-67; dir. surgery Mt. Sinai Hosp., Cleve., 1967-71, asso. clin. prof. surgery Case Western Res. U. Med. Sch., Cleve., 1967-71; prof. surgery La. State U. Med. Sch., New Orleans, 1971—; surgeon Charity Hosp., New Orleans, 1971—, VA Hosp., 1971—, Touro Hosp., 1971—, Hotel Dieu Hosp., 1971—. Named Hunterian Prof., Royal Coll. Surgeons Eng., 1956, Clin. Tchr. of Year, Aesculapian Honor Soc., 1973, 74, 77. Fellow A.C.S., Am. Coll. Cardiology, Royal Coll. Surgeons Eng., Royal Coll. Physicians Edinburgh (hon.), Am. Coll. Chest Physicians, Royal Soc. Medicine; mem. Phi Delta Epsilon. Clubs: New Orleans Lawn Tennis, Cleve. Racquet. Author: Applied Surgical Anatomy, 1972; The Portal Venous System, 1973; A Surgeons World, 1972; Carcinoid Tumors, 1979. Home: 1680 State St New Orleans LA 70118

MARKS, ELIZABETH ANN, advt. agy. exec.; b. Duluth, Minn., Aug. 9, 1950; d. George Meyers and Nancy (Starrett) Marks; student Columbia Coll., 1968-70; B.S., U. S.C., 1972. Art dir. Bob Alexander & Assos., Columbia, S.C., 1971-73; creative dir. Bob Hickman & Assos., Columbia, 1973-74; pres. The Marks Agy., Columbia, 1975-76; pres., creative dir. Elizabeth Marks & Assos., Inc., Columbia, 1976—. Bd. dirs. Moving S. Dance Co., 1979-81. Recipient Internat. Newspaper Execs. award for excellence in newspaper design, 1973; Printing Inst. of Carolinas 1st pl. for brochure design, 1974; Columbia Ad Club silver award of excellence for letterhead design, 1977; Columbia Communicating Arts Soc. silver citation, 1977; Art Direction Mag. Creativity 1975, 76, 77, 78; comml. named to 100 Best IV Commls., Advt. Age. 1976. Mem. Greater Columbia C. of C. Club: Columbia Ad (bd. dirs. 1978-82, pres. elect 1981). Home: 546 Spindrift Ln Columbia SC 29209 Office: 2700 Middleburg Dr Suite 201 Columbia SC 29204

MARKS, HENRY MORTIMER, III, truck dealership exec.; b. Richmond County, Ga., May 15, 1938; s. Henry Mortimer and Virginia (Clark) M.; student Washington and Lee Coll., 1956-59; B.B.A., U. Ga., 1960; m. Anna Augusta Dunbar, Dec. 18, 1977. Vice pres. Marks Surg. Supplies, Augusta, Ga., 1962-66, pres., 1966-70; br. mgr. Owens Minor and Bodeker, Richmond, Va., 1971-76, regional mgr., v.p., 1976-78; pres. Marks GMC Trucks Inc., Augusta, 1978—. Bd. dirs. Boy Scouts Am., 1968-72. Served with U.S. Army, 1960-62. Mem. Nat. Automobile Dealers Assn., Ga. Truck Dealers Assn. Presbyterian. Clubs: Augusta Country, Kiwanis (dir. 1970-72), Pinnacle. Home: 2735 Walton Way Augusta GA 30907 Office: 1269 Gordon Hwy Augusta GA 30904

MARKS, HENRY SEYMOUR, historian, educator; b. Greensboro, N.C., May 26, 1933; s. Benjamin and Florence (Hirsh) M.; B.B.A. in Mgmt. U. Miami (Fla.), 1955, M.A. in History (Food Fair Found. fellow), 1956; postgrad. U. Ala. 1960-61, 62-64; m. Marsha Kass, June 8, 1965; 1 dau., Barbara Carol. Faculty, U. Miami (Fla.), 1955-56, Jacksonville (Ala.) State Coll., 1958-60, U. Ala., 1960-61, Florence (Ala.) State Coll. 1961-62, U. Ala., Huntsville, 1964-68, Ala. A. & M. Coll. 1968-69. Lectr. ednl subjects; judge social sci. fairs, Ala. Co-founder, 1st pres. so. region Popular Culture Assn. of South, also mem. nat. adv. council. Mem. Am., Ala., So., Fla. hist. assns., Orgn. Am. Historians, Huntsville Hist. Soc., Hist. Assn. S. Fla., Hakluyt Soc., Am. Soc. Pub. Adminstrn., Phi Alpha Theta, Phi Delta Kappa. Jewish (past pres. temple brotherhood). Rotarian. Author: The Failure of the United States to Maintain the Independence of Korea and the Effect of the Failure upon Americans in Korea; Who Was Who in Alabama; Who Was Who in Florida; co-author: Rivers of Florida. Contbr. book reviews and abstracts to Huntsville Times and numerous publs. in field. Home: 405 Homewood Dr Huntsville AL 35801 Office: 301 Terry-Hutchens Bldg 102 Clinton Ave W Huntsville AL 35801

MARKS, HERBERT LEE, SR., elec. engr.; b. Alexandria, Va., Oct. 5, 1949; s. Herbert Jasper and Elizabeth Lucille (Winsatt) M.; B.S. in Elec. Engring., N.C. State U., 1975; m. Sharon Ann Spillman, June 12, 1970; one son, Herbert Lee. Project design engr. Naval Surface Weapons Center, Topside Analysis Branch, Dahlgren, Va., 1973—. Mem. King George County Spl. Edn. Adv. Com. Active Boy Scouts Am. Mem. N.C. Vets. Assn., Va. Jaycees (exec. com., program mgr. for community involvement, Luther Lee Allison award 1979), King George Jaycees (past pres., Officer of Yr. award 1978, Keyman award 1979). Baptist. Home: Route 2 55 Willow Tree Ln King George VA 22485 Office: NSWC/DL N-32 Dahlgren VA 22448

MARKS, JAMES JOHN, restaurateur, developer; b. Chgo., Aug. 23, 1911; s. Nicholas John and Stella (Koufoyiani) M.; B.S., U. Mich., 1936; m. Christine Constance Tampary, Nov. 11, 1939; children—Lianna Sandra, James John. Forestry technician U.S. Forestry Service, Ava, Mo., 1934; forest supr. Mich. Conservation Dept., Lansing, 1934-35; cons. forester, Ann Arbor, Mich., 1936-37; owner Martine's Restaurant, Pensacola, Fla., 1942—, Martine's Ice Cream Co., Pensacola, 1942—; pres. Esquire House, Inc., Warrington, Fla., 1934—, Martine's Corp., Pensacola, 1947—, Marwood Motors, Inc., Pensacola, 1955—, Ky. Fried Chicken, Biloxi and Gulfport, Inc., Miss., 1964—, Martines Ky. Fried Chicken Corp., 1964—, New Orleans, 1967—, Col. Sander's Ky. Fried Chicken Corp., Martine's KFC Corp., 1970; sec.-treas. Circle Sanitation, Pensacola, 1959—. Mem. adv. bd. Fla. Hotel and Restaurant Commn., 1961-62; mem. bd. Fla. Hospitality Edn. Program, 1962-63; chmn., pres. Fla. Tourism Council, 1962-63; mem. Fla. Council of 100, 1963—, mem. exec. com. Mem. Fla. Endowment of the Humanities; council advisers U. West Fla.; charter trustee Bapt. Hosp. Health Care Found.; bd. dirs. U. West Fla. Found., 1977—. Served to comdr. USNR, 1937-45. Named Outstanding Fla. Restaurateur, 1964. Mem. Am. Restaurants Hall of Fame, 1961. Paul Harris fellow Rotary Internat. Mem. Nat., Fla. (pres. 1961-62) restaurant assns., Sales Execs. Club. Mem. Hellenic Orthodox Ch. Rotarian (past local pres.). Clubs: Toastmasters; Mobile Country, Pensacola Country. Home: 4002 Marlane Dr Pensacola FL 32506 Office: 4101 Mobile Hwy Pensacola FL 32506

MARKS, JOHN COURTNEY, health systems engr.; b. Harrisburg, Pa., Mar. 1, 1924; s. Courtney B. and Muriel O. (Michael) M.; B.S. in Econs., Villanova U., 1950; B.S. in Bgmt. Engring., U. Scranton, 1953; m. Henrietta Horton, Sept. 25, 1975; children—Barbara, Lynn,

Michael, Paul, Debbie. Asst. chief engr. Air Pollution Control Dist., Louisville, Ky., 1953-56; chief engr. Louisville Med. Center, 1956-63; research engr. Am. Air Filter Co., Inc., Louisville, 1963-67; research engr. Kentec Labs., Louisville, 1967-69; systems engr. Humana, Inc., Louisville, 1969-73; systems engring. cons. Sts. Mary and Elizabeth Hosp., Louisville, 1974-76; adminstr. Shalomwald Hosp., LaGrange, Ky., 1976-77; mgr. support systems Ky. Health Systems Agy., Louisville, 1974-79; mgmt. engr. Bowling Green (Ky.) Med. Center, 1979; instr. systems design Bellarmine Coll., Louisville, 1975; cons. USPHS, Louisville, 1955, Battelle Meml. Inst., Louisville, 1953-55. Mem. Bd. Appeals Jefferson County Bldg. Dept., Louisville, 1957-63, Met. Planning Council, Louisville, 1958. Served with U.S. Army, 1942-44. Recipient Service award Air Pollution Control Assn., 1960. Mem. Am. Soc. Engring. Edn., Nat. Assn. of Power Engrs. (pres. 1958-59), Louisville Engring. and Sci. Council (pres. 1960-61), Hosp. Mgmt. Systems Soc., Am. Assn. for Comprehensive Health Planning, Am. Meteorol. Soc. Contbr. articles on environ. health to profl. jours.; editor Hosp. Environ. Service Guide Humana, Inc., 1972, Hosp. Disaster Program Manuals, 1971-72. Home: Colony Apts M-3 1040 Shive Ln Bowling Green KY 42101 Office: 250 Park St Bowling Green KY 42101

MARKS, MARSHA KASS, historian, educator; b. N.Y.C., May 6, 1935; d. Aaron Z. and Edith (Malkin) Kass; B.A., Hunter Coll., 1956; M.A. (Brinton fellow, Univ. fellow), Yale, 1957, postgrad., 1957-59; m. Henry Seymour Marks, June 8, 1965; 1 dau., Barbara Carol. Mem. faculty Ga. State Coll., Atlanta, 1960-65, Calhoun Jr. Coll., Decatur, Ala., 1965-67; mem. faculty history, Ala. A. and M. U., Normal, 1967—, asst. prof., 1967-79, asso. prof., 1979—. Mem. So. Hist. Assn. (mem. steering com. caucus of women in history 1971-72), Am., Fla., Ala., Huntsville hist. assns., Hist. Assn. of So. Fla., Hakluyt Soc., Orgn. Am. Historians, Am. Studies Assn., Assn. Social and Behavioral Scientists, Western Social Studies Assn., Popular Culture Assn. Phi Beta Kappa, Phi Alpha Theta, Sigma Tau Delta, Phi Sigma Sigma. Jewish religion. Club: Hadassah. Contbr. articles to profl. jours. Home: 405 Homewood Dr S W Huntsville AL 35801 Office: Alabama A and M University Normal AL 35762

MARKS, MEYER BENJAMIN, pediatric allergist; b. Chgo., Feb. 16, 1907; s. Simon and Rose (Block) M.; B.S., U. Ill., 1929, M.D., 1933, M.S., 1934; m. Golda A. Nathan, Sept. 27, 1932; children—Linda, Stephen. Intern Cook County Hosp., 1934-35, resident, 1935-36; practice medicine specializing in pediatrics, 1937-57; cons. pediatric allergist Mt. Sinai Med. Center, Miami Beach; dir. pediatric allergy clinic Jackson Meml. Hosp.; pediatric allergy and gen. allergy, 1957—; chief med. officer Kraver Inst. for Asthmatic Children, North Miami Beach; clin. prof. pediatrics U. Miami Sch. Medicine, also chief div. pediatric allergy. Hon. pres. med. div., Southeastern div. Am. Friends Hebrew U. Pres. Asso. Convalescent Homes and Hosp. for Asthmatic Children, 1971, Kraver Inst. Asthmatic Children, 1978. Bela Schick Meml. lectr., Paris, France, 1974; guest essayist Am. Assn. Orthodontists, Washington, 1979. Diplomate in pediatric allergy Am. Bd. Pediatrics, Am. Bd. Allergy and Immunology. Fellow Am. Acad. Pediatrics (silver award 1975, bronze award 1977), Am. Coll. Allergists (award of merit 1977, Fellow Disting. award 1979), Am. Acad. Allergy; mem. AMA (cert. of merit), Fla., Dade County med. assns., Fla., Miami (pres. 1954-55) pediatric socs., Fla. Allergy Soc. (pres. 1970), Sigma Xi. Jewish. Contbr. articles to med. books and jours. Home: 105 E San Marino Dr Miami Beach FL 33139 Office: 333 Arthur Godfrey Rd Miami Beach FL 33140

MARKS, WALTER FLEMMING, JR., printing co. exec.; b. Greensboro, N.C., Sept. 9, 1946; s. Walter Flemming and Elaine W. M.; B.A. Wofford Coll., 1969; m. Sara Lynn Peeler, Sept. 8, 1973. Vice pres., gen. mgr. Williams Printing Co. div. Craftsman Graphics Co., Spartanburg, S.C., 1969-73; v.p. mktg. Interstate Graphics Co., Charlotte, N.C., 1974-78; exec. v.p. Proctor Press, Dallas, 1978-80; sales mgr. State Printing Co., Columbia, S.C., 1980—; lectr. printing sales Central Piedmont Coll., 1977; lectr. in sales and sales mgmt. J. C. Smith U., 1977, mem. advisory bd. Bus. Sch., 1977; mem. adv. com. Spartanburg Tech. Printing Pubs., 1972-73. Mem. Wofford Coll. Alumni Bd., 1972-74; chmn. printing div. United Way, Charlotte, 1975. Served to 1st lt. U.S. Army, 1969-75. Recipient United Way award, 1975. Mem. Charlotte Sales Mktg. Exec. Club. Methodist. Club: Rotary. Developer curriculum for sales course Central Piedmont Community Coll., 1977. Office: 1305 Sumter St Columbia SC 29204

MARKWALDER, WINSTON ERNEST, educator; b. Talmage, Nebr., Mar. 10, 1923; s. Ernest Alfred and Mary Angeles (Toole) M.; A.B., Drake U., Des Moines, 1947; Ph.D., U. Minn., 1973; m. Terry Rose Lemberg, Sept. 16, 1946; children—James, Terry Ellen, Joy, Matthew, Margaret, Elizabeth, Thomas. Tchr., Iowa and Minn., 1947-48, 53-69; with Daytons, dept. store, Mpls., 1948-53; instr. U. Minn., 1971; mem. faculty U. So. Miss., Hattiesburg, 1971-76, asso. prof. spl. edn., 1977-79; coordinator spl. edn. programs Gulf Coast Regional Campus, U. So. Miss., Long Beach, 1979—; chmn. spl. edn. program La. Tech. U., Ruston, 1976-77; mem. Gov. Miss. Adv. Com. Educating Gifted, 1974-76; dir. So. High Ability Resource Program, 1974-76, La. Adv. Com. Gifted Edn., 1976-77; cons. in field. Served with USAAF, 1942-43. Fellow U.S. Office Edn., 1969-71; recipient Excellence in Teaching award U. So. Miss., 1975. Mem. Am. Assn. Mental Deficiency, Am. Ednl. Research Assn., Council Exceptional Children, Assn. for Gifted, Mid South Ednl. Research Assn., Phi Delta Kappa, Sigma Alpha Epsilon. Roman Catholic. Club: Civitan. Author publs. in field. Home: 2012 W 2d St Apt 1E Long Beach MS 39560 Office: U So Miss Gulf Coast Regional Campus Long Beach MS 39560

MARKWELL, DICK R(OBERT), chemist; b. Muskogee, Okla., Feb. 20, 1925; s. Alex J. and May (Albright) M.; B.S., Wichita State U., 1948, M.S., 1950; Ph.D., U. Wis., 1956; m. Virginia Ann Gass, Aug. 28, 1949; children—Steven R., Scot L., Eric R., Cheryl F. Commd. 2d lt. U.S. Army, 1951, ret. lt. col., 1967, with Office Chief Research and Devel.; asso. prof. chemistry San Antonio Coll., 1967-74; chemist Corpus Christi Dept. Health, 1975-77; supr. chemistry sect. lab. div. San Antonio Met. Health Dist., 1977—. Served with USMC, 1942-45. Mem. Am. Chem. Soc., Sigma Xi. Home: 1406 Haskin Dr San Antonio TX 78209

MARLER, CHARLES HERBERT, journalist, educator; b. Garfield, Ark., Apr. 13, 1933; s. William Owen and Velma Valentine (Poe) M.; A.B., Abilene Christian U., 1955, M.A., 1968; Ph.D., U. Mo., 1974; m. Peggy Lucille Gambill, Dec. 30, 1954; children—David Owen, Todd Alan, Scott Ladd. Asst. dir. publicity Abilene (Tex.) Christian U., 1955-56, sports info. dir., 1958-63, asso. dir. devel., 1963-64, dir. info. and publs., 1964-71, prof. communications, 1974—, editor Horizons mag., 1963-71; publicity dir. Gulf Coast Conf., 1955-56, U.S. Women's Olympic Track and Field Trials, 1960, Pecan Bowl, 1964-65; sports newscaster Sta. KWKC, Abilene, Tex.; news editor Gospel Adv., Nashville, 1978—. Scoutmaster Boy Scouts Am. Served with U.S. Army, 1956-57. Recipient awards for outstanding press brochures Football Writers Assn. Am., 1963, U.S. Basketball Writers Assn., 1962, 63; pub. affairs award Newsweek, 1967; mag. improvement award Time-Life, 1966; 20th Century Christian Mag. Journalism award, 1968; publs. leadership award Am. Coll. Pub. Relations Assn., 1969; yearbook writing award W. Tex. Hist. Assn., 1972; Clinton H. Denman Freedom of Info. award U. Mo. Freedom of Info. Center, 1974; Frank Luther Mott grad. hist. research fellow, 1972-74. Mem. Soc. Profl. Journalists, Assn. Edn. in Journalism, Nat. Council Coll. Publs. Advisers, W. Tex. Hist. Assn., Tex. Journalism Edn. Council, Kappa Tau Alpha. Mem. Chs. of Christ. Home: 818 Radford Dr Abilene TX 79601 Office: ACU Sta Box 7618 Abilene TX 79699

MARLER, EARL ANTHONY, JR., savs. and loan assn. exec.; b. Chattanooga, Nov. 6, 1936; s. Earl Anthony and Mildred M. (Woodlee) M.; B.S., U. Tenn., Chattanooga, 1958, M.B.A., 1963; Advanced Certificate, Am. Inst. Banking, Chattanooga, 1965; grad. Stonier Grad. Sch. Banking, Rutgers, N.J., 1971; m. Carol Patterson, Apr. 11, 1957; children—Margaret, Julie, Sarah. With Hamilton Nat. Bank, Chattanooga, 1954-78, asst. v.p., 1964-69, v.p., 1969-72, sr. v.p., 1973-76; sr. v.p. First Tenn. Nat. Bank, 1976-78; asst. to pres. Chattanooga Fed. Savs. & Loan Assn., 1978—; Am. Inst. Banking instr. Chattanooga State Tech. Coll., 1975—; mem. faculty Tenn. Bankers Assn., 1976—. Vice pres. Cherokee council Boy Scouts Am.; mem. Indsl. Com. of 100, Chattanooga, 1974—; mem. Big Bros. of Chattanooga, 1971—; chmn. bd. dirs. YMCA, Chattanooga, 1975-76; chmn. deacons Duncan Park Baptist Ch., Chattanooga, 1974-75, mem. Christian Radio Fellowship, 1974—, pres., 1978—; mem. Bethel Bible Sch. Bd.; vice chmn. United Fund; mem. athletic com. U. Tenn., Chattanooga. Mem. Am. Inst. Banking (nat. officer 1968-73), Greater Chattanooga C. of C., U. Tenn. at Chattanooga Alumni Assn. (pres. 1979-80), U. Tenn. Alumni Assn. (gov.), Pi Gamma Mu, Sigma Chi. Republican. Clubs: Lions (pres. 1965-66), Kiwanis, Chattanooga Track (charter pres. 1972-73). Home: 111 Ridgeside Rd Chattanooga TN 37411 Office: 701 Market St Chattanooga TN 37411

MARLEY, WILLIAM FRANKLIN, JR., metallurgist; b. Norfolk, Va., Aug. 23, 1941; s. William Franklin and Ila Bernice (Harrell) M.; A.A., Frederick Coll., 1961; B.S., Va. Poly. Inst., 1964; m. Margaret Shawn Rowe, July 24, 1966; 1 son, Brian Lee. Metallurgist, U.S. Army Fgn. Sci. and Tech. Center, Charlottesville, Va., 1969—. Served to capt. USAF, 1964-68. Recipient U.S. Army Sustained Superior Performance award, 1974. Mem. Am. Soc. Metals, Am. Powder Metallurgy Inst., Sigma Gamma Epsilon, Alpha Sigma Mu. Club: Ruritan Nat. Home: Route 1 Box 116 North Garden VA 22959 Office: 220 7th St Charlottesville VA 22901

MARLOW, BILLY HOWARD, chemist; b. Rogers, Ark., Sept. 6, 1941; s. Willard Howard and Nadine Ethyl (Brooks) M.; B.S. in Chemistry, U. Ark., 1964; m. Marjorie Stockdale, July 15, 1967; children—Donna Marie, William Howard. Research chemist animal sci. dept. U. Ark., Fayetteville, 1964-66; research chemist Escambia Chem. Corp., Pensacola, Fla., 1966-68; analytical chemist Kaiser Agrl. Chems., Savannah, Ga., 1968-76, supr. quality control lab., 1976—. Past chmn. chemistry sect. Savannah Sci. Seminar. Mem. Internat. Mgmt. Council (past com. mem.), Am. Chem. Soc., Alpha Chi Sigma. Mem. Ch. of the Nazarene. Home: Rural Route 1 Box 263C Savannah GA 31401 Office: PO Box 246 Savannah GA 31402

MARLOW, H(OBSON) MCKINLEY, lawyer; b. Cookeville, Tenn., Sept. 20, 1931; s. H.M. and Birtha (Bryant) M.; B.S., Tenn. Tech. U., 1954; J.D., Vanderbilt U., 1957; m. Dorothy Fay Teal, June 18, 1960; children—Darryl McKinley, Stephen Teal, Eric Martin. Admitted to Tenn. bar, 1957; practiced in Nashville, 1957—; pres. Motivation Mgmt. Inc., Image Pub. Co., Ashwood Music Co.; treas. Music Industries Corp. Mem. Am. (copyright com.), Nashville bar assns., Bar Assn. Tenn. Mason (Shriner). Author: ABC's of Copyright Law for Songwriters, 1960. Home: Lynn Dr Nashville TN 37211 Office: Parkway Towers Nashville TN 37219

MARONEY, EDGAR ERNST, county adminstr.; b. Germany, Sept. 13, 1938; came to U.S., 1948, naturalized, 1951; s. Edward Arthur and Renate Elizabeth M.; B.A. in Bus. Adminstrn., U. New Haven, also B.A. in Public Adminstrn.; M.A. in Govt., Trinity Coll.; M.S. in Urban Affairs, Yale U.; m. Delores Regina, Feb. 15, 1961; children—Edward, Michele, Robert. Adminstrv. asst. New Haven Dept. Adminstrn., 1963-65, mgmt. analyst, 1965-67, asst. dir. adminstrn., 1967-69; town mgr. City of Plainville (Conn.), 1969-71; city mgr. City of Lexington (Ky.), 1971-72; chief bur. bur. intergovtl. relations, div. state planning Fla. Dept. Adminstrn., Tallahassee, 1972-75; county adminstr. County of Sarasota (Fla.), 1975—; instr. and lectr. various colls., univs. Bd. dirs. Benhaven Sch. for autistic and brain-damaged children; mem. Lexington-Fayette County (Fla.) Bd. Health; bd. dirs. Sarasota County Boys' Club. Served with USAF, 1957-61. Recipient Disting. Service award Plainville Jaycees, 1969, award for adminstrv. excellence Nat. Assn. Counties, 1977. Mem. Nat. Assn. County Ofcls., Internat. City Mgrs. Assn., Nat. League Cities, Am. Soc. Public Adminstrn., Am. Acad. Polit. and Social Sci., U.S. Conf. Mayors. Roman Catholic. Clubs: Yale, Ivy League, Elks. Office: PO Box 8 Sarasota FL 33578

MARPLE, NATHAN BOILEAU, IV, engring. research exec.; b. Portland, Oreg., Sept. 18, 1927; s. Nathan Boileau and Mildred (Fisher) M.; A.B., Kenyon Coll., 1943; B.S., Columbia U., 1951, M.S., 1952; m. Wanda Prokoby, July 19, 1969; children—Mark Schneider, Jeff Schneider. Mgr., Riverside Research Inst., N.Y.C., 1965-69, dir. radar div., 1969-73, asst. v.p. research, 1973—. Home: 1407 Potomac Dr Richardson TX 75081

MARPLES, DONALD ROYAL, physician; b. Furnas County, Nebr., Mar. 8, 1923; s. Frank and Nina Valentine (Davis) M.; B.A., U. Nebr., 1950, M.D., 1953; m. Mary Dell Hecox, Aug. 13, 1949; children—Jon, Gail D. Marples Meadows, Ruth C. Marples Dunnavant, Carole D. Rotating intern Bryan Meml. Hosp., Lincoln, Nebr., 1953-54; practice medicine specializing in family practice and indsl. medicine, Nelson, Nebr., 1954-61, Grant, Nebr., 1961-66, Longview, Tex., 1966—; pres. Don R. Marples, M.D., Profl. Assn., Longview, 1970—, Gregg Profl. Properties, Inc., Longview; mem. staff Good Shepherd Hosp., Longview, Tex. Served with U.S. Army, 1943-46. Diplomate Am. Bd. Family Practice. Fellow Am. Acad. of Family Physicians; mem. AMA, Tex. Med. Assn., Nebr. Med. Assn., Phi Chi. Methodist. Home: 1300 Greenbriar Dr Longview TX 75604 Office: 209 Pinetree Rd Longview TX 75604

MARQUART, BARBARA ANN, musician, educator; b. Dallas, Mar. 1, 1936; d. Ben Leslie and Rosa Bertha (Morris) Marquart; B.Mus., So. Methodist U., 1959, M.Mus., 1969. Organist Temple Emanuel, Dallas, 1959-77; tchr. music The Hockaday Sch., Dallas, 1959-62; organist, choirmaster St. Andrews Episcopal Ch., Ft. Worth, 1968—; adj. prof. organ dept. music So. Methodist U., 1972—; chmn. music commn. Episcopal Diocese of Dallas, 1979—. Mem. Am. Guild Organist (sub dean Dallas chpt. 1973-75, dean 1975-77, chmn. King of instruments recital series 1979—), Pi Kappa Lambda. Democrat. Office: Division of Music Southern Methodist University Dallas TX 75275

MARQUEZ-DIAZ, NESTOR, educator, lawyer; b. Caquas, P.R., Mar. 7, 1936; s. Mario and Angela (Diaz) M.-D.; B.S., U. P.R., 1955; M.A., Ind. U., 1956; Ph.D., U. Madrid, 1958; LL.B., Tulane U., 1961; children—Nestor II, Angela Teresa. Admitted to La. bar, 1961, N.Y. bar, 1975, Supreme Ct. bar, 1975; economist P.R. Treasury Dept., 1954-55; economist P.R. Econ. Devel. Adminstrn., 1956-59; lectr. Loyola U., New Orleans, 1959-61, co-dir. Inter-Am. Labor Mgmt. Center, 1961; partner firm Pilie, Nelson & Limes, New Orleans, 1961-62; prof. bus. adminstrn. Nicholls State Coll., Thibodaux, 1961-70; prof. bus. adminstrn. Tex. A & I U., Laredo, 1970-74; prof. bus. U. North Ala., Florence, 1976—; dir. Office Econ. and Legal Research for Continental and Overseas Ops. Econ. Devel. Adminstrn. P.R., 1974-75; dir. div. econs. and bus. adminstrn. Community Coll. Phila., 1975—; pvt. practice law, New Orleans, 1962-75, N.Y.C., and Phila., Ala., 1975—; sr. partner Marquez-Diaz & Parker, 1967-70; of counsel Stassen, Kostos & Mason, Phila., 1976—; legal and econ. cons.; asst. atty. gen. State of La. Vice pres. Inter-Am. Pub. Corp., New Orleans, 1961-62, Interam. Shipbldg. Corp., La. Rose, La., 1961-63; sec.-treas. All-state Marine & Investment Services, Inc., New Orleans; pres. Marquez-Diaz & Parker Arms Co. Lectr. L. P.R., 1958; tech. adviser to rector U. of Central Am., Managua, Nicaragua, 1961—; indsl. promotion and econ. devel. cons. AID, San Jose, Costa Rica, 1963; econs. cons., New Orleans, 1961—. Spl. agt. La. State Police; dep. sheriff Lafourche Parish; dep. policy insp., Nuevo Laredo, Mexico. Pres. New Orleans West Civic Assn. Vice pres. Spanish Am. Union of La., 1963. Chmn. Seven Eighty Niners Dem. Orgn., 1963; pres. Citizens for Democratic Action. Bd. dirs. U. Coahuila, Torreon, Mexico. Recipient Juarez award Govt. of Mex.; decorated Order of Quetzal medal (Guatemala), Order Isabel la Catolica (Spain). Mem. Am., La., Inter-Am. bar assns., Am. Econ. Assn., Nat. Planning Assn., Acad. Polit. Sci., Phi Alpha Delta, Phi Delta Gamma. Methodist. Clubs: Pass Christian Yacht; International House, New Orleans Press, Import-Export, Young Mens Business; Bayou Country. Author: An Analysis of the Banking System of Costa Rica, 1962; The Furniture Industry of Puerto Rico; Notes and Comments on the Ministry of Industry of Costa Rica; Foreign Capital and Its Role in Economic Development; LAFTA Aims and Achievements, 1973; Puerto Rico, A Study in Political Myths and Economic Realities, 1975. Home: PO Box 87 Killen AL 35645

MARQUIS, EUGENE LEROY, research engr., educator; b. Walker, Mo., June 28, 1926; s. James Winford and Marion Alice (Davis) M.; student S.W. Mo. State U., 1946; B.S. in Civil Engring., U. Mo., 1950, M.S., 1951; Ph.D., Tex. A&M U., 1974; m. Ellen Terry Hausman, Aug. 9, 1952; children—Marion Helen Marquis Poulain, Ellen Terry Marquis Massey, Helen Louise. Research asso. U. Mo., Columbia, 1950-51; design engr. Convair, Ft. Worth, 1951-52; Hazelet & Erdal, Cin., 1952-53, V.L. Beavers, San Antonio, 1953-54, Gullatt Lodal & Assos., San Antonio, 1954-57; partner Johnson & Marquis Engrs. and Consultants, San Antonio, 1957-70; asso. research engr. Tex. Transp. Inst., College Station, 1970—; lectr., asst. prof. civil engring. Coll. Engring., Tex. A&M U., College Station, 1973—; spl. cons. Kirby Forest Industries. Bd. dirs. Greater San Antonio YMCA, 1960-69, chmn. phys. edn. com., 1966-69; mem. ofcl. bd. St. Andrews Meth. Ch., 1957-66, chmn. evangelism commn., 1960-63; mem. ofcl. bd. A&M Meth. Ch., 1972-75, chmn. evangelism commn.; mem. ofcl. bd. A&M Wesley Found., 1974—, chmn. bldg. com.; bd. dirs. College Station United Fund, 1976-79, pres., 1977. Served with USN, 1944-46, 46-52. Registered profl. engr., Mo., Tex. Mem. Nat. Soc. Profl. Engrs., Tex. Soc. Profl. Engrs., ASCE (Arthur M. Wellington award 1977), Am. Concrete Inst. Cons. Engrs. Council, Sigma Xi, Sigma Nu. Clubs: Lions, Aggie, Masons, Royal Arch Masons, K.T., Shrine. Contbr. chpt. to book, articles to profl. jours.; condr. research oil spill booms and highway safety structures. Home: 1018 Guadalupe College Station TX 77840 Office: Civil Engineering Bldg Texas A&M U College Station TX 77843

MARR, GLENDA SUE, speech pathologist; b. Greenville, Tex., Nov. 7, 1938; d. Orville Glen and Sammie Marie (McKinney) Newell; student E.Tex. State U., 1956-57; B.S., Lamar U., 1971; M.A., Our Lady of the Lake U., 1978; m. Billy J. Marr, Dec. 30, 1956; children—Julie Diane, Kenneth Stephen. Stenographer, E.I. duPont de Nemours Co., Beaumont, Tex., 1967-68; clinician Sunnyside Speech and Hearing Center, Port Arthur, Tex., 1972; tchr. lang.-learning disabilities, speech therapist Holy Spirit Catholic Sch., San Antonio, 1972-74; speech, lang., hearing specialist Northside Ind. Sch. Dist., San Antonio, 1974—. Vol. tchr. Cerebral Palsy Center, Beaumont, 1969-70; vol. worker Public Health Well Baby Clinic, Beaumont, 1969-70. Mem. Am. Speech and Hearing Assn. (cert. clin. competence), Tex. Speech and Hearing Assn., San Antonio Speech and Hearing Assn., Assn. Children with Learning Disabilities, NEA, Tex. State Tchrs. Assn., Tex. Classroom Tchrs. Assn., Northside Ind. Tchrs. Assn., Phi Kappa Phi. Methodist. Home: 6307 Rue Sophie San Antonio TX 78238 Office: 519 Clearview St San Antonio TX 78228

MARR, PATRICIA ANN, counselor; b. New Orleans, May 27, 1946; d. Fred J. and Jewel (Fricke) Mauterer; B.S., Loyola U., La., 1977, M.Ed., 1979; m. Charles Chester Marr, June 15, 1965; children—Lisa Ann, Lori Ann. Tchr. lang. arts St. Agnes Sch., Jefferson, La., 1971-74; tchr. English, Our Lady of Divine Providence Sch., Metairie, La., 1974-77, adminstrv. team mem., 1977-78, counselor, 1977-78; counselor Resurrection of Our Lord Sch., New Orleans, 1978-79, St. Charles Parish Schs., Snellville, Ga., 1979-80, Gwinnett County Schs., Snellville, 1980—; mem. acad. evaluation team for sch. improvement program Archdiocese of New Orleans, Office of Edn., 1975-76, 78-79; guest counselor-tchr. Xavier U., 1978. Youth adv. Parkway Presbyn. Ch., 1976-77. Mem. Am. Personnel and Guidance Assn., La. Personnel and Guidance Assn., Am. Sch. Counselors Assn., La. Sch. Counselors Assn., Nat. Cath. Edn. Assn., Nat. Vocat. and Guidance Assn., La. Assn. for Religious and Value Issues in Counseling (v.p. elementary schs. 1977—), Assn. of Religious and Value Issues in Counseling. Presbyterian. Address: 3012 Overwood Ln Snellville GA 30278

MARR, PAULINE, dir. nursing services; b. Newport, N.H., Jan. 24, 1938; d. Bernard and Marie (Dodier) Racicot; R.N., Notre Dame de Lourdes Hosp., Manchester, N.H., 1959; B.S. in Nursing, SUNY, Binghamton, 1976; student Grad. Sch. Nursing Adminstrn. Syracuse U., 1976-77; m. Philip Marr, May 5, 1959; children—Richard, Glenn, Michele, Philip. Med.-surg. nurse Stamford (Conn.) Hosp., 1961-62; emergency room, obstetrical, med.-surg. nurse New Milford (Conn.) Hosp., 1963-71; ICU/CCU nurse Charles S. Wilson Hosp., Johnson City, N.Y., 1971-73, pulmonary nurse specialist, 1973-75; nursing supr. Binghamton (N.Y.) Gen. Hosp., 1975-76, instr. sch. nursing, 1976-77; instr. Daytona Beach (Fla.) Community Coll., 1977; asst. dir. nursing services Fish Meml. Hosp., New Smyrna Beach, Fla., 1978-79, div., 1979—. Cert. coronary care nurse, pulmonary nurse specialist. Mem. Fla. Soc. Nursing Service Adminstrs., Critical Care Nurses Assn., Am. Bus. Women's Assn. Roman Catholic. Home: 1 Waterberry Circle Rural Route 2 Ormond Beach FL 32074 Office: 401 Palmetto St New Smyrna Beach FL 32069

MARRA, DONALD JOHN, sales exec.; b. Newark, Sept. 25, 1945; s. Carmine N. and Anna (Gazzio) M.; ed. Paterson State Coll., 1963-66, Seton Hall Sch. Bus., 1978; mktg. coordinator asso. Research Inst. Am., 1979. Asst. to v.p. ops. natural gas div. Elizabethtown (N.J.) Gas Co., 1965, asst. to pres., 1965-66; salesman, dist. sales mgr. Mid Atlantic Red Devil, Inc., 1969-72, dist. sales mgr. Met. N.Y., 1976, So. sales mgr., Union, N.J., 1976—; v.p. S.E. Mktg. Co., Richmond, Va., 1972-75. Served with U.S. Army, 1966-68. Named Regional Man of Year, Red Devil, Inc., 1970-71, Co. Man of Year, 1972. Mem. Nat. Hardware Assn., Nat. Paint and Decorating

Assn. Home: 765 Argonne Rd NE Atlanta GA 30308 Office: 2400 Vauxhall Rd Union NJ 07083

MARRINSON, RALPH ALAN, health care facility adminstr.; b. Chgo., Feb. 26, 1940; s. George L. and Frieda E. Marrinson; B.S.C., Ohio U., 1962; M.B.A., Xavier U., 1964; m. Jeanine M. Duever, Jan. 14, 1967. Adminstrv. resident Louis A. Weiss Meml. Hosp., Chgo., 1963-64; asst. adminstr. Woodlawn Hosp., Chgo., 1964-66; pres., chief adminstrv. officer Manor Pines Convalescent Center, Independence Hall Retirement Center, Manor Oaks Hosp., Fort Lauderdale, Fla., 1966—. Bd. dirs. Broward County Center for the Blind; pres. Health Planning Council, United Srs. of Am., The Drummers, Ft. Lauderdale Symphony Assn., Service Agy. for Sr. Citizens. Mem. Nat. Assn. Bd. Examiners Nursing Home Adminstrs. (past pres.), Am. Coll. Nursing Home Adminstrs., Execs. Assn. Ft. Lauderdale (dir.). Club: Rotary (pres.). Office: 1701 NE 26th St Fort Lauderdale FL 33305

MARRS, RHEA JEAN TAYLOR, mfg. co. ofcl.; b. Portales, N.Mex., May 6, 1952; d. Otwell Cathey and Kathryn (Evans) Taylor; A.A., N.Mex. Jr. Coll., 1972; B.Bus. Edn., Eastern N.Mex. U., 1974, M.B.A., 1975; m. Robert Dee Marrs, Sept. 30, 1978. With Sears, Roebuck & Co., Lovington, N.Mex., 1970-72; sec. Police Dept Lovington, 1972; with Motor Vehicle Dept. Lovington, 1973; grad. asst. Eastern N.Mex. U., Portales, 1974, adminstrv. asst. Coll. Bus., 1974-75; sales trainee IBM, Amarillo, Tex., 1975, sales rep., Roswell, N.Mex., 1976, mktg. rep., Midland, Tex., 1977, Odessa, Tex., 1978—. Adv. com. vocat. office edn. dept. Goddard High Sch., Roswell, 1975-77. Named Outstanding Student in Bookkeeping, Lovington High Sch., 1970, Outstanding Student in Bus., 1974; Bus. and Profl. Women 29'ers Woman of the Year, 1975. Mem. Bus. and Profl. Women, 29'ers, Phi Gamma Nu, Phi Beta Lambda. Home: 1211 E Tate St Brownfield TX 79316 Office: PO Box 1890 Lubbock TX 79408

MARSDEN, ELIZABETH HARLOW, educator; b. Nashville, Mar. 17, 1923; d. Frank Ernest and Harriet Ellsworth (Rees) Harlow; Mus.B., U. Miami, 1944; M.A., Columbia, 1945; m. Edward Derwood Marsden, Dec. 23, 1946 (div. Jan. 1971); children—Elizabeth Rhys Marsden Marmion, Margaret Lee, Catherine Harlow Marsden Mayhew, Harriet Ann. Tchr., Southeastern La. Coll., 1945-47; asst. prof. music U. Miami, 1947-52; supr. music Penn Hills Sch., Pitts., 1954-59; tchr. piano, voice, Pitts., 1959-61; judge Music Educators Nat. Conf., Miami, 1953, Tampa, Fla., 1953; tchr. Dade County (Fla.) Schs., 1964, Brevard County (Fla.) Schs., 1966-72; minister of music Coral Way Presbyn. Ch., Miami, 1964-66, First Presbyn. Ch., Titusville, 1966-72; music cons. Marietta (Ga.) City Schs., 1972—. Lectr. U. South Fla., 1967-72, Rollins Coll., 1971, U. Ga., 1972—; condr. workshops, music programs for profl. assns., music tchrs., also coll. events; mem. Cobb County Symphony Guild; chmn. Cobb County Artist Series, Cobb County Arts Council, Cobb County Jr. League, Cobb County Parks and Recreation Bd. Mem. AAUP, AAUW, Am. Guild Organists, Music Educators Nat. Conf., NEA, Classroom Tchrs. Assn., Fla. Elementary Tchrs. Assn., Brevard Edn. Assn., Ga. Music Educators Assn. (chmn. 12th dist., mem. study com.), Ga. Assn. Curriculum and Instrnl. Suprs., Ga. Music Edn. Adminstrs. Assn. (pres., steering com. 1977-78, v.p. 1978-79), Brevard Music Edn. Assn. (v.p.), DAR, Internat. Platform Assn., Delta Kappa Gamma, Chi Omega, Sigma Alpha Iota. Clubs: College, Tuesday Music, Mt. Lebanon Women's (Pitts.); Coral Gables Garden, Flamingo Dinner. Home: 2345 Cobb Pkwy Apt L9 Smyrna GA 30080 Office: 145 Dodd St Box 1265 Marietta GA 30061

MARSDEN, ROBERT ALAN, data processing co. exec.; b. N.Y.C., Feb. 3, 1942; s. Frank and Maria (Radice) M.; B.S., Rider Coll., 1963; certificate of computer programming, Ft. Lauderdale Tech., 1969; m. Helen Coulter, Nov. 24, 1965; children—Lisa Marie, Lori Eden. Auditor, County Trust Co., White Plains, N.Y., 1965-68; night mgr. Mayhue's, Ft. Lauderdale, Fla., 1968-70; with Fla. Coast Banks, Inc., Pompano Beach, Fla., 1970—, exec. v.p. ops. group Fla. Coast Bank, 1979—, pres., chief exec. officer subs. FBC Systems, Inc., 1976—, dir., 1973—, also mem. mgmt. com., v.p., sr. ops. officer parent co., 1978—; mem. point of sale coordination com. Fla. Payment Systems, Inc.; mem. point of sale coordination com., dir. Fla. EFTS Inc., 1976—. Served with U.S. Army, 1963-65. Mem. Fla. Bankers Assn., Fla. Bankpac, Rider Coll. Alumni Assn. Democrat. Office: 1471 SW 12th Ave Pompano Beach FL 33060

MARSH, ELEANOR MILLER HACK (MRS. GARNETT S. MARSH), former social worker; b. Indpls., Mar. 23, 1913; d. Oren Stephen and Elizabeth (Miller) Hack; B.S., Butler U., 1934, M.S. in Edn., 1939; M.A. in Social Service, Ind. U., 1947; m. Garnett S. Marsh, Feb. 27, 1972. Elementary sch. tchr., Boggstown, Ind., 1935-39; probation officer Marion County Juvenile Ct., 1939-40, div. spl. services, 1940-42; case worker Children's Bur., Indpls., 1943; supr. med. care and eye treatment pub. assistance div. Ind. Dept. Pub. Welfare, 1944-52; dir. admissions and asst. to med. dir. Ind. U. Med. Center, Indpls., 1953-66; supr. field service sect., div. pub. assistance Ind. Dept. Pub. Welfare, 1966-72. Pres. Ind. Conf. Social Work, 1955, dir., 1952-55, 57-63; chmn. Com. Registration Social Workers, 1950-53; program chmn. Am. Pub. Welfare Assn. Central Regional Conf., 1973. Sec. Women's Aux. YMCA, Henderson County. Mem. Am. Pub. Welfare Assn. (Ind. membership chmn. 1952-55), Indpls. Social Workers Club (pres. 1951-53, chmn. legislative com., 1953-55, James L. Fieser award for distinguished service 1968), Henderson League Women Voters, Kappa Alpha Theta, Phi Kappa Phi, Kappa Delta Pi. Roman Catholic. Editor: Health and Welfare Legislative Information Service, 1949-52. Address: 924 N Main St Henderson KY 42420

MARSH, JOSEPH VIRGIL, research specialist; b. Winston-Salem, N.C., Apr. 28, 1952; s. Gilliam Hughes and Dovie Elizabeth (Watson) M.; student Surrey Community Coll., 1970-72; Coop. Engring. Program, U.S. Govt. Schs., Md., S.C., Washington, 1972-74. With Joint Armed Services Tech. Liaison, Washington, 1974-75; cons. U.S. Govt., 1975-76; corr., cons. individuals, bus. on tech. matters, Ararat, N.C., 1977—. Mem. Internat. Entrepreneurs Assn., VFW (hon.), Armed Forces Assn., Ind. Consultants Assn., Internat. Assn. Sci. Devel., Council Civilian Tech. Advisers. Republican. Address: PO Box 12 R 1 Ararat NC 27007

MARSH, MALCOLM ROY, JR., electronic engr.; b. Bedford, Va., Oct. 12, 1932; s. Malcolm Roy and Mildred (Overstreet) M.; B.E.E., U. Va., 1956; children—Lauranne Ashton, James Overstreet. Elec. engr. Sperry Piedmont, Inc., Charlottesville, Va., 1957-58, Martin Orlando Co., Orlando, Fla., 1958-60; pvt. practice electronic engring. cons., Orlando, 1960-79; electronic engring. cons. IBM Corp., Boca Raton, Fla., 1979—. Served with U.S. Army, 1958. Mem. IEEE. Methodist. Club: Moose. Home: 2609 Tradewinds Trail Orlando FL 32805 Office: 3456 NE 12th Terr Fort Lauderdale FL 33334

MARSH, WARNER GARLAND, civil engr., land surveyor; b. Richmond, Va., Mar. 9, 1924; s. Otis Summers and Mildred Eva (Brown) M.; student Internat. Corr. Schs., 1957; m. Merle Irwin, Jan. 25, 1947; children—Wayne S., Barry I., W. Guy. Chmn. bd., Marsh & Basgier, Inc., engrs., surveyors, planners, Virginia Beach, Va., 1969—. Served with USNR, 1942-45. Registered profl. engr., Va., Fla., N.C.; certified land surveyor, Va., Fla. Mem. ASCE, Nat. Soc. Profl. Engrs., Am. Congress Surveying Mapping, Va. Assn. Surveyors, Soc. Am. Mil. Engrs. Clubs: Norfolk Sports, Cavalier Golf. Home: 2805 N Kings Rd Virginia Beach VA 23452 Office: 1052 Lynnhaven Pkwy M & B Bldg 1 Virginia Beach VA 23456

MARSHALL, BRUCE, artist; b. Athens, Tex., Dec. 23, 1929; s. Lytton Boatner and Myrtis (Hoover) M.; student U. Ariz., 1950-52, (scholar) So. Ariz. Sch. Art, 1952-54, (scholar) Watercolor Guild, 1949-50; m. Ann Randolph Smith, Sept. 30, 1961; children—Susanne, Randolph, Cody. One person shows Tex. Capitol Rotunda, Austin, 1977, Panhandle-Plains Mus., Canyon, 1977, Mus. Big Bend, 1976, Chamizel Nat. Monument, 1977, Confederate Mus., Richmond, 1979, others; exhibited in group shows Smithsonian Instn., 1954, U. Tex., San Antonio, 1973, 74, 75; represented in permanent collection Nat. Inf. Mus., Fort Benning, Ga., U. Tex. Inst. Texan Cultures, San Antonio, Tex. Mil. Mus., Austin, San Jacinto Monument, The Alamo, 1st Cavalry Mus., Fort Hood, Tex. Created knight Peter II Yugoslavia; recipient Jefferson Davis medal UDC, 1976. Mem. Tex. Watercolor Soc., Southwestern Watercolor Soc., Tex. Fine Arts Assn., Co. Mil. Historians, Tex. State Hist. Assn., Former Tex. Rangers Assn., Sons Confederate Vets (past comdr.). Club: Headliners. Home: 903 Loop 360 South Austin TX 78746 Office: Westart PO Box 5512 Austin TX 78763

MARSHALL, DONALD BRUCE, lawyer; b. Pearsall, Tex., July 6, 1947; s. Donald and Dorothy Jane (Medders) M.; B.B.A., St. Edward's U., 1969; J.D., St. Mary's U., 1973; m. Barbara Darlene Browning, Dec. 31, 1976; children—Brittainy Yvonne, Don-Barron. Admitted to Tex. bar, 1973; trial atty. Eichelbaum & Sanders, San Antonio, 1974-76, LeLaurin, Adams, Eichelbaum & Sanders, San Antonio, 1976-77; pvt. gen. practice law, San Antonio, 1977—; instr. adult and continuing edn. San Antonio Coll., 1975—, Tex. Real Estate Commn., 1975—, Tex. Edn. Agy., 1975—; lectr. bus. law Trinity U., San Antonio, 1978—; chmn. bd. Dmarco Mortgage Co., 1975—. Mem. Am. Bar Assn., Tex. Bar Assn., San Antonio Bar Assn., San Antonio Trial Lawyers Assn. Office: 1214 Basse St San Antonio TX 78212

MARSHALL, DONALD IRVING, chem. engr.; b. Houston, Jan. 22, 1924; s. Elmer Daniel and Grace (Crossman) M.; B.S., Sam Houston State Coll., 1944; M.A., U. Tex., 1946, Ph.D., 1948; m. Elaine Ann Kautz, 1948; children—Eric Donald, Scott Alan, Todd Alden; m. 2d, Mary Penton, Feb. 24, 1973 (div. 1977). Devel. asso. plastics div. Union Carbide Corp., Bound Brook, N.J., 1948-58; mem. research staff, research leader Engring. Research Center Western Electric Co., Princeton, N.J., 1958-71, sr. staff devel. engr., Atlanta, 1971—. Com. chmn. George Washington council Boy Scouts Am., 1961. Trustee, treas. Plastics Inst. Am., 1967-72. Recipient Annual Tech. Writing award Western Electric Co., 1966. Mem. Soc. Plastics Engrs. (chmn. program com. elec. and electronics div. 1976, dir. 1976—), Am. Chem. Soc., Soc. Rheology, Sigma Xi. Editor: (Imrich Klein) Computer Programs for Plastics Engineers, 1968. Editorial adv. bd. Polymer Engring. and Sci., 1967-75. Home: 4112 Peachtree Dunwoody Rd Atlanta GA 30342 Office: 2000 NE Expressway Norcross GA 30071

MARSHALL, JOHN MCCLELLAN, judge, lawyer; b. Dallas, Oct. 9, 1943; s. Samuel Wilson, Jr. and Frances Louisa (McClellan) M.; B.A., Va. Mil. Inst., 1965; M.A. (NDEA fellow), Vanderbilt U., 1966; J.D., So. Methodist U. Sch. Law, 1975; m. Mary Lynn Graves, Dec. 28, 1966. Spl. instr. history Memphis State U., summer 1967; instr. history Va. Mil. Inst., 1968-69; research asso. Fla. Inst. Tech., 1970-71; tech. instr. Skylab Program, McDonnell Douglas Astronautical Co., Kennedy Space Center, Fla., 1971-73. judge Municipal Ct., Muenster, Tex. Served to capt. Va. Militia, 1968-69. Decorated officer Most venerable Order of Hosp. of St. John of Jerusalem in Brit. Realm. Mem. State Bar Tex., Am. Bar Assn., Dallas Bar Assn., Soc. of Cin. (founder, pres. Lone Star Assn. 1974-77), SAR (pres. Brevard, Fla. chpt. 1973, Dallas chpt. 1979), Sons Republic Tex., Va. Mil. Inst. Alumni Assn. (pres. N.Tex. chpt.), Phi Alpha Delta, Kappa Alpha. Episcopalian. Mason. Clubs: Rock Creek Barbecue, Dervish, Terpsichorean. Home: 3300 Daniels St Dallas TX 75205

MARSHALL, JOHN RICHARD, opera dir.; b. Schenectady, July 28, 1929; s. Abraham Lincoln and Edith Marion (Lambert) M.; B.A., U. Rochester (N.Y.), 1951; M.Mus., Ind. U., 1953, D.Mus., 1964; m. Jean Deresienski, June 20, 1953. Head opera and choral music U. Buffalo, 1959-62; head opera dept. Boston Conservatory, 1965-68; dir. New Eng. Regional Opera, 1967-76; gen. dir. Charlotte (N.C.) Opera Assn., 1976—; lectr. Longy Sch. Music, Cambridge, Mass., U. Mass., Boston. Served with AUS, 1954-56. Recipient award of merit Assn. Performing Arts; scholar Berkshire (Mass.) Music Center; fellow Harvard U. Inst. Arts Adminstrn. Mem. Nat. Opera Assn., OPERA Am., So. Opera Conf. (founder, pres. 1979—). Office: 110 E 7th St Charlotte NC 28202

MARSHALL, JOHN WEEKS, petroleum distbr.; b. Dallas, Nov. 28, 1933; s. John Walter and Helen Elizabeth M.; B.S. in Geology, So. Meth. U., 1956; postgrad. U. Colo., 1956; m. Sept. 22, 1956; children—Mark, Brent. Ter. mgr. Gulf Oil Corp., San Antonio, 1959-65; pres. Marshall Distbg. Co. Inc., Seguin, Tex., 1965—. Served to capt. USAF, 1956-59. Mem. Tex. Oil Marketers Assn., So. Meth. U. Alumni Assn. Methodist. Clubs: Rotary, Masons, Shriners, Elks. Office: Marshall Distbg Co Inc 2525 N Austin St Seguin TX 78155

MARSHALL, KEITH COOPER, performing arts dir.; b. New Orleans, Nov. 19, 1946; s. Harold Karin and Naomi Vernon (Damonte) M.; B.A., Yale U., 1968; B.Phil., Oxford (Eng.) U., 1970, D.Phil., 1978; postgrad. Courtauld Inst. Art, U. London, 1970-71. Owner, mgr. Downtown Gallery and Dixie Art Supplies, New Orleans, 1970—; founder, dir. Madewood Center Visual and Performing Arts, New Orleans, 1974—; lectr. Victoria and Albert Mus., London, 1971-74; vis. curator New Orleans Mus. Art, 1975. Rhodes scholar, 1968-71. Mem. New Orleans Bd. Trade, Thackeray Soc., Phi Beta Kappa. Republican. Episcopalian. Club: Round Table. Author: Jon McCrady: 1911-1968, 1975. Home: Madewood Plantation House Napoleonville LA 70390 Office: 530 Chartres St New Orleans LA 70130

MARSHALL, MARION AXELL, JR. (BUD), assn. exec.; b. Tucson, Dec. 10, 1942; s. Marion Axell and Barbara Hauser; A.A., Ranger Coll., 1963; B.B.A., Tex. Wesleyan Coll., 1966; m. Patricia Elaine Hall, Mar. 23, 1973; children—Brooke Shannon, Melissa Annette, Meegan Alaine. Sales rep. Crowell, Collier & McMillian and subs.'s, various cities, 1966, field mgr., 1966, nat. trainer, 1967-68, dist. sales mgr., 1969-70, asst. to pres., 1970-71; asst. to pres. and expansion dir. CIC (Cosmetics Internat. Corp.), Dallas, 1971-72; gen. sales mgr. Internat. Psycho-Cybernetics Corp., Dallas, 1973; spl. rep. U.S. C. of C., Dallas, 1974—, dist. membership mgr., 1974—; officer, dir. W.N.D. Inc., Dallas, 1978—; officer, dir. M.D. Labs., Inc., Dallas, Verarex Med. Corp., Dallas. Planning and zoning commr. City of Colleyville (Tex.), 1978—; mem. Conservative Caucus, Nat. Republican Congressional Com. Mem. Tex. Wesleyan Coll. Alumni Assn. (dir. 1978-79), U.S. C. of C., Citizens Choice, Colleyville C. fo C. Republican. Home: 1709 Avondale St Colleyville TX 76034 Office: 4835 LBJ Freeway Suite 750 Dallas TX 75234

MARSHALL, MARION HOWARD, household products mfg. co. exec.; b. Lima, Ohio, Oct. 17, 1937; s. Harry Lee and Melba Hale (Hardin) M.; B.Ch.E., Ohio State U., 1960; student U. Cin., 1964-69; m. Lynne Louise Feigh, Dec. 23, 1960; children—Judith Louise, Melba Anne, Joseph Lee, Jeffrey Lisle. Mech. planning mgr. Procter & Gamble Co., Cin., 1964-65, prodn. planning mgr., 1965-66, dentifrice mfg. mgr., 1966-67, warehouse and shipping distbn. mgr., 1967-68, pkg. soap and detergent mfg. brand mgr., 1968-70, personnel devel. mgr., Jackson, Tenn., 1970—; instr., Jackson State Community Coll., 1972—. Vol. club leader Young Life of West Tenn., 1971—; pres. bd. dirs. Jackson Mental Health Center; trustee Western Mental Health Inst. Served with U.S. Army, 1960-64. Mem. Jackson Area C. of C., Internat. Transactional Analysis Assn. Presbyterian. Club: 4-H (adult advisor, leader). Home: 333 Law Rd Jackson TN 38301 Office: 1306 Hwy 70 Bypass Jackson TN 38301

MARSHALL, MARY AYDELOTTE, state legislator; b. Cook County, Ill., June 14, 1921; d. John Andrew and Nell (Aydelotte) Rice; B.A. with highest honors, Swarthmore (Pa.) Coll., 1942; m. Roger Duryea Marshall, Mar. 3, 1944; children—Nell, Jenny, Alice. Economist anti-trust div. Justice Dept., Washington, 1942-46; mem. Va. Ho. of Dels., 1966-70, 72—, mem. coms. priveleges and elections, rds and internal nav., counties, cities and towns, health, welfare and instns.; mem. Fed. Council on aging, 1978—; chairperson Legis. Study Commn. on Needs of Elderly Virginians, 1973-78; mem. No. Va. Transp. Commn., 1974-80; mem. human services task force Nat. Conf. State Legislatures, intergovtl. relations com., 1974—; dir. Washington Met. Council of Govts., 1977-80; mem. Democratic State Central Com., 1976-78; pres. Va. Fedn. Dem. Women's Clubs, 1971-72; mem. task force on planning Pres.'s Com. on Mental Health, 1978—. Bd. dirs. Nat. Assn. Mental Health, 1972-78; pres. Va. Assn. Mental Health, 1972-78. Recipient numerous achievement awards: Va. Assn. Mental Health, No. Va. Assn. Mental Health, Va. Fedn. Bus. and Profl. Women's Clubs, Va. Assn. Ind. Retail Gasoline Dealers, No. Va. Altrusa No. Va. Retarded Citizens Assn., Arlington Edn. Assn., Arlington County Bd. Mem. Phi Beta Kappa. Congregationalist. Home: 2256 N Wakefield St Arlington VA 22207

MARSHALL, OSA WESLEY, III, psychol. counselor; b. Dallas, Jan. 12, 1952; s. Osa Wesley and Adelle Ellen (Chambers) M.; B.A. (Honors scholar), Southwestern U., 1974; M.S. in Counseling and Guidance (Honors scholar), East Tex. State U., 1975, also postgrad. studies; m. Emily Helen Spessard, May 28, 1973. Program dir. Radio Sta. KGVL, Greenville, Tex., 1974-75; counselor Girls Adventure Trails, Dallas, 1975-76 dir. psychol. counseling, 1977-78; now primary therapist Contemporary Health, Inc., Dallas; cons. in field. Active drive to register underprivileged voters, 1971-72, Faranthold for Gov. campaign, 1972; mem. various ad hoc coms. Tex. Dept. Mental Health and Mental Retardation, Tex. Dept. Pub. Welfare, Youth Services Div., Dallas Police Dept.; mem. exec. com. Substance Abuse Network of Dallas, Dallas Alcohol Assn. Recipient Alumni award Southwestern U., 1975. Mem. Am. Personnel and Guidance Assn., Assn. Specialists in Group Work, Mensa, Blue Key. Presbyterian. Contbr. to Tex. Jazz News, Buddy mag., Tex. Nickelodeon. Home: 6131 Victor St Dallas TX 75214 Office: 6003 Victor Dallas TX 75214

MARSHALL, RICHARD TREEGER, lawyer; b. N.Y.C., May 17, 1925; s. Edward and Sydney (Treeger) M.; student Queens Coll., 1942-43; B.S., Cornell U., 1948; LL.B., Yale, 1951; m. Dorothy M. Goodman, June 4, 1950 (dec. May 1978); children—Abigail Ruth, Daniel Brooks; m. 2d, Sylvia J. Kelley, June 10, 1979. Admitted to Tex. bar, 1952, since practiced in El Paso; asso. firm Fryer and Milstead, 1951-52; sr. partner Marshall and Wendorf, 1959-61. Instr. Am. govt. U. Tex., El Paso, 1961-62; lectr. legal seminars. Chmn. El Paso Vols. for Stevenson, 1956; co-chmn. Tex. Citizens for Kennedy, 1960; mem. Yale U. Alumni Bd., 1959-60; pres. El Paso Jewish Community Council, 1961-62. Served with Signal Corps, AUS, 1943-45; ETO. Fellow Am. Acad. Matrimonial Lawyers; mem. Am. Trial Lawyers Assn. (nat. sec. 1969-70), Tex. Civil Liberties Union (sr. legal counsel 1968-73), El Paso Trial Lawyers Assn. (pres. 1965-66), Am. Arbitration Assn. (panelist 1966—). Editor: El Paso Trial Lawyers Rev., 1973—. Contbr. numerous articles to legal jours. Home: 7133 El Cajon Dr El Paso TX 79912 Office: Marshall & Volk 1214 Montana Ave El Paso TX 79902

MARSHALL, ROBERT GORDON, civil engr.; b. Minden, W.Va., Aug. 28, 1922; s. Thomas Gordon and Luie Bessie (Butrick) M.; student U. Ala., 1946-48; B.C.E., Auburn U., 1950; postgrad. Rensselair Poly. Inst., Washington, 1963-65; M.S., George Washington U., 1972; m. Nina Jean Lawson, Dec. 28, 1946; children—Paul Gordon, Michelle Marie, Glynis Anne. Field engr. Fla. Hwy. Dept., Deland, 1950-53; office engr. firm Cleary Bros. Constrn. Co., West Palm Beach, Fla., 1953-54; staff engr. U.S. Army Engr. Research and Devel. Labs., Ft. Belvoir, Va., 1954-67; civil engr. U.S. Army Material Concepts Agy., Washington, 1969-71, sr. project officer, dir. research and devel., 1967-75, chief Spl. Projects Office, Installations and Services Directorate, Alexandria, Va., 1975—, mem. environ. quality com. U.S. Army Materiel Devel. and Readiness Command, 1975—. Served with C.E. AUS, 1942-46; ETO. Decorated Bronze Star medal; recipient Outstanding Performance awards, 1973, 74, 78, 79, Sustained Performance award, 1974. Registered profl. engr., Ala. Fellow ASCE; mem. Nat., Va. socs. of profl. engrs. Patentee in field. Home: 3308 Lilac Ln Alexandria VA 22308 Office: HDQRS US Army Materiel Devel and Readiness Command 5001 Eisenhower Ave Alexandria VA 22333

MARSHALL, ROBERT JAMES, physician, educator; b. No. Ireland, May 5, 1926; s. Robert James and Margaret (Robinson) M.; came to U.S. 1958, naturalized, 1972; M.B., Queen's U., Belfast, Ireland, 1948, B.Ch., 1948, B.A.O., 1948, M.D., 1952; m. Mabel M. Stevenson, Feb. 16, 1957; children—Stephen, Deirdre, Ian. Intern, Royal Victoria Hosp., Belfast, 1949; asst. lectr. in physiology and pathology Queen's U., 1950-51, tutor dept. medicine, 1951-57; Fulbright scholar, research fellow Melbourne (Australia) U., 1957-58; Edward Wilson meml. fellow Baker Inst., Alfred Hosp., Melbourne, 1957-58; research asso. dept. physiology Mayo Clinic, Rochester, Minn., 1958-61; asso. prof. medicine W. Va. U., 1961-63, prof. medicine, prof. physiology, 1963-76; clin. prof. medicine Marshall U., 1977—, W.Va. U., 1977—; cons. dept. cardiovascular medicine and vis. prof. Oxford (Eng.) U., 1974-75; chmn. cardiovascular study sect. USPHS, 1968-72; v.p. Am. Heart Assn., 1972-73; pres. W. Va. Heart Assn., 1968-69. Recipient Distinguished Service award Am. Heart Assn., 1973. Fellow Royal Coll. Physicians of Ireland (regional adv. for eastern U.S.A. 1977—), Royal Coll. Physicians, London, A.C.P., Am. Coll. Cardiology (gov. for W.Va. 1977—), Pembroke Coll., Oxford U.; mem. Am. Soc. Clin. Investigation, Am. Physiol. Soc., Assn. Univ. Cardiologists, Am. Fedn. Clin. Research, Soc. Exptl. Biology, Medicine. Presbyterian. Author: (with T. D. Darby) Shock: Pharmacological Principles in Treatment, 1966; (with J.T. Shepherd) Cardiac Function in Health and Disease, 1968. Home: 93 Camelot Dr Huntington WV 25701 Office: 1115 20th St Huntington WV 25703

MARSHALL, WALLACE, physician, surgeon, psychiatrist; b. Appleton, Wis., July 19, 1904; s. Victor F. and Fanny (Levy) M.; B.A., U. Wis., 1930; B.M., Northwestern U., 1932, M.D., 1933; m. Louise Marjorie Clayton, Aug. 14, 1953; 1 dau., Victoria Louise. Intern, Wesley Hosp., Wichita, Kan., 1932, Los Angeles County Gen. Hosp., 1932-33; pvt. practice medicine, Two Rivers, Wis., 1949-59, Watertown, Wis., 1959-61, Florala, Ala., 1961-62, Heflin, Ala., 1962, Anniston, Ala.; instr. physiol. chemistry, medicine U. Ala., 1936-37; asso. prof. physiol. chemistry Spring Hill Coll., 1947; lectr. sci. research St. Norbert Coll., 1953; fellow psychiatry La. State U.-Charity Hosp. of La., New Orleans, 1966-67; med. cons. to pharm. firms; prof. emeritus psychology Auburn U., Montgomery, 1971—; staff psychiatrist Bapt. Hosp., Montgomery, Montgomery; staff psychiatrist VA Hosp., Montgomery, 1973—, mem. vocat. rehab. counseling com., 1977—; psychiat. cons. State of Ala., 1978; mem. disability determination com. Vets. Assn., 1978. Recipient certificate of award Med. Econs., 1967. Fellow A.A.A.S., Am. Med. Writers Assn. (life), Miss. Valley Med. Soc. (life dir., Wis. v.p. 1959-61), Nat. Psychiat. Assn. (life), Royal Soc. Health, Acad. Psychosomatic Medicine; mem. Indian Assn. Dermatologists and Venereologists (life), Nat. Writers Club, Southeastern Psychiat. Soc., Am. Fedn. Clin. Research, AMA, Wis. (sec., program chmn. 5th councillor dist., 1956-57), Montgomery County med. socs., Med. Assn. State Ala., So. Med. Assn., Am. Acad. Gen. Practice (past chpt. pres.). Mason (32 deg., Shriner). Author: Noise of Great Waters (1st prize Am. Physicians Literary Guild), 1947; Essentials of Medical Research, 1953; Immunologic Psychiatry and Psychology, 1977. Asso. editor: Med. Times, 1943-63; cons. editor gen. practice of Med. Digest, 1957—; abstract editor Psychol. Reviews, 1938-40; book review editor Mississippi Valley Med. Jour., Clin. Medicine, 1959-61; hon. cons. editor Med. Digest, Bombay, India, 1960—. Contbr. numerous articles to med. and surg. jours. Discovered and produced microcirculatory constrictor from crude liver, Kutapressin, 1950; co-discoverer Marshall-White syndrome, 1965; originator theory of psychoimmunology. Address: 2326 Winchester Rd Montgomery AL 36106

MARSHALL, WILLIAM LEITCH, chemist; b. Columbia, S.C., Dec. 3, 1925; s. William Leitch and Georgia (Kittrell) M.; B.S., Clemson U., 1945; Ph.D., Ohio State U., 1949; m. Joanne Fox, Apr. 16, 1949; children—Nancy Diane, William Fox. Teaching asst. Clemson U., 1944-45, Ohio State U., 1945-46; Naval research fellow Ohio State U., 1947-49; mem. sr. research staff Oak Ridge Nat. Lab., 1949—, research group leader, 1957-75. Plenary lectr., mem. orgn. coms. internat. sci. congresses. Guggenheim fellow van der Waals Lab., U. Amsterdam, 1956-57. Mem. Am. Chem. Soc. (nat. council 1968—, nat. council com. chem. edn., 1970—, chmn. nat. subcom. on high sch. chem. edn. 1970-75, mem. nat. high sch. chemistry com. 1978—, nat. congl. sci. counselor 1974—, nat. com. tchr. tng. guidelines 1975-77, Charles Holmes Herty medal 1977), A.A.A.S., Geochem. Soc., Sci. Research Soc. Am., Sigma Xi (v.p. chpt. 1974-75), Tenn. Acad. Sci. (vis. scientist program 1975), Internat. Assn. for Properties of Steam (working group 1975—), Internat. Platform Assn., Phi Kappa Phi. Contbr. articles to profl. jours. Patentee in field. Home: 101 Oak Ln Oak Ridge TN 37830 Office: Chemistry Div Oak Ridge Nat Lab Oak Ridge TN 37830

MARSHALL, WILLIS HENRY, JR., psychiatrist; b. Covington, Ky., Nov. 28, 1936; s. Willis Henry and Pauline Elizabeth (Murphy) M.; A.B. cum laude, U. Evansville (Ind.), 1958; M.D., Ind. U., Indpls., 1961; m. Carolyn Mae Kowalski, May 5, 1962; children—Louann Lorinda, John Willis. Intern, Detroit Meml. Hosp., 1961-62; resident in psychiatry Mental Health Inst., Cherokee, Iowa, 1965-67, 1969-70; service unit dir. Indian Health Center, USPHS, Ft. Totten, N.D., 1962-64, staff physician Sioux Sanitorium, Rapid City, S.D., 1964-65; staff psychiatrist Mental Health Inst., Cherokee, 1967-69; staff psychiatrist Mental Health Center, Muskegon, Mich., 1970-71; staff psychiatrist Ottawa County Mental Health Center, Grand Haven, Mich., 1971-73; cons. Allegan County (Mich.), Mental Health Center, Allegan, 1973; practice medicine specializing in psychiatry, Muskegon, 1971-74, Madison, Tenn., 1974—; mem. staff Madison Hosp., chmn. dept. psychiatry, 1976-78; courtesy staff Hackley Hosp., Muskegon, Nort Ottawa Community Hosp., Grand Haven, 1971-73, Holland (Mich.) Hosp., 1971-72; mem. staff Muskegon Northshore Hosp., 1970-71; Bd. dirs. Life Services Inc. Recipient Physician's Recognition award for continuing med. edn. AMA, 1969, 79. Mem. Nashville Acad. Medicine, Davidson County (Tenn.), Tenn. med. socs., Loma Linda U. Psychiat. Soc., Am. Psychiat. Assn., Am. Profl. Practice Assn., Nat. Assn. Residents and Interns, Am. Physicians Art Assn., Am. Psychiat. Assn. Art Assn., Nat. Rifle Assn., Laurels, Phi Beta Chi, Alpha Omega Alpha. Clubs: Gallatin Gun; Nashville Gun. Home: 612 Larkin Springs Rd Madison TN 37115 Office: PO Box 1292 Coll Branch Madison TN 37115

MARSIK, FREDERIC JOHN, clin. microbiologist; b. Camden, N.J., June 22, 1943; s. Ferdinand Vincent and Helen Ann (Reidl) M.; B.A., Lebanon Valley Coll., 1965; M.S., U. Mo., 1970, Ph.D., 1973; children—Terri Jean, Kristi Ann. Research asso. Sloan-Kettering Cancer Research Inst., N.Y.C., 1965-66; research asst. Merck Inst. Therapeutic Research, Rahway, N.J., 1966-68; teaching and research asst. microbiology U. Mo., Columbia, 1968-73; postdoctoral trainee clin. microbiology Hartford (Conn.) Hosp., 1974-76; asst. prof. pathology U. Va. Sch. Medicine, Charlottesville, 1976—; cons. microbiologist VA Hosp., Salem, Va., 1977—. Registered microbiologist Am. Acad. Microbiology. Mem. Am. Soc. Microbiology, Conf. Pub. Health Lab. Dirs., Med. Mycological Soc. Ams., Res. Officers Assn. U.S., Sigma Xi. Congregationalist. Club: Toastmasters. Contbr. articles to profl. publs.; researcher virulence factors staphylococcus epidermidis, resistance factors escherichia coli and salmonella. Home: 920 Old Brook Rd Charlottesville VA 22901 Office: Microbiology Dept Pathology U Va Charlottesville VA 22901

MARSTON, JOHN PARK, assn. exec.; b. Montgomery, W.Va., Sept. 21, 1939; s. John Edward and Mary (Nease) M.; student W.Va. Inst. Tech., 1958-60; B.S.J., W.Va. U., 1962; postgrad. U. N.C., Chapel Hill, 1964-66; m. Shelby Delaine Purser, Sept. 11, 1966; children—John Purser, Margaret Ann. Staff writer Charleston (W.Va.) Daily Mail, 1962-64; asst. dir. News Bur., U. N.C., Greensboro, 1966-67; dir. communications N.C. Bd. Sci. and Tech., Raleigh, 1967-68; v.p. N.C. Hosp. Assn., Raleigh, 1968-78; pres. Ga. Hosp. Assn., Atlanta, 1978—. Pres., Young Republicans Fayette County, W.Va., 1959-60. Served with USAF, 1962. Recipient 1st prize for profl. excellence Raleigh Public Relations Soc., 1970; named Outstanding Com. Chmn., Raleigh Jaycees, 1973. Mem. Am. Hosp. Assn., Southeastern Hosp. Conf. (dir.), Sigma Delta Chi. Democrat. Methodist. Club: Kiwanis (Atlanta). Office: 315 Boulevard NE Atlanta GA 30312

MARSTON, JOSEPH GEORGE LANAUX, JR., former cemetery exec.; b. Mobile, Ala., July 13, 1919; s. Joseph George Lanaux and Emily Page (Hereford) M.; student Spring Hill Coll., 1936-37, U. Ala., 1942, Auburn U., 1974; m. Rose Marie Smith, Sept. 28, 1940; children—Joseph Lanaux III, C. Henry, Leila Marston Sanford, Christopher A., Rosemarie Marston Fogarty, Patrick J., Nicholas S., Hereford F. Chief clk. Ala. Drydock & Shipbldg. Co., Mobile, 1941-42; dist. mgr. So. Traffic Assn., Pensacola, Fla., 1945-46; distributor Pensacola Liquor Distbn. Co., 1946-49; clk. Shell Oil Co., Mobile, 1949-51, dist. gen. salesman, Mobile, 1951-52; mcht. rep., Birmingham, Ala., 1952-55; dist. jobber rep., Birmingham, Ala., 1955-58; owner auto service store, Mobile, 1958-61; sales rep. Pitney Bowes, Mobile, 1962-63; dir. Cath. Cemetery of Mobile, 1963-77; ret., 1977. Pres. Conscience Mobile, Inc., 1970-72; pres. Mobile diocesan Holy Name Union, 1970-71, Mobile Diocesan Pastoral Council, 1974-75, Mobile Dist. Bd. Cath. Edn., 1973-74; adminstr., chmn. adv. bd. Cath. Housing of Mobile, Inc., 1973-77; mem. Nat. Cath. Disaster Relief Com., Washington, 1970-76; chmn. disaster preparedness and relief com. Mobile County chpt. ARC, 1968-74. Served with U.S. Maritime Service, 1942-45; PTO, ETO. Recipient Bene Merenti Pope Paul VI, 1967, Humanitarian award Assn. Ala. Cemeteries, 1970, Gavel award Conscience Mobile Inc., 1970, Religious Lay Leader award Mobile Jr. C. of C., 1972, 23 year Service award ARC, 1974; St. Valentine award Cath. Charities, 1978. Mem. Nat. Assn. Holy Name Soc. (regional v.p. 1969-73, treas. 1973-75, pres. 1975-77, Vercelli medal and citation 1977), Nat. Cath. Cemetery Conf. (past diocesan rep., past chmn. rehab. com.), Internat. Platform Assn. SCV (comdr. Raphael Semmes Camp 1206, 1967-68). Democrat. Roman Catholic. K.C. Author: Youth and the Holy Name Society, 1971. Contbr. articles to profl. jours. Home and office: 339 Park Ave Mobile AL 36609

MARSTON, PETER MICHAEL, mfg. co. exec.; b. Pittsfield, Mass., Apr. 22, 1947; s. Fred and Mary Ann (Valenti) M.; B.S., Central Conn. State Coll., 1974; m. Linda Claire Rhoades, Oct. 26, 1968. With Turner & Seymour Mfg. Co., 1974—, prodn. control mgr., Torrington, Conn., 1974-76, with sales dept., 1976-77, div. mgr. Shamrock div., Landrum, S.C., 1977—. Served with USAR, 1969-72. Mem. Water and Pollution Control Assn. S.C., Am. Electroplaters Soc. Home: Carpenter Dr Landrum SC 29356 Office: 300 S Shamrock Ave Landrum SC 29356

MARSTON, ROBERT QUARLES, univ. pres.; b. Toano, Va., Feb. 12, 1923; s. Warren and Helen (Smith) M.; B.S., Va. Mil. Inst., 1943; M.D., Med. Coll. Va., 1947; B.Sc. (Rhodes scholar 1947-49), Oxford (Eng.) U., 1949; hon. degrees from several univs.; m. Ann Carter Garnett, Dec. 21, 1946; children—Ann, Robert, Wesley. Intern Johns Hopkins Hosp., 1949-50; resident Vanderbilt U. Hosp., 1950-51, Med. Coll. Va., 1953-54, asst. prof. medicine, 1954; asst. prof. bacteriology and immunology U. Minn., 1958-59; asso. prof. medicine, asst. dean charge student affairs Med. Coll. Va., 1959-61; dean U. Miss. Sch. Medicine, 1961-66, dir. Med. Center, 1961-65, vice chancellor, 1965-66; asso. dir. div. regional med. programs NIH, 1966-68; adminstr. Fed. Health Services and Mental Health Adminstrn., 1968; dir. NIH, Bethesda, Md., 1968-73; scholar in residence U. Va., Charlottesville, 1973-74; pres. U. Fla., 1974—; dir. Johnson & Johnson; disting. fellow Inst. of Medicine, Nat. Acad. Scis., 1973; mem. exec. council Assn. Am. Med. Coll., 1964-67. Bd. visitors Charles R. Drew Postgrad. Sch., Air U.; mem. Fla. Council of 100. Served to 1st lt. AUS, 1951-53. Markle scholar, 1954-59; hon. fellow Lincoln Coll., Oxford U. Fellow Am. Public Health Assn.; mem. Assn. Am. Rhodes Scholars, Assn. Am. Physicians, Am. Clin. and Climatol. Assn., Am. Hosp. Assn. (hon.), Nat. Med. Assn. (hon.), Soc. Scholars John Hopkins, Inst. Medicine (council), Alpha Omega Alpha. Episcopalian. Author articles in field. Office: Univ Fla Gainesville FL 32601

MARTENS, FRANK HENRY, realtor, cons.; b. Chelsea, Mass., Mar. 28, 1925; s. Henry and Madeline Mary (Tassinon) M.; A.A., Northeastern U., 1951, B.B.A., 1953; M.A., U. Fla., 1955; D.B.A., Ft. Lauderdale U., 1973; grad. Realtors Inst.; m. Katharine Dasher; 1 dau., Janet (Mrs. William Staples). With Frank Martens & Assos., 1955-70; dean Real Estate Inst. of Ft. Lauderdale U., 1961-74; realtor, cons., Ft. Lauderdale, 1970—, also instr. Ft. Lauderdale Bd. Realtors, 1975—; pres. FMA Investments, Inc., Real Estate Inst. Fla., Inc. Served with USNR, 1942-45. Cert. residential specialist, residential broker, property mgr., comml. and investment mem.; accredited farm and land broker. Mem. Nat., Fla. assns. realtors, Internat. Real Estate Fedn., Ft. Lauderdale Bd. Realtors, Inst. Real Estate Mgmt., U.S. Singletons (nat. v.p. 1965-70). Roman Catholic. Author: Florida Real Estate Law, 1969; Florida Supplement, Principles of Real Estate, 1973. Home: 1151 N Atlantic Blvd Fort Lauderdale FL 33304 Office: 370 SE 2d St Fort Lauderdale FL 33301

MARTH, BEATRICE RANGNOW, elem. sch. counselor; b. Victoria, Tex., Apr. 23, 1920; d. Charles Henry and Sophie Louise (Weitzel) Rangnow; student Victoria Coll., 1938-41, U. Tex., 1945-46; B.S., U. Houston, 1954, M.A. in Spl. Edn., 1979, M.A. in Psychology, 1979; M.A. in Edn., Tex. A&I U., 1964; m. Edward Albert Marth, Apr. 3, 1946 (dec. 1966). Elem. tchr. Victoria County (Tex.) Schs., 1941-54, Victoria Consol. Ind. Sch. Dist., 1954-67, elem. counselor, 1967—. Former mem. bd. parish edn. First English Lutheran Ch.; bd. dirs. Girl Scouts U.S.A. Mem. Tex. Tchrs. Assn., Tex. Personnel and Guidance Assn., Am. Personnel and Guidance Assn., Tex. Psychol. Assn., Victoria Classroom Tchrs. Assn. (pres. 1962-63), Victoria Orgn. Civic Endeavors, Delta Kappa Gamma. Democrat. Clubs: Victoria Gem and Mineral (past pres., past sec.), Currier Belle Literary. Research on teaching reasoning lessons to elem. children. Office: 104 Profit Dr Victoria TX 77901

MARTIKAINEN, A(UNE) HELEN, former health edn. specialist; b. Harrison, Maine, May 11, 1916; d. Sylvester and Emma (Heikkinen) Martikainen; A.B., Bates Coll., 1939, D.Sc. (hon.), 1957; M.P.H., Yale, 1941; D.Sc., Harvard U., 1964, Smith Coll., 1969. Health edn. sec. Hartford Tb and Pub. Health Assn., 1941-42; cons. USPHS, 1942-49; chief health edn. WHO, Geneva, Switzerland, 1949-74, now mem. expert adv. panel. Trustee Bridgton Acad., North Bridgton, Maine; bd. dirs. Citizen Involvement Network U.S.A.; mem. N.C. Citizen's Council for Public Health, 1978—; bd. dirs. U.S. Assn. of Club of Rome. Recipient Delta Omega award Yale; Nat. Adminstrv. award Am. Acad. Phys. Edn.; Bates Key award; Internat. Service award, France, 1953; Prentiss medal, 1956; spl. medal, certificate for internat. health edn. service Nat. Acad. Medicine for France, 1959; profl. award Soc. Pub. Health Educators, 1963. Fellow Am. Pub. Health Assn. (chmn. health edn. sect., award for excellence in internat. health 1978); mem. Harvard Pub. Health Alumni Assn. (councillor), AAUW (legis. chmn. N.C. div., rep. N.C. Council on Social Legislation 1979), U.S. Soc. Pub. Health Educators, Internat. Union Health Edn. (Parisot medal, tech. adviser), Acad. Phys. Edn. (asso.), Phi Beta Kappa. Episcopalian. Home: PO Box 3059 Chapel Hill NC 27514

MARTIN, BARBARA BURSA, chemist; b. Oak Park, Ill., Aug. 2, 1934; d. George and Bessie (Zavadil) B.; A.B., Grinnell Coll., 1956; M.Sc., Pa. State U., 1959; m. Dean F. Martin, Dec. 22, 1956; children—Diane, Bruce, John, Paul, Brian, Eric. Vis. lectr. chemistry U. South Fla., Tampa, 1962-74, asst. prof. (courtesy), 1974—. Mem. Am. Chem. Soc., Sigma Xi. Author: Coordination Compounds, 1964; contbr. articles to profl. jours. Home: 3402 Valencia Rd Tampa FL 33618 Office: Dept Chemistry U South Fla Tampa FL 33620

MARTIN, BENJAMIN GAUFMAN, ophthalmologist, air force officer; b. Louisville, Aug. 18, 1931; s. Benjamin Gaufman and Catherine Lucille (Mardis) M.; B.M.E., U. Louisville, 1954, M.Eng., 1973; M.D., U. So. Calif., 1964; m. Caroline Sue Franke, June 23, 1975; children—Benjamin Gaufman, III, Lori, Tamara, Toby, Steven. Served as fighter pilot USNR, 1954-57; design engr. Philco Corp., Palo Alto, Calif., 1958-60; commd. capt. USAF, 1964, advanced through grades to col., 1976; flight surgeon, pilot, 1964-68; chief of ophthalmology, chief of surgery USAF Hosp., MacDill AFB, Tampa, Fla., 1968—; asst. clin. prof. ophthalmology U. S.Fla., 1972-75. Decorated D.F.C., Bronze Star medal, Air medal. Fellow A.C.S., Am. Acad. Ophthalmology. Home: 4912 Bay Way Dr Tampa FL 33608 Office: USAF Hosp MacDill Air Force Base Tampa FL 33608

MARTIN, BENJAMIN ROMIG, social worker; b. Macungie, Pa., July 29, 1944; s. Henry Edward and Jennie May (Hammond) M.; B.A., Berea Coll., 1966; M.S.S., Bryn Mawr Coll., 1972; m. Bonita Louise Brungard, Feb. 14, 1966; 1 dau., Erin Paige. Caseworker, Lehigh County Children's Bur., Allentown, Pa., 1969-70; clin. social worker Orangeburg (S.C.) Mental Health Center, 1972-79; dir. social services and family life S.C. Dept. Mental Retardation Coastal Center, Ladson, 1979—; pvt. practice social work, Orangeburg, 1972-79. Mem. Palmetto Low Country Health Systems Agy., 1977—. Served with U.S. Army, 1966-68. Mem. Nat. Assn. Social Workers, Nat. Council Family Relations, Nat. Register Clin. Social Workers, Acad. Cert. Social Workers. Home: 300 Chessington Circle Summerville SC 29483 Office: Jamison Rd Ladson SC 29456

MARTIN, CARL THOMAS, govt. ofcl.; b. Kemp, Tex., Aug. 7, 1940; s. Orbie Chesley and Bessie Lee (Murchison) M.; A.A., Navarra Jr. Coll., Corsicana, Tex., 1966; B.S., Troy State U., Montgomery, Ala., 1974, M.S., 1975; m. Gloria J. Schroeder, Feb. 13, 1960; children—Clifford Bryan, Melody Ann. With U.S. Postal Service, 1959—, postal insp., Houston, 1967, major projects coordinator, 1979—. Pres. E., Montgomery Dixie Youth Baseball League, 1972-73; Webelo leader Cape Fear council Boy Scouts Am., Fayetteville, N.C., 1970-71; bd. dirs. Village Little League Baseball, Fayetteville, 1970-71. Mem. Ala. Peace Officers Assn., Fed. Law Enforcement Officers Assn., Postal Insps. Mut. Benefit Assn. Democrat. Baptist. Clubs: Franklin Toastmasters (pres. 1980—), Masons, Shriners. Home: 19614 Shinwood Dr Humble TX 77338 Office: 401 Franklin St Houston TX 77001

MARTIN, CAROLE J., ednl. adminstr.; b. Bklyn., Jan. 31, 1946; d. Adee C. and Sophie T. (Wisniewski) M.; B.S. in Spl. Edn., Fla. State U., 1967; M.A. in Audiology, U. Fla., 1973; postgrad. in adminstrn. Fla. State U., 1980—. Speech clinician Seminole County Sch. Dist., 1967-68, 71-72; speech clinician United Cerebral Palsy of Central Fla., 1968-69; hearing clinician Putnam Sch. Dist., 1972-75; audiologist, supr. Sunland Center, 1975-77; tng. project dir. Fla. State Hosp., Chattahoochees, 1977-78; tng. specialist Fla. Dept. Health and Rehab. Service, Tallahassee, 1978-79; staff devel. coordinator Leon County (Fla.) Tchr. Edn. Center, Tallahassee, 1979—; cons. spl. edn., 1976-79. Vice chmn. Dist. Human Rights Advocacy Com., 1979-80; Democratic precinct committeewoman. U.S. Office Edn. fellow, 1970-71; HEW fellow, 1977; Appreciation award Marion County Assn. Children Under Six; recipient cert. Appreciation for Community Service, City of Gainsville, 1977. Mem. Am. Speech, Hearing and Lang. Assn., AAUW, Am. Soc. Public Adminstrs., Council Exceptional Children, NEA, NOW (nat. women and mental health task force 1979, pres. Tallahassee chpt. 1979-80, chpt. public relations chairperson 1977-79, state conf. coordinator). Democrat.

MARTIN, CHARLES BEE, state senator, textile engr.; b. Corona, Ala., July 21, 1931; s. Claud Jasper and Annie (Jones) M.; student U. Ala., Huntsville, 1958-63; m. Daphyne Kimbrell, Oct. 8, 1949; children—Patsy Ann, Joe Bearl, Scarlette, Charles Lee, Treva Jo. Lab. technician Barrow Agee Labs., Decatur, Ala., 1949-50; shipping clk. Goodyear Tire & Rubber Co., Decatur, 1951-52; sr. engr. Monsanto Textiles Co., Decatur, 1952—; city councilman, Decatur, 1968-74; mem. Ala. Ho. of Reps., 1975-78, Ala. Senate, 1979—. Democrat. Methodist. Club: Masons. Home: 1716 Cameilla Dr SW Decatur AL 35601 Office: PO Box 2204 Decatur AL 35602

MARTIN, CHARLES EDWARD, banker; b. Cordova, Ala., July 17, 1940; s. Lonnie L. and Willodean (Love) M.; student Walker State Coll., La. State U.; m. Patricia Clark, June 22, 1958; children—Charles Edward, Melinda. Asst. cashier Dora Bank and Trust (Ala.), 1960-64; exec. v.p. Farmers and Mchts. Bank, Madison, Ala., 1964-66; asst. v.p. 1st Ala. Bank, Huntsville, Ala., 1966-70; pres., chief exec. officer Nat. Bank of Commerce, Birmingham, Ala., 1970—. Mem. Vestavia Park Bd.; bd. dirs. City of Hope, Operation New Birmingham; mem. fund raising com. Birmingham So. Coll. Mem. Ala. Bankers Assn., Am. Bankers Assn., Bank Mktg. Assn., Sales and Mktg. Execs. Am., Ind. Bankers Assn. Baptist. Clubs: Execs. (Birmingham); Downtown Action, Vestavia Country, Riverchase Country. Office: 20 S 20th St Birmingham AL 35233

MARTIN, DALE ALISON, educator; b. Selma, Ala., May 4, 1941; s. Ted Clifton and Omie Lee (Frith) M.; B.S. cum laude, Samford U., 1964; M.S., Fla. State U., 1966, Ph.D., 1970; m. Blanche Waters, June 23, 1962; 1 dau., Alyssa Martin. Tchr. high sch., Panama City, Fla., 1964-65; grad. asst. Fla. State U., Tallahassee, 1966-67; psychometrist VA Guidance Center, Fla. State U., 1967, counselor, dir., 1967-69; dir. univ. counseling services and test center Troy (Ala.) State U., 1969-71; asst. prof. dept. counselor edn. and psychology Troy State U., Montgomery, Ala., 1971-76, asso. prof., chmn. dept. counseling, human devel. and psychology, 1976—; cons. psychol. and ednl. evaluations Ala. Program for Exceptional Children and Youth; cons. vocat. expert panel Montgomery Office, Bur. Hearings and Appeals, Social Security Adminstrn., HEW; cons. psychiat. counseling Prescott Clinic, Fairview Med. Center, Montgomery. Sunday sch. tchr., sec.-treas. bd. deacons, ch. tng. dir., deacon First Bapt. Ch., Montgomery. Mem. Am., Ala. psychol. assns., Nat. Vocat. Guidance Assn., Am., Ala. personnel and guidance assns., Am. Coll. Personnel Assn., Assn. Counselor Educators and Suprs., Ala. Assn. Counselor Educators and Suprs., Phi Delta Kappa, Omicron Delta Kappa, Beta Beta Beta. Home: 3325 Allendale Pl Montgomery AL 36111 Office: Troy State U in Montgomery Whitley Hall Montgomery AL 36101

MARTIN, DANIEL EZEKIEL, lawyer; b. Bluffton, S.C., Apr. 14, 1932; s. John Henry and Rena Aletha (Johnson) M.; B.S., Allen U., 1954; J.D., S.C. State Coll., 1966; m. Ruby Nesbit, Apr. 15, 1960; children—Daniel Ezekiel, Max Maurice. Head phys. edn. dept. Wallace High Sch., Charleston, S.C., 1959-62; tchr. math. W. Gresham Meggett High Sch., 1962-63; admitted to S.C. bar, 1966, U.S. Tax Ct., U.S. Ct. of Customs and Patent Appeals, U.S. Ct. Claims, Fed. Dist. Ct. for S.C., U.S. Supreme Ct.; dir. Neighborhood Legal Assistance Program, Inc., Charleston, 1968-72; partner Moore & Martin Law Offices, 1973-74; asst. solicitor 9th Jud. Circuit, Charleston County, 1974—; pvt. practice law, Charleston, 1972—. Finance chmn. Palmetto Dist. of Coastal Carolina, Boy Scouts Am., 1968-70, Appreciation award, 1974. Vice chmn. Democratic Party for Charleston County, 1970-72. Vice chmn. Mini Parks, Inc., Charleston County Bicentennial Com.; bd. dirs., legal adviser Project Pride, Inc.; bd. dirs. Pub. Defender Corp. of Charleston County, Greater Charleston YMCA, S.C. State Agy. Vocational Rehab.; trustee Allen U. Served with U.S. Army, 1955-57. Recipient certificate of achievement for Porgy and Bess cast, Charleston Symphony Assn., 1970; Scroll of Honor, Omega Psi Phi, 1969; certificate of achievement Alpha Phi Alpha, 1970; Distinguished Service award Alpha Phi Alpha, 1973; Appreciation award Clara D. Hill Missionary

Club, 1974; Jurisprudence Achievement award Omega Psi Phi, 1974. Mem. Am., S.C., Charleston County bar assns., Charleston Trident C. of C. (dir.), Alpha Phi Alpha (life). Mem. A.M.E. Ch. (trustee). Mason (Shriner). Home: 117 Gordon St Charleston SC 29403 Office: 61 Morris St Charleston SC 29403

MARTIN, DAVID EDWARD, educator; b. Green Bay, Wis., Oct. 1, 1939; s. Edward Henry and Lillie (Luckman) M.; B.S., U. Wis., 1961, M.S., 1963, Ph.D., 1970. Ford Found. research trainee Wis. Regional Primate Center, Madison, 1967-70; asst. prof. health scis. Ga. State U., Atlanta, 1970-74, asso. prof., 1974—; collaborating scientist Yerkes Primate Research Center, Emory U., Atlanta, 1970—. U.S. rep. to Internat. Olympic Acad., 1978. Recipient fed. and univ. grants for physiol. research; Distinguished prof., 1975. Mem. AAAS, AAUP, Soc. Study Reprodn., Am. Coll. Sports Medicine, Am. Physiol. Soc., Internat. Primatol. Soc. Clubs: Atlanta Coin, Atlanta Track. Author: Laboratory Experiments in Human Physiology, 2d ed., 1975; The Marathon Footrace, 1979; contbr. articles to profl. jours. Home: 510 Coventry Rd Stonehouse Decatur GA 30030 Office: Dept Respiratory Therapy Ga State Univ Atlanta GA 30303

MARTIN, DWIGHT WESLEY, ret. co. exec.; b. Kalamazoo, June 16, 1910; s. Arba and Virgie (Frantz) M.; A.B., Ohio Wesleyan U., 1931; LL.B., U. Cin., 1934; m. Jeannette B. Nichols, Sept. 7, 1936; children—Sally N., Jeannette F., Dwight Wesley (dec.). Admitted to Ohio bar, 1934; with trust dept. Central Trust Co., Cin., 1934-35; asso. Dinsmore, Shohl, Sawyer & Dinsmore, 1935-45, partner, 1945-46; v.p. Crosley Broadcasting Corp., 1946-52; v.p., dir. Gen. Teleradio, Inc. 1952-55, RKO Teleradio, 1955-56; exec. v.p. Lion Television Corp., 1956-59; chmn. bd. Modern Broadcasting Co. of Baton Rouge, Inc., 1956-64; exec. v.p., treas., dir. Royal St. Corp., 1962-80; chmn. bd., dir. Royal St. Investment Corp., New Orleans, Interchange Realty Co., Inc., 1963-80; dir. Broadcast Music, Inc. Bd. dirs. Bur. Govtl. Research. Served as lt. comdr. USNR, 1943-45. Mem. Nat. Assn. Broadcasters (dir. 1958-62), Order of Coif, Phi Beta Kappa, Omicron Delta Kappa. Home: 415 Park Rd Metairie LA 70005

MARTIN, ERIC WENTWORTH, med. writer; b. Kamloops, B.C., Can., Dec. 6, 1912; s. Wentworth Banger and Ida Magdalen (Coates) M.; came to U.S., 1939, naturalized, 1943; Ph.C., Western Coll. Pharmacy, Vancouver, B.C., 1936; B.Sc., Phila. Coll. Pharmacy and Sci., 1942; M.S., U. Pa., 1948, Ph.D., 1949; m. Ruth Leila Dickson, July 15, 1961; 1 dau., Rosemary. Pharmacist in B.C., and Pa., 1935-42; editor-in-chief Mack Pub. Co., Easton, Pa., 1942-70; asso. dir. LaWall & Harrisson Labs., Phila., 1949-52; asst. prof. Phila. Coll. Pharmacy and Sci., 1949-52; sr. research biochemist U. Pa., 1952-56; editor Jour. Am. Pharm. Assn., 1956-59; exec. editor Pfizer Spectrum, 1959-60; dir. med. communications Lederle Labs., Pearl River, N.Y., 1960-72; adj. prof. biomed. communication Columbia, 1968-70; dep. dir. med. communications FDA, HEW, Rockville, Md., 1973-75, dir. profl. communications, 1975-78, exec. sec. editorial bd., 1978; pres. Provest Inc., 1978—. Founder, 1st pres. Drug Info. Assn., 1965-66. Served to capt. U.S. Army, 1942-45. Fellow Am. Med. Writers Assn. (pres. N.Y. Met. area 1966, nat. pres. 1970-71), Internat. Acad. Law and Sci., AAAS. Author, editor 17 textbooks on hazards, techniques and dispensing of medication. Contbr. articles to profl. jours. Address: 308 Lansdowne Rd Fayetteville NC 28304

MARTIN, FRANCIS AUSTIN, psychologist; b. Louisiana, Mo., Dec. 3, 1941; s. Frances Mae (Davis) M.; A.A., Hannibal LaGrange Coll., 1961; B.A., Okla. Bapt. U., 1963; M.Div., So. Bapt. Theol. Sem., 1969, Ed.D., 1973; m. Martha Virginia Woolf, June 2, 1964; 1 dau., Susan Yvonne. Ordained to ministry Bapt. Ch., 1970; minister youth 1st Bapt. Ch., Bowling Green, Ky., 1968-70; minister edn. Lyndon Bapt. Ch., Louisville, 1970-73; editor pastoral ministries products Bapt. Sunday Sch. Bd., Nashville, 1973-75; asso. prof. psychology Belmont Coll., Nashville, 1975—; counselor Christian Counseling Clinic, Nashville, 1977—; adj. prof psychology Tenn. State U., 1975—; vis. prof. Midwestern Bapt. Theol. Sem., 1975. Mem. Am. Personnel and Guidance Assn., Am. Assn. Pastoral Counselors. Author: Prayers from Where You Are, 1975; Vocational Guidance in a Church, 1975; Facing Grief with Faith, 1976; (with M. Simpson) Coping with Cancer, 1976; The Bible Speaks to Personal Crises, 1980; contbr. articles to profl. jours. Home: 4627 Shys Hill Rd Nashville TN 37215 Office: Dept Psychology Belmont Coll Nashville TN 37203

MARTIN, FRANCIS LINTON, lawyer; b. Chattanooga, Jan. 6, 1891; s. Francis and Lydia (Linton) M.; Ph.B., Yale, 1912; LL.B., Columbia, 1915; m. Emily T. Kelley, Aug. 17, 1933; 1 dau., Caroline T. (Mrs. Erwin Brady Bartusch). Admitted to Tenn. bar, 1916, since practiced in Chattanooga; mem. firm Miller, Martin, Hitching, Tipton, Lenihan & Waterhouse, 1923—. Served as 1st lt., 17th F.A., 2d Div., U.S. Army, 1917-19; AEF in France. Decorated Silver Star (U.S.); Fourragere of Croix de Guerre (France). Mem. Am. Bar Assn., Assn. Life Ins. Counsel. Clubs: Mountain City, Chattanooga Half Century. Home: 1914 Poplar Ave Memphis TN 38104 Office: Volunteer Bldg Chattanooga TN 37402

MARTIN, FREDERICK NOEL, educator; b. N.Y.C., July 24, 1931; s. Philip and Mildred Ruth (Austin) M.; B.A., Bklyn. Coll., 1957, M.A., 1958; Ph.D., City U. N.Y., 1968; m. Mary Catherine Robinson, Apr. 4, 1954; children—David C., Leslie Anne. Clin. instr. U. Ark. Med. Center, Little Rock, 1960-66; dir. audiology Bailey Ear Clinic, Little Rock, 1960-66; asst. prof. speech Bklyn. Coll., 1966-68; prof. speech communication U. Tex., Austin, 1968—. Served with USAF, 1951-55. Fellow Am. Speech and Hearing Assn.; mem. Tex. Speech and Hearing Assn. Club: Masons. Author: Introduction to Audiology, 1975; Pediatric Audiology, 1978; Medical Audiology, 1980; contbr. articles to profl. jours. Home: 8613 Silver Ridge Dr Austin TX 78759 Office: Speech and Hearing Center U Tex Austin TX 78712

MARTIN, GREGORY DEAN, control engr.; b. Oklahoma City, Jan. 21, 1949; s. Howard Burdette and Virginia (Lafalier) M.; B.S., Okla. State U., 1971, M.S., 1973; Ph.D., Purdue U., 1977; m. Janie Sue Batten, June 6, 1970; 1 son, Brian Christopher. Process engr. Whirlpool Corp., Ft. Smith, Ark., summer 1972; research asst. mech. engring. Okla. State U., Stillwater, 1972-73; engr. Union Carbide Chem. & Plastics Tech. Center, South Charleston, W.Va., 1973-75; teaching asst. Purdue U., West Lafayette, Ind., 1975; research engr. Shell Devel. Co., Houston, 1977-80; sr. control engr. Setpoint Inc., Houston, 1980—. Proctor & Gamble fellow, 1975; Cummins Engine fellow, 1975; NSF grantee, 1972-73; Union Carbide grantee, 1975-77. Mem. ASME, IEEE, Instrument Soc. Am., Nat., Okla. socs. profl. engrs., Kappa Alpha, Pi Tau Sigma, Sigma Tau, Phi Kappa Phi. Republican. Home: 12418 Stafford Springs Houston TX 77077 Office: 901 Threadneedle St Suite 150 Houston TX 77079

MARTIN, HARVEY AUGUSTUS, JR., accountant; b. Birmingham, Ala., Aug. 7, 1920; s. Harvey Augustus and Ida Mildred (Ramsey) M.; student U. Ala., 1940-41, Extension Sch. U.S. Army, 1942-45; m. Maria Mathilde Janssen, June 2, 1945; children—Maria Mathilde, Mildred Jane (Mrs. Edward H. Weaver), Harvey Augustus III. Trainee J.J. Newberry Co., Birmingham, 1940-41; salesman Martin Biscuit Co., Birmingham, 1941-42; partner Martin Bros. Food Brokers, Birmingham, 1945-47; pvt. practice pub. accounting, Birmingham, 1947—; v.p., dir. Victory Products Co., Inc. Mem. Jefferson County Movie Review Bd., 1966, Morality in Media of Ala., 1968. Served with AUS, 1942-45; ETO. Mem. Ala. Assn. Pub. Accountants (pres. 1959-60), Nat. Soc. Pub. Accountants. Roman Catholic. Clubs: The Club, Pioneer. Home: 1000 Wildwood Dr Birmingham AL 35235 Office: PO Box 9600 Birmingham AL 35215

MARTIN, HARVEY THOMPSON, JR., univ. adminstr.; b. Rochester, Vt., July 18, 1924; s. Harvey Thompson and Mildred (Stoughton) M.; A.B., Middlebury Coll., 1950; M.S., Wash. State U., 1952, Ph.D., 1957; m. Esther Lee Smith, Aug. 1951; children—Michael Thompson, Lory Lee. Counselor, Student Counseling Center, Wash. State U., 1950-54, head resident counselor, asst. to asso. dean students, 1955-57; psychol. cons. service, asst. prof. mgmt. U. Denver, 1957-59, dir. counseling and testing service, asst. prof. psychology, 1959-63, acting dean students, 1962; dir. Cons. Psychol. Service, Inc., 1961-63; dir. Univ. Counseling Center, asso. prof. psychology U. Fla., 1963-65; dean coll. affairs, prof. psychology U. West Fla., Pensacola, 1965-66, provost, 1966—. Served with USAAF, 1942-46. Mem. Am., Fla. psychol. assns., Am. Coll. Personnel Assn., Nat. Vocat. Guidance Assn., AAUP, Fla. Personnel and Guidance Assn., Fla. Sch. Psychologists Assn., N.W. Fla. Speech and Hearing Assn. (dir. 1972-73), County C. of C. (airport adv. com. 1973-74). Club: Scenic Hills Country. Contbr. articles to profl. jours. Home: 8801 Thunderbird Dr Pensacola FL 32504

MARTIN, HOWARD NATHAN, assn. exec.; b. Livingston, Tex., July 17, 1917; s. Jack Adams and Johnnie Richard (Jones) M.; A.A., Lon Morris Coll., 1937; B.B.A., U. Tex., 1939, M.A., 1941; m. Mavis Valerie Condrey, June 1, 1941; children—Howard, Marylin Gene, Ruth Ann. Bus. mgr. Lon Morris Coll., Jacksonville, Tex., 1941-42; dir. econ. and demographic research Houston C. of C., 1947—; lectr. in field, cons. Ch. bd. trustee Faribanks Meth. Ch., Houston, 1949-53; pres. bd. trustees Cypress-Fairbanks Ind. Sch. Dist. (Tex.), 1953-54. Served with USNR, 1942-46. Decorated Bronze Star medal. Certified Chamber exec. Mem. Am. C. of C. Execs., So. Assn. C. of C. Execs., Tex. C. of C. Mgrs., Am. Statis. Assn. Nat. Assn. Bus. Economists, Am. Mktg. Assn., Am. C. of C. Researchers Assn. (nat. pres. 1961-63), Tex. Hist. Assn., Tex. Folklore Soc., Delta Sigma Pi. Author: Chamber of Commerce Research Activities, 1975; Myths and Folktales of the Alabama-Coushatta Indian Tribes of Tex, 1977. (Book of Year, Tex. Folklore Soc. 1977); other books. Home: 8710 Cedarspur St Houston TX 77055 Office: 1100 Milam Bldg 25th Floor Houston TX 77002

MARTIN, JAMES FLOYD, lawyer; b. Dothan, Ala., Sept. 8, 1922; s. Harry Kennedy and Eleanor (Logan) M.; B.S., U. Ala., 1943, LL.B., 1948; m. Marjorie Fae Jorgensen, Feb. 11, 1946; children—Mabel, Elizabeth. Admitted to Ala. bar; individual practice law, Dothan, 1948—; atty. County of Houston (Ala.), 1962-63, asst. dist. atty., 1963-79, U.S. magistrate, Dothan, 1979—; instr. econs. U. Ala., 1957-58; pres. Houston County Abstract Co. Served with U.S. Army, 1943-46, 51-52. Mem. Am. Bar Assn., Ala. Bar Assn., Houston County Bar Assn., Am. Judicature Soc. Baptist. Home: 702 Wildwood St Dothan AL 36303 Office: 119 S Oates St Dothan AL 36301

MARTIN, JAMES GRUBBS, congressman; b. Savannah, Ga., Dec. 11, 1935; s. Arthur Morrison and Mary Julia (Grubbs) M.; B.S., Davidson Coll., 1957; Ph.D., Princeton, 1960; m. Dorothy Ann McAulay, June 1, 1957; children—James Grubbs, Emily Wood, Arthur Benson. Asso. prof. chemistry Davidson (N.C.) Coll., 1960-72; mem. 93d-96th Congresses from 9th Dist. N.C. Mem. Mecklenburg (N.C.) Bd. County Commrs., 1966-72, chmn., 1967-68, 70-71; founder, 1st chmn. Centralina Council Govts., Charlotte, N.C., 1968-70; v.p. Nat. Assn. Regional Councils, 1970-72; pres. N.C. Assn. County Commrs., 1970-71. Del. Republican Nat. Conv., 1968. Danforth fellow, 1957-60. Mem. Beta Theta Pi (v.p., trustee 1966-69, pres. 1975-78). Presbyn. (deacon). Clubs: Masons, Shriners. Office: 341 Cannon House Office Bldg Washington DC 20515

MARTIN, JAMES GUY, newspaper exec.; b. Birmingham, Ala., Sept. 23, 1931; s. John Rufus and Emma (Meadows) M.; student U. Ala., 1957; m. Vera Elizabeth Grant, Nov. 29, 1952; children—Leslie Anne, James Guy, Catherine Elizabeth, Patricia Lynn. Printer, Outlook Pub. Co., 1949-57; composing room foreman Birmingham News, 1957-62; mech. supt. So. Publs., Cedartown, Ga., 1963, gen. mgr., 1963-64; pres. Ala. Sunday Mag., Birmingham, 1964-66, So. Publ., Montgomery, Ala., 1966-68; pub. Prattville (Ala.) Progress, 1966-68; v.p., gen. mgr. Gadsden (Ala.) Times, 1969-70; personnel, purchasing mgr. The Advertiser Co., Montgomery, Ala., 1970-74, v.p. ops., 1974-77, pres., co-pub., 1977—. Chmn. bd. dirs. St. James Sch., Montgomery; deacon Heritage Baptist Ch., Montgomery. Served with USAF, 1951-53. Named one of Ten Best Dressed Men of Montgomery and State of Ala., 1977; recipient Man of Year award YMCA Youth Program, 1971. Mem. Sigma Delta Chi. Clubs: Lions, Quarterback, Knife and Fork, Capitol City, Masons (32 deg.), Men of Montgomery. Office: 200 Washington Ave Montgomery AL 36102

MARTIN, JAMES PAUL, state legislator La.; b. Lake Charles, La., Mar. 10, 1929; s. Claude A. and Ruth (McLees) M.; B.S., Springhill Coll., Mobile, Ala., 1950; m. Bernardine Fontenot, July 9, 1955; children—Claude A. III, Paul M., Andree M., John S. Field underwriter N.Y. Life Ins. Co., Welsh, La., 1953—, estate mgr., 1956—; mem. La. Ho. of Reps. from 37th Dist., 1972—, chmn. agr. com., 1976; mem. rural devel. com. Nat. Conf. State Legislatures. Mem. S.W. Dist. Law Enforcement Agy., 1970-72, La. Law Enforcement Agy., 1971-72; mem. adv. bd. urban studies La. State U., New Orleans, 1968-72. Mem. Calcasieu area exec. bd. Boy Scouts Am., 1955—. Mem. exec. com. Jefferson Davis Parish Democratic Com., 1956-71; mayor City of Welsh, 1967-72. Served with AUS, 1951-53. Recipient Silver Beaver award Boy Scouts Am., 1967; named Citizen of Year, Welsh, 1964. Mem. Welsh C. of C. (past pres.). K.C. (past grand knight). Rotarian (past pres.). Home: 401 S Elm St Welsh LA 70591 Office: 115 S Adams St Welsh LA 70591

MARTIN, JAMES ROBERT, JR., fed. judge; b. Greenville, S.C., Nov. 30, 1909; s. James Robert and Lyda (Rankin) M.; LL.B., Washington and Lee U., 1931; m. Lydia Prichard, Dec. 19, 1929; children—Belle Mead (Mrs. Robert V. Heckel), Lydia (Mrs. Lydia Martin Sawyer, Jr.), Bobbie Jane (Mrs. Charles W. Traylor). Admitted to S.C. bar, 1931; practice in Greenville, 1931-44; judge 13th Jud. Circuit S.C., 1944-61; U.S. dist. judge Eastern and Western Dists. S.C., 1961-67; chief dist. judge U.S. Dist. S.C., 1967—. Mem. S.C. Ho. of Reps. from Greenville County, 1943-44. Mem. Am., S.C., Greenville Co. bar assns. Presbyterian. Mason, Elk. Home: 401 Crescent Ave Greenville SC 29605 Office: Fed Bldg and US Court House Greenville SC 29601

MARTIN, JESS AARON, educator; b. Picher, Okla., May 2, 1926; s. Corbett Harrison and Sadie Mae (Plank) M.; A.B., San Diego State Coll., 1953; M.S. in L.S., U. So. Calif., 1955; m. Betty Jean Martin, June 20, 1948; children—Robert Kirk, Richard Lewis. Librarian, San Diego (Calif.) County Med. Soc., 1953, 56-57; chief tech. service Convair-Astronautics, San Diego, 1957-58; asst. med. librarian U. Ky., Lexington, 1958-60; dir. Ohio State U. Med. Sch. Library, Columbus, 1960-63; chief Library Br., NIH, Bethesda, Md., 1963-68; dir. Temple U. Med. Library, Phila., 1968-71; dir. U. Tenn. Center for Health Sci. Library, Memphis, 1971—; adj. lectr. U. Md. Library Sch., 1967-68, Memphis State U., 1979. Served with USN, 1944-46. Med. Library Assn. scholar 1954-55. Mem. Med. Library Assn., Spl. Libraries Assn., Tenn. Library Assn., Southeastern Library Assn., AAUP, Beta Phi Mu. Contbr. articles to profl. jours. Home: 6477 Keswick Dr Memphis TN 38138 Office: 800 Madison Ave Memphis TN 38163

MARTIN, JOANNA MAY, educator; b. Jackson County, Mo., Aug. 8, 1938; d. Paul Hobson and Frances Layfield (Clegg) M.; B.S. in Edn., Central Mo. State U., 1960, M.S., 1967; Ed.D., Okla. State U., 1970. Tchr. public schs., North Kansas City, Mo., 1960-62, Banning, Calif., 1962-63, North Kansas City, 1966-68, Warrensburg, Mo., 1966-68; grad. asst. Okla. State U., 1968-70; asst. prof. edn. N. Tex. State U., 1970-73; asso. prof. edn. U. Tex., Tyler, 1973-77, prof., 1977—, dir. field experiences, 1974— Mem. Internat. Reading Assn., Nat. Council Tchrs. English, Assn. Supervision and Curriculum Devel., Phi Delta Kappa, Kappa Delta Pi. Congregationalist. Club: Zonta (v.p. 1977-79). Author: (with I. Lohmann) Open Windows to the World Through the Living Textbook, 1975. Home: 925 E 8th Tyler TX 75701 Office: 3900 University Blvd Tyler TX 75701

MARTIN, JOHN EDWARD), customhouse broker; b. Sharon, Tenn., Jan. 2, 1916; s. Robert Lee and Margaret Ann (Harkey) M.; student Ouachita Bapt. Coll., 1932-34, Tex. Coll. Mines and Metallurgy, 1938-39; m. Mina Ruth Wright, Feb. 28, 1937 (dec. Oct. 1963); children—John L. V., Mina Lynne, Travis Willard; m. 2d, Syble Irene McConnell Aug. 31, 1974. Clk., U.S. Post Office, El Paso, 1936-40; chief insp. U.S. Customs, El Paso, 1940-42, 43-45; owner Martin Brokerage Co., El Paso, 1945-54, pres., 1955-73; pres. Albuquerque Brokerage Co., Inc., 1973—. Mem. U.S. Customs Adv. Com. for Customs Region VI, 1967-72. Dist. chmn. Boy Scouts Am., 1955-58, Bd. dirs. Yucca council, 1958-72. Bd. dirs., v.p. Southwestern Livestock Show. Hon. consul of Guatemala, 1948-53, 1962-75. With AUS, 1942-43. Recipient Carnegie Hero Medal for life saving, 1952. Boy Scouts Am. Honor Medal for live saving, 1952; Silver Beaver award Boy Scouts Am., 1957. Mem. El Paso Customs Brokers Assn. (chmn. 1973-78). Mason. Club: Empire. Home: 209-B Castellano El Paso TX 79912 Office: 1805 Magoffin Ave El Paso TX 79901

MARTIN, JOHN PERRY, JR., chemist, educator; b. Dunbar, Pa., Feb. 19, 1924; s. John Perry and Annette Pearl (Woodmancy) M.; B.S., Carnegie Inst. Tech., 1947, M.S., 1955, Ph.D. (NSF fellow 1961-62, Koppers fellow 1962), 1962; M.H.L. (hon.), Davis and Elkins Coll., 1973. Research asst. metals research lab. Carnegie Inst. Tech., 1947-50, Am. Cyanamide teaching fellow, 1961-62; chemist Dunbar Corp., 1950-52 analyst Duraloy Co., Scottdale, Pa., 1952-54, chief chemist, 1954-59, asst. prof. chemistry Davis and Elkins Coll., 1962-65, asso. prof., 1965-76, prof., 1976—. NSF grantee, 1966. Mem. Am. Chem. Soc. Sigma Xi, Chi Beta Phi. Republican. Baptist. Author: Chemistry: the Study of Substances, 1972, rev. edit., 1976. Home: Teaberry Hills Box 322 Route 3 Elkins WV 26241 Office: Dept of Chemistry Davis and Elkins Coll Elkins WV 26241

MARTIN, JOHN SWANSON, educator; b. Sulligent, Ala., May 7, 1939; s. Judson Roby and Frances Susan (Rutland) M.; A.A., Marion (Ala.) Mil. Inst., 1959 A.B., Livingston U., 1961; M.Ed. (fellow), Auburn U., 1965; Edn Specialist (fellow), U. Ala., 1975; m. Linda Ferrell Isaacs, June 3, 1979. Social studies tchr. W.P. Davidson High Sch., Mobile, Ala., 1961—, chmn. dept., 1962—. Mem. NEA, Ala. Edn. Assn., Mobile County Edn. Assn. (past treas.), Nat. Council for Social Studies, Ala. Council for Social Studies, Mobile County Council for Social Studies (v.p. 1977-78), Ala. Hist. Assn., Phi Delta Kappa. Baptist. Office: WR Davidson High Sch 3900 Pleasant Valley Rd Mobile AL 36609

MARTIN, JOHN THOMAS, architect; b. Norwich, Conn., Jan. 9, 1948; s. Thomas James and Marie (Tracy) M.: B.Arch., U. Houston, 1971; Asso. in Engring., Wentworth Inst., Boston, 1967. Architect, David Butts Assos., Bristol, Conn., 1971-72; asso. McCleary Assos. Architects, Houston, 1972-77; owner Timpke-Martin Constrn. Co., Houston, 1974-77; owner John Martin Assos./Architects, Houston, 1977—. Registered architect, Tex., La., Okla. Mem. AIA, Tex. Soc. Architects, Nat. Council Archtl. Registration Bds. Home: 505 Harvard Houston TX 77007 Office: 506 Heights Blvd Houston TX 77007

MARTIN, KERMIT MARKWOOD, vocat. tchr.; b. Maysville, W.Va., Feb. 10, 1917; s. Hubert and Emily Roberta (Kimble) M.; student Potomac State Coll., 1958-60, Fairmont State Coll., summers 1967-68, Marshall U., summers 1969-70, extension courses; m. Anna Martha Flint, July 16, 1939. With Celanese Corp., Cumberland, Md., 1938-45; tchr. auto body for vets., 1945-48; parts and service mgr. Ridder Motors, Inc., Keyser, W.Va., 1948-60, also owner, operator CATV System, 1951-; rocket researcher Hercules Powder Co., Cumberland, 1960-65; supr. setting up of reflector bead factory Gen. Steel Industries, Keyser, 1967-68; tchr. automotive Mineral County Vocat. Center, Keyser, 1968—, coordinator trades and industries dept.; tchr. woodcarving and sculpture to vocat., civic and Boy Scout groups. Asst. scoutmaster Boy Scouts Am., 1954; lay speaker United Methodist Ch. Recipient cert. of outstanding contbn. to vocat. edn. W.Va. Supt. Schs., 1975. Mem. Am. Soc. Quality Control, W.Va. Edn. Assn., W.Va. Vocat. Edn. Assn., NEA, Nat. Vocat. Assn., Potomac Highlands Council, Potomac State Coll. Alumni, Nat. Carvers Mus. Club: Moose. Illustrator electronic text book, woodcarving manual. Designer rocket measuring devices. Home: New Creek WV 26743 Office: New Creek Dr Keyser WV 26746

MARTIN, LAWRENCE MATTHEW, mag. pub.; b. Chgo., June 10, 1928; s. Max John and Peggy M. (Naegele) M.; student Northwestern U., 1948-49, U. Chgo., 1951; m. Jean E. Thamerus, Nov. 10, 1951; children—Stephanie, Laurence. Projects coordinator mag. and TV advt. Sears, Roebuck, Chgo., 1955-67; account supr. Bloom Advt., Dallas, 1967-72; corp communications dir. Fox & Jacobs, Inc., Dallas, 1972-77; pub. Tex. Bus. mag., Dallas, 1977—; adj. prof. advt. So. Meth. U., Dallas, 1974-77. Vice-pres., chmn. Niles Twp. Human Relations Commn., Niles, Ill., 1962-67; mem. Niles Twp. High Sch. Dist. Bd., 1966-67; chmn. Equal Housing Adv. Com., Dallas, 1976-77. Mem. Assn. Area Bus. Publs. (pres. dir.), Public Relations Soc. Am., Sales and Mktg. Execs. Am., Dallas Advt. League. Home: 903 Creekdale Dr Richardson TX 75080 Office: 3003 LBJ Freeway Suite 115 Dallas TX 75234

MARTIN, LINDA SPENCER, microbiologist; b. New Orleans, May 12, 1946; d. Jack Crow and Edna E. (Hood) Spencer; B.S., U. Ala., 1968; M.S., Ga. State U., 1972; m. Ronald Edwin Martin, Aug. 20, 1976. With parasitology div. Automated Parasitic Serology Lab., Center for Disease Control, Atlanta, 1968-73, research microbiologist in clin. immunology Immunology div., 1974—. Mem. Southeastern Immunology Congress (treas. 1978-79), Southeastern Assn. for Clin. Microbiology, Am. Soc. Microbiologists, Sigma Xi. Methodist. Club: P.E.O. (rec. sec. 1979-80). Home: 3796 Briarcliff Rd Atlanta GA 30345 Office: Center for Disease Control 1600 Clifton Rd 1-2251 Atlanta GA 30333

MARTIN, MARCUS FERREL, veterinarian; b. Pinson, Ala., Aug. 15, 1932; s. George Elliott and Alice Sena (Hughes) M.; student Howard Coll., 1951-52; D.V.M., Auburn U., 1958; m. Leah Ellen

Funderburk, Dec. 8, 1968; children—Pana Jean, George Kenneth, Marcus Ferrel. Practice vet. medicine, Memphis and Birmingham, Ala., 1960—; owner Center Point Animal Clinic, Birmingham, 1960—; chmn. bd. Emergency Animal Clinic, 1976-77; pres. M. & K. Enterprises Inc., Birmingham, 1968-70. Chmn. Ala. Veterinarians for Reelection of Nixon, 1972. Recipient Humanitarian award, 1976; Best Citizen award Birmingham Bar Assn., 1976; Citizen of Yr. award East Birmingham C. of C., 1976. Mem. Ala. Acad. Vet. Practice (first pres. 1972), Ala. (pres. 1974-75), Am. (alt. del. 1973-75), Jefferson County (Ala.) (pres. 1965-66) vet. med. assns., Roebuck Sales Club (pres. 1967), Am. Animal Hosp. Assn. Republican. Baptist. Home: 2424 5th Pl NW Birmingham AL 35215 Office: 1704 Center Point Rd Birmingham AL 35215

MARTIN, MARVIN LAWRENCE, data processing co. exec.; b. Casper, Wyo., Sept. 14, 1935; s. Marvin Lawrence and Verda Jane (Pinny) M.; A.A., Casper Coll., 1959; B.S in Elec. Engring. cum laude, S.D. Sch. Mines and Tech., 1962; m. Mary J. Martin, 1979; children—Larry C., Todd N.; children by previous marriage—Laura Rene, Guy Lawrence, Stacy Nicole. Dist. mgr. Sci. Data Systems, Chgo., 1964-67; regional sales mgr. Control Data Corp., Houston, 1967-72; v.p. Kleinschmidt div. SCM, Deerfield, Ill., 1972-75; pres., dir. Tidelands Data Products Inc., Houston, 1975—. Hon. dep. constable of Harris County; committeeman Go-Texan for Houston Rodeo and Livestock Show; mem. Tex. adv. com. Phil Crain for Pres. Served with U.S. Navy, 1953-57. Named Ky. col. Mem. Assn. for Computing Machinery, Data Processing Mgmt. Assn., IEEE, Houston, Houston N.W. chambers commerce. Republican. Methodist. Clubs: Stage Inc., Playhouse 1960, Lions (charter 1960 club). Home: 12403 Campos Houston TX 77065 Office: 5625 FM 1960 W Suite 419 Houston TX 77069

MARTIN, MERLE DUKE, psychologist: b. Richmond, Va., Nov. 25, 1927: d. Herman Joseph and Irene Emily (Anderson) Duke; student William and Mary Coll., 19

MARTIN, MICHAEL DAVID, lawyer; b. Lakeland, Fla., Jan. 4, 1944; s. E. Snow and Mary Y. (Yelvington) M.; B.A., U. of South, 1964; J.D., U. Fla., Gainesville, 1967; m. Lura Virginia Williams, Dec. 28, 1966; children—Michael David, Mallory Thomas. Admitted to Fla. bar, 1968, U.S. Supreme Ct. bar, 1974; mem. firm Martin & Martin, Lakeland, Fla., 1968—; lectr. estate planning and trial practice pub. seminars, 1974-75. Bd. dirs. Boys Club of Lakeland, 1972-73. Named Outstanding Young Man of Yr., Lakeland Jaycees, 1969. Mem. Am. Bar Assn., Fla. Bar, Acad. Fla. Trial Lawyers, Assn. Trial Lawyers Am., Am. Judicature Soc., Polk County Trial Lawyers Assn. (pres. 1976-77), Lakeland C. of C. (v.p. 1980). Clubs: Rotary (dir. 1972-73), Lakeland Yacht and Country (pres. 1978-79). Home: 403 Palmola Lakeland FL 33803 Office: 400 Florida Fed Bldg Lakeland FL 33801

MARTIN, MONTEZ CORNELIUS, JR., constrn. engr., real estate co. exec.; b. Columbia, S.C., June 11, 1940; s. Montez Cornelius and Elise Lanita (Jones) M.; B.S. in Archtl. Engring., Hampton Inst., 1963; postgrad. Poly. Inst. Bklyn., 1966-67; m. E. Maxine Smith, Mar. 8, 1974; children—Tanya Elayne, Terrie Lanita, Emily Elise. Account exec. Sta. WSB-TV, Atlanta, 1970-73; dir. ops. Sta. WSOK, Savannah, Ga., 1973-74; news reporter Sta. WCBD-TV, Charleston, S.C., 1974-75; dir. constrn. Coll. of Charleston, 1974—; producer, host public affairs program Tempo, Sta. WCBD-TV, Charleston, 1975-76; broker-in-charge Montez Real Estate, Charleston, 1976—. Chmn., Dist. 20 Constituent Sch. Bd., 1974-78; vice chmn. Trident Vol. Action Center, 1976-78; fin. sec. Avery Inst. Afro-Am. History and Culture, 1979-80. Served with U.S. Army, 1963-70. Decorated Meritorious Service medal, Army Commendation medal with oak leaf cluster; named Marketeer of Yr. Atlanta chpt. Nat. Assn. Market Developers, 1972; recipient Living the Legacy award Columbia sect. Nat. Council Negro Women, 1980; cert. energy auditor, S.C. Mem. S.C. Real Estate Brokers, Greater Charleston Bd. Realtors, Soc. Am. Mil. Engrs., Trident C. of C., Alpha Phi Alpha (treas. Beta Kappa Lambda chpt. 1979-80). Mem. African Methodist Episcopal Ch. Home: 176 Peachtree St Charleston SC 29403 Office: College of Charleston Charleston SC 29401 also Montez Real Estate 218 President St PO Box 6087 Charleston SC 29405

MARTIN, NATHAN CLAY, social work adminstr.; b. Amarillo, Tex., Oct. 11, 1933; s. Nathan Eugene and Juanita Eola (Farrell) M.; B.S., W. Tex. State U., 1956; M.S.W., Okla. U., 1967; m. Laura Dell Pierce, Apr. 21, 1961; children—Christopher, Laura, Lewis, Julia. Caseworker, Tex. Dept. Pub. Welfare, Gainesville, 1960-63, supr., Wichita Falls, 1963-65, asst. regional dir., Dallas, 1967-68, dir. field staff, Austin, 1968-72, regional adminstr., Lubbock, 1974—; outpatient social worker VA, Amarillo, 1972-74. Served with USAF, 1956-60. Mem. Nat. Assn. Social Workers (Social Worker of Year 1974), Am. Public Welfare Assn., Tex. Pub. Employees Assn., Panhandle Mental Health Assn. (dir. 1973-75). Democrat. Methodist. Home: 410 S Tennessee St Amarillo TX 79106 Office: 2424 34th St Lubbock TX 79411

MARTIN, NORMA QUIGGLE, real estate broker; b. Cleve., Jan. 2, 1915; d. Carl Frank and Anna Matilda (Burke) Q.; grad. Realtors Inst. Fla., 1973; m. John Robertson Martin, Nov. 26, 1938; children—Douglas, David. Active Welcoming Service Sarasota, Fla., 1950-55; real estate broker, salesman E.J. Bacon Co., Sarasota, 1955-58; owner, operator real estate office Sarasota, 1959-62, partner with husband, 1962—; treas. Sarasota Bd. Realtors, 1962, v.p., 1963. Pres. Osprey (Fla.) PTA, 1951-53, Sarasota County PTA Council, 1952-53; deacon Presbyterian Ch. of Covenant, Sarasota, 1971, elder, 1972—. Mem. Nat. Assn. Real Estate Bds. (pres. Sarasota Women's Council, woman of year 1961), Fla. Assn. Realtors (5th Dist. v.p. Women's Council 1962, council state pres. 1976, corp. sec. 1978), Nat. Assn. Realtors (gov. women's council 1977, 78), Am. Inst. Parliamentarians. Mem. Order of Eastern Star. Home and office: 1700 Vamo Dr Sarasota FL 33581

MARTIN, PATRICIA LINDSEY WARD, corrections ofcl.; b. Paducah, Ky., Nov. 21, 1935; d. Henry and Gladys (Lindsey) Ward; A.B., U. Ky., 1957, M.A., 1971; m. Leslie L. Martin, Oct. 23, 1976; children—Lindsey Richards, Ward Richards, Ellen Richards. Tchr. English, Franklin County, Ky., 1971-72; counselor, Blackburn Correctional Complex, Lexington, Ky., 1972-75, first offender unit dir., 1975-76; dep. commr. career devel., Bur. Corrections, Frankfort, Ky., 1976—. Mem. Am. Correctional Assn., Am. Personnel and Guidance Assn., Ky. Council on Crime and Delinquency (past pres. Bluegrass Chpt.). Democrat. Episcopalian. Club: Kappa Alpha Theta (treas., pres. U. Ky., 1955-56). Address: Route 5 Van Arsdale Pike Harrodsburg KY 40330

MARTIN, PATRICK JOSEPH, coal co. exec.; b. Cin., Mar. 16, 1939; s. Joseph B. and Estelle O. (Fannin) M.; B.A. in History, Centre Coll., Danville, Ky., 1960; children—Christopher, Patrick Joseph. Resident mgr. Liberty Mut. Ins. Co., Cin., 1961-67; prin. P. Martin & Co., Inc., Baton Rouge, 1967-74; area mgr. Grow Chem. Co., Baton Rouge, 1974-76; lease adminstr. Elkhorn Coal Corp. subs. Ethyl Corp., Prestonburg, Ky., 1976—. Bd. dirs. Baton Rouge Salvation Army, 1970-75; mem. exec. bd. Istrouma council Boy Scouts Am., Baton Rouge. Mem. Ky. Coal Assn. (legal and taxation com.). Republican. Roman Catholic. Office: 128 Court St Prestonsburg KY 41653

MARTIN, PHILIP JOE, geophysicist; b. Dewar, Okla., July 26, 1934; s. Buford Pigg and Clarice Vance (Martin) M.; B.S. in Geol. Engring., U. Okla., 1958, B.S. in Physics, 1958; m. Shelia Ann Redd, Oct. 3, 1959 (div.); children—Michael Brent, Kimberly Annette, Susan Yvette. Geol. trainee Shell Oil Co., Oklahoma City, 1956-58; geophys. engr. Mobil Oil Co., Dallas, 1959-60; geophysicist, mathematician Texaco, Inc., Bellaire, Tex., 1960-68; sci. analyst Skelly Oil Co., Tulsa, 1968-75; data processing cons. Sperry Rand Corp., Tulsa, 1975-77; project geophysicist Gulf Oil Exploration & Prodn. Co., Oklahoma City, 1977—; pres. Home Computer Products, Inc. Served with U.S. Army, 1958. Mem. Soc. Exploration Geophysicists, Geophys. Soc. Oklahoma City, Oklahoma City Geol. Soc., Internat. Platform Assn., U. Okla. Assn. Republican. Mem. Ch. of Christ. Home: PO Box 393 Oklahoma City OK 73101 Office: 324 N Robinson Oklahoma City OK 73102

MARTIN, RICHARD BLAZO, chemist; b. Winchendon, Mass., July 1, 1917; s. William Butler and Elizabeth (Ela) M.; A.B., Clark U., 1939, M.A., 1940, Ph.D., 1949; m. Dorothy Mae Holway, Sept. 20, 1941; children—Lawrence Sanborn, Richard Holway, Janet Lois, Jean Leslie. Instr. chemistry Clark U., Worcester, Mass., 1946-49, asst. prof., 1949-53; chemist research br., research and devel. div. AEC, Oak Ridge operations, 1953-56, chief research br., 1956-59, dep. dir. research and devel. div., 1959-66, dep. dir. lab. and univ. div., 1966-72, asst. br. chief waste mgmt. br., research and tech. support div., 1972-73, phys. scientist classification and tech. support br., research and tech. support div., 1973-77; cons. Dept. Energy, 1978—. Pack com. chmn. Great Smoky Mountain council Boy Scouts Am., 1964; pres. Cedar Hill P.T.A., 1963-64, mem. Oak Ridge P.T.A. Council, 1963-64. Served to lt. comdr. USNR, 1941-46; capt. Res. ret., 1968. Mem. Am. Chem. Soc. (treas. Central Mass. sect. 1952-53), Res. Officers Assn. (pres. chpt. 1971-72, sec.-treas. 1973-74, historian 1977-78, Navy v.p. Tenn. dept. 1977-78), Mil. Order World Wars, Am. Nuclear Soc., Sigma Xi, Lambda Chi Alpha. Republican. Clubs: Nat Campers and Hikers Association (pres. 1966-67) (Oak Ridge); Smoky Mountain Coachmen (v.p. 1972-74) (Knoxville). Home: 117 Meadow Rd Oak Ridge TN 37830

MARTIN, ROB (ROBERT) KEITH, pub. relations exec.; b. Pitts., Aug. 9, 1941; s. Wilmer Cope and Ida Irene (Emeigh) M.; B.S., Medill Sch. Journalism Northwestern U., 1963, M.S. in Broadcast News, 1964. Pub. affairs officer Norfolk (Va.) based carrier, USN, Vietnam, 1964-67, Pentagon, 1967-68; newsman sta. WQXI-TV, Atlanta, 1968-69; account exec. div. pub. relations firm Liller, Neal, Battle & Lindsey Inc., advt. and pub. relations, Atlanta, 1969-73; dir. pub. relations firm W. M. Zemp & Assos. Inc., advt., St. Petersburg, Fla., 1973-74; v.p., mgr. ops. for S.E., Carl Byoir & Assos. Inc., internat. pub. relations, Atlanta, 1974—. Instr. journalism and pub. relations Ga. State U., 1971-73; project coordinator Chinese Archaeol. Exhbn., 1975; project dir. N. Am. Indian Exhbn., 1977. Pub. relations adviser Forward St. Peter, urban renewel campaign, 1973, St. Petersburg fluoridation referendum, 1973, March of Dimes, St. Petersburg, 1973. Served with USNR, 1964-68; now comdr. Res. Mem. Pub. Relations Soc. Am., U.S. Naval Inst., Navy League, Naval Res. Assn. Republican. Methodist. Contbr. articles to profl. jours., popular mags., newspapers. Home: 1718 Pine Ridge Dr NE Atlanta GA 30324 Office: 600 W Peachtree St Atlanta GA 30308

MARTIN, ROBERT EARNSHAW, advt. agy. exec.; b. Washington, Oct. 17, 1909; s. Robert Hamilton and Alice King (Earnshaw) M.; B.A., B.Ph. in Journalism, Emory U., 1931; m. Martha Frances Cross, June 17, 1959; children—Robert, Margie Hodges, Gray Rains, Patricia Calvert. Pres., Advt. Center, Atlanta, 1929—; account exec. James A. Greene Advt. Agy., 1931-33; advt. mgr. Muse's Retail Stores, 1934-38; pres. Robert E. Martin & Co., Advt. Agy., Atlanta, 1939—. Former pres. Child Service and Family Counseling Center, Family Service Soc.; mem. Grand Jurors Assn., High Mus. Art; mem. guild Atlanta Symphony Orch.; v.p. Emory U. Alumni Council. Served to lt. USNR, 1944-46. Cert. bus. communicator. Mem. Am. Advt. Fedn. (past dist. gov.), Atlanta Advt. Club (past pres.), Bus./Profl. Advt. Assn., Internat. Yachting Fellowship of Rotarians, Scabbard and Blade, Chi Phi, Omicron Delta Kappa, Tau Kappa Alpha. Republican. Episcopalian. Rotarian. Clubs: University Yacht (founding commodore) (Atlanta); St. Petersburg (Fla.) Yacht. Home: 1914 Ardmore Rd NW Atlanta GA 30309 Office: 1819 Peachtree Rd NE Atlanta GA 30309

MARTIN, ROBERT J(EFFERSON), ins. agt.; b. Dallas, Aug. 16, 1941; s. Robert L. and Sylvia (Fox) M.; student U. Tex., Austin, 1961-63; m. Louise Hoffman, Mar. 25, 1967; children—Jeff, Christy. With N.Y. Life Ins. Co., Dallas, 1970-71; owner Robert J. Martin Ins. Agy., Dallas, 1972-77. Served with USMC, 1963-67. Mem. Ins. Counselors Assn. Tex. (sec. 1976), North Dallas C. of C. Republican. Presbyterian. Home: 8509 Thunderbird Dr Dallas TX 75238 Office: 305 Lake Highlands Village Dallas TX 75218

MARTIN, ROBERT L., ednl. adminstr.; b. Winston-Salem, N.C., May 14, 1921; s. William H. and Jennie E. (Sledge) M.; B.S., Appalachian State U., 1950, M.S., 1952; m. Lou Ann Burleson, Sept. 2, 1950; children—William F., Jenn Sussanne, Melynda, Cynthia, Robert S. Tchr., Forsyth County, N.C., 1952-55, Arlington, Va., 1955-57; prin. Navy Dependents Sch., Midway Island, 1957-59; asst. dir. Navy Dependents Schooling Program, Depf. Def., Washington, 1959-64; dir. NEA Tchrs. Corps, 1964-68; supt. Am. Sch. of Kinshasa (Republic of Zaire), 1968-70; dir. devel. Lees McRae Coll., Banner Elk, N.C., 1970-73; exec. dir. Crossnore (N.C.) Sch. Inc., 1973—. Served with USAAC, 1942-45, USAF, 1950-51. Mem. NEA, Am. Assn. Sch. Adminstrs. Home: PO Box 158 Crossnore NC 28616 Office: PO Box 249 Crossnore Sch Inc Crossnore NC 28616

MARTIN, ROSE GODLOVE (MRS. JOSEPH E. MARTIN, JR.), sec. to U.S. Senator; b. Balt., Dec. 4, 1915; d. Joseph V. and Rosa (Hayward) Godlove; R.N., S. Balt. Gen. Hosp. Sch. Nursing, 1941; postgrad. Davis and Elkins Coll., 1956; m. Joseph E. Martin, Jr., Feb. 19, 1942; children—Joseph Ernest, John Samuel. Exec. dir. Randolph County chpt. ARC, 1943-46; dir. nursing service Meml. Gen. Hosp., Elkins, W.Va., 1955-56; pres., exec. dir. Nat. Assn. Practical Nurse Edn. and Service, Inc., N.Y.C., 1966-74; state sec. to U.S. Senator Jennings Randolph of W.Va., 1974-: mem. adv. commn. to health professions N.Y.C. Bd. Edn., 1967-74. Home nursing instr. ARC, 1943-54; mem. Elkins City Council, 1957-61, Elkins-Randolph County Airport Authority, 1960-66; Randolph County Woman Jury Commr., 1965-68. Served to 2d lt. Nurse Corps, 1941-42. Recipient Woman of Achievement award Elkins Bus. and Profl. Women's Club, 1962, Nat. award for Outstanding Achievement, Nat. Assn. Practical Nurse Edn. and Service, 1967; Ky. col. Mem. Nat. Council Women of U.S., Gen. Fedn. Women's Clubs, Nat. Fedn. Bus. and Profl. Women, W.Va. Assn. Mental Health (exec. com. 1965-67), Nurses Assn. (dist. pres. 1962-66), Am. Pub. Health Assn., Am. Soc. Assn. Execs., Nat. Assn. Practical Nurse Edn. and Service, Nat. Assn. Parliamentarians (registered parliamentarian), Assn. Sch. Allied Health Professions, Bus. and Profl. Women's Clubs. Club: Woman's (pres. 1952-54) (Elkins). Home: Box 450 Elkins WV 26241

MARTIN, THOMAS DAVID, coll. adminstr.; b. Tuscaloosa, Ala., Nov. 21, 1949; s. David T.Z. and Bertha A. (Sandsing) M.; B.S., U. Montevallo, 1972, M.Ed., 1973; m. Peggy Joyce Armstrong, Apr. 9, 1977. Tchr. phys. edn. Columbiana (Ala.) Middle Sch., 1973-75; tchr. traffic, safety edn. W. A. Bell High Sch., Bessemer, Ala., 1975-76; dir. housing, student judiciaries South Ga. Coll., Douglas, 1976-79; asst. dir. univ. housing Middle Tenn. State U., Murfreesboro, 1979—. Mem. So. Coll. Personnel Assn., Assn. Coll. and Univ. Housing Officers, Nat. Assn. Coll. Aux. Services (campus rep. 1977—), Delta Chi. Democrat. Baptist. Office: Housing Office Middle Tenn State U Murfreesboro TN 37132

MARTIN, VERNON DEE, city and regional planner; b. Cushing, Okla., Nov. 13, 1942; s. John Vernon and Julia Maud (Anderson) M.; B.S. in Bus. Econs., Okla. State U., 1965; M. Regional and City Planning, U. Okla., 1975; m. Kanda Kirkwood, Apr. 6, 1968; children—Kanda Paige, John Kirkwood. Planner city planning div. Hudgins, Thompson, Ball and Assos., Oklahoma City, 1965-67; community planner Slash Pine Area Planning and Devel. Commn., Waycross, Ga., 1968-69; law enforcement planner Coastal Area Planning and Devel. Commn., Brunswick, Ga., 1969, dir. planning, 1969-70, asst. dir., 1970, exec. dir., 1970—; mem. Gov.'s Com. on Coastal Zone Mgmt., 1970-73, Coastal Marshland Protection Agency, 1970-72; apptd. by Ga. gov. to Coastal Plains Regional Commn. Marine Adv. Resource Bd., 1973. Div. chmn. Glynn County (Ga.) chpt. Am. Cancer Soc. Crusade, 1971-74. Served with Army N.G., 1969—. Recipient Command Ability award Ga. Mil. Inst., 1969. Mem. Am. Planning Assn., Nat. Assn. Devel. Orgns. (sec. 1976-77, 1st v.p. 1978, pres. 1979), Nat. Assn. Regional Commns., Ga. Regional Exec. Dirs. Assn., So. Indsl. Developers Assn., Ga. Bus. and Industry Assn. (mem. industry resources bd.; participant Leadership Ga. 1976). Methodist. Clubs: Brunswick Toastmasters (pres. 1970), St. Simons Island Jaycees (v.p. 1970-71), Brunswick Kiwanis (dir. 1971-72). Home: 206 Wymberly Rd Saint Simons Island GA 31522 Office: 1503 Newcastle St Brunswick GA 31520

MARTIN, WAYNE A., social worker, health service adminstr.; b. N.Y.C., Jan. 26, 1945; s. Bernard and Juliet (Aurbach) M.; B.A. in Social Sci., Fla. State U., 1966; M.S., Sch. of Social Work, Columbia U., 1968; postgrad. Old Dominion U., 1978—; m. Barbara Jo Goodman, Aug. 16, 1970; 1 son, Jason David. Day camp dir. Jewish Community Center, Norfolk, Va., 1968-71, children's dept. dir., 1968-69, youth dept. dir., 1969-71; psychiat. social worker Psychiat. Assos., Ltd., Portsmouth, Va., 1971-77; clin. social worker Human Resource Inst., Norfolk, 1977-79; caseworker (part-time) Cath. Home Bur., Hampton, Va., 1977-78; pvt. practice clin. social work, Virginia Beach, 1977—; program coordinator for adolescent psychiat. unit Peninsula Psychiat. Hosp., Hampton, Va., 1979-80; field supr. Va. Commonwealth U. Sch. of Social Work, 1978—; chmn. adv. com. Upjohn Health-care Services, 1979—. Chmn., Crisis Center, 1977-78; 1st v.p. B'nai B'rith, Va. State Assn., 1977-78, pres., 1979-80, mem. dist. 5 bd. govs., 1978—; chmn. Hillel Found. for State of Va., 1978-79; bd. dirs. Jewish Community Center, Norfolk, 1973-79. Named Outstanding Lodge Pres., B'nai B'rith, 1977; Man of Yr., Va. State Assn. of B'nai B'rith, 1980; lic. clin. social worker, Va. Mem. Nat. Assn. Social Workers (v.p. Hampton Roads unit 1974-76, state dir. 1977—), Acad. of Cert. Social Workers, ACLU, Kappa Delta Pi, Phi Alpha Theta, Pi Sigma Alpha. Democrat. Jewish. Club: Mogul Ski (v.p. 1970-71) (Norfolk). Home: 419 Sinclair St Norfolk VA 23505

MARTIN, WILLARD FRASER, equipment corp. exec.; b. Litchfield, Ill., July 9, 1931; s. Homer Earl and Nellie Willard (Fraser) M.; student U. Hawaii, 1949-51; A.B. in Bus. Adminstrn., George Washington U., 1964; m. Mary Magdalene Thomas, Aug. 30, 1952 (div.); children—Patricia, Pamela, Willard Fraser, Thomas, Paula. Store mgr. Freeman Shoe Corp., Detroit and Wheeling, W.Va., 1952-55; owner, mgr. Martin's Variety Store, Rockford, Ill., 1955-64; salesman, sales trainer, sales supr., br. mgr., regional mgr. Itek Graphic Products, 1963-76; pres., chief exec. officer Cengraphic Corp., Orlando, Fla., 1976—; v.p. charge N.Am. ops. Madax Graphic Products Inc., Orlando, 1978—. Sec. Wheeling Jr. C. of C., 1953-54; mem. Rockford C. of C., 1955-64, Businessmen's Club. Served with U.S. Army, 1948-52. Mem. Printing Industry Am., Orlando C. of C. (sub-com. chmn. 1976), Printing Industries Fla., Central Fla. Graphic Arts Assn., Nat. Microfilm Assn. Republican. Clubs: Masons, Scottish Rite, Blue Lodge. Home: 43 Sorrento Circle Winter Park FL 32792 Office: 6220 S Orange Blossom Trail Suite 316 Orlando FL 32809

MARTIN, WILLIAM ARTHUR, JR., librarian; b. Burlingame, Kans., May 11, 1922; s. William Arthur and Edna LaVerne (Harris) M.; A.B., Coll. Emporia, 1949; M.L.S., Kans. State Tchrs. Coll., 1953; divorced; children—William Arthur III, Margaret Angela. Stacks supr., undergrad. librarian U. Kan., 1953-58; head circulation dept., dir. reader services U. Mo., 1958-68; dir. library U. Sci. and Arts Okla., Chickasha, 1968—; cons., creative writing program AAUW. Served with AUS, 1942-45. Mem. ALA (life), Okla. (pres. coll. div. 1972-73), Southwestern (v.p. coll. div. 1973-74), Mo. (pres. 1967-68) library assns., Okla. Edn. Assn. (chpt. pres. 1971-72), Grady County, Okla. hist. socs., DAV. Episcopalian (vestry). Lion (Sight Conservation award, dir., pres. 1976-77, zone chmn. 1977-78). Contbr. articles to profl. jours. Home: Route 2 Lot 20 Watsons Mobile Home Estates Chickasha OK 73018

MARTIN, WILLIAM HAYWOOD, III, life scientist; b. Bath Springs, Tenn., Nov. 29, 1938; s. William Haywood and Mary (Isbell) M.; B.S., Tenn. Technol. U., 1960; M.S., U. Tenn., 1966, Ph.D., 1971; m. Sybil Ann Hendrix, Aug. 29, 1965; children—Thomas McMillan, Marianne Hendrix. Prof. biology Eastern Ky. Univ., Richmond, 1969—, dir. div. natural areas, 1977—; dir. initial research Lilley Cornett Woods; postdoctoral fellow dept. agronomy U. Ky., 1974-75, research specialist dept. agrl. engring., 1975; Dir. Ky. Jr. Acad. Sci., 1972-75. Named Ky. Wildlife Conservationist of Yr., 1977. Eastern Ky. Univ. grantee, 1971, 73, 78 Mem. Tenn., Ky. acads. sci., AAAS, Assn. Southeastern Biologists, Ecol. Soc. Am., So. Appalachian Botanical Club, Nat. Wildlife Fedn., Friends of Earth, Nature Conservancy (vice chmn., trustee Ky. chpt.), Sigma Xi. Democrat Methodist. Mason (Shriner, 32 deg.). Home: 403 Springfield St Richmond KY 40475 Office: Div Natural Areas Eastern Ky Univ Richmond KY 40475

MARTIN, WILMA JEAN, hosp. adminstr.; b. Logan County, Va., July 30, 1937; d. Donald Queen and Elberta (Lucas) Queen Ellis; student So. W.Va. Community Coll., 1974; m. James P. Martin, Feb. 1, 1977; children—John F. Cook, J. Michael Cook. Med. sec. to chief of staff Guyan Valley Hosp., Logan, W.Va., 1954-60, asst. to hosp. adminstr., 1960-72, hosp. adminstr., 1972—; v.p., partner Logan Park Care Center Nursing Home; pres., owner Guyan Distb. Co., Logan; sec. Hosp. Corp. Active in community vol. work, including co-chmn. Cancer Soc., Logan. Mem. Smithsonian Instn., Order Ky. Cols. Presbyterian. Home: 171 Nighbert Ave Logan WV 25601 Office: 396 Dingess St Logan WV 25601

MARTINEZ, ALVARO IGNACIO, cardiologist; b. Cartegena, Colombia, Aug. 26, 1936; s. Carlos and Albertina Martinez; came to U.S., 1960, naturalized, 1969; diploma LaSalle U. (Colombia), 1953; M.D., Javeriana U. (Colombia), 1959; m. Gloria Badel, Jan. 14, 1960; children—Alvaro Ignacio, Patricia. Intern, Jefferson Hosp., Roanoke,

Va., 1960-61; resident, Detroit Meml. Hosp., 1961-63; fellow in cardiovascular disease U Ala., Birmingham, 1963-64, U. Miami (Fla.), 1969-70; practice medicine, specializing in cardiology, Hialeah, Fla., 1971—; v.p., chmn. credentials com. Palmetto Gen. Hosp., Hialeah, 1971-72, pres. med. staff, 1973-74, bd. dirs., 1978—; clin. asso. prof. medicine U. Miami Sch. Medicine, Coral Gables, Fla., 1979—. Hon. vice consul, consul for Republic of Colombia, Detroit, 1966-67. Served with M.C., U.S. Army, 1967-69. Fellow A.C.P., Am. Coll. Cardiology, Council Clin. Cardiologists Am. Heart Assn. Roman Catholic. Contbr. sects. to books, articles to profl. jours. Office: 970 W 49th St Hialeah FL 33012

MARTINEZ, DELIA BRONDO, nurse: b. San Luis, Potosi, Mex., Jan. 23, 1928; d. Manuel and Juana (Sanchez) Brondo; came to U.S., 1957; Masters degree, Universidad Autonoma de San Luis, Potosi, 1945; m. Sergio A. Martinez, June 4, 1962; children—Delia Elisa, Sergio Arturo. Staff nurse Am. Smelting Hosp., Rosita, Coahuila, Mex. 1945-47, operating room supr., 1948-57; staff nurse Driscoll Found. Children's Hosp., Corpus Christi, 1953; staff and surg. nurse Vanderbilt U. Hosp., Nashville, 1957-58; staff and surg. nurse Maverick County Hosp., Eagle Pass, Tex., 1959-62; recovery room nurse St. Catherine's Hosp., East Chicago, Ind., 1963-64; operating room supr. Maverick County Hosp., 1967—. Recipient Public Service award Maverick County Hosp., 1977; R.N., Tex., Tenn. Mem. Assn. Operating Room Nurses, Tex. Hosp. Assn., Am. Hosp. Assn., Tex. Soc. Central Service Personnel. Roman Catholic. Home: 508 Pecos St Eagle Pass TX 78852

MARTINEZ, ELENA RAQUEL, physician; b. Pinar del Rio, Cuba, Sept. 4, 1932; d. Maximo and Clara Maria (Aguiar) M.; B.S., U. Pinar del Rio, Cuba, 1950; M.D., U. Madrid (Spain), 1958, U. Havana, Cuba, 1959. Intern, Columbus Hosp., N.Y.C., 1965-66; resident in surgery St. Barnabas Med. Center, Livingston, N.J., 1966-67; resident in orthopaedic surgery USPHS Hosp., S.I., 1967-68, Met. Hosp., N.Y.C., 1969-70, Flower Hosp., N.Y.C., 1969-70, 5th Ave Hosp., N.Y.C., Hosp. Crippled Children, Newark, N.J., 1968-69; clin. instr. orthopedic surgery U. Miami; practice medicine specializing in orthopaedic surgery, Miami, Fla., 1970—. Diplomate Am. Bd. Orthopaedic Surgery. Fellow Am. Coll. Surgeons, Cuban Soc. Orthopaedic Surgery; mem. Am. Acad. Orthopaedic Surgery, Dade County Med. Assn., Fla. Med. Assn., AMA, Miami Orthopaedic Soc., Fla. Orthopaedic Soc., Am. Profl. Practice Assn. Home: 65 Shore Dr W Miami FL 33133 Office: Mercy Professional Bldg Suite 701 3661 S Miami Ave Miami FL 33133

MARTINEZ, IRVING RICARDO, JR., dermatologist; b. New Orleans, Apr. 30, 1935; s. Irving Ricardo and Amelia (Areces) M.; B.S. in Biology, Loyola U., New Orleans, 1958, M.S. in Physiology, 1960; M.D., La. State U., 1965; Ph.D., Boston U., 1971; m. Dolly-Dean Kimball, June 24, 1961; children—Contessa Mariana, Irving Ricardo III. Rotating intern Overlook Hosp., Summit, N.J., 1965-66; USPHS trainee in dermatology N.Y. Hosp.-Cornell U. Med. Center, 1966-67, Univ. Hosp.-Boston U. Med. Center, 1967-70; head electron microscopy lab., div. research Alton Ochsner Med. Found., New Orleans, 1972-74, asst. dir. research, 1973-74, chmn. program com., 1973-74; asso. chmn. dermatology Ochsner Clinic, 1971-74; asst. clin. prof. dermatology and anatomy Tulane U. Med. Sch., 1970—; mem. faculty La. State U. Med. Sch., 1970—, asso. clin. prof. dermatology and anatomy, 1975—; dermatologist E. Jefferson Gen. Hosp., Metairie, La., Lakeside Hosp. for Women, Metairie, St. Charles Gen. Hosp., New Orleans; vis. dermatologist Charity Hosp., New Orleans; cons. USPHS Hosp., New Orleans. Bd. dirs. Delta Festival Ballet Co., 1977—. Served as capt. AUS, 1958-59. Recipient Russell L. Holman Meml. Pathology award La. State U., 1964, Mabel Clair Elmore Research-Essay award, 1965; grantee Nat. Inst. Dental Research, 1974-76. Diplomate Am. Bd. Dermatology. Fellow Am. Acad. Facial, Plastic and Reconstructive Surgery, Am. Acad. Dermatology (Bronze award sci. exhibit 1971), A.C.P., Am. Soc. Dermatol. Surgery, Internat. Acad. Cosmetic Surgery, Royal Soc. Health; mem. Am. Assn. Anatomists, AAAS, Am. Fedn. Clin. Research, AMA, So. Med. Assn., Am. Med. Writers Assn., Am. Soc. Cell Biology, Am. Soc. Dermatopathology, Am. Soc. Zoologists, Assn. Ind. Research Insts., Dermatology Found., Electron Microscopy Soc. Am., Internat. Soc. Tropical Dermatology, La. (sec.-treas. 1972-73), N.Am. Clin. dermatol. socs., La. Soc. Electron Microscopy, La., Orleans parish med. socs., New Orleans Grad. Med. Assembly (chmn. 1976), N.Y. Acad. Scis., Soc. Investigative Dermatology, Thackeray Soc., Sigma Xi, Phi Chi. Democrat. Roman Catholic. Clubs: Metairie Country; Iris; New Orleans Opera (dir., chmn. membership com. 1975—), Empire, Pendennis, Bienville, Semreh (New Orleans). Contbr. numerous articles to med. jours. Home: 1416 Webster St New Orleans LA 70118 Office: 3333 Kingman St Suite M Metairie LA 70002 also 144 Elks Pl Suite 1604 New Orleans LA 70112

MARTINEZ, LUIS OSVALDO, radiologist; b. Havana, Cuba, Nov. 27, 1927; came to U.S., 1962, naturalized, 1967; s. Osvaldo and Felicitas (Farinas) M.; M.D., U. Havana, 1954; m. Norma Rodriguez, Nov. 20, 1955; children—Maria Elena, Luis Osvaldo, Alberto Luis. Intern, Calixto Garcia Hosp., Havana, 1954-55; resident in radiology Jackson Meml. Hosp., Miami, Fla., 1963-65, fellow in cardiovascular radiology, 1965-67; instr. radiology U. Miami, 1965-68, asst. prof., 1968, clin. asst. prof., 1968-70, asso. prof., 1970-76, prof., 1976—; asso. dir. dept. radiology Mt. Sinai Med. Center, Miami Beach, Fla., 1969—, chief div. diagnostic radiology, 1970—, dir. residency program in diagnostic radiology. Mem. Internat. Soc. Lymphology, Internat. Coll. Surgeons, Internat. Coll. Angiology, Internat. Soc. Radiology, Interam. Coll. Radiology (Gold medal 1975), Cuban Med. Assn. in Exile, Am. Coll. Chest Physicians (asso.), AAUP, AMA, Radiol. Soc. N. Am., Am. Coll. Radiology, Am. Roentgen Ray Soc., Am. Assn. Fgn. Med. Grads., Am. Profl. Practice Assn., Am. Thoracic Soc., Pan Am. Med. Assn., Am. Assn. U. Radiologists, Brit. Inst. Radiology, Am. Heart Assn. (mem. council cardiovascular radiology), Faculty Radiologists, Soc. Gastrointestinal Radiologists, Am. Geriatrics Soc., Am. Coll. Angiology, Royal Coll. Radiologists, Am. Soc. Therapeutic Radiologists, Assn. Hosp. Med. Edn., Am. Coll. Med. Imaging, Interasma, So. Med. Assn., N.Y. Acad. Scis., Fla. Thoracic Soc., Fla. Radiol. Soc., Dade County Med. Assn., Greater Miami Radiol. Soc.; hon. mem. numerous med. socs. of Mex., Central and S. Am. Roman Catholic. Reviewer Am. Jour. Radiology, Radium Therapy and Nuclear Medicine, 1978; editor Revista Interamericana de Radiologia, 1975; contbr. articles in field to profl. jours. Office: 4300 Alton Rd Miami Beach FL 33140

MARTINEZ, MILTON EDVARDO, surgeon; b. Matanzas, Cuba, Oct. 13, 1930; came to U.S., 1968, naturalized, 1975; s. Andres V. and Aida R. M.; M.D., U. Havana, 1954; m. Caridad Torres Bauza, Oct. 6, 1956; children—Milton E., Edvardo M., Rebeca C., Ruth M. Intern and resident in gen. surgery Mt. Sinai Hosp., Miami Beach, Fla., 1969-74; resident in surgery Sanitorio La Esperamze, Havana, 1954-60, thoracic surgeon, 1960-67; gen. surgeon Hosp. Covadonga, Havana, 1960-68; practice medicine specializing in gen. and vascular surgery, Miami, 1974—. Mem. AMA, Fla. Med. Assn., Dade County Med. Assn., Cuban Soc. Surgery, Am. Soc. Abdominal Surgeons. Republican. Roman Catholic. Home: 354 SW 20th Rd Miami FL 33129 Office: 2541 SW 27 Ave Miami FL 33133

MARTINEZ, OTTO HERIBERTO, clergyman, counselor psychologist; b. Habana, Cuba, Mar. 16, 1932; s. Abdon and Agnes Helene (Fuchs) M.; came to U.S., 1964, naturalized, 1970; B.A. in Classics and Lit., Colegio S. Estanislao, Havana, 1954; M.A. in Philosophy and Psychology, Colegio Maximo S.F. Borja, Barcelona, Spain, 1957; M.A. in Theology, Coll. L'Immaculee-Conception, Montreal, 1964; M.S. in Counseling and Guidance, Barry Coll., Miami, Fla., 1973; postgrad. Pontificia Universitas Gregoriana, Rome, 1968-70, Barry Coll., 1973-75, U. Miami, 1975—. Joined Soc. of Jesus, 1948; ordained priest Roman Catholic Ch., 1963; asst. prin., tchr. theology and sociology Colegio de Belen, Havana, 1957-60; dir. guidance, tchr. psychology Belen Jesuit Prep. Sch., Miami, 1965-68, 70—; sec., cons. Latin Am. affairs Superior Gen. of Jesuit Fathers, Rome, 1968-70; instr. psychology, counselor psychologist bilingual program Miami-Dade Community Coll., 1973—; cons. to orgns.; cons. Encuentros Familiares; bd. dirs. Cuban Mus. Arts and Culture; cons. WPBS. Recipient award Miami-Dade Community Coll. Student Govt., 1977, Soc. Distinguished High Sch. Students, 1977. Mem. Am. Personnel and Guidance Assn., Nat. Council Family Relations, Internat. Transactional Analysis Assn., Assn. Humanistic Psychology, Am. Specialists in Group Work Assn. Home: 2928 SW 10th St Miami FL 33135 Office: 824 SW 7th Ave Miami FL 33130

MARTINEZ, SAMUEL JOSEPH, JR., editor, educator; b. Chgo., Sept. 20, 1916; s. Samuel Jose and Luzetta (Karst) M.; B.S.in Chemistry, Purdue U., 1937; M.A. in English, U. Tulsa, 1951; m. Alice Louise Roush, Apr. 18, 1943; children—Robert Lee, Luzetta Marie Martinez Ennis, Samuel Joseph III, Alan David, Charles Edwin. Chemist Corn Products Refining Co., Chgo., 1937-40; explosives chemist U.S. Army Ordnance Dept., Charlestown, Ind., 1941-42, Pryor, Okla., 1943-45; research chemist, tech. editor Dow Chem. Co., Tulsa 1946-61; asso. prof. U. Tulsa, 1961—, engring. editor Petroleum Abstracts, 1961—. Mem. Am. Chem. Soc. (chmn. chpt. 1971), Am. Soc. Info. Sci., Soc. Petroleum Engrs., Tulsa Little Theatre, Asso. Artists Philbrook. Methodist. Mason (33 deg.). Club: Spotlight Theatre. Contbr. articles to profl. jours. Home: 1003 E 18th St Tulsa OK 74120 Office: U Tulsa 600 S College Ave Tulsa OK 74104

MARTINEZ, SERGIO ERNESTO, constrn. co. exec.; b. Havana, Cuba, Aug. 4, 1919; s. Sergio and Clara (de la Vega) M.; came to U.S., 1960, naturalized, 1966; B.S. in E.E., M.I.T., 1940, B.S. in Mech. Engring., 1947; M.S. in Indsl. Engring., N.Y. U., 1967; profl. indsl. engr., Columbia U., 1972; m. Adeline Benejam, June 24, 1946; children—Sergio Alberto, Maria Linda. Chief engr. Textilera Ariguanabo, Bauta, Cuba, 1943-49; field supt. Frederick Snare Corp., Venezuela, Cuba and Colombia, 1949-55; mill mgr. Papelera Pulpa Cuba, Trinidad, Cuba, 1955-60; chief project engr., dir. budgeting and planning Parsons & Whittemore, Inc., N.Y.C., 1960-77, v.p., gen. mgr. subsidiary Resources Recovery Constrn. Corp., Miami, Fla., 1977—; parttime instr. N.Y. U. Grad. Sch. Engring., 1969-73. Registered profl. engr., Sask. (Can.). Mem. TAPPI, Am. Assn. Cost Engrs., Cuban Assn. Engrs. Roman Catholic. Author articles in field. Address: 8520 SW 80th Pl Miami FL 33143

MARTINEZ, VICTOR JULIO, surgeon; b. Tampa, Fla., July 27, 1934; s. David and Mary (Fernandez) M.; student U. Fla., 1952-55; M.D., U. Miami, 1959; m. Aline Rheta Guerra, 10, 1956; children—Victor Daniel, Katherine Ann. Intern, Jackson Meml. Hosp., Miami, Fla., 1959-60, resident in thoracic surgery, 1964-66; resident in gen. surgery Tampa Gen. Hosp., 1960-64; comdr. USPHS, S.I., N.Y., also dep. chief of surgery, 1966-68; pvt. practice specializing in thoracic and cardiovascular surgery, Tampa, 1968—; asst. clin. prof. U. South Fla. Sch. Medicine; mem. Hillsborough County Health Planning Council, 1970-74, Fla. Bd. Med. Examiners, 1972—, pres., 1975-76. Bd. dirs. S.W. Fla. Blood Bank, Centro Asturiano Hosp., Tampa Marine Inst., Hillsborough County Med. Found. Mem. AMA (recognition award), Am. Coll. Cardiology, Am. Coll. Chest Physicians, Internat. Coll. Surgeons, Am. Coll. Angiology, Fla., Hillsborough County med. assns., Fla. Soc. Thoracic and Cardio-Vascular Surgeons, Tampa Surg. Soc. Democrat. Roman Catholic. Club: Krewe Sant Yago. Contbr. articles med. jours. Home: 1905 W Orient St Tampa FL 33607 Office: 4530 N Armenia Ave Suite 6 Tampa FL 33603

MARTINEZ-ESTEVE, RAUL JUAN ANTONIO, lawyer; b. Havana, Cuba, Feb. 15, 1945; s. Raul Lazaro and Grethel Ligia (Esteve) M.; came to U.S., 1960, naturalized, 1971; B.S.C.E., U. Fla., 1966; M.B.A., U. Miami (Fla.), 1970, J.D., 1974. Civil engr. Pub. Works Dept. Met. Dade County, Miami, 1969-72; constrn. mgr. New Eng. Oyster House Restaurant Chain, Dania, Fla., 1972; admitted to Fla. bar, 1974; asso. firm Guido A. Aguilera, Coral Gables, Fla., 1974-76, Meyer, Weiss, Rose, Arkin, Sheppard and Shockett, P.A., Miami Beach, Fla., 1976-79, Levine, Reckson, Reed & Geiger, P.A., Miami, 1979—; cons. in field. Mem. ASCE, Am., Dade County, Miami Beach bar assns., Fla. Bar, Am. Trial Lawyers Assn., Cuban-Am. Lawyers Assn., Internat. Law Soc. Asociacion InterAmericana de Hombres de Empresa, U.S. Tennis Assn., Phi Alpha Delta. Democrat. Roman Catholic. Clubs: Kiwanis, Miami Ski. Home: 9204 SW 8th Terr Miami FL 33174 Office: 3501 Biscayne Blvd Miami FL 33137

MARTINEZ-PEREZ, LUIS ARMANDO, educator; b. Toa Alta, P.R., July 19, 1941; s. Melquiades Martinez and Octavia Perez; B.S., U. P.R., 1964; M.S., Fla. State U., 1968, Ph.D. (NDEA fellow), 1973; m. Zaida C. Morales, May 29, 1965; children—Olga Cecilia, Luis Armando. Analytical chemist Gen. Electric Co., Bridgeport, Conn., 1968-70; research asst. Fla. State U., Tallahassee, 1970-73; asso. prof. sci. edn. Fla. Internat. U., Miami, 1973—, dir. Multilingual Intercultural Center, 1979—; cons. sci. edn. and bilingual edn.; chmn. Bilingual Multicultural Consortium, 1978—; adviser Children's TV Workshop Sci. Series, also Office of Hispanic Affairs, HEW. Chmn. bd. dirs. Borinquen Health Care Center. Title VII grantee, 1979—. Mem. Nat. Assn. Research In Sci. Teaching, Nat. Sci. Tchrs. Assn., Am. Ednl. Research, Assn., Bilingual Assn. Fla. Assn. Supervision and Curriculum Devel., Nat. Assn. Bilingual Edn., Southeastern Assn. Tchrs. in Sci., Fla. Assn. Sci. Tchrs., Phi Delta Kappa. Democrat. Roman Catholic. Home: 13239 SW 85th Terr Miami FL 33183 Office: Fla Internat U Tamiami Trail Miami FL 33199

MARTÍN-JIMÉNEZ, LUIS, health service adminstr.; b. Caguas, P.R., Sept. 10, 1925; s. Miguel A. Martín and Marcelina Jiménez; B.S., Syracuse U., 1950; m. Milagros Jimenez, Nov. 22, 1951; children—Milibe, Carmen Luisa, Luis Manuel, Miguel Javier. Adminstr., Mayaguez (P.R.) Tb Hosp., 1950-51, Clinica Dr. M. Julia, Hato Rey, P.R., 1951-53, Auxilio Mutuo Hosp., Hato Rey, 1953-55, Mimiya Hosp., 1955-61; gen. adminstr. Seafarers Internat. Union Welfare and Med. Plan, Santurce, P.R., 1961-67; adminstr. Health Coop., 1967-68; asst. adminstr. Non Fault Auto Accidents Ins., 1968-70; exec. dir. P.R. Bd. Health, 1970-76; adminstr. for asst. secretariat instnl. services P.R. Dept. Health, Hato Rey, 1976—, asst. sec., 1976—; cons. projects in P.R., Santo Domingo. Served with AUS, 1943-46. Mem. Am. Hosp. Assn. (del.), Am. Pub. Health Assn., Am. Assn. Mental Deficiency (del.), P.R. Hosp. Assn. (sec.-treas.), P.R. Hosp. Adminstrn. Assn. (past pres.), Group Health Assn. Am. Roman Catholic. Clubs: Caguas Lions, Berwind Country. Address: 11-I Hato Rey Plaza Hato Rey PR 00918

MARTONE, LUCIA WINIFRED, dietitian; b. Nashville, June 26, 1920; d. Earle Raymond and Lucia Florence (Madden) Hudson; B.S., Loma Linda U., 1941, M.P.H., 1980; M.A., Appalachian State U., 1965; B.A., U. N.C. at Asheville 1977; m. Albert Rocco Martone, Apr. 9, 1943 (dec. 1958); children—Arlene Rae, Linda Marie, Brenda Sharon. Holder various part-time positions as dietitian, art tchr., music tchr., 1943-69; dietitian Fletcher (N.C.) Hosp., 1969-72; dietary cons. Pisgah Manor, Candler, N.C., 1973-76; tchr. art Blue Ridge Tech. Inst., Hendersonville, N.C., 1975-76; tchr., cons. in field. Recipient 2d place award Art in the Bank Show, Asheville, N.C., 1967; Purchase prizes Asheville Art Museum, 1977. The Oct. Show, High Country Crafters, Asheville, 1977. Mem. Am. Dietetic Assn., Hendersonville Art League, Asheville Art Museum, Nat. Audubon Soc.

MARTZ, DAVID MICHAEL, psychiatrist; b. Covington, Ky., July 4, 1937; s. Ralph Joseph and Ruth Barbara (Goshen) M.; B.A. cum laude, Rice U., 1959; M.D., Baylor U., 1963; m. Marilynn Revis, Oct. 17, 1959; children—Laura, Rosalind. Intern surgery Methodist Hosp., Houston, 1963-64; resident psychiatry Baylor Coll. Medicine, Houston, 1964-67, chief resident psychiatry, 1967, clin. asst. prof. psychiatry, 1974—; staff psychiatrist VA Hosp., Houston, 1967-68; practice medicine specializing in psychiatry, Houston, 1968—; mem. staff Rosewood Gen. Hosp., Houston. Mem. honor roll Tex. Bd. Med. Examiners; named Ky. Col. Diplomate Am. Bd. Psychiatry and Neurology. Mem. Am. Psychiat. Assn., Houston Psychiat. Soc., Tex. Med. Assn., Harris County Med. Soc. Office: 9090 Park West Dr Houston TX 77063

MARTZ, GLENN EVERETT, journalist, author, lectr.; b. Livonia, Mo., Sept. 1, 1900; s. Seth Thomas and Lydia Dea (Speak) M.; student Kirksville (Mo.) State Tchrs. Coll., 1924, No. State Tchrs. Coll., S.D., 1926-27; m. Beverly Margaret Smith, June 4, 1936 (dec.); children—Dale Ellsworth, Glenn Eldon, Sally Ann (Mrs. Edward Southgate), Mary Lou (Mrs. Malcolm Minor); m. 2d, Annie Louise Monan, June 2, 1972. Editor Am.-News, Aberdeen, S.D., 1930-36, A.P., Bismarck, N.D., 1945-46, U.P.I., Washington, 1947-53; asso. editor Banner, Nashville, 1965-69; staff writer Look Mag., Des Moines, 1940; pub. Washington News Beat, 1954-63; editorial writer Pensacola (Fla.) New-Jour.; field mgr. Office Def. Transp., Minn., N.D., 1943-45; dir. pub relations Marine Resources div. Ala. Dept. Conservation, 1971-74; editor Baldwin County (Ala.) Independent, also Gulf Coast Farmer, Dixie Farmer, 1979—; mayor City of Summerdale (Ala.), 1976. Republican. Roman Catholic. Home: 212 E Shotwell St Bainbridge GA 31717

MARTZ, WILLARD HARRY, dermatologist; b. Camden, N.J., Dec. 2, 1934; s. Willard Weldon and Lena (Waldner) M.; B.A., Rutgers U., 1956; M.D., Temple U., 1960. Intern, Mt. Sinai of Greater Miami, 1960-61; resident in dermatology VA Hosp., Long Beach, Calif., 1963-66; practice medicine specializing in dermatology, Los Angeles, 1966-67, Fontana, Meml. Hosp., Miami, Fla.; cons. dermatology Miami VA Hosp.; clin. asst. prof. Sch. Medicine, U. Miami. Diplomate Am. Bd. Dermatology. Mem. Am. Acad. Dermatology, Am. Soc. Dermatologic Surgery, Am. Veneral Disease Assn., Pacific Dermatology Assn., Fla., Dade County med. assns., Fla. Soc. Dermatology, Fla. Physicians Assn., Alpha Omega Alpha. Democrat. Cons. editor Jour. Fla. Med. Assn., 1972-75. Home: 301 W San Marino Dr Miami Beach FL 33139 Office: 1688 Meridian Ave Miami Beach FL 33139

MARUTHUR, GOPAKUMAR, physician; b. Calicut, Kerala, India, Mar. 13, 1944; came to U.S., 1971; s. Vasudevan-Nair Muchikkal and Deviamma Maruthur; M.B.B.S., Calicut Med. Coll., Kerala, 1966; m. Peggy Justine Brunner, July 7, 1976; 1 dau., Nisa Marisa. Intern, Calucut Med. Coll., 1967-68; resident in gen. practice West Suburban Hosp., Oak Park, Ill., 1971-72; resident in internal medicine Cook County Hosp., Chgo. 1972-74, fellow in endocrinology and metabolism, 1974-76; attending physician St. Joseph's Mercy Med. Center, Hot Springs, Ark. 1976—, Ouachita Meml. Hosp., Hot Springs, 1976—. Diplomate Am. Bd. Internal Medicine, Am. Bd. Endocrinology and Metabolism. Mem. AMA, A.C.P. Home: 33 Circle Dr Hot Springs AR 71901 Office: Central Tower Suite 805 Hot Springs AR 71901

MARUYAMA, YOSH, physician, educator; b. Pasadena, Calif., Apr. 30, 1930; s. Edward Yasaki and Chiyo (Sakai) M.; A.B., U. Calif., Berkeley, 1951; M.D., U. Calif., San Francisco, 1955; m. Fudeko Tsuji, July 18, 1954; children—Warren H., Nancy C., Marian M., Karen A. Intern, San Francisco Hosp., 1955-56; resident in radiology Mass. Gen. Hosp., Boston 1958-61; Jas. Picker Advanced Acad. fellow Stanford Med. Sch., 1962-64; asst. prof. radiology U. Minn., 1964-67, asso. prof., 1967-70, dir. div. radiotherapy, 1968-70; prof. radiation medicine, chmn. dept. radiation medicine U. Ky., 1970—, dir. Radiation Therapy Oncology Center, 1975—; cons. in field; Jas. Picker traveling fellow, Eng., France, Scandanavia, 1965. Democratic Farm Labor precinct del. Minn. Dem. Conv., 1968. Served as capt., M.C., U.S. Army, 1956-58. Ky. col.; Am. Cancer Soc. fellow, 1960-61. Diplomate Am. Bd. Radiology. Mem. Am. Assn. Cancer Research, Am. Soc. Therapeutic Radiologists, AAUP, AAAS, Am. Assn. Immunologists, Am. Radium Soc., Am. Coll. Radiology, Cell Kinetics Soc., Ky. Med. Assn., Ky. Cancer Commn., Fayette County Med. Soc., Minn. Acad. Scis., N.Y. Acad. Scis., Radiation Research Soc., Soc. Exptl. Biology and Medicine, Soc. Chmn. Acad. Radiation Oncology Programs, Southeastern Cancer Research Assn. (dir.), South Eastern Cancer Study Group, Radiol. Soc. N. Am., Japan Soc. N.Y., Japan Soc. Ky., Phi Beta Kappa, Sigma Xi, Alpha Omega Alpha. Presbyterian. Club: Spindletop Hall (Lexington, Ky.). Contbr. articles to profl. jours.; editor: New Methods in Tumor Localization, 1977; asso. editor Applied Radiology, 1974—; cert. Shodan Judoka, Kodokan Inst. Judo, Tokyo, 1957. Home: 1739 Lakewood Dr Lexington KY 40502 Office: Dept Radiation Medicine Radiation Therapy Oncology Center U Ky Med Center Lexington KY 40536

MARVIN, HELEN RHYNE, state legislator; b. Gastonia, N.C., Nov. 30, 1917; d. Dane Samuel and Tessie Pearl (Hastings) Rhyne; B.A. magna cum laude, Furman U., Greenville, S.C., 1938; M.A., La. State U., 1939; m. Ned Irving Marvin, Nov. 21, 1941; children—Kathryn Andrea, Richard Morris, David Rhyne. Pub. schs. tchr., Gastonia, 1953-65; prof. polit. sci. Gaston Coll., Dallas, N.C., 1965-79, head social sci. dept., 1975-79; mem. N.C. Senate from 25th Dist., 1976—; mem. N.C. Social Services Commn., 1979—, N.C. State Apprenticeship Council, 1978—, N.C. Women's Forum, 1977—. Chmn. N.C. Council Status Women, 1976—; mem. N.C. State Health Coordinating Council, Gov. N.C. Adv. Council Children and Youth, R.J. Reynolds fellow econs. edn., 1964; named Outstanding Tchr., Gaston Coll., 1974. Mem. Am., So., N.C. (pres. 1977-78) polit. sci. assns., N.C. Community Coll. Social Scis. Assn. (chmn. 1976-78), Delta Kappa Gamma, Zeta Tau Alpha. Democrat. Presbyterian. Club: Gastonia Altrusa. Home: 119 Ridge Ln Akers Station Gastonia NC 28052

MARVIN, PHILIP, fin. officer, ins. co. exec.; b. Palatka, Fla., Apr. 17, 1930; s. Constantine Bailey and Sydonia Irene (Wolfe) M.; B.S. in Psychology, U. Fla., 1958, postgrad., 1958-59; m. Velma Ruth Hand, June 4, 1960; children—Ruth Anita, Melissa Anne, Philip Anthony. Staff asst. to congressman from Fla., 1957-59; Ga. state rep. Nat. Found. March of Dimes, 1959, N.Y., 1959, Miss., 1959-62, N.C.,

1962-65; dir. Loyalty Fund, U. Fla., Gainesville, 1965-66; ins. agt. Conn. Mut. & Home Life N.Y., 1966-71; agy. supr. Travelers Corp., Jacksonville, Fla., 1971-75; asst. gen. agt. Thomas & Assos., Jacksonville, 1975—; chief fin. officer Am. Prepaid Profl. Services, Inc., Jacksonville, 1978—, Am. Dental Plan, Inc., Jacksonville, 1978—; instr. ins. courses Fla. Jr. Coll., Jacksonville, 1972-75. Bd. dirs. Nat. Found.-March of Dimes, N.E. Fla. chpt., 1972-77. Served with USN, 1951-55; Korea. Recipient Disting. Vol. Leadership award Nat. Found.-March of Dimes, 1974, H. Laurence Cooper C.L.U. Meml. award, 1975; C.L.U. Mem. Jacksonville Assn. Life Underwriters, Am. Soc. C.L.U.'s, Police Council. Republican. Episcopalian. Club: Sertoma (dir. 1973-77, v.p. 1976-77). Home: 415 Scorpio Ln Orange Park FL 32073

MARYNICK, MARILYN CHASE, botanist; b. Los Angeles, Apr. 25, 1948; d. Mervin McMillan and Emily (Catherman) Chase; B.A. in Botany, Calif. State U., Los Angeles, 1969; Ph.D. in Plant Physiology (Jesse D. Carr fellow), U. Calif., Davis, 1976; m. Dennis Stephen Marynick, June 29, 1975. Research asst., teaching asst. U. Calif., Davis, 1969-74; instr. sci. dept. Bentley Coll., Waltham, Mass., 1976-78; adj. asst. prof. depts. biology and chemistry U. Tex., Arlington, 1978-79; vis. asst. prof. biology dept. U. Tex., Arlington, 1979—; speaker, author. Mem. AAAS, Am. Chem. Soc., Am. Inst. Biol. Scis., Am. Soc. Plant Physiologists, Bot. Soc. Am., N.Y. Acad. Scis., Sigma Xi, Tex. Orgn. for Endangered Species, Phi Kappa Phi. Home: 5622 Valley Meadow Dr Arlington TX 76016 Office: Depts Biology and Chemistry U Tex Arlington TX 76019

MASIKO, PETER, JR., coll. pres.; b. Vera Cruz, Pa., Mar. 18, 1914; s. Peter, Sr., and Sophia (Baker) M.; B.A. with highest honors, Lehigh U., 1936; M.A. (fellow), U. Ill., 1937, Ph.D., 1939; m. Anne E. Fetterolf, July 9, 1932; children—Elaine Irene (Mrs. James Salapatas), Peter III. Instr. U. Ill., 1936-39; with Wright Jr. Coll., Chgo., 1939-56, successively instr., chmn. social sci. dept., asst. dean, became dean, 1950; exec. dean Chgo. City Jr. Coll., 1956-62; pres. Miami-Dade Community Coll., Miami, Fla., 1962—; economist Bd. Investigation and Research, Washington, summer 1942; mem. U.S. Dept. Def. adv. com. on edn. in armed forces; mem. Fla. Post-Secondary Planning Commn.; mem. acad. affairs com. U. Miami; mem. nat. panel Am. Council on Edn. Office Women in Higher Edn.; mem. edn. commn. Dade County Community Relations Bd. Mem. exec. bd. S. Fla. council Boy Scouts Am.; bd. dirs. Dade County Med. Research and Health Services Found., United Way, S. Fla. Comprehensive Health Planning Council; trustee Ednl. Testing Service; mem. Dade County Oceanographic Sci. Park Adv. Com.; mem. steering com. mental health tng. and research So. Regional Edn. Bd. Recipient Outstanding Civilian Service medal Dept. Army. Mem. Am. Econ. Asso., Am. Assn. Sch. Adminstrs. (mem. com. on founds.), Am. Assn. Community and Jr. Colls. (chmn. bd., mem. jr.-sr. coll. com., mem. constl. revision com.; dir., mem. adv. com. new instrs.), N.E.A., N. Central Assn. (commr. commn. on colls., univs. 1956-60), Am. Council on Edn. (dir., sec., mem. commn. on fed. relations), Fla. Community Coll. Pres.'s Council, Greater Miami C. of C., Phi Beta Kappa, Phi Kappa Phi. Lutheran. Kiwanian. Author: (with Atteberry, Auble and Hunt) Introduction to Social Sci., rev. edit., 1951. Home: 10270 SW 102d Terr Miami FL 33176 Office: 11011 SW 104th St Miami FL 33176

MASON, BETTY OXFORD, educator; b. Sikes, La., Oct. 10, 1930; d. Reuben Evan and Della (Killebrew) Oxford; B.S., La. State U., 1950; Ed.D., 1975; M.Ed., U. Fla., 1967; children—David, Paul. Tchr., Jefferson County (Ky.) Schs., Louisville, 1950-52, Atlanta City Schs., 1952-53; curriculum writer So. Bapt. Conv., Nashville, 1957-73; tchr. East Baton Rouge (La.) Parish Schs., 1962-66; asst. prof. Fla. So. Coll., Lakeland, 1967-75; asst. prof. edn., dir. lab. experiences Coll. Edn., North Tex. State U., Denton, 1975—. NDEA fellow, 1966-67. Mem. Assn. Supervision and Curriculum Devel., Internat. Reading Assn., Tex. Assn. Coll. Tchrs., Tex. Elem., Kindergarten and Nursery Educators, Phi Delta Kappa (pres. 1979), Delta Kappa Gamma, Kappa Delta Pi, Phi Theta Kappa, Pi Beta Phi. Democrat. Baptist. Author: The Story of Joseph, 1965; I Go to School, 1971; also articles. Home: 2803 N Bell Ave Denton TX 76201 Office: North Tex State U Denton TX 76203

MASON, CHARLES CULBERSON, JR., petroleum co. exec.; b. Quiriquire, Venezuela, Feb. 25, 1936; s. Charles Culberson and Marjorie (O'Bannon) M. (parents Am. citizens); B.A., U. Tex., 1958, J.D., 1960; postgrad. Grad. Sch. Bus. Adminstrn., Tulane U., 1970; m. Joyce Baldridge, Apr. 17, 1976; children—Stephen, Catherine. Admitted to Tex. bar, 1960; atty., land dept. Exxon Corp., New Orleans, 1963-74; atty., land mgr. Goodhope Refineries, Houston, 1974-75; mgr. of land Amax Petroleum Corp., Houston, 1975-77; exec. Kilroy Co., Houston, 1977-80; pvt. practice law, 1980—. Served to capt. Judge Adv. Gen.'s Corps, U.S. Army, 1961-63. Mem. Am., Tex., Houston bar assns., Am. Assn. Petroleum Landmen, Mid-Continent Oil and Gas Assn., Internat. Platform Assn. Baptist. Home: 12003 Sugar Springs Dr Houston TX 77077 Office: 1200 Commerce Bldg Houston TX 77002

MASON, FRANKLIN HARRELL, edn. cons., musician; b. Dallas, Tex., Dec. 3, 1929; s. Harrell C. and Hazel (Wager) M.; B.A., N. Tex. State U., 1952, M.A., 1957; postgrad. Stephen F. Austin State U., summer, 1972; Litterarum D. (hon.), Sussex Coll. Tech., 1973; pvt. study in harpsichord, 1956; master classes in organ, 1949-71. Instr. in French, Spanish, Latin, Greek and English, Tyler (Tex.) public schs., 1956-74, chmn. div. fgn. langs., 1971-74; profl. church organist, 1946—; numerous organ recitals, Tex., Ga. and Ark., 1955—; asst. organist First Presbyterian Ch., Tyler, 1968—; organist Tex. Fedn. Bus. and Profl. Women's Clubs, 1959; cons. in edn. and langs., since 19—. Served with U.S. Army, 1954-56. Recipient Amicii Latina award, 1969, Hawthorne award, 1972, various awards in religious service, 1947-68. Mem. Am. Guild of Organists (del. to southwest regional conv. 1963, historian, exec. council East Tex. chpt. 1980—), Nat. Council Tchrs. of English (del. to nat. conv. 1966), Tex. Classical Assn., Tex. Fgn. Lang. Assn., Tex. State Tchrs. Assn., East Tex. Latin Assn., Intertel, Am. Mensa Soc., Tyler Citizens League, Pi Delta Phi, Phi Eta Sigma, Sigma Delta Pi. Democrat. Presbyterian. Author: Curriculum Guide for Foreign Languages, 1964; Plot and Characterization in the Episodios Nacionales of Benito Perez Galdos, 1957; contbr. articles to lit. and mus. jours. Address: 505 Sunnyside Dr Tyler TX 75702

MASON, MICHAEL ALAN, fin. broker, graphic designer, illustrator; b. Lenoir, N.C., Feb. 22, 1958; s. Clarence Grey and Bernice (Kiziah) M.; student U. N.C., Wilmington, 1976-77, Washington Sch. Art, 1977-78. Tax shelter cons. Am. Bankers Ins. Group, Miami, Fla., 1977-78; graphic designer, illustrator Clay Printing Co., Inc., Hickory, N.C., 1978—; pres. Capital Mgmt. Assos., Hickory, 1980—; free-lance design cons., polit. cartoonist, 1978—. Mem. Young Ams. for Freedom, Nat. Right To Work Com., Kyokusinkai-Kan Internat. Karate Assn., United Sytlist Karate Assn., Pi Kappa Phi. Republican. Methodist. Designer sr. citizens reference manual Contact. Home: PO Box 3124 Hickory NC 28601 Office: 500 Main Ave Hickory NC 28601

MASON, RAYMOND K., business exec.; b. Jacksonville, Fla., 1927; student U. N.C., 1949. Chmn., pres. Charter Co., Jacksonville; chmn. Charter Mortgage Co., Beach Fed. Savs. & Loan Assn.; dir. Fla. 1st Nat. Bank of Jacksonville. Office: Charter Co Jacksonville Nat Bank Bldg Jacksonville FL 32202*

MASON, ROBERT MCSPADDEN, mgmt. cons.; b. Sweetwater, Tenn., Jan. 16, 1941; s. Paul Rankin and Ruby May (McSpadden) M.; B.S., Mass. Inst. Tech., 1963, M.S., 1965; Ph.D., Ga. Inst. Tech., 1973; m. Betty Ann Durrence, May 9, 1968; children—Michael Dean, Donald Robert. Mem. tech. staff Sandia Labs., Livermore, Calif., 1965-68; teaching asst. Mass. Inst. Tech., Cambridge, 1963-67; research scientist Engring. Expt. Sta., Ga. Inst. Tech., Atlanta, 1971-74, sr. research scientist, head energy mgmt. and policy analysis br., 1975; chmn. Metrics, Inc., Atlanta, 1973-80; pres. Metric Research Corp., 1980—; lectr., cons. in field. NSF grantee, 1973-79. Mem. Inst. Mgmt. Scis., AAAS, Am. Soc. Info. Sci., World Future Soc. Presbyterian. Editor: (with John E. Creps, Jr.) Information Centers: Economics, Management and Technologies. Contbr. articles to profl. jours. Home: 168 Lake Forrest Ln Atlanta GA 30342 Office: 290 Interstate N Atlanta GA 30339

MASON, ROBERT TODD, athletic dir.; b. Greenville, Tex., Aug. 26, 1931; s. Fred Edmund and Eddie Lee (Todd) M.; B.A., Austin (Tex.) Coll., 1956, M.A., 1957; Ed.D., N. Tex. State U., Denton, 1969; m. Ann Biggerstaff, Aug. 30, 1952; children—Richard Todd, Robin Ann. Coach, tchr. high schs. in Gainesville and Marshall, Tex., 1957-61; athletic dir. Austin Coll., 1969—, chmn. phys. edn. dept., 1968—, basketball coach, 1962—; bd. visitors U.S. Sports Acad., 1978, nat. bd. advisers, 1962-78. Deacon, 1st Baptist Ch., Sherman, 1960. Served with USAF, 1952-56. Names to Athletic Hall of Fame, Austin Coll., 1971, Disting. Alumnus, 1977. Mem. Nat. Assn. Intercollegiate Athletics (exec. com.; named to Hall of Fame 1977), Nat. Collegiate Dirs. of Athletics (exec. com. 1974-77), Tex. Assn. Health, Phys. Edn. and Recreation, Tex. Coaches Assn. Democrat. Home: 2206 Tex Cruse Dr Sherman TX 75090 Office: Austin Coll Sherman TX 75090

MASON, RUSSELL ALAN, heavy equipment co. exec.; b. Peoria, Ill., Mar. 11, 1930; s. Frank Russell and Vesta M. (Buck) M.; B.S.B.A., cert. fgn. trade, Bradley U., 1951; m. Virginia C. Jones, Nov. 30, 1957; children—Leslie Anne, Laura Elizabeth. With Caterpillar Tractor Co., 1951-69; founder, pres. Ala. Machinery Co., a John Deere indsl. equipment dealer, Birmingham, Ala., 1969—. Mem. basketball com. Samford U. Served with USN, 1951, U.S. Army, 1954-56. Named Mktg. Man of Yr., 1973. Mem. Associated Builders and Contractors, Associated Gen. Contractors, Ala. Roadbuilders Assn., Ala. Utility Contractors Assn., Central Indsl. Dealers Assn. (pres. 1977), Birmingham C. of C. Republican. Methodist. Clubs: Relay House Dinner, Inverness Country. Office: PO Box 20224 Birmingham AL 35216

MASON, STEPHEN OLIN, coll. adminstr.; b. Fresno, Calif., July 11, 1952; s. Olin James and Mary Edna (Moyer) M.; B.A. in Psychology, Bridgewater (Va.) Coll., 1974; M.Ed. in Counselor Edn., James Madison U., Harrisonburg, Va., 1979. Tech. asst. to dir. Kline Campus Center, Bridgewater Coll., 1974-76, head resident Wardo Hall, 1975-76, asst. to dean student devel., 1977, asst. dean student devel., 1977—; guidance counselor Woodlawn Elem. Sch., Sebring, Fla., 1976-77. Mem. Am. Personnel and Guidance Assn., Am. Coll. Personnel Assn., Assn. Coll. and Univ. Housing Officers, Va. Assn. Student Personnel Adminstrs., Va. Assn. Coll. and Univ. Housing Officers, Va. Personnel and Guidance Assn., Va. Coll. Personnel Assn. (treas. 1980-81). Mem. Ch. of Brethren. Home: 302 E College St Bridgewater VA 22812 Office: Box 100 Bridgewater Coll Bridgewater VA 22812

MASON, WILLIAM ALFRED, physician; b. New Orleans, Aug. 25, 1898; s. William Alfred and Henrietta (Jackson) M.; student Ohio State U., 1918-21; M.D., Meharry Med. Coll., Nashville, 1929; M.P.H., Yale U., 1947; postgrad. Harvard Med. Sch., 1973; m. Virgie Elizabeth Douglas, June 5, 1918; children—Charles Boyd, William Alfred. Boys work dir. YMCA, Nashville, 1919; phys. edn. dir. YMCA, Balt., 1921; intern Provident Hosp., Balt., 1929-30; acting asst. surgeon USPHS, Washington, 1930-32; asso. prof. internal medicine Meharry Med. Coll., 1932-42; pub. health physician Ga. Dept. Pub. Health, Atlanta, 1942-74, now cons.; cons. child health, med. dir. Planned Parenthood Assn., 1974—; vis. lectr. pub. health Atlanta U., Clark Coll., Mercer Sch. Pharmacy. Health and safety dir. Boy Scouts Am.; mem. sch. health com. Atlanta Pub. Schs.; mem. Gov.'s Com. Children and Youth, 1960—; cons. Human Sexuality Edn., 1961—; cons. family planning service Spelman Coll., Atlanta; mem. budget com. Atlanta United Appeal, 1961-62; chmn. Task Force Family Life Edn., Atlanta Met. Council Chs., 1970-73. Pres. bd. Atlanta Planned Parenthood Assn.; bd. dirs. Atlanta Urban League, Ga. State Employees Assn.; lt. col., a.d.c. Gov.'s Staff, 1980. Recipient Service to Youth award Ga. Congress Parents and Tchrs., 1952, Community Service award Atlanta Urban League, 1966, Silver Beaver award Boy Scouts Am., 1974, award for meritorious service Ga. Dept. Human Resources, 1975, W.S. Beaver award for community service WSB Radio and TV, 1972, Alan Guttmacher Internat. award for disting. service Nat. Planned Parenthood Assn., 1980. Cert. sex educator. Fellow Am. Pub. Health Assn., Am. Sch. Health Assn.; mem. Sex Edn. and Info. Council U.S. (asso.), Royal Soc. Health (London, Eng.), AMA, Alpha Phi Alpha, Chi Delta Mu. Methodist. Mason (32 deg., Shriner). Author: An Odyssey In Black and White, 1973. Contbr. articles to profl. jours. Home: 620 Peachtree St NE Atlanta GA 30308 Office: 15 Peachtree St NE Atlanta GA 30303

MASON, WILLIAM CLIFFORD, JR., ednl. adminstr.; b. Athens, Tenn., Aug. 8, 1925; s. William Clifford and Myrtle Elizabeth (Allen) M.; B.A., Emory and Henry Coll., 1946; M.Div., Emory U., 1949; Ed.D., N.Y. U., 1973; m. Laura Lee Frederick, July 9, 1946; children—William, Linda, Bettie. Ordained to ministry United Methodist Ch., 1949; pastor South Bristol Meth. Ch., 1949-53; asso. pastor State St. Meth. Ch., Bristol, Va.-Tenn., 1953-56; asst. prof. religion Emory and Henry Coll., Emory, Va., 1956-79, prof., 1979—, chaplain, 1956-67, dean of students, 1967-79, dir. religious life, 1979—; del. World Meth. Conf., 1966, 71, 76; bd. dirs. Holston Pastoral Counseling Center, Knoxville, Tenn., 1970—. Bd. dirs. Higlands Home for Children, Abingdon, Va., 1973—. Recipient award for campus minister Danforth Found., 1961; named Distinguished Univ. Scholar, N.Y. U., 1974. Mem. Am., Va. (award 1976) personnel and guidance assns., Am., So. Va. coll. personnel assns., Nat., Va. councils family relations, Assn. Mental Health Counselors, Religious Edn. Assn., Assn. Humanistic Psychology, Assn. Sex Educators and Counselors, Acad. Religion and Mental Health. Author: The Church School Workers Handbook, 1955. Home: PO Box 13 Emory VA 24327 Office: Emory and Henry College Emory VA 24327

MASSANISO, PETER ANTHONY, investment counselor; b. Phila., Aug. 18, 1936; s. Frank Paul and Emily Elena (Finocchiaro) M.; A.B., Williams Coll., 1958; M.B.A. in Fin., Wharton Sch. of U. Pa., 1961. Sr. investment analyst, comml. and indsl. loan dept. Prudential Life Ins. Co., 1961-65; v.p. securities Ind. Life and Accident Ins. Co., Jacksonville, Fla., 1965-69; pres. Bus. and Fin. Mgmt., Inc., corp. fin. cons., Jacksonville, 1969-71; v.p. corp. planning, dir. Fisco, Inc., ins., Phila., 1971-74; pres. Profl. Capital Mgmt., Inc., Jacksonville, Fla., 1974—; dir., mem. exec. com. Hickory Furniture Co. (N.C.); dir. Presco Holding Corp., Skokie, Ill. Mem. adv. trust fund com. North Fla. council Boy Scouts Am.; bd. dirs., chmn. investment com. Jacksonville Mus. Arts and Scis. Served with Pa. N.G., 1958-61. Mem. Phila., Jacksonville fin. analysts socs., Nat. Assn. Securities Dealers, Delta Kappa Epsilon. Clubs: Ponte Vedra, River, Sawgrass (Jacksonville); Palm Bay (Miami, Fla.); LeClub (N.Y.C.). Contbr. articles to profl. jours. Home: 17 Lake Julia Dr Ponte Vedra Beach FL 32082 Office: 3303 Independent Sq Jacksonville FL 32202

MASSAY, JACK C., corp. exec.; b. Sandersville, Ga., 1904; grad. U. Fla., 1925. Former chmn., chief exec. officer Hosp. Corp. Am., Nashville, now chmn. exec. com.; chmn. exec. com. Nashville City Bank & Trust Co.; chmn. Vol. Capital Corp.; dir. Thomas Nelson Pubs., Cummings Inc., The Internat. Sign Service, Spectronics, Inc., Enterprise Fabricators, Inc. Trustee, Montgomery Bell Acad. Office: Hospital Corp Am One Park Plaza Nashville TN 37203*

MASSELLO, KATHERINE JANE, speech pathologist; b. Carlisle, Pa., Dec. 4, 1951; d. William and Olga Katherine (Neill) M.; B.A. with honors, Met. State Coll., Denver, 1974; M.A., U. Tex., El Paso, 1975. Speech therapist Ruthe B. Cowl Rehab. Center, Laredo, Tex., 1975-77; speech therapist United Ind. Sch. Dist., Laredo, 1977-79; guest lectr. Laredo State U., 1979, Laredo Jr. Coll., 1976-78; cons. Jim Hogg Webb County Co-op, 1979. Bd. dirs. Laredo Little Theater, 1978-79. Cert. speech therapist, Tex. Mem. Am. Speech and Hearing Assn. (cert. of clin. competence), Tex. Speech and Hearing Assn. Episcopalian. Address: 2316 B 14th St Lubbock TX 79401

MASSETT, WILLIAM AUGUST, JR., educator; b. Monroe, La., Sept. 2, 1941; s. William August and Dolores Margaret (Setze) M.; B.A., La. State U., 1966, M.Ed., 1974, Specialist of Edn., 1976, postgrad. Miss. State U. Welfare visitor La. State Dept. Welfare, 1967; teacher St. Philip Neri Sch., Metairie, La., 1967-68; dist. exec. Boy Scouts Am. Metairie, 1969-70; tchr. St. Francis Xavier Sch., Metairie, 1970-72; tchr. spl. edn. Lutcher High Sch., Lutcher, La., 1974-77; tchr. spl. edn. East Ascension Jr. High Sch., Gonzales, La., 1977-78; tchr. spl. edn. Albany-Springfield Jr. High Sch., Albany, La., 1978—. Served with USN, 1959-62. Mem. Nat., La., Livingston Parish edn. assns., Assn. Classroom Tchrs., Phi Delta Kappa. Democrat. Roman Catholic. Home: 8248 Gladewood Dr Baton Rouge LA 70806 Office: PO Box 347 Miss State U Mississippi State MS 39762

MASSEY, DONALD WAYNE, microfilm cons.; b. Durham, N.C., Mar. 7, 1938; s. Gordon Davis and Lucille Alma (Gregory) M.; student U. Hawaii, 1959, U. Ky., 1965; m. Violet Sue McIlvain, Nov. 2, 1958; children—Kimberly Shan, Leon Dale, Donn Krichele. Head microfilm sect. Ky. Hist. Soc., Frankfort, 1961; dir. microfilm center U. Ky., Lexington, 1962-67; dir. photog. services and graphics U. Va., Charlottesville, 1967-73; pres. Micrographics II, 1973—; pub. Micropublishing Series, 18th Century Sources for Study English Lit. and Culture; instr. U. Va. Sch. Continuing Edn., 1971-72, Central Va. Piedmont Community Coll., 1976; cons. Microform Systems and Copying Centers; owner, Massland Farm, Shadwell, Va.; basketball coach Rock Hill Acad., 1975-77. Pres. Rock Hill Acad. Aux., 1975-76. Served with USMCR, 1957-60. Recipient Key award Workshop V, for handicapped, Charlottesville, Va., pres. bd., 1972-73. Named Ky. Col. Mem. Am., Va. library assns., Soc. Reprodn. Engrs., Nat. (library relations com. 1973—), Va. (Pioneer award 1973, pres. 1971-72, v.p. 1973-74, program chmn. ann. conf. 1974), Ky. (Outstanding award 1967, pres. 1964-67) microfilm assns., Thoroughbred Owners and Breeders Assn. Mem. Christian Ch. (elder, chmn. bd.). Contbg. editor Va. Librarian, 1970-71, Micro-News Va. Microfilm Assn., 1970-71. Contbr. articles to profl. publs. Address: Fairmount Route 1 Box 279 Keswick VA 22947

MASSEY, EARL D., Realtor; b. Killeen, Tex., Aug. 8, 1896; s. Harold Delone and Louise Elza (Bebout) M.; student Rice U., 1917-18, U. Tex., 1916-17, 20-22; m. Josephine Clair Rancier, Dec. 8, 1924; children—Sam Delone, Joe Earl. Owner-mgr. Tex. Theatre, Killeen, 1920-42, Massey Ins. Agy., 1924-29, Massey Appliance Co., 1929-42; postmaster U.S. Post Office Dept., Killeen-Ft. Hood, 1939-66; owner Massey Real Estate Co., Killeen, 1967—. Pres. Ft. Hood Area Bd. Realtors, 1971-72. Sec., Civilian Adv. Com. for Comdg. Gen., Ft. Hood, 1960-66; sec.-treas. Bell County Water Control Improvement Dist. #6, 1968—. City councilman, Killeen, 1935-39; chmn. Bell County Bd. Edn., 1966—. Vice pres., bd. dirs. Killeen Downtown, Inc., 1970—. Served with U.S. Army, 1918. Recipient Distinguished Service award Greater Killeen United Fund, 1964, Golden Deeds award Exchange Club, 1965, Meritorious Service award Post Office Dept., 1966, Dedicated Service award Killeen U.S.O., 1970. Mem. Nat. Assn. Realtors, Nat. Assn. Postmasters of U.S., Greater Killeen C. of C. (pres. 1947; Man of Year 1955), SAR, Nat. Assn. Ret. Fed. Employees (pres. Killeen chpt. 1977-78), Assn. U.S. Army, Tex., Bell County (v.p.) hist. socs., Am. Legion (post comdr.). Democrat. Methodist (adminstrv. bd. 1969-75). Clubs: Masons, K.T., Shriners, Scottish Rite (comdr.), Order Eastern Star, Kiwanis (lt. gov. Tex.-Okla. dist., div. 23, 1961 Exceptional Leadership award Tex.-Okla. dist. 1961), Sojourners. Address: 707 Nolan Ave Killeen TX 76541

MASSEY, HAL, coll. dean; b. Shawnee, Okla., Apr. 10, 1921; s. John Madison and Alberta (Keith) M.; B.S., U. Fla., 1953, M.Ed., 1955; Ed.D., U. Md., 1965; m. Marie Jennings, Apr. 2, 1943. Asst. prof. N.C. State Coll., Raleigh, 1957-58, U. Fla., Gainesville, 1958-62; dir. applied sci. div. Daytona Beach (Fla.) Community Coll., 1962-67, v.p. acad. affairs, 1967-74, recipient Distinguished Service awards, 1962-74; dean Fla. Keys Community Coll., Key West, 1974—. Adviser, Theta Chi Fraternity; adviser U. Fla. Indsl. Arts Assn., recipient Distinguished Service award, 1957. Active Old Island Restoration Found.; mem. exec. bd. Mental Health Assn. Served with C.E., AUS, 1943-46. Mem. Am., Fla. vocational assns., Fla. Assn. Community Colls., Phi Kappa Phi, Phi Delta Kappa, Kappa Delta Pi, Epsilon Pi Tau. Methodist. Club: Fishing of Am. Author: A Research Instrument for Measuring the Unique Contributions of Industrial Arts to the Goals of General Education, 1965. Home: 50 Ave E Big Coppitt Key West FL 33040

MASSEY, HILDA RUTH, accountant; b. Nashville, Feb. 11, 1950; d. Ellis Isaac and Daisy Edith (West) Rader; student Tenn. Tech. U., 1967-71; m. Thomas Ellis Massey, June 6, 1971; 1 dau., Lori Allison. With Control Data Corp., St. Paul, 1971-72; payroll staff Norwalk Furniture Corp., Cookeville, Tenn., 1972-73; acct., Fordham-Bardell Shirt Co., Crossville, Tenn., 1974-76; sec. treas., office mgr. Crossville Mfg. Co., Inc., 1976-78; staff acct. Cumberland Med. Center, Crossville, 1978-79; head acctg. dept. Brandywood Nursing Home, Gallatin, Tenn., 1979—. Mem. Am. Mgmt. Assn., Christian Women's Fellowship, Phi Gamma Nu. Home: Route 2 Box 239 Westmoreland TN 37186 Office: 555 E Bledsoe St Gallatin TN 37066

MASSEY, JAMES LEROY, JR., hosp. adminstr.; b. Stamford, Tex., Nov. 15, 1939; s. James Leroy and Margaret Massey; B.A., McMurry Coll., 1963; M.P.A., U. Mo., Kansas City, 1973; married; 1 dau., Heather. Asst. adminstr. Hillcrest Gen. Hosp., Flushing, N.Y.,

1971-74; administr. Shriners Burns Inst., Cin., 1974-76; exec. dir. Childrens Hosp., New Orleans, 1976-78; exec. v.p. Caobelli & Sever Cons. Co., Metairie, 1978-79; adminstr. Metairie (La.) Gen. Hosp., 1979—. Served with USMC, 1958-59. Mem. Am. Coll. Hosp. Adminstrs., La. Hosp. Assn., Am. Hosp. Assn., Met. Hosp. Council New Orleans. Methodist. Home: Metairie LA Office: 1605 Metairie Rd Metairie LA 70005

MASSEY, MITCHELL COLLINS, radiologist; b. Bruce, Miss., Jan. 14, 1941; s. Lonnie Mitchell and Amy Marie (Collins) M.; B.A., La. State U., 1963, M.D., 1967; dip. in radiology, Confederate Meml. Med. Center, 1973; m. Eleanor Turner Voss, Nov. 22, 1974; 1 son, Mitchell Collins. Intern, Good Samaritan Hosp., Portland, Oreg., 1967-68; resident, Confederate Meml. Med. Center, Shreveport, La., 1970-73; staff radiologist S.W. Regional Med. Center, McComb, Miss., 1973-75, dir. Dept. Radiology and Nuclear Medicine, 1975-77; attending radiologist Walthall County Gen. Hosp., Tylertown, Miss., 1973-76; dir. Dept. Radiology, Nuclear Medicine and Ultrasound, Bogalusa (La.) Community Med. Center, 1977—; clin. asso. in radiology La. State U. Sch. Medicine, Shreveport, 1971-73. Served with U.S. Army, 1968-70. Decorated Bronze Star medal, Army Commendation medal. Diplomate Am. Bd. Radiology. Mem. AMA, Radiol. Soc. N. Am., Soc. Nuclear Medicine, Am. Coll. Radiology, So. Med. Assn., Radiol. Soc. La., La. Med. Soc., Washington Parish Med. Soc. Republican. Presbyterian. Office: 433 Plaza St Bogalusa LA 70427

MASSEY, PEYTON HOWARD, JR., coll. dean; b. Zebulon, N.C., Oct. 4, 1922; s. Peyton Howard and Roselle (Sears) M.; B.S., N.C. State Coll., 1947, M.S., 1951; Ph.D., Cornell U., 1952; m. Elizabeth Lorelei Shumaker, Oct. 3, 1942; children—Elizabeth Howard (Mrs. Curtis Alls), Carol Anne, Suzanne Frances (Mrs. Barry Hughes). Teaching asst. N.C. State Coll., 1947-49; research asst. Cornell U., 1949-52; asso. prof., then prof. horticulture Va. Poly. Inst. and State U., Blacksburg, 1952—, asso. dean Grad. Sch., 1964-65, asso. dean, dir. agronomic and plant scis. div. Coll. Agr., 1966-78, asso. dean, dir. internat. agr., 1978—; cons. to govt. and industry. Past pres. Blacksburg P.T.A. Served with AUS, World War II; ETO. Decorated Purple Heart; recipient certificate and medal City of Paris (France), 1968. Mem. A.A.A.S., Am. Legion (past post comdr.), Sigma Xi, Phi Kappa Phi, Alpha Zeta, Omicron Delta Kappa, Gamma Sigma Delta, Epsilon Sigma Phi. Baptist (past chmn. bd. deacons.). Rotarian (dir., pres.). Author articles. Address: 807 Gracelyn Ct Blacksburg VA 24060

MASSEY, RICHARD WALTER, JR., investment counselor; b. Birmingham, Ala., May 19, 1917; s. Richard Walter and Elizabeth (Spencer) M.; B.S., U. Va., 1939; M.A., Birmingham-So. Coll., 1956; Ph.D., Vanderbilt U., 1960; m. Ann Hinkle, Sept. 4, 1959; children—Richard Walter, Dale Elizabeth. Owner, mgr. Massey Bus. Coll., Birmingham, 1946-56; asst to chancellor Vanderbilt U., 1959-60; chmn. dept. econs. Birmingham-So. Coll., 1960-66; investment trust officer First Nat. Bank of Birmingham, 1966-67; prof. econs. U. Ala., Tuscaloosa, 1967—; v.p., dir. investment research Sterne, Agee & Leach, Inc., Birmingham, 1968-75; pres. Richard W. Massey & Co., Inc., investment counsel, Birmingham, 1975—. Served to maj. AUS, 1941-46. Home: 3000 Cherokee Rd Birmingham AL 35223 Office: 10 Office Park Circle Suite 116 Birmingham AL 35223

MASSEY, SHELBY, corp. exec.; b. 1933. Mgr., Red Hat Poultry Co., Decatur, Ala., before 1970; with Valmac Industries Inc., Memphis, 1970—, v.p., mgr. Foods div., sr. v.p., before 1975, exec. v.p., 1975-76, pres., dir., 1976—. Office: Valmac Industries Inc 2 S Front St Box 3060 Memphis TN 38103*

MASSEY, WILLIAM WALTER, JR., automobile agy. exec.; b. Lawrenceburg, Tenn., Sept. 21, 1928; s. William Walter and Bess Ann (Brian) M.; B.B.A., U. Miami, 1949; B.F.A., U. Fla., 1969; m. Virginia Claire Smith, Aug. 16, 1952; children—William Walter III, Laura Ann, Lynn Smith, Lisa Claire. Vice pres. Massey Motors, Inc., Jacksonville, Fla., 1950—, Atlantic Discount Co., Inc., Jacksonville, 1954-64; pres. Owners Surety Corp., Jacksonville, 1959—, Gen. Services Corp., Jacksonville, 1960-69, Fla. Properties, Inc., Jacksonville, 1961-66; pres. Owners Guaranty Life Ins. Co., Phoenix, 1960-64, Securities Guaranty Life Ins. Co., Phoenix, 1961-64; pres. Chi-Cha, Inc., Jacksonville, 1965-70; v.p., dir. Massey Dodge, Inc., Jacksonville, Regency Dodge, Inc., Jacksonville, Westside Dodge, Inc., Jacksonville, Massey-Mixon Chrysler-Plymouth, Inc., Jacksonville, Biscayne Dodge, Inc., North Miami Beach, Massey-Andrews, Inc., Clearwater, Brooks-Massey, Inc., Tampa, Univ. Dodge, Inc., Tampa, Massey Motors, Inc., Daytona Beach, Massey-Yardley, Inc., Ft. Lauderdale; owner Univ. Sq. Properties; dir. Southside Atlantic Bank, Jacksonville. Exhibited group shows N.Y. Internat. Art Show, 1970; Ball State U., Muncie, Ind., 1972; Artists/U.S.A., 1974. Vice pres. bd. dirs. Southside Country Day Sch., 1963-68. Served to 1st lt. USAF, 1950-52. Mem. Conn. Acad. Fine Arts, Sigma Chi. Methodist. Clubs: River, Deerwood (Jacksonville). Home: 7080 San Fernando Pl Jacksonville FL 32217 Office: 2434 Atlantic Blvd Jacksonville FL 32207

MASSIE, ROBERTA IRIS, draftsman, astrologer; b. Newport News, Va., Oct. 8, 1938; d. George Alexander and Manon Ferea (Reagan) Massie; student Art Instrn., Inc., 1953-56, Newport News Shipyard Apprentice Sch. Drafting, 1957-58; B.S. in Metaphysics, U. Metaphysics, 1978, ordained minister, 1979; m. Billy J. Milhorn, June 17, 1958 (div. 1977); children—Blair Reagan, Feria Ruth Massie Wright, James Edward. Mech. draftsman Newport News Shipbldg. and Dry Dock Co., 1957-58; cartographic draftsman Dept. Hwys. State of Va., Richmond, 1960, Land Office, U.S. Dept. Interior, Fairbanks, Alaska, 1962-63, Blackburn & Blauvelt, Richmond, 1963-64, Ford, Bacon & Davis, Richmond, 1964; draftsman-artist Va. Elec. & Power Co., Richmond, 1964-67; elec. draftsman Elwood F. Holton, Richmond, 1972-75; graphic artist Wilbur Smith & Assos., Richmond, 1977; advanced indsl. design engring. elec. draftsman assigned to Western Electric Co., Richmond, 1977-78, assigned Allied Chem.-Fibers div. Tech. Center, 1979—; pvt. practice cons. astrology, 1975—; tchr. astrology Henrico County Adult Edn. Program, 1977—. Mem. Met. Astrological Research Soc., Nat. Geog. Soc., Assn. for Research and Enlightenment, Nat. Assn. Female Execs., Beta Sigma Phi. Richmond. Home: 14 S Beech Ave Highland Springs VA 23075 Office: 7734 White Pine Rd Richmond VA 23234

MASSIEU, GUILLERMO HELGUERA, research exec.; b. San Luis Potosi, Mexico, Oct. 7, 1920; s. Wilfrido Massieu and Maria Helguera Ceballos; B.Sc., Nat. Sch. Biol. Scis., Nat. Poly. Inst. Mexico, 1945, Sc.D., 1963; m. Yolanda M. Trigo, Aug. 11, 1951; children—Yolanda M., Lourdes M. Mem. research staff Nat. Inst. Nutrition Mexico, 1945-55; prof. Inst. Biology, Nat. U. Mexico, 1956-64; dir. gen. Nat. Poly. Inst. Mexico, 1965-70; prof. biochemistry, dir. Center Research and Advanced Studies, Nat. Poly. Inst., 1971—; cons. Nat. Council Sci. and Tech., Mexico, 1971—; rep. Mexico to exec. com. Interam. Council Sci., Edn. and Culture, Orgn. Am. States, 1969—; apptd. under-sec. for tech. and research, 1978—. Decorated comdr. Order Merit (Italy); comdr. Order Roi Leopold (Belgium); comdr. Order Gt. Cross (West Germany); officer Palmes Academiques (France); recipient Gold medal French Soc. Encouragement Sci. Research and Innovation, 1973. Brit. Council scholar, 1954-55. Mem. Nat. Acad. Medicine Mexico, Acad. Sci. Research Mexico, Mexican Chem. Soc., Mexican Soc. Biochemistry, Internat., Am. socs. neurochemistry, Soc. for Neurosci., Internat. Acad. Environ. Safety. Contbr. articles on nutrition, neurochemistry, sci. policy to profl. jours. Home: 20 Ret P de la Llave 18 Mexico DF Z-22 Mexico Office: Apdo Postal 14-740 Mexico DF Z-14 Mexico

MASSMAN, RICHARD ALLAN, lawyer; b. Beaumont, Tex., Aug. 19, 1943; s. Irwin and Sylvia (Schmidt) M.; B.S. cum laude, U. Pa., 1965; J.D. cum laude, Harvard U., 1968; m. Barbara Elaine Kessler, July 7, 1968; children—Jason, Karen. Admitted to Tex. bar, 1968; asso. firm Coke & Coke, Dallas, 1968-70; asso., partner Hewett, Johnson, Swanson & Barbee, 1970—; lectr. Law Sch., So. Methodist U., 1973. Southwestern regional bd. exec. com. Anti-Defamation League, 1979—. Mem. Am., Dallas (chmn. sect. taxation 1978) bar assns., State Bar Tex. (council sect. taxation 1978—). Club: Dallas. Home: 4950 Mill Run Dallas TX 75234 Office: 4700 First International Bldg Dallas TX 75270

MASSONGILL, BENJAMIN LOYD, city ofcl.; b. Harris, Okla., Jan. 22, 1938; s. Henry Osker and Sarah Jane (Staggs) M.; diploma Tulsa Tech. Coll., 1963; diploma Motorola Tng. Inst., 1967; m. Shirley Jean Johnson, July 13, 1959; children—Mark Henry, Teresa Lorraine. With communications dept. City of Tulsa, 1965—, communications supr., 1972-74, dir. communications, 1974—. Served with USNR, 1955-59. Mem. Asso. Public Safety Communications Officers, Internat. Mcpl. Signal Assn., Nat. Fire Protection Assn. (safety communications com.). Democrat. Home: Rt 3 Box 641 Broken Arrow OK 74120 Office: 200 Civic Center Rm 415 Tulsa OK 74103

MASTEN, MICHAEL KEITH, research engr.; b. Gainesville, Tex., Nov. 11, 1939; s. Raleigh Lee and Dollye (McFarlin) M.; B.S. in Elec. Engring., U. Tex., 1963, M.S. in Elec. Engring., 1965, Ph.D., 1968; m. Roma Yvonne Mayo, June 6, 1964; 1 dau., Rhonda Michelle. Mem. tech. staff Tex. Instruments, Dallas, 1968-79, sr. mem. tech. staff, 1980—, project mgr. pattern recognition study, 1970-73, mgr. Stblzn. Tech. Center, Bus. Devel. Operating Systems div., 1973—. Part-time instr. U. Tex., 1963-67; instr. computer programming I.E.E.E., 1972. Ford Found. fellow, 1964-67. Mem. I.E.E.E. (sec. computer and automatic controls sect. Dallas chpt. 1975-77), Am. Soc. for Engring. Edn. (dir. computers in edn. div. 1976-78), Tau Beta Pi, Eta Kappa Nu. Club: Toastmasters Internat. (v.p. Richardson Noon chpt. 1971, pres. 1972, area ednl. gov. 1973). Mem. Ch. of Christ. Contbr. articles to profl. jours. Patentee pattern recognition area. Office: 13500 N Central Ave Dallas TX 75222

MASTERS, ORLAN VINCENT WADE, physician; b. Corona, Calif., Feb. 29, 1920; s. Francis Wakeman and Grace Elizabeth (Wade) M.; B.A., Stanford U., 1949, M.D., 1953; m. Judy Jay Alves, Aug. 26, 1975; children by previous marriage—Michael Vincent, Martin Wakeman, Susan Lynne, Matthew Christian. Intern, Los Angeles County (Calif.) Hosp., Los Angeles, 1952-53; resident in obstetrics and gynecology Akron (Ohio) City Hosp., 1954-57, chief resident, 1957-58; chief dept. obstetrics and gynecology Beaver Clinic, Redlands, Calif., 1958-73; gynecologist U. Ga. Health Service, Athens, 1973-74, coordinator gynecology service, 1974-75, dir. div. gynecology, 1975—, asst. prof. Sch. Pharmacy, 1975—; asso. prof. obstetrics and gynecology Med. Coll. Ga., 1975—. Spl. cons. Calif. Dept. Health, 1962-67; dir. Gynecology Clinic Northeast Ga. Health Dist., Athens, 1974—; cons. Athens-Clarke County (Ga.) Health Dept., 1975—. Served to lt. col., USAAF, 1942-45. Decorated Air medal, D.F.C., Bronze Star (U.S.); Croix de Guerre (France). Diplomate Am. Bd. Obstetrics and Gynecology. Fellow A.C.S., Am. Coll. Obstetricians and Gynecologists; mem. Riverside-San Bernardino (Calif.) Obstetrics-Gynecology Soc. (pres. 1967), Universal Order Knights of Vine (master knight 1979), Athens Wine Soc. (dir. 1979). Writer wine column Athens newspapers, 1979—. Home: 389 Westview Dr Athens GA 30601 Office: Gilbert Health Center U Ga Athens GA 30601

MASTERS, WESLEY WILL, agribus. exec.; b. Plainview, Tex., Nov. 10, 1937; s. Everett Edison and Melba May (Bandy) M.; B.S., Tex. Tech. U., Lubbock, 1960, M.S., 1962; m. Nancy Tate, Mar. 7, 1959; children—Toni Allison, Wesley Will, Ethel Elise. Sales rep. So. Farm Supply Assn., Amarillo, Tex., 1963-68; founder, pres. Center Plains Industries Inc., Amarillo, 1963—; chmn. bd. W. Tex. Chemco, Amarillo, 1968—; dir. Tex. Bank of Amarillo. Trustee, St. Stephen Meth. Ch., Amarillo, 1968—; active March of Dimes, Am. Heart Assn. Named Boss of Yr., Nat. Secs. Assn., 1971. Mem. Fertilizer Inst., Tex. Plant Food Assn., Nat. Fertilizer Solutions Assn., Am. Soc. Agronomy, Council on Agr., Sci. and Tech., Sigma Xi. Clubs: Masons (32 deg.), Shriners. Home: 3715 Farwell St Amarillo TX 79109 Office: Center Plains Industries Inc 10800 Canyon E-Way PO Box 7988 Amarillo TX 79109

MASTERSON, ADRIENNE CRAFTON, real estate exec.; b. Providence, Mar. 6, 1926; d. John Harold and Adrienne (Fitzgerald) Crafton; student No. Va. Community Coll., 1971-74; m. Francis T. Masterson, May 31, 1947 (div. Jan. 1977); children—Mary Victoria Masterson Powers, Kathleen Joan, John Andrew, Barbara Lynn. Mem. staff Senator T.F. Green of R.I., Washington, 1944-47, 54-60; mem. staff U.S. Senate Com. on Campaign Expenditures, 1944-45; clk. Ho. Govt. Ops. Com., 1948-49, Ho. Campaign Expenditures Com., 1950; asst. appointment sec. Office of Pres., 1951-53; with Hubbard Realty, Alexandria, Va., 1962-67; owner, mgr. Adrienne Investment Real Estate, Alexandria, 1968—. Exec. sec., legis. chmn. Richmond Diocesan Council Cath. Women. Mem. No. Va. Bd. Realtors, Va., Nat. assns. Realtors, Mcht. Broker Exchange (London), Alexandria C. of C., Friends of Kennedy Center (founding), Nat. Hist. Soc., Nat. Trust Historic Preservation. Democrat. Home: 8200 Rolling Rd Springfield VA 22153 Office: PO Box 1271 421 King St Suite 214 Alexandria VA 22313

MASTERSON, THOMAS ROBERT, educator; b. Crystal Lake, Ill., Sept. 17, 1915; s. Peter Aloysius and Isobel Cherry (Woods) M.; Ph.B., U. Chgo., 1946, M.B.A., 1948, Ph.D., 1955; m. Dorothy Jean Mandabach, Aug. 17, 1940; children—Katherine Irene, Judith Amanda, Miriam Alicia. Underwriter, supr. Hartford Accident & Indemnity Co., Chgo., 1935-41; asst. prof. DePaul U., Chgo., 1948-56, asso. prof., 1957-60; asso. prof. mgmt. Grad. Sch. Bus., Emory U., Atlanta, 1960-66, prof., 1967—, exec. officer Center Corporate Policy Direction, 1975—; dir. Mandabach & Simms, Inc., Chgo., 1955-75, also various trusts. Served in USAAF, 1941-45. Mem. Acad. of Mgmt., Am. Mgmt. Assn., Am. Soc. for Personnel Adminstrn. (accredited personnel diplomate), AAUP (pres. DePaul U. chpt. 1955, pres. Emory U. chpt. 1967), So. Mgmt. Assn., Beta Gamma Sigma. Club: Druid Hills Golf. Author books and jour. articles in field. Home: 873 N Superior Ave Decatur GA 30033 Office: Grad Sch Bus Emory U Atlanta GA 30322

MASTRAN, DAVID VINCENT, mgmt. cons.; b. El Paso, Tex., Dec. 14, 1942; s. Joseph Lee and Mary (Black) M.; B.S., U.S. Mil. Acad., 1965; M.S., Stanford, 1966; Sc.D., George Washington U., 1973; m. Shelley Ellen Smith, June 12, 1965; children—David Bruce, Susannah Mary. Commd. 2d lt. U.S. Air Force, 1965, advanced through grades to capt. 1971; ret., 1972; operations research analyst Office Asst. Sec. Def. (Systems Analysis), 1972-73; dir. research Dept. Health, Edn. and Welfare, 1973-75; dir. gen. govt. Arthur Young & Co., 1975—; pres. Maximus, Inc., mgmt. cons., 1975—. Decorated Bronze Star, Air Force Commendation medal. Mem. Operations Research Soc. Am., Sigma Xi. Home: 501 Chesapeake Dr Great Falls VA 22066 Office: Maximus Inc 6723 Whittier Ave McLean VA 22101

MATA, ARMANDO ORTEGA, newspaper editor; b. Cuchillo Parado, Chihuahua, Mex., Apr. 8, 1953; s. Cruz Ortega Padilla and Francisca Mata Ortega; B. in Biol. Scis., Escuela Preparatoria of Universidad Autonoma of Chihuahua, 1970; m. Olga Estela Benavides de Ortega, Dec. 9, 1972; children—Zeida Arlene, Armando. Newspaper reporter Periodico Zocalo, 1978, Periodico El Diario, 1978; newspaper corr. Diario El Coahuileuse, 1978-79; editor La Revista de Piedras Negras, 1979—. Mem. Asociacion Revolucionaria de Periodistas de Coahuila. Mem. Partido Revolucionario Institucional. Author: Los Testi gos de Jehova vs. La Biblia, 1976; 500 Formas de Ganar Dinero, 1978. Home: 214 Oriente Abasolo Piedras Negras Coahuila Mexico Office: 400 Dept 9 Rayon Piedras Negras Coahuila Mexico

MATA, RAMON ALBERTO, educator; b. San Joaquin, Venezuela, Aug. 31, 1949; came to U.S., 1976; s. Miguel Jesus and Mina D. M.; B.Math., Instituto Pedagogico de Caracas, 1972; M. Computer Sci. and Bus. Adminstrn., Fla. Inst. Tech., 1978; m. Anahis Ramos, Aug. 13, 1976; children—Yamileth, Harold, Lys Alejandra. Math. tchr. high sch., Caracas, Venezuela, 1970-75; head dept. math. Fco de Miranda Coll., Caracas, 1975-76; prof. math. and physics Kans. State U., Manhattan, 1980—. Venezuelan Govt. grantee, 1976. Mem. Colegio de Profesores de Venezuela, IEEE, Assn. Computing Machinery.

MATHENY, CHARLES WOODBURN, JR., civil engr., city ofcl.; b. Sarasota, Fla., Aug. 7, 1914; s. Charles Woodburn and Virginia (Yates) M.; B.S. in Civil Engring., U. Fla., 1936; grad. Army Command and Gen. Staff Coll., 1944; m. Jeanne Felkel, July 12, 1942; children—Virginia Ann, Nancy Carolina, Charles Woodburn III. San. engr. Ga. State Dept. Health, 1937-39; civil engr. Fla. East Coast Ry., 1939-41; commd. 2d lt. U.S. Army Res., 1936, 1st lt. U.S. Army, 1941, advanced through grades to col., 1955; gen. staff Dept. Army, 1948-51; arty. bn. comdr., Germany, 1945-46; aviation officer 25th Inf. Div., Korea, 1952; dep. commdt., dir. combat devel. Army Aviation Sch., 1954; dep. dir., research dir., dept. tactics Arty. Sch., 1955-57; aviation officer 7th U.S. Army, 1957-58; Munich sub area comdr. So. Area Command, Europe, 1959, dep. chief staff for info., 1960; Mich. sector comdr. VI Army Corps, 1961-62; ret., 1962; asst. dir. Tampa (Fla.), Dept. Public Works 1963-77, asst. to dir., 1977—. Mem. troop com. Boy Scouts Am., 1965-73; active various community and ch. activities; patron Tampa Mus., 1965—, Tampa Community Concert Series; bd. dirs. Tampa YMCA, 1967-71, Fla. Easter Seal Soc., 1978—; bd. dirs. Easter Seal Soc. Hillsborough County, 1971—, treas., 1973-76, pres., 1977. Decorated Bronze Star with oak leaf cluster, Air medal with three oak leaf clusters. Registered profl. engr. and surveyor, Ga. Fellow ASCE (pres. West Coach br., dir. Fla. sect. 1973, Engr. of Yr. award West Coast br. Fla. sect. 1979); mem. Am. Soc. Profl. Engrs. (sr.), Am. Public Works Assn. (pres. West Coast br. Fla. chpt. 1972, exec. com. Fla. chpt. 1972-77, v.p. 1977, pres. 1978), Ret. Officers Assn., Army Aviation Assn., SAR, Fla. Blue Key, Alpha Tau Omega. Episcopalian. Initiator tactical use of helicopters in Army, 1949, profl. sch. civil engring., 1973. Home: 4802 Beachway Dr Tampa FL 33609 Office: City Hall Plaza 4th Floor North 306 E Jackson St Tampa FL 33602

MATHENY, HERSCHEL ALBERT, sci. and engring. co. exec.; b. Guntersville, Ala., July 28, 1930; s. Ernest Bradford and Martha Ellen (Alexander) M.; student Snead Jr. Coll., 1954-55; B.S., U. Ala., 1957; m. Lynne Shirley Wietfeld, Sept. 27, 1969; children—Ernest Alexander, Herschel Paul Engr., Reynolds Metal Co., Sheffield, Ala., 1957-60; dir. program mgmt. Teledyne Brown Engring. Co., Huntsville, Ala., 1960-74; pres. Dynetics, Inc., Huntsville, 1974—. Served with U.S. Army, 1951-53. Mem. Am. Def. Preparedness Assn. (v.p. 1973-74), Assn. U.S. Army (dir.), Huntsville C. of C., Tau Beta Pi, Alpha Pi Mu. Democrat. Methodist. Home: 3002 Pintail Rd SW Huntsville AL 35802 Office: 306 Wynn Dr NW Huntsville AL 35805

MATHENY, JEANNE FELKEL, artist, educator; b. St. Augustine, Fla., June 6, 1920; d. Herbert and Myrtie Ethel (Warren) Felkel; B.A., Fla. State U., 1942; Nat. scholar Traphagen Sch. Design, N.Y.C., 1941; M.A., Mich. State U., 1963; m. Charles Woodburn Matheny, Jr., July 12, 1942; children—Virginia Ann (Mrs. Iain Stewart Baird), Nancy Caroline, Charles Woodburn, III. Instr. art Tampa (Fla.) Art Inst., 1963-67; instr. painting and art history Tampa Bay Art Center, 1964-68, also bd. dirs., acquistions chmn.; lectr. div. fine arts faculty U. Tampa, 1967-72; owner, operator Matheny Studio, Tampa, 1968—; rep. by Trend House Gallery; exhibited at Hillsborough County Fair (Tri-Color-Best in Show), 1963, Cedar Key Sidewalk Show (1st prize), 1966, Winter Park Sidewalk Show, 1967, Fla. State Fair, 1968. Fine arts chmn. Bid by Phone Auction, WEDU, ednl. TV, 1969; instl. rep. Boy Scouts Am.; designer Easter Seals Christmas Cards, 1967, 68, 69. Mem. Nat. League Am. Pen Women (Davis Island br.), Tampa Bay Art Center, Art Students League of Tampa, Alpha Delta Pi. Democrat. Episcopalian. Designer, dir. constrn. 16 stained glass windows St. Marys Episcopal Ch. Important works include batik banner Offices Aviation Authority, Tampa Internat. Airport, 2 large paintings Lykes Bros., Inc., 2 batik sculptures Merle C. Kelsy Library, U Tampa. Home and office: 4802 Beachway Dr Tampa FL 33609

MATHENY, TOM HARRELL, lawyer; b. Houston; s. Whitman and Lorene (Harrell) M.; B.A., Southeastern La. U., 1954; J.D., Tulane U., 1957; LL.D. (hon.), Centenary Coll., 1979. Admitted to La. bar, 1957; partner firm Pittman & Matheny, Hammond, La., 1957—; trust counsel 1st Guaranty Bank, Hammond; v.p. Edwards & Assos., So. Brick Supply, Inc. Faculty, Southeastern La. U., 5 years, Holy Cross Coll., New Orleans, 3 years; lectr. Union Theol. Sem., Law Sci. Acad.; mem. com. on conciliation and mediation of disputes World Peace through Law Center. Chmn. advancement com. Boy Scouts Am., Hammond, 1960-64, mem. dist. council, 1957-66, mem. exec. bd. Istrouma council, 1966—, adv. com. to dist. area council; pres. Tangipahoa Parish Mental Health Assn.; sec. Chep Morrison Scholarship Found.; mem. men's com. Japan Internat. Christian U. Found.; chmn. speakers com., mem. com. on community action and crime prevention La. Commn. on Law Enforcement and Adminstrn. Criminal Justice. Bd. dirs. La. Moral and Civic Found., Tangipahoa Parish ARC, 1957-67, Hammond United Givers Fund, 1957-68, La. Council Chs., Southeastern Devel. Found., La. Mental Health Assn.; bd. dirs. Wesley Found., La. State U., 1965-68, 70—, chmn. bd.; trustee Centenary Coll., 1964-70, Scarritt Coll.; hon. trustee John F. Kennedy Coll.; hon. sec. U.S. com. Audenshaw Found. Recipient Man of Year award, Hammond, 1961, 64, also La. Jr. C. of C., 1964. Fellow Harry S. Truman Library Inst. (hon.); mem. Am. (com. on probate), La. (past gen. chmn. com. on legal aid, com. prison reform), 21st Jud. Dist. (past sec.-treas., v.p. 1967-68, 71—) bar assns., Comml. Law League Am. (past mem. com. on ethics), La. Alumni Council (pres. 1963-65), Acad. Religion and Mental Health, La. Assn. Claimant Compensation Attys., Southeastern La. U. (dir., pres. 1961-62, dir. spl. fund 1959-62, past dir. Tangipahoa chpt.), Tulane Sch. Law alumni assns., Am. Trial Lawyers Assn., Am. Judicature

Soc., Law-Sci. Inst., World Peace Through Law Acad., Acad. Polit. Sci., Am. Acad. Polit. and Social Sci., Internat. Acad. Law and Sci., Common Cause, Internat. Platform Assn., UN Assn., La. Hist. Assn., Friends of Cabildo, Gideons Internat., Nat. Assn. Conf. Lay Leaders (pres.), Assn. Conf. Lay Leaders South Central Jurisdiction (pres.), Hammond Assn. Commerce (dir. 1960-65), Phi Delta Phi, Phi Alpha Delta. Democrat. Methodist (steward, adminstrv. bd., dist. lay leader 1960-64, past co-chmn. conf. bd. lay activities, lay minister, lay leader La. area conf., numerous other ch. activities). Mason, DeMolay (Legion of Honor), Kiwanian (v.p., dir.). Home: PO Box 221 Hammond LA 70404 Office: 401 E Thomas St Hammond LA 70401

MATHER, LEONARD JOSEPH, educator; b. Nanticoke, Pa., May 30, 1944; s. Leon Edward and Sophia Anna M.; Ph.D., Cath. U. Am., 1971. Asst. prof. Howard U., Washington, 1969-71; prof. psychology No. Va. Community Coll., Annandale, 1971—; pvt. practice psychology, Washington, 1970-77; curator Mus. of Arcane Order, Jacksonville, Fla., 1975-78, preceptor Arcane Order, 1978—; lead tchr. Arlington Alcohol Safety Action Program, 1974-75. Fellow for research in esoteric areas of knowledge, 1975; hon. D.D., Universal Life Ch. Mem. Am. Psychol. Assn., Va. Psychol. Assn., D.C. Psychol. Assn., Mt. Pleasant Assn., AAUP, Council Exceptional Children, NEA, Psi Chi, Phi Delta Kappa, Kappa Phi Kappa. Clubs: K.C., Falcons. Editor Jacksonville Poetry Quar., 1978—; author: Operation: Moving Ahead, 1968; contbr. articles to publs. Office: 3001 N Beauregard St Alexandria VA 22311

MATHERLEE, THOMAS RAY, hosp. adminstr.; b. Dayton, Ohio, Sept. 18, 1934; s. Dennis R. and Eleanor C. Matherlee; B.S. in Bus. Adminstrn. Findlay Coll., 1958; M.B.A., U. Chgo., 1960; m. Phyllis Simmons, July 16, 1960; children—Michael, Jennifer, Craig, Brent, Brian. Adminstrv. resident Shannon Hosp., San Angelo, Tex., 1959-60; asst. adminstr. Richland Meml. Hosp., Olney, Ill., 1960-61; adminstrv. asst., then adminstr. Forsyth Meml. Hosp., Winston-Salem, N.C., 1961-68; exec. dir. Gaston County (N.C.) Hosp., 1968-70, Gaston Meml. Hosp., Inc., Gastonia, 1970—; cons. Sch. Pastoral Care, N.C. Bapt. Hosp., Winston-Salem, 1967-68; mem. sub-area adv. council Health Systems Agy., 1975—. Dir. Olney Ill. CD, 1960-61; mem. fin. com. Piedmont council Boy Scouts Am., 1970; mem. adv. bd. Gastonia Wesleyan Youth Chorus, 1972; mem. joint com. nursing edn. N.C. State Bd. Edn. and Bd. Higher Edn., 1969-71; mem. adminstrv. bd. First United Meth. Ch., Gastonia, 1972-74; bd. dirs. Gaston County Heart Assn., 1968-70, Forsyth County Cancer Soc., 1964-65; trustee N.C. Hosp. Edn. and Research Found., 1966-71, pres., 1970-71; trustee N.C. Blue Cross and Blue Shield, Inc., 1971-77, Southeastern Hosp. Conf., 1971-72, 73—, mem. edn. com., 1978—, mem. program com., 1975-76. Named Boss of Year, Nat. Secs. Assn., 1970-71. Fellow Am. Coll. Hosp. Adminstrs. (chmn. 1977—); mem. N.C. Hosp. Assn. (trustee 1966-72, pres. 1970-71, chmn. council govt. liaison 1978—), N.C. League Nursing, Am. Hosp. Assn. (ho. of dels. 1973-78, trustee 1975-78), Gastonia C. of C. (health affairs com. 1969-72). Club: Kiwanis. Contbr. articles on hosp. adminstrn. to profl. jours.

MATHEWS, CHARLES LOREN, assn. exec.; b. Jackson, Miss., Mar. 1, 1933; s. Clyde Harold and Vivian Margaret (Collins) M.; B.A., La. State U., 1960; m. Phoebe Jane Quaintance, Aug. 1, 1953; children—Charles Loren, John Howard, Lacee Quaintance. Asso. exec. sec. Miss. Med. Assn., Jackson, 1960-69, exec. sec., 1972—; staff asst. in health planning Gov.'s Office, State of Miss., 1969-70; dep. dir. Miss. Medicaid Commn., 1970-71; commr. Miss. Pub. Welfare, 1971-72. Pres., Magnolia Little League, 1969-70; chmn. Miss. Child Devel. Council, 1971-72; mem. exploring com. Area IV, Boy Scouts Am., 1973—. Bd. dirs. Jackson Boys Club, 1972—; trustee Miss. Council on Econ. Edn., 1973—. Served with U.S. Army Security Agy., 1952-55. Named Outstanding Assn. Exec., Miss. Econ. Council, 1964. Mem. So. Med. Assn. (asso.), Pub. Relations Assn. Miss., Am. Assn. Med. Soc. Execs. Club: Rotary. Home: 1951 Hamilton Blvd Jackson MS 39213 Office: 735 Riverside Dr Jackson MS 39216

MATHEWS, DANIEL MONROE, chemist; b. Paris, Ark., Oct. 18, 1926; s. Marion Daniel and Alice Virginia (LeRoy) M.; B.S., U. Ark., 1952, M.S., 1955, Ph.D., 1959; postgrad. Ga. Inst. Tech., 1956; m. Charlene Faye Alexander, Aug. 13, 1977; children—Judy Kay, Janice Carol. Research specialist U. Ark., Little Rock, 1952-55, jr. chemist, 1956-58, asst. prof. Sch. Medicine, 1958-59, asso. prof. Grad. Inst. Tech., 1960-70, prof., 1970—; instr. Ga. Inst. Tech., Atlanta, 1955-56. Served with U.S. Army, 1945-46. Mem. Am. Chem. Soc., Chem. Soc. (London), Health Physics Soc., Ark. Acad. Sci., Sigma Xi. Contbr. articles to profl. jours. Home: 4200 Glenmere St North Little Rock AR 72116 Office: 1201 McAlmont St Little Rock AR 72203

MATHEWS, RAYMOND CLIFFORD, JR., aquatic ecologist; b. Houston, Aug. 8, 1946; s. Raymond Clifford and Betty Lou (Bunting) M.; B.S., Tex. Wesleyan Coll., 1969; M.S., Tenn. Tech. U., 1975; postgrad. Tex. A&M U., 1971-72; U. Tenn., 1977-78; m. Theresa Jo Emerton, Sept. 14, 1974. Zoo keeper Fort Worth Zool. Zoo, 1969-70; marine technician Tex. A&M U., 1970-72; staff biologist Woodward-Envicon Environ. Cons. Co., 1972-73; fisheries biologist Tenn. Wildlife Resources Agy., 1975-76; research biologist Great Smoky Mountains Nat. Park, Gatlinburg, Tenn., 1977—. Mem. Am. Fisheries Soc., Am. Soc. Ichythyologist and Herpetologist, Tenn. Acad. Sci., Assn. Southeastern Biologists, Nat. Speological Soc., Sigma Xi, Beta Beta Beta. Methodist. Clubs: Toastmasters Internat., Masons. Contbr. articles to profl. jours. Home: 353 Circle Dr Gatlinburg TN 37738 Office: Uplands Field Research Lab Great Smoky Mountains Nat Park Gatlinburg TN 37738

MATHEWS, ROBERT CABEEN HOPKINS, JR., contractor; b. Nashville, June 16, 1927; s. Robert Cabeen Hopkins and Mary Olive (Culbert) M.; B.Engring., Vanderbilt U., 1951; m. Alice Walker Casey, May 3, 1952; children—Robert Cabeen Hopkins III, Walker Casey, Mary Alice. With R.C. Mathews Contractor, Inc., Nashville, 1951—, pres., chmn. bd., 1968—; pres. M and M Contractor, Inc., Culbert Constrn. Co.; pres. Met. Indsl. Park, Inc.; partner MetroCenter Properties. Past mem. bd. dirs. Historic Nashville; mem. bd. trust, past pres. Cumberland Mus. and Sci. Center, Ensworth Sch.; trustee George Peabody Coll. for Tchrs., Vanderbilt U.; bd. dirs., mem. exec. com., mem. bldg. com. Tenn. Bot. Gardens and Fine Arts Center; chmn. Met. Nashville Airport Authority. Served with AUS, 1945-47. Named Jr. C. of C. Man of Year, 1954. Mem. Asso. Gen. Contractors Nashville (exec. com.), Nashville C. of C. (bd. govs., past pres.), Phi Delta Theta. Methodist. Clubs: Rotary, Belle Meade Country (Nashville). Home: 4323 Glen Eden Dr Nashville TN 37205 Office: Suite 120 Nashville House One Vantage Way Nashville TN 37228

MATHEY, FRANK ALBERT, JR., state ofcl.; b. Quincy, Ill., July 14, 1935; s. Frank Albert and Elsie Julia (Vandevelde) M.; B.B.A., U. Miami, 1957; m. Agnes Eichler, Aug. 20, 1966; children—Nanette Marie, Frank Albert III. Auditor dept. beverages State of Fla., Miami, 1960-67, dist. auditor, 1967-70, cigarette tax supr., Tallahassee, 1970-72, dir. fin. and acctg. dept. bus. regulation, 1972—; dept. rep. Fla. Gov.'s Revenue Estimating Com., 1974—; project mgr. Manpower Utilization Study, 1978-79. Active, World Wide Marriage Encounter. Served with USAF, 1957-60. Mem. Mcpl. Fin. Officers Assn., Fla. Govtl. Accts. and Mgrs. Assn. Roman Catholic. Home: 7043 Dardwood Ln Tallahassee FL 32312 Office: John's Bldg 725 S Bronough St Tallahassee FL 32304

MATHEY, WILLIAM JOSEPH, veterinarian; b. Chgo., Apr. 1, 1917; s. William Joseph and Theresa (Hagedorn) M.; B.S., U. Notre Dame, 1938; V.M.D., U. Pa., 1943; Ph.D., U. Calif., Berkeley, 1952; m. Mary Dolores Kinney, Feb. 2, 1941; children—William (dec.), Mary (dec.). Veterinarian, Sharp & Dohme, Inc., Glenolden, Pa., 1944-46; mem. faculty U. Calif., 1949-54, U. Ga., 1955; veterinarian Pitman Moore Co., Zionsville, Ind., 1955-57; mem. faculty Mich. State U., 1957-58; mem. faculty N.Y. State Vet. Coll., 1958-59; lab. dir. Whitmoyer Labs., Myerstown, Pa., 1960-62; mem. faculty Wash. State U., Pullman and Puyallup, 1962-74, La. State U., Baton Rouge, 1975-78; vet. cons. Audubon Park Zoo, New Orleans, 1978—. Election commr., 1978-79. Served to capt. U.S. Army, 1943, 46-48. Mem. Am. Assn. Avian Pathologists, Am. Vet. Med. Assn., Am. Assn. Zoo Veterinarians, Wildlife Disease Assn., Poultry Sci. Assn., Conf. Research Workers in Animal Diseases, World's Poultry Vet. Assn., World's Poultry Assn., AAAS, N.Y. Acad. Scis. Roman Catholic. Author: Pet Medicine, 1977. Home: 1944 Nicholson Dr Baton Rouge LA 70802

MATHIS, BETTY, public relations counsel; b. Atlanta, Oct. 5, 1918; d. Walter Rylander and Evelyn Battle (Epting) M.; student Agnes Scott Coll., 1934-36. Sports writer, columnist Atlanta Constitution, 1936-39; gen. news and feature writer, then editor spl. supplements, 1939-40; dir. public relations Atlanta Housing Authority, 1940; feature writer, asst. city editor, daily by-line columnist Atlanta Constitution, 1941-43; asst. regional info. exec. OPA, 1943-45; partner Mathis, Murphey & Bondurant public relations counsel, Atlanta, 1945-50; editor Sun Colony Mag., Fort Lauderdale, Fla., 1950-53; partner Mathis & Bondurant public relations, Fort Lauderdale, 1953—. Bd. dirs. ARC; mem. coms. United Way; sec. vestry All Saints Episcopal Ch., 1974-76, mem. vestry, 1978—, treas., 1979, sr. warden, 1980, del. Diocesan Conv., 1975, 79, 80. Nominee, Pulitzer prize, 1937. Mem. Public Relations Soc. Am., Am. Soc. Hosp. Public Relations (profl. advancement com. 1980), Public Relations Council Fla. Hosp. Assn. (dir. 1977-79, pres. 1977-78), Women in Communications (pres. county 1968, 69, Atlantic Fla. chpt. 1979, named Woman of Yr. 1979), Gold Coast Hosp. Public Relations Council (founding, v.p. 1979-80), Am. Hosp. Assn. Democrat. Club: Tower. Home and office: 1628 NE 15th Ave Fort Lauderdale FL 33305

MATHIS, DAWSON M., Congressman; b. Nashville, Ga., Nov. 30, 1940; s. Marvin W. and Nell Dawson (Abel) M.; student South Ga. Coll., 1958-60; m. Sharon Renee Beavers; children—Anthony Dawson, Craig Steven, Jason Everett, Russell Dean. News dir. sta. WALB-TV, Albany, Ga., 1964-70; mem. 92d-96th congresses from 2d Dist. Ga., mem. Com. Agr., Com. Interior and Insular Affairs. Active Chehaw Boy Scouts Am., 1967-70. Mem. Ga. Assn. Newscasters, Fraternal Order Police. Clubs: Elks, Masons, Toastmasters, Shriners.

MATHIS, GERALD RAY, historian; b. Hattiesburg, Miss., Apr. 2, 1937; s. Paul Monroe and Helen LaVerne (Morris) M.; A.B., Birmingham-So. Coll., 1958; M.Div., Duke U., 1962; M.A., U. Ga., 1963, Ph.D., 1967; m. Mary Kathryn Pugh, Dec. 28, 1958; children—John Paul, Charles Ray. Instr. history Snead Coll., Boaz, Ala., 1964-65; teaching asst. U. Ga., Athens, 1963-64, 65-66; asst. prof. history Ga. So. Coll., Statesboro, 1966-69; prof. history Troy (Ala.) State U., 1969—. Nat. Methodist scholar, 1956-58, 62-63; So. fellow, 1958-59; recipient History award Ga. chpt. Colonial Dames Am., 1964; Am. Philos. Soc. research grantee, 1968. Mem. Orgn. Am. Historians, So., Ga., Pike County hist. socs., Ala. Hist. Assn. (exec. com.), Soc. for Study of So. Lit., Phi Beta Kappa, Phi Kappa Phi, Omicron Delta Kappa, Phi Alpha Theta, Phi Theta Kappa, Alpha Tau Omega. Democrat. Methodist. Author: College Life in Reconstruction South, 1974; T.W. Reed's History of Univ. of Georgia, 1974; J.H. Dent Farm Journals, 1977; J.H. Dent, South Carolina Aristocrat on the Alabama Frontier, 1979; contbr. articles and revs. to profl. jours. Home: Route 1 Mathews AL 36052 Office: Dept History Troy State U Troy AL 36081

MATHIS, JAMES OTTO, educator; b. Monroe, La., July 22, 1929; s. Dewey Otto and Dessie Lee (Williams) M.; B.S., N. Tex. State U., 1951, M.Ed., 1956, Ed.D., 1965; postgrad. N.C. State U., summer 1962; m. Peggy Sue Miller, July 21, 1951; children—Linda Mathis Combs, Elizabeth Ann Mathis Monday, James Allison. Tchr. art Victoria (Tex.) Independent Sch. Dist., 1952-55; tchr. art Andrews (Tex.) Independent Sch. Dist., 1955-59, counselor, 1959-63; grad. fellow North Tex. State U., 1963-65; asso. prof. edn. and psychology East Central Okla. State Coll., 1965-67; asso. prof. edn. Sam Houston State U., Huntsville, Tex., 1967—. Psychologist, Okla. Dept. Health, Ada, 1966-67; cons. Palestine, Aldine and Region 6 Edn. Service Center, Tex. Served with Tex. N.G., 1947-50. Recipient State of Tex. grants for grad. studies, 1963-65. Mem. Am., Tex., Brazos Valley personnel and guidance assns., N.E.A. Tex. Tchrs. Assn., Phi Delta Kappa. Democrat. Baptist. Author: (with David Henderson and Billy Holliman) Evaluation in Secondary Schools-An Activities Approach, 1975. Home: Route 2 Box 140 Huntsville TX 77340

MATHIS, JOEL HENRY, transp. co. exec.; b. Breckenridge, Tex., Nov. 17, 1939; s. Jewell Joseph, Jr. and Lois Marie (Denman) M.; B.B.A., Baylor U., 1962; m. Ellen Louise DuBose, Aug. 4, 1962; children—Michelle Marie, Mark Edward, Susan Rene. Retail supr. Humble Oil Co., Austin, Tex., 1962-66; dir. pub. relations, advt., and personnel Nat. Western Life Ins. Co., Austin, 1966-70; dir. pub. relations and advt. East Tex. Motor Freight, Dallas, 1970—. Tenor soloist Dallas Symphony Orch., Dallas Civic Opera, Dallas First Bapt. Ch., dinner theatres, concerts and TV shows in Dallas area and Southwestern U.S. Served with AUS, 1963. Recipient First place Advt. Program, Am. Trucking Assn., 1974. Mem. Internat. Assn. Bus. Communicators (Outstanding Publ. Design awards 1973, 74, Gold Quill award 1975), Pub. Relations Soc. Am., Tex. Pub. Relations Assn., Dallas Press Club (Outstanding Indsl. Publ. award 1972, mem. trucking industry pub. relations coordinating com.), Dallas Advt. League, Baylor Ex-Students Assn., Dallas Bear Club. Republican. Baptist. Mason. Clubs: Lakewood Country, Dallas Lancers. Home: 13710 Sprucewood Dallas TX 75240 Office: 2355 Stemmons Freeway Box 10125 Dallas TX 75207

MATHIS, LARRY LEE, hosp. adminstr.; b. Lincoln, Nebr., May 29, 1943; s. George and Berneta (Van Laningham) M.; B.A. in Social Sci., Pittsburg (Kans.) State U., 1965; M.H.A., Washington U., St. Louis, 1972; postgrad. program for health systems mgmt. Harvard U., 1978; m. Betty Keith, Aug. 15, 1964; children—Julie, Jennifer. News reporter Pittsburg Sun, 1961-65; adminstrv. resident Meth. Hosp., Houston, 1971-72, adminstrv. asst., 1972, asst. to pres., 1972-74, v.p., 1974-78, sr. v.p., 1978-80, exec. v.p., chief operating officer, 1980—; sec. bd. dirs., mem. fin. com. Greater Houston Hosp. Service Corp.; adj. instr. health care adminstrn. Washington U., 1976, U. Houston, 1979; cons. to minister of edn. and culture Brazil, 1976. Bd. dirs. Houston-Harris County chpt. ARC; vice chmn. bd., treas. St. Luke's United Meth. Ch. Served to capt. U.S. Army, 1965-70; Vietnam. Decorated Bronze Star, others; named Outstanding Young Alumnus, Pittsburg State U., 1976. Mem. Assn. Univ. Programs in Health Adminstrn., Am. Coll. Hosp. Adminstrs., Am. Hosp. Assn., Tex. Hosp. Assn., Greater Houston Hosp. Council (chmn. energy task force com. 1972), Scabbard and Blade, Sigma Chi. Club: Houston Rotary. Home: 3037 Reba Houston TX 77019 Office: 6565 Fannin Houston TX 77030

MATHIS, VIOLA INEZ, ednl. diagnostician; b. Temple, Tex., Jan. 26, 1932; d. Wiley Newman and Velma Imo (Patterson) Berryman; A.A., San Antonio Coll., 1969; B.S. with honors, S.W. Tex. State U., 1971; M.Edn., Trinity U., 1975; m. Herbert Wayne Mathis, Jr., Oct. 22, 1949; children—Larry, Evelyn, Bryan, Kathryn. Tchr. elementary pub. schs., San Antonio, 1971-73; resource tchr., Edgewood Independent Sch. Dist., San Antonio, Tex., 1973-75, ednl. diagnostician, 1975—. Den mother San Antonio council Boy Scouts Am., 1959-64; asst. leader San Antonio Council Girl Scouts U.S.A., 1961-66. Certified ednl. diagnostician. Mem. NEA, Tex. Tchrs. Assn. Ch. of Christ. Address: 9011 Saddle Trail San Antonio TX 78255

MATHIS, WILLIAM HUBERT, ins. co. exec.; b. Madisonville, Tex., Oct. 11, 1933; s. W.J. and Jewel I. Mathis; B.S., U. Houston, 1955; m. Jessie Mae Wells, May, 1955; children—Cherie Kaye, Mark William, Michael Lee. With Gt. So. Life Ins. Co., Houston, 1958—, 2d v.p., asst. sec. and underwriting mgr., 1975-76, 2d v.p., asst. sec. and mgr. policyowner service, 1976-77, v.p., asst. sec. and mgr. policy-owner service, word processing, premium acctg., conservation and records, from 1977, now pres.; dir. Parkway Devel. Corp. Mem. budget com. United Fund. Served with U.S. Army, 1956-58. Mem. Tex. Life Conv., Westador Civic Assn., Houston C. of C. Baptist. Office: PO Box 1972 Houston TX 77001

MATHIS, WILLIAM STEPHAN, coll. dean, musicologist; b. Ft. Meade, Fla., Aug. 22, 1921; s. Arthur William and Jonnie Virgie (Chaffin) M.; Mus.B., Stetson U., 1943; Mus.M., U. Mich., 1946; Ph.D., Fla. State U., 1952; m. Nancy Virginia Boney, Sept. 2, 1949; children—William Stephan, Nancy Nunnery. Asst. prof. music Fla. State U., Tallahassee, 1952-53; prof. music, chmn. div. fine arts Belmont Coll., Nashville, 1953-56; prof., dean Sch. Music, Hardin-Simmons U., Tex., 1956-62, dean acad. affairs, 1962-66; dean acad. affairs Hope Coll., Holland, Mich., 1966-67; prof., dean Coll. Humanities, U. N.C., Charlotte, 1967—. Served with U.S. Army, 1943. Mem. Am. Assn. Higher Edn. Baptist. Author: The Pianist and Church Music, 1962. Office: U NC Charlotte Sta Charlotte NC 28223

MATHUR, VIRENDRA SINGH, cardiologist; b. Kanpur, India, Mar. 7, 1935; s. Ishwari Prasad and Radhika (Rani) M.; came to U.S., 1962; B.Sc. in Zoology, U. Agra, India, 1951; M.B., B.S., King George's Med. Coll., U. Lucknow, India, 1957; M.D., U. Lucknow, 1960; m. Nalini Mathur, Nov. 28, 1966; 1 son, Gaurav. Intern, Lucknow Med. Coll. Hosp., 1957-58; resident in medicine, 1958-59, research fellow in medicine, 1959-60, chief resident in medicine, 1960; chief resident in cardiology All India Inst. Med. Scis., New Delhi, 1961; resident in medicine Meml. Hosp., Worcester, Mass., 1962-63; research fellow in cardiology Harvard Med. Sch., Boston, 1963-65; research fellow in cardiology Boston City Hosp., 1965-67; practice medicine specializing in cardiology, New Delhi, 1967-70; asst. prof. cardiology All India Inst. Med. Scis., New Delhi, 1967-70; asst. prof. medicine Baylor Coll. Medicine, Houston, 1971-73, asso. prof., 1973—; physician VA Hosp., Houston, 1971-75; dir. Clayton Found. Cardiovascular Lab., St. Luke's Hosp., 1976—; investigator Nat. Heart and Lung Inst., 1974—. Recipient Meritorious Service award Baylor Coll. Medicine, 1977. Diplomate Am. Bd. Medicine. Fellow Am. Coll. Cardiology, Am. Coll. Angiology; mem. Am. Fedn. Clin. Research, Tex. Med. Assn., Assn. Physicians India, Am. Heart Assn. Contbr. articles on cardiovascular disease to med. jours. Home: 7707 Braesridge Ct Houston TX 77071 Office: 6720 Bertner St Houston TX 77025

MATLOCK, GIBB BLANKS, system engr.; b. San Angelo, Tex., Nov. 27, 1931; s. William Tillman and Ruth Juanita (Blanks) M.; student Tex. A. and M. U., 1948-50; B.A., U. Tex., 1957, M.S., 1959; Ph.D., So. Meth. U., 1970; m. Mary Jo Hullum, Mar. 30, 1957; children—Gibb B., Jr., Russell Evan, Amy Colleen, Brian Douglass. Research scientist Balcones Research Lab, Austin, Tex., 1958-59; elec. engr. Ling-Temco-Vought, Dallas, 1959-62; sr. mem. tech. staff Tex. Instruments Inc., Dallas, 1962—; instr. probability and statistics So. Meth. U., Dallas, 1973-74. Served with USN, 1951-54. Fellow Inst. for Earth and Man; mem. Am. Statis. Assn., Inst. Navigation, IEEE. Home: 9521 Fieldcrest Dr Dallas TX 75238 Office: Tex Instruments Inc PO Box 226015 Dallas TX 75266

MATSON, JESSIE BALDWIN, ret. govt. ofcl.; b. Omaha, July 18, 1904; d. William Arthur and Elizabeth M. (Bratt) Baldwin; student Grinnell Coll., 1922-25; A.B., U. Nebr., 1926; postgrad. U. Utah, 1945-47; children—John Hanthorn (dec.), Joanne Sandra. Writer Omaha Daily Jour. Stockman, 1926-30; syndicate writer Corn Belt Farm Dailies, 1930-34; state dir. women's div. Iowa Emergency Relief Adminstrn., 1934-40; Iowa dir. women's and profl. projects WPA, Archives Security, Air Force, 1942; faculty mem. U. Utah, 1945-46; tchr. Guam, Mariannas Islands, 1946-47; coordinator women's activities St. Paul Civil Def., 1950-70; now ret.; tchr. So. Cross Sch., Miami, Fla., 1971-78; substitute tchr. Charlotte and Lee County Schs. Former comdr. Ramsey County Cancer Soc.; founder St. Paul Council Human Relations, 1948; former chmn. Nat. Thanksgiving Day Assn.; past v.p. pub. affairs Soroptimist Fedn. Ams.; life mem. past pres. St. Paul Club. State chmn. Luther W. Youngdahl campaign for gov., 1949-50. Recipient certificate of merit Gov. of Minn., 1961, 70, 14 awards on retirement. Mem. VFW Aux., Am. Legion Aux., Nat. Assn. Ret. Govt. Profl. Employees, Inter-Club Council (founder 1944, pres. 1948-49), League Women Voters, PEO, Am. Security Council (adv. bd.), Theta Sigma Phi, Alpha Phi, Gamma Alpha Chi. Clubs: Toastmistress (founder 1st St. Paul and Peace River clubs), River Forest Cultural Exchange (Ft. Myers). Home: 1729 Inlet Dr Waterway Estates North Fort Myers FL 33903

MATSON, ROGER ALLEN, economist; b. Minot, N.D., July 29, 1938; s. Walfred Gustav and Zella Katherine (Martinson) M.; B.A., Concordia Coll., Moorhead, Minn., 1960; Ph.D. (Woodrow Wilson fellow), U. Colo., 1965; m. Sandra Francis Winn, Sept. 2, 1967; children—Todd Allen, Melissa Francis. Instr., U. Mont., 1963-64; USPHS fellow U. N.C., Chapel Hill, 1964-65; chief econ. research staff TVA, Knoxville, 1965-70, chief budget and cost control staff, Chattanooga, 1974—; lectr. U. Tenn., Knoxville, 1969-70; regional economist Dept. Commerce, Washington, 1970-72; asst. prof. U. Wyo., 1970-74; adj. prof. U. Tenn. at Chattanooga, 1974—. Mem. Am. Econ. Assn., Regional Sci. Assn., N.Am. Soc. for Corporate Planning, Nat. Assn. Bus. Economists. Democrat. Lutheran. Contbr. econ. articles to profl. jours. Home: 4944 Willow Lawn Dr Chattanooga TN 37416 Office: Budget and Cost Control Staff TVA Chattanooga TN 37401

MATTESON, LEWIS WHITFORD, JR., automobile dealer, data processing co. exec., cons. engr.; b. Houston, Nov. 24, 1924; s. Lewis Whitford and Lillian (Hall) M.; B.S. in Elec. Engring., Rice U., 1949; m. Betty Irene Dykes, Dec. 16, 1954; children—Sherry Matteson Adelman, Whit, Debbie Matteson Wood, Ricky. Partner, Matteson S.W. Co., Houston, 1950-62, v.p., 1962-67, chmn. bd., 1967-71; owner, chmn. bd., pres. Matteson Transformers Inc., Houston, 1957-72; owner, mgr. Matteson Devel. Co., Houston, 1970—; v.p., sec., treas., dir. Plaza Lincoln-Mercury, Inc., Houston, 1971-79, pres., treas., chmn. bd., 1979—; chmn. bd., pres. Matteson's Motorcycles, Inc., Kerrville, Tex., 1973—. Served with Signal Corps, AUS, 1943-46. Registered profl. engr., Tex. Mem. Am. Theatre Organ Soc., Tex. Motorcycle Roadriders Assn., Phi Theta Kappa. Episcopalian. Club: Racquet (Houston). Home: 211 Paul Revere Dr Houston TX 77024 also Casa del Rio Hunt TX 78024 Office: 9255 Kirby Rd Houston TX 77098

MATTHEWS, ALFRED ST. JOHN, JR., hotel adminstr.; b. Macon, Ga., Dec. 19, 1939; s. Alfred St. John and Willa (Perry) M.; B.A., Randolph-Macon Coll., 1961; m. Pamela Ruth DeYoung, Aug. 19, 1972; children—Alfred St. John, Joseph Douglas, Kristen Elizabeth. Exec. asst. mgr. Saddlebrook (N.J.) Marriott Hotel, 1972-74; resident mgr. Denver Marriott Hotel, 1974-76, Chgo. Marriott O'Hare, 1976-77; gen. mgr. Atlanta Marriott Hotel at Perimeter Center, 1977—. Mem. Ga. Hospitality and Travel Assn., Dekalb County C. of C., Atlanta C. of C. Episcopalian. Club: Atlanta Country. Office: 246 Perimeter Center Pkwy Atlanta GA 30346

MATTHEWS, ANNA (ANN) MAE, hosp. exec.; b. Morehead, Ky., Feb. 20, 1923; d. James and Grace Hollan; cert. New Castle Bus. Coll., 1941; student in bus. mgmt. and psychology Lake Sumter Community Coll., 1977; (div.); children—David E., John W., Jr. Bookkeeper, Farm Bur., New Castle, Ind., 1940; sec. Kelly-Springfield Tire Co., Los Angeles, 1940; clk. World Bestos div. Firestone Co., New Castle, 1941; owner, operator grocery store, New Castle, 1941-69; tchr.'s aide Treadway Elem. Sch., Leesburg, Fla., 1970-71; with Waterman Meml. Hosp., Eustis, Fla., 1971—, bus. office supr., 1973-74, bus. office mgr., 1974—, also mem. job evaluation com. participant profl. workshops. Mem. adv. com. Lake County Vo-Tech Center. Named Employee of Month, Waterman Meml. Hosp., 1972. Mem. Ch. of God. Office: Waterman Meml Hosp Drawer B Eustis FL 32726

MATTHEWS, ANNE LAMB, ednl. adminstr., state ofcl.; b. Florence County, S.C., Nov. 3, 1942; d. Alex B. and Mettie (Nettles) L.; B.S. in Bus. Edn., Coker Coll., 1964; M.A. in Econs., Appalachian State U., 1968; Ed.D. in Ednl. Adminstrn., U. S.C., 1975; m. Glenny Jeff Matthews, Sept. 2, 1967. Tchr. bus. edn. dept. Hannah-Pamplico High Sch., Pamplico, S.C., 1964-67; instr. dept. bus. adminstrn. and secretarial sci. Florence-Darlington Tech. Edn. Coll., Florence, S.C., 1967-69; tchr.-counselor Youth Study Center, Greenville, S.C., 1970-71; dist. cons. Office Occupations Edn., Anderson (S.C.) Dist. Office, 1971-73; adj. prof. Coll. Bus. Adminstrn. U. S.C., Columbia, 1975-78; state supr. bus. and office edn. State Dept. Edn., Columbia, 1973-80, chief supr. program planning, 1980—, mem. various coms., 1975—. Vol. Vets Hosp., Columbia, 1978—. Recipient Hulda Erath award, 1978, 79. Mem. Nat. Bus. Edn. Assn. (chmn. policies com. on bus. and econ. edn. 1979-80), So. Bus. Edn. Assn. (sec. adminstrn. and supervision 1977-78, mem. exec. bd. 1978—), Nat. Assn. State Suprs. of Bus. and Office Edn. (pres. 1977-79), S.C. Office Occupations Assn. (mem. exec. bd. 1973-76), Internat. Soc. for Bus. Edn., Am. Vocat. Assn. (mem. policy and planning com. 1977—), Adminstrv. Mgmt. Soc., S.C. Vocat. Dirs. Assn., S.C. Bus. Edn. Assn. (pres. 1969-70, mem. exec. bd. 1965-77), S.C. Vocat. Assn. (mem. program com. 1975-76), S.C. State Employees Assn., Internat. Word Processing Assn., S.C. Council for Adminstrv. Women in Edn., Delta Kappa Gamma, Phi Delta Kappa. Baptist. Contbr. numerous articles to profl. jours.; author word processing materials; editor and reviewer various manuals and instructional guides on bus. and office occupations programs. Office: 920 Rutledge Bldg State Dept Education Columbia SC 29209

MATTHEWS, BYRON S., writer, lawyer; b. Evanston, Ill., June 2, 1928; s. Thomas A. and Elsie S. (Spears) M.; B.A., Northwestern U., 1949, J.D., 1952; m. Katryna Staunton, Apr. 13, 1951 (dec. Sept. 1977); children—JoAnn Matthews Carpenter, Karen Matthews Martin, Daniel, Jean. Admitted to Ill. bar, 1952, Okla. bar, 1967; atty. for various Ill. municipalities, 1953-66; individual practice law, Tulsa, 1967-70; atty. Legal Aid Soc., Tulsa, 1970-78; individual practice law, free-lance writer, Tulsa, 1978—; author: (with Thomas A. Matthews) Municipal Ordinances, rev. edit., 1979, Local Government, 1970; contbr. articles to legal jours.; mem. faculty John Marshall Law Sch., Lawyers Inst., Chgo., early 1960's. Mem. Am. Bar Assn.

MATTHEWS, CHARLES SEDWICK, cons. petroleum engr.; b. Houston, Mar. 27, 1920; s. Charles James and Zadoc (Sedwick) M.; B.S. in Chem. Engring., Rice U., 1941, M.S., 1943, Ph.D., 1944; m. Miriam Ormerod, June 2, 1945; children—Joan, Wendy. With Shell Devel. Co., San Francisco, 1944-48, Houston, 1948-65, N.Y.C., 1965-67, dir. research, Houston, 1967-72, mgr. engring., 1972-73; cons. petroleum engr., 1974—. Mem. Shell Found., 1967—, engring. adv. council Rice U., Houston, 1971—; chmn. Tex. Engrs. for Conservation, 1973—. Registered profl. engr., Tex. Mem. Soc. Petroleum Engrs. (distinguished lectr.), Am. Petroleum Inst. Clubs: Houston, Meyerland (Houston). Author: (with D.G. Russell) Pressure Buildup and Flow Tests in Wells, 1967. Contbr. articles to profl. jours. Patentee in field. Home: 5307 S Braeswood Blvd Houston TX 77096 Office: PO Box 2463 Houston TX 77001

MATTHEWS, CORNELIA WILLIAMS, business exec.; b. Norene, Tenn., Nov. 16, 1920; d. Horace Vale and Willette (Thompson) Williams; student pub. schs., Watertown, Tenn.; m. William Hayes Matthews, Dec. 13, 1946; 1 son, William Hayes, Jr. With First Am. Nat. Bank, Nashville, 1942-63; mgr. customer service div. Nat. Cash Register Co., Nashville, 1965-71; asst. v.p., tng. coordinator Third Nat. Bank, Nashville, 1971-75; adminstrv. officer, asst. mgr. main office div. First Am. Nat. Bank, 1975-78; v.p., mgr. Bank Systems div. Bus. Machines, Inc., Nashville, 1978—; instr. Am. Inst. Banking, Nashville State Tech. Inst. Past pres. Nashville Mental Health Assn.; bd. dirs. Jr. Achievement Nashville, 1977—; mem. adv. bd. Bus. and Indsl. Inst., Vol. State Community Coll. Recipient Service award Tenn. Bankers Assn., 1976. Mem. Nat. Assn. Bank Women, Am. Inst. Banking, Am. Bus. Women's Assn. (past pres. Tannansie chpt.), Internat. Platform Assn. Republican. Methodist. Club: Capitol (Nashville). Author tng. manuals. Home: 616 Skyview Dr Nashville TN 37206 Office: Bus Machines Inc 304 Space Park S PO Box 110376 Nashville TN 37211

MATTHEWS, DORIS BOOZER (MRS. CHARLES L. MATTHEWS), educator; b. Lexington, S.C., Aug. 18, 1932; d. Otto Raymond and Ruth (Sox) Boozer; B.S., Newberry Coll., 1952; M.Ed., U.S.C., 1955, specialist degree, 1971, Ph.D., 1972; m. Charles L. Matthews, Aug. 20, 1952; children—Shirley Ruth, Carles Ray, Sylvia Ann. Tchr., Brennen Sch., Columbia, S.C., 1952-64; supr. counseling S.C. State Employment Service, Columbia, 1964-66; counseling supr. and basic edn. specialist S.C. Com. for Tech. Edn., Columbia, 1966-68; instr. elementary edn. U. S.C., Columbia, 1968-72; asst. prof. S.C. State Coll., Orangeburg, 1972-75, asso. prof., 1975-79, prof., 1979—. Chmn. Columbians Youth Com., 1968-72, chmn. Cayce Neighborhood Center, 1967-70. Mem. Nat., S.C. edn. assns., Nat., S.C. assns. supervision and curriculum devel., Assn. for Ednl. Communication and Tech., Employment Counselors Assn., Am., S.C. (past pres.) vocational guidance assns., Am., S.C. personnel and guidance assns., S.C. Dept. Audio-Visual Instrn., AAUP (pres. S.C. State Coll. chpt. 1975-79, v.p. state conf. 1979-80), S.C. State Employees Assn., Internat. Platform Assn., Phi Delta Kappa (v.p. S.C. State Coll. chpt. 1978-79, pres. 1979-80). Lutheran. Clubs: Cayce Womens (pres. 1965-67), Fashion Rose Garden (pres. 1962-64). Home: 101 Delisseline Rd Cayce SC 29033 Office: SC State Coll Orangeburg SC 29117

MATTHEWS, ELSIE CATHERINE SPEARS, editor, author; b. Chgo., Aug. 8, 1901; d. Byron Alexander and Catherine (Clark) Spears; A.B., Wheaton (Ill.) Coll., 1923; postgrad. Northwestern U. Law Sch., 1922-24; m. Thomas A. Matthews, June 27, 1925 (dec. Feb. 1977); children—Thomas Alexander, Byron Stewart. Asst. editor, compiler Codes of Ordinances for Ill. communities, 1927-70; asst. editor Current Mcpl. Problems, Callaghan & Co., Chgo., 1959-76; writer Comments for Dept. Agr., Bur. Land Mgmt. Washington County chmn. Keep Okla. Beautiful, 1970, co-chmn., 1971-72; pres. River Forest (Ill.) Ind. Republican Womens Club, 1940-42. Recipient certificate of merit Green County 1971. Fellow Internat. Civic Servants Soc., Internat. Biog. Soc.; mem. Bartlesville C. of C. (anti-litter chmn. 1968—, Bronze medallion for Community Service), Okla. (Johnny Horizon state chmn.), Osage Hills (press and publicity chmn., certificate of merit, chmn. Save the Selenite Crystal Collecting Area) gem and mineral. socs., Rocky Mountain Mineral. Soc., Am. Fedn. Mineral. Socs., Rocky Mountain Fedn. Gem and Mineral Socs. (resolution), Intergalactic Petrology Club (founder, pres.). Persbyn. Club: River Forest Womens (life mem.). Author: (with others) Supplements to Municipal Ordinances; reviser (with Byron Matthews) Municipal Ordinances, 2 vols., 1979; contbr. articles to profl., mineral. jours. Home: 926 Sandstone St Bartlesville OK 74003

MATTHEWS, HENRY JAMES, clergyman; b. Ryswyk, Netherlands, Dec. 13, 1905; s. Hendricus Jacobus and Johanna Petronella (Schoenmaker) Suiker; came to U.S., 1947, naturalized, 1955; student Bishop's Tchrs. Coll., Beverwyk, Netherlands, 1920-21, St. Joseph Studiehuis, Tilburg, Netherlands, Roosendaal, Netherlands, 1927-29, Augustynenklooster, Nymegen, Netherlands; M.A. in Edn., Salem State Coll., 1964; computer programmer diploma Inst. Tech., Miami Beach, Fla., 1971; m. Hilda Milagro Valle, May 23, 1971; 1 stepson, Manuel Lopez. Ordained priest Roman Catholic Ch., 1934, dispensed from monastic and priestly duties, 1970; pastor, missionary priest, Irupana, Quime, Chulumani, La Paz, all Bolivia, 1938-46; Discrete to provincial chpt., Eind Hoven, Netherlands, 1946-47; asst. pastor St. Peter's Ch., N.Y.C., St. Athanasius, Bronx, N.Y., 1947-52; tchr. German Archbishop Stepinac's High Sch., White Plains, N.Y., 1952-54; tchr. Latin and religion Bonner High Sch., Drexel Hill, Pa., 1954-55; tchr. Latin, Spanish, religion, chant Augustinian Acad., S.I., N.Y., 1955-56; asso. prof. philosophies fine arts and religion Merrimack Coll., 1956-63, dir. lang. lab., 1958-63; asso. prof. Spanish, French, German and philosophy of religion Biscayne Coll., 1963-68, dir. guidance and placement, chaplain, 1963-68; asst. pastor St. Mary's, Tampa, Fla., 1968-69, St. Patrick's, Jacksonville, Fla., 1969-70; rehab. coordinator for blind Goodwill Industries, Miami, Fla., 1970-73; interfaith liaison person, staff asst. Adv. Council of Service Programs for Elderly in Dade County (Fla.), Miami, 1973-76; resident mgr. Highland Park Congregate Living for Frail Elderly and Adult Handicapped, Miami, 1976—. Moderator First Friday Club of Our Lady of The Rosary Ch., N.Y.C., 1950-52; instr. English for Brasilians U. South Fla., summer, 1968. Ind. candidate for U.S. Senate from Fla., 1974. Mem. Gerontol. Soc., Smithsonian Inst., Nat. Rehab. Assn., Nat. Conf. Cath. Charities. Composer: The Thief Who Stole Paradise, 1956; Manhattan Swing and Spin, 1957. Inventor ultra high frequency def., solar energy by induction, three-dimensional TV, cinema and X-rays. Home: 455 SW 16th Ave Apt B8 Miami FL 33135 also Box 014018 Miami FL 33101

MATTHEWS, JAY ARLON, JR., publisher, editor; b. St. Louis, Apr. 13, 1918; s. Jay Arlon and Mary (Long) M.; student San Jose State Coll., 1939-41, U. Tex., 1946-47; m. May Clark McLemore, Jan. 16, 1944; children—Jay Arlon III, Emily Cochrane, Sally McLemore. Asst. dir. personnel Adj. Gen.'s Dept. Tex., 1947-53, dept. adj., 1957-65, mil. support plans officer, 1965-69, chief emergency operations, 1965-71; pub. Presidial Press, Mil. History Press; owner Presidial Art Gallery. Past dir. Civil Def., Austin; mem. adv. bd. Confed. Research Center, Hill Jr. Coll.; mil. historian 65th Legislature, Tex., 1977-78. Served with AGC, Tex. N.G., 1946—, brig. gen. ret., 1973. Fellow Co. Mil. Historians; mem. Austin (state v.p. 1951-52), U.S. (chmn. nat. security com. 1952-53) jr. chambers commerce, Tex. Safety Assn. (dir. traffic safety), N.G. Assn. U.S. (chmn. publicity 81st Gen. Conf.), Instituto Internationale de Historia Militar (hon. life), Assn. U.S. Army, Mil. Order World Wars (comdr. Austin chpt. 1980). Episcopalian. Club: Exchange. Editor: Mil. History of Tex. and S.W. Quar. Home: 1807 Stamford Ln Austin TX 78703 Office: 1011 W 31st St Austin TX 78705 also PO Box 5248 Austin TX 78763

MATTHEWS, JAY KAY, petroleum scout; b. Geneva, Tex., Apr. 8, 1933; s. William Quincy and Annie (Howard) M.; student pub. schs., Beaumont, Tex.; m. Mary Patricia Hill, Jan. 15, 1955; children—Steven Mark, Micheal Vernon, Jay Kyle, Jeffery Quin, Lou Anne, Matt Eric, Stanton Hill. Surveyor, Gulf States Utilities Co., Beaumont, 1955-56; sr. draftsman Sun Oil Co., Beaumont and Houston, 1956-69, King Resources Co., Houston, 1969-71; land draftsman Occidental Petroleum Co., Houston, 1971-73; scout Mesa Petroleum Co., Houston, 1973-79, Pogo Producing Co., Houston, 1979—; instr. geol. mapping Houston Community Coll. 1977—. Served with USN, 1951-55; Korea. Mem. Am. Inst. for Design and Drafting (chmn. edn. com.), Internat. Oil Scouts Assn. (dir.), Offshore Oil Scouts Assn. (pres.). Office: 707 McKinney St 17th Floor Houston TX 77002

MATTHEWS, LESLIE AVON, san. engr.; b. Johnson County, N.C., Nov. 4, 1929; s. Joseph Frank and Naomi Lucindy (Nordan) M.; B.S. in Pub. Health, U. N.C., 1957, M.S., 1958; m. Dorothy Jean Coats, Dec. 9, 1951; 1 son, Joseph Michael. Chemist dept. water resources City of Durham, N.C., 1958-60, indsl. waste control engr., 1960-73, supr. process control and devel., water resources div., dept. transp. and utilities, 1973—; cons. in field. Sunday sch. tchr., deacon Sherron Acres Free Will Baptist Ch., Durham, 1962—. Served with USN, 1951-56; Korea. Recipient William D. Hatfield award N.C. Water Pollution Control Assn., 1974. Mem. Am. Water Works Assn. (com. chmn.), Water Pollution Control Assn. (chmn. state coms.), N.Piedmont Water Works Operators Assn. (chmn. 1960-61). Democrat. Contbr. to profl. publs. Home: 2620 Cooksbury Dr Durham NC 27704 Office: 1900 E Club Blvd Durham NC 27704

MATTHEWS, M. D., utility exec.; B.A., U. Ark. Asst. controller Tex. Gas Transmission Corp., 1948-56; v.p., sec., treas. Fish Service Corp., 1956-58; with Internat. Pipeline Constrn. S.A., Panama, 1958-62; pres. Fish Internat. Argentina, 1962; v.p. Valley Gas Prodn. Inc., 1963; asst. to pres. Houston Natural Gas Corp., 1964-65, v.p., 1965-69, asst. treas., 1965-67, treas., 1967-69, sr. v.p., 1969-73, vice chmn. bd. fin. and adminstrn., 1973-74, chmn. exec. com., vice chmn. bd., 1974—, also dir. Office: Houston Natural Gas Bldg 1200 Travis St Box 1188 Houston TX 77001

MATTHEWS, PEGGY JEAN, ry. maintenance equipment mfg. co. exec.; b. Ashville, N.C., June 22, 1945; d. Samuel Clarence and Louise (Jordan) Riley; student Old Dominion U., 1965-67, Tidewater Community Coll., 1976-77; m. Howell Lee Matthews, Nov. 16, 1963; children—Howell Lee, Samuel Mark. Exec. sec. to controller Landmark Communications, Norfolk, Va., 1967-68, sec. to credit mgr., 1971-73; mgr. personnel, adminstrv. services and security Plasser Am. Corp., Chesapeake, Va., 1973—. Mem. Chesapeake Adv. Com. on Employment Practices. Methodist. Mem. Chesapeake C. of C. (women's div.). Club: Great Bridge Swim and Racquet. Home: 528 S Centerville Turnpike Chesapeake VA 23320 Office: 2001 Myers Rd Chesapeake VA 23324

MATTHEWS, PHILLIP WAYNE, telephone co. ofcl.; b. Durham, N.C., May 9, 1941; s. Matthew Mattic and Dorothy May Matthews; student public schs., Durham; m. Jerrilynn Marie Neu, Nov. 22, 1963; children—Gregory Phillip, Karen Marie. With Gen. Telephone Co. of S.E., Monroe, Ga., 1961—, communications cons., 1968, sales tng. adminstr., 1968-70, dist. services mgr., 1970-80, gen. services mgr., Durham, 1980—. Chmn., Heart Fund, 1965; pres. Walton County Hosp. Aux., 1971-72. Served with USMC, 1960-61. Mem. Walton County C. of C. (dir. 1976-78, exec. bd. dirs. 1978). Democrat. Baptist. Clubs: Monroe Rotary, Monroe Golf and Country. Home: 108 Cardiff Pl Durham NC 27712 Office: 1412 Roxboro Rd Durham NC 27712

MATTHEWS, RITA SUE, assn. exec.; b. Durant, Okla., Dec. 18, 1925; d. Edward Sam and Lois (Sharpless) Matthews; A.A., No. Okla. Jr. Coll., 1946; B.A. in Journalism, U. Okla., 1949. News editor Sentinel (Okla.) Leader, 1949-50, Tonkawa (Okla.) News, 1950-51; women's editor radio sta. KWHW, Altus, Okla., 1951-54; health information sec. Tulsa County Pub. Health and Heart Assn., 1954-56; field rep. Okla. affiliate Am. Heart Assn., 1956-64, exec. dir., 1965—. Mem. Gov.'s Com. on Rehab., 1966-67, Gov's Council on Regional Med. Program, 1966-73; mem. nat. com. on rehab. Am. Heart Assn., 1968-70. Bd. dirs. Oklahoma City Vis. Nurse Assn., 1973-76; chmn. Okla. com. Nat. Health Agys., 1975-76, vice chmn., 1976-77, chmn., 1977-78. Mem. Okla. Pub. Health Assn. (v.p. 1969-70), Okla. Health and Welfare Assn., Okla. Assn. Vol. Health Agys. (pres. 1970-72), Nat. Soc. Heart Assn. Profl. Staff Theta Sigma Phi. Republican. Presbyn. Home: 1845 Westminster Pl Oklahoma City OK 73120 Office: 800 NE 15th St Oklahoma City OK 73104

MATTHEWS, TERENCE JAMES, surgeon; b. Rochester, N.Y., Aug. 8, 1945; s. Milton C. and Helen B.; B.S., U. Vt., 1967; M.D., N.Y. Med. Coll., 1971; m. Mar. 21, 1980. Intern, Greenwich (Conn.) Hosp., 1971-72; emergency medicine physician Lynn (Mass.) Hosp., 1972-73; resident in orthopedics U. Pitts., 1973-76; practice medicine specializing in orthopedic surgery, Fort Lauderdale, Fla., 1976—; mem. staff Holy Cross, North Ridge Gen. hosps., North Beach and Imperial Point med. centers. Served with USAR, 1971-77. Diplomate Am. Bd. Orthpedic Surgery. Fellow Am. Acad. Orthopedic Surgery, A.C.S.; mem. Fla. Orthopedic Soc., Broward County Orthopedic Surgery Soc., AMA (Physicians Recognition award), Fort Lauderdale Surg. Soc. Office: 4802 N Federal Hwy Fort Lauderdale FL 33308

MATTHEWS, WILLIAM MCGILL, V, dept. store exec.; b. Gastonia, N.C., July 17, 1940; s. Henry Belk and Evelyn (McArver) M.; B.S., Presbyn. Coll., 1962; m. Frances Augusta Flournoy, Sept. 10, 1966; children—William McGill, Evelyn Flournoy, Carson Henry Belk. With Belk Matthews Co., dept. stores, Macon, Ga., 1964—, sec.-treas., 1966—, v.p., 1972—, also dir.; v.p., sec.-treas., dir. stores in Warner Robins, Milledgeville, Dublin, Cordele and Vidalia, Ga.; dir. First Nat. Bank & Trust Co., Macon. Chmn., Macon Downtown Council, 1971, Macon Mall Mchts. Assn., 1979. Bd. visitors Presbyn. Coll., chmn., 1978—, bd. dirs. Bibb County chpt. Am. Cancer Soc., Macon Mus. Arts and Scis., Macon Goodwill Industries. Served with AUS, 1962-64. Mem. Greater Macon C. of C. (dir. 1972—, treas. 1979—), Presbyn. Col. Nat. Alumni Assn. (pres. 1974), Kappa Alpha. Presbyn. (deacon 1971—, trustee day sch.). Rotarian. Club: Idle Hour Country (Macon). Home: 3185 Vista Circle Macon GA 31204 Office: 3661 Eisenhower Pkwy Macon GA 31206

MATTINGLY, JOSEPH GUY, JR., ednl. adminstr.; b. Rineyville, Ky., Mar. 24, 1930; s. Joseph Guy and Mary Virginia (Pate) M.; B.S., U. Md., 1958, M.B.A., 1966, D.B.A., 1979; m. Olivia Scott Callahan, Apr. 11, 1950; children—Barbara J., R. Keith, Joseph Guy III, Deborah A., N. Kevin. Joined U.S. Army, 1948, commd. lt., 1949, advanced through grades to lt. col., 1966; br. chief USMACV, Saigon, Vietnam, 1966-67; project officer Materiel Command, Washington, 1967-69, U.S. Army Joint Logistics Rev. Bd., Washington, 1969-70; ret., 1970; lectr. transp. and bus. policy U. Md., 1970-73; asst. to dean Coll. Bus. and Mgmt. U. Md., 1973-75, dir. undergrad/studies Coll. Bus. and Mgmt., 1975—. Cubmaster, scoutmaster, com. chmn., instl. rep., merit badge counselor, dist. manpower com. chmn. Boy Scouts Am. Decorated Legion Merit. Mem. Nat. Def. Transp. Assn. (chmn. nat. edn. com.), Nat. Council Phys. Distbn. Mgmt., Ret. Officer Assn., Beta Gamma Sigma Delta Nu Alpha, Delta Sigma Pi. Democrat. Roman Catholic. Club: K.C. Co-editor, Def. Transp. Jour., 1979—. Home: 4804 Bradford Dr Annandale VA 22003 Office: College Business and Management U Md College Park MD 20742

MATTOX, DONALD OTIS, drug co. exec.; b. Welborn, Kans., Jan. 9, 1933; s. Alva Otis and Mary Pearl (Everett) M.; ed. public schs.; m. Beverly Jean Siebert, July 24, 1964 (div. 1978) children—William Edward, Julie Ann, Jennifer Lee; m. 2d, Rebecca Fasha Kingery, Sept. 9, 1978. Dept. mgr. Katz Drug Co., Kansas City, Kans., 1950-57; asst. mgr. Bruce Smith Drugs, Prairie Village, Kans., 1957-63; store mgr. Parkview Drugs, Overland Park, Kans., 1963-65; dist. mgr. Jack Eckerd Drug Co., Deerfield Beach, Fla., 1965—. Mem. South Dade C. of C., Hollywood C. of C., Greater Miami C. of C (trustee), West Palm Beach C. of C. Republican. Baptist. Clubs: Boca Del Mar, Lago Mar, Jacaranda, Center Court. Home: 6820 Tiburon Dr Boca Raton FL 33433 Office: 1471 W Hillsboro Blvd Deerfield Beach FL 33441

MATTOX, JAMES ALBON, congressman; b. Dallas, Aug. 29, 1943; s. Norman and Mary (Harrison) M.; grad. magna cum laude Baylor U., 1965; J.D., So. Meth. U., 1968. Admitted to Tex. bar, 1968; partner firm Crowder & Mattox, Dallas, 1970—; asst. dist. atty., Dallas, 1968-70; mem. Tex. Ho. of Reps., 1972-76; mem. 95th-96th Congresses from 5th Tex. Dist., 1976—. Lay preacher East Grand Bapt. Ch., Dallas, 1970—; mem. Christian Life Commn. Democrat. Home: 5217 Columbia Ave Dallas TX 75214 Office: 1127 Longworth House Office Bldg Washington DC 20515

MATTOX, JOHNNY LYNN, educator; b. Corinth, Miss., Apr. 13, 1951; s. Oliver Lee, Jr. and Margaret Joyce (Mills) M.; A.A., NE Miss. Jr. Coll., 1971 B.A. in Edn. with spl. distinction, U. Miss., 1973, M.C.S., 1974, Ph.D., 1979; m. Glenda Jean Eaton, Aug. 11, 1973; 1 son, Jason Lynn. Sci. tchr. Kossuth (Miss.) High Sch., 1973-75; biology instr. Itawamba Jr. Coll., Fulton, Miss., 1975—. Organist, ch. tng. dir., Sunday sch. tchr. Union Bapt. Ch., Corinth, Miss. Named star tchr. Kossuth High Sch., 1975-76. Mem. Nat. Sci. Tchrs. Assn., Miss. Sci. Tchrs. Assn., Miss. Acad. Scis. (vice chmn. div. sci. edn. 1980), Soc. Coll. Sci. Tchrs., Nat. Assn. Biology Tchrs., U.S. Jaycees, Kappa Delta Pi, Phi Delta Kappa (award 1973), Phi Kappa Phi, Phi Theta Kappa (hon.). Home: Route 5 Box 208 Corinth MS 38834 Office: Itawamba Junior College Fulton MS 38843

MATTSON, JIMMIE WAYNE, educator, clergyman, broadcast engr.; b. Osceola, Ark., Mar. 30, 1938; s. Bill and Gladys Viola (Riley) M.; Asso. in Broadcast Engring., Keegan Tech. Inst., 1960; B.A. in Psychology, Memphis State U., 1975, M.S. in Gen. Counseling, 1977; m. Earnestgean McNabb, June 22, 1956; children—Kathy, Connie. Broadcast engr. WABG-TV, Greenwood, Miss., 1960-61; engring. supr. WKNO-TV, Memphis, 1961-65, WHBQ-TV, Memphis, 1965-75; ordained to ministry, Ch. of God, 1969; minister Ch. of God, West Memphis, Ark., 1969—; head Instructional TV studio Memphis State U., 1975—, dir. Counseling Center, 1978—, adj. prof. dept. theatre and communication arts, 1976—; cons. in field; sports ofcl. in softball and basketball, 1970—. Cert. sex therapist. Mem. Nat. Baseball Congress, Amateur Softball Assn., Am. Personnel and Guidance Assn., Am. Assn. Sex Educators, Counselors and Therapists. Exec. producer: Acceleration, 1978; A New Strategy for Rehabilitation, 1979; One Therapy Approach to Spastic Dysphonia, 1979; Metric System, 1979; producer/dir. Exercises in Sensate Focus, 1978; Parrish Smith Debate, 1977; The 21st Century Teacher, 1977. Home: 605 N Hollywood Memphis TN 38112 Office: Old Brister St Suite 216 Memphis State U Memphis TN 38152

MATULA, RICHARD ALLEN, univ. ofcl., mech. engr.; b. Chgo., Aug. 22, 1939; s. Ludvig A. and Leone O. (Dufeck) M.; B.S., Purdue U., 1961, M.S., 1962, Ph.D., 1964; m. Brenda C. Mather, Sept. 5, 1959; children—Scott, Kristopher, Daniel, Tiffiny. Instr., Purdue U., W. Lafayette, Ind., 1963-64; asst. prof. mech. engring. U. Calif., Santa Barbara, 1964-66, U. Mich., Ann Arbor, 1966-68; asso. prof. mech. engring. Drexel U., Phila., 1968-76, chmn. Environ. Studies Inst., 1972-73, chmn. dept. mech. engring. and mechanics, 1973-76; prof. mech. engring. La. State U., Baton Rouge, 1976—, dean Coll. Engring., 1976—. Vice pres. Wexford Leas Civic Assn., 1969-71. Mem. ASME, Combustion Inst., Am. Soc. Engring. Edn., Soc. Automotive Engrs., Air Pollution Control Assn., AAAS, Sigma Xi, Tau Beta Pi, Pi Tau Sigma, Pi Kappa Phi, Sigma Pi Sigma. Roman Catholic. Contbr. numerous articles to engring. jours. Home: 5536 Valley Forge Ave Baton Rouge LA 70808 Office: Coll Engring 3304-U CEBA La State U Baton Rouge LA 70803

MATURIN, JOSEPH NEWBY, dredging co. ofcl.; b. Abbeville, La., Feb. 3, 1932; s. Sidney and Eva (Romero) M.; m. Theresa Poirier, Aug. 23, 1953; 1 son, Roland Joseph. With Bauer Dredging Co., 1953—, leverman, deck-capt., Coatzacoalcos, Vera Cruz, Mexico, 1967-69, 71—. Founder, Center for Internat. Security Studies, Am. Security Council Edn. Found. Mem. World Dredging Assn., Am. Security Council, La. Intracoastal Seaway Assn., Nat. Trust for Hist. Preservation in U.S., U.S. Capitol Hist. Soc., Smithsonian Assos., Nat. Police Res. Officers Assn., Soc. Confederacy (charter). Democrat. Roman Catholic. Club: K.C. Home: 2710 Pinhook Rd Lafayette LA 70501

MAUCK, HENRY PAGE, JR., educator; b. Richmond, Va., Feb. 3, 1926; s. Henry Page and Harriet Hutcheson (Morrison) M.; B.A., U. Va., 1950, M.D., 1952; m. Janet Garrett Horsley, May 14, 1955; children—Henry Page III, John Waller. Intern, Henry Ford Hosp., Detroit, 1952-53; resident Med. Coll. Va., Richmond, 1953-56, asst. prof. medicine and pediatrics, 1961-66, asso. prof., 1966-72, prof., 1972—. Cons. cardiology Langley Field Air Force Hosp., Hampton, Va., 1970—, McGuire's VA Hosp., Richmond, 1962—; editorial cons. Am. Heart Jour., 1971—. Served with AUS, 1944-46. Diplomate Am. Bd. Internal Medicine. Fellow in cardiology Am. Heart Assn., 1956-57; fellow Am. Coll. Physicians, Am. Coll. Cardiology; mem. Am. Physiol. Soc., So. Soc. Clin. Investigation, Am. Fedn. Clin. Research, So. Soc. Clin. Research. Presbyn. Contbr. chpt. to Pathophysiology, Autonomic Cotrol of Cardiovascular System, 1972. Home: 113 Oxford Circle W Richmond VA 23221 Office: Box 242 Medical Coll of Virginia Richmond VA 23298

MAUDERLI, WALTER, educator; b. Aarau, Switzerland, Mar. 8, 1924; s. Jakob and Bertha (Hofer) M.; M.S. in Physics, Fed. Inst. Tech., Zurich, Switzerland, 1949, D.Sc., 1956; m. Lottie Leuw, Apr. 15, 1950; children—Claudine, Patricia, Priska, Pamela, Walter. Came to U.S., 1956, naturalized, 1962. Research asst. isotope, betatron labs. U. Zurich, 1950-56; asst. prof. isotope lab. U. Ark., Little Rock, 1956-60, also radiation safety officer Med. Center, 1956-60, asst. prof. math., physics Ark. Inst. Tech., 1958-60; asso. prof. dept. radiology U. Fla., Gainesville, 1960-64, prof., 1965—. Served to 1st lt. Swiss Army, 1944-56. Mem. Am. Assn. Physicists in Medicine, Soc. Nuclear Medicine, Societe Helvetique des Naturelles, Soc. Fed. Inst. Tech., Swiss. Soc. Physics, AMA, Sigma Xi. Home: PO Box 13916 Gainesville FL 32604

MAUER, LORETTA JUNE, educator; b. Taylor, Ark., Nov. 12, 1937; d. Rollin Samuel and Helen (McDonald) Lamb; B.S. in Edn., Tex. A&I U., Kingsville, 1970, certificate in Learning, Lang. Difficulties, 1975, M.S. in Special Edn., 1976; m. Tommy Lee Mauer; children—Tommy Lee, Lynn Anne. Tchr. mathematics and sci. Dod Sch., Naha, Okinawa, Japan, 1971-73; resource tchr. mathematics Sinton (Tex.) Ind. Sch. Dist., 1972-74; tchr. special edn. Brush Country Co-op. Sch., Mathis, Tex., from 1974; now tchr. 5th grade Odem-Edroy Ind. Sch. Dist., Odem, Tex. Mem. Council Exceptional Children, Tex. State Tchrs. Assn., NEA, Sinton Edn. Assn., Odem Parent Tchr. Orgn., Corpus Christi Doll Guild, Internat. Piano Guild. Specialist in lang. and learning difficulties. Home: 1001 N Bowie St Sinton TX 78387 Office: Sinton Ind Sch Dist Sinton TX 78387

MAUGER, PAUL ALLAN, clin. psychologist; b. New Haven, Jan. 6, 1946; s. Fred Allen and Grace Lorraine (Buchtenkirch) M.; B.A., Gordon Coll., 1967; Ph.D., U. Minn., 1972; m. Barbara Jean Lovett, Dec. 21, 1968. Asst. prof. psychology Bethel Coll., Arden Hills, Minn., 1968-73, U. South Fla., Tampa, 1973-76, Ga. State U., Atlanta, 1976—; acting chief psychologist Hillsborough County Hosp., Tampa, 1973-76; cons. in field. Mem. citizens adv. bd. Ga. Mental Health Inst., 1977—; ruling elder Presbyn. Ch. U.S., 1975—. Licensed psychologist Fla., Ga. Mem. Bay Region Soc. Clin. Psychologists (pres. 1976), Am., Southeastern, Ga. psychol. assns., Soc. Personality Assessment. Home: 4236 Kings Troop Rd Stone Mountain GA 30083 Office: Dept Psychology Ga State U Atlanta GA 30303

MAUK, BRYANT DOUGLAS, physician, air force officer; b. Troy, Ala., Apr. 4, 1935; s. Harold Douglas and Laura Madeline (Williams) M.; M.D., Emory U., 1960; m. Helen Marie Peters, Mar. 3, 1976; children—Laurie, Leslie, Doug, Bobby. Intern, Emory U.-VA Hosp., Atlanta, 1960-61, resident gen. surgery, 1961-65; commd. 1st lt., 1960, advanced through grades to col., 1975; chief surgery 4780th USAF Hosp., Perrin AFB, Tex., 1965-67, surgeon to chief surgery USAF Hosp., Torrejon (Spain) AFB, 1967-70, chmn. dept. surgery, chmn. aerospace medicine, chief profl. services, dep. comdr. USAF Regional Hosp., also dep. surgeon Air U., Maxwell AFB, Montgomery, Ala., 1970-73, asst. Med. Corps career plans Office Surgeon Gen. USAF, Washington, 1973-78; chief health edn. div. Air Force Manpower and Personnel Center, Randolph AFB, Tex., 1978—. Decorated Meritorious Service Medal. Diplomate Am. Bd. Surgery. Fellow A.C.S.; mem. AMA, Aerospace Med. Assn., Assn. Mil. Surgeons U.S. (Joel T. Boone award 1976), Soc. Air Force Clin. Surgeons, Soc. USAF Flight Surgeons, J.C. Thoroughman Surg. Soc. Methodist. Club: Toastmasters. Home: 606 Moorside Dr San Antonio TX 78239 Office: AFMPC/SGE Randolph AFB TX 78239

MAUNEY, WILLIAM KEMP, JR., state senator; b. Kings Mountain, N.C., Aug. 15, 1917; s. William Kemp and Sarah Jane (Hoffman) M.; A.B., Lenoir Rhyne Coll., Hickory, N.C., 1938; m. Mary Elizabeth Simpson, June 2, 1939; children—Sarah Frances, Mary Leigh, William Kemp, Martha Jane. Pres., dir. Maurey Mills, Inc., Kings Mountain, 1943—, Mauney Hosiery Mills, 1943—; mem. N.C. Ho. of Reps., 1967-73, N.C. Senate, 1973—. Mem. NAM, Nat. Assn. Hosiery Mfrs. Democrat. Lutheran. Clubs: Lions (past pres.), Woodmen of World, Jaycees (pres. Kings Mountain 1952). Home: 200 E Gold St Kings Mountain NC 28086 Office: PO Box 1042 Kings Mountain NC 28086

MAURER, FRED DRY, veterinarian; b. Moscow, Idaho, May 4, 1909; s. Oran J. and Lavina E. (Stone) M.; B.S., U. Idaho, 1934; D.V.M., Wash. State U., 1937; Ph.D., Cornell U., 1948; m. Irene Haworth, Aug. 25, 1935; children—Allen Dry, Linda Janet. Asst. prof. bacteriology U. Idaho, 1937-38; instr. Cornell U., 1938-41; commd. lt. U.S. Army, 1941, advanced through grades to col., Vet. Corps., 1959; research on equine diseases Remount Depot, Front Royal, Va., 1941-43; virus researcher War Disease Control Sta., Grosse Isle, Que., Can., Africa, 1943-46; with Walter Reed Army Inst. Research, Washington, 1946-47, 48-51; research on fgn. animal diseases, Africa, 1951-54; research on virology and pathology Armed Forces Inst. Pathology, Washington, 1954-61; dir. pathology div. Army Med. Research Lab., Ft. Knox, Ky., 1961-64; ret., 1964; asso. dean, dir. Inst. Tropical Vet. Medicine, Coll. Vet. Medicine, Tex. A&M U., 1964-76, emeritus prof., 1976—; cons. numerous govt. agys. and sci. instns.; chmn. bd. Insul-Aid; dir. Bank of A&M. Decorated Army Commendation medal, Legion of Merit; recipient 12th Internat. Vet. Congress award, 1968. Mem. Am. Vet. Medicine Assn., Am. Coll. Vet. Pathologists (diplomate), U.S. Animal Health Assn., Am. Assn. Equine Practicioners. Contbr. numerous articles to profl. publs. Office: Insul-Aid 508 Avondale Bryan TX 77801

MAURER, HAROLD MAURICE, pediatrician; b. N.Y.C., Sept. 10, 1936; s. Isador and Sarah (Rothkowitz) M.; A.B., N.Y.U., 1957; M.D., State U. N.Y., Bklyn., 1961; m. Beverly Bennett, June 12, 1960; children—Ann Louise, Wendy Sue. Intern pediatrics Kings County Hosp., N.Y.C., 1961-62; resident in pediatrics Babies Hosp., Columbia-Presbyn. Med. Center, N.Y.C., 1962-64; fellow in pediatric hematology/oncology Columbia-Presbyn. Med. Center, 1966-68; asst. prof. pediatrics Med. Coll. Va., Richmond, 1968-71, asso. prof., 1971-75, prof., 1975—, chmn. dept. pediatrics, 1976—. Chmn. Intergroup Rhabdomyosarcoma Study; mem. Southwest Oncology Group; mem. Va. Gov.'s Overall Adv. Com. on Care of Handicapped. Served to lt. comdr. USPHS, 1964-66. Diplomate Am. Bd. Pediatrics; NIH grantee, 1974—. Mem. Am. Acad. Pediatrics, Am. Soc. Hematology, Soc. for Pediatric Research, Am. Pediatric Soc., Assn. Med. Sch. Pediatric Dept. Chairmen, Va. Hematology Soc., Am. Cancer Soc., Sigma Xi, Alpha Omega Alpha. Republican. Jewish. Contbr. articles to profl. jours. Home: 405 Berwickshire Dr Richmond VA 23229 Office: Med Coll Va Richmond VA 23298

MAURER, MICHELE LYNNE, ins. co. cons.; b. Canton, Ohio, June 10, 1948; d. Ralph Curtis and Evelyn Margaret (Toohey) M.; student Fla. Presbyn. Coll., 1966-67, John Robert Powers Finishing Sch., 1968; A.B. in Fgn. Lang. Edn., and French, U. Ga., 1970, M. in Mktg. and Bus. Edn., 1972. Hostess on board services Auto Train Corp., Washington, 1972; ins. solicitor Walter C. Wattles, Atlanta, 1973; corp. trainee profl. mgmt. program Aetna Ins. Co., Atlanta, 1974, comml. multi-peril underwriter, 1975-78; comml. multi-peril underwriting supr. Home Office, Aetna Ins. Co., Hartford, Conn., 1979; product cons. Ins. Systems Am., Inc., Atlanta, 1979—. Lic. ins. agt., Ga. Mem. Am. Mktg. Assn., Mariner's Club-A Marine Underwriting Assn., Hist. Soc. Roswell, Nat. Underwriter (certified in property and casualty ins.), Ins. Inst. Am. (cert. gen. ins.), Pi Delta Phi (charter). Republican. Presbyterian. Club: Brookfield West Golf and Country (Roswell). Home: 12005 King Rd Roswell GA 30075 Office: 6855 Jimmy Carter Blvd Norcross GA 30362

MAUTERER, JUDY, speech pathologist; b. New Orleans, Dec. 26, 1951; d. John Victor and Audrey Evelyn (Hartdegen) M.; student La. State U., New Orleans, 1969-70, B.A., Baton Rouge, 1973, M.A., 1976. Cons. speech and hearing La. Div. Health, Communicative Disorders unit, New Orleans, 1976-77; lang. specialist Jefferson Parish Sch. Bd. Title I lang. program, Gretna, La., 1977-79. cons. speech and hearing Spl. Edn. Competent Authority team, 1979—. Fellowship com. Faith Cumberland Presbyn. Ch., Metairie, La., 1978-79, co-dir. vacation bible sch., 1978—. Mem. Am. Speech and Hearing Assn., La. Speech and Hearing Assn. Office: Spl Edn Competent Authority Team 1450 Jefferson St Gretna LA 70053

MAUZY, ANNE ROGERS, investment co. exec.; b. Birmingham, Ala., June 1, 1929; d. H. Olon and Verna Eleanor (Evans) Rogers; B.A., U. Tex., Austin, 1948; M.Ed., U. Houston, 1954: m. Oscar Holcombe Mauzy, Feb. 14, 1976; children—Melanie Rister, Jennifer Rister Tyson, Randy Rister. Tchr. schs. in Tex., 1948-54; tchr. pre-sch. deaf Houston Speech and Hearing Center, 1954-65; adminstr. children's programs Speech and Hearing Inst., U. Tex., Houston, 1965-75; pres. Mauzy Investments Co., Dallas, 1978—. Mem. Am. Speech and Hearing Assn. (cert. audiologist), Tex. Speech and Hearing Assn., NOW, Audiological Rehab. Assn. Democrat. Unitarian. Home and office: 904 Evergreen Hill Dallas TX 75208

MAUZY, OSCAR HOLCOMBE, lawyer, state legislator; b. Houston, Nov. 9, 1926; s. Harry Lincoln and Mildred (Kincaid) M.; B.B.A., U. Tex., 1950, LL.B., 1952; m. Anne Rogers; children—Catherine Anne, Charles Fred, James Stephen. Admitted to Tex. bar, 1951; partner firm Mullinax, Wells, Mauzy & Baab, Inc., Dallas, 1952-79; pres. Oscar H. Mauzy, P.C., Dallas, 1979—; mem. Tex. Senate from 23d Dist., 1967—; pres. pro tem 63d Legislature, 1973—; acting gov. Tex., 1973—. Mem. nat. com. for Tex., Young Democrats, 1954-56; precinct chmn. Dem. party, Dallas, 1962-66; vice-chmn. Dem. Exec. Com. Dallas County, 1964-66. Served with USNR, 1944-46; PTO. Mem. Am., Dallas bar assns., State Bar Tex., Am. Trial Lawyers Assn., Am. Bd. Trial Advocates, VFW, Delta Theta Phi. Home: 904 Evergreen Hill Rd Dallas TX 75208 Office: 1025 Elm St Suite 900 Dallas TX 75202

MAVKO, JACOB JOHN, contractor; b. Painesville, Ohio, Dec. 5, 1950; s. Jacob Frank and Dorothy Barbara (Lauric) M.; B.A., Ohio State U., 1972. Pres., Jones and Mavko Inc., Richmond, Va., 1972-75, J.J. Mavko & Co., Richmond, 1972-75, Mavko Group Ltd., Washington, 1975—, Co-op Property Services, Columbus, Ohio, 1975—. Office: 4785-C Kilcary St Columbus OH 43220

MAVRIS, NICHOLAS BENNIE, pipe line co. exec.; b. Oklahoma City, Nov. 23, 1923; s. George and Ada Virginia (Diles) M.; B.S. in Mech. Engring., Okla. State U., 1948, M.S., 1949; m. Elizabeth Ann Shaver, July 3, 1943; children—Virginia Ann Mavris Humes, George Samuel, Kathryne Ann Mavris Newton, Nicola Ann. Instr., Okla. State U., 1948-49; engr. Interstate Oil Pipeline Co., 1949-51; asst. regional mgr. Rocky Mountain region Continental Oil Co., 1963-67, mgr. transp., 1967-68; with Continental Pipe Line Co., 1951-63, 68—, pres., chief exec. officer, Houston, 1969—, also dir.; v.p., dir. Seaway, Inc.; chmn. bd., dir. Seadock, Inc., 1972—; dir., pres. Yellowstone Pipe Line Co., 1969-76; dir. Platte Pipe Line Co., West Shore Pipe Line Co.; chmn. bd. Explorer Pipeline Co., 1979—, also dir. Bd. dirs. Okla. State U. Devel. Found., 1976-77, trustee, 1975-78. Served with AUS, 1943-46. Named to Engring. Hall of Fame, Okla. State U., 1979. Mem. Rocky Mountain Oil and Gas Assn. (dir.), Am. Petroleum Inst. (div. transp. central com. 1968—), Assn. Oil Pipe Lines (exec. com.), Okla. State U. Alumni Assn. (dir. Houston br. 1973-77). Clubs: Sugar Creek Country, Houston Petroleum. Home: 703 Montclair Blvd Sugarland TX 77478 Office: PO Box 2197 Houston TX 77001

MAWHINNEY, JOHN ALEXANDER, III, health services adminstr.; b. Richmond, Va., Apr. 10, 1943; s. John Alexander and Ellen Elizabeth (King) M.; B.A., Wheaton Coll., 1964; cert. in nursing home adminstrn. Mich. State U., 1969. Adminstr., v.p. Maccabee Gardens Extended Care Center, Saginaw, Mich., 1968-70; cons. N.Y. State Bd. Social Welfare, Syracuse, 1970-72; adminstrv. officer Cayuga County Community Mental Health Center, Auburn, N.Y., 1972-77; exec. dir. Southside Community Mental Health and Mental Retardation Services, South Boston, Va., 1977—; mental health cons. NIMH; chmn. Region IV Mental Health/Mental Retardation Service Provider Consortium. Fellow Am. Coll. Nursing Home Adminstrs.; mem. Am. Mgmt. Assn., Am. Soc. Public Adminstrn., Assn. Mental Health Adminstrs., Nat. Council Community Mental Health Centers, Am. Acad. Med. Adminstrs., Va. Assn. Community Services Bd. (state sec.), Central Va. Health Systems Agy., Va. Human Services Inst. Quaker. Office: Southside Community Mental Health and Mental Retardation Services 2200 Halifax Rd PO Box 586 South Boston VA 24592

MAXFIELD, WILLIAM STREETER, physician; b. Waco, Tex., May 9, 1930; s. James Robert and Marie (Streeter) M.; B.A., So. Meth. U., 1950; M.D., Baylor U., 1954; m. Patricia Jean Carter, Nov. 2, 1957; children—Alice Melissa, Maura Carter, Melinda Marie. Intern So. Pacific Gen. Hosp., San Francisco, 1954-55; preceptor in radiology and nuclear medicine Maxfield Clinic-Hosp., Dallas, Tex., 1955-56; asst. resident in radiology Johns Hopkins U. Hosp., Balt., 1959-60, NIH clin. fellow in cancer, 1960-61; practice medicine specializing in radiation therapy, Balt., 1961-64, New Orleans, 1964-72, Tampa, Fla., 1972—, nuclear medicine, Chelsea, Mass., 1956-57, Bethesda, Md., 1957-59, New Orleans, 1964-72, Bradenton, Fla., 1974-75; instr. in radiology Johns Hopkins U. Sch. of Medicine, Balt., 1961, asst. prof. radiology, 1961-64, chief of radiation therapy sect. dept. radiology, 1961-64; chief of radiation therapy dept., co-chmn. nuclear medicine Ochsner Clinic and Ochsner Found. Hosp., New Orleans, 1964-68; prof., chmn. dept. radiology La. State U. Med. Sch., New Orleans, 1968-72; sr. physician Radioisotope Lab., Charity Hosp., New Orleans, 1968-70; chief of Radioisotope Lab., Earl K. Long Meml. Hosp., Baton Rouge, La., 1970-72; med. dir. Gulf South Radiation Therapy Center of Tampa, 1975—; cons. to Tumor Clinic, USPHS Hosp., Balt., 1961-64, Tumor Clinic, Balt. City Hosps., 1961-64, Tumor Clinic Lafayette (La.) Charity Hosp., 1969-72; clin. prof. radiology Tulane U., New Orleans, 1964-68; vis. physician dept. therapeutic radiology Charity Hosp., New Orleans, 1964-68, sr. physician, 1968-72; prof., chmn. dept. radiology La. State U. Sch. Medicine, New Orleans, 1968-72; rep. for La. to Med. Liaison Officer Network of USPHS and AEC, 1968—; chmn. cancer com. La. Regional Med. Program, 1968-72; cons. in design and equipment of radiation therapy to various labs., hosps., 1968—; mem. cons. staff So. Bapt. Hosp., Community Hosp., New Port Richey, Fla., East Jefferson Hosp., New Orleans; mem. staff Centro Asturiano Hosp., Centro ro Espanol Hosp., Tampa, Fla.; mem. of Sci. Exhibit Sect. of U.S. Med. Delegation to 2d. Internat. Atoms for Peace Chnf., Geneva, Switzerland, 1958, U.S. Delegation, Internat. AEC, Scintillation Scanning Symposium, Salzburg, Austria, 1968; mem. Radiopharm. Advisory com. FDA, 1970-74; chmn. Pub. Health sub-com. So. Govs. Task Force on Nuclear Power, 1970-71; cons., med. coordinator for Radiology, Preventive Health Programs, Falls Church, Va., 1977. Trustee Arthritis Found., La. chpt., 1968-71. Served with M.C., USN, 1956-59. Arthritis Found. grantee, 1965-68, E.R. Squibb & Son grantee, 1964-65, Am. Cancer Soc. grantee, 1965-68; diplomate Am. Bd. Radiology, Am. Bd. Nuclear Medicine. Fellow Am. Coll. Nuclear Medicine (pres. 1974-75), Royal Soc. of Health; mem. Soc. of Nuclear Medicine (v.p. 1968-69, pres. 1972-73), Am. Radium Soc., Fla., Hillsborough County med. assns., AMA, Am. Roentgen Ray Soc., Am. Soc. of Clin. Oncology, Am. Soc. of Thermography, Radiol. Soc. of N.Am. (mem. sci. exhibits com. 1972-76), Am. Cancer Soc. (trustee New Orleans area 1969-71), Assn. of Community Cancer Centers, Am. Coll. of Radiology (mem. sub-com. on resident tng. 1971-73), Am. Soc. of Therapeutic Radiologists. Democrat. Episcopalian. Clubs: Sarasota Yacht; Calyx (Dallas). Contbr. numerous articles on nuclear medicine and radiology to profl. jours. Home: 3304 McFarland Rd Tampa FL 33618 Office: 3000 Medical Park Dr Suite 101 Tampa FL 33612 also 1310 2d Ave Largo FL

MAXWELL, CHESTER ARTHUR, radio exec.; b. San Antonio, Mar. 29, 1930; s. Chester A. and Clara A. (Olle) M.; student Trinity U., San Antonio, 1948-51; student bus. adminstrn. U. Dallas; m. Carolyn King, Aug. 7, 1969; children by previous marriage—Sheryl Ann, Karen Kay (Mrs. Charles Cervantes). With advt. dept. Joskes of Tex., dept. store, San Antonio, 1952-56; account exec., sales mgr. KBAT radio, 1956-63; account exec. KILT radio, Houston, 1964-68; asst. gen. mgr. KBOX/KMEZ radio, Dallas, 1969-71, v.p., gen. mgr., 1972—. Instr. Tex. Assn. Broadcasters Student Clinic Howard Payne U., Abilene, Tex., 1962. Pres., Greater Dallas chpt. Muscular Dystrophy Assn., 1971-73. Vice chmn. Dallas Multiple Sclerosis Soc. Served with USMC, 1946-48. Named One of Dallas' Men of Yr., Women's Equity Action League, 1975, 76; recipient Hope Chest award Nat. Multiple Sclerosis Soc., 1979. Mem. Dallas Advt. League, Assn. Broadcast Execs. Tex. (sec. 1971, pres. 1974), North Tex. Real Estate Investors Assn. Club: Los Colinas Country (Dallas).

MAXWELL, EARL LAVERNE, JR., lawyer; b. Atlanta, Dec. 1, 1942; s. Earl LaVerne and Grace (Rushing) M.; B.A., Fla. State U., 1964; J.D., U. Fla., 1967; m. Lynn Lassetter, Dec. 16, 1967; children—Dacia Lynn, Brent Earl. Admitted to Fla. bar, 1967; legis. aide Fla. State Legislature, Tallahassee, 1967; law clk. to atty. John A. Rudd, Tallahassee, 1967, Kline, Tilker & Lynch, Cheyenne, Wyo., 1967-68; atty. O'Connell & Cooper, West Palm Beach, Fla., 1972-73; partner Farish & Farish, West Palm Beach, Fla., 1973-76; atty. Earl L. Maxwell, Jr., West Palm Beach, 1976—. Pres., North County Choral Soc., Palm Beach County, Fla., 1977-78. Served with JAGC, USAF, 1968-72. Mem. Fed. Bar Assn., Am. Bar Assn., Assn. Trial Lawyers Am., Fla. Acad. Trial Lawyers, Fla. Bar Assn., Palm Beach County Bar Assn. Democrat. Club: Kiwanis (pres.). Office: 414 Comeau Bldg 319 Clematis St West Palm Beach FL 33401

MAXWELL, KATHERINE GANT, ednl. psychologist; b. El Paso, Tex., Nov. 27, 1931; d. Leslie and Lillian Martha (Beard) Gant; B.S., Abilene Christian U., 1955; M.S., Miss. State U., 1967, Ph.D., 1974; m. Fowden G. Maxwell, July 14, 1955; children—Steve, Rebecca, Randy. Teaching asst. Miss. State U., 1969-72, supr. student tchrs., 1973, adminstr. psychol. tests, 1974-75; sch. psychologist Martha Manson Acad., Gainesville, Fla., 1976-77, Community Counseling Center, Bronson, Fla., 1977-78, Gilchrist and Dixie County Schs., 1978-79, Bryan (Tex.) Ind. Sch. Dist., 1979—. Bd. dirs. Child Advocacy and Child Abuse Project, Ocala, Fla.; treas. Citizens' Com. for Mental Health, 1980. Certified tchr., Tex., Miss., Ga.; cert. sch. psychologist, Fla., Tex. Mem. Am. Psychol. Assn., Mental Health

Assn. Alachua County, Miss. Psychol. Assn., Tex. Psychol. Assn., Brazos Valley Psychol. Assn. (publicity chmn. 1980), Council Exceptional Children, AAUW, Mid-South Ednl. Research Assn., Phi Delta Kappa. Club: Buchholtz Band Boosters. Contbr. articles to profl. jours. Address: Redmond Terr Sta PO Box 10027 College Station TX 77840

MAXWELL, OLEN DALE, psychiatrist; b. Tulsa, Oct. 3, 1939; s. Arlie Warren and Edna Pearl (Dees) M.; B.A., Tulsa U., 1962; M.D., Vanderbilt U., 1966; m. Sherry Caumissar, Apr. 2, 1971; 1 dau., Kelly Rebecca. Intern, U. Ky. Med. Center, 1966-67; resident psychiatry Vanderbilt U. Hosp., 1967-70; instr. dept. psychiatry Vanderbilt U., 1970-71; dir. student health psychiatry Okla. State U., Stillwater, 1971-76; psychiat. cons. Payne County Guidance Center, 1971—, Logan County Guidance Center, 1972-73, Psychol. Guidance Center, Okla. State U., 1972—, Logan County Guidance Center, 1974—; dir. psychiat. services Stillwater Municipal Hosp., 1973—; guest lectr. Okla. State Guidance Center Assn., 1972; cons. Community Mental Health Clinic, Okla. Dept. Mental Health, 1974—. Bd. dirs. dist. Am. Contract Bridge League. Diplomate Nat. Bd. Med. Examiners, Am. Bd. Psychiatry and Neurology (examiner 1979). Mem. AMA (Physicians Recognition award 1970-72), Okla., Kay-Nobel Counties med. assns., Am. Psychiat. Assn. (Okla. br. peer rev. com. 1974-78, Champus psychiat. peer rev. 1980—), Payne-Pawnee County Med. Soc. (past pres. elect). Home: 6622 Coventry St Stillwater OK 74074 Office: 2324 W 7th Pl Stillwater OK 74074

MAXWELL, ROBERT EARL, fed. judge; b. Elkins, W.Va., Mar. 15, 1924; s. Earl L. and Nellie E. M.; student Davis and Elkins Coll.; LL.B., W.Va. U., 1949; m. Ann Marie Grabowski, Mar. 1948; children—Mary Ann, Carol Lynn, Ellen Lindsay, Earl Wilson. Practiced in Randolph County, W.Va., 1949; pros. atty. Randolph County, 1952-61; U.S. atty. for No. Dist. of W.Va., 1961-64; judge U.S. Dist. Ct. for No. Dist.; W.Va., after 1965, now chief judge. Del., Democratic Nat. Conv., 1956, 64; chmn. budget com. Judicial Conf. U.S. Recipient award for outstanding community leadership Religious Heritage Am., 1979. Mem. Am., W.Va., Randolph County bar assns., W.Va. State Bar, Am. Legion. Democrat. Roman Catholic. Lion, Moose, Elk. Home: Elkins WV 26241 Office: US Court House PO Box 1275 Elkins WV 26241

MAXWELL, ROBERT RULE, oil co. exec.; b. Greenwood, Miss., Jan. 11, 1943; s. Robert Luther and Isabelle (Rule) M.; B.S., Miss. State U., 1965; m. Martha Ann Lamon, Sept. 15, 1972; children—Robert Rule, Leathe Elizabeth. Pres., R.L. Maxwell Oil Co., Inc., Ruleville, Miss. Past scoutmaster Boy Scouts Am. Mem. Ruleville C. of C. (past pres.), LP Gas Dealers Assn. Miss., Miss Petroleum Marketers Assn., Nat. Fedn. Ind. Bus. Methodist. Clubs: Rotary (past pres.), Drew Ruleville Country, Quiver River Duck, Caulk Island, Merigold Hunting. Office: 121 W Harrison St Ruleville MS 28771

MAY, BETTY JO WHITTEN, educator; b. Hattiesburg, Miss., Oct. 20, 1935; d. Elton Barber and Ethel Duckworth Whitten; B.A., U. Va., 1959; M.A., U. N.C., Greensboro, 1969, Ph.D., 1978; m. Jesse Gaylord May, June 22, 1959; children—Michael Gaylord, Gordon Whitten. Speech pathologist, speech and hearing clinic U. Va., Charlottesville, 1957-61; speech pathologist Children's Rehab. Center, Winston-Salem, N.C., 1963-68, Redding-Speech Psychology Center and Child Guidance Clinic, Winston-Salem, N.C., 1971-77; asst. prof. spl. edn. Winston-Salem State U., 1977-79, Wake Forest U., Winston-Salem, 1971-79; cons. in assessment, remediation of children and adults with learning and communication problems. Bd. dirs. Child Care Council, Urban Coalition, Pre-Sch. for Deaf, Coop. Planning Consortium; mem. adv. bd. Crippled Children's Services. Excellence fellow, 1978; lic. speech pathologist, N.C. Mem. Am. Speech and Hearing Assn. (cert. clin. competence in speech pathology), N.C. Speech, Hearing and Lang. Assn. (pres. 1979-80), Nat. Council Family Relations, Soc. Research in Child Devel., Assn. Children with Learning Disabilities, Speech Hearing and Related Profls. Democrat. Methodist. Contbr. articles to profl. jours. Home: 3318 York Rd Winston-Salem NC 27106 Office: Winston-Salem State U Dept Edn Box 13014 Winston-Salem NC 27106

MAY, DARLENE RAE, educator; b. Akron, Ohio, Feb. 13, 1947; d. James Alva and Bertha Hannah (Graham) May; student (Nat. Merit Scholar 1964-66, Coll. scholar fall 1966) Coll. of Wooster, 1964-66; Degree of Specialization (Colombian govt. fellow spring 1967), Instituto Caro y Cuervo, Bogota, 1967; B.A. summa cum laude (Nat. Merit scholar), Ind. U., 1969, M.A. (Ford Found. Asian Studies fellow), 1971, Ph.D. 1978; postgrad. (Center for Arabic Study Abroad fellow) Am. U., Cairo, Egypt, 1970-71; m. Abdulrahman Ahmed Abdulrahman, Aug. 31, 1974. Asso. instr. in Arabic, Ind. U., 1971-72; asst. prof. Arabic lang. and Islamic studies depts. fgn. langs. and internat. studies Southwestern at Memphis, 1973-76, 78-79, asso. prof., 1979—, Southwestern at Memphis Research and Creative Activity Com. grantee, summer 1976, 80; fellow Summer Coll. Faculty Inst. on Middle East, Hamline U.-Middle East Studies Assn., 1979; Mellon funds research grantee Southwestern at Memphis Faculty Devel. Com., summer 1979; Nat. Endowment Humanities research grantee, 1980-81. Mem. Middle East Studies Assn., Am. Assn. Tchrs. Arabic (exec. bd. 1975-76), Middle East Inst., Assn. Muslim Social Scientists, Muslim Students Assn., Am. Oriental Soc., Panel Am. Women, UN Assn. U.S.A. (bd. dirs. Memphis chpt. 1974—), Mensa, Phi Beta Kappa (pres. Gamma chpt. Tenn. 1980). Home: 1705 Morlye Pl Apt 2 Memphis TN 38111 Office: Southwestern at Memphis 2000 N Parkway Memphis TN 38112

MAY, DARREL LEROY, psychiatric social worker; b. Denver, May 21, 1940; s. Henry Louis and Imogene Lee (Wisdom) M.; B.A., U. Colo., 1963; M.S.W., U. Denver, 1967; m. Rosalyn Ann Balch, Aug. 18, 1963; children—Edward Louis. Program worker Auaria Community Center, Denver, 1963-66; neighborhood area coordinator Neighborhood Centers-Day Care Assn., Houston, 1967-70; psychiatric social worker Mental Health-Mental Retardation Center, Wichita Falls, Tex., 1970-74, Children's Med. Center, Tulsa, 1974—; instr. Tulsa Jr. Coll., 1979. State pres., Colo. Christian Endeavor Union, 1959; mem. Spl. Ministries Commn., Boston Ave. United Meth. Ch., Tulsa, 1977—, chmn., 1980; bd. dirs. Frances F. Willard Home for Girls, 1977—, chmn. services com., 1978—; leader Boy Scouts Am., 1979—. Mem. Nat. Assn. Social Workers, Acad. Certified Social Workers, Okla. Bd. Registration of Social Workers. Democrat. Methodist. Home: 4647 S Winston Ave Tulsa OK 74135 Office: 5300 E Skelly Dr Tulsa OK 74135

MAY, DONALD LYNN, instrument engr.; b. Birmingham, Ala., June 30, 1936; s. Clifford Leon and Ruby Lee (Harris) M.; B.S. in Elec. Engring., Auburn U., 1960; m. Martha Lucretia Owen, Jan. 2, 1960; 1 dau., Martha. Design engr. Phillips Chem. Co., Pasadena, Tex., 1960-62; project mgr. Brown Engring. Co., Huntsville, Ala., 1962-65; sr. instrument engr. Monsanto Textile Co., Pensacola, Fla., 1965—. Served with USNR, 1954-62. Recipient Engring. Achievement award Ellison Instrument Div. of Dieterich Standard Corp., 1973. Registered profl. engr., Ala. Mem. IEEE, Instrument Soc. of Am. (sr.). Republican. Baptist. Contbr. articles to engring. publs. Home: 4170 Bonway Dr Pensacola FL 35204 Office: PO Box 12830 Pensacola FL 32575

MAY, FRANCIS BARNS, educator; b. Cascilla, Miss., Dec. 24, 1915; s. James Marshall and Hallye (Rice) M.; B.B.A. with highest honors, U. Tex., 1941, M.B.A., 1943, Ph.D., 1957; m. Janice Evelyn Christensen, June 9, 1956. Instr. bus. statistics U. Tex., Austin, 1941-43, asst. prof., 1947-58, asso. prof., 1958-61, prof., 1961—, chmn. dept. gen. bus., 1964-68, research scientist Bur. Bus. Research, 1954-57, statistician, 1958-64, cons. statistician, 1964—. Vis. prof. statistics U. Minn., Mpls., 1960; dir. San Antonio br. Dallas Fed. Res. Bank, 1966-71, chmn. bd., 1968, 70. Served from pvt. to capt., USAAF, 1943-46. Mem. Am. Statis. Assn. (council, pres. Austin chpt. 1964-66), Southwestern Social Sci. Assn. (chmn. bus. research sect. 1956-57, editor 1958, pres. 1968-69), Econometric Soc., Ops. Research Soc., Inst. Mgmt. Scis., Phi Kappa Phi, Phi Eta Sigma, Beta Gamma Sigma, Sigma Iota Epsilon, Beta Alpha Psi. Club: Social Science (pres. Austin 1965-66). Author: Introduction to Games of Strategy, 1970. Asso. editor Tex. Bus. Rev., 1963-64. Contbr. numerous articles to profl. jours. Home: 6504 Auburnhill Austin TX 78723

MAY, IRVIN MARION, JR., historian; b. Dallas, Tex., Mar. 20, 1939; s. Irvin M. and Mossie (Thompson) M.; student Kilgore Coll., 1957-58; B.A., U. Tex., 1962; M.A., Baylor U., 1963; Ph.D., U. Okla., 1970; m. Vivian Suzanne Eaton, June 30, 1962; children—Emily Diane, Mary Elizabeth. Instr. history East Central State U., Okla. 1967-68; instr. history Tex. A&M U., College Station, 1968-70, asst. prof., 1970-74; research historian Tex. Agrl. Expt. Station, Tex. A&M U., 1974—; cons. Sam Rayburn House, 1978; project reviewer Nat. Endowment for Humanities, 1977—. McMillan Found. grantee, 1978. Mem. Western History Assn., So. Hist. Assn., W. Tex. Hist. Assn., Red River Valley Hist. Assn., Orgn. Am. Historians, Agrl. History Soc., Tex. State Hist. Assn., Oral History Assn., E. Tex. Hist. Assn. (dir. 1977—, chmn. C.K. Chamberlain award com. 1977—), Western Social Sci. Assn. (1st discipline chmn. agrl. studies 1976), Phi Alpha Theta. Presbyterian. Contbr. numerous essays on Am. agrl. history to scholarly jours.; contbr. numerous revs. to profl. jours.; assoc. editor Red River Valley Hist. Rev., 1974—; author: Marvin Jones: Agrarian Advocate, 1980; Overton; Agricultural Science and Education in Northeast Texas, 1980. Home: 1013 Madera Circle College Station TX 77840 Office: Univ Archives Tex A&M Univ College Station TX 77843

MAY, JOHN LAWRENCE, bishop; b. Evanston, Ill., Mar. 31, 1922; s. Peter Michael and Catherine (Allare) M.; M.A., St. Mary of Lake Sem., Mundelein, Ill., 1945, S.T.L., 1947. Ordained priest Roman Catholic Ch., 1947; asst. pastor St. Gregory Ch., Chgo., 1947-56; chaplain Mercy Hosp., Chgo., 1956-59; v.p., gen. sec. Catholic Ch. Extension Soc. U.S., 1959-67, pres., from 1967; aux. bishop of Chgo., 1967-69; bishop Diocese of Mobile (Ala.), 1969—. Office: 400 Government St PO Box 1966 Mobile AL 36601*

MAY, LAURA JOHNSON, ins. co. exec.; b. Isle of Wight County, Va., Apr. 10, 1922; d. Frank Harvey and Otelia Herndon (Joyner) Johnson; A.S., Keys Comml. Coll., 1940-42; m. Edwin Jackson May, June 27, 1942; 1 son, Edwin Jackson Jr. Sec., U.S. Naval Air Sta., Norfolk, Va., 1942-44; bookkeeper Colonial Stores, Inc., Norfolk, 1946-48; actuarial clk. Home Security Life Ins. Co., Durham, N.C., 1950-60, supr. actuarial dept., 1960-65, personnel asst., 1965-70, personnel dir., 1970-77, asst. v.p. personnel, 1977-78, v.p., planning coordinator, 1978—; past mem. bus. adv. council Durham Coll. Mem. budget com. United Fund, Durham, 1973-75; mem. personnel and blood recruitment coms. ARC, 1972—; deacon, chmn. fin. com. Watts St. Bapt. Ch. Fellow Life Mgmt. Inst.; mem. Triangle Area Personnel and Guidance Assn., Durham Triangle Personnel Assn., Am. Soc. Personnel Adminstrs., Durham C. of C., Durham Mchts. Assn., Life Office Mgmt. Assn. Democrat. Club: Civitan. Home: 2101 Sunset Ave Durham NC 27705 Office: 505 W Chapel Hill St Durham NC 27701

MAY, ROMULUS LEARY, physician; b. Bolton, N.C., Nov. 24, 1917; s. Romulus Leary and Emma (Everett) M.; M.D., Georgetown U., 1942; M.S.S. (fellow), U. Pa., 1953; m. Margaret Mildred Lynn, June 9, 1943; children—Lisa, Leary, Alan. Commd. lt. (j.g.) U.S. Navy, 1942, advanced through grades to capt., 1958; intern Nat. Naval Med. Sch., Bethesda, Md., 1942; resident in gen. surgery U.S. Naval Med. Center, Bethesda, 1947-50; sr. resident in surgery Georgetown U. Hosp., Washington, 1950-51; asst. chief surgery U.S. Naval Hosp., Camp Lejeune, N.C., 1953-55; mem. surg. staff U.S. Naval Hosp., Portsmouth, Va., 1955-56, chief thoracic surgery, 1961-64; resident in cardiovascular surgery St. Francis Hosp., L.I., N.Y., 1955; resident in thoracic surgery U.S. Naval Hosp., St. Albans, N.Y., 1956-58, gen. surgeon, 1956-58, chief cardiopulmonary lab. and surg. staff, 1958-59; cons. on surg. matters to U.S. surgeon gen. Dept. Navy, Washington, 1959-61; ret., 1965; mem. staff Gen. Hosp. of Virginia Beach (Va.), 1965-67; chief gen. and thoracic surgery and gen. practice Hamlet (N.C.) Hosp., 1967—. Diplomate Am. Bd. Surgery, Am. Bd. Thoracic Surgery. Mem. A.C.S., AMA, N.C. Med. Soc. Roman Catholic. Contbr. articles to med. jours. Home: 205 Hylan Ave Hamlet NC 28345 Office: 118 Vance St Hamlet NC 28345

MAY, WINSTON CHARLES, optometrist; b. Cin., Apr. 16, 1943; s. E. Winston and Ann Burnett (Cummings) M.; student Defiance (Ohio) Coll., 1961-64; B.S., M.Optometry, Ind., U., 1967; m. Helen Neumann, Sept. 3, 1966. Pvt. practice optometry, Manassas, Va., 1967—. Diplomate Nat. Bd. Examiners in Optometry. Fellow Am. Acad. Optometry; mem. Am., Va. optometric assns., No.Va. Optometric Soc. (pres. 1973), Optometric Council Nat. Capital Region (pres. 1976-77). Home: 9613 Heather Green Dr Manassas VA 22110 Office: 8721 Digges Rd Manassas VA 22110

MAYALL, MICHAEL MARVIN, educator; b. Spokane, Wash., Apr. 12, 1939; s. Stanley Evans and Mary Doris (Marvin) M.; B.A. in Edn., Central Wash. U., 1961; M.A. in Edn., Eastern Wash. U., 1966; Ed.D., N.Tex. State U., 1976; m. Charlotte E. Bramlett, May 2, 1970; children—Scot, Patrick, Kathleen, Michelle. Tchr., Liberty Sch. Dist., Wash., 1960-63; Spokane (Wash.) Sch. Dist., 1964-65; faculty U. Oreg., Eugene, 1965-66, El Centro Coll., Dallas, 1966-68, Tarrant County Jr. Coll., Dist. Ft. Worth, Hurst, Tex., 1968—, prof., chmn. dept. behavioral occupations and psychology, 1974—; cons. in field. Public health com. City of Ft. Worth; mem. behavior modification and therapy bd. Ft. Worth State Sch., chmn. edn. and info. Am. Cancer Soc., Ft. Worth. Model UN del., 1957-58; recipient disting. service award Wash. Edn. Assn., 1964. Mem. NEA (life), Wash. Dept. Classroom Tchrs. (dir. 1963-65), Wash. Educators Coordinating Council (pres. 1964), Tex. Jr. Coll. Tchrs. Assn., Phi Delta Kappa. Contbr. articles to profl. jours. Home: 1925 Druid Ln Fort Worth TX 76112 Office: 828 Harwood Rd Hurst TX 76053

MAYBERRY, GERALD LEE, chemist; b. Louisville, June 1, 1934; s. Hartford Allen and Anna Louise (Rendon) M.; B.S., Eastern Ky. U., 1956; Ph.D. in Organic Chemistry, U. Louisville, 1961; m. Wanda Frances Lindon, Aug. 24, 1957; children—Susan Carol, David Scott, Daniel Lindon. With Tenn. Eastman Co., Kingsport, 1961—, devel. asso. responsible for process devel., devel. and control dept., organic chems. div., 1976-79, sr. devel. asso., 1979—. Mem. Am. Chem. Soc., Sigma Xi. Presbyterian. Home: 406 Garmon Dr Kingsport TN 37663 Office: Tenn Eastman Co Bldg 231 Kingsport TN 37662

MAYBERRY-CARSON, KATY JANE, microbiologist; b. Cartersville, Ga., Oct. 20, 1939; d. Eugene S. and Katie Lou (Cochran) Carson: B.S., U. Ga., 1962 M.S., 1964, Ph.D. (USPHS fellow), 1966; m. William Roy Mayberry, Jan. 14, 1967. Leverhulme postdoctoral fellow U. Hull (Eng.), 1966; microbiologist Southeast Water Pollution Lab., Athens, Ga., 1967, U. S.D. Med. Sch., Vermillion, 1968-78; microbiologist E. Tenn. State U. Med. Sch., Johnson City, 1979—. Parsons Fund grantee, 1976-77. Mem. Am. Soc. Microbiology, Am. Inst. Biol. Scis., Electron Microscopy Soc., Am. Forestry Assn., Smithsonian Assos., Sigma Xi, Phi Sigma. Democrat. Baptist. Office: Dept Microbiology E Tenn State U Med Sch Johnson City TN 37601

MAYBORN, FRANK WILLIS, newspaper editor and publisher; b. Akron, Ohio, Dec. 7, 1903; s. Ward C. and Nellie C. (Welton) M.; B.A., U. Colo., 1926; H.H.D. (hon.), Mary Hardin Baylor Coll., 1976. With Dallas News, 1926, N. Tex. Traction Co., Ft. Worth, 1927-29; bus. mgr. Temple (Tex.) Telegram, 1929-45, editor, pres., pub., 1945—; founder, pres., 1936-70, operator radio sta. KTEM, Temple; founder, pres., 1953—, operator KCEN-TV, Temple; owner Sherman (Tex.) Democrat, 1945-77; pres., owner, operator Killeen (Tex.) Herald, 1952—, Taylor (Tex.) Press, 1959-74; founder, operator radio sta. WMAK, Nashville, 1947-54; pres., dir. Bell Pub. Co., Temple, 1945—, Bell Broadcasting Co., Temple, 1936-70, Sherman Democrat Co., 1945-77, Killeen (Tex.) Herald Pub. Co., 1952—, Taylor (Tex.) Pub. Co., 1959-62, Channel 6, Inc., 1962—, County Developers, Inc., 1967—, FWM Properties, 1965-75, Community Enterprises, Inc., 1959-74; dir. 1st Nat. Bank, Temple. Mem. Tex. Democratic Com., 1948. Dir. Temple Indsl. Found., 1956, 59-61, 64-66, 68-70, 74-76, pres., 1963; mem. Tex. Hist. Found., 1967-68, Tex. Hist. Survey Com., 1966-69; mem. adv. council U. Tex. Journalism Found., 1964-66, Tex. A. and M. U. Dept. Journalism, 1958-59; mem. adv. and devel. bds. Tex. Indsl. Commn., 1958-64; mem. Ft. Hood Civilian Adv. Com., 1963—, Baylor U. Broadcast Council, 1964-65; mem. adv. bd. Scott and White Hosp. Found., Temple; bd. dirs. Temple Boys Choir, 1969, Waco Symphony Assn., 1968-69, Frank W. Mayborn Found., 1964—; life trustee Vanderbilt U.; trustee Central Tex. Med. Found., 1970—, chmn. bd. trustees Kinsolving Youth Center, 1971-72. Served from pvt. to maj., AUS, 1942-45; ETO. Decorated Bronze Star Medal; recipient Outstanding Citizens award, Temple, 1948, Tex. award for outstanding service V.F.W., 1955, award for contbn. to soil and water conservation Soil Conservation Service, 1959; Citizenship award Jr. C. of C., 1951, Man of Year award, 1971, 4-H award for outstanding service to 4-H Clubs, 1971. Mem. Am. Soc. Newspaper Editors (past dir.), Tex. Daily Press League (dir. Tex. Sunday comic sect.), Temple C. of C. (dir., past pres.), Retail Mchts. Assn. Temple, Tex. Daily Newspaper Assn. (past pres.; award 1946), Am. (fed. laws com.), So. (pres. 1962, chmn. bd. 1963) newspaper pubs. assns., Tex. Council Higher Edn., Assn. U.S. Army (life, mem. mil. affairs com., certificate of achievement 1969), Broadcast Pioneers, Phi Kappa Psi, Sigma Delta Chi. Presbyn. (elder). Mason, Rotarian (hon.). Clubs: Nat. Press (Washington); Advertising (past pres.) (Ft. Worth); Dallas Athletic, Lancers (Dallas); Headliners (Austin); Temple Country. Office: 10 S 3d St Temple TX 76501

MAYDA, JARO, educator; b. Brno, Czechoslovakia, 1918; s. Francis and Maria (Hornová) M.; came to U.S., 1949, naturalized, 1955; Dr. Juris Utriusque, Masaryk U., Brno, 1945; J.D. (Rockefeller fellow 1955-56), U. Chgo., 1957; m. Maruja del Castillo, 1967. Legal counsel export div. Skodaworks, Pilsen-Prague, 1946-48; vis. prof. polit. sci. Denison U., Granville, Ohio, 1949-50, Ohio State U., Columbus, 1950-51; asst. prof. law and polit. sci. U. Wis., Madison, 1951-56; mem. faculty U. P.R., Rio Piedras, 1957—, prof. law and pub. policy, 1958—, dir. Inst. Policy Studies and Law, 1972-75, spl. asst. to pres., 1972; Fulbright research prof. Inst. Comparative Law, U. Paris, 1967-68; Bailey lectr. La. State U., 1969; lectr. Am. specialist program Dept. State, 1960; mem. com. environment policy and law Internat. Union Conservation Nature, 1972—; dep. sec. gen. 42d Conf. Internat. Law Assn., 1947; cons. on environment, mgmt. and law UNESCO, 1972—; cons. Am. Jury project U. Chgo., 1955-56, FAO, 1971—, UN Environment Program, 1977—; adv. panel on Ecosystem Data Handbook, NSF, 1976-77; mem., policy adviser Gov.'s study group P.R. and Sea, 1972; research asso. Center Energy and Environ. Research, U. P.R., Dept. Energy, 1977—; vis. Fulbright prof. Ecole Nationale d'Economie Appliquée, Dakar, Senegal, 1980. Author: Environment and Resources: From Conservation to Ecomanagement, 1967; Introduction to Law, 1974; Francois Geny and Modern Jurisprudence, 1976; also articles. Translator: Geny, Method of Interpretation, 1963; also law treatises. Editorial bd. Am. Jour. Comparative Law, 1958—. Office: Sch Law Univ PR Rio Piedras PR 00931

MAYER, RAYMOND CHARLES, JR., pub. relations exec.; b. Bklyn., Aug. 12, 1921; s. Raymond C. and Sybil (Peacock) M.; student Peddie Prep. Sch., 1939-40; B.A., Colgate U., 1947; m. Grace E. Fleming, Feb. 20, 1949; children—Raymond C., Nancy Ruth, Hollis Elizabeth, Sybil F., Margo G. With Raymond C. Mayer & Assos., Inc., 1947-69, successively, student trainee, exec., staff dir., 1954-60, v.p., 1960-62, exec. v.p., 1962, pres., 1962-69; exec. dir. Elec. Council Fla., Tampa, 1969-76; dir. pub. relations Leesburg (Fla.) Gen. Hosp., 1976-77, Ormond Beach Hosp., 1978—; pub. relations dir. ARC; counsel sci., engring., trade assns. Active Cub and Boy Scouts Am. Mem. council on univ. relations Colgate U.; mem. pub. relations com. United Engring. Trustee, Engrs. Joint Council, Engring. Found. Served from sgt. to lt. AUS, World War II. Mem. Cayuga Heights Assn. (pres.), AAAS, Pub. Relations Soc. Am. (dir. Westchester chpt.), Fla. Mag. Assn., Fla. Soc. Assn. Exec., Fla. Hosp. Assn., Sigma Nu. Republican. Congregationalist. Clubs: Nat. Press; Colgate U. (gov.) (N.Y.C.). Editor Electric Fla. Contbr. articles to trade mags. Home: 470 N Halifax Dr Ormond Beach FL 32074 Office: 264 S Atlantic Ave Ormond Beach FL 32074

MAYER, ROBERT ALLEN, broadcasting co. exec.; b. Melrose Park, Ill., July 23, 1928; s. Lester Edward and Adelaide Marie (Edwards) M.; student Tenn. Temple Coll., 1949-51, Temple Sem., 1951-52; m. Myrtle Mae Harris, Aug. 26, 1950; children—Donna, Sandra Mayer Regal, Stephen, Linda Mayer Burkhart. Ordained to ministry Baptist Ch., 1952; missionary in V.I. and Netherlands, West Indies, 1952-65; founder N.T. Bapt. Enterprises, Chattanooga, 1965, pres., 1965—; founder, owner Radio Paradise, W.I., 1963—; owner Sta. WPGD, Winston-Salem, N.C., 1971-79, Sta. WMOC, Chattanooga, 1974; pres. Mayer Broadcasting Co., Chattanooga, 1974—, Mayer Pub. Co., 1979—; owner Classic Convertible Cars Co., 1979—. Served with USN, 1945-49. Mem. Nat. Assn. Broadcasters, Antique Auto Club Am., U.S. Chess Fedn. Home: 2439 Harbor Ln Sanibel Island FL 33957 Office: PO Box 908 Hixson TN 37343

MAYER, VELIA ANN, lawyer; b. nr. Mt. Pleasant, Tex., Feb. 13, 1943; d. Velia John and Opal (Dale) Mayer; B.A. cum laude, U. Miss., 1965, J.D., 1968. Admitted to Miss. bar, 1968; practiced in Jackson, 1971—; law clk. for judge of Miss. Supreme Ct., Jackson, 1968-69; spl. asst. atty. gen. State of Miss., Jackson, 1969-71; asso. firm Watkins and Eager, attys. at law, Jackson, 1971-75, partner, 1976—. Mem. Am., Miss., Hinds County bar assns., Am. Judicature Soc. Home: 787 Arlington St Jackson MS 39202 Office: Box 650 Jackson MS 39205

MAYES, CLIFFORD GRANT, accountant; b. Springfielo, Tenn., Aug. 16, 1921; s. Mitchell Eugene and Annie Evelyn (Forrester) M.; student higher accounting McKenzie Coll., 1951-54; student Moody Bible Inst., 1949-51, Ga. State Coll., 1964; m. Betty Sue Longley, Sept. 20, 1946; children—Regina Ann Mayes Kelly. Staff auditor McKenzie & McKenzie, C.P.A.'s, Chattanooga, 1952-58; accounting instr. McKenzie Coll., Chattanooga, 1951-54; individual practice accounting, Chattanooga, 1954—; sec.-treas. States-Wide Truck Leasing, Inc., 1971-75; auditor, tax adviser to bd. dirs. McKenzie Coll. Served with U.S. Army, 1942-45. Decorated Purple Heart. Mem. Tenn. Assn. Pub. Accountants, Nat. Soc. Pub. Accountants. Baptist. Home: 208 Hilltop Dr Rossville GA 30741 Office: 3335 Ringgold Rd Chattanooga TN 37412

MAYES, HOYT PATMAN, funeral home exec.; b. Bowie County, Tex., July 8, 1932; s. Hillie Clayton and Willie Ola (Pinkham) M.; student E. Tex. Baptist Coll., 1949-50, Baylor U., 1952-54, Dallas Inst. Mortuary Sci., 1951; m. Mava Geraldine Harris, Jan. 9, 1959; children—Catherine Suzanne, Cynthia Anne. Owner, pres. Mayes Funeral Dirs., Inc., Norman, Okla., 1956—. Mem. Norman Bd. Edn., also pres.; bd. dirs. Norman Alcohol Info. Center, Cleveland County ARC; trustee Acad. Profl. Funeral Service Practice; pres. Fair Sch. Fin. Council Okla., 1979—. Mem. Nat. (dist. gov. 1977-80, treas., 1980—), Okla. (pres. 1975-76) funeral dirs. assns., Order of Golden Rule, Flying Funeral Dirs. Am., Norman C. of C. (dir. 1977-80), Norman Jr. C. of C. (past pres.), Ancient Order of Quiet Birdmen. Republican. Episcopalian. Clubs: Kiwanis, Masons, Shriners, Order Eastern Star. Home: 824 Mockingbird Ln Norman OK 73071 Office: PO Drawer JJ Norman OK 73070

MAYES, SAMUEL HUBERT, JR., lawyer; b. Little Rock, Sept. 6, 1931; s. S. Hubert and Charlotte (McIntosh) M.; J.D., U. Ark., 1954; m. L. Susan Harrell, Dec. 30, 1971; children by previous marriage—Jean, Charlotte, Melissa. Admitted to Ark. bar, 1954; atty. Ark. Revenue Dept., 1954; dep. pros. atty. 6th Jud. Dist., Little Rock, 1957-58; spl. asst. atty. gen. State of Ark., 1963; partner firm Mayes & Murray, Little Rock, 1977—. Asst. sec. Ark. Senate, 1953. Served with USAF, 1955-57. Mem. Delta Theta Phi, Omicron Delta Kappa, Sigma Chi. Democrat. Methodist. Home: 2021 Beechwood St Little Rock AR 72207 Office: 2248 1st Nat Bldg Little Rock AR 72201

MAYES, WENDELL WISE, JR., radio exec.; b. San Antonio, Tex., Mar. 2, 1924; s. Wendell Wise and Dorothy Lydia (Evans) M.; student Schreiner Inst., 1941-42, U. Tex. at Austin, 1942, Daniel Baker Coll., 1946; B.S., Tex. Tech. Coll., 1949; m. Mary Jane King, May 11, 1946; children—Cathey (Mrs. Joe Rollins), Sarah Mayes Yost, Wendell Wise III. Program dir., sta. mgr. KBWD, Brownwood, Tex., 1949-57; mgr. KCRS and KWMJ, Midland, Tex., 1957-63, pres., 1965—; pres. KNOW, Austin, 1970—, KCSW, San Marcos, Tex., 1976—, KVIC and KCWM, Victoria, 1970—; dir. Capital Nat. Bank, Austin. Chmn. bd. Am. Diabetes Assn., 1974-77, mem. nat. diabetes adv. bd., 1977—; pres. Tex. Broadcast Edn. Found., 1973-76; dir. Am. Council Edn. for Journalism, 1977—. Served with USNR, 1943-46. Recipient Addison B. Scoville award Am. Diabetes Assn., 1977. Mem. Tex. Assn. Broadcasters (pres. 1964, Pioneer Broadcaster of Yr. 1978), Nat. Assn. Broadcasters (dir. 1969-72), Broadcast Edn. Assn. (dir. 1973—). Episcopalian (clk. of vestry 1968). Home: 1510 W 24th St Austin TX 78703 Office: Box 2197 Austin TX 78768

MAYFIELD, RALPH, JR., telephone co. engr.; b. Clarkesville, Ga., June 13, 1954; s. Ralph and Lola Mae (Williams) M.; B.B.A., W. Ga. Coll., 1976. Staff asst. in engring. Standard Telephone Co., Baldwin, Ga., 1976-77, planning engr., 1977-79; spl. projects engr. Gen. Telephone Co. of S.E., Durham, N.C., 1979—. Mem. Am. Mktg. Assn., Kappa Alpha Psi (Achievement award 1976, pres. chpt. 1975-76). Democrat. Baptist. Home: 1308 Wyldewood Rd Durham NC 27712 Office: Gen Telephone Co Roxboro Rd Durham NC 27704

MAYFIELD, WILLIAM STEPHEN, lawyer, educator; b. Gary, Ind., Mar. 2, 1919; s. William H. and Elnora E. (Williams) M.; A.B., Detroit Inst. Tech., 1942; J.D., Detroit Coll. Law, 1949; m. Octavia Smith, Feb. 6, 1949; 3 children. Admitted to Mich. bar, 1949; mem. firm Lewis, Rowlette, Brown, Wanzo and Bell, Detroit, 1949-51; atty. U.S. Office of Price Stblzn., Detroit, 1951-53; referee Friend of the Ct., Detroit, 1953-72; prof. law So. U., Baton Rouge, 1972—; vis. prof. law Paul M. Hebert Law Center, La. State U., Baton Rouge, summer 1979; mem. La. State Supreme Ct. Com. on Sci. and Tech. in the Courts, 1978—. Served with U.S. Army, 1942-46. Mem. Nat. Bar Assn., World Assn. Law Profs., Am. Bar Assn., Comml. Law League Am., Wolverine Bar Assn., Ret. Officers Assn., Detroit Coll. Law Alumni Assn., Assn. Henri Capitant, Delta Theta Phi. Baptist. Office: PO Box 73823 Baton Rouge LA 70807

MAYL, NATHAN, plastic and reconstructive surgeon: b. N.Y.C., Sept. 19, 1938; s. George and Fay (Torgovnich) M.; B.S. magna cum laude, U. Pitts., 1960; M.D., Stanford U., 1965; m. Eileen Barbara Freedman, Sept. 4, 1960; children—Merin Leigh, Alexi Drew. Intern, Montefiore Hosp. Med. Center, Bronx, N.Y., 1965-66, resident in surgery, 1966-67; resident in surgery U. Fla., Gainesville, also chief resident, 1969-70; resident, chief resident plastic surgery Emory U., Atlanta, 1970-74; plastic and reconstructive surgeon Atlantic Plastic Surgery Assos., Pompano Beach, Fla., 1974—; chief surgery Cypress Community Hosp., Pompano Beach, 1976—. Served to lt. comdr. USNR, 1967-69. Diplomate Nat. Bd. Med. Examiners. Mem. Am. Soc. Plastic and Reconstructive Surgeons, Southeastern Soc. Plastic and Reconstructive Surgeons, Fla. Soc. Plastic and Reconstructive Surgeons. Club: Rotary. Address: 50 NE 26th Ave Suite 304 Pompano Beach FL 33062

MAYNOR, HAL WHARTON, JR., educator; b. Nashville, Oct. 5, 1917; s. Hal Wharton and Ophelia Abbigail (Hill) M.; B.S., U. Ky., 1944, M.S., 1947, D.Eng., 1954; m. Marjorie Mae Baker, Mar. 16, 1946; children—Sandra (Mrs. Alan Averhart), Susan Lynne (Mrs. Wallace Bromberg), Hal Wharton III. X-ray technician, lab. asst. Henry Vogt Machine Co., Louisville, 1936; lab. asst. Jones Dabney Co., Louisville, 1936-39; asst. prof. mech. engring., asso. engr. atomic research inst. Iowa State Coll., 1947-51; research engr. major appliance div. Gen. Electric Co., Louisville, 1954-57; prin. investigator scaling of titanium and titanium-base alloys USAF contract, dept. mining and metall. engring. U. Ky., 1952-54, asso. prof., 1957-59; prof. dept. mech. engring. Auburn (Ala.) U., 1959-78, prof. emeritus, 1978—, Sch. Engring. rep. Faculty Council, 1962-64, 66-69, supr. Olin Matheison Summer Project Grant Program, 1967-69; project leader fracture of high strength materials Army Missile Command, 1959-70; Cons., Ala. Power Co., 1960-61; engring. faculty cons. Army Rocket and Guided Missile Agy., 1963. Chmn. Auburn High Sch. Kiwanis Career Day, 1961. Bd. dirs. Auburn U. Fed. Credit Union, Friends Auburn Library. Served with USNR, 1943-46. ASTM grantee, 1967-68. Registered profl. engr., Ala., Ky. Fellow Am. Inst. Chemists; mem. Ala., Ky. acads. sci., Am. Inst. Mining, Metall. and Petroleum Engrs., Am. Soc. Engring. Edn., Nat., Ala. (past com. chmn., pres. Auburn chpt. 1964-65) socs. profl. engrs., ASME, Sci. Research Soc. Am., Sigma Xi, Alpha Chi Sigma, Tau Beta Pi, Pi Tau Sigma. Mem. Christian Ch. (elder, bd. dirs., past chmn. ofcl. bd.). Reviewer papers and books for Applied Mechanics Revs. Contbr. articles to profl. jours. Home: 518 Cary Dr Auburn AL 36830

MAYO, CLYDE CALVIN, organizational psychologist; b. Robstown, Tex., Feb. 2, 1940; s. Clyde Culverson and Velma (Oxford) M.; B.A., Rice U., 1961; B.S., U. Houston, 1964; M.S., Trinity U., 1966; Ph.D., U. Houston, 1972; m. Jeanne McCain, Aug. 24, 1963; children—Brady Scott, Amber Camille. Prin., LWFW, Inc., Houston, 1966—; guest lectr. U. St. Thomas; counselor Interface Counselling Center; dir. Diversified Devel. Services. Coach, Fun Football; mgr. Meyerland Little League. Mem. Am., Tex., Houston psychol. assns., Houston Area Indsl. Psychologists, Harris County Mental Health Assn. (edn. com.). Baptist. Club: Meyerland. Co-author: Bi/Polar Inventory of Strengths. Home: 8723 Ferris St Houston TX 77096 Office: 3223 Smith St Houston TX 77006

MAYO, CYNTHIA REED, dietitian; b. Richmond, Va., Feb. 7, 1943; d. John M. and Esterine Reed (Green) R.; B.S., Hampton Inst., 1964; M.S., Va. State Coll., 1973; postgrad. Va. Poly. Inst. and State U., 1979—; m. James R. Mayo Jr., Nov. 25, 1965; children—Keith M., Craig L. Tchr., food service supr. Richmond Public Schs., 1964—; grad. teaching asst. Va. Poly. Inst. and State U., Blacksburg, 1979. Mem. adv. com. Head Start; chmn. fin. com. Baptist Ch. Mem. Am. Dietetic Assn. (registered dietitian), Am. Sch. Food Service Assn., Alpha Kappa Alpha. Office: Richmond Public Schs 6106 Phelps St Glen Allen VA 23060

MAYO, EDWARD BURNETT, mus. ofcl.; b. Houston, July 13, 1918; s. Henry M. and Mary Louise (Sweeney) M.; B.S. in Architecture, Rice U., 1942. Architect firm Thompson McCleary, Houston, 1945-52; draftsman M.D. Anderson Hosp. and Tumor Inst., Houston, 1954-57; sales Coblar Book Stores, Houston, 1959-60, Handmakers Splty. Shop, Houston, 1958-59; mus. registrar Mus. Fine Arts, Houston, 1961—. Served with USAAF, 1942-45. Roman Catholic. Home: 1511 California St Houston TX 77006 Office: 1001 Bissonnet St PO Box 6826 Houston TX 77005

MAYO, EUGENE FRANCIS, ret. naval officer, profl. engr.; b. New Orleans, La., Nov. 30, 1913; s. Eugene Alexander and Frances Catherine (Konitzer) M.; B.S., La. State U., 1942; postgrad. Harvard U., 1942; m. Dorothy Alden Nash, Feb. 1, 1943; children—Richard Alden, Stephen Alden, Thomas Alden. Installer, So. Bell Telephone Co., 1935-42; sales engr. Ins. Mfg. Co., 1946; asst. operating engr. New Orleans Pub. Service Inc., 1947-78; instr. Delgado Jr. Coll. Served to lt. comdr. USN, 1942-46. Registered elec. engr., La. Mem. La. Engring. Soc., Nat. Profl. Engrs. Soc., Kappa Mu Epsilon, Sigma Alpha Epsilon. Democrat. Roman Catholic. Clubs: New Orleans Athletic, Am. Legion, VFW. Home: 5205 Zenith St Metairie LA 70001

MAYO, WALKER PORTER, thoracic surgeon; b. Prestonsburg, Ky., Sept. 20, 1922; s. Walker Porter and Reba (Harkey) M.; M.D., U. Louisville, 1946; M.S. in Physiology, U. Mich., 1950; m. Helen Prevot, June 20, 1952; children—Camille, Walker, Patrice, Lionel. Intern Parkland City-County Hosp., Dallas, 1946-47; resident U. Louisville, VA Hosp., Louisville, 1950-S2, U. Mich., Ann Arbor, 1952-54; practice medicine specializing in thoracic surgery, Lexington, 1954—; chmn. thoracic surgery service Central Bapt. Hosp., Lexington; asso. clin. prof. surgery U. Ky. Med. Sch. Served with USN 1947-49. Recipient distinguished service medal Am. Cancer Soc., 1962. Diplomate Am. Bd. Surgery, Am. Bd. Thoracic Surgery. Fellow Am. Coll. Chest Physicians, A.C.S.; mem. Soc. Thoracic Surgeons, So. Thoracic Surg. Assn., Ky. Surg. Soc., A.M.A. Democrat. Methodist. Contbr. articles to profl. jours. Home: 3325 Braemer Dr Lexington KY 40502 Office: Mayo Long and Saha 168 Burt Rd Lexington KY 40503

MAYO, WALLACE C., dentist; b. Century, Fla., Feb. 10, 1914; s. James Lawrence and Lula Mae (Tompkins) M.; student U. Fla., 1932-33; D.D.S., Emory U., 1937; m. Jean Kingsbery, Jan. 11. 1941; children—Donna Jean, Susan, Clair, Howard. Intern Ft. Oglethorpe, Ga., 1938; pvt. practice dentistry, Pensacola, Fla., 1939-41, specializing in periodonitcs, 1945—. Chmn. adv. council Emory U. Sch. Dentistry, Pensacola Jr. Coll. Sch. Dental Hygiene, trustee coll.; mem. dental adv. com. Dept. Def. Served with Dental Corps, AUS, 1941-45; ETO; NATOUSA. Fellow Internat. Coll. Dentist, Am. Coll. Dentists; mem. Fla. Soc. Peridontology, ADA (ho. of dels.), Fla. (past pres., chmn. council on dental edn.), N.W. Fla. Dist. (past pres.), Pensacola (past pres.) dental socs., Am. (exec. council), So. (past pres.) acads. peridontology, Res. Officers Assn. (past pres. Fla. dist), Pensacola C. of C. (dir.), USCG Aux. (insp. examiner). Methodist. Clubs: Exchange (past pres.), Yacht, Scenic Hills Country. Home: 2920 E Blackshear St Pensacola FL 32503 Office: 901 N 12th Ave Pensacola FL 32501

MAYOZ, RAFAEL, nuclear equipment mfg. co. info. systems exec.; b. Barcelona, Spain, July 6, 1938; s. Rafael and Wenceslada (Valencia) M.; came to U.S., 1957, naturalized, 1967; B.Indsl. Engring., U. Fla., 1962; M. Engring. Systems, U. South Fla., 1967; m. Gloria Alonso, Nov. 22, 1958; children—Rudy, Gloria. Engr., Gen. Telephone & Electronics Co., Tampa, Fla., 1962-65, sr. engr., 1965-67; systems analyst Westinghouse Electric Corp., Tampa, 1967-73, supr. computer ops., 1973-74, mgr. mgmt. info. systems, 1974—; v.p. Fringe Benefit Adminstrs. Fla., Inc., Tampa, 1976—; instr. U. South Fla., 1968-71. Bd. dirs. Centro Asturiano Hosp. Registered profl. engr., Fla. Mem. Am. Inst. Indsl. Engrs. (chpt. devel. dir. 1968). Home: 5021 Homer Ave Tampa FL 33609 Office: 6001 S Westshore Blvd Tampa FL 33616

MAYS, BENITA BANISTER, ednl. coordinator; b. Mt. Vernon, Tex., Mar. 16, 1937; d. Charley Thomas and Maude Eva (Blake) Banister; student Lamar Tech. U., 1955-56, E.Tex. State U., 1957-58; Med. Technologist, Parkland Meml. Hosp., Dallas, 1959; B.S. in Med. Tech., U. Tex., Arlington, 1965; M.A. in Microbiology, U. Tex. Southwestern Med. Sch., 1969; Noyes Found. fellow Tex. A. and M. U., 1974-75, 76-77, Ph.D. in Allied Health Edn., 1977; m. James Edward Mays. Med. technician Parkland Meml. Hosp., Dallas, 1956-58; med. research technician, infectious disease sect. U. Tex. Southwestern Med. Sch., Dallas, 1959-69; ednl. coordinator, instr. Med. Lab. Technician Program, El Centro Coll., Dallas, 1969—; pvt. instr. applied piano, 1955-56, 63-73; faculty Tng. Inst. for Med. Lab. Technician Educators, 1973; adj. clin. instr. Sch. Applied Health Scis., U. Tex. Health Sci. Center, Dallas, 1974—; cons. Task Force of Continuing Edn. for Med. Technologists in N.Tex., 1975. Gen. Diagnostics grad. scholar Am. Soc. for Med. Tech. Edn. and Research Fund, Inc., 1977; recipient spl. recognition award Technicon Instruments Corp., 1977; certified in allied health tchr. edn. and adminstrn. Baylor Coll. Medicine, 1977. Mem. Am. Soc. Clin. Pathologists, Am. Soc. Med. Tech., Am. Soc. Allied Health Professions, AAUP, Am. Acad. Microbiology (specialist in clin. microbiology), Am. Soc. Microbiology, Tex. Soc. Clin. Microbiology, Nat. Guild Piano Tchrs., El Centro Coll. Faculty Assn. Contbr. articles to profl. jours. Home: 5227 Duncanville Rd Dallas TX 75211

MAYS, CARL W., author, editor; b. Humboldt, Tenn., Dec. 6, 1939; s. J. Perry and Hildred H. (Arnold) M.; B.S., Murray State U., 1963; M.A. in Communications and Edn., New Orleans Theol. Sem., 1969; postgrad. Memphis State U., 1963; m. Jean W. Berry, Feb. 9, 1963; 1 son, Carl Wayne. Tchr. speech/drama, sports coach Humes High Sch., Memphis, 1963-64; announcer/writer WFMH Radio, Cullman, Ala. and WHOS Radio, Decatur, Ala., 1964-65; announcer/writer/sportscaster WGAD, Gadsden, Ala., 1965-66; dir. New Orleans Youth Assn., 1967-69; spl. asst. to pastor First Bapt. Ch., Kenner, La., 1967-69; dir. Columbus (Ga.) Youth Assn., 1969-70; spl. asst. to pastor First Bapt. Ch., Columbus, 1969-70; freelance writer/speaker, 1970-72; pres. Creative Living, Inc., Gatlinburg, Tenn., 1972—; chmn. bd. Creative Ministries, Inc., 1972—; editor Creative Living Publs., 1975—; leader in seminars on motivation, creativity, communication, 1972—; spl. cons. in creativity, motivation, communication, 1975—; spl. conv. cons., 1977—. Bd. dirs. Community Counseling Services, Columbus, 1969-70. Mem. ASCAP, Authors Guild, Nat. Speakers Assn. Author: Signs Of The Times, 1971; Mr. Adams: A Parable For Parents and Others, 1975; You Can Do It!, 1977; The Magic of J.B., 1977; Being Joyous (contributing author), 1973; (plays) That Stupid Christmas Play, 1969, Christmas Cousin, 1969, Without A Doubt, 1970, Playing Church, 1970, Celebration: A Writer in Search Of A Play, 1972, GO-LEARN-SHARE, 1973; (musical drama) The Clown, 1975; (film) The Magic Of J.B., 1980; contbr. feature articles to mags. and newspapers. Home: 101 Mountain Dr Gatlinburg TN 37738 Office: PO Box 266 Gatlinburg TN 37738

MAYS, CHARLES RAY, mfg. co. exec.; b. Oak Ridge, Dec. 4, 1946; s. Paul Charles and Irene (Beckner) M.; student Sue Bennett Jr. Coll., 1964-66, Morehead State U., 1966-68; B.S., Oak Ridge U., 1969; M.S., U. Ky. Metals Engring. Inst., 1971; m. Billie Joyce Clemons, June 28, 1975. Asso. prof. physics Morehead (Ky.) State U., 1968-69; engr. A. O. Smith, Mt. Sterling, Ky., 1969-73; with Marathon Electric Co., Nashville, 1973-75; sales engr. Talon div. Textron, Nashville, 1975-76; with Scovill Mfg. Co., Atlanta, 1976—, dist. sales mgr., Fla., Ga., Miss., La., Ala., Atlanta, 1979—. Bd. dirs. Luden Mental Health Center, Nashville, 1977—. Named Salesman of Year Scovill Apparel Fastener, 1978-79, 79-80. Mem. Southeastern Apparel and Textile Mfrs., Sigma Pi Sigma. Office: Scovill Mfg Co 1720 Old Spring House Lane Atlanta GA 30338

MAYS, LARRY WESLEY, civil engr.; b. Pittsfield, Ill., Feb. 7, 1948; s. Fred William and Lola Mae (Myers) M.; B.S., U. Mo., Rolla, 1970, M.S., 1971; Ph.D., U. Ill., 1975; m. Margaret Mary Netemeyer, May 30, 1970. Vis. research asst. prof. civil engring. U. Ill., Urbana, 1976; asst. prof. civil engring. U. Tex., Austin, 1976—; cons. in field; instr. hydraulics, hydrology, water resources; researcher water resource for fed. govt. Served with U.S. Army, 1970-73. Registered profl. engr., Calif., Ill., Tex. Mem. Am. Geophys. Union, Am. Water Resources Assn., ASCE, Sigma Xi, Chi Epsilon, Chi Gamma Iota. Contbr. articles in field to profl. jours. Home: 4111 Columbine Dr Austin TX 78759 Office: Dept Civil Engring U Tex Austin TX 78712

MAYSON, PRESTON BROOKS, JR., radiologist; b. Spartanburg, S.C., June 18, 1932; s. Preston Brooks and Sophie Rowena (Morgan) M.; B.S., U.S. Mil. Acad., 1955; M.D., George Washington U., 1962; m. Sara Dudley Heaton, June 16, 1955; children—Brooks Heaton, James Dudley. Intern, Walter Reed Hosp., Washington, 1962-63; resident in radiology Letterman Hosp., San Francisco, 1963-66; practice medicine specializing in radiology, Roanoke, Va., 1970—; mem. staff Roanoke Meml. Hosp., Community Hosp. Del., Va. Republican Conv., 1977. Served to lt. col. M.C., U.S. Army, 1955-70. Decorated Bronze Star, Meritorious Service Medal. Recipient Hoffman-La Roche award, 1962. Diplomate Am. Bd. Radiology. Mem. AMA, Am. Coll. Radiology, Radiol. Soc. N.Am., Am. Roentgen Ray Soc., Alpha Omega Alpha. Episcopalian. Home: 4906 Buckhorn Dr SW Roanoke VA 24014 Office: 2037 Crystal Spring Ave SW Roanoke VA 24014

MAYTIN, ORLANDO, physician; b. P. Del Rio, Cuba, Aug. 13, 1935; s. Jose and Coralia Maytin; came to U.S., 1962, naturalized, 1967; B.S., Edison Inst., Cuba, 1953; M.D., U. Madrid (Spain), 1963; m. Johanna Cann, Feb. 13, 1970; children—Melanie, Michael, Orlando. Intern, Mt. Sinai Hosp., Miami, Fla., 1964-65, resident, 1965-66; resident Jackson Meml. Hosp.-U. Fla., 1966-67; resident, fellow in cardiovascular surgery Jackson Meml. Hosp., VA Hosp., Miami, 1967-69; practice medicine specializing in cardiology, Plantation, Fla., 1970—; clin. instr. medicine U. Miami, 1970—, Jackson Meml. Hosp., 1970—; attending cons. cardiology VA Hosp., Miami, 1969-71; lectr. Broward Med. Center, Fort Lauderdale, Fla., 1970—; chief medicine Margate Gen. Hosp., 1972-74, chief CCU, 1972-74; treas. staff Plantation Gen. Hosp., 1973-78, vice chief staff, 1975-77, chief staff, 1977—. Diplomate Am. Bd. Internal Medicine. Fellow Am. Coll. Cardiology, Am. Coll. Angiology, Am. Coll. Chest Physicians, A.C.P.; mem. Fla. Med. Assn., Broward County Med. Assn., AMA, Caducean Soc. Contbr. articles to med. jours. Office: 4101 S Hospital Dr Suite 11 Plantation FL 33317

MAYTON, JAMES LAMAR, JR., life ins. co. exec.; b. Carrabelle, Fla., Feb. 4, 1943; s. James Lamar and Mary Ann (Robison) M.; B.S., Fla. State U., 1965; m. Patricia Ann Averhart, June 14, 1969; children—James Lamar III, Rebecca Denise. With Liberty Nat. Life Ins. Co., Birmingham, Ala., 1966—, asst. comptroller, 1974, asso. comptroller, 1975-77, 2d v.p.-accounting, 1977—. Mem. Fin. Execs. Inst., Nat. Assn. Accountants. Republican. Methodist. Home: 5225 Beacon Dr Birmingham AL 35210 Office: PO Box 2612 Birmingham AL 35202

MAZZARULLI, DONALD JOHN, hosp. exec.; b. Camden, N.J., Dec. 12, 1949; s. Anthony Gabriel and Rose Ann (Ferranti) M.; B.S., U. Notre Dame, 1971; M.S., Ohio State U., 1973; m. Judi Kay Ross, June 9, 1973; 1 dau., Melissa. Research asso. Ohio State U., 1971-73; asso. v.p. Cleve. Met. Gen. Hosp., 1973-78; asso. exec. dir. Suburban Hosp., Humana Inc., Louisville, 1978—; adj. prof. bus. Urbana Coll. Mem. Am. Coll. Hosp. Adminstrs., Am. Hosp. Assn. Republican. Roman Catholic. Office: 4001 Dutchmans Ln Louisville KY 40207

MAZZEO, DANIEL PATRICK, navy officer; b. Bklyn., Apr. 18, 1949; s. Gennaro John and Marie Grace (Mazzei) M.; B.S. in Aerospace Engring., Poly. Inst. N.Y., 1971; m. Belva Faye Musick, Sept. 10, 1977. Commd. ensign U.S. Navy, 1971, advanced through grades to lt. comdr., 1980, designated aviator, 1973; project mgr. research and devel. Naval Air Systems Command, Washington, 1973-75; jet flight instr. VT-23, Naval Air Sta., Kingsville, Tex., 1975-77; aircraft comdr. VR-1, Naval Air Sta., Norfolk, Va., 1977-78, VIP transport aircraft comdr. VRC-40, 1978—; tchr. aeronautics Naval Air Systems Sch. Command, Pensacola, Fla., 1972. Recipient numerous awards in field; Sci. grantee Am. Inst., N.Y.C., 1973; rated airline transport pilot. Mem. AIAA, U.S. Naval Inst., Nat. Pilots Assn., Internat. Platform Assn., Tailhook Assn., Aircraft Owners and Pilots Assn. Roman Catholic. Contbr. numerous articles to profl. publs. Home: 2557 Torrey Pl Virginia Beach VA 23454 Office: VRC-40 Naval Air Sta Norfolk VA 23511

MAZZETTI, AUGUST LAWRENCE, govt. ofcl.; b. Aliquippa, Pa., Jan. 5, 1931; s. Carlo Mazzetti and Jean Mazzetti Wilson Ciccanti; B.S. in Engring., Geneva Coll., Beaver Falls, Pa., 1961; m. Elizabeth Gladys Stasny, Oct. 23, 1952; children—Lawrence Lee, Tamara Lynn. Designer, Am. Bridge div. U.S. Steel Co., Ambridge, Pa., 1954-62; sr. facilities project/lead engr. Minuteman/Apollo Space Projects Boeing Co., Cape Canaveral, Fla., 1962-70; supr. engring. services staff TVA, Knoxville, Tenn., 1971-79, chmn. standards bd. of div. engring. design, 1974-79, adminstrv. analyst, 1980—, chmn. mgmt. and planning activities of div., 1975-79, mem. TVA Speakers Bur., 1976-78, strategic planning com., 1979—. Chmn. com. for unification of Knoxville and Knox County govts., 1978. bd. dirs. Grandview Community Assn., 1977—, v.p., 1977-78, pres., 1978-80. Served with U.S. Army, 1952-54. Named to Apollo Saturn Honor Roll Smithsonian Instn., 1969. Mem. Nat. Mgmt. Assn. (public relations mgr.). Republican. Club: Toastmasters Internat. Home: 320 LeConte View Ln Knoxville TN 37920 Office: TVA 400 Commerce Ave Knoxville TN 37902

MAZZOLI, ROMANO LOUIS, congressman; b. Louisville, Nov. 2, 1932; B.S. in Bus. Adminstrn. magna cum laude, U. Notre Dame, 1954; J.D. with honors, U. Louisville, 1960; m. Helen Dillon, Aug. 1, 1959; children—Michael, Andrea. Admitted to Ky. bar, 1960; with law dept. L.&N. R.R., Louisville, 1960-62; pvt. practice law, Louisville, 1962-70; mem. 92d-96th congresses from 3d Ky. Dist.; lectr. bus. law Bellarmine Coll., Louisville, 1963-67. Mem. Ky. Senate, 1968-70. Named Outstanding Freshman Senator, 1968, Best Senator from a Pub. Standpoint, 1970 (both Capitol Press Club). Mem. Am., Ky., Louisville bar assns. Clubs: Notre Dame of Ky.; Notre Dame (Washington). Home: 939 Ardmore Dr Louisville KY 40217 Office: House Office Bldg Washington DC 20515

MC ADAMS, DONALD RAY, coll. adminstr.; b. Havana, Cuba, Mar. 3, 1941; s. Daniel Arthur and Ruth Marie (Gardner) McA.; B.A., Columbia Union Coll., 1963; M.A., Duke U., 1965, Ph.D., 1967; m. Donna Lee Tucker, June 3, 1963; children—Shaun Donald, Daniel Arthur. Mem. history faculty Andrews U., Berrien Springs, Mich., 1967-75, acting chmn. dept., 1974-75; pres. Southwestern Adventist Coll., Keene, Tex., 1975—; sec. Brandom Corp., Keene, 1978—. Bd. dirs. Huguley Meml. Hosp., Fort Worth, Tex., 1975—. NDEA fellow, 1963-67. Mem. Tex. Council of Church-Related Colls. and Univs. (pres. 1978-79), Ind. Colls. and Univs. of Tex. (chmn. public info. commn. 1979), Am. Hist. Assn. Seventh-day Adventist. Club: Rotary. Contbr. articles to profl. jours. Home: 218 Mistletoe St Keene TX 76059 Office: Southwestern Adventist Coll Keene TX 76059

MC ADAMS, HERBERT HALL, banker; b. Jonesboro, Ark., June 6, 1915; s. H.H. and Stella (Patrick) McA.; B.S., Northwestern U., 1937; postgrad. Harvard, 1937-38, Loyola U., Chgo., 1938-39; J.D., U. Ark., 1940; m. Shelia Wallace, Nov. 27, 1970; 1 dau., Nicole Patrick; children by previous marriage—Judith (Mrs. Walter A. DeRoeck), Sandra (Mrs. Robert C. Connor), Hall, Penny (Mrs. Timothy Hodges). Admitted to Ark. bar, 1940; chmn. bd., chief exec. officer Citizens Bank, Jonesboro, 1959—; dir. Ark. La. Gas Co., 1964-73, 76—; chmn. bd., chief exec. officer Union Nat. Bank, Little Rock, 1970—; dir. Fed. Res. Bank, Little Rock br., 1974-76. Mem. Ark. Indsl. Devel. Commn., 1965-72, chmn., 1967-72; mem. exec. com. Nat. Democratic Fin. Com., 1977—; trustee Baptist Med. Center System, 1975—; mem. Ark. Council on Econ. Edn., 1972—, Ark. Bapt. Med. Center System Real Estate Corp., 1977—; exec. com. of bd. govs. Ark. State Fair and Livestock Show Assn., 1975—, chmn., 1976—; chmn. bd. govs. Ark. State U. Found., 1977—; bd. visitors U. Ark., Little Rock, 1978—. Served with USNR, World War II. Decorated Purple Heart; recipient Top Mgmt. award Sales and Marketing Execs. Club, 1972. Mem. Am., Ark. bar assns., Am., Ark. bankers assns., Little Rock C. of C. Baptist. Clubs: Little Rock Country, Little Rock, Pleasant Valley Country, Capital, Rotary (Little Rock). Home: 47 Edgehill Rd Little Rock AR 72207 Office: 1 Union Nat Plaza Little Rock AR 72201 also Citizens Bank Bldg Jonesboro AR 72401

MC ADAMS, KELLY ROY, educator; b. Huntsville, Tex., Feb. 28, 1929; s. Kelly Edgar and Ina (Ogletree) McA.; B.Arch., U. Tex. at Austin, 1951, M.Arch., 1970; m. Nancy Carolyn Reeves, Aug. 12, 1950; 1 dau., Diana Claire. Asso. architect firm R. Gommel Roessner, Austin, 1954-60; prin. firm K.R. McAdams, Austin, 1960-62; staff architect firm Page Southerland Page, Austin, 1962-69; instr. dept. architecture U. Tex., Austin, 1969-71, asst. prof., 1971—; sec.-treas. Solenco Inc., Austin, 1979—. Bd. dirs. Austin Symphony Soc., 1966-69, McAdams Found., Goodwill Industries of Austin, 1977—. Mem. AIA, Tex. Soc. Architects, Constrn. Specification Inst., Assn. Computing Machinery, Nat. Guard Assn. Tex. (dir. 1968-71). Asso. editor: Military History of Texas and the Southwest, 1961. Home: 2607 Great Oaks Pkwy Austin TX 78756 Office: PO Box 7907 Austin TX 78712

MCADAMS, MONA LYNN, educator; b. Ft. Worth, Mar. 13, 1942; d. Jessie Lenoard and Helen (Houx) McDaniel; B.F.A., Tex. Christian U., 1964; M.E., Eastern N.Mex. U., 1975; 1 dau., Melissa Lynn. Tchr., Tech. High Sch., Ft. Worth, 1964-66, Goddard Jr. High Sch., Midland, Tex., 1966-67, Mackenzie Jr. High Sch., Lubbock, Tex., 1967-68, Clovis (N.Mex.) High Sch., 1973-78, Diamond Hill High Sch., Ft. Worth, 1978—; instr. Eastern N.Mex. U., 1977-78. Bd. dirs. Clovis-Portales Arts Council, 1974-75; mem. Friends of Clovis Carver Library, 1973-74. Mem. NEA, Internat. Platform Assn., Clovis Edn. Assn., Speech Communication Assn., Nat. Forensic League, Beta Sigma Phi. Democrat. Methodist. Clubs: Tex. Christian U. Century, Officer's Wives. Home: 8012 Llano Fort Worth TX 76116 Office: 1411 Maydell Fort Worth TX 76106

MCADOO, DAVID LEE, housing component co. exec.; b. Dallas, June 29, 1940; s. Curtis Lee and Mildred Maxine (Bruce) McA.; B.S. in Basic Engring., Southwestern U., Memphis, 1965; B.S. in Indsl. Engring., So. Methodist U., 1966; m. Linnea Anne Minch, Nov. 5, 1966. Line indsl. engr. Collins Radio Co., Dallas, 1965-67, indsl. engring. services mgr., 1967-69; mgmt./engring. cons. LWFW Inc., Dallas, 1969-72; div. mgr., chief engr. Timber Tech., Inc., Arlington, Tex., 1972-78; v.p. engring. Link-Wood Inc., Mansfield, Tex., 1978—. Registered profl. engr., Kans., Tenn., Mo., N.Mex., Ga., Tex., Okla., La., Ark., Ala. Mem. Truss Plate Inst. Republican. Presbyterian. Co-inventor force balance for measuring magnetic hysterisis and curie point in small rock samples. Office: 1703 N Peyco Dr Arlington TX 76017

MC ADOO, DONALD ELDRIDGE, artist; b. Chgo., Feb. 8, 1929; s. Frank Joseph and Marion Louise (Weigler) Kovarik; student pub. schs., Norfolk, Va.; m. Carolyn Westbrook, Oct. 20, 1970. Twenty-four one-man shows, 1969—; one man retrospective exhbn. A Brush with Realism toured 11 So. museums, 1972-74; exhibited in 48 group shows, 1966—, including Hudson Valley (N.Y.) Nat., 1966, Chrysler Mus., Norfolk, Va., 1967, Springfield (Mass.) Mus., 1966, Ball State U., 1969, Watercolor U.S.A. Springfield (Mo.) Mus., 1971-72, Nat. Acad. Galleries, N.Y.C., 1970, Tyler (Tex.) Mus., 1970, U. Okla., 1971, El Paso (Tex.) Mus., 1972; represented in permanent collections Va. Mus., Ga. Mus., Mint Mus., Columbia (S.C.) Mus., Mobile (Ala.) Art Mus., Columbus (Ga.) Mus., Mus. Art and Sci., Macon, Ga., Birmingham (Ala.) Mus., Springfield (Mo.) Mus.; tutor, lectr. to art groups, since 1972—; judge art exhbns., 1968—. Recipient numerous awards for paintings and drawings. Mem. Watercolor Soc. La., Watercolor Soc. Ala., Southeastern Center for Contemporary Arts, Nat. Audubon Soc. Roman Catholic. Co-author: Reflections of the Outer Banks, 1975. Home: 5070 Sunset Trail NE Marietta GA 30067

MC AFEE, CARRIE R. HAMPTON (MRS. JOSHUA O. MC AFEE), educator; b. Galveston, Tex., Dec. 30, 1932; d. Tom and Daisy (Charlton) Hampton; B.A., Tex. So. U., 1952, M.A., 1963; postgrad. Lincoln U., 1958, Columbia, 1960, U. Calif. at Berkeley, 1964; m. Joshua O. Mc Afee, July 31, 1964; children—Rhonda Maria, Roy Bernard. Tchr., Houston Ind. Sch. Dist., 1953-65, counselor, 1965-68, vice prin., 1968-74, prin., 1974—. Counselor, Neighborhood Youth Corps, 1969—; vol. nurses aid ARC, 1964—; active YWCA; bd. dirs. San Jacinto Lung Assn., 1977—; Recipient Outstanding Alumni award Tex. So. U., 1975, Profl. award Houston League of Nat. Assn. Bus. and Profl. Women, 1976, Gov.'s Yellow Rose of Tex. award, 1976. Mem. Am. Personnel and Guidance Assn., Am. Assn. Sex Edn. and Counselors, Nat. Assn. Women Deans, Assn. Supervision and Curriculum Devel., Tex. Tchrs. Assn., Tex. Houston assns. supervision and curriculum devel., Houston Sch. Adminstrs. Assn., Am. Bridge Assn. (dir.), Am. Contract Bridge League, Nat., Tex. (adv. bd. dirs. 1976—, Distinguished Service award 1977) assns. secondary sch. prins., Nat. Assn. Female Execs., Zeta Phi Beta. Roman Catholic. Home: 3618 S MacGregor Way Houston TX 77021 Office: 13719 White Heather St Houston TX 77045

MC AFEE, ELWIN RAY, chemist; b. Huntington, Ind., Sept. 23, 1945; s. Frederick and Miriam Angeline B. McA. B.A., Ball State U., 1967; M.S. in Phys. Chemistry, Iowa State U., 1970; m. Patricia Bledsoe, Aug. 5, 1978; children—Erick R., Todd R.; stepchildren—Helen J. Bledsoe, John T.W. Bledsoe. Med. technologist dept. pathology Mercy Hosp., Des Moines, 1968-70; research asst. Inst. Atomic Research, Iowa State U., 1970; research chemist Organic div. Monsanto Co., Sauget, Ill., 1970; microchem. technician Jewish Hosp., St. Louis, 1970; clin. chemist trainee St. Louis U. Hosp., 1970-71; methods devel. research chemist Verona Dyestuff Corp., Charleston, S.C., 1971-73; prodn. control lab. supr. Mobay Chem. Corp., Charleston, 1973—. Jr. Achievement adv., Charleston, 1976-77. Served alt. mil. duty, 1969-70. Hon. Music scholar Ball State U., 1963. Mem. Am. Chem. Soc., Am. Inst. Chemists. Quaker-Unitarian. Club: Avondale Civic (pres. 1980—). Home: 2 Riverdale Dr Charleston SC 29407 Office: Mobay Chem Corp PO Box 10288 Charleston SC 29411

MC ALISTER, GARY LEE, real estate broker; b. Spruce Pine, N.C., June 4, 1939; s. Earl Andrew and Helen Ethel (Robinson) McA.; student Newport News Shipbldg. and Dry Dock Co. Apprentice Sch., 1957-61; grad. Grad. Realtors Inst., U. Va., 1965; m. Dorothy Louise Keatts, June 11, 1960; children—Laura Lynne, Lisa Anne. Salesman, Carpenter Bros. Real Estate Co., Newport News, 1962-64; sales mgr. Williams Realty, Inc., Newport News, 1964-65; sales mgr., owner McAllister Custom Homes, Newport News, 1963-65; comml. and investment sales McAlister Realty Ltd., Newport News, 1966; comml. and investment mgr. Teagle Realty, Inc., Newport News, 1967-70, v.p., gen. mgr., dir., 1971—. Mem. Newport News-Hampton Bd. Realtors, Gloucester, Mathews, Middlesex Bd. Realtors, Williamsburg Bd. Realtors, Va. Assn. Realtors, Nat. Assn. Realtors, Realtors Nat. Mktg. Inst., Realtors Farm Land Inst. Home: 233 James River Dr Newport News VA 23601 Office: 12284 Warwick Blvd Newport News VA 23606

MC ALLISTER, WALTER WILLIAMS, savs. and loan exec.; b. San Antonio, Mar. 26, 1889; s. Frank Williams and Lena (Stumberg) McA.; E.E., U. Tex., 1910; m. Leonora Alexander, Mar. 26, 1913 (dec. May 1969); children—Elizabeth (Mrs. O. J. Solcher, Jr.), Walter Williams, Gerald N. Chmn. exec. com. San Antonio Savs. Assn., 1921—, South States Oil Co., San Antonio, 1961—; mayor City of San Antonio, 1961-71. Chmn., Fed. Home Loan Bank Bd., Washington, 1953-56. Pres. Tex. Municipal League, 1965; mem. San Antonio River Beautification Commn., 1933, Tex. Finance Commn., 1952-53; hon. co-chmn. Hemis Fair; commr. Urban Renewal Agy. Bd. dirs. Research and Planning Council, Ednl. TV, Channel 9, Austin; chmn. bd. dirs. Witte Mus., 1952-53; trustee Internat. Union Bldg. Socs. and Savs. and Loan Assn.; pres. bd. trustees San Antonio Union Jr. Coll., 1945-60. Recipient Golden Deeds award San Antonio Exchange Club, 1956; Outstanding Citizen award San Antonio Council of Presidents, 1964. Mem. U.S. (mem. legislative com., past pres.), Southwestern (past pres.), Tex. (past pres.) savs. and loan leagues, San Antonio C. of C. (past pres.). Mason (33 deg., Shriner), Kiwanian (past pres. San Antonio). Clubs: Argyle; San Antonio Country. Home: 103 Bushnell Pl San Antonio TX 78212 Office: PO Box 1810 San Antonio TX 78296

MC ALLISTER, WILLIAM ALEXANDER, JR., mktg. co. exec.; b. Phila., Oct. 30, 1928; s. William Alexander and Evelyn Eunice (Kidd) McA.; ed. pub. schs.; m. Jean Carol Dungan, Apr. 22, 1950; children—Martha Jill, Margaret Louise, William Alexander III. Pres., Delaware Asbesto & Rubber Co., Phila., 1946—, Darco So., Inc., Independence, Va., 1976—, McAllister Mktg. Inc., Independence, 1977—. Mem. Am. Arbitration Assn. (arbitrator 1973—), Fluid Sealing Assn. Republican. Methodist. Clubs: Whitemarsh Valley Country, New River Country. Home: PO Box 276 Independence VA 24348 Office: PO Box 454 Independence VA 24348

MCALPINE, CATHERINE ANDERSON, speech clinician; b. Cissna Park, Ill., Mar. 18, 1909; d. Patrick John and Exira Anna (Cameron) Anderson; B.S., S.W. Tex. State U., San Marcos, 1958; m. Gwyn Beaumont McAlpine, Mar. 23, 1929; children—Patricia Ann, John Gwyn. Tchr. elementary grades Victoria (Tex.) Ind. Schs., 1953-58, itinerant speech clinician, 1958-74; speech clinician Victoria Home Health Agy., 1974-80, also Tex. Rehab. Commn., Victoria, 1979—; pvt. practice speech pathology Victoria, 1963-80. Chmn. projects, mem. adv. bd. Victoria Home Health Agy., 1974-79. Mem. Am. Speech and Hearing Assn. (basic clin. cert. speech, cert. clin. competence speech pathology), Victoria (Tex.) Ret. Tchrs. Assn. (chmn. community affairs 1977-78), Nat. Ret. Tchrs. Assn., Tex. Speech and Hearing Assn., Golden Crescent Porcelain Art Club, N. Bon Aire Garden Club, Contract Bridge Club, Phi Sigma Alpha (pres. Tex. Epsilon Iota chpt. 1975-77; Woman of Year 1976-77). Roman Catholic. Home: 1902 E Red River St Victoria TX 77901

MC AMIS, JACK BRUMLEY, JR., advt. agy. exec.; b. Loudon County, Tenn., Sept. 23, 1949; s. Jack Brumley and Daphna Paulene (Malone) McA.; student Freed Hardeman Coll., Henderson, Tenn., 1967-69, U. Tenn., Knoxville, 1969-70; m. Carol Naomi Lloyd, Mar. 14, 1970; 1 dau., Allison Arlene. Lead singer various mus. combos, 1967-76; mgr. trainee group sales Millers Inc., dept. store, Knoxville, 1969-70; gen. store mgr., entertainer Fairfield Glade Resort, Crossville, Tenn., 1972-73; account exec. advt. Sta. WOKI-FM, Oak Ridge, 1973-78; dir.-gen. mgr. So. Mktg. Inc., Knoxville, 1978—. Recipient award Tri Cities Metro Advt. Fedn., 1979. Mem. Greater Knoxville Ad Club, Tri Cities Metro Advt. Fedn. Republican. Mem. Ch. of Christ. Home: 110 Townsend Rd Oak Ridge TN 37830 Office: So Mktg Inc 6408 Papermill Rd Knoxville TN 37919

MC ANDREWS, PATRICK JOSEPH, city ofcl.; b. Omaha, Oct. 18, 1954; s. Thomas Patrick and Kathryn Anne (Degan) McA.; student media arts advt., Tidewater Community Coll., 1974-75, student fire sci., 1977—. With sta. WQRK, Norfolk, Va., 1973-74; firefighter Virginia Beach, Va., 1974-79, fire marshall City of Virginia Beach, 1979—; part time disc jockey. Vol. sgt. rescue squadsman, 1976-77; lifeguard Ocean Rescue of Virginia Beach, summers 1977-79. Cert. state fire edn. instr. Mem. Fire Marshalls Assn. N. Am., Nat. Fire Protection Assn., Va. Record Pool Assn. Roman Catholic. Home: 5716 Bannock Rd Virginia Beach VA 23462 Office: 3610 S Plaza Trail Virginia Beach VA 23452

MC ANINCH, ROBERT DANFORD, educator; b. Wheeling, W.Va., May 21, 1942; s. Robert Danford and Dorothy Elizabeth (Goudy) McA.; A.B., West Liberty State Coll., 1969; M.A., W.Va. U., 1970; M.A., Morehead State U., 1975; postgrad. U. Hawaii; m. Linda Lou Strawderman, Aug. 23, 1975; children—Robert Michael, Christopher Funkhouser. Engring. technician Hydro-Space Research, Inc., Rockville, Md., 1965-66; asso. prof. govt., philosophy Prestonsburg (Ky.) Community Coll., 1970—; dir. Chase-Options, Inc., Calico Corner, Inc. Bd. dirs. Big Sandy Area Community Action Program, Inc., 1973-76; chmn. Floyd County Solid Waste, Inc. Served with AUS, 1962-65. Recipient Great Tchr. award Prestonsburg Community Coll., 1971; named Ky. col., 1977. Mem. Am. Polit. Sci. Assn., Am. Philos. Soc. Ky. Philosophy Assn., Ky. Assn. Colls. and Jr. Colls. Home: Bert Combs Dr Prestonsburg KY 41653

MC ANULTY, BEUNA MAURICE, educator; b. Taylor, Tex., Feb. 18, 1942; d. B.B. and Mary E. (Goff) McA.; B.S. in Edn., Tex. Woman's U., 1965, M.A. in Drama and Tech. Theatre, 1971. Tchr., LaGrange (Tex.) Public Schs., 1965-66, Huto (Tex.) Ind. Sch. Dist., 1966-69; remedial tchr. for mentally retarded students, Florence, Tex., 1971-72; with Point Summer Theatre, Ingram, Tex., summers 1972, 73; faculty Sam Houston State U., Huntsville, Tex., 1972-73; asst. prof. drama and speech, tech. dir. theatre Tarrant County Jr. Coll., Ft. Worth, 1973—; theatre cons. Cedar Valley Coll., Lancaster, Tex., 1976. Recipient Spl. Faculty award for contbns. in all areas of theatre Tex. Woman's U., 1971; Prodn. award Point Summer Theatre, 1973; 5 Yr. Service award Tarrant County Jr. Coll. Dist., 1978. Mem. Tex. Ednl. Theatre Assn. (public relations com. 1979—), Am. Theatre Assn. Children's Theatre Conf., Tex. State Jr. Coll. Tchrs. Assn., Puppeteers of Am., Lone Star Puppet Guild, Hill County Arts Found. Methodist. Club: Rainbow Girls. Contbr. articles to profl. jours.; photographer for books: The Donkey and Mule as a Backyard Pet (Paul and Betsy Hutchins), 1976; The Modern Mule (Paul and Betsy Hutchins), 1978; ofcl. photographer Nat. Am. Donkey and Mule Show, 1978. Home: 3220 Appomattox Dr Fort Worth TX 76119 Office: Drama 155 Tarrant County Jr Coll 5300 Campus Dr Fort Worth TX 76119

MC ANULTY, MARY CATHERINE CRAMER (MRS. CHARLES GILBERT MCANULTY), ret. educator; b. Braddock, Pa., June 26, 1908; d. Albert R. and Sara (Kelly) Cramer; A.B., Fla. So. Coll., 1929; M.A., Tchrs. Coll. Columbia, 1937; postgrad. Fla. State U., 1946-50; m. Charles Gilbert McAnulty, Dec. 25, 1937. Elementary tchr. Lake Ann Sch., Lake Garfield, Fla., 1930-31, elementary prin., 1932-34; prin. South Winter Haven Elementary Sch., Winter Haven, Fla., 1935-55; adminstrv. asst. to supervising prin. Winter Haven Area Schs., 1956-60; prin. Fred Garner Elementary Sch., Winter Haven, 1961-68, Lake Alfred Elementary Sch., 1969-70. Asst. chmn. vols., asst. tng. chmn., local chpt. ARC, 1967-68, 2d v.p., also chmn. vols., 1969-70, bd. mem., chmn. service to mil. families, 1970-71, chmn. coll. youth, 1971-72; v.p. Beymer United Methodist Women, 1973, 74, 75, pres., 1976, 77; pres. Lake Region Extension Homemaker's Club, 1974, 75. Mem. Am. Assn. Supervision and Curriculum Devel., Internat. Reading Assn. (Polk County chmn.), NEA, Fla. Edn. Assn. (dir. dept. elementary sch. prins. 1965-67), Polk County Elementary Prins. Assn. (sec.), League Women Voters (local dir. 1962), AAUW (local br. chmn. status women com. 1963), D.A.R. (chpt. treas. 1967-68, historian 1969-70, regent 1970-72, state chmn. jr. Am. citizens 1972—, dir. dist. VI 1973-74), Fla. So. Coll. Alumni Assn. (sec.), Internat. Platform Assn., P.E.O. (chpt. treas. 1970-74, chaplain 1976, 77, chpt. pres. 1978-79), Pi Gamma Mu, Delta Kappa Gamma (State Achievement award 1964, Fla. pres. 1962-63, chpt. parliamentarian 1968-73, pres., v.p., treas.). Methodist (choir mem. chmn. commn. edn. 1959-60, supt. study program 1969-70, organist 1970-77, pres. Wesley fellowship class 1972-73, chmn. adminstrv. bd. 1980, lay del. ann. conf. 1978, 79). Clubs: Pilot (charter, pres. 1954-55, 61-62), Poinsettia Garden (sec.), Winter Haven Woman's (edn. chmn. 1967-68). Home: 333 W Lake Howard Dr Apt 104D Winter Haven FL 33880

MC ATEE, JEAN FELKEL KINCHEN, nurse; b. Buffalo, Okla., Jan. 18, 1934; d. Harry Eugene and Hilma Alma (Husted) Felkel; B.S. in Nursing, Tex. Christian U., 1957; m. Calvin W. Kinchen, Nov. 26, 1956 (dec.); 1 son, Michael William; m. 2d, Tom E. McAtee, Sept. 1, 1979. Supr. operating room Nix Hosp., San Antonio, 1957; evening supr. Hillandale Hosp., Killeen, Tex., 1957-59; evening supr. labor and delivery services Harris Hosp., Ft. Worth, 1959-61; Ob-Gyn nurse specialist Ft. Worth Woman's Clinic, 1961-66; staff nurse Victoria Pub. Hosp., Fredericton, N.B., Can., 1966-67; dir. nursing Union Meml. Hosp., El Dorado, Ark., 1967-73; primary health care Am. Sch., Kinshasa, Zaire, Africa, 1973-74; adminstrv. dir. nursing services Sparks Regional Med. Center, Ft. Smith, Ark., 1974-79; instr.-trainer Ark. Heart Assn. Lic. nursing home adminstr.; registered nurse, Ark, Tex. Mem. Am. Nurses Assn., Ark. Hosp. Assn., Am. Soc. Hosp. Nursing Service Adminstrs., Gamma Xi, Sigma Theta Tau. Home: 3213 Stratford Pearland TX 77581

MC AULEY, SARAH LONGLEY, psychologist, univ. adminstr.; b. Batesville, Ark., Nov. 21, 1933; d. Nelson Alexander and Ernestine (Smith) Longley; B.A., Ark. Coll., 1954; M.S., U. Central Ark., 1971; postgrad. U. Ark.; 1 son by former marriage, Steven. Tchr. pub. schs. North Little Rock (Ark.) Sch. Dist., 1956-58; tchr. Pulaski County (Ark.) Schs., 1961-70; asst. prof. psychology, counseling, also dir. instl. testing U. Central Ark., Conway, 1971—. Lic. psychol. examiner. Mem. Am., Ark. personnel and guidance assns., Am., Ark. sch. counselors assns., Am., Ark. measurement and evaluation in guidance assns., Ark. Psychol. Assn., Ark. Assn. Counselor Educators and Suprs., AAUW, Delta Kappa Gamma, Sigma Alpha Iota, Phi Delta Kappa. Methodist. Home: 1521 South Blvd Conway AR 72032 Office: U Central Ark Box 918 Conway AR 72032

MC AULEY, VAN ALFON, aerospace mathematician, physicist; b. Travelers Rest, S.C., Aug. 28, 1926; s. Stephen Floyd and Emily Floree (Cox) McA.; student Mars Hill Coll., 1943-44; B.A., U. N.C., 1951; postgrad. U. Ala., Huntsville, 1956-57, 60-63. Mathematician, Army Ballistic Missile Agy., Huntsville, 1956-59; physicist in guidance and control div. NASA-Marshall Space Flight Center, Huntsville, 1960-61, research mathematician in astrionics lab., 1962-70, mathematician in computation lab., 1970—. Served with U.S. Army, 1944-46. Recipient Apollo Achievement award NASA, 1969, Skylab Achievement award, 1974, Certificate of Recognition, 1977; recipient Cost Savs. certificate Marshall Space Flight Center, 1973, Suggestion award, 1974, Outstanding Performance award, 1976. Mem. Phi Beta Kappa. Contbr. articles to profl. jours.; patentee breakthrough control invention; devised new methods of numerical analysis of heat flow equations. Home: 3529 Rosedale Dr Huntsville AL 35810 Office: AH33 Bldg 4663 Marshall Space Flight Center Huntsville AL 35812

MC BEE, J.D., dentist; b. Brady, Tex., July 26, 1932; s. Gussie Daymon and Julia M. (Carlson) McB.; student N. Tex. State Coll., 1949-52, 55-56; D.D.S., U. Tex., 1960; m. Ruth Junell Carlson, Jan.

26, 1952; children—Kay Lynn, Gregory Scott. Practice dentistry, Smithville, Tex., 1960—. Dental cons. Smithville Ind. Sch. Dist.; dir. Smithville Light and Water Dept. Alderman, Smithville, 1963-73. Chmn., Bastrop County Community Action, 1966-67. Trustee Smithville Ind. Sch. Dist., 1975-78, pres., 1977. Served with inf. AUS, 1952-54. Mem. Am., Tex., Tenth Dist. dental assns., C. of C. (dir. 1963-64). Baptist (deacon). Lion (pres. 1962-63). Home: 801 Whitehead St Smithville TX 78957 Office: 601 E 9th St Smithville TX 78957

MC BRAYER, ODELL LAVON, lawyer; b. Lakeview, Tex., Aug. 16, 1930; s. Odell Luke and Ola Lavada (Gregory) McB.; diploma Clarendon Jr. Coll., 1950; B.B.A., U. Tex. at Austin, 1957, J.D., 1958; m. Nelda Renae Morgan, Jan. 5, 1951; children—Scott Alan, Stacy Arlene. Admitted to Tex. bar, 1958; atty. King Fike, Dalhart, Tex., 1958-59, asso. atty. 1958-59; investigator Farmers' Ins. Group, Ft. Worth and Dallas, 1959-62; individual practice law, Ft. Worth, 1962—; city atty. Lakeside (Tex.), 1972-76; municipal judge; Lakeside, 1974-76; lectr. Tex. Alcohol Narcotics Edn., Inc., 1964—; dir. family counseling center, Ft. Worth, 1968—, Teen Challnge Center, Ft. Worth, 1978—. Pres. Union Gospel Mission, Ft. Worth, 1967-73, dir., 1962—; pres. Full Gospel Businessmen's Fellowship, Ft. Worth, 1966-76, Christian Fellowship, Inc., Ft. Worth, 1976—; candidate for Gov. Tex., 1974; precinct chmn., Ft. Worth, 1968—; candidate for dist. judge Tarrant County, 1978; elder Christ Ch. in Wedgewood, 1978—, also dir., tchr., counselor New Hope Singles; mem. Tex. Gov.'s Commn., 1979—. Served with USAF, 1951-55. Mem. Profl. Nat. Alliance for Family Life, Nat. Assn. Christian Marriage Counsellors, Tex., Am., Tarrant County bar assns. Republican. Episcopalian. Clubs: Civitan (editor Club News, Ft. Worth 1969-70; dir., v.p. 1968-71), Lions (treas. Dalhart 1958-59), White Settlement Jaycees (pres. 1961-62, sch. bd. 1960-61), Kiwanis, Men's Club, All Sts. Episcopal, Dist. 10 Senatorial. Contbr. articles in field to profl. jours. Home: 305 Lakeridge Rt Fort Worth TX 76108 Office: 1100 Texas St Fort Worth TX 76102

MC BRIDE, BEVERLEY BOOTH, psychologist; b. Richmond, Va., June 29, 1929; d. Edward Lee and Myrtle Grace (Woodlief) Booth; student Randolph-Macon Woman's Coll., 1949-51; B.S., Va. Commonwealth U., 1951, postgrad., 1951-53; M.S., Va. Poly. Inst. and State U., 1964; postgrad. Ohio U., 1969; m. John William McBride; children—John David, William Stephen, Philip Anthony, James Andrew. Staff psychologist Mountain Empire Guidance Clinic, Radford, Va., 1959-67, acting dir., 1963-65; cons. psychologist Greenbrier Valley Mental Health Clinic, Lewisburg, W.Va., 1964-70, chief psychologist, 1970—, clin. dir., 1976—; dir. clin. services Seneca Mental Health/Mental Retardation Council, 1979—; pvt. practice, Parkersburg, W.Va., 1967-69. Program cons. Headstart-Day Care Program, W. Central W.Va. Community Action Assn., Parkersburg, 1967-70, dir. counseling unit Manpower Program, 1968-70; faculty Radford Coll., 1962-64, W.Va. U., Parkersburg, 1968-70; cons. psychologist Div. Vocational Rehab., Richmond Area, 1953-58, Monroe County Bd. Edn., Union, W.Va., 1965-68, Greenbrier County Bd. Edn., Lewisburg, 1965-72, Monroe County Mental Health Clinic, Union, W.Va., 1970-73. Chmn. fine arts com. Radford Jr. Woman's Club, 1960-61, program chmn., 1961-62, v.p., 1962-63, pres., 1963-64; mem. Gov.'s Study Commn. on Youth, 1962-63, Gov.'s Study Commn. on Mental Health, 1964-65; chmn. Multicounty Interagy. Council, Radford, 1963-64; mem. Parkersburg Fine Arts Center, 1967-70; chmn. conservation dept. Parkersburg Woman's Club, 1968-69; mem. advisory bd. Radford Fine Arts Council, 1963-65, Greenbrier Tng. Center, 1973-75. Mem. Nat. (del. 1971-73), W.Va. (pres. 1975-76) assns. sch. psychologists, W.Va. Psychol. Assn., Assn. Psychiat. Outpatient Centers Am. President-elect, 1979-80 (sec. 1975-78), Assn. Rural Mental Health vice chairman, 1978-80 (bd. 1977-81). Episcopalian. Home: 409 E Washington St Lewisburg WV 24901 Office: 100 Church St Lewisburg WV 24901

MCBRIDE, JAMES SULLIVAN, advt. agy. exec.; b. Cleve., Sept. 13, 1951; s. Lawrence Gordon and Lois Jane McB.; B.S., Slippery Rock State Coll., 1973. Staff announcer WEDA-FM, Grove City, Pa., 1974; mktg. mgr. Gateway Mktg. Service, Pitts., 1974-76; account exec. MARC & Co., Inc., Pitts., 1976-78; account exec./office mgr. Fahlgren & Ferriss, Inc., Lexington, Ky., 1978—; guest lectr. advt. Carnegie Mellon U., 1977-78. Mem. Sales and Mktg. Execs. of Lexington, Lexington C. of C. Republican. Roman Catholic. Club: Lexington Advertising. Office: Fahlgren & Ferriss Inc Suite 2-B 120 Kentucky Ave Lexington KY 40502

MC BRIDE, MICHAEL HANSON, educator; b. Abilene, Tex., Nov. 23, 1944; s. Homer Hanson and Mary Margaret (Farnsworth) McB.; A.A., San Angelo Coll., 1965, B.A., 1967; M.A., Tex. Tech. U., 1973, Ed.D., 1979; 1 dau., Michelle Elaine. Staff writer San Angelo (Tex.) Standard-Times, 1966-67; tchr. Lake View High Sch., San Angelo Ind. Sch. Dist., 1967-73; asso. prof. journalism, dept. chmn. Western Tex. Coll., Snyder, 1973—. Recipient Edith Fox King award, 1972; merit award for journalism teaching profession Tex., 1973; summer grantee Clark Found., 1969, Tex. PTA, 1973; winner 1st place Pineywoods Writers Conf., 1967. Mem. Nat. Council Coll. Publs. Advisors (state chmn., conv. speaker 1977), Community Coll. Journalism Assn., Assn. Edn. in Journalism, Tex. Intercollegiate Press Advisers Assn. (pres. Tex.), Phi Delta Kappa, Phi Kappa Phi, Scurry County Poetry Soc. Republican. Methodist. Author poetry: Silhouettes of Sincerity, 1969; editor 2 edits. description guides to Tex. colls. and univs., 1975, 79; co-editor, sports editor coll. newspaper, 1965-67; copy editor Pensador; contbr. articles and poems to publs. Home: PO Box 561 Snyder TX 79549 Office: Western Texas College Snyder TX 79549

MCBRIER, ELIZABETH, speech-lang. pathologist: b. Leeds, Ala., Nov. 17, 1954: d. James Earl and Mary Nelle McB.; B.A., U. Ala., 1976; M.S., Fla. State U., 1978. Speech-lang. pathologist intern Tallahassee (Fla.) Meml. Hosp. Extended Care Facility, 1978; speech-lang. pathologist Severly Impaired Lang. Class, Brevard County, Fla., 1978-79; speech-lang. pathologist, Fulton County, Atlanta, 1979—. Mem. Am. Speech, Lang. and Hearing Assn., Ga. Speech, Lang. and Hearing Assn. Methodist. Club: Civitan. Home: 8302 Glenwoods Terr Riverdale GA 30274 Office: 2370 Union Rd SW Atlanta GA 30315

MC BROOM, MICHAEL JOHN, state ofcl.; b. Canyon, Tex., Mar. 4, 1948; s. Johnnie Henry and Nettie Odell (Russell) McB.; B.S. in Biology, W. Tex. State U., 1971; doctoral candidate E. Tex. State U., 1974—; m. Joyce Ann Hoover, 1968; children—Michael John II, Jennifer Caley, Timothy Ethan. Grad. teaching asst. biology W. Tex. State U., 1971; dir. staff devel. Tex. Dept. Mental Health and Mental Retardation, Terrell (Tex.) State Hosp., 1976—; project dir. HEW grant. Youth soccer coach. Served to capt. M.S.C., AUS, 1971-73. Decorated Army Commendation Medal; recipient Rotary award, 1966, Danforth award, 1966; named Disting. Mil. Student, U.S. Army, 1968; biology research aide Dept. of Interior, 1968-69. Mem. Dallas Psychol. Assn., Am. Psychol. Assn., Intergovtl. Tng. Council Dallas and Ft. Worth, Lake Highlands Soccer Assn. Home: 9921 Robin Hill Ln Dallas TX 75238 Office: Terrell State Hospital PO Box 70 Terrell TX 75160

MC BURNEY, MILLARD LYLE, educator; b. Athens, Tex., Mar. 10, 1939; s. Millard Jennings and Rinner Mae (Adams) McB.; B.S., E. Tex. State U., 1961, M.S., 1963; m. Ruth Evelyn Percefull, Aug. 13, 1971. Instr. biology Henderson (Ark.) State Tchrs. Coll., 1966-70, asst. prof., 1970-78, asso. prof. Henderson State U., 1978—. Mem. Beta Beta Beta, Sigma Phi Epsilon. Democrat. Methodist. Co-author: Laboratory Exercises in General Biology, 1979. Home: 43 Oakbrook Dr Alexander AR 72002 Office: Henderson State U Box H-1951 Arkadelphia AR 71923

MC CABE, JOHN FRANCIS, pathologist; b. N.Y.C., Dec. 25, 1917; s. Patrick Bernard and Nora Agnes (Murphy) McC.; A.B., Fordham Coll., 1939; M.D., N.Y. U., 1943; m. Margaret E. Bradley, June 24, 1947; children—Patricia Steen, Lily Withrow. Intern U.S. Naval Hosp., Bklyn., 1943-44; resident U.S. Naval Hosp., Phila., 1954-58; commd. lt. (j.g.) U.S. Navy, 1943, advanced through grades to capt., 1964; chief of pathology U.S. Naval Hosp., Phila., 1957; chief pathology U.S. Naval Hosp., Portsmouth, Va., 1958-64; ret., 1964; chief pathology Maryview Hosp., Portsmouth, 1964-74; pathologist Milford (Del.) Meml. Hosp., 1974—. Decorated Bronze star. Fellow Am. Coll. Pathologists; mem. A.M.A., Am. Soc. Clin. Pathologists, Am. Assn. Blood Banks. Lions. Home: 542 S Atlantic Ave Virginia Beach VA 23451

MC CAFFITY, CURTIS LEE, disposal service co. exec.; b. Ft. Worth, Mar. 9, 1934; s. Homer Lee and Vera Mae (Hardisty) McC.; student U. Tex., Arlington, 1962; m. Clara Ruth Wickersham, June 15, 1951 (div.); children—Robert Douglas, Connie Ruth, Sue Ellen. With prodn. control dept. Chance Vought, Grand Prairie, Tex., 1951-54, Gen. Motors, Arlington, Tex., 1954-55, Bell Aircraft, Hurst, Tex., 1955-57; pres. McCaffity Disposal Service, Inc., Bedford, Tex., 1957—, Tarrant County Waste Disposal Inc., Bedford, 1966—; v.p., So. Disposal Inc., Greenville, Tex.; pres., City Garbage Service, Bedford, McCaffity Enterprises Inc., Cleburne, Tex.; owner, McCaffity Farms, Cleburne, Mem. Hurst Euless Bedford C. of C., Nat. Solid Waste Mgmt. Assn., Am. Quarter Horse Assn., Am. Simmental Assn., Tex. Simmental Assn. Republican. Baptist. Clubs: Lions (pres. Bedford club 1961-62), Masons. Home: Route 2 Box 85B Cleburne TX 76031 Office: 2400 Bedford Rd PO Box 98 Bedford TX 76021

MC CAFFREY, JOSEPH EDWIN, paper co. exec.; b. Savannah, Ga., Feb. 27, 1930; s. Joseph Edwin and Ruby Elizabeth (Johnston) McC.; A.A. in Sci., Belmont Abbey Coll., Belmont, N.C., 1951; B.S. in Chemistry, Marquette U., 1953; B.S. in Pulp and Paper Tech., N.C. State U., 1955; postgrad. Ouachita U., 1968-72; M.S. in Counseling Psychology, Henderson State U., 1976, postgrad., 1976—; m. Betty Kimler, Apr. 25, 1953; children—Joseph, Patrick, Michael, Timothy, Shaun, Colleen. With Internat. Paper Co., 1955—, asst. tech. supt., Camden, Ark., 1965-69, supt. quality control, 1969-73, supt. tech. services, 1973-78, mgr. tech. and environ. services, 1978—. Asst. dist. commr. Des DeSota Area council Boy Scouts Am., ElDorado, Ark., 1969-70. Mem. Am. Personnel and Guidance Assn., Pulp and Paper Found., Phi Theta Kappa, Xi Sigma Pi. Republican. Roman Catholic. Clubs: K. C., Kiwanis. Home: 1112 Westwood Rd Camden AR 71701 Office: PO Box 2045 Cullendale Station Camden AR 71701

MC CAIN, GEORGE SPRUCE, owner ins. agy.; b. Denmark, S.C., Aug. 11, 1928; s. Herman Claude and Julia Margaret (Riley) McC.; B.S. in Gen. Bus., U. S.C., 1950; m. Kathryn Ann Rawl, Sept. 12, 1950; children—Richard Sterling, Kathryn Angela, Pamela Margaret. With H.C. McCain Agy., 1953-55, Robinson Realty Co., 1955-57, Comml. Bank & Trust Co., 1957-59; with Penn Mut. Life Ins. Co., 1959—, C.L.U., 1965—; owner, operator McCain & Assos., Columbia, S.C., 1959—; guest lectr. Sch. Law, U. S.C. Tchr. Sunday schs., past mem. fin. com., past bd. dirs. Trenholm Road Methodist Ch.; past pres. bd. Camellia Ball; vice chmn. adv. bd. visitors Mary Baldwin Coll., Staunton, Va.; mem. adv. bd. visitors Luth. Theol. Sem., Columbia. Served with USN, 1950-53. C.L.U. Mem. Nat. Assn. Life Underwriters, S.C. Assn. Life Underwriters, Columbia Assn. Underwriters, S.C. C.L.U. Soc. (past pres.), Columbia Estate Planning Council. Presbyterian. Club: Forest Lake Country. Home: 1393 Kathwood Rd Columbia SC 29206 Office: McCain & Assos 5-202 Calendar Ct Columbia SC 29206

MC CAIN, HAROLD DEAN, printing co. exec.; b. Yanceyville, N.C., July 14, 1938; s. Willie Bill and Pearl Virginia (Barts) M.; student E. Carolina Coll., 1957; m. Faye Cantrell, Jan. 5, 1957; children—Angela, Deana, Lisa. With Caswell Messenger, Yanceyville, 1959-69; owner, mgr. Womack Press., Danville, Va., 1969—. Mem. printing adv. bd. Danville Community Coll., 1971—. Recipient fine printing awards Printing Industries Va., 1973-80. Mem. Danville Printing Assn. (pres. 1974—), Caswell County Jr. C. of C. (pres. 1971-72), Nat. Assn. Printers and Lithographers, Printing Industries Va. Democrat. Baptist. Moose. Home: PO Box 294 Yanceyville NC 27379 Office: 525 Wilson St Danville VA 24541

MC CAIN, JIMMY WAYNE, aerospace engr.; b. Lineville, Ala., Oct. 3, 1950; s. Erdis and Edna Mildred (Carter) McC.; A.S., Gasden State Jr. Coll., 1971; B.A.E., Auburn U., 1973; M.A.S., U. Ala., 1976; m. Kerrilyn Jackson, June 8, 1973; children—John Wyatt, Scott Jackson. Asso. engr. program mgmt. Spartan Missile program Thiokol Corp., Huntsville, Ala., 1974, engr. advanced design sect., 1974-75, engr. igniter systems group, 1975-79; sr. design engr. in charge space shuttle and SRB flight evaluation United Space Boosters, Inc., Huntsville, 1979—. Cardiopulmonary resuscitation instr. Am. Heart Assn., Ala. affiliate, 1976-77. Engr. in training, Ala. Mem. Am. Inst. Aeros. and Astronautics (sec. Ala. sect. 1978—), ASME (young engr. of yr. award 1978), Huntsville Area Rocketry Assn. (pres.), Am. Radio Relay League, Thiokol Mgmt. Club (pres. 1977-78, past program chmn.). Designer safe and arm device and igniter for low cost lightweight missile system. Home: 11312 Crestfield RD SE Huntsville AL 35803 Office: United Space Boosters Inc Huntsville AL 35807

MC CAIN, MAURICE EDWARD, uniform co. exec.; b. Denver, Feb. 14, 1909; s. Thomas C. and Fannie (Burke) McC.; grad. high sch.; m. Florence Inez Snowden, Dec. 27, 1927 (dec. April 1978); m. 2d, Ruth Barnhill Hinkle. With McCain Tailoring Co., 1927-32; mgr. uniform dept. Yielding Bros., 1932-39; with McCain Uniform Co., Inc., Birmingham, Ala., 1939—, pres., 1954—; v.p., dir. Decatur (Ala.) Transit Trucklines, 1954-61; chmn. bd. dirs. Banner Uniform Co., Atlanta, Macon, 1962-78; v.p., dir. Burke Uniform Co., Houston, 1967—. Trustee, Baptist Med. Centers, Birmingham, 1978—. Served with USAAF, 1943-45. Mem. Nat. Assn. Uniform Mfrs. (dir. 1965-78), Birmingham Traffic and Transp. Club, Birmingham Motor Truck Club, Aero Club, Pres.'s Forum of So. Bapt. Radio and TV Commn. Baptist. Clubs: City Salesmen's (pres. 1967-68, Man of Year 1977), Birmingham Aero, Masons, Shriners, Jesters, Vestavia Country, The Club, Downtown, Rotary, Relay House. Home: 3756 Locksley Dr Birmingham AL 35223 Office: 2208 3d Ave N Birmingham AL 35203

MC CAIN, MICHAEL BRYAN, assn. exec.; b. Topeka, Apr. 5, 1951; s. Jack Orrin and Dorothy Joan (Good) McC.; C.deA., U. Complutense Madrid (Spain), 1972; B.A., U. Ala. in Birmingham, 1973, 79; m. Carolyn Ann Massey, Dec. 8, 1972; children—Christopher Michael, Bryan Scott. Internat. rep. 1st Nat. Bank Birmingham, 1973-74; dir. area devel. Met. Devel. Bd. Birmingham, 1974-76; exec. dir. Etowah Expansion Assn. Inc., Gadsden, Ala., 1976—; cons. in field. Chmn. loaned execs. program United Givers Fund Gadsden, 1977—; adminstrv. officer CAP, 1977—; active A.R.C., Big Bros. Am.; mem. Ala. Gov.'s Youth Council, 1972—; mem. adv. com. for vocat. edn. Gadsden Concert Assn., promotion chmn., 1978. Mem. Am. Indsl. Devel. Council, Am. C. of C. Execs., So. Indsl. Devel. Council, Indsl. Developers Assn. Ala. (dir. 1979—), Ala. World Trade Assn., Gadsden Jaycees (publicity dir. 1977—), Godsden Metro C. of C. (exec. v.p. 1979—), Omicron Delta Kappa, Pi Kappa Alpha. Presbyterian. Kiwanian (chmn. internat. relations Gadsden 1976—). Clubs: Gadsden Quarterback; Mountain Top (bd. govs. 1979—). Editor: Birmingham, 1976; editor, pub.: Metropolitan Gadsden at a Glance, 1977. Home: 516 Country Club Dr Gadsden AL 35901 Office: PO Box 271 Gadsden AL 35902

MC CAIN, VIRGIL BOWDEN, JR., educator; b. Oneonta, Ala., Mar. 9, 1910; B.A., Birmingham-So. Coll., 1932; M.A. in Ednl. Adminstrn., U. Ala., 1934; postgrad. (Austin fellow) Harvard U., 1934-35; L.H.D. (hon.), Athens Coll., 1957; LL.D. (hon.), Jacksonville State U., 1973; m.; children—Bobby, Virgil, III. High sch. tchr., coach, Miss. and Ala., 1935-40; prin. Pine Level (Ala.) Schs., 1940-42, Pike Road (Ala.) High Sch., 1942-43; supt., bus. mgr. Meth. Children's Home, Selma, Ala., 1943-48; dean of men, chmn. edn. dept. Huntingdon Coll., Montgomery, Ala., 1948-51; pres. Snead Coll., Boaz, Ala., 1954-59, Athens (Ala.) Coll., 1959-65, Pershing Coll., Beatrice, Nebr., 1965-67, Snead State Jr. Coll., Boaz, 1967-78; pres. Ala. Assn. Ind. Colls., 1963-64. Bd. dirs. Good Samaritan Hosp., Selma, 1944-48; pres. So. Meth. Children's Home Workers, 1945-46; chmn. Limestone-Morgan County com. for planning and opening Calhoun State Jr. Coll., Decatur, Ala., 1959-65; chmn. bd. dirs. Emmanuel Brown Tng. Sch., 1952-64; del. Gen. Conf. Methodist Ch., 1960, 64; pres. Boaz United Fund, 1971; trustee, chmn. bd. stewards St. Paul Meth. Ch., Boaz, 1976-78. Named Man of Yr., Boaz, 1958, Athens, 1960; Virgil McCain Hall at Athens Coll. named in his honor, 1963; Virgil B. McCain Learning Resource Center at Snead State Jr. Coll. named in his honor, 1977.

MCCAIN, WILLIAM DAVID, ret. univ. pres.; b. Bellefontaine, Miss., Mar. 29, 1907; s. Samuel Woodward and Sarah Alda (Shaw) McC.; B.S., Delta State Coll., Cleveland, Miss., 1930; A.M., U. Miss., 1931; Ph.D., Duke U., 1935; Litt.D., Miss. Coll., 1967; m. Minnie Leicester Lenz, Oct. 3, 1931; children—William David, John Woodward (dec.), Patricia. Teaching fellow history U. Miss., 1930-31; head math. dept. East Central Jr. Coll., Decatur, Miss., 1931-32; head social sci. dept. Copiah-Lincoln Jr. Coll., Wesson, Miss., 1932-33; fellow history Duke U., 1933-35; historian Morristown (N.J.) Nat. Hist. Park, 1935; asst. archivist Nat. Archives, Washington, 1935-37; acting asso. prof. history U. Miss., summers 1942, 46, 47; lectr. history Millsaps Coll., 1941-42, 46-48; historian Miss. dept. V.F.W., 1946—; historian dept. Miss., Am. Legion, 1946-55; dir., sec. bd. trustees Miss. Dept. of Archives and History, 1938-55; pres. U. So. Miss., Hattiesburg, 1955-75, pres. emeritus, 1975—. Chmn. Miss. Library Commn., 1941-43, Miss. Hist. Commn., 1948-55; mem. Miss. Geol. Commn., 1938-55. Served as 1st lt. A.A.A., Coast Arty., AUS, 1943-45, 51-53; maj. gen. Res. Mem. Soc. Am. Archivists (founding, council 1939-44, pres. 1951-53), Miss. Hist. Soc., Miss. Library Assn. (pres. 1941-44), Miss. N.G. Assn., Alpha Tau Omega. Baptist. Author: The United States and the Republic of Panama, 1937; The Story of Jackson: A History of the Capitol of Mississippi, 1821-1951, 1953. Editor: Jour. Miss. History, 1939-56. Contbr. to jours. and newspapers. Address: Southern Sta Box 5164 Hattiesburg MS 39401

MC CALEB, FOSTER COLLINS, JR., physician; b. Shreveport, La., May 16, 1922; s. Foster Collins and Ottie Palmer (Powell) McC.; B.S., Tulane U., 1946, M.D., 1951; M.P.H., Johns Hopkins U., 1967; m. Jean Chrissinger, Mar. 28, 1954; children—Geoffrey Alan Ian, Katherine Blaine, Robert Gordon Bruce, Amy Powell. Commd. 1st lt. U.S. Army Med. Corps, 1951, advanced through grades to col., 1968, ret., 1973; intern Walter Reed Gen. Hosp., Washington, 1951-52, resident, 1954-55; dist. dir. Lowcountry Health Dist., S.C. Dept. Health and Environmental Control, Beaufort, S.C., 1973—. Served with AUS, 1942-46. Decorated Legion of Merit with oak leaf cluster, Bronze Star Medal, Army Commendation Medal; Meritorious Service Medal. Diplomate Am. Bd. Preventive Medicine. Fellow Am. Coll. Preventive Medicine, Royal Soc. Health; mem. Am., S.C. pub. health assns., Nu Sigma Nu, Phi Delta Theta. Episcopalian. Clubs: Royal Pines Country, Masons (Shriner). Home: Star Route 5 Box 218G Beaufort SC 29902 Office: PO Box 459 Beaufort SC 29902

MCCALEB, JOHN HENRY, real estate broker; b. Saline County, Ark., Feb. 17, 1934; s. William Harvey and Laura Mildred (McCright) McC.; B.S., U. Ark., 1956; m. Annette Woodard Watts, Oct. 23, 1962; children—Jonathan J., Suzanna E., Sarah L. Engr. U.S. Army C.E., Little Rock, 1958-65; owner John H. McCaleb Constrn. Inc., Little Rock, 1965—. Dir. Quadrangle Enterprises, Inc., Little Rock, 1971-77, Minerva Enterprises, Inc., Little Rock, 1971-77. Webelos scout leader, 1974-75; committeeman Pulaski County Republican Com., 1969-71. Served with USNR, 1956-58. Registered profl. engr., Ark. Mem. ASME, Ark. Mobile Home Park Owners, Operators and Dealers Assn. (dir. 1977), Pulaski County Property Owners Assn. (dir. 1976-77). Home and office: 4600 Annette Ln Little Rock AR 72206

MC CALL, CAROLYN MURPHY, speech pathologist; b. McAllen, Tex., Dec. 10, 1948; d. William Preston and Marjorie LaVonne (Porter) Murphy; B.S., Southwest Tex. State U., 1971; M.Ed., 1973; m. David L. McCall, Aug. 1, 1970; 1 dau., Megan Elizabeth. Speech pathologist Bapt. Meml. Hosp., San Antonio, 1973, Comal Ind. Sch. Dist., New Braunfels, Tex., 1973-74; instr., supr. Southwest Tex. State U., San Marcos, 1974—, dir. Speech, Hearing and Lang. Clinic, 1979—. Mem. Am. Speech-Hearing-Lang. Assn., Tex. Speech and Hearing Assn., Council Exceptional Children, Chi Omega. Baptist. Home: 125 E Sierra Circle San Marcos TX 78666 Office: Dept Spl Edn Southwest Tex State U San Marcos TX 78666

MC CALL, DANIEL THOMPSON, JR., ret. justice Supreme Ct. Ala.; b. Butler, Ala., Mar. 12, 1909; s. Daniel Thompson and Caroline (Bush) McC.; B.A., U. Ala., 1931, LL.B., 1933; m. Mary Edna Montgomery, Apr. 3, 1937; children—Mary Winston (Mrs. Rogers Neilson Laseter), Daniel Thompson III, Nancy (Mrs. John Worrell Poynor). Admitted to Ala. bar, 1933, U.S. Supreme Ct. bar; practiced in Mobile, 1933-60; partner firm Johnston, McCall & Johnston, 1943-60; circuit judge 13th Circuit, 1960-69; asso. justice Ala. Supreme Ct., Montgomery, 1969-75, ret., 1975; mem. Ala. Bd. Bar Commrs., 1957-60. Mem. Mobile County Bd. Sch. Commrs. 1950-56, 58-60; trustee Julius T. Wright Sch. for Girls, 1953-63; trustee U. Ala., nat. alumni pres., 1963. Served to lt. USNR, World War II. Recipient Dean's award U. Ala. Law Sch., 1974, Order of Jurisprudence Cumberland Law Sch., Julius T. Wright Sch. Disting. Service award, 1979. Mem. Am., Ala., Mobile County (past pres.) bar assns., Jr. Bar Assn. Ala. (past pres.), Am. Judges Assn., U. Ala. Law Sch. Found., Am. Judicature Soc., Inst. Jud. Adminstrn., Am. Trial Lawyers Assn., Farrah Law Soc., Nat. Hist. Assn., Ala. Hist. Soc., Ala. Wildlife Fedn., Navy League U.S., Am. Legion, 40 and 8, Mil. Order World Wars, SAR, Sons of Confederacy, Res. Officers Assn., St. Andrews Soc. Mid-South, U. Ala. Sch. Medicine Alumni Assn. (hon.), Sigma Nu,

Phi Delta Phi, Omicron Delta Kappa. Democrat. Episcopalian. Clubs: University (Tuscaloosa); Athelstan, Hickory Hill Hunting. Home: 2253 Ashland Place Ave Mobile AL 36607

MC CALL, JOHN CLARK, ednl. adminstr.; b. Vidalia, Ga., Sept. 6, 1949; s. John Clark and Carolyn Elizabeth (Kay) Mc C.; student U. Ga., 1967-69; Atlanta Sch. Art, 1969; B.A. in Journalism, Ga. State U., 1972. Social host Cloister Hotel, Sea Island, Ga., 1969; program coordinator dept. music Ga. State U., Atlanta, 1972-73, adminstrv. specialist, 1973-75, adminstrv. supr., 1975-76, asst. to dir., office acad. assistance and scheduling Coll. Arts Scis., 1977—; producer (with Eugene List) Keyboard Colossus, 1976. Mem. Save the Fox Theatre com. Atlanta Landmarks, Inc., 1974—; mem. Ga. State Gov.'s Honors Program, 1966. Mem. Am. Theatre Organ Soc., Nat. Trust for Hist. Preservation, Theatre Hist. Soc. Contbr. articles on Atlanta theatre history to profl. jours. Home: 1363 N Decatur Rd NE Atlanta GA 30306

MC CALL, ROBERT EDGAR, JR., surgeon; b. Marion, N.C., Sept. 28, 1911; s. Robert Edgar and Minnie Teleth (Peeler) M.; A.B., Davidson Coll., 1932; certificate in Medicine, U. N.C. Med. Sch., 1934; M.D., Jefferson Med. Coll., 1936; certificate in Otolaryngology, Harvard Med. Sch., 1939; certificate in Surgery, U. Pa., 1948; m. Miriam Joan Aley, Jan. 31, 1952; children—Elizabeth Sarah, Jane. Intern, Grad. Hosp., U. Pa., Phila., 1936-38, resident surgery, 1948-50; resident otolaryngology Mass. Eye and Ear Infirmary, Boston, 1939-41; resident surgery St. Luke's Hosp., Bethlehem, Pa., 1950-51; resident thoracic surgery Episcopal Hosp., Phila., 1951-52, Meml. Hosp., Charlotte, N.C., 1953-55; practice medicine specializing in otolaryngology, Charlotte, 1946-47, specializing in surgery, Kingsport, Tenn., 1952-53, 55-56; surgeon, dept. medicine and surgery VA Hosps., 1956-78; ret., 1978; instr. surgery Med. Coll. Ga., 1956-58, U. Kan. Sch. Medicine, 1958-59. Served with AUS, 1941-46; ETO; col. Res. Decorated Bronze Star medals. Diplomate Am. Bd. Otolaryngology, Am. Bd. Surgery, Am. Bd. Thoracic Surgery. Fellow A.C.S.; mem. Soc. Thoracic Surgeons, S.C. Surg. Soc., Southeastern Surg. Congress, Columbia Med. Soc., Scabbard and Blade, Ret. Officers Assn., Pi Kappa Alpha, Phi Chi. Presbyterian. Clubs: Spring Valley Country (Columbia). Contbr. articles to profl. jours. Home: 4 Tiftgreen Circle Columbia SC 29204

MC CALL, VICKI JO, counselor; b. Ft. Worth, Mar. 30, 1952; d. Forrest R. and Mildred D. McCall; B.A., Baylor U., 1972, M.S. in Spl. Edn. and Supervision, 1975. Tchr. learning disabilities Hill Elementary Sch., Arlington, Tex., 1973-76; tchr. emotionally disturbed Duff Elementary Sch., Arlington, 1976-78, counselor, 1978—. Cert. in elem. edn., spl. edn., counseling, Tex. Mem. Tex. Assn. Autistic Children, Tex. Personnel and Guidance Assn., Council Exceptional Children (pres. Arlington chpt. 1977-78), Tex. State Tchrs. Assn., Arlington Assn. Children with Learning Disabilities, Chi Omega. Home: 1717 Ridgeview Dr Arlington TX 76012 Office: Arlington Ind Sch Dist 1203 Pioneer Pkwy Arlington TX 76010

MC CALLIAN, RICHARD JONES, engring. cons.; b. Dayton, Ohio, Jan. 5, 1913; s. Edwin Lewis and Mary (Marsh) M.; B.S., Tri-State Coll., 1934; postgrad. U. Ga., 1963-65; m. Louise Garnett, Aug. 4, 1969. Metallurgist, U.S. Steel Corp., Gary, Ind., 1936-44; engring. cons., Phila., 1945-48; dist. sales mgr. Stulz-Sickles Co., Elizabeth, N.J., 1949-62; indsl. devel. cons., Port Richey, Fla., 1963—; pres., founder Flore-State Park, Inc., 1972—; pres. Oceanographic Minerals, Inc., Port Richey, 1967—; dir. Chasco Fiesta, Inc., Port Richey. Gideon sec.-treas. Pasco Camp, 1975—; sec.-treas. Withlacoochee River Electric Coop., 1975—. Bd. dirs. Boy Scouts Am., Port Richey. Recipient Distinguished Service award Tri-State Coll., 1975. Mem. Fla. Travel Council, Fla. Indsl. Devel. Council, Am. Mktg. Assn., Fla. C. of C., Port Richey C. of C. (Community Civic Service award 1977), Port Richey Ministerial Assn. (sec. 1976-78), Pioneer Engrs. Club (dir.), Tri-State Coll. Alumni Assn. (dir. 1975-78). Methodist (certified lay speaker 1967—, asso. dist. lay leader 1968—, dir. Meth. Hour Internat. 1975-78). Author: Potential Economic Benefits of Cross Florida Barge Canal, 1965. Patentee in field. Home: 30 Gulf Breeze N Port Richey FL 33568 Office: 19 N Main St Port Richey FL 33568

MC CALLUM, LEONA NICHOLLS, city ofcl.; b. Daviston, Ala., Aug. 13, 1907; d. Ephriam Walter and Lenora (Price) Jones; grad. Jacksonville State Normal Sch., 1928; student U. Ala., 1929; m. John A. Nicholls, Spet. 17, 1932 (div. May 1940); 1 son, John A. III; m. 2d., Clayton F. McCallum, Nov. 13, 1959. Tchr., Childersburg, Ala., 1928-41; clk. U.S. Postal Service, Childersburg, 1941-50, asst. to postmaster, 1951-73; mem. City Council City of Childersburg, 1976-80. Elder, Presbyn. Ch., Childersburg, 1974—; sec. Childersburg United Givers Fund, 1970, bd. dirs., 1977-80; mem. Childersburg Bicentennial Commn., 1976—; mem. Citizens Adv. Council, City of Childersburg, 1973-80; mem. Childersburg Library Bd., 1976-78; mem. Cheaha Regional Library Bd., 1976-78; bd. dirs. Ala. Arthritis Found., 1974-81; vol. ARC, 1950—, disting. service award, 1979: mem. Talladega County Mental Health Bd., 1972-75. Recipient award of merit Ala. Hist. Assn., 1977. Democrat. Presbyterian. Clubs: Garden of Ala. (life); Coosa Garden (3-term pres.), Presbyn. Ch. Women (pres. 1969-70). Home: 420 Forest Hills Dr Childersburg AL 35044

MC CAMMON, JAMES ALLEN, postal service exec.; b. Montgomery, Ala., Jan. 17, 1924; s. Roy Henry and Sarah (Bunkley) McC.; student U. Tex., 1947-49; m. Roberta Ruth Grace, May 18, 1973; children—Allen Lee, Gordon Frederick, Mark Candler; 1 stepdau., Anita Hill Dodson. Office mgr. Yoes Printing & Litho, Fort Smith, Ark., 1948-49; with U.S. Postal Service, 1949—, customer service rep. Fort Smith Sectional Center, 1973-76, mgr. Sta. B Post Office, Fort Smith, Ark., 1976—. Served with AUS, 1943-45. Decorated Purple Heart medal with two oak leaf clusters. Mem. Am. Legion, DAV. Republican. Baptist. Clubs: Masons, Elks, Exchange. Office: US Postal Service PO Box 4366 2417 Midland Blvd Fort Smith AR 72914

MC CANDLESS, CHARLES EMERY, educator; b. Dallas, July 26, 1931; s. Dewey Taylor and Clara (Askins) McC.; B.S., Tex. A. and M. U., 1956, M.Ed., 1958; Ed.D., North Tex. State U., 1966; m. Jeannie Wallace, May 14, 1977; children by previous marriage—Cathy, Sharon, Debra. Head coach Silsbee (Tex.) Jr. High Sch., 1956-58; counselor Silsbee High Sch., 1958-60; part-time instr. health, phys. edn., recreation North Tex. U., Denton, 1960-61; asst. prof. health and phys. edn., intramural athletics dir. Tex. A and M U., College Station, 1963-66, chmn. freshman courses dept. edn. and psychology, 1964-66, dir. adj., chmn. counselor edn., 1966-67, prof. ednl. psychology, 1977—, asso. dean liberal arts, 1966-74, coordinator univ. self study, 1971-73, dir. acad. planning and services, 1974—, dir. planning, 1977—, asso. v.p., acad. affairs, 1979—. Pres., College Station Recreation Council, 1968-73, College Station United Chest, 1973-74; pres. adv. bd. Central Brazos Valley Mental Health Center; bd. dirs. Bryan Boys Club, 1977—; mem. exec. com. Brazos Valley Muscular Dystrophy Assn., 1979—. Served with USAF, 1951-53. Recipient Student-Faculty Relations award Coll. Liberal Arts, 1969. Mem. College Station Progress Assn. (dir. 1969-71), Am., Tex. personnel and guidance assns., Am. Coll. Personnel Assn., Assn. Counselor Edn. and Supervision, Tex. Psychol. Assn. Asso. dir. several profl. jours. Home: 212 Redmond Dr College Station TX 77840

MC CANDLESS, PAUL LESLIE, acctg. co. exec.; b. Omaha, Sept. 27, 1947; s. Ernest Ervin and Eleanor Veronica (McCauley) McC.; B.B.A., U. Notre Dame, 1969; M.B.A., Creighton U., 1977; m. Marjorie Jean Bier, Sept. 13, 1969; children—Erin Elizabeth, Brian Christopher. Acct., Arthur Andersen & Co., Omaha, 1969-72; controller Swanson Enterprises, Omaha, 1972-78; pres., acct. Erin Mgmt. Acctg., Inc., Houston, 1978—. C.P.A., Nebr., Tex. Mem. Nat. Assn. Accountants, Am. Inst. C.P.A.'s, Inst. Mgmt. Accounting. Republican. Roman Catholic. Home: 12310 Pinerock Ln Houston TX 77024 Office: Erin Management Accounting Inc Suite 1177 1177 W Loop S Houston TX 77027

MC CANN, GLENN CROCKER, sociologist, educator; b. Sunnyside, Utah, Apr. 15, 1922; s. John Edward and Clara May (Harvey) McC.; B.A., U. Colo., 1947, M.A., 1949; Ph.D., Wash. State U., 1953; m. Marjorie Maxine Neptune, Jan. 8, 1945 (dec.); 1 son, John Edward; m. 2d, Anne MacRae Perry Stephenson, Sept. 12, 1969; stepchildren—John Boddie Stephenson, Elizabeth Anne Stephenson. Research asst. prof. sociology U. Wash., Seattle, 1952-53; social psychologist Dept. Air Force, Maxwell AFB, Ala., 1953-54, Randolph AFB, Tex., 1954-57; asst. prof. sociology N.C. State U., Raleigh, 1957-60, asso. prof., 1960-65, prof., 1965—; vis. prof. sociology Agrarian U., Peru, 1963-65, Seoul (Korea) Nat. U., 1967; cons. in field. Bd. dirs. Raleigh-Wake County Symphony Devel. Assn., 1978—; mem. Wake County Extension Adv. Com., 1979—; mem. exec. com. Raleigh Area Ministry, Unitarian Ch., 1978—. Served with USAAF, 1943-45; ETO. Decorated Air medal with six oak leaf clusters; Ford Rockefeller grantee, 1963-65; Agrl. Devel. Found. and Asia Found. grantee, 1967. Mem. Rural Sociol. Soc. (chmn. publs. com. 1973-74), Am. Sociol. Assn., So. Sociol. Soc., N.C. Sociol. Soc., Am. Public Opinion Assn., So. Public Opinion Assn., AAUP, Phi Kappa Phi, Pi Gamma Mu, Alpha Kappa Delta. Democrat. Unitarian. Contbr. articles to profl. jours., chpts. to books. Home: 713 Barksdale Dr Raleigh NC 27604 Office: NC State U Raleigh NC 27650

MC CANN, JOSEPH PATRICK, trade assn. exec.; b. N.Y.C., June 14, 1920; s. Patrick Joseph and Bridget Bella (Cullinan) McC.; A.B. in Acctg., Fordham U., 1942, postgrad. Law Sch., 1948-49; m. Veronica Fitzgerald, Sept. 3, 1949; children—Veronica, Colleen, Marybeth, Patrick, John, Kathleen. Spl. agt., supr. FBI, Birmingham and Mobile, Ala., N.Y.C., Miami, 1946-72; dir. Fla. Div. Pari-Mutuel Wagering, Miami, 1973-76; exec. dir. Nat. Assn. Jai-Alai Frontons, Inc., Miami Shores, Fla., 1977—. Chmn. com. drug prevention and control Mayor's Adv. Council, North Miami, Fla., 1973-74. Served as capt. U.S. Army, 1942-46; ETO. Mem. Nat. Assn. State Racing Commrs. (exec. com. 1973-76, chmn. public safety and security com. 1974-75), Soc. Former Spl. Agts. FBI (chmn. Pan Am. chpt. 1978-79), Am. Soc. Assn. Execs. Roman Catholic. Clubs: Lions (3d v.p. 1978-80), Elks, K.C. Home: 780 NE 146th St North Miami FL 33161 Office: Room 207 9999 NE 2d Ave Miami Shores FL 33138

MC CANTS, RALPH SAMUEL, pathologist; b. Woodford, Okla., Nov. 26, 1920; s. James Frank and Pearl (Jones) McC.; B.A., U. Okla., 1941, M.D., 1950; m. Billie Lee Anderson, Nov. 25, 1947; children—Laurie Cathleen, Jeffrey Frank. Intern, Kansas City (Mo.) Gen. Hosp., 1950-51; fellow Mayo Found. for Med. Edn. and Research, Rochester, Minn., 1951-56; asso. pathologist Stormont-Vail Hosp., Topeka, Kans., 1956-58; pathologist, dir. labs. Guthrie Clinic, Sayre, Pa., 1958-62; clin. pathologist St. John's Hosp., Tulsa, 1962-75; asso. pathologist St. Lawrence Hosp., Lansing, Mich., 1975-77; pathologist McCants Clin. Pathology Lab., Tulsa, 1977—; clin. asst. prof. pathology Mich. State U. Served with AC, U.S. Army, 1942-46. Diplomate Am. Bd. Pathology, Am. Bd. Nuclear Medicine. Fellow Nat. Acad. Clin. Biochemistry, Coll. Am. Pathologists, Am. Soc. Clin. Pathologists; mem. Am. Assn. Clin. Chemistry, Okla. Assn. Pathologists (pres. 1970-71), Okla. Heritage Assn., Tulsa Opera Assn., Tulsa Philharmonic Orch. Assn., Phi Beta Kappa, Sigma Xi. Unitarian. Home and office: 6055 E 56th Pl Tulsa OK 74135

MC CARLEY, CAROLYN JOSEPHINE SPENCE (MRS. CLINT WELDON MCCARLEY), shoe store exec.; b. Emporium, Pa., Oct. 16, 1919; d. Charles Burnell and Marguerite (Schoenbohm) Spence; student West Tex. State U., 1938-40; B.A., Tex. Arts and Industries U., 1942; postgrad. U. Guadalajara, 1944; m. Clint Weldon McCarley, June 8, 1945; children—Clint Weldon, Philip Allen, Charles Aubra, Kelvyn Joe. Tchr., Kingsville, Tex., 1942-43, Falfurrias, Tex., 1943-44, Gregory, Tex., 1944-45, Clarkwood, Tex., 1948-49, Harlingen, Tex., 1952-53; co-owner Carolyn's Shoe Store, Harlingen, 1954—. Vice pres. Stephen F. Austin Sch. PTA, Harlingen, 1964-65; sec. St. Paul's Luth Sch. PTA, 1966-68; chmn. Project Goodwill, 1966-68; bd. dirs. Family Emergency Assistance, 1975—, Rio Grande Valley Mus., 1977—; ruling elder Treasure Hills Presbyterian Ch., 1977—, pres. Women in Ch., 1977-78. Recipient citation State Fine Arts Commn., 1966-67. Mem. South Tex. Dist. (pub. affairs dept. chmn. 1968-70, pres. 1970-72, chmn. edn. dept. 1974-76), Tex. (sec. scholarship fund com. 1973-75, chmn. 1975-76, chmn., internat. hostess 1972-74, chmn. gerontology div. 1974-76, chmn. scholarship fund com. 1975-77), Rio Grande Valley (conv. coordinator 1969-71, hospitality chmn. 1971—, cultural affairs chmn. 1975-77, pres. 1979—) fedns. women's clubs, Rio Grande Valley Hist. Mus. Assn. (pres. 1973-75, sec. 1977-79). Clubs: Zonta (pres. 1968-70, service chmn. 1971-72, fin. chmn. 1974-75), Afflatus (sec. 1969-70, pres. 1970-72, 79-80, v.p. 1975-77), City Federation Past Presidents (sec. 1969, treas. 1973-75, pres. 1975-77) (all Harlingen). Home: 102 Wildwood St Harlingen TX 78550 Office: 705 Coronado Village Harlingen TX 78550

MC CARLEY, THOMAS DAVID, data processing cons.; b. Seguin, Tex., Nov. 29, 1942; s. Thomas and Jessie Jewell (Sutherland) McC.; student San Antonio Coll., 1961-67, U. Corpus Christi, 1967, Del Mar Coll., 1968-70, U. Houston, 1976-77; m. Carole Rosene Rowley, June 2, 1962; children—Mark David, Susan Marie. With H.E. Butt Grocery Co., San Antonio, Corpus Christi, 1961-70, computer operator, sr. programmer analyst, 1961-70; mgr. programming and systems J. Weingarten, Inc., Houston, 1970-76; pres. T. McCarley and Assos., Inc., Houston, 1976—, also dir.; gen. partner Bank System Co. Mem. Data Processing Mgmt. Assn. Baptist. Office: 5603 Pinewilde Houston TX 77066

MC CARTHA, WALTER HAYNE, civil engr.; b. Batesburg, S.C., May 13, 1908; s. Walter Jacob and Henryetta (Towill) McC.; B.S. in Civil Engring., The Citadel, 1930, C.E., 1936; postgrad. in econs. George Washington U., 1930-31, in architecture, 34-35; postgrad. U. Mo. at Rolla, 1963, 64, 68, Civil Service Commn., 1966, USPHS, 1969, U. Md., 1962; m. Virginia Jean Ritchhart, June 3, 1957. Valuation engr. aide ICC Washington, 1930-31; archtl. engr. Pub. Bldgs. Service, Washington, 1931-40, engr., chief materials engring. group, 1950-57; chief specifications engr. for constrn. VA, Richmond, Va., 1946-49; archtl. gen. engr. charge specification standards for constrn. Directorate of Civil Engring., Hdqrs. U.S. Air Force, Washington, 1957-74, ret., 1974. Dir. Joint Bd. on Sci. Edn., Washington, 1955-64, 72—, chmn., 1958-59; mem. tri-service com. for constrn. research Nat. Bur. Standards, 1971-74, chmn., 1973-74; materials resource council, bldg. research adv. bd. Tech. Assessment Utilization Program, Washington, 1975-76. Served to col. USAAF, 1940-46. Recipient Civil Engring. Meritorious Achievement award Dept. Air Force, 1962. Registered profl. engr., D.C. Mem. Nat., D.C. (pres. 1954-55, dir. 1963-66) socs. profl. engrs., Soc. Am. Mil. Engrs., Washington Soc. Engrs. (dir. 1969-70, 74-75, 1st v.p. 1972, pres. 1973), D.C. Council Engring. and Archtl. Socs. (chmn. 1956-57), ASTM. Baptist. Mason (32 deg., Shriner). Club: Bolling AFB Officers (Washington). Contbr. constrn. chpts. to Air Force Manuals, 1960, 61, 64-74. Home: 3804 14th St N Arlington VA 22201

MC CARTHY, EDWARD, JR., lawyer; b. Jacksonville, Fla., Jan. 17, 1931; s. Edward and Margaret R. (Durkee) McC.; A.B., Princeton, 1953; LL.B., U. Colo., 1956; m. Julie Beville Fant, May 18, 1962; children—Mitchell Fant, Beville Durkee, Edward III. Admitted to Colo. bar, 1956, Fla. bar, 1959; partner firm Strang & McCarthy, Montrose, Colo., 1956-59, McCarthy, Adams & Foote, Jacksonville, 1959-68, Freeman, Richardson, Watson, Slade, McCarthy & Kelly, P.A., Jacksonville, 1968—; dir. Five Points Guaranty Bank of Jacksonville. Bd. dirs., v.p. Riverside Hosp. of Jacksonville. Mem. Am., Fla., Jacksonville bar assns. Republican. Episcopalian. Clubs: Timuquana Country, Ravines, Florida Yacht, University, River. Home: 4710 Apache Ave Jacksonville FL 32210 Office: 1200 Barnett Bank Bldg Jacksonville FL 32202

MC CARTHY, EDWARD ANTHONY, bishop; b. Cin., Apr. 10, 1918; s. Edward E. and Catherine (Otte) McC.; M.A., Mt. St. Mary Sem. of West, Norwood, Ohio, 1944; Licentiate Canon Law, Cath. U. Am., 1946; D. Canon Law, Lateran U., Rome, Italy, 1947; S.T.D., Angelicum, Rome, 1948. Ordained priest Roman Catholic Ch., 1943; sec. to archbishop of Cin., 1944-65; aux. bishop of Cin., 1965-69; bishop of Phoenix, 1969-76; co-adjutor archbishop of Miami (Fla.), 1976-77, archbishop of Miami, 1977—. Home: St John Vianney Sem 2900 SW 87th Ave Miami FL 33165 Office: 6301 Biscayne Blvd Miami FL 33138

MC CARTHY, JEROME RICHARD, retail co. exec.; b. St. Louis, Apr. 7, 1935; s. Robert Francis and Catherine (Long) McC.; B.B.A., U. Miami, 1959; m. Miriam Jeanette Haury, Nov. 12, 1960; children—Jerome Richard, Jeanne Marie. Accountant, Gen. Motors Corp., Atlanta, 1959-62; controller, Sears, Roebuck and Co., Atlanta, 1962-64, accounting group controller, 1964-71, mgr. sales, use taxes, 1971-74, asst. ter. tax mgr., 1974—. Served with USN, 1956-58. Mem. Nat. Assn. Accountants, Atlanta Tax Club, S.E. Assn. Tax Adminstrs. Roman Catholic. Clubs: Optimist, K.C. Home: 705 Mt Vernon Hwy NE Atlanta GA 30328 Office: 675 Ponce de Leon Ave NE Atlanta GA 30395

MCCARTHY, JUSTIN ANDREW, JR., historian; b. Evanston, Ill., Jan. 27, 1945; s. Justin Andrew and Anita Marie (Gibian) McC.; A.B., John Carroll U., 1967; Ph.D. (NDEA fellow 1973-77), UCLA, 1978; m. Carolyn Beth Lamka, Aug. 17, 1974. Instr., Middle East Tech. U., Ankara, Turkey, 1967-69; tchr. public schs., Chgo., 1969-70; researcher UCLA, 1970-78; asst. prof. history U. Louisville, 1978—; vol. Peace Corps, 1967-69. NSF fellow, 1979-80. Mem. Middle East Studies Assn., Middle East Inst., Am. Hist. Assn., Population Assn. Am. Democrat. Roman Catholic. Contbr. articles to profl. jours. Home: 1701 Rosewood Ave Louisville KY 40204 Office: Dept History U Louisville Louisville KY 40208

MC CARTHY, MARY ELIZABETH, psychologist; b. N.Y.C., Feb. 22, 1937; d. Timothy and Beatrice (Hester) McC.; B.A., Hunter Coll., 1964; M.S., Fordham U., 1965; Ph.D., U. Santo Tomas, Philippines, 1970, M.A., 1971. Supr., job instr. Met. Life Ins. Co., N.Y.C., 1955-60; wage and salary analyst Univac div. Sperry Rand Corp., N.Y.C., 1960-63; tchr. and dir. guidance Notre Dame High Sch., N.Y.C., 1965-66; coordinator student adviser-leadership program Bklyn. Coll., N.Y., 1966-68; asst. prof. edn. Grad. Sch., Ateneo de Manila U., Quezon City, Philippines, 1968-71; dir. Epoch House, Catonsville, Md., 1971-72; lectr. U. of Ife, Ile-Ife, Nigeria, 1972-73; asso. prof. psychology Coll. V.I., St. Thomas, 1973—, chairperson social scis. div., 1977-79; lectr. various schs. and community groups in Thailand, Philippines, Nigeria, Caribbean; spl. lectr. Philippines Air Force, 1970; clin. cons. Parole and Probation Bd., Balt., 1971; dir. Pastoral Guidance Center, St. Thomas, V.I., 1976-79; postdoctoral fellow Fla. State U., Tallahassee, 1979-80; cons. Am. embassy Teen Program in Manila, 1968-69; cons. Golden Grove Correctional Facility, St. Croix, V.I., 1977. Mem. Community Mental Health Planning Com., St. Thomas, 1975; mem. adv. council Community Drug Edn., Dept. Edn., St. Thomas, 1974-75; bd. dirs. St. Dunstan's Episcopal Sch., St. Croix, 1976-77; bd. dirs. V.I. Council on Alcohol, 1975-79, v.p., 1976-78. NDEA grantee, 1967; recipient Appreciation award Philippine Guidance and Personnel Assn., 1968, Philippine Mental Health Assn., 1971; certified vocat. counselor Nat. Vocat. Guidance Assn.; sch psychologist, N.Y. Mem. Am. Assn. Marriage and Family Therapy, Internat. Assn. Group Psychotherapy, Am. Personnel and Guidance Assn., World Fedn. Mental Health, Am. Assn. Sex Educators, Counselors and Therapists (certified), Nat. Council Family Relations, Am. Psychol. Assn., Internat. Graphoanalysis Soc. Assn. Counselor Edn. and Supervision, Acad. Psychologists in Marital and Family Therapy. Contbr. numerous articles on counseling to profl. jours. Office: Dept Psychology Fla State U Tallahassee FL 32306

MC CARTHY, ROSEMARY, educator; b. N.Y.C., June 25, 1948; d. Peter John and Alice Virginia (Berk) Conlon; B.S.N., Niagara U., 1970; M.S.N., Tex. Woman's U., 1979. Pub. health nurse Niagara County Health Dept., Niagara Falls, N.Y., 1970-71; pediatric and pediatric I.C.U. staff nurse Staten Island Hosp., 1971; pub. health nurse Erie County Health Dept., Buffalo, 1971-73; instr. Houston Community Coll., 1973—. Mem. Am. Nurses Assn., Tex. Nurses Assn., Dist. 9 Nurses Assn., Tex-N-Cap. Roman Catholic. Office: 22 Waugh Dr Houston TX 77007

MC CARTHY, THOMAS JAMES, JR., lawyer; b. Pulaski, Va., Nov. 24, 1943; s. Thomas James and M. Jane (Osborne) McC.; grad. The Episcopal High Sch., Alexandria, Va., 1963; B.A. in Econs., Washington and Lee U., 1967; J.D., U. Va., 1970. Admitted to Va. bar, 1970, since practiced in Pulaski; partner firm Gilmer, Sadler, Ingram, Sutherland & Hutton, 1970—; pres. Pulaski Bus. Plaza, Inc., 1969-78, Turnpike Enterprises, Inc., Pulaski, 1970-77; dir. Count Pulaski Realty. Mem. Pulaski County Democratic Com., 1971-74. Served with AUS, 1970; maj. Res. Mem. Pulaski County C. of C. (dir. 1971-74, 77—, v.p. 1978, pres. 1979), Va., Pulaski County (sec.-treas. 1973-74, v.p. 1974-75, pres. 1975-76), 27th Jud. Circuit (pres. 1979) bar assns., Sigma Chi. Episcopalian (vestryman 1979). Elk, Rotarian (pres.-elect 1979). Home: 612 Cardinal Dr PO Box 818 Pulaski VA 24301 Office: Midtown Professional Bldg 65 E Main St Pulaski VA 24301

MC CARTHY, WILLIAM CARROLL, physician, nursing home adminstr.; b. Richmond, Va., Jan. 22, 1948; s. William Oscar and Marianne Eva (Stork) McC.; B.S. magna cum laude, Xavier U., 1969; M.D., Georgetown U., 1973; children—Amanda Beth, Daniel Jason. Intern, U. Wis. Hosp., Madison, 1973-74, resident in family practice, 1974-76; individual practice family medicine, Dumfries, Va., 1976—; dir. continuing med. edn. Potomac Hosp., Woodbridge, Va. Bd. dirs. No. Va. Found. for Med. Care. Mem. Prince Williams County Med.

Soc. (v.p.), Va. Med. Soc., Am. Acad. Family Practice, Am. Geriatric Soc. Roman Catholic. Lectr. in field. Home: 13228 Sturbridge Rd Woodbridge VA 22192 Office: 236 S Fraley Blvd Dumfries VA 22026

MCCARTT, MARGARET LINN (ROBERTS), nurse, med. adminstr.; b. Kanapolis N.C., Oct. 8, 1925; d. John Wertz and Carrie Lee (Redman) Roberts; diploma Cabarrus Meml. Hosp. Sch. Nursing, Concord, N.C., 1946; m. Jack Wilbur McCartt, Aug. 30, 1947; children—Linda Lee, Jack Wilbur, Jane Linn. Staff nurse Montefiore Hosp., Bronx, N.Y., 1946-47, Johnson City (Tenn.) Meml. Hosp., 1947-49; staff nurse, asst. head nurse VA Center, Mountain Home, Tenn., 1949-59; supr. central supply, admission OPC Clinic and Ear, Nose and Throat Clinic, 1959-67, chief spd sect., supply service, 1967—; co-owner, operator Jo-Lyn's Catering Service, Johnson City, 1977—. Mem. Am. Nurses Assn., Tenn. Nurses Assn. (treas. 1972-73), Johnson City Bus. and Profl. Women's Club (treas. 1974-75), E. Tenn. Central Service Suprs. (co-sponsor). Home: Route 4 Box 457-A Johnson City TN 37601 Office: VA Med Center Mountain Home TN 37684

MC CARTY, DORRACE AUDENE, hearing aid specialist; b. Anson, Tex., Sept. 25, 1924; d. James Sanford and Vada Lavena (Hewett) Potts; student S.W. Tex. State U., 1941-43; cert. in audioprosthology U. Tex., El Paso, 1978; m. Owen Henry McCarty, June 22, 1946 (dec. 1973); children—Patricia McCarty Davidson, James Michael. Stenographer, San Marcos AFB, 1943-45; sec. dental div. Tex. Health Dept., Austin, 1945-46; hearing aid cons., 1965-74; owner hearing aid service, 1974—. Mem. San Antonio C. of C., Tex. Hearing Aid Assn., Am. Conf. Audioprosthology, Hearing Aid Specialists S. Tex. Presbyterian. Office: 200 Wonderland Center San Antonio TX 78284

MC CARTY, RAYMOND M., lawyer, poet; b. Council Bluffs, Iowa, July 27, 1908; s. Cecil and Eva Frances (Wilson) M.; student S.W. Mo. State Tchrs. Coll., 1931-33; LL.B., So. Law U., Memphis, 1948, Memphis State U., 1967; m. Margaret Esther Burton, Mar. 23, 1942. Chief clk. State Social Security Commn., Springfield, Mo., 1937-39; admitted to Tenn. bar 1948; with U.S. Army C.E., Memphis, 1939-72, chief planning and control br. Real Estate div., 1953-72; pvt. practice law, Memphis, 1972—. Served with AUS, 1942-43. Recipient Countess d'Esternaux Gold medal award for poetry, 1950. Mem. Poetry Soc. Tenn. (hon. mem., organizer, 1st pres., poet laureate 1977-78), World Poetry Soc. Intercontinental (Distinguished citation for Poetry 1970), Avalon World Arts Acad. (hon.), Ala. Writers Conclave, Nat. Fedn. State Poetry Socs., Acad. Am. Poets, Ala. State Poetry Soc., Am. Legion, Nat. Fedn. Fed. Employees, Fed. Bar Assn. (sec. Memphis chpt. 1971-72), Nat. Assn. Ret. Fed. Employees, Internat. Platform Assn. Baptist (deacon, chmn. deacons 1965-66). Author: Harp in a Strange Land, 1973. Contbr. poems to profl. jours. and popular mags. Home and office: 1247 Colonial Rd Memphis TN 38117

MCCARTY, THOMAS DEAN, hosp. adminstr.; b. Winnfield, La., Sept. 10, 1948; s. Elzie Floyd and Hila Mae (Adams) McC.; B.B.A. in Mgmt., N.E. La. State Coll., 1970; B.S. in Hosp. Adminstrn., Okla. Baptist U., 1971; m. Emily Faye Causey, Jan. 18, 1969; children—Thomas Adam, Joseph David. Adminstrv. asst. Coliseum Park Hosp., Macon, Ga., 1971-72; adminstr. Columbia Heights Med. Center, Columbia, La., 1972-74, Union Gen. Hosp., Farmerville, La., 1974-79; asso. dir. Glenwood Hosp., West Monroe, La., 1979—; cons. in field: officer in investment corps.; chmn. La. Tech. U. Adv. Council to Sch. Nursing. Chmn. Caldwell Parish com. La. Arthritis Found.; sec. Union Parish (La.) Democratic Com.; Union Parish del. to La. Democratic Com. Lic. nursing home adminstr., La. Mem. AMA Pres.'s Assn., Health Systems Agy. (charter dir. North La.), La. Hosp. Assn. (pres. N.E. dist. 1978-79, chmn. legis. com. 1977-79, state trustee 1978-81, trustee devel. com.), Emergency Med. Services (chmn. Union Parish chpt., dir. N.E. Found.), Am. Coll. Hosp. Adminstrs. Baptist. Home: 123 Sunset Dr West Monroe LA 71291 Office: PO Box 1637 West Monroe LA 71291

MC CAULEY, JOHN THOMAS, JR., mfr. modular housing; b. St. Paul, July 20, 1944; s. John Thomas and Helen Reynolds (Campbell) McC.; B.A. in Econs., Guilford Coll., Greensboro, N.C., 1966; M.B.A., Syracuse (N.Y.) U., 1968; m. Pamela Kathryn Sparrow, Aug. 12, 1972; 1 dau., Kathryn Sparrow. With duPont Co., Martinsville, Va., 1968-71; successively planner, dept. dir., acting dir. West Piedmont Planning Dist. Commn., Martinsville, 1972-75; dean fin. and adminstrv. services Patrick Henry Community Coll., Martinsville, 1975-76; asst. to v.p., sec., mgr. processing Nationwide Homes, Inc., Martinsville. Pres. Martinsville-Henry County Soc. Prevention Cruelty Animals, 1979-80. Baptist. Club: Martinsville Rotary (dir. 1977-79, v.p. 1980—). Home: Route 7 Box 439 Martinsville VA 24112 Office: PO Box 5511 Martinsville VA 24112

MC CAULEY, LOYD CECIL, dentist; b. Canton, Tex., Sept. 2, 1913; s. Sidney James and Florence Eva (Prater) McC.; student N. Tex. State Tchrs. Coll., 1930-32; D.D.S., Baylor U., 1936; m. Claudia Alethe Moore, Aug. 30, 1934 (dec. 1976); children—Phillip Ray, Ronald Cecil, Danny Paul; m. 2d, Lila Maxine Smith McCauley, 1978. Pvt. practice dentistry, Alba, Tex., 1938-42, Mt. Pleasant, Tex., 1942—; courtesy staff Titus County Meml. Hosp., Mt. Pleasant. Pres., Mt. Pleasant Ind. Sch. Bd., 1952-56. Fellow Royal Soc. Health; mem. ADA (life), Tex., First Dist. (pres. 1954) dental socs., Pierre Fauchard Acad., Order of Goodfellow. Mem. Ch. of Christ. Home: 1780 Rollin Rd Canton TX 75103 Office: 222 Dallas St Canton TX 75103

MC CAULEY, WINONA ELIZABETH, nurse; b. Houston, Ark., Sept. 3, 1921; d. John and Viola (Summers) McC.; grad. St. Vincent Sch. of Nursing, 1943; m. Jan. 16, 1957 (div.). Head nurse, St. Vincent Infirmary, Little Rock, 1954-58, supr., 1958-65, mgr. central service, 1965-78, dir. central service, 1978—; cons. to various hosp. central service depts. R.N., Ark. Mem. Am. Nurses Assn., Ark. League for Nursing, Ark. Hosp. Purchasing and Materials Mgmt., Internat. Assn. Central Service Mgmt., Am. Hosp. Assn. of Central Service Mgmt. Mem. Assemblies of God Ch. Office: St Vincent Infirmary Markham and University Ave Little Rock AR 72201

MC CLAIN, DAVID H., lawyer, state legislator; b. Macon, Ga., June 4, 1933; s. Joseph A. Jr. and Laura (Burkett) McC.; B.A., Duke U., 1957; M.A. (Scottish Rite fellow 1958), George Washington U., 1961; LL.B., Stetson Coll. Law, 1961; 1 dau., Linda N. (Mrs. Wheeler). Partner, MacFarlane, Ferguson, Allison & Kelly, Tampa, Fla., 1961-73, McClain & Walkley, P.A., Tampa, 1974—; legis. liaison Fla. Gov.'s office, 1967; mem. Fla. Senate, 1970—. Mem. Fla. Law Revision Council, 1970-72, 74-75. Asst. Republican state treas. Fla., 1974—; Rep. state committeeman. Vice chmn. Bd. Pub. Relations and Conf. Facilities, Tampa, 1969-70. Served with AUS. Recipient Outstanding Leadership and Service award Bd. Pub. Relations and Conv. Facilities, 1970, Good Govt. award Tampa Jr. C. of C., 1971, Green Cross award Greater Tampa Safety Council, 1972, award Tampa Hist. Soc., 1974, Spessard Holland Meml. award, 1975, Pro Life award Fla. Right to Life, 1976, 77, 78, 79, numerous others. Mem. Fla., Am., Tampa, Hillsborough County (chmn. unauthorized practice of law com. 1969) bar assns., Beta Theta Pi, Delta Theta Phi. Clubs: Interbay Sertoma (sec. 1970-71), Highlights, Masons, Shriners. Home: 121 S Manhattan St Tampa FL 33609 Office: 605 South Blvd Tampa FL 33606

MC CLAIN, JAMES WILLIAM, coll. ofcl.; b. Shelbyville, Ind., Feb. 27, 1951; s. Chester Lee and Ann (Walker) McC.; B.A., U. Evansville (Ind.), 1973; M.A., Mich. State U., E. Lansing, 1975; m. Marcia Raeber, June 19, 1976. Successively grad. resident adviser, asst. head adviser, head resident adviser Mich. State U., 1973-75; resident inst. U. S.Fla., Tampa, 1975-77; dir. student aid Miss. County Community Coll., Blytheville, Ark., 1977—; condr. career seminars. Mem. Am. Coll. Personnel Assn., Am. Personnel and Guidance Assn., Nat., S.W., Ark. assns. student financial aid adminstrs., S.W. Assn. Placement Officers. Democrat. Methodist. Home: 105-A Amelia Dr Blytheville AR 72315 Office: Miss County Community Coll Blytheville AR 72315

MC CLAIN, MERLE EDWARD, pediatrician; b. Little Rock, Feb. 9, 1947; s. Merle Edward and Merle (Matlock) McC.; B.S., U. Ark., 1969, M.D., 1973. Intern U. Tex. Southwestern Med. Sch., Dallas, also Children Med. Center, 1973, resident in pediatrics, 1973-76; partner in practice pediatrics, Fort Smith, Ark., 1976—; mem. staff St. Edward's Mercy Med. Center, Sparks Regional Med. Center, Fort Smith; clin. instr. U. Ark. Med. Sch., Little Rock, 1976—. Diplomate Am. Bd. Pediatrics. Fellow Am. Acad. Pediatrics; mem. Sebastian County Med. Soc., Alpha Chi Sigma. Office: 312 S 16th St Fort Smith AR 72901

MC CLAIN, PHILLIP DWAYNE, ins. agt., contractor; b. Kingsport, Tenn., Feb. 15, 1953; s. Haskel Alva and Bevelene (Hickman) McC.; student East Tenn. State U., 1971-73; m. Glenna Dean Bryant, Jan. 7, 1977. Sales rep. Sears Roebuck & Co., 1969-74; agt. Allstate Ins. Co., Bristol, Va., 1974—; lic. contractor. Recipient awards Allstate Ins. Co. Mem. Va. Bd. Builders. Baptist. Home: 157 Beechwood Circle Bristol VA 24201 Office: Bristol Mall Bristol VA 24201

MC CLAIN, WILLIAM FRANCIS, mfg. co. owner; b. Abbeville County, S.C., June 14, 1922; s. Clarence Oliver and Ottie Loraine (Davis) McC.; B.S. in Mech. Engring., Clemson U., 1949; m. Mary Edity Stone, Feb. 8, 1946; children—Frances (Mrs. Charles M. Wallace), Randolph Stone. Chief project engr. Studebaker-Packard Corp., Detroit, 1953-56; mgr. engine overhaul Curtiss-Wright Corp., Utica, Mich., 1956-60; owner, pres. McClain Internat., Inc., College Park, Ga., 1962—; also dir.; pres., owner, dir. Tecni Flame Coatings, Inc., College Park, 1970—; partner various real estate ventures. Trustee Arlington Schs., Inc., Atlanta. Served with USAF, 1941-46, 51-53. Decorated D.F.C., Air medal with oak leaf cluster, Purple Heart; named Mr. South Fulton, East Point Moose Club, 1977. Mem. ASME, South Fulton County C. of C. (dir. 1972—, pres. 1974, Man of Year 1974). Elk. Clubs: Lakeside Country (dir., pres. 1975), Commerce (Atlanta). Home: Rt 1 Hwy 74 Box 740 Fayetteville GA 30214

MC CLANAHAN, JAMES ALVA, chemist; b. Charleston, W.Va., Jan. 10, 1922; s. Ollie Washington and Olive Macel (Melton) McC.; B.S. cum laude, B.A. cum laude, Morris Harvey Coll., 1956; m. Thelma G. Harrison, Apr. 6, 1946. Project scientist cellular products Union Carbide Corp., South Charleston, W.Va., 1941—. Served in USNR, 1942-45; PTO. Mem. Soc. Plastics Engrs., Early Am. Soc., Soc. Plastics Industry, Morris Harvey Coll. Alumni Assn. (dir. 1956-62). Democrat. Clubs: University (dir. 1970—), Elks. Home: 25 Norwood Rd Charleston WV 25314 Office: PO Box 8361 South Charleston WV 25303

MC CLANAHAN, JOHN HOWARD, utility exec.; b. Hartselle, Ala., Sept. 22, 1921; s. William Alexander and Trannie (Cooper) McC.; B.E.E., Auburn U., 1943; m. Mary Evelyn Irons, Aug. 3, 1947; children—William Alexander, Timmons Smith. Coop. student Florence (Ala.) Electricity Dept., 1939-43, engr., mgr., 1946—; cons. engr. Bd. dirs. YMCA; mem. exec. bd. Lauderdale-Florence Indsl. Com.; elder, trustee Disciples of Christ. Served with C.E., U.S. Army, 1943-46. Recipient Life Saving Award; registered profl. engr., Ala. Mem. Tennessee Valley Public Power Assn. (dir.), North Ala. Power Distbrs. Assn. (past pres.), Ala. Consumer Owned Power Distbrs. Assn. (past pres.), N.Ala. Indsl. Devel. Assn., Florence Area C. of C. (past pres.), Briareans, Eta Kappa Nu, Tau Beta Pi. Democrat. Clubs: Florence Civitan (past pres., past lt. gov. internat., Outstanding Citizenship award), Tri Cities Quarterback (past pres.), Auburn Alumni (past pres.), Turtle Point Country. Home: 318 Deerpoint Ln Florence AL 35630 Office: 110 W College St Florence AL 35630

MC CLELLAN, CAROLE KEETON, city ofcl.; B.A. in Govt., U. Tex., 1961. Mem. AISD Bd. of Trustees, 1972-77, pres., 1976-77; founding bd. mem., past pres. Austin Community Coll. Bd.; vice chmn. environ. quality com. Nat. League Cities; advisory bd. urban health care fin. U.S. Conf. Mayors; 1st v.p. Tex. Municipal League; mayor City of Austin (Tex.), 1977—; mem. Mayor's Adv. Com. to Gov.; mem. community edn. adv. council HEW. Mem. adv. bd. John F. Kennedy Sch. Govt. Office: Office of Mayor City Hall 124 W 8th St Austin TX 78701

MC CLELLAN, GUY SYDNEY, ret. obstetrician, gynecologist; b. Memphis, Mar. 18, 1906; s. Guy Smith and Nellie Mae (Firth) Mc.; M.D., U. Tenn., 1930; m. Lucy Dell Leathers, June 4, 1935; children—Guy Sydney, Gwen McClellan Laffin. Intern, Rochester (N.Y.) Gen. Hosp., 1930-31, Chgo. Lying-in Hosp., 1931-32, St. Louis Maternity Hosp., 1932-33; resident Vanderbilt U. Hosp., 1933-36; practice medicine specializing in obstetrics and gynecology, Nashville, 1936-75; clin. prof. obstetrics and gynecology Vanderbilt U., Nashville, 1945-76, emeritus, 1976—, acting chmn. dept., 1947-49, 66-67; dir. employee health service Tenn. Dept. Pub. Health, 1971-74, Sumner County Health Dept., 1974-76. Pres. Nashville-Davidson County unit Am. Cancer Soc., 1961-62. Diplomate Am. Bd. Obstetrics and Gynecology. Fellow A.C.S.; mem. AMA, So., Tenn. med. socs., Nashville-Davidson County Acad. Medicine, Tenn. State Pub. Health Assn., Nashville-Davidson County Obstet. and Gynecol. Soc. (pres. 1960-61, dir. 1958-75), Central Assn. Obstetricians and Gynecologists, Alpha Omega Alpha, Alpha Kappa Kappa. Methodist. Club: Nashville Univ. Home: PO Box 446 Slaters Creek Rd Goodlettsville TN 37072

MCCLELLAND, BARBARA GAY, pub. exec.: b. Atlanta, Aug. 3, 1952; d. John Edward and Barbara (Settle) McC.; B.A., U. Hartford, 1974; m. Owen H. Halpern, July 23, 1977. Fashion writer Rich's, Atlanta, 1975-77; free-lance fashion writer, Atlanta, 1977-80; asso. promotion dir. Atlanta Mag., 1978—; women's study tchr. dept. continuing edn. Emory U., 1979—. Club: Atlanta Ad II (v.p. programs).

MC CLELLAND, CLARENCE MARION, mission exec.; b. Quinter, Kans., July 31, 1921; s. Thomas Earl and Martha Marie (Feiler) McC.; ed. public and ins. schs.; m. Phyllis J. Vickers, Nov. 15, 1943; children—Barbara, Roger, Glenn, Charles, Jeffrey. Farmhand, 1936-41; farmer, stockman, 1945-52; grocer, 1952-55; postmaster Studley (Kans.), 1955-73; ins. and securities rep. Columbian Securities Corp., Topeka, 1973-74; bus. mgr. Missionary Tech. Team, Longview, Tex., 1974—. Mem. Bluff Creek (Kans.) Sch. Bd., 1949-52. Served with USN, 1941-45; PTO. Recipient Balanced Farming award Clark County, Tex., 1951. Mem. Nat. Assn. Postmasters, Gideons Internat. Baptist. Home: 2501 Golf Ave Longview TX 75602 Office: 25 FRJ Dr Longview TX 75602

MC CLELLAND, ROBERT NELSON, surgeon, educator; b. Gilmer, Tex., Nov. 20, 1929; s. Robert Hilton and Verna (Nelson) McC.; B.A., U. Tex., 1952, M.D., 1954; m. Connie Logan, May 5, 1958; children—Robert Christopher, Alison, Julie. Intern, U. Kans. Med. Center, Kansas City, 1954-55; resident Parkland Meml. Hosp., Dallas, 1957-62; instr. gen. surgery U. Tex. Southwestern Med. Sch. at Dallas, 1962-63, asst. prof., 1963-67, asso. prof., 1967-71, prof., 1971—; mem. staff Parkland, Presbyn., VA hosps., all Dallas; cons. Baylor, St. Paul, Methodist hosps., Dallas, John Peter Smith Hosp., Ft. Worth, Tex., 4th Army, Ft. Hood, Tex. Served to capt. USAF, 1955-57. Mem. Dallas County Med. Soc., Tex., Am. med. assns., Am., Western surg. assns., Digestive Disease Found., Soc. for Surgery Alimentary Tract (mem. membership com. 1972-73), Am. Gastroenterol. Assn., A.C.S., Tex., Southwestern surg. socs., Phi Beta Kappa, Alpha Omega Alpha, Theta Kappa Psi. Editor: Audio-Jour. Review-Gen. Surgery, 1971—, Selected Readings in Gen. Surgery, 1974—. Contbr. numerous articles, chpts. to surg. med. texts, also jours. Home: 3601 Potomac St Dallas TX 75205 Office: 5323 Harry Hines Blvd Dallas TX 75235

MC CLENDON, FRED VERNON, owner horse ranch; b. Vernon, Tex., Dec. 23, 1924; s. Guy C. and Lexie Marie (Johnson) McC.; B.B.A., Baylor U., 1949; M.B.A. (W.T. Grant fellow), Harvard U., 1951; m. Ethel R. Ling, Sept. 15, 1959; children—Rob Ling, Tracy Wallace, D. Kent, Cathy, Tess Ling, J. T. Ling. Personnel dir. Houston Fire & Casualty Co., Ft. Worth, 1954-55; gen. mgr. Nat. Paper Band Co., Denver, 1952-53, Englander Co., Dallas, 1956; chmn. bd. Lydia-Lynn Button Co., Dallas, 1960; gen. partner, mgr. Allen & McClendon Ins. Agy., Dallas, 1960; owner Ins.-Bank Personnel Agy., Dallas, 1958-60; gen. sales mgr. City Lincoln-Mercury, Dallas, 1957-58; owner, gen. mgr. Eagle Nest Ranch, Roan Mountain, Tenn., 1963—; ranch mgmt. cons.; real estate broker. Served with USN, 1941-45. Mem. C. of C., Australian Appaloosa Assn., Am. Quarter Horse Assn., Am. Charbray Assn., Am. Charolais Assn. Republican. Seventh-day Adventist. Clubs: Masons, Rotary, Appaloosa Horse. Contbr. articles to profl. jours. Home: Box 69 Roan Mountain TN 37687 Office: Heaton Creek Rd Roan Mountain TN 37687

MC CLENDON, JOAN PARSONS, banker; b. Boston, Apr. 21, 1925; d. Jack and Victoria Muriel (Adams) Parsons; student Long Beach Jr. Coll., 1942-43, Los Angeles City Coll., 1944; grad. U. Miss. Sch. Banking, 1973-74; m. Claude M. McClendon, Nov. 17, 1945 (div.); 1 dau., Joan Diane (Mrs. Glenn Wayne Kuykendall). Teller, bookkeeper S.W. Miss. Bank (formerly Magnolia Bank), Magnolia Miss., 1953-59, asst. cashier, 1960—, asst. to pres., 1974—, also exec. sec. Pres., Pike County chpt. Am. Cancer Soc., 1971-72. Del. Democratic State Conv., 1968—; sec. Pike County Dem. Exec. Com., 1966—; asst. chmn. fin. com. Pike County Art Assn., 1977—; bd. dirs. Pike County Mental Health Assn., 1977—. Mem. Nat. Assn. Bank Women (state chmn. 1971-72), Banking Adminstrn. Inst. (dir. S.W. Miss. chpt. 1972—, pres. 1975-76), Am. Inst. Banking (study group chmn.), Miss. Bankers Assn. (v.p. banking edn. com.), Magnolia Area C. of C. (pres., dir.). Episcopalian. Home: Route 4 Magnolia MS 39652 Office: PO Box 191 Magnolia MS 39652

MCCLENDON, MOSES C., developmental engr.; b. Graceville, Fla., Dec. 11, 1934; s. Harry and Virginia McC.; A.A., Edward Waters Coll., 1954; B.A., Morris Brown Coll., 1957; M.S. (NSF grantee), N.C. Agrl. and Tech. State U., 1967; m. Grace Merline Jones, June 24, 1961; children—Chantelle Marsha, Michelle Renee, Moses C. II. Tchr., Washington County Bd. Pub. Instrn., Chipley, Fla., 1960-66; asso. mem. tech. staff Bell Telephone Labs., Winston-Salem, N.C., 1967-71; developmental engr. Western Electric Co., Greensboro, N.C., 1971-73, dept. chief, Richmond, Va., 1973—. Served with U.S. Army, 1957-60. Mem. Am. Chm. Soc., Soc. Plastic Engrs., Inst. Printed Circuits, Beta Kappa Chi, Phi Beta Sigma (vice dir. Eastern region) Democrat. Methodist. Home: 917 Penobscot Rd Richmond VA 23227

MC CLINTOCK, GEORGE DAVISON, architect, planner; b. Texas City, Tex., Jan. 1, 1925; s. Otto Clive and Mary (Davison) McC.; B.Arch., U. Tex., 1951, M.Arch., 1952; m. Nivea Mercedes Hernandez, Oct. 8, 1954; children—Kenneth D., Steven G., Elaine M. Master planner City of San Benito (Tex.), 1951-52; urban renewal planner P.R. Housing Authority, 1952-55; regional planner 3d Air Force in Europe, London, 1955-58; chief planner P.R. Urban Renewal and Housing Corp., 1958-60; pvt. practice architecture and planning, P.R., Virgin Islands, Trinidad and Jamaica, Hato Rey, P.R., 1960—; mem. Fed. Energy Adminstrn. Consumer Affairs Com., 1976-78, Gov.'s Historic Preservation Rev. Bd., 1979—; mem. panel of arbitrators Am. Arbitration Assn. Mem. Am. Inst. Planners (nat. bd. examiners 1971—), Constrn. Specifications Inst. (founding mem., 1st pres. P.R. chpt.), Colegio de Arquitectos de P.R. (charter), Am. Soc. Planning Ofcls., Americans for Democratic Action (founding mem. P.R. chpt.). Democrat. Episcopalian. Club: Caparra Country (Guaynabo, P.R.). Home: 1716 Santa Eduvigis Rio Piedras PR 00926 Office: Suite 524 Fomento Bldg 268 Ponde de Leon Ave Hato Rey PR 00918

MC CLINTOCK, SIMMS, polit. scientist, educator; b. Lake Village, Ark., July 10, 1927; s. William Richey and Lilly (Simms) McC.; B.A., Hendrix Coll., 1951; M.A., Columbia, 1953. Coordinator social studies Crossett (Ark.) High Sch., 1953-65; asso. prof. polit. sci. U. Central Ark., Conway, 1966—, chmn. dept., 1976-77. Faculty adviser Ark. Model UN, 1966—. Faulkner County Hist. Soc. Sec., bd. dirs. Carmichael Found.; rep. Ark. Constl. Conv., 1979-80. Served with USNR, 1945-48, 51-52. Recipient Distinguished award Ark. Jr. C. of C., 1962; named Ark. Tchr. of Year, U.S. Office Edn. and Look Mag., 1963. John Hay fellow Columbia, 1965-66. Mem. Classroom Tchrs. Ark. (pres.), Ark. Edn. Assn., Faulkner County Hist. Soc. (pres.), Phi Delta Kappa. Episcopalian. Author: Guide To Teaching Citizenship, 1961; Guide To Teaching Economics, 1965; A Critical Analysis of the Constitutions of Arkansas for 1836, 1861, 1864, and 1868, 1978; A Critical Analysis of the Constitution of Arkansas for 1868 and 1874 and the Proposed Constitutions of 1918 and 1970, 1978. Home: 120 Baridon St Conway AR 72032

MC CLUNG, JAMES FELTON, JR., mfg. co. exec.; b. Oklahoma City, Sept. 10, 1942; s. James Felton and Mary Agnes McClung; B.A. in Social Sci., San Diego State Coll., 1966; A.A., Pasadena Jr. Coll., 1963; m. Mary Ester Woods, July 1, 1967; children—Kristi Lynn, Todd Allan. Mktg. rep. Texaco, Inc., Burbank, Calif., 1966-68, Bakersfield, Calif., 1968-69; sales rep. Johnson & Johnson, Albuquerque, 1969-70, Ft. Worth, 1971-73, Houston, 1973-74; regional mktg. specialist Cordis Dow Corp., Houston, 1974-76, southwestern div. sales mgr., Houston, 1976—. Bd. dirs. Gulf Coast Kidney Found., Houston, 1979—. Served with U.S. Army, 1968. Republican. Baptist. Club: Masons. Home: 11806 Westmere Dr Houston TX 77077

MC CLUNG, LUTHER THERMAN, oil operator, rancher; b. Kerens, Tex., Oct. 30, 1909; s. Luther T. and Carrie J. (Miller) McC.; student public schs., Dallas; m. Evelyn Louise Loe, Aug. 6, 1927; children—Lucian Louise McClung Richardson, Barbara Ann McClung Wells. Circulation mgr. Courier-Times, Tyler, Tex. and Ft. Worth Press, 1927-40; asst. bus. mgr. Longview (Tex.) News-Jour., 1927-40; gen. contractor Luther T. McClung and McClung Constrn. Co., 1940-48; pres. McClung Oil Corp., 1958—; pres. Western States Equipment Co., Midland, Tex.; owner, operator Luther T. McClung 4M Ranch, Kiowa, Okla. and Comanche County, Tex., 1948—. Mem. Am. (dir. 1950-56), Tex. (pres. 1950, dir. 1948-52) Angus assns. Home: Route 2 Box 99X Comanche TX 76442

MC CLUNG, NORVEL MALCOLM, educator; b. McClungs, W.Va., June 9, 1916; s. Virgil Edward and Mary (Anderson) McC.; A.B., Glenville State Coll., 1936; M.S., U. Mich., 1940, Ph.D., 1949; m. Delia Rainey, Aug. 31, 1945 (div. Sept. 1966); children—Charles E., Margaret L., Ralph A., Susan E.; m. 2d, Hermine Friedson, Oct. 18, 1966. Tchr. Webster Springs (W.Va.) High Sch., 1936-41; asst. prof. biology U. Kans., Lawrence, 1948-57; asso. prof. U. Ga., Athens, 1957-66; prof. U. South Fla., Tampa, 1966—. Vis. prof. Kyoto (Japan) U., 1962-63; cons. Fla. Dept. Health, 1968, Ocean Products, Plant City, Fla., 1968-69. Served to capt. USNR, 1941-46. Decorated Purple Heart, Navy and Marine Corps medal. La. State U. tropical medicine fellow, 1960; Fulbright Research award, Japan, 1961-62; recipient grants U. Kan. Found., 1950-53, NIH, 1954-57, Massengill Corp., 1956-58, NSF, 1960-61, 50-65, travel award Sigma Xi, 1961, Am. Soc. Microbiology, 1963. Mem. Southeastern Electron Microscopy Soc. (chmn. 1970-72), AAAS, AAUP, Am. Inst. Biol. Scis., Am. Soc. Microbiology, Bacteriol. Soc. Japan, Bot. Soc. Am., Internat. Soc. Human and Animal Mycoses, Kans. Acad. Scis., Med. Mycology Soc. Am. (charter), Mycol. Soc. Am., Soc. Gen. Microbiology (Brit.), Am. Acad. Microbiology, Sigma Xi, Phi Kappa Phi, Phi Sigma. Author: (with A.J. Mix) Mycology for Students of Bacteriology and Medicine, 1955; (with R.G. Eagon and W.J. Payne) A Laboratory Manual for Intruductory Bacteriology, 1960. Contbr. sect. on Nocardia to Manual Determinative Bacteriology (Bergey), 8th edit.; also articles to profl. jours. Home: 2701 Varsity Pl Tampa FL 33612

MCCLURE, CHARLES ALFRED, broadcasting exec.; b. Canton, Ga., Mar. 21, 1923; s. Alfred Wright and Kate (Faulkner) McC.; student N. Ga. Coll., 1941, Ga. Evening Coll., 1942; B.A. in Journalism, U. Ga., 1947; m. Dorothy Watson, Sept. 20, 1947; children—Margaret McClure Rogers, Charles Alfred, Joseph Watson. Dir. merchandizing Sta. WSB, Atlanta, 1941-43; sales mgr. Sta. WRFC, Athens, Ga., 1948-53; pres. licensing corps. of the following stas.: WCGQ-FM, Columbus, Ga., WRCG, Columbus, WCHK-AM-FM, Canton, WAGQ-FM, Athens, 1953—; dir. Nat. Bank & Trust. Chmn., Columbus Airport Commn., 1973—; chmn. bd. trustees Spring Theater Co., Columbus; pres. Columbus Boy's Club; mem. Ala.-Ga. council Boy Scouts Am.; bd. dirs. Tb Assn., Columbus. Served with AC, U.S. Army, 1943-46; lt. col. USAF Res. Decorated D.F.C., Air medal with oak leaf cluster. Mem. Ga. Assn. Broadcasters, Nat. Assn. Broadcasters, Radio Advt. Bur., Ga. Alumni Assn., Columbus Bull Dog Club, U.S. Tennis Assn., Sigma Delta Chi, Alpha Kappa Psi, Di Gamma Kappa. Methodist. Clubs: Rotary, Columbus Country, Big Eddy. Office: 1327 Warren Williams Rd Columbus GA 31902

MC CLURE, CHARLES FRANKLIN, JR., data processing exec.; b. Pelzer, S.C., Sept. 26, 1947; s. Charles Franklin and Frances (Saylors) McC.; B.A., U. S.C., 1970, M.A., 1973; M.B.A., Ga. State U., 1978. Asst. store mgr. K-Mart Corp., Atlanta, 1973-74, Greenville, S.C., 1974-77; customer service rep. Nat. Data Corp., Atlanta, 1978-79; account mgr. Policy Mgmt. Systems div. Seibels, Bruce Ins. Co., 1979—. Active Cyclorama Restoration, Inc., Atlanta, 1975—. Mem. Assn. M.B.A. Execs., Am. Mgmt. Assn., Univ. S.C. Alumni Assn., Jaycees. Republican. Presbyterian. Home: PO Box 534 West Columbia SC 29169 Office: 1321 Lady St Columbia SC 29202

MCCLURE, CHARLES RICHARD, supt. schs.; b. Morgantown, W.Va., Apr. 8, 1935; s. C.W. and Alta M. (Cale) McC.; B.A., W.Va. U., 1957, M.A., 1960; m. Shirley Pat Tallman, July 11, 1964; children—Marilyn, Scott, Mary, Marlin. Tchr., Preston County (W.Va.) schs., 1957-60, supr., personnel dir. fed. programs, 1960-67; program coordinator N. Central W.Va., W.Va. Dept. Edn., 1967-73; adminstrv. asst. Harrison County (W.Va.) schs., Clarksburg, 1974, supt., 1974—. Mem. exec. bd. Harrison County United Way. Mem. Am. Assn. Sch. Adminstrs., Nat. Sch. Bd. Assn., Nat. Assn. Supervision and Curriculum Devel., W.Va. Assn. Sch. Adminstrs. (Service award 1979), W.Va. U. Alumni Assn., W.Va. Sch. Bd. Assn., W.Va. Assn. Supervision and Curriculum Devel., Clarksburg C. of C. (edn. com.), Phi Delta Kappa, Phi Mu Alpha Sinfonia. Methodist. Clubs: Clarksburg Lions, Kingwood Rotary, Masons, Shriners. Author papers in field. Home: 402 James St Bridgeport WV 26330 Office: 301 W Main St Clarksburg WV 26301

MC CLURE, DONALD R., city ofcl.; b. Erlanger, Ky., Aug. 14, 1931; s. Howard R. and Anna (Reffitt) McC.; B.A., U. Ky.; M.S.S.W. in Psychiat. Social Work, U. Tenn.; m. Rosa Lee, Jan. 31, 1959. Dir., Ky. Div. Mental Retardation, 1964; dir. instl. services Ky. Dept. Child Welfare, 1964-68; dir. child services City of Jacksonville (Fla.), 1968-71, dir. human resources, 1971-79, chief adminstrv. officer, 1979—. Vice pres. Boys Club; mem. Fla. Gov.'s Task Force on Juvenile Justice and Delinquency Prevention. Served to 1st lt. USAF, 1956-69. Recipient medallion Boys Club, 1977, Basileus award Alpha Kappa, 1978. Mem. Am. Corrections Assn., Acad. Cert. Social Workers, Nat. Assn. Social Workers (pres. N.E. Fla. chpt.). Democrat. Office: City Hall Room 1402 Jacksonville FL 32202

MC CLURE, MICHAEL DESTEWART, profl. football team exec.; b. Chgo., Jan. 23, 1942; s. Charles F. and Janette L. (Lawler) McC.; B.A., DePauw U., 1964; m. Brenda G. Jones, Oct. 24, 1964; children—Michael C., Matthew D. Reporter, City News Bur., Chgo., 1964-65, Chgo. Tribune, 1965-66; public relations cons. Peoples Gas Co., Chgo., 1966-69; sports dir. Sta. WLFI-TV, Lafayette, Ind., 1969-70; service bur. dir. Big Ten Conf., 1970-73; dir. public relations and mktg. Chgo. Bulls, 1973-78; v.p. public relations and mktg. Houston Oilers, 1978—, also dir. Recipient Best in Nation awards Cosida, 1972, 73; named One of 10 Outstanding Young Citizens, Chgo. Jaycees, 1974. Mem. Houston Advt. Fedn., Houston Sportswriters and Sportscasters Assn., DePauw U. Alumni Assn., Sigma Delta Chi, Sigma Chi. Editor Big Ten Records Book, 1970-73; editor Houston Oilers Pro mag., 1979. Home: 3907 Point Clear Dr Missouri City TX 77459 Office: PO Box 1516 Houston TX 77001

MC CLURE, RUTH MARTIN, utility co. exec.; b. Young Harris, Ga., Aug. 14, 1933; d. Sim H. and Ruby (Welch) Martin; student Young Harris Coll., 1950-51; m. Charles R McClure, Dec. 26, 1952; children—Rusty A., Randy, Robby. With Blue Ridge Mountain Electric Membership Corp., Young Harris, Ga., since 1950—, office mgr., 1955-77, adminstrv. asst., 1977-79. Mem. Ga. Electric Membership Office Mgrs. and Bookkeepers (sec.), Power Accts. Assn. (dir. Eastern div. 1979—). Baptist. Eastern Star. Home: Rt 1 Box 18B Blairsville GA 30512 Office: PO Box 8 Main St Young Harris GA 30582

MC CLURG, GENE ROARK, ednl. adminstr.; b. Albuquerque, Sept. 13, 1935; s. Floyd Anderson and Gladys (Roark) McC.; B.S., Tex. Western Coll., 1963; M.S., Tex. A&M U., 1969, Ph.D. (Welch fellow), 1970; m. Ruth Mary Elam, Jan. 30, 1976. Math. tchr. Ysleta public schs. and computer programmer/tchr. El Paso (Tex.) public schs., 1963-66; physics prof. Odessa (Tex.) Coll., 1970-72; owner-promoter San Angelo (Tex.) Raceway, 1971-73; electronics instr. Western Tex. Coll., Snyder, 1974, tech.-vocat. dean, 1974—. Vice pres. Indsl. Found., 1978, sec.-treas., 1979. Served with USAF, 1955-58. Mem. Tex. Jr. Coll. Tchrs. Assn., Tex. Assn. Postsecondary Occupational Adminstrs., Tex. Assn. Jr. Coll. Instructional Adminstrs., Am. Phys. Soc., Sigma Xi, Phi Delta Kappa. Baptist. Club: Rotary (editor 1977, program chmn. 1978). Contbr. articles to Jour. Chem. Physics. Home: 2801 33rd St Snyder TX 79549 Office: Western Texas College Snyder TX 79549

MC COLLAM, JAMES GRAHAM, author, artist, photographer; b. Newburgh, N.Y., Feb. 8, 1913; s. James and Elizabeth (Stolicker) McC.; ed. pub. schs.; m. Lonette Eutzler, Oct. 30, 1937; 1 dau., Ann Lynn (Mrs. Gene Pendl). West coast editor Fla. Boating, Apopka, Fla., 1968-69; editorial cons. So. Sailing, Tallahassee, 1970-71; tech. editor Gondolier mag., Ft. Lauderdale, Fla., 1973-74; furniture forum editor Antique Monthly, Tuscaloosa, Ala., 1969-79; writer for Yachting, Motor Boating, Cruising World, and Sailing, 1971-79; syndicated weekly columnist Antique Furniture, Copley News Service. Served with USAAF, 1943-46. Mem. Antique Appraisal Assn. Am. Club: Dunedin (Fla.) Yacht (gov., vice commodore). Author: The Yachtsman's Weather Manual, 1973; Is It Really an Antique?, 1980; contbr. tech. articles to trade jours. Home: 1003 Egret Ct Dunedin FL 33528

MC COLLOUGH, HELEN LOUISE, marine retail co. exec.; b. Sour Lake, Tex., Mar. 9, 1929; d. Emory Bland and Cora Lee (Frederick) Smith; B.A., Southwestern Bus. Coll., 1952; m. Apr. 30, 1967; children—Harold Wayne Stockdale, Charlotte Elizabeth Stockdale, Thomas Waters. Clk.-steno Humble Oil Refinery, Tomball, Tex., 1956-58; prodn. clk. Superior Oil Co., Conroe, Tex., 1958-63; bus driver Conroe Ind. Sch. Dist., 1967—; owner Conroe Marine Inc., 1967—, owner, pres., 1977—; agt. Tex. Parks and Wildlife, 1974—. Mem. Tex. Tchrs. Assn., Conroe Tchrs. Assn., Bus. and Profl. Club, Internat. CB Radio Operators Assn. Baptist. Home: 413 Oak Hill Dr Conroe TX 77304 Office: Conroe Marine Inc 1100 Wilson Rd Conroe TX 77301

MC COLLUM, SHARON ANN, educator, counselor; b. Oakdale, La., Dec. 24, 1954; d. Walter and Helen Ruth (Lofton) McC.; B.A. (fellow), So. U. New Orleans, 1976; M.A. (grantee), U. Calif., Davis, 1978. Coop. edn. placement Sears, Roebuck and Co., 1971-72; research asst. So. U., New Orleans, 1972, admissions counselor, recruiter, 1978—, instr. dept. sociology, 1979—; sec. La. Wild Life and Fisheries Commn., 1974-76; research and library asst. U. Calif., 1976-78; program analyst Calif. Dept. Health, 1977; cons. in field. Mem. Am. Personnel and Guidance Assn. Democrat. Methodist. Office: So U 6400 Press Dr New Orleans LA 70126

MC COMAS, RONALD EDWARD, computer co. exec.; b. Orlando, Fla., June 11, 1943; s. Roy Leon and Mary Rita (Santry) McC.; student U. Detroit, 1961-63; B.S., Western Mich. U., 1966; postgrad. Wayne State U., 1967-69; m. Donna Sue Frost, Oct. 17, 1969; children—Kelli, Micheal. Systems engr. Gen. Elec. Info. Systems, Inc., Detroit, 1968-70; sales rep. Honeywell Info. Systems, Inc., Detroit, 1970-74; group product mgr., mktg. mgr. Honeywell Info. Systems, Boston, 1974-77; br. mgr. Sperry Univac, Houston, 1977-79; regional mgr. Moore Bus. Systems, Dallas, 1979—; data processing cons. Coordinator high sch. religious program Holy Family Ch.; mem. Bible Study Fellowship; city coordinator Marriage Encounter. Roman Catholic. Home: 3836 Santiago Dr Plano TX 75023 Office: 2974 LB Johnson Freeway Dallas TX 75234

MC CONAGHY, JOSEPH WILLIAM, accountant; b. N.Y.C., Aug. 11, 1932; s. Joseph William and Evelyn (Hartung) McC.; B.S., Fordham U., 1960; postgrad. U.S. Fgn. Service Inst., 1964-65; M.P.H. in Med. Care Adminstrn., U. Mich., 1974; m. Doreen Elizabeth Searle, Nov. 22, 1958; children—Doreen and Dianne (twins), Pamela, Paul. Supervisory officer bond dept. Chase Manhattan Bank, N.Y.C., 1957-60; pvt. practice, N.Y.C., 1958-64; v.p., controller, dir. Glenair Internat. Corp., New Rochelle, N.Y., 1959-64; sr. accountant, tax specialist Price Waterhouse & Co., 1960-64; treas., dir. U.S. Locator Corp., audit and financial specialist U.S. State Dept., AID, Santo Domingo, 1964-67, Viet Nam, 1967-69, Colombia, 1969-70; sr. corporate auditor United Fruit Co., Boston, 1970-72; comptroller dept. community medicine Boston U. Sch. Medicine, 1972; project dir., dir. fiscal affairs Roxbury Comprehensive Community Health Center, Inc., Boston, 1973-74; exec. dir. Econ. Opportunity Family Health Center Inc., Miami, Fla., 1974-76; auditor Dade County, Fla., 1978; pvt. practice accounting, cons., 1976—. Served with USN, 1950-54, USMCR, 1954-57; intelligence officer USNR, 1960-72. C.P.A., N.Y., Mass., Fla. Mem. Nat. Assn. Accountants, Am. Inst. C.P.A.'s, N.Y. State Soc. C.P.A.'s, Fla., Dade County socs. C.P.A.'s, Res. Officers Assn., Nat. Assn. Neighborhood Health Centers, Am. Pub. Health Assn. Roman Catholic (parish council 1972-74). K.C. Home: Miami FL Office: 90 JW McConaghy PO Box 560152 Kendal FL 33156

MC CONKEY, JANICE, nurse; b. McMinn County, Tenn., Nov. 28, 1947; d. Alfred R. and Mary A. (Wood) McC.; R.N., Fort Sanders Presbyn. Hosp., 1969; postgrad. U. Tenn.; 1 dau., Cynthia Dyan. Nurse, Fort Sanders Presbyn. Hosp., Knoxville, Tenn., 1969-70; clin. mgr., nurse Oak Ridge Hosp., 1970—. Mem. Am. Soc. Nursing Service Adminstrs., Tenn. Soc. Nursing Service Adminstrs., E. Tenn. Assn. Nurse Mgrs. Home: 65 Outer Dr Oak Ridge TN 37830 Office: Oak Ridge Hospital 125 W Tennessee Ave Oak Ridge TN 37830

MC CONN, JAMES JOSEPH, mayor Houston; b. Tulsa, Mar. 15, 1928; grad. U. Notre Dame, 1948; m. Margie McConn. Owner, McConn Constrn. Co., Houston; mayor City of Houston, 1978—, mem. city council, 1971-74. Office: City Hall 901 Bagby St Houston TX 77002

MC CONN, JAMES JOSEPH, city ofcl.; b. Tulsa, Mar. 15, 1928; ed. U. Notre Dame; m. Margie. Mayor City of Houston, 1978—. Office: Office of Mayor 900 Brazos St Houston TX 77002

MC CONNELL, BARBARA ANN ROGERS, electric co. adminstr.; b. Pelzer, S.C., July 27, 1939; d. Walter Herbert and Genav (Garrett) Rogers; Asso. Applied Sci., Greenville Tech. Coll., 1973; B.Gen. Studies magna cum laude, U. S.C., 1975; m. William Dendy McConnell, Aug. 24, 1957; 1 son, William Dendy. Gen. acct. J.P. Stevens & Co., Greenville, S.C., 1975-77; gen. acctg. supr. Gear Products plant Reliance Electric Co., Greenville, 1977—. Mem. Nat. Assn. Accts. (asso. dir. membership acquisition Western Carolinas chpt. 1973-74). Club: Order Eastern Star. Home: Route 1 Box 422 Pelzer SC 29669 Office: Reliance Electric Co PO Box 5065 Sta B Greenville SC 29606

MC CONNELL, DOROTHY FRAISER (MRS. FREDERICK EARL MCCONNELL), ret. coll. dean; b. Cocoa, Fla., Sept. 4, 1924; d. Albert Bateman and Norma (Statzer) Fraiser; student U. Tampa, 1949-51, 55; B.A., Pan Am. Coll., 1956; M. Ed., Auburn U., 1960; Ed.D., Baylor U., 1967; m. Fredrick Earl McConnell, Mar. 29, 1947; children—Lester Earl, Ronald Fraiser, Oma Elizabeth. Bookkeeper, Eelbeck Milling Co., Columbus, Ga., 1942-46; elementary tchr. Harligen (Tex.) pub. schs., 1954-59, Colquitt County sch. system, Moultrie, Ga., 1959-61, Connally ind. sch. system, Waco, Tex., 1961-65; prof. edn. Mary Hardin-Baylor Coll., Belton, Tex., 1965-69, dean of students, 1969-75. Bd. dirs. REACH Center, Belton; tchr. sr. citizens First Baptist Ch., Temple, Tex.; treas. Temple Ch. Women. Served with WAVES, USNR, 1946-47. Recipient Exceptional Achievement award Bd. Trustees, Mary Hardin-Baylor Coll., 1975; named Belle of Brazos, State of Tex. Mem. Nat. Ednl. Assn., Tex. State Tchrs. Assn., AAUW, Nat. (recipient Leadership citation), Tex. assns. women's deans, adminstrs. and counselors, Ex-Students Assn. Baylor U. (life), Auburn Alumni Assn. (life), Royal Academia Soc. (hon.), Alpha Delta Kappa, Delta Kappa Gamma. Mem. Order Eastern Star. Editor: Sixty-Six Years Remembered, 1976. Address: 2810 Del Norte St Temple TX 76501

MCCONNELL, FREEMAN ERTON, educator, audiologist; b. West Point, Ind., Apr. 20, 1914; s. Grant Wilson and Alma (Wyman) McC.; B.S., U. Ill., 1939, M.A., 1946; Ph.D., Northwestern U., 1950; m. Grace Boonie Conn, May 31, 1941; children—Conn Michael, Steven Grant. Audiologist, asst. prof. logopedics U. Wichita (Kans.) Inst. Logopedics, 1950-51; cir. Bill Wilkerson Hearing and Speech Center, Nashville, 1951-60, 63-76, dir. emeritus, 1976—; asst. prof. audiology, chmn. div. audiology and speech Vanderbilt U. Sch. Medicine, 1951-53, asso. prof., chmn., 1953-56, prof., chmn., 1956-60, prof. audiology, chmn. div. hearing and spl. scis., 1963-75, asso. prof. otolaryngology, 1969-79, prof. audiology, 1976-79, prof. audiology emeritus, 1979—; prof. head dept. audiology and speech pathology U. Tenn., Knoxville, 1960-63; vis. prof. audiology Syracuse U., 1967; cons. audiology Arnold Engring. Devel. Center, Tullahoma, Tenn., 1953-72; cons. health div. Oak Ridge Nat. Lab., 1963-67; research cons. U.S. Office Edn., 1965-74; mem. U.S.-Can. Adv. Com. Ann. Survey Hearing Impaired Children and Youth, 1970-78, numerous short-term consultantships to health and edn. depts. Bd. dirs. Am. Hearing Soc., 1954-60; trustee Edn. and Auditory Research Found., 1972—. Served with AUS, 1943-46. Nat. Inst. Neurol, Diseases and Stroke grantee, 1957-60, 63-65, 66-74, U.S. Office Edn. grantee, 1965-73. Fellow Am. Speech and Hearing Assn. (honors 1977); mem. Acad. Rehab. Audiology (past pres.), Council on Exceptional Children, AAAS, Acoustical Soc. Am., Tenn. Speech and Hearing Assn. (past pres., honors 1972). Democrat. Episcoplaian. Editor: Deafness in Childhood, 1967; asso. editor: Jour. Speech and Hearing Disorders, 1963-65, Exceptional Children, 1965-71. Contbr. articles to profl. jours. and chpts. to books. Research on hereditary deafness and lang. devel. Home: 3828 Richland Ave Nashville TN 37205

MC CONNELL, JERRY DAVID, collateral control co. exec.; b. Lebanon, Tenn., Feb. 5, 1946; s. Howard David and Hazel Lee (Murray) McC.; B.S., David Lipscomb Coll., 1968; m. Cathy Louise Diane Taylor, Jan. 11, 1975. Mgmt. trainee Nashville City Bank, 1972-73, asst. br. officer, mgr., 1973-76; ops. exam. auditor Lawrence Systems Inc., Nashville, 1976-79, asst. v.p. regional loan adminstrn., fin. cons. Southeast U.S., Atlanta, 1978—. Served as officer AUS, 1968-72; Korea. Recipient award Nashville Area Jaycees, 1979. Mem. Nashville Area Jr. C. of C. (com. chmn.), West Nashville Jaycees (past treas.). Republican. Episcopalian. Home: 3335 Herrenhut Dr Lithonia GA 30058 Office: 51 Executive Park Dr NE Atlanta GA 30329

MCCONNELL, JOHN KNOX, JR., banker; b. McKeesport, Pa., Dec. 13, 1926; s. John Knox and Marie Mary (Rice) McC.; B.S., Waynesburg Coll., 1949; postgrad. Stanford U., 1961. With Pitts. Nat. Bank, 1950-52; pres. Community Bank of Pitts., 1972-75, Micronesia Devel. Bank, Saipan, 1975-77, First Nat. Bank, Keystone, W.Va., 1977—. Served with U.S. Army, 1950. Mem. Nat. Assn. Review Appraisers. Democrat. Presbyterian. Clubs: Univ., Rotary, Masons, Elks. Author: How to Get a Loan, 1975; Micronesia Development Bank, 1976. Address: Drawer AA Keystone WV 24852

MC CONNELL, JOHN MINER, ins. co. exec.; b. Long Branch, N.J., Oct. 14, 1938; s. James Elmer and Marjorie Agnes (Horn) McC.; A.B., U. N.C., 1961; M.B.A., Fla. Internat. U., 1975; student St. John's U., 1959-60; m. Angela Diaz-Serna, July 14, 1968; children—Bridget, Eileen, Maureen. Asst. buyer Coats & Clark, Inc., N.Y.C., 1962-63; mem. staff Jersey Central P & L Co., Allenhurst, N.J., 1962-66; field claims rep. Fla. and Tex., State Farm Ins. Co., 1966-71, claims specialist Corpus Christi, 1971—. Mem. Claims Assn. Corpus Christi, Tex. Claims Assn. Republican. Roman Catholic. Club: Serra (v.p. programs 1979-80) (Corpus Christi). Home: 5302 Bromley Dr Corpus Christi TX 78413 Office: Box 7748 Corpus Christi TX 78415

MC CONNELL, LEWIS H., physician; b. Balt., July 2, 1942; s. William Lewis and Louise Angelus (Llufrio) McC.; A.A., Potomac State Coll., 1962; B.A., W.Va. U., 1964, M.D., 1967; m. Susan Jane Stout, June 12, 1965; children—Amy, David, John, Paul. Intern, Walter Reed Hosp., Washington, 1967-68; resident internal medicine Med. Coll. Wis., Milw., 1968-70, fellow allergy and immunology, 1971-73; practice medicine, specializing in allergy and immunology, Charleston, W.Va., 1973—; asst. clin. prof. W.Va. U. Sch. Medcine, 1973—; mem. staff Charleston Area Med. Center. Served to capt. MC AUS, 1967-68. Diplomate Am. Bd. Internal Medicine, Am. Bd. Allergy and Immunology, Nat. Bd. Med. Examiners. Fellow Am. Acad. Allergy, Am. Coll. Allergy, Am. Coll. Chest Physicians; mem. Am. Coll. Physicians, Am. Assn. Certified Allergists, Am. Thoracic Soc., Southeastern Allergy Soc., So. Med. Assn., W.Va. Med. Assn., Kanawha County Med. Soc. Republican. Contbr. articles to med. jours. Home: 4406 Kanawha Ave SE Charleston WV 25304 Office: 3416 MacCorkle Ave SE Charleston WV 25304

MC CONNELL, MERLE GRANT, personnel adminstr.; b. Henning, Ill., Feb. 25, 1928; s. Grant Wilson and Alma Mahala (Wyman) McC.; student U. Ill., 1946-48; B.S., Northwestern U., 1951; m. Iris May Shreve, June 11, 1950; children—Jeff, Ann, Neal. Tchr. pub. schs. Hillsborough County (Fla.), 1951-52, Cahokia, Ill., 1952-53; with Equifax, Inc. (formerly Retail Credit Co.), 1953—, staff specialist, Atlanta, 1956-59, asst. mgr. br., office, Springfield, Ill., 1959-62, div. head, Atlanta, 1962-70, dir. personnel adminstrn., 1970—. Mem. Am. Soc. Personnel Adminstrn. (past dist. dir., past pres. Atlanta chpt.), Am. Compensation Assn. Republican. Methodist. Club: Civitan. Home: 3002 Marlin Dr Atlanta GA 30341 Office: 1600 Peachtree St Atlanta GA 30302

MC CONNELL, RICHARD LEON, chemist; b. Gate City, Va., Mar. 23, 1926; s. Robert F. and Janie (Broadwater) McC.; student Carson Newman Coll. 1944-45; U. Ill., 1945-46; B.S., Ky., 1948; M.S., U. Va., 1950, Ph.D., 1952; m. Carolyn C. McMeekin, July 17, 1948; children—Richard Leon, Ann Craig, Elizabeth Lee. With Tenn. Eastman Co., Kingsport, Tenn., 1951—, sr. research chemist, 1957-70, research asso., 1970—. Served with USNR, 1944-46. Mem. Am. Chem. Soc., N.Y. Acad. Scis., Sigma Xi, Alpha Chi Sigma. Presbyn. Contbr. to profl. jours. Patentee chemicals. Home: 421

Manderley Rd Kingsport TN 37660 Office: Tenn Eastman Co Kingsport TN 37662

MC CONNELL, RUFUS PAUL, food service adminstr.; b. Mobile, Ala., July 16, 1926; s. Mitchell M. and Fannie (Paul) McC.; student public schs., Mobile, Ala.; m. Edith Harmon, Oct. 11, 1975; children—Wanda, James; stepchildren—Barry, Peggy, Kathy. Line server Morrisons, Inc., Goodman, Miss., 1948-49, storeroom mgr., 1949-53, chief steward, 1953-56, asst. mgr., 1956-58, traveling caterer, 1958-60, mgr., 1960-75, food service dir., 1975—. Served with USN, 1943-46. Decorated Bronze Star (5). Democrat. Baptist. Home: 108 S Washington St Durant MS 39063 Office: Holmes Jr Coll Goodman MS 39079

MC CONOCHIE, WILLIAM MICHAEL, mfg. co. exec.; b. Raleigh, N.C., Nov. 18, 1940; s. Daniel Duncan and Virginia (Duke) McC.; B.Arch., Ga. Inst. Tech., 1968; m. Caroline Kinney, Aug. 21, 1960; children—Elisa, Josh, Micah. Architect, Tomberlin Assos., Architects, Atlanta, 1968-74; prin. William Michael McConochie, Architect, Moultrie, Ga., 1974-75; regional architect Portland Cement Assn., Columbia, S.C., 1975-79; sales mgr. Statesville Concrete Products Co., Statesville, N.C., 1979—. Served with USNR, 1958-64. Mem. AIA. Clubs: Statesville Country, Rotary. Home: 241 Nottingham Circle Statesville NC 28677 Office: PO Box 288 Statesville NC 28677

MC CORD, GUYTE PIERCE, JR., judge; b. Tallahassee, Sept. 23, 1914; s. Guyte Pierce and Jean (Patterson) McC.; student Davidson Coll., 1933-34; B.A., J.D., U. Fla., 1940; m. Laura Elizabeth Mack, Dec. 16, 1939; children—Florence Elizabeth, Guyte Pierce III, Edward LeRoy. Admitted to Fla. bar, 1940; practiced in Tallahassee, 1940-60; dep. commr. Fla. Insl. Commn., 1946-47, pros. atty. Leon County, 1947-48, asst. gen. counsel Fla. Pub. Service Commn., 1949-60; judge 2d Jud. Circuit Fla., Tallahassee, 1960-74; judge Ct. Appeal 1st Dist. Fla., 1974—, chief judge, 1977-79. Pres. Murat House Assn., Inc., 1967-69; bd. dirs. Fla. Heritage Found., 1969-70, mem. exec. com., 1965-69. Served to comdr. USNR, 1942-46, 52-53. Mem. Res. Officers Assn. (v.p. Tallahassee 1961-64), Tallahassee C. of C., Am. Judicature Soc., Fla. Conf. Circuit Judges (sec.-treas. 1970, chmn. 1972), Phi Delta Phi, Sigma Alpha Epsilon. Presbyn. (elder 1960—). Kiwanian (dir. 1958-59). Home: 502 S Ride St Tallahassee FL 32303 Office: PO Box 1028 Tallahassee FL 32302

MC CORGARY, MARVIN VINCENT, pub. co. exec.; b. Arkansas City, Kans., Sept. 24, 1937; s. Thomas Arthur and Devora Agnes (Younger) McC.; B.S., Pittsburg State U., 1963; M.S., Emporia State U., 1966; m. Anita Marie Belew, July 9, 1959; children—Alisa Marie, Michael Grayson. Tchr. printing and journalism Emporia (Kans.) schs., 1963-66; plant supt. Am. Yearbook Co., Topeka, 1966-69; mfg. mgr. Taylor Pub. Co., Dallas, 1969-75, dir. br. plant ops., 1975—. Served with U.S. Army, 1957-59. Roman Catholic. Home: 6247 Los Altos St El Paso TX 79912 Office: Taylor Pub Co 3210 Dyer St El Paso TX 79930

MCCORKLE, ALLAN JAMES, ins. co. exec.; b. Shreveport, La., Aug. 29, 1931; s. Adolphus James and Eugenia Jane (Johnson) McC.; B.S., Fla. State U., 1956; m. Rosemary Louise Hollander, June 15, 1957; children—Kimberly Rae, Scott Allan, Holly Jane. Safety engr., corp. sales rep. Liberty Mut. Ins. Co., Roanoke, Va., and Jacksonville, Fla., 1956-68; founder, pres. various mobile home dealerships, Fla., 1965—; pres. Mobile Am. Corp., Jacksonville, Mobile Am. Ins. Group, Inc., Jacksonville, 1968—, Mobile Am. Village, Inc., Jacksonville, 1969—, Fortune Ins. Co., Jacksonville, 1972—; pres. Fortune Life Ins. Co., Phoenix, 1971—; bd. govs. Fla. Ins. Com. Chmn., Mass Transit, 1971; mem. adv. com. Jacksonville Planning Bd., 1971—. Bd. dirs. Jacksonville Transp. Authority. Served with AUS, 1948-52. Named to Top Producers Club Liberty Mut., 1963-71, Liberty Leaders Club for number 1 sales result in U.S., 1964. Mem. Fla. Mobile Home Assn., Cummer Gallery (life), Jacksonville Art Mus. (life), Fla. State Alumni Assn. (pres. 1964), Jacksonville C. of C., Alpha Tau Omega, Kappa Tau Kappa. Democrat. Roman Catholic. Clubs: Big Tree Racquet; River, Ponte Vedra (Jacksonville). Contbr. articles on mobile home industry to various publs. Home: Box 85 Mandarin Sta Jacksonville FL 32206 Office: Gulf Life Tower Jacksonville FL 32207

MC CORKLE, CHARLES HOWARD, ret. supt. schs.; b. Elizabethton, Tenn., Apr. 8, 1909; s. Arthur Emmert and Bessie D. (Williams) McC.; B.S., Milligan Coll., 1931, LL.D. (hon.), 1972; postgrad. E. Tenn. State U., 1932, State U. Iowa, 1952, George Peabody Coll., 1938; M.A., Vanderbilt U., 1936; m. Elizabeth L. Connell, June 9, 1936; children—Nancy Williams (Mrs. Donald Stivers), Elizabeth Louise (Mrs. Michael Ludwig). Elementary tchr. Johnson City (Tenn.) Pub. Schs., 1932-34, elementary prin., 1934-36, asst. prin. jr. high, 1936-41, prin. jr. high, 1941-42, prin. sr. high, 1942-52, supr., 1952-56, supt., 1956-74, ret., 1974. Mem. exec. com. Assn. Drug Edn., 1969-70; mem. Gov.'s Com. for Mentally Retarded, 1967-70. Bd. dirs. Johnson City United Fund, 1950-60; chmn. bd. dirs. Upper East Tenn. Ednl. Coop., 1970-74; trustee, mem. exec. com. Milligan Coll. Mem. N.E.A. (life), City Supts. Assn. (pres. 1960-62), Tenn. (pres. 1953), E. Tenn. (pres. 1964-65) edn. assns., Tenn. (exec. com. 1974—), Nat. (asst. state dir. East Tenn. 1974-79, state dir. 1979—) ret. tchrs. assns., Tenn. Secondary Sch. Athletic Assn. (legislative council 1958-64), Tenn. Supts. Study Council (chmn. curriculum com. 1963-70), Am., Tenn. (pres. 1964) assns. sch. adminstrs., Kappa Sigma. Mem. Christian Ch. (Bible Sch. supt. 1944-50). Kiwanian. Home: 427 Highland Ave Johnson City TN 37601 Office: S Roan St Johnson City TN 37601

MC CORKLE, JAMES LORENZO, JR., educator; b. Jackson, Miss., May 17, 1935; s. James L. and Lois (Wilson) M.; B.A. (Naval R.O.T.C. scholar), Auburn U., 1957; M.A. (NDEA fellow), U. Miss., 1962, Ph.D., 1966; m. DeAnn O. McCorkle. Asst. prof. history Northwestern State Coll., Natchitoches, La., 1966-75, assoc. prof., 1975-79, prof., 1979—. Served to lt. (j.g.) USNR, 1957-60. Recipient Willie D. Halsell award Miss. Hist. Assn., 1978. Mem. Am., So. hist. assns., Phi Alpha Theta, Phi Kappa Phi. Presbyn. (deacon 1968-72 elder 1972—). Contbr. articles to profl. jours. Home: 615 Marion St Natchitoches LA 71457

MC CORMACK, JOE EDDIE, educator; b. Tipton, Okla., Dec. 6, 1939; s. Ora Elmore and Sarah Joe (Bishop) McC.; B.A., Central State U., 1963; M.A. in Teaching, Southwestern Okla. State U., 1967; postgrad. Okla. State U.; m. Lottie Faye West, Aug. 31, 1958; children—Timothy Kayle, Jeffrey Mark, Steven Todd, Connie Leanne. Tchr. English and speech Carnegie (Okla.) Public Schs., 1963-67; mem. faculty Okla. Christian Coll., Oklahoma City, 1967—, prof. English. Youth minister, chmn. jr./sr. banquet activity Ch. Christ; dir. citizenship seminars Am. Citizenship Center, 1971-77. Mem. MLA, Assn. Depts. English, Nat. Council Tchrs. English, Okla. Council Tchrs. English. Democrat. Author: The Research Paper, 1971. Home: Route 3 Box 307 Edmond OK 73034 Office: Route 1 Box 141 Oklahoma City OK 73111

MC CORMACK, ROBERT EMMETT, JR., candy co. exec.: b. Albany, Ga., June 11, 1923; s. Robert Emmett and Anna Louise (Keller) McC.: B.S., U.S. Naval Acad., 1945; A.S., St. Bernard Coll., 1942; LL.D., St. Bernard Coll., 1976; m. Helen Louise Gross, July 22, 1947; children—Robert Emmett, Mary Helen, William Gregory, Juliana Louise. With Bobs Candies, Inc., Albany, Ga., 1947—, exec. v.p., 1959-62, pres., 1962—, chmn. bd., 1967—; dir. Citizens & So. Bank, Albany, 1965—. Bd. dirs. Dougherty County Dept. Family and Children Services, 1962-73, Albany YMCA, 1964-70; bd. dirs. Albany Urban League, 1968-75, pres., 1973-75; mem. Pres.'s Ga. State Adv. Com. on Edn., 1970-71. Served with USN, 1942-47, 52-53. Mem. Albany C. of C. (dir. 1973-75), Nat. Confectioners Assn., Profit Sharing Council of Am. Roman Catholic. Clubs: Rotary (pres. Albany 1977-78), K.C. Office: PO Box 3170 Albany GA 31706

MC CORMICK, CLYDE REECE, II, air force officer; b. San Francisco, May 31, 1940; s. Clyde Reece and Inez (Gambill) McC.; B.A. in Natural Sci., Hendrix Coll., Conway, Ark., 1964; M.A. in Psychology, St. Mary's U., San Antonio, 1978; Disting. grad. Officer Tng. Sch., 1964, Squadron Officer Sch., 1970; grad. Air Command and Staff Coll., 1979; m. Alice J. Hicks, June 2, 1979; children by previous marriage—Shawna Leigh, Mark Shannon; stepchildren—Richard Reagan Hicks, James Clifton Hicks. Commd. 2d lt. USAF, 1964; advanced through grades to maj., 1976; flight comdr. USAF Pilot Instr. Sch., Randolph AFB, Tex., 1973-76; air ops. officer and behavioral scientist for flying tng. tech. Hdqrs. Air Tng. Command, Randolph AFB, 1976-79; battle dir. Pacific Air Command, Korea, 1979-80. Active local Cub Scouts, 1975-77, Randolph AFB Community Services, 1973-76; counselor troubled youth Bexar County (Tex.) Met. Youth Agy., 1978-79. Decorated Meritorious Service medal, Air Force Commendation medal (2); named an Outstanding Young Man Am., 1974. Mem. Assn. Humanistic Psychology, AAAS, Air Force Assn., Order of Daedalians. Republican. Methodist. Club: Masons. Home: 238 Hillview San Antonio TX 78209

MC CORMICK, DAVID CLEMENT, musician; b. Desterhan, La., Aug. 17, 1930; s. Louis Lafayette and Gertrude Carr (Stephens) McC.; Mus.B.Edn., Southeastern La. U., 1951; Mus.M., Northwestern U., 1952, Ph.D., 1970; m. Lorraine Junette Munger, Oct. 23, 1954; children—Barbara Lynn, James, Carol Ann. Dir. bands and orch. Manchester Coll., 1955-59, 67-70; dir. bands J. S. Morton High Sch. Dist., Cicero, Ill., 1959-67; asso. prof. music Southeastern La. U., 1970—. Served with band U.S. Army, 1952-55. Mem. Nat. Band Assn. (past v.p.), La. Music Educators Assn. (univ. chmn.), Midwest Nat. Band Clinic (adminstrv. staff), La. Alliance Arts Edn. (chmn.). Episcopalian. Office: PO Box 798 Univ Sta Hammond LA 70402

MC CORMICK, EMILY MARIE, educator; b. Austin, Tex., Oct. 23, 1929; d. Helmuth W. and Bertha F. (Duesterhoeft) Zuch; B.S.N., U. Tex., 1951; m. Clifford E. McCormick, Jr., Apr. 25, 1953; children—Janet Deene McCormick Harper, Timothy Wayne. Staff nurse John Sealy Hosp., Galveston, Tex., 1951-52, Baylor Hosp., Dallas, 1952-53, Wadley Blood Center, Dallas, 1953-54, 58-60, Rosewood Hosp., Houston, 1972; staff nurse McAllen (Tex.) Gen. Hosp., 1972, head nurse, 1972-73; instr. nursing dept. nursing Pan Am. U., Edinburg, Tex., 1973—; mem. adv. bd. McAllen Vocat. Nursing Sch., 1977—; mem. procedure com. McAllen Gen. Hosp., 1978—. Vol., Am. Heart Assn., 1978—. Mem. Am. Nurses Assn., Tex. Nurses Assn. (v.p. 1978—), Am. Heart Assn. Lutheran. Home: 1612 Shasta St McAllen TX 78501 Office: 1201 University St Edinburg TX 78501

MCCORMICK, JOHN HOYLE, lawyer; b. Pensacola, Fla., July 30, 1933; s. Clyde H. and Orrie B. (Frink) McC.; B.S., U. Fla., 1955; J.D., Stetson U., 1958. Admitted to Fla. bar, 1958, U.S. Supreme Ct. bar, 1964; practice law, White Springs, Fla., 1958-60, Jasper, Fla., 1960—; mayor White Springs, 1959-60; county judge Hamilton County, Fla., 1960-72; atty. Hamilton County Bank, Jasper, 1966—, v.p., 1968—; also dir.; dir. First Fed. Savs. & Loan Assn., Live Oak, Fla.; local counsel So. Ry. System, 1967—; atty. Hamilton County Devel. Authority, 1966—. Local counsel SCL Ry., 1975—. Mem. Hamilton County C. of C. (pres. 1961), Am. Bar Assn., Fla. Bar, Am. Arbitration Assn., Phi Delta Phi. Methodist. Kiwanian, Mason. Address: PO Drawer O Jasper FL 32052

MC CORMICK, MICHAEL PATRICK, physicist, govt. ofcl.; b. Canonsburg, Pa., Nov. 23, 1940; s. Arthur John and Mary Ann (Nestor) McC.; B.A., Washington and Jefferson Coll., 1962; M.A., Coll. William and Mary, 1964, Ph.D., 1967; m. Judy Kay Moyer, June 30, 1962; children—Lynn Ann, Michael Patrick. Physicist, chief aerosol measurements research br. NASA, Hampton, Va., 1967—; mem. working group on aerosols and climate Global Atmosphere Research Program. Served to capt., Ordnance Corps, AUS, 1968-70. Recipient Arthur S. Fleming award Washington Downtown Jaycees, 1980. Mem. Optical Soc. Am., Am. Geophys. Union, Am. Meteorol. Soc. (com. on laser atmosphere studies), Nat. Wrestling Ofcls. Assn. (sec.-treas. 1973-80, pres. 1980—), Eastern Intercollegiate Wrestling Ofcls. Assn., Washington and Jefferson Coll. Gen. Alumni Assn. (exec. com., 1st v.p. 1978-79, pres. 1979—), Phi Kappa Psi. Contbr. articles on laser radar, satellite and other atmospheric measurements of environ. quality and climate parameters. Home: 354 Level Green Ct Hampton VA 23669 Office: Langley Research Center MS 234 Hampton VA 23665

MC CORMICK, RALPH EUGENE, stationery engraving co. exec.; b. Nashville, May 11, 1948; s. Mildred Marie (Wells) McC.; A.S., King's Coll., 1972, acctg. cert., 1971; m. Eugenia Keitt, Aug. 24, 1974; 1 dau., Darby Eugenia. Acct., Mercy Hosp., Charlotte, N.C., 1972-73; acct. W. A. Buening & Co., Inc., Charlotte, 1973-75, controller, 1975-77, treas., 1977—, also dir. Served with U.S. Army, 1966-69. Mem. Nat. Assn. Accts., Am. Mgmt. Assn., Charlotte Jaycees. Home: 1430 Biltmore Dr Charlotte NC 28207 Office: 2518 Dunavant St Charlotte NC 28203

MC CORMICK, THOMAS HARRY, chemist; b. Corpus Christi, Dec. 20, 1940; s. Robert Lewis and Mildred Virginia (LaRue) McC.; B.A., Okla. State U., 1963; M.S., Kans. State U., 1968; m. Elizabeth Jean Field, June 5, 1964; children—Martha Virginia, Elizabeth Jo. Research and devel. chemist Shell Chem. Co., 1966-68, Tretolite div. Petrolite Co., St. Louis, 1968-75; mgr. research and devel. C-E Natco Chems., Tulsa, 1975—. Mem. Am. Chem. Soc., Nat. Assn. Corrosion Engrs., Sigma Tau. Republican. Presbyterian. Patentee in field. Home: 1820 E 47th Pl Tulsa OK 74105 Office: PO Box 1710 Tulsa OK 74101

MC CORMICK, THOMAS SMITH, printing co. exec.; b. Orangeburg, S.C., Nov. 5, 1952; s. Thomas S. and Rose R. (Dawkins) McC.; B.A. in Govt. and Public Adminstrn., U. S.C., 1975; m. Linda H. Hodges, Mar. 12, 1977; 1 child, Meredith Ashley. Sales trainee State Printing Co., Columbia, S.C., 1975-76, office mgr. in charge customer service, 1976-78, asst. to v.p., 1979—. Baseball coach Little League, 1977; vol. worker United Way, 1978. Republican. Baptist. Home: 2424 Reynolds St Columbia SC 29204 Office: State Printing Co 1305 Sumter St Columbia SC 29202

MC CORMICK, WILLIAM FREDERICK, neuropathologist; b. Riverton, Va., Sept. 9, 1933; s. Jesse Allen and Elizabeth (Hord) McC.; B.S., U. Chattanooga, 1953; M.D., U. Tenn., 1955, M.S., 1957; m. Deanne Bourne Petersen, July 2, 1954; children—William Frederick, Cynthia Anne. Intern, Baptist Meml. Hosp., Memphis, 1956; resident in pathology U. Tenn., 1957-60, asst. in pathology, 1957-60, instr., 1960, asst. prof., 1960-64, mem. exec. com., basic med. scis., 1963-64; spl. fellow, instr. neuropathology Columbia, 1961-62; asso. prof. U. Iowa, 1964-68, prof., 1968-73, chmn. surgery dept. rev. com., 1968-69; prof. pathology, neurosurgery and neurology U. Tex. Med. Br., Galveston, 1973—; cons. VA Hosp., Iowa City, 1964-73, Nat. Cerebral Survival Collaborative Program, 1971-74, sect. on head injuries and stroke Nat. Inst. Neurol. Diseases and Stroke, 1974—; vis. scientist Armed Force Inst. Pathology, Washington, 1965-66; dep. chief med. examiner Galveston County, 1976; mem. head injury study group U.S. Dept. Transp.; vis. prof. U. Tenn., U. Pitts. Scoutmaster, Bay Area council Boy Scouts Am., 1974. Diplomate Am. Bd. Pathology. Mem. Am. Soc. Human Genetics, AAAS, Am. Soc. for Exptl. Pathology, Assn. Am. Med. Colls., Am. Assn. Pathologists, Am. Assn. Neuropathologists, N.Y. Acad. Scis., Am., Tex. med. assns., Nat. Assn. Med. Examiners, Sigma Xi. Author: (with W.E. Bell) Increased Intracranial Pressure in Children, 1972, 2d edit., 1978, Neurologic Infections in Children, 1975; (with S.S. Schochet, Jr.) Syllabus of Neuropathology, 1973, 3d edit., 1978, Atlas of Cerebrovascular Disease, 1976; Neuropathology Case Studies, 1976, 2d edit., 1979; Essentials of Neuropathology, 1979; contbr. articles to profl. jours. Home: 2828 Dominique St Galveston TX 77550

MC CORMICK, WILLIE MAE WARD (MRS. WALTER WITTEN MCCORMICK), city ofcl., ret. tech. specialist; b. Centerville, Tex. Oct. 17, 1908; d. William Sylvester and Lucy (Marshall) Ward; B.A., Mary Hardin Baylor Coll., 1929; M.A., Hardin Simmons U., 1931; postgrad. So. Methodist U., Tex. Woman's U.; m. Walter Witten McCormick, May 29, 1929; 1 dau., Elizabeth Ward (Mrs. Billy Joe Wilcox). Tchr. chemistry and algebra Big Spring (Tex.) High Sch., 1941-44, 45-48; weather observer for Dept. Commerce, Big Spring, 1943-44; analytical chemist Dow Chem. Co., Freeport, 1944-45; calculator Chance Vought (now Ling-Temco-Vought), Dallas, 1951-55, structural engr., 1955-63, sci. programmer, 1963-67, tech. specialist, 1967-69; sr. program analyst Univ. Computing Co., Arlington, Tex., 1970-73; adv. council 1st City Savs. of Euless (Tex.). Mem. Euless City Council, 1973—, mayor pro tem City of Euless, 1975—; chmn. Trinity River Authority Central Wastewater System; mem. Water Resources Council N.Central Tex.; mem. United Way Planning and Research Council. Mem. AAAS, Am. Chem. Soc., Math. Assn. Am., Fedn. Am. Scientists, AAUW, Trainmen's Aux. (pres. 1940-41, Internat. Platform Assn., League Women Voters (publicity chmn.), C. of C. (dir.) Democrat. Baptist (tchr. adult dept. Sunday sch.). Mem. Order Eastern Star (past worthy matron). Club: Oakcrest Woman's. Home: Route 1 Box 66 Euless TX 76039

MC COTTER, BURNEY RICHARD, life ins. co. exec.; b. Grantsboro, N.C., Feb. 9, 1920; s. John Lawrence and Flora (Tingle) M.; A.B., Atlantic Christian Coll., 1941; grad. exec. program U. N.C., 1965; m. Margaret R. Palmer, June 21, 1946; children—Richard, Karen. Tchr. high sch., N.C., 1941-42; agt. Jefferson Standard Life Ins. Co., 1946-47, 48-50; gen. agt. Franklin Life Ins. Co., 1947-48; mgr. Occidental Life Ins. Co., N.C., 1950-52, agy. asst., Raleigh, 1952-55, agy. sec., 1955-60, asst. v.p., 1960-64, v.p., 1964, v.p., sec., 1964-66, v.p. ops., 1966-70, sr. v.p., 1970-77, gen. agt., 1977—. Trustee, exec. dir. Occidental Charitable Found. Served to 1st lt. USAAF, 1942-46. Decorated Air medal with two oak leaf clusters. C.L.U. Mem. Am. Soc. Chartered Life Underwriters (chpt. pres. 1961), Atlantic Christian Coll. Alumni Assn. (past pres.). Democrat. Presbyterian (deacon 1960-64, elder 1969-73). Clubs: Kiwanis, Carolina Country, Capital City. Home: 332 Buncombe St Raleigh NC 27609 Office: 505 Oberlin Rd Raleigh NC 27605

MC COTTER, DINAH WHITE, guidance counselor; b. Windsor, N.C., July 14, 1951; d. Herman Franklin and Elva Una (Leggett) White; B.A., Wake Forest U., 1973; M.Ed., U. N.C., Greensboro, 1975; m. Richard Palmer McCotter, Nov. 25, 1972. Guidance counselor South Fork Elementary Sch., Winston-Salem, N.C., 1975—. Mem. Am. Personnel and Guidance Assn., N.C. Personnel and Guidance Assn., Beech Mountain Assn. Methodist. Am. Sch. Counselors Assn., Home: 8559 Brook Meadow Ln Lewisville NC 27023 Office: 4332 Country Club Rd Winston-Salem NC 27104

MC COTTER, MARGARET ROSEMOND PALMER (MRS. BURNEY RICHARD MCCOTTER), librarian; b. Thomasville, N.C., Nov. 7, 1921; d. Jacob Alexander and Etna (Little) Palmer; A.B., Catawba Coll., 1942; M.S. in L.S., U. N.C., 1944; m. Burney Richard McCotter, June 21, 1946; children—Richard Palmer, Karen Ellen. Librarian So. Pines (N.C.) Sch. System, 1944-47; post librarian Fort Story (Va.), 1950-51; librarian LeRoy Martin Jr. High Sch., Raleigh, N.C., 1959-62, 65—; library cons. N.C. Dept. Pub. Instrn., Raleigh, 1963-65. Mem. N.E.A., United Daus. Confederacy, N.C. Library Assn., N.C. Assn. Educators, N.C. Soc. for Preservation of Antiquities, Beta Phi Mu, Sigma Pi Alpha, Delta Kappa Gamma. Democrat. Presbyn. Clubs: Carolina Country, Capital City (Raleigh). Author: (with others) AV Cataloging and Processing Simplified, 1971. Editor: Reference Materials for School Libraries, 1965. Home: 332 Buncombe St Raleigh NC 27609 Office: 1701 Ridge Rd Raleigh NC 27607

MC COUN, FRED CORBETT, oil and gas producer; b. Campton, Ky., Nov. 9, 1931; s. Glenn Rynolds and Grace Dorcas (Coldiron) McC.; student U. Ky., 1949-51; A.B., Transylvania Coll., 1954; B.D., Lexington Theol. Sem., 1958; m. Margaret Jane Giltner, June 24, 1956; children—Beth, Amy, Laura. Ordained to ministry Christian Ch., 1958; minister Mt. Carmel Christian Ch., Bourbon County, Ky., 1954-56, Floyd's Knobs (Ind.) Christian Ch., 1956; sr. minister Southport Christian Ch., Indpls., 1958-65, Gordon St. Christian Ch., Kinston, N.C., 1965-67, First Christian Ch., Tyler, Tex., 1967-76; chmn. bd., pres. McCoun & Temple Interests Inc.; 1976—; gen. partner McCoun Co., McCoun Petroleum Ltd., various drilling funds. Pres. Perry Twp. Ministerial Assn., 1958-59, Indpls. Ministerial Assn., 1961-62, Ind. Christian Ministers Assn., 1963-64, Christian Ch. Union of Greater Indpls., 1964-65, Tyler Ministerial Alliance, 1971, Northeast Area of Christian Chs. (dist. 14, 16), 1971-73; mem. Gen. Bd. Christian Ch., 1973—. Bd. dirs. East Texas Urban Housing Found. Corp. (chmn. 1969—). Recipient Distinguished Service award Indpls. Jaycees, 1962. Mason, Rotarian. Home: 803 Watkins St Tyler TX 75701 Office: 504 Fair Found Bldg Tyler TX 75702

MC COWAN, OTIS BLAKELY, mathematician, educator; b. Monterey, Tenn., June 17, 1934; s. I. Burton and Martha C. (Phipps) M.; B.S., Tenn. Tech. U., 1959; M.A., La. State U., 1966; Ph.D., George Peabody Coll. Tchrs., 1975; Mathematician, Missile Devel. Center, Holloman AFB, N.Mex., 1962-63; tchr. math. Rhea Central High Sch., Dayton, Tenn., 1963-65; instr. math. Kilgore (Tex.) Coll., 1966-67; asst. prof. math. Belmont Coll., Nashville, 1967-72, asso. prof., 1972-75, prof., 1975—. Served with AUS, 1959-62. Named Outstanding Young Educator Rhea County, Dayton Jr. C. of C., 1964. Mem. Am. Math. Soc., Math. Assn. Am., Nat. Council Tchrs. Math., Tenn. Math. Tchrs. Assn., Tenn. Acad. Sci., Kappa Mu Epsilon, Pi Mu Epsilon, Kappa Delta Pi. Democrat. Baptist. Home: 960 Graybar Ln Nashville TN 37204

MC COWN, HERBERT THOMAS, chem. co. exec.; b. Elkhorn City, Ky., Sept. 28, 1939; s. Herbert Ross and Roxie Irene (Farley) McC.; B.S. in Chem. Engring., U. Ky., 1960; M.S. in Chem. Engring., Washington U., St. Louis, 1968; m. Linda Lee Spaulding, Dec. 27, 1958; children—Steven Thomas, Janet Lynn, Kathryn Ann. Process devel. engr. Procter & Gamble Co., Cin., 1960-63; sr. chem. engr. Monsanto Co., St. Louis, 1963-69; asst. to v.p. research and devel., prodn. supr. Swedlow Inc., Garden Grove, Calif., 1969-70; process engr., prodn. supr. Vulcan Materials Co., Wichita, Kans., 1971-73; prodn. mgr. Vulcan Materials Co., Geismar, La., 1973—. Registered profl. engr., Ill. Mem. Am. Inst. Chem. Engrs. (v.p. Wichita sect. 1973). Republican. Baptist. Home: 13211 Camelot Ave Baton Rouge LA 70815 Office: Vulcan Materials Co PO Box 227 Geismar LA 70734

MC COWN, JAMES KIMBOL, dentist; b. Philadelphia, Miss., Sept. 14, 1915; s. James Monroe and Lou Ada (Green) McC.; student Miss. State U., 1935-37, U. Miss., 1937-38; D.D.S., Loyola U. of South, New Orleans, 1943; m. Mary Victoria Lee, Sept. 8, 1940 (dec. Jan. 1972); m. Mabel Page Yarber, Feb. 24, 1973. Practice dentistry, Amory, Miss., 1946—; pres. Glendale, Inc., Amory, 1970—; owner Glendale Shopping Center, Amory, 1970—. Served with Dental Corps, AUS, 1943-46. Mem. Am. Dental Assn., Miss., Northeast Miss. dental socs. Democrat. Baptist. Home: 808 Town and Country Lane Amory MS 38821 Office: 107 N 3d St Amory MS 38821

MC COY, CAROL LOUISE, lawyer; b. Kingsport, Tenn., Sept. 4, 1947; d. Nelson and Catherine Florence (Barnes) McCoy; B.A., U. South Fla., 1969; J.D., Vanderbilt U., 1973. Admitted to Tenn. bar and Fla. bar, 1973, U.S. Supreme Ct. bar, 1978; staff atty. Legal Service of Nashville, Inc., 1973-75, Tenn. Dept. Revenue, 1975; partner firm Farrell & McCoy, Nashville, 1975—. Bd. dirs. Nashville YWCA, 1973-79, Nashville League Women Voters, 1975, Nashville Consumer Credit Counseling Alliance; vice chmn. Tenn. Commn. on Status of Women, 1974—. Mem. Am., Tenn., Nashville, Fla. bar assns., Am. Judicature Soc., CABLE (pres. 1980; co-founder). Democrat. Roman Catholic. Author: Tennessee Women: Marriage, Property and Divorce, 1978. Office: 921 J C Bradford Bldg Nashville TN 37219

MC COY, DONALD BURCHARD, clergyman, educator; b. Dresden, Tenn., Apr. 22, 1928; s. Albert Austin and Celia Edith (Bass) McC.; B.A., Cumberland U., 1949; B.D., Golden Gate Bapt. Theol. Sem., 1951, Th.D., 1954; M.A., Peabody Coll. for Tchrs., Vanderbilt U., 1959, Ed.S., 1970; Ph.D., St. Louis U. (Philippines), 1979; m. E. Sterline White, Dec. 28, 1951; children—Don David, James Austin, Sterling Mark, Thomas Jefferson. Ordained to ministry Bapt. Ch., 1949; pastor Wrigley (Tenn.) Bapt. Ch., 1949, Calwa (Cal.) Bapt. Ch., 1950-54, Tusculum Hills Bapt. Ch., Nashville, 1959-65; missionary-tchr. to Brazil, 1954-59, Philippines, 1965-72; pastor First Bapt. Ch., Dickson, Tenn., 1972—; prof., chmn. dept. philosophy Am. Bapt. Coll., Nashville, 1964-65, 69, 72—. Mem. Mayoral Adv. Com., City of Dickson, 1975. Trustee Philippine Assn. Bible-Theol. Schs., 1968-71, Bapt. Hosp., Mindanao, Philippines, 1967-69, Belmont Coll., Nashville, 1975—. Recipient Citation of Merit, Am. Bapt. Coll., 1970. Mem. N.E.A., AAUP, Dickson County Fellowship of Ministers (pres. 1972-74), Alumni Assn. Golden Gate Bapt. Theol. Sem. (pres. 1961-63), Alumni Assn. Peabody Coll. for Tchrs., Dickson County Tennis Assn. (pres. 1977-78). Clubs: Tennis, Foreign Language, Book. Contbr. articles to profl. jours. Home: 110 Lee Rd Dickson TN 37055 Office: 1st Bapt Ch Hwy 70E Dickson TN 37055

MC COY, GENE GUY, advt. agy. exec; b. Oskaloosa, Iowa, May 11, 1926; s. Guy Gene and Edith (Seaman) McC.; B.B.A., U. Wis., 1951; M.A. in Marketing, State U. Iowa, 1952; m. Idella Maria Brown, Aug. 8, 1947; children—Gene Guy III, Vicki V., Randi R., S. Sherman. Advt. mgr. W.M. McAllister Co., Sycamore, Ill., 1952-53; account exec. Gerald T. LeFever & Assos., Little Rock, 1953-55, partner, 1956-57; pres. Ad Craft of Ark., Inc., Little Rock, 1958-78, chmn. bd., 1978—; asst. prof., chmn. dept. advt. U. Ark. at Little Rock. Mem. nat. assembly mem. Found. Pub. Relations Research and Edn., 1975. Mem. Ark. Atty. Gen.'s Study Com. for Consumer Protection Legislation; state vice chmn. Ark. Better Bus. Bur., 1973, chmn., 1974; cons. Model Cities Program. Served with AUS, 1944-47. Recipient Advt. Educator of Year award G.D. Crain Found., 1972, Ark. Certificate of Merit, 1974; named Ark. Traveler, 1969. Mem. Am. Advt. Fedn. (dir. 10th dist. 1958—, gov. 10th dist. 1969-70, nat. dir. 1969-70, lt. gov. 1968-69, Advt. Educator of Year 1972, Silver Medal award 1966, Sterling Service award 1974), Internat. Pub. Relations Soc., Pub. Relations Soc. Am. (sec. Ark. chpt. 1972-73, pres. 1975, nat. assembly del. 1980-82), Little Rock Advt. Club (pres. 1958-60), Am. Acad. Advt., A.I.M. (pres. council), Am. Mktg. Assn., Southwestern Assn. Advt. Agys., Am. Acad. Advt., Nat. Fedn. Ind. Bus., Distributive Edn. Clubs Am. (hon. life), Alpha Delta Sigma (nat. v.p. 1971-72), Alpha Kappa Psi, Sigma Alpha Epsilon. Author publs. in field. Home: 12000 Rivercrest Dr Little Rock AR 72212 Office: 3d and Cross St Little Rock AR 72203

MC COY, GLORIA BAKER, guidance counselor; b. Washington, Oct. 19, 1948; d. Milton and Sallie Corrine Baker; B.A., Chatham Coll., 1970; M.Ed., Duquesne U., 1972; postgrad. Tex. So. U., 1976—; m. Walter Jennings McCoy, June 26, 1971. Tchr., Prince George County (Md.) Sch. Dist., 1970-71; guidance counselor West Mifflin Area (Pa.) Sch. Dist., 1972-74; learning facilitator Houston Ind. Sch. Dist., 1975-76, spl. edn. counselor, 1976—. Mem. Am. Personnel and Guidance Assn., NAACP, Phi Delta Kappa. Alpha Kappa Alpha.

MC COY, IDELIA MARIA THERESA BROWN (MRS. GENE GUY MCCOY), bus. exec.; b. Woodriver, Ill., July 21, 1928; d. Mayo Clinton and Loretta (Weisaupt) Brown; student Shurtleff Coll., Ill., 1946-48; m. Gene Guy McCoy, Aug. 8, 1948; children—Gene Guy III, Vicki V., Randall R., S. Sherman. Prodn. mgr. Ad Craft of Ark., Inc., Little Rock, 1958, sec.-treas., 1958-65, exec. v.p., 1965-78, pres., 1978—. Residential chmn. United Fund Pulaski County, 1962-63, pub. relations, 1969. Recipient Ark. Certificate of Merit, 1974. Mem. Am. Advt. Fedn. (dir. S.W. dist.; Silver medal 1975), Little Rock Advt. Club (pres. 1970-71), Southwestern Assn. Advt. Agys., Gamma Alpha Chi (Spl. Service award 1969). Home: 12000 Rivercrest Dr Little Rock AR 72207 Office: 1122 W 3d St Little Rock AR 72201

MC COY, LEE BERARD, paint co. exec.; b. Ipswich, Mass., July 27, 1925; d. Damase Joseph and Robena Myrtle (Bruce) B.; student U. Ala., Mobile, 1958-60; m. Walter Vincent de Paul McCoy, Sept. 27, 1943; children—Bernadette, Raymond, Joan, Richard. Owner, Lee's Letter Shop, Hicksville, L.I., N.Y., 1950-56; mgr. sales adminstrn. Basila Mfg. Co., Mobile, Ala., 1957-61; promotion mgr., buyer Mobile Paint Co., Inc., Theodore, Ala., 1961—. Bd. dirs. Friends of Mus., 1978-80, Monterey Tour House, Mobile, 1972-78; del. Civic Roundtable, 1978-80. Mem. Spectromatic Assos., Nat. Paint Distbrs. Republican. Methodist. Clubs: Quota (Pres. Mobile chpt. 1978-80). Home: 1553 Monterey Pl Mobile AL 36604 Office: 4775 Hamilton Blvd Theodore AL 36582

MC COY, MEDFORD A., oil co. exec.; b. Merkel, Tex., Apr. 18, 1923; s. James A. and Luteenie McCoy; B.S., U. Tex., 1950; m. Margret Dierksen, Dec. 21, 1947; 1 son, Medford Theodore. With Conoco, Inc., 1950—, div. mgr., Lafayette, La., 1967—; dir. Gulf Coast Sch. Drilling Practices. Bd. dirs. United Blood Services, 1976—; pres. United Givers Fund, 1978. Served with USAAF, 1943-46. Mem. Am. Petroleum Inst. (chmn. La. Gulf coast area adv. com.), AIME, Lafayette C. of C. (v.p.), La. Gulf Coast Oil Exposition (chmn.). Clubs: Oakbourne Country (past pres.), Lafayette Petroleum (dir.). Home: 308 Meadow Ln Lafayette LA 70506 Office: 1105 General Mouton Lafayette LA 70505

MC COY, RAYMOND DE PENAFORT, savs. and loan exec.; b. Flushing, N.Y., Oct. 11, 1948; s. Walter Vincent de Paul and Eleanor Elizabeth (Berard) McC.; B.A., U. Ala., 1970; M.B.A., U. South Ala., 1976; m. Rebecca Lee Brown, Sept. 14, 1969; children—Katherine Anne, Melanie Lee. Agt., N.Y. Life Ins. Co., Mobile, Ala., 1970-71; loan officer Mobile Fed. Savs. and Loan Assn., 1971-72, asst. v.p., 1973-74, v.p., 1974—; instr. Inst. Fin. Edn., 1977—. Mem. speakers bur. Mobile Pub. Library, 1974—; bd. dirs. Mental Health Assn. Mobile, 1977—, Mobile Historic Devel. Commn., 1975-76. Served with U.S. Army, 1970-71. Recipient Boss of Year award Am. Bus. Women's Assn., 1977. Mem. Mobile Jaycees (dir. 1972-77, project chmn. Mobile Spl. Olympics 1976), Res. Officers Assn. (treas. 1974—), Inst. Fin. Edn. (chpt. pres. 1977—), Mobile County Bd. Realtors, Mobile Homebuilders Assn., Mortgage Lenders Assn. Methodist. Club: Skyline Country. Home: 6654 Hounds Run S Mobile AL 36608 Office: 3687 Airport Blvd Mobile AL 36616

MC COY, WESLEY LAWRENCE, educator; b. Memphis, Jan. 27, 1935; s. Harlan Eftin and Gladys (Coggin) McC.; B. Music Edn., La. State U., 1957, Ph.D., 1970; M. Music Edn., U. Louisville, 1958; M. Sacred Music, So. Baptist Theol. Sem., 1960; postgrad. George Peabody Coll., 1965; m. Carolyn June Noble, Aug. 26, 1960; children—Jill Laurene, Scott Edward. Minister of music Beechmont Bapt. Ch., Louisville, 1959-62, also instr. music So. Bapt. Theol. Sem., Louisville; asst. prof. music, dir. bands Carson Newman Coll., Jefferson City, Tenn., 1962-67; grad. teaching fellow La. State U., Baton Rouge, 1968-69; asst. prof. music U. S.C., Columbia, 1969-72; asso. prof. music U. Ark., Little Rock, 1972-77, prof., 1977—, condr. Wind Ensemble, River City Community Band, asst. dean Coll. Fine Arts, 1978-79; performer French horn Knoxville (Tenn.) Symphony Orch., 1962-67, Columbia Philharmonic Orch., 1969-72, Ark. Symphony Orch., 1972—; mem. com. to review certification of music tchrs. S.C. Dept. Edn., 1971-72; condr. Die Fledermaus, Ark. Arts Center, Little Rock, 1974. Co-chmn. Jefferson County (Tenn.) Com. for Goldwater for Pres., 1962; mem. Pulaski County Republican Com., 1977—. Mem. S.C. Music Educators Assn. (pres. coll. div. 1971-73), Ark. Music Edn. Assn. (chmn. research and higher edn. 1975-79, sec. 1979—), Music Educators Nat. Conf., Coll. Band Dirs. Nat. Assn. (Ark. chmn. 1976-78), Assn. Concert Bands Am. (dir. 1980), AAUP (Ark. pres. 1979—), Phi Mu Alpha, Pi Kappa Lambda, Phi Delta Kappa, Kappa Kappa Psi. Republican. Baptist. Contbr. to The Ch. Musician, 1974-76. Home: 3200 Imperial Valley Dr Little Rock AR 72212

MC COY, WILLIAM MICHAEL, artist; b. Osceola, Ark., Dec. 20, 1949; s. William Oscar and Helen Mae (Anders) McC.; student So. Bapt. Coll., Walnut Ridge, Ark., 1967-68; B.A. in Christianity, S.W. Bapt. Coll., Bolivar, Mo., 1970; student Southwestern Bapt. Theol. Sem., 1971-73; m. Sharon Kay Blevins, Oct. 17, 1970; 1 son, Michael Nathan. Publs. asst. S.W. Bapt. Coll., Bolivar, 1970-71; sales and advt. mgr. Washer Bros. Clothiers, Ft. Worth, 1973; tech. illustrator Continental Telephone Electronics Co., Euless, Tex., 1974; artist Accelerated Christian Edn., Lewisville, Tex., 1974-76; sales and advt. writer Reliance Telecommunication Electronics Co., Euless, 1976-78; copywriter Radio Shack Nat. Advt. Dept., 1978; artist, owner, founder The Visible Word, Ft. Worth, 1978—; visual exegesis presenter at chs.; tchr. art classes. Mem. Tex. Fine Arts Assn., Internat. Soc. Artists. Baptist. Author: Jesus Christ: 12 Scenes, 1978. Home: 6372 Dorchester Trail Fort Worth TX 76180 Office: The Visible Word PO Box 18721 Fort Worth TX 76118

MC CRACKEN, JAMES BERNARD, JR., govt. ofcl.; b. Huntington, W.Va., Apr. 28, 1947; s. James B. and Elizabeth J. McCracken; B.S. in Mgmt. Scis., Fla. Atlantic U., 1969; M.P.A. in Human Resource Mgmt., Am. U., 1980; m. Jo Ann Wilson, Oct. 30, 1971; children—James Wilson, Joseph Robert. Adminstrv. intern NOAA, 1970-72; employee devel. specialist Smithsonian Instn., 1972-76; tng. officer Bur. Public Debt, Treasury Dept., 1977-78; sr. employee devel. specialist Naval Facilities Engring. Command, Navy Dept., Alexandria, Va., 1978—; chmn. Tng. Officers Conf., Washington, 1975-77. Chmn. tng. com. Alexandria dist. Boy Scouts Am., 1973-78; chmn. Alexandria City CETA Adv. Council, 1977-78; v.p. Strawberry Hill Civic Assn., 1976-78, Virginia Hills Civic Assn., 1980—. Recipient EEO award Smithsonian Instn., 1975; various other letter commendations. Mem. Tng. Officers Conf. (Excellence in Leadership award 1977), Am. Soc. Tng. and Devel., Delta Pi Sigma (life). Office: 200 Stovall St Alexandria VA 22332

MCCRACKEN, JOSEPH HILL, III, lawyer; b. Dallas, June 12, 1927; s. Joseph Hill and Mary Frances (Hall) McC.; B.S., Okla. A. and M. Coll., 1950; LL.B., So. Methodist U., 1956. Admitted to Tex. bar, 1956; asso. firm Carrington, Gowan, Johnson, Bromberg & Leeds, Dallas, 1956-58; partner firm Hughes, Donosky, McCracken & Hunt, Dallas, 1958-63, McCulloch, Ray, Trotti & Hemphill, Dallas, 1963-66; practiced in Dallas, 1966—. Mem. com. edn. Southwestern Law Jour., So. Meth. U., 1955-56, now cons, Mem. S.A.R., Sons Republic of Tex., Tex. Bar, Dallas Bar Assn. (sec.-treas., dir. 1958), Nat. (dir. 1965-69), Tex. (hon. life dir.) skeet shooting assns., Huguenot Soc., Nat. (legis. com. 1966-68), Tex. (legis. com.) rifle assns., Am. Soc. Arms Collectors (dir. 1979-82), Barristers, Sigma Alpha Epsilon, Delta Theta Phi. Methodist. Clubs: Dallas Gun (dir. 1963—), Terpsichorean, Idlewild. Contbg. biog. author Tex. State Hist. Assns.'s. Handbook of Texas-Supplement, 1969; author numerous hist. biographies, 1976—; contbr. to biographies. Home: 3028 Potomac Dallas TX 75205 Office: 211 North Ervay Bldg Dallas TX 75201

MC CRACKEN, MALCOLM DAVID, veterinary pathologist; b. Port Chester, N.Y., Nov. 6, 1942; s. David Patton and Edna Alice (Cobb) McC.; B.S., Kans. State U., 1964, D.V.M., 1966; Ph.D., Purdue U., 1973; m. Therese Marie Wilson, Aug. 15, 1970; children—Daryl, Gail, Richard. Pvt. practice veterinary medicine, Audubon, N.J., 1966-67; grad. instr. Purdue U., 1967-70, NIH spl. fellow, 1971-73; research fellow Merck Inst. for Therapeutic Research, Merck, Sharp & Dohme, West Point, Pa., 1973-74; asso. pathologist Veterinary Diagnostic Lab., U. Ill., Urbana, 1974-77; asso. prof. veterinary pathology U. Tenn., Knoxville, 1977—. Mem. Am. Veterinary Med. Assn., Am. Coll. Veterinary Pathologists (certificate 1977). Home: 221 Crowfield Rd Knoxville TN 37922

MCCRACKEN, WILLIAM EDWARD, II, hosp. exec.; b. Athens, Ala., July 2, 1952: s. William Edward and Martha Evelyn (Beasley) McC.; B.S. in Nursing (Tri-County Regional Planning Bd. scholar 1970-73), U. Ala., Birmingham, 1974, M.S. (NIMH trainee 1976-77), 1977; m. Belinda Gail Mattox, Sept. 14, 1973; 1 son, Samuel Jason. Patient care coordinator Hillcrest Hosp., Birmingham, 1973-75; adminstrv. resident Alton Ochsner Found. Hosp., New Orleans, 1976-77; asso. dir. nursing N.E. Ala. Regional Med. Center, Anniston, 1977-78, v.p. patient services, 1978—; mem. exec. bd. N.E. Ala. Emergency Med. Soc.; mem. N.E. Ala. Regional Perinatal Adv. Com.; preceptor U. Ala. grad. program, Birmingham; operational adv. Hobson City Primary Care Center; mem. state adv. com. continuing edn. nurses U. Ala., Tuscaloosa, 1979. Recipient Outstanding Service award Trans-World Hosp. Cons., 1978; Greater Anniston All-Am. Citizenship award City of Anniston, 1979. Mem. Am. Soc. Nursing Service Adminstrs., Nat. League Nursing, Am. Hosp. Assn., Ala. Soc. Nursing Service Adminstrs. (exec. bd., pres. elect 1979-80), Ala. League Nursing, Ala. Hosp. Assn., Sigma Theta Tau. Democrat. Baptist. Club: Sertoma (v.p. sponsorship 1979). Home: 125 Shannon Ln Anniston AL 36201

MC CRADY, JAMES WARING DE BERNIERES, educator, musician, lay theologian, heraldic designer; b. Sewanee, Tenn., Jan. 13, 1938; s. Edward and Edith May (Dowling) McC.; B.A., U. of South, 1959; M.A., U. N.C., Chapel Hill, 1962, Ph.D., 1971; m. Mazie Morley Vogel, Jan. 30, 1965; children—William Tucker de Bernieres, Elizabeth Allston, Robert Piers de Bernieres. Instr., U. of South, Sewanee, 1962-71, asst. prof., 1971-75, asso. prof. French, 1975—, asst. organist, carilloneur, 1965-71; parish organist, 1971-74; instr. piano, 1968—; mem. Parish Vestry, Episcopal Ch., 1970-74, 76—, sr. warden, 1971-72; del. Convs. of Diocese Tenn., 1972, 73, 76, 77, 78, 79; interpreter Haitian delegation Nat. Convs. Episcopal Ch., 1973; rep. Liturgical Commn. and U. of South, 1976; mem. bishops com. for human and social concerns Diocese of Tenn., 1977—, substitute del., 1979; mem. first services com. Nat. Liturgical Commn., Episcopal Ch., 1973-76, cons. Theol. Commn., 1973-76, mem. com. on hymn book revision, 1977—, com. on French Prayer Book, 1980; heraldic adviser, designer to presiding bishop Upper S.C., Diocese Ala., Diocese Gulf Coast, Diocese Tenn., U. of South. Pres. Community Chest, 1969-70; dist. rep. Town Council, 1975—, treas., 1979. Nat. Endowment for Humanities research grantee Princeton U., 1979. Mem. Modern Lang. Assn., Tenn. Philol. Assn., Sewanee Civic Assn. (pres. 1970), Franklin County Hist. Soc. (dir. 1978-79, pres. 1979-80), Alpha Tau Omega, Delta Kappa Epsilon (hon.). Club: Ecce Quam Bonum Faculty (sec. 1972-73, v.p. 1978-79, pres. 1979-80). Author: Under the Sun, 1967, 79; The Prayer Book Liturgy, 1973. Office: U of South Sewanee TN 37375

MC CRANIE, WILLIAM MARK, economist; b. Miami, Fla., Dec. 27, 1949; s. Lacy Breedlove and Mary (Mayeux) McC.; B.S. in B.A., U. Fla., 1971; M.B.A., U. N.D., 1974; m. Claire Lela Nancy Crews, Dec. 21, 1968; children—Donald Christopher, Anne Catherine, Phillip Lee. Economist, Seaboard Coast Line R.R., Jacksonville, Fla., 1978—. Mem. fin. com. and adminstrv. bd. Arlington United Methodist Ch., Jacksonville; fund devel. chmn. USO Greater Jacksonville; mem. citizens adv. com. Jacksonville's Downtown People Mover, 1979. Served with USAF, 1971-75. Mem. Jacksonville Jaycees (moderator weekly TV show, pres.'s award 1977), Nat. Assn. Bus. Economists. Republican. Club: Toastmasters (pres. Paramount; adminstrv. v.p. Saturday Morning; Toastmaster of Year 1979). Office: 500 Water St Jacksonville FL 32211

MC CRAREY, ROBERT FRANCIS, clin. social worker; b. Erie, Pa., May 16, 1942; s. Harold William and Ann Mary (Connell) McC.; B.A., Gannon Coll., 1959; M.S.W., Va. Commonwealth U., 1973; m. Margaret J. Timmons, Aug. 17, 1968; 1 dau., Karen Marie. Social worker Cath. Social Services, Erie, Pa., 1969-71, Va. Treatment Center for Children, Richmond, 1973-76, Westbrook Psychiat. Hosp. Adolescent Unit, Richmond, 1976—; instr. psychiatry Med. Coll. Va. Served with U.S. Army, 1962-65. Cert. Acad. Cert. Social Workers. Mem. Nat. Assn. Social Workers, Va. Soc. Clin. Social Workers, Inc. (pres.), Greater Richmond Sailing Assn. Democrat. Roman Catholic. Home: 7601 Tanglewood Rd Richmond VA 23225 Office: 1500 Westbrook Ave Richmond VA 23227

MCCRARY, BURMAH MCCRACKEN, farmer, civic worker, former lawyer; b. Dekalb County, Ala., Feb. 3, 1908; d. Joseph Oliver and Mary Elizabeth (Durham) McCracken; student Jacksonville Tchrs. Coll., 1927-29; LL.B., George Washington U., 1939; m. Arthur John McCrary, Nov. 3, 1941. Tchr., Public Schs. Calhoun County, Ala., 1929-34; with IRS, Washington, 1934-39; admitted to D.C. bar, 1939, Ala. bar, 1939; atty., office gen. counsel GAO, Washington, 1939-52; atty. contract liaison officer NASA, Huntsville, Ala., 1952-61; owner, mgr. farm Ft. Payne, Ala., 1962—. Mem. Jury Commn. Dekalb County, Ala., 1979-82; county coordinator gubernatorial campaign Fob James, 1978; pres. Garden Club Ala., Inc., 1979-81. Mem. Fed. Bar Assn., Bus. and Profl. Women's Club, AAUW, Phi Alpha Delta. Democrat. Baptist. Home: Route 3 Box 719 Fort Payne AL 35967

MC CRARY, DENNIE LOCKHART, resort operations and real estate co. exec.; b. Macon, Ga., Mar. 7, 1938; s. Dennie Lockhart and Mary Marguerite (Barksdale) McC.; B.S., U.S. Naval Acad., 1960; M.B.A., Harvard, 1966; m. Frances Roberta Parker, June 24, 1961; children—Jennifer Lane, Thomas Parker, Catherine Barksdale. Asst. to pres. Sea Pines Co. real estate devel., resort operations, Hilton Head Island, S.C., 1966-68, v.p. finance, 1968-70, v.p. finance, gen. mgr., 1970-71, exec. v.p., 1971-72; pres. Hilton Head Beach Properties, 1972-75; v.p. finance Sea Island Co. (Ga.), 1975—, also dir.; dir. Sea Pines Co., First Carolina Bank, Beaufort, S.C. Chmn. bd. trustees Sea Pines Acad. Served to 1st lt. USAF, 1960-64. Decorated Air Force Commendation Medal. Mem. Hilton Head C. of C. (pres.). Presbyn. (deacon, elder). Rotarian, Toastmaster. Home: 305 Wormslow Saint Simons Island GA 31522 Office: Sea Island Co Sea Island GA 31561

MC CRARY, GILES CONNELL, oil operator, mayor; b. Ft. Worth, Nov. 5, 1919; student Washington and Lee U., 1941; m. Helen Louise Luton, May 25, 1940; children—Mary Louise McCrary Prather, Pamela Ann, Giles Connell. Oil operator, Post, Tex., 1958—; mayor, Post, 1968—. Chmn. bd. First Nat. Bank of Post; sec. KVUE-TV, Austin, Tex.; dir. KSEL-TV, Lubbock, Tex. Mem. finance com. Caprock council Girl Scouts Am., 1960-75; mem. at large South Plains council Boy Scouts Am., 1970-75; dir. United Fund Drive, 1968-72; sponsor OS Ranch Roping and Art Exhibit, 1971-75. Chmn. bd. Post Pub. Housing Authority; bd. dirs. Lubbock Symphony Orch., Garza Meml. Hosp., Post Indsl. Found.; trustee Presbyn. Found.-Synod of Sun; trustee, bd. dirs. Presbyn. Found., Denton, Tex.; mem. adv. council Small Bus. Adminstrns. Lubbock. Served with inf., AUS, 1943-46; ETO. Mem. Post (past v.p., dir.), West Tex. (past dir.) chambers commerce, South Plains Assn. Govts. (dir., past pres.), V.F.W. Presbyn. (elder). Mason, Rotarian. Clubs: Lubbock Country, Lubbock; Post Band Boosters. Address: PO Box 790 Post TX 79356

MC CRARY, ROBERT WAYNE, advt. agy. exec.; b. Knoxville, Tenn., Aug. 28, 1946; s. Jack Dean and Helen Elizabeth (Rice) McC.; student U. Tenn., 1965-68, So. W.Va. Community Coll., 1976; Regents B.A., W.Va. State Coll., 1978; m. Mable Darlene Lawson, May 17, 1975; 1 son, Robert Wayne. Actor, dir., designer, writer in profl. theater, N.Y., Calif., Tenn., La., W.Va., Ala., Ohio, Md., 1969-77; adminstrv. aide, asst. dir. Theatre Memphis, 1977; freelance writer, producer TV commls., Memphis, 1977-78; asso. producer Koopman/Taylor Prodns., Memphis, 1978; broadcast prodn. dir. Walker & Assos., Memphis, 1978—; polit., media cons., 1978—. Bd. dirs. Memphis Epilepsy Found., 1978—. Served with USCGR, 1964-65. Recipient Golden award N.Y. Internat. Film Festival, 1972, 1st, 2d, 3d Pl. awards Miami Internat. Film Festival, 1978, Pyramid award for excellence in TV comml. prodn. Memphis Ad Fedn., 1978. Mem. AFTRA, Screen Actors Guild. Clubs: Nat. Writers, Memphis Art Dirs. Home: 2111 Jefferson St Memphis TN 38104 Office: Walker & Assos 2605 Nonconnah Blvd Memphis TN 38132

MC CRARY, THEODORE LORENZA, sanitarian; b. Carbon Hill, Ala., Nov. 19, 1934; s. Archie Theodore and Mary Ellen (McCollum) McC.; student Fisk U., 1952-54; B.S. in Biology, Lane Coll., 1957. With McCrary & Son Cleaners, Jackson, Tenn., 1952-57, Sloan Kettering Cancer Research Inst., N.Y.C., 1958-59; with San Antonio Metro Health Dist., 1968—, quality assurance officer for air pollution control sect., 1976—. Neighborhood commr. Boy Scouts Am. Served with U.S. Army, 1959-68; mem. USCGR. Registered sanitarian, Tex. Mem. Am. Pub. Health Assn., Omega Psi Phi. Methodist. Club: Masons. Research on dog heartworm in South Tex. Home: 1054 H St San Antonio TX 78220

MC CRAW, RONALD KENT, psychologist; b. Houston, Dec. 6, 1947; s. Leon Frank and Lorena Mae (Bailey) McC.; B.A., U. Tex. at Austin, 1970; M.A., U. Tex. Med. Br., Galveston, 1972; Ph.D. candidate U. South Fla., 1974—. Research asst. div. child and adolescent psychiatry U. Tex. Med. Br., 1972-74; grad. asst. div. neuropsychology Fla. Mental Health Inst., Tampa, 1975-76; resident in clin. psychology U. Tex. Health Scis. Center, San Antonio, 1977-78; psychometrician Hillsborough Community Mental Health Center, Tampa, Fla., 1978—. Cert. instr. ARC. Fellow Am. Orthopsychiat. Assn., Am. Psychol. Assn.; mem. Am. Pub. Health Assn., AAAS, Assn. for Advancement Behavior Therapy, Soc. Behavioral Medicine, Soc. for Personality Assessment, U. Tex. Ex-Students Assn. (life), Sigma Xi (asso.), Psi Chi, Nu Sigma Nu. Methodist. Clubs: U. Tex. Longhorn Alumni Band, Order DeMolay (chevalier); Internat. 700. Film reviewer for AAAS Sci. Books and Films, 1977—; contbr. articles to sci. jours. Home: 902 Lindenwood Dr Baytown TX 77520 Office: Dept Psychology U South Fla Tampa FL 33620

MC CREA, WILLIAM GEORGE, banker; b. St. Petersburg, Fla., Mar. 23, 1940; s. William James and Mary Jane (VanFleet) Mc.; B.S., U. Fla., 1965; B.M.A., U. Colo., 1971; postgrad. La. State U., 1975; m. Sara Lynn Alday, June 29, 1963; children—William George, James Trezevant. Community devel. dir., St. Petersburg, 1965-68; v.p. corporate advt. Gen. Telephone Fla., Tampa, 1968-69; v.p., mktg. dir. Charter Bankshares Corp. Fla., St. Petersburg, 1969-73; regional marketing dir. Barnett Banks Fla., St. Petersburg, 1973—; mem. advt. adv. council, Bank Inst. Am. Planning commr. St. Petersburg, 1976; bd. dirs. Jr. Achievement, 1973, Boy Scouts Am., 1973, ARC, 1974, United Way, 1976. Recipient Outstanding Service award St. Petersburg, 1973. Mem. Am. Banking Assn., Bank Mktg. Assn. Democrat. Episcopalian. Clubs: Kiwanis, Suncoasters, Dragons. Home: 1011 Monterey Blvd St Petersburg FL 33704 Office: 3100 Central St St Petersburg FL 33712

MC CREADY, MARY ANN, recording co. exec.; b. Alliance, Ohio, May 28, 1953; d. Byron and Marion Virginia (Saffell) McC.; B.S. cum laude, Vanderbilt U., 1974. With CBS Records, Nashville, 1974—, dir. press and public info., 1977—, dir. artist devel., 1977—; coordinator artist performances. Mem. Country Music Assn., Chi Omega (dir. 1975—). Episcopalian. Contbr. articles to profl. publs.

MCCREARY, EDWARD FLETCHER, sales exec.; b. Dickson County, Tenn., Aug. 21, 1947; s. Benjamin Fletcher and Helen (Hutton) McC.; B.S., U. Tenn., Knoxville, 1969; m. Cheryl Jane Llewellyn, Nov. 26, 1972. Sales rep. John Roberts, Inc., Norman, Okla., 1970-72, sales mgr. S.E., Austin, Tex., 1972-74, dir. market adminstrn., 1974-75; sales specialist Art Carved Class Rings, Inc., Austin, 1975-76; Eastern territorial mgr. Rosenthal, Inc., N.Y.C., 1976—. Republican. Methodist. Office: PO Box 805 Franklin TN 37064

MC CRICKARD, RUBY ASHWELL, nursing adminstr.; b. Huddleston, Va., Apr. 19, 1931; d. Harry O. and Nellie (Cundiff) Ashwell; diploma Riverside Hosp. Sch. Nursing, 1953; B.A., Goddard Coll., 1975; cert. in health care U. So. Calif., Los Angeles, 1976; M.S. in Nursing, Med. Coll. Ga., 1977; m. George T. McCrickard, Aug. 9, 1952; 1 son, George T. Operating room staff nurse Riverside Hosp., Newport News, Va., 1953-54, med. head nurse, 1954-55; staff nurse, acting operating supr. Kecoughtan VA Hosp., Hampton, Va., 1955-61; supr. intensive care and central supply Lynchburg (Va.) Gen.-Marshall Lodge Hosps., 1962-65, asst. dir. nursing services, 1966-69, dir. nursing services, 1969-78, asst. adminstr. in charge respiratory therapy, nursing service, child care center, 1978—; mem. primary care com. SW Va. Health System Agy. Inc., 1979—; chmn. by-laws com. Central Va. Health Planning Emergency Transfer Adv. Com., 1976-77. Mem. Am. Soc. of Nursing Service Adminstrs. (treas. 1977-79), Am. Nurses Assn. (mem. membership com. 1971-72), Va. Nurses Assn. (dir. 1971-75, chmn. by-laws com. 1969-71), Nat. League for Nursing, Va. League for Nursing, Piedmont Heart Assn. (chmn. nursing com. 1971-72, dir. 1973-74), Nat. Soc. Lit. and Arts, AAUW, Riverside Hosp. Sch. Nursing Alumnae (pres. 1958-60), Sigma Theta Tau. Baptist. Clubs: Order Eastern Star, Scottish Rite. Home: Route 1 PO Box 483 Rustburg VA 24588 Office: Lynchburg Gen-Marshall Lodge Hosps Tate Springs Rd Lynchburg VA 24504

MCCROAN, HARVEY HERSHEL, office products co. exec.; b. Grand Ridge, Fla., May 19, 1936; s. William Harvey and Ella McC.; student public schs., Grand Ridge; m. Carolyn Marie Johnson, June 10, 1962; children—Glen, Brenda. Electronics technician Lanier Bus. Products Co., Tallahassee, Fla., 1962-65, service mgr., 1965-70, regional service mgr., Atlanta, 1970-75, nat. service mgr., typing systems, 1975-78, nat. field service mgr., all products, 1978—. Served with USN, 1958-62. Home: 3579 Hermitage Dr Duluth GA 30136 Office: Lanier Bus Products Co 1700 Chantilly Dr Atlanta GA 30324

MC CRORY, ELLANN, radiologist; b. Butler Springs, Ala., Mar. 22, 1936; d. William Bryant and Eva Estelle (Stabler) McCrory; B.S., U. Ala., 1956; M.D., Med. Coll. Ala., 1960. Rotating intern Univ. Hosp., Birmingham, Ala., 1960-61; resident Bapt. Meml. Hosp., Memphis, 1961-64; instr. radiology U. Fla., 1964-65; practice medicine specializing in radiology, Andalusia, Ala., 1965-66, Langdale, Ala., 1966-75, Fort Payne, Ala., 1975—; chief med. staff DeKalb County Hosp., 1977; also lectr. Trustee, Landmark's. Recipient Bausch and Lomb sci. award, 1953. Mem. Am. Coll. Radiology, Radiol. Soc. N.Am., A.M.A., Am. Med. Women's Assn., So. Radiol. Assn., Med. Assn. Ala., DeKalb County (pres. 1977), Chambers County (pres. 1970) med. socs., So. Med. Assn., Ala. Radiol. Soc., Soc. Nuclear Medicine, Am. Roentgen Ray Soc., Ft. Payne C. of C. (dir.), Phi Beta Kappa, Alpha Lambda Delta. Methodist. Home: 1408 Alabama Ave SW Fort Payne AL 35967 Office: Dept Radiology DeKalb County Hosp Fort Payne AL 35967

MC CRORY, MARTHA, educator; b. Quincy, Ill.; d. Joseph W. and Florence (Bastert) McCrory; student Northwestern U., 1937-38; B.M., U. Mich., 1941; M.M., Eastman Sch. Music, 1944, also artists diploma; postgrad. U. London, summer 1955, Berkshire Music Center, 1941, Music Acad. of West, 1952. Cellist, All Am. Youth Orch., 1940, U. Mich. Little Symphony, 1940, Rochester Philharmonic, 1942-46; asst. prof. music Drake U., 1946-47, Trinity U., San Antonio, 1947-52; asst. prin. cello San Antonio Symphony, 1947-53, Chattanooga Symphony, 1955-62, mgr., 1958-62; asst. prof. music U. of South, Sewanee, Tenn., 1962-69, asso. prof., 1969—; dir. Sewanee Summer Music Center, 1963—; cellist Chattanooga, Nashville, Knoxville symphonies. Mem. adv. panel Tenn. Arts Commn. Mem. Nat. Sch. Orch. Assn. (chpt. chmn, chpt. pres.), Tenn. Fedn. Music Clubs (dir.), Tenn. String Tchrs. Assn. (pres.), Pi Beta Phi, Sigma Alpha Iota, Pi Kappa Lambda. Republican. Conglist. Home: Sewanee TN 37375 Office: U of the South Sewanee TN 37375

MC CUE, JAMES CHARLES, research, devel., cons. and publishing co. exec.; b. Jamaica, N.Y., July 1, 1930; s. James John and Adele Anne (Niglutsch) McC.; B.A., Hofstra U., 1952, M.A., 1960; m. Pauline Evelyn Keller, Sept. 6, 1953; 1 dau., Susan Colleen. Sci. specialist EG&G Inc., Boston, 1961-66; sr. physicist Franklin GNO Corp., West Palm Beach, Fla., 1966-69; project physicist Ocean Measurements, Inc., Riviera Beach, Fla., 1969-71; instr. physics Palm Beach Jr. Coll., 1971-78; pres. Radiation Tech. Programs, Inc., Riviera Beach, 1972—. Mem. Am. Nuclear Soc., Soc. for Tec. Communications (sr.). Republican. Lutheran. Home: 500 N Congress Ave 202 West Palm Beach FL 33401 Office: 3601 Blue Heron Blvd Suite E337 Box 10207 Riviera Beach FL 33404

MC CUIN, EARL GOINS, social worker; b. El Dorado, Ark., Dec. 21, 1930; s. Thomas William and Lena Armor (Goins) McC.; B.A., Ouachita Bapt. U., 1952; M.R.E., So. Bapt. Theol. Sem., 1957; M.S. in Social Work, U. Tex., 1971; m. Nancy C. McNeil, Sept. 2, 1956. Minister of edn., youth dir. Shades Mountain Bapt. Ch., Birmingham, Ala., 1957-61, First Bapt. Ch., El Paso, 1962-64; asst. dir. Lee and Beulah Moor Children's Home, El Paso, 1964-69, social worker, 1971-75, dir. social services, 1975—. Served with inf. U.S. Army, 1952-54; lt. col. Res. Mem. Nat. Assn. Social Workers, Acad. Cert. Social Workers. Baptist. Club: Men's Garden. Office: Lee and Beulah Moor Children's Home 1100 E Cliff Dr El Paso TX 79902

MC CUISTON, PAT MICHAUX, banker; b. Kirksey, Ky., Sept. 8, 1917; s. Thomas Montie and Flora (Hamlin) McC.; B.S., Murray (Ky.) State U.; m. Clara Elizabeth Johnson, Nov. 24, 1940; children—Max, Jere, Dale. Tchr., coach in Ky.; exec. C. of C.; personnel dir. mfg. plant; pres. Planters Bank Todd County, Trenton, Ky.; mem. Ky. Senate from 3d Dist. Clubs: Rotary (past local pres.), Woodmen of World (past local pres.). Home: Main St Pembroke KY 42266

MC CULLAH, HARDY NEAL, architect; b. Greenville, Tex., Oct. 17, 1940; s. Rufus Strickland and Willie M. (Weltler) McC.; B.Arch., Tex. Technol. U., 1968; m. Linda McCown, Sept. 31, 1963; children—Kyle B., Clint B. Staff, Thomas E. Stanley, Architects, Dallas, 1968-77, asso. head of design, 1977; partner in charge of design McCullah, Leggett, Manning, Inc., Architects, Dallas, 1977—. Active community redevel. projects. Mem. AIA, Tex. Soc. Architects. Office: McCullah Leggett Manning Inc Architects 12200 Park Central Dr Dallas TX 75251

MCCULLEN, SANDRA RAIFORD, sch. counselor; b. Wayne County, N.C., Feb. 18, 1950; d. Benjamin Braxton and Estelle (Grady) Raiford; B.S. in Home Econs., E. Carolina U., Greenville, N.C., 1972, M.S., 1976; M.A. in Guidance, N.C. State U., 1979; m. Randy Lee McCullen, June 7, 1970; 1 dau., Amanda Kay. Jr. high sch. tchr. Brogden Jr. High Sch., Dudley, N.C., 1972-73; vol. instr. program counselor-coordinator So. Wayne Sr. High Sch., Dudley, 1973-78; guidance counselor Grantham Sch., Goldsboro, N.C., 1978—. Mem. Am. Personnel and Guidance Assn., Am. Vocat. Assn., N.C. Assn. Educators, Mt. Olive Bus. and Profl. Women's Club (v.p. 1979), N.C. Farm Bur. (chmn. conf. meeting 1975; Farm Family of Year award 1979), Delta Kappa Gamma, Phi Upsilon Omicron. Democrat. Methodist. Home: Route 2 Sleepy Creek Dudley NC 28333 Office: Route 1 Goldsboro NC 27530

MC CULLOH, ROBERT LEROY, journalist; b. Oklahoma City, Nov. 21, 1924; s. Robert Andrew and Ruby Gladys (Banta) McC.; B.A., Okla. StateU., 1949, postgrad., 1958-59; m. Gracelyn Allert Harris, June 4, 1948; children—Joicelyn, Richard, Glynden, Kristyn, Scott, Russell. News editor Sequoyah County Times, Sallisaw, Okla., 1949-51; journalist United Press, Oklahoma City, 1951-52; city editor Neosho (Mo.) Daily Democrat, 1952; gen. pub. info. officer Okla. State U., Stillwater, 1952—. Served with A.C., U.S. Army, 1943-45. Mem. Council for Advancement and Support of Edn. (past dir., past sec.-treas. S.W. dist.), Sigma Delta Chi, Kappa Kappa Psi, Kappa Tau Alpha, Phi Eta Sigma. Presbyterian. Home: 214 S Burdick St Stillwater OK 74074 Office: Pub Info Bldg Okla State U Stillwater OK 74078

MC CULLOUGH, JOHN PHILLIP, educator; b. Lincoln, Ill., Feb. 2, 1945; s. Phillip and Lucile Ethel (Ornellas) McC.; B.S., Ill. State U., 1967, M.S., 1968; Ph.D., U. N.D., 1971; m. Barbara Elaine Carley, Nov. 29, 1968; 1 dau., Carley Jo. Adminstrv. mgr. McCullough Ins. Agy., Atlanta, Ill., 1963-68; ops. supr. Stetson China Co., Lincoln, 1967; instr. bus. Ill. Central Coll., East Peoria, 1968-69; home and hosp. instr. Grand Forks (N.D.) pub. schs., 1969-70; research asst. U. N.D., 1970-71; asst. prof. bus. West Liberty (W.Va.) State Coll., 1971-72, asso. prof. mgmt., 1972-74, chmn., prof. mgmt., 1974—; mgmt. cons., Triadelphia, W.Va., 1971—; adj. prof. Wheeling Coll., 1972—; vis. prof. St. Francis Xavier U., 1971; instr. Am. Inst. Banking, 1971—; lect. W.Va. U., 1972—, W.Va. No. Community Coll., 1972—, SBA, 1974—; profl. asso. Inst. Mgmt. and Human Behavior, 1975—; mgmt. cons. Active AFL-CIO Community Services program, Upper Ohio Valley United Fund, Am. Cancer Soc., W.Va. No. Community Coll. Community Service Edn. program. Recipient AFL-CIO community service citation, United Fund Community Service citation, Harris-Casals Found. award. Mem. Soc. Humanistic Mgmt. (exec. com., nat. chmn.), Soc. Data Educators, Cath. Bus. Edn. Assn. (mem. exec. bd. central unit), Am. Soc. Personnel Adminstrn., Adminstrv. Mgmt. Soc., Nat. Acad. Behavioral Sci., Alpha Kappa Psi, Delta Mu Delta, Delta Pi Epsilon, Delta Tau Kappa, Phi Gamma Nu, Phi Theta Pi, Pi Gamma Mu, Pi Omega Pi, Omicron Delta Epsilon. Co-author: Primer in Supervisory Management, 1973. Contbr. articles to profl. jours. Home: 68 Elm Dr Triadelphia WV 26059 Office: Dept Mgmt West Liberty State Coll West Liberty WV 26074

MCCULLOUGH, RICHARD WAYNE, printing, office supply co. exec.; b. Austin, Tex., Sept. 11, 1929; s. William Virgle and Myrtle (Hughes) M.; student U. Tex., 1950-51; m. Elizabeth Janice Pate, July 18, 1952; 1 dau., Cynthia Ann. With hwy. dept. State of Tex., Austin, 1951-59; lab. technician Maverick-Clarke and Clarke Printing Co., Austin, 1959-66; rep. 3M Corp., Austin, 1966; pres. Crawford-Penick, Inc., Austin, 1966—. Mem. Retail Merchants Assn. (dir. 1975), Downtown Optimist Club, Heritage Soc., Austin Sci. Assn., Nat. Office Products Assn., Austin C. of C., Printing Industries Am., Master Printers Am., Printex (dir. local chpt. 1974-76, sec.-treas. 1978). Baptist. Home: 4602 Greystone Dr Austin TX 78731 Office: 112 Congress Ave Austin TX 78767

MC CULLY, RICHARD PHILIP, lawyer; b. Highland Park, Mich., Aug. 4, 1942; s. John M. and Evelyn E. (Richards) Mc C.; B.S., Memphis State U., 1965, J.D., 1968; postgrad. Nat. Coll. Dist. Attys., U. Houston, 1970; M.Pub. Adminstrn., U. Tenn. at Knoxville, 1975; m. Ledra Lynn Massie, Nov. 13, 1971; 1 dau., Colleen Elizabeth. Nat. exec. sec. Phi Alpha Delta Law Fraternity, Granada Hills, Calif., 1968-69; admitted to Tenn. bar, 1968, Fla. bar, 1979; asst. atty. gen., Nashville, 1969-71, exec. asst. atty. gen., 1971-79; asst. state atty., Ft. Lauderdale, Fla., 1976—; instr. Met. Nashville Police Tng. Acad., 1969-79, also Tenn. Law Enforcement Tng. Acad. Served with USN, 1960-62; dist. staff officer and flotilla comdr. USCG Aux., 1971—. Recipient Gold Key award Law Student div. Am. Bar Assn., 1968, also Certificate of Performance award Young Lawyers sect., 1974; U.S. Dept. Justice Law Enforcement Assistance Adminstrn. grantee, 1971-75. Mem. Am. (mem. exec. council young lawyers sect. 1974-75), Tenn. (mem. house dels. 1972-76, gov. 1976-77), Fla. bar assns., Tenn. Young Lawyers Conf. (pres. 1976-77), Barristers Club Nashville (pres. 1973-78), Nat. Dist. Attys. Assn., Fraternal Order Police, Sigma Alpha Epsilon, Omicron Delta Kappa. Club: Harbor Island Yacht. Co-editor The Reporter, nat. mag. of Phi Alpha Delta law fraternity, 1968-69. Home: 2208 NE 18th Ave Fort Lauderdale FL 33305 Office: 640 Broward County Courthouse Fort Lauderdale FL 33301

MC CUMBER, WILLIAM HENRY, JR., systems analyst; b. Midland, Tex., Aug. 21, 1934; s. William Henry and Frances Jeanette (Tyner) McC.; B.S. in Elec. Engring., U. Okla., 1960; M.S. in Engring., U. Ala., 1971; m. Wathena June Word, July 4, 1953; children—Keith, Mark, Kathryn, Deirdre, Matthew, Victoria. With missile and space systems div. Douglas Aircraft Co., Cape Canaveral and Houston, 1960-68; large-scale systems analyst Fed. Systems div. IBM, Huntsville, Ala., 1968—, engring. mgr., 1969-74; instr. electronics Okaloosa County (Fla.) Vocat. Edn. Program, 1962; lectr. solar energy systems; lectr. solar update confs. Dept. Energy, 1978, 79. Mem. Huntsville Edn. Financing Task Force, 1975; founding mem. Huntsville Coalition of Civic Assns., 1978; v.p. Huntsville Seahorses, AAU Swimming Club, 1978; pres. N.W. YMCA Swim Team, 1978. Served with USAF, 1953-57. Registered profl. engr., Okla., Ala.; licensed 1st class radiotelephone operator FCC. Mem. Assn. Folk Musicians (dir., past pres. Huntsville), Mensa, Mt. Charron Homeowners Assn. (chmn.). Contbr. articles on solar energy collector analysis to profl. jours. Address: 11007 Vivian Rd NW Huntsville AL 35810

MC CURRY, JAMES CLIFF, ins. agy. exec.; b. Atlanta, July 8, 1948; s. Arthur J. and Mary Agnes (Lee) McC.; student Armstrong State Coll., 1966-68; B.B.A., U. Ga., 1971; m. Kathryn Hooper, Dec. 5, 1970; 1 son, James Clifford. Account exec. Mercer Ins. Agy., Inc., Savannah, Ga., 1971-73, personal lines mgr., 1973-75, comml. lines mgr., 1975-76, v.p. comml. lines, 1976—. Mem. City of Savannah Fire Prevention Week, chmn., 1972, 73; active United Way, 1976, 77, 78; mem. athletic adv. bd. Savannah Bd. Edn., 1979; sr. warden St. Thomas Episc. Ch., 1979—. Served with Army N.G., 1970-76. C.P.C.U. Mem. Young Agts. of Ga. (exec. com. 1975, chmn. 1979), Savannah Area C. of C., Ind. Ins. Agts. of Savannah (Presdl. award 1976), Ind. Ins. Agts. Ga. (C.P.C.U. Scholarship award 1976), Ind. Ins. Agts. of Am., Profl. Ins. Agts. of Ga. Clubs: Savannah Quarterback, Savannah Yacht, U. Ga., Armstrong State Coll. Big A, Civitan, Debtors. Home: 23 Leary Dr Savannah GA 31406 Office: 7 E Bay St Savannah GA 31412

MC CURRY, JAMES RODNEY, electron microscoptist; b. Asheville, N.C., June 3, 1941; s. James Ray and Dorothy Tommie (Garrison) McC.; B.S. in Zoology, N.C. State U., Raleigh, 1965, B.S. in Sci. Edn., 1966; m. Marsha Taylor Lane, May 29, 1975; 1 son, Michael Rodney. Electron microscope technician N.C. State U., 1966, electron microscope supr. Inst. Biol. Scis., 1967; dir. electron microscope facility, biology dept. Western Ky. U., Bowling Green, 1968—. Active local Cub Scouts, 1975—. Mem. Electron Microscope Soc. Am., Ky. Acad. Scis., AAAS. Democrat. Baptist. Home: 1900 Smallhouse Rd Bowling Green KY 42101 Office: Biology Dept Western Ky Univ Bowling Green KY 42101

MC CURRY, KATHRYN MAREE, educator; b. White Pond, S.C., July 17, 1929; d. William Earle and Mildred Ruth (Owens) McCurry; B.A., Converse Coll., 1950; M.A., U. S.C., 1951; postgrad. Dell Sch. Med. Tech., 1954, U. S.C., 1960-61, 63, 68. Lab. tech. Dr. W.E. McCurry's Clinic, Ridge Spring, S.C., 1952-55; instr. French and English, asst. to dean Greenbrier Coll., Lewisburg, W.Va., 1955-59; tchr. French, Columbia (S.C.) Coll., 1960; tchr. English, Brooklyn-Cayce High Sch., West Columbia, S.C., 1960; tchr. French, A.C. Flora High Sch., Columbia, 1960—. Counsellor Fgn. Lang. Study League, Orsay, France, 1967. Mem. Am. Med. Technologists, S.C. Soc. Am. Med. Technologists (sec., treas. 1961-62), S.C., Richland County edn. assns., S.C. Lang. Assn., Central States Modern Lang. Assn., City French Tchrs. (chmn. 1969-70), AAUW, Colonial Dames XVII Century (chpt. sec. 1974-76, state sec. 1977-79, 1st v.p. 1979—), French Huguenot Soc., Internat. Platform Assn. Home: 6433 Eastshore Rd Columbia SC 29206

MCCUTCHEN, GAY, med. lab. adminstr.; b. Oklahoma City, Sept. 20, 1938; d. Vonly Buel and Wilma Irene (Crosby) McCutchen; B.A., La. State U., 1960; grad. Charity Hosp. Sch. Med. Tech., 1962. Field corr. Horse World Mag., 1961-62; med. technologist in hematology Mercy Hosp., New Orleans, 1962, supr. hematology sect., 1962-67; chief med. technologist U. Tex. System Cancer Center, M.D. Anderson Hosp. and Tumor Inst., Houston, 1967-70, clin. lab. mgr., 1970—; acting adminstr. Inst. Hemotherapy, Houston, 1974-77, cons., 1977—; vis. faculty mem. Mayo Clinic, Rochester, Minn., 1975—; mem. Donor Recruitment Task Force, Am. Blood Commn., 1975-77. Mem. Am. Soc. Med. Tech. (del. 1971-73, 75-80, award 1978, 79), Tex. Soc. Med. Tech. (dir. 1972-75, mem. legis. com. 1973—), Houston Dist. Soc. Med. Tech. (pres. 1971-72), Am. Assn. Blood Banks (mem. com. on planning and action 1976—), S. Central Assn. Blood Banks, Tex. Hosp. Assn., Houston Antibody Club, Tex. Blood Bank Dirs., Omicron Sigma, Alpha Delta Pi. Republican. Methodist. Author: (with B. Wallace) Hematology Procedure Manual, 1975; contbr. articles to profl. jours.; asso. editor Mgmt./Instrumentation sect. Am. Jour. Med. Tech., 1976—. Office: 6723 Bertner St C3001 Houston TX 77030

MCCUTCHEN, JAMES NORMAN, mgmt. cons.; b. Texas City, Tex., Feb. 21, 1949; s. Norman Louis and Marian V. McCutchen; B.S. in Chem. Engring., Purdue U., 1972; postgrad. Bates Coll. Law, 1975—; m. April Allyn Blackburn, Feb. 4, 1978. Ops. engr. Union Oil Co. of Calif., Beaumont, Tex., 1972-74; mgr. econ. analysis Litwin Engring. & Constrn. Co., Houston, 1974-75; sr. cons. Bonner & Moore Assos., Inc., Houston, 1975—. Mem. Am. Inst. Chem. Engrs. Episcopalian. Office: 2727 Allen Pkwy Houston TX 77019

MC CUTCHEON, CHESTER MYERS, investment co. exec.; b. Monroeville, Pa., Oct. 30, 1907; s. William Erwin and Margaret Kelso (Myers) McC.; student Westinghouse Tech. Night Sch., East Pittsburgh, Pa., 1926-30, La Salle Extension U., 1933-35, Am. Savs. and Loan Inst., Atlanta, 1947-54; m. Hellen Sophia Clawson, Nov. 3, 1944; children—Ronald R., Brian L., Brenda (Mrs. Ernest Mosley), Lynn Ellis, Bruce A., Curtis W. Cost accountant Westinghouse Electric & Mfg. Co., Pitts., 1926-33; tax collector No. Huntingdon Twp., Westmoreland County, Pa., 1934-40; examiner Fed. Home Loan Bank Bd., Washington, 1941-47; comptroller Fulton Fed. Savs. & Loan Assn., Atlanta, 1947-73; tech. adviser Bolivian Savs. & Loan

Industry, 1974-75; v.p. Fulton Investment Co., 1958-60, pres., 1960-65; dir. Southeastern Capital Co.; pres. Cherokee Enterprises, Tuxedo, Inc.; office adminstr. Cobb. Jud. Circuit, State of Ga., 1977—. Chmn. Cobb County Republican Exec. Com., Marietta, Ga., 1964-66; co-chmn. finance com. Callaway for Gov. Campaign, 1966. Mem. thesis rev. bd. Grad. Sch. Savs. and Loan, Ind. U., 1960—. Mem. Nat. Soc. Controllers and Financial Officers (past pres.), Nat. Dist. Attys. Assn. Presbyn. (ruling elder). Author: Manual de Contabilidad, 1974. Contbr. articles to profl. jours. Home: 96 Whitlock Ave Marietta GA 30064 Office: Fulton Fed Bldg 11 Pryor St NE Atlanta GA 30303

MC DADE, HIRAM LONSDALE, III, speech pathologist; b. Cleve., Nov. 11, 1947; s. Hiram and Mary Lou (Kishel) McD.; B.A., Baldwin Wallace Coll., 1970; M.A., U. Tenn., 1974, Ph.D., 1976; 1 dau. by previous marriage—Kimberly Walton. Speech pathologist Birth Defects Center, Knoxville, 1973-76; asst. prof. spl. edn. Ind. State U., Terre Haute, 1976-78; asst. prof. pediatrics U. Tex. Med. Br., Galveston, 1978—, dir. communicative disorders, div. child devel. and behavioral pediatrics, 1978—. Mem. Am. Speech Lang. and Hearing Assn., Am. Assn. Mental Deficiency, Council Exceptional Children, Tex. Speech and Hearing Assn. Home: 912 Sealy Galveston TX 77551 Office: Child Development Div U Tex Med Br Galveston TX 77550

MC DANIEL, GERALD CALVIN, accountant; b. Murray City, Ohio, Apr. 28, 1925; s. Ralph and Gladys (Chivers) M.; grad. Tomlinson Vocat. Sch., 1956; m. Catherine P. Haney, May 24, 1947; children—Douglas G., Mark R. Accountant, C. Melton Accounting Service, St. Petersburg Beach, Fla., 1952-55; pvt. practice accounting, St. Petersburg, Fla., 1956—. Served with AUS, 1943-45; ETO. Decorated Purple Heart medal. Mem. Fla. Accountants Assn., Nat. Soc. Pub. Accountants. Lutheran (pres. local ch. 1967). Office: 3012 Central Ave St Petersburg FL 33712

MC DANIEL, GILBERT LEE, social worker; b. Birmingham, Ala., Dec. 19, 1938; s. Renley and Minnie Margaret (Dandridge) McD.; student Jacksonville U., 1960-65; B.S. in Criminology, Psychology and Social Work, Fla. State U., 1966, M.S.W., 1973; m. Margaret Ann Smith, Aug. 16, 1969; children—Baird Lee, Lisa, Leanne, Ronnie, Darren. Program and activity dir. Tampa Heights Hosp., Tampa, Fla., 1973-76; dir. social service, cons. Pinellas Horizon Mental Health Center and Hosp., Clearwater, Fla., 1976; pvt. practice social work, Tampa, 1976-77; mental health program cons. Boys Ranch, Fla., 1977—; unit dir. Fla. Sheriff's Youth Fund, 1977—; cons. psychiat. and gen. hosps. Active Boy Scouts Am., Big Bros., YMCA. Served with AUS, 1957-60. NIMH fellow; VA Social Work grantee; recipient service award in social work, Duval County Sheriff's Dept. Mem. Nat. Assn. Social Work, Hosp. Social Work Dirs., Nat. Parks and Recreation, Child Welfare League, Am. Legion, VFW, Gold Key. Democrat. Methodist. Home: PO Box 20 Boys Ranch FL 32060 Office: Florida Sheriff's Boys Ranch Boys Ranch FL 32060

MC DANIEL, HAYNES A, JR., pharmacist; b. Washington, Aug. 4, 1939; s. Haynes A and Edna (Knowles) McD.; B.S. in Pharmacy, George Washington U., 1961; M.B.A., Fla. Atlantic U., 1972; children by previous marriage—Haynes A III, Dana Elizabeth, Diane Lynn. Intern, Friendship Pharmacy, Washington, 1956-61; pharmacist Peoples Drug Store, Washington, 1961, McClure Drug Co., Vero Beach, Fla., 1962-67; chief pharmacist Indian River Meml. Hosp., Vero Beach, 1967-79, dir. pharmacy, 1979—; cons. pharmacist to Fla. Bapt. Retirement Center Nursing Home, 1973—; asst. prof. pharmacology Indian River Community Coll., 1973; pharmacist for med. assistance team to Antigua, 1975; cert. preceptor U. Fla., 1973—. Mem. Citizens Adv. Com., City of Vero Beach, 1973-75; mem. choir First Bapt. Ch., 1973—; bd. dirs. Am. Cancer Soc., Indian River County, 1968-72, chmn. edn. com., 1970-72. Mem. Am. Pharm. Assn., Am. Soc. Hosp. Pharmacists, Fla. Pharm. Assn. (chmn. edn. com. 1977-78, v.p. 6th dist. 1974-76), Fla. Soc. Hosp. Pharmacists (chmn. profl. placement 1978-79, pres. 1974, Pharmacist of the Year award 1977), Indian River Pharm. Assn., Southeastern Soc. of Hosp. Pharmacists, Vero Beach Jaycees. Club: Treasure Coast Model Railroad (pres. 1975-76). Home: 1835 42d Ave Vero Beach FL 32960 Office: 1000 36th St Vero Beach FL 32960

MCDANIEL, JESSE LOUIE, coll. adminstr.; b. Kinston, N.C., Mar. 21, 1923; s. Leon Dale and Anna Margaret (Oliver) McD.; B.S., E. Carolina U., 1949, M.A., 1950; Ed.D., Duke U., 1965; m. Helen Joyce Perry, Aug. 26, 1950; children—Anna, Ellen. Tchr. public schs., Burlington, N.C., 1949-50; prin. Atlantic (N.C.) High Sch., 1950-51; West Bertie High Sch., Lewiston, N.C., 1952-55, Aycock High Sch., Hillsboro, N.C., 1955-57, Creedmore (N.C.) High Sch., 1957-60; supt. Franklinton (N.C.) City Schs., 1960-63; chmn. edn. dept. U. N.C., Asheville, 1964-67; dean Lenoir Community Coll., Kinston, 1967-71, pres., 1971—. Pres., United Way, Kinston, 1973-74. Served with USNR, 1943-46, 51-52. Mem. Am. Assn. Sch. Adminstrs., N.C. State Employees Assn., N.C. Community Coll. Pres. Assn., N.C. Assn. Colls. and Univs. Democrat. Methodist. Clubs: Rotary, Masons. Home: 1804 St George Pl Kinston NC 28501 Office: PO Box 188 Kinston NC 28501

MCDANIEL, JOHN WILLIAM, hosp. adminstr.; b. Newport News, Va., Mar. 16, 1951; s. Robert Lewis and Mildred Romaine (Brehm) McD.; B.S., Campbell Coll., Buies Creek, N.C., 1973; M.H.A., George Washington U., 1976; m. Dara Melissa Watson, Sept. 3, 1977. Adminstrv. resident Wake County Med. Center, Raleigh, N.C., 1975-76; asst. hosp. adminstr. Craven County Hosp., New Bern, N.C., 1976—; pres. Organizational Performance Techniques, cons., 1978—; mem. New Bern Ednl. Adv. Com., 1976—; past bd. dirs. Eastern Area Health Edn. Center, Craven County United Way, Craven County Mgmt. Assn. Mem. Am. Hosp. Assn., Am. Coll. Hosp. Adminstrs. Republican. Baptist. Clubs: New Bern Golf and Country, River Bend Golf and Country, Masons, Author articles in field. Home: 1309 Green Springs Rd New Bern NC 28560 Office: PO Box 2157 New Bern NC 28560

MC DANIEL, ROBERT MICHAEL, broadcasting co. exec.; b. Lima, Ohio, Feb. 1, 1944; s. Earl E. and Norma McD.; B.S. in Radio-TV Communications, So. Ill. U., 1966; m. Barbara Jo Ann Dudley, July 1, 1966. Program dir. Sta. WCTU-TV, Charlotte, N.C.; gen. mgr. Sta. WATU-TV, Augusta, Ga., Sta. WSPA AM-FM, Spartanburg, S.C., Sta. WPSB, Bridgeport, Conn.; sta. mgr. Sta. WPST, Trenton, N.J.; gen. mgr. Sta. WHEZ, Huntington, W.Va. Chmn., Cabell County (W.Va.) 4-H Found.; W.Va. chmn. Tri State Fair and Regatta Festival. Mem. Nat. Radio Broadcasters Assn. (state dir.), Huntington Ashland Ironton Radio Broadcasters Assn., Advt. Club Huntington (pres.). Office: 3570 Skyview Dr Huntington WV 25701

MC DANIEL, THOMAS JACKSON, coast guard officer; b. Bristol, Va., Feb. 3, 1953; s. Hubert Owen and Sarah Lou (Warner) McD.; B.S., U.S. Coast Guard Acad., 1975; m. Susan Marie Hughes, June 7, 1975; 1 dau., Jennifer Kristina. Commd. ensign U.S. Coast Guard, 1975, advanced through grades to lt., 1979; ops. officer Basswood, Guam, 1975-77; comdg. officer Loran Sta. Jupiter, Hobe Sound, Fla., 1977—. Recipient award for fin. mgmt. U.S. Coast Guard Acad., 1975. Mem. U.S. Coast Guard Acad. Alumni Assn. Methodist. Home: Quarters A Jupiter Lighthouse Rd Jupiter FL 33458 Office: US Coast Guard 13800 SE Federal Hwy Hobe Sound FL 33455

MC DANIEL, WILLIAM YOUNG, radiologist; b. Tuscumbia, Ala., Oct. 31, 1928; s. Dillard Young and Virgie Lee (Holland) McD.; M.D., Tulane U., 1952; postgrad. (fellow) U. Colo., 1970-71; m. Claris Leonora Macon, June 8, 1955; children—William Young, Mark, Paul, Scott, Claris Lynn. Intern, U. Ala. Med. Center, Birmingham, 1952-53; resident in pediatrics Charity Hosp., New Orleans, 1955-57; practice medicine specializing in pediatrics, Mobile, Ala., 1957-70; resident in radiology St. Luke's Hosp., Denver, 1971-73; fellow pediatric radiology Childrens Hosp., Denver, 1973-74; practice medicine specializing in radiology, Mobile, 1974—. Served to capt. M.C., USAF, 1953-55. Diplomate Am. Bd. Pediatrics, Am. Bd. Radiology. Mem. Am. Acad. Pediatrics, Am. Coll. Radiology. Republican. Presbyterian. Home: 314 E Indian Creek St Mobile AL 36607 Office: PO Box 2144 Mobile AL 36601

MC DAVID, JOEL DUNCAN, clergyman; b. Georgetown, Ala., June 10, 1916; s. Harry and Ola Elizabeth (McCaskill) McD.; B.A., Millsaps Coll., 1941, D.D., 1977; B.D., Emory U., 1944; D.D., Birmingham So. Coll., 1959, Fla. So. U., 1973, Bethune-Cookman Coll., 1973; m. Milah Dodd Gibson, Aug. 29, 1942; children—Ben A., Joel G., Karen Anne McDavid Beville. Ordained to ministry Meth. Ch., 1944; pastor, Grand Bay, Ala., 1944-46, Toulminville, Ala., 1946-50, Auburn, Ala., 1950-58, First Meth. Ch., Montgomery, Ala., 1958-66, Dauphin Way Ch., Mobile, Ala., 1966-72; bishop United Meth. Ch., 1972—; faculty Auburn U., 1950-58. Mem. Ala. State Ethics Commn., 1966-67, Bi-racial Com. Montgomery, 1964-66, Mobile, 1970-72; v.p. United Meth. Southeastern Jurisdictional Council, 1968-72; mem. Gen. Bd. Discipleship, 1972—; pres. Southeastern Jurisdiction Council Bishops, 1977—; exec. com. Council Bishops, 1977—. Trustee Fla. So. Coll., Bethune Cookman Coll., Emory U. Named Man of Year, Montgomery, 1965. Mason, Kiwanian. Author: Waiting, 1969. Home: 127 Lake Hollingsworth Dr Lakeland FL 33801 Office: 968 Callahan Ct Lakeland FL 33801

MC DAVID, MARION FOY, lawyer; b. Pelzer, S.C., Sept. 29, 1911; s. James Philip and Nora Dozier (Foy) McD.; A.B., Davidson Coll., 1932; J.D., George Washington U., 1940; postgrad. Fgn. Lang. Sch., U. Pa., 1945; m. Caroline Kelley Okey, Dec. 4, 1943; children—Marion Foy, William Okey. Admitted to D.C. bar, 1940, Tenn. bar, 1946, U.S. Supreme Ct. bar; prin. claims examiner GAO, Washington, 1940-42; practice law, Harriman, Tenn., 1946—. City judge, Harriman, 1951-55. Chmn. Roane County (Tenn.) Democratic Party, 1956-68; alt. del. Nat. Dem. Conv., 1964. Served with CIC, AUS, 1942-45. Mem. Am., Tenn., Roane County (pres. 1959-60) bar assns., Tenn. Assn. Criminal Def. Lawyers, Am. Legion. Presbyn. Home: Tanglewood Rd PO Drawer 436 Harriman TN 37748 Office: PO Drawer 436 Harriman TN 37748

MCDAVID, MARY ELLEN FARRIS, speech pathologist; b. Charleston, W.Va., Nov. 4, 1954; d. Ramon A. and Evelyn May (Starr) Farris; B.S., W.Va. U., 1975, M.S., 1977; m. Daniel James McDavid, June 17, 1978. Speech-lang. pathologist Multicap, Head Start Program, 1978; speech-lang. pathologist Kanawha County Sch. System, South Charleston, W.Va., 1978—. W.Va. Rehab. grantee, 1975. Mem. Am. Speech and Hearing Assn. (cert. clin. competence), W.Va. Speech and Hearing Assn., Beta Sigma Phi. Democrat. Roman Catholic. Clubs: Scarlett Oaks Country. Home: 5 Dairy Rd Poca WV 25159 Office: Office of Exceptional Children C and 3d Sts South Charleston WV 25303

MCDAVID, SARA JUNE, librarian; b. Atlanta, Dec. 21, 1945; d. William Harvey and June (Threadgill) McRae; B.A., Mercer U., 1967; M.L.S., Emory U., 1969; m. Michael Wright McDavid, Mar. 20, 1971. Librarian's asst. Candler Library, Emory U., 1967-68; asst. to librarian Ga. Power Co., Atlanta, 1968-69; head librarian Fernbank Sci. Center, Atlanta, 1969-77; head librarian Research Library, Fed. Reserve Bank of Atlanta, 1977—; bd. dirs. Solinet, 1977—, vice chmn., 1979-80. Pub. relations chmn. Atlanta Humane Soc. Women's Aux., 1976-78, also dir.; mem. Alliance Theater Guild. Recipient HEW Title V-C fellowship, 1968-69; Assn. Sci. and Tech. Centers Project grantee, 1975-76. Mem. Spl. Libraries Assn. (v.p. S. Atlantic chpt. 1974-75, pres. 1975-76, nominating com. chmn. 1977-78, placement officer, 1978—), Ga. Library Assn. (sec.-treas. spl. library sect. 1975-77), Am. Inst. Banking, Southeastern Library Assn., Alpha Gamma Delta. Club: Young Women of the Arts. Mem. editorial bd. Georgia Librarian, 1979—. Home: 2047 Palifox Dr Atlanta GA 30307 Office: Federal Reserve Sta Atlanta GA 30303

MC DAVITT, WILLIAM DONALD, soc. exec.; b. Dallas, May 28, 1945; s. William Early and Mavis Marie (Byrd) McD.; A.A., Tex. Southmost Coll., 1966; B.B.A., S.W. Tex. State U., 1970; m. Linda Kay Fox, June 29, 1968. With Am. Cancer Soc., 1970—, area program dir., Midland, Tex., 1974-76, area dir. program devel., Houston, 1976-77, asst. area exec. dir., 1977-78, area dir., 1978—. Pres., Young Republicans Club, 1964, Rep. precinct del., 1976. Recipient Crusade certification Am. Cancer Soc., 1971, mgmt. certificate, 1974; award of excellence Area Crusade, 1976-77, 78-79. Mem. S.W. Tex. State U. Ex-Students Assn., Alpha Kappa Psi. Baptist. Home: 2110 Malvern Hill Dr Austin TX 78745

MC DERMOTT, JOSEPH EDWARD, petroleum co. mktg. exec.; b. St. Louis, Sept. 23, 1931; s. Albert and Myrtle (Martin) McD.; B.S. in Bus. Adminstrn., S.W. Mo. State U., 1957; m. Doris Gail Bunn, July 30, 1955; children—Timothy Joseph, Robin Jill. Gen. sales mgr. Derby Refining Co., Wichita, Kans., 1957-70; v.p. Vickers Petroleum Corp., Memphis, 1970—, also dir. Pres. bd. trustees Farmington Presbyterian Ch., Germantown, Tenn. Served with U.S. Army, 1951-53. Mem. Am. Petroleum Inst., Soc. Ind. Gasoline Marketers (asso.), Theta Kappa Epsilon (pres. chpt. bd. trustees). Republican. Office: PO Box 18619 Memphis TN 38118

MC DILL, THOMAS HALDANE, educator; b. Little Rock, June 9, 1917; s. Thomas Hemphill and Emmie Gardner (Moody) McD.; A.B., Erskine Coll., 1938, B.D., 1940; postgrad. Princeton Theol. Sem., 1946; M.Div., Columbia Theol. Sem., 1947; M.A., U. Chgo., 1958; Litt.D., Presbyn. Coll., 1968; m. Lila Williams Bost, Dec. 26, 1938; 1 son, Thomas Calvin. Ordained to ministry Asso. Ref. Presbyn. Ch., 1940; pastor, Russellville, Ark., 1940-42; moderator Miss. Valley Presbytery, 1942; chaplain AUS, 1942-46; sr. pastor Highlands Presbyn. Ch., Atlanta, 1946-51; moderator 2d Presbytery, 1950; mem. Presbytery Atlanta Presbyn. Ch. U.S., 1951-54, 72—; mem. Presbytery of Central Miss., 1954-72; prof. pastoral care and counseling Columbia Theol. Sem., 1951-79; interim pastor Highlands Presbyn. Ch., Stone Mountain, Ga., 1979—; sr. group psychotherapist Georgian Clinic, Dept. Pub. Health, Atlanta, 1953-69; sec. bd., chmn. dept. human relations Exec. Edn. Inc., Decatur, Ga., 1970—. Mem. permanent com. on Christianity and health Presbyn. Ch. U.S., 1956-66, chmn., 1960-66; chmn. Joint Office Instnl. Chaplaincies, Council on Ch. Union, 1968-70. Mem. Pres.'s Adv. Com. on Alcoholism, HEW, 1966-67; mem. DeKalb County (Ga.) Mental Health Council, 1962-71, chmn., 1965-71. Bd. dirs. Atlanta Mental Health Found.; bd. dirs., mem. staff Center for Advancement Personal Growth, Atlanta. Mem. Council for Clin. Tng. (nat. accreditation com. 1962-68), Inst. for Pastoral Care, Ga. Assn. Pastoral Care (dir.), Am. Assn. Pastoral Counselors (nat. membership com. 1966-71, chmn. nat. nominating com. 1970-75), Assn. Clin. Pastoral Edn. (ho. of dels. 1968-69), Alcohol and Drug Problems Assn. N.Am. Editorial adv. bd. Pastoral Psychology mag., 1963-73. Home: 1083 Oakdale Rd NE Atlanta GA 30307 Office: Columbia Theol Sem Decatur GA 30031

MC DOLE, HARRY FRANKLIN, JR., marine corps officer; b. Chester, W.Va., Oct. 14, 1954; s. Harry Franklin and Shirley Lillian (Six) McD.; B.S. in Math. The Citadel, 1976; m. Nancy Roberta Adeimy, Nov. 26, 1976. Commd. 2d lt. USMC, 1976, advanced through grades to 1st lt., 1977—; programming officer Depot Maintenance Activity, Marine Corps Base, Albany, Ga., 1977-78; programming officer logistic info. systems, Albany, 1978, programming officer materiel returns program, 1978-79, programming officer Def. Communication Agy., Pentagon, Washington, 1979—. Active Navy Relief, 1977-78, Fed. Combined Campaign funds, 1977-78; v.p. Citadel Religious Council, 1975-76; coach ladies softball, Albany, 1978-79. Recipient Iron Man awards Hdqrs. Bn., Albany. Mem. Citadel Alumni Assn. Republican. Clubs: Flint River Long Rifles, Chess, Math., Running, Summerall Guards. Address: 14746 Tamarack Pl Woodbridge VA 22191

MC DONALD, ALVIS EDWARD, mathematician; b. Clarksville, Tex., June 12, 1935; s. Cecil Edward and Edith Mae (Roberts) McD.; B.S. in Math. (Inst. Alumni Fund scholar), N.M. Inst. Mining and Tech., 1959, B.S. in Petroleum Engring. (Socony Mobil scholar), 1960; M.A., Wash. State U. 1962; Ph.D. (Mobil Oil fellow), U. Tex., 1970; m. JoAnn Roturno, June 4, 1960; children—James Patrick, Belinda Kathleen, Maureen Elizabeth. Tchr. math, physics Socorro (N.Mex.) High Sch., 1960; research technologist Mobil Research & Devel., Dallas, 1963-65, sr. research mathematician, 1968-73, research asso., 1973—. Precinct chmn. Republican party, 1969-70. Ford Found. scholar, 1954-55. Mem. Soc. Petroleum Engrs., Soc. Computer Simulation. Republican. Roman Catholic. Home: 1805 Egyptian Dr Dallas TX 75232 Office: PO Box 900 Field Research Lab Dallas TX 75221

MC DONALD, ANDREW J., bishop, Roman Cath. Ch. Ordained priest Roman Catholic Ch. 1948; apptd. bishop Little Rock, 1972, consecrated, installed, 1972. Address: 2415 N Tyler St Little Rock AR 72210*

MC DONALD, BRUCE BRADFORD, surgeon; b. C.Z., Apr. 27, 1946; s. Donald Fiedler and Virginia (Vail) McD.; grad. (scholar) Colby Coll., 1968; M.D., Bowman Gray Sch. Medicine, 1972; m. Pamela Ann Jones, May 25, 1973; 1 dau., Kelly Vail. Intern in surgery Parkland Meml. Hosp., Dallas, 1972-73; chief surgery and emergency room USPHS Hosp., Crow Agency, Mont., 1973-75; resident in surgery U. Ariz., Tucson, 1975-78; practice medicine specializing in gen. and vascular surgery, Austin, Tex., 1978—; attending staff Seton Hosp., St. Davdid's Hosp. Brackenridge Hosp., and Holy Cross Hosp. Served with USPHS, 1973-75. Diplomate Am. Bd. Surgery. Mem. Tex. Med. Assn., Travis County Med. Soc., Alpha Omega Alpha. Republican. Home: 1613 Preston St Austin TX 78703 Office: Medical Park Tower Suite 515 Austin TX 78705

MC DONALD, CLAIBORNE, IV, lawyer; b. New Orleans, Aug. 6, 1948; s. Claiborne and Edith Lockhart (Rapp) McD.; B.A., Miss. State U., 1970; J.D., U. Ala., 1973; m. Rebecca Mae Crosby, Jan. 8, 1972. Admitted to Miss. bar, 1973; asso. firm William & Smith, Picayune, Miss., 1973-77; partner firm Williams, Smith & McDonald, Picayune, 1977—; city judge, Picayune, 1976—. Mem. exec. com. Pearl River County (Miss.) Democratic party, 1976—; del. Dem. State Conv., 1976. Served with Transp. Corps, U.S. Army, 1974 Mem. Picayune C. of C. (dir. 1976—), Am., Miss., Pearl River County bar assns., Am., Miss. trial lawyers assns., Miss. Municipal Judges Assn., Farrah Law Soc., Phi Alpha Theta, Lambda Chi Alpha, Phi Delta Phi. Democrat. Episcopalian. Clubs: Rotary, Masons, Shriners. Home: PO Box 459 Picayune MS 39466 Office: PO Box 1076 109 N Main St Picayune MS 39466

MC DONALD, CLARENCE JACKSON, mfg. co. exec., lawyer; b. Junction, Tex., Dec. 12, 1926; s. Clarence Grenville and Minnie Ila (Dunning) McD.; B.S., Trinity U., San Antonio, 1950; J.D., So. Meth. U., 1966; m. Barbara June Kennon, Apr. 9, 1950; children—Zane Jay, Laurie Jill. Electronics engr. San Antonio Air Material Command, 1950-54; chief engr. Mathes Co., Marble Falls, Tex., 1955-62; exec. v.p. Folsom Co., Dallas, 1962-66; admitted to Tex. bar, 1966; since practiced in Dallas; pres., co-founder Electric Products Mfg. Corp., Mesquite, Tex., 1968-74; gen. mgr. sun dial plant Square D Co., Mesquite, 1974-78; chmn. bd. Planned Energy Systems Inc., Dallas, 1978—. Served with USNR, 1942-44; PTO. Mem. IEEE, Phi Alpha Delta. Clubs: Masons, Shriners, Kiwanis (pres. 1975). Methodist. Home: 1100 Lakeshore Dr Mesquite TX 75149 Office: 2211 Gross Rd Mesquite TX 75150

MCDONALD, DOROTHY LOVE, educator; b. Arkansas City, Ark., Aug. 18, 1948; d. Frank James and Eliza Jane (Washington) Love; B.S., U. Ark., Pine Bluff, 1970; M.S., Ouachita Bapt. U., 1976; postgrad. Tex. Woman's U., 1977; m. Frisco McDonald, Feb. 19, 1970; children—Kelvin PaShan, Frisco. Tchr., Ark. Farmers Union Tng. Program, Pine Bluff, 1970-71; library asst. U. Ark., Pine Bluff, 1971-76, tchr. English, 1976—. Del., S.W. Workers Fedn., Inc., 1973; sec. United Minority Workers Assn., Inc., 1974, mem. steering com., 1975-76; mem. Title I parent adv. council Broadmoor Elem. Sch., Pine Bluff Sch. Dist. Title III grantee, 1977. Mem. Nat. Council Tchrs. English, South Central MLA, Sigma Tau Delta. Baptist. Office: English Dept U Ark Pine Bluff AR 71601

MC DONALD, FRANCES LEE, health assn. exec.; b. Temple, Tex., Sept. 11, 1930; d. James Jackson and Alice May (Babcock) McD.; A.A., Temple Jr. Coll., 1950; B.A., So. Meth. U., 1953. Program asso. Am. Lung Assn. of Tex., Austin, 1966-72; exec. dir. Am. Lung Assn. of Central Tex., Temple, 1972-76; exec. dir. North Tex. Lung Assn., Ft. Worth, 1976—. Mem. Tex. Gov.'s Regional Council on Aging, 1973-76. Fellow Tex. Public Health Assn. (sec. health edn. sect. 1970-71, chmn. sect. 1971-72); mem. Tex. Soc. Public Health Educators, Congress of Lung Assn. Staff, South Central Users Council (chmn. 1974-75), Kappa Kappa Gamma. Republican. Episcopalian. Club: Altrusa (pres. local club 1973-74, chmn. dist. 9 internat. relations 1976-78, chmn. Altrusa Info. 1977-78, chmn. extension local club 1979-80, pres. 1980). Office: 6000 Camp Bowie Suite 147 Fort Worth TX 76116

MCDONALD, FRANK DOUGLAS, audiologist; b. Cookeville, Tenn., July 15, 1932; s. Frank Thurston and Flora (Harris) McD.: B.S., Middle Tenn. State Coll., 1954; M.S., Vanderbilt U., 1960; Ph.D., U. Okla., 1969; m. Betty Erwin, Jan. 9, 1959; children—Valerie, Kevin, Melinda, Sandra. Chief audiology and speech pathology Wilford Hall USAF Hosp., Lackland AFB, San Antonio, 1962-65; clin. audiologist VA Hosp., Oklahoma City, 1965-69; chief audiology and speech pathology service VA Hosp., Memphis, 1969-70, VA Med. Center, Columbia, S.C., 1970—; adj. prof. audiology U. S.C., Columbia, 1971—; cons. speech and hearing centers. Chmn. S.C. State Bd. Examiners in Speech Pathology and Audiology. 1974-77; elder Trinity Presbyn. Ch., Columbia, 1978—. Served with U.S. Army,

1954-57, 62. Licensed audiologist, S.C. Fellow Am. Speech, Lang. and Hearing Assn.: mem. S.C. Speech and Hearing Assn. (honors 1974, v.p. 1974-75, pres. 1976-77), Acoustical Soc. Am., So. Audiological Soc. (treas. 1972-74). Club: Lions (v.p. Lower Richland 1979). Home: 300 Black Friars Rd Columbia SC 29209 Office: VA Med Center Columbia SC 29201

MC DONALD, FRANK JEVEREE, camp exec.; b. Ocala, Fla., Nov. 28, 1912; s. Oliver Wayne and Nannie Clara (Smith) McD.; student Western Tchrs. Coll., 1933, U. Fla., 1934-35; m. Barbara Hollis Buck Metcalf, Feb. 1, 1952; 1 son, Frank Jeveree. Owner, later co-dir. Camp Nokomis, Lake Winnipesaukee, N.H., 1952-75. Served with USNR, 1942-45, 48-52. Mem. Am. Camping Assn., N.E. Camp Dirs. Baptist. Home: 30 Palm St Weeki Wachee Hills Brooksville FL 33512

MC DONALD, JAMES PATRICK, mcpl. govt. ofcl.; b. Fairmont, W.Va., Mar. 30, 1942; s. Romeo Tell and Ouida Emma (Stonestreet) McD.; B.S. Econs., U. Pa., 1963, M. Govt. Adminstrn., 1964; D.Public Adminstrn., George Washington U., 1976; m. Mary Anne Bevan, Feb. 21, 1969; children—Andrew Bevan, Laura Stonestreet. Asst. city adminstr., College Park, Md., 1964-65; budget analyst, Fairfax County, Va., 1967-68, dir. mgmt. analysis, 1968-70, mgmt. and budget dir., 1970-73, budget and fin. dir., 1973-76, dept. county exec. for mgmt. and budget, 1976—; mem. tech. adv. com. taxation and fin. Nat. Assn. Counties, 1977-79. Trustee, mem. exec. com. Va. Christian Endeavor Union, 1978—; ruling elder Fairlington Presbyn. Ch., Alexandria, Va., 1977-80. Served to capt. Q.M.C., U.S. Army, 1965-67. Decorated Bronze Star medal. Robert Lincoln McNeill scholar, 1959-63, Samuel S. Fels fellow, 1964. Mem. Mcpl. Fin. Officers Assn. Home: 104 W Maple St Alexandria VA 22301 Office: 4100 Chain Bridge Rd Fairfax VA 22030

MC DONALD, JOSEPH DALLAS, hosp. adminstr.; b. Knoxville, Tenn., Oct. 9, 1952; s. James Dallas and Clare-Francis (O'Connor) McD.; B.B.A., U. Tenn., 1975, M.B.A., 1979; m. Penelope A. Wilkinson, June 22, 1974. Dietary supr. St. Mary's Hosp., Knoxville, 1970-73, audio-visual technician, 1973-75, pub. info. officer, 1975-77; evening adminstrv. supr. Nashville Meml. Hosp., Madison, Tenn., 1977-78, exec. asst., 1978-80; v.p. St. Mary's Med. Center, Knoxville, 1980—. Mem. Am. Coll. Hosp. Adminstrs., Planning Execs. Inst., Am. Hosp. Assn., Tenn. Hosp. Assn., Am. Soc. Indsl. Security, U.S. Jaycees, Tenn. Jaycees, Madison/Inglewood Jaycees (v.p. 1978-79, pres. 1979—). Republican. Roman Catholic. Home: 5507 Lake Shore Knoxville TN 37920 Office: St Mary's Med Center Oak Hill Ave Knoxville TN 37917

MC DONALD, KATHLEEN LYNN, mktg. cons.; b. Bklyn., Aug. 3, 1951; d. Robert G. and Patricia Marie (Isaacs) McD.; diploma College d'Europe, Bruges, Belgium, 1972; B.A., George Washington U., 1973. Asso., Washington Cons. Group, Washington, 1973-75; prin. Internat. Devel. Corp., Washington, 1975-76; internat. mktg. and public relations cons., 1977—; lectr. Washington conf. on career devel. Columbia U., 1978-79. Mem. exec. com. Wafa Wa Amal Rehab. Center, Washington, 1978. Mem. Nat. Small Bus. Assn., Nat. Trust Hist. Preservation, Capitol Hill Women's Polit. Caucus, Ripon Soc. (nat. governing bd. 1976—, nat. exec. com. 1976-78, pres. Washington chpt. 1978—), Delta Gamma. Roman Catholic. Home: 408 S Royal St Alexandria VA 22314

MC DONALD, LAURIER BERNARD, lawyer; b. Memphis, Oct. 3, 1931; s. Laurier Bernard and Mary Eva (Covington) McD.; B.A. in History, Tex. Arts and Industry U., 1957; J.D., U. Tex., 1961; m. Juanita Littleton, June 11, 1960; children—James, Rebecca, John, Susan. Admitted to Tex. bar, 1961; spl. agt. FBI, Quantico, Va., 1961, Tampa, Fla., 1961-62, Washington, 1962-63, San Juan, P.R., 1963-65, N.Y.C., 1965-66; partner firm Pena, McDonald, Prestia & Zipp, Edinburg, Tex., 1966—. U.S. commr. So. Dist. Tex., Edinburg, 1966-71; adj. prof. drug abuse and organized crime Pan Am. U., Edinburg, 1972. Chmn. Hidalgo County Hist. Commn., 1966-73. Trustee Haggar Student Fund, Edinburg. Served with USMCR, 1951-53. Mem. Assn. Immigration and Nationality Lawyers (gov.), Edinburg C. of C. (pres. 1973), Alpha Chi, Phi Alpha Theta. Roman Catholic. Club: Rotary of Edinburg. Home: 1027 S 12th St Edinburg TX 78539 Office: PO Drawer 54 Edinburg TX 78539

MC DONALD, LAWRENCE P., Congressman; b. Atlanta, Apr. 1, 1935; pre-med. student Davidson (N.C.) Coll.; M.D., Emory U., 1957; Litt. D. (hon.), Daniel Payne Coll., Birmingham, Ala.; m. Kathryn Jackson, June 1976; children by previous marriage—Tryggvi Paul, Callie Grace, Mary Elizabeth. Resident in gen. surgery Grady Meml. Hosp., Atlanta; tng. in urology U. Mich., Ann Arbor; mem. 94th-96th Congresses from 7th Ga. Dist. Mem. nat. adv. bd. Young Ams. for Freedom; mem. Congl. adv. bd. Am. Conservative Union, Conservative Caucus; mem. nat. adv. bd. Am. Security Council; pres., chmn. bd. Western Goals Found., Alexandria, Va.; mem. citizens cabinet Sec. Def., 1977-80; trustee So. Found. Edn. and Med. Research. Served with M.C., USNR, 1957-61. Recipient Bernardo O'Higgins award (Chile). Mem. Nat. Hist. Soc., John Birch Soc. (nat. council 1967—), Med. Assn. Ga., Med. Assn. Atlanta, Assn. Clin. Urologists, Assn. Am. Physicians and Surgeons, Atlanta Urol. Soc., Reed M. Nesbit Soc., Atlanta Astronomy Club. Methodist. Democrat. Rotarian. Office: 504 Cannon House Office Bldg Washington DC 20515

MCDONALD, MARSHALL, utility exec.; b. Memphis, Mar. 30, 1918; s. Marshall and Nadine (Hardin) McD.; B.S. in Bus. Adminstrn., U. Fla., 1939, LL.B., 1941; M.B.A., Wharton Grad. Sch. U. Pa., 1947; m. Florence Harris, Jan. 10, 1952 (dec. Nov. 1963); m. 2d, Lucille Smoak Collins, May 7, 1965; children—Mary Linda (Mrs. Donald Caton), Charles M. Collins, Cynthia (Mrs. H.T. Langston, Jr.), Marshall III, Roger Collins, Davis, James D. Admitted to Fla. bar, 1941; Tex. bar, 1949; accountant, Houston, 1947-49; atty., Houston, 1950-52; treas. Gulf Canal Lines, 1953-54; pres. Investment Co. Houston, 1955-58; v.p., Sinclair Oil & Gas Co., Tulsa, 1959-61; v.p., gen. mgr. Oil Recovery Corp., Tulsa, 1962-63; asst. to pres. Pure Oil Co., Palatine, Ill., 1964-65; dir. affiliated cos. Union Oil Co., Los Angeles, 1966-68; pres. Sully-Miller Contracting Co., Los Angeles, 1968-71; pres., chief exec. officer Fla. Power & Light Co., Miami, 1971-80, chmn., chief exec. officer, 1980—. C.P.A., Tex. Served with AUS, 1941-46. Mem. Am. Bar Assn., Am. Inst. C.P.A.'s, Alpha Tau Omega. Republican. Presbyn. Mason. Office: 9250 W Flagler St Miami FL 33174 also PO Box 529100 Miami FL 33152

MC DONALD, MICHAEL LEE, food co. exec.; b. Sault Sainte Marie, Mich., Feb. 25, 1949; s. Willis Richard and LaVerne (Carlson) McD.; student U. Notre Dame, 1967-69; B.S., Lake Superior State Coll., 1971; m. Ellen Neelis, Feb. 22, 1969; children—Kimberly, Heather, Ryan. Prodn. team mgr. Procter & Gamble, Inc., Cheboygan, Mich., 1971-73, employee relations specialist, safety engr., 1973-76; plant personnel mgr. Frito Lay, Inc., Vancouver, Wash., 1976-77, personnel mgr., Louisville, 1977-80, Frankfort, Ind., 1980—. Active ARC, Little League. Mem. Louisville Personnel Assn. Republican. Roman Catholic. Home: 8905 Thelma Lane Louisville KY 40220 Office: Frito Lay Inc 1600 Crums Ln Louisville KY 40220

MC DONALD, MILFORD EDGAR, state senator; b. Honea Path, S.C., Apr. 17, 1918; s. Calvin C. and Rosa C. (Hinton) McD.; A.B., Erskine Coll., Due West, S.C., 1943; m. Anne H. Hall, June 16, 1950; children—Rose Marie, Eddie. Prin., Iva Public Schs., 1943-48; personnel and office mgr. Jackson Mills Inc., Iva, 1948—; mem. S.C. Ho. of Reps., 1960-67, S.C. Senate, 1967—. Mem. Iva Sch. Bd.; deacon, Sunday sch. tchr. Baptist Ch. Mem. Iva C. of C. Democrat. Club: Lions. Address: Route 2 Box 9 Iva SC 29655

MCDONALD, MILFORD EDGAR, state senator; b. Honea Path, S.C., Apr. 17, 1918; s. Curtis Calvin and Rosa Cornelia (Hinton) McD.; A.B., Erskine Coll., 1943; m. Anne H. Hall, June 16, 1950; children—Rose Marie, Milford E. II. Tchr., prin., Iva (S.C.) Pub. Schs., 1943-48; office mgr. Jackson Mills, Iva, 1948—; mem. S.C. Ho. of Reps. from Anderson County, 1961-68, S.C. Senate from 1st Dist., 1968—, chmn. Gen. Com., 1976, mem. Election Law Study Com. Trustee Sch. Dist. 3 and Anderson County, 1952-57. Chmn., Anderson County Democratic party, 1962-66. Mem. Iva C. of C. (pres. 1954), S.C. Farm Bur. Baptist (tchr. men's class). Lion, Woodman of World. Home: Route 2 Box 9 Iva SC 29655 Office: Box 8 Iva SC 29655

MC DONALD, MILLER BAIRD, mgmt. cons.; b. Huntsville, Tenn., Feb. 16, 1920; s. Melva Lawson and Bertha Clarence (Baird) McD.; student Lincoln Meml. U., 1939-40, U. Tenn., 1948-49, Cornell U., 1958, U. Wis., 1967, U. Mich., 1971; m. Anna Lois Fox, Nov. 30, 1941; children—Miller Baird, L. Martin, Willard E., Kathryn Lois. Adminstrv. asst. Home Owners Loan Corp., Washington, 1940-41; personnel officer AEC, 1946-51, personnel tng. and security officer, 1953-59; policy devel. ofcl., FAA, 1959-60; chief out-service tng. IRS, Washington, 1960-66; dir. mgmt. tng. Office Sec. of Commerce, Washington, 1966-72; pres. Miller McDonald & Assos., cons.'s to mgmt., Arlington, Va. and La Follette, Tenn., 1972—; instr. U. Ga., 1970, La. State U., 1971. Bd. dirs. Wesleyan Found., 1978; nat. adv. bd. Am. Security Council, 1979—; chmn. Pres. Ford Com., E. Tenn., 1976; mem. Pres.'s Task Force on Career Advancement, 1965; chmn. Campbell County Republican Com., 1976—; mem. Tenn. Commn. Human Devel., 1979—. Served from pvt. to col., U.S. Army, 1942-46, 50-53. Recipient Superior Performance award AEC, 1960, Cert. of Recognition, IRS, 1966; numerous medals. Mem. Am. Soc. Tng. and Devel., Adult Edn. Assn., Inst. Applied Behavioral Sci., Am. Legion. Methodist. Clubs: Rotary, Masons. Address: 109 Crestview Dr LaFollette TN 37766

MC DONALD, PAULINE MILLER, b. Mars Hill, N.C., 1917; d. Hughey O. and Theodosia (Peek) Miller; A.B. in Edn., High Point (N.C.) Coll., 1938; M.A. in Elementary Edn. and Adminstrn., George Peabody Coll. for Tchrs., Nashville, 1956; m. Lawrence Ernest McDonald. Tchr., High Point City Schs., 1951-59, Graner Elementary Sch., Winter Haven, Fla., 1959-61; supt. elementary instrn. Gaston County schs., Gastonia, N.C., 1961-77; ednl. cons. 6th Yr. Program in Advanced Adminstrn., U. N.C., Chapel Hill, 1977—. Active Gaston County chpt. Am. Heart Assn., Community Service Workers Club. Mem. Assn. for Supervision and Curriculum Devel., Am. Childhood Edn. Internat., NEA, N.C. Assn. Educators, Internat. Reading Assn., Nat. Council Tchrs. of English, Fla. Edn. Assn., AAUW, Delta Kappa Gamma. Certified elementary tchr., supr., adminstr., N.C. Office: 221 N Morris St Gastonia NC 28052

MCDONNELL, EDWARD JOHN, energy products mfg. co. exec.; b. Far Rockaway, N.Y., Oct. 19, 1943; s. Edward John and Florence Louise (Bennett) McD.; B.B.A., (Univ. fellow) U. Cin., 1966, M.B.A. cum laude, 1967; m. Carolyn Miller, July 14, 1969; children—Carolyn, Edward John, Molly Margaraet. Sales ter. mgr. Exxon Corp., Orange, Calif., 1971-73; bus. mgr. ITT Co., Lompoc, Calif., 1974-75; contracts mgr. energy systems planning div. TRW Co., Redondo, Calif., 1975—; instr./lectr. Chapman Coll., Golden Gate U., La Verne Coll., Allan Hancock Coll. Served to capt. USAF, 1967-71. Decorated Air Force Commendation medal. Mem. Air Force Assn., Nat. Contract Mgmt. Assn., Beta Gamma Sigma, Alpha Kappa Psi. Republican. Home: 9110 Westerholme Way Vienna VA 22180 Office: Energy Systems Planning Div TRW 7600 Colshire Dr McLean VA 22101

MC DONNELL, JOHN HENRY, found. exec.; b. New Hope, Pa., Apr. 17, 1919; s. Henry Thomas and Eunice (Clark) McD.; A.B., Villanova U., 1942; A.M., Catholic U. Am., 1946, postgrad., 1952-59; m. Ellen Virginia Knight, June 26, 1975. Mem. faculty Villanova (Pa.) U., 1946-48, dean admissions and registrar, 1948-51; tchr., adminstr. Villanova Prep. Sch., Ojai, Calif., 1951, Archbishop Carroll High Sch., Washington, 1951-61; dir. devel. Province of St. Thomas, Roman Cath. Ch., Villanova, 1961-69; pres. Biscayne Coll., Miami, Fla., 1969-75; v.p. City Nat. Bank of Miami, 1975-77; exec. dir. Dade Found., Miami, 1977—. Bd. dirs. Public TV Channel 2, Miami, 1970-79, Miami Mus. Sci., 1975-77. Recipient Silver Medallion Brotherhood award NCCJ, 1974; Distinguished Service award Ind. Colls. and Univs. Fla., 1975. Mem. Council on Founds., Southeastern Council on Founds. Roman Catholic. Clubs: Cosmos (Washington); Miami, Standard (Miami); Riviera Country (Coral Gables, Fla.). Home: 1111 Crandon Blvd Key Biscayne FL 33149 Office: 1177 Brickell Ave Miami FL 33131

MC DONOUGH, DAYLE ANN DAVIS, speech pathologist; b. New Orleans, Aug. 11, 1950; d. Ira Morris and Shirley Mae (Cossé) Davis; B.S., U. Southwestern La., 1972; M.S., U. So. Miss., 1973; postgrad. U. New Orleans, 1974—; m. Edward D. McDonough, Jr., July 11, 1975. Public sch. speech and lang. therapist Orleans Parish Public Sch. System, New Orleans, 1973-76; spl. edn. tchr. children with severe lang. disorders Jefferson Parish Public Schs., Gretna, La., 1976—. U. So. Miss. fellow, 1973. Mem. Council Exceptional Children, Am. Speech Lang. and Hearing Assn., Phi Kappa Phi. Roman Catholic. Home: 401 Crescentwood Loop Slidell LA 70458

MC DONOUGH, THOMAS JOSEPH, archbishop; b. Phila., Dec. 5, 1911; s. Michael Francis and Margaret Mary (Nolnan) McD.; A.B., St. Charles Sem., Phila., 1935; J.C.D., Catholic U. Am., 1941. Ordained priest Roman Cath. Ch. in Cathedral of Phila, May 26, 1938; asst. pastor, Cathedral and St. Charles parish, Phila., 1938-40; vice-chancellor, chancellor, vicar gen. officialis, diocese of St. Augustine, Fla., 1941-48; pastor of Cathedral, St. Augustine, 1943-45; apptd. domestic prelate, 1945; consecrated bishop, St. Augustine, 1947; bishop of St. Augustine, 1947-57; aux. bishop of Savannah, Ga., 1957-60, archbishop, 1960-67; archbishop of Louisville, 1967—. Author: Apostolic Administrators, 1941. Office: PO Box 1073 Louisville KY 40201

MC DOWELL, JEAN LARAMIE, cons. investigator; A.B. Sc. Criminology, Daytona Beach (Fla.) Coll., 1968; B.A. in History, Mercer U., 1975; m. Emily M. McIntire. With accident investigation div. Baton Rouge Police Dept., 1965-66; with Daytona Beach Police Dept., 1966-68; ops. mgr. Versitech Corp., Atlanta, Md. Casualty Co., 1968-79; prin. Craddock & McDowell, Ltd., Kingwood, Tex., 1979—. Mem. Internat. Assn. Arson Investigators, Nat. Fire Protection Assn., Internat. Police Assn., Tex. Safety Assn. System Safety Assos., Served with USMC, 1959-63. Address: Craddock & McDowell Ltd 700 Rockmeade Dr Suite 265 Kingwood TX 77339

MC DOWELL, JOHN WILLIS, educator; b. Honolulu, Dec. 12, 1921; s. James Rhea and Sarah Elizabeth (Willis) McD.; student Loyola U., Chgo., 1939-43; B.S., Colo. State U., 1947, M.S., 1948; postgrad. Okla. State U., 1948-49; M.P.H., U. N.C., 1950; Ph.D., Okla. State U., 1953; m. Hazel Gilchrist, Aug. 6, 1950; children—Jean Carol, Kenneth Edward. Parasitologist, Mut. Security Agy., USPHS, Cambodia, Laos and Vietnam, 1951-53, chief malaria control ICA, Iran, 1954-56, chief malariologist, Philippines, 1956-60, regional malaria adviser Western Pacific region, 1960-61, asst. chief Vector Control Tng. sect. Center for Disease Control USPHS, 1961-64; chief of evaluation Aedes Aegypte Eradication Project, Center for Disease Control, 1964-66, asst. chief of evaluation Malaria Eradication Project, 1966-69; asso. prof. biology Berry Coll., Mt. Berry, Ga., 1969-72, prof. biology, 1972—; cons., WHO, 1964, AID, 1964-69; mem. Joint WHO-AID Task Force on Malaria Tng. in Asia, 1978. Served with AUS, 1943-46. Mem. Ga. Acad. Sci., Nat. Environ. Health Assn., Commd. Officers Assn. USPHS. Contbr. articles profl. jours. Home: 5 Beaver Run Rome GA 30161 Office: Dept Biology Berry Coll Mount Berry GA 30149

MC DOWELL, ROBERT WAYNE, broadcaster; b. Memphis, Feb. 18, 1940; s. James Marvin and Dorothy May (Carney) M.; degree in broadcasting Allied Tech. Sch., 1963; B.B.A., Memphis State U., 1978; m. Marianne Thompson, Apr. 24, 1965; children—Kelli Leigh, Cynthia Shannon. With WDIA Radio, Memphis, 1963—, dir. music, 1963-64, program dir., 1964-68, program dir. FM affiliate WQUD, 1968-74, sta. mgr. Sta. WOUD, 1974-76, gen. mgr., 1976—. Bd. dirs. Memphis Handicapped Inc., 1967-69. Baptist (deacon). Kiwanian. Composer: Our Last Quarrel, 1966. Home: 1439 Whiting St Memphis TN 38117 Office: 2272 Central St Memphis TN 38112

MC DOWELL, WILLIAM LEWIS, JR., archivist; b. Chester, S.C., Sept. 3, 1926; s. William Lewis and Carrie Jane (White) McD.; B.S., Clemson Coll., 1949; M.A. (R. Means Davis fellow), U. S.C., 1953; m. Martha Isabel Rowell, Sept. 10, 1956; children—Martha Ellen, William Lewis III. Archivist, Hist. Commn. S.C. and S.C. Archives Dept., Columbia, 1953-60; asst. dir. S.C. Archives Dept., Columbia, 1961-68; dep. dir. S.C. Dept. Archives and History, Columbia, 1968—. Served with USNR, 1945-46. Recipient award of merit Am. Assn. State and Local History, 1971. Fellow Soc. Am. Archivists; mem. Nat. Assn. State Archivists and Records Adminstrs., Orgn. Am. Historians, S.C. Soc., S.C. Hist. Assn., S.C. Hist. Soc. (archives cons.). Methodist. Editor: Journal of Commissioners of Indian Trade, 1710-18, 1955; Documents Relating to Indian Affairs, 1750-1754, 1958; Documents Relating to Indian Affairs, 1754-65, 1970. Home: 3304 Oakdale Rd West Columbia SC 29169 Office: 1430 Senate St Columbia SC 29201

MCDUFFIE, NEAL LEROY, ins. agy. exec.; b. Washington, Dec. 9, 1940; s. Francis LeRoy and Kathleen L. (Sullivan) McD.; B.B.A., Wake Forest U., 1964; postgrad. exec. program U. N.C., 1977-78; m. E. Rebecca Dail, June 4, 1964; children—Kimberly, Sharon, Patricia. Sales rep. Liberty Mut. Ins. Co., Washington, 1967-69, ins. mgr., 1967-69, account exec., 1969-71; ins. mgr. Collier Cobb & Assos. of Va., Charlotte, N.C., 1971-77, v.p. nat. accounts, 1977—; cons. on risk assumption to various corps., 1977—. Served with U.S. Army, 1965-66; Vietnam. Mem. Washington Bldg. Congress, VFW. Contbr. articles to profl. publs. Home: 2818 Houston Branch Rd Charlotte NC 28105 Office: 317 S Tryon St Charlotte NC 28227

MC EACHNIE, WILLIAM ELLWYN, mech. engr.; b. Buffalo, June 5, 1930; s. Ellwyn and Catherine (Swartz) McE.; B.S.M.E., U. N.Y., 1955; m. Janet L. Vincent, Mar. 21, 1953; children—William Ellwyn, Robert C., Jennifer S. Design engr. Bell Aircraft Co., Buffalo, 1955-59; design engr. Martin Marietta Co., Orlando, Fla., 1959-69, group engr., 1969-77, mgr. computer aided design group, 1977—. Mem. Orange County (Fla.) Republican Exec. Com., 1964-73; coach Little League Baseball, 1965, Pop Warner Football, Orlando, 1970-74. Served with USAF, 1951-55. Mem. Internat. Soc. Hybrid Microelectronics. Republican. Lutheran. Inventor connector adapter. Home: 4833 Betty Sue Terr Orlando FL 32808 Office: Martin Marietta MP111 PO Box 5837 Orlando FL 32855

MCELFRESH, MARY LORRAINE, speech-lang. pathologist; b. St. Joseph, Mo., Aug. 12, 1914; d. Martin Rae and Vena (Clevenger) Leighty; A.Edn., St. Joseph Jr. Coll., 1957; B.S., N.W. Mo. State U., 1961; M.A., U. Kans., 1966; postgrad. Tex. Woman's U., 1974; m. Oles Jack McElfresh, Sept. 11, 1933; 1 son, Samuel Lawrence. Tchr., Stewartsville (Mo.) Sch., 1957-60; speech correctionist Sch. Dist. of St. Joseph (Mo.), 1961-69; speech pathologist Family Guidance Center, St. Joseph, 1969-71; speech-lang. pathologist Plano (Tex.) Ind. Sch. Dist., 1971—, team leader, 1977—; speech pathologist Children's Rehab. Unit, Family Guidance Center, St. Joseph, 1969-71, Youth Center, State Hosp. 2, St. Joseph, 1969-71, Early Childhood Unit, Plano Ind. Sch. Dist., 1976-78. Named Meml. Elem. Sch. Tchr. of the Year, 1975; Certificate of Clin. Competence in speech pathology. Am. Speech and Hearing Assn.; U.S. Office of Edn. fellow, 1965-66; U. Kans. grantee, summer 1966. Mem. Am. Speech-Lang.-Hearing Assn., Tex. Speech-Lang.-Hearing Assn., Speech and Hearing Assn. N. Tex., Tex. Council of Suprs. Lang., Speech and Hearing Programs, NEA, Mo. State Tchrs. Assn., Tex. State Tchrs. Assn., Plano Edn. Assn., Delta Kappa Gamma (Iota Omega chpt.). Baptist. Club: PTO. Home: 1403 15 Pl Apt 105W Plano TX 75074 Office: 1517 Ave H Plano TX 75074

MC ELMURRY, ARTHUR LEE, hosp. adminstr.; b. Maysville, Okla., Mar. 24, 1923; s. Arthur Ernest and Ethel Nita (Alexander) McE.; B.S., U. Okla., 1948; M.S. in Hosp. Adminstrn., Northwestern U., 1952; m. Dorweta Geraldine Wilcox, May 31, 1947; children—Chauna Kay, Leigh Ann. Chief accountant Univ. Hosp., Oklahoma City, 1948-51, bus. adminstrn., 1952-54; adminstr. Nan Travis Meml. Hosp., Jacksonville, Tex., 1954-65; adminstr. Wadley Hosp., Texarkana, Tex., 1965—, pres., 1976—; dir. Blue Cross-Blue Shield Tex.; preceptor Trinity U., Northwestern U.; mem. bd. and exec. com. N.E. Tex. Health System Agency, 1976—. Recipient Earl M. Collier award for disting. hosp. adminstrn., 1978. Fellow Am. Coll. Hosp. Adminstrs. (regent 1975-77, gov. 1977-78); mem. Am. (regional advisory bd.), Tex. (hon.; past pres.) hosp. assns. Contbr. articles in field to profl. jours. Home: 14 Lambeth Circle Texarkana TX 75503 Office: 1000 Pine St Texarkana TX 75501

MC ELREATH, WELDON WAYNE, children's home adminstr.; b. Big Spring, Tex., Dec. 30, 1933; s. Jesse James and Myrtle Estelle (Lancaster) McE.; A.A., Howard County Coll., 1953; B.S., Howard Payne U., 1955; m. Gloria Ann Jackson, Aug. 19, 1955; children—Charles Wayne, James Russell. Public relations Tex. Electric Service Co., Big Spring, 1955-56; acct. Pan Am Oil Co., Ft. Worth, 1958-59; cost acct. U.S. Steel Corp., Dallas, 1959-65; asst. controller Buckner Baptist Benevolences, Dallas, 1965-72, adminstr., Lubbock, Tex., 1972—; cons. in field. Mem. promotions com. United Way, Lubbock, 1977; fund raising com. YMCA, Lubbock, 1975; chmn. communicatons com. Tex. Tech. U. Dad's Assn., 1978-79. Served with U.S. Army, 1956-58. Lic. adminstr. residential child care, Tex. Mem. Nat. Assn. Children's Homes, Southwestern Assn. Execs. Homes for Children, Tex. Assn. Child Care Execs., Tex. Assn. Lic. Children's Services, Tex. United Community Services, Nat. Assn. Social Workers. Baptist. Club: Lions (chaplain Lubbock 1978-79).

Home and Office: Buckner Baptist Home 129 Brentwood Ave Lubbock TX 79416

MC ENTEE, ROBERT BERNARD, internist, nuclear physician; b. Newark, July 21, 1927; s. James Joseph and Marguerite Marie (Hug) McE.; student The Citadel, 1946-49; M.D., Wake Forest U., 1953; m. Anne Blackwell, June 17, 1953; children—Annie Laura, Margaret Marie, Robert Bernard, Joseph Patrick. Intern, Atlantic City Hosp., 1953-54; resident in internal medicine McGuire VA Hosp., Richmond, Va., 1954-57; practice medicine specializing in internal medicine and nuclear medicine, Richmond, 1957—; asso. medicine Med. Coll. Va.; med. dir. U. Richmond; med. cons. C. & P. Telephone Co.; chmn. dept. internal medicine Henrico Drs. Hosp., 1974-75; dir. Suburban Bank of Richmond. Served with USCG, 1945-46. Diplomate Am. Bd. Nuclear Medicine. Mem. Richmond Acad. Medicine, Med. Soc. Va., Am. Coll. Nuclear Physicians, Soc. Nuclear Medicine. Roman Catholic. Club: K.C. Home: 300 El Dorado Dr Richmond VA 23229 Office: Parham and Quioccasin Rds Richmond VA 23229

MC EWIN, JOHN BEN, mech. engr.; b. Paris, Tex., Feb. 22, 1914; s. Fernie Fae and Cora (Weikel) McE.; B.S., Tex. Technol. Coll., 1942. Test engr. Gen. Electric Co., Schenectady, 1942-43; mech. engr. Humble Oil & Refining Co., Baytown, Tex., 1943-46; field engr. Peerless Pump Div., Oklahoma City, 1946-51; project engr. Sandia Corp., Albuquerque, 1951-55; mech., elec. engr. U.S. Army C.E., Perrin AFB, Tex., 1956-57, USAF, 1957-64, Goodfellow AFB, Tex., 1964-76; cons. engr., 1963-76; ret., 1976. Mem. Nat. Rifle Assn. Methodist. Club: San Angelo Gun (treas. 1966). Home: 3354 Cumberland Dr San Angelo TX 76901

MC FADDEN, FRANK HAMPTON, fed. judge; b. Oxford, Miss., Nov. 20, 1925; s. John Angus and Ruby (Roy) McF.; B.A., U. Miss., 1950; LL.B., Yale U., 1955; m. Jane Porter Nabers, Sept. 30, 1960; children—Frank Hampton, Angus Nabers, Jane Porter. Admitted to N.Y. bar, 1956, Ala. bar, 1959; asso. firm Lord, Day & Lord, N.Y.C., 1955-58; asso. firm Bradley, Arant, Rose & White, Birmingham, Ala., 1958-63, partner, 1963-69; judge U.S. Dist. Ct., No. Dist. Ala., 1969—, chief judge, 1973—. Served from ensign to lt. USNR, 1944-49, 51-53. Home: 3015 Briarcliff Rd Birmingham AL 35223 Office: Federal Courthouse Birmingham AL 35203

MC FADDEN, MARVIN RAY, hosp. adminstr.; b. Fulton, Miss., Apr. 26, 1941; s. Elbert Dewey and Gracie (Steele) McF.; student Itawamba Jr. Coll., 1961-62; m. Shirley Ann Shumpert, Apr. 20, 1969; children—Judith, Rose. Supr. central service North Miss. Med. Center, Tupelo, 1967—; tchr. communications classes, 1977. Deacon, Sunday sch. tchr. W. Jackson St. Baptist Ch. Served with U.S. Army, 1963-66. Mem. Am. Soc. Hosp. Central Service Personnel. Clubs: Masons. Shriners. Home: 1206 Rachel St Tupelo MS 38801 Office: 830 S Gloster St Tupelo MS 38801

MCFADDEN, ROBERT LAWRENCE, state legislator; b. Camden, S.C., Aug. 25, 1929; s. Lawrence Walker and Eunice O. (Long) McF.; A.B., Duke U., 1951, LL.B., 1954; m. Martha Anne Stewart, Sept. 24, 1960; children—Larry, Sally. Admitted to S.C. bar, 1954; practiced in Rock Hill, S.C., 1956—; mem. firm Gettys & McFadden. Mem. S.C. Ho. of Reps., 1960—. Served with AUS, 1954-56. Mem. Am., S.C., Rock Hill bar assns. Democrat. Presbyn. Elk, Kiwanian. Home: 949 Beverly Dr Rock Hill SC 29730 Office: PO Box 707 CSS Rock Hill SC 29730

MC FARLAND, FRANK EUGENE, univ. adminstr.; b. Fort Towson, Okla., Sept. 8, 1918; s. Thomas Edward and Sadie Margaret (Gayer) McF.; B.A. cum laude, Baylor U., 1950; M.A., Columbia, 1953, Ed.D., 1959; postgrad. U. Tex., 1956, Tex. A. and M. U., 1956; m. Trudy Hudson Lively, Dec. 20, 1947; children—Marsha Lane, Martha Lynne McFarland Cox. Counselor, Tex. A. and M. U., College Station, 1950-51, acting dir. counseling, 1951, personal and vocat. counselor, 1951-52, 52-53, 53-55, instr., 1951-52, 52-53, asst. prof. psychology, 1953-55, acting dir. testing and research, basic div., asst. prof. psychology, 1955-56, dir. testing and research, basic div., asso. prof. psychology, 1956-59; dir. student personnel Coll. Arts and Scis., asso. prof. psychology Okla. State U., Stillwater, 1959-61, dean student affairs, prof. psychology, 1961-68, prof. applied behavioral studies Coll. Edn., 1968-73, dir. student services, prof. edn., 1973—. First v.p. United Fund Stillwater, Inc., 1963-64, pres., 1964-65; cabinet adviser Will Rogers council Boy Scouts Am., 1961-63; mem. Mayor's Com. on Community Affairs, 1966-70. Bd. dirs., v.p. Stillwater Municipal Hosp. Adv. Bd., 1963-66. Served with AUS, 1941-45. Decorated Purple Heart with oak leaf cluster, Bronze Star medal; recipient Outstanding Service to Students award Okla. State U., 1968; Dean Frank McFarland award for outstanding adminstr. established by Okla. State U. Student Senate, 1968. Columbia U. faculty fellow, 1952-53; lic. psychologist, Okla. Mem. Am. Psychol. Assn., Am. Personnel and Guidance Assn., Am., Okla. coll. personnel assns., Nat. Vocat. Guidance Assn., Southwestern Assn. Student Personnel Adminstrs., Okla. Personnel, Guidance and Counseling Assn., Okla. Deans and Counselors Assn., Okla. Edn. Assn. (pres. 1972-73), Omicron Delta Kappa (Achievement award 1968), Phi Delta Kappa, Kappa Delta Pi, Alpha Chi, Psi Chi, Sigma Epsilon Sigma, Phi Kappa Phi. Rotarian. Author: Compilation of Research Studies from 1953-59, 1959; Student Attitudes Toward the Basic Division, 1958. Contbr. articles to profl. jours. Home: 1224 N Lincoln St Stillwater OK 74074

MC FARLAND, JAMES WILLIAM, real estate devel. co. exec.; b. Montgomery, Ala., Sept. 7, 1948; s. Ward Wharton and Frances Adelia (Morrow) McF.; B.S., U. Ala., 1970; m. Miriam Melinda Webster, Feb. 20, 1971; 1 son, James William. Dir. real estate for Ky., Ind. and Tenn., Winn-Dixie Stores, Inc., Louisville, 1970-72; v.p. Ward McFarland, Inc., Tuscaloosa, Ala., 1972—, also dir. Sustaining mem. Republican Nat. Com., 1977—, mem. nat. Rep. congl. com., 1977; mem. Council for Devel. of French in La., 1976—, Friends of Library, 1975—; young churchmen adviser Episcopal Diocese Ala., 1976—; bd. dirs. Tuscaloosa Kidney Found. Mem. Nat. Assn. Realtors, Tuscaloosa Bd. Realtors, Nat. Small Bus. Assn., U. Ala. Commerce Execs. Soc., U. Ala. Alumni Assn., Nat. Assn. R.R. Passengers, Delta Sigma Pi. Clubs: North River Yacht; Kiwanis of Greater Tuscaloosa. Home: 4714 7th Ct E Tuscaloosa AL 35405 Office: 325 Skyland Blvd E Tuscaloosa AL 35405

MC FARLAND, M. ROBERT, lawyer, state legislator; b. Oskaloosa, Iowa, June 12, 1941; s. Millard Robert and Mildred Fern (VanBibber) McF.; B.B.A., U. Tex. at Arlington, 1963; J.D., So. Meth. U., 1966; m. Helen Jane Highfill, Aug. 10, 1963; children—Theresa Jane, Sandra Diane, Millard Robert. Admitted to Tex. bar, 1966; spl. agt. FBI, Washington, New Orleans and Atlanta, 1966-69; security adminstrv. specialist LTV, Inc., Dallas, 1969; partner Cribbs, McFarland & Holman, Arlington, Tex., 1969—; mem. Tex. Ho. of Reps., 1977—. Bus. chmn. Dallas County United Fund, 1965; mem. adv. bd. Arlington Tarrant County YWCA, 1971-72; pres., 1972, Young Men of Arlington; chmn. profl. sect. Tarrant County United Fund for Arlington, 1971; group leader Tarrant County Cancer Crusade, 1972. Bd. dirs. Arlington Boys Club, 1971—, Young Men of Arlington, 1970—; trustee Arlington Boys Club Endowment Fund, 1973—. Mem. State Bar Tex., Am., Arlington (pres. 1973), Fort Worth-Tarrant County bar assns., Phi Delta Phi. Roman Catholic. Home: 1205 Canterbury Ct Arlington TX 76013 Office: PO Box 13060 Arlington TX 76013

MC FARLAND, MARTHA ANN, educator; b. Natchitoches, La., Aug. 6, 1940; d. Charles I. and Virginia (Watson) McF.; B.A., Northwestern State U., 1967; M.Ed., U. Miss., 1971; postgrad. W.Va. U., 1972-73; Ph.D., Fla. State U., 1979. With Caddo Parish Sch. Bd., Shreveport, La., 1967-70; tchr. W. Shreveport Acad., 1970, Natchitoches (La.) Acad., 1971; regional dir. early childhood Region VI, Ednl. Service, Wheeling, W.Va., 1971-73; instr. edn., dir. kindergarten Berry Coll., Mt. Berry, Ga., 1973-78; asst. prof. edn. Liberty Bapt. Coll., Lynchburg, Va., 1979—; condr. numerous workshops, W.Va., Ga., La. Mem. Assn. Childhood Edn. Internat., Fla. Assn. Childhood Edn., Leon County Assn. Childhood Edn., Nat. Assn. Edn. Young Children, Va. Assn. Young Children, Ga. Assn. Young Children, So. Assn. Children Under Six, W.Va. Assn. Childhood Edn. (v.p. infants 1972-73), Phi Delta Kappa. Contbr. articles to profl. jours. Office: Div Edn Liberty Bapt Coll PO Box 1401 Lynchburg VA 24506

MC FARLAND, WARD MORROW, realty co., shopping center exec.; b. Montgomery, Ala., June 26, 1943; s. Ward Wharton and Adelia Francis (Morrow) Mc F.; B.S. in Commerce, U. Ala., 1965; m. Marion Jackie Westor, Aug. 6, 1965; 1 son, Ward Weston. Pres., Ward McFarland Realty Co., Tuscaloosa, Ala., 1967—; sec. Olympia Mills, textile co., Spartanburg, S.C., 1969-73; owner, mgr. McFarland Mall, shopping center, Tuscaloosa, 1969—; pres. Ward McFarland Inc., 1979—. Active Boy Scouts Am.; trustee Tuscaloosa Acad., 1979—. Served to 1st lt. C.E., AUS, 1965-67. Decorated D.S.M. Mem. Commerce Execs. Soc., U. Ala. Alumni Assn., Tuscaloosa Bd. Realtors (dir. 1970—, bd. dirs. 1977—), Tuscaloosa Homebuilders Assn., Tuscaloosa Jaycees, Soc. Am. Mil. Engrs. (v.p. chpt. 1966-67). Methodist (tchr., mem. bd. stewards 1969-72). Home: Box 5531 Interlaken Tuscaloosa AL 35401 Office: 325 Skyland Blvd Tuscaloosa AL 35401

MC FARLANE, GRAHAM SANDERS, energy co. fin. exec.; b. Bronxville, N.Y., June 29, 1947; s. John A. and Frances Darden (Sanders) McF.; B.S. with honors, Ga. Inst. Tech., 1969; M.B.A., Harvard U., 1971-73; m. Blanche Lee Jemison, June 2, 1973; children—Joshua Jemison, Benjamin Williams. Asst. mortgage officer C & S Nat. Bank, Atlanta, 1973-75; v.p. Modern Diversified Industries, Inc., Memphis, 1975-77; asst. to group v.p. Am. Petrofina, Inc., Dallas, 1977-79; asst. controller Enserch Exploration, Inc., Dallas, 1980—. Served with U.S. Army, 1969-71. Decorated Bronze Star medal. Home: 9414 Gatetrail Dallas TX 75238 Office: 1817 Wood St PO Box 2649 Dallas TX 75221

MC GAHEE, SELVIN CARL, roofing co. exec.; b. Sebring, Fla., Feb. 2, 1954; s. Leroy and Margaret McG.; student Bethel Coll. 1972-73; B.B.A., Eastern Ky. U., 1977. Clerical position Eastern Ky. U., Richmond, 1976-77; purchasing coordinator Barnett Bank of Highlands County, Sebring, Fla., 1978, account rep., 1978-79; part-owner McGahee Roofing Co., Lake Placid, Fla., 1980—. Mem. Highlands County Home Health Adv. Bd.; bd. dirs. Lake Placid (Fla.) Rural Rental Housing Project. Mem. Soc. Advancement Mgmt., NAACP. Democrat. Methodist. Home: Route 6 Box 931 Park St Lake Placid FL 33852

MCGARRY, MICHAEL SHAWN, psychotherapist; b. Tampa, Fla., May 24, 1952; s. Denny J. and Nancy Ann Roy (Sifford) McG.; A.A. with honors, St. Petersburg Jr. Coll., 1972; B.A. magna cum laude, Fla. State U., 1974; M.A., Emory U., 1976. Teaching asst. dept. psychology Fla. State U., 1973-74, Emory U., 1974-76; grad. asst. Emory U. Sch. Medicine, Atlanta, Ga., 1975-76; staff psychologist Psychol. Center, Emory U., 1974-76; psychiat. asst. Peachtree and Parkwood Mental Health Center and Hosps., Atlanta, 1975-77; guest lectr. St. Petersburg (Fla.) Jr. Coll., 1977—; pvt. practice psychotherapy, Clearwater, Fla., 1977—; behavioral programs specialist Pinellas County, Fla., 1973-74. Internat. quarter-finalist Fla. champion barbershop quartet, The Gt. Escape, 1979—; NIH grantee, 1975-76. Mem. Am. Personnel and Guidance Assn., Suncoast Personnel and Guidance Assn., Am. Psychol. Assn., Assn. Advancement Psychology, Soc. Research in Child Devel., Am. Acad. Polit. and Social Sci., Nat. Assn. Retarded Citizens, Assn. to Advance Ethical Hypnosis, Phi Beta Kappa, Psi Chi, Omicron Delta Kappa. Democrat. Mem. United Ch. Christ. Home: 2919-4th Ave North St Petersburg FL 33713 Office: 602 S Greenwood Clearwater FL 33516

MC GAW, JESSIE BREWER, author, educator; b. Clarksville, Tenn., Oct. 17, 1913; d. Lewis Vernon and Birdie (Basford) Brewer; A.B., Duke, 1935; M.A., Peabody Coll., 1940; postgrad. Columbia, 1948-50; student (Fulbright scholar) Am. Acad. Rome, 1959; m. Howard Franklin McGaw, Dec. 28, 1939 (div. 1958); children—Miriam Katherine, Vernon Howard; m. 2d, Harold L. Geis, Aug. 1964 (div. Mar. 1972). Tchr. Latin, Ward Belmont Sch., Nashville, 1938-40; tchr. Lausanne Sch., Memphis, 1940-42; tchr. English and Latin, U. Houston, 1952—. Bd. dirs. YWCA, 1957-59, Day Care Assn., 1956-61, Houston Civic Music Assn., 1958-60, Houston Council Human Relations. Recipient Cokesburg Juvenile award; Theta Sigma Phi lit. award; research grant, 1964; Delta Kappa Theta study grantee, 1972. Mem. Tex. Folklore Soc., South Central Modern Lang. Assn., Houston Council. Tchrs. Fgn. Lang. (treas.), League Women Voters, AAUW, Tex. Inst. Letters, U. Houston Women's Assn. (pres. 1967-68), Kappa Kappa Gamma. Democrat. Methodist. Club: University Houston Woman's (pres. 1954-55). Author: How Medicine Man Cured Paleface Woman, 1956; Painted Pony Runs Away, 1958; Little Elk Hunts Buffalo, 1961; History of Houston YWCA; translator Heptaplus, 1977. Home: 2405 Dickey Pl Houston TX 77019

MC GEACHY, BROOKLYN AUGUSTUS, educator; b. Fayetteville, N.C., Aug. 19, 1922; s. Evander D. and Sallie (Cousar) McG.; B.S., Fayetteville State Tchrs. Coll., 1941; M.A., N.Y. U., 1954; postgrad. N.C. Central U., 1959, Howard U., 1963, Atlanta U., 1969; m. Alice Green; children—Clinton Bernard, Eric Augustus. Prin., Marys Chapel Sch., Scotland Neck, N.C., 1941-45, Hollister (N.C.) Sch., 1945-49, Dawson Sch., Scotland Neck, 1949-51, Jeffries Sch., Rocky Mount, N.C., 1951-52; supervising tchr. Newbold Sch., Fayetteville (N.C.) State Tchrs. Coll., 1952-64; asst. prof. edn. Fayetteville State U., Fayetteville, 1964—. Past pres. Young Peoples League; scoutmaster Occoneechee council Boy Scouts Am., 1952-58, instl. rep., 1958; chmn. Cumberland County (N.C.) Unity Orgn., 1962; ruling elder Haymount Presbyn. Ch., 1964—. Served with arty. U.S. Army, 1942. Recipient Alumnus of Yr. award Fayetteville State U., 1961, Waymon W. Williams Disting. Membership award, 1972. Mem. NEA, Am. Assn. Higher Edn., Assn. of Tchr. Educators, N.C. Assn. of Educators, Assn. of Supervision and Curriculum Devel., AAUP, Omega Psi Phi, Kappa Delta Pi, Phi Delta Kappa. Clubs: Elks (Disting. Service award), Masons (32 deg.) (Disting. Service award 1977, Mason of Yr. award 1965). Home: 1870 Broadell Dr Fayetteville NC 28301 Office: Fayetteville State Univ Fayetteville NC 28301

MC GEE, DEAN ANDERSON, petroleum exec., geologist, engr.; b. Humbolt, Kans., Mar. 20, 1904; s. George Gentry and Gertrude Hattie (Sayre) McG.; B.S. in Mining Engring., Kans. U., 1926; LL.D. (hon.), Oklahoma City U. 1957; D.Sc. (hon.), Bethany Nazarene Coll., 1967; D.Eng. (hon.) Colo. Sch. Mines, 1968; D.H.L., Okla. Christian Coll., 1975; m. Dorothea Antionette Swain, June 28, 1938; children—Marcia Ann, Patricia Dean. Geology instr. Kans. U., 1926-27; petroleum geologist Phillips Petroleum Co., Bartlesville, Okla., 1927; chief geologist, 1935-37; v.p. charge prodn. and exploration Kerlyn Oil Co. (now Kerr-McGee Corp.), Oklahoma City, 1937-42, exec. v.p., 1942-54, pres., 1954-67, chmn. bd., chief exec., 1963—; dir. Sunningdale Oils Ltd., Kerr-McGee Oil (U.K.) Ltd.; pres., dir. Kerr-McGee Bldg. Corp.; v.p. Downtown Airpark, Inc.; dir. Kerr-McGee Resources Corp., Kerr-McGee Iranian Oil Co., Mine Contractors, Inc., Kerr-McGee Australia, Ltd., Kerr-McGee Tunisian Ltd., Kerr-McGee Coal Corp., Kerr-McGee Nuclear Corp., Southwestern Oil & Refining Co., Southwestern Refining Co., Inc., Transworld Drilling Co., Transworld North Sea Drilling Services Ltd., White Shoal Pipeline Corp., Internat. Creosoting & Constrn. Co., Triangle Refineries, Inc., Kerr-McGee Chem. Corp., Fidelity Bank; v.p. Am. Potash & Chem. Corp.; dir. emeritus Gen. Electric Co.; owner McGee-Keesee Ranch. Chmn. Gulf Dist. com. for selection Rhodes Scholarships, Swartmore Coll., 1968-74; mem. Okla. Ambassadors Corps, 1965—. Chmn. exec. com. Okla. Health Scis. Found.; trustee Okla. Industries, Authority; dir. Ark. Basin Devel. Assn., Oklahoma City chpt. NCCJ; trustee Kans. U. Endowment Assn., Midwest Research Inst., Kansas City, Mo.; bd. dirs. Okla. Med. Research Found.; dir., trustee, vice chmn. Okla. Safety Council; dir. Okla. State Fair, Oklahoma City U. Found., Inc.; trustee Calif. Inst. Tech.; pres., dir. Kerr-McGee Found., Inc.; trustee S.W. Research Inst., Sci. and Natural Resources Found. Okla., Presbyn. Hosp., Inc. (hon.), Oklahoma City Indsl. and Cultural Facilities Trust; mem. Okla.'s Future, Inc.; bd. dirs. Okla.-Ark. Presbyn. Found., Inc.; advisory bd. Coll. Bus. U. Okla.; mem. Okla. Med. Scis. Hall Fame, Okla. Hall Fame; trustee, hon. life mem. bd. dirs. Nat. Cowboy Hall of Fame and Western Heritage Center; mem. Okla. City Arts Council, Okla. Hist. Soc.; pres. dir. McGee Found. Inc.; trustee Okla. Eye Found.; founding chmn. U. Okla. Assos.; trustee, vice chmn. exec. com., bd. trustees Oklahoma City U.; trustee emeritus Am. Assn. Petroleum Geologists Found.; mem. governing bd. Okla. Center Scis. and Arts; mem. council Rockefeller U. Recipient Erasmus Haworth Distinguished Alumni award in geology, Distinguished Alumni citation U. Kans., 1951; Outstanding Okla. Oil Man award Okla. Petroleum Council, 1970; Nat. Brotherhood citation NCCJ, 1961; Outstanding Civilian Service award Dept. Army, 1965; Okla. U. Distinguished Service citation, 1966; Industrialist of Year award Headliner award Oklahoma City Press Club, 1958; Golden Plate award Am. Acad. Achievement, 1969; 17th Ann. citation Midwest Research Inst., 1973; Oklahoma City Beautiful award, 1973; Bennett Distinguished Service award Okla. State U., 1974; Distinguished Service award Oklahoma City Advt. Club, 1976, U. Tulsa Coll. Engring. and Phys. Scis. Hall of Fame award, 1976; Disting. Service award Nat. Petroleum Hall of Fame, 1977; Disting. Friend award Oklahoma City U., 1978. Fellow AAAS, U. Okla. Acad. Fellows, Okla. Acad. Scis., Am. Inst. Mining Metall. and Petroleum Engrs. (hon. mem.), Am. Assn. Petroleum Geologists (Pub. Service award 1974, Sidney Powers award 1975, hon. life mem.); mem. Am. Petroleum Inst. (dir.), Ind. Petroleum Assn. Am. (dir.), Nat., Okla. socs. profl. engrs., Am. Inst. Profl. Geologists, Atomic Indsl. Forum, Am. Mining Congress, Okla. Zool. Soc., (trustee), Oklahoma City C. of C. (dir.), Tex. Mid-Continent Oil and Gas Assn. (dir., Disting. Service award 1975), Mid-Continent Oil and Gas Assn. (exec. com.), Nat. Petroleum Council, Oklahoma City Geol. Soc., Soc. Econ. Paleontologists and Mineralogists, AIA (hon. life mem. Okla. chpt.), Navy League U.S., Colo. Sch. Mines Alumni Assn. (hon.), Oklahoma City Symphony Soc. (life), Newcomen Soc. N.Am., Okla. Heritage Assn., All-Am. Wildcatters, Sachem, Sigma Xi, Delta Sigma Pi, Tau Beta Phi, Theta Tau, Pi Epsilon Tau (hon.), Beta Gamma Sigma (Hon.). Democrat. Presbyterian. Mason (Shriner), Acacia. Clubs: Touchdown, Petroleum, Men's Dinner, Sirloin, Whitehall, Beacon, Oklahoma City Golf and Country; Twenty-five Year Club of Petroleum Industry; Oklahoma City Press. Contbr. articles to profl. jours. Home: 7300 N Country Club Dr Oklahoma City OK 73116 Office: Kerr-McGee Center PO Box 25861 Oklahoma City OK 73125

MC GEE, GEORGE JEROME, JR., educator; b. Harvey, Ill., July 30, 1947; s. George Jerome and Evelyn Marie (Cranford) McG.; B.F.A., Ill. Wesleyan U., 1972; M.F.A., Fla. Atlantic U., 1978; m. Catherine M. Gorman, Aug. 7, 1971; 1 dau., Megan Cathleen. Founder, Palm Beach Childrens Theatre, 1973—; dir. Norton Gallery Theatre, West Palm Beach, Fla., 1974—; chmn. speech dept. Palm Beach Atlantic Coll., 1978—, chmn. dept. speech and drama, 1979—; theatre cons. Regional Arts Found., 1978—. Bd. dirs. Palm Beach County Council Arts; chmn. edn. com. Palm Beach Arts Council. Served with AUS, 1967-69; Vietnam. Named An Outstanding Young Man of Am., Jaycees, 1979. Mem. Fla. Theatre Conf., Speech Communication Assn. Roman Catholic. Playwright: Dirt Ho, 1973, Wonderboy, 1974. Home: 5809 Churchill Ct West Palm Beach FL 33405 Office: 1101 S Olive Ave West Palm Beach FL 33401

MC GEE, HALL THOMAS, JR., newspaper, TV exec.; b. Charleston, S.C., Aug. 7, 1913; s. Hall Thomas and Gertrude Wyman (Frampton) McG.; B.S., Coll. Charleston, 1935; postgrad. Harvard U. Bus. Sch., 1936; m. Margaret Anne Pringle, June 29, 1939; children—Margaret Anne McGee McManes, Hall Thomas III. With Evening Post Pub. Co. and The News and Courier Co., Charleston, 1936—, treas., dir., 1945—, gen. mgr., v.p., 1969—; treas., dir. Rochelle Corp., Beaufort. S.C., 1962-75, Aiken Cablevision, Inc. (S.C.), 1965—, The Banner Corp., Cambridge, Md., 1965—, Aiken Communications, Inc., 1968—, Georgetown Communications, Inc. (S.C.), 1973—, Kingstree Communications, Inc. (S.C.), 1973—, Waynesboro Pub. Co. (Va.), 1974—, Portal Communications, Inc., Sta. KDBC-TV, El Paso, Tex., 1974—, Sangre de Cristo Communications, Inc., Sta. KOAA-TV, Pueblo, Colo., 1976—; dir. Editors Press Service Inc., N.Y.C., Buenos Aires (Argentina) Herald. Bd. dirs. Charleston YMCA; v.p. Greater Charleston C. of C.; treas. Charleston Indsl. Assn., 1974—; pres. bd. trustees Grant Home, Charleston, 1975—; trustee Coll. of Charleston, 1952-68, Magnolia Cemetery, Charleston, 1970—; elder Second Presbyterian Ch., Charleston, 1958—. Mem. So. (dir.), Am. (chmn. com. taxation) newspaper pubs. assns., S.C. Press Assn. (pres. 1955-56), St. Cecilia Soc., S.C. Soc., St. Andrews Soc., Agrl. Soc. S.C. Clubs: Rotary (dir. local club), Carolina Yacht. Home: 200 Wentworth St Charleston SC 29401 Office: PO Box 758 Charleston SC 29402

MC GEE, HOWARD VAN BUREN, architect; b. McAlester, Okla., May 21, 1929; s. Loren V. and Margaret Beatrice (Donahue) McG.; B.Arch., U. Okla., 1956; m. Ruth Harriet Smith, Dec. 31, 1950; children—Connie Ellen, Michael Kevin, Patrick Sean. Architect, Collins and Flood, Ardmore, Okla., 1956-72; pvt. practice architecture, Ardmore, 1972—. Chmn., Okla. Arts and Humanities Council, 1974-76; chmn. County Dem. Central Com., 1964-67; bd. dirs. Okla. U. Alumni Devel. Fund, 1968-72. Recipient Service award medallion Alpha Rho Chi, 1956. Mem. Mid-Am. Arts Alliance (dir. 1974-76), Nat. Assembly State Arts Agys. (dir. 1974-76), Ardmore C. of C. (dir. 1971-72), AIA, Lic. Architects Okla. (bd. govs.), Okla. Inst. Architects. Democrat. Baptist. Works include: McCauley House,

McAlester, Okla., 1968; Brady Chapel, Ardmore, 1977; Maureen Office Bldg., Ardmore, 1973; Plainview High Sch., Ardmore, 1974. Home: 113 Country Club Rd Ardmore OK 73401 Office: 225 3rd St NW Ardmore OK 73401

MCGEE, HUMPHREY GLENN, architect; b. Hartsville, S.C., June 26, 1937; s. James Gladney and Elizabeth Adams (Williams) McG.; B.Arch., Clemson U., 1960. Designer, Clark, McCall & Leach, Hartsville-Kingstree, S.C., 1961; Designer prodn. A. G. Odell & Assos., Charlotte, N.C., 1962; chief designer Clark, McCall & Leach, Hartsville-Kingstree, S.C., 1963; sr. designer LBC & W, Inc., Columbia, S.C., 1965-69, pres., 1969-76, sr. v.p. client services and design, 1976; pres. CEDA, Inc., Columbia, S.C., 1976—. Served with U.S. Army Res., 1961-67. Mem. AIA, Nat. Soc. Interior Designers (award 1972), Am. Soc. Interior Designers (chmn. S.C. chpt. com. on Found. Interior Design Edn. and Research 1976), Columbia Council Architects. Home: 415 Harden St Columbia SC 29205 Office: 1605 Blossom St Columbia SC 29201

MC GEE, LAWRENCE PALMER, II, social worker; b. New Orleans, Jan. 8, 1935; s. Lawrence Palmer and Bethel Sunshine (Herr) McG.; B.A., Southeastern La. U., 1960; M.S.W., La. State U., 1966; m. Kay Marie Fussell, July 16, 1960; Welfare visitor Orleans Parish Dept. Public Welfare, New Orleans, 1960-64; family counselor Family Counseling Center, Mobile, Ala., 1966-69, supr. family counseling, 1968-69; counselor Family Counseling Service, Jackson, Miss., 1970; social worker VA Med. Center, Tuskegee, Ala., 1970—, clin. coordinator for undergrad. social work program, 1974—; chmn. bd. Auburn (Ala.) Crisis Center, 1971-73; adj. prof. social work Tuskegee Inst., 1974-79. Delegate Diocesan Conv. Episcopal Diocese of Ala., 1978, 79, 80. NIMH fellow, 1964-66. Lic. social worker, Ala. Mem. Nat. Assn. Social Workers, Acad. Cert. Social Workers. Club: Buccaneer Yacht (Mobile). Home: Apt D-3 650 N Ross St Auburn AL 36830 Office: VA Medical Center Tuskegee AL 36083

MC GEE, LINDA DANNER, guidance dir.; b. St. Louis, Sept. 21, 1948; d. George Julius and Vera Margaret (Purnell) Danner; B.S. in Edn., U. Mo., 1970, M.Ed. in Counseling and Personnel Services, 1973; postgrad. Va. Poly. Inst. and State U., 1976—; m. Kenneth Allen McGee, Sept. 7, 1968; children—Jennifer Lyn, Stephanie Jeanne. Tchr. elementary sci. Jefferson City (Mo.) Pub. Schs., 1970-72; tchr. 7th grade psychology and chemistry, dir. guidance Congressional Schs. Va., Falls Church, 1973—; intern in supervision masters degree practicum students. Certified life elementary tchr., Mo., tchr. chemistry, psychology, guidance and counseling, Va. Mem. Am., Va., No. Va. (exec. bd.) personnel and guidance assns., Am. Sch. Counselors Assn., Kappa Delta Pi (outstanding mem. Mu Delta chpt., 1972), Pi Lambda Theta. Clubs: U. Mo. Geology Wives (pres., 1970-72), No. Va., Loudoun-Fairfax (exec. bd.) Mothers of Twins, U. Mo. Alumni Assn., Alpha Sigma Alpha, Alpha Sigma Alpha Alumni (pres. Columbia, Mo., 1971-72). Home: 116 W Brighton Ave Sterling VA 22170 Office: 3229 Sleepy Hollow Rd Falls Church VA 22042

MC GEE, WESLEY OLEN, consumer products co. exec.; b. Rockingham, N.C., Aug. 25, 1940; s. Cleondrus and Hazel (Williams) McG.; B.S. in Chemistry, N.C. State U., 1962; M.B.A. in Fin., Columbia U., 1969; m. Judith Ann Williams, July 17, 1965; children—Allison, Jennifer, Lance. Chemist, E.I. duPont de Nemours & Co., 1962-64; mktg. rep. Jos. Bancroft div. Indian Head, Inc., 1964-67; asst. v.p. Laird Inc., 1969-70; v.p. planning, treas. Wheelabrator-Frye, Inc. (formerly Equity Corp.), 1970-72; pres. Pargo, Inc., Charlotte, N.C., 1972-73; cons., partner Nathaniel Hill and Assos., Inc., Raleigh, N.C., 1973-76; chmn., chief exec. officer Jones & Presnell Studios, Inc., Charlotte, 1977—, also dir.; dir. G & L Janitor Supply. Mem. Am. Arbitration Assn. Republican. Lutheran. Clubs: Charlotte Athletic, Olde Providence Racquet, Contbr. articles to profl. jours. Home: 5620 Sardis Rd Charlotte NC 28211 Office: 433 Lawton Rd Charlotte NC 28232

MC GEE, WILLIAM SEARS, state justice; b. Houston, Sept. 29, 1917; s. James Butler and Alice (Sears) McG.; student Rice U., Houston, 1934-36; LL.B., U. Tex., 1940; m. Mary Beth Peterson, Mar. 8, 1941; children—James Sears, Mary Gray McGee Neilson, Claire Logan McGee Holmes, Alice Gray McGee Ruckman, George Sears, Erwin Smith. Admitted to Tex. bar, 1940; judge Harris County Ct., Houston, 1948-54, 151st Dist. Ct., Harris County, 1954-55; pvt. practice, Houston, 1955-58; judge 55th Dist. Ct., Harris County, 1958-69; asso. justice Supreme Ct. Tex., 1969—; instr. civil law procedure U. Houston Coll. Law, 1950-52; sec.-treas. Houston Jr. Bar, 1947. 1972-73. Bd. dirs. central br. YMCA, Houston; mem. Houston Community Council; pres. Houston Council Deaf Children; mem. nat. awards jury Freedoms Found. at Valley Forge, 1971. Served with USNR, 1943-46. Mem. Am. Bar Assn., Am. Judicature Soc., State Bar Tex. (past dir.), Sons of Herman, Houston Rose Soc., Phi Delta Theta. Address: Supreme Ct Texas PO Box 12248 Austin TX 78711

MC GEHEE, EDWARD STOKES, elec. equipment mfg. co. exec.; b. Montgomery, Ala., Aug. 17, 1924; s. William Boyd and Ola Juanita (Stokes) McG.; student Auburn U., 1942-43; B.S., U.S. Naval Acad., 1946; m. Gertrude Lanier Gibson, Apr. 16, 1949; children—Edward Stokes, James Hardie. With Vulcan Rivet & Bolt Corp., Birmingham, Ala., 1954-69, works mgr., 1955-59, v.p. prodn., 1959-69; dir. indsl. relations Anderson Electric Corp., Leeds, Ala., 1969-70, asst. plant mgr., 1970-71, exec. asst. to chmn. bd., 1971-73; group dir. indsl. relations Square D Co., Leeds, 1973—; tchr. marine engring. U.S. Naval Acad., 1952-54. Served from ensign to lt USN, 1943-54. Mem. U.S. Naval Inst., Birmingham C. of C., Asso. Industries Ala. (chmn. indsl. relations com. 1969, 75-79), Ala. Bible Soc. (v.p., dir. 1959—), St. Andrew's Soc. Middle South (sec. 1977-78, pres. 1979), Phi Delta Theta. Methodist. Clubs: Capital City (Montgomery); The Club (Birmingham). Home: 2512 Watkins Rd Mountain Brook AL 35223 Office: Square D Co PO Box 455 Leeds AL 35094

MC GEHEE, ROBERT EDWIN, paper co. exec.; b. Vicksburg, Miss., Aug. 19, 1933; s. Clyde and Myrtel (Lammons) McG.; B.S. in Forestry, Miss. State U., 1961; m. Joreen Kay Roselle, July 4, 1954; children—Robert Edwin, Michele, Michael. Operator, Spencer Chem. Co., Vicksburg, 1956-57; forester Dierks Forests, Broken Bow, Okla., 1961-62, pulp foreman, 1962-73; paper mill supt. Weyerhaeuser Paper Co., Pine Bluff, Ark., 1973-76, pulp mill supt., 1976—. Served with U.S. Army, 1954-56. Mem. Paper Industry Mgmt. Assn., La., Ark., Miss., Okla., Tex. Pulp Mill Supt. Com., C. of C. Baptist. Home: 24 Mockingbird Ln Pine Bluff AR 71603 Office: 500 McFadden Rd Pine Bluff AR 71601

MC GETTRICK, WILLIAM JOSEPH JOHN, cons. engr.; b. Whitesboro, N.Y., Nov. 2, 1921; s. William J. and Florence (Avery) McG.; B.S., Fordham U., 1942; postgrad. Stevens Inst., 1948, Tri-State Coll., 1953; m. Ruth Margaret Sheppard, Oct. 17, 1945; children—Judith Ann (Mrs. William Leon Barfield), Craig William. Engr., scientist Norden Bombsight Co., Elmira, N.Y., 1945-48; project engr. Bendix Aviation Co., Teterboro, N.J., 1948-53; pres. Pomac Industries, Alfred, N.Y., 1953-55; program mgr., research staff Link Aviation Co., Binghamton, N.Y., 1955-60; chief scientist Carib-Orient Cons., Largo, Fla., 1960-66; pres. Sci. Pollution Control Co., Orlando, Fla., 1966-72; cons. engr. Am. Cons. Assn., Chgo., 1972—; dir. Jones Constrn. Co., Wilmington, N.C. Partner Craig's Scuba Shop, Burlington, N.C., 1966—. Mem. exec. com. Cherokee council Boy Scouts Am., 1966-70; capt. expansion drive Morton F. Plant Hosp., Clearwater, Fla., 1964-65. Served to lt. comdr. USN, 1941-45. Mem. Marine Tech. Soc., Internat. Oceanographic Found. Kiwanian, Rotarian, Lion. Author: The Second 100 Years War; The Goat Without Horns; The Ultimate War Games. Compiler, editor: Abbreviations and Acronyms of The Space Age. Home: 809 7th St NW Largo FL 33540 Office: Am Cons Assn John Hancock Center Suite 3233 875 N Michigan Ave Chicago IL 60611

MC GILL, EDWIN MILLER, physician; b. Evanston, Ill., May 17, 1922; s. Ernest Charles and Rose (Emerson) McG.; B.S., Northwestern U., 1944, B.M., 1946, M.D., 1947; m. Gladys Maudine Nash, Feb. 14, 1949; children—Mary Sue, Patricia, Michael. Intern, Evanston Hosp., 1946-47; resident St. Francis Hosp., Evanston, 1950-53, formerly mem. staff; pvt. practice Arlington Heights, Ill., 1953-76; chief of staff Northwest Community Hosp., Arlington Heights, 1959-62, now attending and asso. staff; practice medicine, Kerrville, Tex., 1976—; clin. instr. obstetrics and gynecology Med. Sch., Northwestern U. Served from 1st lt. to capt. USAAF, 1947-49. Diplomate Am. Bd. Obstetrics and Gynecology. Fellow A.C.S., Internat. Coll. Surgeons, Am. Coll. Obstetricians and Gynecologists, Royal Soc. Health (London, Eng.), Ill. Obstet. and Gynecol. Soc., Chgo. Gynecol. Soc. (asso.); mem. AMA, Ill., Chgo. med. socs., Tex. Med. Assn., Am. Soc. Abdominal Surgeons, Royal Soc. Medicine (London), Poor Pierre Marching and Chowder Soc. Upper Wabigoon River, Inc. Home: 207 Wild Timber Dr Kerrville TX 78028 Office: Peterson Meml Hosp Bldg Kerrville TX 78028

MC GILL, JOSEPH LEONARD, JR., clin. psychologist; b. Phila., Oct. 30, 1946; s. Joseph Leonard and Esther (Cocito) McG.; B.A., LaSalle Coll., 1968; M.A., U. Ark., 1972, Ph.D., 1975; m. Patti Jo Watson. Outpatient coordinator East Ark. Regional Mental Health Center, West Memphis, 1973-74, asst. dir., 1974-76, dir. research and tng., 1974, center dir., 1976-78; clin. dir. SE Memphis Mental Health Center, Memphis, 1978-79; cons. psychologist Rohrer, Hibler & Replogle, Memphis, 1979—; with VA Hosp., Memphis, also U. Tenn. Center for Health Scis., Memphis. Licensed clin. psychologist, Ark. Mem. Am., Ark. (sec. 1976, council 1977) psychol. assns., Assn. Advancement Behavior Therapy, Ark. Behavior Therapy Assn. (pres. elect 1977). Home: 1101 W Roselawn West Memphis AR 72301 Office: 1201 1st Tennessee Bldg 165 Madison Memphis TN 38103

MC GILL, LYNN DICKSON, educator; b. Springfield, Ill., June 3, 1941; s. Joseph Dixon and Edith Marietta (Dupy) McG.; B.S., Middle Tenn. State U., 1965; M.S., U. Tenn., Knoxville, 1968; m. Linda Faye Branum, June 22, 1963; children—Christopher Alexander, Meredith Lynn. Music tchr. Oak Ridge Public Schs., 1965-67; instr. Tenn. Wesleyan Coll., Athens, 1968-72, asst. prof., 1972-77, asso. prof. music, dir. choral studies, 1977—; founder, dir. Athens Tenn. Wesleyan Community Chorus and Orch., 1971—. Pres., Athens Area Council for Arts, 1979-80. Recipient Spl. award for Choral Conducting, U. Tenn., 1977, U. Tenn. Edward H. Hamilton Conducting scholar, 1967-68. Mem. Am. Choral Dirs. Assn. (life, pres. Tenn. chpt. 1973-75), Coll. Music Soc., Nat. Assn. Tchrs. Singing, Am. Choral Found., Fellowship United Meth. Musicians (pres. Holston Conf. chpt. 1972-74), AAUP, Phi Delta Kappa. Methodist (diaconal minister). Club: Optimist (dir. 1978-80) (Athens, Tenn.). Home: 510 Charlotte St Athens TN 37303 Office: Dept Music Tenn Weselyan Coll Athens TN 37303

MC GILLIVRAY, ROSS TUCKER, geotech. engr.; b. Borinquen AFB, P.R., Apr. 8, 1942; s. Harold Joseph and Jeannette (Campbell) Mc.; B.Civil Engring., Ga. Inst. Tech., 1966; M.S., Mass. Inst. Tech., 1968; m. Marie Josephine Boyle, Dec. 30, 1964; children—Alison Marie, Sandi Sehoy, Alexander Vamie. Research engr. Ga. Hwy. Dept., Atlanta, 1965-66; research engr. Mass. Inst. Tech., Cambridge, 1968-70; staff engr. Lambe & Assos., Concord, Mass., 1970-72; chief engr. Pitts. Testing Lab.-Tampa dist., 1972-74; pres. Armac Engrs., Inc., Tampa, Fla., 1974—, chmn. bd. dirs., 1974—; mem. U.S. com. Internat. Commn. on Large Dams; mem. engring. rev. com. City of Temple Terrace (Fla.). Bd. dirs. program and evaluation com. Northside Community Mental Health Center. Registered profl. engr., Fla., R.I. Mem. Fla. Engring. Soc., Nat. Soc. Profl. Engrs., ASCE (chmn. structual and geotech. group 1974-76), Soc. Mining Engrs. Contbr. articles to profl. jours. Home: 506 Crest Over Dr Temple Terrace FL 33617 Office: 8430 N 40th St Tampa FL 33604

MC GINITY, JAMES WILLIAM, educator; b. Brisbane, Australia, Feb. 10, 1946; s. Andrew and Nora Mary (Sistrom) McG.; came to U.S., 1969, permanent resident, 1972; B.Pharmacy, U. Queensland, 1967; Ph.D., U. Iowa, 1972. Research investigator E.R. Squibb & Sons, 1972-73; asso. prof. pharmacy Tex. So. U., Houston, 1973-76; asst. prof. pharmacy U. Tex., Austin, 1976-79, asso. prof., 1979—. Mem. Am. Pharm. Assn., Acad. Pharm. Sci., Phi Lambda Upsilon, Rho Chi. Home: 4817 Gerona Dr Austin TX 78759 Office: Coll of Pharmacy U Tex Austin TX 78712

MC GINLEY, ANTHONY JOSEPH, educator; b. Centralia, Pa., Sept. 2, 1920; s. Anthony Joseph and Elizabeth Mary (Schoeffler) McG.; B.A., St. Charles Coll., 1941; postgrad. St. Charles Sem., 1942-45; M.A., Cath. U. Am., 1971, Ph.D., 1973. Campus ministry cons. Susquehanna U., Selinsgrove, Pa., 1954-60; advisor/cons. Dickenson Coll. and Dickinson Law Students, Carlisle, Pa., 1960-70; grad. students research dir. Cath. U. Am., Washington, 1971-73; prof. psychology Marymount Coll. of Va., 1979—, Georgetown U., Washington, 1977-79, prof. psychology, dir. dissertations and master theses Georgetown Grad. Sch., Dept. Orthodonics, Washington, 1977-79; doctoral dissertation cons. Hot Line cons., Arlington, 1978-79; active various civic orgns; chaplain VA Hosp., Lebanon, Pa. 1953-54. Named Man of the Year, Carlisle City Com., 1966; recipient Five Year award, Marymount Coll., 1979. Mem. Am. Psychol. Assn., AAUP, Am. Personnel and Guidance Assn. Democrat. Roman Catholic. Clubs: K.C. (hon. life), Washington Golf and Country. Contbr. articles to profl. jours. Home: 2807 N Glebe St North Arlington VA 22207 Office: 4352 A Lee Hwy Apt 103 N Arlington VA 22207

MC GINLEY, EDWARD STILLMAN, II, naval officer, naval engr.; b. Allentown, Pa., June 9, 1939; s. Edward Stillman and Dorothy Mae (Kandle) McG.; student Pa. State U., 1956-57; B.S., U.S. Naval Acad., 1961; S.M. and Engr.'s Degree in Naval Architecture/Marine Engring., M.I.T., 1970; M.S.A. in Mgmt. Engring., George Washington U., 1972; m. Connie Lee Mayo, July 1, 1962; children—Amanda Lee, Edward Stillman, III. Commd. ensign U.S. Navy, 1961, advanced through grades to comdr., 1976; served on submarine, 1961-67, U.S.S. Sea Lion, 1966-67, U.S.S. Runner, 1963-66, U.S.S. Sablefish, 1966-67; head submarine systems analysis div. Naval Safety Center, 1970-73; submarine planning officer Norfolk (Va.) Naval Shipyard, 1973-76; repair officer/overhaul coordinator U.S.S. Simon Lake, 1976-78; head test coordination br., repair officer Charleston (S.C.) Naval Shipyard, 1978—; mem. Navy Spl. Submarine Rev. Team. Mem. Am. Soc. Naval Engrs. (vice chmn. Norfolk chpt. 1976, chmn. Charleston chpt. 1980-81), Soc. Naval Architects and Marine Engrs., Charleston Mus., Charleston Hist. Soc., Tau Beta Pi, Sigma Chi. Republican. Baptist. Contbr. articles to profl. jours., 1970-73; holder naval record for shortest duration of maj. nuclear submarine overhaul, 1975. Home: 602 Indiana Ave Charleston SC 29404 Office: Code 330 Charleston Naval Shipyard Charleston SC 29408

MC GINN, LARRY DEAN, cons. anesthesiologist; b. Sedgwick, Kans., May 4, 1942; s. Hayes Paul and Agnes Agatha (Schaplowsky) McG.; B.A., Kan. U., 1964; M.D., U. Kans., 1968; m. Mary Elaine Moore, June 8, 1968; children—Laura Dean, Michael Thomas, Mary Jane, Janet Lynn. Intern, Good Samaritan Hosp., Phoenix, 1968-69; resident U. Fla. Med. Sch. Hosp., Gainesville, 1971-74; cons. anesthesiologist Anesthesia Cons. of Knoxville (Tenn.), 1974—, pres., chmn. bd., 1976—; chief anesthesia Baptist Hosp., Knoxville, 1976—. Served with AUS, 1969-71. Decorated Army Commendation medal with two oak leaf clusters, Combat Med. badge. Diplomate Am. Bd. Anesthesiology. Fellow Am. Coll. Anesthesiologists; mem. AMA, Am. Soc. Anesthesiologists, Tenn. Soc. Anesthesiologists, Knoxville Anesthesia Soc., Internat. Anesthesia Research Soc., Republican. Methodist. Contbr. articles to profl. jours. Home and office: 9420 Briarwood Blvd Knoxville TN 37923

MC GINNES, FRANKLIN PIERCE, seafood co. exec., automobile dealer; b. Mollusk, Va., Feb. 22, 1927; s. Thomas Dix and Aileen (Poole) McG.; B.S., U. Va., 1947; postgrad. Gen. Motor Inst., Flint, Mich., 1948; m. Nancy Madison Crawford Hubbard, Aug. 14, 1965; 1 stepdau., Anne C. Hubbard Cheek. Gen. mgr. T.D. McGinnes, Inc., Kilmarnock, Va., 1948-64, pres., 1964—; pres. Va. Seafoods, Inc., Irvington, Va., 1964—; pres. MCCO Enterprises, Inc., Kilmarnock, Va. Pet Foods, Inc., Irvington; pres. Kilmarnock Motor Sales, Inc.; mem. No. Neck adv. bd. Bank of Va., 1974—. Mayor Town of Irvington, 1974—. Served with USNR, 1944-46, 52-53. Mem. No. Neck Automobile Dealers Assn. (past pres.), Nat. (chmn. fisheries council 1977), Mid-Atlantic (past pres.) food processors assns., Va. Canners Assns. (past pres.), Shellfish Inst. N.Am. (past pres.), Va. C. of C. (dir. 1975-78). Rotarian. Home: Bell Tower Irvington VA 22480 Office: Irvington VA 22480

MCGINNIS, JOHN SHELDON, mktg. exec.; b. Newburg, W.Va., Feb. 9, 1934; s. Francis Guy and Nola Agnes McGinnis; m. Joyce Bolyard, May 2, 1952; children—Jon, Jo. Joined U.S. Army, 1950, advanced through grades to maj., 1960; div. arty. adviser, 1970; ret., 1970; v.p. mktg. S & S Corp., Cedar Bluff, Va., 1970—. Decorated Legion of Merit, Bronze Star medal, Air medal with oak leaf cluster; Vietnamese Cross of Gallantry with Silver Star. Mem. Am. Mining Congress, Va. Mining Inst., Marion C. of C. (dir. 1976-77). Republican. Methodist. Club: Masons. Home: Route 1 Box 179H Pounding Mill VA 24637 Office: Route 3 Box 70 Cedar Bluff VA 24609

MC GINTY, HELEN, govt. employee; b. Norwood, Ga.; d. Newton Elliott and Susie (Veazey) McGinty; student Tift Coll., Forsyth, Ga., 1932-34; A.B., Shorter Coll., Rome, Ga., 1936; M.S., U. Ga., 1943; NSF fellow, Emory U., 1958-61; postgrad. Ga. State U., Atlanta, 1969-73. Tchr. math., Dalton, Ga., 5 years, Atlanta, 30 years; tchr. math. Ft. McPherson, Atlanta, part-time 1952-59; date transcriber U.S. Dept. Internal Revenue, Chamblee, Ga., 1974-75; clk. HUD, Atlanta, 1975-77, personnel clk., 1977-78, loan processor, 1978—. Pres. Sunday Sch. Class, Grace Meth. Ch., 1976-77. Mem. NEA, Ga. Edn. Assn., Atlanta Edn. Assn. (pres. 1969-70), 5th Dist. Edn. Assn. (v.p. 1969-70), 5th Dist. Classroom Tchrs. Assn. (v.p. 1967-70), Nat. Council Tchrs. Math., Counselors Assn., Bus. and Profl. Women, Nat. Assn. Parliamentarians, Beta Sigma Phi, Alpha Delta Kappa (dist. sec. 1975-76, vice chmn. Atlanta dist. 1976-78), Delta Kappa Gamma (chpt. treas. 1969-70), Kappa Kappa Iota (chpt. pres. 1977-80). Clubs: Atlanta Womans; Pilot Internat. Home: 229 Peachtree Hills Ave NE Apt E Atlanta GA 30305 Office: Atlanta Area Office HUD 75 Spring St SW Atlanta GA 30303

MC GINTY, JEAN LADELLE EPPERSON, educator, historian; b. Houston, Jan. 12, 1927; d. Thomas Marvin and Marguerite LaDelle (Mitchell) Epperson; B.S., U. Houston, 1957, M.Ed., 1973; m. Billy Baten McGinty, Jan. 20, 1947; children—Desiree LaDelle, Mia Colleen, Marla Marie. X-ray technician to pvt. physician, Houston, 1949-51; mem. staff Spectrographic lab. Dickinson Gun Plant, Galena Park, Tex., 1951-53; tchr. Channelview (Tex.) Sch. Dist., 1960-63, tchr., ednl. psychologist Goose Creek Sch. Dist., Baytown, Tex., 1963—. Mem. Am. Psychol. Assn., Tex. State Tchrs. Assn., Chambers County Heritage Soc. (pres. 1976-80), Liberty County Hist. Commn., Houston Archeol. Soc. (sec.-treas. 1979-80), Tex. Archeol. Soc. Democrat. Unitarian. Home: Route 2 Box 162 Dayton TX 77535

MC GLAMERY, ANDREW JOE, advt., newspaper co. exec.; b. Statesboro, Ga., Nov. 1, 1943; s. Walter Elliott and Marguerite Kathleen (Boyd) McG.; A.B. in Journalism, U. Ga., 1965; m. Susan Patricia Vause, Dec. 27, 1967; 1 dau., Nancy Elizabeth. Sales mgr. WWNS, Inc., Statesboro, 1965-73; pres. Advt. Prodn. Assos., Statesboro, 1971—; pres. Southeastern Media of Statesboro, Inc., 1973—, gen. mgr., 1973-75; gen. mgr. Statesboro Herald, 1975-76, pub., 1976—; pub. So. Beacon, 1978—; dir. Statesboro CATV, Inc. Sec., Statesboro City Planning Commn., 1973—; bd. dirs. Bulloch County Heart Unit, 1976, Bulloch County chpt. ARC, 1977. Mem. Ga. Press Assn., So. Newspaper Pubs. Assn., Sigma Delta Chi. Methodist. Club: Kiwanis (lt. gov. 8th div. Ga. dist. 1977-78, editor Ga. Kiwanian 1978—). Office: Statesboro Herald Box 888 8 N Walnut St Statesboro GA 30458

MC GLAMERY, GERALD GARRIS, pollution control engr.; b. North Wilkesboro, N.C., Aug. 31, 1937; s. George Allen and Ruby W. (Landreth) McG.; B.S. in Chem. Engring., Auburn U., 1959; m. Barbara Ann Coggins, Nov. 26, 1960; children—Gerald Garris, George Lee. Tech. service engr. Olin Corp., Brevard, N.C., 1959-62; process design engr. Monsanto Co., Decatur, Ala., 1962-65, sr. planning engr., 1965-67; chem. engr. TVA, Muscle Shoals, Ala., 1967-70, supr. conceptual designs, 1970-73, asst. dir. stack gas emission study staff, 1973-76, asst. mgr. emission control devel. projects, 1976—; lectr. on polution control U. Ala., 1972, U. No. Ala., 1971. Head adviser Jr. Achievement, Florence, 1971-75; baseball coach Underwood Dixie Youth League, Florence, 1971-74; basketball coach Florence City League, 1975-76; com. chmn., dist. camping chmn. troop Boy Scouts Am. Registered profl. engr., Ala. Mem. Am. Inst. Chem. Engrs., Tau Beta Pi, Phi Lambda Upsilon. Presbyn. Clubs: Quad-Cities, Auburn Alumni, Quad Cities Quarterback (Florence). Contbr. papers, reports on air pollution control. Home: 214 Robin Hood Dr Florence AL 35630 Office: TVA Nat Fertilizer Devel Center Bldg Muscle Shoals AL 35660

MC GLAMRY, MAX REGINALD, lawyer; b. Wilcox County, Ga., Sept. 12, 1928; s. Edgar Lee and Allie Bea (Faircloth) McG.; B.S., Auburn U., 1948; J.D. cum laude, Mercer U., 1952; m. Jean Louise Hilyer, Dec. 28, 1950; children—Sharon Kay, Michael Lee. Admitted to Ga. bar, 1953; individual practice law, Columbus, Ga., 1954-64; partner Swift, Pease, Davidson & Chapman, Attys., 1964-70, Swift, Page & Chapman, 1971-73, Page, Scrantom, Harris, McGlamry & Chapman, 1973—. Exec. com. Muscogee County Democratic party, 1956-60. Served with USNR, 1948-49. Fellow Am. Coll. Probate Counsel; mem. Am. Bar Assn., State Bar Ga., Am. Judicature Soc., Blue Key, Phi Kappa Phi, Phi Alpha Delta, Alpha Epsilon Delta, Pi Kappa Alpha. Democrat Baptist. Clubs: Columbus Lawyers (pres.

1964), Lions (pres. 1967), Green Island Hills Country. Home: 2937 Lynda Ln Columbus GA 31906 Office: 1043 3d Ave Columbus GA 31902

MC GLOHON, LOONIS, broadcasting co. exec.; b. Ayden, N.C., Sept. 29, 1921; s. Max Cromwell and Bertha (Andrews) McG.; B.S., East Carolina U., 1942; m. Nan Lovelace, June 19, 1943; children—Reeves, Fan, Laurie. With Jefferson Pilot Broadcasting Co., Charlotte, N.C., 1949—, music dir., 1954—, dir. spl. projects, 1974—; freelance producer, 1950—; composer numerous compositions and works, including many recorded jazz and popular pieces; various commns. for religious works; film scores; new mus. version of Land of Oz, 1970-75; syndicated TV feature mus. scores, including Come Blow Your Horn, 1966, others; score for symphonic drama The Hornets Nest, 1965; guest performer N.C. Symphony. Organizer N.C. agy. Big Bros. Am., 1972, v.p., 1972-75; bd. dirs. Spirit Sq., Historic Bath Commn., Easter Seals Soc., Contact Telephone Counseling, NCCJ. Served with USAAF, 1942-45. Named N.C. Composer of Year, 1974; recipient Peabody award, 1977, 78. Mem. Am. Guild Authors and Composers, Broadcast Music Inc., Pub. Relations Soc. Am. Club: Charlotte Athletic. Home: 222 Wonderwood Dr Charlotte NC 28211 Office: 1 Julian Price Pl Charlotte NC 28208

MC GLOTHIAN, ODELL, SR., publs. exec.; b. Vaiden, Miss., Nov. 11, 1929; s. Earnest and Willie (Moore) McG.; B.A., Judson Coll., 1960; B.D., No. Bapt. Theol. Sem., 1963, M.Div., 1972; M.Ed., Wayne State U., 1967, Ed.D., 1972; m. Gloria D. McDonald, Apr. 16, 1948; children—Della M., Delores, Odell, Doris, Jonathan. With Monark Meat Packing Co., Milw., 1950-54; ordained to ministry, Bapt. Ch., 1950; pastor Mt. Carmel Bapt. Ch., Milw., 1952-57, First Bapt. Ch., East Chicago, Ind., 1957-63, Ch. of Our Father, Detroit, 1963-74; tchr. Detroit Public Schs., 1965-68, counselor, 1968-72; dir. ednl. services Detroit Urban League, 1974-75; dir. publs. Sun. Sch. Pub. Bd., NBC, Nashville, 1975—; instr. Wayne State U., Detroit, 1972-73. Bd. dirs. Council of Chs., Detroit, 1972-75, Detroit Opportunities Industrialization Center, 1972-75, Nashville Opportunities Industrialization Center, 1976—; bd. dirs. Nashville Jr. Achievement, 1978—, Am. Bapt. Theol. Sem., Nashville, 1977—; treas., trustee Todd Phillips Home for Boys, Detroit, 1969-75. Recipient Outstanding Leadership Award in Ch. Affairs, Cotillion Club, Detroit, 1974. Mem. Am. Sch. Counselors Assn., Religious Edn. Assn., Am. Personnel and Guidance Assn., Phi Delta Kappa. Writer Townsend Press Commentary, 1976-79 edits. Home: 134 Riviera Dr Hendersonville TN 37075 Office: 330 Charlotte St Nashville TN 37201

MC GONIGLE, GEORGE LEE, devel. co. exec.; b. Brownsville, Tex., May 6, 1927; s. George and Ruth (Young) McG.; B.S. in Elec. Engring., U. Tex., 1949; postgrad. Columbia, 1966; m. Martha Goss, Nov. 5, 1949; children—Stephen Lee, Catherine Ann, Martha Ellen. With Exxon Co., U.S.A., Houston, 1951—, mgr. gen. services dept., 1965-69, planning mgr. pub. affairs dept., 1971-72; v.p., dir. Friendswood Devel. Co. subs. Exxon Corp., Houston, 1972—. Dir., Model City Dept., Houston, 1970-71; chmn. bd. commrs. Housing Authority of Houston, 1974-77; dep. Gen. Conv., Episcopal Ch., 1976, 79. Served with USNR, 1944-46. Registered profl. engr., Tex.; recipient Distinguished Citizen award, Nat. Municipal League; Recognition award, mayor, City of Houston, 1970. Mem. Nat. Municipal League (v.p. 1974—, exec. com. 1976—). Home: 5243 Birdwood Rd Houston TX 77096 Office: PO Box 2567 Houston TX 77001

MC GOVERN, JOSEPH JAMES, public info. ofcl.; b. N.Y.C., July 15, 1925; s. James and Mary (Ryan) McG.; grad. John Marshall Coll., 1949; m. Marion Jacobs, Feb. 8, 1948. Asst. city editor N.Y. Jour. Am., N.Y.C., 1946-58; news editor The Record, Hackensack, N.J., 1959-69; asst. mng. editor Paterson (N.J.) Morning Call., 1964-66; mng. editor Morning Sentinel and Evening Star, Orlando, Fla., 1969-72; exec. editor Sentinel Star Co., Orlando, 1969-79, ret., 1979; public info. officer Orange County (Fla.), 1980—. Served with USMC, 1943-46. Recipient Pub. Service award N.Y. Silurians Soc., 1967, Sigma Delta Chi, 1967, Nat. Headliners Club, 1967. Home: 138 Country Side Dr Longwood FL 32750 Office: 65 E Central Blvd Orlando FL 32801

MC GOWAN, E(DGAR) L(EON), state ofcl., lawyer; b. Conway, S.C., June 1, 1920; s. Edgar L. and Francis (Mishoe) McG.; student U. Ala., 1938-41; B.S., U. S.C., 1947, M.S., 1950, LL.B., 1957; m. Mildred Parris, Apr. 3, 1941; 1 son, E. Linden. Instr. U. S.C., 1947-50, asst. prof., 1950-57, asso. prof., 1957-71; practice accounting Columbia, S.C., 1947-57; pvt. practice law, 1957—, v.p., dir. Investment Life & Trust Co., Mullins, S.C.; commr. labor State of S.C., 1971—. Sec.-treas. S.C. Democratic Com.; sec. Richland County Dem. Com., 1966-72. Mem. Am., S.C., Richland County bar assns., Nat. Assn. Govt. Labor Ofcls. Methodist. Clubs: Masons, Shriners, Lions. Home: 5067 Hillside Rd Columbia SC 29201 Office: 3600 Forest Dr Columbia SC 29211

MC GOWN, RICHARD ALBERT, III, oil co. exec.; b. Jefferson County, Tex., Nov. 16, 1949; s. Richard Albert and Una Ellen (White) McG.; B.S., Sam Houston State U., 1973. Owner, operator McGown Oil Co., Huntsville, Tex., 1974—. March of Dimes scholar, 1967-68. Mem. So. Gulf Oil Distbrs. Assn., Tex. Oil Marketers Assn., Delta Tau Delta. Methodist. Republican. Club: Rotary. Home: 1523 22d St Huntsville TX 77340 Office: McGown Oil Co PO Box 928 Huntsville TX 77340

MC GRATH, JOHN RAPHAEL, ednl. adminstr.; b. Cleve., Apr. 11, 1941; s. John Raphael and Cora Bell (Grant) McG.; A.S., Miss. Gulf Coast Jr. Coll., 1968; B.S., U. So. Miss., 1970; M.S., So. Ill. U., 1971. Ford Found. intern Forest Park Community Coll., St. Louis, 1971; speech instr. Coahoma Jr. Coll., Clarksdale, Miss., 1971-72; tchr., debate coach Our Lady of Fatima Sch., Lafayette, La., 1972-75; asst. prin., debate coach Our Lady of Victories Central High Sch., Pascagoula, Miss., 1975-76, prin., debate coach, 1976—, exec. sec. bd. dirs., 1976-79, chmn. edn. com. Parish Council, 1979. Vice pres. drug adv. council Singing River Mental Health Center, 1977-78. Served with U.S. Army, 1959-62. Recipient vol. service award Singing River Mental Health Center, 1978; Miss. student-tchr. achievement recognition, 1977, 78. Mem. Am. Forensic Assn., Nat. Forensic League (Double Ruby Coach), Miss. Forensic League (pres., 1976), Nat. Cath. Edn. Assn., Democrat. Roman Catholic. Clubs: Karnival Krew of FAM, K.C. Home: 4303 Willow St Pascagoula MS 39567

MC GRAW, MICHAEL JULIAN, food corp. exec.; b. Louisville, Oct. 29, 1946; s. Woodson Wallace and Mary Elizabeth McGraw; B.S., U. Ky., 1968, J.D., 1972; m. Cheryl Lea Leichhardt, May 25, 1968; children—Kelly Lauren, Brian Patrick. Admitted to Ky. bar, 1973; staff atty. Kingsford Co., Louisville, 1973; staff atty. KFC Corp., Louisville, 1973-75, v.p., gen. counsel, 1975—. Served with USPHS, 1968-70. Mem. Am. Bar Assn., Ky. Bar Assn., Foodservice and Lodging Inst. (dir.), Internat. Franchise Assn., Order of Coif, Tau Beta Phi, Phi Eta Sigma. Mng. editor Ky. Law Jour., 1971-72. Home: 3300 Mt Rainier Dr Louisville KY 40222 Office: KFC Corp PO Box 32070 Louisville KY 40232

MC GRAW, RONALD ALLEN, credit bur. exec.; b. Pasadena, Tex., Dec. 4, 1951; s. Lucius Eltis and Eva Nel (Lade) McG.; student San Jacinto Coll., 1970-72, U. Houston, 1972-74; m. Virginia Ann Milner, Apr. 6, 1974; children—William E., Jamie Nel. Data processing supr. Tex. Commerce Bank, Houston, 1972-74; master operator and supr. data processing Occidental Systems, Inc., Houston, 1974-76; with Associated Credit Services, Inc., Houston, 1976—, systems mktg. mgr., 1978-79, No. regional mgr. Nat. Reporting Services, Inc. subs. Associated Credit Services, 1979—; treas., dir. Southwestern Pretzel Corp. Cert. profl. photographer; cert. profl. diving instr. Mem. Am. Bankers Assn. Republican. Methodist. Club: Masons. Home: 7016 Culmore St Houston TX 77087 Office: 2505 Fannin St Houston TX 77002

MC GREGOR, DONALD THORNTON, journalist; b. McGregor, Tex., Mar. 20, 1924; s. Marshall Thornton and Flora Elvira (Welch) McG.; B.A., Baylor U., 1947; postgrad. Southwestern Bapt. Theol. Sem., 1951-52; m. Alice Carlene Barnhill, Dec. 21, 1946; children—Alice Diane McGregor Tyrone, Robert Thornton, Donald Wayne. Reporter, farm and ranch columnist, asst. wire editor Reporter Telegram, Midland, Tex., 1948-49; continuity dir. Sta. KCRS, Midland, 1949-50; editorial asst. Bapt. Standard, Dallas, 1952-55, asso. editor, 1959-71; bus. news makeup editor Dallas Times Herald, 1956, real estate editor, 1959; publicity dir. Union Bankers Ins. Co., Dallas, 1957-58; editor Calif. So. Bapt., Fresno, 1971-73; editor, pub. Kemp (Tex.) News, Ferris (Tex.) Wheel, Dawson (Tex.) Herald, 1973-74; asso. editor Bapt. Record, Jackson, Miss., 1974-76, editor, 1976—; chmn. public relations adv. com. So. Bapt. Conv., 1979-80. Served with U.S. Army, 1943-45. Mem. So. Bapt. Press Assn. (pres.-elect 1980). Democrat. Home: 202 Turtle Creek Brandon MS 39042 Office: PO Box 530 Jackson MS 39205

MC GREGOR, RAYMOND GENE, chemist; b. New Orleans, Aug. 16, 1948; s. William A. McGregor and Essie M. (Green) Feagin; B.S. McNeese State U., 1970; m. Linda Susann Manuel, Jan. 23, 1971. Tchr., Orleans Parish Sch. Bd., New Orleans, 1971; plant chemist Texaco, Inc., Morgan City, La., 1971-73; analytical chemist Hess Oil Virgin Islands Corp., St. Croix, 1973-75; analytical research and devel. chemist Ciba-Geigy Corp., St. Gabriel, La., 1975-78; sr. chemist Oxirane Chem. Co., Channelview, Tex., 1978—. Mem. Am. Chem. Soc. Methodist. Home: 1314 Littleport Ln Channelview TX 77530 Office: PO Box 580 Channelview TX 77530

MC GREW, JOHN GILBERT, II, chemist; b. Charleston, W.Va., July 30, 1943; s. John Gilbert and Jessie Alma (Given) McG.; B.A., Cornell U., 1965; Ph.D., U. Mich., 1972; m. Barbara Anne Ivy, May 22, 1978. Instr., Macalester Coll., 1971-73; instr., research asso. U. Va., Charlottesville, 1973-75; asst. prof. chemistry Alderson Broaddus Coll., Philippi, W.Va., 1975—. NSF-Nat. Endowment Humanities summer fellow, 1978; faculty research participant Pitts. Energy Tech. Center, 1980—. Mem. Am. Chem. Soc., Sigma Xi, Phi Lambda Upsilon. Home: 219 S High St Philippi WV 26416 Office: Box 1386 Philippi WV 26416

MC GRIGGS, LEE AUGUSTUS, educator; b. Port Gibson, Miss., Feb. 25, 1945; s. Sampson and Lenora McG.; A.B., Jackson State U., 1967; M.S., Tenn. State U., 1969; Ph.D., U. Ill., 1975; m. Virginia Peters, June 20, 1975; 1 son, Lee Augustus. Instr., Ala. A & M U., 1969-71; legis. staff intern Ill. Senate, 1972-73; curriculum devel. specialist Office Supt. Public Instrn., Ill., Springfield, 1973-75; prof. public adminstrn. Tex. So. U., 1975—. Mem. Nat. Assn. Sch. Public Affairs and Adminstrn., Am. Polit. Sci. Assn., Am. Soc. Public Adminstrs. Baptist. Author: Black Legislative Politics in Illinois, 1976; The Odyssey of Martin Luther King, Jr., 1977. Home: PO Box 90083 Houston TX 77090 Office: 3201 Wheeler Ave Houston TX 77004

MCGUFFEY, CARROLL WADE, SR., educator; b. Clinton County, Ky., May 8, 1922; s. Logan Herschel and Kate Ida (Wade) McG.; B.S., Eastern Ky. State U., 1948; M.A., George Peabody Coll. for Tchrs., 1949; D.Ed., Fla. State U., 1957; m. Dorothy Jane Landers, Sept. 2, 1950; children—Carroll Wade, Janie, Linda, Patrick, Donald. Chief office of sch. plant services Ga. Dept. Edn., Atlanta, 1951-58; sch. plant adminstr. Fla. Dept. Edn., Tallahassee, 1958-64; exec. dir. Asso. Consultants in Edn., Tallahassee, 1964-68; prof. ednl. adminstrn. U. Ga., Athens, 1968—; pres. Ednl. Consultants Inc., Athens, 1970—. Served with C.E., U.S. Army, 1943-46, 51-52. Mem. Council of Ednl. Facility Planners Internat. (Planner of Yr. 1978, pres. 1973—), Am. Ednl. Research Assn., Assn. Sch. Bus. Ofcls. U.S. and Can., Phi Delta Kappa, Kappa Delta Pi. Methodist. Contbg. author books; contbr. articles to profl. publs. Home: Route 1 Box 124 Bogart GA 30622 Office: G-10 Aderhold Hall Coll of Edn U Ga Athens GA 30602

MC GUFFIN, WILLIAM LEWIS, JR., physician; b. Memphis, Aug. 13, 1944; s. William Lewis and Valerie (Roach) McG.; B.S. with honors, Ga. Tech. U., 1966; M.D., Duke U., 1970; m. Virginia Sue Rouse, Feb. 13, 1965; children—David, Stephen. Intern, Mass. Gen. Hosp., Boston, 1970-71, resident, 1971-72; clin. asso. clin. endocrinology br. Nat. Inst. Arthritis, Metabolic & Digestive Disease, NIH, Bethesda, Md., 1972-74; fellow nephrology Duke U. Med. Center, 1974-76; asst. prof. medicine U. Ala., 1976-79, U. Tex. Health Sci. Center, Houston, 1979—; dir. dialysis Hermann Hosp., Houston, 1979—. Mem. A.C.P., AMA, Am., Internat. socs. nephrology, Am. Fedn. Clin. Research (councilor So. sect. 1979—), Alpha Omega Alpha. Episcopalian. Home: 5407 Graystone Ln Houston TX 77069 Office: Dept Medicine U Tex Health Sci Center Houston TX 77030

MC GUIRE, FRANKLIN WESLEY, minister, social worker, educator; b. St. Louis, Mar. 15, 1940; s. William Wesley and Reathel Mae McG.; A.B., Central Meth. Coll., 1961; M.Div., Boston U., 1964, M.S. in Social Work, 1967, postgrad., 1974—; m. Judith Kapp, June 10, 1961; children—Scott Gregory, Devin Mathew. Asst. prof. social work and sociology R.I. Coll., Providence, 1974-76; adj. asst. prof. Boston U. Met. Coll., 1973-76; adminstr., dir. The Little House, Dorchester, Mass., 1971-74; coordinator, counselor Preterm Inc., 1974-76; supr., psychiat. social group worker Mystic Valley Mental Health Center, Lexington, Mass., 1970-71; project dir., adminstr. Cambridge Community Services/Dept. Health and Hosp., 1968-70; asst. prof. social work George Mason U., Fairfax, Va., 1976—, Univ. prof., 1978, 79. Mem. Dem. Town Com., Wellesley, Mass., 1975-76; mem. nat. alumni council Boston U., 1974—. Mem. Nat. Assn. Social Workers (nat. adv. bd. policy research network, nat. urban policy task force, nat. task force on housing and social services), Acad. Cert. Social Workers, So. New Eng. Ann. Conf. United Meth. Ch. (nat. task force indsl. chaplaincy), United Neighborhood Centers Am., Council on Social Work Edn., Internat. Assn. Schs. Social Work. Democrat. Methodist. Author: (with others) Worcester, Massachusetts: A Social Profile, 1975. Home: 5161 Linette Ln Annandale VA 22003

MC GUIRE, HUBERT EVERETT, elec. engr.; b. Littlefield, Tex., Dec. 6, 1927; s. Albert Roger and Maude Pearl McGuire; B.S. in Elec. Engring., Tex. Technol. U., 1952; diploma in bus. mgmt. Hamilton Inst., 1957; m. Marilyn Swanson, Sept. 27, 1948; children—Thomas Michael, Dianna Lynn McGuire Wright. Project engr. Melpar, Inc., Fairfax, Va., 1953-58; engring. mgr. Martin Marietta Corp., Orlando, Fla., 1958-66, NASA program mgr., 1966-67; v.p. Ground Data Corp., Ft. Lauderdale, Fla., 1967-72, pres., 1972-76; pres. Charmec Corp., Ft. Lauderdale, 1976—; owner McGuire Properties, Ft. Lauderdale, 1969-71, McGuire Devel. Corp., 1973-75; dir. Atlantic Ventures, Inc., Ft. Lauderdale, 1969-71. Scoutmaster, Boy Scouts Am., 1958; chmn. steering com. Sky Crest Civic Assn., 1964. Served with USN, 1946-48. Recipient Outstanding Achievement award Martin-Marietta Corp., 1964. Mem. AIM (pres.'s council 1971-72, fellow pres.'s council 1972-73). Club: Lions (treas. 1956-58). Patentee in field. Home: 5780 SW 4th Ct Plantation FL 33314 Office: 4750 N Federal Hwy Fort Lauderdale FL 33308

MC GUIRE, JAMES SILAS, agrl. co. exec.; b. Franklin County, Va., Oct. 23, 1925; s. Jack and Elsie (Powell) McG.; student Roanoke Coll., 1947-48; B.S., Va. Poly. Inst., 1951; m. Emily Pearl Cronise, Apr. 5, 1947; children—James Silas, Jeffry Lynn. Dir. membership relations Rockingham Coop. Farm Bur., Harrisonburg, Va., 1951-52; terr. mgr. Hales & Hunter Co., Chgo., 1952-60, dist. sales mgr., 1960-61, dairy feed specialist, 1961-62, dist. gen. mgr., 1963-65; area mgr. A.O. Smith Harvestore Products, Inc., Arlington Heights, Ill., 1965-75, eastern regional mgr., 1976, gen. mgr. so. div., Memphis, 1976-80; v.p., gen. mgr. Tarheel Harvestore Systems, Wilson, N.C., 1980—. Served with USN, 1943-46. Mem. Internat. Sales and Mktg. Execs. Assn., Memphis Sales and Mktg. Execs. Assn. Lutheran. Club: Elks. Home: 1202 Waverly Rd Wilson NC 27893 Office: PO Box 3917 1507 Cargill Ave Wilson NC 27893

MC GUIRE, SHARON GAYLE, guidance counselor; b. McKinney, Tex., Feb. 28, 1948; d. Hubert Preston and Mildred Nona (Braswell) McLeod; B.S. in Home Econs., East Tex. State U., 1970, M.Ed. in Guidance and Counseling, 1974, vocat. supr. cert., 1978; m. Donald James McGuire, Dec. 25, 1970. Tchr. home econs. Princeton (Tex.) High Sch., 1970-73; vocat. counselor Rockwall (Tex.) Ind. Sch. Dist., 1973—. Mem. Am., Tex. personnel and guidance assns., Tex. Vocat. Tech. Assn., Tex. Vocat. Counselors Assn., Am. Vocat. Assn., Tex. Sch. Counselors Assn., Nat. Vocat. Guidance Assn., NEA, Tex. Tchrs. Assn., North Tex. Assn. Dirs., Suprs., and Counselors. Baptist. Home: 103 W Park St Farmersville TX 75031 Office: 1201 High Sch Dr Rockwall TX 75087

MC HENRY, JAMES MELVIN, archtl. and engring. co. exec.; b. Muncie, Ind., Apr. 30, 1940; s. Harry Gail and Mildred Lorane (Lyons) McH.; student Edison Community Coll., Ft. Myers, Fla., 1965, John Wesley Bible Coll., Greensboro, N.C., 1967; m. Norma Lee Bennett, Dec. 23, 1962 children—Sandra, Hope, John, Faith. Archtl. draftsman, 1968-69, 71-76; cable TV draftsman, 1970-71; mgr. tech. services VVKR Inc., Alexandria, Va., 1976—. Sunday sch. tchr. Springfield (Va.) Assembly of God, 1979—; chmn. pack com. local Cub Scouts, 1979—; co. rep. United Way. Served with USAF, 1960-64. Recipient Gold award United Way, 1977, 79. Mem. Romans 8:14 Christian Motorcycle Group (pres.). Republican. Home: 6014 Craig St Springfield VA 22150 Office: 720 N St Asaph St Alexandria VA 22314

MC HENRY, WILLIAM DUNLAP, educator; b. Ridley Park, Pa., June 20, 1932; s. William Rodman and Bonita (Passehl) McH.; B.S. in Commerce, Washington and Lee U., 1954; M.S. in Edn., U. Pa., 1960; m. Joan Cope Acker, Jan. 29, 1955; children—Deborah Joan, Robert Charles. Intramural dir., phys. edn. instr., asst. coach football and track, head coach swimming Pa. Mil. Coll., 1954-58; asst. coach swimming and football, head coach lacrosse, instr. phys. edn. Williams Coll., 1958-61; athletic dir., head football and lacrosse coach Lebanon Valley Coll., Anneville, Pa., 1961-71; dir. athletics, chmn. phys. edn. dept. Washington and Lee U., Lexington, Va., 1971—; mem. football rules com. Nat. Collegiate Athletic Assn., 1976—, mem. lacrosse rules com., 1974-76. Served with U.S. Army, 1954-56. Mem. Am. Football Coaches Assn., U.S. Intercollegiate Lacrosse Assn., Nat. Assn. Collegiate Dirs. Athletics. Presbyterian. Home: 608 Marshall St Lexington VA 24450 Office: Dept Physical Education Washington and Lee U Lexington VA 24450

MC HOLLAND, JOSEPH, mfg. co. exec.; b. Bedford, Ind., Oct. 28, 1934; s. Thad H. and Enid L. (Brock) McH.; B.S., Ball State U., 1959; m. Kathryn Marie Jennings June 6, 1959; children—Teresa, Scott, Jennifer. Cost clk. Infilco div. GATX, Tucson, 1960, budget dir., 1960-61, asst. controller 1961-65; systems analyst Traveler Boat div. Stonray Corp., Danville, Ill., 1965-66, mgr. acctg., 1966-67; asst. controller Roper Alliance div. Roper Corp., Kankakee, Ill., 1967-71, controller Roper Lawn Products, Newark, 1971-75, v.p., controller Roper Lawn Products, Savannah, Ga., 1975—. Treas., Licking County (Ohio) Republican Party, 1972. Served with U.S. Army, 1954-55. Recipient award for tax cons. Ga. Bus. and Industry Assn. Mem. Nat. Assn. Accts., Savannah C. of C. Methodist. Club: Kiwanis. Office: 12052 Middleground Rd Savannah GA 31406

MC ILVAIN, KAREN ELAINE, air force officer; b. Louisville, Sept. 2, 1954; d. Raymond Joseph and Adelie Mae Goeing; student Bellarmine Coll., 1972-74; B.Gen. Studies, U. Ky., 1976; m. Terry Lee McIlvain, Sept. 4, 1976. Commd. 2d. lt. U.S. Air Force, 1976, advanced through grades to 1st lt., 1978; with 4th Aircraft Generation squadron, 1978-79, aircraft maintenance officer 4th Component Repair squadron, Seymour John AFB, Goldsboro, N.C., 1979—; lectr. CPR, ARC. Mem. Air Force Assn., U. Ky. Alumni Assn. Club: Officer's Open Mess. Office: 4th Component Repair Squadron Seymour Johnson AFB Goldsboro NC 27530

MCILVEENE, CHARLES STEELE, clergyman; b. McNeil, Ark., Feb. 11, 1928; s. Bonnie Leonard and Lillian Irene (Owen) McI.; student La. State U., 1945-47; B.A., Hardin Simmons U., 1949; B.D., Southwestern Bapt. Theol. Sem., 1953, M.R.E., 1954, D.Min., 1980; m. Betty Marie Fahlberg, Aug. 12, 1952; children—Carol Ann McIlveene Lemmond, Mary Beth McIlveene Moore, Charles Scott. Ordained to ministry Baptist Ch., 1948; asst. pastor Broadmoor Bapt. Ch., Shreveport, La., 1954-57; pastor Lakeshore Bapt. Ch., Shreveport, 1957-61, Trinity Bapt. Ch., Lake Charles, La., 1961-71, First Bapt. Ch., Lufkin, Tex., 1971—; trustee exec. bd. La. Bapt. Conv., 1961-67, 70-71; 1st v.p. La. Bapt. Conv., 1964; trustee exec. bd. Bapt. Gen. Conv. Tex., 1975—. Trustee La. Coll., 1965-71; trustee E. Tex. Bapt. Coll., 1971—, chmn. bd., 1978-80. Mem. Am. Mgmt. Assn., Angelina C. of C. Club: Rotary. Contbr. articles to various publs. Home: 1305 Woodland St Lufkin TX 75901 Office: First Bapt Ch 106 E Bremond St Lufkin TX 75901

MC ILWRAITH, ISA ROBERTA, organist, composer; b. Paterson, N.J., May 17, 1909; d. Arthur Herriot and Ethel (Williams) McIlwraith; B.A., Barnard Coll., 1931; M.A. (Victor Baier fellow), Columbia U., 1932; M. in Sacred Music, Union Sem., 1936; diploma (fellow) in Orchestral Conducting, Juilliard Grad. Sch. Music, 1937; student of Carl Weinrich, N.Y.C., 1931-35, Ernest White, N.Y.C., 1948-50; m. Arthur Rudolph Plettner, July 12, 1938. Founder and condr. Philomelic Soc., Ridgewood, N.J., 1932-37; organist Plymouth Ch., Bklyn., 1932-34; organist and mus. dir. Ethical Soc., N.Y.C., 1935-38; asst. prof. and condr. Mt. Holyoke Coll. Orch., S. Hadley, Mass., 1937-38; organist Brick Ch., N.Y.C., summers, 1949-55; asso. prof. dept. music U. Chattanooga, 1938-74; guest condr. Juilliard Orch., N.Y.C., 1937, Chattanooga Symphony Orch., 1939; organ recital tours in various states, 1932—; composer of sacred choral compositions including: Appalachian Christmas Carol, 1942; Agnus Dei, 1944; Christians All Rejoice, 1946; Christ Our Passover,

1947; Blessed Art Thou, 1963; Prayer for Peace, 1965; Alleluia, Sing of Gladness, 1969; Behold What Manner of Love, 1970; organ compositions include: Chorale Prelude: O Jesus Christ, Thou Highest Good, 1936; To Us a Child is Born, 1932; Triptych, 1936; Prelude and Fughetta, 1976; book reviewer Chattanooga Times, 1939-64; organist and mus. dir. for various local civic orgns., 1940—. Community activist for proper care of animals, Chattanooga, 1970—. Mem. Am. Guild Organists, Soil and Health Fedn., Animal Protection Inst. Am., Internat. Soc. Protection of Animals, Internat. Fund Animal Welfare, Friends of the Sea Otter, Animal Care of Toms River (N.J.), Defenders of Wildlife, North Shore Animal League, Nat. Health Fedn., African Fund for Endangered Wildlife, Am. Horse Protection Assn., Greenpeace U.S.A., Natural Resources Def. Council, Animal Welfare Inst., United Action for Animals. Contbr. articles to mus. jours. Home and office: 105 Druid Dr Signal Mountain TN 37377

MC INNES, VAL AMBROSE GORDON, clergyman, educator, artist; b. London, Ont., Can., Apr. 21, 1929; came to U.S., 1954; s. Angus J. and Genevieve (Rodgers) McI.; B.A., U. Western Ont., 1952; M.A., U. Windsor, 1954; Dip. Int. Law, Leyden U., 1953; Ph.B., Aquinas Inst., 1958, Ph.L., 1959, Ph.D., 1965. Joined Dominican Order, Roman Catholic Ch., 1954, ordained priest, 1961; lectr. theology St. Thomas Coll., St. Paul, 1962-65; acting chmn. philosophy and theology depts. Kings Coll., London, 1965-66; dir. Cath. Center, Tulane U., New Orleans, 1966-79, exec. sec. chair of Judeo-Christian studies, 1979—; adj. prof. med. ethics Tulane Med. Center, 1969—; prior Dominican Community of St. Anthony of Padua, New Orleans, 1976—; sr. chaplain Order of St. Lazarus of Jerusalem; founding mem. Dominican Province of St. Martin de Porces, 1979; del. to World Conf. on Religion and Peace, 1969-79. Pres. La. Council for Music and the Performing Arts, 1978—, La. Renaissance, Religion and Arts, 1978-79; mem. New Orleans Mayor's Task Force on Arts, 1979. Can. Council grantee, 1966; Nat. Endowment Arts grantee, 1977. Mem. Cath. Philos. Assn., Can. Philos. Assn. Home: 4640 Canal St New Orleans LA 70119 Office: Univ Chapel Tulane U 1229 Broadway New Orleans LA 70118

MC INNIS, HARRY ELWOOD, JR., constrn. co. exec.; b. Shreveport, La., Feb. 21, 1944; s. Harry Elwood and Janie Claire (Burks) McI.; B.B.A., La. State U., 1966, J.D., 1970; m. Nancy Elizabeth Bickham, Aug. 6, 1966; children—Marshall, Katherine, Kyle. Vice-pres. McInnis Bros. Constrn., Inc., gen. contractors, Minden, La., 1969—; dir. UAD Labs., Inc., Minden, Minden Bank and Trust Co. Pres., Dorcheat Hist. Assn., 1976-77, Minden Jaycees, 1972-73, United Givers Fund South Webster Parish, 1974-76, N.W. La. Devel. Center, 1977-78; bd. dirs. Minden Econ. Devel. Corp., La. Polit. Action Council, Norwella council Boy Scouts Am. Named Outstanding Young Man of Year Minden, 1973, Minden Jaycee of Year, 1972. Mem. La. State U. Alumni Assn. (pres. Webster parish 1976-77), Associated Gen. Contractors, Minden C. of C. (dir.), Council for a Better La., Pub. Affairs Research Council La., La. Assn. Bus. and Industry (dir.), Order of Coif, Omicron Delta Kappa. Baptist (deacon). Club: Minden Lions (pres. 1977-78), Mng. editor La. Law Rev., 1968-69. Home: 1113 Broadway Minden LA 71055 Office: 119 Pearl St Minden LA 71055

MC INNIS, JOHN ROBERT, physician, surgeon; b. Moore County, N.C., July 15, 1908; s. James Dalton and Florence Elizabeth (Blue) McI.; student Davidson Coll., 1927-29, U. Okla., 1931; A.B., U. N.C., 1933; M.D., U. Tenn., 1956; m. Esther Alice Hurley, Dec. 26, 1941; children—John Robert, Charles Hurly, Marilyn Esther, Nancy Catherine. Vice pres., mgr. Caroline Handerchief Co., Inc., West End, N.C., 1935-42; accountant, office mgr. Sandhill Furniture Corp., 1947-51; intern, surgery resident Mercy Hosp., Oklahoma City, 1956-58; pvt. practice medicine and surgery, 1956—; mem. staffs Mercy, Bapt. Meml., South Community hosps., McInnis Clinic, Oklahoma City. Chmn. sch. bd. West End (N.C.) Pub. Schs., 1959-61. Served from pvt. to capt. AUS, 1942-47; col. M.C. Res. ret. Mem. A.M.A., Am. Acad. Family Practice, Okla., Oklahoma County med. socs., Oklahoma City Clin. Soc., Ret. Officers Assn., Capitol Hill, Oklahoma City chambers commerce, Am. Assn. Ret. Persons. Presbyterian (elder, trustee). Clubs: Masons (32 deg.), Shriners, Order Eastern Star (worthy grand patron Okla. 1977-78), Rotary. Home: 7008 S Country Club Dr Oklahoma City OK 73159 Office: 4515 S Pennsylvania St Oklahoma City OK 73119

MCINNIS, MARTHA ANN, assn. exec.; b. Montgomery, Ala., July 28, 1937; d. Miles and Rose (Stoner) McI.; B.S., U. Ala., 1959, M.S., 1962; student Huntingdon Coll., 1955-57. Fabric designer Avondale Mills, Inc., Sylacauga, Ala., 1959-62; lectr. Judson Coll., Marion, Ala., 1961-62; instr. U. Miami, Coral Gables, Fla., 1962-63; adult edn. cons. McCall Corp., N.Y.C., 1963-64; asst. prof. Ariz. State U., Tempe, 1964-67: program devel. dir. Ala. Farm Bur. Fedn., Montgomery, 1967-72; exec. v.p. Ala. Environ. Quality Assn., Montgomery, 1972—; pres. Enviro South, Inc., Montgomery, 1975—; editor Enviro South Mag., 1977—; mem. HEW's nat. adv. council on environ. edn., 1975-78. Vice chmn. Auburn U. Sch. of Home Econ. adv. council, 1971-72; chmn. Bartram Trail Conf., 1976—; v.p. Ala. Conf. on Citizenship, 1972-73, pres. 1973-74; mem. Ala. Dem. exec. com., 1979—, Montgomery County Dem. exec. com., 1978—; mem. Ala. Dem. Women's Fedn., 1978—; mem. nat. weather modification adv. bd. U.S. Dept. Commerce, 1977-78). Recipient Mrs. Lyndon B. Johnson award from Keep Am. Beautiful, 1973; Avondale Mills grad. fellow, 1961. Mem. Dixie Zool. Soc. (corporate v.p. 1975-77, bd. dirs. 1975—), U.S. C. of C. (agri-bus. and rural affairs com. 1971-73), AAAS, Am. Soc. Assn. Execs., Ala. Soc. Assn. Execs., Public Relations Council of Ala., Ala. Home Econ. Assn. (pres. 1973-74), Am. Home Econ. Assn., Ala. Hist. Assn., Ala. Acad. Sci. Methodist. Author: Ala. Environ. Edn. Master Plan, 1973; editor: (with others) The Ala. First Lady's Cookbook, 1969; (with others) The Wonderful World of Pork Cookery, 1968. Office: 3815 Interstate Ct Suite 202 Montgomery AL 36109

MC INTOSH, COLIN HUGH ALEXANDER, air transp. cons.; b. Malden, Mass., June 23, 1908; s. Stuart Hugh and Helen (Geddes) McI.; B.A. cum laude, Williams Coll., 1930; m. Anne Magwood, Dec. 17, 1938. Flight supt. Nat. Airways Boston, 1935-37; asst. supr. tng., chief navigator Am. Airlines, 1938-45; spl. asst. v.p. Am. Overseas Airlines, 1946; asso. C.R. Rheinstrom, Aviation Cons., N.Y.C., 1946-48; v.p. ops. Allegheny Airlines, Washington, 1948-52; owner, operator Colin Hugh Mc Intosh Air Transp. Cons., Washington, 1952-73; air transp. cons., Palm Beach, Fla., 1973—; editor Pres.'s Civil Air Policy Report, 1954; spl. asst. to Sec. of Commerce, 1954-55. Mem. Inst. Aeros. and Astronautics, Inst. Nav. (1st pres.), Zeta Psi. Episcopalian. Author: Radio Navigation for Pilots and Long Range Flight, 1942, 43; The Economics of Subsidy, 1965; The Economics of Air Cargo, 1976; contbr. articles to profl. jours.; contbg. econs. editor Air Transport World, 1965-67, 74-77, Airline Exec., 1977—. Home and Office: 3570 S Ocean Blvd Palm Beach FL 33480

MC INTOSH, DONALD KEITH, offshore drilling co. exec.; b. Gadsby, Alta., Can., Dec. 3, 1934; s. William Charles and Laura Ada (Ghent) McI.; m. Dorothy Marie Brinton, Nov. 8, 1958; children—Janet Elaine, Elizabeth Brinton. Accountant, Deloitte, Haskins & Sells, Calgary, Alta., 1954-64; bus. mgr. M.N. Palmer Holdings, Alta., 1964-66; with Reading & Bates Offshore Drilling Co., 1966—, area adminstr., Australia, 1966-67, regional adminstr., London, Eng., 1967-69, area/regional mgr., Lagos, Nigeria, 1969-71, mgr. adminstrn. and fin., Houston, 1971-72, v.p., treas., Tulsa, 1973-75, v.p. fin., treas., Tulsa, 1976—. Home: 5905 S Indianapolis Pl Tulsa OK 74135 Office: Reading & Bates Corp 3800 First Nat Tower Tulsa OK 74103

MC INTOSH, FRANK WESLEY, III, hosp. adminstr.; b. Ft. Dix, N.J., May 28, 1944; s. Frank Wesley and Virginia Ann (Dugger) McI.; A.S., Montreat-Anderson Coll., 1967; B.B.A., Armstrong State Coll., 1971; m. Julia Anne Wright, Aug. 31, 1974; 1 son, Frank Wesley IV. Employee cons. Richmond Corp. subs. Life of Va., 1972-73; employment mgt. Candler Gen. Hosp., Savannah, Ga., 1973-75; personnel dir. N. Fla. Regional Hosp., Gainesville, 1975—; v.p., exec. com., bd. dirs. Civitan Regional Blood Center. Active Gainesville Area C. of C., 1975-77; pres. Gainesville Civitan Club. Served with U.S. Army, 1967-69. Decorated Purple Heart. Mem. Sante Fe Personnel Adminstrn. Assn., Am. Soc. Personnel Adminstrs. (chpt. dir. 1976-77). Presbyterian. Home: 4726 NW 28th St Gainesville FL 32605 Office: PO Box 13494 Gainesville FL 32604

MC INTOSH, JOHN MOHR, JR., bldg. materials co. exec.; b. Savannah, Ga., Apr. 14, 1948; s. John Mohr and Barbara Ann (Neff) McI.; B.S. in Zoology, U. Ga., 1969; m. Sally Madge Ezell, Dec. 23, 1976. Mgmt. assos. Citizens & So. Nat. Bank, Savannah, 1973-74; sales mgr. Performance Sailcraft, Montreal, Que., Can., 1974-76; exec. v.p., treas., sec. Neal-Blun Co., Savannah, 1976—, also dir.; pres. ABJO Inc., Savannah, 1979—. Served to lt. USN, 1969-73. Mem. Nat. Fedn. Ind. Businessmen, Nat. Assn. Home Builders, Nat. Sash and Door Jobbers Assn., Blue Key. Methodist. Clubs: Savannah Yacht, Oglethorpe (Savannah); Charleston Yacht; Corinthian Yacht (Seattle). Home: 7010 Sandnettles Dr Savannah GA 31410 Office: PO Box 22669 Savannah GA 31403

MC INTOSH, PETERSON LINDER, banker; b. Heidelberg, Miss., Feb. 6, 1916; s. Allen Luther and Lee Anna (Linder) McI.; student Ellisville (Miss.) Jr. Coll., 1935-36; B.S., U. So. Miss., 1938; postgrad. U. Ala., 1938-39; m. Bernice Christine Lewis, June 9, 1946. Tchr. bus. edn. pub. schs., Agricola, Miss., 1939-40, Brooklyn, Miss., 1940-42; with Citizens Bank of Hattiesburg, Miss., 1946—, now asst. v.p., bank br. mgr., bank auditor, asst. purchasing and dispersing agent. Trustee, mem. adminstrv. bd. Broad St. United Methodist Ch., Hattiesburg. Served with USAAF, 1942-46; PTO. Mem. Miss. Bankers Assn., Am. Forestry Assn., Internat. Wildlife Assn., Audubon Soc. Am. Clubs: Masons, York Rite, Scottish Rite, K.Y.C.H. Home: 2811 Mamie St Hattiesburg MS 39401 Office: Citizens Bank Hattiesburg PO Drawer 1071 Hattiesburg MS 39401

MC INTOSH, ROBERT JOSEPH, ret. broadcasting exec., performing arts assn. exec.; b. Louisville, Mar. 1, 1910; s. Robert Preston and Rosa Cecilia (Tompkins) McI.; student Harvard, 1956; m. Mary Jo La Copo, Jan. 10, 1951; children—Robert Joseph, David P. Announcer radio sta. WAVE, Louisville, 1934; sports announcer sta. WGRC, Louisville, 1935-42, program dir., 1936-42, comml. mgr., 1946-47; gen. mgr. sta. WJPS, Evansville, Ind., 1948-54; sales mgr. sta. WWJ, Detroit, 1954-56, sta. mgr., 1956-60; pres. sta. WKDL, Clarksdale, Miss., 1960-75. Lectr. on life of Abraham Lincoln, various locations, 1954-60. First v.p. Evansville Mus. of Arts and Scis., 1948-54, chmn. fund raising com., 1951-52; publicity chmn. Community Chest, Evansville, 1949-50; mem. membership com. ARC, Evansville, 1951-52; mem. Evansville Players, 1948-54; chmn. Detroit Civil War Centennial Com., 1954-60; mem. Abraham Lincoln Civil War Round Table, 1954-60, Mich. Civil War Centennial Commn., 1954-60, Ind. Lincoln Found., 1954-60; pres. Clarksdale Theatre Guild, 1965-66; chmn. Bicentennial Commn., Clarksdale, 1975-76; commr. Delta Area council Boy Scouts Am., 1967-68. Served to lt. col. USAAF, 1942-46. Mem. Miss. Hist. Soc., Clarksdale C. of C. (dir. 1963-66), Clarksdale Community Concert Assn. (pres. 1961-78), Advt. Club (pres. 1953-54), Press Club. Republican. Roman Catholic. Clubs: Clarksdale Country, Opera Study (pres. 1966-67); Adcraft of Detroit; Elks. Address: 400 River Rd Clarksdale MS 38614

MC INTURFF, ERNEST ROBERT, aerospace engr.; b. Washington, Feb. 28, 1936; s. Ernest Raymond and Elva Mae (Whitehurst) McI.; B.S. in Aero. Engring., U. Va., 1959, postgrad., 1961-62, 66-68; Aerospace engr. FAA, Washington, 1959-64; aerospace engr., research specialist U.S. Army, Dept. Def., Washington, 1964-67, aerospace engr. propulsion and power systems, 1967-71, supervisory aerospace engr., Charlottesville, Va., 1971—; mem. Interagy. Bd. U.S. Civil Service Examiners, 1967. Served with USN, 1960. Recipient Outstanding Performance award Dept. of Army, 1967; Keyman award United Fund. Mem. Am. Inst. Aeros. and Astronautics, Am. Def. Preparedness Assn. Baptist. Home: 1417 Audmar Dr McLean VA 22101 Office: 220 7th St NE Charlottesville VA 22901

MCINTYRE, DAVID REGINALD, advt. agy. exec.; b. Detroit, July 5, 1937; s. Robert Alexander and Hazel Margaret (Edens) McI.; B.A., Detroit Inst. Tech., 1961; B.F.T., Am. Grad. Sch. Internat. Mgmt., 1968; m. Joan Donna Rompel, Nov. 22, 1965; children—Julia, Shannon, Sean. Tchr., Ministry Edn., Jamaica, W.I., 1961-64; high sch. vice prin., tchr. public and pvt. schs., Honolulu, 1965-67; with 7Up Internat., Inc., N.Y.C., St. Louis, 1968-76, advt. mgr., until 1976; regional account exec. The Marschalk Co., N.Y.C., St. Louis, 1976-78, J. Walter Thompson Co., Miami, Fla., 1978—. Nat. AAU masters swim record holder. Mem. Internat. Advt. Assn., Am. Mgmt. Assn. Club: Florida Masters Swim. Contbr. articles to profl. publs. Home: 17641 SW 75th Ave Miami FL 33157 Office: 1201 Brickell Ave Miami FL 33131

MC INTYRE, JAMES FRANCIS, III, acct.; b. Greensboro, N.C., Sept. 15, 1950; s. James F. and Margarete J. (Ebner) McI.; student E. Carolina U., 1972-76. Pres., partner McIntyre & Gerry, Greenville, N.C., 1976—; faculty Pitt Tech. Inst., Greenville, 1978-79. Capt., Explorer Post's Rifle team, Raleigh, N.C., 1965; chmn. Wake County Teen Age Republicans, 1967; treas. Pitt County Young Reps., 1978, 79, Pitt-Beaufort Conservative Union, 1978; chmn. Pitt County Rep. Party, 1979; regional dir. Young Reps., 1st region, 1979; del. N.C. Young Rep. Conv., 1979, Nat. Young Rep. Conv., 1979, N.C. Rep. Conv., 1979, 1st Dist. Rep. Conv., 1979. Served with USAF, 1968-72. Roman Catholic. Address: PO Box 1693 Greenville NC 27834

MC INTYRE, JAMES HOWARD, coll. adminstr.; b. Birmingham, Ala., Oct. 5, 1946; s. Frank and Inez Margaret (Strickland) McI.; student Bakersfield Coll., 1966-67; B.A., U. Ala., 1975; m. Wanda Letitia Johnson, Apr. 21, 1973; 1 son, Kerry. Receiving clk. U. Ala., Birmingham, 1970, registrar's asst., 1970-74, asst. dir. for registration, 1974—; cons. computer programming. Served with USAF, 1965-69, Calif. Army N.G., 1969-70. Mem. Ala. Assn. Collegiate Registrars and Admissions Officers, So. Assn. Collegiate Registrars and Admissions Officers. AME Zion Meth. Office: 1300 S 8 Ave Birmingham AL 35294

MCINTYRE, ROBERT ALLEN, JR., lighting co. exec.; b. Gettysburg, Pa., Jan. 6, 1940; s. Robert Allen and Leona Hazel (Stoner) McI.; student U. Portland, 1962-63, U. Md., 1963-64, York Coll., 1969-71, U. Wis., 1972-74, also numerous profl. courses; m. Rosemary Holland, Mar. 25, 1967; children—Nicole, Brian. Field salesman L.E. Smith, Inc., Gettysburg, 1958-61; with Black & Decker Mfg. Co., Hampstead, Md. and Beloit, Wis., 1965-75, engring. and service mgr., Beloit, 1974-75; with Dover Corp., Rochester, N.Y. and Beecher, Ill., 1975-78, v.p. engring. Bernard div., Beecher, 1977-78; v.p., gen. mgr. Marvel Lighting div. Am. Brands, Mullins, S.C., 1978, exec. v.p., 1979, pres., 1979—, also dir.; dir. Echelon Corp., Swingline, Inc. Served with USAF, 1961-65; Vietnam. Mem. S.C. C. of C., Florence C. of C., Marion C. of C. Office: 246 SE Front St Mullins SC 29574

MC INTYRE, WAYNE PAUL, insulation mfg. co. exec.; b. Niagara Falls, N.Y., Mar. 21, 1945; s. Eugene James and Alice Louise McI.; Asso. Sci. in Electronic Engring., Bluefield State Coll., 1965; m. Linda Whitt, July 2, 1965; 1 son, Christopher Wayne. Salesman, James McGraw Inc., Richmond, Va., 1965-69; research and devel. mgr. Waco Inc., Newport News, Va., 1969—. Pres. Quail Run Homes Assn., 1966-79. Mem. Am. Soc. Naval Engrs. (asso.). Republican. Roman Catholic. Home: 771 Childress Dr Newport News VA 23602 Office: Waco Inc 814 Chapman Way Newport News VA 23602

MC KANNAN, EUGENE CHARLES, gen. engr.; b. Phila., Apr. 16, 1928; s. Jesse Banks and Dorothy Mabel (Phillips) McK.; B.S., West Chester State Coll., 1949; M.S., U. Ala., Huntsville, 1968; m. Nancy Carolyn Allen, Nov. 23, 1952; children—David, Michael, Gina, Debbie, Jonathon. Test engr. E.I. DuPont Co., Wilmington, Del., 1952-61; with George C. Marshall Space Flight Center, Huntsville, 1961—, chief metallic materials div., 1969-77, project mgr. materials processing in space, 1977—; dir. Allen Mgmt. Corp., Arab, Ala., 1973—. Mem. Ednl. Task Force City of Huntsville, 1973-78. Served with U.S. Army, 1950-52. Recipient Exceptional Sci. Achievement medal NASA, 1972. Mem. Am. Inst. Physics, Am. Soc. Metals, Full Gospel Bus. Men's Fellowship Internat. (dir.). Charismatic Methodist. Author: (with Wainerdi) Analytical Chemistry in Space, 1969; contbr. articles to profl. jours. Home: 2512 Vista Dr Huntsville AL 35803 Office: Marshall Space Flight Center AL 35812

MC KAY, CHARLES FLINT, bus., trade cons.; b. St. Johnsbury, Vt., Nov. 18, 1930; s. Littleton Kirk and Mabel (Flint) McK.; B.B.A., U. Miami, 1954; m. Margaret Eileen Mund, June 14, 1956; children—Lisa Charlene, Sharon Lee. U.S. fgn. service officer Am. embassy, Quito, Ecuador, 1956-57, Am. consulate, Puerto la Cruz, Venezuela, 1957-59, Am. embassy, Uruguay, 1959-62; pres. chmn. bd. North & Latin Am. Devel. Corp., 1962—; pres., founder Charles McKay & Assos., Inc., Miami, Fla., 1964—. Mem. exec. res. U.S. Dept. Commerce, 1967, mem. dist. export council, 1974-75; mem. Regional Export Expansion Council, del. to nat. council conf., Washington, 1970, vice chmn. S. Fla. council, 1971, 72; mem. adv. council U. Miami (Fla.) Sch. Bus., 1974-75; mem. Fla. Metric Commn., 1980—; mem. task force Miami Dept. Trade and Devel., 1980—. Founding mem., bd. dirs. Nat. Fedn. Export Mgmt. Cos., 1972—; founding mem., bd. dirs. Internat. Center, Inc., 1972, pres., 1973, v.p., 1974-75; v.p. Internat. Center Fla. Inc., 1975; bd. dirs., treas. Fla. Council Internat. Devel., 1974-75, chmn., 1979-80, pres., 1979—. Bd. dirs. Bd. Internat. Trade, 1969—. Served to 1st lt. AUS, 1955-56. Mem. Dominican-Am. C. of C. (pres.) Fla. Colombia Alliance, Miami-Dade County C. of C. (bd. dirs.), C. of C. of Ams. (dir. 1970, 71, chmn. world trade com. 1972, pres., then v.p. 1974-75), Center for Advanced Internat. Studies (mem. council), Fla. World Trade Assn. (founder, pres. 1968—). Rotarian. Contbg. author: Guidelines to Operating in Latin America, 1970. Author: A Profile of International Business in Dade County, Florida, 1972; Caribbean Yachting Facilities, 1972; Exporter Profiles, 1973; Florida's World Trade Companies, 1974. Home: 7550 SW 141 St Miami FL 33158 Office: 2550 Douglas Rd Suite 306 Coral Gables FL 33134

MC KAY, GRIFFITH HEAD, cons. engr.; b. Jackson, Miss., Oct. 20, 1907; s. John Peyton and Alice Rose (Strait) McK.; B.S. in Civil Engring., Miss. State U., 1930, Jr. engr. Ark.-La. Gas Co., Shreveport, La., 1930-32, natural gas engr., 1932-42; cons. engr. WPB, Washington, 1942-43; asst. to v.p. Tenn. Gas Transmission Co., Houston, 1943-45, mgr. sales, 1945-47, v.p., 1947-48; v.p., dir. East Tenn. Natural Gas Co., Chattanooga, 1948-49; cons. engr., mgmt., gas, fuels, real estate leasing, rentals, financing, Houston, 1949—. Tchr. gas engring. Centenary Coll., 1939-41. Registered profl. engr., Tex. Mem. Nat., Tex. socs. profl. engrs., Houston Engring, and Sci. Soc. Democrat. Club: Houston. Contbr. articles to trade mags. Designer: (with R.M. Hutchins) Slide Rule-High Gas Transmission. Home: 5217 San Jacinto St Houston TX 77004 Office: 1215 Oakdale St Houston TX 77004

MC KAY, JOHN HARVEY, football coach; b. Everettsville, W.Va., July 5, 1923; s. John Andrew and Gertrude (Lavery) McK.; B.S., U. Oreg., 1950; m. Nancy Jean, June 19, 1950; children—Michele, John Kenneth, Theresa, Richard. Asst. football coach U. Oreg., Eugene, 1950-59; asst. football coach U. So. Calif., Los Angeles, 1959, head football coach, 1959-75, dir. athletics, 1972-75; v.p., head coach Tampa Bay Buccaneers, 1976—. Served with USAAF, 1941-45. Named Football Coach of Year, 1962, 72. Roman Catholic. Office: care Tampa Bay Buccaneers 1 Buccaneer Pl Tampa FL 33607

MC KAY, JOHN JUDSON, JR., lawyer; b. Anderson, S.C., Aug. 13, 1939; s. John Judson and Polly (Plowden) McK.; A.B., U. S.C., 1960, J.D. cum laude, 1966; m. Jill Hall Ryon, June 3, 1961; children—Julia Plowden, Katherine Henry, William Ryon, Elizabeth Hall. Admitted to S.C. bar, 1966; atty. Haynsworth, Perry, Bryant, Marion & Johnstone, Greenville, 1966-70; mem. firm Rainey, Fant & McKay, Greenville, 1970-75, Rainey, McKay, Britton, Gibbes & Clarkson, P.A., 1975-78; individual practice law, Hilton Head Island, S.C., 1978—. Served to lt. (j.g.) USNR, 1961-63; lt. comdr. Res., 1973. Mem. Am., S.C. (sec. young lawyers 1969, pres. 1971, mem. exec. com. 1972), Greenville County bar assns., S.C. Bar Found. (sec. 1975, v.p. 1976, pres. 1977), S.C. Def. Lawyers Assn., Blue Key, Phi Delta Phi, Chi Psi. Episcopalian. Clubs: Poinsett, Greenville Country, Sea Pines. Editor-in-chief S.C. Law Rev., 1965-66. Contbr. articles to profl. jours. Home: 55 Baynard Cove Rd Hilton Head Island SC 29928 Office: PO Box 5066 218 Sapelo Bldg Hilton Head SC 29928

MC KAY, LARRY M., probation services adminstr.; b. Dothan, Ala., Dec. 28, 1945; s. Calvin W., Jr. and Frances Bruce (Granberry) McK.; B.S., Troy (Ala.) State U., 1974, M.S., 1977, now postgrad.; 1 dau., Maggie. Counselor residential treatment center emotionally disturbed adolescents, Montgomery, Ala., 1974; social worker Ala. Dept. Pension and Security, 1974-75; juvenile probation officer Houston County, Dothan, 1975-77, dir. juvenile probation services, 1977—. Mem. Ala. adv. bd. Dept. Youth Services; bd. dirs. Girls Club. Served with USMC, 1966-70. Mem. Child Welfare League Am., Am. Personnel and Guidance Assn., Ala. Council Crime and Delinquency, Ala. Chief Probation Officers Assn., Ala. Juvenile Justice Assn., S.E. Ala. Youth Services Bur. (dir.). Home: 302B N Orange St Dothan AL 36301 Office: PO Box 7071 316 N Oates St Dothan AL 36302

MC KAY, LAWRENCE BRIAN, mktg. and mgmt. cons.; b. Bronx, N.Y., Feb. 19, 1924; s. William Leo and Lillian (Treacey) McK.; student N.Y. U., 1940-43; B.B.A., UCLA, 1949; m. Lola Merle Reagan, Mar. 10, 1948. Partner, Mktg. Innovations Co., Houston, 1979—, planning dir., 1979—. Mem. Republican Nat. Com., 1979—; mem. nat. adv. com. Am. Security Council, 1979—; mem. Nat. Rep.

Congl. Com., 1979—; mem. Gov.'s Com., Tex. Served with USAF, World War II; PTO. Mem. Am. Mktg. Assn., Am. Inventors Assn. Republican. Methodist. Clubs: Chantilly Nat. Golf and Country, Lake Neepaulin Beach, U.S. Senatorial. Patentee in field. Home and Office: 4141 N Braeswood St Houston TX 77025

MC KAY, SAMUEL LEROY, clergyman; b. nr. Charlotte, N.C., Oct. 15, 1913; s. Elmer Ranson and Arlena (Benfield) McK.; A.B. cum laude, Erskine Coll., 1937; B.D. cum laude, Erskine Theol. Sem., 1939; postgrad. U. Ga., 1941-42, Union Theol. Sem., 1957; m. Martha Elizabeth Caldwell, Apr. 29, 1939; children—Samuel LeRoy, Mary Louise, William Ranson. Ordained to ministry of Presbyn. Ch., 1940; pastor Prosperity Asso. Ref. Ch., Fayetteville, Tenn., 1942-46, Bethel Asso. Ref. Ch., Oak Hill, Ala., 1946-50, 1st Asso. Ref. Ch., Salisbury, N.C., 1950-53, 1st Ch. U.S., Dallas, N.C., 1953-60, First Ch., Kernersville, N.C., 1960-66, Cooleemee (N.C.) Presbyn. Ch., 1966-69, Broadway (N.C.) Presbyn. Ch., 1969—. Stated clk. Gen. Synod Asso. Ref. Presbyn. Ch., 1950-53; commr. Gen. Assembly Presbyn. Ch. U.S., 1960, 69; permanent clk. Winston-Salem Presbytery, 1961-69, chmn. leadership edn. com., 1962-66, chmn. Christian edn. com., 1967-68; chmn. nominations com. Fayetteville Presbytery, 1977-79; supr. chaplaincy program Davie County Hosp., 1968-69. Pres. Dallas PTA, 1955-56; bd. mgrs. Kernersville YMCA, 1962-66, chmn. membership com., 1963, treas., 1964, pres., 1965-66; bd. dirs. Winston-Salem-Forsyth County YMCA, 1965-66. Mem. Kernersville Area Ministers Assn. (pres. 1963-64), N.C. Poetry Soc. (dir. 1971—, chmn. poetry contests 1970-72, pres. 1972-74), Clan MacKay Soc. N.Am. (pres. 1971-75). Lion. Contbr. articles and sermons to periodicals and publs. Office: Broadway Presbyn Ch Main at Mcleod Broadway NC 27505

MC KAY, VICKI HIGGASON, educator; b. Haynesville, La., Dec. 29, 1948; d. Victor William and Elba Adis (Walker) Higgason; B.S. in Home Econs., Mary Hardin-Baylor Coll., 1970; tchr. cert. distributive edn. U. Houston, 1974, postgrad., 1976-77; m. Malcolm Stuart McKay, June 11, 1976. With Sanger Harris Dept. Store, Dallas, 1971-72; tchr. distributive edn. Lampasas (Tex.) High Sch., 1972-76, Channelview (Tex.) High Sch., 1977—. Bd. dirs. Capistrano Villas Homeowners Assn., 1977-79. Elected to Distributive Edn. Tchr. Hall of Fame, 1973. Mem. Nat. Assn. Distributive Edn. Tchrs., Am. Vocat. Assn., Tex. Vocat. Tchrs. Assn., Tex. Assn. Distributive Edn. Tchrs. (v.p. area V 1975-76), Nat. Assn. Distributive Edn. Clubs Am., Alumni, Tex. Assn. Distributive Edn. Alumni (life mem., dir. exec. sec., Outstanding Service award 1980). Baptist. Home: 927 Sterling Green South Dr Channelview TX 77530 Office: Channelview High Sch 828 Sheldon Rd Channelview TX 77530

MC KECHNIE, ROBERT MILTON, III, elec. engr.; b. Waco, Tex., Apr. 21, 1937; s. Robert Milton and Margaret Lorene (Frazier) McK.; B.S. in E.E., Tex. A. and M. U., 1959; M.S.E., George Washington U., 1963; postgrad. U. Ariz., 1975—; children—Robert Milton IV, James Garland, John Wesley. Elec. engr. U.S. Navy, Washington, 1959-62, U.S. Army, Ft. Belvoir Va., 1962-65; research scientist Adaptronics Inc., McLean, Va., 1965-68; elec. engr. U.S. Army, Ft. Belvoir, 1968—, group leader leader, 1971-77, devel. project officer Patriot Missile System Support Office, 1977—. Mem. football com. Fairfax Police Youth Club, 1972, athletic dir., 1973, v.p., 1974-75; mgr. Fairfax Little League Baseball, 1969-74, Fairfax Babe Ruth Baseball, 1973, 74. Served with U.S. Army, 1960. Recipient Sci. Achievement awards U.S. Army, 1964, 74. Mem. IEEE, Mil. Ops. Research Soc., Eta Kappa Nu. Methodist. Club: Optimist. Contbr. articles to profl. jours. Home: 3898 Bradwater St Fairfax VA 22030 Office: Army Mobility Equipment Research and Devel Command DRDME-EPAT Fort Belvoir VA 22060

MC KEE, ARTHUR, JR., treasure hunter, museum ofcl.; b. Bridgeton, N.J., Nov. 2, 1910; s. Arthur and Mabel A. (Chain) McK.; grad. Bridgeton High Sch., 1931; m. Janet Gay Bodden; children—Wayne Norris (dec.), Patricia D., Richard A., Arthur III, Terry (dec.), Karen T., Kevin D. Recreational dir., Bridgeton, 1935-36; city recreation dir., Homestead, Fla., 1940-50; deep sea Diver USN pipe line, Fla., 1941-43; organized McKee's Museum Sunken Treasure, Inc., Homestead, 1949; founder, operator McKee's Treasure Mus., Treasure Harbor, Plantation Key, Fla., 1950—; founder, operator divers' tng. sch. underwater archaeology, Treasure Harbor, 1960—; marine archaeologist State of Fla., 1952-62; condr. 32 expdns., Bahamas, Fla. Keys, Caribbean, including McKee-Smithsonian Instn. expdn. to recover treasure from Spanish ship wrecked 1733; excavated Sunken City Port Royal with Link expdn., Kingston Harbor; guest appearances numerous TV shows, Of Land and Seas, To Tell the Truth, Danger is My Business, Mike Douglas Show, others, Named Mr. Treasure Hunter Am. Treasure Trove Club, N.Y.C., 1966, Pioneer in Underwater Archaeology in Western Hemisphere Nat. Geog. Soc., 1973-74. Mem. Islamorada (pres. 1967-68), Upper Keys Fla. (dir. 1973-76, pres. 1977-78) chambers commerce. Elk. Clubs: Ocho Rios Reef (Jamaica); Caribbean Yacht (Grand Cayman). Patentee underwater motion picture camera, underwater metal detector, system excavating wreck sites, others. Recoveries include gold, silver, doubloons, Spanish Coins and artifacts. Home: Treasure Harbor Plantation Key FL 33070

MC KEE, DAVID ELIJAH, mfg. co. exec.; b. Seneca, S.C., Apr. 1, 1928; s. Walter Watson and Floride (Stone) McK.; student RCA Insts., 1956-58; m. Carolyn Lois Freiwald, Aug. 12, 1951; children—Bonnie, David Elijah, Kevin. Served with USN, 1946-50, trans. to USCG, 1950; master chief petty officer U.S. Coast Guard Air Sta., Miami, Fla., 1966-68; ret., 1968; electronic test supr. Sangamo Electric Co., West Union, S.C., 1969-74, design engr. trainee, 1974-75; customer engr. AccuRay Corp., Mobile, Ala., 1975—. Mem. RCA Alumni Assn. Baptist. Home: 130 Ottoway Dr Temple TX 76501 Office: AccuRay Corp First So Fed Tower Suite 702 Mobile AL 36606

MC KEE, JAMES ROBERT, constrn. co. exec.; b. Keokuk, Iowa, Mar. 29, 1939; s. Thomas L. and Mary (Lynch) McK.; B.S. in Civil Engring., Ga. Inst. Tech., 1961; m. Susan Mikell Lovett, Feb. 4, 1966; children—David M., Nancy L. Project mgr. Holder Constrn., Atlanta, 1961-64; project mgr. Caldwell-Scott Engring. & Constrn., Fort Lauderdale, Fla., 1964-66; pres. Creswell-McKee, Inc., Fort Lauderdale, 1966-76; pres. McKee Constrn. Co., Fort Lauderdale, 1977—. Served with USCGR, 1961-62. Mem. Broward Builders Assn., Am. Assn. Gen. Contractors, Beta Theta Phi. Episcopalian. Club: Lauderdale Yacht. Home: 2808 NE 25th Ct Fort Lauderdale FL 33305 Office: 2701 E Sunrise Blvd Fort Lauderdale FL 33304

MC KEE, MARLENE SUE, psychol. service dir.; b. Houston, May 31, 1936; d. Ed Tyndale and Daisy Mae (Bishop) McKee; B.A., Tenn. Temple Coll., 1958; M.Ed., U. Houston, 1970; postgrad. Houston Bapt. U., 1973-75, Baylor Coll. Medicine, 1975-76. Elementary tchr. Blvd. Christian Sch., Pensacola, Fla., 1958-61; adminstr. Tenn. Temple Coll., Chattanooga, 1961-63; tchr. Fairyland Elementary Sch., Walker County, Ga., 1963-64; elementary tchr. Keswick Christian Sch., St. Petersburg, Fla., 1964-68; disseminator psychol. services Harris County Dept. Edn., Houston, 1968-70, psychol. asso., 1970-72, coordinator, 1972-73, dir., 1973—; cons. Summer Inst. Linguistics, Mexico, U.S., 1971—; guest lectr. Lamar U., U. Houston, U. Oklahoma, Norman; condr. workshops at schs. and psychol. assns.; local chpt. pres. Council Exceptional Children, 1978-79. Certified tchr., asso. sch. psychologist, psychol. asso., Tex. Office: 6515 Irvington Blvd Houston TX 77022

MC KEE, MELINDA FRY, educator; b. Austin, Tex., Oct. 30, 1942; d. Judson Gordon and Ruth (Small) Fry Adkins; B.A., Trinity U., 1964; postgrad. Tex. Woman's U., 1966-71, Tarleton State U., 1979; m. June 1966 (div. 1972); 1 dau., Dorothy Elizabeth. Tchr., vocat. counselor for deaf Ft. Worth Public Schs., 1966-67, 69-71, Houston Public Schs., 1968-69; counselor with deaf Tex. Rehab. Commn., Ft. Worth, 1971-78; coordinator deaf student services Tex. State Tech. Inst., Waco, 1978—; cons.; co-chmn. Miss Deaf Tex. Pageant, 1976; pres. Tarrant County Services for the Hearing Impaired, 1971-72. Recipient Disting. Service award Miss Deaf Tex. Pageant, 1977; Outstanding Service award Ft. Worth Silent Club, Inc., 1975; comprehensive skills cert. Nat. Registry Interpreters for Deaf, 1975; deaf edn. tchr. cert., Tex.; high sch. tchr. cert. in Spanish and drama; nat. rehab. counselor cert. Mem. Am. Deafness and Rehab. Assn., Nat. Assn. of Deaf, Tex. Soc. Interpreters for the Deaf (Outstanding Service award, ethics com. 1979-80, pres. 1975-77), Tex. Assn. of Deaf, Conv. Am. Instrs. of Deaf, Conf. Execs. Am. Schs. for Deaf, Central Tex. Council for Deaf. Editor HINTS, 1975, 76. Home: 7008 Country Club Dr Waco TX 76710 Office: Deaf Student Services Tex State Tech Waco TX 76705

MC KEE, MICHAEL DOUGLAS, assn. exec.; b. Oklahoma City, May 28, 1948; s. William Foster and Margie Laverne (Brown) McK.; B.A., Central State U., Edmond, Okla., 1970; m. Janice Marie Thompson, Jan. 25, 1969; children—Michael Jacob, Elizabeth Christin. Program dir. North County br. YMCA Greater St. Louis, 1971-72, program services dir. Kirkwood br., 1972-75, exec. dir. St. Charles County br., 1975-79; pres. Nat. Exec. Search-Okla., Tulsa, 1979—. Served with USAFR, 1969-76. Mem. Assn. YMCA Profl. Dirs. Democrat. Methodist. Home: 7364 S Darlington Tulsa OK 74136 Office: 7060 S Yale Suite 903 Tulsa OK 74177

MCKEE, RICHARD RAY, educator; b. Cin., Nov. 25, 1948; s. Jesse C. and Stella F. (Fryman) M.; B.B.A. in Mgmt., U. Cin., 1972; M.Ed. in Counseling, Xavier U., 1976; m. Trudy A. Eakle, Feb. 24, 1978. Tchr. math. Diocese of Covington (Ky.), 1972-74; tchr. Holmes High Sch., Covington, 1975-78; guidance counselor No. Ky. State Vocat. Tech. Sch., Covington, 1978—. Rep., Ky. Young Democrats Conv. Mem. Nat. Rehab. Assn., Am. Personnel and Guidance Assn., Ky. Personnel and Guidance Assn. (Service award 1979), Ky. Vocat. Guidance Assn., No. Ky. Personnel and Guidance Assn. Presbyterian. Home: 220 Wallace Ave Covington KY 41014 Office: No Ky State Vocational Tech Sch Amsterdam Rd Covington KY 41011

MC KEE, THOMAS LAPSLEY, physician; b. Revere, Mo., Nov. 17, 1902; s. Robert Cleaver and Mary Elizabeth (Lapsley) McK.; student U. Mo., 1919-22, Columbia U., 1923; M.D., State U. Iowa, 1928; m. Mary Lynch, Mar. 16, 1931; children—Alice, James Robert. Intern, St. Lukes Hosp., Chgo., 1928-29; resident Bklyn. Eye and Ear Hosp., 1930-31; pvt. practice medicine, specializing in ophthalmology, Keokuk, Iowa, 1932-41, Ft. Lauderdale, Fla., 1946—; mem. staff Broward Gen. Med. Center, Ft. Lauderdale, 1946—. Served to lt. col., M.C., AUS, PTO. Diplomate Am. Bd. Ophthalmology. Mem. Am. Acad. Ophthalmology and Oto-Laryngology, AMA. Clubs: Masons; Rotary Internat. Contbr. articles to med. jours. Home: 1328 Seminole Dr Fort Lauderdale FL 33304 Office: 918 NE 26th Ave Fort Lauderdale FL 33304

MC KEE, WILLIS PAYNE, JR., surgeon; b. Louisville, Apr. 9, 1939; s. Willis Payne and Mary Evelyn (Miller) McK.; A.B., Centre Coll. of Ky., 1959; M.D., U. Louisville, 1963; m. Mary Ann Wallace Nuttall, Aug. 25, 1960; children—Mary Porter, Willis Payne III. Intern, Ireland Army Hosp., Ft. Knox, Ky., 1963-64; resident surgery Brooke Gen. Hosp., Ft. Sam Houston, Tex., 1964-69; chief surgery 3d Field Hosp., AUS, Saigon, Viet Nam, 1969-70, chief surgery Kenner Army Hosp., Ft. Lee, Va., 1970-71; surgeon Kings Daus. Meml. Hosp., Frankfort, Ky.; pres. Capital Cardiopulmonary Assos., Frankfort, 1974—. Chmn., Franklin County (Ky.) Cancer Soc. crusade, 1974-79. Served to maj. AUS, 1963-71. Decorated Soldiers medal, Bronze Star. Mem. Am., Ky. med. assns., Franklin County Med. Soc. (pres. 1974), A.C.S., Am. Trauma Soc., Ky. Surg. Soc., Société Chirurgical Indochinoise, Phi Delta Theta. Democrat. Episcopalian. Mem. bd. editorial consultants Ky. Med. Assn. Jour., 1975-76. Home: 301 Paul Sawyier Dr Frankfort KY 40601 Office: One Physicians Park Dr Frankfort KY 40601

MC KEEL, CAROLE MEWBORN, educator; b. Goldsboro, N.C., Dec. 19, 1943; d. Ervin Chester and Evelyn Christine (Mozingo) Mewborn; B.S., E. Carolina Coll., 1966; M.Ed., E. Carolina U., 1967; m. Ronald Dow McKeel, Aug. 11, 1974. Tchr., Operation Headstart, Goldsboro, N.C., 1966; instr. phys. edn. Atlantic Christian Coll., Wilson, N.C., 1967-70, asst. prof., coordinator women's athletics, 1970—. Active Spl. Olympics, 4-H. Mem. N.C. Assn. Health, Phys. Edn. and Recreation, N.C. Assn. Intercollegiate Athletics for Women Coaches Assn. (medalist sports adv. bd.). Baptist. Home: Route 4 Box 370-A Wilson NC 27893 Office: Lee St Wilson NC 27893

MC KENDREE, BISHOP DAVIS, petroleum engr.; b. Vega, Tex., Dec. 28, 1919; s. John William and Ellen Tomas (Davis) Mc K.; student West Tex. State Coll., 1947-49; B.S. in Petroleum Engring., U. Tex., 1952; m. Beverly Jean Biery, June 7, 1952; children—Alan Davis, Jean Ellen, Edith Ann. Engring. trainee Gulf Oil Co., Odessa, Tex., 1952-53, petroleum prodn. engr., Andrews, Tex., 1953-60, Buras, La., 1961; engr. Cook Testing and Nitrogen Service Co., Odessa, 1961-62; petroleum engr. oil and gas div. Railroad Commn. of Tex., Austin, 1962—. Served with AUS, 1941-46. Decorated Silver Star, Purple Heart. Mem. Soc. Petroleum Engrs. of Am. Inst. Mining Engrs. Methodist. Home: 4808 W Frances Pl Austin TX 78731 Office: Railroad Commn of Texas Box 12967 Capitol Sta Austin TX 78711

MC KENNA, JOHN DENNIS, pollution cons. co. exec.; b. N.Y.C., Apr. 1, 1940; s. Hubert Guy and Elizabeth Ann (Record) McK.; B.S. in Chem. Engring., Manhattan Coll., 1961; M.S., Newark Coll., 1968; M.B.A., Rider Coll., 1975; m. Christel Klages, Dec. 26, 1964; children—Marc, Michelle. Tech. asst. to pres. Eldib Engring. & Research, Newark, 1964-67; program mgr. Princeton (N.J.) Chem. Research, Inc., 1967-68; projects dir. Cottrell Environ. Systems, Bound Brook, N.J., 1968-72; v.p. Enviro-Systems & Research, Inc., Roanoke, Va., 1973-77, pres., 1978-79; pres. Environ. Testing Services Inc., Roanoke, 1979—. Mem. Am. Inst. Chem. Engrs., Air Pollution Control Assn. Roman Catholic. Contbr. articles to profl. jours. Home: 4118 Chaparral Dr SW Roanoke VA 24018 Office: Environmental Testing Services Inc 3140 Chaparral Dr SW Suite C-103 Roanoke VA 24018

MC KENNA, THOMAS ADAM, JR., analytical chemist; b. Natchez, Miss., Mar. 14, 1922; s. Thomas Adam and Blanche (Korndorffer) McK.; student Copiah-Lincoln Jr. Coll., 1938-39; B.S. in Chemistry, La. State U., 1944; student U. Miss., 1955, Podbielniak Inst., 1956; m. Peggy Marie McCrosky, June 2, 1949; children—Mary Lucille, Thomas Adam III, Michael Gerard, Patrick Joseph. With Motor Fuels Lab., Dept. Revenue, State La.; with Firestone Tire & Rubber Co., Orange, Tex., 1944—, successively shift control chemist, spl. problems chemist, lab. mgr. and chief chemist, 1956—; owner, dir. work Marian Labs., Lake Charles, La., 1955—; lectr. Lamar Coll. Tech., 1963. Mem. dist. advancement com. Boy Scouts Am.; pres. St. Mary's Home and Sch. Assn., 1963-64; mem. council St. Mary's Parish, 1979-80; active Community Concert Assn. Fellow Am. Inst. Chemists; mem. Gulf Coast Spectroscopic Group (chmn.), Am. Soc. Quality Control (area dir. S. Tex. sect. 1959—, chmn. membership com. Sabine subsect., sr. mem.), Am. Chem. Soc. (chmn. S.W. La. 1954—, sec. Tex.-La.-Gulf sect. 1961-62), ASTM (com. chmn.), AAAS, C. of C., Alpha Tau Omega. K.C. Editor: The Newletter, 1949-54. Author numerous articles in profl. jours.; also papers. Home: 312 W Pine St Orange TX 77631 Office: PO Box 1269 Orange TX 77631

MC KENNY, JERE WESLEY, geol. engr.; b. Okmulgee, Okla., Feb. 14, 1929; s. Jere Claus and Juanita (Hunter) McK.; B.S. in Geol. Engring., U. Okla., 1951, M.S., 1952; m. Anne Ross Stewart, May 4, 1957; children—Jere James, Robert Stewart. With Kerr-McGee Corp., 1953—, supt. domestic oil and gas exploration, 1965-68, mgr. oil and gas exploration, 1968-69, v.p. oil and gas, 1969-74, v.p. exploration, 1974-77, vice chmn. bd., 1977—. Mem. alumni adv. council Sch. of Geology and Geophysics U. Okla. Served with U.S. Army, 1953-55. Mem. Am. Assn. Petroleum Geologists, Am. Petroleum Inst. (dir.), Houston Geol. Soc., Oklahoma City Geol. Soc., Sigma Xi, Sigma Gamma Epsilon. Episcopalian. Clubs: Oklahoma City Golf and Country, Whitehall. Office: 123 Robert S Kerr Ave Oklahoma City OK 73125

MC KENZIE, DONALD WILLIAM, ins. co. exec.; b. Catlettsburg, Ky., July 5, 1938; s. James Kenneth and Ruth (Conley) McK.; B.S., U. Ky., 1960. Claim rep. Aetna Life & Casualty, Charlotte, N.C., 1962-65, regional claim supr., Winston-Salem, 1965-69, adminstrv. rep., Hartford, Conn., 1969-71, claim mgr., Des Moines, 1971-74, Dallas, 1974—; instr. ins. Tarrant County Jr. Coll., Ft. Worth, Tex., 1974—. Served to 1st lt., Intelligence Corps, U.S. Army, 1960-62. C.P.C.U., 1973. Mem. Dallas-Ft. Worth Claim Mgrs. Council (pres. 1979—), Tex. Med. Assn. (ins. rep. 1974—). Home: 9901 Smokefeather St Dallas TX 75243 Office: 9229 LBJ Freeway Dallas TX 75243

MC KENZIE, FRANK CHRISTOPHER, educator; b. Madisonville, Tenn., Jan. 13, 1944; s. Donald Penland and William Kate (Best) McK.; A.A., Hiwassee Coll., 1965; B.S., U. Tenn., Knoxville, 1967, M.S., 1971, Ed.D. (Edn. Profl. Devel. Act grantee), 1977; m. Carol Lee Klapser, Mar. 18, 1967; children—Elizabeth, Jennifer. Tchr., Coper Basin (Tenn.) High Sch., 1967-69; dean of students Hiwassee Coll., Madisonville, 1972-73; asst. prof. Cleveland (Tenn.) State Community Coll., 1976—, head bus. careers dept., 1978—; affiliate broker Centry 21 Sloan Realty, Madisonville. Mem. Nat. Bus. Edn. Assn., So. Bus. Edn. Assn., Tenn. Bus. Edn. Assn., Nat. Assn. Realtors, Tenn. Assn. Realtors, Monroe County Realtors, Delta Pi Epsilon, Phi Theta Kappa, Phi Kappa Phi. Home: Route 3 Madisonville TN 37311 Office: Cleveland State Community Coll Box 1205 Cleveland TN 37311

MCKENZIE, JOHN LAWRENCE, III, chemist; b. Nashville, Oct. 26, 1942; s. John Lawrence and Idabel (Mitchell) McK.; B.S., U. Tenn., 1965; M.S., U. N.C., Greensboro, 1971; m. Rebecca Kemp, Mar. 17, 1965; children—Preston, John, Parish. Chemist, R.J. Reynolds Co., Winston-Salem, N.C., 1967-74, group leader, 1974-76, sect. head, 1976—. Served with AUS, 1965-67. Mem. Am. Chem. Soc., Soc. Research Adminstrs., Sigma Xi. Democrat. Episcopalian. Home: 2815 Old Salisbury Rd Winston-Salem NC 27107 Office: RJ Reynolds Tobacco Co Winston-Salem NC 27107

MC KENZIE, MALCOLM LEDBETTER, mfg. co. exec.; b. Cordova, N.C., July 8, 1925; s. Frank Ledbetter and Annie Janette (Reynolds) McK.; B.S. in Engring., N.C. State U., 1950; m. Betty Jeanne Bozeman, Apr. 19, 1952; children—Malcolm David, Catherine Inglis. Application engr. Grinnel Corp., Charlotte, N.C., 1950-51; with Pneumafil Corp., Charlotte, 1951—, dir. engring., 1966-67, dir. mfg., 1967-74, v.p., gen. mgr., 1974—; mem. engring. adv. council U. N.C., Charlotte. Active Boy Scouts Am., United Way, YWCA. Served with USAAF, 1943-45. Decorated Air medal. Mem. Am. Forestry Assn., Woodworking Machine Mfg. Assn., Grain Elevator and Processing Soc., Assn. Operative Millers, Theta Tau. Baptist. Contbr. articles to trade jours.; patentee in field. Office: PO Box 16348 Charlotte NC 28216

MCKENZIE, PHYLLIS DIANN, speech and lang. pathologist; b. Quitman, Miss., June 23, 1953; d. Ray B. and Elizabeth A. (McKenney) McK.; B.S., Miss. U. for Women, 1974, M.S., 1976. Clin. affiliate Univ. Med. Center, Jackson, Miss., 1976: speech and lang. pathologist Oxford (Miss.) City Schs., 1976-78; speech and lang. pathologist Miss. State Dept. Edn., Miss. Lang. Resource System, Jackson, 1978-79; speech and lang. pathologist Water Valley Consol. Schs., 1979—. Mem. Am. Speech, Lang. and Hearing Assn. (cert. clin. competence), Miss. Speech and Hearing Assn. Home: Route 1 Box 370 Water Valley MS 38965 Office: PO Box 608 Water Valley MS 38965

MC KEON, THOMAS LEWIS, univ. dean; b. Yonkers, N.Y., Nov. 14, 1944; s. Thomas Henry and Jane (LaFaye) McK.; B.A., St. Bonaventure U., Olean, N.Y., 1966; M.Ed., U. Va., 1970, Ed.D., 1976; m. Judith O'Grady, June 22, 1968; children—Sarah Linehan, Kathleen Lewis. Mem. staff and faculty U. Va., 1970-77, 79—, asst. dean program devel., div. continuing edn., 1979—; adminstr. Central Va. Consortium Continuing Higher Edn., 1974-75; asso. commr. Va. Employment Commn., 1977-79; mem. Gov. Va. Manpower Services Council, 1977-79, Va. Adv. Com. Community Service and Continuing Edn., 1978—. Served with U.S. Army, 1966-69. Recipient Disting. Service award Ga. Va. Manpower Services Council, 1979. Mem. Am. Soc. Public Adminstrn., Am. Soc. Tng. and Devel., Nat. U. Extension Assn., Kappa Delta Pi, Phi Delta Kappa. Episcopalian. Office: 104 Midmont Ln Charlottesville VA 22903

MC KEOUGH, PAUL KENNETH, JR., hosp. adminstr.; b. Portland, Maine, Dec. 29, 1940; s. Paul Kenneth and Helena Frances (Carleton) McK.; B.A., Boston Coll., 1966, M.A., 1969; M.S., Trinity U., 1977; m. Mary Ruth Gilbert, June 13, 1970; 1 son, Duncan Matthew. Adminstrv. resident Our Lady of the Lake Hosp., Baton Rouge, La., 1976-77, adminstrv. asst., 1977-78, dir. supportive services, 1979; asst. adminstr., dir. gen. services Warner Brown Hosp., El Dorado, Ark., 1979—. Commr., Union County council Boy Scouts Am., 1978-79. Served to maj., M.S.C., U.S. Army, 1966-74. Mem. Am. Coll. Hosp. Adminstrs., Am. Hosp. Assn., Ark. Hosp. Assn., Hosp. Fin. Mgmt. Assn., La. Hospice Fedn., Ark. Shared Purchasing Assn., Am. Mgmt. Assn. Office: 460 W Oak St El Dorado AR 71730

MCKEOWN, JOYCE TAPP, nurse; b. Uniontown, Ky., Nov. 8, 1934; d. Jesse and Laura Dell (Duncan) Tapp; student Greenville (Ky.) Sch. Practical Nursing, 1966-67; A.S., Central Fla. Community Coll., 1974, postgrad., 1975; postgrad. Tampa Gen. Hosp., 1974; children—Harold Clay, II, Curtis Dale, Gracie Marie, Marcia Faye McKeown Buck. Staff nurse Muhlenberg Community Hosp., Greenville, 1967-70, charge nurse Medic Home Health Center, Inverness, Fla., 1970-73; cardiac care charge nurse Marion

Community Hosp., Ocala, Fla., 1974—. Active, CD, 1974—, Fire Rescue, 1974—. Recipient Achievement award Central Fla. Community Coll., 1974. Mem. Am. Nurses Assn., Am. Assn. Critical Care Nurses, Nat. Critical Care Inst. Edn. Republican. Baptist. Home: Rural Route 3 Box 350 Crystal River FL 32639 Office: Marion Community Hosp Ocala FL 32670

MC KERROW, GEORGE WALTER, JR., restaurant exec.; b. Waukesha, Wis., Oct. 13, 1950; s. George Walter and Joann E. McK.; B.A., Ohio State U., 1973; m. Judith Naomi Taylor, May 27, 1973; 1 dau., Ambriel. Owner restaurant, 1973-75; asst. mgr. Victoria Sta., Cin., 1975, gen. mgr., Atlanta, 1975—; gen. mgr. Quinn's Mill, 1976-79, regional mgr. S.E., 1979—. Mem. Hotel Assn., Atlanta C. of C. Republican. Presbyterian. Home: 5686 DeKalb Ln Norcross GA 30093 Office: 3300 Northlake Pkwy Atlanta GA 30345

MC KEY, DELORES DAVIS, coop. exec.; b. Baton Rouge, June 23, 1941; d. Ike N. and Wilma B. (Miller) Davis; student Baton Rouge Vocat. Tech. Sch., 1959; m. Fred A. McKey, Jr., Dec. 21, 1962; children—Emmett Lea, Don Allen. Bookkeeper, Turner Tire Co., Baton Rouge, 1960-64; with Tri Parish Coop., Slaughter, La., 1969—, office mgr., credit mgr., 1976—. Mem. Am. Soc. Women Accountants. Baptist. Home: PO Box 204 Slaughter LA 70777 Office: PO Box 38 Slaughter LA 70777

MC KINLEY, JAMES DANIEL, pharmacist; b. DeQueen, Ark., Jan. 5, 1924; s. James Daniel and Addie Jane (Wood) McK.; A.A., San Angelo Coll., 1943; B.S. with high honors in Pharmacy, U. Tex., Austin, 1948; M.S., U. Md., 1950; m. Patricia Tegart, June 18, 1949; children—Karen Ann, David James, Craig Daniel. Pharmacist, U. Tex. System Cancer Center, M.D. Anderson Hosp. and Tumor Inst., Houston, 1950-57, chief pharmacist, 1957-69, chief pharmacy services, 1969-78, asst. to dir. pharmacy, 1978—; adj. asst. prof. clin. pharmacy U. Tex., U. Houston, Tex. So. U.; chmn. bd. dirs. Unitex Credit Union; mem. Charles Pfizer Nat. Hosp. Pharmacy Adv. Com.; mem. adv. council Pharm. Found. U. Tex.; vis. lectr. hosp. pharmacy U. Tex.; lectr. hosp. pharmacy U. Houston. Pres. Freeway-Pine Valley Civic Club, 1955; mem. Mayor's Adv. Com. Houston's Future, 1956; bd. dirs. Meml. Glen Property Owners Assn., 1964. Served as staff sgt. ordnance, AUS, 1943-46; PTO. Registered pharmacist, Tex., Md.; charter diplomate Am. Bd. Diplomates in Pharmacy. Mem. Am. Pharm. Assn., Am. Soc. Hosp. Pharmacists (exec. com. 1955-56), Tex. Soc. Hosp. Pharmacists (pres. 1958), Houston-Galveston Soc. Hosp. Pharmacists (pres. 1954-55), Rho Chi. Republican. Methodist. Contbr. articles to profl. jours. Home: 14662 G Perthshire Rd Houston TX 77079 Office: M D Anderson Hospital Texas Medical Center Houston TX 77030

MC KINLEY, JIMMIE JOE, business exec.; b. Bertram, Tex., July 23, 1934; s. Joseph Crofford and Velma Anne (Barnett) McK.; B.J. cum laude, U. Tex., 1955; M.S., U. Ky., 1964. Asst. librarian Bethel Coll., McKenzie, Tenn., 1961-63, reference librarian, 1966-70, acting head librarian, 1970-71; owner, mgr. Longview Book Co. (Tex.), 1974—. Bd. dirs. Longview-Piney Woods chpt. ARC; trustee Bethel Coll., 1977—. Mem. ALA, Sigma Delta Chi. Presbyn. Home: PO Box 2106 Longview TX 75606

MC KINNEY, BENJAMIN CALVIN, ret. educator, dentist; b. Ft. Worth, Mar. 18, 1914; s. James Lanehart and Elsie Marie (Dyer) McK.; LL.B., U. Tex. at Austin, 1936; B.S., U. Houston, 1952; D.D.S., U. Tex. at Houston, 1952; m. Kathryn DuRant, Mar. 16, 1941. Admitted to Tex. bar, 1936; practiced law, Dallas, 1936-39; mng. partner Navaway Theater, Houston, 1939-42; mgr. partner O.S.T. Theatre, Houston, 1946-52; adminstrv. asst. U. Tex. Dental Branch, Houston, 1952-53, asst. dean, 1953-65, asso. dean 1965-72, 74-76, acting dean, 1972-74, asso. prof. preventive dentistry, 1956-64, prof., 1964-76, mem. gen. faculty Grad. Sch. Biomed. Scis., 1968-71; hon. prof. Nat. Autonomous U. Mexico Dental Sch., Mexico City, 1972. Mem. Tex. Bar Assn., Delta Chi, Delta Sigma Delta, Omicron Kappa Upsilon. Home: 3410 Hampshire Pearland TX 77581

MC KINNEY, BILLY JACK, chem. engr.; b. Floydada, Tex., Dec. 16, 1938; s. Jack A. and Benja (Johnston) McK.; B.S. in Chem. Engring., Tex. Tech. U., Lubbock, 1961; M.S. in Engring. Adminstrn., U. Tenn., 1976; m. Karen Opal Neyland, Feb. 11, 1961; children—Kim Kayon, Heather Colleen. Engr., E. I. du Pont de Nemours & Co., Inc., 1961-62, 65-68, tech. mktg. rep., Wilmington, Del., 1969-72, sr. process engr., Chattanooga, 1972-78, sr. research engr., 1978—. Pres. Hixson (Tenn.) Elementary Sch. PTA, 1976-77; pres. workshop bd. Chattanooga Dance Theatre Workshop, 1977-80; pres. North Shore Forest Civic Assn., 1979—. Served with USNR, 1961-65. Registered profl. engr., Tenn. Mem. Am. Inst. Chem. Engrs. Republican. Methodist. Clubs: Chattanooga Engrs., Torch, Thursday Thirty Toastmasters (pres. 1976, gov. Dist. 63, 1977-78). Home: 108 Gilmore Ln Hixson TN 37343 Office: 4501 Access Rd Chattanooga TN 37415

MC KINNEY, JAMES CARROLL, ednl. adminstr.; b. Minden, La., Jan. 11, 1921; s. William and Carolyn (Hilman) McK.; student La. Polytech. Inst., 1938-40, Stanford U., 1943-44; B.Mus., La. State U., 1949, Mus.M., 1950; D.M.A., U. So. Calif., 1969; m. Elizabeth Richmond, Aug. 28, 1949; children—James Carroll, Timothy Richmond, John Kevin. Asst. prof. music theory Southwestern Bapt. Theol. Sem., Fort Worth, 1950-54, chmn. dept. theory, 1954-56, dean Sch. Ch. Music, 1956—; vis. prof. U. So. Calif., Los Angeles, 1958, Hong Kong Bapt. Sem., 1971-72; baritone soloist 1st Presbyn. Ch., Hollywood, Calif., 1957-58, 1st Meth. Ch., Fort Worth, 1963-67; solo recitals Bangkok, Thailand, Hong Kong, 1971-72. Bd. dirs. Van Cliburn Internat. Piano Competition, 1962—, Fort Worth Symphony Orch. Assn., 1961-71, Fort Worth Civic Music Assn., 1960-72. Served with U.S. Army, 1941-45. Mem. Am. Choral Dirs. Assn., Nat. Assn. Tchrs. Singing (lt. gov. N. Tex. 1968-72), Music Educators Nat. Conf., Music Tchrs. Nat. Assn., So. Bapt. Ch. Music Conf. (pres. 1977-79), Tex. Assn. Music Schs. (past v.p., past bd. dirs.), Phi Mu Alpha Sinfonia, Phi Kappa Phi, Omicron Delta Kappa, Pi Kappa Lambda. Author: The Beginning Music Reader, 1958; The Progressing Music Reader, 1959; You Can Read Music, 1960; The Advanced Music Reader, 1961; Mastering Music Reading, 1964; Study Guide for Fundamentals of Music, 1964; Vocal Fundamentals Kit, 1976; Vocal Development Kit, 1977. Home: 5604 Wedgmont Circle Fort Worth TX 76133 Office: PO Box 22000-4D Fort Worth TX 76122

MC KINNEY, JAMES DAVID, chemist; b. Gainesville, Ga., Dec. 28, 1941; s. William Boyd and Dorothy Mae (Ferguson) McK.; B.S., U. Ga., 1963, Ph.D. (NIH scholar), 1968; m. Peggy Jean Jones, June 6, 1970; children—Alan, Joseph, Kristen. Pub. health scientist, pesticide toxicology lab. FDA, Atlanta, 1967-69; research scientist, head chemistry sect., environ. biology and chemistry br. Nat. Inst. Environ. Health Scis., Research Triangle Park, N.C., 1969-78, chief environ. chemistry br., 1978-79, chief Lab. Environ. Chemistry, 1979—. Served with USPHS, 1967-69. Mem. Am. Chem. Soc., Am. Inst. Chemists, N.Y. Acad. Scis. Mem. editorial bds., contbr. articles to profl. jours. Home: 7025 Robbie Dr Raleigh NC 27607 Office: Lab Environ Chemistry PO Box 12233 Research Triangle Park NC 27709

MC KINNEY, JARMON CLAYTON, JR., metrology engr.; b. Hawkinsville, Ga., Dec. 27, 1920; s. Jarmon Clayton and Fronie Belle (Cofer) Mc K.; B. in Indsl. engring., Ga. Inst. Tech., 1950; m. Mary Ruth Siegfried, Mar. 11, 1944; children—Philip Michael, William Jarmon, Raymond Allan. Indsl. engr. U.S. Pipe and Foundry Co., Birmingham, 1949-52; production supr. Anderson Elect. Co., Birmingham, 1952-53; chief procurement planning, engr. sec. Birmingham Ordnance Dist., 1953-56; staff engr. Ballistic Missiles U.S. Army Ballistic Missile Agency, Redstone Arsenal, Ala., 1956-58; dep. chief plans div. U.S. Army, Ordnance Missile Commd., 1958-61, chief guided missile br., 1961-62; dep. chief, tech. ops. office Army Missile Support Command, 1962-63, asst. tech. missions, 1963-68; chief Army Standards Lab. U.S. Army Metrology and Calibration Center, Redstone Arsenal, Ala., 1968—; Army mem. Standards Lab. spl. study group Dept. Def., 1978-79; bd. dirs. Nat. Conf. Standards Labs., 1976-80. Coach Little League Baseball, YMCA Basketball; pres. Whitesburg Sch. PTA, Huntsville, Ala., 1960; mem. Huntsville Planning Commn., 1966-67; pres. Huntsville Bd. Edn., 1967-68. Served with USAAF, 1943-45. Decorated Air medal with 5 Oak Leaf clusters. Mem. Assn. U.S. Army, Am. Def. Preparedness Assn., Nat. Conf. Standards Labs., Am. Inst. Indsl. Engrs. Democrat. Baptist. Home: 115 Cole Dr SE Huntsville AL 35802 Office: U S Army Standards Laboratory Redstone Arsenal AL 35809

MC KINNEY, LEONARD LAURENCE, chemist, former govt. ofcl.; b. Siloam Springs, Ark., May 28, 1908; s. Claude Pascal and Maude S. (Leonard) McK.; B.S., U. Ark., 1931; M.S., Bradley U., 1950; m. Alice Ann Rodkey, Aug. 9, 1941; children—Heather Ellen, Carl Stuart, Neil Curtis. Chemist, Tex. Co., 1931-34; insp. FDA, 1935-37; with USDA, 1937—, asst. dir. No. Regional Research Lab., Agrl. Research Ser., USDA, Peoria, Ill., 1958-68, asst. dir. Russel Research Lab., Athens, Ga., 1968-73, emeritus, 1973—; adj. research asso. U. Ga., 1970-73; vis. lectr. Israeli univs., 1963, Indian univs., 1973. Served to lt. col. AUS, 1942-46; PTO. Decorated Legion of Merit, Bronze Star; recipient Superior Ser. award USDA, 1959. Fellow A.A.A.S.; mem. Am. Chem. Soc. (chmn. Peoria sect. 1965), Am. Oil Chemists Soc., Inst. Food Tech., Sigma Xi, Alpha Chi Sigma. Author monographs, articles. Patentee in field. Home: 210 Ponderosa Dr Athens GA 30605 Office: Russell Research Lab PO Box 5677 Athens GA 30604

MC KINNEY, MICHAEL WHITNEY, state ofcl.; b. San Angelo, Tex., Aug. 23, 1946; s. Wallace Luster and Mitzi Randolph (Broome) McK.; B.A. in Govt., U. Tex. at Austin, 1973; m. Martha LaNan Hooker, Feb. 24, 1973; children—Wallace Blake, Lauren Brooke. Adminstrv. asst. to lt. gov. State of Tex., Austin, 1968-69, adminstrv. asst. to gov., 1969-73, asst. to dir. Tex. Water Quality Bd., Austin, 1973-76; chief of staff Tex. Alcoholic Beverage Commn., 1976—. Bd. dirs. Tex. Alpha Ednl. Found., Inc., Austin, 1969. Mem. Phi Kappa Psi. Democrat. Episcopalian. Club: Masons (32 deg., K.T.). Office: PO Box 12115 Austin TX 78711

MC KINNEY, ROBERT EDGAR, police adminstr.; b. Dallas, Oct. 25, 1927; s. Thomas P. and Martha (Hambrick) McK.; B.S., Sam Houston State U., 1970; postgrad. So. Meth. U., 1971-72; m. Noris J. Wilson, Jan. 4, 1949; children—Robert Edgar, James T., Richard W., Elizabeth A., Virginia L., Charlotte M. With Dallas Police Dept., 1952-73, sgt., 1955-61, lt. Criminal Investigation div., 1961-68, watch commdr. homicide, 1968-70, comdr. research and evaluation sect., tng. div., 1970-73, dir. tng. acad., 1973-74; chief police, mem. faculty criminal justice S.W. Tex. State U., San Marcos, 1974—; lectr., mem. adv. bd. S.W. Tex. Regional Police Acad. Mem. Criminal Justice Standards and Goals Com., State of Tex., 1975—; chmn. precinct Hays County (Tex.) Republican party, 1977—; mem. gen. assembly Capitol Area Planning Council, 1975—. Served with USMC, 1945-48, 50-51; Korea. Mem. Tex./N.Mex. Assn. Coll. and Univ. Police Depts. (v.p. 1978—), Internat. Assn. Chiefs Police, Internat. Assn. Coll. and Univ. Security Dirs., Tex. Police Assn., Assn. Tex. Law Enforcement Educators. Baptist. Clubs: Lions, Masons (32 deg.). Home: 1207 Girard St San Marcos TX 78666 Office: 004 Univ Service Center SW Tex State U San Marcos TX 78666

MC KINNIE, NANCY ELLIOTT, bank exec.; b. Jackson, Miss., Feb. 28, 1952; d. Morelle A. and Elaine H. Elliott; B.A. magna cum laude, Memphis State U., 1974; m. William D. McKinnie, May 18, 1974. Pension adminstr. Conn. Gen. Life Ins. Co., Memphis, 1975-77; v.p., trust officer new bus. devel. First Tenn. Bank N.A., Memphis, 1977—. Vice-chmn. ann. fund dr. Memphis State U., 1979-80; active United Way, 1978, 79. Mem. Internat. Assn. Fin. Planners (Memphis chpt.), Am. Inst. Banking, Phi Kappa Phi, Alpha Lambda Delta. Home: 6939 Amberly Rd Germantown TN 38138 Office: First Tennessee Bank Trust Div 4990 Poplar Ave Memphis TN 38117

MC KINNIS, ARCHIE PRICE, textile co. exec.; b. St. Petersburg, Fla., Aug. 24, 1942; s. James Booker and Dorothy Ann (Price) McK.; B.S., Miss. State U., 1964; m. Sidney Ann Faulkner, Dec. 22, 1963; children—Stephen, James. Mgr. internal audit Garan, Ind., Starkville, Miss., 1968-69; controller Thoroughbred Breeding Corp., Ocala, Fla., 1969-71; v.p., controller Allied Foods, Inc., Atlanta, 1971-78; corp. controller, chief acctg. officer Crompton Co., Inc., Waynesboro, Va., 1978—. Pres. Atlanta chpt. Juvenile Diabetes Found., 1976-77. C.P.A., Miss., Ga. Mem. Am. Inst. C.P.A.'s, Miss. Soc. C.P.A.'s, Nat. Assn. Accountants, Miss. State U. Alumni Assn. (pres. Atlanta chpt. 1976). Methodist. Home: 2818 Plantation Ln Waynesboro VA 22980 Office: Crompton Co Inc 400 Race St Waynesboro VA 22980

MC KINSTRY, JOHN ROTHROCK, sem. adminstr.; b. Magnolia, Miss., Sept. 21, 1914; s. John Logan and Margaret Gordon (Rothrock) McK.; B.S., Memphis State U., 1935; postgrad. U. Louisville, 1967; M.A., Samford U., 1974; m. Charlotte Fisher, Sept. 14, 1941; children—Charlotte, Suzanne, John, Margaret, Lynn. With So. Bell Telephone Co., various locations, 1941-78, div. traffic mgr., Louisville, 1956-68, gen. traffic mgr., gen. mktg. mgr., Birmingham, Ala., 1969-78; exec. asst. to minister communications State of Bahrain, 1978-80; adminstr. Birmingham Theol. Sem., 1980—. Pres., Birmingham Crisis Center, 1975. Mem. Birmingham, Ala. chambers commerce, Am. Hist. Assn., Presbyn. Hist. Soc. Ala. (sec.), SCV, Order Stars and Bars, Soc. Cincinnati. Republican. Presbyterian. Clubs: Downtown, The Club, Relay House, Vestavia Country, Kiwanis. Author: History of the Telephone in Birmingham, 1975; editor, pub. The Rothrock Family of Brick Church, Tenn., 1965; The Herron Family of Gibson County, Tenn., 1975; co-editor, co-pub. The Presbyterian Church in Alabama, 1977. Home: 3900 Spring Valley Rd Birmingham AL 35223 Office: Briarwood Presbyn Ch Hwy 280 S Birmingham AL 35243

MC KINSTRY, SAM WESCOAT, educator; b. St. Louis, Mar. 29, 1940; s. Karl and Virginia (Wescoat) McK.; B.A., Westminster Coll., Mo., 1962; M.A., U. Mo., 1969, Ph.D., 1974; m. Carolee Porter, Apr. 2, 1964; children—Sarah Anderson, Lee Wescoat. Asst. v.p. Am. Bank of De Soto (Mo.), 1962-67; asst. prof. polit. sci. East Tenn. State U., 1974-79, asso. prof., 1979—. Treas., Mo. Public Water Supply Dist. 1, 1966-67. Fulbright-Hays fellow, 1971-72. Mem. Am., Mo., Tenn. polit. sci. assns., Assn. Asian Studies, SAR, Phi Alpha Theta, Pi Gamma Mu, Pi Sigma Alpha, Sigma Chi. Mason. Episcopalian (past sr. warden). Home: 910 Grady Dr Johnson City TN 37601 Office: Box 24 517 Dept Polit Sci E Tenn State U Johnson City TN 37601

MC KNIGHT, COLBERT AUGUSTUS, newspaper editor; b. Shelby, N.C., Aug. 19, 1916; s. John Samuel and Norva (Proctor) McK.; B.S., Davidson Coll., 1938; LL.D., Colby Coll.; m. Margaret Belle Henderson, Mar. 29, 1941 (div. 1968); children—John Peter, Margaret C., David P.; m. 2d, Gail Oliver Ehle, Oct. 30, 1968; 1 dau., Colby Augusta. Reporter Charlotte News, 1939-42, news editor, 1944-48, mng. editor, 1948-49, editor, 1949-54; editor San Juan (P.R.) World Jour., also AP war corr., 1942-44; exec. dir. So. Edn. Reporting Service, 1954-55; editor Charlotte (N.C.) Observer, 1955-76, asso. pub., 1976—; v.p., dir. Knight Pub. Co., 1956—. Pres. N.C. Fund, 1963-65; chmn. bd. So. Edn. Reporting Service, 1963-65; trustee Charlotte Coll., 1960-65; bd. dirs. Found. of U. N.C. at Charlotte, 1974—. Mem. Am. Soc. Newspaper Editors (dir. 1965-73, pres. 1971-72, project dir. 1977—), Nat., N.C. confs. editorial writers, N.C. Press Assn. (dir. 1973—). Presbyn. Home: 1627 Beverly Dr Charlotte NC 28207 Office: 600 S Tryon St Charlotte NC 28202

MC KNIGHT, EDGAR VERNON, educator; b. Wilson, S.C., Nov. 21, 1931; s. William G. and Carrie Belle (DeMars) McK.; B.S., Coll. Charleston, 1953; M.Div., So. Bapt. Theol. Sem., 1956, Ph.D., 1960; M.Litt., Oxford U., 1976; m. Shirley Robinson, June 4, 1955; children—Deborah Lynn, Edgar Vernon. Fellow, So. Bapt. Theol. Sem., Louisville, 1956-60; chaplain Chowan Coll., Murfreesboro, N.C., 1960-63; asst. prof. religion Furman U., Greenville, S.C., 1963-67, asso. prof., 1967-74, asso. dean acad. affairs, 1970-73, prof. religion, 1974—, co-dir. faculty devel. programs, 1979—; vis. prof. So. Bapt. Theol. Sem., 1966-67. Recipient Book award for Meaning in Texts: The Historical Shaping of a Narrative Hermeneutics, Conf. on Christianity and Lit., MLA, 1978. Mem. Assn. Bapt. Profs. Religion (pres. 1980), Soc. N.T. Studies, Soc. Bibl. Lit., Am. Acad. Religion, AAUP. Baptist. Club: Torch. Author: (with Oscar Creech) A History of Chowan College, 1964; author: Opening the Bible: A Guide to Understanding the Scriptures, 1967; What is Form Criticism?, 1969; Meaning in Texts: The Historical Shaping of a Narrative Hermeneutics, 1978; author: (with others) Introduction to the New Testament, 1969. Home: 201 Alpine Way Greenville SC 29609 Office: Furman Univ Greenville SC 29613

MC KNIGHT, ESSIE VELMA, artist; b. Spurger, Tex., Oct. 7, 1918; d. Charlie James and Ala May (Durlaney) Spurlock; student pub. schs., Spurger; m. Robert Lee McKnight, Oct. 30, 1937; children—Sharon Marcelle, Robert Lynn. Group shows include: Livingston (Tex.) Folk Festival, HCCA Gallery, Palais Royal Gallery, Sta. KUHT-TV Auction, Houston Nat. Bank (all Houston); represented in pvt. collections, N.Y. and Tex.; work reproduced in Bicentennial issue Artist U.S.A., 1976. Mem. Houston Civic Art Assn., Pasadena Art Club, St. Paul's Altar Guild. Democrat. Episcopalian. Home: 4038 Colgate St Houston TX 77087

MC KNIGHT, JAMES ROSS, rancher, agrl. co. exec.; b. Fort Worth, July 24, 1948; s. James Nance and Mable Beatrice McK.; B.S., Okla. State U., 1970; m. Billie Lea Guskins, Nov. 5, 1973. Rancher, farmer nr. Throckmorton, Tex., 1970—; pres., chmn. bd. Throckmorton Agrl. Products, Inc., 1974—. Bd. dirs. Throckmorton County Hosp., Throckmorton County Livestock Show, Throckmorton Sch. Orgn. Bd., Throckmorton Soil and Water Conservation Dist. Mem. Nat. Cattlemen's Assn., Tex. Cattle Feeders Assn., Tex. Cattle Raisers Assn., Southwestern Cattle Raisers Assn., Throckmorton Stockyards Assn. (dir. 1975-77), Tex. Farm Bur., Throckmorton County Farm Bur. (pres. 1977-80), Throckmorton C. of C. (dir. 1973-75). Home and Office: PO Box 391 Throckmorton TX 76083

MC KNIGHT, ROBERT WAYNE, state senator; b. Port Chester, N.Y., May 11, 1944; s. Joel Roy and Gwendolyn (Crumm) McK.; B.S., Fla. So. Coll., 1966; M.B.A., Fla. State U., 1967; m. Susan Elizabeth Williams, Oct. 3, 1970; children—Michelle Elizabeth, Robert Joel. Vice pres. Planned Devel. Corp., real estate investments, and affiliate Kahn-McKnight Co., Inc., Miami, Fla.; mem. Fla. Ho. of Reps., 1974-78, chmn. mental health and health subcom., chmn. corrections and offender rehab. subcom.; mem. Fla. Senate from 38th dist., 1978—; mem. Gov. Fla. Com. Employment Handicapped, 1972-74, Gov. Fla. Task Force Corrections, 1976-78, Resource Recovery Council Fla., 1978—. Chmn. 15th Congl. Dist. Dade County Democratic Campaign Com., 1976. Served with USAR, 1968-70. Decorated Army Commendation medal; recipient Legis. award S. Dade Bd. Realtors, 1976, Outstanding Legislator Performance award Fla. Epilepsy Found., 1977, Legis. Appreciation award Fla. Assn. Retarded Citizens, 1977, Legis. award City of Miami, Legis. award Fla. Audubon Soc., 1978, Outstanding Legis. award Fla. Assn. Retarded Citizens, 1978. Mem. Coral Gables Jaycees (dir.; Robert L. Searle Leadership award 1972, Good Govt. award 1978), Mental Health Assn. Dade County (dir.), S. Dade C. of C., Coral Gables C. of C., Greater Miami C. of C. (trustee New World Center), Greater Homestead C. of C., Tiger Bay Polit. Club. Mem. Ch. of Christ. Home: 14221 SW 75th Ct Miami FL 33158 Office: 1440 Brickell Ave Miami FL 33131

MC KNIGHT, WILLIAM BALDWIN, physicist, educator; b. Macon, Ga., July 4, 1923; s. Gilbert Franklin and Exie (Baldwin) McK.; B.S., Purdue U., 1950; Ph.D., Oxford (Eng.) U., 1968; m. Helen Mabel Bowling, Oct. 1, 1955; children—Tandy Carol, Linda Kathryn. Physicist, Underwater Sound Reference Lab., Orlando, Fla., 1952-53; physicist U.S. Army Missile Command, Redstone Arsenal, Ala., 1953-61, supervisory research physicist, 1961-74, Sec. of Army research fellow, 1966; cons. Ballistic Missile Def. Advanced Tech. Center, 1975; research prof. physics U. Ala., Huntsville, 1974—. Vice pres. Cotaco Communities League, Somerville, Ala., 1964-65. Served with USAAF, 1943-45. Decorated D.F.C., Air medal with three clusters; recipient Research Devel. award U.S. Army, 1961, 64. Fellow Am. Optical Soc.; mem. IEEE, Am. Phys. Soc., Sigma Xi, Sigma Pi Sigma. Methodist. Club: Huntsville Racquet. Contbr. articles to profl. jours. Inventor missile guidance, lasers for surgery. Home: 7702 Treeline Dr SE Huntsville AL 35802 Office: PO Box 1247 Huntsville AL 35807

MC KOY, VICTOR GRAINGER, artist; b. Fayetteville, N.C., Apr. 21, 1947; s. Adair Morry and Priscilla Claggett (Grainger) McK.; B.S. in Biology, Clemson U., 1970; m. Floride Norris Owens, Jan. 13, 1969; children—Victor Grainger, Elizabeth Floride, Mary Adair. One-man show Hammer Galleries, N.Y.C., 1976; represented various exhbns. including Mus. Natural History, N.Y.C., 1972. Episcopalian. Home and Office: Route 1 Box 42 Wadmalaw Island SC 29487

MC LAFFERTY, CHARLES LOWRY, mfg. co. exec.; b. Evanston, Ill., Apr. 11, 1927; s. Joel Edward and Margaret (Keifer) McL.; B.Sc., U. Nebr., 1949; B.S., Bowling Green Bus. U., 1950; M.B.A., Northwestern U., 1952; m. Dee Hartmann; children—Ardith Ann (Mrs. James P. Zander), Karen Dee, Charles Lowry Jr., Kevin Paul. Sr. accountant Arthur Andersen & Co., Dallas, 1951-54; EDP systems analyst Genesco, Inc., Nashville, 1954-59; controller Martin Stove & Range Co., Florence, Ala., 1959-60; dir. finance Alamet div. Universal Oil Products Co., Selma, Ala., 1961-70; pres. So. Shelter, Inc., Selma, 1970-71; controller Southbridge Plastics div. W.R. Grace & Co.,

1971-72; controller Utica Tool Co. Inc., Orangeburg, S.C., 1972-74; asst. to treas. Triangle Corp., Orangeburg, 1974-75, asst. treas., 1976—; instr. U. Tenn., Nashville, 1959-61. Mem. Gov.'s Com. to Save USS Alabama, 1962-63, treas., commr. USS Ala. Battleship Commn., 1963-74; zone chmn. major gifts Lurleen Wallace Cancer Hosp. Fund, 1969; sec. Dallas County Pvt. Sch. Found., Selma, 1968-70; gen. chmn. S.C. Festival Roses, 1975, bd. dirs., 1975-79; mem. exec. com. Orangeburg Area Human Relations Com., 1975-77, v.p., 1976; del. Ala. Republican Conv., 1962; chmn. bd. trustees John T. Morgan Acad., Selma, 1965-67; mem. bicentennial com. Washington College (Tenn.) Acad., 1979—. Served with USNR, 1944-46. Mem. Fin. Execs. Inst., Nat. Assn. Accountants, Nat. Assn. Homebuilders (nat. dir. 1970-71), Asso. Industries Ala., Mil. Order Loyal Legion (nat. commandery-in-chief), Orton Soc. (v.p. Carolinas br. 1977-79, pres. 1979—), Beta Alpha Psi, Sigma Chi, Beta Pi. Lutheran. Kiwanian, Toastmaster. Club: Orangeburg Country. Home: 1587 Tolly Ganly Circle Orangeburg SC 29115 Office: Cameron Rd Orangeburg SC 29115

MCLAFFERTY, DEE HARTMANN, tchr. learning disabled; d. Henry J. and Ottilie (Truebenbach) Hartmann; B.Sc., U. Nebr.: postgrad. Western Ky. U.; m. Charles Lowry McLafferty; children—Ardith McLafferty Zander, Karen Dee, Charles Lowry, Kevin Paul. Sci. tchr. Franklin-Simpson High Sch., Franklin, Ky., 1949-50; sec. A.B. Dick Co., Niles, Ill., 1950-51; tchr. chemistry A.G. Parrish High Sch., Selma, Ala., 1967-68; tchr. learning disabled children, Orangeburg, S.C., 1975—. Mem. Dogwood Garden Club, Orangeburg, 1974—, pres. 1976-77; mem. Orangeburg Garden Council, 1976—, 2d v.p., 1977-79, pres., 1979-80; mem. hosp. aux. vol. service Greenville Hosp., System, 1979-80; mem., bd. dirs. Orangeburg Festival of Arts, 1976—; mem. Orangeburg Music Club, 1974—, pres., 1977-78; mem., bd. dirs. Orangeburg Attention Home, 1974—; mem. Maude Schiffley chpt. SPCA, Orangeburg, 1976—, treas., 1977—; bd. dirs. Jubilee, Corinth, Miss., 1973; mem. Charity League Selma, 1963—, follies chmn., 1964. Named hon. Ala. adm., 1964, hon. Ala. col., 1968. Mem. Orton Soc. Lutheran. Clubs: Orangeburg Country, Tarantella, Dinner-Dance. Address: 1587 Tolly Ganly Circle Orangeburg SC 29115

MC LAIN, JACK, aerospace co. exec.; b. Jackson, Miss., Nov. 18, 1923; s. Cas Vincent and Tura (Miley) McL.; student Belhaven Coll., 1946, U. Ga., 1946-47; B.S., Millsaps Coll., 1949; M.S. (fellow), U. Miss., 1951; postgrad. Birmingham So. Coll., 1952; m. Hazel Irene Garrett, June 4, 1950; children—Ellen Denise, Sharon Grace. Asso. physicist U. Miss., Oxford, 1950, Philco Corp., Phila., 1951, So. Research Inst., Birmingham, 1952-54; with Kentron Internat., Inc., Dallas, also Hampton, Va., 1954—, div. mgr., Hampton, 1961—. Served with AC, USMCR, 1942-46. Decorated Air medal. Mem. Am. Inst. Aeros. and Astronautics, IEEE, Am. Def. Preparedness Assn. (life), Nat. Contract Mgmt. Assn., Air Force Assn., Peninsula C. of C., Theta Nu Sigma, Omicron Delta Kappa. Baptist. Clubs: Williamsburg Country (York County, Va.), Kiwanis (pres. 1972-73, lt. gov. 1977—). Home: 706 Antrim Dr Newport News VA 23601 Office: 3221 N Armistead Ave Hampton VA 23666

MC LAIN, JOHN HAMILTON, IV, indsl. designer; b. Tallapoosa County, Ala., July 16, 1928; s. John Hamilton and Vivian Iona (Hornsby) McL.; B.S. in Indsl. Design, Auburn U., 1953; m. Mary Elizabeth Jones, May 5, 1959; children—John Hamilton V, Sanford, Wimberley, Matthew, David. Designer, Reynolds Metals Co., Sheffield, Ala., 1953-55; sr. prin. engr. Teledyne Brown Engring. Co., Huntsville, Ala., 1955-59; owner, pres. M.K. Assos., Inc., Huntsville, 1969—; pres. IMP, Inc., Huntsville, 1976—, also dir.; instr. U. Ala., Huntsville, 1955-56. Pres. Madison County Young Democrats, 1962-67; mem. Madison County Dem. Exec. Com., 1968-76. Served in U.S. Navy, 1946-48, U.S. Army, 1950-53. Mem. Soc. Am. Mil. Engrs. Episcopalian. Clubs: Huntsville Golf and Country; Willow Point Golf and Country (Alexander City, Ala.); Madison County Auburn (pres. 1965), Kiwanis. Patentee. Home: 208 Winthrop Dr Huntsville AL 35801 Office: 2607 Leeman Ferry Rd Huntsville AL 35801

MC LAIN, WILLIAM HARVEY, research scientist; b. Chgo., Dec. 18, 1929; s. William Harvey and Claire Cornelius (Shaw) McL.; B.S., U. Chgo., 1950; B.S. in Chemistry, U. Denver, 1952, Ph.D., 1969; M.S., U. Wash., Seattle, 1960; m. Reathie Sarah Ross; children—Cynthia Joan, Rebecca Jean, Priscilla Ann, Dorothy Irene, Virginia Sue, Beverly Kay. Mem. staff U. Wash., 1956-58; engr. Boeing Sci. Research Labs., 1958-61; scientist Martin-Marietta Co., 1961-63; chemist Denver Research Inst., 1963-73; sr. scientist Deutsche Forschung für Luft und Raumfahrt, 1971-72; inst. scientist S.W. Research Inst., San Antonio, 1976—; lectr. mech. engring. U. Denver, 1970. Served with USAF, 1952-56. DuPont fellow, 1956-57. Mem. Am. Chem. Soc., Nat. Fire Protection Assn., Combustion Inst., Nat. Acad. Code Adminstrn., Internat. Council Fabric Flammability, Am. Inst. Aeros. and Astronautics, ASTM, Sigma Xi. Author papers, reports. Home: 6219 War Hawk Dr San Antonio TX 78238 Office: 8500 Culebra Rd San Antonio TX 78238

MC LAIN, WILLIAM RICHARD, plastics co. exec.; b. Huntsville, Ala., Dec. 7, 1916; s. William Walton and Dora Susan (White) McL.; student Ga. Inst. Tech., 1936-41; m. Margaret Jane Copenhaver, Oct. 5, 1941; children—Patricia, Margaret Susan. Chem. engr. Tenn. Eastman Corp., Kingsport, 1941-42; chief civil engr. smoke, incendiary loading div. CWS, Huntsville Arsenal, Ala., 1942-44; pres. Kusan, Inc., Nashville, 1946-69, chmn. bd., chief exec. officer, 1969—; dir. First Am. Nat. Bank, Steel Heddle Mfg. Co., Greenville, S.C. Past pres., bd. dirs. Jr. Achievement of Nashville; past nat. dir. Jr. Achievement, Inc.; past treas., bd. dirs. Family and Childrens Service; past bd. dirs. Council of Community Services. Served to lt. (j.g.) USNR, 1944-46; ETO. Mem. ASME, Am. Chem. Soc., Am. Inst. Chem. Engrs., Soc. Plastics Engrs., Soc. Plastics Industry (past dir.), Young Pres.'s Orgn. (past area v.p., dir.), Toy Mfrs. Am. (past pres.), NAM (dir.), Plastics Pioneers Assn., Newcomen Soc. N.Am., Chief Execs. Forum, Nashville C. of C. (past v.p., dir.), Ga. Inst. Tech. Alumni (mem. nat. alumni adv. bd. 1970—, chmn. 1970-71), Pi Kappa Alpha. Methodist (past trustee). Rotarian. Club: Capital City (Atlanta). Contbr. articles trade jours. Patentee in field. Home: 2814 Kenway Rd Nashville TN 37215 Office: 7 Maryland Farms Brentwood TN 37027

MC LALLEN, MILLARD DANIEL, coll. ofcl.; b. Fowler, Colo., Feb. 24, 1931; s. Samuel B. and Hester Frances (Jones) McL.; B.S., Wayland Bapt. Coll., 1953; M.A. in Speech, W. Tex. State U., 1957; Ph.D., U. Tex., 1975; m. Laura F. Stringer, Aug. 19, 1955; children—Deborah L., Benjamin T. Chief engr. and mgr. Sta. KHBL-FM, Wayland Baptist Coll., Plainview, Tex., 1950-53; propr., mgr. Ben Franklin Variety Store, Hereford, Tex., 1955-57; asst. prof. speech Mary Hardin Baylor Coll., Belton, Tex., 1957-60; instr. (part-time) in speech U. Denver, 1960-61; chmn. dept. speech Mary Hardin-Baylor Coll., 1961-64, prof. communication, 1961-64; tchr. English and math. Englewood (Colo.) High Sch., 1964-65; asso. prof. English, Met. State Coll., Denver, 1965-67, acting chmn. English dept., 1966-67; prof. English and speech So. State Coll. (name changed to U. S.D. at Springfield 1969), 1967-69, chmn. humanities div., 1968-69; edn. specialist Visual Instrn. Bur., U. Tex., Austin, 1969-70, research asso. Center for Sch. Studies, 1970, research asso. computer-assisted instructional lab., 1970-71; dean of instrn. Tarrant County Jr. Coll., Fort Worth, 1971-78, research project dir. indsl. co-op tng., 1974-76; v.p. acad. affairs Wayland Bapt. Coll., Plainview, Tex., 1978—. Program chmn. Heart of Tex. council Boy Scouts Am. 1961-64; bd. dirs. Grad. Career Devel. Center, Arlington, Tex., 1973-76, Horned Frog council Boy Scouts Am., 1974—, merit badge counselor, 1973-76. Served with U.S. Army, 1953-55. NDEA fellow, 1967; NSF research grantee, 1970. Mem. Nat. Council Tchrs. English, Tex. Assn. Jr. Coll. Instructional Adminstrs., Am. Assn. Higher Edn., Am. Assn. Univ. Adminstrs., Gen. Semantics Inst., Am. Tech. Edn. Assn., Nat. Assn. Environ. Edn., Council Occupational Edn., Community Coll. Assn. Instrn. and Tech., Tex. Assn. Tchr. Educators, AAUP, Nat. Council Aging, Nat. Ret. Tchrs. Assn., Nat. Aerospace Edn. Assn., Internat. Narcotics Enforcement Officers Assn., Nat. Council Crime and Delinquency, Phi Delta Kappa, Alpha Psi Omega, Alpha Chi, Tau Kappa Alpha, Phi Theta Kappa. Democrat. Baptist. Contbr. articles on programmed learning and edn. in communications to profl. publs. Home: 1110 Ennis St Plainview TX 79072 Office: Wayland Baptist College Plainview TX 79072

MC LAND, ALBERT CALVIN, ednl. adminstr.; b. Zealandia, Sask., Can., Feb. 3, 1920; s. John and Margaret Leona (Fisher) McL.; B.S. in Bus. Adminstrn., U. So. Miss., 1971, M.S. in Vocat. Tech. Edn., 1972, Ph.D. in Ednl. Adminstrn. and Supervision, 1977; m. Kathryn Rose Chandler, June 20, 1942; children—Margaret Jane, John Albert, Sandra Kay, Colleen Gay. State policeman State of Ind., 1938-40; served as enlisted man U.S. Army, 1940-61; commd. 2d lt. U.S. Army, 1943, advanced through grades to capt., 1958, ret., 1961; dist. scout exec. Council 1, Boy Scouts Am., Anniston, Ala., 1961-63; pastor Stringer (Miss.) Bapt. Ch., 1963-68; clk.-carrier U.S. Postal Service, Auburn, Ind., 1968-69; dir. Manpower Devel. and Tng. Center, Pearl River Jr. Coll., Hattiesburg, Miss., 1974-79; headmaster Lawrence County Acad., Monticello, Miss., 1979—. Scoutmaster, Boy Scouts Am., 1948-68, neighborhood commr., 1968-72. Decorated Silver Star, Bronze Star with oak leaf cluster, Purple Heart with 2 oak leaf clusters, Army Commendation medal; recipient award Boy Scouts Am., 1961, C. of C., 1976; U. So. Miss. fellow, 1974-75. Mem. Asso. Locksmiths Am., La.-Miss. Locksmiths Assn., Profl. Photographers Am., VFW, Am. Legion (post comdr. 1953-55), Res. Officers Assn., Mil. Order of Purple Heart, North-South Skirmish Assn., Nat. Employment and Tng. Assn., Am. Employment and Tng. Assn., Am. Vocat. Assn., Miss. Vocat. Assn., Nat. Rifle Assn., Nat. Muzzleloading Rifle Assn., Miss. Muzzleloading Rifle Assn., Phi Delta Kappa, Delta Kappa Pi. Baptist. Club: Moose. Home: 598 N 25th Ave Hattiesburg MS 39401 Office: PO Box 640 Monticello MS 39654

MC LANE, H. ARTHUR, lawyer; b. Valdosta, Ga., Apr. 2, 1939; s. Carson H. and Philena (Tyson) McL.; B.A., Emory U., 1961; J.D., U. Ga., 1963; m. Jane Campbell Bennet, June 17, 1961; children—Mary Campbell, Paul Corbett. Admitted to Ga. bar, 1963, U.S. Supreme Ct. bar, 1972; practiced in Valdosta, 1963—; county atty. Lowndes County (Ga.), 1965-73; atty. Echols County Bd. Edn., 1966—; judge State Ct., 1974—. Adv. bd. Valdosta Area Vocat. Tech. Sch., 1967—; bd. dirs. Valdosta Boys Club, 1966—, pres., 1971-72; bd. dirs. Valdosta Entertainment Assn., 1968-71; chmn. show div. Valdosta-Lowndes County Bicentennial Celebration, 1975-76; exec. bd. Ga. Sheriffs Boys Ranch, 1979—. Named Outstanding Young Man, 1972. Mem. State Bar Ga., Valdosta Bar Assn. (pres. 1974), Am. Judicature Soc., Valdosta-Lowndes County C. of C. (dir. 1978-80), Blue Key, Sigma Alpha Epsilon, Phi Delta Phi, Phi Kappa Phi. Methodist. Clubs: Rotary (dir. 1973, 76-77, 78-79), Gridiron, Valdosta Country (dir., pres. 1971). Office: 504 N Patterson St Valdosta GA 31601

MCLAUGHLIN, ALEXANDER CHARLES JOHN, oil co. exec.; b. N.Y.C., June 3, 1925; s. Alexander and Margaret (Percival) McL.; B.S., Va. Poly. Inst., 1946; postgrad. Columbia, 1947-48; m. Joan Kosak, June 10, 1950; 1 dau., Jena Hilary. With Standard Vacuum Oil Co., N.Y.C., Shanghai, China, Manila, Saigon, Indochina, Hongkong, Yokohama, Japan, 1946-50; with Trans Arabian Pipeline Co., Turaif, Saudi Arabia, 1951; with Andean Nat. Corp., Cartagena, Colombia, 1952-54; practice civil engring., N.Y.C., 1954-55; chief project engr. mktg. Am. Oil Co., N.Y.C., chief engr. South Atlanta, sr. head engr., Chgo., 1955-64; sr. process engr. mfg. and marketing dept. Amoco Internat. Oil Co., Europe, S.A., Asia, N.Y.C., Chgo., 1969-72; mgr. distbn. Singapore Petroleum Co., 1972-73; constrn. supr. Iran Pan Am. Oil Co., 1973, onshore/offshore supr., 1974-75; sr. staff engr. Amoco Internat. Oil Co., Chgo., 1975—. Vol. fireman Long Beach Fire Dept., 1955-63; tng. officer USCG Aux., 1962; Eagle scout, scoutmaster, troop com. mem. Nassau County N.Y. council Boy Scouts Am., 1946-49. Decorated Order White Cloud. Fellow ASCE; mem. Nat. Soc. Profl. Engrs., Nat. Assn. Corrosion Engrs., Internat. Platform Assn., Omicron Delta Kappa. Republican. Club: Pathfinders (London, Eng.); Columbia Country (Shanghai); Singapore Swim, Singapore Petroleum, Singapore American; Tehran American; Moose. Home: 3106 Cedar Knolls Dr Kingwood TX 77339 Office: 2 Greenspoint Plaza PO Box 4381 1625 Northchase Dr Houston TX 77210

MC LAUGHLIN, (EDWARD) BRUCE, lawyer; b. Omaha, Apr. 2, 1921; s. Charles F. and Margaret (Bruce) McL.; student Mercersburg Acad., 1935-38; B.S., Georgetown U., 1943; postgrad. George Washington U., 1950-51; J.D., U. Miami, 1953. Announcer Sta. KTSM, El Paso, Tex., 1943-44; news editor KFRE, Fresno, Calif., 1944; with McKesson-Robbins, San Francisco, 1945-46; radio prodn. Sta. KOSA, Odessa, Tex., 1947-49, Sta. KPHO, Phoenix, 1949; TV prodn. Sta. WITV, Miami-Ft. Lauderdale, Fla., 1953-55; admitted to Fla. bar, 1955, since practiced in Miami. Served with Signal Corps, U.S. Army, World War II. Mem. Fla. Bar, Am., Dade County bar assns., Lawyers Club Dade County (dir. 1969-70), Screen Actors Guild (pres. Fla. br. 1965-69, mem. Fla. council 1962—, mem. nat. bd. dirs. 1968—), AFTRA (dir. Miami chpt. 1975), Am. Legion, Gamma Eta Gamma. Democrat. Roman Catholic. Clubs: Coral Gables (Fla.) Country; Jockey (Miami, Fla.); University (Washington). Editor: Florida Screen Actor, 1974—; contbr. articles to profl. pubs. Home: 45 Antilla Ave Coral Gables FL 33134 Office: Ainsley Bldg Miami FL 33132

MC LAUGHLIN, JAMES OSCAR, JR., finance co. exec.; b. Atlanta, Aug. 4, 1924; s. James O. and Myrtle Lee (Humphries) McL.; B.A., U. Ga.; grad. Sch. Exec. Devel., U. Ga., 1964; grad. Grad. Sch. Savs. and Loan, Ind. U., 1971; m. Ethyl Velma Pierce, Mar. 2, 1947; children—Vicki Lee, Tracie Elizabeth. Treas. Campbell Coal Co., Atlanta, 1947-57; with Atlanta Fed. Savs. and Loan Assn., 1957—, asst. v.p., 1962-66, v.p. service div., 1966-73, v.p. ops., 1973—; instr. Am. Savs. and Loan Inst., Atlanta, 1964—. Vol. worker various charitable orgns. Served with USAF, 1943. Mem. Am. Savs. and Loan Inst. (pres. 1969). Optimist (sec.-treas. chpt.). Home: 3543 Summitridge Dr Doraville GA 30040 Office: 20 Marietta St NW Atlanta GA 30303

MC LAUGHLIN, MABLE IRENE, nursing home food service adminstr.; b. Livington, La., Apr. 3, 1918; d. William Howard and Ruth Mary (Penn) Hatton; grad. pub. schs.; grad. Am. Dietetic Assn. Course for Food Services Suprs., 1972; m. Ernest Gilbert McLaughlin, June 2, 1939; children—Howard Eugene, Helena Ruth. Mgr. coffee shop 7th Ward Gen. Hosp., Hammond, La., 1960-65, dir. food services, 1965-73; mgr. Snack Bar, Southeastern La. U., 1973-74; food service supr. Belle Maison Nursing Home, Ponchatoula, La., 1974—. Mem. Am. Soc. Food Service Adminstrs. (state nominating com. 1973-76, chmn. nominating com. 1976), Am. Hosp. Assn., Hosp., Instl., Ednl. Foodservice Soc. Baptist (Sunday sch. tchr.). Home: Route 4 Box 54 Hammond LA 70401 Office: PO Box 767 Ponchatoula LA 70454

MC LAURIN, MONTY EARL, hosp. exec.; b. New Orleans, Sept. 21, 1951; s. Julius Ransom and Dorothy Margaret (Montgomery) McL.; B.S. in Sci. Edn., La. Coll., 1974; M.H.A. (Allied Health fellow 1976), U. Ala., Birmingham, 1978; m. Deborah Ann Kirby, Aug. 19, 1972; children—Leigh Erin, Michael Evan. Instr., A. Wettermark High Sch., Boyce, La., 1974-76; asst. v.p. Baptist Meml. Hosp., Gadsden, Ala., 1978—; mem. Etowah County Home Health Care Adv. Council. Mem. LA. N.G., 1970-76. Mem. Am. Coll. Hosp. Adminstrs., Am. Hosp. Assn., Am. Mgmt. Assn., Nat. Fire Protection Assn., Assn. Advancement Med. Instrumentation, Ala. Hosp. Assn., Gadsden Met. C. of C., Alpha Eta. Club: Gadsden Civitan. Home: 105 Argyle Ct Gadsden AL 35901 Office: 1007 Goodyear Ave Gadsden AL 35903

MC LEAN, GAYLA LAPERRIERE, telephone co. exec.; b. Lexington, Ky., Dec. 31, 1936; d. Arthur J. and Ruth P. (Fuller) LaPerriere; student Barry Coll. Model, Burdines Sunshine Fashions Miami, Fla., 1955-58; TV service mgr. Hopkins Smith Co., 1966-67; mem. advt. sales staff So. Bell Telephone Co., Miami, 1961-66; exec. sec. IBM, Boca Raton, Fla., 1966-70, word processing supr., 1971-72, office products sales, 1972-73; owner, mgr. New Look, Inc., real estate, Miami, 1973—; communications cons. So. Bell Telephone Co., Miami, Fla., 1975-77, planner info. processing, 1977-79, word processing/adminstrv. support mgr., Atlanta, 1979—. Recipient Betterment of Edn. award Broward Community Coll., 1978. Mem. Internat. Word Processing Assn. (internat. dir. 1979-81), pres. local chpt. 1978-79, honor soc. award 1979, achievement award 1979), Assn. Records Mgrs. and Adminstrs., Gem. Soc., Future Pioneers. Republican. Club: Toastmasters. Contbr. articles to trade jours. Office: 45 Edgewood Ave SE Atlanta GA 30303

MC LEAN, JAMES HANNIS, educator; b. Grove Hill, Ala., Mar. 25, 1920; s. James Grady and Bertie (Rotch) McL.; B.S., Livingston U., 1941; M.B.A., U. Ala., 1948; J.D., Emory U., 1958; Ph.D., Ohio State U., 1967; m. Mary Owen Van Hoose, Nov. 12, 1942; children—James Hannis, Donald Michael, Janet Kathelaine. Supervisory auditor Office of Auditor Gen., USAF, Atlanta, 1949-52; staff accountant Arthur Young & Co., Atlanta, 1952-55; cost analyst Procurement Office, USAF, Atlanta, 1955-56; asst. prof. accounting Ga. State U., Atlanta, 1956-57; asso. prof. accounting U. Tenn. at Knoxville, 1957-67; asst. dir. edn. Am. Inst. C.P.A.'s, N.Y.C., 1961-62, cons. adv. grading service, 1970—; asst. instr. Ohio State U., Columbus, 1964-65; prof accounting Va. Poly. Inst. and State U., Blacksburg, 1967-76; dean Coll. Bus., East Tenn. State U., Johnson City, 1976—; cons. IRS, 1968-69, Def. Contract Audit Agy., 1969, Audit Agy. of HEW, 1970. Served with USNR, 1942-45. Mem. Am. Inst. C.P.A.'s, Am. Accounting Assn., Tenn. Soc. C.P.A.'s, Ruritan Nat. (pres. local chpt. 1969-70). Baptist. Club: Rotary. Contbr. numerous articles in field to profl. jours. Office: Coll of Business East Tennessee State U Johnson City TN 37601

MC LEAN, MALCOLM DALLAS, historian, editor, educator; b. Rogers, Tex., Mar. 10, 1913; s. Dallas Duncan and Gladys (Robertson) McL.; B.A. with highest honors, U. Tex., 1936, Ph.D., 1951; M.A., Universidad Nacional Autónoma de México, 1938; m. Mary Margaret Stoner, Feb. 11, 1939; 1 son, John Robertson. Field editor in charge Spanish translators Tex. Hist. Records Survey, San Antonio, 1938-39; asst. dir. and archivist San Jacinto Mus. History, Houston, 1939-41; research analyst Mexico and C. Am. desk War Dept., Washington, 1941-46; Spanish translator U. Tex. Library, Austin, 1946-47; instr. Romance langs. U. Tex., Austin, 1947-51; asst. prof. Romance langs. U. Ark., Fayetteville, 1951-55, asso. prof., 1955-56; dir. Binat. Center, Tegucigalpa, Honduras, 1956-59, Guayaquil, Ecuador, 1959-61; asso. prof. Spanish, Tex. Christian U., Fort Worth, 1961-64, prof., 1965-76, asso. dean, 1965-74, prof. emeritus, 1977—; prof. Spanish and history U. Tex., Arlington, 1976—. Recipient citation Mil. Intelligence Div. War Dept., 1945; E.D. Farmer fellow, 1937, 38 Fellow Tex. State Hist. Assn. (Coral Horton Tullis Meml. prize award 1974), Tex. State Geneal. Soc.; mem. Orgn. Am. Historians, Am. Hist. Assn., Am. Assn. State and Local History (award of Merit 1976), Bell County Hist. Assn., East Tex. Hist. Assn., Southwestern Am. Lit. Assn., Tarrant County Hist. Soc., Tenn. Hist. Soc., Western History Assn., Tex. Fgn. Lang. Assn. (pres. 1964-65, hon. mem.), Collector's Inst., Tex. Folklore Soc., Sons of the Republic of Tex. (Disting. Service award 1971, Knights Order of San Jacinto 1973, Summerfield G. Roberts award 1974), Phi Beta Kappa (founding pres. Tex. Christian U. chpt. 1971), Phi Delta Kappa, Phi Sigma Iota, Phi Alpha Theta, Sigma Delta Pi, Phi Eta Sigma. Democrat. Methodist. Author: (with J. Villasana Haggard) Handbook for Translators of Spanish Historical Documents, 1941; contbr. numerous articles on Tex. history and lit. criticism of Spanish lit. to scholarly jours.; compiler and editor Papers Concerning Robertson's Colony in Texas, 6 vols., 1974—; history editor Texas Parade mag., 1948-49; editor Arkansas Fgn. Lang., 1954-56; editorial bd. Boletín Bibliográfico de la Secretaria de Hacienda y Crédito Público, 1969-74, Papers of the Texas Revolution, 10 vols., 1973. Home: 409 Baylor Dr Arlington TX 76010 Office: Univ of Texas PO Box 19099 Arlington TX 76019

MC LEAN, MARGARET STONER (MRS. MALCOLM DALLAS MCLEAN), researcher; b. Victoria, Tex., June 5, 1915; d. Thomas Royal and Mame Victoria (Stoner) Stoner; A.A., Victoria Jr. Coll., 1936; B.S., U. Tex., 1939; m. Malcolm Dallas McLean, Feb. 11, 1939; 1 son, John Robertson. Receptionist, postmaster San Jacinto Mus. History, Houston, 1939-41; microfilm camera operator Library of Congress, Washington, 1942; bibliog. researcher, 1947-53; tchr. elementary sch., Fayetteville, Ark., 1954-55; elementary tchr. Am. Sch., Tegucigalpa, Honduras, 1957-58; tchr. English, U.S. Binat. Center and Am. High Sch., Guayaquil, Ecuador, 1959-61; newspaper microfilm archivist Amon Carter Mus. Western Art, Ft. Worth, 1963-73; microfilm research specialist Spanish Tex. Microfilm Center, Presidio La Bahia, Goliad, Tex., 1973-74; researcher, editorial asst. Papers Concerning Robertson's Colony in Tex., Fort Worth, 1974—. Clubs: Texas Christian University Woman's (Ft. Worth); Faculty Woman's (U. Tex., Arlington). Contbr. articles to profl. jours. Address: 409 Baylor Dr Arlington TX 76010

MC LEAN, VICTOR REED, public relations exec.; b. Troy, Ala., Oct. 19, 1949; s. Horace M. and Leila W. McLean; B.A. in Communications, U. Ala., 1972; m. Judy M. Glass, Mar. 19, 1971. News editor Tallassee (Ala.) Tribune, 1972-73; public relations/info. officer Ala. Dept. Edn., Montgomery, 1973-77; now public relations mgr. Blount Internat., Ltd., Montgomery; cons./instr. Auburn U., Montgomery, 1974-77. Mem. public relations com. United Way, 1978-79. Recipient Ala. Press Assn. award, 1973; Montgomery Assn. Bus. Communicators awards for 4-color mags., 1974, 75, 78; Montgomery Ad Club award, 1978. Mem. Public Relations Council Ala., Internat. Assn. Bus. Communicators, Montgomery Assn. Bus. Communicators. Club: Rolling Hills Golf and Racquet. Editor, Ala.

Vocat. Jour., 1975-77. Office: 4520 Executive Park Dr Montgomery AL 36116

MC LEAN, WILLIAM YOUMANS, architect; b. Vidalia, Ga., Aug. 9, 1927; s. John Archibald and Alma (Tod) McL.; student U.S. Naval Acad., 1945-47; B.S., Ga. Inst. Tech., 1947, B.Arch., 1950; m. Larue Jane Wells, June 9, 1951; children—William Youmans, Jonathan Wells, Amanda Jane. Archtl. draftsman, designer Wm. J.J. Chase & Assos., Atlanta, 1951-52, 55-58; architect Harvey & Elliott, Rome, Ga., 1959-60, M.G. Turner, Rome, 1960-61; partner Turner & McLean, Architects, Rome, 1961-62; asso. Hugh Gaston Assos., Albany, Ga., 1962-63; owner William Y. McLean, Architect, Albany, 1963-67, Tifton, Ga., 1967-75; chief architect Med. Coll. Ga., Augusta, 1975—; project architect Ga. Agrirama. City commr. Tifton, 1972-74, vice mayor, 1972. Served as lt. (j.g.) USNR 1952-55. Mem. A.I.A. (organizer, 1st pres. S.W. Ga. chpt. 1965-66, dir. Ga. council, 1966-67, dir. s. Atlantic regional council 1966). Democrat. Episcopalian (mem. diocesan council 1971-72). Home: 308 Scotts Way Augusta GA 30909 Office: Medical Coll Ga Augusta GA 30902

MC LELLAND, CLAUDE ALLEN, otolaryngologist; b. Ennis, Tex., May 22, 1933; s. Rufus Allen and Claudia Irene (Purdue) McL.; B.A., Southwestern U., 1956; M.D., Southwestern Med. Sch., Dallas, 1960; m. Joyce Ann Allen, June 24, 1961; children—Jaye Alane, Tracy Ann. Rotating intern Methodist Hosp., Dallas, 1960-61; commd. 2d lt. U.S. Air Force, 1961, advanced through grades to lt. col., 1969; chief aerospace medicine Chenault AFB, Lake Charles, La., 1961-63; resident in otolaryngology Baylor U., Houston, 1963-67— chief otolaryngology service USAF Med. Center, Keesler AFB, Biloxi, Miss., 1967-74, ret., 1974; practice medicine specializing in otolaryngology, Corpus Christi, 1974—; mem. staff Meml. Med. Center, Spohn Hosp., Driscoll Found. Children's Hosp.; instr. Tulane U. Med. Sch., 1969; asst. prof. otolaryngology Med. Sch., Baylor U., Houston, 1974—. Bd. dirs. S. Tex. Speech, Hearing and Lang. Center, 1974—, Driscoll Found. Childrens Hosp., 1978—. Decorated Air Force Commendation medal. Diplomate Am. Bd. Otolaryngology. Fellow A.C.S.; mem. Am. Acad. Ophthalmology and Otolaryngology, AMA, Tex. Med. Assn., Tex. Otolaryn. Assn., S. Tex. Otolaryngology Study Club (pres. 1977), Tex. Soc. Ophthalmology and Otolaryngology, Centurian Club of Deafness Research Found., Nueces County Med. Soc., Phi Rho Sigma. Episcopalian. Home: 5002 Royalton St Corpus Christi TX 78413 Office: 2601 Hospital Blvd Suite 117 Corpus Christi TX 78405

MC LEMORE, EUEL PHILLIP, assn. exec.; b. Marietta, Ga., July 2, 1946; s. Euel Smith and Kathreen (Brown) McL.; B.B.A., Ga. State U., 1971, M.B.A., 1974; J.D., Woodrow Wilson Coll. Law, 1979; m. Brenda Carolyn Parkerson, Mar. 17, 1974; 1 stepson, Philip Parkerson. Planner, Atlanta Regional Commn., 1971-73; planning dir. Douglas County, Douglasville, Ga., 1973-74, City of Marietta, 1974—; exec. dir. Downtown Marietta Devel. Authority, 1978—. Served with U.S. Army, 1966-69. Mem. Am. Planning Assn., Nat. Trust for Hist. Preservation, Internat. Downtown Execs. Assn., Ga. Downtown Devel. Assn. Club: Marietta Kiwanis. Home: 306 Kirkpatrick Dr Marietta GA 30064 Office: PO Box 609 Marietta GA 30061

MC LENDON, GORDON BARTON, broadcaster, radio and TV exec.; b. Paris, Tex., June 8, 1921; s. Barton Robert and Jeannette Marie (Eyster) McL.; B.A., Yale U., 1942; postgrad. Harvard U. Sch. Law, 1945-46; children—Janette, Gordon Barton, Kristen, Anna. Founder, Liberty Broadcasting System, 1947, ind. Stas. KABL-FM, San Francisco, KABL, Oakland, Calif., WNUS-AM-FM, Detroit, WYSL-AM-FM, Buffalo, KOST-FM, Los Angeles, WRIT, Milw., KILT, Houston, KTSA, San Antonio, KELP, El Paso, Tex., KEEL, Shreveport, La., WAKY, Louisville, also stas., Winnipeg, Man., Can. and El Paso; owner Sta. KNET, Palestine, Tex.; pres. McLendon Co., Dallas, 1947—. Bd. dirs. Richmond-Freeman Meml. Clinic, Goins Found., Dallas Theatre Center, Dallas Symphony Orch.; past Tex. state chmn. March of Dimes; hon. nat. chmn. VFW Poppy Drive; Democratic candidate U.S. Senate, Tex., 1964; active fund-raising drives Dallas Services for Blind Children. Served with USN, 1942-45; PTO. Named Outstanding Sports Broadcaster, Sporting News, 1951; named to Ten Outstanding Young Men U.S., U.S. Jr. C. of C., 1951; recipient Man of Year award Pulse, Inc., 1967; Betty award Associated Broadcast Execs., 1967; Distinguished Citizen award Harding Coll., 1969. Mem. Nat. Fedn. Ind. Bus. (dist. chmn.), Tex. Law Enforcement Found., Assn. Former Intelligance Officers, Spl. Forces Club London. Clubs: Yale, Brook Hollow Golf, Dallas Country. Author: How to Succeed in Broadcasting, 1961; Correct Spelling in Three Hours, 1962; Style in the Use of English, 1963; Understanding American Government, 1964; 100 Years of America in Sound, 1965; originator Game of Day and Game of Week sports broadcasts, technique of play-by-play sports broadcasting. Home: 2927 Maple Ave Dallas TX 75201 Office: 2119 Southland Center Dallas TX 75201

MC LENDON, MICHAEL JAMES, electronic engr.; b. Wilson, N.C., June 18, 1952; s. James Raymond and Doris Hilda (Tillotson) McL.; student Atlantic Christian Coll., 1970-72, U.S. Army Signal Sch., 1972-73. Technician, Telerent Leasing Corp., Raleigh, N.C., 1975-76; test engr. No. Telecom Co., Creedmoor, N.C., 1976—. Served with White House Communication Agency, U.S. Army, 1972-75. Recipient Presdl. Service medal. Mem. Am. Soc. Quality Control. Republican. Club: Beaverdam. Home: Route 1 Box 201 Creedmoor NC 27522 Office: 12507 Mt Hermon Church Rd Morrisville NC 27560

MC LEOD, ALEXANDER CANADAY, physician; b. Fayetteville, N.C., Jan. 14, 1935; s. Walter Guy and Vida (Canaday) McL.; A.B., Princeton U., 1956; M.D., Duke U., 1960; m. Dorothy Venning Woods, Aug. 21, 1965; children—Alexander Woods, Dorothy Seward. Intern, N.Y. Hosp., 1960-61, resident, 1961-62; resident Vanderbilt U. Hosp., Nashville, 1964-66, fellow in cardiology, instr. medicine, 1966-67, clin. faculty, 1967—, asst. clin. prof. medicine, 1976—; pvt. practice medicine, specializing in internal medicine, Nashville, 1967—. Former jr. warden St. George's Episcopal Ch. Served as flight surgeon USN, 1962-64. Recipient Physicians' Achievement award AMA, 1971, 74, 77; USPHS summer fellow in neurology, 1957-58; Middle Tenn. Heart Assn. fellow, 1966-67; diplomate Am. Bd. Internal Medicine. Fellow A.C.P. (gov.'s council for coll. affairs); mem. Nashville Acad. Medicine (physicians' services com.), Clan MacLeod Soc. U.S.A. (pres.). Republican. Clubs: Princeton of N.Y., Princeton of Nashville and Middle Tenn., Tower, Belle Meade Country, Univ. of Nashville. Contbr. articles on hereditary deafness to med. jours. Home: 203 Evelyn Ave Nashville TN 37205 Office: 300 Mid-State Med Center 2010 Church St Nashville TN 37203

MC LEOD, DANIEL ROGERS, state ofcl.; b. Sumter, S.C., Oct. 6, 1913; s. D. Melvin and Bertie (Guyton) McL.; student Wofford Coll., 1931-32; LL.B., U. S.C., 1948; m. Ellen D. LeBorde, May 20, 1941 (dec.); children—Daniel R., Elizabeth Ann; m. 2d, Virginia B. Hart, July 29, 1962; stepchildren—John E. Hart, Robert S. Hart. Admitted to S.C. bar, 1948; asst. atty. gen. S.C., Columbia, 1950-58, atty. gen., 1958—. Mem. Am., S.C. bar assns. Methodist. Home: 4511 Langrave Rd Columbia SC 29206 Office: Wade Hampton Office Bldg State Capitol Columbia SC 29211

MCLEOD, JAMES EUGENE, real estate co. exec.; b. Atlanta, June 11, 1940; s. James Duncan and Geneva Irene (Ray) McL.; certificate in accounting, LaSalle U., 1961; B.B.A., Ga. State U., 1970; m. Linda Jo Naff, June 17, 1961; children—Lisa Michelle, Sherry Jean. Auditor/accountant Gold Kist, Inc., Atlanta, 1960-63; accountant/asst. controller Terminal Transport, Inc., Atlanta, 1963-66; auditor Am. So. Ins. Co., Atlanta, 1966-69, treas., 1969-73, v.p., 1973-76; corp. accountant Citizens & So. Nat. Bank, Atlanta, 1976-79; asst. controller Citizens & So. Realty Investors, Atlanta, 1979—; tax accountant McLeod & Assos., Conyers, Ga., 1965—; treas. Rate-O-Gram, Inc., Atlanta, 1969-76; cons. corporate accountant Dixie Hauling Co., Inc., Ga. Trucking Co., Inc., Statewide Mgmt. Services, Inc., T&G Systems Control, Inc.; dir., treas. Over & Under Gen. Contractors, Inc. Football coach Midway Youth, 1971-74. Served with USNR, 1957-60. Mem. Ins. Accounting and Statis. Assn. (past pres. Ga. chpt.), Ga. Football Ofcls. Assn., Honey Creek Men's Golf Assn. (sec.-treas.). Democrat. Mem. Christian Ch. Clubs: Masons, Honey Creek Golf and Country, Toastmasters. Home: 886 Sugar Creek Dr Conyers GA 30207 Office: Box 4065 Atlanta GA 30302

MC LEOD, JAMES WILLIAM, orthopaedic surgeon; b. Oklahoma City, July 9, 1947; s. Joseph William and Lucille Elizabeth (True) McL.; M.D., U. Okla., 1972; m. Elaine Fenech, July 11, 1970; 1 son, Matthew James. Intern, Naval Regional Med. Center, Portsmouth, Va., 1972-73, resident in orthopaedic surgery, 1974-77; practice medicine specializing in orthopaedic surgery, Gloucester, Va., 1979—; staff orthopaedic surgeon Walter Reed Meml. Hosp., Gloucester, 1979—, Riverside Hosp., Newport News, Va., 1979—. Served with M.C., USN, 1971-79. Diplomate Am. Bd. Orthopaedic Surgery. Mem. AMA (physicians recognition award 1979), Med. Soc. Va. (physicians recognition award 1979), Mid-Tidewater Med. Soc., Assn. Mil. Surgeons U.S. Republican. Office: PO Box 646 Gloucester VA 23061

MC LEOD, JOHN WOODBURN, packaging co. exec.; b. McAlester, Okla., Mar. 22, 1939; s. Harold James and Katherine Gould (McElroy) McL.; B.B.A., Loyola U., New Orleans, 1961; m. Jean Kearney, June 8, 1961; children—Patricia, John Woodburn, Michael, Kathy. Sales trainee Continental Can Co., New Orleans, 1961-62, sales rep., Atlanta, 1962-65, sales service mgr., 1965-67, regional rep., Phila., 1967-69; sales rep. Consol. Box Co., Tampa, Fla., 1969-78, v.p. sales and mktg., 1978—. Football dir. Immaculate Heart of Mary Sch., 1975-78; pres. United Atlanta Metro League, 1976-78; active St. Vincent de Paul Soc., 1969-78. Mem. Sales and Mktg. Execs. Tampa and Atlanta, Ga. Poultry Fedn., Southeastern Poultry Assn., Ga. Ind. Meat Packers and Processors (v.p. asso. membership), Southeastern Fisheries Assn. Roman Catholic. Club: Toasmasters. Home: 4118 Cypress Bayou Dr Tampa FL 33618 Office: Consol Box Co 410 S Packwood Ave Tampa FL 33606

MCLEOD, PEDEN BROWN, state legislator; b. Walterboro, S.C., Sept. 3, 1940; s. Walton James and Rhoda Lane (Brown) McL.; A.B., Wofford Coll., 1962; J.D., U. S.C., 1967; m. Mary Waite Hamrick, July 7, 1962; children—Mary Carlisle, Peden Brown, Rhoda Lane, John Reaves. Student instr. U. S.C. Law Sch., 1967; admitted to S.C. bar, 1967; law clk. to U.S. dist. judge C.E. Simons, Jr., 1967-69; practice in Walterboro, 1969—; dir. First Nat. Bank in Orangeburg, Walterboro; mem. Walterboro City Council, 1970-72, S.C. Ho. of Reps., from Colleton County, 1972—, mem. ways and means com., rules com. Sec., Colleton County Democratic party, 1967-71. Served with AUS, 1962-64. Recipient Distinguished Ser. award Walterboro Jr. C. of C., 1972. Mem. S.C. State Bar (Ho. of Dels.), Kappa Alpha. Mason, Elk, Moose. Home: 512 Hampton St Walterboro SC 29488 Office: Box 230 Walterboro SC 29488

MCLESKEY, CHARLES HAMILTON, anesthesiologist; b. Phila., Nov. 8, 1946; s. William Hamilton and Marion Alta (Butts) McL.; B.A., Susquehanna U., Selinsgrove, Pa., 1968; M.D., Bowman Gray Sch. Medicine, Winston-Salem, N.C., 1972; m. Nanci Sue Simmons, June 3, 1972; children—Travis Hamilton, Heather Evelyn. Intern, Maine Med. Center, Portland, 1972-73; resident in anesthesiology U. Wash. Med. Center, Seattle, 1973-76, NIH research fellow in anesthesiology, 1974-75; mem. attending staff anesthesia N.C. Baptist Hosp., Winston-Salem, 1978—; asst. prof. Bowman Gray Sch. Medicine, 1978—. Served to lt. comdr. M.C., USNR, 1976-78. Woodruff-Fisher scholar, 1964-68; recipient Lange Med. award, 1972. Diplomate Am. Bd. Anesthesiology. Fellow Am. Coll. Anesthesiologists; mem. AMA, Am. Soc. Anesthesiologists, Am. Soc. Regional Anesthesia, Internat. Anesthesia Research Soc., Soc. Mil. Anesthesiologists, Am. Diabetes Assn., Forsyth County Med. Soc., N.C. Soc. Anesthesiologists, N.C. Med. Assn., So. Med. Assn., So. Soc. Anesthesiologists, Internat. Platform Assn., Alpha Omega Alpha, Tau Kappa Epsilon. Contbr. articles to med. jours. Home: 425 Gloucestershire Rd Winston-Salem NC 27104 Office: 300 S Hawthorne Rd Winston-Salem NC 27103

MC MAHAN, ROBERT CHANDLER, savs. and loan assn. exec.; b. Sevierville, Tenn., June 17, 1940; s. Homer Wright and Cathryn Alexander (Murphy) McM.; student U. Tenn., 1958-61; B.B.A., Ga. State U., 1972; m. Judith Ann Raymer, Dec. 23, 1963; children—Kellie Elizabeth, Alice Marie. Mgr. CrediThrift Fin. Corp., 1961-69; with Decatur Fed. Savs. and Loan Assn. (Ga.), 1969—, v.p., mgr. loan orgination, 1971-73, v.p. South regional mgr., 1973-74, sr. v.p., mgr. loan dept., 1974-75, exec. v.p., chief operating officer, 1975—; pres., dir. CorresponDecatur, Inc., 1976-79, chmn. bd., 1979—. Bd. dirs. YMCA, Decatur-DeKalb, 1974-76, 79—, sec., 1976. Served with U.S. Army, 1962-63. Mem. Home Builders Assn. Met. Atlanta (dir.), DeKalb Bd. Realtors, DeKalb Developers Assn., Goals for DeKalb (dir.), Citizens for Better Govt., DeKalb C. of C. (dir. 1978—), Sigma Phi Omega. Mem. Ch. of Christ. Clubs: Rotary, Masons. Home: 1818 Bedfordshire Dr Decatur GA 30033 Office: 250 E Ponce de Leon Ave Decatur GA 30031

MC MAHAN, ROBERT KENNETH, physicist; b. Concord, N.C., Dec. 5, 1933; s. Henry G. and Clara H. (Hoke) McM.; B.S., Catawba Coll., 1958; M.S., U. Fla., 1963, Ph.D., 1966; m. Barbara Gaines, Dec. 28, 1957; 1 son, Robert Kenneth. Engr., Control Laser Corp., 1967-71; pres., dir. research and devel. McMahan Assos., Inc., Winter Park, Fla., 1971—; cons. to mil. and govtl. research and devel. labs. Served with inf. AUS, 1953-55. Mem. IEEE, Optical Soc. Am. Republican. Lutheran. Patentee in field. Home: 60 E Stovin Ave Winter Park FL 32789 Office: 2160 Park Ave N Winter Park FL 32789

MC MAHON, JOHN MARTIN, physician; b. Buffalo, Dec. 24, 1915; s. Charles A. and Mary (Fox) McM.; B.S., Georgetown U., 1936, M.D., 1940; M.S. in Medicine, U. Minn., 1950; m. Virginia Mary Tracy, Mar. 21, 1942; children—John Martin, Edward, Barbara, Robert, Bruce, Tommy. Intern, Georgetown U. Hosp., Washington, 1940-41; fellow internal medicine Mayo Found., 1945-50; practice medicine specializing in internal medicine, Bessemer, Ala.; asso. Browne-McHardy Clinic, New Orleans, 1950-52; partner Bessemer Clinic, 1952—; prof. clin. medicine U. Ala., 1952—, dir. Arthritis Clinic Med. Center; attending cons. VA Hosp., Birmingham; chief of medicine Bapt. Med. Center-Princeton, Birmingham, also asso. dir. med. edn., 1974—; mem. staff Bessemer Carraway Med. Center. Served to capt. AUS, World War II; PTO. Recipient Benemerenti award Pope Paul VI, 1968. Diplomate Am. Bd. Internal Medicine. Fellow A.C.P., Am. Coll. Gastroenterology (past pres.). Contbr. articles to profl. jours. Home: 106 Waverly Circle Bessemer AL 35020 Office: Bessemer Clinic PO Box 747 Bessemer AL 35020

MC MAHON, RHETT RUSSELL, rental property co. exec.; b. Baton Rouge, Nov. 16, 1916; s. Rhett Gustav and Pearl F. (Fridge) McM.; student La. State U., 1934-35; B.S., Tulane U., 1939; m. Yvonne Marie Barbe, May 29, 1941; children—Rhett, Claudia Barbe, Diane Marie. Owner, mgr. rental properties, Baton Rouge, 1946—; dir. Baton Rouge Water Works Co. Served as m/sgt. M.C., AUS, 1941-45; ETO. Mem. Baton Rouge C. of C., Kappa Sigma. Kiwanian (pres. 1952). Club: Baton Rouge Country. Address: 1645 Perkins Rd Baton Rouge LA 70808

MCMAHON, WILLIAM HERBERT, health systems exec.; b. Chgo., Sept. 6, 1943; s. Ambrose James and Mary Ann (Herbert) McM.; B.A., Eastern Wash. State Coll., 1972; M.P.H., Okla. U., 1974; m. Marian J. Beaty, Aug. 23, 1967; children—Christina, William Herbert, Tracy. Health planner Spokane County (Wash.), 1972-73; asst. adminstr. Univ. Hosp., Oklahoma City, 1974-76; cons. Univ. Hosp., Ann Arbor, Mich., 1976-77; cons. Deloitte, Haskins & Sells, Detroit, 1977-79; pres. Trans-Coastal Health Systems, Terrell, Tex., 1979—; faculty field supr. Okla. U. Grad. Sch. Health, 1975; chmn. Spokane County Emergency Services Planning Com., 1972. Served with USAF, 1965-68. Mem. Hosp. Mgmt. Systems Soc. (chmn. nursing com. Mich. chpt. 1979), Am. Coll. Hosp. Adminstrs., Am. Assn. Hosp. Cons., Am. Hosp. Assn. Home: Box 304 Edgewood TX 75117

MC MANAWAY, HAROLD GENE, banker; b. Hancock County, Ky., Nov. 19, 1942; s. Leslie Virgil ano Eva Dell (Fuqua) McM.; B.S. in Mgmt., U. Louisville, 1975, certificate data processing, 1974; m. Sue Ann Lowery, Jan. 19, 1963; children—Cherie Ann, Douglas Gene. Supr., Profl. Service Bur., Winter Haven, Fla., 1964-65; computer operator Ford Motor Co., Louisville, Ky., 1965-67; supr. data processing Reynolds Metals Co., Louisville, 1967-70; v.p. Bank of Louisville, 1970—; adj. instr. data processing Jefferson Community Coll., Louisville. Served with USAF, 1960-64. Mem. Assn. Systems Mgmt. (officer Louisville chpt.), Kentuckiana Automated Clearing House Assn. Clubs: Jaycees, Optimist. Home: 7308 Wood Rock Rd Louisville KY 40291 Office: Bank of Louisville PO Box 1101 Louisville KY 40201

MC MANIS, JAMES CARL, pathologist; b. Hot Springs, Ark., Jan. 13, 1938; s. Thayne Foster and Reva Ione (Rigdon) McM.; B.S., U. Iowa, 1960, M.D., 1963; m. Linda Ann Bodine, Aug. 18, 1963; children—Steven Patrick, Michael James, Kevin Douglas. Intern, Brooke Gen. Hosp., San Antonio, 1963-64; resident Tripler Army Med. Center, Honolulu, 1964-68; dir. lab. Central Baptist Hosp., Lexington, Ky., 1972—. Served with U.S. Army, 1963-72. Fellow Coll. Am. Pathologists, Am. Soc. Clin. Pathologists; mem. AMA, Ky. Soc. Pathologists (sec. treas. 1977—). Home: 2072 Bridgeport Dr Lexington KY 40502 Office: Central Baptist Hospital and Pathology and Cytology Laboratory Lexington KY 40503

MC MANN, PATRICK THOMAS, govt. ofcl.; b. Queens, N.Y.C., Dec. 6, 1949; s. John and Veronica (Malone) Skelly; B.S., St. Thomas Aquinas Coll., 1973; M.S., E. Tex. State U., 1979. Dir. placement Apex Tech. Sch., N.Y.C., 1973; dir. summer ednl. programs City of St. Louis, summer 1974; vol. Glenwary, Mt. Pleasant, Tex., 1975-76; dir. ednl. programs Dept. Labor, Mt. Vernon, Tex., 1976-77; housing specializing Ark.-Tex. Council of Govts., Texarkana, Tex., 1977—. Mem. Am. Personnel and Guidance Assn., Tex. Personnel and Guidance Assn., Nat. Assn. Housing and Redevel. Ofcls., Tex. Career and Guidance Assn., Nat. Vocat. Guidance Assn., Alpha Chi. Democrat. Roman Catholic. Home: PO Box 1018 Commerce TX 75428 Office: PO Box 5307 Texarkana TX 75501

MC MANUS, LUTHER MITCHELLE, JR., psychologist, hypnotist, educator; b. Washington, Dec. 13, 1921; s. Luther Michell and Hattie (Catoe) McM.; B.S., Miner Tchr.'s Coll., 1943; grad. Command and Gen. Staff Coll., 1963; M.A. in History and Psychology, 1963; Ed.S., George Washington U., 1970, Ed.D., 1973, postgrad., 1976—. Clk., Dept. Navy, 1941-43; served as enlisted man U.S. Army, 1941-45, commd. officer, 1948, advanced through grades to lt. col.; served in Korea, 1950-51; inf. platoon leader, co. comdr., Europe, 1956-59, tank comdr., 1964-67, then sta. Pentagon, Washington; ret., 1968; operative, patrolman Washington Met. Police Vice Squad, 1945-50; dir. admissions and records prof. history Fed. City Coll., U. D.C., 1969-71; asst. chancellor Fayetteville (N.C.) State U., 1971-73, dir. student services center, 1976—, prof. edn. and psychology, 1971—; pvt. practice counseling, hypnotherapy, 1976—. Lay reader, vestryman Episcopal Ch., Diocese of East Carolina; del. Union of Black Clergy and Laity, Washington; chmn. Fayetteville State U. Affirmative Action Com., 1977—. Decorated Disting. Service Cross, Purple Heart, Legion of Merit. Mem. Am. Personnel and Guidance Assn., Am. Psychol. Assn., Soc. Clin. and Exptl. Hypnosis, Assn. Black Psychologists, Phi Delta Kappa. Democrat. Author: The Enigma of Instruction, 1961; (with James Cunningham) The New Breed of Black Activists, 1971. Home: 405 Glen Canyon Dr Fayetteville NC 28303 Office: Fayetteville State U Newbold Sta Fayetteville NC 28301

MC MANUS, PHILIP DANIEL, business exec.; b. Chgo., Apr. 15, 1916; s. Jackson B. and Isabelle (Lewis) McM.; B.A., U. Chgo., 1943, M.B.A., 1946; m. Arvada Belle Roche, July 6, 1935; children—Marilyn McManus Osborn, Bonnie McManus Ruggles, Philip Daniel, Kerry. With A.O. Smith Corp., 1947-63, corporate controller, Milw., 1947-60, gen. mgr. meter and service sta. equipment div., Erie, Pa., 1960-63; v.p. Eagle-Picher Industries, Inc., Cin., 1963-69, group v.p., 1969-73, exec. v.p., 1973-79, also pres. Ohio Rubber Co. div., Willoughby, 1965-69; chmn. bd. McDonough Co., Parkersburg, W.Va., 1979—; dir. Rapoca Energy Corp., Le Blond. Mem. Financial Execs. Inst. Am. (past dir. Milw. chpt.). Clubs: Hyde Park Country; Cincinnati Country, Queen City; Parkersburg Country; Detroit Athletic. Home: 51 Oakwood Estates Parkersburg WV 26101 Office: Box 1774 Parkersburg WV 26101

MC MASTERS, JESSE LOWELL, agrl. engr.; b. Walters, Okla., Oct. 10, 1935; s. Jesse Keith and Francis Lee (Riney) McM.; A.A., Cameron Coll., 1960; B.S., Okla. State U., 1963; postgrad. in soils mechanics engring. Utah State U., 1977; m. Minnie Lou Perkins, June 18, 1955; children—Bobby, Kathy, David. With Soil Conservation Service, 1963—, area engr., Pauls Valley, Okla., 1972—. Dist. commr. Boy Scouts Am., 1973-75, cubmaster Arbuckle council, 1974-75, Webelos leader, 1975, mem. exec. bd. area council, 1976. Served with USAF, 1954-58. Recipient Outstanding Service award Soil Conservation Service, 1969, Certificate of Merit award, 1974. Mem. Am. Soc. Agrl. Engrs., Soil Conservation Soc. Am. (pres. South Central Okla. chpt. 1975), Okla. Soc. Land Surveyors (charter mem.). Elk. Home: 1317 Denson Dr Pauls Valley OK 73075 Office: PO Box 200 Pauls Valley OK 73075

MC MICHAEL JAMES ELMER, state agy. adminstr.; b. Shreveport, La., Mar. 6, 1932; s. Claude Ernest and Tressie (Evans) McM.; B.S., La. Tech. U., 1954; M.A., Northwestern State U., 1958; postgrad. Auburn U., 1960; m. Velma Willene Williams, July 2, 1971. Tchr., coach Webster Parish Schs., Minden, La., 1955-61; employment and benefits mgr. Sperry Rand, Shreveport, 1961-75; personnel supr. Thiokol-La., Shreveport, 1975-79; claims rep. La. State Employment Service, Minden, 1980—; cons. area schs., civic clubs, bus.; notary public. Mem. Minden Citizens Com. for Municipal Devel., 1968-69; Thiokol-La. campaign chmn. United Way, 1975; organizer, chmn. Vol. Blood Donor Campaign, 1977, 78. Mem. Am. Def. Preparedness Assn., Met. Personnel Assn., Nat. Geog. Assn., Norla Mgmt. Assn., NEA, La. Tchrs. Assn., Classroom Tchrs. Assn. Democrat. Baptist. Clubs: Lions, Jaycees. Home: Route 1 Box 47 Minden LA 71055 Office: PO Box 490 Minden LA 71055

MCMICHAEL, ROBERT N., univ. adminstr.; b. Shreveport, La., Oct. 9, 1926; s. Everett Robert and Lola Virginia (Nance) McM.; B.S., La. Tech. U., 1948; M.B.A., La. State U., 1958, Ph.D., 1961; m. Sandra Marie Martin, Dec. 17, 1972; children—Robert, Dennis, Bryan, Cynthia, Michael. Plant engr. Hunt Oil Co., Harleton, Tex., 1948-52; gas engr. Magnolia Petroleum Co., Lake Charles, La., 1952-53; field engr. Socony Mobil de Venezuela, 1953-56; asst. prof. NE La. State U., 1960-61; asso. prof. Lamar U., Beaumont, Tex., 1961-63; asso. prof. U. Ark., Fayetteville, 1963-65; dean Sch. Bus. Adminstrn., Pan Am. U., Edinburg, Tex., 1965—; dir. Nat. Bank of Commerce, Edinburg, 1979—. Chmn. adminstrv. bd. 1st Methodist Ch., Edinburg, 1979-80. Mem. Southwestern Bus. Adminstrn. Assn. (pres. 1978-79), Tex. Council Collegiate Edn. for Bus., Edinburg C. of C. (past dir.). Club: Kiwanis (past pres.). Home: 1111 McKee Dr Edinburg TX 78539 Office: Sch Bus Adminstrn Pan American U Edinburg TX 78539

MC MILLAN, GEORGE DUNCAN HASTIE, JR., lawyer, state ofcl.; b. Greenville, Ala., Oct. 11, 1943; s. George Duncan Hastie and Jean (Autrey) McM.; B.A. magna cum laude, Auburn U., 1966; LL.B. (Southeastern regional scholar), U. Va., 1969; m. Ann Louise Dial, Nov. 20, 1971; children—George Duncan Hastie, Ann Dial. Admitted to Ala. bar, 1969; research asst. dept. agronomy Auburn U., summers 1963-65; law clk. firm Lange, Simpson, Robinson & Somerville, Birmingham, Ala., summers 1967-68; law clk. to judge U.S. Dist. Ct. for No. Dist. Ala., 1969-70; instr. U. Ala. Law Sch., 1969-70; individual practice law, Birmingham, 1970-71; partner firm McMillan & Spratling, Birmingham, 1971—; mem. Ala. Ho. of Reps., 1973, Ala. Senate, 1974-78; lt. gov. State of Ala., Birmingham, 1978—; mem. Permanent Study Commn. on Ala.'s Jud. System, 1975-79. Chmn., Ala. Film Commn.; mem. arts task force Nat. Conf. State Legislatures; mem. Multi-State Transp. Adv. Bd.; mem., com. chmn. So. Growth Policies Bd.; bd. dirs. Campfire, Inc., Met. YMCA, Birmingham, Boys and Girls Ranches, Ala. Served to lt. U.S. Army, 1969. Recipient award Ala. Nurses Assn., 1975; named Legislator of Yr., Ala. Forestry Assn., 1978, Hardest Working Senator, Capitol Press Corps, 1976, One of 4 Outstanding Young Men, Ala. Jaycees, 1977, One of 10 Most Outstanding State Legislators, Assn. Govtl. Employees, 1978; award Birmingham Emancipation Assn., 1977, Ala. Hist. Commn., 1978; James Tingle award, 1979. Mem. Am. Bar Assn., Ala. Bar Assn., Birmingham Bar Assn., Birmingham Jaycees, Ala. Jaycees (dir. 1970-72), Birmingham Urban League, United Negro Coll. Fund. Democrat. Mem. Ch. of Christ. Club: Rotary (Birmingham). Office: 1550 1st Nat So Natural Bldg Birmingham AL 35203

MC MILLAN, HUGH DIX, JR., mfrs. rep. and distbr.; b. Shreveport, La., Sept. 15, 1925; s. Hugh Dix and Edna (Self) McM.; B.S., Tex. A. and M. Coll., 1947; m. Dorothy Jean Sawyer, May 10, 1952; children—Hugh Dix III, Janet Lynn. Design engr. Coastal Equipment Co., Houston, 1947-48; design and sales engr. D & S Sales, Inc., 1948-49; sales engr. J.R. Dowdell & Co., 1949-55; pres. McMillan Equipment Co., 1955—. Dir. F.E. Giesecke Meml. Fund, Austin, Tex. Served with AC, AUS, 1943-45, Res., 1947-61. Mem. Am. Soc. Heating, Refrigerating and Air Conditioning Engrs. (past pres. Houston chpt., past nat. dir., regional chmn., nat. treas. 1976-77, nat. v.p. 1977-78), nat. pres.-elect 1978-79, nat. pres. 1979-80), Houston Engring. and Sci. Soc., Am. Assn. Engring. Socs. (bd. govs. 1980), Nat., Tex. socs. profl. engrs. Baptist. Mason (Shriner). Club: Pine Forest Country. Designed, furnished equipment for heating and ventilating 87 bldgs. for Trans-Alaska Pipeline system from North Slope to Valdez. Home: 13302 Apple Tree Houston TX 77079 Office: 16720 Park Row Houston TX 77084

MCMILLAN, MICHAEL REID, orthopedic surgeon; b. Conway, S.C., Aug. 28, 1941; s. Hoyt and Sara Best (Sherwood) McM.; B.S., The Citadel, 1963: M.D., Duke U., 1967. Intern in medicine Balt. City Hosps., 1967-68; fellow in medicine Johns Hopkins Hosp., Balt., 1967-68; resident in orthopedic surgery Greenville (S.C.) Hosp. Systems and Greenville Shriners Hosp., 1971-75; practice medicine specializing in orthopedic surgery, Conway, S.C., 1975—; mem. staff Conway Hosp., 1975—, chief of orthopedics, 1975—. Trustee Burroughs Found., Conway, 1979. Served to lt. comdr. MC, USN, 1968-71; Vietnam. Diplomate Nat. Bd. Med. Examiners, Am. Bd. Orthopedic Surgery; lic. physician, S.C. Mem. AMA, S.C. Med. Assn., S.C. Orthopedic Assn., Horry County Med. Soc., Assn. of Citadel Men. Baptist. Club: Horry County Citadel. Home and Office: 1400 9th Ave Conway SC 29526

MCMILLIAN, JENNIFER HANNON, speech pathologist; b. Schenectady, Feb. 27, 1954; d. James King and Patricia Cross Hannon; student Tex. Christian U., 1972-73; B.A. in Speech Pathology U. Houston, 1976, M.A. in Speech Pathology, 1977; m. Don Forrest McMillian, Jr., Aug. 17, 1974; 1 dau., Meredith Leigh. Teaching asst., diagnostic testing lab. instr. U. Houston, 1976; speech pathologist, jr. high schs. Spring Branch Ind. Sch. Dist., Houston, 1977-79; pvt. practice speech pathology, Houston, 1978—. Leader handicapped troop Girls Scouts U.S.A., 1976; mem. Nat. Republican Senatorial Com., 1979. Recipient cert. of commendation Spring Branch Ind. Sch. Dist., 1977; tchr. cert., Tex. Mem. Am. Speech and Hearing Assn. (cert. of clin. competence in speech pathology), Tex. Speech and Hearing Assn., Mortar Board, Zeta Tau Alpha. Mem. Christian Ch. (Disciples of Christ).

MC MILLON, RAYMOND CECIL, JR., dentist; b. San Antonio, Tex., Aug. 21, 1943; s. Raymond Cecil and Evelyn Bernice (Reese) McM.; B.S., Baylor U., 1966; D.M.D., U. Louisville, 1972; postgrad. Tex. Tech. U., 1966-68; m. Carol Jean Crush, June 12, 1971; children—Jennifer Lynn, Wendy Raye. Teaching fellow Tex. Tech. U., Lubbock, 1966-68, research fellow, 1967-69; pvt. practice dentistry, Louisville, 1974—; dental cons. Ky. Sch. for the Blind, 1974—; faculty Watterson Community Coll., 1974—. Trustee, Chance Sch., Inc., 1977-82, pres. bd. trustees, 1978-81. Served with U.S. Army, 1972-74. Decorated Army Commendation medal; named hon. Ky. col., 1974. Licensed dentist, Ky. Mem. Ky. Dental Assn., Am. Endodontic Soc., Louisville Dental Soc., ADA, Internat. Coll. Oral Implantology, Am. Orthodontic Soc. (pres. 1978—), Delta Sigma Delta, Alpha Phi Omega. Home: 1901 Lonlipman Ct Louisville KY 40207 Office: 4004 Dutchmans Ln Louisville KY 40207 and 3023 Crums Ln Louisville KY 40216

MC MILLON, REGNAL LUTHER, ins. co. exec., pub. speaker; b. Guion, Tex., Apr. 23, 1921; s. James Luther and Tennessee Jones (Haynie) McM.; student Tarleton State Coll., 1938; m. Elsie Eugenia Roberts, Dec. 14, 1941; children—Toni Karen, Steven Grant. Internat. speaker for convs., clubs, other orgns.; with Bus. Men's Assurance Co., Abilene, Tex., 1946-71, dist. mgr., 1956-60, br. mgr., Abilene, Tex., 1961-71; gen. agt. Washington Nat. Ins. Co., Lubbock, Tex., 1971—. Dir. Nat. Gen. Agts. and Mgrs. Conf.; trustee Life Underwriters Tng. Council U.S., pres., 1965-66. Served with USAAF, 1942-46. Named Ins. Field Man of Yr. in Life Ins. in U.S., 1962; Internat. Health Ins. Man of Yr., 1965; recipient Harold R. Gordon Meml. award Internat. Assn. Health Underwriters, 1965, Distinguished Service award Vocational Agr. Tchrs. Tex., 1965; John Newton Russell award, 1967. Mem. Nat. (pres, 1961-62), Tex. (pres. 1956-57) assns. life underwriters, Tex. Assn. Health Underwriters (pres. 1954-55). Author numerous articles on selling, human relations. Home: 7003 B Hartford St Lubbock TX 79413 Office: 2321 50th St Lubbock TX 79412

MC MINN, MARY INEZ LAMURY, artist; b. Alexandria, La., June 17, 1921; d. Theophile Jean Ferdinand and Alice Inez (Jones) Lamury; student La. State U., 1939-40, 44-45, Charleston (W.Va.) Art Gallery of Sunrise, 1965-76; m. Taylor Howard McMinn, July 15, 1949. Head editor La. State U. Press, 1946-49; free lance editor, 1949-78; tchr. art YWCA, Charleston, 1971—, Charleston Art Gallery, 1975-77, Garnet Adult Edn. Center, 1978—; one-man shows include: Charleston Art Gallery, 1976, Oak Hill (W.Va.) Art Center, 1977, Comml. Bank of Parkersburg (W.Va.), 1978; group shows include: W.Va. Women's Yr. Juried Invitational Exhbn., Charleston, 1977, W.Va. Invitational at Parkersburg, 1977, Pen Women Nat. Biennial, Washington, 1976; represented in permanent collection of State of W.Va. at Cultural Center, Charleston; mem. Gallery Eleven art coop. Mem. Allied Artists of W.Va., Nat. League Am. Pen Women. Clubs: Carbide Tennis, Hilltoppers. Home: 723 Gordon Dr Charleston WV 25303

MC MINN, WILLIAM GENE, architect; b. Abilene, Tex., Aug. 27, 1931; s. Ollie and Mabel (Renfro) McM.; B.A., Rice U., 1952, B.S. in Architecture, 1953; M.Arch., U. Tex., Austin, 1954; m. Joan Gentry, Dec. 10, 1955; children—Kevin, Tracey. Prof. architecture, head dept. architecture Auburn U., 1965-68; dir. design Six Assos., Inc., Asheville, N.C., 1968-71; head dept. architecture La. State U., 1971-74; dean Sch. Architecture Miss. State U., 1974—; mem. public adv. panel GSA, 1978; mem. Nat. Architecture Accrediting Bd., 1980; adv. U. Jordan, Ammon. Mem. Starkville Planning Commn., 1977. Served with U.S. Army, 1953-56. Nat. Endowment for Arts grantee, 1976—. Fellow AIA (N.C. chpt. Design award 1970, honor awards jury for extended use 1979); mem. Assn. Collegiate Schs. Architecture (dir.). Presbyterian. Club: Rotary. Architect: Chem. Research Bldg., Research Triangle Park, N.C., 1970; various bldgs. Mars Hill Coll., 1972. Home: 2206 Plum Rd Starkville MS 39759 Office: PO Drawer AO Miss State U Mississippi State MS 39762

MC MULLAN, JAMES FRANKLIN, ins. cons.; b. Atlanta, Feb. 24, 1928; s. Jesse James and Ruth Guinn (Thomason) McM.; student U. of South, 1945-47; B.B.A., Emory U., 1949; m. Jo Anne Lovern, Sept. 13, 1951; children—Corrie Anne McMullan Cox, Martha Jane (dec.), Ruth Lynn, Robert L., Beth Lovern. Credit reporter Dun & Bradstreet, Inc., Atlanta and Savannah, Ga., 1950-55; agt., asst. gen. agt., gen. agt. State Mut. Life Assurance Co., Worcester, Mass. and Atlanta, 1955-78, gen. agt. emeritus, 1979—, sr. agt., advanced underwriting cons., 1979—. Active United Meth. Ch.; pres. bd. dirs. The Cornerstone, 1976—; sec. New Life Center, Inc., Atlanta, 1978, bd. dirs., 1977-78. Recipient Nat. Mgmt. award for Agency Building, 1972-77, nat. quality award, 1957-78; named to State and nat. Circle of Honor for sales, 1961-63; life mem. Ga. Leaders Round Table; named S. Fulton's Young Man of Year, 1961; hon. lt. col. Ga. Gov.'s Staff. C.L.U. Mem. Atlanta Estate Planning Council, Am. Soc. C.L.U. (Golden Key), Atlanta Life Underwriters Assn., Gen. Agts. and Mgrs. Assn. (pres. 1976). Republican. Methodist. Clubs: Jaycees (bd. dirs. S. Fulton), Optimists (charter pres. Tri-City, lt. gov. Ga. Clubs, life mem.). Home: 2935 Duke of Gloucester East Point GA 30344 Office: 2700 Cumberland Pkwy Suite 500 Atlanta GA 30339

MC MULLEN, LINDA ROYSTER, counselor; b. Macon, Ga., Oct. 20, 1945; d. Floyd Robertson and Elma (Hall) Royster; A.B. in Sociology, Emory U., 1967; M.S. in Counselor Edn., U. Bridgeport, 1976; m. James Clayton McMullen, Sept, 3, 1967; children—James Clayton, Linda Jean. Project Headstart tchr. Union Elem. Sch., Macon, Ga., summer 1966; caseworker Atlanta Employment Evaluation and Service Center, 1967; tchr. social studies Atlanta Public Schs., 1968-69; substitute tchr. Novato (Calif.) Unified Sch. System, 1969-70; tchr. social studies Westmoreland (N.Y.) Central High Sch., 1970-72; tchr. sixth grade Patrician Acad., Butler, Ala., 1972-73, tchr. social studies, dept. chmn., 1973-74; substitute tchr. sch. systems in Bethel, Brookfield and New Fairfield, Conn., 1974-75; guidance intern Brookfield High Sch., 1976; guidance counselor Hartsville (S.C.) Sr. High Sch., 1976-77; counselor Darlington Youth Home, 1978-79; Teen-Peer Counseling Program coordinator Darlington County (S.C.) Sch. Dist., 1977. Vol., Fairhaven Sch. for Mentally Retarded, Atlanta, 1963-67; advisor pep squads, sch. clubs, Future Tchrs. Am., Nat. Beta Club, 1968-74; dir. ACTEENS, First Baptist Ch., Butler, 1973-74; advisor Butler Teen Club, 1973-74; pavilion chmn. Butler Civiettes, 1973-74; tng. union leader older youth Candlewood Bapt. Ch., 1975, youth council, 1975; vol. Snoopy Day Camp, summers 1976-77; Laubach tutor, 1976-77, county coordinator, 1977-79; Mid-Hi counselor Methodist Youth Fellowship, 1976-77; program com. Human Services Assn. Darlington County, 1976-78. Mem. Am., S.C. personnel and guidance assns., Am. Coll. Personnel Assn., Am. Sch. Counselors Assn., Assn. Specialists in Group Work, Internat. Transactional Analysis Assn., NEA, AAUW, Darlington County Tchrs. Assn., S.C. Edn. Assn., Kappa Delta, Emory U., Kappa Delta alumni assns. Methodist. Composer sociology courses syllabus, Atlanta Public School System Curriculum Revision Com., 1969. Home: 116 Schooner Dr Savannah GA 31410

MC MULLIN, LEO FRANCIS, educator; b. Paterson, N.J., Apr. 23, 1919; s. Edward P. and Abby (Martin) McM.; B.A. cum laude, Montclair State Coll., 1940; M.B.A., N.Y. U., 1949; m. Louise M. Willing, Apr. 26, 1947; children—Lawrence W., Amy Louise. Personnel tng. exec. bur. pub. debt U.S. Treasury Dept., Chgo., 1941-45; various positions Andrew Jergens Co., Cin., 1945-61; v.p., dir. media and research Stockton West Burkhart, Inc., Cin., 1961-75, exec. v.p., 1975-79; asst. prof. Lander Coll., Greenwood, S.C., 1979—; adj. asso. prof. mktg. Xavier U., 1956-79. Mem. Am. Mktg. Assn. (pres. Cin. chpt. 1959-60), So. Mktg. Assn., Am. Acad. Advt., Internat. Newspaper Advt. Execs., Am. Assn. Advt. Agys. (newspaper relations com. 1962-63, 67-76). Home: 211 Wellington Dr Greenwood SC 29646 Office: Lander Coll Box 6102 Greenwood SC 29646

MC MURDIE, DENNIS STODDARD, geothermal geologist; b. Logan, Utah, Aug. 16, 1939; s. Neil Hansen and Eva Riggs (Stoddard) McM.; Am. Field Service exchange student, N.Z., 1958; student Brigham Young U., 1958-63; B.S., U. Utah, 1967; M.S., U. So. Calif., 1968; m. Ruth Blanchard, Dec. 27, 1962; children—Neil Deloy, Christina, Celeste, Russell. Devel. geologist THUMS Long Beach (Calif.) Co., 1967-70, Los Angeles Basin, Union Oil Co., Santa Fe Springs, 1970-74; area geologist Union Oil Co., Santa Rosa, Calif., 1974-78; geothermal geologist Western U.S.A., Southland Royalty Co., Ft. Worth, 1978—; instr. Calif. State U., Fullerton, 1973-74. Chmn., Boy Scouts Am. family sustaining membership dr., Santa Rosa, 1978; del. Utah Gov.'s Com. for Student Edn., 1967; chmn. family dr. for Sonoma County (Calif.), Pres. Ford's Dinner, 1978. Registered geologist, Calif. Mem. Geol. Soc. Am., Am. Assn. Petroleum Geologists, Geothermal Resource Council (dir.), Sigma Xi. Republican. Mem. Ch. Jesus Christ of Latter-Day Saints (2d counselor 1st ward bishopric). Club: Country. Contbr. articles to profl. jours.; contbr. to U.S. Geol. Survey maps of geysers. Home: 7620 Skylake Dr Fort Worth TX 76179 Office: 1000 Fort Worth Club Tower Fort Worth TX 76102

MC MURRY, CLAUDIA PAULINE, speech pathologist; b. Pratt, Kans., Feb. 7, 1952; d. Gordon M. and Jean Vee (Vogt) Herr; student Hastings (Nebr.) Coll., 1970-72, U. Salzburg, Austria, 1972; B.A. in Edn. cum laude, Wichita State U., 1974, M.A. in Logopedics, 1975; m. David Lynn McMurry, Apr. 10, 1976: 1 son, Andrew Mitchell. Speech pathologist Dumas (Tex.) Independent Sch. Dist., 1976-79; pvt. practice speech pathology, Dumas, 1979—. Mem. Am. Speech, Lang. and Hearing Assn. (cert. clin. competence), Tex. Speech and Hearing Assn., Panhandle Regional Speech and Hearing Assn., Tex. State Tchrs. Assn., Tex. Profl. Educators, AAUW, Kappa Delta Pi. Republican. Methodist. Address: 610 Belmont St PO Box 272 Dumas TX 79029

MC MURTRY, EDWARD HOYSE, architect; b. Silverton, Tex., July 11, 1912; s. Edward Dawson and Ollie Mae (Smithee) McM.; B.A. in Arch., Tex. Tech. U., 1937; m. Esther Lloyd Jones, Sept. 4, 1938; children—Kathryn (Mrs. Warren E. Hunt), Allan Edward, Steven Lloyd. Draftsman, Robert E. Merrell, architect, Clovis, N.Mex., 1938-41, Wyatt C. Hedrick, Houston, 1941-42, Atcheson & Atkinson, architects, Lubbock, Tex., 1946-51; chief draftsman O.R. Walker, Lubbock, 1951-53; partner McMurtry & Craig, architects and engrs., Lubbock, 1953—. Pres. Friends of Tex. Libraries, 1971-73. Trustee, mem. exhibits com. West Tex. Mus. Assn., Lubbock; bd. dirs. Lubbock Boys Club; mem. camper program com. Tex. Lions Camp for Crippled Children. Served with USAAF, 1944-46. Mem. AIA (pres. Lubbock chpt. 1966), Tex. Soc. Architects, Tau Beta Pi. Democrat. Baptist. Lion (dist. gov. 1972-73). Prin. works: Tulia (Tex.) High Sch., 1956; Evans Jr. High Sch. Lubbock, 1958, Tex. Tech. U. Mus., Lubbock, 1968, Dormitory Bldgs., 1957-63; George and Helen Mahon Library, Lubbock, 1973; Copper Breaks State Park, Quanah, Tex., 1974; Goddard Range and Wildlife Mgmt. Bldg. Tex. Tech. U., 1975; Swisher County Meml. Library, Mus. and Sr. Citizens Center, Tulia, 1979, Telegraph and Telephone Hdqrs., Tulia, 1979; various chs. Home: 3813 27th St Lubbock TX 79410 Office: 3408 32d St Lubbock TX 79410

MC NABB, COLETA PEOPLES, med. clinic adminstr.; b. Marquez, Tex., Sept. 29, 1916; d. James Harmon and Ida Maud (McDaniel) Peoples; student Sam Houston State U., 1932-36, U. Houston, 1962-65; m. Marvin Jackson McNabb, Nov. 26, 1935 (div.); children—Jimanne McNabb Durkee, Michael James; m. 2d, Samuel V. Smith, Aug. 11, 1973. With Gulf Oil Corp., Houston, 1950-53, Hermann Hosp., Houston, 1956-58; with Tellepsen Petrochem. Corp., Houston, 1958-60; with Goodwin, Dannenbaum, Littman & Wingfield, Inc., Houston, 1960-62; with Med. Clinic Houston, 1962—, mgr., 1965-68, adminstr., 1968—. Reader, Taping for the Blind, 1968-70; patron Jr. League Houston, 1977—; editor Houston Heart Assn., 1971-72. Mem. Med. Group Mgmt. Assn., Am. Group Practice Assn., Med. Adminstrs. Tex., Nat. Assn. Female Execs., So. Mgmt. Assn. Republican. Home: 10319 Longmont St Houston TX 77042 Office: 1707 Sunset St Houston TX 77005

MC NABB, NORMAN WARE, ednl. adminstr.; b. Greenwood, Ark., Feb. 15, 1924; s. Charles M. and Eula O. (Thompson) McN.; B.A., U. Okla., 1950, M.S., 1968, Ed.D., 1972; m. Betty Sue Neal, Aug. 1, 1947; children—Scott, Susan, Dana, Bruce. Propr., pres. The Sports Center, Norman, Okla., 1949-65, Midwest Sports Center, Midwest City, Okla., 1952-55; coach freshman football U. Okla., 1951-60, dir. gen. services, 1968-72; dir. personnel Okla. Dept. Wildlife, Oklahoma City, 1965-68; pres. Carl Albert Jr. Coll., Poteau, Okla., 1973-75; dir. adminstrv. services U. Tex., Dallas, Richardson, 1975—, prof. edn., 1972—; cons. bus. mgmt., 1955-72. Scoutmaster, Last Frontier council Boy Scouts Am., 1952-70; chmn. United Cerebral Palsy, 1952-55, United Way, 1977-80; mem. City Council Norman, 1960-61, vice mayor, 1962. Served with USMC, 1943-45. Decorated Purple Heart; recipient Cert. of Appreciation, City of Norman, 1962, Okla. Dept. Wildlife, 1965. Mem. Tex. Assn. Coll. and Univ. Bus. Officers, Higher Edn. Council, Tex. Personnel Assn., Am. Mgmt. Assn., Nat. Assn. Aux. Dirs., Purchasing Mgmt. Assn., In-Plant Printing Mgmt. Assn., Phi Delta Theta. Democrat. Methodist. Clubs: Rotary, Masons. Home: 13 Vista Cliff Pl Richardson TX 75080 Office: 2601 N Floyd Rd Richardson TX 75080

MC NAIR, JOHN WILLIAM, JR., engring. co. exec.; b. Asheville, N.C., June 17, 1926; s. John William and Annie Wilson (Woody) McN.; B.S. in Forestry, Pa. State U., 1950; B.S. in Civil Engring., Va. Poly. Inst., 1955; m. June C. Kratz, Apr. 8, 1950; children—Jeffry L., Marsha L., Cathy G. Forester, U.S. Forest Service, Flagstaff, Ariz., 1950; instr. civil engring. U. Va., Charlottesville, 1955-58; owner, cons. engr. John McNair & Assos., Waynesboro, Va., 1958—. Mem. Indsl. Devel. Commn., 1974—; mem. City of Waynesboro Council, 1968-72, vice mayor, 1970-72. Served with inf. U.S. Army, 1944-46, C.E., 1951-53. Registered profl. engr., Va., W.Va., Md., Pa., N.Y., Ky., N.C. Fellow ASCE; mem. Va. Soc. Profl. Engrs. (pres. 1966-67). Presbyterian. Clubs: Rotary, Rappahannock River Yacht. Home: 1805 W Main St Waynesboro VA 22980 Office: John McNair & Assos LB&B Bldg Waynesboro VA 22980

MC NAMARA, EDWIN THOMAS, textile supply co. exec.; b. Chgo., Feb. 25, 1918; s. John Francis and Veronica Ceck (Gunn) McN.; student parochial schs., Chgo.; m. Kathryn Ann Ely, Feb. 16, 1946; children—Thomas Edwin, Michael William. With Stein Hall & Co., N.Y.C., 1936-72, mgr. sales, Dalton, Ga., 1967-72; exec. v.p., sales mgr. Stevens Textile Supply Co., Dalton, 1972-76, chmn. bd., 1976—; pres. Royce Industries; sec.-treas. Meadowbrook Carpets Co.; v.p. Trueset Yarns, Inc., 1976—, Stermac Realty, 1973—, Southeastern Sales Co., Richco Inc. Served with AUS, 1942-46. Decorated Bronze Star, Purple Heart. Roman Catholic. Clubs: Moose, Dalton Golf and Country (dir.), Battlefield Country. Home: 2124 Haven Crest Dr Chattanooga TN 37421 Office: PO Box 1625 Dalton GA 30720

MCNARY, OSCAR LEE, artist; b. San Antonio, Mar. 23, 1944; student Warren Hunter's Sch. Art, 1963, San Antonio Jr. Coll., 1964-65, Tex. So. U., 1967-68, So. Meth. U., 1973. One-man shows of paintings include: Promenade Nat. Bank, Richardson, Tex., 1976, Phoenix Cultural Arts Center, Atlanta, 1979; group shows include: Witte Mus., San Antonio, 1965, Jewish Community Center, Houston, 1967, Laguna Gloria Art Mus., Austin, Tex., 1975, Nat. Acad. Galleries, N.Y.C., 1976, Gates Gallery, Port Arthur, Tex., 1977, Tex. Technol. U., Lubbock, 1977, Bishop Coll., Dallas, 1977, 78, Tobian

Auditorium, Dallas, 1977, 78, Art Community Center, Corpus Christi, Tex., 1977, Harambee Living Arts Gallery, Atlanta, 1977, Joslyn Art Mus., Omaha, 1978, Ga. Tech. Gallery, Atlanta, 1978, Fort Worth Art Mus., 1978, Sol Del Rio Gallery, San Antonio, 1979; represented in permanent collections: Bishop Mus. African Am. Life and Culture, Phoenix Cultural Arts Center, Atlanta, also private collections. Recipient numerous awards including: Citation award Tex. Fine Arts, 1975. Mem. Tex. Fine Arts Assn., Am. Watercolor Soc., Richardson Civic Art Soc., Dallas Mus. Fine Arts, Artists Coalition Tex. (dir. 1977-79).

MC NEANY, STEVEN ROBERT, nuclear engr.; b. Bklyn., Apr. 1, 1951; s. Charles Raymond and Olga Marie (Lenz) McN.; B.S., Rensselaer Poly. Inst., 1973, M.E., 1974; m. Jeri Ilene Lundin, June 15, 1974. Asso. devel. engr. Oak Ridge Nat. Lab., 1974—. Registered profl. engr., Tenn. Am. Chem. Soc. fellow, 1973-74. Mem. Am. Nuclear Soc., Tau Beta Pi. Methodist. Home: 9427 Ravenwood Circle Knoxville TN 37922 Office: PO Box Y Oak Ridge TN 37830

MC NEER, BUFORD WALLACE, physician; b. Forest Hill, W.Va., Mar. 25, 1915; s. Frank Luther and Sallie Cleveland (Withrowe) McN.; student Roanoke Coll., 1931-33; M.D., W.Va. U., 1935, Med. Coll. Va., 1939; m. Anna Mae Burrow, Feb. 14, 1942; 1 son, Michael Dennis. Intern, Charleston (W.Va.) Gen. Hosp., 1939-40; practice medicine, specializing in med. ophthalmology, Hinton, W.Va., 1940—; mem. staff Summers County Hosp.; commd. 1st lt. U.S. Army, 1939, advanced through grades to col., 1962, ret., 1975; dir. First Nat. Bank, Hinton. Chmn., Civil Rights Commn., Hinton, 1962. Decorated Bronze Star; recipient Pres.'s medal ARC, 1947. Diplomate Am. Bd. Family Practice. Fellow Am. Coll. Family Physicians; mem. AMA, Am. Acad. Family Practice, W.Va. Med. Assn., Summers County Med. Soc., Am. Assn. Ophthalmology and Otolaryngology. Methodist. Address: 220 Ballengee St Hinton WV 25951

MC NEER, MICHAEL DENNIS, physician; b. Hinton, W.Va., Oct. 12, 1943; s. Buford and Anna Mae McN.; B.A. in English, U. Va., 1965; M.D., W.Va. U., 1969; m. Ann Keating Spillers, Aug. 31, 1974; children—James Stirling, Elizabeth Reymann, Lee Forrest. Rotating intern Charleston (W.Va.) Meml. Hosp., 1969-70; resident in psychiatry W.Va. U. Sch. Medicine, Morgantown, 1970-73; group practice Wheeling (W.Va.) Clinic, 1973-75; pvt. practice psychiatry, Beckley, W.Va., 1975—; asst. clin. prof. behavioral medicine and psychiatry W.Va. U. Sch. Medicine, 1973—; cons. psychiatrist Fed. Correctional Instn., Alderson, W.Va., 1979—. Diplomate Am. Bd. Psychiatry and Neurology. Mem. AMA, Am. Psychiat. Assn. Democrat. Methodist. Home: Buck Route Hinton WV 25951 Office: 815 S Kanawha St Beckley WV 25801

MC NEESE, BETTY ALLISON, ednl. adminstr.; b. Shreveport, La., Jan. 26, 1927; d. John Richard Preston and Leora (Byram) Allison; B.A., Northwestern State U., 1947; M.Ed., U. Miss., 1965, Ed.D., 1968; div.; children—Sara Allison, Robert Hilliard. Tchr. English, Rodessa (La.) High Sch., Ida (La.) High Sch., 1947-51, Fair Park High Sch., Shreveport, 1957-66; teaching fellow U. Miss., 1966-67; guidance counselor Oak Terr. Jr. High Sch., Shreveport, 1967-68; parish supr. English-social studies central staff Caddo Parish (La.) Sch. System, Shreveport, 1968-71, dir. secondary edn., 1971-78, asst. supt. for curriculum and instrn., 1979—. Minuteman, Youth Task Force, Bicentennial Com., 1976. Mem. La. Council for Social Studies (pres. 1972-73), La. Council Economic Edn., La. Assn. Educators, La. Div. Arts. Baptist. Author: Stories of the States: Each State's History; The Story of American History; Elementary Story Starters; Advanced Story Starters. Home: 233 Pierremont Rd Shreveport LA 71105 Office: Box 37000 Shreveport LA 71130

MC NEESE, MARSHA DIANE, radiotherapist; b. Bogalusa, La., Feb. 3, 1949; d. John Elmer and Marie (Gann) McN.; B.S., La. State U., 1970, M.D., 1974. Intern, Hermann Hosp., U. Tex., Houston, 1974; resident in radiotherapy M.D. Anderson Hosp., Houston, 1975-77; asst. radiotherapist, asst. prof. radiotherapy U. Tex., M.D. Anderson Hosp. & Tumor Inst., Houston, 1977—. Am. Cancer Soc. fellow, 1977. Diplomate Am. Bd. Radiology. Mem. AMA, Tex. Med. Assn., Harris County Med. Soc., Am. Coll. Radiology, Am. Soc. Therapeutic Radiologists, Am. Radium Soc., Radiol. Soc. N.Am., S.W. Oncology Group, Sierra Club. Democrat. Club: Space City Ski. Home: 924 W Main St Houston TX 77006 Office: 6723 Bertner St Houston TX 77030

MCNEIL, CAROLYN PRUETTE, specialist hearing impaired, educator; b. Memphis, Aug. 21, 1935; d. Thomas Leo and Bernice (Wilson) Pruette; student U. Hawaii, 1955-56; B.S., Memphis State U. 1962, M.A., 1973; div.; children—Michael Kevin, Janice Carol. Copywriter, editor advt. agy. Meth. Pub. House, Nashville, 1958-60; tchr. Memphis City Schs., 1962-72, chmn. English dept., 1965-72, speech and lang. pathologist, 1973-75, cons. tchr. spl. edn., also assessment specialist hearing-impaired program, 1977—; lectr. in field. Mem. City of Memphis Rev. Bd., 1972-75; mem. City of Memphis Drug Abuse Com., 1972-75; sec. Greentrees Civic Assn., 1978-80. Mem. Memphis Edn. Assn., West Tenn. Edn. Assn., Tenn. Edn. Assn., NEA, Am. Speech and Hearing Assn. (cert. clin. competence), Tenn. Speech and Hearing Assn., Council of Exceptional Children, Alexander Graham Bell Assn., Memphis Rose Soc., Am. Rose Soc., Mortar Board, Tau Kappa Alpha, Alpha Gamma Delta. Author, editor: Phase-Sequence Scheduling, 1969. Home: 6780 Messick Rd Memphis TN 38138 Office: Lester Center Memphis City Schs 584 Lester St Memphis TN 38112

MC NEIL, JAMES HENRY, psychologist; b. Blue Ridge, Ga., Dec. 31, 1934; s. Howard Augustus and Elizabeth Orelia (Brittain) McN.; A.A., Young Harris Coll., 1955; A.B., U. Ga., 1957, Ed.D., 1972; M.Div., Emory U., 1961; m. Charlotte Ann Mathis, Aug. 24, 1957; children—Hank, C. Stanley, Cora Elizabeth, Charlotte Ann. Ordained to ministry United Meth. Ch., 1958; pastor chs. Ga., 1955-69; intern in psychology Med. Sch. U. Ill., Chgo., 1969; dir. space utilization U. Ga., 1967-69; prof. edn. and psychology U. Ga., 1969-72; pediatric cons. HEW, State of S.C., 1972-74; clin. psychologist, clin. dir. S.C. Dept. Mental Health, Spartanburg and Union, 1974-76; pvt. practice psychology, Arnoldsville, Ga., 1976—. State v.p. S.C. PTA, 1973-76, Ga. PTA, 1974-78; adviser Explorer Scouts, 1976—, scoutmaster, cub scout master; youth dir., counselor Meth. Ch. Named Jaycee of Yr., 1963, Minister of Year, 1964. Mem. Am., Psychol. Assn., Nat. Assn. Sch. Psychologists, S.C. Mental Health Assn., Assn. Advancement Psychology, Phi Delta Kappa. Club: Masons. Home: Rt 1 Box 75 Arnoldsville GA 30619 Office: Box 774 Athens GA 30602

MC NEIL, JAMES PORTER, JR., obstetrician and gynecologist; b. Aberdeen, Miss., Apr. 19, 1926; s. James Porter and Julia Jordan (Haughton) McN.; B.A., U. Va., 1949, M.D., 1952; m. Anne Butler Yerkes, Oct. 11, 1952; children—James Porter III, Judson Elizabeth, Miranda Yerkes. Intern, U. Va. Hosp., Charlottesville, 1952-53; resident in obstetrics and gynecology N.Y. Lying-In Hosp., Cornell Med. Center, N.Y.C.; instr. Cornell Med. Sch., 1957-58; practice medicine specializing in obstetrics and gynecology, Jacksonville, Fla., 1958—; asst. prof. U. Fla. Med. Sch. Bd. dirs. Jacksonville Mus. Arts and Scis.; trustee Cummer Gallery Art, Jacksonville. Diplomate Am. Bd. Obstetrics and Gynecology. Mem. Fla. (exec. com.), Jacksonville (founding mem.) obstetricians and gynecologists socs., Am. Coll. Obstetrics and Gynecology; Am. Cancer Soc. (bd. dirs. DuVal County), S. Atlantic Assn. Obstetricians and Gynecologists (exec. com.). Episcopalian. Clubs: Fla. Yacht, Ponte Vedra, River. Office: 1820 Barrs St Suite 401 Jacksonville FL 32204

MC NEIL, WALTER HARVE, sales rep.; b. Harlan, Ky., Apr. 21, 1920; s. John Charles and Marie E. (McBrayer) McN.; grad. Pikeville Coll. Acad., 1937; student Pikeville Coll., 1956-59; grad. Squadron Officer Sch., 1955, Air Command and Staff Coll., 1960; m. Nellie Dean, June 1, 1946; children—Kay Francis (Mrs. Barry Runyon), Paula Jean (Mrs. Freddy Branham). With Sycamore Coal Corp., Patterson, Va., 1937-42; enlisted pvt. USAAF, 1942, commd. 2d lt. U.S. Army, 1943, advanced through grades to capt., 1946; staff communication officer Hdqrs. ETO; trans. to USAF Res., 1946, advanced through grades to lt. col., 1967, ret., 1970; liaison officer Air Force Acad. coordinator W.Va., Ky., So. Ohio, 1961-70; with Foster Thornburg Hardware Corp., Huntington, W.Va., 1946-61; sales rep. Tidewater Supply Co., 1961—. Named Outstanding Liaison Officer Coordinator in South, USAF Acad., 1965. Charter mem. Armed Forces Communications and Electronics Assn. (life); mem. Air Force Assn., U.S. Capitol Hist. Soc., USAF Hist. Found. (life), Met. Opera Guild, Ret. Officers Assn. (life), Res. Officers Assn. (life), Mil. Order World Wars. Democrat. Baptist (deacon). Clubs: Masons, Lafayette (Lexington, Ky.). Weekly columnist Pike County News. Home: 508 5th St Pikeville KY 41501 Office: PO Box 2097 Pikeville KY 41501

MC NEILLY, JUANITA ASSEE, counselor; b. Trinidad, W.I.; d. Mary Henrietta Assee; came to U.S., 1968, naturalized, 1973; tchrs. certificate Govt. Tchrs. Coll. Trinidad, 1958; B.A., U. Houston, 1973; M.Ed., U. Houston, 1976; m. D.G. Roy McNeilly, Aug. 8, 1953; 1 son, D.G. Roy. Tchr., asst. prin. Point Fortin Intermediate Roman Catholic Sch., Trinidad, 1951-67; tchr. aide Lantrip Elementary Sch., Houston, 1972; adoption placement worker Catholic Charities, Houston, 1975; psychotherapist Children's Mental Health Services, Houston, 1976—; asst. dir. student and public relations Promes program Cullen Coll. Engring., U. Houston; tchr. English, Houston Ind. Sch. Dist. Asst. treas. PTO, 1965. Cert. in English and psychology Tex. Edn. Agy.; recipient Winfred Garrison award U. Houston, 1973. Mem. Am. Personnel and Guidance Assn. Clubs: Toastmasters, Willowbend Civic. Home: 4834 Warm Springs Houston TX 77035

MC NICHOLS, GERALD ROBERT, mgmt. cons.; b. Cleve., Nov. 21, 1943; s. Charles Wellington and June Beatrice (Kalal) McN.; B.S. cum laude, Case Inst. Tech., 1965; M.S., U. Pa., 1966; Sc.D., George Washington U., 1975; m. Paula Kay Austin, Dec. 26, 1964; children—Gerald Robert, Katherine Lynn, Melissa Sue. Computer cons., Cleve., 1963-65; mgmt. research analyst Wharton Sch., Phila., 1965-66; cons. Corning Glass Works Co. (N.Y.), 1965-67; ops. research analyst Hdqrs. Air Force, Washington, 1967-70; dir. strategic aircraft, office dep. asst. sec. def. Def. Dept., Washington, 1970-72, dir. cost research office sec. def., 1972-76; v.p. GENTECH, Inc., Bethesda, Md., 1976-77, NOAH Assos., Inc., Falls Church, Va., 1977-78; pres. Mgmt. Cons. & Research, Inc., Falls Church, 1978—; professorial lectr. Am. U., Washington, 1967-74; asso. prof. lectr. engring. George Washington U., Washington, 1969—; adj. prof. Southeastern U., 1974-75. Vice pres. Rondelay Civic Assn., 1975-76. Served to capt. USAF, 1967-70. Mem. Washington Ops. Research Council (pres. 1977-78), Inst. Mgmt. Scis. (sec. 1973-74), Ops. Research Soc. Am. (chmn. MAS 1979-80), Assn. Public Program Analysis, Mil. Operation Research Soc., Phi Beta Kappa, Sigma Xi. Presbyterian (elder). Author: (with Ignizio, Gupta) Operations Research in Decision-Making, 1975. Editor Cost-Effectiveness Newsletter, 1972-74; referee Ops. Research, 1968-72, Mgmt. Sci., 1969-71. Home: 8133 Rondelay Ln Fairfax Station VA 22039 Office: MCR Inc 5203 Leesburg Pike Suite 608 Falls Church VA 22041

MC NIEL, GEORGE WILLIAM, state ofcl.; b. San Marcos, Tex., Feb. 21, 1931; s. William and Lora Mae (Riley) McN.; B.B.A., Baylor U., 1952; student S.W. Tex. State U., 1948-50; m. Barbara Jo Metz, June 12, 1953; children—Mark William, Earl Wayne, Glen Daniel. Staff auditor Arthur Andersen & Co., Houston, 1955-56; staff auditor firm Mulholland & Conklin, Austin, Tex., 1956-57; treas. Rich Plan of Austin Inc., 1957-60; partner firm Mulholland, McWhirter & McNiel, Austin, 1960-62; staff auditor Tex. Auditor's Dept., 1962-64, supervising asst., 1964-66, 1st asst., 1966-68, state auditor, 1968—. Served to 1st lt. USAF, 1952-54. Mem. Beta Alpha Psi, Delta Sigma Pi. Baptist (deacon, chmn. bd.). Home: 6507 NE Dr Austin TX 78723 Office: 409 Sam Houston State Office Bldg Austin TX 78711

MC NIEL, NORBERT ARTHUR, agrl. cons.; b. Moody, Tex., Dec. 22, 1914; s. Arthur A. and Gertrude (Burt) McN.; B.S., Tex. A. and M. Coll., 1935, M.Ed., 1952, Ph.D., 1955; m. Jane Edith Richter, Aug. 13, 1939; children—Rebecca McNiel Lindley, Ruth (Mrs. Charles W. Garner, Jr.), Fred, Larkin. Tchr. high sch., Alvin, Tex., 1935-41; supr. McLennan County Vocational Sch., Waco, Tex., 1946-51; adviser fgn. programs Tex. A. and M. Coll. System, Pakistan, 1955-56; mem. faculty Tex. A. and M. U., 1957-79, prof. genetics, 1972-79, ret., 1979; agrl. cons., farmer-stockraiser, 1980—. Del. Tex. Republican Conv., 1968, 70, 72; precinct chmn., 1968—. Served to lt. col. AUS, 1941-46. Decorated Bronze Star; recipient Distinguished Faculty award Assn. Former Students Tex. A. and M. U., 1964. Mem. Am. Genetic Assn., Am. Legion (post comdr. 1946-50). Mem. Ch. of Christ. Kiwanian (lt. gov. div. 9 T-0 dist. 1977-78). Home: 1700 Jersey St Apt 201 College Station TX 77840

MC NUTT, DOLLY HITE, state legislator; b. Henderson, Ky., June 22, 1917; d. Leslie P. and Mary Gladys (Flaherty) Hite; student Paducah Jr. Coll., 1936, Am. Acad. Dramatic Arts, 1938; m. Houston McNutt, Feb. 25, 1941. Partner Royal Crown-Nehi Bottling Co., Paducah, Ky., 1941-73; commr., mayor pro-tem City of Paducah, 1968-70; mayor City of Paducah, Ky., 1972-76; mem. Ky. Gen. Assembly, 1976—; dir. Paducah Bank & Trust Co. Mem. exec. com. Economic Devel. Commn., Commonwealth of Ky.; vol. ARC Paducah; seal chmn. McCracken County Tb Assn., 1969-71; chmn. civic beautification bd. City of Paducah, 1965-66; mem. Home and Neighborhood Devel. Soc. Recipient Distinguished Woman award Fraternal Order of Eagles, 1972; Citizen of Year award Southside Kiwanis Club, 1972; Woman of Year award Bus. and Profl. Women's Club, 1971, Woman of Achievement award, 1977; Meritorious Service award Greater Paducah C. of C., 1974; Community Service award Midway (Ky.) Coll., 1977, others. Mem. Jackson Purchase Hist. Soc., Bus. and Profl. Women's Club, Greater Paducah C. of C. (mem. all Am. city com. 1969-70), Internat. Platform Assn. Democrat. Roman Catholic. Club: Paducah Garden. Home: 105 Country Club Lane Paducah KY 42001 Office: PO Box 891 Paducah KY 42001

MC NUTT, KENNETH LEE, mfg. co. exec.; b. College Springs, Iowa, June 24, 1930; s. Clay Everett and Gladys Fern (Pierce) McN.; A.A., San Diego City Coll., 1956; B.A., San Diego State Coll., 1958; m. Betty Jeanne Gamel, Mar. 11, 1951; children—Judy Charlene, Sandra Lee, Pamela Jeanne, Diana Lynn, Shawn Patrick, Jacqueline Renee, Janette Michelle. With Oroweat Foods Co., Dallas, 1954—, asst. v.p., 1971, gen. mgr. southwest market area, 1971—. Served with U.S. Navy, 1948-54. Cert. adminstrv. mgr. Adminstrv. Mgmt. Soc. Mem. Soc. Cert. Adminstrv. Mgrs., Sales and Mktg. Execs. Club. Presbyterian. Club: Toastmasters Internat. Home: 4609 Woodland Park Blvd Arlington TX 76013 Office: 10701 Harry Hines Blvd Dallas TX 75220

MC PHAIL, BARBARA ANN, greeting ser. exec.; b. Memphis, Feb. 28, 1940; d. George Frederick and Anne Boone (Baggett) Williams; student Memphis State U., 1965-72; m. Prentiss H. McPhail, Apr. 2, 1966; children—Patricia, Terry. Adminstrv. sales mgr. Welcome Wagon, Internat., Memphis, 1965-68, credit mgr., 1969-70, adminstrv. sales mgr., 1971-72, recruiting, tng., promotions mgr., 1973-79, asst. to pres., 1979—; dir., v.p. Gifts Internat., Memphis, 1979—. Home: 4712 Quintell St Memphis TN 38128 Office: 145 Court Ave Memphis TN 38103

MCPHEETERS, EDWIN KEITH, architect, univ. dean; b. Stillwater, Okla., Mar. 26, 1924; s. William Henry and Eva Winona (Mitchell) McP.; B.Arch., Okla. State U., 1949; postgrad. U. Okla., 1952; M.F.A. (Univ. fellow), Princeton U., 1956; m. Patricia Ann Foster, Jan. 29, 1950; children—Marc Foster, Kevin Mitchell, Michael Hunter. Instr. dept. architecture U. Fla., 1949-51; asst. prof. architecture Auburn (Ala.) U., 1951-54, dean, prof. Sch. Architecture and Fine Arts, 1969—; asst. prof. U. Ark., Fayetteville, 1956-58, asso. prof., 1958-65, prof., 1965-66; dean, prof. Sch. Architecture, Rensselaer Poly. Inst., 1966-69; mem. Ala. Bd. Registration for Architects, 1978—; cons. S. Central Bell Telephone Co. Served to 2d lt. AC, U.S. Army, 1943-45. Recipient 4th prize Carson-Pirie-Scott Planning Competition, 1954. Fellow AIA (Ala. council 1975-79, pres. council 1978, Merit award Ala. council 1976); mem. Assn. Collegiate Schs. Architecture (dir. 1970-77). Democrat. Methodist. Office: 202 Fine Arts Center Auburn U Auburn AL 36830

MC PHERSON, ALICE RUTH, physician; b. Regina, Sask., Can., June 30, 1926; d. Gordon and Viola (Hoover) McP.; B.S., U. Wis., 1948, M.D., 1951. Intern, Santa Barbara Cottage Hosp., 1951-52; resident anesthesiology Hartford Hosp., 1952, resident ophthalmology Chgo. Eye, Ear, Nose and Throat Hosp., 1953, U. Wis. Hosp., 1953-55; ophthalmologist Davis & Duehr Eye Clinic, 1956-57, Scott and White Clinic, 1958-60, Houston, 1960-62; fellow retina service Mass. Eye and Ear Infirmary, 1957-58; practice medicine, specializing in ophthalmology, retinal diseases, Houston, 1960—; mem. staffs Meth., St. Luke's, Tex. Children's hosps. (all Houston); clin. instr. U. Wis., 1956-57; clin. asst. prof. ophthalmology Baylor Coll. Medicine, Houston, 1959-61, asst. prof. ophthalmology, 1961-69, clin. asso. prof., 1969-75, clin. prof. ophthalmology, 1975—, chief retina service dept. ophthalmology, 1959—; lectr. ophthalmology U. Tex., 1959—; cons. retinal diseases VA Hosp., 1960—, Ben Taub Hosp., Houston, 1960—. Diplomate Am. Bd. Ophthalmology. Fellow Am. Acad. Ophthalmology, A.C.S.; mem. AMA, Tex., Pan-Am. med. assns., Soc. Cryosurgery, Internat. Coll. Surgeons, Harris County Med. Soc., Houston Ophthal. Soc., Am. Med. Women's Assn., Pan-Pacific Surg. Assn., French Ophthal. Soc., Internat. Med. Assembly Southwest Tex., Am. Assn. Ophthalmology, So. Med. Assn., Assn. Research Ophthalmology, Assn. Am. Physicians and Surgeons, Retina Soc., Soc. Eye Surgeons, Jules Gonin Club. Editor: New and Controversial Aspects of Retinal Detachment, 1968; New and Controversial Aspects of Vitreoretinal Surgery, 1977. Office: 6560 Fannin Suite 2200 Houston TX 77030

MC PHERSON, FRANK ALFRED, corp. exec.; b. Stillwater, Okla., Apr. 29, 1933; s. Younce B. and Maurine Frances (Strauss) McP.; B.S. in Mich. and Petroleum Engring., Okla. State U., 1957; m. Nadine Wall, Sept. 10, 1955; children—David, Craig, Mark, Rebecca. With Kerr-McGee Corp., 1957—, gen. mgr. Gulf Coast oil and gas ops., 1969-73; pres. Kerr-McGee Coal Co., 1973-76, pres. Kerr-McGee Nuclear Co., 1976-77, vice chmn. Kerr-McGee Chem., Coal, Nuclear and Refining Co. and engring. services div., Oklahoma City, 1977—. Adv. bd. Oklahoma City Salvation Army; bd. dirs. YMCA Oklahoma City. Served to capt. USAF, 1957-60. Mem. AIME, Atomic Indsl. Forum (dir.), Am. Mining Congress (dir., exec. com. uranium adv. council), Oklahoma City C. of C. (dir.). Democrat. Baptist. Office: PO Box 25861 Oklahoma City OK 73120

MC PHERSON, GEORGE RAY, home entertainment co. exec.; b. Ft. Worth, Nov. 16, 1949; s. John Ray and Georgia Lucille (Schneider) McP.; B.B.A., Tex. Christian U., 1978, postgrad. (Prof. Devel. scholar), 1978; m. Kathleen Hall, Oct. 8, 1971. Acctg. mgr. Swift & Co., Ft. Worth and Chgo., 1969-77; EDP auditor FFR Co., Ft. Worth, 1977-78; mgr. internal audit Mathes Co., Athens, Tex., 1978—. Mem. Inst. Internal Auditors, Nat. Wildlife Fedn., Fund for Animals. Presbyterian. Club: TCU Century (Ft. Worth). Office: PO Box 151 Athens TX 75751

MC PHERSON, JOSEPH DANIEL, ins. co. exec.; b. Mobile, Ala., Mar. 7, 1918; s. James D. and Annie (Ledkins) McP.; B.A., U. Ala., 1941, LL.B., 1946; m. Betty Jane Johnson, Jan. 22, 1942; children—Megan (Mrs. Harry Van Johnson), Joseph Daniel. Admitted to Ala. bar, 1946; examiner Ala. Ins. Dept., 1946-48, dep. ins. commr., 1952-55; sec. Ala. Ins. Service Co., 1948-49; v.p. Consol. Ins. Co., Nashville, 1950-52; exec. v.p., sec.-treas., dir. Mut. Savs. Life Ins. Co., Decatur, Ala., 1955—; pres., dir. Greater Miss. Life Ins. Co., 1975—; sr. v.p., sec.-treas., dir. United Service Ins. Co., Decatur, Mut. Savs. Fire Ins. Co., Mut. Service Funeral Homes, Decatur; dir. Am. Benefit Life Ins. Co., Lafayette Ins. Co., New Orleans. Dir., chmn. Point Mallard Authority, 1969-72; chmn. Ala.-Miss. Area Council of Boys Clubs Am., 1967-68. Pres., bd. dirs., recipient Distinguished Service award Decatur Boys Club; sec.-treas., bd. dirs. Ala. Mountain Lakes Assn.; founder, past pres. Ala. State Employees Credit Union. Served to maj. Transp. Corps, AUS, 1942-46. Mem. Life Office Mgmt. Assn., Am. Life Ins. Assn., Assn. Ala. Life Cos. (past sec.-treas., dir.), Life Insurers Conf. Episcopalian. Rotarian. Clubs: Wheeler Lake Yacht (past commodore); Decatur Country. Home: 2315 Fairway Circle SE Decatur AL 35601 Office: 2801 Hwy 31 S Decatur AL 35601

MC PHERSON, RAYMOND PAT, pharmacist; b. Cobb County, Ga., July 11, 1943; s. L.M. and Mildred Annie (Westbrooks) McP.; student Oglethorpe U., 1962-63; B.S., Mercer U., 1966; J.D., Woodrow Wilson Coll., 1977; m. Janet Elizabeth Adams, Dec. 16, 1968; children—Sean, Susan, Kimberly. With Atherton Drugs, Inc., Marietta, Ga., 1959-67; pharmacist Kennestone Hosp., Marietta, 1971-72, West Paces Ferry Hosp., Atlanta, 1972-73; founder, pres. Pharmacy Systems, Inc., Smyrna, Ga., 1973—; dir. West Atlanta Indsl. Med. Clinic, Atlanta, 1975-76. Co-founder Homeland Properties, Inc., 1974. Served with USN, 1967-71. Registered pharmacist, Ga., Calif., Fla. Mem. True Historian Soc. (dir.), Ga., Fla., Calif., Am. pharm. assns., Am. Soc. Hosp. Pharmacists. Home: 3750 Woodvalley Dr Smyrna GA 30080 Office: PO Box 654 Austell GA 30001

MC PHILLIPS, JULIAN LENWOOD, JR., lawyer; b. Birmingham, Ala., Nov. 13, 1946; s. Julian L. and Eleanor Elizabeth (Dixon) McP.; A.B. cum laude (McConnell Found. scholar), Princeton U., 1968; J.D., Columbia U., 1971; m. J. Leslie Burton, June 22, 1974; 1 dau., Rachel Sanderson. Admitted to N.Y. bar, 1972, Ala. bar, 1975; asso. firm Davis, Polk & Wardward, N.Y.C., 1971-73; asso.

counsel Am. Express Co., N.Y.C., 1973-75; asst. atty. gen. State of Ala., chief counsel Ala. State Banking Dept., chief counsel Ala. Securities Commn., Montgomery, 1975-77; individual practice law, Montgomery, 1977—. Bd. dirs. Montgomery Crime Prevention Program, 1976—, YMCA, 1977—; candidate for atty. gen. Ala., 1978. Mem. Am. Bar Assn., N.Y. Bar Assn., Bar Assn. City N.Y., Ala. Bar Assn., Montgomery County Bar Assn. Democrat. Episcopalian. Club: Ivy (Princeton). Editor: Columbia U. Law Sch. News, 1970-71, Ala. Traveler, 1979; mem. editorial bd. Columbia U. Jour. Transitional Law, 1970-71. Amateur wrestling champion Ivy League, 1964-68; named All-Am., 1967-68; Eastern AAU wrestling champion, 1971, 73; mem. Nat. AAU team wrestling champions, 1971, 72, 73. Home: 3549 Berkeley Dr Montgomery AL 36111 Office: 516 S Perry St Montgomery AL 36104

MC QUAID, WILLIAM RAVENEL, JR., sales engr.; b. Jacksonville, Fla., July 23, 1924; s. William Ravenel and Henrietta (Murray) McQ.; grad. Hill Sch., 1942; M.E., Stevens Inst. Tech., 1948; m. Elizabeth Ann Tiffany, June 12, 1948; children—William Ravenel III, Elizabeth Lorimier, Douglas Murray. Jr. engr. Am. Locomotive Co., Schenectady, 1948-50; sales rep., also dist. sales mgr. Alco Products, Inc. (formerly Am. Locomotive Co), Chgo., 1950-60; owner Transdustrial Sales Co., Jacksonville, 1960—. Chmn. marine events com. Jacksonville Sesquicentennial Commn., 1971-72. Trustee, past pres. bd. St. Johns Country Day Sch. Served to ensign USNR, 1944-46; PTO. Mem. So. and Southwestern Ry. Club, Fla. Sailing Assn. (past commodore), Delta Tau Delta. Republican. Presbyn. Rotarian (dir. Jacksonville 1973-75, also asst. sec.). Club: Fla. Yacht (past commodore). Home and Office: 3559 Richmond St Jacksonville FL 32205

MC QUEEN, CHARLES RICHARD, lawyer; b. Columbus, Ind., Aug. 25, 1936; s. James Charles and Bertha Ann (Gressel) Mc.; B.A., DePauw U., 1958; J.D., Duke U., 1961; m. Karen Foust, Aug. 24, 1957; children—Katharine, Michael, Lisa. Admitted to Ind. bar, 1961, Ga. bar, 1964; mem. firm Greene, Buckley, Derieux, Jones, Atlanta, 1963—, partner, 1969—. Mem., Atlanta, Ind., Ga., Am. bar assns., Lawyers Club Atlanta, Presbyn. Club: Ansley Golf. Home: 3990 Randall Mill Rd NW Atlanta GA 30327 Office: 1515 Peachtree Center S 225 Peachtree St NE Atlanta GA 30303

MC QUEEN, EDGAR GORDON, automotive parts mfg. co. exec.; b. Billings, Mont., Feb. 24, 1939; s. Edgar A. and Helen F. (Ross) McQ.; B.S. in Engring. Physics, U. Colo., 1961; postgrad. U. Hawaii, 1964-65; m. Karen Darlene Eckloe, June 16, 1961; children—Edgar Gordon, Jeffrey Brian, Kimberle Karen. Elec. systems engr. Litton Industries, Culver City, Calif., 1969-70, systems engr. mgr., 1970-72; mgr. electronic systems, program mgr. Aerojet Gen. Corp. Tacoma, Wash., 1972-74, asst. to pres., El Monte, Calif., 1974-76; pres., dir. Unit Parts Co., Oklahoma City, 1976—. Served to lt. USN, 1961-69; Vietnam. Mem. Automotive Service Industry Assn., Automotive Parts Rebuilders Assn., Oklahoma City C. of C. Home: 1923 Whispering Pines Norman OK 73069 Office: Unit Parts Co PO Box 26021 Oklahoma City OK 73126

MC QUEEN, HORACE FRANKLIN, television agri-bus. news co. exec.; b. Crockett, Tex., July 3, 1938; s. T.F. and F.L. McQueen; B.S. in Agrl. Journalism, Tex. A. and M., 1960; m. Carole Myers, Oct. 11, 1958; children—Dale, Dennis, Debra and Deidre (twins). Editor, Nat. Future Farmer Am. mag., Alexandria, Va., 1960-61, Farm and Ranch mag., Nashville and Dallas, 1961-63; owner, operator Farm and Ranch News Co., Lubbock and Tyler, Tex., 1963—; farm real estate broker; organizer, shipper several New Zealand and Australian ranches to air ship purebred cattle to U.S. and Can. Pres., Troup Taxpayers Assn., 1974-76. Recipient awards Fed. Intermediate Credit Bank of Houston, 1968, numerous agrl. awards Future Farmers Am. and 4-H Clubs. Mem. Nat. Assn. Farm Broadcasters (past v.p.), Order Ky. Cols., Sigma Delta Chi. Baptist. Clubs: Masons (32 deg.), Lubbock A. and M. (past pres.), Tex. A. and M. Century. Home: Box 838 Whitehouse TX 75791 Office: Box 957 Tyler TX 75710

MCQUILKIN, JOHN ROBERTSON, coll. adminstr.; b. Columbia, S.C., Sept. 7, 1927; s. Robert Crawford and Marguerite (Lambie) McQ.; B.A., Columbia Bible Coll., 1947; M.Div., Fuller Theol. Sem., 1950; postgrad. Wheaton Coll., 1945, N. Baptist Theol. Sem., 1947-48, UCLA, 1950; m. Muriel Webendorfer, Aug. 24, 1948; children—Mardi, Robert, David, Virginia, Aimee, Kent. Instr., Greek, theology Columbia (S.C.) Bible Coll., 1950-52, pres., 1968—; headmaster Ben Lippen Sch., Asheville, N.C., 1952-55; missionary, Japan, 1956-68; acting pres. Japan Christian Coll., 1963-64. Mem. Evang. Theol. Soc., Am. Soc. Missiology, Am. Assn. Bible Colls. Home: 7435 Monticello Columbia SC 29203 Office: PO Box 3122 Columbia SC 29230

MCQUIRK, JOSEPH MOORING, retail exec.; b. Wichita Falls, Tex., Apr. 19, 1947; s. Bernard Clair and Florence Madelyn (Mooring) McQ.; student Arlington State Coll., 1965-66, U. Tex., Arlington, 1971, 72-73: B.BA., So. Meth. U., 1976; m. Doris Jean Shaver, Mar. 18, 1972. With Sears Roebuck & Co., Dallas, 1965-67, Austin, Tex., 1970-71; salesman World Stores, Dallas, 1971; mgr. tng. program Gibson Discount Stores, Garland, Tex., 1971; asst. corporate operation mgr. Joske's, Dallas, 1972-76; dir. purchasing Rich's Co., Atlanta, 1976—. Served with USAF, 1967-71. Decorated Bronze Star. Mem. Purchase Mgrs. Assn. Ga., So. Meth. Alumni Assn., Kappa Alpha. Republican. Roman Catholic. Home: 3450 Evans Rd Apt 125-D Atlanta GA 30341 Office: 45 Broad St Atlanta GA 30302

MC RAE, HAROLD WOOTEN, JR., marriage and family therapist; b. Vidalia, Ga., Feb. 2, 1944; s. Harold W. and Virginia (Peacock) McR.; B.B.A., Ga. State U., 1969, Ed.M., 1973; m. Kathryn Thompson, Dec. 3, 1967; children—James Duncan, Laura Kathryn. Office service mgr. Liberty Mut. Ins. Co., Atlanta, 1967-70; adminstrv. mgr. Jud. Service Agy., Albany, Ga., 1970-71; research asst. Social Research Labs., Atlanta, 1971-73; mental health asso. Fulton County Alcohol Treatment Center, Atlanta, 1973-74; adj. counselor Pastoral Inst., Columbus, Ga., 1978-79; pvt. practice marriage and family therapy and human relations, Columbus, 1974—; dir. rehab. Goodwill Industries, Columbus, 1974-79; cons. Mont. Dept. Corrections, 1977. Cert. rehab. counselor, Ga. Mem. Am. Assn. Marriage and Family Therapists, Nat. Rehab. Assn., Am. Personnel and Guidance Assn., Assn. Specialists in Group Work, Ga. Assn. Marriage and Family Therapy (pres. Columbus chpt. 1979), Lower Chattahoochee Council on Alcoholism (dir. 1975). Home: 16435 Chantileer Trail PO Box 18 Upatoi GA 31829 Office: 1661 13 St Suite 102 Columbus GA 31901

MC RAE, JAMES HENDRY, physician; b. Detroit, Aug. 4, 1914; s. Claude F. and Isabelle (Hendry) McR.; B.A., Wayne State U., 1936, M.Biology, 1940, M.D., 1941; m. Luella R. Quick, Sept. 11, 1941; children—James Hendry, Barbara, Catherine, Sandra. Intern, W.A. Foote Meml. Hosp., Jackson, Mich., 1940-41; asst. resident Wayne County Gen. Hosp., Detroit, 1945-46, resident 1947, chief resident, 1948; practice medicine specializing in internal medicine, St. Petersburg, Fla., 1948—; mem. staff St. Anthonys Hosp., Bayfront Med. . Center, Palms Pasadena Hosp., Edward H. White Meml. Hosp., St. Petersburg. Bd. dirs. Rogers Heart Found., St. Petersburg, 1971-76. Served to capt. USAAF, 1941-45. Decorated Legion of Merit; recipient AMA Physicians Recognition award, 1977. Diplomate Am. Bd. Internal Medicine. Mem. Am. Soc. Internal Medicine, So. Med. Assn., Fla. Soc. Internal Medicine, Fla., Pinellas County med. socs., Pi Alpha Kappa. Methodist. Home: 646 17th Ave NE Saint Petersburg FL 33704 Office: 4444 Central Ave Saint Petersburg FL 33711

MC RAE, WILLIAM HOLLAND, lawyer; b. Dallas, June 1, 1937; s. Colin E. and Virginia Saffel (Holland) McR.; B.A. magna cum laude, So. Meth. U., 1959, J.D. cum laude, 1962; m. Lucy Ashcroft Carothers, Nov. 19, 1966; children—Holland Carothers, Ashley Ashcroft. Admitted to Tex. bar, 1962; asso. firm Coon, Dedman, May & Hoffman, Dallas, 1962-64, Strasburger, Price, Kelton, Miller & Martin, Dallas, 1964-66; asso. firm Stroud & Smith, Dallas, 1966-69, partner, 1969—. Mem. Am., Tex., Dallas bar assns., Barristers, Order Woolsack, Phi Beta Kappa, Phi Delta Theta. Republican. Mem. Ch. of Religious Sci. Clubs: Toastmasters (pres. 1970), Terpsichorean, City. Home: 4565 Belclaire Ave Dallas TX 75205 Office: 1407 Main St Dallas TX 75202

MC RAE, WILTON DAVID, otolaryngologist; b. Dothan, Ala., Dec. 5, 1940; s. William Earl and Elizabeth (Sturges) McR.; B.S., U.S. Mil. Acad., 1962; M.D., U. Fla., 1971; children—Charles, Christopher, William. Intern, Fitzsimons Gen. Hosp., Denver, 1971-72; resident in otolaryngology, U. Ala., 1974-78; commd. 2d lt., U.S. Army, 1962, advanced through grades to lt. col., 1974; practice medicine, specializing in otolaryngology, Dothan, Ala., 1978—; staff, Southeast Ala. Med. Center, Flowers Hosp., Dothan, Ala. Decorated Army Commendation medal. Fellow Am. Acad. Otolaryngology; mem. AMA, Ala. Med. Assn., Houston County Med. Soc., Am. Council Otolarngology. Republican. Methodist. Office: 509 W Main St Dothan AL 36301

MC REATH, ANITA HENDERSON, broadcasting co. exec.; b. Birmingham, Ala., June 6, 1949; s. Cyrus Hill and Laura Nell (Wilson) H.; student Auburn U., 1967-69; B.S. in Bus. Adminstrn., U. Ala., Birmingham, 1974; m. John Olen McReath, Dec. 9, 1978. Asst. accountant WBRC-TV, Taft Broadcasting Co., Birmingham, 1975; controller Ala. Ednl. TV Commn., Birmingham, 1975—. Mem. Nat. Assn. Ednl. Broadcasters, Broadcast Fin. Mgmt. Assn., Am. Soc. for Women Accountants, Public Telecommunications Fin. Mgmt. Assn. (sec.), Sports Enthusiasts Assn., Beta Sigma Phi. Baptist. Office: Ala Ednl TV Commn 2101 Magnolia Ave Birmingham AL 35205

MC REE, JOE RICHARD, ret. purchasing agt.; b. Soddy, Tenn., Mar. 21, 1911; s. Frederick Emmett and Winifred (Thomas) McR.; student various armed forces courses, 1938, 42-45, U. Chattanooga, 1947-49; B.S., U. Tenn., 1950; m. Onah Lanave Wilcox, Dec. 12, 1963; 1 dau., Renee Elisabeth (Mrs. David Rhodes Hunter). Engr., Tenn. Hwy. Dept., Chattanooga, 1928-40, 45-50; purchasing agt. TVA, Chattanooga, 1951-72. Served to lt. col. AUS, 1940-45; Res. ret., 1953. Registered engr., Tenn. Mem. Internat. Platform Assn., Am. Security Council (mem. nat. adv. bd.), Am. Mus. Natural History, Ret. Officers Assn. (life), Phi Eta Sigma, Sigma Pi Sigma. Home: 19 Caddy Rd Rotonda West FL 33947

MC REYNOLDS, ELLEN ELIZABETH, dietetic adminstr.; b. Cleveland, Tenn., Feb. 4, 1931; d. Hugh C. McR.; student Tenn. Tech. Inst., 1950-51; B.S., U. Tenn., 1954. Mem. food service staff Phi Beta Phi Sch., Gatlinburg, Tenn., 1954; food prodn. mgr. Ball State U., 1954-57; with Progressive Cafeterias, DuPont, Chattanooga, 1957; therapeutic dietitian Erlanger Hosp. and Children's Hosp., Chattanooga, 1958-59; dir. dietetics Bradley Meml. Hosp., Cleveland, Tenn., 1959—; cons. nursing homes Woods Meml. Hosp., Etawah, Tenn., Copperbasin Hosp., Copperhill, Tenn.; tchr. nutrition Cleveland (Tenn.) Community Coll., 1970; nursing home cons. Registered dietitian. Mem. Am. Dietetic Assn., Chattanooga Area Dietetic Assn. (pres. 1960), Phi Beta Phi. Methodist. Art work exhibited in group shows, represented in pvt. collections. Office: Bradley County Meml Hosp Box 45 Cleveland TN 37311

MC RIGHT, WILLIAM CARDER, engr.; b. McKinney, Tex., Oct. 26, 1948; s. Willie Lester and Erma Lee (Moorehead) M.; B.S. in Mech. Engring., U. Tex., Arlington, 1972; m. Betty Sue Davis, Nov. 24, 1972; children—Laura Lea, Bonnie Gail. Planning engr. City Public Services, San Antonio, 1972-74; project engr. Nichols-Kusan, Inc., Jacksonville, Tex., 1974-76; mech. engr. Data Point Corp., San Antonio, 1976—; tchr. engring. drawing Lon Morris Coll., Jacksonville, 1975; mech. design cons., 1979—. Mem. Tex. Soc. Profl. Engrs., Pi Tau Sigma, Tau Beta Pi, Pi Sigma Epsilon. Republican. Home: 6819 Spring Lark San Antonio TX 78249 Office: 9725 Data Point Dr San Antonio TX 78284

MC SWAIN, RICHARD HORACE, metallurgist; b. Greenville, Ala., Sept. 27, 1949; s. Howard Horace and LaBelle (Henderson) McS.; student Jefferson Davis State Jr. Coll., 1967-68; B.Materials Engring., Auburn U., 1972, M.S., 1974; postgrad. in computer sci. U. Ala., Birmingham, 1974; m. Wanda Lynn Hare, June 9, 1972; 1 dau., Rachel Lynn. Research and teaching asst. Auburn U., 1972-73; asst. metallurgist So. Research Inst., Birmingham, Ala., 1973-74, asso. metallurgist, 1974-76; metallurgist Naval Air Rework Facility, Naval Air Sta., Pensacola, Fla., 1977—. Recipient spl. achievement award U.S. Navy, 1979. Mem. Am. Soc. Metals (edn. chmn. Birmingham chpt. 1975-76), Soc. Advancement Material Process Engring., Sigma Xi, Pi Tau Sigma. Presbyterian. Contbr. articles to profl. publs. Home: 4021 Middlebury Dr Pensacola FL 32504 Office: USN Naval Air Rework Facility Naval Air Sta Pensacola FL 32508

MC SWEEN, JAMES ANGUS, indsl. distbn. corp. exec.; b. Newton, Ala., Sept. 17, 1940; s. Jackson D. and Edna E. (Benton) McS.; B.S., Troy State U., 1966; M.B.A., Auburn U., 1969; m. Mary Ellen Bruner, Mar. 10, 1966; children—Amelia A., Steve A. Fin. analyst West Point Pepperell, Inc. (Ga.), 1966-73; ops. mgr., controller Redman Industries, Inc., Meridian, Miss., 1973-74; v.p. fin., corporate sec. Indsl. Distbrs. Am., Inc., Atlanta, 1974-79; pres. McLeod Cos., Inc., 1980—. Served with USNR, 1958-62. Home: 10 Stone Hedge Dr Greenville SC 29615 Office: PO Box 6588 Congaree Rd Greenville SC 29606

MC SWEENEY, E(LLSWORTH) E(DWARD), cons. chemist; b. Jersey City, Mar. 19, 1914; s. William Joseph and Martha Lillian (Anthony) McS.; A.B., Oberlin Coll., 1934; Ph.D., U. Rochester, 1938; m. Margaret Joy Tewinkel, June 18, 1938; children—Martha Louise McSweeney Powell, Elizabeth Ann McSweeney Gordon, Michael Gordon, Mary Jane McSweeney Piper. Research chemist, div. chief Battelle Inst., Columbus, Ohio, 1938-53, mgr. dept. chemistry and chem. engring., 1953-66; asst. dir. research Union Camp Corp., Princeton, N.J., 1966-70, tech. dir. chem. div., Savannah, Ga., 1970—; pres. Marcam, Inc., 1979—. Mem. Grandview Heights (Ohio) Bd. Edn., 1962-66. Mem. Am. Chem. Soc. (various offices and coms.), Fedn. Socs. for Paint Tech. (Heckel award 1974), Soc. Chem. Industry, ASTM. Republican. Presbyterian. Clubs: Chemists (N.Y.C.); Marshwood (Savannah). Contbr. tech. articles to sci. jours. Home and office: 13 Wesley Crossing The Landings Savannah GA 31411

MC SWIGAN, JAMES ALOYSIUS, JR., lawyer; b. Denver, July 9, 1936; s. James Aloysius and Zella (Parker) McS.; B.S. in History, Xavier U., 1958; J.D., U. Cin., 1962; m. Maureen Conners, June 30, 1962; children—Laura Marie, James Aloysius III, Joy Anne. Admitted to Ohio bar, 1962, Fla. bar, 1977; asso. firm Warren & Young, Ashtabula, 1962-68; partner Warren, Young & McSwigan, Ashtabula, 1969—; dir. Lake Shore Steel Co., Black Gold Coal Corp., Universal Improvement Co., River City Pub. Co., Standard Improvement Co. City solicitor Village of North Kingsville (Ohio), 1970-73; spl. counsel Ashtabula Area Sch. Bd., 1968-70, City of Ashtabula, 1968; founder Ashtabula Legal Aid Corp., 1967. Trustee Ashtabula Fine Arts Center; bd. dirs. Ashtabula Family Service. Mem. Am., Ohio State, Ashtabula County (pres. 1971) bar assns., Ashtabula Area C. of C. (trustee), Phi Alpha Delta. Republican. Roman Catholic. Elk. Clubs: Ashtabula Country, Ashtabula Yacht. Home: 2229 Walnut Blvd Ashtabula OH 44004 Office: Suite 202 Reynolds Securities Bldg 250 Royal Palm Way Palm Beach FL 33480

MC TEE, CLIFFORD RAY, JR., petroleum geologist, rancher; b. Houston, Sept. 1, 1933; s. Clifford Ray and Gladys (Harris) McT.; B.S. in Geology, U. Tex., 1954, postgrad., 1956-57; m. Elsie Mae Wheeler, Dec. 20, 1952; children—Clifford Ray III, Shelly Marie, Charles Dewey. Subsurface geologist Tidewater Oil Co., Lafayette, La., 1957-Midwest Oil Corp., Lafayette, 1962-67; pvt. practice petroleum geology, Houston, 1967-70; dist. exploration mgr. Tex. Oil and Gas Corp., Corpus Christi, 1970-74; pres., chmn. bd. Solana Corp., Corpus Christi, 1974—; pres. Petroleum Data Services, Inc. Served with U.S. Army, 1954-56. Mem. Am. Assn. Petroleum Geologists, Corpus Christi Geol. Soc. (pres.), Am. Assn. Petroleum Landmen, Corpus Christi Assn. Petroleum Landmen. Methodist. Club: Town (Corpus Christi). Contbr. writings to profl. publs. Home: 4322 St George St Corpus Christi TX 78413 Office: Suite 1114 The 600 Bldg Corpus Christi TX 78473

MCVADON, MILNER WAYNE, banker; b. Baton Rouge, Oct. 8, 1938; s. Eric A. and Nita (Gautreaux) McV.; B.A., Tulane U., 1960; grad. Sch. Banking of South, La. State U., 1971, Grad. Inst. Bank Mktg. U. So. Calif., 1978 m. Allison Claire Cook, June 3, 1960; children—Charlotte Marie, Allison Wynne, Susan Claire. Mktg. rep. IBM Data Processing Div., Baton Rouge, La., 1963-67; v.p., dir. mktg. Baton Rouge Bank & Trust Co., 1967-78; v.p., dir. mktg. Am. Bank and Trust Co., Baton Rouge, 1978—. Bd. advisors Grad. Inst. Bank Mktg.; instr. La. Banking Sch. for Supervisory Tng., U. Southwestern La.; cons. TV prodn. of fin. advtg. Finance chmn., bd. dirs. Audubon council Girl Scouts U.S., 1969-71; pres., bd. dirs. Jr. Achievement Inc. of Baton Rouge, 1971-74; mem. Greater Baton Rouge Port Commn., 1971-77, sec., 1972-73, treas., 1973-74, pres., 1974-76. Served with USN, 1960-63. Mem. Bank Mktg. Assn., La. Bankers Assn. (mem. public relations com.), Baton Rouge C. of C. United Methodist. Clubs: Baton Rouge Country, City. Home: 3080 Saratoga Dr Baton Rouge LA 70808 Office: One American Pl Baton Rouge LA 70825

MC WHIRTER, JOHN WALTON, JR., lawyer; b. Tampa, Fla., Sept. 4, 1932; s. John Walton and Murrel Lucille (Hebble) M.; A.B. (Ruge scholar), U. of the S., 1954; J.D. (Root-Tilden scholar), N.Y. U., 1957; m. Camille Crockett, Nov. 24, 1961; children—Camille, John Crockett, Michael Roberts. Admitted to Fla. bar, 1957; pvt. practice law, Tampa, 1959-62, 65—; adminstrv. asst. Fla. Pub. Service Commn., Tallahassee, 1962-63. Exec. dir. Fla. Installment Land Sales Bd., 1963-65. Gen. counsel Hillsborough Community Coll., 1968—. Pres., Fla. Easter Seal Soc., 1967-68, recipient Outstanding Achievement citation, 1968; del. Nat. Easter Seal Soc., Nat. Council Health, 1968-74. Served with USAF Res., 1957-78. Mem. Am., Fla., Hillsborough County Bar assns., Acad. Fla. Trial Lawyers, Fla. Sch. Bd. Attys. Assn., Motor Carrier Lawyers Assn., Tampa Exchange Club (pres. 1969-70). Democrat. Episcopalian. Clubs: Palma Ceia Golf and University (Tampa) (pres. 1974). Home: 10 Ladoga Ave Tampa FL 33606 Office: PO Box 2150 Tampa FL 33601

MC WHORTER, ANDREA ALFREDO, guidance counselor; b. Century, Fla., Oct. 14, 1954; d. Alfred and Priscilla Pearl McWhorter; B.S. (Civitan award 1972), Alcorn U., Lorman, Miss., 1975; M.A. (Guidance/Counseling fellow 1975-76), Ohio State U., 1976. Counselor, Piney Woods (Miss.) Sch., 1976—; coordinator workshops. Mem. Am. Personnel and Guidance Assn., Assn. Non-White Concerns. Address: 1962 Duncan St Mobile AL 36606

MC WILLIAMS, ROBERT WHEALTON, ret. life ins. co. exec.; b. Portsmouth Island, N.C., July 8, 1910; s. Charles S. and Annie T. (Toler) McW.; student U. N.C., 1930-31, Eastman Sch. Bus., 1932-33; m. Dorothy J. Osborne, May 20, 1950; children—Robert Whealton, Ann Cullen. With Life Ins. Co. Va., Portsmouth, 1933-71, successively agt., staff mgr., Portsmouth, mgr. Staunton, Lynchburg, Newport News, Norfolk and Portsmouth, divisional supr., asst. v.p., 1946-50, 2d v.p., 1955-56, dist. mgr., Portsmouth, until 1971, ret., 1971. Past dir. Lynchburg Staunton, Norfolk Life Underwriters. Pres., Norfolk Found., Inc.; trustee Va. Bapt. Homes, 1971—; chmn. bd. deacons, mem. bd. fin. Larchmont Bapt. Ch. Mem. Peninsular Assn. Life Underwriters (past pres., dir.), Norfolk Assn. Life Underwriters, Portsmouth Assn. Life Underwriters (past pres., dir.), Staunton Assn. Life Underwriters, Lynchburg Assn. Life Underwriters. Mason (Shriner, trustee Widows' Fund of Khedive Temple); K.T. Clubs: Cosmopolitan (dir., past pres., trustee Norfolk Found. of Club); Norfolk (Va.) Yacht and Country; Saints and Sinners (charter Staunton). Home: 1215 S Fairwater Dr Norfolk VA 23508

MC WILLIE, NANCY ANN, nurse, med. adminstr.; b. Memphis, Oct. 6, 1920; d. William Compton and Blanche F. (Chapman) McW.; R.N., St. Joseph Hosp., Memphis, 1941; B.S., U. Miami (Fla.), 1954. Nurse operating room St. Joseph Hosp., Memphis, 1941; operating room staff, supr. VA Med. Center, Miami, 1949-57, supr. operating room, Augusta, Ga., 1957-60, St. Petersburg, Fla., 1963-66, coordinator-supr. operating room/recovery room, Gainesville, Fla., 1966—; instr. nursing Dept. Surgery, U. Fla., Gainesville, 1960-63; cons. in field. Served as 2d. lt. Army Nurse Corps, U.S. Army, 1944-46; ETO; col. USAR, 1973—. Mem. Assn. Operating Room Nurses, Res. Officer Assn. Democrat. Roman Catholic. Designer disposable underwater chest drainage system, 1963. Office: VA Med Center Archer Rd Gainesville FL 32602

MEAD, BILL O., food co. exec.; b. 1921. Pres., Mead's Fine Bread, Inc., 1941-59; with Campbell Taggart, Inc. (formerly Campbell Taggart Asso. Bakeries, Inc.), 1959—, chmn. bd., chief exec. officer, 1970—, also dir. Office: 6211 Lemmon Ave Dallas TX 75209*

MEAD, FRANK WALDRETH, entomologist, educator; b. Columbus, Ohio, June 11, 1922; s. Arlington Alfred and Edith May (Harrison) M.; B.S., Ohio State U., 1947, M.S., 1949; Ph.D., N.C. State U., 1968; m. Eileen May Cornwell, Apr. 21, 1945; children—David Harrison, Gregory Scott. Research asst. physiology Ohio State U., summer 1941, research asst. entomology, 1948-50; Japanese Beetle scout U.S. Dept. Agr., Columbus, summer 1948, biol. aid Bur. Entomology and Plant Quarantine, 1950-53; entomologist div. plant industry Fla. Dept. Agr., 1953-58, 1960—; research asst. N.C. State U., 1958-50; adj. asso. prof. U. Fla., Gainesville, 1973—; courtesy asso. prof. Fla. A&M U., Tallahassee, 1977—; state survey entomologist, 1963—. Mem. steering com. Civitan Regional Blood

Bank Found., Gainesville, 1977-79. Served with AUS, 1943-46. Fellow Ohio Acad. Sci.; mem. Am. Mosquito Control Assn., Soc. Systematic Zoology, Entomol. Soc. Am. (bd. dirs. S.E. br. 1978-79), Entomol. Soc. Washington, Fla. Entomol. Soc. (sec. 1968—), Fla. Anti-mosquito Assn., Ga. Entomol. Soc., Am. Registry Profl. Entomologists, SAR, Audubon Soc. (chpt. dir. 1969-75, 77—, treas. 1969-72), Alachua County Hist. Soc. Democrat. Presbyn. Contbr. articles, papers to profl. jours. Home: 2035 NE 6th Terr Gainesville FL 32601 Office: PO Box 1269 Gainesville FL 32602

MEADE, EDWARD GRANT, educator; b. Phila., Apr. 6, 1914; s. Edward and Elizabeth (Grant) M.; A.B., Dartmouth Coll., 1935; M.A., U. Wis., 1936; M.A.L.D., Fletcher Sch. Law and Diplomacy, 1938; Ph.D., U. Pa., 1948; postgrad. Harvard U., 1945, Air War Coll., 1960-61; m. Courtenay Frances Etheridge, Oct. 21, 1949; children—Elise Stokes Meade Kirkland, Courtenay Etheridge Meade Snellings, Sydney Ingram, Elizabeth Grant, Celestia Loyall. Chmn. polit. sci. dept. Haverford Coll., 1946-48; U.S. cultural attache, Bangkok, Thailand, 1955-56, U.S. pub. affairs attache, Thailand, 1956-60, Lagos, Nigeria, 1961-64; coordinator book program USIA, Europe, Africa, Washington, 1964-65; prof., chmn. polit. sci. dept. Old Dominion U., Norfolk, Va., 1965-79, prof. emeritus, 1979—; spl. prof. polit. sci. faculty Chulalongkorn U., Bangkok, Thailand, 1956-60. Dir. pub. relations Norfolk ARC, 1954-55; vice chmn. Fulbright Found., Thailand, 1955-60; bd. dirs. John E. Peurifoy Found., Bangkok, 1956-60, Social Sci. Assn. Thailand, 1957-60, Norfolk Forum, 1969-72. Served with USNR, 1941-46, 48-55. Fletcher fellow, 1936-38. Mem. Am. Hist. Assn., Am. Acad. Polit. and Social Sci., Am. Polit. Sci. Assn., Am. Soc. Internat. Law, Internat. Studies Assn., Am. Soc. Pub. Adminstrn., AAUP, Cum Laude Soc., Mil. Order Fgn. Wars, Pa. Soc., SR, Delta Kappa Epsilon. Clubs: Norfolk Yacht and Country; Pyramid; Merion Cricket (Haverford, Pa.). Author: American Military Government in Korea, 1951. Contbr. articles to profl. jours. Home: 1000 Cambridge Crescent Norfolk VA 23508

MEADOR, BEN FRANKLIN, JR., personnel co. exec.; b. Houston, Apr. 12, 1939; s. Ben Franklin and Martha Reba (Estes) M.; B.B.A., Lamar U., Beaumont, Tex., 1962; m. Dolores Ann Hagerman, Aug. 7, 1961; children—Melinda, Ben Franklin III. Accountant, Armco Steel Corp., Houston, 1962-64; personnel mgr. Diamond Shamrock Chem. Co., Houston, 1964-68; pres. Meador-Brady Personnel Services Inc., Pasadena, Tex., 1968—, Meador-Brady SW Inc., 1970—, Pasadena Honda Motorcycle Dealership, 1976—, Meador-Brady Assos., 1978—, Meador-Brady Temporary Systems, Inc., 1978—; v.p., Meador-Brady Mgmt. Corp., Pasadena, 1976—; dir. Pasadena Nat. Bank; chmn. Intercity Personnel Assos., Appleton, Wis., 1975—. Mem. Pasadena C. of C. (v.p. 1975), Nat. Employment Assn., Nat. Assn. Temporary Services. Methodist. Rotarian. Home: 4012 Paraguay St Pasadena TX 77504 Office: 1414 E Southmore St Pasadena TX 77502

MEADOR, CHARLES EDWIN, accountant; b. Kissimmee, Fla., Nov. 22, 1940; s. Charles Finney and Myrtle Lilly (Thompson) M.; B.A. (scholar), Rice, U., 1963; postgrad. So. Methodist U., 1966-67; m. Mary Carole Pistole, June 2, 1963; children—Kyle Randall, Bret Alexander, Brook Temple. Accountant, Arthur Andersen & Co., Houston and Dallas, 1967-76; controller Gen. Exploration Co., 1976-78; v.p. fin., dir. TBW Industries, Inc., Houma, La., 1978—. Bd. dirs. Am. Diabetes Assn., treas., 1976-77, chmn. bd., 1977-78; bd. dirs. Dallas Lighthouse for Blind, Houston Lighthouse for Blind. Served to lt. (j.g.) USN, 1963-67. C.P.A., Tex., La. Mem. Am. Inst. C.P.A.'s, La. Soc. C.P.A.'s, Tex. Soc. C.P.A.'s. Clubs: Lions (dir.); Ellendale Country (Houma). Home: 206 Oak Alley Houma LA 70360 Office: PO Box 4036 Houma LA 70361

MEADOR, HOWARD KIRKLAND, JR., computer analyst; b. El Dorado, Ark., Nov. 8, 1944; s. Howard Kirkland and Lela Francis (Bowers) M.; B.S. in Math., La. Tech. U., 1967; postgrad. U. So. Miss., Hattiesburg; m. Charlotte Ann Butcher, Aug. 6, 1966. With Tex. Eastern Corp., 1967-68, 71—, lead programmer/analyst, Houston, 1976—. Served with USAF, 1968-71. Mem. Assn. Computing Machinery. Republican. Baptist. Clubs: Toastmasters (pres. 1975), Tanglewild Civic (v.p. 1977). Home: 9650 Val Verde Houston TX 77063 Office: PO Box 2521 Houston TX 77001

MEADOR, JOHN MILWARD, JR., educator, ednl. librarian; b. Louisville, Nov. 4, 1946; s. John Milward and Ruth Inez (Miller) M.; B.A. in English, U. Louisville, 1968; M.A. in English, U. Tex., Austin, 1972, M.L.S., 1973; m. Judith Ann Hay, Dec. 22, 1969; 1 son, John Milward III. Stacks supr. U. Louisville Library, 1965-68; substitute tchr. Austin (Tex.) Ind. Sch. Dist., 1968-69, 71-73; instr., English bibliographer U. Houston Library, 1973-74, asst. prof., also head social scis. and humanities reference, 1974-77, head gen. reference dept. and collection devel., 1977—, asso. prof., 1979—. Served with AUS, 1969-71. Nat. winner essay contest Propeller Club of Am., 1964; English-Speaking Union summer scholar to U. Edinburgh (Scotland), 1968; ALA student grantee, 1973. Mem. AAUP, Am., Southwestern, Tex. library assns., Bibliog. Soc. Am., Modern Lang. Assn. Am., South Central Modern Lang. Assn., English-Speaking Union of U.S., Hon. Order Ky. Cols. Author: (with Covington Rodgers) The Robinson Jeffers Collection at The University of Houston: A Bibliographical Catalog, 1975. Home: 994 Redway Ln Houston TX 77062

MEADOR, ROBERT ALLEN, sporting goods co. exec.; b. Cin., Oct. 15, 1926; s. Fred M. and Florence E. (Overbeck) M.; B.S. in Edn., U. Cin., 1950; m. Joyce A. Biedenharn, Aug. 19, 1950; children—Patti Ann, Teri Jane, Gayle, Robert M. Tchr., coach Cuyahoga Falls (Ohio) High Sch., 1950-51, Montpelier (Ohio) High Sch., 1952, Taylor High Sch., Cleve., 1953; head football coach/swimming coach Withrow High Sch., Cin., 1954-58; sales rep. MacGregor Sporting Goods, W.Va., Ky., Tenn., 1959-62, Ga., Ala., S.C., 1962-71; regional sales mgr. Central Region, MacGregor Golf Co., Dallas, 1972—. Home: 6947 Delmeta Dr Dallas TX 75248 Office: 4825 LBJ Freeway 268 Dallas TX 75234

MEADOWS, DANIEL THOMAS, dentist; b. Salem, Ala., June 5, 1917; s. Daniel Porter and Gemmie Bruce (Browning) M.; B.S., Auburn U., 1939; D.M.D., U. Ala., 1953; m. Agatha Joan Fischer, Mar. 31, 1944; children—Gemma (Mrs. Thomas W. Sanford Jr.), Daniel Thomas. Pvt. practice dentistry, Birmingham, Ala., 1953; resident in prosthodontics U. Ala., 1955-57; staff dentist Birmingham VA Hosp., 1954-55, 57-62, chief dental service, 1962-68, 69—. Prof. clin. dentistry U. Ala., Birmingham, 1968—. Served to col. Dental Corps, AUS, 1942-46, 68-69. Decorated Army Commendation medal with oak leaf cluster; recipient Distinguished Service medal of Ala., 1973. Fellow Am. Coll. Dentists; mem. Am. Prosthodontic Soc., Am., Ala. dental assns., Am. Legion, Southeastern Acad. Prosthodontics, Birmingham Dist. Dental Soc. (exec. council 1968-72), Phi Kappa Phi, Gamma Sigma Delta, Kappa Delta Pi, Xi Psi Phi. Editor: Ala. Farmer, 1939. Home: 4309 Corinth Dr Birmingham AL 35213 Office: 700 S 19th St Birmingham AL 35233

MEADOWS, WADE DEAN, retail co. exec.; b. Charlotte, N.C., 1936; s. John Clayton and Sadie Wray (Britt) M.; A.A., Mars Hill Coll., 1955; B.S. magna cum laude, Appalachian State U., 1960; m. Carolyn Self, Dec. 24, 1964; children—Gregory Dean, Jennifer Lynn. Mgr., Mars Hill Coll. Bookstore and Student Center, 1955-58; asst. mgr. Appalachian State U. Book Store, 1958-64; mdse. mgr. U. N.C. Book Exchange, Chapel Hill, 1964-65; dir. U. Tenn. Book and Supply Store, Knoxville, 1965—. Deacon, Central Bapt. Ch. Recipient Outstanding award Jaycees, 1968. Mem. Nat. Assn. Coll. Stores (trustee 1978—), Tenn. Assn. Coll. Stores (past pres.), Nat. Retail Mchts. Assn., Am. Booksellers Assn., Knoxville Better Bus. Bur. Democrat. Home: 900 Bream Dr Knoxville TN 37720 Office: University Center U Tenn Knoxville TN 37916

MEADS, WALTER FREDERICK, writing inst. exec.; b. Ft. Wayne, Ind., Mar. 11, 1923; s. Frederick C. and Minnie E. Meads; B.S., Kent State U., 1948; M.A., Fairfield U., 1973; m. Mary E. Meads, Mar. 20, 1975. With J. Walter Thompson Co., N.Y.C., 1955-73, corp. sr. v.p., 1965-73; communications cons. Fla. So. Coll., Lakeland, 1974-75; prof. Fla. A&M U., Tallahassee, 1976-77; pres. Meads Inst., Inc., Lakeland, 1978—. Served with USAAF, 1943-45. Recipient numerous awards in field. Mem. Public Relations Soc. Am. (accredited), Am. Soc. for Tng. and Devel. Republican. Unitarian. Home: 4420 Orangewood Loop E Lakeland FL 33803 Office: Lake Morton Profl Center 58 Lake Morton Dr Lakeland FL 33801

MEAGHER, ARNOLD JOSEPH, service co. exec.; b. Longford, Ireland, Mar. 9, 1933; s. Arnold and Mary A. (Reynolds) M.; M.A., U. Calif., Davis, 1969, Ph.D., 1975; m. Jacqueline J. Devlin, Feb. 10, 1973. Teaching asso. U. Calif., Davis, 1967-75; gen. mgr., partner AM Assos., Houston, 1975-77; pres., chief exec. officer Best Writing Services, Inc., Houston, 1977—; lectr. U. Houston, 1977—. Home: 3501 Tangley Houston TX 77005 Office: 2100 W Loop S #600 Houston TX 77027

MEAGHER, CHARLES FRANKLIN, engring. co. exec.; b. Sayreton, Ala., Nov. 29, 1925; s. Arch Webster and Winnie Davis (Layne) M.; B.S. in Mech. Engring., St. Mary's (Calif.) Coll., 1946; postgrad. U. Tenn., 1950, U. Chgo., 1957; m. Francis June Coffman, Dec. 19, 1946 (div. Mar. 1964); children—Vicki Jo, Chareece Lee, David Jonathan; m. 2d, June Elizabeth Jones, Sept. 26, 1964; children—Beth Carol, Nancy Jean, Ellen Lee. Supervising trainee Combustion Engring. Co., Chattanooga, 1950-53; gen. foreman Atlas Powder Co., Tyner, Tenn., 1953-55, engr. in charge layaway, 1955-57; gen. foreman Cramet Titamium Facility, Chattanooga, 1957-58; chief engring. services NASA, Huntsville, Ala., 1960-66; owner, cons. engr. Jonathan Engring. Service, Prospect, Tenn., 1966—. Mil. service, 1944-46. Registered profl. engr., Tenn. Mem. ASME, Am. Rocket Soc., Nat. Soc. Profl. Engrs. Methodist (steward 1953-66, Sunday sch. supt. 1963-65). Mason. Author: Layaway Manual for Decontaminating TNT Plants, 1955; How to Recover Airplanes, 1958. Address: Box 124 Prospect TN 38477

MEALING, ESTHER MORRISON (MOLLIE), artist; b. Corinth, Miss., Aug. 8, 1916; d. Errett Arthur and Marguerite (Adams) Morrison; student Columbus Coll., 1966; grad. Draughons Bus. Coll., 1935; pvt. instruction in art; m. John Pace Mealing, July 20, 1940; children—Robert Adams, Esther Lee Mealing Lehew, Marguerite Anna Mealing Ozley. Cashier, sec. Ace Power Assn., Corinth, 1935-36; clk. typist TVA, Tupelo, Miss., Chattanooga, 1936-41; art tchr. Wynnton Meth. Ch., 1970—; dir. art display Chattahoochee Valley Fair, 1973-76; paintings exhibited Hamilton Art Gallery, That Place, Derium's Antiques, Curio Creations, Kirvens, Talent Tree, others. Asst. den mother Ozark council Boy Scouts Am., 1953-54; leader or co-leader Concharty council Girl Scouts U.S.A., 1952-57, 62-67; sec.-treas. Muscogee County Citizens Assn., 1955-59; bd. dirs. Muscogee County Welfare Dept., 1957-72, chmn. advisory bd., 1971-72, rep. dist. 3, 1971-72; mem. adv. bd. State of Ga., 1971-72. Recipient various prizes in art for water colors, oils, sculptures. Mem. Nat. League Am. Pen Women (past pres. Columbus br., pres. Ga. 1976-78), Columbus Artists Guild (past pres.), Ga. Water Color Soc. (asso.), So. Water Color Soc., Columbus Mus. Arts and Crafts, Hist. Columbus Found. and Hist. Trust for Preservation. Mem. Christian Ch. (former Sunday sch. thcr., substitute organist, choir mem.). Club: Benning Hills Woman's (charter). Author, pub: Sketch Book - Century Old Houses of Columbus and Vicinity, Vol. 1, 1971, Vol. 2, 1975; (Haiku verse) Memories of Studio 10, 1975. Home: 809 Cooper Ave Columbus GA 31906

MEANS, JAMES CLARENCE, JR., ret. sch. prin.; b. Sycamore, Ga., Nov. 4, 1912; s. James Clarence and Caroline Elizabeth (Godard) M.; A.B., Ga. State Coll., 1933; M.Ed., U. Ga., 1967; m. Barbara Alice Birchmore, Dec. 21, 1938; children—Caroline Ann Means Durden, James Clarence, III, John A. Prin., coach Rebecca (Ga.) High Sch., 1933-34; prin., coach Sumner (Ga.) High Sch., 1934-37; prin. Comer (Ga.) High Sch., 1937-40, 42-46; state supr. War Tng. Hdqrs. Atlanta, 1940-42; owner, operator Dairy Farm, Comer, 1946-59; tchr., asst. prin. Madison County High Sch., Danielsville, Ga., 1955-57; prin. Comer Elementary Sch., 1964-75. Mem. Madison County Bd. Edn. 1946-55; chmn. Madison County Planning Commn., 1971-74. Mem. Madison County, Ga., assns. educators, NEA. Democrat. Methodist. Lion, Elk. Author: Nongraded Teachers Manual for Reading, Arithmetic, 1969. Home: 211 Madison St Comer GA 30629

MEANS, RICHARD LAWRENCE, historian; b. Malvern, Ark., Dec. 25, 1945; s. Edward E. and Hazel (Lawrence) M.; B.A., Henderson State Tchrs. Coll., 1966; M.A., U. Ark., 1968; m. Emilia Gay Griffith, Nov. 1, 1969; 1 son, R. Nathaniel Griffith. Instr. history U. Southwestern La., 1968-69, asst. to dean Coll. Liberal Arts, 1969-70; instr. history Mountain View Coll., Dallas, 1970—, chmn. div. social scis., 1970-72. Nat. Endowment for Humanities fellow, 1975. Mem. La. Hist. Soc., Orgn. Am. Historians. Democrat. Presbyterian. Home: 11255 Carissa Circle Dallas TX 75218 Office: 4849 W Illinois Ave Dallas TX 75211

MEANS, WILLERMA FRAZIER, librarian; b. St. George, S.C., Apr. 23, 1947; d. Patrick and Cora Lee (Cohen) Frazier; B.S., S.C. State Coll., 1968; M.S., U. Ill., 1969; m. Paul Allen Means, Aug. 22, 1970. Library asso. Nat. Library of Medicine, Bethesda, Md., 1969-70; reading tchr. Williams Meml. Sch., St. George, 1972-73; area mgr. Field Enterprises Ednl. Corp., St. George, 1974-76; media services coordinator/librarian St. George Elementary Sch., 1973—; mem. Instructional TV Adv. Council, Sch. Fin. Adv. Council; mem. regional planning com. S.C. Gov.'s Conf. on Libraries; part-time auto pruchasing cons., 1978—. Chmn., Dorchester County (S.C.) Polit. Action Com. for Edn., 1974-76, 77—; coordinator for 1st Congl. dist. S.C. Polit. Action Com., 1976; jr. missionary Charleston Dist., 1979—. Recipient Library Service award S.C. State Coll., 1965; USPHS fellow, 1968-69. Mem. NEA (rep. assembly 1975, 77, 78), S.C., Dorchester County edn. assns., ALA, Nat. Assn. for Ednl. Communications and Tech., Internat. Reading Assn., Assn. for Ednl. Communications and Tech. of S.C., S.C. Assn. Sch. Librarians, Assn. for Study Afro-Am. Life and History, Alpha Mu Gamma. Home: PO Box 606 Saint George SC 29477 Office: 201 Johnston St Saint George SC 29477

MEARES, ROMULUS LINNEY, JR., lawyer; b. Knoxville, Tenn., Apr. 15, 1941; s. Romulus Linney and Lucile Elizabeth (Goyne) M.; student U.S. Naval Acad., 1959-61; J.D., U. Tenn., 1964; m. Susan Katherine Harry, June 9, 1963; children—Jennifer Katherine, Judith Price, Romulus Linney. Admitted to Tenn. bar, 1964; practice in Maryville, 1964—. Mem. Am., Tenn., Blount County (pres. 1973) bar assns., Am. Judicature Soc., Tenn. Def. Lawyers Assn., Phi Delta Phi. Office: PO Box 407 111 E Broadway Maryville TN 37801 also 918 State St Knoxville TN 37902

MEAUX, RICHARD CECIL, lawyer; b. Lafayette, La., Dec. 31, 1921; s. Edward and Ida (Girouard) M.; B.S., U. Southwestern La., 1938; J.D., Tulane U., 1948; m. Lillian Breaux, Feb. 9, 1952; children—David, Richard Cecil, Simonette, Daniel, Michelle. Admitted to La. bar, 1948; partner firm Meaux & Meaux, Lafayette, 1948; partner firm Davidson, Meaux, Onebane, Donohoe, Bernard, Torian & Diaz and predecessor firms, Lafayette, 1948-77, Davidson, Meaux, Sonnier & Roy, 1977—; advocate Am. Bd. Trial Advocates. Served with USAAF, 1942-45. Mem. Am. Judicature Soc., Def. Research Inst., La., Lafayette, 15th Jud. Dist., Am. bar assns., Civil Service League, Lafayette C. of C. Home: 318 Beverly Dr Lafayette LA 70501 Office: PO Box 2908 810 S Buchanan St Lafayette LA 70502

MEBANE, GILES YANCEY, family physician; b. Beaufort, N.C., Jan. 10, 1928; s. William Giles and Ruth Amelia (Robinson) M.; B.A., Duke U., 1950, M.D., 1954; m. Charlene Robbins, Mar. 12, 1955; children—Ann, William Giles, Michael Scott, John Anthony. Intern, Duke U. Med. Center, Durham, N.C., 1954; resident in family practice Med. Coll. Va., Richmond, 1954-56; practice medicine specializing in family practice, Mebane, N.C., 1956—; clin. asso. Duke U.; med. advisor Alamance Rescue Service. Diplomate Am. Bd. Family Practice. Fellow Am. Acad. Family Practice; mem. AMA, N.C. Med. Soc., Aerospace Med. Soc., Undersea Med. Soc., Marine Tech. Soc. Research on hyperbaric physiology. Home: Rt 4 Mebane NC 27302 Office: 202 S 5th St Mebane NC 27302

MECOM, JOHN W., JR., oil exec., profl. football team exec.; b. Tex.; ed. U. Okla., U. Tex.; m. Katsy Mullendore, 1962; children—John III, Katsy Kathleen, Mary Elizabeth, Kathleen. Active oil bus., La.; pres. New Orleans Saints profl. football team; also exec. auto and boat racing. Bd. regents Loyola U., New Orleans. Address: care New Orleans Saints 1500 Poydras St New Orleans LA 70112

MEDINA, ARTURO, educator; b. Rio Grande City, Tex., Mar. 1, 1930; s. Estanislado and Arnulfa (Martinez) M.; B.S., Tex. A&I U., 1955, M.S., 1956; Ph.D., Tex. A&M U., 1973; m. Toni O.; children—Dennis Glenn, Keith Allen, Sheryl Amelia, Jacqueline Kim, Edward Samuel, David. Tchr., adminstr. public schs., San Benito and Snook, Tex., 1956-64; supt. schs., LaJoya, Tex., 1964-70; asso. prof. edn. Corpus Christi State U., 1973—. Mem. exec. bd. Jobs-for-Progress; trustee Corpus Christi Ind. Sch. Dist.; mem. Gov.'s Office Blue Ribbon Com. on Edn. Served with U.S. Army, 1950-53. Mem. Coastal Bend Assn. Bilingual Edn. (area pres.), Am. Assn. Sch. Adminstrs., Tex. Assn. Coll. Tchrs. Methodist. Clubs: Masons, Shriners. Home: 5722 Flynn Pkwy Corpus Christi TX 78411 Office: 6300 Ocean Dr Corpus Christi TX 78412

MEDLAND, FRANCIS FREDERIC, psychologist; b. Logansport, Ind., Sept. 22, 1919; s. Francis Sylvester and Nora (Hunt) M.; A.B., U. Dayton, 1942; A.M., U. Chgo., 1948; student Am. U., 1960-63; m. Stephanie Uriniak, Apr. 30, 1949; 1 dau., Mary Elizabeth. Research asst., psychometric Lab., U. of Chgo., 1943-47; research psychologist U.S. Marine Corps Hdqrs., Washington, 1947-59; supervisory research psychologist U.S. Army Personnel Research Office, Washington 1959-74; principal scientist U.S. Army Research Inst. for Behavioral and Soc. Sciences, Alexandria, Va., 1974—. Mem. Am. Psychological Assn., Psychometric Soc., Psi Chi, Sigma Xi. Contbr. research papers in field. Home: 1712 Crestwood Dr Alexandria VA 22302 Office: 5001 Eisenhower Ave Alexandria VA 22333

MEDLEY, DANIEL SPALDING, mktg., mfg. co. exec.; b. Owensboro, Ky., Aug. 23, 1950; s. John Abell and Mary Cecilia (O'Bryan) M.; B.S., Murray (Ky.) State U., 1973; m. Kathleen Ann Slater, Aug. 14, 1976. Mgr., mktg. and advt. Central Bank & Trust Co., Owensboro, 1973-77; dir. public and internal relations Orbco Inc., Owensboro, 1977—, dir. advt. subs. Modern Methods Inc., 1978—, dir. creative sers. in-house agy., August, Benton & Bauer, 1979—; faculty, bd. dirs. Owensboro-Daviess County C. of C. Small Bus. Inst. Chmn. programs Owensboro Hydrofair Inc., 1974-77, chmn. public info., 1977-78; mem. Commn. on Arts Mayor City of Owensboro, 1975-78; bd. dirs. Owensboro Art Guild, 1975-78. Mem. Am. Mgmt. Assn., Owensboro Jaycees. Roman Catholic. Home: 3827 Bowlds Ct Owensboro KY 42301 Office: Orbco Inc 100 1st St E Owensboro KY 42301

MEDLEY, JOHN ABELL, JR., beer distbg. co. exec.; b. Owensboro, Ky., Sept. 8, 1938; s. John Abell and Mary Cecilia (O'Bryan) M.; B.F.A., U. Dayton, 1961; m. Mary Margaret Kiley, Feb. 11, 1961; children—John Abell III, Lisa Ann, Angela Marie. Vice pres., gen. mgr. Quality Beers Distbg. Co., Owensboro, 1962—; dir. Haley-McGinnis Funeral. Bd. dirs. Wendall Foster Center, 1971—, Owensboro Symphony, 1973—, Owensboro Natural Sci. Mus., Hydrofair, 1970—; city commr., Owensboro, 1976—, mayor pro-tem, 1978—. Served with U.S. Army, 1961-62. Mem. Nat. Beer Wholesalers Assn., Nat. League Cities, Ky. Beer Wholesalers Assn. (dir.), Ky. Mcpl. League, Asso. Industries Ky., Ky. C. of C., Owensboro C. of C. (dir. 1976—), S.A.R. Democrat. Roman Catholic. Clubs: Campbell, Moose, Elks, Eagles. Home: 4424 Taylor Dr Owensboro KY 42301 Office: 1010 E 6th St Owensboro KY 42301

MEDLIN, ALLEN, assn. exec.; b. Bauxite, Ark., Sept. 23, 1926; s. James Arthur and Elsie Elizabeth (Sides) M.; B.A., Little Rock U., 1948; m. Lillian Rebecca Gholson, June 16, 1959; children—Clifton Norris, Del Lacy. Asst. mgr. J.H. Hamlen & Son Inc., Little Rock, 1958-70; mgr. lumber procurement and distbn. A. Brandt Co., Ft. Worth, 1970-74; mgr. Little Rock dist. Nat. Hardwood Lumber Assn., 1974—; owner, operator Allen Medlin & Assos., Cons.'s, Little Rock, 1978—. Mem. Am. Mgmt. Assn. Democrat. Baptist. Home: 6717 Rockwood Rd Little Rock AR 72207 Office: Nat Hardwood Lumber Assn PO Box 34518 Memphis TN 38134

MEDLIN, JAMES LOYD, mfg. co. exec.; b. Kings Mountain, N.C., Mar. 25, 1946; s. James Herman and Irene Lula (Gaffney) M.; B.S. in Bus. Adminstrn., Western Carolina U., 1973, M.B.A., 1975; m. Mary Aileen Wright, July 16, 1967; children—Amy Lillian, Seth Wright. Adminstrv. specialist U.S. Air Force, 1967-71; instr. Western Carolina U., Cullowhee, N.C., 1973-75; asso. mgmt. cons. Mgmt. Lead Time, Inc., Pitts., 1974-76; product mktg. mgr. comml. products, planning and research, Gravely div. Clarke-Gravely Corp., Clemmons, N.C., 1976-79, comml. sales mgr. N.Am., 1979—. Pres., dist. dir. Rolling Hills Assn., Winston-Salem, N.C., 1979-80; chmn. social concerns, mem. adminstrv. bd., tchr. Sunday Sch., Mt. Tabor United Meth. Ch., Winston-Salem. Served with USAF, 1967-71. Mem. N.Am. Soc. Corp. Planners, Lambda Chi Alpha. Democrat. Methodist. Home: 600 Kelway Pl Winston-Salem NC 27104 Office: 1 Gravely Ln Clemmons NC 27012

MEDLIN, VIRGIL DEWAIN, historian, educator, lawyer; b. Chickasha, Okla., Feb. 21, 1943; s. Virgil Odell and Beatrice Louise (Fellows) M.; B.A., Oklahoma City U., 1965, M.A.T., 1967, J.D.,

1979; M.A., U. Okla., 1968, Ph.D., 1974. Fine arts editor Okla. Jour., Oklahoma City, 1964-66; columnist Oklahoma City Advertiser, 1964-68; programmer Sta. KFNB-FM, 1965-66; instr. history and govt. Oklahoma City Southwestern Coll., 1966-68, asst. to pres., 1967-69, asso. dean, 1968-69; instr. social scis. Central State U., Edmond, Okla., 1969; asst. prof. history Oklahoma City U., 1969-73, asso. prof., 1973-79, prof., 1980—, chmn. history dept., 1979—, chmn. faculty senate, 1979—; spl. instr. Russian history U. Okla., Norman, 1970-71; dir. Russian and Soviet studies Assn. Colls. and Univs. for Internat. Intercultural Studies, Graz Center, Graz, Austria, 1973-75. Bd. dirs. Wickline United Methodist Ch.; sponsor Explorer post Boy Scouts Am.; Fulbright grantee, 1967-68; French govt. fellow, 1967-68; Oxford U. Extramural scholar, 1967; Russian Studies certificate Institut zur Erforschung UdSSR, Munich, 1965; knight comdr.'s certificate of honor Kappa Alpha Order, 1975. Mem. Am. Bar Assn., Okla. Bar Assn., Okla. Conf., AAUP (exec. sec. 1978—), Am. Hist. Assn., Am. Assn. Advancement Slavic Studies, Assn. Asian Studies, So. Hist. Assn. (life), S.W. Conf. Asian Studies (dir. 1972-73), Rocky Mountain Assn. for Slavic Studies, Southwestern Slavic Assn. (sec.-treas. 1977-79, pres. 1979-80), Okla. Acad. Scis. (social sci. head 1975-76), Blue Key (faculty adviser, 1977—), Phi Alpha Delta, Phi Mu Alpha Sinfonia, Alpha Mu Gamma, Phi Alpha Theta (faculty advisor Sigma Omicron chpt. 1972—), Pi Sigma Alpha, Kappa Alpha Order (province comdr., nat. adv. council 1976-79). Democrat. Author: The Reluctant Revolutionaries, 1974; The Russian Revolution: Democracy or Deference, 1974; V.D. Nabokov and the Russian Provisional Government, 1917, 1976. Mng. editor: Music and Ballet, Soviet Union/Union soviétique, 1974-80; editor S.W. Conf. Asian Studies newsletter, 1973-76; editorial bd. Can.-Am. Slavic Studies, 1977—, Red River Valley Jour. History, 1977—. Home: 2125 Turner Dr Oklahoma City OK 73110

MEDOFF, LAWRENCE RAY, physician; b. Pitts., Dec. 13, 1910; s. David and Rebecca (Kramer) M.; B.S., Mt. Union Coll., 1932; M.D., Chgo. Med. Sch., 1939; m. Thelma Butt, Dec. 29, 1935; children—Mark Howard, Alan Robert. Intern, Jewish Hosp., Louisville, 1938-39, resident, 1948-49; practice medicine, specializing in family medicine, Grayville, Ill., 1939-48; practice medicine specializing in internal medicine, Miami, Fla., 1949-68; med. dir. St. Francis Hosp., Miami Beach, Fla., 1968—, pres. hosp. staff, 1964-68. Bd. dirs. Heart Assn. Greater Miami; mem. bd. edn. Grayville, Ill., 1942-48; mem. Miami Beach Health Planning Commn. Recipient merit award Am. Physicians Art Assn., 1960. Diplomate Am. Bd. Family Practice, Pan-Am. Med. Assn. Fellow Am. Acad. Family Physicians, Am. Coll. Angiology; mem. Fla., Dade County med. assns., AMA (Physicians Recognition award), Am. Geriatric Soc., Am. Acad. Med. Adminstrs. Mason (32 deg., Shriner), Lion (pres. 1945-47). Club: North Shore Tennis (pres. 1963-66). Contbr. articles to profl. jours. Home: 10000 W Bay Harbor Dr Bay Harbor FL 33154 Office: 250 63d St Miami Beach FL 33141

MEEK, EDWIN ERNEST, journalist, educator; b. Jackson, Miss., Sept. 29, 1940; s. Jon F. and Ernestine (Priddy) M.; B.S. in Journalism, U. Miss., 1961, M.A., 1963; Ph.D. in Communications, U. So. Miss., 1974; m. Helen Rebecca Wolfe, June 24, 1960; children—Cynthia Karmen, Kellye Christen. Corr. Birmingham (Ala.) News, 1960-61; staff writer U. Miss., Oxford, 1962-64, dir. pub. info., 1964—, dir. pub. relations, asst. prof. journalism, 1974—; pres. Oxford Advt., 1974—, Ednl. Communications Consultants, 1974—. Rotary Exchange Group fellow to Switzerland, 1967; Am. Council on Edn. fellow in acad. adminstrn. U. Tenn., 1977; recipient Distinguished Service award Oxford civic clubs, 1969; named Outstanding Young Man of Year, Oxford Jr. C. of C., 1969. Mem. Am. Coll. Pub. Relations Assn. (exec. com. 1974-75), Miss. Coll. Pub. Relations Assn. (pres. 1974), Soc. Profl. Journalists (pres. Miss. chpt. 1974), Pub. Relations Soc. Am., Jaycees. Democrat. Methodist. Club: Rotary. Author: E. Percy Howe's Dollar Democrat, 1963; Theora Hamblett Paintings, 1975; Theora Hamblett Dreams and Visions, 1976. Contbr. articles in field to profl. jours. Home: 111 Longest Rd Oxford MS 38655 Office: Box 186 Oxford MS 38677

MEEK, J(OHN) WILLIAM, III, art dealer, cons.; b. Aberdeen, Md., Nov. 8, 1950; s. John William and Margaret Catherine (Etzler) M.; B.A., Fla. So. Coll., 1972; m. Barbara Lynn Hanson, Aug. 14, 1976; 1 dau., Kristine Marie. Asst. dir. Harmon Gallery, Naples, Fla., 1972-77, owner, dir., 1978—; also cons. Served to capt., Signal Corps, U.S. Army Res., 1972-79. Fellow Royal Soc. Arts London; mem. Better Bus. Div. Fla. (dir.), Delta Sigma Pi (pres. 1969-72), Phi Sigma Kappa (sec. 1969-72), Kappa Pi. Republican. Episcopalian. Clubs: Collier County (Fla.) Stamp (pres. 1972), Rotary (mem. bus. exchange program with Naples, Italy 1979). Home: Naples FL 33940 also 511 1/2 Phoenix St South Haven MI 49090 Office: 1258 Third St S Naples FL 33940

MEEK, PAUL DERALD, oil and chem. co. exec.; b. McAllen, Tex., Aug. 15, 1930; s. William Van and Martha Mary (Sharp) M.; B.S. in Chem. Engring., U. Tex., Austin, 1953; m. Betty Catherine Robertson, Apr. 18, 1954; children—Paula Marie, Kathy Diane, Carol Ann, Linda Ray. With tech. dept. Humble Oil & Refining Co., Baytown, Tex., 1953-55; process engr., then pres. Cosden Oil & Chem. Co., 1968-76, dir., 1965—; v.p. parent co. Am. Petrofina, Inc., 1968-76, pres., chief operating officer, 1976—, dir., 1968—; chmn. Engring. Found. adv. council U. Tex., Austin, 1979-80, chmn. chem. engring. vis. com., 1975-76; mem. research com. Tex. Research League, 1979—. Named Disting. Engring. Grad., U. Tex., Austin, 1969; registered profl. engr., Tex. Mem. Am. Petroleum Inst., Am. Inst. Chem. Engrs., Mfg. Chemists Assn. Office: Box 2159 Fina Plaza Dallas TX 75221

MEEKER, NINA LOUISE, nursing adminstr.; b. Arkansas City, Kans., Jan. 23, 1924; d. Robert R. and Ethel A. (King) Clements; R.N., Hillcrest Med. Center, Tulsa, 1945; student various workshops in continuing edn. nursing, 1954-79; m. George Delbert Meeker, Jr., Mar. 8, 1945; children—Sherry Louise, George Delbert, Robert David. Pvt. duty nurse Hillcrest Med. Center, 1945; med. nursing staff Cushing (Okla.) Masonic Hosp., 1946-47, supt. nurses, 1948-49; office nurse, Cushing, Okla., 1949; supt. nurses Kingfisher (Okla.) Hosp., 1950; staff nurse Enid (Okla.) Gen. Hosp., 1951; office nurse, Enid, 1953-54; supr. women's continued treatment service Central State Hosp., Norman, Okla., 1954-56, asst. dir. nursing service, 1957-58, dir. nursing service, 1959-60; staff nurse St. Mary's Hosp., Enid, 1960-61; supr. girls' cottages Enid State Sch., 1961-64, supr. hosp. units, 1964-68, supr. combined hosp. and new intensive care area, 1968-72; team leader nursing unit St. John's Hosp., Salina, Kans., 1972-73, supr. central sterile and material mgtm., 1974-79; house supr. nursing service Enid Meml. Hosp., 1979—. Cub scout mother Norman council Cub Scouts Am., 1955-56; v.p. Exchange Club Aux., 1969-70; pres. Great Plains Soc. Central Service Personnel, 1978-79. Mem. Am. Hosp. Assn., Am. Central Service Assn., Infection Control Orgn., Mental Health Assn., Kans. Hosp. Assn., Kans. R.N. Assn., Midwest Health Congress, Okla. Nurses Assn., Mothers Assn. Southwestern U. Clubs: Lady Elks, White Shriners, Jaycee Janes. Home: PO Box 5205 Enid OK 73701 also 2914 Double Tree Ln Enid OK 73701

MEEKER, RICHARD EDWARD, mfg. exec.; b. Newark, Dec. 8, 1922; s. Charles Augustus and Mary Elizabeth (Thornton) M.; A.S., Central Tech. Coll., 1949; E.E., U. Mich., 1958; m. Catherine Findlay Young, Mar. 24, 1945; With Am. Airlines, Chgo., N.Y.C., Tulsa, 1949-63; mgr. employment and employee relations N.Am. Rockwell, Tulsa and McAlester, Okla., 1963-68; personnel dir. L.T.V. Vought Aeronautics, Dallas, 1968-76; sr. labor relations rep. Johnson div. Eagle Picher Industries, Lubbock, Tex., 1976—, dir. employee and industrial relations. Mem. Nat. Selective Service Bd., Muskogee, Okla., 1962-63, Airport Authority Bd., McAlester, Okla., 1965-68. Served with USN, 1944-46. Recipient U.S. Presdl. Citation for civic duty, Okla., 1967. Mem. C. of C. (dir. 1966-68), Tex. Assn. Bus. Mgmt., Nat. Mgmt. Assn. (sec. 1962-63), Am. Soc. Personnel Adminstrn. (v.p. 1977-78). Presbyterian. Clubs: Order DeMolay, Masons, Shriners, Tulsa Exchange (pres. 1961-62), Nat. Exchange (dist. gov. 1962-63). Home: 2608 Purdue St Lubbock TX 79415 Office: PO Box 2309 Lubbock TX 79408

MEEKER, WILLIAM RAYMOND, JR., surgeon; b. Mobile, Ala., Apr. 10, 1933; s. William Raymond and Isabel (Cowan) M.; student U. Chgo., 1949-52; B.A., Tulane U., 1952-53; M.D., Med. Coll. Ala., 1957; M.S. in Surgery, U. Minn., 1964; m. Winifred Ann Virtue, Oct. 6, 1962; children—William Raymond, David Cowan, Winifred Ann. Intern, U. Minn. Hosp., Mpls., 1957-58, resident, 1958-64; fellow in gastrointestinal cancer surgery Roswell Park Meml. Inst., Buffalo, 1964-65, asso. cancer research surgeon, Buffalo, 1965-69; asst. prof. surgery U. Ky. Med. Center, Lexington, 1969-73, asso. prof., 1973-79, clin. asso. prof., 1979—; on leave with surgery br. div. cancer treatment Nat. Cancer Inst., 1977; practice surgical oncology, Lexington, 1979—; cons. VA Hosp., Lexington; staff Central Bapt., Good Samaritan, St. Joseph's hosps. (all Lexington). Diplomate Am. Bd. Surgery. Mem. AMA, A.C.S., Assn. Acad. Surgeons, Am. Assn. Cancer Research, Am. Soc. Clin. Oncology, Am. Assn. Cancer Edn., Southeastern Surg. Congress, Soc. Surg. Oncology, Central Surg. Assn. Republican. Episcopalian. Research in field. Home: 417 Fayette Park Lexington KY 40508

MEGGINSON, LEON CASSITY, educator; b. Thomasville, Ala., July 26, 1921; s. William A. and Emma Frances (Cassity) M.; student Samford U., 1938-40; B.S., Miss. Coll., 1947; M.B.A., La. State U., 1949, Ph.D., 1953; m. Jayne Margaret Wightman, Sept. 15, 1962; children—Gayle (Mrs. Thomas A. Ross III), William Leon, William Jay. Factory rep. Hershey Chocolate Co., Birmingham, Ala., 1940-42; instr. bus. La. State U., 1949-50, asst. prof., 1951-54, asso. prof., 1954-60, prof., 1960-77, asst. dean Coll. Bus., 1957-60; research prof. mgmt. U. South Ala., 1978—. Fulbright Research scholar, Spain, 1961-62; resident advisor Ford Found., Karachi, Pakistan, 1968-70; cons. in mgmt. devel. for cos. and tng. instns. Mem. La. Adv. Council for Employment Security, 1956-64, chmn., 1960-64; chmn. East Baton Rouge Parish Family Ct., 1958-60. Trustee, mem. personnel com. Baton Rouge Gen. Hosp., 1957-61, 75—; pres. W.A. Hegginson Edn. Found. Served with AC, AUS, 1942-45. Decorated Air medal with 4 oak leaf clusters; recipient Distinguished Faculty Service award La. State U. Alumni Found., 1971. Accredited personnel diplomate Am. Soc. Personnel Adminstrn. Mem. Acad. Mgmt. (dir.), So. Mgmt. Assn. (pres. 1972-73), Southwestern Social Sci. Assn. (pres. 1962-63), So. Case Research Assn. (pres. 1971-75). Republican. Baptist. Author: Personnel, 1967, 4th edit., 1981 (Acad. Mgmt. Book award 1967); Human Resources, 1968; (with Curtis Tate, Jr.) Successful Small Business Management, 1975, rev. edit., 1978; The Complete Guide to Your Own Business, 1977. Home: 166 S Georgia Ave Mobile AL 36604

MEGIAS, SERGIO RAUL, sch. counselor; b. Havan, Cuba, May 25, 1945; s. Sergio M. and Bertha L. (DelPino) M.; came to U.S., 1961, naturalized, 1969; B.A. in Psychology, U. Miami (Fla.), 1967; M.Ed. in Guidance and Counseling, Fla. Atlantic U., 1974; m. Frances Galliano, Sept. 22, 1966; children—Daniel, Eileen. Credit and fin. analyst Dun & Bradstreet Inc., 1969-71, Miami Beach First Nat. Bank, 1971-72; counseling test technician Fla. Employment Service, 1972-74; counselor Dade County Sch. Bd., Miami, 1974—; partner Dr. I. Fitere & Assos., 1978—; v.p. Center Comprehensive Testing and Counseling, 1978—; mem. admissions bd. lic. practical nurse program Lindsey Hopkins Tech. Edn. Center: counselor, profl. cons. Garces Comml. Coll. Recipient cert. recognition Dade County Youth Fair. Mem. Am. Personnel and Guidance Assn., Nat. Vocat. Guidance Assn., Am. Sch. Counselor Assn., United Tchrs. Dade, U. Miami Alumni Assn., Fla. Atlantic U. Alumni Assn. Democrat. Roman Catholic. Club: Sportsrooms. Address: 904 Wallace St Coral Gables FL 33134

MEGIVERN, JAMES JOSEPH, educator; b. Johnson City, N.Y., July 2, 1931; s. John David and Katherine Augusta (Gibbons) M.; Th.D., U. Fribourg (Switzerland), 1962; S.S.L., Bibl. Inst. (Rome), 1966; D.D. (honoris causa), Moravian Theol. Sem., 1966; m. Marjorie L. Smith, July 9, 1977. Bibl. instr. Mary Immaculate Sem., Northampton, Pa., 1962-64; chmn. dept. theology, asso. prof. St. John's U., Jamaica, N.Y., 1965-70; project dir. N.Y.C. Bd. Edn., Dist. 12, 1970-74; chmn. dept. philosophy and religion, prof. U. N.C., Wilmington, 1974—. Mem. AAUP (pres. N.C. Conf. 1979-80), Am. Philos. Assn., Am. Acad Religion, Soc. Philosophy of Religion. Democrat. Roman Catholic. Editor: Bible Interpretation, 1978; Worship and Liturgy, 1978; author: Concomitance and Communion, 1963; co-editor: Catholic Tradition, 14 vols., 1979. Home: Route 3 Box 279A Wilmington NC 28403 Office: Philosophy and Religion Dept U NC Wilmington NC 28406

MEGNA, JOHN COSIMO, mfg. co. exec.; b. Milw., Oct. 22, 1927; s. John Perry and Lenore Susanne (Cripps) M.; B.S. in Chem. Engring., U. Wis., 1951; m. Beverly June Brueggemann, Feb. 4, 1950; children—Karen, Jane Ann, Susan, Nancy, John. Dir. mfg. Bioferm Corp., Wasco, Calif., 1957-63; asst. gen. mgr. ops. Internat. Minerals and Chems., San Jose, Calif., 1963-66; v.p. comml. devel. Bio-Tech. Resources, Manitowoc, Wis., 1966-71; v.p. mfg. Am. Dade div. Am. Hosp. Supply Corp., Miami, Fla., 1971—. Served with U.S. Army, 1946-47. Mem. Am. Chem. Soc., Am. Inst. Chem. Engring., Soc. Indsl. Microbiology. Patentee in field. Office: PO Box 520672 Miami FL 33152

MEHLER, RANDAL ALBERT, mfg. co. exec.; b. Hutsonville, Ill., July 4, 1918; s. Albert Ray and Gretchen Amelia (Maddox) M.; B.S. in Chem. Engring., U. Ill., 1940; LL.B., U. Louisville, 1951; m. Helen Midden, Mar. 2, 1946; children—Fredericka, Linda, Randal Albert, Lawrence. With Joseph E. Seagram Co., Lawrenceburg, Ind., also Louisville, 1940-54; partner Distillers & Bottlers Supply Co., Louisville, 1954-59; southwestern div. sales mgr. Diamond Internat., Louisville, 1959-64; pres. Mo-Vac Internat., LaGrange, Ky., 1964-67, Mo-Vac Corp., Morganfield, Ky., 1959—. Mem. Ky. Bar Assn., Vacuum Coaters Soc. Clubs: Big Spring Country, Breckenridge Golf, Pendennis, N.Y. Athletic. Contbr. articles to profl. jours. Office: Mo-Vac Corp 714 W Main St Morganfield KY 42437

MEHNE, JAMES LEE, automobile co. exec.; b. Louisville, Aug. 28, 1924; s. William John and Anna Mae (Troutwine) M.; student Western Ky. Coll., 1942, Miss. State Coll., 1943; B.M.E., U. Louisville, 1945-48, postgrad. Law Sch., 1950, Div. Adult Edn., 1954-60, M.E., Speed Sci. Sch., 1971; postgrad. Jefferson Sch. Law, 1949-50; m. Marinell Jacobsen, June 12, 1948; children—James Lee, Lesley Carol. Fire prevention engr. Ky. Insp. Bur., Louisville, 1948-50; engr. Ford Motor Co., Louisville, 1953-58, quality control mgr., 1958-63, prodn. mgr., 1963-66, ops. mgr., 1966-68, asst. plant mgr., Atlanta, 1968-70, asst. plant mgr., Louisville, 1970-72, plant mgr., Wayne, Mich., 1972-74, plant mgr., Norfolk, Va., 1974—. Trustee Tidewater Va. Devel. Council. Served with USAAF, 1942-45, USAF, 1950-53. Mem. Norfolk C. of C. (dir.), Mfrs. Council Norfolk (chmn.), Greater Norfolk Corp. (dir.), Theta Tau. Republican. Baptist. Home: 2128 E Kendall Circle Virginia Beach VA 23451 Office: Ford Motor Co PO Box 780 Norfolk VA 23501

MEHTA, JAWAHAR LAL, cardiologist; b. Kahrore, Multan, India, Aug. 10, 1946; s. Mohan Lal and Ishwar (Devi) M.; came to U.S., 1970, naturalized, 1979; M.B., B.S. with honors, Panjab U., Chandigarh, India, 1967; m. Paulette Smedresman, Oct. 20, 1977; 1 dau., Asha. Intern, Inst. Postgrad. Med. Edn. and Research, Chandigarh, 1968-69, Grasslands Hosp., Valhalla N.Y. and N.Y. Med. Coll., 1970, hosp. resident in pediatrics, 1971; resident in internal medicine Beth Israel Hosp., Mt. Sinai Sch. Medicine, N.Y.C., 1971-73; fellow in cardiology SUNY, Stony Brook and L.I. Jewish Hosp., New Hyde Park, N.Y., 1973-75, univ. instr. medicine, 1973-75; instr. medicine U. Minn. Sch. Medicine, attending physician U. Hosp., Mpls., 1975-76; asst. prof. medicine U. Fla., Gainesville, Fla., 1976—; dir. CCU, Shands Teaching, VA hosps., Gainesville, 1976—; staff cardiologist, VA Hosp., 1977—. Diplomate Am. Bd. Internal Medicine with splty. in cardiology; recipient AMA award for continuing med. edn., 1973, 76; Fla. affiliate Am. Heart Assn. grantee-in-aid, 1978-79. Fellow Am. Coll. Cardiology, A.C.P., Am. Heart Assn.-Council on Clin. Cardiology; mem. Am. Fedn. for Clin. Research, AAAS, So. Soc. for Clin. Investigation. Contbr. chpts. to books, numerous articles, abstracts to profl. jours. Home: 6604 NW 18th Ave Gainesville FL 32605 Office: Box J-277 Coll Medicine U Fla Gainesville FL 32610

MEIER, ERNEST ULRICH, traffic engr.; b. Bridgeport, Conn., July 21, 1931; s. Ernest Ulrich and Pauline Geneve (Miller) M.; B.A., U. Conn., 1954; B.S. in Traffic and Transp., LaSalle U., 1968; m. Patricia Ann O'Malley, Nov. 3, 1952; children—Gerald, Ernest Ulrich III, Susan, Eric. Commd. 2d lt. U.S. Marine Corps, 1954, advanced through grades to lt. col., 1974; dir. services div. Camp Pendleton, 1967-68; supply bn. comdr. Vietnam, 1968-69; dir. transp. Hydrqs., Washington, 1969-74; ret., 1974; with Ford Bacon & Davis Inc., engrs., 1974—, v.p., Arlington, Va., 1977-79, corp. v.p., 1979—. Decorated Bronze Star with V, Meritorious Service medal, Vietnamese Honor medal. Mem. Nat. Def. Transp. Assn. (Disting. Service award 1973), Soc. Logistics Engrs., Nat. Def. Transp. Assn., Washington Traffic Club. Republican. Episcopalian. Club: Masons. Home: 8513 Ivybridge Ct Arlington VA 22152 Office: Ford Bacon and Davis 2009 N 14th St Arlington VA 22201

MEIER, KENNETH JOHN, polit. scientist; b. Aberdeen, S.D., Mar. 3, 1950; s. John A. and Elizabeth (Malsam) M.; A.B., U. S.D., 1972; M.A., Syracuse U., 1974, Ph.D., 1975; m. Diane Mae Jones, Dec. 31, 1972. Asst. prof. polit. sci. Rice U., Houston, 1975-77, dir. Ph.D. program, 1976-77; vis. asst. prof. U. Houston, 1976; asst. dir. Bur. Govt. Research, U. Okla., Norman, 1978—; cons. U.S. Hos. of Reps., KTEW-TV, Ednl. Testing Service. Co-chmn. Dem. Precinct, 1979. NSF fellow, 1972-75. Mem. Am. Polit. Sci. Assn., Am. Soc. for Public Adminstrn., Midwest Polit. Sci. Assn., Policy Studies Orgn., Southwestern Polit. Sci. Assn. Democrat. Author: Bureaucracy and Politics, 1979; Measurement and Analysis for Public Administrators, 1979; Organization Theory and Political Science, 1980; contbr. articles to profl. jours. Home: 621 S Flood St Norman OK 57069 Office: Bur Govt Research U Okla Norman OK 73019

MEIGS, WALTER RALPH, lawyer; b. Macon, Ga., Sept. 7, 1948; s. Ralph and Alice Lee (Little) M.; B.A., Birmingham So. Coll., 1970; J.D., U. Ala., 1973; postgrad. Auburn U., Montgomery, 1974; m. Gloria Sharmon Eddins, Sept. 17, 1977; 1 dau., Nancy Sharmon. Admitted to Ala. bar, 1973; research clk. Ala. Judical Br., Montgomery, 1973-74; asso. firm Hubbard, Waldrop & Jenkins, Tuscaloosa, Ala., 1974-75; atty. Ala. Dry Dock & Shipbuilding Co., 1975—, asst. sec., 1978—. Mem. council on young adult ministries Dauphin Way United Meth. Ch. Mem. Mobile Bar Assn., Ala. Bar Assn., Am. Bar Assn. Democrat. Club: Kiwanis. Home: 3505 Springwood Dr E Mobile AL 36608 Office: PO Box 1507 Mobile AL 36601

MEINE, PAUL ANTON, ednl. adminstr.; b. Gainesville, Tex., June 10, 1932; s. Albert R. and Laura M.; B.S. in Indsl. Arts, N. Tex. State U., 1958, M.Ed., 1964; m. Sandra Lou Jennings, Feb. 22, 1972; children—Paul Anton, Jeffrey Lynn, Tonya Gaye, Carla Gayle. Instr., U. Tex., Arlington, 1966-68; vocat. supr. Fort Worth Ind. Sch. Dist., 1972-73, coordinator Tex. telecomputer grid, 1973-74, vocat. supr., 1974-76, project dir., 1976—. Served wtih AUS, 1954-56, 60-61. Named to Tex. Distbv. Hall of Edn. Fame, 1973. Mem. Am. Soc. Cert. Engring. Technicians, Keller Bus. Assn. (chmn. indsl. devel. com.), Fort Worth Public Sch. Adminstrs. Assn., NEA, Tex. Tchrs. Assn., Sales and Mktg. Execs., Counselors and Suprs. Occupational Edn. and Technology. Mem. Ch. of Christ. Clubs: Lions (1st v.p.), Toastmasters. Home: 401 College St Keller TX 76248 Office: 714 Main St Fort Worth TX 76101

MEINECKE, TOMMY JACOB, banker; b. LaGrange, Tex., July 5, 1939; s. Victor Lee and Jessie Juanita (Charles) M.; A.A., San Antonio Coll., 1960; B.B.A., U. Tex., 1962; postgrad. Southwestern Grad. Sch. Banking, 1975; children—Angela Grace, Thomas Christian. Mgmt. trainee Southwestern Bell Telephone Co., Little Rock, 1962-63, unit mgr., 1963-67; personnel interviewer, personnel asst. Trunkline Gas Co., Houston, 1967-69; personnel dir. ADA Oil Co., Houston, 1969-71; personnel dirs., sr. v.p. adminstrv. services First Internat. Bank, Houston, 1971—; instr. U. Houston, 1975-76, Houston Community Coll., 1974-77, Am. Inst. Banking, 1974-77. Mem. Houston Personnel Assn. (pres. 1974), Am. Soc. Personnel Adminstrn. (dist. dir. 1975), Tex. Assn. Bus., Houston C. of C. Republican. Presbyn. Clubs: Houston Metropolitan Racquet, Summit, Greater Houston Toastmasters (pres. 1975). Home: 706-F Bering Dr Houston TX 77057 Office: PO Box 2555 Houston TX 77001

MEINKE, ROY WALTER, elec. engr.; b. Cleve., Aug. 7, 1929; s. George F. and Marie (Reyer) M.; B.S., Miami U., Oxford, Ohio, 1952; postgrad. Ohio State U., 1952-53, 67-68. Asst. instr. dept. math. Ohio State U., Columbus, 1953; tchr. high sch., Edgerton, Ohio, 1953-54, Kingman, Ariz., 1954-56; aerodynamics engr. N.Am. Aviation, Los Angeles, 1956-57; instr. physics dept. Central State Coll., Edmond, Okla., 1957-58; elec. engr. engr. Boeing Co., Seattle, 1958-62, Huntsville, Ala., 1962-74; mem. staff engring. mgmt. Lockheed Corp., Houston, 1974—. Co-pilot Mercy Flight Systems, 1973-74. Recipient Apollo Achievement award NASA, 1970. Mem. IEEE (sr.), AIAA (Outstanding Sect. award Houston 1979), Nat. Soc. Profl. Engrs. Mem. United Ch. of Christ (dir. S.E. conf. 1969-73). Home: 2935 Calder Dr E-8 League City TX 77573 Office: 1830 NASA Rd 1 Houston TX 77058

MEISEL, STUART GODFREY, ednl. adminstr.; b. Phila., June 30, 1941; s. Maxwell Somers and Kathryn (Godfrey) M.; A.B., Franklin and Marshall Coll., 1963; M.A., Temple U., 1968; m. Fyllis S. Lieberman, June 22, 1969; children—Adriane Meredith, Leslie Susan. System controller State N.J. 1969; mktg. specialist RCA Computer Systems, 1971-73; mktg. edn. specialist Univac Mktg., Blue Bell, Pa., 1973-77; adminstr. edn. and standards U. Pa., Phila., 1977-79; dir. tech. edn. Am. Express, Fort Lauderdale, Fla., 1973-77, dir. systems tng., 1979—. Mem. Old Orchard Civic Assn., Cherry Hill, 1974-77; mem. Tax Assessment Bd. Cherry Hill, 1977; treas. South Plantation Homeowners Assn., 1977—. Mem. Am. Mgmt. Assn., Am. Soc. Tng. and Devel., Jr. C. of C. Office: 777 American Express Way Fort Lauderdale FL 33337

MEISTER, JOHN DAVID, diversified mfg. co. exec.; b. Miami, Fla., Apr. 16, 1939; s. Clarence Raymond and Rose E. (Dasch) M.; B.S. in Elec. Engring., U. N.Mex., 1962; m. Martha Elizabeth Terwilliger, June 30, 1962; children—John David, James Christopher. Exploration geophysicist Humble Oil Co., Houston, 1962; mgr. systems engring. TRW, Inc., San Bernardino, Calif., 1965-68; research and devel. program mgr. Tracor, Inc., Austin, Tex., 1968—. Active U. Tex. Internat. Student Host Family Program, 1969—; adult vol. Capitol Area council Boy Scouts Am., 1972—. Served to 1st lt. USAF, 1962-65. Registered profl. engr., Tex. Mem. Armed Forces Communication Electronics Assn. (pres. Austin-Bergstrom chpt.), Tex. Congress Parents and Tchrs. (hon. life), Kappa Alpha. Republican. Presbyn. (deacon 1971-73). Research, publs. in systems engring. field. Home: 6815 Willamette Austin TX 78723 Office: 6500 Tracor Ln Austin TX 78721

MEIXSELL, MELCHIOR FRANCIS, charitable orgn. exec.; b. Easton, Pa., Oct. 31, 1912; s. Melchoir and Elizabeth (Kies) M.; Ph.B., Muhlenburg Coll., Allentown, Pa., 1932; m. Jean Vollmer, Sept. 27, 1951; 1 dau., Jill Elizabeth (Mrs. William DeHoog). Purchasing agt. Canister Co., Phillipsburg, N.J., 1936-46, Lehigh Foundries Inc., Easton, Pa., 1946-50; fund raiser Leewall-Bell Co., Nutley, N.J., 1950-62, United Appeal Lake County, Leesburg, Fla., 1963-78; ret., 1978. Served with USNR, 1944-45. Mem. Alpha Tau Omega. Republican. Methodist. Mason, Elk, Kiwanian. Club: Continental Country. Home: Sandalwood Apts Wildwood FL 32785

MEJIA, ROBERTO, pediatrician; b. Medellin, Colombia, June 8, 1932; s. Roberto Luis and Isabel (Lotero) M.; B.S., Universidad de Antioquia (Colombia), 1950, M.D., 1957; m. Monica Restrepo, May 6, 1961; children—Ana Isabel, Angela M., Juan E., Beatriz E. Intern, Hosp. San Vicente, Medellin, 1957, St. Alexis Hosp., Cleve., 1959-60; resident Charles V. Chapin Hosp., Providence, 1960, U. Nebr. Hosp., Omaha, 1961-62; pub. health officer Colombia Dept. Pub. Health, 1957-59; fellow in child psychiatry Nebr. Psychiat. Inst., Omaha, 1962-63; fellow in cystic fibrosis U. Nebr., Omaha, 1963; pediatrician, med. dir. Harlingen (Tex.) Chest Hosp., 1964-69; med. dir. Corpus Christi (Tex.) State Sch., 1969-75; project dir. C and Y Clinic, Corpus Christi, 1975-77; chief of staff Driscoll Children's Hosp., 1978; pvt. practice medicine specializing in pediatrics Corpus Christi, 1960—; asst. prof. clin. pediatrics U. Tex. Med. Br., Galveston. Mem., sec. Community Action, Corpus Christi. Diplomate Am. Bd. Pediatrics. Fellow Am. Acad. Pediatrics, Am. Coll. Chest Physicians; mem. Nueces County (Tex.) Med. Soc., Corpus Christi Pediatric Soc. (pres. 1976), Tex., Am. So. med. assns., Tex. Pub. Health Assn. Roman Catholic. Club: Rotary. Home: 246 Cape Hatteras St Corpus Christi TX 78412 Office: 3435 S Alameda St Corpus Christi TX 78411

MELANCON, MICHAEL RAY, bus. machines co. exec.; b. Beaumont, Tex., May 29, 1950; s. Joseph Whitney and Hester Dave M.; B.B.A., Lamar U., 1972; postgrad. bus. adminstrn. Tex. So. U., 1977—; m. Gradie B. Hopper, Aug. 12, 1972; children—Leah Michelle, Ray Michael. Counselor, High Sch. Equivalency Program, Beaumont, 1971-72; acct. Ernst & Ernst, Detroit, 1972-75; account rep. IBM, Houston, 1975—. Adviser, Jr. Achievement, 1973-75. Mem. Nat. Assn. Accts., Nat. Assn. Black Accts., Delta Sigma Pi. Roman Catholic. Home: 15830 Valverde Dr Houston TX 77083

MELDER, ELLIS MARIE WEAVER, educator; b. Rayville, La., Oct. 21, 1933; d. Ellis Neely and Marie Estelle (Magee) Weaver; B.A., La. Coll., 1955; postgrad. La. State U., 1957; M.A., Northwestern State Coll., La., 1960; postgrad. U. Wyo., 1977-79; m. Trent Osborn Melder, June 13, 1964; children—Mark Osborn, Sara Marie, James Trent. Tchr. English, Vinton (La.) High Sch., 1955-57; tchr. lang. arts and social sci. Alexandria (La.) Jr. High Sch., 1957-62; instr. dept. langs. Northwestern State U., Natchitoches, La., 1962-73, asst. prof., 1973—. Sec., Mayor's Adv. Council City of Natchitoches, 1975-77; den mother Cub Scouts, 1979—. U. Wyo. grantee, 1978-79. Mem. Nat. Council Tchrs. of English, La. Assn. Educators, P.E.O. (pres. chpt. I, 1976-77), Delta Kappa Gamma. Democrat. Baptist. Home: Route 2 Box 865 Natchitoches LA 71457 Office: Dept Langs Northwestern State U Natchitoches LA 71457

MELGAR, JULIO, mech. engr.; b. Bklyn., July 4, 1922; s. Lorenzo and Maria (Lopez) M.; B.M.E., U. Detroit, 1952. Mech. engr. Chance Vought Aircraft, Dallas, 1952-53, Wyatt C. Hedrick Architects and Engrs., Dallas, 1953, Zumwalt & Vinther, Cons. Engrs., Dallas, 1953-54, Joe Hoppe, Inc., Dallas, 1954-55, A.J. Boynton & Co., Dallas, 1956-57, Wyatt Metal and Boiler Works, Dallas, 1958, Tinker AFB, Okla., 1958-60; mech. engr. FAA, Ft. Worth, 1960—. Mem. Metroplex Recreation Council, 1975—; mem. Tarrant County Mental Health and Mental Retardation, Dallas Soc. Crippled Children, Goodwill Industries; bd. dirs. Fort Worth Opera Assn., Tarrant County Humane Soc., Animal Protection Inst. Served with USMCR, 1943-45. Mem. Nat. Soc. Profl. Engrs., ASME, Am. Soc. Heating, Refrigerating and Air Conditioning Engrs., Profl. Soc. Protective Design, Fed. Bus. Assn., Amateur Athletic Union. Roman Catholic. Home: 6108 Menger Ave Dallas TX 75227 Office: Box 1689 Fort Worth TX 76101

MELHORN, MICHAEL VICTOR, city ofcl.; b. Washington, Mar. 27, 1951; s. Kenneth LeRoy and Harriett Elizabeth (Smullen) M.; student Nat. Crime Prevention Inst., 1975-77, Fla. Inst. for Law Enforcement, 1976-78; m. Sandra Marie Kenady, Jan. 21, 1977; 1 dau., Andrea Sanda. Patrolman, Police Dept., City of Largo, Fla., 1973-75, dir. crime prevention program, 1975—; cons. Law Enforcement Assistance Adminstrn., Nat. Crime Prevention Inst.; instr. police acad., pvt. industry. Mem. State of Fla. Steering Com. on Crimes Against the Elderly, Fla. Com. Armed Robbery Prevention. Recipient Disting. Service award Security World, 1976; named Police Officer of Yr., Largo, 1976. Mem. Internat. Soc. Crime Prevention Practioners (newsletter editor, chmn. media com.), Am. Soc. Indsl. Security, Nat. Crime Prevention Assn., Fla. Crime Prevention Assn. (bd. dirs.), Suncoast Crime Prevention Assn. (pres.). Democrat. Lutheran. Club: Largo Police Brotherhood Assn. Author: Commercial and Industrial Security, 1975. Home: 1310 5th Terr NW Largo FL 33540 Office: 100 East Bay Dr Largo FL 33540

MELITO, CYRUS RAYMOND, JR., retail co. exec.; b. New Orleans, May 16, 1943; s. Cyrus R. and Dorothy A. (Alessi) M.; B.A., Southeastern La. Coll., 1966; m. Dorothy Robin Dawson, Nov. 3, 1978. Auditor, Hartman, Aly Monnint Co., C.P.A.'s, New Orleans, 1966-68; asst. credit office mgr. Shushan Bros. & Co., Inc., New Orleans, 1968-73; office mgr. Wiener Corp., Harahan, La., 1973—. Office: Wiener Corp PO Box 23607 Harahan LA 70183

MELL, WILLIAM SAUNDERS, safety adminstr.; b. Savannah, Ga., Oct. 4, 1942; s. Robert Colding and Louise Nalley N.; student Armstrong Jr. Coll., 1960-63; B.S. in Indsl. Engring., Auburn U., 1966; m. Jeffery Grimm Green, June 13, 1964; children—Michael Jefferson, Megan Judith. Works engr. Westinghouse Co., Hampton, S.C., 1966-69; plant engr. Ingersoll-Rand Co., Mocksville, N.C., 1969-73; lead maintenance supr. Westinghouse Co., Columbia, S.C., 1973-74, mgr. safety, 1974—; dir. Southeastern Occupational Safety Conf., 1978. Served with Army N.G., 1966-72. Mem. Am. Soc. Safety Engrs. (chpt. pres.), Nat. Safety Council (mem. chem. exec. com.), S.C. Occupational Safety Council, S.C. C. of C. (chmn. safety and health com.), Am. Indsl. Hygiene Assn. Democrat. Lutheran. Club: Columbia Country. Home: 906 Kenmore Dr Columbia SC 29209 Office: Westinghouse Electric Corp PO Drawer R Columbia SC 29250

MELLEN, HUGH JOSEPH, mech. engr.; b. Superior, Mont., Sept. 22, 1926; s. Hugh William and Johanna Josephine (Spiekerman) M.; B.S. in Mech. Engring., Mont. State Coll., 1951; postgrad. Mich. State U., 1963, U. So. Ala., 1966; m. Roberta Irene Malm, May 8, 1954; children—Patricia, William, Mary, Anthony, John, Daniel, Theresa, Michael, Cecelia, Elizebeth, Christina, Barbara. Chief mech. engr. Walla Walla (Wash.) C.E., 1955-59; chief engr. Titan I Area Office, Mountain Home, Idaho, 1960-62; chief cryogenics engr. Mobile (Ala.) C.E., 1963-67; chief mech. sect. Huntsville (Ala.) C.E., 1967—; instr. aerospace seminar U. So. Miss., U. So. Ala., 1965. Active Huntsville Civic Club Council, 1976. Served with U.S. Army, 1943-46. Decorated Purple Heart, Bronze Star with Combat V; recipient Meritorious Civilian Service medal Dept. of Army, 1962. Mem. Am. Soc. Profl. Engrs., ASME, Am. Welding Soc., Assn. U.S. Army, VFW, Am. Legion, Phi Sigma Kappa. Roman Catholic. Clubs: Men's 12th Step Group, Columbian, K.C. (dir. 1975-78), Moose. Home: 6110 Sandia Blvd Huntsville AL 35810 Office: PO Box 1600 Huntsville AL 35807

MELLO, HERBERT, data processing adminstr.; b. Cambridge, Mass., Sept. 5, 1924; s. Justino V. and Ligia A. (Periera) M.; student Northeastern U., 1947-48; m. Adeline Kathleen Thomas, June 11, 1944; children—Thomas, Janet, Patricia. Supr. machine accounting Boston Woven Hose & Rubber Co., Cambridge, Mass., 1948-56; EDP analyst, coroporate staff Raytheon Co., Waltham, Mass., 1956-59, sr. analyst systems procedures, govt. equipment div., Wayland, Mass., 1959-60, EDP mgr. missile space div., Waltham, 1960-61, mgr. fin. systems procedures, airborne mfg., , Waltham, 1961-63, mgr. info. processing systems, missile space div., Oxnard, Calif., 1963-69; mgr. info. systems adminstrv. services Taylor Pub. Co., Dallas, 1970—. Mem. Data Processing Mgmt. Assn. Home: 2401 Briarfield Dr Richardson TX 75080 Office: 1550 W Mockingbird Ln Dallas TX 75235

MELNICK, ALICE JEAN, counselor; b. St. Louis, Dec. 25, 1931; d. Nathan and Henrietta (Hausfater) Fisher; B.J., U. Tex., Austin, 1952; M.Ed., N. Texas State U., 1974; m. Harold Melnick, May 24, 1953; children—Susan, Vikki, Patrice. Reporter, San Antonio Light, 1952-53; instr. journalism project Upward Bound, So. Meth. U., Dallas, 1967-71; instr. writing El Dallas County Community Coll., Dallas, part time 1972-74; instr. human devel. Richland Community Coll., Dallas, part-time 1974-79; tchr. English and journalism Dallas Ind. Sch. Dist., 1969—. Mem. Tex., Am. personnel and guidance assns., North Central Tex. Personnel and Guidance Assn. (chmn. human rights com.), Classroom Tchrs. Dallas, Tex. Tchrs. Assn., NEA, Assn. Humanistic Edn. and Devel. Democrat. Jewish. Clubs: Dallas Sports Car, Dallas Camera. Home: 6730 Desco Dr Dallas TX 75225

MELNICK, JOHN LATANE, lawyer, former state legislator; b. Alexandria, Va., Apr. 19, 1935; s. Norbert and Myrtle Gray (Waring) M.; student Roanoke Coll., 1953-55; B.S. in Commerce, U. Va., 1958, J.D., 1961; m. Marjory Mary Helter, Apr. 28, 1962; children—John Latane, Paul Helter, Marjory Kathleen, Laura Elizabeth. Admitted to Va. bar, 1961, since practiced in Arlington; asso. firm Kinney, Whitaker, Smith and Barham, 1961-64; asst. commonwealth atty., 1962-63; mem. firm Ball, McCarthy, Ball and Melnick, 1964-67, Berryman, Melnick and Sanders, 1970-77, Melnick & Holmes, 1977—; mem. Va. Ho. of Dels., 1971-78; asso. prof. forensic sci. George Washington U., Washington, 1978—; dir. Central Fidelity Bank No. Va. Mem. Va. State Crime Commn., 1974—. Democratic committeeman, Arlington, 1964-68; pres. Arlington Young Dems., 1965-66; candidate for atty. gen. Va. Dem. Primary, 1977. Bd. dirs. Arlington YMCA, Boy Scouts Am., 1964-67. Recipient Humane Socs. of Va. award, 1973. Mem. Am., Va., Arlington (pres. 1969-70) bar assns., Am. Judicature Soc. Methodist (dir. 1964—, trustee 1972—). Clubs: Kiwanis (dir. 1965—), Masons. Home: 4710 N Dittmar Rd Arlington VA 22207 Office: 2400 Wilson Blvd Arlington VA 22201

MELOHN, BRENDA DENSON, accountant; b. Jackson, Miss., Sept. 30, 1951; d. Ollie B. and Emma Sue (Stewart) Denson; B.S. in Bus. Adminstrn., Miss. State U., 1972; m. V. Wayne Melohn, Jr., Sept. 4, 1971; 1 son, Michael Wayne. Sr. auditor Ernst & Ernst, 1972-74; audit supr., 1974-76; asst. comptroller Fidelity Bank, Jackson, 1974; dir. budgeting U. Miss. Med. Center, Jackson, 1976-77, comptroller, 1977—. C.P.A. Mem. Am. Assn. Med. Colls., Am. Inst. C.P.A.'s, Miss. Soc. C.P.A.'s, Am. Soc. Women Accountants, Hosp. Fin. Mgmt. Assn. Democrat. Roman Catholic.

MELTON, CHANCELLOR GARLAND, optometrist; b. Fayetteville, Ark., May 22, 1929; s. Josephine (McGill) M.; student U. Ark., 1947-48; B.S., Pacific U., 1951, Dr. Optometry, 1952, M.S., 1957; m. Beverly Joan Brooks Melton, Jan. 22, 1956; children—Marsha Jan, Melissa Jeanne. Individual practice optometry, Fayetteville, Ark., 1957—; pres. Metrocenter Devel. Corp., Fayetteville, 1973-74. Mem. bd. adjustment City of Fayetteville, 1965, mem. bd. dirs., 1966-70, mayor, 1968-70, mem. indsl. park commn., 1970-74, chmn. parking authority, 1973-75, chmn. bd. commrs. Fayetteville Parking Improvement Dist. #1; chmn. N.W. Ark. Regional Planning Commn., 1966-77. Bd. dirs. Fayetteville Boys Club, 1959-65, pres., 1964. Served with USNR, 1952-56; now capt. Res. Recipient State Lions Sight award, 1958, gold medallion Boys Club Am., 1964; Distinguished Service award Fayetteville Jaycees, 1965. Mem. Am. (mem. nominating com. 1966), Ark. (pres. 1966) optometric assns., So. Council Optometry (trustee 1966-67), Am. Optometric Found., Leonardo da Vinci Contact Lens Inst., Fayetteville C. of C. (dir. 1973-75). Democrat. Methodist. Mason (32 deg.), Lion. Home: 927 Applebury Dr Fayetteville AR 72701 Office: 230 N Block St Fayetteville AR 72701

MELTON, DARRELL EVERETT, aerospace engr.; b. Richland, Mo., Dec. 6, 1933; s. William Everett and Agnes Faye Melton; B.S. in Mech. Engring., U. Mo., 1956; m. Dorothy B. Melton; 1 dau., Cynthia R. Mech. engr. U.S. Naval Ordnance Test Sta., Pasadena, Cal., 1956-59; aerospace engr. Marshall Space Flight Center, Huntsville, Ala., 1960—. Mem. Profl. Engrs. of Ala., U. Mo. Alumni Assn., Tau Beta Pi, Pi Mu Epsilon, Pi Tau Sigma. Republican. Patentee in field. Home: 1806 Sherwood Dr SE Decatur AL 35601 Office: Marshall Space Flight Center Huntsville AL 35812

MENAKER, EDWARD GOWARD, elec. engr.; b. Newark, Apr. 10, 1919; s. George and Sara (Goward) M.; A.B., Columbia U., 1938, M.A., 1939; postgrad. Union Coll., Schenectady, 1947-49; m. Elizabeth Dresbold, Sept. 6, 1941; children—Richard Glen, Lawrence James. Tchr. Altaraz Sch., Monterey, Mass., 1940-41; with Gen. Electric Co., Schenectady, also Waynesboro, Va., 1946-79, product reliability and service analyst data communication products dept., 1974-79; mgr. value control Compagnie Bull-Gen. Electric, computers, Paris, 1967; owner Menaker Assos., bus. cons., Waynesboro, 1979—. Pres. Waynesboro Council P.T.A.'s, 1957-58; leader, scouter Boy Scouts Am., 1948—; fencing instr., ofcl. Blue Ridge Fencing Club, 1961-67, Amateur Fencers League Am., 1961—. Chmn. Waynesboro and 15th Legislative Dist. Democratic Com., 1968-72, 76-77; mem. 6th Congressional Dist. and state central Dem. com., 1979—; del. Dem. Nat. Conv., Chgo., 1968; mem., chmn. Waynesboro Recreation Commn., 1972-78. Trustee, chmn. bldg. com. Waynesboro Pub. Library, 1965-67; bd. dirs. Stonewall Jackson Area council Boy Scouts Am., 1961-74, Central Shenandoah Subarea Health Adv. Council, 1978—, Northwestern Va. Health Systems Agy., 1980—; del. Dem. Nat. Conf., Memphis, 1978. Served to maj. USAAF, 1942-46. Decorated Bronze Star medal; recipient Silver Beaver award Boy Scouts Am., 1967. Registered profl. engr., Va., N.Y. Mem. IEEE, Va. Soc. Profl. Engrs., Columbia Alumni Assn., 14th Air Force Assn. Club: Waynesboro (Va.) Country. Home: 1824 Westminster Rd Waynesboro VA 22980 Office: Menaker Assos PO Box 787 Waynesboro VA 22980

MENDEL, JACK GORDON, mktg. exec.; b. West Palm Beach, Fla., July 5, 1929; s. James Coleman and Caroline Elizabeth M.; student U. Fla., 1947-48, Temple Jr. Coll., 1974-76; m. Beth Marie Buckles, Aug. 3, 1970; children—Jack Gordon II (dec.), Jason Gail, Cynthia Marie, James Glenn. Enlisted U.S. Army, 1948; ret. master army aviator, 1974; nat. v.p. mktg. Hydra-Gym Athletics, Inc., Belton, Tex., 1976—. Decorated D.F.C. (3), Bronze Star (3), Air medal (15). Baptist. Club: Masons. Home: 1302 Shady Ln Belton TX 76513 Office: 2121 Industrial Park Rd Belton TX 76513

MENDELL, JAY STANLEY, educator; b. N.Y.C., Mar. 13, 1936; s. Emanuel and Lillian (Danenbaum) M.; M.A., Vanderbilt U., 1958; Ph.D., Rensselaer Poly. Inst., 1964; m. Joan Wilma Brightman, Dec. 17, 1961; children—Risa Sue, Eden Sharon. Sr. staff analyst Pratt & Whitney Aircraft Co., E. Hartford, Conn., 1963-73; asso. prof. Fla. Internat. U., Miami, 1973-76; vis. prof. bus. and public adminstrn. Fla. Atlantic U., Boca Raton, 1976—. Mem. World Future Soc., N. Am. Soc. Corporate Planning, Assn. Sci., Tech. and Innovation, Am. Acad. Polit. and Social Sci. Reform Jewish. Mem. editorial bd. Tech. Forecasting and Social Change, 1972-78, Jour. Internat. Soc. Tech. Assessment, 1973-76; editorial chmn. Bus. Tomorrow mag., 1978—; innovation editor The Futurist mag., 1969—; contbg. editor Planning Review, 1974—; contbr. articles in field to profl. jours. Home: 11295 NW 38th St Coral Springs FL 33065 Office: Fla Atlantic U Boca Raton FL 33431

MENDENHALL, LESLIE WARD, JR., wholesale co. exec.; b. Fort Worth, Sept. 20, 1920; s. Leslie Ward and Viola (Herring) M.; student Tex. Christian U., 1938-41, 45-48; m. June Helen McCord, May 5, 1942; children—Leslie Ward III, June Anne Mendenhall Jenney, Melinda Kaye Mendenhall Blair. Accountant, Patterson, Leatherwood & Miller, Fort Worth, 1945-47; accountant, office mgr. J P. Bowlin Co., Fort Worth, 1947-48; head accounts payable dept., accounting dept., mgr. budget control Montgomery Ward, Fort Worth, 1948-51; accountant, Fort Worth, 1951-59; sec.-treas., controller, dir. Nationwide Advt. Specialty Co. and related cos., Arlington, Tex., 1959—; dir. Arlington Fraternal Builders, Inc.; sec.-treas., dir. Newbern Corp., 1959—, SRI Publ. Co., 1968—, Texad Splty. Co., 1964—, NACO Advt. Splty. Co., 1973—, Nat. Calendar & Advt. Co., 1972—(all Arlington), Heritage Mfg. Corp., Fort Worth, 1959—. C.P.A., Tex. Episcopalian. Elk, Rotarian. Home: 1510 W Lavender Ln Arlington TX 76013 Office: 2025 S Cooper St Arlington TX 76010

MENDENHALL, MELVIN D., metall. co. exec.; b. Bloomingdale, Ind., June 11, 1935; s. Frank H. and Ann Eleanor (Copner) M.; student Purdue U.; m. Lavetta Hutson, June 14, 1959; children—Michael D., Todd Allen. With Linde div. Union Carbide Corp., 1953-55, 63—, field sales rep., Indpls. and Houston, 1970-78, sr. field sales rep., Houston, 1978—. Served with AUS, 1955-57. Mem. Am. Soc. Metals. Mem. Christian Ch. Clubs: Masons, Order Eastern Star. Home: 314 Dawnhill Dr Friendswood TX 77546 Office: 9200 Telephone Rd Houston TX 77075

MENDENHALL, WILLIAM RUSSELL, ednl. adminstr.; b. Terre Haute, Ind., Mar. 24, 1943; s. Russell Heath and Lela Louise (Wright) M.; B.S., Ind. State U., 1965, M.S., 1967; Ph.D. (USOE fellow), Fla. State U., 1975; m. Sue Ellen Bethel, June 18, 1967 (div. 1976). Asst. dir. residence halls Ind. State U., Terre Haute, 1965-67; area dir. office residence hall programs, instr. sociology Ill. State U., Normal, 1967-70; coordinator student affairs Fla. Bd. Regents, Tallahassee, 1972; asso. dean student services, asst. prof. sociology and edn. U. Fla., Gainesville, 1972-77; asso. v.p. student affairs, asso. prof. edn. U. Ga., Athens, 1977—; cons. Sigma Phi Epsilon, 1970—. Active Ind. 4-H Club, 1953-63; bd. dirs. Alachua County div. Fla. Heart Assn.; scoutmaster Boy Scouts Am., 1967-68. Mem. NEA, Am. Personnel and Guidance Assn., So. Coll. Personnel Assn., Nat. Assn. Student Personnel Adminstrs. (annual conf. com., 1976), Am. Sociol. Assn., Sc. Sociol. Soc., SPEBSQSA, Blue Key, Alpha Kappa Delta, Phi Delta Kappa, Alpha Phi Omega, Omicron Delta Kappa, Sigma Phi Epsilon. Republican. Episcopalian. Clubs: Univ. Golf, Masons, Scottish Rite, Shriners, Order of Eastern Star. Home: 157 Woodstone Dr Athens GA 30605 Office: 201 Academics Bldg Univ Georgia Athens GA 30602

MENDEZ, CELESTINO, JR., vet. program adminstr.; b. San Marcos, Tex., Sept. 10, 1930; s. Celestino and Amalia (Cantu) M.; B.S. in Edn., S.W. Tex. State U., 1957, postgrad. in adminstrn., 1958-59; m. Elida Astran, Dec. 27, 1959; children—Jeffrey Wayne, Rose Ana. Instr. primary flight tng., supr. mfg. plant, purchasing agt., material control mgr.; dir. Youth Manpower Program; dir. Vets. Employment Counseling Program, Austin, Tex., 1975—. Mem. San Marcos Consol. Sch. Dist. Sch. Bd., 1963-68, pres., 1966; urban renewal commr., 1972-77, chmn., 1973-77; bd. dirs. South Side Community Center, 1970-76, 78—, also former pres.; active Hispanic rights movement. Served with USAF, 1951-55; Korea. Recipient recognition for sch. bd. service Kiwanis Club, 1966. Mem. Am. G.I. Forum (recipient nat. chmn.'s recognition). Home: 1213 W San Antonio St San Marcos TX 78666 Office: 1209 Rio Grande St Austin TX 78701

MÉNDEZ, FÉLIX GILBERTO, pub. relations exec., pharmacist; b. Lares, P.R., July 31, 1932; s. Edelmiro Mendez and Inocencia Soto M.; B.S., U. P.R., 1954, B.Pharm. Sci., 1977; postgrad. Am. U., Cornell U., Lares Sch. Commerce; m. Antonia Gonzalez, Dec. 21, 1953; children—Felix Antonio, Mercedes, Rosa, Francisco, Marife. Med. rep., supr. numerous pharm. cos., 1956-62; pub. relations dir. Interstate Gen. Contractor, 1962-63; mgr. govt. relations, asst. dir.

pub. relations ITT, 1963-69; dir. Econ. Devel. Adminstrn., P.R. Office Info. and Pub. Relations, 1969-70; pub. relations counsellor Coop. Devel. Adminstrn. and Govt. Housing Bank, 1970—; pres., owner San Juan Pub. Relations, Inc. (P.R.), 1971—, Félix Méndez & Assos., 1975—; pres. Manresa de Aibonito, Inc.; cons. Hill & Knowlton, P.R., 1974-76. Served as 2d lt. AUS, 1954-56. Mem. Pub. Relations Soc. P.R. (past pres.), InterAm. Public Relations Soc. (dir.), Pharmacists Assn. P.R. (past pres.), Coll. Pharmacy Assn. P.R. (pres. 1979-80), Public Relations Soc. Am., Casino de P.R., San Juan Pub. Relations (pres.), P.R. C. of C., Interfraternal Council P.R. (pres. 1966), Alpha Beta Chi (nat. past pres.). Roman Catholic. K.C., Lion (sec.). Home: C-29 Rufino Rodriguez Villa Clementina Guaynabo PR 00657 Office: GPO Box 2114 San Juan PR 00936

MENDIA, CARLOS FERNANDEZ DE, automobile dealership exec.; b. Havana, Cuba, Apr. 14, 1941; s. Eliecer Fernandez de Mendia and Isabel Garces de Marcilla; came to U.S., 1960, naturalized, 1969; student Villanova U., 1958-59, Universidad de Villanueva, Havana, 1959-60; B.B.A., U. Miami (Fla.), 1961, M.A., 1962; m. Irma Maria Alonso, July 22, 1961; children—Carlos, Cristina, Irma. Mgmt. trainee Firestone Tire & Rubber Co., Miami, Akron, Ohio, Tampa, Fla., 1961-69; v.p., treas. Chrysler-Plymouth de Ponce, Inc. (P.R.), 1969-74, pres., 1974—; pres. Chevrolet Del Sur, Inc., Guayama, P.R., 1979—; pres. Mayaguez (P.R.) Chrysler-Plymouth, Inc., 1976-79; pres. CIM Corp., Ponce, 1975—; v.p. Sunshine Chrysler-Plymouth of Miami, 1975-79; del. White House Conf. on Small Bus., 1980; mem. adv. council SBA, Hato Rey, P.R., 1979—. Vice pres. PTA, Sacred Heart Sch., Ponce, 1974-76. Mem. P.R. Automobile Dealers Assn. (pres. 1977-79), Chevrolet Dealers Assn. P.R., C. of C. of P.R., Nat. Assn. Automobile Dealers, So. P.R. Cardiovascular Soc. (dir. 1978—). Clubs: Club Deportivo de Ponce, Ponce Yacht, Bankers (San Juan); Big Five (Miami). Home: 6E556 Extension Rambla Ponce PR 00732 Office: PO Box 7145 Ponce PR 00732

MENDIETA, HEBERTO BERNARDO, chemist, govt. ofcl.; b. Laredo, Tex., Aug. 20, 1919; s. Manuel and Catalina (Valdez) M.; student Tex. A&M U., 1939-40, 46-49; B.A. in Chemistry, U. Tex., 1954; m. Marjorie H. Cantrell, Aug. 26, 1946; children—Sara Bernadine, Hector Edward. Welder, Western Machine Works, Bruni, Tex., 1949-50, salesman, 1950-51; chem. analyst water resources div. U.S. Geol. Survey, Austin, Tex., 1951-62, lab. chief water resources div., 1962-74, supervisory hydrologist for water quality Tex. dist., Austin, 1975—. Treas., PTA, 1957-58, v.p., 1958-59, pres., 1966-68, 74-75; treas. Pleasant Hill Ind. Sch. Bd., 1956-58. Served with M.C., U.S. Army, 1941-45; Life Mem. award PTA. Recipient Scroll of Honor, U.S. Geol. Survey, 1979. Mem. Am. Chem. Soc., AAAS, Garden Writers Assn. Am., Men's Garden Clubs Am. (pres. 1962-63, 69, Bronze medal award 1970). Contbr. weekly garden columns to local newspaper.

MENDOZA, ALICIA, educator; b. N.Y.C., Oct. 14, 1944; d. Alexander Richard and Theresa (Manheimer) M.; B.A., Queens Coll., N.Y.C., 1965; M.Ed., U. Miami (Fla.), 1969, Ed.D., 1972. Classroom tchr., N.Y.C., 1965-68; mem. faculty Clarion (Pa.) State Coll., 1971-74; asst. prof. edn. Fla. Internat. U., Miami, 1974—; cons. Head Start, Pa., Fla.; cons. Tchr. Edn. Center, Dade County Early Childhood Coordinating Council, S.E. Ednl. Consortium. NDEA fellow, 1969-70. Mem. Assn. Tchr. Educators (co-chairperson commn. exploratory field experiences, 1977-80, communications com. 1980—), Fla. Assn. Tchr. Educators (membership chairperson 1979-80), Phi Delta Kappa, Kappa Delta Pi, Gamma Sigma Sigma, Beta Sigma Phi. Contbr. articles to profl. jours. Home: 702 NW 87 Ave Miami FL 33172 Office: 151 St and Biscayne Blvd North Miami FL 33181

MENDOZA, CATALINO BARRERA, JR., surgeon; b. Naic Cavite, Philippines, Mar. 5, 1929; s. Catalino E. and Flavia C. (Barrera) M.; came to U.S., 1955, naturalized, 1965; M.D., Manila Central U., 1955; m. Suzanne Frances Trach, Oct. 10, 1959; children—Debra, Laura, Michael, David. Intern, State U. N.Y. Upstate Med. Center, Syracuse, 1955-56, resident in surgery, 1956-60, staff surgeon W.Va. U. Sch. Medicine, Morgantown, 1963—, instr. surgery, 1963-70, asst. prof., 1970-76, asso. prof. clin. surgery, 1976—; staff surgeon VA Hosp., Clarksburg, W.Va., 1963-71, surg. cons., 1973—; attending surgeon United Hosp. Center, Clarksburg, 1973—; gen. surgeon S.S. Hope, Brazil, 1972. Bd. dirs. W.Va. chpt. Am. Cancer Soc., 1976-79. USPHS research fellow in cancer, 1961-62; recipient Humanitarian Achievements in Research and Surgery award DAV, 1973; Spl. Achievement award Am. Vets. World War II, Korea, Viet Nam, 1973. Diplomate Am. Bd. Surgery. Fellow A.C.S.; mem. AMA, W.Va., Harrison County med. socs., Assn. VA Surgeons, Assn. Mil. Surgeons, Soc. Philippines Surgeons Am. (gov. 1976—), Bernard Zimmerman, Roswell Park surg. socs., Southeastern Surg. Congress, Soc. Surgery Alimentary Tract, Pan Pacific Surg. Assn., Pan Am. Med. Assn., Am. Soc. Gastrointestinal Endoscopy, Collegium Internat. Chirurgiae Digestivae. Roman Catholic. Contbr. articles on surg. to med. jours. Home: 109 Emerson Rd Clarksburg WV 26301 Office: Physicians Office Bldg 4 Hospital Plaza Clarksburg WV 26301

MENDOZA, RUTH JOYCE, counselor; b. San Antonio, Feb. 5, 1941; d. Ignacio Baray and Helen DeLaRosa M.; B.A., U. Tex., Austin, 1965; M.Ed., Our Lady of Lake Coll., 1973. Tchr., Price Elem. Sch., South San Antonio Ind. Sch. Dist., 1963-68; tchr. Francisco Ruiz Elem. Sch., San Antonio Ind. Sch. Dist., 1968-69, tchr. W.J. Knox Elem. Sch., 1970-75, counselor C.C. Ball Elem. Sch., 1975—. Spl. edn. cert., Tex.: system of multicultural pluralistic assessment cert. Inst. Pluralistic Assessment Research and Tng. Mem. Am. Personnel and Guidance Assn., Am. Sch. Counselors Assn., Tex. Personnel and Guidance Assn., San Antonio Dist. Counselors Assn., NEA, Tex. Tchrs. Assn., San Antonio Tchrs. Council Tex. PTA. Home: 4015 Callaghan St Apt 220 San Antonio TX 78228 Office: C C Ball Elem Sch 343 Koehler Ct San Antonio TX 78223

MENEELY, (MARY) LESLIE STEWART, sculptor; b. Amityville, N.Y., July 15, 1911; d. George D. and Ida M. (Robb) Stewart; student of Alexander Archipenko, 1932-35, Heinz Warneke, 1935-37, John Terken, 1966; m. George Rodney Meneely, May 29, 1968; children by previous marriage—Nicole (Mrs. K.L. Demarest, Jr.), Michelle (Mrs. J.H. Limpert, Jr.), Suzanne Van der Leur, Leslie Van der Leur (Mrs. J.M. Derby). Group shows include: Nat. Art Gallery, N.Y.C., 1970, 72, 73; Old State Capitol Gallery, Baton Rouge, La., 1971, 74, Marietta (Ohio) Coll., 1971, 73, 76, Nat. Sculpture Soc. Gallery, 1973; Painters and Sculptors Soc. N.J., Newark, 1973; Catherine Lorillard Wolfe Art Club Gallery, N.Y.C., 1973, 74; Kent (Conn.) Art Assn., 1975; represented in permanent collections La. State U. Med. Center, Shreveport, La., West Paces Ferry Hosp., Atlanta, Mus. Fine Arts, Boston, U. Tex. at Houston, also pvt. collections. Recipient Sam Wiener prize, 1970. Mem. Shreveport Art Guild, Am. Fedn. of the Arts, La. Artists Catherine Lorillard Wolfe Art Club, Mus. of Modern Art, Houston Mus. Fine Arts, Faculty Wives Assn. of La. State U., Met. Mus. of Art (N.Y.), Jr. League (sustainer). Republican. Presbyterian. Clubs: Shreveport, University, Women's Dept. (Shreveport); Cosmos; Princeton of New York. Address: 514 Southfield Rd Shreveport LA 71106

MENÉNDEZ-MONROIG, JOSÉ M., lawyer; b. San Juan, P.R., June 22, 1917; s. Albert Seaman Menendez and Agustina Monroig; B.A., U. P.R., 1939, LL.B., 1941; m. Lyda M. Cortada, Aug. 3, 1946; children—Jose Antonio, Michele Marie. Admitted to P.R. bar, 1941; asso. atty. Pub. Service Commn., 1946; adjudicator VA, 1947; mem. law firm Martínez-Alvarez, Fernández-Paoli, Menéndez-Monroig, Menéndez-Cortada and LeFranc-Romero, 1977—. Mem. P.R. Senate, 1969-72; minority leader New Progressive party, 1973-76; pres. Adelante Estadidad (orgn. promoting statehood for P.R.). Mem. Am. Bar Assn., Colegio de Abogados de P.R. Roman Catholic. Home: 54 Krug St Santurce PR 00911 Office: PO Box 3183 San Juan PR 00904

MENGER, RICHARD ALLEN, banker; b. Victoria, Tex., Apr. 15, 1942; s. James Joffre and Lucille (Livingston) Colglazier; B.A., U. Tex., Austin, 1964; M.B.A., U. Tex., San Antonio, 1975; m. Mary Deborah Bass, June 3, 1966; children—Catherine B., Lucy M. With Frost Nat. Bank, San Antonio, 1968-75, v.p., mgr. mktg. research and planning, 1974-75: sr. v.p., mgr. corporate planning and devel., exec. com. Bexar County Nat. Bank, San Antonio, 1975—; instr. Coll. Bus., San Antonio Coll., 1975—, Am. Inst. Banking, 1971—. Trustee, treas. exec. com. S.W. Tex. Public Broadcasting Council, 1976—; mem. San Antonio Zool. Soc., San Antonio Symphony Soc., San Antonio Art League, San Antonio Mus. Assn.; mem. Arts Council San Antonio, Tex. Arts Alliance; bd. dirs. Bexar County chpt. ARC, 1978-79. Served with USAF, 1960-62. Mem. Bank Mktg. Assn. (dir. Gulf coast chpt.), Houston Advt. Club, Republic Tex. Mktg. Council, Tex. Bankers Assn. (mktg. com.), U. Tex. Ex-students Assn., Harvard Coop. Soc. Republican. Episcopalian. Clubs: St. Anthony, San Antonio German, Christmas Cotillion, Conopus, University. Office: 325 N St Mary's San Antonio TX 78205

MENIUS, ESPIE FLYNN, JR., elec. engr.; b. New Bern, N.C., Mar. 5, 1923; s. Espie Flynn and Sudie Grey (Lyerly) M.; B.E.E., N.C. State U., 1947; M.B.A., U. S.C., 1973; adopted children—James Benfield, Ruben Hughes, James Sechler. With Carolina Power & Light Co., 1947-63, asst. to dist. mgr., Raleigh, Henderson, N.C., Sumter, S.C., 1947-50, elec. engr., Asheville, Southern Pines, Dunn, N.C., 1950-52, dist. engr. Hartsville, S.C., 1952-63; sr. elec. engr. Sonoco Products Co., Hartsville, 1963-74, engring. group leader, 1974—; instr. Florence-Darlington Tech. Ednl. Center. Mem. Hartsville Vol. Fire Dept., 1958—; Eagle Scout, Boy Scouts Am., 1938, scout troop leader New Bern, N.C., 1940-41, Raleigh, 1941-47, Henderson, 1948-49, Asheville, N.C., 1950, Southern Pines, N.C., 1951-52, Sumter, 1949-50, Hartsville, 1952-64. Served with AUS, 1943-46. Recipient Silver Beaver award Boy Scouts Am., 1959; named Hartsville's Citizen of Year, Rotary, 1960. Registered profl. engr., N.C., S.C., Tenn., Ga. Mem. IEEE, AAAS, Nat. Assn. Engrs., Knight of St. Patrick, Scabbard and Blade, Eta Kappa Nu, Pine Burr, Phi Eta Sigma, Theta Tau, Beta Gamma Sigma. Presbyn. (elder, tchr. men's Bible class). Club: Civitan (past dir.). Author articles in field. Home: 423 Richardson Circle W Hartsville SC 29550 Office: Sonoco Products Co N 2d St Hartsville SC 29550

MENSCHER, BARNET GARY, steel co. exec.; b. Laurelton, N.Y., Sept. 5, 1940; s. Samuel and Louise (Zaimont) M.; student Centenary Coll., 1958-59; B.B.A., U. Tex., 1963; m. Diane Elaine Gachman, June 12, 1966; children—Melissa Denise, Corey Lane, Scott Jay. Vice pres. mktg. Ella Gant Mfg., Shreveport, La., 1964-66; warehouse mgr., dir. material control Gachman Steel Co., Fort Worth, 1966-68, gen. mgr., Houston, 1968-70, v.p., sales mgr. Gulf Coast, 1971-77; pres. Menko Steel Service Inc., Houston, 1979—; investment cons. D & L Enterprises, 1966—. Mem. solicitation com. United Fund; mem. Nat. Alliance of Businessmen Jobs Program. Served with AUS, 1963-65. Mem. Assn. Steel Distbrs., Tex. Assn. Steel Importers, Purchasing Agts. Assn. Houston, Credit Assn. Houston, Am. Mgmt. Assn., Phi Sigma Delta, Alpha Phi Omega. Democrat. Jewish religion. Home: 314 Tealwood Dr Houston TX 77024 Office: 6607 Flintlock St Houston TX 77040

MENUTIS, RUTH ANN, mcht.; b. Lafayette, La., Aug. 7, 1939; d. Minus and Annie (Duhon) Pellerin; ed. S.W. La. Inst., Patricia Stevens Sch. Modeling; m. Jimmie Menutis, Feb. 15, 1960; children—Jamie, Marika, Dimitri. Comml. announcer, traffic mgr. KLFY-TV, 1957-58; hostess Tex. Internat. Airlines, also model Dallas Apparel Mart, 1958-68; owner, mgr. Playgril Shop of Am. and Ruth Ann Fashion, New Orleans, 1960—; real estate investor; real estate salesman French Quarter Realty; clothing designer Miss Jane of Miami. Bd. dirs. Better Bus. Bur., 1978: French Market Corp.; del. White House Small Bus. Conf., 1980; chmn. New Orleans Mayor's, French Quar. Task Force. Mem. Vieux Carre Action Assn. (v.p.), Bourbon Mchts. Assn. (pres.), New Orleans C. of C. Greek Orthodox. Office: 108 Royal St New Orleans LA 70130

MENZEL, (MARY) MARGARET YOUNG, educator; b. Kerrville, Tex., June 21, 1924; d. Walter Patterson and Mary (Hightower) Young; B.A. magna cum laude, Southwestern U., 1944; Ph.D., U. Va., 1949; m. Robert Winston Menzel, Apr. 9, 1949; children—Robert Winston, Gary Patterson, Mary Linda. Instr. agronomy Tex. A. and M. Coll., College Station, 1949-54; plant geneticist U.S. Dept. Agr., Tallahassee, 1955-62; research asso. Fla. State U., Tallahassee, 1954-63; asso. prof., 1963-68, prof. dept. biol. scis., 1968—, asso. chmn. dept., 1972-73. Recipient Research prize Assn. of Southeastern Biologists, 1950. Research grantee Sigma Xi, 1954, 55; grantee Am. Philos. Soc., 1954, 66; AEC grantee, 1964-75; Cotton, Inc. grantee, 1974-75; U.S. Dept. Agr. grantee, 1977—; NSF grantee, 1978—. Mem. NOW (pres. chpt. 1972-74), Assn. of Southeastern Biologists (v.p. 1966, editor 1972-77), League Women Voters, Sigma Xi (pres. chpt. 1972-74), Alpha Delta Pi. Methodist. Contbr. articles in field to profl. jours. Office: Dept Biological Science Florida State University Tallahassee FL 32306

MERCADANTE, LUCILLE THERESA, nurse; b. Mt. Vernon, N.Y., Oct. 30, 1925; d. Nicholas and Josephine Veronica (Busetto) M.; grad. Mt. Vernon Hosp. Sch. Nursing, 1946; B.S., Columbia U., 1953, M.A., 1958; D.Ed., Nova U., 1979. Dir. nursing services Shands Teaching Hosp., asst. dean, asst. prof. Coll. Nursing, U. Fla., Gainesville, 1959-67; vis. prof., cons. Rockefeller Found., nursing service adminstrn. Hosp. Universitario del Valle, Cali, Colombia, 1967-68; prof., cons. nursing Coll. Nursing, State U. N.Y., Downstate Med. Center, Bklyn., 1968-69, prof., asso. dean, dir. nursing services, 1969-75; dir. nursing services, asso. dir. Mount Sinai Med. Center, Miami Beach, Fla., 1975-79; mem. nursing adv. com. Miami Dade Community Coll., 1976—; clin. asso. dept. nursing Tchrs. Coll., Columbia U., 1969-70; mem. bd. visitors Duke U. Med. Center, Durham, N.C., 1969-72; cons. com. on nursing U. Rochester, Strong Meml. Hosp., 1968-72; cons. nursing services Macro Systems, Inc., Beverly Hosp., Beverly, Mass., 1970; mem. adv. council on nursing dept. medicine and surgery VA, Washington, 1965-68; cons. nursing services Okla. VA Hosp., Oklahoma City, 1965-69; cons. nursing services Coral Gables (Fla.) VA Hosp., 1963-68; mem. nursing adminstrn. test devel. commn. Am. Nurses Assn. Commn. Nursing Service, 1978-79. Recipient Dean's award Coll. Nursing, U. Fla., 1964. Mem. Am. Nurses Assn. (mem. nominating com. Council Nursing Service Facilitators 1978-80), Nat. League Nursing, Am. Soc. Nursing Service Adminstrs. of Am. Hosp. Assn., Fla. Nurses Assn. (treas. 1977-79). Contbr. articles to profl. jours. Home: 10300 SW 120th St Miami FL 33176

MERCADO-BURGOS, NELSON, biologist; b. Aguada, P.R., Aug. 23, 1939; s. Francisco and Emiliana (Burgos) Mercado; B.S. in Biology, U. P.R., 1962, M.S. in Biology, 1966; M.S. (P.R. Econ. Devel. Corp. scholar) in Environ. Scis., Drexel U., 1972; Ph.D. (P.R. Econ. Devel. Corp. scholar) in Environ. Scis. and Engring., Va. Poly. Inst. and State U., 1975; m. Catalina Castro, Dec. 17, 1966; children—Nelson A., Katia L. Research asst. dept. radiology Albert Einstein Coll. Medicine, Bronx, N.Y., 1962-63; grad. teaching asst. dept. biology U. P.R., Rio Piedras, 1963-65; research asst. P.R. Nuclear Center, San Juan, 1965-67; instr. biology Arecibo Regional Coll., U. P.R., Arecibo, 1967-70, chmn. dept. biology, 1969-70, asst. prof., 1974-76, asso. prof., chmn. dept. natural scis. Aguadilla Regional Coll., U. P.R., Aguadilla, 1976—, faculty rep. Arecibo Regional Coll. to adminstrv. bd. Regional Colls., U. P.R., 1975-76. Mem. edn. com. Environ. Quality Bd., Commonwealth of P.R., 1975-77. HEW grantee, 1977-79. Mem. Internat. Soc. Tropical Ecology, Water Pollution Control Fedn., P.R. Water Pollution Control Assn., Am. Tech. Edn. Assn., P.R. Sci. Tchrs. Assn., Beta Beta Beta. Club: Sertoma (treas. 1969-70). Contbr. articles on effects of pollution on organisms to sci. jours. and books. Home: Urbanizacion Montemar 68 Aguada PR 00602 Office: PO Box 160 Univ of Puerto Rico Aguadilla PR 00604

MERCER, CHARLES VALENTINE, bus. exec.; b. Beaumont, Tex., Dec. 15, 1924; s. Vallie Scott and Bernice Olive (Waugh) M.; B.B.A., So. Meth. U., 1949; m. Betty Genelle Huffaker, Dec. 16, 1950; children—Connie Sue, Penny Lynn. Personnel trainee Pure Oil Co., Port Neches, Tex., 1949-50; salesman Swift & Co., Amarillo, Tex., 1950-51; personnel interviewer Procter & Gamble Pantex Plant, Amarillo, 1951-55; salesman Southwestern Life Ins. Co., Amarillo, 1955-56; personnel asst. Pioneer Corp., Amarillo, 1956-61, personnel dir., 1961—. Bd. dirs. Am. Cancer Soc., 1959-65, pres., 1965; troop leader Amarillo council Girl Scouts U.S.A., 1963-69; bd. dirs. Family Service of Amarillo, 1971-75, v.p., 1974; bd. dir. Salvation Army, 1971-76; bd. dirs. YMCA, 1976-79, v.p., 1977-78, pres., 1979. Served in Tank Corps, U.S. Army, 1943-46; ETO. Recipient Service award So. Gas Assn., 1972; Harry Mays Meml. award YMCA, Amarillo, 1976; named Boss of Yr., Amarillo chpt. Desk and Derrick Club, 1979. Mem. Am. Soc. Personnel Adminstrs., So. Gas Assn., Tex. Assn. Bus., Panhandle Personnel Assn. Methodist. Clubs: Amarillo, Amarillo Country. Home: 3812 Doris Dr Amarillo TX 79109 Office: PO Box 511 Amarillo TX 79163

MERCER, GEORGE RILEY, JR., investor; b. Richmond, Va., Aug. 22, 1946; s. George Riley and Mary Rutherfoord (Rose) M.; grad. St. Christopher's Sch., Richmond, 1964; student U. N.C., Chapel Hill, 1965-67; B.S., U. Ga., Athens, 1968, postgrad., 1968-69; m. Marsha Dale Tatum, Apr. 29 1972; children—Tinsley Randolph, Dabney Winston. Vice pres., dir. Mercer Rug & Carpet Co., Inc., Richmond, 1969—, George-Marshall Real Estate Investment Corp., Richmond, 1970—, Victory Rug & Carpet Co., Inc., Richmond, 1970—; pres., trustee, dir. Airport Properties Co., Richmond, 1974—. Bd. dirs. Va. League Planned Parenthood, 1973—; dir. Richmond br. English Speaking Union; bd. dirs. Friends of Elk Hill Boys Farm, 1977. Recipient Distinguished Vol. Service award Va. League Planned Parenthood, 1974. Mem. Jamestowne Soc. (bd. dirs.), Clan Rose Soc., (historian), Va. Hist. Soc., Assn. Preservation of Va. Antiquities, Order of 1st Families of Va., Descs. of The Order of Knights of the Garter, Baronial Order of Magna Charta, Ams. of Royal Descent, Va. Mus., Valentine Mus., West Richmond Bus. Men's Assn. (dir.), Zeta Psi. Episcopalian. Clubs: Country of Va., Commonwealth (Richmond), Deep Run Hunt (Richmond); Farmington Country (Charlottesville, Va.); Rotary. Home: 4811 Cary Street Rd Richmond VA 23226 Office: 3116 20 W Moore St Richmond VA 23230

MERCER, JAMES LEE, exec. search co. exec.; b. Sayre, Okla., Nov. 7, 1936; s. Fred Elmo and Ora Lee (Davidson) M.; B.S., U. Nev., 1964, M.B.A., 1966; cert. in mcpl. adminstrn. U. N.C., 1971; postgrad. exec. devel. program Cornell U., 1979; m. Carolyn Lois Prince, Nov. 16, 1962; children—Tara Lee, James Lee. Methods and results supr. Pacific Tel. & Tel., Sacramento, 1965-66; prodn. control supr. Gen. Dynamics, Pomona, Calif., 1966-67; nuclear submarine project mgr. Litton Industries, Pascagoula, Miss., 1967-70; asst. city mgr. City of Raleigh (N.C.), 1970-73; nat. program dir. Pub. Tech., Inc., Washington, 1973-76; gen. mgr. Battelle So. Ops., Atlanta, 1976-79; v.p. Korn/Ferry Internat., Atlanta, 1979—; ad hoc prof. N.C. State U., 1972-73. Chmn. Raleigh Mayor's Civic Center Authority Study Commn., 1971. Served with USN, 1955-59. Mem. Internat. City Mgmt. Assn., Am. Soc. for Pub. Adminstrn., Am. Inst. Indsl. Engrs. (past pres.'s award 1970, pres. chpt. 1969-70), Tech. Transfer Soc. (dir. 1978—), U. Nev. Alumni Assn. (exec. com. 1969—). Republican. Clubs: Rotary, Masons, Shriners. Author: Public Management Systems, 1978; contbr. articles to profl. jours. Home: 1119 Aurora Ct Dunwoody GA 30338 Office: 260 Peachtree St NE Atlanta GA 30303

MERCER, SUSAN OSTEEN, educator; b. El Dorado, Ark., Nov. 23, 1942; d. Joseph Robert and Bess (Sample) Osteen; B.A., Baylor U., 1964; M.S.S.W., U. Tex., Austin, 1966; D.Social Work, U. Utah, Salt Lake City, 1978. Asst. clin. prof. social service dept. U. Ark. Med. Center, 1967-68; master social worker Children and Family Services, Carbondale, Ill., 1968-69; chief social worker, asst. clin. prof. maternal and infant care project U. Ark. Med. Center, Little Rock, 1969-72; asst. prof. Grad. Sch. Social Work, U. Ark., Little Rock, 1972-76, asso. prof., 1978—; cons. long term care facilities. Ex-officio mem. Com. on Traffic Court Justice in Ark., 1974—. Named Outstanding Sr. Woman, Baylor U., 1964; NIMH fellow, 1964-66, 76-78, Ark. Endowment for Humanities grantee, 1979-80. Mem. Nat. Assn. Social Workers (mem. exec. com. Ark. chpt.), Council Social Work Edn., Acad. Cert. Social Workers, Ark. Conf. Social Welfare, Phi Kappa Phi, Alpha Kappa Delta. Mem. editorial bd. Jour. Gerontol. Social Work, 1979—. Office: Grad Sch Social Work U Ark 33d and University Sts Little Rock AR 72202

MERCHANT, DONALD JOSEPH, scientist; b. Biltmore, N.C., Sept. 7, 1921; s. Oscar Lowell and Bess (Clark) M.; A.B., Berea Coll., 1942; M.S., U. Mich., 1947, Ph.D., 1950; m. Marian Adelaide Yeager, May 31, 1943; children—Nancy Adele, Barry Scott, Karen Ruth. Instr. bacteriology U. Mich., 1948-51, asst. prof., 1951-58, asso. prof. microbiology, 1958-64, prof., 1964-69; dir. W. Alton Jones Cell Sci. Center, Lake Placid, N.Y., 1969-72; prof. microbiology U. Vt., 1969-72; prof., chmn. dept. microbiology and immunology Eastern Va. Med. Sch., Norfolk, 1973—; cons. research lab. U.S. VA Hosp., Ann Arbor, Mich., 1954-62, Hampton, Va., 1976—; process devel. div. U.S. Army Biol. Labs., Ft. Detrick, Md., 1966-68; mem. sci. adv. bd. Found. for Research on Nervous System, Boston, 1965-69, Masonic Med. Research Lab., Utica, N.Y., 1971-75; mem. adv. com. to animal cell culture collection Am. Type Culture Collection, 1966-70; mem. prostatic cancer task force NCI, 1972-79. Bd. dirs. N.Y. State div. Am. Cancer Soc., 1972, Va. State div., 1974—; mem. Portage Trails council Chippewa dist. Boy Scouts Am., 1965-67; mem. pub. health sect. Detroit Office CD, 1958-62. Served with AUS, 1944-46. Mem. Tissue Culture Assn. (pres. 1964-68), Am. Soc. Microbiology (council 1968), AAAS, Soc. Exptl. Biology and

Medicine, Am., Internat. socs. cell biology, N.Y. Acad. Sci., Sigma Xi, Phi Kappa Phi. Author: (with R.H. Kahn, W.H. Murphy) Handbook of Cell and Organ Culture, 1960, 2d edit., 1964. Home: 2433 Spindrift Rd Virginia Beach VA 23451 Office: Eastern Va Med Sch PO Box 1980 Norfolk VA 23501

MERCHANT, DOROTHY GALLON, counselor; b. Monticello, Fla., Sept. 28, 1948; d. Willie and Frances Gallon; A.A., Daytona Beach Community Coll., 1968; B.A., Bethune Cookman Coll., 1971; postgrad. E. Carolina U.; m. Frank S. Merchant, Jr., Dec. 10, 1976. Employment interviewer Fla. Dept. Commerce, Daytona Beach, 1972-78; career counselor Fayetteville (N.C.) State U., 1978—. Group leader, condr. group sessions Displaced Homemakers Project. Mem. Am. Personnel and Guidance Assn., N.C. Personnel and Guidance Assn., N.C. Vocat. Guidance Assn. Baptist. Office: Fayetteville State U Newbold Sta Fayetteville NC 28301

MERCHANT, WALTER MAYFIELD, orgn. exec.; b. Haskell, Tex., Feb. 1, 1927; s. Walter Herbert and Gladys Adelia (Mayfield) M.; student Southwestern U., 1944-45, 46-47; B.A., U. Tex., 1949; m. Charles Rhea Blocker, Nov. 26, 1947; 1 dau., Donna Rhea. Incorporator, sec. Am. Coll. Musicians, Austin, Tex., 1947-51; salesman Western Auto Co., Austin, 1951-54; owner Self-Merchant's Service Stas., Austin, 1954-59; owner-operator Self-Merchant's Student House for U. Tex. Boys, 1959-62; sales Prudential Life Ins. Co., Austin, 1961-64; editor, v.p. pub. relations, chmn. account schedule Am. Coll. Musicians, 1962—; incorporator Coll. Aid Agy., Austin, sec.-treas., 1969—, editor Piano Guild Notes, 1964—. Served with USNR, 1944-45. Named to Hall of Fame, Am. Coll. Musicians, 1969. Mem. Tex. Ex's, Kappa Alpha. Methodist (treas, 1950-54, mem. bd. 1950—, pres. Sunday sch. class 1969—). Club: Optimist Internat. Home: 5801 Marilyn Dr Austin TX 78731 Office: 808 Rio Grande St Austin TX 78767 Mailing Address: PO Box 2215 Austin TX 78768

MEREDITH, OWEN NICHOLS, pub. relations ofcl.; b. Etowah, Tenn., Mar. 27, 1924; s. Owen Habner and Ora (Nichols) M.; B.A., U. Va., 1946; postgrad. Fla. State U., 1949, U. Mo., 1950, Alliance Francaise (Paris), 1951; M.A., Syracuse U., 1952; m. Mary Virginia Wright, July 19, 1980. Editor, Circuit Rider, sub-features editor Together mag. Meth. Pub. House, Nashville, Chgo., 1953-57; pub. information dir. Nasvhile-Davidson County chpt. ARC, 1957-70; dir. Tenn. State Mus., Nashville, 1970-72; owner, mgr. Gazetteer Typesetters, Nashville, 1973-74; public relations dir. Nashville Area chpt. and Tenn. div. ARC, 1974—. Sec., Tenn. Exec. Residence Preservation Found. Mem. Pub. Relations Soc. Am., Middle Tenn. Bus. Press Club (treas. 1976—), Confederate Meml. Lit. Soc. (Tenn. regent 1972—). Author: (with R.M. McBride) The Hedden Family of North Georgia, 1957, The Nichols Family of North Georgia, 1960; editor: (with McBride and Mary U. Rothrock) Eastin Morris' 1834 Tennessee Gazetteer, 2d edit., 1971; contbr. articles, photographs and revs. to hist. jours. Address 410 Lancaster Ave Nashville TN 37212

MEREDITH, ROBERT FRANKLIN, mfg. engr.; b. McCrory, Ark., July 22, 1945; s. Claud William and Emmer (Isabel) M.; Mech. Drafting degree, Hot Springs Rehab. Center, 1964; m. Lois Jane Taylor, Dec. 31, 1967. Chief draftsman Victor Metal Products Co., Newport, Ark., 1964-66, plant engr., 1969-77; project engr. BMC div. Aerojet Gen. Co., Batesville, Ark., 1966-69; chief engr. Victor Industries Corp., Newport, 1977—; co-owner Oak Bluff Angus Farm; owner Oak Bluff Machine and Equipment Shop; metal working cons. to pvt. industry. Instr. for industry ARC, 1972-74; sec. Jaycees, 1965-66; justice of peace, Independence County, 1975-76; pres., bd. dirs. Oak Bluff Community Center, 1976-79. Mem. Indsl. Services Assn. (dir.), Soc. Mfg. Engrs. (sec. N.E. Ark. sub chpt. 520, 1975, vice chmn. 1976), N.E. Ark. Safety Council, White River Mfg. Adv. Council (chmn.), Metal Tube Packaging Council. Democrat. Mem. Ch. of Christ. Club: Ozark Mountain C.B. (pres. 1967-69). Pioneer article conveyor with accumulating capability. Home: Box 179 Route 2 Batesville AR 72501 Office: Hwy 67N Newport AR 72112

MEREDITH, SARA ELIZABETH, trade assn. exec.; b. Jackson, Miss., Jan. 15, 1912; d. Dexter Ivison and Sallye Belle (Johnson) Meredith; student Miss. Woman's Coll., 1929-30. Sec., St. Louis Bank for Coops., 1934-36; office mgr., cashier Jackson Paper Co., 1937-51; exec. sec.-treas. So. Paper Trade Assn., Inc., Jackson, 1940—; exec. sec. Southerners, Inc., Jackson, 1955—; planner mgmt. seminars Coll. Bus., Fla. State U., Tallahassee, 1955-78. Active church librarian Bapt. Ch. Named mem. Order of Flying Orchid, Delta Air Lines, 1961; honored by Nat. Paper Trade Assn., Inc., N.Y., 1977. Clubs: Bus. and Profl. Women's (treas. 1940-41). Author: A Concert of Favorite Recipes, 1970; only female exec. sec. of regional paper trade assn., 1940-77. Home and office: 5434 Hartsdale Dr Jackson MS 39211

MERIDA, FREDERICK AUSTIN, art dealer; b. Indpls., Mar. 10, 1936; s. Arthur and Lelia Mae (Bristol) M.; student Kansas City Art Inst., 1954-57, New Sch. Social Scis., 1957-59, (Max Beckmann fellow) Bklyn. Mus. Sch., 1957-59; m. Margaret Louise Braden, June 11, 1962; 1 son, Frederick James Craven. Asst. dir. Ky. Guild Artists and Craftsman Train, Berea, 1963; dir. Corner Gallery, Anchorage, Ky., 1964-65, Merida Gallery, Louisville, 1965-69, Frame House Gallery, Inc., Louisville, 1969-77, Merida Gallery Inc., Louisville, 1977—; lectr., U. Louisville, 1969. Served with AUS, 1959-61. Fulbright fellow, 1959. Editor, pub. art Gallery Guide Louisville, 1968-69. Home: 1278 Bassett Ave Louisville KY 40204 Office: Merida Gallery 4156 Westport Rd Louisville KY 40207

MERIN, SIDNEY JULIUS, psychologist; b. Altoona, Pa., Jan. 22, 1927; s. Morris and Lillian (Foreman) M.; B.S., Pa. State U., 1950, Ph.D., 1956, M.A., Temple U., 1952; m. Arlene R. Merrow, Dec. 31, 1945; children—Cheryl Ann, Debra Kay, Michele Lee, Jeffrey Michael. asst. Psychol. Clinic, Temple U., 1950-51; intern Elgin (Ill.) State Hosp., 1952; psychologist Child Guidance Clinic, St. Petersburg, Fla., 1953-54; psychol. asst. supr. Psychol. Clinic, Pa. State U., 1954-55; clin. psychologist Child Guidance Clinic, St. Petersburg, 1955-56; staff psychologist Byron Harless & Assos., Tampa, Fla., 1956-60; sr. psychologist Samuel G. Hibbs, M.D. & Assos., Tampa, 1960-64; pvt. practice as clin. psychologist, Tampa, 1964—. Cons. to Clearwater Adult Mental Health Clinic, 1961—, Reading Edn. and Devel. Clinic, 1962—, dir. Ednl. Services Clinic; faculty U. South Fla., 1962—; dir. psychology, pres. Clin. Center for Reading and Learning, Inc. Mem. profl. services com. Community Resources Council; co-chmn. Mayor's Com. to Investigate Civil Service Practices, 1969. Bd. dirs. Hillsborough County Assn. Mental Health, Inter Profl. Family Council. Served with AUS, 1945-46; ETO. Diplomate Am. Bd. Examiners Profl. Psychology. Mem. Am., Fla. (pres. 1970-71, chmn. standards and ethics com.), Tampa Bay (pres. 1957, chmn. standards and ethics com.) psychol. assns., Council on Exceptional Children, Council on Family Relations, Hillsborough County Soc. Clin. Psychologists, Internat. Acad. Law and Sci., Fla. Bd. Examiners Psychology, Soc. for Neurosci., AAAS, Sigma Alpha Eta, Phi Delta Kappa. Contbr. articles to profl. jours. Research in psychol. factors in indentical twins, wives of men on hazardous duty, psychol. and psychiat. influence in ct. decisions regarding child custody. Home: 4509 San Rafael St Tampa FL 33609 Office: 41 Davis Blvd Tampa FL 33606

MERITZ, NEAL STUART, physician; b. Phila., Nov. 6, 1946; s. Leonard and Rosalyn Meritz (Blum) M.; B.S., Ursinus Coll., 1968; M.D., U. Tex., San Antonio, 1972; m. Patricia Stenger, May 12, 1973; children—Carissa, Darren, Martina. Intern, Los Angeles County/U. So. Calif., 1972-73; resident in family practice Kaiser Found. Hosp., Fontana, Calif., 1975-77; practice family medicine, Sacramento, 1974-75, Ontario, Calif., 1976-77, San Antonio, 1977—; mem. staff S.W. Methodist Hosp., San Antonio Community Hosp., Lutheran Hosp.; asst. clin. prof. U. Tex., San Antonio, 1977—. Med. dir. Cresthaven Children's Center for Mentally Retarded, 1978. Legis. Merit scholar, 1971-72; diplomate Am. Bd. Family Physicians. Mem. Calif. Acad. Family Physicians, Am. Acad. Family Physicians, Tex. Med. Assn., Bexar County Med. Soc. Democrat. Jewish. Office: 314 Oak Hills Med Bldg San Antonio TX 78229

MERIWETHER, CHARLES MINOR, drug co. exec.; b. Memphis, Feb. 15, 1911; s. Charles Minor and Leslie Allen (Stevens) M.; student U. Tenn., 1932; LL.B., Cumberland U., 1933; J.D., Samford U., 1969; m. Beverly Alston, June 7, 1939; children—Leslie Ann (Mrs. Albert M. Shuler, Jr.), Beverly (Mrs. Frank Lockridge, Jr.), Charles Minor. Engaged in ins. law and ins. mgmt., Memphis, 1933-42, in retail and wholesale drug bus., Birmingham, Ala., 1944-58; dir. finance, Ala., 1958-61; bd. dirs. Export-Import Bank Washington, 1961-65; cons. Dewberry Drug Co., Inc., Birmingham, Ala., 1965—. Pres. Ala. Ednl. Authority, 1958-61, Ala. Hwy. Authority, 1958-61; chmn. investment com. Tchr. Retirement Fund and Employees Retirement Fund, Ala., 1958-61; dir. Ala. Adjustment Bd., 1958-61. Chmn. dirs. Ala. chpt. Nat. Multiple Sclerosis Soc., 1958-59. Served with U.S. Mcht. Marine, 1942-43. Mem. Phi Gamma Delta. Methodist. Odd Fellow. Clubs: Nat. Press (Washington); Birmingham Downtown, Birmingham Relay House. Home: 4421 Corinth Dr Birmingham AL 35213 Office: City Fed Bldg Birmingham AL 35203

MERIWETHER, JERRY ABERNATHY, psychologist; b. Clarksville, Tenn., Apr. 4, 1947; d. Howard Jackson and Lillian Mozelle (Crosslin) Abernathy; B.S. in Speech, Theatre and Art, Austin Peay State U., Clarksville, 1977, M.A. in Psychology, 1980; m. Robert Tutwiler Meriwether, III, Nov. 24, 1967. Substitute tchr. Clarksville-Montgomery County Schs., 1973-75; asst. coach forensics for speech team Austin Peay State U., 1977—. Mem. Am. Psychol. Assn., Am. Personnel and Guidance Assn., AAUW, Middle Tenn. Psychol. Assn., Upper Middle Tenn. Humanities Council, Alpha Psi Omega, Pi Kappa Delta. Methodist. Club: Women of Moose. Address: 1001 Ridgecrest Dr Clarksville TN 37040

MERLIN, ALVIN SIMON, urologist: b. New Orleans, June 15, 1936; s. Joseph Boris and Claire (Kamil) M.; student Tulane U., 1952-53, Sch. Elec. Engring., La. State U., Baton Rouge, 1953-55; M.D., La. State U., 1964; m. Carol R. Hochberg, May 14, 1977; children—Shel, Lisa, Kim, Max, Andrew, Ashley. Intern, Charity Hosp., New Orleans, 1964-65: resident Touro Infirmary, VA Hosp., New Orleans, 1965-69; practice medicine specializing in urology, Metairie, La., 1969—; chief sect. urology E. Jefferson Gen. Hosp.; bd. dirs. Jo Ellen Smith Hosp., 1972-74. Exec. com. New Orleans Area Health Systems Agency, 1978; chmn. long range fin. com. Congregation Gates of Prayer, 1976-77; chmn. Jefferson Parish Charter Adv. Bd., 1980. Served with USN, 1955-59. Cert. mortgage loan broker La. Commr. Securities. Diplomate Am. Bd. Urology. Mem. Am. Urol. Assn. (Southeastern sect.), Tuland Soc. Engrs., New Orleans Office Bldg. Assn., La. Restaurant Assn. Jewish. Club: Masons. Home: 4616 Hessmer Ave Metairie LA 70002 Office: 4300 Houma Blvd Metairie LA 70002

MERLIN, JAMES (MERLIN J. JOHNSON), artist; b. Chokio, Minn., Sept. 23, 1906; s. Nels H.K. and Lena (Robertson) Johnson; student Okla. State U., 1930; m. Nola Rogers, Feb. 26, 1931; 1 son, James Roger. Statistician, Gulf Oil Corp., 1950-61; sr. analyst, 1961-68; exhibited one-man shows Galleries I and II, Houston, 1971—, Gallery Cypress, Gallery Woodway, Gallerie Atascocita, Galleri Lewisville; group shows include Community Center, 1967, 68, 69, Dimension Houston IV, Houston Fine Arts, Gulf Fine Arts (1st prize); represented in pvt. and corp. collections. Served with AUS, World War II. Republican. Baptist. Address: 4507 Shetland Ln Houston TX 77027

MERLISS, WILLIAM SIDNEY, architect, engr.; b. Okmulgee, Okla., Sept. 26, 1922; s. Sidney Samuel and Bonnie Bessie (Farr) M.; B.Archtl. Engring., Okla. A. and M. U., 1950; m. Dorothy Halphen Kolb; children—Sherri Lynn, Benjamin Harrison. Architect, engr. Hudgins, Thompson & Ball, Oklahoma City, 1950; engr. Dow Chem. Co., Freeport, Tex., 1953-54; project engr. Walter P. Moore, Houston, 1954-55; cons. engr. W.S. Merliss & Assos., Houston, 1955-61; partner firm Merliss, Jones and Robinson, Houston, 1961-77, Merliss & Jones, 1977—; dir. Modern Savs. and Loan, Pasadena, Tex., 1973—. Democrat precinct chmn., 1968-75. Served with USAF, 1941-45, 51-53. Decorated Purple Heart. Mem. Nat., Tex. socs. profl. engrs., Tex. Soc. Architects, AIA, Prestressed Concrete Inst., Gulf Coast Okla. State Alumni Assn. (pres. 1956-65), Kappa Kappa Psi. Jewish. Clubs: Masons, Shriners, Consistory, Artisans; City (Baton Rouge). Home: 9940 Memorial Dr Apt 27C Houston TX 77024 also 7420 Reinzi Blvd Baton Rouge LA 70809 Office: 2600 Southwest Freeway 300 Houston TX 77027

MERO, MARY WINIFRED, nurse, health adminstr.; b. Bayshore, L.I., N.Y., May 20, 1942; d. Robert Sills and Letitia Florence (Seon) M.; B.S., Pace U., Westchester, N.Y., 1975; postgrad. Adelphi U., 1976-77; M.S. in Nursing, U. Tenn., 1979. Staff nurse Cabrini Health Care Center, Dobbs Ferry, N.Y., 1973-74, acting asst. dir., 1974-75, coordinator primary nursing care unit, 1976-76, inservice instr., 1976-77; asst. dir. nursing for supportive services, also dir. staff devel. dept. Shelby County Health Care Center, Memphis, 1978—. Mem. Nat. Com. Task Force for Mental Health in Elderly, 1979—. Mem. Gerontol. Soc., Tenn. Nursing Assn., Am. Nurses Assn., AAAS. Democrat. Roman Catholic. Home: 6119 Gray Oak Memphis TN 38138 Office: 1075 Mullins Station Rd Memphis TN 38134

MERRELL, CHARLES THOMAS, farm equipment dealer; b. Honey Grove, Tex., Apr. 27, 1948; s. G.C. and Mary E. M.; B.S., East Tex. State U., 1970, M.S., 1978; m. Jane Ann Pope, Mar. 7, 1976; 1 son, Charles Thomas. Tchr., Wolfe City (Tex.) Public Schs., 1969; tchr., head basketball coach Savoy (Tex.) Public Schs., 1970-71; co-owner, mgr. Merrell & Son Tractor Co., Honey Grove, 1972—; asst. instr. history East Tex. State U., 1977. City councilman, Honey Grove, 1976-77; mem. adminstrv. bd. McKenzie United Meth. Ch., 1978—. Mem. Am. Hist. Assn., So. Hist. Assn., Tex. State Tchrs. Assn., SW Hardware and Implement Dealers Assn., Honey Grove C. of C. Home: 204 Spring St Honey Grove TX 75446 Office: 339 S 5th St Honey Grove TX 75446

MERRICK, EUNICE PEACOCK (MRS. GEORGE E. MERRICK), civic worker; b. Coconut Grove, Fla.; d. Alfred and Lillian (Frow) Peacock; student pvt. and pub. schs.; m. George Edgar Merrick, Feb. 5, 1916. Treas. George E. Merrick, Inc., real estate, 1934-42, pres., 1942-45. Active in establishing Dade County Schs., Coral Gables, 1922-25. Recipient Book of Golden Deeds, Exchange Club Coral Gables, 1957. Mem. Hist. Soc. So. Fla., Fla. Hist. Soc., Nat. League Am. Pen Women (patroness), Sigma Alpha Iota (patroness). Christian Scientist. Clubs: Coral Gables Woman's (charter mem., dir.), Coral Gables Garden (past pres.), Coral Gables Music (active hon.). George E. Merrick, the original owner, founder Coral Gables, Fla. Home: 1015 Coral Way Coral Gables FL 33134

MERRIGAN, MARY ELLEN, radio sta. exec.; b. Maryville, Mo., July 7, 1951; d. James Robert and Coletta Marie (Seipel) M.; B.A., N.W. Mo. State U., Maryville, 1973. Sales rep. Sta. WMKC, Miles Kimball Co., Oshkosh, Wis., 1973-74, Sta. KHAK-AM/FM, Communications Properties Inc., Cedar Rapids, Iowa, 1974-77; sales rep. Sta. KARN, Snider Corp., Little Rock, 1977-78, sales mgr., 1978—; lectr. in field. Dir. publicity Miss Oshkosh Pageant, 1974. Mem. Am. Women in Radio and TV, Ark. Advt. Fedn. (dir. 1979—), Am. Bus. Women's Assn. (sec. Triangle '64 chpt. 1975-77). Roman Catholic. Club: Toastmasters (lt. gov. Western div. Dist. 43 1979—, outstanding toastmaster of yr. in dist. 1978, pres. Met. club 1979—). Office: Sta KARN Snider Corp 4021 W 8th St Little Rock AR 72204

MERRILL, GUDRUN WALLGREN, social worker; b. Gothenburg, Sweden, Oct. 31, 1923; came to U.S., 1962; d. Arvid Johan and Elsa Maria (Carlborn) Wallgren; grad. Flicklaroverket Gothenburg, 1943, Sch. for Social Work, Stockholm, 1947, Smith Coll. Sch. Social Work, 1949; M.A., Sch. Social Service Adminstrn. U. Chgo., 1958; postgrad. Vanderbilt U., 1962; m. Joseph M. Merrill, Sept. 16, 1962; children—Maria, Caroline. Child psychiat. social worker Pediatric Clinic Karolinska Sjukhuset, Stockholm, Sweden, 1953-62; instr. Sch. Social Work Stockholm, 1956-60; case worker Family Service Agency, Nashville, 1963-64; vol. social worker psychiat. dept. Harris County Hosp. Dist., Houston, 1978—. Evaluation com. United Way, Houston; mem. sch. com. Alfred C. Glassell, Jr. Sch. Art, Mus. Fine Arts, Houston, 1976—; sec. Tex.-Swedish Cultural Found., 1978—, Linneas of Tex., 1974—. Sweden-Am. Found. scholar, 1957; recipient King Carl XVI gold medal, 1979. Mem. Nat. Assn. Social Workers. Home: 2234 Inwood St Houston TX 77019

MERRILL, MAURICE HITCHCOCK, lawyer; b. Washington, Oct. 3, 1897; s. George Waite and Mary Lavinia (Hitchcock) M.; B.A., U. Okla., 1919, LL.B., 1922; S.J.D., Harvard U., 1925; L.H.D. (hon.), Okla. Christian Coll., 1974; m. Orpha Annita Roberts, June 4, 1922; 1 dau., Jean. Instr. govt. U. Okla., 1919-22; admitted to Okla. bar, 1922; mem. firm Mason & Honnold, Tulsa, 1922-26; asso. prof. law U. Idaho, 1925-26; asst. prof. law U. Nebr., 1926-28, prof., 1928-36; prof. law U. Okla., Norman, 1936-52, acting dean, 1945-46, research prof. law, 1952-68; individual practice law, Norman, 1968—; gen. counsel Okla. Assn. Mcpl. Attys., 1971—; spl. justice Supreme Ct. Okla., 1965-68. Served with U.S. Army, 1918. Mem. Am. Bar Assn., Fed. Bar Assn., Okla. Bar Assn., Cleveland County Bar Assn. (pres. 1964-65), Nat. Acad. Arbitrators. Democrat. Methodist. Author: Law of Notice, 1952; Cases and Materials on Administrative Law, 1953; The Public's Concern with Fuel Minerals, 1960, others; contbr. articles in field to profl. jours. Home: 800 Elm Ave Norman OK 73069 Office: 300 W Timberdell Rd Norman OK 73019

MERRILL, SAMUEL JOHN, obstetrician, gynecologist; b. Brownsville, Tex., Apr. 3, 1917; s. John and Eudosia Merrill; A.A., Brownsville Jr. Coll., 1936; B.S., Tex. Coll. A&I, 1938; B.A., U. Tex., Austin, 1939; M.D., U. Tex., Galveston, 1942; m. Bernice Lucille Hassler, Jan. 23, 1944; children—Samuel Albert, Phyllis Ann Merrill Fontanela. Intern, Santa Rosa Hosp., San Antonio, 1942-43; gen. practice medicine, Brownsville, 1946-51; resident in ob-gyn U. Tex. Postgrad. Med. Div., Houston, 1951-54; resident in gynecol. oncology M.D. Anderson Hosp. and Inst. Cancer Research, Houston, 1953-54; practice medicine specializing in ob-gyn, Brownsville, 1954—; mem. staff Dolly Vinsant Meml. Hosp., San Benito, Tex., 1946—, Valley Bapt. Med. Center, 1946—; mem. staff Brownsville Med. Center, 1946—, chief ob-gyn, 1954-61, pres. staff, 1964-65; mem. staff Valley Community Hosp., Brownsville, 1976—, chief ob-gyn, 1977-78, chief staff, 1978-79, bd. dirs., 1978-80. Pres., Brownsville PTA, 1958-59. Served to capt., M.C., U.S. Army, 1944-46. Diplomate Am. Bd. Ob-Gyn. Fellow A.C.S., Royal Soc. Medicine. Club: Kiwanis (pres. 1963-64) (Brownsville). Home: 3400 Old Alice Rd Brownsville TX 78520 Office: 1134 Los Ebanos Blvd Brownsville TX 78520

MERRIMAN, FRANK ALLEN, telephone co. ofcl.; b. El Paso, Tex., May 12, 1948; s. LeGrand and Helen Elizabeth (Small) M.; B.A. in Journalism, U. Tex., El Paso, 1973, M.A. in English, 1978; m. Susan Gayle Foster, Jan. 12, 1974. Mng. editor, editorial asst. El Burro Mag., U. Tex., El Paso, 1971-72; editor The Prospector, U. Tex., El Paso, 1972-73; wire editor, Sunday city editor, reporter El Paso Times, 1973-74; communications mgr., editor El Paso Today, El Paso C. of C., 1974-78; public relations rep. Mountain Bell Telephone Co., El Paso, 1978—. Served with AUS, 1967-70. Recipient Am. Legion award of merit, 1974, Press Club award for mag. writing 1976. Mem. Pub. Relations Soc. Am. (past pres. Rio Grande chpt.), Tex. Public Relations Assn., Sigma Delta Chi. Home: 210 Rio Tinto Dr El Paso TX 79912 Office: 500 Texas Ave El Paso TX 79901

MERRITT, BORDER RAY, mfg. co. exec.; b. Martha, Okla., Apr. 29, 1931; s. Border and Nola Ann (Coleman) M.; B.B.A., Okla. U., 1953, M.B.A., 1956; m. Crystal LaVeta Carpenter, Sept. 4, 1954; children—David Ray, DeAnn Michelle. Supr. mfg. transistors and diodes Tex. Instruments, Inc., Dallas, 1956-58; indsl. engr. dept. head Western Electric Inc., Oklahoma City, 1964—; pres. Merritt Properties, Inc., Bethany, Hollis and Yukon, Okla., 1964—. Served to 1st lt. USAF, 1954-56. Mem. Soc. Advancement Mgmt. Methodist. Clubs: Downtown Rotary (Oklahoma City), Masons. Home: 1000 Montreal St Yukon OK 73099 Office: 7725 W Reno St Oklahoma City OK 73127

MERRITT, CATHERINE WOZNY, guidance counselor; b. Trenton, N.J., May 30, 1949; d. Alexander Alphonse and Catherine Teresa (Miska) Wozny; B.A., Eastern Ky. U., 1971, M.A., 1972; m. Chelsea Claud Merritt, Oct. 7, 1972; children—Joseph Andrew, Hilary West. Tchr. Palatka (Fla.) Middle Sch., 1972-73; guidance counselor Crescent City (Fla.) Jr.-Sr. High Sch., 1973-74, guidance dir., 1974-77; guidance dir. Palatka (Fla.) High Sch., 1977—. Mem. Am., Fla. personnel and guidance assns., Tri-County Guidance Assn. (pres.), Am. Sch. Counselor Assn., Fla. Sch. Counselor Assn. Republican. Roman Catholic. Home: PO Box 1595 Palatka FL 32077 Office: Palatka High Sch Palatka FL 32077

MERRITT, GARRY ALLAN, ednl. adminstr.; b. Jacksonville, Fla., Oct. 13, 1950; s. Carlin Henry S. and Audrey Alfreda (Washington) M.; B.A., Morgan State U., 1972; postgrad. U. Pitts., 1972-73. Community organizer, Pine Forest Community Sch., Jacksonville, 1974, community sch. coordinator, 1974-75; asst. prin. for community edn. Brentwood Elementary Community Sch., Jacksonville, 1975—; mem. Fla. Gov's. Com. Employment Handicapped, 1977-80; pres. S. Side Neighborhood Advisory Council, Jacksonville, 1974. Mem. Brentwood Local Sch. Adv. Council; chmn. bd. opn. R.E.S.P.E.C.T., 1977; vice chmn. Brentwood Policy Council, 1976-77; bd. dirs. Jacksonville Urban League, 1976-80, Preservation Assn. Tree Hill, Vol. Jacksonville; mem. Leadership Jacksonville '79 Class Alumni. Mem. Duval Assn. Community Edn., Fla. Assn. Community Edn. Democrat. Mem. Holiness Hope Chapel. Clubs: Civitan. Home: 7200 Powers Ave # 8 Jacksonville FL 32217 Office: 3750 Springfield Blvd Jacksonville FL 32206

MERRITT, GEORGE WILLIAM, clergyman; b. Sewanee, Tenn., Aug. 17, 1944; s. James Forest and Mary Louise (Green) M.; student David Lipscomb Coll., 1962-63; m. Wanda Fay Gonce, Sept. 6, 1964; children—Laura Kay, Diana Fay, Maria Gay, Franklin Brown. Ordained to minisitry, Ch. of Christ, 1962; minister chs., Elberton, Ga., 1964-65, Huntland, Tenn., 1965-68, Kimball, Tenn., 1968-74, College Ave. Ch., Enterprise, Ala., 1974—; radio announcer Sta. WCDT, Winchester, Tenn., 1962, 66, Sta. WHAL, Shelbyville, Tenn., 1964, Sta. WBMC, McMinnville, Tenn., 1964; news dir. WZYX, Cowan, Tenn., 1967-70; news editor S. Pittsburg (Tenn.) Hustler Newspaper, 1971-74; daily radio broadcaster, 1970—, TV panelist, 1975. Pres., Franklin County (Tenn.) Volunteer 4-H Leaders Assn., 1967-68; adv. bd. Franklin County Dept. Welfare, 1966-68, Marion County Speech and Hearing Clinic, 1972-74, Marion County Jail Bldg. com., 1973; chmn. E. Coffee County (Ala.) A.R.C. blood program, 1974-76; steering com. E. Coffee County Concerned Citizens for Law and Morality, 1977—; pres. Coppinville Jr. High Sch. PTA, Enterprise, Ala., 1977-78, 79-80; bd. dirs. A.R.C., Ala., 1974—. Recipient Am. Legion Oratorical award, 1962, Nat. 4-H Club award 1962, Four Sq. award, 1962. award AP, 1969, Tenn. Press Assn., 1972, Ala. Press Assn., 1975; award Freedoms Found., 1979; named Enterprise Outstanding Young Religious Leader, 1977. Author: Truth for Today, 1976; weekly newspaper columnist; contbr. articles to profl. jours. Home: 204 Martin St Enterprise AL 36330 Office: PO Box 893 Enterprise AL 36330

MERRITT, HENRY NEYRON, psychotherapist; b. Darlington, S.C., Nov. 9, 1919; s. Henry O. and Lillian (Parrott) M.; B.S., Clemson (S.C.) U., 1941; M.D., Kansas City U., 1944; M.Ed., U. S.C., 1953; Ph.D., Philathea Coll., London, Ont., Can., 1969; D.Sc. (hon.), Western States Coll., Portland, Oreg., 1955; m. Bess Castles, Aug. 15, 1953; children—Henry Neyron, Jo Ann Merritt Jordan. Intern, Gen. Hosp., Columbia, S.C., 1945; resident U.S. Naval Hosp., Jacksonville, Fla.; gen. practice medicine, Columbia, 1958; mem. faculty Frostburg (Md.) State Coll., 1968, Va. Poly. Inst. and State U., 1969; prof., chmn. health U. Wis., La Crosse, 1972; dir. therapy Naval Drug Rehab. Center, 1976; dir. Psychotherapy and Hypnotherapy Clinic, Jacksonville, Fla., 1976—. Fellow AAAS, Am. Orthopsychiat. Assn.; mem. Internat. Soc. Profl. Hypnosis (pres. 1979), Blue Key, Sigma Zeta, Beta Beta Beta. Republican. Mem. Unit Ch. Club: Masons (32 deg.). Home: 6039 Longchamp St Jacksonville FL 32210 Office: 6037 Longchamp St Jacksonville FL 32210

MERRITT, LUCIAN GERALD, instrument mfg. co. exec.; b. Waco, Tex., Aug. 8, 1936; s. Lucian Henry and Hester Novel (Perdue) M.; B.B.A., Baylor U., 1958, M.S., 1960; postgrad. St. Mary's U., 1960-62; m. Tommie Pierce, Dec. 22, 1956; 1 dau., Lezli Diane. Mgr. div. purchasing, space and information systems div. N.Am. Aviation, Inc., Downey, Calif., 1962-67; dir. material services Tracor, Inc., Austin, Tex., 1967-71, dir. mfg. ops., 1971-79, v.p. ops., 1979—; dir. Merritt, Inc. Past pres. Austin Gideon Camp; past bd. dirs. Campus Crusade for Christ. Served from 2d lt. to 1st lt. USAF, 1959-62; capt. Res. Mem. Am. Mgmt. Assn., Nat. Purchasing Mgmt. Assn., Gideons, Order of Artus, Alpha Chi. Home: 98 Wallis St Austin TX 78746 Office: 6500 Tracor Ln Austin TX 78721

MERRIWETHER, JAMES LEWIS, counselor, clergyman; b. Atmore, Ala., Feb. 28, 1914; s. Jacob and Claudia V. (Robinson) M.; B.S. in Agrl. Adminstrn., Auburn U., 1939; M. Div., New Orleans Bapt. Theol. Sem., 1964, M.R.E., 1966; M.S., U. So. Miss., 1971; Ed.D., Luther Rice Sem., 1974; m. Olivia Beatrice Verell, May 29, 1938; children—James Lewis, Claudia Leola, Charles E., Thomas E., David E. County farm supr. Farm Security Adminstrn., Butler and Cullman counties, Ala., 1939-42; propr., mgr. J. Merriwether Livestock, Wagons, Atmore, Ala., 1943-47; farmer, Escambia County, Ala., 1943-58; tractor dealer Merriwether Truck and Tractor Co., Atmore, 1948-58; ordained to ministry So. Baptist Ch., 1958; pastor various So. Bapt. churches in Atmore area, 1958-68; pastor Pleasant View Bapt. Ch., Mobile, Ala., 1968-75; asso. pastor, children's minister, counseling and guidance cons. Manor Bapt. Ch., Mobile, 1976-79; ret., 1979; now guest minister, pastoral counselor; guest speaker various schs. and radio and TV programs, Ala., 1958-79; pastor Home Mission Bd., So. Bapt. Conv., 1961-65; chaplain psychiat. ward Mobile Gen. Hosp., 1973-74. Mem. Mobile Bapt. Assn. (mem. exec. com. 1976-78), Am. Personnel and Guidance Assn., Assn. for Clin. Pastoral Edn., Internat. Assn. of Counseling Services, Am. Mental Health Counselor Assn. Club: Masons. Author: In Quest for Abundant Living, 1977. Home: 406 S Pensacola Ave Atmore AL 36502 Office: 102 S Trammell St Atmore AL 36502

MERRYMAN, ROBERT MILES, social worker; b. Lynchburg, Va., Aug. 23, 1945; s. Emory Hughes and Audrey Elizabeth (Mattox) M.; B.A. in Psychology, Randolph-Macon Coll., 1967; M.S.W., Va. Commonwealth U., 1975; m. Karen Elizabeth Hannell, Mar. 27, 1967; children—Robert Hughes, Christine Elizabeth, Sarah Jo-Anna. Dir. social services Lynchburg (Va.) Tng. Sch., 1971-75, chief adv. Lynchburg Tng. Sch. and Hosp., 1976—; mem. Central Va. Spl. Residences Bd.; asso. faculty Central Va. Community Coll. Chmn. Toys for Tots campaign Friends of Amherst County Library; advisor Blue Ridge Council Boy Scouts Am.; instr. Central Va. Alcohol Safety Action Program. Served with USMC, 1967-71; maj. Res. Recipient outstanding young man of year award, Jaycees, 1973. Mem. Am. Assn. on Mental Deficiency, Acad. Cert. Social Workers, Nat. Assn. Retarded Citizens, Marine Corps Res. Officers Assn. Democrat. Methodist. Club: Coastal Canoeist. Guest lectr. Central Va. Criminal Justice Center; author handbook on rights of mentally retarded, 1977. Home: Box 103X1 Route 1 Rustburg VA 24588 Office: Lynchburg Training School and Hospital Box 1098 Lynchburg VA 24505

MERS, LARRY BUSTER, educator; b. Corpus Christi, Tex., May 11, 1940; s. Kenneth F. and Sara V. (Hill) M.; B.A., U. Corpus Christi, 1962; M.A., Tex. A. and I. U., 1969; postgrad. U. Houston, 1977-78, Sam Houston State U., 1975-76. Tchr., Flour Bluff Schs., 1961-63, Corpus Christi Schs., 1963-69; English coordinator Cy-Fair Schs., Houston, 1970-73; instr. High Sch. for Performing and Visual Arts, Houston Schs., 1973-74; English prof., chmn. arts programs Houston Community Coll., 1974—; owner That Cleaning Co., Inc. Singer, Houston Grand Opera, 1970-79, corp. sales dir., 1977-78. Named Outstanding Tchr. of Year, Cy-Fair Schs., 1973; NDEA grantee, 1965-66. Mem. AAUP, Nat. Council Tchrs. English, Tex. Jr. Coll. Tchrs. Assn., Smithsonian Instn. Democrat. Methodist. Home: 12318 Huntington Venture Dr Houston TX 77099 Office: 320 Jackson Hill Houston TX 77007

MERS, ROY WILLIAM, real estate exec.; b. Carthage, Mo., Jan. 1, 1947; s. Hugh A. and Martha M.; student Franklin and Marshall Coll., 1965-66, So. Meth. U., 1966-72; m. Mary Stewart Hooton, May 23, 1970; 1 son, Roy William. Vice pres. Magnolia Co., Dallas, 1970-72, Hooton & Assos., Dallas, 1972-77; v.p. Robert A. McNeil Corp., Dallas and San Mateo, 1977—. Mem. Dallas Apt. Assn., Tex. Apt. Assn., Nat. Assn. Home Builders, Real Estate Securities Syndication Inst. Methodist. Club: Bent Tree Country. Home: 3324 Southwestern Dallas TX 75225 Office: 13601 Preston Rd Dallas TX 75240

MERTZ, MICHAEL FREDERICK, JR., real estate broker, appraiser; b. Weston, W.Va., May 17, 1931; s. Michael Frederick and Bridget Elizabeth (Mullady) M.; B.S., W.Va. U., 1955, postgrad., 1965; grad. U.S. Army Armor Officers Sch., 1956; postgrad. Rider Coll., 1970, U. Va., 1970; grad. Realtor Inst., Parkersburg Community Coll., 1975; m. Norma Janet Talbott, June 11, 1955; children—Michael, Frank, Gregory, Barbara, Mary Ann; m. 2d, Elizabeth Amy Pierce, Nov. 27, 1970; 1 son, Thomas. Land, coal, oil and gas appraiser, 1957-68, 72—; land agt. Bitner Fuel Co., Uniontown, Pa. 1957-60; comml. farm owner-operator, Jane Lew, W.Va., 1960-68; right of way agt. Ford, Bacon & Davis Constrn. Corp., Monroe, La., 1968-69, 72-73, Coates Field Service, Oklahoma City, 1969-70; appraiser, salesman Joseph H. Martin Appraisal & Real Estate Co., Trenton, N.J., 1970-72; real estate broker, Weston and Bridgeport, W.Va., 1972—; pres. Mertz Land Co., Inc., Weston, 1972—. With Mertz Sch. Real Estate, 1974-79; real estate counselor, 1974—. Mem. Am. Right of Way Assn. (sr. designation), Nat. Assn. Ind. Fee Appraisers (state pres. 1972-73; Ind. Fee Appraisers (sr. designation), Clarksburg Bd. Realtors (pres. 1976), W.Va. Assn. Realtors (dir. 1976-78), Weston Bd. Realtors (Realtor of Yr. 1977; pres. 1977-80), Realtors Nat. Mktg. Inst., Nat. Assn. Realtors. Address: 236 E First St Weston WV 26452

MERZWEILER, ROBERT GLEN, accountant; b. Akron, Ohio, Oct. 13, 1953; s. Leo A. and Ruth G. (Glendenning) M.; B.A., Wittenberg U., Springfield, Ohio, 1976; student European-Am. Study Center, Basel, Switzerland, 1974-75; m. Vicki A. Lombardo, Aug. 7, 1976. With Price Waterhouse & Co., C.P.A.'s, 1976—, sr. accountant, Tampa, Fla., 1979—. C.P.A., Fla. Mem. Am. Inst. C.P.A.'s, Fla. Inst. C.P.A.'s, Lambda Chi Alpha. Office: 2800 First Nat Fla Tower Tampa FL 33601

MESIC, HARRY RANDOLPH, med. technologist; b. Newport News, Va., Dec. 30, 1935; s. Harry Underwood and Evelyn Mae (Hamaker) M.; B.S., U. Richmond, 1959; m. Harriet Lee Bey, Mar. 18, 1956; children—Catherine, Daniel. Chemist, A.H. Robins Co., Richmond, Va., 1960-63; med. technologist, chemist Med. Coll. Va., Richmond, 1963-66; med. technologist Vets Hosp., Charleston, S.C., 1966-74; med. technologist, instr. VA Hosp., Charleston, 1974—; instr. allied health Med. U. S.C., 1970—; clin. instr. allied health Trident Tech. Coll., 1970—; missionary to Puerto Cabasis, Nicaragua, 1974; CPR instr. ARC and Heart Assn., 1977—, Palmetto Low Country Health Systems Agy., 1978—. Sr. adviser Girl Scouts, 1975—, chmn. Assn. VI Carolina Low Country Girl Scouts, 1975-79, bd. dirs., 1975-79; packmaster Coastal Carolina council Boy Scouts Am., 1970-74, Webelo leader, 1973-74. Served with USMC, 1959-60. Mem. Am. Soc. Clin. Pathologists, Internat. Platform Assn. Mem. New Life Ministry Ch. (tchr, deacon). Home: 3103 Hartnett Blvd Isle of Palms SC 29451 Office: 109 Bee St Charleston SC 29403

MESSENGER, STEVE, accountant; b. Friona, Tex., Sept. 24, 1923; s. George C. and Ruth (Kirk) M.; B.B.A., West Tex. State U., 1953; m. Narcia Evelyn Finney, July 18, 1954; children—Michael Brent, Jay Corwin, Troy Wayne. Self-employed accountant Steve Messenger & Co. Mem. Amarillo Area Estate Planning Council, 1966—, treas., 1974-75; chmn. Amarillo Agri-Bus. Com., 1976-78; mem. Fine Arts Council; treas. Tex. Panhandle chpt. Multiple Sclerosis Soc., 1976-79; bd. dirs. Greater S.W. Music Festival, 1973—, pres., 1975-78; mem. council Tex. Panhandle Library System, 1973-79, vice chmn., 1975-77. Recipient Golden Rule award United Fund. C.P.A. Mem. Am. Inst. C.P.A.'s, Tex. (state dir. 1971-75), Panhandle (chmn. pub. affairs com. 1977—) socs. C.P.A.'s, Amarillo C. of C. (dir. 1977), West Tex. C. of C. Baptist. Mason, Lion (pres. Hi-Plains Eye Bank 1969-70; dep. dist. gov. 1974-75). Home: 107 Palomino St Amarillo TX 79106 Office: 709 W 10th St Amarillo TX 79101

MESSER, RICHARD JAMES, automotive parts co. ofcl.; b. Pitts., May 4, 1944; s. Elmer Sykes and Jane Elizabeth (Cleaver) M.; B.S., Okla. State U., 1966; M.B.A., Mich. State U., 1968; m. Carol F. O'Reilly, Sept. 9, 1967; 1 dau., Erin Shawn. Sect. chief Western Electric Co., 1968-70; personnel asst. Williams Pipeline Co., 1970-72; mgr. central personnel services Williams Cos., Tulsa, 1972-74, personnel mgr., 1974; dir. personnel adminstrn. Agrico Chem. Co., Tulsa, 1974-80; mgr. employee relations Maremont Corp., Nashville, 1980—. Chmn., Children's Med. Center; v.p. Cedar Creek Homeowners Assn.; elder Covenant Presbyn. Ch. Accredited personnel mgr. Mem. Am. Soc. Personnel Adminstrn. (regional v.p., dist. dir. 1977-78), S.W. Pension Conf. (dir.), Tulsa Personnel Assn. (pres. 1974-75), Am. Compensation Assn., Pi Kappa Alpha. Republican. Clubs: Oil Capital Toastmasters (pres. 1973), Nicholas (Tulsa). Home: 3430 E 67th St Tulsa OK 74136 Office: 1283 Murfreesboro Rd Nashville TN 37217

MESSIAH, SONCERIA VON, newspaper exec., TV talk; b. Baytown, Tex., Nov. 24, 1953; d. Clyde Joseph and Olivia Mertice (Alfred) M.; B.A. in Polit. Sci., U. Houston. Public relations asst. Creative Concepts, Houston, 1974-75; asst. news dir., reporter Sta. KYOK, Houston, 1975-76; television hostess Sta. KHOU-TV, Houston, 1976-78; sales rep. Forward Times Newspaper, Houston, 1976; TV hostess Sta. KRIV-TV, Houston, 1978—; account exec. Houston Chronicle Newspaper, 1976—; pres. bd. dirs. S-Von Enterprises, Inc. Mem. Harris County Council of Orgns.; mem. Black Leadership Coalition. Mem. Nat. Assn. Market Developers (chpt. award 1979), Black Communicators Assn., Black Coalition for Media Access, NAACP, Houston Citizen C. of C. Roman Catholic. Home: 7624 Richard Baytown TX 77521 Office: 801 Texas Ave Houston TX 77002

MESSICK, WILLIAM JOHN, priest, educator; b. Phila., July 31, 1944; s. William John and Catherine (Olish) M.: A.B., Catholic U. Am., 1968; M.A., Niagara U., 1970, St. Charles Sem., Phila., 1976; Ph.D., U. Md., 1978. Ordained priest Roman Cath. Ch., 1971; tchr. Northeast Cath. High Sch., Phila., 1963-65; counselor, campus minister Georgetown U., 1969-72; dir. pupil personnel services Salesianum Sch., Wilmington, Del., 1974-77; prin. St. Joseph Central Cath. High Sch., Huntington, W.Va., 1977—. Gen. Electric Co. fellow, 1975. Mem. Am. Personnel and Guidance Assn. (dir. 1978—, chmn. public relations com. 1979-80), Assn. Religious and Value Issues in Counseling (treas. and dir. 1975-77, Senator 1977-78, profl. sers. award 1977), Nat. Cath. Edn. Assn. (regional adv. bd. 1978—), Am. Sch. Counselors Assn., Assn. Measurement and Evaluation in Guidance. Democrat. Home: 1216 6th Ave Huntington WV 25701 Office: 600 13th St Huntington WV 25701

MESSINA, JAMES JOHN, mental health adminstr.; b. Niagara Falls, N.Y., Mar. 6, 1945; s. Paul Salvatore and Gilda Marie (Ruffalo) M.; B.A., Cath. U. Am., 1968; Ed.M., SUNY, Buffalo, 1970, Ph.D. in Counseling Psychology, 1973; postgrad. U. Fla., 1974; m. Constance Mayme Giovino, Aug. 4, 1973; children—Melissa Messina, Steven. Instr., counselor Bishop Timon High Sch., Buffalo, N.Y., 1969; sch. counselor Hamburg (N.Y.) Jr. High Sch., 1970-72; head resident Dormitory Authority, SUNY, Buffalo, 1973, grad. asst., 1973; instr. dept. counselor edn. U. Fla., Gainesville, 1974; dir. preventive edn. services Child Devel. Center, Pensacola, Fla., 1974-77; adj. prof. dept. psychology U. West Fla., Pensacola, 1976; faculty counseling dept. Johns Hopkins U., also dir. Evening Coll., Columbia (Md.) Center, 1977-78; project dir., asso. prof. Fla. Mental Health Inst., Tampa, 1978—; cons. Pensacola Edn. Program, 1975-77, nat. office Headstart Mental Health Program, 1977-78; profl. adviser to Childbirth Edn. Assn. NW Fla., 1974-77. Bd. dirs. Mental Health Assn. Escambia County, 1974-77. Mem. Am. Personnel and Guidance Assn. (dir. 1978—), Am. Psychol. Assn., Am. Mental Health Counselors Assn. (dir. 1976—, pres.-elect). Home: 10700 62d St Temple Terrace FL 33617 Office: Fla Mental Health Inst 13301 N 30th St Tampa FL 33612

MESSMORE, PETER BURL, educator; b. Perrysburg, Ind., Apr. 5, 1940; s. Kenneth Eugene and Dorothy Noreen (Brown) M.; B.S., Ind. U., 1966, M.S. in Elem. Edn., 1967; Ed.D. in Reading and Ednl. Psychology (NDEA grantee), Ball State U., 1971; m. Nancy Sue Childers, Aug. 9, 1959; children—Jeffrey, Peter, Scott. Elem. classroom tchr., Kokomo, Ind., 1966-71; prof. reading edn. Fla. Atlantic U., Boca Raton, 1971—, asst. dean curriculum and instrn. Coll. Edn., 1977. Served with USAF, 1958-62. Mem. Nat. Reading Conf., Internat. Reading Assn., Fla. State Reading Council. Author: Letter Sounds All Around, 1976; Phonics Plus Program, 1980; contbr. articles to profl. jours. Home: 719 Pl Chateau Delray Beach FL 33445 Office: Fla Atlantic U Boca Raton FL 33432

MESTAS, GEORGE MARTIN, internist; b. Camaguey, Cuba, Sept. 14, 1951; came to U.S., 1961, naturalized, 1974; s. George William and Mercedes Consuelo (Flores) M.; student U. Kans., 1968-71; M.D., Baylor U., 1974; m. Cynthia Gabriel, Aug. 17, 1971; 1 dau., Nyssa Ann. Intern, Scott & White Hosp., Temple, Tex., 1974-75, resident, 1975-77; fellow in pulmonary disease U. Tex., Houston, 1977-78; practice medicine specializing in pulmonary internal medicine, Fort Myers, Fla., 1979—. Republican. Office: 3800 Evans St Fort Myers FL 33901

METCALF, VERNON, assn. exec.; b. Del Rio, Tenn., Apr. 16, 1932; s. Wesley Garren and Louise Elzora (Ellison) M.; B.S., Tenn. Poly. U., 1955; M.S. in Social Work, U. Tenn., 1966; m. Patty Jean Justice, July 9, 1960; children—Mark Vernon, Melissa Rhea. Cons., adminstr. Tenn. Services for Blind, Nashville, 1958-66; regional cons. for S.E., Am. Found. for Blind, 1966-68; dir. Spl. Services Center, U. Miss., 1968-76; asso. exec. dir. Ark. Enterprises for Blind, Little Rock, 1970-76; exec. dir. Fla. Assn. Workers for Blind, Inc., Miami, 1976—. Chmn. stewardship adminstrv. bd. Perrine Peters United Meth. Ch., Miami; commr. Advancement of Physically Handicapped of Dade County, Fla., 1977—. Served with U.S. Army, 1956-58; Res., 1967. Recipient citation Nat. Accreditation Council of Agencies Serving the Blind and Visually Handicapped; named Dade's Outstanding Rehab. Profl., 1978. Mem. Sunshine State Assn. Workers for Blind (pres. 1978-80), Nat. Assn. Social Workers, Acad. Cert. Social Workers. Democrat. Club: Lions. Mem. editorial bd. New Outlook, 1970-77. Home: 9000 SW 187th Terr Miami FL 33157 Office: 601 SW 8th Ave Miami FL 33130

METCALFE, ALBERT GALLATIN, JR., petroleum co. exec.; b. Greenville, Miss., Dec. 29, 1927; s. Albert Gallatin and Ruth (Reynolds) M.; B.S., Tex. A. and M. U., 1950; m. Catherine Lehnen, Apr. 7, 1951; children—Gail, Albert Gallatin III, Elizabeth. With Tidewater Oil Co., Kilgore, Tex., 1952-53, Conroe, Tex., 1954-57, Victoria, Tex., 1957-61; mgr. James G. Brown & Asso., Corpus Christi, Tex., 1961-63; with Tamarack Petroleum Co., Inc., Midland, Tex., 1963—, v.p. prodn., 1966—. Served to 1st lt. AUS, 1950-52. Named Boss of Yr., Midland Jr. C. of C., 1978; registered profl. engr., Tex. Clubs: Midland Petroleum, Midland Country. Home: 1603 Gulf St Midland TX 79701 Office: Midland Nat Bank Bldg Midland TX 79701

METHVEN, ROBERT JAMES, actuarial cons. co. exec.; b. Flint, Mich., July 4, 1940 s. Harold Ernest and Elizabeth Marie (Cartwright) M.; B.S. U. Mich., 1963; m. Rebecca Ballesta, Dec. 10, 1976; 1 son by former marriage, Robert Joseph. Actuary, Berkshire Life Ins. Co., 1963-64; cons. Wyatt Co., Miami, 1964-65, cons., mgr. Miami and Orlando offices, 1965-79, v.p., 1979—, also dir.; chmn. bd. Blessing-Methven, Inc., Miami, 1974-77. Elks scholar, 1958-59, Fredrick E. Loeb scholar, 1958-63, Regents Alumni scholar, 1958-63; enrolled actuary. Mem. Am. Acad. Actuaries, So. Pension Conf., Internat. Found. Employee Benefit Plans, Sigma Phi Epsilon. Episcopalian. Clubs: Calusa Country, PGA Nat. Golf. Home: 13230 N Calusa Club Dr Miami FL 33186 Office: Wyatt Co Suite 210 10689 N Kendall Dr Miami FL 33176

METTEE, MAURICE FERDINAND, biologist; b. Mobile, Ala., Apr. 28, 1943; s. Maurice Ferdinand and Vivian (Foster) M.; B.S., Spring Hill Coll., 1965; Ph.D., U. Ala., 1974; m. Evelyn Lucille Dunnam, Aug. 31, 1968; children—Meredith Lynn. Cons. biologist Dept. Def., 1974, U.S. Forest Service, 1975, U.S. Fish and Wildlife Service, 1975-78; chief environ. div. Ala. Geol. Survey, University, 1977—. NDEA fellow, 1969-72. Mem. Am. Fisheries Soc., Am. Soc. Ichthyologists and Herpetologists, Southeastern Fishes Council. Roman Catholic. Contbr. articles to profl. jours. Home: 1681 Northwood Lake Northport AL 35476 Office: Univ PO Drawer O University AL 35486

METTS, FREDERICK CHRISTOPHER, JR., educator; b. Branchville, S.C., Mar. 16, 1918; s. Frederick Christopher and Mildred (Garner) M.; B.S., Tex. Wesleyan Coll., 1945; Th.M., Southwestern Bapt. Theol. Sem., 1948; M.A., Tex. Christian U., 1948; M.Ed., U. Ga., 1969; m. Ethel Suzanne Carter, Aug. 30, 1947. Ordained to ministry So. Baptist Convention, 1946; pastor Little Bethel Bapt. Ch., Marion, S.C., 1949-54, Nichols (S.C.) Bapt. Ch., 1954-55, Springvale Bapt. Ch., Lugoff, S.C., 1955-60, Mt. Tabor Bapt. Ch., Anderson, S.C., 1960-62; dean of men, prof. Bible, Anderson (S.C.) Coll., 1962-65, prof. Bible, 1965—, faculty chmn., 1974-75; supply pastor numerous area Bapt. chs. Mem. AAUP. Club: Woodmen of World. Contbr. article to profl. jour. Home: 100 Northgate Dr Anderson SC 29621 Office: Anderson Coll 316 Boulevard Anderson SC 29621

METZ, DONALD PAUL, petroleum landman; b. Creston, Iowa, Apr. 28, 1931; s. Edward Ellery and Irene Honora (Colgan) M.; B.A., U. Iowa, 1952, LL.B., 1956; m. Carolyn Jane Taylor, Aug. 22, 1953; children—Michael G., Patrick T., Suzanne I. Contracts landman Cities Service Oil Co., Bartlesville, Okla., 1956-71, Tulsa, 1971-76; sr. landman Williams Exploration Co., Tulsa, 1976—. Mem. Iowa State Bar Assn., Am. Assn. Petroleum Landmen, Phi Delta Phi. Republican. Roman Catholic. Home: 3913 E 59th St Tulsa OK 74135 Office: PO Box 3102 Tulsa OK 74101

METZ, JOHN RICHARD, pharmacist, hosp. ofcl.; b. Washington, Dec. 21, 1937; s. John Jacob and Edith Virginia (Brown) M.; B.S., Med. Coll. Va., 1964; m. Hilda Theresa Golderos, June 13, 1964; 1 dau., Jennifer Lynne. Asst. mgr. Lloyd's Drug Store, Charlottesville, Va., 1964-67; dir. pharmacy services Martha Jefferson Hosp., Charlottesville, 1967—; clin. instr. pharmacy Med. Coll. Va., Richmond, 1973—. Bd. dirs. Va. Pharm. Ednl. and Research Found., 1977—; deacon 1st Presbyterian Ch., 1980—. Served with USAF, 1961-62. Recipient A.H. Robins Bowl of Hygeia award, 1975, Geigy Leadership award, 1977. Mem. Charlottesville-Albemarle Jaycees (life; dir. 1969-73), Va. Pharm. Assn., Am. Pharm. Assn., Va. Soc. Hosp. Pharmacists, Am. Soc. Hosp. Pharmacists, Am. Assn. Colls. Pharmacy, Va. Hosp. Assn., Nat. Guard Assn. Va., Nat. Guard Assn. of U.S. Club: Masons. Home: 106 Meadowbrook Ct Charlottesville

VA 22901 Office: Martha Jefferson Hosp 459 Locust Ave Charlottesville VA 22901

METZ, LEON CLAIRE, archivist, author; b. Parkersburg, W.Va., Nov. 6, 1930; s. Leon and Velma Mae (Balderson) M.; student U. Tex., 1949-69; children—Velma Marlene, Leon Samuel, Matthew Claire; m. 2d, Cheryl Lynn Schilling, June 12, 1970; 1 son, James David. Patrolman, El Paso Police Dept., 1953; deliveryman Prices Milk Co., El Paso, 1953; operator Standard Oil Co. Tex., El Paso, 1953-67; univ. archivist U. Tex., El Paso, 1967-72, library gift coordinator, 1973-79; exec. asst. to mayor City of El Paso, 1979—; cons. Suncountry Mag., El Paso, 1973-75; editor book page El Paso Times, 1974-79. Pres., Tex. Consortium for Microfilming Mexican Archives, 1970-74, El Paso County Hist. Soc., 1971-72, El Paso Council Arts and Humanities, 1973-74; mem. exec. bd. El Paso Zoo, 1973-76, Soc. S.W. Archivists, 1972-74; treas., 2d v.p. Heritage Found., El Paso, 1974-78, pres., 1978; active United Fund, El Paso, 1970—; v.p. Dowell P.T.A., El Paso, 1973, pres., 1975; chmn. Northeast El Paso Cancer Assn., 1975-76; pres. Mission Heritage Assn. El Paso, 1977-80. Served with USAF, 1948-52. Recipient El Paso C. of C. award, 1973. Mem. Western Writers Am. (v.p. 1978-79), Nat. Soc. Arts and Letters, Soc. Am. Archivists, Border Regional Library Assn. Clubs: Sheriff, Westerners Corral (El Paso). Author: John Selman: Texas Gunfighter (Tex. Writers Roundup prize), 1966; Dallas Stoudenmire: El Paso Marshal, 1969, reprinted, 1979; Pat Garrett: The Story of A Western Lawman (Border Regional Library award for biography), 1974; The Shooters, 1976; contbr. articles to revs. Home: 4513 Cupid Dr El Paso TX 79924

METZGER, PATRICIA ROURKE, speech pathologist; b. Columbia, S.C. Aug. 8, 1942; d. James Lataimer and Lou Emma (Miller) Rourke; B.A., Our Lady of the Lake Coll., 1964; H.A.T., Ind. U., 1968; postgrad. U. Fla., 1978—; m. James William Metzger, Oct. 3, 1970. Speech pathologist Northside Ind. Sch. Dist., San Antonio, Tex., 1964-67; chief speech pathology Munroe Meml. Hosp., Ocala, Fla., 1969-70; chief speech pathology Central Tex. Rehab. Center, Waco, Tex., 1971-77; speech pathologist Marion County Bd. Pub. Instruction, Ocala, 1977—, Marion Community Hosp., Ocala, 1978—; pvt. practice speech pathology, Marion County, Fla., 1977—. Recipient cert. of clin. competence Am. Speech and Hearing Assn. Mem. Daus. of Confederacy. Roman Catholic. Address: 4550 SE 8 St Ocala FL 32670

METZGER, SIDNEY M., bishop; b. Fredericksburg, Tex., July 11, 1902; s. Francis and Ida (Dietz) M.; student St. Mary's Sch., Fredericksburg, 1910-15, St. John's Sem., San Antonio, 1915-22; Th.D., North Am. Coll., Rome, Italy, 1925; Dr. Canon Law, Pontifical Inst. of Canon and Civil Law, Rome, 1928; LL.D., St. Edwards U., 1940. Ordained priest St. John Lateran Basilica, Rome, 1926; prof. St. John's Sem., San Antonio, 1928-33, rector, 1933-40; regent St. Mary's U. Law Sch., San Antonio, 1935-40; consecrated aux. bishop of Santa Fe (titular bishop of Birta), 1940; installed as coadjutor of El Paso, with the right of succession, 1942; succeeded to the See of El Paso, 1942, ret. as bishop, 1978; asst. to Papal Throne, 1965. Decorated Knight Comdr. Equestrian Order of Holy Sepulchre of Jerusalem; Grand Cross of King Alfonso X, The Wise (Spain). Doctor Mundunae Sapientiae of Boswell Soc., 1963; recipient St. Joseph the Worker award Tex. AFL-CIO; John Casey Labor Man of Year award Cath. Labor Inst.; award Amalgamated Clothing Workers Am., 1973. Address: 1200 N Mesa Ave El Paso TX 79902

MEXIC, SIMON, jeweler, realtor; b. New Orleans, Oct. 10, 1931; s. Perry and Rosina (Pulitzer) M.; B.A., Tulane U., 1953; m. Ann Rittenberg, July 17, 1955; children—Scott B., Ginja A. Sec., treas. Mexic Bros. Inc. (retail jewelers), New Orleans, 1953—, sec. A & R Capital; pres. 3 M Mortgage Co.; pres. Frenchmen's Creek Real Estate Devel.; partner Fontainbleau Hotel. Active Vols. of Am. Mem. New Orleans C. of C. Clubs: New Orleans Athletic, Mason, Shriner. Home: 5 Richmond Pl New Orleans LA 70115 Office: 940 Canal St New Orleans LA 70112

MEYBERG, WILLIAM BRAXTON, oil co. exec.; b. Richmond, Va., Mar. 11, 1933; s. L. Otto and Phoebe F. (Ward) M.; B.S. in Engring., Va. Poly. Inst. and State U., Blacksburg, 1954; m. Sara G. Bennett, May 6, 1961; children—James B., Mary B. Constrn. engr. R.F.&P. R.R., Richmond, 1954-59; with Cities Service Co., 1959—, automobile and plants mgr., Phila., 1969-72, transp. mgr., Tulsa, 1975-77, terminal facilities mgr., 1978—. Pres., Cities Service Richmond Fed. Credit Union, 1962-63; sec. Tulsa Cities Service Fed. Credit Union, 1979, pres., 1980; bd. dirs. Tulsa Human Services Agy., 1979—. Served with AUS, 1954-56. Registered profl. engr., Okla. Mem. Nat. Soc. Profl. Engrs. Club: Padre Island Country (Tulsa). Address: 3471 E 75th Pl Tulsa OK 74136

MEYER, FRANZ OSWALD, geologist; b. Rudolstadt, Germany, Apr. 10, 1945; came to U.S., 1953, naturalized, 1968; s. Oswald Franz and Josephine (Stoger) M.; B.A., SUNY, New Paltz, 1973; M.S., U. Mich., 1975, Ph.D., 1979; m. Jeannie Ham, Dec. 28, 1969 (dissolved 1978); 1 son, Peter Oswald. Research asst., N.Y. State Geol. Survey, summers 1971-72, also 1973; geologist Shell Oil Co., New Orleans, 1979—. Served with AUS, 1965-67; Vietnam. Recipient grants Geol. Soc. Am., Scott Turner Earth Sci. Fund, Rackham Found. Mem. Paleontol. Soc. Am., Soc. Econ. Paleontologists and Mineralogists, Ecol. Soc. N.Am., Sigma Xi. Home: 137 Defiance Dr Slidell LA 70456 Office: PO Box 60193 One Shell Sq New Orleans LA 70160

MEYER, GREGORY CHARLES, army officer, social worker; b. Phila., Oct. 6, 1937; s. Franklin B. and Mary R. (Rose) M.; A.B., Gannon Coll., 1959; M.S.W., Catholic U. Am., 1961, D.S.W., 1971; m. Gloria Jean Peterson, Dec. 28, 1963; children—Gregory, Christine, Melissa. Staff social worker Cath. Service League, Akron, Ohio, 1961-62; commd. 1st lt. Med. Service Corps, U.S. Army, 1962, advanced through grades to lt. col., 1976; asst. chief social work service DeWitt Hosp., Ft. Belvoir, Va., 1962-64; chief social work service 56th Gen. Hosp., Verdun, France, 1964-67; project officer computer support in mil. psychiatry Martin Hosp., Ft. Benning, Ga., 1971-73; staff officer Hdqrs. U.S. Army Tng. and Doctrine Command, Ft. Monroe, Va., 1973-76; student U.S. Army Command and Gen. Staff Coll., Ft. Leavenworth, Kans., 1976-77; asst. chief behavioral sci. div. Acad. Health Scis., Ft. Sam Houston, Tex., 1977—; cons. Bayberry Hosp., Hampton, Va., 1973-76. PTA program chmn. Ft. Sam Houston Ind. Sch. Dist., 1978—; mem. budget rev. com. United Way, Columbus, Ga., 1973; bd. dirs. Ft. Monroe Armed Forces YMCA, lay chmn., 1975. Mem. Acad. Cert. Social Workers, Nat. Assn. Social Workers, Assn. U.S. Army. Home: 559 Graham Rd Fort Sam Houston TX 78234 Office: Academy Health Sciences Fort Sam Houston TX

MEYER, HANK, pub. relations and publicity cons.; b. N.Y.C., Mar. 27, 1920; B.B.A., U. Miami; m. Lenore Mittlemark; 3 daus. Owner, operator pub. relations agy., 1946-49; pub. relations dir. City of Miami Beach, Fla., 1949-56; pres., Hank Meyer Assos., Inc., Miami, Fla. and N.Y.C., pub. relations, publicity cons., 1956—, also subs. public relations cons. Former mem. Fla. Council 100; mem. Orange Bowl Com.; founder, trustee U. Miami Symphony Club; former trustee Mt. Sinai Hosp.; hon. trustee Biscayne Coll.; founder, trustee U. Miami Symphony Club; former mem. exec. com. United Fund of Dade County; former mem. bd. govs. Dade Found.; mem. Com. 100, New World Center Action Com., NCCJ, Greater Miami Coalition; former Miami Beach chmn., Dade County chmn. Am. Cancer Soc.; former bd. dirs. Heart Assn. Greater Miami, Nat. Children's Cardiac Home, numerous other civic activities. Served as chief petty officer USNR, World War II. Recipient numerous awards latest including U. Miami First Alumnus of Year award, 1969, Silver medallion NCCJ, 1973; named to Fla. Pub. Relations Hall of Fame. Mem. Am. Municipal Pub. Relations Assn. (v.p. 1950), Govt. Pub. Relations Assn. (pres. 1956), Pub. Relations Soc. Am. (certificate of achievement; pres. Fla. 1958-59), Miami Beach (trustee), Fla., Greater Miami (gov.) chambers commerce, Fla. Pub. Relations Assn., Econ. Soc. S.Fla., Nat. Assn. Travel Orgns., Am. Legion, Omicron Delta Kappa, Sigma Delta Chi. Clubs: Pillars Variety. Address: 2990 Biscayne Blvd Miami FL 33137

MEYER, JACOB JOSEPH, lawyer; b. New Orleans, Dec. 28, 1930; s. Charles and Minnie (Pohl) M.; D.J. with honors, Tulane U., 1955; m. Maria Marguerite Schiro, Sept. 5, 1953; children—Diana R., David C., Paul R., Helen M. Admitted to La. bar, 1955, U.S. Supreme Ct. bar, 1971; partner firm Coleman, Dutrey, Thomson, Meyer & Jurisich, New Orleans, 1955—. Judge Moot Ct. Bd. Tulane U., 1953-55, participant Nat. Tulane Moot Ct. Competition, 1955. Mem. com. fund raising New Orleans Philharmonic Symphony Orch., 1974-75. Mem. Am. Judicature Soc., Am., La., New Orleans, Fed. bar assns., Young Audiences Inc., Lake Vista Property Owners Assn., C. of C. of Greater New Orleans (legis. com. to rev. La. legis. 1963). Home: 15 Wren St New Orleans LA 70124 Office: 321 St Charles Ave New Orleans LA 70130

MEYER, JOHN WILLIAM, drainage and flood control engr.; b. Bismarck, Mo., Sept. 20, 1898; s. George Frederick and Wilhelmina Rosine (Godau) M.; student engring. Internat. Corr. Schs., 1918-20; m. Hazel Fleeman Killian, June 1, 1960; children by previous marriage—Annetta, Severin Poirot. With U.S. Geol. Survey, Wis., 1915-17; resident engr. Drainage Dist. 17, Mississippi County (Ark.), 1918-28, chief engr., 1928-42, cons. engr., 1961-78; chief engr. Lee Wilson & Co., Wilson, Ark., 1942-51; cons. engr., Blytheville, Ark., 1951—. Chmn. Blytheville San. Sewer Commn., 1971—; exec. sec. Blytheville Planning Commn., 1958-67. Chmn. Mississippi County March of Dimes, 1943. Alderman, City of Blytheville, 1963-66. Served with U.S. Army, 1918. Recipient plaque appreciation Nat. Assn. Real Estate Bds., 1955; plaque U.S. C.E. Mississippi River Commn., 1974; Outstanding Civilian Service medal Dept. Army, 1977. Registered profl. engr., Ark. Life mem. Am. Soc. C.E.; mem. Nat. Soc. Profl. Engrs. Club: Blytheville Country (dir. 1966-68). Home: 1800 Country Club Rd Blytheville AR 72315 Office: PO Box 446 Blytheville AR 72315

MEYER, JULIEN H(ERMAN), surgeon, obstetrician, gynecologist; b. Enfield, N.C., May 7, 1914; s. Joseph and Hennye (Lehman); B.S., U. N.C., 1935; M.D., Med. Coll. Va., 1937; m. Dorothy Rose Kahn, July 14, 1940; children—Julien Herman, Carol Joan. Intern. Greater Balt. Med. Center, 1937-38; resident in obstetrics and gynecology St. Joseph's Hosp., Balt., 1938-40; postgrad, course gynecol. pathology Johns Hopkins Hosp., 1940; practice obstetrics and gynecology, Roanoke, Va., 1940—; attending obstetrician, gynecologist Roanoke Meml. Hosps., 1940—, chief obstetrics and gynecology, 1961-62; cons. gynecology VA Hosp., 1946—; attending obstetrician, gynecologist Community Hosp. of Roanoke Valley; attending gynecologist Roanoke Valley Psychiat. Center, 1975—. Fellow A.C.S., Am. Coll. Obstetricians and Gynecologists; mem. A.M.A., Med. Soc. Va., Va. Obstet. and Gynecol. Soc., Roanoke Acad. Medicine, So. Med. Assn., Roanoke Valley Assn. Obstetricians and Gynecologists (pres. 1965-66). Home: 4925 Crossbow Circle SW Roanoke VA 24014 Office: 2118 Rosalind Ave SW Roanoke VA 24014

MEYER, JULIUS FREDERICK, JR., counselor, univ. adminstr.; b. Buffalo, Feb. 1, 1951; s. Julius Frederick and Margaret Edna (Curry) M.; student Flagler Coll., 1972-73; B.A., SUNY at Brockport, 1975; M.A., U. North Fla., 1978; m. Donna Kay Wells, Jan. 12, 1974; 1 dau., Angelic Miranda. Grad. asst. U. North Fla., Jacksonville, 1977-78; counselor, dir. career counseling Fla. Jr. Coll., Jacksonville, 1978; counseling coordinator U. North Fla., Jacksonville, 1978—; counselor career and job-seeking with Sheldon Kaplan, Ph.D., Jacksonville, 1978—. Mem. Am. Personnel and Guidance Assn. Home: 28 Rhode Ave Saint Augustine FL 32084 Office: U N Fla 806 Riverside Ave Jacksonville FL 32204

MEYER, LAWRENCE JOSEPH, lawyer; b. Chgo., July 7, 1927; s. Joseph Benjamin and Sarah (Peilet) M.; student Roosevelt Coll., Chgo., 1948-50; LL.B., U. Miami, 1954; m. Jo Ann Lester, Nov. 6, 1976; children—Sandra Leigh, Janice Beth, Pamela Sue. Admitted to Fla. bar, 1955; individual practice law, Hollywood, Fla., 1955—; small claims judge Broward County, 1963-73. Past chmn. T-Y Park Bd. Broward County. Served with USNR, 1945-48. Mem. Am. Bar Assn., Fla. Bar Assn., Broward Bar Assn. (past mem. exec. com.), South Broward Bar Assn. (past dir.). Mason (Shriner). Home: 3520 N 30th Terr Hollywood FL 33021 Office: 2435 Hollywood Blvd Hollywood FL 33020

MEYER, MARDIS, pharmacist, hosp. ofcl.; b. Canal Point, Fla., Nov. 8, 1924; s. Cecil and Ella Boardman (Taylor) M.; B.S., U. Fla., 1948; m. June 10, 1955 (dec.); children—Melanie Louise, Michelle Laine, Melinda Lee. Asst chief pharmacist Jackson Meml. Hosp., Miami, 1949-53; chief pharmacist Broward Gen. Hosp., Ft. Lauderdale, 1953-58; profl. service rep. Abbott Labs., Jacksonville, Fla., 1958; owner, operator Brentwood Pharmacy Inc., Ft. Lauderdale, 1960-63; chief pharmacist N. Broward Hosp., Pompano Beach, Fla., 1962—. Mem. Fla. Soc. Hosp. Pharmacists (v.p. 1950-51), Broward County Pharm. Assn. (pres. 1965-66), Am. Pharm. Assn., Am. Soc. Hosp. Pharmacists, Fla. Pharm. Assn., E. Central Soc. Hosp. Pharmacists, U. Fla. Alumni Assn., Sigma Phi Epsilon. Democrat. Baptist. Home: 1516 SW 14th Ct Fort Lauderdale FL 33312 Office: N Broward Hosp 201 E Sample Rd Pompano Beach FL 33064

MEYER, NORMAN ISAAC, ophthalmologist; b. Monticello, N.Y., Sept. 10, 1944; s. Ralph and Janice (Cohen) M.; B.A., Cornell U., 1966; M.D., Downstate Med. Center, N.Y.C., 1970; m. Joyce Whitaker, Apr. 29, 1972; 1 son, Gregary Scot. Intern, Emory U., Atlanta, 1970-71, resident in medicine, 1973-74, in ophthalmology Med. Coll. Ga., 1974-77; practice medicine specializing in ophthalmology, Panama City, Fla., 1977—; mem. staff Gulf Coast Community Hosp., Bay Meml. Med. Center. French hornist Gulf Coast Community Coll. Orch. Served with USAF, 1971-73. So. Med. Assn. grantee, 1976. Diplomate Am. Bd. Ophthalmology. Mem. Am. Assn. Ophthalmology, Am. Soc. Contemporary Ophthalmology, Internat. Glaucoma Congress, Am. Acad. Ophthalmology, AMA, Tau Epsilon Phi. Republican. Jewish. Home: 313 W Baldwin Rd Panama City FL 32401 Office: 742 Harrison Ave Panama City FL 32405

MEYER, PAUL JAMES, knowledge/communication co. exec.; b. San Mateo, Calif., May 21, 1928; s. August Carl and Isabel (Rutherford) M.; Dr. Aviation Edn. (hon.), Embry-Riddle Aero. U., Daytona Beach, Fla.; L.H.D. (hon.), Ft. Lauderdale (Fla.) U.; m. Jane Gurley, Nov. 26, 1971; children—James, Larry, Bill, Janna, Leslie. Life ins. agt., Ga., Ala. and Fla., 1949-58; sales mgr. Word, Inc., Waco, Tex., 1958-60; founder, pres. SMI Internat., Inc., Waco, 1960—. Bd. dirs. Waco Boys Club, Nat. Republican Fin. Com., United Negro Coll. Fund, Boy Scouts Am., Waco-Baylor Found.; mem. devel. council Waco Hillcrest Hosp. Served with U.S. Army, 1946-48. Recipient Nat. Sales Leadership award Houston Sales Execs. Club, 1969, Man and Boy award Waco Boys Club, 1977, Americanism award Houston Jr. C. of C., 1970; named hon. v.p. Sales Exec. Club of So. Africa, 1970. Mem. Nat. Speakers Bur., Am. Mgmt. Assn., Internat. Franchise Assn., Waco C. of C. (dir.). Baptist. Author: Sales Manager's Motivation Program, 1966; Dynamics of Personal Motivation, 1968; Executive Motivation Program, 1968; Dynamics of Personal Leadership, 1969; How to Become Financially Independent, 1970; Dynamics of Creative Selling, 1971; Successful Real Estate Selling, 1971; Dynamics of Goal Setting, 1977; Executive Time Management, 1979; Dynamics of Personal Time Control, 1979; co-author: Skills for Dealing with People, 1980; Dynamics of Financial Independence, 1980. Office: 5000 Lakewood Dr Waco TX 76710

MEYER, WILLIS G(EORGE), petroleum geologist; b. Bellwood, Nebr., Jan. 21, 1906; s. George David and Ella V. (Carrigan) M.; A.B., U. Nebr., 1930; A.M., U. Cin., 1933, Ph.D., 1941; m. June Allison, June 26, 1937; children—Nancy Rebecca, Ann Marie. Geologist, Amerada Petroleum Corp., Tex. and Okla., 1934-38, DeGoyler & MacNaughton, Dallas, 1938-48; partner Meyer & Achtschin, Dallas, 1948-57; owner, mgr., cons. petroleum engring. and geology Willis G. Meyer (formerly Willis G. Meyer & Assos.), Dallas, 1957—. Fellow Geol. Soc. Am.; mem. Am. Assn. Petroleum Geologists (v.p. 1969-70), Am. Geophys. Union, AAAS, Soc. Ind. Profl. Earth Scientists (pres. 1966-67), Dallas Geol. Soc. (pres. 1947), Explorers Club, Acacia, Sigma Xi. Unitarian. Clubs: Engrs. of Dallas, Dallas Country, Dallas Petroleum. Contbr. articles on geology to profl. jours. Home: 4590 Rheims Pl Dallas TX 75205 Office: PO Box 7660 Inwood Sta Dallas TX 75209

MEYERS, ANNA BRENNER, lawyer; b. Lodz, Poland, Dec. 18, 1896; d. Joseph and Edith (Gutman) Brenner; came to U.S., 1900, naturalized, 1925; R.N., Bklyn. Jewish Hosp. Nurses Tng. Sch. 1918; student Tchrs. Coll., Columbia, 1920-22, N.Y. Sch. Social Work, 1923-24; LL.B., Bklyn. Law Sch., 1928; LL.D., Bethune-Cookman Coll., 1964, U. Miami, 1972; m. Benjamin Meyers, May 18, 1939 (dec. 1974). Tchr. elementary sch., Stepney, Conn., 1913-14; vis. nurse Henry Street Settlement, 1919-20; nat. dir. farm and rural program Nat. Council Jewish Women, 1922-29; social worker Crime Prevention Bur., N.Y.C. Police Dept., 1929-30; dir. social service Maimonides Hosp., Bklyn., 1924-26; dist. office adminstr. N.Y.C. Emergency Home Relief Bur., 1931-33; admitted to N.Y. State bar, 1934, Fla. bar, 1936, U.S. Supreme Ct. bar, 1941, ICC bar, 1942; practiced in N.Y.C., 1934-35, Miami, Fla., 1936—; social worker Fed. Emergency Relief Adminstrn., Miami, 1935; sec., dir. Miami Bottled Gas, Inc., 1936-60. Former mem. budget com. Community Chest of Dade County, Fla., United Fund; past pres. Jewish Family and Children's Service, Miami; nat. v.p. Am. Jewish Congress, 1958; mem. Dade County Sch. Bd., 1953-71; founder Miami-Dade Jr. Coll.; founder Miami pub. TV channel; founding mem. Miami Jewish Hosp. and Home for Aged; mem. Miami Beach Devel. Commn., 1965-67, Miami Beach Rent Control Commn., 1973; del. White House Conf. on Children, 1970, World Zionist Congress, Zurich, Switzerland, 1937. Trustee, Mt. Sinai Hosp., Miami Beach, 1973—, Miami Beach Pub. Library, 1961-75; past trustee Cedars of Lebanon Hosp.; past chmn. bd. trustees Miami Beach Art Center; past trustee, sec. bd. Greater Miami Jewish Fedn.; mem. bd. Welfare Planning Council. Recipient Outstanding Citizen of Dade County award, 1957; State of Israel medallion, Eleanor Roosevelt-Israel Humanitarian award, 1964, Tower of David award, Jerusalem Liberation award; Man of Year award U. Miami chpt. Delta Kappa, 1969, Abess Human Relations award Anti-Defamation League, 1971; Sch. Bell award Dade County Classroom Tchrs. Assn., 1971; award Greater Miami Jewish Fedn.; Anna Brenner Meyers Hall dedicated in her honor Miami-Dade Community Coll., 1977, also Anna Brenner Meyers Ednl. Telecommunications Center, UHF-TV sta. bldg., 1979, others. Mem. Nat. Assn. Women Lawyers (past treas.), Fla. Fedn. Bus. and Profl. Women's Clubs (past state legislation chmn.), Internat. (v.p., treas.), Fla. (organizer, 1st pres.) assns. women lawyers, Am. Judicature Soc., Phi Theta Kappa. Democrat. Jewish. Home: 5055 Collins Ave Miami Beach FL 33140 Office: PO Box 431157 South Miami FL 33143

MEYERS, GRANT ULYSSES, foundry co. exec.; b. Moline, Ill., May 1, 1913; s. George C. and Lillian (Rommel) M.; B.S.C., Northwestern U., 1933; M.B.A., U. Chgo., 1955; m. Doris M. Fraser, Jan. 23, 1953 (dec. July 1977); children—Stuart, Joan, Glen, Eric, Marcia. Mgr. accounting dept. Wis. Steel Works div. Internat. Harvester Co., Chgo., 1933-55; v.p., comptroller Radiant Mfg. Corp., Morton Grove, 1955-59; sec.-treas. Security-Columbian Banknote Co., N.Y.C., 1959-60, financial v.p., sec., 1960-65; owner, chmn., pres., chief exec. officer Oil City Iron Works, Inc., Corsicana, Tex., 1965—. Mem. Financial Execs. Inst., Nat. Assn. Accountants (internat. pres. 1969-70), Acacia, Beta Gamma Sigma, Beta Alpha Psi. Mason. Clubs: Metropolitan (N.Y.C.); Corsicana Country; Dallas Petroleum; Canyon Creek Country (Richardson, Tex.). Home: 2514 Big Horn Ln PO Box 725 Richardson TX 75080 Office: PO Drawer 1560 Corsicana TX 75110

MEYERS, JOHN HENRY, mech. engr.; b. Annapolis, Md., July 20, 1945; s. Wesley Wilkerson and Ruth Kathryn (Moretz) M.; student N.C. State U., 1963-67, 69-71; B.S., George Washington U., 1973; m. Jane Brooks Turner, Oct. 14, 1973. Engring. technician Naval Surface Weapons Center, Dahlgren Lab. (Va.), 1967-71, mech. engr., 1971—. Trustee, Hanover Ch. Parish, 1976—. Recipient Outstanding Performance award Naval Surface Weapons Center, 1976. Mem. Hist. Fredericksburg Found., Inc., Nat. Trust for Hist. Preservation, ASME, Am. Def. Preparedness Assn. Republican. Episcopalian. Clubs: Masons, Shriners. Home: 18 Farrell Ln Fredericksburg VA 22401 Office: Code DF-56 NSWC/DL Dahlgren VA 22448

MEYERS, MAE ESTELLE, civil engr.; b. Cameron, Tex., Nov. 26, 1908; d. E.L. and Sallie Mae (Hodges) Meyers; B.A., Rice U., 1930; M.A., U. Tex., Austin, 1933; postgrad. Temple U., 1938-40, Air Nav. Instr.'s Sch., USN, 1943, Art Students League, N.Y.C., 1946-49, Columbia Coll. Physicians and Surgeons, 1949-51. Art tchr. pub. schs., Dayton, Tex., 1934-39; advt. artist Mears Advt., N.Y.C., 1946-48; asst. to supr. engring. changes Chance Vought Aircraft Co., Dallas, 1953-56; designer engring., 1956-59; designer, engr. for paving city streets, Dallas, 1959-73, ret., 1973; occupational therapist VA Hosp., McKinney, Tex., 1951-52; pvt. sec. to Caroline Gordon, writer-in-residence U. Dallas, 1977—. Served to lt. USNR, 1943-46, ret. as lt. comdr., 1968. Named One of Top Ten Women in Bus., Am. Bus. Women's Assn., 1970. Mem. U.S. Naval Inst., Am. Bus. Women's Assn. (treas. Tercera chpt. 1969-70, corr. sec. 1977-78, pres. 1979-80), DAR (chpt. regent 1974-76, chpt. parliamentarian 1976—), Colonial Dames XVII Century (1st v.p. chpt. 1975-77, chpt. rec. sec. 1977-79), Magna Charta Dames (rec. sec. Dallas-Ft. Worth colony 1976-82), UDC (chpt. social chmn. 1976—). Roman Catholic. Painted altar pieces, 1935, 37, 39-42. Patentee nav. device. Home: 2038 Mather St Irving TX 75061

MEYERS, RONDELL GRANT, fin. co. exec.; b. Middlesboro, Ky., July 10, 1939; s. Hubert Kyle and Edith Gertrude (Loop) M.; student pub. schs., Tazewell, Tenn.; m. Janna Ruth Carter, Sept. 27, 1961; children—Ronda Lynn, Tonya Renee, Jacqueline Lee. Security clk. FBI, Washington, 1957-58; farmer, Claiborne County, Tenn., 1960-61; privilege tax agt. Tenn. State Revenue Dept., 1961-65; from warehouse mgr. to exec. Butcher Oil Co., Maynardville, Tenn., 1965-71; with So. Indsl. Banking Corp., Knoxville, Tenn., 1971—, pres., 1975—, chmn. bd., 1979—; cons. various banking and fin. orgns. Chmn. Union County Heart Fund, 1971; mem. Tenn. Manpower Service Council, 1975—; mem. Personnel Rev. Bd. for Mayor of Knoxville, 1976; chmn. Union County adv. com. for Gov. Ray Blanton, 1975—. Served with U.S. Army, 1958-60. Recipient Leadership award Union County Heart Fund, 1971; certificate of appreciation Gov. Tenn., 1975. Mem. Tenn. Consumer Fin. Assn. (dir.), Tenn. Manpower Service Council. Democrat. Baptist. Clubs: Jaycees, Elks. Home: Box 51 Route 2 Maynardville TN 37807 Office: 8419 Kingston Pike Knoxville TN 37919

MEYNARD, VIRGINIA DALE GURLEY (MRS. ERNEST BENNET MEYNARD), civic worker; b. Waco, Tex., Nov. 8, 1919; d. Davis Robert and Nell (Whitman) Gurley; B.A., Baylor U., 1941; m. Ernest Bennet Meynard, Dec. 19, 1942; children—Jennifer Nell, Ernest Bennet, Loulie Gurley Meynard Sprague. Reporter Waco (Tex.) News-Tribune, 1938-42, Dayton (Ohio) Herald, 1942-43; pub. relations dir. Vocational Rehab. Center Allegheny County, Pitts., 1966-70. Coordinator, Mid-West Conf. on Effects of Fgn. Aid, 1958; chmn. Citizens Consultations on S.E. Asia for Dayton Area, 1959; del. White House Conf. on Children and Youth, 1960; mem. Jr. com. Children's Hosp. Pitts., 1964-65; mem. agy. operations com. Community Chest Allegheny County, 1964; mem. Pitts. Com. on Employment for Handicapped, 1968-70; mem. Three Rivers Arts Festival Com., 1971-76, Vol. Action Center Adv. Com., 1972-75; mem. adv. com. Show House '76, Pitts.; docent Historic Columbia Found., 1976; docent Columbia Mus. Art, 1977—. Mem. Jr. League Columbia (S.C.), DAR. Presbyn. Republican. Home: 5866 Woodvine Rd Columbia SC 29206

MEYSTEDT, LUCILLE ETHELEN, nurse; b. Jackson, Mo., Nov. 21, 1923; d. Harry Edward and Mary (Collins) Scheper; diploma St. Mary's Sch. Nursing, Cairo, Ill.; divorced. Night supr. Rusk (Tex.) Meml. Hosp., 1970-74, Neuborn Meml. Hosp., Jacksonville, Tex., 1974-76; med./surg. night supr. Rusk State Hosp., 1976—. Mem. Mo., Am. nurses assns., Italian Greyhound Club Houston, Affenpinscher Club Am., Dog Judges Assn. Am., Assn. Canofila Mexican A.C. Republican. Baptist. Home: Rural Route 4 Box 259 Rusk TX 75785

MICA, DANIEL ANDREW, congressman; b. Binghamton, N.Y., Feb. 4, 1944; s. Adeline Mica; B.A. in Edn., Fla. Atlantic U., 1966; m. Martha Fry; children—Christine, Daniel Andrew, Caroline, Paul. Tchr. schs. in Palm Beach County (Fla.) and Montgomery County (Md.), 1966-67; staff aide Congressman Paul Rogers, 1967-78; mem. 96th Congress from 11th Dist. Fla., pres. Democratic freshman group, 1979. Founder, sec. Forum Club Palm Beaches, 1975; bd. dirs. Community Mental Health Center Palm Beach, 1976, Goodwill Industries Palm Beach, 1977. Mem. Palm Beach Jaycees. Roman Catholic.

MICHAEL, JAMES HARRY, JR., lawyer, state senator; b. Charlottesville, Va., Oct. 17, 1918; s. James Harry and Reuben (Shelton) M.; B.S., U. Va., 1940, LL.B., 1942; m. Barbara E. Puryear, Dec. 18, 1946; children—Jarrett, Victoria. Admitted to Va. bar, 1942; since practiced in Charlottesville; mem. firm Michael and Musselman, 1946-54, J.H. Michael, Jr., 1954-59, Michael and Dent, 1959-72, Michael, Dent & Brooks Ltd., 1972-74, Michael and Dent, Ltd., 1974—; asso. judge Juvenile and Domestic Relations Ct., Charlottesville, 1954-68; mem. Va. Senate, 1968—. Exec. dir. Inst. Pub. Affairs, U. Va., 1952; chmn. Council State Govts., 1975-76, also mem. exec. com.; chmn. So. Legis. Conf., 1974-75. Mem. Charlottesville Sch. Bd., 1951-62; bd. govs. St. Anne-Belfield Sch., 1952-76; sec. Charlottesville Com. Fgn. Relations, 1950-75. Served with USNR, 1942-46, comdr. Res. ret. Wilton Park fellow Wilton Park Conf., Sussex, Eng., 1971. Mem. Am., Va. (v.p. 1956-57), Charlottesville-Albemarle (pres. 1966-67) bar assns., C. of C., Am. Judicature Soc., Nat. Consumer Fin. Assn., 4th Jud. Conf., Va., Am. trial lawyers assns., Raven Soc., Sigma Nu Phi, Omicron Delta Kappa. Episcopalian (lay reader). Home: 900 Rugby Rd Charlottesville VA 22903 Office: 414 Park St Charlottesville VA 22901

MICHAELS, JOHN PATRICK, JR., investment investment banker, media broker; b. Orlando, Fla., May 28, 1944; s. John Patrick and Mary Elizabeth (Slemons) M.; grad. Jamaica Coll., Kingston, 1961; B.A. magna cum laude, Tulane U., 1966; M.A. in Communications (ABC fellow), U. Pa., 1968; student London Sch. Econs., U. London, 1964; m. Ingeborg D. Theimer, May 2, 1970; 1 dau., Kimberly Lynn. With Times Mirror Co., 1968-72, v.p. mktg. and devel. TM Communications Co., 1968-72; v.p. Cable Funding, N.Y.C., 1973; founder, sr. partner Communications Equity Assos., cable TV investment bankers, 1973—; co-owner, officer, dir. Sanlando Cablevision, Inc., Altamonte Springs, Fla., Gulfstream Cablevision, Inc., Dunedin, Fla. Tulane scholar, 1962-66; Tulane fellow, 1963-66. Mem. Nat. Cable TV Assn., So. Cable TV Assn., Community Antenna TV Assn., Am. Mktg. Assn., Phi Beta Kappa, Phi Eta Sigma. Clubs: Univ., Tampa Yacht. Contbr. articles to trade jours. Home: 3024 Villa Rosa Park Tampa FL 33611 Office: 851 Lincoln Center 5401 W Kennedy Blvd Tampa FL 33609

MICHAELS, MICHAEL MAGED, urologist; b. Alexandria, Egypt, July 7, 1945; came to U.S., 1969, naturalized, 1975; s. Aziz and Angèle (Grais) Mikhail; M.B., Ch.B., Alexandria U., 1968; m. Debra Ann Bortz, May 5, 1973; children—Kimberley Anne, Bradley Scott. Intern, Alexandria U. Hosp., 1968, Princeton (N.J.) Hosp., 1969-70; resident in surgery N.J. Med. Sch., Newark, 1970-71, resident in urology Geisinger Med. Center, Danville, Pa., 1971-74; attending staff urologist Putnam Community Hosp., Palatka, Fla., 1974—, chief surgery, 1979—. Served with U.S. AR, 1978. Diplomate Am. Bd. Urology. Fellow A.C.S.; mem. Putnam County Med. Soc., Fla. Med. Assn., Am. Urol. Assn. Contbr. articles in field to profl. jours. Home: 3204 Blair Dr Palatka FL 32077 Office: 700 Zeagler Dr Suite 4 Palatka FL 32077

MICHEL, HARRY ALBERT, office systems cons. and analyst; b. Alexandria, La., Apr. 19, 1938; s. Jacob Bernard and Marion (Marrus) M.; B.S. in Acctg., La. State U., 1959; m. June Aaron, Sept. 1, 1963; children—Robin, David. Programmer, systems analyst IBM Corp., Poughkeepsie, N.Y., 1962-67, Boca Raton, Fla., 1967-69, programming mgr., 1969-71, office systems cons., analyst, 1976-79. Mem. exec. bd., v.p. Palm Beach County Muscular Dystrophy Assn., 1978-79; mem. Boca Raton Youth Adv. Bd., 1971-74, vice chmn., 1972-74; pres. local AAU Swim Orgn., 1976-78. Served with U.S. Army, 1959-61. Recipient Boca Raton Community Service award, 1976. Mem. Boca Raton Jaycees (pres. 1970-71, Presdl. award of Leadership 1971), Alpha Kappa Psi. Jewish. Home: 2772 NE 4th Dr Boca Raton FL 33431 Office: PO Box 1328 Boca Raton FL 33431

MICHELSON, AARON IVAN, librarian; b. Cleve., Oct. 3, 1927; s. William and Florence Beatrice (Slesnick) M.; B.S., Case Western Res. U., 1949; M.S.L.S., Case Western Res. U., 1950; postgrad. U. Chgo., 1958-59; m. Dorothy Marie Lund, Apr. 12, 1975; children—Katherine, Mary, Sarah. Librarian, Detroit Public Library, 1950-51, N.D. State Coll., Ellendale, 1954-56; project dir. Okla. Library-Community Project, 1959-60; asst. prof. U. Okla. Sch. Library Sci., 1960-65; chief librarian Scott, Foresman & Co., 1965-66; library dir. U. S. Ala., Mobile, 1966—; cons. in field. Served with U.S. Army, 1951-54. Mem. ALA, Southeastern Library Assn., Ala. Library Assn., Bay Area Library Assn., NEA. Unitarian. Contbr. articles to profl. jours. Home: 6427 Airport Blvd #107 Mobile AL 36608

MICHELSON, DONALD DAVID, historian; b. Balt., Dec. 31, 1913; s. Aaron Adolph and Amalia Mary (Sussman) M.; A.B., Eastern Ky. U., 1936; M.A., George Peabody Coll., 1937; Ph.D., Peabody-Vanderbilt U., 1940; m. Dorothy Murchison, July 2, 1941; children—Jan Deborah Michelson Higbie, David Nathaniel, Joseph Darryl. Asst. prof. history George Peabody Coll., Nashville, 1940-46; chmn. div. social sci., prof. history Austin Peay State U., Clarksville, Tenn., 1946-48; adj. prof. U. Miami (Fla.), 1948-67; dir. B'nai B'rith Hillel Found., U. Miami, 1948-68; asso. dean div. humanities Miami Dade Community Coll., 1967-69, prof. history, 1969—. Dir. religious edn. Temple Israel, Miami, 1951-52, Congregation Beth David, Miami, 1972-73; discussion leader White House Conf. on Youth, 1960; dir. research Dade County Council Community Relations, 1952-56. Served with USCGR, 1942-46; ETO, MTO, PTO, to comdr., 1942-73. Mem. Am. Hist. Assn., Am. Acad. Polit. and Social Sci., Nat. Council Social Studies, Jewish War Vets, Am. Zionist Assn., Phi Delta Kappa, Kappa Delta Pi. Democrat. Author: Biography of William Franklin Phelps, 1941; Images of America; others. Home: 10525 SW 114th Terr Miami FL 33176 Office: 11011 SW 104th St Miami FL 33176

MICHELSON, EDITH MAXINE, realtor; b. Wichita Falls, Tex., Nov. 19, 1927; d. Charlie Clifton and Emmer Pearl (Williams) Putnam; student Jolly's Sch. Bus., Long Beach, Calif., 1950-51; grad. Tex. Realtors Inst., 1972, Dale Carnegie Inst.; m. Robert A. Michelson, Apr. 1, 1947; children—Roberta, Gayle. Credit mgr. W.T. Grant Co., Fairfax, Va., 1963-64; real estate sales rep. Jim West & Co., Houston, 1971-72; partner Red Carpet Real Estate, Houston; owner, mgr. income properties. Mem. Nat. Mktg. Inst., Tex. Assn. Realtors, Houston Bd. Realtors. Home: 13123 Berkwood Ct Houston TX 77038 Office: 1746 W Mt Houston Houston TX 77038

MICHELSON, RONALD KEITH, oral surgeon; b. San Francisco, July 10, 1936; s. Charles Dean and Mary (Bettencourt) M.; student Coll. San Mateo, 1954-56, Georgetown U. Coll. Arts and Scis., 1959-61; D.D.S., Georgetown U., 1965; m. Susan Valarie Michelson; children—David Keith, Douglas Michelson. Intern oral surgery Norfolk (Va.) Gen. Hosp., 1965-66; individual practice dentistry, Virginia Beach, Va., 1967-71; 2d year resident oral surgery Jackson Meml. Hosp., U. Miami, 1971-72, chief resident, 1972-73; oral and maxillofacial surgeon, Virginia Beach, 1973—. Served with AUS, 1956-59. Diplomate Am. Bd. Oral Surgery. Mem. Tidewater, Va., Am. dental assns., Am. Assn. Oral and Maxillofacial Surgeons, Va. Soc. Oral Surgeons, Virginia Beach Dental Soc., Am. Bonsai Soc., Va. Bonsai Soc., Bonsai Clubs Internat., Nat. Chrysanthemum Soc., Norfolk Bot. Garden Soc., Delta Sigma Delta. Episcopalian. Contbr. articles to profl. jours. Home: 233 Bridgeview Circle Chesapeake VA 23320 Office: 816 Independence Blvd Virginia Beach VA 23462 also 200 Medical Pkwy Suite 301 Chesapeake VA 23320

MICHERO, WILLIAM HENDERSON, retail trade exec.; b. Ft. Worth, June 19, 1925; s. William Alvin and Lela Belle (Henderson) M.; B.S., Tex. Christian U., 1948; m. Nan Elaine Henderson, July 9, 1948; children—Jane Elaine (Mrs. Stephen A. Christie), William Sherman, Thomas Edward. With Tandy Corp., 1948—, sec., 1960-75, v.p., 1970-75, v.p., sec., treas. Tandycrafts, Inc., Ft. Worth, 1975—, also dir. Served with USNR, 1943-46. Named Valuable Alumnus Tex. Christian U., 1969. Mem. Am. Soc. Corporate Secs., Newcomen Soc. N.Am., Fin. Execs. Inst. Clubs: Fort Worth, Colonial Country. Home: 213 Crestwood Dr Fort Worth TX 76107 Office: 1700 One Tandy Center Fort Worth TX 76102

MICHIE, LUCILE EASTHAM (MRS. J. TEVIS MICHIE), sch. psychologist; b. Charlottesville, Va., Jan. 22, 1907; d. Rosser J. and Helen H. (George) Eastham; student Coll. William and Mary, 1924-26; B.S. in Edn., U. Va., 1929, M.Edn., 1960, advanced grad. student, 1963-72; m. J. Tevis Michie, Aug. 6, 1929; children—Robert Kinloch, Martha Tevis. Tchr. pub. schs. Wakefield, Va., 1929-30, Clark Sch., Charlottesville, 1931-39; sec.-treas., dir. Helen G. Eastham Shop, Inc., 1931-50; tchr. Lane High Sch., Charlottesville, 1931-45, counselor, 1957-60, counselor-psychometrist, 1960-63; sch. psychologist Charlottesville Pub. Schs., 1963-72; cons. Children and Youth Center, Pediatric Dept., U. Va. Hosp., 1972—; sch. psychologist Fluvanna County (Va.) Pub. Schs.; supr. sch. psychology practicum students, 1968; cons. Nat. Guidance Inst., U. Va., Charlottesville, 1960-61; treas. Country Day Sch., 1948-54; v.p. Va. Assn. Mental Health Parliamentarian; mem. Va. Bd. Psychology, 1976—. Pres. bd. dirs. Children's Service Center, Charlottesville, 1954-56, bd. dirs., 1954-57; bd. dirs. Charlottesville, Albemarle County community chests. Recipient service award Charlottesville Mental Health Assn., 1959; Scribinen-Garnett mental health award, 1977. Mem. Nat., Va., Charlottesville (past pres., dir., parliamentarian) edn. assns., Nat. Vocational Guidance Assn., Va., Piedmont (past pres.), Am. personnel and guidance assns., U. Va. Edn. Alumni Assn., Am. Assn. U. Women, League Women Voters, Bus. and Profl. Women's Club (pres. Charlottesville 1939-41, pres., dir. Va. Fedn. 1944-46; dir. nat. fedn.), Charlottesville Mcht. Assn. (treas. 1946-49), Alumni Assn. Coll. William and Mary, U. Va. Alumni Assn. (life mem.), Am. (asso.), Va. psychol. assns., Va. Assn. Sch. Psychologists (mem. profl. affairs com. 1970-72), Nat. Assn. Sch. Psychologists, Delta Kappa Gamma, Kappa Delta Pi (life mem., chpt. treas. 1959-69, service award 1969), Phi Delta Kappa (Disting. Service award U. Va. 1979). Republican. Episcopalian. Club: 2300 (Richmond, Va.). Author articles on mental health and handling children's problems. Home: PO Box 3445 Charlottesville VA 22903

MICHIELS, RAYMOND VICTOR, JR., architect; b. Charlotte, N.C., Mar. 18, 1938; s. Raymond Victor and Verda Letha (Miller) M.; B.S., La. State U., 1963, B.Arch., 1966; m. Bettye Smith, June 8, 1962; children—Raymond Victor III, Shahn L., Channing L. With Locatell, Inc., Atlanta, 1966-68; project architect Toombs, Amisano & Wells, Atlanta, 1968-70; asso. Saggus, Vaught, Spiker & Howell, Atlanta, 1970-76; pres. Architects Plus, Atlanta, 1976—; vis. design critic Ga. Tech., 1969-72; cons. in field; cons. Ga. Conservancy, 1970-80, DeKalb Heritage Trust, 1970—; spl. design cons. Atlanta Meml. Arts Center, 1968-70. Served with U.S. Army, 1963-65. Registered architect, Ga., Ala., S.C., Fla., Okla. Mem. Ga. Assn. of Architects (dir. 1975-76, 78-79), AIA (Service award Atlanta chpt. 1977). Home: 1476 Indian Forest Trail Stone Mountain GA 30083 Office: 1800 Century Blvd NE Suite 800 Atlanta GA 30345

MICKEY, GEORGE HENRY, cytogeneticist; b. Claude, Tex., Jan. 26, 1910; s. Luke Ross and Clara Alice (Pennington) M.; B.A., Baylor U., 1931; M.S., U. Okla., 1934; Ph.D., U. Tex., 1938; m. Alwilda Editha Davis, Aug. 20, 1932; children—Wilda Rhea, Don Davis. Teaching fellow botany Baylor U., 1931-32; grad. asst. zoology U. Okla., 1932-34; research asst. genetics U. Tex., 1934-35, instr. zoology, 1935-38; instr. zoology La. State U., Baton Rouge, 1938-42, asst. prof., 1942-44, asso. prof., 1944-48; research fellow in biology Calif. Inst. Tech., 1948; asso. prof. biology Northwestern U., 1949-56; prin. biologist Oak Ridge Nat. Lab., 1953; prof., chmn. zoology La. State U., 1956-59, dean grad. sch., 1959-60; sr. scientist New Eng. Inst., Ridgefield, Conn., 1960-70, dean Grad. Sch., 1970-74; vis. prof. U. Bridgeport (Conn.), 1971; clin. asso. dir. cytogenetics Duke U. Med. Center, Durham N.C., 1975—. Guggenheim fellow, 1948; research grantee Sigma Xi, Rockefeller Found., AEC, Wallace Genetic Found., NSF, Wood Found., Population Council, John A. Hartford Found., Office Naval Research. Fellow AAAS; mem. Am. Inst. Biol. Scis., Am. Naturalists, Am. Genetic Assn., Am. Soc. Human Genetics, Am. Soc. Study Evolution, Am. Soc. Zoologists, AAUP, Genetics Soc. Am., Assn. Southeastern Biologists, Okla., N.Y., Ill., La. (pres. 1948) acads. sci., Sigma Xi, Beta Beta Beta (nat. pres. 1957-60). Asst. editor Proc. La. Acad. Sci., 1943-45, asso. editor, 1945-48. Co-author manual studies gen. zoology, 1947. Home: 2404 Perkins Rd Durham NC 27706 Office: 3062 Duke U Med Center Durham NC 27710

MIDDENDORF, KAREN LEIGH, developmental disabilities serivces co. exec.; b. Columbus, Ohio, July 21, 1941; d. Paul E. and Olga (Logan) Bean; B.S. Geneva Coll., 1969; M.Ed., Morehead State U., 1974; m. Charles P. Middendorf, June 17, 1958: children—Teresa, Charles, Mason. Tchr., Western Beaver County Schs., Fairview, Pa., 1968-70: tchr. Mason County Schs., Maysville, Ky., 1970-71; coordinator mental retardation services Comprehend, Inc., 1971-73, dir. developmental disabilities services, 1973—; pvt. cons. developmental disabilities services, 1974—. Chmn., Maysville Cystic Fibrosis Drive, 1976; cons. Council for Handicapped Citizens, 1972—; mem. adv. bd. Headstart's Resource Access Project, Ala., Tenn., Ky., 1976-78; mem. Ky. Gov.'s Spl. Legis. Commn. on Comprehensive Care Centers, 1977-78; mem. statewide task force on specialized foster care; chmn. human resources coordinating com. Buffalo Trace Area Devel. Dist., 1973-74; mem. subcom. on plan devel. for long term care E. Ky. Health Systems Agy., 1978—. Mem. Am. Assn. on Mental Deficiency chmn.-elect Southeast region 1979-80, chmn. constn. and bylaws com. 1978-79, mem. nominating com. Southeast region 1976-78, pres. Ky. chpt. 1977-78, editor 1975-77). Club: Maysville River Runners. Home: Route 5 Box 273 Maysville KY 41056 Office: PO Box G Maysville KY 41056

MIDDLETON, CLYDE WILLIAM, state senator; b. Cleve., Jan. 30, 1928; s. Edward George and Eleanor Genevieve (Mertz) M.; B.S., U.S. Naval Acad., 1951; M.B.A., Xavier U., 1962; J.D., No. Ky. State Coll., 1974; m. Mary Ann Janke, Aug. 14, 1954; children—Ann Eleanor, David Edward, Richard Carl, John Clyde. Mfg. dept. mgr. Procter & Gamble Co., Cin., 1955-57, buyer, 1957-64; field underwriter N.Y. Life Ins. Co., Covington, Ky., 1964-74; mem. firm Theissen, Middleton & Wohlwender, and predecessor, 1974—; mem. Ky. Senate from 24th Dist., 1967—, minority whip, 1978—. Dist. chmn. Young Republicans, 1962-63; chmn. Kenton County Rep. party, 1961, Ky. State Rep. party, 1975-76; candidate for U.S. Ho. of Reps., 1962, 64. Mem. No. Ky. Mental Health Bd., 1968-70; chmn. Ky. Comprehensive Health Planning Council, 1968-72. Served from ensign to lt. (j.g.) USN, 1951-55, now comdr. Res. Recipient Pub. Ser. awards Ky. Pub. Health Assn., 1969, Newport Elks Club, 1970, No. Ky. Tchrs. Assn., 1972, Ky. Comprehensive Health Planning Council, 1973. Mem. No. Ky. C. of C. (dir. 1969-72). Lutheran. Optimist (pres. Covington 1969-70). Address: PO Box 546 Covington KY 41012

MIDDLETON, DOUGLAS DELANO, land surveyor; b. Plains, Ga., Apr. 8, 1942; s. Shelton Taft and Iva Lee (Rigsby) M.; A.S. in Civil Engring., So. Tech. Inst., 1965, B. Civil Engring., 1975; J.D., John Marshall Law Sch., Atlanta, 1978; m. Judy Catherine Nickelson, Aug. 1, 1964; children—Amy LaVerne, Brian Scott, Rebecca Catherine. Chief field services Keck and Wood, Inc., Atlanta, 1967-69; project mgr. J.F. Denny Constrn. Co., Rome, Ga., 1969-71; pvt. practice land surveying, Rome, 1971-72; pres. Cadastral & Land Surveys Ltd., P.C. (formerly Douglas D. Middleton and Assos.), Marietta, Ga., 1972—; instr. surveying law So. Tech. Inst., 1975—; admitted to Ga., U.S. Dist. Ct. and U.S. Ct. Appeals bars, 1978, since practiced in Marietta; mem. firm Kaley & Middleton. Candidate for County Surveyor, Cobb County, Ga., 1976. Served with USN, 1966-67. Mem. State Bar Ga., Cobb County Bar Assn., Atlanta Bar Assn., Am. Bar Assn., Surveying and Mapping Soc. Ga. (past v.p., past chmn. ethics and practices com.), Am. Congress on Surveying and Mapping. Democrat. Baptist. Club: Mason. Home: 740 Teague Dr NW Kennesaw GA 30144 Office: Suite #550 1st Nat Bank Bldg 100 Cherokee St Marietta GA 30061

MIDDLETON, DOUGLAS FRANK, petroleum engr.; b. Sedalia, Mo., July 24, 1928; s. Douglas Miles and Florence Elizabeth (Youse) M.; B.S. in Mining Engring., U. Mo., 1950; m. Grace Alice Brigham, Oct. 20, 1956; children—Jane, Grace. Reservoir engr. Texaco Co., 1959; reservoir and prodn. engr. Aramco, 1959-63; engring. cons., 1964-65; dist. reservoir engr. Mobil Oil Co., Venezuela, 1965-67; sr. reservoir engr. Coastal States Gas Producing Co., Houston, 1967-74; mgr. reservoir engring. Charter Exploration and Prodn. Co., Houston, 1975-76; sr. reservoir engr. Oxy Petroleum, 1976-77; mgr. engring. Con Vest Energy Corp. 1977—. Mem. sch. bd. Escuela Araco, Venezuela, 1965-66. Served with AUS, 1950-52. Registered profl. engr., Tex., Okla., La. Mem. Soc. Petroleum Engrs., Colegio Ingenieros de Venezuela. Methodist. Mason. Home: 4434 Twinkle Ct Houston TX 77072 Office: 1700 West Loop S Suite 1000 Houston TX 77027

MIDDLETON, ELWYN LINTON, lawyer; b. Pomona, Fla., Oct. 16, 1914; s. William Spencer and Lizzie A. (Williams) M.; LL.B., Stetson U., 1939; m. Annie L. Fielding, Dec. 7, 1942; children—Elwyn Linton, Mary Ann, John David, Phillip Fielding. Admitted to Fla. bar, 1939, since practiced in Palm Beach; asso. E. Harris Drew, 1939-42; mem. firm Burns, Middleton, Farrell & Faust (formerly Burns, Middleton, Rogers & Farrell), 1946—; town atty., Palm Beach, 1953—. Dir. Bank of Palm Beach & Trust Co., Palm Beach. Trustee Eckerd Coll. Served from ensign to lt. USNR, 1942-46. Mem. Am., Palm Beach County (pres. 1951) bar assns., Fla. Bar (gov. 1954-56), Phi Alpha Delta. Democrat. Presbyn. Home: 242 Dunbar Rd Palm Beach FL 33480 Office: 205 Worth Ave Palm Beach FL 33480

MIDDLETON, HARRY JOSEPH, govt. ofcl.; b. Centerville, Iowa, Oct. 24, 1921; s. Harry Joseph and Florence Genevieve (Beauvais) M.; student Washburn U., 1941-43; B.A., La. State U., 1947; m. Miriam Miller, Oct. 29, 1949; children—Susan, Deborah, James Miller, Jennifer. Reporter AP, 1948-49; editor Archtl. Forum Mag., 1949-53; writer March of Time, 1953-55; free lance writer, 1955-66; staff asst. to Pres. Lyndon B. Johnson, Washington, 1966-69, spl. asst., 1969-70; dir. Lyndon B. Johnson Library, GSA, Austin, Tex., 1970—. Served with Armed Forces, 1943-46, 50-52. Decorated Bronze Star. Mem. Sigma Delta Chi. Author: Compact History of the Korean War. Home: 2201 Exposition Blvd Austin TX 78703 Office: LBJ Library Austin TX 78705

MIDDLETON, HERMAN DAVID, educator; b. Sanford, Fla., Mar. 24, 1925; s. Arthur Herman and Ruby Elmerry (Hart) M.; B.S., Columbia, 1948, M.A., 1949; Ph.D., U. Fla., 1964; postgrad. N.Y. U., summer 1950, Northwestern U., summer 1951; m. Amelia Mary Eggart, Dec. 1, 1945 (dec. 1976); children—Herman David, Kathleen Hart. Instr., dir. drama and speech Maryville (Tenn.) Coll., 1949-50; instr., designer-tech. dir. theatre U. Del., 1951-55; stage mgr. Unto These Hills, Cherokee (N.C.) Hist. Assn., summers 1952-56; asst. prof., head dept. drama U. N.C., Greensboro, 1956-59, asso. prof., head dept. drama and speech, 1959-65, prof., head dept., 1965-74, prof., 1974—, Excellence Fund prof. communication and theatre, 1979—; designer Chucky Jack, Great Smokey Mountains Hist. Soc., Gatlinburg, Tenn., 1956, designer, dir., 1957; tech. dir. The Confederacy, Tide Water Hist. Assn., Virginia Beach, Va., summer 1958. Communications cons. N.C. Nat. Bank, 1968, Jefferson Standard Life Ins. Co., Greensboro, 1969, Gilbarco, Inc., Greensboro, 1969-70, 73; dir. region X (S.E.) and mem. central com. Am. Coll. Theatre Festival, 1977-79. Mem. N.C. Arts Council Commn., 1964-66, Guilford County Bi-Centennial Celebration Commn., 1969-70. Pres., Shanks Village Players, Orangeburg, N.Y. 1947-48, Univ. Drama Group, Newark, Del., 1954-55; bd. dirs. Broadway Theatre League of Greensboro, 1958-60; bd. dirs. Southeastern Theatre Conf., 1963-68, pres., 1965, pres. pro-tem, 1966; bd. dirs. Greensboro Community Arts Council, 1964-67, 69-72. Recipient O. Henry award for distinguished artistic contbns. to Greensboro, 1966, Gold medallion Am. Oil Co., 1973, Suzanne M. Davis award Southeastern Theatre Conf., 1975. Mem. Del. (dir. 1950-55), Carolina 1958-59) dramatic assns., Am. Nat. Theatre Acad. (exec. v.p. Piedmont chpt. 1957-60), N.C. Drama and Speech Assn. (pres. 1966-67), Am. Theatre Assn. (chmn. bd. nominations 1971-72), Am., So. speech communication assns., N.C. Theatre Conf., Nat. Collegiate Players, Phi Delta Kappa, Phi Kappa Phi, Theta Alpha Phi, Alpha Psi Omega. Democrat. Methodist. Drama critic, columnist The Sunday Star, Wilmington, Del., 1952. Theatre editor Players mag., 1959-61. Theatre columnist Sunday edits. Greensboro Daily News, 1959-62. Home: 203-A Village Ln Greensboro NC 27409

MIDDLETON, MERRILEE RUTH, counselor; b. Hazelhurst, Ga., July 12, 1932; d. Ruth (Bussell) Montmery; B.S., Stetson U., 1953; M.A., Peabody Coll., 1960; Ed.S., Fla. Atlantic U., 1974. Tchr./counselor Fairfax (Va.) High Sch., 1953-56; counselor coordinator Apopka (Fla.) High Sch., 1956-60; program specialist Palm Beach County (Fla.) Schs., 1960-66; counselor Stetson U., Deland, Fla., 1968, also instr.; counselor Psychol. and Consultation Services Inc., Boca Raton, Fla., 1969—; dir. Center for Group Counseling, Boca Raton, 1973-76; dir. Project Peace, community counseling program Boca Raton, 1977—. Bd. dirs. Palm Beach County Mental Health Assn., Faulk Found. Named outstanding young woman of yr. Boca Raton, Soroptomist Internat., 1977. Mem. Palm Beach County Psychol. Assn., Am. Personnel and Guidance Assn., Am. Sch. Counselors Assn., Am. Assn. for Specialists in Group Work. Democrat. Episcopalian. Club: Soroptimist. Home: 499 S Ocean Blvd Boca Raton FL 33432 Office: Psychol and Consultation Services Inc 168 E Boca Raton Rd Boca Raton FL 33432

MIDDLETON, MOZELLE JOHNSON, educator; b. Orangeburg County, S.C., Dec. 5, 1928; d. Carey and Carrie Elizabeth (Cleckley) Johnson; B.S., Claflin U., 1950; M. Ed., S.C. State Coll., 1964; postgrad. U. S.C., 1970-77; m. James Benjamin Middleton, June 17, 1977; children—Earline, Karine, Marion, Donnie Michael; stepchildren—Charlene, Anthony, Lagiya, Darlynn, Patrica, Agatha. Tchr., St. George (S.C.) Elementary Sch., 1950-52, Estill (S.C.) High Sch., 1954-57, Fairfield High Sch., Winsboro, S.C., 1957-59; guidance coordinator Jenkins High High Sch., Harleyville, S.C., 1960-69; dir. curriculum devel. social studies, English, guidance and counseling S.C. State Coll., Orangeburg, 1969-77; dir. guidance services, curriculum devel., 1958—; cons. in field, lectr. lang. arts Gen. Electric fellow, 1974-75. Mem. Nat., S.C. edn. assns., Columbia Adlerian Soc., Edisto Reading Council, Nat. Council Negro Women, NAACP, Partners Program, Zeta Phi Beta. Democrat. Clubs. Order Eastern Star, Dau. Elks. Home: 124 Strickland St Walterboro SC 29488 Office: Box 2076 SC State Coll Orangeburg SC 29117

MIDDLETON, NORMAN GRAHAM, social worker, counselor; b. Jacksonville, Fla., Jan. 21, 1935; s. Norman Graham and Betty (Quina) M.; B.A., U. Miami (Fla.), 1960; M.S.W., Fla. State U., 1962; m. Judy Stephens, Aug. 1, 1968; stepchildren—Monty Stokes, Toni Stokes. Casework counselor Family Service, Miami, 1962-64; psychiat. social worker asso. firm Drs. Warson, Steele, Wiener, Sarasota, Fla., 1964-66; marriage, family counselor, Sarasota, 1966—. Instr. Manatee Jr. Coll., Bradenton, Fla., 1973-76; psychiat. social work cons. Sarasota Meml. Hosp. Pres. Council on Epilepsy, Sarasota, 1969-70. Served with USAF, 1954-58. Fellow Fla. Soc. Clin. Social Work (pres. 1978-80); mem. Nat. Assn. Social Workers, Am. Assn. Marriage and Family Counselors, Am. Group Psychotherapy Assn., Am. Assn. Sex Educators and Counselors (cert. sex educator), Acad. Cert. Social Workers. Democrat. Episcopalian. Home: Route 2 Box 18 Winburn Dr Sarasota FL 33582 Office: 1857 Floyd St Sarasota FL 33579

MIDDLETON, RICHARD TEMPLE, III, educator; b. Jackson, Miss., Jan. 17, 1942; s. Richard Temple, II, and Johnnie Mae (Beadle) M.; B.S. in Edn., Lincoln U. of Mo., 1963, M. Ednl. Adminstrn., 1965; Ed.D. in Secondary Edn., U. So. Miss., 1972; m. Brenda Marie Wolfe, Aug. 10, 1968; children—Jeanna Elizabeth, Richard Temple. Instr. in edn. Tougaloo (Miss.) Coll., 1967-70; asso. prof. Jackson (Miss.) State U., 1970—, dir. student teaching, 1978—; cons. in edn. Chmn. bd. dirs. St. Mark's Day Care. Mem. various polit. campaign coms. Served to 1st lt. U.S. Army, 1965-67. Woodrow Wilson-King fellow, 1969-72. Mem. Assn. Miss. Tchr. Educators (pres.), Alpha Phi Alpha, Sigma Pi Phi. Episcopalian (lay reader). Clubs: Elks, Masons. Contbr. articles to publs. Home: 1104 Arbor Vista Blvd Jackson MS 39209 Office: Student Teaching Office Jackson State U Jackson MS 39217

MIDKIFF, MARY ELIZABETH MATZKE (MRS. PATRICK CLAYTON MIDKIFF), editor; b. Galveston, Tex., Dec. 3, 1920; d. August and Uarda Caroline (Butts) Matzke; grad. high sch.; m. Patrick Clayton Midkiff, Apr. 1, 1945. Reporter, feature writer, society editor Galveston (Tex.) News & Tribune, 1938-42; reporter, feature writer, asst. night city editor Houston Post, 1943-47; editor Action, Houston C. of C., 1947-49, editorial asst., 1964-66, asso. editor, 1966-69, exec. editor, 1969-72, editor, mgr. Houston mag., 1972-74, mgr. information publs. Houston C. of C., 1974—; copy editor Houston Chronicle, 1949-53; co-owner Waller County Record, weekly newspaper, Waller, 1952-59. Cons. publs. Am. C. of C. Execs. Communications Council, 1973—. Mem. adv. panel in pub. affairs Houston-Harris County chpt. A.R.C., 1971-72; mem. pub. relations com. Houston-Galveston Regional Transp. Study, 1972-73; mem. info. com. Houston chpt. Am. Heart Assn., 1978-79. Recipient Headliner award Houston profl. chpt. Women in Communications, 1973. Mem. Am. C. of C. Execs., Am. C. of C. Exec. Communications Council (chmn. 1974-75, steering com. 1975-77), Am. Assn. Commerce Publs. (dir. 1970-72), Tex. C. of C. Mgrs. Assn., Women in Communications, Press Club Houston, Am. Soc. Assn. Execs. Democrat. Methodist. Home: 908 E Whitney Dr Houston TX 77022 Office: 1100 Milam Bldg Houston TX 77002

MIELE, ANTHONY WILLIAM, state librarian; b. Williamsport, Pa., Feb. 12, 1926; s. Harry John and Louise Casale (Troyano) M.; B.S., Marquette U., 1951; M.L.S., U. Pitts., 1966; m. Ruth Cassidy, Jan. 29, 1955; children—Terri Ann, Anthony, Robert John, Elizabeth Ann. Partner, mgr. restaurant, Williamsport, 1960-66; dir. Elmwood Park (Ill.) Pub. Library, 1967-68; asst. dir. Oak Park (Ill.) Pub. Library, 1968-70; asst. dir. for tech. services Ill. State Library, Springfield, 1970-75; dir. Ala. Pub. Library Service, Montgomery, 1975—. Served with USNR, 1944-46. Mem. ALA (mem. com. Nat. Library Week 1971-74), Ill., Ala. library assns., Internat. Fedn. Libraries, Nat. Microfilm Assn., Chief Officers State Library Agencies, Beta Phi Mu. Roman Catholic. Club: Kiwanis. Asso. editor Govt. Publs. Review, 1974. Home: 103 Saccapatoy Dr Montgomery AL 36117 Office: 6030 Monticello Dr Montgomery AL 36130

MIELZAREK, ROLF HERBERT, psychologist; b. Elizabeth, N.J., July 2, 1932; s. Wilhelm and Julie Pauline (Laur) M.; B.A., Wagner Coll., 1954; B.D., Luth. Sem., Gettysburg, Pa., 1957; Ph.D., U. Md., 1976; m. Lee Anna Hammond, May 29, 1969; children—Lori Kristine, Erik Paul, Kara Lynn. Exec. dir. Montgomery Workshop, sheltered workshop for handicapped, Kensington, Md., 1965-68; asso. dir. Commn. Govtl. Efficiency and Economy, Balt., 1968-69; dir., owner Camp Shenandoah, residential camp for mentally retarded, Winchester, Va., 1969—; psychologist Hope Center, Temple Hills, Md., 1971-73; psychologist Great Oaks Center, state inst. for mentally retarded, Silver Spring, Md., 1974-75; psychologist, dir., owner Concord, residential community for mentally retarded, Yellow Spring, W.Va., 1974—. Chief cons. Cons. on Programs for Mentally Retarded Persons, Yellow Spring, 1974—; operator Shenandoah Adventures, travel programs for mentally retarded, Yellow Spring, 1974—; instr. psychology Shenandoah Coll., Winchester. Named Man of Year, Silver Spring Jaycees, 1968. Mem. Council for Exceptional Children, Am. Assn. Mental Deficiency, Am. Camping Assn. (pres. sect. 1972-74, dir. region, chmn. conv. 1975), Nat. Assn. Pvt. Residential Facilities for Mentally Retarded (dir. 1977—). Home: Concord Yellow Spring WV 26865 Office: Camp Shenandoah Mountain Falls Route Winchester VA 22601 also Concord Yellow Spring WV 26865

MIERS, HARRIS WOOD, JR. (BUDDY), health care co. exec.; b. Dallas, Oct. 5, 1939; s. Harris Wood and Sally Grace (Richardson) M.; student U. Tex., Arlington, 1959-61; B.B.A., N. Tex. State U., 1963, M.B.A., 1965; m. Wanda Wilson, Oct. 4, 1963; children—Harris Wood, Clare Ellan. With Frito-Lay, Inc. div. Pepsico, Dallas, 1965-69, nat. tng. coordinator; pres. Univ. Mgmt. Services, Inc., Dallas, 1969-75; pres. Lifemark Dental Services, Inc. div. Lifemark, Inc., Houston, 1975—; guest instr. N. Tex. State U. Mem. adminstrv. bd., past tchr. Terrace Methodist Ch. Mem. Am. Dental Trade Assn., Am. Mgmt. Assn., Dental Lab. Conf. Am. (dir.). Home: 6919 Alderney St Houston TX 77055 Office: 3800 Buffalo Speedway Houston TX 77098

MIESCH, DAVID CHEATHAM, physician; b. Clarksville, Tex., July 6, 1928; s. Raymond John and Mamie (Cheatham) M.; M.D., U. Tex. at Galveston, 1951; m. Jo Peevey, Mar. 22, 1956; children—Margaret Louise, Mary Gail. Intern, Hosp. of U. Pa., Phila., 1951-52; resident in internal medicine Parkland Hosp., Dallas, 1952-53, John Sealy Hosp., Galveston, Tex., 1953-55; pvt. practice internal medicine, Paris, Tex., 1973—; mem. staff McCuiston Regional Med. Center. Mem. devel. bd. U. Tex. Med. Sch. at Galveston, 1973—; mem. Chancellor's Council U. Tex., 1975—. Diplomate Am. Bd. Internal Medicine. Fellow A.C.P.; mem. Am., Tex. med. assns., Tex. Soc. Internal Medicine, Alpha Tau Omega. Episcopalian. Home: 665 31st St SE Paris TX 75460 Office: 2850 Lewis Ln Paris TX 75460

MIESSE, MARY ELIZABETH (BETH), educator; b. Amarillo, Tex.; M.Ed. in Guidance and Counseling, W. Tex. State U., Canyon, 1952, M.B.A., 1960; M.Personnel Service, U. Colo., Boulder, 1954. With various bus. firms and radio stas., 1940-47; prof. Amarillo (Tex.) Coll., 1947-63; tchr. pvt. and pub. schs., also TV work, 1963-74; spl. edn. tchr. Cal Farley's Boys Ranch Sch. System, Boys Ranch, Tex., 1974-78; spl. edn. cons., writer, 1978—. Mem. NEA, Tex. State Tchrs. Assn., Tex. Diagnosticians, Am. Psychol. Assn., North Plains Assn. for Children with Learning Disabilities. Pioneered in ednl. TV in West Tex.; recipient awards in typewriting and ednl. TV. Certified in spl. edn. supr., spl. edn. counselor, edn. diagnostician, spl. edn. (lang. and/or learning disabled, mentally retarded) tchr., profl. counselor, profl. tchr., supt., prin., Tex. Home and Office: 2219 Van Buren St Amarillo TX 79109 also PO Box 31 Channing TX 79018

MIGDALIA, A. HERNANDEZ, hosp. exec.; b. Guanica, P.R., July 6, 1936; d. Francisco Antonio Almodovar and Alejandrina Tirado; diploma Bayamon Dist. Hosp., 1957; m. Rafael Hernandez Cardona, July 23, 1961: children—Rafael Antonio, Jose Alberto. Neurosurgical nurse Dept. Health Bayamon Dist. Hosp., 1957-59; operating rm. nurse Univ. Dist. Hosp., Rio Piedras, 1959-60, supr. intensive care unit, 1960-61; operating rm. nurse Presbyn. Hosp., Santurce, P.R., 1966-67, instr. nursing, 1967-70, instr. inservice, 1967-70, asst. dir. nursing dept., 1976-77, dir. inservice edn., 1975—. Mem. Coll. Profl. Nurses, Am. Legion Aux. (sec. 1970-72, 77—) Damas Columbinas (treas.), Inservice Assn. (sec.) Roman Catholic. Home: PR 11 Via 19 Villa Fontana Carolina PR 00630 Office: Presbyterian Hospital San Juan PR 00902

MIGHELL, RICHARD HENRY, elec. engr.; b. Aurora, Ill., Mar. 18, 1907; s. Ray and Ouida Lillian (Henry) M.; B.S., U. Denver, 1929; m. Ruth Aline Simon, June 12, 1930; children—Kenneth, Donald, Robert. Meter and instrument design engr. Gen. Electric Co., Lynn, Mass., 1935, salesman, Schenectady, 1935-38, meter and instrument specialist, Dallas, 1938-43, meter and instrument transformer sales engr., 1943-71; lectr. in field. Instr. electric meter schs. Tex. A. and M. U., 1938-71, U. Ark., 1938-71. U.S.O. counselor, 1941-42; committeeman Boy Scouts Am., 1946-47; capt. United Fund, Dallas, 1966. Mem. Dallas Electric Club, Southwest Metermen's Assn., Indsl. Electric Heating Engrs., Illuminating Engring. Soc., IEEE, Am. Assn. Ret. Persons (dir. N. Dallas chpt. 1977—), Lambda Chi Alpha, Tau Beta Phi, Phi Beta Sigma. Methodist (mem. ofcl. bd. 1971-73). Club: Brookhaven Country (Dallas). Contbr. articles to profl. publs. Home: 6705 Golf Dr Dallas TX 75205

MIHALAP, LEONID ISAAKOVICH, Slavic studies specialist, educator; b. Bobruisk, USSR, Apr. 10, 1924; s. Isaak V. and Tatiana D. (Shcherbich) M.; came to U.S., 1952, naturalized, 1958; B.S., Georgetown U., 1961, M.S., 1963; Ph.D., U. N.C. at Chapel Hill, 1973; m. Hope Christopoulos, Nov. 26, 1964; children—Penelope, Tamara, Nicolai. Asst. prof. Russian lang. and lit. Old Dominion U., Norfolk, Va., 1963-76, asso. prof., 1976—. Served with AUS, 1952-57. Mem. Am. Assn. Advancement Slavic Studies, Am. Acad. Polit. and Social Sci., Nat. Slavic Honor Soc., Omicron Delta Kappa, Alpha Epsilon Pi. Democrat. Greek Orthodox. Translator: The Last Tsar, History of Reign of Nicholas II, 4 vols., 1975. Home: 1316 Graydon Ave Norfolk VA 23507 Office: Old Dominion U Norfolk VA 23508

MIHALIK, GLORIA ROSE, educator; b. N.Y.C., Apr. 14, 1935; d. Anthony R. and Rose Mary (Iulo) Catalano; B.S., City U. N.Y., 1956; M.S., St. John's U., 1958, Ph.D., 1963; m. John A. Mihalik, June 29, 1963; children—Mary Beth, Margaret Rose; stepchildren—John A., Nancy Elizabeth. Lab. technician N.Y. State Psychiat. Inst., N.Y.C., 1958-59; tchr. sci. and mathematics Fairfax County pub. schs., J.F. Cooper Intermediate Sch., McLean, Va., 1974—; cons. in field. Pres., PTA, Springhill Elem. Sch., McLean, Va., 1972-73; PTA adv. council J.F. Cooper Intermediate Sch., McLean, 1978—. St. John's U. assistantship, 1956-58, 59-63. Mem. N.Y. Acad. Sci., Am. Fedn. Tchrs., Sigma Xi. Roman Catholic. Club: Goebel Hummel Collector's. Contbr. articles in field to profl. jours. Home: 8370 Greensboro Dr Bldg #4 Apt 222-224 McLean VA 22102 Office: 977 Balls Hill Rd McLean VA 22101

MIHALYKA, EUGENE ERNST, surgeon, bus. exec.; b. Richmond, Va., Nov. 21, 1917; s. Daniel A. and Elizabeth R. (Kristopher) M.; A.B., Johns Hopkins, 1940; M.D., Med. Coll. Va., 1950; m. Jean Beaumont Merritt, Mar. 25, 1942; children—George Kristopher, Jane Beaumont. Intern, Sewickley Valley Gen. Hosp., Pitts., 1950-51; resident Crile VA, Western Res. U. hosps., Cleve., 1953-57; practice medicine specializing in surgery, Cleve., 1953-71; head and neck surgeon, sr. clin. instr. Case Western Res. U. Sch. Medicine, 1953-71, now sr. vis. lectr.; asso. staff head and neck surgery Fairview Gen. Hosp., Cleve., 1957—; dir. med. edn. and med. affairs Edward McCready Meml. Hosp., Crisfield, Md., 1972—, chief of staff, 1978—, also mem. active surg. staff; instr. dept. surgery Eastern Va. Med. Sch., Norfolk, 1975—; cons. med. programs State Md. Chmn. bd. Chesapeake Systems Corp., 1964—. Tru-Har Products Inc., Lakewood, O.; dir. Pandor Coal Corp. Physician, Met. Opera Assn. Northeastern Ohio, 1960—; chmn. bd. SSS local bd., 1971—. Fellow Internat. Oceanographic Found. Served to maj. USAAF, 1941-46. Research grantee for head and neck cancer work, 1960. Diplomate Am. Bd. Otorhinolaryngology. Fellow Am. Coll. Otorhinolaryngology (v.p. 1974-75), Am. Coll. Cryosurgery; mem. AMA, Ohio, Va., Md. med. socs., Cleve. Acad. Medicine, Johns Hopkins Surg. Assn., Ohio Surg. Soc., Am. Mgmt. Assn., Save the Chesapeake Bay Found., Gt. Lakes Found. Presidents Club. Contbr. articles to profl. jours. Home: Cherry-Core Cheriton VA 23316 Office: Cheriton VA 23316

MIHELICH, DONALD LOUIS, engring. co. exec.; b. Lake Linden, Mich., Mar. 26, 1926; s. Lodi Mathew and Evelyn Ann (Thouin) M.; B.Indsl. Engring., Gen. Motors Inst., 1950; M.Indsl. Engring., Okla. State U., 1971; m. Wilma Tuma, Dec. 20, 1947; children—Michael, Kenneth, Thomas, Anne Marie. Foreman, Chevrolet div. Gen. Motors Corp., St. Louis, 1951-53; sr. mfg. engr. N. Am. Aviation Co., Los Angeles, 1953-57; prodn. mgr. Bobrick Mfg. Co., Los Angeles, 1957-59; v.p. prodn. Barber Webb Inc., Los Angeles, 1959-65; indsl. engring. specialist N.Am. Rockwell Corp., 1965-68, mgr. indsl. and facilities engring., Tulsa, 1968-71; mgr. Urban Ore div. Williams Bros. Engring. Co., Tulsa, 1971—. Bd. dirs. Neighbor for Neighbor. Served with USAAF, 1944-46. Decorated Air medal. Registered profl. engr., Okla., Calif. Mem. Am. Inst. Indsl. Engrs. (v.p. Los Angeles 1956, dir. 1956-59, treas. Tulsa 1974-76), ASTM (chmn. com. resource recovery 1978—), Engrs. Soc. Tulsa, Okla. Soc. Profl. Engrs. Patentee plastic cell liners. Home: 4344 E 72d St Tulsa OK 74136 Office: 6600 S Yale Ave Tulsa OK 74177

MIHM, DAVID JAMES, pharmacist, med. adminstr.; b. Borger, Tex., Dec. 13, 1945; s. Clifford Henry and Adeline (Cleary) M.; B.S. in Chemistry, Tex. Tech. U., 1968; B.S. in Pharmacy, Southwestern Okla. State U., 1976; m. Linda Maria Brockman, Sept. 7, 1967; 1 son, David Anthony. Analytical chemist CAMEX Inc., Borger, 1968-73; intern pharmacist St. Anthony Hosp., Oklahoma City, 1976-77; pharmacist Presbyn. Hosp., Oklahoma City, 1977-78; pharmacist Baptist Med. Center Okla., Oklahoma City, 1978, asst. dir. pharmacy, 1978—, acting dir., 1978; clin. faculty Okla. U. Sch. Pharmacy, 1978—. Registered pharmacist Okla., Wash. Mem. Okla. Soc. Hosp. Pharmacists, Am. Soc. Hosp. Pharmacists. Kappa Psi. Republican. Roman Catholic. Office: Baptist Med Center Okla 3300 NW Expressway 9klahoma City OK 73112

MIKEMAN, CARL HARMON, physicist; b. Seminole, Okla., Apr. 9, 1942; s. Kenneth Carl and Ernestine (Rinard) M.; B.S. in Physics, City U. N.Y., 1967; postgrad. Washington U., St. Louis, 1959-60; m. Nona Marcel Weinberg, Dec. 7, 1963 (div. Dec. 1976); children—Lynn Chara, Kenneth Reese. Tech. mgr. Cons.'s & Designers, N.Y.C., 1962-63; research technician JFD Electronics, Bklyn., 1963-64; biophysicist N.Y. State Psychiat. Inst., N.Y.C., 1965-68; physicist, project engr. U.S. Army Night Vision and Electro-Optics Lab., Ft. Belvoir, Va., 1968—; photographer, owner Image Masters Studio, Springfield, Va., 1974—. Pres., Orange Hunt Estates Civic Assn., 1972-73; chmn. Planning and Land Use Task Force, Fairfax County, Va., 1973-74; mem. Springfield Dist. Council, 1972-74; mem. Fairfax County Fedn. Civic Assns., 1972-74. Decorated Bronze medal for combat area service Army Material Command, 1973; NSF grantee, 1967; recipient Spl. Act and Service award Night Vision Lab., 1971. Mem. Optical Soc. Am. (v.p. sect. 1978-79), Soc. Photog. Instrumentation Engrs., Am. Physics. Soc., Art League, Springfield Art Guild, Friends of Matthew Brady Soc. Clubs: Morgan Car, Austin-Healy, Washington Rally. Patentee apparatus for and method of testing direct view image intensifiers. Home: 910 Neal Dr Alexandria VA 22314 Office: DRSEL-NVVI Fort Belvoir VA 22308

MIKESELL, STELLA MARIE, nursing adminstr.; b. Chgo., Nov. 15, 1930; d. Henry Robert and Josephine Marie (Klapper) Friebe; B.S.N., U. Ill., 1967; M.S.N., St. Xavier Coll., 1971; children—James W., Deana Louise Emery. Staff nurse, ednl. instr. State Ill. Dept. Mental Health, 1967-69, supr., 1971; staff nurse psychiatry, psychol. generalist VA, Bay Pines, Fla., 1971-74; asso. chief nursing service VA, Memphis, Tenn., 1974-75; asso. chief nursing service/edn., Dayton, Ohio, 1975-77, Dublin, Ga., 1977-79, Alexandria, La., 1979—; chmn. Nurse Profl. Standards Bd., Dayton and Dublin, 1975-79; mgr. Fed. Women Program, Dublin, 1977-79, mem. EEO adv. com., 1977-79; mem. subcom. Writing Affirmative EEO Plan of Action, 1977-78; chmn. disaster planning com. VA, Dublin, 1977-79, chmn. learning resource com., 1977-79; asso. instr. Wright State U., Dayton, 1977-78. Mem. Ga. Adult Edn. Assn. Episcopalian. Clubs: Toastmasters, Order Eastern Star. Office: VA Med Center Alexandria LA 71301

MIKLAS, PAULINE ROBINSON (MRS. MICHAEL J. MIKLAS), clubwoman, writer; b. Balt., Nov. 15, 1913; d. Emmanuel Ellinger and Mary Alice (Dunn) Robinson; grad. Inst. de Notre Dame; m. Michael J. Miklas, Dec. 23, 1946; children—Patricia (Mrs. Rudolph Henning), Joanne P. Free-lance advt. and pub. relations, Balt., Miami Beach, Fla., Tampa, Fla.; dir. pub. relations Miami Beach Pub. Co., 1946-49, Coppertone, Inc., Coconut Grove, Fla., 1947-48. Chmn. TV and communications Mother's March of Dimes, 1955-58; pres. Women of Gallery, Tampa Art Inst., 1956-58; cons. Clearwater (Fla.) Symphony League, 1957-60; pres. Tampa Philharmonic Women's League, 1957-60; United Cerebral Palsy Assn., Tampa, 1958, Sunstate Opera Guild, Tampa, 1965-69; Eastern U.S. chmn. Am. Art Week, Am. Artists Profl. League, 1965. Bd. dirs. Tampa Gen. Hosp. Women's Aux., 1955-58, Tampa Philharmonic Assn., 1952-63, Multiple Sclerosis Assn., 1962-64, Religious Arts Theatre, Tampa, 1964-66. Named Outstanding Woman of Fla., 1960. Mem. Nat. League Am. Pen Women (pres. Davis Island br. 1960-64, Fla. pres.

1970-72, nat. biennial chmn. 1972-74, founder, pres. Tallahassee br. 1978-80), Internat. Platform Assn., UDC (chpt. v.p. 1968-70, 78-79, pres. Winnie Davis chpt. 1979—), Fla. Fedn. Music Clubs (dir. 1955-62, Tampa C. of C. (chmn. edn. for Davis Island 1958), League Women Voters (dir. 1960-64), Hillsborough County Fedn. Women's Clubs (chmn. 1962-66), Friday Morning Musicale (artistic dir. 1962-66). Clubs: Tampa Women's (certificate of recognition 1976), Davis Island Garden (Tampa); May Oaks Garden (pres. 1980—). Editor Crescendo mag., 1963-65. Home: 2555 Marston Rd Tallahassee FL 33303

MIKRONIS, CHRISTOS EDGAR, hydraulic valves mfg. co. exec.; b. Baton Rouge, Apr. 16, 1921; s. Christos B. and Mary Elizabeth (Rawlins) M.; student La. State U., 1938-41; m. Winnie V. Whitehead, Feb. 13, 1943; children—Edgar Andrew, Robert Tucker, Gary Eugene. Mgr. truck and fleet sales Ford Dealership, Jackson, Miss., 1945-48; owner, mgr. Western Auto Asso. Store, Purvis, Miss., 1949-51; gen. contractor, egg rancher, Sarasota, Fla., 1951-59; design engr. Sarasota Precision Products Inc., 1959-62; chief sales engr. Rexnord Inc., Sarasota, 1959-65, 1962-65, v.p. ops., 1965-67, exec. v.p., 1967-68, pres., 1968-78, mgr. mobile mktg., 1978—, Osprey, Fla., 1977—; dir. Sarasota Precision Products Inc., Pan Am. Bank, Sarasota. Second v.p. Sarasota chpt. Am. Cancer Soc., 1978, crusade chmn., 1st v.p., 1979; bd. dirs. Sta. WEDV-TV, public TV. Served with USNR, 1941-45. Decorated Purple Heart, Silver Star. Mem. Sarasota County C. of C. (pres. 1979), Nat. Fluid Power Assn., Sarasota Area Mfrs. Assn. (pres. 1978). Republican. Presbyterian. Clubs: Univ. Sarasota (gov. 1975—), Rotary (pres. Sarasota Bay 1973). Design contbn. in hydraulic componentry for power transmission. Home: 2572 Tulip St Sarasota FL 33579 Office: Rexnord Inc 838 S Tamiami Trail Osprey FL 33559

MILANO, JOHN LOUIS, credit co. exec.; b. Bklyn., July 20, 1945; s. John E. and Ann M.: B.A., S.I. Community Coll., 1967; m. Barbara Lewis, May 12, 1975; 1 dau., Jennifer Lynn. Vice-pres. fin. Primer Co., N.Y.C., 1967-72; v.p. fin. Pro Recovery Ser., Jacksonville, Fla., 1972-78; pres. Am. Med. Credit Corp., Jacksonville, 1978—; pres. Am. Profl. Consultants, Jacksonville, 1979—: cons. fin. audit, billing, credit collection data processing systems. Office: 2121 Corporate Square Blvd Suite 266 Jacksonville FL 32216

MILAZZO, MILDRED MARYANN, statistician; b. N.Y.C., Dec. 21, 1912; d. Paul Zachary and Laura Virginia (Manzo) Milazzo; B.C.S., Columbus U., 1951, postgrad., 1951-52; postgrad. U.S. Dept. Agr. Grad. Sch., 1943-66, George Washington U., 1963-64. Statis. clk. WPB, Washington, 1943-44, econ. statistician, 1944-45; cost accounting clk. OPA, Washington, 1945-47; fiscal accounting clk. VA, Washington, 1948-51, Dept. Commerce, Bur. Pub. Rds., Washington, 1951-54, engring. aide, 1954-56, statis. asst., 1956-66; statistician in social sci. Dept. Justice, Washington, 1966-68; fiscal analyst Rehab. Services Adminstrn., HEW, Washington, 1968-76. Mem. Am. Statis. Assn., Internat. Platform Assn., Alpha Chi Upsilon. Home: 200 Branch Rd SE Vienna VA 22180

MILBRODT, PAUL EUGENE, electronic engr.; b. Wilson, Ark., Mar. 21, 1923; s. Paul and Ola (Sanders) M.; student Ark. State Coll., 1946-49; B.S. in Elec. Engring., U. Ark., 1951; M.S., George Washington U., 1969; m. Edna Louise Lindenberg, Aug. 3, 1951; 1 dau., Cathy Louise. Electronic engr. Nat. Union, 1951-54, Melpar Inc., 1954-57; prin. electronic engr. Budd Co., 1963-65; sr. electronic engr. Control Sci. Corp., 1965-67; engring. mgr. Airtronics, Inc., Chantilly, Va., 1968-75; engring. and mktg. cons., Va., 1967—. Served with USAAF, 1941-45. Registered profl. engr. Home: 12001 Central Dr Fairfax VA 22030

MILBURN, JAMES WILLIAM, JR., concessions co. exec.; b. Chgo., Oct. 29, 1939; s. James William and Margaret E. (Grundmann) M.; student Lyons Twp. Jr. Coll., 1957, 59, So. Ill. U., 1961; B.S. in Bus. Adminstrn., U. Denver, 1963; m. Dinah Sue Rogers, Apr. 6, 1974; children—Bradley Neal, James Temple. Gen. office and control staff Nat. Park Concessions, Inc., Mammoth Cave, Ky., 1961, mgmt. trainee food and beverage controls Sherman House Ltd., Chgo., 1964-65; mgmt. trainee Isle Royale Nat. Park, Nat. Park Concessions, Inc. Mich., 1965, asst. mgr. Big Bend Nat. Park, Tex., 1965-66, asst. mgr. ops., 1968-69, mgr., 1970—; mgr. Sol Due Hot Springs Olympic Nat. Park, Wash., 1966-68. Pres., Terlingua Ranch Property Owners Assn., 1978-79; active Tex. Tourist Devel. Agy., 1969—. Served with U.S. Army, 1963-64. Recipient Award of Merit, Nat. Restaurant Assn., 1963; Outstanding Achievement award, Chgo. Tribune, 1965. Mem. Discover Tex. Assn., Nat. Restaurant Assn., Alpine C. of C., W. Tex. C. of C., Hwy. 67 Assn. Democrat. Lutheran. Address: Basin Rural Station Big Bend Nat Park TX 79834

MILBURN, WILLIAM ISAAC, banker; b. Washington County, Ky., Mar. 15, 1914; s. John and Pearl (Sparrow) M.; student in bus. Campbellsville Coll., 1932-33; m. Theresa Holtzclaw, Aug. 15, 1945; 1 dau., Theresa Sue Milburn Sallee. With Old Bank of Perryville (Ky.), 1933-76, exec. v.p., 1966-76, dir., 1960-76. Sec., Boyle Sch. Bd., 1973-76; chmn. Community Drive, Cemetery Bd., 1973-74. Served with AUS, 1943-45. Named Ky. col. Mem. Am. Legion, VFW, 40 and 8. Democrat. Baptist. Address: Route 1 Harmon Heights Danville KY 40422

MILDREN, JACK, oil co. exec.; b. Kingsville, Tex., Oct. 10, 1949; s. Larry and Mary Glynne (Lamont) M.; B.B.A., Okla. U., 1972; m. Janis Susan Butler, Jan. 14, 1972; children—Leigh Dresden, Laureen. Pres., Regency Exploration Co., Dallas. Mem. Am., Dallas assns. petroleum landmen, Permian Basin Landmen Assn., Nat. Football League Players Assn. Clubs: Bent Tree Country, Bay Hill, Petroleum (Midland), Okla. Alumni Assn. Home: 7145 Manor Oaks Dallas TX 75248 Office: 16950 Dallas Parkway Dallas TX 75248

MILER, GEORGE GIBBON, JR., electronics co. exec.; b. Sumter, S.C., Jan. 21, 1940; s. George Gibbon and Coralie (Bland) M.; B.S., Clemson U., 1962; postgrad. Oak Ridge Inst. Nuclear Studies, 1965; M.S., Fla. Inst. Tech., 1968; m. Jennie Lou McGee, Aug. 8, 1964; children—George Bland, Elizabeth Lucretia, Wyatt Hamilton. Research engr. Coll. Arts and Scis., Clemson (S.C.) U., 1963-67; engr. Harris Semiconductor, Palm Bay, Fla., 1968-72; founder, pres. George Miler, Inc., Greenville, S.C., 1972—. Mem. Brevard County Govt. Study Commn., 1971-72, chmn. goals and alternatives com. and data processing com., 1971-72; bd. dirs. Cape Kennedy Young Reps., 1971-72. Mem. IEEE (Piedmont sect. treas. 1979; sr. mem.), Aircraft Owners and Pilots Assn., Nat. Fedn. Ind. Bus., C. of C. U.S., Greater Greenville C. of C. Baptist. Contbr. articles to profl. jours. Home: 305 Sasanqua Dr Greenville SC 29615 Office: 303 Airport Rd Greenville SC 29607

MILES, ALAN CLARENCE, gen. contracting exec.; b. Norfolk, Va., Oct. 24, 1947; s. Joseph Dudley and Alma Julia (Noland) M.; student Randolph Macon Coll., 1965-67; Asso. Sci. in Bus., Chesapeake Coll., 1967-70; student Old Dominion U., 1967-70; m. Evelyn Miller, Mar. 9, 1979. Vice pres. J.D. Miles & Sons, Chesapeake, Va., 1967-73, J.D. Miles Roofing, Inc., Chesapeake, 1971-73; pres., chmn. bd. A.C. Miles Bldg. Systems, Inc., Norfolk, 1973—, Remi Properties, Norfolk, 1974—, ACM Investments, Norfolk, 1975—; mem. pres. adv. council Varco-Pruden Mfg. Co., 1976, outstanding dealer award, 1976; mem. pres. adv. council Star Mfg. Co., 1975, outstanding dealer award, 1974. Contact worker Teleministry Counseling Program, 1977. Served with Va. N.G., 1967. Mem. Nat. Assn. Gen. Contractors, Builders and Contractors Exchange Norfolk, Tidewater Roofing Assn. (past treas.), Metal Bldg Assn. (pres. Va. Chpt.). Republican. Methodist. Clubs: Chesapeake Better Bus. (pres. 1970), Chesapeake Coll. Athletic (pres. 1971), Norfolk Kiwanis (dir. 1977—, v.p. 1978, 79), Moose. Address: 898 Widgeon Rd Norfolk VA 23513

MILES, BENJAMIN BOWLER, radio sta. exec.; b. Richmond, Va., Feb. 19, 1943; s. William Haywood and Virginia (Bowler) M.; student Va. Union U., 1961-65, Va. Commonwealth U., 1972-73; m. Jacqueline Elaine Hughes, Aug. 24, 1968; children—Jacques, Jamal, Jason. Announcer Sta. WANT, Richmond, 1964-66, 68-69, program dir., 1969-73, ops. mgr., 1973-77, gen. mgr., 1977—; tchr. J. Sargeant Reynolds Community Coll. Vice-pres., Met. Athletic Scholarship Fund, Richmond, 1976—. Served wtih U.S. Army, 1966-68. Mem. Black Music Assn., Laurel Athletic Assn. (dir. 1977-78), Nat. Assn. TV and Radio Announcers (sgt. at arms 1976). Roman Catholic. Office: 1101 Front St Richmond VA 23222

MILES, CHARLES EWING, corp. exec., biochemist; b. Granite City, Ill., Sept. 29, 1929; s. Finis Ewing and Lela (Robertson) M.; student U.S. Armed Forces Inst., 1947-49; B.S., St. Louis U., 1950; M.S., Tex. Tech. U., 1954, Ph.D. in Polit. Sci., U. Tex., 1967; m. Jane Frances Kallus, June 6, 1964; children—Karen, Kevin, Jonathan, Alyson, Joshua. Chmn. dept. bacteriology USPHS, 1949-51; cons. biochemist St. Louis County Hosp., 1951-58; biochemist, chmn. bd. Stanbio Labs. Inc., San Antonio, 1958—; chmn. bd. Best Leasing Co., San Antonio, 1970—, Green Mountain Corp., San Antonio, 1973—, Prince Edward Inc., Rockport, Tex., 1975—; dir. numerous other cos. Tex. awards chmn. Boy Scouts Am., 1953-62; pres. San Antonio Symphony, 1969—; trustee St. Mary's Hall, San Antonio, 1977. Served with USN, 1947-49. Recipient award K.C., 1960. Mem. Am. Med. Technologists (award 1955), Am. Assn. Clin. Chemistry, Am. Bacteriol. Assn., San Antonio C. of C. Republican. Roman Catholic. Patentee in field. Contbr. articles to profl. jours. Home: 3506 Mary Mont San Antonio TX 78217 Office: 2930 E Houston St San Antonio TX 78202

MILES, JOHN E., state senator; b. Florence County, S.C., July 13, 1939; s. McSwain and Lucille (Sims) M.; B.A. in Polit. Sci. cum laude, U. S.C., 1978, B.A. in English magna cum laude; m. Rachel Delores McCaskill, Sept. 28, 1962. Tchr. piano, 1963-71; organist Clarendon Baptist Ch., 1962-66, 1st Bapt. Ch., 1966-69; pres., gen. mgr. stas. WFIG and WWDM, Columbia, S.C., 1968-76; tchr. English, Sumter (S.C.) High Sch.; mem. S.C. Ho. of Reps., 1973-74, S.C. Senate, 1976—. Chmn., Sumter County Democratic Party; mem. Sumter County Devel. Bd.; pres. Manning Jaycees, 1965; bd. dirs. S.C. Jaycees, 1967. Served with AUS, 1955-58. Recipient various service awards; named Jaycee Boss of Year, 1973. Mem. Sumter C. of C. (dir.). Baptist. Club: Shriners. Home: 602 W Calhoun St Sumter SC 29150 Office: 501 Gressette Bldg Columbia SC

MILES, OSCAR LANDON, III, engring. and constrn. co. exec.; b. Monroe, La., Apr. 5, 1920; s. Oscar Landon and Gladys (Skinner) M.; B.S., La. Tech. U., 1940; m. Virginia Anita Vaughan, Dec. 9, 1944; children—Margaret Ann (Mrs. Oscar P. Barnes), Michael Landon. Mgr. payrolls U.S. Contrn. Q.M., Alexandria, La., 1940; chief project accountant Ford, Bacon & Davis, Monroe, La., 1941-61, mgr. sealants dept., 1962-67, v.p. bus. devel., 1968-77, v.p. corporate mktg., 1977—, v.p. sealants dept., 1979—; pres., dir. Sealants Internat., Inc., West Chester, Pa., 1965—; dir. Engenharia E Construcoes Ltda., Sao Paulo, Brazil. Exec. adviser Jr. Achievement, Monroe, 1970-71; pres. Little League Baseball, Joliet, Ill., 1960; speaker United Fund, 1973-75; chmn. council Boy Scouts Am., 1975-76. Served with USNR, 1942-46; lt. comdr. Res. (ret.). Mem. T.A.P.P.I., Am., New Eng., Southeastern gas assns., N.C. Pulp and Paper Found., Am. Inst. Chem. Engrs. (speakers bur. 1975), La. Engring. Soc., So. Indsl. Devel. Assn., Nat. Def. Transp. Assn., Alpha Phi Omega. Episcopalian. Mason (32 deg., Shriner, K.T.). Clubs: New York Athletic (N.Y.C.); Lotus (pres. 1969-70), Bayou De Siard Country (Monroe). Home: 4405 Belle Terre Monroe LA 71201 Office: 3901 Jackson St Monroe LA 71201

MILES, SHARRON SUE BOLDING, ednl. adminstr.; b. Temple, Tex., Oct. 20, 1946; d. Teddy Wayne and Charlotte Josephine (Murray) Bolding; A.A., Temple Jr. Coll., 1966; B.S.Ed., S.W. Tex. State U., 1968, M.Ed., 1969; postgrad. Baylor U., 1979—; m. Danny Roy Miles, May 30, 1969; children—Daniel Adam, Amy Cenée. Speech therapist San Marcos (Tex.) Ind. Sch. Dist., 1969-70, Alamo Heights Ind. Sch. Dist., San Antonio, 1970-72; spl. edn. tchr., speech therapist Temple Ind. Sch. Dist., 1972-75, supr. spl. edn., 1975-76; dir. spl. edn. Bell County Coop. for Exceptional Children, Bartlett, Tex., 1976—. Bd. dirs. Child Care Coordinating Council; program chmn. Holland PTA, 1978; Sunday sch. dir. First Baptist Ch., Holland, Tex., 1979-80. Mem. Am. Speech and Hearing Assn., Tex. Tchrs. Assn., Council Exceptional Children, NEA, Tex. Speech and Hearing Assn., Tex. Assn. Children with Learning Disabilities, Assn. Childhood Edn., Jaycee Wives, Gamma Phi Beta, Phi Delta Kappa. Club: Holland Women's Study. Office: PO Drawer S Bartlett TX 76511

MILES, STEPHEN WARREN, chem. bulk storage co. exec.; b. East Boston, Mass., June 5, 1935; s. Frederick E. and Josephine D. (Romasko) M.; B.M.E., Cornell U., 1958; postgrad. N.Y. U., 1963-65; m. Marilyn Ross, Oct. 20, 1962; children—Stephen Warren, Edward, Thomas. Engr., mktg. exec. GATX, Chgo. and N.Y.C., 1958-65; pres. chem. div. Steuber Co., N.Y.C., 1965-69; v.p. Burgess Industries, Houston, 1969-72; founder, pres. Terminal Specialists Internat., Houston, 1969—, Intercontinental Bulk Systems, Inc., 1975—, Stemil, Inc., 1972—; co-founder, partner, pres. Intercontinental Terminals Co., 1972—; dir. Allied Deer Park Bank, Intercontinental Bulk Systems, Inc. Served to 1st lt. U.S. Army, 1959-60. Mem. Ind. Liquid Terminals Assn. (dir., v.p.), Southwest Chem. Assn., Nat. Petroleum Refiners Assn., Chem. Mktg. Research Assn., Houston Port Bur., Houston C. of C. (community adminstr. Terra Oaks). Republican. Clubs: Univ., Houston Racquet, Plaza. Home: 10622 Tarleton St Houston TX 77024 Office: 17 Briar Hollow Houston TX 77027

MILES, THEO FRANKLIN, chemist; b. Thomaston, Ga., Feb. 4, 1940; s. John Franklin and Ruby Lee (Sargent) M.; A.B., Mercer U., 1963; m. Linda Faye Holmes, June 16, 1963; children—Kelley, Karen. Chemist, Thomaston Mills (Ga.), 1966-72, mgr. quality assurance, 1972-79, tech. supt., 1979—; instr. Gordon Jr. Coll. Deacon, treas. E. Thomas Bapt. Ch. Served to 1st lt. AUS, 1964-66. Mem. Am. Assn. Textile Chemists and Colorists. Club: Kiwanis. Home: 505 Nelson Dr Thomaston GA 30286 Office: Thomaston Mills Thomaston GA 30286

MILES, THOMAS PEYTON, lawyer, judge; b. Appling County, Ga., Dec. 20, 1921; s. Thomas Peyton and Elizabeth (Faulkner) M.; LL.B., Mercer U., 1950, A.B., 1951; m. Mary Jacqueline Fennell, Sept. 2, 1944; children—Mary Cathy, Constance Ann, Elizabeth Paulette, Thomas Peyton Miles III. Admitted to Ga. bar, 1950; practice law, Baxley, 1950—; solicitor State Ct. of Appling, 1955-58, judge, 1959—; judge Juvenile Ct., Appling County, 1963—. Dir. Appling Devel. Corp. Mayor, Surrency, Ga., 1953-60. Served with USAAF, 1940-45. Decorated Air medal with 10 oak leaf clusters, Purple Heart. Mem. Am., Ga., Brunswick (pres. 1963-64) bar assns., V.F.W., Am. Legion, Delta Theta Phi. Mason, Moose, Elk, Kiwanian (past pres. Baxley, past lt. gov. 4th div.). Home: PO Box 412 Baxley GA 31513 Office: PO Box 412 Baxley GA 31513

MILGRAM, ABRAHAM SAMUEL, constrn. exec.; b. Tel-Aviv, Palestine, Sept. 25, 1936; s. Jaime and Esther (Reich) M.; came to U.S., 1952; B.S., U. Tex., 1958; postgrad. Central U. Venezuela, 1958-59, Northwestern U., 1958; m. Zelma K. Milgram; 1 son, Andrew Scott. Field engr. Atlantic Refining Co., Port Arthur, Tex., 1958; design engr. Orinoco Mining Co., Port Ordaz, Venezuela, 1958-63; gen. mgr. Bella Co., Beaumont, Tex., 1963-66, exec. v.p., 1966—, also dir.; exec. v.p., dir. Hurco, Inc., Beaumont, 1967—; dir. Tex. Bank Beaumont. Trustee, Sabine Area Laborers Tng. Trust, Sabine area Carpenters Apprenticeship Tng. Fund. Mem. ASTM, Am. Concrete Inst., ASCE. Home: 680 Heritage Ln Beaumont TX 77706 Office: PO Box 5421 Beaumont TX 77702

MILHOUSE, PAUL WILLIAM, bishop; b. St. Francisville, Ill., Aug. 31, 1910; s. Willis Cleveland and Carrie (Pence) M.; A.B., Ind. Central Coll., 1932; D.D., 1950; B.D., Am. Theol. Sem., 1937, Th.D., 1946; L.H.D., Westmar Col., 1965; S.T.D., Oklahoma City U., 1969; D.D., So. Meth. U., 1969; m. Mary Frances Noblitt, June 29, 1932; children—Mary (Mrs. R.L. Hauswald), Pauline (Mrs. Arthur Vermillion), Paul Davic. Ordained to ministry United Brethren Ch., 1931; pastor, Birds, Ill., 1928-29, Mt. Vernon, Ill., 1932, Elliott, Ill., 1932-37, Olney, Ill., 1937-41, Decatur, Ill., 1941-51; asso. editor Telescope-Messenger, Harrisburg, Pa., 1951-59; exec. sec. Gen. Council of Adminstrn., Dayton, Ohio, 1959-60; bishop, Kansas City, 1960-68, Oklahoma City, 1968—. Pres., Decatur (Ill.) Council of Chs., 1945-49, Bd. of Arbitration, Decatur, 1946, Bd. of Evangelism, Dayton, 1960-68; pres. Council Bishops United Meth. Ch., 1977-78. Trustee So. Meth. U., Oklahoma City U., Meth. Manor, Meth. Home, Boys Ranch; v.p. Council Fin. and Adminstrn., 1976-80. Recipient Alumnus award Ind. Central U., 1978; Disting. Friend award, 1979, Disting. Service award, 1980 (both Oklahoma City U.). Mem. Epsilon Sigma Alpha. Author: Enlisting and Developing Church Leaders, 1946; Come Unto Me, 1946; Doorways to Spiritual Living, 1950; Except the Lord Build the House, 1949; Christian Worship in Symbol and Ritual, 1953; Lift Up Your Eyes, 1955; Laymen in the Church, 1957; At Life's Crossroads, 1959; Philip William Otterbein, Pioneer Preacher to German Speaking Americans, 1968; Nineteen Bishops of the Evangelical United Brethren Church, 1974. Editor: Facing Frontiers, 1960; Organizing for Effective Ministry, 1980; Theological and Historical Roots of United Methodists, 1980. Contbr. articles to profl. jours. Home: 2213 NW 56th Terr Oklahoma City OK 73112 Office: 2420 N Blackwelder Oklahoma City OK 73106

MILIAN, EMILIO, broadcaster; b. Sagua la Grande, Cuba, Sept. 8, 1931: s. Emilio and Maria M.; came to U.S., 1965, naturalized, 1973; student U.Havana, 1948-52; B.A., Biscayne Coll., 1974; m. Emma Maria Milian, Nov. 16, 1958; children—Emilio, Alberto, Mirtha Mary. Broadcaster, journalist, radio and TV producer, Havana, 1948-59; columnist Excelsior newspaper, Mex., 1965: radio announcer, newsman, sports commentator Sta. WMIE, Miami, Fla., 1965-71; owner off-set printing bus., 1966-70; editor El Rotograbaado, Miami, 1970; advt. dir. Miamco Advt., 1970; columnist, asso. mgr. El Dia, Miami, 1971; program and news dir. Sta. WQBA, Miami, 1971-76, v.p., 1976-77; pres. New Continental Broadcasting Co., Miami, 1978—. Vice pres. Leukemia Soc. Am. So. Fla. chpt., 1976—; mem. community relations bd. Dade County, Fla., 1975-78; mem. Hispanic-Am. Bicentennial U.S.A., 1976; active voter registration, human rights; founder Worldwide Assn. Relief of Refugees; creater Ann. Parade of the Three Magi; condr. radiothons for charitable causes. Named Freedom Fighter of Year, Fla. Broadcasters Assn., 1976, Broadcaster of Year, Greater Miami Broadcasters Assn., 1976; recipient spl. citation Pres. Gerald Ford, 1976. Mem. Nat. Broadcast Editorial Assn. (spl. award). Roman Catholic. Clubs: Lions, Sertoma, Optimist. Office: 1015 N American Way Suite 113 Miami FL 33132

MILK, RICHARD GEORGE, economist; b. Munnsville, N.Y., Sept. 28, 1915; s. Lee B. and Martha Priscilla (Hendricks) M.; B.S., Cornell U., 1936; M.S. (Univ. fellow), U. Tenn., 1939; Ph.D., Ia. State U., 1959; m. Juliet Ruth Chick, Aug. 25, 1940; children—Richard, Robert, Carol, Martha, Ann With U.S. Dept. Agr., 1936-37, 39-41; farm mgmt. Scarritt Coll., Nashville, 1940-46; agrl. missionary Bd. Missions United Meth. Ch., Cuba, Jamaica, Mexico, Vietnam, 1946-70; asst. prof. econs. N.E. La. U., 1970-73; asso. prof. econs. Va. State Coll., Petersburg, 1973-76; lay pastor United Meth. Ch., Stony Creek, Va., 1976-78; asso. prof. econs Va. Commonwealth U., Richmond, 1978—. Chmn. Commn. on rural ch. Cuban Council Chs., 1954-56; teaching fellow Iowa State U. at Ames, 1957-59. Mem. Am. Econs. Assn., So. Va assns. econs., Omicron Delta Epsilon. Methodist. Author: Responsibilism, 1952; contbr. articles to profl. jours. Home: 343 Greenwood Dr Petersburg VA 23803

MILLARD, DAVID RALPH, JR., physician; b. St. Louis, June 4, 1919; s. David Ralph and Florence Nightingale (Hamilton) M.; B.A., Yale, 1941; M.D., Harvard, 1944; m. Barbara Lou Rene Smith, Apr. 7, 1956. Intern, Boston Children's Hosp., 1944-45; resident Vanderbilt U. Hosp., 1945-47; plastic surgery trainee under Sir Harold Gillies, London, Eng., 1948-49; resident Barnes Hosp., St. Louis, 1949; fellow in plastic surgery Straith Clinic, Detroit, 1950; resident in plastic surgery Jefferson Davis Hosp., Houston, 1951; instr. plastic surgery Baylor Med. Sch., Houston, 1951-52; practice medicine, specializing in plastic surgery, Miami, Fla., 1955—; chief dept. plastic surgery Variety Children's Hosp., 1967—; mem. staff Jackson Meml. Hosp., VA Hosp., Mt. Sinai Hosp., Kingston (Jamaica) Pub. Hosp., Univ. Coll. of West Indies, Kingston, Children's Hosp., Kingston; clin. prof. surgery U. Miami, 1967—, Light-Millard prof. plastic surgery, 1974—, chief div. plastic surgery, 1967—; chmn. South Fla. Cleft Palate Clinic, Miami, 1957—. Served to lt. (j.g.) USNR, 1945-46, to maj. USMCR, 1954; Korea. Diplomate Am. Bd. Plastic Surgery. Fellow A.C.S.; mem. Am., Fla., Dade County, So. med. assns., Am. Cleft Palate Assn., Am. (pres. Ednl. Found. 1970-72, 1st prize sr. div. Internat. Scholastic Contests Ednl. Found. 1965, 68), Southeastern socs. plastic and reconstructive surgeons, Am., Fla., Brit. (corr.) assns. plastic surgeons, Internat. Fedn. Plastic Surgeons, Soc. Head and Neck Surgeons, Am. Soc Aesthetic Plastic Surgery. Author: (with Sir Harold Gillies) The Principles and Art of Plastic Surgery, 3 vols., 1957; Cleft Craft: The Evolution of Its Surgery in Lip, Nose, Alveolus and Palate, 3 vols. (Hawkins award), 1976; editor: Corrective Rhinoplasty, 1976; contbr. articles to profl. jours. Home: 4501 Lake Rd Bay Point Miami FL 33137 Office: 1444 NW 14th Ave Miami FL 33125

MILLEDGE, SARAH FRANKLIN (MRS. STANLEY MILLEDGE), civic worker; b. Melrose, Mass., July 8, 1906; d. Albert Barnes and Edith (Bradbury) Franklin; B.A., Wellesley Coll., 1927; m. Stanley Milledge, Sept. 1, 1928 (dec. Oct. 1965); children—Allan Francis, Sarah Woodman (Mrs. Harold S. Nelson), Eleanor Franklin (Mrs. Barry Decker). Producer, Woman's Place, Sta. WCKT-TV, Miami, Fla., 1962—. Pres. Miami Shores PTA, 1938-39; pres. Girl Scouts U.S.A., Dade County, 1948-50, chmn. region 6, 1952-56, nat. dir., 1952—, chmn. nat. nominating com., 1963-66, mem. nat. exec.

com., 1958, council pres., 1961-62; pres. Children's Service Bur., 1950-52, Vis. Nurse Assn., 1952-54; chmn. Dade County recreation div. Welfare Planning Council, 1949-51, chmn. health div., 1956-60; mem. Children's Com., 1951-56; sec. Community Chest, 1953-55; v.p. Council Community Relations, 1954-56, Civil Liberties Assn., 1954-57; sec. Protestant Service Bur., 1955-56 (all Dade County); v.p. James E. Scott Community Assn., 1957-70; mem. state bd. Fla. Council Human Relations, 1958-62; sec. Fla. Co-operating Council Children and Youth; chmn. Fla. Com. for Children and Youth, 1968; bd. St. Petersburg Community Welfare Council, 1958-62; sec. South Pinellas Mental Health chpt., 1959-62; bd. dirs. Dade County Mental Health Assos., 1975-78; bd. dirs. Girl Scouts Tropical Fla., Dade County Welfare Planning Council, Vis. Nurse Assn., Miami Travellers Aid, United Cerebral Palsy Assn., United Ch. Women Greater Miami; pres. Miami Wellesley Club, 1979—; sec. Wellesley Class of 1927; trustee Everglades Sch. Girls, Miami, Fla., 1955-60; bd. dirs. Miami YWCA, pres., 1968-72; treas. Women's Com. of 100, Miami; chmn. Miami Council for Continuing Edn. of Women, 1971-72. Recipient Fla. regional award NCCJ, 1957, Media award, Beautiful Activist award Miami chpt. N.O.W., 1974; named Woman of Achievement, Dist. 12 Fla. Bus and Profl. Women, 1967; Community Service award Fla. Internat. U., 1978; award Miami chpt. Am. Women in Radio-TV, 1979. Mem. AAUP (chpt. bd. 1958—, local chpt. treas. 1959-62, vice chmn. Miami 1971-72), Am. Women in Radio and TV (v.p. chpt.), UN Assn. (pres. chpt. 1972-75), Soc. Mayflower Descs., Women in Communications. Congregationalist. Club: Miami Wellesley (pres. 1947-49). Home: 1600 S Bayshore Ln Miami FL 33133 Office: Station WCKT Miami FL 33138

MILLER, ALBERT HENDERSON, cons. engr.; b. Newport, Ark., Nov. 30, 1932; s. Albert Jackson and Dovie (Murphy) M.; student Ark. State Tchrs. Coll., 1950-51; B.S. in Agrl. Engring., U. Ark., 1955; M.S. in Agrl. Engring., U. Mo., 1957; m. Lynette Alexander, Dec. 31, 1957; children—Alison Lyn, Albert Alexander. Sales engr. Delta Irrigation Co., Memphis, 1956; grad. asst. U. Mo., 1955-57; field engr. Short & Brownlee Constrn. Co., Inc., Newport, Ark. and Kansas City, Mo., 1957-59; br. mgr. Browntee & Rogers, Inc., El Dorado, Ark., 1960; v.p. H.D. Kantor & Son, Inc., Clarksdale, Miss., 1961; pres. Miller Engring. Co., Inc., Clarksdale, 1961-63, Miller-Newell Engrs., Ltd., Newport, Ark., 1963—; owner A.H. Miller Farms, Newport, 1973-75; pres. Miller-Newell Farms, Inc., Newport, 1975—; sec.-treas. Miller-Newell Abstract Co., Inc., Newport, 1967—; partner Village Realty & Devel. Co., Newport. Registered profl. engr., Ark., Miss., Mo., Ala., Tenn. Mem. Am. Soc. Agrl. Engrs. (chmn. Ark. chpt. 1971), Nat. Soc. Profl. Engrs., Cons. Engrs. Council Ark. (pres.), Newport Area C. of C. (pres. 1971), Phi Delta Theta (chpt. pres. 1954, pres. alumni club 1967), Gamma Sigma Delta, Kappa Kappa Psi, Gamma Alpha (chpt. pres. 1957). Episcopalian. Clubs: Rotary (dir. 1964-68, pres. 1973), Newport Country (dir.). Home: 1001 Walnut St Newport AR 72112 Office: 308 Walnut St Newport AR 72112

MILLER, ALVIN JULIUS, ret. chem. engr.; b. Corsicana, Tex., Oct. 8, 1910; s. Mose Mayer and Raye (Daniels) M.; B.S., Tex. A. and M. U., 1933, M.S. in Chem. Engring., 1934; m. Ernestine Elam, June 21, 1942; 1 son, Larry D. Gas process engr. Phillips Petroleum Co., Bartlesville, Okla., 1934-40, chief process engr., 1947-50, industry tech. adviser, 1951-75; chief chemist Butadiene plant, Phillips Def. Dept., 1941-46. Recipient Hanlon award Gas Processors Assn., 1965; award of merit Am. Gas Assn., 1975. Mem. Nat. Soc. Profl. Engrs., Am. Chem. Soc., ASTM (com. on gaseous fuels award 1977), Am. Inst. Chem. Engrs. Contbr. articles to profl. jours.; patentee in field. Home: 1318 Melmart Dr Bartlesville OK 74003

MILLER, ANDREW LAMAR, state ofcl.; b. Repton, Ala., Oct. 8, 1939; s. Aubrey Alfred and Lois (Turnipseed) M.; B.S. in Pharmacy, Auburn U., 1970; M.S., Troy State U., 1976; m. Judith O'Neal Wallace, Dec. 14, 1964; children—Andrew Lamar, Patrick O'Neal. Cons. in civil and criminal litigation, 1967—; instr. Enterprise Jr. Coll., 1970—, Troy State U., 1971—; dir. Enterprise (Ala.) Regional Crime Lab., 1970-75; examiner questioned documents Hdqrs. Tech. Staff, Ala. Dept. Toxicology, Auburn, 1975—. Diplomate Am. Bd. Forensic Document Examiners. Mem. Am. Soc. Questioned Document Examiners, Am. Acad. Forensic Scis., So. Assn. Forensic Sci. Methodist. Research on effects of drugs and diseases on handwriting. Home: 101 Carter St Auburn AL 36830 Office: PO Box 231 Auburn AL 36830

MILLER, BRUCE RICHARD, jewelry store exec.; b. Hazleton, Pa., Mar. 16, 1944; s. Robert Joseph and Marguerite Marie (Fritz) M.; B.A. in Polit. Sci., Pa. State U., 1971. Supr. salary adminstrn. Govt. Employees Ins. Co., Chevy Chase, Md., 1971-73; asst. to personnel dir. MCI Telecommunications, Inc., Washington, 1973-74; wage and salary adminstr. Kay Jewelers, Inc., Alexandria, Va., 1974, dir. personnel, 1974—. Served with U.S. Army, 1966-70. Mem. Am. Soc. Personnel Adminstrn., Met. Washington Bd. Trade, Alexandria C. of C., Pa. State U. Alumni Assn. Club: Pa. State U. Nittany Lion. Contbr. articles to profl. jours. Home: 400 Madison St Alexandria VA 22314 Office: 320 King St Alexandria VA 22314

MILLER, CHARLES LEO, accountant; b. Lambert, Miss., May 28, 1931; s. Louis David and Sybil (Claussen) M.; B.S., Memphis State Coll., 1953; certificate Memphis Coll. Accountancy, 1956; m. Wanda Lee Trudel, Feb. 14, 1963; 1 dau., Crystal Ann. Staff accountant Minor & Moore, Memphis, 1955-57, Edward C. Wirotious & Co., Memphis, 1957-58; office mgr. Standard Welders Supply Co., Memphis, 1959-63; staff accountant Speer, Chavez, Ruggenberg & Wright, Bakersfield, Calif., 1963-65; pvt. practice accounting C. Leo Miller, Columbia, Tenn., 1965-76; partner Miller & York, Columbia, 1977-79, Miller Stutts & York, 1979—; sec. Recreation Enterprises Inc., Columbia, 1973—; pres. Crystal Clear Water Co., Columbia, 1977—; sec., treas., Funway Products Inc., Columbia, 1977-79; dir. Morgan Bros. Electric Co. Inc. Adviser Jr. Achievement Columbia, 1970-72, bd. dirs., 1972-74; scoutmaster Boy Scouts Am., 1966-74, asst. dist. commr., 1972-73, chmn. Duck River dist., 1977-79; treas., adviser, also bd. dirs. Maury County Creative Arts Guild, 1972-74; founder, pres. Duck River Humane Soc., 1973-75, 77-79, bd. dirs., 1973-79; bd. dirs. Big Bros. Columbia. Served with U.S. Army, 1953-55. C.P.A. Mem. Am. Inst. C.P.A.'s, Tenn. Soc. C.P.A.'s, Am. Legion, Nat. Assn. Accountants, Nat. Rifle Assn., Delta Sigma Pi. Methodist. Clubs: Shriners, Elks, Masons. Author: Campfire Ghost Stories (And How to Tell Them), 1975; Ghost and Crazy Horse Hollow, 1978. Home: Route 8 Columbia TN 38401 Office: 305 W 8th St Columbia TN 38401

MILLER, CHARLES RICKIE, thermal analyst; b. New Albany, Ind., Oct. 4, 1946; s. Marshall Christian and Thelma Virginia M.; B.A., DePauw U., 1969; postgrad. Rice U., 1969-70, U. Houston, 1972-76; m. Janel Howell, Nov. 24, 1968; children—Kimberly, Brian, Audrey, Rachel. Tech. editor Fed. Electric Corp., ITT, Houston, 1970-71, Service Tech. Corp., LTV, Houston, 1971; system safety engr. Boeing Aerospace Co., Houston, 1971-76; thermal analyst space div. Rockwell Internat. Co., Houston, 1976—. Rector scholar DePauw U., 1964-68; Rice fellow, 1969-70. Mem. AIAA, Nat. Space Inst. L-5 Soc., Air Force Assn., ASME, Am. Inst. Physics, Sigma Pi Sigma. Mem. editorial teams preliminary sci. reports Apollo 14 and 15, 1971-72. Home: 806 Walbrook Dr Houston TX 77062 Office: Space Div Rockwell Internat Co 1840 NASA Rd One Houston TX 77058

MILLER, CHARLES VALENTINE, physician; b. Omaha, Apr. 23, 1915; s. Lloyd Herman and Jennette L. (Wiegand) M.; B.S., U. Wyo., 1938; M.D., U. Rochester, 1942; m. Ann Clark, Apr. 28, 1945; 1 son, John Allyn. Intern U. Neb. Hosp., 1942-43, fellow U. Rochester Sch. Medicine, 1946-48; resident and instr. U. Tenn. Coll. Medicine, 1948-51; fellow hematology Pratt Diagnostic Clinic, Boston, 1958-59; practice medicine, Chattanooga, 1954-58, Ft. Worth, 1959-61; dir. labs., hematologist Mary Washington Hosp., Fredericksburg, Va., 1961-77; asst. public health officer Prince William County (Va.), 1979—. Bd. dirs. Fredericksburg chpt. A.R.C.; mem. med. adv. com. D.C. Blood Program; bd. dirs. Fredericksburg bd. Am. Cancer Soc.; med. bd. Va. chpt. Leukemia Soc. Am. Served from 1st lt. to maj., AUS, 1943-46; as maj. USAF, 1951-53; ETO. Diplomate Nat. Bd. Med. Examiners, Am. Bd. Pathology. Fellow Am. Soc. Clin. Pathologists, Internat. Soc. Hematology, Assn. Clin. Scientists, Soc. Nuclear Medicine; mem. AMA, Va. Med. Assn., Mid-Atlantic Assn. Blood Banks, Am. Coll. Nuclear Medicine, Internat. Platform Assn., Ducks Unltd., Am. Security Council, Va. Soc. Hematology, Sigma Chi, Gamma Sigma Epsilon. Presbyn. Club: Fredericksburg Rod and Gun. Research in field. Home: 1109 Westwood Dr Fredericksburg VA 22401

MILLER, CLEMON THERON, JR., textile co. exec.; b. Erwin, N.C., June 15, 1945; s. Clemon Theron and Dorothy Ann (Denning) M.; B.S. in Engring. Ops., N.C. State U., Raleigh, 1967; m. Judith Lee Strickland, July 31, 1966; children—Theron, Cathy. Div. staff engr. Burlington Industries, Durham, N.C., 1967-68, staff engr., Greensboro, N.C., 1968-71; chief engr. Boiler Equipment Co., Raleigh, 1971-76; environ. air systems engr. Burlington Industries, Greensboro, 1976-77, environ. air systems sect. mgr., 1977—. Bd. dirs. Woods of Guilford Neighborhood Assn., Greensboro, 1979—, Guilford Coll. Youth Athletic Assn., Greensboro, 1979—; youth football coach, jr. deacon First Baptist Ch., Greensboro. Clubs: Wolfpack, Masons. Home: 5303 King George Ct Greensboro NC 27410 Office: PO Box 21207 Greensboro NC 27420

MILLER, DALE DON, utility co. exec.; b. Bibb County, Ga., Dec. 12, 1941; s. John Thomas and Margaret Louise (Young) M.; Asso. Sci., So. Tech. Inst., 1963; student Oglethorpe Coll., 1968; grad. So. Tech. Inst., 1973; M.B.A. in Fin., Ga. State U., 1974; m. Brenda Joyce Lancaster, Dec. 5, 1964; children—Dawn Lynn, Robyn Lorene, Geoffrey Dale. Engring. asso. Wgstern Electric Co., Atlanta, 1963-64; field engr. Engring. Assos., Atlanta, 1964-65; project engr. J.B. McCrary, Atlanta, 1965-66; engring. asst. Ga. Power Co., Atlanta, 1966-67, sr. engring. asst., 1967-69, asst. div. trouble supr., 1969-71, dist. engr., Forest Park, Ga., 1971-72, asst. div. meter supt., 1972-74, distbn. staff engr., Atlanta, 1974-76, field ops. supr., 1976-77, mgr. skills devel., Tucker, Ga., 1977—. Active mem. DeKalb County PTA. Certified engring. technician. Mem. Internat. Assn. Elec. Inspectors, IEEE (sr.), Nat. Fire Protection Assn., Power Engring. Soc., Am. Soc. Tng. Dirs., Ga. Power Engring. Assn. Republican. Methodist. Home: 736 Valley Creek Dr Stone Mountain GA 30083

MILLER, DAVID EDMOND, physician; b. Biscoe, N.C., June 6, 1930; s. James Herbert and Elsie Dale (McGlaughon) M.; A.B., Duke U., 1952, M.D., 1956; m. Marjorie Willard Penton, June 4, 1960; children—Marjorie Dale, David Edmond. Intern, Duke Med. Center, Durham, N.C., 1956-57, resident in internal medicine, 1957-58, 59, 60, research fellow cardiovascular disease, 1958-59, 61, asso. internal medicine and cardiology, 1963-79, clin. asst. prof. medicine (cardiology), 1979—; practice medicine, specializing in internal medicine and cardiology, Durham, 1964—; attending physician internal medicine div. cardiology Watts Hosp., Durham, 1964-76, chief medicine, 1975-76; attending physician cardiology div. internal medicine Durham County Gen. Hosp., 1976—, chmn. dept. internal medicine, 1976—. Mem. adv. com. Physician's Asso. Program, Duke Med. Center. Trustee Meth. Retirement Home, Durham. Served to lt. comdr., USNR, 1961-63. Diplomate Am. Bd. Internal Medicine, Supsplty. bd. cardiovascular disease. Fellow A.C.P., Am. Coll. Cardiology; mem. Am., So. med. assns., Am. Heart Assn. (fellow council clin. cardiology 1963—), N.C., Durham-Orange County med. socs., Am., N.C. socs. internal medicine, Am. Fedn. Clin. Research. Methodist (mem. chancel choir, adminstrv. bd., chmn., 1979; lay del. N.C. ann. conf.). Clubs: Capitol City, Hope Valley Country. Contbr. articles profl. jours. Home: 1544 Hermitage Ct Durham NC 27707 Office: 2609 N Duke St Suite 403 Durham NC 27704

MILLER, DAVID FREELAND, mktg. cons. exec.; b. Elizabeth, N.J., Apr. 6, 1928: s. Alan Baldwin and Margaret Hazard M.; A.B., Princeton U., 1950; M.A. in Psychology, U. Mich., 1951, Ph.D. in Psychology, 1955; m. Florence Latitia Pierce Durbin, July 3, 1967; 1 son, David Scott; 1 stepdau., Latitia Margaret Durbin. Dir. mktg. research J. Walter Thompson Co., Detroit, 1953-62; mgr. mktg. research Chrysler Corp., Detroit, 1962-68; exec. v.p. Louis Harris & Assos., N.Y.C., 1968-69; dir. SelectaVision mktg. RCA, N.Y.C. and Indpls., 1969-74; dir. pub. affairs research and programs Gulf Oil Corp., Pitts., 1975; mgr. mktg. research Gulf Refining and Mktg. Co., Houston, 1975-79; v.p., dir. research R.D. Doubleday Co., Little Rock, 1979—; dir. Consumer Communications Inc., Am. Home Video Corp. Served with U.S. Army, 1955-57. Mem. Am. Mktg. Assn. (v.p. 1967-68, 77-78), Princeton Alumni Assn. Ark. Office: R D Doubleday Co 1630 Worthen Bank Bldg Little Rock AR 72201

MILLER, EDMOND TROWBRIDGE, civil engr., educator; b. Pitts., Dec. 9, 1933; s. George Ellsworth and Billie (Watson) M.; B.C.E., Ga. Inst. Tech., 1955, M.S.C.E., 1957; C.E., Mass. Inst. Tech., 1963; Ph.D., Tex. A. & M. U., 1967; m. Nancy Lee Cooper, July 21, 1956; children—Carol Anne, Nancy Ruth, Laura Elizabeth. Found. engr. Law Engring. Testing Co., Atlanta, 1956-57, found. engr., br. mgr., Tampa, Fla., 1957-61; asst. prof. civil engring. U. Ala., 1963-64; instr. civil engring. Tex. A. & M. U., 1965-67; asso. prof. civil engring. U. Ala., 1967-71, prof., 1971-75, acting head dept., 1973; v.p. William S. Pollard Consultants, Inc., Memphis, 1975-77; chmn. civil engring. dept. U. Louisville, 1977—. Mem. Tuscaloosa Urbanized Area Transp. Study Tech. Coordinating Com., 1967-75. Served with AUS, 1967. Automotive Safety Found. fellow, 1964-65. Mem. ASCE, Transp. Research Bd., Nat., Ky. socs. profl. engrs., Inst. Transp. Engrs., Am. Soc. Engring. Edn., Sigma Xi, Tau Beta Pi, Phi Kappa Phi, Chi Epsilon, Scabbard and Blade, Phi Gamma Delta. Mem. Ch. Christ Scientist. Home: 2404 Northfield Ct Louisville KY 40222 Office: Speed Sci Sch U of Louisville Louisville KY 40208

MILLER, ERNEST BARGER, III, energy exec.; b. Tyler, Tex., May 15, 1938; s. Ernest Barger Jr. and Dorothy (Bryan) M.; B.S., Stanford U., 1960; M.B.A. (fellow), Northwestern U., 1962; m. Dale Porter, June 25, 1966; children—Ernest Barger IV, Margaret Dale. Engr., analyst Humble Oil Co., Baton Rouge, La., 1962-66; staff economist, Houston, Tex., 1966-68; portfolio mgr., security analyst Funds, Inc., 1968-69; portfolio mgr., security analyst, v.p., dir. Investment Advisors, Inc., 1969-79; pres., dir. Charterhouse Japhet Tex., Inc.; pres. Glenda Exploration and Devel. Corp., Houston, 1979—. Mem. Am. Chem. Soc., Am. Inst. Chem. Engrs., Financial Analysts Fedn., Houston Soc. Security Analysts, Nat. Assn. Petroleum Investment Analysts, Am. Petroleum Inst., Baton Rouge Jr. C. of C. (dir. 1963-65, v.p., 1964-65), Stanford Houston Alumni Assn. (dir., pres. 1966), Kappa Sigma. Clubs: Houston City, River Oaks Country, Coronado (Houston). Home: 3250 Huntingdon St Houston TX 77019 Office: Suite 604 3700 Buffalo Speedway Houston TX 77098

MILLER, ESTELLE LEE (MRS. T.E. MILLER), lawyer, polit. cons.; b. N.Y.C., Nov. 30, 1929; d. Jacob and Theresa (Smith) Lieberman; A.B., Bklyn. Coll., 1949; postgrad. U. Miami, 1952-53; LL.B., U. Wis., 1954; m. Robert M. Ague, Jr., Mar. 28, 1952 (div. Jan. 1966); children—Robert M. III, Lindajean Duff; m. 2d, T. E. Miller. Tchr. pub. schs., N.Y.C., 1949-51; admitted to Wis. bar, 1954; practiced in Janesville, Wis., 1955-56; research asst. U. Wis. Law Sch., 1954; trial lawyer FTC, Washington, 1956-58, FPC, 1958; opinion writer CAB, Office of Gen. Counsel, Washington, 1958-61; spl. cons. Republican Nat. Com., Washington; guest participant White House Conf. Internat. Cooperation, 1962; coordinator local casting and community liaison Walt Disney Prodns. Million Dollar Dixie Deliverance, 1977; participant Gov.'s Pre-White House Conf. Libraries, 1977; instr. congl. campaign workers, Va., Tex., Okla., Ga. Regional coordinator Pres.'s Environ. Merit Awards Program; trustee Chattahoochee Valley (Ga.) Regional Library Bd.; chmn. Nat. Bicentennial Commn., Lumpkin, Ga.; chmn. Stewart County (Ga.) Rep. Party; vice chmn. 2d Congl. Dist. of Ga.; casting dir. films Long Riders, 1979, Mother Seton, 1980. Recipient Ga. Vol. Service award, 1976, Meritorious Service award Am. Revolution Bicentennial Adminstrn., 1976. Mem. Am., Fed., Wis. bar assns., Nat. (dir. 1965—, chmn. nat. ednl. advisory com.), Ga. (dir. 1964—, pres. 1965-67), Cobb County (founder, pres. 1964) fedns. Rep. women, D.C. League Rep. Women. Episcopalian. Clubs: Columbus (Ga.) Country; Capitol Hill (Washington). Author: Dinner at the Bedingfield Inn, 1975; Women in The White House, 1976. Contbr. articles to profl. jours. Home: Longview Farms Lumpkin GA 31815

MILLER, F(REDERICK) DEWOLFE, educator; b. Rogersville, Tenn., Aug. 2, 1907; s. Samuel Powel and Sarah Foard (Wendel) M.; A.B., Davidson Coll., 1930; M.A., U. Va., 1935; Ph.D., 1942; m. Wilhelmina Livingston, Mar. 20, 1939; children—F(rederick) DeWolfe, Lee Miller Goldfeld. Master, Stuyvesant Sch., Warrenton, Va., 1930-32, acting headmaster, 1935-40; instr. English, Bucknell U., 1945-46; spl. agt. FBI, 1942-45; vis. instr. Lehigh U., summer 1946; asst. prof. U. Tenn., Knoxville, 1946-52, asso., 1952-62, prof., 1962-78, prof. emeritus, 1978—; Fulbright lectr. U. Oslo, 1963-64; exchange prof. U. Hawaii at Hilo, 1976-77. Pres., Planned Parenthood Knox County, 1975-76. Grantee Am. Philos. Soc., 1954, 55, 60, Am. Council of Learned Socs., 1961. Mem. Modern Lang. Assn., South Atlantic Modern Lang. Assn., Nat., Tenn. edn. assns., Phi Beta Kappa, Phi Kappa Phi. Author: Christopher Pearse Cranch, 1951. Editor: Walt Whitman's Drum-Taps, 1959. Contbr. articles to profl. jours. Home: 3834 Sequoyah Ave Knoxville TN 37919

MILLER, FANNIE CAROLYN ROLL (MRS. WILLIAM PEOPLES MILLER), educator; b. Kansas City, Mo.; d. Edward Francis and Louisa Caroline (Chambers) Roll; B.A., U. Buffalo, 1927; postgrad. U. State N.Y., State Tchr. Coll., Buffalo, Canisius Coll., Buffalo, Beaver Coll., Jenkintown, Pa.; Temple U.; m. William Peoples Miller, Nov. 24, 1937 (dec. May 1961); children—Frances Roll (Mrs. Robert Alan Barnett), Janet Peoples (Mrs. Harold Robert Crooks). Tchr. Pub. Schs., Clarence, N.Y., 1927-28; tchr. English and social studies, librarian Lewiston High Sch., Lewiston, N.Y., 1928-32, Buffalo Sch. System, 1932-38; tchr., English and social studies St. Basil Acad., Phila., 1959-70, chmn. social studies dept., 1965-70. Mem. Nat. League Am. Pen Women, Internat. Platform Assn. Republican. Roman Catholic. Contbr. Verses and poems to childrens publications, also original radio plays for amateur childs productions. Home: 7719 Jansen Dr Springfield VA 22152

MILLER, FREDERICK WARREN, chem. co. exec.; b. Pitts., Nov. 19, 1935; s. Warren Jennings and Grace Elizabeth (Sawhill) M.; B.S. in Chem. Engring. (H.H. Geist scholar, Pa. Senatorial scholar), Pa. State U., 1957; Ph.D. (fellow), Rice U., 1965; m. Ann Louise Sutton, Jan. 30, 1960; children—Karinne Adele, David Sutton, Diane Elizabeth. With E.I. du Pont de Nemours & Co., Inc., 1957—, research supr., Old Hickory, Tenn., 1970—; pres., co-owner Wine Celler, Inc., Hendersonville, Tenn., 1973—. Com. chmn. Brandywine Hundred Republican Orgn., 1967; mem. exec. com. Sumner County (Tenn.) Rep. Exec. Com., 1969—, county chmn., 1972-78; regional dir. Henderson Rep. Party, 1970-78; vice chmn. Tenn. 4th Congl. Dist., 1972-76; mem. Capitol Club Tenn., 1973-76. Bd. dirs. Nashville Aquatic Center, Inc. Mem. Am. Inst. Chem. Engrs., Hendersonville C. of C. Clubs: Nashville Aquatic (pres. 1976-78, chmn. 1979—); Toastmasters (pres. Wilmington, Del. 1967, Distinguished Achievement award 1967); Hendersonville Seroma (sec. 1970-71). Author, patentee in field. Home: 313 Appomattox Dr Brentwood TN 37027 Office: Research and Devel Lab Du Pont Co Old Hickory TN 37138

MILLER, GEORGE DUNBAR, electronics technician; b. Guyton, Ga., Mar. 3, 1923; s. Jackson Emanuel and Susie Agustus (Shellman) M.; B.S. in Indsl. Mgmt., Va. State U., 1944; cert. in electronics Brunswick Vocat. Sch., 1949; m. Albertha Mae Baker, Dec. 31, 1954; children—George Dunbar, Shirley Ruth. Electric welder/metalsmith U.S. Navy Dept., Portsmouth, Va., 1942-44; partner King Radio Service Co., Darien, Ga., 1949-55; owner G.D. Miller, Electronic Equipment Repair Co., Brunswick, Ga., 1953—; dir., sec. Camden, Glynn & McIntosh Corp.; cons. King Radio & TV Co., Darien, 1955-75, Wrice's Radio Studio, 1975—, Penn Community Services, Beaufort, S.C., 1968. Mem. adv. com. Urban Renewal Brunswick, 1963; dir. voter edn., citizenship tng. Glynn County (Ga.) NAACP, 1964-72, 73-74, chmn. ednl. com., 1978—; moderator radio broadcast Voice of People, 1965-72, 77—; sec. Community Action Com., Brunswick, 1965-66, editor community newsletter, 1979—; mem. polit. adv. com. Glynn County, 1966-72, 77—. Served with USNR, 1944-46. Recipient Service award NAACP, 1971; Citizen's award First Down Club, 1978; named Father of Year Zion Bapt. Ch., 1967, 69. Mem. Am. Legion. Baptist (sec. finance 1955-65, trustee 1976—, ch. bldg. com. 1968-73). Home: 2400 Albany St Brunswick GA 31520

MILLER, GEORGE OTHA, SR., cleaning services firm exec.; b. Campbellsville, Ky., Dec. 18, 1924; B.S. in Civil Engring., U. Ky., 1948; postgrad. in Mgmt. for Engrs. Ga. Inst. Tech., spring 1968; children—Claudia (Mrs. Robert Bartlett), Debbie (Mrs. Rayburn Taylor), George Otha. Jr. instrumentman, draftsman L & N R.R. Co., Louisville, 1948-49, 52-53; hydraulic engr. water resources U.S. Geol. Survey, Louisville, 1949-52; jr. engr. Girdler Corp., Louisville, 1953-54; supr. engring. and maintenance planning Ford Motor Co., Louisville, 1954-59; group engr. Martin-Marietta Corp., Orlando, Fla., 1959-64; aerospace technician NASA, Kennedy Space Center, Fla., 1964-67; sr. design engr. Dow Chem. Co., Titusville, Fla., 1967; asso. engr. firm Clark, Dietz & Assos., Sanford, Fla., 1967; gen. engr. Warner Robins Air Material Area USAF, Robins AFB, Ga., 1967-69, 70-71, 69-71, supervisory civil engr. 49th Combat Support Group, Holloman AFB, N.Mex., 1971-72, civil engr., 1972-73, Bergstrom AFB, Tex., 1973-74; civil engr. officer in charge of constrn. USN, Saigon, Vietnam, 1969; owner Domesticare of Punta Gorda (Fla.), 1974—. Served with USN, 1944-46. Registered profl. engr., Ky. Mem.

Charlotte County (Fla.) C. of C. Address: PO Box 1253 Punta Gorda FL 33950

MILLER, GLENN CURREY, credit union exec.; b. Chattanooga, Oct. 13, 1946; s. Willard and Fonza (Swafford) M.; student U. Tenn., 1964-66. With Vol. State Life Ins. Co., Chattanooga, 1967—, advt. asst., 1967-68, mgr. advt. and promotion, 1968-70, dir. advt. and promotion, 1970-75; advt. dir. Chattanoogan, 1975-78; dir. advt. and pub. relations Continental Film Prodns., Chattanooga, 1975-76; dir. advt. Crown Crafts, Inc., 1976-78; dir. mem. relations Fed. Employees Credit Union, Atlanta, 1978—; creative cons., copywriter. Mem. pub. relations com. United Fund, 1969-70; spl. gifts com. Am. Cancer Soc., 1971; actor Chattanooga Little Theatre, 1967—. Mem. campaign staff U.S. Sen. Albert Gore, 1970. Mem. Chattanooga (pres. 1972-73), Am. (treas. 7th dist. 1974-75, sec. 1975-76) advt. fedns., Chattanooga Assn. Bus. Communicators (pres. 1969-70), Greater Chattanooga C. of C. (jr. achievement adviser, mem. pub. relations com. 1973-74). Democrat. Episcopalian. Home: 2254 Virginia Pl NE Atlanta GA 30305

MILLER, HARVEY ALFRED, educator; b. Sturgis, Mich., Oct. 19, 1928; s. Harry Clifton and Carmen (Sager) M.; B.S., U. Mich., 1950; M.S., U. Hawaii, 1952; Ph.D., Stanford U., 1957; m. Robin Bovard Huck, Jan. 25, 1980; children—Valerie Yvonne, Harry Alfred, Emily Luce Huck. Instr. in botany U. Mass., 1955-56; instr. botany Miami U., 1956-57, asst. prof., 1957-61, asso. prof., curator herbarium, 1961-67; prof., chmn. program in biology Wash. State U., 1967-69; vis. prof. botany U. Ill., 1969-70; prof., chmn. dept. biol. scis. Fla. Tech. U., 1970-75, prof., 1975—; v.p. Marine Research Assos. Ltd., Nassau, 1962-65; asso. Lotspeich & Assos., natural systems analysts, Winter Park, Fla., 1979—; botanist U. Mich. Expdn. to Aleutian Islands, 1949-50; prin. investigator Systematic and Phytogeol. Studies Bryophytes of Pacific Islands, NSF, 1959; prin. investigator Miami U. Expdn. to Micronesia, 1960; dir. NSF-Miami U. Expdn. to Micronesia and Philippines, 1965; research asso. John Young Mus., Orlando; vis. prof. U. Guam, 1965; cons. tropical botany, foliage plant patents, also designs for sci. bldgs. Recipient Acacia Order of Pythagoras; Acacia Nat. award of Merit; Guggenheim fellow, 1958. Mem. Pacific Sci. Assn. (chmn. sci. com. for botany 1975—), Assn. Tropical Biology, Council Biology Editors, Am. Inst. Biol. Scis., A.A.A.S., Am. Bryol. Soc. (v.p. 1962-63, pres. 1964-65), Brit. Bryol. Soc., Bot. Soc. Am., Bot. Soc. Japan, Assn. Southeastern Biologists, Internat. Assn. Plant Taxonomists, Internat. Assn. Bryologists, Mich. Acad. Sci. Arts and Letters, Hawaiian Acad. Sci., Am. Soc. Plant Taxonomists, Fla. Acad. Sci. (exec. sec. 1976—, rep. to Assn. Acads. Sci. 1974—, pres.-elect 1979, pres. 1980), Nordic Bryol. Soc., Acacia, Sigma Xi, Phi Sigma, Explorers Club. Author: (with H.O. Whittier and B.A. Whittier) Prodromus Florae Muscorum Polynesiae, 1978; editor: Florida Scientist, 1973-78. Contbr. numerous articles to sci. jours. Home: Box 4413 Winter Park FL 32793 Office: U Central Fla Orlando FL 32816

MILLER, HERBERT DELL, petroleum engr.; b. Oklahoma City, Sept. 29, 1919; s. Merrill Dell and Susan (Green) M.; B.S. in Petroleum Engring., Okla. U., 1941; m. Rosalind Rebecca Moore, Nov. 23, 1947; children—Rebecca Miller Friedman, Robert Rexford. Field engr. Amerada Petroleum Corp., Houston, 1948-49, Hobbs, N.Mex., 1947-48, dist. engr., Longview, Tex., 1949-57, sr. engr., Tulsa, 1957-62; petroleum engr. Moore & Miller Oil Co., Oklahoma City, 1962-78; owner Herbert D. Miller Co., Oklahoma City, 1978—. Served to maj., F.A., AUS, 1941-47; ETO. Decorated Bronze Star with oak leaf cluster, Purple Heart (U.S.); Croix de Guerre (France). Registered profl. engr., Okla., Tex. Mem. AIME, Petroleum Club. Republican. Episcopalian (pres. Men's Club 1973). Clubs: Oklahoma City Golf, Country. Home: 6708 NW Grand Blvd Oklahoma City OK 73116 Office: 603 First Life Assurance Bldg Oklahoma City OK 73102

MILLER, HOWARD GEORGE, JR., structural, agrl. engr.; b. Richlands, Va., Sept. 3, 1947; s. Howard George and Doris Polk (Reed) M.; B.S. in Agrl. Engring., Va. Poly. Inst., 1969, M.S. in Structural Engring., 1974. Bridge design engr. Va. Dept. Hwys., Richmond, 1970-72; agrl. engr. Southside Electric Coop., Crewe, Va., 1972-73; facility engr. Kroger Co., Salem, Va., 1974-75; store engr. Malone & Hyde, Salem, 1975-79; mgr. store engring. Richfood, Inc., Richmond, Va., 1979—. Served with AUS, 1970. Mem. ASHRAE, Assn. Energy Engrs., ASCE. Home: 8737 Kilpeck Ct Richmond VA 23229

MILLER, IDELLE BLOCK, counselor; b. Bklyn., May 18, 1950; d. George L. and Sarah (Shane) Block; A.B. magna cum laude, U. Miami, 1972, M.Ed., 1973; grad. work Biscayne Coll. Human Resources Inst., 1975. Counselor, Office of Vocat. Rehab., Miami, Fla., 1973-79; vocat./ednl. specialist Spectrum Programs, Miami, 1979—. Parent aide com. Parent Resource Center, 1979—. Mem. Am. Personnel and Guidance Assn., Nat. Assn. Social Workers, Nat. Vocat. Guidance Assn., Nat. Rehab. Assn., Mental Health Assn. Dade County, U. Miami Alumni Assn., Mortar Bd. Alumni, Phi Sigma Sigma, Phi Kappa Phi. Democrat. Jewish. Office: 1 NW 67 St Miami FL 33150

MILLER, ILAH MAE, nurse; b. Delavan, Kans., Dec. 6, 1914; d. Earl Cecil and Lola Edna (Watkinson) M.; B.S., Emporia State U., 1941; R.N., Johns Hopkins U., 1947; M.Gen. Edn. and Guidance, Tex. Christian U., 1967. Tchr. public schs., Kans. and Iowa, 1932-44; staff nurse Johns Hopkins Hosp., Balt., 1947-48, Wesley Hosp., Chgo., 1949-50, St. Joseph's Hosp., Ft. Worth, Tex., 1950-51; instr. pediatrics Johns Hopkins Hosp., Balt., 1952; dir. nursing edn. Cook Children's Hosp., Ft. Worth, 1953-56, dir. nursing services, 1956-78, dir. community relations, 1978—; mem. faculty Baylor U. Sch. Nursing, 1953-56. Mem. nursing adv. com. Tarrant County Jr. Coll., 1976-79; mem. planning com. Lucy Harris Linn Inst., 1976—, treas., 1978—; adv. Pvt. Duty Nurses Bur., 1970-76; active ARC; mem. All Saints Hosp. Sch. Vocat. Nursing adv. com., 1970—. Mem. Tex. Nursing Assn., Am. Nursing Assn., Nat. League for Nursing, Nursing Service Adminstrs. (sec. 1967-68), Am. Soc. Hosp. Nursing Services Adminstrs., Tex. Soc. Hosp. Nursing Service Adminstrs., Southwestern Soc. Fund Raisers, Nat. Soc. Fund Raising Execs., South Ft. Worth Bus. and Profl. Women's Club. Methodist. Home: 3915 W 4th St Fort Worth TX 76107 Office: 1212 W Lancaster St Fort Worth TX 76102

MILLER, ISRAEL BERNARD (BUDDY), scrap metal co. exec.; b. Huntsville, Ala., June 11, 1926; s. Louis and Elsie (Ratner) M.; B.S. in Indsl. Mgmt., Ga. Inst. Tech., 1948; m. Dolores Evelyn Katz, Feb. 6, 1947; children—Joy (Mrs. Kenneth Jay Greenberg), Solomon Ira, Sara Gayle. Partner, L. Miller & Son, Inc., Huntsville, 1948-58, treas., mgr., 1958-66, pres., 1966—; bus mgr. Technique, Ga. Inst. Tech., 1947. Mem. Huntsville United Jewish Appeal Com., 1948-59, Huntsville United Jewish Fund, 1959—, Nat. Joint Distbn. Com., 1964—, pub. relations com. Huntsville Jewish Community Council, 1975—. Bd. dirs. regional Anti-Defamation League, B'nai B'rith, 1967—. Served with USNR, 1944-46. Mem. Indsl. Mgmt. Soc., Inst. Scrap Iron and Steel, Am. Welding Soc., Nat. Welding Supply Assn., Alpha Epsilon Pi, Pi Delta Epsilon. Jewish (pres. temple 1957-58, trustee temple 1959, 68-69, 73-74). Clubs: Masons, Shriners, B'nai B'rith (pres. 1956, 67), Rotary. Home: 1101 Fraser Ave SE Huntsville AL 35801 Office: PO Box 1207 Huntsville AL 35807

MILLER, J. D., textile mfg. co. exec.; b. Albemarle, N.C., Jan. 14, 1931; s. Mumpford C. and Nellie (Almond) M.; student pub. schs.; m. Blanche Ruby Page, Sept. 2, 1950; 1 dau., Joy Darlene. Electrician, Snuggs Electric Co., Albemarle, 1954-56, Stanly Electric Co., Albemarle, 1956-59; electrician Collins & Aikman Corp., Albemarle, 1969—, maintenance mgr., Charlotte, N.C., 1969—; elec. foreman Superior Stone Co., Raleigh, N.C., 1967-69. Served with U.S. Army, 1952-54. Democrat. Baptist. Home: 1491 Hilltop St Albemarle NC Office: Collins & Aikman Corp 701 McCullough Dr PO Box 32665 Charlotte NC 28232

MILLER, JACK EVERETT, lawyer; b. Monroe, La., Dec. 10, 1921; s. Herman M. and Syble (Harrison) M.; student Ga. Tech., 1942-43; grad. Gilbert Johnson Law Sch., 1948; m. Vivian Geraldine Bagby, May 13, 1945 (div.); children—Jack E., John A.; m. 2d, Kathryn Woodard Garriss, Dec. 23, 1970. Admitted to Ga. bar, 1948; formerly mem. firm Duffy, Miller, Duffy; now individual practice, Savannah. Served with USAAF, 1943-45, with USAF, 1951-53, lt. col. Res. Judge Adv. Gen. Dept. Mem. Am. Trial Lawyers Assn., Am., Ga., Savannah bar assns. Club: American Business (chpt. pres. 1959, dist. gov. 1964-65). Home: 2 Stillwood Ct S Savannah GA 31406 Office: 122 E Oglethorpe Ave Savannah GA 31401

MILLER, JAMES EDWARD, broadcasting exec.; b. Oklahoma City, Oct. 7, 1927; s. John Edward and Willie (Myrth) M.; student Xavier U., 1946-49; m. Betty Lou Douglas, 1966; children—James, John, Michelle, Monte, Garbielle, Nicollette, Mark, Christopher, St. Paul, James Edward. Mgmt. specialist FAA, 1967; mgr. Bryant Center Bowl & Oasis Club, 1967-69; pres. All Am. Broadcasting Corp., Oklahoma City, 1969—; gen. mgr. sta. KAEZ, 1971—. Democrat. Roman Catholic. Home: 3204 N Bryant St Oklahoma City OK 73111 Office: 4240 NE 23d St Oklahoma City OK 73136

MILLER, JAMES HOWARD, govt. rehab. program exec., educator; b. English, W.Va., Feb. 15, 1934; s. Howard Loney and Martha Mary (De Bord) M.; B.S., Concord Coll., 1959; M.S., W.Va. U., 1961; Ed.D., Auburn (Ala.) U., 1971; m. Wanda Faye Porter, Apr. 7, 1957; children—James Howard, Joseph Lee. Rehab. counselor Dept. Edn., Nashville, 1961; rehab. supr. dept. edn. Milledgeville (Ga.) State Hosp., 1961-67; prof., asst. dept. head spl. edn. and rehab. U. Tenn., Knoxville, 1967—; dir. rehab. continuing edn. program Region IV HEW, Knoxville, 1974—; cons. in field. Pres. East Tenn. Children's Rehab. Center, Knoxville, 1970-71. Served with USN, 1951-55. Recipient Counselor of Year award Ga., 1963, 64, 65. Mem. Am. Psychol. Assn., Nat. Rehab. Assn., Nat., Am. rehab. counseling assns. Methodist. Club: Knoxville Boat. Contbr. articles to profl. jours. Home: 1604 Arrow Wood Rd Knoxville TN 37919 Office: 1814 Lake Ave Knoxville TN 37916

MILLER, JAMES RICHARD, computer scientist; b. Mt. Clemens, Mich., Mar. 13, 1930; s. William Glen and Martha Elizabeth (Hubble) M.; B.S., U.S. Mil. Acad., 1955; M. Engring. Adminstrn., George Washington U., Washington, 1963, D. Bus. Adminstrn., 1970; m. Diane Alden Franklin, Dec. 21, 1955; children—Elizabeth Ann, Melanie Lynn. Commd. 2d, lt., U.S. Army, 1955, advanced through grades to col., 1975, adviser S. Korean Army, 1963-64, bn. comdr. combat, Vietnam, 1970-71, mem. Gen. Staff, Washington, 1965-67, Office of Joint Chiefs of Staff, 1973-76, dir. planning, world-wide mil. command, control sytem automatic data processing program, 1975-76, ret., 1976; sr. scientist Rosslyn office Sci. Applications Inc., Arlington, Va., 1976-78; dir. EPD, Am. Med. Labs., Inc., Fairfax, Va., 1978-79; EDP program mgr. Sci. Applications, Inc., Arlington, 1979—; asso. prof. computer sci. George Washington U., Washington, 1972—; lectr. in field. Decorated Legion of Merit, Bronze Star, Medal for Valor, Vietnamese Cross Gallantry with Gold Star. Mem. Assn. Computing Machinery, IEEE, West Point Alumni Assn., Armed Forces Communications and Electronics Assn. Episcopalian. Contbr. articles electronic computers, nat. def. to profl. publs. Home: 2519 Fowlers Ln Reston VA 22091 Office: 11091 Main St Fairfax VA 22030

MILLER, JAMES RONALD, univ. ofcl.; b. Houston, May 2, 1941; s. William Otto and Ruby Zelda M.; B.B.A., Lamar U., 1966; m. Pherris Sylvia Nichols, July 30, 1966; 1 dau., Christine Sylvia. Mgmt. trainee Firestone Tire & Rubber Co., Houston, 1966-67; with Brown & Root, Inc., Houston, 1967-69, buyer, 1967-68, traffic coordinator, 1968-69; purchasing agt. U. Houston, 1969—; regional adv. Tex.-Okla.-Ark. Regional Group, Ednl. and Instl. Coop. Service, Inc., 1980—. Named Boss of Year, Space City chpt. Am. Bus. Women's Assn., 1971-72. Mem. Nat. Assn. Ednl. Buyers (2d vice chmn. Tex.-Okla.-Ark. Regional Group 1978-79, 1st vice chmn. 1979-80). Roman Catholic. Office: Purchasing Dept U Houston Houston TX 77004

MILLER, JAMES THOMAS, personnel consultant co. exec.; b. Ithaca, N.Y., Dec. 1, 1949; s. John Ivan and Viola (Henry) M. Exec. v.p. search div. JBA Inc., Houston, 1972; founder, pres. JTM Assos., Houston, 1973—. Mem. Nat. Fedn. Ind. Businessmen. Office: 6250 Westpark Suite 227 Houston TX 77057

MILLER, JANEL HOWELL, psychologist; b. Boone, N.C., May 18, 1947; d. John Estle and Grace Louise (Hemberger) Howell; B.A., DePauw U., 1969; postgrad. Rice U., 1969; M.A., U. Houston, 1972; Ph.D., Tex. A. and M. U., 1979; m. C. Rick Miller, Nov. 24, 1968; children—Kimberly, Brian, Audrey, Rachel. Asso. sch. psychologist Houston Ind. Sch. Dist., 1971-74; research psychologist VA Hosp., Houston, 1972; asso. sch. psychologist Clear Creek Ind. Sch. Dist., Tex., 1974-76; instr. psychology Tex. A. and M. U., 1976-77; clin. psychology intern VA Hosp., Houston, 1977-78; coordinator psychol. services Clear Creek Ind. Sch. Dist., 1978—; cons. in field. DePauw U. Alumni scholar, 1965-69; NIMH fellow U. Houston, 1970-71; cert. psychologist, asso. sch. psychologist, licensed social psychotherapist, Tex. Mem. Am., Tex., Houston psychol. assns., Am., Tex., Houston assns. marriage and family therapists, Tex. Psychotherapy Assn., Tex. Sch. Psychol. Affiliates, Houston Behavior Therapy Assn. Home: 806 Walbrook Dr Houston TX 77062 Office: Clear Creek Ind Sch Dist 2301 E Main St League City TX 77573

MILLER, JEFFREY HAROLD, designer; b. Wilkes-Barre, Pa., Aug. 27, 1942; s. Milton and Irma (Ganz) M.; B.A., Pa. State U., 1964, postgrad., 1964-65; m. Sally Ann Fitzpatrick, Oct. 10, 1972; children—Erin Fitzpatrick, Jacob Milton, Benjamin David Ganz, Jonathan Peter Desmond. Pres., Jeff Miller Assos., 1964-65, MG Assos., Alexandria, Va., 1969-71, Hunter/Miller & Assos., Design Cons., Alexandria, 1971—; mem. fed. portfolio rev. panel U.S. CSC; cons. Nat. Endowment for Arts; mem. Fed. Hwy. Adminstrn. Task Force on Transp. Graphics and Communications; mem. adv. panel Interior Design Mag. Served to lt. USNR, 1965-69. Decorated Navy Achievement medal; recipient Achievement award Va. Travel Council, 1973, Design Rev. award Indsl. Design Mag., 1970. Mem. Fed. Design Council, Constrn. Specifications Inst., Washington Bd. Trade, Am. Craftsmen's Council. Club: Belle Haven Country. Home: 117 Prince St Alexandria VA 22314 Office: 110 S Lee St Alexandria VA 22314

MILLER, JOHN CHARLES, corp. exec.; b. Wilkes-Barre, Pa., Jan. 20, 1940; s. John C. and Delia F. (Hardy) M.; A.B., U. Pa., 1964; m. Linda C. Williams, Apr. 22, 1967; children—Susan, Elizabeth Ann. Fin. mgr. Philco-Ford, Phila., 1961-69; div. controller Hitchiner Mfg. Co., Milford, N.H., 1969-70; corporate controller Kleer-Vu Industries, Inc., N.Y.C., 1970-74; v.p., treas. Fed. Express Corp., Memphis, 1974—. Gov. U. Pa., 1964. Mem. Nat. Accounting Assn. (sec. 1974), Memphis Area U. Pa. Alumni Assn. (pres. 1976), Fin. Execs. Inst. Office: 2837 Sprankle Ave Memphis TN 38130

MILLER, JOHN DAVID, agronomist; b. Todd, N.C., Aug. 9, 1923; s. Reuben Patterson and Chessie (Graham) M.; B.S., N.C. State U., 1948, M.S., 1950; Ph.D., U. Minn., 1953; m. Frances McCollum, June 9, 1946; children—John David, Glenn, Mary. Research fellow U. Minn., 1953; asst. prof. Kans. State Coll., 1953-57; research agronomist Agrl. Research Service, U.S. Dept. Agr., Blacksburg, Va. and Tifton, Ga., 1957-75, research leader, 1972-79, sr. agronomist, 1975—. Dist. commr. Boy Scouts Am., 1971-74. Served with AUS, 1943-46. Decorated Bronze Star medal. Mem. Am. Soc. Agronomy, Phi Kappa Phi, Sigma Xi. Clubs: Toastmasters, Lions. Home: Rt 3 Box 49-1 Tifton GA 31794 Office: Agrl Research Service USDA Coastal Plain Sta Tifton GA 31794

MILLER, JOHN EDWARD, ednl. adminstr.; b. McKeesport, Pa., Dec. 9, 1921; s. Thomas and Millie (Price) M.; B.S. in Math., Randolph Macon Coll., 1948; M.A., in Physics, U. Va., 1950, Ph.D., 1952; m. Virginia Lee Bazile, Feb. 25, 1943 (dec. Mar. 1972); 1 dau., Renee (Mrs. Stuart Holmes); m. 2d, Patricia Gonzalez-Rubio, Aug. 24, 1974; 1 son, John Paul. Prof. physics Clemson U., 1952-62, 63-66; v.p. academic affairs Fla. Inst. Tech., Melbourne, 1966—, now also exec. v.p. Served with AUS, 1943-47. Mem. V.F.W., Phi Beta Kappa. Contbr. articles on physics to sci. publs. Home: 801 Atlantic St Melbourne Beach FL 32951

MILLER, JOHN ELDON, state legislator; b. Melbourne, Ark., Mar. 2, 1929; s. Greene Hightower and Annie Margaret (Gray) M.; B.S., Ark. State U., 1949; m. Ruby Lenora Robertson, Nov. 5, 1949; children—David Eldon, Martha Marie, Naomi. County and circuit clk. Izard County (Ark.), 1953-56; with Reynolds Metals Co., Benton, Ark., 1957; owner, mgr. John E. Miller Agy., Melbourne, Ark., 1957—; mem. Ark. Legislature, Little Rock, 1959—. Chmn. ARC, Melbourne, 1958—; state chmn. Ark. Easter Seals, 1976—. Registered land surveyor. Mem. Ark. Ins. Assn., Ark., Am. real estate assns., Nat. Soc. State Legislators, Ark. Title Assn. Democrat. Baptist. Clubs: Lions (pres. 1960-61), Masons (master 1956-57). Address: PO Box 436 Melbourne AR 72556

MILLER, JOSEPH BAYARD, lawyer; b. Highland, La., Feb. 25, 1920; s. Harrison Coleman and Wilbur Jeannette (Donaldson) M.; A.B., Tulane U., 1939, LL.B., 1941; m. Gloria Mae Berthelot, Dec. 31, 1950; children—Joseph Bayard, Melinda May. Admitted to La. bar, 1941; mem. firm Milling, Benson, Woodward, Hillyer, Pierson & Miller, New Orleans, 1941—, partner, 1948—; pres. Continental Land & Fur Co., Inc., 1974—, also dir. Served to maj. USAAF, 1941-46; PTO. Decorated Bronze Star. Mem. Am., La., New Orleans bar assns. Episcopalian. Clubs: New Orleans Country, Boston, La., Internat. House, Petroleum, Stratford. Home: 7399 Agate St New Orleans LA 70124 Office: 1100 Whitney Bldg New Orleans LA 70130

MILLER, KEITH LICHTENBERGER, petroleum engr.; b. Terre Haute, Ind., Aug. 21, 1940; s. Herman Jacob and Joy (Lichtenberger) M.; student Purdue U., 1958-61; B.S., Ind. State U., 1963; M.S., Okla. U., 1971, postgrad., 1971-73; m. Linda Sue Mitchell, June 12, 1965; children—Molly Anne, Mitchell Keith Lichtenberger. Petroleum geophysicist Mobile Oil Corp., Dallas, 1973-74; asso. research geophysicist Sun Co., Richardson, Tex., 1974-75, staff petroleum engr., Oklahoma City, 1975-77; sr. ops. engr. Grace Petroleum Corp., Oklahoma City, 1977-79; dist. engr. J-W Operating Co., 1979—. Chmn. Republican Precinct, 1979; del. Rep. County and State Conv., Okla., 1979; mem. sci adv. council George Lynn Cross Acad., Norman, Okla., 1979. Served with USAF, 1963-68. NDEA Title IV fellow, 1969-72. Mem. Soc. Petroleum Engrs., Am. Petroleum Inst., Nat. Eagle Scout Assn., Sigma Xi, Sigma Pi Sigma. Methodist. Home: 216 N Mercedes Norman OK 73069 Office: PO Box 19319 Oklahoma City OK 73119

MILLER, LAURENCE ALAN, librarian; b. Bloomsburg, Pa., Jan. 19, 1940; s. Harold R. and Muriel M. (Marshall) M.; B.S., Kutztown State Coll., 1962; M.S., Fla. State U., 1963, A.M.D., 1970, Ph.D., 1971; m. Carole A. Bissinger, Jan. 12, 1963; children—Julia Denise, Sylvia Kristin. Acquisitions librarian Bucknell U., 1963-65; area dir. libraries Inter Am. U., P.R., 1966-69; dir. library services California (Pa.) State Coll., 1971-74; dir. univ. library E. Tex. State U., 1974—; vice chmn. and chmn.-elect Tex. Council State Univ. Librarians, 1979—. Mem. exec. bd. Common Cause of Tex., 1976-80, vice chmn., 1979-80. Mem. ALA, Tex. Library Assn. (chmn. com. intellectual freedom 1978-79), Freedom to Read Found., Steamship Hist. Soc., World Ship Soc., Tex. Assn. Coll. Tchrs. Democrat. Unitarian. Club: Rotary. Office: James Gee G Library E Tex State U Commerce TX 75428

MILLER, LAWRENCE MICHAEL, computer co. exec.; b. Grand Rapids, Mich., Nov. 29, 1936; s. Lawrence E. and Mable M. (Bieber) M.; student Grand Rapids Jr. Coll., 1957, Colo. Coll., 1959; A.A., Pueblo Jr. Coll., 1958; B.S. in Elec. Engring., U. Mich., 1962, M.S. in Elec. Engring., 1963; m. Donna Rae Headlee, May 5, 1959; 1 dau., Michelle Annette. Sr. engr. advanced design Tex. Instruments Inc., Dallas, 1963-69; mgr. systems engring. Recognition Equipment Inc., Dallas, 1969-74; mgr. product mktg. Recognition Products Inc., Dallas, 1974-77; v.p. Recognition Bus. Systems, Inc., Dallas, 1977—; lectr. systems engring. Associometrics Inc., Dallas, 1970—. Mem. IEEE (systems, man and cybernetics group), Am. Mgmt. Assn., Mensa, Triple Nine Soc., Phi Theta Kappa. Club: Toastmasters Internat. Home: 7311 Wintergood Ln Dallas TX 75248

MILLER, LOUIS H., JR., golf profl., golf club exec.; b. Washington, Ga., Nov. 8, 1943; s. Louis H. and Leta Jane M.; B.S. in Edn., Ga. So. Coll., 1966; m. Beverly G. Golson, Aug. 3, 1969; children—Shannon, Cory, Brent. Dir. golf John's Island Club, Vero Beach, Fla., 1972-76; dir. golf Pinehurst Hotel and Country Club (N.C.), 1976-79; v.p., dir. golf Pinehurst, Inc., 1979—; cons. in field. Named Profl. of Year, Country Club Golfer Mag., 1979. Mem. Profl. Golf Assn. Am., Nat. Golf Found., N.C. Young Republicans. Baptist. Club: Kiwanis. Contbr. articles to golfing mags. Home: 106 James Creek Rd Southern Pines NC 28387 Office: PO Box 4000 Pinehurst NC 28374

MILLER, LOUIS OLEMAN, JR., assn. exec.; b. Portsmouth, Va., July 18, 1940; s. Louis Oleman and Mary Virginia (Snyder) M.; B.A. in Journalism, U. S.C., 1970, postgrad., 1971; postgrad. Inst. Orgn. Mgmt., 1977—; m. 2d, Mary Ann Griffin, Dec. 27, 1974; children—L. Paul, Andrea Lynn, David K. Public relations dir. S.C. Bar Assn., Columbia, 1968-69; grad. asst U. S.C., Columbia, 1970-71, program dir./exec. producer coll. FM sta., 1969-70; broadcaster WDZ Radio, Decatur, Ill., 1971-72; promotion dir./public affairs dir. WCBD-TV, Charleston, S.C., 1972; sta. mgr./gen. sales mgr. WKHJ Radio, Holly Hill, S.C., 1972-73; account exec. (radio)/sportscaster (TV) WCSC-Radio/TV, Charleston, 1973; promotion dir. WSPA-TV,

Spartanburg, S.C., 1973-76; membership and communications mgr. Asheville Area (N.C.) C. of C., 1976-79; mktg. mgr. Orlando (Fla.) Area C. of C., 1979—. Sub-deacon The Cathedral of St. Luke Episcopal Ch., 1979—, lay adminstr., 1977—; pres., sec.-treas. Asheville Tourist Assn., 1977-79, bd. dirs., 1976-79; bd. dirs. Nat. Found. March of Dimes, 1978-79; adv. council Asheville Health Adventure Mus., 1976-77. Served with U.S. Army, 1963-67. Mem. Nat. Pilots Assn., Aircraft Owners and Pilots Assn., Am. C. of C. Execs., So. Assn. C. of C. Execs., Asheville Advt. Fedn. (dir. 1977-79), Alpha Epsilon Rho (nat. pres. 1971-73), Sigma Delta Chi, Alpha Delta Sigma, Kappa Tau Alpha. Club: Beech Aero. Office: Box 1234 Orlando FL 32802

MILLER, MARY RUTH, educator; b. Bartow, Fla., Dec. 22, 1926; d. Willie Boyd and Ruth (Anderson) Miller; A.B. in Edn., Fla. State U., 1948; M.A., George Peabody Coll., 1951; Ph.D., Duke, 1966; postgrad. Columbia, summer 1953, U. So. Calif., summer 1954, Shakespeare Inst., Stratford-on-Avon, Eng., summer 1955, U. Edinburgh (Scotland), summer 1969. Tchr. elementary sch., Palatka, Fla., 1948-49; tchr. high schs., Bell, Fla., 1949-50, Brandon, Fla., 1950-51, Webster, Fla., 1951-53; tchr. English, dir. pub. relations Reinhardt Coll., 1953-59; asst. prof. English, Fla. So. Coll., 1962-67; prof. English and chmn. dept. Tenn. Wesleyan Coll., Athens, 1967-76; prof. English, head dept. N. Ga. Coll., Dahlonega, 1976—. Recipient Lewis State Tchr.'s Scholarship, Fla. State U., 1945-48; Danforth Tchrs. Summer Scholarship, U. So. Calif., 1954; Cokesbury award in Coll. Teaching, Duke U., 59-60, 61-62, grad. research assistantship, 1960-61. Mem. South Atlantic Modern Lang. Assn., Coll. English Assn., Modern Lang. Assn., Nat. Council Tchrs. English, Research Soc. Victorian Periodicals, S.E. Renaissance Conf., Ga.-S.C. Coll. English Assn. Democrat. Methodist. Author: Thomas Campbell. Home: 605 N Hall Rd Dahlonega GA 30533

MILLER, MORTON LARRIMORE, physician; b. Cleve., Oct. 14, 1921; s. Maurice Louis and Goldie (Joseph) M.; B.A., Ohio State U., 1943, M.D., 1946; m. Alice Fellerman; 4 children. Intern, Kings County (N.Y.) Hosp., Bklyn., 1946-47; gen. practice medicine, Cleve., 1948-53; mem. staffs Euclid, Glenville, Women's hosps.; resident obstetrics and gynecology Cleve. Met. Gen. Hosp., 1953-55, Jackson Meml. Hosp., Miami, Fla., 1955-57; practice medicine specializing in obstetrics, gynecology, Miami, 1957—; mem. staffs Jackson Meml., North Miami Gen., Parkway hosps.; chief obstetrics, gynecology North Shore Hosp., 1974-75; asst. clin. prof. U. Miami. Served with AUS, 1943-46, to 1st lt. M.C., AUS, 1946-48. Diplomate Am. Bd. Obstetrics and Gynecology. Fellow A.C.S., Am. Coll. Obstetrics and Gynecology, Am. Fertility Soc., Miami Obstetrics and Gynecology Soc.; mem. Am., Fla., Dade County med. assns., Fla. Obstetrics and Gynecology Soc., Obstetrics and Gynecology Travel Soc., Am. Assn. Gynecologic Laparoscopists, Phi Delta Epsilon. Office: 111 NW 183d St Miami FL 33169

MILLER, NATHAN ANDERSON, educator; b. Dandridge, Tenn., May 24, 1914; s. Thomas Norman and Leutitia (Davis) M.; A.B. magna cum laude, Carson-Newman Coll., 1936; M.S., U. Tenn., 1944; m. Alfreda Rowena Reed, July 5, 1949; children—Gwenna, Thomas. Tchr. grammar sch., Jefferson City, Tenn., 1936-38, prin. high sch., 1943-44; tchr. O'Keefe High Sch., Atlanta, 1938-43; dir. tchr. internes Carson-Newman Coll., 1944; dean Little River Sch., Miami, Fla., 1945-55; dean of boys Madison Jr. High Sch., 1955-56; cons. Reader's Digest, Pleasantville, N.Y., 1956-58; tchr. North Miami (Fla.) High Sch., 1958-65; asst. prin. North Dade High Sch., 1965-67, Miami Springs (Fla.) Jr. High Sch., 1967—; owner, dir. Camp Sky-Top, Rosman, N.C., 1950—; cons. Ednl. Testing Service, Princeton, N.J., 1955—; chmn. interviewing com. for Exchange Tchrs., U.S. Office Edn., 1952—. Chmn., Jefferson County A.R.C. Fund, 1943-44; v.p. Little River Youth Center Found.; bd. dirs. Fla. Youth Found. Mem. Nat. Council Tchrs. English (dir., chmn. audio visual aids com. 1942-50, co-editor Speak-Look-Listen 1943), Dade County Classroom Tchrs. Assn. (hon. life; pres. 1948-49), Nat. Soc. for Study Communication (charter mem.), Jefferson County Bapt. Assn. (Sunday sch. supt.), Phi Kappa Phi, Phi Delta Kappa. Rotarian. Editor: Atlanta Teacher, 1941-43; co-founder, editor: Dade County, Fla. Teacher, 1946-48; editorial collaborator Reading Skill Builders, 1957-58. Home: 570 Hunting Lodge Dr Miami Springs FL 33166 Office: 150 Royal Poinciana Blvd Miami Springs FL 33166

MILLER, NATHAN HUFF, state senator Va.; b. Rockingham County, Va., July 4, 1943; s. Garland F. and Edith L. (Huff) M.; B.A., Bridgewater (Va.) Coll., 1965; LL.B., U. Richmond, 1969. Admitted to Va. bar, 1969; partner firm Conrad, Litten, Sipe & Miller, Harrisonburg, Va., 1969—; mem. Va. Ho. of Dels. from 16th Dist., 1972-75, Va. senate, 1975—; judge Timberville (Va.) Mcpl. Ct., 1971. Bd. dirs. Project Concern, 1971—, Harrisonburg-Rockingham County Mental Health Assn., 1974—; hon. bd. dirs. Shenandoah Valley Music Festival Com., 1974—; mem. Bridgewater Indsl. Devel. Commn., 1975—; mem. vol. sers. council Western State Hosp., Staunton, Va., 1972—. Named Outstanding Young Man, Bridgewater Jaycees, 1972. Mem. Am., Va., Harrisonburg bar assns., Bridgewater Coll. Alumni Assn., Harrisonburg Jaycees, Rockingham Male Chorus, Omicron Delta Kappa. Republican. Mem. Ch. of Brethren. Rotarian. Home: Route 2 Bridgewater VA 22812 Office: 218 E Market St Harrisonburg VA 22801

MILLER, R(ONALD) BAXTER, educator; b. Rocky Mount, N.C., Oct. 11, 1948; s. Marcellus C. and Elsie B. (Bryant) M.; B.A. magna cum laude, N.C. Central U., 1970; M.A., Brown U., 1972, Ph.D., 1974; m. Jessica Garris, June 5, 1971; 1 son, Akin Dasan. Asst. prof. English, Haverford Coll. (Pa.), 1974-77; asso. prof., dir. Black lit. program U. Tenn., Knoxville, 1977—; cons. Nat. Endowment for Humanities sponsored TV series The South, 1977-78, evaluator div. public programs Harlem Renaissance, 1978—. Recipient Faculty awards Haverford Coll., 1975, 76, U. Tenn., 1977, 78-80; Nat. Endowment for Humanities grantee, summer 1975; Am. Council Learned Socs. Conf. grantee, 1978. Mem. MLA (exec. com. Black lit. discussion group 1980—), AAUP, English Inst., Coll. Lang. Assn., Nat. Minority Assn. Interdisciplinary Studies (charter). Democrat. Author: Define the Whirlwind: Reference Guide to Langston Hughes and Gwendolyn Brooks, 1978; editor, contbr. Black American Literature and Humanism, 1980; contbr. articles and revs. to scholarly jours. Home: 1433 Pine Springs Rd Knoxville TN 37922 Office: Dept English U Tenn Knoxville TN 37916

MILLER, RICHARD EUGENE, educator, family and marriage counselor; b. Howell, Mich., Jan. 13, 1931; s. Raymond and Mildred (Ketchum) M.; B.A., Eastern Mich. U., 1954; B.D., No. Bapt. Theol. Sem., 1958; M.A., Mich. State U., 1963, Ph.D., 1968; children—Sherry Miller Pruitt, Richard Lyle, David Paul. Asst. prof. Mich. State U., 1968-70, Calif. Poly. State U., 1970-72; asso. prof., dean of students Universidad de las Americas, 1972-74; asso. prof. U. Tex., Permian Basin, 1974-77; prof. edn. Navarro Coll., Corsicana, Tex., 1977—; family and marriage counselor. Nat. Endowment for Humanities grantee, 1979. Mem. Am. Jr. Coll. Assn., Am. Assn. for Marriage and Family Therapy, Tex. Psychotherapy Assn., Am. Personnel and Guidance Assn., Nat. Fgn. Policy Conf. Am. Educators. Baptist. Home: 700 Madison Ave Corsicana TX 75110 Office: Navarro College Corsicana TX 75110

MILLER, RICHARD KENDALL, acoustic engring. cons.; b. Muncie, Ind., Oct. 16, 1946; s. Robert K. and Ruth (Beinke) M.; B.M.E., Purdue U., 1970; m. Marcia Lee Drummond, May 20, 1979. Design engr. Electro-Voice, Inc., 1965-70; cons. Goodfriend-Ostegaard Assos., 1970-72; founder Richard K. Miller & Assos., Inc., Atlanta, 1972, pres., 1972—; pres. Fairmont Press, Atlanta, 1973—, also dir.; cons. acoustical engring. to various govt. agys. including U.S. Dept. Labor, 1975—, EPA, 1974—, USN, 1976, U.S. Army, 1974, HUD, 1971—, also to over 400 indsl. firms, 1973—; dir. Hearex Corp., Tampa, Fla.; guest lectr. in acoustics various colls. and univs., 1972—. Bd. dirs. Southeast Acoustics Inst., 1974—. Mem. Acoustical Soc. Am. (v.p. Ga. chpt.), Assn. Energy Engrs. (co-founder, dir. 1977-79), Archtl. Acoustics Soc. (dir.), ASME, Ga. Soc. Engrs. and Architects, Madison Hist. Soc., Purdue Alumni Assn., Phi Kappa Sigma (Outstanding Mem. award 1969, past pres.). Methodist. Author: Secrets of Noise Control (with Albert Thumann), 1974; Handbook of Industrial Noise Management, 1976; (with Wayne V. Montone) Acoustical Enclosures and Barriers, 1977; Basic Industrial Hearing Conservation, 1979; contbr. numerous articles in field to tech. jours.; instrumental in developing technique for surveying environ. noise of cities. Office: 464 Armour Circle NE Atlanta GA 30324

MILLER, ROBERT DWIGHT, mfg. co. exec.; b. Saskatoon, Can., Aug. 24, 1944; s. Robert Calvin and Kathleen (O'Connor) M.; B.S., Tex. A&M U., 1967; m. Randee Jane Lindsay, Apr. 5, 1969; 1 son, Reed Lindsay. Sales rep. Bucyrus Eric Co., Houston and South Milw. 1967-73, product analyst, 1970-71, product mgr., 1971-73, regional mgr., Houston, 1978—; v.p. Weatherford/AAI, Houston, 1974-76. Deacon, Presbyterian Ch., Houston. Served with U.S. Army, 1968-69. Club: Univ. Home: 2107 Elmgate St Houston TX 77080

MILLER, ROBERT ELMER, energy and environ. co. exec.; b. Kansas City, Mo., Sept. 4, 1920; s. Harold Elmer and Henrietta Mary (Mersch) Miller; student Am. U., 1949-50, Kans. U., 1951-52, U. N.Mex., 1953-54; grad. U.S. Army Command and Gen. Staff Coll., 1963, Indsl. Coll. Armed Forces; m. Louise Isabelle Hartman, Nov. 3, 1940; children—Sharron Louise Miller Hughes, Antoinette Lynn Miller Reed, Theresa Beth. Enlisted as pvt. U.S. Army, 1940, commd., 1942, advanced through grades to col., 1964; ret. 1968; nuclear planner AEC, Las Vegas, Nev., 1952-57, test planner, 1957-60, dir. nuclear test plans, 1960-67, dep. mgr. test ops., 1968-69, mgr. nuclear tests, 1969-72, mem. AEC On-Off Continent Test Planning Bd., 1962-69; v.p. plans Resource Scis. Corp., Tulsa, 1972-73, v.p. ops., 1973-74, exec. v.p., 1974-79; former vice chmn. bd. Alaskan Resource Scis. Corp.; pres. REM Mgmt. Corp., 1977—; exec. v.p. Williams Bros. Engring. Co., 1979; v.p. U.S. Filter Corp., 1980—; former dir. Williams Bros. Waste Control, Inc., Williams Bros. Process Services, Inc., Williams Bros. Engring. Co., East-West Co.; dir. NUSAC Corp., 1979—. Pres., Indian Springs Homeowners Assn., 1974-75. Decorated Bronze Star, Purple Heart. Mem. Am. Nuclear Soc., Assn. Am. Mil. Engrs., Ret. Officers Assn. Republican. Clubs: Tulsa, Indian Springs Country. Home: 841 Millwood Rd Broken Arrow OK 74012 Office: PO Box 192 Broken Arrow OK 74012

MILLER, RUBY ANDERSON, public relations exec.; b. Spartanburg County, S.C., July 31, 1944; d. Johnny J. and Gladys Anderson; B.S. in Bus. Edn., Livingstone Coll., Salisbury, N.C., 1968; m. Horace L. Miller, May 11, 1964; children—Anthony, Darryl, Latasha. Sci. sec. chem. tech. div. Oak Ridge (Tenn.) Nat. Lab., 1968-71; tech. asst. public relations dept. Union Carbide Corp. nuclear div., Oak Ridge, 1971-72, public relations rep., 1972-78, asst. dir. public relations, 1978—; instr. journalism/public relations U. Tenn., Knoxville, 1978-80. Bd. dirs. Knoxville Area Urban League, Anderson County United Way; mem. personnel adv. bd. Oak Ridge Schs.; mem. human studies com. Oak Ridge Associated Univs./Oak Ridge Nat. Lab. Mem. Public Relations Soc. Am. (award 1979, pres.-elect vol. chpt., accredited), NAACP (publicity chmn. Oak Ridge br.), Alpha Kappa Alpha. Democrat. Baptist. Club: Altrusa (Oak Ridge). Office: Union Carbide Corp Nuclear Div PO Box X Oak Ridge TN 37830

MILLER, RUTH SHIRLEY, standards review cons.; b. Chgo., July 6, 1930; d. Frank Joseph and Ella J. (Stanek) Polacek; grad. St. Lukes Sch. Nursing, 1951; student U. Minn., 1952-53; A.A., Miami-Dade Community Coll., 1967; B.S. in Health Sci., Fla. Internat. U., 1974; m. Lester John Miller, Feb. 7, 1956; children—Richard Frank, David Lester. Staff, North Miami (Fla.) Gen. Hosp., 1964-67; asst. dir. nursing Parkway Gen. Hosp., North Miami Beach, 1967-70; emergency dept. supr. Community Hosp. of S. Broward, Hollywood, Fla., 1971-73, asst. dir. nursing, 1973-74, dir., 1974-75; instr. dept. critical care and allied health scis. Miami-Dade Community Coll., Mt. Sinai campus, 1973-74; standards review cons. Lifemark, Houston, 1975—. Mem. Fla. Emergency Med. Services Adv. Com., 1973-75; mem. ednl. adv. com. for adv. com. and steering com. for devel. Intermediate EMT Tng. Curriculum for Fla., 1973-74; mem. governing bd. and exec. com. various hosps. and med. centers. Registered nurse, Ill., Tex., Fla., La., Mo., Ky.; State of Fla. grantee, 1973-74. Mem. Am. Nurses Assn., Fedn. Am. Hosps., Nat. Emergency Dept. Nurses Assn. Lutheran. Home: 103 Carriage Ln Conroe TX 77302 Office: 3800 Buffalo Speedway Houston TX 77098

MILLER, STUART MALCOLM, service bur. exec.; b. San Antonio, Apr. 25, 1938; s. George B. and Henrietta (Sircus) M.; B.S. in Bus. Adminstrn., U. Fla., 1959; m. Dorothy Elizabeth Miller, Nov. 15, 1959; children—Donald, Sharon. Systems analyst CBS, N.Y.C., 1966-69; project mgr. REA Express, N.Y.C., 1969-70; systems devel. mgr. GAC Corp., Miami, Fla., 1970-72; mgmt. cons. Systems Tech. Unlted., Chattanooga, 1972-74; v.p., dir. Accountant's Computer Service, Inc., Nashville, 1974—; data processing cons. to govt., real estate bds. Certified data processor. Mem. Data Processing Mgmt. Assn., Am. Mgmt. Assn., Amateur Softball Assn. Am., Soc. Mgmt. Info. Systems. Jewish. Contbr. script to Twilight Zone TV series, novels to Fantasy and Sci. Fiction mag. Home: 5524 Hill Rd Brentwood TN 37027 Office: 1451 Elm Hill Pike 150 Nashville TN 37210

MILLER, THOMAS ALLEN, surgeon; b. Harrisburg, Pa., July 7, 1944; s. Joseph Edgar and Marion Ruth (Corpman) M.; B.S. in Zoology, Wheaton (Ill.) Coll., 1966; M.D., Temple U., 1970; m. Janet Ruth Walters, Dec. 28, 1968; children—David Allen, William James, Laurie Ann. Surg. intern U. Chgo. Hosp., 1970-71; resident in surgery U. Mich. Hosps., Ann Arbor, 1971-75; postdoctoral research fellow in gastrointestinal hormone physiology dept. surgery U. Tex. Med. Br., Galveston, 1975-76; postdoctoral research fellow in gastrointestinal physiology, dept. physiology U. Tex. Med. Sch., Houston, 1976-77, asst. prof. surgery, 1977-79, asso. prof. surgery, 1979—; attending surgeon Hermann Hosp., Houston; mem. pharmacy, therapeutics and tissue coms. U. Tex. Med. Sch. and Hermann Hosp., Houston. Ruling elder Presbyn. Ch., 1979—. Recipient Conrad Jobst award, 1973, Frederick A. Coller award, 1974; Frederick A. Coller traveling scholar, 1974-75; NIH grantee, 1979—. Fellow A.C.S.; mem. AMA, AAAS, Am. Fedn. Clin. Research, Assn. for Acad. Surgery (chmn. legis. action com., 1979—), Soc. Surgery of the Alimentary Tract, Am Gastroent. Assn., Am. Physiol. Soc. Republican. Contbr. articles, abstracts in field to profl. publs. Office: 6431 Fannin #4162 Houston TX 77030

MILLER, THOMAS LLOYD, galvanizing co. exec.; b. Wilmington, Del., June 30, 1915; s. Thomas W. and Katharine Marie (Tallman) M.; grad. Choate Sch., 1933; B.S., U.S. Naval Acad., 1937; m. Madeleine Bridgeford Russel, Oct. 7, 1939 (dec. Jan. 1975); children—Russel T., Lloyd, Lindsay, Bruce W.; m. 2d, Elizabeth Cooper Joy, July 18, 1975. Commd. ensign USN, 1937, advanced through grades to comdr., 1947; with submarine forces Atlantic and Pacific, 1940-47; ret., 1947; pres. Miller Ford Co., Inc., Stonington, Conn., 1950-62; pvt. investor, 1962-70; v.p., sec. U.S. Mfg. & Galvanizing Corp., Miami, 1970—. Founder, pres. Pine Point Sch., Stonington, Conn., 1948-52. Justice of the Peace, Stonington, Conn., 1950-63. Trustee Marine Hist. Assn., Mystic Seaport, Conn., 1948—. Mem. Am. Legion, V.F.W., U.S. Naval Acad. Alumni Assn. (trustee 1950-52). Clubs: New York Yacht; Storm Trysail (Larchmont, N.Y.); Ocean Reef (Key Largo, Fla.); Biscayne Bay Yacht, Coral Reef Yacht (Miami); Ocean Racing Am. (founder). Home: 3570 Matheson Ave Coconut Grove FL 33133 Office: US Manufacturing & Galvanizing 7320 NW 43d St Miami FL 33166

MILLER, THOMAS WAINWRIGHT, JR., county ofcl.; b. Clearwater, Fla., Nov. 28, 1927; s. Thomas Wainwright and Grace Ellen (Gilbert) M.; B.C.E., Ga. Inst. Tech., 1952; m. Mavis Stinson, Dec. 25, 1952; 1 son, Thomas Wainwright III. With Fla. State Bd. Health, 1952-56; dir. Lee County Mosquito Control Dist., Ft. Myers, Fla., 1956—, dir. Gulf Fed. Savs. and Loan Assn. Bd. dirs. Goodwill Industries, 1978—; pres.-elect United Way, 1980; bd. dirs. SW Fla. council Boy Scouts Am., 1978-79. Served with AUS, 1946-47. Registered profl. engr., Fla., La., Mass. Mem. Fla. Anti-Mosquito Assn. (pres. 1962, sec.-treas. 1976—), Am. (dir. 1963-72; policy council 1964-72, rec. sec. 1965-72), Calif., Tex., La., Va., N.J., Utah, Ill., Ohio, Mid-Atlantic, Northwestern mosquito control assns., Am., Fla. pub. health assns., Fla. Engring. Soc. (pres. Calusa chpt. 1967; chmn. engrs. in govt. 1968; v.p. 1969), Nat. Soc. Profl. Engrs., Am. Soc. C.E., Fla. Entomol. Soc., Entomol. Soc. Am., Aquatic Plant Mgmt. Soc. (pres. 1961, sec. 1973—, editor jour. 1965), Weed Sci. Soc. Am., S.W. Fla. Conservation Clearinghouse (sec. 1966-74), Ft. Myers-Lee County C. of C. (dir.). Baptist. Clubs: Rotary (chpt. pres. 1975, now dir.), Fort Myers Rod and Gun (pres. 1969, now dir.); Royal Palm Yacht (dir. 1978—), Rangoon, Masons, Shriners. Home: 1314 Florida Ave Fort Myers FL 33901 Office: Lee County Mosquito Control Dist PO Box 06005 Fort Myers FL 33906

MILLER, TOM POLK, architect; b. Houston, Nov. 17, 1914; s. Enoch Lester and Willie Elvie (Chumley) M.; B.A., Rice U., 1936, B.S. in Arch., 1937; m. Isabel Mount, Aug. 10, 1947; children—Crispin Mount, Abigail Mount. Architect, Salisbury & McHale, Houston, 1937-38, H.B. Tucker, Nacogdoches, Tex., 1938, Nunn & McGinty, Houston, 1939-40, Robert & Co., Corpus Christi, Tex., 1940-41, Kemper Nomland, Los Angeles, 1946-48, DeWitt & Swank, Dallas, 1952-54; pvt. practice architecture Mount-Miller, Denton, Tex., 1954—. Mem. Denton Municipal Research League, 1958-61; mem. Denton County Democratic Exec. Com., 1962-68. Mem. A.I.A. (chmn. historic preservation com. Dallas chpt. 1965, mem. Tex. hist. preservation com. 1965-68), Interfaith Forum on Religion, Art and Architecture, Fellowship of Reconciliation, War Resisters League, A.C.L.U. (pres. Denton chpt. 1974-75), Nat. Trust for Hist. Preservation, Soc. Archtl. Historians, Am. sect. Internat. Solar Energy Soc., North Tex. Assn. Unitarian Universalist Socs. (pres. 1968-69), Denton Forum, Denton County Arkwork, Anthropology Club Dallas. Unitarian Universalist (pres. Denton fellowship 1962-63). Mem. editorial bd. The Voice, 1970-73; editor Arkwork Rev., 1979—. Home and Office: 711 W Sycamore St Denton TX 76201

MILLER, WALLACE DYETT, educator; b. Granger, Wyo., Apr. 2, 1927; s. David Dyett and Dorothy (Buck) M.; A.A., S.W. Baptist Coll., 1952; B.A., S.W. Mo. State Coll., 1954; M.A., N.E. Mo. State Coll., 1961; Ph.D., So. Ill. U., 1966; m. Frances Lois Hobson, Mar. 1, 1953; children—Lorraine, Wally Dee, David Edwin, Letitia Kay. Tchr., Chester (Mont.) Pub. Schs., 1954-55; elementary prin., tchr. Fordland (Mo.) Pub. Schs., 1955-58; bldg. prin., tchr. Sullivan (Mo.) Pub. Schs., 1958-60; tchr. Jennings (Mo.) Jr. High Sch., 1960-63; grad. asst. So. Ill. U., Carbondale, 1963-65, asst. prof. NDEA Reading Inst., 1967; dir. Title I Reading Program, Woodland Pub. Schs., Lutsedale, Mo., 1966-67; asso. prof. S.W. Bapt. Coll., Bolivar, Mo., 1967-71; asso. prof. U. So. Miss., Hattiesburg, 1971-74, prof. curriculum and instrn., 1974—, dir. 32d-39th Ann. Reading Confs., 1972—; dir. 1st ann. interdisciplinary forum on troubled youth, 1980. Cons. pub. schs., Scott County, Kemper County, Jasper County and Perry County, Miss., 1971—; pastor, deacon Bapt. Chs., 1950—. Served with USMCR, 1943-45, with USAF, 1947-50. Decorated Bronze Star medal, Victory medal with Combat V; recipient reading grants U. So. Miss., 1972-74. Mem. NEA, Miss. Edn. Assn., Am. Psychol. Assn., Miss. Psychol. Assn., Coll. Reading Assn. (bd. dirs. 1974—, dir. research commn. 1974—, treas. 1976—), Internat. Reading Assn., Miss. Reading Assn., S.Miss. Reading Council Internat. Platform Assn., Nat. Reading Conf. (editor Yearbooks 1975, 76), Am. Reading Conf., Ednl. Research Assn., Assn. for Supervision and Curriculum Devel., Nat. Assn. Sch. Psychologists, Miss. Assn. Sch. Psychologists, Assn. Advancement of Ethical Hypnosis, Phi Delta Kappa, Phi Rho Pi. Republican. Masons (32d degree), Lions. Contbr. articles to profl. jours. Office: So Sta Box 8209 U So Miss Hattiesburg MS 39401

MILLER, WESLEY, lawyer; b. Jay, Okla., Mar. 28, 1918; s. William W. and Leah (Boyd) M.; B.A., Northeastern State Coll., 1939; postgrad. U. Okla. Sch. Law, 1939-41; m. Louise Heflebower, Mar. 30, 1963; children—Teresa Lynn, Mark Wesley. Admitted to Okla. bar, 1945; practice law, Tahlequah, Okla., 1945—. Referee, Nat. Mediation Bd., Kansas City, Mo., 1961, Honolulu, 1961, Mpls., 1965, Nat. R.R. Adjustment Bd., Chgo., 1962-71; vice chmn. Council Judicial Complaints, State of Okla., 1974—. Pres., Okla. League Young Democrats, 1949-50. Served to capt. AUS, 1941. Recipient 20 Year Selective Service medal, 1969. Mem. Am., Okla. (mem. exec. council 1951, ho. of dels. 1967—), Cherokee County (pres. 1952-55) bar assns., Tahlequah C. of C., Am. Legion, V.F.W., Phi Beta Epsilon, Phi Delta Phi. Democrat. Methodist. Kiwanian (pres. 1955). Home: 100 Bluff Ave Tahlequah OK 74464 Office: 214 S Muskogee St Tahlequah OK 74464

MILLER, WILLIAM (BILL) E., JR., transp. industry cons.; b. Bonham, Tex., July 27, 1948; s. William E. and Iva Jo (Smith) M.; B.A., Tex. Tech. U., 1971; m. Linda Riek, June 16, 1973. With T.I.M.E.-DC, Inc., Lubbock, Tex., 1970-73; partner Transportation Credit Services, Inc., and predecessor, Lubbock, Tex., 1973-76, pres., 1976—. Deacon, First Christian Ch.; unit commr. Boy Scouts Am. Mem. Nat., Tex. (dir.) acctg. and fin. councils, Am. Trucking Assn., Nat. Freight Claim Council, Traffic Clubs Internat., Comml. Law League Am., Alpha Tau Omega, Delta Nu Alpha. Home: 2401 20th St Lubbock TX 79401 Office: 1515 13th St Lubbock TX 79413

MILLER, WILLIAM FRANKLIN, engring. cons.; b. Houston, Oct. 27, 1942; s. Robert William and Edith Grace (Bell) M.; student U. Tex., Austin, 1961-63; M.E., U. Houston, 1970; m. Joyce Kay Sams, Aug. 27, 1966; children—Robert William, Christina Elizabeth, Paul Alan. Instrument designer and engr. S.I.P., Inc., Houston, 1966-73; instrument engr. Ehrhart div. Procon, Houston, 1973-74; sr. instrument engr. Tellepsen Constrn. Co., Houston, 1974-75; v.p.

strong Engring., Inc., Houston, 1975-78; instrument cons. W.F. Miller Co., Houston, 1978—. Com. chmn. Cub Scouts, 1971-72, den leader, 1977-78; asst. scoutmaster Boy Scouts Am., 1978—. Registered profl. engr., Tex. Mem. Nat., Tex. socs. profl. engrs., Instrument Soc. Am., ASME, Houston Engring. and Sci. Soc., U. Houston Alumni Fedn., Nat. Eagle Scout Assn. Episcopalian. Contbr. to Applied Instrumentation in the Process Industries (W.G. Andrew), 1974. Home: 9243 Rowan Ln Houston TX 77036 Office: PO Box 42343 Houston TX 77042

MILLER, ZELL BRYAN, lt. gov. Ga.; b. Young Harris, Ga., Feb. 24, 1932; s. Stephen Grady and Birdie (Bryan) M.; student Young Harris Jr. Coll., 1951; A.B., U. Ga., 1957, M.A., 1958, also postgrad.; m. Shirley Ann Carver; children—Murphy Carver, Matthew Stephen. Mayor, Young Harris, 1960; mem. Ga. State Senate, 1961-64; mem. State Bd. Children and Youth, 1965; personnel officer Ga. Dept. Corrections, 1968; exec. sec. to Gov. of Ga., 1969, to Lt. Gov. of Ga., 1971; mem. Bd. Pardons and Paroles, 1973; lt. gov. of Ga., 1975—. Del., Democratic Nat. Conv., 1972, 76; exec. dir. Dem. Party Ga., 1971-73. Served with USMC, 1953-56. Methodist. Mason. Author: The Administration of E.D. Rivers as Governor of Georgia; The Mountains Within Me; The Legend of Hiawassee. Home: Young Harris GA 30582 Office: 418 State Capitol Atlanta GA 30334

MILLICAN, KATHERINE VERONICA, computer programmer; b. Jacksonville, Fla., Sept. 23, 1953; d. Francis John and Joan Eleanor (Anderson) Miller; B.A. in Math., Huntingdon Coll., 1975; postgrad. U. Ala., Birmingham; m. Charles Wayne Millican, Aug. 11, 1979. Programmer, State Ala., Med. Services Adminstrn., Montgomery, 1975-78; programmer U. Ala. Rust Computer Center, Birmingham, 1978-79; progressive farmer, programmer analyst, Birmingham, 1979—. Methodist. Home: 1509 16th Ave S 5 Birmingham AL 35205 Office: 820 Shades Crest Pkwy Birmingham AL 35202

MILLIGAN, J(OHN) BRUCE, JR., synthetic rubber co. exec.; b. Milw., Dec. 24, 1941; s. John Bruce and Barbara Jane (Black) M.; B.S. in Bus. Adminstrn., Marquette U., 1965; M.B.A., Washington U., St. Louis, 1966; m. Barbara Ann Groll, June 16, 1962; children—John Bruce III, Karoline Ann. With Enjay Chem. subs. Exxon Chem. Co. U.S.A., various locations, 1966-75, product planner, econ. coordinator synthetic rubber div., Houston, 1971-75; exec. v.p. Peter Heard & Assos., Houston, 1975—. Pres. Cypress Creek Estates Civic Club. Recipient Am. Prodn. and Inventory Control Soc. award, 1965. Mem. Am. Chem. Soc. (rubber div.), Los Angeles Rubber Group, So. Rubber Group. Republican. Roman Catholic. Clubs: Gulf Coast Arabian Horse (pres.), Am. Horse Shows Assn. Home: 12703 E Shadowlake Cypress TX 77429 Office: 9800 Northwest Freeway Houston TX 77092

MILLIGAN, W(INFRED) O(LIVER), chemist; b. Coulterville, Ill., Nov. 5, 1908; s. John Winfried and Millie Mae (McMillan) M.; A.B., Ill. Coll., Jacksonville, 1930, Sc.D., 1946; M.A., Rice Inst., Houston, 1932, Ph.D., 1934; D.Sc., Tex. Christian U., 1960, Tenn. Tech. U., 1980; LL.D., Baylor U., Waco, Tex., 1979. Research chemist Harshaw Chem. Co., Cleve., 1934; cons. Houdry Process Corp., 1936-45, Humble Oil & Refining Co., 1946-62, Oak Ridge Nat. Lab., 1950—; prof. chemistry Rice U., 1930-63, Baylor U., 1965—; dir. research Robert A. Welch Found., 1955—; chmn. Nat. Colloid Symposium, 1952-59; mem. coms. application x-ray and electron diffraction Nat. Acad. Sci.-NRC, 1938-41, mem. panel permanent magnet materials, 1952—, panel clay mineralogy, 1953—; mem. Tex. Adv. Com. Atomic Energy, 1955—. Postdoctoral fellow Nat. Acad. Sci.-NRC, 1954-59. Mem. Am. Inst. Chemists, Am. Phys. Soc.; mem. Crystallographic Assn., Am. Chem. Soc. (dir. 1961-66, past chmn. coms.), Southwest Sci. Forum (pres. 1976-77), Faraday Soc., Phi Beta Kappa, Sigma Xi, Phi Lambda Upsilon, Alpha Chi Sigma. Author articles in field; editor various conf. proc.; asso. editor Jour. Phys. Chemistry, 1952. Address: 2010 Bank of S W Bldg Houston TX 77002

MILLIN, HENRY ALLAN, lt. gov. V.I.; b. St. Thomas, V.I., Mar. 17, 1923; grad. Nat. Sch. Real Estate Fin.; m. Graciela Millin; 5 children. Former exec. dir. V.I. Housing Authority; lt. gov. V.I., Charlotte Amalie, 1978—. Mem. St. Thomas-St. John C. of C. (past pres.). Democrat. Anglican. Club: Rotary (St. Thomas). Office: Office of Lt Gov State Capitol Charlotte Amalie VI 00801

MILLING, ROBERT NICHOLSON, psychiatrist; b. Greenwood, S.C., July 5, 1933; s. Robert Lyon and Sarah Elizabeth (Marbert) M.; B.S., U. S.C., 1954, M.D., 1958; m. Marjorie Jean Snell, Sept. 30, 1961; children—Julia Frances Otken Pearson, Melanie J. Otken, Marjorie Jean Otken, Deborah Marie Milling, Mary Margaret Milling, Evelyn Elizabeth Milling, Melissa Brooks Milling. Intern, Ga. Baptist Hosp., Atlanta, 1958-59; fellow in cardiology Sch. Medicine, U. Tenn., Memphis City Hosps., 1959-61; resident in psychiatry William S. Hall Psychiat. Inst., Columbia, S.C., 1961-64; dir. Sumter-Clarendon-Kershaw (S.C.) Mental Health Center, 1964-66; practice medicine specializing in psychiatry, Columbia (S.C.) Psychiat. Assos., 1966—; clin. asso. prof. psychiatry, William S. Hall Psychiat. Inst., Sch. Medicine, U. S.C., Columbia, 1977—; cons. in psychiatry, Columbia VA Hosp., 1974—; bd. trustees, Columbia Area Mental Health Center, 1972—, vice chmn., chmn. bd. Served with USPHS, 1959-61. Recipient Ravenel award in Pub. Health, Med. U. S.C., 1958. Diplomate Am. Bd. Psychiatry. Fellow Am. Psychiat. Assn. (pres. S.C. Dist. Br., 1977), Southeastern Group Psychotherapy Assn. (pres., 1975-76), Carolinas Soc. Adolescent Psychiatry (pres. 1976-77), AMA, S.C. Med. Assn., Columbia Med. Soc. Episcopalian. Club: Columbia Rotary. Editorial bd. Medical Audit Review; contbr. articles on psychophysiologic mechanisms epidemiology of various cardiovascular diseases to profl. pubs. Home: 1627 Woodlake Dr Columbia SC 29206 Office: 1401 Laurel St Columbia SC 29201

MILLION, E. Z., data processing cons.; b. Moscow, Idaho, Dec. 13, 1940; s. Elmer Mayse and Zenna Belle (Clark) M.; B.S. in Math., U. Okla., 1961, M.S. in Computer Sci., 1964; m. Janice Elsie Mager, Sept. 12, 1961; children—J. Scott, Tedder Clark. Systems engr. IBM, Oklahoma City, 1962-68; prof. stats. and mgmt. Oklahoma City U., 1968-70; cons. FCC, Washington, antitrust div. Dept. Justice, N.Y.C., 1975-77; prof. computer mgmt. Okla. State U. Tech., Norman, 1977—; cons. electronic data processing. Mem. Ops. Research Soc. Am., Soc. Mgmt. Info. Systems. Republican. Methodist. Club: Optimists. Author: (with others) The Petroleum Management Game, 1961. Office: PO Box 950 Norman OK 73070

MILLIS, GEORGE ALSTON, veterinarian; b. Tuscaloosa, Ala., Oct. 18, 1948; s. Lancelot Burton and Louise (Alston) M.; D.V.M., Auburn (Ala.) U., 1973; m. Mary Ellen Trawick, Feb. 28, 1976. Resident, Small Animal Clinic, Auburn U., 1972-73; asso. veterinarian Eastmont Animal Clinic, Montgomery, Ala., 1973-77, 78—, Pell City (Ala.) Animal Hosp., 1977-78. Sr. advisor Vet. Explorers Post 109, Montgomery, 1973-77; campaign worker United Appeal, Montgomery, 1974-76; bd. dirs. Ala. Jr. Miss Pageant, St. Clair County Humane Soc., Montgomery Riverboat Commn., 1979—, Jimmy Hitchcock Com., 1977—. Served with Army N.G., 1976—. Recipient Borden award Sch. Vet. Medicine, Auburn U., 1973. Mem. Ala., Am., Central Ala. (sec.-treas. 1973-78) vet. med. assns., Montgomery Jaycees (adminstrv. v.p. 1974, Spoke of Year 1975). Republican. Episcopalian. Clubs: Montgomery Auburn, Auburn Tip Off. Home: 555 Farmington Rd Montgomery AL 36109 Office: 5630 Atlanta Hwy Montgomery AL 36117

MILLS, GEORGE THOMAS, physician; b. Memphis, Sept. 25, 1920; s. Charles Gilbert and Ina Ruby (Davis) M.; M.D., Loma Linda U., 1949; m. Fay Adele Vaughan, Sept. 10, 1946; children—George Thomas, Joan Marie, Robert Charles, Carolyn Elizabeth. Intern, Nashville Gen. Hosp., 1948-49; practice medicine with Dr. B.E. McLarty, Memphis, 1949—, Mills, McLarty and McLarty, 1973—; mem. staff Meth., Le Bonheur, Children's, St. Joseph, John Gaston hosps. Bd. dirs. Highland Acad., Portland, Tenn., 1967-72, Madison (Tenn.) Acad., 1967-72; Memphis dir. Five-Day Plan to Stop Smoking. Served with USNR, 1955-57. Fellow Am. Assn. Abdominal Surgeons. Seventh Day Adventist (elder). Home: 1600 Peabody Ave Memphis TN 38104 Office: 220 S Claybrook St Memphis TN 38104

MILLS, HUGH MILTON, JR., jr. coll. adminstr.; b. Albany, Ga., Oct. 24, 1922; s. Hugh Milton and Johnnie (West) M.; diploma, N.Ga. Coll., Dahlonega, 1943; B.S., U. Ga., 1945, M.Ed., 1947, Ed.D., 1956; m. Evelyn Heath, Oct. 6, 1944; children—Hugh Milton, Ralph West, Rebecca Ann. Prin., Rockmart (Ga.) Jr. High Sch., 1945-47; tchr., coach Albany (Ga.) High Sch., 1947-48; instr. Coll. Edn., U. Ga., Athens, 1948-49, asst. prof., 1949-51; supervising prin. Rockmark (Ga.) Schs., 1951-53; instr. Coll. Edn., U. Ga., Athens, 1953-56, asst. prof., 1956-62, asso. prof., 1962-65; pres. Gainesville (Ga.) Jr. Coll. Deacon, Blackshear Pl. 1st Baptist Ch. Mem. Ga. Assn. Colls. and Jr. Colls. (past pres.), Ga. Psychol. Assn., Ga. Assn. Sch. Counselors, NEA, Ga. Assn. Educators, Phi Beta Kappa, Phi Kappa Phi, Psi Chi, Phi Delta Kappa, Kappa Delta Pi. Club: Rotary (past pres.). Office: PO Box 1358 Gainesville GA 30503

MILLS, MAURICE, chemist, educator; b. Henderson, Tex., Jan. 8, 1938; s. Jobe and Margie (Jones) M.; B.S., Tex. Coll., 1960; Ph.D., Howard U., 1972; m. Ola Marie Reese, June 16, 1962; children—Tenisa, Carita, Enil and Nikenya. Tchr., Tatum (Tex.) Ind. Sch. Dist., 1960-68; research chemist Bishop Coll., 1972-73; chmn. dept., prof. chemistry Prairie View (Tex.) A&M U., 1973-78, Wiley Coll., Marshall, Tex., 1978—; cons. in field. Active Boy Scouts Am., 1962—. NDEA fellow, 1968; NSF grantee, 1974; Tex. Coll. awardee in chemistry, 1960; Dept. Energy grantee, 1978; U.S. Army grantee, 1973. Mem. Am. Chem. Soc., Tex. Acad. Sci., AAAS, Nat. Assn. Profl. Advancement of Black Chemists and Chem. Engrs. Mem. Ch. of Christ. Research in isomerization of exo tricyclic system, synthesis of antimalarial drugs. Home: 404 West End Blvd Marshall TX 75670 Office: Dept Chemistry and Physics Wiley Coll Marshall TX 75670

MILLS, ROLLIN WILLIAM, sch. prin.; b. Dayton, Ohio, Feb. 17, 1954; s. Rollin Wilson and Helen Maye (Carter) M.; B.S., Bob Jones U., 1966; M.Ed., Western Carolina U., 1969; Ed.S., U. S.C., 1976; m. Sharon Lee Polk, June 18, 1966; children—Jason Andrew, Brent Allen. Supr. McClaren Sch. for Boys, Woodburn, Ore., 1966; tchr. social studies Greenville (S.C.) Jr. High Sch., 1966-69; asst. prin. Slater-Marietta (S.C.) High Sch., 1969-70; asst. prin. Dent Sr. High Sch., Columbia, S.C., 1970-71; prin. Harbor Christian Sch., West Columbia, S.C., 1971-72; prin. Lexington (S.C.) Intermediate Sch., 1972—. Mem., S.C. Assn. Sch. Prins., Nat., S.C., Lexington County (S.C.) edn. assns., Nat. Assn. Elementary Sch. Prins. Baptist (deacon 1974). Home: 1417 Whipporwill West Columbia SC 29169 Office: 420 Hendrix St Lexington SC 29072

MILLS, VERENT JOHN, charitable orgn. exec.; b. Birmingham, Eng., May 12, 1913; s. John William and Ruth (Timms) M.; grad. Western Bible Coll., Winnipeg, Man., Can., 1938; Ph.D., Ewha U., Korea, 1971; m. Alma Eunice Kenney, Apr. 2, 1932; children—Ruth (Mrs. Gale Erickson), Muriel (Mrs. Donald Strum), Beverley (Mrs. Donald MacLeod). Came to U.S., 1949, naturalized, 1956. Ordained to ministry Baptist Ch., 1937; with Missions in China, 1931-40, Am. Adv. Com. in China, 1940-47; overseas dir. Christian Children's Fund, Richmond, Va., 1947-70, exec. dir., 1970—. Mem. Welfare Adv. Com. to Hong Kong Govt.; bd. examiners for Hong Kong Govt. Recipient citations Govts. of China and Japan, 1947-54; decorated Order of Cultural Merit Nat. Award, Order of Camelia (Korea); Order of Sacred Treasure (Japan). Republican. Rotarian. Club: Downtown. Home: 507 Ridge Top Rd Richmond VA 23229 Office: 203 E Cary St Richmond VA 23219

MILLS, WILLIAM ANDREW, ret. accountant; b. nr. Sandersville, Ga., Apr. 7, 1910; s. Oscar L. and Willie Mae (Griffin) M.; B.S. in Commerce, U. Ga., 1934; m. Ruth H. Waters, Aug. 31, 1940 (dec. Jan. 1974). Staff accountant M.H. Barnes & Co., C.P.A.'s, Savannah, Ga., 1934-43; partner Barnes, Askew, Mills & Co., C.P.A.'s, Savannah, 1947-61, Haskins & Sells, pub. accountants, Savannah, 1961-73, ret., 1973. Served to capt. U.S. Army, 1943-46, C.P.A., Ga., La., N.C. Mem. Am. Inst. C.P.A.'s, Ga. Soc. C.P.A.'s, Beta Gamma Sigma, Phi Kappa Phi, Beta Alpha Psi. Kiwanian. Home: 802 E 41st St Savannah GA 31402 Office: Suite 618 C & S Bank Bldg Savannah GA 31402

MILLS, WILLIAM EDWARD, safety engr.; b. Cin., Jan. 10, 1935; s. William Francis and Loretta Emma (Greber) M.; A.S., U. Cin., 1955; B.S. in Indsl. Tech., Fla. Internat. U., 1979; m. Linda D. Conley; children—Lory Ann, Larry William, Linda Kay. With Formica Corp., Cin., 1953-62; div. mgr. safety and occupational health Trailmobile div. Pullman Co., Chgo., 1962-66; corp. safety dir. Consol. Foods Corp., Chgo., 1966-70; corp. staff rep. Borden's Inc., Columbus, Ohio, 1971-72; safety and ins. officer U. South Fla., Tampa, 1973-76; mgr. safety and security foods div. Coca-Cola Co., Auburndale, Fla., 1976—. Bd. dirs. N.W. Mental Health Assn., 1970; mem. spl. bus. gifts com. United Fund, 1970. Registered profl. safety engr., Calif. Mem. Am. Soc. Safety Engrs., Risk Ins. Mgmt. Soc. Republican. Christian. Club: Masons. Office: PO Box 247 Auburndale FL 33528

MILLS, WILLIAM HAROLD, gen. contractor; b. Birmingham, Ala., Feb. 19, 1911; s. Charles W. and Mary (Parker) M.; student Woodberry Forest Sch. (Va.), 1928-29, U. Fla., 1929-30; B.S. in Civil Engring., Mass. Inst. Tech., 1934; m. Helen D. Cooper, Nov. 16, 1963; children—William Harold, Susan Ann, Caroline Bridget, Mary Danforth. Partner Clarson & Mills, St. Petersburg, Fla., 1935-46; pres., chief exec. officer Mills & Jones Constrn. Co., 1946—; dir. Gen. Telephone Co. Fla., Fla. Fed. Savs. and Loan Assn., Founders Life Assurance Co. Mem. corp. Mass. Inst. Tech.; bd. dirs. St. Petersburg Episcopal Community. Mem. Fla. Council 100, Newcomen Soc., Tampa Horse Show Assn., Greater St. Petersburg C. of C. (past pres.), Suncoasters, Delta Tau Delta. Episcopalian. Clubs: St. Petersburg Yacht, Dragon (past pres.), Feather Sound Country (dir.), Mass. Inst. Tech. Central Fla. (past pres.). Home: Bayfront Tower One Beach Dr SE Saint Petersburg FL 33701 Office: PO Box 1257 Saint Petersburg FL 33731

MILLS, WILLIAM HAROLD, JR., bldg. exec.; b. St. Petersburg, Fla., July 24, 1939; s. William Harold and Caroline (Bonfoey) M.; B.C.E., U. Fla., 1961; children—William Harold III, Robert Michael, Leslie Anne. Vice pres. bus. devel. Mills & Jones Constrn. Co., St. Petersburg, 1964-68; v.p. Wellington Corp., Atlanta, 1968-71; exec. v.p. Mills & Jones Constrn. Co., 1971—; pres. Fed. Constrn. Co., 1979—; dir. 1st Nat. Bank St. Petersburg. Pres. Pinellas Marine Inst. Chem. blue ribbon zoning com., City St. Petersburg, 1965-68; mem. Tampa Bay Aviation Adv. Com., 1967-68. Bd. dirs. United Fund, Pinellas County, 1966-68. Served to lt. (j.g.) USPHS, 1962-64. Mem. St. Petersburg C. of C., ASCE, Nat. Soc. Profl. Engrs., Am. Mgmt. Assn., Am. Inst. Contractors, Mensa, Sigma Alpha Epsilon. Democrat. Episcopalian. Clubs: St. Petersburg Yacht, Dragon, Suncoasters (St. Petersburg); Feather Sound Country, Jockey (Miami, Fla.). Home: 1705 Bayfront Tower One Beach Dr SE Saint Petersburg FL 33701 Office: PO Box 1257 Saint Petersburg FL 33731

MILLS, WILLIAM HAYNE, cons. civil engr.; b. North Augusta, S.C., Oct. 29, 1903; s. William H. and Emma Louise (Pressley) M.; B.S., Clemson U., 1923; postgrad. U. S.C.; m. Elizabeth Legaré McCarley, Nov. 28, 1925; children—William Hayne III, Elizabeth Ann Mills Callaway. Draftsman, S.C. State Hwy. Dept., from 1923, later testing engr.; with Airport Constrn. CAA, 1947-49; dist. engr. Asphalt Inst., 1949-52; cons. civil engr. Brazil, 1954-58, Egypt, 1956, Atlanta, 1958—. Partner Atlanta Testing and Engring. Co., 1969, 70, 71. Served to lt. col., C.E., AUS. Registered profl. engr. Fellow Am. Soc. C.E. (pres. Ga. sect.); mem. S.C. Soc. of Engrs. (pres.), Tau Beta Pi. Presbyn. (elder). Club: Buckhead Men's Garden (pres.). Pioneer in devel. of soil cement and mech. soil stabilization for paving in Brazil. Address: 2496 Dellwood Dr NW Atlanta GA 30305

MILNER, CHARLES FREMONT, JR., mfr.; b. Durham, N.C., July 21, 1942; s. Charles Fremont and Eloyse (Sargent) M.; B.A., Guilford Coll., 1963; M.B.A., Harvard, 1965; m. Molly Franc Wakefield, Aug. 28, 1965; children—Bernadette Ann, Eloyse Lee. Asst. to comptroller Harvard, 1965-66; instr. Northeastern U., Boston, 1965-66; with Burlington Hosiery Co. div. Burlington Industries (N.C.), 1966-71, asst. v.p., 1970-71; exec. v.p. Parklane Hosiery Co., Inc., Great Neck, N.Y., 1971-74, also dir.; pres. Rudin & Roth, Inc., N.Y.C., 1974-75, also dir.; v.p. apparel group M. Lowenstein and Sons, Inc., N.Y.C., 1975-76; pres., chief exec. officer Bacon Baker Commack and Camp divs., pres. hosiery group Genesco, Inc., N.Y.C., 1976-79, gen. mgr. Johnston & Murphy Shoe Co., Jarman Shoe Co., Fortune Shoe Co., Pvt. Label Sales, pres. Hosiery Group subsidiaries, Nashville, 1979—. Trustee, Friends Acad., Locust Valley, N.Y., 1974-79. Home: 612 Belle Meade Blvd Nashville TN 37205 Office: Genesco Park Nashville TN 37202

MILNER, JOSEPH FREEMAN, JR., ednl. adminstr.; b. Chattanooga, Jan. 3, 1935; s. Joseph Freeman and Ethel M.; B.A., U. Tenn., Chattanooga, 1974, M.A., 1979. Employment counselor Chattanooga Concentrated Employment Program, 1968-71; supr. scheduling Chattanooga Human Services Dept., 1971-73, mgr. human service dept. project for the elderly, 1973-75, chief of psycho-motivation, human services dept., 1975-76; supt. building services U. Tenn., Chattanooga, 1976—. Cert. pest control supr. Mem. Am. Personnel and Guidance Assn., U. Tenn. Nat. Alumni Assn., U. Tenn. Group Facilitation. Seventh-day Adventist (elder, lay minister). Home: 2210 Milne St Chattanooga TN 37406 Office: 833 Fortwood St Chattanooga TN 37402

MILSTEAD, WILLIAM CLYDE, bldg. materials co. exec.; b. San Antonio, Apr. 30, 1926; s. Earl L. and Mattie Lee (Brown) M.; B.S., Rice Inst., 1946; m. Jacqueline Wheeler, July 16, 1955; children—William Mark, Matthew Earl. With Austin Industries, Inc. (formed by merger Calcasieu Lumber Co. and Milstead Co. 1975), Austin, Temple, Waco, Tex., 1946—, v.p. sales, 1953-56, v.p., gen. mgr., 1956-64, pres., treas., 1964-75, chmn. bd., 1975—; dir. Am. Nat. Bank Austin, First Fed Savs. & Loan Assn., Austin. Mem. planning commn. City Austin, 1963-74, chmn., 1972-74; vice commodore Austin Aqua Festival, 1968-69; trustee St. David's Hosp.; founding trustee Austin Community Found., 1976-77, treas., 1978-79; pres. Capitol Area Council Boy Scouts Am. Served as ensign USNR, 1943-46, lt. (j.g.), 1952. Mem. Am. Inst. Supply Assn. (past dir.), S.W. Air Conditioning and Refrigeration Wholesalers Assn. (past chmn.), Am. Soc. Heating, Air Conditioning and Refrigeration Engrs. (pres. Austin 1966), Wholesale Distbrs. Assn. Tex. (pres. 1955-56), Austin C. of C. (pres. 1971), Tex. Assn. Bus. (chpt. chmn. 1979), Young Men's Bus. League (pres. 1957). Episcopalian (vestryman 1959-61). Mason (32 deg., Shriner), Rotarian (pres. Austin 1971). Home: 2516 Tanglewood Trail Austin TX 78703 Office: Box 1827 Austin TX 78767

MILTIER, THOMAS WILSON, JR., mfg. co. exec.; b. Suffolk, Va., Jan. 15, 1947; s. Thomas Wilson and Mary Orlander (McClenney) M.; student Elon Coll., 1965-68; B.S. in Bus. Adminstrn., Old Dominion U., 1974; m. Mary Lee LaRue, Aug. 17, 1968. Asst. to budget dir. Royster Fertilizer Co., Norfolk, Va., 1975; asst. personnel mgr. Texfi Industries, Knitwear Group, Kinston, N.C., 1976-79; personnel mgr. L'Eggs Products div. Hanes Co., Hartsville, S.C., 1979—. Served with USAF, 1968-72. Decorated 3 air medals, Vietnam Campaign Medal, Republic of Vietnam Service Medal. Democrat. Mem. United Ch. of Christ. Office: L'Eggs Products Hartsville SC 29550

MILTON, ROGER GRANTHAM, elec. engr.; b. Memphis; s. Edgar Newell and Lottie Breba (Wilmouth) M.; B.S. in Elec. Engring., Christian Bros. Coll., 1971; student Coll. William and Mary, 1971-73; M.B.A., Boston U., 1975, cert. in data processing, 1978; m. Elizabeth Gillum, Apr. 9, 1972. Design engr. Newport News (Va.) Shipbuilders, Inc., 1971-73; planning coordinator Stone & Webster, Boston, 1973-75; staff asst. Touche Ross & Co., Memphis 1975-76, programmer analyst, 1976; communications engr. Cook Industries, Memphis, 1976-77, communications mgr., 1977-78; sr. systems rep. Burroughs Corp., Memphis, 1978—. Advisor, Jr. Achievement, Memphis, 1976-77, recipient Exec. award, 1967. Mem. IEEE, Gama Theta Phi. Roman Catholic. Home: 5359 Maple Ridge Cove Memphis TN 38134 Office: 5384 Poplar Ave Memphis TN 38117

MIMS, DAVID LATHAN, editor; b. Sumter, S.C., Apr. 29, 1916; s. Joseph Wright and Emma Curtis (Lathan) M.; A.B., Wofford Coll., 1936; postgrad. Harvard U. Law Sch., 1946; m. Lurline Shirley Stovall, Mar. 29, 1942; children—David Lathan, Diane Mims Langhorst, Sandra Mims Rowe, William C. Reporter, Florence (S.C.) Morning News, 1936, Spartanburg (S.C.) Herald-Jour., 1936-40; Carolinas state editor AP, Charlotte, N.C., 1946-54; alumni and pub. relations dir. Wofford Coll., 1954-56; editor, gen. mgr. Daily News-Record (Copeland award 1957, 1968), Harrisonburg, Va., 1956; pres. Page-Shenandoah Newspaper Corp., pub. Page News & Courier, Luray, Va., and Shenandoah Valley/Herald, Woodstock, Va.; chmn. adv. com. Old Dominion Savs. & Loan Co., Harrisonburg; mem. adv. com. ARA Va. Sky-line Co.; commr. Va. Port Authority. Pres. Harrisonburg-Rockingham County United Way, 1965, Va. United Way, 1972-73; pres. Shenandoah Valley, Inc., Staunton, Va., 1960; active senatorial and gubernatorial campaigns, including state chmn. Virginians for Byrd, 1976. Served with U.S. Army, World War II; ETO. Decorated Croix de guerre (France); named Boss of Yr., Harrisonburg Secs. Assn., 1968; recipient Service award Va. United Way, 1973. Mem. AP Assn. Va. (pres. 1962-63), Va. Press Assn. (pres. 1974-75, Service award 1975), Va. State C. of C. (1st v.p. 1976-77, Service award 1977), Am. Soc. Newspaper Editors, Sigma Delta Chi, Sigma Alpha Epsilon. Episcopalian. Clubs: Rotary (pres. club 1961-62) (Harrisonburg); Spotswood Country. Contbr. articles to Commonwealth Mag. Home: 560 S Mason St Harrisonburg VA 22801 Office: PO Box 193 Daily News-Record Harrisonburg VA 22801

MIMS, JAMES LUTHER, JR., ophthalmologist; b. Austin, Tex., May 21, 1920; s. James Luther and Evelyn Bell (Hornsby) M., Sr.; B.A., U. Tex., 1941, M.D., 1943; m. Mary Charline McGehee, Dec. 31, 1941; children—James L., III, Charles Lee, Robert Lewis. Intern, Wichita Falls (Tex.) Clinic Hosp., 1943-44; preceptor in ophthalmology, San Antonio, 1946-48; resident in ophthalmology Tulane U. Eye Ear Nose Throat Hosp., New Orleans, 1948-50; chief ophthalmology Robert B. Green Hosp., San Antonio, 1960-65, Bapt. Meml. Hosp. 1969-71; pvt. practice medicine specializing in ophthalmic surgery, San Antonio, 1950—; staff Bapt. Meml. Hosp., SW Tex. Meth. Hosp., Santa Rosa Hosp.; clin. prof. ophthalmology U. Tex. Med. Sch., San Antonio, 1967—. Lectr. on boating safety, skills, San Antonio Power Squadron, 1955—. Served with U.S. Army, 1944-46. Diplomate Am. Bd. Ophthalmology. Fellow A.C.S., Am. Acad. Ophthalmology; mem. San Antonio Soc. Ophthalmology and Otolaryngology, Bexar County Med. Soc., Tex., Am. med. assns., Am. Intra Ocular Implant Soc. Contact Lens Assn. of Ophthalmologists, Tex. Ophthalmological Assn. (pres. 1967-68). Methodist. Clubs: Alamo Kiwanis, San Antonio Squadron, U.S. Power Squadron. Clin. investigator contact lenses, intra-ocular implants; contbr. articles in field to profl. jours. Home: 311 Camden St Sta 206 San Antonio TX 78215 Office: 311 Camden St Suite 206 San Antonio TX 78215

MIMS, JULIAN LANDRUM, records mgmt. cons.; b. Edgefield, S.C., July 20, 1941; s. Matthew Hansford and Nancy (Crockett) M.; student Archives Inst., U. Ill., 1964; M.A. in History, U. S.C., 1969; m. Paulette Champy, Dec. 30, 1965; children—Stuart Crockett, Julian Landrum, Florence Adams. Asst. dir. local records S.C. Dept. Archives and History, Columbia, 1968-79; adj. prof. U. S.C., 1973—; instr. 6th Inst. Records Mgmt., Am. U., 1980; mem. history adv. com. S.C. Office Instructional TV; now records mgmt. cons. Recipient certificate in Archival Adminstrn., Am. U./Nat. Archives and Records Service, 1970. Mem. Assn. Records Mgrs. and Adminstrs. (nat. v.p. 1975-79, Disting. Service award S.C. chpt. 1980), Soc. Am. Archivists (state and local records com., records mgmt. com., micrographics com., program com.), S.C. Hist. Assn. Presbyn. (chmn. Diaconate 1974, ruling elder 1979—). Contbr. articles, revs. to profl. jours.; mem. staff The Am. Archivist, 1972-79. Home: 1522 Shady Ln Columbia SC 29206 Office: Data Mgmt Capitol Sta Box 11212 Columbia SC 29211

MIMS, LAMBERT C., mayor; b. Uriah, Ala., Apr. 20, 1930; m. Reecie Phillips; children—Dale, Danny. Commr. public works City of Mobile (Ala.), 1965-68, 69—, mayor, 1968-69, 72—. Bd. dirs. Mobile Rescue Mission; pres. Ala. Baptist State Conv., Mobile Bapt. Brotherhood, Ala. Bapt. Brotherhood; trustee Judson Coll., Marion, Ala. Mem. Am. Public Works Assn. (pres. 1979—), Ala. Public Works Assn. (pres.), Ala. League Municipalities (past mem. exec. com.), Nat. League Cities (com. employment and income security), U.S. Conf. Mayors (com. on transp.), Mobile Area C. of C., Mobile County Mcpl. Assn. (past pres.). Clubs: Kiwanis, Masons, Shriners. Author: For Christ and Country, 1969. Office: PO Box 1827 Mobile AL 36601

MIMS, LAMBERT CARTER, city ofcl.; b. Uriah, Ala., Apr. 20, 1930; s. Jeff and Carrie (Lambert) M.; grad. high sch.; m. Reecie Philips, Aug. 17, 1946; children—Dale, Danny. Engaged in retail and wholesale food bus., 1949-65; owner Mims Brokerage Co., Mobile, Ala., 1958-70; pub. works commr. City of Mobile, 1965-68, 69—, mayor, 1968-69, 72—; mem. transp. com. Ala. League Municipalities, 1966-68; mem. human resources com. Nat. League Cities; lectr. in field. Former trustee Judson Coll., Marion, Ala. Named Mobile's Most Outstanding Young Man, 1965. Mem. Ala. (pres. 1969-70, 72—), Am. (pres. 1979—), public works assns., Mobile C. of C. Baptist (deacon; chmn. bd. 1950-65; 1st v.p. Ala. Bapt. State Conv. 1969-70, pres. 1970-71; mem. Mobile Camp Gideons, pres. 1962-65; mem. Christian businessmen's com. internat. 1965-70; bd. dirs. Mobile rescue mission; past pres., now dir. Mobile Bapt. Brotherhood). Clubs: Masons, Shriners, Kiwanis. Author: For Christ and Country, 1969. Address: PO Box 1827 Mobile AL 36601

MIMS, THOMAS JEROME, ins. co. exec.; b. Sumter, S.C., Dec. 12, 1899; s. Lazarus and Sarah Rebecca (White) M.; A.B., Furman U., 1921; m. Valma Gillespie, Dec. 14, 1926; children—Thomas Jerome, George Franklin. Apprentice, Rec. & Statis. Corp. of N.Y., Detroit, 1921, N.Y.C., 1921-22, asst. mgr., Phila., 1922-25, mgr., Indpls., 1925-27, Boston, 1927-29; salesman Burroughs Adding Machine Co., Detroit, Boston, 1929-31; ins. spl. agt. State N.J., Morley Gen. Agy., Camden, 1931-32; mgr. William R. Timmons Agy., Greenville, S.C., 1933—; v.p., sec. Canal Ins. Co., Greenville, 1942-48, pres., treas., dir., 1948—; dir., pres. Canal Indemnity Co.; dir., mem. bd. mgmt., bd. govs. Internat. Ins. Seminar; bd. electors Ins. Hall of Fame. Bus. mgr. Greenville Little Theater, 1951-53, 64-66, council, 1951—, v.p., 1956-57, pres., 1957-58, 72-75; pres. Rotary Charities, Inc., 1964-65; mem. adv. bd. S.C. Safety Council, 1969-70, pres., 1970-75; past dir. Met. Arts Council; bd. dirs. United Way Greenville, 1970—, chmn. bd., 1979, campaign chmn., 1976, v.p., 1977-78, pres., 1978; vice chmn. Found. Modern Liquor Regulations and Control; adv. council Furman U. Named Boss of Year Greenville Jr. C. of C., 1964, Greenville Assn. Ins. Women, 1966; Spl. award S.C. Assn. Ins. Women, 1977; S.C. Vol. of Year, United Way, 1979. Mem. Nat., S.C., Greenville (past pres.) assns. ins. agts., S.C. Motor Transp. Assn. (chmn. ins. com. 1951-63, dir. 1973-75), S.C., U.S. (ins. com. 1959-61, 64-68), Greenville (chmn. community relations com. 1964-69, dir. 1969-74, pres.-elect 1972, pres. 1973, pres. found. 1973) chambers commerce, Am. Mgmt. Assn. (pres.'s assn.), AIM (fellow pres.'s council), Truck and Heavy Equipment Claims Council (charter mem., chmn. membership com.), Assn. S.C. Property and Casualty Ins. Cos. (pres. 1962-63, 72-73, mem. exec. com. 1963-68), Internat. Platform Assn., Pres.'s Assn. Baptist (past pres. men's Bible class, past mem. fin. com.). Clubs: Elks, Rotary (pres. Rotary Charities, Inc. 1964-65; dir. Greenville 1957-58, pres. 1963-64, v.p. 1964-65), Touchdown (charter mem.; pres. 1963-64), Greenville City (dir. 1964, pres. 1965, chmn. bd. dirs. 1966-67), Poinsett, VIP (Greenville); Palmetto, Summit (Columbia, S.C.). Home: Knollwood Dr Route 6 Greenville SC 29607 Office: 417 E North St Greenville SC 29602

MINAHAN, JOSEPH JAMES, JR., constrn. co. exec.; b. Houston, July 31, 1951; s. Joseph James and Jane P.; B.S. in Archtl. Engring., U. Tex., Austin, 1975; m. Leslee Kay Murray, May 22, 1976. Mgmt. trainee Oilwell div. U.S. Steel Corp., Houston, 1975-76, sales rep., 1976-79, mgr. Mexico and S. Am., Houston, 1979; v.p. Baxter Constrn. Co., Inc., Houston, 1979—. Mem. Republican Nat. Com., 1976-80. Am. Iron and Steel Inst. fellow, 1978-79. Mem. Am. Petroleum Inst., Soc. Petroleum Engrs. of AIME, Sigma Nu. Episcopalian. Clubs: Plaza, Walden Yacht, Raveneaux Country. Home: 9123 Herts Spring TX 77373 Office: PO Box 7744 Houston TX 77007

MINCH, VIRGIL ADELBERT, civil and san. engr.; b. Cleve., Dec. 24, 1924; s. Henry Joseph and Mary (Terlaak) M.; B.S., N.D. State U., 1946; S.M. in San. Engring., Mass. Inst. Tech., 1948; m. Elma Queen, Jan. 6, 1947; children—David, Philip. Research asso. Mass. Inst. Tech., 1948-49; sr. asst. san. engr. USPHS, Cin., 1949-53; staff engr. Mead Corp., Chillicothe, Ohio, 1953-55, group leader, 1956-59, mgr. pollution control activities, 1960-65, asso. dir. tech. services, 1966-68, coordinator environmental resources, 1969-73; v.p., dir. Asso. Water and Air Resources Engrs., Nashville, 1972-74; project mgr. Stanley Cons., Muscatine, Iowa, 1974, v.p., 1974-77; v.p. John J. Harte Assos., Inc., Atlanta, 1977-78; S.E. regional mktg. mgr. Environ. Research and Tech., Atlanta, 1978—. Recipient Indsl. liaison service award Ohio River Valley Water Sanitation Commn., 1959. Registered profl. engr. Ga. Mem. Scioto Conservancy dist. (v.p., dir. 1959—), Am. Meteorol. Soc., Am. Water Works Assn., Water Pollution Control Fedn., Air Pollution Control Assn., T.A.P.P.I., Ga. Pulp and Paper Assn. (sec. 1955-65), Nat. Council Air and Stream Improvement (chmn. S. Central region 1963—), Nat. Rivers and Harbors Congress (chmn. S.E. Ohio sect. 1968-72), Sigma Xi, Tau Beta Pi, Sigma Phi Delta. Contbr. articles profl. jours. Patentee plastic film trickling filter. Home: Main St Union Mills NC 28167 Office: 2028 Powers Ferry Rd Atlanta GA 30339

MINGE, JERRY LEE, lawyer; b. Rome, Ga., Sept. 23, 1934; s. Willie Lee and Mary (Moore) M.; B.B.A., U. Ga., 1959, LL.B., 1959; m. Carol Bland, Mar. 27, 1958; children—Mary Angela, Jennifer Bland, Anne Marquerite. Admitted to Ga. bar, 1958; partner Scoggin & Minge, Attys., Rome, 1959-63, Hamilton & Minge, Attys., Rome, 1963—; judge City Ct. of Floyd County, Ga., 1967-69. Mem. Ga. Ho. of Reps., 1965-67. Mem. Am., Ga., Rome (pres.) bar assns., Jr. C. of C. (past pres.), Phi Delta Phi, Sigma Nu. Baptist. Clubs: Coosa Country, Nine O'Clock Cotillion, Masons, Elks. Home: 10 Saddle Mountain Rd Rome GA 30161 Office: PO Box 746 237 N 5th Ave Rome GA 30161

MINKLEY, SUZANNE SAWYER (MRS. CARL H. MINKLEY), educator; b. Middletown, Ohio, May 15, 1915; d. Clifford Louis and Harriett May (Logan) Sawyer; A.B., John B. Stetson U., 1937, M.A., 1942; B.L.S., George Peabody Coll. Tchrs., 1940; postgrad. Manatee Jr. Coll., 1960, Fla. So. Coll., 1966, U. South Fla., 1966-67; m. Carl Henry Minkley, Apr. 3, 1943; children—Elizabeth Suzanne Minkley Jarrard, Philip Carl. Tchr., librarian Mt. Dora High Sch., 1937-41, Leesburg High Sch., 1941-43, Delray Beach High Sch., 1943-45, Samsula Elementary Sch., 1955-56; tchr. Spanish, Sarasota High Sch., 1956-57; reading specialist, chmn. lang. arts Bayshore Jr. High Sch., 1963-74; tchr. social studies Bradenton Middle Sch., 1974—; cons. tchr. tng. program Edn. Professions Devel. Act of U.S. Dept. Edn., 1970-71; parliamentarian Manatee County Edn. Assn., 1968-72, Bradenton Middle Sch. PTA, 1976—. Chmn. bd. Deland (Fla.) Children's Mus., 1954-56, Volusia County Continuing Council on Edn., 1954-56; state bd. dirs. Am. Cancer Soc., 1954-61, v.p., crusade chmn. Volusia County unit, 1952-55. Recipient citation Am. Cancer Soc., 1952-55; various radio and newspaper awards; certificate of profl. acceptance NEA, 1966-67. Mem. Volusia County Fedn. Women's Clubs (legis. chmn. 1952-54), Fla. Fedn. Women's Clubs (chmn. radio and TV 1962-66), D.A.R., NEA, Nat. Council Tchr. of English, AAUW (chmn. edn. com. 1943-45, 60-62), Am. Inst. Parliamentarians, Nat. Assn. Parliamentarians (pres. Sarasota unit 1973-77, 79—), Fla., Manatee County edn. assns., Fla. Assn. Parliamentarians, Gen. Fedn. Women's Clubs, DAR, Joan Ortiz Soc. (sr. pres. 1961-63), Leonardy Gaveliers (pres. 1972-73), Mu Omega Xi, Sigma Kappa. Democrat. So. Baptist. Clubs: Primrose Garden (founder, pres. 1953-55), Orange Blossom Garden (pres. 1962-63), DeLand Women's (pres. 1951-53), Woman's of Sarasota (pres. 1960-61), Fla. Fedn. Women's Clubs (dist. dir. 1960-63, parliamentarian dist. 1963-65). Coordinator Have Gavel, Will Travel panels for civic and social orgns., 1959-65. Author: (booklet) Parliamentary Procedure for Teen-Agers. Home: 2540 Hibiscus St Sarasota FL 33579

MINNIEAR, WALTER COLLINS, symphony conductor; b. Chgo., Apr. 17, 1911; s. Harry Hilemon and Dorothy Ruhamy (Mullen) M.; B.S. in Music, Columbia, 1931; M.Mus.Edn., VanderCook Sch. Music, Chgo., 1947; m. Mary Elizabeth Mohr, Oct. 28, 1932; children—Robert Lee, Thomas Collins, John Mohr, Mary Jane (Mrs. Joe Allen Recer), Kathryn Ruhamy. Music tchr., Lombard, Ill., 1929-35, Monroe (La.) Quachita parish schs., 1936-49, Lamar Tech. U., Beaumont, Tex., 1949-52, Caddo (La.) parish schs., 1952-69; chmn. humanities div. Westark Community Coll., Ft. Smith, Ark., 1969-79, instr., 1969—, also dir. Breedlove Gallery; violinist, percussionist Shreveport Symphony, 1952-69, also condr. youth symphony; condr. Ft. Smith Symphony, 1969—. Pres. La. Music Educators Assn., 1958-62, mem. exec. com., 1962-69. Named La. Bandmaster of Year, La. Bandmasters Assn., 1964; elected to 1st Chair of Am., 1962, Order Silver Horn, 1969; NACUBO grantee, 1978. Life mem. Music Educators Nat. Conf. (mem. bd. So. div. 1958-62); mem. ASCAP. Club: Rotary. Home: 6800 South W St Fort Smith AR 72901

MINNIS, MHYRA SCHWAY, educator, sociologist; b. Dvinsk, Latvia; d. Hersh and Beth Ann Schway; B.A., Oberlin Coll., 1939, M.A., 1940; Ph.D., Yale, 1951; m. Dean Hugh Minnis, June, 1932 (div. Nov. 1945). Instr. sociology Bowling Green (Ohio) State U., 1946-48; asst. prof. sociology U. Idaho, 1954-56, asso. prof., 1957-60; asst. prof. Skidmore Coll., Saratoga Springs, N.Y., 1956-57, San Fernando Valley State Coll., 1960-62; asso. prof. sociology Tex. Tech. U., 1962-65, prof., 1965-76, prof. emeritus, 1976—, research grantee, 1970-71. Research analyst adminstrv. div. Plans and Reports br. USPHS, Washington, 1951; sr. research analyst Library of Congress, 1951-54. Recreational social worker, asst. program dir., head recreation worker A.R.C., 1943-46; occupational and recreational dir. County Tb Hosp., Amherst, Ohio, 1940-41. Trustee Lubbock City-County Child Welfare Bd., Council on Alcoholism. Recipient Merit award A.R.C., Tex. 1946; scholarships Case Western Res. U., Oberlin Coll., Yale; Tex. Tech. U. research grantee 1964-65, Hogg Found. for Mental Health grantee, 1964-65. Fellow Am. Sociol. Assn.; mem. Am. Assn. U. Profs., Tex. Assn. Coll. Tchrs., Soc. Internat. Criminology, So. Sociol. Assn., S.W. Sociol. Assn. (v.p., program chmn. 1972-73, pres. 1973-74), Tex. Acad. Sci., T.A.C.T. Sr. editor: Sociological Perspectives: Readings in Social Problems and Deviant Behavior 1968; Tornado: The Voice of the People in Disaster and After, A Study in Residential Integration, 1971. Contbr. articles to profl. jours. and books. Home: 4512A 65th St Lubbock TX 79414

MINOR, CARL LESTER, broadcasting exec.; b. Lewisville, Tex., Oct. 7, 1922; s. Carl Lester and Frances M.; student indsl. mgmt. Tex. Tech. U., Lubbock, 1947; m. Amy Sue Way, Sept. 7, 1947; children—Susan Elaine, Carl Jefferson. Tchr., Floydada, Tex., 1950-52; sales announcer, sta. mgr. Sta. KFLD, Floydada, Tex., 1951-57; various sales positions Sta. KCBD-TV, Lubbock, 1957—, gen. sales mgr., 1974—. Bd. dirs. S. Plains Dist., Boy Scouts Am., 1960-75. Served with USMCR, 1943-46, 50-51. Mem. Lubbock Advt. Fedn. (pres. 1969-70). Democrat. Methodist. Clubs: Masons, Rotary (pres. Floydada chpt. 1956-57, SW Lubbock chpt. 1959-60). Home: 3602 61st St Lubbock TX 79413 Office: Sta KCBD-TV 5600 Ave A Lubbock TX 79408

MINOR, MARGIE NELL, accountant; b. Dallas, Nov. 21, 1945; d. King and Lena Mae (Kimbrough) Huff; student public schs., Wilmer-Hutchins, Tex.; m. Alvie Monroe Minor, Jr.; children—Tommy Lee Sturgeon, Jr., Teressa Marie, Michael King. Unit head acctg. office Southwestern Life Ins. Co., Dallas, 1964-67; accounts receivable clk./receptionist Marriott Motor Hotel, Dallas, 1967-68; bookkeeper Jensen Co., Dallas, 1971; acctg. supr. Tecon Enterprises, Inc., Dallas, 1971—. Baptist. Home: 1714 Novel Dr Garland TX 75040 Office: 1300 Expressway Tower Dallas TX 75206

MINTO, GEORGE DENNIS, logistics engr.; b. Butler, Pa., June 15, 1941; s. George and Katherine Elizabeth (Lesnik) M.; grad. electronics engring. DeVry Inst. Tech., Chgo., 1963; postgrad. N.Y. Inst. Tech., 1974-75; m. Charlotte Muriel Johnson, Apr. 30, 1971; children—Tanya Lesnik, Heidi Kristin. Electronics designer, research technician Argonne Nat. Labs. (Ill.), 1963-65; field engr. Calif. and Philippines, Kay & Assos., Chgo., 1965-68; field engr. Cape Kennedy, Fla. and W. Ger., Martin Marietta Corp., Orlando, Fla., 1968-72, logistics engr., Orlando, 1972-74, ops. analyst, cost analyst, 1974-77, logistics engring. supr., 1977-78, chief logistics/product support, 1978-79, mktg. mgr., 1980—; mem. workshop teaching staff Soc. Logistics Engrs., Los Angeles, fall 1977. Mem. Soc. Logistics Engrs. (officer, newsletter editor Orlando chpt.), Am. Def. Preparedness Assn. Roman Catholic. Home: 3900 LeJune Ave Titusville FL 32780 Office: Box 5837 MP 486 Orlando FL 32855

MINTON, CAROLYN GRACHIA BROCK, educator; b. Erie, Pa., Nov. 3, 1926; d. O. Carlyle and Grachia May (King) Brock; A.B., U. Tex., Austin, 1948; A.B., Angelo State U., 1971, M.A., 1976; student Eastman Sch. Music, 1943, Emerson Sch. Dramatic Art, 1944; m. Robert Marion Minton, Jr., Dec. 30, 1947; children—Cynthia Maureen, Rhonda Carolyn, Robert Brock, Randall Mark. Tchr. Episcopal Day Sch., Midland, Tex., 1962-66; tchr. orthopedically handicapped and lang. learning disabled, Central High Sch., San Angelo, 1967—. Vice pres. Midland County TB Assn.; pres. Experiment in Internat. Living, 1960. NDEA fellow, 1968. Mem. AAUW (pres. 1958-60), Tex. Classroom Tchrs. Assn., Tex. Joint Council Tchrs. English, Sigma Tau Delta, Kappa Delta Pi, Delta Kappa Gamma. Republican. Episcopalian. Home: 2500 Douglas Dr San Angelo TX 76901 Office: Central High School San Angelo TX 76901

MINTON, KEVIN LEWIS, mech. engr.; b. Canton, Ohio, Sept. 3, 1952; s. Lewis Gray and Marie Elizabeth (Miller) M.; B.S. in Mech. Engring., Ohio No. U., 1974; postgrad. U. Akron, 1974-75; m. Gloria Kristine Kastner, June 8, 1974; 1 son, Jason Abram. Quality control engr. Hoover Co., N. Canton, Ohio, 1972; asst. plant engr. Belden Brick Co., Canton, 1973; mfg. engr. Babcock & Wilcox Co., Barberton, Ohio, 1974-75, plant engr., West Point, Miss., 1975-79; indsl. engr. Michelin Tire Corp., Sandy Springs, S.C., 1979—. Registered profl. engr., Miss., S.C. Mem. ASME, Tau Beta Pi, Phi Kappa Phi. Mem. First Brethren Ch. Home: 413 Pine Bark Rd Anderson SC 29621 Office: PO Box 308 Sandy Springs SC 29677

MINTZ, ALBERT, lawyer; b. New Orleans, Oct. 19, 1929; s. Morris and Goldie (Goldblum) M.; B.B.A., Tulane U., 1948, J.D., 1951; m. Linda Barnett, Dec. 19, 1954; children—John Morris, Margaret Anne. Admitted to La. bar, 1951, since practiced in New Orleans; partner firm Montgomery, Barnett, Brown & Read, 1956—; partner Hurwitz-Mintz Realty Cos., New Orleans, 1945—; mem. bd. advisers Law Sch., Tulane U., 1972—. Bd. dirs. Jewish Community Center, New Orleans, 1965-72, Jewish Fedn., New Orleans, 1968-73, Home for Jewish Aged, New Orleans, 1968-71, Jewish Family Service, New Orleans, 1968-72; trustee bd. mgrs. Touro Infirmary Hosp. Mem. Am., La. (lectr., publ. on corp., tax, real estate law), New Orleans (exec. com. 1971-74) bar assns., Am. Law Inst., New Orleans C. of C. (chmn. com. state legis. 1968-69), Phi Delta Phi (v.p. 1951), Omicron Delta Kappa, Zeta Beta Tau. Jewish. Home: 2017 Jefferson Ave New Orleans LA 70115 Office: 806 First Nat Bank Commerce Bldg New Orleans LA 70112

MINTZ, HOWARD, hosp. adminstr.; b. N.Y.C., Aug. 16, 1949; s. Sidney and Sylvia (Bienstock) M.; B.E., Cooper Union, 1970, M.S., 1973; postgrad. Poly. Inst. Bklyn., 1970-73; m. Ruth Lea Forman, June 13, 1971; children—Alyson Helene, Seth Ian. Systems analyst Cumberland Hosp., N.Y.C., 1973; quantitative analyst N.Y.C. Transp. Adminstrn., 1973-74; mgmt. engr. Lenox Hill Hosp., N.Y.C., 1974-76; dir. mgmt. service Mercy Hosp., Miami, Fla., 1976—. Recipient Frank H. Tallman Meml. award, 1969. Mem. Am. Inst. Indsl. Engrs. (sr.), Hosp. Mgmt. Systems Soc. of Am. Hosp. Assn. (S.E. regional dir.; Lit. award 1977, 79), Tau Beta Pi, Eta Kappa Nu. Contbr. articles to publs. in field. Home: 7984 SW 146th Ct Miami FL 33183 Office: Mercy Hosp 3663 S Miami Ave Miami FL 33133

MINYARD, JAMES PATRICK, JR., chemist, educator; b. Greenwood, Miss., May 11, 1929; s. James Patrick and Mary Lou (Duke) M.; B.S. in Chemistry, Miss. State U., 1951, Ph.D., 1967; postgrad. Calif. Inst. Tech. (Gen. Edn. Bd. scholar), 1951-52; m. Mary Louise Whitesell, Aug. 11, 1956; children—Mary Susan, Thomas James, Barbara Lynn, Carol Ann, William Patrick. Field engr. Minyard Well Co., Belzoni, Miss., 1954-58; asst. chemist Miss. State Chem. Lab., 1958-59, chemist, 1959-64, state chemist, 1967—; research chemist Boll Weevil Research Lab., Agrl. Research Service, Dept. Agr., 1964-67; faculty Miss. State U., 1961—, prof. chemistry, 1967—. Served with U.S. Army, 1952-54. Mem. Am. Chem. Soc. (chmn. 1977; fellow div. pesticide chemistry), AAAS, Miss. Acad. Scis., Newcomen Soc. Am., Am. Oil Chemists Soc., Assn. Ofcl. Analytical Chemists (chmn. editorial bd., dir. 1977—), Assn. Am. Feed Control Ofcls. (pres. 1975-76), Am. Assn. Fertilizer Control Ofcls., Assn. Am. Pesticide Control Ofcls., Assn. Food and Drug Ofcls., Sigma Xi, Phi Lambda Upsilon. Democrat. Methodist. Editorial advisory com. Jour. Agrl. and Food Chemistry, 1977—; contbr. to profl. jours. Home: Box 2198 Mississippi State MS 39762 Office: Miss State Chem Lab Box CR Mississippi State MS 39762

MIRABAL-NAVEIRA, GUSTAVO, social worker; b. Ponce, P.R., Sept. 4, 1945; s. Rafael and Emma (Naveira) M.; B.B.A., Cath. U. P.R., 1967; M.S.W. cum laude, U. P.R., 1970; prof. cert. Ohio State U., 1975; m. Edda V. Colon, Nov. 28, 1968; children—Gustavo A., Daniel R., Kendra E. Social worker Dept. Social Services, Ponce, 1971-72; social worker St. Lukes Home Care Program, Ponce, 1973-79; zone supr. Juvenile Ct. Justice, Ponce, 1979—; prof. Interamerican U., Ponce, part time 1974—; mem. profl. adv. bd. St. Lukes Home Care Program; mem. Christian Edn. Bd., Episcopal Ch. P.R., 1976-77. Recipient grants Govt. P.R., P.R. Dept. Social Services, 1969-70; named Layman of Yr., Ponce 1st Bapt. Ch., 1977. Mem. Nat. Assn. Social Work, Colegio de Trabajadores Sociales de Puerto Rico. Home: H-22 D St Jardines de Ponce Ponce PR 00731

MIRABILE, JACK JAMES, counselor; b. Bklyn., July 5, 1952; s. Jack William and Jean Marie (DiStefano) M.; B.S., Ga. State U., 1974, M.Ed., 1977; postgrad. U. Ga., 1978—; m. May 30, 1975. Counselor, trainer Dept. Offender Rehab., Women's Work Release Center, 1975-76; counselor trainer dept. counseling and psychol. services Ga. State U., Atlanta, 1976-77; bd. dirs. South DeKalb Counseling Center, Decatur, Ga., 1976—; pvt. practice counseling and psychol. services Century Center Clinic, Atlanta, 1979—. Mem. Am. Personnel and Guidance Assn., Am. Psychol. Assn., Democrat. Roman Catholic. Office: 1780 Century Circle Suite 8 Atlanta GA 30345

MIRABILE, THOMAS KEITH, lawyer; b. Lancaster, Ohio, May 11, 1948; s. Joseph Anthony and Marie Johanna Mirabile; B.A., No. Ill. U., 1972; M.A., Northeastern Ill. U., 1973; J.D., Oklahoma City U., 1975; m. Cathy Louise Willing, June 9, 1971. Admitted to Okla. bar, 1976, Ill. bar, 1977; spl. eligibility reviewer Ill. Dept. Pub. Aid, Chgo., 1972-73; govt. intern-legal Okla. Dept. Consumer Affairs, Oklahoma City, 1974-76; prin. Thomas K. Mirabile, P.C., Oklahoma

City, 1976—; of counsel firm Speiser and Bedoya, Chgo.; adj. prof. dept. sociology Oklahoma City U.; adj. prof. law Central State U.; adj. prof. dept. human affairs S. Oklahoma City Jr. Coll. Vice-pres. bd. dirs. Community Counseling Center of Oklahoma City. Mem. Ill., Okla., Am., Oklahoma County bar assns., Comml. Law League Am., Am., Okla. trial lawyers assn. Home: 2536 NW 25 St Oklahoma City OK 73107 or 3337 N Page Ave Chicago IL 60634 Office: 706 Park Harvey Center 200 N Harvey St Oklahoma City OK 73102

MIRANDA, CARLOS ROLANDO, surgeon; b. Juarez, Chihuahua, Mex., Dec. 5, 1939; s. Carlos and Carmen (Rueda) M.; came to U.S., 1968, naturalized, 1973; B.S., Chihuahua State U., 1958; M.D., Chihuahua Med. Sch., 1968; m. Dolores Ortega, May 15, 1965; children—Carlos, Luis, Adriana. Intern surgery Mount Sinai Hosp., N.Y.C., 1968-69; resident surgery Scott and White Meml. Hosp., Temple, Tex., 1969-73; practice medicine specializing in surgery, El Paso, Tex. and Juarez, Mex., 1973—; asso. prof. surgery Juarez Sch. Medicine, 1973—. Diplomate Am. Bd. Surgery. Mem. A.C.S., Internat. Coll. Surgeons, Southwest, El Paso surg. socs., El Paso County, Tex. med. assns., Am. Soc. Abdominal Surgeons, Sociedad Medica de Juarez. Clubs: Vista Hills Country, Juarez Country. Home: 10541 Tomwood St El Paso TX 79925 Office: 1100 N Stanton St El Paso TX 79902

MIRANDA, OSMUNDO AFONSO, educator; b. Araguary, Minas Gerais, Brazil, Dec. 23, 1926; came to U.S., 1956, naturalized, 1977; s. Olympio Afonso Miranda de and Laurinda Ferreira Nascimento; M.Div., Campinas Theol. Sem., Campinas S.P., Brazil, 1954; Th.M., Princeton Theol. Sem., 1957, Ph.D., 1962; children—Laurinisa, Georgeolimpio A., Cheyenne A. Ordained to ministry Presbyterian Ch., 1956; pastor Presbyn. chs., Brazil, U.S. 1955; prof. Bibl. criticism, dean Sem. Campinas (Brazil), 1962-65; instr. modern langs. Midwestern Coll., Denison, Iowa, 1966-68; prof. religion and philosophy Stillman Coll., Tuscaloosa, Ala., 1968—. Mem. Am. Acad. Religion, Soc. Bibl. Lit., AAUP. Contbr. articles and book revs. to theol. jours. Home: 80 E Lake St Tuscaloosa AL 35405

MIRANTI, VINCENT JOSEPH, container leasing co. ofcl.; b. New Orleans, Oct. 6, 1939; s. Gandolfo Joseph and Mildred Josephine M.; A.A., St. Joseph Coll., La., 1960; m. Judith Goodwyne, Dec. 20, 1974; 1 son, Vincent Joseph Goodwyne. Container control coordinator U.S. Gulf, Container Transport Internat., New Orleans, 1973-77, dist. mgr., 1977—. Mem. Intermodal Club Greater New Orleans (sec. 1978, dir. 1977), World Trade Club. Roman Catholic. Home: 1628 Dante St New Orleans LA 70118 Office: Suite 1940 International Trade Mart New Orleans LA 70130

MIRISCIOTTI, JOSEPH PAUL, ednl. adminstr.; b. Muskogee, Okla., Apr. 28, 1945; s. Frank Paul and Jessie Inez (Standifer) M.; B.S. (Peter Linehart scholar), E. Tex. State U., 1971, M.Ed., 1973; now postgrad. N. Tex. State U.; children—Lisa, Lacy. Park recreation dir. City of Commerce, Tex., 1969-72; coordinator phys. edn. program Commerce Ind. Sch. Dist., 1969-70, coordinator spl. edn., 1971-72; lead tchr. Ft. Worth Ind. Sch. Dist., spl. edn., 1972-74; coordinator devel. services Ft. Worth State Sch., 1974-75, adminstr. community based services, 1975-78, dir. program services, 1978—; coordinator, coach Tex. Spl. Olympics; mem. Action NOW Com. Mem. adv. bds. Camp Hope, reorganization of Ft. Worth ARC, United Univ. Meth. Ch. Served with U.S. Army, 1965-71. Decorated Soldiers Medal for Heroism; medal of honor (Republic of Vietnam); recipient award Mental Retardation Mgmt. Program, U. Ala., 1976; Clark Found. grantee, 1979. Mem. Council for Exceptional Children (pres. 1974-75), Ft. Worth Council for Exceptional Children, Ft. Worth Council of Adminstrs. Spl. Edn., Nat. Assn. for Retarded Citizens (Ft. Worth and Arlington), Nat. Teachers Assn., Am. Assn. on Mental Deficiency. Home: 3825 Bluegrass Ln Fort Worth TX 76133 Office: 5000 Campus Dr Fort Worth TX 76119

MISHELEVICH, DAVID JACOB, computer center exec., physician; b. Pitts., Jan., 1942; s. Benjamin and Sarah (Bachrach) M.; B.S., U. Pitts., 1962; M.D. (Henry Strong Denison scholar), Johns Hopkins, 1966, Ph.D. in Biomed. Engring., 1970; m. Elaine Carol Grumer, Aug. 18, 1963. Post-sophomore research fellow Johns Hopkins Sch. Medicine, 1964-65, NIH spl. fellow in biomed. engring. and medicine, 1969-71; intern in medicine Balt. City Hosps., 1966-67; sr. asst. surgeon USPHS, 1967-68, surgeon, 1968-69; staff asso. NIH, Bethesda, Md., 1967-69; v.p. Nat. Ednl. Cons., Inc., Balt., 1970-71, chief computing and profl. records div., 1970-72, exec. v.p., 1971-72; dir. Med. Computing Resources Center, U. Tex. Health Sci. Center at Dallas, 1972—, asst. prof. med. computer sci., 1972-74, asso. prof., 1974-79, prof., 1979—, chmn. dept., 1973—, asst. prof. internal medicine, 1972—, mem. Grad. Faculty, 1973—; adj. asso. prof. math. scis. U. Tex. at Dallas, 1974-79, adj. prof., 1979—; adj. asso. prof. math. U. Tex., Arlington, 1974-79, adj. prof., 1979—, adj. asso. prof. biomed. engring., 1975-79, adj. prof., 1979—; attending physician Dallas County Hosp. Dist., 1973—, tech. adviser info. services, 1975—, acting dir. info. services, 1975, dir., 1978-79; mem. biomed. library rev. com. Nat. Library of Medicine, NIH, 1978—; cons. hosp. info. systems and med. computing. Mem. AAAS, Am., Tex. hosp. assns., Am. Soc. Info. Sci., Assn. for Computing Machinery, Digital Equipment Corp. Users Soc., Electronic Computing Health Oriented, IEEE, Johns Hopkins Med. and Surg. Assn., Soc. Computer Medicine, MUMPS Users Group, Tex. Assn. State-Supported Computer Centers, Tandem Computer Users Group (past pres.), Tex. Hosp. Info. Systems Soc., Tex. Inst. for Med. Assessment, Phi Beta Kappa, Omicron Delta Kappa. Jewish. Contbr. articles and abstracts to profl. jours. Home: 4390 Shady Bend Dallas TX 75234 Office: Dept Med Computer Sci Univ Tex Health Sci Center at Dallas 5323 Harry Hines Blvd Dallas TX 75235

MISKIMEN, GEORGE WILLIAM, biologist, educator; b. Appleton, Wis., May 21, 1930; s. George Oscar and Gladys Matilda (Burns) M.; B.S., Ohio U., 1953, M.S., 1955; Ph.D., U. Fla. at Gainesville, 1966; m. Carmen Milagros Rivera-Batlle, Apr. 19, 1963; children—Kathryn Ann, Teresa Marie, Elizabeth Joan, Carmen Mildred. Entomologist V.I. Agrl. Program U.S. Dept. Agr., St. Croix, 1958-61; research entomologist, investigations leader entomology research div. U.S. Dept. Agr. Mayaguez, P.R., 1962-66; dir., prof. biology Entomol. Pioneering Research Lab. U. P.R. at Mayaguez, 1966-74, prof. biology, research dir., 1975—. Served with AUS, 1947-51. U. Fla. Academic fellow; Hatch Scientific grantee, NSF grantee, NIH grantee. Mem. Soc. for Neuroscis., Entomol. Soc. Am., Internat. Orgn. Biol. Control, Coleopterist's Soc., Assn. Tropical Biology, U.S. Coast Guard Aux. (Flotilla comdr. 1968—, div. tng. officer 1970), Explorers Club, Sigma Xi, Gamma Sigma Delta, Delta Upsilon (sec. 1954, pledge pres. 1953). Episcopalian. Mason, Rotarian. Clubs: Boqueron Yacht (Boqueron, P.R.); Deportivo del Oeste (Mayaguez, P.R.); Casino de Mayaguez (P.R.). Contbr. articles to scientific jours. Home: Box 1420 Km 4 0 Miradero Rd Villa Sonsire Mayaguez PR 00708 Office: Dept Biology University PR at Mayaguez Mayaguez PR 00708

MISKOVSKY, GEORGE, lawyer, ex-state senator; b. Oklahoma City, Feb. 13, 1910; s. Frank and Mary (Bourek) M.; LL.B., U. Okla., 1936; m. Nelly Oleta Donahue. Dec. 30, 1932; children—George, Gary, Grover, Gail Marie. Admitted to Okla. bar, 1936, since practiced in Oklahoma City; sr. mem., head firm Miskovsky, Sullivan & Miskovsky, Oklahoma City; pub. defender Oklahoma City, 1936; county atty. Oklahoma County, 1943-44; mem. Okla. Ho. of Reps., 1939-42; mem. Okla. Senate, 1950-60. Pres. Economy Square, Inc. and Penn 74 Mall Inc. Shopping Centers. Mem. Am., Okla., Oklahoma County bar assns., Am. Judicature Soc., C. of C., Am., Okla. trial lawyers assns., U. Okla. Law Assn., Order of Coif, Pi Kappa Alpha, Phi Alpha Delta. Democrat. Episcopalian. Clubs: Lions, Oklahoma City Golf and Country, Oklahoma City Press, Masons, Shriners. Sooner Dinner. Home: 1511 Drury Ln Oklahoma City OK 73116 Office: Hightower Bldg Oklahoma City OK 73102

MISOVEC, ANDREW PETER, research engr.; b. N.Y.C., Aug. 22, 1936; s. Charles Vincent and Mary Elizabeth (Trojack) M.; B.S. in Aerospace Engring., Poly. Inst. Bklyn., 1962, M.S. in Applied Mechanics, 1964, Ph.D. in Applied Mechanics (fellow), 1968; m. Margaret Smith, Sept. 2, 1961; children—Kathleen, Andrew, Margaret, Michael. Research technician Poly. Inst. Bklyn., 1958-62, research asst., 1962-64, research asso., 1964-68, asst. prof. applied mechanics, 1968-71; mech. engr., ship protection br. David Taylor Naval Ship Research and Devel. Center, Carderock, Md., 1971-74, mech. engr. submarine survivability group, underwater explosions research div., Portsmouth, Va., 1974-76, head submarine survivability group, 1976-78; asso. partner Weidlinger Assos., Portsmouth, Va., 1978—; asst. prof. civil engring. Howard U., Washington, 1971-74; adj. asst. prof. Old Dominion U., Norfolk, Va., 1975, 76. Served with U.S. Army, 1954-57. Mem. Sigma Xi, Sigma Gamma Tau. Home: 4337 Meadowwood Dr Chesapeake VA 23321 Office: 1801 Airline Blvd Portsmouth VA 23707

MISRA, RAGHUNATH PRASAD, pathologist; b. Calcutta, India, Feb. 1, 1928; s. Guru Prasad and Anandi (Devi) M.; came to U.S., 1964, naturalized, 1971; B.Sc., Calcutta U., 1948; M.B.B.S., Med. Coll. Calcutta, 1953; Ph.D., McGill U., Montreal, Que., Can., 1965; m. Therese Rettenmund, Sept. 12, 1963; children—Sima, Joya, Maya, Tara. Intern, Med. Coll. Hosp., 1953-54; resident in pathology Univ. Hosp., Cleve., 1973-76; instr., asst. prof., dir. kidney lab. U. Louisville, 1966-68; asst. to asso. investigator, dir. kidney lab. Mt. Sinai Hosp., Cleve., 1968-73; asst. prof. exptl. pathology Case Western Res. U., Cleve., 1971-76; asst. prof. pathology La. State U. Sch. Medicine, Shreveport, 1976—. Trustee Bengali Cultural Soc. Cleve., 1973-76; pres. India Assn. Shreveport, 1979; bd. govs. India House, Cleve., 1976. Jean Tallisman fellow, 1971-73; Canadian Heart Found. fellow, 1960-64; USPHS research fellow, 1964-66. Mem. Am. Soc. Nephrology, Am. Soc. Exptl. Pathologists, Internat. Acad. Pathology, Am. Soc. Clin. Pathologists. Hindu. Author: Molecular Structure of Biological Membranes, 1971. Contbr. articles to profl. jours. Home: 6153 River Rd Shreveport LA 71105 Office: PO Box 33932 Shreveport LA 71130

MISTRY, FIROZ RUSTOM, architect; b. Bombay, India, Nov. 28, 1927; came to U.S., 1957, naturalized, 1967; s. Rustom and Meher Bhikhaji (Gotla) M.; student Khalsa Coll., 1944-46; diploma Royal Inst. Brit. Architects, 1952; student Sir J.J. Sch. Art, 1946-51, Frank Lloyd Wright Found., 1957-58; M.Sc. Edn., Fla. Internat. U., Miami, 1975; m. Bernice Faye Andries, May 2, 1959; children—Chand-Lloyd, Roshan Paree, Carlos Keith, Carmen Faye. Architect, Decora Studio, Bombay, 1952-55; partner Mohenjodaro Architects, 1955-57; architect apprentice Frankl Lloyd Wright Found., Taliesin, Wis., Taliesin West, Ariz., 1957-58; designer Roberts & Barksdale, Alexandria, La., 1958-61; project designer Lester C. Haas Architect, Shreveport, La., 1961-62, Edward Durell Stone Architect, N.Y.C., 1962-68; design dir. Bodman & Webb Architects, Baton Rouge, 1968-69; pvt. practice architecture, South Miami, Fla., 1969—; asst. prof. architecture Miami-Dade Community Coll., 1970—, mem. senate, 1977—. Adv., explorer Boy Scouts Am.; past pres. Miniplayers Inc. Recipient Prof. Robert W. Cable Meml. Prize, Sir J.J. Sch. Art, 1948, Prof. Claud Batley Commemoration Prize-Design award 1948-51; Citation award Profl. Group, U.S. Nat. Design Competition for Med. Center, 1951; traveling scholar Frankl Lloyd Wright Found., 1957. Registered architect, N.Y., Fla., La. Mem. AIA (corp.), Nat. Council Archtl. Registration Bds. (cert.), Fla. Assn. Community Colls. Republican. Jarathosti Parsee. Home: Coral Gables FL 33134 Office: 7211 SW 62d Ave South Miami FL 33143

MISTRY, VITTHALBHAI DAHYABHAI, med. physicist; b. Vesma, India, Sept. 30, 1942; came to U.S., 1965, naturalized, 1976; s. Dahyabhai Jivanji and Jamnaben Dullabhbhai M.; B.S. with great distinction, Haile Selassie I U., 1964; Ph.D. in Nuclear Physics, U. Tex., Austin, 1969; m. Padmaben K. Prajapati, May 18, 1974; 1 dau., Vandana. Asst. prof. Haile Selassie I U., 1964-65; teaching asst. U. Tex., 1965-67, research asso., 1967-69; postdoctoral fellow Tex. Christian U., Ft. Worth, 1969-71; X-ray physics instr. Austin State Hosp. (Tex.), 1974-78; med. physicist Capital Area Radiation and Research Center, Austin, Tex., 1971—. Diplomate Am. Bd. Radiology. Mem. Am. Phys. Soc., Am. Assn. Physicists in Medicine, Am. Soc. Therapeutic Radiology, Soc. Tex. Regional Med. Physicists, Sigma Xi, Sigma Pi Sigma. Hindu. Office: 2600 E M L K Blvd Austin TX 78702

MITCHELHILL, JAMES MOFFAT, indsl. adminstr., b. St. Joseph, Mo., Aug. 11, 1912; s. William and Jeannette (Ambrose) M.; B.S., Northwestern U., 1934, C.E., 1935; m. Maurine Hutchason, Jan. 9, 1937 (div. 1962); children—Janis Maurine Mitchelhill Johnson, Jeri Ann Mitchelhill Riney. Engring. dept. C., M., St. P. & P.R.R. Co., Chgo. and Miles City, Mont., 1935-45; asst. mgr. Ponce & Guayama R.R. Co., Aguirre, P.R., 1945-51, v.p., gen. mgr., 1969-70; mgr. Central Cortada, Santa Isabel, P.R., 1951-54; r.r. supt. Braden Copper Co., Rancagua, Chile, 1954-63; staff engr. Coverdale & Colpitts, N.Y.C., 1963-64; asst. to exec. v.p. Central Aguirre Sugar Co., 1964-67; v.p., gen. mgr. Coddea, Inc., Dominican Republic, 1967-68; asst. to gen. mgr. Land Adminstrn. of P.R., La Nueva Central Aguirre, 1970-71, for Centrals Aguirre Lafayette and Mercedita, 1971-72; asst. to gen. mgr. Corporacion Azucarera de P.R., 1973-76, asst. to exec. dir., 1977-79, asst. exec. dir. for environ., 1979—. Registered profl. engr., Mont.; licensed civil engr., P.R. Fellow ASCE, Am. Geog. Soc. N.Y.; mem. Am. Ry. Engring. Assn., Colegio de Ingenieros y Agrimensores de P.R., Asociacion de Technicos Azucareros de P.R., Aguirre Recreation Assn., Sigma Xi, Tau Beta Pi. Club: Explorers (N.Y.C.). Home: PO Box 137 Aguirre PR 00608 Office: Central Aguirre Aguirre PR 00608 also PO Box 9477 Santurce PR 00908

MITCHELL, ALFRED TAYLOR, univ. adminstr., cons.; b. Rockford, Iowa, Mar. 10, 1912; s. Theron Harmon and Bessie (Hanchett) M.; student Iowa State U., 1929-30; B.A., U. Iowa, 1946; m. Hazel Margaret Ashley, July 7, 1942; children—Peter Ashley, John Harmon. Mng. editor Student Publs. Inc., Iowa City, Iowa, 1931-33; sports and news dir. Mason City (Iowa) Globe-Gazette, KGLO Radio, 1933-40; asst. dir. news service Iowa State U., 1940-42; news editor Iowa City Press-Citizen, 1946-52; sr. tech. writer, publs. mgr. Collins Radio Co., Cedar Rapids, Iowa, 1952-57, Dallas, Tex., 1957-62; devel., univ. relations dir. U. Tex. at Dallas, 1962-75, univ. editor, 1975-77; cons., 1977—. Served with USNR, 1942-62. Mem. Council for Advancement and Support of Edn., Ret. Officers Assn., Iowa State U., U. Iowa Alumni assns., Pi Kappa Alpha, Scabbard and Blade. Methodist. Mason. Kiwanian (dist. editor, pub. relations chmn. Tex.-Okla. dist. 1971-76, internat. pub. relations com., counselor 1972-73, 76-78). Author numerous tech. handbooks for Collins Radio; editor Ki-Notes, 1971-72, 74-75; editor Advance U. Tex. at Dallas, 1964-77. Home: 628 Sherwood Dr Richardson TX 75080 Office: U Tex at Dallas Box 688 Richardson TX 75080

MITCHELL, ARTHUR HERBERT, historian; b. Boston, June 23, 1936; s. Francis Herbert and Alice Helen (Gallagher) M.; B.A., Boston U., 1961; Ph.D., U. Dublin (Ireland), 1968; m. Marie J. O'Donoghue Leahy, July 5, 1966; 1 dau., Grainne Maire. Asst. prof. history Curry Coll., Milton, Mass., 1967-70, Ill. State U., 1970-72; editor, rep. Mass. Soc. Profs., 1972-74; asst. prof. history U. S.C., Allendale, 1976—; grant reviewer Nat. Endowment Humanities. Served with U.S. Army, 1958. Research grantee Am. Philos. Soc., 1973, U. S.C., 1977-79. Mem. Am. Hist. Assn., Am. Com. Irish Studies, Conf. Brit. Studies, S.C. Hist. Soc., S.C. Hist. Assn., Irish Labor History Soc. (bd. editors). Author: Labour in Irish Politics, 1890-1930, 1974; editor: Ireland and Irishmen in the American War of Independence, 1975; The History of the Hibernian Society in Charleston S.C., 1977-78, 1980. Home: 11a Maner Dr Allendale SC 29810 Office: Salkehatchie Campus Univ SC Allendale SC 29810

MITCHELL, BOBBY GLEN, assn. exec.; b. Bonham, Tex., June 3, 1932; s. Jimmy T. and Maggie Belle (Davis) M.; student McNeese State U., 1960-62; Midwestern U., 1970-71; m. Jo Ann Herriage, July 26, 1952; children—Ronald Glen, Linda Susan, Steven Paul, Laura Ann. Enlisted U.S. Air Force, 1952, promoted to master sgt., 1969, ret. 1972; environ. engring. tech. instr. Water and Wastewater Tech. Sch., Neosho, Mo., 1973-74; tng. coordinator N. Central Tex. Council Govts., Arlington, 1974—; chmn. tech. edn. com. NW Dist. Tex. Water Utilities, Wichita Falls, 1966-67. Recipient Bronze Zero Defects award, 1964; SAC Ednl. Achievement award, 1964; USAF Commendation medal, 1969, 72. Mem. Air Force Sgts. Assn., Tex. Water Utilities Assn., Water Pollution Control Fedn., Tex. Water Pollution Control Assn., Clean Water Tchrs. and Instrs. of Our Nation. Democrat. Baptist. Home: 3105 Hanover Dr Arlington TX 76014 Office: PO Box COG Arlington TX 76011

MITCHELL, CARLTON TURNER, educator, minister; b. Richmond, Va., Sept. 27, 1920; s. Lester Hall and Annie Sophia (Merritt) M.; A.A., Campbell Coll., 1941; A.B., Wake Forest U., 1943; B.D., Yale U., 1945; S.T.M., Union Theol. Sem., 1956; Ph.D., N.Y. U., 1962; m. Miriam Grace Sexton, Jan. 31, 1921; children—Grace, Betty Mitchell Morgan, John. Ordained minister Baptist Ch., 1944; asso. pastor First Bapt. Ch., St. Joseph, Mo., 1946-47; pastor Zebulon (N.C.) Bapt. Ch., 1947-52, First Bapt. Ch., Ridgefield Park, N.J., 1955-61; prof. religion Wake Forest U., Winston-Salem, N.C., 1961—. Chmn. Community Council, Zebulon, 1950-52; v.p. Zebulon Rotary, 1952; bd. dirs. YMCA, Ridgefield Park, N.J., 1956-61, N.C. Sch. Pastoral Care Found., Winston-Salem, 1974—. Served as chaplain USNR, 1944-46, 1952-54. Recipient Man of Year award, Zebulon, 1951, Distinguished Alumnus award Campbell Coll., 1975. Mem. Campbell Coll. Nat. Alumni (pres. 1966-68), AAUP (N.C. conf. pres. 1969-71), Am. Acad. Religion, Am. Soc. Ch. History, Religious Edn. Assn., Soc. for Sci. Study Religion, Assn. Clin. Pastoral Edn., Am. Catholic Sociology Soc., Am. Cath. Histo. Soc., Bapt. Hist. Soc., Assn. Bapt. Profs. Religion, Religious Research Assn., Inst. Religion and Health, Assn. Research in Religious Edn., Phi Delta Kappa. Democrat. Baptist. Club: Humanities. Author, editor numerous documents on baptism and ch. membership. Home: 3121 Shannon Dr Winston-Salem NC 27106 Office: PO Box 7363 Winston-Salem NC 27109

MITCHELL, CHARLIE HOWARD, JR., mech. engr.; b. Pittsylvania County, Va., July 10, 1930; s. C.H. and Nannie Mae (Waller) M.; B.S. in Mech. Engring., Va. Poly. Inst., 1952; postgrad. Richmond Profl. Inst., 1967-68; m. Malinda Beryl Branscome, June 15, 1963; children—Laura Carol, Karen Eileen, Sarah Kate. Test engr. Wright Aero. div., Woodridge, N.J., 1952-53; with Wiley & Wilson, Inc., Lynchburg, Va., 1955—, asso., 1966—, project mgr., 1972—; owner lumber mill, 1977—. Adviser to wood harvesting firm, 1972—. Bd. dirs. Central Va. Diabetes Assos., Inc., co-founder, 1972, pres., 1972-73. Served with C.E., AUS, 1953-55. Registered profl. engr., Va. Mem. Nat., Va. (dir. 1965-66, pres. chpt. 1965-66) socs. of profl. engrs., Va. Assn. of Professions, Isaac Walton League, Nat. Rifle Assn. Baptist (Sunday sch. tchr. 1960—, deacon 1965—). Home: 3414 Plymouth Place Lynchburg VA 24503 Office: 2310 Langhorne Rd Lynchburg VA 24501

MITCHELL, DAVID LEE, geophysicist; b. Dallas, Nov. 3, 1949; s. Buel Lee and Irene Cora (Barber) M.; B.S., Baylor U., 1972; M.S., Purdue U., 1974, Ph.D., 1976; m. Gesina Patrick Roach, Aug. 6, 1971; children—Stephen Adam, Paul Michael. Research scientist Conoco, Inc., Ponca City, Okla., 1976-78; research scientist geophysics Getty Oil Co., Houston, 1978—. Violinist, Community Orch. Soc. Greater Houston, Inc., Houston Met. Symphony. Purdue U. research fellow, 1974-76. Mem.AAAS, Am. Meteorol. Soc., Am. Geophys. Union, Soc. Exploration Geophysicists, Geophys. Soc. Houston, Sigma Xi, Phi Eta Sigma, Sigma Pi Sigma. Episcopalian. Home: 10734 Shannon Hills Houston TX 77099 Office: PO Box 42214 Houston TX 77042

MITCHELL, EDWARD LEE, physician, ins. co. exec.; b. Corning, N.Y., Sept. 26, 1932; s. Edward Henry and Bessie (Dail) M.; B.S., U. N.C., 1955, M.D., 1959; m. Doris McKinney, Aug. 23, 1958; children—Gregory, Ted. Intern Moses H. Cone Hosp., Greensboro, N.C., 1959-60; practice medicine, Liberty, N.C., 1962-66; asst. med. dir. Jefferson Standard Life Ins. Co., Greensboro, N.C., 1967-70, asso. med. dir., 1970-71; v.p., new bus. adminstrn. Commonwealth Life Ins. Co., Louisville, 1972-77, exec. v.p. adminstrn., med. dir., 1977—. Active March of Dimes, Kidney Found., Heart Fund. Served with USAF, 1960-62. Certified Bd. Life Ins. Medicine. Mem. Am., Ky. med. assns., Jefferson County Med. Soc., Assn. Life Ins. Med. Dirs., Home Office Life Underwriters Assn., Midwestern Med. Dirs. Club. Republican. Presbyn. Club: Hunting Creek Country. Home: 6110 Tidewater Ct Prospect KY 40059 Office: Box 32800 Louisville KY 40232

MITCHELL, FAYE ELIENE, ins. agt.; b. Cressmont, Ky., July 13, 1915; d. Daniel Thomas and Ida Belle (Moore) M.; ed. bus. coll. Asst. to personnel mgr. O. Ames Co., Parkersburg, W. Va., 1944-50; with S. Byrl Ross Enterprises. Inc., Parkersburg, 1950—, treas., 1955—; ins. agt. 1950—. Pres. Parkersburg Young Women's Christian Assn., 1953-54; del. UN Seminar Status Women, 1957; bd. dirs. W. Va. Baptist Young People's Union, 1939-45. C.P.C.U. Mem. Parkersburg Assn. Ins. Women (pres 1958-59), Nat. Soc. C.P.C.U.'s. Republican. Episcopalian. Home: 1806 Avery St Parkersburg WV 26101 Office: 929 Market St Parkersburg WV 26101

MITCHELL, GEORGE ERNEST, JR., nutritionist, educator; b. Duoro, N.Mex., June 7, 1930; s. George Ernest and Alma Thyrza (Hatley) M.; B.S., U. Mo., 1951, M.S., 1954; Ph.D., U. Ill., 1956; m. Billie Carolyn McMahan, Mar. 14, 1952; children—Leslie Dianne, Karen Leigh, Cynthia Faye. Asst. prof. U. Ill., 1956-60; asso. prof. U. Ky., Lexington, 1960-67, prof., 1967—, also dir. grad. studies and coordinator beef cattle and sheep. Partner, Mitchell Livestock Farms, Green Forest, Ark. Served to capt. USAF, 1951-53. Recipient Sang award for contbns. to grad. edn., 1966, Ky. Research Found. Research award, 1969, Thomas Poe Cooper Agrl. Research award, 1969. Sr. Fulbright Research scholar to New Zealand, 1973-74. Mem. Am. Soc.

Animal Sci. (sec. So. sect. 1969-70, v.p. 1970-71, pres. 1971-72), Am. Dairy Sci. Assn., Am. Inst. Nutrition, A.A.A.S. (life), Sigma Xi, Gamma Sigma Delta, Phi Eta Sigma, Omicron Delta Kappa, Alpha Zeta. Methodist. Contbr. articles to profl. jours. Home: 690 Hill'n'Dale Lexington KY 40503

MITCHELL, GLENN WHITTAKER, physician, data processing co. exec.; b. New Haven, Feb. 23, 1946; s. Roy Glenn and Bernice Wakelee (Jacobs) M.; Sc.B. in Physics, Brown U., 1967, Sc.M. in Elec. Engring. (NDEA fellow), 1969, M.D. (Univ. fellow), 1975; 1 dau. by previous marriage, Heather Flynn; m. Jane Ann Hathaway; 1 son, Bradford Roy. Instr. in elec. engring. U. Bridgeport, 1968-69; dir. test facility Technik, Inc., N.Y.C., 1969-71; intern R.I. Hosp., Providence, 1975-76; resident Butler Hosp., Providence, 1976-77; emergency physician Warwick and North Providence (R.I.) Emergency Rooms, 1977-78; mem. staff gen. medicine and emergency medicine Venice (Fla.) Hosp., 1978—; pres. Microcomputer Engring. Inc., Venice, 1979—; med. dir. Sarasota County (Fla.) Emergency Med. Services, 1979—; mem. Sarasota County Emergency Med. Services Adv. Bd., 1979—. Mem. AMA (Physician's Recognition award 1978), Fla. Med. Assn., Sarasota County Med. Soc., AAAS, Am. Coll. Emergency Physicians, Sigma Xi, Zeta Psi (elder.). Home: 208 Bayshore Circle Venice FL 33595 Office: 100H W Venice Ave Venice FL 33595

MITCHELL, GORDON TERRENCE, constrn. co. exec.; b. Johnson City, Tenn., Aug. 27, 1921; s. Lynn A. and Anna N. (Missimer) M.; ed. pub. schs.; m. Phyllis Moyer, May 26, 1957; children—Susan Mitchell Cummings, Katherine Mitchell Manning, Mark C., David C., Alison B. Supt., Perrin Co., Richmond, Va., 1941-48; partner Howard-Mitchell Constrn. Co., Richmond, 1948-56; project mgr. Charles H. Tompkins Co., Washington, 1956-58; field supt. Tester & Son, Inc., Clinton, Md., 1959-60; with J.A. Jones Constrn. Co., 1960—, gen. supr. various comml. and indsl. constrn. projects in New Orleans area, 1964-65, supt. constrn. N.C. br. Tex. Gulf Sulphur Co. project, 1965-66, project mgr. Tampa regional office, 1966-73, project mgr. on Carolando Center project, Orlando, Fla., 1971-73, v.p., mgr. regional office, Atlanta, 1973—. Mem. membership com. Richmond Builders Exchange, 1953; mem. Washington Bldg. Congress, 1957; pres. Va. br. Asso. Gen. Contractors, 1955. Bd. dirs. Family Service Soc., 1954-56; mem. adv. bd. Sch. Bldg. Constrn., Va. Poly. Inst., 1952-55. Mem. Am. Inst. of Constructors. Democrat. Episcopalian. Clubs: River Bend Gun, Century II, Atlanta Athletic. Home: 446 Angie Way Lilburn GA 30247 Office: 805 Lambert Dr NE Atlanta GA 30324

MITCHELL, HAROLD DEE, architect; b. Floydada, Tex., July 9, 1924; s. A.J. and Lena May (Stagner) M.; B.Arch., Tex. Tech. U., Lubbock, 1952; m. Dorothy Jane Lucas, May 1, 1954; children—Steven Craig, Kelly Diane. Owner, prin. Harold Mitchell & Assos., Amarillo, Tex., 1959—. Chmn. Amarillo Planning and Zoning Commn., 1968, Community Devel. Amarillo, 1974; mem. Amarillo Bldg. Bd. Appeal, Amarillo Airport Zoning Bd. Served with USN, 1942-46. Mem. AIA (pres. Amarillo chpt. 1972), Constrn. Specification Inst. (pres. Amarillo chpt. 1975), Am. Bus. Club (pres. elect Amarillo chpt. 1979), Amarillo Exec. Assn. (pres. 1978-79). Home: 1502 S Alabama St Amarillo TX 79102 Office: 1408 S Jefferson St Amarillo TX 79101

MITCHELL, HAZEL MAE, nursing adminstr.; b. Lillian, Tex., Jan. 24, 1922; d. John Sidney and Laura (Gentry) Tutt; R.N., Valley Baptist Med. Center, Harlingen, Tex., 1958; A.S. in Nursing, Pan Am. U., Edinburg, Tex., 1969; m. Lynn Evans Mitchell, July 24, 1938; children—Lynn Mitchell, Robert, Sidney, David, Catherine M. Mitchell Rochell. Staff nurse Valley Bapt. Med. Center, 1958-59, emergency room supr., 1959-66, clin. coordinator Sch. Vocat. Nursing, 1966-67, staff nurse, 1967-69, asst. dir. nursing, 1969-75, dir. nursing, 1975-76, v.p. patient care services, 1976—; adv. bd. Tex. Southmost Coll. Sch. Nursing. Mem. Nat. League Nursing, Tex. League Nursing, Am. Hosp. Assn., Tex. Hosp. Assn., Am. Mgmt. Assn., Am. Soc. Law and Medicine, Nat. Forum Adminstrs. Nursing Services, Nursing Service Dirs. Lower Rio Grande Valley of Tex. Health Care Instns. Mem. Ch. of Christ. Home: 4206 Bluebonnet St Harlingen TX 78550 Office: PO Drawer 2588 Harlingen TX 78550

MITCHELL, JERRY DON, psychologist; b. Coleman, Tex., Dec. 24, 1940; s. Wilbur Robert and Mary Lena (Moore) M.; B.A., Howard Payne Coll., 1963; M.Ed., Sul Ross State U., 1970; Ed.D., E. Tex. State U., 1974; m. Margaret Cloean Walker, May 15, 1971. Tchr. history Pasadena (Tex.) High Sch., 1969; counselor Tex. Rehab. Commn., San Angelo, 1970-73, cons., Commerce, Tex., 1974-75; psychologist Big Springs State Hosp., Big Spring, Tex., 1975-76; clin. dir. David Mountain Achievement Center, Ft. Davis, Tex., 1976—; cons. Tri-County Mental Health Center, Alpine, 1977. Justice of Peace, Coleman, Tex., 1962-63. Certified history tchr., sch. counselor, Tex.; certified and lic. psychologist, Tex.; lic. childcare adminstr., Tex. Mem. Am., Tex. personnel and guidance assns., Am., Tex. psychol. assns., Kappa Delta Pi, Psi Chi. Club: Masons. Home: 806 N 10th St Alpine TX 79830 Office: Davis Mountain Achievement Center Box 1455 Fort Davis TX 79834

MITCHELL, JOHN BISHOP, coach, educator; b. Ft. Stockton, Tex., July 1, 1937; s. Bishop Evans and Mary E. (Oates) M.; B.S., Baylor U., 1959, cert. of advanced study in counseling, 1972; M.S., Tex. A. & I. U., 1966; m. Marsha Striedel, May 28, 1960; children—Cara Jean, John. Coach, Marshall (Tex.) Jr. High Sch., 1959-60, Cuero (Tex.) Jr. High Sch., 1960-61; ranch mgr. John S. Oates Ranch, Ft. Stockton, 1962-64; head coach, athletic dir. Rio Hondo (Tex.) High Sch., 1964-67; track coach McAllen (Tex.) High Sch., 1967-70; asst. track coach Baylor U., Waco, Tex., 1970-72; counselor Sweeny (Tex.) High Sch., 1972-75; trach coach Austin Travis High Sch., Austin, Tex., 1975-77; track coach, social studies tchr. Luling (Tex.) High Sch., 1977—. Mem. Tex. Tchrs. Assn., Tex. High Sch. Coaches Assn., Tex. Social Studies Council, Am. Personnel and Guidance Assn. Methodist. Club: Kiwanis. Home: 700 E Bowie St Luling TX 78648

MITCHELL, JOSEPH BRADY, mil. historian, author; b. Ft. Leavenworth, Kans., Sept. 25, 1915; s. William A. and Margery (Brady) M.; B.S., U.S. Mil. Acad., 1937; m. Vivienne French Brown, Aug. 20, 1938; children—Sherwood N., J. Bradford. Mem. ops. div. War Dept. Gen. Staff, 1945-49; chief historian Am. Battle Monuments Commn., 1950-61, hist. cons., 1969—; curator Ft. Ward Mus. and Park, Alexandria, Va., 1964-77. Trustee Nat. Temple Hill Assn. Served from 2d lt. to lt. col., 5th inf. div., AUS, 1937-45; ETO. Decorated Bronze Star; recipient Am. Revolutionary Round Table prize for best book in field, 1962. Mem. Soc. of Cin., Civil War Round Table Alexandria and D.C. (past pres.), Am. Revolution Table D.C. (past pres.), SCV (lt. comdr.-in-chief). Episcopalian. Author: Decisive Battles of the Civil War, 1955; Decisive Battles of the American Revolution, 1962; Twenty Decisive Battles of the World, 1964; Discipline and Bayonets, 1967; The Badge of Gallantry, 1968; Military Leaders in the Civil War, 1972; contbr. articles to encys. and mags. Home: 625 Pommander Walk Alexandria VA 22314

MITCHELL, LANSING LEROY, fed. judge; b. Sun, La., Jan. 17, 1914; s. Leroy A. and Eliza Jane (Richardson) M.; B.A., La. State U., 1934, LL.B., 1937; m. Virginia Jumonville, Apr. 18, 1938; children—Diane Mitchell Parker, Lansing Leroy. Admitted to La. bar, 1937; practice law, Pontchatoula, La., 1937-38; spl. agt. FBI, 1938-41; atty. SEC, 1941-42; asst. U.S. atty. Eastern Dist. of La., 1946-53; practice law, New Orleans, 1946-53; partner firm Deutsch, Kerrigan & Stiles, New Orleans, 1953-66; judge U.S. Dist. Ct., Eastern Dist. La., 1966—. Vice chmn. New Orleans Armed Forces Day, 1964, 65, New Orleans Heart Fund campaign, 1959-60; mem. Small Bus. Adv. Council La., 1963-66; pres. Camp Fire Girls Greater New Orleans, 1965-67. Mem. Orleans Mcpl. Com. Finance, 1955-67; La. chmn. Lawyers for Kennedy-Johnson, 1960. Served to lt. col. AUS, 1942-46; col. Res. Mem. Am., Inter-Am., La., New Orleans bar assns., Maritime Law Assn. U.S., Judge Adv. Assn., Soc. Former Spl. Agts. FBI, Am. Legion, Mil. Order World Wars, V.F.W., Navy League, Assn. U.S. Army (pres. La. 1964-65), New Orleans C. of C. (chmn. nat. security com. 1963-66), Scabbard and Blade, Pi Kappa Alpha, Phi Delta Phi, Theta Nu Epsilon. Mason. Clubs: Press, Paul Morphy Chess, Bienville, Southern Yacht, Pendennis (New Orleans); Tchefuncta Country (Covington, La.). Home: 6027 Hurst St New Orleans LA 70118 Office: 500 Camp St New Orleans LA 70130

MITCHELL, LAWRENCE DU-WAYNE, physician; b. Henderson, Ky., Feb. 23, 1925; s. Edward Preston and Martha Alma (Martin) M.; B.B.A., Sam Houston U., 1948; B.A., U. Tex., 1952; M.D., Baylor U., 1956; M.A., Sam Houston U., 1966; m. Ethel Clark, July 3, 1964; children—Michael Warren, Melissa Ann. Intern Midstate Baptist Hosp., Nashville, 1957; practice of gen. medicine, San Jacinto County, Tex., 1957-65, Grimes County, 1965—; med. staff Tex. Dept. Corrections, Huntsville, 1967-74; mem. staffs Grimes Meml. Hosp., Navesota, Tex., Huntsville Meml. Hosp., Tex. Served with USNR, 1943-46. Decorated with Bronze Star medal. Mem. Am., Tex. med. assns., Nat. Occupational Research Soc., Postgrad. Med. Nutrition Today Soc., Internat. Acad. Preventive Medicine, Tri-Med. Soc., Royal Soc. Health, The Smithsonian Assos., Acutherapy Soc., Nat. Ret. Tchrs. Assn., Orthohygenics Soc. (v.p.), Tex. Farm Bur., Lambda Alpha Epsilon, Phi Chi. Mason. Home: Route 2 Box 35 Huntsville TX 77340 Office: Navasota Hwy Box 160 Anderson TX 77830

MITCHELL, MARY LOU, dept. store exec.; b. Cherry Ridge, La., July 25, 1934; d. W.C. and Ora Mae (Henderson) Webb; student St. Louis Bus. Coll., 1961; m. Bill H. Mitchell, May 15, 1966. Women's dir., hostess Noon Show, Sta. KTHV-TV, Little Rock, 1964-73; v.p. account service Holland & Assos., advt. agy., Little Rock, 1973-76; dir. corp. broadcast advt. Dillard Dept. Stores, Inc., Little Rock, 1973—. Active United Fund, Ark. Heart Assn.; bd. dirs. Better Bus. Bur. Ark. Mem. Nat. Sales and Mktg. Execs. Assn., Little Rock Sales and Mktg. Execs. Assn., Ark. Advt. Assn. Office: Dillard Dept Stores Inc 900 W Capitol St Room 214 Little Rock AR 72203

MITCHELL, MICHAEL WESLEY, hosp. central service adminstr., naval non-commissioned officer; b. Mansfield, Ohio, May 7, 1955; s. Wesley Acey and Ethyl Maria (Strong) M.; operating room technician cert. Naval Regional Med. Center, Portsmouth, Va., 1977, emergency med. technician cert., 1979; lic. practical nurse diploma Ohio State U., 1978; A.S., Tidewater Community Coll., 1979, R.N. diploma, 1979; m. Mary Theresa Siurano, Nov. 18; children—Karen, Moses, Tina. Enlisted U.S. Navy, 1973; asst. supr. surg. ward Naval Regional Med. Center, Roosevelt Rds., P.R., 1973-74, supr. pediatrics ward, 1974-75; physician asst. 3d Bn. 6th Marines, 1975-76, supr. physician assts., 1976-77; operating room technician Naval Regional Med. Center, Portsmouth, Va., 1977-78, asst. supr. central supply room, 1978—; cons. Va. Assn. Hosp. Central Service Practitioners. Mem. Am. Soc. Hosp. Central Service Personnel, Internat. Assn. Hosp. Central Service Personnel (registered central supply technician), Assn. Practitioners in Infection Control, Va. Assn. Central Service Practitioners, Hosp. Fin. Mgmt. Assn., Nat. Assn. for Nurse Edn. and Service. Roman Catholic. Research on hazards of ethylene oxide. Home: Route 1 LT 4403 Wren St Ches VA 23322 Office: CSR Naval Regional Med Center Portsmouth VA 23708

MITCHELL, R(ICHARD) GLEN(WOOD), land planner, landscape architect, urban designer; b. Oxford, Miss., Oct. 3, 1940; s. Jefferson George and Mary Taylor (Jones) M.; B.S., La. State U., 1966; m. Margaret Gaynell Montagnino, Sept. 1, 1962; children—Glenna, Melissa, Jeff. Planner, landscape architect Ewald Assos., land planners and landscape architects, Memphis, 1966-67; project planner Ellers & Reaves, Inc., engrs. and planners, Memphis, 1967-68; project planner Reynolds, Smith & Hills, Architects-Engrs.-Planners, Inc., Jacksonville, Fla., 1968-70, head dept. urban and devel. design, 1970-73, asso. v.p. planning, dir. design, 1973-78, dir. land planning and environ. design, 1978, mgr. planning div., 1978—; land planning instr. landscape design Nat. Council State Garden Clubs, 1973; vis. evaluator Bd. Landscape Archtl. Accreditation, 1977-80. Served with USNR, 1962-63. Recipient award of excellence in land planning for maj. center Fla. chpt. Am. Soc. Landscape Architects, 1969, merit award in community planning for maj. center, nat. soc., 1970, award of excellence for Crystal Lake, Fla. chpt., 1973. Mem. Am. Soc. Landscape Architects (exec. com. Fla. chpt. 1980—), Am. Planning Assn., Nat. Trust Historic Preservation, Delta Sigma Phi. Home: 108 Janelle Lane Jacksonville FL 32211 Office: 4019 Boulevard Center Dr Jacksonville FL 32207

MITCHELL, ROY DEVOY, mgmt. engr., govt. ofcl.; b. Hot Springs, Ark., Sept. 11, 1922; s. Watson W. and Marie (Stewart) M.; B.S., Okla. State U., 1948, M.S., 1950; B.Indsl. Mgmt., Auburn U., 1960; m. Jane Caroline Gibson, Feb. 14, 1958; children—Michael, Marilyn, Martha, Stewart, Nancy. Instr., Odessa (Tex.) Coll., 1953-56; prof. engring. graphics Auburn (Ala.) U., 1956-63; field engr. HHFA, Community Facilities Adminstrn., Atlanta, Jackson, Miss., 1963-71; area engr. Met. Devel. Office, HUD, 1971-72, chief architecture and engring., 1972-75, chief program planning and support br., 1975, dir. archtl. br., Jackson, 1975—; cons. Army Balistic Missile Agy., Huntsville, Ala., 1957-58, Auburn Research Found., NASA, 1963; mem. state tech. action panel Coop. Area Manpower Planning System. Mem. Central Miss. Fed. Personnel Adv. Council. Served USNR, 1943-46. Commended by Sec. HUD, Outstanding Achievement award HUD; registered profl. engr., Ala., Miss. Mem. Nat. Soc. Profl. Engrs., Am. Soc. for Engring. Edn., Miss. Soc. Profl. Engrs., Nat. Assn. Govt. Engrs. (charter mem.), Jackson Fed. Execs. Assn., Central Miss. Safety Council, Am. Water Works Assn., Iota Lambda Sigma. Methodist (trustee, mem. bd. 1959-60). Clubs: River Hills, University (Jackson). Home: 706 Forest Point Dr Brandon MS 39042 Office: HUD 100 W Capitol St Jackson MS 39201

MITCHELL, RYAN DUNNAHOO, constrn. co. exec.; b. Belton, S.C., Aug. 1, 1935; s. Ryan Dunnahoo and Laura Haynie (Boyce) M.; B.S., Clemson U., 1958; postgrad. Ga. So. U., 1965, Manhattan Coll., 1966; m. Barbara Jean Zimmer, Sept. 16, 1954; children—Elizabeth Anne, Pamela Jean, Ryan Dunnahoo. Engr., R. M. Angas & Assos., Jacksonville, Fla., 1958-63; mgr. engring. Davco Mfg. Co., Thomasville, Ga., 1963-66; dir. Rhodes Corp., Oklahoma City, 1966-69; pres. Mitchell Engring., Inc., Georgetown, Guyana, S.Am., 1969-71; v.p. Lang Engring., Coral Gables, Fla., 1971-72; div. mgr. Daniel Internat., Greenville, S.C., 1972-77, dir. mktg., 1977—. Profl. engring. tech. Thomas County Vocat. Sch., 1965. Registered profl. engr., Ark., Okla., S.C., Tex. Mem. ASCE, ASME, Nat., S.C. socs. profl. engrs., Am. Inst. Plant Engrs., So. Indsl. Devel. Council, Am. Chem. Soc., U.S. C. of C. (subcom. internat. econ. devel. 1979). Patentee in field. Home: 307 Sassafras Dr Taylors SC 29687 Office: Daniel Bldg Greenville SC 29602

MITCHELL, SYDNEY HENRY, illumination engr.; b. Cleve., Sept. 23, 1918; s. Samuel H. and Lillian Rebecca (Mannheim) M.; Sc.B., Western Res. U., 1940; m. Mary J. Montana, Dec. 11, 1941; children—Michael David, Suzanne. Cons., engr., economist various U.S. govt. agencies, 1940-49; adminstrv. dir. Rader & Assos., Engrs. and Architects, Miami, Fla., 1949-58; cons. engr. IVX Corp., Ft. Lauderdale, Fla., 1958—; partner T. Billman Assos., 1960-68; dir. Lighting Design Group, Apogee Internat. Served with USAF, 1942-49. Mem. Am. Mil. Engrs.' Assn., Am. Inst. Elec. Engrs., Nat. Soc. Profl. Engrs., Illuminating Engring. Soc. Democrat. Roman Catholic. Club: Presidents'. Designer pyramid lighting fixtures. Office: 1040 Bayview Dr Suite 201 Fort Lauderdale FL 33304

MITCHELL, WILLIAM GRANT, JR., broadcasting adminstr.; b. Social Circle, Ga., Mar. 1, 1921; s. W. Grant and Inez (Williams) M.; B.A., Emory U., 1942; M.A., U. Fla., 1956; Ph.D., Mich. State U., 1970; m. Mary Sue Sims, June 27, 1944; children—Patricia Alice Mitchell DeWitt, John William. Freelance writer, 1945-51; editor Ga. Experiment Sta., Griffin, Ga., 1951-52; asst. editor Fla. Agrl. Extension Service and Exptl. Sta., Gainesville, 1952-56, asso. editor, 1956-61; asst. dean, Div. Radio and TV, Fla. Inst. Continuing Univ. Studies, Gainesville, 1961-65; coordinator instructional resources No. Mich. U., Marquette, 1965-68; dir. instructional resources No. Mich. U., 1968-74; dir. ednl. resources U. South Fla., also gen. mgr. WUSF-TV and FM, Tampa, 1974—; cons. in field. Served with USAAF, 1942-45. Acad. proficiency scholar, W. Ga. Coll., 1938-40; Whitehead scholar, 1940-41. Recipient Nat. Farm Film Found. award excellence film prodn., 1958. Decorated Air Medal with clusters, D.F.C. Mem. Nat. Assn. Ednl. Broadcasters, Assn. Ednl. Communication and Tech., Fla. Assn. Media in Edn., Fla. Pub. Broadcasting Service (dir. 1976—, vice-chmn. 1979—), Sigma Delta Chi, Phi Delta Kappa, Kappa Tau Alpha. Methodist. Home: 715 Rob Roy Pl Temple Terrace FL 33617 Office: Div Ednl Resources U South Fla Tampa FL 33620

MITCHELL, WILLIAM L., marketing exec.; b. Columbus, Ohio, Nov. 3, 1920; s. Arthur R. and Mary E. M.; B.A., Ohio State U., 1948; m. Eloise Johnson, Sept. 16, 1953; children—Jacquelyn, Debra, William L. Commd. officer U.S. Army, advanced through grades to lt. col., 1957; systems engr. Raytheon Service Co., Colorado Springs, Colo., 1970-72; dir. investment mgmt. Equity Control Corp., 1972-73; mktg. mgr. Antonio J. Bermudez Indsl. Park, Juarez, Mex., 1973—. Chmn., Community Relations Commn., El Paso, Tex., 1968-70; bd. dirs. El Paso chpt. ARC, Yucca council Boy Scouts Am., NCCJ; mem. ad hoc com. El Paso Sister Cities; vice-chmn. bd. Aliviane; bd. dirs. Vista Hillsbank. Mem. Internat. Mgmt. Assn., El Paso C. of C. (dir.). Home: 1636 Tommy Aaron El Paso TX 79936 Office: KM 7 Carr Panamerican Hwy Juarez Chihuahua Mexico

MITTENDORF, THEODOR HENRY, paper mfg. cons.; b. Clay Center, Kans., Jan. 14, 1895; s. Theodor Henry and Antonie (Carls) M.; B.S., Okla. State U., 1917; m. Dorothy E. Solger, May 18, 1919; 1 dau., Laone M. (Mrs. D. R. Hoerl). Lectr. extension div. Okla. State U., 1917; lectr., free-lance writer, 1919-20; dept. supt. Armour & Co., Chgo., 1920-22; sec., dir. sales and advt. Mid-States Gummed Paper Co., Chgo., 1922-38; v.p. charge sales Indsl. Tng. Inst., 1938-39, v.p., gen. mgr. Gummed Products Co., Troy, Ohio, 1940-48; v.p. charge sales Hudson Pulp and Paper Corp., N.Y.C., 1948-56, exec. v.p., 1956-58, cons., 1958—; pres. Mitt Industries, Inc., 1973—; dir. 5 East 71st St. Corp. Bd. dirs. Muscular Dystrophy Assn. Served from 2d lt. F.A. to 1st lt. AS, U.S. Army, World War I, AEF. Named to Okla. State U. Alumni Hall of Fame, 1961. Mem. Kraft Paper Assn. (dir., mem. exec. com. 1951-58), Gummed Industries Assn. (pres. 1955-56). Paper Bag Inst. (pres. 1955-56), Paper Club N.Y., Am. Legion, Symposiarchs, Kappa Sigma, Alpha Zeta, Pi Kappa Delta. Republican. Methodist. Mason; mem. Order Eastern Star. Clubs: Mt. Dora (Fla.) Golf, Mt. Dora Yacht; Ponte Vedra (Fla.); African Safari of Fla. Home: PO Box 1138 Mount Dora FL 32757

MITTENTHAL, FREEMAN LEE, lawyer; b. Dallas, Dec. 29, 1917; s. Albert Harry and Rae (Goldstein) M.; student U. Tex., 1934-36; LL.B., So. Methodist U., 1940; m. Evelyn Naomi Gates, May 3, 1947; children—Richard Charles, Brian Lee. Admitted to Tex. bar, 1940, U.S. Supreme Ct., U.S. Ct. Mil. Appeals, 1954; pvt. practice law, Dallas, Tex., 1940-42; enforcement atty. Office of Price Adminstrn., Dallas, 1946-47; lawyer U.S. VA, Dallas, 1947-49; pvt. practice law, Dallas, 1949—. Mem. Young Democrats State Exec. Com., 1940; mem. Tex. Economy Commn., 1950. Served to maj. USAAF, 1942-46. Mem. Dallas Bar Assn. (mem. publs. com. 1965-74, bicentennial and civic affairs com. 1975—), State Bar of Tex., Am., Fed. bar assns. Mason (32 deg.). Clubs: Dallas Athletic, Metropolitan, Elks. Home: 820 Overglen Dr Dallas TX 75218 Office: 2560 Main Tower Dallas TX 75202

MITTS, CLIFFORD ALLEN, III, banker; b. Grand Rapids, Mich., Apr. 10, 1932; s. Clifford Allen and Doris Bonfield (McKeon) M.; A.B., U. Mich., 1954; M.B.A., Northwestern U., 1961; m. Martha Hill, Sept. 1, 1954; children—David Clifford, Douglas Lawrence, Russell Allen. Asst. cashier No. Trust Co., Chgo., 1954-64; v.p. Am. Nat. Bank, Beaumont, Tex., 1964-66, sr. v.p., 1966-72, sr. trust officer, 1968-72; sr. v.p. Continental Nat. Bank, Fort Worth, 1972-74, exec. v.p., 1974—; dir. Big River Industries, Baton Rouge. Pres., Community Council, Beaumont, 1961-64; chmn. bd. trustees Tex. State Library, 1963-65; chmn. Beaumont Public Library Bd., 1958-64; chmn. Fort Worth Public Library Bd., 1973-79; pres. Fort Worth-Tarrant County Arts Council, 1977-79; treas. Fort Worth Devel. Corp.; pres. Fort Worth Opera Bd., 1979-80. Served to capt. USAF, 1955-57. Mem. Robert Morris Assos. Episcopalian. Office: PO Box 910 Fort Worth TX 76101

MIXON, ALVIN, farmer, mcht., cattleman; b. Georgiana, Ala., Dec. 19, 1908; s. Samuel Henderson and Lela (Cook) M.; grad. Massey Bus. Sch., Birmingham, Ala., 1930; m. Frances Brassell, May 15, 1936; 1 son, Alvin. Salesman, interior decorator Morgan Bros. Dept. Stores, Birmingham, Georgiana and Evergreen, Ala., 1930; founder, owner S. H. Mixon's Store, Gin & Milling Co., Georgiana, Alvin Mixon Merc., Harper Merc. Co., Belleville; cattleman, Georgiana, 1952—; adv. bd. Georgiana Bank; organizer So. Pine Electric Co-op, Brewton, Ala., 1938; pres. So. Electric Co-op, Brewton, 1957—, So. Pine Electric Coop., Brewton; dir. Ala. Electric Power Generation Plants and High Voltage Transmission Lines, Andalusia; mem. Ala. Energy Adv. Council. Asso. dir. SSS, Conecuh County, 1938-42; organizer Conecuh County United Fund; organizer Conecuh County Hosp., 1954, bd. dirs., 1954—. Mem. Ala. Forest Products Assn., Am., Ala. Angus assns., Ala., Conecuh County cattlemens assns., Conecuh County Hist. Soc., Conecuh Farm Bur. (dir.), Georgiana, Evergreen chambers commerce, Internat. Platform Assn., Woodmen of World. Methodist (steward, layman). Clubs: Masons, Shriners, Rotary, Kiwanis, Quarterback (Georgiana). Address: Route 1 Georgiana AL 36033

MIXSON, JOHN WAYNE, lt. gov. Fla.; b. Coffee County, Ala., June 16, 1922; s. Cecil Marion and Mineola (Moseley) M.; student Columbia U., 1944, U. Pa., 1945; B.S. in Bus. Adminstrn., U. Fla., 1947; m. Margie Grace, Dec. 27, 1947. Acct., So. Bell Telephone Co., Jacksonville, Fla., 1947-48; farmer, cattleman, Jackson County, Fla., 1948—; dir. orgn. Fla. Farm Bur., Gainesville, 1954-59; dir. field services So. region Am. Farm Bur., 1959-61; mem. Fla. Ho. of Reps., 1967-78; lt. gov. Fla., Tallahassee, 1979—. Served with USNR, 1942-46. Named Legislator of Yr., Fla. Assn. Community Colls., 1975, Man of Yr. in Fla. agr. Progressive Farmer mag., 1976; recipient award from numerous So. agrl. group. Mem. Fla. Farm Bur., Fla. Cattlemen's Assn. Democrat. Methodist. Club: Rotary. Office: Lt Gov's Office The Capitol Tallahassee FL 32304

MIYAGAWA, ICHIRO, physicist, educator; b. Hiratsuka, Japan, Mar. 5, 1922; s. Shigejiro and Tsuma (Itoh) M.; B.S., Nagoya U., 1945; D.Sc., U. Tokyo, 1954, postgrad., 1954-56; postgrad. Duke U., 1956-59; m. Mitsuko Yamada, Feb. 10, 1950; children—Shigeru, Haruyo, Mari. Came to U.S., 1962. Asst. prof. chem. physics U. Tokyo, 1959-62; vis. asst. prof. Duke U., 1963-65; asst. prof. U. Ala., University, 1965-66, asso. prof., 1966-70, prof. physics, 1971—. Cons. to Redstone Arsenal, 1966-72. Chmn. Southeastern Magnetic Resonance conf., 1973. USPHS grantee, 1967. Fellow Am. Phys. Soc.; mem. AAAS, Sigma Xi. Contbr. articles on magnetic resonance to sci. jours. Home: 4905 10th Ct E Tuscaloosa AL 35401 Office: Box 1921 University AL 35486

MIZE, EARL JACK, JR., iron and steel co. exec.; b. Trussville, Ala., Jan. 7, 1946; s. Earl Jack and Doris (Allen) M.; B.S.B.A., Jacksonville State U., 1968; M.B.A., Samford U., 1972; m. Dianne Atkins, June 3, 1967; children—David, Jonathan, Jill. With U.S. Pipe & Foundry Co., Birmingham, Ala., 1968—, controller, 1976-78, v.p., controller, 1978—; dir. Wedlo, Inc. Mem. Fin. Execs. Inst. Republican. Episcopalian. Club: Exchange (Birmingham). Author: Economic Impact of Football on the Birmingham Area. Office: 3300 First Ave N Birmingham AL 35202

MIZE, JAN LEE, educator; b. Americus, Ga., Apr. 6, 1938; s. Hugh Milton and Annie Ruth (Barton) M.; B.S.M.E., Duke U., 1960; M.B.A., Emory U., 1961; Ph.D., Ga. State U., Atlanta, 1968; m. Linda Ruth Greene, Sept. 22, 1960; children—Jonathan Lee, Jessica Dorothy. Systems analyst Lockheed-Ga. Co., Marietta, Ga., 1961-63; asst. prof. of econs. Ga. State U., Atlanta, 1964-68, asst. prof. info. systems, 1971-77, dir. computer center, 1977—; systems analyst IBM Corp., Jacksonville, Fla., 1968-70; dir. Hypersystems, Inc., Atlanta, 1971—; contract instr. U.S. Civil Service Tng. Center, Atlanta, 1971—. Served with AUS, 1963-64. U. Chgo. Econometric Studies grantee, 1966-67. Mem. Assn. Computing Machinery, Am. Econ. Assn., AAAS. Club: Atlanta Athletic. Author: An Econometric Analysis of the Demand for Airline Passenger Transportation-Domestic Routes, 1968; (with W.W. Cotterman) Essentials of Structured Cobol Programming, 1978. Home: Box 23 Rt 6 Cumming GA 30130

MIZE, JOANNE PAGE, counselor; b. Lumberton, N.C., Aug. 22, 1930; d. Joseph and Gertrude (Rooney) Page; B.A., U. N.C., Chapel Hill, 1952; M.A.T., Rollins Coll., Winter Park, Fla., 1970, M.A., 1979; children by former marriage—Debra Ann, Sandra Leigh. Part-time instr. Seminole Community Coll., Sanford, Fla., 1977—; pvt. practice individual, marriage and family counseling, Sanford, 1978—. Bd. dirs. Central Fla. chpt. ARC, 1968-70; bd. dirs. Orange-Seminole-Osceola chpt. Easter Seal Soc., 1970-72. Mem. Am. Personnel and Guidance Assn., Am. Assn. Marriage and Family Therapy (asso.), Central Fla. Family and Marriage Assn., Assn. Family Conciliation Cts., Order of Old Well, Kappa Delta Pi, Pi Sigma Alpha, Delta Kappa Gamma, Kappa Delta. Republican. Presbyterian. Club: P.E.O. Office: 209 San Carlos Ave Sanford FL 32771

MIZE, WILLIAM KENNETH, apparel mfg. co. exec.; b. Santiago, Chile, July 19, 1930; s. Theron Neal and Rachel (McInnes) M.; B.S., Ga. Inst. Tech., 1952; postgrad. N.E. La. U.; m. Dollene Monte, Apr. 9, 1955; children—Cynthia Lynn, William Kenneth. Internat. engr., cons. Blue Bell, Inc., Greensboro, N.C., 1951-62; distbn. mgr. Oxford Industries, Inc., Atlanta, 1963-72; mfg. mgr. Levi Strauss & Co., Memphis, 1972-78; v.p., gen. mgr., part owner LaSevilla Fashions, Inc., Mangham, La., 1978—. Stephens County (Ga.) chmn. Republican Party, 1972; participant Ga. Tech. Today, 1977. Mem. Am. Apparel Mfrs. Assn., La. Assn. Bus. and Industry, Aircraft Owners and Pilots Assn., Ga. Tech. Nat. Alumni Assn. Presbyterian. Clubs: West Paces Racquet (Atlanta); Moose, Elks. Inventor curing oven safety malfunction indicator, automatic carton compression sealer, automatic overedge operating system. Home: 308 Spencer St Rayville LA 71269 Office: 317 Main St Mangham LA 71259

MIZELL, ANDREW HOOPER, III, concrete co. exec.; b. Franklin, Tenn., Sept. 26, 1926; s. Andrew Hooper and Jennie McEwen (Fleming) M.; B.A., Vanderbilt U., 1950; m. Julia Yolanda Mattei, Dec. 20, 1947; children—Andrew Hooper, Julia Fleming. Supt., Wescon Constrn. Co., Nashville, 1950-52; accountant McIntyre & Assos., Nashville, 1952-55; credit mgr. Ingram Oil Co., Nashville, 1955-56, v.p., dir., 1956-60; v.p., dir. Comml. Sign and Advt. Co., Nashville, 1957-59, Gen. Properties Co., New Orleans, 1957-62, Minn. Barge and Terminal Co., St. Paul, 1957-62; mgr. real estate and devel. Murphy Corp., El Dorado, Ark., 1962-63, mgr. retail sales, 1962-63; pres., chmn. bd. Transit Ready Mix, Inc., Nashville, 1963—. Active United Givers Fund, 1965-66; chmn. Concrete div. Office Emergency Planning, 1965—; mem. Nat. UN Day Com. Served with USNR, 1944-46. Named Ark. traveler, 1966, Ky. col., 1969. Mem. Nat. Ready Mix Concrete Assn. (chmn. membership com. Tenn. sect. 1971—, chmn. mktg. com. Tenn. sect. 1973—), Assn. Gen. Contractors (legis. com.), Tenn. Bldg. Material Assn. (concrete com., mktg. com.), Nat. Fedn. Ind. Businessmen, Portland Cement Assn., Nat. Area Bus. and Edn. Radio, Assn. Builders and Contractors, Spl. Indsl. Radio Service Industry, Tenn. Road Builders, Boat Owners U.S., Am. Concrete Inst., Nashville, U.S. chambers commerce, Phi Delta Theta. Presbyterian. Clubs: Nashville Yacht, Nashville City, Belle Meade Country, Commodore Yacht (past commodore). Home: 4340 Beekman Dr Nashville TN 37215 Office: 2319 Crestmoor Rd Nashville TN 37215

MLOTT, SYLVESTER ROMAN, clin. psychologist, educator; b. Chgo., Dec. 17, 1925; s. Roman and Mary Margaret (Haber) M.; B.S., Roosevelt U., 1950, M.A., 1953; Ph.D., U. Miss., 1963; m. Mildred Yvonne Dunaway, Jan. 25, 1964; children—Brent Allan, Bruce Wayne. Psychologist Oak Park (Ill.) Neuropsychiat. Clinic, 1953-55; psychologist Neuropsychiat. Clinic Chgo., 1955-57; practice psychol. counseling, Oak Park, 1957-58; psychologist U. Miss. Med. Center, Jackson, 1963-64; chief clin. Psychologist Southeast Psychiat. Clinic, Lincoln, Neb., 1964-65; asso. prof. Med. U. S.C., Charleston, 1965—; cons. Geneva Tng. Sch. Girls, Hastings (Neb.) Mental Hygiene Clinic, North Platte (Neb.) Mental Hygiene Clinic, Charleston VA Hosp., Mid-wifery Nursing Program Med. U. S.C. Served with USAF, 1944-46. Mem. Am., S.C., Charleston Area (trea. 1972-73, pres. 1973-74) psychol. assns., Nat. Assn. Vocat. Rehab. Contbr. articles to profl. jours. Home: 745 Creekside Dr Mount Pleasant SC 29464

MMAHAT, JOHN ANTHONY, lawyer; b. New Orleans, Sept. 5, 1931; s. Joseph and Mary (Bertucci) M.; B.A., Tulane U., 1956, J.D., 1958; m. Arlene Cecile Montgomery, Aug. 12, 1967; children—Arlene Cecile, Amy Montgomery, John Anthony. Admitted to La. bar, 1958, since practiced in Metairie; sr. partner Mmahat, Gagliano, Duffy & Giordano, 1958—; chmn. bd. Medallion Mgmt., Inc.; pres. Gulf Fed. Savs. & Loan Assn., Exec. Office Center, Inc. Vice chmn. New Orleans Aviation Bd., 1964—. Served with USAF, 1951-53. Recipient Glendy Burke medal for oratory Tulane U., 1956. Mem. Am., La., New Orleans (chmn. pub. relations com.) bar assns., La. Landmarks Soc., New Orleans Mus. Art. Club: K.C. Home: 1239 1st St New Orleans LA 70130 Office: 5500 Veterans Meml Blvd Metairie LA 70003

MO, LUKE WEI, physicist; b. Shantung, China, June 3, 1934; came to U.S., 1959, naturalized, 1972; s. Si Leng and Shu Feng (Lo) M.; B.S. in Elec. Engring., Nat. Taiwan U., 1956; Ph.D. in Physics, Columbia U., 1963; m. Doris Chang, Dec. 31, 1960; children—Curtis L., Alice. Research asso. Columbia U., 1963-64; research scientist Stanford Linear Accelerator Center, 1963-69; asst. prof. physics U. Chgo., 1969-76; prof. physics Va. Poly. Inst. and State U., Blacksburg, 1976—. Served with Chinese Air Force, 1956. NSF grantee. Mem. Am. Phys. Soc. Contbr. articles to Phys. Rev., Phys. Rev. Letters; research on high energy physics. Home: 219 Price St Blacksburg VA 24061 Office: Dept Physics Robeson Hall Va Poly Inst and State U Blacksburg VA 24061

MOBERLY, OSCAR BURNS, JR., aircraft mfg. co. exec.; b. Kearney, Mo., Feb. 25, 1931; s. Oscar Burns and Lena Maxa (Bradley) M.; student Westminster Coll., 1949-50, William Jewell Coll., 1950-51, U. Calif. at Los Angeles, 1955-56, Tex. Christian U., 1956-62; m. Margaret Morgan Bohart, May 17, 1952; 1 dau., Melissa Morgan (dec.). Accountant, Southwestern Portland Cement Co., Los Angeles, 1955-56; dept. asst. Gen. Dynamics Corp., Ft. Worth, 1956-58, tooling analyst, 1959-62, mfg. project analyst, 1963-66, mfg. control group supr., 1967-73, mfg. project analyst, 1973-76, mfg. control gen. supr., 1977—. Served with U.S. Army, 1952-53. Mem. Nat. Mgmt. Assn., Am. Prodn. and Inventory Control Soc., Nat. Assn. Accountants, Air Force Assn. Mem. Christian Ch. Home: Rt 1 Box 77A Aledo TX 76008 Office: PO Box 748 Fort Worth TX 76101

MOBERLY, ROBERT BLAKELY, arbitrator, lawyer, educator; b. Madison, Wis., Sept. 17, 1941; s. Russell Louis and Hildegarde (Reimer) M.; B.S., U. Wis., 1963, J.D., 1966; m. Jeanne Clinton, 1962; children—Laura, Richard. Admitted to Wis. bar, 1966, Tenn. bar, 1977; law clk. Wis. Supreme Ct., 1966-67; arbitrator, trial examiner, mediator Wis. Employment Relations Commn., 1968-71; practice law, Milw., 1971-73; prof. law U. Tenn. Coll. Law, Knoxville, 1973-77, U. Fla., 1977—; vis. prof. U. Louvain (Belgium), 1975; mem. arbitration panels Fed. Mediation and Conciliation Service, Am. Arbitration Assn., Nat. Mediation Bd. Mem. Nat. Acad. Arbitrators (past chmn. S.E. region), Am. Bar Assn., Indsl. Relations Research Assn., Soc. Profls. in Dispute Resolution. Co-author: Public Employment Labor Relations, 1974; Arbitration and Conflict Resolution, 1979; contbr. articles to profl. jours. Office: U Fla Coll Law Gainesville FL 32611

MOBLEY, CARROLL WADE, supt. schs.; b. Williamston, N.C., Jan. 1, 1927; s. William Leonard and Fonnie (Harrison) M.; B.A., Atlantic Christian Coll., 1950; M.Ed., U. N.C., 1954, advanced adminstrn. certificate, 1964; m. Jean Ewing Bellingrath, Mar. 12, 1949; children—Larry Wade, Julia Elizabeth. Athletic dir., coach, Bolivia (N.C.) High Sch., 1950-52; prin. Long Creek Grady Sch., Rocky Point, N.C., 1953-54; prin. Red Springs (N.C.) Schs., 1954-59; prin. Aberdeen Dist. Schs. (N.C.), 1959-63; supt. Montgomery County (N.C.) schs., 1963-71, Rowan County (N.C.) schs., 1971—. Served as sgt. AUS, 1945-46; ETO. Mem. Nat., N.C. (life mem., past pres. div. prins.) edn. assns., Nat. Assn. Secondary Sch. Adminstrs. (life), Phi Delta Kappa. Presbyn. (elder). Mason, Rotarian. Address: 227 Camelot Dr Salisbury NC 28144

MOBLEY, J. DAVID, environ. engr.; b. Winterville, N.C., June 27, 1948; s. James Hughie and Bessie Christine (Allen) M.; B.S. with honors, N.C. State U., 1970; m. Peggy Lucy Smith, July 12, 1970; children—Diane Christine, Sarah Catherine. Mgr. computer ops. Mobile Source Pollution Control Program EPA, Ann Arbor, Mich., 1970-73; environ. engr. Air Pollution Control Bur., City of Richmond, Va., 1973-76; environ. engr. Indsl. Environ. Research Lab., EPA, Research Triangle Park, N.C., 1976—. Served with USPHS, 1970-73. Registered profl. engr., Va. Mem. Air Pollution Control Assn., ASME, Pi Tau Sigma, Tau Beta Pi, Phi Kappa Phi. Baptist. Home: 909 Thoreau Dr Raleigh NC 27609 Office: US EPA Research Triangle Park NC 27711

MOBLEY, JOHN HOLMER, II, lawyer; b. Shreveport, La., Apr. 28, 1930; s. John H. and Beulah (Wilson) M.; A.B., U. Ga., 1951, J.D., 1953; m. Sue Lawton, Aug. 9, 1958; children—John Lawton, Anne Davant. Admitted to Ga. bar, 1952; practiced in Atlanta, 1955; mem. firm Kelley & Mobley, 1956-63, Gambrell & Mobley, 1963—. Served as 1st lt. Judge Adv. Gen. Corps, USAF, 1953-55. Mem. Am., Atlanta bar assns., State Bar Ga., Am. Judicature Soc., Phi Delta Phi, Kappa Alpha Order. Episcopalian. Clubs: Laywers, Atlanta Athletic, N.Y. Athletic, Piedmont Driving, Atlanta Country, Commerce. Home: 4348 Sentinel Post Rd NW Atlanta GA 30327 Office: 1st Nat Bank Bldg Atlanta GA 30383

MOCK, DAVID BENJAMIN, ins. agt.; b. Eustis, Fla., June 8, 1951; s. Benjamin Franklin and Margarette Ellen (Starnes) M.; A.A., Lake-Sumter Community Coll., 1971; B.A., Fla. State U., 1973, M.A., 1978; M.A. in Edn., Pepperdine U., 1975; m. Marie Bisignano, Dec. 28, 1974. Tutor dept. history Fla. State U., Tallahassee, 1972-73; grad. asst. dept. history, 1977-78; ins. agt. Ind. Life Ins. Co., Leesburg, Fla., 1978—. Served with U.S. Army, 1974-76. Mem. Am. Hist. Assn., Res. Officers Assn., Eustis Jr. C. of C. (dir. 1979—), Scabbard and Blade, Phi Alpha Theta, Phi Theta Kappa, Kappa Delta Pi. Democrat. Baptist. Home: 3701 B Aksarben Dr Tallahassee FL 32301 Office: PO Box 879 Leesburg FL 32748

MODISETTE, BARBARA JANE, ednl. diagnostician, special edn. counselor; b. Jacksonville, Tex., Oct. 14, 1938; d. R.G. and Kathaleen (Williams) Hensley; A.A., Kilgore Coll., 1959; B.S., Stephen F. Austin U., 1962, M.Edn., 1970; postgrad. E. Tex. State U., 1972-73, 80—, U. Calif. Extension, 1978, Tex. Eastern U., 1979; m. James H. Modisette, Oct. 4, 1958; children—John Philip, James Bret, Jay Hensley. Tchr. kindergarten Spring Hill Public Sch., Longview, Tex., 1964-75; ednl. diagnostician, special edn. counselor, Gregg County Plan A Cooperative, Longview, 1975—; cons. spl. edn. tchrs. tng. program, 1975-76. Charter mem., oboist Longview Symphony Orchestra, 1956-57; mem. Longview Civic Music Assn., 1974-77; pianist children's choir Spring Hill Presbyn. Ch., 1972-75; sponsor, tchr. jr. high sch. youth group, Spring Hill, Tex., 1975-78; officer Missionary Auxiliary, Spring Hill Presbyn. Ch., 1974-76, tchr. Bible Sch. and Youth Camp. Certified kindergarten, elementary tchr., Tex., sch. counselor at all levels, special edn. counselor, ednl. diagnostician, Tex.; winner Civitan Club Essay Contest, 1957; winner 1st place, oboe solo, 1st div., Regional UIL Solo & Ensemble contest, 1952-56. Mem. Tex. State Tchrs. Assn., NEA (council for exceptional children), Tex. Assn. Ednl. Diagnosticians (local officer), Assn. Children with Learning Disabilities, Gregg County, Am. assns. for retarded citizens, Am. Personnel and Guidance Assn., Am. Sch. Counselors Assn., Assn. Measurement and Evaluation in Guidance Counsel for Diagnostic Services, PTA. Alpha Delta Kappa, Phi Theta Kappa, Alpha Chi, Kappa Delta Pi. Author: The Appraisal Process for Gregg County Co-op, 1977; co-author position paper presented to Commnr. of Special Edn., 1977; former mem. Kilgore Rangerettes, Tex., 1958-59. Home: 102 Crystal St Longview TX 75604 Office: Route 1 Box 189 Sabine ISD Gladewater TX 75647

MOE, JOHN LOCKWOOD, electronics engr.; b. Flushing, N.Y., Feb. 29, 1928; s. Franklin Lockwood and Helen Langdon (Bates) M.; B.Indsl. Elec. Engring., Pratt Inst., 1948; m. Marcia Irene Campbell, Feb. 17, 1979. Mgr. Midwestern div. Filtron Co., Inc., 1953-63; chief electromagnetics Gen. Dynamics, Ft. Worth, 1963—. Chmn. USAF/SAE Internat. Conf. on Lightning and Static Electricity. Served with AUS, 1951-53. Recipient certificate of appreciation Soc. Automotive Engrs., 1973. Mem. Soc. Automotive Engrs. (nat. vice chmn. electromagnetic compatibility com. 1965-75, nat. chmn. 1976—), Nat. Mgmt. Assn., Air Force Assn., S.A.R. Congregationalist. Clubs: Fort Worth Boat, Catalina 22 Sailing Assn. (nat. rear commodore). Masons, Shriners, Elks. Contbr. articles to sci. jours. Home: 2933 Softwind Trail Fort Worth TX 76116 Office: Gen Dynamics PO Box 743 Fort Worth TX 76101

MOEHLMAN, ROBERT STEVENS, oil co. exec.; b. Rochester, N.Y., Feb. 23, 1910; s. Conrad Henry and Bertha (Young) M.; B.A., U. Rochester, 1931; M.A., Harvard, 1932, Ph.D. in Geology, 1935; m. Lillian Johnson, Sept. 17, 1934; children—Karen, Linda Gail. Exploration geologist for mining cos. in Can., Mex., Colo., summers, 1929-35; mine geologist Anaconda Copper Mining Co., 1936-38, at Butte, Mont., exploration geologist, Inspiration, Ariz., 1938-40, Reno, 1941-44; chief geologist S Am. Mines Co., N.Y.C., 1945-50; exec. v.p., dir. Austral Oil Co., Inc., Houston, 1951-62; pres. Newmont Oil Co., 1962-77, dir., 1962—; pres. Newmont Oil Co. Internat., 1971-77, dir., 1971—; chmn. bd., dir. Yucca Water Co., 1962—, Can. Export Gas & Oil, 1974-76; mem. Nat. Petroleum Council, Washington, 1973-79. Fellow Geol. Soc. Am.; mem. Ind. Petroleum Assn. Am. (v.p. 1966-68), Am. Inst. Mining Metall. and Petroleum Engrs., Am. Assn. Petroleum Geologists, Houston Geol. Soc. Clubs: Houston Petroleum; Harvard, Canadian, Mining (N.Y.C.). Home: 242 Maple Valley Rd Houston TX 77056 Office: 9th Floor 600 Jefferson St Houston TX 77002

MOEHLMAN, WILLIAM FREDERICK, metals co. exec.; b. Madison, Wis., Aug. 7, 1897; s. William Frederick and Dorothea (Niederer) M.; B.S., U. Wis., 1922; m. Constance Kennedy, Sept. 3, 1969. Dist. engr. Armco Drainage & Metal Products, Middletown, Ohio, 1927-30, municipal and airport engr., 1930-33; sales mgr. Tenn. Metal Culvert Co., Nashville, 1934-45, v.p., mgr., dir., 1945-62, chmn., sec., 1962—; dir. Home Fed. Savs. & Loan Assn., Knoxville, Tenn., 1950—; chmn., sec Knox Concrete Products Inc., Knoxville, 1962-76, Southeastern Inc., Knoxville, 1962—. Served with AUS, 1918-19. Mem. Gt. Smoky Mountain Conservation Assn. (pres.), Nat. Soc. Profl. Engrs., Am Soc. C.E., Knoxville C. of C. (pres. 1947-50), Am. Heart Assn. (dir. 1959-62), Tau Beta Pi. Mason. Home: Route 5 Sevierville TN 37862 Office: Box 10765 Knoxville TN 37919

MOENSSENS, ANDRE ACHILLES, legal educator, cons.; b. Belgium, Jan. 13, 1930; s. Frans A. and Leontine M. (De Meulenaere-Moenssens) M.; came to U.S., 1956, naturalized, 1961; J.D. with honors, Chgo.-Kent Coll. Law, 1966; LL.M., Northwestern U., 1967; m. Susan Gedney, Mar. 6, 1974; children—Suzanne Marie, Mark Andre; children by previous marriage—Monique J., Jacqueline R., Michele Lee. Cons criminalist, 1950—; admitted to Ill. bar, 1966, Va. bar, 1974, fed. cts., 1966; prof. law Chgo.-Kent Coll. Law, 1967-73; prof. law, dir. Inst. Criminal Justice, U. Richmond (Va.), 1973—; cons. in forensic scis. Fellow Am. Acad. Forensic Scis. (sec.-treas. 1974-76); mem. Va., Ill., Richmond bar assns., Richmond Criminal Bar Assn., Can. Identification Soc., Internat. Assn. Identification. Baptist. Author: Fingerprints and the Law, 1969; Fingerprint Techniques, 1971; sr. co-author: Scientific Evidence in Criminal Cases, 1973, 78; Cases on Criminal Procedure, 1979; co-author: Cases and Comments on Criminal Law, 1973-79; Scientific Police Investigation, 1972, others. Address: TC Williams Schs Law PO Univ Richmond VA 23227

MOFFAT, CHARLES ELWOOD, public accountant; b. Lawrenceville, Va., July 4, 1919; s. Elwood Barkley and Florence Olivia (Ivey) M.; B.B.A., U. Richmond, 1950; m. Mary Elizabeth Crockett, June 5, 1948; 1 dau., Pamela Moffat Saunders. Accountant, Am. & Efird Mills, Inc., Mt. Holly, N.C., 1950-52; asst. head accountant, then comptroller Mooresville Mills, Inc. (N.C.), 1952-55; asst. adminstrn. mgr., then accounting coordinator Burlington Industries, Inc., 1955-59; partner accounting practice, Draper, N.C., 1960-62; pvt. accounting practice, Eden, N.C., 1963-71, Reedville, Va., 1972—. Served with AUS, 1943-46. Mem. Nat. Soc. Pub. Accts., Am. Legion (fin. officer), Lambda Chi Alpha. Republican. Baptist (ch. treas.). Clubs: Masons, Shriners, Moose, Lions (Northumberland County). Home: PO Box 300 Reedville VA 22539 Office: Bayview Rd Reedville VA 22539

MOFFAT, DAVID CARL, theatrical dir. and actor; b. Chatham, Ont., Can., June 1, 1943; s. Carl Emerson and Velma (Armentrout) M.; A.B., So. Methodist U., 1964, B.B.A., 1965; M.A., Northwestern U., 1969. Stage mgr. Peter Pan with Sandy Duncan, 1979, Cabaret with George Chakiris; dir. forensics Sunset High Sch., Dallas, 1966-69; dir. drama Richmond (Calif.) High Sch., 1970-71; asst. prof. speech and drama Sauk Valley Coll., Dixon, Ill., 1971-72; prodn. mgr. Orpheum Theater, San Francisco, 1972-73; numerous roles in plays, motion pictures, commercials; founding mem. Dallas Repertory Theatre; chmn. regional conf. for Actor's Equity, Dallas-Fort Worth, 1974-76. Treas. Screen Actors Guild Actors Lab., Dallas-Fort Worth, 1974-75. Mem. Actors Equity Assn., Screen Actors Guild, AFTRA, Speech Communication Assn., Am. Theatre Assn., Nat. Thespians, Am. Forensic Assn., Nat. Forensic League, Delta Sigma Phi, Blue Key, Delta Psi Omega.

MOFFETT, ANDERSON GRANT, state ofcl.; b. Belvoir, Va., May 8, 1919; s. Anderson Franklin and Lucy (Grant) M.; B.S. in Agrl. Edn., Va. Poly. Inst., 1941; postgrad. N.C. State Agr. Policy Inst., 1962, U. Richmond, 1963; m. Anne Fielding, Apr. 25, 1942; 1 son, Grant Lower. Tchr. vocational agr. pub. schs., Warrenton, Va., 1946-48; poultry marketing agt. Va. Dept. Agr., Richmond, 1948-49, supr. market expansion, 1949-63, asst. dir. div. markets and market devel., 1963—; dir. program devel. and field services Va. Farm Bur. Fedn., Richmond, 1968—. Program chmn. Va. World Trade Com., 1977; mem. Shenandoah Community Assn., Va. Mus.; bd. dirs. Richmond Met. Authority, Blue Cross-Blue Shield of Va.; adv. com. Med. Coll. Va. Sch. Nursing; mem. task force Va. Assn. Continuing Edn. for Med. Profls.; mem. nursing liaison com. Va. Commonwealth U.; sec. Va. Council Health and Med. Care. Served to maj. AUS, 1941-46; PTO. Recipient Recognition award Va. Poultry Fedn., 1951, award Nat. Safety Council, 1954, U.S. Dept. Agr., 1965. Mem. Am. Mktg. Assn., Am. Security Council, Smithsonian Assos., Alpha Zeta.

Baptist. Home: 9400 Highgate Rd Richmond VA 23235 Office: Va Farm Bur Fedn 200 W Grace St Richmond VA 23220

MOFFETT, HENRY CLAY NICK, former public relations exec., floraculturist; b. Camden, N.J., Nov. 30, 1908; s. Charles Chauncey and Melissa Lawrence (Arthur) M.; student Fordham U., 1946, Rutgers U., 1947-48; m. Betty Lee Sloan-Sherman, Jan. 15, 1979; 1 dau., Betty Marie Moffett Terres. Free-lance accountant, Camden, 1931-39; sales mgr. staff Met. Life Ins. Co., Camden and Haddonfield, N.J., 1939-63; chief fin. officer City of Woodbury (N.J.), 1963-72; v.p. pub. relations firm Most Co., Inc., 1972-79; pres. N.Am. Gladiolus Council, 1962-64; judge, dir. All Am. Gladiolus Selections, 1962—; lectr. gladiolus culture; TV and radio commentator gladiolus culture; gladiolus hybridist with 35 new varieties in commerce under name Walker-Moffett orgn. Chmn. Gloucester County (N.J.) Econ. Stblzn. Bd., 1968—; commr. Gloucester County Tax Bd., 1972; pres. Woodbury Republican Club, 1958; Rep. campaign mgr. Gloucester County, 1958-71; trustee, adminstr. treas. Woodbury Pub. Library, 1963-72. Served with AUS, World War II; PTO. Named Man of Year 4-H Gloucester County, 1968; recipient Gold medal award N.Am. Gladiolus Council, 1964. Mem. N.J. Gladiolus Soc. (pres. 1960-62), Gloucester County Holy Name Soc., St. Patrick's Soc., St. Vincent de Paul Soc. (pres. 1948-67), Met. Vets. Assn. N.J., Royal Brit. Hort. Soc. (hon.), Gloucester County Hist. Soc. (trustee 1972—), Am. Legion, VFW. Clubs: Rotary (pres. 1968-69), Woodbury Men's Catholic (pres. 1946-69). Home: Route 11 Box 125Q Fort Myers FL 33908

MOFFETT, THOMAS ROBERT, anesthesiologist; b. Center, Tex., June 23, 1933; s. Ferdie Leo and Rosa Lenore (Janes) M.; B.S., Baylor U., 1953, M.D., 1956; m. Jean Marie Morrow, Aug. 13, 1955; children—Thomas Robert, Cheryl Jean, Elizabeth Ann. Intern, Hermann Hosp., Houston, 1956-57; gen. practice meidicine, Mt. Home, Idaho, 1957-59; resident in anesthesiology Lackland AFB Hosp., Tex., 1959-61; practice medicine specializing in anesthesiology, Shreveport, La., 1963—; mem. staff Willis Knighton Meml. Hosp. Served with M.C., USAF, 1956-63. Diplomate Am. Bd. Anesthesiology. Fellow Am. Coll. Anesthesiologists; mem. AMA, So. Med. Assn., La., Shreveport med. socs., Am., La. socs. anesthesiologists, Internat. Anestheseia Research Soc. Presbyterian. Home and office: PO Box 3740 Shreveport LA 71103

MOFFIT, WILLIAM C., musician, educator; b. New Philadelphia, Ohio; B.A. cum laude, Baldwin-Wallace Coll.; Masters Degree, U. Mich.; Mus.D. (hon.), Otterbein Coll. Tchr. pub. schs. in Mich. and Ohio, 10 years; mem. faculty Mich. State U., East Lansing; now mem. faculty, dir. marching band U. Houston; condr. Patterns of Motion workshops at numerous colls. and univs.; adjudicator music festivals; guest condr. at major band events; pres. Moffit ShowPower, Inc., Houston. Recipient George Washington medal Freedoms Found. at Valley Forge, 1978; Distinguished Service to Music medal; named Top Prof., U. Houston Mortar Board. Mem. Am., Tex. (pres., condr. Dirs. Band) bandmasters assns., Nat. Band Assn. (bd. dirs.), ASCAP, Kappa Kappa Psi (dist. gov.). Author: Patterns of Motion. Arranger: Soundpower Series; published works include numerous arrangements of patriotic music. Office: School of Music Office of Univ Bands U Houston Houston TX 77004

MOFFITT, ROY BRATTON, lawyer, engr.; b. Greensboro, N.C., Sept. 11, 1927; s. Royall Brower and Janet (Bratton) M.; B. Geol. Engring., N.C. State U., 1952, profl. degree in Ceramic Engring., 1957, B.S. in Chem. Engring., 1961; J.D., George Washington U., 1966; m. Hilda Marie Geide, July 8, 1967. With coal mine works U.S. Steel Co., Fairfield, Ala., 1952-54; instr. engring. N.C. State U., Raleigh, 1955-57, asst. prof. research, 1957-63; with Office Legislative Planning, U.S. Dept. Commerce, Patent Office, Washington, 1963-68; coordinator patent activities Superior Continental Corp., 1968-69, patent counsel, 1969-73, sec., legal counsel, 1973-77; pvt. practice, 1977—. Admitted to D.C. bar, 1967, N.C. bar, 1968; engring cons., 1957-63. Republican precinct capt., Birmingham, Ala., 1952. Served with USMC, 1946-47. Registered Profl. Engr. N.C., Miss. Mem. D.C., N.C., Catawba bar assns. Kiwanian. Contbr. articles to profl. jours. Patentee in field. Home: Box 675 Route 10 Hickory NC 28601 Office: 1928 Main Ave SE Hickory NC 28601

MOFIELD, WILLIAM RAY, coll. adminstr.; b. Hardin, Ky., July 3, 1921; s. Kelzie E. and Zela (Irvan) M.; A.B., Murray State Coll., 1943; M.A., Columbia, 1958; Ph.D., So. Ill. U., 1964; LL.D., Ida. Christian Coll., 1962; m. Janie Belle Bloomingburg, July 24, 1953; 1 dau., Ruth Ann. Tchr., Vienna (Ill.) High Sch., 1944-45; with WPAD-AM-FM, Paducah, Ky., 1945-59, mgr., 1959; mgr. WCBL-AM-FM, Benton, 1959; dir. acad. affairs radio-tv dept. So. Ill. U., 1959-64; exec. pres. Murray (Ky.) State U., 1964-68, chmn. dept. communications, 1968—; stringer CBS News, 1945-64; sportscaster Ashland Oil Network, 1946-59; radio-tv mgmt. cons., 1945—; alt. mem. Ky. Commn. Higher Edn., 1965—. Bd. dirs. to Assn., Paducah, Ky., 1956-59; commr. Boy Scouts Am., 1965, 66—, bd. dirs., 1965—; bd. dirs. Benton (Ky.) Hosp., Ky. State Penitentiary, Eddyville. Served with USNR, 1942-43. Recipient Duke of Paducah Civic award Mayor Paducah, 1956; named Ky. Communication Tchr. of Year, 1977; Ky. Col.; CBS Found. News fellow, 1958. Mem. Nat. Assn. Broadcasters, Am. Soc. Disk Jockey Newscasters and Sportscasters, Ky. Broadcasters Assn., Internat. Radio and TV Soc., Ky. Edn. Assn., Alpha Phi Omega, Alpha Phi Gamma, Sigma Delta Chi, Tau Kappa Alpha, Sigma Beta Gamma. Democrat. Mem. Ch. of Christ. Club: Rotary (pres. local club). Home: RFD 1 Hardin KY 42048 Office: Murray State U Murray KY 42071

MOGEL, RONALD DWIGHT, accountant; b. New Orleans, Sept. 4, 1951; s. Wallace W. and Faye Elizabeth (Taylor) M.; student U. Southwestern La., 1970; B.S. in Acctg., U. New Orleans, 1974; m. Sharon Lynn Scisco, Feb. 6, 1971; children—Marcus Oedipus, Ronald Dwight. Asst. personnel mgr. Deansgate, New Orleans, 1972-75; acct. Odeco, New Orleans, 1975-76; purchasing mgr. prodn. systems Deansgate, Inc., New Orleans, 1976—; instr. acctg. Jefferson Parish West Bank Vo-Tech Sch., 1978—. Res. officer New Orleans Police Dept. Recipient letter of commendation (2) New Orleans Police Dept. Mem. Nat. Assn. Accts., La. Soc. Public Accts., Am. Inst. C.P.A.'s, Beta Alpha Psi. Democrat. Lutheran. Home: 4041 S Woodbine St Harvey LA 70058 Office: 950 Poeyfarre St New Orleans LA 70150

MOGGE, HARRIET MORGAN, ednl. assn. exec.; b. Cleve., Jan. 2, 1928; d. Russell VanDyke and Grace (Wells) Morgan; B.M.E., Northwestern U., 1959; postgrad. Ill. State U., 1969; m. Robert Arthur Mogge, Aug. 17, 1948 (div. 1977); 1 dau., Linda Jean. Instr. piano, Evanston, Ill., 1954-58; instr. elementary music pub. schs., Evanston, 1959; editorial asst. archivist Summy-Birchard Co., Evanston, 1964-66, asst. to editor-in-chief, 1966-67, cons., 1968-69, ednl. dir., 1969-74, also historian, 1973-74; asst. dir. profl. programs Music Educators Nat. Conf., Reston, Va., 1974—. Supr. vocal music jr. high sch., Watseka, Ill., 1967-68. Active various community drives. Mem. Music Educators Nat. Conf., Am. Choral Dirs. Assn., In and About Chgo., Music Educators Assn. (dir.), Suzuki Assn. Ams. (exec. sec. 1972-74), Mu Phi Epsilon, Kappa Delta (province pres. 1960-66, 72-76, regional chpts. dir. 1976-78). Republican. Presbyterian. Clubs: Bus. and Profl. Women's (dir. 1968-70) (Watseka); Antique Automobile Club, Model T Ford Internat. (v.p. 1971-72, 76, 77, dir. 1971—). Mng. editor Am. Suzuki Jour., 1972-74; display advt. mgr. Model T Times, 1971—. Home: 1554 Northgate Sq Apt 21B Reston VA 22090 Office: 1902 Association Dr Reston VA 22091

MOHAMED, ADEL WAGDI, urologist; b. Mehalla, Egypt, Jan. 10, 1943; came to U.S., 1970, naturalized, 1977; s. Abdel-Aziz and Naeima (Kadoos) M.; M.B., B.Ch., Cairo U., 1965, diploma of surgery, 1968; m. Amina Nour-Eldin, Jan. 11, 1968; children—Mona, Adam, Ameer. Intern, Cairo U., 1965-66, resident in surgery, 1967-69; sr. house officer, London, 1969-70; intern U. Conn., Hartford, 1970-71, resident in surgery, 1971-72; resident in urology U. Pa. Grad. Hosp., Phila., 1972-75; urologist Johnston Meml. Hosp., Smithfield, N.C., 1975—. Diplomate Am. Bd. Urology. Mem. Eastern Carolina Urol. Soc., AMA, Am. Urol. Assn., Am. Urol. Assn.-S.E., Egyptian-Am. Scholars. Republican. Moslem. Contbr. articles to med. jours. Home: 4 Lakeview Plaza Smithfield NC 27577 Office: 415 N 7th St Smithfield NC 27577

MOHAMED, MANSOUR HUSSEIN, mech. engr., textile technologist; b. Alexandria, Egypt, Jan. 9, 1937; s. Hussein M. and Faika Mahmoud (Soliman) M.; B.Sc., Alexandria U., 1959; postgrad. diploma Manchester (Eng.) U., 1962, Ph.D., 1965; m. Soad Aly Abou-Youssef, Nov. 23, 1960; children—Mohamed, Medhat, Mae. Instr. mech. engring. Alexandria U., 1959-61, lectr. textile engring., adj. prof. High Inst. Cotton, 1965-69; vis. lectr., researcher Sch. textiles N.C. State U., Raleigh, 1969-72, asso. prof., 1972-76, prof. textile materials and mgmt., 1976—; cons. to textile industry. Recipient Oustanding Extension Service award N.C. State U., 1974. EPA grantee, 1972. Fellow Textile Inst. Eng.; mem. Fiber Soc., Am. Soc. Mech. Engrs. (exec. com. and chmn. textile engring. div.), Sigma Xi, Delta Kappa Phi. Muslim. Co-author textile books; contbr. articles to profl. jours. Home: 1926 Highland Pl Raleigh NC 27607 Office: Sch Textiles NC State Univ Raleigh NC 27650

MOHAMMED, M. HAMDI ABDELHAKIM, dentist; b. Egypt, May 10, 1940; s. Abdelhakim Mohammed and Enayat Abdelhakim (Abdelsamad) El-tahawi; D.D.S., U. Alexandria, 1963, M.S., 1965; M.Sc., Northwestern U., 1967; Ph.D. (Grad. fellow), U. Mich., 1971; m. Assma Abdelwahab, Sept. 24, 1964; children—Karim, Eman. Came to U.S., 1965, naturalized, 1975. Oral surgeon, instr. oral surgery U. Alexandria (Egypt) Hosp. and Dental Sch., 1963-65; research asso. dental materials, instr. dental anatomy and occlusion U. Mich., Ann Arbor, 1969-71; asst. prof. gen. dentistry U. Conn., Farmington, 1971-72, asso. prof., 1972-74; prof. biomaterials U. Fla., Gainesville, 1974—, chmn. dept., 1975—. Recipient UAR medal sci. achievement, 1963. Fellow Internat. Coll. Dentists, Royal Soc. Health (London), Internat. Coll. Oral Implantology; mem. Internat., Am. assns. dental research, Am. Assn. Dental Schs., Am. Dental Implant Soc., ADA, Am. Soc. Metals, Soc. Exptl. Stress Analysis. Contbr. articles to profl. jours.; author: Basic Dental Biomaterials Science; Material Science in Dentistry I and II. Office: Dept Dental Biomaterials Coll Dentistry U Fla Box J446 MSB Gainesville FL 32610

MOHLHENRICH, JOHN SIDNEY, govt. ofcl.; b. Balt., Oct. 12, 1931; s. Eugene and Marjorie (Moss) M.; A.A., Towson State Coll., 1950; B.S., U. N.Mex., 1957, M.S., 1959; postgrad. George Washington U., 1966-67; m. Sherry Livermore, Nov. 24, 1955; children—David John (dec.), Eugenia, Mark Moss. With Nat. Park Service, U.S. Dept. Interior, 1959—, chief naturalist Lassen Volcanic Nat. Park, Mineral, Calif., 1968-72, chief park interpreter Natchez Trace Pkwy., Tulepo, Miss., 1972—. Exec. sec. Loomis Mus. Assn., Lassen Volcanic Nat. Park, Mineral, 1968-72; scoutmaster Boy Scouts Am., Mineral, 1967-68. Served with USAF, 1950-54. Mem. Assn. Interpretive Naturalists, Phi Sigma. Club: Toastmasters (Hungry Horse, Mont.). Home: Rural Route 1 NT-34 Tupelo MS 38801 Office: Rural Route 1 NT-143 Tupelo MS 38801

MOHON, ROBERT TROY, ins. co. exec.; b. Cleveland, Miss., Jan. 18, 1939; s. Beauregard Lucas and Lois (O'Dell (Wheeler) M.; B.A. with distinction, Miss. Coll., 1960; m. Joy Earlene Mann, Apr. 21, 1961; children—David Kyle, Chadwick Troy. Mgmt. trainee, asst. mgr. W.T. Grant Co., Tyler, Longview, Tex., 1961-63; mcpl. bond salesman D.D. Starnes Co., Mineola, Longview, 1963-64, Cooper & Co., Longview, 1964-65; asst. trust investment officer Deposit Guaranty Nat. Bank, Jackson, Miss., 1965-74; 2d v.p. securities Protective Life Ins. Co., Birmingham, Ala., 1974—. Chartered fin. analyst. Past chmn. asso. deacons Mountain Brook Baptist Ch. Served with U.S. Army, 1960, 61-62. Mem. Inst. Chartered Fin. Analysts, Southeastern Life Ins. Bond Club, Ala. Security Dealers Assn., Mensa. Home: 3516 Crestbrook Rd Birmingham AL 35223 Office: 2801 Hwy 280 S Birmingham AL 35223

MOHR, BOULTON DIXON, pub. co. exec.; b. Phila., May 26, 1933; s. Joseph Ferguson and Louise (Dixon) M.; B.A., Kenyon Coll., 1955; m. Margaret Catherine Quinn, June 14, 1976. Mgmt. trainee TV Guide mag., div. Triangle Publications, Inc., Radnor, Pa., 1961-62, promotion rep., Cin., 1963-64, Seattle, 1965, regional mgr., Salt Lake City, 1966, Kansas City, 1967-70, Atlanta, 1971—; pres. Advt. Roundtable of Kansas City, 1970. Served with USN, 1955-60. Mem. Atlanta Advt. Club, Sales and Mktg. Execs. Atlanta. Club: Winter Harbor (Maine) Yacht. Office: 2600 Century Pkwy Suite 480 Atlanta GA 30345

MOHR, G(LENN) ROBERT, educator; b. Glidden, Iowa, Feb. 15, 1922; s. Leon Henry and Adella Isophene (Carter) M.; B.S., State U. Iowa, 1948, M.A., 1950; m. Wilma Louise Purdie, Oct. 1, 1942; children—Robert K., Deborah Mohr Foster, Loretta Mohr Reuss. Asst. prof. econs. Memphis State U., 1950-53; fin. analyst Harris Trust & Savs. Bank, Chgo., 1954-58; evening lectr. Ill. Inst. Tech., Chgo. and No. Ill. U., DeKalb, 1958-64; asst. prof. fin. and statistics Mankato (Minn.) Coll., 1964-67; asso. prof. fin. and statistics Ferris State Coll., Big Rapids, Mich., 1967-72; asso. prof. Central State U., Edmond, Okla., 1972-77; prof., area coordinator Bethune-Cookman Coll., Daytona Beach, Fla., 1977—; vis. prof. econs. Rockford (Ill.) Coll., summers 1966, 68, 70. Chmn. bus. and profl. chpt. Am. Vets. Com., Chgo., 1958-60; treas. Unitarian Ch., Park Forest, Ill., 1959-62, Mankato, 1965-67, Big Rapids, Mich., 1969-70, Ormond Beach, Fla., 1978—; pres. Big Rapids Fellowship, 1971. Served with USCG, 1941-45. Econs. in Action fellow, Case Western Res. U., 1953. Fellow Fin. Analysts Fedn.; mem. Jacksonville Soc. Fin. Analysts, Fin. Mgmt. Assn., S.E. Fin. Assn., S.E. Aids, Am. Inst. Decision Scis. Club: Elks. Author: Beginning Statistics, 1966. Home: 247 Brookline Daytona Beach FL 32018 Office: Div Bus Bethune-Cookman Coll Daytona Beach FL 32015

MOHR, JAY PRESTON, neurologist; b. Mar. 5, 1937; s. John G. and Marguerite F. M.; A.B., Haverford Coll., 1958; M.S., U. Va., 1963, M.D., 1963; m. Joan L. Seal, Mar. 10, 1962; children—Thea, Gregory. Intern, asst. resident in medicine Mary Imogene Bassett Hosp., Cooperstown, N.Y., 1963-65; asst. resident neurology N.Y. Neurol. Inst., Columbia-Presbyn. Med. Center, N.Y.C., 1965-66; fellow in neurology Mass. Gen. Hosp., Boston, 1966-69; instr. neurology Johns Hopkins U., U. Md., 1969-71; asso. neurologist Mass. Gen. Hosp., 1972-78; asst. prof. neurology Harvard Med. Sch., 1972-78; prof. neurology, chmn. dept. U. South Ala. Sch. Medicine, Mobile, 1978—. Served to maj., M.C., U.S. Army, 1969-72. Diplomate Am. Bd. Neurology and Psychiatry. Fellow Am. Acad. Neurology; mem. Stroke Council Am. Heart Assn., Sigma Xi. Democrat. Quaker. Contbr. articles to med. jours. Home: 2447 River Forest Dr Mobile AL 36605 Office: 2451 Fillingim St Mobile AL 36617

MOISE, FRANCIS DAVIS, brokerage co. exec.; b. Sumter, S.C., Dec. 31, 1935; s. Francis Marion and Ella Pauline (Blanding) M.; B.S., U. S.C., 1958; postgrad. Wharton Inst. Fin., 1972-74; m. Helen Frances Fisher, June 30, 1960; children—Helen Penina, Francis Davis. Registered rep. Bache & Co., Inc., Charlotte, N.C., 1959-70, resident mgr., Fort Worth, 1970-76, Columbia, S.C., 1976-77; v.p. instl. sales Bache Halsey Stuart Inc., 1977—; mng. partner Moise & Haritt, Sumter, S.C., 1978—; pres. The Moise Co., Sumter, 1978—, Eastside, Inc., Sumter, 1978—; advisor in field, 1978—. Solicitor United Fund, 1968-72; sect. chmn. United Way, 1973, div. dir., 1977; deacon Presbyn. Ch., 1970-76; bd. dirs. Boystown, Charlotte, 1968—, founder, 1968. Mem. Leadership Ft. Worth, 1972. Served with inf. U.S. Army, 1958. Mem. Nat. Assn. Securities Dealers, Greater Columbia C. of C. (chmn. transp. com., dir. 1977-79), Sigma Nu. Baptist. Clubs: Palmetto (Columbia, S.C.); Petroleum Ft. Worth, Charlotte Athletic. Home: 936 Wisteria Way Sumter SC 29150 Office: Executive Bldg 410 W Liberty St Suite 200 Sumter SC 29150

MOIZE, JERRY DEE, lawyer, govt. ofcl.; b. Greensboro, N.C., Dec. 19, 1934; s. Dwight Moody and Thelma T. (Ozment) M.; A.B. cum laude, Elon Coll., 1957; J.D., Tulane U., 1960; m. Margaret Ann Wooten, Aug. 13, 1976; 1 son, Jerry Dee. Admitted to Colo. bar, 1961, N.C. bar, 1965, U.S. Ct. Mil. Appeals bar, 1962, U.S. Supreme Ct. bar, 1965; legal clk. Army Air Def. Command, Colorado Springs, Colo., 1960-61, legal assistance officer, 1962-63, chief legal assistance div. 2d Army, Ft. Meade, Md., 1964-65; staff JAG, Indiantown Gap Mil. Reservation, 1965; law clk. to U.S. Dist. judge Middle Dist., N.C., Winston-Salem, 1965-66; dir. Legal Aid Soc. Forsyth County (N.C.), 1966-69; exec. dir. Forsyth Ball Project, Winston-Salem, 1968-69; dir. Lawyer Referral Service of Bar of 21st Jud. Dist. N.C., 1968-69; staff atty. Office of Gen. Counsel, FAA, Washington, 1969-70, acting chief Adminstrn. and Legal Resources br., 1970-71; staff atty. Office of Gen. Counsel, HUD, Washington, 1971, area counsel Jackson (Miss.) Area, Miss., 1971—; mem. Project Adv. Group, Legal Services Program, Office of Econ. Opportunity, 1968-69. Mem. Pilot Mountain (N.C.) Preservation and Park Com., 1968-70; mem. adv. com. Miss. Law Research Inst., 1980—. Served to capt. U.S. Army, 1960-65. Decorated Army Commendation medal. Mem. N.C. State Bar, Res. Officers Assn., Pi Gamma Mu. Democrat. Methodist. Clubs: Whitworth Hunt (pres. 1973-76), Austin Hunt (joint-master of hounds 1976—), Friends of Nat. Sporting Library, Inc. Contbr. to law revs.; contbr. articles on foxhunting, horses, motion pictures to periodicals; editor North Carolina Legal Aid Reporter, 1968-69; North Carolina Legal Aid Directory, 1968. Home: Houndhill Route 2 Box 185B Canton MS 39046 Office: 1016 Fed Bldg 100 W Capitol St Jackson MS 39201

MOKRASCH, LEWIS CARL, neurochemist, educator; b. St. Paul, Mar. 9, 1930; s. Lewis and Anna (Dvorak) M.; B.S. magna cum laude, Coll. of St. Thomas, 1952; Ph.D., U. Wis., 1955; m. Jane Carolyn Church, Apr. 21, 1974. Research asso. dept. psychiatry and neurology La. State U. Med. Center, New Orleans, 1956-57, asso. prof. dept. biochemistry, 1971-76, prof., 1976—, named Most Outstanding Prof., 1975, 76; instr. medicine U. Kan. Med. Center, Kansas City, 1957-59, asso. in medicine, dir. neurochemistry lab., 1959-62; asst. biochemist McLean Hosp., Belmont, Mass., 1960-64, asso. biochemist, 1964-71; asso. dept. biol. chemistry Harvard Med. Sch., Boston, 1964-67, asst. prof., 1967-71; adj. asso. prof. biology Hellenic Coll., Brookline, Mass., 1969-71; staff scientist Neurosciences Research Programs, Brookline, 1970-71. Mem. New Orleans Mus. Art, Friends of Cabildo; founding mem. River Rd. Hist. Soc.; mem. New Orleans Jazz Club, La. Art Found.; pres. Belmont Preservation Soc., 1969. Candidate for town selectman, Belmont, 1969. Recipient Bausch and Lomb award, 1948. Spl. fellow Nat. Inst. Neurol. Diseases and Blindness, Harvard Med. Sch., 1960-62. Fellow Am. Assn. Clin. Chemists; mem. AAUP, Am. Chem. Soc., Am. Soc. for Neurochemistry (local chmn. 1974), Am. Soc. Biol. Chemists, Internat. Soc. Neurochemistry, Soc. for Neuroscience (pres. local chpt. 1974-75), Soc. Research Adminstrs. (membership chmn. New Eng. sect.), Mensa. Universalist. Contbr. articles to profl. jours. Home: 6342 Pratt Dr New Orleans LA 70122 Office: La State U Med Center New Orleans LA 70112

MOLINA, ADOLFO, JR., ins. and real estate exec.; b. San Benito, Tex., Sept. 6, 1949; s. Adolfo G. and Maria Molina; student Pan Am. U., 1973-77; m. Blanca Estela Mireles, July 23, 1969; children—Francisco E., Stephanie D. Ins. agt. Mut. of N.Y. Ins. Co., McAllen, Tex., 1974-77; owner, pres. Molina & Assos., McAllen, 1975—, gen. agt. Gt. Nat. Life Ins. Co. Served with U.S. Army, 1970-73. Mem. Nat. Assn. Life Underwriters, Million Dollar Round Table, Tex. Leaders Round Table, Nat. Assn. Realtors, Ins. Econs. Soc. Am., Tex. Assn. Realtors. Office: Suite 1607 McAllen Allen State Bank Tower McAllen TX 78501

MOLINS, MARIO PABLO, JR., city ofcl.; b. Havana, Cuba, Jan. 11, 1947; came to U.S., 1960, naturalized, 1970; s. Mario P. and Clara M. (Perez) M.; B.A., cert. Latin Am. studies, U. Fla., 1967; M.S. in Mgmt. and Public Adminstrn., Fla. Internat. U., 1973; cert. govt. project mgmt. N.Y. U., 1978; m. Virginia Menendez, Aug. 24, 1968; children—Michael Paul, Tanya Cecilia. Tng. dir. Metro Dade County Public Employment Program, Miami, Fla., 1971-72; spl. asst. to exec. dir. Comprehensive Manpower Program Met. Dade County, 1972-74; city liaison to Manpower Planning Council/Consortium, Miami, 1974-77; exec. manpower coordinator City of Miami, 1974—; v.p. Energy Wholesalers, Inc., 1980—; mgmt. cons., 1980—; cons. Montal Edn. Assn., 1974; part-time asst. prof. polit. sci. Biscayne Coll., 1974-75. Mem. adv. com. Dade County Public Schs., 1976-77; chmn. Spanish speaking bilingual vocat. adv. com. Miami Dade Community Coll., 1978—; chmn. econ. panel Bilingualism in Pluralistic Soc. Conf., 1975; treas. Spanish Am. League Against Discrimination, 1978—. Served with U.S. Army, 1969-70; Vietnam. Recipient Bilingual Conf. award Metro Dade County, 1975. Mem. Am. Soc. Public Adminstrn., Internat. Personnel Mgmt. Assn., Pan Am. C. of C. (v.p. 1977-80). Democrat. Roman Catholic. Club: Professional (Miami). Home: 801 NW 47th Ave Apt 516 Miami FL 33126 Office:

MOLISH, HERMAN BARRY, psychologist, educator; b. Phila., Oct. 15, 1914; s. Morris and Clara (Bush) M.; A.B., Temple U., 1936; M.A., Ohio State U., 1936; Ph.D., U. Chgo., 1955; m. Ellen Anne Elste, Aug. 23, 1949; children—John Ronald, Carol Anne, Margaret Beth, Nancy Ellen. Commd. ensign U.S. Navy, 1941, advanced through grades to comdr., 1966; chief psychologist Abraham Ribicoff Research Center, Norwich (Conn.) Hosp., 1966-68; chief psychol. services Tex. Children's Hosp., Houston, 1968—; asso. prof. psychology Baylor Med. Sch., Houston, 1968—, also asso. prof. pediatrics and psychology. Fellow Am. Psychol. Assn., Am. Orthopsychiatry Assn. (life), Am. Group Psychotherapy Assn.; mem. Am., Houston (pres. 1975-77) group psychotherapy assns. Author: (with Dr. S.J. Beck) Rorschach Test, 1967. Editorial bd. Am. Jour. Orthopsychiatry, 1958-68, Jour. Clin. Psychology, 1966-69. Home:

1347 Country Place Dr Houston TX 77079 Office: Texas Children's Hosp 6621 Fannin St Houston TX 77030

MOLL, WILLIAM GENE, broadcasting co. exec.; b. Sikeston, Mo., Dec. 25, 1937; s. John Alexander and Letha Ann (McDowell) M.; student So. Ill. U., 1955-57, Anderson (Ind.) Coll., 1957-58; B.A. in Edn., S.E. Mo. State Coll., 1961; M.A., U. Tex., Austin, 1963; m. Marilyn Lewis, Aug. 2, 1957; children—David William, Craig Lewis. Announcer, program dir. Sta. KSIM, Sikeston, Mo., 1954-57; announcer Sta. WCBC, Anderson, 1957; announcer, program dir. Sta. KSIM, Sikeston, 1958-59; announcer, writer, dir. Sta. KFVS-TV, Cape Girardeau, Mo., 1959-62; producer, dir., writer Sta. KLRN-TV, Austin, Tex., 1962-64, mgr. sta. ops., San Antonio, 1964-69; v.p., gen. mgr. Sta. WSMW-TV, Worcester, Mass., 1969-72; v.p., gen. mgr. Sta. KENS-TV, San Antonio, 1972—; pres., chief exec. officer Harte-Hanks TV Group, San Antonio, 1979—; spl. instr. U. Tex., Austin, 1963-64. Chmn., San Antonio Art Inst., 1978—; bd. dirs., v.p. Goodwill Rehab. Service, San Antonio, 1973-79, v.p., 1979—; bd. dirs. United Way, San Antonio, 1979—, Friends of McNay, San Antonio, 1979—, San Antonio Symphony Soc. Mem. Tex. Assn. Broadcasters (dir. 1976—). Club: Torch of San Antonio. Office: Box TV 5 San Antonio TX 78299

MOLLENHOFF, CLARK RAYMOND, journalist, educator; b. Burnside, Iowa, Apr. 16, 1921; s. Raymond Eldon and Margaret Pearl (Clark) M.; LL.B., Drake U., 1944; m. Georgia Giles Osmundson, Oct. 13, 1939 (div. 1978); children—Gjore Jean, Jacqueline Sue, Clark R. Investigative reporter Des Moines Register, 1941-70, bur. chief, Washington, 1970-76; Nieman fellow Harvard U., 1949-50; syndicated columnist, 1970-78; spl. counsel to the Pres., 1969-70; now prof. journalism Washington and Lee U., Lexington, Va., 1976—. Served with USNR, 1944-46. Recipient Pulitzer prize, 1958, Raymond Clapper award, 1956, Heywood Broun award, 1956, John Peter Zenger award, 1962, William Allen White award, 1964, Drew Pearson Investigative Reporting award, 1973. Mem. Am., Iowa, D.C. bar assns., Investigative Reporters and Editors, Sigma Delta Chi (vice chmn. Freedom and info. com. 1956-66, chmn. 1966-69). Roman Catholic. Club: Nat. Press (past bd. govs.). Author 10 books on govt. and politics. Home: 805 McMath Circle Lexington VA 24450 Office: 207 Reid Hall Washington and Lee U Lexington VA 24450

MOLLOHAN, ROBERT H., congressman; b. Grantsville, W.Va., Sept. 18, 1909; s. Robert P. and Edith (Witt) M.; student Glenville Coll., Shepherd Coll.; m. Helen M. Holt; children—Robert H., Alan B., Kathryn (Mrs. Moats). Successively chief miscellaneous tax div., cashier U.S. Internal Revenue Bur. W.Va.; dist. mgr., W.Va. personnel dir. Works Projects Adminstr.; W.Va. dir. Census, 1940; supt. W.Va. Indsl. Sch. for Boys; U.S. marshal for No. Dist. W.Va.; clk. U.S. Senate Com. on D.C.; mem. 83d, 84th, 91st-96th congresses from 1st W.Va. dist. Democrat. Baptist. Elk, Eagle, Moose. Office: House Office Bldg Washington DC 20515

MOLONEY, LOUIS CAREY, univ. adminstr.; b. Trenton, N.J., Nov. 26, 1920; s. Louis Carey and Florence (Smith) M.; B.S. in Edn., Trenton State Coll., 1942, B.L.S., 1948; postgrad. U. Chgo., 1950-51; M.S., Tex. A. and I. U., 1958; D.L.S., Columbia U., 1970; m. Doris Lee Pettit, Nov. 30, 1944; children—Doris Lee, Evelyn Estabrook, Louis Carey III. Head librarian Bishop Meml. Library, Toms River, N.J., 1947-50, Trenton Jr. Coll., 1951-52; asst. librarian Tex. A. and I. U., Kingsville, 1952-64; asso. librarian Southwest Tex. State U., San Marcos, 1964-65, head librarian, 1965-75, dir. Learning Resources Center, 1975—. Bd. dirs., chmn., sec. Southside Community Center, 1973-79. Served with USAAF, 1942-43, USNR, 1943-45. Mem. ALA, Tex. Library Assn. (past publicity chmn., past dist. chmn.), Tex. Council State Univ. Librarians (chmn.), Council Research and Acad. Libraries (past pres.), Phi Delta Kappa (treas.). Democrat. Methodist. Club: Lions (pres. 1976-77). Home: 604 Dale St San Marcos TX 78666 Office: Learning Resources Center Southwest Tex State U San Marcos TX 78666

MOLONY, MICHAEL JANSSENS, JR., lawyer; b. New Orleans, Sept. 2, 1922; s. Michael Janssens and Marie (Perret) M.; J.D., Tulane U., 1950; m. Jane Leslie Waguespack, Oct. 21, 1951; children—Jane Leslie, Michael Janssens III, Megan, Kevin, Sara, Brian, Ian, Duncan. Admitted to La. bar, 1950, since practiced in New Orleans; partner Molony & Baldwin, attys., 1950; asso. partner Jones, Flanders, Waechter & Walker, 1951-56; partner Jones, Walker, Waechter, Poitevent, Carrere & Denegre, 1956-75, Milling, Benson, Woodward, Hillyer, Pierson & Miller, 1975—; instr., lectr. Med. Sch. and Univ. Coll., Tulane U., 1953-59. Asst. sec.-treas. La. Law Inst., 1958-70. Mem. Eisenhower Legal Com., 1952; chmn. La. Gov.'s Task Force on Space Industry, 1971-73; chmn. Gov.'s Adv. Com. Met. New Orleans Transp. and Planning Program, 1971-77; mem. La. Gov.'s Task Force Natural Gas Requirements, 1971-72; mem. Mayor's Adv. Com. on City Charter; mem. Goals Found. Council and ex-officio mem. Goals Found. Met. New Orleans Goals Program, 1969-72; vice chmn. ad hoc planning com. Goals for Met. New Orleans, 1969-73; vice chmn. Port of New Orleans Operation Impact, 1969-70; mem. Met. Area Com., New Orleans, 1970-74; trustee Public Affairs Research Council La., 1970-73, Acad. Sacred Heart, 1975-77; mem. corp. bd. Boys Clubs Greater New Orleans, 1969-74; bd. dirs., exec. com. New Orleans Tourist and Conv. Com., 1973-75, chmn. family attraction com., 1973-75; bd. commrs., 2d v.p. Port of New Orleans, 1976—, pres. bd. commrs., 1978. Served with AUS, USAAF, 1942-46; PTO. Mem. Am. (mem. anti-trust law com. 1968, mgmt. co-chmn. com. devel. law union adminstrn. and procedures 1969, mem. com. equal employment opportunity practice and procedure labor relations law sect.), La. (past sec.-treas., gov. 1959-60, editor jour. 1957-59, sec. spl. Supreme Ct. com. on drafting code jud. ethics), New Orleans (dir. legal aid bur. 1954, vice chmn. standing com. pub. relations 1970-71), Fed. bar assns., La. Law Inst. (asst. sec.-treas. 1958-70), Am. Judicature Soc., Internat. House (dir. 1978), So. Inst. Mgmt. (a founder), U.S. (labor relations com. 1965, urban and regional affairs com. 1970-72, blue-ribbon com. lawyers), La. (dir. 1963-66), New Orleans Area (v.p. met. devel. and urban affairs 1969, dir. 1963-78, pres.-elect 1970, pres. 1971, exec. com. 1972) chambers commerce, Sigma Chi (pres. New Orleans alumni chpt. 1956). Roman Catholic. Clubs: Pickwick, So. Yacht, Serra, Plimsoll, Bienville, Lakewood Country (New Orleans). Home: 3039 Hudson Pl New Orleans LA 70114 Office: 1100 Whitney Bldg New Orleans LA 70130

MOLPUS, HELEN REILY, singer, educator; b. Meridian, Miss., Mar. 8, 1917; d. Abel N. and Bessie Lee (Shealey) R.; student in piano East Miss. Jr. Coll., 1931, in voice and piano Miss. Synodical Coll., 1932, Cin. Conservatory Music, 1936; student (Coll. scholar) Miss. Woman's Coll., 1937-38, So. Bapt. Theol. Sem., 1970-74; diplomas in music Ohio State U., 1969, U. S.C., 1972; pupil Rellie Mae Still, Meridian, 1933-36, Inmann Johnson, Louisville, 1938-39, Louise Bave, N.Y.C., 1940-41, Charles McCool, Jackson, Miss., 1956-64, Elizabeth Newell, 1970—; m. Chester A. Molpus, June 16, 1938; children—C. Manly, Frank Reily, David Lee. Soloist, choir dir. First Bapt. Ch., Taylorsville, Ky., 1941-44; dir. choirs First Bapt. Ch., Belzoni, Miss., 1943-64, soloist, 1932-72; pvt. tchr. piano and voice, Taylorsville, Belzoni, Yazoo City, Miss., Chesterfield, S.C.; vocalist in religious and classical recitals, 1950-64. Recipient vocal award Fedn. Music Clubs, 1936, recognition for outstanding contbn. to mus. devel. U. S.C., 1972. Mem. S.C. Music Tchrs. Assn., Nat. Assn. Tchrs. Singing, Nat. Music Council, Nat. Fedn. Music Clubs, Nat. Music Tchrs. Assn., Nat. Music Educators Assn., Sigma Pi Mu. Democrat. Baptist. Home and office: Rt 1 Box 116 Chesterfield SC 29709

MOLPUS, JOHN KINDRED, JR., utility co. exec.; b. Daytona Beach, Fla., Nov. 9, 1929; s. John Kindred and Katherine Elizabeth (Bond) M.; B.S. B.A., U. Fla., 1950; M.B.A., N.Y. Inst. Tech., 1976; m. Rachel May Garrett, June 22, 1957; children—J. Lane, Kelly L., Brantley K. With Fla. Power & Light Co., Daytona Beach, Fla., 1950—, comml. rep., 1964-71, div. claims mgr., 1971-74, div. personnel mgr., 1974-79, div. adminstrv. services mgr., 1979—. Treas., United Way of East Volusia, Fla., 1970-72; mem. Juvenile Ct. Merit Bd., Volusia County, 1968-73; mem. Volusia County Sch. Bd. Adv. Com., 1973-75. Bd. dirs. Mental Assn. Volusia County; v.p. Volusia County Assn. for Gifted, 1970-71. Mem. Am. Soc. Personnel Adminstrn., Asso. MBA Execs., Mental Health Assn. Volusia County, Am. Soc. Indsl. Security, Daytona Beach C. of C., Daytona Beach chpt. U. Fla. Alumni Assn., Halifax Hist. Soc., Sigma Phi Epsilon. Republican. Baptist. Club: Daytona Beach Jaycees (dir. 1954-56). Home: 846 Lemon Rd Daytona Beach FL 32019 Office: PO Box 151 Daytona Beach FL 32015

MONAGHAN, ROBERT LEE, oil operator; b. Ft. Worth, Sept. 16, 1923; s. Johnnie Edgar and Ruby Joyce (Ferguson) M.; B.S. in Petroleum Engring., U. Tex., 1948, J.D., 1951; m. Virginia Fay Phipps, Jan. 4, 1964; children—Cullen S., Patrick Kevin, Robert Lee. Roustabout, Roughneck Magnolia Petroleum Co., 1948-49; with land dept. Standard Oil Co. Tex., 1951-53; gen. mgr. Tex. Crude Oil Co., 1953-54; gen. partner C & M Oil Mgmt. Co., 1954-56; pres. Cal-Mon Oil Co., Midland, Tex., 1956—. Mem. Midland County chpt. Tex. Criminal Justice Council; pres. Midland County Republican Men's Clubs, 1969-70; chmn. Midland County Rep. Com., 1970-76; del. Rep. Nat. Conv., 1972, 76, mem. permanent com. on rules, 1976; dist. committeeman Tex. Rep. Exec. Com.; mem. City of Midland Planning and Zoning Commn., 1973-74. Served to 2d lt. USAAF, World War II. Mem. Am. Assn. Petroleum Landmen (Citizenship award 1979), W. Tex. Geol. Soc., Soc. Petroleum Engring., State Bar Tex., Permian Basin Landmen's Assn., Midland County Bar Assn. Episcopalian (vestry 1970-73). Home: 2007 Country Club Dr Midland TX 79701 Office: PO Box 2066 Suite 1200 Midland Nat Bank Tower Midland TX 79702

MONAHAN, STEPHEN MARTIN, publisher, composer; b. Detroit, Mar. 13, 1944; s. Martin Oliver and Maybelle (Valine) M.; student Henry Ford Coll., 1962-65. Pres. Free Breeze Pub. Co., Nashville, 1968—, Charlie Boy Pub. Co., 1969—; v.p. Moonworld Pub. Co., Inc., 1969—; pres. Smile Music Co., 1974—, Mondoman Music Co., Nashville, 1975—, Monahan Music Pub. Co., Inc., 1977—; owner Red Clay Music Co., 1977—; advisor Dick Clark Caravan of Stars. Mem. ASCAP, Broadcast Music, Inc., AFTRA, Nashville Song Writers Assn. Home: 419 A Anastasia Blvd Saint Augustine FL 32084 Office: 3926 Blanding Blvd Jacksonville FL 32210

MONAS, SIDNEY, educator; b. N.Y.C., Sept. 15, 1924; s. David Joseph and Eva (Kiener) M.; A.B., Princeton U., 1948; A.M., Harvard U., 1951, Ph.D., 1955; m. Carolyn Babcock Munro, Sept. 5, 1948; children—Erica Beecher Monas Clements, Deborah Gardner, Stephen Sidney. Instr. history Amherst (Mass.) Coll., 1955-57; asst. prof. history Smith Coll., 1957-62; prof. history and lit., dir. Russian Studies Center, U. Rochester (N.Y.), 1962-69; prof. Slavic lang. and history U. Tex., Austin, 1969—, chmn. dept. Slavic langs., 1969-75; Fulbright prof. Russian history Hebrew U., Jerusalem, 1966-67; chmn. adv. bd. Nat. Transl. Center, 1969-70; vis. fellow Humanities Research Centre, Australian Nat. U., 1977; fellow Nat. Inst. Humanities, U. Chgo., 1977-78. Served with AUS, 1943-45. Ford fellow, 1954-55; Nat. Endowment for Humanities fellow, 1973-74. Mem. Am. Hist. Assn., Am. Assn. Advancement Slavic Studies, Modern Lang. Assn. Author: The Third Section, 1961; editor: Selected Works of N. Gumilev, 1972; Complete Poems of Osip Mandelstam, 1973; editorial bd. Jour. Modern History, 1967-70, Soviet Studies in Literature, 1968—; translator: Scenes from the Bathhouse, 1961; Crime and Punishment, 1968; editor, translator: Selected Essays of Osip Mandelstam, 1977. Home: 2200 Trail of Madrones Austin TX 78746

MONCARZ, ELISA, educator, accountant; b. Havana, Cuba, Oct. 10, 1947; came to U.S., 1960, naturalized, 1966; d. Benjamin and Felicia (Steinberg) Shafran; B.B.A., Bernard Baruch Sch. Bus., CUNY, 1966; m. Raul Moncarz, May 31, 1973; children—Felippe Henley, Roger Jonathan. Asst. acct. to supr. acct. S.D. Leidesdorf & Co. C.P.A.'s (merged with Ernst & Ernst 1978), N.Y.C., 1966-72; audit review mgr. Spear, Sheldon, Safer & Co., Miami, Fla., 1972-74; asst. prof. sch. of hospitality mgmt., acctg. and fin. program Fla. Internat. U., Miami, 1974-79, asso. prof., 1979—; cons. to banks, hospitality firms, mfg. cos. Founding bd. dirs. CTA, Inc., 1969-72; alt. chmn. Hispanic Employees Assn., Fla. Internat. U., affirmative action officer sch. of hospitality mgmt., 1975-78. Steering com. nat. symposium on Hispanic Bus. and Economy, Miami, 1979. C.P.A., N.Y., Fla. Mem. Am. Inst. C.P.A.'s, N.Y. State Soc. C.P.A.'s, Fla. Inst. C.P.A.'s, Ernst & Ernst Alumni, Am. Acctg. Assn. Council Hotel and Restaurant Instl. Edn., So. Fin. Assn., Southwestern Fin. Assn., Beta Alpha Psi. Contbr. articles to profl. publs.; researcher on hospitality acctg. and tourism. Office: Florida Internat U Sch Hospitality Mgmt Tamiami Trail Miami FL 33199

MONCURE, CONWAY BAGWELL, public accountant; b. Richmond, Va., Aug. 15, 1941; s. William Irby and Sue Seay (Bagwell) M.; B.S. in Bus., Va. Poly. Inst. and State U., 1963; m. Linda Day Harrison, Nov. 28, 1963; children—James Harrison, Susan Conway. Staff accountant A.M. Pullen & Co., C.P.A.'s, Richmond, 1966-68; accountant in pvt. practice, Blackstone, Va., 1968-73, C.P.A. in pvt. practice, 1973—. Sec. Indsl. Devel. Authority Blackstone; drive chmn. Blackstone Boy Scouts Am. Fund, 1970. Mem. Nottoway County Republican Com., 1972—. Bd. dirs. Blackstone Ednl. Found., 1968-71, Va. Ind. Sch. Assn., 1970-71; treas. Bill Willis Meml. Found., 1975. Served to 1st lt. AUS, 1964-66. C.P.A., Va. Mem. Va. Soc. C.P.A.'s, Nat. Soc. Pub. Accountants, Blackstone C. of C. (dir. 1971-74), Va. Poly. Inst. and State U. Alumni Assn. (chpt. sec.-treas. 1975), Blackstone Jaycees (pres. 1970-72; Outstanding Young Man award 1973, Key Man award 1970), Alpha Phi Omega. Methodist (adminstrv. bd. 1974-76). Rotarian (dir. Blackstone), Mason. Club: Blackstone Ruritan. Home: 605 College Ave Blackstone VA 23824 Office: 205 S Main St Blackstone VA 23824

MONDAY, GORDON VICTOR, architect; b. Grosse Pointe, Mich., Mar. 5, 1943; s. George A. and Marguerite L. (Maes) Hugelier; student U. W. Fla., 1968-69, Valencia Community Coll., 1969-70; B.A., U. Central Fla., 1976. With Howell Hopson, Architects, Leesburg, Fla., 1961-62, McCloud Nigel, Leesburg, 1962-64, Robert Ford, Architects, Leesburg, 1964-66, Danial Hart, Architects, Pensacola, Fla., 1968-69, Donald Hampton, Architect, Orlando, Fla., 1969-73; with Hampton & Monday, Architects, Winter Park, Fla., 1973—, partner, 1979—; architect for Orange County (Fla.) Public Works Facility. Served with U.S. Army, 1966-68. Decorated Bronze Star medal, Air medal. Mem. Nat. Council Archtl. Registration Bds., AIA. Club: Citrus. Office: 1460 W Fairbanks Ave Winter Park FL 32789

MONELL DE SANTIAGO, CARLOS RAFAEL, indsl. mgr.; b. Fajardo, P.R., Apr. 16, 1939; s. Carlos Monell Gauthier and Flor Maria De Santiago; B.S. in Indsl. Edn., U. P.R., 1961; m. Adita Mercado, Jan. 31, 1962; children—Zaida, Astrid, Vanessa, Clarissa, Carlos Raefael Monell. Product engr. Gen. Electric Co., 1961-63; plantation indsl. engr. C. Brewer, 1963-66; civilian utilities engr. U.S. Navy, 1966-67; quality control mgr. Kelvin Industries, 1967-71; quality control dir. Technicon Electronics Corp., 1971-75; plant mgr. Gen. Electric Co., 1975-77; gen. mgr. Bose Products, Inc., Toa Baja, P.R., 1977-79, Monell & Assos., engring. cons. firm, Santiago, P.R., 1979—, Systems Corp. P.R., Humacao, 1980—, Monell Shell Service, Humacao, 1980—; dir. Empresas Agricolas, Rumoll Corp., El Batey Devel. Corp. Registered profl. engr., P.R. Mem. Nat. Soc. Profl. Engrs., Am. Inst. Indsl. Engrs. (chpt. pres. 1973-74, 77—; named Outstanding Treas. 1969-71, Outstanding Pres. 1974), Am. Soc. of Tool and Mfg. Engrs., P.R. Mfrs. Assn., Am. Soc. for Quality Control. Roman Catholic. Clubs: P.R. Exchange (pres. 1970-72, 74-75; named Outstanding pres. 1971), Anasco Shooting, Humacao Shooting. Home: Box 114 Punta Santiago PR 00741 Office: Box 698 Humacao PR 00661

MONEY, JOHN MARSHALL, constrn. co. exec.; b. Carrollton, Miss., June 20, 1900; s. John Clark and Annie Laura (Marshall) M.; student Massey Bus. Coll., 1916-17, U. Va., 1918-21; m. Lorraine Lloyd, June 26, 1923; 1 dau., Betty Anne (Mrs. Robert Frances Arenz). With Hardaway Contracting Co., Columbus, Ga., 1921—, engr., 1921-25, supt., 1925-37, v.p., 1937-42, v.p. and gen. mgr., 1942-52, pres., 1952-69 chmn. bd., 1969-79, chmn. emeritus; chmn. bd. emeritus Internat. Incinerators, Inc., Atlanta, Cone Bros. Contracting Co., Tampa Fla. Served with AUS, 1918; Mem. Am. Soc. Civil Engrs. Meth. Clubs: Columbus Country, Atlanta Commerce. Home: 2222 Wildwood Ave Columbus GA 31906 Office: 300 Eleventh St Columbus GA 31902

MONROE, BETTY JOHNSON, ednl. evaluator; b. Cokedale, Colo.; d. Nils A. and Elsie A. (Eakins) Johnson; B.A. in English, Newcomb Coll., New Orleans, 1954; M.Ed., Tulane U., 1969; m. Charles A. Monroe (dec.); children—Neil R., Carla M. Posey, Gayle M. Goodwin, Philip L. Tchr. Orleans Parish Pub. Schs., New Orleans, 1964-69, cons. in English, 1970-74, dist. cons., 1974-76, acting evaluation Specialist Dept. Staff Evaluation, Div. Human Resources Mgmt., 1976—. Chairperson Innovative Worship Services Com. St. Charles Ave. Presbyn. Ch., 1970—, dir. youth div., 1975—, ruling elder, 1977—. Mem. Nat. Council Tchr. English, Adolescent Lit. Assembly (dir.), La. Council Tchrs. English (pres.), New Orleans Council Tchrs. English (pres.), Am. Assn. Sch. Adminstrs., La. Assn. Sch. Adminstrs., La. Assn. Supervision and Curriculum Devel. Internat. Reading Assn., Assn. Supervision and Curriculum Devel., Profl. Personnel Assn., Presbyn. Assn. Musicians. Contbr. articles to profl. jours. Curriculum cons. Scope English Program, Scholastic Book Services, Grades 7-9, 1979 Certified as tchr., guidance counselor, prin., adminstr. Home: 2830 Soniat St New Orleans LA 70115 Office: 4100 Touro St New Orleans LA 70122

MONROE, DORIS DRIGGERS, editor, author; b. Mt. Pleasant, Tex., July 11, 1916; d. Samuel Wyatt and Leola (Harris) Driggers; student Mary-Hardin Baylor Coll., 1934-35, William Jewell Coll., 1935-37, Southwestern Bapt. Theol. Sem., 1937-38, So. Bapt. Theol. Sem., 1938-39, 44-45, George Peabody Coll., 1947-50; m. Edwin Ulys Monroe, Aug. 6, 1937; children—Leola Fran (Mrs. Dudley B. Burton), Billie Barbara (Mrs. William F. Hardy, Jr.). Music dir., pastor's asst. Bethany Bapt. Ch., Kansas City, Mo., 1945-47; asso. editor Story Hour Leader, Bapt. Sunday Sch. Bd., Nashville, 1947-50, editor Primary Leader, Every Day with Primaries, 1950-68, cons. Work with Exceptional Persons, 1968—. Mem. Sunday sch. bd. So. Bapt. Conv. Mem. Nat. Assn. for Retarded Children, Am. Camping Assn., Am. Pen Women, Beta Lit. Soc. Author: When Marcia Goes to Church, 1966; The Come-and-Go Village, 1967; A Church Ministry to Retarded Persons, 1971; Reaching and Teaching the Mentally Retarded through the Sunday School, 1980; co-author: The Primary Leadership Manual, 1957; co-author, co-editor Adventures in Christian Living and Learning, Exploring Life Curriculum Series, 1968-72. Home: 2308 Donna Hill Ct Nashville TN 37214 Office: 127 9th Ave N Nashville TN 37203

MONROE, EDWIN PAUL, resort services exec.; b. Galion, Ohio, Apr. 5, 1915; s. Edwin P. and Georgia (Pavey) M.; student Ohio Wesleyan U., 1933-34; B.A., Rollins Coll., 1937; m. Virginia Lorene Hocker, Oct. 12, 1940; children—Edwin Paul III, Frederic Alan. Sales promotion mgr. Hercules Steel Products Co., Galion, 1938-42; pres., dir. Monroe Standard, Inc., Galion, 1946-65; v.p. Monroe Enterprises, Inc., Clearwater, Fla., 1968—; pres. Sea Chest Resort Properties, Treasure Island, Fla., 1949—. Vice mayor, commr. City of Treasure Island, 1951-54, chmn. planning and zoning bd., 1955-61. Served with USAAF, 1942-46. Mem. Sigma Alpha Epsilon, Pi Gamma Mu. Republican. Clubs: Rotary; St. Petersburg Yacht. Home: 8350 40th Ave N St Petersburg FL 33709 Office: 11780 Gulf Blvd Treasure Island FL 33706

MONROE, MATTHEW THEODORE, cardiologist; b. Warsaw, Poland, Aug. 6, 1941; s. Maria Malecki; came to U.S., 1967, naturalized, 1973; M.D., Sch. Medicine, Wroclaw, Poland, 1965; Ph.D. (Dowdle fellow, 1967-70), U. Calif., San Francisco, 1970; m. Beth Edeiken, Nov. 12, 1972; children—Douglas Perry, Brett Justin. Intern, Northeastern Hosp., Phila., 1970-71; resident in internal medicine Lankenau Hosp., Phila., 1971-73; Southeastern Pa. Heart Assn. fellow in cardiology Thomas Jefferson U. Hosp., Phila., 1973-75; practice medicine specializing in cardiology, Houston, 1975—; asst. clin. prof. U. Tex., Hermann, 1976—; MPM staffs Hermann Hosp., 1976—, Park Plaza Hosp., 1975—, Diagnostic Center Hosp., 1975—, Houston N.W. Med. Center, 1977—; courtesy staff in cardiology St. Luke's Episcopal Hosp., 1978—. Exchange student Orsett (Essex, U.K.) Hosp., 1963. Diplomate Am. Bd. Internal Medicine. Fellow Am. Coll. Angiology; mem. AMA, Am. Soc. Internal Medicine, A.C.P., Harris County Med. Soc., Am. Heart Assn., Houston Cardiology Soc. Contbr. articles in field to profl. publs. Office: 1213 Hermann Dr Suite 655 Houston TX 77004

MONTAGUE, BURT CHESLEY, obstetrician and gynecologist; b. Elgin, Okla., May 10, 1934; s. Bruce and Annie Laurie (Smith) M.; B.S., U. Okla., 1957, M.D., 1965; m. Jeannie Gay Lee, Dec. 11, 1976; children—Dorothy Lynn, Marjorie Ann, Sharon Elise, Susan Kelly, Chesley Burt. Rotating intern St. Anthony Hosp., Oklahoma City, 1965-66; asst. resident Okla. Sch. Medicine and Affiliated Hosps., Oklahoma City, 1966-69, resident, 1969-70; chief phys. therapy Community Hosp., Elk City, Okla., 1958-61; practice medicine specializing in Ob-Gyn, Lawton, Okla., 1970—; staff Comanche County Meml. Hosp., Lawton, 1970—, Great Plains Women's Clinic, Lawton, 1970—, Lawton Women's Center, 1980—; chief Ob-Gyn, Comanche County Meml. Hosp., 1974-76, chief med. staff, 1976-78. Served to capt. USNG, 1958-68. Am. Cancer Soc. fellow, 1969-70. Fellow Am. Coll. Obstetricians and Gynecologists, Am. Soc. for Colposcopy and Colpomicroscopy; mem. Am. Fertility Soc., AMA (Physicians Recognition award 1970-73) Okla. Med. Assn., Am.

Assn. Gynecol. Laparascopists, Comanche, Cotton, Tillman County Med. Soc. Club: Elks. Office: 93 NW 24th St Lawton OK 73505

MONTAGUE, ROBERT LATANE, III, lawyer; b. Washington, Sept. 18, 1935; s. Robert Latane and Frances Breckinridge (Wilson) M.; B.A., U. Va., 1956, LL.B., 1961; m. Prudence Mason Darnell, June 20, 1964; children—Anne Steele Mason, Robert Latane. Asst. atty. gen. State of Ky., Frankfort, 1961-64; asso. law with Howard W. Smith, Alexandria, Va., 1964-66; asso. firm Lambert, Broun & Furlow, Washington, 1965-69; asso. John Howard Joynt, Alexandria, 1970-79, Johns Breckinridge, Lexington, Va., 1979—. Pres., Historic Alexandria Found., 1968-70, exec. sec., 1971-74; pres. Conservation Council Va., 1979—; chmn. Alexandria Environ. Policy Commn., 1970-74; chmn. Nat. Capital Area chpt. Nat. Found., 1972-75; pres. No. Va. Conservation Council, 1973-74, 78-79; vice chmn. Nat. Health Agys. Council, 1977-78, chmn., 1978-79; Democratic nominee Alexandria city council, 1973; trustee Assn. Preservation Va. Antiquities, Richmond. Served to comdr. USNR. Mem. Am., Va. (chmn. spl. com. environ. law 1973—), Ky., D.C. bar assns., Am. Judicature Soc., Soc. Cin., Aircraft Owners and Pilots Assn. Clubs: Army and Navy Town; Antique Automobile Am. Contbr. articles to legal jours. Home: 207 Prince St Alexandria VA 22314 also Box 327 Urbanna VA 23175 Office: 1007 King St Alexandria VA 22314

MONTANARI, MARION GOODRUM, treatment center adminstr.; b. McKeesport, Pa., Apr. 20, 1935; d. John Thomas and Edith (Lutz) Goodrum; B.A. in Psychology, Carlow Coll., Pitts., 1962; M.Ed. in Counseling, Duquesne U., Pitts., 1969; m. Adelio J. Montanari, Dec. 20, 1971; stepchildren—Gary, Adele. Tchr., then prin. pvt. elem. and jr. high sch., Pitts.; child care counselor, Pitts.; asso. dir. Montanari Residential Treatment Center, Hialeah, Fla., 1970—, also inservice staff tng. dir.; co-owner Hialeah Homes News, Las Noticias de Hialeah; cons. Troubled Children's Found., 1971—. Trustee Greater Miami Opera Assn. Mem. Am. Personnel and Guidance Assn., Fla. Group Child Care Assn., Am. Orthopsychiatric Assn., Inc., Dade County Mental Health Assn. Roman Catholic. Office: 291 E 2d St Hialeah FL 33010

MONTANTI, JOHN CHARLES, speech pathologist, clin. audiologist; b. Jersey City, May 10, 1947; s. Charles and Rose Rivita (Catino) M.; B.B.A. cum laude, Fort Lauderdale U., 1970; B.A. cum laude, Jersey City State Coll., 1974; M.A., Kean Coll. N.J., 1975; Ed.D., Nova U., 1980; m. Angela LaCognata, Dec. 18, 1971; children—Jennifer Rose, John David. Vice pres. Bruce MacIntyre A.R.P., Inc., Cliffside Park, N.J., 1971-72; dir. speech, lang. and hearing services Aviva Manor, Ft. Lauderdale, Fla., 1978—, Pinehurst Convalescent Center, Pompano Beach, Fla., 1979—; pres. Communicative Learning Dynamics, Inc., Ft. Lauderdale, 1976—; cons. in field. Exec. dir., v.p. H.E.A.R. Found. S. Fla., 1976-79. Served with USAR, 1971. Mem. Am. Speech Lang. and Hearing Assn., N.J. Speech Lang. and Hearing Assn., Fla. Speech Lang. and Hearing Assn., Am. Acad. Pvt. Practice in Speech Pathology and Audiology. Republican. Presbyterian. Home: 3321 NE 17th Way Fort Lauderdale FL 33334 Office: 701 S 21st Ave Hollywood FL 33020

MONTES DE OCA, PEDRO F., agribus. co. exec.; b. Ferrol, Spain, Aug. 1, 1924; came to U.S., 1961; s. Pedro and Angela (Abella) M. de O.; LL.D., U. Havana, Cuba, 1949; m. Alicia Beruff, Feb. 7, 1948; children—Alicia, Pedro. Pres., Vallejo Steel Works, Havana, 1956-61; partner De La Fuente & Montes, Miami, Fla., 1961-66; gen. mgr. Gold Kist S.A., Lima, Peru, 1967-74, proteins and oils sales mgr. Gold Kist Internat., Atlanta, 1974—. Mem. Cuban Lawyers Assn. in Exile, NAM (chmn. steel producers com. 1956-61). Roman Catholic. Clubs: Atlanta Cuban (dir. 1977—), Am. in Miami. Home: 5304 Winters Chapel Rd Doraville GA 30360 Office: Gold Kist Internat PO Box 2210 Atlanta GA 30301

MONTGOMERY, CLARENCE DANIEL, health facility adminstr.; b. Uniontown, Ala., Oct. 31, 1934; s. Elbert and Bessie (Hopkins) M.; L.P.N., Shapero Sch. Practical Nursing 1963; A.D.R.N., Highland Park Community Coll., 1968; B.A. (scholar), Mich. State U., 1970; M.P.H. (Nat. Assn. Neighborhood Health Centers and U. Mich. Grad. scholar), U. Mich., 1974; children—Lisa Deniel, Darryle Kevin, Paul Ivan. Exec. dir. Saginaw (Mich.) Community Clinic, 1971-72; asst. project dir. Family Health Center, Miami, Fla., 1972-75; dir. nurses N. Dade Hosp., Opa Locka, Fla., 1975-76; adminstr. Doris Ison S. Dade Community Health Center, Miami, 1976—. Served with arty. U.S. Army, 1956-58. Mem. Am. Public Health Assn., Am. Acad. Health Adminstrn. Home: 529 SW 80th Ave Miami FL 33144 Office: Doris Ison S Dade Community Health Center 10300 SW 216th St Miami FL 33170

MONTGOMERY, DOUGLAS CLAYTON, mgmt. cons.; b. Sunderland, Vt., Apr. 13, 1917; s. Douglas Clayton and Winifred Mary (Grout) M.; B.S. in Mech. Engring., U. Ill., 1939, also various extension courses; m. Frances Helen Hall, Sept. 14, 1946; children—Edith Frances Montgomery Barrett, Mary Margaret. Refinery pump engr. Lummus Co., N.Y.C., 1939-40; ballistic engr. Ind. Ordnance Works, DuPont Co., 1941, Ala. Ordnance Works, 1942-43, atomic reactor operating engr. Hanford (Wash.) Engr. Works, 1944-46; atomic reactor operating engr. Hanford Engr. Works, Gen. Electric Corp., 1947-49, atomic propulsion test engr. Knolls Atomic Power Lab., Schenectady, 1950-55; mgmt. cons. Douglas Montgomery Consultants, Columbia, S.C., 1956—; pres. Palmetto Safety Consultants, Milmont Shores, Inc.; partner Hallmont Investors. Bd. dirs. Indsl. Services, Inc.; active PT. Mem. S.C. Soc. Profl. Engrs., S.C. C. of C. (congl. action com.). Republican. Baptist. Clubs: Masons, Civitan. Home: 1411 Belmont Dr Columbia SC 29205 Office: 516 Beltline Blvd Columbia SC 29205

MONTGOMERY, ELIZABETH FLANAGAN (MRS. STEWART MAGRUDER MONTGOMERY), ch. and civic worker; b. Cary, Miss., July 25, 1898; d. Robert Edward Lee and Annie May (Purdy) Flanagan; grad. Northwestern Sch. Speech, 1918; A.B., Miss. State Coll. for Women, 1924; summer study Peabody Coll., U. Cal., Columbia; m. Stewart Magruder Montgomery, Jan. 5, 1935. Instr. elementary grades, high sch. English and dramatics, Cary, Miss., 1924-51. Mem. King's Daus. and Sons, state pres. 1949-51, 55-56, dir. Indian work, speaker internat. conv.; state pres. Miss. Women's Cabinet, 1954-55; mem. adv. council Miss. Children's Code Commn.; edn. com. Miss. Assn. Mental Health, 1958—, dir., exec. com., nominating com., 1963-66, dir., 1966—, sec., 1973—; chmn. Miss. Mental Health Conv., 1964; county commr. Fifth Region Mental Health Center, 1967—; commr. Delta Mental Health Service; del. Nat. Mental Health Conv., 1963, meeting, N.Y.C.; dir. State Mental Health Bd.; sec. Miss. Mental Health Assn., 1971-73; county campaign chmn. A.R.C., 1962. Mem. pub. relations com. Miss. Women's Cabinet, 1961—, now also recreation chmn.; mem. Gov.'s Ladies Staff, Miss., 1960-64; sec. Miss. Mental Health, 1969—; mem. Sharkey County Mental Health Commn., 1967—. Trustee King's Daus. Home, Natchez, Miss., 1948-52, pres. gov.'s bd., 1956—, gov.'s bd. trustees, 1965—; pres. gov.'s bd. Recipient Woman of Achievement award Rolling Fork Bus. and Profl. Women, 1965; named Outstanding Civic leader Am., 1967. Mem. Miss. King's Daus. and Sons (historian 1969—, parliamentarian), Internat. Platform Assn., Daus. Am. Colonists, Order of Washington, Daus. of 1812, Colonial Dames of XVII Century (chpt. pres. 1971-73, state 1st v.p. 1971-73, state pres. 1973—), Dames of Court Honor, Daus. Confederacy, Soc. Magna Charta Dames, Ams. Royal Descent, Zeta Phi Eta. Episcopalian (state pres., women's orgn., 1952-55; pres. IV province Episcopal Ch. 1957-60). Clubs: Sharkey County Home Makers (sec.), Highland (pres. aux. 1963-64), Delta Debutante (patron 1961—). Home: Route 2 Rolling Fork MS 39159

MONTGOMERY, GILLESPIE V., congressman; b. Meridian, Miss.; s. Gillespie M. and Emily (Jones) M.; B.S., Miss. State U. Mem. Miss. Senate, 1956-66; mem. 90th-96th congresses from 3d Dist. Miss.; chmn. select com. on missing persons in S.E. Asia, 94th Congress; mem. Presdl. Commn. on MIA's, 1977. Mem. Miss. Agrl. and Indsl. Bd., 1957-60; pres. Miss. N.G. Assn., 1959; pres. Miss. Heart Assn., 1967-68. Served with AUS, World War II, Korean War. Decorated Bronze Star, Combat Inf. Badge; recipient Miss. Magnolia award, 1966; certificate of merit for saving a life ARC, 1947. Mem. VFW, Am. Legion, 40 and 8, Miss. Farm Bur., Congressional Prayer Breakfast Group (pres. 1970), Miss. State U. Alumni Assn. (past pres.), Kappa Alpha. Episcopalian. Clubs: Masons, Shriners, Moose. Home: PO Box 5618 Meridian MS 39301 also 1200 N Nash St Apt 1135 Arlington VA 22209 Office: 2367 Rayburn House Office Bldg Washington DC 20515

MONTGOMERY, HENRY EDWARD, JR., naval officer; b. Lexington, Ky., July 7, 1946; s. Henry Edward and Agnes Luella (Callebs) M.; B.A., Berea Coll., 1968; Ph.D., U. Ky., 1971. Instr. chemistry U. Ky., 1968-71; commd. ensign U.S. Navy, 1971, advanced through grades to lt. comdr., 1979; instr. Naval Nuclear Power Sch., Bainbridge, Md., 1971-76; asst. prodn. engring. officer Phila. Naval Shipyard, 1976; instr. chemistry U.S. Naval Acad., Annapolis, Md., 1976-78; ship supt. Charleston (S.C.) Naval Shipyard, 1978—. Mem. Am. Chem. Soc., Am. Inst. Physics, Am. Soc. Naval Engrs., Am. Parachute Assn., Sigma Xi, Phi Kappa Phi. Contbr. articles to profl. jours. Home: BOQ Rm 4-207 Naval Station Charleston SC 29408 Office: Code333 Charleston Naval Shipyard Charleston SC 29408

MONTGOMERY, JAMES ALFRED, athletic dir.; b. Birmingham, Ala., Jan. 12, 1929; s. Lucius Shirley and Essie Louise (Bagley) M.; A.B. in English, Birmingham So. Coll., 1953; A.M., George Peabody Coll., Nashville, 1956, Ed.D., 1960. Tchr., coach Hewitt-Trussville (Ala.) High Sch., 1953-54, Haleyville (Ala.) High Sch., 1954-55, Athens (Ala.) Coll., 1955-57; mem. athletic staff and faculty Millsaps Coll., Jackson, Miss., 1959—, chmn. dept. phys. edn., dir. athletics, tennis coach; pres. Hunters Mountain Tennis Group. Mem. AAHPER, Intercollegiate Tennis Coaches Assn., Phi Delta Kappa, Kappa Phi Kappa. Republican. Methodist. Home: 819-D Euclid St Jackson MS 39202 Office: Millsaps Coll Jackson MS 39210

MONTGOMERY, JOHN DENNY, lawyer; b. Hobart, Okla., June 27, 1928; s. Robert Place and Theitis (Curreathers) M.; B.A., U. Okla., 1950, LL.B., 1955; m. Martha Carolyn Flow, June 9, 1950; children—John Denny, Mary Ann. Admitted to Okla. bar, 1955; since practiced in Hobart, Okla.; mem. firm Montgomery & Montgomery, 1955—. Pres., United Fund, Hobart, 1959; chmn. Kiowa County chpt. ARC, 1967—; sec. Hobart Planning Commn., 1964-65. Dir. S.W. Okla. Devel. Council, 1964; dir. Hobart Industries, Inc., 1965, pres., 1977-79; trustee Kiowa County Indsl. Trust, 1970-80; trustee Washita Presbytery, 1977—, elder local Presbyterian Ch. Served from ensign to lt. (j.g.) USNR, 1950-53; capt. Res. Mem. Am., Okla., Kiowa County (pres. 1960) bar assns., S.W. Okla. Bar Inst. (v.p. 1965), S.W. Okla. Legal Inst. (pres. 1966-67), Okla. Bar. Found. (trustee), C. of C. (pres. 1962, 73), Kappa Alpha, Phi Alpha Delta. Republican. Clubs: Rotary (pres. 1958-59), Hobart Country (pres. 1959), Quarterback (sec. 1965). Home: 107 E Dogwood St Hobart OK 73651 Office: Montgomery Bldg 325 S Main St Hobart OK 73651

MONTGOMERY, MELVIN BOYCE, musician; b. Richards, Tex., Jan 3, 1925; s. Henry Lester and Mary Frances (Welch) M.; B.S., Sam Houston State U., 1948; M.A., 1955; postgrad Tex. Tech. U., 1965-68; m. Virginia Faye Harrington, May 22, 1948; children—Donald Glenn, Jill Ann. Band dir. Stephen F. Austin High Sch., Port Arthur, Tex., 1948-52; dir. instrumental music Snyder (Tex.) Public Schs., 1952-68; dir. bands, asso. prof. music Stephen F. Austin State U., Nacogdoches, Tex., 1968—; guest condr., clinician, cons., adjudicator. Served with AUS, 1943-46. Mem. Am. Bandmasters Assn., Tex. Music Educators Assn., Tex. Bandmasters Assn., Coll. Band Dirs. Nat. Assn., Percussive Arts Soc., Leblanc Music Educators Adv. Bd., Phi Beta Mu, Phi Mu Alpha, Kappa Kappa Psi, Tau Beta Sigma, Phi Delta Kappa. Democrat. Methodist. Home: 2416 Twin Oaks St Nacogdoches TX 75961 Office: Dept Music Stephen F Austin State U Nacogdoches TX 75962

MONTGOMERY, ROBERT PLACE, lawyer; b. Washington, Nov. 15, 1902; s. Denny and Cora (Johnson) M.; LL.B., U. Okla., 1925; m. Theitis Curreathers, July 6, 1927; children—John Denny, Robert Place. Admitted to Okla. bar, 1925; practiced in Hobart, Okla., 1925—; mem. firm Montgomery & Montgomery, 1955—; U.S. conciliation commr., 1934—; atty. City of Hobart, 1941-43; speaker Law Insts., Okla., 1940—; spl. justice Okla. Supreme Ct., 1964, 67. Dir. 1st Nat. Bank, Hobart. Dist. chmn. Boy Scouts Am., Hobart, 1941; chmn. Kiowa County chpt. A.R.C., 1940-46; co-chmn. Am. Cancer Soc., Hobart, 1948; adv. bd. Selective Service, 1940, 71—, appeal agt., 1950-71; acting postmaster Hobart, 1927-28; chmn. Kiowa County Election Bd., 1928-34. Chmn., Kiowa County Republican Com., 1928-58, dist. chmn., 1934-58; del. Rep. Nat. Convs., 1936, 44. Bd. dirs. Okla. Soc. Crippled Children, pres., 1972-73; bd. dirs. Westminster Found., Okla.-Ark. Synod Found. Mem. Am., Okla. (central com. 1952—, exec. council 1951-53, v.p. 1954, asso. editor Jour. 1961, award for outstanding community service 1975) bar assns., Phi Delta Phi, Alpha Sigma Phi. Presbyn. Mason (32 deg.), Rotarian. Home: 126 W Dogwood St Hobart OK 73651 Office: 325 S Main St Hobart OK 73651

MONTGOMERY, ROYCE LEE, educator; b. Hartsville, Tenn., Nov. 8, 1933; s. Erby Lee and Jimmie (Belcher) M.; A.B., U. Va., 1955; M.S., W.Va. U., 1960, Ph.D., 1963; m. Jane Hansford, Oct. 3, 1966; children—Royce Todd, Scott Hansford, Jill Harriet. Asso. prof. anatomy W.Va. U., 1964-65; with U. N.C., 1965—. Served to lt. U.S. Army, 1955-57. Home: 728 Shadylawn Ct Chapel Hill NC 27514 Office: Dept Anatomy U NC Chapel Hill NC 27514

MONTGOMERY, WILLIAM SHEARIN, amusement co. exec.; b. Nashville, Jan. 16, 1941; s. Luke Hamilton and Virginia Love (Shearin) M.; B.S., U. Tenn., 1963; m. Sue Billips, July 25, 1964; children—Phillip, David. Personnel mgr. footwear div. Genesco, Inc., Nashville, 1964-66, asst. dir. selection and placement corporate manpower, 1966, asst. dir. mgmt. devel., 1967-69, dir. corporate mgmt. devel., 1969-71, dir. corporate mgmt. manpower, 1971-73, dir. ops. analysis, 1973-76, v.p. corporate human resources, 1976-79; pres. M & W Amusements, Inc. Chmn. consumer advisory bd. Parkside Hosp. Recipient Superior Achievement Recognition award Genesco, Inc., 1977. Mem. Am. Soc. Tng. and Devel., U. Tenn. Davidson County Alumni Assn. (dir. 1971-73). Republican. Home: 611 W Meade Dr Nashville TN 37205 Office: 111 7th Ave N Nashville TN 37202

MONTIN, JOHN ERNEST, mech. contractor; b. Alexandria, Va., Aug. 3, 1918; s. Alfred Constance and Mary Marie (Ceppi) M.; B.S., Okla. A. and M. Coll., 1947; m. Lillian Stout, June 23, 1945; children—John, Jean, Robert. With Frigidaire Sales Corp., Oklahoma City, 1948-49; v.p. W.A. Landers Co., Oklahoma City; v.p. Mid Continent Constructors. Scoutmaster, Boy Scouts Am., 1956-62. Served with AUS, 1941-45; PTO. Decorated Legion of Merit; registered profl engr., Okla. Mem. Am. Soc. Heating, Refrigerating and Air Conditioning Engrs., Nat. Soc. Profl. Engrs., C. of C., Okla. State U. Alumni Assn. Methodist (trustee). Clubs: Masons, Shriners, Jesters, Kiwanis, Beacon. Home: 66 West Shore Dr Lake Hiwassee Arcadia OK 73007 Office: 100 NE 25th St Oklahoma City OK 73105

MONTZ, GLEN NORMAN, botanist; b. New Orleans, May 25, 1941; s. Guy and Alma Gertrude (Babin) M.; B.S., Southeastern La. U., 1963, M.Ed., 1967; Ph.D. (NDEA fellow), La. State U., 1970; m. Joanna Dee Jordan, July 25, 1969; children—Jason Christopher, Jennifer Adele. Tchr. high sch. chemistry St. Bernard Parish, La., 1963-65; asst. prof. botany U. New Orleans, 1970-72; environ. resources specialist U.S. Army C.E., New Orleans, 1972-77, botanist, 1977—. Mem. La. Acad. Sci., So. Appalachian Bot. Club, So. Weed Sci. Soc., Aquatic Plant Mgmt. Soc., La. Pesticide Applicators Assn., Sigma Xi. Democrat. Roman Catholic. Club: Hill Heights Country (Destrehan, La.). Contbr. articles to profl. jours. Home: 219 Murrayhill Dr Destrehan LA 70047 Office: PO Box 60267 New Orleans LA 70160

MONYEK, MILTON S., physician; b. Elizabeth, N.J., Aug. 10, 1914; s. Frank and Esther (Blau) M.; grad. cum laude, Brandeis U., 1935; M.D. cum laude, Middlesex U., 1939; LL.B., U. Miami, 1961; children—Fredi Cynthia, Debra, Roberta, Mari Beth. Intern, resident in surgery Alexian Bros. Hosp., Elizabeth, 1939-41; resident surgeon St. Francis Hosp., Miami Beach, Fla., 1953-54; grad. in cardiology and internal medicine Harvard Med. Sch., 1948; practice medicine specializing in family practice, Miami Beach, 1954—; clin. asst. prof. U. Miami Sch. Medicine; chief dept. family practice North Miami Gen. Hosp., 1974-76, now sr. attending physician; med. adviser Travelers Ins. Co.; sr. examiner FAA, 1952—; physician-adv. Dade Monroe Peer Rev. Service Orgn., Palmetto, Palm Spring, King, Christian, Miami Internat. hosp., HEW. Served with M.C., AUS, 1941-45. Diplomate Am. Bd. Family Practice. Fellow Internat. Coll. Surgeons; mem. Dade County, Fla. med. assns., AMA, Am. Acad. Family Practice, Am. Assn. Trial Lawyers. Cons. editor Fla. Acad. Family Practice, Current Medicine for Attorneys. Office: 16200 NE 13th Ave North Miami Beach FL 33162

MOODY, JOHN COMPTON, JR., mfg. co. exec.; b. Clearwater, Fla., Nov. 22, 1951; s. John Compton and Nedra (Carper) M.; B.S. in Acctg., Va. Poly. Inst. and State U., 1974; postgrad. in bus. Radford U., 1980—; m. Patricia Elaine Hill, Mar. 3, 1979. Cost acct. Harvey Hubbell Inc., Christiansburg, Va., 1975-77; cost acct. Electro-Optical Products div. ITT, Roanoke, Va., 1977-78, sr. fin. analyst, 1978—. Mem. Christiansburg Vol. Rescue Squad, 1972-79. Mem. Nat. Assn. Accts., Inst. Mgmt. Acctg. Methodist. Office: 7635 Plantation Rd Roanoke VA 24019

MOODY, JOHN PETER, obstetrician and gynecologist; b. Rochester, N.Y., Aug. 20, 1934; s. John Crosby and Edna Mae (Schreib) M.; B.S. in Chemistry, Tufts Coll., Medford, Mass., 1956; M.D., N.Y. Med. Coll., 1961; m. Linda Carol Eagon, Nov. 2, 1973; children—Cynthia Jean, John David, James Christopher. Intern, Easton (Pa.) Hosp., 1962; resident William Beaumont Gen. Hosp., El Paso, Tex., 1966; pvt. practice, El Paso, 1969—; chief staff Newark Methodist Maternity Hosp., 1970-72. Chmn. med. adv. com. Planned Parenthood El Paso; mem. S.W. regional med. com. Planned Parenthood Assn. Am. Served to maj. M.C., AUS, 1962-69; decorated Combat Med. badge, Bronze Star. Fellow Am. Coll. Obstetricians and Gynecologists, A.C.S.; mem. Am., Pan Am., Tex., El Paso County med. assns. Club: Internat. (El Paso). Contbr. papers profl. jours. Home: 6006 Balcones Ct 24 El Paso TX 79912 Office: 1900 N Oregon St El Paso TX 79902

MOODY, JOHN WILLIAM, lawyer; b. Miami, Okla., Oct. 23, 1943; s. Benjaman Nicholas and Bonnie Irene (Gadberry) M.; A.A., Northeastern A. and M. Jr. Coll., 1963; student Kans. U., 1963; B.A., Okla. State U., 1967; J.D., U. Tulsa, 1968; children by previous marriages—Gerald Brent, Robert Floyd, Melissa Ann, John Heath. Planning analyst Tulsa Met. Area Planning Commn., 1966-67; asst. to pres. Morland Devel. Co. Inc., Tulsa, 1967-69, also dir.; admitted to Okla. bar, 1969; asso. firm Spillers, Tucker, Boyd & Parks, Tulsa, 1969-71; asso. firm Boyd & Parks, Tulsa, 1971-73, partner, 1973-78; asso. firm Hall, Estill, Handurick et. al., 1979—. Lectr. law Tulsa U., 1974, Okla. State U., 1973. Mem. Tulsa City-County Environ. Adv. Council, 1974—, chmn., 1976—. Mem. Am., Okla., Tulsa County (chmn. com. zoning 1974) bar assns. Democrat. Presbyn. Asso. editor Tulsa Law Jour., 1967-68. Home: 5045 S Hudson St Tulsa OK 74135 Office: 4100 Bok Tower Tulsa OK 74103

MOODY, LAMON LAMAR, JR., cons. engr.; b. Bogalusa, La., Nov. 8, 1924; s. Lamar Lamon and Vida (Seal) M.; B.C.E., U. Southwestern La., 1951; m. Eve Thibodeaux, Sept. 22, 1954; children—Lamon Lamar, Jennifer Eve, Jeffrey Matthew. Engr., Tex. Co., N.Y.C., 1951-52; project engr. African Petroleum Terminals, West Africa, 1952-56; chief engr. Kaiser Aluminum & Chem. Corp., Baton Rouge, 1956-63; pres., owner Dyer & Moody, Inc., Cons. Engrs., Baker, La., 1963—, also chmn. bd., dir. Chmn., Baker Planning Commn., 1961-63. Served with USMCR, 1943-46. Decorated Purple Heart; registered profl. engr., La., Ark., Miss., Tex. Fellow ASCE; mem. La. Engring. Soc. (dir., Charles M. Kerr award for pub. relations 1971), Profl. Engrs. in Pvt. Practice (state chmn. 1969-70), Am. Congress Surveying and Mapping (award for excellency 1972), La. Land Surveyors Assn. (pres. 1968-69), Cons. Engrs. Council, Engrs. Joint Council, Nat. Soc. Profl. Engrs., Greater Baker Assn. Commerce (dir. 1974, chmn. indsl. devel. com. 1974-75), Baker C. of C. (v.p. 1976, pres. 1977, Outstanding Bus. Leader of Year award 1975), Blue Key. Democrat. Baptist. Clubs: Masons (32 deg.), Kiwanis (dir. 1964-65). Home: 3811 Charry Dr Baker LA 70714 Office: 2845 Ray Weiland Dr Baker LA 70714

MOODY, MAX DALE, microbiologist; b. Onaga, Kans., Sept. 29, 1924; s. Harry F. and Cora (Deveny) M.; A.B., U. Kans., 1948, M.A., 1949, Ph.D., 1953; m. Mildred B. Brooks, Apr. 30, 1950; children—Steven, Janet, Marcia. Commd. in USPHS, 1954, advanced through grades to scientist dir., 1971; chief streptococcus unit Center for Disease Control, Atlanta, 1966-70, chief reagents evaluation unit, 1970-71; ret., 1971; tech. dir. reagents div Burroughs Wellcome Co., Research Triangle Park, N.C., 1971—; area com. chmn. for microbiology Nat. Com. Clin. Lab. Standards, 1977—; chmn. Conf. Pub. Health Lab. Dirs., 1979; mem. expert com. bacterial disease WHO, 1966—. Served with USNR, 1943-46. Co-recipient Kimble Methodology Research award, 1967. Diplomate Am. Bd. Med. Microbiology (bd. govs. 1979—). Fellow Am. Acad. Med. Microbiology (sec. internat. subcom. streptococci and pneumococci 1960-77); mem. Am. Soc. Microbiology (pres. N.C. br. 1977; bd. govs. 1979—). Home: 115 Dunedin Ct Cary NC 27511 Office: 3030 Cornwallis Rd Research Triangle Park NC 27709

MOODY, MILDRED GEAN STOREY, counselor, ednl. adminstr.; b. Clarksville, Tex., Apr. 1, 1927; d. Louis Richard and Tommie Lena (Taylor) Storey; B.A., N. Tex. State U., 1947; M.Ed., Tex. Technol. U., 1973; m. Eldon Golden Moody, Feb. 3, 1951; children—Richard, David, Linda, Susan. Tchr. pub. schs., Ft. Stockton, Tex., 1947-51; tchr. English, social studies Union Sch., Lamesa, Tex., 1964-71; tchr. spl. edn. Lamesa Pub. Sch., 1971-72, vocat. adjustment coordinator, 1972-74, ednl. diagnostician, 1974-76, spl. edn. counselor, ednl. diagnostician, 1976—; tchr. child care devel. Lamesa campus Howard Coll., 1978—; cons. in field. Active 4-H Clubs, Boy Scouts Am., United Fund; del. Democratic State Conv., 1952. Recipient Tchr. of Handicapped award Rotary Found., 1977-78. Mem. Am. Personnel and Guidance Assn., NEA, Tex. State Tchrs. Assn., Lamesa Edn. Assn., Am. Sch. Counselors Assn., Council for Exceptional Children, Council for Ednl. Diagnostic Services, Delta Kappa Gamma. Methodist. Contbr. articles to profl. jours. Home: Box 56 306 Terrace Circle Lamesa TX 79331

MOODY, WILLIS ELVIS, JR., engr.; b. Raleigh, N.C., Mar. 30, 1924; s. Willis Elvis and Inez Marie (McDade) M.; B.S. in Ceramic Engring., N.C. State U. at Raleigh, 1948, M.S., 1949, Ph.D., 1956; postgrad. in nuclear metallurgy Iowa State U., 1957; J.D., Woodrow Wilson Coll. Law, 1979; m. Mary Susan McAfee, Mar. 22, 1947 (div. June 1967); children—Susan E., Michael T., Peggy A., Willis Elvis, III, William S. Ceramic engr. Spark Plug div. Electric Auto Lite Co., Fostoria, Ohio, 1949-50; ceramic engr. Lab. Equipment Corp., St. Joseph, Mich., 1950-51; instr. ceramic engring. and metallurgy N.C. State U. at Raleigh, 1951-56; faculty Ga. Inst. Tech., Atlanta, 1956—, prof. ceramic engring., 1960—; research participant Oak Ridge Nat. Lab., summers 1954, 55; cons. to clay and ceramic industries, 1951—. Served with AAC, 1943-46; ETO. Decorated Air medal with two oak leaf clusters; registered profl. engr., Ga. Fellow Orton Ceramic Found.; mem. Am. Ceramic Soc. (trustee 1965-68, dir. Southeastern sect. 1962), Ceramic Ednl. Council (pres. 1963), Am. Soc. Engring. Edn. (chmn. materials div. 1971), Am. Phys. Soc., AAAS, Assn. Applied Solar Energy, Nat. Inst. Ceramic Engrs. (pres. 1980), Clay Minerals Soc. (councillor 1969-71), Keramos, Sigma Xi, Sigma Pi Sigma, Tau Beta Pi. Contbr. articles to tech. jours. Patentee in field. Home: 4545 Northside Pkwy Apt 13K Atlanta GA 30339 Office: Sch Ceramic Engring Ga Inst Tech Atlanta GA 30332

MOOK, BARBARA HEER HELD, assn. adminstr.; b. Akron, June 9, 1919; d. Harold Edward and Helen Wilhelm (Heer) Held; student Coll. Wooster, 1937-39; diploma Actual Business Coll., 1941; m. Conrad Payne Mook, Sept. 6, 1941; children—Patricia Ann Mook Harris, Mary Ann Mook Barnum. Tchr., lectr. DAR Museum, Washington, 1973—; sr. nat. asst. organizing sec. Children of the Am. Revolution, Washington, 1974-76, hon. sr. nat. v.p., 1977-80. Troop leader Girl Scouts U.S.A., Arlington, Va., 1951-53, neighborhood chmn., 1953-55, mem. program com. Arlington County council, 1955-56; rec. sec. Thomas Nelson chpt. DAR, Arlington, 1963-65, 73-75, librarian, 1967-69, regent, 1965-67. Mem. Va. Hist. Soc., Ohio Geneal. Soc., Washington's Army at Valley Forge (charter v.p. 1976-78), Daus. of Union Vets. of Civil War 1861-65 (sr. v.p. 1978-80), Children of Am. Revolution (sr. nat. officers club), Potomac Regent's Club DAR (treas. 1974-75), Smithsonian Resident Assos., Assos. of Nat. Archives, Am. Mus. Natural History, Aux. Sons of Union Vets. of Civil War, Internat. Platform Assn. Home: 5222 26th Rd N Arlington VA 22207

MOOK, CONRAD PAYNE, meteorologist, ret. govt. ofcl.; b. Titusville, Pa., May 2, 1914; s. Raymond L. and Ella (Payne) M.; A.B., Coll. of Wooster, 1939; M.S., N.Y. U., 1943; m. Barbara Heer Held, Sept. 6, 1941; children—Patricia Ann Mook Harris, Mary Ann Mook Barnum. Instr., N.Y. U., 1941-43; meteorologist U.S. Weather Bur., Washington, 1943-57; geophysicist Harry Diamond Labs., Washington, 1957-61; hurricane forecaster U.S. Weather Bur., Washington, 1961-62; program mgr., space vehicle thermal control and vacuum tech. NASA Hdqrs., Washington, 1962-70; del. 11th gen. assembly Internat. Union Geodesy and Geophysics, Toronto, 1957; mem. commn. IV, U.S. nat. com. Internat. Sci. Radio Union, 1958-65; chmn. Govt.-Industry Com. on High Powered Light Source Devel., 1969-70. Mem. Am. Meteorol. Soc., Am. Geophys. Union, Am. Inst. Aeros. and Astronautics, Order Founders and Patriots Am. (treas. D.C. Soc. 1977—), D.C. Mayflower Soc. (editor Pilgrim News 1976—), Soc. Mayflower Desc., SAR (pres. George Mason chpt. 1979—, Va. SAR-Children Am. Revolution coordinator 1980—), Internat. Platform Assn., Va., Valley Forge hist. socs., Sons Union Vets. Civil War, Ohio Geneal. Soc. Presbyterian (fin. sec., trustee 1977-78). Editor for Meteorology Trans., Am. Geophys. Union, 1956-58; asso. editor Jour. Geophys. Research, 1959-65; contbr. articles to profl. publs. Home: 5222 26th Rd N Arlington VA 22207

MOOKHERJEE, HARSHA NATH, sociologist; b. Calcutta, India, Sept. 1, 1935; came to U.S., 1967, naturalized, 1977; s. Kanai Lal and Saibalini (Chakrabarty) M.; B.S., U. Calcutta, 1954, B.A. in English, 1961, B.S. with honors, 1963, M.S., 1966; Ph.D., Miss. State U., 1971; m. Ira Gangopadhyay, May 28, 1966; 1 dau., Paramita. Research asso. Anthrop. Survey of India, Calcutta, 1960-67; grad. research asst. Social Sci. Research Center, Miss. State U., Starkville, 1967-70; asst. prof. sociology Tenn. Tech. U., Cookeville, 1970-74, asso. prof., 1974—, dir. alcohol safety program, 1974—. Mem. Am. Sociol. Assn., Internat. Rural Sociology Assn., Rural Sociol. Soc., So. Sociol. Soc., So. Assn. Agrl. Scientists, Southwestern Sociol. Assn., Mid-South Sociol. Assn., Indian Anthrop. Soc., Inst. Social Studies (India), Inst. Social Research and Applied Anthropology (India). Hindu. Club: Civitan. Editor: Rural Sociology in the South, 1977. Home: 1505 E 7th Cookeville TN 38501 Office: Box 5191 Tenn Tech Univ Cookeville TN 38501

MOON, BRYDEN EARL, educator; b. Houser, Md., June 8, 1918; s. Ellsworth G. and Oda Hope (Gnegy) M.; B.A. cum laude, U. Alaska, 1960; M.Ed., U. Ark., 1965, Ed.D., 1970; m. Sally Nitsche, July 31, 1943; children—Crystal Ann, Bryden Earl. Prof. aerospace studies U. Ark., Fayetteville, 1961-66, asst. dean men, 1967-68, graduate asst. to v.p. student affairs, 1968-69; prof. psychology, dean students Coll. of the Ozarks, Clarksville, Ark., 1969-80. Served to lt. col. USAF, 1937-66. Decorated Bronze Star. Mem. Am., Ark. personnel and guidance assns., Am. (state membership chmn. 1974-77), Ark. (pres. 1977-78) coll. personnel assns., Nat. Assn. Fgn. Student Advisors (state chmn. 1970-71), Phi Delta Kappa, Lambda Chi Alpha. Democrat. Roman Catholic. Club: K.C. Home: 1415 Buckingham Rd Winter Park FL 32789

MOON, EUNICE GRAFTON, hotel chain exec.; b. Atlanta, Sept. 22, 1925; d. George Farrington and Eunice (Hawes) Grafton; student John Marshall Law Sch., 1948; m. J. W. Moon, June 16, 1955; children—George Dennis, Robert Michael, James Lee. Group chief ops. So. Bell System, 1955-60; office mgr. Ansering Atlanta, 1960-67; dir. communications Hyatt Corp., Atlanta, 1967—. Home: 540 No 18 Old Front St Stone Mountain GA 30083 Office: 265 Peachtree St Atlanta GA 30302

MOON, GAIL JONES, librarian; b. Hawkinsville, Ga., Feb. 27, 1947; d. Algie Julian and Marcia (Perry) Jones; A.A., Middle Ga. Coll., 1966; B.A., U. Ga., 1968; M.L.S., Fla. State U., 1971; m. James Clinton Moon, May 8, 1976; 1 dau., Marcia Louise. Reference librarian Fling River Regional Library, Griffin, Ga., 1971-73; reference/acquisitions librarian Middle Ga. Coll., 1973-74; head reference dept. Washington Meml. Library, Macon, Ga., 1974-77, head librarian, 1977—. Mem. Ga. Library Assn., Southeastern Library Assn. Baptist. Office: 1180 Washington Ave Macon GA 31201

MOON, GERALD REX, banker; b. Atlanta, Aug. 16, 1936; s. Raymond Slaughter and Elizabeth Hempealey M.; B.S., Ga. Inst. Tech., 1959; grad. Stonier Sch. Banking, 1969; m. Mary Ellen Burtz, Apr. 21, 1963; children—LaTrelle, Rex, Alan. With 1st Nat. Bank of Atlanta, 1959-69, regional mgr. corp. banking, 1966-69; with Bank of Va., Richmond, 1969-74, exec. v.p., mgr. corp. banking, 1973-74; pres. City and County Banking Group, Knoxville, Tenn., 1974; pres. United Am. Bank in Knoxville, 1974—. Campaign chmn., dir. United Way of Knoxville, 1979; dir. U. Tenn. Sch. Bus., 1978—. Mem. Tenn. Banking Assn., Am. Bankers Assn., Robert Morris Assn., Knoxville C. of C. (dir.), Downtown Knoxville Assn. (dir.). Republican. Baptist. Clubs: Cherokee Country, Club LeConte (Knoxville); Cherokee Town and Country (Atlanta). Home: Route 4 Box 299 Beals Chapel Rd Lenoir City TN 37771 Office: PO Box 280 United American Plaza Knoxville TN 37901

MOON, JERRY ALTON, broadcasting co. exec.; b. Garden Valley, Tex., May 11, 1933; s. Homer Lee and Billie Viola (Nation) M.; student San Antonio Coll., 1964-68; m. Camilla Faith Kelley, Dec. 28, 1950; children—Tommy Dalton, Jerry Alton. Sales mgt. Sta. KEYE, Perryton, Tex., 1957-58; producer, announcer, dir., account exec. Sta. KFDA-TV, Amarillo, Tex., 1958-60; newsman, mng. editor Sta. KTSA, San Antonio, 1960-68; account exec. Sta. KONO, San Antonio, 1968-70, Sta. KBAT, San Antonio, 1970-71; v.p., gen. mgr. Gibson Broadcasting Co., Tyler and Beaumont, Tex., 1971-75; v.p., gen. mgr. Sta. KAPE-AM and KTUF-FM, San Antonio, 1975—. Bd. dirs. Project F.R.E.E. Recipient Fred D. Patterson award United Negro Coll. Fund, 1973; State of Tex. Merit award, 1977; M.K. Curry Extra Mile award, 1978. Mem. Nat. Assn. Broadcasters, Tex. Assn. Broadcasters, San Antonio Radio and Advt. Execs., Sales Mktg. Execs. San Antonio, Appliance Assn. San Antonio. Republican. Club: Masons. Home: 8318 Delphian St Universal City TX 78148 Office: 3900 ML King PO Box 20107 San Antonio TX 78220

MOON, JOHN HENRY, SR., banker; b. Van Buren, Ark., Aug. 19, 1937; s. B.R. and Alma (Witte) M.; A.A., Delmar Coll., Corpus Christi, 1956; B.B.A. cum laude, Tex. A. and I. Coll., 1958; m. Agnes Rose Dickens, Aug. 16, 1958; children—John Henry, Randall Allen. Sr. accountant Tex. Eastern Transp. Co. and subs.'s, 1958-63; exec. v.p., dir. Houston Research Inst., 1963-68; sr. v.p., asst. to chmn. bd., dir. Main Bank, 1968; vice chmn. bd., dir. N.E. Bank, 1969; chief exec. officer, chmn. bd., dir. Pasadena (Tex.) Nat. Bank, 1970—; gen. partner Moon and Assos., Ltd.; chmn. bd., pres. Interservice Life Ins. Corp., Phoenix, Community Ins. Co., Tex.; adv. dir., chmn. bd. Community Bank; adv. dir., adv. chmn. bd. Interstate Bank, Houston; adv. chmn. bd., dir. Tex. Independence Bank, Pasadena. Bd. dirs. Pasadena Heart Assn., Salvation Army, Tex. Assn. Prevention of Blindness; chmn. City of Pasadena Bd. Devel. Named Outstanding Young Man of Year, Pasadena Jr. C. of C., 1973, Outstanding Young Man of Am., 1973. Mem. Pasadena C. of C. (dir.), Am. Inst. C.P.A.'s, Tex. Soc. C.P.A.'s, Tex. (legis. affairs com.), Ind. bankers assns. Club: Rotary (dir.). Home: 3914 Peru Circle Pasadena TX 77504 Office: PO Box 992 Pasadena TX 77501

MOON, ROBERT ALLEN, JR., energy co. exec.; b. Eudora, Ark., Feb. 14, 1929; s. Robert Allen and Lillian (Hunnicutt) M.; student U. Tex., 1947-49; B.S. in Chem. Engring., La. Inst. Tech., 1952; m. Barbara J. Emerson, Jan. 26, 1952; children—Allen, Alicia, Joel, Nancy. Process engr. Gulf Oil Corp., Port Arthur, Tex., 1952-57; dir. planning and economics Venezuela Gulf Refining Co., 1957-65; mgr. ops. Caribbean Gulf Refining Co., Puerto Rico, 1965-67; mgr. ops. Gulf Oil U.S., Alliance Refinery, La., 1968-72; staff engr. Gulf Research and Devel. Co., Pitts., 1967-68, 72-73; tech. mgr. Panhandle Eastern Pipe Line Co., Houston, Tex., 1973-78; mgr. coal industry mktg. and mgmt. dept. Brown & Root Inc., Houston, 1978—. Served with USMC, 1952-54. Mem. Am. Inst. Chem. Engrs. Republican. Methodist. Holder gasoline treating patents. Home: 5611 Pebble Spring Dr Houston TX 77066 Office: PO Box 3 Houston TX 77001

MOONEY, JOSEPH FRANCIS, JR., flood control engr.; b. Boston, Feb. 6, 1929; s. Joseph Francis and Margaret Gertrude (Clements) M.; student Memphis State Coll., 1950-51; B.S., Miss. State U., 1954; m. Bobbie Katheryn Spencer, May 23, 1948; children—Marilyn Lee, Joseph Spencer. Asst. engr. St. Francis Levee Bd., West Memphis, Ark., 1954-63; chief engr. Yazoo-Miss. Delta Levee Bd., Clarksdale, Miss., 1964—. Mem. Sunflower River Devel. Commn., 1970—, Gov.'s Com. on Long Range Water Planning, 1969; treas. Clarksdale-Coahoma Airport Bd., 1976—; dist. dir. Delta Area council Boy Scouts Am., 1970, 71; deacon Oakhurst Bapt. Ch. Served with USNR, 1946-48, with USAF, 1951-52. Registered profl. engr., Ark., Miss. Mem. Miss. Engring. Soc. (chpt. pres. 1970), Lower Mississippi Valley Flood Control Assn. (chmn. engring. com. 1974), Water Resources Congress (nat. dir., chmn. region 5). Club: Rotary (pres. 1979). Home: 506 Catalpa St Clarksdale MS 38614 Office: PO Box 610 Clarksdale MS 38614

MOONEY, MARLIESE ELIZABETH, hosp. adminstr.; b. Bonn, Germany, June 25, 1929; came to U.S., 1949, naturalized, 1952; B.S., Concord Coll., 1964; M.A., W.Va. U., 1968; diploma Harvard U.; postgrad. U. Tex., Dallas; children—Barbara, Evelyn, Vivian, Charles. Tchr., Mercer County Bd. Edn., Princeton, W.Va., 1964-68; dir. nursing Princeton Community Hosp., 1969-72, asst. adminstr., 1972-73; adminstr. Garland (Tex.) Community Hosp., 1973-75, regional mgr., 1975-76; exec. dir. Med. City Dallas Hosp., 1976—. Mem. W.Va. Planning Commn. for Nursing, 1971-72; mem. Gov.'s Task Force for Legislation and Public Relations of Emergency Med. Care Com., 1971-73; bd. dirs. Home Health Care, So. W.Va. Regional Health Council, 1971-73. Recipient Outstanding Accomplishment award Humana Inc., 1974, Adminstr. of Yr. award, 1975; R.N., W.Va., Tex. Mem. Tex. Hosp. Assn., Concord Coll. Alumni Assn., W.Va. U. Alumni Assn., Harvard U. Alumni Assn. Club: Soroptimist Internat. Democrat. Roman Catholic. Office: 7777 Forest Ln Dallas TX 75230

MOOR, RALPH CARL, JR., economist; b. Atlanta, Jan. 2, 1941; s. Ralph Carl and Ruth Mavis (Sanders) M.; B.S., Ga. Inst. Tech., 1962; M.B.A., Ga. State U., 1967, Ph.D., 1971; m. Mary Carter Irving, Aug. 14, 1961; children—Wayne Tift, Tamara Sanders. Methods and cost analyst Citizens & So. Nat. Bank, Atlanta, 1964-67; adminstrv. asst., instr. Ga. State U., Atlanta, 1967-69; asst. prof. bus. adminstrn. Fla. Atlantic U., 1969-74, asst. dean coll. bus. and public adminstrn., 1972-74, asst. to pres., 1974-78, asso. prof., 1974—; mgmt. cons. Served with AUS, 1962-64. Mem. So. Econ. Assn. Author: (with others) Business Policy: A Framework for Analysis, 1972. Home: 1101 SW 4th St Boca Raton FL 33432 Office: Dept Bus Fla Atlantic U Boca Raton FL 33431

MOORE, ALICE EVELYN, social scientist; b. Washington, N.C., Feb. 16, 1933; d. Willie and Lillie Belle (Barrow) M.; B.S., Tuskegee Inst., 1955; M.A. (Coe fellow), N.Mex. Highlands U., 1962. Instr., Friendship Jr. Coll., Rock Hill, S.C., 1962-71, Elizabeth City (N.C.) State U., 1971-73; asst. prof. social scis. Claflin Coll., Orangeburg, S.C., 1974—. Dir. teenage program YWCA, Norfolk, Va., 1955-56; adv. Campus Gold Scouts; editor newsletter Treadwell St. Ch. Lilly scholar, 1977-78. Mem. NAACP, S.C. Literacy Assn., Black Social Workers Assn., Assn. for Study Afro-Am. Life and History (co-founder, sec.-treas.), S.C. Sociol. Assn., S.C. Social Welfare Forum, N.C. Sociol. Assn., Pi Gamma Mu. Home: 255 Treadwell St Orangeburg SC 29115 Office: Claflin Coll College St Orangeburg SC 29115

MOORE, ALLEN HOYT, JR., air force officer, hosp. adminstr.; b. New Market, Va., Mar. 19, 1923; s. Allen Hoyt and Faye (Alltsatt) M.; B.A. in Journalism, U. N.C., 1950, M.D., 1962; m. Martha Nell Cope, Nov. 6, 1965; children—Benjamin, Marcus, Joseph, Christopher, Kay. Served as flight instr., fighter pilot man U.S. Army Air Corps, 1942-46; sales mgr. typewriter div. Bus. Equipment Corp., Greensboro, N.C., 1950-54; researcher USPHS, 1954-58; intern Meml. Mission Hosp., Asheville, N.C., 1962-63; practice medicine specializing in family practice, Bryson City, N.C., 1963-65, Branson, Mo., 1965-75; commd maj. M.C., U.S. Air Force, 1975, advanced through grades to col., 1979; chief aeromed. services, Cannon AFB, N.Mex., 1975-76; comdr. USAF Hosp., Lajes, Azores, 1976-78, Reese AFB, Tex., 1978—; Clin. asst. prof. medicine U. Mo., 1970-76; asst. prof. health scis. Eastern N.Mex. U., 1975-76; clin. asso. prof. Tex. Tech. U. Sch. Medicine, 1978—; bd. dirs. Found. for Restoration of Physically Disfigured, 1975—. Decorated D.F.C., Meritorious Service medal, Air medal with oak leaf cluster; recipient Honor medal Soc. Portuguese Orthopaedic and Traumatological Surgeons, 1978. Mem. Am. Acad. Family Practice, Order of Daedalians (dir. 1979—). Home: 3006 69th St Lubbock TX 79413 Office: USAF Hosp Reese AFB TX 79489

MOORE, ALVIN EDWARD, patent lawyer; b. Auburn, La., Sept. 3, 1904; s. William Absalom and Mahala (Scoggins) M.; student U.S. Naval Acad., 1921-24, George Washington U. Law Sch., 1925, John Marshall Law Sch., Atlanta, 1945; B.S. in History and Engring., Am. U., 1949, M.A. in History, 1958; postgrad. U. Fla., 1955-56, La. State U., 1958-61, Tulane U. 1961-62; m. Laura Belle Van Zandt, May 26, 1925. Seaman, U.S. Shipping Bd., 1924; nautical scientist U.S. Hydrographic Office, 1924; patrol insp. U.S. Border Patrol, 1926-27, immigration insp. U.S. Immigration Service, 1927-28; Am. vice consul, Guaymas, Mex., 1928-29; examiner U.S. Patent Office, 1924-25, 30-42, 45-49, 56-58; intelligence officer CIA, 1949-50, 53-56; admitted to Ga. bar, 1945, U.S. Ct. Customs and Patent Appeals bar, 1947; patent atty. Army Ordnance Missile Command, 1958-60; practice as patent atty., Miss., 1960—. Co-founder Friends U.S. of Latin Am., 1950. Served with USN, 1921-24; from lt. to lt. comdr. USNR, 1942-46, comdr., 1950-53. Mem. Fed. Bar Assn., U.S. Naval Acad. Alumni Assn., Ret. Officers Assn. Clubs: Nat. Travel; Diamondhead Country and Yacht. Author: The World Republic, 1942; History of Hardy County, 1963; Mystery of the Skymen, 1979; contbr. articles, short stories, poems to various mags. Inventor with over 50 patents in various fields. Address: 8712 Manini Way Diamondhead Bay St Louis MS 39520

MOORE, BERNICE MILBURN (MRS. HARRY E. MOORE), mental health cons., author; b. San Antonio, June 17, 1904; d. Ted Hatton and Carrie (Cobey) Milburn; B.J., U. Tex., 1924, M.A., 1932; Ph.D., U. N.C., 1937; m. Harry Estill Moore, Nov. 27, 1924 (dec. July 1966). Reporter, Austin Am. and Statesman, 1924-26; dir. Child Welfare Survey Tex., Tex. Relief Commn., 1933-34; asst., Inst. Research Social Sci., U. N.C., 1934-37; asst. dir. Austin Regional Office, Profl. Projects, Work Projects Adminstrn. Tex., 1938-41; cons., Hogg Found. Mental Hygiene (name now Hogg Found. Mental Health), U. Tex., 1941-55, asst. to pres. community programs, 1955-72, exec. asso., spl. cons., 1972—, asso. dir. philanthropy in S.W., 1964-71; cons. home and family edn., counseling Tex. Edn. Agy., 1941-64, state adv. com. innovation and assessment edn., 1968-76; cons. inter-disciplinary program Nat. Inst. Child Health and Human Devel., NIH, 1965-67. Task force on youth Joint Commn. Mental Health of Children; coordinator Tex. Coop. Youth Study; dir. seminars for chaplains in counseling human factors USAF, sponsored by Hogg Found. Mental Health, 1956-66; spl. cons. research utilization br. Nat. Inst. Mental Health, 1963-64; adv. bd. children Children's Bur., U.S. Office Health, Edn., and Welfare, 1963-66, ad hoc com. for youth services, 1968-69. Chmn. adv. com. on med. and dental edn., coordinating bd. Tex. Coll. and U. System, 1973-74. Recipient Nat. Headliner award Theta Sigma Phi, 1956; Spl. Service award Tex. Soc. Mental Health, also Ft. Worth-Tarrant County Soc. Mental Health; spl. merit award Am. Vocational Assn., 1963; Distinguished Alumna award Ex-Students Assn. U. Tex., 1974; Bernice Milburn Moore Scholarship established U. Tex. at Austin, 1970. Fellow Am. Sociol. Assn., Am. Assn. Marriage and Family Counselors (hon.); mem. Nat. Assn. Mental Health, Am. Home Econs. Assn., Southwestern Social Sci. Assn., Tex. Assn. Mental Health, Tex. Council Mental Health (past pres.), Tex. Council Mental Health Research, Future Homemakers Am. (nat. hon. mem.), Alpha Kappa Delta, Theta Sigma Phi, Omicron Delta Kappa (hon. mem.), Delta Kappa Gamma, Phi Upsilon Omicron. Democrat. Mem. Disciples of Christ Ch. Author: (with Harry Estill Moore) Through Your Own Front Door, 1945; (with Dorothy M. Leahy) You and Your Family, 1948, rev. 1954; (with Robert L. Sutherland) Family, Community and Mental Health, 1950: Juvenile Delinquency, Research, Theory, Comment, 1959; (with W. H. Holtzman) Tomorrow's Parents, 1965; (with Robert L. Sutherland) Our Youngest Children, 1971; pamphlets and study guides on mental health and the family. Contbr. to edn. yearbooks. profl. jours. Home: 1215 W 22 1/2 St Austin TX 78705 Office: Hogg Found Mental Health Will C Hogg Bldg U Tex Austin TX 78712

MOORE, BRENDA FAYE, ednl. counselor; b. Martin, Tenn., Apr. 14, 1948; d. Paul Edward and Ruby Nell (Brock) Moore; B.S., U. Tenn., 1970; M.Ed., Memphis State U., 1976; m. William Bryant Bondurant, Sept. 7, 1968 (div.). Tchr., Collierville (Tenn.) High Sch., 1970-73; tchr., counselor Collierville (Tenn.) Middle Sch., 1973—. Mem. Nat., Collierville edn. assns., Nat. Sci. Tchrs. Assn., Nat. Assn. Environ. Edn., Am. Personnel and Guidance Assn., Phi Kappa Phi. Methodist. Author: Curriculum Guide for Environmental Education, grades 4-8, 1973. Developer drug and sex edn. programs. Home: 5941 Lucy Crest Memphis TN 38118 Office: Ross Elementary Sch 4890 Ross Rd Memphis TN 38138

MOORE, CHARLES EDWARD, steel co. ofcl.; b. Carnegie, Pa., Aug. 30, 1924; s. Charles Edney and Elizabeth Viola (McBride) M.; A.S.I.E., Pitts. Tech. Inst., 1950; m. Georgia Belle Mann, Nov. 20, 1948. Armature coil winder Pa. Elec. Coil Corp., Pitts., 1946-48; indsl. analyst Bethlehem Steel Co., Rankin, Pa., 1950-55, chief indsl. analyst, 1955-63; supr. indsl. engring. Fla. Steel Corp., Tampa, 1963-66, wage and salary adminstr., 1966-71, mgr. compensation, 1971—; instr., speaker, writer on wage and salary adminstrn.; compensation cons. Fla. Baptists, Univ.-Community Hosp., So. Assn. Steel Fabricators; ordained deacon Calvary Baptist Ch. Served with USAAF, 1943-46. Mem. Am. Compensation Assn., Adminstrv. Mgmt. Soc. Republican. Club: Feather Sound Country. Home: 13845 Whisperwood Dr Clearwater FL 33520 Office: PO Box 23328 Tampa FL 33623

MOORE, CHARLES ROBERT, ophthalmologist; b. Ill., Aug. 26, 1938; s. Robert R. and Marion Elizabeth Moore; B.S., Tex. A&M U., 1959; M.D., U. Tenn., 1962; children—Charles Robert, Kistal Michelle. Intern, Hermann Hosp., Houston, 1962-63; resident in ophthalmology U. Tex., Houston, 1969-72; practice medicine specializing in ophthalmology, Moultrie, Ga., 1972—; propr. Moore Eye Clinic, Moultrie, 1973—; gen. partner Moore and Moore, Oil and Gas Ventures, 1976-77; chmn. bd., exec. v.p. Moore Oil and Gas Inc., 1978—; pres. Spec Optical Inc.; nat. med. dir. Intermedics Intraocular, Inc., 1978-79; pres. Implant Tech. Inc.; mem. staff Colquitt County Meml. Hosp. Deacon, United Presbyn. Ch. U.S.A., Moultrie, 1977—. Served to capt. M.C., USAR, 1963-66. Decorated Air medal, Army Commendation medal; diplomate Am. Bd. Ophthalmology. Mem. AMA, Low Vision Clin. Soc. (charter), Am. Intraocular Lens Implant Soc., Am. Assn. Ophthalmology, So. Med. Assn., Ga. Med. Assn., Colquitt County Med. Soc. Club: Elks. Home: PO Box 1339 Moultrie GA 31768 Office: 2907 S Main St Moultrie GA 31768

MOORE, CHARLES WILSON, JR., cement mfg. ofcl.; b. Monahans, Tex., July 26, 1940; s. Charles Wilson and Natalie Ruth (Rash) M.; B.S. in Indsl. Engring., Tex. A&M U., 1963; M.B.A., Baylor U., 1974; grad. U.S. Steel Basic Mgmt. Program, 1977; m. Nancy Anita McNatt, Nov. 7, 1964; children—Collin Roberts, Derek James, Reagan Anita. Indsl. engr., project engr. Owens-Ill., Waco, Tex., 1965-68; mill operating engr., supt. operating Universal-Atlas div. U.S. Steel Corp., Waco, 1968—. Mem. City of Woodway Planning and Zoning Commn., 1976-78, chmn., 1978-79; capt. United Way of Waco, 1969-79, loaned exec., 1972, recipient award; active fin. drive St. Paul's Episcopal Ch., 1966-79, chmn., 1978. Served to capt. arty. U.S. Army, 1963-65, with USAR, 1965-69. Recipient award Tex. A&M Century Club, City of Woodway. Mem. Am. Inst. Indsl. Engrs. (past pres. local chpt.), Tex. A&M Alumni Assn., Baylor Alumni Assn., Assn. M.B.A. Execs. Clubs: Waco Hedonia (pres.), Woodland West Country. Home: 8264 Forest Ridge Dr Waco TX 76710 Office: PO Box 8176 Waco TX 76710

MOORE, CHRISTOPHER BARRY, mfg. co. exec.; b. Deal, Kent, Eng., Feb. 25, 1938; s. Ernest Stanley and Millicent Lillian (Harris) M.; diploma mgmt. studies Barking Regional Coll. Tech., Eng., 1966; m. Jill Irene Porter, July 6, 1963; came to U.S., 1977; children—Andrew, Stephen, Jeremy, Jennifer. Prodn. unit mgr. Plessey Co. Ltd., Ilford, Eng., 1968-70, productivity mgr., Upminster, 1970-72, regional indsl. engr., Ilford, 1972-74; mgr. mfg. devel. Northern Telecom Ltd., Montreal, Que., Can., 1974-77, dir. indsl. engring., Nashville, 1977—. Served with RAF, 1956-59. Mem. Am. Inst. Indsl. Engrs. (sr.), Inst. Electronic and Radio Engrs., Brit. Inst. Mgmt., Am. Mgmt. Assn., Soc. Mfg. Engrs. (sr.). Clubs: Indian Lake Forest Swim and Tennis, Middle Tenn Youth Soccer Assn. (dir.). Home: 293 Raintree Dr Hendersonville TN 37075

MOORE, CONARD DEA, ophthalmologist; b. Okmulgee, Okla., July 8, 1928; s. Conard Milton and Mildred Ezelle (Fenno) M.; B.A., Baylor U., 1950, M.D., 1955; m. Kitzia Poniatowska, Dec. 20, 1975; children—Pablo, Sean, Alex, Jeff, Kevin, Santiago, Constance, Kitzia. Intern, Meth. Hosp., Houston, 1956; resident in ophthalmology Baylor Coll. Medicine, 1960, asst. prof. ophthalmology, 1957-72; practice medicine, specializing in ophthalmology, Houston, 1980—; chief dept. ophthalmology Center Pavilion Hosp., Houston, 1980—, chief med. staff, 1980—. Served with U.S. Navy, 1948-53. Diplomate Am. Bd. Ophthalmology. Fellow A.C.S., Internat. Coll. Surgeons; mem. Soc. Eye Surgeons, Mil. Ophthalmol. Soc. Republican. Roman Catholic. Club: River Oaks Country. Office: 1700 E Holcombe Blvd Houston TX 77030

MOORE, DALTON, JR., petroleum engr.; b. Snyder, Tex., Mar. 25, 1918; s. Dalton and Anne (Yonge) M.; diploma Tarleton State U., 1938; B.S., Tex. A. and M. U., 1942; diploma U.S. Army Command and Gen. Staff Sch., 1945. Field engr. Gulf Oil Corp., 1946; dist. engr. Chgo. Corp., 1947-48, chief reservoir engr., 1949; mgr. Burdell Oil Corp., N.Y.C. and Snyder, Tex., 1950-52; mgr. Wimberly Field Unit, 1953-55; profl. petroleum cons., Abilene, Tex., 1956—; pres. Dalton Moore Engring. Co., 1957-67, First Oil Co., 1960-67, Second Oil Co., 1960-72, Petroleum Engrs. Operating Co., 1967—, Evaluation Engr. for Investment Bankers Corp., 1968—, Investment Bankers Oil Co., Inc., 1968—. Pres., Sweetwater (Tex.) Jr. C. of C., 1938; precinct chmn. Taylor County Democratic Com., 1956-76; bd. Bd. dirs. Taylor County chpt. ARC, 1956-62, Preini Log Library. Served from 2d lt. to maj., AUS, 1940-46. Eagle Scout, Boy Scouts Am. Mem. Am. Inst. Mining, Metall. and Petroleum Engrs. (chmn. W.Central Tex. sect. 1954), Abilene Geol. Soc., VFW. Address: 4065 Waldemar Dr Abilene TX 79605

MOORE, DIANE WHITT, med. technologist; b. Person County, N.C., Sept. 25, 1941; d. Elmer Lambeth and Hilda Franklin (Allen) Whitt; A.A. (Nat. Methodist scholar), Louisburg Jr. Coll., 1961; grad. Watts Hosp. Sch. Med. Tech., Durham, N.C., 1961-62; postgrad. U. N.C., Chapel Hill, 1962; B. Health Scis. (Univ. Continuing Edn. grantee), Duke U., 1981; m. Harry Daniel Moore, Oct. 29, 1966; 1 dau., Julie de Anne. Chief technologist Person County Meml. Hosp., Roxboro, N.C., 1963-65; clin. chemistry supr. Duke U. Med. Center, 1966-69, staff supt. STAT lab., microchemistry, lab. collection service, 1970-78, clin. lab. mgr., hosp. labs., 1978—. Treas. local PTA, Durham, 1976-78. Named Bus. and Profl. Woman of Year, Roxboro Club, 1965. Mem. Am. Soc. Med. Technologists, Am. Soc. Clin. Pathologists (affiliate; cert.). Contbr. articles to profl. jours.; research in multi-channel autoanalyzer; editor Unitarian Newsletter, 1979—. Home: 4602 Regis Ave Durham NC 27705 Office: PO Box 2902 Duke U Med Center Durham NC 27710

MOORE, DONALD EARL, educator; b. Meridian, Miss., Feb. 18, 1938; s. Claude Melton and Elsie Mae (Higginbotham) M.; B.S., Miss. So. Coll., 1961; M.Ed., U. So. Miss., 1971, postgrad., 1975-76; postgrad. U. Miss., 1976-78; m. Nancy Carole Adams, Sept. 18, 1966; 1 son, Donald Christopher. Tchr. math. Choctawatchee Sr. High Sch., Shalimar, Fla., 1961-65, Petal (Miss.) Sr. High Sch., 1965-66; geol. asst. Chevron Oil Co., New Orleans, 1967-69; instr. speech and theatre Jeff Davis campus Miss. Gulf Coast Jr. Coll., Gulfport, 1969-77, media coordinator, 1977—; lighting and sound cons. Exec. v.p. Biloxi (Miss.) Little Theatre; cubmaster Cub Scouts, 1978—. U. So. Miss. Summer Theater Scholar, summer 1966. Mem. Am. Theatre Assn., Miss. Theatre Assn., Mississippians for Ednl. TV, Southeastern Theatre Conf., Miss. Assn. Media Educators, Assn. Edn. Communication and Tech. Democrat. Baptist. Home: 3 Lexington Pl Gulfport MS 39501 Office: Jeff Davis Campus Miss Gulf Coast Jr Coll Switzer Rd Gulfport MS 39501

MOORE, FRED HENRY, lawyer; b. Chattanooga, July 24, 1943; s. Alvin O'Brien and Annie Kate (Rebman) M.; A.B. in Math., Duke U., 1965; J.D., Duke U., 1968; m. Diane Campbell, July 1, 1967; children—Fred Henry, Andy Rebman. Admitted to Tenn. bar, 1968, Ga. bar, 1974; asso. firm Spears, Moore, Rebman & Williams, Chattanooga, 1968-73, partner, 1973—; spl. prof. bus. law U. Tenn., Chattanooga, 1969; mem. Estate Planning Council; officer Antique Armory, Inc.; officer, treas. Blue Springs, Inc. Dir. Girls Club, Inc., Lookout Mountain Meml. Fund, St. Barnabas Nursing Home, Inc., St. Barnabas Apts., Inc. Served with U.S. Army, 1968-69. Mem. Am. Bar Assn., Tenn. Bar Assn., Fed. Bar Assn., Ga. Bar Assn., Chattanooga Bar Assn., Lookout Mountain Bar Assn., Am. Soc. Hosp. Attys., Am. Law and Med. Soc., Tenn. Soc. Hosp. Attys. Presbyterian. Clubs: Mountain City, Fairyland. Home: 109 Glenview St Lookout Mountain TN 37350 Office: 8th Floor Blue Cross Bldg Chattanooga TN 37402

MOORE, GEORGE MILTON, ednl. adminstr.; b. Seneca, S.C., Aug. 11, 1931; s. Thomas S. and Irene (Elrod) M.; student U. Tex., 1951; B.S., Clemson U., 1958; postgrad. Brakely/John Price Jones Inst. in Mgmt., 1972, Nat. Fund Raising Inst. U. Chgo., 1978; m. Sara Elizabeth (Betty) Mason, Nov. 31, 1959; 1 dau., Allison Lyn. Sports dir. Blue Ridge Broadcasting Co., Seneca, 1953-58; field rep. Clemson (S.C.) U alumni relations staff, 1959-67, asst. dir. alumni and public relations, 1967-69, asso. dir. alumni relations 1969-76, dir. alumni relations, 1976—, univ. devel. coordinator, 1978—. Exec. dir. Tri City area Heart Fund Unit, Clemson, 1973-77; mem. Mayor's Council for Community Improvement, Clemson, 1974-75. Served with SAC, USAF, 1949-53; Korea, Japan, Eng., N. Africa. Recipient Disting. Service award Clemson U., 1976, Disting. Service award Heart Fund, 1977; Named Man of Yr. Fort Hill Clemson U. Club, 1971. Mem. Am. Alumni Council, Council for Advancement and Support of Edn., Blue Key, Pi Kappa Alpha. Republican. Methodist. Club: Lions (dir. 1966-68, 2d v.p. 1969, 1st v.p. 1970, dist. gov.'s cabinet 1967-69). Contbr. articles on edn. to profl. publs. Home: 200 Willow St Clemson SC 29631 Office: University Alumni Center Clemson Univ Clemson SC 29631

MOORE, GEORGE WILSON, III, microbiologist, hosp. lab. adminstr.; b. Berea, Ky., Sept. 19, 1947; s. George Wilson and Katherine (Stith) M.; B.A. in Chemistry, Berea Coll., 1969; M.T., Good Samaritan Hosp., Lexington, Ky., 1970; M.S. in Microbiology, Eastern Ky. U., 1973; Ph.D. in Med. Parasitology, U. N.C., 1978. Med. technologist Good Samaritan Hosp., 1969-70; chief med. technologist Mary Chiles Hosp., Mt. Sterling, Ky., 1970-71; dir. clin. parasitology and urinalysis, adminstrv. dir. labs. dept. pathology Baylor U. Med. Center, Dallas, 1978—, instr. Sch. Med. Tech., 1978—; cons., co-investigator Millipore Corp., Bedford, Mass.; Nat. Inst. Allergy and Infectious Diseases research grantee, 1973-78. Mem. AAAS, Am. Soc. Microbiology, Am. Soc. Parasitologists, Am. Soc. Tropical Medicine and Hygiene, Am. Soc. Zoologists, Clin. Radioassay Soc., N.Y. Acad. Scis., Sigma Xi. Mem. Christian Ch. (Disciples of Christ). Home: 5746 Caruth Haven Ln Apt 3-208 Dallas TX 75206 Office: Dept Pathology Baylor U Med Center 3500 Gaston Ave Dallas TX 75246

MOORE, GERALD JASON, ins. co. exec.; b. Lancaster, Pa., Dec. 31, 1935; s. Jason Hess and Helen Elizabeth (Griel) M.; B.S. in Econs., Franklin and Marshall Coll., 1957; M.B.A., St. Mary's U., San Antonio, 1976; children by previous marriage—Scott Eric, David Brian. Asst. mgr. claims United Services Auto Assn., San Antonio, 1972-73, mgr. customer service, 1973-78, dir. mgmt. devel. tng., 1978—; bd. dirs. United Services Auto Assn. Fed. Credit Union; prof. ins. St. Mary's U., 1978-79. Bd. dirs. continuing edn. program U. Tex., San Antonio. Served with USAF, 1957-60. Mem. C.P.C.U.'s (dir. Alamo chpt.), Air Force Assn., Am. Soc. Tng. Dirs., Greater San Antonio C. of C. (ambassador team capt. 1973-76). Club: Masons. Home: 3006 Briarfield San Antonio TX 78230 Office: USAA Bldg San Antonio TX 78288

MOORE, GLOVER, educator; b. Birmingham, Ala., Sept. 22, 1911; s. Glover and Maud (Mims) M.; B.A., Birmingham-So. Coll., 1932; M.A., Vanderbilt U., 1933, Ph.D., 1936. Teaching fellow Vanderbilt U., 1935-36; instr. history Miss. State U., 1936-38, asst. prof., 1938-46, asso. prof., 1946-53, prof., 1953-77, prof. emeritus, 1977—. Pres. Miss. Hist. Soc., 1970-71. Served with Adj. Gen.'s Dept., AUS, 1942-46. Mem. Am., So. hist, assns., Orgn. Am. Historians. Episcopalian. Author: The Missouri Controversy, 1819-1821, 1953; William Jemison Mims, Soldier and Squire, 1966; editor: A Calhoun County, Alabama, Boy in the 1860s, 1978. Home: 404 Myrtle St Starkville MS 39759 Office: Box 5326 Mississippi State MS 39762

MOORE, HARRY VANE, mgmt. cons.; b. Charlotte, N.C., July 27, 1927; s. Lloyd W. and Verla Jane M.; B.B.A., U. Ga., 1954; m. M. Clarice Cooper, July 6, 1974; children—James David, John Jeffery, Kon-tiki McGravy. Account exec. Gen. Foods Inc., White Plains, N.Y., 1959-61; nat. sales mgr. vending and wholesale div. Gordon Foods Co. div. Sunshine Biscuit Inc., Atlanta, 1961-69; chmn. bd., pres. Moore Brokerage Co., Inc., Lithonia, Ga., 1969-75; chmn. bd., v.p., sec. treas. Lithonia Execs. Services, Inc., 1974—; cons. regional v.p., mem. exec. com. Integrated Control Systems, Inc., Litchfield, Conn., 1975-78; cons. v.p. Am. Mgmt. Systems Co., Inc., Washington, 1978-79. Served with USN, 1945-49; PTO. Mem. Nat. Wholesale Candy Assn., So. Candy and Tobacco Assn., VFW, Am. Legion. Republican. Lutheran. Club: Fairington Golf and Tennis. Office: PO Box 236 Lithonia GA 30058

MOORE, HOWARD VICTOR, concrete co. exec.; b. Kingsville, Tex., Oct. 22, 1948; s. Howard Victor and Marjorie Dolores (Alsup) M.; B.S., Tex. A&M U., 1971; m. Martha Day Risdon, Sept. 30, 1972; children—Mary Christine, Victoria Day. Jr. engr. Heldenfels Bros., Corpus Christi, Tex., 1971-72, estimator horizontal constrn., 1972-74, salesman-estimator precast concrete, 1974-77, sales mgr. precast div., 1977-79, operation dir., 1980—. Served with C.E., USAR, 1971—. Mem. Am. Concrete Inst., Soc. Am. Mil. Engrs., Am. Mgmt. Assn., Prestressed Concrete Inst. (mem. hollowcore com.), Tex. Precast Concrete Mfrs. Assn. (pres.). Republican. Presbyterian. Home: 541 Greenway St Corpus Christi TX 78412 Office: 521 McBride St Corpus Christi TX 78408

MOORE, HUGH JACOB, JR., lawyer; b. Norfolk, Va., June 29, 1944; s. Hugh Jacob and Ina Ruth (Hall) M.; B.A., Vanderbilt U., 1966; LL.B., Yale, 1969; m. Jean Garnett, June 10, 1972; children—Lela Miller, Sarah Garnett. Admitted to Tenn. bar, 1970, U.S. Supreme Ct. bar, 1973; law clk. U.S. Dist. Court, Middle Dist. of Tenn., Nashville, 1969-70; asst. U.S. atty., Eastern Dist. of Tenn., Chattanooga, 1973-76; asso. Witt, Gaither & Whitaker, Chattanooga, 1976-77, partner, 1977—. Mem. bd. dirs. Adult Edn. Council, Chattanooga, 1976—, pres., 1977—; mem. alumni council McCallie Sch. Mem. Am., Tenn., Chattanooga, Fed. bar assns., Baptist. Home: 315 Hemphill Ave Chattanooga TN 37411 Office: 1100 American National Bank Bldg Chattanooga TN 37402

MOORE, JACK MICHAEL, engr.; b. Enid, Okla., July 16, 1913; s. John and Rose Ellen (Reynolds) M.; B.S., U. Okla., 1939; m. Frances Elizabeth Clark, Sept. 6, 1941; With Dowells div. Dow Chem. Co., service engr., Flora, Salem and Grayville, Ill., 1939-43, sta. mgr., Levelland, Tex., 1943-46, devel. engr., Midland, Tex., 1946-47, dist. engr., 1947-58, asst. dist. mgr., 1958-68; dir. personnel City of Midland (Tex.), 1968-79; cert. instr. Defensive Driving Course and multimedia 1st aid. Bd. executors Permian Basin Mus., Library and Hall of Fame; mem. cabinet United Way of Midland. Named Citizen of Year Midland Kiwanis Club, 1973. Mem. Assn. City Personnel Dirs. (life), C. of C., Am. Soc. Safety Engrs., Am. Assn. Petroleum Geologists, Soc. Petroleum Engrs., Am. Soc. Tng. and Devel. Clubs: Permain Toastmasters, Downtown Kiwanis (pres. 1972). Co-author various tech. papers. Home: 1905 W Tennessee St Midland TX 79701

MOORE, JAMES CLAYTON, III, retail exec.; b. Washington, Apr. 5, 1949; s. James Clayton and Charlotte Elizabeth (Hopkins) M.; student Emory U., 1967-69; B.A., U. S.C., 1971. With Jim Moore Cadillac-Oldsmobile, Inc., Columbia, S.C., 1969—, bus. mgr., 1975-76, gen. mgr., 1976—. Mem. Columbia Auto Dealers Assn. (past v.p., pres.; treas. 1979—), Central S.C. Alumni Assn. (past pres.), Sales Mktg. Execs. Internat. Clubs: Kiwanis, WildeWood, Columbia Sailing. Home: 220 Raintree Dr Irmo SC 29063 Office: 2222 Main St Columbia SC 29201

MOORE, JAMES FRANCIS, II, marine surveyor; b. Bklyn., Dec. 14, 1949; s. James Francis and Dorothy Ann (Grennan) M.; B.S. in Marine Engring., Tex. Maritime Acad., Tex. A. and M. U., 1973; m. Louisa May Sikes, Feb. 27, 1976. Marine engr. Designers & Planners, Inc., Galveston, Tex., 1973-74; pres. Matthews Daniel Marine, Inc., Houston, 1974—. Mem. Tex. Soc. Profl. Engrs. (engr.-in-tng.), Soc. Naval Architects and Marine Engrs., Galveston C. of C. (commerce oceanography com. 1971-72). Roman Catholic. Clubs: Galveston Rugby Football, Port of Galveston Propeller. Home: 1186 Sailfish Hitchcock TX 77563 Office: PO Box 26836 Houston TX 77207

MOORE, JAMES KENNETH, SR., computer scientist; b. Franklin, Ky., Oct. 3, 1943; s. James Turnie and Hassie Cleon (Coley) M.; B.E., Vanderbilt U., 1965; postgrad. U. Md., 1968-70; M.B.A., Va. Tech., 1980; m. Cherie Faye Meyer, Nov. 10, 1973; children—James Kenneth, Aimee Catherine, David Michael. Commd. ensign U.S. Navy, 1965, advanced through grades to lt. comdr., 1973; with Naval Security Group, Ft. Meade, Md., 1968-70; electronic engr. Nat. Security Agy., Ft. Meade, 1970-75; computer scientist Def. Communications Agy., Reston, Va., 1976—. Mem. IEEE, Armed Forces Communications and Electronics Assn., Naval Res. Assn., Am. Mgmt. Assn., St. Bernard Fanciers Assn. Republican. Presbyterian. Home: 12345 Coleraine Ct Reston VA 22091 Office: 11440 Newton Sq N Reston VA 22090

MOORE, JAMES WALLACE, educator; b. Birmingham, Ala., Feb. 19, 1923; s. Felix Tyre and Mary (Ingraham) M.; student Berea Coll., 1941-42; B.A., Tenn. Poly. Inst., 1951; M.S., U. Ky., 1952; Ph.D., Purdue U., 1962; m. Doris Jean Livingston, Sept. 3, 1948; children—Karen Sue, Joyce Ann, James Wallace II. Project engr. Carbide and Carbon Chem. Co., South Charleston, W. Va., 1952-55; sr. project engr. Allison div. Gen. Motors Corp., Indpls., 1955-57; research asst. Purdue U., West Lafayette, Ind., 1958-62; sr. research engr. Jet Propulsion Lab., Cal. Inst. Tech., summers 1960-61; asso. prof. U. Va., Charlottesville, 1962-67, prof., 1967—, mem. univ. senate, 1967-71, U. Va. Sesquicentennial fellow, Barcelona, Spain, 1971-72. Co-chmn. Automatic Control Group, 1967—; cons. automatic controls U.S. Army; cons. automobile accident and failure analysis, various legal and ins. firms. Pres., Woodbrook PTA, 1966; mem. Albemarle County Planning Commn., 1976—; mem. Albemarle County Republican Com., 1966-71. Served with AUS, 1943, 45-46; USAF, 1944. Fellow ASME (chmn. exec. com. automatic control div. 1971, paper rev. chmn. automatic control div. 1965-67, mem. exec. com. automatic control div. 1967-72, chmn. honors com. 1973-74, del. policy bd. basic engring. dept. 1976—, chmn. mem. interests 1976); mem. Am. Automatic Control Council (dir. 1972-73, program chmn. 1965 Joint Automatic Control Conf., gen. chmn. 1981 Conf.), N.Y. Acad. Sci., Soc. Automotive Engrs., Internat. Platform Assn., Sigma Xi, Pi Tau Sigma, Tau Beta Pi. Baptist (deacon 1969-72). Contbr. articles to profl. jours. Patentee automotive safety screen, jet engine variable nozzle; research in reading machine for the blind, learning control and patterns, indsl. robots. Home: 3409 Indian Spring Rd Charlottesville VA 22901

MOORE, JAMES YOUNG, mcht.; b. Florence, Ala., Jan. 24, 1913; s. Charles Wallace and Ada Jane (Young) M.; student U. Tenn., N.Y. U.; m. Elizabeth Lumpkin, Jan. 8, 1938; children—James Young, Mary Jane (Mrs. Timothy J. Cambias), Elizabeth Diane (Mrs. James D. Cone), Susan Wallace (Mrs. Danny Wilson), Molly Ann. Mfg. rep. Schloss Bros., Balt., 1936-39; organizer, chmn. bd. Jim Moore Co., Lawrenceburg, Tenn., 1939—; organizer Quality Cleaners, 1940—; owner Double M Ranch, 1972—; organizer Lawrence County Bank, Lawrenceburg. Rep. exec. seminar men's wear store mgmt. N.Y. U., 1967. Past Internat. dir. Boy Scouts Am.; past dir. Am. Cancer Soc.; exec. com. Citizens for Ct. Modernization; sponsor Citizens for Decent Lit., Help Hospitalized Vets.; nat. adv. bd. Am. Security Council; participant First Nat. Conf. on Jud. selection and Tenure Am. Judicature Soc. and U. Denver Coll. Law, 1974; hon. citizen Boys Town. Presdl. elector at large for Tenn., 1936; nat. committeeman Young Republican Fedn., 1938-48; del. Rep. Nat. Conv., 1940; campaigner, mem. Republican Nat. Com., mem. finance com. for re-election Pres., 1972. Fellow Menninger Found. Named Valuable Human Resource of U.S. by Am. Bicentennial Research Inst. Mem. C. of C. (past nat. counselor, past dir.), Internat. Platform Assn., Am. Judicature Soc., Farm Bur., Men's Wear Retailers Am., Tenn. Conf. to Improve Adminstrn. Justice, U.S. Senatorial Club (founding mem.), Delta Tau Delta (life). Republican. Mem. Ch. of Christ. Club: Wally Byam Caravan. Home: 5 Locust St Hwy 43 Lawrenceburg TN 38464 Office: 39 NW Public Square Lawrenceburg TN 38464

MOORE, JEFF ROBERTSON, plastic surgeon; b. Jackson, Miss., Nov. 19, 1928; s. George Hyer and Ruth Caroline (Robertson) M.; B.A. cum laude, Vanderbilt U., 1950, M.D., 1953; m. Virginialee Hoffman, May 30, 1953; children—Ruthann, Jeff Robertson, Christina Jane. Intern, U. Minn. Hosp., 1953-54, resident surgery, 1954; resident surgery U. Tex. Med. Br., Galveston, 1957-59; resident plastic surgery Kansas City (Mo.) Gen. Hosp., 1959-61; pvt. practice plastic surgery, Amarillo, Tex., 1961—; mem. staff St. Anthony's, N.W. Tex., High Plains Baptist hosps.; cons. VA Hosp., Amarillo; asso. clin. prof. Tex. Tech. U. Sch. Medicine, 1973—. Trustee Amarillo Ind. Sch. Dist., 1970-76, pres., 1973. Served with AUS, 1955-57. Diplomate Am. Bd. Plastic Surgery, Am. Bd. Surgery. Mem. Am., Tex., Potter-Randall County med. assns., Am. Soc. Plastic and Reconstructive Surgery, A.C.S., Am. Cleft Palate Assn., Tex. Soc. Plastic Surgeons (pres. 1975-76), Amarillo Surg. Soc. (pres. 1974), Am. Assn. Hand Surgery, Am. Soc. Aesthetic Surgery, Phi Beta Kappa. Baptist (deacon). Club: Amarillo. Home: 8 Woodstone Amarillo TX 79106 Office: Medical Plaza 5211 W 9th St PO Box 3755 Amarillo TX 79106

MOORE, JOHN ISHAM, JR., mathematician, computer scientist, educator; b. Camden, S.C., May 25, 1948; s. John Isham and Hazel (Adams) M.; B.S. in Math., The Citadel, 1970; Ph.D. in Math., U. S.C., 1975; M.S. in Computer Sci., Ga. Inst. Tech., 1979; m. Kayran Leary Cox, June 6, 1970; children—John Isham III, Robert Leary. Asst. prof. Coll. Charleston (S.C.), 1975-76; asst. prof. dept. math. The Citadel, Charleston, 1976-80, asso. prof., 1980—. Served with USAR. Daniel scholar, 1966-70; NASA trainee, 1972. Mem. Math. Assn. Am., Assn. Computing Machinery, Ops. Research Soc. Am., AAUP. Methodist. Contbr. articles to math. jours. Home and Office: The Citadel Charleston SC 29409

MOORE, JOHN NORTON, diplomat, lawyer; b. N.Y.C., June 12, 1937; s. William Thomas and Lorena (Norton) M.; A.B., Drew U., 1959; LL.B., Duke, 1962; LL.M., U. Ill., 1965; fellow Yale Law Sch., 1965-66. Admitted to Fla. bar, 1962, Ill. bar, 1963, Va. bar, 1969, D.C. bar, 1973, U.S. Supreme Ct. bar, 1972; asst. dean, asso. prof. law U.

Fla. Sch. Law, 1963-65; prof. law, dir. grad. program U. Va. Sch. Law, 1966—, sesquicentennial asso. Center for Advanced Studies, 1971-72, dir. Center for Oceans Law and Policy, 1976—, Walter L. Brown prof. law, 1976—; counselor on internat. law Dept. State, 1972-73; chmn. NSC Interagy. Task Force on Law of the Sea, dep. spl. rep. of Pres. (with rank ambassador) for Law of Sea Conf., 1973-76; fellow Woodrow Wilson Internat. Center for Scholars, 1976; U.S. rep. UN Seabeds Com., 1973, 3d UN Conf. on Law of the Sea; mem. U.S. del. UN Gen. Assembly; cons. Naval War Coll., Nat. War Coll., Fgn. Service Inst., Judge Adv. Gen. Sch., Dept. State. Mem. Am. Bar Assn. (vice chmn. sect. internat. law), Council Fgn. Relations, Phi Beta Kappa, Order of Coif. Clubs: N.Y. Yacht; Fgn. Service, Cosmos (Washington). Author: Law and the Indo-China War, 1972; editor: Law and Civil War in the Modern World, 1974; The Arab-Israeli Conflict, Vol. I-III, 1974, 1-vol. edit., 1977; bd. editors Am. Jour. Internat. Law, 1970, Marine Tech. Soc. Jour., 1977—. Home: Route 10 Box 824 Charlottesville VA 22901 Office: U Va Sch Law Charlottesville VA 22901

MOORE, JOHN STERLING, JR., clergyman; b. Memphis, Aug. 25, 1918; s. John Sterling and Lorena (Bounds) M.; student Auburn U., 1936-37; A.B., Samford U., 1940; Th.M., So. Baptist Theol. Sem., 1944; m. Martha Louise Paulette, July 6, 1944; children—Sterling Hale, John Marshall, Carolyn Paulette. Ordained to ministry Bapt. Ch., 1942; pastor in Pamplin, Va., 1944-48, Amherst, Va., 1949-57, Manly Meml. Bapt. Ch., Lexington, Va., 1957—. Mem. hist. commn. So. Bapt. Conv., 1968-75, vice chmn., 1973-74; mem. sesquicentennial com. Bapt. Gen. Assn. Va., 1972-73; pres. Va. Bapt. Pastor's Conf., 1963. Chmn. Lexington Mayor's Com. Race Relations, 1962-65. Bd. dirs. Rockbridge Mental Health Assn., 1962-72; bd. dirs. Rockbridge Mental Health Clinic, 1967—, treas., 1971—; bd. dirs. Stonewall Jackson Hosp., Lexington, 1967-71, pres., 1969-70. Mem. Va. Bapt. Hist. Soc. (exec. com. 1964—, pres. 1977-78), So. Baptist Hist. Soc. (dir. 1972, pres. 1975-76, sec. 1977—). Club: Masons. Co-author: Meaningful Moments in Virginia Baptist Life, 1972. Contbr. articles to profl. jours. Editor: Va. Bapt. Register, 1972—; Va. editor Ency. So. Bapts., vol. 3, 1971. Home: 463 2444 30 Sellers Ave Lexington VA 24450 Office: 463 4181 Main at Preston Sts Lexington VA 24450

MOORE, JOYCE WEST, psychiat. social worker; b. Anadarko, Okla., Nov. 18, 1936; d. Carl Edwin and Alma Hunter (Pulis) West; B.S., U. Okla., 1958; M.S. in Social Work, U. Tex., Arlington, 1973; children—Richard Britain, Cynthia Jane. Pub. welfare worker Tex. Dept. Welfare, Dallas, 1971-72; clin. social worker Med. Center, Baylor U., Dallas, 1972-76, rehab. team, 1973-76; field practicum supr. dept. rehab. sci. U. Tex. Health Scis. Centers at Dallas, 1974-75; psychiat. social worker, instr. dept. psychiatry Sch. Medicine, Tex. Tech. U., Lubbock, 1976-78, also mem. child psychiatry treatment and teaching team, cons. alcoholism treatment program and emergency room Health Scis. Centers Hosp., also chmn. edn. com. dept. social work, 1976-78, coordinating council for staff devel., ambulatory clinic, 1977-78; coordinator out-patient services, psychiat. social worker Mental Health Services So. Okla., Ada, 1978-79, program cons. outpatient and follow-up services, 1979—, field supr. dept. nursing and dept. human resources; adv. com. Okla. Dept. Mental Health; bd. dirs. Gestalt Inst. Dallas; adv. bd. Project Provide, No. Tex.; speaker bur. for parent edn. YWCA and Tex. Dept. Human Resources, Lubbock, 1977-78; mem. adv. council social work concentration dept. human resources East Central U., Ada. Bd. dirs. Am. Cancer Soc., sec.-treas. Montague County, Tex., 1963-64; bd. dirs. Planned Parenthood Assn. Am., treas. Cleveland County, Okla., 1966-67; Panel Am. Women, Wichita, Kans., and Dallas, 1959-73; vol. tchr. YWCA pre-sch., Wichita, 1967-68; pres. Women's Soc. Christian Service, West Heights United Methodist Ch., Wichita, 1969-70, exptl. worship com., 1968-70, dir. Lay Acad., 1967-70, dir. vacation ch. sch., 1967; lay leader Casa View United Meth. Ch., Dallas, 1971-74, chmn. adminstrv. bd., 1971-74, dist. del., 1971-73, del. ann. conf., 1971-73, mem. nominating com., 1973-75, mem. pastor-parish relations com., 1971-74, adminstrv. bd., commn. on social concerns; mem. adminstrv. bd., chancel choir 1st United Meth. Ch. Registered social worker, Okla.; lic. social psychotherapist. Mem. Acad. Certified Social Workers, Nat. Assn. Social Workers (speaker profl. symposium 1977, dir. Okla. chpt., chmn. S.E. Okla. unit), Nat. Rehab. Counseling Assn., U. Okla. Alumni Assn., Beta Sigma Phi, Chi Omega Alumnae Assn. Clubs: Amity (Bowie, Tex., pres. 1962-63), Tex. Fedn. Women's Clubs, Ada (Okla.) Tennis. Office: Mental Health Services Southern Oklahoma 111 E 12th St PO Box 1965 Ada OK 74820

MOORE, KENNETH LEE, indsl. engr.; b. Fayetteville, N.C., Jan. 10, 1947; s. Raymond Lee and Ruth Virginia (Kirby) M.; B.S., N.C. State U., 1969; m. Janice Lynne Williford, May 31, 1975; 1 dau., Suzanne. Indsl. engr. U.S. Steel Co., Johnstown, Pa., 1969-71; with civil service U.S. Army, 1971—, indsl. engr., Fort Bragg, N.C., 1973-76, chief indsl. engr., 1976—. Deacon MacPherson Presbyterian Ch., chmn. bd. deacons, 1974-75, elder, 1978—; active Boy Scouts Am. Mem. Am. Instn. Indsl. Engrs., Nat. Eagle Scout Assn., N.C. State U. Alumni Assn. Democrat. Club: Masons. Home: 403 Roxie Ave Fayetteville NC 28304 Office: Indsl Engr Office Materiel Maintenance Div Fort Bragg NC 28307

MOORE, KENNETH LIGHT, food mfg. co. exec.; b. Calhoun, Ga., Nov. 22, 1930; s. Luther Lafay and Grace Clare (Henderson) M.; B.S., Clemson U., 1955; m. Mary Marcia Poole, Sept. 10, 1955; children—Margaret Grace, Marcia Leigh, Kenneth Light. Sales trainee, dist. sales, mktg. dept. chain rep., sales mgr., Sealtest Foods Co., Knoxville, Tenn., 1960-64; dist. mgr. Kinnett-Dairles, Pie Co., 1962-64; br. mgr. Pine State Dairy, 1964-71; gen. mgr. Kinnett-Dauvies, 1964-69; dist. mgr. Flav-o-Rich Inc., Columbus, Ga., 1971-72, asst. mgr. div., 1972-73, mgr. div., 1973-74, mgr. corp. mktg. and sales dept., 1974-79, group v.p., 1979—. Active Fellowship Christian Athletes, Jr. Achievement Columbus. Served with USMCR, 1950-52. Mem. Milk Industry Found., Ga. Dairy Assn., Atlanta Food Sales Exec. Club, Clemson Alumni Assn. Democrat. Presbyterian. Clubs: Columbus Country, Fox Den Country, Kiwanis. Home: 733 Whirlaway Circle Knoxville TN 37919 Office: 315 Erin Dr Knoxville TN 37919

MOORE, KENT OAKLEY, audiovisual cons.; b. San Antonio, Aug. 9, 1930; s. John Douglas and Lela Rebecca (Oakley) M.; B.A., St. Mary's U., 1969; student Southwestern U., U. Tex.; m. Barbara Leah Barbee, Jan. 29, 1952; children—Mark, Kevin, Julie, Janette. With Channel 5, San Antonio, 1952-67; dir. ops. Sta. KLRN, U. Tex., Austin, 1967-68; program dir. Acad. Health Scis., U.S. Army, San Antonio, 1969-78; audio visual officer Am. Forces Radio and TV, Panama, 1978—; audio visual cons.; owner Jill's Costume Shops, San Antonio. Recipient Public Service awards Health Edn. Media Assn., 1977. Mem. Press Assn., Nat. Assn. Ednl. Broadcasters, Nat. Costumers Assn., Health Edn. Media Assn., Navy League. Clubs: Lions, Rotary, San Antonio Media. Home: 2460 Harry Wurzbach St San Antonio TX 78209 Office: PO Box 1789 APO Miami 34004

MOORE, LEON, bank auditor; b. Raymond, Miss., June 22, 1952; s. Jimmie and Willie Mae M.; B.S. cum laude in Bus. Adminstrn., Alcorn State U., 1974; M.B.A., U. Minn., 1978. Asst. store mgr. K Mart Stores, 1974-76; summer intern IBM, Mpls., 1978; internal auditor Mercantile Nat. Bank, Dallas, 1978—. Vol. counselor Muscle Shoals (Ala.) Mental Health Center, 1977. Mem. Nat. Assn. Accts., Nat. Assn. Black Accts., Assn. M.B.A. Execs., Am. Inst. Banking, Alpha Phi Alpha. Methodist. Home: Route 1 Box 146 Raymond MS 39154

MOORE, LEWIS EDWARD, JR., polit. scientist; b. Nashville, May 1, 1932; s. Lewis Edward and Mary Eunice (Campbell) M.; B.A., Vanderbilt U., 1954, M.A., 1959; D.Arts, U. Miss., 1974; m. Lilybel Lewis, Apr. 24, 1954; children—Bonnie Kathleen, Melinda Lew, Lewis Edward. Mem. faculty Columbia (Tenn.) Mil. Acad., 1960-66, chmn. social studies dept., 1961-66; mem. faculty Columbia State Community Coll., 1966—, prof. polit. sci., 1980—, chmn. social sci. div., 1973-80. Mem. Maury County Democratic Exec. Com. Served with AUS, 1954-56. Falk fellow, 1957-58. Mem. So., Tenn. (pres.) polit. sci. assns., NEA, Tenn. Edn. Assn., Biennial Conf. Tchrs. Social Sci. in Tenn. Pub. Colls. and Univs. (pres. 1974-76), Assn. Preservation Tenn. Antiquities (dir. 1976-79), Pi Sigma Alpha. So. Baptist. Clubs: Maury County Tennis Assn. (pres. 1968); Columbia Civitan (v.p. 1965). Author: Past Progress-Future Potential: An Economic Study of Maury County, Tenn., 1970; Using the Computer in the Social Sciences: A Non-Technical Approach, 1974; Gen. Education for Two-Year College Graduates, 1978. Home: 1107 Sunnyside Dr Columbia TN 38401

MOORE, LUTHER EUGENE, equipment mfg. co. exec.; b. Tulsa, Dec. 13, 1948; s. Roy Eugene and Violet G. (Hays) M.; student Okla. State U., 1967-71; m. Diana Gail Bowman, May 25, 1977. With Deckard Mfg. Co. Inc., Tulsa, 1971—, v.p. sales, 1978—. Mem. Sigma Alpha Epsilon. Office: 2601 Dawson Rd PO Box 50008 Tulsa OK 74150

MOORE, MAMIE JOHNSON, accountant; b. Hamilton, Ga., Feb. 12, 1919; d. William Moses and Vola Lee Cornett Jones; grad. Truman-Smith Bus. Coll., 1938; student U. Ga. Continuing Coll., 1954-56, Columbus Coll., 1965-68; m. Duncan F. Johnson, Sept. 24, 1938 (dec. Sept. 1953); 1 dau., Kathy Johnson Riley; m. 2d, Herman Moore, Sept. 16, 1956 (dec. Sept. 1963). Sec. to sec.-treas. Muscogee Mfg. Co., Columbus, Ga., 1939-44; supr. gen. accounting Gas Light Co., Columbus, Ga., 1948—, corporate sec., 1973—. Chmn. work Area Commn. on Missions St. Luke United Methodist Ch. Mem. Nat. Assn. Accts. (sec. 1976-77), Assn. U.S. Army, Bus. and Profl. Women's Club (pres. 1959-61). Republican. Methodist. Clubs: Pilot (pres. 1971-72), Country (Columbus, Ga.); Executive. Editor: Blessed Be My Rock (Herman Moore), 1963. Home: 1949 Wildwood Ave Columbus GA 31906 Office: PO Box 1657 Columbus GA 31902

MOORE, MARION EDWARD, educator; b. Boise City, Okla., May 22, 1934; s. Floyd Ollie and Bobbie Edith (Bivens) M.; B.S., W.Tex. State U., 1957; M.S., Tex. Tech. U., 1960; Ph.D., U. N.Mex., 1968; m. Cleta Joy Sappenfield, Jan. 24, 1953; 1 dau., Leslie Ann. Instr., W.Tex. State U., Canyon, 1958-61; instr. U. N.Mex., 1961-66; asst. prof. U. Tex., Arlington, 1966-70, asso. prof. math., 1970—. Dir. State Com. on History Math. Served with U.S. Army, 1953-55. Mem. Am. Math. Soc., Math. Assn. Am., Sigma Xi, Alpha Chi. Contbr. articles to profl. jours. Home: 3207 Canongate Dr Arlington TX 76015

MOORE, MARTIN SASSEEN, advt. exec.; b. Dallas, July 12, 1930; s. Marsline K. and Susy W. Moore; B.S.C., Tex. Christian U., 1953; m. Barbara Johnson, May 21, 1956; children—Martin Sasseen, Karen. Vice pres. Tex. United Outdoor Advt., Inc., Ft. Worth, 1956-75, pres., 1975—; chmn. bd. Trinity Nav. Corp. Mem. exec. com. Tarrant County Democratic Party, 1979-80; pres. Ft. Worth Jaycees, 1963-64; bd. dirs., trustee Miss Tex. Pageant, 1965-66; bd. dirs. Ft. Worth Opera Assn., 1965. Served with USAF, 1954-56, lt. col. USAFR. Mem. Advt. Club Ft. Worth, Air Force Assn., Outdoor Advt. Assn. Am., Arnold Air Soc. (treas. 1952-53). Mem. Christian Ch. (Disciples of Christ). Club: Colonial Country. Home: 6317 Wakeland St Fort Worth TX 76133 Office: PO Box 11511 Fort Worth TX 76109

MOORE, MORGAN JACKSON, physician; b. Montgomery, Ala., May 19, 1934; s. William Manning and Georgia Lane (Morgan) M.; B.S., U. Ala., 1956; M.D., Med. Coll. Ala., 1959; m. Betty Jean Wise, Sept. 2, 1956; children—Sandra Katheryn, Linda Charlene, Michael Steven. Intern, U.S. Naval Hosp., Jacksonville, Fla., 1959-60; resident U.S. Naval Sch. Aviation Medicine, Pensacola, Fla., 1960; practice medicine specializing in family practice, Andalusia, Ala., 1964—; active med. staff Columbia Gen. Hosp., Andalusia, also bd. dirs. Served with M.C., USN, 1959-63. Diplomate Am. Bd. Family Practice. Fellow Am. Acad. Family Physicians; mem. AMA, Andalusia Civitan Club (pres. 1969). Baptist. Home: 505 3rd St Andalusia AL 36420 Office: Med Center PO Drawer 370 601 By-Pass W Andalusia AL 36420

MOORE, PATRICIA A. T., real estate exec.; b. Cambridge, Mass., June 11, 1939; d. John F. and Harriet M. Thompson; B.S., Fla. State U., 1961, M.S., 1965; m. Fred Moore, June 3, 1961; children—Hilde, Snow, Fritz, Holly Polly. Pres., Associated Sci. Industries, Austin, Tex., 1975—; partner M&B Assos., 1979—; cons. field real estate acquisition and mgmt. Address: 300 W 33d St Austin TX 78705

MOORE, RAYBURN SABATZKY, educator; b. Helena, Ark., May 26, 1920; s. Max Sabatzky and Sammie Lou (Rayburn) M.; A.B., Vanderbilt U., 1942, M.A., 1947; Ph.D., Duke U., 1956; m. Margaret Elizabeth Bear, Aug. 30, 1947; children—Margaret Elizabeth, Robert Rayburn. Vice pres. Interstate Grocer Co., Helena, 1947-50; research asst. Duke U., 1952, grad. asst., 1952-54; asst. prof. English, Hendrix Coll., Conway, Ark., 1954-55, asso. prof., 1955-58, prof., 1958-59; asso. prof. English, U. Ga., Athens, 1959-65, prof., 1965—, dir. grad. studies in English, 1964-69, chmn. Am. studies program, 1968—, chmn. div. lang. and lit., 1975—; vis. scholar Duke U., 1958, 64. Mem. troop com. Boy Scouts Am., Athens, 1973-75. Served to capt. AUS, 1942-46. Mem. Soc. for Study So. Lit. (exec. com. 1968, 74-80), Modern Lang. Assn. Am. (exec. com. Gen. Topics VI 1972-75), South Atlantic Grad. English Coop. Group (exec. com. 1969-79, chmn. 1971-72), S. Atlantic Modern Lang. Assn. (exec. com. 1975-77), Blue Key, Phi Beta Kappa, Sigma Chi. Presbyterian (deacon, elder 1962—). Author: Constance Fenimore Woolson, 1963; For the Major and Selected Short Stories of Constance Fenimore Woolson, 1967; Paul Hamilton Hayne, 1972; contbr. articles to profl. jours.; editorial bd. U. Ga. Press, 1972-74, Ga. Rev., 1974—. Home: 106 St James Dr Athens GA 30606

MOORE, RAYMOND THOMAS, state health ofcl.; b. Searcy County, Ark., July 16, 1919; B.S., Ark. Tchrs. Coll., 1939; M.D., U. Ark., 1944; m. Melba McNeil, July 31, 1948; children—Rosemary, Maureen, Ranelle, Lois. High sch. sci. tchr., West Memphis, Ark., 1939-41; intern Bapt. Meml. Hosp., San Antonio, 1945, resident, 1948; gen. practice medicine, Seguin, Tex., 1949-58; commd. surgeon USPHS, 1959, served as med. dir. until 1974, discharged, 1974; dep. dir. spl. health services Tex. Dept. Health, 1974-75, dep. commr., 1977-78, commr. of health, 1978-80, dep. commr. spl. health services, 1980—; acting dep. dir. Tex. Dept. Health Resources, 1975-76, dep. dir., 1976-77. Served with U.S. Army, 1945-47. Mem. AMA, Indsl. Medicine Assn., Health Physics Soc., Am. Public Health Assn., Am. Acad. Occupational Medicine. Baptist. Club: Rotary. Office: Tex Dept Health 1100 W 49th St Austin TX 78756

MOORE, REID FRANCIS, JR., lawyer; b. Chattanooga, Sept. 27, 1934; s. Reid Francis and Corinne (Milton) M.; B.A., Yale U., 1956; LL.B., U. Va., 1959; m. Janice Griffin, July 20, 1963; children—Allyson, Ramsey, Carter. Admitted to Fla. bar, 1959; practiced in Palm Beach, 1959—; mayor, West Palm Beach, 1967-68; commr. West Palm Beach, 1965-69; mem. Fla. Ho. of Reps., 1976-78. Recipient Disting. Service award West Palm Beach Jr. C. of C., 1965, Good Govt. award, 1967. Mem. Am., Palm Beach County (chmn. TV program 1972-73) bar assns., Fla. Bar, C. of C. (dir.), West Palm Beach Jr. C. of C. (pres. 1963-64), Phi Alpha Delta. Episcopalian. Republican. Mason (Shriner). Home: 343 Seabreeze Ave Palm Beach FL 33480 Office: 350 Royal Palm Way Palm Beach FL 33480

MOORE, RICHARD CARROLL, JR., physician; b. Balt., Nov. 24, 1946; s. Richard Carroll and Virginia Mae (Clark) M.; B.A., Johns Hopkins U., 1968; M.D., UCLA, 1972; m. Jeremy Pierson, Jan. 27, 1973; children—Peter Gregory, Laura Alexandra. Intern, South Baltimore Gen. Hosp., 1972-73; commd. med. officer USPHS, HEW, 1976; chief med. div. U.S. Coast Guard Aviation Tng. Center, Mobile, Ala., 1976—; mem. exec. bd. Emergency Med. Services Council Mobile County, 1979—, Med. and Chirurg. Faculty Md. Served wtih USN, 1973-76. Diplomate Am. Bd. Family Practice. Mem. Assn. Naval Aviation, Soc. U.S. Naval Flight Surgeons, Johns Hopkins U. Alumni Assn., Commd. Officers Assn. USPHS, Alpha Omega Alpha, Sigma Phi Epsilon. Republican. Home: 324 Hadrian St Mobile AL 36606 Office: USCG Aviation Tng Center Mobile AL 36608

MOORE, ROBERT BRENT, JR., agribus. exec.; b. Wytheville, Va., Dec. 5, 1941; s. Robert Brent and Jane Courtney (Oewel) M.; B.S., Va. Polytech. Inst. and State U., 1964, M.S., 1965; m. Connie Jo Catron, July 2, 1964; children—Karen Elizabeth, Robert Brent III. Mech. engr. research and devel. Tenn. Eastman Co., Kingsport, 1965-73; v.p. Wythe Lumber Co., Inc., Wytheville, 1973—; gen. mgr. Glencoe Farms, Wytheville, 1973—; owner, operator SW Va. Bull Evaluation Center; dir. Wythe County (Va.) Farm Bur., 1976. Mem. exec. bd. Diocese S.W. Va. Protestant Episcopal Ch. U.S.A., 1974-76; jr. warden St. John's Epis. Ch., Wytheville, 1973-74, sr. warden, 1975-76; chmn. Wythe County Library Assn., 1975-78, co-chmn. building program, 1976—; bd. dirs. Wythe County Dept. Social Services, 1979—. Mem. Nat. Fedn. Ind. Businesses, Am., Va. (state del. 1976, 77) farm bur. assns., Contbr. articles to profl. jours. Home: Route 2 Box 94 Wytheville VA 24382 Office: PO Box 54 Wytheville VA 24382

MOORE, ROBERT CALEB, univ. ofcl.; b. Danville, Ill., July 5, 1922; s. Caleb Randolph and Mattie Ellen (Smith) M.; student U. Md., 1951, U. Mass., 1952; m. Cathryn Clare Kokosko, Nov. 13, 1948; children—Nancy Ann, Ellen Lee, Bridget Kay. Commd. pvt. U.S.Air Force, 1940, advanced through grades to sgt.; ret., 1962; store mgr. Mr. M Corp., San Antonio, 1965-70; asst. dir. supply and procurement Trinity U., San Antonio, 1973—; editor, pub. Tex. Defiance, 1965-66. Ind. candiadate San Antonio City Council, 1964; Conservative Party candidate for Congress, 20th Dist. Tex., 1966; state exec. com., presdl. elector Am. Party of Tex., 1968; pres. San Antonio Citizens Assn., 1966. Recipient award for dedication Am. Women for Constnl. Govt. 1968, honor award Am. Patriot's Hall of Fame, 1968. Mem. U.S. Strategic Inst., Am. Security Council, Assn. Former Intelligence Officers, Nat. Mil. Intelligence Assn., Am. Def. Preparedness Assn. Author: One Man's Agony, 1969. Home: 535 Mount Vernon Ct San Antonio TX 78223 Office: 715 Stadium Dr San Antonio TX 78284

MOORE, ROBERT GARVICE, educator; b. Lamar County, Ala., Oct. 8, 1910; s. James Charles and M. Glo Vina (Stacy) M.; B.S., U. Ala., 1952, M.A., 1956, postgrad., 1965-73; m. Ola Grace Holliday, May 2, 1931; 1 dau., Betty Jo (Mrs. Bobby Gene Morris). Tchr. pub. schs., Lamar County, 1942-53, supt. edn., 1955-63; instr. phys. edn. N.W. Ala. State Coll., 1963—, chmn. div. arts and skills, 1970—. Mem. NEA, Ala., Franklin County edn. assns. Democrat. Methodist. Clubs: Lions, Masons, Shriners. Composer: Our Government. Home: Route 3 Box 250 Phil Campbell AL 35581

MOORE, ROBERT WAYNE, coll. adminstr.; b. Piner, Ky., Oct. 3, 1933; s. Robert Sharon and Lena Blanche (Pribble) M.; B.M.E., Georgetown Coll., 1955; M.R.E., So. Bapt. Theol. Sem., 1958; M.S., Ind. U., 1959; Ed.D., U. Miss., 1968; m. Carolyn Ann Chick, Aug. 7, 1954; children—Kathryn Ann, Steven Wayne. Minister of recreation Crescent Hill Baptist Ch., Louisville, Ky., 1956-58, Calvary Baptist Ch., Jackson, Miss., 1960-62; dir. admissions Mississippi Coll., 1962-65; mem. faculty Georgetown Coll., 1969-72, dir. student devel. center, 1973-79, dir. alumni affairs and student devel., 1979—. Mem. Am. Personnel and Guidance Assn., Am. Coll. Personnel Assn., Coll. Personnel Assn. Ky., So. Coll. Placement Assn., Phi Delta Kappa. Baptist. Home: 1001 Mojave Trail Georgetown KY 40324 Office: Georgetown Coll Georgetown KY 40324

MOORE, ROY WALKER, lawyer; b. Novasota, Tex., Oct. 14, 1938; s. Clarence and Massey (Lott) M.; B.B.A., So. Methodist U., 1960; J.D., S. Tex. Coll. Law, 1971; m. Pene Pettit, June 9, 1961; 1 son, Royal Lott. Engaged in investments and farming, Navasota, 1960-71; admitted to Tex. bar, 1971, since practiced in Houston; co-chmn. bd., dir. Alvarado State Bank (Tex.), 1973-75. Agt. class of 1960, So. Meth. U., 1963—. Mem. Am., Houston bar assns., Tex. State Bar (chmn. grievance com.), Phi Delta Theta, Phi Alpha Delta. Methodist. Club: River Oaks Country. Home: 2432 Inwood St Houston TX 77019 Office: 914 Main St Suite 1717 Houston TX 77002

MOORE, W. HENSON, congressman; b. Lake Charles, La., Oct. 4, 1939; s. Mr. and Mrs. W.H. Moore, Jr.; B.A., La. State U., 1961, J.D., 1965, M.A., 1973; m. Carolyn Ann Cherry; children—William Henson, Jennifer Lee, Cherry Ann. Admitted to bar; mem. firm Dale, Owen, Richardson, Taylor & Matthews, 1967-74, mng. partner, 1969-74; mem. 94th-95th Congresses from 6th La. Dist. Mem. La. Republican State Central Com., 1971-75, past chmn. state research and issues com. Served with U.S. Army, 1965-67. Mem. Am. Bar Assn., La. Bar Assn. Jaycees, Am. Legion. Episcopalian. Club: Rotary. Office: 2444 Rayburn Office Bldg Washington DC 20515

MOORE, WINFRED BOBO, JR., historian; b. Spartanburg, S.C., Nov. 24, 1949; s. Winfred Bobo and Corinne Ethel Moore; B.A., Furman U., 1971; M.A., Duke U., 1972, Ph.D., 1975. Research historian Liberty Corp., Greenville, S.C., 1976; mem. faculty The Citadel, Charleston, S.C., 1976—, asst. prof. history, 1978—, co-dir. conf. on South, 1978-79. Served with USAR, 1975. Citadel Devel. Found. grantee, 1978. Mem. Am. Hist. Assn., Orgn. Am. Historians, So. Hist. Assn., S.C. Hist. Assn. Democrat. Baptist. Home: 4296 Congress St Charleston SC 29409 Office: Dept History The Citadel Charleston SC 29409

MOORHEAD, ROLANDE ANNETTE REVERDY, artist; b. Périgueux, France, Sept. 24, 1937; d. Rémy Jean and Andrée Marcelle (Lavollee) Reverdy; came to U.S., 1959; student College Technique, Nice, France, 1950-54; m. Elliott Swift Moorhead, III, Sept. 30, 1960; children—Edward Marc, Roland Elliott, Rémy Bruce. Bi-lingual sec. French embassy, Washington, 1959-60, 1968-70, Ft. Lauderdale, Fla., 1970—; one-woman shows Ocean Club Art Gallery, 1971, 72, 73, 74, Pier 66 Art Gallery, 1972, 74, 76, Am. Nat. Bank, 1973, Science of the Mind Ch., Ft. Lauderdale, 1973, Ft. Lauderdale City Hall, 1974, 77, 78, spl. exhbt. Ft. Lauderdale C. of C., 1976, St. Basil Cath. Orthodox Ch., N. Miami Beach, 1977, Galerie Vallombreuse, Biarritz, France, 1977, Galerie du Palais des Fêtes, Perigueux, 1978, Le Club Internat., Ft. Lauderdale, 1979, spl. exhbn. Indsl. Expo 1979, Pompano Beach; group shows: St. Coleman Cath. Ch., Pompano Beach, Fla., 1971, Point of Am. Gallery, Ft. Lauderdale, 1971, Gold Coast Spring Art Festival, 1972, 73, Inverrary Art Festival, 1973, Boca Raton C. of C. Art Show, 1973, Broward Art Guild, 1973, Christ Meth. Ch., Lauderdale/by/the/Sea, 1974, Jackie Gleason Environ. Art Festival, 1974, Internat. Salon, Biarritz, 1977, Paris, 1977, Galerie Mouffe, Paris, 1977, Long Galleries, Ft. Lauderdale, 1979, Spl. Bicentennial Exhbn., Fla., 1976; represented in permanent collections: DAV Hdqrs., Washington, Air Force Mus., Ohio, Ft. Lauderdale City Hall, Asso. Aircraft Co., Fla., Mayor Virginia Young, Ft. Lauderdale, Creditreform, Dusseldorf, W. Ger., March of Dimes Bldg., Ft. Lauderdale, Cathedrale St. Front, Perigueux, Cathedrale of Sarlat (France); also numerous pvt. collections; demonstrator various schs. and chs., Fla.; donor numerous paintings to charitable fund drs.; v.p. Lauderdale/by/the/Sea Art Guild, 1972-74, chmn. exhibit com., 1972-75. Recipient best in show awards Internat. Salon, Biarritz, 1977, various others; accepted Internat. Salon, Paris, 1977. Mem. Broward, DelRay Beach, Lauderdale/by/the/Sea art guilds, Boca Raton Center for Arts, Fla. League Arts, Gold Coast Watercolor Soc., Alliance Francaise Dade County (treas., dir. 1973-75), Internat. Platform Assn. Holder 1st one-woman show in France at age 16; subject of articles in various Fla. newspapers and mags. Address: PO Box 8692 Fort Lauderdale FL 33310

MOORMAN, LEWIS CHARLES, mfg. co. exec.; b. Lynchburg, Va., Mar. 30, 1922; s. Lewis Charles and Lillian Ann (Whitten) M.; student Lynchburg Coll., 1959, U. Iowa, 1955, U. Mich., 1962, Randolph-Macon Women's Coll., 1960; married; 1 dau., Faye Presley. Lithographer, Piedmont Label Co., Bedford, Va., 1941-42; meteorologist U.S Weather Bur., Richmond and Lynchburg, Va., 1950-54; timestudy engr. Griffin Pipe Products Co., Lynchburg, 1954-56, indsl. relations supr., 1956-62, plant personnel mgr., 1962—. Served with USN, 1942-46; ETO. Recipient Citations for service, United Givers Fund of Lynchburg, 1959, 70; citation Vocat. Indsl. Clubs Am., 1970. Mem. Am. Soc. for Personnel Adminstrn., Am. Meteorol. Soc., Indsl. Mgmt. Council. Methodist. Office: PO Box 740 Lynchburg VA 24505

MOORMAN, MARVIN ROY, govt. health ofcl.; b. Glen Dean, Ky., July 30, 1923; s. Earl and Myra Elma (Shelton) M.; A.B., Western Ky. U., 1950; M.P.H., U. N.C., Chapel Hill, 1962. Secondary sch. tchr. Breckenridge County (Ky.) Bd. Edn., 1950-54; agrl. rep. Reynolds Aluminum Co., Louisville, 1954-58; sales and sales promotion F. A. Ames Co., Owensboro, Ky., 1958-59; local public health educator Ky. Dept. Health, Leitchfield, 1959-63, sr. health educator, Lexington and Bowling Green, 1965-72; health edn. coordinator Pike County (Ky.) Health Dept., Pikeville, 1963-65; dir. health edn. Green River Dist. Health Dept., Owensboro, 1972—; mem. bd. Owensboro-Daviess County Council on Aging, 1973—, Ky. Coalition on Teenage Pregnancies, 1978—. Served in USCGR, 1943-46. USPHS grantee, 1961. Mem. Am. Public Health Assn., Ky. Public Health Assn., Soc. Public Health Edn., Western Ky. Health Edn. Consortium (dir.). Democrat. Methodist. Club: Masons. Office: 3520 New Hartford Pike PO Box 1094 Owensboro KY 42301

MOOSE, JOHN WADSWORTH, parasitologist; b. Fort Leavenworth, Kan., Sept. 29, 1925; s. Frank McAlpin and Dolores May (Bezold) M.; B.S., Randolph-Macon Coll., 1947; M.S., George Washington U., 1953; m. Hildegard Goebel, Oct. 18, 1956; children—Bryan Francis, Corinna Dolores. Commd. 2d lt. Med. Service Corps, U.S. Army, 1950, advanced through grades to lt. col.; various assignments as parasitologist U.S. Army Med. Labs., P.R., Germany, Japan, U.S., 1950-71, ret., 1971; parasitologist Bur. Labs., S.C. Dept. Health and Environ. Control, Columbia, 1971—; instr. in parasitology Acad. of Health Scis., Fort Sam Houston, Tex., 1966-71. Certified as specialist microbiologist in pub. health, med. lab. microbiology Am. Acad. Microbiology. Mem. Am. Soc. Parasitologists, Am. Soc. Tropical Medicine and Hygiene, S.C. br. Am. Soc. Microbiology, Am. Soc. Med. Technology, South Eastern Assn. for Clin. Microbiology, Kappa Alpha, Beta Beta Beta. Roman Catholic. Author: The Application of Comparative Morphology in the Identification of Intestinal Parasites, 1973. Contbr. articles to profl. jours. Home: 7733 Castleton Ln Columbia SC 29206 Office: 2600 Bull St Columbia SC 29201

MORALES, HONORIO, health care cons.; b. Guayama, P.R., Jan. 25, 1938; s. Juan and Emilia (Cadiz) M.; M.S. in Hosp. Adminstrn., U. P.R., 1970; m. Aracelis Cortes, July 1, 1961; children—Ruth A., Edwin H. Comptroller, Badrena & Perez, Inc., Hato Rey, P.R., 1966-68; pres. Las Americas Med. Mgmt. Services, San Juan, P.R., 1971-77; cons. Hosp. Mimiya Inc., Santurce, P.R., 1970—; pres. Saludhos, Inc., San Juan, 1978—; prof. acctg. EDP Jr. Coll., Hato Rey, 1975—. Mem. P.R. Hosp. Adminstrs. Assn. (pres. 1974-75), P.R. Hosp. Assn. (past dir.), Am. Coll. Hosp. Adminstrs., Am. Hosp. Assn., P.R. Fedn. Newsmen and Writers. Roman Catholic. Club: Lions (del. internat. conv., past 1st v.p., past treas., past dir., pres. several coms., past tail twister). Editor, pub., Saludhos, mag.; editor NotiAccion, 1974. Office: Domenech 400 Suite 202 Hato Rey San Juan PR 00919

MORALES-CARRION, ARTURO, adminstr.; b. Havana, Cuba, Nov. 16, 1913; s. Arturo Morales and Agripina Carrion; B.A., U. P.R., 1935; M.A., U. Tex., 1936; Ph.D., Columbia U., 1950; LL.D., Temple U., 1976; m. Ines Arandes; children—Arturo, Edgardo, Inex. Instr., U. P.R., 1936-38, asst. prof., 1944-46, chmn. dept. history, 1946-52, dir. history research center and latin Am. seminar, 1970-73, pres. univ., 1973-79; exec. dir. P.R. Endowment for Humanities, San Juan, 1979—; cultural affairs office Dept. of State, 1939-43, dep. asst. sec. of state for Inter-Am. affairs, Washington, 1961-63; lectr. in history Columbia U., 1947-49; undersec. of state Commonwealth of P.R., 1953-60; spl. adviser to sec. gen. OAS, 1964-69; mem. U.S. del. inter-Am. confs., 1954-63; mem. Linowitz Comm. on U.S.-Latin Am. Relations, 1974-77. Recipient Eugenio Maria de Hostos award N.Y. State, 1962, Inst. Puerto Rican Lit. awards, 1968, 72; Nat. Found. Humanities grantee, 1972-73. Mem. Am. Council on Edn. (dir. 1977—), Nat. Assn. State Univs. and Land Grant Colls. (council of presidents 1974—), Assn. Caribbean Univs., Research Insts., Am. History Assn., Am. Acad. Polit. Scis., Ateneo Puertorriqueno. Democrat. Roman Catholic. Author: Puerto Rico and the Non-Hispanic Caribbean, 2d edit., 1971; Historia del Pueblo de Puerto Rico, 1968; (in Spanish) Glimpses of the Historical Process in Puerto Rico and Other Essays, 1971; The Rise and Fall of 19th Century Slave Trade in Puerto Rico, 1978; contbr. articles to profl. publs., Ency. Brit. Office: Apartado S-4307 San Juan PR 00904

MORAN, ANGELA CLARE, hosp. adminstr.; b. Aughavas, Ireland; B.A., Incarnate Word Coll., 1950; M.H.A., St. Louis U., 1960. Joined holy order, Roman Catholic Ch.; supr. nursing St. Joseph Hosp., Ft. Worth, 1951-54; asst. adminstr. Spohn Hosp., Corpus Christi, Tex., 1954-55, adminstr., 1955-58, 59-60; adminstrv. resident St. Vincent Hosp., Erie, Pa., 1959; dir. health service Sisters of Charity of the Incarnate Word, San Antonio, 1960-72; exec. dir. Santa Rosa Med. Center, San Antonio, 1972-79, pres., 1979—. Fellow Am. Coll. Hosp. Adminstrs.; mem. Am., Tex. nurses assns., Cath., Tex. hosp. assns., Nat., Tex. leagues nursing. Author books. Office: 519 W Houston St San Antonio TX 78275

MORAN, ANN ELIZABETH, librarian; b. Franklin, Tenn.; d. James Walker and Emma Mai (Fly) Moran; B.S., Middle Tenn. State U., 1940; B.S. in L.S., George Peabody Coll. for Tchrs., 1943, M.A., 1953. Librarian various schs., Tenn., 1943-61; tchr. Franklin City Schs., 1961-65; tchr., librarian Williamson County (Tenn.) Schs., Franklin, 1940-43, library supr., 1965—. Chmn. fund drive Heart Assn., Franklin, 1969, 77, chmn. bus., 1970, co-chmn. rural fund dr., 1972; vice-chmn. Williamson County Heart Council, 1974-75, chmn., 1976-78. Mem. Nat. Tenn., Middle Tenn. edn. assns., Am., Tenn. (sec. sch. sect. 1978, vice chmn. 1979, chmn. 1980) library assns., Mid-State Library Assn. (exec. council 1978—), Bus. and Profl. Women's Club (sec. 1969-70), Women's Nat. Book Assn. (sec. 1971-73, treas. 1977-78), Delta Kappa Gamma (treas. 1972-74). Home: Route 11 Franklin TN 37064 Office: Columbia Ave Franklin TN 37064

MORAN, HAROLD JOSEPH, lawyer; b. N.Y.C., Feb. 21, 1907; s. Thomas J. and Leonore M.F. (Geoghegan) M.; A.B. cum laude, Holy Cross Coll., 1928; LL.B., Fordham U., 1932; J.D., 1968; m. Geraldine D. Starkey, July 12, 1956. Admitted to N.Y. bar, 1934; practiced in N.Y.C., 1934-42, Bklyn., 1949-57, Malverne, N.Y., 1977—; law dept. Title Guarantee & Trust Co., Bklyn., 1945-48; sr. atty. real property bur. N.Y. State Law Dept., Albany, 1957-63, N.Y.C., 1963-77, ret., 1977; spl. dep. atty. gen. election frauds, 1973. Title closer City Title Co., Bklyn., 1949-52; U.S., P.R. mortgage loan examiner Cadwalader, Wickersham & Taft, N.Y.C., 1952-56, 63—, 9th Fed. Savs. & Loan Assn., N.Y.C., 1971—; instr. law St. John's U. Sch. Commerce, Jamaica, N.Y., 1956-57; disbursing agt. under bankruptcy law U.S. Dist. Ct. for So. Dist. N.Y., 1978—. Served with AUS, 1942-45. Knight Holy Sepulchre. Mem. Am. Bar Assn., Bar Assn. Nassau County, Am. Judicature Soc., N.Y. County Lawyers Assn., Catholic Lawyers Guild, Am. Assn. Ret. Persons (chmn. legis. com. Boynton Leisureville chpt.). Democrat. Roman Catholic. Clubs: Hempstead Golf and Country, Southward Ho Country. Home: 1509 Alfred Dr Boynton Beach FL 33435 Office: 277 Hempstead Ave Malverne NY 11565

MORAN, MARLENE JUNE YORDAN, food service exec.; b. Martins Ferry, Ohio, Mar. 17, 1939; d. Joseph Ronald and Helen Louise (Baumann) Yordan; student U. Fla., 1974-75; food service supr. cert. Nat. Inst. Food Service, 1975; san. mgr. cert. W.Va. No. Community Coll., 1977; student W. Liberty State Coll., 1969—; m. Fred Moran, Mar. 9, 1957; children—Roy Louis, Fred. Dietary aide Ohio Valley Med. Center, Wheeling, W.Va., 1967-71, sec., 1971-75, food service supr., 1975; food service mgr. Peterson Hosp., Ohio Valley Med. Center, Wheeling, 1975—. Mem. Hosp. Instn., Ednl. Food Service Soc., W.Va. Hosp., Inst. Ednl. Food Service Soc. (editor bull.). Republican. Methodist. Home: 34 Walnut Ave Bethlehem WV 26003 Office: Peterson Hosp Homestead Ave Wheeling WV 26003

MORASKI, ROBERT LEO, research and devel. exec.; b. Joliet, Ill., June 26, 1933; s. Leo John and Teresa (Stytz) M.; B.S., U. Md., 1964; M.S., George Washington U., 1972; m. Laura Frances Vann, Apr. 11, 1959. Enlisted in USAF, 1952, advanced through grades to lt. col.; reconaissance staff officer, Shaw AFB, S.C., 1967-68; research and devel. officer Hdqrs. USAF, Washington, 1968-73; ret. 1973; mgmt. trainee Prudential Ins. Co., Montgomery, Ala., 1973-74; mktg. cons. Edutronics Systems Internat. Mktg. Co., Dallas, 1975-76; project mgr. Computer Aided Mfg. Internat., Inc., Arlington, Tex., 1977—. Decorated D.F.C., Meritorious Service medal, Air medal (2). Mem. Am. Mgmt. Assn., Am. Inst. Indsl. Engrs., Soc. Mfg. Engrs. Republican. Home: 111 McCullar Rd Burleson TX 76028 Office: 611 Ryan Plaza Dr #1107 Arlington TX 76011

MORE, BERKELEY DAVIS, army officer; b. N.Y.C., Oct. 21, 1921; s. Morgan Berkeley and Lucinda Davis (Bateson) M.; B.A., B.S., Harvard U., 1943; postgrad., Command Gen. Staff Coll., 1956-57, Armed Forces Staff Coll., 1960; 1 dau., Kathleen Ann. Commd. 2nd lt. U.S.Army, 1943, advanced through grades to col., 1968; forward air observer, Germany, World War II; corps arty. adviser to I Republic Korea Corps, 1952-53; chief, G-4 plans, Ryukus Islands, Okinawa, 1959-60; comdr. 1/83d F.A.Bn., Germany, 1960-61; with Army Concept Team, Vietnam, 1967-68; with U.S.Army Forces Command, 1973-76; ret., 1976. Decorated Legion of Honor, Bronze Star medal with 3 oak leaf clusters, Air medal with 4 oak leaf clusters (U.S.); Croix de Guerre (France). Mem. Nat. Aviation Club, Am. Helicopter Soc., Assn. U.S.Army. Republican. Clubs: Toastmasters Internat.; Harvard (Boston, Atlanta). Home: 2383 Akers Mill Rd Apt J-20 Atlanta GA 30339

MORE, EDUARDO ANGEL, motion picture and TV exec.; b. Havana, Cuba, Feb. 17, 1919; s. Angel and Maria Luisa (Rodriguez) M.; came to U.S., 1960, naturalized, 1968; Agrl. Engr., U. Havana, 1943; grad. real estate U. Miami (Fla.), 1969; m. Carmelie de Ribas, Dec. 21, 1945; children—Carmen L., Eduardo J. Pres. Producciones Kinart, Havana, 1947-48; dir. motion picture prodn. CMQ-TV, Havana, 1948-60; gen. mgr. Film and Dubbing Prodns. Co., San Juan, P.R., 1960-61; adviser motion picture prodn. and TV recording Producciones Argentinas de Television, 1961-64; pres. Soundlab Inc., Coral Gables, Fla., 1961—, Internat. Prodns. Investment Inc., Miami, 1971—, Internat. TV and Film Distbrs., Inc., Coral Gables, 1974—; real estate broker, 1970—; chmn. intra-bd. relations com. Coral Gables Bd. Realtors, 1974—. Pres. Ballet Concerto Co. of Miami, 1971—. Mem. Interam. Bus. Men's Assn., Soc. Motion Picture and TV Engrs. (chmn. Cape Kennedy sect.). Clubs: Coral Gables Country; Am., Big Five (Miami). Home: 400 Sansovino Ave Coral Gables FL 33146 Office: 4130 Aurora St Coral Gables FL 33146

MORE, PHILIP JEROME, arts and antiques co. exec.; b. Chgo., Dec. 11, 1911; s. Louis Eli and Anna Leah (Kahn) M.; B.S., Heidelberg (Germany) U., 1933; postgrad. Ill. Inst. Tech., 1936; LL.D. (hon.), Roosevelt U., 1967; m. Sylvia Sally Bernstein, Oct. 16, 1937 (div. 1977); children—Andrea More Williams, Michael E., William M. Owner, pres. Feris Flying Service, Chgo., 1936-38; metallurgist Standard Dental Labs., Chgo., 1938-39; project design engr. Birtman Electric Co., Chgo., 1939-41; sr. design engr. Hotpoint div. Gen. Electric Co., Cicero, Ill., 1950-68; dir. purchasing Modern Maid, McGraw Edison, Chattanooga, 1968-76; pres. Choo-Choo Indsls. Inc., 1976-79; pres. Things of Beauty, 1979—; mem. indsl. and sci. conf. Appliance Design and Mfg. Adv. Council; cons. primitive monies, museums and univs.; sponsor numismatic studies Roosevelt U., Chgo., 1966-67, chmn. Numismatic Library Project; Presdl. appointee Assay Commn., 1965. Chmn. Engrs. for Senator Baker, 1972—, Engrs. for Sasser for Senator, 1976, Engrs. for Carter for Pres., 1976. Served to comdr. USNR, 1950-58. Decorated Navy Cross; recipient Gen. Electric citation for cost saving, 1966. Mem. Gas Appliance Engrng. Soc. (pres. 1970-71), Am. Soc. Gas Engrs. (nat. pres. 1975—). Clubs: North Shore Coin (founder, pres. 1950-58), Chgo. Coin (pres. 1964-65) (Chgo.); Central States Numismatic Soc. (pres. 1965-66). Author: The Lure of Primitive Money, 1960; Odd and Curious Monies of the World, 1963; purchasing editorial adv. bd. Appliance mag.; contbr. articles on monies and engrng. design to profl. jours. Patentee in field. Home: 404 Tunnell Blvd #H9 Chattanooga TN 37411 Office: PO Box 8211 Chattanooga TN 37411

MOREHEAD, CHARLOTTE ROSE, educator; b. Christopher, Ill., Aug. 8, 1950; d. Daulton Hugo and Lela Pearl (Hammers) Anthony; B.S. Elem. Edn., Lee Coll., 1973; M.S. in Edn., U. Tenn., 1977; m. Joel Alan Morehead, June 25, 1971. First grade tchr. Bradley County, Cleveland, Tenn., 1971—. Pres., Enetha Circle, 1976-77; troop leader Girl Scouts U.S.A., 1978. Mem. NEA, Tenn. Edn. Assn., Am. Personnel and Guidance Assn., Bradley County Edn. Assn. (sec. 1975-76, editor 1976). Home: 3605 Crestwood Dr NW Cleveland TN 37311 Office: Valley View Sch Spring Pl Rd Cleveland TN 37311

MOREHEAD, SAMUEL, guidance counselor; b. Hopkinsville, Ky., Nov. 24, 1938; s. Jodia Alexander and Katie Bell (Poston) M.; B.A., Ky. State U., 1960; M.A. in Edn., Murray (Ky.) State U., 1966. Classroom tchr., then Title VI-B coordinator Christian County Sch. Systems, Hopkinsville, 1961-77; guidance counselor Christian County Middle Sch., Hopkinsville, 1977—. Mem. Am. Personnel and Guidance Assn., NEA, Ky. Personnel and Guidance Assn., Ky. Edn. Assn., Western Ky. Personnel and Guidance Assn., Ky. Edn. Polit. Action Com., 2d Region Ky. Assn. Sch. Adminstrs., Christian County Edn. Assn. Democrat. Baptist. Home: 7007 Forest Park Blvd Hopkinsville KY 42240 Office: Christian County Middle Sch Glass Ave Hopkinsville KY 42240

MORELAND, CARL DONALD, newspaper editor; b. Scott County, Ky., July 23, 1934; s. Roy Guy and Edith Irene (Wright) M.; B.A., U. Ky., 1956, M.Public Affairs, 1979; m. Linda Austin Hockensmith, June 20, 1971; children by previous marriage—Catherann, R.D., Lawrence, Edith. Mem. staff Harlan (Ky.) Daily Enterprise, 1956-57, Frankfort (Ky.) Morning Times, 1957-58, Princeton (Ind.) Daily Clarion, 1958-60, Lexington (Ky.) Herald, 1960-65, Roswell (N.M.) Record, 1965-67; with Frankfort (Ky.) State Jour., 1967—, news editor, 1968—. Pres. Bur. Vol. Services, Frankfort, 1975-76. Mem. Ky. Press Assn. (awards), Sigma Delta Chi. Democrat. Baptist. Club: Frankfort Civitan (pres. 1974-75, dir. communications Ky. dist. 1975-76, dir. William N. Dryden Scholarship Fund 1975-77). Home: 234 Leawood Dr Frankfort KY 40601 Office: 321 W Main St Frankfort KY 40601

MORELAND, RALPH ROWNTREE, restaurant chain exec.; b. Stamford, Tex., Jan. 8, 1927; s. Patrick Dacus and Sara Elizabeth (Rowntree) M.; B.B.A., U. Tex., 1950; m. Lono Pauline Saunders, July 15, 1952 (div. 1969); children—Michelle Ann, Jean Marie; m. 2d, Essie Marie Payne, July 10, 1971. Pres., owner Ralph Moreland, Inc., operators 24 restaurants, Austin, Tex., 1952—; dir. Chase Nat. Bank, Austin. Vice pres. Austin Aqua Festival, 1966. Served with USNR, 1944-46. Mem. Tex. (dir. 1962-66), Austin (pres. 1962) restaurant assns., Sigma Iota Epsilon, Lambda Chi Alpha. Office: 1400 Timberline Office Park Austin TX 78746

MORELLI, HENRY ERNEST, JR., electronic mfg. co. exec.; b. N.Y.C., Jan. 14, 1944; s. Henry E. and Grace R. (Cinelli) M.; A.A.S., Pace U., 1965, B.B.A., 1967, M.B.A., 1970; m. Catherine Marie Slager, Dec. 28, 1978; children—John, Paul, Christine, Henry Ernest, Timothy. Dir., Hudson River Mus. and Planetarium, Yonkers, N.Y., 1966-67; systems specialist IBM, White Plains, N.Y., 1967-71; corp. staff cons. Burndy Corp., Norwalk, Conn., 1971-72; cons. Informatics, Inc., communications systems div., River Edge, N.J., 1972-75; dir. mgmt. info. systems Racal-Milgo, Inc., Miami, 1975—; bd. govs. Univac Computers Users Group, Inc. 1979—. Mem. Assn. Computing Machinery, Data Processing Mgmt. Assn. Republican. Roman Catholic. Clubs: Miami Country, Costa Del Sol Golf and Raquet, Miami Lakes Raquet. Office: 8600 NW 41st St Miami FL 33166

MORELOCK, JAMES CRUTCHFIELD, mathematician; b. Martin, Tenn., Feb. 7, 1920; s. Joseph Fletcher and Lura Martha (Crutchfield) M.; student Bethel Coll., McKenzie, Tenn., 1937-39; B.S., Memphis State Coll., 1941; M.A., U. Mo., 1948; Ph.D. (fellow), U. Fla., 1952; m. Eugenia Scott Browne, Apr. 29, 1945 (dec.); children—Elinor Morelock Smith, Constance Morelock Grear, Diana Morelock Brown. Instr. astronomy and math. U. Fla., Gainesville, 1949-52; asst. prof. math. Auburn (Ala.) U., 1952-56; head math. dept. King Coll., Bristol, Tenn., 1956-60; mathematician U.S. Naval Computation Lab., Dahlgren, Va., 1960-61; mem. staff Computation Center Gen. Electric, Huntsville, Ala., 1961-63; mathematician computation lab. Marshall Space Flight Center, Huntsville, Ala., 1963-78, ret., 1978. Instl. rep. to Boy Scouts, Civitan Club, Auburn, 1952-56; v.p. Huntsville Concert Band, 1963—. Served with USAAF, 1941-45; PTO. Manning scholar, 1940-41; recipient U.S. Treasury award, 1968, NASA 10 year Achievement award, 1969, NASA Apollo Achievement award, 1969. Mem. Am. Math. Soc., Math. Assn. Am., Assn. Computing Machinery, Bristol Astronomy Soc. (pres. 1956-60). Methodist. Club: Pistol. Home: 2917 Garth Rd SE Huntsville AL 35801

MORENO, FRANKLIN RIVERA, psychologist; b. Mayaguez, P.R., Jan. 2, 1945; s. Robustiano Rivera and Rosa Moreno; B.A. with high honors, U. P.R., 1965; M.A., Interam. U. P.R., 1971; M.Div., Northgate Grad. Sch., 1976; Ph.D. in Ednl. Counseling, Walden U., 1978; postgrad. George Washington U., 1978. Tchr. English public schs., P.R., 1964-71, guidance counselor, 1972-79; mem. faculty Inter-Am. U. P.R., 1974-79; field dir. Northgate Grad. Sch., Edmonds, Wash., 1978-79; instr. Inst. de Hipnologia Exptl., P.R., 1975-79; vocat. counseling psychologist Hostos High Sch., Mayaguez, P.R., 1979—; public lectr. on human behavior, P.R., 1973-79. Sec. religious liberty Bella Vista Seventh-Day Adventist Ch., Mayaguez, 1976-77. Cert. clin. mental health counselor; cert. sex counselor. Mem. Am. Personnel and Guidance Assn., Nat. Assn. Christian Marriage Counselors, Am. Mental Health Counselors Assn., Federación de Maestros de P.R., Nat. Geog. Soc. Jewish. Author: Personalidad Para el Exito, 1975. Office: Hostos High School Mayaguez PR 00708

MORENO, LEOPOLD SEGISMUNDO, physician; b. Corrientes, Argentina, Feb. 6, 1927; s. Leopoldo Sixto and Espectacion Blasia (Saling) M.; B.S., Colegio Nacional Gen. San Martin, 1944; M.D., Buenos Aires Med. Sch., 1951; m. Susan Elizabeth Kinne, May 27, 1972; chilren—Karen, L. Bryan, Mark, Francis L. Came to U.S., 1952, naturalized, 1957. Practicante Adscripto, Hosp. Alvarez, Buenos Aires, 1950-51; practicante Hosp. Espanol, Buenos Aires, 1950-52; resident tng. Tampa (Fla.) Gen. Hosp., 1952, St. Marys Hosp., Troy, N.Y., 1953, Suffolk Sanatorium, L.I., N.Y., 1954, Jackson Park Hosp., Chgo., 1955, Lincoln (Ill.) State Sch., 1956; practice medicine, specializing in family practice, Norfolk, Va., 1957—; mem. staff, asst. dir. dept. family practice DePaul Hosp.; mem. staff Med. Center Hosp. Mem. faculty Eastern Va. Med. Sch. Diplomate Am. Bd. Family Practice, Pan Am. Med. Assn. Charter fellow Am. Acad. Family Practice; mem. AMA, Am. Thoracic Soc., Va., Norfolk County med. socs., Tidewater Acad. Family Practice (corr. sec. 1970-71, pres. 1977-78) Am. Geriatric Soc., Va. Tb Assn. Home: 441 Harriton Ct Norfolk VA 23505 Office: 7927 Old Ocean View Rd Norfolk VA 23518

MORETON, ROBERT DULANEY, radiologist; b. Brookhaven, Miss., Sept. 24, 1913; s. Robert D. and Lena (Durfey) M.; student Tulane U., 1931-32; B.S., Millsaps Coll., 1934; student U. Miss. Med. Sch., 1934-36; M.D., U. Tenn., 1938; fellow radiology Mayo Found., 1940-42; m. Alma Williamson, Sept. 21, 1945. Intern Lloyd Nolan Meml. Hosp., Fairfield, Ala., 1938-39; instr. physiology U. Miss. Med. Sch., 1939-40; staff radiologist Scott and White Clinic and Hosp., also Santa Fe Hosp., Temple, Tex., 1942-50; sr. partner Bond Radiol. Group, Ft. Worth, 1950-65; chmn., dir. dept. radiology Harris Hosp., 1960-65, Ft. Worth Childrens Hosp., 1961—; cons. St. Joseph, USPHS, John Peter Smith hosps.; prof. clin. radiology Southwestern Med. Sch., Dallas, 1958-65; asst. to dir. U. Tex.-M.D. Anderson Hosp. and Tumor Inst., Houston, 1965-69, asst. dir., 1969-70, prof. radiology, 1965—, v.p. for profl. and pub. affairs, 1969—. Mem. Tex. Bd. Health, 1961-75, vice chmn., 1963-75, chmn., 1977—; mem. Tex. Adv. Com. Atomic Energy, 1955-61; mem. Tex. Bd. Health Resources, 1975-77, chmn., 1975-77; founding mem. Carter Blood Bank, Ft. Worth, 1959; founding mem. Radiation and Research Found. Southwest, 1957, exec. com. Radiation Center, 1958—; mem. Tech. Electronic Products Radiation Safety Standards Com. Recipient gold medal Assn. Mil. Surgeons, 1949; certificate merit exhibit Chgo. Med. Soc., 1950; Brotherhood award Ft. Worth chpt. Nat. Conf. Christians and Jews, 1967; Distinguished Citizen award Goodwill Industries Houston, 1968. Fellow Geriatrics Soc. (chmn. ins. com. 1962), Am. Coll. Radiology (exec. com. 1957-59); mem. Tarrant County (pres. 1959, chmn. trustees 1963), N.W. Tex. (pres. 1963) med. socs., Am. (chmn. radiology sec. 1964-65; gold medal exhibit 1949, del. Tex. 1969), So. (chmn. bd. councilors and exec. com., 1959-60, chmn. ins. com. 1956-63, pres. 1964), Tex. (chmn. sect. radiology 1950, council med. jurisprudence 1958-62), Indsl. med. assns., Ft. Worth Acad. Medicine (past trustee), Am. Registry X-ray Technicians (pres. 1959, 62), Tex. Soc. X-ray Technicians (hon.), Tex. (pres. 1950-51), Dallas-Ft. Worth (pres. 1963), Rocky Mountain (past councilor) radiol. socs., Am. Roentgen Ray Soc. (certificate of merit exhibit 1949), Radiol. Soc. N. Am. (dir. 1959, chmn. bd. 1963, pres. 1965; certificate of merit exhibit 1949, gold medal 1973), Harris County Acad. Medicine (trustee 1966-76), Sigma Chi (life), Phi Chi (pres. chpt. 1937). Mason (K.T.). Contbr. profl. jours. Home: 1600 Holcombe Blvd Houston TX 77030 Office: 6723 Bertner Ave Houston TX 77030

MORFORD, CATHERINE ANNE, educator; b. El Paso, Tex., Aug. 3, 1945; d. Daniel Leroy and Edna Louise (Shaw) Morford; B.S., Hardin-Simmons U., 1967; M.S., Ind. U., 1972. Tchr. pub. schs., Ft. Worth, 1967-71, Ft. Worth Schs. Outdoor Learning Center, 1972-78; grad. teaching asst. Lorado Taft campus No. Ill. U., 1978-79; dir. Camp Waluta, Port Arthur Council Camp Fire Girls, summers 1973-75, Camp Tyogin, Camp Fire Girls' resident camp, Tyler, Tex., 1977. Recipient Perot award for teaching excellence Ft. Worth Sch. Bd., 1976; scholar Ind. U. Sch. Health, Phys. Edn. and Recreation, summer 1972, Ft. Worth Sch. Bd., Richmond Coll., London, Eng., summer 1976. Certified profl. educator. Mem. Tex., Ft. Worth classroom tchrs. assns., Tex. State Tchrs. Assn., NEA, Am. Camping Assn., Nat. Wildlife Fedn., Ind. U. Alumni Assn., Am. Inst. Fgn. Study, Delta Kappa Gamma. Co-author: Middle School Mathematics Continuum, 1970. Home: 9220 Shaver Dr El Paso TX 79925 Office: 3210 W Lancaster St Fort Worth TX 76107

MORFORD, WILLIAM JACOB, service co. exec.; b. Phila., Mar. 18, 1931; s. Herbert Northrup and Laura Bertha (Neef) M.; B.A., Hobart Coll., 1953; postgrad. in Hosp. Adminstrn., U. Minn., 1953-55; m. Jean Carter, May 4, 1956; children—Carter, Scott, Margo. Adminstrv. resident San Jose (Calif.) Hosp., 1954-55; mgmt. analysis supt. Parks AFB Hosp. (Calif.), 1955-56; salesman, dist. sales mgr. Vestal Labs. div. W.R. Grace, Calif., N.C., Fla., Md., 1958-71; dir. hosp. services Bldg. Services div. Macke Co., Cheverly, Md., 1971-72; dir. contract services Marriott Corp., Bethesda, Md., 1972-74; pres., prin. stockholder Health Environs, Inc., Lexington, S.C., 1974—; cons. in field. Served wtih U.S. Army, 1956-58. Mem. Bldg. Service Contractors Assn., Internat. Fabricare Inst. Episcopalian. Club: Lexington County Saddle. Home: Route 11 Box 285-A Lexington SC 29072 Office: 125 Parker St Lexington SC 29072

MORGAN, ALBERT RICHARD, JR., industrial exec.; b. Oakland, Calif., Feb. 1, 1922; s. Albert Richard and Genevieve Henrietta (Overman) M.; B.S. in Chemistry, U. Calif. at Berkeley, 1943, postgrad., 1947-48; m. Alice Marie Hill, Jan. 5, 1944; children—Richard John, Jacqueline Diane. Dir. research FMC Corp., Princeton, N.J., 1948-68; v.p. Panacon Corp., Cin., 1968-72; asst. to pres. Jim Walter Corp., Tampa, Fla., 1972-73; exec. v.p. Amicor, Inc., Tulsa, 1973—. Served to capt., Ordnance Corps, AUS, 1943-46. Mem. Am. Inst. Chem. Engrs., Am. Chem. Soc. Patentee in field. Home: 145 Center Plaza Tulsa OK 74119 Office: 424 N Boulder Tulsa OK 74101

MORGAN, ALMA DEURENE, ednl. adminstr.; b. Shamrock, Tex., Jan. 8, 1919; married, 2 children. B.S.L.S., North Tex. State U., 1950; M.S. in Curriculum, Houston U., 1955. Library tchr. Victoria (Tex.) Ind. Sch. Dist., 1948-60; curriculum coordinator pub. schs., Brownsville, Tex., 1962-68; supr. N.E. Ind. Sch. Dist., San Antonio, 1968—. Pres. Univ. Women, 1965-66. Mem. Tex. Assn. Sch. Librarians (pres.), Assn. Lang. Arts Suprs. (chmn.), Tex. Joint English Assn. (chmn.), Am. Assn. Supervision and Curriculum Devel., Tex. Assn. Supervision and Curriculum Devel., Internat. Reading Assn., Tex. Secondary Reading Council (pres. 1978-80), Tex. Joint Council Tchrs. English (v.p. 1977), ALA, Tex., Library Assn., Nat. Council Tchrs. English, Tex. Council Tchrs. English, Delta Kappa Gamma (pres. elect 1966-68). Home: 1118 Curlew Dr San Antonio TX 78213 Office: 10333 Broadway San Antonio TX 78286

MORGAN, ANTONIA BELL (MRS. WILLIAM J. MORGAN), psychologist; b. London, Oct. 5, 1914; d. James Young and Jean (Macnair) Bell; B.A., U. Oxford, 1936, M.A., 1945; tchrs. diploma U. London, 1938; m. William James Morgan, Nov. 2, 1944; children—William James, Jean Elizabeth, Robert Macnair. Came to U.S., 1946, naturalized, 1948. Chmn. dept. classical studies St. Albans Sch., Hertfordshire, Eng., 1938-41; Walter Hines Page scholar, lectr. English-Speaking Union, 1941-42; lectr. Brit. Ministry of Info., 1942-43, asst. prin., India Office, 1943-45; sec. Aptitude Assos., 1946-49, asso. dir. 1949-57; pvt. practice clin. psychology, 1951—; cons. ch. schs. Diocese Va.; lectr. mental health topics to civic groups, schs. Vice pres. No. Va. Mental Health Assn., 1959-61; trustee The Schefer Schs., 1972-77. Lic. clin. psychologist, Va. Mem. Am. Psychol. Assn., Va. Psychol. Assn., AAAS, Am. Personnel and Guidance Assn., English Speaking Union, Nat. Assn. Sch. Psychologists. Episcopalian. Author psychol. articles on edn. of gifted children, projective tests. Home and office: 2816 Gallows Rd Vienna VA 22180

MORGAN, BARBARA ANN, real estate broker; b. Owen County, Ky., Dec. 27, 1937; d. Lester James and Gladys Marie M.; student U. Ky., 1955-57; m. William R. Jones, Feb. 25, 1967 (div. Feb. 1971); m. 2d, John H. Gilliam, May 19, 1973 (div. Aug. 1977); 1 son, John H. II. Real estate salesman Dan Long Real Estate, Lexington, Ky., 1960-65; real estate broker Bill Jones Real Estate, Lexington, 1965-71; owner, mgr. Morgan Real Estate Co., 1971-78; partner, owner Century 21 Morgan-Gilliam Realtors, Lexington, 1978—. Mem. Lexington Bd. Realtors (dir.), Nat. Assn. Realtors, Ky. Assn. Realtors, Women's Council (past pres.). Baptist. Home: 703 Bullock Pl Lexington KY 40508 Office: 139 Walton Ave Lexington KY 40508

MORGAN, CARLISLE LEE, JR., radiologist; b. Wilmington, Del., July 9, 1944; s. Carlisle Lee and Loretta Theresa (Dzielakowski) M.; B.S. magna cum laude (Presdl. scholar), Villanova U., 1966; M.Phil. (Gibbs fellow), Yale U., 1968, Ph.D. in Physics, 1971; M.D. (Jesse Smith Noyes Found. scholar), U. Miami (Fla.), 1972; m. Joanne Pierson, Aug. 20, 1966; children—Eva Anastasia, Alexander Edmund, Ursula Joanne. Intern in internal medicine Duke U. Med. Center, Durham, N.C., 1973, resident in diagnostic radiology, 1974-76, asst. prof. radiology, co-dir. ultrasound and computed tomography, 1977-79; practice medicine specializing in radiology, Richmond, Va.; mem. staff St. Mary's Hosp. James Picker scholar, 1977-79. Diplomate Am. Bd. Med. Examiners, Am. Bd. Radiology. Mem. Interam. Coll. Radiology, Am. Coll. Med. Imaging, Am. Inst. Ultrasound in Medicine, Radiol. Soc. N. Am., Am. Coll. Radiology, Computerized Tomography Soc. Republican. Roman Catholic. Home: 8918 River Rd Richmond VA 23229 Office: Saint Mary's Hospital 5801 Bremo Rd Richmond VA 23226

MORGAN, CECIL, JR., urologist; b. Shreveport, La., Mar. 13, 1933; s. Cecil and Margaret Harriet (Geddes) M.; B.A., Tulane U., 1954, M.D., 1959; m. Jane Headley, Aug. 11, 1965; children—Philippa, Cecil, Delia, Alison Lockridge (stepdau.). Intern, Touro Infirmary, New Orleans; resident urology Ochsner Found. Hosp., New Orleans, 1959-63; asst. prof. urology U. Ala. Med. Sch., Birmingham, 1963-68; staff urologist Lloyd Noland Clinic, Birmingham, 1967-70; pvt. practice urology, Birmingham, 1970—; mem. staff Baptist Med. Center, St. Vincent's, Brookwood, U. Ala. hosps.; pres. surg. staff Children's Hosp., 1974, pres. gen. staff, 1976-77, asst. chief pediatric urology, 1977—; cons. Social Security Adminstrn.; asst. clin. prof. U. Ala. Med. Center, 1967—. Bd. dirs. Birmingham Opera. Fellow A.C.S.; asso. fellow urology Am. Acad. Pediatrics; mem. AMA, Am. Urol. Assn., Ala. Urology Soc. (past pres.), Soc. Pediatric Urology, Jefferson County Med. Soc. (trustee 1974-76, censor 1978-80), Newcomen Soc. N.Am., Delta Kappa Epsilon, Nu Sigma Nu. Clubs: Birmingham Country; Boston (New Orleans). Contbr. articles to med. jours. Chmn. bd. Ala. Med. Rev., 1974-78. Home: 4 Pine Ridge Ln Birmingham AL 35213 Office: 2660 10th Ave S Birmingham AL 35205

MORGAN, CLAYTON AQUILLA, educator; b. Jones County, Miss., Mar. 16, 1917; s. Aquilla Q. and Eleanor (Hinton) M.; student Jones County Jr. Coll., 1935-37; B.A., Millsaps Coll., 1940; M.Ed., U. Tex., 1949, Ed.D., 1953; m. Eleanor Frances Hoving, Aug. 1, 1950; children—Jane Eleanor, Clayton Aquilla. Tchr., Ellisville Jr. High Sch., 1940-41, 46-47; vocat. rehab. counselor Tex. Edn. Agy., Corpus Christi, 1952-58; instr. night classes Del Mar Jr. Coll., Corpus Christi, 1955-58; prof. psychology, coordinator rehab. counselor edn. Okla. State U., Stillwater, 1958—. Cons., VA. Vice pres., then pres. Corpus Christi Council for Retarded Children, 1955-57; mem. Okla. Gov.'s Com. on Employment Handicapped, 1972—. Mem. adv. com. Ark. Rehab. Research and Tng. Center, nat. adv. com. to develop model for tng. counsellors to place handicapped in employment. Served with USAAF, 1941-45. Recipient 50th Anniversary Commemorative medallion Rehab. Services Adminstrn., HEW, 1970. Distinguished lectr. spl. edn. and rehab. U. So. Calif., 1971; Lou P. Ortele lectr. Nat. Rehab. Assn. Ann. Conf., 1972. Mem. Nat. Rehab. Assn. (Presdl. citation for distinguished service adminstrv. and supervisory practices div. 1974), Nat. Rehab. Counseling Assn., Am. Personnel and Guidance Assn., Am. Rehab. Counseling Assn., Am. Assn. Workers for Blind, Creative Edn. Found., Rehab. Internat., Okla. Edn. Assn., Council Rehab. Counselor Educators, Omicron Delta Kappa, Phi Delta Kappa. Methodist. Contbr. articles to profl. jours. Home: 2004 W 11th Ave Stillwater OK 74074

MORGAN, DENNIS FRANKLIN, utility co. ofcl.; b. Youngstown, Ohio, Sept. 30, 1941; s. John B. and Lela Mae Morgan; A.A., A.S., Brevard Jr. Coll., 1964; B.S., Fla. State U., 1966; M.B.A., Nova U., 1979; m. Lynn Carol Harris, Sept. 20, 1975; children—Mark Eugene, Troy Thomas. Acctg. clk. Fla. Power & Light Co., 1966-68, office asst., 1968-70, acctg. supr., 1970-73, adminstrv. acctg. supr., 1973-78, corp. records adminstr., 1978—, instr. acctg. and public utility fin., 1972—. Mem. Assn. Records Mgrs. and Adminstrs. (dir. 1976-79), Nuclear Records Mgmt. Assn. (mem. com. 1978-79), Nat. Micrographics Assn., Delta Sigma Pi. Republican. Baptist. Home: 5200 Thoroughbred Ln Fort Lauderdale FL 33330 Office: 9250 W Flagler St Miami FL 33174

MORGAN, DOUGLAS GERALD, computer programmer; b. Houston, Dec. 9, 1952; s. Kay and Mary Francis (Douglas) M.; student Robert E. Lee Coll., 1968-70, Stephen F. Austin Coll., 1970-71, U. Houston, 1974-75. Computer operator, asso. programmer Exxon Corp. U.S.A., Houston, 1972-74; programmer-analyst Seismic and Digital Concepts, Inc., Houston, 1974-77; systems programmer-analyst Digital Resources Corp., Houston, 1977-79; geophys. programmer-analyst Digicon Inc., Houston, 1977-79; counselor East Garner Middle Sch., Garner, N.C., 1979—. Mem. Soc. Exploration Geophysicists, Geophys. Soc. Houston, Assn. Computer Programmers and Analysts, Instrumentation Soc. Am. Home: 115 Byron Pl Raleigh NC 27609

MORGAN, EDWIN BUFORD, hosp. adminstr.; b. Marlow, Okla., Dec. 11, 1918; s. William Pruitt and Sarah Elizabeth (Nevins) M.; student Ark. Tech. Coll., 1938-39, U. Okla., 1940; m. Mary Merle Arline, Sept. 30, 1944; children—Edwin Buford, Dennis Wayne, William Randolph. Asst. adminstr. Angus Hosp., Lawton, Okla., 1945-49; mgr. Double-Cola Bottling Co., Ardmore, Okla., 1949-51; adminstr. Lawton Clinic, 1951-66, John Buist Chester Hosp., also Chester Clinics, Dallas, 1966—. Vice pres. Dallas Hosp. Council, 1971, pres., 1972; dir. Regional Health Planning Council of N. Central Tex. Council Govts., exec. com., 1973-75. Mem. Dallas Fire Council, 1969-74; adv. com. Dallas Health Planning Council, 1970-74. Served with USCG, 1941-44. Recipient Silver Beaver award Boy Scouts Am. Fellow Am. Acad. Med. Adminstrs.; mem. Tex. Hosp. Assn. (chmn. Blacklands div. 1971), Okla. Anthrop. Soc. (pres. S.W. chpt. 1961, 65-66), Southwestern Okla. Hist. Soc. (sec.-treas. 1963-66). Author: Wichita Mountains, Ancient Oasis of the Prairie, 1973. Home: 1540 Driftwood Dr Dallas TX 75224 Office: 3330 S Lancaster St Dallas TX 75216

MORGAN, ELIZABETH, plastic surgeon; b. Washington, July 9, 1947; d. William James and Antonia (Bell) M.; B.A., Harvard U., 1967; postgrad. Somerville Coll., Oxford U., 1967; M.D., Yale U., 1971. Practice medicine specializing in plastic surgery, Vienna, Va., 1978—; columnist, med. cons. Cosmopolitan mag., 1973—; Author: The Making of a Woman Surgeon, 1980; also numerous articles on surgery and plastic surgery; columnist Ask Dr. Elizabeth, Register and Tribune Syndicate, 1977. Diplomate Am. Bd. Surgery, Am. Bd. Plastic Surgery. Fellow Internat. Coll. Surgeons; mem. AMA, So. Surg. Soc., Am. Med. Women's Soc., Va. Med. Soc., Washington Med. Soc. Club: Yale of D.C. Office: 2816 Gallows Rd Vienna VA 22180

MORGAN, EVAN, chemist; b. Spokane, Wash., Feb. 26, 1930; s. Evan and Emma Anne (Klobucher) M.; B.S., Gonzaga U., 1952; M.S., U. Wash., 1954, Ph.D. 1956; m. Johnnie Lu Dickson, Feb. 14, 1959; 1 son, James. Staff chemist IBM, Poughkeepsie, N.Y., 1956-60; group supr. Olin Mathieson Co., New Haven, 1960-64; asso. prof. chemistry High Point (N.C.) Coll., 1964-65; sr. research chemist Reynolds Metals Co., Richmond, Va., 1965-72; group supr. Babcock & Wilcox Co., Lynchburg, Va., 1972—. Mem. Am. Chem. Soc., ASTM. Home: 5128 Wedgewood Rd Lynchburg VA 24503 Office: PO Box 1260 Lynchburg VA 24505

MORGAN, GEORGE ROBERT, petroleum corp. exec.; b. Baton Rouge, Oct. 30, 1897; s. Thomas O. and Mattie H. (Joor) M.; student La. State U., 1920-21; m. Nell M. Boddeker, Aug. 5, 1925 (dec. Feb. 1978). Stenographer traffic dept. Gulf Coast Lines, 1916-17; chief clk. land dept. Sinclair Oil & Gas Co., 1918-19; clk.-stenographer Am. Petroleum Co., Tex., 1921-22, asst. sec., 1922—, dir., 1940—; asst. treas. Am. Republics Corp., 1932-51, chief communications div., 1951-56, ret., 1956. Democrat. Methodist. Home: 7248 Joor Rd Baton Rouge LA 70805

MORGAN, GEORGE TERRELL (TERRY), lawyer; b. Columbia, Miss., Sept. 7, 1937; s. Herbert Ramsay and Flossie (Sylvest) M.; A.A., Pearl River Jr. Coll., Poplarville, Miss., 1962; B.S.P.H., U. Miss., 1965, J.D., 1972; m. Sara Elizabeth Land, June 7, 1970; children—Michael Land, Elizabeth Jean. Pharmacist Lucedale Drug Co. (Miss.), 1965-66, Frisch's Drug Store, Mobile, Ala., 1966-69; admitted to Miss. bar, 1972; asso. firm Reeves & Reeves, McComb, 1972-73; partner firm Ratcliff & Morgan, McComb, 1973-74, Morgan & Price, McComb, 1975—. Served with USN, 1956-60. Mem. Tri-County, Miss. State, Am. bar assns., Delta Theta Phi, Phi Theta Kappa. Roman Catholic. Rotarian. Club: Fernwood Country. Home: Pinehurst Estates McComb MS 39648 Office: PO Box 694 McComb MS 39648

MORGAN, GRETCHEN MARIE, counselor coordinator; b. Okemah, Okla., May 14, 1948; d. Eugene M. and Suzanna (Tiger) Harjo; B.S., Northeastern State Coll., Tahlequah, Okla., 1971; M.Ed., Northeastern Okla. State U., Tahlequah, 1976; m. Ronnie Morgan, Nov. 10, 1973; children—Kevin (Scott), Tasha Suzanne. Elementary tchr. phys. edn. U.S. Bur. Indian Affairs, Concho, Okla., 1971-72, Headstart tchr. Deepfork Community Action, Henryetta, Okla., 1972-73; adult edn. tchr. U.S. Bur. Indian Affairs, Warner, Okla., 1973-74; bus. faculty, dir. adult edn. Connors State Coll., Warner, Okla., 1974-77, counselor, coordinator, Upward Bound 1977—; sec. local com. Johnson O. Malley Indian Edn. Com., 1978-79, v.p. Title IV Indian Edn., 1979-80. Mem. Okla. Edn. Assn. (local sec. 1976), Okla. Div. Student Assistance, Okla. Personnel and Guidance Assn., S.W. Assn. Student Assistance Programs, NEA, Nat. Indian Edn. Assn. Republican. Baptist. Home: 325 Faculty St Connors State Coll Warner OK 74469 Office: PO Box 304 Connors State Coll Warner OK 74469

MORGAN, HARCOURT ALEXANDER, JR., physician; b. Knoxville, Tenn., Aug. 20, 1909; s. Harcourt Alexander and Sara Elizabeth (Fay) M.; B.A., U. Tenn., 1931, M.D., 1933; M.P.H., Johns Hopkins U., 1941; m. Sarah Lanier Stone, Aug. 9, 1934; children—Harcourt Alexander, Sarah Lanier Morgan Davis, Lucy Fay Morgan Hinds. Intern, Memphis Gen. Hosp., 1933-35; resident, commd. officer U.S. Marine Hosp., Balt., 1936-37, Detroit, 1937; gen. practice medicine, Sparta, Tenn., 1937-39; pub. health physician Tenn. Dept. Pub. Health, 1939-78; pvt. practice medicine, Lewisburg, Tenn., 1978—; mem. staff Lewisburg Community Hosp.; dir. Bank Belfast, Tenn., Middle Tenn. Heart Assn., Nashville, 1970—; med. adviser Selective Service, Lewisburg, 1948—; dir. Marshall County Farm Bur., Lewisburg, 1955—. Served to 1st lt. AUS, 1935-36; served with USPHS, 1936-37. Diplomate Am. Bd. Preventive Medicine. Fellow Am. Pub. Health Assn.; mem. Am. Assn. Pub. Health Physicians (charter), Marshall County Med. Soc., Tenn. Med. Assn., AMA, Delta Omega. Methodist (ofcl. bd. 1948-72). Clubs: Elks, Lions (pres. 1956-57). Home: 1525 White Dr Lewisburg TN 37091 Office: 1525 White Dr Lewisburg TN 37091

MORGAN, HERMAN WILTON, educator; b. Brooksville, Fla., Apr. 13, 1925; s. Soloman Arleigh and Alice (Lee) M.; B.S., Fla. So. Coll., 1949; M.S., Fla. State U., 1958; m. Florence Harrison, Sept. 7, 1949 (dec. 1964); children—Laura Ann, Herman Wilton; m. 2d, Willette Phillips, Feb. 27, 1965. Linotype operator Dade City (Fla.) Banner, 1949-52; asso. editor Zephyrhills (Fla.) News, 1952-54; printing instr. Brewster Vocational Sch., Tampa, Fla., 1954-62; evening trade extension coordinator Evening Vocat. Sch., Tampa, 1962-63; prin. Adult Tech. Sch., Tampa, 1963-79, Brewster Vocat.-Tech. Center, Tampa, 1979—. Pres., Printing Industry Tampa, 1960-62; bd. dirs. Printing Industries Fla., 1960-62. Served with USNR, 1943-46. Mem. Fla. Vocational Assn. (v.p. 1961-63, 73-75, sec.-treas. 1963-66, 68-71, pres. 1967, Carl Proehl award 1977), Indsl. Edn. Assn. Fla. (pres. 1961-62, 73-75), Am. Vocat. Assn., Am. Assn. Sch. Adminstrs., Theta Chi, Phi Delta Kappa, Iota Lambda Sigma. Democrat. Methodist. Home: 410 Island Rd Temple Terrace FL 33617 Office: 3606 10th Ave Tampa FL 33605

MORGAN, HUGH JACKSON, JR., natural gas exec.; b. Nashville, Aug. 10, 1928; s. Hugh Jackson and Robert Ray (Porter) M.; A.B., Princeton U., 1950; LL.B., Vanderbilt U., 1956; m. Ann Moulton Ward, Aug. 28, 1954; children—Ann, Grace, Caroline, Hugh Jackson III. Admitted to Tenn. bar, 1956; practiced in Chattanooga, 1956-60; with So. Natural Gas Co., Birmingham, Ala., 1960—, asst. gen. counsel, asst. sec., 1965-66, gen. atty., asst. sec., 1966-70, asst. v.p., gen. atty., asst. sec., 1970-71, v.p. pipeline affairs, 1971-73, sr. v.p., 1978—, v.p. So. Natural Resources, Inc., 1973-79, sr. v.p., 1979—; dir. S.Ga. Natural Gas Co., Thomasville, Offshore Co., Houston, Sea Robin Pipeline Co., Houston. Trustee Children's Hosp., Birmingham. Served from ensign to lt. (j.g.) USNR, 1950-53. Recipient Bennett Douglas Bell Meml. award Vanderbilt Law Sch., 1956. Mem. Am., Tenn. bar assns., Am., So. gas assns., Ind. Natural Gas Assn. Am., Order of Coif. Episcopalian. Clubs: Mountain Brook, Downtown (Birmingham); Boston (New Orleans); Army-Navy (Washington); University Cottage (Princeton); Linville (N.C.) Golf. Home: 3121 Brookwood Rd Mountain Brook AL 35223 Office: First Nat-So Natural Bldg PO Box 2563 Birmingham AL 35202

MORGAN, JACK COCHRAN, lawyer; b. Sweetwater, Tex., Mar. 17, 1928; s. John Franklin and Tommie Lee (Cochran) M.; B.A., Tex. U., 1948, LL.B., 1950; m. Millicent Edmunds, Jan. 24, 1953; children—Millicent, Jack C. Admitted to Tex. bar, 1950, practiced in Kaufman, 1950—; asst. county atty., Kaufman, 1951; mem. firm Morgan and Mosley; dir. Farmers & Merchants Nat. Bank, Kaufman. Dem. county chmn., 1965; mem. Tex. legislature, 1955. Mem. State Bar Grievance Com. Chmn. bd. regents Tex. Eastern U., 1973-74; regent Tex. Eastern U. Found., 1970-79. Mem. Kaufman County, (past pres.), Tri-County bar assns., Sigma Chi. Mason, Rotarian. Home: 1506 S Houston St Kaufman TX 75142 Office: 201 W Mulberry St Kaufman TX 75142

MORGAN, JAMES BAKER, lawyer; b. Fort Worth, Tex., Dec. 14, 1940; s. James N. and Ruth Alice (Baker) M.; B.B.A., Baylor U., 1963, J.D., 1964; m. Sherry Diane Rawls, Dec. 28, 1962; children—James

Michael, Marshall Wayne. Admitted to Tex. bar, 1964; asst. city atty. Fort Worth, 1964; atty. Office Chief Counsel, IRS, Washington, 1965-66, Jacksonville, Fla., 1966-69; partner Handy, Morgan & Meeks, Hurst, Tex., 1969—; dir. Tex. Commerce Bank, Hurst. Mem. sch. bd. Hurst Euless Bedford Ind. Sch. Dist., 1971-79, pres., 1977-79; bd. mgrs. YMCA, 1971—, chmn., 1979—. Mem. Am., Tex., N.E. Tarrant County bar assns., Phi Delta Phi. Clubs: Rotary (pres. 1973-74), Woodhaven Country (Fort Worth). Baptist. Home: 6212 Camelot Ct Fort Worth TX 76118 Office: 1409 Precinct Line Rd Hurst TX 76053

MORGAN, JAMES LELAND, palynologist; b. Gatesville, Tex., Nov. 9, 1914; s. William Pruit and Sarah Elizabeth (Nevins) M.; student So. Meth. U., 1950-51; B.S., U. Okla., 1953, M.S., 1955; m. Blanche Therese Williams, Aug. 14, 1954; children—Karen Michelle, Paul Timothy. Palynologist research div. Humble Oil & Refining Co., Houston, 1955-64, Esso Prodn. Research Co., Houston, 1964-74, Exxon Prodn. Research Co., Houston, 1974—. Served with inf. AUS, 1941-46; ETO. Recipient Bronze Star (3), 5 service medals, Silver Star. Mem. Am. Assn. Petroleum Geologists, Soc. Econ. Paleontologists and Mineralogists, Paleontol. Soc., Am. Assn. Stratigraphic Palynologists, Sigma Xi, Sigma Gamma Epsilon. Republican. Methodist. Author: Spores of McAlester Coal, 1955; contbr. articles to profl. jours. Pioneer in using fossil spores and pollen for stratigraphic correlations, geologic age determinations, and as an aid in oil exploration; pioneer microscopic analysis of kerogen to predict hydrocarbon source potential of sedimentary rocks. Home: 2205 Nantucket Dr Houston TX 77057 Office: PO Box 2189 Houston TX 77001

MORGAN, JAMES WILLIAM, civil engr.; b. Jackson, Tenn., Oct. 3, 1946; s. James Edward and Emma Anne (Timbes) M.; student U. Tenn., Martin, 1964-66; B.S.C.E., Tenn. Tech. U., 1968; M.S. in Civil Engring., U. Tenn., Knoxville, 1975; m. Sherry Jean Ward, Dec. 17, 1967; children—Stacey Renee, Jeremy Ward. Civil engr., tech. supr. TVA, Knoxville, Tenn., 1968—. Registered profl. engr., Tenn. Mem. Chi Epsilon, Alpha Tau Omega. Democrat. Presbyterian. Home: 1016 Rennboro Rd Knoxville TN 37923 Office: 400 Commerce Ave Knoxville TN 37902

MORGAN, JIMMY DALE, electronic engr.; b. Dallas, July 28, 1944; s. James Middleton and Bennie Frances (Holman) M.; B.S.E.E., U. Tex., 1969; A.S. in Aviation Adminstrn., Mountain View Coll., 1974; B.S. in Mech. Engring., U. Houston, 1978; m. Mary Ellen Turner, May 23, 1964; children—La Dawn Babette, Brigitte Monique. With Tex. Instrument Co., Dallas, 1965-67, LTV Corp., Dallas, 1967-76; elec. project engr. DFW Regional Airport Bd., DFW Airport, Tex., 1976—. Precinct chmn. Democratic Party, 1968. FCC licensed, 19. Mem. ASME, Nat. Soc. Profl. Engrs., Tex. Soc. Profl. Engrs., Soc. Logistics Engrs. Contbr. articles in field to profl. jours. Home: 714 SW Dallas St Grand Prairie TX 75051 Office: PO Box 61204 DFW Airport TX 75261

MORGAN, JOE LEE, librarian; b. nr. Marshall, N.C., May 14, 1931; s. Frank Woodard and Effie Mae (McDaris) M.; A.B. in History and Polit. Sci., Berea Coll., 1954; postgrad. No. Ill. U., 1955, U. Hawaii, 1956, U. Colo., 1957, 58, U. N.C., 1957-58, Asian Affairs Inst., Duke, summer 1959; M.A. (Title II-B grantee), East Tenn. State U., 1975; J.D., Woodrow Wilson Law Sch., 1978; diploma hotel-motel tng. LaSalle Extension U.; diploma Atlanta Sch. Apt. Mgrs., 1976. Farmer, Marshall, 1945-75; tchr. pub. schs., Mendota, Ill, 1954-55, Charlotte, N.C., 1957-59; tchr.-librarian Madison County (N.C.) Schs., 1959-65; librarian Truett-McConnell Coll., Cleveland, Ga., 1965-67; tchr. history Capt. Riverside Mil. Acad., Gainesville, Ga., 1967-69; librarian Vardell Hall Girls' Prep. Sch., Red Springs, N.C., 1969-72; mgr. Cavalier Motel, Asheville, N.C., 1972-73; librarian Cloverleaf Sch., Cartersville, Ga., 1973-78. Owner, Circle A Motel, Cedartown, Ga., 1976-79. Regional rep. N.C. Sch. Performing Arts; mem. library council, chmn. adult lit. program French Broad Bapt. Assn., 1964-67, clk., 1965-69, contbr. minutes, 1965-69; Sunday Sch. sec., tchr., supt., librarian Peek's Chapel Bapt. Ch., Marshall, 1946-66; mem. Arts and Humanities Commn., Council So. Mountains, 1966-69, edn. commn., 1970-73; mem. Citizens Com. for Free Cuba; bd. policy of Liberty Lobby; mem. Am. Friends Vietnam, Inc.; mem. Civic Arts Council, Inc. Asheville, N.C., 1964-67; active A.R.C. Broadcasting bd. sponsors Radio Free Asia. Precinct chmn., mem. Mecklenburg County Republican Exec. Com., 1958-59; temporary chmn. White County (Ga.) Rep. Conv., 1966; 1st vice chmn. White County Rep. party, 1966-67; del. Ga. congl. and state convs., 1966, 75, N.C., 1958, 62, 64, 70, 71, 73, 74, 75, 79; mem. United Reps. Am.; chmn. Robeson County Young Reps., 1970-71; chmn. community services com. N.C. Fedn. Young Reps., 1971, also mem. exec. bd.; del. Young Reps. Fedn. nat. conv., Phoenix, 1971; chmn. Madison County Rep. Com., 1971-73; mem. 11th Dist. N.C. Rep. exec. com., 1971-73; del. So. Rep. Conf., 1973; mem., sec. Madison County Bd. Elections, 1974-77; mem. Mitchell County Bd. Health, 1980—; parliamentarian project rev. com. Western N.C. Health Systems Agy.; nat. adv. council Nat. Right to Work Found. Served with AUS, 1955-57. Recipient certificate appreciation N.C. Rep. party, founding supporter's certificate Radio Free Asia; named Young Am. of Day radio sta. WWNC, Asheville, N.C.; commd. Ky. col. Mem. N.E.A. (del. assembly), N.C. Edn. Assn., N.C. Librarians Assn., Ga. Assn. Educators (del. rep. assembly 1973, del. state conv. 1975), Korean Cultural and Freedom Found., Young Ams. for Freedom, N.C. Literary and Hist. Assn., RCA Victor Soc. Great Music (founding mem.), N.C. Farm Bur., Nat. Congress Parents and Tchrs., Western N.C. (chmn. awards com. 1973-76), Roanoke Island (chmn. Madison County 1971-72) hist. assns., Madison County Classroom Tchrs. Assn. (sec.-treas. 1959-63), N.C. Soc. Preservation Antiquities, U.N. Assn. U.S., Asheville (N.C.) Community Concerts Assn., Am.'s Future, Inc., Am. Econ. Found., Internat. Platform Assn., Common Cause, United Taxpayers Am. Author: A Librarian's Handbook, 1964; Reflection on the Scopes Evolution Trial, 1965; North Carolina and the Admission of Kansas, 1966; Jeter Conley Pritchard, Senator and Jurist, 1975; weekly column Profiles and Flashbacks, Tri-County News, Spruce Pine, N.C., 1980—. Contbr. to profl. publs. Home: East Fork Route 2 Marshall NC 28753

MORGAN, JOHN CAMPBELL, JR., architect; b. Richmond, Va., Aug. 5, 1939; s. John Campbell and Lillian Virginia (Jones) M.; student Va. Commonwealth U., 1963, 64, Va. Inst. Tech., 1965-66; m. Marilyn Gill Williams, July 15, 1967; children—Anne Wesley, John Campbell. Draftsman, Ben R. Johns Jr., Architect, Richmond, 1967-70, Alan McCullough, Architect, 1970-71, Ernie Rose, Architect, 1971-72, Budina & Freeman, Architects, 1972-75; partner, architect Freeman & Morgan, Architects, Richmond, 1975—. Served with USAF, 1961-62. Mem. Constrn. Specifications Inst. (sec. 1977-80), Va. Soc. Architects, AIA, Engrs. Club Richmond. Home: 2355 Brookwood Rd Richmond VA 23235 Office: 6716 Patterson Ave Richmond VA 23226

MORGAN, JULIA ELIZABETH, chemist; b. Asheville, N.C., Oct. 18, 1922; d. Clyde Terrell and Ada Angeline (Anders) Morgan; A.A., Asheville Biltmore Jr. Coll., 1941; student N.C. State U., 1942-43; B.S. in Chemistry, U. N.C., 1944. Research chemist Ecusta Paper Corp., Pisgah Forest, N.C., 1944-49; toxicological chemist Bowman Gray Sch. of Medicine, Winston-Salem, N.C., 1949-51; toxicological chemist Cabarrus Meml. Hosp., Concord, N.C., 1951-52; blood chemist VA Hosp., Oteen, N.C., 1952-53; research chemist Am. Enka Co. Akzona, Inc., Enka, N.C., 1953-59, mgr. rayon research analytical lab., 1959-62, research chemist, 1962-63, mgr. polymer control lab. and analytical devel. lab., 1964, head, research analytical sect., 1965-78, mgr. analytical and testing research dept., 1978—; tchr. chemistry Cabarrus County Hosp. Sch. Nursing, 1951, Asheville-Biltmore Coll., 1959-62. Troop leader Pisgah council Girl Scouts U.S.A., 1956-60. Mem. Am. Chem. Soc., (Western Carolinas sect. sec. 1962), Am. Assn. Textile Chemists and Colorists, U. N.C. Alumni Assn. Baptist. Home: Hartshorn Rd Route 6 Box 310 Candler NC 28715 Office: Research Center Enka NC 28728

MORGAN, KARL ZIEGLER, health physicist; b. Enochsville, N.C., Sept. 27, 1907; s. Jacob Levi and Elizabeth Virginia Clay (Shoup) M.; student Lenoir Rhyne Coll., 1925-27; B.A., U. N.C., 1929, M.A., 1930; Ph.D., Duke U., 1934; D.Sc. (hon.), Lenoir Rhyne Coll., 1967; m. Helen Lee McCoy, Aug. 2, 1937; children—Karl Ziegler, Eric Lee, Joan Elen, Diana. Chmn. physics dept. Lenoir Rhyne Coll., 1934-43; with metall. lab. U. Chgo., 1943; dir. health physics div. Oak Ridge Nat. Lab., 1943-72; prof. nuclear engring. Ga. Inst. Tech., Atlanta, 1972—; witness 15 Congressional hearings on radiation protection. Recipient 1st gold medal for radiation protection Royal Acad. Sweden, 1962. Fellow Am. Coll. Radiology, Am. Phys. Soc., Am. Nuclear Soc.; mem. Health Physics Soc. (founding pres.), AAAS, Am. Indsl. Hygiene Soc., Internat. Comm. Radiol. Protection, Radiation Research Soc., Nat. Council Radiation Protection, Sigma Xi. Democrat. Lutheran. Contbr. numerous articles to profl. jours.; editor: Principles of Radiation Protection, 1967; patentee in field. Home: 1984 Castleway Dr Atlanta GA 30345 Office: Sch Nuclear Engring Ga Inst Tech Atlanta GA 30332

MORGAN, MARIANNE, bus. exec.; b. Muncie, Ind., Oct. 13, 1940; d. Clarence Wilson and Mary Estle (Shafer) M.; student Ball State U., 1958-61; B.A., Calif. State U., 1962; M.S., U. So. Calif., 1968; postgrad. U. Calif. at Long Beach, 1962-63, U. Calif. at Irvine, 1970-74, So. Fla. U., 1974—. Library asst. Anaheim (Calif.) Pub. Library, 1963-65, sr. library asst., 1965-68; librarian Orange Coast Coll., Costa Mesa, Calif., 1968-74, exec. v.p., dir. F.E. Brady Products, Inc., Clearwater, Fla., 1974—; dir. Brady Air Controls, Inc., Muncie, 1976—; partner Pine Meadow Ranch, Inverness, Fla. Alice M. Kitselman scholar, 1958. Mem. Calif. Library Assn., Faculty Assn. Calif. Community Colls., Wilderness Soc., ACLU, NOW, Sierra Club, Common Cause, Gamma Theta Upsilon, Beta Phi Mu. Republican. Home: Route 1 1331 Appaloosa Rd Tarpon Springs FL 33589 Office: PO Box 5304 2151 Logan St Clearwater FL 33515

MORGAN, MARY FRANCISCO, ednl. counselor; b. Madison, Ind., Jan. 22, 1918; d. Van Edwin and Alice Joyce (Millar) Francisco; A.B., Hanover Coll., 1940; M.Ed., N.C. State U., 1973; m. Douglas Morgan, Nov. 24, 1951; children—Ann, Leonard, Paul, Alice, Joseph. Social worker Jefferson County (Ind.) Welfare Dept., Madison, 1940-41; sec., personnel rep., shipping supr. Seagram Distillers, Ind., Ky. and Pa., 1941-43; clk.-sec. Brit. Mcht. Shipping Mission, Washington, 1943-44; research asst. Office Inter-Am. Affairs, Voice of Am., Washington and N.Y.C., 1944-47; fgn. service staff, Santiago, Chile, 1947-51; tchr. English, Wake County and Raleigh (N.C.) schs., 1965-66, 67-68, 69-70; mem. staff N.C. Gen. Assembly, 1955-73; guidance counselor Wake County Schs., 1974—, N. Garner (N.C.) Jr. High Sch., from 1974, now E. Garner Middle Sch. Tri Kappa scholar, 1939-40. Mem. NEA, N.C. Assn. Educators, Am., N.C. personnel and guidance assns., Raleigh Panhellenic, Wake County Democratic Women, Ch. Choir and Altar Soc., Phi Mu. Democrat. Roman Catholic. Home: 115 Byron Pl Raleigh NC 27609 Office: E Garner Middle Sch Garner NC 27529

MORGAN, MILDRED IMOGENE, speech pathologist, ednl. adminstr.; b. La Grange, Ga., Sept. 12, 1947; d. James Marshall and Mildred Lillian (Strickland) M.; B.A., Trinity U., 1969; M.A., Our Lady of Lake U., 1974. Tchr. remedial/clerical skills San Antonio Neighborhood Youth Corps, 1969-70; speech pathologist San Antonio Ind. Sch. Dist., 1970-73, lead speech pathologist, 1974-78, supr. spl. edn., 1978—; lectr., cons. in field. Recipient P.L. McAnear medal, 1967; Bd. Nat. Missions scholar, 1965-69; cert. speech, history, spl. edn. supr. lang. and learning disabilities mid-mgmt. Mem. Am. Speech and Hearing Assn. (cert. clin. competence), San Antonio Speech, Lang. and Hearing Assn. (pres. 1977-78), NEA, Tex. Tchrs. Assn., Tex. Council Suprs., San Antonio Adminstrs. and Suprs. Assn., Public Sch. Caucus. Baptist. Chief editor: Comprehensive Special Education Plan: A Guide for Speech, Hearing and Language Therapists, 1976. Home: 742 McDougal St San Antonio TX 78223 Office: San Antonio Ind Sch Dist 1910 Rigsby St San Antonio TX 78210

MORGAN, NEVILLE NEWTON, sociologist; b. Guyana, S. Am., Nov. 18, 1937; came to U.S., 1964, naturalized, 1973; s. Edgar Messiah and Leonie M.; B.A., St. Francis Coll., N.Y., 1969; M.A., U. Cin., 1974, Ph.D. candidate, 1974—; m. Constance Eileen Denney, Apr. 25, 1964; children—Dawn Michelle, Michael Neville, Nicole Rene. Acctg. clk. Govt. Guyana, 1956-64; instr. sociology Central State U., Wilberforce, Ohio, 1970-73; asst. prof. Ky. State U., Frankfort, 1975—. NIH fellow, summers 1978—. Mem. Am. Sociol. Assn., Guyana Sociol. Soc., Caribbean Studies Assn., Alpha Kappa Delta. Democrat. Methodist. Home: Route 9 Poe Ln Frankfort KY 40601 Office: Dept Sociology Ky State U Frankfort KY 40601

MORGAN, RICHARD MICHAEL, chemist; b. Daytona Beach, Fla., Dec. 29, 1946; s. Richard Talford and Mildred Ann (Makatura) M.; B.S. in Biology, Youngstown State U., 1974, M.S. in Chemistry, 1976; m. Georgiann Williams, Aug. 23, 1975. Materials research engr. Packard Electric, Warren, Ohio, 1974-76; research chemist Dow Chem. Co., Plaquemine, La., 1976—. Lab. supr. Community Free Clinic; adv. Jr. Achievement; mem. Baton Rouge Jaycees. Served with USMC, 1965-69. Decorated Bronze Star, Purple Heart. Mem. Am. Chem. Soc., Soc. Plastics Engrs., Internat. Wire Assn., IEEE, Power Engring. Soc., Insulated Conductors Com., ASTM, Sigma Xi. Roman Catholic. Club: K.C. Home: 15934 Malvern Hill Baton Rouge LA 70816 Office: Hwy 1 Bldg 2307 Plaquemine LA 70764

MORGAN, ROBERT BURREN, senator; b. Lillington, N.C., Oct. 5, 1925; s. James Harvey and Alice (Butts) M.; B.S., E. Carolina Coll., 1947; LL.B., Wake Forest Coll., 1950; m. Katie Owen, Aug. 1960; children—Margeret Ann, Mary Elizabeth, Alice Jean (dec.), Rupert. Admitted to N.C. bar, 1950; clk. Superior Ct. Harnett County, N.C., 1950-54, also judge probate, juvenile cts.; practiced in Lillington, from 1954, mem. firm Morgan Jones; mem. N.C. Senate, 1955-68, pres. pro tem, 1965-68; atty. gen. N.C., Raleigh, 1969-75; senator from N.C., 1975—. Served as ensign USNR, 1944-46, lt. comdr., 1952-53; Korea. Mem. Am. Bar Assn., N.C. Bar Assn., Am. Trial Lawyers Assn., Am. Legion, VFW, E. Carolina Gen. Alumni Assn. (pres. 1956-59), Phi Alpha Delta, Phi Sigma Pi. Baptist. Rotarian (past pres.), Mason; mem. Order Eastern Star. Home: Morgan Dr Lillington NC 27546

MORGAN, ROBERT EARLE, educator; b. Rutherfordton, N.C., Mar. 2, 1935; s. Roy Gilbert and Sue Belle (Hampton) M.; A.B., Lenoir Rhyne Coll., 1956; M.Ed., U. N.C., Chapel Hill, 1961, Ph.D., 1971; Tchr. math. and French, Wadesboro (N.C.) High Sch., 1956-59, Wingate (N.C.) Coll., 1959-67; prof. French and math. Gardner-Webb Coll., Boiling Springs, N.C., 1967—. Recipient J.R. Anderson Meml. Math. award Rutherfordton-Spindale Central High Sch., 1952. Mem. Am. Assn. Tchrs. of French, S. Atlantic MLA, Phi Delta Kappa. Democrat. Baptist. Author: Portrait of Myself, 1965. Home: PO Box 903 Boiling Springs NC 28017 Office: Gardner-Webb Coll Boiling Springs NC 28017

MORGAN, THEAOSTER CARL, educator; b. Memphis, Nov. 12, 1929; s. Otis V. and LouAnna (Judy) M.; M.S., U. N.D., 1962; Ed.D. (fellow), Ball State U., 1972. Tchr., McNair High Sch., Belzoni, Miss., 1959-61; asst. prof. bus. Ala. A&M U., Huntsville, 1962-66; prof. bus. edn. S.C. State Coll., Orangeburg, 1966—. Served with U.S. Army, 1948-55. Mem. Nat. Bus. Edn. Assn., Am. Assn. Sch. Adminstrs., Nat. Orgn. Legal Problems in Edn., Phi Delta Kappa, Delta Pi Epsilon, Phi Beta Lambda, VFW (quartermaster Post 8166, 1978—). Democrat. Presbyterian. Home and Office: PO Box 1642 SC State Coll Orangeburg SC 29117

MORGAN, WILLIAM JAMES, psychologist; b. Rochester, N.Y., Apr. 30, 1910; A.B., U. Rochester, 1933; Ph.D., Yale, 1937; m. Antonia Mary Farquharson Bell, Nov. 2, 1944; children—William James, Jean Elizabeth, Robert Macnair. Chief clinician Vineland (N.J.) Tng. Sch., 1936-38; psychologist Bd. Edn., Rochester, N.Y., 1939-41; dir. Psychol. Test Bur., Rochester, 1941-42; dep. chief tng., chief psychol. assessment CIA, 1947-52; mem. Psychol. Strategy Bd., White House, 1952-53; pres. Aptitude Assos., Merrifield, Va., 1953—; mem. Army Research Com.; cons. Dept. Justice, Dept. Def., other agys. Mem. Va. Bd. Certification Clin. Psychologists. Served from pvt. to maj. AUS, 1942-47; OSS, ETO. Diplomate in clin. psychology Am. Bd. Examiners Profl. Psychology. Mem. Va. Psychol. Assn. (pres. 1957-58), Sigma Xi. Author: Spies and Saboteurs (Gollancs-London), 1955; The O.S.S. and I, 1957; numerous articles and tests. Home: 2816 Gallows Rd Vienna VA 22180

MORGAN, WILLIAM JAY, coll. pres.; b. Huntington, W.Va., Dec. 15, 1929; s. Fred Joseph and Mabel Clare (Gill) M.; B.A., Ky. Christian Coll., 1951; M.A., U. Tex., El Paso, 1973; postgrad. Nova U.; m. Dorothy Clay, Aug. 30, 1951; s. William David, Dennis James, Beverly Jean. Ordained to ministry Ind. Christian Ch., 1950; minister chs., W.Va., Ohio, Va., Tex., 1950-71; evangelist Kyowva Evang. Assn., 1955-56; instr. Grundy Bible Inst., 1956-60, So. Christian Coll., 1960-61; dir. Spanish Am. Evangelism, Inc., El Paso, Tex., 1964-74; instr. El Paso Community Coll., 1973-77; pres. El Paso Christian Coll., 1974—; instr. U.S. Sgt. Major Acad., 1974-77. Served with USNG, 1947-48. Mem. Nat. Missionary Conv. (pres. 1977), Am. Assn. Univ. Adminstrs. Club: Lions. Contbr. articles to religious jours. Home: 5716 Prince Edward Ave El Paso TX 79924 Office: 7412 Mundy Dr El Paso TX 79902

MORGAN, WILLIAM JOSEPH, JR., educator; b. Boston, Sept. 17, 1924; s. William Joseph and Mabel Agnes (Cheney) M.; B.S. with distinction, Cornell U., 1959, Ph.D. (Heinz-Nat. Restaurant Found. Tchr. tng. fellow 1969-70), 1971; M.S., SUNY, Albany, 1967; m. Beatrice Ellen Streets, Aug. 30, 1943; children—Virginia Ilene, Michael. Asst. prof., then asso. prof. SUNY, Delhi, 1962-67; instr. St. Petersburg (Fla.) Jr. Coll., 1967-69; lectr. Cornell U., 1969-71; prof. hotel and restaurant mgmt. Fla. Internat. U., Miami, 1972—; cons. in field. Served to lt. comdr. USN, 1942-62; service in ETO, Africa, Italy, Korea. Hospitality Edn. fellow Fla. Restaurant Assn., 1969-70. Mem. Council Hotel, Restaurant and Instl. Edn., Am. Soc. Hosp. Food Service Adminstrs., Cornell Soc. Hotelmen, Cornell U. Sch. Adminstrn. Ye Hosts Soc. Republican. Roman Catholic. Author textbooks, articles in field. Home: 170 Velma Dr Largo FL 33540 Office: Sch Hospitality Mgmt Fla Internat Univ Tamiami Trail Miami FL 33199

MORGAN, WILLS NAPIER, advt. agy. exec.; b. Nashville, Apr. 2, 1916; s. Edwin Scruggs and Mary Lee (Napier) M.; student Vanderbilt U., 1932-34; m. Eloise Hanley, Oct. 5, 1940; children—Wills Napier, Mary Lisa (dec.), Eloise Hanley. Auditor, U.S. Govt., Nashville, 1934-36; purchasing agt. Genesco, Inc. (formerly Gen. Shoe Corp.), Nashville, 1936-46; partner Morgan Enterprises, Nashville, 1946—. Served with U.S. Army, 1944-46. Mem. Splty. Advt. Assn. Internat., Advt. Splty. Inst., Soc. Plastics Engrs. Baptist. Club: Downtown Nashville Lions. Home: 4325 Signal Hill Dr Nashville TN 37205 Office: 116 16th Ave N Nashville TN 37203

MORGAN, YOWELL SPANN, banker; b. Dublin, Tex., Feb. 16, 1907; s. Robert Morris and Minerva Allene (Jones) M.; student Abilene Christian Coll., 1927-28, 42-43; m. Margarette Allene Lowery, Apr. 2, 1926; children—Flora Merle Morgan Gobbel, Joy Sandra Morgan Larson, Judy Ann. Supr., Southwestern Bell Telephone Co., Ft. Worth, 1924-72; v.p. Northwest Bank, Ft. Worth, 1972—, also adv. dir. Mem., past chmn. Burleson Ind. Sch. Dist. Tax Equalization Bd.; treas. White Settlement-West Worth unit Am. Cancer Soc.; past pres. White Settlement Hist. Soc.; hon. commr. Tarrant County; mem. Service Corps Ret. Execs. of SBA; chmn., election judge Precinct 24 Democratic Party; mem. Tarrant County Dem. Exec. Com.; bd. dirs. 1st Tex. council Camp Fire Inc.; treas. Hist. Preservation Council for Tarrant County Texas Inc. Recipient Disting. Service award Kiwanis Internat., 1975, Tex. Ho. of Reps. Mem. White Settlement C. of C. (past mgr., pres. 1975, Man of Year 1974, Outstanding Community Service award 1975), Telephone Pioneers Am. (past pres. life mem. club, treas., mem. exec. council Ft. Worth). Mem. Ch. of Christ. Clubs: Lions (past pres. Burleson, Lion of Year award 1970-71, 78-79, past zone chmn., past dep. dist. gov., past dist cabinet sec.-treas., now dist. found. chmn.), Masons, White Settlement Kiwanis (dir.), Burleson Band Boosters (past pres.). Home: Route 3 1016 Oak Grove Rd E Burleson TX 76028 Office: 101 Jim Wright Freeway Fort Worth TX 76108

MORGANSTERN, ARTHUR LEON, electronics co. exec.; b. Lublin, Poland, Nov. 25, 1931; came to U.S., 1938, naturalized, 1943; s. Kay and Anna (Lerman) M.; B.S. in Bus. Adminstrn., U. Louisville, 1954; B.S. in Elec. Engring., Ill. Inst. Tech., 1960; M.S. in Elec. Engring., N.Y. U., 1962, Ph.D., 1970; m. Annette Appel, Feb. 1, 1953; children—Deborah, Rhoni. Mem. tech. staff Bell Labs., Whippany, N.J., 1960-65; research engr. Grumman Aircraft, Bethpage, N.Y., 1965-67; sr. engr. Resalab, Los Angeles, 1970-72; sr. specialist E-Systems, Garland, Tex., 1972-75; mgr. engring. Bell Tech. Ops., Killeen, Tex., 1975-79; mgr. info. systems Kentron Internat., Dallas, 1979—. Mem. Plano Human Relations Council, 1972-73. Served with U.S. Army, 1955-57. Mem. IEEE (IEEE Outstanding Student award, 1960), Optical Soc., Am. Contract Bridge League, Tau Beta Pi, Eta Kappa Nu. Democrat. Jewish. Contbr. articles in field to profl. jours. Home: 1112 Longworth St Plano TX 75075 Office: 2345 W Mockingbird Dallas TX 75235

MORGENSTERN, PAULINE CECILE, accountant; b. Houston, May 7, 1916; d. Gilbert Cecil and Sarah Mae (Hirsch) Lechenger; B.A., Rice U., 1936; B.B.A., U. Houston, 1962, M.B.A., 1965; m. Gerard Joseph Morgenstern; children—Margery, Carol, Joan, Patsy. Office mgr. Laufman's, Houston, 1965; accountant Stop & Go Co., Houston, 1965-69, internal auditor, 1970-71; pvt. practice accounting, Houston, 1972—; v.p. L. Lochenger, Inc., 1952-60. C.P.A., Tex. Mem. Tex. Soc. C.P.A.'s, S.W. Civic Assn., Am. Contract Bridge

League, Council Jewish Women. Home: 3706 Dumbarton St Houston TX 77025 Office: 3700 Buffalo Speedway Suite 403 Houston TX 77098

MORGRET, ANDREW JACOB, univ. adminstr.; b. Napoleon, Ohio, Aug. 1, 1941; s. Frank Clay, Jr., and Ruth Shepard (Love) M.; B.S. in Edn., Memphis State U., 1968, M.Ed., 1971; m. Jane Gay Hoskins, Nov. 22, 1967; 2 children—Ann Marie, Mimi Gay. Quality control mgr. Header Products, Inc., Romulus, Mich., 1968-70; grad. research asst. Memphis State U., 1970-71, asst. dir. records, 1975-78, asso. dean admissions and records, 1978—; guidance counselor Wonder Jr. High Sch., West Memphis, Ark., 1971-75; mem. ESEA Needs Assessment Com., West Memphis public schs., 1974. Served with USMC, 1961-63. Mem. Am. Coll. Personnel Assn., Am. Ednl. Studies Assn., Am. Personnel and Guidance Assn., Am. Assn. Coll. Registrars and Admissions Officers, So. Assn. Coll. Registrars and Admissions Officers, Tenn. Assn. Coll. Registrars and Admissions Officers, Mensa, Kappa Delta Pi, Phi Delta Kappa. Episcopalian (lay reader). Clubs: Royal Sch. Church Music, Phi Kappa Psi (charter mem. Tenn. Zeta chpt., Colony pres.). Co-author research evaluation reports, bus. and procedure manuals. Home: 4301 Powell Ave Memphis TN 38122 Office: Asso Dean Admissions and Records Memphis State Univ Memphis TN 38152

MORI, PAUL ALBERT, radiologist; b. Amherst, Ohio, May 5, 1925; s. Paul Albert and Mattie Melissa (Cummings) M.; B.A., Ohio State U., 1947, M.D., 1948; m. Minna Lee Conn, Aug. 30, 1947; children—Mark Waggoner, Kurt Wick, Thorpe Stuart, Meredith Dea. Intern, Blodgett Meml. Hosp., Grand Rapids, Mich., 1948-49; resident in radiology U. Mich. Hosp., 1952-55; sr. clin. instr. radiology U. Mich., 1955-56; dir. radiology Bapt. Meml. Hosp., Jacksonville, Fla., 1956-68; pvt. practice medicine specializing in radiology, Jacksonville, 1968—; pres. med. staff Meml. Hosp. of Jacksonville, 1977-78; chmn. adv. com. to health program office Fla. Dept. Health, 1977—. Bd. dirs., exec. com., chmn. civic affairs com. Am. Bicentennial Commn. of Jacksonville, 1973-77. Served to lt. USNR, 1950-52. Recipient certificate of merit Am. Cancer Soc., 1960; diplomate Am. Bd. Radiology, Am. Bd. Nuclear Medicine. Fellow Am. Cancer Soc., Am. Coll. Radiology (Fla. councilor); Fla. Radiology Soc. (pres. 1975-76), Am. Coll. Nuclear Medicine, AMA, Radiol. Soc. N.Am. (councilor for Fla.), Fla. Assn. Nuclear Physicians (dir. 1977—), Nu Sigma Nu, Phi Eta Sigma, Alpha Epsilon Delta. Presbyterian. Club: Rotary of South Jacksonville (dist. gov. internat. 1972-73). Home: 4836 Yacht Club Rd Jacksonville FL 32210 Office: 3599 University Blvd Jacksonville FL 32216

MORIAL, ERNEST NATHAN, mayor; b. New Orleans, Oct. 9, 1929; s. Walter Etienne and Leonie Viola (Moore) M.; B.S., Xavier U. of La., 1951; J.D., La. State U., 1954; m. Sybil Gayle Haydel, Feb. 18, 1955; children—Julie Claire, Marc Haydel, Jacques Etienne, Cheri Michele, Monique Gayle. Admitted to La. bar, 1954; auditor Keystone Life Ins. Co., New Orleans, 1951, partner firm Tureaud, Trudeau & Morial, New Orleans, 1954-60; gen. counsel Standard Life Ins. Co. of La., 1960-70; asst. U.S. atty., New Orleans, 1965-67; juvenile Ct. judge, New Orleans, 1970-74; judge La. Ct. of Appeal, New Orleans, 1974-77; dir. Liberty Bank & Trust Co., 1972—, Gourmet Services, Inc., 1974—; prof. law Tulane U. Law Sch., 1973—. Mem. La. Ho. Reps., 1968-70; mayor New Orleans, 1978—. Bd. govs. Tulane U. Med. Center; bd. dirs. Loyola U.; formerly trustee Xavier U. Served with U.S. Army, 1954-56. Fellow Inst. Politics Harvard U., 1978. Named one of 100 Most Influential Blacks, Ebony mag., 1971, 72, 73, 78; recipient certificate for Distinguished Service, Links, Inc., 1972. Mem. Am., La. State bar assns., Am. Judicature Soc., Alpha Phi Alpha (gen. pres. 1968-72); Knights of Peter Claver. Home: 1101 Harrison Ave New Orleans LA 70122 Office: Office of Mayor City Hall 1300 Perdido St New Orleans LA 70112

MORIN, BRUCE LEONARD, mgmt. cons.; b. Worcester, Mass., July 31, 1949; s. Leo P. and Rita G. (McNeil) M.; B.A. in Mgmt., Park Coll., 1978; postgrad. Samford U., Birmingham, Ala., 1978—. Mgmt. engr. Baptist Med. Centers, Birmingham, 1978-79; sr. mgmt. cons. Brookwood Health Services, Homewood, Ala., 1979—. Served with USAF, 1970-78. Decorated Joint Services Commendation medal, Air Force Commendation medal. Mem. Am. Inst. Indsl. Engrs., Hosp. Mgmt. Systems Soc., M.B.A. Assn. Roman Catholic. Home: 1217 River Rd Birmingham AL 35244 Office: 2022 Brookwood Medical Center Dr Homewood AL 35209

MORING, FELIX CLEVELAND, lawyer; b. Soperton, Ga., June 9, 1941; s. Joel Josephus and Johnie Will (Winge) M.; B.A., Emory U., 1963; M.A., U. Tenn. at Knoxville, 1971, J.D., 1973. Admitted to Ga. bar, 1973; individual practice law Atlanta, 1973—; instr. law John Marshall Law Sch., Atlanta, 1975—; adj. instr. law DeKalb Community Coll., Decatur, 1975—. Served to capt., inf., USMCR, 1964-67; Vietnam. Mem. Altanta, Ga., Am. bar assns., Am. Soc. Judicature, Am. Internat. Law Soc., Atlanta Com. Fgn. Relations, Atlanta C. of C., Ga. C. of C., Atlanta Hist. Soc., Ga. Forestry Assn., Marine Corps Res. Officers Assn. (pres. Atlanta chpt. 1976—), So. Council Internat. and Pub. Affairs. Home: 1101 Collier Rd NW Atlanta GA 30318 Office: 1512 Peachtree Center 230 Peachtree St Atlanta GA 30303

MORITZ, WALLACE ALBERT, realtor; b. Milw., Apr. 21, 1913; s. Leopold and Theresa (Bauer) M.; student Marquette U., 1931; m. Ruth Kalle, Jan. 2, 1945; children—Judith Moritz Phillips, Diana M. Hill, Arthur Lee. Founder Wallace Labs. Inc., San Angelo, Tex., 1940, now pres.; pres. W. Tex. Bus. Music Co., San Angelo, 1953; owner Wallace A. Moritz and Assos., San Angelo, 1960—. Chmn. Nat. Wool Pageant, 1958-59; pres. Crippled Children's Center, San Angelo, 1958, United Fund, San Angelo, 1963, Lighthouse, San Angelo, 1965; trustee Tex. Scottish Rite Found., Tex.-Okla. Kiwanis Found. Named San Angelo Citizen of Year, 1958. Mem. Nat. (dir.), Tex. (dir. 1969, 1st v.p. 1977, sec. 1975, treas. 1976, pres. 1978) assns. realtors, San Angelo Bd. Realtors (pres. 1967). Presbyterian. Clubs: San Angelo Country, Masons, Kiwanis. Home: 166 Moritz Circle San Angelo TX 76901 Office: 1900 Sherwood Way San Angelo TX 76901

MORKOVSKY, JOHN LOUIS, clergyman; b. Moulton, Tex., Aug. 16, 1909; s. Alois Joseph and Marie (Raska) M.; grad. St. John's Sem., San Antonio, 1930; student N. Am. Coll., Rome, Italy, 1930-36; attended lectures Pontifical Univ. of Propagation of Faith, 1930-32; S.T.D., Pontifical Gregorian U., 1936; A.M., Cath. U. Am., 1943; LL.D., St. Edward's U., 1958. Ordained priest Roman Catholic Ch., 1933; asst. pastor St. Michael's Ch., Weimar, Tex., 1936-39, St. Ann's Ch., San Antonio, 1940; prof. canon law St. John's Sem., San Antonio, 1940-41; archdiocesan supt. of schs., 1941-56; pastor St. Leo's parish, San Antonio, 1945-54, St. Mary Magdalen parish, 1954-56; titular bishop Hieron and aux. bishop Amarillo, 1956-58, vicar gen., chancellor Amarillo Diocese, 1957-58, bishop, Amarillo, 1958-63; coadjutor bishop, apostolic administrator, Galveston-Houston, 1963-74: bishop, 1975—. Judge on Archdiocesan Tribunal, 1946-56; mem. Archdiocesan Bd. Consultors, 1947-56; pres. Tex. Conf. Christian Chs., 1971-72. Papal chamberlain with title very reverend monsignor, 1944, domestic prelate with title right rev. monsignor, 1954. K.C. (4 deg.). Address: Catholic Chancery 1700 San Jacinto Houston TX 77002

MORLAND, ALVIN WESLEY, assn. exec.; b. Birmingham, Ala., July 29, 1914; s. Howard Canon and Ethel May (Cowan) M.; B.S., Auburn U., 1937; postgrad. Acad. Orgn. Mgmt., U. Notre Dame, 1972; m. Gretchen Bickelhaupt, Feb. 15, 1947; children—Douglas Verne, Timothy Easton. With U.S. Steel Corp., Birmingham, 1937-41, 46-47; adminstrv. asst. U.S. Congressman L.C. Battle, 1947-49; city mgr. Mountain Brook, Ala., 1949-51; mgr. trade devel. Birmingham C. of C., 1951-53; mgr. Dothan (Ala.) C. of C., 1953-55, Ft. Pierce (Fla.) C. of C., 1955-62; exec. v.p. Pompano Beach (Fla.) C. of C., 1963—. Served with AUS, 1941-46. Decorated Purple Heart, Bronze Star. Mem. Am. C. of C. Execs. (Fla. del. 1975-78), So. Assn. C. of C. Execs. (dir. 1971-72, 76-78), Am., Ala. (dir. 1954), Fla. (pres. 1964-65) chambers commerce execs., Spades, Sigma Alpha Epsilon, Omicron Delta Kappa (pres. Auburn U. chpt. 1936-37). Republican. Rotarian (dir. Pompano Beach club 1967, officer, dir. 1969-71). Home: 2326 N E 29th St Lighthouse Point FL 33064 Office: Chamber of Commerce 2200 E Atlantic Blvd Pompano Beach FL 33062

MORLAND, JESSIE PARRISH, educator; b. Parrish, Fla., Dec. 3, 1924; d. Jonah and May (Lowry) Parrish; B.A., Fla. Southern Coll., 1947; m. Richard B. Morland, Mar. 17, 1949; 1 dau., Laura. Dir. publicity Fla. Southern Coll., 1948-50; editor Dun's Bulletin, Dun and Bradstreet, N.Y.C., 1950-52; feature writer Deland Sun News, Daytona Beach (Fla.) News Jour., 1952-65; tchr. English, journalism Deland (Fla.) Jr. High Sch., 1967—. Bd. dirs. Deland Mus., 1957-62, Democratic Women's Club, 1952-65. Mem. AAUW (dir. 1955-62), Nat. League Am. Pen Women, Alpha Delta Pi. Democrat. Methodist. Club: Garden. Home: 524 McDonald Ave N Deland FL 32720 Office: 210 Clara Ave N Deland FL 32720

MORLAND, JOHN KENNETH, educator; b. Huntsville, Ala., July 4, 1916; s. Howard Cannon and Ethel Mae (Cowan) M.; B.S., Birmingham So. Coll., 1938; B.D., Yale U., 1943; Ph.D., U. N.C. at Chapel Hill, 1950; m. Margaret Louise Ward, Feb. 26, 1949; children—Carol, Katherine, Evelyn. Instr., Yale in China Middle Sch., Changsha, Hunan, 1943-46; exec sec. Yale in China Assn., New Haven, 1946-47; asst. prof. Coll. William and Mary, Williamsburg, Va., 1949-53; Charles A. Dana prof., chmn. dept. sociology and anthropology Randolph Macon Woman's Coll., Lynchburg, Va., 1953—; cons. U.S. Dept. Edn., Dept. Commerce, Nat. Endowment for Humanities, So. Regional Council, NSF. Pres. bd. nat. ministries Am. Bapt. Churches U.S.A., 1973-79. Fulbright scholar Chinese U. Hong Kong, 1966-67; recipient grants NSF, Taiwan, 1975, U.S. Dept. Edn., 1972. Fellow Am. Anthrop. Assn.; mem. Am., So sociol. socs., Va. Social Sci. Assn. (pres. 1963), AAUP (pres. 1962). Author: Social Problems in the United States, 1975; Millways of Kent, 1958; (with John Williams) Race, Color and the Young Child, 1976; contbr., editor: The Not So Solid South, 1971. Home: 1619 Dogwood Ln Lynchburg VA 24503 Office: Box 477 Randolph Macon Woman's Coll Lynchburg VA 24503

MORLAND, MARGARET WARD, poet, civic leader; b. Birmingham, Ala., Apr. 28, 1923; d. James Alto and Linda Belle (Heacock) Ward; B.A. with honors, Samford U., 1944; M.A., U. N.C., 1951; m. John Kenneth Morland, Feb. 26, 1949; children—Margaret Carol, Katherine Louise, Evelyn Ward. Research chemist Spies Nutrition Clinic, Birmingham, 1945-46; tchr. English Samford U., 1946-47; asst. to dean of women U. N.C., Chapel Hill, 1947-49; instr. English Lynchburg (Va.) Coll., 1965-66; poetry readings, lectures, 1969—. Bd. dirs. League Women Voters, 1960-75; bd. dirs. Am. Field Services, 1971-73; bd. dirs. Ch. Women United, 1970-73; bd. Deacons Peakland Baptist Ch., 1964-67, 75-78; mem. music bd. Lynchburg Fine Arts Center, 1975-78. Recipient 1st prize Nat. Bicentennial Poetry Contest, 1st prize Poetry Contest Va. Fedn. Women's Clubs, 1976, 1st and 2d prizes Writers' Forum Poetry Contest, 1977, 1st prize Va. Fedn. Women's Clubs Poetry Contest, 1977. Mem. Poetry Soc. Va. (v.p. 1970-73, exec. com. 1976—, recipient 1st prize 1976, 2d prize poetry contest 1977), Poetry Workshop of Lynchburg, Poetry Soc. Am., Acad. Am. Poets, Nat. League Am. Pen Women (1st prize nat. poetry contest San Diego br. 1977, 2d prize nat. poetry contest Knoxville br. 1977). Club: Lynchburg Woman's (pres.). Poetry pub. in mags., newspapers, anthologies. Home: 1619 Dogwood Ln Lynchburg VA 24503

MORLAND, RICHARD BOYD, educator; b. Huntsville, Ala., June 27, 1919; s. Howard Cannon and Ethel May (Cowan) M.; A.B., Birmingham-So. Coll., 1940; M.Ed., Springfield Coll., 1947; Ph.D. (So. Fellowships Fund fellow 1957-58), N.Y. U. 1958; m. Jessie May Parrish, Mar. 17, 1949; 1 dau., Laura. Phys. dir. YMCA, Frankfort, Ky., 1940-41; dir. athletics, head basketball coach Fla. So. Coll., 1947-50; lectr. in edn., N.Y. U., 1950-51; chmn. dept. phy. edn., Stetson U., Deland, Fla., 1952-60, head basketball coach, 1952-57, asso. prof., 1958-63, prof., 1963—, chmn. grad. council, 1962-69, chmn. dept. edn., 1969-75. Served to lt. USNR, 1941-45. Named to Stetson U. Sports Hall of Fame. Mem. Philosophy of Edn. Soc. (pres. region 1963-64), Fla. Council Deans and Dirs. Tchr. Edn. (pres. 1974-75), Am. Ednl. Research Assn., Am. Edn. Studies Assn., Omicron Delta Kappa, Phi Alpha Theta, Kappa Delta Pi, Phi Delta Kappa (pres. region 1977-78, editorial bd. Phi Delta Kappan 1978—), Kappa Alpha. Democrat. Methodist. Contbr. articles to profl. jours. Home: 524 N McDonald St DeLand FL 32720

MORLANG, CHARLES, JR., biologist; b. N.Y.C., Apr. 21, 1935; s. Charles and Florence (Livingston) M.; B.S. cum laude, Coll. City N.Y., 1956; Ph.D. in Pure Sci., Columbia U., 1965. Substitute tchr. N.Y.C. high schs. (part-time), 1957-64; lab. instr. in botany Columbia U., N.Y.C., 1957-59, Grad. Morphology Lab., 1959-60, lectr. in botany, 1957-59; coordinator biol. methods sects. Columbia U. High Sch. Sci. Honors Program, N.Y.C., 1961-64; lectr. in biology Coll. City N.Y., 1964-65; asst. prof. biol. scis. Mass. State Coll. at Westfield, 1965-67; asso. prof. biol. scis. Hollins Coll., Va., 1967—, chmn. dept. biology, 1978—; lectr. to various schs., clubs and civic groups; appeared on various radio and TV lectr. programs; cons. Population Inst., Roanoke City Sch., Blue Ridge Nat. Park. Mem. AAAS, Bot. Soc. Am., Nat. Parks Assn., Am. Inst. Biol. Scis. (editorial bd. 1974-76), Sci. Mus. Assn. Roanoke Valley, Torrey Bot. Club, Nat. Rifle Assn., AAUP (chmn. Hollins chpt. 1976-77), Nat. Assn. Biology Tchrs. (editorial bd. 1975-80), Sigma Xi. Contbr. articles on ecology, plant morphology, applications of photography to biology to profl. jours. Office: Dept Biology Hollins Coll Hollins College VA 24020

MORLEY, CARL F., chem. co. exec.; b. Marfa, Tex., May 6, 1948; B.B.A. (hon.), N.Mex. State U., 1974; m. Sandi G., June 8, 1968. Salesman, United Auto Store, Carlsbad, N.Mex., 1965-70; indsl. painter welder Potash Co. Am., Carlsbad, 1970-72; buyer, Duval Corp., Carlsbad, 1974-77; personnel/communications mgr. Miss. Chem. Corp., Carlsbad, 1977-79, corp. mgr. human resource devel., Yazoo City, Miss., 1979—; instr. bus. adminstrn. N.Mex. State U., Carlsbad, 1977-78. Named Jaycee of Month, 1976. Mem. Am. Mgmt. Assn., Am. Soc. Personnel Adminstrs., Am. Soc. Tng. and Devel. Democrat. Baptist. Club: Elks. Home: Route 3 Box 102A Yazoo City MS 39194 Office: PO Box 388 Yazoo City MS 39194

MOROCK, JAMES ANDREW, internist; b. Coral Gables, Fla., Sept. 1, 1945; s. Emil Peter and Marion Alice (Moore) M.; B.S. in Chemistry, Tulane U., 1967, M.D., 1971; m. Cheryl Lee Gregoratti, Mar. 2, 1974; 1 son, James Andrew. Intern, Charity Hosp. of La., New Orleans, 1971-72, resident, 1972-75; fellow in nephrology Ochsner Hosp., New Orleans, 1975-77; practice medicine specializing in internal medicine and nephrology, New Orleans, 1977—; mem. staff Meth. Hosp., New Orleans. Diplomate Am. Bd. Internal Medicine. Mem. AMA, A.C.P., Am. Soc. Nephrology, Am. Soc. Internal Medicine, Orleans Parish Med. Soc. Presbyterian. Club: Krewe of Pegrasus. Home: 319 30th St New Orleans LA 70124 Office: Suite 300 Med Center of East New Orleans 5640 Read Blvd New Orleans LA 70127

MORONEY, CHARLES CURTIS, architect; b. Natchez, Miss., Oct. 2, 1937; s. Charles Louis and Jennie Elizabeth (Reed) M.; B.Arch., Auburn U., 1960; m. Felicity Ann Brady, Sept. 3, 1960; children—Ross Brady, Curtis Lee, Kari Suzanne. Architect, Curtis & Davis, Architects, New Orleans, 1963-67; prin. Charles Curtis Moroney, Architect, Natchez, Miss., 1967—. Served to lt. (j.g.), USN, 1960-63. Registered architect, Miss., La. Mem. Nat. Council Archtl. Registration Bds., AIA, Scarab. Home: Route 6 Box 126A Natchez MS 39120 Office: 24 Green St Natchez MS 39120

MOROSANI, GEORGE WARRINGTON, warehousing co. exec.; b. Cin., July 20, 1941; s. Remy Edmond and Virginia Caroline (Warrington) M.; B.A., Rollins Coll., 1964, M.B.A., 1965; div.; children—Katherine Carmichael, Elizabeth Warrington. Fin. mgr. Lunar Orbitor and Minuteman Programs, Boeing Co., Cape Canaveral, Fla., 1965-68; controller Equitable Leasing Co., Asheville, N.C., 1968-69; founder, pres., treas. Western Carolina Warehousing Co., Asheville, 1969—. Bd. dirs. Jr. Achievement Greater Asheville Area, 1977—. Mem. Sales and Mktg. Execs. Asheville (dir. 1974-76, chmn. membership com. 1976-77), Western N.C. Traffic Club (dir. 1973-74, sec.-treas. 1974-76, pres. 1976-77, dir. 1977-79), Asheville Bd. Realtors, Am. Warehousemen Assn., Southeastern Warehousemen's and Movers Assn. (dir. 1977-79), N.C. Merchandise Warehousemen's Assn. Nat. Council Distbn. Mgmt., Affiliated Warehouse Cos., Asheville Area C. of C. (chmn. indsl. relations 1978-79), Western Carolina Horse Show Assn. (co-chmn. 1969-70, treas. 1968-71, 73-75). Episcopalian. Clubs: Biltmore Forest Country, Asheville Downtown City, Asheville Racquet, Civitan (dir. 1975-77). Home: PO Box 858 Fletcher NC 28732 Office: PO Box 858 Fletcher NC 28732

MORPHOS, DIANE BELOGIANIS (MRS. PANOS PAUL MORPHOS), civic worker; b. Chgo.; d. Demetrios and Alice (Rousseas) Belogianis; B.S., U. Chgo., 1937, M.A., 1938; m. Panos Paul Morphos, Dec. 11, 1948; children—Evangeline, Paul. Mem. faculty U. Chgo. Orthogenic Sch., 1938-45, U. Chgo. Remedial Reading Clinics, 1945-48; vis. lectr. Tulane U., 1947. Bd. dirs. S.E. La. council Girl Scouts U.S. New Orleans, 1959-65, v.p., 1965-68, pres., 1968—; mem. bd. AAUW, New Orleans, 1969, v.p., 1970-75, pres., 1975—; chmn. legis. com., bd. Reading is Fundamental program, New Orleans. Mem. Athenee Louisianais, France-Amerique, Maison Hospitaliere, League Women Voters. Mem. Greek Orthodox Ch. Clubs: Greek Women's Univ. (Chgo.); Tulane U. Women's (New Orleans, La.). Home: 1404 Audubon St New Orleans LA 70118

MORREL, REECE BOONE, lawyer; b. Macomb, Okla., Mar. 20, 1940; s. John Dalton and Zula (Lavada) M.; B.S., Central State U., 1961; J.D., Tulsa U., 1966; m. LaReta Martin, Aug. 6, 1960; children—Reece Boone, LaRhea Susan. Admitted to Okla. bar, 1966; trust officer Bank of Okla., 1967-68; partner firm Ellison, Morrel, Hays and Nelson, Tulsa, 1968-74, Morrel, Herrold, West, Hodgson, Shelton & Striplin, Tulsa, 1975—; agt. IRS, 1961-67. Bd. dirs. Tulsa Christian Home, Inc. Mem. Am. Bar Assn., Okla. Bar Assn., Tulsa County Bar Assn., Tulsa C. of C. Republican. Mem. Ch. of Christ. Club: Rotary. Home: 4223 E 74th St Tulsa OK 74136 Office: 4111 S Darlington St Suite 600 Tulsa OK 74135

MORREY, JOHN WILLIAM, III, engring. technician; b. Denver, Mar. 24, 1947; s. John William, Jr. and Bonnie Bell (Paxton) M.; diploma in archtl. drafting Nixon Clay Coll., 1966; m. Sue Stamper, Jan. 8, 1977; 1 stepson, Michael W. Hancock. Tech. coordinator Freese & Nichols, Inc., Cons. Engrs., Austin, Tex., 1970—. Vol. mem. police depts. Lakeway, Tex., West Lake Hills, Tex., 1975—. Served with USN, 1966-70; Vietnam. Cert. civil engring. technician Inst. for Cert. Engring. Technicians. Mem. Tex. Surveyors Assn., Am. Inst. Design and Drafting, Am. Soc. Cert. Engring. Technicians (sec.-treas., nat. dir.), Res. Law Officers Assn. Am. Home: 2503 Oak Meadow Round Rock TX 78664 Office: 314 Highland Mall Blvd Suite 560 Austin TX 78752

MORRIS, ANDERSON ASHE, JR., data processing mgr.; b. Columbia, S.C., Apr. 23 1943; s. Anderson Ashe and Sara Christine (Ruff) M.; B.S. in Bus. Mgmt., U. S.C., 1965; m. Willie Lee Graham, May 30, 1965; children—Anthony Kevin, Timothy Shane. Account mgr. Burroughs Corp., 1965-77; dir. info. services Lexington County Hosp., West Columbia, S.C. 1977—. Mem. Hosp. Fin. Mgmt. Assn. Methodist. Clubs: Mt. Pleasant Hunting, Pomaria Ruritan (pres. 1972), St. Andrews Rotary Home: Route 2 Box 167 Pomaria SC 29126 Office: 2720 Sunset Blvd West Columbia SC 29169

MORRIS, BARTON WISTAR, JR., newspaper publisher; b. Roanoke, Va., Oct. 10, 1922; s. Barton Wistar and Mary Wilkinson (Buckner) M.; A.B., Washington and Lee U., 1943; m. Margaret Jarrett, May 7, 1949 children—Anna Jarrett, Barton Wistar. Reporter, Roanoke World-News, 1945-50; asst. to gen. mgr. Times-World, Roanoke, 1950-52, corp. sec., promotion mgr., 1952-69, pres., 1978—; exec. editor Roanoke Times and World-News, 1955-73, v.p., 1960-73, pub., 1973—. Chmn., Roanoke Community Fund, 1954; bd. dirs. United Way Roanoke, Roanoke Symphony Orch., Roanoke Fine Arts Center, Guidance Center Roanoke. Served with USAF, 1945. So. Nieman Travel fellow, 1958. Mem. Am. Newspaper Pubs. Assn., So. Newspaper Pubs. Assn. (dir. 1978, chmn. editorial com. 1978-79). Va. AP (past chmn.), Va. Press Assn. (dir. 1958-59). Presbyterian. Clubs: Shenandoah, Roanoke Country. Office: 201 W Campbell Ave Roanoke VA 24010

MORRIS, BEN RANKIN, publishing co. exec.; b. Gastonia, N.C., Nov. 12, 1922; s. Theodore Page and Nancy (Rankin) M.; B.S., N.C. State U., 1948; m. Henriette Dargan Hampton, Dec. 20, 1946; children—Ben Rankin, Wade Hampton, Henriette Dargan, Frank Page. Prodn. dept. head Textiles Inc., Gastonia, 1948-50; with Aldrich Machine Works of Greenwood, S.C., Atlanta, Ga., 1950-70, v.p., dir., 1953-70; pres. State Record Co., publishers Columbia Newspapers, Inc., State and Columbia Record, State Printing Co., Bestway Express, Gulf Pub. Co. Inc., publishers The Daily Herald, State Telecasting Co. Inc., Charleston, S.C. also Lubbock, Tex., Roswell, N.M.; chmn. bd. dirs. all subsidiaries; dir. C. & S. Nat. Bank. Chmn. S.C. Found. for Modern Liquor Regulations and Controls, 1971; mem. Greater Columbia Community Relations Council, 1972, S.C. Commn. on Human Affairs, 1972-74. Mem. bd. dirs., exec. com. S.C. Safety Council; trustee Richland County Pub. Library; bd. dirs. Allen U.; mem. advisory bd. dirs. Aurora Center for Blind. Served with USAAF, 1943-46. Mem. S.C. C. of C. (chmn. 1975). Episcopalian. Clubs: Forest Lake, Summit, Palmetto, Capital City, Piedmont Driving Club (Atlanta). Home: 5025 Radcliffe Rd Columbia SC 29206 Office: The State-Record Co Stadium Rd PO Box 1333 Columbia SC 29202

MORRIS, BEN TILLMAN, JR., oil co. exec.; b. Dallas, Apr. 8, 1946; s. Ben Tillman and Edna Earle (Hilley) M.; B.B.A., North Tex. State U., 1967; m. Margaret Ann Williams, June 30, 1966; children—Sharla Laine, Steven Michael, Lindsey Margaux. With Price Waterhouse & Co., Fort Worth, Cin., Houston, 1967-73, mgr. audit staff, to 1973; sr., chief operating officer, dir. Mid Am. Oil & Gas, Inc., Houston, 1973—. Republican. Methodist. Clubs: Athletic, Houston Met. Racquet. Home: 63 Williamsburg Ln Houston TX 77024 Office: 1200 Milam Suite 3323 Houston TX 77002

MORRIS, CARLOSS, lawyer, title guaranty co. exec.; b. Houston, June 7, 1915; s. W.C. and Willie (Stewart) M.; B.A. with distinction, Rice Inst., 1936; J.D. with highest honors, U. Tex., 1939; m. Doris Poole, Dec. 2, 1939; children—Marietta Morris Maxfield, William Carloss, Malcolm Stewart, Melinda Louise (Mrs. Glen Ginter). Admitted to Tex. bar, 1938; with Stewart Title Guaranty Co., Houston, 1939—, pres., 1951-75, chmn. bd., chief exec. officer, 1975—, also dir.; sr. chmn. bd., co-chief exec. officer Stewart Info. Services Corp.; stockholder, dir. Morris, Harris, McCanne, Tinsley, Snowden & Ellis, P.C., Houston. Pres. Star of Hope Mission, 1951—, Tex. Safety Assn., 1950-51; chmn. Adv. Commn. on Housing and Urban Growth; bd. dirs. Goodwill Industries; bd. dirs., mem. exec. com. Billy Graham Evangelistic Assn.; trustee Baylor U., 1952-72, vice chmn., 1971-72, chmn. bd. Coll. Medicine, 1968-69; trustee Oldham Little Church Found., B.M. Woltman Found., Baylor Coll. Medicine. Fellow State Bar Tex. Found., Am. Bar Assn.; mem. Tex. Bar. Baptist (trustee, deacon). Clubs: Downtown Kiwanis (atty. 1945—), River Oaks Country, Sugar Creek Country, University. Home: 3996 Inverness Dr Houston TX 77019 Office: 2200 W Loop S Houston TX 77027

MORRIS, CELITA LAMAR, educator; b. Miami, Fla., Aug. 21, 1939; d. Carlos Perez and Celia Maria (Fernandez) Lamar; B.A., U. Miami, 1960, M.A., 1967; postgrad. (Woodrow Wilson fellow), U. Calif., Berkeley, 1960-61; m. James H. Morris, June 4, 1960; children—Linda Lamar, Kathleen Elizabeth. Instr. French, U. Miami, 1966-73, asst. prof., 1973—; coordinator Fla. Task Force on Fgn. and Biblical Langs., 1972—. Mem., chmn. subcom. Policy Council for State of Fla. Course Numbering Project, 1976—. Mem. AAUP (pres. Fla. conf. 1974-75, 77-79), Modern Lang Assn., S. Atlantic Modern Lang. Assn., Am. Assn. Tchrs. French, Am. Assn. Tchrs. Spanish and Portuguese, Asociacion de Literatura Femenina Hispanica, ACLU, Mus. Sci., Women's Caucus for Modern Langs., Vizcayans, Mortar Bd., Confrerie de la Chaine des Rôtisseurs, Phi Kappa Phi. Democrat. Roman Catholic. Contbr. articles to profl. jours. Home: 520 Castania Ave Coral Gables FL 33146 Office: Dept Fgn Langs Box 248093 U Miami Coral Gables FL 33124

MORRIS, CLETUS EUGENE, chemist; b. Alcorn County, Miss., Jan. 30, 1935; s. Van Buren and Jessie Ray (Green) M.; A.S., N.E. Miss. Jr. Coll., 1954; B.S., Auburn U., 1959, Ph.D. (NDEA fellow, NSF fellow), 1966; m. Nancy Carole Mitchell, June 5, 1962; 1 son, Kendall Eugene. Research chemist So. Regional Research Center, Dept. Agr., New Orleans, 1965—. Served with U.S. Army, 1954-57. Mem. Am. Chem. Soc. (treas. La. sect. 1975-77, chmn. La. sect. 1979), Am. Assn. Textile Chemists and Colorists, Orgn. Profl. Employees of U.S. Dept. Agr., Sigma Xi (pres. New Orleans chpt. 1976), Phi Lambda Upsilon. Contbr. articles to profl. jours.; patentee in field. Home: 3816 Metairie Ct Metairie LA 70002 Office: PO Box 19687 New Orleans LA 70179

MORRIS, DONAL FRANKLIN, chem. engr.; b. Bixby, Okla., June 8, 1932; s. Troy Franklin and Mary Belle (Mulkey) M.; A.S., Connors State U., 1952; B.S. in Chem. Engring., Okla. State U., 1955; m. Delores Joan Marshall, July 31, 1953; children—Randall, Karen, Ron. Process engr. Phillips Petroleum, Borger, Tex., 1955-58; process engr. Dresser Engring. Co., Tulsa, 1958-68, chief process and project engr., 1968-75, v.p., 1975—. Registered profl. engr., Okla., Tex., Colo., Kans. Mem. Nat., Okla. socs. profl. engrs., Am. Inst. Chem. Engrs., Engrs. Club Tulsa. Home: 11262 S 89th East Ave Bixby OK 74008 Office: PO Box 2968 Tulsa OK 74101

MORRIS, EARL DOUGLAS, JR., social worker; b. Cleve., Oct. 31, 1925; s. Earl Douglas and Viola (Mau) M.; B.S., Western Res. U., 1949; M.S.W., Boston U., 1952; M.B.A., Old Dominion U., 1976; m. Helen N. Alcott, June 28, 1952; children—David, Brenda, Martha. With Children's Services, Cleve., 1952-54; exec. dir. Family Service Soc., Youngstown, Ohio, 1954-60; with Family Service/Traveler's Aid, Norfolk, Va., 1960—, exec. dir. 1960—. Mem. Va. Bd. Social Work, 1976—, chmn. 1977-79; pres. Am. Assn. State Social Work Bds., 1979—. Served with USN, 1944-46. Mem. Nat. Assn. Social Workers. Lutheran. Home: 2201 Bayville Rd Virginia Beach VA 23455 Office: Family Service/Traveler's Aid 222 19th St W Norfolk VA 23517

MORRIS, EARLE ELIAS, JR., state ofcl., bus. and ins. exec.; b. Greenville, S.C., July 14, 1928; s. Earle Elias and Bernice (Carey) M.; B.S., Clemson Coll., 1949; m. Carol Telford Morris; children—Lynda Lewis, Carey M., Elizabeth, Earle Elias, David Earle. Owner, operator Morris & Co., Inc., wholesale grocers, Pickens, S.C., 1949-56; v.p., dir. Pickens Bank, 1956-68, Bankers Trust S.C., 1968-75; pres. Gen. Ins. Agy.; comptroller gen. State of S.C., 1975—; chmn. bd. Santee Cooper Fisheries (Far East) Ltd., Hong Kong; sec. Carolina Investors, Inc.; partner Morris Realty Co., Pickens; dir. Brunswick Worsted Mills, Pickens Savs. & Loan Assn.; chmn. bd. Tai Pan Screen Printing Co., Hong Kong; mem. S.C. Ho. of Reps., 1950-54, S.C. Senate, 1954-70; lt. gov. S.C., 1971-75. S.C. rep. So. Regional Council Mental Health; mem. Crippled Children's Soc. S.C.; mem. S.C. Gov.'s Adv. Group Mental Health Planning; mem. Nat. Adv. Mental Health Council, 1965-66; mem. S.C. Interagy. Council Mental Retardation, S.C. Mental Health Commn., 1975-76; del. S.C. Democratic Convs., 1950-78, Nat. Dem. Convs., 1952, 56, 68, 72; state chmn. S.C. Dem. Com., 1966-68. Recipient Distinguished Alumnus award Clemson U. Mem. Jr. C. of C., S.C. Vocat. Rehab. Assn. (v.p.), SAR, Blue Key, Phi Kappa Phi, Sigma Alpha Epsilon. Presbyterian. Clubs: Masons (32 deg.), Shriners, Elks, Moose, Lions. Home: 1137 Baywater West Columbia SC 29169 Office: Box 11228 St Columbia SC 29211

MORRIS, EVANGELINE FELICIA (BECKY), counselor; b. Altoona, Wis., June 27, 1922; d. Floyd Milo and Eva Ann (Feight) Sharp; student Ill. Wesleyan Sch. Music, 1938; B.A., U. Dubuque, 1941; M.A., U. South Fla., 1967; Ed.D., Ariz. State U., 1973; m. Fred Harold Morris, July 26, 1968; children by previous marriage—Robert M., Jon Floyd, Philip Alan Stoneburner. Tchr. high schs., Casper, Wyo., Opp, Ala., Ashland, Ky., Gastonia, N.C., 1948-52; instr. Rio Grande Coll., 1947-48; tchr. Boca Ciega High Sch., St. Petersburg, Fla., 1958-66; chmn. dept. English, Lakewood High Sch., St. Petersburg, 1966-68; instr. Edison Jr. Coll., Ft. Myers, Fla., 1968-70, Scottsdale (Ariz.) Community Coll., 1970-72; counselor Clearwater (Fla.) High Sch., 1974-79; pvt. counseling, Clearwater. Mem. Nat., Fla., Pinellas edn. assns., Am., Fla. personnel and guidance assns., Am., Fla. (v.p. 1977-79) sch. counselors assns., Phi Delta Kappa. Mormon. Home: 2352 Timbercrest Circle S Clearwater FL 33515

MORRIS, GEORGE ALAN, III, orthopedic surgeon; b. Memphis, Sept. 3, 1935; s. George Alan and Caroline (Hogue) M.; B.A., Southwestern U., 1957; M.D., U. Tenn., 1960. Intern, Charity Hosp. of La., New Orleans, 1960-61; resident in orthopedics Bowman-Gray Med. Sch., Winston-Salem, N.C., Baptist Hosp., Winston-Salem, 1965-68; practice medicine specializing in orthopedic surgery, Clearwater, Fla., 1968—; past chief orthopedics Clearwater Community Hosp.; chief surgery, chief orthopedics Morton Plant Hosp., chmn. emergency room and disaster com., chmn. operating room personnel com.; chief orthopaedics Med. Center Hosp., Largo, Fla.; advisor med. explorers. Served with USN, 1961-65. Diplomate Am. Bd. Orthopedic Surgery. Fellow A.C.S., Am. Acad. Orthopedic Surgeons; mem. Pinellas County, Fla. med. socs., Eastern Orthopedic Assn., Fla., Upper Pinellas County orthopedic socs. Republican. Episcopalian. Clubs: Clearwater Yacht (dir.). Contbr. articles in field to med. jours. Home: 228 Bluffview Dr Belleair Bluffs FL 33540 Office: 1011 Jeffords St Clearwater FL 33516

MORRIS, HAROLD GERARD, JR., fin. co. exec.; b. Elizabeth, N.J., Feb. 23, 1948; s. Harold Gerard and Bernadine Mary (LeHota) M.; B.S., St. Peter's Coll., 1970; m. Dorothy B., Apr. 18, 1970; children—Robert Adam, Timothy Ryan. Staff auditor Main LaFrentz & Co., N.Y.C., 1971-76; sr. auditor, supr. internal audit dept. Foster Wheeler Corp., Livingston, N.J., 1976-78; controller Chem. Separations Corp., Oak Ridge, 1978-79, treas., 1979—. Capt., Voluntary Crime Prevention Program, Knox County, Tenn., 1979—. Served with USAF, 1970-76. Mem. Am. Mgmt. Assn. Home: 11631 S Monticello Dr Concord TN 37922 Office: Chemical Separations Corp 795 Oak Ridge Turnpike Oak Ridge TN 37830

MORRIS, HORTON HAROLD, pigment co. exec.; b. Post, Tex., May 26, 1922; s. Max Lindsay and Ida (Nelson) M.; B.S. in Chemistry, Tex. Technol. U., 1949; M.S. in Chemistry, U. Maine, 1953; m. Annie May Martin, Dec. 17, 1945; children—Karen, Lindsay, Larry. Tchr. sci. Lockney (Tex.) High Sch., 1949-50; asso. prof. chemistry U. Maine, Orono, 1953-57; research dir. So. Clays, Inc., Gordon, Ga., 1957-62; v.p. research and devel. Freeport Kaolin Co., Gordon, 1963-74, 79—; pres. SSI Consultants, Macon, Ga., 1974-79. Served with U.S. Army, 1943-45. Mem. Am. Chem. Soc., Clay Minerals Soc., ASTM, Am. Inst. Chemists, Am. Ceramic Soc., N.Y. Acad. Sci., AAAS, TAPPI, Sigma Xi. Contbr. articles to profl. jours. Home: 4684 Twin Oaks Dr Macon GA 31210 Office: Freeport Kaolin Co Gordon GA 31031

MORRIS, JAMES ALLEN, systems co. exec.; b. Vienna, Ga., Jan. 18, 1929; s. Clyde Center and Gladys (Taylor) M.; student Ga. Mil. Coll., 1945-46, U.S. Naval Acad., 1946-49; B.S., Mass. Inst. Tech., 1952; postgrad. U. Tenn., 1957-68; m. Annabel Cheney Trapp, Sept. 30, 1950; children—James Allen, Linda Carol, Glenn Perry. Tchr. advanced sci. Lanier High Sch., Macon, Ga., 1949-50; engr. Robins AFB, Ga., 1950-51; test engr. U.S. Naval Engring. Exptl. Sta., Annapolis, Md., 1952-55; project engr. Ford Sci. Lab., Ford Motor Co., Dearborn, Mich., 1955-57; project engr. ARO, Inc., Arnold Engring. Devel. Center, Arnold Air Force Sta., Tenn., 1957-68; dept. mgr. Planning Research Corp., Huntsville, Ala., 1968-73; mgr. printer mech. sect. SCI Systems, Inc., Huntsville, 1973—; instr. steam engring. Tenn. Agrl. and Indsl. State U., Nashville, 1962-68. Served with USN, 1946-49. Registered profl. engr., Tenn. Asso. fellow Am. Inst. Aeros. and Astronautics; mem. Am. Ordnance Assn., Am. Legion. Baptist (deacon). Contbr. articles to profl. jours. Home: 8018 Navios Dr SE Huntsville AL 35802 Office: 8600 S Memorial Pkwy Huntsville AL 35802

MORRIS, JAMES AVON, banker; b. Tuscaloosa County, Ala., Jan. 9, 1939; s. Harvey Anderson and Rosie Bell (Tingle) M.; student Berry Coll., 1957-59, Bank Adminstrn. Inst. Sch., U. Wis., 1968-70; m. Shelby J. Nolen, Nov. 28, 1959; children—John Mark, James Edward. Photostat clk. First Nat. Bank, Atlanta, 1959-60, asst. mgr. office services, 1960-62, mgr. office services, 1962-64, bldg. coordinator, 1964-68, mgr. space planning, 1968-69, mgr., purchasing dir., 1969-75, mgr. office planning and constrn. dept., 1975—; tchr. facilities planning Bank Adminstrn. Inst. Sch., U. Wis., 1978-79. Pres., Elementary Sch. PTA, 1973-74, Middle Sch. PTA, 1975, Powders Springs Youth Orgn., 1975, 78, 79. Mem. Bldg. Owners and Mgrs. Assn. Methodist. Clubs: Lions (sec. 1969), Kiwanis. Home: 5161 Blunschi St Powder Springs GA 30073 Office: 2 Peachtree St Atlanta GA 30303

MORRIS, JAMES BADGETT, chiropractor; b. Oxford, N.C., May 21, 1912; s. Asa Younger and Ellie Ray (Badgett) M.; student Wake Forest Coll., 1933-35; Dr. Chiropractic, Logan Chiropractic Coll., St. Louis, 1939; postgrad. Nat. Chiropractic Coll., Chgo., 1954; m. Eloise Emma Chappell, Dec. 3, 1941; children—Anita Rose (Mrs. Grover Dale), Jon Byron, James Douglas. Chiropractor, Durham, N.C., 1942—. Vice pres. Chiropractic State Bd. Examiners, 1953, pres., 1954; mem. N.C. Bd. Chiropractic Examiners, 1979—; mem. Adv. Com. on Med. Assistance for State Medicaid Program, 1970. Named Chiropractic Dr. of Year in N.C., 1954. Hon. fellow Internat. Coll. Chiropractors; mem. Am. (mem. posture council; N.C. liaison chmn. spl. com. on polit. edn.), N.C. (pres. 1947, chmn. council on posture 1954-59, 68—, mem. Speakers Bur., past pres. Gavel Club, Journalistic Achievement award 1961) chiropractic assns., Durham Chiropractic Soc., Internat. Platform Assn., Durham C. of C. Baptist (chmn. fin. com. 1978, chmn. bd. deacons). Clubs: Durham Exchange (pres. 1950, Man of Year 1950, pres., dir. Sheltered Workshop 1969-70), N.C. State Exchange (pres. 1951), N.C. Dist. Exchange (N.C. Exchangite of Year 1970). Home: 1709 Vista St Durham NC 27701 Office: 219 N Gregson St Durham NC 27701

MORRIS, JAMES EDWARD, engring. co. exec.; b. Dallas, Mar. 25, 1952; s. William B. and Virginia C. M.; B.S. in Engring., U. Tex., Arlington, 1976. Fed. insp. Parson/McKee, Inc., Dallas/Ft. Worth Airport, 1971-73; constrn. mgr. Engrs.-Designers, Inc., Cons. Engrs., Dallas, 1975—. Republican. Episcopalian. Home: 3903 Pipeline St Euless TX 76039 Office: PO Box 20871 Dallas TX 75220

MORRIS, JAMES KENNETH, psychologist, clergyman; b. Bessemer, Ala., Jan. 26, 1896; s. Charles Ellis and Rosa (Allenton) M.; B.A., U. Ala., 1917; postgrad. Columbia U., 1923; M.Div., Episcopal Theol. Sem., 1925, D.D., 1965; postgrad. Japanese Lang. Sch., Tokyo, 1925-28; M.A., U. S.C., 1957; L.H.D., St. Augustine Coll., 1964; D.Hum., Voorhees Coll., 1972; m. Esther Jones, Sept. 9, 1925; children—Elizabeth Morris Feltus, James Kenneth, John Robert. Partner, Morris-Howard Lumber Co., Camden, Ala., 1920-22; ordained to ministry Episc. Ch., 1925; missionary, Kyoto, Japan, 1925-40; rector St. Johns Episc. Ch., Columbia, S.C., 1941-43, 45-60; psychologist, marriage and family counselor, lectr., Columbia, 1960—; mem. Council of Advice, trustee Missionary Dist. of Kyoto; pres. Central Japan Missionary Assn., mem. Kagawa Fellowship; sec. Fellowship of Christian Missionaries in Japan, 1925-40, Diocese of Upper S.C., 1941—; mem. Diocesan Exec. Council; chmn. Dept. Christian Social Relations, Com. on State of Ch., Com. on Ch. Architecture, Com. on Constn. and Canons; dean Central Convocation; dep. Provincial Synod; del. Gen. Conv., 1945-60, N.Am. Conf. on Ch. and Family, 1961, 66. Chmn. merit system council S.C. Bd. Health, 1970-74; mem. Interagy. Merit System Council, 1974-77; hon. mem. S.C. Planned Parenthood; adviser Parents without Partners; past chmn. Meml. Youth Center. Trustee Voorhees Coll., Denmark, S.C., 1951—, chmn. bd., 1961-71; trustee Episc. Ch. Home for Children, Heathwood Hall Sch., Episc. Ch. Found. Diocese Upper S.C. Served to 1st lt. U.S. Army, World War I; to lt. col. AUS, World War II. Decorated Army Commendation medal with pendant. Diplomate Am. Assn. Pastoral Counselors. Fellow Am. Assn. Marriage and Family Therapy; mem. Assn. Clin. Pastoral Edn., Am., S.C. psychol. assns., Nat. Council Family Relations, Phi Beta Kappa, Phi Gamma Delta. Clubs: Masons, Rotary. Author: Noda, A Story of Redemption, 1938; Premarital Counseling-A Manual for Ministers, 1960; My Strength and My Shield, 1963; Marriage Counseling-A Manual for Ministers, 1965; The Windows of St. John's, 1971; Source Material on Life of Elizabeth Evelyn Wright, 1977; contbr. articles to profl. jours. Home: 2433 Monroe St Columbia SC 29205

MORRIS, JANE EMELIA, health planner; b. Texarkana, Tex., Oct. 5, 1950; d. Samuel John and Mabel (Martin) Morris; B.F.A., U. Tex., 1973; M.Ed., E. Tex. State U., 1974. Curriculum/career devel. specialist Cameron U., Lawton, Okla., 1975-76; grant coordinator, asst. to city adminstr. City of New Boston (Tex.), 1976-77; claims rep. Social Security Adminstrn., Monroe, La., 1977-78; dir. N.E. La. Emergency Med. Services, Monroe, 1978—; co-dir. colloquium in changing roles of women, Denton, Tex., 1971, symposium on women in non-traditional career fields, Lawton, 1976. Staff counselor Tex. Youth Conf., 1969; recommendation com. Okla. regents for higher edn. seminar on women in higher edn., 1976; gov.'s commn. on higher edn. and E.R.A., Okla., 1976. Recipient Tex. Agrl. Products Fashion award, 1971. Mem. Am. Personnel and Guidance Assn., Am. Coll. Personnel Assn., Southwestern Assn. Student Personnel Adminstrs., Nat. Vocat. Guidance Assn., Alpha Kappa Delta, Psi Chi, Omega Rho Alpha, Alpha Lambda Delta. Republican. Methodist. Clubs: Bus. and Profl. Women, D.A.R. Author: Employment Outlook for Selected Occupational Fields Requiring A College Degree, 1976; contbr. article to Am. Sch. Counselor Jour. Home: Rt 2 Box 1 New Boston TX 75570 Office: NE Found for Emergency Med Services Monroe LA 71201

MORRIS, JOANN J., nurse; b. Eunice, W.Va., July 7, 1930; d. Percy E. and Leola Jarrell; R.N., Charleston (W.Va.) Gen. Hosp. Sch. Nursing, 1951; B.S. in Nursing, Eastern Ky. U., 1975, M.A., 1976; cert. nursing adminstrn., 1980; m. Enos R. Morris, Apr. 22, 1953; 1 son, John Wood. Staff nurse Charleston (W.Va.) Gen. Hosp., 1951-52, VA Hosp., Chillicothe, Ohio, 1952-53; charge nurse Ince Meml. Hosp., Twentynine Palms, Calif., 1955-57, Trinity Meml. Hosp., Cudahy, Wis., 1958-60; emergency room charge nurse Miners' Meml. Hosp., Beckley, W.Va., 1960-61; staff nurse VA Hosp., Atlanta, 1962-68; coordinator home health services Beckley, 1969; staff nurse VA Hosp., Beckley, 1970-73; clin. nurse specialist, asst. chief nurse trainee VA Hosp., Lexington, Ky., 1976-78; asst. chief nursing service VA Med. Center, Waco, Tex., 1978-80; asst. chief nursing service VA Med. Center, Columbia, S.C., 1980—. Mem. Ky. Nurses Assn. (recipient Cert. Recognition for Leadership and Continued Edn. 1975, 76, 77), Am. Nurses Assn., ARC, Am. Soc. Nursing Service Adminstrs. Presbyn. (bd. deacons 1976-78). Contbr. articles to nursing jours. Office: VA Med Center Columbia SC 29201

MORRIS, JOSEPH WILSON, chief justice; b. Rice County, Kans., Apr. 28, 1922; s. J.B. and Hazel (Sluder) M.; A.B., Washburn U., 1943, J.D., 1947; LL.M., U. Mich., 1948, S.J.D., 1955; m. Dorothy Deane Conklin, Nov. 6, 1948; children—Jeffrey David, Marilyn, Cynthia. Admitted to Kans. bar, 1947, Okla. bar, 1949; with Shell Oil Co., Tulsa, N.Y.C., 1948-60; asso. gen. counsel Amerada Petroleum Corp., Tulsa, 1960-67, gen. counsel, 1967-69, v.p., gen. counsel, 1969-72; adj. prof. law U. Tulsa, 1960-72, dean Coll. Law, 1972-74; chief judge U.S. Dist. Ct., Eastern Dist. Okla., 1974—. Mem. Okla. State Regents Higher Edn., 1970-73. Mem. Tulsa County (pres. 1971), Muskogee County, Okla., Am. bar assns., Am. Judicature Soc., Am. Law Inst. Episcopalian. Contbr. articles to legal jours. Office: PO Box 828 Muskogee OK 74401*

MORRIS, KENNETH WAYNE, dentist; b. Lynchburg, Va., Mar. 12, 1939; s. Ulysses Bernice and Louise Elvira (Adams) M.; B.A., U. Va., 1961; D.D.S., Med. Coll. of Va., 1965; m. Judy Faye Atkins, May 31, 1964 (dec. Dec. 7, 1976); children—Jeffrey Wayne, Kenneth Christian; m. 2d, Robin Marie Crutchlow, June 19, 1977; 1 son, Kendall Wayne. Gen. practice dentistry South Hill, Va., 1967—; mem. staff Community Meml. Hosp., South Hill, 1967—. Served to lt., USNR, 1965-67. Mem. Gideons Internat. (pres. S.Central camp 1969-72, meml. bible sec.), Am., Va. dental assns., Southside Dental Soc., Alumni Assn. Med. Coll. Va., Alumni Assn. U. Va., South Hill C. of C. (dir. 1971—). Baptist (deacon, tchr. Sunday sch.). Clubs: Woodfield, Tanglewood Shores Golf and Country. Home: 509 Raleigh Ave South Hill VA 23970 Office: 604 N Thomas St South Hill VA 23970

MORRIS, KENNETH WAYNE, electronic engr.; b. Blountsville, Ala., Aug. 31, 1937; s. William Ernest and Agnes Vera (Palmer) M.; B.S. in Elec. Engring. Auburn U., 1959; M.S. in Elec. Engring., U. Pa., 1962; children—Anthony Dewayne, Sheila Renee. Asst. dir. engring. TV Communications Corp., N.Y.C., 1970-71; chief engr. Capital Cable Vision, Albany, N.Y., 1971-72; project engr. Martin Marietta Corp., Orlando, Fla., 1967-69, 74, Gen. Electric Co., Daytona Beach, Fla., 1974-75; group leader Ancillary Equipment Design, Repco, Inc., Orlando, Fla., 1975—. Mem. Eta Kappa Nu, Tau Beta Pi. Repuplican. Mem. Assemblies of God Ch. Inventor in field. Home: 912 Wrenwood Ln Altamonte Springs FL 32701 Office: PO Box 7065 Orlando FL 32804

MORRIS, LASZLO DANIEL, JR., lawyer; b. Jacksonville, Fla., Nov. 21, 1939; s. Laszlo Daniel and Claudine Judin (Mumaw) M.; B.C.E., Auburn U., 1961; J.D., Georgetown U., 1968; m. Melanie Monk, June 5, 1965; children—Melanie Michele, Leigh Danielle. Project engr. Farnsworth & Chambers, Birmingham, 1961-62; engr. Indsl. Service Co., Birmingham, 1962-63, Rust Engring. Co., Birmingham, 1963-66; patent examiner U.S. Patent Office, Washington, 1966-68; admitted to Ill. bar, 1969, Ala. bar, 1970, U.S. Patent Office, 1969; asso. firm Wolfe, Hubbard, Volt & Osann, Rockford, Ill., 1968-69; atty. Vulcan Materials Co., Birmingham, 1970-74, atty., asst. sec., 1974-78, gen. atty., asst. sec., 1978—. Mem. Homewood Planning Commn., 1976-79, chmn. subdiv. com., 1977-79; bd. dirs. Jefferson County div. Am. Heart Assn., 1974—; bd. control Shades Valley YMCA, 1974—. fin. chmn., 1977, bd. chmn., 1978; trustee Children's Hosp. Birmingham, 1976—, sec. bd. trustees, 1978, 79. Served with U.S. Army, 1963. Mem. Am., Ala., Birmingham bar assns. Episcopalian. Club: Racquet (Birmingham). Home: 4415 Briar Glen Circle Birmingham AL 35243 Office: PO Box 7497 Birmingham AL 35223

MORRIS, LEWIS S., corp. exec.; b. Salisbury, N.C., 1915; A.B., U. N.C., 1936; B.S., N.C. State Coll., 1937; married. With Cone Mills Corp., Greensboro, N.C., 1937—, sec., asst. treas., 1956-58, with Revolution div., 1958-59, v.p., 1959-63, sr. v.p. mgr., 1963-65, pres., chief exec. officer, mem. exec. com., 1965-72, chmn. bd., chief exec. officer, 1972—, also dir. Served with USNR, 1941-46. Office: Cone Mills Corps 1201 Maple St Greensboro NC 27405

MORRIS, MARVIN LEON, psychologist; b. Fort Worth, Aug. 24, 1940; s. Lewis Don and Emma Faye (Cole) M.; B.A., U. Tex. at Arlington, 1966; M.S., N. Tex. State U., 1967, Ed.D., 1971; m. Leslie Anne Bradshaw, Aug. 24, 1965; children—David Gregory, Julie Christine. Pvt. practice psychology Wichita Falls Neuropsychiat. Center (Tex.), 1972—. Mem. Am. Group Psychotherapy Assn., Am., Tex., Southwestern, Wichita County (v.p.) psychol. assns., Assn. Advancement Psychology, Nat., Tex. rehab. assns., Soc. Personality Assessment, Southwestern Group Psychotherapy Soc., Soc. Police and Criminal Psychology. Home: 2711 Elmwood Ave Wichita Falls TX 76308 Office: 1714 10th St Wichita Falls TX 76301

MORRIS, OWEN GLENN, govt. ofcl.; b. Shawnee, Okla., Feb. 3, 1927; s. Vestus and Myrtle (Lindsey) M.; B.S. in Mech. Engring., U. Okla., 1947, M. Aero. Engring., 1948; postgrad. U. Va., 1952-53, Va. Poly. Inst., 1955-56, Coll. William and Mary, 1957-58; m. Clifton Moree Glover, Aug. 4, 1948; children—Deborah Moree, Janine Inez. With NASA, Houston, 1948—, aero. research scientist, 1948-61, mgr. mission engring. Apollo, 1961-64, mgr. reliability and quality assurance Apollo, 1964-66, chief project engr. Lunar Module, 1966-69, mgr. Lunar Module, 1969-72, mgr. Apollo Spacecraft Program, 1972-73, dep. mgr. Space Shuttle Orbiter, 1973, mgr. Space Shuttle systems integration, 1974-79; pres. Eagle Engring., Inc., 1980—. Mem. Tex. Water Control Improvement Dist. Bd., 1969-78. Served with USNR, 1943-46. Recipient U.S. Medal of Freedom, NASA, 1972, Distinguished Service medal, 1973, Exceptional Service medal, 1969. Fellow Am. Inst. Aeros. and Astronautics (asso.); mem. Am. Aviation Hist. Soc., Am. Soaring Soc., Acad. Model Aeros., Tau Beta Pi, Tau Omega. Presbyn. (elder 1964—). Rotarian. Home: 130 Driftwood Dr Seabrook TX 77586 Office: 17629 El Camino Real Suite 125 Houston TX 77058

MORRIS, RANDY JOE, chemist; b. Princeton, Ill., Nov. 24, 1952; s. Joseph Oscar and Annabelle Marie (Plumley) M.; B.S. in Chemistry, Tex. Christian U., 1974; M.B.A., Okla. State U., 1980; m. Cathe Mae Nawa, July 6, 1974. Chemist, Phillips Petroleum Co., Bartlesville, Okla., 1974-77, market research analyst, 1977-79, sr. strategy analyst, 1979—. Mem. Am. Chem. Soc., Assn. M.B.A. Execs., Jaycees. Republican. Presbyterian. Club: Toastmasters (pres. 1979). Home: 1231 Harris Dr Bartlesville OK 74003 Office: 16 C1 Phillips Bldg Bartlesville OK 74004

MORRIS, ROBERT CROCKETT, audiologist; b. Inman, Va., June 24, 1931; s. James Walker and Martha Virginia (Ireson) M.; B.S., U. Va., 1957, M.Ed., 1959; postgrad. U. Va.-Gallaudet Coll., 1959-60; m. Alice Jo Gilliam, Dec. 20, 1953; children—Virginia, Rebecca, Robert Crockett, Joseph, James, Paul, Glenn, Jonathan, Sonny, Timothy, Victor, Norman, Felicia, Bart. Speech therapist, hearing cons. Roanoke (Va.) City Schs., 1960-61; clin. audiologist, acting dir. Hampton Roads Speech and Hearing Center, Newport News, Va., 1961-65; exec. dir., clin. audiologist Roanoke Valley Speech and Hearing Center, Roanoke, 1965-69; asst. prof. speech pathology and audiology James Madison U., Harrisonburg, Va., 1969—, coordinator clin. services, 1973—; cons. indsl. audiology. 1st v.p. Sedgefield PTA, 1964-65; mem. profl. adv. com. Roanoke Total Action Against Poverty, 1966-69; mem. Roanoke Valley Regional Health Planning Council, 1968-69; chmn. profl. adv. council United Cerebral Palsy Va., 1970-71; chmn. research com. Va. Council for Deaf Commn., 1972-76; Mem. stake high council Ch. Jesus Christ Latter-day Saints, Charlottesville, Va., 1978—. Served with USAF, 1950-54. Mem. Speech and Hearing Assn. Va. (past pres.), Am. Speech and Hearing Assn. (cert. in audiology and speech pathology, Va. legis. councilor 1976-79), Kappa Delta Pi. Home: 165 New York Ave Harrisonburg VA 22801 Office: Speech and Hearing Center James Madison U Harrisonburg VA 22807

MORRIS, ROGER DALE, banker, artist; b. Huntington, W.Va., Feb. 23, 1947; s. Guy Robert and Corena (Irby) M.; student Art Instrn. Schs., Mpls., 1965-68. With Gary (Ind.) Nat. Bank, 1965-70; asst. cashier The Peoples Bank, Marion, Ky., 1971—; free-lance artist, 1975—; paintings exhibited at Gallery LaLuz (N.Mex.), 1979, Overland Trail Gallery, Laramie, Wyo., 1979, Kapok Tree Inn, Clearwater, Fla., 1979; works represented in pvt. collections; painting reproduced in Artists, USA, 1977-78. Recipient hon. mention Red Wing Pottery, Mpls., 1967, 1st place award Art Instrn. Schs., 1968, 2d place award, 1969. Mem. Internat. Soc. Artists. Home: PO Box 183 Carrsville KY 42030 Office: PO Box 231 Marion KY 42064

MORRIS, STEPHEN MICHAEL, assn. exec.; b. Bklyn., Feb. 3, 1938; s. Lester J. and Gladys M.; B.S., Alfred U., 1959; cert. fin. planner Coll. Fin. Planning, 1975; m. Carla A. Williams, Oct. 17, 1975; children—Andrew B., Jonathan J. Devel. engr. Ferro Corp., JFD and IBM, Ohio, N.Y., Va., 1960-71; personal fin. sales Elba Corp., Waddel & Reed, Va., 1972-73; pres., DMR Ltd., Fairfax, Va., 1974-75; asst. dir. Nat. Automobile Dealers Assn. Retirement Trust, McLean, Va., 1975—; producer, moderator cable TV program Money Mgmt., 1974—. Served with U.S. Army, 1959. Mem. Inst. Cert. Fin. Planners, Internat. Assn. Fin. Planners, Internat. Found. Employee Benefit Plans. Home: 1545 Scandia Circle Reston VA 22090 Office: Nat Automobile Dealers Assn Retirement Trust 8400 Westpark Dr McLean VA 22102

MORRIS, WILLIAM OTIS, lawyer; b. Fairmont, W.Va., Dec. 2, 1922; s. William Otis and Flora (Preston) M.; B.A., Coll. William and Mary, 1944; LL.B., U. Ill., 1946, J.D., 1965; m. Hazel I. Kolbus, May 28, 1948; children—Barbara Ann Morris Jabbur, Melinda Morris Grant. Admitted to Va. bar, 1945, Ill. bar, 1946, U.S. Supreme Court bar, 1948; faculty Coll. Commerce, U. Ill., Urbana, 1946-55; asso. prof. law Stetson U., St. Petersburg, Fla., 1955-58; prof. law W.Va. U., Morgantown, 1958—; Disting. prof. U. Miss., Oxford, 1979. Served with U.S. Army, 1941. Mem. Va. Bar Assn., Order of Coif. Lutheran. Club: Masons. Author: Dental Litigation, 1972, rev. edit., 1977; The Law of Domestic Relations, 1973; Veternarian in Litigation, 1976; Statutes and Cases on Domestic Relations, 1973; contbr. articles in field to profl. jours. Home: 644 Bellaire Dr Morgantown WV 26505 Office: WVa U Law Center Morgantown WV 26506

MORRISON, ALEXANDER NORMAN, wire mfg. co. exec.; b. Johnson City, Tenn., July 7, 1951; s. John Joseph and Latrell Wilma (Caudel) M.; student Ga. Tech. Inst., 1969-72; B.Mech. Tech., So. Tech. Inst., 1977; m. Consuelo Ravelo, May 15, 1976. Engring. draftsman Nat. Linen Service, Atlanta, 1972-74, project engr., 1974-77; engr. Southwire Co., Carrollton, Ga., 1977—. Mem. ASME, Ga. Soc. Profl. Engrs., Greater Atlanta Philippine-Am. Assn., So. Tech. Inst. Nat. Alumni Assn. (bd. dirs.). Baptist. Home: 5705 Macedin Dr Douglasville GA 30135 Office: Southwire Co Fertilla St Carrollton GA 30117

MORRISON, FRANCIS SECREST, physician; b. Chgo., July 29, 1931; s. Clifton B. and Marie B. (LaPierre) M.; student U. Ill., Chgo., 1949-51; B.S. with honors, Miss. State U., 1954; M.D., U. Miss., 1959; m. Dorothy Daniels, Nov. 29, 1957; children—Francis, Thomas, Kenneth. Intern, Hosp. of U. Pa., Phila., 1959-60, resident in internal medicine, 1960-62; trainee in hematology Blood Research Lab., Tufts-New Eng. Med. Center, Boston, 1962-64, research fellow, 1964-65; vis. investigator St. Mary's Hosp., London, 1966; attending physician and dir. Div. Hematology and Oncology U. Hosp., Jackson, Miss., 1969—; dir. U. Hosp. Blood Bank, Jackson, 1974—; cons. in hematology Miss. Meth. Rehab. Center, Jakcson, 1976; asst. prof. medicine U. Miss. Sch. Medicine, Jackson, 1969-70, dir. div. hematology, 1969—, asso. prof. medicine, 1970-76, prof. medicine, 1976—, mem. faculty Grad. Sch. Medicine, 1971—; profl. adviser Jackson Community Blood Bank, Inc., 1973-75; dir. Regional Cancer Program, Miss. Regional Med. Program, 1971-75; exec. dir. Miss. Regional Blood Center, 1975—; mem. adv. bd. Jackson-Hinds Comprehensive Health Center, 1973—; research cons. Alcorn A. and M. Coll., Lorman, Miss., 1973-74; guest lectr. various health orgns. and TV programs; mem. hemophilia adv. bd. Miss. Bd. Health, 1974—; chmn. task force on regionalization Am. Blood Commn., 1978-79. Mem. Miss. Gov.'s Council on Aging, 1976—; pres. parish council St. Peter's Cathedral, Jackson, 1972-74; chmn. Diocesan Commn. for Community Services, Diocese of Natchez, Jackson, 1972-76; pres. sch. bd. St. Joseph High Sch., 1974-76; bd. dirs. Miss. Opera Assn., 1973—. Served to comdr., M.C., USN. Diplomate Am. Bd. Internal Medicine. Fellow A.C.P.; mem. Am., Internat. socs. hematology, Am. Fedn. Clin. Research, Am. Assn. Blood Banks, Internat. Soc. Blood Transfusion, Jackson Acad. Medicine (pres. 1976), Am. Coll. Nuclear Medicine (alt. del. for Miss. 1975), Am. Assn. Cancer Edn. (exec. com. 1978—), Am. Assn. Cancer Research, N.Y., Miss. acads. sci., World Fedn. Hemophilia, Internat. Soc. Thrombosis and Haemostasis, Central Med. Soc., So., Miss. (com. on blood transfusion 1976-78) med. assns., Am. Soc. Nuclear Medicine, Am. Soc. Clin. Oncology, S.W. Oncology Group (prin. investigator), Soc. Cryobiology, AMA, Am. Cancer Soc. (pres. Miss. div. 1977), S. Central Assn. Blood Banks (program chmn. 1975, v.p. 1977-79), AAUP, Council Community Blood Centers (trustee 1975-79), So. Blood Club (pres. 1977), Internat. Platform Assn., Sigma Xi, Phi Kappa Phi, Omicron Delta Kappa. Contbr. numerous articles on hematology and cancer to med. jours. Home: 771 Belhaven St Jackson MS 39202 Office: Univ Medical Center Jackson MS 39216

MORRISON, GLENN, neurol. surgeon; b. Phila., June 16, 1940; s. James Thomas and Naomi (Partridge) M.; A.B., Colgate U., 1962; M.D., Case Western U., 1967; m. Jane Ellen Linke, July 6, 1963; children—Tom, Ted, Tim. Intern, Cleve. Met. Gen. Hosp., 1967-68; resident Univ. Hosps., Cleve., 1970-74; practice medicine specializing in neurol. surgery, Coral Gables, Fla., 1974—; asst. clin. prof. dept. neurol. surgery U. Miami (Fla.), 1974—; neurol. surgeon Perlmutter, Dooley & Morrison, Neurol. Assos., P.A., Coral Gables, 1974—. Served to lt. comdr. USPHS, 1968-70. Diplomate Am. Bd. Neurol. Surgeons. Fellow A.C.S. Office: 4685 Ponce de Leon Blvd Coral Gables FL 33146

MORRISON, ROBERT HARRY, restaurant chain exec.; b. Charleston, W.Va., Dec. 12, 1943; s. Harry Cylde and Everitte May (Dawson) M.; B.S. in Acctg., Ill. State U., 1973; postgrad Columbia-So. Sch. Law, 1978—. Mgmt. trainee McDonalds, Oak Brook, Ill., 1973-74, asst. acctg. supr., 1974, acctg. supr., Oklahoma City, 1974-75, regional controller, N.Y.C., 1975-77, controller Southeastern zone, Atlanta, 1977—. C.P.A., Ga. Mem. Am. Inst. C.P.A.'s, N.J. Soc. C.P.A.'s, Ill. C.P.A. Soc., Phi Theta Kappa, Iota Gamma Phi. Baptist. Home: 1999 Glacier Dr Stone Mountain GA 30087 Office: 1740 Century Circle Atlanta GA 30345

MORRISON, ROBERT HAYWOOD, investment co. exec.; b. Hickory, N.C., Mar. 27, 1927; s. Charles Tyson and Rebecca Grace (Tuttle) M.; A.B., U. N.C., 1946, M.A., 1947. Asst. in bus. English U. Ill., 1947-48; chmn. bus. communication, sec. of faculty Sch. Bus., U. Kans., Lawrence, 1948-51; editor Daily News Enterprise, Newton, N.C., 1952-54; pres. Morrison & Co., Charlotte, N.C., 1955—, Catawba Capital Corp., 1961—, Investors Corp. S.C., 1961—. Prof. journalism Winthrop Coll., Rock Hill, S.C., 1955-59. Justice of peace, Catawba County, 1951-59; Republican chmn. 1st precinct Mecklenburg County, N.C., 1971—. Mem. Nat. Assn. Realtors, Phi Beta Kappa, Sigma Phi Epsilon, Delta Sigma Pi. Rotarian. Author: A Guide to Bank Correspondence, 1949; Problems and Cases in Business Writing, 1951; Better Letters, 1952; Profit Making Letters, 1959; Modern Journalism, 1962; Bank Correspondence Handbook, 1964. Home: 1333 Queens Rd Charlotte NC 28207 Office: 1409 E Boulevard Charlotte NC 28203

MORRISON, WALTON S., lawyer; b. Big Spring, Tex., June 16, 1907; s. M. H. and Ethel (Jackson) M.; student Texas A. and M. Coll., 1926-28; J.D., Texas U., 1932; m. Mary Bell, Dec. 19, 1932. Admitted to Tex. bar, 1932; asso. Morrison & Morrison, Big Spring, 1932-37; county atty. Howard County, Tex., 1937-39; county judge Howard County, 1941-42; pvt. practice, 1946-47; county judge Howard, 1947-48; partner Morrison & Morrison, 1949-53; pvt. practice, 1953—; city atty. Big Spring, 1949-58. Pres., Tex. City Attys., 1955-56. Served with USAF, 1942-46; lt. col. Res. ret. Fellow Am. Coll. Probate Counsel; mem. Am., Tex. (mem. taxation council 1967-76), local bar assns. Rotarian; Mason (Shriner). Home: 1501 E 11th Pl Big Spring TX 79720 Office: 113 E 2d St Big Spring TX 79720

MORROW, ARCHIBALD HALDANE, phys. edn. adminstr.; B.S., N.C. A&T U., 1934; M.A., Columbia U., 1940; postgrad., Ind. U., 1967. Tchr. sci. public schs., Asheboro, N.C., 1934-35, also athletic coach, 1934-35; instr. phys. edn. Fayetteville (N.C.) State U., 1935, also asst. librarian, track coach; tchr. sci., athletic coach Smith High Sch., Fayetteville, 1940-41; dir. phys. edn. N.C. A&T U., Greensboro, 1941-43; dir. phys. edn. Tulsa Public Schs., 1943-46, also asst. basketball and track coach; dir. health, phys. edn. and recreation Winston-Salem (N.C.) State U., 1946-52, boxing, tennis and golf coach; dir. health, phys. edn. and recreation Philander Smith Coll., Little Rock, 1942-67, head football coach, 1952-60; asso. prof. health, phys. edn. and recreation, dir. intramural sports Grambling (La.) State U., 1967—; chmn. athletics Grambling Recreation Center, 1976-77. Supt., Sunday sch. local ch., Grambling, also chmn. bd. Christian edn. Mem. Am. Sch. Health Assn., AAHPER, Nat. Intramural Recreation Sports Assn., Phi Delta Kappa, Omega Psi Phi, Phi Epsilon Kappa. Office: Dept Phys Education Grambling State Univ Grambling LA

MORROW, PHILLIP STANLEY, systems analyst; b. Clarksville, Tenn., Nov. 5, 1941; s. Clyde Lawson and Mary Virginia (White) M.; B.S. in Bus. Adminstrn., Austin Peay State U., 1964; M.P.A., U. Tenn., 1975; m. Betty Sue Freeman, Apr. 15, 1965; children—Virginia Leigh, Mary Catherine. Caseworker, Tenn. Dept. Human Services, Clarksville, 1964-65; computer programmer Tenn. Dept. Transp., Nashville, 1965-66; computer specialist Tenn. Dept. Finance and Adminstrn., Nashville, 1966-73; systems analyst Tenn. Dept. Safety, Nashville, 1973-79, mgr. systems analysis, 1979—. Mem. fin. com. St. Paul's United Methodist Ch., 1977—, mem. men's club, treas., 1979-80. Recipient certificate for service State of Tenn., 1974. Mem. Assn. Systems Mgrs., Am. Soc. Pub. Adminstrn. (sec.-treas. 1976-77, pres. 1978-79), Capitol Hill Jaycees (sec. 1977-78), Tenn. State Employees Assn., Data Processing Mgmt. Assn. Club: YMCA Athletic (Nashville). Home: 432 Rembrandt Dr Old Hickory TN 37138 Office: 1201 Andrew Jackson Bldg Nashville TN 37219

MORROW, R. BARRY, fastener mfg. co. exec.; b. Statesville, N.C., May 25, 1950; s. Ralph Settle and Pauline Harriet M.; B.S., N.C. State U., 1972; M.B.A., Wake Forest U., 1974. Cost acct. Owens-Corning Fiberglas, Anderson, S.C., 1974-75; fin. budget analyst Sea-Land Service, Menlo Park, N.J., 1975-76; budget mgr. NL Fasteners, Statesville, N.C., 1976—. Mem. Nat. Assn. Accts. Baptist. Home: 425 Walnut St Statesville NC 28677 Office: Barkley Rd Statesville NC 28677

MORSE, EUGENIA MAUDE, architect, educator; b. Houston, Feb. 23, 1920; d. Robert Emmett and Eugenia Elizabeth (Maddox) Morse; B.A. in Architecture, Rice U., 1941, B.S. in Architecture, 1942. Practicing architect, 1949—; asso. prof. U. S.W. La., 1954-59; prof. architecture Tex. Tech U., Lubbock, 1959—. Pres. bd. dirs. Storm Def. Club, 1970-73. Mem. Am. Forestry Assn. (life), West Tex. Watercolor Assn. (treas., cir. 1971-72), Nat. Geog. Soc., Museum Natural History, Smithsonian Instn. Prin. works include Seitter Photography Bldg., Corpus Christi, Tex., Miles Ramagosa Clinic, Lafayette, La., Haltom Optical Co. Office and Lab., Corpus Christi, Buccaneer Gardens Housing Project, Corpus Christi, others, also residences. Home: 2621 33d St Lubbock TX 79410 Office: 1008 F Architecture Bldg Tex Tech U Lubbock TX 79409

MORSE, F. D., JR., dentist; b. Glen Lyn, Va., Apr. 5, 1928; s. Frank D. and Ida Estell (Davis) M.; B.S., Concord Coll., 1951; D.D.S., Med. Coll. Va., 1955; m. Patsy Lee Apple, Feb. 4, 1967; children—Fortis Davis, Pamela Marie. Free lance photographer, 1950-56; practice dentistry, Pearisburg, Va., 1958—; mem. staff Giles Hosp., Pearisburg, 1958—. Served from asst. dental surgeon to sr. asst. dental surgeon USPHS, 1955-57; assigned to USCG, 1957-58. Mem. Am., S.W. Va. dental assns., Assn. Mil. Surgeons, A.A.A.S., Nat. Assn. Advancement Sci., Fedn. Dentaire Internat., Internat. Platform Assn., W.Va. Collegiate Acad. Sci., Beta Phi. Kiwanian. Home: Bicuspid Acres Pearisburg VA 24134 Office: Giles Profl Bldg Pearisburg VA 24134

MORSE, FREDERICK WHITTON, advt. agency exec., writer; b. Gordonsville, Va., Sept. 10, 1915; s. Frederick Anderson and Rosa Belle (Yancey) M.; A.B., Hampden-Sydney Coll., 1940; m. Linda Firestone, 1977; children by previous marriage—Frederick Anderson, Ann Dabney. Reporter, sports editor, city editor Daily Progress, Charlottesville, Va., 1935-36; publicity dir. Hampden-Sydney (Va.) Coll., 1936-40; reporter, feature writer Richmond (Va.) Times-Dispatch, 1940-42; news specialist, dir. radio and TV office covering five states and Washington, VA, 1946-49; pub. relations dir. Richmond Area Community Chest and Council, 1949-51; dir. pub. relations, account exec. Cabell Eanes Advt. Agy., Richmond, 1951-55, sec., 1955-57, exec. v.p., 1957-66, pres., 1966-79; pres. Communications Assos., Inc., Richmond, 1979—; treas. Bill Muller, The Toymaker, Inc., Oak Hall, Va., 1978—; author: (with Linda Firestone) Virginia's Favorite Islands, Chincoteague and Assateague, 1976, Florida's Enchanting Islands, Sanibel and Captiva, 1976, Jefferson's Country, Charlottesville and Albemarle County, 1977; contbr. articles to trade mags. Served with USN, 1942-46; served to lt. comdr. USNR, 1946-63; lt. comdr. Res. ret. Office: 713 N Courthouse Rd Richmond VA 23235

MORSE, GENEVIEVE FORBES (MRS. FREDERICK TRACY MORSE), club woman; b. New Rochelle, N.Y., June 8, 1905; d. James and Mabel (Sabin) Forbes; B.A., La. Poly. Inst., 1932; m. Frederick Tracy Morse Jan. 1, 1926; 1 son, Robert Frederick. Pres., U. Va. Hosp. Circle, 1947-49, bd. dirs., 1945-66; Va. corr. sec. DAR, 1953-56, editor Va. News Bull., 1953-59, vice regent, 1956-59, regent, 1959-62, v.p. gen. from Va., 1962-64, curator gen. nat. soc., 1965-68, adviser DAR Museum, 1968—, state chmn. Va. Room in Washington, 1968-71, mem. com., 1971-77, nat. chmn. resolutions com., 1971-74, nat. chaplain gen., 1974-77; Va. rec. sec. Daus. Colonial Wars, 1953-56, chaplain, 1959-62, pres., 1956-59; nat. chmn. nat. def. com., 1959-62, nat. pres., 1962-65, nat. chmn. historic research and preservation com., 1968-71, chmn. by laws com., 1971—. Ky. col. Mem. Colonial Daus. 17th Century (pres. Jamestown chpt. 1976-79, nat. council 1979—), Order of Crown Am., Daus. Am. Colonists, Daus. Barons Runnemede (registrar 1978—), Order Descs. Colonial Clergy, Hereditary Order Descs. Colonial Govs. (registrar gen. 1961-67, gov. gen. 1967-70), Order of Three Crusades (registrar gen. 1978—), Soc. Descs. of William the Conqueror, Order of Washington, Albemarle Hist. Soc., Nat. Soc. Am. Royal Descent (corr. sec. gen. 1974-80, 1st v.p. gen. 1980—), Nat. Trust Hist. Preservation, Nat. Gavel Soc. (pres. 1977-80), Colonial Dames Am., Dames of Guild of St. Margaret of Scotland, Sigma Tau Delta, Kappa Delta (nat. council 1953-67, nat. editor The Angelos 1953-59, pres. Alpha South province 1950-54, nat. pres. 1959-67, nat. historiographer 1967-73, nat. dir. archives 1973—). Episcopalian. Editor: Monticello Cook Book, 3d edit., 1950; author: Through the Years, and Other Poems, 1945; A History of Kappa Delta Sorority, 1897-1972, 2 vols., 1973; contbr. poetry to various anthologies. Home: Retreat Albemarle County Charlottesville VA 22906

MORSE, RICHARD HOWARD, psychiatrist; b. Milw., Sept. 16, 1935; s. Herbert and Frieda B. (Wineman) M.; A.B., Harvard U., 1959; M.D., U. Wis., 1967; M.P.H., U. Minn., 1975. Intern, U. Wash., 1967-68; resident in psychiatry U. Minn., 1971-75; instr. Harvard U., asst. psychiatrist McLean Div. Mass. Gen. Hosp., fellow Inst. Law and Psychiatry, 1975-76; dir. consultation-liaison La. State U. Med. Sch., 1976-77; dir. pain unit New Eng. Rehab. Hosp., 1976, Mercy Pain Center, New Orleans, 1977—; asst. prof. psychiatry La. State U.; practice medicine specializing in adult, child and adolescent psychiatry, New Orleans, 1977—. Served with M.C., Spl. Forces, AUS, 1969-71. Decorated Army Commendation medal, 2 Bronze Stars, Air medal; diplomate Am. Bd. Psychiatry and Neurology. Mem. Am. Cath. Hosp. Assn. (chmn. adv. com. med. affairs 1979). Jewish. Editorial bd. Obesity and Metabolism, 1979—. Home and Office: 4417 Danneel St New Orleans LA 70115

MORSE, SAMUEL ALTON, med. services adminstr.; b. Bryan, Tex., Feb. 24, 1943; s. Samuel A. and Dorothy Mae (Thomas) M.; B.S. in Bus. Adminstrn., Abilene Christian U., 1966; M.S., Trinity U., 1971; M.B.A., St. Mary's U., 1973; D. Bus. Adminstrn., Ind. No. U., 1974; Ph.D., U. Tex., 1977—; m. Neville J. Stromquist, Sept. 4, 1965; children—Joshua, Jeremy, Mary Ann. Youth phys. dir. East End YMCA, Houston, 1967-69, Town North YMCA, San Antonio, 1969-70; mgmt. cons., San Antonio, 1970-72; asst. adminstr. Bexar County Hosp. Dist., San Antonio, 1972-74; exec. dir. Daytona Community Hosp., Daytona Beach, Fla., 1974-77; adminstrv. asst. to v.p. eastern div. Am. Medicorp, Inc., Atlanta, 1977, dir. mgmt. systems, Dallas, 1978-79; asso. hosp. dir. Hermann Hosp., Houston, 1977-78; exec. v.p. Brookhaven Med. Center, Farmers Branch, Tex., 1979—; clin. instr. dept. surgery U. Tex., Houston, 1977-78; asst. adj. prof. health care adminstrn. Tex. Women's U., 1977—; asst. adj. prof. U. Dallas, 1978—; preceptor health care adminstrn. various univs., 1974—; guest lectr. Sch. Health Scis., Sheppard AFB, Tex., 1977—. Asst. patrol leader Sam Houston council Boy Scouts Am., 1956-57, sr. patrol leader, 1957-58, scout master, 1963-64; song leader Westbury Ch. of Christ, Houston, 1977-78; tchr., song leader Holly Hill (Fla.) Ch. of Christ, 1974-76; bd. dirs. Daytona Beach Community Coll., 1974-76, YMCA Daytona Beach, 1974-76, Mus. Arts and Scis., Daytona Beach, 1974-76, Am. Cancer Soc., Daytona Beach, 1974-76, Am Mended Hearts Assn., Daytona Beach, 1974-76, United Way, Daytona Beach, 1974-76, Houston, 1967-69, YMCA Houston, 1967-69, chmn. jr. dirs. com., 1968-69. Served with USAFR, 1966—. Recipient Gold Palm award Boy Scouts Am., 1958; Spark Plug award Daytona Beach Jaycees, 1975. Fellow Am. Acad.

Med. Adminstrs., Soc. Public Health Educators, Royal Soc. Health; mem. Am. Coll. Hosp. Adminstrs., Am. Hosp. Assn., Tex. Hosp. Assn., Fla. Hosp. Assn., Am. Inst. Indsl. Engrs., Hosp. Fin. Mgmt. Assn., Am. Public Health Assn., Assn. M.B.A. Execs., Fedn. Am. Hosps., Air Force Assn., Res. Officers Assn., Assn. Mil. Surgeons, Inst. Health Service Adminstrs., Trinity U. Alumni Assn. (editor 1974-76), Eagle Scout Assn. Am. Clubs: Lions, Rotary. Home: 3620 Cross Bend Plano TX 75023 Office: 12100 Webb Chapel Rd Farmers Branch TX 75234

MORSE, TED ALLAN, computer and electronics co. exec.; b. Toledo, June 7, 1947; s. Leroy Eugene and Bessie Marie (Jacobs) M.; student Elmhurst Coll., 1966-67; B.B.A., U. Toledo, 1970; student exec. mgmt. seminars Harvard U., 1977-78, U. Western Colo., 1980; m. Lorraine K. Moore, 1966; children—Julie, Jenny, Ted Allan. Corp. systems analyst Owens Corning Fiberglas Co., 1968-69; asst. to v.p. mktg. Am. Warming and Ventilating Co., Toledo, 1970-72; sr. sales rep. Olivetti Co., Toledo, 1970-72; sales mgr. Toledo Metal Fabricators Co., 1972-74; dist. sales mgr. Docutel Corp., Toledo, 1974-76; S.E. regional sales mgr. TRW, Inc., Longwood, Fla., 1976-79; central ops. mgr. Datatrol Inc., Altamonte Springs, Fla., 1979—; tchr., cons. in electronic funds transfer. Republican. Baptist. Clubs: Tennis, Ski, Investment. Research in future direction of electronic funds transfer. Home: 102 Ridgewood Ct Longwood FL 32750 Office: Cranes Roost Office Park 159 Whooping Loop Dr Altamonte Springs FL 32701

MORSE, YVONNE LINSERT, librarian; b. Portsmouth, Va., Dec., 1928; d. Ernest Edward and Dorothy (Tenney) Linsert; B.A., U. S.Fla., Tampa, 1972, M.A., 1974. Dental asst., 1947-50; computer operator, 1961-69; asst. librarian Coll. of Medicine, U. S. Fla., 1974-76; chief librarian VA Hosp., Fayetteville, N.C., 1976—; exhibited in one-woman art show, 1978. William and Marie Selby grantee, 1971; VA work-study trainee, 1973-74. Mem. Southeastern Library Assn., Med. Library Assn., Spl. Libraries Assn., Library Sci. Alumni Assn. U. S.Fla. (pres. 1975-76), Sarasota Art Assn., Kappa Delta Pi, Phi Kappa Phi. Democrat. Contbr. chpts. to books in field. Home: 127 E Tree Top Dr Fayetteville NC 28301 Office: VA Hosp 2300 Ramsey St Fayetteville NC 28301

MORTON, CAROLINE JULIA, devel. co. exec.; b. N.Y.C.; B.S. in Edn., U. Pa.; M.B.A., N.Y. U.; grad. cert. in profl. writing and effective communication, CCNY. Vice pres. mktg. mgmt. V-TEC Corp., Hopewell, Va.; pres. CMR Co., Hopewell; past cons. Advt. Women of N.Y. Mem. Am. Mktg. Assn. (past dir.), Advt. Women of N.Y., Fedn. Profl. Bus. Women, Am. Mgmt. Assn., AAUW. Contbr. articles to profl. jours. Address: PO Box 841 Hopewell VA 23860

MORTON, CHARLES BRINKLEY, clergyman, former state rep. and state senator; b. Meridian, Miss., Jan. 6, 1926; s. Albert Cole and Jean (Brinkley) M.; J.D. with distinction, U. Miss., 1949; M.Div. optime merens, U. South, 1959; m. Virginia Roseborough, Aug. 26, 1948; children—Charles Brinkley, Mary Virginia. Admitted to Miss. bar, 1949, also Tenn. bar; practiced in Senatobia, Miss., 1949-56; mem. firm Thomas & Morton, 1952-56; ordained to ministry P.E. Ch. as deacon and priest, 1949; priest-in-charge Ch. of Incarnation, West Point, Miss., 1959-62; rector Grace-St. Luke's Ch., Memphis 1962-74, Ch. of Advent, Birmingham, Ala., 1974—. Mem. Miss. Commn. Interstate Cooperation, 1952-56, Miss. State Hist. Commn., 1952-56. Chmn. N. Miss. Polio Fund, 1954; active numerous civic and cultural groups. Mem. Miss. House of Reps., 1948-52, Miss. Senate, 1952-56. Served with AUS, World War II, Korea; now col., chaplain Res. Decorated Silver Star, Bronze Star medal with cluster, Purple Heart, Combat Inf. Badge; recipient Freedoms Found. Honor medal, 1967, 68, 72. Mem. Miss. State Bar (complaint commr. 1953), Internat. Soc. Bibl. Lit. and Exegesis, Mil. Order World Wars. Am. Legion (past post comdr.), Phi Delta Phi, Tau Kappa Alpha, Omicron Delta Kappa, Phi Delta Theta. Democrat. Rotarian. Contbr. articles law and hist. jours. Home: 3538 Lenox Rd Birmingham AL 35213 Office: 524 21st St N Birmingham AL 35203

MORTON, ELIZABETH CRAFT, guidance counselor; b. Cullman, Ala., Apr. 27, 1953; d. Hershel Eugene and Ruth (Pruett) Craft; B.S. in Family and Child Services, Auburn (Ala.) U., 1974; M.A. in Community Agy. Counseling, U. Ala., Birmingham, 1976, postgrad., 1978-79; m. Randyal S. Morton, Aug. 26, 1972. Probation aide Lee County Juvenile Ct., Opelika, Ala., 1974; female juvenile offender counselor Ala. Dept. Youth Services, Chalkville, 1974-75; individual and family guidance counselor Community Intensive Treatment Youth Program, Birmingham, 1975-78; therapeutic program counselor Underwood Treatment Program Juvenile Offenders, Ala. Dept. Youth Services, Birmingham, 1978—; tutor, counselor adolescents King's Acres, Opelika, 1973; cons. in field. Mem. adminstrv. bd. Taylor Meml. United Methodist Ch., Chalkville, 1976—, chmn. social concerns com., chmn. urban and minorities concerns com., 1976—. Recipient cert. of merit Ala. Dept. Youth Services, 1977; named Outstanding Alumni, Auburn U. Sch. Home Econs., 1978. Mem. Am. Personnel and Guidance Assn., So. States Correctional Assn., Ala. Juvenile Justice Assn., Ala. Council Crime and Delinquency, Ala. Fedn. Bus. and Profl. Women (pres. elect Center Point club 1979; Outstanding Young Career Woman award Center Point club 1978). Home: 903-A Valley Ave Birmingham AL 35209 Office: 8950 Roebuck Blvd Birmingham AL 35206

MORTON, JAMES HARRY, tax and bus. cons.; b. Charlotte, N.C., Feb. 18, 1939; s. John Harry and Mary Elizabeth (Stikeleather) M.; grad. Am. Inst. Banking, 1964; m. Yvonne Marie Haigler, Nov. 14, 1958; children—Tina Marie, Tressa Yvonne. Staff accountant N.C. Nat. Bank, Charlotte, 1955-65; pub. accountant Conrad, Hoey, East & Co., C.P.A.'s, Charlotte, 1965-69; controller, sec.-treas. Aabco Industries, Inc., Gaffney, S.C., 1969-71, pres. AABS/Assos. Bookkeeping and Tax Service, Gaffney, 1971—, Gaffney Distbg. Co., Inc., 1971-73, Morris Constrn. & Devel. Corp., Gaffney, 1971-72; controller Power-Pak Products, Inc., Spartanburg, S.C., 1974-76; enrolled to practice before IRS. Nat. v.p. pub. relations Distributive Edn. Clubs Am., 1955-57, pres. N.C. State, 1955-57, pres. N.C. Western Region, 1955-57; treas. Gaffney Day Sch., 1969-72, chmn. bd., 1972-73. Mem. Nat. Assn. Tax Consultors, Am. Accounting Assn. Methodist (mem. adminstrv. bd., fin. com.). Club: Cherokee Sertoma (Gaffney). Home: 418 Barclay Dr Gaffney SC 29340 Office: PO Box 1116 1203 Floyd Baker Blvd Gaffney SC 29340

MORTON, JEAN SLOAT, biologist; b. Blountville, Tenn., Apr. 2, 1926; d. Charles V. and Cora (Taylor) Sloat; B.S., D.C. Tchrs. Coll., 1958; M.S. in Sci. Teaching, Am. U., 1962; M.A., 1964; postgrad. U. Oslo, Norway, 1963; M.P.S., George Washington U., 1969, Ph.D., 1970; m. Clyde Dulaney Morton, Aug. 3, 1947; 1 dau., Jennifer Sue. Chmn. dept. sci. Hart Jr. High Sch., Washington, 1958-60; teaching fellow American U., Washington, 1960-61, instr. biology, 1961-64, asst. professorial lectr., 1964-70, instr., part-time, 1967-70; cons. in toxicology and microbiology, 1974—. King research fellow, 1965-69; NSF research fellow, 1962; Smithsonian research fellow, 1969-70. Mem. N.Y. Acad. Scis., Miss. Acad. Sci., The Guild, Sigma Xi, Beta Beta Beta, Phi Delta Gamma, Phi Epsilon Phi, Kappa Delta Pi. Democrat. Baptist. Club: Newcomer (Picayune, Miss.). Author: Science in the Bible, 1978; various instructional manuals and handbooks in sci. Home: 2208 Millswood Rd Picayune MS 39466 Office: PO Box 597 Picayune MS 39466

MORVANT, HENRY FERDINAND, elec. engr.; b. Crowley, La., Nov. 3, 1925; s. Henry F. and Madeline (Jeanis) M.; B.S., U. Southwestern La., 1951; m. Connie Stewart, June 20, 1959; children—Michael, Michelle. Electronic engr. Michoud plant Chrysler Corp., New Orleans, 1951-52; elec. engr. Kaiser Aluminum & Chem. Corp., Chalmette, 1952—, sr. engr., power dept., 1955—. Served with USNR, 1944-46. Mem. I.E.E.E. (asso.). Home: 76 Carolyn Ct Arabi LA 70032 Office: PO Box 1600 Chalmette LA 70043

MOSBY, JOHN OLIVER, inventory mgmt. specialist; b. Trenton, N.J., Mar. 6, 1917; s. John Oliver and Florence (Stewart) M.; A.A., St. Philips Coll., 1949; B.B.A., St. Mary's U., 1956, M.A., 1966; m. Eddie Mae Harris, Mar. 2, 1946 (dec. Nov. 1978). Civilian staff U.S. Army, Fort Sam Houston, 1952—, inventory mgmt. specialist Fifth Army, 1966—. Instr. St. Philips Coll., San Antonio, 1968—. Served with AUS, 1942-46, USAF, 1950-52; ETO. Decorated Bronze Star medal. Mem. Am. Accounting Assn., Am. Econ. Assn., Am. Assn. Social Economy, A.A.U.P., San Antonio Soc. Bus. and Econs., Tex. Jr. Coll. Alamo C. of C., Assn., Omicron Delta Epsilon, Omega Psi Phi (basileus 1976—, Man of Yr. 1976). Mem. A.M.E. Ch. (steward). Optimist (charter, pres. 1973-74, membership award), Mason (Shriner). Home: 4922 Stoneleigh Dr San Antonio TX 78220 Office: Office of Dep Chief Staff (Logistics) Hdqrs Fifth US Army Fort Sam Houston TX 78224

MOSELEY, DAVID BARTON, JR., lawyer; b. Dallas, Dec. 16, 1946; s. David B. and Madge (McGraw) M.; A.S., Dallas Bapt. Coll., 1967; B.A., Baylor U., 1969; J.D., So. Meth. U., 1974; m. Judy Bob Evans, Dec. 30, 1966; 1 son, Joe Thomas. Admitted to Tex. bar, 1974; partner firm Moseley, Jones, Enoch & Martin, Dallas, 1974—. Served to 1st lt. U.S. Army, 1969-70. Mem. Am. Bar Assn., Assn. Trial Lawyers Am., Tex. Assn. Young Lawyers, Tex. Criminal Def. Lawyers Assn., Tex. Trial Lawyers Assn., State Bar of Tex., Dallas County Criminal Bar Assn., Dallas Estate Planning Council, Dallas Assn. Young Lawyers, Dallas Trial Lawyers Assn., Dallas Bar Assn. Office: 6060 N Central St Dallas TX 75206

MOSELEY, EMORY FRANKS, agrl. equipment sales co. exec.; b. Ebony, Va., Dec. 20, 1928; s. James Branford and Fannie H. (Reid) M.; grad. Indsl. Tng. Inst., 1948; m. Virginia Sunday, Jan. 27, 1950; children—Gary Wayne, Donna Lea, Terri Lynn. Refrigeration engr. Jones, Tompkins & Wright Co., Boydton, Va., 1948-49; with sales and service dept. Gen. Mills, Inc., Richmond, Va., 1950-53; treas. Superior Equipment & Supply Co. Inc., Richmond, Va., 1953—; pres. Dairymen's Supply Co., Inc., Richmond, 1957—, Superior Equipment & Supply Co. Inc., 1979—, Garber & Moseley Inc., 1979—; v.p. Garber & Moseley, Inc., Richmond, 1964—. Served with USN, 1946-47. Baptist. Club: Varina Charles City Sportsman and Ducks Unltd. Home: Route 5 Box 287A Richmond VA 23231 Office: 13 N 24th St Richmond VA 23223

MOSELEY, JAMES FRANCIS, lawyer; b. Charleston, S.C., Dec. 6, 1936; s. John Olin and Kathyrn (Moran) M.; A.B., The Citadel, 1958; J.D., U. Fla., 1961; m. Anne McGehee, June 10, 1961; children—James Francis, John McGehee. Admitted to Fla. bar, 1961, U.S. Supreme Ct. bar, 1970; partner firm Toole, Taylor, Moseley & Joyner, Jacksonville, Fla., 1963—. Pres. Civic Round Table, Jacksonville, 1974; pres. United Way, Jacksonville, 1979; chmn. Southeastern Admiralty Law Inst., 1980; vice chmn. bd. trustees Jacksonville Libraries, 1979. Fellow Am. Coll. Trial Lawyers; mem. Jacksonville Bar Assn. (pres. 1975), Maritime Law Assn. (exec. com. 1978—), Fedn. Ins. Counsel, R.R. Trial Lawyers Assn. Clubs: Deerwood, River. Contbr. articles on admiralty law to legal jours. Home: 7780 Hollyridge Rd Jacksonville FL 32217 Office: Toole Taylor Moseley & Joyner Barnett Bank Bldg Jacksonville FL 32202

MOSELEY, MICHAEL, mental health adminstr.; b. Kinston, N.C., Jan. 28, 1953; s. Emanuel and Mamie Lee (Albritton) M.; B.A., U. N.C., 1974; postgrad. East Carolina U., 1978—; m. Cassandra Gail Lane, July 20, 1975. Recreation specialist Kinston Recreation Commn., 1975-76; vol. services rep. Caswell Center, Kinston, 1976, resident advocate, 1976-78, asst. to dir., 1978—. Mem. Mayor's Com. for Employment of the Handicapped, Kinston, 1976-77; trustee, mem. chancel choir St. Augustus A.M.E. Ch., 1975—; mem. Lenoir Community Band, 1974-76; organizer and coordinator Lenoir County Spl. Olympics, 1975-76; bd. dirs. Lenoir County chpt. ARC, 1977-78, Our Homes, Inc., 1976-77. Recipient Cert. for Faithful Service, St. Augustus Ch., 1977. Mem. Nat. Therapeutic Recreation Soc., N.C. State Employees Assn., Am. Assn. on Mental Deficiency, Kinston Jaycees (Jaycee Rookie of the Yr. 1976), Lenoir County Assn. for Retarded Citizens (dir. 1975-77, v.p. 1975-67), NAACP, Gov.'s Sch. Alumni Assn., Easter Seal Soc., Nat. Recreation and Parks Assn., N.C. Recreation and Parks Soc., Lenoir County Interagy. Council, Carolina Wheelchair Athletic Assn., N.C. Assn. Vol. Adminstrs. Democrat. Club: Masons (sec. 1977-79, Meritorious cert. 1979). Home: 2412 Linden Ave Kinston NC 28501 Office: 2415 W Vernon Ave Kinston NC 28501

MOSELEY, NINA RANDOLPH, oil co. adminstr.; b. Oakville, Tex., Oct. 15, 1924; d. Parker Charles and Ella Jeannette (Brawner) Randolph; student S.W. Tex. State U., 1941-43; m. Jeryl Richard Moseley, May 28, 1976; 1 son by previous marriage, William Jefferson Bridges; stepchildren—Cheryl Moseley Jaksha, Martha Ann Moseley, James Edward Moseley, John Earl Moseley. With Standard Oil Co. of Tex., Houston, 1947-70; with Chevron Geophys. Co., Houston, 1970—, supr. secretarial services, 1974—; cons., lectr. in field. Mem. Spring Valley City Council, 1957-58. Mem. Internat. Word Processing Assn., (internat. dir. 1976-79, pres. Houston chpt. 1974-76, pres. emeritus 1979—, Honor Soc. Achievement award 1979), Adminstrv. Mgmt. Soc. (functional dir. word processing div. 1976-77). Republican. Baptist. Home: 1202 Antoine St Houston TX 77055 Office: 8435 Westglen St PO Box 36487 Houston TX 77036

MOSELEY, VINCE, physician; b. Orangeburg, S.C., Oct. 29, 1912; s. William Lawrence and Jessie George (Vince) M.; student Clemson Coll., 1930-31; A.B., Duke U., 1933, M.D., 1936, L.H.D., 1977; m. Matilda Holleman, Oct. 11, 1938; children—Robert Dwight, Julia Moseley Brandon, Kelsey Moseley Cattles, William Vince, Matilda Moseley Height, Lawrence Holleman, Esther Jane, Selma Jessica. Intern, N.C. State Tb Sanitarium, Sydenham Hosp., Balt., Duke U. Hosp., Durham, N.C., 1937; resident Duke U. Hosp., 1938-40, U. Pa. Hosp., Phila., 1940-41; practice medicine specializing in internal medicine, Charleston, S.C., 1947-48; asso. in medicine, asst. prof. of medicine, asso. prof., prof. medicine Med. Coll. of S.C., Charleston, 1947-49, co-chmn. dept. of medicine, 1949-61, dean of clin. medicine, 1961-66; prof. medicine Med. U. of S.C., Charleston, 1939-79, dir. div. continuing edn., 1969—, asst. academic v.p. for extramural affairs, 1975-79, prof. emeritus, 1979—; chief of med. service Charleston VA Hosp., 1966-68; mem. cons. staff Charleston County Hosp., Roper Hosp. Chmn. Goodwill Industries of Lower S.C., Inc., 1977—; mem. S.C. State Commn. for Mental Retardation, 1968—; mem. Gov.'s Advisory Com., Vocat. Rehab., State of S.C., 1965-67; chmn. Trident Forum for the Handicapped, S.C., 1957-66; trustee Presbyn. Coll., Clinton, S.C., Palmer Coll., Charleston, 1970-75. Served to col. M.C., U.S. Army, 1941-47. Recipient Humanitarian award Lake City, S.C., 1963, Durkee award for Outstanding Contbns. to Care of the Retarded, 1974, Distinguished Faculty award Med. U. of S.C., 1973; diplomate Am. Bd. Internal Medicine. Fellow A.C.P., Royal Soc. Health; mem. S.C., Charleston (pres. 1953-54) med. socs., Soc. for Exptl. Biology and Medicine, Am. Fedn. for Clin. Research, N.Y., S.C. acads. sci., AMA, AAAS, So., S.C. med. assns., Am. Clin. and Climatological Assn., Am. Geriatrics Soc., Am. Rheumatism Assn., Am. Therapeutic Soc., So. Soc. for Clin. Research. Episcopalian. Club: Kiwanis. Contbr. articles on internal medicine and health programs to profl. jours. Home: 51 E Bay St Charleston SC 29401 Office: 51 E Bay Charleston SC 29401

MOSER, HAROLD DEAN, historian; b. Kannapolis, N.C., Oct. 31, 1938; s. Walter Glenn and Angie Elizabeth (Allen) M.; A.A., Wingate Coll., 1959; B.A. cum laude, Wake Forest U., 1961, M.A. (Univ. fellow), 1963; Ph.D. (Ford fellow), U. Wis., 1977; m. Carolyn Irene French, Mar. 28, 1964; children—Andrew Paul, Anna Elizabeth. Tchr., Robert B. Glenn High Sch., Winston-Salem, N.C., 1961-62; instr. history Coll., Murfreesboro, N.C., 1963-65; teaching asst. dept. history U. Wis., Madison, 1967-69; research asso., history of Wis. project State Hist. Soc. Wis., Madison, 1968-71; Nat. Hist. Publ. Commn. fellow The Papers of Daniel Webster, Dartmouth Coll., Hanover, N.H., 1971-72, asst. editor, 1972-73, asso. editor, 1973-76, co-editor, 1976-77, editor corr. series, 1978-79; editor, dir. The Papers of Andrew Jackson, 1979—. Mem. Am., So. hist. assns., Orgn. Am. Historians, Phi Alpha Theta, Eta Sigma Phi, Phi Theta Kappa. Democrat. Contbr. articles to profl. jours. Home: 2547 Lakeland Dr Nashville TN 37214 Office: Box D The Hermitage Hermitage TN 37076

MOSER, PAUL HOMER, geologist; b. Burity, Brazil, July 23, 1931 (parents Am. citizens); s. Homer Oliver and Edith (Lahr) M.; B.A., Berea Coll., 1954; M.S., U. Ky., 1961; m. I. Delphine Cody, June 7, 1954; 1 son, Cody. Cons. geologist, co-owner Carser Cons.'s, Lexington, Ky., 1959-60; engring. geologist Stokley & Assos., Lexington, 1960-64; petroleum geologist Texaco Inc., Midland, Tex., 1964-66; environ. geologist, geohydrologist Geol. Survey Ala., University, 1966—. Served with C.E., AUS, 1954-56. Registered profl. engr., Ala. Mem. Ky., Ala. socs. profl. engrs., Am. Assn. Profl. Geologists (v.p. Ala. chpt.), Geol. Soc. Am., Ala. Geol. Soc. (v.p.), Sigma Xi, Sigma Gamma Epsilon. Presbyterian. Home: 10-T Northwood Lake Northport AL 35476 Office: Geological Survey Ala PO Box O University AL 35486

MOSER, ROYCE, JR., physician; b. Versailles, Mo., Aug. 21, 1935; s. Royce and Russie Frances (Stringer) M.; B.A. summa cum laude, Harvard U., 1957, M.D., 1961, M.P.H., 1965; m. Lois Anne Hunter, June 14, 1958; children—Beth Anne, Donald Royce. Commd. capt. U.S. Air Force, 1962, advanced through grades to col., 1974—; dir. aerospace medicine, Schilling AFB, Kans., 1962-64, resident aerospace medicine, 1964-67; chief aerospace medicine Aerospace Def. Command, Ent AFB, Colo., 1967-70; dir. base med. services Phan Rang AB, Republic Vietnam, 1970-71; supr. aerospace medicine primary course U.S. Air Force Sch. Aerospace Medicine, Brooks AFB, Tex., 1971-74, supr. aerospace medicine residency program and chief aerospace medicine br., 1974-77; comdr. USAF Hosp., Tyndall AFB, Fla., 1977-79; dep. dir. clin. scis. div. USAF Sch. Aerospace Medicine, Brooks AFB, Tex., 1979—; sr. cons. aerospace medicine Surgeon Gen., U.S. Air Force, 1974. Decorated Bronze Star, Legion of Merit, Air medal with 2 oak leaf clusters, Air Force Commendation medal. Diplomate Am. Bd. Preventive Medicine, Am. Bd. Family Practice. Named Mil. Scientist of Year, Air Force Assn., 1973; Instr. of Year, U.S. Air Force Sch. Aerospace Medicine, 1974. Fellow Am. Coll. Preventive Medicine, Aerospace Med. Assn.; mem. Soc. U.S. Air Force Flight Surgeons (pres. 1978-79), Am. Acad. Family Physicians, Air Force Assn., SAR, Phi Beta Kappa, Delta Omega. Republican. Baptist. Contbr. articles to profl. jours. Home: 8803 Cattail Creek San Antonio TX 78239 Office: USAF Sch Aerospace Medicine/NG Brooks AFB TX 78235

MOSES, JOHN HERRICK, JR., state ofcl.; b. N.Y.C., Mar. 15, 1939; s. John Herrick and Katharine Dieterich M.; B.A., Bowdoin Coll., 1960; M.Ed., Va. Commonwealth U., 1976; m. Sara Ann Woolford, Oct. 12, 1978. With Dept. State, Washington, 1961-62; tchr. Waldorf Schs., Germany, N.Y. and Washington, 1962-69, trustee Waldorf Schs. Fund Inc., 1965-69; tchr. St. Christopher's Sch., Richmond, Va., 1971-72; purchase officer Commonwealth of Va., Richmond, 1973—. Bd. dirs. Richmond Community Action Program, 1976—, treas., 1979-80. Mem. Va. Assn. Govtl. Purchasing, Alpha Delta Phi. Episcopalian. Club: Richmond First. Home: 17 N Nansemond St Richmond VA 23221

MOSIER, BENJAMIN, chemist; b. Corsicana, Tex., July 15, 1926; s. Philip and Fannie (Zulauf) M.; B.S., Tex. A. and M. U., 1949, M.S., 1951; Ph.D. (NSF fellow), U. Ill., 1957; m. Doreen Zidel, Aug. 22, 1954; children—Marc, David, Linda, Adam. Instr. chemistry Kilgore (Tex.) Coll., 1949-50; research scientist Gen. Dynamics Corp., Ft. Worth, 1951-52; research scientist Humble Oil & Refining Co., Houston, 1957-60; pres. Inst. for Research, Inc., Houston, 1960—, also dir.; guest lectr. Rice U., 1961-68, 72—, Signal Oil Co., Houston, 1964—; cons. M.D. Anderson Hosp. and Tumor Inst., 1966-68, 73—; pres. Encap, Inc., 1968—; v.p. and dir. Tech. Research, Inc., 1968—; adj. research asst. prof. dept. pathology Baylor Coll. Medicine, Houston, 1974—, research asst. prof., 1975—; sr. research asso. Rice U., Houston, 1975—; adj. prof. dept. chemistry Kans. State U., Manhattan, Kans., 1977. Served to 1st lt. USAF, 1944-46, 52-54. Registered profl. engr., Calif.; recipient numerous NASA awards. Fellow Am. Inst. Chemists; mem. AAAS, Am. Council Ind. Labs., Am. Chem. Soc., Electrochem. Soc., Ill. State Acad. Sci., Nat. Assn. Corrosion Engrs., N.Y. Acad. Scis., Research Sci. Assn., Tex. Acad. Sci., Sigma Xi. Contbr. articles to profl. jours.; holder many patents in field. Home: 5139 S Braeswood St Houston TX 77063 Office: 8330 Westglen Dr Houston TX 77096

MOSKOWITZ, RITA JOYCE, Realtor; b. Little Rock, Aug. 31, 1928; d. Sam and Celia (Granoff) Schlesinger; X-ray technician, radiation therapist, U. Ark., 1947; m. Frank David Moskowitz, Oct. 28, 1951; children—Marcy Ann, Mitchell Ben, Shelley Rae. X-ray technician, radiation therapist Mo. Pacific Hosp., St. Louis, 1947-48; radiation therapist Jewish Hosp., St. Louis, 1948-49; X-ray technician for pvt. physician, Kansas City, Mo., 1949-50, Mt. Sinai Hosp., Miami Beach, Fla., 1950-51; sec.-treas. Moskowitz Realty Co., Tulsa, 1963—; also free lance writer. Chairperson Okla. Real Estate Commn. 1973-76; mem. Okla. Personnel Bd., 1976-83. Mem. NCCJ, Nat. Council Jewish Women (life), NOW, Met. Tulsa Bd. Realtors, Nat., Okla. assns. Realtors, Real Estate Securities and Syndication Inst., Internat. Real Estate Fedn., Realtors Nat. Mktg. Inst., Nat. Assn. Real Estate License Law Ofcls., Okla. Writers Fedn., Tulsa Night Writers. Jewish. Home: PO Box 2875 Tulsa OK 74101 Office: 3530 E 31 St Suite 100 Tulsa OK 74135

MOSLEY, BILLY RAY, urologist; b. Gilbertown, Ala., Apr. 25, 1937; s. Hubert Marvin and Clara Ann (Lewis) M.; M.D., U. Ala., 1962; m. Virginia Amacker, Apr. 4, 1958; children—Emily Claire, George Lyles. Intern U. Fla., 1962-64; resident U. Ala., 1964-67;

faculty urologic surgery U. Ala., 1967; practice medicine specializing in urology, Mobile, Ala., 1969—. Asst. prof. U. S. Ala. Served to maj. AUS, 1967-69. Mem. Alpha Omega Alpha. Baptist. Clubs: Country, Bienville (Mobile). Home: 71 Byrnes Blvd Mobile AL 36608 Office: 1720 Center St Mobile AL 36604

MOSLEY, IVAN SIGMUND, JR., financial exec.; b. Jasper, Ga., Sept. 15, 1946; s. Ivan Sigmund and Estelle (Kelly) M.; A.A., Emory U., 1966, B.B.A., 1968; m. Dianna Griffin, June 26, 1969; children—Anna Louise, Karen Elizabeth. Staff accountant Peat, Marwick, Mitchell & Co., Atlanta, 1968-69, Mgmt. Sci. Am., Inc., Atlanta, 1969-72, controller, 1972-78, sec.-treas., 1972—; dir. LAS Assos., Inc., Atlanta, 1975—, sec.-treas., 1974—. Recipient Campbell Accounting medal, 1968. Mem. Am. Accounting Assn., Nat. Assn. Accountants, Nat. Assn. Credit Mgrs., Fin. Execs. Inst. Democrat. Baptist. Home: 315 Saddle Horn Circle Roswell GA 30076 Office: 3445 Peachtree Rd Atlanta GA 30326

MOSLEY, JAMES P., electronics engring. technician; b. Van Dyke, Va., July 15, 1922; s. Franklin M. and Louise (Bucklen) M.; B.E.E., U. Ala., 1949, M.E.E., 1959; D.D.S., St. John's Acad., 1971; m. Theresa Firetti, June 30, 1945; children—Franklin, Theresa, Josephine, James; m. 2d, Pansy Ornbaum, Sept. 19, 1970. Engr. div. nuclear electronics RCA, Cape Kennedy, 1961-66; field supr. compliance div. Fed. Security Agy., Washington and Charleston, W.Va., 1952-59; adv., cons., tech. project engr., 1972, 73-79; design engr. bank security systems, 1979—. Served with USNR, 1940-46. Mem. Profl. Engrs. Soc., Nat. Pilots Assn., VFW, DAV, Nat. Bus. Assn., Nat. Assn. Electronic Engrs., Sons of Italy. Episcopalian. Clubs: Moose, Elks.

MOSLEY, WILLIAM FIELDING, III, accountant; b. Munich, Germany, Mar. 2, 1948; s. William Fielding, Jr., and Martha Frank (Bufkin) M. (parents Am. citizens); student U.S. Air Force Acad., 1966-67; B.A., N. Tex. State U., 1970; m. Pamela Jane Fox, Aug. 1, 1970; 1 son, Ryan Scott. C.P.A., Coopers & Lybrand, 1970-73, A.H. Gardes & Co., C.P.A.'s, Houston, 1973-76, Ernest E. Leavitt C.P.A.'s, 1976-77; v.p., sec. Leavitt, Mosley & Co., C.P.A.'s, Houston, 1977—; pres., dir. Scottson, Inc.; v.p., sec., dir. Hilmar's Hot House Farms, Inc.; dir. Inter Continental Personnel Consultants, Inc.; instr. acctg. N. Tex. State U., 1971. Served with USAFR, 1967-73. Recipient 2d place award for paper Inst. Internal Auditors, 1970; C.P.A., Tex. Mem. Am. Inst. C.P.A.'s, Tex. Soc. C.P.A.'s, Houston Soc. C.P.A.'s, Pi Kappa Phi. Episcopalian. Clubs: Houston Indoor Tennis, Kiwanis. Home: 11323 Chevy Chase St Houston TX 77077 Office: 2000 S Post Oak St Suite 1625 Houston TX 77056

MOSS, BARBARA ANN, human services adminstr.; b. Midway, Pa., Sept. 23, 1939; d. Edgar Wilson and Isobel Ann (Massey) Dowler; B.S., N. Tex. State U., 1965, M.S., 1967; postgrad. Internat. U. Switzerland, 1974, U. Tex., Arlington, 1979; m. James Donald Moss, Aug. 23, 1958; children—James Richard, Scott David. Group worker Dallas County Juveniles, 1959-65; speech pathologist Irving (Tex.) Ind. Schs., 1966-68; Title specialist Dallas County Children's Emergency Shelter, Dallas, 1968-69; dir. speech and hearing Denton (Tex.) State Sch., 1969-71; adminstr. tech. programs Dallas County Mental Health-Mental Retardation Center, Dallas, 1971-77, dir. central adminstrn. planning and evaluation div., 1977—; instr. Dallas County Community Coll., 1978; mem. planning com. Tex. Evaluation Network, 1979. Gen. bd. dirs. First Christian Ch., 1976-79. Mem. Am. Speech and Hearing Assn., Am. Assn. Mental Deficiency, Family Therapy Assn. Tex., Tex. Evaluation Network. Co-author: Radea, 1974; editor: Sail, 1979. Office: 2710 Stemmons Freeway 1100 Tower St N Dallas TX 75207

MOSS, DAVID ARNOLD, state ofcl.; b. S. Charleston, W. Va., Sept. 3, 1950; s. Robert Hugh and Norma Jean (Williams) M.; B.A. in Pol. Sci., Morris Harvey Coll., 1973; m. Margaret Ann Mills, May 19, 1973. Field rep. W. Va. Human Rights Commn., Charleston, 1974-75, conciliator, 1975-76, chief of conciliations, 1976-77, asst. compliance dir., 1977—, also agency records officer and compliance officer; chmn. S. Charleston Human Rights Commn., 1975-76, spl. adviser, 1976—. Mem. Pocatalico-Sissonville Jaycees (external activities dir. 1977-78), NAACP, Nat. Assn. Human Rights Workers. Democrat. Roman Catholic. Home: PO Box 25B Allens Route Sissonville WV 25320 Office: 215 Profl Bldg 1036 Quarrier St Charleston WV 25301

MOSS, ELIZA WALLER EASLEY, former educator, physiologist; b. Martinsville, Va., Mar. 26, 1928; d. Owen Randolph and Cassie Louise (DuVal) Easley; B.S., Longwood Coll., Farmville, Va., 1950; M.S., U. Fla., 1957; Ph.D., N.Y. U., 1967; m. Charles George Gordon Moss, July 22, 1972. Tchr. biochemistry Va. Poly. Inst., 1953-55, 58-59; tchr., research physiology Boyce-Thompson Inst., 1960-62; tchr., researcher cytology Harvard, 1962-63; jr. adminstrv. asst. phys. chemistry Rockland State Hosp. Research Facility, Orangeburg, N.Y., 1963-64; tchr., researcher cell physiology Rockefeller U., 1967-69; asst. prof. biology St. Paul's Coll., Lawrenceville, Va., 1970-72, coordinator natural sci., 1971-72. Mem. Farmville Council Human Relations; bd. dirs. Prince Edward County Central Piedmont Community Action Com., 1973—. Mem. Am. Chem. Soc., Harvey Soc., Am. Inst. Chemists, ACLU, NAACP. Home: 507 Buffalo St Farmville VA 23901

MOSS, JAMES BURKE, ins. co. exec.; b. Clarksburg, W.Va., Apr. 29, 1933; s. Hayward B. and Edith E. (Reeder) M.; student Defience Coll., 1951-52, Ohio State U., 1953; m. Carol M. Kuck, July 26, 1952; children—Robert, Steven, Rebecca, Kathy, Donald, Mark. Agt., Nat. Life and Accident Ins. Co., Lima, Ohio, 1953-54, staff mgr., Springfield, Ohio, 1954-57; prin. James B. Moss Ins. Agy., Lima, Springfield, Ohio, South Bend, Ind., Huntington, Ind., 1957-76; v.p. mortgage banking/savs. and loan bus. Am. Bankers Life Assurance Co., Miami, Fla., 1976-78, v.p. fin. manpower devel., 1978—. Dist. chmn., bd. dirs. council Anthony Wayne Area council Boy Scouts Am., 1973-74, dist. fin. chmn. South Fla. council, 1976, dist. chmn., 1978, council tng. dir., exec. bd., 1979. Recipient numerous sales awards. Office: 600 Brickell Ave Miami FL 33131

MOSS, JAMES MERCER, physician; b. Bradley, Ga., Dec. 15, 1917; s. Fred August and Rosa (Mercer) M.; M.D., U. Va., 1941; m. Rachel Scott Bybee, Sept. 6, 1941; children—James Marion, Fred Aubrey (dec.), William Wallace, Robert Edward. Intern, U. Va. Hosp., 1941-42, resident medicine, 1947-49; fellow, instr. endocrinology Duke U., 1946-47; pvt. practice internal medicine, Alexandria, Va., 1949—; instr. clin. medicine Georgetown U., 1949-51, clin. asst. prof., 1952-56, clin. asso. prof., 1956-62, clin. prof., 1962—; dir. diabetic clinic Georgetown U. Hosp., 1949-75, D.C. Gen. Hosp., 1950-55; active staff Circle Terrace Hosp., pres., 1965-68; dir. City Bank & Trust, 1963-71, Circle Terrace, Inc., 1965-75 (all Alexandria); mem. pub. adv. com. on endocrine drugs FDA, 1974-78; mem. Health Manpower Commn. Va., 1973-77. Treas. No. Va. Med. Com. Good Govt., 1960, 62; chmn. Va.-Med. Polit. Action Com., 1966-67; chmn. Va. Physicians for Reelection of Pres., 1972; mem. Alexandria Republican Com., 1972-75. Served from lt. to maj., M.C., AUS, 1942-46. Recipient awards for sci. exhibits. Diplomate Am. Bd. Internal Medicine. Fellow A.C.P. (gov. Va. 1979—), Am. Coll. Cardiology; mem. Am. (chmn. pharms. com. 1974-78), Va. (pres. 1962-63) socs. internal medicine, Am. Heart Assn., Am., Va. (pres. 1971-72) diabetes assns., Endocrine Soc., So. Med. Assn. (asso. counselor 1975, chmn. sect. on medicine 1979-80, mem. com. sci. work 1976—), Med. Soc. Va. (pres. 1970-71), AMA (council on continuing edn. 1971-77, chmn. exhibit com. 1975-76, chmn. audiovisual com. 1976-77), Diabetes Assn. D.C. (pres. 1956-57), Med. Council Washington Met. Area (pres. 1958-59), Heart Assn. No. Va. (pres. 1964-65), Am. Assn. Physicians and Surgeons (del. from Va. 1974-76), Am. Podiatry Assn. (hon.), Am. Med. Writers Assn., Alexandria Med. Soc. (pres. 1958-59), Med. Alumni Assn. U. Va. (pres. 1965-66), Phi Chi, Alpha Omega Alpha. Editorial bd. Va. Med. Monthly, 1961-70; editorial cons. Am. Acad. Family Practice, 1969—; author: Fundamentals of Diabetic Management, 1962; Monograph on Diabetes, 1974; contbr. articles to profl. jours. Home: 319 Mansion Dr Alexandria VA 22302 Office: 1707 Osage St Alexandria VA 22302

MOSS, MIKE, ins. co. exec.; b. N.Y.C., Feb. 6, 1943; s. Edward and Rose M.; student Miami Dade Coll., 1961-63, U. Miami, 1963-65; m. Laurie Judd, May 4, 1969. Div. Mgr. Nat. Cash Register Co., Miami, Fla., 1964-69; asst. gen. agt. Mass. Mut. Ins. Co., Miami, 1969-74; mgr. Home Life Ins. Co. of N.Y., Coral Gables, Fla., 1974—. Recipient Nat. Mgmt. award Gen. Agts. and Mgrs. Assn., 1976, 77, 78; RAM award Fla. State Gen. Agts. and Mgrs. Assn., 1979; C.L.U. Mem. Gen. Agts. and Mgrs. Assn. Miami (pres.), Greater Miami Estate Planning Council, Miami Assn. Life Underwriters, Life Underwriters Polit. Action Com. Club: Standard (Miami). Home: 212 W DiLido Dr Miami Beach FL 33139 Office: Home Life Ins Co of NY 2600 Douglas Rd Coral Gables FL 33134

MOSS, RACHEL SCOTT BYBEE, civic worker; b. Charlottesville, Va., Feb. 2, 1920; d. Aubrey Walker and Wirtle (Williams) Bybee; R.N., U. Va. 1941; m. James Mercer Moss, Sept. 6, 1941; children—James Marion, Fred Aubrey (dec.), William Wallace, Robert Edward. Head nurse on medicine U. Va. Hosp., 1941-42. Dir. Security Savs. and Loan Assn., Alexandria. Mem. ladies bd. Georgetown U. Hosp., 1954—, Heart Assn. No. Va., 1963—; treas. Alexandria Crew Booster's Club, 1965-67; sec. Va. Med. Polit. Action Com., 1967-68; pres. Mansion Drive Club, 1968-69, treas., 1977-78; chmn. Alexandria Tiny Tots Concert, 1965; mem. nurses com. on continuing edn. Va. Heart Assn., 1969—; mem. ARCS Found., Inc., 1969—; mem. Va. Med. Polit. Action Com. Mem. Alexandria (Va.) Democratic com., 1954-55; mem. Fin. Com. to Re-elect Pres. Nixon, 1972; mem. Pres. Ford Com., 1976. Mem. Woman's Aux. Med. Soc. Va. (pres. 1963-64, dir. 1964-67, fin. chmn. 1972-73), Am. Med. Edn. Found., Woman's Aux. So. Med. Assn. (v.p. 1965-66), Woman's Aux. AMA (del. from Va. 1954-64), Woman's Aux. Alexandria Med. Soc. (pres. 1961-62), Alumni Assn. U. Va. Hosp. Sch. Nursing. Presbyterian. Clubs: Mansion Drive Garden, Beverly Hills Woman's (pres. 1973-74). Home: 319 Mansion Dr Alexandria VA 22302

MOSS, STEPHEN CRAIG, banker; b. Milledgeville, Ga., Mar. 27, 1950; s. William Hugh and Rosalyn Elizabeth (Shouse) M.; B.S. in Mgmt. Sci., Ga. Inst. Tech., 1972. Indsl. engr. Collins & Aikman Corp., Charlotte, N.C., 1972-73; cost analyst First Union Nat. Bank, Charlotte, 1973-76, cost analysis mgr., 1976-77, direct compensation mgr., 1977—. Mem. Am. Compensation Assn. Republican. Presbyterian. Home: 1200 Meadowood Ln Charlotte NC 28211 Office: First Union Nat Bank 301 S Tryon St Charlotte NC 28288

MOSTELLER, BETTE VAUGHAN, librarian; b. Amelia County, Va., Feb. 1, 1937; d. Lawson Paul and Rosa Vaughan (Mottley) M.; B.A., Longwood Coll., 1958; M.L.S. (Va. State Library fellow), George Peabody Coll., 1959; now postgrad. Coll. William and Mary. Cataloger, Va. State Library, Richmond, 1959-62; readers adviser Richmond Pub. Library, summer 1962; dir. library Christopher Newport Coll., Newport News, Va., 1962—; library adv. com. State Council Higher Edn., 1971—; library dir.'s com. Tidewater Consortium for Continuing Edn., 1976—, vice-chmn. com., 1978—, mem. steering com. for Tidewater network, 1979—. Mem. Eastern Va. Hist. Orgn. for Bi-Centennial Celebration, 1970—; mem. Task Force for State Library Plan, 1975-76, Task Force to Plan State Library Storage Facility, 1977. Mem. ALA, Va. (exec. asst. nat. library week com. 1969-71), Southeastern library assns. Home: 163 Yeardley Dr Newport News VA 23601 Office: PO Box 6070 Newport News VA 23606

MOTHERSHED, GEORGE LLOYD, oil co. exec., lawyer; b. Phoenix, June 12, 1943; s. Caldwell C. and Elizabeth Louise (Jagow) M.; B.S., No. Ariz. U., 1965; J.D., U. Okla., 1968; m. Carri Abernathy, Apr. 11, 1963; children—Robert Stuart, Kelsey Ann. Admitted to Okla. bar, 1968, U.S. Supreme Ct. bar, 1973; atty. Big Chief Drilling Co., Oklahoma City, 1968-72; pres., dir. Post Oak Oil Co., Oklahoma City, 1972—; dir. Southwestern Bank & Trust Co. Mem. Gov.'s. Energy Adv. Com., 1975—; vice-chmn., gov.'s rep. Interstate Oil Compact Commn., 1975—; mem. Okla. Housing Authority, 1977—, Okla. Personnel Bd., 1977—. Mem. Am. Bar Assn., Okla. Bar Assn., Oklahoma County Bar Assn., Nat. Assn. Mfrs., Am. Petroleum Inst., Oklahoma City All-Sports Assn., Ind. Petroleum Assn. Am. (dir. 1978—), Okla. Ind. Petroleum Assn., Southwestern Legal Found., Oklahoma City C. of C. Presbyterian. Office: Post Oak Oil Co 800 City Center Bldg Oklahoma City OK 73102

MOTOS, RAMON AVIS, physician; b. Naga City, Philippines, Oct. 26, 1941; came to U.S., 1967; s. Cipriano Balid and Asuncion Tena (Avis) M.; M.D., Far Eastern U., 1966; m. Louella F. Lasala, May 16, 1970; children—Rosel, Ramon, Renelle. Intern, E. Deaconess Hosp., Milw., 1967-68; resident in gen. surgery Huron Rd Hosp., Cleve., 1968-69, Elyria (Ohio) Meml. Hosp., 1969-70, Hamot Med. Center, Erie, Pa., 1970-71; attending physician Clinch Valley Community Hosp., Richlands, Va., 1971—, also attending staff. Diplomate Am. Bd. Family Practice. Fellow Am. Acad. Family Physicians; mem. Va. Med. Soc., Tazewell County Med. Soc., S.W. Va. Filipino Practicing Physicians, C. of C. Roman Catholic. Home: Route 1 Box 410 Pounding Mill VA 24637 Office: 2949 W Front Richlands VA 24641

MOTT, BOBBY RICSHAN, home improvement co. exec.; b. Church Point, La., July 4, 1941; s. Lester and Eulia (Collins) M.; student public schs., Crowley, La.; m. Mary Kelly, Oct. 26, 1964; children—Bobbie Rayshea, Ricshan Kelly. Owner, pres. Bob Mott Inc., Columbia, S.C., 1976—. Served with U.S. Army, 1962-64. Mem. Painting and Decorating Contractors of Am. Baptist. Home: 3927 Webb Ct Columbia SC 29204 Office: Bob Mott Inc 2531 Main St Columbia SC 29201

MOTT, CHARLES DAVIS, civil engr.; b. Phila., Aug. 30, 1914; s. Charles Hilliard and Emma (Davis) M.; B.S. in Civil Engring., U. Pa., 1936; M. Engring. Adminstrn., George Washington U., 1967; m. Ellen Mary Hooge, July 15, 1938; children—Ellen H., Charles H., Joseph W. H. With Cruse Kemper Co., Ambler, Pa., 1936-37, Central Aircraft Mfg. Co., 1941-45; commd. ensign USN, 1937, advanced through grades to capt., 1959; dir. missile, ammunition, astronautics prodn. Navy Dept., Washington, 1960-63; ret., 1963; dep. mgr. Analytic Services, Inc., Arlington, Va., 1963—. Decorated Purple Heart, Navy Commendation medal, Cloud and Banner (China). Mem. AIAA, Am. Def. Preparedness Assn., Mil. Ops. Research Soc., Naval Inst., Flying Tiger Assn., U.S. Chess Fedn. Home: 2522 Rocky Branch Rd Vienna VA 22180 Office: 400 Army Navy Dr Arlington VA 22202

MOTT, CHARLES JAMES, geologist; b. Dansville, N.Y., Oct. 9, 1941; s. Charles E. and Cornie (Burgio) M.; B.S., SUNY, Geneseo, 1963; M.S., U. Fla., Gainesville, 1967; Ed.D., Nova U., 1975; m. Donna Jeanne Warren, Sept. 19, 1969; children—Thomas, Maryellen. Tchr., Central Sch. Dist., Dansville, 1963-65; mem. faculty St. Petersburg Jr. Coll., Clearwater, Fla., 1968—, prof. natural sci., 1979—; geol. cons., 1970—. Mem. Citizens Coastal Environ. Adv. Com., 1976. Mem. Nat. Assn. Geology Tchrs., S.E. Geol. Soc., Ga. Geol. Soc., Fla. Paleontol. Soc., Fla. Acad. Scis., Phi Delta Kappa. Author: Earth Science 1975, 2d edit., 1980; Audio-Tutorial Earth Science, 1972; contbr. articles to profl. jours. and popular mags. Home: 1856 Belmont Dr E Clearwater FL 33515 Office: 2465 Drew St Clearwater FL 33515

MOTT, DENNIS LEE, educator; b. O'Neill, Nebr., Feb. 21, 1944; s. George Joe and Laura (Hulda) M.; B.A. in Bus. Edn., Wayne (Nebr.) State Coll., 1965; M.S. in Ednl. Adminstrn., U. Nebr., Omaha, 1969, Ed.D., Lincoln, 1972; m. Karen Rae Wehenkel, May 15, 1965; children—Nicole, Bryan. Instr. bus. edn. Missouri Valley (Iowa) High Sch., 1965-68, Omaha Central High Sch., 1968-70; prof. bus. U. Wis., 1971-74; prof. Okla. State U., 1974—, head dept. adminstrv. services and bus. edn., 1979—; pres. Innovative Mgmt. Systems, Inc., Stillwater, Okla., 1979. Chmn. budget com. United Way, Stillwater. Recipient Outstanding Teaching award Okla. State U. Mem. Am. Vocat. Assn., Nat. Bus. Edn. Assn., Am. Bus. Communication Assn., Adminstrv. Mgmt. Soc., Okla. Bus. Edn. Assn. (pres. 1979; Outstanding Tchr. award 1978), Mountain Plains Bus. Edn. Assn. (pres. 1980), Okla. Edn. Assn. (Outstanding Tchr. award 1976, 79). Republican. Lutheran. Editor: National Business Education Forum, 1976-77. Home: 1824 W Liberty Ave Stillwater OK 74074 Office: 332 Coll Bus Okla State U Stillwater OK 74074

MOTT, JAMES RANDOLPH, counselor; b. Norman, Okla., Sept. 26, 1944; s. James Joshua and Anita Reppeard (Motsenbocker) M.; B.A., U. Okla., 1967, M.A. P.A., 1973; postgrad. Chapman Coll., 1973-74; M.A. (Research grantee 1977), U. Tex., 1976, postgrad., 1976—; m. Susan Rice, Aug. 27, 1965 (div. 1975); children—Paul Christopher, Samantha Beth; m. 2nd, Janet Marie Luther Green, May 15, 1979. Psychometrist, Counseling-Psychol. Services Center, U. Tex., Austin, 1974-76, psychology intern/counselor, 1976-78, telephone counselor Telephone Counseling and Referral Service, 1976-78; psychology trainee VA Hosp., Temple, Tex., 1976; counselor Career Choice Info. Center, U. Tex., Austin, 1978; counselor Student Services Office, Austin Community Coll., 1978—, instr., 1979—. Served with USAF, 1967-74. Mem. Am. Psychol. Assn. (student), Am. Personnel and Guidance Assn. (student), Am. Coll. Personnel Assn. (student), Nat. Vocat. Guidance Assn. (student), Phi Kappa Phi. Home: 5818-B Highland Pass Austin TX 78731 Office: Austin TX 78767

MOTTNER, MICHAEL ERIC, writer; b. Seattle, June 8, 1945; s. Robert Louis and Patricia Jane (Dudley) M.; B.A. in Communications, Wash. State U., 1969; m. Sandra Ann Slover, Sept. 7, 1968. Copywriter Nordstroms Inc., Seattle, 1969, Lamonts, Seattle, 1970, Sears, Roebuck & Co., Chgo., 1970-76; direct mail copywriter Brand Edmonds Advt. Agy., Salem, Va., 1976-78; copy dir. Associated Advt., Roanoke, 1978-79; author: Death Winds, 1978; Someday, 1979; The Prez, 1979; Welcome to Fear, 1979; The Marmotville Incident, 1979; The Missing Part, 1979; Choices, 1979; Therapy, 1979; Only One Way To Deal with a Bike Thief, 1979; Murder on the Mereer Street Off-Ramp, 1979; The Borrowed Motorcycle, 1979; Swedish Secrets and Black Leather, 1980; Tiny's Tap, 1980; The Tired Freedom Fighter, 1980; Impressions of the Factory, 1980; Instincts, 1980; The Man Who Ran over the Biker, 1980; Mindreach, 1980; I Just Don't Love You No More, Harley, 1980; Pleasures of the Highway, 1980; The Bad Joke, 1980; A Nice, Quiet Neighborhood, 1980; A Second Chance, 1980; Now an Outlaw, 1980; Lips That Touch Liquor, 1980; The July 4th Confrontation, 1980; Biker's Image, 1980; The Collector's Dream, 1980; The Late Movie, 1980; The Rescue, 1980. Mem. Am. Motorcylist Assn. Home: 2912 Guilford Ave SW Roanoke VA 24015

MOULDEN, TREVOR HOLMES, educator; b. Leicester, Eng., Oct. 13, 1939; came to U.S., 1966; s. George Harry and Olive May (Holmes) M.; B.S. with honors in Engring., Imperial Coll., London, 1961; M.Phil., London U., 1968; Ph.D., U. Tenn., 1973. Scientist, Nat. Phys. Lab., Teddington, Eng., 1961-66; research engr. Lockheed Ga. Co., Marietta, 1966-69; research fellow U. Tenn. Space Inst., Tullahoma, 1970-73, asst. prof., 1973-78, asso. prof., 1978—. Mem. Am. Acad. Mechanics, AIAA, Royal Aero. Soc., Calcutta Math. Soc., Sigma Xi. Co-editor: Handbook of Turbulence, vol. I, 1977. Office: U Tenn Space Inst Tullahoma TN 37388

MOULTRIE, VELMA THOMAS, coll. fin. adminstr.; b. Perry, Ga., Dec. 19, 1947; s. Velmon and Jimetta (Oliver) Thomas; B.B.A., Albany State Coll., 1969; M.B.A., Atlanta U., 1974; m. Alton J. Moultrie, Aug. 14, 1970. Adminstrv. asst. to dean/dir. student activities Albany (Ga.) State Coll., 1965-69; asst. coordinator, sec., fellow Atlanta U., 1969-70; auditor Arthur Andersen & Co., C.P.A.'s, Atlanta, 1970; payroll acct., asst. to chief acct. Spelman Coll., Atlanta, 1971; student fin. aid dir., counselor Atlanta U., 1971-78; student affairs and fin. aid officer Sch. Medicine, Morehouse Coll., Atlanta, 1978—. Recipient Past Pres. award Am. Bus. Women, 1975; Center for Manpower Studies fellow, 1969-70. Mem. Nat. Assn. Student Fin. Aid Adminstrn., So. Assn. Student Fin. Aid Adminstrs., Ga. Assn. Student Aid Adminstrs., Mktg. Assn., Soc. for Advancement of Mgmt. and Adminstrn., NAACP, Atlanta Silhouettes (pres. 1978—), Squaws (charter), Nat. Council Black Women, Delta Sigma Theta, Phi Beta Lambda. Baptist. Home: 3415 Ethan Allen Dr College Park GA 30349 Office: Sch Medicine Morehouse Coll PO Box 86 830 Westview Dr SW Atlanta GA 30314

MOUNTAIN, CLIFTON FLETCHER, physician; b. Toledo, Apr. 15, 1924; s. Ira Fletcher and Mary (Stone) M.; A.B., Harvard U., 1947, postgrad., 1946-47; M.D., Boston U., 1954; postgrad. U. Chgo., 1954-59; m. Marilyn Isabelle Tapper, Feb. 28, 1945; children—Karen Lockerby, Clifton Fletcher, Jeffrey Richardson. Dir. dept. statis. research Boston U., 1947-50; cons. research analyst Mass. Dept. Pub. Health, 1951-53; intern U. Chgo. Clinics, 1954, resident, 1955-58, instr. surgery, 1958-59; practice medicine, specializing in thoracic surgery, Houston, 1959—; mem. staff M.D. Anderson Hosp. and Tumor Research Inst.; asst. prof. thoracic surgery U. Tex., 1960-63, chmn. program in biomath. and computer sci., 1962-64, asso. prof. surgery, 1963-76, prof. surgery, 1976—, chief sect. thoracic surgery, 1973—, also chmn. thoracic oncology; Mike Hogg vis. lectr. in S. Am., 1967; mem. sci. mission on cancer USSR and Japan, 1974—; mem. com. health, research and edn. facilities Houston Community Council, 1964—; cons. Am. Joint Com. for Cancer Staging and End Result Reporting, 1966—, chmn. lung task force; mem. NIH Working Party on Lung Cancer, 1971-76 chmn. com. surgery, 1971-76, mem. plans and scope com. cancer therapy Nat. Cancer Inst., 1972-75, mem. lung cancer study group, 1977—, chmn. steering com., 1973-75, mem. bd. sci. counselors, div. cancer treatment, 1972-75. Chmn. profl. adv. com. Harris County Mental Health Assn.; bd. dirs. Harris County chpt. Am. Cancer Soc. Served to lt. (j.g.) USNR, 1942-46. Diplomate Am. Bd. Surgery. Fellow Am. Coll. Chest Physicians (chmn. com. cancer 1967-72), Inst. Environ. Scis., N.Y. Acad. Sci., A.C.S.; mem.

AAAS, Am. Assn. Cancer Research, Am. Assn. for Thoracic Surgery, Am., So. med. assns., Am. Thoracic Soc., Soc. Thoracic Surgeons, Soc. Biomed. Computing, Biomed. Info. Processing Orgn., Am. Fedn. Clin. Research, Internat. Assn. for Study Lung Cancer (pres. 1976-79), Am. Radium Soc., Pan-Am. Med. Assn., Am. Congress Rehab. Medicine, Houston Surg. Soc., Soc. Surg. Oncology, James Ewing Soc., Sigma Xi. Editor: The New Physician, 1955-59; editorial bd. Yearbook of Cancer, 1960—; contbr. articles to profl. jours. Home: 1612 South Blvd Houston TX 77006 Office: 6723 Bertner Ave Houston TX 77025

MOURGLEA, GERALD LEE, acct.; b. Valdese, N.C., Dec. 1, 1946; s. Archllio and Carrie Pauline (Clark) M.; A.A.S. in Acctg., Western Piedmont Community Coll., 1972; m. Aloma Kay McCracken, June 30, 1972; children—Jeremy, Daniel, Amanda. Acct., bookkeeper Brinkley Lumber Co., Valdese, 1971-74; acct. Inform, Inc., Hickory, N.C., 1974-75, comptroller, 1975—. Served with USAF, 1965-69. Mem. Hickory-Catawba Valley Home Builders Assn., Catawba Valley Hosiery Assn., Nat. Rifle Assn. Republican. Baptist. Home: PO Box 98 Rutherford College NC 28671 Office: 415 1st Ave NW Hickory NC 28601

MOURSUND, ALBERT WADEL, III, lawyer; b. Johnson City, Tex., May 23, 1919; s. Albert W. and Mary Frances (Stribling) M.; LL.B., U. Tex., 1941; m. Mary Allen Moore, May 8, 1941; children—Will S., Mary M. Admitted to Tex. bar, 1941; practice in Johnson City, 1946—; mem. firm Moursund & Moursund, 1963—; county judge Blanco County, 1953-59. Pres., dir. Moore State Bank, Llano, Tex., 1963—, also dir.; pres. Arrowhead Co., Lakeland Investment Corp., Ranchlander Corp.; pres., dir. Tex. Am. Moursund Corp., Southwest Moursund Corp.; dir. Scott Corp., Scott Plaza, Inc., Las Vegas. Mem. Tex. Parks and Wildlife Commn., 1963-67. Mem. Tex., Ho. of Reps. 1948-52. Served with USAAF, 1942-46. Mem. Am., Tex., Hill County (past pres.), bar assns., Blanco County Hist. Soc. (charter), Sons of Hermann. Democrat. Clubs: Masons, Woodman of World. Home: Johnson City TX 78636

MOURSUND, KENNETH CARROLL, grocery co. exec.; b. Austin, Tex., Oct. 21, 1937; s. Leif Erickson and Ethel Alberta (Aiken) M.; B.A., U. Tex., Austin, 1963; m. Claudia Frances Reifel, Dec. 21, 1963; 1 son, Kenneth Carroll. Mgmt. trainee Am. Warehouses, Inc., 1963-64; with Kroger Co., Houston, 1964—, transp. supr., 1964, distbn. mgr. charge all warehousing and transp. Houston div., 1969—. Life mem., mem. group ticket com. Houston Livestock and Rodeo Assn. Served with USAR, 1960-66. Mem. Houston C. of C., Houston Symphony Soc., Delta Nu Alpha; life mem. Ex-Student Assn. U. Tex., Nat. Rifle Assn. Episcopalian. Club: Pine Forest Country. Home: 2315 Dryden St Houston TX 77030 Office: PO Box 1309 Houston TX 77001

MOUSOURAKIS, IOANNIS NIKOLAOS, fin. co. exec.; b. Canea-Crete, Greece, Aug. 5, 1944; s. Lambros and Erasmia (Lambrinakis) M.; came to U.S., 1962, naturalized, 1974; B.A., West Liberty State Coll., 1968; M.A., Vanderbilt U., 1970; J.D., Woodrow Wilson Sch. Law, 1980; m. Donna Rose, Aug. 15, 1969; children—John Steven, Mary Ann, Erasmia Elena. Officer, mgr. internat. banking dept. Commerce Union Bank, Nashville, 1969-74; v.p., mgr. internat. banking dept. Hamilton Nat. Bank, Chattanooga, 1974; internat. treas. Tuftco Corp., Chattanooga, 1975—, internat. v.p., 1978—; cons., dir. several comml. or pvt. banking cos. Served with M.C., USNR, 1963-69. Vanderbilt U. grantee, 1968-70. Mem. Internat. Law Assn., Am. Soc. Internat. Law, Middle East Inst., U.S.-Arab, U.S. Brazilian/French chambers commerce, UN Assn., Pan Am. Assn., others. Greek Orthodox. Home: Somerset Estates 9307 Wyndover St Ooltewah TN 37363 Office: 2318 Holtzclaw Ave Chattanooga TN 37404

MOUTON, JANE SRYGLEY, indsl. psychologist; b. Port Arthur, Tex., Apr. 15, 1930; d. Theodore and Grace (Stumpe) Srygley; B.A. in Edn., U. Tex., 1950, Ph.D. in Psychology (Univ. fellow 1954-55), 1957; M.S. (Lewis fellow) U. Fla., 1951; m. Jackson C. Mouton, Jr., Dec. 22, 1953; children—Jane, Jacquelyn. Research asst. U. Tex., Austin, 1953-57, social sci. research asst., 1957-59, instr. in psychology, 1957-59, asst. prof. psychology, 1959-62; v.p. Scientific Methods, Inc., Austin, 1961—. Diplomate Am. Psychol. Assn. Licensed, certified Tex. State Bd. Examiners of Psychologists. Mem. Internat. Assn. Applied Social Scientists, N.Y. Acad. Scis., Southwestern Psychol. Assn., Interam. Soc. Psychology. Author: The Marriage Grid, 1971; The Grid for Sales Excellence, 1970; Corporate Excellence through Grid Organization Development, 1968; How to Assess the Strengths and Weaknesses of a Business Enterprise, 1972; Corporate Darwinism, 1966; Managing Intergroup Conflict, 1964; The Managerial Grid, 1964; Consultation, 1976; Instrumented Team Learning, 1975; The Supervisory Grid, 1975; The New Managerial Grid, 1978; The Social Worker Grid, 1979; The Real Estate Grid, 1980; contbr. articles to profl. jours. Home: 2305 Hartford Rd Austin TX 78703 Office: PO Box 195 Austin TX 78767

MOUTZ, JOSEPH, sales exec.; b. East McKeesport, Pa., Aug. 29, 1929; s. Joseph and Emma (Shaner) M.; diploma Transylvania Coll., Freeport, Pa., 1952; postgrad. U. Okla., 1952; A.B., Asbury Coll., 1965, postgrad., 1966; children—Mary, Joseph. Tchr., Am. Coll., Eritrea, Ethiopia, 1954-59, high sch. prin., sch. dir., 1957-59; tchr. Jessamine County (Ky.) High Sch., 1966-67, Ky. Village Reformatory, Lexington, 1968; salesman Chem. Assos., Wilmore, Ky., 1968—. Supt., Asbury Ministerial Chs., Wilmore, 1963-66; pastor Peoples Ch., Shelbyville, Ky., 1964-65, Trinity Chapel, Ky., 1966-67; mem. Christian and Missionary Alliance Ch.; asst. scoutmaster Boy Scouts Am., 1946-48; bd. dirs. Wildwood Chapel Missions, 1975—. Recipient D.C. Corbitt Social Sci. award, 1962. Mem. Am. Sci. Affiliation, Evang., Wesleyan theol. socs. Home: 104 Asbury Dr Wilmore KY 40390

MOWAT, JOHN JACOB, brokerage co. exec.; b. Dallas, July 21, 1920; s. Oliver Cromwell and Maude Isabella (Harvey) M.; student So. Meth. U., 1938-39, 47-48; B.B.A., Huntingdon Coll., 1957; M.B.A., U. Okla., 1960; m. Orinda Dobbin, Feb. 26, 1942; children—Donna Marie, Orinda Lee, Juanita Gail. Commd. U.S. Army Air Force, 1942, advanced through grades to col. U.S. Air Force, 1966, ret., 1969; exec. v.p., dir. R.L. Stewart & Co., Inc., San Antonio, 1972—. Decorated D.F.C., Air medal. Mem. Nat. Assn. Security Dealers, Ret. Officers Assn., Air Force Assn., Hump Pilots Assn., Ret. Profls. Assn. Methodist. Clubs: Masons, Shriners, Oak Hill Country. Home: 2502 Danbury Dr San Antonio TX 78217 Office: R L Stewart & Co Inc 5140 Broadway San Antonio TX 78209

MOWBRAY, JAMES ARTHUR, social agy. adminstr.; b. Evansville, Ind., Jan. 7, 1941; s. John Alexander and Wilma Louise (Kronberg) M.; Ph.B., Monteith Coll., 1964; M.A., Wayne State U., 1966; Ph.D. (W.T. Laprade fellow), Duke U., 1975; m. Paulette Anne Rosbury, Aug. 27, 1966; children—Renée Anne, Danielle Elizabeth. Instr., U. S.W. La., Lafayette, 1971-73; exec. coordinator Office of Mayor, City of Lafayette, 1973-74; dir. plan devel. Acadiana Health Planning Council, Lafayette, 1974-76; asst. exec. dir. Mid-La. Health Systems Agy., Baton Rouge, 1976-77; dir. E. Central Fla. Area Agy. on Aging, Winter Park, Fla., 1977—; adj. prof. history Fla. So. Coll., Orlando, 1978—. Co-founder, pres. Lafayette Historic Preservation Soc., 1974-76; co-founder, mem. Acadiana Com. for Twining and Franco-Acadiana Relations, Lafayette, 1976-77; mem. Crimes Against the Elderly Task Force, City of Orlando (Fla.), 1977—; maj. CAP, 1957—, dir. of tng. Fla. wing, 1979—; mem. Wayne State U. Fund, 1976—. Co-recipient E. Davis CD award Lafayette Parish-City of Lafayette, 1977; recipient Bronze Medal of Valor, CAP, 1978. Mem. Am. Planning Assn. (asso.), Fla. Assn. Area Agys. on Aging, Am. Hist. Assn., Armor Assn., Nat. Assn. Search and Rescue, So. Hist. Assn., Mil. History Soc. (U.K.). Democrat. Lutheran. Club: Univ. (Winter Park). Home: 371 Radebaugh Ct Longwood FL 32750 Office: E Central Fla Regional Planning Council 1011 Wymore Rd Winter Park FL 32789

MOWER, JAY MASON, food co. exec.; b. Cin., Sept. 14, 1937; s. Charles Mason and Helen Madge (Bishop) M.; B.A. cum laude, Harvard Coll., 1959; M.B.A., Stanford U., 1964; m. Vivian Evans Locker, June 22, 1964; children—Jason, Andrew, Matthew. Account exec. Benton & Bowles Advt., N.Y.C., 1964-67; market planner Marschalk Advt., Atlanta, 1968-69; brand mgr., group brand mgr. foods div. Coca-Cola Co., Houston, 1969-77, dir. new product devel., 1977—. Served to lt. USN, 1959-62. Mem. Assn. Nat. Advertisers (mem. new product com.). Episcopalian. Office: PO Box 2079 Houston TX 77001

MOWERY, WILLIAM EDWARD, dentist; b. Cairo, Ill., Apr. 20, 1919; s. Hugh Lloyd and Adah Belle (Little) M.; student U. Louisville, 1937-40, D.M.D., 1943; postgrad. U. Mich., Ohio State U., U. Pa., Georgetown U.; diploma in ch. music So. Bapt. Theol. Sem., 1979; m. Nancy Wilds Baskett, June 21, 1942; children—Marilyn Elizabeth (Mrs. David W. Bryant), James Taylor, Lois Evelyn (Mrs. Larry W. Roberts). Pvt. practice dentistry, Richmond, Ky., 1946-47; staff dentist VA regional office, Louisville, 1947-50; VA guest worker, dental research labs. Nat. Bur. Standards, Washington, 1950-52; chief Central Dental Lab., VA Regional Office, Louisville, 1952-56, VA West Side Hosp., Chgo., 1956-63; asst. chief dental service VA Center, Dayton, Ohio, 1963-71; chief Central Dental Lab., VA Hosp., Washington, 1971-72; asst. chief dental service VA Hosp., Louisville, 1972-75. Mem. faculty U. Louisville Sch. Dentistry, 1953-56, 72—, Loyola U., Chgo., 1956-63, Ohio State U., Columbus, 1964-71. Served with USNR, 1943-46; capt. res. (ret.). Diplomate Am. Bd. Prosthodontics. Fellow Am. Coll. Prosthodontists (life); mem. Louisville (life), Ky. dental assns., ADA, Am. Prosthodontic Soc., Gideons Internat., Omicron Kappa Upsilon. Baptist (deacon). Contbr. articles to profl. jours. Home: 2250 Wynnewood Circle Louisville KY 40222

MOXLEY, THOMAS IRVIN, SR., chemist; b. Louisville, July 11, 1922; s. Wilford Irvin and Safronia Alma (Sewell) M.; B.S., U. Louisville, 1949; m. Winefred Georgette Wise, Feb. 14, 1952; children—Thomas Irvin, Norman Alan. Chem. technician Health Scis. Center, U. Louisville, 1951-55, sr. chem. technician, 1955-60, research asst., 1960-68, sr. research asst., 1968-76, organ transplant technologist, 1976-77, sr. research technologist, 1977—; lectr. Watterson Coll. Instnl. rep. Boy Scouts Am.; chmn. mini bd. edn. Parkland Jr. High Sch.; pres. advisory com. Male High Sch.; mem. Louisville Philharmonic Chorus. Served with U.S. Army, 1943-46; ETO. Recipient Pres.'s award Boy Scouts Am., 1970; Mayor's award City of Louisville, 1975; named Ky. col. Mem. Sigma Xi (asso.), Beta Kappa Chi, Kappa Alpha Psi. Mem. United Ch. of Christ. Contbr. article to profl. jours. Home: PO Box 11061 Louisville KY 40211 Office: U Louisville Health Scis Center 511 S Floyd St Louisville KY 40201

MOYE, CHARLES ALLEN, JR., fed. judge; b. Atlanta, July 13, 1918; s. Charles Allen and Annie Luther (Williamson) M.; A.B., Emory U., 1939, J.D., 1943; m. Sarah Ellen Johnston, Mar. 9, 1945; children—Henry Allen, Lucy Ellen. Admitted to Ga. bar, 1943; practice in Atlanta, 1943-70; partner firm Gambrell, Russell, Moye & Killorin, and predecessors, 1955-70; judge U.S. Dist. Ct. for No. Dist. Ga., Atlanta, 1970—, chief judge, 1979—. Chmn. DeKalb County Republican Exec. Com., 1952-56, Rep. Exec. Com. 5th Congl. Dist. Ga., 1956-64; mem. Ga. Rep. Central Com., 1952-64; Rep. candidate for Congress, 1954; del. Rep. Nat. Conv., 1956, 60, 64; chmn. Rep. Exec. Com. 4th Congl. Dist. Ga., 1964; Rep. presdl. elector, 1964. Mem. Am., Fed., Atlanta bar assns., State Bar Ga., Lawyers Club Atlanta, Assn. Bar City N.Y., Am. Law Inst., Am. Judicature Soc., Delta Tau Delta. Baptist. Clubs: Atlanta Athletic, Atlanta City; Nat. Lawyers (Washington). Contbr. articles to legal jours. Home: 1317 Council Bluff Dr NE Atlanta GA 30345 Office: Old Post Office Bldg Atlanta GA 30303

MOYER, REBECCA S., real estate broker; b. Spartanburg, S.C., Aug. 8, 1951; d. Eugene Frederick and Gladys Louise (Clary) Moyer; student pub. schs., Spartanburg, S.C.; grad. Realtors Inst., U. S.C., 1976. Real estate sales agt. Moyer Realty Co., Spartanburg, S.C., 1974—; sec., asst. treas., bookkeeper Moyer Constrn. Co., Inc., Spartanburg, 1968—; pres. Moyer Investment Co., Inc., 1979—. Lic. real estate broker, S.C. Mem. Spartanburg Bd. Realtors. Home: PO Box 2741 Spartanburg SC 29304 Office: 659 E Main St Spartanburg SC 29302

MOYER, REX C., oncologist, educator; b. Elkhart, Ind., Dec. 8, 1935; s. Carl E. and Evelyn (Wenger) M.; B.S., Purdue U., 1957; M.S., U. Nebr., Lincoln, 1961; Ph.D. (USPHS trainee 1961-65), U. Tex., Austin, 1965; m. Mary Pat Sutter, Dec. 26, 1974; children—Gina, Sonja, Pamela, Amy. Asst. bacteriologist Miles Labs., Elkhart, 1957-58; Nat. Acad. Sci., NRC research asso., Ft. Detrick, Md., 1965-66, research microbiologist, 1966-69; asso. prof., dir. Thorman Cancer Lab., Trinity U., San Antonio, 1969—; Bd. trustees Met. San Antonio March of Dimes, 1972-74. Internat. Agy. for Research on Cancer travel fellow, Hammersmith Hosp., London, 1967. Mem. Am. Soc. Microbiology, Nat. Tissue Culture Assn., Tex. Tissue Culture Assn., Internat. Study Group for Detection and Prevention of Cancer, N.Y. Acad. Sci., SW Sci. Forum (vice-chmn. molecular biology sect. 1977—), Tex. Acad. Sci., Rare Fruit Council Internat., Palm Soc., Sigma Xi. Contbr. articles to sci., profl. jours.; asso. editor: Tex. Jour. of Sci., 1978—. Home: Route 3 Box 662 San Antonio TX 78218 Office: Trinity U 715 Stadium San Antonio TX 78284

MOYER, ROBERT ALEXANDER, oil co. ofcl.; b. Joplin, Mo., Nov. 12, 1944; s. Benjamin Michael and Rita Marguerite (Scheurich) M.; B.S. in Mktg., Okla. State U., 1967; m. Kathleen Ann Moore, June 3, 1967; children—Richard, David, Michael and Steven (twins). With Cities Service Co., Tulsa, 1967, 69—, coll. recruitment mgr., 1978-79, spl. projects mgr., personnel resources dept. for energy resources group, 1979—. Served with USNR, 1967-69. Mem. Mid-Atlantic Placement Assn., Eastern Coll. Personnel Assn., Tulsa Personnel Assn., Work Edn. Council Tulsa. Republican. Roman Catholic. Home: 7034 E 52d Pl Tulsa OK 74145 Office: 110 W 7th St Tulsa OK 74012

MOYNAHAN, BERNARD THOMAS, JR., fed. judge; b. Akron, Ohio, Dec. 29, 1918; s. Bernard Thomas and Mayme (Turner) M.; A.B., U. Ky., 1935, LL.B., 1938; m. Mary Thomas Parks, Dec. 19, 1942; children—Mary Patricia, Bernard Thomas III. Admitted to Ky. bar, 1940; practice law, Nicholasville, 1940-42, 54-61; county atty., Jessamine County, 1946-54; U.S. atty. Eastern Dist. Ky., 1961-63, judge U.S. Dist. Ct., 1963—, now chief judge. Served to 1st lt. USAAF, 1942-45. Recipient award of merit Ky. State Bar Assn., 1974. Home: Rural Route 2 Nicholasville KY 40356 Office: 113 Court Row Nicholasville KY 40356

MUCHOW, RANDALL EUGENE, ceramic engr.; b. Lockport, N.Y., Dec. 6, 1949; s. Eugene Karl and Adele Marie (Szafranski) M.; B.S. in Ceramic Engring., Alfred (N.Y.) U., 1971; m. Deborah Gail McMillan, June 30, 1973; children—Holly Michelle, Keri Andrea. Applications engr., then product engr. Carborundum Co., Niagara Falls, N.Y., 1971-74, sales engr., Atlanta, 1975—; ceramic engr. Gen. Electric Co., St. Petersburg, Fla., 1974-75; owner Superamics, 1972—. Mem. Am. Ceramic Soc. Republican. Roman Catholic. Author articles. Home: 5155 Sunburst Dr Norcross GA 30092 Office: 5785 Peachtree Ind Blvd Atlanta GA 30341

MUDD, JOHN PHILIP, lawyer, real estate exec.; b. Washington, Aug. 22, 1932; s. T. Paul and Frances M. (Finotti) M.; B.S., Georgetown U., 1954, J.D., 1956; m. Barbara E. Sweeney, Aug. 10, 1957; children—Laura, Ellen, Philip, Clare, David. Admitted to Fla. bar, 1964, Md. bar, 1956, D.C. bar, 1963, Calif. bar, 1973; practice law, Upper Marlboro, Md., 1956-66; chief corporate counsel Deltona Corp., Miami, Fla., 1966-68, chief corporate counsel, sec., 1968-72, v.p., 1972-73; sec. Nat. Community Builders, San Diego, 1972-73; gen. counsel Continental Advisers, adviser to Continental Mortgage Investors, Coral Gables, Fla., 1973-75, v.p., 1975—; pres. Tropic Devel. Corp., 1974—; dir. Commonwealth Continental Corp., St. Petersburg, Nationwide Bldg. & Devel. Corp., Ft. Lauderdale, Fla., L.E.C., Inc., Silver Spring, Md., H.M.F. Inc., Honolulu. Gen. counsel Continental Mortgage Investors; sec. Marco Island Devel. Corp., Miami, 1968-72; mem. internat. land devel. adv. com. N.Y. State, 1971-74. Alumni interviewer Georgetown U.; bd. dirs. Palomaores Nursing Center, Pomona, Calif. Mem. Fla., Calif., D.C., Md., Am., Dade County bar assns. Republican. Roman Catholic. Home: 1211 Hardee Rd Coral Gables FL 33146 Office: 5915 Ponce de Leon Blvd Coral Gables FL 33146

MUELLER, HAROLD O., farm equipment dealer; b. Clayton, Mo., Dec. 10, 1931; s. Erich G. and Meta M. (Kropp) M.; B.S., U. Mo., 1953; m. Jean Crabtree, June 25, 1955; children—Stephen Lynn, Stacy Lee, Amy Beth. Agrl. technician A. Reich & Sons Gardens, Inc., Kansas City, Mo., 1953-56; field rep. Packer Pub. Co., Kansas City, 1956-58; partner Valley Equipment Co., Pauls Valley, Okla., 1958-64, pres., mgr., 1964—. Bd. dirs. Carvin County Rural Water Dist.; mem. adv. bd. Mid. Am. Vo-Tech. Sch. Served with U.S. Army, 1953-55. Mem. Pauls Valley C. of C., Okla. Hardware and Implement Assn. (dir.), Nat. Farm and Power Equipment Dealers Assn., Alumni Assn. Farm House Frat., Alpha Zeta. Methodist (chmn. bd. trustees). Home: Route 1 Box 241A Pauls Valley OK 73075 Office: Box 288 Pauls Valley OK 73075

MUELLER, MARK CHRISTOPHER, lawyer, accountant; b. Dallas, June 19, 1945; s. Herman August and Hazel Deane (Hatzenbuehler) M.; B.A. in Econs., So. Meth. U., 1967, M.B.A. in Accounting, 1969, J.D., 1971; m. Linda Jane Reed. Admitted to Tex. bar, 1971, since practiced in Dallas; accountant A.E. Krutilek, Dallas, 1968-71, Arthur Young & Co., Dallas, 1967-68; asso. L. Vance Stanton, Dallas, 1971-72. Instr. legal writing and research So. Meth. U., 1970-71, instr. legal accounting, 1975. C.P.A., Tex. Mem. Am., Tex. bar assns., Tex. Soc. C.P.A.s, Order of Coif, Beta Alpha Psi, Phi Delta Phi, Sigma Chi. Mason (32 deg., Shriner). Club: Nat. Rifle Assn. Home: 7310 Brennans St Dallas TX 75214 Office: 400 Adolphus Tower Dallas TX 75202

MUELLER, ROBERT LOUIS, physician; b. Granite City, Ill., Sept. 2, 1929; s. Louis Jacob and Mildred (Fegley) M.; A.B. magna cum laude, Carthage Coll., 1951; M.D., U. Ill., 1955; m. Dorothy Jane Grant, Apr. 28, 1956; children—Deborah Jean, Mary Jane, Allan Louis, Catherine Grant. Intern Ill. Central Hosp., Chgo., 1955-56; resident obstetrics and gynecology U. Tenn. and City of Memphis Hosps., 1957-60; practice medicine, specializing in obstetrics and gynecology, Morristown, Tenn., 1964-74, Knoxville, Tenn., 1975—; mem. staff Morristown Hamblen Hosp., chief staff, 1969-70, 73-74; mem. attending staff Park West Hosp., 1975—, U. Tenn. Meml. Research Hosp., 1975—; courtesy staff Ft. Sanders Presbyn. Hosp., E. Tenn. Baptist Hosp.; med. dir. Knoxville Center for Reproductive Health, 1975—; clin. instr. obstetrics and gynecology U. Tenn. Served to maj. AUS, 1956-64. Diplomate Am. Bd. Obstetrics and Gynecology. Fellow Am. Coll. Obstetrics and Gynecology; mem. AMA, Tenn., So. med. assns., Hamblen County Med. Soc. (pres. 1974), Knoxville Acad. Medicine, So. Obstet. and Gynecol. Seminar, East Tenn. Obstet. and Gynecol. Soc. (pres. 1979), Am. Assn. Gynecol. Laparoscopists, Am. Fertility Soc. Lutheran. Club: Optimists. Home: 313 Heritage Dr W Knoxville TN 37922 Office: 8609 Kingston Pike Knoxville TN 37919

MUELLER, ROY CLEMENT, graphic arts co. exec.; b. Weehawken, N.J., Aug. 15, 1930; s. Adam and Bertha Mueller; student Rochester Inst. Tech., 1976; m. Patricia Robinson, Sept. 3, 1970; children—Eric, Janet, Debra, Gregory. Mgr. estimating/billing dept. Editors Press, Hyattsville, Md., 1962-66; v.p., gen. mgr. Peninsula Press div. A.S. Abell Corp., Salisbury, Md., 1968-70; owner, mgr. Crown Decal & Display Co., Bristol, Tenn., 1972—; pres. Bristol Screen Inc. (Va.), 1977—. Recipient Ad award Tri City Advt. Fedn., 1975; internat. exhbn. award Screen Printing Assn., 1977. Mem. Screen Printing Assn., Am. Philatelic Soc.. Republican. Lutheran. Home: Route 5 Box 455A Bluff City TN 37618 Office: 1608 Edgemont Ave Bristol TN 37620

MUELLER, WILLIAM ANTON, chemist; b. Dortmund, Germany, Feb. 27, 1911; came to U.S., 1923, naturalized, 1930; s. Anton Franz and Kate Tietje (Reitsma) M.; B.S., U. Wis., 1933, Ph.D., 1938; m. Maggie Ruth Thomas, July 23, 1953; children—(William) Thomas, Margaret L(ei). Asso. prof. chemistry SE Mo. State Coll., 1938-43; asso. prof. chemistry and physics Southwestern U., Memphis, 1943-44; research chemist Buckeye Cotton Oil Co., Memphis, 1944-49, head research, 1949-53; asso. dir. research Buckeye Cellulose Corp., Memphis, 1954-57; research specialist Procter & Gamble, Memphis, 1957-76; cons. chemist, 1976—. Mem. Am. Chem. Soc., AAAS, TAPPI, Textile Research Inst., Am. Forestry Assn. Contbr. articles to profl. jours.; patentee cellulose products. Home and Office: 4494 Princeton Rd Memphis TN 38117

MUELLER, WILLIAM FEGLEY, clergyman; b. East St. Louis, Ill., Jan. 19, 1936; s. Louis J. and Mildred E. (Fegley) M.; A.B., Carthage Coll., 1958; B.D., Northwestern Luth. Theol. Sem., 1962, M.Div., 1971; m. Patty Ann Cleveland, Aug. 16, 1958; children—Kurt, Elizabeth, Steven, James, Cherylyn. Ordained to ministry Lutheran Ch., 1962; pastor Christ Luth. Ch., Shelbyville, Ind., 1962-64; asst. pastor Unity Luth. Ch., Milw., 1964-67; pastor Emmanuel Luth. Ch., Atlanta, 1967-76, Redeemer Luth. Ch. and St. Peter's Luth. Ch., Augusta County, Va., 1978—; chaplain, maj. USAR; exec. com. Billy Graham's Atlanta Crusade; ecumenical service com. ground breaking Martin Luther King Center for Social Change; former pres. Atlanta Luth. Council. Mem. Legion of Honor of Chapel of Four Chaplains. Mem. UN Assn., Res. Officers Assn., Smithsonian Instn. Assos., West Augusta County Ministers for United Way (chmn. 1979), Nat. Geog.

Soc., Nat. Trust Hist. Preservation, Cousteau Soc., Nat. Small Bus. Assn., Tau Sigma Chi. Author devotional writings for denominational booklets.

MUENCH, STEPHEN ROBERT, agrl. co. exec.; b. Spokane, Wash., Feb. 2, 1943; s. Charlie Robert and Leola Winfred (Coultas) M.; B.A., Eastern Wash. U., 1965; M.S., Wash. State U., 1971, Ph.D., 1975; m. Linda Jean Warren, Aug. 22, 1964; children—Eric Christopher, Kimberlie Lynn. Product devel. rep. Monsanto Agrl. Products Co., McAllen, Tex., 1975—. Asst. coach Boys Club Football, 1978; asst. leader Webelos troop Boy Scouts Am., 1978-79. Served with AUS, 1965-68. Decorated D.F.C., Air medal, Purple Heart. Mem. Weed Sci. Soc. Am., Am. Soc. Agronomy, Council Agrl. Sci. and Tech., So. Weed Sci. Soc., Rice Tech. Workers Group, Am. Soc. Agronomy Tex., Sigma Xi. Home: 413 Hibiscus St McAllen TX 78501

MUES, FLAVIO JORGE, elec. engr.; b. Mexico City, Mexico, Aug. 26, 1930; s. Eric and Marta (Becker) M.; M.S., Nat. U. Mexico 1963; student Grad. Sch., U. Ibero Americana, 1971-73; m. Teresa Zepeda, Jan. 5, 1966; 1 dau., Astrid. Project engr. Continental Engring. N.V., Amsterdam, Holland, 1965, Ingenieria Continental S.A., Mexico City, 1966-67; project mgr. Condumex S.A., wire and cable mfrs., Mexico City, 1968-73; project mgr. Ludwig Saenger Cons., Mexico City, 1974; new enterprises orgn. dept. head Nacional Financiera, 1974—. Tchr. systems Grad. Sch., U. Ibero Americana, 1973-74. Mem. I.E.E.E., Nat. Geog. Soc., Roda Automobile Club. Club: de Golf Vallescondido. Contbr. articles to profl. jours. Home: 791 Cali Ave Mexico City DF 14 Mexico Office: 51 Isabel la Católica Ave Mexico 1 DF Mexico

MUGNIER, CLIFFORD JOHN, cons. cartographer; b. New Orleans, Jan. 15, 1944; s. Clifford Alphonse and Anna Irma (Schedler) M.; B.A., Northwestern State Coll., Nachitoches, La., 1967; m. Diane Marie Mars, June 28, 1969; children—Gus, André, Jacques, Monique, Théodore. Cartographer, USAF Aero Chart and Info. Center, St. Louis, 1967-68; applied photogrammetry chief Raytheon/Autometric Co., Wayland, Mass., 1972-73; mgr. photogrammetry div. Owen and White, Inc., Baton Rouge, 1973-77; pres. M-Squared Systems, Inc., New Orleans, 1977—; instr. surveying Baton Rouge Vocat.-Tech. Sch.; guest lectr. La. State U.; instr. cartography and geodesy U. New Orleans. Served to capt. C.E., U.S. Army, 1968-72. Mem. Photogrammetric Soc. London, Am. Soc. Photogrammetry (regional dir.), Am. Congress Surveying and Mapping (sect. dir.). Democrat. Roman Catholic. Contbr. articles to profl. jours. Address: 4489 Baccich St New Orleans LA 70122

MUGNO, MARJORIE JANE (MARJIE), writer; b. Mar. 17, 1935; d. John A. and Mildred Norton M.; B.J., U. Tex., Austin, 1957. Editor, Hwy. News travel and info. div. Tex. Hwy. Dept., 1957-72, asst. editor Tex. Hwys., until 1972; free-lance writer, 1973—. Dallas Press Club Katy award finalist for Oak Cliff mag., 1974. Mem. Women in Communications, 500 Inc. Republican. Methodist. Club: Dallas Ski. Home: 6761 Larmanda St Apt 138 Dallas TX 75231

MUHLENDORF, DAVID MILTON, accountant; b. Sheffield, Ala., Mar. 23, 1950; s. Jack and Beatrice Muriel (Israel) M.; B.S., U. Ala., 1972; m. Lizabeth Fabian Levy, Nov. 3, 1974. Audit mgr. Price Waterhouse & Co., Birmingham, Ala., 1972—. Active Jr. Achievement Jefferson County, 1978-79. C.P.A., Ala. Mem. Am. Inst. C.P.A.'s, Ala., Birmingham socs. C.P.A.'s, Nat. Assn. Accountants, Commerce Exec. Soc., Asso. Industries Ala. (edn. com. 1979), Birmingham Jaycees (treas. 1975, dir. 1975), Zeta Beta Tau, Omicron Delta Kappa, Alpha Kappa Psi. Democrat. Jewish. Clubs: B'nai B'rith, Met. Kiwanis (dir. 1978-79), Toastmasters, Relay House, Pinetree Country, Beth-El Men's. Home: 3664 Northcote Dr Birmingham AL 35223 Office: 1200 First Nat So Natural Birmingham AL 35203

MUIR, HELEN, author; b. Yonkers, N.Y., Feb. 9, 1911; d. Emmet A. and Helen T. (Flaherty) Lennehan; student Yonkers pub. schools; m. William Whalley Muir, Jan. 23, 1936; children—Mary (Mrs. Frederick W. Burrell), William Torbert. With Yonkers Herald Statesman, 1929-30, 31-33, N.Y. Eve. Post, 1930-31, N.Y. Eve. Jour., 1933-34, Carl Byoir & Assos., 1934-35; syndicated columnist Universal Service, 1935-38, Miami Daily News, 1935-39; broadcaster stas. WIOD, WQAM, 1935, 42; columnist Miami Herald, 1941-42; woman's editor Miami Daily News, 1943-44; free lance mag. writer, Sat. Eve. Post, This Week, Nations Bus., Woman's Day, 1944—; children's book editor Miami Herald, 1949-56; drama critic Miami News, 1960-65. Trustee Coconut Grove Library Assn., Friends U. Miami Library, Met. Dade County Library Bd., State Library Adv. Council, Friends Miami-Dade Pub. Library Inc. Recipient award Delta Kappa Gamma, 1960; Trustees and Friends award Fla. Library Assn., 1973; award Dade County Library Assn., 1977. Mem. Women in Communications (Community Headline award 1973). Club: Fla. Women's Press (award 1963). Author: Miami, U.S.A., 1954. Home: 3855 Stewart Ave Miami FL 33133

MUIRHEAD, JANE ANN, audiologist; b. Shreveport, La., Apr. 30, 1953; d. Robert Lloyd and Donna Jane (Gauthier) Muirhead; student So. Meth. U., 1971-73, U. Nev., summers 1972, 73; B.S., U. Tex., Austin, 1975, M.A., 1977. Speech and hearing cons. La. Dept. Health and Human Resources, Baton Rouge, 1977; dir. audiology Highland Clinic, Shreveport, La., 1977-79; clin. audiologist Drs. Pou, Quinn & Watkins, Shreveport, 1979—; clin. audiologist La. State U. Med. Sch., Shreveport, 1979—, clin. practicum supr., 1979—. Lic. audiologist, La. Mem. Am. Speech and Hearing Assn. (cert. of clin. competence), La. Speech and Hearing Assn., So. Audiological Soc., La. Hearing Rehab. Assn., Am. Auditory Soc., Phi Kappa Phi. Republican. Methodist. Home: 10122 Carlsbad St Shreveport LA 71115 Office: 2121 Line Ave Shreveport LA 71104

MULDOON, WILLIAM HENRY, III, newspaper publisher; b. San Antonio, June 14, 1935; s. Wilfrid Edward and Laurie Elizabeth (Battersby) M.; A.B., Dartmouth Coll., 1957; postgrad. U. Tex., 1958; m. Nancy Knight Achning, Aug. 23, 1958; children—William Henry, IV, Shevaun Elaine. Pres. Virgin Islands Printing Corp., St. Thomas, 1961-72, Press, Inc., St. Thomas, 1972-76, Mt. Top Estates, St. Thomas, 1968-76, North Star Village, Inc., St. Thomas, 1968-76; pres., pub. Commerce (Tex.) Jour., 1976—; pub. Cooper (Tex.) Rev., 1977—; regional cons. Graphic Arts Tech. Found. Chmn. Commerce United Way Fund, 1976-77; mem. Hunt County Com. Crime Prevention/Drug Edn.; mem. exec. bd. Boy Scouts Am.; mem. bd. presdl. advisers East Tex. State U. Served to capt. USMCR, 1958-61. Mem. Commerce C. of C., Nat. Newspaper Assn., Tex., N. and E. Tex. press assns., Am. Newspaper Pubs. Assn., Underwater Soc. Am., Internat. Oceanographic Found., Marine Corps Assn., Air Force Assn., Nat. Rifle Assn. (life), Internat. Wine and Food Soc., Order Arrow, Commerce Band Boosters, Delta Tau Delta. Republican. Episcopalian (sr. warden). Clubs: Kiwanis (pres.-elect), Sand Hills Country, Am. Sportsmen's. Home: 3009 Washington St Commerce TX 75428 Office: 1210 Main St Box 1291 Commerce TX 75428

MULFINGER, GEORGE LEONIDAS, JR., educator, musician, author; b. Syracuse, N.Y., June 21, 1932; s. George Leonidas and Elizabeth Claire (Bartenslager) M.; B.A. summa cum laude, Syracuse U., 1953, M.S., 1962, postgrad., 1963-66; postgrad. Harvard U., 1954, U. Ga., 1967; m. Joan Elizabeth Wade, June 24, 1956; children—Linda, Ruth, Mark, Rachel, Sara, Julia, Martha, Daniel, Mary, Sharon, Joanna. Head math. and sci. dept. Elbridge (N.Y.) Central Sch., 1955-57; instr. sci. Syracuse (N.Y.)-Central Tech. High Sch., 1957-65, chmn. sci. dept., 1962-65; prof. physics and phys. sci. Bob Jones U., Greenville, S.C., 1965—, prof. cello, 1965—; lectr. in field. Mem. Creation Research Soc., Sigma Pi Sigma, Pi Mu Epsilon, Phi Beta Kappa. Baptist. Club: Nat. Radio. Co-author earth sci. textbook, 1980, phys. sci. textbook, 1974, various sci. textbooks, 1975-77. Home: 25 Springdale Dr Greenville SC 29609 Office: Bob Jones U Wade Hampton Blvd Greenville SC 29614

MULHEARN, THOMAS EDWIN, mfg. co. exec.; b. Washington, Jan. 28, 1952; s. Rupert Albert and Era Louise (Gresham) M.; B.A. cum laude, James Madison U., 1974; postgrad. U. Va., 1976-77, Lynchburg (Va.) Coll., 1979—; m. Carole Daughton, June 3, 1978. Personnel adminstr. Value Engring. Co., Alexandria, Va., 1974-76, 77-78; employment coordinator Babcock & Wilcox Co., Lynchburg Research Center, 1978-80; profl. staffing rep. Gen. Electric, Lynchburg, 1980—; speaker. Mem. Am. Soc. Personnel Adminstrn., Employment Mgmt. Assn., Central Va. Personnel Assn., Washington Tech. Personnel Forum. Home: 309 Rainbow Forest Dr Lynchburg VA 24502 Office: Gen Electric Mountain View Rd Lynchburg VA 24502

MULKEY, SIDNEY WAYNE, counselor, educator; b. Dayton, Tenn., Aug. 14, 1938; s. James Henry and Bessie Elizabeth (Sharp) M.; B.S., E. Tenn. State U., 1963; M.S., U. Tenn., 1970; postgrad. Fla. State U.; m. Elizabeth Ross (Betty) Powers, Nov. 28, 1970; 1 dau., Lauren Ross. Welfare worker Tenn. Dept. Human Services, Chattanooga, 1964-66; counselor service for Blind, Knoxville, Tenn., 1966-69, registrar, Nashville, 1970-71; counselor-tchr. U. Tenn. Dept. Edn., Knoxville, 1971-77; bd. dirs. E. Tenn. Children Rehab. Center, Knoxville, 1973-77. Cert. rehab. counselor. Mem. Nat. Rehab. Assn., Nat. Rehab. Counseling Assn., Am. Assn. Workers for the Blind, Am. Personnel and Guidance Assn., Am. Rehab. Counseling Assn. Republican. Baptist. Home: 229 Westridge Dr Tallahassee FL 32304

MULLEN, ANDREW JUDSON, physician; b. Selma, Ala., June 23, 1923; s. Andrew J. and Helen (Johnson) M.; A.B., Vanderbilt U., 1948; M.D., Jefferson Med. Coll., 1952; children—J. Thomas, Debbie, Gail, Andrea, Shawn, Connie, Beth. Intern, U.S. Marine Hosp., Galveston, Tex., 1952-53; resident Tex. Med. Center, Houston, 1954-57; chief neurology and psychiatry service VA Hosp., Jackson, Miss., 1957; dir. Mobile (Ala.) Mental Health Center, 1957-58; practice medicine, specializing in psychiatry and neurology, Shreveport, La., 1958—; chief female service Confederate Meml. Med. Center, 1959-63, bd. dirs., chmn. pub. relations com., 1964; med. dir. Shreveport Child Guidance Center, 1961—; mem. med. adv. bd. Extendicare Corp.; cons. psychiatry and neurology Barksdale AFB, VA Hosp.; chief staff Brentwood Neuro-Psychiat. Hosp., Shreveport, 1970-73; clin. prof. psychiatry La. State U. Sch. Medicine, 1975—. Dep. coroner, cons., Caddo Parish, La., 1964; chmn. mental health com. Community Council, 1964—. Served with RCAF, 1941-42, AUS, 1942-45. Decorated Purple Heart with oak leaf cluster, Bronze Star. Diplomate Am. Bd. Psychiatry and Neurology (asso. examiner). Fellow Am., So. psychiat. assns., Am. Coll. Psychiatrists; mem. AMA, So. Med. Assn., Shreveport Med. Soc. (dir. 1971-72), Flying Physicians Assn., Alpha Tau Omega, Nu Sigma Nu. Episcopalian. Home: 333 Berkshire Pl Shreveport LA 71101 Office: 902 Olive St Shreveport LA 71104

MULLEN, DAVID EDWARD, clergyman, psychologist; b. Omaha, Sept. 6, 1938; s. Edward Francis and Gretchen Louise (Schultz) M.; B.A., Davidson Coll., 1960; M.Div., Union Sem., 1963; M.A. in Psychology, W.Ga. Coll., 1974; m. Sandra Little, June 26, 1961; children—Lynn, Michael. Ordained to ministry Presbyn. Ch., 1963; pastor Faith Presbyn. Co., Greensboro, N.C., 1965-68; dir. Carroll County Alcoholism Clinic, Carrollton, Ga., 1973-74; staff psychologist Marian-Citrus Mental Health Center, Ocala, Fla., 1974-76; dir. Episcopal Pastoral Counseling Center, Sarasota, Fla., 1976—. Bd. dirs. Career and Counseling Center, Eckerd Coll., 1976. Mem. Am. Assn. Marriage and Family Counselors, Am. Assn. Sex Educators and Therapists, Am. Personnel and Guidance Assn., Internat. Transactional Analysts Assn., Am. Orthopsychiat. Assn. Home: 2108 41st St W Bradenton FL 33505 Office: 222 S Palm Ave Sarasota FL 33577

MULLEN, ELISA CELESTE CAVAZOS, speech pathologist; b. Brownsville, Tex., Sept. 15, 1939; d. Raul Alfredo and Eliza (Zepeda) Cavazos; B.S. in Elem. Edn., Incarnate Word Coll., San Antonio, 1961; M.Ed. in Speech Pathology, U. N.C., Greensboro, 1972; m. Patrick Anthony Mullen, July 22, 1978. Tchr. spl. edn. Harlingen (Tex.) Ind. Sch. Dist., 1961-63; tchr., spl. edn. coordinator Brownsville (Tex.) Ind. Sch. Dist., 1963-69; reading tchr. Remedial Program, High Point (N.C.) City Schs., 1969-72; speech pathologist Colonial Hills Elem. Sch., North East Ind. Sch. Dist., San Antonio, 1972—, named Bilingual Tchr. of Year, 1978, Outstanding Tchr. Employee, 1979; instr. Monolingual Inst. Spanish Instrn. for Tchrs., 1975-76; research assessor S.W. Tex. State U., 1977—; supr. H. Jersig Speech and Hearing Center, Our Lady of the Lake U., 1975—. Recipient Am. Legion award, 1957; Duke U. Speech Pathology summer program trainee, 1972; U. Tex., Austin, trainee, 1973. Mem. Am. Speech and Hearing Assn. (cert. clin. competence), Nat. Tchrs. Assn., Tex. Tchrs. Assn., N.E. Dist. Tchrs. Assn., Tex. Assn. for Bilingual Edn., San Antonio Assn. for Bilingual Edn. Democrat. Roman Catholic. Author bilingual program: Hablando Español con los niños. Home: 14623 Reigh County San Antonio TX 78248 Office: 10333 Broadway San Antonio TX 78217

MULLEN, JOHN O'KEEFE, ch. interior designer; b. New Haven, Mar. 13, 1919; s. Arthur Daniel and Katherine Leola (O'Keefe) M.; grad. Phillips Andover Acad., 1936; B.Engring., Yale, 1940, M.E., 1948; m. Ann McNally, Apr. 14, 1956; children—Mark, Christopher, John O'Keefe, Kate, Desmond. Engr., Fed. Shipbldg. & Dry Dock Co., 1940-41; asso. prof. naval architecture U. Tampa, 1941-42; cons. engr. Westcott & Mapes, New Haven, 1946-51; research and devel. engr. Am. Paper Goods Co., Kensington, Conn., 1953-55; gen. mgr. research and devel. Continental Can Co., 1955-56; owner Mullen Religious Supplies, Tampa, Fla., 1956—. Active Tampa Bay Art Center, Tampa Symphony; mem. devel. council St. Joseph's Hosp., Tampa. Served as comdr. USNR, World War II. Mem. Mil. Order World Wars. K.C. Clubs: Bay Area Yale (dir.), Tampa Yacht and Country, Tampa Torch. Devel. 1st plastic lined paper cup, 1954. Home: 901 S Delaware St Tampa FL 33606 Office: 1413 S Howard Ave Tampa FL 33606

MULLEN, JOSEPH, fin. mgmt. cons.; b. St. Louis, Mar. 24, 1921; s. Joseph and Elizabeth Welsh (Cocke) M.; B.S. in Chemistry, Va. Mil. Inst., 1942; m. Edith Talmage Donnan, Dec. 19, 1942; children—Edith Talmage, Joseph, William Cocke, Janet Randolph, Elizabeth Horner, Christopher Louis. With So. Acid & Sulphur Co. (merged with Mathieson Chem. Co. 1949, Olin Corp. 1954), Pasadena, Tex., St. Louis and Little Rock, 1946-58, gen. mgr. agrl. div., 1954-58; cons. Wheat & Co., Richmond, Va., 1958-60; partner A.G. Edwards & Sons, Inc., St. Louis, 1960-64; cons. fin. mgmt., Little Rock, 1965—; mgr. corp. devel. Ramteck Industries, Inc., Houston; pres. Exec. Travel; dir. numerous cos. Served with USN, World War II. Mem. Ark. Assn. Fin. Mgrs., Little Rock Fgn. Relations Assn., Ark. Tennis Assn. (pres. 1976). Roman Catholic. Clubs: Little Rock Country, Westside Tennis (pres.), Serra. Home and Office: 6209 Greenwood Rd Little Rock AR 72207

MULLEN, PHILIP EDWARD, artist; b. Akron, Ohio, Oct. 10, 1942; B.A., U. Minn., 1964; M.A., U. N.D., 1966; Ph.D., Ohio U., Athens, 1970. Artist, David Findlay Galleries, N.Y.C., 1975—, Dubin's Gallery, Los Angeles, 1977—; painter-in-residence U. S.C., 1979—; one-man exhbns. include David Findlay Gallery, 1976, 78, 80, Dubin's Gallery 1979; group exhbns. include Biennial Contemporary Art, Whitney Mus., N.Y.C., 1975, 21st Nat. Print Exhbn., Bklyn. Mus., 1978. Recipient 46 awards, including Russell award, 1976. Home: 1611 Hollywood Dr Columbia SC 29205 Office: Art Dept Univ SC Columbia SC 29208

MULLEN, SANFORD ALLEN, physician; b. Tampa, Fla., Jan. 16, 1925; s. Earl and Edith (Allen) M.; student Mercer U., 1943-45; M.D., Columbia, 1949; m. Minnie Lucille Woodall, Dec. 23, 1945; children—Sanford Allen, Henry Woodall, Michael Hill. Intern, Grady Meml. Hosp., Atlanta, 1949-50, resident anatomic pathology, 1950, 53-54; fellow clin. pathology U. Minn. Hosps., Mpls., 1954-56; practice medicine specializing in pathology, Jacksonville, Fla., 1958—; mem. staff, co-chief dept. pathology U. Hosp. of Jacksonville; mem. staff Bapt. Med. Center, St. Vincent's Med. Center, Hope Haven Children's Hosp., Meml. Hosp.; chief med. staff Cathedral Health and Rehab. Center (all Jacksonville), Putnam Community Hosp., Palatka, Fla., Lake Shore Hosp., Lake City, Fla. Nat. bd. govs. Arthritis Found., 1963-64, pres. Duval County div., 1960-61, pres. Fla. chpt., 1963-64; chmn. Jacksonville Mayor's Citizens Adv. Com. on Water Pollution Control, 1965-66, United Fund Campaign; vice chmn. Jacksonville Water Quality Control Bd., 1971-73, Health Planning Council N.E. Fla., 1976—; exec. v.p., med. dir. Jacksonville Blood Bank, 1970—; mem. various adv. coms. Fla. Bd. Health, Fla. Dept. Edn., Fla. Jr. Coll., Jacksonville; mem. adv. bd. Fla. div. Salvation Army, 1971-76; pres. Civic Round Table, 1967-69; rep. Greater Jacksonville Econ. Opportunity, Inc., 1966-68. Bd. dirs. Jacksonville Symphony Assn., 1970-77, v.p., 1971-73, sec., 1976-77; bd. dirs. Northeast Fla. region Kidney Found., Inc., 1972-74; bd. dirs. Jacksonville Area chpt. ARC, 1972-77, treas., 1974-75; vice chmn., 1975-77; bd. dirs. Cathedral Found., 1972-76, exec. vice chmn., 1972-76; bd. dirs. Jacksonville Exptl. Health Delivery System, Inc., 1973-76, pres., 1973-76; trustee Jacksonville Hosps. Ednl. Program, 1971-76. Served with M.C., USNR, 1950-52; on loan to AUS in Korea; comdr. Res. Ret. Recipient Service to Mankind award West Jacksonville Sertoma Club, 1974. Diplomate Am. Bd. Pathology. Fellow Coll. Am. Pathologists (gov. 1966-69, 70-73, chmn. state legis. com. 1969-72); mem. AMA, AAAS, Jacksonville Acad. Medicine (pres. 1963, dir. 1966-68, 72-77), Fla. Soc. Pathologists (pres. 1964-66, 72-73, v.p. 1966-67, 73-74), Am. Soc. Clin. Pathologists (councilor Fla. 1962-66), Duval County Med. Soc. (chmn. legislative council 1967, 70-72, dir. 1972—, pres. 1974), Fla. (ho. of dels. 1964—, chmn. com. state legis. 1969-75, vice speaker ho. of dels. 1976-78, speaker 1978—, A.H. Robins award 1973), So. (vice-chmn. sect. pathology 1967-68) med. assns., N.E. Fla. Heart Assn. (dir. 1967-69), Fla. (dir. 1968-76, pres. 1973-74), Am. (state rep. for Fla. 1971-72) assns. blood banks, Am. Cancer Soc., Fla. Med. Polit. Action Com. (dir. 1964-65), Jacksonville Zool. Soc. (dir. 1971-77), Jacksonville Area C. of C. (gov. 1966-68, 72-74, chmn. pub. health com. 1965-66, v.p. membership affairs, membership devel. award 1969), Jacksonville Art Mus., Cummer Gallery Art, Ye Mystic Revellers, Blue Key, Sigma Mu, Gamma Sigma Epsilon, Phi Eta Sigma, Alpha Tau Omega (pres. Jacksonville alumni 1958-59). Episcopalian (vestryman 1967-69, sr. warden 1969). Rotarian (pres. Jacksonville 1970-71). Clubs: Fla. Yacht, Timuquana Country, River, St. Johns Dinner (dir. 1967-70, pres. 1969-70), Torch (dir. 1968-72, pres. 1971-72). Home: 5171 Yacht Club Rd Jacksonville FL 32210 Office: Box 2921 Jacksonville FL 32203

MULLEN, WESLEY GRIGG, civil engr., educator; b. Richmond, Va., Nov. 30, 1922; s. Clary Sutton and Helen (Drummond) M.; B.S. in Civil Engring., Va. Mil. Inst., 1949; M.S. in Civil Engring. (Stephen Stepanion fellow 1949-51), U. Md., 1951; Ph.D. (Portland Cement Assn. fellow, 1961, ASTM doctoral fellow, 1962-63), Purdue U., 1963; m. Eloise Barton Morgan, June 23, 1951; children—Wesley Grigg, Melissa Morgan. Concrete engr. field contract adminstrn. Madigan-Hyland, Cons. Engrs., 1951-59, Pier 57, Haverstraw, N.Y., 1951-52, Tappan Zee Bridge, 1952-56, New Eng. Thruway, 1956-57, Berkshire Thruway, 1957-59; instr. U. Md., College Park, 1959-61, Purdue U., West Lafayette, Ind., 1961-62; research engr. Md. State Roads Commn., Brooklandville, 1963-65; asso. prof. N.C. State U., Raleigh, 1965-70, prof. civil engring., coordinator hwy. research program, 1970—; prof. Fredrik Wachtmeister chair for Eminent Scientists and Engrs., Va. Mil. Inst., Lexington, spring 1980. Vol. unit leader cub scouts, scouts, explorers Oconeechie council Boy Scouts Am., 1963-77; lay reader Episcopal Ch. Served with U.S. Army, 1943; served to lt. USMCR, 1943-46. Named to Acad. Outstanding Tchrs., N.C. State U., 1969; Asphalt Inst. fellow U. Minn., 1960; registered profl. engr. Md., N.C., N.J., N.Y., Va. Fellow ASCE (student chpt. advisor, Outstanding Service award 1979); mem. Am. Concrete Inst., Transp. Research Bd., Nat. Acad. Sci. (univ. liaison rep.), ASTM (Charles B. Dudley medal, 1966, mem. various coms.), Assn. of Asphalt Paving Technologists, Sigma Xi, Tau Beta Pi, Phi Kappa Phi, Chi Epsilon. Republican. Contbr. articles to profl. jours.; researcher in field; inventor apparatus in field. Home: 1203 Trailwood Dr Raleigh NC 27606 Office: NC State U PO Box 5993 Raleigh NC 27650

MULLER, CHARLES JULIUS, architect; b. Commerce, Tex., Feb. 24, 1918; s. Charles Julius and Nora Bradley (Cockerham) M.; B.S., East Tex. State U., 1938 B.Arch., Mass. Inst. Tech., 1941; postgrad. U. Tex., 1939; M.Ed., East Tex. State U., 1962; m. Linda Moody, May 18, 1943; children—Charles Julius, Jamie Muller Lassiter. Gen. mgr. Muller Ice Co., Commerce, Tex., 1945-58; pvt. practice architecture, 1946—; dir. First Nat. Bank. Chmn., Commerce Bd. Adjustment, 1967—, Housing Authority of Commerce, 1949-74. Served to maj. AUS, 1941-45. Mem. A.I.A., Tex. Soc. Architects. C. of C. (pres. 1951), E. Tex. State U. Alumni Assn. (bd. dirs. 1970—), Phi Delta Kappa. Episcopalian. Lion (pres. 1951). Home: 2505 Washington St Commerce TX 75428 Office: 2507 Washington St Commerce TX 75428

MULLER, FREDERICK LAWRENCE, investment counselor; b. Memphis, Apr. 25, 1938; s. Louis Frederick and Martha (McFadden) M.; B.A., U. Pa., 1960; M.B.A., George Washington U., 1966; m. Elizabeth Anne Healy, Feb. 11, 1961; 1 son, Frederick Reynolds. Sales, research staff Drexel Harriman Ripley, Atlanta, 1968-69, Faulkner Dawkins & Sullivan, N.Y.C., 1969-70; v.p., sr. investment officer Citizens and So. Nat. Bank, Atlanta, 1970-72; pres. Atlanta Capital Mgmt. Co., 1972—. Co-chmn. gifts program Atlanta Arts Alliance, 1976—; trustee Ga. Found. for Ind. Colls. Served to lt. (j.g.), USNR, 1961-65. Chartered financial analyst, certified investment counselor, Ga. Mem. Atlanta Soc. Financial Analysts (pres. 1974-75), Financial Analysts Fedn., Atlanta Econs. Club. Clubs: Piedmont Driving, Capital City, St. Anthony N.Y. Home: 18 Palisades Rd Atlanta GA 30309 Office: 230 Peachtree St Atlanta GA 30303

MÜLLER, GENE ALAN, historian; b. Grand Island, Nebr., Jan. 10, 1943; s. Ludwig Frederick and Erma Gertrude (Gorin) M.; B.A. cum laude, Midland Lutheran Coll., Fremont, Nebr., 1965; N.Y. U. in Spain scholar, U. Madrid, 1963-64; Fulbright-Hays scholar, U. Nacional Tucuman (Argentina), 1965-66; M.A. (NDFL Title VI fellow), U. Kans., Lawrence, 1969, A.B.D., 1970; OAS fellow to Guatemala, 1973; m. Diana June Curry; 1 dau., Michelle Nicole. Asst. instr. U. Kans., 1967-73; asst. prof. history Ft. Hays (Kans.) State U., 1973-74; bilingual historian El Paso (Tex.) Community Coll., 1974—; project reviewer Nat. Endowment Humanities, 1978—. Mem. council Good Shepherd Luth. Ch. Am., El Paso, 1974-78, St. Timothy's Luth. Ch., El Paso, 1980—. Mem. Am. Hist. Assn., Am. Cath. Hist. Assn., Latin Am. Studies Assn., Conf. Latin Am. Studies, Tex. Cath. Hist. Assn., Rocky Mountain Council Latin Am. Studies, Midwest Assn. Latin Am. Studies, AAUP. Democrat. Author articles, book revs., chpts. in books. Home: 10708 Vista Lomas El Paso TX 79935 Office: El Paso Community Coll PO Box 20500 El Paso TX 79998

MULLER, RICHARD LOUIS, govt. ofcl., bus. exec., artist, ednl. adminstr.; b. Chgo., Jan. 26, 1935; s. Ludwig Oboe Muller and Lilyan (Gershan) Muller Richter; student U. Ark., 1958-59; B.S. with highest honors, U. Central Ark., 1961; M.Ed. (Gilman fellow), Johns Hopkins, 1965; postgrad. George Peabody Coll. Tchrs., 1965; D.Sc., London Insts., 1973; m. Norma Marie Estes, Aug. 7, 1960; 1 son, Richard Louis. Tchr. sci. Gwynn Falls Jr. High Sch., Balt., 1961-62, Balt. City Coll., 1962-65, No. High Sch., Balt., 1965-66; edn. specialist U.S. Army Ordnance Center and Sch., Aberdeen, Md., 1966-71; ednl. adviser Navy Fleet Sonar Sch., Key West, Fla., 1971-73; edn. specialist Chief Naval Edn. and Tng., Pensacola, Fla., 1973-76, head standards, procedures and appraisal br., research and program devel. div., chief naval edn. and tng., 1976-78, head systems specific tng. program devel. br. and audiovisual program coordinator, chief Naval Edn. and Tng. Command, 1978—; owner, dir. Muller's Fine Arts, Pensacola. Mem. WEBB radio panel show Educators Look At, Balt., 1963. Mem. Edgewood Meadows (Md.) Civic Assn., 1966-71, Key Haven (Fla.) Civic Assn., 1973; pres. Edgewood Jaycees, 1967-71; mem. nominating caucus Harford County (Md.) Sch. Bd., 1968-70; mem. Md. Council on Edn., 1967-71, Citizens' Goals for Escambia County (Fla.), 1976-77; basketball coach Pensacola Christian Recreation Council, 1978-80; active Boy Scouts Am. Served with USN, 1953-58. NIH grantee, 1961, NSF fellow, 1965. Recipient Chem. Rubber Co. Physics Achievement award, 1960-61, U.S. Jr. C. of C. Distinguished Service award, 1968, certificate appreciation State Md., 1968, Presdl. award Honor, 1969, certificate achievement U.S. Army, 1971, Outstanding Performance awards U.S. Navy, 1975-77; named Edgewood (Md.) Jaycee of Year, 1968-69, Young Man Md., 1968; award Pensacola Christian Recreation Council, 1979. Mem. Nat. Sci. Tchrs. Assn. (life), Am. Assn. Sch. Adminstrs., Council Ednl. Facility Planners Internat., Am. Ednl. Research Assn., Am. Med. Technologists, Assn. Supervision and Curriculum Devel., Md. Acad. Sci., Mil. Testing Assn., U. Central Ark. Alumni Assn., Johns Hopkins Alumni Assn., Alpha Chi, Phi Delta Kappa (exec. bd., historian, life mem.). Methodist (asst. ch. sch. supt., fin. com.). Clubs: Arturus, Fleet of Chesapeake, Carriage Hills Golf and Country, Kiwanis. Author: A Cry for Help!; the City-Tomorrow; also research pamphlets, articles in profl. jours. Home: 5576 Charbar Dr Pensacola FL 32506 Office: Chief Naval Edn and Tng Naval Air Sta Pensacola FL 32508

MULLIGAN, MARIE LOWE, broadcaster; b. Parker, Colo., Mar. 13, 1925; d. Willis and Iva Mae (Brown) Lowe; ed. Bay City (Tex.) public schs., corr. courses Massey Coll.; m. James A. Mulligan, July 3, 1945; children—James A., Gregory Paul, Michael David, Patrick Joseph. With Dow Chem. Co., 1943-45; legal sec., 1945-49; sec., accountant Long Theatres, Inc., 1951-76; mgr. Sta. KIOX, Bay City, 1976—. Mem. Nat. Assn. Broadcasters, Tex. Assn. Broadcasters. Democrat. Clubs: Bus. and Profl. Women's, Eagles Aux. (past sec.). Home: 4220 Doris St Bay City TX 77414 Office: PO Box 1391 Bay City TX 77414

MULLIKEN, JOHN HALLETT, JR., news correspondent; b. Chgo., July 17, 1922; s. John Hallett and Pauline (Miller) M.; A.B., Darmouth Coll., 1944; m. Barbara Haenschen, 1947; children—Stephanie C., Cynthia P., John Hallett; m. 2d, Helen Abbott, May 4, 1968. Reporter, Life Mag., N.Y.C., 1950-52, corr., London, 1952-55, bur. chief, Bonn, W. Ger., 1956-61, corr., Washington, 1961-63, corr. Time mag., Pentagon and State Dept., Washington, 1963-75; dep. press sec., press sec. to Vice Pres. Nelson A. Rockefeller, Washington, 1975-77. Served with AUS, 1943-46. Decorated Bronze Star Medal, Silver Star. Named Man of the Year, Culver Mil. Acad., 1971. Mem. Nat. Press Club. Democrat. Clubs: The Island, F. St., Internat. Contbr. to mags. including Life, Time, Sports Illustrated, Story Mag., Washingtonian. Home: Snail's Pace PO Box 863 Hobe Sound FL 33455

MULLIN, FREDERICK WILLIAM, pharmacist; b. Dodge City, Kans., Sept. 13, 1948; s. Frederick William and Antoinette (Fesi) M.; student Nicholls State U., 1966-68; B.S. in Pharmacy, N.E. La. U., 1972. Resident in hosp. pharmacy U. Tex. Med. Br., Galveston, 1972-73, staff pharmacist, 1973, pharmacy supr., 1973—. Officer, USAR. Registered pharmacist, Tex., La. Mem. Am., Tex. (treas.), Houston-Galveston socs. hosp. pharmacists. Democrat. Roman Catholic. Contbr. research paper in field. Home: 219 N Tarpey Rd Texas City TX 77590 Office: 8th and Mechanic Sts Galveston TX 77550

MULLINAX, OTTO B., lawyer; b. Clearwater, Tex., June 28, 1912; s. Claxton Napoleon and Essie Ruth (Shelby) M.; B.A., U. Tex., 1937; LL.B., 1937; m. Ernestine Maxey, July 20, 1941; 1 son, Michael Lewis. Admitted to Tex. bar, 1937; with firm Mandell & Combs, Houston, 1938-40; sr. partner firm Mullinax, Wells, Morris and Mauzy, Dallas, 1947-71; pres. Mullinax, Wells, Mauzy & Baab Inc., Dallas, 1971-72. Dir. Capital Eye Co., 1970-72; trustee KERA-Channel 13, Dallas, 1973-75. Pres. Dallas UN Assn., 1971-72. Bd. dirs. Americans for Dem. Action, 1952-71. Served to maj. AUS, 1941-46. Fellow Am. Law-Sci. Acad.; mem. Internat. Acad. Law and Sci., Dallas Trial Lawyers Assn. (pres. 1956), Tex. Trial Lawyers Assn. (dir.). Asso. editor N.A.C.C.A. Law Jour., 1952-65. Home: 11806 Cheswick St Dallas TX 75218 Office: 8204 Elmbrook Dr Dallas TX 75247

MULLINS, CHARLES BROWN, physician, hosp. adminstrn. ofcl.; b. Rochester, Ind., July 29, 1934; s. Charles E. and Mary Ruth B. (Bamberger) M.; B.A., N. Tex. State U., 1954; M.D., U. Tex., 1958; m. Stella Churchill, Dec. 27, 1955; children—Holly, David. Intern, U. Colo. Med. Center, Denver, 1958-59; resident medicine Parkland Meml. Hosp., Dallas, 1962-64; USPHS research fellow U. Tex. Southwestern Med. Sch., Dallas, 1964-65; chief resident medicine Parkland Meml. Hosp., 1965-66; USPHS spl. research fellow cardiology br. Nat. Heart Inst., Bethesda, Md., 1967-68; practice medicine specializing in cardiology, Dallas, 1966—; mem. sr. attending staff Parkland Meml. Hosp., dir. med. affairs, 1977-79; mem. cons. staff Presbyn. Hosp., VA Hosp.; asst. prof. medicine U. Tex. Southwestern Med. Sch., Dallas, 1968-71, asso. prof., 1971-75, dir. clin. cardiology, 1971-77, prof., 1975-79, clin. prof. medicine, 1979—; clin. prof. medicine U. Tex. Health Sci. Center, Dallas, 1979—; chief exec. officer Dallas County Hosp. Dist., 1979—. Served with M.C., USAF, 1959-62. Diplomate Am. Bd. Internal Medicine. Fellow A.C.P., Am. Coll. Cardiology (Tex. gov. 1974-77, chmn. bd. govs. 1976), Am. Heart Assn. Council on Clin. Cardiology; mem. Am. Fedn. Clin. Research, Pan Am. Med. Assn., Assn. U. Cardiologists, Laennec Soc., AMA, AAUP, Alpha Omega Alpha. Contbr. articles on cardiology to med. jours. Home: 6475 Norway St Dallas TX 75230 Office: 5201 Harry Hines Blvd Dallas TX 75235

MULLINS, EDWARD WADE, JR., lawyer; b. Columbia, S.C., Jan. 17, 1936; s. Edward W. and Katherine (Clarke) M.; B.S., U. S.C., 1957, LL.B. cum laude, J.D., 1959; m. Andrea Robertson, Aug. 1968; children—Edward Wade III, Andrew Robertson. Admitted to S.C. bar, 1959; partner Nelson, Mullins, Grier & Scarborough, and predecessor firms, Columbia; mem. nat. adv. council Comml. Union Ins. Co., 1978-79. Chmn. bd. Columbia Area Mental Health Center, 1976. Served as 2d lt. USAF, 1960-61. Mem. Am., S.C., Richland (exec. com. 1970) bar assns., Fedn. Ins. Counsel (regional v.p., dir.), Def. Research Inst. (regional v.p., dir.), S.C. Def. Attys. Assn. (pres. 1973), Am. Judicature Soc., Phi Delta Phi, Kappa Alpha Order (sec. 1956), Kappa Sigma Kappa (v.p. 1957), Omicron Delta Kappa. Clubs: Richland Sertoma (pres. 1975), Tarentilla (pres. 1969), Wildewood Country (dir., v.p.), Columbia Cotillion (mem. exec. com. 1973-75), Forest Lake Country, Centurion. Home: 1413 Milford Rd Columbia SC 29206 Office: Keenan Bldg 1310 Lady St Columbia SC 29201

MULLINS, JACK SIMPSON, state ofcl.; b. Cherokee County, S.C., June 7, 1933; s. Dever Victor and Mary Elizabeth (Talley) M.; B.A., Furman U., 1954; M.A., U. S.C., 1961, Ph.D., 1963; m. Mary Eva Bruce, Aug. 14, 1959; children—Robert Bruce, Michele Ann, Michael Alan, Melissa Annette. Asst. prof. Houston Baptist Coll., 1963-64; asst. prof. U. Richmond, 1964-65; asst. editor Papers of John C. Calhoun, Columbia, S.C., 1965-67; dep. dir. State Commn. for Tech. Edn., Columbia, 1967-71; exec. dir. S.C. Commn. on Higher Edn. Facilities, Columbia, 1972-73; state personnel dir. State of S.C., Columbia, 1973—. Served with U.S. Army, 1955-57. Mem. Nat. Assn. State Personnel Execs. (sec.-treas. 1976, v.p. 1977, pres., 1978), Internat. Personnel Mgmt. Assn., Am. Soc. Personnel Adminstrs. Baptist. Editor Proceedings S.C. Hist. Assn., 1966-68. Office: 1205 Pendleton Columbia SC 29201

MULLINS, LARRY EDWARD, furniture co. exec.; b. Denver, Sept. 18, 1935; s. Hershel Edward and Josephine Ida (Maestas) M.; diploma Famous Artists Schs. (Conn.), 1957-60; student Corcoran Art Sch., Washington, 1960-61, Connecticut Ave. Sch. Art, 1961-63, Southeastern U., 1961; m. Coleen V. Holden, Dec. 29, 1977; 1 dau., Kathleen Diane. Staff, Western Electric Co., Washington, 1955-62; staff Art Designers Studios, Va., 1962; chief layout Kann's Dept. Store, Washington, 1962-64; art dir. Curtis Bros. Furniture Co., Washington, 1964-67, advt. dir., 1964-65, dir. public relations, 1965-66, asst. v.p., 1966-67; creative chief Basic Inc., Santa Barbara, Calif., 1967-69; v.p. advt., promotion and public relations Lawhon Furniture Co., Tulsa, 1969—; lectr. in field. Recipient Real Mench award Jewish Brotherhood Temple Israel, 1979. Mem. Advt. Club Tulsa, 1st Urantia Soc. Okla. (v.p. 1979—). Roman Catholic. Author: Jesus: God and Man, 1978. Home: 1602 S Gary Ave Tulsa OK 74104 Office: Lawhon Furniture Co 4530 Sheridan Ave Tulsa OK 74145

MULLINS, WILLIAM BROWNING, finance co. exec.; b. Cin., Aug. 15, 1943; s. LeCompt Browning and Mary Louise (Clark) M.; student Internat. Data Processing Inst., 1963, Internat. Accountants Soc., 1966; m. Linda Sue Duchemin, Aug. 3, 1963 (div.); children—Michelle Lynn, Monica Lee; m. 2d, Mollie Sue Powell, Oct. 9, 1976; 1 son, Maclain Talton. Computer operator Cin. and Suburban Bell Telephone Co., 1961-63; supr. data processing Robert Becht Co., Cin., 1963-64; dir. data processing Ky. Finance Co., Inc., Lexington, 1964—; tchr. future data processors Fayette County (Ky.) pub. high schs., 1966-69. Active youth work in baseball and basketball. Mem. Data Processing Mgmt. Assn., Univac Users Assn. Republican. Mem. Ch. Christ. Club: Rotary. Home: 543 Laketower Unit 129 Lexington KY 40502 Office: Kincaid Towers Lexington KY 40508

MULLON, CHRISTOPHER GRAY, advt. agy. exec.; b. Rockville Center, N.Y., Aug. 31, 1947; s. Franklin G. and Marjorie W. (White) M.; B.S., U. Fla., 1969; postgrad. Nova U., 1973-78; m. Katy Klipp, Mar. 29, 1975; 1 son, Jeremy Christopher. Account exec. Maimi (Fla.) Herald, 1970-74; v.p., gen. mgr. Jacoby & Co., Pompano Beach, Fla., 1974-79; pres. C. Gray Mullon, Inc., Pompano Beach, 1979—. Mem. Greater Ft. Lauderdale Advt. Fedn. (bd. dirs. 1976, pres. 1979), Fla. Public Relations Assn. (treas. Gold Coast chpt. 1977-79 pres. 1980—), Pompano Beach C. of C., Better Bus. Div. Broward County (bd. dirs. 1979). Democrat. Roman Catholic. Club: Rotary. Home: 808 NE 5th Ave Pompano Beach FL 33060 Office: 1800 SW 3d St Pompano Beach FL 33060

MUNCIE, DOUGLAS JENNINGS, physician; b. Bklyn., Oct. 8, 1916; s. Curtis Hamilton and Louise (Jennings) M.; student U. N.C., 1937-38; D.O., Kirksville Coll. Osteopathy and Surgery, 1942; M.D., Kansas City U., 1944; m. JoAnn Tenney, Dec. 22, 1966; children (by previous marriage)—Curtis Hamilton, Douglas Newson. Intern, Orange Meml. Hosp., Orlando, Fla., 1944; practice medicine, specializing in deafness, Miami, Fla., 1946—; founder Muncie Inst. for Hearing, Miami, 1946. Served with AUS, 1945. Recipient Optimist Club award, Lakeland, Fla., 1958. Mem. Am. Acad. Osteo. Surgeons, Am. Acad. Medicine and Surgery, Am. Osteo. Assn., Nat. Health Fedn., Miami Shores C. of C. Research and publs. on treatment of deafness. Home and Office: 150 NE 96th St Miami Shores FL 33138

MUNCY, DOROTHY KATHRYN, nurse; b. Knoxville, Tenn., July 4, 1924; d. Robert Ernest and Ethel Margaret (McDonald) Davis; diploma Knoxville Gen. Hosp., 1945; student Carson-Newman Coll., 1956-58, U. Tenn., 1968—; certificate in Acute Coronary Care, St. Mary's Hosp., Knoxville, 1977; m. Estle Pershing Muncy, Dec. 31, 1946 (div. Feb. 1980); children—Robert Hilton, Teresa Ann, Estle Pershing, Dorothy Jean, James William. Surg. nurse Oak Ridge (Tenn.) Hosp., 1946-47, Dallas Methodist Hosp., 1947-48; med. records librarian Milligan Clinic, Jefferson City, Tenn., 1965-70; head nurse med. unit Jefferson Meml. Hosp., Jefferson City, 1976—. Mem. adv. bd. Jefferson City Library, 1970-77; mem. adv. bd. Jefferson County Dept. Human Services, 1971-74; mem. Jefferson County Heart Council. Recipient Certificate of Recognition, E. Tenn. Heart Assn., 1977. Mem. Am., Tenn., Dist. 18 nurses assns., Am. Assn. Critical Care Nurses, Smokey Mountain Hist. Soc. Republican. Episcopalian. Clubs: Jefferson City Friday Luncheon. Home: 7273 Cresthill Dr Knoxville TN 37919 Office: PO Box 577 Jefferson City TN 37760

MUNDAY, STEPHEN DALE, journalist; b. Haskell, Tex., Mar. 10, 1949; s. Charles Houston Munday and Edna Mae (Rainey) Munday Moody; B.A. in English, W. Tex. State U., 1970; m. Lois Reed, Mar. 16, 1974. Farm and ranch editor Abilene (Tex.) Reporter-News, 1971-72; field editor Cattleman mag. Tex. and Southwestern Cattle Raisers Assn., Ft. Worth, 1972-74, editorial dir. Cattleman mag., 1976-78, news dir. of assn., 1978—; info. dir. Tex. Cattle Feeders Assn., Amarillo, 1974; freelance writer, Arlington, Tex., 1974-76; dir. field services Simmental Shield mag., Arlington, 1975; livestock advt. cons. to purebred cattle breeders. Served with U.S. Army, 1971. Mem. Am. Agrl. Editors Assn., Western Writers Am. Republican. Club: Press (Ft. Worth). Contbr. articles to mags. Home: 620 Haltom Rd Fort Worth TX 76117 Office: 410 E Weatherford St Fort Worth TX 76102

MUNIER, RONALD ALAN, mfg. co. exec.; b. St. Louis, Nov. 4, 1933; s. Joseph Charles and Margaret Flora (Wilde) M.; B.S., U. Miami, 1959; M.Mech. Engring., Stevens Inst. Tech., 1967, M.Mgmt. Sci., 1970; m. Mary Jane Lewis, Sept. 18, 1954; children—Jonathan Lewis, Christopher Alan, Valerie Anne. Designer, Newport News Shipbldg. & Dry Dock Co. (Va.), 1959-60; air-conditioning and refrigeration engr. York div. Borg-Warner Corp., York, Pa., 1960-63; project engr. Worthington Corp., Harrison, N.J., 1963-65, asst. chief engr., 1965-67, mgr. engring. Gamon meter div., 1967-69; v.p. engring. Gamon-Calmet Industries, Inc. subs. Studebaker-Worthington Corp., Florence, Ky., 1969-71, pres., 1971-73, also dir.; pres. NL-Shaffer div. NL Industries, Inc., Houston, 1973-78; v.p.-adminstrn. NL Petroleum Services, Houston, 1978-79, group pres. prodn. equipment, 1979—. Served with AUS, 1953-55. Registered profl. engr., Pa. Mem. Am. Mgmt. Assn., ASME, Tau Beta Pi. Patentee in field. Home: 9617 Longmont Houston TX 77063 Office: 1717 Saint James Suite 333 Houston TX 77056

MUNK, MINER NELSON, physicist; b. Napa, Calif., Nov. 17, 1934; s. Eugene Nelson and Virginia Mary (Barker) M.; A.B. with honors, U. Calif., Berkeley, 1957, M.A., 1959, Ph.D., 1967; m. Helen Suzanne McBride, Jan. 28, 1955; children—Marilyn Sue, Warren Nelson. Physicist, Aerojet Gen. Co., Sacramento, 1959-62; nuclear engr. Aerojet Nucleonics Co., San Ramon, Calif., 1962; sr. physicist Varian Assos., Walnut Creek, Calif., 1967-75; research scientist Milton Roy Co., St. Petersburg, Fla., 1975, chief scientist Lab. Data Control div., Riviera Beach, Fla., 1975—. Mem. Optical Soc. Am., Instrument Soc. Am., Assn. Advancement Med. Instrumentation, Sigma Xi. Contbr. articles to profl. jours. Patentee analytical instrumentation. Home: 4579 Square Lake Dr Lake Park FL 33404 Office: PO Box 10235 Riviera Beach FL 33404

MUNN, RICHARD EUGENE, oil co. exec.; b. Sciotoville, Ohio, Mar. 6, 1932; s. Charles Gilbert and Alma Jane (Shaffer) M.; student U. Ky., 1951, 56-58. m. Marilyn Jean Rowland, Dec. 30, 1952; children—Richard Eugene, Kathy Lynn, Charles Rowland. Lab. tech. Our Lady of Bellefonte Hosp., Russell, Ky., 1956; Cabell-Huntington (W.Va.) Hosp., 1956-57; lab. tech. Ashland (Ky.) Oil Co., 1957-68, safety supr., 1967—. Lay speaker United Meth. Ch., Ashland, 1976—, mem. Chancel Choir and soloist, 1972—; leader Boy Scouts Am., 1961-63, merit badge counselor. Cert. first aid instr., emergency med. technician, asso. safety profl. Served with USN, 1951-56. Mem. Am. Soc. Safety Engrs., Nat. Mgmt. Assn. Methodist. Home: 3224 Holt St Ashland KY 41101 Office: PO Box 391 Ashland KY 41101

MUNN, SETH WILLIAM, psychologist, ednl. adminstr.; b. Burnet County, Tex., Dec. 1, 1908; s. William Roy and Jennie Elizabeth (McDaniel) M.; student Southwestern U., 1927-28, S.W. Tex. State U., 1929, 30; B.A., U. Tex., Austin, 1935, M.A., 1937, postgrad. 1949-64; postgrad. Tulane U., 1938, U. Chgo., 1952; m. Cumi Graham Munn, Aug. 6, 1938; children—Graham William, Roy Daniel. Prin. rural schs. Burnet County, Tex., 1928-30, 32-34; tchr. Cuero (Tex.) High Sch., 1935-38; field worker Tex. Dept. Pub. Welfare, Columbus and Cuero, 1938-41, asst. area supr., then supr., 1941-45; counselor Rehab. Div., San Antonio and San Angelo, 1945-49; dir. Oaks unit Brown Schs. for Exceptional Children, Austin, 1949-51; counselor State Orphans Home, Corsicana, Tex., 1951-54; counselor Killeen (Tex.) High Sch., 1954-70, dir. guidance, 1970-76. Pvt. practice psychol. evaluation and psychotherapy, 1953—. Mem. state legis. com. to Study Handicapped, 1968-70. Bd. dirs. Bell County Mental Health/Mental Retardation Center, 1964-68. Lic. Psychologist Nat. Council Health Service Providers in Psychology. Mem. Am., Tex., Mid-Tex. (pres. 1960-71, citation Contbg. to Outstanding Chpt. in State 1972) personnel and guidance assns., Am., Tex., Bell County (clin. mem.) psychol. assns., Am., Tex. assns. marriage and family therapy, Rational Emotive Therapy Assn., N.E.A., Tex. State Tchrs. Assn., Greater Killeen C. of C. (edn. com.). Mem. Christian Ch. (bd. dirs. 1956-76). Clubs: Masons (Most Excellent High Priest 1979-80), Kiwanis (pres. 1964; chmn. vocat. guidance com. 1958-62, dist. chmn. 1962—; chmn. youth services com. 1965-73). Home: 1706 White Ave Killeen TX 76541 Office: 623 Blake St Killeen TX 76541

MUNN, YVONNE LORAINE MOGEN, hosp. adminstr.; b. Sask., Can., July 19, 1928; d. Henry Oscar and Gertrude (Lund) Mogen; came to U.S., 1956, naturalized, 1961; B.S. in Nursing, U. Alta., 1951; M.S. in Nursing, U. Calif., San Francisco, 1969; m. Roger Vincent Munn, Dec. 19, 1970. Sci. instr. Edmonton (Alta.) Gen. Hosp. Sch. of Nursing, 1951-53; ednl. dir. Sch. of Nursing, asst. dir. nursing service Medicine Hat (Alta.) Hosp., 1953-56; asst. dir. nursing service Sharp Meml. Community Hosp., San Diego, 1956-68; asst. v.p., asso. dean. Coll. of Nursing, Rush Presbyn.-St. Luke's Med. Center, Chgo., 1969-77; v.p. patient services Meth. Hosps. of Dallas, 1977—; asst. prof. U. Ill., 1970-77; asso. prof. Rush Coll. of Nursing, 1972-77. Mem. Am. Nurses Assn., Nat. League for Nursing, Am. Hosp. Assn. Soc. for Nursing Service Adminstrs. Office: Meth Hosps of Dallas 301 Colorado St Dallas TX 75208

MUNNA, RAYMOND JOSEPH, lawyer; b. New Orleans, Aug. 9, 1941; s. Leonard and Anna (Lovoi) M.; B.A. (Furuseth scholar 1959-63), U. New Orleans, 1963, M.B.A., 1979; J.D., Loyola U., New Orleans, 1969; LL.M. in Corp. Law, N.Y. U., 1971. Systems rep. IBM, New Orleans, 1964-65; systems analyst, Pan Am. Life Ins. Co., New Orleans, 1965-68, counsel, 1975—; admitted to La. bar, 1969; individual practice law, New Orleans, 1969-70; trial atty. SEC, Arlington, Va., 1971-75. Bd. dirs., sec. Am.-Italian Renaissance Found., 1978—. Mem. La. Bar Assn., Fed. Bar Assn., Am. Bar Assn., Greater New Orleans Italian Cultural Soc. Roman Catholic. Clubs: Young Men's Bus. of Greater New Orleans, Young Men's Bus. of Jefferson, Toastmasters (pres. chpt. 1169 1978). Office: 2400 Canal St New Orleans LA 70119

MUNO, RICHARD CARL, museum ofcl.; b. Arapaho, Okla., July 2, 1939; s. Randolph and Julie Josephine (Jelinek) M.; certificate comml. art Okla. State U., 1959; m. Norma Faye Simpson, Oct. 14, 1960; children—Iris Amanda, Will Randolph. Preparator, Thomas Gilcrease Inst. Am. Art, Tulsa, 1960-64; curator Nat. Cowboy Hall of Fame and Western Heritage Center, Oklahoma City, 1965-69, art dir., 1970-76, dep. dir., 1977-78, mng. dir., 1978—; sculptor Western art; lectr. art and lost wax process of casting. Trustee Nat. Acad. Western Art. Home: 6300 E Danforth Edmond OK 73034 Office: 1700 NE 63d St Oklahoma City OK 73111

MUNOZ, EDWARD, plastics mfg. co. exec.; b. Brownsville, Tex., Jan. 7, 1944; s. Cipriano R. and Consuelo H. (Hernandez) M.; A.A., Tex Southmost Coll., 1964; B.S. Chemistry, U. Tex., Austin, 1967; M.B.A., Tex. A. and I. U., 1979; m. Diane G. Gomez, June 22, 1967; children—Katherine Marie, Robert Edward, Michael Anthony, Deborah Ann. Process chemist Celanese Chem. Co., 1967-69, analytical supr., 1970; process engr. Celanese Plastics Co., Bishop Tex., 1971-73, research chemist, 1973, supr. facilities planning, 1974, tech. supt., 1975-76, ops. supt., 1977-79, tech. mgr. Celanese plastics and spltys., 1979—. Loaned exec. United Way, 1969. Mem. Am. Chem. Soc., Am. Mgmt. Assn. Patentee in field. Home: 4102 Nicklaus St Corpus Christi TX 78413 Office: PO Box 428 Bishop TX 78343

MUÑOZ DE RIVERA, ANA LUISA, counselor; b. Juana Diaz, P.R., June 28, 1949; d. Antonio J. and Ana (Bermudez) Muñoz; B.A., U. P.R., 1970; M.A., Catholic U. P.R., 1973; postgrad. Centro Caribeño Estudios, 1979—; m. Jorge A. Rivera, July 24, 1971; children—Jorge Antonio, Criselid Joanna, Fernando Jose. Social worker Dept. Edn., Santa Isabel, P.R., 1971-72; counselor Dept. Edn., Ponce, P.R., 1972-73, Juana Diaz, P.R., 1973-75; counselor Guidance Center, Cath. U. P.R., Ponce, 1975—. Fund collector Asociacion Cardiovascular del Sur, Ponce, Colegio San Ramon Juana Diaz. Mem. Am. Personnel and Guidance Assn., Univ. Counselors Assn., P.R. Personnel and Guidance Assn., Assn. Ex Alumnos Colegio San Ramon, Assn. Ex Alumnos U. P.R. Roman Catholic. Clubs: Rotary (Lady Rotarian 1968), Ponce Yacht and Fishing, Deportivo de Ponce, Juana Diaz Country. Home: 2F-20 Urb Las Flores Juana Diaz PR 00665 Office: Guidance Center Catholic U PR Ponce PR 00731

MUNOZ-DONES DE CARRASCAL, ELOISA (MRS. JOSE DANIEL CARRASCAL), physician; b. San Lorenzo, P.R., Oct. 25, 1922; d. Pedro and Maria (Dones) Munoz; B.A. cum laude, U. P.R., 1943, B.S. cum laude, 1943; M.D., Tulane U., 1948; m. Jose Daniel Carrascal, Dec. 7, 1962; children—Lilia, Maria Eloisa. Intern Arecibo Charity Dist. Hosp., 1948-49, resident, 1949-51; resident in pediatrics San Juan City Hosp., 1949-51; practice medicine specializing in pediatrics, Rio Piedras, P.R., 1951—; chief newborn service San Juan City Hosp., 1951—, pres. med. faculty, 1976-77; instr. clin. pediatrics U. P.R., Med. Center Sch. Medicine, 1951-69, asst. prof., 1969-77, asso. prof., 1977—; cons. in neonatology Tchrs. Hosp., 1976—. Recipient Bronze plaque P.R. Med. Women Assn., 1969, Silver plate, 1973; Bronze plaque distinguished med. services Pediatric Residents Assn. San Juan City Hosp., 1973; award Brazilian Acad. Humanities, 1975. NIH grantee, 1962. Diplomate Am. Bd. Pediatrics, Pan Am. Pediatric Sect. Fellow Am. Acad. Pediatrics (chpt. treas. 1964-69), A.M.A.; mem. Am. Med. Womens Assn. (chpt. pres. 1962-66), Royal Soc. Health, Pan Am. Med. Women Alliance, Dominican Pediatric Soc., Tulane Med. Alumni. Democrat. Roman Catholic. Home: C 12 Duke Esquire Tulane Rio Piedras PR 00927 Office: 400 Domenech St Rio Piedras PR 00918

MUNRO, (HARRIET) BERNICE, mathematician, former educator; b. Detroit, June 17, 1916; d. George Thomas and Viola Banghart (McCormick) Proctor; B.A., Mich. State U., 1938; M.Ed., Wayne State U., Detroit, 1961; m. Donald McAlpine Munro, Oct. 23, 1942; children—Douglas Roy, David McAlpine. Tchr. pub. schs., Detroit, Clare, Mich., 1940-63; NSF aide, instr. Applied Mgmt. Tech. Center, Wayne State U., 1960-68; tchr. Ann Arbor (Mich.) pub. schs., 1963-71, math. coordinator, 1971-78; cons. in field. Mem. Nat., Mich. (past pres.), Detroit (past pres.) councils tchrs. math., Math. Assn. Am., Nat. Council Suprs. Math., Kappa Delta, Delta Kappa Gamma, Alpha Delta Kappa. Clubs: Ann Arbor Women's City, Order Eastern Star. Editor Math Mots, 1971-78. Home: Route 7 Box 284C Franklin NC 28734

MUNS, BETTY BELL, psychotherapist; b. Dallas, Dec. 24, 1931; d. Robert S. and Katharine (Tubb) Bell; B.S. with honors, Abilene Christian U., 1953; M.Ed., Worth (Tex.) State U., 1970; m. James Nelson Muns, June 17, 1952; children—Katharine, Marla, Greg, John. Elem. sch. tchr., then spl. edn. tchr., 1954-67; supr. pre-sch. dept. Walnut Hill Ch. of Christ Sch., Dallas, 1960-70; counselor Counseling Center, Tex. Women's U., Denton, 1976-78, Walnut Hill Ch. of Christ, Dallas, 1977-78; pvt. practice psychotherapy, Dallas, 1978—; leader workshops and seminars, lectr. in field. Election judge, Collin County, 1976-79. Mem. Am. Assn. Marriage and Family Therapists, Am. Assn. Sex Educators, Counselors and Therapists, S.W. Council Hypnosis. Republican. Author mag. columns. Home: 3420 Ranchero Rd Plano TX 75074 Office: 13999 Goldmark St Dallas TX 75240

MUNS, GEORGE EHRMAN, educator; b. Chgo., June 9, 1921; s. George E. and Florence Isobel (Leedy) M.; A.B., U. Mo., 1943; postgrad. Southwestern-at-Memphis, 1947-46; M.A., U. N.C., 1951, Ph.D., 1955; m. Carolyn Louise Brantley Holland, July 8, 1944; children—George Ehrman, Richard Lee, Marilyn Ruth. Asst. supt. chartered service St. Louis Public Service Co., 1945-46; asst. prof. Ariz. State Coll., Tempe, 1951-52, Bradley U., Peoria, Ill., 1952-54, Ohio U., Athens, 1954-55; minister of music Christ Meth. Ch., Memphis, 1955-57; head dept. music Delta State Coll., Cleveland, Miss., 1957-69; chmn. dept. music Eastern Ky. U., Richmond, 1969—, also prof. music. Served with U.S. Army, 1943-45. Mem. Miss. Music Tchrs. Assn. (pres. 1963-65), Miss. Music Educators Assn. (pres. 1966-69), Ky. Assn. Coll. Music Depts. (pres. 1972-73), Music Educators Nat. Conf., Nat. Assn. Schs. Music (instl. rep.), Ky. Music Educators Assn., Phi Mu Alpha. Republican. Presbyterian. Club: Rotary. Home: Route 7 Hickory Hills Richmond KY 40475 Office: Dept Music Eastern Ky Univ Richmond KY 40475

MUNSON, DON BURNELL, entrepreneur; b. Houston, Sept. 28, 1944; s. Willard B. and Verna I. Munson; B.A., Houston Bapt. U., 1968. Computer programmer, analyst Dept. Def., Arlington, Va., 1968-73; pvt. practice acctg. and computer services, Colorado Springs, Colo., 1973-74, Houston, 1974—; acctg. services cons., Houston, 1974-75; Realtor and sports car dealer, 1975-78; mem. controller's staff Rice U., Houston, 1978—. Served with U.S. Army, 1968-70. Mem. Houston Bd. Realtors. Baptist. Home: 406 Kyle St Sugar Land TX 77478 Office: 4800 Calhoun St Houston TX 77004

MURAKAMI, MASANORI, plasma physicist; b. Ohmasu-cho, Ashiya, Hyogo, Japan, May 16, 1940; came to U.S., 1965; s. Shohei and Chiyoko Tani M.; B.S. in Elec. Engring., Nagoya (Japan) Inst. Tech., 1963; M.S. in Elec. Engring., Kyoto (Japan) U., 1965; Ph.D. in Nuclear Engring., M.I.T., 1970; m. Keiko Takechi, June 6, 1968; children—Tsuyoshi, Megumi, Hiro. Mem. sr. research staff, fusion energy div. Oak Ridge Nat. Lab., 1969—, coordinator ISX-B Tokamak expt., 1978—; U.S. del. Internat. Atomic Energy Agy. Conf., 1974, 1978. Fellow Am. Phys. Soc.; mem. Sigma Xi. Contbr. articles to profl. jours. Home: 150 Cumberland View Dr Oak Ridge TN 37830 Office: 9201-2 Oak Ridge Nat Lab PO Box Y Oak Ridge TN 37830

MURASECCO, MARIA STEFANINA (SISTER MARY ERNESTINA), guidance counselor; b. San Luca-Montefalco, Perugia, Italy, Mar. 18, 1937; came to U.S., 1964, naturalized, 1967; d. Settimio and Santina (Rambotti) M.; degree in teaching Regina Victoriae, Rome, Italy, 1958; B.A. in Social Work, Dominican Coll., New Orleans, 1972; M.A. in Counseling, Xavier U., New Orleans, 1978; postgrad. in religious edn. Loyola U., New Orleans. Joined Daus. of Divine Providence, Roman Catholic Ch., 1955; tchr. kindergarten Udine, Italy, 1959-63; tchr. elem. sch., Chalmette, La., 1966-70; social worker, Metairie, La., 1971-72; tchr. religion, Metairie, 1972-74; tchr. elem. sch., Camden, N.J., 1974-77; counselor Our Lady of Divine Providence Sch., Metairie, 1977—; cons. in social work; counselor in religion. Mem. Am. Personnel and Guidance Assn., Nat. Cath. Edn. Assn. Research in youth field. Home: 1029 N Atlanta St Metairie LA 70003 Office: 917 N Atlanta St Metairie LA 70003

MURATTI, DALIANA, univ. ofcl.; b. Mayaguez, P.R., Oct. 15, 1948; d. Santiago Muratti and Amelia Nieves; diploma secretarial sci., U. P.R., 1968, Ed.M., 1978; B.A. magna cum laude, Inter-Am. U., 1973, M.A. in Edn., 1975. Sec., Inter Am. U., Hato Rey, P.R., 1968-70, adminstrv. asst., 1970-72, dir. students activities, 1972-73, acad. counselor, 1973-77; dir. women residence hall U. P.R., Rio Piedras, 1977-78, asst. dean students, 1979—; dir. admissions P.R. Jr. Coll., Cupey, 1978-79. Recipient Merit Cert., Biol. Sci. Student Assn. of Inter-Am. U., 1976. Mem. Am. Personnel and Guidance Assn., P.R. Personnel and Guidance Assn. Home: 811 21 St SO Las Lomas Rio Piedras PR 00921 Office: Univ of Puerto Rico Rio Piedras PR 00931

MURAYAMA, TAKAYUKI, physicist; b. Tokyo, Mar. 29, 1932; s. Tokijiro and Asa (Yamauchi) M.; came to U.S., 1960, naturalized, 1970; B.S., Tokyo U. Agr. and Tech.; M.S., U. Lowell (Mass.); Ph.D., Kyushu U., 1968. From mech. engr. to sr. research physicist Chemstrand Research Center, Research Triangle Park, N.C., 1962-77; fellow Monsanto Research Center, Research Triangle Park, 1977—; adj. asso. prof. N.C. State U., Raleigh. Mem. Am. Inst. Physics, Am. Chem. Soc. Author: Dynamic Mechanical Analysis of Polymeric Material, 1978. Home: 3004 Devonshire Dr Raleigh NC 27607 Office: PO Box 12274 Research Triangle Park NC 27709

MURDICK, ROBERT GORDON, educator; b. Phila., Aug. 26, 1920; s. Philip Pierce and Mary Myrtle (Heath) M.; A.B. magna cum laude, Duke U., 1941; M.S. in Mgmt., Rensselaer Poly. Inst., 1960; Ph.D. (Ford Found. doctoral fellow), U. Fla., 1962; m. Emily B. Beckstedt, Jan. 1, 1942; children—William Maxwell, Kent Gordon. Engring. adminstr. Gen. Elec. Co., 1946-62; prof. mgmt. U. Louisville, 1962-63, SUNY, Albany, 1963-68, Fla. Atlantic U., Boca Raton, 1968—; cons. Dominican Republic, Incolda, Colombia, IBM. Served wtih USAAF, 1943-46. Recipient research grants Fla. Atlantic U.; registered profl. engr., N.Y. Mem. Acad. Mgmt., U.S. Tennis Assn. (life). Republican. Club: Laver's Racquet. Author: (with others) Sales Forecasting, 1967, The Management of Capital Expenditures, 1968; Business Research: Concepts and Practice, 1969; Mathematical Models in Marketing, 1971; (with others) Management Update, 1973, Information Systems for Modern Management, 1975, Business Policy: A Framework for Analysis, 1976, 3d edit., 1980, Introduction to Management Information Systems, 1977, Human Resources Management, 1978, Accounting Information Systems, 1978, The Management of Capital Expenditures, 1980; MIS: Concepts and Design, 1980; (with others) Managing Engineering and Research, 3d edit., 1980; editor: (with others) MIS in Action, 1975; contbr. articles to profl. jours. Patentee in field. Home: 4189 NW 4th Ave Boca Raton FL 33431 Office: Florida Atlantic Univ Boca Raton FL 33431

MURDOCH, BRUCE THOMAS, nuclear engring. physicist; b. Prague, Okla., Mar. 15, 1940; s. Thomas J. and Mary E. Murdoch; B.A. in Physics, Carleton Coll., 1962; postgrad. U. Rochester, 1962-64; M.A. in Physics, Rice U., 1966, postgrad., 1966-67; Ph.D. in Physics, Utah State U., 1975; m. Carol Ann Heggblom, June 28, 1969; children—Vanessa J., Robert W. Devel. engr. Goodyear Aerospace Corp., Litchfield Park, Ariz., 1967-70; grad. research fellow Utah State U., 1970-74; profl. asso. in physics U. Man. (Can.), Winnipeg, 1974-78; project devel. engr. Schlumberger Well Services, Houston, 1978—. Mem. Am. Phys. Soc., Phi Beta Kappa, Sigma Xi, Sigma Pi Sigma. Contbr. articles on nuclear physics to profl. jours. Home: 12607 Hunting Briar Houston TX 77099 Office: 5000 Gulf Freeway Houston TX 77023

MURDOCK, ALVIN EDWIN, counselor; b. Sand Springs, Tex., Jan. 3, 1918; married, 5 children. M.S. in Agr., Sam Houston State U., Huntsville, Tex., 1947, M.A. in Agr., 1949. Counselor, Victoria (Tex.) Ind. Sch. Dist., 1960-61, Tyler (Tex.) Ind. Sch. Dist., 1961-64, Llano (Tex.) Ind. Sch. Dist., 1964-66, Anderson County Coop., Palestine, Tex., 1966—. Scout master Boy Scouts Am., 1953-55. Mem. Tex. Small Schs. Assn., Tex. Personnel and Guidance Assn. Test cons. for Tex. Edn. Agy.; coop. coordinator for crime prevention and drug edn. Tex. Edn. Assn. Office: PO Box 428 Frankston TX 75763

MURDOCK, GORDON ROBERT, biologist, marine resources adminstr.; b. Redlands, Calif., Jan. 4, 1943; s. Glenn Evert and Doris G. (Marsh) M.; A.B., Reed Coll., 1965; Ph.D., Duke U., 1972; m. Barbara Jane Scott, Sept. 3, 1968; children—Caitlin Elizabeth, Evan Andrew. Asst. prof. zoology Ariz. State U., Tempe, 1970-75; vis. scholar U. Manchester (Eng.), 1974-75; postdoctoral fellow in biology Duke U., Durham, N.C., 1975-77; vis. faculty W. Indies Lab., Fairleigh Dickinson U., 1976; vis. asso. prof. zoology Clemson (S.C.) U., 1977-78; adj. asso. prof. biology U. N.C., Wilmington, 1979—; dir. N.C. Marine Resources Center/Ft Fisher, Kure Beach, N.C., 1978—. NSF predoctoral fellow, 1969-70; Cocos Found. postdoctoral fellow, 1974-77. Mem. AAAS, Am. Soc. Zoologists, Soc. Exptl. Biology, Nat. Marine Edn. Assn., Sigma Xi. Researcher structure and function of animals. Home: 2318 Mimosa Pl Wilmington NC 28403 Office: NC Marine Resources Center Ft Fisher Gen Delivery Kure Beach NC 28449

MURDOCK, JAMES DOUGLAS, mfg. co. exec.; b. Cleve., Aug. 25, 1942; s. Milton Edward and Mary Elizabeth (Wismar) M.; B.A. in Philosophy, Wittenberg U., Springfield, Ohio, 1964; m. Barbara Crace, June 21, 1975; children by previous marriage—Jennifer Elizabeth, Laura Jean; 1 son, James Douglas II. With Am. Can Co., 1964—, successively mktg. trainee, sales rep., Chgo., terr. sales rep., Mpls., nat. account exec., Miami, Fla., dist. sales mgr., Orlando, Fla., 1976-79, nat. accounts sales mgr., Orlando, 1979—. Bd. dirs., chmn. edn., lake environ. coms. Butler Chain Conservation Assn. Mem. The Southerners (dir.), So. Paper Trade Assn. Republican. Home: 198 Ron Den Ln PO Box 349 Windermere FL 32786 Office: 2479 Eunice Ave Orlando FL 32808

MURDOCK, LOUINE MURRAY, med. services adminstr.; b. Oklahoma City, Mar. 4, 1931; d. James M. and Lula F. (Tracy) Murray; grad. Elliott Bus. Coll., Okla., 1949, Dallas Bible Coll., 1952; m. Lyall Gordon Murdock, Jr., Aug. 1, 1952; children—Lyall Gordon III, Melissa Faye, Veda Lynn. Sec. dept. pathology U. Okla. Hosp., Oklahoma City, 1948-49; sec. to pres. Dallas Bible Coll., 1950-52; sec. to personnel dir. Am. Optical Co., Dallas, 1952-53; sec. group life div. Great S.W. Life Assurance Co., Dallas, 1953; housemother, sec. Cal Farley's Boys Ranch, Amarillo, Tex., 1953-56; Boys Haven, Beaumont, Tex., 1958-59; sec., fund raiser Boys Village, Lake Charles, La., 1956-58; tchr. Boys Harbor, La Porte, Tex., 1959-60; sec. Trinity Bapt. Ch., Dallas, 1960-61, Dale Carnegie Franchise, New Orleans, 1961-63, McNeff Industries, Dallas, 1964, Dallas Ind. Sch. Dist., 1965; substitute tchr. Mineola (Tex.) Ind. Sch. Dist., 1966; ch. sec. 1st Bapt. Ch., Mineola, 1967; recruitment supr. Baylor U. Med. Center, Dallas, 1968-70, dir. vol. services dept., 1970—; chmn. vol. services Metroplex Hosp., 1976-79; guest speaker on community orgns. at various civic and church groups, 1970—. Mem. adv. bd. Ret. Sr. Vol. Program, Dallas, 1971—; bd. dirs. Vol. Center of Dallas County, 1979—, mem. recruitment and referral com., 1979—. Mem. Am. Hosp. Assn., Tex. Hosp. Assn. (historian 1977-78, pres. 1979—), Assn. of Dirs. of Vols. (pres. 1978-79), Am. Cancer Soc., Vol. Mgmt. Edn. Coalition. Baptist. Office: 3500 Gaston Ave Dallas TX 75246

MURDOCK, ROBERT ERNEST, textile co. exec.; b. Abbeville, S.C., Dec. 8, 1948; s. James Arthur and Lillie Beryl (Burton) M.; student Forrest Coll., 1966-68; m. Martha Ann Godwin, Mar. 15, 1975. With Riegel Textile Corp., Ware Shoals, S.C., 1969-73; with Standard Textile Mills Inc., Paw Creek, N.C., 1973—, now controller; dir. M & M Fin. Corp , Paw Creek. Mem. Nat. Assn. Accts. Baptist. Home: 8537 Hammonds St Paw Creek NC 28130 Office: Standard Textile Mills Inc PO Box 67 Paw Creek NC 28130

MURFF, CLARENCE YUALPA, JR., educator; b. Ft. Worth, Mar. 26, 1918; s. Clarence Yualpa and Evalyn (Rector) M.; student Tex. Christian U., 1935-36; D.D.S., Baylor U., 1940; m. Eldred Ferguson Wells, Jan. 17, 1945; children—Bruce Wells, Joclyn Dianne. Gen. practice dentistry, Seminole, Tex., 1940-42, Ft. Worth, 1945-47; served with USNR, 1942-45; commd. lt. comdr. U.S. Navy, 1948, advanced through grades to capt., 1955; instr. U.S. Naval Dental Technicians Sch., San Diego, 1948-50, officer-in-charge, Bainbridge, Md., 1951-54, San Diego, 1956-62, ret., 1964; prof. operative dentistry and dental anatomy Baylor Coll. Dentistry, Dallas, 1964. Fellow Am. Coll. Dentists; mem. Am., Tex., Dallas County Dental Assns., Delta Sigma Delta, Omicron Kappa Upsilon (pres. 1974). Presbyn. (elder) Home: 9728 Lanshire Dr Dallas TX 75238

MURIEL, ROBERT, data processing mgr.; b. San Juan, P.R., Dec. 31, 1946; s. Aniceto and Diomedes Muriel; student Bronx Community Coll., 1964-67; m. Kay Garcia, Aug. 12, 1967; children—Andre, Kristine. Tab operator Hartford Fed. Savs.; console operator Iso, 1966-69; supr. Am. Express Co., Ft. Lauderdale, Fla., 1969-76, Ryder Trucks, Miami, Fla., 1977-78; data center mgr. M. Lowenstein & Sons, Lyman, S.C., 1978-79, project mgr., 1979, data center mgr., Rock Hill, S.C., 1979—. Office: PO Box 10232 Rock Hill SC 29730

MUROFF, LAWRENCE ROSS, physician; b. Phila., Dec. 26, 1942; s. John M. and Carolyn (Kramer) M.; A.B. cum laude, Dartmouth Coll., 1964, B.M.S., 1965; M.D. cum laude, Harvard U., 1967; m. Carol Renee Savoy, July 12, 1969; children—Michael Bruce, Julie Anne. Intern, Boston City Hosp./Harvard, 1968; resident in radiology Columbia Presbyterian Med. Center, N.Y.C., 1970-73, instr., asst. radiologist, 1973-74; dir. dept. nuclear medicine Univ. Community Hosp., Tampa, Fla., 1974—; clin. asst. prof. radiology U. South Fla., 1974-79, clin. asso. prof., 1979—. Served to lt. comdr. USPHS, 1968-70. Diplomate Am. Bd. Radiology, Am. Bd. Nuclear Medicine. Fellow Am. Coll. Nuclear Medicine (Distinguished fellow; Fla. del.), Am. Coll. Nuclear Physicians (bd. regents 1976—, pres.-elect 1978, pres. 1979); mem. Am. Assn. Acad. Chief Residents Radiology (chmn. 1973), Am. Coll. Radiology (nuclear commn.), AMA, Boylston Soc., Fla. Assn. Nuclear Physicians (pres. 1976), Fla., Hillsborough County med. assns., Radiol. Soc. N.Am., Soc. Nuclear Medicine (council 1975—), Fla., West Coast/Radiol./Socs., Phi Beta Kappa, Alpha Omega Alpha. Contbr. articles to profl. jours. Home: 10531 Homestead Dr Tampa FL 33618 Office: 13505 N 31st St Tampa FL 33612

MURPH, JOHN HAROLD, JR., constrn. mgmt. co. exec.; b. Brownwood, Tex., June 23, 1945; s. John Harold and Margaret (Hamilton) M.; B.S.M.E., U. Houston, 1968, M.B.A., 1972; m. Linda Joyce Flowers, Mar. 17, 1967; children—Mori Leigh, Marcus Hamilton, Matthew Hamilton. Engr., planning coordinator Texaco Inc., Houston, 1966-72; bus. mgr., sec./treas., v.p. CM Inc., Houston, 1972-77; pres. MNF Inc., Houston, 1977—. Registered profl. engr. Mem. ASME. Office: 2801 S Post Oak Suite 394 Houston TX 77036

MURPHEY, ARTHUR GAGE, JR., educator; b. Macon, Miss., June 16, 1927; s. Arthur Gage and Jennie Elizabeth (Crutcher) M.; student Vanderbilt U., 1947-48; A.B., U. N.C., 1951; J.D., U. Miss., 1953; postgrad. London Sch. Economics, U. London, 1953-54; LL.M., Yale U., 1962; m. Linda Chaney, May 17, 1975; children—Mason Alexander, Arthur Nesbit. Asso. law firm Satterfield, Ewing Williams and Shell, Jackson, Miss., 1953; admitted to Miss. bar, 1953, Ohio bar, 1964, Ark. bar, 1979; asst. prof. U. Ga., Athens, 1956-58; asst. prof. Emory U., Atlanta, 1958-61; asst. prof. U. Akron (Ohio), 1962-63, asso. prof., 1963-67; prof. U. Ark., Little Rock, 1967-75, asst. dean Little Rock Div. Sch. Law (now U. Ark. Little Rock Sch. Law), 1970-73, prof. law, 1975—; vis. lectr. Case Western Res. U., Cleve., 1966; vis. prof. U. Miss., 1977; mem. Ark. Com. on Reparations for Auto Accident Victims, 1968-69; mem. Juvenile Code Rev. Com. Ark., 1974-75; mem. Ark. Adv. Com. for Legal Services for the Indigent, 1970-73. Served with USAAF, 1945-47. Fulbright scholar, 1953-54; Stirling fellow, 1961-62; Ford Found. grantee, 1964. Mem. Phi Delta Phi, Beta Theta Pi, Phi Beta Kappa. Episcopalian. Club: Grande Maumelle Sailing. Faculty editor Jour. Public Law, 1958-61; faculty adv. Ga. Bar Jour., 1958-61; contbr. articles to profl. jours. Home: 1917 Old Forge Dr Little Rock AR 72207 Office: Sch Law U Ark 400 W Markham St Little Rock AR 72201

MURPHEY, R. BRITT, truck parts mfg. co. exec.; b. Elkhart, Ind., Dec. 25, 1945; s. Robert Leroy and Frances Kay (Phillips) M.; student public schs., Elkhart; m. Judy Lynne Zellmer, Apr. 12, 1969; children—Bradly Micheal, Jamie Lee. Asst. metallurgist La Bour Pump Co., Elkhart, 1964-65; fireman N.Y. Central R.R., Elkhart, 1965-68; salesman Battjes Pontiac, Elkhart, 1968-70; with Kelsey Axle & Brake div. Kelsey Hayes Co. subs. Fruehauf Corp., 1971—, regional sales mgr., Seminole, Okla., 1979—. Mem. Mobile Housing Mfrs. Assn., Recreational Vehicle Inst., Nat. Assn. Farm and Ranch Trailer Mfrs. Lutheran. Club: Elks. Office: Kelsey Axle Div 307 A St Seminole OK 74868

MURPHREE, DENNIS EUGENE, real estate developer, banker, constrn. co. exec.; b. Bryan, Tex., Dec. 10, 1946; s. Samuel Eugene and Marian Joyce (Alessandra) M.; B.A., So. Methodist U., 1969; M.B.A., U. Pa., 1971; m. Penelope Anne Mize, Dec. 27, 1969; 1 son, Patrick Eugene. Asso., Shindler Cummins Inc., Houston, 1971-72; founder, chmn., pres. Murphree Interests Inc., Houston, 1973—; founder, chmn. Brazos Mgmt. Co., Houston, 1974—; founder, co-chmn. Commonwealth Bank, Houston, 1975—, also dir.; founder, sec.-treas. Brazos Constrn. Co., 1976—; founder, chmn. Treptow, Murphree & Co., Houston, 1976—; founder, chmn. Vail Nat. Bank (Colo.), 1977—, also dir.; instr. U. St. Thomas, Houston; dir. Gene Murphree Corp., Pameo Constrn. Corp. Trustee Tex. Inst. Family Psychiatry, 1975—; bd. dirs. Childrens Fund, 1973—, March of Dimes, 1977—, F.O.L.L.O. Found., 1977—, Houston Heart Assn., 1971-74; chmn. West Houston Voters for Bentsen, 1976; mem. finance council Democratic Nat. Com., Washington, 1975-76. Served with USAF, 1969-70. Mem. Wharton Grad. Alumni Assn., River Oaks Tennis Assn (dir. 1973-77), So. Methodist U. Alumni Assn., Bldg. Owners and Mgrs. Assn., Houston Bd. Realtors, So. Methodist U. Mustang Club, Sigma Alpha Epsilon. Methodist. Clubs: River Oaks Country, Coronado, Brazos, River Oaks Breakfast, Houstonian. Home: 11030 Greenbay Houston TX 77024 Office: 2425 Fountainview Houston TX 77057

MURPHREE, JAMES WALLACE, radiologist; b. Pratt, Kans., Jan. 26, 1924; s. Charles O. and Beatrice L. (Durham) M.; M.D., U. Okla., 1947; m. Melrose Kelly, Oct. 10, 1948; children—Paula, Kathy, Jim, Melanie. Intern, St. Josephs Hosp., St. Paul, 1947-48, resident in radiology, 1948-49, Cleve. Clinic, 1951-53; practice medicine specializing in radiology, Ponca City, Okla., 1954-76, Clovis, N.Mex., 1976-77, Abilene, Tex., 1977—; mem. staff Ponca City Hosp., 1954-76, chief staff, 1963; mem. staff Hendrick Meml. Hosp., Abilene W. Tex. Med. Center, 1977—; vis. lectr. radiology U. Okla. Coll. Medicine, 1970, admissions com., 1975; dir. Pioneer Nat. Bank of Ponca City. Bd. dirs. Community Concerts Assn., 1957. Served to lt. USNR, 1949-51. Diplomate Am. Bd. Radiology, Am. Bd. Nuclear Medicine. Fellow Am. Coll. Radiology; mem. Am., Tex., Okla. med. assns., Tex. Radiol. Assn., Okla. Radiol. Soc., Radiol. Soc. N.Am., Soc. Nuclear Medicine, Am. Coll. Nuclear Medicine, Am. Coll. Nuclear Physicians. Republican. Presbyterian. Club: Rotary. Contbr. editor Jour. Okla. Med. Assn., 1967. Home: 41 W Townsend McAlester OK 74501

MURPHREE, JOHN WILSON, JR., educator; b. Waverly, Tenn., Dec. 29, 1939; s. John Wilson and Olive Pearl (Duncan) M.; B.A., David Lipscomb Coll., 1962; M.A., George Peabody Coll. for Tchrs., 1964; Ed.D. (Fellow 1970-72), Ball State U., 1975; m. Gillerene Samons, June 6, 1965; 1 son, John Gilbert. Faculty, Christina Jr. Coll., Rochester, Mich., 1962-68, No. Va. Community Coll., Annandale, 1968-70, Ball State U., Muncie, Ind., 1970-75; asst. prof. English S.Ga. Coll., Douglas, 1975—. Nat. Endowment for Humanities seminar grantee, 1978. Mem. MLA, S. Atlantic MLA, Nat. Council Tchrs. of English, Conf. on Coll. Composition and Communication, Am. Dialect Soc., Southeastern Conf. on Linguistics. Democrat. Mem. Church of Christ. Contbr. papers in field to profl. publs. Home: 1101 Karen Ln Douglas GA 31533 Office: Ga Coll Douglas GA 31533

MURPHY, BEN CARROLL, engring. co. exec.; b. Rome, Miss., Aug. 21, 1931; s. Benjamin Franklin and Effie (Lett) M.; B.S., Delta State U., 1969, M.B.A., 1974; grad. United Electronic Inst., 1972; m. Vivian Inez Hancock, Mar. 3, 1950; children—Lanny Carroll, Debra Kay Murphy Snead, Kathy M. Murphy David, Gregory Lynn, Jon Patrick. With U.S. Gypsum Co., Greenville, Miss., 1951-54, Atlantic & Pacific Tea Co., Greenville, 1954-55, U.S. Gypsum Co., Greenville, 1955-66; cost acct. Baxter Labs., Cleveland, Miss., 1966-69; project engr. mfg. U.S. Gypsum Co., Danville, Va., 1969-72; plant personnel and safety mgr. Cook Industries, Inc., Memphis, 1972-73, div. safety dir., plant personnel mgr., 1973-75, corp. compensation sr. analyst, 1976, div. indsl. relations and personnel mgr., 1975-76, corp. compensation mgr., 1976-79; div. asst. personnel mgr. Mitchell Engring. Co., Columbus, Miss., 1979—; night instr. bus. and econs. N.W. Jr. Coll., Southaven, Miss., 1975-79; cons. in compensation S.E. Memphis Mental Health Center, 1978-80. Mem. Mid-South Compensation and Benefits Assn. (dir. 1977-80, mem. organizing team 1976), Am. Compensation Soc., Miss. Mfg. Assn., Am. Mgmt. Compensation Soc. Baptist. Club: Masons. Home: PO Box 1103 Batesville MS 38606 Office: PO Drawer 911 Columbus MS 39701

MURPHY, BILLY JACK, athletic dir.; b. Lorenzo, Tex., Jan. 13, 1921; s. Ernest Columbus and Mattie Elizabeth (Fullingum) M.; B.A., Miss. State Coll., 1947; m. Elizabeth Parrish, Feb. 14, 1947; children—Michael Norwood, Elizabeth Ann. Asst. football coach Memphis State U., 1947-52, Miss. State Coll., 1952-53, U. Minn., 1954-57; head football coach Memphis State U., 1958-71, dir. athletics, 1966—; charter mem. Metro Seven Athletic Conf.. Served to lt. USMCR, 1943-45. Decorated Bronze Star; recipient Nat. In-Print award, 1963; named Nat. Football Coach of Year, 1963, Tenn. col., Ky. col.; named to Miss. State U. Hall of Fame, 1975, Tenn. Hall of Fame, 1977, Nat. Football Found. and Hall of Fame, 1976. Mem. Nat. Assn. Coll. Dirs. Athletics, Shelby County Sheriff's Assn. Methodist. Clubs: Colonial Country, Highland Hundred, Asst. Coaches. Home: 5301 Pecan Grove Memphis TN 38117 Office: FH 108 Athletic Dept Memphis State Univ Memphis TN 38152

MURPHY, CHARLES JOSEPH, ins. broker, cons. engr.; b. N.Y.C., June 17, 1921; s. Francis Joseph and Eva (Smith) M.; student Gen. Motors Inst., 1937-40; B.S., McNeese State U., 1973; m. M. Patricia Farrell, July 24, 1948; children—Kathleen, Clare, Frank, Daniel, Maureen, Michael, Thomas, Veronica, Christopher, Madeline. Cons. indsl. engr., Ill., Ark., La., 1952-72; econ. cons., Lake Charles, La., 1973—; ins. broker, Lake Charles, 1972—. Served with AUS, 1943-46; PTO. Decorated Purple Heart. Mem. La. Engring. Soc., Am. Soc. Metals, Instrument Soc. Am., Kappa Sigma. Clubs: K.C. (grand knight 1967-68, dist. dep. 1971-73), Rotary, Optomist. Home: 1306 Louisiana Ave Lake Charles LA 70601

MURPHY, CHARLES WILLOUGHBY, financial planner; b. Richmond, Va., June 22, 1944; s. Francis Patrick and Mary Reginia (Morgan) M.; B.S. magna cum laude, Va. Commonwealth U., 1973; M.B.A., U. S.C., 1977; postgrad. Coll. Fin. Planning, 1978—; m. Judith Becker Jensen, Apr. 6, 1974. Sales rep. in computer sales Burroughs Corp., 1966-70; asst. dir. U. S.C. Fin. Center, 1973-74; account exec. Merrill Lynch, Columbia, S.C., 1974-75, Bache Halsey Stuart Shields, Columbia, 1975-78; asst. office mgr. E.F. Hutton & Co., 1978—; lectr. in ins. and fin. planning Va. Commonwealth U., U. S.C. Served with U.S. Army, 1967. Recipient Scholarship award Va. Commonwealth U., 1973, Leadership award, 1973; Wall St. Jour. award, 1973; certified fin. planner. Mem. Internat. Assn. Fin. Planners, Nat. Assn. Accountants, Delta Sigma Pi (Outstanding Bus. Student 1973), Omicron Delta Epsilon. Republican. Methodist. Club: Palmetto. Research on a comparison of employee benefits in brokerage firms, 1976, on fixed income securities, 1977. Home: 107 Boulters Lock Rd Irmo SC 29063 Office: 2700 Middleburg Dr Suite 200 Columbia SC 29204

MURPHY, EMMA GRACE, assn. exec.; b. Carter County, Tenn., Oct. 29, 1917; d. William Hicks and Alice Elizabeth (Pierce) Elliott; student pub. schs., Elizabethton, Tenn.; m. Leonard Clarence Peters, 1934 (div. 1944); m. 2d, Odell Murphy, 1946 (div. 1970); children—Rebecca Lee, Leonard, Margaret Elizabeth. With Sears, Roebuck & Co., Altanta, 1946-54, dept. mgr., 1950-54; with Holiday Inns., Am., Jacksonville, Fla., 1958-71; exec. dir. Carter County (Tenn.) chpt. ARC, Elizabethton, 1971-77; speaker on health and safety, pub. schs. Founder, charter mem. Community Services Council, 1974; founder, bd. dirs. Carter County Care and Share, 1975-76; bd. dirs. Boys Club, 1975-76; charter mem., sec. Concerned Citizens Carter County; bd. dirs., founder child abuse center; active Rape Crisis Task Force. Named Outstanding Female Citizen of Carter County, 1975. Mem. Bus. and Profl. Women's Club, NOW, Council on Appalachian Women, Inc., Ladies Aux. VFW. Home: Route 2 Box 522 Elizabethton TN 37643 Office: 205 Sycamore St Elizabethton TN 37643

MURPHY, HAROLD LOYD, fed. judge; b. Haralson County, Ga., Mar. 31, 1927; s. James Loyd and Georgia Gladys (McBrayer) M.; student West Ga. Coll., 1944-45, U. Miss., 1945-46; LL.B., U. Ga., 1949; m. Jacqueline Marie Ferri, Dec. 20, 1958; children—Mark Harold, Paul Bailey. Admitted to Ga. bar, 1949; practiced law, Buchana, Ga., 1949-58; partner firm Howe and Murphy, Buchanan and Tallapoosa, Ga., 1949-71; judge Superior Cts., Tallapoosa Circuit, 1971-77, U.S. Dist. Ct., No. Dist. Ga., 1977—; asst. solicitor gen. Tallapoosa Jud. Circuit, 1956; mem. Ga. Jud. Qualifications Commn., 1977. Mem. Ga. Gen. Assembly, 1951-61. Served with USN, 1945-46. Mem. Am. Bar Assn., State Bar Ga., Tallapoosa Circuit Bar Assn., Dist. Judges Assn. Fifth Circuit, Am. Judicature Soc. Democrat. Methodist. Clubs: Lions, Masons, Gridiron Secret Soc. Office: Fed Bldg 600 E 1st St Rome GA 30161

MURPHY, JAMES JOSEPH, mfg. co. exec.; b. Phila., Aug. 1, 1929; s. John Tilden and Marion M.; student U. Pa., 1947-50; m. Betty Jane Lawson, Nov. 1, 1952; children—James Joseph, Michael John. With Honeywell, Inc., Richmond, Va., 1958—, now account exec., sales mgr. Mem. Washington Jaycees (1st v.p. 1961-62), Am. Soc. Indsl. Security (sec. 1973-74, chmn. 1974-75), Nat. Fire Protection Assn., Soc. Fire Protection Engrs., Elec. League, Va. State Crime Clinic, Va. Fire Prevention Assn., Constrn. Specifiers Inc. Republican. Lutheran. Club: Lions. Home: 511 Ironington Rd Richmond VA 23227 Office: Honeywell 1500 Forest Ave Richmond VA 23288

MURPHY, JAMES LEONARD, nursing adminstr.; b. Keokuk, Iowa, Feb. 25, 1949; s. Russell Dee and Margaret Norine (Johnson) M.; B.S. in Nursing, N.E. Mo. State U., 1971; M.A. in Nursing Adminstrn., U. Iowa, 1974; m. Patricia Ann Fridley, Aug. 22, 1970; children—Rachel, Christa. Teaching asst. U. Iowa, Iowa City, 1973-74; asst. dir. nursing Decatur (Ill.) Meml. Hosp., 1974-76; asst. prof. Tex. Woman's U., Denton, 1976-78; dir. nursing St. Joseph Hosp., Ft. Worth, 1978—; adj. asst. prof. U. Tex., Arlington, 1979. Chmn. bd. dirs. Colony Child Center, 1977-78; trustee Colony United Meth. Ch., 1978-79. Served to 1st lt. U.S. Army, 1970-73. Mem. Am. Nurses Assn., Tex. Nurses Assn., Soc. Nursing Service Adminstrs., Sigma Theta Tau. Democrat. Home: 648 Caduceus St Hurst TX 76053 Office: St Joseph Hosp 1401 S Main St Fort Worth TX 76104

MURPHY, JAMES WOODYARD, mfg. co. exec., clergyman; b. Pennsboro, W.V., May 24, 1932; s. Donald C. and Ruth (Emrick) M.; B.A., Glenville (W.Va.) State Coll., 1974; LL.D. (hon.), Clarksville Sch. Theology, 1978; m. Norma Jean Eschbacher, Jan. 17, 1954; children—Steven, Kevin, Cheryl, Robb. Tng. supr. for mgmt., employee relations dept. E.I. DuPont Corp., Parkersburg, W.Va., 1954—; ordained to ministry Baptist Ch., 1967; dir. 11 tours of Holy Land, 1967-80. Served with USN, 1951. Mem. Am. Soc. for Tng. and Devel. Home: Box 105 Davisville WV 26142 Office: EI DuPont Corp Box 1217 Parkersburg WV 26101

MURPHY, JERROLD VAUGHN, ins. co. exec.; b. Swandale, W.Va., Oct. 13, 1938; s. Colonel and Dorothy Barbara (Westfall) M.; student Glenville State Coll., 1955-58; A.B., Marshall U., 1961; postgrad. Ins. Inst. Am., 1978; m. Marilyn Kay Watkins, Sept. 1, 1958; children—Jerrold Vaughn, John Edward, JoAnna Lynne. Tchr., Clay County Schs., 1956-57, 59-60, Putnam County Bd. Edn., 1961-63; sales mgmt. Ravens Metal Products, 1963-67, 69-70; sales rep. Pitney-Bowes Co., 1967-68; field claim rep. State Farm Ins. Co., 1968-69; asst. v.p., br. mgr. Erie Ins. Exchange, Parkersburg, W.Va., 1970—. Mem. exec. com. Troop 21, Boy Scouts Am., 1977—. Mem. Nat. Assn. Life Underwriters, Jaycees (named Chmn. of Yr., Parkersburg Area chpt. 1971, senator, Jaycee of Yr. 1972). Republican. Methodist. Club: Promenaires Western Square Dance (pres. 1979-80). Home: 1215 20th St Vienna WV 26105 Office: Erie Ins Exchange 906 Grand Central Ave Vienna WV 26105

MURPHY, JOHN EDWARD, govt. agy. ofcl.; b. Lancaster, Ohio, Jan. 9, 1947; s. John Richard and Frances Louise (Bolhman) M.; B.S., Ohio U., 1971; M.A., Central Mich. U., 1976; m. Zola Marie Peters, Dec. 19, 1970; children—Kelly Louise, Carey Ann. Work/study coordinator Bloom Carroll High Sch., Carroll, Ohio, 1970-73; mgmt. analyst Def. Logistics Agy., Richmond, Va., 1973—. Served with USAF, 1969-70. Recipient award for sustained superior performance Def. Logistics Agy., 1979. Roman Catholic. Author tech. reports in field. Home: 1041 Robmont Dr Richmond VA 23235 Office: Def Performance Standards Support Office Jefferson Davis Hwy Richmond VA 23297

MURPHY, JOHN MICHAEL, mfg. co. exec.; b. Cambridge, Mass., Apr. 22, 1940; s. Joseph Edward and Alice Mary (Murphy) M.; A.B., Dartmouth Coll., 1961; M.B.A., Harvard U., 1966; m. Carol Ann Stroud, July 16, 1966; children—Brian Stroud, Erin Elizabeth. Gen. mgr. Drum Service Co. Fla., Zellwood, 1966-71, v.p., 1971-77, owner, pres., 1977—. Bd. dirs. Butler Chain Conservation Soc. Served with AUS, 1961-63. Mem. Dartmouth Club Central Fla. (pres. 1975-77), Nat. Barrel and Drum Assn. (dir. 1980—), Fla. Citrus Processors Assn. Club: Orlando Country. Home: 525 2d Ave Windermere FL 32786 Office: 803 Jones Ave Zellwood FL 32798

MURPHY, JOSEPH FRANCIS, clergyman, educator; b. Chattanooga, Dec. 1, 1910; B.A., St. John's U., Collegeville, Minn., 1932; M.A., U. Okla., 1942, Ph.D., 1961. Joined Benedictine order Roman Catholic Church, 1930, ordained priest, 1936; mem. faculty St. Gregory's Coll., Shawnee, Okla., 1936—, instr. in history and govt., 1936—, treas., 1939-42, chmn. dept. social scis., 1960-77, headmaster St. Gregory Coll. and High Sch., 1942-49, v.p., 1949-54; civilian chaplain Ft. Sill, Okla., 1941—. Recipient Archival award D.A.R., Okla., 1961, cert. of achievement, commanding gen. Ft. Sill, 1966; service award Okla. Cath. Edn. Assn., 1975; named Tchr. of Yr., St. Gregory's Coll.; Kellog Found. grantee to UCLA, 1962; Ford Found. grantee to U. Tex., Austin, 1964. Mem. Am. Cath. Hist. Soc. Democrat. Author: Tenacious Monks, 1975; contbr. articles to New Catholic Ency. Home and office: St Gregory's College 1900 MacArthur St Shawnee OK 74801

MURPHY, JOSEPH PATRICK, III, elec. engr.; b. Jackson, Miss., May 25, 1934; s. Joseph Patrick and Dorothy Elizabeth (Cooper) M.; B.S. in E.E., Ariz. State U., 1964, M.S. in E.E., 1965; m. Dolores Lynn Murphy, Aug. 1, 1957; children—Michael Patrick, Patricia Ann. Commd. 2d lt. U.S. Air Force, 1956; advanced through grades to maj., 1967; comdr. Grand Turk AAF, BWI, 1967-68; fgn. tech. div., Wright-Patterson AFB, Ohio, 1968-69; 1st Tactical Fighter Wing, Macdill AFB, Fla., 1969-74; ret., 1974; power systems engr. Westinghouse Electric Co., Tampa, Fla., 1974—. Registered profl. engr., Fla. Mem. IEEE, Tau Beta Pi, Eta Kappa Nu. Republican. Roman Catholic. Office: 8507 Adamo Dr Tampa FL 33619

MURPHY, JUDSON BOYNTON, land devel. exec.; b. Clinton, Mo., Apr. 12, 1916; s. Andrew Judson and Susie Bell (Boynton) M.; student Maryville Coll., 1934-35; m. Lois Sarah Brown, June 15, 1940; 1 son, Robert Judson. Auto salesman Davis Motor Co., Maryville, Tenn., 1936-39, partner (name changed to Murphy-West Motor Co. 1955), 1939-47, dealer, 1947-67; owner Murphy Oldsmobile, Maryville, 1967-74; prin. Murphy Motor Manors, Alcoa, Tenn., 1967-74, partner, chmn. bd., 1974—; pres. Murphy Enterprises, Inc., Alcoa, 1967—; sec.-treas. Scenic Point, Inc., 1964-78. Chmn. Blount County chpt. ARC, 1947; mem. Maryville Planning Commn., 1950; advanced gift chmn. Maryville Coll., 1977; bd. dirs. Better Bus. Bur., Knoxville, Tenn., 1973, Maryville Coll., 1978—; ordained deacon and elder United Presbyn. Ch. in U.S.A. Served with USNR, 1943-46. Named Young Man of Year Jr. C. of C., 1947. Mem. Tenn. Automobile Dealers Assn. (dir. 1955), E. Tenn. Auto Club, Blount County C. of C. (dir. 1963), Am. Legion. Clubs: Kiwanis (pres. Maryville 1947); Green Meadow Country. Home: Route 1 Scenic Point Louisville TN 37777 Office: 3163 Airport Hwy Alcoa TN 37701

MURPHY, KATHERINE CLANCY, dietitian; b. Knoxville, Tenn., Feb. 26, 1922; d. Arthur Vincent and Ilene Mary (McDaniel) Clancy; B.S., U. Tenn., 1944; m. Paul Joseph Murphy, Jr., May 10, 1947; children—Josephine, Patrick, Katherine, Mary Ann, John Arthur, Michael Lawrence, Paul Joseph. Dietetic intern St. Mary's Hosp., Rochester, Minn., 1945; dir. dietetics St. Mary's Hosp., Knoxville, 1946-47; therapeutic and teaching dietitian St. Mary's Hosp. and Sch. of Nursing, Knoxville, 1956-66; dir. dietary Eastern State Psychiat. Hosp., Knoxville, 1966-72; metabolic support nutritionist, asst. dir. dietary dept. E. Tenn. Bapt. Hosp., Knoxville, 1972—; cons. in field. Asst. leader Girl Scouts U.S.A., Knoxville, 1956-57; den mother Boy Scouts Am., Knoxville, 1958-60; conductor diabetic workshop Knox County Health Dept., 1964; dietary cons. Sweetwater (Tenn.) Hosp., 1972—. Named Tenn.'s Outstanding Dietitian, Tenn. Dietetic Assn./Southeastern Hosp. Conf., 1966. Mem. Knoxville Dist. Dietitian Assn. (pres. 1963-64), Tenn. Dietetic Assn. (pres. 1966-67), Am. Dietetic Assn., Am. Soc. Parenteral and Enteral Nutrition, Am. Soc. for Hosp. Food Service Adminstrs., Knoxville Dist. Cons. Dietitians Practice Group (chmn. 1980—). Roman Catholic. Home: 5504 Meadow Glenn Dr Knoxville TN 37919 Office: PO Box 1788 Knoxville TN 37901

MURPHY, LIZETTE LUNCEFORD, educator; b. Berry, Ala., Oct. 16, 1922; d. David Winfield and Lola B. (Jones) Lunceford; B.S., U. Ala., 1946, M.A., 1952; m. Thomas F. Murphy, Aug. 6, 1955; children—Thomas F., II, Daniel Gribbin, Lizanne Kelly, Joseph Winfield. Tchr., Ind. pub. schs., 1947-52; instr., dir. home econs. tchr. intern program U. Miami, Coral Gables, Fla., 1952-53; program dir. spl. services U.S. Army Dept. Civilians, Tokyo, 1953-55; instr. home econs., asst. dean U. Ala., 1955-56; instr. consumer edn. U. Calif., Berkeley, 1956-61; mem. faculty U. Fla., Gainesville, 1970—, asso. prof. food buying and consumer edn., 1975—; adv. bd. to edn. relations staff J.C. Penney, Inc., 1974—; cons. in field. Vol., Shands Teaching Hosp., Gainesville, 1969-70; mem. parent com. Gainesville Boys Choir, 1974. Home econs. fellow U. Ala., 1951-52; grantee Dairy Farmers, Inc., 1976-78. Mem. Am. (del. 1974), Fla. (chmn. consumer interest com. 1974-76, chmn. pub. info. com. 1977) home econs. assns., Fedn. Internat. Home Econs., Am. Council Consumer Interest, So. Home Mgmt. and Family Econs. Assn., Inst. Food Tech., U. Fla. Agrl. Women's Assn., Gamma Sigma Delta, Epsilon Sigma Phi. Republican. Presbyterian. Clubs: U. Fla. Univ. Women's (chmn. Coll. Bus. Adminstrn. sect. 1970-71), Gainesville Women's. Author articles, curriculum materials, newspaper columns. Home: 1300 NW 50th Terr Gainesville FL 32605 Office: Extension Home Econs Univ Fla Gainesville FL 32611

MURPHY, MARVIN LORRAINE, cardiologist; b. Woodston, Kans., June 2, 1930; s. Rollen E. and Esther Mae (Cook) M.; B.A., U. Kans., 1952, M.D., 1956; m. Rosanne Drake, Aug. 15, 1954; children—Julie, Ronnie, Susan, Cheryl. Intern, Indpls. Gen. Hosp., 1956-57; resident U. Kans. Hosps., Kansas City, 1957-59, U. Ark. Hosps., Little Rock, 1961-62; practice medicine specializing in cardiology, Siloam Springs, Ark., 1959-61; instr. medicine U. Ark. Sch. Medicine, Little Rock, 1963-65, asst. prof. medicine, 1965-69, asso. prof. medicine, 1969-74, prof. medicine, 1974—, dir. div. cardiology, 1977—; staff physician Little Rock VA Med. Center, 1963-65, asst. chief cardiology, 1965-69, chief cardiac catheterization lab., 1965-71, chief cardiology sect., 1969—. Active, Community Concert Assn. Diplomate Am. Bd. Internal Medicine. Fellow Am. Coll. Cardiology, A.C.P., Council Clin. Cardiology (council rep.); mem. Internat. Soc. Heart Research, So. Soc. Clin. Investigation, Ark. Heart Assn., Ark. Med. Soc., Nat. Wildlife Assn., Phi Beta Kappa, Sigma Xi, Alpha Omega Alpha, Phi Beta Pi. Methodist. Club: Univ. Home: 25 Nob View Circle Little Rock AR 72205 Office: 300 E Roosevelt Rd Little Rock AR 72206

MURPHY, MARY JULIA, guidance counselor; b. Augusta, Ga., June 29, 1944; d. Wiley Simeon and Mary Elizabeth (Dickson) Murphy; A.B., Mercer U., 1966; M.Ed., U. Ga., 1971. Tchr., Cobb County Bd. Edn., Marietta, Ga., 1966-68, Richmond County Bd. Edn., Augusta, 1968-70; part-time assc. tchr. Beaufort (S.C.) campus U. S.C., 1972—; guidance counselor Laurel Bay (S.C.) Elementary Schs., 1971—. Bd. dirs., sec. Coastal Speech and Hearing Clinic, Beaufort, Vols. for Youth, Beaufort. Mem. Am., S.C. personnel and guidance assns., Am., S.C. sch. counselor assns., Beaufort Bus. and Profl. Women's Club. Baptist. Home: 809 Mystic Dr E Beaufort SC 29902 Office: Laurel Bay Schs Laurel Bay SC 29902

MURPHY, MARY KATHLEEN CONNORS (MRS. MICHAEL C. MURPHY), ednl. adminstr., writer; b. Pueblo, Colo.; d. Joseph Charles and Eileen E. (McDermott) Connors; A.B., Loretto Heights Coll., 1960; M.Ed., Emory U., 1968; Ph.D., Ga. State U., 1980; m. Michael C. Murphy, June 6, 1959; children—Holly Ann, Emily Louise, Patricia Marie. Tchr. of English, pub. schs. of Moultrie, Ga., 1959, Sacramento, 1960, Marietta, Ga., 1960-65, Atlanta, 1966; tech. writer Ga. Dept. Edn., 1966-69; editorial asst. So. Regional Edn. Bd., Atlanta, 1969-71; dir. alumni affairs The Lovett Sch., Atlanta, 1971-75, dir. publs. and info. services, 1975-77; free lance edn. writer, 1968—; contbr. and contbg. editor numerous articles on teaching and secondary edn. to profl. publs.; columnist Marietta Daily Jour., 1963-67, The Atlanta Constn., 1963-68; cons. Ga. Postsecondary Edn. Commn., 1977. NDEA fellow, 1965-66, Adminstrn. of Aging fellow, 1977-79. Mem. Council for Advancement and Support of Edn. (publs. com.), Edn. Writers Assn., AAUW, Nat. Assn. Women Deans, Adminstrs., and Counselors, Gerontol. Soc., Nat. Assn. Ind. Schs. (publs. com.), Assn. Supervision and Curriculum Devel., Phi Delta Kappa, Kappa Delta Pi (pres.-elect chpt. 1980—). Author: College After Fifty: 26 Who Enrolled; co-author: Fitting in as a New Service Wife, 1966. Home: 2892 Castlewood Dr NW Atlanta GA 30327

MURPHY, MATTHEW EDWARD, ins. co. exec.; b. S.I., Oct. 1, 1944; s. John David and Mary Louise (McKeever) M.; B.S., St. John's U., Jamaica, N.Y., 1976; grad. spl. intensive course in Chinese, Yale U., 1965; m. Beverly Marie Auriemma, Feb. 4, 1978; 1 son, Matthew McKeever. Programming systems rep. IBM, N.Y.C., 1969-75; mgr. systems programming team Atlantic Co., Roanoke, Va., 1975—. Served with USAF, 1964-68, USNR, 1973-75, USAR Spl. Forces, 1976-79. USMCR, 1979—. N.Y. State Regents scholar, 1962. Mem. Data Processing Mgmt. Assn., Am. Mgmt. Assn., Am. Radio Relay League, VFW. Roman Catholic. Club: K.C. Home: 2738 Greggin Dr Roanoke VA 24012 Office: 1325 Electric Rd SW Roanoke VA 24028

MURPHY, MEREDITH KATHLEEN, govt. ofcl.; b. Oak Park, Ill., Nov. 23, 1948; d. Frank Desmond and Ruth Marie (McNally) M.; B.A., Duke U., 1970; M.S.A., George Washington U., 1977. Procurement intern U.S. Army Aviation Systems Command, St. Louis, 1970-71; contract specialist U.S. Army Mobility Equipment Command, St. Louis, 1971-72; contract adminstr., Defense Contract Adminstrv. Services Office, Collins Radio, Dallas, 1972-73, E-Systems, Greenville, Tex., 1973-75; price analyst, procurement analyst U.S. Army Mobility Equipment Research Devel. Command, Ft. Belvoir, Va., 1975-78; procurement analyst Fed. Acquisition Regulation Project Office, Rosslyn, Va., 1978—. Mem. Nat. Contract Mgmt. Assn., Am. Def. Preparedness Assn, Kappa Alpha Theta.

Home: 429 Hampton Ct Falls Church VA 22046 Office: 1815 N Lynn St Rosslyn VA 22209

MURPHY, MICHAEL DENNIS, boarding kennel owner; b. Princeton, N.J., July 13, 1947; s. William Harold and Shirley Bell (Rodgers) M.; student pvt. schs., N.J. and Fla. Real estate mgr. Wenonah Corp., Palm Beach, Fla., 1963-68, 71-74; show dog breeder (Lhasa Apso's), Palm Beach County, Fla., 1971-74; owner Wenonah Kennels, Stuart, Fla., 1974—. Bd. dirs. Animal Rescue League of Martin County (Fla.), 1978—; mem. Animal Birth Control of Martin County, 1976—. Served with USN, 1968-71. Mem. Am. Boarding Kennel Assn. Republican. Roman Catholic. Club: Stuart-Ft. Pierce Kennel. Address: 4976 SW Leighton Farm Ave Stuart FL 33494

MURPHY, MICHAEL GORDON, banker; b. Dallas, Jan. 26, 1939; s. Elbert Gordon and Mary Emma (Ford) M.; B.B.A., So. Meth. U., 1960; J.D., U. Tex., Austin, 1963; m. Charlotte Head, Aug. 31, 1965; children—Shannon, Marshall. Admitted to Tex. bar, 1963; atty. Tenneco, Inc., 1964-66, Tex. Eastern, 1966-70; individual practice law, Houston, 1970-73; pres., chief exec. officer Chem. Bank, Houston, 1973—. Mem. Pres.'s Assn. Am. Mgmt. Assn. Methodist. Office: PO Box 66549 Houston TX 77006

MURPHY, MICHAEL PURDON, cons. engr.; b. Gainesville, Fla., Oct. 8, 1950; s. David Purdon and Ella Maude (Jones) M.; student Clemson U., 1968-70; B.S. in Civil Engring., U. Fla., 1972, M.Engring., 1975. Project engr. William Bishop Engrs., 1972-73, charge West Palm Beach (Fla.) office, 1977-78, co-dir. engring., Tallahassee, 1978—. Registered profl. engr., Fla. Mem. Nat. Soc. Profl. Engrs., Fla. Engring. Soc., ASCE, Water Pollution Control Fedn. Democrat. Episcopalian. Contbr. to profl. publs. Home: 410 Victory Garden Tallahassee FL 32301 Office: PO Box 3407 Tallahassee FL 32303

MURPHY, RAYMOND JOSEPH, JR., engr.; b. Bexar County, Tex., Oct. 11, 1938; s. Raymond Joseph and Betty (Godwin) M.; A.Sc., San Antonio Coll., 1963; B.E.E., U. Tex., Arlington, 1971; m. Mary Noah, Nov. 25, 1963; children—Kathryn, Karen, Kristin. Instrument technician City Pub. Service Bd., San Antonio, 1963-66; systems design engr. Forney Engring. Co., Addison, Tex., 1966-70, sr. systems design engr., 1970-72, supr. elec. engring. and final systems depts., 1972-75, dept. mgr., 1975-80, v.p. power and process div., 1980—. Served with USN, 1959-63. Mem. Instrument Soc. Am. (award 1972). Republican. Lutheran. Club: Chess (Forney). Patentee burner control system. Home: 3200 Gail Ct Irving TX 75060 Office: 3405 Wiley Post Rd Addison TX 75001

MURPHY, TERRY ALAN, mortgage banker; b. Ft. Wayne, Ind., Oct. 16, 1941; s. Benjamin Franklin and Esther Joanetta (Braun) M.; B.A., Ind. U., 1964; M.A. in Bus. Adminstrn., Ball State U., 1979; m. Kathleen Diane Armstrong, June 13, 1964; children—Todd Alan, Ryan Kirke. Asst. regional mgr. mortgage loans Lincoln Nat. Life Ins. Co., Co., Ft. Wayne, Ind., 1964-68; asst. mgr. mortgage loans Pan-Am. Life Ins. Co., New Orleans, 1969-72; pres., partner Mortgage Corp. Am., North Miami Beach, Fla., 1972—. Mem. Christian Businessmen's Com., S. Fla. Christian Bus. Men; cert. trainer Evangelism Explosion Internat., also mem. com. of 100; past pres. Young Men's Activities Com. New Orleans. Lic. real estate salesman, Fla. Mem. Mortgage Bankers Assn., Internat. Council Shopping Centers (registered mortgage solicitor). Republican. Home: 2100 Middle River Dr Fort Lauderdale FL 33305 Office: 17071 W Dixie Hwy North Miami Beach FL 33160

MURPHY, THOMAS B., state legislator; b. Bremen, Ga., Mar. 10, 1924; s. W. H. and Leita (Jones) M.; grad. N. Ga. Coll., 1943; LL.B., U. Ga., 1949; m. Agnes Bennett, July 22, 1946; children—Michael L., Martha L., Marjorie Lynn, Mary Jane. Admitted to Ga. bar; partner firm Murphy & Witcher, since 19—; mem. Ga. Ho. of Reps., 1961—, adminstrv. floor leader, 1969-70, speaker pro-tem, 1971-74, speaker, 1973—. Served with USNR, World War II. Mem. Ga. Bar Assn., Am. Legion, VFW, Gridiron Soc.; hon. mem. Ga. Peach Officers Assn., Ga. Frat. Order Police, Ga. Sheriffs Assn. Democrat. Baptist. Club: Moose. Home: PO Box 163 Bremen GA 30110 Office: Room 332 State Capitol Atlanta GA 30334

MURPHY, THOMAS DAVIDSON, JR., ins. exec.; b. Cordell, Okla., Mar. 20, 1920; s. Thomas Davidson and Anna Christine (Murphy) M.; A.B., Austin Coll., 1941; m. Dorothy Lee Kimes, Nov. 7, 1941 (dec. Aug., 1962); children—Bonnie Bowers Hines, Thomas Davidson, Julie Murphy Booth, Lawrence Deane, Paula Bowers Landry, Catherine Ann; m. 2d, Rubye Prokish Bowers, Dec. 5, 1964. Vice chmn. bd. Murphy & Rochester, Inc., real estate, 1951—; dir. Ector Shopping Center Inc., 1958—; co-chmn. bd. Colonial Food Stores, San Angelo, Tex., 1968—; vice chmn. bd. 1st Nat. Bank, Olney, 1966—; pres. Kimur, Inc. real estate rental, 1955—; owner, prin. Thomas D. Murphy, Jr. Ins. Agy., Odessa, 1975—. Chmn. adv. bd. Salvation Army Odessa, 1966; chmn. bd. James G. Matthews Scholarship Trust, 1973—. Served to lt. (j.g.) USCGR, 1943-45; ETO. Mem. Ins. Counselors Assn. Tex. (sec. 1974-75), Odessa Assn. Ins. Agts. (pres. 1955-56), Austin Coll. Alumni Assn. (pres. 1956-58). Clubs: Masons (33 deg.), K.T., Shriners, Odessa Country. Home and Office: 1712 W Crescent Dr Odessa TX 79761

MURPHY, WILLIAM HINTZ, hosp. adminstr.; b. Oak Ridge, Tenn., May 16, 1945; s. Jack Tullus and Virginia (Hintz) M.; B.A., U. Minn., 1968; M.Internat. Mgmt., Am. Grad. Sch. Internat. Mgmt., 1971; M.H.A., George Washington U., 1978; married. With bond dept. Northwestern Nat. Bank of Mpls., 1968-70; loan officer Export-Import Bank of U.S., Washington, 1972-74; asst. v.p. Internat. Dept., Rep. Nat. Bank of Dallas, 1974-76; adminstr. Coryell Meml. Hosp., Gatesville, Tex., 1978—. Mem. Gatesville Civic Theatre, 1979. Recipient Dept. Health Care Adminstrn. award George Washington U., 1977. Mem. Am. Hosp. Assn., Tex. Hosp. Assn. Episcopalian. Club: Lions. Contbr. articles to profl. jours. Office: 1507 W Main St Gatesville TX 76528

MURR, GWENDOLYN ROCHELLE COOK, nurse; b. Roanoke, Ala., Nov. 14, 1935; d. Holly Bishop and Dorothea Pearl (Weathers) Cook; diploma in nursing Carraway Meth. Hosp., Birmingham, Ala., 1956; student So. Union State Jr. Coll., Wadley, Ala., 1965-79, Auburn U., 1979; m. Jim Murr, Dec. 17, 1956; children—Doreen, James Holly, John Benjamin. Staff nurse Carraway Meth. Hosp., Birmingham, Ala., 1956-59; staff nurse, 3-11 supr. Randolph County Hosp., Roanoke, Ala., 1960-62, dir. nursing services, 1967—; staff nurse Randolph County Health Dept., Wedowee, Ala., 1962-67. Instr. first aid, home nursing ARC; merit badge counselor Boy Scouts Am.; mem. adv. com. for spl. edn. Roanoke City Schs.; mem. Roanoke City Schs. Edn. Study Task Force. Registered nurse, Ala. Mem. Am. Nurses Assn., Nat. League Nursing, Ala. State Nurses Assn., Ala. League Nursing, Ala. Soc. Nursing Service Adminstrn. Methodist. Home: Route 4 Box 153 Roanoke AL 36274 Office: Randolph County Hosp 1000 Wadley Hwy Roanoke AL 36274

MURRAH, WILLIAM FITZHUGH, III, ophthalmologist; b. Memphis, Jan. 14, 1945; s. William Fitzhugh and Esther (Gavin) M.; B.A., Southwestern U., Memphis, 1967; M.D., U. Tenn., Memphis, 1970; m. Ann Dickey, Mar. 21, 1970. Rotating intern Meth. Hosp., Memphis, 1971; ophthalmology resident U. Tenn., Memphis, 1974-77; fellow phacoemulsification and intraocular lenses James H. Little, M.D., Oklahoma City, 1977-78; practice medicine specializing in ophthalmology Murrah Eye Clinic, Fairhope, Ala., 1978—. Served with USPHS, 1971-74. Diplomate Am. Bd. Ophthalmology. Mem. Am. Assn. Ophthalmology, Am. Acad. Ophthalmology, Am. Intraocular Implant Soc., AMA, Med. Assn. State Ala., Baldwin County Med. Soc. Roman Catholic. Club: Lions. Home: 710 S Mobile St Fairhope AL 36532 Office: 150 S Ingleside Fairhope AL 36532

MURRAY, DERRICK DUANE, data processing service bur. exec.; b. Oakland, Calif., Sept. 1, 1947; s. Lloyd Pershing and Elma Gertrude (Derrick) M.; B.A. in Math., East Central U., 1972; m. Linda Kay Durham, Aug. 30, 1969; children—Sean, Zac, Scott. Computer operator Computer Utility Corp., Ada, Okla., 1972-73, ops. mgr., 1973-74, v.p., controller, 1974-75, owner, 1975—; founder, pres. Ada Siding Inc. Pres., Ada Softball Assn., 1976-77; precinct chmn. Pontotoc County Democratic Central Com., 1977-78. Served with U.S. Army, 1969-70. Mem. S.E. Okla. Devel. Assn., Ada C. of C. (dir.), Okla. Amateur Softball Assn. (Commr. of Year 1978). Democrat. Methodist. Clubs: Oak Hills Golf and Country, Kiwanis (treas. 1974-76, pres. 1977). Home: 2423 Timber Terr Ada OK 74820 Office: Box 608 Ada OK 74820

MURRAY, ELIZABETH DAVIS REID, writer, lectr.; b. Wadesboro, N.C., June 10, 1925; d. James Matheson and Mary Kennedy (Little) Davis; A.B. cum laude, Meredith Coll., Raleigh, N.C., 1946; postgrad. N.C. State U., 1957-58, 74-75; m. James William Reid, Feb. 7, 1948 (dec. June 1972); children—Michael Ernest, Nancy Kennedy, James William; m. 2d, Raymond L. Murray, May 12, 1979; stepchildren—Stephen, Ilah Garton, Marshall. Continuity writer Sta. WPTF, Raleigh, 1946-47; program mgr., women's commentator Sta. WADE, Wadesboro, 1947-48; dir. news bur. Meredith Coll., 1948-51; state woman's news editor, columnist Raleigh News and Observer, 1951-52; exec. sec. Gov.'s Coordinating Com. on Aging, 1959-61; research asst. to Dr. Clarence Poe, Raleigh, 1963-64; contbg. editor Raleigh Mag., 1969-72; local history corr. Raleigh Times and News and Observer, Spectator of Raleigh; lectr. art and local history; research cons. Wake County Pub. Libraries, Mordecai Historic Park, State Visitor Center, Exec. Mansion; resource person Wake Public Schs.; dir. Capital County Pub. Co.; writer; books include: From Raleigh's Past (certificate of commendation Am. Assn. State and Local History), 1965; editor, compiler: North Carolina's Older Population: Opportunities and Challenges, 1960; editor, contbr. Wake County Hist. Soc. newsletter, 1965-69; History of Raleigh Fire Dept., 1970; guest editor Raleigh Mag. Wake County Bicentennial Issue, 1971; author, photographer filmstrip for Wake Pub. Schs., 1971; author sect. Windows of the Way, 1964; Am. arts slide lectures for pub. library; author instructional materials State Exec. Mansion and Mordecai Hist. Park docents; author monthly history page Raleigh Mag., 1969-72; contbr. to newspapers and mags. Mem. Raleigh City Council, 1973; pres. Jr. Woman's Club, 1956-57; organizing pres. Arts Council Raleigh, 1965; exec. com. N.C. Humanities Found., 1974-76; dir., officer North Carolinians for Better Libraries, 1965-69; mem. Meredith Bd. Assos., 1976-79; trustee Pub. Libraries, 1956-67, Meredith Coll., 1966-69; pres. Wake Meml. Hosp. Aux., 1962-63; mem. Raleigh Hist. Sites Commn., 1969-73; trustee Pullen Meml. Bapt. Ch., 1975-78, chmn., 1977-78, also deacon; chmn. Mayor's Com. to Preserve Hist. Objects, 1965—; mem. Tryon Palace Commn., 1967-78; adv. council WUNC-FM, 1976—, N.C. Art Soc.; vis. lectr. N.C. Mus. History Assos., 1980; docent, lectr. State Capitol, Exec. Mansion, Mordecai Hist. Park, N.C. Mus. Art; bd. dirs. Raleigh-Wake County Symphony Orch. Devel. Assn., 1979—, Estey Hall Found., 1980—, Friends of Meredith Library, 1980—. Recipient Outstanding Community Service award, 1952, best all-round Jr. Woman's Club mem., 1955, Distinguished Alumna award Meredith Coll., 1970, recognition for service award Raleigh Hist. Sites Commn., 1973, Raleigh City Council, 1973. Mem. N.C. Soc. County and Local Historians (life), N.C. Lit. and Hist. Assn., N.C. Art Soc. (Disting. Service citation 1979), Docents N.C. Mus. Art (pres. 1980-81), Friends of N.C. State U. Library, Friends of Carlyle Campbell Library (charter, life), Kappa Nu Sigma. Democrat. Clubs: Carolina Country, Capital City (charter mem.). Home: 108 Lord Ashley Rd Raleigh NC 27610

MURRAY, ERNEST DON, educator; b. Asheville, N.C., Apr. 21, 1930; s. Ernest Burgin and Daisy Anne (Bishop) M.; B.F.A., U. Tenn., 1952; student Art Students League, N.Y.C., 1952-54; M.F.A., U. Fla., Gainesville, 1957, M.Ed., 1958; m. Catherine Ann Fields, Dec. 11, 1978. Prof., head dept. fine arts Chipola Jr. Coll., Marianna, Fla., 1958-68, chmn. div. humanities and fine arts, 1964-68; prof. humanities U. Fla., 1968-79, asso. chmn. dept., 1974-77, prof. fine arts, 1979—; textbook cons. to publishers, 1965—; painter and sculptor, 1950—; one-man and group exhbns., 1951—; represented in public and pvt. collections. Served with C.E., U.S. Army, 1954-56. Named Tchr. of Year, Chipola Jr. Coll., 1968. Mem. AAUP, Fla. Artists Group, So. Highlands Craftsmen's Guild, Phi Beta Kappa, Phi Theta Kappa, Phi Kappa Phi, Omicron Delta Kappa. Unitarian. Home: 1854 NW 41st Ave Gainesville FL 32605 Office: 209 Fine Arts Bldg U Fla Gainesville FL 32611

MURRAY, GEORGE EDWARD, physician, lawyer; b. Bklyn., Sept. 4, 1917; s. Joseph Francis and Mary (Hanley) M.; student Notre Dame U., 1936-38, Georgetown U., 1938-40; M.D., L.I. Coll. of Medicine, 1943; J.D., U. Tenn., 1964; m. Rosaura Esteva, June 27, 1941; 1 son, Michael Joseph. Intern, Nassau Hosp., Mineola, N.Y., 1944; resident in urology L.I. Coll. Hosp., Bklyn., 1944-46; practice medicine specializing in urology, Bklyn., 1948, P.R., 1948-50, 51-53, Oak Ridge, 1954-55, Knoxville, Tenn., 1955—; admitted to Tenn. bar, 1964; individual practice law, Knoxville, 1964—. Served with M.C., USN, 1946-48, with M.C., U.S. Army, 1950-54. Mem. Knoxville Bar Assn., Tenn. Trial Lawyers Assn., Tenn. Urol. Assn. Roman Catholic. Clubs: Elk, K.C. Contbr. articles to med. jours. Home: 112 Killarney Rd Knoxville TN 37919 Office: 5612 Kingston Pike Knoxville TN 37923

MURRAY, HELEN HOLLOWAY, state tng. supr.; b. Monroe, N.C., Nov. 5, 1945; d. Claude Robert, Jr., and Rose (Purdy) H.; B.A. in Psychology, Winthrop Coll., Rock Hill, S.C., 1967; postgrad. in counseling U. S.C., Columbia, 1970-72; m. Emery Graham Murray, July 21, 1979. Tchr., Morningside Elementary Sch., Charleston, S.C., 1967-70, Wallace Primary Sch., S.C., 1970-71; employment counselor, office supr. S.C. Employment Security Commn., Kingstree, 1971-73, job bank supr., Florence, 1973-74, state tng. supr., Columbia, 1974—; mem. S.C. Employees Grievance Com. Mem. adv. council Ednl. Resources Found. Cert. instr. ARC; vol. Contact Help. Gen. Elec. Found. Guidance fellow, 1972; recipient state award for student research S.C. Psychol. Assn., 1966. Mem. Am., Carolina socs. tng. and devel., Internat. Assn. Personnel in Employment Security (exec. bd. S.C. chpt.), S.C. State Employees Assn. Club: Columbia Altrusa (corr. sec. 1977-79, 2d v.p. 1979-80, pres. 1980—). Home: Route 4 Box 158 Chapin SC 29036 Office: 1550 Gadsden St PO Box 995 Columbia SC 29202

MURRAY, JAMES LEE, physician; b. Indpls., Jan. 27, 1946; s. James L. and Marjorie A. (Geupel) M.; B.A., Colo. Coll., 1968; M.D., U. Ind., 1972; m. Georgia Anne Thomas, June 17, 1978. Rotating intern St. Joseph's Hosp., Denver, 1972-73; resident internal medicine U. Ind., Indpls., 1973-75; hematology and oncology fellow Ohio State U., 1975-78; practice medicine specializing in internal medicine, Columbus, Ohio, 1975-78, Oklahoma City, 1978—; asst. mem. Okla. Med. Research Found., 1978—; asst. prof. medicine U. Okla. Health Scis. Center, Oklahoma City, 1978—; mem. staff Univ., Presbyn., VA hosps. Am. Cancer Soc. research grantee, 1976-78. Diplomate Am. Bd. Internal Medicine. Mem. Okla. County Med. Soc., AMA, Delta Epsilon. Contbr. articles on hematology to med. jours. Home: 1604 Ridgecrest Edmond OK 73034 Office: 825 NE 13th St Oklahoma City OK 73104

MURRAY, LANE (JOYCE ELAINE STONE) (MRS. THOMAS FRANCIS MURRAY), educator; b. Celina, Tex., Nov. 6, 1921; d. Esibbious Jefferson and Elise (Porter) Stone; B.A., Tex. Tech. Coll. 1942; M.Ed., Sam Houston State Tchrs. Coll., 1952; Ed.D., U. Houston, 1962; m. Dr. Thomas Francis Murray, Dec. 16, 1941; children—Stone Thomas, Joyce Elaine, Mark Vincent. Secondary sch. English and and Spanish tchr., Barstow, Tex., 1942-43; job analyst U.S. Govt., Rome, N.Y., 1944-47; journalism and English tchr. secondary schs., Huntsville, Tex., 1954-58; exec. v.p. Essential Edn., Huntsville, 1957—; also asst. prof. edn., coordinator student teaching, Tex. A. and M. U., College Station, 1960-69, dir. instructional media lab., 1968-69; supt. schs. Windham Sch. Dist., Tex. Dept. Corrections, 1969-79, dir. edn., 1979—; mem. Nat. Adv. Council on Adult Edn., 1976-79; chmn. adv. council to adult performance level porject U. Tex. at Austin, 1976—. Dir. Guidiance Filmstrips (Houston). Dep. county clk. Walker County, Tex., 1952-54. Recipient blue ribbon award Am. Film Festival, 1962, red ribbon award, 1972. Mem. Am. Assn. Sch. Adminstrs., NEA, Am. Correctional Assn. (bd. govs.), Correctional Edn. Assn. (past pres.), D.A.R., Kappa Delta Pi. Roman Catholic. Author: Preparation of Manuscripts for Reproduction by Diazo, 1962; The Development of a Secondary-Level Student Teaching Handbook for the University of Houston, 1962. Author filmstrip series: (with Dr. Thomas Murray) The Student Council in Action, 1957; Getting Ready for College, 1957; Getting Ready for High School, 1958; The Physical Education Series, 1960; The Library Series, 1959; The Group Guidance Series, 1961. Documentary (with Dr. Thomas Murray) 16 mm film, color, sound Tattoo My Soul; Make Straight My Mind, 1971. Home: PO Box 1575 Huntsville TX 77340 Office: Windham School Dist Texas Dept Corrections Box 99 Huntsville TX 77340

MURRAY, LOWELL LEWIS, city ofcl.; b. Oneida, Ky., May 9, 1942; s. Gordon and Florence K. (Lewis) M.; B.A. in Physics, Berea Coll., 1964; m. Peggy Sue Baird, Sept. 5, 1965; children—Melissa, Margaret. Owner, Murray Electric, Berea, Ky., 1964-68; mem. Berea Fire Dept., 1968—, fire chief, chief elec. insp., 1972-80; codes enforcement officer City of Berea, 1980—; dir. civil def. City of Berea, 1972—; instr. Eastern Ky. U. Mem. Internat. Assn. Fire Chiefs, Internat. Assn. Elec. Insps., Nat. Fire Protection Assn. (charter mem. fire service sect.), Central Ky. Firemen's Assn. (v.p. 1976-77). Democrat. Mem. Ch. of Christ. Clubs: Kiwanis. Masons. Home: Box 434 Route 5 Berea KY 40403 Office: City of Berea Box 8 Berea KY 40403

MURRAY, MAL CHARLES, broadcast syndication co. exec.; b. White Plains, N.Y., June 12, 1934; s. Malachy T. and Juliette (Smith) M.; B.S., Lehigh U., 1956; children—Mal Charles, Christine, Patricia, Michele, Geraldine. Vice pres. Batten, Barton, Durstine & Osborn, N.Y.C. and Atlanta, 1960-76; dir. mktg. WB Tanner Co., Memphis, 1976-77; v.p. Vitt Media Co., Atlanta, 1977-78; sr. v.p. MCA, Atlanta, 1978—; lectr. mktg. Ga. State Coll., Massey Jr. Coll. Mem. Atlanta Broadcast Execs. (past pres., dir.), Atlanta Media Planners (pres.), Southeastern Lehigh Alumni Club (pres.). Roman Catholic. Clubs: N.Y. Athletic, Westchester Country; West Paces Ferry Racket, Chatahoochee Plantation. Contbg. editor So. Advt. and Mktg., 1977-78. Home: 200 26th St Atlanta GA 30309 Office: 1800 Peachtree Rd Atlanta GA 30309

MURRAY, NEVILLE, psychiatrist; b. Dundee, Scotland, Jan. 31, 1923; s. Samuel and Frances (Rothfield) M.; came to U.S., 1951, naturalized, 1954; M.D., U. St. Andrews, Scotland, 1945; m. Betty Lee Fatheree, Feb. 13, 1954; children—Melissa, Dundee. Intern St. Bartholomew's Hosp., Rochester, Eng., 1945-46; postgrad. tng. psychiatry, London and Scotland, 1946-50; tchr. U. Tex. Med. Sch. at Galveston, 1951-54; practice medicine specializing in psychiatry, San Antonio, 1956—; asso. prof. U. Tex. Med. Sch. at San Antonio, 1968-77; cons. USAF Hosp., Wilford Hall, Social Security Adminstrn.-HEW; dir. psychodrama Moreno Inst., 1960. Pres. San Antonio Little Theatre, 1970-72. Served to capt. M.C., USAF, 1954-56. Diplomate Am. Bd. Psychiatry and Neurology. Fellow Am. Psychiat. Assn.; mem. A.M.A., Brit. Med. Assn., Titus Harris Assn. Democrat. Club: Argyle. Contbr. articles to profl. jours. Home: 1402 700 E Hildebrand San Antonio TX 78212 Office: Suite C 2727 Babcock Rd San Antonio TX 78229

MURRAY, RICHARD GEORGE, educator; b. Omaha, Jan. 24, 1934; s. George Roy and Margaret Leona (Ormsby) M.; B.S., So. Meth. U., 1959; M.S., U. Mo. at Rolla, 1962; Ph.D. (Pan Am. Petroleum fellow), Okla. State U., 1970; m. Nancy Lou Rhoads, Aug. 3, 1957; children—Justin Roy, George Edwin. Co-op engr. Convair Aircraft, Fort Worth, 1955-59; asst. prof. mech. engring. U. Mo. at Rolla, 1959-64; asst. prof. Western Mich. U., Kalamazoo, 1964-65; adviser mech. engring. edn. Tech. Coll., Ibadan, Nigeria, 1965-68; asso. prof., mech. power tech. Okla. State U. at Stillwater, 1970—. Pres. Murray Devel. Co., Camdenton, Mo., 1959—; cons. mech. equipment, engine and aircraft failure, legal firms and ins. cos. Served with AUS, 1953-55; Korea. NSF scholar, summer 1969; NASA-Am. Soc. Engring. Edn. fellow, summer 1973, 74, 75. Registered profl. engr., Okla. Mem. Soc. Automotive Engrs. (vice chmn. edn. 1973), Am. Soc. Engring. Edn., ASME, Sigma Xi, Kappa Mu Epsilon, Pi Tau Sigma. Author: Instructors Guide-Course in Applied Heat for 2d Year Mechanical and Electrical Students, 1968; A Student Text in Small Engines Laboratory, 1968. Contbr. articles to profl. jours. Patentee hydrogen fueled engine. Home: PO Box 398 Perkins OK 74059 Office: Sch Technology Oklahoma State U Stillwater OK 74074

MURRAY, ROBERT CROCKER, instnl. adminstr.; b. Wakefield, Mass., Jan. 9, 1939; s. Donald Mason and Natalie (Rowe) M.; B.A. in Sociology, U. N.C., 1950; M.Ed. in Public Sch. Adminstrn., S.W. Tex. State U., 1966; m. Eloise Cowles, Aug. 11, 1962; children—Sarah, David. Tchr., Judson Ind. Sch. Dist., San Antonio, 1963-66, prin. elem. sch., 1966-72; exec. dir. Boysville, Inc., San Antonio, 1972-73; v.p. Tiffany Stone & Brick Co., San Antonio, 1973-76; exec. dir. Mission Road Developmental Center, San Antonio, 1976—. Vice pres. San Antonio Urban Council, 1977, pres. bd., 1978, 79; bd. dirs. Christian Assistance Ministry, 1977—, Youth Alternatives, 1977—; ruling elder, past chmn. bd. deacons First Presbyterian Ch., San Antonio. Served with U.S. Army, 1960-62. Mem. Am. Assn. Mental Deficiency, Council for Exceptional Children, Nat. Assn. for Retarded Citizens, Nat. Assn. Pvt. Residental Facilities for Mentally Retarded. Republican. Club: Kiwanis (San Antonio). Home: 1032 Garraty Rd San Antonio TX 78209 Office: PO Box 14038 San Antonio TX 78214

MURRAY, ROGER GOODMAN, JR., state legislator; b. Jackson, Tenn., Mar. 3, 1931; s. Roger Goodman and Agnes (Bradford) M.; B.A., Union U., Jackson, 1958; LL.B., Cumberland Law Sch., 1960; m. Judith Ann Ligon, Sept. 9, 1960; children—Thomas David, Mona Melissa, Roger Goodman III, Luanne, William. Admitted to Tenn. bar, 1961; practiced in Jackson, 1962-73; asst. city atty., Jackson, 1963-67; pres., chmn. bd. Murray Guard, Inc., Jackson, 1968—; mem. Tenn. Ho. of Reps., 1972—. Chmn., Madison County chpt. A.R.C., 1972-73. Served with Signal Corps, U.S. Army, 1953-55. Mem. Jackson-Madison County Bar Assn., Am. Legion, Delta Theta Phi, Alpha Tau Omega. Democrat. Methodist (adminstrv. bd. 1973). Elk, Moose. Club: Jackson Exchange. Home: 30 Royal Oaks St Jackson TN 38301 Office: 425 E Baltimore St Jackson TN 38301

MURRAY, SYLVIA ANNETTE, biologist; b. Sacramento, July 17, 1937; d. Frederick Paul and Marie Katherine (Pennachio) Murray; B.A., U. Calif., Berkeley, 1962; M.A., San Francisco State U., 1967. Lab. technician Lawrence Berkeley (Calif.) Lab., 1960-66; head botanist Frederic Burke Found. Research Center, San Francisco, 1965-69; plant physiologist San Francisco Bay Marine Research Center, Inc., Richmond, Calif., 1968-75; cons. in stats. and marine biology, 1968-75; biologist TVA, Muscle Shoals, Ala., 1976—. Mem. Am. Inst. Fisheries Biologists, Sigma Xi. Republican. Mormon. Contbr. articles to sci. jours.

MURRAY, THOMAS MCKELVAN, JR., educator; b. Guston, Ky., Apr. 23, 1927; s. Thomas McKelvan and Violet Francis (Shumate) M.; B.A. in Physics, U. Louisville, 1953; M.S. in Mgmt. Sci., U. Mich., 1958, postgrad. 1963-66; m. Patricia M. Blankenbaker, Mar. 2, 1951; children—Thomas McKelvan III, Sharon Ann. Served to 2nd lt. U.S. Army, 1945-47; commd. 1st lt. U.S. Air Force, 1950, advanced through grades to lt. col., 1966, ret., 1972; sr. systems analyst Health Scis. Computing Center, U. Louisville, 1973-74, lectr. elec. engring., 1974-78, asst. prof. elec. engring., 1978—. Energy commr. Jefferson County, Louisville, 1978—. Decorated D.F.C., Air medal. Mem. IEEE, Am. Soc. Elec. Engrs., Internat. Solar Energy Soc., Solar Energy Industries Assn., Sigma Xi, Eta Kappa Nu. Contbr. articles in field to profl. jours. Home: 1045 Alta Vista Rd Louisville KY 40205 Office: Dept Elec Engring U Louisville Louisville KY 40208

MURRAY, VINCENT D'ARCY, psychologist, educator; b. N.Y.C., Mar. 3, 1947; s. Warren Taylor and Carolyn Faye (Ward) M.; A.B., Morehouse Coll., 1969; M.A., U. Ga., 1971; Ph.D., Boston U., 1975; m. Renée Camille Hubert. Supply tchr. elementary schs., Atlanta, 1968-72; tchr. perceptually handicapped, Cambridge, Mass., 1972; social worker Lindemann Mental Health Center and Boston-Mass. Mental Health Center, summer 1973; master tchr. spl. edn., behavioral therapist Hayden Goodwill Inn for Boys, Dorchester, Mass., 1974-75; dir. counseling center, asst. prof. psychology Morehouse Coll., Atlanta, 1975—; instr. spl. edn. Atlanta U., 1976—; cons. dean of students office, resident dormitory counselors, 1977; active Bur. Educationally Handicapped, 1977—, Encampment for Citizenship, San Juan, P.R., summer 1967. Recipient award, psychology dept. Morehouse Coll., 1976, community services award Sta. WSB, 1975, Nat. Soc. Easter Seal Assn., Alpha Gamma Delta scholarship, 1974; Boston U. teaching fellow, 1972-73; licensed marriage and family counselor, Ga. Mem. Atlanta U., Ga. student personnel assns., AAUP, Am. Personnel and Guidance Assn., Assn. Black Psychologists, Nat. Orgn. Legal Problems in Edn., Council for Exceptional Children, Assn. for Children with Learning Disabilities, Assn. for Children with Behavior Disorders, Phi Delta Kappa, Pi Lambda Theta. Episcopalian. Contbr. papers to confs. Home: 734 Shorter Terrace NW Atlanta GA 30318 Office: PO Box 84 Morehouse College Atlanta GA 30314

MURRAY, VINCENT THOMAS, business exec.; b. N.Y.C., July 22, 1923; s. Thomas William and Gwin (LeMassena) M.; B.S. in Biology, Rutgers U., 1944; postgrad. Columbia U.; m. Septima Porcher, Oct. 14, 1950; children—Allison, Vincent Thomas, Jack. Salesman, Sayford Corp., N.Y.C., 1946-49, regional sales mgr., Atlanta, 1949-62; owner Murray Sales, Inc., paper and plastic products, Atlanta, 1963—, Buccaneer Brokerage, Inc., Atlanta, 1967—. Lay reader, vestryman All Saints Episcopal Ch., Atlanta; 1st pres. Big Bros. Atlanta, 1960, nat. bd. dirs., 1963-66. Served with USMCR, 1942-45; PTO. Recipient award NCCJ, 1967, Spl. Father of Year award, 1977. Mem. Mfrs. Reps. Am. (dir.), Fulton County Grand Jurors Assn. Republican. Clubs: Cherokee Town and Country, Optimists (life; past pres. N. Fulton chpt.). Home: 2874 Alpine Rd NE Atlanta GA 30305 Office: 491 Armour Circle NE Atlanta GA 30324

MURRAY, WILLIS LYNN, theatre adminstr., designer; b. Texarkana, Tex., Oct. 15, 1934; s. Henry Felix and Eva Fay (Birmingham) M.; B.F.A. with honors, U. Tex. at Austin, 1957, postgrad., 1966—; m. Patricia Ann Cousins, May 31, 1958; children—Robin, Amy, Byron, Loren. Dir./designer summer workshops U. Tex. at Austin, 1963-79, asst. prof. drama, 1970-76; asst. prof. drama Sam Houston State U., Huntsville, Tex., 1957-70; profl. cons. and speaker; state drama dir. Univ. Interscholastic League, Austin, 1970—. Served with Tex. Army N.G., 1951-62. Mem. S.W. Theatre Conf. (dir. 1976-77), Tex. Ednl. Theatre Assn. (past pres.), Tex. Theatre Council (dir. 1974-78, past pres.), Am. Theatre Assn. (Tex. rep. to assembly of states 1976-77), Tex. Alliance for Arts in Edn., Secondary Sch. Theatre Assn. (dir. 1978—), Univ. and Coll. Theatre Assn., Phi Delta Kappa, Delta Phi Omega, U.S. Inst. Theatre Tech. Democrat. Presbyterian. Home: 7524 Glenhill Austin TX 78752 Office: Univ Interscholastic League Box 8028 Univ Sta Austin TX 78712

MURRELL, HAROLD DEAN, SR., coach, educator; b. Lawrenceburg, Tenn., Feb. 14, 1942; s. Jessie Daniel and Gertrude M.; student Martin Jr. Coll., 1962; A.A., Athens State Coll., 1962, B.S. in Edn., 1964, M.A.T., 1968; m. Patricia Ann Powell, July 11, 1964; 1 son, Harold Dean. Head basketball coach, asst. football coach Ardmore (Ala.) High Sch., 1965-70, 72-74; head basketball, head baseball, athletic dir. N.W. Ala. Jr. Coll., 1970-72; asst. coordinator Madison County Vocat. and Tech. Sch., Huntsville, Ala., 1974-75; head baseball coach, asst. prof. phys. edn., 1974—, head basketball coach, 1979—; cons. on guidance counseling Limestone County; cons. on rules com. Nat. Assn. Intercollegiate Athletics, 1978-79; play off dir. So. States Conf. Baseball, 1978-79. Named Coach of Year in Basketball, Ala. Jr. Coll. Conf. 1966, 68, 71. Mem. Ala. Edn. Assn., NEA, Nat. Coaches Assn., So. States Conf. Coaches Assn. Baptist. Office: Dept Phys Edn Athens State Coll Athens AL 35611

MURRELL, JAMES ROBERT, III, lawyer; b. Dallas, Feb. 22, 1942; s. James Robert, Jr., and Zora Wyndoleen (Watson) M.; B.A., La. State U., 1966, J.D., 1968. Admitted to La. bar, 1968; mem. polit. unit ABC, 1968; with Jones, Walker, Waechter, Poitevent, Carrere & Denegre, New Orleans, 1969—, partner, 1974—. Dir., gen. counsel Bay Broadcasting Corp. Mem. Am., Fed., La. bar assns. Democrat. Episcopalian. Home: 4319 Hamilton St New Orleans LA 70118 Office: 225 Baronne St New Orleans LA 70112 also 1020 First Southern Tower Mobile AL 36616

MURRELL, SAM E., JR., lawyer; b. Sarasota, Fla., Sept. 28, 1927; s. Sam E. and Myrtle (Hailey) M.; J.D., U. Fla., 1948; m. Mercerdees Lawrence, Oct. 6, 1955; children—Joan Mercedees, Katherine Jean, Sarah Elizabeth, Sam E. Admitted to Fla. bar, 1948, D.C. bar, 1975; partner firm Sam E. Murrell & Sons, Orlando, Fla., 1948—; mem. N.Y. Cotton Exchange, N.Y. Merc. Exchange, Mid-Am. Commodity Exchange, New Orleans Commodity Exchange. Served to lt. Judge Adv. Gen.'s Corps, U.S. Army, 1951-52. Mem. Am. Bar Assn., Fed. Bar Assn., Am. Trial Lawyers Assn., Fla. Trial Lawyers Assn., Nat. Assn. Criminal Def. Lawyers, Internat. Bar Assn., Assn. Immigration and Nationality Lawyers, Inter-Am. Bar Assn. Presbyterian. Clubs: Elks, Moose, Woodman of World Office: 1 N Rosalind Orlando FL 32802

MURREY, JOSEPH HENNING, JR., newspaper editor; b. Nashville, Aug. 14, 1929; s. Joseph Henning and Margaret (Harwell) M.; B.A., George Peabody Coll., 1960. With Gen. Shoe Corp., 1956-58, Sales Realty Co., Nashville, 1958-60, Murrey Realty Co., Lewisburg, Tenn., 1960-63; editor Lewisburg Tribune, Inc., 1963—. Mem. Lewisburg Mayor's Advisory Council, 1974, Marshall County Sr. Citizen Bd., 1974—, Blue Grass Regional Bd., 1974—; mem. Marshall County Library Bd., 1964-70, chmn., 1968; mem. City of Lewisburg Re-apportionement Bd., 1977-78. Served with USAF, 1951-55. Recipient best of show award Marshall County Art Guild, 1977, best pastel, 1977, best graphic, 1979; hon. mention for best editorial Tenn. Press Contests, 1974. Mem. Tenn. Press Assn. (dir. 1979—). Methodist. Club: Elks. Home: 412 Forrest St Lewisburg TN 37091 Office: 116 E Ewing St Lewisburg TN 37091

MURRILL, PAUL WHITFIELD, univ. adminstr.; b. St. Louis, July 10, 1934; s. Horace Williams and Grace (Whitfield) M.; B.S., U. Miss., 1956; M.S., La. State U., 1962, Ph.D., 1963; m. Nancy Williams, May 17, 1959; children—Paul Whitfield, John Parham, William Britton. Instr. chem. engring. La. State U., 1961-62, spl. lectr. chem. mech., indsl. and aerospace engring., 1962-63, asst. prof., 1963-65, asso. prof., 1965-67, asso. prof., head dept. chem. engring., 1967-68, prof., head dept. chem. engring., 1968-69, prof., 1968—, vice chancellor, dean acad. affairs, 1969-70, provost, 1970-74, chancellor, 1974—. Trustee Gulf South Research Corp.; cons. to bus., project mgr. Dept. Def. project THEMIS, 1967-74. Bd. dirs. local Boy Scouts Am., United Givers. Served to lt. comdr. USNR, 1956-59. Recipient Faculty Service award Nat. U. Extension Assn., 1968; Halliburton Found. award for excellence in engring. teaching, 1966; named one of Top 100 Educators in U.S., Change mag., 1978. Registered profl. engr., La. Mem. La. Engring. Soc. (Tech. Accomplishment medal 1970), Am. Soc. Engring. Edn., Am. Inst. Chem. Engrs., Instrument Soc. Am., Sigma Xi, Omicron Delta Kappa, Tau Beta Pi, Pi Kappa Pi, Phi Kappa Phi, Phi Eta Sigma, Phi Lambda Epsilon. Baptist (deacon). Club: Rotary. Author: Automatic Control of Processes, 1967; co-author: FORTRAN IV Programming for Engineers and Scientists, 1968; The Development and Utilization of Mathematical Models, 1970; An Introduction to FORTRAN IV Programming: a General Approach, 1970; COBOL Programming, 1970; Basic Programming, 1970; PL/I Programming, 1973; Introduction to Computer Science, 1973; cons. editor Chemical Engineering Series, 1966-72. Home: 206 Sunset Blvd Baton Rouge LA 70808

MURROW, WAYNE LEE, educator; b. Alva, Okla., Jan. 23, 1935; s. Everett Emmet and Stella (McGlothlin) M.; B.A., Bethany Nazarene Coll., 1956; student Northwestern State U., summers, 1954-55; M. Teaching in Lang. Arts, Central State U., 1968; Ph.D., Okla. U., 1972; m. Nila Arlene West, Jan. 19, 1968; children—Sherri, Randal, Cynthia, Jeffrey. Ordained to ministry, Ch. Nazarene, 1963; pastor Ch. of the Nazarene, Tex. and Okla., 1956-61; asso. minister Ch. of the Nazarene, Oklahoma City, 1961-70; teacher, dept. head Choctaw (Okla.) Pub. Schs., 1962-68; with Bethany Nazarene Coll., 1968—, asst. prof., 1968-72, asso. prof., 1972-74, prof., 1974—, grad. coordinator, 1971—, chmn. dept., 1976—, div. chmn., 1978—, dir. grad. studies, 1980—. Mem. Okla. Edn. Assn., NEA, Central State Speech Communication Assn., Internat. Communication Assn., Okla. Speech Communication Assn. (pres.-elect 1979-80, pres. 1980-81). Home: 2100 Flamingo St Bethany OK 73008 Office: Bethany Nazarene Coll Bethany OK 73008

MURTAGH, FREDERICK REED, neuroradiologist; b. Phila., Nov. 20, 1944; s. Frederick and Mary (Shaner) M.; B.A., Coll. William and Mary, 1966; M.D., Temple U., 1971; m. Donna Carol Day, Aug. 23, 1968; children—Ryan David, Kevin Reed. Intern in surgery N.C. Meml. Hosp., U. N.C., Chapel Hill, 1971-72; resident in neurosurgery U. Fla., Gainesville, 1974; resident diagnostic radiology U. Miami, Jackson Meml. Med. Center, Miami, Fla., 1975-78, fellow in neuroradiology, 1978, chief resident radiology, 1977; practice medicine, specializing in neuroradiology, Tampa, Fla., 1978—; instr. radiology U. Miami (Fla.) Sch. Nursing, 1976-77; chief neuroradiology sect. U. South Fla. Coll. Medicine, Tampa, 1978—, asst. prof., 1978—. Served with M.C., USN, 1972-74. Diplomate Am. Bd. Radiology. Mem. Am. Coll. Radiology, Southeastern Neuroradiology Soc., Fla. West Coast Radiol. Soc., Radiol. Soc. N. Am., AMA, Fla. Med. Assn., Hillsborough County Med. Assn. Contbr. articles to med. jours. Office: 12901 N 30th St Tampa FL 33612

MURTHY, VADIRAJA VENKATESA, biochemist, educator; b. Bombay, India, Mar. 27, 1940; came to U.S., 1961, naturalized, 1974; s. Ramanathpur Venkatesa and Saroja Venkatesa M.; B.Sc. with honors (Merit scholar), Bombay U., 1959, M.Sc. First Rank, 1961; Ph.D. (Birla Edn. Trust scholar, J. N. Tata Endowment scholar, U. Md., 1968; m. Jayashree Deshpande, Sept. 21, 1969; children—Deepti, Seema. Research fellow dept. biochemistry U. Md. Med. Sch., 1963-68; sci. officer Govt. of India at St. John's Med. Coll., Bangalore, 1968-70; sr. research biochemist/asst. group leader, div. biol. research USV Pharm. Corp., Yonkers, N.Y., 1970-71; research asso. Toxicology Center, U. Iowa, 1971-72; vis. scientist Nat. Inst. Environ. Health Sci., NIH, Research Triangle Park, N.C., 1972-74; sr. research asso. dept. pharmacology Emory U., 1974-75; adj. asst. prof. chemistry Atlanta U., 1975-76; asso. prof. biochemistry Talladega Coll., 1976-80, prof., 1980—, co-dir. MBS research program, 1976-78, 78-81. NIH grantee, 1976-78, 78-81. Mem. Am. Assn. Cancer Research, Am. Chem. Soc., N.Y. Acad. Scis., Am. Fedn. Clin. Research, AAAS, Southeastern Cancer Research Assn., Sigma Xi. Democrat. Hindu. Contbr. articles to profl. publs. Home: 121 Willman Rd Talladega AL 35160 Office: Chemistry Dept Talladega Coll Talladega AL 35160

MURTHY, YELAMELI SATYANARAYANA, obstetrician and gynecologist; b. India, Sept. 23, 1938; s. Y. Seshachar and Anasuya (Bai) M.; came to U.S., 1963; naturalized, 1972; M.B.B.S., Bangalore Med. Coll., 1961; m. Suguna Rao, May 13, 1963; children—Rohini S., Ramesh, Roopa S. Lectr. anatomy Bangaloer Med. Coll., India, 1962-63; intern St. Margaret Meml. Hosp., Pitts., 1963-64; resident Union Meml. and Johns Hospkins hosps., Balt., 1964-68; fellow in infertility and endocrinology Royal Victoria Hosp. and McGill U., Montreal, Que., Can., 1968-70; sci. pool officer St. John's Med. Coll., Bangalore, 1970-71; practice medicine specializing in obstetrics and gynecology, Richlands, Va., 1972—; mem. staff Clinch Valley Community Hosp., Mattie Williams Hosp., Tazewell Community Hosp. Recipient research award Canadian Fertility Soc., 1970. Diplomate Am. Bd. Obstetrics and Gynecology. Fellow Royal Coll. Physicians and Surgeons of Canada, Am. Coll. Obstetricians and Gynecologists, Internat. Coll. Surgeons; mem. Tazewell County Med. Soc., Med. Soc. Va. Club: Tazewell County Country. Contbr. articles to med. jours. Home: 721 Cresswood Richlands VA 24641 Office: SW Va Med Center Box 226 Cedar Bluff VA 24609

MUSE, PATRICIA ALICE, writer, educator; b. South Bend, Ind., Nov. 27, 1923; d. Walter L. and Enid (Cockerham) Ashdown; B.A., Principia Coll., 1947; student Columbia U., 1946, Seminole Community Coll., 1977, U. Central Fla., 1978—; m. Kenneth F. Muse, Dec. 2, 1950; children—Patience Eleanor, Walter Scott. Substitute tchr. pub. schs., Key West, Fla., also Brunswick, Ga., 1962-68; free lance writer, Casselberry, Fla., 1968—; novels: Sound of Rain, 1971, The Belle Claudine, 1971, paperback, 1973, Eight Candles Glowing, 1976; creative writing instr., Valencia Community Coll., 1974-75; instr. various writers confs. Community resource vol. Orange County (Fla.) Sch. Bd. (recipient certificates appreciation 1975, 76, 77). Mem. Nat. League Am. Pen Women, Mysteries Writers Am., Dixie Council Authors and Journalists, Southeastern Writers Assn. Clubs: Naval Tng. Equipment Wives.

MUSELLA, JOSEPH ANTHONY, govt. ofcl.; b. N.Y.C., Sept. 4, 1942; s. John and Louise Olympia (Russo) M.; B.B.A., Iona Coll., 1964; postgrad. Baruch Coll., 1965-67; M.A., Central Mich. U., 1979; m. Phyllis Rose Mascolo, Jan. 15, 1966; children—Joseph Michael, Catherine Elizabeth, Marie Louise. Auditor, U.S. Air Force Auditor Gen., N.Y.C., 1964-65; sr. auditor Def. Contract Audit Agy., L.I., N.Y., 1965-70, staff auditor N.Y. Regional Office, N.Y.C., 1970-73, program mgr. Alexandria, Va., 1975-76; auditor, instr. Def. Contract Audit Inst., Memphis, 1973-75, mgr. tng. br., 1976—. Mem. Fed. Exec. Assn., Assn. Govt. Accts. (pres. Memphis chpt. 1978-79), Am. Soc. Tng. and Devel. Home: 7912 Ashbrook Cove Memphis TN 38138 Office: Def Contract Audit Inst Defense Depot Airways Blvd Memphis TN 38114

MUSGRAVE, RAY SIGLER, ret. psychologist; b. Mt. Lake Park, Md., Feb. 3, 1911; s. Pinkney Z. and Mary Sigler M.; B.A., Bethany Coll., 1933; M.A., Ohio Wesleyan U., 1935; Ph.D., Syracuse U., 1937; postgrad. Columbia U., 1950-51; m. Anna Myrtle Phair, July 27, 1935; 1 dau., Rae Ann. Acting head psychology dept. Birmingham Southern Coll., 1937-38; instr. psychology Russell Sage Coll., 1938-39; prof. psychology Millsaps Coll., Jackson, Miss., 1939-54, dean students, 1946-54; prof. psychology, dir. student personnel services Tex. Womens U., Denton, 1954-56; prof., chmn. dept. psychology U. Southern Miss., Hattiesburg, 1956-75, distinguished univ. prof., 1975—; pvt. psychol. cons., 1951-77. Served with AUS, 1942-46. Recipient research grants State Miss., U. South Miss. Mem. Miss. Bd. Psychol. Examiners, 1968-70, 70-73. Fellow Am. Psychol. Assn.; mem. Am. Personnel and Guidance Assn., Southeastern Psychol. Assn., Miss. Psychol. Assn., Sigma Xi, Methodist. Club: Kiwanis. Contbr. articles to profl. jours. Home: Lux Community Route 7 Box 193A Hattiesburg MS 39401

MUSGRAVE, TERESA WACHTER, speech and lang. therapist; b. Greensboro, N.C., Mar. 10, 1953; d. John Francis and Margaret Elizabeth (McRorie) Wachter; B.S. in Speech Pathology, E. Carolina U., 1975; M.Ed. in Speech Pathology, U. N.C., Greensboro, 1977; m. John Newbould Musgrave, Sept. 17, 1977. Staff speech pathologist Nash Gen. Hosp., Rocky Mount, N.C., 1975-76, Guilford County Head Start, Greensboro, 1976-77; dir. Martin County Speech and Hearing Clinic, Williamston, N.C., 1977-78; staff speech pathologist Devel. Evaluation Center, N.C. Dept. Human Resources, Raleigh, 1978—; cons. in field. Lic. speech and lang. pathologist, N.C., 1975. Mem. Am. Speech and Hearing Assn., Council Exceptional Children, Child Advocacy Council, N.C. Speech, Hearing and Lang. Assn., N.C. Public Health Assn. Roman Catholic. Home: 446 Westcliffe Ct Raleigh NC 27606 Office: 3325 Executive Dr Suite 110 Raleigh NC 27610

MUSHUNG, LANCE JOSEPH, aerospace engr.; b. Chgo., Nov. 24, 1950; s. Anton Joseph and Marie (Pellettiere) M.; B.Aerospace Engring., Ga. Inst. Tech., 1973. Aerospace engr. Martin Marietta Aerospace, Orlando, Fla., 1973-74, Singer Link, Houston, 1974-77, Pullman Kellogg, Houston, 1977-79, OAO Corp., Houston, 1979—. Registered profl. engr., Tex. Mem. AIAA, Nat. Soc. Profl. Engrs. Home: 1110 Camino Vig Dr Houston TX 77058 Office: 1730 NASA Road One Suite 204 Houston TX 77058

MUSSELMAN, GEORGE ABRAHAM, oil operator, rancher, farmer, real estate investor; b. Salem, Tex., June 5, 1914; s. David G. and Rose (Lambert) M.; B.A., U. Tex., 1938, M.A., 1940; student Victoria Jr. Coll., 1929-31, Bluffton Coll., 1931-32; m. Josephine Boothe, Aug. 28, 1940; children—George, Jr. (dec.), Jo Lynne Musselman Meador, Joyce Musselman Mayfield, Larry Jack, Carol Jean Musselman Kirkwood, Jamie Boothe, Jan Musselman Marchbanks. Geologist, Carter Oil Co., Tulsa, 1939-48, chief geologist, 1948-50; ind. oil operator, San Antonio, 1950—; partner Musselman Cattle Co., San Antonio, 1957—; pres. Musselman Ranches, Inc., San Antonio, 1975, Musselman Investments, Inc., San Antonio, 1978—; dir. Francitas Gas Co., First Internat. Bank San Antonio. Asso. trustee Bapt. Meml. Hosp. System, San Antonio, 1973—, chmn. bd. trustees, 1963-73; trustee Baylor U., Waco, Tex., 1973—, Keystone Sch., San Antonio, 1974—; exec. com., bd. dirs. Greater San Antonio C. of C., 1960; mem. Research and Planning Council of San Antonio, 1968—, KLRN Channel 9 Ednl. TV, San Antonio, Austin, 1972-78; mem. Alamo Area Council of Govts., San Antonio, 1971—; trustee, treas. Cancer Therapy and Research Found. S. Tex., 1977—; bd. dirs., pres. Minnie Stevens Piper Found. and Ingenio Oil Co., 1975; v.p., mem. exec. bd. Alamo Area council Boy Scouts Am., pres., 1962-63, recipient Silver Beaver award, 1964. Mem. Ind. Petroleum Assn. Am. (exec. com. 1960-65), Tex. Ind. Producers and Royalty Owners Assn., Tex. Rice Producers Assn., Tex. and Southwestern Cattlemen's Assn., Am. Simmental Assn., Am. Petroleum Inst. Baptist. Clubs: Northern Hills Country (pres., bd. govs. 1971—), San Antonio Knife and Fork (pres. 1968), Alamo Kiwanis (pres. 1965), Oak Hills Country, San Antonio, St. Anthony, Flaza. Home: 440 Morningside Dr San Antonio TX 78209 Office: 1920 Alamo Nat Bldg San Antonio TX 78205

MUSTAIN, DONALD, II, furniture corp. exec.; b. Independence, Mo., Apr. 12, 1935; s. Donald and Alice Margaret M.; children—Donald, Blake Edward, Michelle Nicholette, Nicole Renee. Mgr., Hecht Co., Washington, 1962-65; store mgr., nat. buyer Reliable Stores, 1965-68; br. ops. mgr., regional v.p. Levitz Furniture Corp., Miami, Fla., 1968-77, sr. v.p., 1977—, mem. scholarship com. Bd. dirs. United Way Campaign; active Am. Cancer Soc., Boys Club Am. Mem. Am. Mgmt. Assn. Home: 820 Mockingbird Ln Plantation FL 33324 Office: Levitz Furniture Corp 1317 NW 167th St Miami FL 33169

MYER, JOHN HYSON, aerospace co. exec.; b. Iola, Kans., July 6, 1949; s. Isaac William and Myra Cecile (Chawluk) M.; B.S.B.A., U. Fla., 1971, M.B.A., 1972; m. Faith Tulino, July 5, 1975. Mgr., Medicare, Blue Cross & Blue Shield Fla., Jacksonville, 1972-77; mgmt. cons. govt. products div. Pratt & Whitney Aircraft, West Palm Beach, Fla., 1977—. Adv., Jr. Achievement, Jacksonville, 1974, 75, 76. Mem. Am. Inst. Indsl. Engrs. (dir.), Phi Kappa Tau. Democrat. Roman Catholic. Home: 4219 Oak St Palm Beach Gardens FL 33410 Office: PO Box 2691 West Palm Beach FL 33402

MYERBURG, ROBERT JEROME, physician; b. Balt., Jan. 22, 1937; s. Maurice M. and Minna (Strumwater) M.; student Johns Hopkins U., 1954-57; M.D. magna cum laude, U. Md., 1961; m. Wilhelmina M. Sluis, Sept. 2, 1974; children—Michael William, Laura Ann. Intern, U. Md. Hosp., 1961-62; resident in internal medicine Charity Hosp.-Tulane U., New Orleans, 1964-66; fellow in cardiology Emory U.-Grady Meml. Hosp., Altanta, 1966-68; research fellow Columbia U. Coll. Physicians and Surgeons, N.Y.C., 1968-70; asst. prof. medicine Sch. Medicine, U. Miami (Fla.), 1970-72, asso. prof., 1972-74, prof. medicine and physiology, dir. div. cardiology, dept. medicine, 1974—; chief of cardiology Miami VA Hosp., 1970-74. Served with USPHS, 1962-64. Diplomate Am. Bd. Internal Medicine. Fellow A.C.P., Am. Coll. Cardiology; mem. Am. Heart Assn. (fellow council on clin. cardiology, dir. Greater Miami affiliate 1971—, v.p. 1977—), Am. Soc. Clin. Investigation, Am. Fedn. for Clin. Research, Assn. Univ. Cardiologists, Alpha Omega Alpha. Contbr. numerous articles to profl. publs. Office: U Miami PO Box 016960 Miami FL 33101

MYERS, DON ARDEN, hosp. adminstr.; b. Findlay, Ohio, Sept. 11, 1928; s. Lehr Ira and Lucille (Lance) M.; B.S., Toledo U., 1956; M.S., Northwestern U., 1958; D. Pharmacy, U. Mich., 1967; m. Dortha Jean Wilson, July 30, 1956; children—Don Arden, Dianna Kay. Adminstrv. researcher Maury County Hosp., Columbia, Tenn., 1957-58, asst. adminstr., 1958-61; asst. adminstr. Glynn-Brunswick Meml. Hosp., Brunswick, Ga., 1961—. Served with Hosp. Corps, USNR, 1948-52. Fellow Am. Coll. Hosp. Adminstrs.; mem. Am., Ga. hosp. assns., Am., Ga., Glynn County (pres. 1966-67) pharm. assns., Am., Ga. (pres. 1977-78), Southeastern socs. hosp. pharmacists, Ga. Acad. Preceptors in Pharmacy, Am. Bd. Diplomates in Pharmacy, S.E. Hosp. Council (pres. 1972-73), Kappa Psi, Alpha Delta Mu. Presbyn. Lion (pres. 1968-69). Home: 4323 6th St East Beach St Simons Island GA 31522 Office: Box 1518 Glynn Brunswick Meml Hosp Brunswick GA 31520

MYERS, DONALD RAY, bank exec.; b. Harrisonburg, Va., Mar. 23, 1943; s. Garold Rolston and Katie Francis (Wiseman) M.; B.S., Bridgewater Coll., 1965; M.B.A., James Madison U., 1979; m. Nancy Mohler, June 24, 1965; children—Robin Carole, Kimberly Ann. Sales specialist, cost accountant Kawneer/Amax Co., Harrisonburg, 1969-71; with Rockingham Nat. Bank, Harrisonburg, 1971—, v.p. personnel, 1974—; dir. personnel benefits and policies Valley of Va. Bankshares, Inc., Harrisonburg, 1976—. Elder, Cooks Creek Presbyterian Ch., 1971—. Served to 1st lt. M.C., U.S. Army, 1966-69. Mem. Am. Soc. Personnel Adminstrs., Va. Bankers Assn. Club: Masons (past master Rockingham Union Lodge). Home: 112 Clement Dr Harrisonburg VA 22801 Office: Rockingham Nat Bank Harrisonburg VA 22801

MYERS, DONNY PAUL, hosp. adminstr.; b. Greensville, Ky., June 22, 1943; s. David Paul and Cora Mae (Harris) M.; student in health adminstrn. U. Ala., 1976; m. Mary Grimes, July 21, 1966; children—David, Howard. Chief lab. and x-ray technician Clay County Hosp., Ft. Gaines, Ga., 1964-76; purchasing agt. Abernethy Hosp., Flomaton, Ala., 1976, asst. adminstr., 1976-77, hosp. adminstr., 1977—. Mem. Emergency Med. Service Council, 1976—. Mem. Ala. Assn. Hosp. Execs., Ala. Hosp. Assn. Club: Lions. Home: Karen St Flomaton AL 36441 Office: Wilkerson St Flomaton AL 36441

MYERS, FREDERICK CLARENCE, ceramic engr.; b. Union City, N.J., May 5, 1928; s. Clarence and Margie Relyea (Conklin) M.; B.S. in Ceramic Engring., Alfred U., 1950; m. Barbara Jean Teetsell, Aug. 15, 1953; 1 son, Grant F. Project engr. U.S. Army Engr. Research and Devel. Labs., Fort Belvoir, Va., 1951-56, sr. project engr., 1956-61; chief Graphic Scis. br. U.S. Army Engr. Topographic Labs., 1961-73, sr. cons. engring., 1973—. Mem. research com. Graphic Arts Tech. Found. Served with U.S. Army, 1950-52. Mem. Soc. Photog. Scientists and Engrs., Sigma Xi. Contbr. articles to profl. jours. Home: 4209 Adrienne Dr Alexandria VA 22309 Office: USAETL ETL-TD-EC Fort Belvoir VA 22060

MYERS, GEORGE, advt. agy. exec.; b. Pitts., Feb. 5, 1939; s. George C. and Elizabeth (Doran) M.; B.A., U. Pitts., 1962, M.A., 1963; m. Jo Anne Diehl, Oct. 5, 1973. Supr. lit. Copperweld Steel Co., Pitts., 1963-64; copywriter Kenyon & Eckhardt, Providence, 1964-65; group head Harold Cabot & Co., Boston, 1965-67; creative dir. Howard Advt. Agy., Raleigh, N.C., 1967-69; v.p. Interface, Inc., Pitts., 1969-71; dir. mktg. and communication Southeastern Printing, Stuart, Fla., 1971-73; pres., creative dir. The Impact Group, Stuart, 1973—; condr. seminars in advt. Indian River Community Coll., 1975—. Served with U.S. Army, 1958-60. Recipient various advt. awards. Mem. Phi Beta Kappa. Republican. Episcopalian. Clubs: Advt. of Palm Beach, Treasure Coast Advt., Exchange (pres. 1976-77). Home: 9203 Angler's Cove Stuart FL 33494 Office: 951 Colorado Ave Stuart FL 33494

MYERS, GEORGE EMIL, trade assn. exec.; b. Leland, Ill., Feb. 28, 1911; s. Emil Louis and Laura May (Spray) M.; B.S. in Journalism, U. Ill., 1933; m. Edna Irene Twait, Aug. 14, 1943; children—Ellen Kay, Susan Ann Myers Caiazza, Laura Lee Myers Hurter. Editor, pub. Leland Times, 1940-43; served to col. U.S. Army; ret., 1966; dir. pub. relations Credit Union Nat. Assn., Inc., Washington, 1966-76, dep. dir., 1974-76; exec. dir. Def. Credit Union Council, Washington, 1974—; apptd. by Pres. Gerald Ford to Consumer Adv. Council, 1975-77. Decorated Legion of Merit, Bronze Star with cluster. Mem. Nat. Press, Exchequer. Republican. Presbyterian. Club: Masons. Writer commentary column Credit Union Nat. Mag., 1966-77, recipient Nat. Credit Union Adminstrn. merit award, 1977. Home: 2834 Lafora Ct Vienna VA 22180 Office: 1730 Rhode Island Ave NW Washington DC 20036

MYERS, HERBERT LEWIS, JR., coll. adminstr.; b. Okeana, Ohio, Mar. 16, 1919; s. Herbert Lewis and Margerite A. (George) M.; B.S., Ohio State U., 1940; M.B.A., Harvard U., 1942, D.B.A., 1960; m. Vera Lorene St. Clair, Dec. 24, 1941; children—Herbert Lewis, Marilyn Jane, Elizabeth Carol, James Frederick. Dir., Center for Mgmt. Devel., prof. mgmt. Frostburg (Md.) State Coll., 1970-75; chmn. mgmt. faculty, dir. mgmt. programs Shenandoah Coll. and Conservatory of Music, Winchester, Va., 1975—. Mem. Soc. Advancement of Mgmt., Am. Acctg. Assn., AAUP. Home: Rt 2 Box 557 Ridgeley WV 26753 Office: 904 Allen Dr Winchester VA 22601

MYERS, JAMES CLARK, advt. exec.; b. Chgo., Aug. 26, 1941; s. Herbert George and Lenore Levi (Goldberg) M.; B.A., Washington U., St. Louis, 1964; m. Judy Schnitzer, Feb. 9, 1964; children—Jeffrey Stephan, Jeremy H. Account exec. Nahas, Blumberg, Zelikow Advt. Agy., Houston, 1967-69; mgr. spl. events Houston Post, Houston, 1969-73; pres. Motivators, Inc., pub. relations and advt., Houston, 1972—. Vice chmn. Internat. Sci. and Engring. Fair Council, Washington, 1972-73; dir. Sci. Engring. Fair Houston, 1969-73, Houston Spring Art Festival, 1969-73; dist. Cub Scout commr. Boy Scouts Am.; mem. Jewish Community Council. Cert. bus. communicator. Mem. Houston C. of C., Pub. Relations Soc. Am. (accredited). Jewish. Home: 8006 Duffield Ln Houston TX 77071 Office: 5622 Southwest Freeway Houston TX 77057

MYERS, JOANNE KISSEL, publisher; b. N.Y.C., July 7, 1941; d. Charles and Clara (Strachman) Kissel; B.A., N.Y. U., 1963; m. Lewis Goodkin; 1 dau., Deborah Lynne. Founder, 1974, since owner, pub. Broward Life mag., Ft. Lauderdale, Fla.; pres., pub. Brenda Pub. Co., 1974—; adv. bd. W. Broward Nat. Bank; bd. dirs. Greater Ft. Lauderdale Advt. Fedn., 1976-79. Bd. dirs. United Way Broward County, 1979, Broward Center Blind, 1977. Mem. Women in Communications (named Woman of Yr. in Broward County 1978), Savs. and Loan Mktg. Soc., Fla. Mag. Assn., Ft. Lauderdale Bus. and Profl. Women's Club. Jewish. Clubs: Inverrary Country, Le Club Internat., Marina Bay. Office: 3081 E Commercial Blvd Fort Lauderdale FL 33308

MYERS, JOHN ALBERT, piston ring mfg. co. exec.; b. Two Rivers, Wis., Oct. 9, 1929; s. Alvin H. and Ada C. (Karhs) M.; m. Helen Jenkins, Dec. 20, 1952; children—Cynthia Kay, Kenneth John. Wholesale mgr. E.C. Blackstone Co., Memphis, 1975-77; asst. shipping mgr., then asst. prodn. supr. Continental Piston Ring Co., 1954-74, prodn. supr., Hernando, Miss., 1977—. Served with USN, 1950-54; Korea. Baptist. Home: 1631 Killarney Ln Memphis TN 38116 Office: 800 Memphis St Hernando MS 38632

MYERS, LEON E., educator; b. Georgetown, S.C., July 31, 1946; s. Shirley Myers; M.A., S.C. State Coll., 1972; postgrad. U. S.C. Instr. math. S.C. State Coll., Orangeburg, 1972-76, instr. and coordinator basic skills math., 1976—; mem. evaluation team Nat. Tchrs. Exam., Charleston, S.C., 1976. Mem. Nat. Council Tchrs. Math., Math. Euclidean Club, Phi Delta Kappa, Kappa Mu Epsilon, Omega Psi Phi. Office: Dept Math South Carolina State College Orangeburg SC 29115

MYERS, LEWIS ALBERT, educator; b. Florence, S.C., Aug. 11, 1930; s. John Monroe and Ehrin Mae (Hyman) M.; B.A., Wake Forest Coll., 1956; B.D., Southeastern Bapt. Theol. Sem., 1959; postgrad. Union Theol. Sem., 1962-63; M.A., Vanderbilt U., 1970; Ph.D., N.Y. U., 1980; m. Rebecca Diane Davis, Nov. 19, 1977. Ordained to ministry Bapt. Ch., 1958; asst. pastor First Bapt. Ch., Knoxville, Tenn., 1963-65; asst. prof. philosophy and religion Stetson U., DeLand, Fla., 1968-74; prof. Westminster Schs., Atlanta, 1974—. Served with AUS, 1951-53. Home: 2666 Ridge Valley Rd NW Atlanta GA 30327 Office: 1424 W Paces Ferry Rd NW Atlanta GA 30327

MYERS, MARCEAU CHEVALIER, music educator; b. Ottawa, Ill., Oct. 9, 1929; s. St. Clair and Marcella (Chevalier) M.; B.S., Mansfield State Coll., 1954; M. in Music Edn., Penn State U., 1957; Ed.D., Columbia U., 1972; postgrad. Ind. U., 1954-55; m. Judith May Kleine, Dec. 23, 1954; 1 dau., Daraugh Anne. Instrumental music instr. Bronxville (N.Y.) public schs., 1957-60; asst. prof. music Western Conn. State Coll., Danbury, 1960-70, chmn. dept. music, 1965-69; dean of Conservatory of Music, Capital U., Columbus, Ohio, 1970-74; dean Sch. of Music, N.Tex. State U., Denton, 1974—; mem. adv. bd. Music Found., 1976—, Tex. Girls Choir, 1978—. Chmn. Cultural Commn., City of Danbury, Conn., 1965-70; bd. dirs. Ft. Worth (Tex.) Symphony. Served with USMC, 1950-52. Mem. Nat. Assn. Schs. of Music, Tex. Assn. Music Schs., Tex. Council of Arts in Edn., Music Tchrs. Nat. Assn., Coll. Music Soc., Phi Mu Alpha Sinfonia (Orpheus award 1974). Contbr. articles to profl. publs. Home: 1614 Highland Park Rd Denton TX 76201 Office: PO Box 13887 NT Station Denton TX 76203

MYERS, MARILYN, cooking sch. propr.; b. Michigan City, Ind., July 25, 1943; d. Budd Arthur and Agnes Helen (Orzech) Myers; A.B., Ind. U., 1965; postgrad. Inst. for Ednl. Mgmt., Harvard U., 1974. Program asst. OEO, Washington, 1965-67; legis. asst., select subcom. on labor Com. on Edn. and Labor, U.S. Ho. of Reps., Washington, 1967-68; mng. editor Poverty and Human Resources, Inst. Labor and Indsl. Relations, U. Mich., Ann Arbor, 1968-71; free-lance writing, editing and pub. relations work, 1971-72; legis. specialist Mass. Econ. Opportunity Office, Boston, 1972-73; spl. asst. to pres. Hood Coll., Frederick, Md., 1973-75; coordinator equal opportunity and affirmative action Ark. State U., State University, 1975-78; propr., tchr. cooking sch. Marilyn Myers Kitchen, Little Rock, 1978—; dir. Acad. Travel Abroad, Inc. Mem. adv. com. Capital Zoning Dist. Commn. Mem. Am. Assn. Cooking Schs., AAUW, ACLU, NOW. Author pamphlets in field. Home and Office: 115 S Victory St Little Rock AR 72201

MYERS, ROBERT LAWRENCE, pharm. co. exec.; b. Elkhart, Ind., May 13, 1945; s. Lawrence Myrl and Frances Alice (Thunander) M.; B.S. in Pharmacy, Butler U., 1968; m. Kimberly Junius, Aug. 29, 1970; children—Robert Bradley, Meghan Waldorf. Staff pharmacist Jack Eckerd Corp., Clearwater, Fla., 1970-72, pharm. buyer, 1972-75, mdse. mgr. pharms., 1975-77, dir. pharmacy services, 1977—; mem. adv. bd. Roche Labs., 1977—. Served with U.S. Army, 1969-70. Mem. Am. Pharm. Assn., Fla. Pharm. Assn., Nat. Assn. Chain Drug Stores (pharmacy affairs com.), Sigma Chi. Methodist. Club: Carlouel Yacht. Home: 221 Ocala Rd Belleair FL 33516 Office: 2120 US 19 S Clearwater FL 33518

MYERS, WILLIAM CHAMBERS, athletic dir.; b. St. George, S.C., Feb. 3, 1926; s. Alexander Coke and Ruby (Westbury) M.; B.S., Erskine Coll., 1950; postgrad. U. S.C.; m. Marcellene Leslie, July 27, 1950; children—William Chambers, Leisa Weston, Melissa Westbury, Laurie Leslie. Tchr., football and track coach Dreher High Sch., Columbia, S.C., 1950-57; dir. alumni affairs Erskine Coll., 1957-58, dir. athletics, basketball coach, 1958—; del. World Univ. Games, Mexico City, 1979; cons. in field. Served with USMCR, 1944-46. Named S.C. High Sch. Football Coach of Year, 1954, 56, S.C. Coll. Basketball Coach of Year, 1978. Mem. Nat. Assn. Intercollegiate Athletes (pres. elect 1979, exec. com. 1972—; named Dist. Coach of Year Baseball, Dist. Basketball Coach of Year), Nat. Assn. Collegiate Athletic Dirs. Mem. Reformed Presbyn. Ch. Home: Box 206 Due West SC 29639 Office: Erskine Coll Due West SC 29639

MYERS, WILLIAM ROBERT, banker; b. Cin., July 25, 1946; s. Robert Jackson and Sara Ann (Huber) M.; B.A., Rollins Coll., 1969, M.B.A., 1970; grad. Nat. Comml. Lending Sch., Am. Banker's Assn., 1973, Nat. Comml. Lending Grad. Sch., 1974; m. Pamela Ann Hodges, Aug. 2, 1969; children—Barbara Ann, Sara. With Barnett Bank, Jacksonville, 1970—, asst. cashier, 1972-73, asst. v.p., 1973-75, v.p., 1975—. Vice pres. Big Bros. Jacksonville, 1975; bd. dirs. Jr. Achievement of Jacksonville, 1976—; trustee Jacksonville Marine Inst., 1975, treas., 1976-79, pres., 1979—. Mem. Am. Bankers Assn., Robert Morris Assos., Jacksonville C. of C. Republican. Presbyterian. Office: PO Box 990F Jacksonville FL 32231

MYERS, WILLIAM SIMS, JR., dist. judge; b. Tulsa, Feb. 6, 1924; s. William Sims and Grace Viola (Gardner) M.; B.S., U. Okla., 1947; postgrad. Fordham U., 1943; J.D., Harvard, 1949; m. Audrey J. Lewis, Sept. 4, 1969; children—Kathryn, Victoria, Elizabeth Ann, Susan Marie. Admitted to Okla. bar, 1949; pvt. practice law, 1949-60; mem. firm Berry, Myers & Weiss, Oklahoma City, 1960-66; judge Oklahoma County, 1966-67; judge 7th Jud. Dist. Okla., 1967—. Spl. lectr. U. Okla. Coll. Law, 1954-55, 57-58. Served with AUS, 1943-45; col. USAFR. Mem. Oklahoma County Bar Assn. (dir.), Oklahoma County Mental Health Assn., Phi Delta Theta, Beta Gamma Sigma, Kiwanian. Club: Oklahoma City Golf and Country. Home: 7204 Lancelot Pl Oklahoma City OK 73132 Office: 807 Oklahoma County Courthouse Oklahoma City OK 73120

MYERS, WOODROW HORACE, transp. adminstr., ret. army officer; b. Munday, Tex., July 2, 1919; s. Robert Lee and Sally Eizabeth (Ford) M.; B.S. in Petroleum Engring., Agr. and Mech. Coll. Tex., 1942; m. Katherine Barbara Kullman, June 20, 1942; 1 dau., Linda Elizabeth Myers Self. Commd. 2d lt. U.S. Army, 1942; sr. prodn. and drilling engr. Pan Am. Prodn. Co., Houston and Franklin, La., 1945-47; re-entered U.S. Army, 1947, advanced through grades to col., 1965; ordnance advisor U.S. Inf. Bd., Ft. Benning, Ga., 1958-61, ordnance officer 2d Inf. Div., 1962; maintenance officer Hdqrs. 8th Army, Korea, 1963; supply officer Hdqrs. 3d Army, Ft. McPhearson, Ga., 1964-66, Hdqrs. U.S. Communication Zone, Germany, 1967-69, Army Inf. Center, Ft. Benning, 1970-72; ret., 1972; exec. dir. S. Ga. Transp. Corridor Advisory Bd., Columbus, 1974—. Mem. County Planning Commn., 1973—; mem. Harris County Tax Assessor Bd.; supr. Pine Mt. Soil and Water Conservation Dist. Ga. Decorated Legion of Merit. Mem. Nat. Rifle Assn., Nat. Def. Preparedness Assn., Ret. Officers Assn. Home: 213 Pike Dr Ellerslie GA 31807 Office: PO Box 923 Columbus GA 31902

MYHRE, TRYGVE CHATHAM, metallurgist; b. Sheboygan, Wis., May 1, 1937; s. Roy Ernest and Dorothea Constance (Chatham) Tanney; B.Mgt.E., Rensselaer Poly. Inst., 1958, M.Metall. Engring., 1960; m. Elizabeth Halsted, June 14, 1958; children—Elise, Glen Scott, Kari. Grad. asst. Rensselaer Poly. Inst., 1958-60; prodn. engr. Washington Equipment Co., Paterson, N.J., 1960-65; metall. specialist nuclear div. Union Carbide Corp., Oak Ridge, 1965-72, spl. projects engr., 1972—. Treas. project concern Oak Ridge Walk for Mankind. Mem. Am. Soc. Metals, Nat. Soc. Profl. Engrs. Elevated temperature tensile properties of rolled ingot beryllium sheet; described manufacture of 97 percent tungsten alloy rods, effect of hot isotatic pressing on tungston composite penetrator. Home: 100 Greenbriar Ln Oak Ridge TN 37830 Office: Union Carbide Corp Nuclear Div Y-12 Plant 9103/3 Oak Ridge TN 37830

MYINT, HLA, psychiatrist; b. Mandalay, Burma, Sept. 14, 1921; s. U San Kyu and Daw Ma Ma Lay; M.D., U. Rangoon, 1942; I.Sc., Rangoon Med. Coll., 1945; M.B., B.S., Grant Med. Coll., Bombay, India, 1947; m. Sofie Noronha, May 18, 1947; children—Fleur, David, Cherie, Dean, Desmond, Twinkle, Christina. Intern, Rangoon (Burma) Gen. Hosp., 1947-49; resident, postgrad. trainee in gen. surgery J.J. Hosp., Bombay, 1949-54; gen. practice medicine, Mandalay, Burma, 1954-72; resident in psychiatry Terrell (Tex.) State Hosp., 1972-73, staff psychiatrist, 1975-78, unit dir., unit A, 1978—; resident in psychiatry Southwestern Med. Sch.-Parkland Hosp., Dallas, 1973-75, mem. staff, 1975—; clin. asst. instr. dept. psychiatry Southwestern Med. Sch., U. Tex., Dallas; chmn. mental health quality assurance com. Tex. Dept Mental Health and Retardation, Austin, 1980—. Served as capt. Burmese Army Med. Corps, 1963-66. Diplomate Am. Bd. Psychiatry and Neurology. Mem. Am. Psychiat. Assn., Tex. Med. Assn. Buddhist. Home: 7130 Winedale St Dallas TX 75231 Office: PO Box 70 E Brin St Terrell TX 75160

MYKKELTVEDT, ROALD Y., polit. scientist; b. Tracy, Minn.; s. Nels Larsen and Nora Emily (Dahle) M.; B.A., St. Olaf Coll., 1951; M.A., Fla. State U., 1955, Ph.D., 1966; m. Montrell Sessions, Oct. 11, 1952; children—Lauren, Melissa, Jeffrey. Lectr., instr. Fla. State U., 1957-66; asst. prof. polit. sci. West Ga. Coll., Carrollton, 1966-69, asso. prof., 1969-73, prof., 1973—. Served with USAF, 1951-53. NSF grantee, 1966; Nat. Endowment Humanities grantee, 1977; Inst. on Am. Freedoms grantee, 1966. Mem. Ga. Polit. Sci. Assn., So. Polit. Sci. Assn., Am. Polit. Sci. Assn. Democrat. Lutheran. Contbr. articles to profl. jours. Office: West Georgia Coll Carrollton GA 30117

MYNATT-AXAMETHY, CONSTANCE VIRGINIA, educator; b. Knoxville, Tenn., Nov. 7, 1921; d. Everette E. and Ettra L. (Mynatt) Mynatt; B.S., Carson-Newman Coll., 1943; M.S., U. Tenn., 1946; Ph.D., U. Mich., 1955; m. William Emery Axamethy, June 5, 1977. Mathematician, Nat. Adv. Com. Aeronautics, Langly Field, Va., 1943-44; dir. women's phys. edn. Milligan (Tenn.) Coll., 1945-56; teaching fellow U. Mich., 1956-57; dir. women's phys. edn. and athletics E. Tenn. State U., Johnson City, 1957-73, prof. phys. edn., 1957—. Recipient Honor awards, Tenn. Assn. Health, Phys. Edn. and Recreation, 1962, Tenn. Coll. Assn., 1966, AAHPER, So. Dist., 1971; gov. citation Tenn. Commn. on Status of Women, 1978. Mem. E. Tenn. Assn. Health, Phys. Edn. and Recreation (pres. 1958), Tenn. Coll. Phys. Edn. Assn. (pres. 1958-59), Tenn. Assn. Health, Phys. Edn. and Recreation (pres. 1960-61), So. Assn. Phys. Edn. for Coll. Women (sec. 1961-62), AAHPER (past dist. chmn. div. girls' and women's sports, So. dist. chmn. internat. council 1975), NEA, Tenn. Edn. Assn. Author: Folk Dancing for Teachers and Students, 1968, 2nd edit. 1975; contbr. articles in field to profl. jours. Home: 2202 Ridgefield Dr Johnson City TN 37601 Office: PO Box 21340A E Tenn State Univ Johnson City TN 37601

MYNETT, JACK WILLIAM, corp. exec.; b. Council Bluffs, Iowa, Aug. 7, 1924; s. Charles William and Edna (Burke) M.; B.B.A., So. Methodist U., 1949, M.B.A., 1951; m. Jo Nell Stubblefield, Mar. 1, 1946; children—Judy Lynne, Charles William II. Dir. personnel Hartford Ins. Group, Dallas, 1951-63; v.p. planning, devel. and gen. services Gulf Ins. Group, Dallas, 1963-68; sr. v.p., dir. UCC Financial Corp., 1968-72; resident mgr. Boyden Assos., Inc., 1972-73; pres. Jack W. Mynett & Assos., 1973—. Active various community drives. Trustee, Amigos de las Ams., 1971—. Served with AUS, 1942-46. Mem. Adminstrv. Mgmt. Soc. (Diamond Merit award 1967, Mem. of Year Dallas chpt. 1965, internat. v.p.-treas. 1967-68, chpt. pres. 1964-65), Dallas Mgmt. Assn. (pres. 1963-64), Dallas Personnel Assn. (pres. 1963-64), So. Methodist U. Bus. Sch. Alumni Assn. (pres. 1957), Dallas C. of C. (pres., life mem. club 1965-66, Triple Life mem. 1962, 63, 67). Address: 4308 Alta Vista Ln Dallas TX 75229

MYRICK, CHARLES NORMAN, financial cons.; b. Jacksonville, Fla., Jan. 11, 1935; s. Charles Nathaniel and Vernice (Simmons) M.; student Ga. Inst. Tech., 1953-57, DeKalb Community Coll., 1962, LaSalle U., 1974-75; m. Mary Esther Rowell, Oct. 10, 1957; children—Mary Beth, Charles Jeffrey. Bookkeeper, Universal Carloading & Distbg Co., Atlanta, 1955-61; auditor Armour Agrl. Chem. Co., Atlanta, 1961-63; pres. James R. Wilson, Inc. cons., Atlanta, 1963—. Trustee, Carriage Hill, Inc., 1970-72. Mem. Nat. Soc. Pub. Accountants, Nat. Assn. Enrolled Agts. (state membership chmn., 1975, pres. 1976—, nat. dir. 1977—, treas. 1978), Nat. R.R. Soc. Baptist. Club: Carriage Hill. Founder, pub. Yardstick, 1963—. Home: 1152 Old Coach Rd Stone Mountain GA 30083 Office: 525 William Oliver Bldg Atlanta GA 30303

MYRICK, DEAN KENT, speech pathologist; b. Hammond, La., May 15, 1938; d. John Raines and Emily Corinne (Guess) M.; B.S., La. State U., 1960; M.S., Tulane U., 1966. Speech pathologist Davison Sch., Atlanta, 1960-61; speech cons.-in-residence Ford Found. Project Opportunity, 1967-70; speech and lang. pathologist Orleans Parish schs., New Orleans, 1961—; pvt. practice speech and lang. therapy, 1977—. Mem. Am. Speech and Hearing Assn., La. Speech and Hearing Assn., La. Colonials, Kappa Kappa Gamma.

Episcopalian. Home: 3221 Plymouth Pl New Orleans LA 70114 Office: 703 Carondelet St New Orleans LA 70130

MYRICK, FRED LEE, JR., mktg. info. service exec.; b. Ft. Worth, Sept. 24, 1946; s. Fred Lee and Molly Melinda (Tipton) M.; B.B.A., U. Tex., 1969, M.B.A., 1970, Ph.D., 1972. Instr. bus. adminstrn. U. Tex., Austin, 1971-72; asst. prof. mktg. U. Ariz., Tucson, 1972-73; asso. prof. bus. adminstrn. U. Ala., Birmingham, 1973-78; exec. dir. Mktg. Info. Service, Atlanta, 1979—. Mem. Am. (pres. Birmingham chpt. 1977—), So., Southwestern mktg. assns., Am. Bus. Communication Assn., Am. Trauma Soc. (dir. 1977—). Home: 1977 Gotham Way Atlanta GA 30324 Office: PO Box 4402 Atlanta GA 30302

NABERS, JOSEPH LYNN, state legislator; b. Brownwood, Tex., Mar. 31, 1940; s. Joseph D. and Ima Lou (Littlefield) N.; B.S., Howard Payne Coll., 1962; J.D., Baylor U., 1967; m. Mary Scott, Oct. 3, 1959; children—Joseph Scott, Timothy Lynn. Admitted to Tex. bar, 1967; mem. Tex. Ho. of Reps. from 55th Dist., 1969—. Named Distinguished Alumni, Howard Payne Coll., 1973; recognized for outstanding service in State Legislature, Tex. Bar Assn., 1973. Mem. Am., Tex., Brown County (pres.) bar assns., Brownwood C. of C. Democrat. Baptist. Club: Rotary. Home: 4 Quail Creek Rd Brownwood TX 76801 Office: 308 N Broadway Brownwood TX 76801

NACLERIO, NICHOLAS JOSEPH, mgmt. cons.; b. N.Y.C., July 22, 1932; s. Nicholas Joseph and Gemma (Milo) N.; B.A., N.Y. U., 1954; M.A., Eastern Mich. U., 1965, S.P.A., 1966; m. June Ann Zimany, Aug. 13, 1955; children—Susan, Nicholas, Jean, Anne. Commd. 2d lt. U.S. Army, 1954, advanced through grades to lt. col., 1954, served chief staff mgmt. Office Asst. Chief of Staff for Intelligence, 1974-76, dir. personnel and adminstrn. Criminal Investigation Command, 1971-74, adj. gen. U.S. Army, Thailand, 1970-71, civil affairs officer, Panama, 1967-70, ret., 1978; pres. N.J. Naclerio & Assos. Inc., Washington, 1979—; asst. prof. mil. sci. Eastern Mich. U., 1963-66. Participant various civic action projects C. and S. Am., 1968-70. Decorated Legion of Merit. Mem. Am. Personnel and Guidance Assn., Am. Coll. Personnel Assn., Internat. Word Processing Assn. (v.p. programs Nat. Capitol chpt. 1978-79, chmn. edn. com. 1979—), Word Processing Soc. Roman Catholic. Developer word processing systems; organizer, lectr. workshops, confs. in field. Home: 4407 Evergreen Dr Woodbridge VA 22193 Office: Suite 201 7830 Backlick Rd Springfield VA 22150

NADLER, BURTON JAY, career counselor, edn. coordinator; b. Newark, Nov. 24, 1953; s. Roy and Audree Weil (Savino) N.; B.A. in Psychology, B.A. in Sociology cum laude, U. Pa., 1975, M.S. in Psychol. Services, 1978; M.A. in Edn., Stanford U., 1977; m. Teri Albright, Aug. 5, 1978. Program asst. counselor ACT 101 Program, U. Pa., Phila., 1977-78; career counselor Career Center, So. Meth. U., Dallas, 1978—, M.B.A. placement coordinator, 1979—; career edn. coordinator Tejas Girl Scout Council, Dallas, 1978-79; substitute tchr. social scis., asst. coach freshman lacrosse, Maplewood, N.J., 1975-76; student tchr. Mountain View (Calif.) High Sch. and Fremont High Sch., Sunnyvale, Calif., 1976-77; asso. Mood Clinic-Center for Cognitive Therapy, U. Pa., Phila., 1977-78, counselor reading clinic, 1977-78. Mem. Am. Personnel and Guidance Assn., Am. Psychol. Assn., Phi Delta Kappa. Home: 7743 Willow Tree Ct Apt 126 Dallas TX 75230 Office: SMU Career Center 208 Clements Hall Southern Methodist U Dallas TX 75275

NAGAPRASANNA, BANGALORE RANGASWAMY, indsl. engr.; b. India, June 25, 1940; s. Bangalore N. and Bangalore R. (Kamalamma) R.; M.B.A., St. Johns U., 1972; M.P.S., L.I. U., 1974; m. Lalitha Nagaprasanna, Aug. 15, 1970; 1 dau., Shobha. Indsl. engr. Montefiore Hosp., N.Y.C., 1970-71; dir. mgmt. engring. Mary Immaculate Hosp., N.Y.C., 1971-76, South Chgo. Community Hosp., Chgo., 1976-77; project indsl. engr. Eastern Airlines, Miami, Fla., 1977—; adj. prof. Fla. Internat. U., Miami, 1979—. Registered profl. engr., Fla. Mem. Am. Inst. Indsl. Engrs., Airline Group Ops. Research Soc., Fla. Engring. Soc. Office: Eastern Airlines Miami Internat Airport Miami FL

NAGLEE, ELFRIEDE KURZ, nursing adminstr.; b. Phila., Mar. 13, 1932; d. Emil K. L. and Frida (Keppler) Kurz; R.N., Phila. Gen. Hosp., 1952; m. David I. Naglee, Sept. 6, 1952; children—David Stephen, Joanna Jane, Deborah Ruth, Miriam Louise, Joy Ann. Staff nurse, Princeton, N.J., obstet. nurse, Cuba, N.Y., 1952; staff nurse, Salamanca, N.Y., 1953-54, Springville, N.Y., 1955-56; obstet. nurse, Woodbury, N.J., summer 1956; nurse Bridgeton (N.J.) Hosp., 1957-62, pvt. duty nurse, 1963-64; part time staff nurse, Millville, N.J., 1965; part-time staff nurse, West Ga. Med. Center (formerly City County Hosp.), LaGrange, Ga., 1966-70, head nurse, 1970-71, acting dir. nursing, 1971-72, surg. supr., 1972-79, clin. supr. surg. unit, 1979—. Recipient First Employee of Yr. award, 1973. Mem. Am., Ga. State nurses assns. Democrat. Methodist. Club: Faculty Wives LaGrange Coll. Pianist, organist church, concerts. Home: 804 Piney Woods Dr LaGrange GA 30240

NAGY, STEVEN, biochemist; b. Fords, N.J., Apr. 7, 1936; s. Steven and Martha (Moberg) N.; B.S. in Chemistry, La. State U., 1960; M.S. in Physiology and Biochemistry, Rutgers U., 1962, Ph.D. in Biochemistry, 1965; M.Engring. in Indsl. Engring., U. South Fla., 1977. Analytical chemist USPHS, Metuchen, N.J., 1962-65; research asso. Lever Bros., Edgewater, N.J., 1965-67; research chemist Dept. Agr., Winter Haven, Fla., 1968-79; research scientist Fla. Dept. Citrus, Lake Alfred, 1979—; adj. prof. U. Fla., 1979—. Mem. Am. Chem. Soc., Phytochem. Soc. N. Am., Am. Oil Chemists Soc., Am. Soc. for Hort. Sci., Internat. Soc. Citriculture, Fla. Hort. Soc., Sigma Xi. Republican. Author: Citrus Science and Technology, 2 vols., 1977; Tropical and Subtropical Fruits, 1980; contbr. articles to profl. jours. Home: 61 Circle Dr Winter Haven FL 33880 Office: PO Box 1088 Lake Alfred FL 33850

NAHAI, FOAD, plastic surgeon; b. Teheran, Iran, Sept. 23, 1943; came to U.S., 1970; s. Rouhallah and Marcelle N.; B.S. with honors, Bristol (Eng.) U., 1966, M.B., Ch.B., 1969; m. Shahnaz Mossanen, Aug. 4, 1969; children—Farzad, Fariba. Intern, Balt. City Hosps., 1970-71; resident Johns Hopkins Hosp., Balt., 1971-72, Emory U. Affiliated Hosps., Atlanta, 1972-75; practice medicine specializing in plastic surgery, Atlanta, 1978—; mem. staff VA, St. Joseph's, Crawford W. Long Meml., Grady Meml., Emory U. hosps., Henrietta Egleston Hosp. for Children, Scottish Rite Hosp. for Crippled Children; asst. prof. surgery Emory U., 1978—. Mem. Brit. Med. Assn., Southeastern Surg. Conf., Southeastern Soc. Plastic Surgeons, AMA, Ga. Soc. Plastic Surgeons, Med. Assn. Atlanta, Med. Assn. Ga. Author: (with S.J. Mathes) Clinical Atlas of Muscle and Musculocutaneous Flaps, 1979; contbr. articles to med. jours. Office: 25 Prescott St NE Atlanta GA 30308

NAIL, BILLY RAY, ednl. adminstr.; b. Roby, Tex., Jan. 19, 1933; s. Radney Harmon and Helen Juanita (Parker) N.; B.A., Hardin-Simmons U., 1956; A.M., U. Ill., 1962, Ph.D., 1967; m. Glenda Fern Campbell, July 12, 1952; children—Marsha Lynn, Vicky Rae, Penny Suzanne. Tchr. math., coach Merkel (Tex.) High Sch., 1957-61; instr. math. Wayland Bapt. Coll., 1962-64; prof., head dept. math. Morehead (Ky.) State U., 1967-72; dean coll. Clayton Jr. Coll., Morrow, Ga., 1972—. Chmn., Fed. Revenue Sharing Adv. Com., Clayton County, Ga., 1976—; chmn. Clayton County unit Am. Cancer Soc., 1976-79, pres., 1975-76, dir. Ga. div., 1977—. NSF fellow, 1961-62, 65-67. Mem. Conf. Acad. Deans of the So. States, Nat. Assn. Staff, Program and Organizational Devel., Math. Assn. Am. Baptist. Home: 2201 Carmen Ct Morrow GA 30260 Office: 5900 Lee St Morrow GA 30260

NAIL, ZELMA ELAINE, sch. counselor; b. San Angelo, Tex., Feb. 26, 1933; d. Clannie Albert and Eva Lena (Coulter) Fairbanks; B.A., Trinity U., San Antonio, 1954, M.Ed., 1957; m. James C. Nail, Aug. 25, 1957; children—Ronald James, Daniel Albert. Secondary sch. tchr., San Antonio, 1954-57; sec. B'nai B'rith Hillel Found., College Station, Tex., 1957-58; bookkeeper Terry Farm Supply Co., Brownfield, Tex., 1965-68; elementary sch. tchr., Brownfield, 1968-70; secondary sch. counselor Matthews Jr. High Sch., Lubbock, Tex., 1970—. Pres. Friends of Library, Terry County, Tex., 1966-68, United Presbyn. Women's Orgn., Brownfield, 1967; mem. Lubbock County Emergency First Aid Team, 1974-76. Life mem. NEA, Tex. State Tchrs. Assn., Tex. Classroom Tchrs. Assn.; mem. Am., Tex., W. Tex. (sec.-treas. 1976-78, pres. 1979-80) personnel and guidance assns., Am., Tex. sch. counselors assns., AAUW, Lubbock Classroom Tchrs. Assn., Lubbock Educators Assn., Friends of Lubbock County Library. Baptist. Home: 5426 80th St Lubbock TX 79424 Office: 417 N Akron St Lubbock TX 79415

NAKAHARA, HIROO, internat. trading co. exec.; b. Japan, May 8, 1924; s. Chikanosuke and Kuni (Ueda) N.; came to U.S., 1955; B.S. in Econs., Kyoto (Japan) U., 1950; m. Akiko Iida, Apr. 13, 1955; children—Asuka, Luke, Kane. With Nichimen Co., Ltd., Osaka, Japan, 1950-55; with Japan Cotton Co., Dallas, 1955—, exec. v.p., 1962-64, pres., 1964—, also dir.; dir. Nichimen de Mex., Indsl. de Tuberias, San Salvador, Plasticio Eslon de Mex. Vice pres. Japan-Am. Soc. Dallas, 1973; deacon E. Dallas Christian Ch., 1972—. Served with Japanese Army, 1943-44. Office: PO Box 1247 Dallas TX 75221

NAKAMOTO, TETSUO, dentist, nutritionist; b. Kure, Japan, Dec. 20, 1939; s. Takamori and Masae N.; predental student Nihon U., 1958-60, D.D.S., 1964; M.S. in Prosthodontics, U. Mich., 1966, M.S. in Physiology, 1971; M.S. in Physiology, U. N.D., 1969; Ph.D. in Nutritional Biochemistry and Metabolism, M.I.T., 1978. Asst. prof. physiology La. State U., New Orleans, 1978—. Nat. Inst. Dental Research postdoctoral fellow, 1969-78. Mem. Internat. Assn. Dental Research, Am. Assn. Dental Research, Soc. Exptl. Biology and Medicine, AAAS, Am. Assn. Dental Schs., Soc. Nutrition Edn., Sigma Xi. Catholic. Research in growth and devel., infant nutrition, bone and tooth growth. Office: 1100 Florida Ave New Orleans LA 70119

NAKARAI, CHARLES FREDERICK TOYOZO, musicologist; b. Indpls., Apr. 25, 1936; s. Toyozo Wada and Frances Aileen N.; B.A. cum laude, Butler U., 1958, Mus.M., 1967; postgrad. U. N.C., Chapel Hill, 1967-70. Organist, dir. choirs Northwood Christian ch., Indpls., 1954-57; minister music Broad Ripple Christian Ch., Indpls., 1957-58; asst. prof. music Milligan Coll., Tenn., 1970-72; pvt. instrn. organ, piano, Durham, 1972—. Served with USAF, 1958-64. Mem. Am. Musicol. Soc., Coll. Music Soc., Am. Guild Organists, Music Tchrs. Nat. Assn. Composer: Three Movements for Chorus, 1971, Bluesy, 1979. Address: 3520 Mayfair St Apt 205 Durham NC 27707

NAKARAI, TOYOZO WADA, educator; b. Kyoto, Japan, May 16, 1898; s. Tosui and Wakae (Harada) N.; A.B., Kokugakuin U., Tokyo, 1920; A.B., Butler U., 1924, A.M., 1925; Ph.D. (fellow Sch. Religion), U. Mich., 1930, also post-doctorate studies; grad. student Nippon U., Tokyo, U. Chgo., Hebrew Union Coll., N.Y. U.; m. Frances Aileen Yorn, June 22, 1933; children—Charles Frederick Toyozo, Frederick Leroy. Came to U.S., 1923, naturalized, 1953. Instr. Tokyo Fourth High Sch., Sei Gakuin Mission Sch., Matsumiya Lang. Sch., Tokyo, 1920-23; instr. Coll. of Missions, Indpls., 1923-25; instr. Semitics, Butler U., Indpls., 1927-28, asst. prof., 1928-29, asso. prof., 1929-31, prof., head dept. Semitics, 1931-65, prof. emeritus, 1965—; prof., head dept. Semitics, Emmanuel Sch. Religion, 1965-71, hon. prof. Old Testament, 1971—; profl. appointee Am. Sch. Oriental Research, Jerusalem, 1947-48, hon. asso., 1962-63; alumni lectureship Ky. Christian Coll., 1956, T. H. Johnson Meml. lectr. Manhattan Bible Coll., 1957; lectr. Sch. Ministry, Milligan Coll., 1957, 66; vis. prof. Tainan Theol. Coll., Formosa, 1963; faculty lectr. Christian Theol. Sem., 1964; lectr. Ashland Theol. Sem., 1974, Westwood Christian Consortium, 1976, Lincoln Christian Sem., 1977. Mem. Gov.'s Abraham Lincoln Commn. to Orient, 1960. Recipient Baxter Found. award, medal and scroll Internat. Order B'rith Abraham, Nat. Assn. Profs. Hebrew; J. I. Holcomb prize Butler U.; citation and scroll Histadrut Ivrit. Mem. AAUP, Am. Oriental Soc., Am. Sch. Oriental Research (chmn. cast investigation com. 1941-42), Am. Acad. Religion, Soc. Sci. Study Religion, Soc. Bibl. Lit. (v.p. Midwest br. 1949-51, pres. 1951-52), Nat. Assn. Profs. Hebrew (pres. 1956-58, editor Iggeret, 1974-77, asso. editor Hebrew Studies 1974-77, recipient citation scholarship and merit), Israel Exploration Soc., Nippon Kyuyaku Gakkai, Israel Soc. for Bibl. Research, Internat. Inst. for Study Religions, Eta Beta Rho, Phi Kappa Phi, Theta Phi, Author: A Study of the Kokinshu, 1931, Biblical Hebrew, 1951, rev. edit., 1976; (with others) To Do and To Teach, 1953; Shin Tosa Nikki, 1962; An Elder's Public Prayers, 1968, rev. enlarged edit., 1979; (with others) The Mind of a Faculty, 1973; (with others) Essays on New Testament Christianity, 1978; The Dead Sea Scrolls and Biblical Faith, 1980. Home: Route 4 PO Box 240 Elizabethton TN 37643 Office: Drawer Q Milligan College TN 37682

NAKASHIMA, TADAYOSHI, biochemist; b. Yokkaichi-city, Japan, Dec. 1, 1922; s. Chunosuke and Hina (Kato) N.; came to U.S., 1962; B.P., Nagoya Pharm. Coll., 1943; B.S., Taihoku Imperial U., 1946; Ph.D. in Biochemistry, Kyushu U., 1961; m. Fukuko Kondo, Nov. 15, 1947; 1 child, Rieko. Postdoctoral fellow in biochemistry U. Hawaii, 1962-64; research scientist Inst. Molecular and Cellular Evolution, U. Miami, Coral Gables, Fla., 1964-73, research asst. prof., 1973-77, research asso. prof., 1977—; vis. researcher Inst. Animal Physiology, U. Bonn (W. Ger.), 1966-69. Japanese Nat. Sci. Found. grantee, 1957. Mem. Am. Chem. Soc., Internat. Soc. Study of Origin of Life, Japanese Soc. Food and Nutrition, Sigma Xi. Methodist. Contbr. articles to profl. jours. Home: 7400 SW 159th Terr Miami FL 33157 Office: U Miami 521 Anastasia Ave Coral Gables FL 33134

NALL, JAMES OTHO, physician; b. nr. Clay, Ky., Dec. 17, 1897; s. James Webster and Harriet Truman (Smith) N.; student U. Ky., 1919-21; M.D., Washington U., St. Louis, 1925; m. Florence Phillips, June 4, 1932; children—Peggy and Patricia (twins). Intern, Evang. Deaconess Hosp., St. Louis, 1925-26; asst. editor Jour. of AMA, Chgo., 1928-29; physician Murray (Ky.) State Tchrs. Coll., 1931-32, 35-36; med. writer E.R. Squibb & Sons, N.Y.C., 1930, Abbott Labs., North Chicago, Ill., 1933; practice medicine, Marion, Ky., 1942-73; health officer Crittenden, Caldwell, Lyon, Livingston Counties, Ky., 1940-42, 1953-55, 1963-68; practice medicine, Owensboro, Ky., 1973—. Mem. AMA, Ky. Med. Assn. Republican. Presbyn. Kiwanian (pres. 1945). Author: The Tobacco Night Riders of Kentucky and Tennessee, 1905-1909, 1939; Kentucky Derby Poems, 1875-1975, 1975; Venture in Verses, 1979. Home: 1019 E 21st St Owensboro KY 42301 Office: 2414 E 4th St Owensboro KY 42301

NAMBOODIRI, THRIVIKRAMAN M. S., mathematician, coll. adminstr.; b. Kerala, India, May 11, 1932; came to U.S., 1963, naturalized, 1979; s. M.T. Sankaran and Arya Devi N.: B.Sc., U. Kerala, 1957; M.A., Boston U., 1965; Ph.D., So. Ill. U., Carbondale, 1968; postgrad. N. Tex. State U., 1977-80; m. Saraswathy Namboodiri, Apr. 22, 1961; children—Maya, Indu. Project asso. U. Wis., 1971-72; asst. prof. math. Wis. State U. System, 1968-71, Coll. Racine (Wis.), 1972-74; asso. prof. math. Tex. Coll., Tyler, 1974-78, dir. computer center, 1978—. Recipient research cert. Oak Ridge Nat. Lab., 1976, certs. IBM, 1978, 79. Mem. Math. Assn. Am., Nat. Ednl. Computing Conf., Tex. Assn. Math. Tchrs. Club: Tennis. Contbr. articles in field to profl. jours. Home: 708 Oxford Circle Tyler TX 75703 Office: 2404 N Grand Ave Tyler TX 75702

NAMEY, THOMAS CURTIS, rheumatologist, nuclear physician, educator; b. Sharon, Pa., Sept. 22, 1948; s. John Thomas and Lorena Juanel (Curtis) N.; B.A. summa cum laude, Thiel Coll., 1969; M.D., Washington U., St. Louis, 1973; m. Anne M. Sexton, Oct. 7, 1978; 1 son, Thomas Anthony Curtis. Intern, Montreal Gen. Hosp.-McGill U., 1973-74, resident, 1974-75; fellow in rheumatology and nuclear medicine Med. U. S.C., 1975-76, U. Ala. Med. Center, 1976-78; instr. dept. medicine U. Ala., 1977-78; postdoctoral research fellow Arthritis Found., 1977-80; dep. dir. La. State U.-NIH Multipurpose Arthritis Center, New Orleans, 1978—; asst. prof. medicine and radiology La. State U. Med. Center, New Orleans, 1978—, asso. dir. sect. rheumatology and rehab. La. State U. Sch. Medicine, 1979—; cons. physician Mercy Hosp. Med. Center and Pain Unit; cons. rheumatologist Hotel Dieu and Touro Infirmary, New Orleans. Mem. council Arthritis Found. New Orleans. Diplomate Am. Bd. Nuclear Medicine; Pharm. Mfrs. Assn. trainee, 1972. Fellow Am. Acad. Neurologic Orthopedic Surgery (chief Coll. of Rheumatology); mem. AMA, N.Y. Acad. Scis., Orthopedic Research Soc., Soc. Nuclear Medicine, Am. Roentgen Ray Soc., AAAS, Am. Rheumatism Assn., Am. Coll. Nuclear Physicians, Am. Fedn. for Clin. Research, Am. Soc. for Clin. Pharmacology and Therapeutics, Am. Coll. Sports Medicine, Am. Geriatrics Soc., A.C.P., Orleans Parish Med. Soc., Sigma Xi. Republican. Developer nuclear medicine technique for evaluating causes of low back pain. Home: 107 Beverly Gate Metairie LA 70001 Office: La State U Med Center 1542 Tulane Ave New Orleans LA 70112

NANCE, MARY JOE, educator; b. Carthage, Tex., Aug. 7, 1921; d. F. F. and Mary Elizabeth (Knight) Born; B.B.A., N. Tex. State U., 1953; postgrad. Northwestern State U. La., 1974; M.E., Antioch U., 1978; m. Earl C. Nance, July 12, 1946; 1 son, David Earl. Tchr., Port Isabel (Tex.) Integrated Sch. Dist., to 1979; tchr. English, Splendora (Tex.) High Sch., 1979—. Served with USAAF, 1942-45. Cert. bus. educator. Mem. Nat. Bus. Edn. Assn., NEA, Tex. Tchrs. Assn., Tex. Bus. Tchrs. Assn., Nat. Women's Army Corps Vets. Assn., Air Force Assn., Assn. Supervision and Curriculum Devel., Council for Basic Edn. Baptist.

NANCE, NOLLEY TOLAR, architect; b. Sanford, Fla., Sept. 2, 1936; s. Murray Elmer and Mary Elizabeth N.; B.Design, U. Fla., 1973, M.Arch., 1974; m. Brenda Nancy Barnes, Apr. 29, 1972; children—Jason Rawdon, Jennifer Elizabeth. Project architect Mudano Assos., Architects, Inc., Clearwater, Fla., 1976-77; architect in charge prodn. and design Paras Assos., Tampa, Fla., 1977-78; prin./owner Nolley T. Nance, AIA, Dunedin, Fla., 1978—; cons. architect Ken L. King & Assos., cons. civil engrs., Clearwater, 1978—. Interim chmn. Dunedin Adv. Com. on Environ. Quality, 1977, chmn., 1978. Served with U.S. Army, 1959-62. Registered architect, Fla. Mem. AIA, Fla. Assn. Architects (sec./treas. Clearwater sect. Fla. Central chpt. 1978-79). Democrat. Baptist. Address: Nolley T Nance AIA Architect 234 Park Circle N Dunedin FL 33528

NANCE, TIMOTHY HAMILTON, elec. engr.; b. Columbia, S.C., Dec. 1, 1952; s. Robert Brown and Edna Earl (Burriss) N.; B.S. in E.E., The Citadel, 1975; m. Rosemary Price, Apr. 1, 1978. Design engr. Owen Electric Steel of Columbia (S.C.), 1975-78, elec. maintenance engr., 1978-80; project engr. Square D Co., Columbia, 1980—. Served with USAF, 1976. Mem. IEEE. Presbyterian. Home: 51 Orchard Circle Columbia SC 29206 Office: PO Box 9247 Columbia SC 29290

NAPIER, JAMES VOSS, telephone co. exec.; b. Ellsworth, Kans., Feb. 2, 1937; s. Nial Voss and Leonillia (Seus) N.; B.A., St. Benedict's Coll., 1959; postgrad. U. Kans., 1959; m. Mary Louise Hocke, July 18, 1959; children—Laura, Lisa, Miriam, Suzanne, Cynthia, Amy. With Continental Telephone Corp., Atlanta, 1965—, pres., 1976—. Mem. U.S. Ind. Telephone Assn. (sci. dir. Atlanta, 1978—), Young Pres.'s Orgn. Address: 56 Perimeter Center E Atlanta GA 30346

NAPIER, JOHN HAWKINS, III, historian; b. Berkeley, Calif., Feb. 6, 1925; s. John Hawkins and Lena Mae (Tate) N.; B.A., U. Miss., 1949; M.A., Auburn U., 1967; postgrad. Georgetown U., 1971; m. Cameron Mayson Freeman, Sept. 11, 1964. Journalist, tchr. Picayune (Miss.) High Sch., 1946; commd. 2d lt. U.S. Air Force, 1949, advanced through grades to lt. col., 1966, ret., 1977; staff dir. Congressional Com. on S.E. Asia, 1970; faculty Air War Coll., 1971-74; Air U. Command historian, 1974-77; asst. to exec. dir. Ala. Commn. on Higher Edn., Montgomery, 1977-78; lectr. in field. Pres., Montgomery Opera Guild, 1974-75, Montgomery Community Concert Assn., 1974-76, Old S. Hist. Soc., 1977-78. Served with USMC, 1943-46. Decorated Legion of Merit, also others; recipient award of Merit, Ala. Hist. Commn., 1976; Taylor Medal and grad. fellow U. Miss., 1949; Storrs scholar Pomona Coll., 1942-43. Mem. English-Speaking Union (pres. 1978—), Newcomen Soc., Ala. Hist. Assn. (pres. 1979-80), Soc. Pioneers Montgomery (pres. 1980—), Soc. Colonial Wars, SCV (vice comdr. Ala. 1979—), Soc. War of 1812 (v.p. Ala. 1978—), St. Andrews Soc., S.R., SAR, Order 1st Families Va., Jamestowne Soc., Sigma Chi, Phi Kappa Phi, Omicron Delta Kappa, Phi Alpha Theta, Pi Sigma Alpha, Scabbard and Blade. Democrat. Episcopalian. Clubs: Montgomery Country, Capital City, Aztec 1847, Mil. Order Carabao. Contbr. articles to profl. jours. Home: Kilmahew Box 193 Route 2 Ramer AL 36069

NARANJO, DANIEL ALBERTO, lawyer; b. San Antonio, Aug. 16, 1939; s. Joe Abel and Alice (Morales) N.; B.A., U. Tex., Austin, 1962, J.D., 1963; 1 dau., Cecilia Miriam. Admitted to Tex. bar, 1967, U.S. Supreme Ct. bar, 1971; partner firm McDonald, Karam, Naranjo & Guyer, San Antonio, 1980—; mem. grievance com. 10th Bar Dist., 1979-80. Mem. San Antonio Areawide Planning Adv. Com., 1976-77; insp. state elections State of Tex., 1976-77; bd. dirs. Camp Fire Girls, Inc., San Antonio, 1969, v.p., 1970, pres., 1971; bd. dirs. Drug Abuse Central, San Antonio, 1972-74, Citizens for Better Environment, San Antonio, Greater San Antonio Youth Symphony, 1977-79; chmn. intercultural coordinating com. San Antonio Symphony, 1979-80. Served to capt. USAF, 1967. Mem. Am. Bar Assn. (chmn. drug abuse com. Tex. 1972-73), Am., Fed., Inter-Am., San Antonio (dir. 1974-75, sec.-treas. 1975-76) bar assns., Tex. Jr. Bar (state dir. 1972-74, chmn. drug abuse program com. 1972-74, steering com. vol. parole aid com. 1973-74), San Antonio Jr. Bar (v.p. 1970-71, state bar dir. 1972-74, dir. 1972-74, participant Conf. on Delivery Legal Services to Spanish

Speaking 1977), Cath. Lawyer's Guild (v.p. 1971, pres. 1972), Bus. and Econ. Soc. San Antonio, State Bar Tex. (chmn. com. increase minority participation in bar 1975-76, com. legal services to poor, dir. 1976-77), Tex. Criminal Def. Lawyers Assn., Tex., San Antonio (dir. 1980—) trial lawyers, U. Tex. Law Sch. Alumni Assn. (dir. 1978—), Internat. Platform Assn., Common Cause, Delta Theta Phi, Phi Kappa Theta. Club: San Antonio Bachelor's. Home: 907 Fabulous St San Antonio TX 78213 Office: 442 Dwyer San Antonio TX 78204

NARASIMHAN, SEETHARAMA LAKSHMI, educator; b. Mohanur, Tamil Nadu, India, June 1, 1936; s. Seetharaman and Rukmani; B.S.M.E., U. Madras (India), 1959; M.S.I.E., U. Tenn., 1963; Ph.D., Ohio State U., 1973; m. Vethanayaki, Sept. 8, 1967; children—Priya, Ram Anand; came to U.S., 1962; Lectr., Nachimuthu Poly., 1960-62, head mech. engring. dept., 1962-63; process engr. Ford Motor Co., 1963-66; indsl. engr. Western Electric Co., Columbus, Ohio, 1967-72, mem. research staff, 1973-74; program fin. mgr. NCR Corp., Dayton, Ohio, 1974-75; asst. prof. N.C. Central U., Durham, 1976-78, asso. prof. bus. adminstrn., 1978—; adj. prof. N.C. State U., Raleigh, 1977—; vis. asso. prof. dept. mgmt. sci. U. R.I., Kingston, 1979-80; cons. Mgmt. Devel. Corp., Durham, 1978. Mem. Am. Inst. Indsl. Engrs. (chpt. v.p.), Ops. Research Soc. Am., Am. Inst. Decision Scis., Am. Prodn. and Inventory Control Soc., Sigma Xi, Alpha Pi Mu. Clubs: Toastmasters (v.p.), Optimist.

NARAYAN, KALMAN SRINIVASA, gastroenterologist; b. Madras, India, Nov. 19, 1946; s. Kalmanje Srinivasa and Upadhyaya (Indira) Upadhyaya; came to U.S., 1970; M.D., Govt. Stanley Med. Coll., Madras, 1962-70; m. Kusuma Malini Rao, Aug. 18, 1973; 1 child, Navin. Intern, Wayne State U., Detroit, 1970-71, resident in internal medicine, 1971-73, fellow in gastroenterology, 1974-76; emergency room physician Detroit Gen. Hosp., 1973-74; practice medicine specializing in gastroenterology, Ft. Worth, 1976—; cons. in gastroenterology Ft. Worth area hosps. Diplomate Am. Bd. Internal Medicine, Am. Bd. Gastroenterology. Fellow Am. Coll. Gastroenterology, Internat. Acad. Proctologists; mem. A.C.P., Tex. Med. Assn., Tarrant County Med. Soc. Home: 4301 Cumberland St N Fort Worth TX 76116 Office: 909 8th Ave Suite 7 Fort Worth TX 76104

NARDO, NORA, restaurant and hotel supply co. exec.; b. Havana, Cuba, Dec. 9, 1940; came to U.S., 1962, naturalized, 1970; d. Anselmo Amado and Zenaida (Valdes) Llizo; B.S., U. Havana, 1960; m. Juan A. Nardo, Dec. 9, 1960; children—Ana Maggie, Tony. Teller, ofcl. charge savs. accounts Trust Co. Havana, 1957-62; with Edward Don & Co. Fla., Miami, 1962—, office mgr., 1972—, br. budget coordinator, 1979—. Republican. Roman Catholic. Home: 100 NW 40th Ave Miami FL 33126 Office: 1550 N Miami Ave Miami FL 33136

NARINS, CHARLES SEYMOUR, lawyer, instrument co. exec.; b. Bklyn., Mar. 12, 1909; s. Joshua and Sarah E. (Levy) N.; J.D., Yale, 1932; B.S., N.Y. U., 1929; m. Frances D. Kross; children—Lyn Ross, Joyce Hedda. Admitted to N.Y. bar, 1933, Mass. bar, 1955; atty. Curtin & Glynn, N.Y.C., 1932-34, Glynn, Smith & Narins, 1934-37, Probst & Probst, 1937-47; pres., dir., counsel C.L. Berger & Sons, Inc., Boston, 1947-68; chmn. Berger Instruments div. High Voltage Engring. Corp., 1968-74. Past bd. dirs., mem. corp. Norfolk House Centre, Boston, 1957. Trustee Boston Opera, Boston Ballet Co.; chmn. med. planning com., bd. dirs. New Eng. Sinai Hosp.; mem. men's com. Boston Symphony Ball, 1965; bd. dirs. Boston Civic Symphony Orch., 1975—; v.p., bd. dirs. Greater Palm Beach Symphony: law sch. rep. Assn. Yale Alumni. Mem. Am., N.Y. State, Mass., Boston bar assns., Assn. Bar City N.Y., N.Y. County Lawyers Assn., Am. Congress Surveying and Mapping, Am. Mgmt. Assn., Am. Judicature Soc., Boston C. of C., Advt. Club N.Y., Pi Lambda Phi. Clubs: University, Yale (Boston); Yale, N.Y. U. (N.Y.C.); Yale, Poinciana (Palm Beach); Harvard (Boston); Kernwood Country (Salem, Mass.); Palm Beach (Fla.) Country (bd. govs., sec.). Home: 100 Sunrise Ave Palm Beach FL 33480 also Rockyledge Rd Swampscott MA 01907

NARVAEZ, JOSE LUIS, pharm. mfg. co. exec.; b. Naranjito, P.R., Jan. 8, 1942; s. Jose and Filomena (Marrero) N.; B.B.A., U. P.R., 1964; m. Virginia Ortiz, Sept. 5, 1964; 1 son, Jose Luis. Adminstrv. asst. Blue Cross, San Juan, P.R., 1967-69; personnel mgr. Texaco P.R., San Juan, 1969-73; personnel adminstr. Warner Lambert Co., N.Y.C., 1973-79; personnel mgr. Bristol Alpha Corp., Barceloneta, P.R., 1979—. Treas., Cruzada Civica Pro Seguridad de Transito, 1972-73. Served to 1st lt., inf. U.S. Army, 1964-66. Mem. Personnel Mgrs. Assn. Pharm. Industry, Queens Personnel Mgrs. Assn. (v.p. 1978-79), Mu Tau Sigma. Democrat. Roman Catholic. Office: Bristol Alpha Corp Rd 2 Cruze Davila Barceloneta PR 00617

NASCHOLD, ERIC THEODORE, JR., cons. engring. firm exec.; b. Erie, Pa., Nov. 3, 1927; s. Eric Theodore and Clara Maria (Wolff) N.; B.S., Va. Mil. Inst., 1950; student in Bus., Alexander Hamilton Inst., 1968; m. Janice Marylyn Hoover, Jan. 29, 1950; children—Frederick Theodore, Marylyn Jane. Elec. engr. E.I. DuPont Co., Camden, S.C., 1950-51; partner, elec. engr. Hayes, Seay, Mattern & Mattern, Salem, Va., 1951—; profl. engring. mem. City of Salem Bldg Code Appeals Bd., 1975—, State Bd. Architects, Profl. Engrs. and Land Surveyors, 1978—. PTA pres. Mt. Vernon Elem. Sch., 1966-67, Broad St. Sch., 1973-74; regional v.p. Roanoke County Council, 1974-75; 2d v.p. Salem High Sch., 1978-79, 1st v.p., 1979—. Served with AUS, 1946-47. Mem. IEEE (sr.), Cons. Engr. Council Va., Nat. Soc. Profl. Engrs. (pres. Roanoke chpt. 1957-58, state pres. Va. 1965-66, nat. dir. 1968-73). Baptist. Clubs: Roanoke Country; Salem Kiwanis. Home: 133 Bartley Dr Salem VA 24153 Office: Hayes Seay Mattern & Mattern 1315 Franklin Rd S W Roanoke VA 24034

NASH, ROBERT TAYLOR, coll. dean; b. Dickson County, Tenn., Dec. 9, 1936; s. James H. and Karleen E. (Martin) N.; B.S. in Econs., Austin Peay State U., 1965; Ph.D., Tex. A&M U., 1971; m. Evelyn Joyce Morris, Jan. 6, 1961; children—Lori Michelle, Jennifer Sheree. Program analyst Exec. Office, Tenn. State Govt., 1965-67; chmn. dept. econs. Tex. A&I U., Kingsville, 1971-78, acting dean Coll. Bus., 1978, dean, 1978—; cons. Gas Finders Inc., 1976, City of Kingsville, 1977-79. Served with U.S. Army, 1955-58. NDEA fellow, 1967-71. Mem. SW Bus. Adminstrn. Assn., Southwestern Soc. Economists, Nat. Assn. Realtors, Soc. of Real Estate Appraisers, Kingsville Assn. Realtors, Tex. Assn. Realtors, Delta Sigma Pi, Omicron Delta Epsilon. Office: PO Box 182 Tex A&I Kingsville TX 78363

NASIM AKHTAR, cardiologist; b. Jamshedpur, India, June 30, 1944; came to U.S., 1967, naturalized, 1976; s. Mohammad and Saeedun (Nessa) Mohsin; student Notre Dame Coll. (Pakistan), 1961; M.D., King Edward Med. Coll. (Pakistan), 1966; m. Suzanne Chatham, Oct. 24, 1970; children—Jamiel Andrew, Sarah Meredith, Jehan Mohsin. Intern, Crozier-Chester Med. Center, Chester, Pa., 1967; resident in medicine Grad. Hosp., U. Pa., 1968-69, fellow in cardiology, 1970-71; fellow in cardiology Baylor U. Med. Center, Dallas, 1971-72; research trainee and clin. asso. in cardiovascular physiology and pharmacology VA Hosp., Washington, 1972-73; chief cardiac catheterization lab. Phila. Gen. Hosp., 1973-74; practice medicine specializing in med. cardiology Med. and Surg. Clinic Assn., Ft. Worth, 1974-75; pvt. practice cardiology, Ft. Worth, 1975—; mem. staff St. Joseph Hosp., Harris Hosp., Med. Plaza Hosp.; asst. prof. medicine U. Pa. Sch. Medicine, 1973-74. Fellow Am. Coll. Cardiology, Am. Coll. Chest Physicians, Clin. Council in Cardiology; mem. AMA, A.C.P., Tex. Med. Assn., Tarrant County Med. Soc., Am. Heart Assn. Islam. Contbr. articles in field to profl. jours. Office: 800 8th Ave Suite 506 Fort Worth TX 76104

NASON, DORIS ELNORA, educator; b. North Girard, Pa., Apr. 25, 1913; d. Roy B. and Emma (Dean) Nason; student Edinboro State Coll., Pa., 1930-32; B.S. in Edn., Boston U., 1947, M.Ed., 1948, Ed.D., 1951. Elementary tchr. Union Twp., Pa., 1932-35, Union City, Pa., 1935-42, Millcreek Twp., Pa., 1942-43, 45-47; Link Trainer instr. USN, Sanford, Fla., 1943-45; teaching fellow elementary edn. Boston U., 1948-50, lectr. edn., summers 1948-50; asst. prof. edn. U. Conn., 1950-61, asso. prof. edn., 1961-70, prof., 1970-75, prof. emeritus, 1975—, acting dir. reading-study center, 1969-72, dir., 1972-75; vis. prof. Stetson U., 1978—; dir. Reading Resources Network Center in Conn., 1970-75; cons., lectr. in field. Mem. Conn. State Adv. Council Right to Read. Mem. Conn. Assn. Reading Research, Nat. Conf. Research English, Internat., New Eng. (mem. exec. bd., 1964-68, pres. 1966-67, pres. Eastern Conn. council 1974-75) reading assns., Fla. Reading Council, AAUW, Pi Lambda Theta, Phi Delta Kappa. Author (with Robert Norris, Herbert Tag and Richard Neville) Foundations for Elementary School Teaching, 1963; cons. Reading Diagnosis: A Scholastic In-Service Audio Cassett Program, 1975. Editor: Teacher Education Quar., 1957-58. Editorial bd. 1952-66. Contbr. articles to profl. jours. Home: 95 Seminole Ave Ormond Beach FL 32074

NASRALLAH, NASEEM HANI, surgeon; b. Karaba, Syria, Jan. 21, 1940; s. Hani Gerues and Helen (Ghates) N.; came to U.S., 1971, naturalized, 1980; M.D., Med. Sch. Cairo, 1965; m. Hilda Ajailate, Feb. 5, 1971; children—Caroline, Ruba, Hani, Lauria. Intern, New Hanover Hosp., Wilmington, N.C., 1971-72, resident, 1972-74; resident U. N.C., Chapel Hill, 1974-76; practice medicine, specializing in surgery, Mathews, La.; active staff St. Anne Gen. Hosp., Raceland, La., 1976—; cons. staff St. Charles Hosp., St. Charles Parish, La., 1979, Lady of the Sea Hosp., Galliano, La., 1978—. Diplomate Am. Bd. Surgery. Mem. Am. Soc. Abdominal Surgery, So. Med. Assn., La. Med. Assn., Lafourche Parish Med. Assn. Home: 215 Church St Raceland LA 70394 Office: Central Lafourche Dr Mathews LA 70375

NASSAU, MARIAN EVELYN, social worker; b. Columbus, Ohio, Apr. 4, 1924; d. Joseph Mason and Fay (Levy) N.; A.B., Berea (Ky.) Coll., 1946; Univ. scholar U. Louisville, 1946-47; M.S.W. (ARC study scholar), Fla. State U., 1955. Caseworker, Children's Agy., Louisville, 1946-47; asst. dir. recreation center Louisville Dist. Recreation, 1948-49; receptional therapist Child Guidance Home, Cin., 1949; mgr. Miller's Gift Shop, Orlando, Fla., 1950-52; caseworker Orange County chpt. ARC, 1952-54; asst. dir. social service Fla. State Hosp., Chattahoochee, 1955-58; asst. dir. Mental Health Resource Council, Tampa, Fla., 1958-63; program dir. adult day treatment center Hillsborough Community Mental Health Center, Tampa, 1963-79, sr. psychiat. social worker, 1979—; cons., pub. health nurse, 1958-64; cons. Tampa County Welfare, 1966-69, Fla. Welfare Mental Health Unit, 1967-74. Active Nat. Council Jewish Women. Mem. Nat. Assn. Social Workers, Acad. Certified Social Workers (chpt. sec. 1957), Fla. Soc. Clin. Social Workers (charter), Marquis Soc., Internat. Platform Soc. Democrat. Jewish. Home: 4414 Paxton Ave Tampa FL 33611 Office: 5707 N 22d St Tampa FL 33610

NATANSON, GEORGE, fgn. news corr.; b. Chgo., 1928; student Pomona (Calif.) Jr. Coll., UCLA, U. San Marcos, Lima, Peru; married; 2 children. Radio, then TV reporter NBC News, Buenos Aires, 1952-54; fgn. press adv. to pres. Bolivia, La Paz, 1954; free-lance writer, La Paz; advt. rep. N.Y. Times; v.p. public relations for U.S. bank, Bolivia; Latin Am. editor Bus. Internat., 1958; spl. features editor, co-editor Sunday mag. Caracas (Venezuela) Daily Jour., 1959; econ. editor Vision, Spanish lang. news mag., N.Y.C., 1960-62; Mexico City bur. chief Los Angeles Times, 1962-66, Buenos Aires bur. chief, 1966-68; dep. coordinator fgn. press Mexican Organizing Com., Olympic Games, 1968; Latin Am. corr. CBS News, Mexico City, 1969—. Recipient journalism award for best fgn. story Los Angeles Times. Mem. Overseas Press Club, Fgn. Press Assn. Mexico City (past pres.).

NATCHER, WILLIAM HUSTON, congressman; b. Bowling Green, Ky., Sept. 11, 1909; s. J. M. and Blanche (Hays) N.; A.B., Western Ky. State Coll., Bowling Green, 1930; LL.B., Ohio State U., 1933; m. Virginia Reardon, June 17, 1937; children—Celeste, Louise. Admitted to Ky. bar, 1934, pvt. practice, Bowling Green, 1934—. Fed. conciliation commr. Western Dist. Ky., 1936-37; atty. Warren Co., 1937-49; commonwealth atty., 8th Jud. Dist., 1952-53; elected to 83d Congress (to fill unexpired term of Garrett L. Withers), 1953; mem. 84th to 96th Congresses, 2d Ky. Dist. Served as lt. USNR, 1942-45. Mem. Bowling Green Bar Assn. (pres.), Am. Legion, 40 and 8. Democrat. Odd Fellow, Kiwanian. Home: 638 E Main St Bowling Green KY 42101 Office: 414 E 10th St Bowling Green KY 42101

NATELSON, STEPHEN ELLIS, neurosurgeon; b. N.Y.C., Dec. 23, 1937; s. Samuel R. and Ethel D. (Nathan) N.; B.A. magna cum laude, Carleton Coll., 1958; Fulbright scholar in Math., Westfälische-Wilhelms U., Germany, 1958-59; M.D., U. Rochester, 1963; m. Marcia Gail Glidewell; children—Lea Jane, Jamie Ann, Jessica Ilana, Benjamin Henry. Intern, USAF Hosp., Wright-Patterson AFB, 1963-64; resident in neurosurgery Ohio State U., 1967-71; chief resident in neurology U. N.Mex., 1971-72; pvt. practice specializing in neurosurgery, Knoxville, Tenn., 1972—; clin. asso. prof. U. Tenn. Served with USAF, 1962-67. Decorated Air Force Commendation medal; diplomate Am. Bd. Neurol. Srugery. Fellow ACS; mem. Am. Assn. Neurol. Surgeons, Congress Neurol. Surgeons, AMA, Knoxville Acad. Medicine, Am. Physicians Fellowship, Undersea Med. Soc., Phi Beta Kappa, Sigma Xi, Alpha Omega Alpha. Republican. Jewish. Contbr. articles to profl. jours. Office: 505 Fort Sanders Professional Bldg Knoxville TN 37916

NATH, SUNIL BARAN, planner, researcher, adminstr.; b. Silchar, Assam, India, Mar. 31, 1937; s. Sarat Chandra and Sarada (Devi) N.; came to U.S., 1968, naturalized, 1977; B.A., Visva-Bharati Internat. U., Sriniketan, India, 1960; M.A. in Sociology, Agra (India) U., 1964, Ph.D. candidate in Sociology, 1967; M.A. candidate in Pub. Adminstrn., Fla. State U., 1978, Ph.D. candidate in Criminology, 1978—, student in Bus. Law, 1978—, grad. cert. in pub. adminstrn., 1978; m. Abha Rani Barua, Dec. 3, 1967; children—Subrata (Bobby), Sunita, Lipika. Asst. prof. sociology B.V. Rural Higher Inst., Agra, 1964-67; instr., field dir. Survey Data Center, Polit. Research Inst., Fla. State U., Tallahassee, 1969-70, research asso., field dir., 1970-71; statistician Fla. Parole and Probation Commn., Tallahassee, 1971, project dir. Fla. intensive probation and parole projects, 1971-73, dir. research planning and statistics, 1973-74, dir. planning and evaluation, 1974-76; planner, evaluator Dept. Offender Rehab., Tallahassee, 1976-79; civil rights adminstr. Fla. Dept. Transp., Tallahassee, 1979—; co-dir. Fla. Conf. on Evaluation Research; owner Nath Auto Super Mktg. Services, Tallahassee, 1977—; cons. Human Research & Devel. Services, Inc., Univ. Research Corp., Inc., Washington; a founding mem. Good Life Gen. Store, Tallahassee, 1979—; sub-agt. A Tour Travel Agy., Chgo. and Travel Connection, Inc., Miami, 1978—. Cubmaster Cub Scouts, 1979-80; active Boy Scouts Am., 1976—; mem. Gov.'s Adult Reform Plan, 1972-73; project dir. L.E.E.A. grant, 1972-74; 4-H Club community leader, 1979—. Mem. Am., Fla., So. States correctional assns., Am., So. sociol. assns., Am. Judicature Soc., Am. Acad. Polit. and Social Scis., Internat. Platform Assn., Nat., Fla. councils on crime and delinquency, Assn. for Correctional Research and Statistics, Internat. Howard League for Penal Reform (Eng.), Am. Soc. Pub. Adminstrn., Conf. Minority Pub. Adminstrs., Nat. Assn. Ams. of Asian Indian Descent (nat. exec. bd. 1980—), Delta Tau Kappa, Alpha Kappa Delta. Democrat. Hindu. Clubs: Toastmasters (pres. 1979-80), Internat. (Tallahassee). Contbr. articles to profl. jours. Home: 431 Victory Garden Dr Tallahassee FL 32301 Office: 605 Suwannee St Tallahassee FL 32301

NATHAN, DANIEL EVERETT, physician, surgeon; b. Tifton, Ga., May 8, 1916; s. Max and Edith (Lease) N.; B.S., U. Ga., 1936, M.D., 1940; m. Muriel Halprin, Jan. 24, 1942; children—David Harris, Sherrie Halprin. Intern St. Elizabeth Hosp., Elizabeth, N.J., 1940-41, City Hosp., N.Y.C., 1941-42, resident, 1945; practice medicine and surgery, Ft. Valley, Ga., 1946—; chief staff Peach County Hosp., 1962, 71-72, 76—; dir. Citizens Bank of Fort Valley; pres. Westview Devel. Corp. Lt. Col. Staff Gov. Ernest Vandiver of State of Ga., 1959, 62, lt. col. staff Carl Sanders, 1963-67; vice pres., dir., Ft. Valley Med. Nursing Home, 1967—. Co-ordinating com., Fort Valley; mem. Continental Air Command Res. Forces Policy Council, Surgeon Gen. Air Res. Forces Med. Adv. Council. Bd. dirs. Fedn. Jewish Charities Macon and Middle Ga., 1948-58. Med. adviser Local Draft Bd. 115, Ft. Valley, 1948; citizen's adv. council Robins AFB, Ga., 1963-67. Served from 1st lt. to maj. USAAC, 1942-45. Decorated Air medal, Soldier's medal. Diplomate Am. Bd. Family Practice. Fellow Am. Acad. Family Practice; mem. C. of C., Peach Belt, 6th Dist. med. socs., Med. Assn. Ga., Am. (Physician's Recognition award 1977-80), So. Aerospace med. assns., Assn. Mil. Surgeons, Ga. Heart Assn. (mem. profl. edn. com. 1961-66, Am. Cancer Soc., Am., (dir.-at-large), So. Calif., Middle Ga. (pres. 1973-75) camelia socs., Air-Medics Med. Aviation Assn., Ga. Alumni Soc., Am. Legion, Alpha Epsilon Pi, Phi Delta Epsilon, Jewish (dir. temple). Mason (Shriner). Club: Pine Needles Country. Home: 501 Westview Dr Fort Valley GA 31030 Office: 401 Park Ave Fort Valley GA 31030

NATHAN, IRA CLIFFORD, govt. ofcl.; b. N.Y.C., June 4, 1930; s. Abraham E. and Lillian (Rubin) N.; B.S., Rensselaer Poly. Inst., 1951; m. Tama Ripps, June 6, 1954; children—Keith, Bonnie, Shari. Mgr. quality assurance and metallurgy Taylor-Wharton, Harsco Corp., High Bridge, N.J., 1964-68; project mgr. Sperry-Rand, La. Army Ammunition Plant, Shreveport, 1968-74; project mgr. Thiokol Corp., La. Army Ammunition Plant, Shreveport, 1975-79; U.S. govt., ARRADCOM liaison officer Miss. Army Ammunition Plant, 1979—; metall. cons. Secondary sch. chmn. Rensselaer Poly. Inst. Served to lt. USAF, 1952-53. Mem. Am. Def. Preparedness Assn., Am. Soc. Metals, Epsilon Delta Sigma. Jewish. Mason. Clubs: East Ridge Country, Red River Stamp Soc. (pres. 1970-71). Home: Penthouse Garden Apts C-12 1550 E 2d St Pass Christian MS 39571 Office: Miss Mall 200 Hwy 43 E Picayune MS 39466

NATION, ROSALIND JOAN, social worker; b. LaGrange, Ga., Apr. 16, 1952; d. Jasper Newton and Margaret N.; B.A., LaGrange Coll., 1974; M.S.W., U Louisville, 1977. Tchr. adult basic edn. Troup Vocat. Tech. Sch., LaGrange, 1974-76, also social worker technician II Troup County Mental Health Center; psychiat. aide Norton's Children Hosp., Louisville, 1976-77; sr. social worker N.W. Ga. Mental Health Center, Fort Oglethorpe, 1977-78; social worker Peachford Hosp., Atlanta 1978-79, Comprehensive Care Center, 1979—. Mem. Nat. Assn. Social Workers, Atlanta Group Psychotherapy Soc. Baptist. Home: 1423-B Druid Valley Dr Atlanta GA 30329 Office: 2355 Bolton Rd NW Atlanta GA 30318

NATIONS, JOHN DREWRY, wholesale firm exec.; b. Fayette County, Ga., June 1, 1918; s. James Andrew and Birdie Elizabeth (Edmondson) N.; student Ga. Tech., 1935-37; m. Nancy Johnson, Sept. 21, 1940; children—Michael T., Nancy (Mrs. Clifford Ray Davis), Andrew H. Salesman Pye-Barker Supply Co., Atlanta, 1937-43; partner Cotton Gin, Turin, Ga., 1946-48; pres., chmn. bd. Bearings and Drives, Inc., indsl. distbn. firm, Macon, Ga., 1948—. Mem. nat. distbr. adv. council Dayco Mfg. Co., 1966, 70, sr. adviser, 1975; mem. nat. distbr. adv. council Diamond Chain Co., 1970, 73. Served to 1st lt. pilot, USAF, 1943-45. Mem. Bearing Specialists Assn. (dir. 1975—), Power Transmission Distbrs. Assn., C. of C. Methodist (finance chmn. 1960-66, chmn. ofcl. bd. 1962-65). Kiwanian, Elk. Club: Idle Hour Golf and Country (Macon, Ga.). Home: 4416 Old Club Rd Macon GA 31204 Office: 607 Lower Poplar St Macon GA 31208

NAUGLE, THOMAS CALVERT, JR., ophthalmologist, ophthalmic plastic surgeon; b. Gadsden, Ala., Nov. 30, 1939; s. Thomas Calvert and Mildred Annette N.; B.A., U. Miss.; M.D., Tulane U., 1967. Intern, Sch. Medicine, Baylor U., Houston, 1967-68; resident in ophthalmology with honors Sch. Medicine, Tulane U., New Orleans, 1968-71, asso. clin. prof. dept. ophthalmology, 1976—, dir. ophthalmic plastic surgery services; Heed Found. fellow in ophthalmic plastic surgery Eye Found. Hosp., Birmingham, Ala., 1971, Manhattan Eye/Ear Hosp., N.Y.C., 1972; co-dir. ophthalmic residency tng. program, dir. ophthalmic plastic surgery service Doctor's Hosp., Washington, 1974-75; practice medicine specializing in ophthalmology and ophthalmic plastic surgery, New Orleans, 1975—; cons. ophthalmic plastic surgery USPHS Hosp., New Orleans; cons. ophthalmology and ophthalmic plastic surgery VA Hosp. and Charity Hosp., New Orleans; chmn. surgery com. Eye, Ear, Nose and Throat Hosp., 1977, chmn. program com., 1978, exec. com., 1980; guest lectr. Chinese Acad. Sci., 1979. Sect. chmn. United Fund, 1976. Served to maj., M.C., USAF, 1972-74. Recipient USAF Med. Achievement award, 1973. Diplomate Am. Acad. Ophthalmology. Mem. Byron Smith Ophthalmic Plastic Surgery Club (treas. 1977—), New Orleans Grad. Med. Assembly (vice chmn. ophthalmology sect. 1977, chmn. 1978), New Orleans Acad. Ophthalmology (co-chmn. host com. 1977, chmn. 1978), So. Eye Bank (trustee), Tulane Ophthalmol. Alumni Club (v.p.), Napoleon Surg. Facility (chief ophthalmic surg. sect.), La.-Miss. Otolaryngol. and Ophthalmol. Soc., La. Opthalmol. Assn., Orleans Parish Med. Soc., Physicians Edn. Network, Sigma Delta Pi, Phi Delta Theta. Republican. Methodist. Clubs: France-Amerique de la Louisiane, Mem.'s Opera Guild New Orleans. Author pamphlet Emergency Ocular Care, 1972; contbr. articles to profl. publs. Home: 5420 Camp St New Orleans LA 70115 Office: 2620 Jena St New Orleans LA 70115

NAVARRO, CESAR OSWALD, mfg. co. exec.; b. Lima, Peru, Feb. 3, 1943; came to U.S. 1964; naturalized, 1971; m. Saturnino and Sara G. (Gallegos) N.; B.A. in Indsl. Engring., N.Y. U., 1967; postgrad. U. Houston, 1979-80; divorced; children—Cesar, Alex. Jr. engr. Western Electric Co., Kearny, N.J., 1968-71; personnel asst. Holly Stores-S.S. Kresge, N. Bergen, N.J., 1971-73; personnel mgr. Petro-Peru, Houston, 1973-77; dir. personnel and safety Proler Internat., Houston, 1977-79; personnel mgr. Veeco-Lambda Electronics, Corpus Christi, Tex. 1980—; instr. time and motion studies Piura (Peru) U., 1976; mem. staff Inst. Internat. Edn., World Trade Center,

Houston, 1977-80. Mem. Houston C. of C., Am. Mgmt. Assn., Houston Hispanic C. of C., Am. Inst. Indsl. Engrs., Am. Inst. Safety Engrs. Democrat. Baptist. Club: Hurricane Soccer. Home: 802 Barry St Corpus Christi TX 78411 Office: 121 International Dr Corpus Christi TX 78410

NAWROCKI, ALOYSIUS DAVID, scientist; b. Gary, Ind., Mar. 27, 1936; s. Aloysius David and Mary Eleanore (Stolarz) N.; A.B., Ind. U., 1963, M.S., 1965; Ph.D., U. Ill., 1973; m. Susanna Hunt; children—Sarah Marie, Elizabeth Hunt, Michael David. New products devel. engr. 3M Co., St. Paul, 1966-68; biophysics trainee U. Ill., 1968-72; post-doctoral fellow Rockefeller U., 1972-74; research scientist Brooks AFB, San Antonio, 1974-76; energy cons., San Antonio, 1976-78; asso. prof. physics Our Lady of the Lake U., San Antonio, 1978—; tech. adv. seminars Tex. Gov.'s Office Energy Resources, 1979; cons. S.W. Research Inst., San Antonio, 1978-80. Mem. Solar Task Force, Tex. Energy Adv. Council, 1977—; bd. dirs. I.D.E.A., Inc., 1977—. NSF grantee, 1978-79. Mem. AAAS, World Future Soc., Tex. Solar Energy Soc. (dir. 1978), Am. Soc. Public Adminstrs. Home: 1101 Wiltshire Dr San Antonio TX 78209 Office: Office of Spl Programs Our Lady of the Lake U 411 SW 24th St San Antonio TX 78285

NAYEEM, MOHAMMED ABDUL, physician; b. Shadnagar, India, Sept. 25, 1940; came to U.S., 1970, naturalized, 1972; s. Mohammed Abdul and Ahmadi (Begum) Raheem; B.Sc., Nizam Coll., 1958; M.B.,B.S., Osmania U., India, 1963, M.S. in surgery, 1969; m. Wanda I. Richey, Sept. 25, 1973; children—Anisa, Sara, Alia, Asma. Intern, Osmania Gen. Hosp., Hyderabad, India, 1963-64; resident Ill. Central Community Hosp., Chgo., 1972-75; practice family medicine and surgery Shelby Meml. Hosp., Alabaster, Ala. Mem. AMA, Tenn. Med. Assn., Am. Coll. Emergency Physicians. Home: 344 Adams St NW Rainsville AL 35986

NAYLOR, GEORGE LEROY, lawyer; b. Bountiful, Utah, May 11, 1915; s. Joseph Francis and Josephine Chase (Wood) N.; student U. Utah, 1934-36; student George Washington U., 1937; J.D. (Bancroft Whitney scholar, 1950-51, 52), U. San Francisco, 1953; m. Maxine Elizabeth Lewis, Jan. 18, 1941; children—Georgia (Mrs. Ralph E. Price), RoseMaree (Mrs. Glenn B. Hammer), George LeRoy II. Admitted to Calif. bar, 1954, San Francisco bar, 1954, Ill. bar, 1968, Chgo. bar, 1968; v.p., sec., legis. rep. Internat. Union of Mine, Mill & Smelter Workers, CIO, Dist. Union 2, Utah-Nevada, 1942-44; examiner So. Pacific Co., San Francisco, 1949-54, chief examiner, 1955, asst. mgr., 1956-61; carrier mem. Nat. R.R. Adjustment bd., Chgo., 1961-77, chmn., 1970-77; atty. Village of Fox River Valley Gardens, Ill., 1974-77; gen. counsel for Can-Veyor, Inc., Mt. View, Calif., 1959-64. Served with AUS, World War II. Mem. Am. Bar Assn. Mem. Ch. of Jesus Christ of Latter Day Saints. Author: Defending Carriers Before the NRAB and Public Law Boards, 1969; Choice Morsels in Tax and Property Law, 1966; Underground at Bingham Canyon, 1944; Nat. R.R. Adjustment Bd. Practice Manual, 1978. Home: 8417 Klondike Rd Pensacola FL 32506

NAZAR, JOSE L., publishing co. exec.; b. Santiago De Chile, Chile, Aug. 8, 1948; came to U.S., 1972; s. Jose and Eliana M. (Yrarrazaval) N.; A.A. in Bus. Adminstrn., Miami Dade Community Coll., 1976; B.A., Fla. Internat. U., 1980. Sales mgr. La Enciclopedia De Cuba, Coral Gables, Fla., 1976-77, regional mgr., 1977-78, chief exec. dir., 1978—; exec. cons. Nat. Fin. Co. Club: Masons. Home: 5401 Collins Ave Suite 319 Miami Beach FL 33140 Office: 801 Madrid St Coral Gables FL 33134

NAZARIO, LUIS ADAM, dentist; b. Sabana Grande, P.R., Sept. 25, 1909; s. Antero and Ramona N.; B.A., Inter Am. U., 1930; M.Th., Evang. Sem. P.R., 1934; M.S.W., Tulane U., 1943; D.D.S., Loyola U., New Orleans, 1946; m. Rosaline Rodriguez Alonso, Oct. 27, 1936; children—Yolanda Nazario Wagner, Nilda Nazario Brown, Alma Nazario Lax. Pvt. practice dentistry, Santurce, P.R., 1947—. Pres., founder Health Coop. P.R., 1960-65, Retirement City, P.R., 1963-78; pres. bd. trustees Evang. Hosp. Assn. P.R., 1955-78; bd. dirs. Geriatric Commn. P.R., 1966-76; pres. founder Club Sebaneno P.R., 1953-60, Gideons Internat. Assn. P.R., 1965-68, Assn. Elderly Persons of P.R., Inc., 1972-73; v.p. Council Chs. P.R., 1968-73. Served with AUS, 1943-44. Fellow Internat. Acad. Law and Sci.; mem. Coll. Dentists P.R., Am., Ohio dental assns. Presbyterian (elder 1955—). Clubs: Masons (32 deg.), Shriners, Order Eastern Star (Grand rep. 1970—, gen. grand lectr. 1973-77, writer laureate 1976). Author: Principles of Dental Health, 1960; My Student Life in New Orleans, 1971; What is Masonry?, 1974; Manual of Instruction in Masonry. Contbr. articles to dental and cultural mags. Home: Cond Condado Real Santurce PR 00914 Office: 184 Loiza St Box 6244 Loiza Sta Santurce PR 00914

NAZARIO-BLAS, AMADEO, TV exec.; b. Mayaguez, P.R., Feb. 7, 1943; s. Amadeo Nazario-Janer and Paquita Blas-Vera; B.A., U. P.R., Mayaguez Campus, 1966; m. Idabell Colon, May 29, 1969; children—Aline, Astrid Michelle. Ins. investigator Retail Credit Co., San Juan, P.R., 1969-71; pres., owner Creative Communications Co., Mayaguez, 1971-72; gen. mgr. Sta. WOLE-TV, Channel 12, Mayaguez, 1972—. Named exec. of yr. in TV, Sales and Mktg. Execs., 1976. Mem. C. of C. of West (dir. 1979), Nu Sigma Beta (dist. v.p. 1976-77). Roman Catholic. Clubs: Rotary, Deportivo del Oeste (social pres. 1978-79). Home: B-28 Picachos Mayaguez PR 00708 Office: Sta WOLE-TV Channel 12 Box AQ Mayaguez PR 00708

NAZEMI, MALEK M., physician, biochemist; b. Teheran, Iran, July 5, 1935; came to U.S., 1967, naturalized, 1976; M.D., U. Heidelberg (Germany), 1962; Ph.D., U. Giessen (Germany), 1967. Biochemist, U. Giessen, 1964-67; intern Tucson Med. Center, 1968-69; resident Baylor Coll. Medicine, Houston, 1969-74; practice medicine specializing in internal medicine, El Paso, Tex., 1974—; mem. staff Sierra Med. Center, Providence, Sun Tower infectious disease cons. Diplomate Am. Bd. Internal Medicine. Fellow A.C.P.; mem. AMA, Am. Soc. Microbiology, Am. Fedn. Clin. Research, El Paso County Med. Soc., Tex. Med. Assn., Am. Thoracic Soc., Sierra Club. Contbr. articles to profl. jours. Patentee in field. Office: 1501 Arizona Blvd El Paso TX 79902

NAZZARO, SAMUEL GERALD, hosp. adminstr.; b. Dover, N.J., May 30, 1929; s. Alfonso L. and Mafalda I. (Miranda) N.; B.S., St. Louis U., 1951, M. Hosp. Adminstrn., 1953; m. Della Mustacciuolo, Oct. 9, 1956; children—Rosemary, Samuel Gerald, Delores, Michael. Asst. adminstr. Wheeling (W.Va.) Hosp., 1955-61, asso. adminstr., 1962-65, adminstr., 1965—. Served with Med. Service Corp., U.S. Army, 1953-55. Mem. W.Va. Hosp. Assn., Am. Hosp. Assn., Am. Coll. Hosp. Adminstrs. Club: Civitan. Home: 6 Hawthorne Ct Wheeling WV 26003 Office: Med Park Wheeling WV 26003

NEAL, PATRICK K., builder, state senator; b. Des Moines, Iowa, Mar. 4, 1949; s. Paul and Patricia K. N.; B.S. in Econs., U. Pa., 1971; m. Charlene Lovingood, Aug. 12, 1978. Pres., Neal Communities, Inc., Longboat Key, Fla., 1977—; broker Neal & Neal Realtors, Longboat Key, 1972—; mem. Fla. Ho. of Reps., 1974-78, Fla. Senate, 1978—. Trustee, New Coll. Found., Sarasota, Fla. Mem. Nat. Bd. Realtors, Fla. Bd. Realtors, Nat. Homebuilders Assn., Gulf Coast Builders Assn. Democrat. Roman Catholic. Club: Kiwanis. Office: PO Box 500 Longboat Key FL 33548

NEAL, RUTH ELIZABETH, radiologist; b. New Orleans, Nov. 16, 1948; d. Carroll Osborne and Eola Lyons (Lyons) Reid; B.S., Xavier U., 1969; M.D., Howard U., 1973; (class sec. 1971-72, 72-73, recipient health service certificate, Fredrick D. Drew award, 1973); m. Alimam Butler Neal, Jan. 3, 1976; 1 son, Alimam Butler. Intern, Howard U. Hosp., Washington, 1973-74, resident in diagnostic radiology, 1974-77 (recipient 3d. pl. resident presentation, 1977, 2d. pl. 1976); practice medicine specializing in radiology Augusta, Ga., 1977—; mem. staff Eugene Talmedge Meml. Hosp.; asst. prof. diagnostic radiology Med. Coll. Ga. Augusta, 1977—. Mem. Nat. Assn. Resident, Internes, Am. Coll. Radiology (jr. mem.), Am. Med. Womens' Assn., Stoney Med. Assn., Student Nat., Am. (Physicians Recognition award 1978) med. assns., Alpha Kappa Alpha. Democrat. Methodist. Contbr. articles to profl. jours. Home: 540 Hillwood Circle Augusta GA 30909

NEAL, STEPHEN LYBROOK, congressman; b. Winston-Salem, N.C., Nov. 7, 1934; s. Charles H. and Mary Martha (Lybrook) N.; student U. Calif., Santa Barbara; B.A. in Psychology, U. Hawaii, 1959; m. Rachel Landis Miller, June 13, 1964; children—Mary Piper, Stephen Lybrook. Mortgage banker, hotel mgr., until 1966; pres. Community Press, Inc., Winston-Salem, 1966-75; mem. 94th-96th Congresses from N.C. 5th Dist.; chmn. subcom. internat. trade, investment and monetary policy, select com. task force on marijuana, ranking majority mem. subcom. on domestic monetary policy. Democrat. Presbyterian. Office: 331 Cannon House Office Bldg Washington DC 20515

NEAS, DIXON VALMORE, govt. ofcl.; b. Abilene, Tex., Aug. 10, 1944; s. Otis Bertram and Latayne (Kendrick) N.; student U. Tex., 1962-64; B.S. in Indsl. Engring., Tex. Technol. U., 1967; postgrad. U. Okla., 1968-69; M.B.A., Central State U., 1977; m. Judy Carole Fletcher, May 22, 1970; children—Holly Laughlin, Heather Suzanne. Indsl. engr. U.S. Air Force Logistics Command, Oklahoma City Air Logistics Center, Tinker AFB, 1967-77, cost analyst, 1977-79; sr. cost analyst Hdqrs. USAF Logistics Command, 1980—. Cons., Clean Community Commn., Oklahoma City Beautiful, Inc. (Excellence award, 1977); exec. com. Last Frontier council Boy Scouts Am., 1979. Mem. Am. Inst. Indsl. Engrs. (Sr.), Soc. Profl. Engrs. and Scientists, Air Force Assn., Internat. Material Mgmt. Soc. (certified), Tinker Mgmt. Club. Mem. Ch. of Christ. Club: Toastmasters Internat. Home: 8304 Glenwood Ave Oklahoma City OK 73114 Office: 2854th ABG/ACM Tinker AFB Oklahoma City OK 73145

NEAS, JOHN THEODORE, petroleum co. exec.; b. Tulsa, May 1, 1940; s. George and Lillian J. (Kasper) N.; B.S., Okla. State U., 1967, M.S., 1968; m. Sally Jane McPherson, June 10, 1966; children—Stephen, Gregory. With accounting dept. Rockwell Internat., 1965; with controller's dept. Amoco Prodn. Co., 1966-67; mem. audit and tax staff Haskins & Sells, 1968-75; pres. Nat. Petroleum Sales, Inc., Tulsa, 1975—, Port City Bulk Terminals, Inc., Tulsa, 1976—; owner John Neas Tank Lines; asst. instr. U. Tulsa, 1974. C.P.A., Okla. Mem. Nat. Assn. Accountants (v.p. membership 1976-77), Am. Inst. C.P.A.'s, Okla. Soc. C.P.A.'s, Port of Catoosa C. of C. Republican. Lutheran. Clubs: Petroleum, Oil Marketers, Transportation (Tulsa); Propeller; Oaks Country. Home: 7840 S College Pl Tulsa OK 74136 Office: 3105 S Skelly Dr Suite 509 Tulsa OK 74105

NEAVES, WILLIAM BARLOW, cell biologist; b. Spur, Tex., Dec. 25, 1943; s. William Fred and Revvie Lee (Hefner) N.; A.B. magna cum laude with highest honors in Biology, Harvard U., 1966, Ph.D., 1969; m. Priscilla Elizabeth Wood, Jan. 25, 1965; children—William Barlow, Clarissa d'Laine. Teaching fellow in biology Harvard U., 1965-66; lectr. vet. anatomy U. Nairobi, Kenya, 1970-71; lectr. anatomy Harvard U. Med. Sch., 1972; asst. prof. cell biology U. Tex. Southwestern Med. Sch., Dallas, 1972-74, asso. prof., 1974-77, prof., asso. dean Grad. Sch., 1977—; research asso. Los Angeles County Mus., 1970-73; cons. Ford Found., 1973-74; vis. prof. U. Nairobi, 1978. Rockefeller Found. postdoctoral fellow, 1970-71; recipient numerous research grants USPHS, nat. and internat. founds. Mem. Am. Assn. Anatomists, AAAS, Soc. Study of Reprodn., Sigma Xi. Methodist. Asso. editor Anatomical Record, 1975—; contbr. numerous articles to profl. jours., chpts. to books. Home: 3510 Sheffield Ct Arlington TX 76013 Office: Dept of Cell Biology University of Texas Southwestern Medical School 5323 Harry Hines Blvd Dallas TX 75235

NEBEL, WILLIAM ARTHUR, physician; b. Charlotte, N.C., Dec. 23, 1936; s. Arthur E. and Marie G. (Hunter) N.; A.B. in History, U. N.C., 1958, M.D., 1962; m. Ann Elizabeth Bonner, June 30, 1959; children—William Arthur, Ann Marie. Intern in medicine Duke U. Med. Center, Durham, N.C., 1962-63, asst. clin. prof. dept. obstetrics and gynecology, 1973—; resident in obstetrics and gynecology U. N.C., Chapel Hill, 1963-67, instr. dept. obstetrics and gynecology, 1969-70, clin. instr., 1970—; practice medicine specializing in obstetrics and gyencology, Chapel Hill, 1969—; mem. staff N.C. Meml. Hosp.; chmn. dept. Ob-gyn. Durham County Gen. Hosp.; mem. steering com. Chapel Hill Health Maintenance Orgn. Planning Project, 1973. Chmn. troop com. Oconeeche council Boy Scouts Am., 1975-78; basketball coach Boys Recreation League, Chapel Hill, 1975-79; mem. Orange County (N.C.) Health Bd., 1977—; vestryman Ch. of Holy Family, 1973-76. Served to lt. comdr. M.C., USNR, 1967-69. Recipient Tchr. Recognition award Am. Acad. Family Physicians, 1976; Chapel Hill-Carrboro Father of Year award, 1977. Diplomate Am. Bd. Obstetrics and Gynecology. Fellow Am. Coll. Obstetrics and Gynecology; mem. N.C., South Central, Robert A. Ross (pres. 1976) obstet. and gynecol. socs., Am. Fertility Soc., South Atlantic Assn. Obstetricians and Gynecologists, N.C., Durham-Orange County med. socs., Am. Cancer Soc. (pres. Orange County unit 1975-76, dir. N.C. div. 1977-78), Internat. Platform Assn., Alpha Omega Alpha, Phi Alpha Theta, Phi Chi, Pi Kappa Alpha (pres. 1958). Episcopalian. Clubs: Rotary (pres. 1975-76), Chapel Hill Country, Chapel Hill Cotillion, Seven Lakes Country. Contbr. articles to profl. jours. Home: 1030 Torrey Pines Pl Chapel Hill NC 27514 Office: Conner Dr Profl Bldg Chapel Hill NC 27514

NECHAY, BOHDAN ROMAN, pharmacologist, toxicologist; b. Prague, Czechoslovakia, Nov. 26, 1925; s. Simon M. and Maria (Malewicz) N.; student U. Innsbruck (Austria), 1945, Sch. Veterinary Medicine, Munich, Germany, 1946-47; Cand. Med. Vet., Sch. Veterinary Medicine, Giessen, Germany, 1947-49; D.V.M., U. Minn., 1953; m. Birgitta Singhild Ahlm, July 14, 1961; children—Nicholas, Peter. Poultry pathologist Hilltop Labs., Mpls., 1951-53; practice veterinary medicine, Mpls., 1954-56; asst. prof. dept. pharmacology and therapeutics U. Fla. Coll. Medicine, 1961-66; asst. prof. div. pharmacology and urology Duke U. Sch. Medicine, 1966-68; asso. prof. dept. pharmacology and toxicology U. Tex. Med. Br., Galveston, 1968-78, prof., 1978—; vis. scientist Inst. Pharmacology and Toxicology Biomed. Center, Uppsala U., Sweden, 1972-73. NIH fellow, 1960-61; Am. Heart Assn. fellow, 1959-60. Mem. Am. Soc. Pharmacology and Exptl. Therapeutics, Am. Soc. Nephrology, Southwestern Assn. Toxicologists, So. Salt, Water and Kidney Club, Soc. Toxicology, Sigma Xi. Club: Lions. Patentee in field. Contbr. articles to profl. jours. Home: 29 Dansby Dr Galveston TX 77550 Office: Dept Pharmacology and Toxicology U Tex Med Br Galveston TX 77550

NEEB, DAVID LYNN, assn. exec.; b. Bossier City, La., Oct. 30, 1952; s. George W. and Iris Neeb; B.A., La. Tech. U., 1974. Research analyst Harvey (La.) Canal Indsl. Assn., 1975-76; membership dir. Associated Builders and Contractors, Gretna, La., 1976, dir. edn., 1977-78; exec. dir. Assn. Diving Contractors, Gretna, 1978—. Mem. Algiers Jaycees (Jaycee of Yr. 1978-79, external v.p. 1979-80, pres. 1980—). Home: 203 Linda Ct Gretna LA 70053 Office: 1799 Stumpf Blvd Bldg 7 Suite 4 Gretna LA 70053

NEEDHAM, CHRISTINA WHITTEN, educator; b. Sayre, Okla., July 7, 1921; d. Commodore D. and Ora M. (Brown) Whitten; B.Ed. cum laude, U. Miami, 1961, M.Ed., 1967; Ed.S., Fla. Atlantic U., 1970, postgrad. 1971—; m. Francis J. Needham. Owner-operator LaCima Apts., Miami, Fla., 1955—, resort apt. hotel, Hampton Beach N.H., 1946-54; mgr. hotel, Miami Beach, Fla., 1946-48; newspaper reporter, advt. salesperson, 1939-42; team leader, tchr. Dade County Schs., Miami, 1961-64, supr. central adminstrn., 1964-66, lead project asso. Center for Self-Instrn., 1966-69; asst. prof. edn. Fla. Atlantic U., Boca Raton, 1969—. Coe Found. fellow Am. studies, 1961. Mem. Am. Acad. Polit. and Social Sci., Nat. Soc. Study Edn., Am., Fla. ednl. research assns., Am., Fla. assns. tchr. educators, Internat. Platform Assn., Am., Fla. assns. for supervision and curriculum devel., Friends of Everglades, Herstory, Phi Alpha Theta, Phi Delta Kappa, Delta Kappa Gamma, Kappa Delta Pi, Epsilon Tau Lambda. Author: (with Betty C. Morris) A Competency-Based Student Teaching and Internship Program, 1974; A Systems Model Approach to Accountability, 1976, Spanish edit., 1976. Home: 8865 SW 83d St Miami FL 33173 Office: Fla Atlantic U Coll Edn Boca Raton FL 33431

NEEF, HAZEL EVE MOUTON, dietitian; b. Scott, La., July 4, 1926; d. Rene F. and Leah Marie (Martin) Mouton; B.S., U. Southwestern La., 1946; postgrad. Nichols State U., 1965-66, La. State U., 1970; m. William Granville Neef, Jan. 19, 1951; children—Patricia Ann, Pamela Joan, Janette Lynn, Geralyn, William Stephen, Dorothy Marie, Thomas Michael. Dietitian, Touro Infirmary, 1947-48; asst. chief dietitian VA Hosp., Alexandria, La., 1948-51; head therapeutic dietitian Hermann Hosp., Houston, 1952-53; head dietary dept. St. Joseph Hosp., Thibodaux, La., 1964-67; dir. dietary dept. Our Lady of Lourdes, Lafayette, La., 1967—. Bd. dirs. Acadiana Health Planning Council, 1972-76, Dist. IV Area Agy. on Aging, 1976—; mem. Council on Alcoholism, 1976-78; mem. Mid La. Health Systems Agy. Mem. Lafayette Dist. Dietetic Assn. (chmn. legis. com.), La. Dietetic Assn. (pres. elect), Am. Dietetic Assn., Nutrition Today Soc., Kappa Omicron Phi. Roman Catholic. Home: Route 1 Box 35 Scott LA 70583 Office: 611 St Landry Lafayette LA 70502

NEELY, J(AMES) WINSTON, plant breeder; b. Cotton Plant, Ark., Feb. 4, 1906; s. James William and Daisy (Holland) N.; B.S., U. Ark., 1928; Ph.D., Cornell U., 1935; m. Elsie Norris, June 13, 1935 (dec.); 1 son, Eugene Trahin; m. 2d, Betty J. Goodman, Jan. 13, 1973. Asst. in agronomy U. Ark., 1929-30, Cornell U., 1930-35; geneticist U.S. Dept. Agr., 1935-46; plant breeder Stoneville (Miss.) Pedigreed Seed Co., 1946-51; v.p., dir. plant breeding Coker's Pedigreed Seed Co., Hartsville, S.C., 1951-71, cons., 1971-78; exec. v.p. S.C. Soybean Assn., 1971-72; adviser Clemson Coll., U.S. Dept. Agr., assns. and orgns.; pres. S.C. Agronomy Soc., 1973-74. Fellow A.A.A.S., Am. Soc. Agr.; mem. Phi Kappa Phi, Sigma Xi. Presbyn. Home: 203 Holly Dr Hartsville SC 29550

NEELY, MATTHEW MANSFIELD, II, educator; b. Fairmont, W.Va., Feb. 11, 1933; s. John Champ and Mary (Faust) N.; B.A., Ohio State U., 1957, M.A., 1961, B.S., 1962, Ph.D., 1967; m. Lahna Rogene Runck, Mar. 9, 1962; 1 son, Matthew Mansfield III. Reporter, Dun & Bradstreet, Inc., Columbus, O., 1957-59; tchr. pub. schs., Columbus, 1962-64; instr. Ohio State U., Columbus, 1967; asst. prof. edn. and philosophy Shepherd Coll., Shepherdstown, W.Va., 1967-70; prof. history Lord Fairfax Coll., Middletown, Va., 1970—. Fellow in residence in ancient Nr. Eastern history, 1974. Served with AUS, 1952-55. Decorated Bronze Star; Sigmund Rhee medal for valour (South Korea). Mem. Am. Hist. Assn., Winchester Hist. Soc., W.Va. Philos. Soc. (past pres.), Va. Social Sci. Assn., Preservation Historic Winchester, Phi Alpha Theta, Tau Kappa Epsilon, Phi Theta Kappa (founder local chpt.). Reviewing editor for history Va. Social Sci. Jour. Contbr. articles to profl. jours. Home: 419 Jefferson St Winchester VA 22601 Office: Lord Fairfax Coll Middletown VA 22645

NEELY, RALPH HENRY, accountant, fin. cons.; b. Hornell, N.Y., Aug. 5, 1922; s. Lynn J. and Nellie A. (Crippen) N.; B.A., Drake U., 1948; m. Donna M. Blaney, Dec. 21, 1945; 1 son, Lawrence E. Asso. editor, sports editor Allegany County Democrat, Wellsville, N.Y., 1941-42; mem. prodn. engring. dept. Worthington Corp., 1942-43; with Garner Pub. Co., 1943-56; sr. accountant Nelson & Co., Oviedo, Fla., 1957—; columnist, editorial writer Outlook, Oviedo, 1977—; dir., fin. cons. NPN Corp., 1977—. Mem. Charter Revision Com. for Oviedo, 1977—; mem. grants com. City of Oviedo, 1978—; dir. Oviedo Athletic Assn. Mem. Fla. Sheriffs Assn. Nat. Trust Hist. Preservation. Democrat. Methodist. Home: PO Box 549 Oviedo FL 32765 Office: PO Box 836 Oviedo FL 32765

NEELY, RICHARD, chief justice W.Va. Supreme Ct.; b. Aug. 2, 1941; s. John Champ and Elinore (Forlani) N.; A.B., Dartmouth, 1964; LL.B., Yale, 1967; m. Carolyn Elmore. Admitted to W.Va. bar, 1967; practiced in Fairmont, W.Va., 1969-73; chmn. Marion County Bd. Pub. Health, 1971-72; mem. W.Va. Ho. of Dels., 1971-72; justice W.Va. Supreme Ct. of Appeals, Charleston, 1973—. Chmn. bd. Kane & Keyser Co., Belington, W.Va. Served from 1st lt. to capt., U.S. Army, 1967-69. Decorated Bronze Star medal, Vietnam Honor medal 1st Class. Mem. W.Va. Bar Assn., Am. Econ. Assn., V.F.W., Am. Legion, Phi Delta Phi, Phi Sigma Kappa. Episcopalian. Moose. Home: Pinelea Country Club Rd Fairmont WV 26554 Office: E-306 State Capitol Bldg Supreme Ct of Appeals Charleston WV 25305

NEELY, ROBERT ALLEN, physician; b. Temple, Tex., Mar. 1, 1921; s. Jubal A. and Almeida (Fordtran) N.; B.A., U. Tex., 1942, M.D., 1944; postgrad. Washington U., 1951-52; m. Eleanor V. Stein, June 29, 1944; children—Byron D., Warren F. Intern, also resident Hermann Hosp., Houston, 1944-45, 55-57; gen. practice medicine, 1946-51, specializing in ophthalmology, Bellville, Tex., 1955—; trustee, staff mem. Bellville Hosp., Inc.; pres. Mid-Tex. Nursing Homes, Inc.; dir. 1st Nat. Bank of Bellville. Mem. Bellville Ind. Sch. Dist. Sch. Bd., 1948-53; past pres. Bellville Area United Fund; adv. bd. mem. Sam Houston Area council Boy Scouts Am., past mem. nat. council. Served with USNR, 1943-46, 53-55. Recipient Silver Beaver award Boy Scouts Am. Fellow Am. Acad. Ophthalmology; mem. AMA, Austin-Grimes-Waller Counties (past pres.), Ninth Dist. (past pres.) med. soc., Tex. Med. Assn., Tex. Ophthal. Assn., Houston Ophthal. Soc., Tex. Soc. Opthalmology and Otolaryngology, Bellville C. of C. Republican. Lutheran. Clubs: Bellville Golf (past pres.), Champions Golf, Doctors, Lions (past pres.). Home: 105 E Hacienda Ln Bellville TX 77418 Office: Bellville Clinic Bldg Bellville TX 77418

NEESE, URBAN EARL, geophysicist; b. Fayette County, Tex., July 19, 1914; s. Earl Conrad and Edna (Schott) N.; student U. Tex., 1933-34, St. Mary's U., 1934-35, U. Alaska, 1935-36, U. Tex., 1936-37; m. Dorothy Louise Finck, Apr. 17, 1937; children—Patricia

Anne, Robert Urban. Geophys. computer Stanolind Oil & Gas Co., Tulsa, 1937-45; geophys. supr. N.Am. Geophys. Co., Houston, 1945-46; geophysicist, v.p. Tidelands Exploration Co., Houston, 1946-53; geophysicist, owner Neese Exploration Co. and Gravity Map Service, Richmond, Tex., 1953—. Mem. Soc. Exploration Geophysicists, Am. Assn. Petroleum Geologists. Roman Catholic. Author geol. and geophys. reports. Home: Route 1 Box 205-D Richmond TX 77469 Office: PO Box 146 Richmond TX 77469

NEFF, BARBARA LEE, govt. exec.; b. Lincoln, Nebr., Oct. 19, 1940; d. Richard Gilmer and Esther Lucile (Papik) Beeler; student Colo. Woman's Coll., Denver, 1958-59; m. 1959 (div. 1964); children—Deborah Kay, David Bryan. Personal sec. to Congressman John Paul Hammerschmidt, Washington, 1969-74; personal sec. to sr. partner Kirkland, Ellis & Rowe, 1974-75; personal sec. to gen. counsel Nat. Oceanic and Atmospheric Adminstrn., Washington, 1975-77; asst. to chmn. Climate Research Bd., Nat. Acad. Scis., Washington, 1978-79; asst. to adminstr. NRC, 1979-80; asst. to pres. Univ. Corp. for Atmospheric Research, 1980—. Named Outstanding Citizen of Year, 1958. Mem. Future Bus. Leaders Am. (pres. schs. chpt.), Alpha Pi Epsilon. Home: 6827 Dina Leigh Ct Springfield VA 22153

NEFF, HELEN MARGARET OSTERHOLM, writer, editor; b. Superior, Wis.; d. Albin N. and Ellen (Julien) Osterholm; student U. Neb., 1925-27, U. Cal., Berkeley, 1929-30; A.B., Washington U., St. Louis, 1933, Rensselaer Poly. Inst.-Tech. Writers' Inst., 1962; m. Carroll Forsyth Neff, Feb. 1, 1930, (div. 1957); children—Charlotte (Mrs. Walter Newman), Carroll. Sch. reporter Omaha World-Herald, 1923-27; sec. Swedish Vice Consul, Omaha, 1927-29; case worker St. Louis Relief Adminstrn., 1935-36; med. writer dept. surgery Emory U. Sch. Medicine, Atlanta, 1951-55; writer-editor Center for Disease Control USPHS, Atlanta, 1955-79, chief, editorial sect. Info. Office, 1960-79; ret., 1979. Bd. dirs., editor newsletter Druid Hills Civic Assn., 1949-70. Fellow Am. Med. Writers Assn. (nat. sec. 1967-70, chmn. organizing com., 1st pres. S.E. chpt. 1975-76); mem. Am. Pub. Health Assn., A.A.A.S., League Women Voters, Internat. Platform Assn., Am. Bus. Women's Assn. Methodist. Contbr. articles to profl. jours. Home: 400 Princeton Way NE Atlanta GA 30307

NEFF, WILLIAM, JR., clergyman, lawyer; b. Muskogee, Okla., May 22, 1925; s. William and Arnetas (Zink) N.; B.A., U. Tulsa, 1945; M.Div., Garrett Theol. Sem., 1947; J.D., U. Tulsa, 1976; m. Margie Fisk, June 19, 1946; children—William, Naomi, Jonathan, David. Ordained to Meth. ministry, 1947; pastor Sheridan Ave. Ch., Tulsa, 1947-49, Pilgrim Presbyn. Ch., Vinita, Okla., 1949-55, St. Andrews Presbyn. Ch., Tulsa, 1955-77, Congl. Ch. of the Pilgrimage, Tulsa, 1978—. Chaplain Okla. legislature, Tulsa County Bar. Dep. Gov. Okla. Mayflower Soc. Mem. Am., Okla. bar assns., Assn. Trial Lawyers Am., Soc. Mayflower Descs. (elder gen.), Descs. Colonial Clergy, Lambda Chi Alpha, Phi Gamma Kappa, Pi Gamma Mu, Pi Kappa Delta. Mason. Clubs: Tulsa Farm, Westerners. Home: Rural Route 3 Broken Arrow OK 74012 Office: 5600 S 257th St E Broken Arrow OK 74012

NEGUS, ALAN GRANT, mgmt. cons.; b. Boston, May 29, 1924; s. Harry Caswell and Esther Mildred (Grant) N.; student U.S. Naval Acad., 1948; B.S., N.Y. U., 1950; m. Barbara Moseman, Apr. 24, 1975. With Nat. Records Mgmt. Council, N.Y.C., 1950-58; v.p. Naremco Services, N.Y.C., 1958-76; founder, owner Alan Negus Assos., Inc., Sarasota, Fla., 1976—. Served with USN, 1943-48. Mem. Am. Arbitration Assn., Assn. Records Mgrs. and Adminstrs. (exec. v.p. 1979-80). Episcopalian. Clubs: Sarasota U., Mattituck Yacht. Contbr. articles in field to profl. jours. Office: PO Box 15226 Sarasota FL 33579

NEHLS, GERALD JOSEPH, mathematician; b. Dubuque, Iowa, Dec. 20, 1941; s. Earl Joseph and Helen Marie (Junkersdorf) N.; B.S. in Math., Iowa State U., 1964; M.S. in Statistics, U. Iowa, 1966. With EPA, 1966—, chief system devel. sect., monitoring and data analysis div., Research Triangle Park, N.C., 1972-76, chief data mgmt. staff, health effects research lab., 1976—. Served with USPHS, 1966-68. Recipient Spl. Achievement award EPA, 1975. Mem. Am. Mgmt. Assn., AAAS. Democrat. Roman Catholic. Author articles, chpts. in books. Home: 704 Godwin Ct Raleigh NC 27606 Office: MD-55 EPA Research Triangle Park NC 27711

NEIGHBORS, RONALD JOE, mgr.; b. Hominy, Okla., Jan. 4, 1937; s. Joseph Andrew and Ruth Mae (Jordan) N.; student Hardin-Simmons U., 1954-55; B.B.A., Tex. Tech. U., 1958; m. Glenda Cherie Smith, May 18, 1972; children from previous marriage—Norman Bradley, Bryan Devin, Brooks Daron; stepchildren—Krista d'Ann, Mindy Gay. Budget officer City of Lubbock, Tex., 1956-58; asst. city mgr. Snyder, Tex., 1958-60; dir. of finance City of Arlington, Tex., 1960-63; asst. city mgr. Wichita Falls, Tex., 1963-66; city mgr. Carrollton, Tex., 1966-68, Odessa, Tex., 1968-77; gen. mgr. Harris-Galveston Coastal Subsidence Dist., 1977—. Bd. dirs. Odessa United Fund, 1968-74, v.p., 1975—. Mem. Odessa C. of C. (dir. 1968-77), Tex., West Tex. (pres. 1972), Internat. city mgrs. assns, Tex. Indsl. Devel. Council, Texas City Mgmt. Assn., Groundwater Dists. Mgmt. Assn. (dir., v.p. 1978, pres. 1979), Tex. Water Conservation Assn. (dir. 1979). Baptist (deacon 1968-71). Club: Space Center Rotary. Home: 1314 Crawford Friendswood TX 77546 Office: 1730 NASA Rd 1 Bldg II Houston TX 77058

NEILL, ROLFE, newspaperman; b. Mount Airy, N.C., Dec. 4, 1932; s. Kenneth A. and Carmen (Goforth) N.; A.B. in History, U. N.C., 1954; m. Rosemary Clifford Boney, July 20, 1952; children—Clifford Randolph, Sabrina Ashley, Dana Catlin, Jessica Rosemary Ingrid, Quentin Roark Robinson. Reporter, Franklin (N.C.) Press, 1956-57; reporter Charlotte (N.C.) Observer, 1957-58, bus. editor, 1958-61; editor, pub. Coral Gables (Fla.) Times and The Guide, 1961-63, Miami Beach (Fla.) Daily Sun, 1963-65; asst. to pub. N.Y. Daily News, 1965-67, suburban editor, 1967-68, asst. mng. editor, 1968-70; editor Phila. Daily News, 1970-75; v.p., dir. Phila. Newspapers Inc., 1970-75; pres., pub. Charlotte (N.C.) Observer, Charlotte News, 1975—. Served with AUS, 1954-56. Home: 2238 Pinewood Circle Charlotte NC 28211

NEIMAN, NORMAN, aerospace corp. exec.; b. Phila., May 23, 1935; s. Harry and Clara (Schuller) N.; B.S. in M.E., U. Miami, Coral Gables, Fla., 1957; m. Sandra Elaine Berk, Sept. 8, 1956; children—Nadene Lori, Andrea Leslie, David Michael. Launch ops. engr., supr. Gen Dynamics, Douglas Aircraft and Grumman Aerospace Corp., Kennedy Space Center, 1959-66; chief of ground systems and facilities engring. for Lunar Module Apollo program Grumman Aerospace Corp., Kennedy Space Center, 1966-73, mgr. Central Fla. ops., 1973-79; dir. Central Fla. ops. Advanced Tech., Inc., 1979—; pres. Neiman & Co. Consultants, 1980—; pres. Sunshine State Realty Investments, Inc. Served with USAFR, 1954-62. Registered real estate broker, Fla. Mem. Mensa, Intertel. Republican. Jewish. Designer waveguide quick-disconnect coupling, 1958. Home: 239 Salvador Sq Winter Park FL 32789 Office: 3191 Maguire Blvd Orlando FL 32803

NEKHOM, MARC, mathematician; b. Paris, Dec. 14, 1931; s. Michel and Esther (Carnier) N.; came to U.S., 1964, naturalized, 1969; degree in agrl. engring. Sorbonne, U. Paris, 1957; M.S. in Petroleum Engring., U. Tulsa, 1959; m. Lisa C. Moyano, June 7, 1959; children—Alan Victor, Deborah Lis. Petroleum engr. Cities Service Co., Mendoza, Argentina, 1960-64, computer engr., Bartlesville, Okla., 1964-70, sr. cons. analyst, Tulsa, 1970-74, optimization techniques mgr., 1974-79, sr. research mathematician, 1979—. Mem. Soc. Petroleum Engrs., Inst. Mgmt. Scis. Republican. Club: Tulsa Econs.

NELDNER, ROBERT FLATER, communications and advt. co. exec.; b. Bklyn., Apr. 17, 1949; s. Curtis Edward and Yvonne Katherine N.; B.A., Hofstra U., 1973; m. Peggy Ann Moleno, Dec. 16, 1972; children—Susan Michelle, Michael Robert. With St. Regis Paper Co., Jacksonville, Fla., 1973-79, regional public affairs rep., 1976-77, public relations rep., corp. communications dept., 1977-79; exec. v.p., dir. corp. communications Caraway, Kemp Communications, Jacksonville, 1979—. Bd. dirs. N. Fla. Multiple Sclerosis Soc. Recipient Anvil award So. Public Relations Fedn., 1977. Mem. Fla. Public Relations Assn., So. Public Relations Assn., Jacksonville C. of C. (bd. dirs., Com. 100), Am. Polit. Sci. Assn., Fla. Forestry Assn., Ga. Forestry Assn., Miss. Forestry Assn., Forest Farmers Assn., Nat. Wildlife Fedn. Home: 3907 Buckskin Trail E Jacksonville FL 32211 Office: PO Box 18020 Jacksonville FL 32229

NELIUS, SIGRID JOHANNA VON RENNER (MRS. ALBERT ARNOLD NELIUS), physician; b. Pirna, East Germany, Mar. 22, 1924; d. Sigmund Georg and Susanne Hertha (Schmidt) von Renner; M.D., U. Munich (Germany), 1949; m. Albert Arnold Nelius, June 19, 1955; 1 son, Alexander Stefan von Renner. Came to U.S., 1953, naturalized, 1960. Fellow in pathology U. Munich, 1949-50, resident medicine, 1950-52; staff physician medicine 98th Gen. Hsop., U.S. Army, Munich, 1952-53; rotating intern St. Thomas Hosp., Nashville, 1953-54, resident medicine, 1954-56; resident medicine Watts Hosp., Durham, N.C., 1961-62; staff physician medicine John Umstead Hosp., Durham, 1962-67, unit dir. med.-surg. unit, 1967-73; asso. dept. community and family medicine Duke Med. Center Durham, 1973-79, clin. asst. prof., 1979—, med. dir. dietary rehab. clinic dept. community health scis., 1973—, program dir. dietary rehab. clinic dept. community health scis., 1977—. Mem. AMA, Med. Soc. N.C., Durham Orange County Med. Soc. Address: 3112 Sprunt St Durham NC 27705

NELL, O. LESLIE, banker; b. Indpls., Feb. 7, 1932; s. Owen B. and Helen M. (Burgan) N.; A.B., Wabash Coll., 1956; M.B.A., Stonier Grad. Sch. Banking, Rutgers U., 1966; grad. Stanford Exec. Program, 1978; m. Oct. 10, 1952; children—Deborah, Steven, Laura. With Ind. Nat. Bank, Indpls., 1956-74, v.p. nat. div., 1964-67, v.p. met. div., 1967-69, sr. v.p. consumer banking div., 1969-72, exec. v.p., 1972-74, chmn. bd. affiliates Monument Life Ins. Co., 1972-74, Consumer Mktg. Services, Inc., 1972-74; exec. v.p. Southeast Banking Corp., Miami, Fla., 1974-79; pres., chief exec. officer, dir. Gulfstream Banks, Inc., Boca Raton, 1979—; dir. Am. Bankers Ins. Co. of Fla. Trustee U. Miami; chmn. bd. Greater Miami, Inc., 1977-78, Greater Miami Free Trade Zone, Inc., 1977-78. Mem. Am. Bankers Assn., Fla. Bankers Assn., Beta Theta Pi. Republican. Clubs: Meridian Hills Country, Columbia (Indpls.). Office: Gulfstream Banks Inc 150 E Palmetto Park Rd Boca Raton FL 33432

NELLER, ARTHUR AUGUSTUS, JR., sewing thread mfg. co. exec.; b. Greensboro, N.C., Feb. 28, 1937; s. Arthur Augustus and El Phrieda L. (Physioc) N.; B.S., U. N.C., 1959; m. Barbara A. Eichhorn, Aug. 11, 1962; children—Mary Victoria, Anne Markel. Pres., High-Speed Threads, Inc., Greensboro, 1968—, also dir. Served as ensign USNR, 1959-63. Mem. Thread Inst. (dir. 1979). Democrat. Episcopalian (warden). Home: 610 Myers Ln Greensboro NC 27408 Office: PO Box 6154 Greensboro NC 27405

NELSON, BILL, Congressman; b. Miami, Fla., Sept. 29, 1942; B.A., Yale U., 1965; J.D., U. Va., 1968; m. Grace H. Cavert, 1972; children—C. William, Nan Ellen. Admitted to Fla. bar, 1968; practiced law; mem. Fla. Ho. of Reps., 1972-78; mem. 96th Congress from 9th Dist. Fla.; vol. asst. to gov. Fla., 1971. Served to capt. U.S. Army, 1968-70. Named One of 5 Outstanding Young Men in Fla., 1975, Fla. Democrat of 1975. Mem. Fla. Bar Assn., Fla. Wildlife Sanctuary, Melbourne Jaycees. Democrat. Mem. Christian Ch. Clubs: Kiwanis, Masons. Office: Room 1513 Longworth House Office Bldg Washington DC 20515

NELSON, CAROLYN BERYHILL, lawyer; b. Guin, Ala., June 27, 1933; d. Lonnie and Bertha Beryhill; B.A., Samford U., Birmingham, Ala., 1967; J.D., Cumberland Sch. Law, Birmingham, 1969. Admitted to Ala. bar, 1969; atty. firm Lange, Simpson, Robinson & Somerville, Birmingham, 1971-76; sr. v.p., gen. counsel Brookwood Health Services, Inc., Birmingham, 1976—; v.p., dir. numerous affiliated health care companies. Mem. Am. Bar Assn., Am. Soc. Hosp. Attys., Nat. Health Lawyers Assn., Ala. Bar Assn., Birmingham Bar Assn., Exec. Women Internat., Phi Alpha Delta. Home: 1200 Wickford Rd Birmingham AL 35216 Office: 2000-D Brookwood Med Center Dr Birmingham AL 35209

NELSON, CHARLES LAMAR, guidance counselor; b. Lafayette County, Miss., June 9, 1917; s. Charles Robert and Willie Aline (Welch) N.; B.A., U. Miss., 1946, M.A., 1947; postgrad. (Scholar), Auburn U., 1957, Shorter Coll., 1967; m. Lena Reaves, Oct. 1, 1940; 1 son, Timothy Lamar. Tchr. high sch., Blue Springs, Miss., 1940-41, elem. sch., Taylor, Miss., 1941-42; high sch. prin., Batesville, Miss., 1948-49, Tyronza, Ark., 1949-50; supt. high sch., Ripley, Miss., 1950-51; high sch. prin., Middleton, Tenn., 1951-52; tchr., Pearson, Ga., 1952-53; high sch. guidance counselor, Hazlehurst, Ga., 1953-54, Douglas, Ga., 1954-55, Washington, Miss., 1955-58; welfare agt., Natchez, Miss., 1958-59; elem. prin., Bell City, Mo., 1962-63; high sch. prin., Bloomfield, Mo., 1962-63; high sch. guidance counselor, Jackson, Miss., 1963-65, Orange Park, Fla., 1965-66, Adairsville, Ga., 1966-67; jr. high sch. tchr., Rome, Ga., 1967-72; high sch. guidance counselor, Caledonia, Miss., 1972—. Local chmn. Vocat. Rehab. Div., Lowndes County, Miss.; registrar Selective Service Commn., Lowndes County, 1975-76. Served with USNR, 1942-45; PTO. Recipient Cert. of Appreciation, Pres. Gerald Ford, 1976. Mem. NEA, Miss. Assn. Educators, Lowndes County Assn. Educators, Miss. Personnel and Guidance Assn., Internat. Platform Assn., Miss. Poetry Soc. (past sec.), Natchez Poetry Soc. (co-founder, pres. 1959). Democrat. Author: (with David Goforth) Our Neighbor, William Faulkner, 1977; (poetry) The Marble Urn, 1941; William Faulkner: The Anchorite of Rownan Oak, 1973; A Chain That Breaks a Man, 1975; contbr. to Faulkner edit. of Oxford (Miss.) Eagle, 1965, Faulkner: A Biography (Joseph Blotner), 1974, Nat. Poetry Anthology, 1949, Mid-Century Prose and Verse, 1951. Home and Office: PO Box 57 Caledonia MS 39740

NELSON, CLOTIEL RILEY, educator; b. Torras, La., Dec. 21, 1937; d. Prince Henry and Prestener (Johnson) Riley; B.S. cum laude, Grambling Coll., 1960; M.A., Xavier U., 1970; Ph.D. (fellow) Kans. State U., 1974; m. Ivory Vance Nelson, Sept. 9, 1960; 1 dau., Karyn Renee. Tchr. Leavenworth (Kans.) pub. schs., 1961-63, East Baton Rouge (La.) parish schs., 1963-69; guidance counselor Xavier U., New Orleans, 1970; tchr. Houston Independent Sch. Dist., 1970-72; instr. continuing edn. So. U., Baton Rouge, La., 1974—, clin. prof. Office Profl. Lab. Experiences, 1974—, asso. prof. dept. of elementary edn., 1974—, also coordinator elem. student tchrs.; cons. to U.S. Office of Human Devel., 1972—, State of La. Community Services Adminstrn., Baton Rouge, 1974—; hon. mem. La. Ho. of Reps., 1975. Vol. March of Dimes, Baton Rouge, 1974-76, Arts and Humanities Council of Greater Baton Rouge, 1975—; mem. choir Bethel A.M.E. Ch., 1963-69, 74—, chmn. layman's newsletter com., 1975—; bd. dirs. Community Assn. for Welfare of Sch. Children, 1975—, Community Coordinated Children's Council Baton Rouge, 1976—, Arthritis Found., Baton Rouge chpt., 1976—; mem. Mayor-President's Commn. on Needs of Women. Mem. La. State Reading Council, Nat. Assn. U. Women, Assn. Coll. Tchrs. of Reading, Nat. Assn. Edn. of Young Children, Day Care and Child Devel. Assn., La. Assn. Childhood Edn., La. Assn. Tchr. Educators, Baton Rouge Pre-Sch. Assn., Capital Area Reading Assn., Delta Sigma Theta, Phi Delta Gamma, Phi Delta Kappa Kappa Delta Pi. Democrat. Club: Jack and Jill Am. Contbr. articles on edn. to profl. jours. Home: 5622 Congress Blvd Baton Rouge LA 70308 Office: Profl Lab Experiences Southern Univ Baton Rouge LA 70813

NELSON, DANIEL JOEL, educator; b. North Loup, Nebr., Sept. 27, 1938; s. Loren Benjamin and Grace Leola (Sheldon) N.; B.A. (Boettcher Found. scholar), Wheaton Coll., 1960; postgrad. (Fulbright scholar), U. Bonn (Germany), 1960-62; M.A., U. Mich., 1963; Ph.D. (N.Y. State regents fellow), Columbia, 1970. Instr. polit. sci. Auburn (Ala.) U., 1969-70, asst. prof., 1970-76, asso. prof., 1976—. Distinguished lectr. Air U., Montgomery, Ala., 1972-73; Fulbright-Hays prof. Nat. U. Nepal, Kathmandu, 1973-74; vis. asso. prof. Boston U., 1978-80. Mem. Am. Polit. Sci. Assn., Am. Soc. Internat. Law, Acad. Polit. Sci., AAUP. Author: Wartime Origins of the Berlin Dilemma, 1978. Home: 516 E Glenn Ave Apt 219 Auburn AL 36830 Office: Dept Political Science Auburn Univ Auburn AL 36830

NELSON, DAVID STEPHEN, physician; b. N.Y.C., Dec. 16, 1935; s. William and Winnie (Walker) N.; B.S., Geneva Coll., 1957; M.D., Bowman Gray Sch. Medicine, 1961; m. Patricia Ann Clark, Dec. 14, 1970. Intern, Bellevue Hosp. Center (Cornell), N.Y.C., 1961-62; resident in gen. and thoracic surgery N.C. Baptist Hosp., Winston-Salem, 1962-67 v.p. Forsyth Emergency Services Profl. Assn., Winston-Salem, 1970—; clin. asst. prof. surgery Bowman Gray Sch. Medicine, Winston-Salem; mem. Forsyth Health Planning Council, 1972-76, Forsyth Hosp. Authority, 1973-74, N.C. Emergency Med. Services Council, 1973-75, N.C. Med. Care Commn., 1975—, Fed. Interagy. on Emergency Med. Services, 1974—. Fellow Internat. Coll. Surgeons, Am. Coll. Emergency Physicians, Univ. Assn. Emergency Med. Services; mem. AMA, Am. Trauma Soc., Southeastern Surg. Congress, Pan Am. Med. Assn., Am. Soc. Abdominal Surgeons, Internat. Coll. Agiology, N.C., Forsyth County med. socs. Democrat. Jewish. Clubs: Masons (Shriners), Elks. Home: 248 Flintshire Rd Winston-Salem NC 27104 Office: 3333 Silas Creek Pkwy Winston-Salem NC 27103

NELSON, DONALD DEWEY, assn. exec.; b. San Francisco, June 8, 1938; s. Dewey Francis and Leila (Crabtree) N.; B.S., Calif. State U., Fresno, 1962; M.S., U. Calif., Davis, 1964; Ph.D., Ohio State U., 1969; m. Suzanne A. Phister, Dec. 30, 1958; children—Stuart, Heather, Montgomery, Holly. Prof. animal sci. Calif. State U., Fresno, 1964-74; gen. mgr. agrl. ops. Bixby Ranch Co., Los Angeles, 1974-77; exec. dir. Am.-Internat. Charolais Assn., Houston, 1978—; mem. internat. com. Houston Livestock Show, 1978. Named Outstanding Tchr. in Sch. Agr. (Salgo-Noren award), Calif. State U., 1970; recipient Outstanding Teaching and Counseling award Sch. of Agr., Calif. State U. at Fresno, 1972. Mem. Houston C. of C., Am. Soc. Animal Sci., Calif. Agrl. Leadership Assn., Am. Soc. Assn. Execs., Western Stock Show Assn., U.S. Beef Breeds Council (dir. 1978—), Agriservices Found. (adv. 1978—), Nat. Cattlemen's Assn. (purebred adv. council 1978—), Gamma Sigma Delta. Republican. Presbyterian. Contbr. articles in field to profl. jours. Home: 32731 Wright Rd Magnolia TX 77355 Office: 1610 Old Spanish Trail Houston TX 77054

NELSON, DONALD ROBERT, orgn. devel. cons.; b. Ellendale, N.D., Dec. 25, 1939; s. Ray E. and Marion (Hall) N.; B.S., N.D. State U., 1961; M.Div., Andover Newton Sem., 1965; m. Joyce Harris, Dec. 27, 1961; children—Christopher, Cheri. Youth dir. Newton (Mass.) YMCA, 1962-66; youth work exec. Providence YMCA, 1966-68; dir. community services Ga. Inst. Tech., Atlanta, 1968-72, dir. student programs, 1972-76; dir. student center So. Tech. U., 1976-77; adminstr. DeKalb County Health Dept., 1977; dir. Ga. tng. office, adminstr. children, youth and families HEW, Atlanta, 1977—; pres. bd. Golden Age Enterprises, Inc.; orgn. devel. cons.; sec. bd. dirs. Humanics Assos. Chmn. Community Devel. Commn., 1974-77; vice chmn. Community Relations Commn., 1975—; chmn. evaluation com. United Way, 1978-79; bd. dirs. YMCA. Recipient R.I. Youth Service award, 1967 Esral award, 1961, Outstanding Community Service award, 1976, Recognition award in community devel., 1977. Mem. Assn. Profl. Dirs., Nat. Friends of Head Start, Ga. Head Start Assn., Am. Soc. Tng. and Devel., Orgnl. Devel. Network, Chi Psi. Republican. Mem. United Ch. of Christ. Author: How to Get a Grant, 1975. Home: 1283 Bramble Rd Atlanta GA 30329

NELSON, EDWARD SHEFFIELD, utility co. exec.; b. Keevil, Ark., Feb. 23, 1941; s. Robert Ford and Thelma Jo (Mayberry) N.; B.S., State Coll. Ark., 1963; LL.B., Ark. Law Sch., 1966; J.D., U. Ark., 1968; m. Mary Lynn McCastlain, Oct. 12, 1961; children—Cynthia, Lynn, Laura. Mgmt. trainee Ark. La. Gas Co., Little Rock, 1963-64, sales engr., 1964-67, sales coordinator, 1967-69, gen. sales mgr., 1969-71, v.p., gen. sales mgr., 1971-73, pres., dir., 1973—, chmn., chief exec. officer, 1979—. Chmn., United Way, 1975. Bd. dirs. Better Bus. Bur. Named Ark.'s Outstanding Young Man, Ark. Jr. C. of C., 1973; One of Am.'s Ten Outstanding Young Men, U.S. Jr. C. of C., 1974. Mem. Am., Ark., Pulaski County bar assns., Ark. (dir.), Little Rock (dir.) chambers commerce, Sales and Mktg. Execs. Assn. (pres. 1975), So. Gas Assn. (dir. 1974). Democrat. Methodist. Home: 11210 Shenandoah Valley Dr Little Rock AR 72207 Office: 400 E Capitol St Little Rock AR 72201

NELSON, EDWINA WILLIAMS, guidance counselor; b. Columbus, Miss., Sept. 14, 1937; d. Daniel and Ollie Mae (Owen) Williams; B.A. in English and Bus. Adminstrn., Bennett Coll., Greensboro, N.C., 1958; M.A. in Internat. Relations, Boston U., 1969; M.A. in Guidance and Counseling, Wayne State U., 1973; m. William E. Nelson, Dec. 27, 1964; children—Melva Reneee, Edwina Michelle. Tchr. English and stenography Harwood Sch., Albuquerque, 1958-59; adminstrv. asst. Com. for Free Asia, San Francisco, 1955; tchr. elem. edn. Chgo. Public Schs., 1959-63, U.S. Dependent Schs., France and Germany, 1963-66; area coordinator Cultural Awareness Program, Aviano, Italy, 1971-75; staff devel. officer Ga. Dept. Human Resources, 1976-77; guidance counselor DeKalb County Schs., Decatur, Ga., 1977—; cons. staff devel. and tng. Ga. Dept. Human Resources, Family and Children's Services Div. Active Nat. Urban League. Recipient Albuquerque Kiwanis Club grant, 1963, award for superior teaching U.S. Dependent Schs., 1976-77. Mem. AAUW, Bus. and Profl. Women's Assn., Am. Personnel and Guidance Assn., Am. Sch. Counselors Assn., DeKalb Assn. Educators, Alpha Kappa Alpha. Methodist. Club: Columbia

Valley Women's. Home: 3698 Oregon Trail Decatur GA 30032 Office: 5036 Lavista Rd Tucker GA 30084

NELSON, ERIC, investment counselor; b. Charleston, W.Va., Jan. 13, 1930; s. Oscar and Harriet (Engstrom) N.; grad. Reppert Sch. Auctioneering, 1949; B.S. in Econs., U. Pa., 1951; postgrad. Washington and Lee U. Sch. Law, 1951-52; m. Ann Cabell Patrick, Oct. 10, 1959; children—Eric, Mary Elizabeth, William C. Southeastern rep. Am. Hereford Jour., Memphis, 1954-56; asst. chemist Monarch Rubber Co., Canton, Ohio, 1956; sales rep. United Carbon Co., Memphis, 1956-58; supr. advt. and public relations Greyhound Corp., Charleston, W.Va., 1958-59; pres. Nelson Enterprises, Charleston, 1959—; v.p. Nelson & Co. Inc., Charleston, 1961—; dir. South Hills Bank, Morlunda Farms, Viking Exploration, Coralynn Corp., NAPCO, Inc. Mem. W.Va. Legislature, 1966-70; alt. del. Republican Nat. Conv., 1968, 76; mem. Rep. State Fin. Com., 1966—; chmn. W.Va. Conservative Union, Sunrise Found. Permanent Endowment Fund; trustee St. Paul's Lutheran Ch. Served to cpl. U.S. Army, 1952-54. Mem. Ind. Oil and Gas Assn. W.Va., W.Va. Polled Hereford Assn., Future Farmers Am., Navy League of U.S. (life), Phi Kappa Psi. Clubs: Lions (dir.), W.Va. Bond (pres. 1974-75), Shriners, Masons, Elks, Edgewood Country. Home: 748 Myrtle Rd Charleston WV 25314 Office: PO Box 186 Charleston WV 25321

NELSON, ERNEST JACOB, bank exec.; b. Binghamton, N.Y., Mar. 16, 1918; s. Thomas J. and Pearl Gertrude (Sherman) N.; student in social sci. Harper Coll., 1945; student in mech. engring. Cornell U., 1946; m. Constance E. Springer, July 19, 1969. With IBM Corp., Endicott, N.Y. and Boca Raton, Fla., 1937-75, personnel mgr., 1958-75; pres., personnel and mgmt. cons. E. C. Co., Inc., Boca Raton, Fla., 1975—; personnel officer, personnel cons. First Bank and Trust of Boca Raton, 1975—; instr. Palm Beach Jr. Coll., 1977—. Chmn. bd. Ethics, City of Boca Raton, 1977; mem. selection com. for Selection of City Mgr. for Boca Raton, 1979; bd. dirs. United Way Greater Boca Raton, 1972—, pres., 1973-74; bd. dirs. Florence Fuller Child Devel. Center, 1977—. Mem. Palm Beach County Personnel Assn. (pres. 1968-69), Boca Raton C. of C. (dir. 1973-79, Man of Yr. 1979). Republican. Clubs: Rotary Internat. (v.p. 1977-78), Boca Raton Hotel and Club, Gulf Stream Yacht, English Speaking Union, Fla. Atlantic Music Guild, Golden Harbor Yacht, Bankers, Royal Palm Yacht and Tennis. Home: 714 Coquina Ct Boca Raton FL 33432 Office: 150 E Palmetto Park Rd Boca Raton FL 33432

NELSON, GEORGE AGLE, cons. structural engr.; b. Kansas City, Mo., Mar. 29, 1931; s. Gordon Vernon and Myrtle (Agle) N.; B.C.E., Kans. State U., 1953; M.S., 1957; m. Marcia Janyce Bailey, June 22, 1957; children—Jennifer Elaine, Eugene Gordon. Engr. Black & Veatch, Cons. Engrs., Kansas City, Mo., 1957-63; engr. Weitz-Hettelsater Engrs., Kansas City, Mo., 1963-64; engr. Patchen-Mingledorff & Assos., Augusta, Ga., 1965-71; owner George A. Nelson, P.E., cons. engr., North Augusta, S.C., 1971-75; v.p., dir. Willowwick, Inc., North Augusta, 1970-78, Williams, Nelson & Assos., cons. engrs., Augusta, Ga., 1975-79; owner George A. Nelson, P.C., cons. engr., Augusta, 1979—. Mem. North Augusta Planning and Zoning Commn., 1970-77, chmn., 1972-73; dir. Central Savannah River council Girl Scouts U.S.A., 1972-78, exec. bd., 1974-78. Served with USAF, 1953-55. Mem. ASCE (pres. S.C. sect. 1978), Nat. Soc. Profl. Engrs. (pres. Augusta chpt. 1973), Joint Council Engring. and Sci. Socs. (chmn. 1969), Greater Augusta C. of C., Acacia, Sigma Tau. Lutheran. Mason. Club: North Augusta Country. Home: 802 Springdale Rd North Augusta SC 29841 Office: 1220 D'Antignac St Augusta GA 30901

NELSON, H(OWARD) ROICE, JR., geophysicist; b. Cedar City, Utah, Nov. 3, 1949; s. Howard Roice and Pauline (Hafen) N.; B.S. in Geophysics, U. Utah, 1974; postgrad. So. Methodist U., 1977—; m. Martha Ellyn Sharp, Sept. 5, 1973; children—Howard Roice III, Benjamin Bengt, Paul Frederick, Melanie Robbyn. Profl. asst. Pan Am. Petroleum, Denver, 1970; vol. missionary Ch. of Jesus Christ of Latter-day Saints, Eng., 1970-72; profl. asst. Amoco Production Co., Denver, 1973, Applied Geophysics, Salt Lake City, 1973; with dept. geol. and geophys. scis. U. Utah, 1974; geophysicist IV Mobil Exploration and Producing Services, Dallas, 1974-80; sr. researcher Seismic Acoustics Lab., U. Houston, 1980—; co-founder, pres. Computer Geneal. Services, 1978-79. Active Ch. of Jesus Christ of Latter-day Saints. Mem. Soc. Exploration Geophysicists, Dallas Geophys. Soc., Phi Sigma Kappa, Phi Eta Sigma. Republican. Home: 8403 Blue Quail St Missouri City TX 77459 Office: Seismic Acoustics Lab U Houston Houston TX 77004

NELSON, HAZEL FOWLER (MRS. BOWEN CRESTON NELSON), civic worker; b. Mulhall, Okla., May 16, 1905; d. Oscar Frederick and Belle Virginia (Lowe) Fowler; B.A., U. Okla., 1927; postgrad. U. Wis., 1928; m. Bowen Creston Nelson, Oct. 26, 1941; 1 dau., Creston Annette. Tchr. journalism, English, sponsor publs. Chickasha (Okla.) High Sch., 1927-30; reporter Norman (Okla.) Transcript, 1930-37; feature writer Oklahoma City Times, 1937-41; mil. editor Miami (Fla.) Herald, 1942-45; officer Nelson Mortgage Co., Inc., Miami, 1941-69, sec., dir., 1942-69. Mem. bd. Childrens Service Bur., Miami, 1952; pres. Franklin Bush chpt. U. Miami Women's Cancer Assn., 1969. Recipient silver award for assistance through newspaper series Miami's Fgn. War Brides, 1946. Mem. Vizcayans Soc. So. Families, Fla. Hist. Assn., Internat. Platform Assn., Women in Communications, (pres. U. Okla. chpt. 1927, Miami chpt. 1952-53). Democrat. Mem. Christian Ch. Club: Coral Gables Country. Home: 10255 SW 53d Ave Miami FL 33156

NELSON, IVORY VANCE, ednl. adminstr.; b. Curtiss, La., June 11, 1934; s. Elijah Henderson and Mable (Tyler) N.; B.S. magna cum laude (T. H. Harris scholar 1959), Grambling Coll., 1959; Ph.D. summa cum laude (DuPont Teaching fellow 1962), U. Kans., Lawrence, 1963; m. Clotiel Riley, Sept. 9, 1960; children—Cherlyn Yvette, Karyn Renee. Tchr. chemistry Grambling (La.) Coll., summer 1961; research chemist Am. Oil Co., summer 1962; mem. dept. chemistry So. U., Baton Rouge, 1963-67, chmn. div. natural scis., Shreveport, 1967-68; asst. dean coll. Prairie View (Tex.) A. and M. U., 1968-71, v.p. for research and spl. programs, 1971—; Fulbright lectureship U. Autonomous de Guadalajara, 1966; vis. prof. Loyola U., New Orleans, 1967; sr. research chemist Union Carbide, 1969; cons. Oak Ridge Asso. Univs., 1969-72; mem. exec. com. for grad. edn. and research policy Nat. Assn. Land-Grant Colls. and Univs.; mem. exec. adv. com. for energy and mineral resources Tex. A. and M. U. System. Mem. Houston, Galveston Area Council Goals Study, Agrl. Research Inst., 1971; mem. adv. com. Tex. Ho. of Reps., 1970; trustee S.E. Consortium for Internat. Devel. Served to s/sgt. USAF, 1951-55. Mem. Tex. Acad. Sci., A.A.A.S., Am. Assn. Coll. Tchrs., Am. Chem. Soc., Nat. Council U. Research Adminstrs., N.Y. Acad. Scis., Phi Beta Kappa, Sigma Xi, Phi Lambda Upsilon, Sigma Pi Sigma, Beta Kappa Chi, Alpha Mu Gamma, Kappa Delta Pi, Phi Delta Kappa. Contbr. articles to sci. jours. Home: 5622 Congress Blvd Baton Rouge LA 70808

NELSON, JOHN C., energy co. exec.; b. McKinney, Tex., 1913; B.S., Tex. A&M U., 1935, M.S., 1937; married. With United Gas Pipeline Co., exec. v.p. planning and ops., 1973-77, also dir.; exec. v.p. planning and ops. United Energy Resources, Inc., Houston, 1977, vice chmn., 1978—, also dir.; dir. United Tex. Transmission Co.; group v.p., dir. United Offshore Co. Served to maj. U.S. Army, 1941-48. Office: PO Box 1478 Houston TX 77001*

NELSON, JOHN PETTIT, lawyer; b. Gulfport, Miss., Aug. 5, 1921; s. John P. and Stella (Foret) N.; student La. State U., 1938-40; B.S., Loyola U., 1947, LL.B., 1950; m. Marie Anna Murphy, June 5, 1946; children—Marie Anna, Jennie, Cesyle, Stephanie. Admitted to La. bar, 1950; asso. Dodd, Hirsch & Barker, 1950-54; asst. dist. atty. Parish of Orleans, 1953-58; sr. partner firm Nelson & Nelson, 1958—; dir. Law Clinic, Loyola U., New Orleans. Served to capt. AUS, 1940-45. Decorated Silver Star, Bronze Star medal, Purple Heart. Mem. Am., La., New Orleans bar assns., Am. Legion, Nat. Cath. Conf. of Interracial Justice. Home: 2432 Jay St New Orleans LA 70122 Office: Law Clinic Loyola U New Orleans LA 70130

NELSON, KENNETH EDWARD, communications cons.; b. Chgo., Mar. 23, 1949; s. Wilbur T. and Catherine Ruby (Johnson) N.; student U. Dallas, 1975; B.A., Ill. Wesleyan U., 1971; m. Nancy Coleman, Mar. 18, 1972; 1 dau., Christine Lynn. Mfrs. rep. Vogel Peterson Co., Elmhurst, Ill., 1971-73; sales rep. Albert Ladymon Co., Dallas, 1973; communications cons. Southwestern Bell Telephone Co., Dallas, 1973-78; Dallas County field dir. Clements for Gov. Campaign, 1978; pres. Nelson Telecom Cons., Dallas, 1978—. Commr., Interstate Compact on Red River, 1979—; mem. state exec. com. Republican Party, 16th Dist. committeeman, 1978—, mem. Dallas County exec. com., 1974—, exec. campaign com., 1979-81; nat. committeeman Tex. Young Republicans, 1976-78. Mem. Tex. State Farm Bur., Ill. Wesleyan U. Alumni Assn., E. Dallas C. of C., Pi Kappa Delta. Republican. Home and Office: 11723 Cimarec St Dallas TX 75218

NELSON, KENWYN GORDON, thoracic surgeon; b. San Francisco, July 9, 1926; M.D., U. Va., 1948; B.A., U. Tex., El Paso, 1965. Intern, Bellevue Hosp., N.Y.C., 1948-49, resident in gen. surgery, 1949-50, 53-55; Commd. 1st lt. U.S. Army, 1951, advanced through grades to col., 1968; comdr., sr. thoracic surgeon 71st Evacuation Hosp., Vietnam, 91st Evacuation Hosp., 1970-71; chief surgery William Beaumont Gen. Hosp., El Paso, 1971, dep. comdr., chief profl. services, dir. med. edn., chief thoracic surg. service services, 1971-75, ret., 1975; clin. prof. thoracic surgery, chief dept. surgery U. Tex. Health Center, Tyler, 1975—. Decorated Legion of Merit with oak leaf cluster. Diplomate Am. Bd. Thoracic Surgery, Am. Bd. Surgery. Fellow A.C.S., Am. Coll. Cardiology; mem. Soc. Thoracic Surgeons, So. Thoracic Surg. Assn. Home: 609 Purdue St Tyler TX 75703 Office: U Tex Health Center Tyler TX 75710

NELSON, LEONARD ALLEN, geologist; b. Norfolk, Nebr., Mar. 28, 1923; s. William Arthur and Margaretha Minna Maria (Andersen) N.; B.Sc., U. Nebr., 1950, M.Sc., 1951; postgrad. U. Zulia (Venezuela), 1960; m. Dorothy Faye Smith, June 5, 1946; children—Byron Eric, Cynthia Faye, Laura Jean. Devel. geologist The Calif. Co., various locations, 1951-53; geologic observer, Mont., N. and S.D., 1953-54, lead geophysicist, Mont., N.D., S.D., 1954-55; structural geologist Colo., Utah, Ariz., 1955-56; regional geologist Richmond Exploration Co., Eastern and Western Venezuela, 1956-60; lead geologist, Venezuela, 1960-62; subsurface geologist Standard Oil Co. Tex., N.Mex., 1962-65; div. geophysicist gravity and magnetics, Okla., W. Tex., Ariz., N.Mex., 1965-71; geophysicist div. staff Chevron Oil Co., Okla., Tex., 1971-72, geologist div. staff spl. assignments, various locations, 1972-74, geologist exploration staff, remote sensing, Ala., Ariz., Colo., La., Mont., Nebr., N.Mex., N.D., S.D., Tex., Utah, Wyo., 1974-76; geologist Chevron U.S.A., Colo., Utah, Mont., N.Mex., 1976-77; sr. staff evaluations geologist Enserch Exploration Inc., Dallas, 1977—; grad. asst. geology U. Nebr., 1950-51. Account exec. United Way Campaign, Denver, 1972-73; chmn. Aquatics-W. Tex. Assn. AAU, 1970-71. Served with USAAF, 1941-45. Registered profl. geologist. Mem. Soc. Exploration Geophysicists, Am. Assn. Petroleum Geologists, Dallas Geol. Soc., Dallas Geophys. Soc., Explorers Club, Sociedad Geologica de Venezuela Occidental (v.p. 1961, pres. 1962), U. Nebr. Alumni Assn., Sigma Gamma Epsilon, Am. Legion. Republican. Methodist. Home: 11601 McRae Rd Dallas TX 75228 Office: 1817 Wood St Suite 509W Dallas TX 75201

NELSON, MICHAEL, data processing co. exec.; b. Bklyn., Dec. 28, 1948; s. Ira and Ethel N.; B.S., CCNY, 1970; postgrad. Baruch Coll., 1974-75, Fla. Atlantic U., 1977-; m. Sharon Elaine Wolf, June 20, 1970; children—Marti Suzanne, Ian Matthew. Programmer, analyst Dun & Bradstreet, N.Y.C., 1972-73; sr. systems analyst Am. Express Co., Plantation, Fla., 1973—; pres. Computer Resource Asso., Coral Springs, Fla., 1979—. Mem. Assn. Computing Machinery, Data Processing Mgmt. Assn., Am. Mgmt. Assn., Assn. M.B.A. Execs., Eastern Users Group for Software Internat. Office: 777 American Expressway Plantation FL 33337

NELSON, RALPH ERWIN, land planner; b. Chgo., July 30, 1946; s. Vernon Leslie and Astrid Lorraine (Seagren) N.; B.S., McPherson Coll., 1971; m. Elarie Marie Fletcher, Oct. 14, 1967; 1 dau., Anne Marie. Chief planning dept. Roberts & Zoller Inc., Bradenton, Fla., 1971-76; v.p., supr. planning div. Dan Zoller Engring. Inc., Bradenton, 1976-78; pres. R.E. Nelson, Inc., planning and archtl. consultants, Bradenton, 1978—. Mem. Am. Soc. Planning Ofcls., Met. Assn. Urban Designers and Environ. Planners, Fla. Planning and Zoning Assn., Am. Soc. Certified Engring. Technicians, Am. Inst. Planners (asso.), Am. Forestry Assn. Republican. Baptist. Home: PO Box 8564 Bayshore Branch Bradenton FL 33507 Office: PO Box 8564 4630 5th St W Bradenton FL 33507

NELSON, RUSSELL GENE, electronic engr.; b. Ada, Minn., Mar. 15, 1943; s. Clarence Orlando and Ida Caroline (Anderson) N.; B.E.E., U. N.D., 1966; M.E.E., U. Houston, 1972; m. Judith Ann Knight, Aug. 2, 1970. Electronic engr. Naval Ship Missile Systems Engring. Sta., Port Hueneme, Calif., 1966-70; engr. Tex. Instruments, Houston, 1972-75; sr. scientist Baroid Petroleum Services, Houston, 1975—. Adviser, Jr. Achievement, 1976-77; sec. Friend's Theosophical Study Center; radio chmn. Radio Theosophy for So. Calif., 1969-70. Mem. IEEE, Instrument Soc. Am., Am. Fedn. Human Rights, Theosophical Soc. in Am., Am. Radio Relay League, Theosophical Research Inst., Ancient and Mystical Order Rosae Crucis. Republican. Liberal Catholic. Home: 708 Stoneledge St Friendswood TX 77546 Office: PO Box 1675 Houston TX 77001

NELSON, STUART OWEN, agrl. engr.; b. Pilger, Nebr., Jan. 23, 1927; s. Irvin Andrew and Agnes Emilie (Nissen) N.; B.S., U. Nebr., 1950, M.S., 1952, M.A. in Physics, 1954; Ph.D., Iowa State U., 1972; m. C. Joye Fricke, Dec. 27, 1953 (dec. 1975); children—Richard Lynn, Jana Sue; m. 2d, Ellen White Fuller, Apr. 8, 1979. Grad. asst. U. Nebr., 1952-54, research asso., 1954-60, asso. prof., 1960-72, prof., 1972-76; project leader, farm electrification research U.S. Dept. Agr., 1954-59, research investigations leader, Agrl. Research Service, 1959-72, research leader Agrl. Research Service, 1972-76, research agrl. engr. Russell Research Center, Sci. and Edn. Adminstrn., Athens, Ga., 1976—; adj. prof. U. Ga., 1976—; mem. sci. adv. council Am. Seed Research Found. Served with USN, 1946-48. Mem. Am. Soc. Agrl. Engrs. (sr.), IEEE (sr.), AAAS, Internat. Microwave Power Inst., Orgn. Profl. Employees of Dept. Agr., Sigma Xi, Sigma Tau, Gamma Sigma Delta, Tau Beta Pi. Club: Optimist (v.p. Lincoln, Nebr. 1975; v.p. Athens, Ga. 1978, 79, pres. 1980). Asso. editor Jour. Microwave Power, 1975—; contbr. articles to profl. jours. Home: 270 Idylwood Dr Athens GA 30605 Office: US Dept Agr Sci and Edn Adminstrn Russell Research Center Box 5677 Athens GA 30604

NELSON, THOMAS EDWARD, scientist, educator; b. Altus, Okla., Aug. 18, 1937; s. Jackson Milton and Honor (Etheridge) N.; B.S., Abilene Christian Coll., 1960; M.S., Okla. State U., 1967, Ph.D., 1970; m. Maredda Rose Nelson, Sept. 28, 1963; children—Christopher Thomas, Kenneth Edward, Carter Tray. Med. technician Civil Aeromed. Research Inst., Oklahoma City, 1960-61; instr. St. Anthony's Sch. Nursing, Oklahoma City, 1961-62; research asso. Oklahoma City U., 1962-63, Harding Coll., Searcy, Ark., 1963-65; chief technician dept. animal sci. Okla. State U., 1965-69, research asso. Coll. Vet. Medicine, 1970-74; postdoctoral fellow Australian Nat. U., Canberra, 1974-76; asst. prof. dept. anesthesiology U. Tex. Med. Br., Galveston, 1976—. NIH grantee, 1977—. Mem. Internat. Anesthesia Research Soc., Am. Soc. Anesthesiologists, Am. Physiol. Soc. Contbr. chpts. to books; contbr. articles to profl. jours. Office: Dept Anesthesiology U of Tex Med Branch Galveston TX 77550

NELSON, VIRGINIA ANNE, speech pathologist; b. Siloam, Tex., Mar. 18, 1939; d. Woodrow and Edith Louise (Powell) Mosely; B.S., E. Tex. State U., 1960, M.S., 1977; children—Leigh-Ashley, Norman L. III. Speech therapist Dallas Ind. Sch. Dist., 1960—, N.E. sub-dist. area resource clinician, 1978—. Mem. Am. Speech and Hearing Assn., Council Exceptional Children, Tex. Speech and Hearing Assn., Dallas Speech and Hearing Assn., Dallas Assn. Retarded Children. Methodist. Democrat. Office: 9720 Waterview St Dallas TX 75218

NELSON, WALLACE JAY, govt. ofcl.; b. Patrick County, Va., Aug. 1, 1926; s. Willie Everitt and Mollie Jane (Tudor) N.; B.S. in Biology, Va. Poly. Inst. and State U., Blacksburg, 1950; J.D., Am. U., 1961; m. Helen Nixon Blount, Oct. 25, 1951; children—Jane Elizabeth, Wallace Jay. Analytical chemist, chem. lab. technician Dept. Army Ordnance, Radford (Va.) Arsenal, 1951-55; patent examiner U.S. Patent Office, Commerce Dept., Washington, 1955-61; admitted to Va. bar, 1961; patent atty. Langley Research Center, NASA, Hampton, Va., 1961—. Vice pres. Fox Hill-Harris Creek (Va.) Civic League, 1970-72; coach Little League basketball, football and baseball, 1957-63. Served with USNR, 1944-46; PTO. Methodist (adminstrv. bd., chmn. commn. evangelism). Mason (past master). Home: 34 Salt Pond Rd Hampton VA 23664 Office: MS 313 Langley Research Center NASA Hampton VA 23669

NELSON, WILLIAM ROY, audiologist; b. St. George, Utah, July 20, 1940; s. LeRoy Bleak and Nola (Lang) N.; student Utah State U., 1963-66, B.S., 1966, postgrad. 1966-67, M.S., 1972; m. Donna Toye MacPherson, May 7, 1970; children—Marnie, Roydon Bleak, William Aaron, Camron Blair. Audiologist Southeastern Utah Community Action Programs, Price, 1967-71; commd. 1st lt. U.S. Army, 1972, advanced through grades to capt., 1974, chief audiology clinic Ear, Nose, Throat Service Moncrief Army Hosp., Ft. Jackson, S.C., 1973-75; chief audiometrics br. Bioacoustics Div. U.S. Army Aeromed. Research Lab. Ft. Rucker, Ala., 1975-78; chief audiology clinic U.S. Army Med. Dept. Activity, Panama, S.Am., 1979—; U.S. Army Surgeon Gen's. ad hoc com. on hearing protective devises. Dir. summer neighborhood youth corps, San Juan and Grand Counties, Utah, 1969-71; instl. rep. Wiregrass Council Boy Scouts Am., 1973-74. Served with USMC, 1963. Certified course dir. Council for Accreditation in Occupational Hearing Conservation; Neurol. and Sensoral Disease Service Project fellow, HEW, 1966-67. Mem. Am. Speech and Hearing Assn. (cert., Mil. Audiology and Speech Pathology Soc., Soc. Med. Audiologists. Mormon. Researcher, contbr. article in field to profl. publ. Home: Box 645 Fort Clayton CZ APO Miami FL 34004 Office: Audiology Clinic US Army MEDDAC Fort Clayton CZ APO Miami FL 34004

NEMETH, PETER, elec. engring. co. exec.; b. Hungary, Oct. 15, 1949; came to U.S., 1965, naturalized, 1967; s. Steve and Sarolta N.; B.A., U. Louisville, 1972; married; two children. Pres., Nemeth Engring. Assos., Inc., Crestwood, Ky. Office: Nemeth Engring Assos Inc 7450 Hwy 329 Crestwood KY 40014

NEMITZ, WILLIAM CHARLES, educator; b. Memphis, July 27, 1928; s. Emil Charles and Grace (Corwine) N.; B.S., Southwestern at Memphis, 1950; M.S., Ohio State U., 1956, Ph.D., 1959. Instr. math. Ohio State U., 1959-60; asst. prof. U. Kans., 1960-61; asst. prof. Southwestern at Memphis, 1961-62, asso. prof., 1962-70, prof., 1970—, dir. computer centers, 1968-78. Served with USNR, 1951-54. NSF grantee, 1964, 71-73. Mem. Am. Math. Soc., Math. Assn. Am. Democrat. Unitarian. Contbr. articles to profl. jours. Home: 181 N Merton #1 Memphis TN 38112 Office: Dept Math Southwestern at Memphis Memphis TN 38112

NEMUTH, HAROLD ISAAC, physician; b. Norfolk, Va., Mar. 12, 1912; s. Marcus Cohen and Rose (Lasdan) N.; B.A., Columbia, 1934; M.D., Med. Coll. Va., 1939; m. Doreen Graham, Mar. 22, 1947; children—Mark Graham, Karen Lasdan, William Benson. Intern, Med. Coll. Va., 1938-39, Knickerbocker, N.Y., 1939-40; Sheltering Arms, Richmond, Va., 1940-41, St. Elizabeth Hosp., Richmond, 1941-42; practice medicine, Richmond, 1947—; asso. in medicine Med. Coll. Va., 1956—, asso. prof. preventive medicine, 1958-74, clin. prof. preventive medicine, 1974—, acting chmn. dept. preventive medicine, 1959-62; chief of staff Sheltering Arms Hosp., 1956-57. Mem. Va. Commn. Human Resources Priorities, Va. Drug Abuse Council, Va. Council on Aging. Bd. dirs. Capital Area Comprehensive Planning Council, Instructive Vis. Nurse Assn.; bd. visitors Va. Commonwealth U., 1978—. Served with M.C., USNR, 1942-46. Fellow Royal Soc. Health; mem. A.M.A., Med. Soc. Va. (v.p. 1970-71, chmn. com. on aging), Richmond Acad. Medicine (v.p. 1970-71), Am. Pub. Health Assn., Assn. Am. Med. Colls., Assn. Tchrs. Preventive Medicine, Pan Am. Med. Assn., Am., Internat. gerontological socs. Jewish. Home: 5518 Riverside Dr Richmond VA 23225 Office: 2012 Monument Ave Richmond VA 23220

NEMZEK, THOMAS ALEXANDER, constrn. co. exec.; b. Fargo, N.D., Mar. 22, 1926; s. Alexander Jerome and Anne Jane (Hagen) N.; B.S., U.S. Naval Acad., 1949; M.S., N.C. State U., 1953; m. Margaret Clare Peters, June 18, 1949; children—Paula, Alexandra, Thomas, Michael. Commd. 2d. lt. U.S. Air Force, 1949, advanced through grades to capt., 1953, served as pilot, instr. pilot, research and devel. officer, ret., 1957; dir. nuclear reactor div. U.S. AEC, asst. mgr. tech. op., Chgo., 1957-64, dep. mgr., San Francisco, 1964-69, asst. dir. Pacific NW Programs, Richland, Wash., 1964-71, mgr. Richland ops., 1971-73, dir. reactor devel. div., Washington, 1973-76; v.p., energy adv. J.A. Jones Constrn. Co., Charlotte, N.C., 1976-78, v.p. spl. projects, 1978—; pres. J.A. Jones Applied Research Co., also dir.; dir. J.A. Jones Constrn. Services Co. Recipient Disting. Service award U.S. AEC, 1972; Spl. Achievement award U.S. ERDA, 1976. Mem. Am. Nuclear Soc., Atomic Industry Forum, Associated Gen. Contractors Dept. Energy Com. Republican. Roman Catholic. Home: 5718 Bentway Dr Charlotte NC 28211 Office: PO Box 30247 Charlotte NC 28230

NESBETT, BILLY CURTIS, physician; b. Jonesville, Tex., Jan. 1, 1933; s. Curtis Badgett and Dorris (Grant) N.; A.A., Cumberland U., 1960; student Middle Tenn. State U., 1960-61; M.D., U. Tenn., 1964; m. Barbara Ann Spear, Aug. 5, 1969; 1 dau., Susan Michelle. Intern, Bapt. Hosp., Pensacola, Fla., 1964-65; physician Cumberland Clinic Found., Crossville, Tenn., 1965-66; pvt. practice family medicine, Celina, Tenn., 1966-70, pres., Billy C. Nesbett M.D. Corp., Jena, La., 1970-77; mem. staff LaSalle Gen. Hosp., Jena, 1970-77; mem. staff White County (Tenn.) Hosp., 1977—, bd. dirs., 1978—; mem. faculty La. State U. Med. Sch., New Orleans, 1975—. Trustee, LaSalle Gen. Hosp., 1972-77; bd. dirs. Clay County Hosp., 1966-70, Cumberland Psychiat. Hosp., Cookeville, Tenn., 1968-70. Served with USAF, 1953-56. Mem. White County Med. Soc. (sec. 1978—), Tenn. Med. Assn., AMA, Alpha Kappa Kappa. Republican. Methodist. Home and office: 615 W Bockman Way Sparta TN 38583

NESBITT, FRANK WILBUR, lawyer; b. Miami, Okla., Dec. 26, 1916; s. Frank Wilbur and Nelle May (Grayson) N.; B.A., Okla. U., 1937; J.D., U. Tex., 1939; children—Mary Nelle (Mrs. Bruce Ralston), Kathleen Marie (Mrs. Dan Smith). Admitted to Tex. bar, 1939; pvt. practice law, Corpus Christi, 1939-40; asst. city atty. Corpus Christi, 1941-42; partner King & Nesbitt, Corpus Christi, 1946-53; partner Wood, Burney, Nesbitt & Ryan, Corpus Christi, 1954—. Served as capt. F.A., AUS, 1942-45. Decorated Bronze Star. Fellow Tex. Bar Found., Am. Coll. Trial Lawyers; mem. Am. Nuces County bar assns., State Bar Tex., Order of Coif, Sigma Nu, Phi Delta Phi. Home: 929 Miramar St Corpus Christi TX 78411 Office: Petroleum Tower Corpus Christi TX 78401

NESBITT, SAMMY RICHARD, canning co. exec.; b. Mableton, Ga., May 30, 1948; s. Herman Wilson and Montie Arizona (Reece) N.; student Ga. State U., 1966-68; m. Edith Delores Crawford, Nov. 3, 1968; children—Richard, John, Daniel. Sr. systems analyst So. Motor Carriers Rate Conf., Atlanta, 1967-72; transp. coordinator Gulf Atlantic Distbn. Services, Forest Park, Ga., 1972-78; distbn. services mgr. Calif. Canners & Grwoers Co., Atlanta, 1978—. Served with AUS, 1969-71. Mem. Transp. Club Atlanta, Delta Nu Alpha. Home: 5815 Hiram Powder Spring Powder Springs GA 30073 Office: 4601 Welcome All Rd Atlanta GA 30349

NESER, WILLIAM BERNARD, educator; b. Balt., Apr. 20, 1927; s. Bernard William and Ernestine Albertine (Hagedorn) N.; B.A., U. Md., 1952; M.S., Case Western Res. U., 1954; M.S. in Public Health, U. Mo., 1966; D. Public Health, U. N.C., 1971; m. Priscilla Jean Rose, June 26, 1954; children—William Bernard II, Robert A. Caseworker, supr., instr. Highland View Hosp., Cleve., 1954-61; instr., asst. prof., asso. prof. community health and social work U. Mo., Columbia, 1961-71; asso. prof., dir. health care research Meharry Med. Coll., Nashville, 1971-77, prof., 1977—; asso. clin. prof. preventive medicine Vanderbilt U., Nashville, 1973—. Mem. Nat. Assn. Social Workers, Nat. Conf. Social Welfare, AAAS, Am. Public Health Assn., Royal Soc. Health. Contbr. articles in field to profl. jours. Home: Route 3 Box 62 Fairview TN 37062 Office: Meharry Med Coll 1005 18th Ave N Nashville TN 37208

NESHYBA, VICTOR PETER, govt. ofcl.; b. Frelsburg, Tex., Oct. 8, 1922; s. Peter and Anna (Zietz) N.; B.S. in Elec. Engring., U. Calif. at Berkeley, 1949; M.S., Mass. Inst. Tech., 1968; postgrad. U. Houston, 1973; m. Mary C. Gwazdac, Jan. 6, 1945; children—Victor Peter, Ronald S., Janice J., Marylee, Val J., Keith, David, Dolores, Michele. Enlisted as pvt. USMC, 1941, advanced through grades to col., 1956; assigned Korea, 1950; attache embassy, Iran, 1952-54; ret., 1956; project engr. Gen. Dynamics Corp., 1956-62; with NASA, 1962—, chief instrumentation and data processing Gemini, Skylab and Apollo missions, tech. mgr. shuttle engine system integration Shuttle Program Office, 1972-73; pres., dir. Energ-Eco-Engring., Inc., 1973—. Mem. sch. bd. O'Connell High Sch., Galveston, Tex., 1969-73; mem. bd. Republican Party Galveston County. Recipient Superior Achievement award NASA, 1966, citation, 1971; Presdl. citation, 1972; Dryden award, fellow NASA, 1968. Mem. I.E.E.E., Soc. Geol. Engrs. Roman Catholic (parish and diocesan councils). Home: 3339 E Bayou Dr Dickinson TX 77539 Office: Box 530 Dickinson TX 77539

NESMITH, FRANCES JANE, educator; b. Tulsa, Nov. 6, 1926; B.A. in History and Edn., U. Houston, Tex., 1947; M.A. in History, Columbia, N.Y.C., 1951, Ed.D. in History of Edn., 1968. Tchr., Houston Ind. Sch. Dist., 1947-58; tchr. Austin (Tex.) Ind. Sch. Dist., 1958-69, coordinator secondary social studies, 1969—. Mem. Austin Bicentennial Com., 1973-76, Travis County Hist. Commn., 1978—. Mem. Am., Tex. hist. assns., NEA, Tex. State Tchrs. Assn., Nat. Council for Social Studies, Social Studies Suprs. Assn., Am. Assn. for State and Local History, Orgn. Am. Historians, Phi Delta Kappa, Delta Kappa Gamma. Author: Challenging the Abler Student in American History, 1957, The Story of Texas, 1963. Home: 2605 Salado St Austin TX 78705 Office: Austin Ind Sch Dist 6100 N Guadalupe Austin TX 78752

NETER, JOHN, statistician; b. Germany, Feb. 8, 1923; B.S., U. Buffalo, 1943; M.B.A., U. Pa., 1947; Ph.D., Columbia U., 1952; m. Dorothy Rachman, June 24, 1951; children—Ronald J., David L. Asst. prof. Syracuse (N.Y.) U., 1949-55, chmn. dept. bus. statistics, 1952-55; prof. U. Minn., 1955-75, chmn. dept. quantitative analysis, 1961-65; supervisory math. statistician U.S. Bur. Census, 1959-60; distinguished prof. mgmt. sci. and statistics U. Ga., Athens, 1975—; cons. in field. Chmn. citizens adv. com. City of St. Louis Park, Minn., 1972, mem. planning commn., 1974-75. Served with AUS, 1943-45. Ford Found. faculty research fellow, 1957-58. Fellow Am. Statis. Assn. (council 1963-64, 67-70, dir. 1975—), AAAS; mem. Am. Inst. Decision Scis. (pres. 1978-79), AAUP (chpt. pres. 1969-70), Inst. Mgmt. Scis., Inst. Math. Statistics, Am. Soc. Quality Control. Co-author: Statistical Sampling for Auditors and Accountants, 1956; Fundamental Statistics for Business and Economics, 4th edit., 1973; Applied Linear Statistical Models, 1974; Applied Statistics, 1978; editor Am. Statistician, 1976—; asso. editor Decision Scis., 1973-74. Contbr. profl. publns. Home: 310 St George Dr Athens GA 30606 Office: Coll Bus Adminstrn Univ Ga Athens GA 30602

NETHERCUT, WILLIAM ROBERT, educator, baritone; b. Rockford, Ill., Jan. 11, 1936; s. Robert C. and Constance E. (Stanley) N.; A.B. magna cum laude, Harvard, 1958; M.A. (Henry Drisler fellow, Pres.'s fellow), Columbia, 1961, Ph.D., 1963; student New Eng. Conservatory of Music, 1959-60; m. Jane Lillian Swann, July 27, 1977; children—William Andrew, Amanda Jane. Instr. Greek and Latin, Columbia, 1961-66, asst. prof., 1966-67, Lawrence H. Chamberlain fellow, 1967; asso. prof. Classics U. Ga., Athens, 1967-72, prof., 1972-75; prof. Classics U. Tex., Austin, 1975—. Announcer radio sta. WROK, Rockford, 1957-58; soloist New Eng. Opera Theatre, Boston, 1958-59, debut as Figaro in Barber of Seville, 1958; soloist recital Carnegie Hall, N.Y.C., 1966; soloist Atlanta Opera Co., 1968; appearance ednl. program TV sta. WGTV, Athens, Ga., 1970-72. Lectr. 1st Internat. Conf. on Ovid, Constanta, Rumania, 1972, Internat. Soc. Homeric Studies, Athens, Greece, 1973, 74, 2d Internat. Congress Cypriot Studies, Nicosia, 1974, 3d Internat. Congress S.E. European Studies, Bucharest, 1974, Conf. on Ancient Novel, Bangor, Wales, 1976. Am. Council Learned Socs. grantee, 1972. Mem. Am. Philol. Assn., Archaeol. Inst. Am. (pres. Athens chpt. 1972-74), Vergilian Soc. Am. (trustee 1974—). Clubs: Harvard, University, Explorers of New York City. Translator: De Praestigiis Daemonum (Johan Weyer), 1964, Almanach Perpetuum Celestium Motuum (Rabbi Abraham Zacuto), 1973. Editor: The World and Its Peoples, Italy, 1964; asso. editor Latina et Graeca, 1974—. Contbr. articles on classic lit. and antiquity to profl. jours. Home: 1003 High Rd Austin TX 78746

NETHERLAND, JOEL BERNARD, broadcasting co. exec.; b. Vaughn, Miss., Oct. 11, 1935; s. Marvin E. and Cecil Fields N.; student Cook's Radio Sch., 1957-58; m. Shirley Dixon, Aug. 16, 1953; 1 dau., Dale Yvonne. Program dir. Sta. WDDT, Greenville, Miss., 1960-61, Sta. WJPR, Greenville, 1961-64; mgr. Sta. KPBA, Pine Bluff, Ark., 1965; sales mgr. WABG-TV, Greenville, 1966-68; pres., gen. mgr. Gateway Broadcasting Co., Inc., WJNS-WYAZ, Yazoo City, Miss., 1968—; mem. adv. bd. radio Holmes Jr. Coll., Goodman, Miss., 1977—. Chmn., Yazoo County CD; bd. dirs. Indsl. Found. Yazoo County. Recipient Good Citizenship award Yazoo Civitan Club, 1971. Mem. Nat. Assn. Broadcasters, Delta Council, Miss. Mfrs. Assn., Miss. Broadcasters Assn. (sec.-treas. 1979-80), Yazoo County C. of C. (dir., retail mchts. com.). Methodist. Clubs: Lions (past pres.) (Greenville); Rotary, Masons (Yazoo City); Yazoo County Young Farmers. Office: Enchanted Drive Box 1048 Yazoo City MS 39194

NETTLES, GAYLON JAMES, mental health counselor, army non-commd. officer; b. Detroit, Jan. 16, 1947; s. Lemuel James and Florence Junell (Morrow) N.; student Kans. State U., 1964-67; B.S. in Social Sci., Campbell (N.C.) Coll., 1974; M.S. in Counseling, Am. Tech. U., Killeen, Tex., 1978; m. Bungon Sook-Ka, May 18, 1970; children—Linda Ann, Catherine Junell. Enlisted U.S. Army, 1967, advanced through grades to sgt. 1st class, 1979; behavioral sci. specialist Ft. Knox Confinement Facility, 1974-75, U.S. Army Drug and Alcohol Program, Korea, 1975-76, Ft. Hood, Tex., 1976-78; instr. behavioral sci. U.S. Army Acad. Health Scis., Ft. Sam Houston, Tex., 1978—. Decorated Army Commendation medal. Home: 2603 Lake Altair St San Antonio TX 78222 Office: Academy of Health Sciences Behavioral Science Div Fort Sam Houston TX 78234

NETTLES, JOHN BARNWELL, physician, educator; b. Dover, N.C., May 19, 1922; s. Stephen A. and Estelle (Hendrix) N.; B.S., U. S.C., 1941; M.D., Med. Coll. S.C., 1944; m. Eunice Anita Saugstad, Apr. 28, 1956; children—Eric, Robert, John Barnwell. Intern Garfield Meml. Hosp., Washington, 1944-45; research fellow in pathology Med. Coll. Ga., Augusta 1946-47; resident in obstetrics and gynecology U. Ill. Research and Ednl. Hosps., Chgo., 1947-51; instr. to asst. prof. obstetrics and gynecology U. Ill. Coll. Medicine, Chgo., 1951-57; asst. prof., asso. prof., prof. obstetrics and gynecology U. Ark. Med. Center, Little Rock, 1957-69; dir. grad. edn. Hillcrest Med. Center, Tulsa, 1969-73; prof. U. Okla. Coll. Medicine, Oklahoma City, 1969—; prof., chmn. dept. gynecology and obstetrics U. Okla. Coll. Medicine, Tulsa, 1975—, mem. council on residency edn. in obstetrics and gynecology, 1974—; dir. Tulsa Obs. and Gynecol. Edn. Found., 1969—. Coordinator med. edn. for Nat. Def., Ark., 1961-69; mem. S.W. regional med. adv. com. Planned Parenthood Fedn. Am. Served as lt. (j.g.) M.C., USNR, 1945-46, as lt., 1953-54. Diplomate Am. Bd. Obstetrics and Gynecology. Fellow Am. Coll. Obstetricians and Gynecologists (dist. sec.-treas., dist. chmn. exec. bd. 1970-73, v.p. 1977-78), A.C.S. (bd. govs. 1969-71), Royal Soc. Health, Royal Soc. Medicine; mem. Ark. Obstet. and Gynecol. Soc. (exec. sec. 1959-69), Central Assn. Obstetrics and Gynecology (exec. com. 1966-69, pres. 1978-79), Internat. Soc. Advancement Humanistic Studies in Gynecology, Assn. Mil. Surgeons U.S., Am. (sect. council on obstetrics and gynecology 1975—), So. (chmn. obstetrics 1973-74) med. assns., Okla., Tulsa County, Chgo. med. socs., Am. Assn. for Maternal and Infant Health, Assn. Am. Med. Colls., Am. Pub. Health Assn., Assn. Hosp. Med. Edn., Assn. Planned Parenthood Physicians, Am. Assn. Sex Edn. Counselors and Therapists (SW regional bd. 1976—), N.Y. Acad. Sci., Soc. for Gynecol. Investigation, A.A.A.S., Am. Soc. for Study Fertility and Sterility, Internat. Soc. Gen. Semantics, Aerospace Med. Assn., So. Gynecol. and Obstet. Soc., Sigma Xi, Phi Rho Sigma. Lutheran. Research and main publs. on uterine malignancy, kidney biopsy in pregnancy, perinatal morbidity and mortality, sch. age pregnancy. Address: Univ Okla at Tulsa Med Coll 2727 E 21st St Suite 408 Tulsa OK 74114

NETTLETON, GARY STEPHEN, anatomist; b. Albert Lea, Minn., May 7, 1946; s. William Warner and Mildred Luella (Greenwood) N.; B.S. cum laude, McPherson Coll., Kans., 1968; Ph.D., U. Minn., 1976; m. Rose Ann Sink, Aug. 24, 1968; 1 dau., Sarah Louise. Teaching asst. McPherson Coll., 1965-68, U. Minn., 1968-70, 72-76; surgery technician Elkhart (Ind.) Gen. Hosp., 1970-72; mem. faculty U. Louisville Med. Sch., 1976—, asst. prof. anatomy, 1977—. USPHS scholar, 1968-70, 72-76. Licensed minister Ch. of Brethren. Named Tchr. of Yr. freshman med. class U. Louisville, 1979. Mem. Soc. Applied Spectroscopy, Histochem. Soc., Biol. Stain Commn., Sigma Xi. Editorial asst. Stain Tech., 1977—; contbr. to profl. jours. Home: 2115 Blvd Napoleon Louisville KY 40205 Office: Dept Anatomy PO Box 35260 Univ Louisville Louisville KY 40232

NEU, HOWARD MITCHELL, lawyer, mayor; b. Chgo., Mar. 22, 1941; s. Maurice A. and Phyllis (Spector) N.; student U. Fla., 1958-61; B.B.A., U. Miami, 1962, J.D., 1968; m. Beverly Block, July 3, 1977; children—Carol Deborah, Wendy Joy; stepchildren—Sandra Block, Alan Block. C.P.A., Weber, Thompson & Lefcourt, 1962-63, Morgan, Altemus & Barrs, 1963-68; admitted to Fla. bar, 1968; mem. firms William J. Goldworn, Miami, Fla., 1968-69, Goldworn & Neu, Miami, 1969-70, Neu & Hertz, 1971-73, Neu & Sanderhoff, 1977—; practiced in North Miami, 1970-71, 1973-77. Asso. judge, North Miami, 1971-75; councilman City of North Miami, 1975-79, mayor, 1979—; founder North Miami Mayor's Econ. Task Force; interim instr. U. Miami Sch. Law, 1969-70; instr. Miami Edn. Consortium, 1971-72. Chmn., Metro-Dade County Library Adv. Bd., 1968-69; chmn. Fla. Library Devel. Council, 1971-74; vice chmn. small cities adv. council Nat. League Cities; bd. dirs., 1st v.p. Dade League of Cities; pres. Gold Coast League Cities; bd. govs. Abbey Hosp.; musical dir. The Chosen Children. C.P.A., Fla. Mem. Fla. Inst. C.P.A.'s, North Miami C. of C., Am. Fla., Dade County, N. Dade (dir., 1st v.p.) bar assns., Am. Arbitration Assn. Kiwanian; mem. B'nai B'rith (past pres. Council So. Fla. lodges). Jewish (temple choir dir. 1966—). Elk. Club: Tiger Bay Political (Miami). Home: 1766 NE 142d St North Miami FL 33181 Office: 12955 Biscayne Blvd North Miami FL 33181

NEUCERE, NAVIN JOSEPH, chemist; b. Hessmer, La., Feb. 21, 1932; s. Xavier and Rose Marie (Rachal) N.; B.S., La. State U., 1960; postgrad. Tulane U., 1964-65, U. New Orleans, 1967-68; m. Martha June Froeba, Apr. 8, 1971; 1 child—Susan Dymphna. Research chemist So. Regional Research Center, U.S. Dept. Agr., New Orleans, 1961—. Served with USAF, 1951-55. Mem. Am. Chem. Soc., AAAS, Inst. Food Technologists, Am. Assn. Cereal Chemists, Sigma Xi. Democrat. Contbr. articles to profl. jours. Home: 8455 Beechwood Ct New Orleans LA 70127 Office: PO Box 19687 New Orleans LA 70179

NEUHOUSER, DAVID JEROME, ins. agt.; b. Ft. Wayne, Ind., Aug. 27, 1929; s. Melvin Ray and Leona Viola (Herbst) N.; B.S., Ball State U., 1953; m. Ellen F. Frohm, Mar. 10, 1956; 1 dau., Mary Susan. Ins. agt. Lincoln Nat. Life Ins. Co., Ft. Wayne, 1946-48, 53-64, Provident Life and Accident, Ft. Wayne, 1964-66, Sentry Ins. Co., Stevens Point, Wis., 1966-68, INA Life & Security Corp., Phila., 1968-72, Houston, 1972-76; owner, mgr. Comdr. Ins. Agy., Houston, 1976—; cons. ins. and pension, 1975—. Bd. dirs. Ashford Civic Assn., 1974-75. Served with USAF, 1948-49. Mem. Nat., Tex., Houston assns. life underwriters, Am. Soc. C.L.U.s Lutheran (elder). Home: 12053 Champion Forest Dr Houston TX 77066 Office: 5950 FM 1960 West Houston TX 77069

NEUMANN, DONALD LESTER, computer service exec.; b. Highland, Ill., Jan. 14, 1931; s. Lester H. and Cornelia R. (Wiedner) N.; B.S.C.E., U. Ill., 1953; postgrad. U.S. Air Force Communications Sch., 1953-54, Washington U., 1957, Miss. Coll., 1960-61, Miss. State U., 1965-66; m. Marjorie Ann Stelbrink, Sept. 3, 1955; children—Mark, Heidi. Mgr. Automatic Data Processing Center, U.S. Corps Engrs., Vicksburg, Miss., 1957—; cons. on computer mgmt. to govt., bus. and industry. Served to maj. USAF Res.; Korea, 1953-54. Registered profl. engr., Miss. Mem. Data Processing Mgmt. Assn., Aircraft Owners and Pilots Assn., ASCE, CAP. Clubs: Vicksburg Engrs., Lions (pres. local club 1969) (Vicksburg). Contbr. articles on computers to profl. jours. Home: 5 Bugle Ridge Dr Vicksburg MS 39180 Office: PO Box 631 Vicksburg MS 39180

NEUMANN, PEGGY-ANN, coll. adminstr.; b. Balt., Sept. 13, 1927; d. Walter Edward and Wanda (Monath) Neumann; B.A. magna cum laude, N.Y. U., 1966, M.A., 1968. Asst. to dir. Va. Poly. Inst., Danville, 1952-59; area supv. census bur. Dept. Commerce, Danville, 1960; project dir. for exec. dean arts and scis., N.Y. U., N.Y.C., 1962-64; asst. to dean Washington Sq. Coll. N.Y. U., 1970-72, instr. English, 1970-72; dir. career counseling and lectr. English, Hollins Coll., Roanoke, Va., 1972—; lectr., cons. in field. Bd. dirs., chmn. membership drive Danville Concert Assn., 1956-62; sec. ch. council Lutheran Ch. of Ascension Danville, Va., also mem. choir, ch. visitors com., Sunday sch. tchr., comm. edn. com., 1952-62; Recipient Lena Kastle award, 1966. Mem. Coll. Placement Assn., So., Va., Middle Atlantic coll. placement assns., Assn. for Sch. Coll. and Univ. Staffing, Middle Atlantic Assn. for Sch., Coll. and Univ. Staffing, Nat. Assn. for Women, Deans, Adminstrs. and Counselors, Catalyst, Roanoke Valley Bus.-Educators Consortium, Roanoke Network for Profl. and Managerial Women (founder). Working Women on Their Own (founder), Am. Soc. for Tng. and Devel. Contbr. articles to profl. jours. Home: PO Box 9565 Roanoke VA 24020 Office: Career Counseling Center Hollins Coll Roanoke VA 24020

NEVILS, BOBBY GENE, physician; b. Lake Charles, La., Aug. 5, 1938; s. Henry Murray and Ellen Martha (Blessing) N.; B.S., La. State U., 1959, M.D., 1963; m. Linda Louise Houston, June 6, 1964; children—Julia, Robert Mark. Intern, U.S. Naval Hosp., Charleston, S.C., 1963; resident in obstetrics and gynecology U.S. Naval Hosp., Great Lakes, Ill., 1965-69; practice medicine, specializing in obstetrics and gynecology, Kinder, La., 1971—. Served with USN, 1963-71. Diplomate Am. Bd. Obstetrics and Gynecology. Fellow Am. Coll. Obstetricians and Gynecologists; mem. Parish Med. Soc. (pres.), La. Med. Soc., La. Assn. Obstetrics and Gynecology. Democrat. Address: Drawer E Kinder LA 70648

NEWBERN, COPELAND DAVIS, citrus and vegetable grower, cattleman; b. Powells Point, N.C., Aug. 22, 1911; B.S. in Agr., U. Fla., 1933, postgrad., 1936-37; m. Edna Creekmore, Aug. 24, 1935; children—Caroline (Mrs. John Shepard), Nancy (Mrs. Peter Skemp). Tchr. vocat. agr., coach, Moyock, N.C., 1933-34; tchr. vocat. agr. Hernando County, Brooksville, Fla., 1935-38; agrl. agt., Hernando and Manatee County, 1938-45; pres., owner Newbern Groves, Inc., 1946-76, chmn. bd., 1976—; pres., owner Fancy Fresh Farms, Inc., Tampa, Fla., 1967—; dir. Jacksonville br. Fed. Res. Bank; mem. Fla. Citrus Commn., 1960-67; pres. Fla. Agrl. Council, 1973-76; mem. citrus shippers adminstrv. com. U.S. Dept. Agr. Chmn. SHARE council U. Fla., 1975-76, mem. president's adv. bd.; bd. curators Stephens Coll., 1970—; bd. dirs. Poultry Fedn., 1973-74; mem. Fla. Pari-Mutual Commn. 1979—. Mem. Greater Tampa (bd. govs. 1970-73), North Tampa chambers commerce, Fla. Fresh Citrus Shippers Assn. (pres. 1971-73), United Fresh Fruit and Vegetable Assn. (dir. 1972-74), Gamma Sigma Delta, Lambda Chi Alpha. Clubs: Kiwanis, Tampa Yacht and Country, University (Tampa); Ye Mystic Krewe of Gasparilla; River (Jacksonville, Fla.). Home: 912 S Himes Ave Tampa FL 33609 Office: Newbern Groves Inc PO Box 17237 Tampa FL 33682

NEWBERRY, JOSEPH ORION, fund raising corp. exec.; b. New Orleans, Jan. 19, 1915; s. Joseph Orion and Stella Eola (Smith) N.; B.S., Stephen F. Austin Coll., 1934; m. Harriette Rachel Baldion, Nov. 28, 1948; children—Joseph Orion, Patricia Ann, Linda Chell. With J.J. Collins Law Firm, Lufkin, Tex., 1938-39; asst. mgr. Lufkin C. of C., 1939-40; mgr. Gladewater (Tex.) C. of C., 1940-42, Texarkana (Tex.) C. of C., 1942-43; founder, pres., chmn. bd. Community Service Bur., Inc., 1946—; chmn. bd. Nat. Community Devel. Services, Inc.; lectr. seminars on fund raising. Bd. dirs. Dallas Health and Sci. Mus., Dallas County Community Coll. Dist. Found.; chmn. City Planning Commn. Served with U.S. Army, 1943-46. Mem. Am. Assn. Fund-Raising Counsel (pres. 1971-72), Press Club of Dallas, Am. Assn. C. of C. Execs., So. Assn. C. of C. Execs., Tex. C. of C. Mgrs., Nat. S.W. Socs. Fund Raisers, Coalition of Nat. Voluntary Orgns., Sigma Delta Chi. Democrat. Methodist. Clubs: Rotary, Brookhaven Country, City, Lancers, 2001, Cipango 21. Contbr. articles to publs. in philanthropic field. Home: 11349 Crest Brook St Dallas TX 75230 Office: 505 N Ervay Suite 806 Dallas TX 75201

NEWBERRY, ROBERT ALAN, hosp. ofcl.; b. Greenville, Tenn., Jan. 16, 1949; s. Roy Fred and Georgia Rose Newberry; B.S., E. Tenn. State U., 1971; m. Linda Joyce Thompson, Sept. 7, 1970; children—Robert Alan, II, Amiee Elizabeth. Customer service rep. Comml. Credit Co., Morristown, Tenn., 1972-73; life ins. salesman, 1973; asst. personnel dir., employee devel. officer Lakeshore Mental Health Inst., Knoxville, Tenn., 1973-78; personnel dir. Central Baptist Hosp., Lexington, Ky., 1978—. Accounts chmn. Knoxville United Way, 1977. Mem. Tenn. N.G., 1971-78. Mem. Am. Soc. Personnel Adminstrn., Am. Hosp. Personnel Assn., Ky. Hosp. Personnel Assn. (sec. 1979), Blue Grass Area Personnel Assn. Home: 2410 Tulsa Dr Lexington KY 40503 Office: 1740 S Limestone St Lexington KY 40503

NEWBY, CHARLES DAVID, auto parts co. exec.; b. Fort Worth, Tex., Dec. 15, 1953; s. Milas E. and Ruth L. (Echols) N.; B.B.A. in Mgmt., Tex. Christian U., 1976. With Greenfield Sales Co., Fort Worth, 1969—, v.p. mktg., 1974, exec. v.p., 1979—, pres. subs. Dave's Auto Parts and Tools, 1974—. Mem. Nat. Right to Work Com. Mem. Am. Mgmt. Assn., Ind. Garagemens Assn. Democrat. Mem. Ch. of Christ. Home: 1517 Byrd St Fort Worth TX 76114 Office: 509 E 3d St Fort Worth TX 76101

NEWBY, DAVID HENRY, aerospace mfg. co. exec.; b. Chickamauga, Ga., Feb. 12, 1920; s. Henry Burdick and Lucile (Williams) N.; B.S. in Elec. Engring., Ga. Inst. Tech., 1942; m. Lillian Marjorie Robinson, Nov. 17, 1942; children—David Henry, III, Donna Carol Newby Newman. Head instrumentation br. NACA, Langley Field, Va., 1942-51; chief test and evaluation lab. Army Rocket and Guided Missile Agy., Huntsville, 1951-59; liaison officer to U.S. Army, NASA, Huntsville, 1959-60; staff mem. Marshall Space Flight Center, Huntsville, 1960-73, dir. adminstrv. and tech. services, 1968-73; self-employed mgmt. cons., 1973-78; procurement mgr. United Space Boosters, Inc., Huntsville, 1978—; dir. Redstone Fed. Credit Union; mem. Ala. Space Sci. Commn. Gen. campaign chmn. Huntsville United Givers Fund, 1966; mem. Madison County Jud. Commn., 1974-77, Huntsville Minimum Housing Bd., 1965-75; chmn. adv. bd. Huntsville Civic Center, 1969-70; bd. dirs. Huntsville YMCA. Recipient Exceptional Service medal NASA, 1969; also numerous certs. appreciations, service awards. Mem. Nat. Contract Mgmt. Assn., Huntsville C. of C. Baptist. Club: Huntsville Rotary. Home: 2817 Garth Rd Huntsville AL 35801 Office: 220 Wynn Dr Huntsville AL 35801

NEWBY, HI EASTLAND, physician; b. Del Rio, Tex., Dec. 8, 1929; s. Byron Elvel and Amanda (Eastland) N.; student Schreiner Inst., 1947-48; B.A., Baylor U., 1951, M.D., 1957; postgrad. Sul Ross State U., 1948, 51-52; m. Ona Darlene Northcutt, Apr. 25, 1959; children—Byron Edgar, Hi Eastland. Intern, Bexar County Hosp., Dist., San Antonio, 1957-58; practice family medicine, Del Rio, 1958-77; chief staff Val Verde Meml. Hosp., Del Rio, 1968-69; med. cons. Tex. Rehab. Agy., San Antonio area, 1966-73; examining physician So. Pacific Co., 1959-77; med. dir. Dowell div. Dow Chem. U.S.A.; clin. asso. prof. dept. family practice U. Tex. Med. Sch., San Antonio, 1974—; asst. clin. prof. dept. family practice U. Tex. Med. Sch., Houston, 1979—. Mem. charter commn., City of Del Rio, 1966-67. Mem. Del. Rio Ind. Sch. Dist. Bd., 1968-71, pres., 1969-71; pres. San Felipe Del Rio Consol. Ind. Sch. Dist., 1971-72; mem. Val Verde County Sch. Bd., 1972-77; v.p. Cypress Creek Utility Dist., Houston, 1979-80, pres., 1980—. Diplomate Am. Bd. Family Practice. Mem. AMA, Tex. Med. Assn., Tex. Acad. Gen. Practice (dir. 1966-70), Tex. Acad. Family Physicians (chmn. membership and credential com. 1971-72, mem. edn. com. 1977—). Mason (Shriner). Home: 10523 Cypresswood Dr Houston TX 77070 Office: 400 West Belt South Houston TX 77042

NEWBY, JOHN MELVIN, coll. ofcl.; b. Westfield, Ind., Jan. 31, 1928; s. James Edwin and Mary Augusta (Williams) N.; diploma Union Bible Sem., 1948; A.B., LaVerne Coll., 1952; M.S., U. So. Calif., 1958; Ph.D., Mich. State U., 1972; m. Rebecca Jean Hall, Apr. 15, 1949; children—Sharon Jean, Karen Jane, Becky Lynette, John Melvin. Ordained to ministry Pilgrim Holiness Ch., 1951; minister Pilgrim Holiness Ch., San Dimas and Pasadena, Calif., 1950-59; instr. music Upland (Calif.) Coll., 1951-52; mgr. of schs. Pilgrim Holiness Ch., Zambia, Africa, 1959-63, acting field supr. and edn. sec., 1963-64; registrar, instr. Owosso (Mich.) Coll., 1964-66, dir. bus. affairs, 1966-67, registrar, 1967-68; registrar Spring Arbor (Mich.) Coll., 1968-73, dir. instl. research and planning, 1972-79, acting dean acad. affairs, 1973-74, v.p. adminstrv. affairs, 1974-79; mem. Free Methodist Ch., 1974-79, minister music Spring Arbor Free Meth. Ch., 1970-73; examiner N. Central Assn. Colls. and Schs., 1977-79; mem. Wesleyan Ch., 1950-74, 79—; pres. Central (S.C.) Wesleyan Coll., 1979—. Sec. Owosso Library Bd., 1966-68; bd. dirs. David Livingston Tchr. Tng. Coll., Zambia, 1963-64; trustee Western Pilgrim Coll., sec., 1951-58; trustee Mich. Library Consortium; bd. dirs. Mich. Heart Assn. Mem. Assn. for Instl. Research, Council for Advancement Small Colls. (chmn. student learning outcomes task force and student attrition task force, 1975-78), Am. Assn. for Affirmative Action, Am. Assn. Higher Edn., Phi Delta Kappa, Phi Kappa Phi. Republican. Club: Rotary (dir. 1966-71). Home: Central SC 29630 Office: Central Wesleyan Coll Central SC 29630

NEWCOMB, NOEL EDGAR, ins. exec.; b. Campbellsville, Ky., Apr. 13, 1928; s. Isaac Tate and Harriet Susan (Richerson) N.; student public schs., Campbellsville; m. Lois Irene Harrison, June 4, 1949; children—Bonnie Sue, Paula Ann, Lana Jill. Store mgr. Motor & Electric Supply Co., Campbellsville, 1950-57, Interstate Auto Supply, Campbellsville, 1957-60; store owner G & N Automotive, Campbellsville, 1960-64; ins. agt., Campbellsville, 1964-68; agy. owner Newcomb Ins. Co., Campbellsville, 1968-72; regional sales mgr. Fed. Kemper Ins. Co., Campbellsville, 1972—; dir. Ambulance Services, 1975-78. Deacon, Campbellsville Bapt. Ch.; scoutmaster Boy Scouts Am., 1949-50. Served with USAAF, 1945-48. Mem. Ind. Ins. Agts. Republican. Baptist. Clubs: Optimist, Holiday Ramblers (Past Pres. award, state council, pres. 1979), Masons, Good Sams.

NEWDORP, JOHN, physician; b. Chgo., Apr. 29, 1910; s. James and Katie (Vellenga) Nieuwdorp; A.B., Calvin Coll., Mich., 1931; M.D., U. Chgo., 1936; m. Eloise A. Beckham, Feb. 22, 1943. Intern, St. Luke's Hosp., Chgo., 1936-37; practice gen. medicine, Benham, Ky., 1937-39; resident in ob Chgo. Lying-In Hosp., 1939-40; with Ala. Health Dept., 1941-42; dep. exec. med. dir. UMWA Welfare Retirement Fund, 1947-52; dep. med. adminstrn. Mines Meml. Hosp. Assn., 1952-57, med. adminstr., Washington, 1957-64; dep. exec. med. dir. UMWA Welfare and Retirement Fund, Washington, 1964-69, exec. med. officer, 1969-76; med dir. Group Health Assn., Washington, 1977-78, cons., 1978—. Served with USPHS, 1942-47. Mem. Am. Public Health Assn., Group Health Assn. Am., Am. Med. Joggers Assn., U.S. Ski Assn. (pres. Eastern div., dir.). Clubs: Washington Canoe, other athletic clubs. Home: 2809 Oakton Manor Ct Oakton VA 22124

NEWELL, JAMES THAXTON, govt. engr.; b. Vernon, Ala., Dec. 31, 1939; s. Ernest Clovis and Welthey (Younghance) N.; A.A.S. with honors, DeVry Tech. Inst., 1960; B.S. in Engring. summa cum laude, U. Central Fla., 1975, M.S. in Engring., 1979; m. Sylvia Ellen Thomas, Mar. 9, 1963; children—Karen Lynn, James Thomas, Kelly Elizabeth, Jonathan Michael; m. 2d, Susan Gail Malone, Oct. 9, 1973; 1 son, Jason Roy. Reliability engr. McDonnell Douglas Aircraft Co., St. Louis, Mo., 1960-66; reliability program mgr. Emerson Electric Co., St. Louis, 1966-67; engring mgr. Naval Plant Rep. Office, St. Louis, 1967-68; mgr., also reliability and maintainability engr. Naval Tng. Equipment Center, Orlando, Fla., 1968-77, ops. research analyst, 1977—. Founder, dir. AstroCel Research Inst., Inc.; instr. Seminole Community Coll., 1974—. Registered profl. engr., Mo., Fla. Mem. Am. Fedn. Astrologers, Alpha Pi Mu. Baptist (Sunday sch. tchr. 1962-63). Home: 575 E Jessup Longwood FL 32750 Office: Naval Training Equipment Center Code N434 Orlando FL 32813

NEWELL, WILLIAM THOMAS, bus. exec.; b. Rochester, N.Y., July 5, 1936; s. Earl Edward and Ruth Hazel (Dorsey) N.; student Rochester Inst. Tech., 1955; m. Margret Anne Laurash, July 10, 1971. Owner, operator ChemMark Chem. Co., Miami, Fla., 1965-67, Newell & Co., sales and mktg. cons. and sales agts., Atlanta, Dallas, Ft. Lauderdale, Fla., 1967—, Keynote Music Studios, Ft. Lauderdale, 1974—; pres. Sytlewood Industries, Inc., mfg. and sales of insulated bldg. panels, Gainesville, Fla., 1977—. Served with U.S. Army, 1959-61. Democrat. Episcopalian. Home: 2500 NE 48th Ln Fort Lauderdale FL 33308 Office: 5130 N Federal Hwy Fort Lauderdale FL 33308

NEWLAND, MARY JANE, dietitian; b. Huntington, W.Va., Feb. 18, 1937; d. Land H. and Jessie Marble (Nelson) Smith; B.S. in Dietetics and Instl. Mgmt., Marshall U., 1959; dietetic intern Vanderbilt U. Hosp., Nashville, 1960; M.A. in Health Care Adminstrn., Central Mich. U., 1977; m. Daniel Rhea Newland, May 25, 1974. Asst. chief dietitian VA Hosp., Huntington, 1960-67; dir. dietetics Meml. div. Charleston (W.Va.) Area Med. Center, 1963—, co-dir. dietetic traineeship, 1967—; cons. Bronco Junction, summer camp asthamatic children; instr. nutrition for nurses Charleston U. Named Outstanding Dietitian for W.Va., Southeastern Hosp. Conf. Dietitians, 1972; recipient Silver Plate award Hosps. and Health Care Establishments, 1979. Mem. Am. Dietetic Assn. Democrat. Baptist. Home: 612 Burkewood Pl Charleston WV 25314 Office: 3200 MacCorkle Ave SE Charleston WV 25304

NEWMAN, BURTON CHEVIS, fleet services exec.; b. Covington, Tenn., Aug. 6, 1941; s. Nathaniel Rives and Kathrine (Hill) N.; student U. Tenn., 1960-62; B.A. in History, Memphis State U., 1965; m. Patricia Hall, Jan. 7, 1965; children—Burton Chevis, Langdon, Shannon. Mgr. sales analyst Plough, Inc., Memphis, 1969-73; sales analyst Mid Continent Systems, Inc., West Memphis, Ark., 1973-74, v.p. sales, 1975-78, exec. v.p. fleet service, 1978—. Served to lt., USNR, 1965-69; Vietnam. Methodist. Club: Holly Hills Country. Office: PO Box 1370 West Memphis AR 72301

NEWMAN, CHARLES FORREST, lawyer; b. Grenada, Miss., Jan. 15, 1937; s. Wiley Clifford and Lurene (Westbrook) N.; B.A. magna cum laude, Yale, 1959, J.D., 1963; postgrad. (Adenauer fellow) U. Bonn (Germany), 1959-60; m. Jeannette Kay Bailey, May 26, 1973. Admitted to Tenn. bar, 1964; law clk. U.S. Dist. Judge Bailey Brown, Western Dist. Tenn., 1963-64; mem. firm Burch Porter & Johnson, Attys., Memphis, 1965—, partner, 1966—; vis. prof. Memphis State Law Sch., spring 1976, 77; mem. faculty environ. litigation seminar Am. Law Inst.-Am. Bar Assn., fall 1979. Past bd. dirs. Tenn. Conservation League; bd. dirs. Memphis Acad. Arts, Tenn. Environ. Council, Art Today, Environ. Action Fund, Inc., USO; adv. council Mid-South Water Quality Council; chmn. legal com. Memphis State U. Neighborhood Assn.; mem. president's Council Southwestern Coll.; mem. class council Class of '59, Yale Coll.; patron Arts Appreciation, Inc. Mem. Am., Tenn., Memphis and Shelby County (discipline and ethics com. 1976, pub. relations com. 1976—, Memphis State U. Law Sch. liaison com. 1980—) bar assns., Am. Judicature Soc., Am. Assn. Trial Lawyers, Wilderness Soc., Soaring Soc. Am., Airplane Owners and Pilots Assn., L.Q.C. Lamar Soc., Environmental Action Council, Sierra Club, Phi Beta Kappa. Clubs: Tennessee, Yale of Memphis (past pres.), Yale of N.Y. Home: 3880 Poplar Ave Memphis TN 38112 Office: 130 N Court Memphis TN 38103

NEWMAN, DAVID, psychologist; b. N.Y.C., Nov. 1, 1938; s. Joseph and Mollie (Greengold) N.; B.S., Coll. City N.Y., 1960; M.A. (Alvin Johnson scholar), New Sch. Social Research, 1963; Ph.D. (honor grad.), N.Y. U., 1969; m. Carol Lea Rosenbaum, Aug. 26, 1962; children—Elisabeth, Mara, Richard. Dir. psychology Children and Adolescent Unit, S. Fla. State Hosp., Hollywood, 1973—; pvt. practice psychology, Margate, Fla., 1975—; adj. prof. psychiatry Med. Sch., U. Miami, 1973—; dir. Community Mental Health Clinic, Va., 1973. Mem. Broward County Child Abuse Task Force, 1977—. Served with U.S. Army, 1960. Mem. Am., Southeastern, Broward County (sec. 1976-77, v.p. 1977-78, pres. 1978—) psychol. assns., Fla. Psychol. Assn. Contbr. articles to profl. publs. Home: 1684 NW 81st Ave Coral Springs FL 33065 Office: 5750 Margate Blvd Margate FL 33063

NEWMAN, EMMETT WAYNE JACK, lawyer; b. Smith County, Tex., Sept. 22, 1917; s. Frank M. and Pearl (Miller) N.; LL.B., Houston Law Sch., 1938; postgrad. U. Tex., 1945, S. Tex. Coll. Law, 1946, U. Houston, 1950-54; m. Grace U. Love, June 6, 1953; 1 son, Paul W. With Archer Grain Co., Houston, 1935-46; admitted to Tex. bar, 1948; mem. firm Bracewell & Tunks, Houston, 1948-49; practiced in Houston, 1949—. Vice pres. Cedar Bayou Park, Inc., Houston, 1964—, F.N.N. Co., Inc., Houston, 1965—, Cedar Bayou Water Supply Co., Inc., Houston, 1966—. Pres. Armand Yramategui Meml., Inc., Houston, 1970—, Armand Bayou Fund, Houston, 1972-74. Bd. dirs. Tex. Conservation Council of Tex., 1959-70, pres., 1970—. Mem. Am., Tex., Houston bar assns., Am., Tex. trial lawyers assns., Tex. Soc. Practising Lawyers, Bass Anglers Sportsman Soc. Am., Nat. Rifle Assn., Bayou Rifles, Inc. Republican. Methodist. Mason (Shriner). Clubs: Sportsmen's of Tex. (dir. 1962-64, v.p. 1965-67), Bayshore Rod, Reel and Gun (dir. 1964-68). Home: 5015 Jason St Houston TX 77035 Office: 711 Fannin St Room 816 Houston TX 77002

NEWMAN, FLETCHER CAMPBELL, librarian; b. El Paso, Tex., Dec. 21, 1929; s. Simeon Harrison and Willie Lea (Montague) N.; B.A., Tex. Western Coll., 1954; M.A. in L.S., Immaculate Heart Coll., Los Angeles. Monk, Trappist Abbey of Our Lady of Guadalupe, Lafayette, Oreg., 1955-67; librarian Los Angeles Pub. Library, 1969; librarian sci. library U. Tex., El Paso, 1969—, head circulation and reference dept., 1974-77, head sci./engring./math. library, 1978—; cons. El Paso Natural Gas Co., 1975-76. Served with AUS, 1951-53. Mem. Tex., Border Regional (editor newsletter 1973) library assns. Democrat. Roman Catholic. Home: 6105 Fiesta Dr El Paso TX 79912 Office: Univ Tex Library El Paso TX 79968

NEWMAN, JAMES HEFLIN, univ. cons.; b. Lafayette, Ala., June 3, 1908; s. James R. and Sara Dean (Mathews) N.; A.B., U. Ala., 1929, M.A., 1930, LL.D. (hon.), 1957; m. Dixie Ann Jones, June 6, 1940; children—Ann Newman Dickson, James Blair. Dir. student activities U. Ala., 1930-32, asst. dean of men, 1932-37, asso. dean of men, 1937-38, dean of men, 1938-42, dean adminstrn., 1950-56; interim pres., 1957-58, exec. v.p., 1958-65; dean of students U. Va., Charlottesville, 1946-50; pres. Longwood Coll., Farmville, Va., 1965-67; v.p. acad. affairs Samford U., Birmingham, Ala., 1968-70, asst. to pres. for planning and research, 1970-73, univ. cons., 1973—. Served from lt. (j.g.) to lt. comdr. USN, 1942-45. Recipient Algernon Sydney Sullivan award, 1930. Mem. Nat. Assn. Deans and Advisers of Men (pres. 1948-49), Assn. Ala. Coll. Adminstrs., Newcomen Soc., Phi Beta Kappa, Phi Eta Sigma, Phi Kappa Phi, Phi Gamma Delta, Alpha Phi Omega, Omicron Delta Kappa. Episcopalian. Club: Rotary. Home: PO Box 743 Pell City AL 35125 Office: Samford U 800 Lake Shore Dr Birmingham AL 35209

NEWMAN, JAMES SAMUEL, chem. engr.; b. Sevier County, Tenn., Sept. 25, 1922; s. Sim O. and Lola A. (Romines) N.; B.S. in Chem. Engring., U. Tenn., 1951; m. Sarah K. Miller, Sept. 7, 1947; children—Jerry F., Jama R. Shift supr. Belding Heminway Co., Hendersonville, N.C., 1951-69, colorist and chemist, 1969-72, shift supr., chemist, 1972-76, chemist, chem. engr., 1976—. Vol. fireman; instr. fire service; crewman vol. Rescue Squad. Served with AUS, 1942-46. Named man of year Henderson County Community Devel., 1975; recipient CD commendation, 1971; cert. of appreciation U.S. Dept. Agr., 1974. Mem. Am. Inst. Chem. Engrs., Am. Assn. Textile Chemists and Colorists, Am. Chem. Soc., VFW, Am. Legion, Am. Security Council (nat. adv. bd.), Am. Def. Preparedness Assn. Baptist. Clubs: Woodmen of the World, Masons. Home: 410 Glover St Hendersonville NC 28739

NEWMAN, JERRY OKEY, agrl. engr.; b. New Martinsville, W.Va., May 9, 1936; s. James Okey and Hazel Edna (Howell) N.; B.S., W.Va. U., 1958, M.S., 1960; Ph.D., U. Md., 1972; m. Patricia Grace Devericks, May 25, 1958; children—Tamrah M., Lucetta R., Symantha C., Onika M. Grad. asst. W.Va. U., 1958-60; with VA, Clarksburg, W.Va., 1960-62; with Dept. Agr., 1962—, research leader housing for rural families program Rural Housing Research Unit, Sci. and Edn. Adminstrn., Clemson, S.C., 1978—; cons. in field. Bd. dirs. S.C. Retarded Citizens Assn., 1978-79; pres. Pickens County Assn. Retarded Citizens, 1975-77, bd. dirs., 1975-79; bd. dirs. Better Skills, 1975-79; leader 4-H Club, 1974-79. Recipient Superior Performance awards VA, 1960, 61; Danforth summer fellow, 1957; registered profl. engr., W.Va. Mem. Am. Soc. Agrl. Engrs., Internat. Assn. Housing Specialists, Orgn. Profl. Employees, Sigma Xi, Tau Beta Pi. Author papers in field, Dept. Agr. reports and bulls. Home: Route 1 Box 375 Central SC 29630 Office: PO Box 792 Clemson SC 29631

NEWMAN, LOUIS EDWARD, III, veterinarian, pathologist, educator; b. Schenectady, N.Y., Nov. 14, 1930; s. Louis Edward and Ruth (Sensenbrenner) N.; B.S. in Agr., U. N.H., 1952; D.V.M., Cornell U., 1956; M.S. in Pathology, Mich. State U., 1975, Ph.D., 1978; m. Leslie Williams, June 9, 1955; children—Lise, Kathryn, Janet, Tracy, James, Richard; m. 2d, Jane Anne Yarhouse, Jan. 2, 1972; 1 adopted dau., Elaine. Practice vet. medicine, Worland, Wyo., 1956-57; founder, owner, operator Glasgow (Mont.) Vet. Clinic, Glasgow Vet. Supply & Flying N Ranch, 1957-69; extension project leader dept. large animal surgery and medicine Coll. Vet. Medicine, Mich. State U., 1969-79; dir., pathologist dept. vet. sci. Livestock Disease Diagnostic Center, Coll. Agr., U. Ky., Lexington, 1979—. Cons. herd health Miss. State U., Starkville, 1975-76. Mem. adv. bd. Valley County (Mont.) Devel. Council, Glasgow, 1966-69; chmn. LeRoy Twp. (Mich.) Zoning Bd., Webberville, 1975-76, Planning Commn., 1976-79, Zoning Bd. Appeals, 1976-79. Trustee Williamston (Mich.) Community Schs. Bd. Edn., 1975-79. Mem. Nat. Mastitis Council (dir., chmn. com. coliform mastitis research 1975-76), Am., Mich., Ky. vet. med. assns., Am. Vet. Soc. for Study Breeding Soundness (chmn. bd. 1966), Am. Assn. Bovine Practitioners, Am. Assn. Vet. Clinicians, Am. Assn. Vet. Nutritionists, Am. Assn. Extension Veterinarians, Soc. Theriogenology, Alhpa Zeta, Phi Zeta, Epsilon Sigma Phi. Research on neonatal calf mortality, intestine of gnotobiotic calves, role of sawdust bedding in etiology of coliform mastitis in dairy cattle. Home: 2108 Tamarack Dr Lexington KY 40504 Office: Livestock Disease Diagnostic Center 1429 Newtown Pike Lexington KY 40511

NEWMAN, MAURICE STANLEY, accountant, educator; b. Southchurch, Eng., July 12, 1917; came to U.S., 1931, naturalized, 1939; s. David S. and Mabel (Campbell-Everden) N.; B.B.A., CCNY, 1947; M.B.A., N.Y. U., 1966, Ph.D., 1972; m. Ann Marie Schwartz, July 22, 1943; children—James William, David Frederick, Nancy Louise, Susan Catherine Newman Schmierer, John Campbell, Sarah Jane. Asst. office mgr. Bank Manhattan Co., N.Y.C., 1936-43; chief acct. consumer fin. div. Irving Trust Co., N.Y.C., 1945-47; mgr. Arthur Andersen & Co., N.Y.C., 1947-51; mgmt. cons. Cresap, McCormick & Paget, N.Y.C., 1952-56; partner Haskins & Sells, N.Y.C., 1956-76; bd. visitors research prof. Coll. Commerce and Bus. Adminstrn., U. Ala., University, 1976—. Served to lt. (j.g.) USN, 1943-46. C.P.A., N.Y., Calif., Ill., Wis., Iowa, La. Mem. Am. Inst. C.P.A.'s, Ala. Soc. C.P.A.'s, Calif. Soc. C.P.A.'s, Nat. Assn. Accts., Am. Mgmt. Assn. Presbyterian. Clubs: Masons, Shriners; North River Yacht; Va. Hot Springs Golf and Tennis. Hills Country. Home: 38 Ridgeland Tuscaloosa AL 35406 Office: PO Drawer AC University AL 35486

NEWMAN, MICHAEL KEITH, social worker; b. Martinsville, Va., Dec. 26, 1944; s. Coy Homer and Ruby Newman; student Smithdeal-Massey Bus. Coll., 1963-65; B.S., Va. Commonwealth U., 1969; M.S.W., 1971. Caseworker, Family and Children's Service of Richmond (Va.), 1971-74; clin. social worker Richmond County Mental Health Clinic, Rockingham, N.C., 1974-76; dir. partial hospitalization program Guilford County Mental Health Center, Greensboro, N.C., 1976-77; dir. area prevention, consultation, edn. and tng. Guilford County Area Mental Health, Mental Retardation and Substance Abuse Program, Greensboro, 1977-80; co-founder, co-dir. Wholistic Living Center, Greensboro, 1978-80; cons. psychotherapy and leadership devel. Maultsby Orthopaedic Clinic, 1979-80; dir. community and family services DeJarnette Center for Human Devel., Staunton, Va., 1980—; rep. IDS, Greenville, S.C., 1980—. Vice pres. N.C. Alliance for Primary Prevention, 1979-80; bd. dirs. Crisis Control Center, 1979-80. Mem. Nat. Assn. Social Workers, Nat. Assn. Prevention Profls., Am. Soc. Tng. and Devel., Acad. Cert. Social Workers, Am. Assn. Marriage and Family Therapy. Home: 304 Timberlake Dr Anderson SC 29621 Office: Koger Exec Center Chesterfield Bldg Suite 114 Greenville SC 29615

NEWMAN, SAMUEL WILLIAM, ret. air force officer, educator; b. Marcelina, Tex., Oct. 10, 1910; s. James R. and Clara E. (Callaway) N.; B.A. in Secondary Edn., History and Spanish, Baylor U., Waco, Tex., 1964, M.A. in History, 1967; m. Elizabeth Ann Beahan, Jan. 26, 1942; children—John P. (dec.), William A., Robert A. Enlisted in U.S. Army, 1932, advanced through grades to col. USAF, ret., 1960; exec. officer 27th Air Depot Group, New Guinea, 1942-45; dir. personnel Barksdale AFB, La., 1946-50; dir. mil. personnel Hdqrs. Flying Tng. Air Force, Waco, Tex., 1951-52; labor liaison officer NATO, London, 1953-55; assigned USAF Insp. Gen.'s Office, Washington, 1955-60; classroom tchr. Waco Ind. Sch. Dist., 1964-69, asst. prin., 1969-70, supr. social studies, 1970-71, 73-76; ret., 1976; cons. edn. and geneal. research, 1977—; vis. prof. edn. Baylor U., 1972-73. Mem. McLennan County Alcoholism Com., 1972-75; mem. adv. com. Dist. Juvenile Ct., 1975—; adv. com. teaching techniques Tex. Hist. Assn., 1969-72; chmn. ann. fund drive McLennan County unit Am. Cancer Soc., 1979-80; pres. Heart O' Tex. Study Am. Heritage, 1973-76. Decorated Legion of Merit; recipient Jr. Historian Leadership award, 1977. Mem. NEA, Tex. State Hist. Assn., Ret. Officers Assn. (pres. elect Heart of Tex. chpt.), Waco C. of C. (edn. com. 1974—), Central Tex. Geneal Soc. (editor 1979—), VFW, DAV, Sons Confederate Vets., Pi Gamma Mu, Phi Delta Kappa, Sigma Delta Pi. Author: The Post-Civil War Career of James Harrison Wilson, 1967; Texas and Its History, 1972; American Free Enterprise Curriculum Guide, 1974; History of the Waco Public Schools, 1875-1975, 1975; compiler: Readings in Texas History, 3 vols., 1976. Home: 5413 Lake Lindenwood Dr Waco TX 76710 Office: PO Box 27 Waco TX 76703

NEWMAN, WAYLAN WILLIAM, food distbn. co. exec.; b. Mobeetie, Tex., Sept. 17, 1934; s. Johnie William and Lillie Marie N.; student Clarendon (Tex.) Jr. Coll., 1954-55; m. Nelda Barton, Aug. 6, 1954; children—Ann, Larry. Retail positions, 1955-65; with Waples Platter Co., Lubbock, Tex., 1965—, v.p. sales, 1979—. Deacon, Meml. Baptist Ch., Lubbock. Club: Lions. Office: PO Box 1530 Lubbock TX 79408

NEWMAN, WILLIAM WASHINGTON, JR., cons. elec. engr., farmer; b. Cullman, Ala., Feb. 7, 1919; s. William Washington and Ossie (Daniel) N.; B.S., Auburn U., 1941; student U.S. Dept. Agr. Grad. Sch., 1959; m. Charlotte J. Windsor, May 5, 1944; children—Rose Marie, Margaret Patricia, William Washington. Jr. engr. TVA, Cherokee Dam, Tenn., 1941; engr. Birmingham Electric Co. (Ala.), 1946-48; elec. engr. Rural Electrification Adminstrn., Columbia, Tenn., 1949-53, asst. chief telephone engring. div., Washington, 1955-59, dir. Western Area Telephone, 1959-60; gen. mgr. Millington Telephone Co. (Tenn.), 1954-55; chief elec. ground support equipment design br. SD & D Lab. Army Ballistic Missile Agy. Redstone Arsenal, Huntsville, Ala., 1960; formerly dep. dir.

Launch and Ancillary Equipment Lab., Army Ordnance Missile Command, dep. dir. Ground Support Equipment Lab., chief Research and Tech. Office, supervising engr. GSE Lab, chief missile design and aircraft weaponization group Gen. Engring. and Missile Directorate, ret. 1973; cons. engr. Lincoln County (Tenn.); farmer, 1973—; owner, operator Willchar Angus Farm, Dellrose, Tenn. Past alderman, Millington; vice chmn. Lincoln County (Tenn.) Planning Commn.; chmn. Lincoln City Pub. Utilities Bd. Served from 2d lt. to maj. C.E., U.S. Army, 1941-46. Named Engr. of Year Huntsville IEEE, 1966; registered profl. elec. engr., Ala., Tenn. Mem. IEEE (chmn. engring. mgmt. sect. Huntsville sect.), Ala. Acad. Sci., Am. Ordnance Assn., Assn. U.S. Army, Am. Angus Assn., Tenn. Livestock Producers Assn., Eta Kappa Nu, Tau Beta Pi. Club: Lions (past pres. Millington, Tenn.). Author: A New Device for Sagging Telephone Wires, 1955; (with C.R. Ballard) Standard Colors and Color Deviations for Communications Wires and Cables, 1959. Contbr. articles to profl. jours. Home: RFD 1 Dellrose TN 38453

NEWMARK, EMANUEL, ophthalmologist; b. Newark, May 25, 1936; s. Charles M. and Bella (Yoskowitz) N.; B.S., Rutgers U., 1959; postgrad. U. Amsterdam, 1960-63; M.D., Duke U., 1966; m. Tina Steinberg, Aug. 25, 1957; children—Karen Beth, Heidi Ellen, Stuart Jeffry. Intern, George Washington Hosp., Washington, 1966, resident in ophthalmology, 1967-70; instr. ophthalmology U. Fla. Coll. Medicine, Gainesville, 1970, U. Tex. Med. Sch., San Antonio, 1971-72; practice medicine specializing in ophthalmology, West Palm Beach, Fla., 1972—; mem. staff Good Samaritan, St. Mary's, Doctors, J.F. Kennedy, Palm Beach Gardens Community hosps., Bascom Palmer Eye Inst.; cons. Gainesville VA Hosp., 1970; clin. instr. ophthalmology U. Miami Coll. Medicine. Served to maj. U.S. Army, 1970-72. Diplomate Am. Bd. Ophthalmology. Fellow Am. Acad. Ophthalmology and Otolaryngology, A.C.S.; mem. AMA, So., Fla. med. assns., Soc. Mil. Ophthalmologists, Assn. Research in Vision and Ophthalmology, Am. Intra-Ocular Implant Soc., Palm Beach County ophthal. socs., Palm Beach County Med. Soc., Duke U. Med. Sch. Alumni Assn., Palm Beach County Jewish Fedn., Palm Beach Jewish Community Center. Clubs: Hineni, B'nai B'rith. Contbr. articles to books and jours. Home: 1707 W Terrace Dr Lake Worth FL 33460 Office: 1500 N Dixie Hwy West Palm Beach FL 33401

NEWMASTER, THOMAS WALTER, lawyer; b. Stillwater, Okla., Aug. 16, 1947; s. Walter Henry and Louise Agnes (Brandewiede) N.; B.A., St. Ambrose Coll., 1969; J.D., U. Okla., 1972: m. Karolis Kay Jones, Sept. 28, 1974. Admitted to Okla. bar, 1973; asso. firm Harold Hall, Ada, Okla., 1973-75; individual practice law, Ada, 1975-77; partner firm Benson and Newmaster, Ada, 1978—. Chmn. Pontotoc County (Okla.) chpt. Nat. Found. for Birth Defects/March of Dimes, 1976-79; ballot security officer, precinct chmn. Pontotoc County Republican Party, 1976-79. Mem. Am., Okla. (mem. ho. of dels. 1976-77), Pontotoc County (sec.-treas. 1976, pres. 1977) bar assns., Okla. Trial Lawyers Assn., Ada C. of C., Phi Alpha Delta. Roman Catholic. Clubs: Ada Tennis, Elks. Home: 721 W 20th St Ada OK 74820 Office: American Bldg Suite 308 Ada OK 74820

NEWSOM, DOUGLAS ANN JOHNSON, journalist; b. Dallas, Jan. 16, 1934; d. J. Douglas and R. Grace (Dickson) Johnson; B.J. cum laude, U. Tex., 1954, B.F.A. summa cum laude, 1955, M.J., 1956, Ph.D., 1978; m. L. Mack Newsom, Jr., Oct. 27, 1956 (separated); children—Michael Douglas, Kevin Jackson, Nancy Elizabeth, William Macklemore. Gen. publicity State Fair Tex., 1955; advt. and promotion Newsom's Women's Wear, 1956-57; publicity Auto Market Show, 1961; lab. instr. radio-tv news-writing course U. Tex., 1961-62; local publicist Tex. Boys Choir, 1964-69, nat. publicist, 1967-69; pub. relations dir. Gt. S.W. Boat Show Dallas, 1966-72, Family Fun Show, 1970-71, Horace Ainsworth Co., Dallas, 1966-76; pres. Profl. Devel. Cons.'s, Inc., non-profit seminar prodn.; asso. prof. dept. journalism, chmn. dept., former adviser yearbook and mag. Tex. Christian U., Ft. Worth, 1970—. Sec.-treas., Public Relations Found. Tex., 1979-80, also trustee; public relations chmn. local Am. Heart Assn., 1973-76, state public relations com. 1974—, vice chmn. bd. dirs., 1979-80, chmn., 1980—. Mem. Assn. Edn. in Journalism (pres. pub. relations div. 1974-75), Women in Communications (nat. conv. treas. 1967, nat. pub. relations chmn. 1969-71), Pub. Relations Soc. Am. (nat. edn. com. 1975, chmn. 1978, nat. faculty adv.), Tex. Public Relations Soc. (dir. 1976—, v.p. 1980—), Am. Women in Radio and TV, Delta Delta Delta, Mortar Bd. Alumnae (adviser Tex. Christian U. 1974-75). Baptist. Author: (with Alan Scott) This is PR, 1976, 2d edit., 1980; (with Tom Siegfried) Writing for Public Relations Practice, 1981; editorial bd., book rev. editor Pub. Relations Rev. Home: 4237 Shannon Dr Fort Worth TX 76116

NEWSOM, MICKEY BRUNSON, bus. exec.; b. Columbia, Miss., July 26, 1941; s. James Hezzie and Opal Eugenia (Prescott) N.; A.A., Hartnell Coll., 1961; B.B.A., Golden Gate U., 1964, M.B.A., 1976; m. Rose Marie Christensen, May 25, 1963. Mgr., Roy's Restaurants, Salinas, Calif., 1964-67; prin. Humboldt County Schs., Redcrest, Calif., 1967-69; educator Bur. Indian Affairs, Wide Ruins, Ariz., 1969-71; owner Western Auto Store, Columbus, Miss., 1971-76; owner Mickey Newsom & Co., 1976—; col. on staff gov. of Miss., 1976-80. Polit. cons. various state and nat. candidates; mem. Columbus Municipal Democratic Exec. Com., 1977—; bd. dirs. Lowndes County Assn. Retarded Citizens, 1979—. Mem. Am. Polit. Sci. Assn., E. Miss. Council (dir. 1977—), Am. Acad. Polit. and Social Sci., Mid-Continent Oil and Gas Assn., New Orleans Mus. Art, Golden Gate U. Alumni Assn. Tower Club. Democrat. Lutheran. Clubs: Columbus Civitan (pres. 1977-78, lt. gov. Miss. North dist. 1978-79); Commonwealth of Calif. Home: PO Box 241 Columbus MS 39701 Office: PO Box 241 Columbus MS 39701

NEWSOM-CLARK, SANDRA KAY, speech pathologist; b. Paintsville, Ky., June 1, 1950; d. George and Ida (Bentley) Newsom; student Prestonsburg Community Coll., 1967-68, U. Ky., 1968-69; B.S. with honors, Eastern N.Mex. U., 1971; M.S., Vanderbilt U., 1971, postgrad., 1973; postgrad. U. Tenn., 1977—; m. James Howard Clark, Jr., June 17, 1978. Speech-lang. pathologist Mountain Comprehensive Care Center, Paintsville, 1972-73, VA Center, Johnson City, Tenn., 1973-74; dir. Speech and Hearing Clinic, asst. prof. Appalachian State U., Boone, N.C., 1974-77; clin. supr. U. Tenn. Hearing and Speech Center, Knoxville, 1977-78; speech-lang. pathologist Neuropathology Services dept. audiology and speech pathology, Knoxville, 1979—; cons. speech-lang. pathologist Patricia Neal Rehab. Center, Knoxville, 1979—; dir. Summer Easter Seals Speech Clinics, 1975-77. Congl. action contact Rep. Carl D. Perkins, 1972-73; regional bd. dirs. Easter Seals, 1974-77, Outstanding Service award, 1977, grantee, 1974-77. Mem. Am. Speech-Lang. and Hearing Assn., Council Univ. Suprs. Speech and Lang. Pathology, Council Exceptional Children, Ky. Speech and Hearing Assn., N.C. Speech, Lang. and Hearing Assn., Tenn. Speech and Hearing Assn. (mem. com. on aging). Baptist. Home: 151 Walnut Ave Paintsville KY 41240 Office: South Stadium Hall Room 444 U Tenn Knoxville TN 37916

NEWTON, DENNIS ELBERT, JR., constrn. co. exec.; b. Slidell, La., Aug. 14, 1918; s. Dennis Elbert and Ausie (Culley) N.; grad. Tex. A. and M. U., 1939; m. Mary Virginia Collins, Jan. 4, 1941; children—Dennis, Denise, Marianne. Works purchasing agent Carbide & Carbon Chem. Co., Texas City, Tex., 1940-54; div. purchasing agent Union Carbide Corp., N.Y.C., 1954-56, mgr. materials and services, chem. and plastic div., Houston, 1956-73; dir. purchasing Brown & Root, Inc., Houston, 1974-75, v.p. procurement, 1975—; sec., treas., dir. Cheena Investment Co., Houston, 1969. Pres., Houston Regional Minority Purchasing Council, 1977-78. Served with USN, 1944-46. Named Man of Year, Houston Indsl. Distbrs. Assn., 1975. Mem. Nat. Assn. Purchasing, Am. Mgmt. Assn., Purchasing Mgmt. Assn. Houston (pres. 1967-68), Houston Engring. and Sci. Soc. Republican. Roman Catholic. Club: Houston City. Home: 6106 Sanford Houston TX 77096 Office: Brown & Root Inc 4100 Clinton St Houston TX 77001

NEWTON, JEAN CAROL MCCORMICK, advt. agy. exec.; b. Norwalk, Conn., June 13, 1938; d. John Millard and Dorothy Florence (Bennett) McCormick; B.S., U. R.I., 1960; children—Gregory, Stefanie, Geoffrey. Copywriter, Montgomery Ward & Co., N.Y.C., 1960-61, WGHQ, Kingston, N.Y., 1962-63; asst. advt. mgr. Advertiser-Democrat, Norway, Maine, 1963-65; copywriter, woman's editor WMTW-TV, Poland Spring, Maine, 1965-67; continuity dir. WEAT-TV, West Palm Beach, Fla., 1967-70; creative dir. Haselmire Advt., West Palm Beach, 1970—, v.p., 1977—. Mem. Am. Advt. Fedn., Advt. Club Palm Beaches (pres. 1976-77), Sigma Kappa. Republican. Home: 314 Minnesota St Lantana FL 33462 Office: 324 Datura St Suite 212 West Palm Beach FL 33401

NEWTON, KENNETH ALAN, elec. engr.; b. Portsmouth, Va., Mar. 4, 1948; s. Ernest C. and Juanita (Cundiff) N.; B.S. in Engring., Old Dominion U., 1974; children—Kenneth A., Troy W., Gina Vachel. Electrician apprentice Navy Public Works Center, Norfolk, Va., 1966-69, electric power controller, 1969-75, elec. utilities engr., 1975-78, supervisory gen. engr., 1978—. Vice pres. Little Creek Community Baseball, Norfolk, 1976-78, pres., 1978—; athletic dir. Azalea Athletic Assn., Norfolk, 1977—. Mem. IEEE. Methodist. Home: 1740 N Lakeland Dr Norfolk VA 23518 Office: Utilities Dept Navy Public Works Center Bldg P-71 Norfolk VA 23511

NEWTON, LILLIAN HINSON, writer; b. Templeman, Va., Apr. 17, 1921; d. Geroge Washington and Mary Marks H.; student Am. U., 1960-63, Charles County Community Coll., 1968-71; m. John Norton Newton, Jan. 31, 1943 (dec.); children—Norton Byrd, Wanda Newton Atkins. Computer systems analyst Naval Weapons Surface Center, Dahlgren, Va., 1946-76; mgr. Profl. Mgmt. Services, Fredericksburg, Va., 1976-77; engring. writer Sperry Univac, Dahlgren, Va., 1977—. Vice chmn. King George County Planning Commn.; chmn. King George County Med. Services; past pres. missionary group Potomac Bapt. Ch., Oakland Bapt. Ch.; past pres. Potomac and King George PTA. Mem. Am. Assn. Ret. Persons (pres.), King George C. of C. Clubs: Toastmistress (past pres.), Garden (past pres.). Home: Forrest Rd Dahlgren VA 22448 Office: Sperry Univac Dahlgren VA 22448

NEWTON, MARY K., guidance counselor; b. Bennettsville, S.C., May 24, 1947; d. Willard Perry and Mary Elizabeth (McLaurin) W.; A.A., Spartanburg Meth. Coll., 1967; B.S., Coker Coll., 1974; M.Ed., U. S.C., 1977, postgrad., 1979—; m. Lawrence Dewey Newton, III. Sec., dir. admissions St. Andrews Presbyn. Coll., Laurinburg, N.C., 1967, sec., 1967-68, sec., dir. devel., 1968-72; asst. to dir. finance and devel. Coker Coll., Hartsville, S.C., 1972-73, acting dir. placement, 1973-74, dir. placement, 1974-75; career counselor Chesterfield-Marlboro Tech. Coll., Cheraw, S.C., 1976, dir. admissions, 1976, counselor, 1976—. Coker Coll. scholar, 1975. Mem. Am. Coll. Personnel Assn., Am. Personnel and Guidance Assn., S.C. Personnel and Guidance Assn., Carolinas Assn. Collegiate Registrars and Admissions Officers, S.C. Tech. Edn. Assn. (instl. v.p.), So. Coll. Personnel Assn. Baptist. Home: Route 1 Box 320 McColl SC 29570 Office: Chesterfield-Marlboro Tec Coll Cheraw SC 29520

NEWTON, ROBERT PARK, III, automotive service equipment mfg. co. exec.; b. Orangeburg, S.C., Oct. 6, 1943; s. Robert Park and Elizabeth (Edwards) N.; student Clemson U., 1963-64; m. Francine Herack, Jan. 4, 1969. Asst. dir. mktg. Western Heritage U.S.A., Ocala, Fla., 1964-66, dir. mktg., 1966-68; owner retail automotive service center, Tampa, Fla., 1968—; pres., founder Autodynamics, Inc., Tampa, 1970-78; pres., treas., chmn., founder Ride Control Systems, Inc., Tampa, 1978—; founder C.U.B.S., Inc., Tampa, 1975—. Served with USAR, 1962-70. Mem. Equipment and Tool Inst., Nat. Tire Dealers and Retreaders, Motor Equipment Mfrs. Assn., Tampa C. of C. Republican. Episcopalian. Club: Elks. Home: 4011 Priory Circle Tampa FL 33624 Office: PO Box 15276 Tampa FL 33684

NEYLAND, DIETRICH ALLEN, architect; b. Shreveport, La., Nov. 26, 1914; s. Junius Charles and Mary Rulfs) N.; B.Arch., Tulane U., 1938; m. Linda R. Halbert, Dec. 21, 1968. Asst. to Richard Neutra, 1940; architect camouflage devel., Fort Belvoir, Va., 1941; prin. Van Os & Flaxman, 1946-50; asso. Ginocchio Cromwell, 1950-57; with Cromwell, Neyland, Truemper, Levy & Gatchell, Architects and Engrs., Inc., Little Rock, 1957—, chmn. bd., 1974—, dir. design, 1960—. Vestryman, sr. warden Christ Episcopal Ch., 1972. Served to lt. USN, 1942-46. Mem. AIA, Gargoyle, Alpha Tau Omega. Clubs: Tulane T, Little Rock, Westside Tennis. Architect: Little Rock Air Terminal, U. Ark., Little Rock, prince's palace Riyadh, Saudi Arabia, State Dept. Housing, Delhi, Madras, India. Home: 12140 Rivercrest St Little Rock AR 72212 Office: 1 Spring Bldg Little Rock AR 72201

NGUYEN, NGOCLINH, fast food co. exec.; b. Vietnam, Aug. 29, 1930; s. TrongTan and ThiSuu N.; B.A., Bowdoin Coll., Brunswick, Maine, 1952; m. Pham Thi Thu, Oct. 24, 1953; children—MyChau, QuocHung, QuocAnh, MyLinh, QuocViet. Gen. mgr. Cong Dan Pub. Co., Saigon, Vietnam, 1956-60; pres. Nat. Broadcasting System, Republic of Vietnam, 1964-65, Vietnam Press Agency, 1965-68; dir. gen. info., mem. Cabinet, Govt. of Republic of Vietnam, 1968; pres., chmn. bd. Mekong Group Cos., 1969-75; pres. LTH of Tex. Corp., Houston, 1977—; prof. journalism Dalat U., 1967-72, Mekong U., 1973-75. Sec. gen. Vietnam Council on Fgn. Relations, 1970-75; chmn. bd. trustees Mekong U., 1973-75. Served to 1st lt. Vietnamese Army, 1960-64. Recipient Merit medal 1st class, 1968, Info. medal 1st class, 1968, Labor medal 1st class, 1967 all from Govt. Republic Vietnam. Buddhist. Author: English Idioms for Vietnamese, 1960; translator: Economics by Samuelson, 1960; editor: Cong Dan Information Please Almanac, 1960, Vietnam Journalism Quar., 1970-73, Vietnam Mag., 1970-75. Office: 800 Sharpstown Center Houston TX 77036

NIBLOCK, WILLIAM ROBERT, paint co. exec.; b. Phila., Aug. 15, 1928; s. William and Grace (Rennie) N.; B.S., Drexel U., 1951; M.B.A., U. Chgo., 1956; m. Barbara Parsons, Sept. 22, 1956; children—Elizabeth Ann, Christopher Parsons. Chem. engr. Atlantic Refining Co., Phila., 1951-56; mgr. planning and analysis Pitts. Coke & Chem. Co., 1956-60; dir. comml. devel. and licensing USS Chems. div. U.S. Steel, Pitts., 1960-70; v.p., Porter Paint Co., Louisville, 1970—. City trustee City of Northfield, Ky., 1976—; alumni bd. U. Chgo., 1974—; bd. dirs. Jr. Achievement Louisville, Camp Piomingo, Met. YMCA Louisville. Served with USNR, 1952-55. U. Chgo. Teaching fellow, 1955-56. Mem. Licensing Execs. Soc., Comml. Devel. Assn., Am. Chem. Soc. Republican. Episcopalian. Clubs: Wynn-Stay, Jefferson (Louisville). Home: 2210 Wynnewood Circle Louisville KY 40222 Office: PO Box 1439 Louisville KY 40201

NICELEY, GILLON TRUETT, furniture store owner, farmer; b. Bellevue, Ky., June 5, 1923; s. Curtis Lafayette and Trailing Arbutus (Broome) N.; grad. Union Coll., 1942; m. Mary Ellen Oyer, Dec. 24, 1943; children—Gillon Truett, Richard Dyer, Nelle Dyer. Owner, Niceleys Home Furnishings, Elizabethtown, Ky., 1945—; farmer, Elizabethtown; bus. cons. Elizabethtown Community Coll., 1979—. Served with USAF, 1942-45. Decorated Air medal with 2 clusters. Mem. Farm Bur., Nat. Furniture Owners Assn., Downtown Mchts. Assn. (pres.), Sigma Alpha Epsilon. Democrat. Baptist. Clubs: Masons, Shriners, Elizabethtown Country. Home: Rural Route 2 Gaither Station Rd Elizabethtown KY 42701 Office: 131 W Dixie Elizabethtown KY 42701

NICHOLAS, ALLAN WRIGHT, forensic chemist; b. Harrisonburg, Va., Feb. 8, 1946; s. Carlyle Koiner and Winifred (Wright) N.; B.A., Bridgewater Coll., 1968; M.S. in Organic Chemistry, U. Va., 1973, Ph.D., 1974; m. Mardine Judith Thompson, Oct. 16, 1976; children—Eric, Robin, Greg. Postdoctoral fellow in medicinal chemistry U. Iowa, Iowa City, 1974-75; postdoctoral asso. in bio-organic chemistry Research Triangle Inst., Research Triangle Park, N.C., 1975-79; forensic drug chemist State Bur. Investigation, Raleigh, N.C., 1979—. Served with U.S. Army, 1969-70; Vietnam. Decorated Army Commendation medal; NDEA fellow, 1971-74. Mem. Am. Chem. Soc., N.C. Acad. Scis., N.C. Assn. for Advancement of Sci., Sc. Assn. Forensic Scientists, Sigma Xi. Republican. Lutheran. Contbr. articles to profl. jours. Home: 1001 Millbrook Rd Raleigh NC 27609 Office: 3320 Old Garner Rd Raleigh NC 27610

NICHOLAS, JAMES ERNEST, paper co. exec.; b. Montgomery, Ala., Feb. 28, 1922; s. Ernest Elmore and Mazie (Broughton) Nicholas; B.S. in Civil Engring., Auburn (Ala.) U., 1947; m. Molly Geneva Ford, Feb. 23, 1944; 1 son, James Ernest. With Internat. Paper Co., 1947—, constrn. mgmt., Texarkana, Tex., 1969-72, Mobile, Ala., 1972—. Served with USMCR, 1943-46. Registered profl. engr., Ala. Mem. Soc. Am. Mil. Engrs. Home: 1050 Westbury Dr Mobile AL 36609 Office: PO Box 160707 Mobile AL 36616

NICHOLAS, NICKIE LEE, indsl. hygienist; b. Lake Charles, La., Jan. 19, 1938; d. Clyde Lee and Jessie Mae (Lyons) Nicholas; B.S., U. Houston, 1960, M.S., 1966. Tchr. sci. Pasadena (Tex.) Ind. Sch. Dist., 1960-61; chemist FDA, Dallas, 1961-62, VA Hosp., Houston, 1962-66; chief biochemist Baylor U. Coll. Medicine, 1966-68; chemist NASA, Johnson Spacecraft Center, 1968-73; analytical chemist TVA, Muscle Shoals, Ala., 1973-75; indsl. hygienist, compliance officer Occupational Safety and Health Adminstrn., Dept. Labor, Houston, 1975-79, Tulsa area dir., 1979—; mem. faculty VA Sch. Med. Tech., Houston, 1963-66. Recipient award for outstanding achievement German embassy, 1958, Suggestion award VA, 1963, Group Achievement award Skylab Med. Team, NASA, 1974, certificate appreciation Dept. Labor, 1977. Mem. Am. Chem. Soc. (dir. analytical group Southeastern Tex. and Brazosport sects. 1971, chmn. elect 1973), Am. Assn. Clin. Chemists, Am. Harp Soc., Kappa Epsilon. Office: US Dept Labor OSHA 717 S Houston Ave Suite 304 Tulsa OK 74127

NICHOLS, CHARLES JOSEPH, ch. constrn. cons.; b. Pitts., Dec. 31, 1943; s. Albert Charles and Margaret Kathryn (Meyers) N.; E.E., Penn Tech. Inst., 1964; spl. courses Ga. State U., 1978, Elkins Inst., Miami Inst. Fin., 1974. Cons. and quality control engr. Union Switch & Signal Co., Braddock, Pa., 1964-74; v.p. constrn. S.E. region Niehaus Bldg. Systems, West Mifflin, Pa., 1974-79; pres. So. Heritage, Inc., New Smyrna Beach, Fla., 1979—; dir. Fellowship of Christian Love (Orlando, Fla.); tchr. ann. seminars on fundamentals of ch. design, fin. and constrn. Lic. Class A gen. contractor, Fla.; lic. radio-telephone operator 1st class, pvt. pilot, FAA. Mem. Nat. Assn. Bldg. Scis. (cons. com.), So. Standard Bldg. Code Congress, Constrn. Specification Inst., Aircraft Owners and Pilots Assn. Author: Fundamentals of Design, Finance and Construction for Today's Churches, 1979; patentee E-Z fill aid to self-service gas station users. Office: 161 N Causeway Suite 5 New Smyrna Beach FL 32069

NICHOLS, DUANE GUY, chem. engr.; b. Tyler, W.Va., July 18, 1937; s. Guy L. and June G. N.; B.S. in Chem. Engring., W.Va. U., 1959; M.Chem. Engring., U. Del., 1963, Ph.D., 1968. Asst. prof. Del. State Coll., Dover, 1963-68; asst. prof. W.Va. U., Morgantown, 1968-75, asso. prof., 1975-78; sr. chem. engr. Research Triangle Inst., Research Triangle Park, N.C., 1978—, head fossil energy sect., 1979; mem. fossil energy com. So. States Energy Bd., 1979-80; tech. chmn. 5th and 6th Nat. Confs. on Energy and Environ., also editor Proc. Recipient Whitehill Chemistry award, 1956. Mem. Am. Chem. Soc., Am. Inst. Chem. Engrs., Air Pollution Control Assn., Sigma Xi, Tau Beta Pi, Omega Chi Epsilon, Phi Lambda Upsilon (chemistry award). Democrat. Unitarian. Club: Kiwanis. Office: PO Box 12194 Research Triangle Park NC 27709

NICHOLS, EDWARD TYLER, surgeon; b. Montgomery, Ala., Feb. 9, 1938; s. Grover Tyler and Ruby (Rogers) N.; grad. Auburn U., 1959; M.D., Med. Coll. Ala., 1962; children—Edward Tyler, David Spencer, Carol Ann. Intern, Univ. Hosp., Birmingham, Ala., 1962-63; resident Mobile (Ala.) Gen. Hosp., 1963-65, 67-69; practice surgery, Mobile, 1969-71, Bay Minette, Ala., 1971-76, Foley, Ala., 1976—; mem. teaching staff dept. surgery Mobile Gen. Hosp., 1969-71. Served with USAF, 1963-65. Diplomate Am. Bd. Surgery. Fellow A.C.S.; mem. Med. Soc. Ala., So. Surg. Assn., Baldwin County Med. Soc. (pres. 1972-73, 73-74). Methodist. Club: Rotary. Home: Orange Beach AL 36533 Office: Medical Arts Center Foley AL 36535

NICHOLS, HORACE ELMO, state justice; b. Elkmont, Ala., July 16, 1912; s. William Henry and Louella (Bates) N.; B. Mus., Columbia, 1933, postgrad., 1934; LL.B., Samford U., 1935; m. Edith Bowers, Oct. 20, 1945; children—Nancy Bates (Mrs. James Lewis Glenn), Carol Elizabeth, Horace Elmo. Admitted to Ga. bar, practiced in Canton, 1938-40, Rome, after 1940; judge superior ct. Rome Jud. Circuit, until 1955; judge Ga. State Ct. Appeals, 1955-66; justice Ga. Supreme Ct., Atlanta, 1966—, now chief justice. Mem. Rome, Ga., Am. bar assns., State Bar Ga. Elk. Club: Coosa Country (Rome). Home: 13 Virginia Circle Rome GA 30161 Office: Judicial Bldg Atlanta GA 30334

NICHOLS, IRBY COGHILL, JR., historian; b. Baton Rouge, Apr. 10, 1926; s. Irby Coghill and Pauline (Wright) N.; B.A., La. State U., 1947; M.A., U. N.C., 1949; Ph.D., U. Mich., 1955; m. Margaret Sunshine Irby, Apr. 18, 1953; children—Nina Keith, Irby Coghill, III. Instr., Catawba Coll., 1949; teaching fellow U. Mich., 1949-52; instr. N.Mex. Mil. Inst., 1952-55; asst. prof. European history North Tex. State U., 1955-57, asso. prof., 1957-67, prof., 1967—, also dept. grad. adv.; vis. asso. prof. La. State U., summer 1962. Served with USMC, 1944-46. Recipient Louis Knott Koontz award Pacific Hist. Assn., 1968, First Ann. Jo Houston Shelton award North Tex. State U., 1976; 15 N. Tex. State U. Faculty Research Grants, 1956—. Mem. Am. Acad. Arts, Scis., So. Hist. Assn., Soc. French Hist. Studies, Southwestern Soc. Sci. Assn. (chmn. sessions 1971—, chmn. history sect. 1969-70), Smithsonian Instn., World Future Soc., Phi Kappa Phi. Democrat. Episcopalian. Author: The European Pentarchy and the Congress of Verona, 1822, 1971; (with Paul Smith and Dwane Kingery) North Texas State University A Self-Study, 1962; history asso. editor Social Sci. Quar. (formerly Southwestern Social Sci. Quar.), 1961-64; contbr. articles to profl. publs. Home: 2514 Royal Ln Denton TX 76201 Office: Box 6212 North Tex Sta Denton TX 76203

NICHOLS, JAMES OLIVER, univ. adminstr.; b. Corpus Christi, Tex., July 29, 1941; s. James Walton and Lorraine (Patteson) N.; B.S., Trinity U., 1963; M.A. in Teaching, Alaska Meth. U., 1968; Ph.D., U. Toledo, 1971; m. Karen Lynn Wentz, Jan. 26, 1963; children—Patricia Lorraine, Barbara Ellen, Elizabeth Diane, James Walton. Dir. instl. research Concord Coll., Athens, W.Va., 1971-73; coordinator instl. studies Bluefield (W.Va.) State Coll. and Concord Coll., 1973-76; dir. instl. research and planning Marshall U., Huntington, W.Va., 1976-79; asst. prof. higher edn. and dir. instnl. research and planning U. Miss., Oxford, 1979—; cons. in field. Served to capt. U.S. Army, 1963-68. Mem. Assn. Instl. Research, Soc. Coll. and Univ. Planning. Episcopalian. Club: Exchange. Contbr. articles to ednl. jours. Home: 109 Lakeway Dr Oxford MS 38677 Office: 204 Lyceum U Miss University MS 38677

NICHOLS, JAMES RICHARD, civil engr.; b. Amarillo, Tex., June 29, 1923; s. Marvin Curtis and Ethel N.; B.S. in Civil Engring., Tex. A. & M. U., 1949, M.S. in C.E., 1950; m. Billie Louise Smith, Dec. 24, 1944; children—Judith Ann, James R., Jr., John M. Pres., Freese and Nichols, Inc., Ft. Worth, 1977—; farm operator Chisholm, Tex., 1969—; dir. Continental Nat. Bank, Fort Worth. Bd. dirs. Panther Boys Club, Fort Worth, 1969—; trustee All Saints Episcopal Hosp., Ft. Worth. Served with AUS, 1943-46. Registered profl. engr., Tex., Okla., N.Mex. Mem. Cons. Engrs. Council, ASCE, Nat. Soc. Profl. Engrs. Methodist. Mason, Rotarian. Clubs: Fort Worth, Colonial Country (Fort Worth). Home: 3024 Tanglewood Park E Fort Worth TX 76109 Office: 811 Lamar St Fort Worth TX 76102

NICHOLS, JEANNETTIE DOORNHEIN, artist, educator, cons.; d. Jacob Lenard and Caroline (Hauk) Doorhein; B.A.E., Art Inst. Chgo., 1934; s. Charles Martin Nichols, Apr. 21, 1941; 1 dau., Jean Lawson. Art supr. Belvidere Pub. Schs., 1930-31; tchr. comml. art Crane Evening Sch., 1933-36; tchr. art Chgo. Pub. Schs., 1933-71, art dept. head, 1948; studio for pvt. students, 1935-74; chmn. art dept. Washington High Sch., Chgo., 1962-71; exhibited Pa. Nat. Acad., Phila., Chgo. Asso. Galleries, Mandels Art Gallery, Conrad Hilton Hotel, 1952, Ind. State Fair, 1954, 55, Gary Extension U. Ind., also So. Shores Juried Ann., Gary, Ind., 1961, Lynn Kotler Galleries, N.Y.C., 1973; one-man shows, Waukazoo, Holland, Mich., 1952, Cottage Studios, Chgo., 1953, Gary Hotel, Gary, Ind., 1957, Crespi Gallery, N.Y.C., 1959, Krieg Art Gallery, Lombard, Ill., 1970-74, Lord Fairfax Community Coll., Middletown, Va., 1975, Dallas Artist Equity, 1977; invitational exhbn. Mpls. Mus. Art. Recipient 1st prize, enamel on copper, Gary Craftsman Guild, 1955, 2d prize, mixed-medium, Chesterton Ann., 1955; 1st prize water color, Gary Artists League, 1955; 2d watercolor award, Southern Shores Exhibit, 1956, 1st, 2d, 3d purchase awards, Ann. Ceramic Show, South Bend, Ind., 1956; Tri Kappa award, 1967. Life fellow Internat. Inst. Arts and Letters; mem. Artists and Craftsmen Porter County (past pres.), Art Educators Chgo. (past pres., bd. mem.), Art Inst. Alumni Assn., Western Arts Assn., Gary Artists League (1st v.p., past pres., bd. mem.), Nat. Art Edn. Assn., Ellis County Art Assn. (1st award 1978), Artists Equity, Woodbridge Art Guild (v.p. 1975). Studio: Route 1 Buttonwood Village Waxahachie TX 75165

NICHOLS, LYNN DAVID, educator; b. Hawkins County, Tenn., Sept. 11, 1933; s. Charles Seviere and Ruby (Carter) N.; B.S., M.E., Carson Newman Coll., 1955; dip. Wurzburg Conservatory, 1957-58; D.Higher Edn. (hon.), Memphis State U., 1956. Band dir. McNairy County, Tenn. Bd. Edn., 1955-56; music dir. Morristown (Tenn.) City Schs., 1958-60, Knoxville (Tenn.) City Schs., 1960-62; entertainment dir. U.S. Army Spl. Services, Stuttgart and Augsburg, Ger., 1962-68; band and music supr. Greene County Bd. Edn., Mosheim, Tenn., 1969—; choir dir., soloist Church St. Meth. Ch., Knoxville, 1960-62. Served with U.S. Army, 1956-58. Tenn. Bur. Transp. scholar, 1978-79. Mem. Music Educators Nat. Conf., NEA, Tenn. Edn. Assn., Tenn. Choral Soc., Tenn. Band Assn., Am. Guild Organists. Democrat. Methodist. Club: Exchange (bd. dirs. 1978-79, pres.-elect 1979-80), European Recreation Soc. Home: 135 Woodbine Ave Bulls Gap TN 37711 Office: Union at Charles St Greenville TN 37743

NICHOLS, MARY KATHRYN, educator; b. Baldwin, Fla., Dec. 11, 1927; d. Grady Dee and Alma E. (Clements) Taylor; B.S., Tex. Christian U., 1962; M.S., Tex. Woman's U., 1968; m. Charles S. Nichols, Jr., Jan. 31, 1948; children—Linda Kathryn Nichols Zakaryan, Michael Stephenson, Dan Charles. Staff nurse Harris Hosp., Ft. Worth, 1958-59, head nurse, 1960-62; mem. faculty Harris Coll. Nursing, Tex. Christian U., Ft. Worth, 1962—, asso. prof. nursing, 1968—; mem. adv. com. extra-mural programs M.D. Anderson Tumor Clinic, Houston, 1976—; mem. adv. com. to nursing div. Fort Worth City Health Dept., 1976—. Mem. Am. Nurses Assn., Nat. League Nursing, Nat. Assn. Mental Health, Tex. Nurses Assn. (pres. 1975-76, named Nurse of Year, Dist. III 1978), Sigma Theta Tau. Mem. Ch. of Christ. Home: 3724 Westcliff Rd N Fort Worth TX 76109 Office: Tex Christian U Fort Worth TX 76129

NICHOLS, N. B., constrn. co. exec.; b. Floydada, Tex., Mar. 23, 1932; s. Burette and Elva Callie (Jeter) N.; B.S., Midwestern U., 1954; postgrad Midwestern U., U. Houston; m. Lettie Faye Nichols, Sept. 18, 1964; children—Lisa Kaye, Jeffery Scott. Tchr. sci. Bandera (Tex.) High Sch., 1954-55; with Armco Steel Corp., Houston, 1955-74, field sales engr., 1968-72; gen. mgr. sales M.C. White Constrn. Co., Memphis, 1972-74; v.p. Abbott & Williams Constrn. Co., Shreveport, La., 1974—. Mem. La. Indsl. Devel. Exec. Assn., Shreveport C. of C. (pres. indsl. devel. group 1979), Metal Bldg. Dealers Assn., Shreveport Econ. Devel. Found., Kappa Kappa Psi, Beta Beta Beta. Republican. Methodist. Club: Kiwanis.

NICHOLS, ROBERT LEIGHTON, engring. co. exec.; b. Amarillo, Tex., June 24, 1926; s. Marvin Curtis and Ethel N.; B.S. in Civil Engring., Tex. A&M U., 1947, M.S., 1948; m. Ida Frances Hardison, June 8, 1948; children—Frances Eileen, William Curtis, Michael Lynn. Instr., Tex. A & M U., College Station, 1947-48; with Freese & Nichols, Inc., Ft. Worth, 1948—, v.p., 1977—; dir. 1st State Bank, Rockwall, Tex., 1967—. Registered profl. engr., Tex., La., N.Mex., Colo., Okla. Mem. Nat. Soc. Profl. Engrs. (pres. 1978-79), Am. Water Works Assn., ASCE, Tex. Soc. Profl. Engrs. (pres. 1965-66), Am. Public Works Assn., Tex. Water Conservation Assn., Water Pollution Control Fedn., Tex. Water Pollution Control Assn. (pres. 1962-63), Tex. Water Utilities Assn., Tex. Public Works Assn., Tau Beta Pi, Chi Epsilon. Methodist. Clubs: Masons, Ft. Worth. Home: 2410 Stadium St Fort Worth TX 76109 Office: Freese and Nichols Inc 811 Lamar St Fort Worth TX 76102

NICHOLS, RONALD LEE, psychologist; b. McKinney, Tex., Nov. 12, 1950; s. Elmer Lee and Wandalene (Cook) N.; B.A., E. Central U., Ada, Okla., 1973; M.S., Okla. State U., Stillwater, 1974, postgrad., 1975—; m. Maj-Brit Karen Melugin, Aug. 7, 1971; 1 dau., Erin Michelle. Psychologist, Hillcrest Med. Center, Tulsa, 1975-78; psychologist, clin. asst. prof. psychiatry U. Okla. Med. Coll., Tulsa, 1978—, instr. dept. Ob-Gyn, 1978—. Mem. Okla. Gov's. Com. on Employment of Handicapped; asso. mem. Mayor's Com. on Employment of Handicapped, Tulsa, 1975—. Recipient state of Okla. Handicapped Citizen of Yr. award, 1980. Mem. Nat. Rehab. Assn., Nat. Rehab. Counseling Assn., Am. Personnel and Guidance Assn., Am., Okla. (asso.) psychol. assns. Democrat. Mem. Christian Ch. (Disciples of Christ). Office: U Okla at Tulsa Med Coll 2727 E 21st St Tulsa OK 74104

NICHOLS, RONALD LEE, surgeon, educator; b. Chgo., June 25, 1941; s. Peter Raymond and Jane Eleanor (Johnson) N.; M.D., U. Ill., 1966, M.S., 1970; m. Elsa Elaine Johnson, Dec. 4, 1964; children—Kimberly Jane, Matthew Bennett. Intern U. Ill. Hosp., Chgo., 1966-67, resident surgery, instr., 1967-72; asst. prof. surgery U. Ill. Med. Sch., 1972-75; asso. prof. U. Health Scis. Chgo. Med. Sch., 1975-77, dir. surg. edn., 1975-77; Henderson prof. surgery Tulane U. Sch. Medicine, New Orleans, 1977—, prof. microbiology and immunology, 1979—; attending surgeon Tulane Med. Center Hosp., Charity Hosp. La.; cons. surgeon VA Hosp., Alexandria, La., Huey P. Long Hosp., Pineville, La., Lollie Kemp Charity Hosp., Independence, La., Touro Infirmary, New Orleans; mem. VA Coop. Study Rev. Bd. and Merit Rev. Bd. in Surgery, 1978—. Mem. exec. bd. Westminster House, Chgo., 1974—. Recipient Med. Council Teaching award U. Ill. Med. Sch., 1972; Bd. Trustees award for research U. Health Scis./Chgo. Med. Sch., 1977, Clin. Prof. of Year award, 1977; Clin. Prof. of Yr. award Tulane U. Sch. Medicine, 1979. Diplomate Am. Bd. Surgery, Nat. Bd. Med. Examiners. Fellow A.C.S. (core com. operating room environ.), Infectious Disease Soc. Am.; mem. Central, Midwest surg. assns., Ill., Chgo. surg. socs., AMA, Assn. VA Surgeons, N.Y. Acad. Sci., Inst. Medicine of Chgo., Soc. Surgery Alimentary Tract, Assn. Acad. Surgery, Collegium Internationale and Chirurgiae Digestivae, Soc. Univ. Surgeons, Surg. Soc. La., Southeastern Surg. Congress, New Orleans Surg. Soc., Warren H. Cole Soc., Sigma Xi. Episcopalian. Mem. editorial adv. bd. Guidelines to Antibiotic Therapy; editorial bd. Rev. Surgery. Contbr. chpts. to med. books, articles to med. jours. Home: 1521 7th St New Orleans LA 70115 Office: Dept Surgery Tulane Med Sch 1430 Tulane Ave New Orleans LA 70112

NICHOLS, WILLIAM (BILL), Congressman; b. nr. Becker, Miss., Oct. 16, 1918; B.S. in Agr., Auburn U., 1939, M.A., 1941; m. Carolyn Funderburk; children—Memorie, Margaret, Flynt. Vice pres. Parker Fertilizer Co., Sylacauga, Ala., 1947-66; pres. Parker Gin Co., Sylacauga, 1947-60; mem. Ala. Senate, 1963-66; mem. 90th to 92d congresses from 4th Ala. Dist., 93d to 95th Congresses, 3d Ala. Dist.; mem. Armed Sers. Com. Former mem. Sylacauga Bd. Edn. bd. govs. Nat. Hall of Fame; trustee Auburn U. Served to capt. U.S. Army, 1942-47; ETO. Decorated Bronze Star, Purple Heart; named Outstanding Mem. Ala. Senate, Montgomery Press Corps, 1965, Man of Year in Agr., Progressive Farmer mag., 1965. Mem. Am. Legion, V.F.W., D.A.V., Ala. Cattlemens Assn., Ala. Farm Bur., Blue Key, Scabbard and Blade, Gamma Sigma Delta. Democrat. Methodist (steward). Home: Sylacauga AL 35150 Office: 2417 Rayburn House Office Bldg Washington DC 20515

NICHOLSON, HAROLD JACKS, JR., transp. exec.; b. Atlanta, Apr. 4, 1942; s. Harold Jacks and Carolena N.; student U. Ga., 1960, Ga. State Coll., 1961-63, 76—; m. Elizabeth Gower, Oct. 12, 1972; children—Michael Edwin, Jason Samuel. Vice pres. ops. Central Transfer Co., Inc., Atlanta, 1959—; pres. Nicholson Machinery Movers, Inc. Baptist. Home: 3136 Bruckner Blvd Snellville GA 30278 Office: 14 SCL Terminal NW Atlanta GA 30313

NICHOLSON, LUTHER BEAL, accountant; b. Sulphur Springs, Tex., Dec. 15, 1921; s. Stephen Edward and Elma (McCracken) N.; B.B.A., So. Meth. U., 1942, postgrad., 1946-47, Tex. U., 1947-48; diploma Southwestern Grad. Sch. Banking, 1967; m. Ruth Wimbish, May 29, 1952; children—Penelope Elizabeth, Stephen David. Controller, Varo, Inc., Garland, Tex., 1946-55, dir., 1947-72, v.p. fin., 1955-66, sr. v.p., 1966-67, exec. v.p., 1967-70, pres., 1970-71, chmn. bd., 1971-72, cons. to bd. dirs., 1972-75. Gen. mgr. Challenger Lock Co., Los Angeles, 1956-58; dir. Varo Inc. Electrokinetics div., Varo Optical, Inc., Biometrics Instrument Corp., Varo Atlas GmbH, Micropac Industries, Inc., Gt. No. Corp., Garland Bank & Trust Co., Garland Enterprises, Inc., Newan Oil Co., Inc. Bd. dirs., exec. v.p. Harriett Stanton-Edna Murray Found. Served with AUS, 1942-46. Mem. Financial Execs. Inst. (past pres.), Am. Inst. C.P.A.'s, A.I.M., Am. Mgmt. Assn., N.A.M. Home: 1917 Melody Ln Garland TX 75042 Office: 610 W Garland Ave Garland TX 75040

NICKEL, PRISCILLA EDITH (PENNY), educator; b. Chgo., June 12, 1948; s. Eugene Byron and Alta Harriett (Deahl) N.; B.S. in Phys. Edn., Wheaton Coll., 1970; M.S. in Experiential Edn., Mankato State U., 1974. Leader wilderness trips Honey Rock Camp, Three Lakes, Wis., 1969-79, dir. girls' camp, 1980; tchr. phys. edn. Homewood Flossmoor High Sch., Flossmoor, Ill., 1970-73; prof. health, phys. edn. and recreation Montreat-Anderson Coll., Montreat, N.C., 1974—, varsity tennis and volleyball coach, 1978-80; mem. asso. staff Young Life, Inc.; tchr. Upward Bound Sch., Austria, summer 1979. First aid, water safety instr. ARC, Asheville, N.C. Recipient 10-yr. vol. pin ARC, 1978. Mem. AAHPER, Christian Camping Internat. Presbyterian. Office: Montreat-Anderson Coll Montreat NC 28757

NICKELL, WILLIAM BOYD, plastic surgeon; b. Birmingham, Ala., Nov. 13, 1937; s. K. V. and Ann N. (Bailey) N.; M.D., Princeton U., 1959; M.D., Med. Coll. Ala., 1963; m. Cindy Lee Farrar, Sept. 12, 1972; children—Kimberly, Robin, Ryan, Lori. Intern, U. Fla., 1966-67, asst. resident, 1967-68, 1st yr. plastic surgery fellow, 1968-69, chief resident, 1968-70, instr. in gen. and plastic surgery, 1970-71; asst. prof. plastic surgery U Tex., Dallas, 1971-72; chief plastic surgery Dallas VA Hosp., 1971-72; cons. John Peter Smith Hosp., Ft. Worth, 1971-72; cons. Baylor Med. Center, Dallas, 1971-72; co-dir. combined hand service Parkland Meml. Hosp., Dallas, 1971-72; chief plastic surgery East End Meml. Hosp., Birmingham, 1972—. Served to capt. U.S. Army, 1964-66. Recipient Harvard Book award, 1956; NIH grantee, 1972. Fellow A.C.S.; mem. AMA, So. Med. Assn. (tng. grantee 1969-70), Ala. Med. Assn., Am. Soc. Plastic and Reconstructive Surgeons, Jefferson County Med. Soc., Am. Burn Assn., Southeastern Soc. Plastic and Reconstructive Surgeons, Southeastern Surg. Assn., Am. Soc. Aesthetic Plastic Surgery. Contbr. articles to med. jours. Office: 7722 2d Ave S Birmingham AL 35206

NICKERSON, GIFFORD SPRUCE, anthropologist; b. Pawtucket, R.I., July 17, 1931; s. John Edward and Laura Alice (Goodwin) N.; diploma Barrington (Ill.) Coll., 1952; A.B., Wheaton (Ill.) Coll., 1954; M.A., Northwestern U., 1957; Ph.D., U. N.C., Chapel Hill, 1973; m. Janet Anna Crooker, Aug. 29, 1953; children—Paula, John, Karen. Instr. anthropology Seattle Pacific Coll., 1959-61; asst. prof. sociology and anthropology Rocky Mountain Coll., 1961-64; research asso. dept. community medicine U. Ky. Coll. Medicine, 1964-66; NIMH fellow in med. anthropology U. N.C., Chapel Hill, 1966-68; instr. N.C. State U., Raleigh, 1968-73, asst. prof. anthropology, 1973-75, asso. prof., 1975—. Ann. campaign worker YMCA, Raleigh, 1976-79. Fellow Am. Anthropol. Assn., Soc. Applied Anthropology; mem. So. Anthropol. Soc., Soc. Med. Anthropology, Council on Anthropology and Edn., Assn. Am. Indian Affairs. Editor: Perspectives on Culture, 1969; Man's Cultural Dimension, 1970; editor Rocky Mountain Rev., 1963-64. Home: 409 Stacy St Raleigh NC 27607 Office: PO Box 5535 Raleigh NC 27650

NICKEY, LAURANCE NOYES, pediatrician; b. Ft. Worth, Tex., May 25, 1931; s. Laurance N. and Jennie Maye (Langston) N.; student Vanderbilt U., 1948, Tex. Western Coll., 1949-51; M.D., Baylor U., 1955; m. Janis Jones; children—Deborah Ann, Laurance Noyes, Donna Lynn, Stephen Harrison; stepchildren—Harold Foxworth, Susan Foxworth, Grant Foxworth. Intern, Jefferson Davis Hosp., Houston, 1955-56; resident in pediatrics Baylor U. Coll. Medicine Affiliated Hosps., Houston, 1956 58; practice medicine specializing in pediatrics, El Paso, Tex., 1960—; instr. in pediatrics Baylor Coll. Medicine, 1956-58; mem. teaching staff William Beaumont Gen. Hosp., 1959-60, R.E. Thomason Gen. Hosp., 1960—; pediatrician in-charge Children's Tb Clinic, El Paso City-County Health Unit, 1960—; chief of pediatrics Hotel Dieu Hosp., 1965; chief of staff Providence Meml. Hosp., 1972; cons. pediatrics N.Mex. Crippled Children's Hosp., Truth or Consequences, 1963-76, Headstart Program of El Paso County, 1968-76; gen. chmn. Oral Polio Immunization Program, So. N.Mex. and W. Tex., 1963; mem. med. adv. com. Father Rahm Family Health Center, 1973-76; asso. clin. prof. dept. pediatrics Tex. Tech. U. Sch. Medicine, 1975—; mem. Tex. Bd. Health, 1979—. Campaign chmn. Nat. Found. March of Dimes, 1972-74; co-chmn. human needs com. Goals for El Paso, 1975-76, mem. steering com., 1975-76; chmn. El Paso City-County Bd. Health, 1970-71; campaign chmn. Christmas Seals, El Paso County Tb Assn., 1964; chmn. El Paso County Child Welfare Bd, 1966-69; trustee St. Clement's Episcopal Parish Sch., 1962-63. Served to capt., M.C., U.S. Army, 1958-60. Named Outstanding Ex-Student, El Paso High Sch., 1974. Diplomate Am. Bd. Pediatrics. Mem. Tex. Pediatric Soc. (Distinguished Service award 1973), Am. Acad. Pediatrics, (pediatric practice com. Tex. chpt. 1968—, mem. fetus and newborn com. Tex. chpt. 1973-76), So., Southwestern (pres. 1968-70), Tex. (cons. council on tax-financed health care programs 1974-77) med. assns., AMA, El Paso County Med. Soc. (sec. 1965-66, Tb com. 1966-72, diabetes com. 1970-72), El Paso (pres. 1969), Tex. diabetes assns., AAAS, Am., Tex. thoracic socs., Tex. Perinatal Assn., Baylor Coll. Medicine Pediatric Alumni Assn. (pres. 1966), Alpha Chi, Sigma Alpha Epsilon. Baptist. Contbr. articles on pediatrics to med. jours.; instrumental in securing legislation which permits health ins. coverage for newborn babies in Texas.

NICKLE, DENNIS EDWIN, electronics co. exec.; b. Sioux City, Iowa, Jan. 30, 1936; s. Harold Bateman and Helen Cecilia (Killackey) N.; B.S. in Math., Fla. State U., Tallahassee, 1961. Reliability mathematician Pratt & Whitney Aircraft Co., W. Palm Beach, Fla., 1961-63; br. supr. Melpar Inc., Falls Church, Va., 1963-66; prin. mem. tech. staff Xerox Data Systems, Rockville, Md., 1966-70; sr. tech. officer WHO, Washington, 1970-76; software devel. mgr. Melpar div. E-Systems Co., Falls Church, 1976—; ordained deacon Roman Catholic Ch., 1979. Chief judge for math. and computers Fairfax County Sci. Fair, 1964-78; scoutmaster, commr. Boy Scouts Am., 1957—; youth custodian Fairfax County Juvenile Ct., 1973—; chaplain No. Va. Regional Juvenile Detention Home, 1978—. Served with arty. U.S. Army, 1958-60. Recipient Eagle award, Silver award, Silver Beaver award, other awards Boy Scouts Am.; Ad-Altare Dei St. George Emblem, Diocese of Richmond. Mem. Assn. Computing Machinery, Old Crows Assn., Rolm Users Group (Eastern v.p.), Hewlett Pakcard Users Group, Nat. Rifle Assn. (life), Alpha Phi Omega (life), Sigma Phi Epsilon. Club: K.C. (4 deg.). Home: 4925 Van Walbeek Pl Annandale VA 22003 Office: 7700 Arlington Blvd Falls Church VA 22046

NICKLEBERRY, L. PATRICIA, state ofcl.; b. Longview, Tex., Sept. 14, 1944; d. John W. and Katherine M. Brown; B.A., Prairie View A&M Coll., 1964; M.B.A., U. Dallas, 1980; m. David Lee Nickleberry, May 6, 1978; children—Micehlle A., David Eric. Dir. personnel Dallas Community Action, 1965-72; personnel asst. So. Meth. U., Dallas, 1972-74; regional civil rights dir. Tex. State Dept. Human Resources, 1974-75, regional personnel officer, 1975-78, personnel officer III, Arlington, 1979—. Mem. personnel com. Vis. Nurses Assn. Mem. Sigma Iota Epsilon. Democrat. Baptist. Home: Route 1 Box 856 Cedar Hill TX 75104 Office: 714 N Watson Rd Arlington TX 76011

NICKOLES, EDDIE RAY (NICK), accountant; b. Gordo, Ala., Dec. 3, 1948; s. Clarence Albert and Ella Earline N.; B.S., U. Ala., 1971. Jr. acct. Haskins & Sells, Birmingham, Ala., 1971-72, sr. acct., 1972; sr. acct. Blankenship, Bouton & James, Birmingham, 1972-74; surp. Cherry, Bekaert & Hollard, Birmingham, 1974-77, mgr., 1977-79, partner, 1979—, health care cons. Mem. Nat. Assn. Accountants (asso. dir. membership South Birmingham chpt. 1977), Am. Inst. C.P.A.'s, Hosp. Fin. Mgmt. Assn., Commerce Execs. Soc. U. Ala., Ala. Soc. C.P.A.'s (audit standards and procedures com.), Homebuilders Assn. Ala. (asso.). Home: 110 Sunapee Dr 209 Homewood AL 35209 Office: 600 Brown-Marx Bldg Birmingham AL 35203

NICKOLS, MARCIA ANNE, psychologist; b. Rahway, N.J., Nov. 29, 1932; d. George Joseph and Emma Marie-Louise (Michels) Ceremsak; B.A., Antioch Coll., 1954; M.A., Cornell U., 1957; postgrad. U. Ky., 1960-61; postgrad. Case Western Res. U., summer 1959, U. Md., 1964-73; children—Kurt Allan, Liese Elaine. Psychologist, Kanawha County Schs., W.Va., 1958-60; psychologist Child Guidance Clinic, Lexington, Ky., 1960-61, Arlington County Schs., Arlington, Va., 1962-64, Montgomery County Schs., Md., 1964-71; cons. human relations Curber Assoc., Washington, 1969-73; cons. career edn. Aries Corp., McLean, Va., 1972-73; fed. women's program coordinator/dep. dir. equal employment opportunity Alchol, Drug Abuse and Mental Health Adminstrn., McLean, Va., 1973-77, acting dir. equal employment opportunity, 1977-79; mgr. fed. Women's Program NASA, 1980—; pvt. practice clin. psychology, McLean, 1967—; faculty Navy Race Relations Sch., Key West, Fla., 1973; mem. nat. adv. council to regional coalitions on drugs, alcohol and women's health, 1977; mem. No. Va. Community Bd. on Mental Health Problems of Minority Groups. Licensed psychologist, Va., D.C.; named Outstanding Profl. in human services Am. Acad. Human Services, 1974. Mem. Nat. Register of Health Service Providers in Psychology, Va. Acad. Clin. Psychologists, Am. Psychol. Assn., D.C., Va. psychol. assns. Democrat. Unitarian. Author: Brief Forms of the WAIS, 1962; 1962; contbr. articles in field to profl. jours. Home: 1736 N Albemarle St McLean VA 22101 Office: Room 6115 Code NASA Washington DC 20546

NICOLL, JAMES MURPHY, recreation center exec.; b. New Orleans, June 19, 1946; s. James Joseph and Ethel (Murphy) N.; student La. State U., 1964-66, 66-68; B.A., U. New Orleans, 1970; m. Lynn Colomb, Aug. 3, 1968; children—Jimmy, Jennifer, Jack. Sales rep. S.C. Johnson & Son, New Orleans, 1972-74, Nat. Cos. Associated Ins. Agy., New Orleans, 1974, sales mgr., 1974-75, regional mgr., Dallas, 1975-76, asst. v.p., 1976-77; partner, pres. Nautilus Health Centers, Inc., New Orleans, 1977—. Mem. Internat. Phys. Fitness Assn., C. of C., AAU. Roman Catholic. Club: Over the Mountain Athletic. Home: 5 Traminer St Kenner LA 70062 Office: 921 Canal St Suite 620 New Orleans LA 70112

NICOULIN, POLLY ANNA, hosp. exec.; b. Louisville, Jan. 7, 1934; d. Ralph Herbert and Evelyn Vivian Graves; diploma Bryant and Stratton Bus. Sch., Louisville, 1952; m. Frederick Anthony Nicoulin, Oct. 17, 1953; children—M. Patricia, Karen, Frederick Anthony,

Joseph, Stephen, Christopher. Various secretarial positions, 1952-54, 70-73; chmn. residential crusade Jefferson County chpt. Am. Cancer Soc., 1962-70; dir. vol. services and community relations Suburban Hosp., Louisville, 1973—. Democratic precinct committee-woman, 1976—; mem. sch. bd. Louisville Roman Cath. Archdiocese, 1977-80; past chmn. parish council St. Margaret Mary Roman Cath. Ch., Louisville; mem. Ky. Ednl. TV Mini-Board. Recipient President's award Boy Scouts Am., 1976. Mem. Am. Hosp. Assn., Ky. Council Adminstrs. Vol. Services, Ky. Soc. Dirs. Vol. Services, St. Matthews Bus. and Profl. Woman's Club, Women's C. of C. Office: 4001 Dutchmans Ln Louisville KY 40207

NIEBRUEGGE, EDWARD LUDY, ins. co. exec.; b. Washington, Mo., Feb. 18, 1947; s. Edward Ludy and Marion (Vitt) N.; B.E. magna cum laude in Elec. Engring., Vanderbilt U., 1969; m. Sherry Landis, May 28, 1967; children—Christina, Tonya, Bryant. Systems engr. Electronic Data Systems, Dallas, 1973-75; sr. systems analyst Nat. Life & Accident Co., Nashville, 1975-77; systems mgr. E.D.S. Fed. Co., Nashville, 1977—. Mem. Goodlettsville (Tenn.) Bd. Zoning Appeals, 1979—. Served with USN, 1969-73. Mem. Assn. Systems Mgrs., Tau Beta Pi, Eta Kappa Nu. Democrat. Baptist. Home: 220 Engel Ave Goodlettsville TN 37072 Office: 1101 Kermit Dr Suite 300 Nashville TN 37217

NIEDERER, KURT WILLY, mfg. co. exec.; b. Rheinau, Switzerland, Aug. 4, 1934; came to U.S., 1961, naturalized, 1968; s. Willy and Hedwig (Luescher) N.; B.S., State Coll. Zurich, 1960; m. Rebecca Johanna Luedi, Sept. 10, 1960; children—Nicole, Monique, Kevin. Staff engr. Leesona Corp., Warwick, R.I., 1961-69; v.p. Am. Artos, Charlotte, N.C., 1969-70; project mgr. Am. Schlafhorst, Charlotte, 1970-76; research mgr. Terrell Machine Co., Charlotte, 1976—. Elder, Calvary Presbyterian Ch., Charlotte, 1975—, chmn. planning com. Served to 1st lt. Swiss Army, 1959-61. Mem. Am. Soc. Knitting Technologists, Am. Assn. Textile Tech. Contbr. articles to profl. jours.; patentee in field. Home: 3021 Mountainbrook Rd Charlotte NC 28210 Office: PO Box 240868 Charlotte NC 28224

NIEDERGESES, JAMES D., bishop; b. Lawrenceburg, Tenn., Feb. 2, 1917; ed. St. Bernard Coll., St. Ambrose Coll., Mt. St. Mary Coll., Sem. of West, Athenaeum Coll. Ordained priest Roman Catholic Ch., 1944; bishop, 1975; tchr. pvt. schs.; chaplain Newman Club; pastor Our Lady of Perpetual Help, Chattanooga, 1962-73, Sts. Peter and Paul parish, 1973-75; bishop of Nashville, 1975—; mem. personnel bd., cons. Diocese of Nashville. Office: 2400 21st Ave S Nashville TN 37212*

NIEHOFF, FRED HAROLD, JR., indsl. engr.; b. Fairview Village, Ohio, Aug. 17, 1930; s. Fred Harold and Helen Marie (Champ) N.; B.I.E., Gen. Motors Inst., 1952; M.A. in Edn., Appalachian State U., 1973; m. Vivien Margarite Park, Sept. 10, 1949 (dec. 1973); children—Margaret, Fred Harold, III; m. 2d, Caroline Wheeler Cooper, Apr. 4, 1975. Supr. new departure div. Gen. Motors Corp., Sandusky, Ohio, 1947-53; quality control mgr. Colson Corp., Elyria, Ohio, 1953-57, The Barden Corp., Danbury, Conn., 1957-70; instr. engring., chmn. engring. and human services div. Blue Ridge Tech. Inst., Hendersonville, N.C., 1970—. Chmn., United Way, 1973; pres. YMCA, 1974. Mem. N.C. State Employees Assn., Flat Rock C. of C. (dir. 1979). Methodist. Clubs: Hendersonville Country, Rotary (pres.), Elks, Masons. Home: 1351 Asheville Hwy Hendersonville NC 28739 Office: Route 2 Flat Rock NC 28731

NIELSEN, KURT THORKILD KUDSK, elec. engr.; b. Horsens, Denmark, Mar. 19, 1936; s. Ejnar Thorkild and Margrethe N.; came to U.S., 1965, naturalized, 1976; B.S. in Elec. Engring., Aarhus Elektroteknikum, Denmark, 1964; m. Elise Iversen, Feb. 7, 1959; children—Brian, Kenneth. Engr., Kirk Tlp Mfg., Inc., Denmark, 1964-65; mfg. engr. Gen. Electric Co., Phila., 1965-66; prodn. engr., Morrison, Ill., 1966-67; engr. ECI, St. Petersburg, Fla., 1967-70; facility engr. NCR, Dayton, Ohio, 1970-72; prin. engr. ECI div. E-Systems, St. Petersburg, 1972—. Served with Danish Navy, 1958-59. Home: 8888 95th St N Seminole FL 33543 Office: ECI Div E-Systems 1501 72d St N Saint Petersburg FL 33733

NIELSEN, LARRY ANDREW, educator; b. Chgo., Aug. 29, 1948; s. Warren Eugene and Edna A. (Andersen) N.; B.S., U. Ill., 1970; M.S. (Love fellow 1972-74), U. Mo., 1974; Ph.D., Cornell U., 1978; m. Sharon Kay Florini, Sept. 26, 1970; children—Jennifer Elizabeth, Amanda Kathleen. Asst. prof. dept. fisheries and wildlife Va. Poly. Inst. and State U., Blacksburg, 1977—; tech. adv. com. Va. Water Resources Research Center, 1978—. Served with U.S. Army, 1970-72. Recipient Bronze Tablet, U. Ill., 1970. Mem. Am. Fisheries Soc. (pres. educator's sect. 1980—), Va. Acad. Sci., N. Am. Benthological Soc., Phi Beta Kappa, Sigma Xi, Phi Kappa Phi, Gamma Sigma Delta, Phi Eta Sigma. Editor: (with R.T. Lackey) Fisheries Management, 1980; contbr. articles in field to profl. jours. Home: 704 Elizabeth Dr Blacksburg VA 24060 Office: Cheatham Hall Dept Fisheries and Wildlife Sci Va Poly Inst and State U Blacksburg VA 24061

NIEMAN, WILLIAM LOUIS, color TV sales exec.; b. Cin., July 22, 1927; s. Frank and Blanche (Walsh) N.; B.S. in Bus. Adminstrn., Xavier U., 1950; m. Elaine H. Toerner, Aug. 28, 1948; children—Robert, Ronald, Nancy, Janice, William, Jill, Michael, James, Christopher. Office mgr. Rainbo Bread Co., Aurora, Ill., 1951-52, v.p., Saginaw, Mich., 1952-57, Cin., 1957-64; controller Manor Baking Co., Dallas, 1964-69; v.p., controller Curtis Mathes Sales Co., Athens, Tex., 1964—. Pres., Henderson County United Way, 1974-75; v.p. Athens Indsl. Found., 1979, pres., 1980; chmn. Blackeyed Pea Jamboree, 1975, 79; bd. dirs. Region VII Edn. Service Center. Served with U.S. Navy, 1945-46. Named Athens Citizen of Yr., Athens C. of C., 1977. Mem. Am. Mgmt. Assn., Athens C. of C. (pres. 1976-78). Roman Catholic. Clubs: Kiwanis (pres. 1976), K.C. Home: 213 Trailridge Rd Athens TX 75751 Office: One Curtis Mathes Pkwy Athens TX 75751

NIEMEYER, KATHERINE AGNES, dietitian, food service ofcl.; b. Chgo., June 26, 1925; d. Edwin Frederick and Katherine (Hemmila) N.; B.S., U. Ill., 1960; M.A., Seton Hall U., 1970. Clin. dietitian VA Hosp., Saginaw, Mich., 1960-63, Butler, Pa., 1963-66; chief dietitian VA Hosp., East Orange, N.J., 1966-74; asst. mgr. food service Lee Meml. Hosp., Ft. Myers, Fla., 1974—; adj. prof. nutrition U. S.Fla. and Edison Community Coll. Mem. President's com. on employment of handicapped, 1968—, chmn. com. on physically handicapped, 1975-78. Named Outstanding Handicapped Fed. Employee, 1968, Handicapped Profl. Woman of Year, Pilot Club Internat., 1976. Mem. Am. Dietetic Assn., Am. Soc. Hosp. Food Service Adminstrs., Phi Upsilon Omicron. Clubs: Zonta Internat., U. Ill. Alumni Assn., USCG Aux., Delta Sigma Omicron. Contbr. papers to profl. confs. and publs. in field. Home: 5326 Cocoa Ct Cape Coral FL 33904 Office: 2776 Cleveland St Fort Myers FL 33902

NIEMEYER, RONALD (DUANE), accountant; b. Sweet Springs, Mo., Mar. 3, 1941; s. Walter Hugo and Flora (Langewisch) N.; B.S. in Acctg., Central Mo. State U., 1964, M.B.A., 1965; D.B.A. in Acctg., Miss. State U., 1974; m. Mollie Michelle Dinwiddie, June 28, 1975; 1 dau., Elise Claire. Staff accountant Johnson and Fleet Co., C.P.A.'s, Kansas City, Mo., 1962-63; asst. prof. acctg. Wis. State U., Whitewater, 1965-66; asst. prof. Western Ky. U., 1966-67; lectr. accountant series Miss. State-Miss. Valley State U., 1967-71; asso. prof., head dept. acctg., Jackson (Miss.) State U., 1972—, dir. master of profl. accountancy program, 1977—; cons. in field; dir. U.S. Office of Edn. Grad. and Profl. Opportunities Program; chmn. Jackson Community Tax Forum Series. Del., Luth. Ch. Council Miss., 1977-78; chmn. evangelism bd. Our Redeemer Luth. Ch., Jackson, 1977-78, chmn. expansion and future needs council, 1978-79. Miss. State U. research fellow, 1967; recipient Outstanding Leadership award Jackson State U. Acctg. Soc., 1975; named Outstanding Young Man of Am., U.S. Jaycees, 1978; U.S. Office of Edn. grantee, 1978—. Mem. Nat. Assn. Accountants, Adminstrs. Acctg. Programs Group, Am. Acctg. Assn., Nat. Assn. Public Accountants, Beta Alpha Psi, Delta Sigma Pi. Home: 720 Laney Dr Clinton MS 39056 Office: Sch of Bus and Econs Jackson State U 1400 J R Lynch St Jackson MS 39217

NIEMI, ALBERT WILLIAM, JR., economist; b. Worcester, Mass., Aug. 30, 1942; s. Albert William and Helen Josephine (Powers) N.; A.B., Stonehill Coll., 1964; M.A., U. Conn., 1965, Ph.D., 1969; m. Maria Theresa DiSano, Feb. 4, 1967; children—Albert William, Edward Charles. Research asst. U. Conn., 1965-68; faculty U. Ga., Athens, 1968—, prof. econs., 1975—, dir. research Coll. Bus. Adminstrn., asso. dean coll., 1976-79. Active Cedar Creek Civic Assn., Boy Scouts Am. Mem. Am. Econ. Assn., Assn. Univ. Bus. and Econ. Research, Econ. History Assn., So. Econ. Assn., Western Econ. Assn., Atlantic Econ. Soc., Phi Kappa Phi, Delta Epsilon Sigma, Beta Gamma Sigma. Author: State and Regional Patterns in American Manufacturing, 1974; Gross State Product and Productivity in the Southeast, 1975; U.S. Economic History, 1975; Understanding Economics, 1978. Home: 190 Rolling Wood Dr Athens GA 30605 Office: Div Research Coll Bus Adminstrn U Ga Athens GA 30602

NIES, ROBERT JOHN, JR., financial planner; b. Syracuse, N.Y., Jan. 25, 1943; s. Robert John and Eula M. (Markert) N.; student U. Pitts., 1961-68; m. Cheryl C. Carter, Sept. 25, 1975; children—Brian Robert, Gregory Robert, Carter Robert, Jacqueline Mae. Registered rep. 1st Investors Corp., N.Y.C., 1968, dist. mgr., 1969, br. mgr., 1970-72, regional mgr., 1971-72, asst. v.p., 1972-73; pres. Nies Fin. Systems, Inc., St. Petersburg, Fla., 1974—; pres. Forerunner's, Inc. 1975—. Pres. Free Enterprise Ednl. Fund. Certified fin. planner; registered fin. prin., fin. advisor, mortgage broker. Mem. Nat. Assn. Securities Dealers, Internat. Assn. Fin. Planners, Sales and Mktg. Execs. St. Petersburg, St. Petersburg C. of C. (com. of 100), Internat. Platform Assn. Republican. Episcopalian. Clubs: St. Petersburg Stock and Bond (v.p., dir.), St. Petersburg Yacht. Home: 1300 52d Ave NE Saint Petersburg FL 33703 Office: 5401 Central Ave Saint Petersburg FL 33710

NIEVES ORTIZ, HERIBERTO, police ofcl.; b. Mayaguez, P.R., Jan. 11, 1944; s. Heriberto Nieves Caro and America Ortiz Acosta; B.A., U. P.R., 1966, M.A. in Public Adminstrn., 1975; m. Miriam Nieves, Dec. 25, 1966; children—Heriberto, Mireyda, Jose. Programming dir. Police Acad., Gurabo, P.R., 1973; prof. Interam. U., Fajardo, P.R., 1973—; with recruiting sect. P.R. Police Dept., San Juan, 1967—, personnel dir., 1977—; mem. Personnel Council, Govt. of P.R. Bd. dirs. Govt. Employees Assn. Mem. Police Assn. (exec. bd. 1976), N.G. Rifle Club, Phi Alpha Chi. Club: Lions. Home: Cst Block C 37 Urb Jards de Carolina Carolina PR 00630 Office: Personnel Bur Police Dept Hdqrs Franklin D Roosevelt Ave Hato Rey PR 00917

NIGH, GEORGE PATTERSON, gov. Okla.; b. McAlester, Okla., June 9, 1927; s. Wilbur Roscoe and Irene (Crockett) N.; student Okla. Eastern A. and M. Coll., 1946-48; B.A., Central State Tchr.'s Coll., Ada, Okla., 1950; m. Donna Faye Skinner, Oct. 14, 1963; children—Mike, Georgeann. Tchr. history and polit. sci. McAlester High Sch., 1951-58; mem. Okla. Ho. of Reps., 1951-59; lt. gov. Okla., Oklahoma City, 1959-63, 67-79, gov., 1963, 79—. Served with USNR, 1945-46. Recipient Distinguished Service awards McAlester Jr. C. of C., 1952, 54, 55. Mem. Am. Legion. Clubs: Masons (32 deg.), Shriners. Home: 8321 Picnic Ln Oklahoma City OK 73127 Office: State Capitol Bldg Oklahoma City OK 73105

NIGRO, FRANK JOSEPH, systems analyst; b. Bklyn., Sept. 8, 1948; s. Benjamin P. and Florence M. Nigro; B.S., Fordham U., 1970, M.B.A., 1973. With J.C. Penney Co., N.Y.C., 1971-73, Warner Communications Co., N.Y.C., 1973-74, Citibank, N.Y.C., 1974-76; systems analyst Amerifirst Fed. Savs. and Loan Assn., Miami, Fla., 1976—. Served with USMCR, 1970-71. Office: Amerifirst Fed Savs and Loan Assn 1 SE 3d Ave Miami FL 33131

NIGRO, VINCENT JAMES, art dir., illustrator; b. N.Y.C., Mar. 29, 1952; s. Vincent James and Ann Joan (Pisapia) N.; A.A., N.Y.C. Community Coll., 1973; student Julliard Sch., 1975. Graphic designer Dell Publ. Co., N.Y.C., 1975-76; asst. art dir., mech. artist Ross Roy Advt., N.Y.C., 1976-78; art dir. H. J. Kaufman & Assos. Advt., Washington, 1978-79; freelance art dir., Washington and N.Y.C., 1979—; cons. Booz Alan & Hamilton, N.Y.C., 1976-78; pvt. instr. art, N.Y.C., 1978-79. Mem. Washington Ad Club (print advt. award 1979), Am. Mgmt. Assn., Soc. Illustrators N.Y. Democrat. Roman Catholic. Address: 1011 Arlington Blvd Arlington VA 22209 also 43-08 41st St Long Island City NY 11104

NILL, CARL JONATHAN, publishing exec.; b. Dayton, Ohio, Sept. 7, 1938; s. Carl M. and Winifred N.; student Wheaton Coll., 1957-58; grad. Am. Inst. Banking, Chgo., 1964; m. Suzanne Jacobsen, July 1, 1960; children—Kevin, Jonathan. Asst. cashier Bank of Naperville (Ill.), 1960-64; asst. v.p. Am. Nat. Bank Jacksonville, 1964-68; v.p. State Bank Jacksonville, 1968-71; chmn., pres. Fla. Equity and Mortgage Investors, Jacksonville, 1972-73; pvt. investments, Jacksonville, 1973-74; partner, sr. v.p., co-owner Home & Land Publ. Corp., Jacksonville, 1974—; pres. Homes & Land Southeast, Inc., Jacksonville, 1978—. Chmn., officer Christian Bus. Men's Com., Campus Crusade for Christ, Youth for Christ. Republican. Baptist. Clubs: Sertoma, Deerwood, Univ., Bent Tree, Ionosphere. Tenor, vocal rec. artist Crescendo Records; also TV and radio appearances. Home: 7540 Hollyridge Rd Deerwood Jacksonville FL 32216 Office: 5740 Spring Park Rd Jacksonville FL 32216

NILSEN, ANDERS MALLABAR, coll. dean; b. N.Y.C., July 13, 1946; s. Alfred Emile and Elizabeth (Mallabar) N.; B.S. in Bus. Adminstrn., U. So. Miss., Hattiesburg, 1974, M.B.A., 1975; m. Cathy Stallworth Ware, June 17, 1972. Instr., dean academics Phillips Coll., Gulfport, Miss., 1975-79, dean fin., 1979—; mem. accreditation teams Assn. Ind. Colls. and Schs. Served with USN, 1967-71; Vietnam; lt. Res. Republican. Episcopalian. Club: Optimist. Home: PO Box 714 Gulfport MS 39501 Office: 0942 E Beach St Gulfport MS 39501

NIMMO, OTIS DALE, fire equipment co. exec.; b. Fair Grove, Mo., June 26, 1936; s. Otis Gustus and Iverene Mahala (Gallion) N.; student S.W. Mo. State Coll., 1954-55; m. Cora Lee Batson, Mar. 24, 1956; children—Steven Anthony, Michael Andrew, Deborah Ann, Mark Allen. With Otis G. Nimmo, Springfield, Mo., 1955-56, Caterpiller Tractor Co., Joliet, Ill., 1956-57; sales mgr. A & W Appliances, Springfield, 1957-58; route salesman Manor Bread, Topeka, 1958-59, Taystee Bread Co., Topeka, 1959-60; partner L.L. Letterman Meat Co., Springfield, 1960-63; mgr. Ozark Fire Extinguisher Co., Springfield, 1963-64; pres., gen. mgr. Mozark Fire Extinguisher Co., Springdale, Ark., 1964—, also dir. Profl. chmn. Fire Extinguisher Serviceman and Installer adv. bd., Ark. Gov. David Pryor, 1978. Served with Mo. N.G., 1952-56. Mem. Nat. Fire Protection Assn. Mem. Ch. of Christ. Home: 2201 S 40 St Springdale AR 72764 Office: 705 E Robinson Ln Springdale AR 72764

NIMS, DONALD READ, counselor; b. Winchester, Mass., Jan. 6, 1947; s. Donald Farwell and Freda Randle (Read) N.; B.A., Wright State U., 1968; M.P.S. in Counseling, Western Ky. U., 1973, Ed.S. in Counseling, 1978; m. Peggy Ann Bunnell, June 12, 1976. Peace Corps vol. as tchr. rural primary sch., Fiji Islands, 1968-70; instr. reading, math. and GED, Great Onyx Job Corps Center, Mammoth Cave, Ky., 9171-76, head counselor, 1976—, also staff cons. Corpsmen, Welfare Fund. Mem. Am. Personnel and Guidance Assn., Am. Assn. for Marriage and Family Therapy, SAR. Democrat. Mem. Ch. of Christ. Club: Civitan. Home: Route 3 Box 15 Cave City KY 42127 Office: Great Onyx Job Corps Center Mammoth Cave KY 42259

NIRSCHL, ROBERT PHILIP, surgeon; b. South Milwaukee, Wis., Aug. 28, 1933; s. Bord August and Helen (Wozny) N.; M.D., Marquette U., 1958; M.S., U. Minn., 1965; m. Mary Ann Oleniczak, June 21, 1958; children—Suzanne Marie, Robert Christopher, Julie Ann. Intern, St. Marys Hosp., Duluth, Minn., 1959; resident Mayo Clinic, Rochester, Minn., 1959-63; practice orthopedic surgery, Arlington, Va., 1965—; mem. staff No. Va. Doctors Hosp., Arlington Hosp., Georgetown U. Hosp. Asst. prof. Georgetown U., 1974—; cons. VA Hosp., Washington, 1966—; med. adviser Zimmer, Warsaw, Ind., 1974—; pres. Med Sports Inc. Mem. Arlington County Commn. on Human Resources, 1969-72; med. cons. Arlington Sch. Health Com., 1972—; mem. Arlington Health and Welfare Council, 1968-70; trustee No. Va. Med. Found., No. Va. med. Polit. Action Com.; bd. dirs. Arlington YMCA, 1972-76, No. Va. Heart Assn., 1977—; mem. adv. council Republican Nat. Com. Served to lt. comdr. USNR, 1963-65. Diplomate Am. Bd. Orthopedic Surgery. Fellow Am. Acad. Orthopedic Surgery; mem. A.C.S., A.M.A., Eastern, Va. orthopedic assns., Arlington County Med. Soc. (pres. 1976), Phi Chi. Republican. Roman Catholic. Club: Washington Golf and Country. Patentee Nirschl tennis elbow support. Contbg. editor World Tennis mag.; contbr. articles to profl. jours. Office: 3801 N Fairfax Dr Arlington VA 22203

NISSLER, CHRISTIAN WILLIAM, III, constrn. co. exec.; b. Phila., Aug. 27, 1923; s. Christian William and Anna Haynes (Fitzgerald) N.; B.S., U. Mich., 1949; m. Sara Betty Kelly, May 13, 1961. Estimator Walter L. Couse & Co., Detroit, 1949-59, Dunn Constrn. Co., Birmingham, Ala., 1959-63; v.p., estimator Stuart Constrn. Co., Bay Minette, 1963—. Served with USNR, 1943-46, PTO. Recipient Honorable Mention in Sculpture, Spring Hill Coll., 1966. Fellow Am. Soc. C.E.; mem. Phi Delta Theta. Episcopalian (vestryman 1966-70). Club: Holly Hills Country (pres. 1969) (Bay Minette). Home: 105 Chalet Ridge Bay Minette AL 36507 Office: PO Box 570 Bay Minette AL 36507

NISWONGER, JEANNE DU CHATEAU (MRS. JOSEPH K. NISWONGER), wildlife biologist, writer; b. Indpls.; d. Simon Nicholas and Portia (Reeves) Du Chateau; A.B., Miami U., Oxford, Ohio; postgrad. Washington Sch. Psychiatry; M.A., Ph.D., Calif. Western U.; m. Joseph K. Niswonger; children—Kenneth Arnold, Laura Elaine, Nancy Jo. Research asso. HEW and W.Va. Dept. Health, Charleston; research biologist Bio-Research Inst., Fla. So. Coll., Lakeland, 1958-61; writer Tampa (Fla.) Tribune, 1960-70. Mem. bd. dirs. Polk Pub. Museum; dir. pub. relations Polk County Council Parents and Tchrs.; pres. Fla. chpt. Nature Conservancy. Mem. Fla. Audubon Soc. (mem. adv. bd. 1960-72), Lake Region Audubon Soc. (pres. 1960-65), AAUW (br. sec. 1962-64), Wildlife Soc., Wilderness Soc., Am. Soc. Mammalogists, Am. Assn. Zool. Parks and Aquariums, Izaak Walton League, Fla. Wildlife Fedn. (dir. 1974—), Nat. Wildlife Fedn., Am. Museum Natural History, Fla. Zool. Soc., Defenders of Wildlife, Nat. Parks and Conservation Assn., Woman's Aux. Fla. Med. Assn., Tampa Doll Club (pres.), Tropical Doll Study Club (pres.), United Fedn. Doll Clubs (bd. mgmt.), Ginny Doll Club (pres.). Asso. editor Fla. Medaux, 1963-65; editor Lake Region Naturalist, 1959-69; asst. editor Fla. Naturalist, 1964-70; editor Fla. Wilderness Calendar, 1964-67; author: That Doll Ginny. Home: 305 W Beacon Rd Lakeland FL 33803

NIVEN, DAVID CLARK, info. systems planner; b. Attleboro, Mass., Nov. 28, 1943; s. David Wallace and Olive (Clark) N.; student Syracuse U., 1961-62, U. Mass., 1962-65; m. Linda Sue Tynan, Oct. 30, 1965; children—Kimberly Douglas, Nancy. Trainee, Honeywell Info. Systems, Wellesley Hills, Mass., 1965-66, ops. analyst, 1966-67, systems rep. Fed. Systems div., Rosslyn, Va., 1967-70, systems supr., McLean, Va., 1970-73; exec. v.p. Passage Marine, Inc., Gwynn, Va., 1973-75; property mgr. Dickinson Mgmt. Co., Inc., Charlottesville, Va., 1975-76; mgr. systems services U. Va., Med. Computing Center, Charlottesville, 1976-77, mgr. user services, 1977-78, planning coordinator, 1978—; mem. U. Va., Arbitration Bd., 1975-79; dir. U. Va. Employees Credit Union, 1979. Mem. Mathews County Wetlands Commn., 1974. Served with Air N.G., 1965. Mem. Data Processing Mgmt. Assn. (pres. 1979). Club: Lions. Home: Route 3 PO Box 420 Crozet VA 22902 Office: U Va Med Computing Center Med Center Box 282 Charlottesville VA 22908

NIVEN, KURT NEUBAUER, art appraiser; b. Vienna, Austria, July 19, 1922; s. Salmon and Julia (Waldmann) Neubauer; ed. Austria; 1 dau., Dorit. Came to U.S., 1958, naturalized, 1963. Certified appraiser Albert Einstein Coll. Medicine, Bronx, N.Y., 1959-61, buyer constrn. dept., 1959-61; pres. Visual Art and Gallery, Inc., Dallas, 1964-77; pres. K. Niven Sales Corp., Dallas, 1974—; appraiser of art World Trade Center, 1974— collector graphic art. Served with Brit. Army, 1939-45, Israeli Army 1948-49. Mem. Am. Soc. Appraisers, Tex. Art Assn. Odd Fellow. Home: 13319 Kit Ln Dallas TX 75240 Office: WTC 330-1 World Trade Center Dallas TX 75258

NIX, CHRISTINE MARIE WARD, social worker, hosp. ofcl.; b. East St. Louis, Ill., Aug. 11, 1950; d. Claude Homer and Sadie Eleanor (Walsh) Ward; B.A., LaVerne (Calif.) Coll., 1975; M.S.W., U. Ala., 1977. Counselor, Family Counseling Service, Tuscaloosa, Ala., 1976-77; nephrology social worker Petersburg (Va.) Gen. Hosp., 1978, dir. social service, 1978—. Active Contact Tri-City Inc., telephone crisis intervention service. Mem. Nat. Assn. Social Workers, Soc. for Hosp. Social Work Dirs. of Am. Hosp. Assn., Nat. Kidney Found. Council of Nephrology Social Workers, Alpha Gamma Sigma. Club: Toastmasters. Office: Petersburg Gen Hosp 801 S Adams St Petersburg VA 23803

NIX, JOSEPH NELSON, JR., advt., pub. relations and mktg. exec.; b. Atlanta, Dec. 18, 1942; s. Joseph Nelson and Era Marguerite (Parks) N.; B.A., U. Ga., 1965, M.A., 1970; postgrad. Yuba Coll., 1968-69; m. Carole Norfolk, Oct. 5, 1974. News dir. Sta. WJJC, Commerce, Ga., 1969-70; corporate pub. relations coordinator Citizens and So. Nat. Bank, Atlanta, 1971; dir. pub. relations Mead Packaging, Atlanta, 1972; comml. broadcast cons., Atlanta, 1973; field account exec. N. W. Ayer ABH Internat., N.Y.C., 1973-79, regional account supr., Richmond, Va., 1979—. Mem., co. rep. Atlanta Internat. Council, 1972, Ga. Bus. and Industry Assn., Atlanta, also

Keep Am. Beautiful, Inc., N.Y.C., Nat. Center for Resource Recovery, Washington, Jr. Achievement, Atlanta, 1971-72; committeeman United Way, Atlanta, 1971. Served to capt. USAF, 1965-69. Mem. Atlanta C. of C. (mem. com. 1972), Pub. Relations Soc. Am. (Old Dominion chpt.), Atlanta Press Club, Ga. Press Assn., Atlanta Ad Club, Air Force Assn., Ga. Assn. Newscasters, Sigma Delta Chi, Advt. Club Richmond, DiGamma Kappa. Baptist. Home: 1706 Chevelle Dr Richmond VA 23235 Office: 1706 Chevelle Dr Richmond VA 23235

NIX, MARY MCDOUGLE, nutritionist; b. Calhoun, Ga., Nov. 3, 1936; d. Lewis Richard and Beatrice Estelle McDougle; B.S. in Food Prodn. Mgmt., Morris Brown Coll., Atlanta, 1969; M.Ed. in Food Service, U. Ga., 1975; m. Bailey Eugene Nix, Dec. 3, 1955. Sch. lunch mgr. N. Cobb High Sch., Marietta, Ga., 1967-69; dir. sch. food and nutrition program Bartow County Bd. Edn., Cartersville, Ga., 1969-70, Cobb County Bd. Edn., Marietta, 1974—; area cons. Ga. Dept. Edn., Atlanta, 1970-74. Mem. Am. Sch. Food Service Assn. (pres. 1980—; undergrad. scholarship 1968), Ga. Sch. Food Service Assn. (pres. 1977-78; grad. scholarship 1974), Cobb County Sch. Food Service Assn., Am. Home Econs. Assn., Ga. Home Econs. Assn., Ga. Nutrition Council, Ga. Assn. Sch. Bus. Ofcls., 7th Dist. Home Econs. Assn., Cobb County Assn. Adminstrd. Baptist. Home: 203 Parkwood Dr Kennesaw GA 30144 Office: PO Box 1088 Marietta GA 30061

NIXON, AUSTIN ERNEST, food processing co. exec.; b. Thomas County, Ga., Mar. 5, 1939; s. Charlie Dawson and Estelle Gertrude (Owen) N.; student Austin Peay U., Clarksville, Tenn., 1969-72; m. JoAnne Jones Southerland, Jan. 19, 1979; children by previous marriage—Karen, Richard (dec.), Jennifer (dec.); stepchildren—Christa, Joe, John, Emily, Susan. Salesman, Frosty Morn Meats, Inc., Quincy, Fla., 1959-62, sales mgr., Quincy, 1962-69, Clarksville, Tenn., 1969-72; pres. Mr. Sam's Pecans, Inc., Hawkinsville, Ga., 1972—; v.p. Young Pecan Shelling Co., Inc., Florence, S.C., 1979—. Mem. Nat. Pecan Shellers and Processors Assn., Southeastern Pecan Growers Assn., Ga. Pecan Growers Assn. Episcopalian. Clubs: Kiwanis, Elks. Home: 911 Lorraine Dr Florence SC 29501 Office: Young Pecan Shelling Co Inc 1200 Pecan St PO Box 5779 Florence SC 29502

NIXON, FRANK EDWIN, newspaper exec.; b. Lincolnton, N.C., Sept. 23, 1943; s. Colvert Edwin and Dorothy M. (Pratt) N.; student Western Carolina U., 1961-64; m. Ann Karen Fackelman, Apr. 26, 1969; 1 dau., Laura Moseley. Asst. to N.C. Congressman, 10th Dist., 1966; advt. dept. Atlanta Jour.-Constitution, 1968-69; pub. Crowley (La.) Daily Signal, 1969-74; pub. Tarpon Springs (Fla.) Leader, 1974—; dir. Washington County (Fla.) News, 1972—; sec.-treas. Ruston (La.) Pubs. Inc., 1971—, also dir.; v.p., treas. Crowley Post-Signal, Inc., 1974—; dir. Slidell (La.) Daily Times, Roane County (Tenn.) Pub. Co. Adminstrv. bd. 1st. Meth. Ch., Crowley, 1969-74, Tarpon Springs, Fla., 1975—; mem. bd. indsl. devel. City of Crowley, 1969-74; mem. bd. econ. devel., Tarpon Springs, 1974—; mem. community adv. panel Gen. Telephone Co.; mem. Pinellas County (Fla.) and Tarpon Springs chpt. Adv. Bd., Distributive Tech. Coop. Edn. 1977—. Mem. Fla. Press Assn., Tarpon Springs C. of C. (dir. 1975—, sec.). Democrat. Clubs: Kiwanian, Tarpon Racquet. Home: 1005 Bay Vista Dr Tarpon Springs FL 33589 Office: 11 E Orange St Tarpon Springs FL 33589

NIXON, GWINN HUXLEY, lawyer; b. Augusta, Ga., Jan. 17, 1906; s. Gwinn H. and Eliza Huxley (Scott) N.; B.S., U. Ga., 1926, J.D., 1929; m. Nora Palmer Fortson, Apr. 30, 1930; children—Eleanora N. Hoernle, Sally N. Hand, Gwinn Huxley; m. 2d, Caroline Stavely Fortson, May 14, 1954; children—Nelson Alexander, John Maddox. Admitted to Ga. bar, 1929, since practiced in Augusta; sr. partner Nixon, Yow, Waller & Capers; hon. dir. First R.R. & Banking Co. Ga.; dir. First Ga. Devel. Corp. Former pres. Augusta Citizens Union; former co-chmn. Augusta Round Table, Nat. Conf. Christians and Jews; chmn. Com. for Good Govt., 1939-40, Augusta Pub. Forum, 1938-41. Dir. Augusta Library, 1947-73, pres., 1951-54; chmn. bd. trustees Gertrude Herbert Inst. Art., 1964-74; former bd. dirs. Augusta Opera Assn. Served with AUS, 1942-46; lt. col. O.R.C., 1953-66; lt. col. AUS, ret., 1966. Fellow Am. Coll. Probate Counsel; mem. Am., Ga., Augusta (pres.) bar assns., Judge Advocates Assn., U. Ga. Alumni Soc. (v.p. 1940-41), Am. Legion, 40 and 8, Res. Officers Assn., S.R., Phi Kappa Phi, Chi Psi. Democrat. Episcopalian (sr. warden; chancellor Diocese of Georgia, 1972-76; lay dep. gen. conv. 1964, bd. officers of corp. 1978—). Elk, Kiwanian. Clubs: Art (pres. 1932-40; dir.), Augusta Sailing (commodore 1957, dir.), Augusta Country; Pinnacle. Home: 3285 Wheeler Rd Augusta GA 30909 Office: 1500 Ga Railroad Bank Bldg Augusta GA 30902

NIXON, MARY ELLEN, banker; b. Tulsa, July 5, 1934; d. George F. and Annie Catherine Shrier; student Southwestern Grad. Sch. Banking, So. Meth. U., 1978-79; m. John E. Nixon, Feb. 4, 1954; children—John E., Jeffrey R. With Peoples State Bank, Tulsa, 1952-71, loan sec., 1969-71; with Am. Bank of Tulsa, 1971—, cashier, 1978—. Mem. Nat. Assn. Bank Women, Am. Inst. Banking, Bank Adminstrn. Inst. (dir.) Okla. Bankers Assn. (women's div.). Democrat. Roman Catholic. Club: Toastmistress. Office: 6465 S Yale Tulsa OK 74177

NIXON, ROBERT KENWOOD, data processing exec.; b. Des Moines, July 25, 1936; s. Paul Wesley and Ruth Louise (Gore) N.; B.S., Iowa State U., 1959; M.B.A., Temple U., 1972; m. Donna Rae Ploth, Sept. 7, 1958; children—Frederick, Robert Kenwood, Randolph. Served as maj. USMC, 1959-79; officer recruiter Commonwealth Va., 1963-66; sta. in Viet Nam, 1967-68; data systems analyst, Phila., 1968-71; asst. prof. U. Louisville, 1971-74; dir. USMC Computer Center, Okinawa, Japan, 1974-75; dir. USMC ADP Procurement and Budgeting, Washington, 1975-77, dir. ADP Mgmt. Standards, 1977-79; ret., 1979; sr. tech. account rep. Tesdata Corp., McLean, Va., 1979; mktg. project mgr. Fed. Data Corp., Chevy Chase, Md., 1980—. Mem. central com. Ky. Derby Festival, 1972-74; dist. commr. Boy Scouts Am., 1973-74. Decorated Navy Commendation medal, Navy Achievement medal, Purple Heart. Mem. Assn. Computer Machinery, Phi Delta Theta. Methodist. Home: 6708 Reynard Dr Springfield VA 22152 Office: 4601 North Park Ave Chevy Chase MD 20015

NIXON, TAMARA FRIEDMAN, economist; b. Cleve., June 3, 1938; d. Victor and Eva J. (Osteryoung) Friedman; B.A. with honors in econs. (Wellesley scholar), Wellesley Coll., 1959; M.B.A. (fellow), U. Pitts., 1961; m. Daniel D. Nixon, June 14, 1959; children—Asa Joel, Naomi Devorah, Victoria Eva. Asst. economist Fed. Res. Bank, N.Y.C., 1959-60, 61-62; economist R.P. Wolff Econ. Research, Miami, Fla., 1972-75; econ. cons., Miami, 1975-79; economist Washington Savs. & Loan Assn., Miami Beach, Fla., 1979—; real estate feasibility cons.; investment adminstr. Land use chmn. Dade County chpt. LWV, 1975-76. Mem. Econ. Soc. S. Fla. (v.p. programs), Am. Econ. Assn. Office: Washington Savings and Loan 1701 Meridian Ave Miami Beach FL 33139

NIXON, WILLIAM CARSON, publishing exec.; b. Portsmouth, Va., Feb. 9, 1948; s. John Layfette and Frances (Yates) N.; B.A. in History, U. Md., 1972; m. Phyllis Dae Rountree, June 23, 1979. Sales exec. Pierce Printing Co., Inc., Ahoskie, N.C., 1972-73; bus. sales dir. Parker Bros., Inc., Ahoskie, 1973—, also sec. and dir.; instr. area tech. schs.; cons. various area pubs. Mem. regional adminstrv. bd. CETA, 1979—. Served with U.S. Army, 1966-68; ETO. Mem. Am. Press Inst., Mid-Atlantic Advt. Execs. Assn., Nat. Agri-Mktg. Assn. Club: Jaycees. Home: 805 W Church St Ahoskie NC 27910 Office: PO Box 1325 Ahoskie NC 27910

NOAH, SHIRLEY JEAN, nurse, hosp. adminstr.; b. Corinne, W.Va., May 15, 1941; d. Powell James and Ida Marie (Beverly) Ellis; B.A., Stephens Coll., Columbia, Mo., 1975; R.N., St. Mary's Sch. Nursing, Huntington, W.Va., 1962; m. Kenneth Eugene Noah, Dec. 13, 1968; 1 son, Jeffrey. Staff nurse Appalachian Regional Hosp., Beckley, W.Va., 1962-65; instr. practical nurse edn. Raleigh County Vocat. Sch., Beckley, 1965-67, Appalachian Sch. Practical Nursing, Lexington, Ky., 1967-68; instr. Frankfort (Ky.) Dept. Vocat. Edn., 1976-78; adminstr. nursing service Garrard County Meml. Hosp., Lancaster, Ky., 1968—; adj. faculty Eastern Ky. U., Richmond, and Berea (Ky.) Coll. of Nursing; clin. faculty, cons. Joint Commn. on Accreditation of Hosps., Chgo., 1975—. Active, Am. Heart Assn., Am. Cancer Soc. Mem. Ky. Soc. Hosp. Nursing Service Adminstrs., Nat. League Nursing, Ky. League Nursing, Ky. Nurses Assn. (dist. pres. 1975-76), St. Mary's Hosp. Alumni Assn. Presbyterian. Club: Order of Eastern Star. Home: Route 1 Windswept Subdiv Lancaster KY 40444 Office: Garrard County Meml Hosp 308 W Maple Ave Lancaster KY 40444

NOBES, CHARLES JAY, govt. def. ofcl.; b. Regina, Sask., Can., Jan. 19, 1942; s. Charles William and Jayleen (Reniker) N.; student Case Western Res. U., 1959-63; A.A., N.E. Okla. A. and M. U., 1963; B.S. in Bus. Adminstrn., Pittsburg State U., 1965; M.B.A. (Dept. Army tng. grantee), U. Okla., 1972; m. Patricia Anne Carey, Dec. 20, 1969; 1 son, Charles William. Electronic technician Miami Sales Co. (Okla.), 1964-65; procurement analyst Tank-Automotive Command, U.S. Army, Warren, Mich., 1965-70, dep. dir. procurement ops. Procurement Agy. Vietnam, Saigon, 1970-71, contract specialist Tank-Automotive Command, 1972-73, dep. chief contract adminstrn. U.S. embassy Def. Attache Office, Saigon, 1973-74, procurement, prodn. officer, project mgr. for tng. devices, Ft. Benning, Ga., 1974-76; dir. contracts USMC Logistics Base, Albany, Ga., 1976—. Recipient Outstanding Employee Performance award USMC, 1977, 80. Mem. Nat. Contract Mgmt. Assn. (organizer Albany Area chpt.), Armed Forces Communications and Electronics Assn., Am. Def. Preparedness Assn. (life), Am. Radio Relay League (life), Albany C. of C. (mem. small bus. adv. council), Alpha Kappa Psi (life). Presbyterian. Club: Albany Amateur Radio (dir.). Home: 5024 Sears Ct Columbus GA 31907 Office: PO Drawer 18 MCLB Albany GA 31704

NOBILE, HUGH BELANGER, psychiatric social worker; b. Lutcher, La., Nov. 29, 1949; s. Anthony J. and Hester (Belanger) N.; B.A., La. State U., 1971, M.S.W., 1973; m. Catherine Elizabeth Smith, Aug. 2, 1975. Clin. social worker Donaldsonville (La.) Mental Health Center, 1973-75, acting adminstr., 1975-77, clin. coordinator, 1977—. Mem. Nat. Assn. Social Workers, Acad. Cert. Social Workers, Mid La. Health Systems Agy. Democrat. Roman Catholic. Home: 263 Rue De Laplace Baton Rouge LA 70810 Office: Donaldsonville Mental Health Center 419 Memorial Dr Donaldsonville LA 70346

NOBLE, DENNIS RAY, audiologist; b. Little Rock, Feb. 3, 1948; s. Carl, Jr. and Helen Faye (Moon) N.; B.A. in Speech, Harding Coll., Searcy, Ark., 1970; M.A. in Audiology and Speech Pathology, Memphis State U., 1973; m. Molly Marie Mason, Apr. 13, 1971; 1 son, Nathan Scott. Speech therapist New London (Conn.) public schs., 1970-71; audiologist Central Ga. Speech and Hearing Center, Macon, 1973-75; salesman, audiologist Beltone Hearing Aid Service, Hot Springs, Ark., 1975-76; audiologist Albany (Ga.) Ear, Nose & Throat, P.C., 1976—; mem. part-time faculty Albany State Coll.; CPR instr.-trainer mem. Ga. CPR com. Am. Heart Assn. Mem. Am. Speech, Lang. and Hearing Assn., Ga. Heart Assn., Dougherty County Heart Assn., Alpha Psi Omega. Mem. Ch. of Christ. Club: Dougherty County Kiwanis (dir. 1977-78, v.p. 1979-80). Home: 906 Rosedale Ave Albany GA 31701 Office: 804 14th Ave Albany GA 31701

NOBLE, DOUGLAS ROSS, museum adminstr.; b. Sturgis, Ky., Jan. 19, 1945; s. Roscoe and Robbie Rae (Martin) N.; B.S., Okla. State U., 1967; M.P.A., Ga. Coll., 1978; m. Catherine Ann Richardson, Nov. 3, 1973; 1 dau., Kate Faxon. Asst. to dir. Savannah (Ga.) Sci. Mus., 1970-72, acting dir., 1972; dir. Mus. Arts and Scis., Macon, Ga., 1972—; cons., trustee Nat. Sci. for Youth Found. Vice-pres., Macon Area Community Theatre. Served with U.S. Army, 1967-70. Decorated Bronze Star; recipient Elsie M.B. Naumburg award, 1978. Mem. Southeastern Mus. Conf. (council 1977-80), Ga. Assn. Museums and Galleries (sec.-treas. 1978-80), Kappa Sigma. Office: 4182 Forsyth Rd Macon GA 31210

NOBLE, JOHN LORING, lawyer; b. Columbus, Ohio, Apr. 28, 1941; s. James Paul and Mary Louise (Pfening) N.; B.S. in Bus. Adminstrn., Ohio State U., 1963; J.D., St. John's U., 1970; m. Frances Patricia Shuler, Oct. 14, 1978. Tax acct. Abex Corp., N.Y.C., 1964-66, Mobil Oil Corp., N.Y.C., 1966-68; tax supr. Lever Bros. Co., N.Y.C., 1968-70; admitted to N.Y. State bar, 1971, U.S. Supreme Ct. bar, 1976; tax counsel Exxon Corp., N.Y.C., 1970-72; with Coca-Cola Co., Atlanta, 1972—, asst. dir. taxes, 1976—, sr. tax counsel, 1978—. Mem. Tax Execs. Inst. (v.p. and dir.; past pres. southeastern chpt.), Am. Bar Assn., Internat. Fiscal Assn., Internat. Tax Assn. Home: 3793 Paces Ferry W Atlanta GA 30339 Office: Coca Cola Co PO Drawer 1734 Atlanta GA 30301

NOBLES, BENNIE PETER, obstetrician, gynecologist; b. New Orleans, Mar. 10, 1944; s. Bennie Peter and Doris Marie (Benedict) N.; B.S. in Biology, Loyola U., New Orleans, 1967; M.D., La. State U., 1971; children—Lisa Marie, Leslie Ann, Kimberly Denise. Intern, Charity Hosp., New Orleans, 1971-72, resident in Ob-Gyn, 1972-74; practice medicine specializing in Ob-Gyn, Drs. George, Seese and Nobles, Metairie, La., 1974—; mem. vis. staff, instr. Ob-Gyn, La. State U., 1974—. Bd. dirs. Lakeside Hosp. for Women. Served with USAR, 1971-77. Fellow Am. Coll. Ob-Gyn; mem. Jefferson Soc. Ob-Gyn, Jefferson Parish Med. Soc., Am. Assn. Gynecol. Laparoscopists, Am. Fertility Soc., Am. Legion. Democrat. Club: New Orleans Track. Home: 1504 Hickory Ave Harahan LA 70123 Office: 4740 I-10 Service Rd Metairie LA 70001

NOBLES, LEWIS, coll. pres.; b. Meridian, Miss.; B.S., M.S., U. Miss.; Ph.D. in Pharm. Chemistry, U. Kans.; postgrad. U. Mich.; m. Joy Ford; children—Sandra Nobles Nash, Suzanne (dec.). Successively asst. prof., asso. prof., prof. U. Miss., dean Grad. Sch., 1960-68, coordinator univ. research, 1964-68; pres. Miss. Coll., 1968—; mem. Nat. Adv. Council on Regional Med. Programs, HEW, 1976-79. Deacon, lay speaker Baptist Ch.; mem. bd. grants Am. Found. Pharm. Edn.; bd. dirs. Miss. Found. Med. Care; trustee New Orleans Bapt. Theol. Sem. Mem. Am. Pharm. Assn. (found. award for stimulation of research 1966), Am. Chem. Soc., Chem. Soc. (Gt. Brit.), AAAS, N.Y. Acad. Sci., Acad. Pharm. Scis. (past pres. medicinal chemistry sect.), Internat. Platform Assn., Sigma Xi, Kappa Psi, Rho Chi. Co-author: Physical and Technical Pharmacy; contbr. numerous tech. articles to profl. jours.; editorial adv. bd. Jour. Pharm. Scis., 1966.

NOE, RANDOLPH, lawyer; b. Indpls., Nov. 2, 1939; s. John H. and Bernice (Baker) Reiley; student Franklin Coll., 1957-60; B.A., Ind. State U., 1964; J.D., Ind. U., 1967; m. Anne Will, Mar. 2, 1968; children—John Henry Reiley, Anne Will, Randolph, Jr., Jonathan Baker. Admitted to Ind. bar, 1968, Ky. bar, 1970; trust officer Citizens Fidelity Bank and Trust Co., Louisville, 1969-71; practice law, Louisville, 1971—; asst. Jefferson County (Ky.) atty., 1979—. Mem. exec. bd. Louisville Area Muscular Dystrophy Assn., 1971-73; bd. dirs. Holy Rosary Acad., 1978—; chmn. Eagle Scout Assn. Old Ky. Home council Boy Scouts Am., 1975-77; mem. Louisville Estate Planning Council. Mem. Am., Ky. (probate and trust law com.), Ind., Louisville bar assns. Democrat. Clubs: Pendennis, Bachelors, Wranglers. Author: Kentucky Probate Methods, 1975, Supplement, 1979. Home: 3222 Crossbill Rd Louisville KY 40213 Office: 100 N 6th St Louisville KY 40202

NOEL, MARK GERARD, housing devel. co. exec.; b. Louisville, Mar. 12, 1942; s. Noah and Sarah Collins Mc Dowell; B.A. in Sociology, Wofford Coll., 1964; m. Milner McAdory Smith, June 26, 1965; children—Mark McDowell, Martha Milner. Sales and mktg. staff Perkins Real Estate Co., Birmingham, Ala., 1967-70; founder, pres. Municipal Devel. Co., Birmingham, 1970-76; pres. Kesler Co., Birmingham, 1976—; founder, owner Noel. Mfg. Co., Birmingham, 1978—; cons. in field. Served to capt. U.S. Army, 1964-66. Mem. Birmingham Bd. Realtors, Inst. Property Mgmt. Episcopalian. Clubs: Kiwanis (dir.), Mt. Brook Swim Tennis (dir.). Home: 2910 Westmoreland Dr Birmingham AL 35223 Office: 2607 Commerce Blvd Birmingham AL 35210

NOEL, THOMAS ELBERT, distbn. services co. exec.; b. Flora, Ind., May 22, 1938; s. Thomas Elbert and Mary Lou (Colvin) N.; B.S., U.S. Mil. Acad., 1960; M.A., Duke U., 1968; m. Geraldine Bochnowski, June 24, 1961; children—Lisa, Kelly. Commd. 2d lt. U.S. Army, 1960, advanced through grades to lt. col., 1974, ret., 1974; exec. asst. Fed. Energy Adminstrn., Washington, 1974-75, asst. adminstr., 1975-77; asst. sec. U.S. Dept. Energy, Washington, 1977-78; pres. DSI Terminals, Inc., Houston, 1978—. Decorated Legion of Merit, Bronze Star, Air medal. Mem. Assn. of Petroleum Engrs. Club: Univ. Home: 201 Kensington Ct Houston TX 77024 Office: PO Box 1505 Houston TX 77001

NOELL, PAUL MARCUS, businessman, planter, educator; b. Burlington, N.C., July 1, 1937; s. Edward Speed and Mary Foster (Horne) N.; student N.C. State U., 1955-57, B.S., 1963, M.S., 1973. Social worker N.C. State Commn. for Blind, 1965-67, Alamance County Dept. Social Services, Burlington, 1967-71; research asst. N.C. State U., Raleigh, 1971-72, teaching asst., 1973, instr., 1974; instr. Western Carolina U., Cullowhee, 1974, Gardner-Webb Coll., Boiling Springs, N.C., 1975-76; child support enforcement officer Rowan County (N.C.), Salisbury, 1977-79; tobacco planter, Haw River, N.C., 1970—; businessman, Haw River, 1979—. Active ACLU. Served with USN, 1957-61. Mem. Am. Sociol. Assn., Rural Sociol. Soc., AAUP, N.C. Social Services Assn., Am. Assn. Workers for the Blind, Soc. King Charles the Martyr, Alpha Kappa Delta. Democrat. Episcopalian. Author: The Blind: Acquisition of a Deviant Identity, 1972; The Goliards: Deviants of the Dark Ages, 1972; Selected Characteristics of Rural Law Enforcement Officers: An Exploratory Inquiry, 1973; A Conflict Model and Analysis of School Teachers as a Minority Category, 1975. Home and Office: Noell's Folly-on-the-Haw Box 93 Haw River NC 27258

NOETZEL, GROVER ARCHIBALD JOSEPH, educator; b. Greenwood, Wis., June 14, 1908; s. August Herman and Coralie Marie (Van Den Bossche) N.; A.B., U. Wis., 1929, Ph.D., 1934; certificate in econs., U. London, 1930, U. Geneva, 1936; D.Aviation Edn. (hon.), Embry Riddle U., 1975; fellow Social Sci. Research Council, 1935-36; m. Anna B. Dobbins, June 11, 1953. Instr. econ. U. S.D., 1930-32; instr. econ. U. Wis., 1934-35; economist Nat. Bur. Econ. Research, 1936-37; asst. prof. Temple U., 1937-40, asso. prof., 1940-46; pvt. cons. econ. and investment counselor, Phila. and N.Y.C., 1939-46; prof. econ. U. Miami, 1946-48, dean Sch. Bus. Adminstrn., 1948-61, prof. econs., 1961-72, dean emeritus and prof., 1972—, cons. economist, 1961—; dir. Am. Bankers Ins. Co. Fla.; chmn. investment and finance com. Coral Gables Fed. Savs & Loan Assn.; Bd. dirs. Goodwill Industries, Inc., Med. Service Bur. Miami. Mem. Econ. Soc. South Fla. (dir., pres. 1956), Phi Kappa Phi, Alpha Phi Omega, Alpha Delta Sigma, Delta Sigma Pi, Artus, Beta Gamma Sigma. Clubs: Rotary (Miami, Fla.); Coral Gables Country, Rivieria Country, Century (Coral Gables). Author: Recent Theories of Foreign Exchange, 1934; Cooperation Entre L'Universite et Les Milieux Economiques, 1956; Objectives of a Management Center, 1956; Decisions That Affect Profits, 1957; Today's Economy, 1974; Housing: How Sick is the Patient, 1975; also articles in field. Home and office: 2845 Granada Blvd Apt 1A Coral Gables FL 33134

NOHRNBERG, JAMES CARSON, educator; b. Berkeley, Calif., Mar. 19, 1941; s. Carson and Geneva Gertrude (Gibbs) N.; student Kenyon Coll., 1958-60; B.A. magna cum laude, Harvard Coll., 1962; Ph.D., U. Toronto, 1970; m. Stephanie Payson Lamport, June 14, 1964; children—Gabrielle Lamport, Peter Carson Lamport. Jr. fellow Soc. Fellows, Harvard U., Cambridge, Mass., 1965-68; instr., lectr. Yale U., New Haven, 1968-70, asst. prof., 1970-75; prof. English U. Va., Charlottesville, 1975—. Woodrow Wilson fellow, 1962-63; Queen Elizabeth II scholar, 1964-65; Morse fellow, 1974-75; mem. Center for Advanced Studies, U. Va., 1975-78. Mem. MLA, Spenser Soc. (founding). Presbyterian. Author: The Analogy of The Faerie Queene, 1976; contbr. articles to profl. jours. Home: 1874 Wayside Pl Charlottesville VA 22903 Office: Dept English U Va Charlottesville VA 22903

NOLAN, DAVID THOMAS, public assembly facility mgr.; b. Little Rock, Jan. 9, 1943; s. William Thomas and Ruth Ann (Tisdale) N.; student Little Rock U., 1961-62, U. Ark., 1962-65; m. Laura Elizabeth Winburn, Sept. 3, 1965. Graphic designer Environ. Design, Inc., Little Rock, 1971-73; sr. research analyst Dept. Parks and Tourism, State of Ark., Little Rock, 1973-74; event coordinator Little Rock Conv. Center, 1974-76; asst. dir. Montgomery (Ala.) Civic Center, 1976—. Served with USN, 1966-70. Mem. Internat. Assn. Auditorium Mgrs., Travel Research Assn., Ala. Hotel/Motel Mfrs. Assn., Montgomery Hotel/Motel Assn. Methodist. Club: Dixie Sailing. Office: 300 Bibb St Montgomery AL 36104

NOLAN, EDWIN JOSEPH, univ. adminstr.; b. Jamaica, N.Y., July 22, 1945; s. Raymond Richard and Margaret Joan (Dempsey) N.; B.S. in Psychology, Eastern Ky. U., 1970, M.A. in Counseling, 1972; Ed.D. in Counseling, U. Va., 1977; m. Joan Renne Kennedy, Aug. 28, 1971; 1 son, Michael Bradley. Dir. counseling So. W.Va. Community Coll., Logan, 1972-74; grad. asst. U. Va. Charlottesville, 1974-76; staff counselor Central Va. Coll., Lynchburg, 1976-78; dir. counseling U. Tampa (Fla.), 1978—, adj. prof. psychology, 1978—. Served with U.S. Army, 1968. Recipient various fellowships; cert. group leader in human potential seminars. Mem. Am. Psychol. Assn., Am. Personnel and Guidance Assn., Am. Coll. Personnel Assn., Fla. Personnel and Guidance Assn., Fla. Coll. Personnel Assn. Contbr. articles to profl.

jours. Home: 8304 W Elm St Tampa FL 33615 Office: U Tampa W Kennedy Blvd Tampa FL 33606

NOLAN, RAYMOND PAUL, physician; b. Tullow, Ireland; s. Stephen John and Elizabeth (O'Brien) N.; came to U.S., 1923, naturalized, 1929; B.S., Columbia, 1948; M.D., N.Y. U., 1951; m. Mildred Geiger, Feb. 11, 1957; children—Robert Paul, Kenneth Joseph. Intern St. Vincent's Hosp., N.Y.C., 1951-52; resident Bellevue Med. Center, N.Y. U., 1952-56; practice medicine, specializing in obstetrics and gynecology, Hollywood, Fla., 1960—; asst. prof. obstetrics and gynecology N.Y. U. Coll. Medicine, 1957-60; attending obstetrician and gynecologist, chief dept. Meml. Hosp., Hollywood, Fla., 1970-72. Served with USAAF, 1943-46. Fellow A.C.S.; mem. Am., Fla., Broward County med. assns., Am. Coll. Obstetricians and Gynecologists, Fla., Broward County obstet. and gynecol. socs. Home: 5555 SW 61st Ave Davie FL 33314 Office: 3711 Garfield St Hollywood FL 33021

NOLAN, RICHARD CHARLES, football coach; b. Pitts., Mar. 26, 1932; s. Vincent John and Agnes (Sharples) N.; B.A. in Bus. Adminstrn., U. Md., 1954; m. Elizabeth Ann Tullis, Apr. 19, 1954; children—Richard Charles, Nancy, Michael, Kelly, Lisa, James. Profl. football player N.Y. Giants, 1954-57, 59-61, Chgo. Cardinals, 1958; player-coach Dallas Cowboys, 1962, asst. coach, 1963-67; head coach San Francisco 49'ers, 1968-75; personnel scout Oakland Raiders, 1976-77; asst. coach New Orleans Saints, 1977-78, head coach, 1978—. Named Nat. Football Conf. Coach of Year, 1970; recipient Disting. Alumni award U. Md., 1971; inducted into Westchester Sports Hall of Fame, 1978. Mem. Phi Delta Theta. Republican. Roman Catholic. Club: U. Md. M. Office: New Orleans Saints 6928 Saints Dr Metairie LA 70003

NOLAN, WILLIAM CARL, polit. scientist; b. Las Vegas, Jan. 28, 1922; s. Carl Peter and Helen (Fowler) N.; B.S., N.Mex. Western Coll., 1946; M.A., U. N.Mex., 1948; postgrad N.Y. U., 1947-50, U. Miss., 1968; m. Naoma Reynolds, Nov. 26, 1942; children—Mary Brenda, Linda, Patrick. Research asso. Bur. Public Adminstrn., U. Tenn., 1950-51, asst. prof. polit. sci., 1955-56; mgmt. analyst U.S. Signal Agy., White Sands Proving Grounds, N.Mex., 1956-57; indsl. engr. Chino Mines div. Kennecott Copper Corp., N.Mex., 1957-62; asst. prof. polit. sci. So. Ark. U., Magnolia, 1962-64, asso. prof., 1964-70, prof., 1970—, chmn. social sci. div., 1964—. Del., Democratic County Conv., 1976, State Conv., 1976. Served with USAAF, 1943-45, USAF, 1951-55. Mem. Am. Polit. Sci. Assn., So. Polit. Sci. Assn., Ark. Polit. Sci. Assn., NEA, Ark. Ednl. Assn., Res. Officers Assn. Mormon. Office: Dept Polit Sci So Ark U Magnolia AR 71753

NOLF, CHESTER FRANKLIN, JR., engr.; b. St. Louis, Feb. 26, 1948; s. Chester F. and Janet M. (Bremer) N.; B.S., U. Ariz., 1971, M.S., 1974; m. Karen Louise Herr, Aug. 28, 1971; 1 son, Christopher Lee. Researcher, U. Ariz., Tucson, 1971-74; reliability engr. Burr Brown Research, Tucson, summer 1973; system effectiveness engr. Navy Electronic System Command, Washington, 1974—. Served with U.S. Army, 1971-74. Gen. Resident scholar, 1966-67. Mem. ASME, Res. Officers Assn., Sigma Xi, Theta Tau. Contbr. articles in field to profl. jours. Address: 14221 Fallbrook Ln Woodbridge VA 22193

NOLL, ARTHUR WILLIAM, banker; b. San Antonio, July 22, 1930; s. Arthur Gordon and Dorothea Virginia (Young) N.; B.S., Tex. A&M U., 1951; M.B.A., Oklahoma City U., 1973; M.Banking, So. Meth. U., 1976; m. Marcia Sue Deutch, Dec. 18, 1976; children—Arthur W., Russell Thomas. Asst. ranch mgr. 711 Ranches, Boerne, Tex., 1953-68; sr. v.p. mktg. Union Bank & Trust Co., Oklahoma City, 1973—. Served with U.S. Army, 1951-53, 68-73. Decorated Bronze Stars, Purple Heart, Air medal, others. Mem. Bank Mktg. Assn. (pres. Oklahoma chpt.), Oklahoma City C. of C., Okla. Bankers Assn., Res. Officers Assn., Am. Bankers Assn., Nat. Rifle Assn. Republican. Roman Catholic. Clubs: Lions, Oklahoma City Farm. Home: 2745 NW 111th St Oklahoma City OK 73120 Office: 4921 N May Ave Oklahoma City OK 73112

NOLTE, GEORGE WASHINGTON, investment co. exec.; b. nr. Woodbury, N.J., Apr. 2, 1904; s. Harry Kircher and Anna (Porch) N.; B.S., U. Pa., 1924. Accountant, Lybrand, Ross Bros. & Montgomery, Phila., 1924-32; comptroller Atwater Kent Mfg. Co., Phila., Wilmington, Del., 1932-49, v.p., dir., 1949-67, pres., 1972—; v.p. Kent Co., Wilmington, 1972—; treas., dir. Kent Elec. Mfg. Corp., 1949-71. Cons. parks, recreation com. Bd. Chosen Freeholders, Gloucester County, N.J., 1965-66. Pres., trustee Etlon Found., 1959—; comdr. USNR, 1942-46. Recipient Distinguished Service award for outstanding community service Woodbury Jr. C. of C., 1965. C.P.A., Pa. Home: 801 Lake Shore Dr Lake Park FL 33403 Office: 3411 Silverside Rd Wilmington DE 19810

NOMEIR, ABDEL-MOHSEN AMIN, cardiologist; b. Edku, Egypt, Mar. 16, 1926; came to U.S., 1971, naturalized, 1978; s. Amin Mohammed and Zakiah Mohammed N.; B.A., Abbasiah Sch., 1945; M.B., B.Ch., Faculty of Medicine, U. Alexandria, 1952, D.M., 1956, M.D., 1960; m. Charlotte Freckwinkel, Apr. 2, 1965; 1 dau., Selina. Fellow, Bowman Gray Sch. Medicine, Winston-Salem, N.C., 1972-73, instr., 1973-76, asst. prof. medicine, 1976—; NSF lectr. Faculty of Medicine, Cairo U., 1976. Diplomate Am. Bd. Internal Medicine. Fellow A.C.P.; mem. Am. Inst. Ultrasound in Medicine, Forsyth County Med. Soc., Piedmont Med. Found. Contbr. articles in field to profl. jours. Home: 3219 Pensby Rd Winston-Salem NC 27106 Office: Dept Medicine Bowman Gray School of Medicine 300 S Hawthorne Rd Winston-Salem NC 27103

NORAN, WILLIAM HAROLD, neurologist; b. Mpls., June 22, 1943; s. Harold Hans and Kathryn Mae (Anderson) N.; B.S., U. Minn., 1965, M.D., 1968; m. Sally Ann Blackburn, Mar. 14, 1969; 1 dau., Nicole Yvette. Intern, Los Angeles County Gen. Hosp., 1968-69; resident U. Minn., Mpls., 1969-72; neurologist Jacksonville (Fla.) Neurol. Clinic, 1974—. Served with M.C., USAF, 1972-74. Diplomate Am. Bd. Psychiatry and Neurology. Mem. AMA, Fla. Med. Assn., Am. Acad. Neurology. Office: Suite 601 3599 University Blvd S Jacksonville FL 32217

NORD, GORDON LUDWIG, JR., geologist; b. Cin., Apr. 3, 1942; s. Gordon Ludwig and Barbara (Kohn) N.; B.S. in Geology, U. Wis., 1965; M.S. in Geology, U. Calif., Berkeley, 1971, Ph.D. in Geology, 1973; m. Dec. 23, 1965 (div. 1978); 1 dau., Elizabeth; m. 2d, Ann Chandler Veltri, May 24, 1980. Research asso. dept. metallurgy and materials sci. Case Western Res. U., 1971-74; geologist, br. exptl. geochemistry and mineralogy U.S. Geol. Survey, Reston, Va., 1974—. Mem. Geol. Soc. Am., Mineral. Soc. Am., Am. Geophys. Union, AAAS, Electron Microscopy Soc. Am. Democrat. Office: 959 Nat Center US Geol Survey Reston VA 22092

NORDBY, HAROLD EDWIN, chemist; b. New England, N.D., Nov. 3, 1931; s. Edward C. and Olga (Benson) N.; B.A., Concordia Coll., Moorhead, Minn., 1953; postgrad. U. Iowa, 1956-57; M.A., U. Ariz., 1959, Ph.D., 1963; m. Marlene Ann Dirks, Aug. 23, 1958; children—Paul, Mark. Jr. scientist Hormel Inst., U. Minn., Austin, 1953-56; research asso. U. Ariz., 1959-63; research chemist, citrus and subtropical products lab. U.S. Dept. Agr., Winter Haven, Fla., 1962—. Rep., Nat. Assn. Stuttering, 1978-79. Mem. Am. Chem. Soc., Am. Oil Chemists Soc., Fla. Hort. Soc., Soc. Preservation Barbershop Quartet Singing in Am., Sigma Xi. Republican. Lutheran. Clubs: Toastmaster, Sertoma (v.p.). Contbr. articles to profl. jours. Home: 804 Lake Jessie Dr Winter Haven FL 33880 Office: 600 Ave S NW Winter Haven FL 33880

NORDER, EARL HENRY, engring. cons.; b. Clinton, Iowa, Feb. 25, 1932; s. Earl George and Ethel Lulu (Schluter) N.; B.A. in Arch., Iowa State U., 1955; m. Garita Josephine Woods, July 27, 1960; children—Steven, Camilla. Chief engr. Air Force European Exchange, Wiesbaden, Germany, 1958-61; chief engring. U.K. Region, London, 1961-64; chief engring. designs European Exchange System, Nuernberg, Germany, 1964-68; chief engring. standards and criteria Army and Air Force Exchange Service, Dallas, 1968-74, chief engring. cons. services, 1977—; dep. for engring. Pacific Exchange System, Honolulu, 1974-77. Served to capt. USAF, 1956-58. Recipient AIA 1st prize in archtl. design, Iowa State U., 1955; Army and Air Force Exchange Service Achievement award, 1968, Excellence award, 1972, Superior Accomplishments award, 1977. Mem. Soc. Am. Mil. Engrs., Questors. Republican. Methodist. Club: Toastmasters. Contbr. articles to profl. jours. Home: 3022 Cortez Ct Irving TX 75062 Office: 3911 S Walton Walker Blvd Dallas TX 75222

NORDLING, KARL INGMAR, computer cons. co. exec.; b. Brando, Finland, Mar. 26, 1935; s. John Axel and Sanny Maria (Soderstrom) N.; came to U.S., 1954, naturalized, 1960; B.S., Heald's Coll., 1958; M.S., U. Pa., 1963; m. Anne-Berit Vik, Dec. 6, 1974; children—Eric, Leif. Applications engr. Beckman Instruments Co., Fullerton, Calif., 1961-62, 63-65; mgr. product planning Control Data Corp., San Diego, 1965-69; dir. product mgmt. Paradyne Corp., Largo, Fla., 1969-77; pres., founder Kinex Corp., Largo, 1977—. Mem. IEEE. Patentee in field. Author: (with others) Basics of Data Communications, 1976. Home and office: 9280 119th Ave N Largo FL 33543

NORDQVIST, STAFFAN ROLF BJÖRNSON, obstetrician, gynecologist; b. Lund, Sweden, July 16, 1936; s. Bjorn R.B. and Liv (Wicksell) N.; M.D., U. Lund, 1963, Ph.D., 1969; children by previous marriage—Joakim, Jesper, Jonas. Intern, U. Lund, 1963-64, resident in ob-gyn, 1964-67, asso. prof. ob-gyn, 1970-71; asso. prof. ob-gyn Cornell U. Med. Sch., N.Y.C., 1972-74; asso. prof. U. Miami (Fla.) Med. Sch., 1974-77, prof. obstetrics, gynecology and oncology, 1977—; asso. Meml. Sloan Kettering Cancer Center, N.Y.C., 1972-74. Bd. dirs. Am. Cancer Soc., Dade County, 1978—. Served with Swedish Army, 1955-71. Mem. Fla. Med. Assn., Dade County Med. Assn., Fla. Ob-Gyn Soc., Am. Coll. Ob-Gyn, Miami Ob-Gyn Soc., Soc. Gynec. Oncologists, Am. Soc. Colposcopy and Cervical Pathology, Internat. Soc. Gynec. Pathologists, Continental Gynec. Soc. Lutheran. Club: Coral Reef Yacht. Contbr. articles to profl. jours. Home: 6815 Edgewater Dr Coral Gables FL 33133 Office: Dept Obstetrics Gynecology PO Box 016960 Miami FL 33101

NOREM, RICHARD FREDERICK, SR., musician, educator; b. Joliet, Ill., June 28, 1931; s. Oscar Lewis and Mabel Vera (Meyer) N.; B.M., U. Rochester, 1953, M.M., 1958; postgrad. Guildhall Sch. Music, London, 1974; m. Sally Lou Jarvis, July 24, 1954; 1 son, Richard Frederick II. Tchr., Rochester (N.Y.) Public Sch. System, 1956-57; faculty La. State U., Baton Rouge, 1957—, asst. dean, prof. music, 1970—; performer Jackson (Miss.) Symphony Orch., 1961-65, U.S. Marine Band, 1953-56, Lake Charles (La.) Symphony Orch., 1965-70; prin. horn player Baton Rouge Symphony Orch., 1957—, bd. dirs., 1958-68. Bd. dirs. Bengal A.A.U. Swim Team, 1972, 73, 75, 76, 78; chmn. Episcopal High Parents Fund Drive; mem. music com. St. Lukes Episcopal Ch. Served with USMC, 1953-56. George Eastman scholar, 1953; Govs. honors grantee, 1970, 71, 76; recipient Outstanding Educator of Am. award, 1971, 72. Mem. Internat. Horn Soc. (dist. dir.), Music Educators Nat. Conf., Nat. Assn. Coll. Wind and Percussion Instrs., Am. Fedn. Musicians, La. Music Educators Assn., Phi Mu Alpha Sinfonia, Omicron Delta Kappa, Kappa Kappa Psi, Pi Kappa Lambda. Democrat. Episcopalian. Clubs: Camelot, Rolls-Royce Owners, Bengal Swim. Home: 4821 Sweetbriar Pl Baton Rouge LA 70808 Office: Sch Music La State U Baton Rouge LA 70803

NORFLEET, MICHELE MCCLURE, speech pathologist; b. Louisville, July 4, 1949; d. Rush Delbert and Molly Karnes (Hill) McClure; B.S. in Speech Pathology, So. Ill. U., Carbondale, 1970, M.S. in Speech Pathology, 1971; m. John Michael Norfleet, May 6, 1972; children—Dana Christine, Erin Lee. Speech pathologist Jewish Hosp. of St. Louis, 1971-72, St. Lucie County Schs., Ft. Pierce, Fla., 1972-73, Columbia (S.C.) Hearing and Speech Center, 1972-73, Charleston (S.C.) Speech and Hearing Center, 1973-75; speech pathologist Charleston County Public Schs., 1976—; supr. clin. fellowship year applicants in speech pathology. HEW fellow, 1970-71; lic. speech pathologist, S.C. Mem. Am. Speech, Lang. and Hearing Assn. (cert.), S.C. Speech and Hearing Assn. Roman Catholic. Home: 1022 Grand Concourse Charleston SC 29412 Office: 3 Chisolm St Charleston SC 29412

NORIEGA, RUDY JORGE, hosp. adminstr.; b. Havana, Cuba, Apr. 23, 1937; s. Rodolfo and Iris (Santini) N.; came to U.S., 1961; naturalized, 1966; B.S., Masonic U., 1960; m. Rosa E. Del Castillo, Jan. 2, 1960; children—Rudy A., George. Accountant, Continental Can Co., Havana, Cuba, 1961, Am. Fgn. Ins. Assn., N.Y.C., 1961-62, North Miami Gen. Hosp., Miami, Fla., 1962-64; asst. controller Jackson Meml. Hosp., Miami, 1964-65; asst. adminstr. Plantation (Fla.) Gen. Hosp., 1965-72, adminstr., trustee, 1972—. Mem. Am. Coll. Hosp. Adminstrs., So. Fla. Hosp. Assn. (pres. 1979-80), Broward County Hosp. Assn. (pres. 1978—), Fla. League Hosps. (pres. 1974-75), Fedn. Am. Hosps. (dir. 1973-74), Hosp. Fin. Mgmt. Assn. (dir. 1971-72), Plantation C. of C. (pres. 1978-79). Club: Kiwanis (v.p. 1978-79) (Plantation).

NORMAN, DAVID MICHAEL, social work exec.; b. Providence, May 3, 1945; s. Nathan and Dorothy Rose (Cohen) N.; B.A., U. R.I., 1967; M.S.S.W., U. Louisville, 1971; M.P.A., Old Dominion U., 1979; m. Carolyn Frances Vine, Aug. 18, 1968; children—Perri Naomi, Nathan Aron. Social worker Family Service/Travelers Aid, Norfolk, Va., 1971-73; dir. Portsmouth (Va.) Mental Health/Mental Retardation Services Bd., 1973—; instr. Eastern Va. Med. Sch.; mem. Va. Mental Health Adv. Council. Pres., Temple Sinai of Portsmouth. Served with AUS, 1967-69. Cert. Acad. Cert. Social Workers. Mem. Nat. Assn. Social Workers, Am. Soc. Public Adminstrn. Office: 334 Effingham St Portsmouth VA 23704

NORMAN, MARGIE IRENE, counselor; b. Nixon, Tex., Jan. 24, 1930; d. Alexander Edmund and Alta Patricia (Childress) Hall; B.A., Mary Hardin-Baylor Coll., 1949; M.Ed., Our Lady of the Lake, 1970; m. Gene Franklin Norman, Aug. 31, 1951; children—Dale Alan, James Thomas, Stephen Wayne. Tchr., Stonewall Elementary Sch., San Antonio, 1949-51, Briscoe Elementary Sch., 1955-67; tchr. Long Creek Elementary Sch., Charlotte, N.C., 1967-68; tchr. Travis Elementary Sch., San Antonio Sch. Dist., 1968-70; spl. edn. counselor, 1970-71, media specialist, 1971-73, spl. edn. counselor, Fenwick/Lamar Elementary Schs., San Antonio, 1973-75, Austin Elementary/Opportunity Sch., 1975—, dir. Project Prime, San Antonio Sch. Dist., 1971-72; cons. for tchr. tng. in spl. edn. Certified profl. teacher, profl. counselor, profl. spl. educator in mental retardation, profl. supr., profl. ednl. diagnostician, profl. spl. edn. counselor, profl. spl. edn. supr., Tex. Mem. Am. (award 1977), Tex. (Research award 1977) S.Tex. personnel and guidance assns., Am., Tex., San Antonio Dist. (pres.) sch. counselors assns., Tex., Bexar County psychol. assns., Council for Exceptional Children, San Antonio Assn. for Children with Learning Disabilities, NEA, Tex. State Tchrs. Assn. (life), San Antonio Adminstrs. and Suprs. Assn., San Antonio Women Deans and Counselors, Delta Kappa Gamma, Kappa Pi, Sigma Tau Delta, Hist. Phila Soc. Managing editor: Texas Personnel and Guidance Jour., 1977—; editor: Guide-Write Newsletter; contbr. articles to profl. jours. in field. Home: 5402 Rolling Wood San Antonio TX 78228 Office: 621 W Euclid St San Antonio TX 78212

NORMAN, MICHAEL EDWARD, research and devel. chemist; b. Ft. Worth, Oct. 27, 1953; s. Delmer E. and Laney L. (Lahman) N.; B.S. in Chemistry, Stephen F. Austin U., 1975; M.B.A., U. Tex., Arlington, 1979; m. Regina Diane Brown, Oct. 10, 1971; 1 son, David Edward. Trainee, Western Co. N. Am., Kermit, Tex., 1976-77, applied chemist, Ft. Worth, 1977, research chemist, Ft. Worth, 1977-79, sr. research chemist analytical services, 1979—. Mem. Soc. Petroleum Engrs., Am. Chem. Soc., Assn. M.B.A.'s. Republican. Developer products for enhanced recovery of oil from marginal/depleted reservoirs. Home: 7640 Blue Carriage Ln Fort Worth TX 76112 Office: PO Box 186 Fort Worth TX 76101

NORMAN, THERON JESSE, JR., packaging mfg. co. exec.; b. Gainesville, Ga., Nov. 3, 1915; s. Theron Jesse and Mary Lewis (Butler) N.; student in bus. adminstrn. U. N.C., 1957-58; m. Jane Ellen Taylor, Aug. 23, 1938; children—James Theron, Thomas Edmund, David Taylor, Richard Calhoun. Sales rep. Herald Press, Inc., Charlotte, N.C., 1933-40, v.p., 1941-45; founder, pres. Package Products Co., Inc., Charlotte, N.C., 1946-73; pres. Engraph, Inc., Charlotte, 1973-77, chmn., 1977—, chief exec. officer, 1978—; dir. 1st Union Nat. Bank, Charlotte, 1966—. Trustee, Mint Museum of Art, 1966-72, pres., 1971-72 dir. Arts and Scis. Council, 1977—. Mem. Nat. Flexible Packaging Assn. (dir. 1955-62, pres. 1958-59), Charlotte C. of C. (dir. 1970-72, 74-78). Republican. Baptist. Clubs: Charlotte City (pres. 1977), Charlotte Country, Quail Hollow Country, Grandfather Golf and Country. Color landscape photographer; one-man shows include Wingate Coll., 1973, Queens Coll., 1974, 76, 78, Queens Coll., 1978. Home: 3906 Seminole Ct Charlotte NC 28210 Office: 6060 St Alban's St Charlotte NC 28233

NORMAN, WALLACE, pipe co. exec.; b. Houlka, Miss., Feb. 5, 1926; s. Leland Fleming and Alma Lucile (Brown) N.; student East Central Jr. Coll. 1942, U. Miss., 1946, Millsaps Coll., 1946; B.S., Oklahoma City U., 1948; m. Maurene Collums, Dec. 26, 1950; children—Wallace, Karen Jean, Emily June, Lauren Beth, John Crocker. Owner, operator Wallace Norman Ins. Agy., Houston, Miss., 1949—; pres. Norman Oil Co., Houston, 1956—, Nat. Leasing Co., Houston, 1969—, U.S. Plastics, Inc., Houston, 1969—, Calhoun Nat. Co., 1974—, Norman Trucking Co., 1975—. Chmn. Running Bear dist. Boy Scouts Am., 1971-73. Served with USNR, World War II. Mem. Miss. Assn. Ins. Agts., Miss. Mfrs. Assn., Am. Waterworks Assn., DAV, VFW, Am. Legion. Methodist. Club: Exchange. Address: PO Box 208 Houston MS 38851

NORMENT, JACQUELIN BOYKIN, glass co. exec.; b. Richmond, Va., Sept. 16, 1916; d. Robert Hunt and Miriam Taylor (Boykin) Norment; B.S., Hampden-Sydney Coll., 1938; 1 son, Robert Hunt. Sales rep. Church & Dwight Co., Inc., N.Y.C., 1938-42, Binswanger & Co., Richmond, Va., 1946-49; gen. mgr. Warren Bros. Co. Inc., Nashville, 1949-52; pres. Norment Industries Inc., and predecessors, Montgomery, Ala., 1959—. Chmn. United Appeal, Montgomery, 1958; bd. dirs. Fellowship House, 1977. Served to lt. USNR, 1942-46. Mem. Flat Glass Mktg. Assn. Republican. Episcopalian. Clubs: Montgomery Country; San Destin (Fla.); Kiwanis. Home: 335 Clanton Ave Montgomery AL 36104 Office: 3224 Mobile Rd Montgomery AL 36108

NORRELL, OLIVER LEWIS, III, lawyer; b. Frankfurt, W. Ger., Feb. 6, 1953; s. Oliver Lewis, Jr. and Ida (Hunter) N.; came to U.S., 1954, naturalized, 1965; B.A., U. Va., 1974; J.D., U. Richmond (Va.), 1976; m. Ruth Arleathia Scott, Sept. 24, 1977. Admitted to Va. bar, 1976; asso. firm Ealey & Norrell, Richmond, 1976-78; asst. commonwealth's atty. Henrico County, Va., 1978-79, Richmond, 1979—; vol. probation officer Richmond Juvenile Ct., 1977—. Mem. Am. Bar Assn., Nat. Bar Assn., Va. State Bar, Va. Assn. Commonwealth Attys., Va. Juvenile Officers Assn., Old Dominion Bar Assn., Richmond Bar Assn., Alpha Phi Alpha. Democrat. Baptist. Home: 10221 Sauna Dr Richmond VA 23235 Office: John Marshall Cts Bldg 800 E Marshal St Richmond VA 23219

NORRIS, ELWIN LAMAR, systems analyst; b. Noxapater, Miss., July 5, 1930; s. Grover Cleveland and Effie Matilda (Breazeale) N.; B.S., Anderson (Ind.) Coll., 1953; m. Esther May Thorsen, Aug. 29, 1957; children—Linda Kay, David Elwin. Accountant, Summerford, Wicker, Helvering & Hunter, C.P.A.'s, Houston, 1955-56, Tenn. Gas Transmission Co., Houston, 1956-61; sr. accountant Tenneco Oil Co., Houston, 1961-63, supr. Atlanta, 1963—. Treas. Gulf Coast Bible Coll., Houston, 1955-57, 1st Ch. of God, Houston, 1960-63. Served with U.S. Army, 1953-55. Cert. in data processing. Mem. Assn. Systems Mgmt. Republican. Home: 3265 Tulip Dr Decatur GA 30032 Office: 6600 Powers Ferry Rd Atlanta GA 30329

NORRIS, FRANKLIN GRAY, surgeon; b. Washington, June 30, 1923; s. Franklin Gray and Ellie Narcissus (Story) N.; B.S., Duke U., 1947; M.D., Harvard U, 1951; m. Sara Kathryn Green, Aug. 12, 1945; children—Gloria Norris Sales, Franklin Gray. Resident, Peter Bent Brigham Hosp., Boston, 1951-54, Bowman Gray Sch. Medicine, 1954-57; practice medicine, specializing in thoracic and cardiovascular surgery, Orlando, Fla., 1957—; mem. staff Brevard Meml. Hosp., Melbourne, Fla., Waterman Meml. Hosp., Eustis, Fla., West Orange Meml. Hosp., Winter Garden, Fla.; Orange Meml. Hosp., Fla. Hosp., Lucerne Hosp., Holiday Hosp., Mercy Hosp. (all Orlando). Bd. dirs. Orange County Cancer Soc., 1958-64, Central Fla. Respiratory Disease Assn., 1958-65. Served to capt. USAAF, 1943-45. Decorated Air medal with 3 oak leaf clusters. Diplomate Am. Bd. Surgery, Am. Bd. Thoracic and Cardiovascular Surgery. Mem. Fla. Heart Assn. (dir. 1958—), Orange County Med. Soc. (exec. com. 1964-75, pres. 1971-75), A.C.S., Soc. Thoracic Surgery, So. Thoracic Surg. Assn., Am. Coll. Chest Physicians, Phi Kappa Psi. Presbyterian (deacon). Clubs: Citrus, Orlando Country. Home: 1801 Bimini Dr Orlando FL 32806 Office: 55 W Columbia St Orlando FL 32806

NORRIS, GAYLIN, counselor; b. Kansas City, Mo., May 18, 1946; d. Clinton Karl and Mary Lou (Rosener Lampe) Norris; B.A., St. Marys U., 1969; M.A., San Jose State U., 1973. Community organizer, Project FREE, San Antonio, 1968; tchr. Harlandale Ind. Sch. Dist. San Antonio, 1969-70, Opn. SER, San Jose, Calif., 1970-71, M.C. Perry Sch., Iwakuni, Japan, 1971-72; counselor high sch., Cupertino, Calif., 1972, Job Corps, San Jose, 1972; ednl. cons. Edn.

Service Center, Region 20, San Antonio, 1972-75; ednl. cons., psychotherapist, marriage and family counselor, San Antonio. Mem. Internat. Transactional Analysis Assn., Alamo Area Assn. Supervision and Curriculum Dirs., Am. Personnel and Guidance Assn., Am. Assn. Marriage and Family Therapists, Kappa Sigma Phi. Home and Office: 421 Howard St San Antonio TX 78212

NORRIS, JAMES SCOTT, endocrinologist; b. Selma, Ala., Aug. 6, 1943; s. Richard R. and Marjorie R. (Jennings) N.; student U. N.H., 1961-64; B.S., Keene State Coll., 1966; Ph.D., U. Colo., 1971; m. Gloria Jean Ackerson, July 2, 1966. NIH fellow, U. Ill., 1972-73; instr. dept. cell biology Baylor Coll. Medicine, Houston, 1973-77; asst. prof. depts. medicine and physiology U. Ark., Little Rock, 1977—. Fellow Tissue Culture Assn. (pres. Gulf Coast br. 1975-76); mem. Endocrine Soc., Am. Soc. Cell Biology, AAAS, Sigma Xi. Contbr. numerous articles on cell biology to sci. jours. Home: 11201 Bainbridge Dr Little Rock AR 72212 Office: Univ Arkansas 4301 W Markham Little Rock AR 72201

NORSTOG, KNUT JONSON, educator; b. Grand Forks, N.D., June 11, 1921; s. Jon and Inga (Bredesen) N.; B.A., Luther Coll., 1943; Ph.D., U. Mich., 1955; m. Nona Evensen, Mar. 17, 1944; children—Jon, Eric, Paul. Asso. prof. Wittenburg Coll., Springfield, Ohio, 1954-63; asso. prof. U. South Fla., Tampa, 1963-66; prof. No. Ill. U., DeKalb, 1966-77, prof. emeritus, 1977—; research asso. Fairchild Tropical Garden, Miami, Fla., 1978—. Served with U.S. Army, 1943-46. NSF fellow, 1952-54. Mem. Bot. Soc. Am., Linnean Soc. London (fellow), Assn. for Trop. Biology, Internat. Soc. Plant Morphologists, Sigma Xi. Contbr. articles to profl. jours.; author: Plant Biology, 1976; editor-in-chief Am. Jour. Botany, 1980—. Home: 11935 Old Cutler Rd Miami FL 33156 Office: 10901 Old Cutler Rd Miami FL 33156

NORTELL, GUIA PARADERO, radiologist; b. Aloran, Philippines, Oct. 23, 1940; s. Victorino Paradero and Julieta T. Madula; came to U.S., 1965; M.D., Far Eastern U., Manila, 1964. Intern, St. Joseph's Hosp., Chgo., 1966-67; resident in pediatrics Cook County Hosp., Chgo., 1967; resident radiology U. Chgo., 1967-70; practice medicine specializing in radiology, Nashville, 1974-76, Punta Gorda, Fla., 1976—; instr. radiology Emory U., Atlanta, 1970-72; lectr. Vanderbilt U., Nashville, Tenn., 1974-76; staff radiologist Med. Center Hosp., Punta Gorda, 1976—. Diplomate Am. Bd. Radiology. Fellow Am. Coll. Chest Physicians; mem. Fla. Med. Assn., Charlotta County Med. Soc. Roman Catholic. Home: 940 Santa Brigida Punta Gorda FL 33950 Office: 809 E Marion Punta Gorda FL 33950

NORTH, MICHAEL RAY, real estate broker; b. Corpus Christi, Mar. 12, 1949; s. Jack Lane and Betty Lou (Pemberton) N.; student Tex. A&M U., 1967-70; m. Delilah Sue Womack, Nov. 20, 1978; children—Mitzi Jean, Eric Ryan Jones. Engaged in real estate sales and land devel., 1970—; broker, mgr. Jack North & Assos., Alpine, Tex., 1974—; gen. mgr. N & N Land and Cattle Co., Alpine, 1976—; cons., appraiser, 1976—. Mem. Nat. Assn. Realtors, Tex. Assn. Realtors. Home: Terlingua Route Box 221 Alpine TX 79830 Office: Terlingua Route Box 200 Alpine TX 79830

NORTH, PHIL RECORD, corp. exec.; b. Fort Worth, July 6, 1918; s. James M. and Lottie R. N.; A.B., U. Notre Dame, 1939; m. July 28, 1944; children—Phillip Kevin, Kerry Lawrence, Mairin Kathleen, Deirdre Anne. With Fort Worth Star-Telegram, to 1962; v.p. Carter Publs., Inc., exec. editor, asst. gen. mgr.; chmn. bd., chief exec. officer, pres. Tandy Corp., Fort Worth. Served with AUS, 1940-46. Decorated Bronze Star. Roman Catholic. Clubs: Fort Worth, River Crest, Shady Oaks, Little Bay, Life Oak. Home: 6141 Locke Fort Worth TX 76116

NORTHROP, SANDRA KREY, psychotherapist; b. New Orleans, Oct. 12, 1937; d. Philip J. and Olga (Walker) Krey; B.A., Newcomb Coll., New Orleans, 1959; M.S., Tulane U., 1975; m. Jerry F. Northrop, June 27, 1959; children—Jerry F., Douglas K. Pvt. practice behavior therapy and counseling, Metairie, La. 1965—; psychol. cons. New Orleans public schs., 1975; instr. Our Lady of Holy Cross Coll., New Orleans, 1975; instr. psychol., career/life planning, counselor Women's Center for Greater New Orleans, Loyola U.; speaker in field; seminar leader, 1976—. Mem. Am. Personnel and Guidance Assn., Nat. Inst. Hypnotherapy, Am. Psychol. Assn., Psi Chi. Home: 136 Glenwood Dr Metairie LA 70005 Office: Loyola U Women's Center 6322 Cromwell Pl Box 36 Loyola U New Orleans LA 70118

NORTHUP, JOHN DAVID, JR., physician; b. Bridgeton, N.J., Aug. 1, 1941; s. John David and Ruth (Bender) N.; A.B. in Biology cum laude, Amherst Coll., 1963; M.D., Yale U., 1967; m. Mildred Pasker, June 5, 1971; 1 son, John David. Intern in internal medicine N.Y. Hosp-Cornell U. Med. Center, N.Y.C., 1967-68, jr. asst. resident in internal medicine, 1968-69; sr. asst. resident in internal medicine Duke U., 1971-72, advanced clin. resident in gastroenterology Mayo Clinic and Mayo Grad. Sch. Medicine, Rochester, Minn., 1972-74; practice medicine, specializing in internal medicine, Savannah, Ga., 1974—, also in gastroenterology; mem. staffs St. Joseph Hosp., Meml. Med. Center, Candler Hosp. (all Savannah). Served with USPHS, 1969-71. NSF grantee, 1962; NIH grantee, 1965, 66. Diplomate Am. Bd. Internal Medicine. Mem. A.C.P., AMA, Ga. Med. Soc., Am. Soc. Gastrointestinal Endoscopy, Health Services Assn. Southeastern Ga., Ga. Lung Assn., Clean Air Com. Savannah, Ga. Wild Life Found., Sierra Club, Ga. Conservancy, Sigma Xi (asso.), Psi Upsilon, Nu Sigma Nu. Student editor Jour. History of Sci. and Medicine, 1966-67; contbr. articles to med. jours. Home: 507 Old Mill Rd Savannah GA 31406 Office: Suite 125 Exec Court 5105 Paulsen St Savannah GA 31405

NORTON, BARRY LEE, accountant; b. Augusta, Ga., Oct. 19, 1952; s. Odell and Marion Jennings (King) N.; B.B.A., Augusta Coll., 1974; m. Susan Presley, June 21, 1974; children—Barry Lee, Dana Presley. Lab. technician Wren Optical Co., Augusta, 1972-73; mill acct. Ga.-Pacific Corp., Augusta, 1973-77, 79—, asst. credit mgr. So. div., 1977-79, loan officer credit union, 1978-79. Mem. fin. com. St. John United Meth. Ch., Augusta, 1975—, treas., 1977-78. Mem. Nat. Assn. Accts., Augusta Jaycees (pres. 1978-79), Ga. Jaycees (treas. 1979-80), Augusta Coll. Alumni Assn. (dir. 1978—). Methodist. Club: North Augusta Country. Home: 1112 Glenwood Dr Augusta GA 30904 Office: Ga Pacific Corp PO Box 1808 Augusta GA 30902

NORTON, DICKIE, ins. co. exec.; b. Athens, Tenn., Nov. 25, 1947; s. Waid Henderson and Grace (McCall) N.; B.S. in Bus., U. Chattanooga, 1969; m. Janice Shelton, June 27, 1975; 1 son, David Shelton. Sales mgr. Aetna Life & Casualty Co., Atlanta, 1969-71; founder, pres. Cleveland Ins. Center (Tenn.), 1974-79; v.p. Ins. Inc., Cleveland, 1979—. Bd. dirs. Child Shelter Home, 1975. Mem. Profl. Ins. Agts. Tenn., Insurors of Tenn. Baptist. Clubs: Elks, Cleveland Country, Rolling Hills Country, Sertoma (v.p. 1974-75, dir. 1975-76, Man of Yr. 1974). Home: Rockland Ct Cleveland TN 37311 Office: 154 Central Ave Cleveland TN 37311

NORTON, KENNETH EDWARD, accountant; b. Tampa, Fla., July 1, 1932; s. Iva Edward and Loretta Doris (Bocash) N.; B.S., Fla. State U., 1959; M.B.A., U. Santa Clara, 1965; m. Judith Fern Jones, Oct. 3, 1959; children—Theresa, John, Michael. Program accountant Honeywell, Inc., St. Petersburg, Fla., 1959-60, 62-63; cost accountant, personnel dir. Pinellas County, Clearwater, Fla., 1961; subcontract cost adminstr. Lockheed Missile and Space Co., Sunnyvale, Calif., 1963-66; bus. control mgr. advanced communications tech. R.C.A., Camden, N.J. and N.Y.C., 1966-68; audit/resident mgr. Harry C. Pratt & Co., C.P.A.'s, Bradenton and Palmetto, Fla., 1968-69; with Norton and Troup, C.P.A.'s, St. Petersburg, Fla., 1969—; dir. Kraft Color Labs., Inc., St. Petersburg, 1970—; trustee MFL Housing, Inc.; mem. Pinellas County Contractors Pre-Qualification Bd. Trustee Martin Luther Found.; bd. dirs. Pinellas County chpt. Fla. Conservative Union, 1st Christian Fin. Corp., Faith Halfway House; fin. adviser Blessed Trinity Cath. Ch., 1969—. Served with USN, 1950-55. C.P.A., Fla. Mem. Am., Fla. insts. C.P.A.'s, Am. Accounting Assn., Greater St. Petersburg C. of C., Delta Tau Delta, Beta Alpha Chi, Alpha Kappa Psi. Republican. Clubs: St. Petersburg Exchange, St. Petersburg Yacht; K.C. Home: 1 Beach Dr Apt 1102 Saint Petersburg FL 33701 Office: 4620 Central Ave Saint Petersburg FL 33711

NORTON, PHILIP LESTER, paper mill ofcl.; b. Kankakee, Ill., July 28, 1940; s. Charles Lester and Lois Janet (Warren) N.; student public schs., Kankakee; m. Jayne Rea Cahan, Sept. 14, 1963. Apprentice printer Adcraft Advt., Kankakee, 1957-62; asst. supr. printing dept. Gen. Foods Corp., Kankakee, 1962-64; offset pressmen Carton Plant, Olinkraft Corp., Kankakee, 1964-66, leadman, 1966-68, printing foreman, 1968-70, gen. plant foreman, 1970-75, plant supr., 1975-77, asst. customer service mgr., West Monroe, La., 1977—. Mem. Am. Mgmt. Assn., Graphic Arts Tech. Found., Litho-Tech. Forum, TAPPI Paper Makers Assn. Methodist. Clubs: Highland Country, Cleanwater Bass, Bass Masters. Office: PO Box 488 West Monroe LA 71291

NORTON, RICHARD W(ILEY), retail security exec.; b. Ennis, Tex., Oct. 3, 1933; B.A. in Advt., Arlington State Coll., 1953; m. Charlsye Ann Schwalbe, May 16, 1952; children—Jennifer, Elaine. Dep., Dallas County, Tex., 1954; mem. Irving (Tex.) Police, 1955-56; lt. Mesquite (Tex.) Police, 1956-58; security dir. Montgomery Ward, Dallas, 1958-61; corp. security dir. Sanger-Harris div. Federated Dept. Stores, Dallas, 1961—; instr. So. Meth. U., Tex. A&M U., Tex. U. Recipient Courageous Citizen award City of N.Y., 1978. Mem. Am. Soc. Indsl. Security (cert. appreciation 1968-77), Cert. Protection Profls. (chmn. Norht Tex. chpt. 1970-71), Internat. Acad. Criminology, Police Law Soc., Am. Polygraph Assn., Internat. Assn. Chiefs of Police, Tex. Assn. Polygraph Examiners, Nat. Assn. Chiefs of Police, Nat. Retail Merchants Assn. (vice chmn. bd.). Democrat. Presbyterian. Conbtr. articles to profl. jours. Office: 303 N Akard St Dallas TX 75221

NORTON, ROBERT DEAN, SR., indsl. cons.; b. Mobridge, S.D., June 6, 1932; s. Bertram Albert and Anna Bertine (Nordahl) N.; A.A., Troy State U., 1974, B.S. magna cum laude, 1975, M.S., 1977; m. Carolyn Maude Ahern, June 23, 1954; children—Robert Dean, David Richard, Thomas Michael. Enlisted in USAF, 1950; air transp. supt. Takhli Royal Thai Air Base, Thailand, 1966-67; maintenance support officer SAC, Offutt AFB, Nebr., 1967-68; air transp. supt., Clark Air Base, Philippines, 1968-70, Charleston AFB, S.C., 1970-71; research analyst Air Force Data Systems Design Center, Air Force Hdqrs., Pentagon, Washington, Air Force Logistics Mgmt. Center, Gunter AFB, Ala., 1971-79; ret., 1979; indsl. cons., Tacoma, 1979—. Counselor, Ala. Pardons and Paroles Halfway House, 1976—; vol. counselor and probation officer Family Ct. and Montgomery County Youth Facility, 1977-79. Decorated Meritorious Service medal, Air Force Commendation medal with 3 oak leaf clusters; recipient Mil. Airlift Command Superior Performance award, 1970. Mem. Soc. Logistics Engrs., Am. Personnel and Guidance Assn., Am. Rehab. Counseling Assn. Republican. Lutheran. Pioneer, Mode Decision Facilitator for Air Force shipments. Home: 9317 70th St Tacoma WA 98498

NORTON, SAMUEL STUART, JR., elec. engr.; b. Birmingham, Ala., May 31, 1933; s. Samuel S. and Thelma (Thomas) N.; B.S. in Elec. Engring., Auburn U., 1960; m. Shirley Hall, Jan. 31, 1958; children—Sheryl Renee, Stacy, Stuart Lee. Test engr. Atlanta div. Ga. Power Co., 1960-63, sr. engr. protective relaying, 1963-66; sr. engr. substa. design control Ala. Power Co., 1966-71, sr. engr. substa. design-preliminary plans and estimates, 1971-75, asst. mgr. substa. design control, 1975—. Chmn. bldg. and grounds com. PTA, Pleasant Grove, Ala., 1972-74; pres. Band Boosters, 1977. Served with U.S. Army, 1954-56. Registered profl. engr., Ala. Mem. Power Engring. Soc. of IEEE. Home: 504 2d Way Pleasant Grove AL 35127 Office: Alabama Power Co 600 N 18th St Birmingham AL 35202

NORVELL, JOHN EDMONDSON, III, anatomist; b. Charleston, W.Va., Nov. 18, 1929; s. John Edmondson, Jr., and Mathilde L. (Wood) N.; B.S., Morris Harvey Coll., 1953; M.S., W.Va. U., 1956; Ph.D., Ohio State U., 1966; m. Rosemary Justice, June 2, 1962; children—John Edmondson, Scott Justice. Instr. dept. biology Johnstown (Pa.) Coll., U. Pitts., 1956-60; asst. prof. dept. biology Otterbein Coll., Westerville, Ohio, 1960-62; asst. instr. dept. anatomy Ohio State U., Columbus, 1962-65; asst. prof., asso. prof. dept. anatomy Med. Coll. Va., Richmond, 1966-76; prof., chmn. dept. anatomy Oral Roberts U., Tulsa, 1976—; chmn. State Anatomical Bd. Okla., 1978—. Named one of outstanding tchrs. of year by freshman class Sch. Medicine, Med. Coll. Va., 1970, 71, 72, 75. Mem. Am. Assn. Anatomists, Assn. Anatomy Chmn., Soc. for Neurosci., So. Soc. Anatomists, Transplantation Soc., Okla. Acad. Sci. Contbr. articles to profl. publs. Office: 7777 S Lewis Ave Tulsa OK 74171

NORVILLE, RICHARD GEROW, aluminum mfg. co. exec.; b. Mobile, Ala., Jan. 23, 1917; s. Thomas Peyton and Annie Angela (Gerow) N.; B.M.E., Ala. Poly, Inst., 1939; B.E.E., Auburn U., 1940; m. Kathleen Taylor Brannen, Nov. 8, 1941; children—Angela (Mrs. Philip Peemelin), Richard Gerow. Mech. engr. Alcoa Smelting plant, 1940-42, project engr. new def. plant corp. smelters, 1942-46, staff mech. engr. to smelting div. mgr., Pitts., 1946-47, project engr. Point Comfort (Tex.) Smelter, 1948-49, chief mech. engr. constrn., 1949, chief plant engr. Point Comfort Works, 1949-52, asst. mech. supt. Alcoa (Tenn.) smelter, 1953-63, div. engr. Tenn. Albron ingot and smelting plants, 1964-69, div. mech. engr. smelting, 1969—; asso. prof. mech. engring. Auburn U., 1939-40. Pres. Alcoa Elementary PTA, 1955, high sch., 1961, Blount County PTA, 1962; chmn. Our Lady of Fatima Cath. Ch., 1965-70, bd. dirs., 1965—; chmn. Alcoa Bd. Bldg. Code Appeals, 1968—. Served to 2d. lt., C.E. U.S. Army, 1940-45. Registered profl. engr., Pa., Tex. Mem. ASME, Tau Beta Pi. Clubs: Alcoten Mgmt. (pres. 1967), Toastmasters (pres. Alcoa 1952—), Kiwanis (dir. Alcoa 1959—), K.C. (dist. dep. 1959). Home: 1772 Nobel St Alcoa TN 37701 Office: Box 9128 Hall Rd Alcoa TN 37701

NORVILLE, WARREN RAYMOND, author; b. Mobile, Ala., Oct. 20, 1923; s. Thomas Peyton and Angela (Gerow) N.; student Millsaps Coll., 1943-44; B.S., Spring Hill Coll., 1947; m. Harriet Durant, May 22, 1948; children—Harriet Durant, Warren Raymond, Mary Jane. Owner, mgr. Norville Constrn. Co., Mobile, 1948-50; civilian employee, trainee U.S. Air Force, Mobile, 1955; specifications writer C.E., U.S. Army, Mobile, 1956-58; mgr. Norville Bros. Ins. Agy., Inc., Mobile, 1958-70; owner, operator Warren Norville Marine Cons., Mobile, 1970—. Served with USN, 1943-46, 50-52. Mem. Authors Guild. Author: Storm Jib and Running Sails, 1970; Celestial Navigation Step by Step, 1973; Coastal Navigation Step By Step, 1975; (with Gerald Hoffman and Fred Townsend) Nautical Education for Offshore Extractive Industries, 1977; Death Tide, 1979. Home: 327 Dalewood Dr Mobile AL 36608

NORWOOD, THOMAS LOCKE, engr.; b. Siler City, N.C., Jan. 5, 1952; s. Archie Franklin and Margaret Elizabeth (Campbell) N.; B.S. in Chem. Engring., N.C. State U., 1975; m. Mary Phylis Williamson, May 18, 1974; 1 dau., Emily Elizabeth. Phys. sci. aide EPA, Research Triangle Park, N.C., 1973-74; chem. engr. Northrop Services, Research Triangle Park, 1975-76; asst. field mgr. Rockwell Internat., Research Triangle Park, 1976-77; tech. writer Xonics Inc., Research Triangle Park, 1977-78; plutonium process engr. Rockwell Internat., Richland, Wash., 1978-79; staff engr. Acurex, Inc., Morrisville, N.C., 1979—. Mem. Am. Inst. Chem. Engrs., Raleigh Amateur Radio Soc. Republican. Lutheran. Contbr. articles to profl. jours. Home: PO Box 661 Cary NC 27511 Office: Rt 1 Box 423 Morrisville NC 27560

NOVACK, JOHN MICHAEL, architect; b. Denver, Dec. 11, 1941; s. John Michael and E. Jane (Butler) N.; B.Arch., U. Colo., 1965; m. Janis Ellen Beeson, Dec. 30, 1978; 1 son, Kurtis Riordan. Prin., in charge design and planning C.F. Murphy Assos., Chgo., 1965-75; propr. Urban Design Group, Architects & Planners, Tulsa, 1975—. Mem. AIA. Democrat. Designer Hilton Hotel, parking facility and other Phase II projects O'Hare Airport, Chgo., 1966-73; Kennedy Atrium Bldg., Tulsa, 1979. Home: 1500 S Frisco St Tulsa OK 74119 Office: Urban Design Group Architects & Planners 320 S Boston St Suite 1102 Tulsa OK 74103

NOVAK, ALBERT JOHN WITTMAYER, electronic parts mfg. co. exec.; b. Grand Rapids, Mich., Mar. 30, 1921; s. Albert Joseph and B. Joan (Wittmayer) N.; A.B. magna cum laude in physics, Harvard, 1941; postgrad. Mass. Inst. Tech., 1954, Case Inst. Tech., 1946-48; m. Patricia M. Henline, Mar. 25, 1950; children—Patricia Joan, Albert John Wittmayer, David Bruce, Loren Lee. Indsl. engr. RCA, Camden, N.J., 1941-42; sales mgr. Brush Instruments div. Clevite Corp., Cleve., 1946-53, gen. mgr. Tex. div., Houston, 1955-57; mgr. sales and engring. Ansonia Wire & Cable Co., Ashton, R.I., 1957-59; gen. mgr. Electronics div. Hoover Co., Balt. and Pompano Beach, Fla., 1959-65; founder, pres., chmn. bd. Novatronics, Inc., Pompano Beach, 1965—; chmn. bd. Novatronics East Inc., Dover, N.H., Novatronics South, Inc., Ft. Lauderdale, Fla.; founder, chmn. bd. Novatronics of Can., Ltd.; dir. Fla. Coast Bank of Broward County. Chmn. Broward Indsl. Bd., 1967, 75, now dir.; chmn. Broward County Community Relations Commn., 1974, Center for Pastoral Counseling and Human Devel.; v.p. United Way of Broward County, 1975—; pres. Fort Lauderdale (Fla.) Symphony Assn., 1970-72; bd. dirs. South Fla. Edn. Center, 1963—, pres., 1970—; mem. Fla. Gov.'s Mgmt. Adv. Council Health and Rehab. Services, 1977—, Dist. X Health and Rehab. Services Adv. Council, 1977—, also others. Served to lt. comdr. USNR, 1942-46. Named Industrialist of Year Pompano Beach, 1966-67, 75-76; recipient Outstanding Service award Nat. Elec. Mfrs. Assn., 1967; named Small Bus. Person of 1977. Mem. South Fla. Mfg. Assn. (pres. 1966-67), Pompano Beach C. of C., Greater Ft. Lauderdale C. of C. (dir. 1973—), Opera Guild, Phi Beta Kappa. Club: Harvard of Broward County (pres. 1976, 77). Home: 2500 NE 48th Ln Fort Lauderdale FL 33308 Office: 500 SW 12th Ave Pompano Beach FL 33061

NOVAK, DONALD C., hosp. adminstr.; b. New Brunswick, N.J., July 7, 1934; s. Chester Novak and Stacia Novak; B.S., U. W.Va., 1957; M.B.A., Xavier U., 1967; m. Janet Lee Mallonee, Aug. 24, 1957; children—Stacie Lee, Laura Lee, Kara Lee. Public relations dir. St. Peter's Gen. Hosp., New Brunswick, 1962-64; adminstrv. resident, asst. adminstr. Methodist Evang. Hosp., Louisville, 1966-68; asst. adminstr. Mercy Hosp., Altoona, Pa., 1968-69, Washington Hosp. Center, Washington, 1969-73; adminstr. George Washington U. Med. Center, Washington, 1973-78; adminstr., chief exec. officer Talmadge Meml. Hosp.-Med. Coll. Ga., Augusta, 1978—; adj. asst. prof. George Washington U., 1977-78; mem. E. Central Ga. Health Systems Agy. Task Force on Hosps. Served with U.S. Army, 1959-62. Mem. Am. Coll. Hosp. Adminstrs., Ky. Hosp. Assn., D.C. Hosp. Assn. (pres. 1978), Am. Hosp. Assn., Ga. Hosp. Assn. Office: 1120 15th St Augusta GA 30912

NOW, JOSEPH R., athletic dir.; b. Mercer County, Ohio, June 23, 1938; s. James W. and Naomi M. Now; B.S., Heidelberg Coll., Tiffin, Ohio, 1960; M.S., Ind. U., 1964; diploma phys. edn., Springfield (Mass.) Coll., 1973; m. Evelyn A. Aller, Apr. 22, 1962; children—Jodi, Lori, Susan, Karen. Secondary tchr., coach Lima (Ohio) Public Schs., 1960-63; dir. recreation Borough of Wyomissing (Pa.), 1964-69; asst. prof. phys. edn., athletic coach Albright Coll., 1964-69; dir. phys. edn. Children's Study Home, Springfield, 1972; coordinator student teaching Springfield Coll., 1971-72; supt. student teaching Kent (Ohio) State U., 1973-77; dir. athletics, chmn. health, phys. edn. and safety Glenville (W.Va.) State Coll., 1977—. Mem. AAHPER, AAUP, Nat. Assn. Intercollegiate Athletics Athletic Dirs. Assn., Nat. Assn. Coll. Dirs. Assn., W.Va. Assn. Health, Phys. Edn. and Recreation, W.Va. Intercollegiate Athletic Assn., Nat. Basketball Hall of Fame (life). Lutheran.

NOWICKI, MICHAEL, hosp. adminstr.; b. Munich, Germany, Oct. 25, 1952; s. John Stanley and Kay N.; came to U.S., 1953, naturalized, 1958; B.A. in Polit. Sci., Tex. Tech. U., 1974; M.A. in Health Care Adminstrn., George Washington U., 1977. Adminstrv. asst. Lubbock (Tex.) Med. Center Hosp., 1973-74; adminstrv. analyst Valley Med. Center of Fresno, Calif., 1977, dir. profl. services, 1978; lectr. Inst. for Profl. Devel., St. Mary's U., Moraga, Calif., 1977-78; process mgr. Humana, Inc., Louisville, 1979—. Mem. Am. Coll. Hosp. Adminstrs., Am., Western hosp. assns., Health Care Execs. Central Calif., Hosp. Fin. Mgmt. Assn., Pi Sigma Alpha, Sigma Tau Delta, Eta Sigma Phi. Contbr. analysis in field.

NOWLIN, JAMES ROBERTSON, state legislator; b. San Antonio, Nov. 21, 1937; s. William Forney and Jeannette (Robertson) N.; B.A., Trinity U., 1959, M.A., 1962; J.D., U. Tex. at Austin, 1963. Admitted to Tex. bar, 1963, U.S. Supreme Ct. bar, 1969; atty. Kelso, Locke & King, San Antonio, 1963-65; asso. legal counsel U.S. Senate Labor and Pub. Welfare Com., Washington, 1965-66; individual practice, San Antonio, 1967—; mem. Tex. Ho. of Reps., 1967-71, 73—. Instr. Am. history and govt. evening div. San Antonio Coll., 1964-65, 71-73. Served with U.S. Army, 1959-60. Mem. Am., D.C., Tex., San Antonio bar assns., Am. Judicature Soc., San Antonio C. of C. Author: A Political History of the Texas Prison System, 1962; Legislative Ethics, 1973. Home: 254 Tuxedo Ave San Antonio TX 78209 Office: 8918 Tesoro Dr Suite 545 San Antonio TX 78217

NOWLIN, WILLIE, JR., ins. exec.; b. Florence, S.C., Feb. 14, 1933; s. Willie and Fannie N.; B.S., S.C. State Coll., 1955; m. Sarah Deas, June 1, 1963; children—Leon, Brenda, Andre, Kervin, Sharon. Agt., N.C. Mut. Life Ins. Co., Washington, 1958-63, staff mgr., Chgo., 1963-65, staff mgr., Washington, 1966-70, dist. mgr., Charleston, 1971-75, dist. mgr., Goldsboro, N.C., 1976—. Bd. dirs. Goldsboro Downtown Assn. Commn.; mem. Goldsboro Park and Recreation Com. Mem. Wayne County Underwriters Assn., Nat. Underwriters Assn., Goldsboro Credit Union (dir.). Democrat. Baptist (Sunday sch.

tchr. 1976—). Mason. Home: 303 MacArthur St Goldsboro NC 27530 Office: 301 S James St Goldsboro NC 27530

NOZAKI, MASAKO, pharmacologist; b. Eniwa, Hokkaido, Japan, Mar. 24, 1941; came to U.S., 1974; s. Kennosuke and Sumi Nozaki; Ph.D., Hirosaki U. Med. Coll., 1976. Vis. asso. Nat. Inst. on Drug Abuse Addiction Research Center, Lexington, Ky., 1974-77; research asso. dept. pharmacology Cornell U. Med. Coll., N.Y.C., 1977-78; vis. asst. prof. dept. pharmacology U. Ky. Coll. Medicine, Lexington, 1978-79, med. research scientist, 1979—. Mem. AAAS, Sigma Xi. Contbr. articles to profl. publs. Home: 3640 Bold Biddler Dr Lexington KY 40502 Office: Dept Pharmacology U Ky Coll Medicine Lexington KY 40536

NUDO, RUDOLPH, plant engr.; b. Greenvale, N.Y., June 2, 1925; s. Rocco and Angela (Fillippone) N.; Cert. in Communications, U. Fla., 1965; student Fla. Jr. Coll., 1975-76; m. Elizabeth Hommerson, Jan. 30, 1949; children—Alida, Rudolph, Gerrit, Eva, Leesa. Operating engr. L.I. Lighting Co., 1948-54; watch engr. Gibbs Corp., Jacksonville, Fla., 1954-55, tech. supr., Dominican Republic, 1955-57; terminal supt. The Tex. Co., Dominican Republic, 1957-59; chief engr. Pan Am Air, U.S. Missle Program, Caribbean and S. Am. range, 1959-61; asst. bldg. engr. City of Jacksonville, 1961-67; dir. plant services Univ. Hosp., Jacksonville, 1967-76; dir. engring. Meml. Hosp. of Jacksonville, 1976—. Mem. planning and grounds com. Central YMCA, Jacksonville, 1964-71; pres. Southside Estates Civic Assn., 1965; adv. com. Fla. Jr. Coll., 1975-76. Served with USAAF, 1943-46. Named Engr. of Year, Fla. Hosp. Engrs. Assn., 1977; cert. plant engr., Fla. Mem. Nat. Assn. Power Engrs. (nat. treas. 1971-72), Fla. Hosp. Engrs. Assn. (pres. 1975-76), Am. Inst. Plant Engrs., Am. Soc. Hosp. Engrs., Fla. Hosp. Engrs. Assn., Southeastern Assn. Hosp. Engrs., Am. Assn. of Advancement of Med. Instrumentation, ASHRAE, Nat. Fire Protection Assn. Club: Ga. Bulldog Alumni. Home: 9751 Lily Rd Jacksonville FL 32216 Office: 3625 University Blvd S Jacksonville FL 32216

NUEHRING, ELAINE MAE, sociologist; b. Butte, Mont., Feb. 20, 1943; s. Emil Leonard and Mae E. (Lynchehan) Fredrickson; B.A., Gonzaga U., 1965; M.S.W. (NIMH fellow), U. Wis., Madison, 1967; Ph.D. (NIMH fellow), Fla. State U., 1975; m. Ronald E.E. Nuehring, Sept. 26, 1967. Clin. social worker Mendota State Hosp., Madison, 1967-69; research asso. Inst. for Social Research, Fla. State U., Tallahassee, 1973-76; sr. cons. Behavioral Sci. Research Inst., Coral Gables, Fla., 1976—; asso. prof. social work Barry Coll., Miami, Fla., 1976—, Coll. Profl. Devel. grantee, 1976-78; mental health cons. to fed., state agys., 1973—. Mem. instl. rev. com. Miami Center for Dialog. Mem. Am. Sociol. Assn., So. Sociol. Soc., Soc. for Study Social Problems, Council on Social Work Edn., Tropical Audubon Soc. (exec. bd.). Contbr. articles to profl. jours.; editorial reviewer Jour. Social Service Research, 1978—. Home: 6290 S W 86th St Miami FL 33143 Office: Barry Coll 11300 N E 2d Ave Miami FL 33161

NUESCH, FREDERICK CHARLES, sports journalist, ednl. adminstr.; b. Malvern, Ark., July 10, 1938; s. James Charles and Charlene (Hudson) N.; B.A., Henderson State U., 1960; M.A., U. Mo., 1962; m. Joan Isabel Howe, Dec. 27, 1969. Sportswriter, Ark. Democrat, Little Rock, 1962-63; sports editor Malvern (Ark.) Daily Record, 1962, Paris (Tex.) Daily News, 1964-68; sports info. dir., publs. dir., journalism instr. Tex. A&I U., Kingsville, 1968—. Served with Air N.G., 1963-69. Elected to Nat. Assn. Intercollegiate Athletics Hall of Fame, 1979, also recipient numerous All-America certs., awards of merit, 1969—; recipient numerous All-America certs. Coll. Sports Info. Dirs. Am., 1968—. Mem. Coll. Sports Info. Dirs. Am. (sec.), Nat. Assn. Intercollegiate Athletics, Sports Info. Dirs. Assn. (mem. exec. bd.), Football Writers Am., U.S. Basketball Writers Assn., U.S. Track and Field Writers Assn., Tex. Sports Writers Assn. Roman Catholic. Club: Rotary Internat. Editor numerous Tex. A & I U. athletic brochures, programs. Home: 1601 Santa Cecelia St Kingsville TX 78363 Office: Tex A & I U Campus Box 114 Kingsville TX 78363

NUGENT, CLARENCE JOHN, acctg. co. exec.; b. New Orleans, Mar. 7, 1943; s. Arnold Joseph and Lillian Marie (Babin) N.; B.S. in Acctg., Southeastern La. U., 1972; m. Karen Leggio, Feb. 3, 1979; children by previous marriage—Joseph, Samuel, Phyllia. Internal auditor Maison Blanche, New Orleans, 1966-67; office mgr. Celotex Corp., New Orleans, 1969-70; asst. bus. mgmt. mgr. Internat. Auto Sales & Service, Inc., New Orleans, 1970-72; bus. mgr. Robertson Porsche-Audi, New Orleans, 1972-73; office mgr. Ernst & Whinney, C.P.A.'s, New Orleans, 1973—. Adv. coordinator Jr. Achievement, New Orleans; tribal chief YMCA Indian Guides, New Orleans. Served with La. Air N.G., 1966-72. Mem. Nat. Assn. Accts., Adminstrv. Mgmt. Soc., Inst. Internal Auditors. Democrat. Roman Catholic. Home: 4405 Chenet St Metairie LA 70001 Office: 920 One Shell Sq New Orleans LA 70139

NUGENT, DONALD YORK, photographer; b. Oklahoma City, Apr. 24, 1939; s. Leroy Homer and Elma Anne (Brundage) N.; B.S., La. State U., 1967; student U. New Orleans, 1958-60; With Sch. Geosci., La. State U., Baton Rouge, 1967—, now sci. research photog. specialist; founder, mgr. DNP Visual Products Co. Pres., Apt. Renters Civic Assn. Tigerland, Baton Rouge, 1972-76. Served with U.S. Army, 1961-64. Recipient Silver bowl award Photography Council La., 1972, 74, honor award Univ. Profl. Photographers Assn., 1975. Mem. Am., La. profl. photographers assns., Fortier Astronomy Club (pres.). Democrat. Contbr. articles to profl. and popular mags. Home: 12414 Parkknoll Ave Baton Rouge LA 70816 Office: Geology Bldg La State U Baton Rouge LA 70803

NUGENT, JOHN HILLIARD, fin. exec.; b. Paterson, N.J., Aug. 20, 1944; s. James Joseph and Jacqueline Anne (Storms) N.; B.A., Columbia U., 1970; M.S., Southeastern U., 1978; postgrad. Internat. Inst. Advanced Studies, 1979; m. Mary Elizabeth Maher, June 3, 1967; 1 dau., Jill Frances. Sr. personal trust adminstr. Chase Manhattan Bank, N.Y.C., 1970-71; analyst U.S. Dept. Army, Washington, 1971-72; sr. auditor Fin. Gen. Bankshares, Inc., Washington, 1972-73; corp. auditor Internat. Trust Co. of Liberia, Monrovia, 1973-75; asst. treas. Liberian Services, Inc., N.Y.C., 1975-76; v.p., dir. Adminstrv. Control Services, Inc., Reston, Va., 1976—; chmn. bd. Strategic Planning & Research Corp.; mem. faculty dept. acctg. No. Va. Community Coll. Served with USMC, 1962-66. Mem. Nat. Assn. Accountants, Computer Security Inst. Home: 2327 Archdale Rd Reston VA 22091 Office: 1870 Michael Faraday Dr Reston VA 22090

NUGENT, OLAN ANDREW, mgmt. analyst; b. Shanghai, China; s. Olan and Tatianna Nugent; B.S. in Bus. Adminstrn., U. Ark., 1971, M.S., 1979; m. Nancy Carol Vogel, June 16, 1973; 1 dau., Allison Carol. Service officer Ark. Vets. Service Office, 1972-73; community services coordinator Ark. Dept. Social and Rehab. Services, Little Rock, 1973-74, planning specialist services for youth, 1974-76; supr. policy analysis sect. Ark. Dept. Human Services, 1978—. Served with USAF, 1970-72. Mem. U. Ark. Alumni Assn. Baptist. Club: Arkansas Razorback. Home: 6311 Osage North Little Rock AR 72116 Office: Dept Human Services 1408 Donaghey Bldg Little Rock AR 72201

NULL, DONALD MORLEY, JR., neonatologist; b. Abington, Pa., Jan. 17, 1944; s. Donald Morley and Mildred Dorothy (Prifold) N.; student U. Pitts., 1961-65; M.D., W.Va. U., 1969; m. Kathy Rae Briggs, Nov. 19, 1974; children—Mildred Dorothy, JulieAnn. Intern, Wilford Hall Med. Center, San Antonio, Tex., 1969-70; commd. 2d lt. USAF, advanced through grades to lt. col., 1977; gen. med. officer Rhein Main AFB, Germany, 1970-73; resident in pediatrics Columbus Childrens Hosp., 1973-75; fellow in neonatology Wilford Hall Med. Center, San Antonio, 1975-77, staff neonatologist, 1977—; clin. asst. prof. pediatrics U. Tex. Health Sci. Center, San Antonio, 1978—. Diplomate Am. Bd. Pediatrics, Am. Bd. Neonatology. Mem. Bexar County Med. Soc. Republican. Contbr. articles to profl. jours. Home: 6735 Peachtree St San Antonio TX 78238 Office: Wilford Hall USAF Med Center Lackland AFB San Antonio TX 78238

NUMAJIRI, SATORU SAM, organic chemist; b. Mito-shi, Ibaraki, Japan, Feb. 22, 1930; s. Misao and Katsumi (Tsunoda) N.; came to U.S., 1952, naturalized, 1973; B.A., Harding Coll., 1955; B.A., Tex. Christian U., 1959, M.A., 1963; m. Ayako Kato, Dec. 6, 1962; 1 son, Akira S. Research fellow 1959-63, jr. scientist Alcon Labs., Inc., Ft. Worth, 1963-64, scientist, 1964-65, section head, 1965-68, sr. scientist 1968-73, group leader, 1973-74, sr. scientist, head mfg. and chem. synthesis, 1974-75, head chem. synthesis, 1975-76, sr. scientist, head of medicinal chemistry, 1976—. Recipient leadership award, Ft. Worth Central YMCA, 1961, appreciation award, Lena Pope Home, Ft. Worth, 1962, recognition award, City of Ft. Worth, 1975; cert. profl. chemist. Fellow Am. Inst. Chemists; mem. Am. Chem. Soc. (div. medicinal chemistry), AAAS, Pharm. Soc. of Japan, U.S. Judo Fed. Mem. Ch. of Christ. Clubs: Ft. Worth Judo (pres.), Tex. Judo Black Belt Assn. Researcher and patentee in field. Home: 2821 Southgate Dr Fort Worth TX 76133 Office: Alcon Labs 6201 S Freeway PO Box 1959 Fort Worth TX 76101

NUNEZ, EUGENE CLAUDE, oil mktg. exec.; b. Chgo., Nov. 11, 1923; s. Alcide Patrick and Hilda Freda (Badaghn) N.; student bus. adminstrn. Tulane U., 1957; cert. maritime law U. New Orleans, 1976; m. Shirley Marie Giglio, Sept. 27, 1941; children—Susan Nunez (Mrs. William Belsom), Eugene C. With Shell Oil Co., 1952-72; pres., chief exec. officer Plaquemines Oil Sales Corp., Belle Chasse, La., 1972—; pres., chief exec. officer H.R. & W. Marine Corp., New Orleans, 1972—; pres., chief exec. officer Hi Le. Nu. Inc., Belle Chasse, 1976—; mng. partner Gene's Towing Co., New Orleans, 1975—. Served with USNR, 1942-46. Decorated Purple Heart medal. Notary Public. Mem. Nat. Oil Jobbers Council (mem. steering com.), La. Oil Marketers Assn. (past pres., mem. exec. com.). Democrat. Roman Catholic. Mason. Clubs: Lakewood Country, Offshore Marine Assn., Westbank Petroleum, Mercedes Benz Club of Am., Green Wave, Stadium, Superdome. Office: 110 Belle Chasse Hwy S Belle Chasse LA 70037

NUNEZ, LOYS JOSEPH, educator; b. New Orleans, Mar. 18, 1926; s. Loys J. and Claylia C. (Coleman) N.; B.S. in Chemistry, Tulane U., 1947; M.S., La. State U., 1955, Ph.D., 1960. With Cities Service Refining Corp., Research and Devel. Co., Lake Charles, La., 1947-53, 59-60; supr. phys. research sect. Jefferson Chem. Co., Austin, Tex., 1960-61; asso. prof. chemistry U. Tenn. Center for Health Scis., Memphis, 1971—. Fulbright fellow U. Tübingen (W. Ger.), 1957-58. Mem. Am. Chem. Soc., AAAS, N.Y. Acad. Scis., AAUP, Am. Public Health Assn., Tenn. Acad. Scis. Roman Catholic. Asso. editor Forum for Advancement Toxicology, 1979—. Office: 847 Monroe St Room 237 Memphis TN 38163

NUNEZ-PORTUONDO, RICARDO, investment co. exec.; b. N.Y.C., June 9, 1933; s. Emilio and Maria (Garcia) N.-P.; LL.D., U. Havana, 1958; postgrad. in law U. Fla., 1975; m. Dolores Maldonado, Sept. 7, 1963; children—Ricardo José, Emilio Manuel, Eduardo Javier. Press attache Cuban embassy, Madrid, 1958-59; editor The American, Madrid, 1959-60; writer, editor news dept. Latin Am. div. USIA, Miami and Washington, 1961-71; exec. v.p. Gramco Sales Ltd., dir. Gramco Mgmt. Ltd., Nassau, Bahamas, 1968-71; chmn. bd. NBS Devel. Inc., Miami, Fla., 1971—, also dir.; dir. Numar Enterprises Inc., Miami Nat. Bank; nat. dir. Cuban Refugee Program, Washington and Coral Gables, Fla., 1975-77; pres. Central Investment Trust Corp., 1977—. Trustee, mem. founders council Fla. Internat. U.; mem. citizens bd. U. Miami Latin Am. Adv. Bd.; mem. planning com. City of Coral Gables; mem. council of advisors Fla. State U. System. Clubs: Met. (N.Y.C.); Lyford Cay (Nassau); Big Five (Miami). Home: 675 Solano Prado Coral Gables FL 33156 Office: 200 Country Club Rd Fort Lauderdale FL 33326

NUNGESSER, WILLIAM AICKLEN, food co. exec.; b. New Orleans, Sept. 30, 1929; s. Harold John and Isabel (Aicklen) N.; m. Ruth Amelia Marks, May 5, 1956; children—Nancy, William, Eric, Heidi. Founder, Algiers Canning & Sales Co., New Orleans, 1954—, also pres., chmn. bd.; pres., chmn. bd. Gen. Marine Catering Co., Inc., 1971—; chmn. bd. Nunco Food Co., Inc. Pres. Adv. Com. on Fisheries; treas. Orleans Parish Republican Polit. Action Com., 1972-76; bd. dirs. Met. New Orleans Crime Commn., 1974-76, Internat. House, New Orleans; mem. La. Republican Central Com.; treas. Dave Treen for Gov. Served with USMCR, 1950-53. Mem. U.S. C. of C., New Orleans Tourist Commn., La. Shrimp Assn. (dir.) La. Restaurant Assn., New Orleans Hotel Assn. Home: 5740 Durham Dr New Orleans LA 70114 Office: 300 Homer St New Orleans LA 70114

NUNLEY, GLORIA JEAN, nurse, med. adminstr.; b. Portsmouth, Ohio, Mar. 23, 1927; d. Robert Newton and Nellie (Hensley) N.; diploma King's Daus. Hosp. Sch. Nursing, Portsmouth, Va., 1948; B.S., U. Cin., 1961; M.S., Ohio State U., Columbus, 1965. Staff nurse supervision VA Hosp., Dublin, Ga., 1950-53, Durham, N.C., 1953-55, staff nurse, head nurse supervision, Chillicothe, Ohio, 1955-67, asst. chief nursing service, Gulfport, Miss., 1967-70, chief nurse trainee, N.Y.C., 1970-71, chief nursing service, Livermore, Calif., 1971-74, Ann Arbor, Mich., 1974-76, chief nursing service VA Med. Center, Gainesville, Fla., 1976—; adj. asst. prof. nursing U. Mich., Ann Arbor, 1974-76, U. Fla., Gainesville, 1976—. Active ARC. Recipient Exceptional Service award, adminstr. VA, 1969. Mem. Am. Nurses Assn., Nat. League Nursing, Res. Officers Assn., Ohio State U. Alumni Assn., Assn. Mil. Surgeons, Am. Hosp. Assn., Fla. Soc. Nursing Service Adminstrs. Office: VA Med Center (118) Archer Rd Gainesville FL 32602

NUNN, SAM, U.S. senator; b. Perry, Ga., Sept. 8, 1938; s. Samuel Augustus and Elizabeth (Canon) N.; A.B., Emory U., 1960, LL.B., 1962; m. Colleen O'Brien, 1964; children—Mary Michelle, Samuel Brian. Lawyer; farmer; mem. Ga. Ho. of Reps. from Houston County, 1968-72; U.S. senator from Ga., 1972—. Chmn. Mid Ga. Planning Com., 1967-68. Served with USCG, 1959-60. Recipient Dist. Atty.'s award as outstanding legislator Ga. Dist. Attys. Assn., 1972; named One of Five Outstanding Young Men in Ga., Jr. C. of C., 1971. Mem. Perry C. of C. (dir. 1964-65, pres. 1964), Emory U. Com. of 100, Bryon Honor Soc., Phi Delta Theta. Methodist. Office: 3241 Dirksen New Senate Office Bldg Washington DC 20510*

NUNNALLY, JOHN WARREN, JR., computer programming exec.; b. Stillwater, Okla., July 14, 1951; s. John Warren and Marian Jane (Songer) N.; B.S., Harding Coll., 1973; M.S., Fla. State U., 1975; m. Kathryn Faye Green, Aug. 6, 1972; children—John Matthew, Adrienne Joy. With Ellers & Reeves Cons. Engrs., Memphis, 1974; computer programmer Harding U., Searcy, Ark., 1975, dir. computer programming, 1976—; teaching asst. Fla. State U., 1975. Ch. of Christ. Home: 129 Western Hills Searcy AR 72143 Office: Sta A PO Box 890 Searcy AR 72143

NUNNALLY, STEPHENS WATSON, civil engr., educator; b. Gadsden, Ala., Nov. 30, 1927; s. John Marshall and Mae Louise (Watson) N.; B.S., U.S. Mil. Acad., 1949; M.S., Northwestern U., 1958, Ph.D., 1966; m. Joan Marie Arel, May 29, 1957; children—Stephens Watson, Janine, John. Commd. 2d lt. C.E., U.S. Army, 1949, advanced through grades to lt. col., 1966, asst. dist. engr. Canaveral Dist., 1969-70; dir. logistics U.S. Army Engring. Command Europe, 1966-69; force engr. U.S. Forces, Dominican Republic, 1966; ret., 1970; asst. prof. civil engring. U. Fla., Gainesville, 1971-75; asso. prof. civil engring. N.C. State U., Raleigh, 1975—; cons. in field. Decorated Legion of Merit. Mem. Am. Soc. for Engring. Edn. (vice chmn. constrn. engring. com. 1979—), ASCE (constrn. research council 1977—), Am. Rd. and Transp. Builders Assn. (dir. ednl. div. 1978—), Soc. Am. Mil. Engrs. Republican. Episcopalian. Club: North Hills. Author: Managing Construction Equipment, 1977; Construction Methods and Management, 1980. Contbr. articles to tech. publs. Home: 4406 Pitt St Raleigh NC 27609

NUREYEV, JAIMÉ LEE, computer and parapsychocybernetics researcher; b. Phila., Mar. 11, 1956; d. Ellis Harold and Jeanette (Bachrach) Tollin; student U. Chgo., 1972-74; m. Steven Fishman, Oct. 11, 1976; children—Arielle Haze, Michael Evan. Dir. artificial intelligence computation div. Neuronics, Inc., Chgo., 1972-74; dir. computer and cybernetics research METRA Corp., Pompano Beach, Fla., 1975, 77—; asso. to James Schlesinger Sec. Def., Washington, 1975-76. Mem. Southeast Computer Conf., Internat. Soc. Applied Cybernetics. Democrat. Jewish. Club: Woodlands Country and Golf. Artwork shown Sokolsky Galleries, Miami.

NUTSCH, JAMES GEORGE, historian; b. Morrowville, Kans., Jan. 6, 1930; s. George August Nutsch and Marvel Bessie (Burton) Nutsch Stoker; B.S. in Social Scis., Kans. State U., 1952; M.A. in History, U. Kans., 1965, Ph.D. in Russian and Soviet History, 1968; m. Donna Rae Dewey, July 26, 1959; children—James George, II, Jana Sue. Commd. 2d lt. U.S. Air Force, 1952, advanced through grades to capt., 1958; flight crew mem. Nfld. and U.S., 1955-61; resigned regular commn., 1961; field underwriter N.Y. Life Ins. Co., Washington, Kans., 1961-63; asst. prof. history Calif. State Col., San Bernardino, 1968-71; asso. prof. N.C. Agrl. and Tech. State U., 1971—. Kans. State U. Inst. Citizenship scholar, 1948-49; U. Kans. scholar, 1964-65. Mem. So. Conf. Slavic Studies, Am. Hist. Assn., Phi Kappa Phi, Phi Alpha Theta, Lambda Chi Alpha. Democrat. Unitarian. Contbr. to Modern Ency. Russian and Soviet History, also articles to profl. publs.; editor: Readings in Contemporary Problems, Issues, and Values, 1974. Home: 505 Rocky Knoll Rd Greensboro NC 27406 Office: Dept History NC A&T State U Greensboro NC 27411

NUTT, REX LYNN, phys. therapist; b. Tipton, Okla., June 30, 1933; s. Lacy Brackston and Nell (Smith) N.; B.S., Abilene Christian U., 1956; m. JoAnn Ewing, Aug. 28, 1953; children—Robert Lynn, Ronald Lee. Staff phys. therapist Gonzales Warm Springs Found. Crippled Children, 1955-57, 59; asst. ednl. adminstr. Hermann Sch. Phys. Therapy, 1959-62, ednl. adminstr., 1962-65; dir. phys. therapy Spring Branch Meml. Hosp. Houston, 1964—; pres. Houston Phys. Therapy Service, Inc., 1969—. Mem. bd. African Christian Hosp. Found.; bd. dirs. Herod Sch. Parent Tchrs. Orgn., 1967-69; mem. subcom. edn. of schs. and orgn. Am. Heart Assn., 1972; mem. adv. com. spl. services. Houston Indsl. Sch. Dist., 1975-78; mem. Tex. State Bd. Phys. Therapy Examiners. Served with USAF, 1957-59. Mem. Am. Phys. Therapy Assn., Tex. Phys. Therapy Assn., Am. Coll. Sports Medicine. Mem. Churches of Christ.

NUTT, WELLS EDWARD, paper co. exec.; b. Hensley, Ark., June 25, 1939; s. William Edward and Lois Ernestine (Wells) N.; B.S. with honors in Chem. Engring., U. Miss., 1962, M.S. in Chem. Engring., 1963; m. Mary Ellen Woodburn, June 2, 1962; children—Douglas Allen, Sandra Diane, Angela Karen. Process engr. Union Camp Corp., Savannah, Ga., 1963-64, supr. process engring., 1965-74, overall asst. supt. pulp/power, 1975-77, tech. dir. unbleached paper and board div., 1977—. Mem. Am. Inst. Chem. Engrs., TAPPI (past chmn. Southeastern sect.), Miss. Registered Profl. Engrs. Baptist. Mem. editorial bd. TAPPI mag., 1980—. Home: 721 Windsor Rd Savannah GA 31406 Office: Union Camp Corp PO Box 570 Savannah GA 31402

NUTTER, CHARLES WILLIAM, city ofcl.; b. Kansas City, Mo., Sept. 17, 1937; s. Charles Perry and Eleanor (Haldeman) N.; student Rice U., 1956-58; B.B.A., Tulane U., 1961; m. Dawna Beth Eukel, Oct. 18, 1974. Dist. exec. New Orleans council Boy Scouts Am., 1962-67; classification analyst New Orleans Civil Service Commn., 1967-69; asst. ops. adminstr. New Orleans Adminstrv. Office, 1969-71; dir. recreation City New Orleans, 1971-78, supt. Parkway and Parks Commn., 1978—. Troop scoutmaster New Orleans council Boy Scouts Am., 1963-74, v.p. exec. bd., 1977—. Bd. dirs. Greater New Orleans Fedn. Chs., 1970-72, La. Nature Center. Served to 2d lt. AUS, 1961-62. Recipient Silver Beaver award Boy Scouts Am., 1971; Nat. Disting. Community Service award Nat. Recreation and Park Assn., 1979; Monte M. Lemann award La. Civil Service League, 1979. Mem. SAR. Episcopalian (vestryman). Club: Rotary (New Orleans). Home: 6325 Clara St New Orleans LA 70118 Office: 2829 Gentilly Blvd New Orleans LA 70122

NUTTER, JAMES IRVING, conveyor belting mfg. co. exec.; b. Lawrence, Mass., Sept. 4, 1935; s. Lester Cyril and Gertrude Agnes (Fraughton) N.; student Mass. Inst. Tech., 1953-54; B.S., Northeastern U., 1959; M.S., Iowa State U., 1961, Ph.D., 1963; m. Marion Nancy Hennion, Aug. 29, 1959; children—Michael, Charles, Elizabeth, Laura. Teaching asst. chem. engring. Iowa State U., Ames, 1959-63; research engr. W.R. Grace Co., Clarksville, Md., 1963, 64-68; supr. kinetics group Marshall Space Flight Center NASA, Huntsville, 1963-64; supr. process devel. Lord Corp., Erie, Pa., 1968-70; tech. dir. Robin Industries, Cleve., 1970-75; mgr. research and devel. Scandura Inc., Charlotte, N.C., 1975—. Served to capt. Signal Corps, U.S. Army, 1953-64. Uniroyal scholar, 1957-59; Dow Chem. Co. fellow, 1961—, Ford Found. grantee, 1961-63. Mem. Am. Chem. Soc., ASTM, N.Y Acad. Scis., Sigma Xi. Researcher adsorption, permeation and diffusion processes polymers; patentee in field. Home: 8033 Rising Meadow Matthews NC 28105 Office: PO Box 30606 1801 N Tryon St Charlotte NC 28230

NYBERG, KENNETH LANGELAND, educator; b. St. Paul, Feb. 15, 1947; s. R. Gerald and Katherine (Langeland) N.; B.A., St. Cloud U., 1969; M.A., U. Maine, 1971; Ph.D., U. Utah, 1973; m. Janice Lynn Nyberg, Aug. 2, 1969; 1 dau., Kjerstie. Grad. teaching asso. U. Maine, Orono, 1969-71, grad. teaching and NDEA fellow U. Utah, Salt Lake City, 1971-73; asst. prof. sociology Tex. A. and M. U., 1973—, coordinator Office Human Resources Research and Devel., 1978—; cons. Mitre Corp., NIMH, Nat. Inst. Drug Abuse, Indian Health Service. Nat. Inst. Drug Abuse grantee, 1977-79; NIMH grantee, 1978-79; U.S. Dept. Agr. grantee, 1978-81; Tex. Commn. Alcoholism grantee, 1979-80; NDEA fellow, 1971-73. Mem. Am.

Sociol. Assn., Soc. Study Social Problems, Rural Sociol. Soc., Assn. Rural Mental Health, Soc. Advancement Social Psychology, Southwestern Sociol. Assn. Office: Office Univ Research Tex A and M U College Station TX 77843

NYE, NANCY HAMILTON, univ. adminstr.; b. Harnett County, N.C., May 6, 1937; d. Robert W. and Vernie S. Hamilton; A.B., U. N.C., 1959; A.A., Campbell Coll., 1957; m. Kemp Battle Nye, Oct. 9, 1960; children—Plummer Battle, Scarlett Elizabeth. Tchr., Raleigh City Schs., 1959-60; typist dept. biochemistry U. N.C., Chapel Hill, 1967-74, acctg. technician, 1974-77, bus. mgr., 1977—. Pres., Episcopal Churchwomen, Chapel of the Cross, Chapel Hill, N.C., 1974-75. Democrat. Episcopalian. Office: Biochemistry Dept U NC Chapel Hill NC 27514

NYMAN, ARNOLD SIGURD, mfg. co. exec.; b. Chgo., Apr. 7, 1938; s. Sigurd and Thyra Olivia (Tholen) N.; student Monmouth Coll., 1957-58, Ill. Inst. Tech., 1959-60; m. Carol Sue Wiltse, Oct. 8, 1960; children—Scott Arnold, Mark Allen. Mgr. prototype engring. Chgo. Rawhide Co., Elgin, Ill., 1960-69; v.p. Robert G. Regan Co., Joliet, Ill., 1969-73; plant mgr. Burgess-Norton Mfg. Co., Geneva, Ill., 1973-76, Claremore, Okla., 1976—. Mem. industry adv. com. Claremore Coll.; bd. dirs. Rogers County United Way, 1978-80, drive chmn., 1979. Recipient plaque United Way, 1979. Mem. Claremore C. of C. (chmn. govt. affairs com. 1978). Republican. Clubs: Elks, Rotary (chmn. 75th anniversary com. 1980) (Claremore). Home: Route 3 Box 248 Claremore OK 74017 Office: PO Box 1S8 Claremore OK 74017

OAKES, DONALD WESLEY, mfg. co. exec.; b. Sebastian, Tex., Aug. 10, 1938; s. Charles Ernest and Juanita Dale (Bray) O.; student Brazosport Coll., 1974-75, S.W. Motivation Inst., 1972-73, Tex. A. and M. U., 1966-71; m. Marlene C. Willy, Mar. 23, 1979; children by previous marriage—Donna, Dinah. With Offshore Exploration Co., Houston, 1963-65; owner, mgr. Brazoria (Tex.) Farm & Ranch Supply, 1965-69; mgr. personnel and safety Gulf States, Inc., Freeport, Tex., 1970—; mgr. Merit Contractors subs. Gulf States, Inc., Freeport, 1979—. Pres., Brazosport Safety Council; active Boy Scouts Am., 1969; pres. Jr. Achievement, 1977; mem. Indsl. Comml. Electricity Curriculum adv. com., Brazosport Coll., Clute, Tex., 1975-79; precinct chmn. Dem. Party, 1976-77; del. Dem. State Conv., 1976. Served with U.S. Army, 1959-62. Named Outstanding State V.P., Jr. C. of C., 1974. Mem. Asso. Builders and Contractors, Tex. Safety Assn., Soc. to Prevent Blindness, Nat. Assn. Builders and Contractors (bd. dirs.), Am. Mgmt. Assn. Democrat. Baptist. Home: 121 Poppy St Lake Jackson TX 77566 Office: 304 N Gulf Blvd Freeport TX 77541

OAKES, HERBERT CHARLES, diversified industries exec.; b. Manhattan, Kans., Nov. 17, 1927; s. Herbert Lafern and Loraine Lillian (Coppedge) O.; B.S., U. Okla., 1950; M.B.A., Harvard U., 1955; m. Suzanne Vinson, Aug. 16, 1951; children—Bailie Vinson, Herbert Charles. Treas., Vinson Steel & Aluminum Co., Dallas, 1955-59; pres. Southwestern Match Co., Ft. Worth, 1957-60; chmn. bd. Nashville State Bank (Ind.), 1961; pres. Johnston Bearing & Supply Co., Houston, 1961-66, Republic Drug Co., Denver, 1967-70; chmn. bd. R.B. Clouse Lumber Co., Houston, 1971—; pres. Cigarette Sales Inc., Houston, 1975—, Sundries Wholesale Inc., Houston, 1975—; dir. Valhi Inc., Dixie Rice Agrl. Co., Republic Rice Mill Inc. Mem. nat. bd. field advisers SBA, 1955-61. Served to lt. (j.g.) USNR, 1950-53; Korea. Mem. Nat. Assn. Tobacco Distbrs., Phi Dalta Theta. Republican. Methodist. Clubs: Warwick, Houston Racquet, Toastmasters, Rotary. Home: 1736 Milford St Houston TX 77098 Office: 1601 Live Oak St Houston TX 77003

OAKES, JAMES LOYS, JR., mgmt. cons.; b. Lake Charles, La., Nov. 15, 1946; s. James Loys and Doris Dean (Morgan) O.; B.S. in Indsl. Engring., Ga. Inst. Tech., 1969, M.S. in Indsl. Mgmt., 1976; m. Margaret Ina Lane, Mar. 4, 1972; 1 dau., Liisa Catherine. System engr. Med. Coll. Ga., 1969-70; co-founder Ga. Hosps. Shared Services, Atlanta, 1974-76; regional mgr. Spectra Med. Systems, Atlanta, 1976—; preceptor Ga. Inst. Tech. Sch. Health Systems. Elder, Morningside Presbyn. Ch., Atlanta, 1976—, ch. treas., 1978—. Served as officer USAF, 1970-74. Decorated Air Force Commendation medal. Mem. Hosp. Mgmt. Systems Soc., Am. Inst. Indsl. Engrs. Office: 1175 Peachtree St Atlanta GA 30361

OAKLEY, T. J., gambling co. exec.; b. Washington, Feb. 23, 1948; s. A. John and M. Theresa O.; B.S., Georgetown U., 1975. Pres., chmn. Gamble, Inc., Palm Beach, Fla., 1979—; inventions cons., product devel., mktg. Served with USN, 1966-70. Author: Strategies of Exotic Multiple Pari-Mutuel Betting, 1979. Invented the Bettors Box (computer). Office: Gamble Inc PO Box 1950 West Palm Beach FL 33402

OAKLEY, WILLIAM MELVIN, pharmacist, hosp. ofcl.; b. Durham, N.C., May 16, 1945; s. William Melvin and Mabel Christine (Robbins) O.; B.S., U. N.C., 1968; children—Loren Elizabeth, William Melvin III. Dir. pharmacy Craven County Hosp., New Bern, N.C., 1968—, dir. pharmacy services, 1978—; practitioner, instr. U. N.C. Sch. Pharmacy, Chapel Hill, 1975—. Mem. adv. com. N.C. Drug Commn., 1974-76; past bd. dirs. Craven County Cancer Soc. Eckerds scholar, 1963-68. Mem. N.C. Soc. Hosp. Pharmacists (past pres., chmn. bd. dirs. 1975, dir. 1972, 73, 75, 79-80), N.C. Pharm. Assn., Am. Soc. Hosp. Pharmacists, Am. Pharm. Assn. Democrat. Methodist. Club: New Bern Golf and Country. Home: 3515 Canterbury Rd New Bern NC 28560 Office: Craven County Hosp 2000 Neuse Blvd New Bern NC 28560

OATES, CARL EVERETTE, lawyer; b. Harlingen, Tex., Apr. 8, 1931; s. Joseph William and Grace (Watson) O.; student Schreiner Inst., 1948-49, Tex. A. and I. Coll., 1949-50; B.S., U.S. Naval Acad., 1955; LL.B., So. Meth. U., 1962; m. Janet Carolyn Stone, Jan. 1, 1977; children—Michael George, Carol Jan, Carl William, Patricia Janet. Admitted to Tex. bar, 1962; mem. firm Akin, Gump, Hauer & Feld (and predecessor firm), Dallas, 1962—; dir. Valley View Bank, Dallas, Equitable Bank, Dallas. Bd. dirs. Park Cities YMCA, 1973, Kiwanis Wesley Dental Center, Dallas; chmn. adv. council Dallas Health and Sci. Mus., 1972-75, trustee, 1975—. Served as pilot USN, 1955-59. Mem. Am., D.C., Tex., Dallas bar assns., Barristers, N. Dallas C. of C. (dir., exec. com. 1973), Sons of Republic of Tex., Delta Theta Phi. Presbyn. (deacon). Kiwanian (past pres.), Mason (32 degree). Clubs: Northwood, Dallas Country, Dallas, Engineers; Argyle (San Antonio); Home: 7256 Ashington Dr Dallas TX 75225 Office: 2800 Republic Nat Bank Bldg Dallas TX 75201

OATES, WILLIAM HALL, civilian army ofcl.; b. White Plains, Ky., Feb. 4, 1916; s. Racean Clea and Ruby Lee (Allen) O.; student Ordnance Auto. Sch., 1942; m. Dec. 5, 1975; children—Catherine Lee, William Robert. Foreman, Gen. Motors Truck & Coach Co., Pontiac, Mich., 1936-39; commd. pvt., U.S. Army, 1939, advanced through grades to lt. col., 1961, ret., 1961; civilian, chief ops. review div. Milan (Tenn.) Army Ammunition Plant, 1961-71, civilian ops. officer, 1979—. Mem. VFW. Democrat. Roman Catholic. Clubs: Milan Golf and Country, Elks, Moose. Home: 215 Tanglewood St Milan TN 38358 Office: Milan Army Ammunition Plant Milan TN 38358

O'BANION, JOHN WILLIAM, surgeon; b. Ennis, Tex., Sept. 25, 1925; s. John William and Minnie (Wilkinson) O'B.; B.S. with honors, So. Methodist U., 1954; M.D., Southwestern Med. Sch., U. Tex., Dallas, 1954; m. Eleanor Ruth Mendenhall, Nov. 23, 1949; children—Patricia, Kathleen, John III. Intern, Riverside County (Calif.) Hosp., 1954-58; resident in surgery Parkland Hosp., Dallas, 1955-59, teaching fellow, 1958-59; practice medicine specializing in surgery, Snyder, Tex., 1959—; staff surgeon Cogdell Meml. Hosp., Snyder, 1959-61, chief surgery, 1961—, chief med. staff, 1965-68, sec. med. staff, 1968—. Mem. bldg. com. Snyder Christian Ch., 1959-77; mem. Snyder Zoning Bd., 1973-76. Served with U.S. Army, 1944-48, 51. Recipient Recognition award City of Garland, Tex., 1973; diplomate Am. Bd. Surgery; Am. Cancer Soc. grantee, 1958-59. Fellow A.C.S.; mem. Am., Tex. med. assns., Colo. Basin Med. Soc. (pres. 1976-77), Am. Abdominal Surgery Assn., Am. Soil Conservation Soc., Alpha Omega Alpha, Kappa Sigma. Home: 2717 32d St Snyder TX 79549 Office: Cogdell Center Clinic Snyder TX 79549

O'BANNON, EMILY BELLE WOOD, pianist, educator; b. Woodville, Miss., Oct. 28, 1906; d. Carroll Lee and Bennie Edwin (McCearley) Wood; student Newcomb Coll., Tulane U., 1933-34, Meissner Inst. Music, Chgo., 1937-39, New Orleans Conservatory Music; m. Harris Lynwood O'Bannon, Aug. 19, 1927; children—Ernest L., Douglas W., Emily O'Bannon Benson, Martha O'Bannon Rickerson. Mem. piano faculty Ridgewood Prep. Sch., Metairie, La., 1950-72; tchr. piano, Metairie, 1950—. Mem. Nat. Music Tchrs. Assn., Music Educators Nat. Assn. (sec. S. Central div.), La. Music Tchrs. Assn. (pres., award 1970), Met. Piano Tchrs. Assn. (pres. 1978—), New Orleans Music Tchrs. Assn. (past pres.), Nat. Guild Piano Tchrs. (faculty, adjucator, Hall of Fame), Nat. Fedn. Music Clubs, Am. Coll. Musicians (Hall of Fame). Democrat. Baptist. Home: 1708 Belmont Pl Metairie LA 70001

O'BARR, WILLIAM MCALSTON, anthropologist, educator; b. Sylvania, Ga., Dec. 1, 1942; s. William J. and Mary Walter (Clark) O'B.; B.A., Emory U., 1964; M.A., Northwestern U., 1966, Ph.D., 1969; student UCLA, 1963, U. Ams., 1964, U. Mich., 1973; m. Jean Fox, Sept. 4, 1965; children—Claire Anne, Emily Catherine. Research sociologist USPHS, Atlanta, 1964—; asst. prof. anthropology Duke U., Durham, N.C., 1969-74, asso. prof., 1974-79, prof., 1979—; cons., lectr. in field. Recipient award for disting. teaching Duke U. Alumni Assn., 1972; research grantee NSF, 1974-76, NIMH, 1967-69, Wenner Gren Found., 1966, 70. Mem. Am. Anthrop. Assn., Linguistic Soc. Am., Royal Anthrop. Inst. Gt. Britain and Ireland, Am. Ethnological Soc., African Studies Assn., Internat. African Inst. Author: Survey Research in Africa, 1973; Tradition and Identity in Changing Africa, 1974; Language and Politics, 1976; Student Africanists's Handbook, 1976. Office: Dept Anthropology 104 North Bldg Duke U Durham NC 27706

OBÉN, JOSÉ MANUEL, counselor, educator; b. Santurce, P.R., Nov. 3, 1952; s. Marcelo José and María Esperanza (Martínez) O.; B.A., U. P.R., 1975; M.Ed., Cath. U. P.R., 1977. Counselor U. Ponce (P.R.), 1977-78, Cath. U. P.R., Ponce, 1978—, asst. dir. continued edn., evening session, 1979—; active convs., workshops, seminars, confs. Mem. Am. Personnel and Guidance Assn., P.R. Personnel and Guidance Assn., Circulo Orientadores Nivel Universitario, Assn. for Specialists in Group Work, Assn. for Humanistic Edn. and Devel. Roman Catholic. Clubs: Rotary, Guayama Nautic. Contbr. research in field. Home: Cond El Senorial Apartamento 1006 Salud #10 Ponce PR 00731 Office: Counseling Center Catholic University of PR Ponce PR 00731

O'BENAR, JOHN DEMARION, neurophysiologist; b. Chgo., Apr. 10, 1943; s. Jack J. and Geraldine Agnes (Light) O'B.; B.A., Cornell Coll., 1964; M.S., U. Ill., 1968, Ph.D., 1971; postdoctoral fellow U. Calif., Berkeley, 1971-72; m. Mary Caroline Teal, June 18, 1970. Surg. research technician Billings Hosp., U. Chgo., 1960-66; research physiologist U.S. Naval Weapons Support Center, Crane, Ind., 1972-75, Naval Aerospace Med. Research Lab., Pensacola, Fla., 1976-78; chemist Army Aviation Center, Ft. Rucker, Ala., 1978—; faculty U. Ill., Urbana, 1968-69; NIH traineeship Marine Biol. Lab., Woods Hole, Mass., 1967-68; cons. U.S. Navy Project Sanguine, 1976-78. USPHS traineeship, 1967-68; NIH fellow, 1969-71; Nat. Eye Inst. fellow, 1971-72; NIH traineeship, 1971-72. Recipient Best Group in Chgo. award Downbeat mag., 1961. Mem. AAAS, Am. Optometric Assn. (sci. fellow), Sigma Xi, Phi Sigma. Club: L.C.O. Neurophilosophy (pres. 1969-70). Contbr. articles in field to profl. jours. Home: 5 Richardson Dr Daleville AL 36322 Office: DIO/S&S US Army Aviation Center Fort Rucker AL 36362

OBENSHAIN, WILEY SHACKFORD, III, lawyer; b. N.Y.C., Jan. 1, 1946; s. Wiley Shackford and Barbara Jeanne (Williams) O.; A.B., U. N.C., 1967; J.D., U. Ga., 1970; m. Gretchen Zane Williams. Admitted to Ga. bar, 1970; asso. mem. firm Fulcher, Hagler, Harper & Reed, Augusta, 1970-73, partner, 1973—. Mem. Am., Augusta bar assns., State Bar Ga. (exec. council of young lawyers sect. 1975—, gov. 1979—), Am. Judicature Soc., Young Lawyers Club Augusta (exec. com. 1974-75, v.p. 1976-77, pres. 1977-78), Ga. Def. Lawyers, Assn. Ins. Attys., Phi Delta Phi, Sigma Nu (nat. div. comdr.). Democrat. Clubs: Capital City (Atlanta); Augusta Country; Exchange of Richmond County (dir. 1979—). Mem. editorial bd. Ga. State Bar Jour., 1969-70. Home: 913 Littleton St Augusta GA 30904 Office: 520 Greene St Augusta GA 30903

OBERGFELL, SANDRA CHESHIRE, educator; b. Indpls., Feb. 24, 1947; d. Frank Taylor and Edna (Malicoat) Cheshire; B.A., Butler U., 1968; M.A., Ind. U., 1970, Ph.D., 1974; m. Philip Kent Obergfell, July 27, 1968; 1 dau., Stephanie Christina. Asso. instr. French, Ind. U., Bloomington, 1968-72; exchange lectr. of English, U. Lille, France, 1972-73; lectr. French Marian Coll., Indpls., 1974; asst. prof. Purdue U., West Lafayette, Ind., 1975-76; asst. prof. French, Wabash Coll., Crawfordsville, Ind., 1976-79; asst. prof. French, Mars Hill (N.C.) Coll., 1979—. Mem. Mediaeval Acad., MLA, Internat. Studies Assn., Am. Council Teaching Fgn. Langs., Am. Assn. Tchrs. French, Ind. Fgn. Lang. Tchrs. Assn., Kappa Delta Pi, Phi Kappa Phi, Alpha Lambda. Methodist. Home: Box 645 Mars Hill NC 28754 Office: Dept Modern Fgn Langs Mars Hill Coll Mars Hill NC 28754

OBERNDORFER, JAMES EDWIN, retail trade exec.; b. Harlingen, Tex., Jan. 27, 1934; s. Arnold Edwin and Ethel O.; student Tex. A&M U., 1952-55; m. Thelma Synatschk, Aug. 23, 1958; children—Doris, Claire, Helen Ruth, James Arnold. Draftsman, Dale S. Cooper and Assos., Houston, 1955-62; designer Exxon Co., Houston, 1962-69; sr. mech. engr. Recognition Equipment Inc., Irving, Tex., 1969-71; project mgr. Sears Roebuck and Co., Dallas, 1971—. Mem. Tex. Retail Fedn. Subcom. on Energy, 1976-79; mem. Mo. Task Force on Energy Codes for Bldgs., 1977-79. Served with U.S. Army, 1957. Mem. ASHRAE. Republican. Lutheran. Home: 3819 Echo Brook Ln Dallas TX 75229 Office: Sears Roebuck and Co 1000 Belleview St Dallas TX 75295

O'BERRY, LISTON CHARLES, govt. planner; b. Jacksonville, Fla., May 27, 1946; s. Liston Cleveland and Susan Mildred O'B.; B.S.E.E., U. Fla., 1969. Elec. engr. Martin Marietta Corp., Orlando, Fla., 1969-71; facility engr. Boeing Aerospace Co., Kennedy Space Center, Fla., 1971-73; pollution control engr. City of Jacksonville Civil Service, 1973-75; pres. Pollution Control Co., Jacksonville, 1975-78; planner U.S. Fed. Govt./USN, U.S. Naval Air Sta., Jacksonville, 1978—. Mem. Methodist Youth Group. Served with U.S. Armed Forces, 1964-66. H. Harold Hart Meml. scholar; EPA scholar. Mem. IEEE (sec.), Soc. Mil. Engrs., NEA, Am. Inst. Planners, Am. Mgmt. Assn. Democrat. Baptist. Club: Spanish Lang. (pres.). Author: Your Subconscious Mind.

OBERT, GENE MADALENE SAULSBURY (MRS. PAUL M. OBERT), nurse; b. Oklahoma City; d. Claude and Elizabeth (Young) Saulsbury; R.N., St. Anthony Hosp. Sch. Nursing, 1947; B. Nursing Arts, Okla. U., 1947; m. Paul M. Obert, Apr. 27, 1947; children—Mary (Mrs. James Leita), Jeanne, Paul, Elizabeth, Catherine. Supr. nurses Wesley Hosp., Oklahoma City, 1948; directress nursing McCurdy Hosp., 1948-50; dir. Red River Med. Center Corp., Victoria, Tex., 1968-72. First aid instr. ARC, 1958—. Bd. dirs. Fine Arts Assn., Victoria. Republican. Roman Catholic. Mem. Tex. Mem. Profl. Nurses Assn., Victoria-Calhoun-Goliad Tri-County Med. Aux. Club: Victoria Country. Home: 303 Tampa St Victoria TX 77901 also Rockport TX Office: Box 3784 Victoria TX 77901

OBERT, PAUL MICHAEL, physician; b. Apache, Okla., Apr. 25, 1924; s. Joseph M. and Mary (Fitter) O.; B.Sc., Stanford, 1944; M.D., U. Okla., 1947; m. Gene Salisbury, Apr. 27, 1947; children—Mary, Jeanne, Paul, Elizabeth. Catherine. Intern, St. Anthony Hosp., Oklahoma City, 1947-48; practice gen. medicine, Purcell, Okla., 1948-50, resident U. Hosp. Oklahoma City, 1950-52, cancer research fellow, 1951-52; practice medicine, specializing in pathology Victoria, Tex., 1956—; chief staff McCurdy Hosp., Purcell, 1949-50; asst. prof. pathology U. Okla. Sch. Medicine, Oklahoma City, 1952-56; attending pathologist VA Hosp., Oklahoma City, 1953-56; pathologist-in-chief USPHS Hosp., Galveston, Tex., 1953-56; asst. prof. pathology U. Tex. Sch. Medicine, Galveston, 1954-57; dir., owner Regional Med. Lab., Victoria; pres. Citizen Profl. Bldg.; dir. Dr. Obert's Diagnostic Lab., Victoria; chief pathologist, dir. labs. Citizens Meml., Calhoun County Meml. Victoria, Nightengale hosps., all 1956—; cons. pathologist Cuero, Wagner, Yorktown, Palacious City hosps., 1956—; dir. labs. Meml. Hosp., Beeville, Tex., 1963—; vis. pathologist M.D. Anderson Hosp., 1962—; dir. lab Goliod County Hosp., 1963—, Kleberg Hosp., Kingsville, Tex., 1968—, Edna. Hosp., El Campo Hosp.; forensic pathologist South Tex., 1968; bd. dirs. Victoria Med. Center, 1963—, pres., 1969—; bd. lab. cons. Carizo Springs, Youens, Eagle Lake hosps.; bd. dirs. Tex. Rehab. Center, Gonzales, 1970—, Tex. div. Cancer Soc., South Tex. Health Systems Agy.; trustee, med. dir. South Tex. Regional Blood Bank. Trustee Victoria Ednl. Found.; bd. dirs. Victoria Fine Arts Assn. Served with AUS, 1943-46; comdr., USPHS, 1953-56. Diplomate Am. Bd. Pathology. Fellow Coll. Am. Pathologists, Am. Soc. Clin. Pathologists; mem. Am., Tex., Victoria-Calhoun-Coliad County med. assns., Internat. Acad. Pathology, Tex. Assn. Pathologists, N.Y. Acad. Scis., AAAS, Soc. Exptl. Biology and Medicine, Am. Assn. Blood Banks. Roman Catholic. Clubs: Victoria Country, Serra (trustee). Contbr. articles to profl. publs. Home: 303 Tampa Dr Victoria TX 77901 Office: 2602 Houston Hwy Victoria TX 77901

OBEY, FAYE DORIS, nurse; b. Birmingham, Ala., June 26, 1946; d. Paul William and Mildred Lillian Bailey; B.S., Prarie View A. and M. U., 1969; M.S., Tex. Woman's U., 1973; children—Sheena Faye, Michelle Yvette. Staff nurse Methodist Hosp., Houston, 1969-71, neurol. nurse specialist, 1971; staff charge nurse VA Hosp., Houston, 1971-73, head nurse neuro-surg. ward, 1973-76, nursing instr. nursing edn., 1976—; faculty continuing edn. dept. Tex. Woman's U., Coll. Nursing, Houston, intermittently 1976—.

O'BRIEN, FRANCIS WILLIAM, educator; b. Willmar, Minn., July 27, 1917; s. John Edward and Lauretta Catherine (Carroll) O.; B.A., Gonzaga U., 1941, M.A., 1942; M.A., Boston Coll. Grad. Sch., 1952; Ph.D., Georgetown U., 1956; certificat d'Etudes Françaises, U. de Poitier, Tour, France, 1961; postgrad. Harvard U., 1952-53, U. Geneva (Switzerland), 1962, U. de Marseilles (France), 1965-66. Instr. polit. sci. Georgetown U., Washington, 1956-61; instr. law U. Fribourg (Switzerland), 1961-62; instr. polit. sci. Seattle U., 1963-65; instr. law U. Lausanne (Switzerland), 1966-67, Aix-en-Provence Inst., France, 1965-66; prof. govt. Emory U., Atlanta, 1967-68; prof., chmn. dept. polit. sci. Rockford (Ill.) Coll., 1968-71; dir. acad. programs Hoover Presdl. Library, West Branch, Iowa, 1972-75; Tower prof. polit. sci. Southwestern U., Georgetown, Tex., 1975—. Mem. Georgetown Community Theater. Relm Found. grantee for research in Switzerland, France, 1965-67; Earhart grantee for research in Ireland, 1970. Hoover Assn. grantee for Wilson-Hoover papers, 1971-72. Mem. Am. Polit. Sci. Assn. Republican. Roman Catholic. Author: Justice Reed and the First Amendment, 1958; Was Justice Done? Historic Trials on Review, 1971; Divided Ireland, The Roots of the Problem, 1971; The Hoover-Wilson Wartime Correspondence, 1974; Two Peacemakers in Paris, 1978; Contbr. numerous articles to profl. jours. Home: 1703 Elm St Georgetown TX 78626 Office: Southwestern Univ Georgetown TX 78626

O'BRIEN, JAMES MATHEW, ednl. adminstr.; b. Rockford, Ill., Apr. 13, 1924; s. Charles Mathew and Adah Mae (Breeding) O'B.; B.S., Iowa State U.; M.S., Troy State U., also postgrad.; m. Patricia Ann Smith, May 4, 1958; 1 son, James Mathew. Joined U.S. Air Force, 1942, advanced through grades to lt. col.; course dir. Officer Electronics Sch., Keesler AFB, Miss., 1964-66; chief editorial-document research Aerospace Studies Inst., Montgomery, Ala., 1967-69; dep. chief of staff for communications electronics Air U., Maxwell AFB, Ala., 1969-70; ret., 1970; cons. and tchr. Montgomery (Ala.) Schs., 1970-71; asst. to v.p. Troy State U., Montgomery, 1971-73; chmn. sci. dept., tchr. Glenwood Sch., Phenix City, Ala., 1973-78; headmaster Lee Acad., Auburn, Ala., 1978—; ednl. cons. Ch. organist; asst. scoutmaster Boy Scouts Am. Decorated Bronze Star, Air medal; medal of Honor (Vietnam); certified tchr. and headmaster, Ala.; advanced class radio amateur. Mem. Soc. Tech. Communications (sr.), Ala. Pvt. Sch. Tchrs. Assn. (pres. dist. VI, dist. rep. to state assn.), Dadaelian Soc., Ala. Acad. Scis., Ala., Nat. sci. tchrs. assns., Ala. Headmasters Assn., Armed Forces Communications Electronics Assn., Air Force Assn. Club: K.C. (4 deg). Author air force manuals. Home: 3801 Brookwood Dr Phenix City AL 36867 Office: 2307 E Glenn Ave Auburn AL 36830

O'BRIEN, JAMES MICHAEL, pathologist; b. Newton, Iowa, Nov. 14, 1936; s. Earle James and Berl Keithel (Braley) O'B.; B.S., U. Notre Dame, 1959; M.D., Creighton U., 1963; m. Sara Jane Ryan, Aug. 4, 1962; children—Mary Katherine, James Richard, Mary Margaret, Mary Sarajane, Kevin Earle. Intern, St. Joseph's Hosp., Omaha, 1936-64, resident, 1964-67; resident St. Francis Hosp., Wichita, Kans., 1967-68; practice medicine specializing in pathology, 1968—; asso. dir. pathology John Peter Smith Hosp., Fort Worth, 1970-76, dir., 1976—; clin. asso. prof. pathology U. Tex. Southwestern Med. Sch., Dallas, 1972—. Served to maj. M.C., USAF, 1968-70. Diplomate Am. Bd. Pathology. Fellow Coll. Am. Pathologists, Am. Soc. Clin. Pathologists; mem. Tarrant County Med. Soc., Am., Tex. med. assns., Tex. Soc. Pathologists. Roman Catholic. Club: Rotary. Home: 3805 Lands End Fort Worth TX 76109 Office: 1500 S Main St Fort Worth TX 76104

O'BRIEN, JOHN EDWARD, mktg. exec.; b. St. Louis, May 30, 1929; s. Edward Joseph and Norma Mary (Yaw) O'B.; A.B., Notre Dame U., 1952; m. Marilyn Jean O'Brien, Aug. 15, 1953; children—Mary Pat, Cathryn Jean, Lynn Marie. Asso. advt. mgr. paper div. Procter & Gamble, 1954-67; v.p., dir. Campbell-Muthun Advt. Agy., Chgo., 1967-72; v.p. mktg., dir. Calgon Consumer Products, Pitts., 1972-77; pres. NoNonsense Fashions, Inc., Greensboro, N.C., 1977—. Served with USNR, 1952-54. Republican. Roman Catholic. Home: 3023 Lake Forest Dr Greensboro NC 27408 Office: PO Box 77057 Greensboro NC 27407

O'BRIEN, JOHN FRANCIS, dermatologist; b. Bklyn., Sept. 21, 1940; s. John Joseph and Margaret Bradford (Preston) O'B.; B.S., Fordham U., 1962; M.S., U. Conn., 1964; M.D., N.Y. Med. Coll., 1968; m. Virginia Catherine Leith, Sept. 9, 1967; children—Kristen Elizabeth, Matthew John. Rotating surg. intern Flower and Fifth Ave hosps., N.Y.C., 1968-69; resident in dermatology N.Y. Med. Coll.-Met. Hosp. Center, N.Y.C., 1969-70, 72-74; individual practice medicine specializing in dermatology Staten Island, N.Y., 1974-78; asst. clin. prof. dermatology N.Y. Med. Coll.-Met. Hosp. Center, 1975-78, Emory U. Sch. Medicine; clin. asst. DeKalb Gen. Hosp.; Served to lt. comdr., M.C., USNR, 1970-72. Diplomate Am. Bd. Dermatology. Mem. AMA, Soc. Investigative Dermatology, N.Y. State Soc. Dermatology, Am. Acad. Dermatology, Dermatology Found., Am. Geriatrics Soc., So. Med. Soc., DeKalb County Med. Soc., Atlanta Dermatol. Assn., Southesstern Dermatol. Assn., Internat. Soc. for Tropical Dermatology, Am. Dermatol. Soc. for Allergy and Immunology, Ga. Soc. Dermatologists, Nat. Psoriasis Found. Home: 5581 Stapleton Dr Dunwoody GA 30338

O'BRIEN, PAUL HERBERT, surgeon, educator; b. Evanston, Ill., Sept. 12, 1930; s. Maurice Edward and Nellie (Fitzgerald) O'B.; B.S., Northwestern U., 1950, M.D., 1954; m. Ann Hope Miller, Aug. 28, 1965; children—Jennifer, Paul Edward. Intern, Wesley Meml. Hosp., Chgo., 1954-55; resident Cook County Hosp., Chgo., 1957-62; sr. resident Meml. Hosp. for Cancer and Allied Diseases, N.Y.C., 1962-65; asst. prof. surgery Northwestern U. Med. Sch., Chgo., 1967-69; asso. prof. surgery Med. U. S.C., Charleston, 1970-72, prof., 1972—, Am. Cancer Soc. prof. clin. oncology, 1974-79; Am. Cancer Soc. clin. fellow, 1965-67. Served with M.C., U.S. Army, 1955-57. Diplomate Am. Bd. Surgery; Schweppe fellow, 1967-70. Fellow A.C.S.; mem. AMA, Charleston County Med. Assn., S.C. Med. Assn., Chgo. Surg. Soc., Am. Cancer Soc., James Ewing Soc., Am. Assn. Cancer Edn., Soc. Surgery Alimentary Tract, AAUP, Assn. Acad. Surgery, Southeastern Surg. Congress, Halsted Soc., Allen O. Whipple Surg. Soc. Roman Catholic. Contbr. articles to med. jours. Home: 1467 Burning Tree Rd Charleston SC 29412 Office: Med U SC 171 Ashley Ave Charleston SC 29412

O'BRIEN, RICHARD DENNIS, JR., communications exec.; b. Dallas, July 23, 1927; s. Richard D. and Rose O. (McGilligan) O'B.; B.A., So. Meth. U., 1951; m. Apr. 14, 1951; children—Bridget, Shannon, Sean. With Chance Vought Aircraft, Dallas, 1952-54; pub. editor Champlin Oil & Refining Co., Ft. Worth, Tex., 1954-62; free lance writer, photographer, 1962; with Wyatt & Williams Advt., Dallas, 1963-68, v.p., account supr., 1965-68; dir. advt. Ling-Temco-Vought, Dallas, 1968, dir. corporate communications, 1969-70; with Richard O'Brien & Assos., Dallas, 1970-73; dir. corporate communications LTV Corp., Dallas, 1973—. Served with USMC, 1945-46. Mem. Dallas Advt. League. Roman Catholic. Home: 2416 Skyline Dr Irving TX 75062 Office: PO Box 225003 Dallas TX 75265

O'BRIEN, THOMAS JOHN, SR., assn. exec.; b. Battle Creek, Mich., May 12, 1947; s. Joseph Duane and Rose Helen (Mangan) O'B.; B.S. in B.A., Central Mich. U., 1970; m. Carolyn Ruth Winton, Aug. 1, 1970. Field claims rep. Farmers Ins. Group, Southfield, Mich., 1970-74; exec. sec. Livingston-Overton County C. of C., Livingston, Tenn., 1975—. Mem. Upper Cumberland Devel. Dist. Bd., 1975—; chmn. Overton County Girl Scouts U.S.A., 1975; adv. bd. Overton County ARC, 1976—; mem. Livingston City Park Improvement com., 1975—, Overton County Indsl. Park Land Bd., 1975—, Upper Cumberland Transp. Com., 1976—; mem. Upper Cumberland Devel. Dist. Housing Adv. com., 1977—; mem. Overton County Indsl. Bond Bd., 1975—, Livingston City Airport Authority Bd., 1977—, U.S. Tourist Council, 1976—; organizing mem. Overton County United Way Agy., 1977; Overton County chmn. Tenn. Gov.'s Com. on Employment of Handicapped; adv. bd. Pacesetters, Inc. Recipient Southeastern Community Devel. Assn. award for Tenn., 1977. Mem. So. Assn. C. of C. Execs., U.S. C. of C., Tenn. C. of C. Execs., Cordell Hull Hwy. Assn., Upper Cumberland Tourist Assn. Office: PO Box 354 Livingston TN 38570

O'BRIEN, THOMAS KEVIN, research scientist; b. Balt., Dec. 5, 1949; s. Raymond Anthony and Shirley Ann O'Brien; B.S. in Engring. Mechanics, Va. Poly. Inst. and State U., 1972, M.S., 1976, Ph.D., 1978; m. Mary Sandra Huwalt, Mar. 15, 1970; children—Sean Kevin, Melissa Ann. Research asso. Va. Poly. Inst. and State U., Blacksburg, 1977-78; research scientist U.S. Army Research and Tech. Labs., NASA Langley Research Center, Hampton, Va., 1978—. Recipient J. Shelton Horsley award Va. Acad. Sci., 1978. Mem. ASTM, Soc. for Exptl. Stress Analysis, AIAA. Contbr. articles to profl. jours. Office: MS 188E Structural Integrity Br NASA Langley Research Center Hampton VA 23665

O'BRYANT, JAMES ARTHUR, acct.; b. Erath County, Tex., June 1, 1923; s. Arthur and Suejette (Cherry) O'B.; student U. N.Mex., 1940-41, Durham Coll., 1946-47; m. Billie Louise Birdwell, Apr. 6, 1946; children—Betty Joyce, Jimmy Bruce. Commd. capt. USAF, 1967, advanced through grades to lt. col., 1972; personnel officer-insp. gen., Europe, Africa, Middle East, 1942-45; personnel br. chief, Korea 5th Army, 1951-53; various assignments SAC; gen. mgr. Kleen-Air Tex., Inc., Dallas, 1962-64; pres. Chem. Exhaust, Dallas, 1964-65; sales mgr. Guardian Fire Protection, Dallas, 1965-69; sec.-treas. Whitel Music Co., Dallas, 1969-75; pres. O'Bryant & Machtley, Inc., Dallas, 1975—; mem. action com. Nat. Fedn. Small Bus., 1979—. Lt. col., exec. officer MP Group Tex. State Guard, 1971-79. Decorated Bronze Star medal. Mem. Nat. Soc. Public Accts., Nat. Soc. Mgmt. Cons., Tex. Assn. Public Accts., Tex. Nat. Guard Assn., Tex. State Guard Assn. Republican. Baptist. Home: 5215 Clubview Dr Dallas TX 75232 Office: 3626 N Hall St Suite 620 Dallas TX 75219

OCAMPO-BAEZ, RAUL, architect; b. N.Y.C., Feb. 3, 1949; s. Raul and Olga Alejandra (Baez-Benjamin), Ocampo-Cabrera; B.Arch. with high honors, U. Fla., Gainesville, 1973; student archtl. engring. U. Miami (Fla.), 1968-70, postgrad. in urban planning and design, 1975-77; m. Ninfa Emma Anton, Aug. 26, 1972; children—Kassandra Moné, Kristen Venessa. Structural draftsman, project coordinator Lawrence F. Brill, Cons. Engrs., Inc., Coral Gables, Fla., 1965, 66, 67, 68-70; draftsman, job capt. Marchesani, Cohen & Assos., Architects, Inc., Miami Springs, Fla., 1970-71, 72; architect, planner, project mgr. Greenleaf/Telesca Planners, Engrs., Architects, Inc., Miami, 1973-75; prin. architect Ocampo & Assos., Miami, 1975-76; partner Kotkin & Ocampo, Architects/Planner, Miami, 1976—; prin. Ocampo, Fernandez, Renaud, Inc., Fort Lauderdale, Fla., 1976—; instr. dept. architecture U. Miami, Coral Gables, 1974-77. Recipient First Place Prize, Singer Island Urban Design Competition, 1976. Mem. AIA, Constrn. Specifications Inst. Author: A New City, 1973; also regional planning reports. Home: 1601 SW 99th Ct Miami FL 33165 Office: 7221 Coral Way Suite 202 Miami FL 33155

O'CARROLL, BEATINA ALEXANDER, health services adminstr.; b. Wilmington, Del., Jan. 26, 1927; d. John R. and Beatina Marie (Wilkinson) Alexander; B.A., Barnard Coll., 1948, postgrad. 1948-49; postgrad. La. State U., 1979—; m. Thomas K. O'Carroll, Apr. 23, 1960; 1 son, Thomas A. Reporter, El Panama America, Republic of Panama, 1949-51; research analyst Office Naval Intelligence, Balboa, C.Z., 1951-53; vol. mem. publicity staff Am. Cancer Soc., Washington, 1956-59; vol. publicity dir. ARC, Andrews AFB, Washington, 1963-65, mem. aerospace med. evaluation team, 1966-68, editor family page The Gateway weekly, 1967-68; tchr. English, La Purisma Sch., Lompoc, Calif., 1971; exec. dir. S.W. La. chpt. Epilepsy Found. Am., Lake Charles, La., 1971-74, S.W. La. Health Counseling Service, Lake Charles, 1974—. Mem. Commn. on Justice and Peace, Diocese of Lafayette, 1979; mem. Gov.'s Conf. on Handicapped Individuals, 1975, Commn. on Community Residential Alternatives, State of La., 1979-80. Mem. Am. Acad. Cerebral Palsy, Nat. Rehab. Assn., Nat. Soc. Autistic Children, United Cerebral Palsy Assn., Nat. Assn. Epilepsy Execs. Contbr. articles on rehab. of handicapped and disabled to profl. jours.

OCCHETTI, ARMAND EDWARD, social work agy. exec.; b. Iron Mountain, Mich., Jan. 3, 1943; s. Alfred and Josephine (Paulson) O.; B.A., Heidelberg Coll., 1965; M.S.S.A., Case Western Res. U., 1967; m. Dianne Reavis, June 10, 1979; children by previous marriage—Aimee Elizabeth, Armand Edward. Social worker Summit County Children's Services Bd., Akron, Ohio, 1965-67, Family and Children's Service Soc., Akron, 1967-68, Akron Child Guidance Clinic, 1968-71; asso. prof. Ohio No. U., Ada, 1971-75; exec. dir. Family Services of Wake County, Raleigh, N.C., 1975—; bd. dirs. Wake County Council on Aging, 1978—. Mem. Nat. Assn. Social Workers, Acad. Cert. Social Workers, Am. Assn. Marital and Family Therapists. Democrat. Home: 105 Carriage Trail Raleigh NC 27614 Office: Family Services of Wake County 3803 Computer Dr Raleigh NC 27609

OCHIAI, SHINYA, control engr.; b. Kofu City, Japan, June 6, 1935; s. Shinroku and Takako (Ichikawa) O.; came to U.S., 1960; B.S. in M.E., Waseda U., Tokyo, 1960; M.S. in M.E., Rice U., 1962; Ph.D., Purdue U., 1966; m. Hisako Ozawa, May 21, 1966; 1 dau., Mari. Instrumentation devel. engr. Celanese Fibers Co., Narrows, Va., 1965-67; research and devel. engr. Fibers Industries, Inc., Charlotte, N.C., 1967-68; sr. process systems engr. Celanese Chem. Co., Corpus Christi, Tex., 1968-74, engring. asso., 1974—; vis. asso. prof. Tex. A. and I. U., Kingsville, 1974-75. Registered profl. engr., Tex.; recipient O. Hugo Schuck Best Paper award Joint Automatic Control Conf., 1974. Mem. Instrument Soc. Am., Soc. Instrument and Control Engrs. Japan, Sigma Xi. Contbr. articles to profl. jours. Patentee automatic controls. Home: 7010 Southhaven Dr Corpus Christi TX 78412 Office: Box 9077 Corpus Christi TX 78408

OCHS, MATTHEW EDWARD, rheumatologist; b. Allentown, Pa., Jan. 29, 1948; s. Milton George and Joyce Anna (Fetzer) O.; B.S., Franklin and Marshall Coll., Lancaster, Pa., 1969; M.D., Temple U., Phila., 1973; m. Judith Jacqueline Shallow, July 10, 1971; 1 son, Joshua Edward. Intern, then resident in internal medicine SUNY Hosp., Buffalo, 1973-76, fellow in immunology, 1976-77; fellow in rheumatology U. Tenn. Hosp., Memphis, 1977-79, NIH postdoctoral research fellow, 1979—; cons. rheumatologist Tipton County Meml. Hosp., Covington, Tenn. Diplomate Am. Bd. Internal Medicine. Mem. Am. Rheumatism Assn. Home: 3357 Sycamore View Rd Bartlett TN 38134 Office: BECEG-24 USVA Hosp 1030 Jefferson Ave Memphis TN 38134

OCHSE, DANIEL ROGER, health care exec.; b. Newark, July 27, 1941; s. Daniel C. and Mildred Elizabeth (Shoemaker) O.; B.A., Dickinson Coll., 1963; M.A., U. Rochester, 1966; m. L. Ann Estes, Jan. 24, 1973; children—Weston, Ingrid, Karl, J. Daniel. Instr. English, Ripon (Wis.) Coll., 1967-70; asst. prof. English, Sioux Falls (S.D.) Coll., 1970-72; adminstrv. intern House of the Good Shepherd, Hackettstown, N.J., 1972-73, asst. dir., 1973-76; adminstr. Alexian Bros. Rest Home, Signal Mountain, Tenn., 1976-78; v.p. Health Futures Investment Corp., Cleveland, 1978-79; pres. Seniorcenters of Am., Cleveland, Tenn., 1979—. U. Rochester grad. fellow, 1966-67. Fellow Am. Coll. Nursing Home Adminstrs.; mem. Tenn. Health Care Assn. (dir. 1979-80), Gerontol. Soc., Chattanooga Health Care Assn. (pres. 1979—), Am. Assn. of Homes for the Aging. Episcopalian. Club: Masons. Home: 4916 Lake Haven Dr Chattanooga TN 37416 Office: 2640 Peerless Rd NW Cleveland TN 37311

OCMOND, WILBERT JOSEPH, JR., ednl. adminstr.; b. New Orleans, Jan. 17, 1949; s. Wilbert Joseph and Theresa Thelcide (Oubre) O.; B.A., Francis T. Nicholls State U., 1971; M.A.T., Tulane U., 1973; m. Dolly Ann Boudreaux, Jan. 24, 1970. Speech pathologist St. James Parish Sch. Bd., Lutcher, La., 1971-74, St. John Parish Sch. Bd., Reserve, La., 1974-76, prin. John L. Ory Elemen. Sch., LaPlace, La., 1976-78, supr. spl. edn. parish, 1978—. Mem. Am. Speech and Hearing Assn., La. Speech and Hearing Assn., NEA, La. Edn. Assn., St. John Edn. Assn., Council Exceptional Children, Nicholls Reading Council, Assn. Gifted/Talented Students. Extraordinary lay minister Roman Catholic Ch. Clubs: Laca, K.C. (dist. dept.). Home: 4 Hickory St LaPlace LA 70068 Office: W 10th St Reserve LA 70084

O'CONNELL, JAMES PATRICK, microbiologist; b. Washington, Sept. 22, 1946; s. James A. and Adelaide M. (Milner) O'C.; B.S., Va. Poly. Inst., 1968; M.P.H., U. N.C., Chapel Hill, 1975, D.P.H., 1977; m. Jeannette A. Reeder, Aug. 21, 1971; children—James Patrick, Matthew. Microbiologist, Microbiol. Assn., Inc., Bethesda, Md., 1968; vol. Peace Corps, Philippines, 1968-69; research asso. Georgetown U., Washington, 1970; bacteriologist Commonwealth Va., Arlington, 1972-73; sr. microbiologist Becton, Dickinson & Co., Research Triangle Park, N.C., 1975—; adj. asst. prof. U. N.C., Chapel Hill, 1978-79. Congressional intern, 1964-68. Served with U.S. Army, 1971-72. Becton Dickinson research fellow U. N.C., Chapel Hill, 1974-77. Mem. Am. Soc. Microbiology, Am. Public Health Assn., AAAS, Sigma Xi, Delta Omega. Republican. Home: 1909 White Plains Rd Chapel Hill NC 27514 Office: Box 12016 Research Triangle Park NC 27709

O'CONNELL, ROBERT WEST, astronomer; b. San Francisco, Mar. 22, 1943; s. William Wallace and June (Curts) O'C.; A.B. with Gt. Distinction, U. Calif., Berkeley, 1964; Ph.D. (NSF fellow), Calif. Inst. Tech., 1970; m. Ruth Vega Landean, Dec. 20, 1976; 1 son, Stephen Robert. Postgrad. research astronomer Lick Obs., U. Calif., 1969-71; asst. prof. astronomy U. Va., 1971-76, asso. prof., 1976—, chmn. dept. astronomy, 1979—, dir. Leander McCormick Obs., 1979—; team leader STARLAB Facility Definition Team, NASA. Mem. Am. Astron. Soc., Royal Astron. Soc. (London), Internat. Astron. Union, Phi Beta Kappa, Sigma Xi. Research, publs. in extragalactic astronomy; producer film: The Invisible Universe, 1974. Home: 1809 Wakefield Rd Charlottesville VA 22901 Office: PO Box 3818 Univ Sta Charlottesville VA 22903

O'CONNOR, JOHN CHRISTOPHER, JR., cons. petroleum engr.; b. New Orleans, Feb. 13, 1920; s. John Christopher and Adelaide Pauline (Estopinal) O'C.; B.S., La. State U., 1941; m. Olivia Hortense Cazayoux, Dec. 27, 1944; children—Maureen Judith, Karen Inez, Rebecca Frances (Mrs. James Franklin Russo, Jr.), Denise Olivia (Mrs. Michael Allen Harris). Petroleum engr. The Calif. Co., Gulf of Mexico, La., Okla., Wyo., Colo., Utah, 1946-56; v.p. charge operations Continental Shelf Drilling Corp., New Orleans, 1956-59; cons. petroleum engr., New Orleans, 1959—. Served with C.E., AUS, 1941-45; CBI, ETO. Named knight Holy Sepulchre. Mem. Soc. Petroleum Engrs., La. Engring. Soc., Nat. Soc. Profl. Engrs., Am. Petroleum Inst., Phi Kappa Theta, Roman Catholic. Clubs: K.C., Plimsoll, Petroleum, Serra (New Orleans). Home: 801 Marguerite Rd Metairie LA 70003 Office: 1729 Nat Bank Commerce Bldg New Orleans LA 70112

O'CONNOR, KEVIN THOMAS, elec. engr.; b. Reading, Pa., Mar. 14, 1949; s. Irving and Genevieve (McGloin) O'C.; B.S. in Elec. Engring., Va. Poly. Inst. and State U., 1973; M.B.A., Marshall U., 1977; m. Mary Martha Mapes, Mar. 15, 1975. Elec. engr. Appalachian Power Co., Huntington, W.Va., 1973-77, area supr., Milton, W.Va., 1977—. Registered profl. engr., W.Va. Democrat. Roman Catholic. Club: Engrs. (Huntington). Home: 169 Iroquois Trail Ona WV 25545 Office: Appalachian Power Co 1046 Pike St Milton WV 25541

O'DAY, BUCKLEY EARL, JR., oil co. exec.; b. Victoria, Tex., Dec. 15, 1942; s. Buckley Earl and Hilda (Vyvial) O'D.; student Southwestern U., 1960-61, Alvin Jr. Coll., 1963, U. Md., 1967; B.A., U. Tex., 1974; m. Katie Belle Shirey, Oct. 26, 1965; children—Hilda, Anna, Buckley Earl III, Julia. Asst. to cost engr. Bechtel Corp., San Francisco, 1961-63; lab. technician U. Tex. Med. Br., Galveston, 1964, Clayton Found., Austin, Tex., 1968; lab., x-ray technician Austin (Tex.) State Sch., 1969-71; air pollution research div. Tex. Air Control Bd., Austin, 1971-73; tchr. Houston Ind. Sch. Dist., 1974; drilling fluids engr. Dresser Industries, Houston, 1975-77; offshore supr. drilling dept. Union Oil Co. of Calif., Houston, 1977—. Served with U.S. Army, 1965-68. Mem AIME, V.F.W. Home: PO Box 776 Van TX 75790 Office: Union Oil Co of Calif 4615 SW Freeway Houston TX 77023

ODDSON, TERRENCE ANDREW, diagnostic radiologist; b. Dallas, May 3, 1943; s. Texas Melbourne and Louise Cordelia (McCamey) O.; B.S., Tex. A. & M. U., 1965; M.D., Southwestern Med. Sch., 1969; m. Dachiell Harding Ahlschlager, July 29, 1968. Intern, Southwestern Med. Sch., Dallas, 1969-70; resident in diagnostic radiology Duke U. Med. Center, Durham, N.C., 1973-76, asst. prof. radiology, 1976—. Served with USAF, 1970-73. Diplomate Am. Bd. Radiology. Mem. Am. Coll. Radiology, Radiol. Soc. N. Am., Soc. Gastrointestinal Radiology, Am. Inst. Ultrasound in Medicine, AMA, N.C. Med. Soc., Ark. Med. Soc. Home: 4808 Crestwood Little Rock AR 72207 Office: 500 S University Ave Little Rock AR 72205

ODEGARD, GREGORY JAMES, gas co. exec.; b. Mpls., Sept. 4, 1947; s. Gerald Edwin and Christine (Christensen) O.; B.A. (Scholar), Ariz. State U., 1969, M.S., 1972; Ph.D., Colo. State U., 1974; m. Mamiko Martinez, July 30, 1972. Grad. teaching asst. Ariz. State U., 1969-71; grad. research asst. Colo. State U., 1971-74; environ. scientist Columbia Gas System Service Corp., Wilmington, Del., 1974-78; mgr. environ. scis. El Paso Natural Gas Co. (Tex.), 1978—. Mem. AAAS, Ecol. Soc. Am., Am. Inst. Biol. Scis., Audubon Soc., Wilderness Soc., Sigma Xi, Beta Beta Beta, Kappa Delta Pi, Gamma Sigma Delta. Home: 5400 Connors Ln El Paso TX 79932 Office: PO Box 1492 El Paso TX 79978

O'DELL, CHARLES LEVENDAR, engring. reprographics ofcl.; b. Knoxville, Tenn., Aug. 10, 1945; s. Oscar Levendar and Mossie (England) O'D.; B.S. in Indsl. Tech., East Tenn. State U., 1972; m. Sylvia Juanita Sharpe, Dec. 16, 1967; children—Amanda Beth, Adam Russell. Engring. aide TVA, Knoxville, 1972-73, asst. mgr. engring. reprographics unit, 1974, mgr., 1974—; instr. photog. facility mgmt. Served with USAF, 1966-70. Recipient numerous certifications and awards in mgmt. and engring. reprographics. Mem. Nat. Mgmt. Assn. (dir. TVA Knoxville chpt. 1978—, chmn. bd. dirs. 1979, Profl. Devel. award TVA Knoxville chpt. 1976), Nat. Micrographics Assn., Am. Engring. Model Soc. (dir. 1978—), Epsilon Pi Tau. Republican. Baptist. Clubs: Masons, Shriners. Home: 7732 Cranley Rd Powell TN 37849 Office: TVA SL Comml Realty Mgmt Bldg 400 Commerce Ave Knoxville TN 37902

ODELL, GLADYS HARPER, educator; b. Walton, W.Va., Jan. 18, 1917; d. Lenzy Ernest and Dona (Coon) Harper; A.B. in Home Economics, Sci., English, Marshall Coll., Huntington, W.Va., 1957; M.Ed. in Supervision, U. Va., Charlottesville, 1962; M.S. in Biology, Syracuse (N.Y.) U., 1963; m. Challens B. Odell; children—Ernest, Sue. Sci. specialist Erie Regional Lab., Syracuse, 1966-67; research specialist Pace Center, Parkersburg, W.Va., 1967-69; tchr. Tucker County (W.Va.) schs., Parsons, 1969-72, dir. fed. programs, 1972—. Vol. leader 4-H Club, 1954-61. Mem. NEA, W.Va. Edn. Assn., Assn. Supervision and Curriculum Devel., Am. Ednl. Research Assn., AAUW, Delta Kappa Gamma. Office: Box L Parsons WV 26287

ODELL, JOAN ELIZABETH, lawyer; b. Jo Davies County, Ill., May 3, 1932; d. Peter Emerson and Olive Isabelle (Bonnet) Odell; A.B. cum laude, U. Miami, 1956, J.D., 1958; children—Dominique Rosalyn, Nicole Laurienne. Admitted to Fla. bar, 1958, D.C. bar, 1974, Ill. bar, 1977; trial atty. U.S. SEC, 1959-60; asst. state atty., Dade County, Fla., 1960-64; asst. county atty., Dade County, 1964-70; county atty., Palm Beach County, Fla., 1970-71; regional counsel U.S. EPA, Regional IV, Atlanta, 1971-73; asso. gen. counsel U.S. Environmental Protection Agy., Washington, 1973-77; v.p. Angel Mining, Inc. Bd. dirs. Mental Health Assn. Palm Beach County. Named among Outstanding Young Women in Am., 1965. Mem. Fed. Fla., Dade County, D.C., Chgo. bar assns., Nat. Assn. County Civil Attys. (sec.-treas.), Fla. Assn. County Attys. (dir.), AAUW. Home and office: 720 NE 69th St Suite 4B Miami FL 33138

ODEN, GARY LEE, univ. ofcl.; b. Amity, Ark., Nov. 16, 1944; s. Garvin Lesley and Retha Winnie (Burchfield) O.; B.S., U. Ark., 196B; M.S., So. Ark. U., 1977; m. Glenda Sue Minor, Jan. 21, 1967; children—Gregory Lee, Angela Susan, Lance Christopher. Instr., program dir. dept. architecture and bldg. constrn., tech. br. So. Ark. U., Camden, 1968-73, asst. to the chancellor for devel. and community relations, 1973—. Recipient C. William Brownfield Meml. award U.S. Jaycees, 1977, Jaycee of Yr. award, 1978, Outstanding Local Pres. award Ark. Jaycees, 1978, Disting. Ser. award Camden Jaycees, 1979. Mem. Camden C. of C. (pres. 1980). Baptist. Home: 208 Ingram St Camden AR 71701 Office: Box 3048 Camden AR 71701

ODEN, JAMES CLEVELAND, hobby kit and game mfr.; b. Floydada, Tex., Dec. 6, 1945; s. Conner and Berniece Opal (Avent) O.; B.B.A., So. Meth. U., 1968; J.D., 1973; m. Debrah Lee Dunn, May 17, 1969; children—Heather Ann, Hollie Michelle. Pres., Miniature-Figurines U.S.A. Inc., Dallas, 1973-79; Heritage Models, Inc., Dallas, 1975-79, Royal Guardsman, Inc., Dallas, 1975-79; mng. dir. Heritage Models UK Ltd., Newcastle, No. Ireland, 1979; mfg.

mgr. Commodore Optoelectronics, Dallas, 1980—; admitted to Tex. bar; mem. European Crossroads Shopping Center Adv. Com. Served with USN, 1968-70. Mem. Hobby Industry Assn. Am., Tex. Bar Assn., Am. Mgmt. Assn. Republican. Club: Rotary. Home: 1407 Tierra Calle Carrollton TX 75006 Office: Commodore Optoelectronics 4350 Pkwy S Beltwood Dallas TX 75240

ODEN, KENNETH, lawyer; b. Yoakum, Tex., Sept. 5, 1923; s. J.D. and Lena (Upchurch) O.; student Kilgore Jr. Coll., 1941-42, U. Tulsa, 1943, Navarra Coll., 1946; A.B., LL.B., Baylor U., 1950; m. Frances Walker, May 29, 1948; children—Kenneth, Theresa Lynne, Patricia Marie. Admitted to Tex. bar, 1950, since practiced in Alice, Tex.; mem. firm Perkins, Oden, Warburton, McNeill & Adami, 1950—. Sec.-treas., dir., mem. John G. and Marie Stella Kennedy Meml. Found., 1963—. Served to maj. USAAF, 1944-46; ETO. Decorated Air medal with 5 oak leaf clusters. Mem. Am., Coastal Bend (past pres.) bar assns., State Bar Tex. (past mem. prosecuting grievance com.), Tex. Assn. Def. Counsel. Baptist. Home: 1821 Walker St Alice TX 78332 Office: 601 E Main St Alice TX 78332

ODEN, WALDO TALMAGE, JR., lawyer; b. Altus, Okla., May 17, 1929; s. Waldo Talmage and Lily (Clark) O.; B.A., U. Okla., 1950, LL.B., 1952, J.D., 1970; m. Rebecca Jane Hazlitt, Mar. 25, 1951; children—Waldo Talmage III, Timothy Patrick, Amy Germaine, Jonathan Andrew. Admitted to Okla. bar, 1952. U.S. Supreme Ct. bar, 1960; practiced in Altus, 1952—; mem. firm Robinson & Oden, 1952-53, Oden & Oden, 1954-67; mng. partner Oden, Oden & Derryberry, 1967—; asst. atty. Jackson County, 1953-54; dir. Farmers & Mchts. Bank; instr. bus. law Altus Coll., 1956-59; instr. criminology Altus AFB, 1958; instr. masters degree program Webster Coll., Altus AFB, 1975—; mem. Okla. Jud. Nominating Commn., 1967-71; lectr. in agrl. law. Bd. dirs. Jackson County CD, 1959-68; chmn. Kicking Bird dist. Boy Scouts Am., 1969-78; del. Methodist Jurisdictional Confs., 1964, 68, 72, 76, 80, Meth. Gen. Confs., 1964, 66, 68, 70, 72, 76, 80; sec. exec. com. Meth. Series of Protestant Hour, 1968-72; chmn. dept. communications and pub. relations Okla. United Meth. Conf.; mem. exec. com. W.W. and Rosa Woodworth Estate; pres. U. Okla. Wesley Found., 1947, Okla. Meth. Student Movement, 1948; mem. Okla. Humanities Com., 1976-79; campaign chmn. Jackson County Democratic Com., 1954-60; trustee Altus Library Bd., 1965-72. Mem. Am. (chmn. agrl. law com. gen. practice sect. 1975-80, mem. council gen. practice sect. 1978—), Okla., Jackson County bar assns., Am., Okla. trial lawyers assns., Phi Delta Phi. Methodist (chmn. ofcl. bd. 1960-61). Mason, Rotarian (pres. 1959-60). Mem. staff Okla. Law Rev., 1950-52. Home: 913 E Elm St Altus OK 73521 Office: PO Drawer J 209 N Hudson St Altus OK 73521

ODOM, ELLEN PAYNE (MRS. JAMES M. ODOM), civic worker; b. Blossburg, Ala., July 5, 1906; d. Turner Ashby and Annie Ellen (Ancell) Payne; A.B. summa cum laude, Judson Coll., 1926; M.A., U. Ala., 1931; B.S., Howard Coll., 1932; m. James Malcolm Odom, Aug. 25, 1935. Tchr. French, Spanish, Italian, Judson Coll., 1926-30, U. Ala., 1930-31; head dept. romance langs. Norman Coll., Norman Park, Ga., 1933-35. Chmn. Colquitt County March of Dimes, 1953; sec. Colquitt County Civic Music Assn., 1959-65; mem. adv. bd. Ga. Extension Service, 1957-63; dir. Ga. Tb Assn., mem. exec. com., 1963-66, sec., 1965-66; trustee Colquit-Thomas Regional Library, 1963-71, 75—, mem. regional bd. of trustees, 1964-71, 75—; pres. Colquitt County Tb Assn., 1961-62; adviser 4-H Club, 1936—, state adviser 1961-62. Mem. 2d Congl. Dist. Dem. Exec. Com., 1965-66. Recipient Colquitt County Woman of Year, 1961. Mem. UDC (parliamentarian Ga. div. 1958—, exec. bd., 1948—, v.p. 1968-70), Huguenots (nat. corr. sec. 1948-49), D.A.R. Clubs: Woman's (pres. 1957-58); Golden of Judson Coll. (organizing pres. 1977-78). Author: A History of the Library of Moultrie, Ga., 1966. Home: Odomfarms RFD 5 Moultrie GA 31768

ODOM, FLOYD CLARK, surgeon; b. Cisco, Tex., Mar. 24, 1946; s. Olin Otis and Betty Elda (Clark) O.; A.A., Cisco Jr. Coll., 1966; postgrad. So. Methodist U., 1966; B.A. magna cum laude, McMurry Coll., Abilene, Tex., 1968; M.D., U. Tex., San Antonio, 1972; m. Rebecca Reich, Dec. 27, 1969; children—Brendon Clark, Erin Christine, Justin Ernest. Intern, Bexan County (Tex.) Hosp., 1972-73, resident in surgery, 1973-77; fellow in colon and rectal surgery Baylor U. Med. Center, Dallas, 1977-78; practice medicine specializing in colon and rectal surgery, San Antonio, 1978-79, Dallas, 1979—; asst. clin. prof. surgery U. Tex., San Antonio, 1978-79. Diplomate Am. Bd. Surgery, Am. Bd. Colon and Rectal Surgery. Mem. Alpha Chi. Democrat. Lutheran. Home: 12617 Hornbeam St Dallas TX 75243 Office: 8220 Walnut Hill Ln Dallas TX 75231

ODOM, FRANKLIN CURRIE, public relations exec.; b. Jacksonville, Fla., Jan. 8, 1948; s. John Duncan and Anneliese Odom Ponfickl. B.A., Ga. So. Coll., 1970; M.A., U. Ga., 1973. Freelance writer, public relations, Roswell, Ga., 1974-78; pres. Odom Public Relations, Inc., Roswell, 1978—. Mem. Public Relations Soc. Am. Methodist. Club: Horseshoe Bend Country.

ODOM, JAMES CHRISTIE, JR., oil field rental equipment co. exec.; b. Shreveport, Jan. 27, 1949; s. James Christie and Marilyn (McKaskle) O.; B.B.A., Stephen F. Austin State U., 1972. Salesman, Tex Tan Welhausen Co., 1972; with Prodn. Rentals Inc., Harvey, La., 1972—, div. mgr., cons., 1975-79, spl. sales and Tex. regional sales mgr., 1980—; pres. In-Filco, 1980—. Mem. Soc. Petroleum Engrs., Am. Petroleum Inst., Delta Sigma Phi. Republican. Methodist. Office: 2510 Lester Ave Harvey LA 70058

ODOM, JOYCE RACKLEY, speech pathologist; b. Pontotoc, Miss., Nov. 11, 1941; d. James Calvin and Kathlyn (Purdon) Rackley; B.S., Miss. State Coll. for Women, 1963; M.A., U. Ill., 1974; m. Reginald W. Odom, Nov. 29, 1963; children—Reginald W., Audra Michelle. Speech therapist Regional Rehab. Center and Child Devel. Clinic, Tupelo, Miss., 1966-67, Dept. Air Force, Raney AFB, P.R., 1967-69; speech therapist and pathologist Thomasboro-Flatville Schs., Thomasboro, Ill., 1971-76; speech pathologist San Felipe Del Rio Consol. Ind. Sch. Dist., Del Rio, Tex., 1976—; speech, lang. and voice cons. and therapist Tex. Rehab. Commn. Recipient cert. in Laryngectomy Therapy, Am. Cancer Soc., 1973. Mem. Am. Speech and Hearing Assn., Council Exceptional Children, Beta Sigma Phi. Democrat. Presbyterian. Club: Del Rio Music. Home: 8120A Hall St Laughlin AFB Del Rio TX 78840 Office: San Felipe Del Rio Consol Ind Sch Dist Meml Sch Main St Del Rio TX 78840

ODOM, LINDA JACOB, mfg. co. exec.; b. Nashville, Dec. 10, 1947; d. William Gilbert and Margaret Lou (Long) Jacob; B.S. in B.A., U. Tenn., 1977, postgrad. 1978-79; m. Sam Houston Odom, July 26, 1979. Adminstrv. asst. Commerce Union Bank, Nashville, 1973-74; exec. asst. Stanley D. Lindsey & Asso., Ltd., Nashville, 1974-77; office services mgr., mgr. managerial controls No. Telecom, Nashville, 1978—; cons. mktg. Active Buddies of Nashville affiliate Big Bros. Internat., 1974—. Served to 2d lt. USAR, 1976—. Mem. Jr. C. of C. Ch. of Christ. Home: 1321 Meridian St Nashville TN 37207 Office: 640 Massman Dr Nashville TN 37210

ODOM, WILLIAM MCBRIDE, educator; b. Hodge, La., Sept. 23, 1939; s. Roy Harris and Willie Mai (Tolar) O.; B.A., La. State U., 1961; postgrad. Free U. Berlin, 1961-63, 67-68; Ph.D., Tulane U., 1973; m. Margaret Rosemary Fullick, July 26, 1964; 1 son, Stewart. Instr., asst. prof. Loyola U., New Orleans, 1970-74; asst. prof. fgn. langs. U. So. Miss., Hattiesburg, 1974-78, asso. prof., 1978—; ednl. cons. German Ednl. TV Network, N.Y.C. Fulbright fellow, 1961-63, 76. Mem. Am. Assn. Tchrs. German, Am. Council Teaching Fgn. Langs., Nat. Assn. Learning Lab. Dirs. Home: 810 N 31st Ave Hattiesburg MS 39401 Office: Box 5038 U So Miss Hattiesburg MS 39401

O'DONNELL, CHARLES PATRICK, JR., newspaper exec.; b. Cleve., Dec. 12, 1945; s. Charles Patrick and Mary Rita (Monroe) O'D.; B.A. magna cum laude, Harvard Coll., 1968; Ph.D., Princeton U., 1973; m. Kendra Stearns, Dec. 22, 1978. Asst. prof. Princeton (N.J.) U., 1973-75; reporter Charlotte (N.C.) Observer, 1975-77, Wall St. Jour., Detroit, 1977-78; dir. corporate relations Knight-Ridder Newspapers, Inc., Miami, Fla., 1978—. Author: (with T.D. Roche, Jr.) Edmund Spenser's Faerie Queene, 1978. Home: 418 Savona Ave Coral Gables FL 33146 Office: 1 Herald Plaza Miami FL 33101

O'DONOGHUE, DON HORATIO, orthopaedic surgeon; b. Storm Lake, Iowa, Nov. 13, 1901; s. James Horatio and Janet (Fairbairn) O'D.; student Buena Vista Coll., Storm Lake, 1919-20; B.S., Iowa U., 1923, M.D., 1926; D.S., Morningside Coll., 1944; m. Ragnhild Christensen, Jan. 4, 1928; 1 son, Donald Patrick. Surgery resident Iowa U. Hosps., 1926-27; orthopaedic surgery resident Okla. U. Hosp., 1927-30; gen. practice specializing in orthopaedic surgery, Oklahoma City, 1930—; prof., chmn. emeritus dept. orthopaedic surgery and fractures U. Okla. Med. Sch., dir. div. sports medicine Health Scis. Center, past chmn. bd. trustees U. Hosp.; past chief orthopaedics St. Anthony's Hosp., Vets Hosp.; mem. staff Presbyn., Mercy, Bapt. hosps.; orthopedic team physician, athletic dept. U. Okla. Chmn. profl. adv. com. Dept. Pub. Welfare. Bd. dirs. YMCA; trustee United Fund. Recipient Distinguished Service award U. Okla., 1969, U. Iowa, 1971, Buena Vista Coll., 1979; Wisdom award, 1971; President's Challenge award Nat. Athletic Trainers Assn., 1978; named to Okla. Hall of Fame, 1970. Fellow Internat. Coll. Surgeons, Sicot, A.C.S.; mem. Am. Acad. Orthopaedic Surgeons, Am. Orthopaedic Assn. (past pres.), Internat. Soc. Knee (founding mem., pres.), AMA, So., Okla. State, Oklahoma County med. socs., Clin. Orthopaedic Soc., Western Surg. Assn., S.W. Surg. Congress, Pan-Pacific Surg. Soc., Mid-Central State Orthopaedic Soc., Am. Assn. for Surgery of Trauma, Am. Trauma Soc., (founding mem.), Am. Orthopaedic Soc. Sports Medicine (founding mem., first pres.). Author: Treatment of Injuries to Athletes, 1962, rev. edit., 1970, 76; also articles in profl. jours. Editorial bd. Orthopaedic Review. Home: 1403 Glenwood Ave Oklahoma City OK 73116 Office: 1111 N Lee Oklahoma City OK 73103

OEHLSCHLAGER, FREDERICK KEITH, physician; b. Kansas City, Mo., Apr. 16, 1911; s. Henry George and Lillie Marie (Kaltenbach) O.; A.A., Kansas City Jr. Coll., 1930; B.S., U. Kans., 1933; M.D., 1935; m. Helen Mae Poulson, May 10, 1935 (dec. 1960); children—Richard, Susan, Robert; m. 2d, Jimmie Nell Lietzow, Mar. 10, 1965; stepchildren—Cynthia, Matthew, Celeste, Colleen. Intern, U.S. Marine Hosp., New Orleans, 1935-36; pvt. practice Lees Summit, Mo., 1936, Yale, Okla., 1936-51, Odessa, Tex., 1951—; chief of staff Cushing Meml. Hosp., Okla., 1950-51; mem. staff Med. Center Hosp., Odessa, 1951—, chmn. dept. obstetrics and gynecology, 1962-63, 72-73; staff, mem. exec. com. Women's and Children's Hosp., Odessa; sec. Permian Basin Investment Corp.; founder, sec.-treas., med. dir. Permian Basin Life Ins. Co., 1954-63; pres. Nat. Sun-Well Corp., Odessa, Sherwood Bldg. Corp., Odessa; partner Decision Support Corp., Santa Monica, Calif., Pan-Africa Corp., Sierra Leone, West Africa. Med. dir. Permian Basin Planned Parenthood, 1971—. Pres. Permian Playhouse, Inc., Odessa, 1962-64; dir. Permian Basin Ballet Assn., 1968-70, Midland-Odessa Symphony Assn., 1968-71; mayor City of Yale, Okla., 1948-50; chmn. Ector County-City of Odessa, Tex. Dept. Parks and Recreation, 1954-62; chmn. Ector County Child Welfare Bd., 1952-56; dir. Tri-County Group Foster Home Bd., 1951-57, ARC, 1954-57; pres. Permian Basin Civic Ballet Assn., 1969-70, Midland-Odessa Symphony Assn., 1969-70; bd. dirs. Tex. Abortion Rights Action League, 1979-80. Pres. Payne-Pawnee County Med. Soc. (Okla.), 1944. Recipient Margaret Sanger award Planned Parent Fedn. Am., 1976. Mem. Am. Cancer Soc. (dir. 1955, Ector County pres. 1967-68, dist. dir. 1968—), Odessa C. of C., AMA, So. (life), Tex. med. assns., Andrews and Ector County Med. Soc., Am. Soc. Study Fertility, Internat. Fertility Assn., Internat. Soc. Obstetrics and Gynecology, Am. Soc. Colposcopy and Colpomicroscopy, Am. Assn. Gynecol. Laparoscopists, Nat. Abortion Rights Action League, Nat. Abortion Fedn., Permian Basin Petroleum Assn., Am. Rose Soc. Methodist. Mason (Shriner). Clubs: Odessa Country, Rotary (pres. 1963-64), Men's Garden (pres. 1970-71). Home: 316 Casa Grande Odessa TX 79760 Office: Sherwood Med Center 42d and Everglade Sts Odessa TX 79762

OESTERLING, MICHAEL JAMES, marine biologist; b. Columbus, Ohio, Jan. 4, 1949; s. Donald Oswald and Ann (McDowell) O.; B.S. in Biology, U. Miami, 1970; M.S. in Zoology, U. Fla., 1976; m. Barbara Louise Green, Sept. 2, 1975. Marine sci. technician Center for Aquatic Scis., U. Fla., Gainesville, 1973-74, marine biologist resource mgmt. systems program, 1974-77, asst. in marine research C.V. Whitney Lab. for Exptl. Marine Biology and Medicine, St. Augustine, 1977-78; marine extension agt., Sea Grant marine adv. program Fla. Coop. Extension Service, Inverness, 1978—. Mem. Fedn. Aquatic Resource Technologists, Nat. Blue Crab Industry Assn., Shellfish Inst. N.Am., Nat. Shellfisheries Assn., Southeastern Estuarine Research Soc., Sigma Xi. Democrat. Lutheran. Home: Route 2 Box 130 Floral City FL 32636 Office: Fla Coop Extension Service 3600 S Florida Ave Inverness FL 32650

OFFUTT, WILLIAM NELSON, IV, ophthalmologist; b. Lexington, Ky., May 3, 1939; s. William Nelson and Marie Celeste (Lyons) O. III; student Washington and Lee U., 1957-60; B.A. in Econs., U. Ky., 1963, M.D., 1968; m. Jane Allen Tullis, June 11, 1966; children—Jane Scott, William Nelson V. Intern, Charity Hosp., Tulane Service rotating intern, New Orleans, 1968-69; ophthalmic resident Wills Eye Hosp. & Research Inst., Phila., 1969-72; Heed Found. postgrad. fellow in corneal and transplant surgery and ophthalmic plastic surgery U. Ky. Coll. Medicine, Lexington, 1972-73, clin. instr. dept. ophthalmology, 1972-74, asst. clin. prof., 1974-79, asso. clin. prof., 1979—, chief ophthalmic plastic surgery sect., 1974—; attending ophthalmic surgeon VA Hosp., 1973-75, cons. ophthalmic surgeon, 1975—; ophthalmic plastic and corneal transplant surgeon Ophthalmol. Assos., Lexington, Ky., 1973—. Bd. mem. Kidney Found. Central Ky., 1976-79; mem. Scott County Bd. Health, 1975-77. Served with USAFR, 1961-67. Am. Cancer Soc. grantee, 1965, NIH tng. grantee, 1969-71. Diplomate Am. Bd. Ophthalmology. Fellow Am. Acad. Ophthalmology and Otolaryngology, A.C.S.; mem. AMA, Heed Ophthalmic Soc., Soc. R.R. Surgeons, Soc. Prevention Blindness, Wills Eye Hosp. Soc., Fayette County Med. Soc. (mem. utilization and rev. com. 1975-79), Ky. Med. Assn., Ky. Acad. Eye Physicians and Surgeons, Lexington Acad. Eye Physicians and Surgeons (pres. 1978-80). Presbyterian. Clubs: Idle Hour Country (Lexington); Boston (New Orleans). Home: 336 E Main St Georgetown KY 40324 Office: Suite 200 Profl Arts Center 135 E Maxwell St Lexington KY 40508

OGDEN, FREDERIC DORRANCE, polit. scientist, univ. ofcl.; b. Orange County, N.Y., Oct. 11, 1915; s. Fred D. and Florence Caroline (Young) O.; A.B., Tusculum Coll., Tenn., 1938; Ph.D., Johns Hopkins U., 1951; m. Jessie Cupitt, June 10, 1943; children—Elisabeth J. Ogden Churchill, Katharine J. Ogden Cornell. Clk., Edgewood Arsenal, Md., 1940-41; asst. mgr. Civilian Personnel Field Office, Wright-Patterson Field, Ohio, 1941-42; instr. polit. sci. U. Ala., 1946-47, 48-51, asst. prof., 1951-58, asso. prof., 1958-61; Fulbright lectr. Indian Sch. Internat. Studies, New Delhi, India, 1957-58; prof. polit. sci. Eastern Ky. U., Richmond, 1961—, chmn. dept. polit. sci., 1961-65, dean Coll. Arts and Scis., 1965-79, asso. v.p. for planning, 1977—; dir. workshop internat. relations Appalachian State U., N.C., summer 1960, 61; mem. nat. screening com. South Asia, Inst. Internat. Edn., 1975, 76, chmn., 1976. Mem. com. to select city mgr. Richmond, Ky., 1971; mem. Citizens Adv. Subcom. on Compensation of Ky. Legislators, 1974; bd. dirs. Am. Conf. of Acad. Deans, 1974-77, sec.-editor of proc., 1975-77. Served with USAAF, 1942-45. Commonwealth fellow Duke U., summer, 1959. Mem. Am. Polit. Sci. Assn., So. Polit. Sci. Assn., Ky. Polit. Sci. Assn., Council Colls. Arts and Scis., AAUP, Phi Kappa Phi, Pi Sigma Alpha. Democrat. Episcopalian. Author: The Poll Tax in the South, 1958; editorial bd. Univ. Press of Ky., 1969-79. Home: 212 College View Dr Richmond KY 40475 Office: Eastern Ky Univ Richmond KY 40475

OGDEN, JOHN MORRIS, JR., wholesale food co. exec.; b. Phila., Dec. 19, 1916; s. John Morris and Irene (Kelly) O.; B.S. in Bus. Adminstrn., U. Pa., 1938; m. Dorothy May Graves, Sept. 15, 1945; children—Susan Graves, John Morris. Dept. mgr. So. States Coop., Richmond, Va., 1945-53; life underwriter Mut. Life Ins. Co. N.Y., Richmond, 1953-55; accountant Richmond Food Stores, Inc., 1955-61, office mgr., 1961-64, dir. personnel, 1964-75; dir. personnel Richfood, Inc., Richmond, 1974—. Rep. Hanover County Henrico-Chesterfield-Hanover C.E.T.A. Consortium, 1974—; bd. dirs. Jr. Achievement Richmond, Inc., 1966-76, United Givers Fund Richmond, 1964-69, Pvt./Industry Council, 1979; trustee Richfood Ednl. Trust, 1964—. Served with USAAF, 1941-45. Mem. Am. Soc. Personnel Adminstrn. (dir. Richmond chpt.), Va. State C. of C. (mgmt. relations com.), Southside Richmond Civitan Club (pres. 1964-65, Am. Soc. Tng. and Devel., Am. Mgmt. Assn., U.S. Power Squadron. Clubs: Fishing Bay Yacht, Va. All-Weather Tennis, Masons. Home: 8405 Michael Rd Richmond VA 23229 Office: PO Box 26967 Richmond VA 23261

OGDEN, ROBERT GLENN, computer service co. exec.; b. Cooks Run, Pa., Apr. 20, 1941; s. Robert Glenn and Elizabeth Sarah (Albert) O.; B.S. in Math., Pa. State U., 1963; m. June 11, 1969; children—Robert A., Sherri L., Deanna L., David G. Tchr., Harrisburg (Pa.) city schs., 1963-66; instr. NCR Corp., Dayton, Ohio, 1966-70, systems analyst, 1970-73; auditor Town of Wallaceton (Pa.), 1974-75; mgr. tech. support unit Wachovia Services, Winston-Salem, N.C., 1975-78; pres., dir. advanced systems Customized Acctg. Systems House, Inc., Winston-Salem, 1978—. Mem. Data Processing Mgmt. Assn. (cert. data processor), Assn. Computing Machinery. Democrat. Home: 1308 Watson Ave Winston-Salem NC 27103 Office: Customized Acctg Systems House Inc 897 Peters Creek Pkwy Winston-Salem NC 27103

OGG, JACK CLYDE, state senator; b. Kansas City, Mo., Sept. 7, 1933; s. William Jewell and Annie Mildred (Owens) O.; B.S., U. Houston, 1957; LL.B., J.D., S. Tex. Coll. Law, 1962; m. Constance Sue Harner, Jan. 1, 1959; children—Kimbra, Jon. Admitted to Tex. bar, 1962, since practiced individually in Houston; former mem. Tex. Ho. of Reps.; mem. Tex. Senate, 1972—; dir. Katy Savs. & Loan Assn., Nat. Title Co. Mem. Tex. N.G. Mem. Tex. Bar Assn., Houston Bar Assn., Spring Branch Bar Assn. Democrat. Episcopalian. Club: Masons. Home: 761 Kuhlman St Houston TX 77024 Office: 2223 W Loop South Suite 333 Houston TX 77027

OGG, WADE MASON, III, chem. co. exec.; b. Richmond, Va., Aug. 11, 1944; s. Wade Mason and Virginia (Delp) O.; B.S. in Bus. Adminstrn., Va. Poly. Inst. and State U., 1967. Dealer rep. Shell Oil Co., Clifton, N.J., 1967-72; mgr. Am. Alchemy Co., Richmond, 1972—. Active Young Republicans; mem. Chester Recreation Assn., 1977—. Mem. Va. Paint and Coatings Assn. (chmn. bd.), Chester Jaycees, U.S. Power Squadron, Alpha Kappa Psi. Republican. Baptist. Home: 12716 Richmond St Chester VA 23831 Office: PO Box 34189 Richmond VA 23234

OGILVIE, DOUGLAS SIKES, health facility and urban planning exec.; b. Aurora, Mo., July 17, 1940; s. Elmer E. and Charlotte L. O.; B.Arch., Tex. A&M U., 1965, M.Arch., 1967; m. Barbara Wetherell, Nov. 11, 1972; children—Kimberly Shawn, Donal Shannon, Christine Charlotte, Michael Douglas. Health facility planner and cons. Tufts-New Eng. Med. Center, Boston, 1967-69, NIMH, Boston, 1969-70, Booz, Allen & Hamilton, Inc., Chgo., 1970-72; dir. health and med. div. Bernard Johnson, Inc., Houston, 1972-74; dir. N. Am. health Llewelyn-Davies Assos., Houston, 1974-78; pres. Ogilvie Assos., Inc., Houston, 1978—. USPHS fellow, 1966-67; recipient grad. research award Tex. A&M U., 1967. Mem. Am. Hosp. Assn., Am. Inst. Planners, A.I.A., Am. Assn. Hosp. Planning, Tex. Soc. Architects, Tex. Hosp. Assn., Phi Kappa Phi. Editor: Architecture Plus, 1963; art editor Tex. A&M Engr., 1963-64. Home: 17807 Mid Oaks Ct Spring TX 77379 Office: 2411 Fountainview St Suite 212 Houston TX 77057

OGILVIE, MARGARET PRUETT, counselor; b. McKinney, Tex., Jan. 8, 1922; d. William Walter and Ida Mae (Houk) Pruett; B.A., Baylor U., 1943; M.Ed., Hardin Simmons U., 1968; m. Frederick Henry Ogilvie, May 13, 1943; children—Ida Margaret, James William. Tchr. pub. and pvt. schs., Tex., Calif., Alaska, W.Ger., 1944, 53-65; guidance counselor Dentsville High Sch., Columbia, S.C., 1968-69, Northwest H.S., Clarksville, Tenn., 1970-72; personal and marital counselor, Fairfield Glade, Tenn., 1972—; co-owner F & M Gems & Jewelry. Chmn. vols. ARC, Ft. Irwin, Calif., 1965; pres. Women's Golf Assn., Ft. Irwin, 1965-66; v.p. Ch. Women United, Crossville, Tenn., 1972-74; bd. dirs. Cumberland County Mental Health Assn., 1975—; mem. legis. com. and pub. affairs com. Tenn. Mental Health Assn., 1976—, mem. exec. bd., 1977—; mem. Middle Tenn. com. Internat. Women's Yr., 1975. Mem. Am. Personnel and Guidance Assn., Nat. Ret. Tchrs. Assn., Bus. and Profl. Women's Club (chmn. 1973-75), DAR, Pi Gamma Mu. Democrat. Baptist (choir dir., organist 1972—). Clubs: Fairfield Glade Women's (parliamentarian 1974-77), Fairfield Glade Women's Golf Assn. (pres. 1973), Fairfield Glade Sq. Dance. Home: 240 Snead Dr Fairfield Glade TN 38555

OGILVIE, PHYLLIS ANNE, oil co. exec.; b. Dover, Ohio, Aug. 1, 1953; d. Siegel Louis and Betty Ann (Garan) Tschappat; B.S. in Mgmt. Sci., Okla. State U., 1975; m. Clark David Ogilvie, May 24, 1975. Systems analyst Cities Service Co., Tulsa, 1975-79, tech. systems analyst, 1979—, instr. fundamentals of applied systems techniques, 1978. Mem. Am. Bus. Women's Assn. (treas., rec. sec., hospitality chmn. 1977-79), Assn. for Systems Mgmt. (growth and retention chmn. 1978-79), Chi Omega. Republican. Roman Catholic. Office: PO Box 300 Tulsa OK 47102

OGLE, EDWARD GERALD, data processing exec.; b. DeQueen, Ark., May 15, 1940; s. Paul Evert and Bonnie Sahra (Davis) O.; student Wash. State U., 1972; m. Renate Elisibeth, Sept. 4, 1959; children—Michaela Yvonne, Patricia B., Edward Gerald, Gregory S. Enlisted in U.S. Army, 1958; assigned to Germany, 1958-70, S.E. Asia and Vietnam, 1970-71, U.S. Army Air Def. Bd., Ft. Bliss, Tex., 1977-79; personnel data systems adminstr. E.G. Ogle Co., El Paso, Tex., 1979—. Office: 5205 Sweetwater St El Paso TX 79924

OGLE, MARTHA SMOAK, public relations exec.; b. Colleton, S.C., Aug. 4, 1939; d. Guy Lynwood, Jr. and Uldean (Kinsey) Smoak; B.A. in English, Columbia (S.C.) Coll., 1960; m. Carroll Gordon Ogle, Aug. 4, 1971; children—Don, Scott, Ginger, Kelly. Media asst. Southeastern Galleries, Charleston, S.C., 1964-66; media buyer Lavidge & Assos., Greensboro, N.C., 1966-68; media dir. Harry Gianaris and Assos., Greensboro, 1968-70; para-legal asst. firm Deal, Hutchins and Minor, Winston-Salem, N.C., 1970-73; media dir. Kal, Merrick and Salan, Inc., Raleigh, N.C., 1973-79; account exec. Carmichael, McKneely, Dusenbury & Alban Advt., Durham, N.C., 1979—. Mem. Am. Advt. Fedn. (nat. awards rev. bd. com., 3d dist chmn. Addy awards), Triangle Advt. Fedn., N.C. Tarheels Roundtable. Democrat. Lutheran. Author: A Gathering Tension, 1976, A Myth in Progress, 1976, The Snow Owl, 1977, Gingerbread Iceing, 1978; also poems, articles, short stories. Home: 928 Bluestone Rd Research Triangle Park NC 27709 Office: Cedar Terr Office Park Chapel Hill Blvd Durham NC 27702

OGLESBY, VICTORIA DIANE, coll. adminstr.; b. Sulphur Springs, Tex., Aug. 6, 1952; d. Robert Lynn and Patricia Ann (Woods) Mallory; B.A. with honors, E. Tex. State U., 1974, M.A., 1976; m. Donald H. Oglesby, Feb. 16, 1973. With Paris (Tex.) Jr. Coll., 1975—, coordinator for spl. courses. Fund raising capt. Public TV, Dallas. Mem. Tex. Jr. Coll. Tchrs. Assn., Tex. Assn. Vocat. Educators for Spl. Needs Personnel, Tex. Adminstrs. Continuing Edn. for Community Colls., Bus. and Profl. Women. Democrat. Methodist. Contbr. poetry to mags. Home: 870 40th St SE Paris TX 75460 Office: Paris Junior College Paris TX 75460

OGLETREE, DAVID, clergyman; b. Perry, Ga.; student Emory U., Oxford, Ga.; B.A. in History, LaGrange Coll.; attended Columbia Sem., Decatur, Ga., Candler Sch. Theology, Emory U.; Mem. staff Trinity and Kirkwood Methodist chs., Atlanta, Sam Jones Meml. Meth. Ch., Cartersville, Ga., 1st United Meth. Ch., Gainesville, Ga.; now youth minister 1st Meth. Ch., Atlanta. Bd. counselors Oxford Coll., Emory U. Named Young Man of Yr., Cartersville Jaycees, 1964; Poet of Yr., Dixie Council Authors and Journalists, 1977. Mem. Atlanta Writers Club (1st v.p.), Ga. Poetry Soc. (charter mem., librarian), Hist. Soc. of S. Ga. Conf. United Meth. Ch. (hon.), Am. Guild Organists (asso.) Dixie Council of Authors and Journalists, Poetry Soc. of Ga. in Savannah, Village Writers Group, also Lincoln Group and many others. Author: Steeples, A Volume of Verse; Landscapes; Weavings; co-author: Noel Poems of Christmas. Address: First Methodist Ch 360 Peachtree St Atlanta GA 30308

OGLIARUSO, MICHAEL ANTHONY, organic chemist; b. Bklyn., Aug. 10, 1938; s. Andrea and Anna (Bianco) O.; B.S., Poly. Inst. N.Y., 1960, Ph.D., 1965; m. Basila E. Gallo, Apr. 2, 1961; 1 son, Michael Dana. Asst. prof. chemistry UCLA, 1965-67; asst. prof. chemistry Va. Poly. Inst. and State U., Blacksburg, 1967-72, asso. prof. chemistry, 1972-78, prof. chemistry, 1978—. Served with AUS, 1960-61. Revlon scholar, 1959-60. Mem. Am. Chem. Soc., Phi Lambda Upsilon, Sigma Xi. Roman Catholic. Contbr. numerous articles to sci. jours. Office: Dept Chemistry Davidson Hall Blacksburg VA 24061

OGLUKIAN, RAYMOND LEVON, engr., chemist; b. Pasadena, Calif., Mar. 24, 1930; s. Levon Mardiros and Ruth (Gertmenian) O.; A.B., Duke U., 1952; M.S. in Phys. Chemistry, Tulane U., 1955, Ph.D. in Phys. Chemistry, 1968; m. Mary Lucille Williams, May 27, 1960; children—Mercedes, Portia. Commd. cadet U.S. Air Force, 1955, advanced through grades to lt. col., 1977; navigator 5th Air Commando Squadron, Vietnam, 1967-68; chief chem. laser br. Air Force Weapons Lab., Kirtland AFB, N.Mex., 1969-73; sci. exchange officer U.S. Army Laser Program, Redstone Arsenal, Ala., 1973-75; program mgr. Advanced Research Project Agy., Washington, 1975-77; ret., 1977; sr. project engr. Pratt and Whitney Aircraft Co., West Palm Beach, Fla., 1977—. Decorated D.F.C., Air medal with 11 oak leaf clusters, Meritorious Service medal with oak leaf cluster, Air Force Commendation medal. Mem. Am. Chem. Soc., Combustion Inst., Air Force Assn., Sigma Xi. Pesbyterian. Home: 600 Shore Rd North Palm Beach FL 33408 Office: Pratt & Whitney Aircraft West Palm Beach FL 38403

O'GRADY, TIMOTHY PORTER, nursing adminstr.; b. Edmonton, Alta., Can., Mar. 29, 1947; s. Thomas Joseph and Margaret Mary (Porter) O'G.; came to U.S., 1969; Asso. Nursing Sci., Lower Columbia Coll., Longview, Wash., 1973; B.S. in Nursing, Seattle U., 1975; M.N. in Nursing Adminstrn., U. Wash., 1977; 1 foster child. Clin. and adminstrv. supr. Providence Med. Center, Seattle, 1973-76; dir. nursing Alleghany Regional Hosp., 1977-79; nursing cons. Hosp. Affiliates Internat., Nashville, 1977—; nursing adminstr. Henrico Doctors Hosp., Richmond, Va., 1979—; mem. Va. Joint Practice Com., Richmond. HEW grantee, 1976-77. Mem. Am., Va. Dist. 5 nurses assns., Am. Soc. Nursing Service Adminstrs., Sigma Theta Tau. Republican. Roman Catholic. Author: (with M. Elizabeth West and Nancy Stamey) The Nursing Administrator's Guide to Manpower Control, 1979; contbr. articles to profl. jours. Office: Henrico Doctors Hosp Richmond VA 23229

O'GRADY, TOM, poet; b. Balt., Aug. 26, 1943; s. Thomas Joseph and Sallie Mapp (Dennis) G.; B.A., U. Balt., 1966; M.A., Johns Hopkins U., 1967; m. Bronwyn Southworth, July 28, 1971. Poet in residence Hampden-Sydney (Va.) Coll., 1974—; owner, mgr. The Rose Bower Vineyard & Winery, Hampden-Sydney, 1974—; works include: Establishing A Vineyard, 1977; The Farmville Elegies, 1979; Photo-Graphs, 1980; editor, founder Hampden-Sydney Poetry Rev., 1975—. Served with U.S. Army, 1967-69. Recipient Homeland award for lit., 1966, Leache prize, 1977, Fels prize, 1978; Nat. Endowment Poetry residency, 1976-77. Office: Dept English Hampden Sydney Coll Hampden-Sydney VA 23943

OH, HEE YONG, physician; b. Haenam, Korea, Apr. 15, 1942; s. Man Tae and Yuk Yun (Park) O.; came to U.S., 1972, naturalized, 1978; M.D., Chonnam U. Med. Sch., 1968; m. Vivian Okcha Park, Jan. 10, 1971; children—Hae Su, Jean Vera, Annie Wuhyun. Public health physician, Jindo, Korea, 1971-72; intern St. Francis Gen. Hosp., Pitts., 1973-74; resident in internal medicine VA Med. Center, Dayton, Ohio, 1974-76; staff physician Montgomery (Ala.) VA Med. Center, 1976—, preceptor internal medicine residency program, 1976—. Served with Korean Army, 1968-71. Diplomate Am. Bd. Internal Medicine. Mem. A.C.P. Christian. Home: 680 Hillsboro Rd Montgomery AL 36109 Office: 215 Perry Hill Rd Montgomery AL 36109

O'HAIR, SHEILA SUE, acctg. firm exec.; b. Lubbock, Tex., Mar. 1, 1950; d. Roy James and Kathryn Ray (Millsap) O'H.; B.B.A., Tex. Tech. U., 1972. With Blue Cross-Blue Shield of Tex., Lubbock, 1972-78, mgr., 1975-78; audit supr. (health care) Mason, Nickels & Warner, Lubbock, 1978—; cons., speaker health care related topics, 1976—. Mem. Am. Inst. C.P.A.'s, Am. Women's Soc. C.P.A.'s, Am. Soc. Women Accts., Tex. Soc. C.P.A.'s. Home: Apt 202 5208 11th St Lubbock TX 79416 Office: Mason Nickels & Warner Suite 400 Tower of the Plains 5010 University St Lubbock TX 79452

O'HARA, JOHN STEPHEN, state ofcl.; b. Emmet, Mich., Sept. 28, 1918; s. John C. and Mable Catherine (Mittig) O'H.; B.S. in Bus. Adminstrn., U. Fla., 1946; m. Ann Theresa Rhoads, Feb. 26, 1949; children—John Stephen, Janis Elaine, Victoria Louise, Deborah Ann, David Bruce, Ellen Carol, Suzanne Denise, Cathy Elizabeth, Rebecca Alayne. Statistician, Fla. Indsl. Commn., Tallahassee, 1946-55, asst. dir. research and stats., 1955-68; dir. research and analysis Fla. Dept. Labor and Employment Security, Tallahassee, 1968—. Cubmaster and com. mem. Sewannee River council Boy Scouts Am., 1958-70. Served with USN, 1942-45. Mem. Internat. Assn. Personnel in Employment Security, Fla. State Employee's Assn. Democrat. Roman Catholic. Clubs: Tallahassee Twirlers, Capitol City Cloggers, Apalachee Canoe, K.C. Home: 1021 Carrin Dr Tallahassee FL 32301 Office: 1720 S Gadsden St Tallahassee FL 32301

O'HARA, NORBERT WILHELM, geoscientist, educator; b. Youngstown, Ohio, Oct. 7, 1930; s. Thomas Norbert and Vineta Louise (Wilhelm) O'H.; student Adrian Coll., 1949; B.S., Mich. State Coll., 1952; M.S., Mich. State U., 1954, Ph.D., 1967; m. Fran Louise Allen, Apr. 14, 1967; children—Michael, Kathleen, Colleen, Margaret, Majel, Shannon. Asst. prof. geology Eastern Mich. U., Ypsilanti, 1960-63; asst. prof. geophysics Mich. State U., East Lansing, 1963-67; asso. prof. oceanography World Campus Afloat, Orange, Calif., 1967-68; research asso. in marine geophysics U. Mich., Ann Arbor, 1968-71; research geophysicists U.S. Navy, China Lake, Calif., 1971-76; prof. geosci., head dept. oceanography and ocean engring., Fla. Inst. Tech., Melbourne, 1976—. Dir. Center for Coastal Zone Research, 1977—. Served as naval aviator USMCR, 1954-58. Hinman fellow, 1959-60; Herrick fellow, 1959-60; NSF grantee, 1964-67. Registered geologist, geophysicist, Calif. Mem. Geol. Soc. Am., Soc. Exploration Geophysicists (chmn. U.S. and N. Am. gravity map programs 1977—), Am. Geophys. Union, Soc. Econ. Paleontologists and Mineralogists, Am. Soc. Engring. Edn. Contbr. articles to profl. publs. Home: 1300 S Ramona Ave Indialantic FL 32901 Office: Dept Oceanography and Ocean Engring Fla Inst Tech PO Box 1150 Melbourne FL 32901

OHLENDORF, HAROLD FRED, banker, farmer; b. Freeburg, Ill., Feb. 7, 1909; s. Diedrich and Annie (Schmidt) O.; B.A., Southwestern at Memphis, 1931; m. Frances Margaret Jones, May 2, 1934; children—Nancy (Mrs. Lindsey Fairley), June. Engaged in farming, Mississippi County, Ark., 1935—; pres., dir. Ohlendorf Farms, Osceola, Ark., 1943—, Ohlendorf Milling Co., Osceola, 1943—, Ohlendorf Corp., 1943—, Ohlendorf Investment Co., 1951—, Osceola Broadcasting Corp., 1949—, Ark. Casualty Investment and Ins. Co., 1960—, Farm Bur. Mut. Ins. Co. of Ark., Little Rock, 1960—, So. Farm Bur. Casualty Co., Jackson, Miss.; v.p., dir. First Nat. Bank, Osceola, 1946—; chmn. bd. 1st Nat. Bank, West Memphis, 1954—; pres., dir. So. Farm Bur. Casualty Ins. Co., Jackson, Miss.; dir. Delta Products Co. (Wilson, Ark.), Southwestern Bell Telephone Co. (St. Louis). Pres. Ark. Farm Bur. Fedn., Little Rock, 1954—, also bd. dirs., mem. devel. council U. Ark., Fayetteville; bd. dirs., treas. Nat. Cotton Council. Mem. Osceola Sch. Bd., 1948—; pres., dir. Osceola Indsl. Devel. Corp., 1957—; dir. Ark. Dept. Econ. Devel. Commn., Little Rock, 1970—; trustee Ark. Coll., Batesville; chmn. bd. govs. Osceola Meml. Hosp., Chicksawba Hosp., Blythville Ark.; trustee Mississippi County Library. Recipient Outstanding Citizens award Osceola C. of C., 1950; named Master Farmer of Year, 1950, Ark. Mem. Sigma Nu. Presbyn. (deacon). Clubs: University, Summit, Memphis Country (Memphis). Five Lake Outing (Hughes, Ark.), Greasy Slough Outing (Jonesboro, Ark.); Menesha (Turrell, Ark.); Memphis Country. Home: Ohlendorf Farms Hwy 61 Osceola AR 72370

OHLINGER, WAYNE LAURANCE, ceramic engr.; b. Lake Wales, Fla., Oct. 3, 1944; s. Robert Hayes and Elizabeth (Wirt) O.; B.Ceramic Engring., Ga. Inst. Tech., 1968, M.S., 1974, Ph.D., 1977; m. Lynn Ann Contway, Aug. 23, 1969. Asso. scientist Control Data Corp., Mpls., 1968-71; chief engr. Semicon Asso., Inc., Lexington, 1977—; adj. asso. prof. dept. metall. engring. and materials sci. U. Ky., Lexington, 1978—. Mem. Am. Ceramic Soc., Nat. Inst. Ceramic Engrs., Am. Soc. Metals, Am. Powder Metallurgy Inst., IEEE, Keramos, Sigma Xi. Home: 2983 Shirlee Dr Lexington KY 40502 Office: PO Box 832 Lexington KY 40587

OHMER, MERLIN MAURICE, mathematician, univ. ofcl.; b. Napoleonville, La., Mar. 15, 1923; s. Tobias A. and Elvina M. (mayon) O.; B.S., Tulane U., 1944, M.S., 1948; Ph.D., U. Pitts., 1954; m. Beverly C. Landwerlin, Aug. 30, 1947; children—Carol Ann, Merlin Paul, Susan Stephanie. Asst. prof. math. U. S.W. La., Lafayette, 1948-53, asso. prof., 1953-56, prof., 1956-66; prof. math. Nicholls State U., Thibodaux, La., 1966-69, dean Coll. Scis., 1969—, dir. Metric Edn. Center; vis. asst. prof. Tulane U., New Orleans, 1949-50; vis. asso. prof. U. Pitts., 1953-54; vis. scientist La. Acad. Scis., 1961-67; guest speaker various profl. meetings, civic clubs, parent-tchr. groups and radio stations, 1959—; demonstration class tchr. various levels various schs. in La., 1960—; chmn. adv. bd. Mt. Carmel High Sch., Lafayette, 1962-66; dir. spl. pilot program in metric edn. Lafourche Parish, 1975—; chmn. career edn. com. for high schs. State of La., 1974-77; mem. metric speakers bur. U.S. Bur. Standards. Chmn. budget com. Our Lady of Wisdom Chapel and Student Center, Lafayette, 1960-66; pres. Hamilton PTA, Lafayette, 1962-64; mem. Mayor's Adv. Com., Thibodaux, 1971—; pres. First St. Joseph Parish Council, Thibodaux, 1970-74. Served with USN, World War II. Mem. Am. Math. Soc., Math. Assn. Am. (v.p. 1956-57), Nat. Council Tchrs. Math., La. Acad. Scis., La. Tchrs. Assn., La. Acad. Scis. (dir. vis. scientists program 1965-67), La. Assn. High Edn., Kappa Mu Epsilon, Pi Mu Epsilon. Club: Thibodaux Rotary (dir.). Author: (with others) Elementary Contemporary Mathematics, 1964, Elemtary Contemporary Algebra, 1965; The Real Number System, 1965; (with others) College Algebra, 1966, Modern Mathematics for Elementary School Teachers, 1966; Elementary Geometry for Teachers, 1969; Mathematics for a Liberal Education, 1971; contbr. articles on math. to sci. publs. Home: 106 Acadia Ln Thibodaux LA 70301 Office: Nicholls State Univ Thibodaux LA 70301

O'KEEFE, MICHAEL HANLEY, lawyer, state senator; b. New Orleans, Dec. 1, 1931; s. Arthur J. and Eleonora (Gordon) O'K.; B.A., LL.B., Loyola U., 1955; m. Jean Ann Van Geffen, June 18, 1955; children—Michael H., Erin Elizabeth. Admitted to La. bar, 1955; partner O'Keefe, O'Keefe & Berrigan, 1955—; mem. La. Senate, 1959—, Senate floor leader, 1963-67, pres. pro tem, 1971-76, pres., 1976—; chmn. La. Commn. on Intergovtl. Relations; mem. Council State Govts., La. Fiscal Authority; chmn. Goals for La. Vice pres. Council for Music and Performing Arts, Archdiocesan Commn. on Housing and Community Life; hon. chmn. La. Commn. Status of Women; chmn. Gov.'s Com. Correctional Treatment and Rehab.; chmn. adv. com. La. Planning Office; pres.'s council Loyola U.; bd. dirs. Methodist Hosp., La. Expo, Inc., trustee United Way. Served from 2d lt. to 1st lt., AUS, 1955-57. Mem. C. of C., Am., La., New Orleans bar assns., Res. Officers Assn., Blue Key (hon.). Roman Catholic. Clubs: K.C., Kiwanis. Home: 4 Gull St New Orleans LA 70124 Office: 2623 Canal St New Orleans LA 70119

OKEL, BENJAMIN BOYD, physician; b. Montgomery, Ala., Apr. 18, 1929; s. Edward and Laura Lucile (Boyd) O.; B.S., Tulane U., 1951, M.D., 1954; m. Deborah Westcott, Oct. 26, 1957; children—James L., Thomas W., Susan B. Intern, U.S. Naval Hosp., Bethesda, Md., 1954-55; resident Grady Meml. Hosp., Atlanta, 1958-59; practice medicine specializing in internal medicine, Decatur, Ga., 1961—; mem. Ga. Bd. Human Resources. Served with USNR, 1954-57. Diplomate Am. Bd. Internal Medicine. Fellow A.C.P.; mem. AMA, So. Med. Assn., Med. Assn. Ga., DeKalb Med. Soc. Home: 147 Mount Vernon Dr Decatur GA 30030 Office: 2193 N Decatur Rd Decatur GA 30033

O'KELLEY, WILLIAM CLARK, fed. judge; b. Atlanta, Jan. 2, 1930; s. Ezra Clark and Theo Dosia (Johnson) O'K.; A.B., Emory U., 1951, LL.B., 1953; m. Ernestine Allen, Mar. 28, 1953; children—Virginia Leigh Wood, William C. Admitted to Ga. bar, 1952; practiced law, Atlanta; partner firm O'Kelley, Hopkins & Van Gerpen, 1961-70; asst. U.S. atty. for No. Dist. Ga., 1959-61; U.S. dist. judge, 1970—. Mem. finance com. N.W. Ga. council Girl Scouts, 1958-70. Gen. counsel Republican Party of Ga., 1968-70. Served as 1st lt. USAF, 1953-57. Mem. Dist. Judges Assn. 5th Circuit (pres. 1979-80), Omicron Delta Kappa, Phi Delta Phi, Sigma Chi (grand praetor 1967). Baptist. Kiwanian (past pres. Peachtree-Atlanta). Editorial bd. Ga. Bar Jour., 1952-53. Home: 550 Ridgecrest Dr Norcross GA 30071 Office: 1942 US Courthouse 75 Spring St SW Atlanta GA 30303

O'KOREN, MARIE LOUISE, nurse, univ. dean; b. Eveleth, Minn., Mar. 10, 1926; diploma Sch. Nursing, U. Minn., 1946; B.S.N., Long Beach State Coll., 1957; M.S.N., U. Ala., 1958, Ed.D., 1964. Staff nurse, asst. supr. operating rm. Seaside Meml. Hosp., Long Beach, Calif., 1947-57; instr. med.-surg. nursing Sch. Nursing, U. Ala., Tuscaloosa, 1958-61, asst. prof., 1961-62, asst. dean, chmn. grad. program, asso. prof., 1964-67, asst. dean, prof. nursing, Birmingham, 1967-69, asso. dean, 1969-70, dean, 1970—, prof. nursing, 1967—, chmn. grad. program, 1967—; mem. acad. health affairs com. VA Region 14; mem. nursing and health programs com. ARC; past adv. com. Ida V. Moffett Sch. Nursing; bd. advs. Seymour Ednl. and Vocat. Guidance Assn.; mem. chmn. exec. com. council of deans of schs. of nursing Ala. Commn. Higher Edn.; nat. adv. council nurse tng. Health Resources Adminstrn.; rev. com. on fin. distress div. nursing NIH. Bd. dirs. Vol. Bur., Birmingham; past chmn. Ch. Ministry Bd. Bixler scholar, 1963-64. Mem. Nat. League Nursing (doctoral fellow, 1962-63), Ala. League Nursing (past dir.), Am. Nurses Assn., AAUP, Am. Assn. Colls. Nursing, Assn. Suprs. and Curriculum Devel., World Edn. Fellowship, Jefferson County Mental Health Soc., Ala. Nurses Assn. (chmn. dist. scholarship com.), Sigma Theta Tau, Sigma Chi Nu, Delta Kappa Gamma, Kappa Delta Pi, Omicron Delta Kappa, Phi Delta Kappa, Alpha Tau Delta. Mem. editorial bd. Health Care Dimensions; cons. Nurse Educator, Jour. Nursing Adminstrn.; research and publs. in field. Office: U Ala Sch Nursing Univ Sta Birmingham AL 35294

OLDHAM, DOROTHY CLOUDMAN (MRS. ROBERT PRICE OLDHAM), advt. agy. exec.; b. Detroit; d. Philip Horace and Mabel (Rigg) Cloudman; student Albion Coll., Mich.; B.A., U. Mich.; m. Robert Price Oldham; 1 dau., Carol Cloudman. Jewelry advt. service mgr. Simons Michelson Advt. Co., Detroit; fashion editor Detroit Free Press; account exec. W. B. Doner & Co., Detroit; owner-pres. Cloudman Oldham Advt. and Pub. Relations Agency, Inc., 1947-72, owner, 1975—; editor Detroit & Suburban Life, 1967-71; dir. pub. relations advt. agy., Miami, 1974-75; writer Fla. Architecture Mag., 1975, Miami Mag., 1976; v.p. NHFL Jour. Sales, 1975-76, 77—. Chmn., Fashion Careers Lectr. Series, Wayne U., 1965; mem. pub. affairs com. Greater Detroit Bd. Commerce, 1967-72. Chmn., Women Out Working for Romney for Gov., 1966; pres. Republican Bus. and Profl. Women, 1966-67. Mem. Women in Communications, Fashion Group of Miami, Adv. Fedn. Greater Miami, Nat. Home Fashions League (v.p. NHFL Jour. sales 1977-78, v.p. edn.-consumer 1979-80). Home and office: 261 Bal Cross Dr Bal Harbour FL 33154

OLDHAM, HENRY NEVEL, aerospace engr.; b. Athens, Ga., Apr. 29, 1943; s. Arthur S. and Florrie M. (Phillips) O.; B.S., U. Ga., 1963; B.Aerospace Engring., Ga. Tech., 1965; M.Aerospace Engring., U. Va., 1968; m. Frances Wynn Hamilton, May 27, 1978; 1 son, John Nevel. Rocket propulsion design engr. Pratt & Whitney div. United Aircraft, W. Palm Beach, Fla., 1965; research asso. U. Va. Research Labs., Charlottesville, 1966-68; aerospace engr. systems engring. directorate U.S. Army Missile Command, Redstone Arsenal, Ala., 1971-76; aerospace engr. Multiple launch rocket system project office Redstone Arsenal, Ala., 1977—; mem. community adv. com. Solar Energy Research Inst. 1975-76. Mem. Civic Club Council, 1975—, pres., 1977-79; bd. dirs. N.Ala. Kidney Found., 1975—, Madison County Heart Assn., 1979—, fund drive co-chmn., 1979—. Served with Ordnance Corps, U.S. Army, 1968-71. Recipient cert. of achievement U.S. Army, 1975, 77, 78. Mem. AIAA, Assn. of U.S. Army, Res. Officers Assn., Aircraft Owners and Pilots Assn., Madison County C. of C., Jaycees (pres. Huntsville 1975-76, internat. senator 1977), Phi Mu Alpha Sinfonia. Methodist. Composer instrumental music for Punch and Judy Puppet Show, Fantasy Playhouse Children's Theatre, 1977. Home: 8801 Willow Hills Dr Huntsville AL 35802 Office: DRCPM-RSES Redstone Arsenal AL 35809

OLDSON, WILLIAM ORVILLE, educator; b. Hampton, Va., Jan. 23, 1940; s. James Orville and Kathryn Francis (Zephir) O.; B.A. magna cum laude, Spring Hill Coll., 1965; M.A., Ind. U., 1966, Ph.D., 1970; m. Judith Ann Kinsinger, June 11, 1967; children—Scott Ryan, Darren Randall. Asst. prof. history dept. Fla. State U., Tallahassee, 1969-74, asso. chmn. history dept., 1973-75, asso. prof., 1974-79, prof., 1979—; dir. grievances and arbitrations United Faculty Fla., 1978—. Russian and East European Inst. fellow, 1965-66, grantee, 1967-68, Nat. Def. Fgn. Lang. fellow, 1966-67; Fulbright fellow, 1967-68; Internat. Research and Exchanges Bd. fellow, 1973. Mem. Am. Hist. Assn., Am. Assn. Advancement Slavic Studies, Soc. Romanian Studies, Am. Assn. S.E. European Studies, Conf. Slavic and East European History, Delta Tau Kappa. Democrat. Roman Catholic. Author: The Historical and Nationalistic Thought of Nicolae Torga, 1973; Contract Adminstration: From Grievance to Arbitration, 1978. Home: 1116 Sandhurst Dr Tallahassee FL 32312 Office: History Dept Fla State U Tallahassee FL 32306

OLDZIEJ, BARBARA ELIZABETH, mfg. co. exec.; b. Ft. Lauderdale, Fla., Nov. 18, 1950; d. Gerard Stanley and Regina Josephine (Sudziarski) O.; B.A., Fla. State U., 1972; M.B.A., N.Y. Inst. Tech., 1976. Tchr. history Broward County Sch. System, Ft. Lauderdale, 1972-74; mem. public relations staff Saxon Bus. Products, Inc., Miami, 1976-77, mgr. mktg. communications, 1977—. Mem. fin. div. Big Bros., Big Sisters. Republican. Roman Catholic. Home: 1607 Park Rd Hollywood FL 33021 Office: 13900 NW 57th Ct Miami Lakes FL 33014

O'LEARY, JOHN GREGORY, JR., mgmt. info. systems co. exec.; b. Bklyn., Aug. 9, 1944; s. John Gregory and Helen Elizabeth (Doran) O'L.; B.A. in Econs., Fordham U., 1967; M.S. in Mgmt., U. Tex., Dallas, 1976; m. Jane Roberts, Nov. 10, 1968; children—John G.,

Michael. Electronic data systems engr. Electronic Data Systems, N.Y.C., 1973-74, Dallas, 1974-75; programmer/analyst Tex. Instruments, Dallas, 1975-76, sr. tech. analyst, 1976-77, prodn. services bus. group mgr., 1977-78, mgr. prodn. ops. control, 1978—; tchr. U. Tex., Dallas, 1976—. Served with USAF, 1968-73. Mem. Am. Mgmt. Assn., Assn. Computing Machinery, Soc. Computer Simulation. Home: 2304 Covinton Ln Plano TX 75023 Office: PO Box 225621 M/S 963 Dallas TX 75265

O'LEARY, WILLIAM COLDEN, JR., psychologist; b. Savannah, Ga., Mar. 9, 1941; s. William Colden and Julia Margaret (Chapman) O'L.; A.A., Armstrong State Coll., 1961; A.B., Columbia Bible Coll., 1965; M.Div., Trinity Div. Sch., 1968; M.Ed., U. Ga., 1972; Ph.D., U. S.C., 1974; m. Bonnie Jan Tyner, Sept. 3, 1966; children—William Colden, Ronald Tyner, David Brian. Vocat. rehab. counselor Ga. Dept. Edn., Augusta, 1968-71; counseling psychologist VA Med. Center, Augusta, 1971—; pvt. practice psychology, North Augusta, S.C., 1975—; adj. faculty, depts. psychology and edn. Augusta Coll.; psychol. cons. Easter Seals Center, Augusta Reading Found., S.C. and Ga. depts. vocat. rehab., Ga. Office Offender Rehab., 1975. Vice chmn. Augusta Mayor's Com. on Employment of Handicapped, 1976—; del. Pres.'s. Com. Conf. on Employment of Handicapped, Washington, 1976, 77, 78; bd. dirs. Broad Oaks Sch., Augusta, 1976-78; adv. bd. Augusta Shelter for Abused Children, 1979. Recipient Dir's. commendation VA, 1976. Licensed psychologist, S.C. Mem. Am., Ga., Southeastern, S.C., Central Savannah River (sec.-treas. 1980) psychol. assns., Southeastern Behavior Therapy Assn., Nat. Register Health Service Providers in Psychology, Phi Delta Kappa. Baptist. Clubs: Lions (pres. Augusta Club), Able-Disabled. Contbr. papers to symposia, Med. Coll. Ga., 1976, 80, Internat. Assn. Personnel in Employment Security, 1977; Southeastern Psychol. Assn. Conv., 1978. Home: Route 1 Hereford Farm Rd Evans GA 30809 Office: VA Med Center Augusta GA 30904

OLEJAR, PAUL DUNCAN, former info. sci. adminstr.; b. Hazelton, Pa., Sept. 13, 1906; s. George and Anna (Danco) O.; A.B., Dickinson Coll., 1928; m. Ann Ruth Dillard, Jan. 6, 1933 (dec. Oct. 1978); 1 son, Peter; m. 2d, Martha S. Ross, Sept. 8, 1979. Dir. edn. W.Va. Conservation Commn., 1936-41; coordinator U.S. Fish and Wildlife Service, 1941-42; chief press and radio Bur. Reclamation, Dept. Interior, 1946-47; editor Plant Industry Sta. AGRI, 1948-51; chmn. spl. reports Agrl. Research Adminstrn., 1951-56; dir. tech. info. Edgewood Arsenal, Md., 1959-63; chief, tech. info. plans and programs Army Research Office, Washington, 1963-64; chmn. chem. info. unit NSF, Washington, 1965-70; dir. drug info. program Sch. Pharmacy, U. N.C., Chapel Hill, 1970-73, ret. Served with AUS, 1942-46. Decorated Army Commendation medal. Mem. Am. Soc. Info. Sci., Drug Info. Assn., Ravens Claw, Theta Chi, Omicron Delta Kappa. Methodist. Home: 664 SW Port Malabar Blvd Palm Bay FL 32905

OLINGER, RONALD DEAN, chemist; b. Chattanooga, Apr. 2, 1948; s. Herbert Telford and Frances Elizabeth (Sotherland) O.; B.S., U. Ala., 1970, M.S., 1978. Tchr. math. Madison County (Ala.) schs., 1970-73; tchr. chemistry Huntsville (Ala.) city schs., 1973-76; grad. lab. asst. U. Ala., Huntsville, 1976-77; chemist PPG Inc., Lake Charles, La., 1977—. Class B tchr.'s certificate, Ala. Mem. Am. Chem. Soc., Sigma Xi. Democrat. Methodist. Home: 2960 Lake St Apt 215 Lake Charles LA 70601 Office: PPG Inc Box 1000 Lake Charles LA 70602

OLIPHINT, ROBERT ERSKINE, technology co. exec.; b. Austin, Tex., June 1, 1941; s. Joseph and Helen (Rhodes) O.; B.B.A., U. Tex., 1964; children—Joseph, Patricia. Jr. engr. White Instrument Labs., Austin, 1961-63; successively cost acct., materials mgr., sales mgr., ops. mgr., gen. mgr., div. v.p. Tracor, Inc., Austin, 1963-75, corp. v.p., gen. mgr., 1975—; pres. Westronics, Inc., Ft. Worth, 1971—, also dir. Active Austin United Way, Austin Heritage Soc. Mem. Instrument Soc. Am. (sr.), Austin C. of C. (dir. diplomat), IEEE, Austin Amateur Radio Club, Longhorn Corvette Club. Republican. Episcopalian. Contbr. articles to profl. jours. Home: 8503 Appalachian Austin TX 78759 Office: 6500 Tracor Ln Austin TX 78721

OLIVA, RALPH ANGELO, electronics co. exec.; b. Tarrytown, N.Y., July 1, 1946; s. I. Ralph and Raechel (Pisacano) O.; B.S. in Physics, Fordham U., 1966; M.S. in Physics, Rensselaer Poly. Inst., 1973, Ph.D. in Solid State Physics, 1973. Staff physicist U.S. Army Electronics Command, Ft. Monmouth, N.J., 1965-68; doctoral asst. Rensselaer Poly. Inst., 1966-73; mem. tech. staff Tex. Instruments Inc., 1973-75, mgr. ednl. merchandising devel., 1975-77, dir. Learning Center, 1977—; founder Learning Factors Engring. Lab., 1978; bd. vis. advs. UCLA Grad. Sch. Edn.; adv. Congressional Congress of Future, 1979. Recipient Sun and Balance award Rensselaer Poly. Inst., 1973; NSF study and research grantee, 1959, 64. Mem. Am. Phys. Soc., Am. Assn. Physics Tchrs., Nat. Council Tchrs. Math., Nat. Council Suprs. Math. Roman Catholic. Author books, the most recent being: Sourcebook for Programmable Calculators, 1978. Home: 4301 Country Club Dr Plano TX 75074 Office: PO Box 225012 M/S 84 Dallas TX 75265

OLIVER, CLIFTON, JR., educator; b. Amarillo, Tex., Dec. 3, 1915; s. Clifton and Laura Pearl (Hudson) O.; B.A., Tex. Tech U., 1935, M.A., 1936; postgrad. La. State U., 1937-38, U. Wis., 1938-39. Prof. mgmt. Tex. Christian U., Ft. Worth, 1939-43; prof. U. Fla., Gainesville, 1946—, dir. Mgmt. Center, 1959-71; cons. in field. Served to lt., AUS, 1943-46. Recipient service award U. Fla. Athletic Assn., 1977; elected to Fla. Track and Field Hall of Fame, 1979. Mem. Acad. Mgmt., Am. Personnel Assn., Am. Soc. Tng. Dirs., Nat. Panel Am. Arbitration Assn., Mgmt. Assn. Gainesville (pres. 1969—), Nat. Police Assn., Fla. Purchasing Assn. (life), Fla. Blue Key, Alpha Kappa Psi (Service award 1968), Alpha Tau Omega (trustee, Service award 1971), Alpha Chi, Pi Sigma Alpha, Pi Gamma Mu. Elk, Kiwanian. Home: PO Box 14505 Gainesville FL 32604

OLIVER, ERNEST BINGHAM, physician; b. Birmingham, Ala., Oct. 8, 1912; s. William George and Eula (Bingham) O.; A.B., U. Ala., 1934; M.D., Harvard, 1938; m. Barbara Schroeder, May 24, 1965; children—Jane, Bingham, Margaret, William; stepchildren—Carter, Taylor, Clay. Intern, Springfield (Mass.) Hosp., 1938-40; house officer in obstetrics and gynecology Boston Lying-in Hosp., 1940; practice medicine specializing in gynecology, Birmingham, 1946—; clin. asso. prof. obstetrics and gynecology U. Ala., Birmingham, 1977—; chief obstetrics and gynecology Bapt. Med. Center-Princeton, Birmingham, 1968-75. Served to lt. col. USAF, 1940-46. Decorated Air Medal, Bronze Star with oak leaf cluster. Diplomate Am. Bd. Obstetrics and Gynecology. Mem. Am. Coll. Obstetrics and Gynecology; Ala., Southeastern obstet. and gynecol. socs., AMA. Episcopalian. Club: Birmingham Country. Home: 3276 Overton Manor Dr Birmingham AL 35243 Office: 801 Princeton Ave Birmingham AL 35211

OLIVER, FREDERICK CARLTON, JR., internist; b. Spartanburg, S.C., Nov. 19, 1949; s. Frederick Carlton and Betty Sue (Thomas) O.; B.A. cum laude, Wofford Coll., 1971; M.D., Med. U. S.C., 1975; m. Susan Ayers, Dec. 31, 1972; 1 son, Frederick Carlton. Intern, Erlanger Med. Center, Chattanooga, 1975-76, resident in internal medicine, 1976-78, chief resident in medicine, 1978-79; practice medicine specializing in internal medicine, Cary, N.C., 1979—; chief staff Western Wake Hosp.; med. examiner Wake County, 1980—. Diplomate Am. Bd. Internal Medicine, Nat. Bd. Med. Examiners. Mem. ACP, AMA, N.C. Med. Soc., Wake County Med. Soc., Am. Soc. Internal Medicine, N.C. Soc. Internal Medicine, C. of C. Methodist. Home: 115 Overview Ln Cary NC 27511 Office: 901 Kildaire Farm Rd Cary NC 27511

OLIVER, GEORGE JOSEPH, nuclear engr.; b. Kinston, N.C., Sept. 4, 1947; s. George Melvin and Carrie Jean (Eason) O.; B.S., N.C. State U., 1969, M.S., 1971, Ph.D., 1973, M.S. in Econs., 1976; m. Vicki Lynn Sexton, Feb. 12, 1977; 1 son, George Brandon. Research asso. N.C. State U., Raleigh, 1971-73; scientist Carolina Power & Light, Raleigh, N.C., 1973-75, sr. engr. radiation control, 1975-78, project engr. health physics, 1978-79, prin. engr. health physics, 1979—; mem. grad. faculty U., N.C., 1979—; adj. prof. nuclear engring. N.C. State U., 1980—. USPHS fellow, 1969-71. Mem. Health Physics Soc., Am. Nuclear Soc. Democrat. Methodist. Home: 287 High Meadow Dr Cary NC 27511 Office: Box 1551 Raleigh NC 27602

OLIVER, JAMES RUSSELL, ednl. adminstr., computer scientist; b. Egan, La., Sept. 12, 1924; s. Jack and Edna (Trumps) O.; B.S. in Chemistry, U. Southwestern La., 1950; M.S., Tulane U., 1951, Ph.D. in Chemistry, 1955; m. Betty Jean Truax; children—Cynthia Louise, James Russell, Mary Ellen. Asso. prof. chemistry U. Southwestern La., 1954-59, prof., 1959-69, prof. computer sci., 1969—, dir. Computing Center, 1960-70, 72, chmn. adv. com. Computing Center, dean Grad. Sch., 1961-73, v.p. adminstrv. affairs, 1973—; asst. state supt. edn. for mgmt. research and fin. La. Dept. Edn., 1972-73, exec. dir. La. Bd. Edn., 1972; cons., adv. in field; moderator Inside USL, TV series; mem. tchr. cert. appeals com. La. Bd. Elem. and Secondary Edn.; chmn. bd., chief exec. officer Mgmt. Systems Design, Inc., Lafayette, La.; cons./adv. in data processing Commr. of La. Health and Human Resources Adminstrn.; mem. La. Data Processing Coordinating and Adv. Council; chmn. edn. task force Lafayette region La.: Priorities for Future; bd. dirs. S.W. Ednl. Devel. Lab. Bd. dirs., chmn. U. Southwestern La. relations com. Lafayette C. of C.; sec. U. Southwestern La. Newman Found.; mem. pastoral council Roman Catholic Diocese of Lafayette, chmn. pastoral council, ordained permanent deacon, 1977, asso. chancellor; mem. exec. bd. Evangeline Area council, chmn. Live Oak dist. Boy Scouts Am.; mem. Lafayette Bicentennial Commn. Served with USAAF, 1943-45, USAF, 1951-53. Decorated knight St. Gregory Vatican; recipient Frank G. Brewer Meml. Aerospace award CAP, 1974. Fellow AAAS; mem. Am. Chem. Soc., AAUP, La. Acad. Scis. (pres., editor newsletter), La. Edn. Assn. (chmn. com. human relations), Assn. Computing Machinery (nat. chmn. com. student membership and student chpts.), Soc. Indsl. and Applied Math., Soc. Automation Bus. Edn., Data Processing Mgmt. Assn. (regional Computer Sci. Man of Yr.), La. Assn. Ednl. Data Systems (pres., dir.), Sigma Xi, Phi Kappa Phi, Sigma Pi Sigma, Omicron Delta Epsilon. Club: Rotary (club Rotarian of Yr., dir. Internat. Chess Fellowship). Author Diocesan Newspaper series Current of Life; research, publs. in field; abstractor, sect. editor Chem. Abstracts; reviewer Computing Revs.; dept. editor Computers and Soc., also editor. Office: PO Box 133 USL Sta Lafayette LA 70501

OLIVER, JAMES WENDELL, city ofcl.; b. Southern Pines, N.C., Feb. 20, 1928; s. Samuel Hudnell and Eula Leora (Inge) O.; B.S. in Civil Engring., N.C. State U., 1956; m. Lois Irene Ray, Feb. 2, 1952; children—James, Charles, Julia. Design engr. City of Greensboro (N.C.), 1956-61; constrn. engr. City of Burlington (N.C.), 1962-65; city engr. City of High Point, 1966—. Served with U.S. Army, 1950-53. Mem. Am. Public Works Assn., Am. Water Works Assn. Home: 1901 Beaucrest Ave High Point NC 27260 Office: 211 S Hamilton St High Point NC 27261

OLIVER, JOHN PHIN, mfg. co. exec.; b. Houston, May 20, 1923; s. Harold Wellesley and Elizabeth (Phin) O.; B.S. in Mech. Engring., Rice U., Houston, 1948; M.B.A., U. Houston, 1954; m. Pilialoha Hopkins Robertson, June 23, 1973; children by previous marriage—John Phin, James Robert. With Cameron Iron Works Inc., Houston, 1948-74, tech. mgr. valve and oil tool products, 1972-74; engring. and mgmt. cons., Houston, 1974-75, 78—; v.p., gen. mgr. Vetco Valve Corp., Houston, 1975—. Served to capt. USAAF, 1943-46. Registered profl. engr., Tex. Mem. Am. Soc. Metals, ASME, Am. Petroleum Inst., Houston Engring. and Sci. Soc., Nat. Soc. Profl. Engrs. Club: Houston Racquet. Patentee in field. Home and Office: 37 Stillforest St Houston TX 77024

OLIVER, MARY WILHELMINA, law librarian, educator; b. Cumberland, Md., May 4, 1919; d. John Arlington and Sophia (Lear) Oliver; A.B., Western Md. Coll., 1940; B.S. in Library Sci., Drexel Inst. Tech., 1943; J.D., U. N.C., 1951. Asst. circulation librarian N.J. Coll. Women, 1943-45; asst. in law library U. Va., 1945-47; asst. reference, social sci. librarian Drake U., 1947-49; research asst. Inst. Govt., U. N.C., 1951-52, asst. law librarian, 1952-55, asst. prof. law, law librarian, 1955-59, asso. prof. law, law librarian, 1959—, prof. law and library sci., law librarian, 1969—; admitted to N.C. bar, 1951. Mem. Am. Assn. Law Libraries (pres. 1972-73), Spl. Libraries Assn., Am., N.C. bar assns., Assn. Am. Law Schs. (exec. com. 1979—), Am. Soc. Legal History, Law Alumni Assn. U. N.C., Inc., Internat. Assn. Law Libraries, Seldon Soc., Order of Coif. Home: Box 733 Chapel Hill NC 27514

OLIVIER, HENRI GASTON, mktg. exec.; b. Ougree, Belgium, Oct. 7, 1954; came to U.S., 1954, naturalized, 1960; s. Gaston Pierre and Fernande Sylvie (Chartier) O.; B.B.A., U. Tex., 1975. With Mitsui & Co., Inc., Houston, 1977—, sr. staff. Mem. Tex. Assn. Steel Importers (dir. 1978—), Acacia. Roman Catholic. Home: 3928-8 W Alabama St Houston TX 77027 Office: 5000 One Shell Plaza Houston TX 77001

OLMSTEAD, GLORIA KATHERINE, univ. ofcl.; b. Somerville, Mass., Feb. 18, 1932; d. Perley Bernard and Delia Teresa (Lynskey) Welch; student Boston Coll., 1951, U. Pa., 1975, U. Calif., Santa Barbara, 1976; m. Robert Douglas Olmstead, July 12, 1952; children—Robert Douglas, Diane Frances, David. Dir. federally insured loan program U. Pa., 1972-77, asst. treas., officer of corp., 1977; acct. facilities planning and constrn. U. Houston, 1977-78, mgr. fiscal services facilities planning and constrn., 1978—; Pa. state trainer Basic Edn. Opportunity Grant Program; cons. collection agy.; nat. rep. higher edn. on legislation and regulations, Washington; performer featured roles in Lil Abner, Fiorello and Mame. Active Huntwick Civic Assn., Pitman Choral Soc., Washington Stage Scripteasers; bd. dirs. N.J. State Pageant for Miss Am.; cantor, trainer extraordinary ministers Prince of Peace Community Ch. Mem. Nat. Assn. Coll. and Univ. Bus. Officers, Eastern Assn. Fin. Aid Adminstrs., Nat. Assn. Fin. Aid Adminstrs., Tex. Assn. State Sr. Coll. and Univ. Bus. Officers, Am. Work Edn. Found., U. Houston Acad. and Profl. Women's Assn., AAUW. Office: 4211 Elgin St Houston TX 77004

OLSEN, CARL EDWIN, mfr.; b. Clifton, Tex., Aug. 3, 1902; s. Petter and Helene (Fjaestad) O.; B.S., Tex. A. and M. U., 1923; m. Elsie Duncan, Oct. 3, 1923; 1 son, Carl Edwin. Profl. baseball player, 1923-26; pres., gen. mgr., dir. Gearench Mfg. Co., Clifton, 1927—; pres. Mgmt. Info. Systems Inc., 1973—. Recipient award of honor Am. Assn. Coll. Baseball Coaches, cert. of appreciation Am. Legion Baseball; mem. Hall of Fame, Tex. A&M U.; registered profl. engr., Tex. Tex. A. & M. U. Baseball Field named in his honor. Mem. ASME, Am. Soc. Tool Engrs. Clubs: Houston Petroleum, Nomad. Masons, Lions, Yankee Alumni. Patentee in field. Home: PO Box 9140 Houston TX 77011 Office: PO Box 192 Clifton TX 76634

OLSEN, CLIFFORD EUGENE, lawyer; b. Morgan City, La., Dec. 6, 1944; s. Clifford Danna and Lucille (Bergeron) O.; B.S., U. Southwestern La., Lafayette, 1966; J.D., Loyola U. New Orleans, 1970. Staff acct. Voorhies, Davis & Clostio, Lafayette, 1964-66; lectr., lab. teaching asst. U. Southwestern La., Lafayette, 1964-66; staff acct. Peat, Marwick & Mitchell, New Orleans, 1966; tax. acct. Ernst & Ernst, New Orleans, 1966-67; admitted to La. bar, 1971; tax atty. Shell Oil Co., New Orleans and Los Angeles, 1967-72; gen. counsel, sec.-treas. Euro-Pirates, Internat., Inc., (Europe and S. Am.), Euro-Pirates Ltda. (Brazil and Panama), Slater Farms, French Quarter Inn, Inc., Charles Slater Enterprises, New Orleans, 1972-74; tax and ins. mgr., counsel Diamondhead Corp., New Orleans, 1974-76; mem. firm Gegenheimer & Bienvenu, Gretna, La., 1974-77; pres. Landura Co., Harvey, La., 1976-79; atty., counselor at law Clifford E. Olsen, Harvey, 1979—; pres., chmn. bd. Delta Internat. Investor Corp., Delta Internat. Constrn. Corp., New Orleans. Mem. Am. Bar Assn., Fed. Bar Assn., La. Bar Assn. Office: 2150 Westbank Expressway Oil Center Suite 516 Harvey LA 70057

OLSEN, GARY KENT, realty co. exec.; b. Titusville, Pa., May 26, 1938; s. Harold George and Mary Eyla (Herring) O.; B.A., Haverford Coll., 1961. Sales rep. Control Data Corp., Washington, 1968-69; exec. dir. Nat. Jogging Assn., Washington, 1968—; v.p. sales Cumberland Corp., Front Royal, Va., 1972-75; pres. Homestead Properties of Front Royal, Inc., 1974—; instr. Lord Fairfax Community Coll., 1977. Served to maj., USAF, 1962-67. Mem. Nat., Va. assns. realtors, Blue Ridge Rd. Realtors, Farm and Land Inst., Am. Med. Joggers Assn., Am. Numis. Assn., Nat. Geneal. Soc., SAR, Sigma Xi. Republican. Presbyterian. Club: Rotary. Editor: Guidelines to Successful Jogging, 1972. Home and office: 501 S Royal Ave Front Royal VA 22630

OLSEN, ROBERT JON, mgmt. cons.; b. Port Chester, N.Y., Jan. 25, 1943; s. Clarence O. and Grace Louise (Sofield) O.; B.S. in Chem. Engring., Lehigh U., 1964; M.S. in Mgmt. Sci., 1965. Vice pres., dir. Summit Ins. Co. N.Y., Houston, 1971-75; chmn. bd. Sunshine Energy Systems, Inc., Houston, 1976—; mgmt. cons. Gulf Oil Corp., Houston, 1976—; founder Chicago Pizza Corp., Houston, 1976, dir., 1976—. Mem. Am. Inst. Chem. Engrs., Inst. Mgmt. Sci., Tex. Ski Council (pres. 1976-77). Rocky Mountain Ski Assn. (dir. 1976—). Club: Space City Ski (pres. 1975-76, dir. 1977—). Office: Gulf Oil Corp PO Box 2100 Houston TX 77001

OLSEN, ROGER LESLIE, lighting fixture co. exec.; b. Ashland, Wis., Feb. 24, 1935; s. Leon W. and Amy Desideria (Melstrand) O.; B.B.A., U. Wis., Madison, 1960; m. Barbara Ann Tlusty, Oct. 1, 1960; children—Robert, Thomas, Karin. With Price Waterhouse & Co., Chgo. and Mpls., 1960-64; controller Preway Inc., Wisconsin Rapids, Wis., 1964-67; comptroller, mgr. acctg. A.O. Smith Corp., Milw. and Louisville, 1967-73; comptroller ITT-Nesbitt, Jackson, Tenn., 1973-75; v.p., divisional comptroller ITT Lighting Fixture Div., Southaven, Miss., 1975—. Served with U.S. Army, 1954-56. Mem. Nat. Assn. Accts., Fin. Execs. Inst. Republican. Home: 2576 Overlook Dr Germantown TN 38138 Office: PO Box 100 Southaven MS 38671

OLSON, HARRY CHANDLER, electronics distbn. exec.; b. Des Moines, Jan. 27, 1918; s. Harry Sigfred and Lulu Clara (Mollenhoff) O.; B.A., Drake U., 1941; M.B.A., George Washington U., 1964; grad. Indsl. Coll. Armed Forces, 1964; m. Betty Jane Graham, Dec. 25, 1941; children—Penny Suzanne Olson Haan, Jill Ann Olson Monroe, Jon Chandler, Graham Donald. Commd. 2d lt. U.S. Marine Corps, 1941, advanced through grades to maj. gen., 1967; with installations and logistics Hdqrs. USMC, 1972-73; ret., 1974; dir. central ops. Am. Handicraft Co. div. Tandy Corp., 1974-78, dir. adminstrn. distbn. operation Radio Shack div., Ft. Worth and Charleston, S.C., 1978—; asso. prof. U. So. Calif., 1946-49; Keynote speaker NATO Logistics Conf., Naples, Italy, 1973. Decorated Legion of Merit (4), Bronze Star with Combat V, Navy Commendation medal; recipient meritorious service award Dept. Def., 1963; named one of ten outstanding grads. for last 100 yrs. East High Sch., Des Moines, 1978. Mem. Soc. Automotive Engrs., Marine Corps Assn., Delta Theta Phi, Sigma Alpha Epsilon. Lutheran. Clubs: Ft. Worth Boat, Lake Country Estates Golf and Country, Optimists, Toastmasters, DeMolay (past master, Legion of Honor, Legion of Merit). Home: 322 Shaftsbury Ln King's Grant Summerville SC 29483 Office: PO Box 9163 Hanahan Br Charleston SC 29410

OLSON, HERBERT THEODORE, trade assn. exec.; b. Bridgeport, Conn., Feb. 9, 1929; s. Herbert Theodore and Inez Evelyn (Lindahl) O.; student Heidelberg Coll., 1947-49; A.B., Ohio U., 1951, postgrad., 1951-52; m. Ethel Victoria Cross, Oct. 29, 1960; 1 dau., Christina Victoria. Asst. to dean of men Ohio U., 1951-52; with Union Carbide Corp., 1952-71, mgr. employee relations, coordinator public affairs, Chgo., 1967-69, corp. mgr. public affairs, N.Y.C., 1969-71; exec. v.p. Am. Assn. for Aging, Washington, 1971-75; dir. spl. projects Am. Health Care Assn., Washington, 1975-79; pres. Splty. Advt. Assn. Internat., Irving, Tex., 1979—; mem. long-term care for elderly research rev. and adv. com. Dept. Health, 1972-77; mem. Longterm Care grant rev. com. HEW, 1972-77. Mem. planning commn. City of Torrance (Calif.), 1962-64, city councilman, 1964-67; mem. nat. Exploring com., mem. nat. events com., mem.-at-large nat. council Boy Scouts Am. Served with USAR. Recipient Disting. Eagle award Boy Scouts Am., 1974, Silver Beaver award, 1968. Mem. Meeting Planners Internat. (charter), Am. Soc. Assn. Execs., U.S. C. of C., Washington Soc. Assn. Execs., Am. Advt. Fedn., Tex. Soc. Assn. Execs. Lutheran. Clubs: Rotary, Las Colinas Country, Nat. Assn. Execs., Masons, Shriners. Office: 1404 Walnut Hill Ln Irving TX 75062

OLSON, JAMES ROBERT, naval officer; b. Columbus, Nebr., Nov. 23, 1940; s. Robert August and Jean Elizabeth Olson; student U.S. Naval Acad.; B.A., U. Nebr., Lincoln, 1965; M.A., Central Mich. U.; divorced; 1 son, Eric Robert. Commd. ensign U.S. Navy, 1965, advanced through grades to comdr., 1980; service in S.W. Pacific, Philippines and Vietnam; operational intelligence mgr. Task Force #168, Alexandria, Va., 1977—; mem. faculty Def. Intelligence Sch., 1970-71. Decorated Bronze Star with combat V, Air medal (5); recipient various certs. appreciation. Mem. Naval Res. Assn., U.S. Naval Acad. Alumni Assn., Nat. Rifle Assn. (life), Colo. R.R. Hist. Found. (life), Phi Alpha Theta. Methodist. Club: Econ. of Detroit. Home: 6416 Bluebill Ln Alexandria VA 22307 Office: NIC-03 RN 2461 Eisenhower Ave Alexandria VA 22314

OLSON, JOHN DAVID, pathologist; b. Willison, N.D., Sept. 22, 1944; s. Arnold Floyd and Emily S. O.; B.A., U. Colo., 1966; B.S., U. N.D., 1968; M.D., Georgetown U., 1970; Ph.D., U. Minn., 1976; m. Lorraine Louise Boos, June 29, 1968; children—Emily Carolyn, Sara Catherine. Intern, Mayo Grad. Sch. Med., Rochester, Minn., 1970-71, resident, 1971-75; instr. in pathology, 1974-75; asst. dir. clin. pathology Naval Regional Med. Center, Oakland, Calif., 1975-77;

asst. prof. pathology U. Tex. Med. Sch., Houston, 1977—. Served to lt. comdr. M.C., USN, 1975-78. Am. Heart Assn. Tex. Affiliate grantee, 1978-80. Mem. Am. Fedn. Clin. Research, Am. Soc. Hematology, Am. Soc. Clin. Pathology, Coll. Am. Pathologists, Am. Assn. Blood Banks. Contbr. articles to profl. jours. Office: U Tex Med Sch at Houston PO Box 20708 Houston TX 77025

OLSON, JOHN VICTOR, dentist, coll. dean; b. Kibbie, Mich., June 24, 1913; s. John Leonard and Elizabeth Johanna (Ytterberg) O.; D.D.S., U. Mich., 1936; m. Margaret Pray; 1 dau., Nancy. Pvt. practice dentistry, South Haven, Mich., 1938-42; asst. prof. prosthetics St. Louis U. Sch. Dentistry, 1947-49, asso. prof., 1949-50, dir. postgrad dental edn., 1948-50; prof. dentistry U. Tex., Houston, 1950—, dean, 1952—, dean Dental Sch., San Antonio, 1969-72, acting pres. Health Sci. Center, Houston, 1972-74. Served to maj. AUS, 1942-46. Fellow Am. Coll. Dentists, Internat. Coll. Dentists. Mem. ADA, Tex. Dental Assn., Houston Dist. Dental Soc., Phi Kappa Phi, Omicron Kappa Upsilon, Xi Psi Phi. Club: Rotary. Home: 2725 Pemberton St Houston TX 77005 Office: PO Box 20068 Houston TX 77025

OLSON, RICHARD FLOYD, engring. co. exec.; b. Chgo., May 3, 1932; s. Obert Edwin and Viola Cymanthe (Wolfgram) O.; student Mankato (Minn.) State Coll., 1949-50, Milw. Sch. Engring., 1955-57, U. Wis., 1957; m. Sharon JoAnn Freed, Aug. 9, 1953; children—Julia Christine, Rebecca Lynn, Beth Ann. Designer, McCulloch Corp., Mpls., 1957-59; project engr. Cornelius Co., Anoka, Minn., 1959-68; engring. mgr. Pharmaseal Labs., Johnson City, Tenn., 1967-71, Arrow Automotive Industries, Spartanburg, S.C., 1971-74; founder, 1975, since pres. Applied Tech., Inc., Spartanburg; cons. in field. Mem. council Our Saviour's Luth. Ch., Johnson City, 1968-71, St. John's Luth. Ch., Spartanburg, 1979-80. Served with AUS, 1953-55; Korea. Mem. Soc. Mfg. Engrs. (sr., v.p. 1978, pres. 1980), Nat. Tool, Die and Precision Machinery Assn. Club: Piedmont. Patentee dispensing valve and spout structure, beverage tank, refrigerated cabinet for beverage dispensing. Home: 129 Sunline Pl Spartanburg SC 29302 Office: 8202 Maxwell Circle Spartanburg SC 29303

OLSON, STEVEN ARTHUR, ins. co. exec.; b. Orange, N.J., Feb. 24, 1949; s. John Arthur and Mary Katherine (Wyrick) O.; B.A., Lafayette Coll., 1971; m. Susan Maxfield, May 29, 1971; children—Cynthia Diane, David John. With Prudential Ins. Co., Newark, 1972-76, sales promotion specialist; coordinator sales promotion services Country Cos., Bloomington, Ill., 1976-78; dir. sales promotion and advt. Am. Gen. Life Ins. Co., Houston, 1978—. Legis. press aide, assemblyman N.J., 1973-74. Mem. Life Advertisers Assn. (excellence award, 1973, 77, 78, 79), Assn. Multi-Image, Ins. Advt. Conf. Presbyterian. Composer radio jingles, 1973-76. Home: 4814 Lost Oak Dr Spring TX 77373 Office: 2727 Allen Pky Houston TX 77019

OLSON, WALTER JUSTUS, JR., utility co. exec.; b. Paterson, N.J., July 27, 1941; s. Walter Justus and Viola P. (Trautvetter) O.; Sc.B., A.B., Brown U., 1964; M.B.A., Columbia U., 1967. Design engr. Rockwell Internat., Inc., Downey, Calif., 1964-65; fin. officer CIA, Washington, 1969-73; sr. cons. Booz, Allen & Hamilton, Inc., Washington, 1973-77; corp. planning coordinator Washington Gas Light Co., Springfield, Va., 1977—. Served with USAF, 1967-69. C.P.A., Md. Mem. Am. Inst. C.P.A.'s, D.C. Inst. C.P.A.'s, No. Am. Soc. Corp. Planning, Republican. Episcopalian. Home: 7348 Dartford Dr McLean VA 22102 Office: Washington Gas Light Co 6801 Industrial Rd Springfield VA 22151

OLSSON, PETER ALAN, physician; b. Bklyn., June 26, 1941; s. John Berger and Doris O.; B.S., Wheaton Coll., 1963; M.D., Baylor U., 1967; m. Pamela Nicholson, Nov. 24, 1976; 1 son from previous marriage—Nathaniel Jeffrey. Intern, U. Vt. Hosps., 1967-68; resident in psychiatry Baylor Coll. Medicine Hosps., 1968-71; staff psychiatrist VA Hosp., Houston, 1973—; pvt. practice psychiatry, Houston, 1973—; clin. and tng. dir. Tex. Inst. Family Psychiatry, Houston, 1975-79; clin. asst. prof. psychiatry U. Tex. Houston Med. Sch., 1974—; asst. clin. prof. Baylor Coll. Medicine, 1973-79, asso. clin. prof., 1979—. Served with USN, 1971-73. Fellow Am. Psychiat. Assn.; mem. Am. Group Psychotherapy Assn., Tex. Med. Assn., Am. Assn. Psychotherapy, Houston Group Psychotherapy Soc. Contbr. articles to profl. jours. Home: 1648 Banks St Houston TX 77006 Office: 1128 Bissonnet Houston TX 77005

OLSTOWSKI, FRANCISZEK, chem. engr.; b. N.Y.C., Apr. 23, 1927; s. Franciszek and Marguerite (Stewart) O.; A.A., Monmouth Coll., 1950; B.S. in Chem. Engring., Tex. A. and I. U., 1954; m. Rosemary Sole, May 19, 1952; children—Marguerita Antonina, Anna Rosa, Franciszek, Anton, Henryk Alexander. Research and devel. engr. Dow Chem. Co., Freeport, Tex., 1954-56, project leader, 1956-65, sr. research engr., 1965-72, research specialist, 1972—. Lectr. phys. scis. elementary and intermediate schs., Freeport, 1961—. Vice chmn. Freeport Traffic Commn., 1974-76, chmn., 1976—. Served with USNR, 1944-46. Fellow Am. Inst. Chemist; mem. Electrochem. Soc. (sec. treas. South Tex. sect. 1963-64, vice chmn. 1964-65, chmn. 1965-67, councillor 1967-70), AAAS, Am. Chem. Soc., N.Y. Acad. Sci. Patentee in synthesis of fluorocarbons, natural graphite products, electrolytic prodn. magnesium metal and polyurethane tech. Home: 912 N Ave A Freeport TX 77541 Office: Dow Chemical Co U S A Bldg B 4810 Freeport TX 77541

OLSZEWSKI, EDWARD THEODORE, priest; b. Detroit, Apr. 17, 1933; s. Stanley and Stella (Ziolkowska) O.; B.A., St. Mary's U., 1956, St. John's Provincial Sem., 1960; M.S.W., Barry Coll., 1978; M.P.A., Nova U., 1979. Ordained priest Roman Catholic Ch., 1960; asso. pastor, dir. Detroit Urban Regional Analysis Inst., 1960-72, pastor; program coordinator, social services dept., equal opportunity officer City of Hallandale, Fla., 1976-79; asso. pastor St. Mary Magdalen Ch., Miami Beach, Fla., 1979—. Treas., Pembroke Towers Condominium Assn., 1976—. Mem. Nat. Assn. Social Workers, Fla. Assn. Health and Social Services, Fla. Assn. Community Action Agencies, Am. Inst. Polish Culture. Democrat. Home: 17775 N Bay Rd Miami Beach FL 33160

OLTMAN, JOHN HAROLD, patent lawyer; b. Grand Rapids, Mich., Nov. 18, 1929; s. Peter Harold and Hazel Evelyn (Kelly) O.; B.S. in Chem. Engring., U. Mich., 1952, J.D., 1957; m. Lita Marilyn Hagen, Aug. 16, 1952; children—David K., Laura G., John K. Admitted to Ill. bar, 1957, Ariz. bar, 1964, Mich. bar, 1965, Fla. bar, 1968; mem. firms Mueller & Aichele (Attys.), Chgo., and Phoenix, 1957-64, Barnes, Kisselle, Raisch & Choate (Attys.), Detroit, 1964-65, Settle, Batchelder & Oltman (Attys.), Detroit, 1965-67, Settle & Oltman (Attys.), Detroit and Ft. Lauderdale, Fla., 1967-72, Oltman and Flynn (Attys.), Ft. Lauderdale, 1972—. Trustee for pvt. trust. Served with USMCR, 1952-54. Mem. Am., Fla., Broward County bar assns., Am. Patent Law Assn., Am. Judicature Soc., Fla. Engring. Soc., IEEE, Phi Eta Sigma, Tau Beta Pi. Kiwanian (dir. Ft. Lauderdale Club 1972-74, 77-78, treas. 1979, chmn. Key Club com. 1970-78). Home: 2130 NE 55th St Fort Lauderdale FL 33308 Office: 915 Middle River Dr Fort Lauderdale FL 33304

O'MALLEY, MICHAEL FRANCIS, state ofcl.; b. Grand Island, Nebr., Dec. 2, 1950; s. Thomas L. and Patricia Ann (Swoboda) O'M.; B.S., Colo. State U., 1972, M.S.; m. Sharon Jane Tollett, Aug. 20, 1977. Wildlife communications coordinator Region III, Tenn. Wildlife Resources Agy., Nashville, 1974-77, info. supr. statewide, 1977—. Recipient U.S. Jaycees Outstanding Young Man award, 1979; Ernest Thompson Seton award, 1979. Mem. Outdoor Writers Assn. Am., Southeastern Outdoor Press Assn., Tenn. Outdoor Writers Assn., Assn. Conservation Info., Tenn. Jaycees (regional dir. 1977-78), Crossville Jaycees (pres. 1976-77). Editor Tenn. Wildlife Mag., 1977—. Home: 710 Hollendale St LaVergne TN 37086 Office: Tenn Wildlife Resources Agy Box 40747 Nashville TN 37204

O'MARA, RICHARD JOHN, state ofcl.; b. Bronxville, N.Y., Feb. 24, 1920; s. William F. and Emily M. O'M.; A.B., U. Miami, 1952; M.Ed., U. Fla., 1966; m. May 1, 1954. With Fla. Dept. Labor and Employment Security, Tallahassee, 1958—, state counseling supr., 1958—. Served with USCGR, 1941-45, USNR, 1952-54. Mem. Nat. Employment Counselors Assn. (pres. 1978-79), Internat. Assn. Counseling Services (v.p. and chmn. public and pvt. accrediting bd. 1978—), Internat. Assn. Personnel in Employment Security. Editorial bd. Jour. Employment Counseling, 1972-80. Home: 2061 Taylor Rd Tallahassee FL 32308 Office: Fla Dept Labor and Employment Security 308 Caldwell Bldg Tallahassee FL 32301

OMIZO, MICHAEL MASAMI, educator; b. Honolulu, Mar. 1, 1949; s. Masaaki and Sue Teruko (Teruya) O.; B.E., U. Hawaii, 1971, M.Ed., 1973; Ph.D., U. So. Calif., 1978; m. Sharon Ann, Aug. 5, 1978. Instr., Olympic Coll., Honolulu, 1973-74; instr. U. Hawaii, 1975-78, counselor, coordinator, 1975-77; asst. prof. guidance and counseling U. Houston, 1978—; cons. Ednl. and Indsl. Testing Services, Program for Minority Engring. Studies. Served with Army N.G., 1971-77. Recipient grant U. Houston, 1979. Mem. Am. Personnel and Guidance Assn., Am. Psychol. Assn., Tex. Personnel and Guidance Assn., Am. Ednl. Research Assn., So. Ednl. Research Assn., Nat. Council Evaluation and Measurement, Phi Delta Kappa. Contbr. articles to profl. jours. Home: 7311 Brompton St #B 245 Houston TX 77025 Office: Dept Guidance and Counseling U Houston/Central 4800 Calhoun St Houston TX 77004

O'MORE, ELOISE PITTS, designer; b. Fayetteville, Tenn., June 7, 1911; d. William Woodruff and Josephine Martin (Diemer) Pitts; student Ward-Conley Art Sch., 1928-30, Ward-Belmont Coll., 1930-32; Baccalaureat d'Art Decoratif, Le College Feminin, Paris, 1937; m. James Robert Muratta, Oct. 4, 1929; 1 dau., Donna Maria; m. 2d, Rory O'More, IV, Dec. 26, 1940; 1 son, Rory V. Self-employed designer and muralist, 1938-60; dir. design Stoddards Office Designs, Nashville, 1960-66; partner Mitchell & O'More, designers, Nashville, 1966-69; founder, dir. O'More Sch. of Design, Franklin, Tenn., 1970—; executed historic murals 3d Nat. Bank, Nashville, 1963, First Franklin Fed., 1964, First Nat. Bank, Centerville, 1972, United Am. Bank, Nashville, 1972, Harpeth Nat. Bank, Franklin; lectr. design and decoration for various schs., clubs and bus. orgns. Bd. dirs. Heritage Found. Franklin; mem. Cheekwood Fine Arts Center, Nashville; mem. Nashville Hist. Commn. Mem. Am. Soc. Interior Designers, Nat. Trust Historic Preservation, Williamson County Hist. Soc., Societe des Arts, Alliance Francaise. Roman Catholic. Office: 423 S Margin St Franklin TN 37064

OMURA, GEORGE ADOLF, med. educator; b. N.Y.C., Apr. 30, 1938; s. Bunji K. and Martha (Pilger) O.; B.A., magna cum laude, Columbia U., 1958; M.D., Cornell U., 1962; m. Emily Fowler, Dec. 27, 1962; children—June Ellen, Susan, Ann, George Fowler. Intern, Bellevue Hosp., N.Y.C., resident, 1965-67; fellow Meml. Sloan-Kettering Cancer Center, N.Y.C., 1967-70; asst. prof. medicine U. Ala., Birmingham, 1970-73, asso. prof. medicine, 1973-78, prof., 1978—; cons. Nat. Cancer Inst., 1975—. Served with USNR, 1963-65. Am. Cancer Soc. jr. faculty clin. fellow, 1971-74. Fellow A.C.P.; mem. Southeastern Cancer Study Group, Gynecol. Oncology Group, Leukemia Soc. Am. (chpt. med. adv. bd., trustee 1973-77), Am. Soc. Clin. Oncology, Am. Soc. Hematology, Am. Assn. Cancer Research, Phi Beta Kappa, Alpha Omega Alpha. Club: Relay House. Contbr. articles to profl. jours. Home: 3621 Crestside Rd Mountain Brook AL 35223 Office: University Sta Birmingham AL 35294

ONEAL, DENNIS JAY, educator; b. Paxton, Ill., Aug. 22, 1944; s. Jay Raymond and Zella Edriss (Rutledge) O.; B.S., So. Ill. U., 1966; M.A., U. Ark., 1972; Ph.D., U. So. Miss., 1979; m. Carol Ann Acree, July 12, 1968; children—Christopher Jay, Timothy Patrick. Announcer, engr. Sta. WJPF-AM, Herrin, Ill., 1965-66; scriptwriter, dir. instructional TV U.S. Army, Ft. Sill, Okla., 1966-69; sales mgmt. trainee Procter & Gamble, Ft. Smith, Ark., 1969-71; asst. prof. broadcast journalism and gen. mgr. Sta. KUAF-FM, U. Ark., Fayetteville, 1972-80; asso. prof. journalism Northwestern State U., Natchitoches, La., 1980—, head mass communications dept., 1980—; free-lance announcing and prodn. Mem. Fayetteville Mcpl. Parking Authority, 1979—; founding mem. Fayetteville Soccer Assn., 1978—, cert. referee, 1979—. Served with U.S. Army, 1966-69. Mem. Soc. Profl. Journalists, Ark. Broadcasters Assn., Pub. Radio in Mid-Am., Sigma Delta Chi. Contbr. articles to profl. jours. Home: 121 Isadore St Natchitoches LA 71457 Office: Kyser Arts and Sci Bldg 103 Northwestern State U Natchitoches LA 71457

O'NEAL, OBIE WASHINGTON, JR., educator; b. Union Mills, N.C., June 17, 1925; s. Obie Washington and Annie Mae (Long) O'N.; B.S. magna cum laude, Bluefield State Coll., 1948; M.S., W.Va. U., 1950; student Ind. U., summers 1957, 59, 60-65, 68; m. Rosa Marie Griffin, Aug. 31, 1951; children—Phyllis, Denise, Roger Kevin. Tchr., McDowell County (W.Va.) Pub. Schs., 1950-51; with Albany State Coll., 1951—, prof., chmn. phys. edn. dept., 1968—, head coach football, basketball and track, dir. athletics, 1951-58, head football and track coach, dir. athletics, 1958-68, dir. athletics, 1968-72; football and basketball ofcl. Bd. dirs. Albany chpt. ARC, 1967-69; mem. Albany Citizens Advisory Council, 1974-76. Bd. dirs. Boys' Clubs of Albany; bd. dirs., chmn. bd. dirs. Cedar St. Unit, Boys Clubs of Albany; mem. Ga. Gov.'s Phys. Fitness Council. Served with USAAF, 1943-46. Named Football Coach of Year, Southeastern Athletic Conf., 1955, 57, 59, 60, 63. Mem. AAHPER, Gas Assn. for Health, Phys. Edn. and Recreation, Nat. Coll. Phys. Edn. for Men, Ga. High Sch. Assn., Kappa Alpha Psi. Democrat. Baptist (deacon). Mason (32 deg.). Home: 905 Odon Ave Albany GA 31701 Office: 504 College Dr Albany GA 31705

O'NEAL, ROBERT PALMER, marine corps officer; b. Tonapah, Nev., Sept. 20, 1912; s. Robert McWilliam and Aimee (Ford) O'N.; A.B., Occidental Coll., 1935, M.A., 1936; m. Nancy Monroe, June 10, 1935; children—Robert M., Nancy B. (Mrs. Thomas Arthur), Patricia M. (Mrs. Marvin Colyer), Peggy F. (Mrs. Ray Perry). Eastern sales mgr. Monroe Chem. Co., Manchester, Conn., 1937-41; insp. naval aircraft, engines Pratt & Whitney Aircraft Corp., East Hartford, Conn., 1941-43; joined USMC, 1944, advanced through grades to lt. col.; aircraft maintenance officer, Japan, 1958-59; material and aircraft maintenance officer, Cherry Point, N.C., 1959-62; mem. Atlantic Task Force Team, 1962-64; coordinator weapons demonstration SEATO reps., Kadena AFB, Okinawa, 1964, coordinator movements 1st Marine Jet Squadron in combat, South Viet Nam, 1965; prodn. officer Japan Aircraft Corp., Ltd., Atsugi, Japan, 1967-69; aircraft maintenance officer, Chu Lai, Viet Nam, 1969-70; staff AWSS aircraft maintenance officer, Norfolk, Va., 1971—; pres. Piksco Corp., Pine Knoll Shares. Dir. CD. Recipient Adm. Coates Outstanding award, 1966. Fellow Internat. Biog. Assn.; mem. Am. Chem. Soc., AAAS, Soc. Am. Mil. Engrs., Am. Ordnance Assn., Engrs. Joint Council Inc., Am. Inst. Aeros. and Astronautics, Internat. Platform Assn., N.C. Acad. Scis., Am. Mgmt. Assn., Optimists Internat., Delta Upsilon. Address: Route 1 Morehead City NC 28557

O'NEAL, RUTH, pediatrician, educator; b. Dunn, N.C., June 7, 1915; d. Joseph Bryan and Jane (Wilson) O'N.; A.B., Transylvania U., 1939; M.D., Med. Coll. Va., 1943; M.S. in Pediatrics (Mayo Found. fellow), U. Minn., Rochester, 1948. Intern, Med. Coll. Va., Richmond, 1944; fellow Mayo Clinic, Rochester, Minn., 1944-48; practice medicine specializing in pediatrics, Winston-Salem, N.C., 1948-69; instr. pediatrics Bowman Gray Sch. Medicine, Winston-Salem, 1948-51, asst. prof. pediatrics, 1951-69, asso. prof. pediatrics, 1969—; asso. dir. pediatrics Reynolds Meml. Hosp., 1969-72, dir. pediatrics, 1972-77; served with S.S. Hope, 1968. Diplomate Am. Bd. Pediatrics. Fellow AMA; mem. Mayo Found. Alumni Assn., Soc. for Research in Child Devel., Forsyth County Med. Soc., Med. Soc. State of N.C., N.C. Pediatric Soc., N.C. Mental Hygiene Soc., So. Med. Assn., Am. Acad. Pediatrics, Ambulatory Pediatric Assn., So. Soc. Pediatric Research, Internat. Coll. of Pediatrics, Am. Women's Med. Assn., Internat. Soc. for Prevention of Child Abuse and Neglect. Republican. Mem. Christian Church (Disciples of Christ). Club: Forsyth Country. Contbr. papers, articles in field to profl. publs. Home: 445 Springdale Ave Winston-Salem NC 27104 Office: Bowman Gray School of Medicine 300 Hawthorne Rd Winston-Salem NC 27103

O'NEIL, JOHN JOSEPH, artist, educator; b. Bklyn., Apr. 20, 1932; s. John J. and Elizabeth (Grady) O'N.; grad. in Comml. Art, N.Y. State U.; B.S., SUNY, Buffalo; M.A., Ed.D., Columbia U.; postgrad. Hunter Coll., Kans. State U., U. Florence (Italy); m. Robin Harmon, Dec. 3, 1977; children—Virginia, Johnny, Tommy. Asst. art dir. Mut. Broadcasting Co., N.Y.C., 1952, graphic designer; art dir. Stamps Conhaim and Whitehead, N.Y.C., 1952, B. Altman, N.Y.C., 1953; creative mgr. Givandan Advt., N.Y.C., 1955; free lance artist for Blue Cross Blue Shield, Time, Inc., Look Mag.; prof., chmn. dept. art U. S.C., Columbia; one-man shows drawings, paintings and/or ceramics; numerous group shows in museums and galleries of eastern U.S. including: Columbia Mus. Art, N.Y.C., Ithaca (N.Y.) Coll., Columbia U., N.Y.C., Beaufort Mus., Mint Mus., Greenville Mus., Florence (Italy) Mus., Mobile Art Gallery, Gallery of Contemporary Art; represented in permanent collections: Columbia U., N.Y.C., Beaufort Mus., Artist Guild Columbia, Columbia Mus. Art, N.Y.C., S.C. Commn. Arts, Florence Mus., Laurel Gallery. Served with U.S. Army, 1953-55; Korea. Mem. Columbia Art Mus. Assn., Columbia Artist Guild (v.p.), Guild S.C. Artists (dir. 1976), S.C. Craftsmen (founding mem.), S.C. Art Edn. Assn., Southeastern Print Council, Coll. Art Assn., Sigma Epsilon, Kappa Delta Phi. Roman Catholic. Contbr. graphic designs to various mags. including Newsweek, Time, Look, Fortune and U.S. News; contbr. articles and revs. to various jours. Home: 4225 Sequoia Rd Columbia SC 29206 Office: Dept Art U SC Columbia SC

O'NEILL, PAUL JOHN, psychologist; b. Taunton, Mass., Apr. 12, 1936; s. Clarence Bernard and Edna Mary (Burke) O'N.; B.A., St. Bonaventure U., 1960; M.A., Boston U., 1961; Ed.D., U. Ga., 1973; m. Avis Bernson Kelly, Apr. 24, 1973. Research asso. Met. Life Ins. Co., N.Y.C., 1961-69; research asst. Inst. Behavioral Research, Athens, Ga., 1969-71; instr. dept. psychology U. Ga., 1970-71; research asst. Bur. Ednl. Studies, Athens, 1972; asso. prof. psychology Jackson (Miss.) State U., 1972—; cons. Skill Advancement, Inc., N.Y.C., 1968, Human Resources Devel. Tng. Inst., West Monroe, La., 1974-77. Served with U.S. Army, 1954-56. Licensed psychologist, Miss. Mem. Am. Ednl. Research Assn., Am., Southeastern, Miss. psychol. assns., Nat. Council on Measurement in Edn., Miss. Acad. Scis., Southeastern Indsl. and Orgnizational Psychology Assn., Sierra Club. Democrat. Contbr. articles to profl. jours. Home: 956 Valley Falls Rd Jackson MS 39212 Office: Psychology Dept Jackson State U Jackson MS 39217

ONEY, ROBERT LEIGHTON, pub. co. exec.; b. Charleston, W.Va., July 9, 1942; s. James Leighton and Faith Tandy O.; B.S., Marshall U., 1965; m. Kay Marie Sage, July 30, 1965; children—Jeffrey Leighton, Robin Linn. Retail advt. salesman Gazette & Daily Mail, Charleston, 1965-72; retail advt. salesman News & Observer Pub. Co., Raleigh, N.C., 1972-74, retail advt. mgr., 1974-79, research/mktg. dir., 1980—. Mem. Raleigh All-America City Com., 1975; mem. adv. council com. N.C. Symphony; bd. dirs. Triangle Cities Better Bus. Bur., 1975—; mem. citizens action com. Sertoma Arts Center, 1978—. Mem. Internat. Newspaper Advt. Execs., Mid-Atlantic Newspaper Advt. Execs. Assn., Raleigh C. of C., Triangle Advt. Fedn. (pres. 1977-78). Democrat. Presbyterian. Club: Sertoma (pres. 1977-78). Home: 1309 Shady Side Dr Raleigh NC 27612 Office: News & Observer Pub Co 215 S McDowell St Raleigh NC 27601

ONI, CLAUDIUS ADESINA, counselor; b. Lagos, Nigeria, Feb. 8, 1953; s. Samuel Folarin and Tanimowo Omoseri (Aiyede) O.; B.S. in Psychology, Bethany Coll., 1976; M.A. in Counseling and Rehab., Marshall U., 1978. Adminstrv. aide W.Va. Research Coordinating Unit for Vocat. Edn., Marshall U., Huntington, W.Va., 1977-78; emergency counselor Community Mental Health Center, Huntington, 1978-79; counselor, asst. dir. spl. student services Bluefield (W.Va.) State Coll., 1979—; chmn. Commn. on Counseling; mem. W.Va. Task Force on Licensure. Mem. Am. Personnel and Guidance Assn., W.Va. Personnel and Guidance Assn., Am. Coll. Personnel Assn., W.Va. Coll. Personnel Assn., Assn. Humanistic Edn. and Devel., Mid-Eastern Assn. Edn. Opportunity Program Personnel. Author articles in field. Home: 116 Gott Rd Priceton WV 24740 Office: Bluefield State College Special Services Bluefield WV 24701

ONORATO, ROBERT CARDINAL, real estate devel. co. exec.; b. N.Y.C., Apr. 20, 1931; s. Victor Martin and Christine Marie (Cardinal) O.; B.S., U. Ariz., 1952; m. Patricia Joanne Davis, June 22, 1956; children—Robert Victor, Patricia Constance. Asst. v.p., mgr. Ariz. Bank, Tucson, Phoenix, 1957-63; exec. v.p. U.S. Land Inc., Indpls., 1965-67; v.p. western ops. Boise Cascade Properties, Palo Alto, Calif., 1967-70; pres., dir. Palmetto Dunes Resort, Inc., Hilton Head Island, S.C., 1972—; sr. v.p. Phipps Land Co., Inc., Atlanta, 1972-79; dir. Bank of Beaufort. Chmn. United Fund Campaign, Hilton Head Island, 1975; bd. dirs Soc. for the Arts, Hilton Head Island, 1975—; chmn. bd. dirs. May River Acad.; trustee, bd. dirs. Hilton Head Hosp. Served with AUS, 1952-54. Recipient Order of Palmetto, State of S.C. Mem. Hilton Head Island C. of C. (dir.), Hilton Head Island Mktg. Council (dir.). Presbyn. Home: 8 Man-O-War Palmetto Dunes Hilton Head Island SC 29928 Office: Palmetto Dunes Resort Inc PO Box 5628 Hilton Head Island SC 29928

ONYEBERECHI, SYDNEY EMEH, educator; b. Emekuku, Owerri, Nigeria, Nov. 29, 1942; came to U.S., 1966; s. Stephen Amanze and Theresa Ayozieuwa O.; B.A., U. Oreg., 1970, M.A. in English, 1971; m. Francisca Nlemuwa Obioma, Dec. 4, 1971; children—Chinedu, Onyeali-Dike, Odunze. Sch. master Owerri, former Eastern Nigeria Ministry of Edn., 1960-66; bilingual public interpreter, English-Ibo Emekuku, Owerri, Nigeria, 1962-66; now asst. prof. langs. and lit. Va. State U., Petersburg; lectr. in field. Sec. Emekuku, Owerri Town Council, 1961-63. Mem. African Lit. Assn. in U.S. (speaker), African Studies Assn. U.S., Va.-N.C. Assn. Coll. Tchrs. of English, Phi Beta Sigma. Roman Catholic. Author: Africa: Melodies and Thoughts, 1979; African Influence on the New Negro Renaissance Literature, 1979; Hemingway: The River and the Heroes, 1979; Some Hints on African Literature, 1973. Home: 20712 #M 4th Ave Ettrick VA 23803 Office: Box 393 Virginia State Univ Petersburg VA 23803

OOLEY, RONALD LEE, personnel exec.; b. Salem, Ind., Oct. 16, 1945; s. Glenn Forrest and Freda Pearl (Montgomery) O.; B.S. in Bus. Adminstrn., Ind. U., 1970; postgrad. Mercer U.; m. Phyllis June Wade, July 3, 1966; children—Kimberly Dawn, Kevin Scott. With Brown & Williams Tobacco Corp., 1966—, prodn. supr., Louisville, 1966-70, staff asst., 1970-72, prodn. dept. mgr., 1973-74, prodn. supr., 1974-75, mgr. tng. and devel., 1976-77, personnel mgr., Macon, Ga., 1977—. Mem. Ga. C. of C., Macon C. of C., Am. Soc. Personnel Adminstrs. Christian Ch. Home: 5620 Kentucky Downs Dr Macon GA 31210

OOSTERHUIS, HERMAN HENDRIK, diesel engine co. exec.; b. Amsterdam, Holland, Apr. 1, 1926; s. Folkert and Clasina Elisabeth (Morlang) O.; came to U.S., 1963, naturalized, 1969; degrees in marine engring. Amsterdam Marine Engrs. Coll., 1946, 54; m. Adriana Theresa VanRoey, Mar. 26, 1956; 1 son, Patrick Herman. Engr., Netherlands Navigation Co., Rotterdam, 1946-56, chief engr., 1956-58; supervising engr. Vinke & Co., Rotterdam, 1958-60, asst. to pres., 1960-62; pres., mgr. Power Engring. Inc., New Orleans, 1963-66, Oosterhuis Industries, Inc., Belle Chasse, La., 1966—; dir. Marine Engring. Inc., Marine Financing Corp., Am. Brons Corp. Recipient Albert Galatin Certificate of Merit, 1974. Mem. Soc. Naval Architects and Marine Engrs., Vereniging Technici Scheepvaart Gebied (Netherlands). Clubs: Propeller (New Orleans); Whitehall (N.Y.C.) Home: 51 Park Timbers Dr New Orleans LA 70114 Office: 1800 Engineers Rd Belle Chasse LA 70037

OPALA, MARIAN PETER, justice Supreme Ct. Okla.; b. Lodz, Poland, Jan. 20, 1921; s. Antoni and Antonia (Chrobot) O.; came to U.S., 1947, naturalized, 1953; J.D., Oklahoma City U., 1953, B.S. in Econs., 1957; LL.M., N.Y. U., 1968; divorced; 1 son, Joseph Anthony. Admitted to Okla. bar, 1953; asst. county atty. Okla. County, 1953-56; pvt. practice, Oklahoma City, 1956-60, 65-67; referee Supreme Ct. Okla., 1960-65; prof. law Oklahoma City U. Sch. Law, 1965-69; asso. prof. law U. Okla., 1969—; legal asst. to Justice McInerney, Okla. Supreme Ct., 1967-68; adminstrv. dir. Cts. of Okla., 1968-79; justice Okla. Supreme Ct., Oklahoma City, 1979—. Mem. N.Y. U. Inst. Jud. Adminstrn., Okla. Crime Commn., Okla. Jud. Council; mem. permanent faculty Am. Acad. Jud. Edn.; chmn. Nat. Conf. Ct. Adminstrv. Officers; pres. N.Y. U. Summer Program Law Tchrs. Alumni Assn. 1973; mem. Council Juvenile Delinquency Planning. Mem. Am., Okla., Oklahoma City bar assns., Am. Soc. Legal History, Oklahoma City Title Lawyers Assn., Order of Coif, Phi Delta Phi. Co-author: Oklahoma Court Rules for Perfecting a Civil Appeal, 1969. Contbr. articles to legal jours. Home: 5709 NW 64th St Oklahoma City OK 73132 Office: 202 State Capitol Oklahoma City OK 73105

OPP, CHRISTINE ANNE, lawyer; b. Sandusky, Ohio, Jan. 21, 1950; d. Donald Philip and Irene Rita (Owen) O.; student Heidelberg Coll., 1968-69; B.A. with honors in History, Northwestern U., 1972; J.D., U. N.C., 1975. Restaurant mgmt. positions Interstate United, Cedar Point, Ohio, 1968-72; admitted to N.C. bar, 1975, U.S. Dist. Ct. bar Middle Dist. N.C., 1975; adminstrv. asst. S.E. Regional Session, Nat. Inst. Trial Advocacy, Chapel Hill, N.C., 1975-76, S.E. regional dir., 1977-79, devel. dir., 1977-79; individual practice law, also mem. firm Eifort, Jabbs & Opp, Chapel Hill, 1975-77; project dir. expanding trial skills Consortium Profl. Edn., Am. Bar Assn., 1979-80; vis. prof. N.C. Central Sch. Law, Durham, 1980; lectr. Occupational Safety and Health Edn. Center; cons. EEO Commn. Bd. dirs. ACCESS, Inc., 1976-79, chairperson, 1979; city chmn. Heart Fund, Chapel Hill, 1976; leader Girl Scouts U.S.A., 1979. Mem. N.C. Bar Assn., Am. Bar Assn. Editor The Docket, 1977-79, Adminstrv. Guides for Teaching Nita-Style Courses, 1979. Home: 52C Davie Circle Chapel Hill NC 27514 Office: PO Box 2026 Chapel Hill NC 27514

O'QUINN, APRIL GALE, physician; b. Columbia, Miss., Apr. 21, 1936; d. R.V. and Anna Pauline (Cook) O'Q.; diploma Scott and White Hosp. Sch. Nursing, 1965; A.A., Temple Jr. Coll., 1965; B.S. with honors, Baylor U., 1968; M.D., U. Tex. Med. Br., 1971. Intern, U. Tex. Med. Br., Galveston, 1971-72, resident ob-gyn., 1972-75; fellow in oncology M.D. Anderson Hosp., Houston, Tex., 1976-78; practice medicine specializing in ob-gyn., Galveston, 1978—; asst. prof. dept. ob-gyn. U. Tex. Med. Br., Galveston, 1975—; mem. staff John Sealy Hosp. Diplomate Am. Bd. Ob-Gyn. Fellow Willard R. Cooke Obstetrical and Gynecologic Soc., Am. Coll. Ob-Gyn.; mem. Tex. Assn. Obstetricians and Gynecologists, Houston Gynecol. and Obstetrical Soc., Tex. Med. Assn., Galveston County Med. Soc., Felix Rutledge Soc. Republican. Baptist. Home: 1401 Ball Ave Galveston TX 77550 Office: Dept Ob-Gyn Univ Tex Med Br Galveston TX 77550

ORBE, LAWRENCE FRANCIS, III, investment banker; b. Paterson, N.J., Sept. 20, 1938; s. L. F. and V.A. (Scola) O.; B.S., Lafayette Coll., 1960; M.B.A., Harvard U., 1962; m. Dinah K. Williams, Aug. 31, 1978; children (by previous marriage)—Lance, William, Robert. Partner, Glore Forgan & Co., N.Y.C., 1962-68; gen. partner L.F. Orbe & Co., N.Y.C., 1968-72; v.p. Cantor, Fitzgerald & Co., N.Y.C., 1972-75; head corporate fin. dept. L.F. Orbe & Co., Investment Bankers, Pensacola, Fla., 1975—; cons. Dept. Commerce, 1969-70, various senators, congressmen. Republican. Roman Catholic. Home: PO Box 305 Gulf Breeze FL 32561 Office: PO Box 12686 Pensacola FL 32574

ORBEN, ROBERT, writer; b. N.Y.C., Mar. 4, 1927; s. Walter August and Marie (Neweceral) O.; m. Jean Louise Connelly, July 25, 1945. Humor and speech writer for entertainment personalities, bus. execs., politicians, 1946—; TV writer Jack Paar Show, 1962-63, Red Skelton Hour, 1964-70; cons. Vice Pres. Gerald R. Ford, 1974; speechwriter Pres. Gerald R. Ford, 1974-75, spl. asst. to Pres., dir. White House speechwriting dept., 1976-77; editor Orben's Current Comedy, Orben's Comedy Fillers, Wilmington, Del., 1971—. Mem. Writers Guild Am. Unitarian. Club: Nat. Press (Washington). Author 44 books of humor for public speakers and performers. Address: 1200 N Nash St Arlington VA 22209

ORCUTT, BEN AVIS, educator; b. Falco, Ala., Oct. 17, 1914; s. Benjamin A. and Emily Olive Adams; A.B., U. Ala., 1936; M.A., Tulane U., 1939, M.S.W., 1942; D.S.W., Columbia U., 1962. Social worker, acting field dir. ARC, LaGarde Gen. Hosp., New Orleans, Fort Benning (Ga.) Regional Hosp., 1942-46; chief social work service VA regional office, Phoenix, 1946-51, chief social work service unit outpatient office, Birmingham, Ala., 1954-57, 58; research asst. Research Center Sch. Social Work, Columbia U., N.Y.C., 1960-62, field adv. social work, 1962, asso. prof. social work, 1965-76; asso. prof. social work La. State U., Baton Rouge, 1962-65; prof. social work, dir. doctoral program U. Ala., University, 1976—; research cons. Tavistock Centre, London, 1972. NIMH fellow, 1957-60. Mem. Council Social Work Edn., Nat. Assn. Social Workers, Am. Assn. Orthopsychiatry, Found. Thanatology, Arts and Humanities Council, Ala. Conf. Social Welfare (exec. bd.), Tuscaloosa County Mental Health Assn., Bus. and Profl. Women's Guild. Episcopalian. Club: Zonta (mem. exec. bd.). Author: (with Harry P. Orcutt) America's Riding Horses, 1958; (with Elizabeth R. Prichard, Jean Collard, Austin H. Kutscher, Irene Seeland, Nathan Lefkowitz) Social Work with the Dying Patient and the Family, 1977; editor: Poverty and Social Casework Services, 1974; contbr. articles to profl. jours. Home: 222 Fox Run Tuscaloosa AL 35406 Office: PO Box 1935 University AL 35486

ORELL, TERRENCE MICHAEL, shipping container mfg. co. ofcl.; b. Eugene, Oreg., Jan. 21, 1945; s. Bernard Leo and Helen Margaret (Kirchoff) O.; B.A., U. Santa Clara, 1967, M.B.A., 1969; m. Margery Ann Lemire, Dec. 28, 1968; children—Maureen Elizabeth, Michael Terrence. Personnel rep. Weyerhaeuser Co., Tacoma, Wash., 1969-70, asst. mgr. personnel, corp. support functions, 1972, personnel mgr., 1972-74, mgr. manpower planning, 1974-75, mgr. corp. staffing, 1975-76, shipping container mktg. mgr. So. region, 1976-77, gen. mgr. Charlotte shipping container plant, N.C., 1977—. Dist. council, Charlotte, Boy Scouts Am., 1977-78, bd. dirs. Charlotte-Mecklenburg council, 1980; group chmn. United Way, 1978. Served as 1st lt., U.S. Army, 1970-71. Decorated. Mem. Charlotte C. of C., Fiber Box Assn. Republican. Roman Catholic. Home: 1133 Berkeley Ave Charlotte NC 28203 Office: Weyerhaeuser Co 5419 Hovis Rd Charlotte NC 28266

ORELLANA, WALTER A., mgmt. cons. co. exec.; b. San Salvador, El Salvador, June 22, 1946; came to U.S., 1965, naturalized, 1980; s. Augusto and Nadina Lopez (Loucel) O.; B.S. in Indsl. Engring., La. State U., 1971; M.S. in Indsl. Engring. and Ops. Research, Purdue U., 1973; m. Ruby Moreno, Apr. 27, 1973; 1 dau., Carla. Teaching asst. Purdue U., Lafayette, Ind., 1972; sr. mgmt. systems analyst, project leader Burroughs Corp., Detroit, 1973-76; mgr. mgmt. cons. Arthur Young & Co., Detroit, 1976-78, mgr. mgmt. cons. and Latin Am. coordinator, Dallas, 1980—; sr. mgmt. cons. Booz, Allen & Hamilton, Caracas, Venezuela, 1978-80. Served with USAF, 1965-69. Named hon. citizen City of Baton Rouge, 1970. Mem. Am. Inst. Indsl. Engrs. (sr., v.p. 1977-78), Assn. for Systems Mgmt. (profl. mem.), Planning Execs. Inst., Am. Prodn. and Inventory Control Soc., U.S. Jaycees (dir. 1977-78), Phi Kappa Phi, Tau Beta Pi (pres. 1970-71), Pi Mu Epsilon, Pi Kappa Phi (past pres.). Home: 6534 La Manga Dr Dallas TX 75248 Office: 2900 Republic Nat Bank Bldg Dallas TX 75201

ORF, PEGGY ANN, audiologist; b. Dallas, Nov. 5, 1952; d. Henry Charles and Pauline (Sellers) Vogelpohl; student U. Tex., 1970-71; B.S., N. Tex. State U., M.S., 1978; m. David Charles Orf, Aug. 23, 1974. With Dallas Ind. Sch. Dist., 1971-72, summer 1973; audiologist Drs. Gay and Johnstone, P.A., Sherman, Tex., 1978—. Certified tchr., Tex. Mem. Am. Speech and Hearing Assn. Home: Route 2 Box 82 Sanger TX 76266 Office: 809 Gallagher St Suite B Sherman TX 75090

ORGLER, GORDON KENT, physician; b. Neptune, N.J., Dec. 8, 1946; s. S. Fred and Rosemary (Van Dyke) O.; B.S., Wagner Coll., S.I., N.Y., 1969; M.S. in Occupational Medicine, U. Cin., 1976; M.D., Creighton U., 1973; m. Mary E. Hart, May 12, 1973. Resident in occupational medicine U. Cin., 1974-76, AT&T, Basking Ridge, N.J., 1976-77; corp. med. dir. Torrington Co. (Conn.), 1977-78, M. Lowenstein Corp., Lyman, S.C., 1978—; cons. staff Spartanburg Gen. Hosp. Diplomate Am. Bd. Preventive Medicine. Mem. Am. Occupational Medicine Assn., Am. Acad. Occupational Medicine, AMA, Am. Coll. Preventive Medicine, Carolina Occupational Med. Assn., Spartanburg County Med. Assn., Am. Textile Mfrs. Inst. (med. subcom.). Author: Mercury Intoxication, 1976. Office: M Lowenstein Corp Lyman SC 29365

ORIO, EDWARD BENNETT, ednl. adminstr.; b. Ft. Bragg, N.C., Sept. 29, 1942; s. Harry Bennett and Edith (Brooks) O.; B.S. in Polit. Sci., Sociology, Memphis State U., 1964, M.A. in Curriculum 1967. Tchr. Fayette County Schs., Somerville, Tenn., 1964-67, supr., 1967-75, dir. div. spl. services, 1975—; mem., chmn. steering com. Tenn. Suprs. Study Council, 1974-78, pres., 1976; chmn., vice chmn. S.W. Memphis Suprs. Study Council, 1974-75; mem., chmn. numerous accreditation teams So. Assn. Colls. and Schs., 1974—. Mem. NEA, Tenn., W.Tenn. edn. assns., W.Tenn. Suprs. Assn. (chmn. 1974), Early Childhood Edn. Assn. W. Tenn. (sec., vice chmn., chmn. 1976-79), Tenn. Assn. Supervision and Curriculum Devel. Home: 585 E Parkway S Memphis TN 38104 Office: 207 Arcade Somerville TN 38068

ORLESH, DIANNE POWERS, speech pathologist; b. New Orleans, July 10, 1940; d. Austin B. and Freda Marie (Michel) Powers; B.A., St. Mary's Dominican Coll., 1962; M.S., Tulane U., 1968; m. Joseph Michael Orlesh, Jr., June 7, 1962; children—Jennifer Marie, Jan Margaret. Itinerant public sch. speech therapist Livingston (La.) Parish Sch. System, 1962-63; research asst. speech and hearing dept. Crippled Children's Hosp., New Orleans, 1965-67; speech pathology trainee VA Hosp., New Orleans, 1965-68; pvt. practice speech pathology, New Orleans, 1965-70; itinerant public sch. speech therapist Jefferson Parish Sch. System, Gretna, La., 1968-70, head speech therapy dept., 1970—; clin. instr. dept. otolaryngology Tulane U. Sch. Medicine, New Orleans, 1977—; mem. La. Bd. Examiners for Speech Pathology and Audiology, 1976—, chmn., 1978-79. Cert. tchr., La.; cert. speech pathologist, La. Mem. Am. Speech and Hearing Assn. (cert.), La. Speech and Hearing Assn., Jefferson Parish Spl. Edn. Tchrs. Assn., Delta Kappa Gamma. Democrat. Lutheran. Home: 213 Norland New Orleans LA 70114 Office: 1450 Jefferson St Gretna LA 70053

ORLOFF, DAVID IRA, mech. engr.; b. Bklyn., Mar. 14, 1944; s. Michael and Miriam Anna (Schwartz) O.; B.S., Drexel U., 1966, M.S., 1968, Ph.D., 1974; m. Susan Nessa Schriber, June 18, 1972; children—Jenny Rebecca, Rachel May. Research and teaching asst. mech. engring. Drexel U., Phila., 1966-73; engr. project devel. Ford Motor Co., Dearborn, Mich., 1973-74; asst. prof. mech. engring. U. S.C., Columbia, 1974-79, asso. prof., 1979—; v.p. Engring. Design and Testing Corp., Columbia, 1979—; cons. combustion, fires, explosions. Bd. dirs. Tree of Life Temple, Columbia, 1976-79. Faculty research participant Savannah River Lab., Aiken, S.C., summers 1975-77. Danforth asso., 1977—. Mem. Soc. Automotive Engrs. (Ralph R. Teetor award 1977), ASME (exec. bd. Midlands sec. 1975-76, treas. 1978-79, vice chmn. 1979-80), Combustion Inst., AAAS, Omicron Delta Kappa (Chi circle). Home: 4658 Pamlico Circle Columbia SC 29206

ORNDORFF, JACK COVER, devel. co. exec.; b. Winchester, Va., Jan. 13, 1922; s. Ernest Cover and Anna Bell (Newlin) O.; B.C.S. in Acctg., Strayer Jr. Coll., 1949; postgrad. Am. U., 1949-50; m. Lucile May Hake, June 2, 1951; children—Eugene, Deborah. Treas., Air Survey Corp., Arlington, Va., 1951-60; promoter various research and devel. cos., Md., Va., Washington, 1960-63; treas. F. W. Berens Sales, Inc., Washington, 1964-67; pres. F.D.S. Inc., St. Petersburg, Fla., 1968-71; treas. Grandoff Investments Inc., Tampa, Fla., 1971-74; pres. Fla. Devel. Enterprises Inc., Tampa, 1974—; dir. Mangrove Systems, Inc., Cad-Fis-Chuk-R Inc., Westomatic Mfg. Inc., Crowson Printing Service Inc. Founder, treas. Family Housing Inc.; pres. Woodmoor Civic Assn.; dist. coordinator Common Cause; trustee Town & Country Civic Assn., hon. dir.; bd. dirs. Washington Cathedral Housing Corp.; mem. D.C. Crime Commn., 1967, Arlington Dem. exec. com.; vestryman, treas. St. Agnes Ch. Served with U.S. Army, 1943-46. Recipient cert. of appreciation N. Tampa C. of C., Family Housing Inc., Town and Country Civic Assn. Mem. Nat. Assn. Accts., Greater Town and Country Area C. of C. (pres.). Episcopalian. Club: Kiwanis (Tampa Bay). Home: 8103 W Powhatan Ave Tampa FL 33615 Office: 5700 Memorial Highway Tampa FL 33615

ORNSTEIN-GALICIA, JACOB LEONARD, linguist, educator; b. Cleve., Aug. 12, 1915; s. Joseph and Bertha (Schwarcstein) Ornstein; B.S. in Edn., Ohio State U., 1936, M.A. in Spanish, 1937; Ph.D. in Hispanic Studies, U. Wis., 1940; 1 dau., Dena. Grad. asst. U. Wis., 1937-40, instr. Spanish, 1940-41; instr. Spanish and Latin Am. civilization Washington U., St. Louis, 1941-42; civilian intelligence officer OSS, Washington, 1942-45; asst. prof. langs. Waldorf Coll., Iowa, 1947-51; asst. prof. Spanish lang. and lit. N.Mex. State U., Las Cruces, 1949-51; asso. Russian Research Center, Dept. Def., Washington, 1951-68, sci. linguist, dept. head, 1951-68; tchr. Grad. Sch., U.S. Dept. Agr., 1951-63; lectr. linguistics Georgetown U., 1964-68; prof. modern langs. and linguistics U. Tex., El Paso, 1968-75, prof. emeritus, 1975—; vis. asso. prof. Catawba Coll., N.C., 1948; cons. U.S. Office Edn., 1967-68, SW Coop. Ednl. Lab., Albuquerque, 1970, Ednl. Testing Service, Princeton, N.J., 1974, others. Mem. Linguistic Soc. Am., Linguistic Assn. of SW, Linguistic Assn. Can. and U.S., Am. Dialect Soc., Border Linguistics Circle, Assn. Tchrs. of Spanish and Portuguese, Asociación de Lingüística y Filología de América Latina, MLA (exec. com. lang. change devel. 1975-77), Assn. Borderland Scholars. Author: (with W.W. Gage) The ABC's of Language and Linguistics, 1964; other books, monographs, articles; spl. regional contbr. N.Y. Times Edn. Page, 1960-64; co-editor, founder Studies in Lang. and Linguistics, 1969—; asst. mng. editor Modern Lang. Jour., 1961-64; editorial bd. Lang. Problems and Lang. Planning.

O'ROURKE, FRANKLYN SEWALL, orthopedic surgeon; b. N.Y.C., May 15, 1929; s. Bart James and Harriet (Decker) O'R.; A.B., Lafayette Coll., 1950; M.D., George Washington U., 1955; m. Eleanor Jean McKinley, June 22, 1957; children—Franklyn Sewall, Lisa Jean, Stephanie Lyn. Intern, St. Vincent's Hosp., N.Y.C., 1956-57; resident Walter Reed Hosp., Washington, 1958-62; commd. 1st lt. U.S. Army, 1957, advanced through the ranks to maj., 1965, ret., 1965; chief orthopedic surgery 121st Hosp., Korea, 1962-63; cons. 8th U.S. Army, 1962-63; chief orthopedic surgery U.S. Army Hosp., Ft. Jay, N.Y., 1963-65; practice medicine specializing in orthopedic surgery, Livingston, N.J., 1965-77, Georgetown, S.C., 1977—; attending orthopedic surgeon St. Barnabas Med. Center, Livingston, 1965-77, Georgetown County Meml. Hosp., Georgetown, S.C.; clin. asso. N.Y. Med. Coll., 1963-77; asst. prof. surgery Seoul (Korea) Nat. U., 1962-63; lectr. in trauma N.J. Coll. Medicine also Rutgers U. Coll. Medicine; chmn. N.J. Commn. on Transport Injured; disaster cons. Newark Airport; cons. West Essex Gen. Hosp., Livingston. Trustee, ARC, 1978—; cons. in trauma Pee Dee Area Regional Emergency Med. Care, 1979—. Diplomate Am. Bd. Orthopedic Surgery. Fellow A.C.S. (N.J. sec. com. trauma 1965-69), Am. Acad. Orthopedic Surgery; mem. S.C. Med. Assn. (ho. of dels. 1977—), N.J., Essex County, Georgetown County med. socs., AMA, Soc. Cryosurgery, Pan Am. Med. Assn., Soc. Contemporary Medicine in Surgery, Am. Trauma Soc. (founding mem.; mem. ho. of dels.; pres. NE unit) N.J. Soc. Surgeons, Eastern Orthopedic Assn. (charter), S.C. Orthopaedic Assn. (Boyd cup 1978), Livingston Orthopedic Group (pres.), Georgetown County Hist. Soc., Nat. Assn. Accts., Phi Chi. Clubs: Rotary; Belle Isle Yacht (commodore 1978—) (Georgetown); Winnah Bay Country (trustee 1978); Wedgefield Country (charter). Author: Palliative Use of Cryosurgery in Bone Tumors, 1973; also papers. Home: Route 2 Box 16D Belle Isle Rd Georgetown SC 29440 Office: 551 Black River Rd Georgetown SC 29440

ORR, ALEXANDER STEPHENS, obstetrician, gynecologist; b. Atlanta, Dec. 31, 1938; s. Wilson Fred and Cynthia (Nance) O.; student Emory U., 1956-59, M.D., 1963; m. Judith E. Priddy, Nov. 25, 1978; children—Stephen Lee, William Fred, David Paul. Intern, Atlanta VA Hosp., Emory U. Hosp., Atlanta, 1963-64; resident in Ob-Gyn, Ga. Baptist Hosp., Atlanta, 1966-68, C.W. Long Hosp., Atlanta, 1970-71, asst. dept. obstetrics and gynecology, 1975-78, acting chief residency tng. program, 1978—; practice medicine specializing in Ob-Gyn, Atlanta, 1972—. Served with USPHS, 1964-66. Diplomate Am. Bd. Ob-Gyn. Mem. Med. Assn. Atlanta, Med. Assn. Ga., Am. Coll. Ob-Gyn, Am. Fertility Soc., Ga. State Ob-Gyn Soc., Atlanta Ob-Gyn Soc. Unitarian. Club: Druid Hills Golf. Office: 490 Peachtree St Atlanta GA 30308

ORR, CHARLES WESLEY, JR., electronics engr.; b. Kerrville, Tex., July 26, 1938; s. Charles Wesley, Sr. and Mary Catherine (Farrell) O.; B.S. in Elec. Engring., U. Tex., 1961, M.S., 1973; children—John Wesley, Robert William. Project engr. Tracor Inc., Austin, Tex., 1966-71, Naval Air Test Sta., Patuxent River, Md., 1971-76; supervisory engr. U.S. Naval Oceanographic Office, Bay St. Louis, Miss., 1976—; mem. underwater group Range Comdrs. Council, 1975-76; sec. Soc. Engrs. and Scientists, Naval Air Test Center, 1975-76. Lay leader Hollywood United Methodist Ch., 1974-75. Served as aviator USNR, 1961-66; Vietnam. Mem. IEEE, Acoustical Soc. Am., Naval Res. Assn. Mem. Christian Ch. (Disciples of Christ) (chmn. ch. bd. 1979-80, elder 1979—). Home: 103 Carolyn St Route 1 Gulfport MS 39503 Office: NSTL Station Bay St Louis MS 39522

ORR, DAVID WESLEY, bus. exec.; b. Des Moines, Jan. 10, 1944; s. Will W. and Eloise (Reid) O.; B.A., Westminster Coll., 1965; M.A., Mich. State U., 1966; Ph.D., U. Pa., 1973; m. Elaine Carol Brainard, June 18, 1966; children—Michael David, Daniel Wade. Asst. prof. polit. sci. Agnes Scott Coll., Atlanta, 1971-76, asso. prof., 1976; asst. prof. polit. sci. U. N.C., Chapel Hill, 1976-79; co-dir. Meadowcreek Project, Inc., Fox., Ark., 1979—. Mem. World Futurest Soc., N.E. Polit. Sci. Assn., AAAS. Contbr. articles on energy and environ. policy to various profl. jours. Co-editor: The Global Predicament - Ecological Perspectives on World Order, 1979. Address: care Meadowcreek Project Fox AR 72051

ORR, ROBERT WINN, systems analyst; b. Richmond, Va., June 8, 1954; s. George Frederick and Helen Wray O.; student public schs., Highland Springs, Va. Programmer, J. Robert Carlton Assos., Richmond, 1974-76; systems and procedures analyst Va. Farm Bur. Mut. Ins. Co., Richmond, 1976—. Mem. Assn. Systems Mgmt., Adminstrv. Mgmt. Assn. Methodist. Office: Va Farm Bur Mut Ins Co 200 W Grace St Richmond VA 23261

ORTEGA, RODOLFO, psychiatrist, psychoanalyst; b. Sonora, Mex., July 22, 1924; s. Anatolio and Elisa (Borbon) O.; M.D., U. Mex., 1952; postgrad. U. Ill., 1956. Psychiatrist, State U. N.Y., 1959; psychoanalyst, Mexico's Inst. for Psychoanalysis, 1960-65; m. Ann Turgeon, Nov. 26, 1955; children—Daniel, Robert, Julia, Jenny, Nancy, Susan, Natalia. Chief resident, ward adminstr. Syracuse (N.Y.) Psychiat. Hosp., 1957-59; fellow child psychiatry Kansas City

(Mo.) Mental Health Found., 1959-60; practice medicine specializing in psychiatry and psychoanalysis, Mexico City, Mex., 1960—; psychology instr. U. Americas, Mexico City, 1960-66; prof. child psychiatry Nat. U. Mex.; cons. psychiat. residents admission Dept. Health, Kansas City, Mo., 1960. Mem. Am. Psychiat. Assn., N.Y. Acad. Sci., AAAS, Internat., Mexican (dir.) psychoanalytic assns., Assn. Psicoanali Tica Mexicana, Sociedad Mex de Psiquiatria, Mexican Assn. Child Psychiatry, Mexican Council Psychiatry. Club: Mundet Park (Mexico City). Author: El Aparato Psiquico Apreciacion Metodologica Cuadernos de Psicoanalisis, III, 1967; Crisis de Identidad del Padre: Memorias del II Congreso Mexicano de Psiquiatria Infantil, 1979; contbr. article to profl. jour. Home: Morvan 200 Mexico 10 DF Mexico Office: 92-403 Guanajuato Mexico DF 7 Mexico

ORTEGA, TEODORO KALAW, physician; b. Lipa, Phillippines, Apr. 1, 1939; s. Enrique M. and Felisa R. (Kalaw) O.; A.A., U. Santo Tomas, 1957, M.D., 1962; m. Feb. 27, 1965; children—Marcos, Melissa. Intern, Elyria (Ohio) Meml. Hosp., 1965; resident in gen. surgery Hamot Med. Center, Erie, Pa., 1966-70; resident in head and neck surgery Roswell Park Meml. Inst., Buffalo, 1970; resident in plastic surgery Phoenix Childrens Hosp., 1971-73; practice medicine specializing in plastic surgery, Pensacola, Fla., 1973—. Diplomate Am. Bd. Plastic Surgery. Fellow A.C.S. Roman Catholic. Office: 5149 N 9th Ave Suite 309 Pensacola FL 32504

ORTEGA, WALTER TELMO, export co. exec.; b. Quito, Ecuador, May 24, 1934; came to U.S., 1955, naturalized, 1967; s. Edward N. and Judith Maria (Mediavilla) O.; B.S. in Engring., U.S. Naval Acad., 1959; m. Nella M. Ghiglione, Nov. 11, 1961; children—Anna Maria, Edward. Elec. engr. Bechtel Power Corp., Gaithersburg, Md., 1962-67; Latin Am. mktg. mgr. Sola Basic Industries, Caracas, Venezuela, 1967-69, mng. dir. Sola Basic TYF S.A. subs., Bogota, Colombia, 1969-76; dir. internat. ops. Saxon Export Corp. subs. Saxon Industries, Miami, Fla., 1976—; dir. Mercandisa S.A., Bogota. Served to lt. Ecuadorian Navy, 1959-62. Mem. IEEE, U.S. Naval Acad. Alumni Assn., U.S. Naval Inst. Republican. Roman Catholic. Club: Orange Brook Golf (Hollywood, Fla.). Home: 3201 N 47th Ave Hollywood FL 33021 Office: 13900 NW 57th Ct Miami FL 33014

ORTIZ, ADAM JOSEPH, musician, educator; b. Abilene, Tex., Sept. 2, 1934; s. Adam Longoria and Luisa (Gonzalez) O.; B.Mus. Edn., U. So. Miss., also M.Mus.; m. Margaret Lynne Perkins, July 4, 1973; children—Margo, Mark, Daniel. Choral condr. male chorus Keesler AFB, Miss., 1956-58, condr. annual Messiah presentations, 1977—; choral music coordinator CBS, New Orleans, 1956-58; prof. music, vocal therapist Miss. Gulf Coast Jr. Coll., Jefferson Davis Campus, Gulfport, 1959—. Singer leading roles operas and musical prodns.; condr. community chorus, Gulfport; choral master Community Opera Assn., Gulfport; music dir. First United Meth. Ch., Gulfport; guest condr. New Orleans Symphony, 1956. Served with USAF, 1955-58. Named hon. citizen, key to city New Orleans, 1956. Mem. Choral Condrs. Nat. Assn. Methodist. Author workbook: Fundamentals of Writing/Reading Music, 1977. Office: Dept Music Miss Gulf Coast Jr College Gulfport MS 39501

ORTIZ, ARACELI, oral pathologist, educator; b. Culebra, P.R., Jan. 15, 1937; d. Jesus M. and Pura (Martinez) O.; B.S., U. P.R., 1958, D.M.D., 1962; M.Dental Sci., Ind. U., 1967; m. Jesus Latimer, Feb. 7, 1976; 1 son, Paul S. Resident in gen. dentistry Univ. Dist. Hosp., U. P.R., 1962-65; asso. prof. dept. oral pathology and diagnosis McGill U. Sch. Dentistry, Montreal, Que., Can., 1967-73; cons. oral pathology and diagnosis VA Hosp., P.R., Hosp. Sociedad Auxilio Mutuo y Beneficencia, P.R., Univ. Dist. Hosp. Med. Center, 1973—; cons. forensic dentistry Inst. Forensic Medicine, 1979—; guest lectr. forensic odontology Interam. U. Law Sch., 1975; prof. pathology and oral medicine sect. Sch. Dentistry, U. P.R., 1973—; producer, moderator TV program Smile P.R., 1978—; mem. clin. cancer tng. commn. NIH, 1972. Diplomate Am. Bd. Oral Pathology, Am. Bd. Oral Medicine. Recipient numerous awards. Mem. ADA, Coll. Dental Surgeons P.R., Am. Acad. Oral Pathology, Am. Acad. Oral Medicine, Can. Soc. Forensic Sci., Am. Soc. Forensic Odontology, Puerto Rican Soc. Periodontology, P.R. Assn. Women Dentists, Beta Beta Beta. Roman Catholic. Club: Zonta. Home: Condominio Segovia Apt 410 Hato Rey PR 00918 Office: Med Scis Campus Sch Dentistry Rio Piedras PR 00936

ORWIG, HERBERT LEES, engring. exec.; b. Pitts., Oct. 17, 1931; s. Herbert I. and Lela M. (Groves) O.; student U. Pitts., 1949-50; B.S. in Mech. Engring., Letourneau Tech. Inst., 1955; m. Lois M. Gienow, Jan. 26, 1957; children—Lorrel, Linda, Gwen, Gail. Design project engr. Clark Equipment Co., Benton Harbor, Mich., 1955-58; successively chief design engr., acting chief engr., devel. engr. Trojan div. Yale & Towne, Mfg. Co., Batavia, N.Y., 1958-63; mgr. project engring. Mixing Equipment Co., Rochester, N.Y., 1963-64; dept. engr. J.I. Case Co., Racine, Wis., 1964-67, chief engr., Terre Haute, Ind., 1967-70, chief engr., Burlington, Iowa, 1971-72, mgr. engring. adminstrn., Racine, Wis., 1973; chief engr. Dynahoe Products Bucyrus-Erie Co. (Pa.), 1973-75; v.p. engring. ATO Constrn. Equipment Div., Marion, Ohio, 1975-77, Charleston, S.C., 1978—. Served with Chem. Corps, AUS, 1957. Recipient Lincoln Arc Welding award, 1959. Mem. Soc. Automotive Engrs., ASME, Constrn. Industry Mfrs. Assn. Republican. Contbr. articles on design and equipment maintenance to mags. Patentee in field. Home: 104 Kendall Ct Summerville SC 29483 Office: ATO Construction Equipment Div PO Box 10263 Charleston SC 29411

ORY, HOWARD WILLIAM, epidemiologist; b. Worcester, Mass., Oct. 1, 1944; s. Albert J. and Belle (Lederman) O.; B.S., U. Wis., 1966; M.D., Tufts U., 1969; M.S. in Epidemiology, Sch. Public Health, Harvard U., 1974; m. Carole Feldman, June 26, 1966; children—Michael, Jill. Intern and resident Met. Hosp., N.Y.C., 1969-71; commd. med. officer USPHS, 1971, med. epidemiologist Family Planning Evaluation div. Center for Disease Control, Atlanta, 1971-73, chief fertility control epidemiology br., 1973—. Recipient commendation medal USPHS, 1978. Contbr. articles to med. publs. Office: 1600 Clifton Rd NE Atlanta GA 30333

O'RYAN, JULIO CANDIDO, pediatrician; b. Bayamo, Cuba, Feb. 24, 1943; came to U.S., 1962, naturalized, 1978; s. Candido and Eulalia (Esteva) O'R.; B.S. and B.A., Holguin Inst. (Cuba), 1961; B.S., Zaragoza U., 1965, licenciature in medicien and surgery, 1971; m. Maria Isabel Rivas, July 1967; children—Alex, Maria Pilar, Julio Candido. Intern in internal medicine U. Zaragoza (Spain), 1970-71, intern in pediatrics, 1969-70; rotating intern Perth Amboy (N.J.) Hosp., 1972; jr. resident pediatrics Children's Hosp. Med. Center, Harvard Med. Sch., Boston, 1972-73, asst. resident in medicine, 1973-74, teaching fellow in pediatrics, 1973-74; sr. pediatric resident Driscoll Children's Hosp., Corpus Christi, Tex., 1974-75; practice medicine, specializing in pediatrics, Kingsville, Tex., 1976—; chief of nursery and pediatrics Kleberg County Hosp., Kingsville, 1976—, sec. med. staff, 1976-77. Harvard Med. Sch. fellowship in pediatrics, 1973-79. Diplomate Am. Bd. Pediatrics; lic. physician, Tex., Mass. Fellow Am. Acad. Pediatrics; mem. AMA, Nueces County Pediatric Soc., Harvard U. Alumni Assn. Democrat. Roman Catholic. Home: 1409 Brenda St Kingsville TX 78363 Office: 500 Caesar St Kingsville TX 78363

OSAKI, SHIGEMASA, biochemist; b. Tokyo, May 1, 1928; s. Koziro and Shigeko (Osaki) Nakazawa; M.S., U. Tokyo, 1953, Ph.D., 1961; m. Shizuko Morita, Dec. 11, 1956; 1 son, Isaac S. Research asso. Fla. State U., 1961-66; sr. research fellow Norwegian Council for Sci. and Humanity, U. Oslo, 1966-68; sr. research asso. Fla. State U., 1968-74; dir. enzyme lab. U. Kans., Lawrence, 1974-76; prof. biochemistry, 1975-76; mgr. research HYCEL, Inc., Houston, 1976—. NSF grantee, 1976-78. Mem. Japanese-Am. Citizen League Houston (pres. 1979—), Am. Soc. Biol. Chemists, Am. Chem. Soc., Am. Assn. Clin. Chemists, AAAS, Sigma Xi. Contbr. chapters to books, articles to profl. jours. Office: PO Box 36329 Houston TX 77036

OSBORN, GENE EDWARD, engr.; b. Willard, Ohio, Sept. 27, 1945; s. Dale Edward and Hermina (Kruger) O.; student Ohio No. U., 1963-67; m. Maureen Sue Harvey, Mar. 24, 1967; 1 dau., Michelle Lynn. Elec. engr. Marion Power Shovel Co. (Ohio), 1967-71; project engr. North Elec., Galion, Ohio, 1971-74; gen. contractor, Waldo, Ohio, 1974-77; bldg. engr. United Telephone Systems, Altamonte Springs, Fla., 1977—. Mem. Five County Builders and Contractors Assn., YMCA, Sigma Phi Epsilon. Lutheran. Clubs: Moose, Elks. Home: 1530 Palmer Ave Winter Park FL 32789 Office: PO Box 5000 151 Wymore Rd Altamonte Springs FL 32701

OSBORN, GLENN RICHARD, audio engr.; b. Los Angeles, Oct. 25, 1928; s. Glenn Litz and Nellie (Hoffman) O.; B.S. in Audio Engring., U. Hollywood, 1949; m. Joyce Elise Hughes, Feb. 15, 1963; children—Eric William, John Howard. Head transmission engr., 1352 Motion Picture Squadron, Hollywood, 1953-60; head sound dept. Sandia Corp., Albuquerque, 1960-65; supr. sound dept. A-V Service Corp., Seabrook, Tex., 1965—; owner G.R. Osborn & Co., Audio Engrs., Seabrook, 1975—. Served with AUS, 1950-52. Mem. Audio Engring. Soc., Acoustical Soc. Am., Soc. Motion Picture and TV Engrs. Home: 2117 Willow Wisp Dr Seabrook TX 77586 Office: LBJ Space Center Bldg 2 Room 145 Houston TX 77058

OSBORN, PRIME FRANCIS, III, lawyer, r.r. ofcl.; b. Greensboro, Ala., July 31, 1915; s. Prime Francis and Anne (Fowlkes) O.; J.D., U. Ala., 1939, LL.D., 1970; m. Grace Hambrick, Aug. 30, 1939; children—Prime Francis IV, Mary Anne. Admitted to Ala. bar, 1939, Ky. bar, 1952, N.C. bar, 1959, also Fed. Cts., ICC, U.S. Supreme Ct. bar; asst. atty. gen., Ala., 1939-41; atty. G., M. & O. R.R., 1946-51, commerce atty., 1950-51; gen. solicitor L. & N. R.R., 1951-57; v.p., gen. counsel, dir. A.C.L. R.R., 1957-67, S.C. Pacific R.R. Co., Atlantic Land & Improvement Co.; v.p. law Seaboard Coast Line R.R. Co., 1967-69, pres., 1969-78, chief exec. officer, 1977—, also dir.; pres. SCL Industries, Inc., 1970—, chief exec. officer, 1977—; pres., chief exec. officer Louisville & Nashville R.R. Co., 1972—; chmn. bd. Haysi R.R., pres. Columbia, Newberry & Laurens R.R. Co., Winston-Salem Southbound Ry. Co.; vice chmn., dir. Alico Land Devel. Co.; pres. Duval Connecting R.R.; dir. Winston-Salem Terminal Co., Clinchfield R.R. Co., Atlantic & East Coast Terminal Co., Richmond, Fredericksburg & Potomac R.R., S.C. Pacific Ry. Co., First Nat. Bank Louisville, Fla. Fed. Savs. & Loan Assn., Ethyl Corp., Jacksonville, Carrollton R.R., Monon Transp. Co., S.C.L. R.R. Co., Central R.R. S.C., Tampa & Gulf Coast R.R. Co., Richmond-Washington Co. Exec. reservist Office Emergency Transp. Dept. Transp.; nat. council, nat. exec. bd., 1965-78, nat. chmn. exploring regional chmn. Boy Scouts Am., 1965-69. Bd. overseers, bd. dirs. Sweet Briar Coll., Barry Coll., Jacksonville U.; provincial chmn. Episcopal Ch. Found. Served from 2d lt. to lt. col. atty., AUS, 1941-46. Decorated Bronze Star. Named Man of Year, Duval County, Fla., 1962; recipient Silver Beaver and Antelope, Boy Scouts Am. Mem. Am. Bar Assn., Bar Assn. City N.Y., ICC Practitioners Assn. (past v.p.), Soc. Confederate Vets., Newcomen Soc. N. Am., So. Soc. N.Y., Nat. Def. Transp. Assn., Episcopal Men of Ky. (past pres.), Episcopal Men of Ala. (past pres.), Jacksonville Area (pres. 1971—, com. of 100), Louisville Area (dir. 1972-74) chambers commerce, Sigma Alpha Epsilon, Omicron Delta Kappa, Tau Kappa Alpha, Alpha Kappa Psi (hon.). Democrat. Episcopalian (nat. exec. counsel vestryman). Clubs: Rotary, Ponte Vedra (Fla.) Beach; River, Florida Yacht, Timuquana Country, Union League (N.Y.C.); Metropolitan (Washington); Pendennis, Jefferson, Harmony Landing, Louisville Country (Louisville); Augusta Nat.; Laurel Valley Country (Ligonier, Pa.). Home: 5005 Yacht Club Rd Jacksonville FL 32210 Office: 500 Water St Jacksonville FL 32202 also 908 W Broadway

OSBORN, THOMAS NOEL, II, economist; b. Danville, Ill., May 22, 1940; s. Thomas Noel and Georgia (Bagnetto) O.; B.A., U. Colo., Boulder, 1963, M.A., 1970, Ph.D. (univ. grantee 1973), 1973; m. Diana L. Bergerhouse, Dec. 28, 1966; children—Elise Brailliard, Aaron-Emile Worrel. Founding dir., prof. Center Econs. and Bus. Research, Autonomous U., Guadalajara, Mex., 1970-73, Fulbright-Hays lectr., 1970-71; Fulbright prof. Coll. Bus., Nat. U. Mex., 1973-76, prof. econs., researcher, 1973—, founding dir. doctorate program in bus. adminstrn., 1976—; adj. prof. econs. U. Colo., 1976—; cons. in field. Served as officer USNR, 1963-67; Vietnam. Rockefeller grantee, 1971-72; named chmn. U.S. Bicentennial, Am. C. of C., 1977-78. Mem. Am. Econ. Assn., N.Am. Econ. Studies Assn., Blue Key, Omicron Delta Epsilon (past chpt. pres.), Pi Kappa Alpha (past chpt. pres.). Author: Higher Education in Mexico, 1976; co-editor: U.S.-Mexico Economic Relations, 1979; El Dilema de Dos Naciones, 1980; also articles. Home: Ave Leon Felipe 42 Col San Angel Mexico 20 DF Mexico Office: Apartado Postal 70-552 Mexico 20 DF Mexico

OSBORNE, GERALD EDWARD, educator; b. Evergreen Park, Ill., Nov. 25, 1938; s. Herbert Edward and Genevieve Frances (Meehan) O.; B.A., DePaul U., 1959, M.A., 1966; Ph.D., Purdue U., 1970; postgrad. Chgo. U., 1960-62, U. Ill., 1964, Harvard, 1975; m. Mary Patricia Brittain, Oct. 1, 1960; children—Kurtiss, Kristin. Counselor DePaul U., Chgo., 1965-68; lectr., clinic asst. Purdue U., W. Lafayette, Ind., 1968-70; coordinator counseling U. Houston, 1970-73, dir. and asso. prof. counseling, 1974—; vis. prof. Ball State U., Europe, Eng., Germany, 1973-74; vis. prof. U. Guadalajara (Mexico), 1974. Cons. N.Y. State Dept. Mental Health, 1973-75, Harris County Probation Services, 1974-75, Learning Devel. Found., Houston, 1974; presiding officer exec. com. Southwest region Coll. Bd. Recipient Merit award, U. Guadalajara (Mexico), 1975. Mem. Am. Coll. Personnel Assn., Am. Psychol. Assn., Kappa Delta Pi, Phi Delta Kappa. Contbr. chpt. to Group Procedures (R. Diedrich and H. Dye), 1972. Home: 10314 Metronome St Houston TX 77043

OSBORNE, JOHN ARTHUR, accountant, univ. business officer; b. Denver, Feb. 7, 1931; s. Harold Humphrey and Erma (Allison) O.; A.A., Coffeyville (Kans.) Jr. Coll., 1954; B.S. with honors, U. Tulsa, 1956, law student, 1956-58; short course (scholarship student) U. Omaha, 1962. Accountant Pan. Am. Petroleum Corp., 1956-57; sr. accountant Frazer & Torbet, C.P.A., Tulsa, 1957-61; asst. sec.-treas. U. Tulsa, 1961—, comptroller, 1968—. Gen. chmn. Southwest Bus. Equipment Show of Tulsa, 1965; mem. planning com. Tulsa Conf. Accountants, 1965—, mayor's system study com., Tulsa, 1967; asst. treas. St. John's Episcopal Ch., 1977-79; mem. Epis. Ch. Council of Tulsa, 1980—. Served with USAF, 1951-52. C.P.A., Okla., 1959. Recipient Scholarship key Delta Sigma Pi, 1956; Gold medal award Okla. Soc. C.P.A.'s, 1956; certificate of merit Coll. Bus. Adminstrn., U. Tulsa, 1956, Merit award, Tulsa chapter Systems and Procedures Assn., 1967; named One of Outstanding Young Men in Am., 1966. Mem. Central Assn. Coll. and Univ. Bus. Officers (exec. com. 1963-64, 75-76, treas 1979—), Okla. Assn. Coll. and Univ. Bus. Officers (sec. treas. 1973-74, v.p. 1974-75, pres. 1975-76), Assn. Coll. and Univ. Auditors, Am. Inst. C.P.A.'s, Okla., Tulsa socs. C.P.A.'s, U. Tulsa Alumni Assn. (treas. 1960-70), Systems and Procedures Assn. (treas. Tulsa chpt. 1962-64, pres. 1965-66), Nat. Assn. Accountants (chpt. dir. 1971—, chpt. v.p. 1973-74, chpt. pres. 1974-75, nat. membership com. 1975-76), Fin. Execs. Inst., Assn. Coll. and Univ. Research Adminstrs., Coll. and U. Personnel Assn., Photog. Soc. Am. Tulsa Camera Club (treas. 1976—), Tulsa Council Camera Clubs (chmn. 1979), Phi Gamma Kappa (treas. 1962-76), Alpha Kappa Psi (charter mem. U. Tulsa chpt.). Club: University (incorporator, sec.-treas. 1963-69). Home: PO Box 4614 4639 E 58th St Tulsa OK 74104 Office: 600 S College St Tulsa OK 74104

OSBURN, CARROLL DUANE, educator; b. Arkansas City, Kans., Sept. 2, 1941; s. Jessie Gorman and Mattie Lee O.; B.A., Harding Coll., 1963; M.Th., Harding Grad. Sch. Religion, 1968, M.A., 1969; D.D., Vanderbilt U., 1970; Ph.D., U. St. Andrews, Scotland, 1974; m. Linda Carol Moore, July 31, 1966; children—Heather Denise, Valerie Michelle. Asst. prof. N.T., Harding Grad. Sch. Religion, Memphis, 1973-76, asso. prof., 1976—; Greek trans. cons. Wycliffe Bible Translators. Mem. Soc. Bibl. Lit., N.Am. Patristic Soc., Am. Acad. Religion, Memphis Oratorio Soc. Mem. Ch. of Christ. Contbr. articles to profl. jours. Office: 1000 Cherry Rd Memphis TN 38117

OSGOOD, FRANK WILLIAM, econ. planning cons.; b. Williamston, Mich., Sept. 3, 1931; s. Earle Victor and Blanche Mae (Eberly) O.; B.S., Mich. State U., 1953; M.C.P., Ga. Inst. Tech., 1960; children—Ann Marie, Frank William. Prin. planner Tulsa Met. Area Planning Commn., 1958-60; sr. asso. Hammer and Co. Assos., Washington, 1960-64; econ. cons. Marvin Springer & Assos., Dallas, 1964-65, Gladstone Assos., Washington, 1965-67; prof. in charge urban planning program Iowa State U., 1967-73; pres., econ. cons. Frank Osgood Assos., Inc., Dallas, Tulsa, 1973—; pres. Internat. Lang. Cons.'s, Inc., Tulsa, 1975-78; v.p., dir. Myrick-Newman-Dahlberg Inc., Dallas, 1979—; adj. prof. U. Tulsa, 1974-76; lectr. U. Tex., Dallas, 1979. Pack awards chmn. Cub Scouts Am., 1971-73. Served as officer USAF, 1954-56. Mem. Am. Planning Assn. (v.p. Okla. br. 1975-77), Okla. Soc. Planning Cons.'s (sec.-treas. 1976-79), Am. Econ. Assn., Am. Soc. Planning Ofcls., Am. Mktg. Assn., Nat. Assn. Bus. Economists, Nat. Assn. Housing and Redevel. Ofcls., Council Urban Econ. Devel., Urban Land Inst. Republican. Presbyterian (deacon). Club: Le Club. Author: A Program for Continuous Renewal of Our Cities and Metropolitan Regions: A Design for Improved Management, Decision-Making and Action, 1970; contbr. numerous articles to profl. jours. Home: 6918 Charade Dr Dallas TX 75214 Office: 5207 McKinney Ave Dallas TX 75205

O'SHAUGHNESSY-LEWISON, NINA ELIZABETH, speech-lang. pathologist; b. Amber, Okla., Sept. 18, 1941; d. Edmond Varner and Dora Emma Littlefield; B.A. (Alumni scholar), U. Okla., 1974, M.S. (stipendee), 1976; m. James M. Lewison, Sept. 25, 1978; 1 stepson, Christopher Todd. Dept. head speech and hearing unit Okmulgee (Okla.) Rehab. Center, 1976—; adj. instr. Okla. State U. 1976—; cons. in field; condr. workshops for nurses. Mem. Am. Speech and Hearing Assn., Okla. Speech and Hearing Assn. (chmn. planning com. 1978—), Phi Beta Kappa. Republican. Presbyterian. Club: Lioness (3d. v.p. 1979—). Home: 804 S Alabama St Okmulgee OK 74447 Office: Okmulgee Rehab Center Okla State Tech PO Box 677 Okmulgee OK 74447

O'SHIELDS, JERRY WOFFORD, systems analyst; b. Joanna, S.C., May 27, 1935; s. William Ernest and Sara Lois (Duckett) O'S.; student pub. schs., Clinton, S.C. Programmer, Park Seed Co., Greenwood, S.C., 1966-67; programmer analyst Systems & Programming Cons., Inc., Columbia, S.C., 1967-69; programmer analyst City of Columbia, 1969-70; programmer analyst/cons. Dept. Health & Environ. Control, Columbia, 1970-72, part-time, 1972-74; sr. systems analyst Blue Cross & Blue Shield of S.C., Columbia, 1970—, dir. fed. credit union, 1977, chmn. policies manual com., 1977. Served with U.S. Army, 1958-59. Certified data processor, 1977. Mem. Data Processing Mgmt. Assn. (dir. 1976), Mensa.

O'SHIELDS, RICHARD LEE, natural gas co. exec.; b. Ozark, Ark., Aug. 12, 1926; s. Fay and Anna Mae (Johnson) O'S.; B.M.E., U. Okla., 1949; M.S., La. State U., 1951; m. Shirley Isabelle Washington, Nov. 8, 1947; children—Sharon Isabelle, O'Shields Boles, Carolyn Jean O'Shields Turney, Richard Lee. Instr. petroleum engring. La. State U., 1949-51; prodn. engr. Pure Oil Co., Fort Worth, 1951-53; sales engr. Salt Water Control, Inc., Fort Worth, 1953-54, chief engr., 1955-59, v.p., 1956-59; cons. engr. Ralph H. Cummins Co., Fort Worth, 1959-60; with Anadarko Prodn. Co. and parent co. Panhandle Eastern Pipe Line Co., Houston, 1960—, pres. Anadarko Prodn. Co., 1966-68, dir., 1966—, exec. v.p., Panhandle Eastern Pipe Line Co., 1968-70, pres., chief exec. officer, 1970-79, chmn., chief exec. officer, 1979—; pres., chief exec. officer Trunkline Gas Co., Houston, 1970-79, chmn. chief exec. officer, 1979—; dir. 1st City Bancorp. of Tex., Nat. Distillers and Chem. Corp. Bd. dirs. Tex. Research League, Midwest Research Inst. Served with USAAF, 1945. Registered profl. engr., Kans., Tex. Mem. Am. Petroleum Inst. (dir. 1972—), Mid Continent Oil and Gas Assn. (dir. 1968—), Soc. Petroleum Engrs., Interstate Natural Gas Assn. (dir. 1970-79, chmn. 1976-77), Am. Gas Assn. (dir. 1974-79), Ind. Petroleum Assn. Am. (dir. 1971—), So. Gas Assn., Nat. Petroleum Council (dir. 1971—). Republican. Baptist. Clubs: Houston, Ramada, River Oaks Country, Masons. Office: PO Box 1642 Houston TX 77001

OSIAS, RICHARD ALLAN, internat. financier, investor, real estate investment exec., city ofcl.; b. N.Y.C., Nov. 13, 1936; s. Harry L. and Leah (Schenk) O.; student Columbia U., 1951-63; m. Alexandra Stuart Currey, Sept. 22, 1962; children—Alexandra Stuart Kimberly, Alexandra Elizabeth. Founder, Osias Orgn., Inc., N.Y.C., also Ft. Lauderdale, Fla., St. Clair, Mich., San Juan, P.R., 1953, chmn. bd., chief exec. officer, 1953—. Mem. North Lauderdale (Fla.) City Council, 1967—; vice-mayor and police commr. North Lauderdale, 1967—. Active Royal Dames Nova U., Ft. Lauderdale Mus. Art, Ft. Lauderdale Symphony Soc., Tower Council of Pine Crest Prep. Sch., Ft. Lauderdale, Boys Clubs Broward County. Served with USAF, 1953. Recipient Am. House award Am. Home Mag., 1962, Westinghouse award, 1958; named Builder of Year, Sunshine State Info. Bur. and Sunshine State Sr. Citizen, 1967-69. Mem. Ft. Lauderdale Better Bus. Bur., Offshore Power Boating Assn., Lauderhill (Fla.) Fraternal Order Police Assn. (pres.), Fla., Margate, Ft. Lauderdale chambers commerce. Clubs: Tower, Bankers Top of First (San Juan); Quarter Deck (Galveston, Tex.); Boca Raton (Fla.) Hotel and Country; Jockey, Le Club Internat. (Miami). Prin. works include city devel., residential and apt. units, residential housing communities, shopping centers, country clubs, golf courses, hotel chains, comprehensive housing communities. Home: Bay Colony 71 Compass Island Ft Lauderdale FL 33308 also Chateau de Vincy Gilly Switzerland

OSSI, MANIER BENJAMIN, food co. exec.; b. Mosul, Iraq, Sept. 27, 1929; s. Tobia George and Janie (Zebouni) O.; came to U.S., 1930, naturalized, 1941; B.S., Tulane U., 1951, postgrad., 1952-54; postgrad.

Jacksonville U., 1971-73; m. Alexandra Rizk Moore, May 29, 1965; children—Gregory, Jonathan, Madeleine, Christina. Sales rep., trainer Schering Corp., Kenilworth, N.J., 1954-66; v.p. Bingham Coffee Co., Jacksonville, Fla., 1966-68, sec.-treas., controller, 1971—; v.p., gen. mgr. J.B.C. Food Spltys., Inc., St. Augustine, Fla., 1968-71; pres. Suwannee Foods Inc., Lake City, Fla., 1978—. Pres., Gateway Center Half Way House, Jacksonville, 1968, Mental Health Clinic Jacksonville, 1976; chmn. Congressional Action Com., 3d Dist. Fla., 1977. Served with USNR, 1946-48. Mem. So. Coffee Assn. (pres. 1976-77). Democrat. Roman Catholic. Home: 2433 Segovia Ave Jacksonville FL 32217 Office: PO Box 5824 Jacksonville FL 32207

OSSWALD, KARL HANS, engr.; b. Garmisch, Germany, June 26, 1930; s. Karl and Maria (Schickl) O.; came to U.S., 1950, naturalized, 1954; student high sch. and tech. coll., Ulm, Germany; m. Gerdi Waltraud Krepp, Jan. 29, 1966; 1 dau., Catherine Marcelle Baugh. Sr. process engr. Avco-Lycoming Corp., Stratford, Conn., 1955-65, Charleston, S.C., 1968-70, contract engr., 1966-68; contract engr. Sikorsky Aircraft Corp., Stratford, 1966; mfg. engr. Mayer & Cie., Orangeburg, S.C., 1970-73; supr. engring. adminstrn. Robert Bosch Corp., Charleston, 1973—; metric cons., 1970—; tchr. metric and blue print reading, 1976—; mem. Bethel (Conn.) Police Dept., 1959-61. Served with AUS, 1952-55. Registered profl. engr., S.C. Mem. Am. Inst. Design and Drafting, Soc. Mfg. Engrs. (Certificate Outstanding Service 1970-71, Appreciation 1974-75, 75-76, treas. 1974-75, sec. 1975-76). Democrat. Roman Catholic. Co-inventor automotive anti-skid device. Home: 4343 Evanston Blvd Charleston Heights SC 29405 Office: Robert Bosch Corp PO Box 10347 Charleston SC 29411

OSTENDORF, CHARLES EDWARD, mfg. co. exec.; b. Vincennes, Ind., Jan. 27, 1938; s. Joseph Edward and Edna Helen (Tredez) O.; B.S., U. Notre Dame, 1959; M.B.A., Ind. U., 1960; m. Judith Ann Stachura, June 24, 1961; children—Andrea Lynn, Amy Leigh. Indsl. engr. Owens Corning Fiberglas, Newark, Ohio, 1960-61, Barrington, N.J., 1961-63, process and methods technologist, Waxahachie, Tex., 1963-64, indsl. engring. mgr., 1964-65, prodn. supt., 1965-66; gen. mgr. Trinity Coach Co., Dallas, 1966-67; dir. planning and systems Baifield Industries, Dallas, 1967-68, gen. mgr., Shreveport, La., 1968-69; with Beaunit Corp., 1969—, corp. dir. adminstrn., Raleigh, N.C., 1976-79, dir. ops., 1979—; lectr. in field. Active PTA. Mem. Am. Inst. Indsl. Engrs., Am. Ordnance Assn. (dir. 1968), Notre Dame Alumni Assn. (chmn. Eastern N.C.). Republican. Roman Catholic. Home: 2004 Eagleton St Raleigh NC 27609 Office: PO Box 12400 Raleigh NC 27605

OSTERHAUS, LEO BENEDICT, educator; b. Fargo, N.D., Jan. 19, 1920; s. Bernard and Carolyn (Wiltz) O.; B.S., Kans. State U., 1942; M.S., Trinity U., 1961; Ph.D., U. Tex., 1966; m. Edna Reichle, Mar. 9, 1943; children—Susan A., Annette R. Commd. 2nd lt. U.S. Army, 1943, advanced through grades to lt. col., 1964; with Philippine Command Hdqrs., Manila, 1946-48; stationed Heidelberg, Germany, 1954-57; with Brook Army Med. Center, Med. Field Service Sch., Ft. Sam Houston, 1959-64; ret. 1964; asst. prof. hosp. adminstrn. Baylor U., San Antonio, 1959-64; teaching, adminstrv. asst. U. Tex. at Austin, 1964-66; prof. bus. adminstrn. St. Edwards U., Austin, 1966-69, dir., dean. Holy Cross Coll., 1969-70, dean Center Bus. Adminstrn., 1970—; vis. prof. mgmt. U. Tex., 1966—, U. Md. European div., 1972-73; vis. prof. U. Carabobo, Valencia, Venezuela, 1978; cons. to industry and hosps. Recipient Gilbreth Mgmt. award U. Tex., 1966. Mem. Am. Mgmt. Assn., Acad. Mgmt., S.W. Social Sci. Assn., Austin Personnel Assn., Am. Accounting Assn., Sigma Iota Epsilon, Delta Mu Delta. Contbr. articles to profl. jours. Home: 8307 Tecumseh Dr Austin TX 78753

OSTERMILLER, RONALD DANIEL, JR., chem. engr.; b. Sterling, Colo., Dec. 18, 1938; s. Ronald Daniel and Argyle Viola (Horton) O.; B.S. in Chem. Engring., U. Colo., 1961; 1 dau. from previous marriage, Susan Annette. Mem. prodn. supervision staff Monsanto Co. chem. mfrs., Cin., 1961-62, process design staff, Columbia, Tenn., 1962-65, project mgmt. staff, Soda Springs, Idaho, 1965-66; mem. process design staff Union Carbide Corp., Houston, 1966-68; sr. process design engr. Pace Co., Cons., Engrs., Houston, Baton Rouge, 1968-70; founded Chem-Tran, Inc., Cons., Engrs., Houston, Baton Rouge, 1970, exec. v.p., dir., 1970-74; owner R.D. Ostermiller Intervest, Houston, 1975—; v.p., dir. T.A. Short and Assos., Inc., Houston, 1979—. Served with USMCR, 1956-64. Registered profl. engr., Idaho, Tex., La., Ala. Mem. Houston Engr. and Sci. Soc., Nat., Tex., La. socs. profl. engrs., Aircraft Owners and Pilots Assn., Pipeliners Club Houston. Home: 10502 Hammerly Blvd Houston TX 77043 Office: 902 Cohn St Houston TX 77007 also PO Box 42439 Houston TX 77042

OSTROFF, AARON JOEL, aero. engr., b. Fall River, Mass., Oct. 2, 1939; s. Sydney and Ruth (Taylor) O.; B.S., Northeastern U., 1962; M.S. in Elec. Engring., George Washington U., 1971; m. Gloria Spivak, Sept. 5, 1965; children—Stuart Alan, Sacha Michelle. Aerospace engr. NASA Langley Research Center, Hampton, Va., 1962—. Chmn. edn. com. Jewish Fedn. Newport News, 1979-80; bd. dirs. Jewish Community Center, 1979—. Recipient Group Achievement award NASA, 1965, 79, Cert. of Recognition, 1978, Certificate of Outstanding Performance, 1972, 73, Spl. Achievement award, 1973, 78 (all Langley Research Center). Mem. IEEE. Jewish (dir. temple 1971-73, sec. 1973-75, v.p. 1975-77, pres. 1977-79, pres. Men's Club 1972-73, named man of year 1974). Elk. Author tech. articles. Patentee star image motion compensator. Home: 560 Viking Dr Newport News VA 23602 Office: M S 494 Langley Research Center Hampton VA 23665

OSTROFF, DONALD HOWARD, clergyman; b. Brattleboro, Vt., Aug. 18, 1949; s. Alexander and Lucille (Howard) O.; B.S. in Econs. cum laude, U. Pa., 1971; postgrad. Sch. Theology, Internat. Grad. Christian U., San Bernardino, Calif., 1973-76; m. Barbara Anne Banks, June 2, 1973; children—Michelle, Jennifer. Asst. dir. Explo '72 Conv., Dallas, 1971-72; coordinator Great Jesus Rally, Dallas, 1972; nat. coordinator nat. confs. on ch. mgmt. Campus Crusade for Christ, San Bernardino, 1973-74; asst. dir. Here's Life, Dallas Evangelistic Outreach, 1974-76; asst. dir. Discipleship Counseling Services, 1977—. Club: Dallas Downtown Men's (dir.). Founder, editor Way of Life newsletter, 1973—, People Reaching People mag., 1979—; author: Bible Study Leaders Guide, 1979; author curricula on ch. evangelism and discipleship tng. Office: PO Box 503 Dallas TX 75221

OSTROFSKY, BENJAMIN, indsl. engr., educator; b. Phila., July 26, 1925; s. Eli and Edith (Segal) O.; B.S. in Mech. Engring., Drexel U., 1947; M.Engring., UCLA, 1962, Ph.D. (Ford Found. grantee 1962-65), 1968; m. Shirley Marcia Welcher, June 2, 1956; children—Keri Ellen, Marc Howard. Project engr. George C. Lewis Co., Phila., 1948-50; chief engr., prodn. mgr. Generator Equipment Co., Los Angeles, 1953-54; research test engr. Douglas Aircraft Co., Santa Monica, Calif., 1954-57; sr. engr. Northrop Corp., Hawthorne, Calif., 1957-61; sr. staff engr. TRW Systems, Redondo Beach, Calif., 1961-69; prof. systems and ops. mgmt. Coll. Bus. Adminstrn. and Indsl. Engring., U. Houston, 1969—; lectr. engring. design UCLA, 1962-68; cons. various indsl. firms and govt. agys., 1969—; mem. ad hoc com. long range planning for automated data processing USAF Sci. Adv. Bd., 1979—. Served with USAAF, 1943-45, USAF, 1950-53. Registered profl. engr., Calif., Tex.; recipient Armitage medal, 1978. Fellow Soc. Logistics Engrs. (nat. v.p. tech. 1974-75), AAAS, AIAA; sr. mem. Am. Inst. Indsl. Engrs., Nat. Soc. Profl. Engrs., Am. Inst. Decision Scis., Ops. Research Soc. Am., Am. Soc. Engring. Edn., Sigma Xi, Phi Kappa Phi, Alpha Iota Delta, Tau Beta Pi. Author: Design, Planning and Development Methodology, 1977; contbr. articles on engring. design and systems mgmt. to profl. jours. Home: 14611 Carolcrest Dr Houston TX 77079 Office: Mgmt Dept Univ Houston Houston TX 77004

OSTROWSKI, RONALD STEPHEN, univ. adminstr., biologist; b. Chgo., Mar. 3, 1939; s. Stephen Paul and Julia A. (Sulinski) O.; A.A., Wright Jr. Coll., 1964; B.S., No. Ill. U., 1966, M.S., 1968; Ph.D., U. Notre Dame, 1971; m. Carol Dressel, July 28, 1968; 1 dau., Beth. Asst. prof. biology U. N.C., Charlotte, 1971-77, asso. prof., 1977—, acting chmn. dept. biology, 1975, asst. to vice chancellor, 1976—, dir. evening program, 1976—, acting dir. Grad. Studies, 1979—. Served with USNR, 1957-61. Mem. Genetics Soc. Am., Am. Soc. Psycho-Prophylaxis in Obstetrics, AAAS, Assn. Southeastern Biologists, Sigma Xi. Contbr. articles to profl. jours. Office: Dept Biology U NC Charlotte NC 28223

OSTWALT, JAY HAROLD, educator; b. Iredell County, N.C., Jan. 28, 1913; s. Jay Loyd and Lottie Jane (Robbins) O.; A.B., Davidson Coll., 1935; Ph.D., Duke U., 1952; m. Adeline Hill, Apr. 19, 1957. Tchr., Glade Valley (N.C.) High Sch., 1935-37, prin., 1936-37; asso. prof. edn. Flora MacDonald Coll., Red Springs, N.C., 1937-39; tchr., dir. guidance Kannapolis (N.C.) High Sch., 1940-41; asso. prof. edn. and psychology Davidson (N.C.) Coll., 1948-60, asso. prof. edn., 1961-66, prof. edn. and psychology, 1966-67, asso. dean and registrar, 1967-71, dir. instl. devel., 1971-72, prof. edn. and psychology, 1972-78, prof. emeritus, 1978—; profl. psychology, dean students Med. Coll. Va., Richmond, 1960-61. Asso. dir. Bur. Testing and Guidance, Duke U., Durham, N.C., 1946-48; vis. prof. edn. U. N.C., Chapel Hill, 1956-57. Mem. N.C. community coll. adv. council, 1963—; dir. Mecklenburg County (N.C.) pub. sch. curriculum study, 1961-64; chmn. humanities study com. Charlotte-Mecklenburg (N.C.) schs., 1973-74; dir. health services study United Community Services, Davidson, 1971-72; mem. coll. coordinating council United Methodist Ch., 1968-75, council for higher edn., 1975—, chmn., 1978—; dir. joint higher edn. planning and strategy com. N.C. and Western N.C. ann. confs., also editor study, 1975, dir., editor study com. on ministry to campus. Served with USAAF, 1941-46. Decorated Bronze Star medal. Methodist. Home: PO Box 387 Davidson NC 28036

OSWALD, ELIZABETH LOUISE, ins. co. mgr.; b. Little Rock, Apr. 3, 1938; d. Andrew William and Elsie Irene O.; student public schs., Little Rock. With First Pyramid Life Ins. Co. Am., Little Rock, 1956—, asst. sec., 1974-76, asst. v.p., mgr. policyowners service, file, and word processing dept., 1976—. Loaned exec. United Way, 1977, 78. Cert. profl. ins. woman Nat. Assn. Ins. Women. Mem. Ins. Women of Little Rock (Boss of Yr. 1975, Ins. Woman of Yr. 1978, pres. 1978-79). Mem. Adminstrv. Mgmt. Soc. Democrat. Lutheran. Home: 5413 Westminster Dr Little Rock AR 72209 Office: First Pyramid Life Ins Co Am 650 Shackleford Rd Little Rock AR 72201

OSWALD, WILLIAM JACK, financial investor; b. Chgo., Feb. 10, 1927; s. Jeho and Maria Jeanette (Van Calcar) O.; student Ill. Inst. Tech., 1943-44, U. Wis., 1944-45; B.S., Barry Coll., 1978; m. Delores Jean Kipple, Dec. 6, 1958; 1 son, William Randolph. Pres. Star Corps., Chgo., 1953-74, chmn. bd., 1964-74; pres. Holiday Rent-A-Car Internat., 1976—; chmn. bd. Capital & Devel. Control Corp., Coral Gables, Fla., 1975—; dir. Ostar, Inc., Am. Autolet Corp. Served with USAAF, 1945-46. Cert. employment cons. Am. Inst. Employment Counseling. Home: 2200 S Ocean Ln Fort Lauderdale FL 33316

OSWALT, EUGENE TALMADGE, SR., ednl. adminstr.; b. Tuscaloosa County, Ala., Sept. 3, 1935; s. James Carl and Ethel (Kemp) O.; B.S., U. Ala., 1958; M.A., Montevallo U., 1963; Ed.D., Auburn U., 1975; m. Katherine Johnson, Apr. 2, 1954; 1 son, Eugene Talmadge. Tchr., counselor, adminstr. jr. high sch. level Montgomery, Ala., 1958-62; instr. sci. Troy (Ala.) State U., 1962-63; instructional supr., adminstr. Montgomery (Ala.) Public Schs., 1963-70, asst. supt. for instruction and curriculum, 1970—; adj. asst. prof. edn. Auburn U., Montgomery, 1974—. Mem. Ala. Suprs. and Dirs. Instrn. (pres. 1976-77), Assn. Supervision and Curriculum Devel., NEA, Ala. Edn. Assn., Montgomery County Edn. Assn., Montgomery Jr. League (adv. bd.), Urban League of Montgomery (adv. bd.), Phi Delta Kappa, Kappa Delta Pi, Alpha Beta Alpha. Democrat. Baptist. Active in devel. of competencies and testing for minimal skills in Ala. students, 1977—. Home: 3435 S Water Mill Rd Montgomery AL 36116 Office: Montgomery Public Schs PO Box 1991 Montgomery AL 36103

OSWALT, JOHN MACON, clergyman; b. Fayette, Ala., Mar. 19, 1921; s. Andrew C. and Pearl (Patterson) O.; B.A., U. Ala., 1943; Th.M., Southwestern Bapt. Theol. Sem., 1945; m. Lois Elaine Thornton, June 16, 1943; children—Lynn Thornton, Lonn Macon, Lewis Earle, Lori Elaine. Ordained to ministry Bapt. Ch., 1942; student pastor, Royse City, Tex., Palestine, Tex., 1943-45; pastor Blanchard (La.) Bapt. Ch., 1945-50, Main St. Bapt. Ch., Bogalusa, La., 1950-54, 1st Bapt. Ch., Hammond, La., 1954—. Trustee Baton Rouge Gen. Hosp., 1957-64, So. Bapt. Sunday Sch. Bd., 1978—, La. Moral and Civic Found., 1957-64, 65-77; So. Bapt. Annuity Bd., 1962-68; pres. trustees S.E. Bapt. Assembly, Mandeville, La., 1967-68; mem. interocular adv. com. Seventh Ward Gen. Hosp., Hammond; bd. dirs. Hammond United Way; chaplain-on-call Holiday Inn Hammond, 1974—; pres. Tangipahoa chpt. ARC, 1976—. Mem. La. Bapt. Conv. (mem. exec. bd. 1956-63, 69-77), Dist. 11 Bapt. Conv. (pres. 1953-54, 59-60), La. Poetry Soc. Mason, Kiwanian (pres. 1957). Contbr. articles to profl. jours. Home: Puma Dr Hammond LA 70401 Office: 200 S Pine St Hammond LA 70401

OTERO, CARLOS, found. exec.; b. Ciudad Guzman, Jalisco, Mex., Sept. 22, 1942; s. T. and Aurora (Villanueva) Otero-Pablos; B.A., Our Lady of the Lake U., San Antonio, 1971, M.S., 1973. Asst. dir. Minnie Stevens Piper Found., San Antonio, 1968—; cons. Tex. Coordinating Bd., City Arts Panel, Nat. Endowment Arts; officer, sec., dir. Family Life Center. Bd. dirs. Funding Info. Library. Mem. Council Internat. Relations (1st v.p.), Am. Personnel and Guidance Assn., Tex. Personnel and Guidance Assn. (recognition award 1977), S. Tex. Personnel and Guidance Assn. (officer, recognition award 1978), Am. Sch. Counselors Assn., Nat. Assn. Student Fin. Aid Adminstrs., Nat. Assn. Fgn. Students Assns. Roman Catholic. Club: K.C. Co-author: Mini-Course on College Admissions. Office: 201 N Saint Marys St Room 100 San Antonio TX 78205

OTHMER, MURRAY EADE, chem. engr.; b. Muscatine, Iowa, Aug. 6, 1907; s. Harry Roger and Mary Louise (Eade) O.; B.S., Grinnell Coll., 1929; postgrad. U. Rochester, 1930-32; M.S. in Engring., U. Mich., 1933; m. Mary Magdalene Artman, Sept. 30, 1937; 1 son, David Artman. Chem. plant supr. Eastman Kodak Co., Rochester, N.Y., 1929-32; chem. engr. Am. Cyanamid Co., Bound Brook, N.J., 1933-36; tech. dir. C.A.I. Prod. de Grasas, Caracas, Venezuela, 1936-40, 59-74; asso. prof. chem. engring. Tufts Coll., 1940-47; prof. chem. engring. U. P.R., 1947-48, 57-59; tech. dir. Valores Guatemaltecos, Guatemala City, 1948-53; prodn. supr. for S. Am., Sterling Drug Co., Rio de Janeiro, Brazil, 1953-57; cons. in field, 1974—. Fellow AAAS; mem. Nat. Inst. Oilseed Processors (quality control com.), Triangle Meml. Soc. (dir. 1977—), Am. Chem. Soc., Am. Inst. Chem. Engrs., Am. Oil Chem. Soc., Am. Soc. Engring. Edn., Sigma Xi, Alpha Chi Sigma. Club: Chapel Hill Country. Contbr. articles in field to profl. jours. Home and Office: 1087 Burning Tree Dr Chapel Hill NC 27514

OTIS, JOHN JAMES, civil engr.; b. Syracuse, N.Y., Aug. 5, 1922; s. John Joseph and Anna (Dey) O.; B.Chem. Engring., Syracuse U., 1943, M.B.A., 1950, postgrad., 1951-55; m. Dorothy Fuller Otis, June 21, 1958; children—Mary Eileen, John Leon. Jr. process engr. Gen. Motors Corp., Syracuse, 1951-53, prodn. engr., 1954-58, process control engr., 1958-59, process engr., 1960-61; engr., writer Gen. Electric Co., Syracuse, 1961-63, configuration control engr., Phila., 1969; asso. research engr. Boeing Co., Huntsville, Ala., 1963-65; asso. Planning Research Corp., Huntsville, 1965-67; prin. engr. Brown Engring Co. subs. Teledyne Co., Huntsville, 1967-69; mech. designer, Drever Co., Beth Ayres, Pa., 1970-71; civil engr. U.S. Army Corps Engrs., Mobile, Ala., 1971-74, Galveston, Tex., 1974—. Lector, lay minister Roman Catholic Ch. Served with USNR, 1944-46. Registered profl. engr., Ala., Tex. Mem. Am. Inst. Indsl. Engrs. (past v.p. Syracuse and Huntsville chpts.), Tex. Soc. Profl. Engrs. (dir. Galveston County chpt. 1976-79, sec.-treas. 1979-80), Tau Beta Pi, Phi Kappa Tau, Alpha Chi Sigma, Chi Eta Sigma. Home: 2114 Yorktown Ct N League City TX 77573 Office: 400 Barracuda St Galveston TX 77553

OTLEY, ALAN CHARLES, traffic and transp. engr.; b. London, June 1, 1946; s. John Arthur and Iris Laura (Pflanz) O.; B.S., Wayne State U., 1968, M.S., 1972; postgrad. St. Edwards U., 1977; m. Janey Davis, July 19, 1976. Traffic engr. Goodell, Grivas & Assos., Southfield, Mich., 1971-72; traffic systems engr. Eagle Signal Corp., Davenport, Iowa, 1972-76, traffic control product specialist, Austin, Tex., 1976—; lectr. in field. Served with U.S. Army, 1969-71. Registered profl. engr.; State of Ill. scholar, 1977. Mem. Tex. Soc. Profl. Engrs., Inst. Transp. Engrs. (asso.), Chi Epsilon, Tau Beta Pi. Episcopalian. Home: 5000 Smoky Mountain Dr Austin TX 78759 Office: Eagle Signal Corp 8004 Cameron Rd Austin TX 78753

OTTE, FREDERICK LEWIS, educator; b. Amite County, Miss., Mar. 25, 1934; s. Harry Clifford and Janie Estelle (Lewis) O.; B.A., Miss. Coll., 1955; M.S., U. So. Miss., 1960; Ph.D., Ga. State U., 1972; m. Joan Elizabeth Alford, June 28, 1974; 1 son by previous marriage—Paul Frederick. Speech tchr. Biloxi (Miss.) Pub. Schs., 1960-62; dir. student services Durham (N.C.) Tech. Inst., 1964-65; cons. Ga. Dept. Edn., Atlanta, 1966-69; asst. prof. career devel. Ga. State U., Atlanta, 1969-73, asso. prof., 1973—; cons. career devel. to various agencies. Served with AUS, 1955-58. Mem. Am., Ga. ednl. research assns., Am., Ga. personnel and guidance assns., Am., Ga. vocational assns., Am., Ga. sch. counselor assns., Nat. Vocational Guidance Assn., Assn. Counselor Edn. and Supervision. Democrat. Office: Georgia State University University Plaza Atlanta GA 30303

OTTEN, JAMES ARNOLD, microbiologist; b. Sioux Falls, S.D., Mar. 23, 1939; s. Albert and Rena (Viet) O.; student Augustana Coll., Sioux Falls, S.D., 1957-58; B.S., S.D. State U., 1961; M.S., U. Tenn., 1969; m. Ardith Marie Benney, June 30, 1962; children—Jeffrey Lynn, Jeanne Marie. Microbiologist, Oak Ridge Nat. Lab., 1965—, Ft. Sanders Hosp., Knoxville, Tenn., 1973—. Mem. adminstrv. bd. First United Methodist Ch., Oak Ridge, 1976—; bd. dirs. Clinch Valley Campfire Girls, Oak Ridge, 1976—; pres. Woodland Sch. PTA, Oak Ridge, 1976-77. Served with U.S. Army, 1961-64. Mem. Am. Soc. Microbiology, Am. Indsl. Hygiene Assn., Tenn. Soc. Clin. Microbiology, U.S. Power Squadrons, Sigma Xi. Republican. Club: Elks. Contbr. articles to profl. jours. Home: 127 Baltimore Dr Oak Ridge TN 37830 Office: Oak Ridge Nat Lab PO Box Y Oak Ridge TN 37830

OTTEN, JAMES THEODORE, educator; b. Pearl River, N.Y., Jan. 30, 1945; s. John Henry and Constance E. (Terwilliger) O.; B.A. in History, Clemson U., 1966; M.A. in History, U. S.C., 1970, Ph.D., 1976; m. Ramoth Kay Shetley, Nov. 19, 1965; children—Jennifer, Lanny. Asst. dir. U. S.C., Union, 1971-72, asst. dir. student personnel services, 1972-73, 74-75, acting dir., 1973-74, asst. dir. instructional services, 1975-77, acting dir., 1977, asso. prof. history, 1977—. Exec. bd. Broad River Br. S.C. Lung Assn., 1976—; bd. dirs. Union County Cancer Soc., 1975; mem. quality of life com. City of Union Great Towns Program, 1978—; trustee Union Carnegie Library, 1979—. Served with U.S. Army, 1967-69. Mem. So. Hist. Assn., S.C. Hist. Assn., Union County Hist. Found. (v.p. 1976-77). Methodist. Asso. editor WPA Interviews with Union County Ex-Slaves, 1979; contbr. articles to profl. publs. Home: 100 Birchwood Dr Union SC 29379 Office: E Main St Union SC 29379

OTTINGER, M(ARVIN) GERALD, ins. co. exec.; b. Stamford, Tex., Nov. 17, 1929; s. Almer Marvin and Alma Ruby (Felts) O.; B.S., Tex. A&M U., 1953; M.S., U. So. Calif., 1971; m. Dorothy Jeanne Crozier, Apr. 12, 1966; children by previous marriage—M. Gerald II, Kimberly Ann Ottinger Givens, Bryan Clark, Tammy Lynn; stepchildren—Jeannetta Jo Polasek Acklin, Houston George Polasek. Commd. 2d lt. USAF, 1953, advanced through grades to maj., 1968; flyer jet fighters/bombers, 1954-60; aircraft maintenance officer, 1960-72; maintenance control officer, 1973; wing comdr.'s staff adminstr., 1974-75; ret., 1975; Tex. Gov.'s Office Traffic Safety traffic safety mgmt., coordinator Weatherford (Tex.) Coll., 1975-76; safety cons. Employers Ins. of Wasau, Ft. Worth, 1978—. Decorated Bronze Star medal. Mem. Am. Soc. Safety Engrs. Republican. Mem. Ch. of Christ. Home: 7520 Circle Dr Fort Worth TX 76118 Office: Employers Ins of Wausau Suite 818 2001 Beach St Fort Worth TX 76103

OTTINGER, MARIANN FANNIN, speech therapist; b. Cambridge, Ohio, May 15, 1948; d. Carl Albert and Juanita Marie (Romans) Fannin; B.A., U. Akron, 1970, M.A., 1973; m. Gary Keith Ottinger, Dec. 16, 1967; 1 son, Jason Robert. Speech therapist Hillsborough County Schs., Tampa, Fla., 1971—. Fla. Dept. Edn. grantee, 1973. Mem. Am. Speech and Hearing Assn. Methodist. Office: Dept Exceptional Students 411 E Henderson Ave Tampa FL 33602

OTTMANN, HAROLD GEORGE (HARRY), JR., advt. exec.; b. Ft. Worth, Nov. 10, 1925; s. Harold George and Lucie Stout (Waddell) O.; B.B.A., U. Tex., Austin, 1949; m. Nadine Louise Line, Sept. 8, 1950; children—Harold George III, Jerri Jo. Advt. mgr. Ellison Furniture and Carpet Co., Ft. Worth, 1950-52, Ft. Worth Steel & Machinery, 1952-53; retail advt. rep. Ft. Worth Press Newspaper, 1953-55; v.p.-mgr. Thomas L. Yates Advt. Agency, Ft. Worth, 1955-65; pres. Ottmann Advt. Agency, Inc., Ft. Worth, 1965—; advt. instr. evening coll. Tex. Christian U. Served with USAF, 1944-46. Recipient disting. ser. award to edn. Journalism dept. Tex. Christian U., 1974. Mem. Affiliated Advt. Agencies Internat. (trustee 1971-74), Southwestern Assn. Advt. Agencies (pres. 1976-77), Am. Advt. Fedn. (Silver medal, 1973, gov. SW Dist. 1972-73, exec. sec. treas.), Advt. Club Ft. Worth (pres. 1964-65), Ft. Worth C. of C., Sigma Alpha Epsilon. Democrat. Methodist. Clubs: Colonial Country, Ft. Worth Kennel (pres., 1960-63, 71-73, bd. dirs.), Shrine, Scottish Rite, Masons. Home: 21 Crosslands Rd Fort Worth TX 76132 Office: PO Box 2056 1020 Summit Ave Fort Worth TX 76113

OTTO, DONALD RAY, museum dir.; b. N.Loup, Nebr., Oct. 7, 1943; s. Leonard R. and Lorraine E. (Lindsay) O.; B.A., Hastings (Nebr.) Coll., 1967; m. Sylvia D. Cook, Aug. 7, 1965; 1 dau., Allison Lindsay. With Kans.-Nebr. Natural Gas Co., Hastings, 1967-68; exhibits dir. Hastings Museum, 1968-72; asst. dir. Kans. State Hist. Soc., 1972-75; program dir. Ft. Worth Mus. Sci. and History, 1975-77, exec. dir. 1977—; pres. Kans. Mus. Assn., 1974, 75; officer Mountain Plains Mus. Conf., 1976-79, pres., 1977-78; spl. cons. mus. curriculum planning Coll. Liberal Studies, U. Okla., 1980. Mem. adminstrv. bd. 1st Meth. Ch., 1978, 80. Mem. Am. Assn. Museums (accreditation on site com. 1974—), Am. Assn. State and Local History, Tex. Mus. Assn., Am. Assn. Sci. and Tech. Centers, Assn. Sci. Mus. Dirs. Methodist. Clubs: Masons, Ridglea Country, Rotary (Ft. Worth). Office: 1501 Montgomery St Fort Worth TX 76107

OTTO, SISTER MARY VINCENT, counselor, nun; b. Scotland, Tex., Aug. 5, 1932; d. Edward H. and Margaret M. (Meurer) O.; B.A., Our Lady of the Lake U., 1965, M.S. in Counseling, 1979. Joined Sisters of St. Mary of Namur, 1949; various teaching and adminstrv. positions in parochial elem. and jr. high schs. by Sisters of St. Mary, Tex., 1949-75; asst. prin. Resurrection Sch., Houston, Tex., 1954-58; prin., 1969-73; field dir. Office of Camp Fire Girls, Wichita Falls, Tex., 1968-69; guest lectr. mental health to civic and church groups, 1976—; pvt. practice family and rehab. counseling, Houston, 1979—. Vol. southwest unit, bd. dirs. Bexar County Mental Health Assn., 1977-79; bd. dirs. Vol. Services Council of San Antonio (Tex.) State Hosp., 1978-79, Mental Health Assn. Harris County; bd. sponsors Houston Holistic Health Assn., 1979—. Mem. Am. Assn. for Marriage and Family Therapy, Am. Personnel and Guidance Assn., Tex. Personnel and Guidance Assn., Mental Health Assn., Nat. Assembly of Women Religious, Nat. Rehab. Counseling Assn. Address: 5918 Wigton Houston TX 77096

OUALLINE, VIOLA JACKSON, psychologist; b. Edna, Tex., Oct. 17, 1927; d. S.R. and Myrtle Mae (Wood) Jackson; B.S., U. Houston, 1949; M.S., N. Tex. State U., 1962, Ph.D., 1975; m. Charles Morris Oualline, Jr., Sept. 3, 1949; children—Stephen, Susan, Shari. Phys. therapist Hermann Hosp., Houston, 1948-49; pvt. practice phys. therapy, Austin, Tex., 1949-54; phys. therapist Miller Orthopedic Clinic, Charlotte, N.C., 1956-57; psychologist Dallas Soc. for Crippled Children, 1963—; ind. cons. in psychology to spl. edn. depts. of sch. dists.; condr. workshops on House-Tree-Person, Bender, Vineland; condr. workshops on parenting. Mem. Am. Psychol. Assn., Southwestern Psychol. Assn., Tex. Psychol. Assn., Am. Personnel and Guidance Assn., Council Exceptional Children. Baptist. Office: 5701 Maple Dallas TX 75222

OUDKERKPOOL, FRITS, airline exec.; b. Amsterdam, Netherlands, Sept. 9, 1930; came to U.S., 1965; s. Karel Johannes and Saartje (Ledoe) O.; Engring. degree Royal Dutch Airline Coll., Dynselburg, 1956; m. Beauchampet, July 17, 1953; children—Joyce J., Claudia P. Mgr. line maintenance Royal Dutch Airlines, Rome, Budapest, Hungary and Zurich, Switzerland, 1947-65; maintenance instr. United Air Lines, San Francisco, 1965-67; maintenance supt. Saturn Airways, Oakland, Calif., 1967-72; dir. line maintenance Braniff Internat. Airlines, Miami, Fla., 1972—. Served with Royal Dutch Air Force, 1950-52. Club: Kings Ct. Tennis. Office: PO Box 2013 Miami FL 33159

OUSTALET, JOHN AUGUSTIN, JR., physicist; b. New Orleans, Apr. 11, 1935; s. John Augustin and Mafalda Grace (Favalora) O.; B.S. in Physics, Loyola U., New Orleans, 1957; M.S. in Physics, U. Tenn., Knoxville, 1966; M.B.A., Tulane U., 1973; m. Julia Anne Garitty, June 8, 1957; children—John Augustin, Jeffrey Arthur. Project engr. nuclear div. Union Carbide Corp., Oak Ridge, 1962-67; mfg. research engr. space div. Chrysler Corp., New Orleans, 1967-68; control systems engr. Union Carbide Corp., Taft (La.) plant, 1968-75, control systems/elec. engring. group leader, 1975-79, head computer systems dept., 1980—. Served with Ordnance Corps, U.S. Army, 1957-62. Mem. La. Assn. Bus. and Industry. Democrat. Roman Catholic. Home: 608 Fairfield Ave Gretna LA 70053 Office: Union Carbide Corp Taft Plant PO Box 50 Hahnville LA 70057

OUTTEN, JOSEPH FENDALL, dentist; b. Lynchburg, Va., Aug. 19, 1928; s. Clarence Fendall and Mary Jane (Wolf) O.; B.S., Va. Poly. Inst., 1949; postgrad. U. Richmond, 1949-50; D.D.S., Med. Coll. Va. 1954; m. Mildred Lacey Wright, Aug. 2, 1952; children—Joseph Fendall, Mary Cornelia, Samuel Wright, Thomas Hobson. Individual practice dentistry, Greenville, S.C., 1956—; pres. Hosa, Inc., Greenville, 1966—; sec.-treas. Composite Enterprises, Greenville, 1958-72; chmn. dental dept. Greenville County Hosp. System. Mem. exec. council Officer Econ. Opportunity, 1968—, treas., 1971—. Bd. dirs. United Fund, Greenville, YMCA, Greenville. Served to capt. USAF, 1954-56. Recipient Service to Youth award YMCA, 1971. Mem. Dental Assos. of Greenville (sec.-treas. 1971-72), Am., S.C. dental assns., Am. Soc. Dentistry for Children, Southeastern Acad. Prosthetics, Greenville County Dental Assn. (pres. 1966-67), Piedmont Assn. (dir. 1968-69), Am. Legion, Theta Chi, Psi Omega. Mason. Clubs: American Business, Greenville Country (Greenville); Port Royal Country (Hilton Head, S.C.); Caroline Caribean Corp. (Banner Elk, N.C.). Home: 130 Rockingham St Greenville SC 29607 Office: 10 Sevier St Greenville SC 29604

OUTTEN, L(ORA) M(ILTON), educator; b. Pocomoke City, Md., Aug. 17, 1913; s. L(ora) P(rettyman) and D. Elizabeth (Blades) O.; A.B., Western Md. Coll., 1934, M.A., 1937; M.S., Cornell U., 1950, Ph.D., 1956; postgrad. U. Mich., 1958, Harvard U., 1961, Oxford (Eng.) U., 1967, Cambridge (Eng.) U., 1971, U. Calif., Berkeley, 1975. Tchr. secondary schs., Md. and Va., 1934-36, 37-46; instr. Mars Hill (N.C.) Coll., 1946-56, prof. biology, 1956—, chmn. dept. biology, 1966-71, Chair for Ecol. Research, 1971—. Fellow AAAS; mem. Am. Soc. Ichthyologists and Herpetologists, Am. Soc. Naturalists, Am. Soc. Zoologists, Am. Inst. Biol. Sci., Ecol. Soc. Am., Am. Soc. Limnology and Oceanography, Internat. Soc. Limnology, Freshwater Biol. Assn. (Gt. Britain), Am. Fisheries Soc., Soc. Systematic Zoology, Assn. Southeastern Biologists, Am. Nature Study Soc., Assn. for Edn. Tchrs. Sci., Genetics Soc. Am., Gulf and Caribbean Fisheries Inst., Inst. Environ. Sci., N.C. Acad. Sci., NEA, N.C. Edn. Assn., Sigma Xi, Beta Beta Beta. Baptist. Club: Civic. Contbr. articles in field to profl. jours.

OVERBEY, EDWARD ALEXANDER, railroad exec.; b. Mobile, Ala., Sept. 9, 1923; s. Edward V. and Elizabeth (Neely) O.; student Citadel, 1941-42, Springhill Coll., 1946-50, U. Ala., 1952; m. Oct. 18, 1947; children—Edward Alexander, Michael D., Lynn M., C. Eric. With Gulf Mobile & Ohio R.R., 1947-72; with Ill. Central & Gulf R.R., Mobile, 1972—, asst. mgr. data processing, 1964-67, auditor disbursements, 1967-72, dir. acctg., 1974—. Served with USMC, 1943-46; PTO. Mem. Assn. Am. R.R.'s, Southeastern Ry. Assn., Mobile Traffic Club, Internat. Trade Club. Roman Catholic. Club: Friendly Sons St. Patrick. Office: PO Box 1828 Mobile AL 36624

OVERBY, GEORGE ROBERT, univ. pres.; b. Jacksonville, Fla., July 21, 1923; s. Taylor Earl and Virginia (Hewett) O.; B.A., Fla. State U., 1951, Ph.D., 1966; M.Ed., U. Fla., 1959, S.Ed., 1963. Tchr., Lake Forest Hills Elementary Sch., 1956-59, Ribault Secondary Sch., 1961-64; prin. Jacksonville Christian Schs., 1959-61; asso. prof. Slippery Rock (Pa.) State Coll., 1966-68; asso. prof. Youngstown (Ohio) State U., 1968-71; prof., chmn. dept. edn. Shelton Coll., Cape Canaveral, Fla., 1971-74; pres. Freedom U., 1973—. Cons pvt., pub. edn., 1958—. Pres. bd. trustees Christian Enterprises, Inc., 1962-66; pres. bd. dirs. Christian Warriors for Christian Edn., Inc., 1972-76; nat. bd. Decency Through Law; adv. bd. Am. Security Council. Served as aviator USNR, 1943-46. Life fellow Internat. Inst. Community Service, Intercontinental Biog. Assn.; mem. Internat. Assn. Christian Edn. (founder, dir., past pres.), William Holmes McGuffey Hist. Soc., Am. Assn. Higher Ed. (life, charter), NEA (life), AAUP, Am. Assn. Sch. Adminstrs., Nat. Assn. Elementary Sch. Prins., Assn. Childhood Edn. Internat., Nat. Council for Social Studies, U. Profs. for Acad. Order (charter), Christian Educators Assn. of S.E., Widows for Christ, Christian Community Internat., Am. Assn. Christian Schs., Soc. Study Edn., Am. Biog. Research Assn. (life patron), Internat. Biog. Assn. (life patron), U.S. Naval Aviation Mus. (life), Kappa Delta Pi (life), Phi Delta Kappa (life). Home: 5927 Windhover Dr Orlando FL 32805

OVERHOLT, JOHN LOUGH, ops. analyst; b. Estherville, Iowa, May 28, 1909; s. Jonas Ira and Lilly May (Lough) O.; B.S. in Chem. Engring., Iowa State Coll., 1932; M.S. in Chem. Engring., Lehigh U., 1935; m. Marguerite Eloise Harkness, July 15, 1939; children—John Harkness, Regina Jane, Georgia Deborah. Research fellow Archer Daniel Midland, 1933-34; research investigator N.J. Zinc Co., Palmerton, Pa., 1934-55; ops. research analyst M.I.T.'s Ops. Evaluation Group, U.S. Navy, 1955-62; mem. staff Center for Naval Analyses, Arlington, Va., 1962-75, cons., 1975—. Active Boy Scouts Am., 1934-62; bd. dirs. Palmerton Meml. Park Assn., 1950-55; vestry Wicomico Episcopal Ch., 1978—. Fellow AAAS; mem. Am. Chem. Soc., Ops. Research Soc. Am., Am. Statis. Soc., Sigma Xi, Tau Beta Pi. Episcopalian. Home: Rural Route 1 Box 173 Kilmarnock VA 22482

OVERMAN, FRANCES ELIZABETH HENSON, writer, civic worker; b. Eddyville, Ky.; d. John Napoleon and Ida Belle (Koon) Henson; student Union U., 1930-32; A.B., Murray State U., 1937; postgrad. Northwestern U., 1940, U. Wis., 1941, 44; m. Ralph Theodore Overman, June 30, 1945 (div. Jan. 1968); children—Ralph Theodore, Ann Frances. Tchr. elementary schs., Ballard County, Ky., secondary schs., LaCenter, Cadiz, Maysville, and Benton, Ky., 1937-44; tchr. Oak Ridge Schs., 1944-45, 57-59; free lance writer; contbr. to Fact and Fiction, Internat. (Oak Ridge). Active Cub Scouts, Brownies; adviser Y-Teens; active Oak Ridge Civic Music Assn., Oak Ridge Community Playhouse, Oak Ridge Community Art Center. Recipient Community Service award, 1972, other awards. Fellow Intercontinental Biog. Assn.; mem. Internat. Platform Assn., League Women Voters, Centro Studi E Scombi Internazionali (internat. com. fine arts 1970-71), Internat. Acad. Leonardo Da Vinci, Tau Kappa Alpha. Contbr. articles to profl. jours. Address: 107 E Vanderbilt Dr Oak Ridge TN 37830

OVERMAN, STEVEN JOE, educator; b. Lafayette, Ind., May 28, 1943; s. Joe B. and Doris (Snyder) O.; B. Phys. Edn., Purdue U., 1965; M.S., Eastern N.Mex. U., 1968; Ph.D., Wash. State U., 1971; M.A., Jackson State U., 1979; m. Linda Lou Hege, Dec. 28, 1963; children—Arthur Joe, Christopher Ross, Penelope Elaine. Instr., coach Los Alamos Public Schs., 1966-68; asso. prof. phys. edn. Jackson (Miss.) State U., 1971—. Mem. AAHPER, Nat. Assn. Phys. Edn. in Higher Edn., Phi Delta Kappa, Phi Epsilon Kappa. Author: The Student in Medieval and Modern Times, 1977. Office: Dept Physical Edn Jackson State U Jackson MS 39217

OVERSTREET, JAMES CARLISLE, lawyer; b. Augusta, Ga., Mar. 31, 1945; s. John Olan and Jean (Carlisle) O.; student U. Ga., 1963-65; A.B., Augusta Coll., 1967; J.D., Mercer U., 1970; m. Shara Baker, July 31, 1971; 1 son, James Carlisle. Admitted to Ga. bar, 1971, U.S. Supreme Ct. bar, 1975; asso. firm Sanders, Hester, Holley, Askin & Dye, Augusta, 1970-72, partner, 1972-76; partner firm Hester, Dye, Overstreet, & Williams, Augusta, 1976-77; individual practice law, Augusta, 1978—; mem. faculty Augusta Coll. Trustee, Augusta Coll. Found.; bd. dirs. Augusta Coll. Athletic Assn.; bd. visitors Walter F. George Sch. Law, Mercer U. Mem. Am. Bar Assn., Ga. Bar Assn., Augusta Bar Assn., Augusta Trial Lawyers Assn. (treas. 1979-80), Augusta Coll. Alumni Assn. (past pres., treas. and dir.). Home: 3024 Lake Forest Dr Augusta GA 30905 Office: 206 7th St Augusta GA 30902

OVERSTREET, JAMES SYLVESTER, educator; b. Jewel Ridge, Va., May 28, 1944; s. Earl Watson and Carmella Jane O.; B.A., U. Fla., 1966; M.B.A., Fla. State U., 1975, D.B.A., 1980; m. Johanna Jean Romano, June 17, 1973; stepchildren—Victor, Annette. Adminstrv. ops. mgr. IBM Corp., Savannah, Ga., 1967-70; v.p., dir. constrn. Miller Bros., Tamarac, Fla., 1971-73; project supt. Cenvill Corp., Deerfield, Fla., 1973-74; asst. prof. mgmt. Appalachian State U., Boone, N.C., 1979—. Mem. Acad. Mgmt., So. Mgmt. Assn., Sigma Iota Epsilon. Home: Route 1 Box 270 Boone NC 28607 Office: Appalachian State U Boone NC 28608

OVERSTREET, PAUL ALEXANDER, JR., med. technologist; b. Chattanooga, Sept. 15, 1950; s. Paul Alexander and Virginia Ellen (Leeper) O.; B.S., U. Ala., 1972; student Holy Name of Jesus Sch. Med. Tech., 1974; m. Elaine McDonald, Mar. 28, 1974. Staff technologist Baptist Meml. Hosp., 1974, supr. hematology, 1975-77; chief technologist, lab. mgr. Northeast Ala. Regional Med. Center, Glencoe, Ala., 1977—. Cert. med. technologist. Mem. Am. Soc. Clin. Pathologists, Am. Soc. Med. Technologists, Ala. State Soc. Med. Tech., Ala. Assn. Lab. Mgrs. Methodist. Home: 205 Del Mar Glencoe AL 35905 Office: 400 E 10th St Anniston AL 36202

OVERSTREET, ROBIN MILES, parasitologist, marine biologist; b. Eugene, Oreg., June 1, 1939; s. Robin M. and Laura (McGinty) O.; B.A., U. Oreg., 1963; M.S., U. Miami (Fla.), 1966, Ph.D., 1968; m. Kim Bunton, Mar. 31, 1964; children—Brian, Eric. NIH fellow parasitology Tulane Med. Sch., New Orleans, 1968-69; parasitologist Gulf Coast Research Lab., Ocean Springs, Miss., 1969—, head parasitology sect., 1970—; adj. prof. marine biology U. So. Miss., U. Miss., other univs., 1969—. Served with USNR, 1957-59. Mem. Am. Fisheries Soc., Am. Microscopical Soc., Am. Soc. Parasitologists, Am. Soc. Tropical Medicine and Hygiene, Helminthological Soc. Washington, Marine Biol. Assn. U.K., Sigma Xi, others. Author book; contbr. articles to research publs. Home: 14 Paraiso Rd Ocean Springs MS 39564 Office: Gulf Coast Research Lab East Beach Ocean Springs MS 39564

OVERTON, BEN FREDERICK, state justice; b. Green Bay, Wis., Dec. 15, 1926; s. Banjamin H. and Esther M. (Wiese) O.; B.S. in Bus. Adminstrn., U. Fla., 1951, J.D., 1952; LL.D. (hon.), Stetson U., 1975, Nova U., 1977; m. Marilyn Louise Smith, June 9, 1951; children—William Hunter, Robert Murray, Catherine Louise. Admitted to Fla. bar, 1952; with Office Fla. Atty. Gen., 1952; with firms in St. Petersburg, 1954-57; circuit judge 6th Jud. Circuit Fla., 1964-74, chief judge, 1968-71, chmn. Fla. Conf. Circuit Judges, 1973; justice Supreme Ct. Fla., Tallahassee, 1974—, chief justice, 1976-78; mem. exec. council Conf. of Chief Justices, 1977-78; mem. exec. com. Appellate Judges Conf.; past mem. faculty Stetson U. Coll. Law; mem. faculty Nat. Jud. Coll.; also mem. bd. dirs.; mem. Fla. Bar Continuing Legal Edn. Com., 1963-74, chmn., 1971-74; 1st chmn. Fla. Inst. Judiciary, 1972. Past reader, vestryman, sr. warden St. Albans Episcopal Ch., St. Petersburg, Fla. Served as officer U.S. Army, 1945-47, USAR, 1950-74 active duty, 1961-62. Fellow Am. Bar Found.; mem. Am., Fla. bar assn., Am. Judicature Soc. (dir.). Democrat. Club: Rotary. Contbr. articles to legal publns. Office: Supreme Ct Bldg Tallahassee FL 32301

OVERTON, HELEN PARKER (MRS. SAMUEL WATKINS OVERTON), real estate broker; b. Memphis, Dec. 30, 1920; d. William and Pearl (Pinkston) Parker; m. Samuel Watkins Overton, Sept. 3, 1952; children—Helen Parker (Mrs. William Barron Brown), Napoleon Hill. Exec. sec. Memphis State U., 1941-43, Chgo. and So. Air Lines, 1943-46, Memphis Bd. Edn., 1948-50; dir. women's program Sta. WHBQ-TV, Memphis, 1950-52. Pres., Beethoven Club, 1960-66, 72-78; mem. Tenn. Arts Commn., 1967-74, chmn., 1967-69; pres. Mid-South Opera Guild, 1966—; dir. auditions Mid-South region Met. Opera, 1961-71, mem. nat. council, 1961-72; bd. dirs. Memphis Arts Council, Opera Memphis, Arts Appreciation. Mem. Sigma Alpha Iota, Alpha Gamma Delta. Club: Memphis Country. Home: 5476 Collingwood Cove Memphis TN 38117

OVERTON, KENNETH, human resources cons.; b. Port Arthur, Tex., Nov. 15, 1908; s. Ellis Andrew and Myrtle Amelia (Morgan) O.; Asso. Sci. in Economics, U. Houston, 1946; student U. Mo., Peabody Coll., Baylor U., Sam Houston U.; m. Mary Lou Johnson, July 17, 1932; 1 dau., Carey O. Randall. Tchr. phys. edn. Port Arthur (Tex.) Pub. Schs., 1928-32; supr. indsl. relations mgmt. and oil ops. Texaco Inc., Port Arthur, 1933-50; supt. Central/Western Arabia mgmt. Arabian Am. Oil Co. (Aramco), Saudi Arabia, 1951-63; exec. cons. to Jean Paul Getty, Getty Oil Co., Kuwait, 1963-65; sr. cost engr. Pipeline Technologists, Inc., Houston/Alaska, 1967-75; resources cons., Saudi Arabia, Houston, 1977, EG&G, Saudi Arabia, Houston, Rockville, 1976, 80. Mem. Am. Petroleum Inst. Clubs: Port Arthur Country, USAF Officers (hon.), Press.

OVERTON, NANCY JANE, stockbroker; b. Pikeville, N.C., July 17, 1940; d. James Hardy and Ola Esther (Morris) O.; B.A., Duke U., 1962. Research analyst N.Y. Life Ins. Co., N.Y.C., 1962-63; asst. to office mgr. Conf. Bd., N.Y.C., 1963-66; sec. to com. on Harvard U. Computing Center, Cambridge, Mass., 1966-67; adminstrv. asst. instl. trading dept. Paine Webber Jackson & Curtis, Boston, 1967-70; sales asst. Reynolds Securities, Inc., Jacksonville, Fla., 1970-75; account exec. Dean Witter Reynolds, Inc., Jacksonville, 1975—. Bd. dirs. N. Fla. council Camp Fire Girls, 1976-79, 2d v.p., 1978-79; bd. dirs. Riverside Avondale Preservation Assn. Nat. Methodist scholar, 1958-59. Mem. Jacksonville Area C. of C., Jacksonville Stock and Bond Club. Episcopalian. Club: University. Home: 1846 Margaret St Unit 9D Jacksonville FL 32204 Office: 54 W Forsyth St Jacksonville FL 32202

OVERTON, ROBERT ELTING, petroleum co. exec.; b. GlenRidge, N.J., Sept. 19, 1936; s. Elting Fillmore and Velma (Bird) O.; B.S., Widener U., 1958; m. Carolyn Ingrid Johnson, Nov. 8, 1958; children—Cheryl Lynn, Susan Elaine, Lori Ann. With Shell Oil Co., 1960-71, mgr. direct mail, Houston, 1960-71; dir. mail mktg. Sperry & Hutchinson Co., N.Y.C., Cin., 1971-74; pres. Gulf Consumer Services Co. and Gulf Auto Club, Inc., Houston, 1974—. Pres., Meml. Drive Luth. Ch. Council; v.p. Am. Field Services, Houston chpt. Served with U.S. Army, 1958-60. Mem. Direct Mail Mktg. Assn., Nat. Premium Sales Execs., Am. Mgmt. Assn. Republican. Lutheran. Club: Houston. Home: 13723 Butterfly Ln Houston TX 77079 Office: 909 Fannin Rm 2232 Houston Center Houston TX 77001

OVERTURF, R. CRAIG, real estate co. exec.; b. Yankton, S.D., Nov. 5, 1933; s. Chester F. and Mary J. O.; B.A., Harvard U., 1955, M.B.A., 1959; m. Rosalie Hodges, Dec. 30, 1969. Dir. mktg. Janss Corp., Los Angeles, 1965-69; sr. v.p. Bankamerica Realty Services, San Francisco, 1970-73; pres. Bankamerica Internat. Realty Co., San Francisco, 1974-75; pres. Sugarland Properties, Inc., Houston, 1976-79; chmn. bd. Wilma, Inc., Atlanta, 1980—. Served with U.S. Army, 1955-57. Mem. Urban Land Inst. (council), Mensa. Clubs: St. Francis Yacht, Univ. Office: 233 Peachtree St NE Atlanta GA 30303

OWAIS, MUHAMMAD, physicist, educator; b. Pakistan, Apr. 16, 1942; came to U.S., 1966, naturalized, 1977; s. Abdul and Saleha Khatoon (Quaim) Aziz; B.S., U. Karachi, Pakistan, 1961, M.S., 1964; M.S., U. Ga., 1970, Ph.D., 1973; m. Zahra Ahmad, Nov. 21, 1965; children—Huma, Seema, Saba. Lectr. in physics Habib Inst. Tech., Nawabshah, Pakistan, 1964-66; teaching asst. U. Ga., Athens, 1966-71, Fulbright fellow, 1966, research fellow, 1970-73, research asst. summers 1967, 68, grad. research asst., 1971-73; vis. asst. prof. dept. physics SUNY, Potsdam, 1973-74, asst. prof. physics SUNY Agrl. and Tech. Coll., Canton, 1974; asst. prof. physics Paine Coll., Augusta, Ga., 1975-78, asso. prof., 1978-79, chmn. dept. physics, 1975-79; asso. prof. physics Alcorn State U., Lorman, Miss., 1979—; with Oak Ridge (Tenn.) Nat. Lab., 1967-69; faculty research participant Savannah River Lab., Reactor Physics Div. E.I. DuPont & Co., Aiken, S.C., 1978; cons. Dept. Energy; vis. physicist Lawrence Livermore (Calif.) Lab. summer 1979. Pres. Pakistan Student Assn. Am., U. Ga. Chpt., 1970. NASA grantee, 1976-77. Mem. Am. Phys. Soc., AAUP (pres. Paint Coll. chpt., 1978), Muslim Student Assn. Am. and Can., Miss. Acad. Sci., Sigma Xi, Sigma Pi Sigma. Contbr. articles, abstracts to profl. publs. Home: 310 Linda St Vicksburg MS 39180 Office: Dept Physics Alcorn State U Lorman MS 39096

OWEN, DAVID WESLEY, children's service exec.; b. Kansas City, Mo., Nov. 17, 1934; s. Harry J. and Irene P. (Rogers) O.; B.A., William Jewell Coll., 1957; M.A., Carver Sch. Missions and Social Work, 1963; D.D., Kansas City Bible Inst., 1974; m. Nancy Ailene Bentley, Aug. 20, 1954; children—David D., Wesley Vincent, Christopher Bentley. Ordained to ministry Baptist Ch., 1954; pastor chs., Mo., Kans., Ind., 1954-65; pioneer missionary, Hoisington, Kans., 1961; settlement house missionary, Louisville, 1961-62; teaching fellow U. Kansas City (Mo.), 1958-60; juvenile ct. adminstr., Louisville, 1961-65; children's home adminstr., Salem, Va., 1965-71; fund raising cons., Tulsa, 1978—; exec. dir. Tulsa Boys' Home, 1971-80. Mem. Okla. Assn. Child Welfare (dir. 1976-79), Nat. Assn. Social Workers, Nat. Assn. Homes for Children, Okla. Health and Welfare Assn., Am. Assn. Marriage and Family Therapists. Republican. Clubs: Rotary Internat. (dir. Tulsa 1977, chmn. student loan fund 1977, 78), Masons. Home: 3925 E 59th St Tulsa OK 74135 Office: PO Box 1101 Tulsa OK 74101

OWEN, DUNCAN SHAW, JR., physician, educator; b. Fayetteville, N.C., Oct. 24, 1935; s. Duncan Shaw and Mary Gwyn (Hickerson) O.; B.S., U. N.C., 1957, M.D., 1960; m. Irene Lacy Rose, Oct. 22, 1966; children—Duncan Shaw, Robert Burwell, Frances Gwyn. Med. intern Med. Coll. Va. Hosp. Richmond, 1960-61, asst. med. resident, 1964-65, NIH fellow in rheumatic diseases, 1965-66, instr. in medicine, 1966-67, asst. prof. medicine, 1967-71, asso. prof. medicine, 1971-78, prof., 1978—; asst. med. resident N.C. Meml. Hosp., Chapel Hill, 1961-62; attending physician Med. Coll. Va. Hosp. and Richmond VA Hosp., 1966—; chief pvt. med. service Med. Coll. Va., Richmond, 1967-74; chmn. MCV Pvt. Practice Group, Richmond, 1972-75. Chmn. med. and sci. com. The Arthritis Found., 1975-77; bd. dirs. Blue Shield of Va., 1975-77; diaconate First Presbyn. Ch.,

Richmond, 1973-77, chmn., 1975-77, elder, 1977—. Served with M.C., U.S. Army, 1962-64. Decorated Army Commendation medal; recipient Distinguished Service award Arthritis Found., 1971; Gerard B. Lambert award for effective implementation of innovative ideas regarding patient care and costs, 1974-75; Certificate of Merit, AMA, 1975. Fellow A.C.P.; mem. Richmond Acad. Medicine (v.p. 1978, trustee 1979), Med. Soc. Va. (v.p. 1973, 75), AMA, Richmond Soc. Internal Medicine, Am. Rheumatism Assn. (exec. com. 1979—). Presbyterian. Asso. editor: Va. Med., 1978—; contbr. articles in field to med. jours. Home: 8910 Brieryle Rd Richmond VA 23229 Office: 1200 E Broad St Richmond VA 23298

OWEN, EDWIN LEWIS, tech. co. exec.; b. Evanston, Ill., Aug. 8, 1942; s. Oliver L. and Ruby E. O.; B.S., Colo. Sch. Mines, 1965; Ph.D., Ohio State U., 1970; m. Kristina K. Owen, Aug. 28, 1965; children—Justin, Sean. Asst. prof. metallurgy Pa. State U., State College, 1970-73; sr. metallurgist Kennecott Copper Co., Lexington, Mass., 1973-76; mgr. quality assurance, tech. lab. Chromalloy Turbine Support Div., San Antonio, 1976—; cons. in field. Active Roughrider Soccer Club, San Antonio. Registered profl. engr., Tex. Mem. Am. Soc. Metals, Nat. Assn. Corrosion Engrs., Am. Electroplaters Soc. Contbr. articles on corrosion and diffusion to profl. publs. Home: 601 Crestway St San Antonio TX 78239 Office: Turbine Support Div Chromalloy Co PO Box 20148 San Antonio TX 78220

OWEN, EVA VATTER, artist; b. Shreveport, La.; d. Henry and Josephine E. (Hayes) Vatter; student La. State Normal Coll., 1934-35, La. State U., 1945, Tulane U., 1961-66, San Miguel de Allende, Mexico, 1968-69, Art Students League, N.Y.C., 1971; student of Don Brown, 1939-40, James L. Steg, others; 1 son, Ralph. Co-founder, Galerie d'Or, New Orleans, 1971, sec., 1971-73; condr. student field trips, 1971; portrait artist Astroworld, Houston, 1980; one-woman shows paintings at galleries and banks in New Orleans, also Pierremont Mall, Shreveport, 1968; group shows at various galleries in New Orleans, Galerie Paula Insel, N.Y.C., 1971, Bertrand Russell Mus., Nottingham, Eng., 1973, Galerie Mouffe, Paris, 1974; represented in permanent collections: St. Vincent's Acad., Shreveport, Schumpert Meml. Hosp., Shreveport, Haughton (La.) United Pentecostal Ch.; paintings include: St. Louis Cathedral, 1975, Louisiana Moon, 1978, Cypress Swamp, 1976, Idlewylde, 1976, Murex shell, 1979, California View, 1979. Mem. New Orleans Art Assn., La. Watercolor Soc. (sec. 1972-73), La. Landmarks Soc., Am. Fedn. Arts of N.Y.C., New Orleans Mus. Art, Crescent City Needlework Guild, Art League Houston. Roman Catholic.

OWEN, GAYLE BLASIUS, ednl. counselor; b. Terrell, Tex., Mar. 8, 1944; d. Carl Curtis and Martha Helen (Pipes) Blasius; B.A., E. Tex. State U., 1969, M.Ed., 1972; m. Joe McQuary Owen, Aug. 7, 1965; children—Kathy Jan, Paul Curtis (dec.), Julie Helen. Tchr. 2d grade Dallas Ind. Sch. Dist., 1969-70; tchr. 1st and 6th grades and learning disabilities, Mesquite, Ind., 1971-76, counselor, kindergarten-12, 1976—; counselor parent groups. Mem. Am., Tex. personnel and guidance assns., Assn. Children with Learning Disabilities, Tex. Assn. Children with Learning Disabilities, Mesquite Edn. Assn., Phi Delta Kappa. Baptist. Home: 4754 Snow Dr Mesquite TX 75150 Office: 405 E Davis St Mesquite TX 75149

OWEN, GEORGE TREZEVANT, III, lawyer; b. Baton Rouge, Dec. 3, 1926; s. George Trezevant and Kate Louise (Borron) O.; B.A., La. State U., 1949, J.D., 1955; m. Anna Christine Stanard, Dec. 23, 1950; children—Christine Trezevant, George Trezevant, Georganna Faser. Admitted to La. bar, 1955, also U.S. Supreme Ct.; partner firm Borron, Owen, Borron & Delahaye, Baton Rouge, 1955-68; partner firm Dale, Owen, Richardson, Taylor & Mathews, Baton Rouge, 1968—; dir. City Nat. Bank of Baton Rouge. Lectr. negotiable instruments law Nat. Banking Inst., 1960-61. Bd. dirs. Cancer Radiation Research Found., Inc.; chmn. Baton Rouge Assembly. Served with USNR, 1944-46, AUS, 1950-53. Decorated Bronze Star medal, Air medal with four oak leaf clusters. Mem. Phi Delta Phi. Rotarian. Clubs: Baton Rouge City (pres.), Baton Rouge Country (pres.). Office: PO Box 3177 Baton Rouge LA 70821

OWEN, GUY, author, educator; b. Clarkton, N.C., Feb. 24, 1925; s. Guy and Ethel (Elkins) O.; B.A., U. N.C., 1947, M.A., 1949, Ph.D., 1955; student U. Chgo., 1947, U. Utah, 1943-44. Instr., Davidson (N.C.) Coll., 1949-52, Elon (N.C.) Coll., 1954-55; asst. prof. dept. English, Stetson U., DeLand, Fla., 1955-62; prof. English, N.C. State U., Raleigh, 1965—; writer-in-residence U. N.C., Greensboro, 1968, Appalachian State U., 1968; dir. N.C. Poetry Circuit, 1962-68; poetry readings various colls. and univs. Recipient N.C. award for lit., 1972, Brown Hudson Folklore award, 1977. Mem. MLA, N.C. Folklore Soc., Soc. Study of So. Lit. Author: (fiction) Season of Fear, 1960; The Ballad of the Flim-Flam Man, 1965; A Journey for Joedel (Sir Walter Raleigh award; nominated for Pulitzer prize), 1970; The Flim-Flam Man and the Apprentice Grifter, 1972; The Flim-Flam Man and Other Stories, 1979; (poetry) Cape Fear County and Other Poems, 1958; The Guilty and Other Poems, 1962; The White Stallion, 1969; contbr. short stories and poetry to various lit. jours.; founder, editor Impetus, 1958-64; editor So. Poetry Rev., 1964-75, Modern American Poetry: Essays in Criticism, 1972; contbg. editor Books Abroad, 1963-67; co-editor New Southern Poets, 1974, Contemporary Poetry of North Carolina, 1977, Contemporary Southern Poetry, 1979; editorial bd. Pembroke Mag., 1974—, Appalachian Jour., 1974-78. Home: 105 Montgomery St Raleigh NC 27607 Office: Dept English NC State Univ Raleigh NC 27607

OWEN, JAMES LEE, JR., Realtor, auctioneer; b. Princeton, W. Va., Jan. 5, 1950; s. James Lee and Corrinne Elizabeth (Wheeler) O.; grad. Realtors Inst., U. Va., 1970, Mendenhall Sch. Auctioneering, 1972; m. Lisa J. Peraldo, Jan. 24, 1976; 1 dau., Elizabeth Darby. Salesman real estate, Princeton, 1968—, broker, 1971—; auctioneer Princeton, 1971—; expert witness as real estate appraiser Mercer County (W. Va.) Cts., 1968—; instr. Mendenhall Sch. Auctioneering, High Point, N.C. Pres. Mercer County Bd. Realtors, 1971-72, 77. Bd. dirs. Greater Princeton Athens United Fund. Mem. W. Va. (sec. 1972-73), Nat. assns. Realtors, Nat., W. Va. auctioneers assns., Mercer County Bd. Realtors. Democrat. Methodist. Club: Elks. Home: Sandlick Rd Princeton WV 24740 Office: 234 New Hope Rd Princeton WV 24740

OWEN, JOHN REES, audiologist; b. White Plains, N.Y., Feb. 7, 1945; s. John Walker and Virginia (Thompson) O.; B.A. in Psychology, Alderson Broaddus Coll., Philippi, W.Va., 1967; M.A. in Speech Pathology, Marshall U., Huntington, W.Va., 1971; equivalent M.A. in Audiology, W.Va. U., 1972; m. Barbara Ann Pownall, Sept. 4, 1974; children—Elizabeth L., Kimberly Ann. Speech therapist, then head speech and hearing program Mason County (W.Va.) schs., 1971-73; audiologist W.Va. Sch. Deaf and Blind, Romney, 1973-75, dir. child study center, 1975—; cons. in field. Pres. Hampshire County Council PTA, 1976. Mem. Am. Speech and Hearing Assn., W.Va. Speech and Hearing Assn. (pres. 1978). Presbyterian. Office: Child Study Center WVa Sch Deaf and Blind Romney WV 26757

OWEN, KENNETH DALE, orthodontist; b. Charlotte, N.C., May 9, 1938; s. Olin Watson and Ruth (Watlington) O.; B.S., Davidson Coll., 1959; D.D.S., U. N.C., 1963, M.Sc. in Orthodontics, 1967; m. Lura Aven Carnes, Feb. 14, 1958; children—Kenneth Dale, Aven Anna. Individual practice orthodontics, Charlotte, 1966—. Asst. clin. prof. U. N.C. Sch. Dentistry, 1969-72. Bd. dirs. N.C. Dental Found., 1973—, exec. com., 1974—, v.p. 1976-77, pres., 1978-79. Served with Dental Corps, AUS, 1963-65. Fellow Internat. Coll. Dentists, Am. Coll. Dentists; mem. ADA, Am. Assn. Orthodontists, So. Soc. Orthodontists, N.C. Orthodontic Soc. (chmn. long range objectives com. 1975-79, sec.-treas. 1976-78, pres. 1979-80), N.C. (ho. dels. 1969-77, chmn. coms.), 2d Dist. (editor 1967,69, sec.-treas. 1971-74, pres. 1975-76, exec. com. 1971-77), Charlotte (chmn. various coms., dir. 1978-79), Stanly County dental socs., U. N.C. Orthodontic Alumni Assn. (sec.-treas. 1971, v.p. 1972-73, pres. 1974-75, exec. com. 1971-76), Orthovista Orthodontic Study Group (pres. 1968; treas. 1972, sec. 1973, pres. 1974), Delta Sigma Delta (pres. N.C. grad. chpt. 1970-71), Omicron Kappa Upsilon, Kappa Sigma, Alpha Epsilon Delta. Methodist (steward 1968-69, adminstrn. bd. 1969-71, 74-75, 77—). Clubs: Olde Providence, Foxcroft Hills. Home: 3724 Pomfret Ln Charlotte NC 28211 Office: 1201 E Morehead St Charlotte NC 28204 also 119 Vadkin St Albemarle NC 28001

OWEN, LARRY THOMAS, social worker; b. Alexandria, La., Mar. 9, 1946; s. Thomas Earl and Sarah Lucille (Coker) O.; student La. State U., Alexandria, 1964-66; B.A., La. Coll., Pineville, 1969; M.S.W., La. State U., 1974 (HEW fellow); m. Rita Katheryn Herrington, Aug. 14, 1971; 1 dau., Amanda Kay. Counselor, Donaldsonville (La.) Mental Health Clinic, 1972; social work supr., asst. dir. div. adolescent services Central La. State Hosp., Pineville, 1974—; adj. asst. prof. Northwestern State U. La., 1977—. Served with AUS, 1969-71; Korea. Mem. Acad. Cert. Social Workers, Nat. Assn. Social Workers. Democrat. Baptist. Home: 104 Lake Dr Pineville LA 71360 Office: PO Box 31 Pineville LA 71360

OWEN, LAURA ELLEN, elec. engr.; b. Tucumcari, N.Mex., Nov. 26, 1939; d. Luther Moody and Ida Floy (Hutchens) O.; B.S. Geophysics, N.Mex. Inst. Mining and Tech., 1961; B.S.E.E., U. Tex., Austin, 1969. Engr., Schlumberger, Houston, 1961-66; project engr. Zapata, Houston, 1972-74; sales rep. Ocean Research Equipment, Falmouth, Mass., 1974-75; engr., mgr. power and controls TOC, Houston, 1968-72, 75-76; power plant supr. Mobil Oil Corp., Beaumont, Tex., 1976—; dir. Taza De Oro, Inc., Beaumont. Bd. dirs. Rape Crisis Center S.E. Tex.; campaign mgr. Alice Marie Andrews campaign; mem. coordinating com. Bob Krueger campaign; asst. to chmn. Tex. Women's Polit. Caucus. Mem. IEEE, AAUW, Instrument Soc. Am., Assn. Desk and Derrick Clubs, Tex. Restaurant Assn., Bus. and Profl. Women's Club. Democrat. Home: 9550 Doty Beaumont TX 77707 Office: PO Box 3311 Beaumont TX 77704

OWEN, ROBERT BARRY, physicist; b. Chgo., Oct. 16, 1943; s. Jack Saunders and Dorothy Orleen (Riley) O.; B.S. in Physics, Va. Poly. Inst. and State U., 1966, Ph.D. in Physics, 1972; m. Lyn Irvin, Oct. 31, 1970; children—Catherine Anne, Ruth Riley. Grad. coop. student NASA Marshall Space Flight Center, Huntsville, Ala., 1966-72, exptl. research scientist, 1972—; tchr. physics Va. Poly. Inst. and State U., Blacksburg, 1966-69; cons. to fed. agys. Recipient sect. prize IEEE, 1978. Mem. Optical Soc. Am., Soc. Photo-Optical Instrumentation Engrs., Sigma Xi, Sigma Pi Sigma. Republican. Unitarian. Contbr. articles to profl. jours.; spl. editor SPIE, 1979. Home: 703 Clinton Ave NE Huntsville AL 35801 Office: ES 74 Marshall Space Flight Center AL 35812

OWEN, ROBERT DALE, zoologist; b. Tulsa, Oct. 16, 1948; s. Edgar Lyle and Mary K. Owen; B.S., U. Okla., 1976, postgrad., 1976—; m. Susan Allison Miller, Apr. 15, 1975; 1 son, William Wildcat Owen-Miller. Research asst. Techrad Inc., Oklahoma City, 1975, environ. zoologist, 1975-76; grad. research asst. life scis. div. Stovall Mus. Sci. and History, U. Okla., Norman, 1976-78, grad. teaching asst. dept. zoology, 1978—. Chmn., Okla. U. Com. to End War in Viet Nam, 1968-69. Recipient Travel award Phi Sigma, 1973; NSF grantee, 1978—. Mem. Am. Soc. Mammalogists, Soc. for Study of Evolution, Soc. Systematic Zoology, Sigma Xi, Phi Sigma. Home: Route 6 PO Box 139 Norman OK 73071 Office: Dept Zoology Univ Okla Norman OK 73019

OWENS, BOB RAY, coll. dean, educator; b. Dallas, Nov. 7, 1933; s. William E. and Gladys C. (Cox) O.; B.B.A., N. Tex. State U., 1959, M.B.A., 1960; Ph.D., U. Ark., 1966; m. Johnie Rae Reed, Feb. 4, 1961; children—Julie Dianne, Michael Jeffrey. Acct., Shell Oil Co., Houston, 1960-62; instr. U. Ark., 1962-65; asst. prof. mgmt. La. Tech. U., Ruston, 1965-66, asso. prof., 1966-68, prof., 1968—, dean Coll. Adminstrn. and Bus., 1975—; mgmt. cons. Served with USN, 1953-57. Mem. So. Bus. Adminstrn. Assn., Southwestern Bus. Adminstrn. Assn., Ruston C. of C. (dir. 1976-78), Alpha Kappa Psi, Phi Kappa Phi, Beta Gamma Sigma, Sigma Iota Epsilon, Delta Pi Epsilon. Episcopalian. Office: PO Box 5796 Ruston LA 71272

OWENS, CLINTON EVAN, food co. exec.; b. Pasadena, Calif., Aug. 6, 1941; s. Herbert E. and Jean Virginia (Helm) O.; B.A., U. Redlands, 1963; m. Mary Ann Welch, Aug. 18, 1962; children—Todd, Douglas. With Procter & Gamble, 1963-74, dist. mgr., Milw., 1971-74; dir. nat. sales R.J. Reynolds Foods Co., 1975-78; v.p. consumer sales foods div. The Coca Cola Co., Houston, 1978—. Mem. Am. Mgmt. Assn. Republican. Episcopalian. Home: 11118 Smithdale Houston TX 77024 Office: PO Box 2079 Houston TX 77001

OWENS, DAVID BRUCE, data processing adminstr.; b. Sharon, Pa., Nov. 2, 1945; s. Melvin Harold and Doris Eileen (Bender) O.; B.S. in Bus. Adminstrn., Wheeling Coll., 1978; m. Barbara Rae Carpenter (div., 1977); children—Tracy Linn, Robin Dean. Sr. systems analyst Nat. Cash Register Co., Columbus, Ohio, 1968-71, Clarksburg, W.Va., 1971-73, Wheeling, W.Va., 1973; data processing mgr., Stone and Thomas, Wheeling, 1973-75; dir. data processing adminstr. Valley Camp Coal Co., Wheeling, 1975—; mem. data processing advisory com. Belmont Tech. Coll., St. Clairsville, Ohio. Served with USAF, 1964-68. Mem. Data Processing Mgmt. Assn. (v.p. Greater Wheeling chpt.). Republican. Methodist. Home: 108 Carmel Rd Wheeling WV 26003 Office: Valley Camp Coal Co Data Center PO Box 7005 Wheeling WV 26003

OWENS, ETTA MAE HARRIS (MRS. GEORGE W. OWENS), rehab. exec.; b. Pontotoc, Miss., Apr. 30, 1911; d. Jesse Seale and Viola (Abernethy) Harris; student Blue Mountain Coll., 1928-31; B.S., U. So. Miss., 1940; M.Ed., Miss. State U., 1967, ednl. specialist, 1971; postgrad. U. Miss., 1941; m. George W. Owens, Dec. 20, 1937. Tchr. elementary sch., Ecru, Miss., 1931-34; county supr. adult edn., Pontotoc, 1934-37; sec. to registrar U. So. Miss., Hattiesburg, 1938-40, instr., 1940-42; instr. Itawamba Agr. High Sch., Fulton, Miss., 1944-46; counselor Rehab. Div. for Blind, Pontotoc, Miss., 1955-66, supr., 1967-76. Co-chmn. Pontotoc Bicentennial Commn., 1974-76. Mem. Nat. Rehab. Assn. (chpt. sec. 1963-70, 73-75, divisional dir. 1968-71, nat. chmn. awards com. 1971-72, pres. Miss. adminstrv. and supervisory practices unit 1973-74), Am. Assn. Workers for Blind (nat. dir. 1969-72, pres. S.E. region 1974-76), Miss. Assn. Workers Blind (pres. 1969-72), Miss. Women's Cabinet Pub. Affairs, Am., Miss. heart assns., Rehab. Assn. Miss. (sec. 1973-74), Miss. Fedn. Women's Clubs (chmn. 1958—). Baptist. Clubs: Pontotoc Woman's (pres. 1961-64, 74-77), Miss. Women's (ofcl. 1937-44, 62-70), Am. Assn. Ret. Persons (pres. Pontotoc chpt. 1979-80), Colonial Dames XVII Century. Home: 115 Brooks St Pontotoc MS 38863

OWENS, EVERETTE, JR., ednl. adminstr.; b. Slagle, La., Aug. 28, 1928; s. David Everette and Cleo Patra (Franklin) O.; B.S., U. Tex., Austin, 1970; M.Ed., SW Tex. State U., 1974; m. Doris Elaine Trotti, June 4, 1949; children—Rosalind E., Rodney E. Joined USAF, 1947, advanced through grades to master sgt., 1962; ret., 1967; tchr. social studies Austin (Tex.) Ind. Sch. Dist., 1970-73; dir. student life and tng. Travis State Sch., Austin, Tex., 1974—. Mem. U. Tex. Ex-Student Assn., Am. Assn. Mental Deficiency, Tex. Public Employee Assn., Tex. State Tchrs. Assn. Democrat. Mem. Ch. of God.

OWENS, FREDRIC NEWELL, animal scientist; b. Baldwin, Wis., Sept. 1, 1941; s. Fred Newell and Stell Elvera (Jorstad) O.; B.S., U. Minn., 1964, Ph.D., 1968. Asst. prof. animal sci. U. Ill., Urbana, 1968-73, asso. prof., 1973-74; asso. prof. animal sci. Okla. State U., Stillwater, 1974-79, prof. animal sci., 1979—. Served with AUS, 1961-62. Mem. Am. Soc. Animal Sci., Am. Dairy Sci. Assn., Am. Inst. Nutrition. Lutheran. Sect. editor ruminant nutrition Jour. Animal Sci., 1975-78. Home: 121 W 35th St Stillwater OK 74074 Office: Dept Animal Sci Okla State U Stillwater OK 74074

OWENS, HILDA FAYE, educator; b. Fountain, N.C., Mar. 23, 1939; d. Floyd Curtis and Essie Lee (Gay) O.; B.S., E. Carolina U., 1960, M.A. in Edn., 1965; Ph.D., Fla. State U., 1973. Tchr. pub. schs., New Bern, N.C., 1960-65; dean of women Mt. Olive (N.C.) Coll., 1965-66, dir. counseling services, 1966-71, dean of students, 1973-77; coordinator for student affairs State U. System of Fla., Tallahassee, 1971-73; asso. prof. of higher edn. U. S.C., Columbia, 1977—; mem. Gov.'s. Task Force Career Edn., Fla., 1972-73. Mem. exec. bd. Tuscarora council Boy Scouts Am.; mem. adv. com. Wayne Community Coll., Goldsboro, N.C.; active fund drives various local charitable orgns. Smith Reynolds fellow, 1962; Gen. Electric fellow, 1967. Mem. S.C. Council Adminstrv. Women in Edn. (treas.), Nat. Assn. Student Personnel Adminstrs. (dir. research region III, 1978—), Am., So., S.C. coll. personnel assns., Am. Personnel and Guidance Assn., Am. Assn. Higher Edn., Nat. Council on Student Devel., Nat., N.C. fedns. bus. and profl. women's clubs, Mt. Olive Bus. and Profl. Women's Club (charter pres. 1975-77, named Outstanding Bus. and Profl. Women of Year 1976), Columbia Bus. and Profl. Women's Club (2d v.p. 1979—). Club: So. Wayne Country. Mem. editorial bd. Jour. Nat. Assn. Student Personnel Adminstrs., 1977—. Home: 346 Rutledge Pl Columbia SC 29210 Office: Dept Higher Edn Coll Edn U SC Columbia SC 29208

OWENS, J. LYNN, plumbing and heating co. exec.; b. Portales, N.Mex., Oct. 14, 1936; s. Burnis Franklin and Nellie Florence (Van Noy) O.; student U. N.M., 1954-55; m. Virginia Lee Campbell, July 25, 1959; 1 dau., Suzan Lynnette. Price clk. Brown Pipe & Supply of Albuquerque, N.Mex., Inc., 1954-55; bookkeeper, office mgr. Brown Pipe & Supply of Artesia, Inc. (N.Mex.), 1956-62; gen. mgr. Brown Pipe & Supply of Pecos, Inc. (Tex.), 1962—, sec.-treas., 1962—; chmn. Plumbing Adv. Com., Pecos. Bd. dirs. Pecos Vol. Fire Dept., 1974-77; asst. chief, tng. officer Pecos Vol. Ambulance Service, 1970—; emergency med. service instr. Tex. Dept. Health; emergency med. technician instr. Odessa (Tex.) Coll.; basic life support instr. Am. Heart Assn. Mem. Tex. Assn. Emergency Med. Technicians (charter). Baptist. Home: 1923 S Park St Pecos TX 79772 Office: 2134 W Hwy 80 Pecos TX 79772

OWENS, JEAN WAREHAM, investments exec.; b. Kearney, Nebr., Oct. 4, 1925; d. Charles Richard and Laverne Anna (Anstine) Wareham; B.A., Kearney Coll., 1947; m. W. R. Owens, Aug. 11, 1944 (div. 1975); children—Marguerite Ann, Debra Kay. With Security Bank, 1949; asst. comptroller B.L. Shoes, Tex. and La., 1950-52, Internat. Life Ins. Co., Austin, Tex., 1952-55; with Wareham Investments, Ft. Worth, 1955—. Treas. League Women Voters, 1956-59, Ft. Worth Geneal. Soc., 1968-73; sec. Civic League, 1965; founder Log Cabin Village Guild, 1964, Peter Smith Aux., 1960. Author: Cedar County Iowa Historical Index; Ft. Kearney 1860; 1870 Diary of John Wareham; Where Buffalo Roam; Old Grandad; Linn County Marriages. Home: 6209 Calmont Fort Worth TX 76116

OWENS, KENNETH, JR., architect; b. Chattanooga, May 23, 1939; s. Kenneth and Lydia Mary (Alexander) O.; B.S., Tenn. State U., 1963; m. Shelby Jean Woodruff, June 9, 1963; children—Kevin L., Keith L. Draftsman, U.S. C.E., 1963-66, Rust Engring., 1966-68; archtl. job capt. C. H. McCauley Architects, Birmingham, Ala., 1968-71; owner, partner Owens Devel. Co., Birmingham, 1971—; partner Owens and Woods Partnership, Architects, Birmingham, 1974—. Chmn., Birmingham Public Bldg. Authority; bd. dirs. United Community Centers, Inc.; mem. Birmingham Bicentennial Exec. Com.; chmn. sustaining membership drive Boy Scouts Am., Birmingham. Mem. AIA, Omega Psi Phi. Democrat. Methodist. Club: Masons. Office: 1905 Bessemer Rd Birmingham AL 35208

OWENS, LEWIS MARSDEN, broadcasting co. adminstr.; b. Russell County, Ky., May 23, 1929; s. Clifford Marsden and Lola Pearl (Robertson) O.; m. Marilyn Ann Hammond, June 18, 1950; children—Cathie Ann, Judy Lynn Owens Pelfrey, L. Michael. Radio-communications engring. technician, Columbia, Ky., 1953-63; dist. service rep. Motorola Communications and Electronics, Inc., Nashville, 1963-65, dist. service mgr., 1966-71; tech. dir. Sta. WLAP, Sta. WLAP-FM, Lexington, Ky., 1971—. Mem. IEEE, Soc. Broadcast Engrs., Ky. Hist. Soc., SAR (v.p. Ky.). Republican. Presbyterian. Home: 2824 Dan Patch Dr Lexington KY 40511

OWENS, WILLIAM HENRY, info. processing specialist; b. Atlanta, May 12, 1942; s. Andrew Gay and Lucille (Stargell) O.; B.S., Morehouse Coll., 1964; M.S., Ga. Inst. Tech., 1972; 1 son, Sean Chevalier. Instr., Morehouse Coll., Atlanta, 1964; tchr. Cherokee County Bd. Edn., Canton, Ga., 1964-65; cartographer USAF, St. Louis, 1965; programmer, analyst Lockheed Aircraft Corp., Marietta, Ga., 1965-72; sr. planning analyst So. Co. Services, Inc., Atlanta; info. processing cons. Pres. high sch. class reunion; peanut brigader presdl. campaign, Miss., 1976; bd. dirs. Sandtown Recreation Assn., 1977. Mem. Nat. Mgmt. Assn., Internat. Word Processing Assn. (pres. Atlanta chpt.; Honor Soc. award 1979), Adminstrv. Systems Assn. (pres. 1978-79), Assn. Records Mgrs. and Adminstrs., Morehouse Alumni Assn., Ga. Inst. Tech. Alumni Assn., L.J. Price Alumni Assn. (pres.). Democrat. Baptist. Club: The 1980 (chmn.). Home: 879 Beryl St Atlanta GA 30310 Office: So Co Services 64 Perimeter Center E Atlanta GA 30346

OWENS, WILLIAM LIONEL, clergyman; b. Waycross, Ga., May 21, 1935; s. Harry William and Audrey Lee (Riddle) O.; A.S., So. Tech. Coll., 1959; P.D., Luther Rice Sem. Internat., 1968, M.Div., 1968, Th.D., 1970; m. Mary Anne Gray, Feb. 8, 1958; 1 son, William Lionel II. Indsl. engring. positions, research and mfg. firms, southeastern U.S., 1959-63; ordained to ministry So. Bapt. Conv., 1963; pastor New Providence Bapt. Ch., Hartsville, S.C., 1963, Boulougne (Fla.) Bapt. Ch., 1966, Good Hope Bapt. Ch., Saluda, S.C., 1968, Coll. Park Bapt. Ch., Rock Hill, S.C., 1969, Village Dr. Bapt. Ch., Fayetteville, N.C., 1970-79, Woodlawn Bapt. Ch., Charlotte, N.C., 1979—; pres. Cape Fear Sch. Theology, Fayetteville, 1973—. Mem. Evang. Theol. Soc., Christos Soc. for Bibl. Exposition (founder, pres.). Democrat. Author: Reality of Evil Spirits, 1970; Spiritual

Growth Manual, 1974. Home: 6300 Wheeler Dr Charlotte NC 28210 Office: 4622 Nations Ford Rd Charlotte NC 28211

OWENS, WILLIAM RALPH, physicist; b. Fort Worth, Jan. 3, 1931; s. Phil and Alma Leigh (Word) O.; B.S., U. Tex., 1953, M.S., 1956; m. Barbara Nadean Houston, Sept. 22, 1975; children—Marguerite Ann, Debra Kay. With underwater sound studies Def. Research Lab., U. Tex., Austin, 1951-56; supr. Gen. Dynamics, Fort Worth, 1956-73, sr. quality control engr., radar tng. systems, 1973—. Mem. Am. Assn. Phycists in Medicine, Phys. Measurements Assn., Sigma Pi Sigma, Sigma Xi. Methodist. Contbr. articles to profl. jours. Home: 6501 Banbury Dr Fort Worth TX 76119 Office: General Dynamics PO Box 748 Fort Worth TX 76101

OWENSBY, DAVID EUGENE, physician; b. Pittsburg, Kans., Aug. 3, 1927; s. Oscar Monroe and Mary Frances (Cook) O.; B.S., U. Ala., Tuscaloosa, 1948, M.D., Birmingham, 1952; m. Mary Louise Clark Lyon, May 1, 1971; children—Barbara, Jim, Dan, Mary Kay, Will, Mary Margaret, Gene. Intern, Orange County Gen. Hosp., Orange, Calif., 1952-53; resident in gen. surgery Calif. Luth. Hosp., Los Angeles, 1953-55; gen. practice medicine, rural Ala., 1955-70, Ventura, Calif., 1970-75, Sonora, Tex., 1975—; mem. staff Lillian M. Hudspeth Meml. Hosp., Sonora, Shannon-West Tex. Hosp., San Angelo, Community Hosp., San Angelo. Chmn. bd. Ala. Heart Assn.; mem. adv. bd. Am. Heart Assn., 1955-59; bd. dirs. Tex. Heart Assn., 1977—. Served with USN, 1945-46. Diplomate Am. Bd. Family Practice; cert. in psychosomatic medicine and sexology. Fellow Am. Acad. Family Practice, Internat. Coll. Surgeons (jr.); mem. AMA, Tex. Med. Assn., Tom Green Eight County Med. Soc., Am. Soc. Bariatric Physicians, Am. Psychosomatic Soc., Am. Acad. Med. Hypnoanalysts, Faculty Am. Inst. Hypnosis. Republican. Episcopalian. Club: Lions. Home: 121 Edgemont St Sonora TX 76950 Office: Box 435 Sonora TX 76950

OWENSBY, PHOEBE THERESSA, psychiat. nurse; b. Meade, Kan., Mar. 4, 1918; d. Jasper Miles and Alice Pearl (Taggart) Singley; diploma St. Luke's Sch. Nursing, 1941; B.A. in Eng. Lit., Stanford U., 1950; m. Archie Francis Owensby, Mar. 19, 1956; children—Alice, Stepson Dean. Nurse therapist S.W. Guidance Center, Liberal, Kans., 1968-73; psychiat. nurse coordinator Dept. Community Mental Health, Coundersport, Pa., 1973-78, East Ark. Regional Mental Health Center, Helena, Ark., 1978-80; cons., ednl. adv. on mental health to rural areas, 1968-80. Served as lt. USN, 1943-46, 50-56. Decorated UN Service medal. Mem. Bus. and Profl. Women Orgn., Am. Orthopsychiat. Assn. Home: 119 Valley Dr Helena AR 72342 Office: 305 Valley Dr Helena AR 72342

OWINGS, FRANCIS BARRE, surgeon; b. McColl, S.C., Mar. 9, 1941; s. Ralph Seer and Antoinette (Moore) O.; B.S., U. Miss., 1963, M.D., 1966; m. Judith Myers, Feb. 14, 1976; 1 child, F. Patterson. Intern, San Francisco Gen. Hosp., 1966-67; resident in surgery U. Calif., San Francisco, 1969-74; surg. registrar Norfolk and Norwich Hosp., Norwich, Eng., 1971-72; practice medicine specializing in surgery, Atlanta, 1974—; mem. staff Crawford Long Hosp., Piedmont Hosp., St. Joseph Hosp.; clin. instr. surgery Emory U. Served to capt. USAF, 1967-69. Diplomate Am. Bd. Surgery. Fellow A.C.S., Southeastern Surg. Congress; mem. Med. Assn. Atlanta, Med. Assn. Ga., Ga. Surg. Soc., Naffziger Surg. Soc., Alpha Epsilon Delta, Sigma Chi, Phi Chi. Republican. Methodist. Home: 365 Brentwood Terr Atlanta GA 30305 Office: 478 Peachtree NE Atlanta GA 30308

OWINGS, WILLIAM JENNINGS BRYAN, ret. physician, surgeon; b. nr. Ashland, Ala., Feb. 25, 1908; s. Thomas Harvey and Josephine (Morris) O.; A.B., U. Ala., 1929, B.S., 1930; M.D., Tulane U., New Orleans, 1932; postgrad. Vanderbilt U., 1936; m. Lena Mae Thompson, Sept. 17, 1930; children—Clyde Lacy, William Orange, Joseph Lee, John and Alice (dec.), Thomas Gene and Linda Kay (twins). Health officer Lamar Co., Ala., 1934-36; asso. USPHS, Hot Springs, Ark., 1940; dir. Bibb. Co. Venereal Disease Clinic, 1940-47, Bibb Co. Pediatric Clinic, 1940-47, Bibb Co. Prenatal Clinic, 1940-47; gen. practice medicine, Brent, Ala., 1936-63; owner, dir. Owings Clinic, 1940-63; sec. staff Bibb County Hosp., Centreville, Ala., 1959-60, v.p., 1962-63. Local surgeon Ill. Central Gulf R.R., Ill. Central Hosp. Assn. Chmn. Bibb County Bd. Health, 1940-63, Bibb County Board Censors, 1937—; med. adviser local bd. Selective Service System, 1941-72; bd. dirs. East End Meml. Hosp., Birmingham, 1944-47; exec. bd. Black Warrior council Boy Scouts Am., 1943-63, v.p., 1946-50. Recipient Selective Service System medal, Wisdom award, 1972. Fellow Am. Inst. Chemists, (life), Royal Soc. Health (life), Am. Geriatric Soc., Am. Acad. Family Physicians (charter); mem. Ala. Acad. Gen. Practice (pres. 1959, chmn. bd. dirs. 1960), Am., So. (asso. counsellor 1959-60, life mem.), Ala. (counsellor 1941—) med. assns., Black Belt Med. Assn. (pres. 1953), Aero-Med. Assn., Am. Pub. Health Assn., Am. Acad. Gen. Practice (pres. elect 1958, pres. Ala. chpt. 1959-60), Mo. Pacific Hosp. Assn., Bibb County Med. Soc. (pres. 1977), Soc. (pres.), Phi Chi, Sigma Phi Epsilon. Baptist (deacon), Woodman World (council Comdr.), Mason (32 deg., Shriner), Elk. Clubs: Tuscaloosa Amateur Radio, Ala. Amateur, Civitan. Amateur radio operator. Home: 101 Wilson St Brent AL 35034

OWINGS, WILLIAM ORANGE, physician, surgeon; b. Selma, Ala., Sept. 18, 1936; s. William Jennings Bryan and Lena Mae (Thompson) O.; B.S. in Chemistry, U. Ala., 1956; M.D., Tulane U., 1958; m. Elizabeth Joyce Grimsley, Apr. 6, 1957; children—William Donovan, Robert Thompson, Bradley Gene, Elizabeth Patton. Intern, St. Francis Hosp., Wichita, Kans., 1958-59, resident gen. surgery, 1959-61, 63-65; practice medicine specializing in family medicine and surgery, Centreville, Ala., 1965—; asso. prof. family and community medicine Coll. Community Health Scis. U. Ala. at Tuscaloosa, 1973—. Bd. dirs. W. Ala. Dist. Health Bd., W. Ala. Health Council, W. Ala. Emergency Med. Services, Inc. Served to maj. U.S. Army Res., M.C., 1961-63. Diplomate Am. Bd. Family Practice. Fellow Am. Acad. Family Physicians; mem. A.C.S. (com. trauma Ala. chpt.), Bibb County (Ala.) Med. Soc. (past pres., chmn. bd. censors), Ala. Lung Assn. (dir.), AMA, Med. Assn. Ala., Am. Burn Assn., So. Med. Assn., Ala. Acad. Family Physicians (dir.), Civitan Club, CAP. Mason (Shriner, K.T.). Home: Brent AL 35034 Office: 136 Hospital Dr Centreville AL 35042

OWNBY, CHARLOTTE LEDBETTER, anatomist; b. Amory, Miss., July 27, 1947; d. William Moss and Anna Faye (Long) Ledbetter; B.S., U. Tenn., 1969, M.S., 1971; Ph.D., Colo. State U., 1975; m. James Donald Ownby, Sept. 6, 1969; children—Holly Ruth, Mary Faye. Instr. physiol. sci. Okla. State U., Stillwater, 1974-75, asst. prof., 1975—, dir. electron microscope lab., 1976—. NSF fellow, 1968; NIH grantee, 1979—. Mem. Am. Assn. Anatomists, Electron Microscope Soc. Am., Okla. Soc. Electron Microscopy (founder, pres. 1979), Sigma Xi, Phi Beta Kappa, Phi Kappa Phi. Contbr. articles to profl. jours. Home: 2413 Tanglewood Circle Stillwater OK 74074 Office: Dept Physiol Sci Okla State U Stillwater OK 74078

OWNBY, HELEN LOUISE ENGELBRECHT, microbiologist; b. Frederick, Md., Feb. 7, 1940; d. Lincoln Dittmar and Effie Pearl (Moore) Engelbrecht; B.A., Wittenberg U., Springfield, Ohio, 1962; M.S., Mich. State U., E. Lansing, 1966, Ph.D., 1968; m. Dennis Randall Ownby, May 24, 1970; children—David Randall, Kathryn Louise. Biologist, Nat. Cancer Inst., 1962-64; instr. Mich. State U., 1968-69; instr., then asst. prof. Med. Coll. Ohio, Toledo, 1969-72; vis. asst. prof. U. N.C., Chapel Hill, 1972; research asso. dept. medicine Duke U. Med. Center, 1974-76, research asso. div. allergy and immunology, dept. pediatrics, 1976—. Mem. Am. Soc. Microbiology, AAAS, Sigma Xi, Phi Kappa Phi. Author research papers in field. Office: PO Box 3050 Duke Med Center Durham NC 27710

OWSLEY, WILLIAM CLINTON, JR., radiologist; b. Austin, Tex., Oct. 6, 1923; s. William Clinton and Lois (Lamar) O.; B.A., U. Tex., 1944; M.D., U. Pa., 1946; m. Betty Pinckard, 1949; 2 children. Intern, Hermann Hosp., Houston, 1946-47; resident Hosp. of U. Pa., Phila., 1949-52; instr. radiology U. Pa., 1950-52; practice medicine specializing in radiology, Houston, 1952—; mem. staffs Hermann, Twelve Oaks, Bellville, Waller County hosps., Sealy Hosp. Found.; asso. clin. prof. radiology U. Tex. Served with USNR, 1947-48. Diplomate Am. Bd. Radiology. Fellow Am. Coll. Radiology, Am. Roentgen Ray Soc., Radiol. Soc. N.Am. Republican. Baptist. Office: 214 Hermann Profl Bldg Houston TX 77030

OWUSU, JOSHUA KWASI, process engr.; b. Accra, Ghana, Oct. 2, 1948; came to U.S., 1971; s. John Kwabena and Esther Kwama (Ankrah) O.; B.S., Angelo State U., 1974; M.S., Tex. Technol. U., 1976; m. Doris Obeng-Benne, July 20, 1974; 1 child, Drexell Kwaku. Process engr. Cosden Oil & Chem., Big Spring, Tex., 1976-79, group leader refinery tech. support, 1979—. Recipient Community Service award San Angelo (Tex.) C. of C., 1974. Mem. Am. Inst. Chem. Engrs., Am. Chem. Soc., Sigma Xi. Club: Optimists. Home: 2208 Merrily Dr Big Spring TX 79720 Office: Box 1311 I-20 Big Spring TX 79720

OXLEY, PHILIP, oil co. exec.; b. Utica, N.Y., Feb. 1, 1922; s. Chester Jay and Beatrice (Heller) O.; B.A., Denison U., 1943; M.A., Columbia U., 1948, Ph.D., 1952; m. Patricia Jane Kienker, Aug. 27, 1946; children—Christopher, Jonathan, Timothy, Philip, Patricia. Instr., asst. prof., chmn. dept. geology Hamilton Coll., Clinton, N.Y., 1948-53; geologist Calif. Co., 1953-57; dist. and div. exploration mgr. Tenn. Gas Transmission Co., 1957-61; div. exploration mgr., v.p. exploration, dir. Signal Oil & Gas Co., 1961-69; exec. v.p. Tex. Crude Oil, 1969-71; mgr. geology, v.p. Tenneco Oil Co., Houston, 1971-74, sr. v.p., 1974-79, exec. v.p. oil exploration and prodn., 1980—. Chmn. bd. dirs. Geology Found., U. Houston; mem. So. regional bd. Inst. Internat. Edn. Served witb USNR, 1943-46. Fellow Geol. Soc. Am.; mem. Am. Assn. Petroleum Geologists, Sigma Xi. Presbyterian. Club: Houston. Home: 153 Hickory Ridge Houston TX 77024 Office: 1010 Milam Houston TX 77001

OYEKAN, SONI OLUFEMI, chem. engr.; b. Aba, Nigeria, June 1, 1946; s. Theophilous Adebayo and Emilia Uduak (Inyang) O.; came to U.S., 1966; B.S., Yale U., 1970; M.S., Carnegie-Mellon U., Pitts., 1972, Ph.D., 1977; m. Priscilla Ann Parker, June 2, 1970; 1 child, Oluranti Alvita. Instr. phys. scis. Univ. Community Edn. Programs, U. Pitts., 1972-75, coordinator, 1976-77; engr. Exxon Research and Devel. Labs., Baton Rouge, 1977-78, research engr., 1978-79, sr. engr., 1979—. Mem. Baton Rouge Jaycees, Am. Inst. Chem. Engrs., Am. Chem. Soc., AAAS, Nat. Orgn. Black Chemists and Chem. Engrs., Soc. Applied Spectroscopy, Yale Sci. and Engring. Assn., Manuscript Soc., Sigma Xi, Phi Kappa Phi. Home: 1051 Knollhaven Baton Rouge LA 70810 Office: Exxon Research and Devel Labs PO Box 2226 Baton Rouge LA 70821

OZUNA, GEORGE, JR., cons. engr.; b. San Antonio, Nov. 22, 1930; s. George G. and Stella Graciano O.; student St. Mary's U., 1949-50; B.S.C.E., U. Tex., 1956; m. Yolando B. Perez, Dec. 22, 1956; children—George A., Kenneth L., Jessica L., Jocelyn A. Engrs. asst. Tex. Hwy. Dept., 1956-60; profl. engr. City of San Antonio, 1960-63; city mgr. Crystal City (Tex.), 1963-64; project engr. Brown & Root, Inc., Houston, 1964-66; pres. Ozuna & Assos., Inc., cons. engrs., San Antonio, 1966—. Trustee, San Antonio Community Coll.; dir. Jobs for Progress, Inc.; chmn. Mexican-Am. Unity Council. Served with USMC, 1950-52. Mem. Res. Officers Assn., ASCE, Soc. Am. Mil. Engrs., Am. Water Works Assn., Tex. Soc. Profl. Engrs. Democrat. Roman Catholic. Home: 5118 Vance Jackson Rd San Antonio TX 78230 Office: 8118 Broadway San Antonio TX 78209

PACE, CAROLINA JOLLIFF (MRS. JOHN MCIVER PACE), ednl. media cons.; b. Dallas, Apr. 12, 1938; d. Lindsay Gafford and Carolina (Juden) Jolliff; student Holton-Arms Jr. Coll., 1956-57; B.A. in Comparative Lit., So. Meth. U., 1960; m. John McIver Pace, Oct. 7, 1961. Fashion cons., lectr. Nancy Taylor Sch., Dallas, 1959-61; promotional adv., dir. season ticket sales Dallas Theatre Center, 1960-61; exec. sec. Dallas Book and Author Luncheon, 1959-63; promotional and instnl. cons. Henry Regnery-Reilly & Lee Pub. Co., Chgo., 1962-65; pub. trade rep. various cos., institutional rep. Don R. Phillips Co., Southeastern area, 1965-67; Southwestern rep. Ednl. Reading Service, Inc.-Troll Assos., Mahwah, N.J., 1967-72; v.p., dir. multimedia div. Melton Book Co., Dallas, 1972-79; dir. mktg. Webster's Internat., Inc., Nashville, 1980—; mem. nat. adv. bd. Nat. Info. Center Spl. Edn. Materials; speaker seminar Nat. Media Center for Severely and Profoundly Handicapped, 1980. Mem. Women's Nat. Book Assn., Nat. Audio Visual Assn. (speaker 1979 conf.), Assn. Ednl. and Communications Tech., Council Exceptional Children (chmn. publicity and public relations com. 1979 conf.), ALA (AASL arrangements coordinator 1979 conf.), Assn. Spl. Edn. Tech. (nat. dir., v.p.), DAR, Downtown Dallas Central Bus. Assn. Dallas Civic Opera Assn., Friends of Dallas Pub. Library, Dallas Art Assn., Alpha Delta Pi. Presbyterian. Club: Dallas Press. Home: 4524 Lorraine Ave Dallas TX 75205

PACE, CHARLES MILLS, lawyer; b. Spartanburg, S.C., May 19, 1911; s. Otis Leroy and Amanda (Blackwood) P.; B.S., Clemson U., 1932; LL.B., U. S.C., 1935, J.D., 1969, Ph.D., 1970; m. June Cannington, July 23, 1966. Admitted to S.C. bar, 1935, practiced in Spartanburg, 1935-36, 71—; probate judge, Spartanburg, 1939-42; judge Superior County Ct., Spartanburg County, 1947-71. Mem. S.C. Ho. of Reps., 1937-38; mem. citizens com. Spartanburg County Council, 1963-66; chancellor Brotherhood of St. Andrew, St. Francis Episcopal Ch. Served from 2d lt. to maj. AUS, 1942-46; col. Res. ret. Mem. S.C. Bar Assn. (pres. county judges assn. div. 1969-70), Pace Soc. Am. (1st v.p. 1963-68), Burns Hist. Soc. (pres. 1977-79, chmn. bd. trustees 1979-80), SAR (v.p. Daniel Morgan chpt. 1979-80, pres. 1980-81), Phi Delta Phi, Omicron Delta Kappa, Pi Kappa Alpha. Clubs: Spartanburg Country, Piedmont, Elks. Home: 1166 Woodburn Rd Spartanburg SC 29302 Office: 248 N Church St PO Box 2413 Spartanburg SC 29304

PACE, JANYCE AKARD, educator; b. Moyers, Okla., Dec. 7, 1929; d. Thomas Henry and Willie Christine (Rea) Akard; B.A. in Edn., E. Central State U., 1958, M.A. in Edn., 1962; Ed.D. in Higher Edn., Okla. State U., 1974; m. Jewel Henry Pace, Aug. 14, 1947; children—Thomas Henry, Susan Lynette, David Wayne. English tchr. Tupelo (Okla.) High Sch., 1958-61, Byng High Sch., Ada, Okla., 1962-65; English instr. Connors State Coll., Warner, Okla., 1965—. Title III Higher edn. grantee, 1968-69. Mem. Okla. Edn. Assn., NEA, Higher Edn. Alumni Assn. Okla., Okla. Assn. Community and Jr. Colls. (pres. 1967-68), Okla. Assn. Higher Edn. (pres. 1969-70), SW Regional Assn. English Tchrs. in Two Year Colls., Melville Soc., Kappa Kappa Iota (nat. scholar 1968), Delta Kappa Gamma (scholar 1973-74, state rec. sec., chpt. pres.). Home: 1103 Connors Rd Warner OK 74469 Office: Connors State College Warner OK 74469

PACE, WARREN MAXWELL, ins. co. exec.; b. Glen Ridge, N.J., Apr. 14, 1920; s. William and Vallie (Gunn) P.; B.S. in Bus., U. Richmond, 1943; m. Wanda W. Walton, Feb. 14; children—Warren Maxwell, Judith A., Janet A., Stephen J. From sales rep. to agt. dir. Guardian Life Ins. Co. Am., N.Y.C., 1946-54; asst. v.p., then agt. v.p., dir. Atlantic Life Ins. Co., Richmond, Va., 1954-61; with Life Ins. Co. Va., Richmond, 1961—, exec. v.p., then pres., 1963-73, chmn. bd., 1973—, also dir.; pres. Richmond Corp., 1968—, chief exec. officer, 1968-77; pres. Continental Fins. Services; exec. v.p. Continental Group, Inc.; dir. United Va. Bankshares, Thalmeimer Bros., Western Employers Co., Lawyers Title Ins. Co., Old Equity Ins. Co. Trustee, U. Richmond; dir. fund raising Va. Soc. Blind; mem. captial fund bd. Richmond United Fund; chmn. Richmond Bus. Devel. Corp. Served to lt. USNR, World War II Recipient Nat. Alumni Council Disting. Service award U. Richmond; C.L.U. Mem. Life Underwriters Assn., Omicron Delta Kappa, Alpha Soc., Beta Gamma Sigma. Clubs: Commonwealth, Country of Va.; Duckwoods (N.C.); Met. (N.Y.C.). Address: Life Ins Co Virginia 6610 N Broad St Richmond VA 23261

PACENZA, FRANKLIN JOSEPH, lawyer; b. Rome, N.Y., Nov. 9, 1945; s. John Eugene and Maria Rose (DiCristo) P.; B.A., Tulane U., 1967; J.D., U. Tulsa, 1976. Admitted to Okla. bar, 1976; asst. dist. atty. Osage and Pawnee counties, Pawhuska, Okla., 1975-79. Bd. dirs. Green County chpt. Nat. Multiple Sclerosis Soc., 1976-80; state dir. Pawhuska Jaycees, 1977-78. Served as aviator USN, 1967-73; Korea, Vietnam. Kerr Found. grantee, 1977. Mem. Am., Okla., Osage County (treas. 1977, law day chmn. 1977, v.p. 1978) bar assns., Nat., Okla. dist. attys. assns., Order Barristers, Delta Tau Delta. Home: PO Box 86 Prue OK 74060 Office: 110 N Broadway Cleveland OK 74020

PACH, RAYMOND PETER, bldg. contractor; b. N.Y.C., Dec. 26, 1914; s. Walter and Magdalene (Frohberg) P.; B.S., Bowdoin Coll., 1936; postgrad. U. N.C., 1943-44, Paris Conservatory Music, 1947-48, Rome Conservatory, 1950-52, San Francisco Conservatory Music, 1946-47; m. Ruth Nantkes, Dec. 21, 1946; children—Michael, Christina, Marc, Tjode. Pres., Fgn. Cars SRL, Rome, 1957-66; dir. fgn. export sales Chiasso, Switzerland, 1959-66; pres. Office Fgn. Liquidation Commn., U.S. State Dept., Paris; v.p. Cagle Constrn., Inc., Candler, N.C., 1966-68; pres. Peter Pach, Inc., Waynesville, N.C., 1968—. Del., Haywood County State Library Conf., 1978, chmn. book com., 1979; alt. del. to pres. Nat. Library Conf., 1979. Served to maj. USMCR, 1943-68; ETO. Mem. Res. Officers Assn. (pres. Rome chpt.), Western Carolina Contractors Assn. Democrat. Lutheran. Home and Office: 247 Norman Heights Waynesville NC 28786

PACKARD, JOHN MALLORY, physician; b. Saranac Lake, N.Y., Sept. 25, 1920; s. Edward Newman and Mary Bissell (Betts) P.; B.A., Yale U.; M.D., Harvard U., 1945; m. Ann Maurine Schoonover, June 15, 1944; children—Michael David, John Mallory, Ann Maurine, Mary Betts, Charles Edward, Frank Schoonover, Charlotte Mellen. Intern, Presbyn. Hosp., N.Y.C., 1945-46; resident Peter Bent Brigham Hosp., Boston, 1948-49 pvt. practice medicine specializing in internal medicine and cardiology, Pensacola, Fla., 1954-68; exec. dir. Ala. Regional Med. Program, 1968-73; asso. dean, prof. medicine U. Ala. Sch. Medicine, Birmingham, 1968-73, asso. dean, prof. medicine Coll. Community Health Scis., 1973-76, clin. prof., 1976—; dir. med. edn. Baptist Med. Centers, Birmingham, 1976—; chief of staff Escambia Gen. Hosp., 1959-61, Baptist Hosp., 1964, Hale Meml. Hosp., Tuscaloosa, Ala., 1972-73; cons. aviation medicine Surgeon Gen., U.S. Navy, 1954-68; cons. VA Hosps., Tuskegee and Tuscaloosa, 1970—; mem. staff Bapt. Med. Centers, Birmingham. Served with USNR, 1943-45, 46-54. Diplomate Nat. Bd. Med. Examiners, Am. Bd. Internal Medicine. Fellow ACP, Am. Coll. Cardiology, Council on Clin. Cardiology, Royal Soc. Medicine, Royal Soc. Health; mem. Jefferson County Med. Soc. Med. Assn. State Ala., AMA, Am. Heart Assn., Boylston Med. Soc. Ala., Am. socs. internal medicine, Ala. Pub. Health Assn., Assn. Am. Med. Colls., Assn. Hosp. Med. Edn., Soc. Health and Human Values. Democrat. Episcopalian. Contbr. articles, editorials, med. jours. Office: 3201 4th Ave S Birmingham AL 35222

PACKARD, PHILIP CHARLES, psychiat. social worker; b. Lodi, Ohio, Mar. 10, 1943; s. Charles D. and Elsie (Block) P.; B.A. in Psychology, St. Mary's U., 1971; M.S.W., Our Lady of Lake U., 1973; m. Kathryn Anne Bilger, May 21, 1977. Clin. social worker Mercy Hosp., Watertown, N.Y., 1973-74, Dept. Econ. Security, Phoenix, 1974-75; clin. dir. psychiat. programs South Ark. Regional Health Center, El Dorado, 1974—. Served with U.S. Army, 1968-70. Decorated Bronze Star. Mem. Nat. Assn. Social Workers, Ark. Behavior Therapy Assn. (mem. exec. council), Assn. for Advancement Behavior Therapy. Lutheran. Office: 715 N College St El Dorado AR 71730

PACKWOOD, WILLIAM THEODORE, III, state ofcl.; b. Biloxi, Miss., Oct. 25, 1942; s. William Theodore, Jr. and Julia Estelle (Moore) P.; B.A., Yale U., 1964; Ph.D., U. Minn., 1970; m. Virginia Mary Markell, Dec. 23, 1967; children—Kirk David, Theodore Joseph, Matthew William. Instr. psychology, counselor U. Minn., Mpls., 1965-70; asst. prof. counselor edn. and coll. student personnel U. Iowa, Iowa City, 1970-73, asso. prof., coordinator, 1973-75; asst. dir. Office Social Service Policy, State of La. Dept. Health and Human Resources, Baton Rouge, 1975-76, dir. evaluation and research, 1976—; mgmt. cons. Joint Legis. Com. Reorgn. Exec. Br., 1977-78. Del., European Christian Youth Assembly, Lausanne, Switzerland, 1960. Fulbright tutor to India, 1964-65. Mem. Am. Personnel and Guidance Assn., Am. Coll. Personnel Assn. Author: Drugs and the School Counselor, 1972; College Student Personnel Services, 1977, also articles. Home: 7543 Watford Ave Baton Rouge LA 70808 Office: La Dept Health and Human Resources PO Box 3776 Baton Rouge LA 70821

PADDEN, DONALD JOSEPH, govt. ofcl.; b. Scranton, Pa., June 23, 1936; s. John Francis and Sylvia Ann (Moran) P.; B.S., U. Scranton, 1958; postgrad. Chapman Coll., 1976-78. Commd. 2d lt. U.S. Army Res., 1958, advanced through grades to lt. col., 1980; sta. in Europe, Vietnam, Thailand, U.S.; civil instr. U.S. Army Logistics Mgmt. Center, Ft. Lee, Va., 1975-78, systems analyst, 1978—. Roman Catholic. Home: PO Box 481 Petersburg VA 23803 Office: US Army Logistics Center Fort Lee VA 23801

PADDOCK, AUSTIN JOSEPH, business exec.; b. Washington Court House, Ohio, July 18, 1908; s. Leon A. and Nellie (Hare) P.; B.S. in Civil Engring., U. Mich., 1929; m. Janet Nevin, Aug. 3, 1934 (dec. Aug. 1964); children—Larry C. and Linda M. (twins), Jane M.; m. 2d, JoAnn Rourke May 1966; 1 dau., Jennifer-Jo. With Am. Bridge div. U.S. Steel Corp., 1929-56, successively timekeeper erecting dept., to pres., 1929-61, adminstrv. v.p. fabrication and manufacture U.S. Steel Corp., 1961-69; pres., chief exec. officer Blount Inc., 1969-74; cons. Blount, Inc. 1974—, also dir.; chief operating officer, exec. v.p. Pa. Engring. Corp., 1975-78, vice-chmn. bd., 1978—, also dir.; dir. Birdsboro Corp., Pitts.-Des Moines Steel Co. Bd. dirs., mem. exec. com. Allegheny council Boy Scouts Am.

Mem. Men of Montgomery. Clubs: Duquesne, Longue Vue Country (Pitts.); Montgomery Country; Rolling Hills Country, Capital City. Home: Route 1 Box 56C Pike Road AL 36064 Office: 32d St and AVRR Pittsburgh PA 15201

PADDOCK, MARGARET JACQUELINE SPARKS, dietitian; b. Maryville, Tenn., Mar. 24, 1932; d. Allen McTeer and Margaret Gaynelle (Russell) Sparks; B.S., Maryville Coll., 1954; m. Patric W. Paddock, Mar. 22, 1958. Intern, Univ. Hosp., Duke U., Durham, N.C., 1954-55; with U. Md. Hosp., Balt., 1955-58, D.C. Gen. Hosp., Washington, 1959-60, Columbia Hosp. for Women, Washington, 1963-65, Fairfax Hosp., Falls Church, Va., 1960-62, 68—, asst. dir. dietetics, 1968—; mem. Fairfax County Nutritional Com.; mem. adv. com. dietetics program No. Va. Community Coll. Mem. Am. Dietetic Assn., Va. Dietetic Assn. (pres.-elect no. dist.), Am. Soc. Hosp. Food Service Adminstrs. Home: 9722 Fonda Dr Vienna VA 22180 Office: Fairfax Hosp 3300 Gallows Rd Falls Church VA 22046

PADGETT, CHARLES HENRY, city ofcl.; b. Mosselle, S.C., Oct. 11, 1943; s. Willie E. and Pearline K. (King) P.; student U. S.C., 1965-69, U. No. Fla., 1975—. Technician, Jacksonville (Fla.) Dept. Air Pollution Control, 1970-77, specialist, 1977—; seminar lectr. U. Fla. Grad. Sch. Environ. Engring., 1979. Bd. dirs. Fla. Kidney Found., 1978-79; tech. dir. Jacksonville Acting Co., 1977—. Recipient Cert. in Environ. Achievements, EPA, 1973, 77. Mem. Audubon Soc., Nat. Wildlife Fedn., Nat. Geog. Soc., Am. Math. Assn. Home: 5578 Plymouth St Jacksonville FL 32205 Office: 515 W 6th St Jacksonville FL 32206

PADILLA, SHARRON KAY, GILLETT, home economist; b. Tekamah, Nebr., Dec. 27, 1939; d. Kenneth L. and Viola V. Gillett; B.S. in Vocat. Home Econs., Kearney State Coll., 1962; M.A. in Edn., Interam. U. P.R., San German, 1974; postgrad. (Interam. U. P.R. grantee) U. Nebr., Lincoln, 1976-77; m. Jose R. Padilla, June 18, 1966; children—Tania R., Natalie V. Peace Corps vol., Colombia, S. Am., 1963-65; mem. faculty Interam. U. P.R., San German, 1965—, now asso. prof. home econs., 1977—; chmn. dept. home econs., 1971-75. Mem. Am. Home Econs. Assn., Am. Vocat. Assn., Phi Delta Kappa (sec. local chpt.), Alpha Delta Kappa, Nat. Fedn. Bus. and Profl. Women's Clubs (2d v.p. local chpt.). Club: Altrusa (pres. internat. com. local chpt.). Office: Dept Econ Econs Interamerican U PR San German PR 00753

PADON, WILLIAM TUNSTALL, museum dir.; b. Longview, Tex., July 12, 1921; s. Jesse Shaw and Cathrine Elizabeth (Tunstall) P.; B.S. in Edn., Tex. Christian U., 1949, M.Ed., 1950; postgrad. Sacramento State Coll., Tulane U., N. Tex. State U.; m. Mildred Leona Armstrong, Dec. 20, 1952; 1 son, William Jesse. Instr. phys. edn. Tex. Christian U., 1951-52; tchr. bus. Grandview (Tex.) High Sch., 1969-72; dir. Jr. Coll. Campus, Cleburne, Tex., also tchr. bus. adminstrn., 1972—; chmn. Layland Mus., Cleburne, 1974—. Served as aviator USNR, 1942-46, 52-69; ETO, PTO, Vietnam. Decorated Air medal, Air Force Commendation medal. Mem. Tex. Jr. Coll. Tchrs. Assn., Johnson County Hist. Survey Com., Tex. Hist. Commn., Mid-Tex., Tex. Angus assns. Democrat. Methodist. Clubs: Shriners, Elks. Home: 902 Prairie Cleburne TX 76031 Office: PO Box 853 Cleburne TX 76031

PAETRO, SIDNEY, health educator, hypnotherapist; b. Bklyn., Oct. 29, 1923; s. Abraham and Frances (Newman) P.; B.A., U. Miami, 1949; M.P.H., Tulane U., 1954; Ph.D., Heed U., 1975; m. Jessie Goris, Oct. 30, 1964; 1 son, Victor. Sanitarian, Broward County Health Dept., Ft. Lauderdale, Fla., 1950-68, health educator, 1968—, dir. health edn., 1968—; hypnotherapist, instr. hypnosis and self-hypnosis; instr. Broward County DWI Counter Attack Program, Ft. Lauderdale, 1972—. Mem. Am. Pub. Health Assn., Am. Personnel and Guidance Assn., Nat. Environ. Health Assn., Assn. to Advance Ethical Hypnosis (chmn. Fla. chpt. 8, Joseph H. Makfka Award 1973, trustee, pres. 1973, 74), Fla. Assn. Sanitarians (pres. dist. chpt. 1958). Contbr. articles on barracuda poisoning to profl. jours. Home: 2818 Mayo St Hollywood FL 33020 Office: PO Box 14608 Fort Lauderdale FL 33302

PAGAN-DEL TORO, RAFAEL, accountant; b. Guerra, Dominican Republic, Feb. 4, 1931; s. Jesus and Josefa (del Toro-Perez) Pagan-Rodriguez; B.B.A. magna cum laude, U. P.R., 1959; M.B.A. summa cum laude, Fairleigh Dickinson U., 1962; m. Teresita Suarez, July 25, 1954; children—Marlene, Rafael, Ariel. Prof., U. P.R., Rio Piedras, 1959-61, 62-66, Fairleigh Dickinson U., Rutherford, N.J., 1961-62; pvt. practice accounting, Hato Rey, P.R., 1962-66; v.p. Radio Amers. Corp., Mayaguez, P.R., 1966-71; treas. Banco Comercial, Mayaguez, 1968-71; partner Rafael Pagan del Toro & Co., C.P.A.'s, Mayaguez, 1971—. Served to 1st lt. AUS, 1959-65. Named Man of Year, Mayaguez, Jaycees, 1971. Mem. Coll. C.P.A.'s of P.R. (pres. 1976-77), Am. Inst. C.P.A.'s, Nat. Assn. Accountants, P.R. C. of C. Democrat. Roman Catholic. Lion (chmn. bd. govs. 1975—). Club: Deportivo del Oeste. Home: 17 Valladolid Urb Ponce de Leon Mayaguez PR 00708 Office: Cond Las Nereidas Mayaguez PR 00708

PAGE, CAREY PRYOR, surgeon; b. Childress, Tex., Jan. 7, 1943; s. Jo and Opal (Fox) P.; B.S., Sul Ross State Coll., Alpine, Tex., 1964; M.D., Baylor U., Houston, 1968; m. Marilyn Alma, Apr. 24, 1965; children—Thomas, Amy, Jana. Intern in surgery Johns Hopkins Hosp., Balt., 1968-69; resident Wilford Hall USAF Med. Center, Lackland AFB, Tex., 1971-75; asst. prof. surgery U. Tex. Health Sci. Center, San Antonio, 1978—; staff physician gen. surgery Audie Murphy VA Hosp., San Antonio, 1978—; instr. U. Tex. Med. Sch., San Antonio. Served with USAF, 1967-78. Diplomate Am. Bd. Surgery. Mem. Assn. Acad. Surgery, Assn. Mil. Surgeons U.S., Am. Soc. Parenteral and Enteral Nutrition, Soc. Air Force Clin. Surgery, AMA, J. B. Aust Surg. Soc., S.W. Surg. Soc., Tex. Med. Assn., Bexar County Med. Soc., San Antonio Surg. Soc., Alpha Omega Alpha. Roman Catholic. Contbr. articles to profl. jours. Office: Dept Surgery U Tex Health Sci Center 7703 Floyd Curl Dr San Antonio TX 78284

PAGE, DANIEL EUGENE, electronics engr.; b. Junction City, Kans., June 18, 1932; s. Belton and Irene Ada (Smythe) Pyle; B.S. in Engring., C.W. Post Coll., 1967, M.S. in Math., 1967. Asst. service mgr. Link Aviation Co., Binghamton, N.Y., 1953-57; project sales engr. Condec Corp., Stamford, Conn., 1957-60; engring. group leader Grumman Aerospace Corp., Bethpage, N.Y., 1960-73; instr. elec. engring. Westark Community Coll., Fort Smith, Ark., 1973—; electronics design cons. biomed. applications, 1970—. Served with USAF, 1949-52. Mem. IEEE, Am. Soc. Engring. Educators, Am. Radio Relay League. Roman Catholic. Home: Rt 4 Box 137W Fort Smith AR 72901 Office: Westark Community Coll Fort Smith AR 72901

PAGE, GARY WAYNE, comml. banking exec.; b. Wilmington, N.C., Feb. 2, 1944; s. Daniel and Edith (Graham) P.; student Asheville-Biltmore Coll., 1962-64; B.S., U. Tenn., 1966; m. Cynthia Carolina Cash, Jan. 13, 1979; children—Karen Elaine, David Patrick. Asst. cashier Valley fidelity Bank & Trust Co., Knoxville, Tenn., 1964-67; asst. cashier Bankers Trust S.C., Columbia, 1967-71, asst. v.p., 1971-73, v.p., corp. planning div., 1973—; chmn. Bank Fin. Mgmt. Forum; mem. faculty Midlands Tech. Coll. Treas., Carolinians Good Govt. Fund, Columbia, 1977—; mem. Smithsonian Inst., Council on Child Abuse. Mem. Bank Adminstrn. Inst. (pres. chpt. 1977-78), Planning Execs. Inst., Am. Inst. Banking, N. Am. Soc. Corp. Planners. Baptist. Office: PO Box 448 Columbia SC 29202

PAGE, HENRY CLAY, chem. co. exec.; b. Newport News, Va., July 11, 1938; s. Henry C. and Edla (Davis) P.; B.S., Va. Poly. Inst. and State U., 1960; m. Margaret Kathrine Tolson, June 20, 1964; children—Teresa, David. Personnel rep. Union Carbide Corp., Oak Ridge, 1963-67; supr. employee relations Fibers div. Allied Chem. Corp., Chester, Va., 1967-70, 70-72, area mgr. employee relations, 1972-74, mgr. employee relations, N.Y.C., 1974-77, dir. employee relations, Agrl. div., Houston, 1977-79, v.p. employee and community relations, 1979—. Served with U.S. Army, 1961-63. Decorated Army Commendation Medal. Mem. Chester (Va.) Jaycees (v.p. 1979—), Agrl. Chem. Indsl. Relations Assn. Methodist. Clubs: Pine Firest Country, Masons, Lions (v.p. 1973-74). Office: Union Tex Petroleum div Allied Chem Corp One Riverway Houston TX 77056

PAGE, LARRY KEITH, neurosurgeon; b. Rayville, La., July 7, 1933; s. Ardie Lee and Edris Estelle (Chaney) P.; B.S., La. State U., 1955, M.D., 1958; m. Joan Marie Doherty, Aug. 27, 1960; children—Matthew, Elizabeth, Jennifer. Intern, Grad. Hosp., U. Pa., Phila., 1958-59; resident Children's Hosp. and Peter Bent Brigham Hosp., Boston, 1962-66; clin. instr. neurosurgery Harvard U., Boston, 1966-71; asso. prof. neurosurgery U. Miami (Fla.), 1971—, chief div. pediatric neurosurgery, 1971—; mem. staff Jackson Meml. Hosp., VA Hosp., Miami; neurol. cons. FDA, 1977—. Served in USN, 1959-62. Mem. ACS, Am. Assn. Neurol Surgeons, Congress Neurol. Surgeons, Internat. Soc. for Pediatric Neurosurgery, Fellowship of Acad. Neurosurgeons, Royal Soc. Medicine, New Eng., Fla. neurosurg. socs., Mass. Med. Soc., Dade County Med. Assn. Methodist. Mem. editorial bd. Neurosurgery, 1976—. Home: 13845 SW 73d Ct Miami FL 33158 Office: U Miami Sch Med PO Box 016960 Miami FL 33101

PAGE, LAUREL EDWARD, educator; b. Ozark, Ark., Aug. 14, 1929; s. Joseph Whitwill and Elizabeth (Pattillo) P.; student Okla. U., 1963-66; B.A. A.S. in Indsl. Edn., Tarleton State U., 1976, M.A.T.S. in Public Adminstrn., 1979; m. Dorothy Lucile, June 3, 1950; children—Jacquelyn Ann, Michael Edward, Timothy Laurel. Enlisted U.S. Air Force, 1948, advanced through grades to master sgt., 1965; ret., 1969; sales John Hancock Ins. Co., Waco, Tex., 1970; with Gen. Dynamics, Waco, 1970; faculty Tex. State Tech. Inst., Waco, 1970—; cons. field of aircraft maintenance. Decorated Air Force commendation. Mem. Order of the Red Red Rose. Democrat. Nazarene. Home: Route 5 Box 1253 Waco TX 76705 Office: Dept of Aviation Texas State Technical Institute Waco TX 76705

PAGE, WILLIS, condr.; b. Rochester, N.Y.; grad. with distinction Eastman Sch. Music, Rochester. With Boston Symphony Orch.; prin. bass Boston Pops; condr. Cecilia Soc. of Boston; organizer, condr. New Orchestral Soc. of Boston (name now Boston Festival Orch.); music dir.-condr. Nashville Symphony Orch., 8 years; asso. condr. Buffalo Philharmonic; condr. Yomiuri Nippon Symphony, Tokyo, Japan, 1962-63; prof. conducting Eastman Sch. Music, 1967-69; prof. conducting, dir. orchestral activities Drake U., Des Moines, 1969-71; condr. Des Moines Symphony, 1969-71, Jacksonville (Fla.) Symphony Orch., 1971—. Guest condr. with Boston Pops, Toronto, Rochester Civic, Eastman-Rochester, Denver, Muncie, Kol Israel, St. Louis, Colorado Springs, Memphis, Hartford orchs.; condr. all-state orchs. of N.Y., Ia., Ky., Tenn., Fla., also regional festivals. Ford Found. European travel award, 1967. Address: 46 W Duval St Jacksonville FL 32202 also Jacksonville Symphony Assn 333 Laura St Jacksonville FL 32202

PAILIN, JAMES EDWARD, rest home adminstr.; b. Elizabeth City, N.C., July 23, 1924; s. James E. and Felecia P.; B.Sc. in Elem. Edn., Elizabeth City State U., 1953; M.Sci. in Edn., Agrl. and Tech. State U., Greensboro, N.C., 1958; driver edn. certificate U. S.C., Conway, 1960; m.; 2 children. Tchr. Bladen County schs., Elizabethtown, N.C., 1954-56; prin., tchr. Columbus County schs. Tabor City, N.C., 1956-73; asst. prin. Whiteville (N.C.) Sr. High Sch., 1973-79; adminstr. Sunny View and Spring Valley rest homes, Fairmont, N.C., 1979—. Past pres. Club 15 civic club. Pres. Bladen County Classroom Tchr. Assn., 1955-56. Mem. NEA, N.C., Columbus County tchrs. assns., N.C. Assn. Educators, N.C. Assn. Long Term Care Facilities. Club: Gentlemen's of Whiteville. Recipient spl. award for outstanding work with young sch. bus drivers. Home: 809 School St Tabor City NC 28463 Office: PO Box 86 Fairmont NC 28340

PAINTER, JOHN HOYT, elec. engr.; b. Winfield, Kans., Mar. 27, 1934; s. John Paul and Marjorie Marietta (Slack) P.; B.S., U. Ill., 1961, M.S., 1962; Ph.D., So. Meth. U., 1972; m. Joy Lou Vaughan, June 7, 1955; children—John Mark, Paul Burton, William Vaughan, Joy Lynn. Electronic engr. Apollo Project, NASA, Houston, 1962-65; sr. engr. Motorola Corp., Scottsdale, Ariz., 1965-67; research engr. NASA Langley Research Center, Hampton, Va., 1967-74; prof. elec. engring. Tex. A&M U., College Station, 1974—; pres., dir. Altair Corp., College Station, 1979—. Served with USAF, 1953-58. Registered profl. engr., Tex. Mem. IEEE (sr.), Radio Tech. Commn. for Aeros., Sigma Xi, Tau Beta Pi, Eta Kappa Nu, Pi Mu Epsilon. Club: Masons (Scottish Rite). Contbr. articles to profl. jours.; patentee in field. Office: Elec Engring Dept Tex A&M U College Station TX 77843

PAJON, EDUARDO RODRIGUEZ, lawyer; b. Ciego de Avila, Camaquey, Cuba, Nov. 22, 1917; s. Francisco Rodriguez Ubals and Maria Luisa Pajon; J.D., U. Havana (Cuba), 1941, U. Miami, 1964; m. Olga M. Fernandez, Jan. 31, 1942 (div. Apr. 1973); children—Olga (Mrs. Ignacio G. del Valle), Eduardo R.; m. 2d, Maribel Maxwell, Dec. 1973 (div. Jan. 1977); m. 3d, Leah Munoz, Sept. 1977. Came to U.S., 1959, naturalized, 1965. Admitted to Fla. bar, 1965; partner firm Helio R. Ecay, Havana, 1941-59, Salley, Barns, Pajon & Immer (now Salley, Barns & Pajon), Miami, 1967—; head legal dept., sec. Cuban subsidiaries The Cuban Am. Sugar Co. (name changed to N.Am. Sugar Industries, Inc. 1960), N.Y.C., 1952-60; sec., counsel Talisman Sugar Corp., Miami, 1965-72; v.p., dir. Fla. Sugar Corp., Belle Glade, 1960-62, Sunshine Farms, Inc., South Bay, Fla., 1960-72; dir. Intercontinental Corp. Miami Beach, Fla. Mem. adv. bd. Fla. Meml. Coll., Miami, 1970—, endowment com. U. Miami, 1969—. Mem. Am., InterAm., Fla., Dade County bar assns. Republican. Roman Catholic. Clubs: Miami, LaGorce Country (Miami Beach); Jockey (North Miami, Fla.); American, Big Five, Bankers (Miami). Home: 6518 Kendale Lakes Dr #810 Miami FL 33183 Office: Suite 700 100 Biscayne Blvd Miami FL 33132

PAKE, DONALD GORDON, printing co. exec.; b. Chgo., Jan. 14, 1929; s. Lawrence Amos and Agnes Mary (Hosek) P.; ed. public and army schs.; m. Rolene Slate, Dec. 13, 1952; children—Mary Elizabeth, Donald Gordon. Pressman, Am. Ticket Corp., Chgo., 1943-50; plant supt. Arrow Printers, Clarksville, Tenn., 1953-64; head instr. Printing Industries Tech. Inst., 1964-67; plant supt. Printers Service Co., Inc., Nashville, 1967-69, prodn. mgr., 1969-71, v.p., dir., 1971—; show judge Printing Industry of Fla., Printing Industry of South, So. Graphic Arts Assn. Scoutmaster Boy Scouts Am., recipient Scouters Key. Served with AUS, 1950-53. Mem. Gideons Internat., Internat. Assn. Printing House Craftsmen, Nat. Hist. Soc., Lay Witness Missions (youth coordinator). Democrat. Methodist. Home: 808 Curtis Dr Nashville TN 37207 Office: Printers Service Co Inc 1940 Elm Hill Pike Nashville TN 37202

PAL, DILIP KUMAR, orthopedic surgeon; b. Balasore, India, Mar. 3, 1933; came to U.S., 1970; s. Nilmani and Santosh (Bhar) P.; I-Sc., St. Xavier Coll., U. Calcutta (India), 1951; M.D., Prince of Wales Med. Coll., Patna, India, 1957; m. Sumita Gue, Dec. 14, 1959; 1 dau., Anita. Intern, Highland Park Gen. Hosp., Detroit, 1970-71; resident Akron (Ohio) City Hosp., 1971-72, Albert Einstein Med. Center, Phila., 1972-74; practice medicine specializing in orthopedic surgery, Daytona Beach, Fla., 1974-76, Lubbock, Tex., 1976—; mem. staffs Meth. Hosp., Highland Hosp., St. Mary's Hosp., Univ. Hosp., W. Tex. Hosp., Health Scis. Center Hosp.; asso. clin. prof. orthopedics Sch. Medicine, Tex. Tech. U., Lubbock. Fellow Internat. Colls. Surgeons, Royal Coll. Surgeons; mem. Am. Acad. Orthopedic Surgeons, AMA, Tex. Med. Assn., Lubbock-Crosby-Garza County Med. Soc., Brit. Orthopedic Assn. Home: 3202 81st St Lubbock TX 79423 Office: 3702 21st St Lubbock TX 79410

PALM, JOHN WILLIAM, chem. engr.; b. Blackwell, Okla., Oct. 10, 1921; s. John William and Flora Alice (Winter) P.; B.S., Okla. State U., 1943; M.S., U. Mich., 1951; m. Fran Doretta Bocox, June 4, 1943; children—James Donald, David Eugene, Nancy Carol. Research engr. Cities Service Research & Devel. Co., Tallant, Okla., 1943-52; sr. research engr. Amoco Prodn. Co., Tulsa, 1952-63, staff research engr., 1964-71, research asso., 1971-79, spl. research asso., 1979—; lectr. Okla. State U., 1969. Scoutmaster, Boy Scouts Am., 1968; pres. Oil Capital Concert Band, 1967; mem. Tulsa Community Orch., 1969-72, Tulsa Community Band, 1967—. Registered profl. engr., Okla. Mem. Am. Inst. Chem. Engrs., Soc. Petroleum Engrs., Phi Lambda Upsilon, Sigma Tau, Phi Kappa Phi. Republican. Methodist. Patentee in field (16); contbr. articles to profl. jours. Home: 3713 E 48th Pl Tulsa OK 74135 Office: PO Box 591 Tulsa OK 74102

PALMER, CHARLES KENT, educator; b. Pittsfield, Maine, Oct. 26, 1927; s. Charles Alton and Ruth Hazel (Whitten) P.; student Coburn Class. Inst., Waterville, Maine, 1941-45, Balt. Sch. Navigation, 1959, U.S. Navy Sch. Amphibious Operations, 1966; m. Betty Lucille Higgs, July 30, 1950; children—Deborah Lucille, Bonnie Ruth, Margaret Ellen. Enlisted as pvt. U.S. Army, 1945, advanced through grades to chief warrant officer, 1966; vessel master, asst. harbor master, pilot, Korea and Ft. Eustis, Va., 1955-59; tugboat master, platoon leader, operations officer, Ft. Eustis and Can., 1959-61; terminal operation plans and coordination officer, Ft. Eustis and Okinawa, 1962-66; ret., 1966; sr. instr. terminal ops. U.S. Army Transp. Sch., Ft. Eustis, 1966—; cons. in field. Scout master Peninsula council Boy Scouts Am., Newport News, Va. Decorated Bronze Star. Mem. Am. Security Council, Res. Officer Assn., Nat. Def. Transp. Assn. Republican. Methodist. Home: 575 Viking Dr Newport News VA 23602 Office: US Army Transportation School Fort Eustis VA 23604

PALMER, CHARLES MILLER, natural gas prodn. exec.; b. Hannibal, Mo., Apr. 15, 1938; s. Charles R. and Evelyn M. (Bagby) P.; B.S. in Journalism, U. Nebr., Omaha, 1962; A.A., Casper (Wyo.) Coll., 1959; m. Kathryn Jacklyn Walters, Aug. 24, 1959; children—Cynthia Lee, Jennifer Lynn, T. Scott. TV news reporter, broadcast mgr., writer and pub., Nebr., Mont. and Okla., 1958-70; campaign asst. Bellmon for U.S. Senate Com., Oklahoma City, 1968; legis. asst. to Sen. Henry Bellmon, Washington, 1970-74; exec. asst. CAB, Washington, 1974-77; v.p. public affairs Sun Gas Co. div. Sun Co., Dallas, 1977—. Founder, dir. Grand Nat. Quail Hunt, 1967—; pres. Okla. State Soc. of Washington, 1965-66; chmn. heavy industry group Dallas United Way, 1978-79; cons. polit. campaigns. Recipient Panko Journalism Scholarship award Omaha Press Club, 1961, numerous awards from UPI and Nat. Press Photographers for TV news reporting and documentaries. Mem. Internat. Assn. Bus. Communicators, Ind. Petroleum Assn. Am., Okla. Mid-Continent Oil and Gas Assn., Nat. Gas Supply Assn., Am. Petroleum Inst., Dallas C. of C. Republican. Methodist. Clubs: Internat. Aviation, Grand Nat. Quail, Nebr. One Box Pheasant Hunt, Dallas Friday Group, Okla. State Soc. Home: 7667 Fallmeadow Ln Dallas TX 75248 Office: PO Box 20 3 Northpark E Dallas TX 75221

PALMER, CHARLES WILLIAM, architect; b. Watertown, S.D., Dec. 23, 1908; s. Charles H. and Helen B. (Barrett) P.; degree in archtl. engring. Wash. State U., 1933; postgrad. U. Va., 1966; m. Ethel M. Puckett, June 9, 1937; children—Charles G., Carol Ann. Pvt. practice, arch., Tacoma, 1927-39, Seattle, 1940-42; civil architect U.S. Navy, Washington and Guam, 1943-50; chief architect USAF, Far East, Tokyo, 1950-55; architect USAF/Dept. Def., Washington, 1950-72; owner Charles W. Palmer, AIA, Arlington, Va., 1972—. Recipient Civilian Cert. of Service USAF, Pentagon, 1972. Mem. Fed. Architect Council (pres. 1962-65), Far East Architects & Engrs. (dir. 1954), AIA. Episcopalian. Clubs: Masons (32 deg., Shriner). Archtl. works include Ch. of Blessed Sacrament, Guam, Hawthorne House, Waterford, Va.; hist. restoration: Ft. Nisqually, Tacoma.

PALMER, CHESTER DELACY, III, food service co. exec.; b. Orangeburg, S.C., Dec. 28, 1948; s. Byron Anthony and Annette Louise (Ducker) P.; B.A. in History, N.C. State U., Raleigh, 1971; M.A. in Social Scis., No. Colo. U., Greeley, 1976. Dir. purchasing and property Bamberg County (S.C.), 1977-78; asst. food service dir. Morrison, Inc., assigned to Stetson U., Deland, Fla., 1978—; county rep. S.C. Assn. Govtl. Purchasing Ofcls., 1977-78; adv. Bamberg County Planning Commn., 1977-78. Vice chmn. N.C. Fedn. Coll. Republicans, 1969-70; scoutmaster local Boy Scouts Am., 1974-76. Served to 1st lt. USAF, 1971-76. Mem. USAF Assn. Episcopalian. Clubs: Columbia (S.C.) Ski, Masons. Home: 515B E Church St Deland FL 32720 Office: Stetson U N Woodland Blvd Deland FL 32720

PALMER, EDWINNA LOPEZ COLLINS, univ. adminstr.; b. Chgo.; d. Curtis Harlee and George Esta (Jacobs) Collins; B.A., Huston-Tillotson Coll., Austin, Tex., 1965; M.Ed., Stephen F. Austin State U., Nacogdoches, Tex., 1969; children by previous marriage—Esta Ayanna, Crystal Rehema. Tchr., Center (Tex.) Ind. Sch. Dist., 1966-69; guidance counselor Stephen F. Austin State U., 1969—, dir. minority affairs, 1977—. Sec.-treas. bd. dirs. Nacogdoches Heart Assn., 1973-77. Mem. Am., Tex. personnel and guidance assns., Nat. Orientation Dirs. Assn., Alpha Kappa Alpha. Home: 3609 SE Stalling Dr Nacogdoches TX 75961 Office: Stephen F Austin State U Box 3032 Nacogdoches TX 75962

PALMER, HARRY ALLEN, metal bellows mfg. co. exec.; b. Goldthwaite, Tex., Apr. 12, 1930; s. Harry Wafford and Alma Mary (Allen) P.; grad. Cal-Aero. Tech. Inst., 1951, Tex. Tech. Coll., 1948-55; m. Trula Jean Adams, Dec. 23, 1951; children—Harry E., Laura K., David A., Morris W. Service mgr. Champs Aviation Inc., Lubbock, Tex., 1955-58; v.p. service Vroman Aviation, Inc., Midland, Tex., 1958-68; dept. mgr. Woolley Tool & Mfg. Co. div. Chromalloy Am. Corp., Odessa, Tex., 1969-79, v.p., 1979-80; pres. Bellows Systems, Inc., Dallas, 1980—; pres. Permian Basin Aviation Assos., Midland, 1964. Asst. scoutmaster Buffalo Trails council Boy Scouts Am., 1963-68, Explorer Scout leader, 1968-74. Served to 1st sgt. USAF, 1951-55; Korea. Recipient Nat. Aviation Mechanics Safety award FAA, 1963, 64, State and Regional Aviation Mechanics Safety award, 1972. Mem. Am. Welding Soc. (chpt. pres. 1973), ASME (chpt. pres. 1978), Soc. Mfg. Engrs., Champion Aviation Mechanics

Club, Order of Arrow. Republican. Methodist. Clubs: Knife & Fork, Am. Legion, Royal Order of Forty and Eight (Odessa). Papers presented to Gen. Aviation Maintenance Seminar, 1968, Automotive Engrs. Symposium, 1969. Home: 3932 E Everglade St Odessa TX 79762 Office: PO Box 3643 Odessa TX 79760

PALMER, HUBERT BERNARD, dentist, ret. air force officer; b. San Antonio, Sept. 6, 1912; s. Hubert Victor and Rosemary (Garvey) P.; student St. Mary's U., 1931-34; D.D.S., Baylor U., 1938; postgrad. George Washington U., 1946-47, U. Md., 1950-53; m. Elizabeth Harriet McAlary, Aug. 16, 1945; children—Hubert Bernard II, Robert Leldon. Commd. 1st lt. USAAF, 1938, advanced through grades to col. USAF, 1971; chief dept. dental research U.S. Army, 1946-50; chief dept. exptl. dentistry, USAF, 1953-54, chief research dentistry div. 1954-56; command dental surgeon, 1958-59, 63-65, 65-68; dental staff officer, 1959-62, dir. dental services, 1968-71; dir. Eastside Dental Clinic San Antonio Met. Health Dist., 1972—; clin. asst. prof. U. Tex. Dental Sch., San Antonio, 1973-76. Decorated Legion of Merit, Commendation medal First Oak Leaf Cluster. Fellow AAAS; mem. Am. Dental Assn., Internat. Assn. Dental Research, Soc. Gen. Microbiology, Am. Soc. Microbiology, Omicron Kappa Upsilon. Contbr. articles to profl. jours. Research reduction decalcification tooth enamel. Home: 6115 Forest Timber San Antonio TX 78240 Office: 210 N Rio Grande San Antonio TX 78202

PALMER, LEE, pediatrician; b. Washington County, Ala., Dec 26, 1897; s. Randson Dabney and Margaret (Lee) P.; student U. Auburn, 1915-18; M.D., U. Louisville, 1923; m. Adele Albrecht, Dec. 18, 1922; children—Lee, Carolyn Palmer Bland, Adele Palmer Joyes; m. 2d, Donna W. Ezell. Intern, Louisville City Hosp., 1922, resident in pediatrics, 1927-28; intern Ky. Tb Sanitarium, 1923; postgrad. in pediatrics Harvard Med. Sch., Boston Children's Hosp.; practice medicine specializing in pediatrics, Louisville, 1927—; mem. staffs Children's, Louisville Gen., Kasair Crippled Children's, Bapt., St. Anthony's hosps. (all Louisville); clin. prof. pediatrics U. Louisville Med. Sch., 1947—; pres. Louisville-Jefferson County Bd. Health, 1950-54. Served with U.S. Army, 1918-19, to col., M.C., 1942-47. Decorated Army Commendation medal. Diplomate Am. Bd. Pediatrics. Mem. Am. Acad. Pediatrics (life mem., chmn. Ky. chpt. 1953-55), AMA, Ky., Jefferson County med. socs., Ky. Pediatric Soc. Presbyterian. Clubs: Louisville Country, Pendennis (Louisville); Coral Ridge Country (Ft. Lauderdale, Fla.); Masons, Shriners. Home: 5801 Creighton Hill Rd Louisville KY 40207 Office: 518 Medical Towers N Louisville KY 40202

PALMER, MICHAEL HAMILTON, educator; b. Lenoir, N.C., Dec. 6, 1932; s. Lawrence Narvel and Faye Land (Crisp) P.; A.A., Charlotte Coll., 1953; A.B., U. N.C., Chapel Hill, 1954; M.A., Appalachian State U., 1960; postgrad. Duke U., 1962-64, N.C. State U., Raleigh, 1970, 72-73, Ariz. State U., 1968; Ph.D., George Peabody Coll., 1975; m. Patricia Ann Greene, June 16, 1962; children—Michael, Patrick. Tchr. English, Gamewell High Sch., Lenoir, N.C., 1954-55, 57-60; instr., asst. dir. public relations Gardner-Webb Coll., Boiling Springs, N.C., 1960-62; instr. No. High Sch., Durham, N.C., 1963-65; mem. faculty Louisburg (N.C.) Coll., 1965—, prof. English, 1965—, head dept., 1978—. Served with AUS, 1955-57. Recipient Tchr. of Yr. award Hardbarger Jr. Coll. Bus., 1978, 79; Nat. Endowment for Humanities fellow, 1980-81. Mem. AAUP, Philol. Assn. Carolinas, Coll. English Assn., N.C. English Tchrs. Assn., Conf. on Coll. Composition and Communication, Nat. Council Tchrs. English. Democrat. Unitarian. Club: Lions (past gov. council). Home: 1700 Banbury Rd Raleigh NC 27608 Office: PO Box 737 Louisburg Coll Louisburg NC 27549

PALMER, OWEN THACKARA, JR., lawyer; b. Gulfport, Miss., July 15, 1920; s. Owen Thackara and Lula (Barksdale) P.; B.A., U. Miss., 1942, LL.B., 1947; m. Joanne Melton, Apr. 5, 1947; children—Jan Barksdale, Wawice Eugenia. Admitted to Miss. bar, 1947; with firm Eaton & Cottrell, Gulfport, Miss., 1947-48; individual practice law, Gulfport, 1948-64; sr. partner, Palmer & Stewart, Gulfport, 1965-73, Palmer, Stewart & Gaines, 1973-79, Palmer & Gaines, 1980—. Instr. Am. history U. Miss., 1947. Disaster chmn., Gulfport chpt. A.R.C., 1949-51; coach Gulfport Recreation Dept., 1954-68. City pros. atty., asst. city atty. Gulfport, 1953-69; atty. Gulfport Mcpl. Separate Sch. Dist., 1957—. Dir., past pres. Gulfport-Harrison County Library, 1954-68; bd. dirs., 1st v.p., mem. exec. com. Miss. Safety Council, 1971—, pres., 1972-73; past pres. Gulfport Little Theatre; atty., mem. exec. com. Greater Gulf Coast Arts Council, 1972—. Served with USNR. Mem. Miss. State Bar (chmn. traffic ct. com. 1962—), Am. (rep. State Miss. on adv. com. to traffic ct. com. 1966—), Harrison County (past pres.) bar assns., Am. Trial Lawyers Assn., Am. Judicature Assn., Delta Kappa Epsilon, Phi Delta Phi. Episcopalian. Rotarian. Club: Gulfport Yacht (past commodore). Home: 1308 E Beach St Gulfport MS 39501 Office: 2209 14th St Gulfport MS 39501

PALMER, SIDNEY J(EWELL), television producer, condr.; b. Houston, Nov. 18, 1928; s. Jewell S. and Lizzette M. (Shilling) P.; grad. Houston Conservatory Music, 1940; B. Mus., U. Tex., 1947, Mus.M., 1949; postgrad. (fellow) Juilliard Sch. Music, 1947-48, Berkshire Music Center, Tanglewood/Lenox, Mass., 1947-49; m. Lanny Sullivan, Aug. 19, 1967; children—Margaret Ann, Mary Elizabeth. Concert pianist, composer, condr., opera stage dir., 1947—; radio dir., producer, various locations 1945-58; producer KARK-TV, Little Rock, 1952-60; exec. producer, prodn. supr. WIS-TV, Columbia, S.C., 1960-73; exec. producer, dir. nat. program prodn. and devel. and cultural affairs S.C. Ednl. Television Network, Columbia, 1973—; pres. Nat. Photo Enterprises; owner strictly Glamour and Talent. Condr., New Braunfels (Tex.) Symphony Orch., 1947-48, Houston Symphonette, 1949-51, Ark. State Symphony, 1950-54, Hot Springs (Ark.) Lyric Theatre, 1951-59, Little Rock Philharmonic, 1955-58; artistic dir. Columbia Lyric Theatre, Columbia, 1960-70; artist-in-residence Columbia Coll., 1972—; head, theory and composition depts. Houston Conservatory Music, 1949-50; condr., lectr. U. Ark. Grad. Center, 1954-56. Nat. sec. Television Program Conf., 1973—. Bd. dirs. Russell George Found. Recipient mus. composition awards, including Harold J. Abrams award, 1950, Tex. Composers' Contest award, 1949, several Nat. Fedn. Music Clubs award, Los Angeles Internat. competition, 1955, Mid-South competition, 1958; Broadcast Media awards San Francisco State Coll., 1969, 70; Roy W. Howard award S.C. Ednl. TV, 1975. Author: Color Television Manual, 1962; (with others) Creativity in Media, 1977. Home: 3101 Barnes Spring Rd Columbia SC 29204 Office: 2712 Millwood Ave Columbia SC 29205

PALMER, STEPHEN DONALD, pediatrician; b. Spartanburg, S.C., Mar. 30, 1924; s. Leon Carlos and Lala Keith (Caldwell) P.; B.A. U. South, 1948; M.D., Med. Coll. Ala., 1953; children—Kathryn Love, James Gordon, Stephen Leon, Anne Caldwell. Intern, VA Hosp., McKinney, Tex., 1953-54; resident Univ. Hosp., Birmingham, Ala., 1956-58; physician in charge Hudson Stuck Hosp., Ft. Yukon, Alaska, 1954-55; dir. clin. lab. Univ. Hosp., Birmingham, 1957-60; practice medicine specializing in pediatrics, Birmingham, 1960-79; pres. med.-dental staff Children's Hosp., Birmingham, 1976; clin. prof. pediatrics Med. Coll. Ala., 1979—; asst. clin. prof. U. Ky., 1980—; med. dir. Frontier Nursing Service, Hyden, Ky., 1979—. Served with USNR, 1943-46. Diplomate Am. Bd. Pediatrics. Mem. AMA, Am. Acad. Pediatrics, Am. Assn. Blood Banks, Jefferson County Pediatric Soc., Jefferson County Med. Soc., Med. Assn. State Ala., So. Med. Assn., So. Soc. Pediatric Research, So. Perinatal Assn., Ky. Med. Assn., Ky. Primary Care Assn. Episcopalian. Home: Hyden KY 41749 Office: Frontier Nursing Service Hyden KY 41749

PALMER, THOMAS L, univ. pres.; b. Breckenridge, Tex., Mar. 31, 1925; s. Thomas L. and Grace P.; B.S., Okla. Southwestern State U., 1949; M.S., Okla. State U., 1953, Ed.D., 1966; m. Dorothy Mae Corley, Dec. 26, 1944; children—Corley Mark, Patti Jo, Stacy Yvonne, Tracy Yvette. Pres., Panhandle State U., Goodwell, Okla., 1971—; dir. Bank of the Panhandle, Profl. Investors Corp. Served with USNR, World War II. Mem. Am. Assn. State Colls. and Univs., Am. Assn. Sch. Adminstrs., Am. Assn. Higher Edn., Okla. Assn. Sch. Adminstrs., Guymon (Okla.) C. of C. Baptist. Clubs: Rotary (past pres.), Masons, Elks. Home: Box 640 Aggie Ave Goodwell OK 73939 Office: Box 430 Aggie Ave Goodwell OK 73939

PALMER, THOMAS WILLIAM, utility exec.; b. Birmingham, Ala., Feb. 11, 1924; s. Lewis William and Agnes Mae (Thomas) P.; B.A., Birmingham-So. Coll., 1950; m. Nancy Ann Stone, Sept. 6, 1947; children—Debra Palmer Reid, Lee Ann, Lisa. Staff acct. J.J. Scarborough & Co., Birmingham, 1949-50; acctg. analyst UNIVAC div. Sperry Rand Co., Birmingham, 1950-51; mgmt. engr. Thomas & Assos., mgmt. cons., 1952-53; internal auditor So. Co. Services, Inc., Birmingham, 1953-57, chief. acct., 1957-61, asst. to comptroller, 1961-63, asst. treas., 1963-64, treas., asst. comptroller, Atlanta, 1964-77, treas., asst. sec. The So. Co., Atlanta, 1971-77, dir. internal auditing, 1977—. Served with USAAF, 1942-45; with USAF, 1951-52. Mem. Inst. Internal Auditors. Baptist. Home: 9475 River Lake Dr Roswell GA 30075 Office: PO Box 720071 Atlanta GA 30346

PALMORE, JOHN STANLEY, JR., state chief justice; b. Ancon, C.Z., Aug. 6, 1917; s. John Stanley and Antoinette (Gonzalez) P.; student Western Ky. State Coll., 1934-36; LL.B. cum laude, U. Louisville, 1939; student Harvard Grad. Sch. Bus. Adminstrn., 1942-43; m. Eleanor Gertrude Anderson, July 31, 1938; 1 son, John W. Admitted to Ky. bar, 1938; asso. firm King & Flournoy, Henderson, Ky., 1939-42; chief legal br. Jeffersonville (Ind.) O.M. Depot, 1946-47; partner firm Hunt & Palmore, Henderson, 1947-52, Palmore & Mitchell, Henderson, 1956-59; pvt. practice, 1952-56; Commonwealth's atty. 5th Jud. Dist. Ky., 1955-59; city atty. Henderson, 1954-55; pros. atty. Henderson, 1949-53; city atty. Sebree, Ky., 1954-59; judge Ct. Appeals Ky., 1959-76, chief justice, 1966, 73; justice Supreme Ct. Ky., 1976—, chief justice, 1977—. Served to lt. Supply Corps, USN, 1942-46, 51-52. Mem. Am., Ky. bar assns. Democrat. Episcopalian. Home: Owensboro KY 42301 Office: State Capitol Frankfort KY 40601

PALMS, JOHN MICHAEL, physicist, coll. ofcl.; b. Rijswijk, Holland, June 6, 1935; s. Peter Joannes and Mimi Adele (De Yong) P.; came to U.S., 1941, naturalized, 1957; B.S., The Citadel, 1958; M.S., Emory U., 1959; Ph.D., U. N.Mex., 1966; m. Norma Lee Cannon, June 2, 1958; children—John Michael, Daniele Maria, Lee Cannon. Physicist, Sandia Lab., Albuquerque, 1962-63, Los Alamos (N.Mex.) Sci. Lab., 1963-66; mem. staff Oak Ridge Nat. Lab. Instrumentation div., summer, 1966; asst. prof. dept. physics Emory U., Atlanta, Ga., 1966-68, asso. prof., 1968-73, chmn. dept. physics, 1969-73, prof., 1973, dean Coll. Arts and Scis., 1974-79, v.p. arts and scis., 1979—, asso. prof. radiology Sch. Medicine, 1969—; cons. to various sci. labs., indsl. firms and govt. agys., 1963—; mem. Savannah River Lab. Nuclear Edn. Com., 1969—. Served to capt. USAF, 1958-62. Mem. Am. Phys. Soc., Am. Assn. of Physics Tchrs., Soc. of Nuclear Medicine, AAAS, IEEE, Am. Nuclear Soc., Sigma Xi, Sigma Pi Sigma, Phi Beta Kappa. Contbr. numerous articles on nuclear physics, environ. sci. and medicine to sci. jours. Home: 334 Durand Falls Dr Decatur GA 30030 Office: Emory College Emory Univ Atlanta GA 30322

PALUMBO, MARIO JOSEPH, state senator; b. N.Y.C., Apr. 13, 1933; s. Jack and Nancy (Alfonso) P.; A.B., Morris Harvey Coll., Charleston, W.Va., 1954; LL.B., W.Va. U., 1957; m. Louise Corey, May 10, 1969; children—Christopher, Corey Lee. Admitted to W.Va. bar, 1957; partner firm Love, Wise, Robinson & Woodroe; mem. W.Va Senate, 1969—. Served to lt. col. W.Va. Air N.G. Mem. Am., W.Va. bar assns., Order of Coif. Clubs: Exchange (pres. 1969), Tennis (Charleston). Home: 1838 Louden Heights Rd Charleston WV 25314 Office: 1200 Charleston Nat Plaza Charleston WV 25301

PANCHOK, FRANCES, educator; b. N.Y.C., Nov. 9, 1946; d. Andrew Henry and Philomena (Grygalin) P.; B.A., St. Joseph's Coll., Bklyn., 1968; M.A. (tuition grantee), Cath. U. Am., 1970, Ph.D., 1976; m. John M. Berry, June 8, 1974. Grad. teaching asst. Cath. U. Am., Washington, 1969-72, instr. history, 1972-73; asso. prof. history, dept. chmn. Sch. Theology, U. of St. Thomas, Houston, 1973—; instr. religious history permanent diaconate tng. program Cath. Diocese Galveston-Houston, community adult edn. programs. Com. on lay theol. edn. Council of Southwestern Theol. Sch.; mem. commn. for ecumenism and interreligious affairs Cath. Diocese of Galveston-Houston; water safety instr. vol. ARC. Grantee to spl. inst. Bklyn. Coll., 1969. Mem. Am. Hist. Assn., Am. Studies Assn., Am. Soc. Ch. History, Orgn. Am. Historians, Am. Cath. Hist. Assn., AAUP, Tex. Cath. Hist. Soc. Roman Catholic. Asst. to editor John Carroll Papers, 1976; contbr. articles in field to publs. Office: 9845 Memorial Dr Houston TX 77024

PANICALI, LOUIS VINCENT, elec. engr.; b. Buffalo, July 20, 1932; s. Angelo Joseph and Clorinda Rose (Godani) P.; B.S. in Elec. Engring., Tenn. Tech. U., 1973, M.E.E., 1977; m. Emma Sue Pickens, Mar. 8, 1961; children—Michael Joseph, Deborah Sue. Enlisted U.S. Marine Corps, 1951, advanced through grades to capt., 1968, ret., 1971; elec. engr. power distbn. Cookeville (Tenn.) Electric Dept., 1975-79, chief engr., 1979—. Mem. power bd. Tenn. Tech. U. Registered profl. engr., Tenn. Mem. IEEE, Tenn. Valley Public Power Assn., Am. Public Power Assn. Roman Catholic. Club: Rotary. Home: Route 10 Box 221 Cookeville TN 38501 Office: 45 E Broad St Cookeville TN 38501

PANKEY, GEORGE EDWARD, educator; b. Charlotte Court House, Va., Dec. 2, 1903; s. John Wesley and Cora Smith (Daniel) P.; B.A., U. Richmond, 1926; M.A., U. N.C., 1927; m. Annabel Atkinson, Mar. 6, 1931; 1 son, George Atkinson. Mem. faculty Ogden Coll. and Western Ky. State Tchrs. Coll., 1927-28, La. Poly. Inst., 1928-43; with land dept. Gulf Oil Corp., 1944-46; currently in research work. Mem. Huguenot Soc., S.A.R., Sons Am. Colonists, Sigma Tau Delta. Baptist. Mason. Author: John Pankey of Manakin Town, Virginia and His Descendants, Vol. I, 1969, Vol. II, 1972; co-author: Five Thousand Useful Words, 1936. Address: PO Box 84 Ruston LA 71270

PANKEY, GEORGE STEPHEN, dentist; b. Durham, N.C., Dec. 3, 1922; s. Edwin Wilburn and Julia (Bender) P.; A.B., U. N.C., 1948; D.D.S., Emory U., 1954; m. Christina R. Curry, Jan. 17, 1959 (div. Feb. 1967); children—Julia Gay, Crista Merry; m. 2d, Diane Joy Flaim, Oct. 14, 1967; adopted children—Laura Jean, Julia Ann, George Stephen. Practice dentistry, Winter Garden, Fla., 1954-58, North Miami Beach, Fla., 1958-59, St. Cloud, Fla., 1959—; dir. Fla. United Investment, Inc. Served with U.S. Army, 1943-46; ETO. Mem. Am. Dental Assn., Fla. State, Central Dist. dental socs., V.F.W., St. Cloud C. of C (pres. 1961-62), Sigma Chi. Republican. Episcopalian. Mason (worshipful master 1965, Shriner), Rotarian (pres. 1962-63). Home: Pine Lake Estates Saint Cloud FL 32769 Office: 1216 10th St Saint Cloud FL 32769

PANKOWSKI, MARY LAWRENCE, educator; b. N.Y.C., Oct. 28, 1940; d. David G. and Nancy Wemple (Bissell) Lawrence; B.A. in Edn., U. Fla., 1963, M.Ed. in Counseling and History, 1964; Ph.D. (Competetitive fellow), Fla. State U., 1972; m. Joseph Michael Pankowski, June 30, 1962; children—Joseph Michael, Mark S., Anne-Marie. Measurement and evaluation cons. U. Fla., Gainesville, 1964-69; instr. corr. study Lively Vocat.-Tech. Sch. and Santa Fe Community Coll., 1968-73; instr. social studies evening sch. Fla. State U., Tallahassee, 1967-70, instr., research asst. dept. adult edn., 1970-71, instr. dept. adult edn., summer 1972, adminstr. spl. programs div. continuing edn., 1972-73, asst. dir. spl. programs, dir. program devel. div. continuing edn. asst. prof. adult edn., 1973-75, dir. Center for Profl. Devel. and Public Service, asso. prof. adult edn., 1975—; Fla. State U. rep. Nat. Council Extension and Continuing Edn., 1977—. Mem. Blessed Sacrament Sch. Bd., 1976-78; mem. Leon County Tourist Devel. Council, 1978-79; participant Inst. Mgmt. of Lifelong Edn., 1979. Mem. Am. Soc. Tng. and Devel. (pres. Fla. chpt. 1975-76), Nat. Univ. Edn. Assn. Democrat. Roman Catholic. Home: 744 Duparc Circle Tallahassee FL 32312 Office: Florida State University Hecht House 325 Tallahassee FL 32306

PANTANA, JOHN JOSEPH, educator; b. Goshen, Ind., July 19, 1947; s. Joseph Thomas and Alma Ogatha (Shank) P.; B.S. in Secondary Edn., Bob Jones U., 1970; M.Ed. in Ednl. Adminstrn., Ga. State U., 1974; postgrad. U. Va., 1974-80; m. Linda Kay Smith, June 13, 1970; children—Krista, Lisa, Matthew. Tchr., Hammond (Ind.) Bapt. High Sch., 1970-72; prin. Forrest Hills Christian High Sch., Atlanta, 1972-74; secondary edn. coordinator Liberty Bapt. Coll., Lynchburg, Va., 1974—, asso. prof. edn., 1974—. Mem. Am. Ednl. Research Assn., Assn. of Tchr. Edn. Baptist. Mem. mixed quartet Pantana Family appearing Jerry Falwell's Old Time Gospel Hour TV. Home: 420 Oakridge Blvd Lynchburg VA 24502 Office: Liberty Bapt Coll Box 1111 Lynchburg VA 24514

PAOLINI, GILBERTO, scholar Spanish lit., educator; b. L'Aquila, Italy, Dec. 22, 1928; s. John and Assunta A. (Turavani) P.; came to U.S., 1949, naturalized, 1954; Classical Maturity, Liceo Classico D. Cotugno, L'Aquila, 1949; B.A., U. Buffalo, 1957, M.A., 1959; postgrad. (Italian Sch. scholar) Middlebury Coll., summers 1960, 61, Ph.D., U. Minn., 1965; m. Claire Jacqueline Landro, June 18, 1960; children—Angela Janet, John Frank. Teaching fellow Spanish, U. Buffalo, 1957-58; lectr. Spanish, Rosary Hill Coll., Buffalo, 1957-58; instr. Italian and Latin lit. U. Mass., Amherst, 1958-60; teaching asst. Spanish and Italian, U. Minn. at Mpls., 1960-62; instr. Spanish and Italian, Syracuse (N.Y.) U., 1962-65, asst. prof., 1965-67; asso. prof. Spanish lit. Tulane U., New Orleans, 1967-76, prof., 1976—, Grad. Sch. research grantee, 1968, 78, 79; co-founder La. Conf. on Hispanic Langs. and Lits., 1979. Originator Spanish Culture Week, New Orleans. Served with AUS, 1952-54. Mem. Modern Lang. Assn., Am. Assn. Tchrs. Spanish and Portuguese, Am. Assn. Tchrs. Italian, Am. Soc. 18th Century Studies, Southeastern Am. Soc. 18th Century Studies (exec. bd.), South Central Modern Lang. Assn., S. Atlantic Modern Lang. Soc., Asociación Internacional de Hispanistas, Sigma Delta Pi (pres. 1956), Phi Sigma Iota. Author: Bartolome Soler, novelista: procedimientos estilisticos, 1963; An Aspect of Spiritualistic Naturalism in the Novels of B. P. Galdos: Charity, 1969. Mem. editorial bd. Forum Italicum, 1967-71, Crítica Hispánica, 1979—; asso. editor South Central Bull., 1978-80; contbr. articles and revs. in field to prof. jours. Home: 1823 S Carrollton Ave New Orleans LA 70118

PAQUETTE, DEAN RICHARD, computer co. exec.; b. Detroit, July 15, 1930; s. William Roy and Neta Norine (Hadder) P.; B.A., U. Md., 1970; M.S., George Washington U., 1971; m. Emma Shirley Jones, July 2, 1952; children—Neta E., Diane R., Kingsley W. Commd. 2d lt. U.S. Army, 1946, advanced through grades to col., 1972; dep. dir. facilities engring. Chief of Engrs., 1975-76; div. chief, support requirements, 1973-75; sr. Army rep. in Australia, 1971-73; sr. Army liason Internat. Civil Aviation Orgn., FAA, 1965-68; chief, research and devel. facilities constrn., 1969-71; chief of ops., mem. faculty Army Engr. Sch., 1958-61; ret., 1976; mgr. govt. requirements and planning Control Data Corp., Arlington, Va., 1977—. Vice pres. Waynewood (Va.) PTA, 1967. Decorated D.F.C., Purple Heart, Legion of Merit with 2 oak leaf clusters. Mem. Soc. Am. Mil. Engrs., Order of Purple Heart, Daedalions, Order of Carabao, Assn. U.S. Army, Am. Def. Preparedness Assn., Army Aviation Assn. Club: Bolling AFB. Home: 1117 Priscilla Ln Alexandria VA 22308 Office: 3717 Columbia Pike Arlington VA 22204

PARDUE, HOWARD MONROE, mfg. co. exec.; b. Jonesville, N.C., Aug. 10, 1942; s. William Donald and Celtia Victoria (Nicks) P.; B.S., Va. Tech., 1964; M.Ed., U. N.C., 1968; m. Linda Chamberlin, May 11, 1962; children—Mark, Lori. Mng. tng. and personnel devel. R.J.R. Industries, 1970-74; asst. dir. personnel Appalachian State U., Boone, N.C., 1974-75; corp. EEO/personnel mgr. Mead Corp., 1975; dir. personnel and indsl. relations Stewart-Warner Corp., 1975-76; dir. personnel Reliance Universal, Inc., High Point, N.C., 1976—; part-time instr., personnel mgr. Forsyth Tech. Inst., Winston-Salem, N.C. Exec. dir. Area Youth Athletic Program, High Point, 1979. All-Am. coll. basketball player, 1961-64; cert. tchr., N.C. Mem. Am. Soc. Personnel Adminstrn. (dir. career devel. 1978), Va. Tech. Alumni Assn. (v.p. 1980), Am. Soc. Tng. and Devel., Am. Mgmt. Soc. (com. of 500), Coll. and Univ. Personnel Assn., Am. Soc. Safety Engrs. Republican. Methodist. Address: Reliance Universal Inc 1431 Progress St High Point NC 27263

PARDUE, ROBERT LOUIS, biologist; b. Boston, Nov. 21, 1946; s. Robert Wright and Theresa Rota P.; B.S., Wayland Baptist Coll., Plainview, Tex., 1968; M.S. (Teaching fellow), N. Tex. State U., 1972; Ph.D., U. Houston, 1973; married, Aug. 18, 1972. Research asso. in cell biology U. Tex. Med. Br., Galveston, 1972-76; teaching fellow U. Houston, 1976-78; research asso. in cell biology Baylor U. Coll. Medicine, Houston also part-time faculty, 1978—. Mem. AAAS, Tex. Soc. Electron Microscopy, Electron. Microscopy Soc. Am., Am. Soc. Cell Biology, AAU, Sigma Xi. Researcher microtubules, cancer. Home: 3302 Bishopton Circle Pearland TX 77581 Office: Dept Cell Biology Baylor U Coll Medicine 1200 Moursand St Houston TX 77030

PAREDES-GIL, ABEL, pediatrician; b. Guatemala City, Guatemala, Sept. 11, 1944; s. Abel and Lilia (Gil) Paredes-Luna; came to U.S., 1970; M.D., U. San Carlos of Guatemala, 1970; m. Donna Chadwell, Feb. 7, 1975; 1 step-son, Eric A. Ellington; 1 dau., Amy Michelle. Intern, Children's Meml. Hosp., Omaha, 1970-71; resident in pediatrics Baylor U. Coll. Medicine, Houston, 1971-73, pediatric infectious disease fellow, 1973-75, instr. dept. pediatrics, dept. microbiology and immunology, 1975-76, asst. prof., 1976-77, clin. asst. prof. dept. pediatrics, 1977—; practice medicine specializing in pediatrics, infectious disease, Houston, 1977—; chmn. pediatric sect. Meml. City Med Center, Houston, 1979. Mem. Am. Acad.

Pediatrics, So. Soc. Pediatric Research, Infectious Disease Soc. Houston, Coll. Physicians and Surgeons of Guatemala, Am. Soc. Microbiology, Harris County (Tex.) Med. Soc. Roman Catholic. Contbr. articles, abstracts to profl. jours. Office: Suite 163 902 Frostwood St Houston TX 77024

PARHAM, CHARLES ELLIOT, serologist; b. Chipley, Ga., Oct. 25, 1932; s. John Dewey and Annie Martin P.; B.A., Paine Coll., 1957; m. Daisy Benita Porter, Oct. 25, 1958. Tchr. sci. Meriwether County Bd. Edn., Greenville, Ga., 1957-63; pub. health lab. technologist Center for Disease Control, USPHS, HEW, Atlanta, 1963—; cons. verereal disease test reagents prodn. Served with U.S. Army, 1950-53. NSF grantee, 1958. Mem. Nat. Geog. Soc., NAACP, Paine Coll. Alumni Assn., Sigma Xi. Home: 2669 Black Forest Trail SW Atlanta GA 30331 Office: Center for Disease Control 1600 Clifton Rd NE Atlanta GA 30333

PARHAM, DONALD ALBERT, athletic dir.; b. Atoka, Okla., Apr. 3, 1930; s. Carl Albert and Louella Mae (Prosper) P.; B.S., Southeastern Okla. State U., Durant, 1952; M.S., Okla. State U., 1955; Ed.D., Peabody Coll., 1956; m. Kay Baker, Dec. 26, 1954; children—David William, Brent Donald, Warren Gene. Asst. prof. phys. edn. So. Ark. U., 1956-59; prof. phys. edn., chmn. dept. health, phys. edn. and recreation, dir. athletics, baseball coach Southeastern Okla. State U., 1959—. Chmn., Durant City Planning Com., 1963-70. Served with AUS, 1952-54. Mem. AAHPER, Am. Assn. Coll. Baseball Coaches. Baptist. Clubs: Elks, Lions (past pres. Durant). Address: Southeastern Okla State Univ University Blvd Durant OK 74701

PARHAM, GUY HENRY, JR., ret. educator; b. Knoxville, Tenn., Oct. 4, 1913; s. Guy Henry and Rose (Morrison) P.; B.S., U. Cin., 1939; m. Dorothy Duggan, Oct. 11, 1939; 1 son, Guy Henry III. Faculty, U. Tenn., Knoxville, 1941-43, 46—, prof., 1947-74; individual practice architecture, Fla., Tenn., 1945-46; lectr. safe boating Coast Guard Aux.; pres. Par-D Navigational Co., Knoxville, 1965—. Col., staff Gov. Tenn., 1974-79. Served with USAAF, 1943-45. Mem. U.S. Naval Inst., Inst. Navigation, Sigma Phi Epsilon, Omicron Delta Kappa. Author: Celestial Navigation, 1964; Oceanic Navigation, 1965; Map and Chart Reading, 1966; Star Identification, 1966; Advanced Celestial Navigation, 1967; Graphical Analysis of Navigation, 1969. Designer navigational computers. Home: 241 Hawthorne Ave Knoxville TN 37920 Office: PO Box 2012 Knoxville TN 37901

PARHAM, ROBERT RANDALL, writer, editor; b. Takoma Park, Md., Apr. 21, 1943; s. Orion Lee and LaVon Louise P.; B.A., Belmont Coll., 1965; M.S., Fla. State U., 1970, postgrad., 1976-79; m. Anne Van Hook, July 31, 1965; children—Misty Dawn, Thomas Orion. Tchr. pub. schs., New Port Richey, Fla., 1965-69; instr. in English, Francis Marion Coll., 1970-76, 78-79, editor Francis Marion Rev., 1975-77; resident S.C. Poets-in-the-Schs. Program S.C. Arts Commn., 1974-77; author chapbook: Sending The Children for Song, 1975; contbr. numerous poems, stories, essays to lit. jours. Recipient William Gilmore Simms poetry prize, 1971. Mem. Nat. Council Tchrs. English, Blue Key. Home: 233 Creek Dr Quincy SC 29501 Office: Dept English Box 7500 Florence SC 29501

PARIKH, SHRIDMAR VAIKUNTHLAL, chem. engr.; b. Surat, India, Oct. 19, 1939; s. Vaikunthlal D. and Devkiben V. P.; came to U.S., 1961, naturalized, 1971; M.S., Kans. State U., 1963; m. Carmina S. Parikh, June 7, 1968; children—Dev S., Monica Debki. Chem. engr. E.I. DuPont de Nemours & Co., Inc., Wilmington, Del., 1965-70; chief chemist trailblazer div. Olin Corp., Statesville, N.C., 1970-74; sr. devel. chemist plastics div. Stauffer Chem. Co., Anderson, S.C., 1974—; cons. in field. Mem. Am. Chem. Soc., Am. Assn. Textile Chemists and Colorists, Info. Council on Fabric Flammability, Flame Retardant Chem. Assn. Contbr. articles in field to profl. jours. Office: Stauffer Chem Co PO Box 5288 Anderson SC 29621

PARIS, JANET FRESCH (MRS. MAURICE THATCHER PARIS), library cons.; b. Balt., July 29, 1911; d. George Oliver and Jane (Grady) Fresch; A.B., Wilson Coll., 1933; B.S. in L.S., Drexel Inst. Tech., 1934; M.L.S., Columbia U., 1940; m. Maurice Thatcher Paris, June 19, 1943; 1 dau., Katrina Van Buskirk Douglass (Mrs. Eugene Salmon Napier Lawrimore). Cataloger, Enoch Pratt Free Library, Balt., 1934-41; cataloger, descriptive cataloging div. Library of Congress, Washington, 1941-52; cataloger N.Y. Pub. Library Reference Div., 1953-56; instr. library sci. Nazareth Coll., Louisville, 1956-60; cataloger in charge book catalog project Montgomery County (Md.) Dept. Pub. Libraries, Gaithersburg, 1960-66; cataloger S.C. State Library, Columbia, 1966-68; dir. Georgetown County Meml. Library, Georgetown, S.C., 1968-74; library cons., free lance writer, 1974—. Recipient Superior Accomplishment award Library of Congress, 1950. Mem. Southeastern, S.C. library assns., Georgetown County Hist. Soc. Republican. Episcopalian. Home: Wicklow Hall Plantation Georgetown SC 29440

PARISH, BETTY ROSS HAYES, city ofcl.; b. Atlanta, Dec. 16, 1927; d. Ross Jackson and Myrtle Lester (Skinner) Hayes; student public schs., Wrens, Ga.; m. Randall Reeves Parish, Aug. 9, 1946; children—Randall Reeves, Joy Elizabeth, Molly Evelyn, Jerry Ross, John Huff. Teller, Thompson Banking Co., Wrens, 1944-46; sec. Metro. Life Ins. Co., Augusta, Ga., 1946-48, 8th Army Procurement Sect., Yokohama, Japan, 1949; bookkeeper Pace Foods Co., San Antonio, 1961-63; city clk. City of Wrens, 1963—, clk. of recorders ct., 1963—. Sec., Wrens Planning Commn., 1966—; sec.-treas. Wrens Med. Authority, 1978—. Cert. mcpl. clk., Ga.; cert. emergency med. technician, Ga. Mem. Ga. Mcpl. Clks. and Fin. Officers Assn. (dir. 1978-79), Mcpl. Fin. Officers Assn., Internat. Inst. Mpcl. Clks., E. Central EMT Assn., N. Jefferson EMT Assn. Baptist. Home: 104 Center St Wrens GA 30833 Office: 401 Broad St Wrens GA 30833

PARISH, MARION ROBBINS, speech pathologist; b. Houston, Feb. 2, 1944; d. Walter Alvis and Maude Marion (Robbins) P.; B.A., U. Tex., Austin, 1966; M.A., Our Lady of Lake Coll., 1967. Speech pathologist Corpus Christi (Tex.) Speech and Hearing Center, 1966; instr., supr. undergrads. Our Lady of Lake Coll., San Antonio, 1967-72; co-dir. Speech Pathology Assos., Houston, 1972—; cons. in field. Active, Jr. League Houston. Mem. Houston Area Assn. Communication Disorders, Am. Speech-Lang.-Hearing Assn., Tex. Speech-Lang.-Hearing Assn., Council for Exceptional Children, Orton Soc. Office: Speech Pathology Assos 11211 Katy Freeway Suite 490 Houston TX 77079

PARISH, SYDNEY SIMON, accountant, govt. ofcl.; b. Bayonne, N.J., Aug. 15, 1909; s. William and Ida (Lazarus) P.; certificate in accountancy, bus. admistrn. Pace Inst., 1935, asso. Applied Sci., 1961; m. Ruth Eleanore Kapiloff, May 27, 1934; children—David Monroe, Fern, William, Daniel, Donna, Paula, Steven. Accountant, Sol & Orans, C.P.A.'s, N.Y.C., 1937-42; C.P.A., Bayonne, N.J., 1972—; internal revenue agt. treasury dept. Internal Revenue Service, Newark, 1942-72; tax accountant, N.Y.C., 1973-77. Bd. dirs. Hebrew Youth Acad., Newark. C.P.A., N.Y., N.J. Recipient Albert Gallatin award Sec. Treasury, 1972. Mem. Am. Inst. C.P.A.'s, N.Y., N.J. socs. C.P.A.'s, Internat. Platform Assn., Religious Zionists Am., Zionist Orgn. Am., Internat. Biog. Assn., Knights of Khorassan. Jewish religion (trustee, v.p. treas., lay cantor congregation). Mason (32 deg., Shriner), K.P. Address: Ramblewood East 4129 NW 88th Ave Coral Springs FL 33065

PARISI, WILLIAM EDWARD, hosp. adminstr.; b. Chicago Heights, Ill., Nov. 27, 1944; s. Patrick M. and Monica (Kidd) P.; B.A., U. Iowa, 1966, M.A., 1968; m. Sharon Ann Parisi, Aug. 19, 1967; 1 dau., Erin Nicole. Food service cons. Ruth Presbyn. St. Lukes Med. Center, Chgo., 1968, dir. housekeeping services, 1968-69, dir. rental properties, 1969-72, asst. adminstr., dir. rental properties, 1972-73, asst. adminstr. for patient support services, 1973-74; asso. health and med. div. Booz, Allen & Hamilton, Inc., Chgo., 1974-76; asso. exec. dir., adminstr. Methodist Hosps. of Dallas, 1976, exec. v.p., chief operating officer, 1976—. Bd. dirs. Am. Diabetes Assn. Recipient award Am. Legion. Mem. Am., Tex. hosp. assns., Am. Coll. Hosp. Adminstrs., Dallas Hosp. Council, Dallas Teaching Hosp. Council, Oak Cliff C. of C. (dir. 1977). Roman Catholic. Club: Rotary Internat. Office: PO Box 5999 Dallas TX 75222

PARK, HARRY RAY, mgmt. cons.; b. Columbus, Ga., Aug. 12, 1921; s. Harry Lee and Annie (Seay) P.; B.S. in Econs., Trinity U., 1953; M.A. in Econs., U. Calif. at Berkeley, 1956; postgrad. N.Y. U., 1960—; m. Juanita Martin, Feb. 10, 1943 (div. 1965); children—Harry Ray, Alton Lee; m. 2d, Jean M. Masterson, Mar. 2, 1965; children—Melissa Lorien, Steven Craig. Served to maj. USAF, 1940-57, ret.; air transport pilot USAF, 1942-48; dir. adminstrn., Frankfurt, Germany, 1948-49; staff dir. adminstrn., San Antonio, 1949-51, dir. personnel, 1951-53; asst. dir. operations and tng., Calif., 1953-55; staff dir. operations and tng., Iceland, 1956-57; asso. prof., asst. dept. chmn. aerospace sci. N.Y. U., N.Y.C., 1959-62; supr. tng. div. Job Orientation in Neighborhoods, N.Y.C., 1963-67; asso. dir. Mgmt. Center, Inst. for Bus. and Community Devel., also asst. prof. U. Richmond (Va.), 1967-73; mgr. human resources devel. Control Systems div. Robertshaw Controls Co., Richmond, 1973—. Lectr. mgmt. Hofstra U., L.I., N.Y., 1963-64. Mem. Am. Econ. Assn., Am. Personnel and Guidance Assn., Am. Mgmt. Assn., Am. Soc. Tng. and Devel., ACLU, Am. Humanist Assn., Orgn. Devel. Network, Internat. Registry Orgn. Devel. Profls., Mensa. Home: 7617 Marilea Rd Richmond VA 23225

PARK, LELAND MADISON, coll. librarian; b. Alexandria, La., Oct. 21, 1941; s. Arthur Harris and Jane Rebecca (Leland) P.; student McCallie Sch., 1957-59; A.B., Davidson Coll., 1963; M.L.S., Emory U., 1964; postgrad. Simmons Coll., 1968; Adv. M. in L.S., Fla. State U., 1973, Ph.D., 1974. Reference librarian Pub. Library of Charlotte and Mecklenburg County (N.C.), 1964-65; head of reference and student personnel Davidson (N.C.) Coll. Library, 1967-70, asst. dir., 1970-75, dir., 1975—; vis. lectr. Emory U., summer 1972; temporary instr. Fla. State U., 1973; library cons.; bd. dirs. Southeastern Library Network, 1978—; conf. speaker; chmn. adv. com. Library Services and Constrn. Act. Mem. Wake County (N.C.) Citizens for Better Libraries, 1965-67; sec. com. library affairs Piedmont U. Center, 1969-70, chmn., 1970-72; mem. nat. bd. consultants Nat. Endowment Humanities, 1976—. Served to capt. AUS, 1965-67. Recipient periodical award H.W. Wilson Library, 1979. Mem. Am., Southeastern (chmn. coll. and univ. sect. 1976-78, exec. bd. 1976-78), N.C. (2d v.p. 1975-77, chmn. membership com. 1975-77), Metrolina (pres. 1969-71), Mecklenburg County (treas. 1969-70) library assns., Soc. of Cin., S.A.R., Davidson Coll., McCallie Sch. alumni assns., Mil. Order World Wars, Raleigh Jaycees (chmn. library com. 1965-67), Res. Officers Assn., S.C.V., AAUP, Soc. Colonial Wars, S.C. Huguenot Soc., Beta Phi Mu, Sigma Nu (chpt. alumni comdr. 1967—), Omicron Delta Kappa. Democrat. Episcopalian (treas. 1975—). Editor, Southeastern Librarian, 1976-78; acad. sect. editor N.C. Libraries, 1972-77; contbr. articles to profl. jours. Home: 235 Ney Circle PO Box 2201 Davidson NC 28036

PARK, YONG KYUN, physician; b. Seoul, Korea, Dec. 25, 1943; s. Woo Pyung and Soon Hi (Chu) P.; B.D., Korea U., 1971; m. Miyoung Lee, Mar. 10, 1970; children—Changwon, Nicholas. Intern, Baylor Coll. Medicine, Houston, 1972; resident U. Tex. Med. Sch., Houston, 1972-75; practice medicine, specializing in ob-gyn, Plano, Tex., 1975—; mem. staff Plano Gen., Richardson Gen., Collin Meml. hosps. Diplomate Am. Bd. Ob-Gyn. Fellow Am. Coll. Ob-Gyn, Korean Natural Sci. Assn. Dallas (pres.), Collin County Med. Soc., AMA, Tex. Med. Assn., Plano C. of C. Club: Los Rios Country. Home: 1800 Lake Hill Plano TX 75023 Office: 3900 W 15 St Suite 505 Plano TX 75075

PARKENING, TERRY ARTHUR, anatomist; b. Omaha, Jan. 24, 1943; s. Arthur Albert and Kathryn Helena (Schultz) P.; B.S., Midland Coll., 1965; M.A., U. S.D., 1968; Ph.D., U. Oreg., 1974; m. Miriam Amrah Mosey, Nov. 24, 1965; 1 son, Aaron Amain. Postdoctoral fellow Worcester Found. for Exptl. Biology, Shrewsbury, Mass., 1974-76; asst. prof. anatomy U. Tex. Med. Br., Galveston, 1976-79, asso. prof., 1979—. NIH grantee, 1977—. Mem. Am. Assn. Anatomists, Soc. Study Reproduction, Soc. Exptl. Biology and Medicine, Gerontol. Soc., Am. Assn. Tissue Banks, Am. Aging Assn., Sigma Xi. Democrat. Lutheran. Office: Dept Anatomy U Tex Med Br Galveston TX 77550

PARKER, ALTON BROOKS, JR., pub. relations exec.; b. San Antonio, Sept. 30, 1930; s. Alton Brooks and Hazel Florence (Lyons) P.; B.A., U. South, 1957; postgrad., U. Tenn., 1960-61; m. Anne Smith, July 30, 1959; children—Carrie Malissa, Christopher, Alexander. Account exec. Ellis Shapiro Agy., San Antonio, 1955-56; research asst. U. of South, 1956-57; pub. relations supr. So. Bell Telephone Co., 1958-60; account exec. Robert H. Horsley Assos., 1960-63; dir. pub. relations, v.p. Buford Lewis Co., 1963-68; dir. Tenn. Health Careers Program and v.p. Tenn. Hosp. Assn., Nashville, 1968-72; dir. communications Vanderbilt U. Regional Med. Program, 1973; dir. communications State of Tenn. and press sec. to gov., 1974-78; pres. The Parker Group, mktg. communications consultants, Nashville, 1979—; commr. Tenn. Dept. Employment Security, 1978—. Bd. dirs. Tenn. Com. for the Humanities, 1976-78, Tenn. Commn. Status of Women, 1977-78, Tenn. Performing Arts Center, 1978—; mem. Nashville Bicentennial Commn. Served with USN, 1951-53. Mem. Pub. Relations Soc. Am. (accredited, past pres. Middle Tenn. chpt.). Home: Sycamore Terrace Farm Route 1 Box 85 Ashland City TN 37015 Office: 1514 B South St Nashville TN 37219

PARKER, ARCHIE DAVID, JR., state ofcl.; b. West Monroe, La., Aug. 23, 1929; s. Archie David and Ethel (Crowell) P.; B.A., Northeast La. U., 1956, M.A., 1969; student U. Ark., 1951-53; certificate social work La. State U., 1959, M.S.W., 1974; m. Gail Annette Hargrove, May 1, 1976; children by previous marriage—Daniel, Mark, Barbara. Probation officer, Monroe, La., 1959-62; dist. supr. probation Monroe dist. State of La., 1962-70, correctional instn. supt., Baker, La., 1970-75; asst. dir. for adult corrections La. Dept. Corrections, 1975-76, asst. sec. corrections, 1976—. Pres. Parker-Bergeron Distbg. Co., Monroe, 1963-66. Northeast La. U. dir. Students for Morrison, Barnham for Gov., 1955. Served to lt. col. AUS, 1945-48, 53-58. Recipient Northeast La. Alumni Assn. President's Service award, 1969; named Optimist of Yr., Greater Monroe chpt., 1970. Mem. Nat. Assn. Social Workers, Nat. Council on Crime and Delinquency, Nat. Assn. Correctional Supts., Am. Soc. Criminology, La. Assn. Criminal Justice Social Workers (dir. 1977), Northeast La. U. Alumni Assn. (1st v.p. 1967-68). Episcopalian. Mason (Shriner). Optimist (state bldg. chmn. 1972, pres. Tigertown chpt. 1973). Home: 9024 S Riveroaks Dr Baton Rouge LA 70815 Office: PO Box 44304 State Capitol Baton Rouge LA 70804

PARKER, CARL, state senator; b. Port Arthur, Tex., Aug. 6, 1934; B.A., U. Tex., 1955, LL.B., 1958; m. Beverly Steigler Parker; children—Valerie Lynn, Christian Ann, Carl Allen. Admitted to Tex. bar, 1958; partner firm Long & Parker, Doyle & Murphy, Port Arthur; mem. Tex. Ho. of Reps., 1963-77; mem. Tex. State Senate, 1977—; speaker pro tempore Tex. Ho. Reps., 1973. Served with USNR. Mem. Tex. Bar, Port Arthur C. of C., South Jefferson County Mental Health Soc., Sabine/Neches Conservation Club. Club: Lions. Home: 3549 6th St Port Arthur TX 77640 Office: One Plaza Sq Port Arthur TX 77640

PARKER, CARLOS DALE, allergist; b. Killeen, Tex., July 6, 1933; s. Carlos G. and Rose Ellen (Culp) P.; B.S., Baylor U., 1955; M.D., U. Tex. Med. Sch., 1960; m. Marilyn Burns, July 8, 1955; children—Susan Burns, Mary Jane. Intern, St. Joseph's Hosp., Ft. Worth, 1960-61; resident U. Hosp., Madison, Wis., 1961-64, Milwaukee County Hosp., Milw., practice medicine specializing in allergies, Austin, Tex., 1964—; mem. staffs Seton, St. David's hosps. (both Austin); cons., instr. Brackenridge Hosp.; dir. First Taylor Nat. Bank. Diplomate Am. Bd. Allergy and Immunology. Fellow Am. Acad. Allergy, Am. Assn. Certified Allergists, Am. Coll. Allergy; mem. ACP, S.W. Allergy Forum, Assn. Allergists for Mycological Investigation. Republican. Presbyterian. Office: 1301 W 38th St Suite 107 Austin TX 78705

PARKER, CHARLES SCOTT, oilwell servicing co. exec.; b. San Antonio, Aug. 27, 1935; s. Horatio Maxwell and Francis Page (Venable) P.; B.S. in Petroleum Engring., U. Tex., 1958; m. Barbara Joan Dresslar, Aug. 31, 1956; children—Jeffrey Scott, Gregory Maxwell. Area engr. Texaco, Inc., various locations, Tex., 1958-62; partner Poynor & Parker, Cons. Engrs., Liberty, Tex., 1962-65; v.p., gen. mgr. Bertman Well Service Co., Liberty, 1965-71; v.p. ops. Bertman Gas & Oil Corp., Goodale Bertman & Co., Inc., Liberty, 1969-71; partner, v.p., sec., treas. Adkins-Parker Well Service, Inc., Liberty, 1971-72; owner-pres. Parker Well Service, Inc., Liberty, 1973—; dir. First Liberty Nat. Bank. Sec. Liberty (Tex.) Zoning and Planning Commn., 1969-75, chmn., 1975-76; chmn. Liberty Bd. Equalization, 1971-72; mem. Liberty City Council, 1977—; bd. dirs. Lower Trinity Valley Assn., 1977—; mem. Tex. Gov.'s Trinity Basin Adv. Commn., 1977-79; mem. grievance com. dist. III-A, Tex. Bar Assn.; pres. Liberty County Indsl. Commn., 1979-80. Served to 1st lt. C.E., USA, 1959-60. Registered profl. engr., Tex. Mem. Liberty-Dayton Area C. of C. (charter pres. 1977-78), Liberty C. of C. (dir. 1969-77, sec. 1974-75, v.p. 1975-76 pres. 1976-77), Am. Inst. Petroleum Engrs., Gulf Coast Assn. Oilwell Servicing Contractors (chmn. 1968-69), Order Alamo. Methodist (bd. stewards 1969-72, 78—). Rotarian (dir. 1972, pres. 1974-75). Club: Magnolia Ridge Country (dir. 1962-75, pres. 1969-72) (Liberty). Home: 2415 Hollywood St Liberty TX 77575 Office: PO Box 407 Liberty TX 77575

PARKER, CLYDE H., fiberglass mfg. co. exec.; b. Phila., July 12, 1943; s. Clyde H. and Mary Josephine (Barefoot) P.; B.S., N.C. State U., 1971; m. Carole Perteet, Jan. 31, 1980; children by previous marriage—Kelly Jo, Christopher Keith. Supr. production N.C. Textiles & Chems. Co., Fuquay Varina, 1968-71; supr. Deering Milliken Co., Williamston, S.C., 1971-73; safety adminstr. Chicopee Mfg. Co., Gainesville, Ga., 1973-74, indsl. relations mgr., Athens, 1974-78; indsl. relations mgr. CertainTeed Corp., Athens, 1978—. Served with USN, 1962-64. Mem. Am. Soc. of Personnel adminstrn., Am. Mgmt. Assn., Am. Soc. of Safety Engrs. (registered profl. safety engr.), Athens Area Indsl. Mgmt. Group (past pres.), Am. Soc. Indsl. Security, Athens Area C. of C. (ex-officio bd. dirs.). Republican. Home: 240 University Circle Athens GA 30605 Office: PO Box 1967 Athens GA 30603

PARKER, DANIEL FRANKLIN, mfg. co. exec.; b. Ludowici, Ga., May 2, 1947; s. William H. and Carrie W. (Weathers) P.; B.S., U. Ga., 1969, M.S., 1971; m. Carol Roberts, Aug. 15, 1970; 1 dau., Claudia Weathers. Cashier, Citizens Nat. Bank, Montezuma, Ga., 1971-72; dir. personnel So. Frozen Foods, Inc., Montezuma, Ga., 1972-75; mgr. employee relations Aladdin Industries, Inc., Nashville, 1975-77; dir. employee relations Samsonite Corp., Murfreesboro, Tenn., 1977—. Mem. mayor's council for manpower planning, Nashville, 1977; chmn. Heart Fund, Montezuma, 1972-73; campaign chmn. Macon County for Gov. George Busbee, 1974. Recipient Meritorious Service award, Am. Heart Assn., 1972. Mem. Am. Soc. Personnel Adminstrn., Tenn. Indsl. Relations Soc. Baptist. Clubs: Lions (pres. 1973), Rotary. Home: 2048 Woodside Ct Murfreesboro TN 37130 Office: Samsonite Blvd Murfreesboro TN 37130

PARKER, FREDERICK MICHAEL, banker; b. Charleston, S.C., July 17, 1947; s. Simpson Martin and Susie (Sugg) P.; student U. S.C., 1965-70; grad. Sch. Banking of the South, 1976; m. Barbara Eilene Addy, July 24, 1976. With bank card center S.C. Nat. Bank, Columbia, 1968-70, ops. mgr., 1970-71, asst. cashier, 1972-74, asst. v.p., 1974-77, project leader check guarantee study and implementation group, mgr. honest face services, 1977—; instr. bank card course Am. Inst Banking, 1976. Mem. Data Processing Mgmt. Assn., Am. Inst. Banking. Lutheran. Home: 408 Beechwood Dr Columbia SC 29210 Office: PO Box 750 Columbia SC 29202

PARKER, GEORGE OTIS, architect, land planner; b. Savannah, Ga., Jan. 18, 1943; B.Arch., Auburn U., 1968; m. Froydis Heltveit, Oct. 15, 1965; children—Christopher, Ingrid, George. Architect-planner Ministry of Housing, Beersheva, Israel, 1964-65; architect Poole-Pardue-Morrison, Anniston, Ala., 1969-71; dir. city planning E. Ala. Regional Commn., Anniston, 1971-74; prin., owner George O. Parker, AIA, Architect-Planner, Anniston, 1974—. Bd. advisors Ala. Hist. Commn.; mem. Com. of Unified Leadership; bd. dirs. Ala. Shakespeare Festival State Theatre. Served with AUS, 1968-69. Yale-Towne & Eaton Urban Design award finalist; Ala. Hist. Commn. award of merit. Mem. Scarab, Am. Inst. Architects, Calhoun County Engring. Assn., Alpha Tau Omega. Presbyn. Clubs: Anniston Country; Rotary (dir.). Home: 715 Maplewood Ave Anniston AL 36201 Office: 900 Leighton Ave Anniston AL 36201

PARKER, GLORIA TERRY, med. center adminstr., educator; b. Bessemer, Ala., Oct. 23, 1921; d. Ellis Griffin and Lula Audrey (Craig) Terry; B.A. (Scholar), U. Ala., 1942, M.A. in Speech Pathology, 1949; postgrad. Feagin Sch. Drama, N.Y.C., 1943, Johns Hopkins U., 1970, Auburn U., 1973; m. Thomas F. Parker, Jan. 10, 1944; children—Thomas F., Jack Terry, Gloria Alleta. Speech therapist Chgo. Public Schs., 1945-46; instr. speech U. Ala., Montgomery, 1949-54; asso. prof. speech Huntingdon Coll., Montgomery, 1955—; asso. prof. spl. edn. Ala. State U., Montgomery, 1972—; supr. speech pathology services VA Med. Center, Montgomery, 1974—; instr. bio-communications Sch. Medicine, U. Ala., Birmingham, 1975—; alt. del. White House Conf. on Handicapped Individuals, 1977. Bd. dirs. Jr. League of Montgomery, 1959-62, March of Dimes, Montgomery, 1971-77; pres. Cloverdale Sch. PTA, Montgomery,

1967-68. Mem. Am. Speech, Lang. and Hearing Assn., Speech and Hearing Assn. Ala., Montgomery Assn. Speech and Hearing, Women in Communication, U. Ala. Alumni Assn. (v.p. 1956-57), Chi Omega, Zeta Phi Eta. Democrat. Baptist. Home: 2515 Hermitage Dr Montgomery AL 36111 Office: Huntingdon Coll Fairview Ave Montgomery AL 36105 also VA Med Center Perry Hill Rd Montgomery AL 36109

PARKER, HARRY S., III, museum dir.; b. St. Petersburg, Fla., Dec. 23, 1939; s. Harry S. and Catherine (Baillie) P.; B.A., Harvard, 1961; postgrad. U. Utrecht (Netherlands); M.A., N.Y. U., 1966; m. Ellen Margaret McCance, May 23, 1964; children—Elizabeth Day, Thomas Baillie, Samuel Ferguson, Catherine Allan. With Met. Mus. Art, N.Y.C., 1963-74, chmn. edn. dept., 1967-69, vice dir. edn., 1970-74; dir. Dallas Mus. Fine Arts, 1974—. Trustee Am. Fedn. Arts, N.Y.C., Greenhill Sch., Dallas, Corning (N.Y.) Mus., Museum Collaborative, N.Y.C. Fulbright fellow, 1961-62. Mem. Am. Assn. Museums (trustee, accreditation com.). Office: Dallas Mus Fine Arts Fair Park Dallas TX 75226

PARKER, HERBERT GERALD, state ofcl.; b. Fayetteville, Ark., May 13, 1929; s. Otis James and Anna Berthina P.; B.S., U. Nebr., Omaha, 1962; M.S., A&T State U., Greensboro, N.C., 1971; postgrad. Fla. State U., Tallahassee, 1977—; m. Florida Fisher, June 27, 1959; 1 dau., Christie Lynne. Commd. 2d. lt. U.S. Army, 1947, advanced through grades to col., 1969; served advisor mil. assistance advisory group Republic of China, Taiwan, 1962-65; prof. mil. sci. N.C. A&T State U., Greensboro, 1965-68; comdr. all U.S. Spl. Forces units the Delta, S. Vietnam, 1968-69; dir. non-resident instrn. U.S. Army Civil Affairs Sch., Ft. Gordon, Ga., 1969-71, commandant and dir., Ft. Bragg, N.C., 1971-74; prof. mil. sci., dept. head Fla. A&M U., Tallahassee, 1974-77; ret., 1977; exec. dir. Crimes Compensation Commn. State of Fla., 1978—. Bd. dirs. Opportunities Industrialization Centers, Leon County United Way, 1977—; mem. Nat. Urban League. Decorated Silver Star, Legion of Merit (2), Bronze Star (3), Purple Heart, Air Medal (3). Recipient distinguished service award Boy Scouts Am., 1969. Mem. Nat. Assn. Social Scientists, Res. Officers Assn., U.S. Army Civil Affairs Assn. (Disting. Service award, 1973), Assn. Parents and Teachers, Tallahassee C. of C., Phi Kappa Phi. Democrat. Methodist. Clubs: Jack and Jill of Am., Am. Bowling Congress (pres. Univ. Men's League), Fla. A&M Credit Union Bowling League (sec.), Bass Anglers Sportsman Soc., Winewood Men's Golf Assn. (v.p.), Toastmasters Internat. (pres., 1971-73), Nat. Geog. Soc. Co-author article in Internat. Jour. of Social and Behavioral Scientists. Home: 3510 Tullamore Ln Tallahassee FL 32308 Office: Fla Crimes Compensation Commn 2562 Executive Center Circle E Montgomery Bldg Suite 201 Tallahassee FL 32301

PARKER, ISRAEL FRANK, labor union ofcl.; b. Sylvania, Ga., Oct. 29, 1917; s. Cornelius Dean and Mary Eunice (Lewis) P.; student Ga. So. U., 1935-36, U. Ala., Birmingham, 1942-43, 49-50; m. Mary Alice, Dec. 26, 1938; 1 dau., Rebecca Gaye. Bus. mgr. United Bakery Workers Local 441, 1941-42; internat. rep. Retail, Wholesale and Dept. Store Union, 1942-52, regional dir., 1952-56, asst. So. area dir., Brimingham, 1957-70, So. area dir., 1970-76, internat. sec.-treas., 1976—. Mem. bd. appeals Ala. Unemployment Compensation, 1955—; chmn. Ala. Trade Union Council for Histadrut, 1970—; bd. mgrs. Birmingham Retirement and Relief System, 1970-73; bd. dirs. Internat. Found. Employee Benefit Plans; founder, trustee Ratail, Wholesale and Dept. Store Union-Industry Pension Fund and Health Ins. Fund. Served with USN, 1944-46. Decorated Letter of Commendation; named Man of Year, Birmingham Fraternal Order Police, 1972. Methodist. Club: Altadena Valley Golf and Country. Home: 745 Bentley Dr Birmingham AL 35213 Office: 101 W 31st St New York City NY 10001

PARKER, JAMES LEE FITZGERALD, sch. social worker; b. Frederick, Md., Jan. 25, 1949; s. Lee Thomas Fitzgerald and Kitty (Simpson) P.; B.A. in History, Va. Polytech. Inst., State U. Va., 1971, M.A. in Edn., 1975; m. Rita Elizabeth Cox, Aug. 5, 1972; children—George Michael Fitzgerald Christina Lee. Clk. computer div. GSA, Washington, 1967; with Va. Hwy. Dept., Farifax, 1969; salesman Hecht Co., 1969, Woodward & Lothrop Co., 1971-72 (both Fairfax); social studies tchr. Bath County Schs., Warm Springs, Va., 1972-74; vis. tchr., counselor, supr., adminstr. Galax (Va.) City Schs., 1975—. Pres. Carroll County Young Democrats, 1976—; dir. ch. choir. Served to 2d lt. F.A., U.S. Army, 1971; capt. Res. Mem. NEA, Va., Galax edn. assns., U.S. Res. Officers Assn., Va. Poly. Inst. Corps Cadets, Va. Poly. Inst., State U. Va. alumni assns. Democrat. Methodist. Home: Route 1 Box 217 Hillsville VA 24343 Office: Galax City Schs PO Box 855 Galax VA 24333

PARKER, JAMES MONROE, investment counselor; b. Alexandria, La., Dec. 5, 1945; s. James Roy and Mildred Eunice (Hamilton) P.; B.S. with honors, La. State U., 1967; M.B.A., Harvard U., 1970; children—Christine, Jennifer. Vice pres., portfolio mgr. Am. Gen. Capital Growth Fund, Am. Gen. Ins. Co., N.Y.C., 1970-73, Houston, 1973-74; v.p., office dir. Scudder, Stevens & Clark, Houston, 1976—; dir. Clean Cotton Corp. Mem. fin. com. San Jacinto council Girl Scouts U.S.A. Chartered fin. analyst, investment counselor. Mem. Inst. Chartered Fin. Analysts, Fin. Analysts Fedn., Houston Soc. Fin. Analysts (exec. com., pres.), Fin. Analysts Research Found., Pi Tau Pi, Beta Gamma Sigma, Phi Kappa Phi, Kappa Sigma. Democrat. Episcopalian. Clubs: Houston, Rotary, Greater Houston Toastmasters (adminstrv. v.p.), Harvard Bus. Sch. Home: 2300 Augusta St Houston TX 77057 Office: 1530 Bank of Southwest Bldg Houston TX 77002

PARKER, JIMMIE CHOATE, army officer, social worker; b. Alpine, Tex., Mar. 18, 1933; s. Frank and Effie (Choate) P.; B.A. in Govt., U. Tex., Austin, 1957, M.S. in Social Work, 1973; children—Judith Ann, John Franklin. Commd. 2d lt. U.S. Army, 1959, advanced through grades to maj., 1969, served platoon leader, exec. officer 1st Battle Group 13th Inf., 1st Inf. Div., Ft. Riley, Kans., 1959-61, transp. career officer course, Ft. Eustis, Va., 1962, platoon leader, hdqrs. comdt. 55th Aviation Maintenance Battalion, Korea, 1963, exec. officer Mobile Tng. Team, Colombia, 1964, co. comdr. 71st Aviation Co. Air Mobile, Ft. Amador, C.Z., 1965-66, exec. officer 56th Aviation Recovery and Maintenance Co., Vietnam, 1967-68, div. aviation officer 2d Armored Div., Ft. Hood, Tex., 1968-69; public welfare worker Austin (Tex.) State Hosp., 1970; adminstrv. technician Tex. Dept. Public Welfare Regional Office, Austin, 1971, program cons. services to aged blind and disabled, social services br., Austin, 1973-74; state program mgr. alt. care services to aged, blind and disabled Tex. Dept. Human Resources, Austin, 1975-80; v.p. Tex. Human Services Assos., Inc., Austin and Vidor, 1980—; pres. Parker and Wilson Human Services, Inc., Austin and Vidor, 1980—. Bd. dirs. Community Devel. Corp. Austin, 1971-73. Decorated Bronze Star, Air medal with 5 oak leaf clusters. Mem. Nat. Assn. Social Workers, Acad. Cert. Social Workers, Am. Public Welfare Assn. (nat. policy com. on long-term care 1978), Tex. Public Employees Assn. Unitarian. Clubs: Masons, Scottish Rite. Hon. pilot Colombian Air Force. Home: 1801 Ullrich Ave Austin TX 78756 Office: 132 N Main St Vidor TX 77662

PARKER, JOHN MALCOLM, utility co. exec.; b. Halifax, N.S., Can., June 13, 1920; s. Charles Fisher and Mabel (Hennigar) P.; came to U.S., 1936, naturalized, 1942; m. Irene Wilson Davis, Oct. 11, 1942; 1 dau., Bette Elane (Mrs. William E. Sewell). Accounting clk. Standard Oil Co. N.J., Charlotte, N.C., 1941; accounting supr. Duke Power Co., Charlotte, 1941-42; office mgr. So. Bell Tel. & Tel. Co., Charlotte, 1946-50, Atlanta, 1950-60, gen. internal auditor, 1960-68; gen. internal auditor South Central Bell Telephone Co., Birmingham, Ala., 1968—. Chmn. Empty Stocking Fund, Atlanta, 1952-54; bd. mgrs. Birmingham YMCA. Served with AUS, 1942-46. Mem. Nat. Assn. Accountants (pres. chpt. 1972-73, nat. dir. 1974-78), Am. Mgmt. Assn., Inst. Internal Auditors (pres. chpt. 1978-79, internat. v.p., 1977—), Internat. Platform Assn. Republican. Presbyterian (commr. gen. assembly Presbyn. Ch. of U.S. 1968, 76). Home: 3520 Belle Meade Lane Birmingham AL 35223 Office: 600 N 19th St Birmingham AL 35201

PARKER, JOSEPHUS DERWARD, limestone co. exec.; b. Elm City, N.C., Nov. 16, 1906; s. Josephus and Elizabeth (Edwards) P.; A.B., U. South, 1928; postgrad. Tulane U., 1928-29, U. N.C., 1929-30, Wake Forest Med. Coll., 1930-31; m. Mary Wright, Jan. 15, 1934 (dec. Dec. 1937); children—Mary Wright (Mrs. Mallory A. Pittman, Jr.), Josephus Derward; m. 2d, Helen Hodges Hackney, Jan. 24, 1940; children—Thomas Hackney, Alton Person, Derward Hodges, Sarah Helen (Mrs. Michael R. Smith). Founder, chmn. bd. J. D. Parker & Sons, Inc., Elm City, N.C., 1955—, Parker Tree Farms, Inc., 1956—; founder, pres. Invader, Inc., 1961-63; pres., dir. Brady Lumber Co., Inc., 1957-62; v.p., dir. Atlantic Limestone, Inc., Elm City, 1970—; owner, operator Parker Airport, Eagle Springs, N.C., 1940-62. Served to capt. USAAF, 1944-47. Episcopalian. Moose, Lion. Club: Wilson (N.C.) Country. Address: PO Box 905 Elm City NC 27822

PARKER, LYNNE CATHERINE, records adminstr.; b. New Orleans, July 13, 1947; d. Robert Lyon and Barbara Catherine (Martin) P.; B.A., La. State U., Baton Rouge, 1969, M.S., 1970. Librarian, Tulane U. Med. Sch., New Orleans, 1970-73; librarian med. records St. Charles Gen. Hosp., New Orleans, 1973-74; records adminstr. J. Ray McDermott & Co. Inc., New Orleans, 1974—. Mem. Assn. Records Mgrs. and Adminstrs. (v.p. Greater New Orleans chpt. 1977), Am. Mgmt. Assn., Nat. Micrographics Assn., Phi Mu. Episcopalian. Office: J Ray McDermott & Co Inc 1010 Common St New Orleans LA 70160

PARKER, MARGARET MEBANE (MRS. CARL P. PARKER), psychiat. social worker; b. Burlington, N.C.; d. Sidney Robert and Margaret (Murphy) Mebane; B.A., U. N.C., 1954, M.S.W., 1960; m. Carl Putnam Parker. Case work asst. Lee County Dept. Pub. Welfare, Sanford, N.C., 1954-56, Alamance County Dept. Pub. Welfare, Burlington, 1956-58; psychiat. social worker, social service VA Hosp., Salem, Va., 1960-64; social work unit coordinator, social service VA Hosp., Salisbury, N.C., 1964—. Field work instr. U. N.C. Sch. Social Work, 1965-70, Livingstone Coll., 1971-72, 76—, U. S.C., 1972-73. Mem. Nat. Assn. Social Workers, Acad. Certified Social Workers, D.A.R. Methodist. Home: 803 Wesley Dr Brentwood Acres Salisbury NC 28144

PARKER, MARY EVELYN DICKERSON (MRS. W. BRYANT PARKER), state ofcl.; b. Fullerton, La., Nov. 8, 1920; d. Racia E. and Addie (Graham) Dickerson; B.A., Northwestern State Coll., 1941; diploma of social welfare, La. State U., 1943; m. W. Bryant Parker, Oct. 31, 1954 (dec. May 1965); children—Mary Bryant, Ann Graham. Social worker, Allen Parish, La., 1941-42; personnel adminstr. War Dept., Camp Claiborne, La., 1943-47; editor Oakdale (La.) Jour., 1947-48; exec. dir. La. Dept. of Commerce and Industry, Baton Rouge, 1948-52; with Mut. of N.Y., Baton Rouge, 1952-56; chmn. State Bd. of Pub. Welfare, Baton Rouge, 1950-51; commr. La. Dept. of Pub. Welfare, Baton Rouge, 1956-63; commr. Div. of Adminstrn., State of La., Baton Rouge, 1964-67; state treas. State of La., Baton Rouge, 1968—. Chmn. White House Conf. on Children and Youth, 1960; pres. La. Conf. of Social Welfare, 1959-61. Nat. Democratic Committeewoman, 1948-52. Bd. dirs. Woman's Hosp., Baton Rouge. Baptist. Home: 9309 Hill Trace Ave Baton Rouge LA 70809 Office: PO Box 44154 Capitol Sta Baton Rouge LA 70804

PARKER, MOLLIE DERONE, counselor; b. Phillip, Miss., Jan. 9, 1930; d. Ed and Estella (Ringold) P.; B.S., Tuskegee Inst., 1949; M.Ed., U. Miss., 1970. Prin., Avent Elem. Sch., Minter City, Miss., 1949-50; tchr. Leflore County Tng. Sch., Itta Bena, Miss., 1950-52, Brooks High Sch., Drew, Miss., 1952-54; tchr., basketball coach T. Y. Fleming Sch., Minter City, 1954-70; counselor, student council advisor Leflore County High Sch., Itta Bena, 1970—. Sec. Greenwood Dist. Conf.; treas. Missionary Soc., Miss. Ann. Conf. Recipient Miss. Econ. Council awards for star tchr., 1967, 72. Mem. Leflore County Assn. Educators, Miss. Assn. Educators, NEA, Delta Personnel and Guidance Assn., Miss. Personnel and Guidance Assn., Am. Personnel and Guidance Assn. Clubs: Leflore High Courtesy, Order Eastern Star (worthy matron). Home: 1006 Broad St Greenwood MS 38930 Office: PO Box 564 Itta Bena MS 38941

PARKER, NATHANIEL BOWDITCH, biologist; b. Newport, R.I., Nov. 1, 1954; s. Jefferson David and Louisa Bowditch (Barbour) P.; B.A., Bowdoin Coll., 1977; M.S., George Washington U., Washington, 1980. Legal asst. Baker and McKenzie, Washington, 1977-78; environ. scientist Pollutant Evaluation sect., EPA, Washington, 1978; environ. systems scientist Metrek div. The MITRE Corp., McLean, Va., 1978—, also cons. use of pesticides. Mem. Union of Concerned Scientists, Internat. Oceanographic Found. Republican. Episcopalian. Home: 10710 Fred's Oak Ct Burke VA 22015 Office: Metrek div MITRE Corp 1820 Dolley Madison Blvd McLean VA 22102

PARKER, R. DENSON, loose leaf binder mfg. co. exec.; b. Birmingham, Ala., Aug. 8, 1944; s. Ralph Jerry and Robbie LaVerne (Wood) P.; B.S. indsl. Relations, U. Ala., 1967; m. Joyce Ann Seagraves, Sept. 3, 1966; children—Brian, Craig. With Vulcan Binder and Cover div. EBSCO Industries Inc., Birmingham, 1969—, purchasing mgr., 1972-73, adminstrv. asst., 1973-75, gen. mgr., 1975-77, v.p., 1977—; mem. advisory bd. Nunnelley State Tech. Coll. Served with U.S. Army, 1967-69. Mem. Binding Industries Am., Internat. Tape Assn., Nat. Office Products Assn., Birmingham C. of C. Mem. Ch. of Christ (deacon). Home: 4926 Windwood Circle Birmingham AL 35243 Office: Box 29 Vincent AL 35178

PARKER, ROBERT GORDON, equipment co. exec.; b. Scotland County, N.C., Aug. 9, 1941; s. Earl Gibson and Mable Evelyn (Gibson) P.; student Presbyn. Jr. Coll., 1960; A.S. in Bus. Adminstrn., King's Coll., Charlotte, N.C., 1962; m. Betty Jean Seals, Mar. 1, 1963; children—Gary Robert, Rodney Wayne. Ins. accountant Presbyn. Hosp., Charlotte, N.C., 1962; gen. sales mgr. Pate's Allis-Chalmers and Massey Ferguson, Laurel Hill, N.C., 1963-74; v.p., corp. dir., gen. mgr. Parker Equipment Co., John Deere dealer, Laurinburg, N.C., Lumber Bridge, N.C., 1974—. Recipient Distinctive Honor award State of N.C. Mem. Nat. Farm and Power Equipment Dealers Assn., John Deere Br. Council, Avco New Idea Key Dealer Council. Methodist. Club: Lions (sec. 1968-69). Office: PO Box 1569 1100 N 401 Bypass Laurinburg NC 28352

PARKER, ROBIN MERRILL, bus. services co. exec.; b. Chattanooga, June 1, 1938; s. Arthur Harry and Sarah Belle (Tittle) P.; B.S., Auburn U., 1960; m. Helen Kay Blackburn, Jan. 26, 1968; children—Sarah, Shirley. Project engr. Gt. Lakes Chem. Corp., El Dorado, Ark., 1969-72. Mich. Chem. Corp., El Dorado, 1972-74; v.p. Control Systems Engring. Co., Shreveport, La., 1974-75; project engr. LLLL Constrn. Co., Shreveport, 1975-77; pres. design/build constrn. Indsl. Consultants & Contractors, Inc., Alvin, Tex., 1977—; dir. J.A. Reece Co., Inc., Clarksville, Tenn. Registered profl. engr., Tex. Mem. Am. Inst. Chem. Engrs , Nat. Soc. Profl. Engrs. Republican. Mem. Ch. Christ. Home: League City TX 77573 Office: Alvin TX 77511

PARKER, RUTH MARSHALL, state ofcl.; b. Dallas, Feb. 11, 1931; d. Thomas Edward and Nell Annette (Norris) Marshall; B.A., So. Meth. U., 1963; M.S.W., Our Lady of Lake Coll., 1966; 1 son, Frank Edward. Field worker, supr., tng. specialist Tex. Dept. Public Welfare, 1957-68; dir. social service Travis State Sch., Tex. Dept. Mental Health and Mental Retardation, Austin, 1968-73, dir. state sch. admissions, 1973-77, dir. quality assurance Lufkin (Tex.) State Sch., 1977—. Mem. Acad Cert. Social Workers, Nat. Assn. Social Workers, Am. Assn. Mental Deficiency. Episcopalian. Club: Zonta. Address: PO Drawer 1648 Lufkin TX 75901

PARKER, SARAH LUCILLE, educator, artist; b. Sumrall, Miss., Mar. 31, 1911; d. William Grady and Myrtle (Wood) Parker; student (Scholar) U. So. Miss., 1931-32, B.F.A., 1966; M.A. (Scholar), U. Ala., 1968; postgrad. in painting Pietro Venucci Acad. Art, Perugia, Italy, 1972. Continuity writer Sta. WFOR, Hattiesburg, Miss., 1947-64; chmn. art dept. Judson Coll., Marion, Ala., 1964-74; prof., chmn. art dept. William Carey Coll., Hattiesburg, 1974—; art cons. Miss. Ednl. TV; art lectr. Miss., Ala.; chmn. art Ala. Consortium for Devel. of Higher Edn., 1971-74; 25 one-man art shows Miss., Ala., Ga.; designer posters, catalogs, book covers; illustrator Mississippi Cook Book, 1972. Mem. AAUW, Delta Kappa Gamma. Baptist. Club: Colonial Dames of 17th Century. Author: Mississippi Wildflowers, 1980. Home: 1508 Mamie St Hattiesburg MS 39401 Office: William Carey Coll Hattiesburg MS 39401

PARKER, STEVEN COUNCIL, ins. co. exec.; b. Jackson, Miss., Mar. 28, 1953; s. Harry and Grace Barton (Council) P.; student Eastfield Coll., 1972-74, So. Meth. U., 1978—. With Union Bankers Ins. Co., Dallas, 1974—, mgr. marketing services, 1975-78, dir. public relations and communications, 1978—. Mem. Internat. Assn. Bus. Communicators (dir.), Life Advertisers Assn., Dallas Advt. League, Ad/2, Public Relation Soc. Am., Dallas C. of C., Dallas Friday Group. Editor, Wings mag., 1979—. Office: 2551 Elm St Dallas TX 75226

PARKER, WALTER ENNIS, JR., architect; b. Emory, Ga., Mar. 17, 1942; s. Walter Ennis and Martha Rogers (Chapman) P.; B.Arch., Ga. Inst. Tech., 1965; M.B.A., Ga. State U., 1973; m. Ann McKee, Oct. 9, 1971; 1 son, Walter Ennis. With Heery & Heery, Architects & Engrs., Inc., Atlanta, 1967—, asst. to pres., 1973-76, exec. v.p., 1976-78, pres., 1978—. Chmn. architects/engrs. div. United Way Campaign, 1976; bd. dirs. Atlanta Community Design Center, 1979. Served with USNR, 1965-67; Vietnam. Registered architect, Ga., La.; cert. Nat. Council Archtl. Registration Bds. Mem. AIA (dir. Atlanta chpt. 1978-79), Profl Services Bus. Mgmt. Assn. (nat. dir. 1979—), Atlanta C. of C. Office: Heery & Heery Architects & Engrs Inc 880 W Peachtree St NW Atlanta GA 30309

PARKER, WILLIAM DALE, business exec.; b. Portsmouth, Va., Apr. 13, 1925; s. Otis Durie and Eva Estelle (Dempsey) P.; student Coll. William and Mary, 1946; grad. indsl. engr., Internat. Corr. Schs., 1956; student U. Del., 1959-60, Calif. Western U. 1961-62, U. Calif., 1964, Stetson U., 1969; D.Sc., Jame Balmes U., Saltillio, Mex., 1968; Ph.D. in Edn., Fla. Inst., 1970; D.D., Univ. of Life, 1971; m. Frances Ross Jennings, Feb. 2, 1946 (dec.); children—Frances Lea, Elizabeth Dale, Kim Carolyn Jane, Penny Jo Ann, Jacquelyn Susan; m. 2d, Boots Lee Farthing, 1968. Layout, process and prodn. engr. engr. Gen. Motors Corp., Wilmington, Del., 1949-59, asst. dir. salaried personnel pub. relations, 1959-61; mfg. engr., lectr. Gen. Dynamics/Astronautics, San Diego, 1961-64; dir. Internat. Inst. Human Relations, La Jolla, Calif., 1964—; aerospace scientist, mgmt. specialist Gemini and Expts. Program Office, NASA, Houston, 1964-67, Cape Kennedy, Fla., 1967-69; family and marriage counselor, Titusville, Fla., 1967-71; mgmt. cons., pres. Multiple Services, Inc., Titusville and Boone, N.C. 1969—; dir., v.p. in charge franchising Am. and Internat. Model Festivals, Spangler Television, N.Y.C., 1969-73; chmn. bd. Travel Internat., Inc., Titusville, 1971-74, N.W. N.C. Shopping City, Inc., Boone, 1978—; guest lectr. Appalachian State U., 1979—. Founder Monroe Park Civil Def. Orgn., 1951; mem. Wilmington council Boy Scouts Am., 1953-55; chmn. Varions Agy. Fund, 1954-60; co-chmn. Del. Dept. Civil Def. TV Shows, 1956-57; mem. Middle Atlantic States Conf. Correction, 1956-60; chmn., pres. Del., Md., Pa. Tri-State Hosp. Com., 1957-59; mem. Wilmington Inner-City Study Commn., 1957-60; chmn. Del. Civil Def. Evacuation Commn., 1958-59, Del. Hwy. Safety Campaign, 1959-60; active PTA; faculty adviser Mensa Coll. Mem. Democratic Exec. Com., 1975-77; polit. adv. Congress, Pres. U.S., 1974—; bd. dirs. Boys and Girls Aid Soc. San Diego, 1962-64; bd. advisers Salvation Army. Served with USCGR, World War II. Named Del. Outstanding Young Man of Year, U.S., Wilmington, jr. chambers commerce, 1957; recipient Silver award Del. Vol. Bur., 1957; ann. awards Va. Jr. Achievement Inc., 1959; speech award U.S. Jr. C. of C., 1960; Gemini award NASA, 1967; Internat. Distinguished Service to Humanity award 1969, Internat. Humanitarian award, 1971, Keys to City, Wilmington, Del., 1959, 61, 72, Titusville, Fla., 1970, Miami, 1973, named Hon. Sheriff of Portsmouth, Va., 1973. Mem. Am. Legion (life), Wilmington Indsl. Mgmt. Club, Mensa Internat. (life), Monroe Park Civic Assn. (pres. 1952-53), Nat. Space Inst. (charter, life), Vols. Speakers Bur. (San Diego), Coll. William and Mary Alumni Soc., S.A.R., Authors Guild, Authors League Am., VFW (life). Mason (32 deg.), Elk (life), Moose (life). Clubs: Royal Oak Golf and Country, Mexican Turf, S.Am. Turf (life); Hound Ears Golf, Ski and Country. Author: Philosophy of Genius; American Values, Solutions to Family and Marriage Problems, Gutless America, 1973. Columnist, Sentinal Newspapers, 1963-64, Campers Illustrated Mag., 1964-65, Star Adv., 1968, INSIGHT, 1969-72, Challenge, 1970—; hon. mem. editorial adv. bd. Am. Biog. Inst., 1975—. Patentee peanut dolls, copyrights to sports clubs, other medallions. Home: Deck Hill PO Box 246 Boone NC 28607 also 724 Jamestown Dr Winter Park FL 32792 Office: PO Box 246 Boone NC 28607 also PO Box 1441 Titusville FL 32780

PARKERSON, PHILLIP TAYLOR, historian; b. Eastman, Ga., July 23, 1946; s. Avery Felton and Anne Maxine (Taylor) P.; A.B. in Journalism, U. Ga., 1968, M.A., 1973; Ph.D., U. Fla., 1979; m. Maria Alicia Crespo Quintanilla, Sept. 22, 1970; children—Nicolas Mallory, Maria Alicia, John Phillip. Coordinator Latin Am. Colloquium, U. Fla., 1976-77, project historian Bolivian coca leaf study Nat. Inst. Drug Abuse, 1977-79; asst. prof. history Middle Ga. Coll., Cochran, 1979—; v.p. public relations The Aymara Found., Gainesville, Fla., 1977. Served with USN, 1968-70. Fulbright-Hays grantee, 1972-74. Mem. Sociedad Boliviana de Historia, Am. Hist. Assn., Latin Am. Studies Assn., Ga. Assn. Higher Edn. (exec. council 1980-81, rep.-at-large), Alpha Delta Sigma, Phi Alpha Theta, Lambda Chi Alpha. Roman Catholic. Home: 305 Palm Dr Eastman GA 31023 Office: Box 124 Middle Georgia Coll Cochran GA 31014

PARKMAN, JAMES N., JR., assn. exec.; b. Columbus, Ga., Dec. 14, 1931; stepson L.D. and Gertrude Hollingsworth; ed. Ga. State U., 1972; m. Hazel W. Wilkinson, June 26, 1976; children—James N. III, Matthew Dow. Partner Macon Venetian Blind Co. (Ga.), 1959-60; dir. indsl. relations Anaconda Aluminum Co., Atlanta, 1960-67; exec. v.p. Ga. Bus. Industry Assn., Atlanta, 1968—. Mem. Ga. Employment and Tng. Council; mem. adv. council Ga. Dept. Labor; vice chmn. So. Govs. Conf.; mem. Gov.'s Conf. on Career Devel.; mem. Ga. Metrication Com.; met. dir. Nat. Alliance of Businessmen; mem. Ga. Energy Conservation Adv. Council; dir. Navy Recruiting Council, Atlanta. Served with USNR, 1950-54. Certified assn. exec. Mem. Am. Soc. Assn. Execs., Ga. Soc. Assn. Execs., (pres.), Fontaine Owners Assn. (dir.), Am. Soc. Personnel Adminstrn., Cosma Indsl. Relations Com., Internat. Dietary Info. Found. (trustee). Club: Horseshoe Bend Country. Home: 400 Sassafras Rd Roswell GA 30076 Office: 181 Washington St SW Atlanta GA 30303

PARKS, BERNARD HARRISON, credit union ofcl.; b. Chesterfield, S.C., May 31, 1940; s. Lonnie Lee and Cora Mae (Lee) P.; student Southeastern Regional Credit Union Sch., 1971-74; A.S., Central Piedmont Community Coll., 1976. Enlisted U.S. Air Force, 1958, served as ground safety supr., air policeman, ret., 1967; asst. mgr. Thrift Loan Co., Greensboro, N.C., 1967-68; field rep. N.C. Credit Union League, Greensboro, 1968-71; mgr. J.M.L. Fed. Credit Union, Charlotte, N.C., 1971-75; asst. mgr. customer service, spl. projects adminstr. Data Processing of the South, Charlotte, 1976; gen. mgr., treas. Pope (AFB, N.C.) Fed. Credit Union, 1977—; mgr. ex-officio Carolina MAC Fed. Credit Union, 1972-74. Lic. real estate broker, N.C. Mem. Credit Union Exec. Soc. (pres. N.C. council 1978—), N.C. Credit Union League (bd. dirs. 1973-75, treas. 1974-75, v.p. Piedmont chpt. 1972-75), League Central Credit Union (chmn. supervisory com. 1971-73). Democrat. Baptist. Home: 411 Homestead Dr Fayetteville NC 28303 Office: Pope Fed Credit Union Pope Air Force Base NC 28308

PARKS, DAVID HALL, mfg. co. ofcl.; b. Talladega, Ala., Nov. 25, 1918; s. Lee Otis and Kate Moss (Freeze) P.; student Jacksonville State U., 1953-55; B.B.A., Auburn U., 1956; m. Minnie Lou Henley, May 31, 1941. Adminstrv. asst. Ala. Mil. Dept., Talladega, 1949-51; cost analyst Am. Cast Iron Pipe Co., Birmingham, Ala., 1956-63, systems analyst, 1963-67, mgr. systems and procedures, 1967—. Served with USAAF, 1940-46, U.S. Army, 1951-53, lt. col. ret. Recipient certificate of appreciation Goodwill Industries, 1964. Mem. Nat. Mgmt. Assn., Birmingham Mus. Art, Nat. Assn. Accountants, Ret. Officers Assn., Phi Kappa Phi. Democrat. Baptist. Clubs: Masons (32 deg.), Shriners. Home: 2220 Gay Way Birmingham AL 35216 Office: PO Box 2727 Birmingham AL 35202

PARKS, DAVID LEWIS, clergyman; b. Asheville, N.C., Dec. 23, 1926; s. June Leonidas and Leta Mae (Burroughs) P.; B.E.E., Ga. Inst. Tech., 1950; B.D., Columbia Theol. Sem., Decatur, Ga., 1954, M.Div., 1974; m. Anna Rue Osteen, May 30, 1954; children—David Lewis, James, Walter, Leta, Anna. Elec. engr. Oerlikon Corp., Swannanoa, N.C., 1953; ordained to ministry Presbyn. Ch. U.S., 1954; pastor chs. in Ga., Miss. and N.C., 1954-56, 67-74; overseas missionary in Korea, Bd. World Missions, Presbyn. Ch. U.S., 1956-67; prof. Bible, Montreat (N.C.)-Anderson Coll., 1974—; supply minister Lakey Gap Presbyn. Ch., Black Mountain, N.C., 1974—; trustee Montreat-Anderson Coll., 1971-73, Presbyn. Home for Children, Black Mountain, 1976—; chmn. commn. on the minister Asheville Presbytery, 1979; dir. Grace Fuel Co. Served with U.S. Army, 1943-46. Named Tchr. of Year, Montreat-Anderson Coll., 1975-77. Mem. Aircraft Owners and Pilots Assn., Eta Kappa Nu. Club: Lions. Home: Route 1 Box 86-E Black Mountain NC 28711 Office: Montreat-Anderson Coll Montreat NC 28757

PARKS, ELIZABETH ANN ROSE, acctg. services exec.; b. McKinney, Tex., Dec. 6, 1943; d. Byron Ray and Othelia Jane (Worley) Rose; B.F.A. with honors, So. Meth. U., 1979; 1 son, Mitchell Randolph. Intern, Case Advt., Dallas, 1978; office adminstr. Jim Jacobs Studio, Inc., Dallas, 1978-80; staff Walker/Fuld & Assos., Inc., Dallas, 1980—. Bd. dirs., treas., mem. planning and telephone coms. Merriman Park Estates Home Owners Assn., Inc., 1972—. Mem. LWV (unit league 1971-77). Home: 6939 Colfax Dr Dallas TX 75231 Office: The Quadrangle 2800 Routh St Suite 235 Dallas TX 75231

PARKS, JACKELEE ANTHONISE, bus. woman; b. Chgo., Oct. 16, 1935; d. Herbert Frank and Dorothy Irene (Lovgren) Anthonise; student U. Houston, 1954-55; m. James Marshall Parks, Jr., June 17, 1954 (div. 1958); 1 son, Joel David. Singer, dancer Joyce Rolland Dancers, 1958-59; exec. Pan Am. Ins. Co., Houston, 1958-60; ins. investigator Internat. Service Ins. Co., 1961; exec. sec. J. Ray McDermott Co., Houston, 1961-62; owner Parks Reporting, Houston, 1962—. Mem. Nat., Tex., Houston shorthand reporters assns., Ecumenical Soc. Psychorientology. Democrat. Methodist. Office: Astro Sta Box 20393 Houston TX 77030

PARKS, LARGENT, JR., exec. search and mgmt. cons.; b. Dallas, Nov. 29, 1934; s. Largent and Laura (Mayo) P.; B.B.A., So. Meth. U., 1957; student Inst. Ins. Mktg., 1969; m. Patsy Lavercombe, May 13, 1977; children—Dorothy Dee, Largent III. With various ins. cos., 1957-76; founder, owner, pres. Largent Parks & Partners, Inc., Dallas, 1976—. Mem. Soc. Exec. Recruiting Consultants (founder, pres.), Intertel, Mensa. Author syndicated column Fin. Fiction and Fact. Home: 13112 Copenhill Rd Dallas TX 75240 Office: 402 Carillon Tower E Dallas TX 75240

PARKS, LLOYD LEE, oil co. exec.; b. Kiefer, Okla., Dec. 9, 1929; s. Homer H. and Avis Pearl (Motes) P.; student Okla. State U., 1948-50, Tulsa U., 1951; A.M.P., Harvard Bus. Sch., 1965; m. Mary Ellen Scott, Aug. 20, 1948; children—Connie, Karyn, Becky. Accountant, Deep Rock Oil Co., Tulsa, 1951-54; sec., treas. Blackwell Oil & Gas Co., Tulsa, 1954-62; v.p. finance Amax Petroleum Corp., Houston, 1962-68, pres., 1969—, v.p. Amax Inc., Houston, 1975—; dir. Adobe Oil Co., Midland, Tex. Bd. dirs. Town & Country Bank, Houston. Served with U.S. Army, 1946-48. Republican. Clubs: Cherry Hills Country (Denver), Lakeside Country (Houston), Houston. Home: 11321 Greenvale Houston TX 77024 Office: 1300 West Belt PO Box 42806 Houston TX 77042

PARKS, PAUL FRANKLIN, univ. ofcl., agronomist; b. Opelika, Ala., Nov. 9, 1933; s. James W. and Annie R. (Edwards) P.; B.S., Auburn U., 1956, M.S., 1959; Ph.D., Tex. A&M U., 1962; m. Martha Gaynell Bailey, July 17, 1953; children—Paul, Angelia, Amy, Carrie. Research asst. Tex. A&M U., 1959-62, asst. prof., 1962-65; asso. prof. dept. animal and dairy scis. Auburn (Ala.) U., 1965-68, prof., 1974—, asst. dean Grad. Sch., 1968-72, dean Grad. Sch., 1972—. Pres., Lee County Council for Neglected and Dependent Children; bd. dirs. Presbyn. Community Ministry, Interagy. Day Care Center; bd. dirs., pres. Lee County Youth Devel. Center. NIH grantee, 1965-73. Mem. Am. Inst. Nutrition, Am. Assn. Univ. Adminstrs., AAAS, Sigma Xi, Alpha Zeta, Phi Kappa Phi, Gamma Delta Sigma. Home: 209 Bibb Ave Auburn AL 36830 Office: Grad Sch 211 Martin Hall Auburn Univ Auburn AL 36830

PARKS, WILLIAM EDWARD, telephone co. ofcl.; b. Butler, Ala., Oct. 3, 1946; s. Snethen Neil and Charlotte Elizabeth (Porter) P.; B.S., U. Ala., 1970; m. Gene Gayle Butts, Aug. 24, 1973; 1 dau., Anna Elizabeth. With South Central Bell, Co., Birmingham, Ala., 1972—, mgr. corp. hdqrs., 1974, staff specialist automotive ops., 1978—. Sunday Sch. tchr. First Methodist Ch., Birmingham. Served to 1st lt. U.S. Army, 1970-71; Korea. Cert. autosense operator. Mem. Bell System Assn. Motor Vehicle Suprs. Club: Goodfellows. Home: 337 Linda Ave Birmingham AL 35226 Office: 600 N 19th St Birmingham AL 35201

PARKS, WILLIAM HARRISON, JR., lumber and bldg. products co. exec.; b. Memphis, Apr. 11, 1948; s. William Harrison and Nora Kay (Tatum) P.; B.B.A., Memphis State U., 1972; m. Cynthia Leigh Rogers, May 28, 1967; children—Angela Dawn, William Brian, Amy Marie. Regional adminstr. Evans Products Co., Memphis, 1968-75; div. mgr. Slaughter Bros., Inc., Memphis, 1975-77, mgr. ops. SE region, Atlanta, 1977-80; v.p., chief operating officer Baldwin Lumber, Inc., Atlanta, 1980—; chmn. bd. Metro Mktg., Inc., Memphis, 1974-75. Mgr., coach Little League, Atlanta, 1978-79. Served with USMC, 1966-67. Named Jaycee of Yr., 1972. Mem. Am. Mgmt. Assn., Nat. Assn. Credit Mgmt. Republican. Methodist. Clubs: Ho-Ho Internat., PWMC Recreation Assn. Home: 3499 Meadowchase Dr Marietta GA 30062 Office: 5780 Peachtree Dunwoody Rd Atlanta GA 30342

PARL, EIKE LUDWIG, obstetrician and gynecologist; b. Chemnitz, Germany, Jan. 1, 1938; s. Helmuth and Annie (Kraatz) P.; came to U.S., 1966, naturalized, 1970; student medicine Free U. Berlin, 1959-62; M.D., U. Goettingen (Germany), 1964, Ph.D., 1966; m. Sieghilde Heinz, Aug. 28, 1962; children—Silke, Fenja, Haiko. Rotating intern Pa. Hosp., 1966-67, resident in obstetrics and gynecology, 1967-70; instr. gynecology Grad. Hosp. U. Pa., 1970-72; pvt. practice specializing in obstetrics and gynecology, infertility, Plantation, Fla., 1972—; speaker; police surgeon; mem. Sexual Assault Investigating Team of Broward County. Recipient certificate of recognition Broward County Sch. Bd., 1974, 75, Bennett Community Hosp., 1977. Fellow Am. Coll. Obstetrics and Gynecology; mem. AMA (Physicians Recognition award 1976), Am. Assn. Gynecol. Laparoscopists, Broward County Med. Assn., Pan Am. Med. Assn. Lutheran. Home: 241 Holly Ln Plantation FL 33317 Office: 4101 NW 4th St Plantation FL 33317

PARMER, WALTER RAY, hosp. adminstr.; b. Greenville, Ala., Dec. 6, 1937; s. James Franklin and Katye V. (Rhodes) P.; B.A., Vanderbilt U., 1960; m. Mary LeGrand Parks, July 7, 1962; children—Mary Kathryn, Walter. Exec. mgmt. trainee Ford Motor Co., Dearborn, Mich., 1962-64; area mgr. Profl. Mgmt., Southern Pines, N.C., 1967-70; dept. supr. Citizens and So. Nat. Bank, Savannah; pres. Parmer-Little & Assos., Inc., Savannah; chief exec. officer L. V. Stabler Meml. Hosp., Greenville, Ala., 1977—; sec.-treas. S.E. Ala. Emergency Med. Council, 1978—; mem. S.E. Ala. Health System Agy., 1977. Served with U.S. Army, 1960-67. Mem. Central Ala. Hosp. Council (sec.-treas. 1978—), Ala. Hosp. Assn. Episcopalian. Clubs: Greenville Country, Chatham (Savannah). Home: 857 Forest Dr Greenville AL 36037 Office: 424 Oak St Greenville AL 36037

PARNABY, GARY REDELLE, bank exec.; b. Jacksonville, Fla., Nov. 15, 1945; s. Frank Ernest and Doris (Darden) P.; B.A., Fla. State U., 1969; postgrad. U. N. Fla., Grad. Sch. Bank Investments U. Ill., 1979; m. Janice Creamer, June 14, 1969; children—Gary Redelle, Laura. Mgmt. trainee Atlantic Nat. Bank of Jacksonville, 1972, bond officer, 1973-74, asst. v.p., 1974-76; dir. bond portfolio mgmt. div. Fla. Nat. Banks of Fla., Jacksonville, 1976, v.p. div., funds mgmt., 1976—. Mem. ad hoc adv. com. Jacksonville Housing Authority, 1978—. Served with U.S. Army, 1969-72. Decorated Bronze Star medal. Mem. Am. Bankers Assn., Nat. Assn. Bus. Economists, Fla. Bankers Assn., Dealer Bank Assn., Fla. Bankers Investment Com. Republican. Baptist. Clubs: University, Jacksonville Racquetball, PGA Tournament Players. Home: 8315 Hidden Lake Dr S Jacksonville FL 32216 Office: Fla Nat Banks PO Box 689 Jacksonville FL 32201

PARNELL, DAVID RUSSELL, retail co. exec., legislator; b. Parkton, N.C., Nov. 16, 1925; s. John Quincy and Clelia (Britt) P.; B.S., Wake Forest U., 1949; m. Barbara Johnson, June 11, 1948; children—David Russell, Anne, Timothy. With J.Q. Parnell, Inc., Parkton, 1949—, mgr., exec. v.p., 1952-70, pres., 1970—; mgr. Parnell Oil Co., 1954—, pres., 1961—; dir. First Union Nat. Bank, St. Pauls, N.C., 1955—. Mem. Robeson County Indsl. Devel. Commn., 1964—, chmn., 1968; mem. N.C. State Hwy. Commn., 1969—, chmn. secondary roads com., 1969-73. Democratic precinct chmn., Parkton, 1964-70; mem. N.C. Ho. of Reps., 1974—; bd. dirs. N.C. Cancer Inst., Lumberton; trustee Meredith Coll., Raleigh, N.C., 1977—; mem. commn. trustees N.C. Ind. Colls. and Univs. Served with AUS, 1945-46. Baptist. (treas. 1950—, deacon 1951—, chmn. bd. deacons 1961-70). Club: Parkton Ruritan (pres. 1954). Home: PO Box 190 Parkton NC 28371 Office: Parkton NC 28371

PARNELL, KELLY PRESTON, educator; b. Carroll County, Va., June 24, 1943; s. Elmer Preston and Eulalia Florence (Easter) P.; student Berea Coll., 1961-62, Wytheville Community Coll., 1963-64; B.S. in Distributive Edn., Va. Poly. Inst. and State U., 1967, M.S. in Edn., 1977; m. Sandra Joyner Dalton, June 17, 1967; children—Patrick Kelly, Timothy Heath, Jamie Preston. With Leggett Co., Christiansburg, Va., 1965-67; coordinator distributive edn. Kempsville High Sch., Virginia Beach, Va., 1967-74; supervising coordinator distributive edn. E.C. Glass High Sch., Lynchburg, Va., 1974—; part-time asso. prof. bus. div. Central Va. Community Coll. Served with USMCR, 1961-67. Named Tchr. of Yr., Kempsville High Sch. Tri-Hi-Y, 1970; elected to Nat. and Va. Distributive Edn. Halls of Fame. Mem. NEA, Va. Edn. Assn., Lynchburg Edn. Assn., Am. Vocat. Assn., Va. Vocat. Assn., Nat. Assn. Distributive Edn. Tchrs., Va. Assn. Distributive Edn. Tchrs., Distributive Edn. Clubs Am. (trustee Va. orgn.). Baptist. Club: Lions (dir.). Office: E C Glass High Sch 2111 Memorial Ave Lynchburg VA 24501

PARNELL, SARA MAE, med. asst.; b. Peachland, N.C., May 20, 1938; d. Marshall and Evelyn Frances (Campbell) Carpenter; student pub. schs., N.C.; student med. lab. and x-ray dept., Richmond County Hosp., Rockingham, N.C., 1956-57; grad. Am. Booksellers Sch., 1970; m. Billy Parnell, Sept. 1, 1957; children—William Michael, Sara Kimberly, Stacey Marshall, Mark Leonard. Lab. asst., x-ray asst. Richmond County Hosp., 1956-57; with ARC, Green Cove, Springs, Fla., 1957-59; doctor's asst., New Orleans, 1961-69; mgr. Bayou Books, Gretna, La., 1968-76; lab. supr., med. asst. Dr. George Pettit, Gretna, 1976—; book reviewer, 1975—. Mem. Am. Assn. Med. Assts., Am. Booksellers Assn. Democrat. Baptist. Home: 2634 Behrman Way New Orleans LA 70114

PARRAMORE, DEBORAH JEANNE, aquatics dir.; b. Quincy, Fla., Sept. 6, 1945; d. Alton E. and Frances Leone (Quinn) P.; A.A., Chipola Jr. Coll., 1967; B.S., Fla. State U., 1969, M.S., 1973. Coach, Wilson (N.C.) Swim Club, summers, 1964-70; temporary instr., head coach women's swim team Fla. State U., Tallahassee, 1971-72; dir. aquatics, instr. phys. edn. and recreation Columbia (S.C.) Coll., 1972-79; dir. aquatics Trenholm Park Pool, Columbia, 1979—; faculty mem. Nat. Red Cross Aquatic Sch., 1975, 77, 79. Water safety instr., trainer Carolina's div. ARC, 1975—; 1st chmn. SCAIAW swimming, 1975-77. Mem. Nat. Inst. for Creative Aquatics (dir. S.E. Technique seminar 1977-78), AAHPER, Am. Swim Coaches Assn., Nat. Assn. Girls' and Women's Sports. Clubs: Tarpon, Posideon (coach 1972-79). Address: Route 2 Box 61D Ridgeway SC 29130

PARRAMORE, JOSEPH VERNON, JR., state ofcl.; b. Tallahassee, May 1, 1947; s. Joseph Vernon and Jamie Kathleen (Cottingham) P.; B.S. in Mgmt., Fla. State U., 1973; m. Patricia Gayle Tankersley, June 14, 1969; 1 son, Joseph Michael. File clk. Fin. Responsibility Bur., Fla. Dept Hwy. Safety, Tallahassee, 1966-68; warehouseman, receiving clk., salesman Southeastern Surg. Supply Co., Tallahassee, 1968-70; student asst. dept. sci. edn. Fla. State U., 1972-73; tax examiner Intangible Tax Bur., Fla. Dept. Revenue, Tallahassee, 1973-78, budget analyst, div. ad valorem tax, 1978—. Served with USMC, 1970-71; Vietnam. Mem. Tallahassee Jaycees. Democrat. Baptist. Club: Order of DeMolay. Home: 2811 Nepal Dr Tallahassee FL 32303

PARRISH, BUFORD BRIAN, anesthesiologist; b. Houston, Aug. 26, 1946; s. Buford and Marjorie Mae (Culpepper) P.; B.A., Baylor U., 1968; M.D. (Jesse H. Jones scholar, Schlumberger scholar), U. Tex. Med. Br. at Galveston, 1972. Intern, U. Tex. Med. Br. Hosp. at Galveston, 1972-73, resident in anesthesiology, 1973-75; anesthesiologist John Sealy Hosp., Galveston, 1973-75, also lectr. respiratory subjects for nurses and anesthesiologists; anesthesiologist Scott AFB, Ill., 1975-77, Park Plaza Hosp., Houston, 1977—. Fellow Am. Coll. Anesthesiologists; mem. Am., So., Tex. med. assns., Am., Tex. socs. anesthesiologists, Alpha Chi. Baptist. Contbg. author: Communications in Anesthesiology, Vol. 7. Home: 5353 Institute Ln #38 Houston TX 77005 Office: Park Plaza Hosp Suite 270 Houston TX 77004

PARRISH, CLIFFORD MARION, structural and civil engr.; b. Bellview, N.Mex., June 21, 1919; s. Bonnie and Sallie Wade (Shore) P.; B.S., Tex. Tech Coll., 1941; M.S., U. Ill., 1948; m. Patricia Ann Pollock, Feb. 7, 1945; children—Robert C., Patrick W., Michael K. San. engr. Tex. Health Dept., 1941; civil engr. Corps of Engrs., 1941-43; instr. Tex. Tech Coll., 1949-52; pvt. practice structural and civil engring., 1952-61; asso. prof. civil engring. Tex. Tech U., Lubbock, 1961—; cons. structural engr.; works include: tornado proof bldg. for AEC, Fed. office and court house, Porter Exchange Tower for S.W. Bell Telephone Co., equipment and office tower for S.W. Bell Telephone Co., Univ. Center Theatre, Univ. Center Recital Hall, Home Econs. Classroom Tower. Served with San. Corps, AUS, 1943-45. Registered profl. engr., Tex. Mem. Tex. Soc. Profl. Engrs., Tau Beta Pi. Republican. Home: 2713 54th St Lubbock TX 79413 Office: Dept of Civil Engineering Texas Tech University Lubbock TX 79409

PARRISH, EDWARD, lawyer; b. Adel, Ga., Nov. 21, 1911; s. C.E. and Nona (Rountree) P.; grad. Young Harris (Ga.) Coll., 1930; m. Jeannette Crane. Admitted to Ga. bar, 1931, since practiced in Adel; county atty. Cook County, Ga., 1938-42; city atty. City of Adel, Ga., 1940-42, 46—, also city atty. Sparks, Ga.; solicitor-gen. Alapaha Jud. Circuit, 1949—. Dir. Cook-Berrien Service Corp., Cook County Fed. Savs. & Loan Assn., Adel. Served with AUS, 1942-45. Mem. Am. Legion, V.F.W., Woodmen of the World. Lion. Home: 201 E 8th St Adel GA 31620 Office: Sowega Bldg and County Ct House Adel GA 31620

PARRISH, HENRY HOWARD, JR., elec. engr.; b. Gainesville, Fla., Feb. 6, 1944; s. Henry Howard Parrish and Margaret (Adkins) Parrish Blodgett; student U. Fla., 1961-62, 66-67. With Racal-Milgo Electronics, Inc., Miami, Fla., 1968—, design specialist, 1977—. Served with USN, 1962-66. Mem. IEEE (asso.). Home: 600 Westward Dr Miami Springs FL 33166 Office: 8600 NW 41st St Miami FL 33166

PARRISH, HENRY MACK, physician; b. Ocala, Fla., June 21, 1927; s. Joseph Gid and Winnifred (Hunt) P.; B.S., Wake Forest U., 1949; M.D., U. Pa., 1953; M.P.H., Yale U., 1956, Dr.P.H. (Am. Cancer Soc. fellow), 1959; m. Carole Anne Carr, Dec. 21, 1957; children—Cynthia Marie, Catherine Anne, Cheryl Lynne. Asst. in biology and psychology Wake Forest U., 1948-49; intern Pa. Hosp., Phila., 1953-54; asst. resident obstetrics N.C. Baptist Hosp., Winston-Salem, 1954-55; asst. instr. obstetrics Bowman Gray Sch. Medicine, 1954-55; fellow in pub. health Yale U., 1955-56, asst. physician U. Health Dept., 1955-57, fellow in epidemiology, 1956-57; research fellow epidemiology U. Pitts., 1957-58; asst. prof. preventive medicine U. Vt., 1958-59; epidemiology cons. Vt. Health Dept., 1958-59; dir. med. edn. Marion County Gen. Hosp., Indpls., 1959-61; instr. pub. health Ind. U., 1959-61; pvt. practice medicine, Ocala, 1961-62, 73—; asso. prof. community health U. Mo., 1962-64, prof., 1965-69, chmn. community health Sch. Medicine, 1965-67, asso. prof. vet. microbiology and pub. health Sch. Vet. Medicine, 1964-69, dir. grad. studies in pub. health, 1963-69; cons. in chronic disease Div. Health of Mo., 1962-67; asso. dean, prof. community medicine U. S.D., 1969-71, v.p. for health affairs, 1971-73; acting dir. S.D. Regional Med. Program, 1971. Served with USNR, 1945-47. Research fellow in epidemiology U. Pitts., 1958. Diplomate Am. Bd. Preventive Medicine. Fellow ACP, Am. Pub. Health Assn., Am. Coll. Preventive Medicine; mem. Am., Fla., So. med. assns., Contbr. articles to med. jours. Home: 1909 SE 13th St Ocala FL 32670 Office: 111 SW 8th St Ocala FL 32670

PARRISH, JOHN ASTOR, JR., environ. co. exec.; b. Henderson, N.C., Oct. 16, 1948; s. John Astor and Mae Gillian (Denton) P.; A.A.S., Southwood Coll., 1968, Wake Tech. Inst., 1971; m. Jackie Dorsey, June 27, 1971. Engring. tech. N.C. Air Quality Div., Raleigh, 1971-72; mgr. air guard div. So. Testing and Research Labs., Inc., Wilson, N.C., 1972-74; mktg. mgr. Entropy Environmentalists Inc., Research Triangle Park, N.C. Mem. Carolinas Air Pollution Control Assn. (sec.), TAPPI, Air Pollution Control Assn. Democrat. Baptist. Clubs: Raleigh Jaycees (sec. 1977, v.p. 1978). Home: 1623 Beechwood Dr Raleigh NC 27609 Office: PO Box 12291 Research Triangle Park NC 27709

PARRISH, PRESTON ROYD, accountant; b. Charleston, S.C., May 21, 1943; s. James Thomas and Mamie LaTrelle (Carter) P.; B.B.A. magna cum laude, Armstrong State Coll., 1971; m. Ruth Earldine Hand, June 5, 1966; children—Schaunell Earldine, Preston Royd. With Union Camp Corp., various locations, 1961—, asst. to plant acct., Montgomery, Ala., 1974-76, plant acct., Savannah, Ga., 1976—; instr. Armstrong State Coll. Served with Air NG, 1961-67. Mem. Nat. Assn. Accts., Am. Mgmt. Assn. Mem. Ch. of God. Home: 721 Leaning Oaks Dr Savannah GA 31410 Office: PO Box 8 Savannah GA 31404

PARRISH, ROBERT VERNON, real estate broker; b. Jackson, Tenn., Apr. 7, 1934; s. Robert Edwin and Tommie Lucille (Pearson) P.; student Union U., 1952-54; B.S., Belmont Coll., 1956; m. Dorothy Greene, Sept. 10, 1954; children—Robert Lee, Jennifer Annette, Toby Greene. Mgmt. trainee So. Bell Telephone and Telegraph Co., Nashville, 1956-58, office mgr., 1958-59, mgr., 1959-62; v.p. ops. Guaranty Bond & Securities Corp., Nashville, 1962-70; pvt. practice fin. cons. colls. and hosps., Nashville, 1971-73; affiliate broker Mid-South Realty Co., div. First and Mid-South Cos., Nashville,

1973—; instr. in real estate Belmont Coll., Nashville, 1975, 76. Deacon, Sunday Sch. tchr., mem. personnel, building plans, building fin. coms. Brentwood (Tenn.) Bapt. Ch. Served with USAR, 1957-63. Named to Million Dollar Sales Club, 1975, 76, 77, 78, 79. Mem. Nashville Bd. Realtors (legis. com.), Tenn. Bd. Realtors. Republican. Club: Optimist of Nashville-Downtown (pres. 1962-63). Home: 6017 Foxland Dr Brentwood TN 37027 Office: 315 Union St Nashville TN 37219

PARROTT, BARBARA MARIE, geophysicist; b. Astoria, Oreg., June 6, 1940; d. John B. and Vera Louise (Johnston) P.; B.A., U. Baylor U., 1962. With Shell Oil Co., 1962-79, sr. geophys. asst., Midland, Tex., 1973-74, geophysicist, party chief, Houston, 1974-77, geophysicist, 1977-78, sr. geophysicist, 1978-79; geophysicist, mktg. rep. Seismic Reflections, Inc., Houston, 1979—. Mem. Soc. Exploration Geophysicist, Houston Geophys. Soc. Republican. Baptist. Office: 3303 Louisiana Suite 211A PO Box 66963 Houston TX 77006

PARROTT, LAWRENCE HUITT, pathologist; b. N.Y.C., Nov. 9, 1935; s. Warley Lawrence and Helen (Huitt) P.; B.S., Davidson Coll., 1956; M.D., Duke U., 1960; m. E. Joy Buffaloe, Dec. 19, 1959; children—David, Stephen, Holly, Amy. Intern, Vanderbilt U. Hosp., Nashville, 1960-61; resident in pathology U. Miami (Fla.) Hosp., 1963-67; asso. pathologist Presbyterian Hosp., Charlotte, N.C., 1967-73; pathologist Kershaw County Meml. Hosp., Camden, S.C., 1973—; faculty pathology Med. U. S.C., 1976—. Coach, YMCA Swimming Team, Camden, 1973—. Served to capt. USAF, 1961-63. Mem. AMA, S.C. Med. Assn., S.C. and N.C. Soc. Pathologists, Coll. Am. Pathologists, Am. Soc. Clin. Pathologists, Phi Beta Kappa. Presbyterian. Clubs: Camden Country, Rotary, Wateree Sailing. Home: 412 Bruce Dr Camden SC 29020 Office: Kershaw County Meml Hosp Camden SC 29020

PARSLEY, BRANTLEY HAMILTON, librarian; b. Balt., Oct. 15, 1927; s. Clarence Elroy and Florence Sally (Barnes) P.; A.A., Balt. Jr. Coll., 1950; B.A., U. Md., 1952; B.D., New Orleans Bapt. Theol. Sem., 1955, M.R.E., 1958; M.Librarianship, Emory U., 1965; m. Loyce Marie Franklin, Apr. 18, 1951; children—Linda Marie, Brantley Hamilton. Ordained to ministry Baptist Ch., 1956; pastor Calvary Bapt. Ch., Albany, Oreg., 1955-57; library asst. New Orleans Pub. Library, 1958-61; supt. night circulation and stacks Theology Library, Emory U., 1961-65; dir. library Campbellsville (Ky.) Coll., 1965—; dir. Genealogy Workshop. Bd. dirs. Taylor County Community Concerts; pres. Central Ky. Arts Series, 1975-78; dir. Sch. Merger Workshop, 1976. Recipient Sch. award Am. Legion, 1947. Mem. Am., Southeastern, Ky. (chmn. coll. and research sect. 1970-71, sec. treas. edn. sect. 1972-73) library assns., Council Ind. Ky. Colls. (chmn. 1970-75), Taylor County Hist. Soc. (dir. 1970), Taylor County Bapt. Assn. (dir. 1968-70), Taylor County Bapt. Sunday Sch. Assn. (supt. 1968-70). Dir. radio broadcast series: Ky. Authors, 1976; Study of Black Lit., 1978. Home: 114 Longview Dr Campbellsville KY 42718

PARSONS, DAVID HAROLD, translator; b. Burlington, Vt., Nov. 10, 1940; s. Stanton A. and Dorothy C. (Thomas) P.; B.A. in Physics, U. Vt., 1965, M.S., 1967; postgrad. U. N.H., 1967-69; children—Arthur, Susan. Prin., Dave Parsons & Assos., translators, Gainesville, Fla., 1969—. Served with AUS, 1960-63. Mem. Am. Phys. Soc., AAAS. Club: Fla. Track. Translator: Stellarators, 1975; Microwave-Plasma Interactions, 1975; Neutral Sheets in Plasmas, 1976; Soviet Jour. Plasma Physics, 1976—, Soviet Tech. Physics Letters, 1976—, Soviet Physics-Tech. Physics, 1976—; Review of Plasma Physics, Vol. 8, 1977; Methods of Digital Holography. Home: 4240 NW 69th St Gainesville FL 32601 Office: 4040 Newberry Rd Gainesville FL 32607

PARSONS, FLOYD W., assn. exec.; b. Andice, Tex., Oct. 16, 1909; s. William Culberson and Ida A. (Davis) P.; B.A., U. Tex., 1935, M.A., 1945; m. Christina Fowler, Dec. 25, 1932; children—Lou Anne (Mrs. William Raymond Smoot), Floyd W., Paul. High sch. prin., tchr., coach Johnson City (Tex.) Pub. Schs., 1932-33; elementary prin., tchr. Orangedale (Tex.) Common Sch. Dist., 1933-36; supt. schs., Calallen, Tex., 1936-46, Bishop, Tex., 1946-52, Beeville, Tex., 1952-56, Big Spring, Tex., 1956-61, Little Rock Sch. Dist., 1961-72; exec. sec. Assn. Advancement of Internat. Edn., 1973—. Instr. dept. sociology U. Tex., summer 1945; instr. Hardin-Simmons U., summer 1959; participant Columbia Workshop, summer 1958. Trustee Ark. State Tchrs. Retirement System; bd. dirs. Salvation Army, YMCA, United Fund, Pulaski County Assn. Mental Health, Boy Scouts Am. Mem. N.E.A. (life), Tex. Tchrs. Assn. (life), Tex. (life), Ark. (life) congresses parents and tchrs., Ark. Edn. Assn., Econ. Edn. Bd., Am. Assn. Sch. Adminstrs. (pres. 1972-73, exec. com.), Council Ednl. Facility Planners, Horace Mann League U.S. (dir.), C. of C. (bd.), Phi Delta Kappa, Alpha Kappa Delta. Kiwanian (past pres. Little Rock). Home and Office: 31 Nob View Circle Little Rock AR 72205

PARSONS, FRANK RAYMOND, JR., hosp. adminstr.; b. Salisbury, Md., Jan. 25, 1928; s. Frank Raymond and Ruth (Hearne) P.; B.S., U. Md., 1950; M.B.A., George Washington U., 1966; m. Barbara Hughes, June 9, 1951; children—David, Diane, Mary, Nancy. Commd. officer USAF, advanced through grades to col.; assigned Hdqrs. USAF, Washington, 1966-71, Pacific Air Forces, 1971-73, ret., 1973; asst. adminstr. Gen. Hosp., Charleston, W.Va., 1973-75, adminstr., 1975—. Bd. dirs. Am. Cancer Soc., Kanawha County, 1977—; mem. exec. com. Buckskin council Boy Scouts Am., Charleston, 1977—. Mem. W.Va. Hosp. Assn., Am. Hosp. Assn., Am. Coll. Hosp. Adminstrs., W.Va. Health Systems Agy. Methodist. Club: Optimist (v.p. 1975-76, pres. 1976-77, lt. gov. Ky-W.Va. dist. 1977-78). Home: 1418 Mount Vernon Rd Charleston WV 25314 Office: PO Box 1393 Charleston WV 25325

PARSONS, JANET ELIZABETH, ednl. cons.; b. Utica, N.Y., July 9, 1940; d. Addison Kimberly and Mary Alice (Shearer) P.; B.A., SUNY, 1968; M.S., Canisius Coll., 1976. Tchr. pvt. schs., Wis., Ill., 1961-64; guidance counselor Nardin Acad., Buffalo, 1976; owner J. Parsons Ednl. Cons., Stuart, Fla., 1978—. Cert. tchr., guidance counselor, Fla., N.Y.; cert. tchr. sch. psychology, Fla. Mem. Am. Personnel and Guidance Assn., Fla. Reading Assn., Internat. Reading Assn., Am. Horse Shows Assn. Roman Catholic. Home and office: 75 Maple Ridge Ln Asheville NC 28806

PARSONS, JOE MAX, educator; b. nr. Lexington, Tenn., June 20, 1915; s. Cleff and Myrtle (White) P.; student U. Tenn. Jr. Coll., 1935-36, Union U., 1937-39, Syracuse U., 1942-44; B.S., George Peabody Coll. for Tchrs., 1947, M.A., 1948; m. Elizabeth Davis, Mar. 22, 1947. Tchr., sch. prin. Henderson County (Tenn.) pub. schs., 1936-42; instr. math. George Peabody Coll. for Tchrs., 1948, U. Tenn., 1948-52; chief instr. Tenn. Radio Service Sch., Knoxville, 1951-52; dean, head dept. math. Asheville-Biltmore Coll., 1952-63, dean of students, head dept. math., 1963-68, dean men, 1967-69; dean men, asso. prof. U. N.C., Asheville, 1969—, head dept. math., 1976—. Bd. dirs. Humane Soc., Asheville, Buncombe County (N.C.) Dept. Pub. Welfare. Served to sgt. AUS, 1942-46. Mem. N.C. Coll. Conf., N.C. Edn. Assn. (v.p. div. higher edn. 1959—), Kappa Phi Kappa, Phi Delta Kappa. Democrat. Baptist. Clubs: School Masters of Western N.C. (pres. 1962), Asheville Executives, Asheville City, Lions (pres. 1976-77). Home: 110 Stuyvesant Rd Asheville NC 28803

PARSONS, NOLAN CHARLES, JR., dermatologist; b. Parkersburg, W.Va., Nov. 19, 1945; s. Nolan Charles and Lorena Mae (Kelly) P.; B.A. cum laude, W.Va. U., 1967, M.D., 1971; m. Brenda Mae Board, June 8, 1968; 1 dau., Sarah Paige. Intern, W.Va. U. Hosp., Morgantown, 1971-72; resident in dermatology W.Va. U. Med. Center, Morgantown, 1972-75; practice medicine specializing in dermatology, Charleston, W.Va., 1977—; mem. staff Charleston Area Med. Center, St. Francis Hosp., Charleston; asst. prof. medicine W.Va. U., Morgantown, 1977—. Served with USAR, 1975-77. Mem. So. Med. Assn., Am. Acad. Dermatology, W.Va. Dermatol. Assn., Phi Beta Kappa, Alpha Omega Alpha. Home: 2306 S Walnut Dr St Albans WV 25177 Office: 1200 Quarrier St Charleston WV 25301

PARSONS, TARLTON FLEMING, II, mgmt. cons. co. exec.; b. Independence, Mo., Dec. 5, 1927; s. Tarlton Fleming and Elinor (Flournoy) P.; B.S., U.S. Mil. Acad., 1950; M.B.A. with highest distinction, Babson Coll., 1965; Hon. D.Sc., London Inst. Applied Research, 1973; D.D. (hon.), Phoenix Sem., 1969; m. Joan Norwood Ferguson, June 10, 1950; children—Aileen-Elinor, Tarlton Fleming III, Dawn Parsons Kearnes. Enlisted in U.S. Army, 1945, commd. 2d. lt., 1950, advanced through grades to lt. col., 1966; chief Logistics and Surface Mobility br. Combat Devels. Command, Fort Belvoir, Va., 1972-73; ret., 1973; property mgr. Star Realty, Inc., Falls Church, Va., 1972-74; vice-chmn. Internat. Equity Corp., Silver Spring, Md., 1972-74; property mgr. Tysons Realty, Inc., McLean, Va., 1974-78; distbr. Amway Corp., 1976—; chmn., pres. Cumbernalud Ltd., Alexandria, Va., 1974—. Co-chmn. Seminar on Aging, The Lepers of Today, 1977. Decorated Bronze Star medal with oak leaf cluster, Meritorious Service medal, Army Commendation medal with three oak leaf clusters; Legion of Honor, Croix de Gerre with Palm (France); N.Y. State Conspicuous Service Cross, others. Fellow Augustian Soc., Soc. Antiquaries of Scotland, Royal Soc. Arts, Augustan Soc., Truman Library Inst.; mem. Internat. Mensa, Am. Def. Preparedness Assn., Assn. U.S. Army, Nat. Geog. Soc., Va. Hist. Soc., Smithsonian Assos., No. Va. Bd. Realtors, Ret. Officers Assn. Episcopalian. Clubs: Army and Navy, Jefferson Islands, St. Andrews Soc. of Washington, Farmington Country, The Murray Clan Soc. N.Am. (pres. 1972—). Contbr. articles to profl. jours. Home and office: Swansholm 2500 Culpeper Rd Alexandria VA 22308

PARSONS, WARD CHESTER, environ. cons. engr.; b. Bristol, Conn., Mar. 28, 1923; s. Ward C. and Cloffie S. (St. Cyr) P.; B.M.E., La. State U., 1951; M.S. in Mgmt., Advanced Mgmt. Inst., 1977; m. Katie Cecilia Bridges, Sept. 4, 1943; children—Ward C., Richard G., Debra Cloffie. Asst. to maintenance supt. Philips Petroleum Co., Sweeney, Tex., 1951-52; plant engr. Jefferson Island Salt Co. (La.), 1952-53; asst. plant engr. Colonial Sugars Co., Gramercy, La., 1953-57; sr. utilities engr. Kaiser Aluminum & Chem. Co., Gramercy, 1957-58, supr. utilities, 1958-59, supr. tech. services, 1959-60, supr. adminstrn., 1960-62; chief engr. Houston Chem. Corp., Houston, 1962-63; plant engr. CIBA-GEIGY Chem. Corp., McIntosh, Ala., 1963-66; mgr. utilities engring. Masonite Corp., Chgo., 1966-72; v.p. Roy F. Weston, Inc., Wilmette, Ill., 1972-77; v.p. Metcalf & Eddy Inc., Atlanta, 1977-79, CHZM-Hill, Gainesville, Fla., 1979—. Served with USN, 1942-46. Mem. ASME, Am. Inst. Chem. Engrs., TAPPI, Air Pollution Control Assn., Water Pollution Control Fedn., Nat. Soc. Profl. Engrs., Profl. Engrs. in Pvt. Practice. Episcopalian. Contbr. articles to profl. jours.

PARTIN, BURKE FRED, JR., psychologist; b. Raleigh, N.C., June 14, 1942; s. Burke Fred and Eloise S. (Stallings) P.; B.A., N.C. State U., 1968; M.Ed., U. N.C., Chapel Hill, 1971, Ph.D., 1974; m. Kathryn Jean Weeks, Mar. 23, 1967; 1 dau., Kelli Elizabeth. Grad. instr. Sch. Edn., U. N.C., Chapel Hill, 1972-73; cons. sch. psychology Raleigh Guidance Center, 1973-76; dir. psychol. services Wake County Pub. Schs., Raleigh, 1974-76, sch. psychologist, 1976-78; dir. pupil support services Alamance County Schs., Graham, N.C., 1978—. Mem. Alamance County Arts Council, 1979—. Served to 1st lt. USAR. Lic. psychologist, N.C.; cert. sch. psychologist, sch. counselor, spl. edn. tchr. Mem. Internat. Sch. Psychology Com., So. Assn. for Counselor Edn. and Supervision, N.C. Assn. for Counselor Edn. and Supervision (pres. elect 1979—), Am. Personnel and Guidance Assn., Assn. Humanistic Edn. and Devel., Assn. for Counselor Edn. and Supervision, Am. Psychol. Assn., N.C. Assn. for Research in Edn., N.C. Assn. Sch. Psychologists, N.C. Psychol. Assn., N.C. Personnel and Guidance Assn. (exec. council 1976—, chmn. ethics com. 1977-78, chmn. profl. services com. 1977—), N.C. Assn. Humanistic Edn. and Devel., N.C. Mental Health Assn. (exec. com. 1976-77), Phi Delta Kappa. Club: Soaring Soc. Am., Inc. Office: 609 Ray St Graham NC 27253

PARTON, ALBERT CLARENCE, JR., nursing home adminstr.; b. Covington, Ky., Mar. 24, 1940; s. Albert C. and Rosemary (Cutter) P.; B.A., Xavier U., 1962, M.Ed., 1966; m. Patricia Ann Brunen, Aug. 22, 1964; children—Mark, David, Adam, Blake. Spl. edn. tchr. Hamilton County Council for Retarded Children, Cin., 1962-69, exec. dir., 1969-70; adminstr. Three Rivers Convalescent Center, Miami Heights, Ohio, 1970-74, Woodspoint Nursing Home, Florence, Ky., 1975—; owner P-S & Assos., Cons., Florence, 1978—. Mem. Am. Nursing Home Assn., Ky. Health Care Facilities, No. Ky. Mental Health Assn., Xavier Univ. Alumni Assn. Roman Catholic. Author: Winter Moods (poetry), 1979; Changing Scenes, 1976. Office: Woodspoint Nursing Home 7300 Woodspoint Dr Florence KY 41042

PARTRIDGE, MARY, coll. adminstr.; b. St. Louis, Aug. 31, 1929; d. Leslie Elridge and Ann (Schoenemann) Prichard; B.A., Mt. Holyoke Coll., 1950; m. Edwin M. Partridge, Jr., June 24, 1950; children—Edwin M. III, Stephen Bradford. Reporter, Ridgewood (N.J.) News, 1952-54; editor Vienna and Fairfax (Va.) News, 1973; coll. relations officer Marymount Coll. Va., Arlington, 1974-79, public relations dir., 1979—. Regional chmn. N.J., Mt. Holyoke Alumnae Fund, 1962-63; Wyckoff chmn. Bergen County (N.J.) Heart Assn. Dr., 1966; bd. dirs. Wyckoff (N.J.) YMCA, 1958-64, McLean (Va.) Chamber Orch., 1976-78. Mem. Council Advancement and Support Edn. Clubs: Mt. Holyoke Bergen-Passaic Counties (hon., pres. 1963-65), Mt. Holyoke Washington (chmn. ways and means 1976). Editorial bd. Mt. Holyoke Alumnae Quar., 1976-79. Home: 7706 Falstaff Rd McLean VA 22101 Office: 2807 N Glebe Rd Arlington VA 22207

PASCHAL, JAMES ALPHONSO, coll. adminstr.; b. Americus, Ga., Aug. 11, 1931; s. Bouie Lee and Mary (Jackson) P.; B.A., Xavier U., 1957; M.S., Ft. Valley State Coll., 1963; Ed.D., U. S.C., 1977; m. Mimia Lafavor, Nov. 2, 1957; 1 dau., Maret Elvara. Elem. tchr., librarian, counselor E. View Sch., Americus, Ga., 1957-65; sch. social worker Americus City Sch. System, 1965-67; coordinator student services Augusta (Ga.) Tech., 1967-77; dir. Bridge (counseling center), Benedict Coll., Columbia, S.C., 1978—. Served with U.S. Army, 1951-53. Recipient citation Am. Legion, 1975. Mem. Am. Legion (comdr. 1971-73), Am. Personnel and Guidance Assn., S.C. Personnel and Guidance Assn., S.C. Assn. for Counselor Edn. and Supervision, S.C. Assn. for Non-White Concerns, S.C. Coll. Personnel Assn., Alpha Phi Alpha. Democrat. Roman Catholic. Clubs: Optimist (pres. 1976-77), K.C. (grand knight 1974-75), Lambda Enterprises. Home: 3109 Bellemeade Dr Augusta GA 30906 Office: Benedict Coll PO Box 42 Columbia SC 29204

PASK, RODNEY HARRISON, hosp. ofcl.; b. Washington, Feb. 18, 1946; s. Chester James and Nancy Elizabeth (Harrison) P.; A.B.A., Benjamin Franklin U., 1966, B.C.S., 1968; m. Nancy Hartwell Thompson, June 5, 1971; children—Amanda Harrison, Nancy Ellen Hartwell, Rebecca Louise Thompson. Cost acct. Nat. Orthopaedic and Rehab. Hosp., Arlington, Va., 1970-71, asst. controller, 1971-72, controller, 1972; controller Barcroft Inst., Falls Church, Va., 1972-74; controller, adminstrv. coordinator Warren Meml. Hosp., Front Royal, Va., 1974—. Pres., Warren County Heart Assn., 1978-79, bd. dirs., 1975—; treas. Calvary Episcopal Ch., 1977, 78, vestryman, 1976-78; chmn. profl. div. United Way, 1975, 77. Served with U.S. Army, 1968-70; Vietnam. Mem. Hosp. Fin. Mgmt. Assn., Va. Health Care Assn., Va. Hosp. Assn. Club: Front Royal Rotary. Office: 1000 Shenandoah Ave Front Royal VA 22630

PASLEY, JAMES LAWRENCE, JR., mfg. co. exec.; b. Hemingway, S.C., Feb. 2, 1953; s. James Lawrence and Sadie R. (Cooper) P.; B.S. in Bus. Adminstrn. and Acctg., Bapt. Coll., 1974; student S.C. State Coll., 1970. Asst. dir. Pee Dee Area Day Care Center, Hemingway, 1975; asst. Summer Food and Recreation Program, Waccamow Econ. Opportunity Council, Conway, S.C., 1975; ednl. coordinator Williamsburg County Substance Abuse Council, Hemingway, 1976; asst. personnel mgr., recreation dir. and pub. relations dir. Tupperware Co., an Internat. Div. of Dart Industries, Hemingway, 1976—. Mem. S.C. Statewide Health Coordination Council, 1977-81, S.C. Social Services Adv. Com., 1979; v.p. Williamsburg County Grassroots Citizen Adv. com., 1976-80; chmn. The Donnelly Community Devel. Council, 1974-80. Served with USAFR, 1972-74. Recipient Nat. Sojourner award, USAF, 1972; Disting. Commodant award, USAF, 1972. Mem. Pee Dee Personnel Assn., Nat. Indsl. Recreation Assn., NAACP, Arnold Air Soc., Afro-Am. Soc. Democrat. A.M.E. Ch. Clubs: Masons (32 deg., Shriner), Order Eastern Star. Home: Route 1 PO Box 327 Hemingway SC 29554 Office: Drawer 668 Hemingway SC 29554

PATE, JACQUELINE HAIL, equipment co. mgr.; b. Amarillo, Tex., Apr. 7, 1930; d. Ewen and Virginia Smith (Crosland) Hail; student Southwestern U., Georgetown, Tex., 1947-48; children—Charles, John Durst, Virginia C., Christopher. Exec. sec. Western Gear Corp., Houston, 1974-76; adminstr., treas., dir. Aberrant Behavior Center, Personality Profiles, Inc., Corp. Procedures, Inc., Dallas, 1976-79; br. facilities mgr. Digital Equipment Corp., Dallas, 1979—. Active PTA, Dallas, 1958-73. Methodist. Home: 14500 Dallas Pkwy #210 Dallas TX 75240 Office: 12100 Ford St Suite 200 Dallas TX 75234

PATE, JOHNNY RAY, engr.; b. Memphis, July 17, 1942; s. Stoy and Edith (Sawyer) P.; B.E., Vanderbilt U., 1966; B.S., David Lipscomb Coll., 1965; m. Sandra Snell, Dec. 16, 1961; children—Phil, Eric. Engr. Trane Co., LaCrosse, Wis., 1966-73; pres. Environ. Enterprises, Inc., Little Rock, 1973—, Pate Energy Systems, 1980—; contract trainer of energy auditors Ark. Energy Office: instr. dept. engring. U. Ark., Little Rock, 1975-76, mem. Engring. Bd. Bd. dirs. Ark. Engring. Found.; mem. Ark. State Energy Task Force. Mem. Am. Soc. Heating, Refrigerating and Air Conditioning Engrs. (chpt. pres. 1971-72, nat. membership com., Ernest N. Pettit award 1973, Lincoln Boullioun award 1975), Little Rock Engrs. Club, Little Rock C. of C. (mem. environ. improvement com. 1975—), Ark. Council Engring. and Related Socs. (chmn. 1979), Ark. Fedn. Water and Air Users, Assn. Energy Engrs. Club: Little Rock Engrs. Home: 4115 Cooper Orbit Rd Little Rock AR 72210 Office: 423 N University Ave Little Rock AR 72205

PATE, WANDA ARLENE (WHALEY), nurse; b. Mt. Pleasant, Iowa, Mar. 29, 1942; d. Ernest Leslie and Alice Marie (Edwards) Whaley; R.N., Broadlawns Polk County Sch. Nursing, 1963; B.S.N., U. Iowa, 1966; M.S., U. So. Miss., 1976; m. William A. Pate, Feb. 2, 1973. Supr., Iowa Psychopathic Hosp., Iowa City, 1963-67; staff nurse DePaul Hosp., New Orleans, 1969-70; milieu therapist Riveroaks Hosp., New Orleans, 1970-73; dir. nursing Garden Park Community Hosp., Gulfport, Miss., 1973-74; dir. staff devel. Meml. Hosp. at Gulfport, 1977—. Mem. Saucier Vol. Fire Dept., Miss., 1975—; bd. dirs. Miss. Bd. Nursing, Coastal Family Health Center, Biloxi. Served to capt. Nurse Corps, USAF, 1967-69. Recipient Mary Scott Trust award in Mental Health, 1964. Mem. Am. Nurses Assn., Miss. Nurses Assn., Dist. 5 Nurses Assn. (pres.), Nurses Coalition for Action in Politics, Soc. for Hosp. Educators of Miss. Hosp. Assn., Miss. Gulf Coast Continuing Edn. Inc. Democrat. Clubs: Gulfport Yacht, Order Eastern Star. Home: Route 1 Box 132 Saucier MS 39574 Office: Meml Hosp at Gulfport PO Box 1810 Gulfport MS 39501

PATEL, AMRUT RANCHHODJI, engr.; b. Navsari, India, Jan. 4, 1944; s. Ranchhodji Naran and Bhikhiben (Ranchhodji) P.; came to U.S., 1967, naturalized, 1977; B.E.E., Sardar Patel U., Anand, India, 1966; M.M.E., Villanova U., 1971; M.B.A., Miss. Coll., 1978; m. Hansa Chhotubhai Govindji, May 5, 1973; 1 dau., Nirali. Devel. engr. ITE Imperial Corp., Phila., 1967-68, research engr. Haberlin Research Center, Chalfon, Pa., 1968-72; sr. engr. Siemens-Allis Inc., Jackson, Miss., 1973—. Recipient 6 patent awards Siemens-Allis Inc., 1974-76. Mem. IEEE. Hindu. Club: Swimming and Racket. Home: 332 Bay Park Dr Brandon MS 39042 Office: Box 6289 Jackson MS 39208

PATEL, SHIVABHAI ISHWARLAL, horticulturist; b. Mahadevpura, India, Feb. 22, 1944; s. Ishwarlal Amulakhdas and Puriben Ishwarlal P.; B.Sc., Gujarat U., Ahmedabad, India, 1966; M.Sc., U. Baroda, 1968; M.S., U. Ga., 1971, Ph.D., 1977; m. Shardaben S. Patel, May 29, 1966; 1 son, Tarak Shivu. Research fellow U. Baroda, India, 1968-70; teaching asst. U. Ga., 1970-74; quality control and research mgr. Leaf Nurseries, Miami, Fla., 1974-77, sr. mgr. prodn. ops. research and devel., 1977; research and devel. dir. growing div. Florafax Internat., Inc., 1978; pres., treas. Agri Horticulture Corp., Miami, 1978—. Mem. Internat. Soc. Hort. Sci., Am. Soc. Hort. Sci., Internat. Plant Propagators Soc., Botanical Soc. Am., Internat. Plant Tissue Culture Soc., Fla. Hort. Soc., Internat. Platform Assn., Sigma Xi. Contbr. articles to profl. and trade jours. Home: 20300 SW 105th Ave Miami FL 33189 Office: 11460 N Kendall Dr Miami FL 33176

PATIL, MILIND, state ofcl.; b. Bombay, India, June 8, 1948; s. Dattaram and Hirabai (Pathare) P.; came to U.S., naturalized, 1974; B.S.E.E., Indian Inst. Tech., 1970; M.S.E.E., Carnegie Mellon U., 1971; M.S. in Pub. Affairs, U. Tex., 1973; v.p. prodn. planning Air Frame Products, Bombay, 1969-70, v.p. world mktg., 1970-73; dir. mgmt. Tex. Dept. Human Resources, Austin, 1973-76; sr. project mgr. Tex. Comptroller's Office, Austin, 1976-77, asst. dir. data services, 1977—; v.p. UBQ Imports; sr. partner Rational Systems, Mgmt. Assistance Assos.; cons. in field. Campaign worker state and nat. elections, 1972-76. L.B.J. fellow. Mem. IEEE, AAAS, Am. Pub. Health Assn., Am Polit. Sci. Assn., Am. Statis. Assn. Author numerous publs. Research in field. Home: 2708 Pegram Austin TX 78723 Office: 111 E 17th St Austin TX 78701

PATILLO, LEONARD SYLVESTA, assn. exec.; b. Paducah, Ky., Jan. 25, 1923; s. Prentice Sylvester and Mallie Louise (Hill) P.; certificate Paducah Jr. Coll., 1942; m. Mary Kathryn Kindred, Jan. 15, 1943; children—Patricia (Mrs. Robert Estes), Dennis Lynn. Reporter, photographer Paducah Sun Democrat, 1942-43, 45-46; editor, publicity dir. Houston C. of C., 1946-52, mgr. publs. dept., 1954-59, bus. mgr., 1959-70, gen. mgr., 1970-72, exec. v.p., gen. mgr., 1972—; dir. pub. relations Tex. Mfrs. Assn., 1952-54. Instr. Inst. Orgn. Mgmt., 1973-75. Exec. v.p. Greater Houston Community Found., 1971—; dir. Korea-Tex. Trade Promotion Council, 1973—, Houston Port Bur., 1969—. Bd. dirs. Tex. Soc. Prevention Blindness, 1963-70. Served to 1st lt. USAAF, 1942-45. Decorated Purple Heart with oak leaf cluster. Mem. Am. C. of C. Execs. (v.p. profl. programs 1974-76, chmn. bd. 1975-76), Am. Assn. Commerce Publs. (pres. 1965-66), C. of C. U.S. (mem. community and urban affairs com. 1973-77, internat. trade subcom. 1977—, mem. working group on overseas bus. practices 1979-80), C. of C. Mgrs. and Secs. Assn. S. Tex. (pres. 1968-69), Houston Jr. C. of C. (hon.), So. Assn. C. of C. Execs. (pres. 1978-79), Inst. Dirs. (London), Japan-Am. Soc. Houston (dir. 1976—). Rotarian. Clubs: Houston, Advertising (dir. 1956). Contbr. articles to profl. jours. Home: 5402 Rutherglenn St Houston TX 77096 Office: 1100 Milam Bldg 25th Floor Houston TX 77002

PATRICK, DON ALVA, oil and gas co. exec.; b. Tulsa, Sept. 8, 1942; s. C.A. and Bessie (Woodward) P.; B.B.A., SW Tex. State U., 1969; 1 dau., Donna Jo. Joint interest acct. Sunray Dx Oil Co., Houston, 1966-68; auditor Sun Oil Co., Dallas, 1968-75; owner, operator Patrick Cons. Service, Dallas, 1975—, auditor, 1977—; pres. Patrick Enterprises, Inc., Dallas, 1977—; instr. acctg. N. Tex. State U., 1976—. Mem. Council of Petroleum Accts. Soc., Permian Basin Petroleum Assn. Baptist. Author: Audit of Joint Interest, Contracts and Reports, and Sample Audit Cases, 1976. Home: 3108 Lindbergh Dr Dallas TX 75228 Office: Patrick Enterprises Inc 3727 Dilido St Suite 102 Dallas TX 75228

PATRICK, JOHN MONNICH, steel co. exec.; b. Tucson, Nov. 21, 1936; s. Walter Wellington and Delia (Monnich) P.; student U. Ariz., 1956; m. Dianna Sue Kaiser, May 19, 1972; children by previous marriage—John Michael, Scott Michael; stepchildren—Julie Joline Ward, John Maline Ward. Owner, operator Engine Specialists Inc., Shalimar, Fla., 1966-69, Ft. Walton Beach, Fla., 1969—, Dianna Steel Products Inc., Ft. Walton Beach, 1977—; faculty Okaloosa Walton Jr. Coll. Clubs: Moose, Elks. Home: 131 Virginia Dr Fort Walton Beach FL 32548 Office: 1306 N Beal Pkwy Fort Walton Beach FL 32548

PATRICK, MARY ERLINE ENGLAND, librarian; b. Huntland, Tenn., Aug. 30, 1921; d. William Edward and Sara Ellen (Gamble) England; B.S., Middle Tenn. State U., 1952, M.A., 1954; postgrad. George Peabody Coll., 1958, 63, U. Tenn., 1969, U. S.C., 1970; m. Harold Shelton Patrick, May 30, 1941; children—Don (dec.), Gary. Tchr., Robert E. Lee Elementary Sch., Fayetteville, Tenn., 1955-68; librarian Fayetteville Jr. High Sch., 1968—. Tchr. Sunday sch. First United Methodist Ch., Fayetteville, also mem. adminstrv. bd. Freedom's Found. scholar, 1970. Mem. NEA, ALA, Tenn., Middle Tenn. (past pres.) library assns., Fayetteville City Tchrs. Edn. Assn. (past pres.), Tenn. Edn. Assn. (del. to rep. assembly), Delta Kappa Gamma (past pres. local chpt.). Clubs: Eastern Star, Am. Legion Aux. (past pres.). Home: 812 W College St Fayetteville TN 37334 Office: Fayetteville Jr High Sch Wilson Pkwy Fayetteville TN 37334

PATTEN, ZEBOIM CARTTER, state senator, banker; b. Chattanooga, Feb. 2, 1903; s. Z.C. and Sarah (Key) P.; grad. Asheville Sch. for Boys, 1921; B.S., Cornell U., 1925; D.C.L., U. of South, 1962; m. Elizabeth Bryan, Aug. 19, 1931; children—Sarah Patten Gwynn, Emma Patten Casey, Zeboim Cartter III and W. A. Bryan (twins). Asst. treas. to v.p. Vol. State Life Ins. Co., 1928-39, now dir.; chmn. bd. First Fed. Savs. & Loan Assn. of Chattanooga. Mem. Tenn. Ho. of Reps., 1958-60, Tenn. Senate, 1961—. Mem. Tenn. Hist. Commn. Trustee U. Chattanooga; chmn. bd. Bonny Oaks Sch. Served to lt. USCGR, 1942-44. Recipient Distinguished Service award Kiwanis Club, 1969; named Tenn. Conservationist of Year, 1970. Mem. Chattanooga Hist. Assn. (pres. 1949; treas. 1949-56). Episcopalian. Author: A Tennessee Chronicle, 1953; Signal Mountain and Walden's Ridge, 1962; So Firm a Foundation, 1968. Home: 406 N Palisades Dr Signal Mountain TN 37377 Office: 33 Patten Pkwy Chattanooga TN 37402

PATTERSON, ALVIN LYNN, educator; b. Sweetwater, Tex., July 22, 1950; Asso. Applied Sci., Tex. State Tech. Inst., 1970, B.Tech. Edn., 1971; m. Janice Howington, Aug. 23, 1969; children—Michelle, Keith. Laborer, Wolfe Greenhouses, Waco, Tex., 1969, Northhaven Gardens, Dallas, 1969; plant maintenance supr., land foreman N.W. Garden Center, Austin, Tex., 1971; garden supt. G. H. Pape, Waco, Tex., 1972; horticulture instr. Tex. State Tech. Inst., Waco, 1976—. Served with Army N.G., 1970-76. Recipient Magnolia Scholarship award Tex. Assn. Nurserymen, 1969. Mem. N.G. Assn. Tex., Central Tex. Zool. Soc. Republican. Baptist. Club: Order Red Red Rose. Office: Dept Hort Tech Tex State Tech Inst Waco TX 76705

PATTERSON, ANDY JAMES, educator, composer; b. Gordon, Tex., Feb. 20, 1929; s. Andrew Ebenezer and Ida Kate (Fulferi) P.; B.A. in Music, Tex. Christian U., 1948, Mus.M., 1951; Mus.D., Fla. State U., 1969; m. Beverly Jane Shaw, Jan. 25, 1963; children—Andy James, Michael, Philip. Adminstrv. asst. to dean fine arts, instr. music Tex. Christian U., Ft. Worth, 1948-51, 53-56; grad. asst. music Fla. State U., Tallahassee, 1956-58; asst. prof. music Fla. A and M U., 1967-68; asst. prof. music Ga. Tchrs. Coll., Statesboro, 1958-59; mem. faculty Hardin-Simmons U., Abilene, Tex., 1959—, asso. prof. music, 1959-69, prof., 1969—, chmn. dept. theory and composition, 1959—, also chmn. grad. studies in music. Served with AUS, 1951-53. Andy J. Patterson award named in his honor Theta Lambda chpt. Phi Mu Alpha-Sinfonia at Hardin-Simmons U.; recipient 1st place award orchestral composition Tex. Composers League Competition Contest, 1969. Mem. Am. Soc. U. Composers, Am. Music Center, Inc., Am. Assn. U. profs. (chpt. pres. 1964-66), Nat. Assn. Coll. Wind and Percussion Instrs., Southeastern Composers League, Pi Kappa Lambda, Phi Mu Alpha-Sinfonia (province gov. 1962-66; Orpheus award Theta Lambda chpt. 1979). Composer large works for orch., sonatas, songs and choral works, piano and organ works, concerti for various instruments, others; 113 compositions printed in 23 vols. in Smith Music Library. Home: 1642 Swenson St Abilene TX 79603

PATTERSON, BENNETT BURR, lawyer; b. McCrory, Ark., Aug. 14, 1899; s. Marshall H. and Ethel E. (Lippman) P.; B.A., Hendrix Coll., 1918; postgrad. U. Ark., 1918; LL.B., Georgetown U., 1922; m. June Barbarin, Aug. 13, 1940; children—Sandra (Mrs. L.C. Woods), Kathleen June (Mrs. Wayne Marek). Admitted to Tex. bar, 1922, D.C. bar, 1922, U.S. Supreme Ct. bar, 1951; mem. firm Patterson, Boyd, Lowery & Aderholt, and predecessor, Houston, 1922-48, sr. partner, 1948—. Prof. Houston Sch. Law, 1926-34; spl. lectr. Rice U., 1956-57, U. Houston, 1957, 45-66. Bd. dirs. Houston Sch. for Deaf Children. Served with U.S. Army, 1918-19. Recipient 1st award Am. Acad. Pub. Affairs Los Angeles, 1956. Mem. Am., Tex. bar assns., Am. Judicature Soc., C. of C. Episcopalian. Mason (33 deg., Shriner). Clubs: Sertoma (past pres. Houston); Racquet. Author: The Forgotten Ninth Amendment, 1955. Office: Suite 601 609 Fannin St Houston TX 77002

PATTERSON, BOB, JR., personnel psychologist; b. Oklahoma City, Okla., Nov. 20, 1947; s. Bob and Lou Ellen (Graham) P.; B.A., Central State U., 1974, M.Ed., 1979; m. Carol Jean Ison, Feb. 1980. Computer operator First Nat. Bank, Okla. City, 1967-69; computer specialist Tinker AFB, Okla., 1969-76, equal employment opportunity specialist, counselor, 1976—. Served with USAF, 1966-67. Recipient awards, USAF, 1972, 76. Mem. Am. Personnel and Guidance Assn., Assn. Specialist Group Work. Republican. Baptist. Clubs: Okla. City Corvette, Nat. Council of Corvette. Home: 1511 Glenwillow St Midwest City OK 73110

PATTERSON, CHARLES DAROLD, librarian, educator; b. Wahpeton, N.D., Aug. 8, 1928; s. Charles Irwin and Inez Fern (Slagg) P.; B.Sc., Bemidji (Minn.) State Coll., 1950; M.A., U. Minn., 1956; M.Mus., W.Va. U., 1964; advt. certificate U. Pitts., 1968, Ph.D., 1971. Tchr., Fargo (N.D.) pub. schs., 1950; jr. reference librarian U. Minn., 1954-55; head librarian Bemidji State Coll., 1955-58; head librarian, asst. prof. Glenville (W.Va.) State Coll., 1958-62; asst. prof. library sci. W.Va. U., 1962-66; from lectr. to asst. prof. Grad. Sch. Library Sci. and Info. Sci., U. Pitts., 1966-72; asso. prof. Grad. Sch. Library Sci., La. State U., Baton Rouge, 1972-77, prof., 1978—, mem. univ. senate, 1972-76; del. La. Gov.'s Conf. on Libraries, 1978; cons., lectr. in field. Served with AUS, 1950-52; Japan, Korea. Decorated Combat Inf. badge. Mem. ALA (chmn. scholarship jury 1973, mem. reference and subscription books review com. 1975-77), W.Va. (chmn. coll. and univ. library sect. 1960-61, chmn. indexing and publns. com. 1962-66, chmn. nomination com. 1965, exec. bd. 1960-61, 64-66), La., Southwestern, Music library assns., Assn. Coll. and Research Libraries (pres. Tri-State chpt. 1972), Assn. Am. Library Schs. (chmn. interest group on continuing library edn. 1973, exec. bd. 1980—), AAUP, Am. Guild Organists, Univ. Chamber Music Soc. (dir., chmn. bd. dirs. 1978-80), Pitts. Bibliophiles, Beta Phi Mu. Methodist. Editor: West Virginia Libraries, 1963-66; Analysis of the Library of Congress Music Subject Headings, 1971, JEL Cumulative Index, 1979; editorial bd. Jour. Edn. for Librarianship, 1975-79, editor, 1980—; contbr. articles to profl. jours. Home: 1480 Kenmore Ave Baton Rouge LA 70808 also Birchmont Beach Bemidji MN 56601 Office: Grad Sch Library Sci La State Univ Baton Rouge LA 70803

PATTERSON, CURTIS RAY, artist; b. Shreveport, La., Nov. 11, 1944; s. Charley and Lizzie Lee (Pogue) P.; B.S., Grambling State U., 1967; M.Visual Arts, Ga. State U., 1975; m. Gloria M. Morris, Dec. 31, 1967; children—Curtis Ray, Chari Raneice. Tchr., Muscogee County Schs., 1967-68, Caddo Parish Schs. 1968-70, Atlanta Public Schs., 1970-77; instr. sculpture Atlanta Coll. Art, 1977—; one-person show Ga. State U., 1975; exhibited in group shows: Festival Arts and Culture, Lagos, Nigeria, 1977, High Mus. Art, Atlanta, 1979, Gt. Atlanta-N.Y. Sculpture Exchange, 1979; represented in pvt. collection. Recipient Bronze Jubilee award Sta. WETV, 1979. Mem. Black Artists Atlanta, Thirteen Minus One. Baptist. Office: Dept Art Atlanta Coll Art Atlanta GA 30309

PATTERSON, GLORIA SWANSON ABBOTT, ednl. counselor; b. Memphis, Tenn., Aug. 1, 1925; d. Ira E. and Sadie S. Abbott; B.A. with distinction, Miss. Coll., 1947; M.S. in Guidance, U. Tenn., 1972; postgrad. Middle Tenn. State U., Tenn. State U., 1975-77; m. Robert Benton Patterson, Jr., Dec. 27, 1944 (div. 1970); children—Robbie Anne Patterson Williams, Philip Wayne. Tchr. elem. schs., Clinton, Miss., 1947-48, Pittsboro, Miss., 1948-49, Nashville, Tenn., 1957-60; tchr. English, Central High Sch., Nashville, 1967-71; sch. counselor Apollo Jr. High Sch., Nashville, 1971-74, Wright Jr. High Sch., Nashville, 1974—, faculty rep. to Met. Nashville Edn. Assn., 1976-79; mem. curriculum adv. council Met. Public Schs., Nashville, 1978—. Mem. adv. bd. Hickory Valley Condominiums, Nashville, 1974-76. PTA scholar, 1958; cert. tchr., Miss., Tenn. Mem. Am. Personnel and Guidance Assn., Tenn. Personnel and Guidance Assn., NEA, Middle Tenn. Edn. Assn. (sec. treas. guidance sect. 1977-78), Middle Tenn. Personnel and Guidance Assn. (human rights chmn. 1976-77, sec. 1977-79), Tenn. Edn. Assn., Am. Sch. Counselors Assn., Tenn. Sch. Counselors Assn. (pres.-elect 1979-80, pres. 1980-81), Tenn. Assn. Middle Schs. Democrat. Baptist. Home: PO Box 445 Antioch TN 37013 Office: 180 McCall Nashville TN 37211

PATTERSON, JAMES NELSON, pathologist; b. Onnalinda, Pa., Feb. 15, 1902; s. Joseph S. and Catherine (Nelson) P.; B.S., Bucknell U., 1924; B.M., U. Cin., 1928, M.D., 1929, M.S. in Pathology, 1932; m. Viola Townsend Davis, Sept. 30, 1939; 1 son, Joseph R. Intern, Conemaugh Valley Meml. Hosp., Johnstown, Pa., 1928-29; resident in pathology Cin. Gen. Hosp., 1929-31; practice medicine specializing in pathology, Cin., 1931-38, Jacksonville, Fla., 1938-42, Tampa, Fla., 1946—; pathologist to coroner Hamilton County (Ohio), 1931-35; chief of lab. service Kennon Dunham Tb Hosp., Cin., 1936-38; dir. Bur. Labs., Fla. State Bd. Health, 1938-42; asst. state health officer State of Fla., 1941-42; partner Mills & Patterson Labs., Tampa, 1946-52; sr. partner Patterson & Leonard Labs., Tampa, 1952-54, Patterson & Catanzaro Labs., Tampa, 1955-61, Patterson & Eckert, Tampa, 1961-64, Patterson & Coleman & Assos., Tampa, 1964-70, cons. Patterson Coleman Labs., Tampa, 1970—; asst. prof. pathology U. Cin. Coll. Medicine, 1934-38; prof., head dept. pathology Eclectic Med. Coll., Cin., 1932-34; clin. prof. pathology U. South Fla. Coll. Medicine, Tampa, 1973—; mem. staff Centro Asturlano, Centro Espanol, Citrus Meml. hosps., Community Hosp. of New Port Richey (Fla.), DeSoto Meml., Jackson Meml., St. Joseph, Tampa Gen., Tarpon Springs (Fla.) Gen., Univ. Community, West Posco, G. Pierce Wood Meml. hosps.; asso. med. dir. S.W. Fla. Blood Bank, 1946-48, med. dir., 1949-69, med. dir. emeritus, 1970—. Served from maj. to lt. col., USAAF, 1942-46. Recipient Pvt. Practioner of Year award Am. Pathology Found., 1968, Placque awards Franciscan Sisters of St. Hosp., 1974, Cuban Med. Assn. in Exile, 1975; adm. Tex. Navy, 1977. Diplomate Am. Bd. Pathology (trustee 1952-66, pres. 1966). Fellow Am. Coll. Pathologists; mem. Am., Fla. (pres. 1954) assns. blood banks, Am., Internat., Fla. (pres. 1949) socs. pathologists (pres. 1949), Internat. Acad. Pathology, Fla. (editorial bd. 1952-61, research com. 1956-58, gov. 1959), Hillsborough County (pres. 1956, mem. exec. com. 1950-70) med. assns., AMA, Am. Soc. Clin. Pathologists (chmn. com. on clin. chemistry 1960-62), Assn. Clin. Pvt. Practitioners Pathology Found. (trustee 1963-64), Am. Cancer Soc. (dir. Fla. div. 1967-75, v.p. 1969-70, Placque award 1975), Tampa C. of C. (health com. 1968-70), Fla. West Coast Assn. Pathologists, So. Assn. Clin. Nutrition (hon.). Republican. Episcopalian. Clubs: Rotary, Fla. Coll. Country. Editorial bd. Progress in Clin. Pathology, 1972—; contbr. articles on pathology and hematology to profl. jours. Home: 900 Golfview Ave Tampa FL 33609 Office: 4807 N Armenia Ave Tampa FL 33603

PATTERSON, JOHN H., steel co. exec.; b. Chgo., June 27, 1922; s. Howard Lorraine and Isabel Mary (Cronin) P.; B.B.A., U. Richmond, 1950; m. Sara Powers, May 27, 1967; children—John Howard (dec.), Patrick C. (dec.), Tralene L., Cheryl A., Meredith L. Gen. mgr., Reco Tanks, Inc., West Columbia, S.C., 1950-58, v.p., 1958-62; pres. Midland Steel Corp., Columbia, 1962—; mem. nat. indsl. adv. bd. Underwriters Lab., Inc. Bd. dirs. Cola ARC. Served with USNR, 1942-45. Mem. Soc. Heating, Ventilating and Refrigerating Engrs., S.C., Columbia, West Columbia-Cayce chambers commerce. Presbyterian. Clubs: Kiwanis (chmn. vocat. guidance com.), Palmetto (Columbia). Home: 14 Ludwell Rd Columbia SC 29209 Office: 1940 Shop Rd Columbia SC 29201

PATTERSON, LLOYD DALE, bus. cons.; b. Chgo., May 23, 1934; s. Ralph Stevens and Estelle Mary (Witek) P.; B.S., Western Mich. U., 1956; D.M.D., McCarrie-Temple U., 1959; postgrad. U. Wis., 1962; m. Mary Ann Schlicher, July 27, 1957 (dec.); 1 son, Jeffrey Wynn. Pvt. practice prosthetic dentistry, Kalamazoo, Mich., 1959-60; asso., v.p. Dr. Dvorkovitz & Assos., Ormond Beach, Fla., 1967-75; pvt. practice cons. internat. licensing, Ormond Beach, 1976—. Served with U.S. Army, 1957-60. Mem. Internat. Law Licensing Assn., Internat. Med. Prosthetic Assn., Sigma Xi. Home: 135 Pine Cone Trail Ormond Beach FL 32074 Office: PO Box 994 Ormond Beach FL 32074

PATTERSON, RICKEY LEE, clergyman; b. Indpls., Sept. 24, 1952; s. William Irving and Wanda Lou (Calbert) P.; B.A., Ind. U., 1976; M.B.A., U. Miami, 1980; m. Sharon Rose Leonard, May 4, 1974. Sales mgr., rep. Louisville Courier-Jour., Bloomington, Ind., 1974-76; sales rep. Novar Electronics, Plantation, Fla., 1976-77; sales mgr. Spartan Security, Miami, Fla., 1977—; pres. Pat-Cat Enterprises, Inc., Miami, 1977—; pastor, 1972—; founder, pres. Jesus Student's Fellowship, Inc., 1973—, pastor, 1979—, radio broadcast speaker, 1978—, dir. J.S.F. Cassette Ministries, 1978—; ordained to ministry Internat. Conv. Faith Chs. and Ministers, Inc., 1980; spl. coll. agt. Northwestern Mut. Life Ins. Co., Milw., 1979—; instr. Bible, Ind. U., 1973-76; instr. Bible, U. Miami, 1976—, also guest lectr. dept. religion; sales rep. Bell & Howell Corp., South Fla. area, 1978-79; guest lectr. Miami North Community Correctional Center, Dade County Correctional Inst., Fed. Inst. Corrections; dir. Testimony, Christian rock band; campus minister Ind. U., U. Miami, Fla. Internat. U., Miami-Dade Community Coll. Mem. Bur. Bus. Practice, Nat. Audubon Soc., Am. Mktg. Assn., Full Gospel Businessmens Fellowship Internat., Ind. U. Alumni Assn., Sigma Pi. Democrat. Home: 11311 SW 200th St Apt 310-D Miami FL 33157 Office: 255 Alhambra Circle Suite 650 Coral Gables FL 33134

PATTERSON, ROBERT, real estate broker; b. Chgo., Nov. 6, 1905; s. Robert and Mabel (Prior) P.; Ph.B., Yale U., 1929; m. Isabel G. Carter, May 16, 1941; children—Shirley C., Robert Rush. Partner stock exchange firm Greene & Ladd, Dayton, Ohio, 1934-47; mem. N.Y. Stock Exchange, 1953-60; pres. Patterson & Co., Tucson, Dayton, N.Y.C., 1953-60; pres. Hulman Realty Corp., Dayton, 1945-78; dir. Gagel Realty, Dayton; dir. Fidelity Am. Bank Va. Mem. Albemarle County Republican Com., 1960-70; chmn. bd. dirs. Lee Jackson Found. Served with USNR, 1940-45. Republican. Episcopalian. Clubs: Nantucket (Mass.) Yacht, Sankaty Golf (Nantucket); Buz Fuz (Dayton, Ohio), St. Andrew's Golf and Tennis (DelRay Beach, Fla.).

PATTERSON, SOLON PETE, investment counselor; b. Atlanta, Nov. 11, 1935; s. Pete G. and Frances (Marinos) P.; B.B.A., Emory U., 1957, M.B.A., 1958; m. Marianna Reynolds, Oct. 29, 1960; children—John Solon, Joseph Peter. With Piedmont Adv. Corp., N.Y.C., 1958-62; pres. Montag & Caldwell, Inc., Atlanta, 1962—; chmn., pres. Alpha Research Corp., Atlanta, 1968—, Alpha Fund, Inc.; chmn. Alpha Income Fund; chmn. Alpha Tax-Exempt Bond Fund. Past pres. United Greek Orthodox Charities Atlanta, Inc.; bd. visitors Emory U., mem. Bus. Sch. Mgmt. Conf. Bd.; trustee Gammon Theol. Sem. Named Atlanta's Outstanding Young Man of Year in Bus., 1968. Chartered investment counselor. Mem. Inst. Chartered Fin. Analysts, Atlanta Soc. Financial Analysts (past pres., trustee), Atlanta C. of C., Financial Analysts Fedn. (chmn., chief exec. officer 1977-78), Leadership Atlanta Alumni Assn. Clubs: Atlanta Economics (past pres.), Commerce, Piedmont Driving. Home: 1360 Barron Ct NW Atlanta GA 30327 Office: Two Piedmont Center Atlanta GA 30305

PATTERSON, STEVEN LEROY, phys. oceanographer; b. Waco, Tex., Oct. 2, 1947; s. Jacob Claud and Edith Roberta (Landtroop) P.; B.S., Tex. A and M U., 1970, M.S., 1972, Ph.D., 1978. Research asso. dept. oceanography Tex. A&M U., 1978; phys. oceanographer Sci. Applications, Inc., McLean, Va., 1979—. Co-recipient Sun Oil Co. award, 1973; recipient Disting. Grad. Student award Assn. Former Students-Grad. Coll. Tex. A. and M. U., 1978. Mem. Am. Geophys. Union, Sigma Xi. Research in descriptive phys. oceanography. Home: 601 Four Mile Rd Apt 511 Alexandria VA 22305 Office: 8400 Westpark Dr McLean VA 22102

PATTERSON, VIRGINIA GOODWIN, social worker; b. Nashville, Feb. 21, 1917; d. Marsh and Lena Grace (Givens) Goodwin; B.S., Peabody Coll., 1968; M.S.W., U. Tenn., 1970; m. Fletcher Woodall Patterson, June 17, 1940; 1 dau., Judith Ellen Patterson Murphy. Various secretarial positions, 1934-43; dir. day camp Cumberland Valley Girl Scout council, Nashville, summers 1953-62; sec. Centenary Methodist Community Center, Nashville, 1961-64; dir. resident camp Sycamore Hills, Ashland City, Tenn., summers 1963-65; case worker United Methodist Community Center, 1970-71; social case worker, dir. day care for elderly Sr. Citizens, Inc., Nashville, 1971—; v.p. Cumberland Valley Girl Scout council, 1963-64; youth tchr., counselor Dalewood Meth. Ch., 1950—. Pres. Isaac Litton High Sch. PTA, Nashville, 1959-61. Recipient Thanks badge Girl Scouts, 1961. Mem. Nat. Assn. Social Workers (past chpt. corr. sec.), Am. Camping Assn., Nat. Geront. Assn., Tenn. Fedn. Aging, Pi Gamma Mu (past chpt. sec.). Club: Soroptimist (program chmn. 1979-80). Republican. Contbr. articles to profl. jours. Home: 1709 Sherwood Ln Nashville TN 37216 Office: 1801 Broadway Nashville TN 37203

PATTERSON, WARREN RICHARDSON, otolaryngologist; b. Waverly, Tenn., Mar. 18, 1937; s. Malcolm Rice and Ruby Claire (Richardson) P.; B.A., Vanderbilt U., 1960; M.D., U. Tenn., 1964; m. Mary Theresa Rauen, 1962; children—Karen Elizabeth, Jeffrey Richardson. Intern, Balt. City Hosps., 1964-65; head physician minor trauma Los Angeles County/U So. Calif. Med. Center, 1968-70; jr. surg. resident U. Calif. at Irvine, 1970-71; resident in otolaryngology Vanderbilt U. Hosp., Nashville, 1971-72; resident Yale U., New Haven, 1972-73, chief resident and instr. otolaryngology, 1973-74; clin. instr. otolaryngology Vanderbilt U., Served as flight surgeon USNR, 1965-67; Vietnam. Diplomate Am. Bd. Otolaryngology. Fellow A.C.S., Am. Acad. Otolaryngology; mem. AMA, Tenn. Med. Assn., Nashville Acad. Medicine, Tenn. acads. ophthalmology and otolaryngology. Methodist. Home: 401 Bowling Ave Nashville TN 37205 Office: Mid-State Med Center 2010 Church St Suite 211 Nashville TN 37203

PATTERSON, WILLIAM H., univ. pres. emeritus; b. Charleston, S.C., April 10, 1913; s. William H. and Leacadia (Dawson) P.; A.B., U. S.C., 1934, M.A., 1949, Ph.D., 1952; summer student Columbia, U. Wis.; H.H.D., Francis Marion Coll., 1973; m. Frances Rhude Meetze, May 29, 1942 (div. Oct. 1970); m. 2d, Mary Alice Copeland, July 6, 1971. Draftsman FCA, 1934-37; topog. draftsman S.C. Hwy. Dept., 1937-40; archtl. engr. C.E., War Dept., 1940-43; instr. U. S.C., 1943-47, asst. prof. 1947-50, asst. to pres., 1950-52, dean adminstrn., bus. mgr. 1952-61, dean univ., 1961-66, sr. v.p., 1966-68, provost regional campuses, 1967-72, sec. bd. trustees, 1964-74, provost, 1968-74, pres., 1974-77. Mem. Am., So., S.C. hist. assns., S.C. Soc. Engrs., Newcomen Soc. Eng. Episcopalian. Clubs: Summit, Nassau (Princeton, N.J.). Home: 8-E The Heritage 1829 Senate St Columbia SC 29201

PATTON, ALMEDA JANE VANDIKE, ret. librarian; b. Elberon, Ia., May 17, 1914; d. Frank Allen and Clara Marie (Tarvestad) VanDike; student Culver Stockton Coll., U. Ia., 1931-36, B.S., Fla. State U., 1957, M.S., 1967; m. John Henry Patton, Feb. 20, 1937 (div.); children—Jon, Judith, Joanna. Librarian, Springfield (Fla.) Elementary Sch., 1956-57, Bay County Pub. Library, Panama City, Fla., 1957-79; dir. N.W. Regional Library System, Panama City, 1960-79, ret., 1979. Work-study grantee Fla. State Library, 1965-66. Bd. dirs. Bay County Credit Union, 1978, Health Edn. Resource Center, 1978. chmn. natural, scenic and historic com. W.Fla. Resource Conservation and Devel. Project, 1977—. Mem. Am., Southeastern, Fla. (mem. standards com. 1969—; mem. interlibrary cooperation com. 1975-76, chmn. public library sect. 1979—) library assns., Aubudon Assn., Panama Art Assn., World Future Soc., Bay County Hist. Soc. (pres. 1974—), Fla. Hist. Soc., Archives Soc. Clubs: Country (Panama City); Woman's, Garden. Home: 1613 Dewitt St Panama City FL 32401 Office: 25 W Government St Panama City FL 32401

PATTON, CELESTEL HIGHTOWER, educator; b. Nacogdoches, Tex., July 14; d. Felix and Martha Jane (Turner) Hightower; D.H., Meharry Med. Coll., 1947; B.S., Tenn. A. and I. State U., 1952; M.A., Columbia U., 1954; M.A. in Spanish, Interam. U., Saltillo, Mex.; m. Ural L. Patton, Feb. 1, 1930. Dental hygienist pub. schs., Tex., 1947-52; dean women and tchr. health Bishop Coll., Marshall and Dallas, 1954-60; dir. phys. edn. for women Wilberforce (Ohio) U., 1960-62; asso. prof. health edn. So. U., Baton Rouge, 1962—. Active Community Chest, Dallas, 1950-58. Recipient Meharry Pres.'s award, 1967, Alumni's Award for Outstanding Achievement in the Area of Dental Hygiene, 1972. Mem. Dental Hygienists Soc., Meharry Coll. Alumni Assn. (pres. 1952), AAUP, AAUW, Am. Dental Hygienists Assn., Tex. Dental Hygienist Assn., Am. Pub. Health Assn., AAHPER. Democrat. Christian Ch. Contbr. articles to profl. jours. Address: Dept Health Safety Southern Univ Baton Rouge LA 70813

PATTON, DAVID A., JR., mgmt. cons.; b. Yakima, Wash., Aug. 15, 1951; s. David A. and Belen (Asumendi) P.; B.S. in Commerce, U. Va., 1973; postgrad. Va. Theol. Sem., Georgetown U. Cons., Peat, Marwick, Mitchell & Co., Washington, 1973-76, Arthur Andersen & Co., Washington, 1976; budget dir. Pres. Ford Com., Washington, 1976; mgr. Program Resources, Inc., 1977—. Adv. del. Presbyn. Nat. Gen. Assembly, 1974, candidate Va. Ho. of Dels., 1975; patron Jefferson Soc. U. Va.; treas., dir. Circle Condominiums, 1974-76; exec. bd. Arlington County Republican Com., 1976-77, also rep., 1977-80; bd. dirs. Companions in World Mission, 1978—; treas. No. Va. Young Reps., 1979-80; pres. Arlington Young Reps., 1976-77. Recipient Jefferson Soc. award 1973. Mem. Data Processing Mgmt. Assn., EDP Auditors Assn., English Speaking Union, Jefferson Soc., U. Va. Alumni Assn. (life), Mensa. Contbr. articles to profl. jours. Home: 2030 N Adams St Arlington VA 22201

PATTON, HAGER, advt. agy. exec.; b. Fallsburg, Ky., May 21, 1936; s. Hager and Mary Edna (Cochran) P.; B.A., Marshall U., 1958; m. Dorothy Kay Salter, Oct. 21, 1978. Acct. exec. Advt., Inc., Boulder, Colo., 1958-62; v.p. Varicom Internat., Inc., Boulder, 1962-65; account exec. Fahlgren Advt., Parkersburg, W.Va., 1965-68; v.p., account supr. Buchen Advt., Denver, 1968-70; v.p., account group supr. Frye-Sills/Young & Rubicam, Denver, 1970-76; v.p. mgmt. supr. Glenn, Bozell & Jacobs, Houston, 1976-79; sr. v.p. Poole Advt., Inc., Houston, 1979—. Served with USNR, 1954. Mem. Bus./Profl. Advt. Assn. (cert. bus. communicator). Republican. Club: Plaza (Houston). Home: 10750 Boardwalk Houston TX 77042 Office: 7700 San Felipe Houston TX 77063

PATTON, HUGH WILSON, chemist, research adminstr.; b. Lebanon, Tenn., Dec. 2, 1921; s. Hugh and Lois (Massey) P.; B.S. in Chemistry, Middle Tenn. State U., 1945; Ph.D. in Phys. Chemistry, Vanderbilt U., 1952; m. Martha Major, Aug. 18, 1950; children—Ann Patton Henley, Paige Patton Edwards, Elizabeth Major, Barbara M. Prof. chemistry Ark. State Tchrs. Coll., 1950-53; research chemist Tenn. Eastman Co., Kingsport, 1953-56, sr. research chemist, 1956-63, research asso., 1963-66, acting div. head physics research div., 1966-67, head phys. and analytical chemistry research div., 1967-70, asst. dir. research labs., 1970-73, dir. research labs., 1978-79, v.p., 1979—; v.p. Eastman Chem. Products, Inc., Kingsport, 1973-78. Served with USN, 1943-45. Mem. Am. Chem. Soc., Am. Assn. Textile Chemists and Colorists, Am. Phys. Soc., Am. Assn. Textile Technologists, AAAS, Sigma Xi. Presbyterian. Contbr. articles on gas chromatography to sci. jours. Home: 939 Lookout Dr Kingsport TN 37663 Office: Tenn Eastman Co Kingsport TN 37662

PATTON, LARRY DIXON, lawyer; b. Shawnee, Okla., Oct. 8, 1943; s. Guy Dixon and Eliene Leona (McCaskey) P.; B.A., U. Okla., 1965, LL.B., 1967; m. Nanette Jordan, July 17, 1971. Admitted to Okla. bar; asso. firm McClelland, Collins, Sheehan, Bailey & Bailey, 1967, firm G. M. Fuller, 1967-68, firm Kerr, Davis, Irvine & Burbage, 1968-72; partner firm Tomerlin, High & Patton, 1972-77; U.S. atty. Western Dist. Okla., Oklahoma City, 1978—; chmn., founder Okla. State Fed. Law Enforcement Coordinating Com. Co-chmn. Oklahoma County Democratic Party, 1974-76; chmn. Oklahoma County campaign, Carter-Mondale Campaign, 1976. Mem. Oklahoma County Bar Assn., Okla. Bar Assn., Fed. Bar Assn., Am. Bar Assn., Am. Trial Lawyers Assn., Okla. Dist. Attys. Assn. Episcopalian. Clubs: Jaycees (past v.p.), Lawyers (v.p.). Office: 200 NW 4th St Oklahoma City OK 73102

PATTON, LEWIS KAY (L.K.), advt. agy. exec.; b. Lima, Ohio, Nov. 18, 1932; s. Edgar Armon and Betty Eva (Oberdier) P.; B.A., U. Cin., 1954; B.F.A., Conservatory Music, Cin., 1955; M.Ed., Xavier U., Cin., 1956. Pres., L.K. Patton Enterprises, Inc., Ft. Thomas, Ky., 1960—; tchr. Thomas More Coll., Wellman Sch., 1966—; tchr. Vogue Coll., 1966—, also pres.; appeared with Cin. Symphony, Cin. Opera and nat. cos. of Jesus Christ, Superstar and Godspell; recorded album with Dave Brubeck; free lance radio-TV announcer; founder, exec. dir. Ky. Covered Bridge Assn., 1964—; co-chmn. Ky. Gov's. Adv. Council Libraries, Library Bd.; notary pub., 1963—; bd. dirs. No. Ky. Chiropractic Center, New Concepts, Inc. Mem. AFTRA, Cin. Advertisers Club (dir.), Pub. Relations Soc. Am., Internat. Platform Assn., Ky., No. Ky. (past pres.), Christopher Gist hist. socs., Ky. Civil War Roundtable, N.Ky. Heritage League, Filson Club, Am. Assn. for State and Local History (award of merit), Ind., Zumbrota, Ohio, So. covered bridge assns., Phi Delta Theta, Omicron Delta Kappa, Rho Tau Delta, Alpha Delta Sigma. Democrat. Clubs: Masons (32 deg.; past high priest, grand rep.); K.T.; Shriners; Order DeMolay (dep. for Ky., chevalier Legion of Honor). Author: Kentucky Legends, 1963; Kentucky's Vansihing Landmarks, 1976. Contbr. articles on history to profl. publs. Home: 62 Miami Pkwy Fort Thomas KY 41075

PATTON, LYDIA PETTIS, vocat. counselor; b. Ft. Lauderdale, Fla., Nov. 8, 1947; d. Cyrus Rembert and Sara Louise Pettis; B.S. in Health and Phys. Edn., Ky. State U., 1969; M.Ed. in Coll. Personnel Counseling, U. Louisville, 1972; m. James Marlin Patton, Aug. 24, 1968; children—Asha Jamila-Louise, Ade Jabari-James. Vocat. counselor Hampton (Va.) public schs., 1976-78; adminstrv. asst. facilitative environments encouraging devel. project Ind. U., Bloomington, 1975-76; partner Patton & Patton Assos., cons., Petersburg, Va., 1978—. Mem. Am. Personnel and Guidance Assn., Nat. Vocat. Guidance Assn., Va. Personnel and Guidance Assn., Delta Sigma Theta. Roman Catholic. Author: Developing Your Job Search Skills, 1978. Home: 1142 W Washington St Petersburg VA 23803

PATTON, MICHAEL LEE, auto dealer; b. San Francisco, Dec. 28, 1947; s. William Francis and Helen Vivian (Griffin) P.; B.B.A., U. Tex., 1971. Aide to State Senator Charles Herring, Austin, Tex., 1966-71; asst. br. mgr. Will Ross Inc., Dallas, 1971-72; gen. mgr. San Antonio Auto Dealers Assn., 1972-76; sec.-treas. Corpus Christi Franchised New Car Dealers Assn., San Antonio, 1972-76; v.p., gen. mgr., dir. Mission Volkswagen-Honda Co., San Antonio, 1976—. Vol. juvenile probation officer, San Antonio, 1972-74; dir. Beautify San Antonio Assn., 1974—. Mem. Nat., Tex., San Antonio auto dealers assns., Research and Planning Council, Econ. Devel. Found., San Antonio C. of C., Am. Imported Auto Dealers Assn. Democrat. Baptist. Contbr. articles to profl. jours. Home: 2600 NE Loop 410 Apt 1504 San Antonio TX 78217 Office: 1300 SE Military Dr San Antonio TX 78214

PATTON, MICHAEL PATRICK, personnel exec.; b. Tulsa, Mar. 10, 1949; s. S. E. and Marthyne Wanda (Hunt) P.; B.S. in Edn./Psychology, Okla. State U., 1971, M.S. in Psychology/Edn., 1975; m. Carolyn Diane Hildebrand, Aug. 14, 1975; 1 dau., Melanie Renee. Employment interviewer Pepsico Corp., Tulsa, 1971-72; employment rep. Crest div. Combustion Engring., Tulsa, 1975-77; corporate personnel adminstr. Resource Scis. Corp., Tulsa, 1977; mgr. employment-employee devel. div. resource scis. Williams Bros. Engring., Tulsa, 1977—; psychology instr. Tulsa Jr. Coll., 1975—. Recipient Service award Students for Higher Edn., 1977, Recognition cert. U. Tulsa, 1979. Mem. Am. Soc. Tng. and Devel., Am. Soc. Personnel Adminstrn., Am. Personnel Assn., Applied Behavioral Scis. (asso.), Tulsa EEO Coordinators Assn. (v.p. 1978), Tulsa Personnel Assn., Okla. State U. Alumni Assn. Methodist. Club: Shadow Mountain Racquet. Office: 6600 S Yale St Tulsa OK 74197

PATTON, THERESA HENDLEY, med. center adminstr.; b. Ponca City, Okla., Sept. 25, 1948; d. Charles Wesley and Janelle (Weimar) Hendley; student E. Central State U., 1966-68; B.S. in Edn., Central State U., 1970; postgrad. UCLA, 1979; m. Joe B. Patton, Oct. 5, 1968; 1 son, Charles Aaron. Elem. edn. tchr. Walters (Okla.) Sch. System, 1968-69, Oklahoma City public schs., 1970-72; tchr. Children's World of Baptist Med. Center, of Okla., Oklahoma City, 1973-74, asst. dir. public info. Med. Center, 1974, coordinator of vols., 1976-77, dir. vol. services, 1977—; 5th year center instr. Oklahoma City public schs., 1974-76, math. cons., 1974-76. Chmn. March of Dimes, Oklahoma City, 1970-72; dr. chmn. Cerebral Palsy, 1971-72; chmn. Okla. Kidney Assn., 1978—; parent adv. com. Children's World, 1976-78; coordinator Central Dist. of Okla. Cancer Center, 1978—; mem. citizen's com. to combat cancer, 1978—; participator Fed. Coop. Urban Teach Edn. program, 1969-70. Recipient George Washington Medal of Freedom award Sertoma Club of Oklahoma City, 1970; Outstanding Young Artist award Drumright Hist. Soc., 1966. Mem. Okla. Soc. for Dirs. of Vol. Services of Okla. Hosp. Assn. (legis. chmn. 1979—), Am. Soc. Dirs. Vol. Services of Am. Hosp. Assn., Central Okla. Dirs. Hosp. Vols. Council of Okla. Hosp. Assn., Postal Council of Oklahoma City, Am. Contract Bridge League, Bridge Studio of Okla., Zeta Tau Alpha. Democrat. Methodist. Clubs: Order of Rainbow Grand Cross of Color. Home: 6125 N May Ave Apt 215 Oklahoma City OK 73112 Office: 3300 NW Expressway Oklahoma City OK 73112

PATTON, WILLIAM ALFRED, TV sta. exec.; b. El Dorado, Ark., Aug. 20, 1927; s. Joseph Alfred and Carolea (Hayes) P.; student Tex. A & M U., 1944-45, La. State U., 1947; B.S., U. Southwestern La., 1949; m. Carol Leah Conover, Apr. 8, 1950; children—William David, Jack Andrew, Catherine Ellen. Sportscaster Sta. KVOL-FM, Lafayette, La., 1948-49; sportscaster, salesman Sta. KLFY, Lafayette, 1950-52, gen. mgr., 1952-54, gen. mgr. TV, 1955; acct. exec. Sta. KTBS-TV, Shreveport, La., 1955-56; sta. mgr. Sta. KSIX-TV, Corpus Christi, Tex., 1956-57; v.p., gen. mgr. Sta. KPEL, Lafayette, 1957-62; v.p., gen. mgr. Acadian TV Corp., Lafayette, 1962—, also dir.; dir. Actel Corp. Bd. dirs. Lafayette Parish Harbor Terminal and Indsl. Devel. Dist., 1970-74, v.p., 1970-74. Served with USN, 1945-46. Mem. Greater Lafayette C. of C. (dir. 1969-72, v.p. 1970, pres. 1971), La. Assn. Broadcasters (dir. 1970-73, 79—, v.p. 1972, pres. 1973-74), Nat. Assn. Broadcasters, TV Bur. Advt., Southwest La. Mardi Gras Assn. Democrat. Presbyterian. Clubs: Krewe of Gabriel (commodore), Beaver of Lafayette (dir. 1968-70). Home: 504 White Oak Dr Lafayette LA 70506 Office: 1103 Eraste Landry Rd Lafayette LA 70506

PATURIS, E(MMANUEL) MICHAEL, lawyer; b. Akron, Ohio, July 12, 1933; s. Michael George and Sophia (Cacomanolis) P.; B.S. with honors, U. N.C., 1954, J.D. with honors (Block award 1959, staff law rev. 1957-59), 1959; m. Mary Ann Toompas, Feb. 28, 1965; 1 dau., Sophia Elena. Admitted to N.C. bar, 1959, D.C. bar, 1969, Va. bar, 1973; tax atty. Chief Counsel's Office, IRS, Washington, 1964-66, sr. tax atty. Regional Counsel's Office, Richmond, Va., 1966-69; partner firm Reasoner, Davis & Vinson, Washington, 1969-78; practice law, Alexandria, Va., 1978—; speaker, tchr. in field. Served with U.S. Army, 1954-56. C.P.A., N.C. Mem. Am. Assn. Atty.'s-C.P.A.'s (pres. Potomac chpt. 1977-79), D.C. Inst. C.P.A.'s, Va. Soc. C.P.A.'s, Am. Bar Assn., N.C. Bar Assn., Va. Bar Assn., D.C. Bar Assn., Phi Beta Kappa, Beta Gamma Sigma. Republican. Greek Orthodox. Clubs: Washington Golf and Country, Fairfax Hunt. Home: 2732 N Radford St Arlington VA 22207 Office: Lee St Square 431 N Lee St PO Box 511 Alexandria VA 22313

PATYK, CHARLES DENNIS, broadcasting sta. exec.; b. Detroit, July 7, 1947; s. Joseph and Harriet (Makowski) P.; student Mich. State U., 1965-70; m. Linda Joyce Maddox, Sept. 13, 1968; 1 dau., Sandra Marilyn. News reporter, announcer WILS Radio, Lansing, Mich., 1966-70; state capitol corr., TV anchorman WILX-TV, Lansing and Jackson, Mich., radio news anchorman Mich. News Network, Lansing, 1971; news producer, asst. news dir., TV anchorman WILX-TV, 1971-73; sr. radio news editor, asst. news dir. WHAS/WNNS-FM, Louisville, 1973-76; press sec. to county judge/exec., dir. public info. Jefferson County Govt., Louisville, 1976-78; founder Publicast Communications, 1975—, pres., gen. mgr. WZZX-FM, Louisville, 1978—; instr. Public Relations Soc. Am. TV Techniques Sch., U. Lousville, 1976—. Media adv. Louisville/Jefferson County Carter for Pres. campaign, 1976; media cons. aldermanic campaign, 1976, county commr. campaign, 1979; campaign communication coordinator T. Hollenbach re-election campaign, 1977; in-house talent coordinator WHAS Crusade for Children telethons, 1973-75; mem. Lansing Mayor's Artificial Ice Rink Study Com., 1972; Recipient Louisville Ad Club/AFTRA spl. awards, 1974-77. Mem. Am. Meteorol. Soc., AFTRA, Nat. Assn. Broadcasters, Nat. Radio Broadcasters Assn., Louisville Area Radio Stas., Sigma Delta Chi. Office: WZZX-FM Publicast Communications Inc 10000 Shelbyville Rd Louisville KY 40223

PAUL, GABRIEL GABE, profl. baseball club exec.; b. Rochester, N.Y., Jan. 4, 1910; s. Morris and Celia (Snyder) P.; ed. public schs., Rochester; m. Mary Frances Copps, Apr. 17, 1939; children—Gabriel, Warren, Michael, Jennie Lou, Henry. Reporter, Rochester Democrat and Chronicle, 1926-28; publicity mgr., ticket mgr. Rochester Baseball Club, 1928-34, traveling sec., dir., 1934-36; publicity dir. Cin. Baseball Club, 1937, traveling sec., 1938-48, asst. to pres., 1948-49, gen. mgr., 1951-60, v.p., 1949-60; v.p., gen. mgr. Houston Baseball Club, 1960-61; gen. mgr. Cleve. Baseball Club (Cleve. Indians), 1961-63, pres., treas., 1963-72, v.p., gen. mgr., 1972-73; pres. N.Y. Yankees, 1973-77; pres., chief exec. officer Cleve. Indians, 1978—. Dir. or trustee various charitable instns. Served with inf. AUS, 1943-45. Named Major League Exec. of Yr., Sporting News, 1956, 74, Milw. chpt. Baseball Writers Assn., 1976, Sports Exec. of Yr., Gen. Sports Time, 1956, Baseball Exec. of Yr., Boston chpt. Baseball Writers Assn., 1974, 76, Maj. League Exec. of Yr., United Press, 1976; recipient J. Lewis Comiskey Meml. award Chgo. chpt. Baseball Writers Assn. Am., 1961, Judge Emil Fuchs Meml. award Boston chpt., 1967, Bill Slocum Meml. award N.Y. chpt. Baseball Writers Assn. Am., 1975, Sports Torch of Learning award, 1976. Clubs: Palma Ceia Country (Tampa); Skyline Country (Tucson); Shaker Heights (Ohio) Country; Cleve. Athletic. Home: 5700 Mariner Dr Tampa FL 33609 also 2112 Acacia Park Dr Lyndhurst OH 44114 Office: Cleveland Indians Cleveland Stadium Cleveland OH 44114

PAUL, GEORGE HAROLD GOFF, clergyman, historian, educator; b. Vancouver, B.C., Can., May 25, 1910; s. George Stewart and Ella May (Goff) P.; B.A. with honors in History, U. B.C., 1930, M.A., 1931; asso. cert. Toronto Conservatory Music, 1935; Ph.D., U. Okla., 1965. Ordained to ministry Pentacostal Holiness Ch., 1937; pastor, evangelist, denominational ofcl., Can., S. and S.E. U.S. and N.Y., Pa., 1935-48; evangelist, Western and Southwestern states, also Alta. and B.C., 1960—; prin. Pacific Coast Bible Inst., Chillwick, B.C., 1945-49; v.p., dean SouthWestern Coll., Oklahoma City, 1956-65; chmn. history, humanities and polit. sci. dept. Oral Roberts U., Tulsa, 1967—. Named Faculty Mem. of Yr., Oral Roberts U., 1970. Mem. Okla. Assn. Coll. History Profs. (past pres.), Am. Hist. Assn., So. Hist. Assn., NEA, Okla. Edn. Assn., 16th Century Hist. Assn., Faith and History Soc., Okla. Hist. Assn., various ministerial assns., Phi Alpha Theta. Author: Dan T. Muse: From Printer's Devil to Bishop, 1976; contbr. articles to Pentecostal Holiness Advocate. Home: 1524 E 58th St Tulsa OK 74105 Office: Dept History Oral Roberts U 7777 S Lewis St Tulsa OK 74171

PAUL, GRACE, ret. med. technologist, author; b. Liberal, Kans., Mar. 12, 1908; d. David and Myrtle Helen (Brewer) P.; student Tulsa U., 1930-36, Auburn U., 1948, Columbia U., 1949-51. Med. technologist St. Johns Hosp., Tulsa, 1930-36, VA Hosp., Wadsworth, Kans., 1947-48; plant quarantine insp. U.S. Dept. Agr., N.Y.C., 1948-51; claims examiner Social Security Adminstrn., Balt., 1956-71; market research interviewer Response Analysis, Princeton, N.J., 1973-79. Vol. worker United Way of Temple (Tex.), 1974—, Cultural Activities Center, RSVP, Office Citizen Involvement, Youth Services Bur.; active Humanities Council of Temple, 1972—. Served with WAC, 1944-46. Mem. Am. Soc. Med. Technologists, Entomol. Soc. Am., Internat. Platform Assn. Presbyterian. Club: Bus. and Profl. Women's. Author: Your Future in Medical Technology, 1962; A Short Course in Skilled Supervision, 1965; contbr. to Environ. Engr.'s Handbook, vol. III, 1975. Address: 705 N Main St Temple TX 76501

PAUL, JAMES ROBERT, energy co. exec.; b. Wichita, Kans., Sept. 10, 1934; s. Harold Robert and Zona Belle (Marlatt) P.; B.S., Wichita State U., 1956; m. Julia Ann Haigh, Aug. 14, 1955; children—John Robert, Jeffrey James, Julie Renee. With Boeing Co., Wichita, 1956-67, mgr. systems dept., 1966-67; mgmt. cons. Peat, Marwick, Mitchell and Co., Houston, 1967-70; v.p. fin. and adminstrn. Robertson Distbr. Systems, Inc., Houston, 1970-73; treas. Colo. Interstate Gas Co., Colorado Springs, 1973-74; treas. Coastal States Gas Corp., Houston, 1974-75, v.p. fin., 1975-78, sr. v.p. fin., 1978—. Mem. Am. Petroleum Inst., Fin. Execs. Inst. Republican. Methodist. Office: 9 Greenway Plaza Houston TX 77046

PAUL, ROBERT, lawyer; b. N.Y.C., Nov. 22, 1931; s. Gregory and Sonia (Rijock) P.; B.A., N.Y. U., 1953; J.D., Columbia, 1958; m. Christa F. Holz, Apr. 6, 1975; 1 dau., Gina. Admitted to Fla. bar, 1958, N.Y. bar, 1959; partner Paul Landy Beiley & Harper, Miami, 1964—, Morrison Paul & Beiley, N.Y.C., 1970—, Landy Paul & Morrison, London, 1974—; counsel, dir. Republic Nat. Bank Miami, 1968—. Vice pres. exec. com. Citizens' Bd. U. Miami, 1977; bd. dirs., former pres. Fla. Philharmonic Inc., 1976-78. Mem. Am., N.Y., Fla., Inter-Am. bar assns. Home: 700 Alhambra Circle Coral Gables FL 33134 Office: 200 SE 1st St Miami FL 33131

PAUL, RONALD E., Congressman, physician; b. Pitts., Aug. 20, 1935; B.A., Gettysburg Coll., 1957; M.D., Duke U., 1961; m. Carol Wells, 1957; children—Ronald, Lori, Randal, Robert, Joy. Practice medicine specializing in ob-gyn; mem. 94th and 96th Congresses from 22d Congl. Dist. Tex. Served to capt., M.C., USAF, 1963-65. Mem. Brazoria County Med. Soc. Republican. Clubs: Kiwanis, Eagles, 94th. Office: Room 1234 Longworth House Office Bldg Washington DC 20515*

PAUL, WILLIAM DEWITT, JR., artist, educator; b. Wadley, Ga., Sept. 26, 1934; s. William DeWitt and Sonoma (Tinley) P.; student Emory U., 1952, Ga. State Coll., 1953-56; B.F.A., Atlanta Art Inst., 1956; A.B., U. Ga., 1958, M.F.A., 1959; m. Dorothy Hefling, Sept. 2, 1962; children—Sarah Elizabeth, Barbara Susan, Dorothy Ann. Grad. asst. dept. art U. Ga., Athens, 1958-59, asst. prof., 1965-69, curator Ga. Mus. of Art, 1967-69, dir., 1969—, asso. prof. art, 1969—; instr. art and art history dept. Park Coll., Parkville, Mo., 1960-61; instr. art history Kansas City (Mo.) Art Inst., 1959-64; curator study collections, 1964-65, asst. prof. art, 1964-65; one-man exhbns. include: Ga. Mus. Art, 1959, Atlanta Art Assn., 1959, Unitarian Gallery, Kansas City, 1960, Palmer Gallery, Kansas City, 1965, Health Gallery, Atlanta, 1976, Hunter Mus. Art, Chattanooga, 1976, Forum Gallery, N.Y.C., 1977, Madison-Morgan Cultural Center, Ga., 1980, Columbus (Ga.) Mus. Arts and Scis., 1980, Banks-Haley Gallery, Albany, Ga., 1980, Macon Mus. Arts and Scis., 1980, Augusta-Richmond County (Ga.) Mus., 1980; group exhbns. include: New Arts Gallery, Atlanta, 1961, Kansas City Art Inst., 1960-64, Park Coll., 1960, Mulvane Art Center, Topeka, 1965; represented in permanent collections: Ga. Mus. Art, Little Rock Arts Center, U. Ga., Gen. Mills, Hallmark Cards; chmn. visual arts rev. panel Ga. Council for Arts and Humanities, 1976-77. Mem. Am. Fedn. Arts (trustee 1969—), Coll. Art Assn., Am. Assn. Museums, Ga. Alliance for Arts Edn. (past bd. dirs.), Assn. Art Mus. Dirs., Phi Kappa Phi. Home: 150 Bar H Ct Rural Route 3 Athens GA 30605 Office: Ga Mus Art Univ of Ga Athens GA 30602

PAULK, JAMES LANE, state ofcl.; b. Fitzgerald, Ga., Mar. 26, 1949; s. Milton Lane and Madge Elizabeth (Harper) P.; B.B.A., U. Ga., 1972; C.L.U., Am. Coll., 1977. Agt. Nationwide Ins., Fitzgerald, 1972—; senator State of Ga., 1977—; founder, v.p. The Bank of Fitzgerald, 1976—, also dir.; dir. The Paulk Funeral Home, Inc. Mem. exec. bd. Alaphaha council Boy Scouts Am.; trustee Fitzgerald Carnegie Library; vice chmn. Ga. Baptist Christian Life Commn. Mem. Am. Soc. C.L.U.'s, Am. Legis. Exchange Council. Democrat. Clubs: Rotary, Masons, Shriners. Office: PO Box M 212 S Grant St Fitzgerald GA 31750

PAVLISH, ANTHONY STEPHEN (TONY PACE), prodn. co. exec., entertainer; b. Cleve., June 18, 1940; s. Steven John and Anna Marcella P.; student F.M.I. Inst., Stamford, Conn., 1965, Brown Inst., Ft. Lauderdale, Fla., 1978; m. Linda Zabiega, Nov. 1, 1970; 1 son, Steven Francis. Musician, singer, actor, N.Y.C., 1961-67; actor and model, N.Y.C., 1967-70; ind. producer and promoter, Ft. Lauderdale, 1970-74; radio show host, entertainment news editor Sta. WEXY, Ft. Lauderdale, 1975-77; pres. Great Prodns. Inc., Ft. Lauderdale, 1974—; tech. dir. news and engring. WHFT-TV, Miami, Fla., 1979—. Lic. by FCC. Democrat. Christian. Home and Office: 2248 SW 35th Ave Fort Lauderdale FL 33312

PAWLUK, JOHN, JR., club mgr.; b. Watervliet, N.Y., June 15, 1933; s. John Samuel and Anna (Fritz) P.; student pub. schs., Watervliet; m. Marie Eleanor Lattanzi, Apr. 22, 1957; children—Karen Ann, Nadine Marie, Lisa Michele. Entered U.S. Air Force, 1952; mgr. clubs Ent AFB, Colorado Springs, 1955-61, Lajes AFB, Protugal, 1961-63, Westover (Mass.) AFB, 1963-66, Cam Rahn Bay, Vietnam, 1966-67, Otis (Mass.) AFB, 1967-69, Kinchelle (Mich.) AFB, 1969-70, Seoul, Korea, 1970-71, Otis (AFB) Mass., 1971-72, Incirlik AFB, Adana, Turkey, 1972-74, NCO Club Shaw (S.C.) AFB, 1975-77, ret., 1977; civilian club mgr. NCO Club Shaw (S.C.) AFB, 1977—. Decorated Meritorious Service medals, 1971, 77, Commendation medals, 1963, 70, 73. Named Outstanding Club Mgr. Europe, 1974, Outstanding Club Mgr. Tactical Air Command, 1977. Mem. Club Mgrs. Assn. Am., Am. Legion. Russian Orthodox. Club: Shriners. Home: 2371 Hunt Club Rd Sumter SC 29150 Office: Box 524 Shaw AFB SC 29152

PAYNE, ARNOLD PERSHING, b. Williamsburg, Ky.; s. Joseph S. and Sallie Kidd (Wilder) P.; B.S. in Phys. Edn., Math., U. Tex., Austin, 1948, M.Ed. in Phys. Edn., Ednl. Adminstrn., 1950; Ph.D. in Ednl. Adminstrn., Ednl. Psychology, Curriculum, Tex. A & M U., Coll. Sta., 1973; m. Beverly Donahoe Greer; children—Johanna, Joseph, Lucy, Mary, Ray. Prin., Aldine Jr. High Sch., Houston, Tex., 1954-65; grad. asst. Tex. Agrl. and Mech. U., Coll. Sta., 1969-70; curriculum coordinator Windham (Tex.) Pub. Schs., 1970-71; adminstrv. asst., curriculum Gonzales (Tex.) Ind. Sch. Dist., 1973—. Chmn. edn. com. Don Yarborough campaign for gov., 1967-68; bd. dirs. Gonzales United Fund, 1978-79, Gonzales Crippled Children's Soc., 1979-80. Mem. Am., Tex. Assns. Sch. Adminstrs., Am. Assn. Supervision and Curriculum Devel., Gonzales Tchrs. Assn. (pres. 1978-79), Tex. Assn. Secondary Sci. Prins., Tex. State Tchrs. Assn., PTA, Phi Delta Kappa. Certified in gen. elementary, secondary edn., sch. adminstrn., Tex. Contbr. articles to profl. jours. Home: PO Drawer H Gonzales TX 78629 Office: PO Box 157 Gonzales TX 78629

PAYNE, C(ALVIN) LEE, JR., indsl. designer; b. Lowell, Mass., June 28, 1934; s. Calvin Lee and Helen J. (Hennessey) P.; student fine arts U. Ga., 1952-55; B.S. in Indsl. Design, U. Cin., 1958; m. Jennie Hardaway McBride, Sept. 11, 1954; children—Louise Deming, Calvin Lee. Design supr. Walter Dorwin Teague Assos., N.Y.C., 1960-64; dir. product devel. and research Tudor Metal Products Corp., N.Y.C., 1964-68; pres. Lee Payne Indsl. Design Inc., Hastings-on-Hudson, N.Y., Hilton Head Island, S.C. and Atlanta, 1968-80; pres. Payne-Gambello, Inc., Atlanta, 1980—; dir. indsl. design, asso. prof. Ga. Inst. Tech., Atlanta, 1976—. Served as 1st lt. U.S. Army, 1959. Recipient Product Design awards Indsl. Design Mag., 1972, 73; Package Design awards Packaging Design Mag., Folding Paper Box Assn., 1966, 74. Mem. Indsl. Designers Soc. Am. Episcopalian. Holder 12 patents relating to games, plastic devices, and furniture; designer industry prototype soft margarine package, 1963. Home: 801 Durant Pl Atlanta GA 30308 Office: Ga Inst Tech Coll Architecture Atlanta GA 30332

PAYNE, DELORES BECK, educator; b. Loranger, La., Oct. 12, 1919; d. Buren Arnold and Frances D'Maris (Jones) Beck; B.A., La. Coll., 1940; M.Ed., N.E. La. U., 1967; Ed.D., Northwestern State U., Natchitoches, La., 1971; m. Howard Devone Payne, Aug. 25, 1940 (dec. Mar. 1958); children—Devone, Robert Charles, Joe Beck, Andy. Tchr. elem. schs. Madison Parish, La., 1948-52, Monroe, La., 1958-62; prof. elem. edn. Northwestern State U., Natchitoches, 1971—, dir. reading lab., 1971—. Mem. Assn. Preservation Hist. Natchitoches, PEO, Colonial Dames, DAR, Daus. Am. Colonialists, Internat. Reading Assn., Internat. Congress Individualized Instrn., Assn. Tchr. Edn., La. Tchrs. Assn., Genealogy Assn., Delta Kappa Gamma (Disting. Faculty Chair nominee). Baptist. Contbr. articles in field to profl. jours. Home: 214 Bird Ave Natchitoches LA 71457 Office: Northwestern State U Sch Edn Natchitoches LA 71457

PAYNE, EUGENE EDGAR, univ. adminstr.; b. San Antonio, Aug. 9, 1942; s. Eugene Edgar and Louise (Speer) P.; B.S., Tex. A&M U., 1964, M.S., 1965; Ph.D. (research fellow 1968-70), U. Okla., 1970; m. Karen S. James, June 10, 1978; children—Kelly Lynn, Katherine Louise, Mary Patricia, Kerry Erin, Kimberley Ann, Thomas Julius. Mgmt. cons. E.I. DuPont de Nemours Co., Del., 1965-68; dir. mgmt. info. systems, spl. cons. Electronic Data Systems Corp., Dallas, 1970-71; dir. planning and mgmt. systems U. Tex., Dallas, 1971-74; v.p. for fin. and mgmt. SW Tex. State U., San Marcos, 1974—; exec. dir. SW Tex. State U. Found.; cons. in field. Mem. vestry, fin. com. St. Marks Episcopal Ch. NDEA fellow, 1969. Mem. Am. Inst. Indsl. Engrs., Inst. Mgmt. Scis., Ops. Research Soc. Am., Assn. Computing Machinery, Assn. Instl. Research, Soc. Coll. and Univ. Planning, Nat. Assn. Coll. and Univ. Bus. Officers. Club: Kiwanis. Contbr. articles to profl. jours. Home: 303 W Sierra San Marcos TX 78666 Office: SW Tex State U San Marcos TX 78666

PAYNE, FRED J., physician; b. Grand Forks, N.D., Oct. 14, 1922; s. Fred J. and Olive (Johnson) P.; student U. N.D., 1940-42; B.S., U. Pitts., 1948, M.D., 1949; M.P.H., U. Calif., Berkeley, 1958; m. Dorothy J. Peck, Dec. 20, 1948; children—Chris Ann, Roy S., William F., Thomas A. Intern, St. Joseph's Hosp., Pitts., 1949-50; resident Charity Hosp., New Orleans, 1952-53; med. epidemiologist Center Disease Control, Atlanta, 1953-60; prof. tropical medicine La. State U. Med. Center, New Orleans, 1961-66; epidemiologist Nat. Nutrition Survey, Bethesda, Md., 1967-68; chief public health professions br. NIH, Bethesda, 1971-74, med. officer, sr. research epidemiologist Nat. Inst. Allergy and Immunologic Diseases, 1974-78; ret., 1978; asst. health dir. Fairfax County (Va.) Health Dept., 1978—; clin. prof. La. State U., 1966—; cons. NIH, 1979—. Served with AUS, 1942-46, 49-52. Decorated Combat Medic Badge. Diplomate Am. Bd. Preventive Medicine. Fellow Am. Coll. Preventive Medicine; mem. Am. Public Health Assn., Am. Soc. Microbiology, AAAS, Internt. Epidemiology Assn., Soc. Epidemiologic Research, USPHS Commd. Officers Assn., Sigma Xi. Contbr. articles to profl. jours. Home: 1820 Saint Roman Dr Vienna VA 22180 Office: 4080 Chain Bridge Rd Fairfax VA 22030

PAYNE, JAMES CHRIS, II, univ. adminstr.; b. St. Petersburg, Fla., Jan. 8, 1938; s. James Chris and Elsie (Slater) P.; B.A., Fla. A&M U., 1965; M.S., Fla. State U., 1969, Ph.D., 1973; m. Anne Ruth Robinson, May 17, 1963; children—Lisa, Rodney, Nicole. Mgr. evaluation center Dept. Health and Rehab. Services, Tallahassee, 1970-72; criminal justice planner Gov.'s Council on Criminal Justice, Tallahassee, 1972-73; chief bur. research and evaluation Fla. Parole and Probation Commn., Tallahassee, 1974-76; adminstr. planning Social and Econ. Services program office Dept. Health Rehab. Services, Tallahassee, 1976-79; research asso., office of pres. Fla. State U., Tallahassee, 1979—. Served with M.C., U.S. Army, 1958-62. Alpha Kappa Alpha scholar, 1956. Home: PO Box 5981 Tallahassee FL 32301 Office: Office of Pres Fla State U Tallahassee FL 32306

PAYNE, ROBERT LAMAR, petroleum land mgmt. co. exec.; b. Crane, Tex., Mar. 27, 1932; s. Lyle Leroy and Bernice Lorine (Martin) P.; B.B.A., Baylor U., 1954; postgrad. U. Houston, 1957-58, So. Methodist U., 1958-59; m. Wanda Lu Payne, Aug. 15, 1953; children—Robert Mark, Michael Lyle, Sally A. Rock Mountain regional land mgr. San Jacinto Petroleum, Houston, 1957-60; pres. Acoustron Corp., Houston, 1960-70, also dir.; pres. Landlock Petroleum Co., Houston, 1962-71; v.p., land legal mgr. McRae Consol. Oil and Gas Corp., Houston, 1971—. Served to capt. USAF, 1954-57. Mem. Houston, Am., Ark-La-Tex, E. Tex. assns. petroleum landmen. Methodist. Clubs: Houston Athletic, Pres. Health, Bear Creek Golf. Home: 14739 Kellywood Houston TX 77079 Office: 800 Dresser Tower 601 Jefferson St Houston TX 77002

PAYNE, VIRON ERNEST, SR., research co. exec.; b. Corsicanna, Tex., Aug. 14, 1918; s. William Rufus and Aletha (Hocker) P.; B.S., Tex. A. and M. U., 1941; postgrad. U. Ala., 1962-63; m. Willodean Davis, Aug. 11, 1957; children—William E., Barry D., Viron Ernest. TV technician RCA, Hollywood, Cal., 1948-49; self-employed as mfr. TV antennas, Los Angeles, 1949-50; field engr. with USAF, Philco Corp., Guam, Korea and U.S.A., 1950-54; project engr. John I. Thompson & Co., Key West, Fla., 1954-55; project engr. Naval Ordnance Unit, Key West, 1955-56, chief analysis div., 1956-62; electronic engr. Future Missile Systems div., Redstone Arsenal, Ala., 1962-63; aerospace mgr., tech. staff to dir. tech. support Kennedy Space Center, Fla., 1963-69; pres. Viron E. Payne & Co., Inc., Merritt Island, Fla., 1955—; dir. Spaceport Flyers, Inc., Merritt Island, 1964-69. Bd. dirs. N. Merritt Island Little League, 1973-74, sec., 1974. Served to 1st lt. USAF, 1941-48. Registered investment adviser. Mem. IEEE, Mensa, Brevard Geneal. Soc. (pres. 1976-78, permanent mem.). Republican. Mem. Ch. of Christ. Contbr. articles to profl. publs. Patentee in field. Address: 200 Juniper Ave Merritt Island FL 32952

PAYNE, WILLIAM HAYDON, broadcasting exec.; b. Washington, July 3, 1939; s. William Howard and LoRena Elizabeth (Haydon) P.; B.A., Oklahoma City U., 1961; m. Gail Ann Curtis, July 3, 1960; children—Anne Marguerite, Kelly Gail, Haydon Michelle, William Haydon, II. Announcer Radio Sta. KOMA, Oklahoma City, 1959-61; technician FAA, Oklahoma City, 1961-62; owner, gen. mgr. Radio Sta. KWHP, Edmond, Okla., 1962-79; editor, pub. Graphic Newspaper, 1973-77; owner, gen. mgr. Radio Sta. KTFX, Tulsa, 1977—; pres. Central Broadcast Co. Deacon, First Presbyn. Ch., Edmond, 1962-65. Recipient award of appreciation Central State U., Edmond, 1974, FAA certificate award, 1963, awards of recognition VFW, 1967, Muscular Dystrophy, 1967, Lt. Gov.'s award for outstanding service in Kiwanis, 1970, Distinguished Service award Edmond Jr. C. of C., 1972, USN award for appreciation in assistance in Bicentennial, 1976, certificate of appreciation for outstanding accomplishment rendered as permanent group leader Dale Carnegie Sales Courses, 1977. Mem. Better Bus. Bur., Nat., Okla. broadcasters assns., Okla. Press Assn., Radio Advt. Bur., Nat. Assn. Broadcasters, Oklahoma City Advt. Club, Edmond C. of C. (medal of merit 1979), Sigma Tau Gamma (past pres.). Democrat. Mem. Metrochurch. Clubs: Kiwanis of Edmond (pres. 1969-70); Dale Carnegie Sales. Pioneer Time of Day machine; pub. Edmond Map, 1964-80. Home: 5 Trail Ridge Rd Edmond OK 73034 Office: PO Box 686 Edmond OK 73034 also The Falls Center 5840 S Memorial Tulsa OK 74145

PAYSINGER, FRANCES KNOX, educator; b. Bainbridge, Ga., Sept. 12, 1918; B.S. in Home Economics, Ga. State Coll. Women, Milledgeville, 1939; M.S. in Edn., U. Ga., Athens, 1971; married, 3 children. Home economist Gulf Power Co., Panama City, Fla., 1948-51; tchr. Bay County Pub. Schs., Panama City, 1954-60; tchr. Terry Parker High Sch., Jacksonville, Fla., 1960-71; supr. home economics edn. Duval County Schs., Jacksonville, 1971. Mem. Fla. Jr. Coll. Home Economics Adv. Com. Mem. Am. Home Economics Assn., Fla. Home Economics Assn. (v.p. 1974-76), Nat. Assn. Local Suprs. Home Economics, Am., Fla., Duval vocat. assns., Home Economics Ednl. Assn., Fla. Assn. Supervision and Curriculum Devel., AAUW, Phi Kappa Phi, Kappa Delta Pi. Home: 4705 Morris Rd Jacksonville FL 32225 Office: 1450 Flagler Ave Room 17 Jacksonville FL 32207

PAYTON, ALBERT LEVERN, chemist, educator; b. Hattiesburg, Miss., Feb. 8, 1944; s. Leroy and Alma Jean (Bady) Peyton; B.S., Alcorn State U., Lorman, Miss., 1965; M.S., So. U., Baton Rouge, 1969; Ph.D., U. So. Miss., Hattiesburg, 1976; m. Maggie Belle Smith, Oct. 21, 1965; children—Andriae Monique, Al Michaelis. Tchr. high sch. chemistry, physics and math. Hattiesburg (Miss.) Public Schs., 1965-67; instr. chemistry, math. Dillard U., New Orleans, 1969-71; asso. prof. chemistry Miss. Valley State U., Itta Bena, 1974—. Active Leflore County (Miss.) Unified PTA, 1979; supt. New Bethel Missionary Baptist Ch., Itta Bena, 1976—. Recipient Disting. Service award L.S. Rogers PTA, 1979, Khem Klub award Alcorn State U., 1979; NSF grantee, 1978—. Mem. Am. Chem. Soc., Nat. Inst. Sci., Beta Kappa Chi, Omicron Delta Kappa. Home: 703 Magnolia Ave Hattiesburg MS 39401 Office: Dept Chemistry and Physics Miss Valley State U PO Box 131 Itta Bena MS 38941

PEACE, WILLIAM KITTRELL, librarian; b. Rusk, Tex., Mar. 25, 1925; s. George Wesley and LaVada May (Meltabarger) P.; B.A., Tex. Christian U., 1950; M.Ed., U. Tex., 1960; M.S. in Library Sci. (grad. fellow 1966-67), La. State U., 1964; certificate county and regional librarianship Rutgers U., 1954. Library asst. Fort Worth Pub. Library, 1948-49, U. Tex. Library, Austin, 1950-53; asst. legislative ref. librarian Tex. State Library, Austin, 1952-53, extension librarian, 1953-55, asst. state librarian, 1955-60, 1962-66, acting state librarian, 1960-62; librarian Lee Coll., Baytown, Tex., 1967—. Cons. Pub. Library Insts., Tex. State Library, 1954-66, library services Tex. Dept. Corrections for coll. programs, 1969-71, So. Assn. Colls. and Schs., 1972—. Served with USNR, 1943-46. Mem. Baytown C. of C., Tex. Library Assn. (dist. chmn. 1969), Am. Assn. U. Profs. (chpt. pres. 1968-69), Tex. Jr. Coll. Tchrs. Assn. (chpt. pres. 1969-71 sect. chmn. 1970), Assn. Ednl. Tech. Communications. Author: History of the Texas State Library With Emphasis on the Period, 1930-59, 1959. Home: 611 N Whiting St Baytown TX 77520 Office: Box 818 Lee Dr Baytown TX 77520

PEACHEE, CHARLES ANDREW, JR., psychologist; b. Detroit, Sept. 16, 1927; s. Charles Andrew and Bessie Louise (Sullivan) P.; B.A., U. Richmond, 1949; M.S. in Clin. Psychology, Richmond Profl. Inst. of Coll. William and Mary (now Va. Commonwealth U.), 1952; m. Nancy Jane Wagner, Aug. 8, 1953; children—Carol Lynne, Barbara Lee. Psychol. asst. Western State Hosp., Staunton, Va., 1949-50; staff psychologist Central State Hosp., Petersburg, Va., 1952-55; chief psychologist Westbrook Psychiat. Hosp., Richmond, Va., 1955-57, Mobile Psychiat. Clin, Richmond, 1952-62; sr. psychologist Meml. Guidance Clinic, 1962-67; clin. psychologist, dir. Personal and Family Guidance Center, Richmond, 1967—; pvt. practice clin. psychology, Richmond, 1967—; lectr. Va. Commonwealth U., 1961-68 John Tyler Community Coll., 1974-75; appeared on weekly psychology program Sta. WXEX-TV, 1971-76; bd. dirs. Richmond Area Mental Health Assn., 1966—, chmn. edn. com., 1974—, mem. profl. adv. com., 1979—. Served with U.S. Army, 1946-47; PTO. Recipient award, plaque for therapy service Meml. Guidance Clinic, 1967; licensed psychologist, clin. psychologist, Va.; registered Nat. Register Health Service Providers in Psychology. Mem. Va. (charter, newsletter editor 1957-58, chmn. public relations com. 1966-78, chmn. ad hoc com. on freedom-of-choice health ins. legis. 1973, chmn. bd. profl. affairs 1975—), Am., Southeastern, Richmond Area psychol. assns., Va. Acad. Sci., Va. Acad. Clin. Psychologists (charter), Mid-Atlantic Group Psychotherapy Assn. (charter), AAAS, Am. Soc. Psychologists in Pvt. Practice, Richmond Alumni Assn. Sigma Alpha Epslion. Club: Salisbury Country (Midlothian, Va.). Home: 9961 Oldfield Dr Richmond VA 23235 Office: 3026 W Cary St Richmond VA 23221

PEACOCK, CONARD BERNELL, army noncommissioned officer; b. Brewton, Ala., Jan. 30, 1942; s. Conard Cleveland and Myrtle Louise (Joiner) P.; B.B.A., Campbell Coll., 1974; M. in Guidance and Counseling, U. Ala., 1976; postgrad. U. Md., 1970-75, U. Fla., 1971-72; m. Priscilla Costene Duncan, Dec. 21, 1961; 1 son, Steven Conard. Enlisted U.S. Army, 1959, advanced through grades to master sgt., 1978; truck driver, 1959-62; Morse Code intercept operator, 1962-66; mem. Spl. Forces, 1967-69; crypto technician, 1969-73, 74-76; platoon sgt., 1976; co. operations sgt., 1977; 1st sgt., 1977, group operations sgt., Ft. Hood, Tex., 1978—. Asst. scoutmaster Boy Scouts Am., 1966, den leader, 1972-73; vol. preventive child abuse Tex. Dept. Human Resources, 1978—; group facilitator Systematic Tng. for Effective Parenting, 1979. Decorated Bronze Star, Army Commendation Medal; recipient Giordano Bruno Italian Masonic award, 1972; cert. group facilitator. Mem. Non-Commd. Officers Assn. (life), Am. Personnel and Guidance Assn. Democrat. Clubs: Colosseum Lodge (Rome); Masons (master 1971-72), Shriners (pres. 1976). Home: 6223 Louisville Ave Pensacola FL 32505

PEACOCK, HARRY, ins. agy. exec.; b. Barnwell, S.C., Oct. 16, 1919; s. Furman and Idalue Wright P.; student pub. schs., Blackville, S.C.; m. Jan. 5, 1942; children—Waller L., Furman I. Owner, operator ins. agy., Blackville, 1963—; also owner night club, Blackville, 1940—. Vice chmn. Barnwell County Democratic Com.; mem. Lower Savannah River Council of Govt.; mem. Devel. Bd. S.C., 1978—. Served with USAF, 1943-51. Mem. NAACP (life), Am. Legion (post comdr., dist. comdr. Dist. 17, zone comdr. Zone 5, Graham Cup award 1970, Shirley Cup award, 1970, Nat. Achievement award 1971, Outstanding Zone Comdr. award 1972-78), VFW. Democrat. Clubs: Masons, Shriners. Office: Blackville Town Box 278 Blackville SC 29817

PEAK, DORIS JEAN, editor; b. Covington, Ga., Oct. 30, 1932; d. Edward Harold and Sadie Elizabeth (Hayes) Gast; B.A., Huntingdon Coll., 1955; m. Willie Drew Peak, Jr., Aug. 24, 1955; children—Beth, Jeanne, Lee Anne. Tchr., Dalraida Elem. Sch., Montgomery, Ala., 1955-57; research editor Bellwether, Inc., Montgomery, 1972—; officer Prologue Press, Inc., Montgomery, 1978—. Active Girl Scouts U.S.A., Montgomery, 1966—; mem. Diaconate, Westminster Presbyterian Ch., Montgomery, 1978—; mem. Community Council, United Way of Montgomery, 1974—; pres. Robert E. Lee High Sch. PTA, 1978-80. Democrat. Home: 507 Karen Rd Montgomery AL 35109 Office: PO Box 3052 Montgomery AL 36109

PEAKE, LOUIS ARTHUR, historian, educator; b. Huntington, W.Va., Nov. 17, 1946; s. Woodrow Wilson and Lucille Mae (Bowes) P.; A.B. in Social Studies, Marshall U., 1972, M.A. in History, 1976; m. Linda Sue Sams, Aug. 5, 1972. Tchr. South Point (Ohio) Jr. High Sch., 1972-74, 76; instr. So. W.Va. Community Coll., Logan, 1977; tchr. Am. and Black history Edgemeade of Ohio, Ironton, 1977-78; coordinator Lawrence County (Ohio) Joint Vocat. Sch., Chesapeake, 1978—; grad. asst. dept. history Marshall U., 1976. Chmn. Human Services Council, 1979—; disaster vol. ARC; mem. Nat. Human Rights Com. for POW/MIA's, U.S. Olympic Soc. Served with U.S. Army, 1966-69. Advanced research fellow U.S. Army Mil. History Inst., Army War Coll., 1980; Herschel Heath scholar, 1978-79. Mem. Am. Hist. Assn., Orgn. Am. Historians, Am. Mil. Inst., Co. Mil. Historians, Ohio Vocat. Assn. (chmn. S.E. Ohio region 1980), Nat. Hist. Soc., Nat. Trust Hist. Preservation, Assn. Smithsonian, Nat. Fourth Inf. Div. Assn., Assn. Am. Indian Affairs, Marshall U. Alumni Assn. Speaker conf. profl. assn.; contbg. author: Dictionary of American Military Biography. contbr. articles to profl. publs. Home: 3602 Skyview Dr Huntington WV 25701 Office: Lawrence County Joint Vocational School Route 2 Getaway Chesapeake OH 45619

PEAKE, TERRENCE MERWIN, banker; b. Des Moines, Feb. 27, 1938; s. Merwin Rollin and Allace Virginia (Westgaard) P.; B.B.A., So. Meth. U., 1965, M.B.A., 1967; postgrad. Southwestern Grad. Sch. Banking, 1977-80; m. Ina Murel Lee, Mar. 14, 1964; children—Karen Michelle, Christopher Terrence. Circulation promotion mgr. Dallas Times Herald, 1956-61; indsl. engr. Tex. Instruments, Inc., Dallas, 1961-68; sr. indsl. engr. ITT Telecommunications, Milan, Tenn., 1968-69; v.p. Republic Nat. Bank of Dallas, 1969—; instr. Dallas County Community Coll. Dist., Eastfield Coll., 1974-75. Mem. Am. Inst. Indsl. Engrs. (pres. Dallas chpt. 1974-75), Methods-Time-Measurement Assn. for Standards and Research (dir. 1975-78). Methodist. Home: 6923 Kingsbury Dr Dallas TX 75231 Office: PO Box 225961 Dallas TX 75265

PEAKER, WELDON KENDRICK, constrn. corp. exec.; b. Minden, La., Oct. 14, 1939; s. Arthur Phillip and Myra Winslow (Mims) P.; B.S., N.E. La. U., 1974; children—Kenneth Wayne, Terresa Anne, Lawrence Edward. Instrumentman, H.H. Hardeman, Minden, 1958, Demopulos & Ferguson Cons. Engrs., 1959; instrumentman, party chief, draftsman Wayne E. Williamson, 1959-62; draftsman, drafting supr. So. Mapping & Engring. Co., 1962-64; draftsman, party chief Aillet, Fenner, Jolly & McClelland, Cons. Engrs., 1964-65; project chief draftsman Ford, Bacon & Davis Constrn. Corp., Monroe, La., 1965-69, project engr., 1969-75, asst. project mgr., 1976-78, project mgr. offshore, 1978—; with W.R. Baggett & Assos., Monroe, part-time 1968-70. Mem. La. Engring. Soc., Nat. Soc. Profl. Engrs., Inst. Certification Engring. Technicians. Democrat. Methodist. Home: 119 Ada St West Monroe LA 71291 Office: Ford Bacon & Davis Constrn Corp 3901 Jackson St Monroe LA 71201

PEARCE, CHARLES WELLINGTON, surgeon; b. Ballinger, Tex., Nov. 2, 1927; s. Francis Marion and Fannie (Brown) P.; student Rice U., 1945-46, 48-49, U. Tex., 1948; M.D., Cornell U., 1953; m. Dorothy Andree DeLorenzo, Apr. 2, 1955; children—Charles Wellington, Andrew F., Margaret E., John Y., III. Intern, resident N.Y. Hosp.-Cornell U. Med. Center, N.Y.C., 1953-55, 56-60; resident Baylor U. Affiliated Hosps., 1955-56, Charity Hosp., New Orleans, 1960-61; practice medicine specializing in cardiovascular and thoracic surgery, New Orleans, 1961—; mem. staff Touro Infirmary, So. Bapt. Hosp., Hotel Dieu, Mercy Hosp., East Jefferson Hosp. (all New Orleans); mem. faculty Tulane U., New Orleans, 1960—, asso. prof. surgery, 1966-69, head sect. cardiovascular and thoracic surgery, 1967-69, asso. prof. clin. surgery, 1969—; vis. surgeon Charity Hosp., New Orleans, 1961—; cons. surgery Huey P. Long Charity Hosp., Pineville, La., 1961-70, Lallie Kemp Charity Hosp., Independence, La., 1961-70, VA Hosp., Alexandria, La., 1961—, Keesler Air Force Hosp., Biloxi, Miss., 1967-70; cons. cardiac sect. crippled children program La. Dept. Health. Served with AUS, 1946-48. La. Heart Assn. grantee, 1961-62. Diplomate Am. Bd. Surgery, Bd. Thoracic Surgery. Fellow A.C.S., Am. Coll. Chest Physicians, Am. Coll. Cardiology; mem. Am. Assn. Thoracic Surgery, Soc. for Vascular

Surgery, Am. Heart Assn. (established investigator 1962-65), Soc. Thoracic Surgeons, Internat. Cardiovascular Soc., Internat. Surg. Soc., So. Med. Assn., Orleans Parish, La. med. socs., La., New Orleans surg. socs., La. Heart Assn., New Orleans Postgrad. Med. Assembly, Soc. Mayflower Descs. (La. gov. 1975—), SAR, New Orleans Opera House Assn. (dir. 1976—), New Orleans Spring Fiesta Assn., New Orleans Opera Club, Fgn. Relations Assn., La. Landmark Soc., New Orleans Mus. Art, New Orleans Area C. of C., Internat. Platform Assn., R Assn. Rice U., Phi Chi, Alpha Omega Alpha. Republican. Presbyn. Contbr. articles to profl. jours. Home: 1662 State St New Orleans LA 70118 Office: 2633 Napolean Ave New Orleans LA 70115

PEARCE, DOROTHY ANDREE DE LORENZO, civic worker; b. N.Y.C., Mar. 22, 1927; d. Andrew John and Margaret (Robilotti) De Lorenzo; B.A., Barnard Coll., 1947; m. Charles W. Pearce, Apr. 2, 1955; children—Charles W., Andrew Francis, Margaret Elizabeth, John Y. III. Research asst. cardiac catherization lab. Bellevue Hosp., 1948-50, Cornell Med. Coll., 1950-55; exec. research librarian Shell Chem. Co., 1955-57. Thrift shop rep. Soc. N.Y. Hosp. Women's Aux., 1959-60; bd. govs. New Orleans Opera House Assn. Women's Guild, 1965-73, social hostess, 1966-71, historian, 1969—; chmn. uptown subscription com., 1967-69, mem. children's concerts com., 1964-66; mem. tour com. New Orleans Springs Fiesta Assn., 1966-67; mem. opera orientation com. New Orleans Opera House Assn., 1964-72, registrar, hostess, 1965; active New Orleans Symphony Previews, 1968—; mem. fund raising com. De Paul Hosp. Women's Aux., 1968—; vol. Crippled Children's Hosp. Guild, 1965-66; mem. La. Council for Performing Arts, 1967—; mem. Gallier Hall Women's Com., 1967; mem. bd. Community Concerts Assn., New Orleans; mem. fund raising com. Hotel Dieu Women's Aux., 1968—. Bd. dirs. Mercy Hosp. Women's Aux., 1965-72, pres., 1970; bd. dirs. Sara Mayo Hosp. Guild, 1964—, chmn. hospitality com., 1967-72; bd. dirs. Orleans Parish Med. Soc. Women's Aux., 1969-71, chmn. A.M.A. edn. and research fund com., 1969-71; bd. dirs. Vis. Nurses Assn. Mem. New Orleans Garden Soc. (chmn. Christmas decorations 1969-70), Fgn. Relations Assn., Am. Assn. U. Women, La. Landmark Soc. Republican. Roman Catholic. Club: New Orleans Country. Home: 1662 State St New Orleans LA 70118

PEARCE, HARLEE JOSIE, JR., accountant; b. Florence, S.C., Aug. 15, 1940; s. Harlee Josie and Ida Lois (Utsey) P.; B.S. in Bus. Adminstrn., The Citadel, 1962; m. Mary Jacquelyn McNeill, Apr. 15, 1961; children—Rebecca Olivia, Mary Josie, Lee David. Rental mgr. Bel-Aire Realty, Cherry Grove, S.C., 1962; account exec. Dixon Mktg., Inc., Kinston, N.C., 1965-69; bus. mgr. WIS-TV, Columbia, S.C., 1969-71; sales agt. Pilot Life Ins., Columbia, 1971; dir. fiscal ops. S.C. State Govt., Hwy. Safety, Columbia, 1971—. Served with U.S. Army, 1962-65. Decorated Army Commendation medal. Mem. St. Andrews-Irmo Jaycees (Key Man 1974, 76, Jaycee of Year 1974, Senator 1977). Presbyterian. Clubs: Kinston Lions, Meth. Men. Home: 3208 Bush River Rd Columbia SC 29210 Office: Edgar Brown Bldg Room 477 1205 Pendleton St Columbia SC 29201

PEARSON, BILLY GENE, mfg. co. exec.; b. Amory, Miss., Jan. 6, 1933; s. Carl and Claude (Kyle) P.; student Itawamba Jr. Coll., 1956; B.S., Miss. State U., 1958, M.Ed., 1961; m. Bonita Dawn Nash, July 4, 1953; children—Bill Alan, Vicky Lee, Suzanne. Tchr., coach Lynville High Sch., Preston, Miss., 1958-60, Maben (Miss.) High Sch., 1960-61; coach, guidance counselor Aberdeen (Miss.) High Sch., 1961-63; employment mgr. Walker Mfg. Co., Aberdeen, 1963-69; mgr. employee relations True Temper Corp., Amory, Miss., 1969—. Mem. Hatley Sch. Bd., 1973-75, pres., 1975. Served with U.S. Army, 1953-55. Mem. Monroe County C. of C. (dir. 1978, Am. Soc. Personnel Adminstrn., N. Miss. Indsl. Relations Assn., Tombigbee Indsl. Club. Mem. Ch. of Christ. Home: Route 3 Box 304 Amory MS 38821 Office: PO Box E Hwy 25 Amory MS 38821

PEARSON, DANIEL S., judge; b. N.Y.C., Oct. 9, 1930; s. Joseph and Lee (Epstein) P.; B.A., Amherst Coll., 1955; J.D., Yale U., 1958; m. Beverly Ann Danto, July 1, 1956; children—Elizabeth, William, Charles. Admitted to Fla. bar, 1959; asso. firm Boardman, Bolles, Davant & Lloyd, Miami, Fla., 1959-61; asst. U.S. atty., Miami, 1961-63; pvt. practice law, Miami, 1963-67; partner firm Pearson & Josefsberg, Miami, 1967-80; judge Dist. Ct. Appeal 3d Dist. Fla., 1980—; adj. prof. U. Miami Law Sch.; lectr. Nova Law Sch., Practising Law Inst., Acad. Fla. Trial Lawyers, Continuing Legal Edn. Fla. Bar. Served with USCG, 1951-54. Mem. Am., Fla., Dade County bar assns. Home: 9266 SW 136th St Circle Miami FL 33176 Office: PO Box 650307 Miami FL 33165

PEARSON, JUDITH ELIZABETH, psychologist; b. Kansas City, Mo., June 19, 1950; d. Richard and Lois Jane (Dyer) Curtis; B.S., Kans. State Coll., 1972; M.A., East Carolina U., 1977; postgrad. Cath. U.; m. Craig Edwin Pearson, June 10, 1972. Social worker Dept. Social Services, Cumberland County, N.C., 1973; psychologist asst. Children's Treatment Center, Fayetteville, N.C., 1973-76; child screening specialist N.C. Developmental Evaluation Centers, Fayetteville, 1976-78; psychologist, psychol. services staff CIA, 1978—. Mem. Am. Psychol. Assn., Alpha Kappa Delta. Home: 8504 Richmond Ave Alexandria VA 22309

PEARSON, KENNETH GEORGE, JR., med. center exec.; b. Clarksdale, Miss., Mar. 4, 1950; s. Kenneth George and Rosemary Catherine (Lane) P.; B.B.A., Delta State U., 1972; m. Debra Francis Brown, Aug. 19, 1972; 1 dau., Rachel Melody. Creditman, Nat. Data Corp., Atlanta, 1972-74; coordinating mgr. ServiceMaster Industries, Inc., Atlanta, 1974-77; instl. dir. services N. E. Ala. Regional Med. Center, Anniston, Ala., 1977—. Asst. scoutmaster, cubmaster Boy Scouts Am., 1969-70, scoutmaster, cubmaster, 1970-72, cubmaster, Webelows leader, 1972-75, scoutmaster, 1975-77, neighborhood commr., 1979—; instl. chmn. United Way campaign, 1978. Recipient Outstanding Ch. Laymen award Chamblee/Doraville Jr. C. of C., 1973-74. Mem. Am. Mgmt. Assn., Ala. Hosp. Assn., Nat. Fire Protection Assn., Am. Inst. Maintenance, Nat. Assn. Instl. Laundry Mgrs., Nat. Exec. Housekeepers Assn. Methodist. Office: N E Ala Regional Med Center 400 E 10th St Anniston AL 36201

PEARSON, MARGARET DONOVAN, educator; b. Nashville, Oct. 29, 1921; d. Timothy Graham and Nelle Ligon (Schmidt) Donovan; B.A., George Peabody Coll., Nashville, 1944, M.A., 1950; M.S., U. Tenn., Knoxville, 1954; widow. Cryptanalysist, U.S. Govt., Washington, 1944-45; tchr. Nashville city schs., 1945-46, White County schs., Sparta, Tenn., 1946-57; specialist div. edn. handicapped Tenn. Dept. Edn., Cookeville, 1957—; mem. part-time faculty Tenn. Tech. U., Cookeville, 1970—; guest lectr. St. Louis U., Vanderbilt U., U. Tenn., Knoxville, Middle Tenn. State U., Memphis State U. Fellow Am. Speech and Hearing Assn.; mem. Tenn. Council Exceptional Children (pres. 1960, Outstanding Mem. award 1961), Council Exceptional Children (pres. chpt. 1959), NEA, Assn. Supervision and Curriculum Devel., Tenn. Speech and Hearing Assn. (v.p. 1972), Bus. and Profl. Women (dist. dir. 1971), Delta Kappa Gamma. Methodist. Home: 114 Highland Dr Sparta TN 38583 Office: Box 5077 Tenn Tech Univ Cookeville TN 38501

PEARSON, OLEN RAYMOND, mathematician, physicist; b. Americus, Ga., Oct. 5, 1946; s. Olen and Pearl Lowe (Hanner) P.; B.S., Emory U., 1967, M.S., 1969; M.Ed., Columbus Coll., 1978. Grad. teaching asst. Emory U., 1968-70; tchr. math. and sci., high sch. Columbus (Ga.) Christian Schs., 1971-74; asst. prof. math. and physics Ga. Mil. Coll., 1974-77, Piedmont Coll., 1978—; instr. in chemistry Columbus Coll., 1978; state sci. fair judge; mem. conv. rev. coms.; sci. speaker to local groups. Named Outstanding Young Man of Am., U.S. Jaycees, 1979; NSF research fellow, 1969; cert. tchr. math., physics, chemistry and sci., Ga. Mem. Ga. Acad. Sci., Nat. Sci. Tchrs. Assn., Am. Inst. Physics, Am. Assn. Phyics Tchrs., Sigma Xi, Sigma Pi Sigma. Baptist. Revising author: Physics Laboratory Experiments, 1970; reviewer introductory physics manuscripts Wadsworth Pub. Co. Home: PO Box 668 Demorest GA 30535 Office: Piedmont Coll Demorest GA 30535

PEARSON, SUSAN WINIFRED, coll. adminstr.; b. Wasco, Calif., Oct. 8, 1941; d. Gerald T. and Maxine K. (Jensen) Pearson; B.S., Tex. Christian U., 1963; M.Ed., Tex. Christian U., 1971; postgrad. U. Houston, 1973—. Tchr., chmn. dept. Spring Branch Ind. Sch. Dist., Houston, 1963-68; personnel asst. Tenneco Inc., Houston, 1969-70; grad. asst. Tex. Christian U., Ft. Worth, 1970-71, instr., 1971—; dir. student activities Navarro Jr. Coll., Corsicana, Tex., 1972-73; dir. counseling services N. Harris County Coll., Houston, 1973—. Mem. Am. Personnel and Guidance Assn., Am. Coll. Personnel Assn., Nat. Assn. Women Deans, Adminstrs. and Counselors, Tex. Assn. Coll. and Univ. Student Personnel Adminstrs., So. Coll. Personnel Assn., S.W. Assn. Student Personnel Adminstrs., Delta Gamma, Phi Kappa Phi. Presbyterian. Office: 2700 W W Thorne Dr Houston TX 77073

PEAVOY, SHARON ANN, counselor; b. Bridgeport, Conn., Mar. 11, 1951; d. Edward Ellis and Ann Marie (Von Dietsch) P.; B.A., Pfeiffer Coll., 1973; M.A.E., E. Carolina U., 1979. Asst. coordinator learning disabilities Albermarle (N.C.) City Sch., 1973; tchr. basic psychology Anson County Tech. Inst., Ansonville, N.C., 1976; ct. counselor 20th Jud. Dist., Wadesboro, N.C., 1973-76; juvenile intake counselor II 12th Jud. Dist., Fayetteville, N.C., 1976—; co-therapist family counseling; condr. ednl. workshops on hyperactivity, panel on group counseling. Chmn. Children's Service Com., City of Wadesboro, 1974-75; chmn. Anson County Youth Adv. Bd., 1975-76; sec. Anson County Inter-Agy. Council, 1975-76; sec. Anson County Child Find Task Force, 1976; mem. Anson County Family Planning Com., 1976. Mem. N.C. Juvenile Services Assn., Am. Personnel and Guidance Assn., Public Offender Counselor Assn. Democrat. Roman Catholic. Home: 3102-A Beckham Pl Fayetteville NC 28304 Office: 12th Jud Dist PO Box 363 Fayetteville NC 28302

PEAVY, DON EZZARD, SR., newspaper editor, credit union mgr.; b. Ft. Worth, Dec. 2, 1950; s. Dan Aubrey, Sr., and Roxie Mae (Dawson) P.; A.A. with honors, Tarrant County Jr. Coll., 1974; B.A., Tex. Christian U., 1976; m. Pattie Jo Clark, Aug. 31, 1974; children—Cheryl Lynn, Don Ezzard. Dir. Vets. Upward Bound Project, Tarrant County Jr. Coll., Ft. Worth, 1974-76; pres. Donepe Co., Ft. Worth, 1976—; editor Tex. Vets. News, Ft. Worth, 1974—; treas., mgr. Tex. Vets. Fed. Credit Union, Ft. Worth, 1977—, treas. bd. dirs.; cons. AMVETS. Pres. Maddox Neighborhood Council, 1979; exec. v.p., asso. editor A Galaxy of Verse Lit. Found., 1977-79; bd. dirs. 12th Dist. Conservative Caucus, 1978-79. Served with U.S. Army, 1970-72. Mem. Press Club Ft. Worth, Nat. Writers Club, Tex. Press Assn., Tex. Credit Union League, AMVETS. Baptist. Author: Brotherhood of the Battlefield, 1976; Without Humor or Grief, 1979. Home: 4820 El Rancho Rd Fort Worth TX 76119 Office: PO Box 15356 Fort Worth TX 76119

PECERI, MICHAEL BERNARD, resort exec.; b. Schenectady, Apr. 9, 1926; s. Michael and Bernadette P.; B.S., Rider Coll., 1951; M.S., George Washington U., 1968; P.M.D., Havard U. Bus. Sch., 1967; m. JoAnn Bennett, Oct. 31, 1970. Diplomatic service Dept. State, Vienna, Moscow, Buenos Aires, 1954-69; fgn. service officer Edison Nat. Bank, Fort Myers, Fla., 1969-72; mgr. Mariner Group, Inc., Sanibel, Fla., 1972—; v.p., gen. mgr. South Seas Plantation, Captiva, Fla., 1976—. Bd. dirs. Edison Community Coll. Endowment Fund; pres. Fla. Assn. Orchestras, Fort Myers Symphony and Opera Assn. Served with USN, World War II. Recipient Meritorious award for service Nat. Security Council, White House, Dept. State, 1970. Mem. Am. Hotel and Motel Assn., Fla. Hotel and Motel Assn. (dir. 1980), Nat. Restaurant Assn., Met. Fort Myers C. of C., Sanibel-Captiva Islands C. of C. (pres.). Roman Catholic. Clubs: Lions, Harvard. Home: 1143 Sand Castle Rd Sanibel FL 33957 Office: South Seas Plantation PO Box 194 Captiva FL 33924

PECHACEK, RAYMOND EDWARD, engring. co. exec.; b. Flatonia, Tex., Oct. 13, 1915; s. Frank Fred and Emma (Hajek) P.; B.S. in Mech. Engring., U. Tex., 1939; m. Marie Pfluger, Sept. 7, 1940; children—Patsy Pechacek Klaus, Jane Pechacek Moller, Linda Pechacek Andron, Raymond, Debbie. Job engr. Fluor Corp., Kansas City, Mo., 1939-40; chief engr. Wyatt, Industries, Houston, 1940-46; product engr. A.O. Smith Corp., Houston, 1946-54; v.p. Hahn & Clay, Houston, 1954—. Pres., Gethsemy Lutheran Ch., Houston, 1966-68, bd. elders, 1977—. Mem. ASME, Tex. Soc. Profl. Engrs. (past pres. local chpt.; chmn. state employment practices com. 1976-80; named Engr. of Note, N.W. Houston chpt. 1976; Order of Engr., 1977), Am. Nuclear Soc., Houston Engring. and Sci. Soc. Patentee pressures seals and closures, ocean diving equipment; contbr. articles to profl. jours. Home: 1846 Latexo Houston TX 77018 Office: 5100 Clinton St Houston TX 77020

PECK, DIANNE KAWECKI, architect; b. Jersey City, June 13, 1945; d. Thaddeus Walter and Harriet Ann (Zlotkowski) Kawecki; B.A., Carnegie-Mellon U., 1968; m. Gerald Paul Peck, Sept. 1, 1968; children—Samantha Gillian, Alexis Hilary. Staff, Berry, Rio & Assos., Annandale, Va., 1968-70, Kohler-Daniels Co., Vienna, Va., 1970-71; asso. Beery, Rio & Assos., Annandale, 1971-73; partner Peck & Peck, Occoquan, Va., 1973-74, Peck, Peck & Williams, Occoquan, 1974—; lectr. in field; cons. Active Republican party; v.p. Vocat. Edn. Found., 1975. Mem. AIA, Prince William C. of C. (dir. 1975—), Washington Profl. Women's Coop. (chairwoman Indsl. Devel. Authority 1976), Health Systems Agency No.Va., AAUW (community rep. 1975), Roman Catholic. Soroptimist (del. Woodbridge 1977). Registered architect, Va., Md. Home: 11510 Wildflower Ct Woodbridge VA 22192 Office: 1986 Opitz Blvd Woodbridge VA 22191

PECK, JOSEPH RICHARD, racquetball complex mgr.; b. Lexington, Ky., Oct. 1, 1947; s. Bob K. and Joy (Freeman) P.; B.A., U. Ky., 1969; m. Susan Pelton, May 18, 1968; children—Mercedes Kirsten, Robert Richard. Product mgr. Sight & Sound Internat., Milw., 1971-72; dir. mktg. Hal Leonard Publ. Corp., Milw., after 1972, then dir. product devel.; gen. mgr. Sturgeon Constrn., Pompano Beach, Fla., to 1979, Quadrangle Racquetball Complex, Coral Springs, Fla., 1979—. Mem. U.S. Racquetball Assn., Am. Amateur Racquetball Assn. Baptist. Contbr. articles to profl. jours. Office: 8414 NW 35 St Coral Springs FL 33065

PECK, PAUL SCOTT, mayor; b. Sutton, W.Va., Sept. 28, 1948; s. Benjamin William and Lucile (Bosely) P.; B.A., Glenville State Coll., 1970; postgrad. W.Va. U., 1972, 76-77. Tchr., Braxton County High Sch., 1970-76, Gassaway Middle Sch., 1977-80; recorder Town of Burnsville (W.Va.), 1973-75, 76-77, acting mayor, 1975, councilman, 1975, mayor, 1977—; lectr. math. W.Va. U., 1980—. Mem. NEA, W.Va. Edn. Assn., Nat. Council Tchrs. Math. Democrat. Methodist. Club: Burnsville Lions. Home: Academy St Burnsville WV 26335 Office: Municipal St Burnsville WV 26335

PECK, RICHARD HYDE, hosp. adminstr.; b. Fort McClelland, Ala., Aug. 30, 1941; s. Robert H. and Elizabeth M. P.; A.B., U. N.C., 1963; M.H.A., Duke U., 1966; m. Barbara Mansfield, Dec. 27, 1964; children—Catherine, Nancy, Joanne. Adminstrv. asst. Univ. Hosps. of Cleve., 1966-67, asst. adminstr., 1967-69; asst. dir. Duke U. Hosp., Durham, N.C., 1969-71, asso. dir., 1971-73, adminstrv. dir., 1973—, asso. prof. Duke U. Health Adminstrn. Program. Mem. exec. com. Durham chpt. ARC, 1976-79. Mem. Am. Coll. Hosp. Adminstrs., N.C. Hosp. Assn. Democrat. Presbyterian. Home: 2833 McDowell Rd Durham NC 27705 Office: Box 3708 Duke Hosp Durham NC 27710

PEDDADA, ANANDARAO VENKATA, environ. engr.; b. Eluru, Andhrapradesh, India, Feb. 28, 1935; s. Syamala Das and Sanjeevamma (Rayasam) R.; came to U.S., 1971, naturalized, 1978; B.Sc., Andhra U., India, 1954; B.Tech. with honors, Indian Inst. Tech., Kharagpur, 1958, M.Tech., 1961; Ph.D., W.Va. U., 1975; m. Jalaja Revuru, Oct. 1, 1960; children—Abhinand, Anuj, Arvind. Design asst. Central Water and Power Commn., Govt. of India, Delhi, 1958-60; asst. engr. Hochtief-Gammons, Rourkela Steel Plant, India, 1961-62; asst. exec. engr Nat. Indsl. Devel. Corp., New Delhi, 1962-68; design engr. Engrs. India Ltd., New Delhi, 1968-71; project engr., research asst. civil engring. dept. W.Va. U., 1971-75; sr. environ. engr. H.K.S. Inc., Beckley, W.Va., 1975-77; chief environ. engr. L.J. Daigre Assos., Alexandria, La., 1977-80; owner A.V.P. Cons. Engrs., 1980—. Founding mem., sec. So. W.Va. India Cultural Assn., Beckley, 1975-76. Registered profl. engr., W.Va., Ohio, Tex., S.C., Calif., La.; diplomate Am. Acad. Environ. Engrs. Mem. Water Pollution Control Fedn., Nat. Soc. Profl. Engrs., ASCE, La. Soc. Engrs. Author tech. studies. Home and Office: 4121 Mayflower Blvd Alexandria LA 71301

PEDDICORD, HERSCHEL QUINTON, JR., educator; b. Macon, Ga., June 26, 1927; s. Herschel Quinton and Mamie Gertrude (Johnson) P.; B.A., Presbyterian Coll., Clinton, S.C., 1951; M.Ed., U. S.C., 1957; Ed.D., Duke U., 1967; m. Mary Evelyn Hill, June 1, 1949; children—Herschel Quinton III, Wallace Dean. Elem., high sch. prin. Cordova (S.C.) Schs., 1951-53; tchr., coach Edisto High Sch., Cordova, 1953-54; coach, high sch. prin. Harleyville (S.C.) - Ridgeville Schs., 1954-56; prin. Allendale-Fairfax (S.C.) High Sch., 1956-62, Palmetto High Sch., Williamston, S.C., 1964-72; faculty U. So. Miss., Hattiesburg, 1971—, asso. prof. dept. curriculum and instrn., 1973—. Served with USMCR, 1942-45. Mem. Assn. Tchr. Educators, Nat. Assn Secondary Sch. Prins., Miss. Assn. Higher Edn., Assn. for Supervision and Curriculum Devel., Council Basic Edn., Kappa Delta Pi, Phi Delta Kappa. Home: 109 Tanglewood Dr Hattiesburg MS 39401 Office: U So Miss Box 8432 Southern Sta Hattiesburg MS 39401

PEDDICORD, MARY EVELYN HILL, ednl. adminstr.; b. Laurens, S.C., Oct. 21, 1932; d. Robert Lee and Eunice Lenora (Culbertson) Hill; A.A. summa cum laude, Anderson Coll., 1969; A.B. with honors, Clemson U., 1971; M.S., U. So. Miss., 1972, postgrad. (Grad. fellow 1976-77), 1973—; m. Herschel Q. Peddicord, Jr., June 1, 1949; children—Herschel Q., Wallace D. Tchr., Laurel (Miss.) City Schs., 1972-74, Hattiesburg (Miss.) City Schs., 1974-75; instr. U. So. Miss., Hattiesburg, 1976-77; instr., chmn. humanities dept. Pearl River Jr. Coll., Poplarville, Miss., 1977—. Mem. Nat. Council Tchrs. English, SE Conf. on English in Two Year Coll., South Central MLA, English Commn. for Miss., Kappa Delta Pi. Baptist. Club: Kappa Kappa Iota. Home: 109 Tanglewood Dr Hattiesburg MS 39401 Office: Academic Bldg Office 133 Pearl River Junior College Poplarville MS 39470

PEDEN, RALPH KENNETH, educator; b. Owings, S.C., Apr. 11, 1934; s. William Ralph and Ida Beatrice (Curry) P.; B.S., Presbyn. Coll., Clinton, S.C., 1956; M.A., Middle Tenn. State U., 1965; Ed.D., U. Miss., 1972; m. Greeta Granger, Mar. 7, 1959; children—Cindy Ann, David Ralph. Sci tchr., prin. Hebron (S.C.) High Sch., 1955-56; chmn. sci. dept. Blue Ridge High Sch., Greer, S.C., 1960-71; prof. health edn. for future tchrs. Clemson (S.C.) Coll., 1972—; cons. in field. Bd. dirs., v.p. S.C. Lung Assn., v.p. Piedmont br.; bd. dirs. local Am. Cancer Soc.; v.p. Cancer Soc. Pickens, 1979—; bd. dirs. Anderson County chpt. ARC; chmn. Pendleton City United Way. Served with USAF, 1956-60. NSF grantee, summers 1963-68; NDEA fellow, 1971-73; named Ruritan Club Tchr. of Year, 1969, Outstanding Kappan of Yr., 1979; Star Tchr., Greenville County, S.C., 1970. Mem. Am. Sch. Health Assn. (chmn. safety and emergency care sect.), AAHPER, S.C. Pub. Health Assn., S.C. Assn. Health Educators, Diabetic Assn., Am. Personnel and Guidance Assn., NEA, Nat. Sci. Tchrs. Assn., Nat. Biology Tchrs. Assn., AAUP. Methodist. Clubs: Exchange (pres Clemson 1977-78, dist. dir.), Masons. Author curriculum materials, articles. Home: Route 2 Shannon Dr Pendleton SC 29670 Office: Dept Elementary and Secondary Edn Clemson Univ Clemson SC 29631

PEDEN, ROBERT F., JR., lawyer; b. Ft. Worth, July 26, 1911; s. Robert F. and Laura (Phillips) P.; LL.B., Cumberland U., 1933; m. Virginia LeTulle, May 25, 1939. Admitted to Tex. bar, 1934; practice law, Bay City, 1934—; city atty., Bay City, 1935-38, 65-79; atty. Matagorda County, Tex., 1939-46, 50-54. Bd. dirs. Bay City Library Assn. Mem. State Bar Tex., Am., Matagorda (pres. 1961-62, v.p. 1967-68) bar assns., Am. Judicature Soc., Lambda Chi Alpha. Democrat. Presbyterian (clk. session 1969-71). Rotarian (v.p. 1968-69, pres. 1969-70). Club: Knife and Fork (dir. 1968-69, pres. 1970-71). Home: 1916 Austin St Bay City TX 77414 Office: 1212 7th St PO Box 1245 Bay City TX 77414

PEDRICK, ALLEN REID, mfg. co. exec.; b. Pleasantville, N.J., Dec. 26, 1929; s. Charles Allen and Margaret (Reid) P.; B.S., Lehigh U., 1951, M.S., 1952; m. Daisy Lee Pedrick, June 22, 1968; children—Allen Reid, Robin Reid, Cinda Irene. Contracts and mktg. staff RCA, N.J. and Calif., 1951-58, mgr. southeastern region, 1958-60, contract mgr., 1960-61; exec. asst. NASA-Kennedy Space Center, 1961-68; dir. contracts and mktg. Bendix Corp., Cocoa Beach, Fla., 1969-78; dep. gen. mgr. Applied Devices Corp., Kissimmee, Fla., 1978—; cons. in field Bd. dirs. Retarded Children's Assn. Brevard County (Fla.), 1961—, pres., 1973-75. Served with U.S. Army, 1948-51. Recipient Silver Snoopy award NASA. Mem. Nat. Contracts Mgmt. Assn., Am. Radio Relay League. Democrat. Presbyterian (elder). Author (under name Allen Reid): R.F. Propagation, 1960; The Golden Spheres, 1970; Short Stories, 1973. Patentee in field. Home: 1446 Hagen Ln Rockledge FL 32955 Office: 2931 N Poinciana Blvd Kissimmee FL 32741

PEDRO, CLIFFORD TONY, Indian tribal govt. exec.; b. Concho, Okla., Aug. 7, 1936; s. John and Rose (Charcoal) P.; student Okla. State U., 1955-56; A.E.E., DeVry Tech. U., 1962; m. Janis Mary Hammermeister, Oct. 23, 1971; children—Francis Joseph, Joanna Michelle, Sean Anthony. Seismic instr., engr. Geophys. Service Internat., Middle East, SE Asia, Far East, 1963-71; with Petty-Ray Geophys., Geophys. Service Internat., Rocky Mountain Area,

1972-76; resource devel. coordinator Cheyenne-Arapaho Tribal Govt., Concho, 1977—; cons. Bur. Indian Affairs, Dept. Interior, Andrew Skeeter, Inc., Adminstrn. for Native Ams., Dept. Health and Human Services. Served with U.S. Army, 1956-60. Mem. U.S. Indian Planners Assn., Nat. Congress Am. Indians, Nat. Indian Edn. Assn., Am. Acad. Polit. and Social Sci., Am. Mgmt. Assn. Democrat. Home: PO Box 181 Calumet OK 73014 Office: PO Box 93 Concho OK 73022

PEEBLES, EMORY BUSH, JR., stevedoring co. exec.; b. Mobile, Ala., Dec. 17, 1918; s. Emory Bush and Geraldine (Hill) P.; B.A., The Citadel, 1939; m. Augusta Lee Baldwin, June 3, 1941; children—Emory Bush, Laura Peebles Rutherford, John D. With Ryan Stevedoring Co., Inc., Mobile, 1939—, v.p., 1956-65, exec. v.p., 1965-74, sr. exec. v.p. Ryan-Walsh Stevedoring Co., Inc. (merger Ryan Stevedoring Co. and Walsh Stevedoring Co. 1974), 1974—, also dir.; pres., dir. Stevedores, Inc.; v.p., dir. Marine Bulk Handling Corp.; sr. exec. v.p., dir. So. S.S. Agy., Inc.; chmn. bd., dir. Eastern Shore Nat. Bank; exec. v.p., dir. So. Marine Service, Inc., Container Services Internat., Inc.; dir. 1st Nat. Bank Mobile, First Bancorp, Ala. Dry Dock & Shipbldg. Corp., Mobile Gas Corp. Vice pres. Sr. Bowl Com.; past pres. Am.'s Jr. Miss Pageant; mem. Regional Export Expansion Council, 1969-71. Served with AUS, 1941-46; PTO. Decorated Bronze Star, Purple Heart. Mem. Mobile Arts and Sports Assn. (v.p., trustee), Mobile Area C. of C. (past dir.), Newcomen Soc. N.Am. Republican. Episcopalian. Clubs: Mobile Touchdown (past pres.), Country; Athelstan, Lakewood Country, Bienville, Internat. Trade, Fairhope Yacht. Home: Peeblesshire Point Clear AL 36564 Office: 150 N Royal St PO Box 2188 Mobile AL 36601

PEEBLES, LARRY MASON, radiologist; b. Fayetteville, Tenn., Aug. 3, 1938; s. Milton H. and N. Katherine (McQuiddy) P.; B.A., Harding U., 1960; M.D., U. Ark., 1965; m. Tish Maynard, June 3, 1960; children—Laura, Angie Beth, Mason. Intern, U. Hosp., Little Rock; gen. practice medicine, Texarkana, Tex., 1966-73; resident in radiology U. Hosp., Little Rock, 1973-76; practice medicine specializing in radiology, Texarkana, 1976—; clin. prof. radiology U. Ark., 1976—. Mem. president's devel. council Harding U., Searcy, Ark.; deacon Nash Ch. of Christ. Served with USAF, 1968. Mem. Tex. Med. Assn., AMA, Am. Coll. Radiology. Home: Route 3 Box 258 Texarkana TX 75503 Office: 3300 Rhozine St Texarkana TX 75503

PEEL, WILLIAM LAURIE, JR., architect; b. Memphis, Mar. 21, 1952; s. William Laurie and Dorothy Allene (South) P.; B. Environ. Design, Tex. A&M U., 1974, M.Arch., 1975; m. Sansa Headrick, May 25, 1974; 1 son, Christopher William. Research asst. Tex. A&M U., 1974-75, adminstrv. asst., 1975-76; project architect, project designer 3D/Internat., Austin, Tex., 1976-79, bus. devel. specialist Houston, 1979—. Registered architect, Tex. Mem. AIA, Constrn. Specifications Inst., Tex. Soc. Architects, Alpha Tau Omega. Home: 11755 Southlake Dr Apt 121 Houston TX 77077 Office: 1900 West Loop S Suite 200 Houston TX 77027

PEELER, RAY DOSS, JR., lawyer; b. Bonham, Tex., May 4, 1929; s. Ray Doss and Opal (Porter) P.; B.A. with high honors, U. Tex., 1948, LL.B., 1951; children—William Bryan, Maribel Porter. Admitted to Tex. bar, 1951; practiced law, Bonham, 1953—, dist. and county atty., Fannin County, 1960-61; pres. Fannin Nat. Bank, Windom, Tex., 1963-70, chmn. bd., 1970—; chmn. bd. 1st Nat. Bank, Bonham, 1972—. Del. Democratic Nat. Conv., 1960; trustee S.B. Allen Meml. Hosp., Bonham, 1962—; chmn. Bonham United Fund, 1959; pres. Bonham Indsl. Found., 1965-75. Served to capt. USAF, 1951-53. Mem. State Bar Tex., Am. Bar Assn., State Jr. Bar Tex. (v.p. 1959-60), Tex. Horticulture Soc. (pres. 1974-76), Tex. Pecan Growers Assn. (pres. 1974-76), Bonham C. of C. (pres. 1958), Fannin County Hist. Soc. (hon. life, sponsor 1954-60), Phi Beta Kappa, Phi Gamma Delta, Phi Alpha Delta. Mem. Christian Ch. Clubs: Bonham Rotary (pres. 1957), Bonham Golf (dir. 1958-61), Quail Hollow Country. Home: 400 W 5th St Bonham TX 75418 Office: 302 Peeler Bldg Bonham TX 75418

PEER, GARY GAIL, coll. dean; b. Hoisington, Kans., Nov. 14, 1940; s. Glenn E. and Genevieve G. (Balch) P.; B.A. in History, Washburn U., 1963; M.S., Emporia Kans. State Coll., 1967; Ed.D. in Counseling and Guidance, Ind. U., 1971; m. Beverly Pedigo, June 23, 1958; children—Teri, Mike, Duke. Tchr., Spring Hill (Kans.) pub. schs., 1963-65; counselor Unified Sch. Dist. 330, Eskridge, Kans., 1966-67; asst. prof. edn. Emporia (Kans.) State Coll., 1967-69; vis. asst. prof. edn. Ind. U., Bloomington, 1971-72; asst. prof. edn. U. Tulsa, 1972-74, asso. prof., 1974—, asso. dean Coll. Edn., 1976—. Mem. Am. (chmn. Midwest region 1979-80, dir. 1980-83), Okla. (pres. 1976-77) personnel and guidance assns., Rocky Mountain Ednl. Research Assns., Okla. Edn. Assn., Assn. Counselor Educators and Supervisors, Phi Delta Kappa. Democrat. Contbr. numerous articles on counseling to profl. jours. Home: 4152 E 47th St Tulsa OK 74135 Office: 600 S College St Tulsa OK 74104

PEERY, CHARLES MARTIN, publisher, Angus breeder; b. Tazewell, Va., Aug. 1, 1920; s. Charles Clarence and Irene P.; B.S. in Animal Husbandry, Va. Polytechnic Inst., 1941; m. Mildred C. Bilhardt, May 25, 1943; children—Irene M., Barbara A., Charles M. Field rep. Eastern Breeder Mag., 1948-49; sec. Md. Angus Assn., 1949-51; mgr. Glenangus Farm, Bel Air, Md., 1951-55, Forest Grove Farm, Sparaland, Ill., 1956-57; pres. Angus Topics, Inc., also publisher, editor Angus Topics Mag., New Market, 1959—; owner Senendoa Farm, New Market, 1966—. Served to capt. U.S. Army, 1941-46. Mem. Am. Angus Assn., Va. Angus Assn., Va. Beef Cattle Assn., New Market C. of C., South Bus. Assn. Republican. Methodist. Home and Office: PO Box 4 New Market VA 22844

PEERY, WILLIAM ROBERT, architect; b. Gardner, Va., July 31, 1917; s. James Harve and Eva Leona (Hurt) P.; B.F.A., Ohio U., 1951; B.S., Morris Harvey Coll., 1952; m. Mary Jo Ritchie, July 24, 1942; children—Kathryn Peery Rollins, Elizabeth Peery Mays; m. 2d, Carrie Elizabeth Brown, Jan. 1, 1954; children—Alfred M., Robert B., Patricia L. Cons. architect Union Carbide Corp., South Charleston, W.Va., 1956—; pres. William R. Peery, Architect-Engr., South Charleston, 1967-71, Modern Builders Inc., South Charleston, 1959-67; partner Peery and Dunn, Architects and Engrs., South Charleston, 1966-68. Mem. Municipal Planning Commn. of South Charleston, 1962-71; chmn. Bldg. Code Com. of South Charleston, 1966-68; pres. Ridgewood Pool Inc., 1958-60. Served with U.S. Army, 1942-45. Registered architect, certified Nat. Council Archtl. Registration Bds.; registered profl. engr., W.Va. Recipient Archtl. Soc. Ohio U. award, 1951. Fellow AIA (dir. 1974-77); mem. W.Va. Soc. Architects (pres. 1974), Archtl. League Greater Charleston, Constrn. Specifications Inst. (pres. W.Va. chpt. 1968-69, pres.'s award 1970). Republican. Presbyn. Home: 1016 Knob Way South Charleston WV 25309 Office: PO Box 8361 South Charleston WV 25303

PEEVY, LEWIS JACKSON, county adminstr.; b. Atlanta, Feb. 18, 1942; s. Edwin J. (stepfather) and Ruth (Spence) Wills; B.S. in Bus. Adminstrn., N. Ga. Coll., 1964; M.S. in Mgmt., Fla. Internat. U., 1974; postgrad. U.S. Army Command and Gen. Staff Coll., 1974. Dept. mgmt. staff J.C. Penney Co., North Miami Beach, Fla., 1970-72; tng. officer Office of Dade County Elections, Miami, Fla., 1975-76; adminstr. Office of Dade County Med. Examiner, Miami, 1976—, Served to capt. U.S. Army, 1964-69; maj. Res.; Vietnam. Decorated Bronze Star, Purple Heart. Mem. Res. Officers Assn., N. Ga. Coll. Alumni Assn., Civil Affairs Assn., Porsche Club Am. Democrat. Methodist. Contbr. articles to profl. jours. Home: 4241 SW 62d Ct Miami FL 33155 Office: Dade County Med Examiner 1050 NW 19th St Miami FL 33136

PEEVY, MARY ROSE HAROLD, mfg. co. exec.; b. East Brewton, Ala., Feb. 4, 1926; d. William Henry and Eula Belle (Grice) Harold; student Massey Draughn Bus. Coll., 1945; m. Jack James Peevy, Apr. 18, 1947; children—Waylon James, Amanda Grace. Sec., bookkeeper Harold Bros. Lumber Co., East Brewton, 1945-51, partner, 1951-71; v.p., sec., treas. Harold Bros. Veneer Co., Inc., 1971-80; also dir. Vol., co chmn. United Fund, Heart Fund, Leukemia Fund; chmn. East Brewton Bicentennial Action Com., 1975-76, East Brewton-Fort Crawford Park Recreational Com., 1977-79; mem. East Brewton Library Bd., 1979; mem. Escambia County Courthouse Hist. Com., 1979-80; treas. Cedar Hill United Meth. Ch. Mem. Escambia County Hist. Soc. Home: 1239 Forrest Ave East Brewton AL 36426 Office: 500 Ashton St East Brewton AL 36426 Died Feb. 13, 1980

PEGG, PHILLIP OLIVER, data processor, govt. ofcl.; b. Bayard, Nebr., Aug. 24, 1929; s. Harley Thomas and Gretna Lois (Gray) P.; B.S., Am. U., 1956, M.B.A., 1958; student U. Nebr., 1947-49; m. Ursula Anna M. Frank, July 26, 1954; children—Linda Marie, Phillip Oliver. With U.S. Steel Corp., Fairless, Pa., 1957-61, cost analyst, 1960, methods analyst, 1961; systems cons. CBS, N.Y.C., 1961-63; systems cons. Fawcett Publs., Louisville, 1963-66, mgr. systems design and data processing Fawcett Printing, 1966-69; asst. v.p. data processing Life of Ky. Ins. Co., Louisville, 1969-70; mgr. data processing Dairymen Inc., Louisville, 1970-75; computer specialist fed. order no. 4 Middle Atlantic milk mktg. area dairy div. Agrl. Mktg. Service, USDA, Alexandria, Va., 1975—. Served to 1st lt. USMCR, 1950-54. Mem. Assn. Systems Mgmt. (pres., dir. 1966-67). Home: 8617 Old Mt Vernon Rd Alexandria VA 22309 Office: 300 N Lee St Alexandria VA 22314

PEGUES, WENNETTE OSCEOLA WEST, univ. dean; b. Pitts., Nov. 25, 1936; d. Wilbur Brown and Mary Josephine (Cutts) West; B.S. in Nursing, Carlow Coll., Pitts., 1958; C.C.S. in Sociology, U. Tulsa, 1974, Ed.D. in Ednl. Adminstrn., 1978; m. Julius Pegues, June 21, 1958; children—Mary Pamela, Michael David, Angela Suzette. Mem. nursing staff hosps. in Okla., Mo., Calif. and Nev., 1959-67; dir. nursing services N. Tulsa Comprehensive Health Center, 1968-70; asst. head nurse med.-surg. Okla. Osteopathic Hosp., 1970-71; dir. nursing services ARC, Tulsa, 1971-72; asst. to dean, then asst. dean Henry Kendall Coll. Arts and Scis., U. Tulsa, 1976-79; asso. acad. dean Langston U. Urban Center, Tulsa, 1979—. Bd. dirs. Family and Children Services, Tulsa, 1969-78, Margaret Hudson Program Teenage Parents, Tulsa, 1970-73, Tulsa YWCA, 1974-75, Magic Empire council Girl Scouts U.S.A., 1975; mem. Okla. Welfare Commn., 1978—, Dependent Sch. Bd. Dist. 55, 1979-80. Served with Army Nurse Corps, 1956-59. Grad. asst. U. Tulsa, 1974-75, grad. research fellow, 1975-76. Mem. Am. Personnel and Guidance Assn., Nat. Assn. Acad. Affairs Adminstrs. (dir. 1975-79), Nat. Assn. Women Deans, Adminstrs. and Counselors, AAUW, Nat. Conf. Acad. Advisers (chmn. regional publicity and orgn. 1977—, exec. steering com. 1977—), Am. Public Welfare Assn., Tulsa League Nursing (dir. 1969-71), Tulsa Dist. Nurses Assn. (dir. 1970-72), Alpha Kappa Delta, Kappa Delta Pi, Phi Delta Kappa. Author papers in field. Home: 1741 W Virgin St Tulsa OK 74127 Office: 440 S Houston St Tulsa OK 74127

PEIRCE, ROBERT VINCENT, state govt. ofcl.; b. Middletown, Ohio, Sept. 20, 1925; s. Robert Arthur and Ethel Marguerite (Fisher) P.; A.B., Miami U., Oxford, Ohio, 1947; A.M., U. Ill., 1950; M.B.A. (Jason S. Bailey scholar), Harvard U., 1956; m. Miriam Louise Bauer, July 2, 1950; children—Catherine, Carolyn. Staff controller Tex. Instruments, Inc., Dallas, 1959-67; controller So. Meth. U., Dallas, 1967-70, also lectr. bus. adminstrn.; v.p. adminstrn. Fla. State U., Tallahassee, 1970-74, also prof. mgmt.; pres. Certified Automotive Warehouse, Inc., Tallahassee, 1974-75; dep. asst. sec. Fla. Dept. Health and Rehab. Services, 1975—; vice-chmn. over-all concepts group of Project NOBSKA, Nat. Acad. Scis.-NRC, 1956. Served with USAAF, 1944-46. Recipient Culler prize in Physics, Miami U., 1946. Mem. Phi Beta Kappa, Gamma Alpha, Pi Mu Epsilon, Pi Kappa Alpha, Sigma Pi Sigma. Methodist (adminstrv. bd. 1971—). Prin. author, editor: Atomic Energy and Business Strategy, 1956; Robinson-Patman Act: Principles of Cost Justification, 1962; also articles. Home: 2731-174 Blairstone Rd Tallahassee FL 32301 Office: 1317 Winewood Blvd Tallahassee FL 32301

PEK, ING TIEN, liquid paper co. exec.; b. Surabaya, Indonesia, Dec. 18, 1933; came to U.S., 1954, naturalized, 1970; s. Poo Liat and Tjhay Nio (Soema) P.; B.A., Baylor U., 1958; M.B.A., Fairleigh Dickinson U., 1977; m. Alice Choo Neo Tan, Sept. 17, 1965; children—Zelah Giok Lan, Jackson Kian Kie. With Louis Harris & Assos., N.Y.C., 1966-68, J. Walter Thompson, N.Y.C., 1968-71, Burlington Industries, N.Y.C., 1971-72, Ciba-Geigy, Summit, N.J., 1972-78; with mktg. dept. Liquid Paper Corp., Dallas, 1978—. Mem. Am. Mktg. Assn. Home: 1127 Grassmere Dr Richardson TX 75080 Office: Liquid Paper Corp PO Box 225909 7515 Greenville Ave Dallas TX 75265

PELEZO, CHRIS ALFORD, polymer chemist; b. Greenville, Miss., Sept. 1, 1930; s. John Arthur and Margaret Earline (Cothran) P.; B.S., U. W.Fla., 1970; m. Doris Rose Ferrell, Apr. 17, 1965; children—Stephen Glenn, Joanna Lynn. Research chemist then devel. engr. textiles Monsanto Co., 1970-74, polymer research chemist, Pensacola, Fla., 1974-78, analytical chemist, Fayetteville, N.C., 1978—. Active local Boy Scouts Am.; chmn. Cumberland County adv. bd. Girl Scouts U.S.A.; chmn. Monsanto N.C. campaign United Way, 1979-80. Served with AUS, 1954-56. Mem. Am. Chem. Soc., Freelance Model Railroaders, Model Railroaders of South, Nat. Model Railroaders Assn., Cape Fear Railroaders Assn. Democrat. Baptist. Patentee in field. Home: 3526 Clearwater Dr Fayetteville NC 28301 Office: PO Box 2307 Fayetteville NC 28302

PELFREY, JAMES ASA, JR., communications services exec.; b. Lexington, Ky., Apr. 24, 1932; s. James Asa and Viola (Perkins) P.; B.A., U. Ky., 1954; student U. Calif., Los Angeles, 1957; m. Bettie Marie Swope, Aug. 7, 1953; children—Stephanie, Sharon, James Asa. Sales cons. GTE, Lexington, 1959-61, service supr., 1961-63, asst. div. mgr., 1963-64; mgr. communications U. Ky., 1964—. Instr., Command and Gen. Staff course, U.S. Army Res. Sch., 1968-77. Served with AUS, 1954-56, now col. Res. Mem. Assn. Coll. and Univ. Telecommunications Adminstrn. Democrat. Baptist (deacon). Clubs: Exchange (pres. Lexington chpt. 1966-67), Kiwanis. Home: 1612 Ft Sumter Dr Lexington KY 40505 Office: U Ky S Lime St Lexington 40506

PELFREY, WILLIAM VIRGIL, criminologist; b. Dotha, Ala., Feb. 17, 1947; A.A., Marion Mil. Inst., 1967; B.A., Auburn U., 1969; M.S., U. Ala., 1975; Ph.D., Fla. State U., 1978. Lectr. criminal justice U. Ala., Birmingham, 1976-78, asst. prof. criminal justice, 1978—; cons. Birmingham Police Dept., Jefferson County Sheriff Dept., 1976-78. Served with U.S. Army, 1970-74. Mem. Acad. Criminal Justice Scis., Am. Soc. Criminology, So. Assn. Criminal Justice Educators. Office: Dept Criminal Justice U Ala Birmingham AL 35294

PELL, BEN EARL, pharmacist; b. Mt. Airy, N.C., July 10, 1949; s. Joe Bill and Lucille Alene (Childress) P.; B.S. in Pharmacy, U. N.C., Chapel Hill, 1972. Medication asst. Duke U. Med. Center, 1972; staff pharmacist Morehead Meml. Hosp., Eden, N.C., 1972-73, N.C. Meml. Hosp., Chapel Hill, 1973-75; dir. pharmacy services Johnston Meml. Hosp., Smithfield, N.C., 1975—. Mem. Southeastern Soc. Hosp. Pharmacists, N.C. Soc. Hosp. Pharmacists, Phi Delta Phi. Baptist. Clubs: Jaycees, Masons. Home: 202 W Langdon Ave Smithfield NC 27577 Office: PO Box 1376 Johnston Meml Hosp Smithfield NC 27577

PELLON, HUMBERTO JUAN, real estate broker; b. Havana, Cuba, May 15, 1936; s. Humberto and Zoila P.; came to U.S., 1964; naturalized, 1969; student U. Havana, 1959-60, U. Miami, 1972-73; m. Jackie Pellon, Aug. 23, 1978; 1 son, Humberto Juan. children by previous marriage—Ivan, Lisette. With Merrill Lynch, Pierce, Fenner and Smith, 1964-66, Ace Letter Co., 1966-68; v.p. Comml. Ins. Co., Miami, Fla., 1968-69; pres. Miami Properties Realty Inc., 1974—. Mem. Nat. Assn. Realtors, Nat. Soc. Fee Appraisers, Asociacion Interamericana de Hombres de Empresas. Republican. Roman Catholic. Home: 6502 Kendale Lake Dr Apt 204 Miami FL 33183 Office: Miami Properties Realty Inc 1429 SW 1st St Miami FL 33135

PELOQUIN, GARRY WAYNE, hosp. adminstr.; b. Welch, La., Feb. 7, 1937; s. Joseph Lud and Darlene (Langford) P.; B.S., U. Ala., 1964; m. Margaret Ann Nelson, Oct. 25, 1958; children—Jerry W., Garry L. Adminstr., Macon County Hosp., Tuskegee, Ala., 1966-72; adminstr. N. Ala. Hosp., Russellville, 1972-74; exec. dir. Doctors Hosp. Augusta (Ga.), 1974—; adj. asst. prof. U. Ala.; asst. clin. prof. Med. Coll. Ga. Served with U.S. Army, 1955-58. Mem. Am. Coll. Hosp. Adminstrs., Southeastern Hosp. Conf., Ala. Hosp. Assn., Am. Hosp. Assn., Central Hosp. Council, Ala. Soc. Radiol. Technologists. Baptist. Club: Rotary (pres.). Home: 3505 Pebble Beach Rd Augusta GA 30909 Office: 3651 Wheeler Rd Augusta GA 30904

PELSINGER, FRED, internat. transp. cons.; b. Bklyn., Feb. 8, 1943; s. Harold and Hortense (Etkin) P.; student So. Ill. U., 1961-62; B.A., Bklyn. Coll., 1964; m. Elena S. Wiesel, Mar. 26, 1967; children—Mindy Robyn, Shara Simmone, Janna Bari. Asst. to pres. Fashion Park Stein Bloch, N.Y.C., 1967-69; prodn. mgr., asst. v.p. Golding Upholstery Fabric div., W. R. Grace & Co., N.Y.C., 1969-73; head European Consolidation Service ECCA, N.Y.C., 1973-76; regional sales mgr., br. mgr. Express Forwarding & Storage Co., Inc., Houston, 1976-79; pres. F.P. Internat., Houston, 1979—. Served with USN, 1965-67. Mem. South Houston C. of C. (sec., Achievement award), Nat. Customs Brokers and Forwarders Assn. Am., Fort Worth World Trade Club (bd. mem.), Houston World Trade Club. Jewish. Clubs: K.P., Masons, B'nai B'rith. Home and Office: 15810 Laurel Heights Dr Houston TX 77084

PELTON, MARGARET MARIE, ednl. adminstr.; b. Charlotte, N.C.; d. William Andrew and Helen Marie (Cook) Miller; B.A., U. Miami, 1956; M.S., Fla. State U., 1957; Ed.D., Nova U., 1979; m. Donald W. Pelton Jr.; 1 son, Charles F. Art tchr. Dade County Public Schs., Miami, Fla., 1957-70; asso. prof. South Campus, Miami-Dade (Fla.) Community Coll., 1970—, chmn. art dept., 1971-79, asso. dean humanities div., 1979—. Participant Nat. Identification Program for Advancement Women in Higher Edn. Adminstrn. Mem. Nat. Art Edn. Assn., Fla. Art Edn. Assn., Am. Crafts Council, Nat. Assn. Humanities Edn., Am. Assn. Women in Community and Jr. Colls., Fla. Assn. Community Colls., Nat. Council Art Adminstrs., Delta Kappa Gamma. Home: 11725 SW 82nd Rd Miami FL 33156 Office: Dept Fine Arts Miami Dade Community College Miami FL 33167

PELUSO, GLORIA MCDONALD, coll. adminstr.; b. Louisville, Ga., Oct. 22, 1948; d. George Thomas and Hazel Walden McDonald; B.A. Sociology, Augusta (Ga.) Coll., 1971, M.Ed. Spl. Edn., 1979; m. Paul Renato Peluso, Sept. 21, 1969 (dec.). Lab. technician Med. Coll. Ga., Augusta, 1968-69; social caseworker Dept. Family and Children Services, Gibson, Ga., 1970; tchr. Richmond County Bd. Edn., Augusta, 1971; prodn. control asst. Townsend Textron, Santa Ana, Calif., 1972-75; product mgr. J. O. King, Inc., Atlanta, 1975-76; program specialist Augusta Coll., 1976-79; spl. edn. tchr. Columbia County Bd. Edn., Harlem, Ga. and instr. Ga. Mil. Coll., Ft. Gordon, 1979—; ednl. testing cons., 1978—. Bd. dirs. personnel com. Augusta Open Door Kindergarten, 1978—. Mem. Am. Assn. Mental Deficiency, Augusta Coll. Alumni Assn., Alpha Delta Pi. Home: 3935 Willowwood Dr Martinez GA 30907 Office: Harlem High Sch Harlem GA 30907

PENAFIEL, LORENZO VILLA-REAL, accountant; b. Manila, Philippines, Oct. 22, 1921; came to U.S., 1967; B.S.C., Far Eastern U., Manila, 1947; M.B.A., Tex. Tech. U., 1961, D.B.A., 1970; m. Cora Suarez, Sept. 9, 1944; children—Tessie, Antonio, Roland, Rosalie, Nenette. Acct., Oceanic Med., Inc., Manila, 1949-50, treas., 1950-59; supr. Zialcita & Assos., C.P.A.'s, Manila, 1959-60; partner Penafiel & Assos., C.P.A.'s, Manila, 1961-67; owner, mgr. Felor Enterprises, Manila, 1964-67; asst. prof. Far Eastern U., 1950-66; also Philippine Women's U., both Manila; instr. Tex. Tech. U., Lubbock, 1967-70; prof. acctg. Angelo State U., San Angelo, Tex., 1970—; dir. Oceanic Medical, Inc.; cons. Small Bus. Bur., Ateneo de Manila U., Philippine Center for Profl. Devel. Mem. Am. Acctg. Assn., Tex. Soc. C.P.A.'s, Tex. Assn. Coll. Tchrs., Nat. Assn. Accountants, Philippine Inst. C.P.A.'s, Beta Gamma Sigma, Delta Sigma Pi. Roman Catholic. Home: 3605 Honeysuckle St San Angelo TX 76901 Office: Dept Acctg Angelo State U San Angelo TX 76901

PENCE, LUDLOW MAYS, neurologist; b. Dallas, Feb. 16, 1916; s. Camden Preston and Gertrude Juliet (Mays) P.; M.D., Baylor Med. Coll., 1941; m. Erika M. Mitchell, June 16, 1967; 1 son, Michael M. Mitchell. Intern, St. Paul Hosp., Dallas, 1941-42; resident Duke U. Hosp., Durham, N.C., 1946-48; dir. Epilepsy Clinic, Parkland Meml. Hosp., Dallas, 1948-74; chief neurology service Dallas VA Hosp., 1961-74, coordinator hosp. based home care, 1974—; clin. asso. prof. neurology Southwestern Med. Coll. Served with M.C., USAF, 1942-46. Diplomate Am. Bd. Psychiatry and Neurology. Fellow Am. Acad. Neurology; mem. Tex., Dallas County med. socs., Tex. Neurol.-Psychiat. Soc., So. EEG Soc. Presbyterian. Home: 1416 Union Bower Irving TX 75061 Office: 4500 S Lancaster St Dallas TX 75216

PENDERGAST, RICHARD JOSEPH, ins. co. exec.; b. Newburg, W.Va., June 12, 1933; s. Thomas Leo and Edith (Gibson) P.; A.A., Potomac State Coll., 1953; B.S. in Journalism, W.Va. U., 1959; children by previous marriage—Mary Elizabeth, Jennifer Ann, Kathryn Lesley. Newsman, AP, New Orleans, 1959; editor Pan-Am. Life Ins. Co., New Orleans, 1959-65, asst. dir. pub. relations, 1965-73, dir. pub. relations, 1973—; mem. pub. relations com. United Way, New Orleans; communications adviser New Orleans Pub. Schs. Served with USMC, 1953-57. Recipient Distinguished Service award Internat. Council Indsl. Editors, 1968; named Communicator of Year Indsl. Editors La., 1964. Mem. Pub. Relations Soc. Am. (accredited, pres. New Orleans chpt. 1975-76), Life Advertisers Assn. (exec. com.), La. Press Assn., New Orleans C. of C., Marine Corps Combat

Corr. Assn. Club: New Orleans Press. Editor Life Advertiser, 1976-77. Home: 4229 Maple Leaf Dr New Orleans LA 70114 Office: Pan-Am Life Center New Orleans LA 70130

PENDERGRAFT, NORMAN ELVEIS, museum dir., art historian; b. Durham, N.C., Mar. 4, 1934; s. Harvey Wilson and Essie Mae (Wilson) P.; A.B., U. N.C., Chapel Hill, 1962, M.A.C.T., 1967; doctoral candidate Ohio U., 1969-71; profl. studies Conservatorio di Musica G. Rossini, Pesaro, Italy, 1962-65; student Museum Mgmt. Inst., U. Calif., Berkeley, summer 1979. Tchr., N.W. High Sch., Greensboro, N.C., 1962-63; tchr. English, The English Centre, Ancona, Italy, 1964-65; mem. faculty N.C. Central U., Durham, 1966—, dir. Mus. Art, 1976—, prof. art history, 1967—; lectr. Bd. dirs. Durham Arts Council, 1976-78, Durham Art Guild, 1976-79, Durham Theatre Guild, 1975-78, N.C. Symphony, 1980—. Served in USN, 1954-58. Mem. Am. Assn. Museums, Am. Coll. Art Assn., AAUP, N.C. Museums Council, Southeastern Museums Council. Democrat. Episcopalian. Author: Durham Chautauqua: The Black Man in Art, 1974; Heralds of Life: Artis, Bearden and Burke, 1977; contbr. revs. to art jours. and newspapers; N.C. corr. Art Voices/South, 1978—. Home: 208 Watts St Durham NC 27701 Office: Museum of Art NC Central U Durham NC 27707

PENDERGRASS, HENRY PANCOAST, physician, educator; b. Bryn Mawr, Pa., Jan. 29, 1925; s. Eugene and Rebecca (Barker) P.; A.B., Princeton U., 1948; M.D., U. Pa., 1952; M.P.H. (Nat. Inst. Gen. Med. Scis. fellow 1968-69), Harvard U., 1969; m. Carol L. Dodson, Aug. 27, 1960. Intern, Pa. Hosp., Phila., 1952-53; resident U. Pa. Hosp., 1953-56; clin. asst. Nat. Hosp., London, 1959-60; staff radiologist U. Pa. Hosp. and asst. prof. radiology U. Pa., 1953-58, 60-61; radiologist Mass. Gen. Hosp., Boston, 1958-59, 61-76; prof. radiology, vice chmn. radiology Vanderbilt U., Nashville, 1976—; mem. cancer control rev. com. NIH, 1975—; bd. dirs. Tenn. div. Am. Cancer Soc., 1976—. Served with U.S. Army, 1943-44, USN, 1944-46. Am. Cancer Soc. trainee, 1956-57; Nat. Cancer Inst. fellow, 1957-58; Nat. Inst. Neurol. Diseases and Blindness fellow, 1959-60. Mem. Radiol. Soc. N.Am. (dir. 1972-78, pres. 78), Am. Coll. Radiology (counselor and counselor-at-large 1969-73, chancellor 1976—), AMA, Eastern Radiol. Soc. (pres., trustee 1968-72), Am. Roentgen Ray Soc. Presbyterian. Contbr. numerous articles to profl. jours. Editorial bd. Internat. Skeletal Soc., 1976—. Office: Dept Radiology and Radiol Scis Vanderbilt U Nashville TN 37232

PENDLETON, WILLIAM HARRY, trucking co. exec.; b. Seminole, Okla., Sept. 4, 1938; s. William Ordell and Clara Nadine (Herndon) P.; student U. Md., 1957-60; B.B.A., Washburn U., 1965; m. Joan C. Francis, Feb. 21, 1958; children—Terry L., William D., Laura L. Ops. mgr. Roadway Express Inc., Chgo., 1965-68; asst. to v.p. Spector Freight System, Chgo., 1969; terminal mgr. Spector Freight, Nashville, 1970; gen. mgr. Lewisburg Transfer Co. (Tenn.), 1971; pres., owner Dyersburg Express Inc. 1972—, Delta Drayage & Distbn. Co., Dyersburg, 1977—; owner Sartain Truck Line, 1977—, Pendleton Enterprises, Roadmasters, 1979—; chmn. bd. Tenn. Connecting Line, Inc.; v.p. Motor Carrier Corp., 1979—. Chmn. Dyer County Election Commn., 1975—; bd. dirs. Parkview Hosp.; campaign mgr. Rep. James O. Lanier; mem. Conservative Caucus; col., a.d.c. staff gov. Tenn.; mem. consumer adv. council Tenn. Public Service Commn., 1978. Served with USAF, 1956-64. Mem. Am. Trucking Assn. (gov., com. of 100), Small Carriers Labor Relations Assn. (dir.), Dyersburg C. of C. (chmn. transp. com.), Assn. Election Commrs. (v.p.), Nat. Small Bus. Assn. (action council), Tenn. Intrastate Rate Com., Delta Sigma Pi. Democrat. Baptist. Clubs: Lions, Rotary, Masons, West Tenn. Traffic Club. Home: Route 3 Dyersburg TN 38024 Office: PO Box 1298 Dyersburg TN 38024

PENFOUND, MARY ELEANOR SHARON, nurse; b. Chatham, Ont., Can., Jan. 28, 1942; d. John Henry and Bernice Eileen (Deighton) P.; came to U.S., 1965, naturalized, 1971; R.N., Providence Hosp., Detroit, 1973; student U. Detroit, 1975—. Head nurse Henry Ford Hosp., Detroit, 1975-77, project nurse, 1977-79, supr. dept. emergency medicine, 1978-79; asst. adminstr. nursing Baptist Med. Center-DeKald, Ft. Payne, Ala., 1979—. Mem. Emergency Dept. Nurses Assn. Baptist. Designer peritoneal dialysis delivery system utilizing Gorman-Rupp blood warmer. Office: Bapt Med Center-DeKald 1400 N Forrestt Fort Payne AL 35967

PENG, GEORGE TSO-CHIH, educator, planner, urban designer, architect; b. Yuhsien, Hunan, China, Feb. 25, 1928; s. Tsu-Wen and Hwei-Yien P.; came to U.S., 1952, naturalized, 1965; B.S., Sun Yat-sen U. (China), 1951; M.S., U. Ill., 1954; Dr.-Ing., Technische Hochschule Aachen (Germany), 1960; m. Marianne H. Gerads, Nov. 11, 1960; children—Georgianna, Sonia, Claudia. Chief planner Shenango Valley Regional Planning Commn., Pa., 1960-62; planning dir. City of Allentown (Pa.), 1962-64; prof. U. Nebr., Lincoln, 1965-71; pres. Urban-Rural Planning and Design, Inc., Lincoln, also Tampa, Fla., 1971-75; prof. Tex. Tech. U., Lubbock, 1975—; vis. lectr.; planning cons. Mem. Am. Planning Assn., Inst. for Urban Design, Am. Inst. Cert. Planners, Internat. Fedn. Housing and Planning, AAUP. Author books, articles, pamplets and project reports; founder Organicdualism. Home: 5403 16th Pl Lubbock TX 79416 Office: Tex Tech U Lubbock TX 79409

PENLAND, MICHAEL, trade co. exec.; b. Dalton, Ga., July 5, 1951; s. Pledger William and Nettie Lou (Ballew) P.; student public schs., Dalton, Ga.; m. Sherrie Starlene Ogles, Jan. 5, 1979. Owner, pres. Michael Penland Enterprises, Inc., Dalton, 1969—; v.p. World Tours, Inc., Chattanooga, 1976-80; owner, pres. Motivational Dynamics Internat., Inc., Dalton, 1975—, GO Tours Internat., Dalton, 1979—; exec. dir. Travel Clubs Internat., Dalton, 1980—; pub. Impex Internat. Confidential Newsletter, Dalton, 1980—; sales/mktg., franchise sales; airline cons.; lectr. in field. Recipient award World Traders Success Club, Los Angeles, 1969. Mem. Internat. Traders, Impex Internat., Am. Tour Host Assn., Nat. Splty. Mdse. Assn. Author: Believe and be Great, 1974; Dynamics of the Master Salesman and Dynamics of the Master Motivator, 1980. Home: Dalton GA 30720 Office: 104 N Easterling St Dalton GA 30720

PENN, HUGH FRANKLIN, postmaster, restaurant owner; b. Morgan County, Ala., Aug. 15, 1917; s. Charles Franklin and Bessie Melinda (Praytor) P.; student U. Ala., 1936-37; m. Marynelle Walter, Nov. 12, 1939; children—Hugh Franklin, Charles Phillip, Beverly Ann. Owner, mgr. Hugh Penn Lumber Co., Hartselle, Ala., 1946-60, C.F. Penn Hamburgers, Hartselle, 1958—; postmaster Hartselle, 1957—. Chmn. Hartselle Bd. Zoning Adjustment, 1956-76; founder, bd. dirs. Hartselle Downtown Action Com., 1971—; dir. Morgan County Combined Fed. Campaign, 1971—. Mem. Nat. Assn. Post Masters U.S., Hartselle C. of C. (pres. 1976-77). Republican. Baptist. Club: Kiwanis (Legion of Honor award 1977). Home: 204 Short St Hartselle AL 35640 Office: PO Box 8 Hartselle AL 35640

PENNING, HERBERT WILLIAM, JR., retail store exec.; b. St. Louis, Spet. 21, 1938; s. Herbert William and Wilma Leona (Tumbrink) P.; B.A., Okla. State U., 1960; m. Sara L. Wulff, Sept. 16, 1961; children—Herbert William III, Bruce Stephens; m. 2d, Barbara R. May, Dec. 28, 1978; stepchildren—Leslie Yvonne May, Stacey Lynn May. Trainee, Boyd Richardson Co., St. Louis, 1960, Graham Paper Co., St. Louis, 1960-61, Genesco, Nashville, 1960-61; with Bonwit Teller, N.Y.C., 1961-66, buyer, 1963-66; asst. to pres. T. Jones, N.Y.C., 1966-72, store mgr., Chgo., 1967-70, Beverly Hills, Calif., 1970-71; group sales mgr. Famous Barr, St. Louis, 1972-73, br. store gen. mgr., 1973-77; gen. mgr. Saks Fifth Ave, Houston, 1977—. Chmn. Citizens Action Com., Oak Park, Ill., 1969. Served with USAF, 1961. Mem. Retail Mchts. Assn. Houston (dir., exec. com.), City of Post Oak Assn. (dir.). Clubs: Fedn. Fly Fishers, Ozark Fly Fishers (exec. com.), Tex. Fly Fishers (pres.). Home: 14203 Appletree Ln Houston TX 77079 Office: 1800 S Post Oak Rd Houston TX 77056

PENNINGTON, BUFORD TIMOTHY, chemist; b. Jackson, Miss., Sept. 2, 1948; s. Buford James and Doris June (Palmer) P.; A.A., E. Central Jr. Coll., Decatur, Miss., 1968; B.S., U. So. Miss., 1968, Ph.D. (NDEA fellow), 1974; m. Esther Kennedy, Aug. 15, 1970; 1 dau., Laurie Elizabeth. NRC research asso. Dept. Agr., Phila., 1974-76; Robert A. Welch postdoctoral research grantee U. Tex., Arlington, 1976-77; prof. chemistry Navarro Coll., Corsicana, Tex., 1977-79; research chemist Cities Service Co., Lake Charles, La., 1979—. Mem. Am. Chem. Soc., Tex. Jr. Coll. Tchrs. Assn., Sigma Xi. Contbr. articles to chem. jours.; also videotape in gen. chemistry for NSF. Home: 2215 St Francis St Sulphur LA 70663 Office: Cities Service Co PO Box 1562 Lake Charles LA 70602

PENNINGTON, CLAUDE LEE, physician; b. Macon, Ga., Nov. 20, 1927; s. Claude L. and Evelyn (Adams) P.; B.S. in Medicine, Mercer U., 1951; M.D., Med. Coll. of Ga., 1949; m. Kay Ricks, Nov. 8, 1976; children—Evely Arlene, Claude Lee III. Intern, Med. Center of Central Ga., 1949-50; resident internal medicine U. Hosp., Augusta, Ga., 1950; asst. resident otolaryngology Columbia-Presbyn. Med. Center, N.Y.C., 1953, resident, 1954-55; fellow Lempert Endaural Hosp., N.Y.C., 1956; practice medicine specializing in otolaryngology, Macon, Ga., 1956—; sr. partner ENT Med. Group, Macon, 1969—; mem. staff Middle Ga. Hosp., Med. Center of Central Ga., chmn. dept. otolaryngology, 1971-80; mem. staff Coliseum Park Hosp.; founder Central Ga. Speech and Hearing Center, 1963, pres., 1963-64; Bd. Examiners Speech Pathology and Audiology, 1974-77. Served to capt., M.C., U.S. Army, 1951-52. Recipient Ga. Vocat. Rehab. Physicians award, 1964; diplomate Am. Bd. Otolaryngology (bd. examiner 1972-73). Mem. Am. Otologic Soc., Am. Acad. of Otolaryngology and Head and Neck Surgery, Am. Council of Otolaryngology (pres. 1972-74), Am. Laryngol. Assn., Am. Laryngol., Rhinological and Otological Soc., Am. Bronchoesophagological Assn., AMA, So. Med. Assn., Med. Assn. of Ga., Ga. Soc. of Otolaryngology (pres. 1969-70), Bibb County Med. Soc. Republican. Episcopalian. Clubs: Idle Hour Country, Elks, Kiwanis. Author: (with others) Otorhinolaryngology: Manpower Resources and Needs, 1975; contbr. numerous articles on otolaryngology to profl. jours. Home: 1161 Nottingham Dr Macon GA 31201 Office: 800 1st St Macon GA 31201

PENNINGTON, HARRY LUCAS, bldg. material co. exec.; b. Wetumpka, Ala., Sept. 3, 1919; s. William M. and Bernadine (Williams) P.; A.B., U. Ala., 1941, LL.B., 1950; m. Mary Evelyn Higgins, May 30, 1964 (dec.); children—Harry L., Mary Melanie. Admitted to Ala. bar, 1950; individual practice law, Huntsville, Ala., 1950-51, 52-55; circuit solicitor 23d Jud. Circuit, 1951-52, circuit judge, 1955-61; pres. Huntsville Lumber Co., Inc., 1959-79, chmn. bd., 1979—; pres. Pennington-Dawkins Volkswagen, Gulfport, Miss., 1961-63; chmn. bd. Bank of Huntsville, 1968-76; exec. sec. to Ala. Gov. George C. Wallace, 1971-75; mem. Ala. Ho. of Reps., 1963-70. Vice chmn. Ala. Space Sci. Exhibit Commn., 1970—; trustee U. North Ala., 1968-76, Ala. A&M U., Huntsville, 1976-79; dir. N.Ala. Council Boy Scouts Am., 1975-78; bd. dirs. Huntsville-Madison County Mental Health, 1975—, United Way of Huntsville and Madison County, 1976—, Salvation Army, Huntsville, 1977—, Family Found. Am., 1977—. Served to maj. U.S. Army, 1941-46. Mem. Am. Mgmt. Assn., Huntsville-Madison County Bar Assn., V.F.W., Am. Legion. Democrat. Methodist. Clubs: Masons, Shriners, Elks. Home: 5807 Lenlock Circle Huntsville AL 35802 Office: 809 Shoney Dr SW Huntsville AL 35801

PENNINGTON, HILDA BRADY, bus. services co. ofcl.; b. Atlanta, Sept. 22, 1942; d. Hollis and Myrtle Mindora (Smith) B.; sec. II degree Greenleaf Bus. Coll., 1961; gen. degree Truett McConnel Coll., 1963; m. Fonia R. Pennington, Dec. 14, 1975. Encoding operator 1st Nat. Bank, Atlanta, 1963; bookkeeping clk. King Hardware Co., Atlanta, 1963-66; supr. Rollins Inc., Atlanta, 1966—. Cert. profl. sec. Mem. Nat. Secs. Assn. Baptist. Home: 4586 Peachtree Dunwoody Rd Atlanta GA 30342 Office: 2170 Piedmont Rd NE Atlanta GA 30324

PENNINGTON, LUCY SIMMONS, soft drink mfg. co. ofcl.; b. Hancock County, Ga., Aug. 1, 1923; d. Grover Cleveland and Lizzie (Wells) Simmons; B.A., Morris Brown Coll., 1944; M.A., Atlanta U., 1963; m. Thomas Maurice Pennington, Feb. 2, 1952. Auditor, Atlanta Life Ins. Co., 1944-46; tchr. Rockdale County Bd. Edn., Conyers, Ga., 1947-48; caseworker, supr. caseworkers Fulton County Dept. Family and Child Service, Atlanta, 1960-65; dir. Neighborhood Youth Corps, Atlanta, 1965-70; mgr. social devel. Model Cities Program, Atlanta, 1970-72; chief civil rights unit Ga. Dept. Human Resources, 1972-75; dir. personnel City of Atlanta, 1975-79; program analyst for adminstrn. Coca-Cola Co., Atlanta, 1979—. Bd. dirs. Atlanta Women's Network, 1980; mem. Intergovtl. Council, 1976-79; mem. better infant birth storks nest Nat. March of Dimes; mem. personnel com. YWCA. Recipient Community Service award Sta. WSB, 1975; cert. of recognition Ga. Assn. Human Relations, 1974; Image Maker award Big Bethel A.M.E. Ch. Mem. Am. Soc. Personnel Adminstrn. (cert. of achievement 1976), Assn. Non-White Counselors, Am. Personnel and Guidance Assn., Intergovtl. Personnel Assn., Internat. Personnel Mgmt. Assn., Atlanta C. of C. (area wide council for career devel. 1978-79), NAACP, Nat. Conf. Negro Women, Zeta Phi Beta (v.p. 1977-79, Community Service award, cert. of merit in edn.). Methodist. Home: 150 Old Fairburn Close SW Atlanta GA 30331 Office: Coca-Cola Co 310 North Ave NW Atlanta GA 30313

PENNOCK, DAVID HAROLD, musician, educator; b. Winnipeg, Man., Can., Aug. 24, 1947; s. Harold Charles and Patricia (King) P.; B.M.Ed., Abilene Christian U., 1969, M.Ed., 1974; m. JoAnn Jameson, Dec. 27, 1968; 1 dau., Holly Joanna. Asst. band dir., orch. dir., jazz ensemble dir. Central High Sch., San Angelo, Tex., 1969-74; asso. dir. bands, jazz ensemble dir. Coronado High Sch., Lubbock, Tex., 1974-75; asst. prof. music, dir. jazz studies, asso. dir. bands Abilene (Tex.) Christian U., 1975—; adjudicator, condr. clinics for jazz ensembles, bands, orchs. Mem. Abilene Community Band, Abilene Jazz Septet. Mem. Tex. Music Educators Assn., Tex. Bandmasters Assn., Nat. Assn. Jazz Educators, Phi Delta Kappa, Phi Beta Mu. Mem. Ch. of Christ. Home: 2426 Brentwood St Abilene TX 79605 Office: Box 8196 Station Abilene Christian Univ Abilene TX 79601

PENNY, JAMES EDWARD, broadcasting co. exec.; b. Lubbock, Tex., May 20, 1944; s. E.P. and Emma Mundine P.; student Elkins Inst., Dallas, 1972; B.A. in Telecommunications, Tex. So. U., 1977; m. Wanda Pearl Williams, Sept. 16, 1966; children—Shawn Conrad, Semaj Carmen. Announcer Sta. KOZA, Odessa, Tex.; announcer, music dir. Sta. KAPE, San Antonio; announcer, news reporter Sta. KBER, San Antonio; announcer Sta. KRLY, Houston; engr., cameraman Sta. KHTV, Houston; exec. producer, host program Sta. KDOG-TV, Houston; now gen. mgr. Sta. KTSU-FM, Houston. Served with USAF, 1963-67. Mem. Nat. Assn. Ednl. Broadcasters, Nat. Assn. Broadcasters. Office: 3201 Wheeler Ave Houston TX 77004

PENNY, JAMES NELSON, printing press mfg. co. exec.; b. Far Rockaway, N.Y., Aug. 10, 1934; s. Robert E. and Eva Rose (March) P.; B.A., Rutgers U., 1955; m. Mary Ann Foley, June 22, 1957; children—Kathleen, John, Matthew. Supr. employment and tng., dir. tng. Brown & Sharpe Mfg. Co., North Kingstown, R.I., 1964-69; mgr. employee relations Web Press div. Harris Corp., Westerly, R.I., 1969-70, personnel mgr., Fort Worth, 1971-79; mgr. devel. and tng., 1979—. Mem. Gov.'s Adv. Commn. Vocat. Rehab., 1967; mem. Regional Vocat. Tech. Adv. Bd., 1967; chmn. adv. bd. Fort Worth Vocat. Office Edn., 1973-74. Served with USN, 1956-60. Mem. Fort Worth Personnel Indsl. Relations Assn. (pres. 1974), Am. Soc. Personnel Adminstrn. Club: Woodhaven Country. Home: 4609 Weyhill Dr Arlington TX 76013 Office: PO Box 15247 Fort Worth TX 76119

PENNYPACKER, DEBORAH ANN, speech pathologist; b. Wichita, Kans., Oct. 26, 1942; d. Raymond Wills and Margaret Alice Snyder; B.A., U. Wichita, 1964; M. Ed., S.W. Tex. State U., 1970; m. B. Frank Pennypacker III, July 3, 1964; 1 dau., Tiffany Ann. Speech pathologist Temple (Tex.) Ind. Sch. Dist., 1964-67, 68-69, New Braunfels (Tex.) Ind. Sch. Dist., 1967-68, 69-70, Cerebral Palsy Treatment Center, San Antonio, 1970-74, San Antonio Ind. Sch. Dist., 1974—. Cert. tchr. speech and hearing therapy, elem. edn., Tex. Mem. Am. Speech and Hearing Assn. (cert. clin. competence), Tex. Speech and Hearing Assn., San Antonio Speech, Lang. and Hearing Assn. (pres. 1975-76), Tex. Edn. Assn. Episcopalian. Home: 8326 Babe Ruth St San Antonio TX 78240 Office: San Antonio Ind Sch Dist 106 N Las Moras St San Antonio TX 78207

PENROSE, GILBERT QUAY, financial planning co. exec.; b. Robinson, Pa., Sept. 8, 1938; s. Albert Snyder and Olive Jeanette (Boring) P.; B.S. in Chem. Engring., Pa. State U., 1960; m. Anna Mae Riffle, Aug. 22, 1959; children—Kim Denise, Kevin Lee, Kara Lynn. Registered rep. Investors Diversified Services, 1969-70, div. mgr., Huntington, W.Va., 1972-73, Miami, 1973-76; regional mgr. S. Fla., Westamerica Fin. Corp., Miami Lakes, 1976—; pres. Gilbert Penrose & Assos., Inc., Certified Fin. Planners, Miami, 1976—; pres., chmn. Penrose Internat.; pres. So. Fla. Mgmt. Co. Inc., S. Pitts. Mgmt. Co. Inc. Bd. dirs. Miami Lakes Civic Assn., 1975-76. Certified fin. planner. Mem. Internat. Assn. Fin. Planners, Assn. Certified Fin. Planners. Home: 7353 Loch Ness Dr Miami Lakes FL 33014 Office: Suite 510 1840 W 49th St Hialeah FL 33012

PENROSE, WILLIAM O., educator; b. Hunter, Ark., Nov. 23, 1914; A.B., U. Ark., Fayetteville, 1937, A.M., 1945; Ed.M., Harvard U., 1941, Ed.D., 1943; diplomate Inst. Social Studies The Hague, Netherlands, 1958; postgrad. Columbia U., 1950-51, U. Pitts, 1951-52, Rutgers U., 1952-53, Ursinus Coll., 1953; m. Georgia McLaughlin, Mar. 22, 1979; children—Elizabeth H., Charles H. Tchr. public schs., Ark., 1933-34, 37-39; prof. U. Del., Point Park Coll., Pa. State U., U. Pitts.; adj. prof. Stetson U.; dean Sch. Edn., dir. Summer Sch., U. Del., 1949-59. Served to maj., inf., U.S. Army, 1942-46; PTO. Mem. NEA, Internat. Orgn. Writers, Phi Beta Kappa, Pi Kappa Alpha, Omicron Delta Kappa, Pi Alpha Theta. Presbyterian. Author books, including: Freedom Is Ourselves, 1952; Structure of Higher Education, 1959; A Primer on Piaget, 1979; How To Teach The Piaget Way, 1979.

PENTICUFF, MARGARET STANFIELD, nurse; b. Waverly, Tenn., Sept. 29, 1934; d. James and Maybelle (Smith) Stanfield; R.N., Nashville Gen. Hosp. Sch. of Nursing, 1955; student Baylor U. Med. Center, 1967-68; m. James P. Penticuff, Nov. 22, 1968; 1 dau., Cynthia Sue Penticuff Chazarra. Staff nurse Nashville Gen. Hosp., 1955-56; office nurse Miami, Fla., 1957-59; staff nurse, operating room Bapt. Hosp., Nashville, 1959-67, operating room dir., 1978-80. R.N., Tenn. Mem. Assn. Operating Room Nurses. Democrat. Mem. Ch. of Christ. Home: 536 Starliner Dr Nashville TN 37209 Office: Bapt Hosp 2000 Church St Nashville TN 37203

PEOPLES, NAPOLEON LEE, counselor, educator; b. Phila., Jan. 17, 1947; s. Leola Peoples; B.A., Wilberforce U., 1968; Ed.M., Kent State U., 1969, Ed.S., 1970, Ph.D., 1977. Field rep. and counselor Akron (Ohio) Urban League, 1969-70; counselor, asst. prof. edn. Student Devel. Counseling Center, Va. Commonwealth U., Richmond, 1970—; cons. Fla. A&M U., Knoxville Coll., Hampton Inst., St. Paul's Coll., Cuyahoga Community Coll., Cleve. State U.; gen. aptitude test battery adminstr. Ohio Bur. Employment Services, Columbus, 1969. Little League coach Met. Baseball League, 1976; chmn. ad hoc com. on prison youth, Richmond, 1970-71; mem. adv. bd. Rubicon Alcoholism program, Richmond, 1979—. Lic. profl. counselor, cert. sex therapist, Va. Mem. Black Edn. Assn. (pres. 1974), Am. Psychol. Assn., Nat. Rehab. Assn. (cert. rehab. counselor), Assn. Black Psychologists, Am. Personnel and Guidance Assn., AAUP, Phi Delta Kappa, Omega Psi Phi. Mem. A.M.E. Ch. Clubs: Shriners, Masons. Contbr. articles on ednl. adminstrn. to profl. publs. Office: 913 W Franklin St Richmond VA 23284

PEPITONE, JOSEPH PHILIP, beverage co. exec.; b. Bklyn., Oct. 22, 1944; s. Philip Anthony and Santina Teresa (LoGelfo) P.; student Fullerton Jr. Coll., 1965-66, Nassau Community Coll., 1966-67; B.B.A., Hofstra U., 1969; m. Ellen Shaw, July 31, 1969; children—Jason Scott, Morgan Lance. Budget coordinator/asst. account exec. Ogilvy & Mather Advt., Inc., N.Y.C., 1970-71; account exec. Schweppes U.S.A. Ltd., Ogilvy & Mather Advt., Inc., N.Y.C., 1971-72; pres. Beverage King, Inc., beverage-convenience store franchise chain, Ft Lauderdale, Fla., 1972—; pres. World of Beverages Inc., Ft. Lauderdale, 1978—, Subway Systems of Oakland Park Inc. (Fla.), 1979—; v.p. Diversified Beverages Inc., Ft. Lauderdale, 1977—, Equipment Solution Group Inc., Ft. Lauderdale, 1979—; cons. in field. Voting mem. Boca Raton (Fla.) Acad., 1976—. Mem. Nat. Hist. Soc., Nat. Geog. Soc., Sigma Alpha Mu. Club: Boca Del Mar Golf and Country. Contbr. articles in field to profl. jours. Home: 22247 Alyssum Way Boca Raton FL 33432 Office: 1545 E Commercial Blvd Fort Lauderdale FL 33334

PEPPARD, FELIX PRUNTY, surgeon; b. Wichita, Kans., Feb. 6, 1934; s. Richard Kenneth and Bonnie Helen (Prunty) P.; B.S., U. Tex., 1958; M.D., Southwestern Med. Sch., 1962; m. Sylvia Joyce Gilder, June 9, 1967; children—Richard Mark, Kelton Denise, William Felix. Intern, John Peter Smith Hosp., Fort Worth, 1962-63; resident in surgery Baylor U. Med. Center, Dallas, 1963-67; practice medicine specializing in surgery, pres. Peppard, Halloran & Small, Assos., Dallas, 1967—; asso dir surg. edn. Med. Center, Baylor U., 1968—; clin. asso. prof. surgery Southwestern Med. Sch., 1969—; med. dir. Buckner Bapt. Benevolences, 1967—. Served with AUS, 1954-56. Diplomate Am. Bd. Surgery. Mem. ACS, Southwestern Surg. Congress, Royal Soc. Medicine Eng., Tex. Surg. Soc., So. Med. Assn. Democrat. Roman Catholic. Home: 4529 Glenleigh St Dallas TX 75220 Office: 3600 Gaston Ave Dallas TX 75246

PEPPER, CLAUDE DENSON, congressman; b. Dudleyville, Ala., Sept. 8, 1900; s. Joseph Wheeler and Lena (Talbot) P.; A.B., U. Ala., 1921; J.D., Harvard, 1924; LL.D., McMaster U., 1941, U. Toronto, U. Ala., 1942, Rollins Coll., 1944; Sc.D., U. Miami, 1974; m. Irene Mildred Webster, Dec. 29, 1936. Instr. law U. Ark., 1924-25; admitted to Ala. bar, 1924, Fla. bar, 1925; practice law, Perry, Fla.; mem. Fla. Ho. Reps., 1929; practice law, Tallahassee, 1930; mem. Fla. Bd. Pub. Welfare, 1931-32, Fla. Bd. Law Examiners, 1933; mem. U.S. Senate from Fla., 1936-51, mem. coms. on small bus. and fgn. relations, on mil. affairs, small bus., reorgn. of congress, chmn. com. on inter-oceanic canals, Middle East sub-com. of senate fgn. relations com., 12 yrs.; mem. 88th-89th Congresses 3d Dist. Fla., 90th-92d congresses 11th Dist. Fla., 93d-96th Congresses from 14th Dist. Fla. Officer, dir. Washington Fed. Savs. & Loan Assn. Chmn., Fla. delegation Democratic Nat. Conv., 1940-44, del., 1948, 52, 56, 60, 64, 68. Served with Armed Forces, 1918. Recipient Albert Lasker Pub. Service award, 1967. Mem. Internat., Inter-Am., Am., Fla. (exec. com.), Tallahassee, Miami Beach, Coral Gables, Dade County bar assns., Bar Assn. City N.Y., Am. Legion, 40 and 8, Vets. World War I, Blue Key, Gold Key. Phi Beta Kappa, Omicron Delta Kappa, Phi Alpha Delta, Sigma Upsilon, Kappa Alpha. Baptist. Elk, Mason (Shriner), Moose, Kiwanian, Woodman of World. Clubs: Harvard (Washington, Miami); Jefferson Island, Army and Navy (Washington); Coral Gables Country; Miami Shores Country; Columbia Country (Chevy Chase, Md.); Burning Tree (Bethesda, Md.). Contbr. to periodicals. Office: 1701 Meridian Ave Miami Beach FL 33139 also 2239 Rayburn House Office Bldg Washington DC 20515

PEPPER, JOHN CLAYTON, counselor; b. Lincoln County, Tenn., Nov. 11, 1928; s. J.C. and Minnie Odell (Baker) P.; student pub. schs., Taft and Blanch, Tenn.; m. Sarah Maxie Cherry; children—Randal, Rhonda, John, Ronnie, Anita. Ch.-sponsored counselor Juvenile Ct., Nashville, 1959—; ct. counselor, dir. outreach Hermitage Ch. of Christ, Hermitage, Tenn., 1979; pres. Christian Lighthouse, Inc., 1964—, editor, pub. Personal Evangelism mag., 1964—; co-founder Happy Hills Boys Ranch, 1970, Great Commn. Sch., Nashville, 1971; speaker Three Unusual Days program. Recipient plaque Tenn. Juvenile Ct. Services Assn., 1977. Author: Ye Are the Light of the World, 1964; Jesus Sent Them Two by Two, 1964; Go Preach the Gospel to Every Creature, 1965; We Persuade Men, 1965. Home: 745 Cedarcrest Ave Madison TN 37115 Office: Met Office Bldg 802 2d Ave S Nashville TN 37210

PEPPERS, LOUISE JAMES, spl. edn. tchr.; b. Daingerfield, Tex., July 8, 1916; widowed, 2 children. B.S. in Home Econs. cum laude, Bishop Coll., Marshall, Tex., 1947; M.Ed. in Spl. Edn., Prairieview Coll (Tex.) 1964. Primary tchr. Daingerfield Schs., 1941-46; tchr. Linden (Tex.) Schs., 1948-57; tchr. Hooks (Tex.) Schs., 1961-78. Leader Boy Scouts Am., 1963-68. Mem. NEA, CTA, Tex. State Tchrs. Assn., Bowie County Local Tchrs. Assn. Certifications, Tex.; specialist in spl. edn. for mentally retarded. Home: Route 1 Box 126C Hooks TX 75561 Office: E Hooks Elementary Sch Box 217 Hooks TX 75561

PEREIRA, RONALD MANUEL, petroleum co. exec.; b. Sandusky, Ohio, Sept. 20, 1938; s. Antonio and Helen (Miller) P.; B.A., Cornell U., 1960; M.B.A., Columbia U., 1965; B.S. in Acctg., U. Miami (Fla.), 1976; m. Carolyn Kenney, Mar. 28, 1962; children—Charles Manuel, William Wyatt. Corporate internal auditor The Singer Co., N.Y.C., 1965, cost acctg. supr., Power Tool Div., Pickens, S.C., 1966; fin. analyst Esso InterAm., Coral Gables, Fla., 1967-69; fin. mgr. Esso Paraguay, Asuncion, 1970-72; sr. acct. Esso Caribbean, Coral Gables, 1973-76; ops. acct., 1977—. 1977—. Active Coconut Grove Civic Club, Miami, 1972-79. Served with USN, 1960-63; to lt. comdr., USNR, 1977-79. Recipient Danforth Found. award, 1956; Delta Upsilon Leadership award, 1960; Navy ROTC scholar, 1956-60; C.P.A., Fla. Mem. Coconut Grove C. of C., Nat. Assn. Accts., Fla. Soc. C.P.A.'s, Am. Inst. C.P.A.'s, Naval Reserve Assn., Fla. Hort. Soc., Rare Fruit and Vegetable Council Broward County, Delta Upsilon. Republican. Episcopalian. Clubs: Rare Fruit Council, Internat. Fairchild Tropical Garden; Miami Men's Garden Home: 111 Prospect Dr Coral Gables FL 33133 Office: 396 Alhambra Circle Coral Gables FL 33134

PEREZ, LAZARO M., airline exec.; b. Cartagena, Colombia, S.Am., Feb. 21, 1937; s. Lazaro M. and Mary (Martinez) P.; B.S. in B.A., Georgetown U., 1959; M.B.A., N.Y. U., 1961; m. Rosario Lozano, Sept. 6, 1958; children—Lyllian, Lazaro, Carlos, Juan. Sr. acct./auditor Arthur Young & Co., N.Y./Colombia, 1959-63; asst. comptroller Sinclair Oil Co., Colombia, 1964-65, comptroller, 1965-68; comptroller Ganso Azul, Arco-Sinclair Oil, Peru, 1968-76; spl. acct. Arco, Los Angeles, 1976-77; fin. mgr. N.Am., Avianca Airlines, Miami, Fla., 1977—; dir. Avianca, Inc. C.P.A., D.C. Mem. Inst. Internal Auditors, Am. Mgmt. Assn., Nat. Assn. Accts. Roman Catholic. Clubs: Los Lagartos (Bogota, Colombia); Cartagena, Cartagena Country (Colombia), Diners (dir. 1965-68-Colombia); Lima Golf (Peru). Home: 13835 SW 73 Ave Miami FL 33158 Office: 4299 NW 36 St Suite 419 Miami FL 33166

PEREZ, MANUEL ROBERT, urologist; b. Arecibo, P.R., Nov. 3, 1934; s. Manuel and Virgilia (Varela) P.; B.S., U. P.R., 1955, M.D., 1959; m. Geraldine Helen Szymanski, June 1, 1963; children—Manuel Robert, Kevin Paul. Resident, Albert Einstein Med. Center, Phila., 1964-68; commd. 2d lt. U.S. Air Force, 1960, advanced through grades to lt. col., 1963-64; chief urology service, pres. med. evaluation bd. Scott AFB Med Center, St. Louis, 1968-72; hon. discharged, 1972; practice medicine specializing in urology, Bowling Green, Ky., 1973—; mem. staff Greenview Hosp., 1973—, chief of surgery, 1975-76; budget dir. Graves-Gilbert Med. Clinic Corp., 1977; mem. staff Bowling Green City-County Hosp. Leader Boy Scouts Am., 1975-76; mem. Ky. Med. Polit. Action Com. Diplomate Nat. Bd. Med. Examiners, Am. Bd. Urology. Mem. AMA (Physician Recognition award 1971, 74, 77), Am. Urol. Assn., Ky. Med. Assn., Aerospace Med. Assn., Soc. Mil. Surgeons, Ky. Urol. Soc., Bowling Green Tri-County Med. Soc. Republican. Roman Catholic. Clubs: Bowling Green Country, Warren-Simpson Sportsmans. Home: 2045 McCubbin Dr Bowling Green KY 42101 Office: 1109 State St Bowling Green KY 42101

PEREZ-ANZALOTA, JOSE RAFAEL, surgeon, educator; b. Toa Alta, P.R., Oct. 23, 1931; s. Antidio and Josefa (Anzalota) Perez; B.S., U. P.R., 1952, M.D., 1956; m. Antonia Quiros, July 10, 1954; children—Mary Jo, Jose, Carmen, Madelaine. Intern, Allentown (Pa.) Hosp., 1956-57; resident in gen. surgery Univ. Hosp., San Juan, P.R., 1959-63; resident thoracic and cardiovascular surgery Baylor Coll. Medicine Affiliated Hosps., Houston, 1968-70; practice medicine, specializing in thoracic and cardiovascular surgery, San Juan, 1970—; mem. staffs Univ., Tchrs., Auxilio Mutuo hosps.; asst. prof. surgery U. P.R., 1970—. Served with M.C., AUS, 1957-59. Diplomate Am. Bd. Surgery, Am. Bd. Thoracic Surgery. Fellow A.C.S., Am. Coll. Cardiology; mem. Soc. Thoracic Surgeons, Am., P.R. med. assns. Rotarian. Home: B-16 Adams St Guaynabo PR 00657 Office: GPO Box 2286 San Juan PR 00936

PEREZ-COMAS, ADOLFO, physician; b. Mayaguez, P.R., Nov. 27, 1941; s. Adolfo and Alma Luz (Comas-Lugo) Perez-Sosa; B.S., U. P.R., 1961; M.D., U. Barcelona (Spain), 1967, Ph.D., 1975; m. Alba Valles-Formosa, Oct. 3, 1965; children—Adolfo, Alberto. Intern, San Juan City Hosp., 1968, fellow in endocrinology, 1970-72; resident in pediatrics San Juan City Hosp., P.R. Med. Center, Rio Piedras, 1969-70; practice medicine specializing in endocrinology and med. genetics, Mayaguez, P.R., 1972—; asst. prof. physiology and biochemistry Sch. Medicine, U. Barcelona, 1963-67; dir. pediatric endocrinology and med. genetics sect. Mayaguez Med. Center, 1972—, sec. of faculty, 1972-73, chief of staff, 1975-79; lectr. physiology U. P.R., Mayaguez, 1973—, clin. instr. pediatrics, 1974—. Counselor Growth Hormone Fund, Inc., 1974—. Named Citizen of the Year, Mayaguez, 1974, Most Distinguished Young Man in Fields of Sci. and Medicine, Rio Piedras Jaycees, 1974. Fellow Superior Council on Sci. Investigations (hon.) (Spain); mem. Am. Acad. Pediatrics (ann. award 1968), Am. Soc. Human Genetics, Am. Soc. of Andrology, Internat. Diabetes Fedn., Fedn. Latinoam. de Assns. de Lucha Contra la Diabetes (exec. council) (Venezuela), Am. Diabetes Assn., Latinam. Assn. of Diabetes (dir.) (Colombia), AAAS, N.Y. Acad. Sci., Am. Med. Writers Assn., Soc. Nuclear Medicine P.R., Western Dist. Med. Soc. (dir. med. edn.), Govtl. Physicians Assn. of P.R. (pres. 1979—), Craniofacial Genetics Assn. N.Am., P.R. Med. Assn., Endocrine Soc., Dominican Republic Acad. Sci. (hon.), Peru Diabetic Assn. (hon.), Nu Sigma Beta. Roman Catholic. Contbr. articles on research in endocrinology and med. genetics to med. jours. Home: 90 Alhambra Mayaguez PR 00708 Office: 22 N Dr Basora Mayaguez PR 00708

PEREZ THILLET, WILLIAM, C.P.A., hosp. ofcl.; b. Ponce, P.R., Dec. 31, 1939; s. Fernando Perez and Ramona Thillet; B.B.A., Cath. U. P.R., 1962, postgrad., 1972; m. Andrea Gomez, July 21, 1962; children—Luis Guillermo, Edith, Michael, Jose Fernando. Owner, mgr. Boricua Superette, 1962-66; cost acct. Commonwealth Oil Refining Co., Inc., Ponce, 1966-73; asst. controller Presbyn. Community Hosp., Inc., Santurce, P.R., 1973-75; controller St. Luke's Episcopal Hosp., Ponce, 1976—; sec. treas. Ortho-Medic, Inc., 1978—; mem. dist. com. Ponce Consumers Coop.; tchr. acctg. World U. Bd. dirs. Obra Familiar de Schoenstant de Maraguëz, Ponce. Mem. Am. Inst. C.P.A.'s, Colegio de Contadores Publicos Autorizados de P.R. Roman Catholic. Home: B-18 W24A Glenview Gardens Ponce PR 00731 Office: PO Box 2027 Ponce PR 00732

PERKEL, ROBERT SIMON, photojournalist; b. Jersey City, Apr. 23, 1925; s. Louis Leo and Flora Sonia (Levin) P.; B.S., N.Y. U., 1948; M.S., Barry Coll., 1964. Owner, operator Gulfstream Color Labs., Miami Beach, Fla., 1955-61; graphic instr. Dade County Pub. Schs., 1962-66; free lance photojournalist, 1967—; rep. News Events Photo Service, Ft. Lauderdale, Fla.; contbr. photo stories, and photographs to numerous mags. and indsl. trade publs. including Women's World, Nat. Utility Contractor, Mainstream, Nat. Jewish Monthly and Delta Digest. Dir. publicity Council for Internat. Visitors of Greater Miami. Served with AUS, 1943-46; ETO. Mem. Am. Photog. Artisans Guild, N.Y. U. Alumni Assn., Barry Coll. Alumni Assn., Nat. Press Photographers Assn., Profl. Photographers Am. Photog. Soc. Am., DAV (nat. citation for distinguished service 1969), Royal Photog. Soc. Gt. Britain, Alpha Mu Gamma. Clubs: L'Alliance Francaise de Dade County, B'nai B'rith. Home: 20500 W Country Club Dr North Miami Beach FL 33180 Office: 16336 W Dixie Hwy North Miami Beach FL 33160

PERKINS, CARL D., Congressman; b. Hindman, Ky., Oct. 15, 1912; s. J.E. and Dora (Calhoun) P.; grad. Jefferson Sch. Law, Louisville, 1935; m. Verna Johnson; 1 son, Christopher. Practice law, Hindman, 1935; commonwealth atty. 31st Jud. Dist., 1939; mem. Ky. Gen. Assembly from 99th Dist., 1940; Knott County atty., 1941-48; counsel Ky. Dept. Hwys., Frankfort, 1948; mem. 81st to 96th congresses 7th Dist. Ky., chmn. edn. and labor com., 1969—. Served with AUS, World War II; ETO; participated in battles No. France, Battle of the Bulge, Rhineland, Central Europe. Democrat. Home: Hindman KY 48122 Office: 2328 Rayburn House Office Bldg Washington DC 20013

PERKINS, GUINN LAMONT (MONTE), speech pathologist; b. Abilene, Tex., June 8, 1949; s. Robert DeWitt Perkins and Alta Geraldine Perkins Reece; B.A. in Speech, Tex. Tech. U., 1974; M.S. in Speech Pathology, North Tex. State U., 1975; m. Judith Anne Durham, May 24, 1975; 1 son, Corbin Durham. Staff speech pathologist West Tex. Rehab. Center, San Angelo, 1975-77, center dir., 1977-79, coordinator speech/lang. therapy and edn., 1979—; cons. speech and lang., behavior mgmt.; condr. workshops in non-verbal communication, behavior mgmt.; bd. dirs. Inst. Cognitive Devel., San Angelo. Pres. bd. dirs. Unity Ch. of Christianity, San Angelo, 1979—. Mem. Am. Speech/Lang. and Hearing Assn.

PERKINS, JAMES FRANCIS, physicist; b. Hillsdale, Tenn., Jan. 3, 1924; s. Jim D. and Laura Pervis (Goad) P.; A.B., Vanderbilt U., 1948, M.A., 1949; Ph.D., 1953; m. Ida Virginia Phillips, Nov. 23, 1949; 1 son, James F. Sr. engr. Convair, Fort Worth, Tex., 1953-54; scientist Lockheed Aircraft, Marietta, Ga., 1954-61; physicist Army Missile Command Redstone Arsenal, Huntsville, Ala., 1961-77; cons. physicist, 1977—. Served with USAAF, 1943-46. AEC fellow, 1951-52. Mem. Am. Phys. Soc., Sigma Xi. Contbr. articles to profl. jours. Home and office: 102 Mountainwood Dr Huntsville AL 35801

PERKINS, MARION LOUISE, pianist, educator; b. Mpls., Mar. 21,1927; d. Roscoe Davis and Pearl Marion (Stephenson) P.; B.A., U. Minn., 1948, M.A., 1955; Ph.D., U. So. Calif., 1961; pvt. piano study with Artur Schnabel and Karl Ulrich Schnabel. Instr. U. Mo., Columbia, 1958-60; asst. prof. Ball State U., Muncie, Ind., 1961-62; asst. prof. Sam Houston State Coll., Huntsville, Tex., 1962-63; asso. prof. Colo. Woman's Coll., Denver, 1963-68; prof. music James Madison U., Harrisonburg, Va., 1968—; concert pianist, including recitals in Town Hall, N.Y.C., Nat. Gallery, Washington; concert tours of Europe and Mex. Mem. Music Tchrs. Nat. Assn., Sigma Alpha Iota. Home: 66 Hope St Harrisonburg VA 22801 Office: Dept Music James Madison U Harrisonburg VA 22801

PERKINS, MARY JOANNE, hosp. supply adminstr.; b. Cornelius, N.C., Apr. 30, 1932; d. John M. and Mary W. Hager; student med. specialist course U.S. Army, 1959. North State Bus. Coll., 1961-62. Nurse aide, unit sec. Cabarrus Meml. Hosp., Concord, N.C., 1960-65; with N.C. Baptist Hosp., Winston-Salem, 1965—, asst. dir. central service, 1967-75, dir. central service, 1975—. Served with M.C., U.S. Army, 1958-60. Mem. N.C. Assn. Central Service Personnel. Democrat. Baptist. Home: 114 Creekwood Dr Advance NC 27006 Office: Central Service Dept NC Bapt Hosp 300 S Hawthorne Rd Winston-Salem NC 27103

PERKINS, PERCY HAROLD, JR., architect; b. Metter, Ga., Sept. 8, 1905; s. Percy Harold and Bertha Mae (Warwick) P.; student Ga. Sch. Tech., 1923-27; grad. The Infantry Sch., 1932, Command and Gen. Staff Sch., 1942, Gemological Inst. Am., 1966; m. Mary L. Martin, Nov. 5, 1933 (dec. June 1962); m. 2d, Estelle B. Bennett, Jan. 25, 1963; 1 stepson, James Gordon Bennett. Archtl. draftsman, 1927-41, Atlanta, 1946-51; asso. architect Barili & Humphreys, Atlanta, 1946-51; architect Percy H. Perkins Jr. & Assos., Atlanta, 1951—; past pres. Am. Equipment Co.; past v.p. Paramount Real Estate Trust Fund. Gemologist, 1966—; lectr. gems and gemology. Served from 2d lt. to col., USAR, 1927-65; ETO; NATUSA; col. Res. (ret.). Aide-de-camp Gov.'s staff, 1971-75. Decorated Bronze Star with V, Army Commendation medal, Purple Heart; Czechoslovakia War Cross; Ouissam Alauite Cherifien (Morocco). Mem. Ga. Mineral Soc., Ga. Gem Soc., Res. Officers Assn. (life mem., pres. Greater Atlanta chpt. 1947, medal), Fulton County Grand Jurors Assn., Am. Legion, AIA (emeritus mem., past dir. Ga. chpt.), Am. (affiliate), Ga. gem socs., Ga. Mineral Soc., Ret. Officers Assn. (life), 16th Armored Div. Assn. (life), 760th Tank Bn. Assn. (life), Men's Garden Club, Atlanta and Buckhead, Scabbard and Blade, Pi Kappa Alpha. Presbyterian (elder). Mason (Shriner), Kiwanian. Author: Gem Stones of The Bible. Former newspaper columnist. Home: 5450 Peachtree-Dunwoody Rd NE Atlanta GA 30342 Office: 3110 Maple Dr NE Atlanta GA 30305

PERKINS, RICHARD BURLE, real estate broker; b. Rockville, Ind., July 1, 1923; s. Walter Mac and Olevia Maude (Vinson) P.; student Ball State U., 1941-42, Oberlin Coll., 1944-45, U. Mich., 1946; B.A., DePauw U., 1947; m. Mariam Catherine Jamail, Aug. 1, 1959; children—Richard Burle II, Mele Angelique. Territory mgr. P & G Edible Oils, Tex., La., Okla., 1947-53; dist. mgr. Southwest U.S. DCA Food Industries, spl. flours, mixes and machinery, Houston, Tex., 1953-62; pres. Gold Seal Donuts, Houston, 1962-63; div. mgr. Nat. Oats Co., Houston, 1963-68; mgr. apt. mng. systems Office Services, Inc., Houston, 1970—; owner Dick Perkins Co., realtor, Houston, 1970—; registered securities rep. Waddel & Reed, Houston, 1970-71; gen. mgr. Seven-Up Bottling Corp., Houston, 1969. Chmn. orgn. and extension com. Sunset dist. Boy Scouts Am., 1970; com. chmn. Cub Scout Pack 855, 1968—; coach, sponsor Spring Branch Little League Baseball, 1967—. Served with USMC, 1942-46. Mem. Pi Sigma Alpha. Club: Memorial Plaza Civic (pres. 1968) (Houston). Home: 6503 Rippling Hollow Spring TX 77379 Office: 5211-YFM 1960 West Houston TX 77069 also 13027 Champions Dr Suite C Houston TX 77069

PERL, ARNOLD EDWIN, lawyer; b. Beaumont, Tex., Dec. 16, 1939; s. Joe G. Perl and Cecil (LeVine) Berman; B.A., U. of Ill., 1961, LL.B., 1963; m. Mary Lynn Perlman, Aug. 8, 1965; children—Stephanie, Laurie. Admitted to Tenn. bar; lawyer NLRB, Memphis, 1964-65; advisor to Gen. Counsel, Appellate Ct. Branch, NLRB, Washington D.C., 1965-66; mem. firm McDermott, Will & Emery, Chgo., 1967-68; sr. partner firm Young & Perl, 1969—. Mem. Am. (Labor Law Section), Tenn., Memphis, Shelby County bar assns. Editor U. of Ill. Law Forum, 1962-63; contbr. articles in field to profl. jours. Home: 1265 Calais St Memphis TN 38138 Office: 1 Commerce Square Suite 2380 Memphis TN 38103

PERLEY, JAMES DWIGHT, indsl. relations cons., arbitrator, educator; b. Durham, N.H., Oct. 11, 1911; s. George A. and Mary (Foster) P.; student U. N.H., 1928-30; B.S. in Mech. Engring., Pa. State U., 1932; postgrad. U. Pa., 1932-33; m. Cecil E. Pendleton, May 4, 1943; 1 dau., Kent P. (Mrs. Charles A. Porter). Personnel mgr. Seth Thomas Clocks, 1936-39; personnel dir. Supplee Wills, & Jones Milk Co., 1939-41; personnel coordinator Gen. Tire & Rubber Co., 1945-46; dir. employee relations Ingersoll Products div., 1946-52, asst. v.p.-employee relations Westinghouse Air Brake Co., 1952-59; v.p. employee relations Consol. Natural Gas Service Co., Inc., 1959-74; indsl. relations cons., arbitrator, 1974—; prof. Coll. Bus., Appalachian State U., Boone, N.C., 1974—. Served from lt. to lt. col. AUS, 1941-45. Decorated Legion of Merit Mem. Indsl. Relations Research Assn., Am. Arbitration Assn., Nat. Def. Exec. Res., Nat. Wildlife Fedn. Alpha Tau Omega. Episcopalian. Clubs: Duquesne, Beech Mountain Country. Home: 256 Rhododendron Dr Banner Elk NC 28604 Office: Appalachian State U Boone NC 28608

PERLINSKI, JEANNETTE DAVIS, fed. agy. exec.; b. N.Y.C., June 24, 1920; d. Ben and Mary (Rosenbloom) D.; student Ga. State U., 1938-40, U. Denver, 1944-45; m. Julius Alfred Perlinski, May 5, 1942; 1 dau., Emily P. Friedman. With Internal Revenue Service, Atlanta, 1963—, selective placement coordinator for handicapped, 1974-79, equal employment officer, 1974—, mgr. Fed. Women's Program, 1974—. State chmn. Nat. Fed. Task Force for Women, 1977; mem. Ga. Com. for Status of Women, 1976-77; adv. council Metro Atlanta Task Com. for Handicapped. Served with WAC, 1944-45. Mem. Atlanta Federally Employed Women (pres. 1976-78), Fed. Womens Program Mgrs. Council, Equal Employment Officers Council, IRS Nat. Speakers, NOW, Nat. Orgn. Public Adminstrs. Democrat. Jewish. Clubs: Hadassah, B'nai B'rith Women, Federally Employed Women, Inc. Home: 1087 Cumberland Rd Atlanta GA 30306 Office: 4800 Buford Hwy Chamblee GA 30006

PERLMAN, EILEEN ELEANOR, civic worker, investor, former restaurant chain, hotel exec.; b. Chgo., Oct. 31, 1935; d. Bennett Viggo and Eleanor Lucille Christensen; student Northwestern U., nights 1954, Patricia Stevens Modeling Sch., 1955, Liberty Baptist Coll., 1977-79; m. Clifford Seely Perlman, July 30, 1959 (div. 1969); children—Jason, Clayton, Ivy. Co-founder, Lum's, Inc., Miami Beach, Fla., 1958; fin. sec., treas. Christian Womens Club, South Fla., 1973-75; visitation chmn. Granada Presbyn. Ch., 1973-75, circle chmn., 1978; active Protect Our Children, Anti-ERA campaign, ARC; corr. sec., bd. dirs. S. Fla. chpt. Women for Responsible Legis. and Polit. Action, 1978-79; active Floridians Against Casino Takeover, Christian Broadcasting Network, Inc., 700 Club; mem. coms. Westminster Christian Sch., Jews for Jesus; mem. nat. adv. com. Am. Security Council; sustaining mem. Republican Nat. Com.; mem. Nat. Rep. Congressional Com. Mem. U.S. Lawn Tennis Assn., U.S. Figure Skating Assn. (dir. Miami chpt.), Interfaith Commn. Against Blasphemy, Am. Biog. Inst., Am. Bridge Club. Presbyterian. Home: 6401 Cellini St Coral Gables FL 33146

PERRET, ROLAND FRANCIS, JR., chemist; b. New Iberia, La., Feb. 18, 1946; s. Roland Francis and Anita Marie (Ducote) P.; B.S., U. Southwestern La., 1968. Asst. chemist Murphy Oil Corp., New Orleans, 1969-70; mgr. Roland Perret Distbg., Inc., Jeanerette, La., 1974—. Mem. Am. Chem. Soc. Roman Catholic. Home: 2810 W Main St Jeanerette LA 70544 Office: Roland Perret Distbg Inc S Canal St Jeanerette LA 70544

PERRIN, SARAH ANN, lawyer; b. Neoga, Ill., Dec. 13, 1904; d. James Lee and Bertha Frances (Baker) Figenbaum; LL.B., George Washington U., 1941, J.D., 1964; m. James Frank Perrin, Dec. 24, 1926. Admitted to D.C. bar, 1942; asso. atty. Mabel Walker Willebrandt, law office, Washington, 1941-42; atty. various fed. housing agys., 1942-69, asst. gen. counsel FHA, Washington, 1959-60, asst. gen. counsel HUD, Washington, 1960-69; sec. Nat. Housing Conf., Washington, 1970—; research cons. housing and urban devel., Palmyra, Va., 1970—; acting sec. Nat. Housing Research Council, Washington, 1973—; bd. dirs. Nat. Housing Conf., 1972—. Trustee Found. for Coop. Housing, 1975—; mem. Blue Ridge Presbytery Div. Mission, Presbyterian Ch., 1979—. Mem. Am. Bar Assn., Fed. Bar Assn., Women's Bar Assn. D.C. (pres. 1959-60), Nat. Assn. Women Lawyers, Phi Delta Delta, Fluvanna County Hist. Soc. (pres. 1973-75). Club: Order Eastern Star. Home: Solitude Plantation Palmyra VA 22963

PERRIN, SHEPARD FRANCIS, JR., state ofcl.; b. New Orleans, June 3, 1922; s. Shepard Francis and Leila Winans (Joffrion) P.; B.S. in Chem. Engring., Tulane U., 1942; m. Elizabeth Rice, June 20, 1947; children—Leila Joffrion, Cidette St. Martin, Shepard Francis. Supr. petroleum refining Esso Standard Oil, Baton Rouge, 1946-57; head splty. products sales Esso & Humble Oil, N.Y.C., 1957-66; sr. adviser Esso Inter Am., Coral Gables, Fla., 1966-70; head lube oil sales Exxon Internat., N.Y.C., 1970-72; sr. advisor Esso Asia, Singapore, 1972-74; exec. dir. La. Superport Authority, Baton Rouge, 1975—. Chmn. com. United Way, Baton Rouge, 1977, 78; adv. council Gulf South Research Inst.; adv. bd. La. State U. Sea Grant Program; mem. Tulane Engring. Bd. Advs., past pres. Served to lt. USNR, 1942-46. Registered profl. engr., La. Mem. SAR, Tulane U. Nat. Alumni Assn. (past pres.). Presbyterian. Clubs: N.Y. Yacht, Biscayne Bay Yacht, Storm Trysail, Baton Rouge City, Baton Rouge Country, New Orleans, Plimsoll. Home: 7465 Boyce Dr Baton Rouge LA 70809

PERRINE, REBECCA ANN, retail exec.; b. Lyons, Ga., Dec. 14, 1934; d. Julius Russell and Martha Inez (Horton) Clark; student Accounting Manatee Jr. Coll., 1960-62; m. Gary Raymond Perrine, June 12, 1962; 1 son, Raymond Clark. Accountant, Electro Mech. Systems, Titusville, Fla., 1963-66; head internal accounting dept., Kelley, Drye, Newhall, McGuiness & Warren, 1967-70; co-owner, mgr. Perrine Mobile Homes Sales, Naples, Fla., 1972—, Palm River Mobile Home Park, Naples, 1971—, Chokoloskee Island Park (Fla.), 1972—, Shady Acres Travel Park, Estero, Fla., 1977—, also Harmony Shores Mobile Home Port. Republican. Home: 2470 Tarpon Rd Naples FL 33942 Office: 3078 Tamiami Trail S Naples FL 33942

PERRITT, R. T., clergyman; b. Winnsboro, Tex., May 20, 1926; s. James Hogg and Clara (White) P.; A.A., Jacksonville (Tex.) Coll., 1948; B.D., Bible Bapt. Sem., Arlington, Tex., 1958; Th.M., Okla. Missionary Bapt. Inst. and Sem., 1960, Th.D., 1961; m. Betty Ruth Powell, Nov. 23, 1944; children—Robert Lynn, John Mark, Ruth Ann, James Lance. Ordained to ministry Bapt. Ch., 1945; pastor Calvary Missionary Bapt. Ch., Sherman, Tex., 1949-51, Liberty Missionary Bapt. Ch., Ft. Worth, 1951-56, Cavanaugh Missionary Bapt. Ch., Fort Smith, Ark., 1956-59, 5th St. Missionary Bapt. Ch., Marlow, Okla., 1959—; dean Okla. Missionary Bapt. Coll., Inst. and Sem., 1961-63, pres., 1963—; asst. moderator Bapt. Gen. Assembly Okla., 1970-72, moderator, 1973-75. Pres., Unique Christian Ministries, Inc., 1974-79; chmn. bd. Leisure Village, Norman, Okla., 1976-79; pres. Myrtle Springs Perpetual Care Cemetary Assn., Quitman, Tex., 1977—. Pres., Cavanaugh Baseball Club, 1957-59. Served with U.S. Maritime Service and Mcht. Marine, 1944-45. Named Community Leader Am., 1969. Mem. Am. Bapt. Assn. (v.p. 1970—, chmn. missionary com. 1966-75). Democrat. Lion. Author: The Natural and the Spiritual, 1960; Kindling Fires for Church Growth, 1965; Mastery in Sorrow, 1969; Studies in Daniel, 1973; also numerous religious tng. course quars. Home: 610 W Kiowa St Marlow OK 73055 Office: 415 W Cherokee St Marlow OK 73055 also 9th and Caddo Sts Marlow OK 73055

PERRY, EDWARD BELK, civil engr.; b. Oxford, Miss., Sept. 29, 1939; B.S.C.E., U. Miss., 1962; M.S., Miss. State U., 1968; Ph.D., Tex. A&M U., 1973; married; 3 children. With Miss. State Hwy. Dept., Grenada, summers 1957-61, asst. office engr. testing div., Jackson, 1962-63; civil engr. soil dynamics div. soils and pavements lab. U.S. Army C.E. Waterways Exptl. Sta., Vicksburg, Miss., 1963-69, research civil engr., 1969-75, research civil engr. soil mechanics div., 1974—, instr. courses, 1978—; adj. asst. prof. civil engring. Jackson Engring. Grad. Program, Univs. Center, 1977—; chmn. Interagy. Research Coordination Com. on Identification Dispersive Clays, 1978; chmn. Streambank Erosion Subcom. on Tech. transfer, 1980. Recipient Spl. Act award Waterways Exptl. Sta., 1976, Dir.'s Research and Devel. Achievement award, 1979, Army Research and Devel. award, 1979; registered profl. engr., Miss. Mem. ASCE (com. soil properties), ASTM (mem. coms.), Am. Soc. Engring. Edn. (ocean and marine engring. com.), Transp. Research Bd., Deep Founds. Inst. (com. geotech. research), U.S. Com. on Large Dams, Internat. Soc. Soil Mechanics and Found. Engring., Chi Epsilon. Author publs. in field.

PERRY, HORACE RANDOLPH, JR., biologist, educator; b. Bertie County, Colerain, N.C., Sept. 3, 1946; s. Horace Randolph and Helen Clair (Castello) P.; B.S. (Univ. scholar), N.C. State U., 1969, Ph.D. (Nat. Wildlife Fedn. fellow), 1974; M.S., La. State U., 1971; m. Linda Dare Gray, June 1, 1969. Vector control aid USPHS, Mobile, Ala., summer 1965; field asst. N.C. Wildlife Resource Commn., Raleigh, summer 1966; research biologist, technician U.S. Fish and Wildlife Service, McBee, S.C., summers 1968, 69, 71; wildlife biologist-environ. cons. Coastal Zone Resources Corp., Wilmington, N.C., 1974-75; asst. unit leader La. Coop. Wildlife Research Unit, La. State U., Baton Rouge, 1975—. Active Boy Scouts Am. Served to capt., inf. U.S. Army, 1972. Edn. Opportunity grantee, 1966; N.C. Wildlife Fedn. grantee, 1969; Nat. Wildlife Fedn. postdoctoral grantee, 1977-78. Mem. Wildlife Soc. (parliamentarian Southeastern sect. 1979—), Am. Soc. Mammalogists, AAAS, La. Wildlife Biologists Assn. (pres. 1977-78), Nat. Wildlife Fedn., N.C. Wildlife Fedn., Assn. Southeastern Biologists, Sports Car Club Am., Sigma Xi, Xi Sigma Pi, Phi Kappa Phi, Gamma Sigma Delta. Baptist. Researcher ecology of coastal plain swamps; contbr. articles to profl. jours., popular mags. Home: 9259 High Point Rd Baton Rouge LA 70810 Office: Sch Forestry and Wildlife Mgmt La State U Baton Rouge LA 70803

PERRY, JEANNETTE LARUE, govt. agy. adminstr.; b. Fairfax, Okla., July 29, 1945; d. Joseph Paul and Ida Minnie (Moses) Zelinski; student Okla. State U., 1963-64; children—Ann Lynette, Susan Lizabeth. Clk.-typist, Soil Conservation Service, U.S. Dept. Agr., Cherokee, Okla., 1965-67; clk.-typist, design br. C.E., Tulsa, 1967-69, mgmt. asst. office adminstrv. services, 1969-74; cert. and rev. clk. HEW, Dallas, 1975-78; mgmt. asst. office adminstrv. services C.E., Tulsa, 1978, grants mgmt. asst. EPA grants, 1978-79, gen. services supr., 1979—. Mem. Tulsa Fed. Women's Com., 1978—, program mgr. Tulsa dist., 1979—. Mem. Am. Records Mgmt. Assn. (past chmn. publicity com.). Republican. Office: PO Box 61 224 S Boulder St Tulsa OK 74121

PERRY, JESSE LAURENCE, JR., investment mgr., financier; b. Nashville, Oct. 15, 1919; s. Jesse Laurence and Mamie Lucretia (White) P.; B.A. magna cum laude, Vanderbilt U., 1941; M.B.A., Harvard U., 1943; postgrad. edn. retarded children George Peabody Coll., summer 1953; m. Susan Taylor White, Nov. 5, 1949 (dec. Mar. 1972); children—Robert Laurence, Judith Foulds; m. 2d, Sarah Kinkead Stockell, Apr. 6, 1974. Treas., J.L. Perry Co., Nashville, 1947-48, v.p., 1949-54, pres., 1954-73, also dir.; pres. Perry Enterprises, Nashville, 1973—; chmn. 1st So. Savs. and Loan, 1975—; pres. Porters Field, Inc., Nashville, 1971—. Pres., Police Assistance League, 1973-74; mem. Tenn. Dept. Agr. Pest Control Licensing Bd., 1971-76; a.d.c. gov.'s staff, 1962-76; 1st v.p. Tenn. Assn. Retarded Children, 1954-62; mem. Tenn. Mental Retardation Adv. Council, 1966-72; bd. advisers Salvation Army, 1958-72; founder, sec. Tenn. Bot. Garden and Fine Arts Center, 1958—; hon. col., staff Gov. Tenn., 1962-76; chmn. 5th dist. Republican Exec. Com., 1950-54; vice chmn. Tenn. Rep. State Exec. Com., 1956-70; Middle Tenn. campaign mgr., 1956, 60, 66; state mgr. Pub. Service Com. Campaign, 1964; mem. spl. com. on urban devel. Rep. Nat. Exec. Com., 1962; del. Rep. Nat. Exec. Com., 1960, vice chmn. Tenn. del., 1960, alt. del., 1968; dist. mem. Rep. State Exec. Com., 1954-75; state chmn. Rep. Capitol Club, 1971-73; Tenn. Rep. party state committeeman, 1956-74; bd. govs. U. So., 1968-76, Sewanee Acad. Served with AUS, 1943-46. Decorated chevalier Order Constantini Magni, 1978, Order St. John of Jerusalem, 1978. Mem. Episcopal Churchmen Tenn. (v.p. 1956), Am. Ch. Union (v.p. 1958), SAR (pres. chpt.), Young Pres.'s Orgn., U.S. C. of C., Nat. Office Mgmt. Assn. (pres. Nashville chpt. 1958-59), Am. Legion, English Speaking Union, Westerners Internat. (sheriff Nashville chpt.), Phi Beta Kappa, Omicron Delta Gamma, Pi Kappa Alpha. Clubs: Elks; Nashville Exchange, Nashville Sewanee, Harvard, Nashville City, Cumberland, Lakeside Country (Nashville); Capitol Hill (Washington); Magna Charta Barons. Home: Rokeby 3901 Harding Rd Nashville TN 37205 Office: Executive Sq 16th Floor First Am Center Nashville TN 37238

PERRY, MARCELLA ELLEN DONOVAN, banker; b. Yorktown, Ind.; d. James Garfield and Elizabeth (Jones) Donovan; student Rice Inst., 1922-24; m. Glenn Arthur Perry, Nov. 10, 1930 (div. 1958); 1 dau., Gayle Donovan (Mrs. Fredric Milam Saunders). Debut as solo dancer Carnegie Hall; owner, Donovan Dance Studio, Houston, 1932-54; sec.-treas. Heights Savs. Assn., Houston, 1954-61, pres., 1961—; chmn. bd. 1st Pasadena State Bank, now sr. chmn. bd.; chmn. bd. First City Bank of Almeda-Genoa; dir. Reagan Commerce Bank. Del. Democratic Nat. Conv., 1960, 64; mem. State Dem. exec. com. 6th Senatorial Dist. Tex.; mem. state adv. bd. Small Business Adminstrn., 1965-67, mem. nat. adv. bd., 1969-70; sec. Harris County (Tex.) Grand Jury Assn., 1965-72; port commr. Port of Houston Authority of Harris County, 1973—; vice chmn. Am. Revolution Bicentennial Commn. of Tex.; pres. Allegro Ballet of Houston, 1966; mem. Houston-Harris County Economic Opportunity Bd., 1965; mem. Exec. Res. Office Emergency Planning; chmn. Houston Municipal Art Commn., 1971-72; bd. dirs. Boy Scouts Am., Beautify Tex. Council, Houston-Harris County chpt. ARC, Blue Cross-Blue Shield of Tex.; chmn. Houston Parks Bd.; commr. Houston Clean City Commn. Chmn. bd. regents Tex. Woman's U., 1973—. Recipient Gold medallion B'nai B'rith, Mylie E. Durham award. Mem. Nat. Assn. Bank Women (chmn. Houston 1965-66, regional v.p., 1965-66), Houston Zool. Soc. (dir.), Harris County Savs. and Loan League (pres. 1969), Houston C. of C. (dir.), U.S. C. of C. Home: 503 Bolton Pl Houston TX 77024 Office: PO Box 7483 Houston TX 77008

PERRY, MARK DANIEL, vehicle mfg. co. exec.; b. Tulsa, July 6, 1948; s. John David and Dorthy Ruth P.; B.S., Ball Ball State U., 1973; m. Norma Stephanie Hamilton, Jan. 29, 1979. Brick layer Pierson Constrn. Co., Eaton, Ind., 1971-73; retail indsl. equipment salesman Hartford (Ind.) Indsl. Corp., 1973-74, Weiss Machinery, Inc., Daleville, Ind., 1974-76; dealer devel. mgr. Holiday Rambler Corp., Sweetwater, Tex., 1976—. Republican. Mormon. Home: 10101 Roark Rd Houston TX 77099 Office: Holiday Rambler Corp PO Drawer 768 Sweetwater TX 79556

PERRY, RONALD HOWARD, physician; b. Chgo., Nov. 21, 1933; s. Howard Petty and Anne (Rochkes) P.; M.D., U. Tenn., 1956; m. Janice Lynn Schubert, June 19, 1954; children—Mark E., Donna L., Dana M., M. Darlene. Intern, St. Luke's Hosp., Jacksonville, Fla., 1956-57, resident, 1957-58; resident gen. radiology Fitzsimons Hosp., Denver, 1961-64; chief radiology service Kenner Hosp., Ft. Lee, Va., 1964-66; fellowship radiation therapy Walter Reed Hosp., Washington, 1966-68; chief radiation therapy Letterman Hosp., San Francisco, 1968-69; dir. radiation oncology Fort Sanders Presbyn. Hosp., Knoxville, Tenn., 1969—; asso. prof. clin. radiology U. Tenn., 1970—. Served with AUS, 1958-69. Diplomate Am. Bd. Radiology. Mem. Knoxville Acad. Medicine, Tenn., Am. med. assns., Radiol. Soc. N.Am., Am. Soc. Therapeutic Radiologists. Republican. Club: Lions. Home: 316 Seven Oaks Trail Knoxville TN 37922 Office: Radiation Oncology Center Fort Sanders Presbyn Hosp Knoxville TN 37916

PERRY, RUSSELL H., ins. exec.; b. Cornell, Ill., Nov. 8, 1908; s. Walter O. and Mabel (Hilton) P.; student N.Y. U., 1937; J.D. cum laude, Bklyn. Law Sch., 1940; D.C.L., Atlanta Law Sch.; m. Phoebe Sherwood, June 2, 1956. Clk., Chgo. Fire & Marine Ins. Co., 1925-32; underwriter Republic Ins. Co., N.Y.C., 1934-38, charge eastern dept. underwriting, 1939-42, asst. to v.p., 1942-43, spl. agt. for L.I. and Westchester, 1934, mgr. eastern dept., 1945-47, resident sec., 1947-49, v.p., 1949-59, exec. v.p., 1959-61; pres. Republic Financial Services, Inc., holding co. for Republic Ins. and Allied Finance Groups Dallas, 1961-71, chmn. bd., pres., 1971-72, chmn. bd., chief exec. officer, 1972—; trustee Murray Mortgage Investors; dir. Bonanza Internat., Met. Savs. & Loan Assn., Dallas, TACA, Inc., Union Bank & Trust, Dallas. Bd. dirs. Ins. Info. Inst., N.Y.C.; bd. dirs., chmn. Dallas Council on World Affairs; bd. dirs. Dallas Postal Customers Council; pres. Trinity Improvement Assn.; bd. dirs., exec. com. Dallas Citizens Council; mem. devel. bd. Dallas Bapt. Coll.; mem. exec. adv. council Coll. Bus. Adminstrn., North Tex. State U.; adv. chmn. Salvation Army, Dallas, nat. bd. dirs.; mem. exec. com. Dallas Community Chest; nat. bd. dirs. Am. Cancer Soc.; bd. dirs. Big Bros./Big Sisters Am., Citizen's Choice, Dallas UN Assn., Texas Research League, KERA-TV, Dallas, Dallas County Community Coll. Found., Inc.; pres. Tex. Bur. Econ. Understanding, Inc.; adv. council Airline Passengers Assn.; bd. dirs. Dallas Summer Musicals, Greater Dallas Planning Council; chmn. Tex. Right To Work Com. Recipient G. Mabry Seay award Dallas Assn. Ins. Agts., 1970, Headliner of Yr. award Press Club Dallas, 1975, Orchid for Uncommon Support Free Enterprise, Students in Free Enterprise, So. Meth. U., 1977, Person of Vision award Tex. Soc. for Prevention Blindness, 1977, Linz award for public service Linz Bros. Jewelers-Dallas Times Herald, 1978, Torch of Liberty award Anti-Defamation League, 1979; named Boss of Yr., Ins. Women Dallas, 1976, Disting. Salesman of Dallas 1976, Sales and Mktg. Execs. Dallas, 1977. Mem. Philonomic Soc., Am., N.Y., Dallas bar assns., State Bar Tex., Tex. Good Roads Assn. (exec. com.), Am. Ins. Assn. (dir.), Nat. Assn. Casualty and Surety Execs. (exec. com.), Tex. Assn. Taxpayers (dir.), Newcomen Soc. N.Am., Delta Theta Phi. Clubs: Lawyers of N.Y. U. (N.Y.C.); Ins. (dir.), Knife and Fork, Dallas Petroleum, Dallas Country, Rotary, Lancers, 2001 (Dallas); Austin. Home: 3437 Gillespie Dallas TX 75219 Office: 2727 Turtle Creek Blvd Dallas TX 75219

PERRY, SAMUEL LLOYD, oil mktg. exec.; b. N.Y.C., Dec. 11, 1917; s. John P. Hazen Perry and Augustine (Lloyd) Perry Gifford; A.B., U. Mich., 1940; m. Marion Wagner Fahey, Feb. 23, 1946; children—Samuel Lloyd, Elizabeth M. Various mktg. positions Texaco Inc., 1940-62; pres. Comer Oil Inc., Fort Myers, Fla., 1962—; dir. 1st Nat. Bank of Ft. Myers, S.W. Fla. Banks, Inc. Bd. dirs. Com. of 100, 1974—, Edison Pageant of Light, 1973-76, Ft. Myers Symphony Orch. and Chorus Assn., 1975-76. Served to lt. comdr. USNR, 1941-46. Mem. Fla. Petroleum Marketers Assn. (dir. 1964-66). Republican. Episcopalian. Clubs: Royal Palm Yacht, Cypress Lakes Country, Met. Dinner (dir. 1970—, pres. 1975-76). Home: 1388 Wales Dr Fort Myers FL 33901 Office: PO Box 1389 Fort Myers FL 33902

PERRY, SHIRLEY BIRD, univ. ofcl.; b. Stockdale, Tex., Aug. 18, 1936; d. Homer S. and Laura B. (Stevenson) Bird; B.S., U. Tex., 1958, M.A., 1967; m. Sam R. Perry, July 13, 1963. Program dir. Tex. Union, U. Tex., Austin, 1958-59, 60-73, dir. Tex. Union, 1973-76; coordinator ednl. programs and services Assn. Coll. Unions Internat. 1976-79; asst. to pres., centennial coordinator U. Tex., Austin, 1979—; tchr. Cajon Valley Ind. Sch. Dist., El Cajon, Calif., 1959-60; cons., lectr. in field. Mem. Austin Bicentennial-Horizons Com., 1974-76. Mem. Assn. Coll. Unions Internat. (v.p. 1969-70, pres. 1972-73, chmn. ednl. program com. 1975-76, Butts-Whiting award 1976), Council Student Personnel Assns. in Higher Edn. (exec. com. 1971-75), Am. Coll. Personnel Assn., Am. Personnel and Guidance Assn., U. Tex. Ex-Students Assn. (exec. council 1977—, sec. 1979—), U. Tex. President's Assos., U. Tex. Chancellor's Council, Am. Assn. Higher Edn., English Speaking Union. Democrat. Methodist. Contbr. articles to profl. publs. Home: 1906 Matthews Dr Austin TX 78703 Office: Office of Pres U Tex at Austin Austin TX 78712

PERRY, VINCENT, accountant; b. Riverside, N.J., Jan. 5, 1943; s. John Vincent and Florence Catherine (O'Rourke) P.; A.A., Orlando Jr. Coll., 1965; B.A., U. South Fla., 1967; postgrad. Rollins Coll., 1970—; m. Carol Ann McCarroll, Feb. 14, 1969; children—Cherie, Laurie. With Ernst & Ernst, Orlando, Fla., 1967-70; asst. comptroller Rollins Coll., Winter Park, Fla., 1970-74, adj. instr. accounting, 1970—; partner Perry, Tomlinson, Weinstein & McMillen, C.P.A.'s, Winter Park, 1975—; dir. Ellman Battery Co., Inc. Treas., E. Central Fla. Regional Planning Council, 1971-72; bd. dirs. Parent Resource Center, Inc., Orlando, 1976; chmn. Seminole County Republican exec. com., 1980. C.P.A. Mem. Am., Fla. insts. C.P.A.'s, Nat. Fedn. Ind. Bus., Altamonte-Casselberry C. of C., Winter Park C. of C., Fla. Conservative Union, Council of Arts and Scis., Central Fla. Zool. Soc. Clubs: Sertoma, Rotary Register of Greater Orlando. Home: 1092 Dyson Dr Maitland FL 32751 Office: PO Box 426 Winter Park FL 32790

PERSON, WILLARD DALE, chemist; b. New London, Jan. 27, 1934; s. Amos and Ethel Ora (Honeycutt) P.; student Kilgore Coll., 1952-54; B.S., East Tex Bapt. Coll., 1957; m. Mae Dean Bechtold, Aug. 1963; children—Rebecca, Sheila, Sarah, Terry, Kelly, Brenda. Chemist, ICI Ams., Inc., Marshall, Tex., 1957-63, lab. supr. research and devel. lab., 1964—. State bd. dirs. Am. Heart Assn., 1977-78; bd. dirs. ARC, 1971-76, United Fund, 1972-74. Mem. ASTM, Am. Chem. Soc. Democrat. Baptist. Home: 3107 Acadia St Marshall TX 75670 Office: ICI Ams Inc W University Ave Marshall TX 75670

PERULLO, LOUIS CHRISTOPHER, JR., retail splty. chain exec.; b. Boston, July 23, 1939; s. Louis Christopher and Ferma Florence (Fiore) P.; B.A., Dartmouth Coll., 1960; m. Karen Telesco, May 7, 1976; 1 dau., Laura. Asst. media buyer Grey Advt., N.Y.C., 1960-63; media dir. Chirurg & Cairns, Boston, 1962-64; account supr. Arnold & Co., Boston, 1964-66; dir. advt. Thom McAn Shoe Co., Worcester, Mass., 1966-74; v.p. advt., display and constrn. Kay Jewelers, Alexandria, Va., 1974—; performing mem. Potomac River Jazz Club. Served with U.S. Army, 1960-62. Recipient cert. of appreciation USMC-Toys for Tots, 1970, 73, cert. of merit for lyric composition Am. Song Festival, 1976; named Outstanding Driver, Md. Internat. Raceway, 1976. Mem. Nashville Song Writers Assn., Art Dirs. Club Washington, Nat. Hot Rod Assn., Am. Fedn. Musicians. Roman Catholic. Club: Italian Am. Citizens (life). Poem Bix Beiderbecke included in Best Loved Contemporary Poems, 1979. Home: 707 S Lee St Alexandria VA 22314 Office: 320 King St Alexandria VA 22314

PESCE, ROBERT JOSEPH, architect; b. Chgo., Aug. 4, 1928; s. Carlo and Mary (Pesci) P.; cert. in archtl. design and constrn. Pratt Inst., 1953; B.S., Columbia U., 1963; m. Joan Nemetz, June 23, 1956; children—Teresa A., Robert B., Catherine M., Christopher C. With aviation dept. Port of N.Y. Authority, N.Y.C., 1957-69; v.p. Brodsky Hopf & Adler, Dallas, 1969-70; resident architect Brodsky Hopf Adler Hellmuth, Obata & Kassabaum for constrn. Dallas-Fort Worth Regional Airport, 1970-73; prin. Gossen Livingston Pesce, Dallas and Wichita, Kans., 1973-75; owner, architect Robert J. Pesce & Assos., Dallas, 1975-78; partner Pesce Clendening Assos., Dallas, 1978—. Mem. zoning bd. adjustment City of Richardson, Tex., 1979—. Served with USN, 1946-48. Mem. AIA, Am. Planning Assn., Tex. Soc. Architects, Sales and Mktg. Execs. Dallas. Roman Catholic. Home: 2802 Valley Ridge Dr Richardson TX 75080 Office: Pesce Clendening Assos 13771 N Central St Suite 606 Dallas TX 75243

PESCHEL, RANDAL CHARLES, real estate developer; b. Austin, Tex., Oct. 27, 1948; s. Calvin Charles and Amanda Lea (Ponder) P.; B.B.A., U. Tex., Austin, 1971; m. Sue Alison Wright, Aug. 1, 1970; children—Lea Alison, Melissa Carolyn. Asst. cashier Capital Nat. Bank, Austin, 1972-73, asst. v.p., 1974-76, v.p., 1977; v.p. City Nat. Bank, Austin, 1977-79; pres. Select Constrn. Co., Austin, 1979—. Bd. dirs. Young Men's Bus. League, 1976; active Com. to Re-Elect J.J. (Jake) Pickle, 1978, Com. to Re-Elect John Tower, 1978. Mem. Austin Assn. Home Builders, Soc. Real Estate Appraisers, Nat. Assn. Credit Mgrs., Austin C. of C. (dir./diplomat 1979). Baptist. Clubs: Longhorn, Austin Woods and Waters, Austin Country, Admirals. Home: 5924 Fairlane Dr Austin TX 78731 Office: 812 San Antonio Suite 220 Austin TX 78707

PESHEL, BARBARA BARNES, librarian; b. Oklahoma City, May 18, 1929; d. James Thurman and Gladys (Hadley) B.; A.A., Ward-Belmont Jr. Coll., 1948, B.A., Grinnell Coll., 1950; M.L.S., U. Okla., 1972; m. Robert Lee Peshel, Sr., Aug. 27, 1949 (div. 1968); children—Elizabeth Gladys, Dolores Ann, Richard Dean, Robert Lee. Reference librarian NASA, Ames Research Center, Moffett Field, Calif., 1967-68; instr. Health Scis. Center Library, U. Okla., Oklahoma City, 1973-76, asst. prof., 1976—. Mem. ALA, Med. Library Assn., Spl. Libraries Assn., Okla., South Western, Okla. Health Scis. library assns., Higher Edn. Alumni Council Okla., U.S. Coast Guard Aux., Phi Delta Gamma. Republican. Episcopalian. Co-editor Life Scis. Publs., 1964-69. Home: 1507 Eisenhower St Norman OK 73069 Office: Library U Okla Health Sci Center PO Box 26901 Oklahoma City OK 73190

PETER, JOHN EDWARD, architect, educator; b. Oklahoma City, Dec. 23, 1934; s. Maurice Lyle and Claribel Elizabeth (Oldfield) P.; B.Arch., Okla. State U., 1958; M.Arch., U. Okla., 1979; m. Judith Louise Rice, Jan. 26, 1957; children—David Mark, Kevin Andrew, Anita Deborah. With various archtl. firms, Oklahoma City, 1958-62; pvt. practice architecture, Oklahoma City, 1962-68, Woodward, Okla., 1968-76, Clinton, Okla., 1975-80; asst. prof. Coll. Architecture and Environ. Design, Tex A&M U., College Station, 1980—; prin., owner John E. Peter, AIA, Architect. Bd. advs. Goodwill Industries of Oklahoma City, 1964-68; v.p. Boiling Springs dist. Great Salt Plains council Boy Scouts Am.; chmn. N.W. Guidance Center, Woodward, Okla., 1973-75; pres. S.W. Playhouse, 1978-79. Served with USAR, Air N.G., 1958-64. Lic. architect, Okla., Tex., Kans.; cert. Nat. Council Archtl. Registration Bds. Mem. AIA. Clubs: Rotary, Masons, K.T. Home: 1405 Skrivanek Ct College Station TX 77840 Office: Tex A&M U Coll Architecture College Station TX 77840

PETER, LILY, plantation operator, writer; b. Marvell, Ark.; d. William Oliver and Florence (Mobrey) Peter; B.S., Memphis State U., 1927; M.A., Vanderbilt U., 1938; postgrad. U. Chgo., 1930, Columbia,

1935-36; L.H.D., Moravian Coll., Bethlehem, Pa., 1965; LL.D., U. Ark., 1975. Owner, operator plantations, Marvell and Ratio, Ark., writer poetry, feature articles pub. in S.W. Quar., Delta Rev., Cyclo Flame, Etude, Am. Weave, others; mem. staff S.W. Writers Conf., Corpus Christi, Tex., 1954—, sponsor Ark. Writers' Conf. Chmn., Poetry Day in Ark., 1953—; chmn., sponsor music Ark. Territorial Sesquicentennial, 1969. Bd. dirs. Ark. Arts Festival, Little Rock, Grand Prairie Festival Arts; chmn. bd. Phillips County Community Center, 1969-71. Hon. trustee Moravian Music Found. Recipient Moramus award Friends of Moravian Music, 1964; Distinguished Alumni award Vanderbilt U., 1964, Gov.'s award as Ark. Conservationist of Year, Ark. Wildlife Fedn., 1975; named Poet Laureate Ark., 1971; Democrat Woman of Year, 1971. Mem. D.A.R., (hon. state regent), Nat. League Am. Pen Women, Ark. Authors and Composers Soc., Poets' Roundtable Ark., poetry socs. of Tenn., Tex., Ga., Met. Opera Assn., So. Cotton Ginners Assn. (dir. 1971—), Big Creek Protective Assn. (chmn. 1974—), Sigma Alpha Iota. (hon.). Democrat. Methodist. Clubs: Pacaha (Helena, Ark.); Woman's City (Little Rock). Author: The Green Linen of Summer, 1964; The Great Riding, 1966; The Sea Dream of the Mississippi, 1973. Home: Route 2 Box 69 Marvell AR 72366

PETERS, CALVIN RONALD, plastic surgeon; b. New Orleans, Jan. 27, 1940; s. Arthur Henry and Christine Cecile (Moldaner) P.; M.D., La. State U., 1964; m. Pamela Alice Orth, Sept. 4, 1965; children—Brandon Scott, Kendall Kyle. Intern, U.S. Navel Hosp., Portsmouth, VA, 1964-65; resident in surgery Ochsner Clinic, New Orleans, 1968-72; resident in plastic surgery Duke U., Durham, N.C., 1972-75; Christine Kleinert fellow in hand surgery U. Louisville Hosp., 1973; craniofacial fellow, Paris, France, 1975; asst. prof. plastic and maxillofacial surgery Duke U. Med. Center, Durham, 1975-78, dir. craniofacial clinic, 1975-78; program dir. Cleve. Clinic, 1978-79. Served in USNR, 1964-68. Diplomate Am. Bd. Surgery, Am. Bd. Plastic Surgery. Fellow ACS; mem. Am. Soc. Plastic and Reconstructive Surgeons, Am. Assn. Hand Surgery, Am. Soc. Maxillofacial Surgeons, Am. Soc. Head and Neck Surgeons, Am. Burn Assn., C. of C. Durham. Republican. Episcopalian. Contbr. articles to profl. jours. Home: 337 Turkey Run Circle Winter Park FL 32789 Office: 1355 Orange Ave Winter Park FL 32789

PETERS, CHARLES WILLIAM, phys. scientist; b. Pierceton, Ind., Dec. 9, 1927; s. Charles Frederick and Zelda May (Line) P.; A.B., Ind. U., 1950; postgrad. U. Md., 1952-58; m. Katharine Louise Schuman, May 29, 1953; 1 dau., Susan Kay. Supervisory research physicist Naval Research Lab., Washington, 1950-71; phys. scientist EPA, Washington, 1971-76; mgr. Advanced Systems div. Consol. Controls Corp., Springfield, Va., 1976—; chmn. bd. Spectrum Techs., Ltd. Chmn. Fed. Interagency Task Force Emergency Instrumentation for Nuclear Incidents, 1974-76. Served with AUS, 1945-47. Mem. AAAS, Am. Mgmt. Assn., Am. Phys. Soc., IEEE, Internat. Platform Assn. Contbr. articles to profl. jours. Home: 8525 Cyrus Pl Alexandria VA 22308 Office: PO Box 726 7213 Lockport Pl Springfield VA 22150

PETERS, GEORGE THOMAS, educator; b. Poplar Bluff, Mo., Nov. 24, 1930; s. Emery Thomas and Opal Thusnelda (Steward) P.; B.S. in Edn., Southeast Mo. State U., 1952; M.S., U. Mo., 1953, Ed.D., 1960; m. Mary Helen Lichtenegger, May 25, 1952; children—Jennifer, Greg, Doug. Tchr., N. Kansas City (Mo.) Pub. Schs. System, 1956-57; prof. edn. SE Mo. State U., 1957-65; prof. counselor edn. dept. Ark. State U., 1965—. Served with U.S. Army, 1953-55. Danforth asso. (life). Mem. Am. Personnel Guidance Assn., Nat. Vocat. Guidance Assn., NEA, Ark. Psychol. Assn., Ark. Assn. for Counselor Edn. and Supervision, Ark. Sch. Counselors Assn., Phi Delta Kappa, Dappa Delta Pi, Sigma Tau Delta. Club: Elks. Home: 2804 Turtle Creek Jonesboro AR 72401 Office: PO Box ZZ State University AR 72467

PETERS, HENRY BUCKLAND, optometrist, univ. dean, educator; b. Oakland, Calif., Nov. 2, 1916; s. Thomas Henry and Eleanor Bernice (Hough) P.; A.B., U. Calif. at Berkeley, 1938; M.A., U. Nebr., 1939; D.O.S., So. Coll. Optometry, 1971; m. Anne Zara Ledin, Feb. 3, 1968; children—Lynn Peters MacDonald, Thomas Henry, James Clifton, Christopher Patrick, Elizabeth Anne. Practice optometry, Chico, Calif., 1939-40, Oakland, 1946-59; clin. asst. prof. optometry U. Calif. at Berkeley, 1947-62; asso. prof., asst. dean Sch. Optometry, 1962-69; prof., dean Sch. Optometry, U. Ala. in Birmingham Med. Center, 1969—; dir. Calif. Vision Service, Oakland, 1953-59; v.p. Children's Vision Center of East Bay, Oakland, 1963-69; bd. dirs. Community Service Council, 1972-76; mem. com. acad. health affairs VA Hosp., Birmingham, 1969—; mem. Council on Hypertension Ala. Dept. Pub. Health, 1974—; v.p. Nat. Health Council, 1976-77, pres. elect, 1977-78, pres., 1978-79, also bd. dirs.; bd. dirs. Am. Optometric Found., Birmingham Regional Health Systems Agy., 1976-79; chmn. nat. adv. com. on health promotion Nat. Health Council. Served to lt. USNR, 1942-46. Named Optometrist of Year Calif. Optometric Assn., 1960, Ala. Optometric Assn., 1973. Fellow Am. Pub. Health Assn., Am. Acad. Optometry (Carel C. Koch Meml. medal 1974, pres. 1972-74); mem. Assn. Schs. and Colls. Optometry (pres. 1967-69, dir.), Am. Optometric Assn. (Ala. del. ho. of dels. 1969—), Am. Found. Blind. Contbr. numerous articles to profl. publs. Home: 712 Vestavia Lake Dr Birmingham AL 35216

PETERS, JAMES MARTIN, environ. engr.; b. San Antonio, Tex., Dec. 19, 1940; s. Martin A. and Mary F. (Field) P.; B.S., U.S. Mil. Acad., 1965; M.S. in Environ. Engring., U. Tex., 1971; m. Judith Ann Hardcastle, June 15, 1974; children—Jill Marie, James Martin, Susan Michelle. Environ. engr. El Paso Natural Gas Co. (Tex.), 1972-73; environ. mgr. Amoco Chem. Corp., Texas City, 1974-78; vis. instr. U. Tex., El Paso, 1972-73; environ. cons., 1978—. Served to capt. U.S. Army, 1965-69; Vietnam; to capt. Tex. N.G., 1979—. NDEA fellow, 1969; registered profl. engr., Tex. Mem. Am. Inst. Chem. Engrs., Air Pollution Control Assn., Houston C. of C. (environment com. 1974-78, award 1979), U.S. Mil. Acad. Assn. Grads. Contbr. articles on air pollution control to profl. jours. Home: Route 5 Box 141B Austin TX 78748 Office: PO Box 501 Manchaca TX 78652

PETERS, JO ANN, health service assn. adminstr.; b. Sherman, Tex., Oct. 1, 1936; d. Joe B. and Gladys Ruth Deaton; B.J., U. Tex., 1958. Editorial asst. Tex. Jour. Medicine, Austin, 1957-61; asst. public relations dir. Dallas County (Tex.) United Fund, 1961-64; customer service rep. Texas Instruments, Inc., Dallas, 1964-65; publicity rep. Lone Star Gas Co., Dallas, 1965-69; public relations dir. Dallas Community Chest Trust Fund, 1970-76; exec. dir. N.Tex. div. Tex. Soc. to Prevent Blindness, Dallas, 1976—. Mem. Public Relations Soc. Am., Dallas Press Club, Dallas Indsl. Editors, Southwest Fundraising Assn., Alpha Chi Omega, Theta Sigma Phi. Republican. Methodist. Contbr. articles and news reports to med. jours., periodicals. Home: 6136 Oram Dallas TX 75214 Office: 3610 Fairmount St Dallas TX 75219

PETERS, OTTO FREDERICK, JR., univ. adminstr.; b. Galveston, Tex., Nov. 1, 1920; s. Otto Frederick and Hazel Christine (Smith) P.; B.S., Tex. A&M U., 1943; m. Frances Augusta Malitz, Dec. 1, 1945; children—Frances Peters Stone, Suzanne Peters Lawrence, Otto Frederick, III, Diane Peters Robinson, Deborah Peters Goodwill. Vice pres., gen. mgr. LaMarque (Tex.) Lumber Co., 1946-64; adminstr. dept. pathology U. Tex. Med. Br., Galveston, 1964—. Mem. La Marque Sch. Bd., 1961-67; pres. Twelve Oaks Civic Assn., 1979-80. Served with U.S. Army, 1942-46; ETO. Decorated Purple Heart. Fellow Am. Coll. Med. Group Adminstrs. (sec. 1978-80); mem. Med. Br. Credit Union (pres. bd. dirs. 1975-77), Mainland Lumberman's Assn. (past pres.), Med. Group Mgmt. Assn. (1st v.p. so. sect.), Med. Adminstrs. of Tex. (past pres.), Am. Mgmt. Assn., Methodist. Clubs: Kiwanis (past pres.), Masons, Shriners. Office: Dept Pathology U Tex Med Br Galveston TX 77550

PETERS, RONALD GREGORY, oil co. ofcl.; b. Tulsa, Sept. 28, 1944; s. Stanley Ray and Margie (Smith) P.; B.S. in Bus. Adminstrn., Tulsa U., 1966, cert. in mgmt., 1974; m. Bonnie LaVerne Swenke, June 12, 1965; children—Gregory James, Ronda JoAnn. Market analyst Sunray DX Oil Co., Terre Haute, Ind., 1966, mgr. planning and analysis LP Gas div., Tulsa, 1967, mktg. research and econs. analyst, Tulsa, 1968, mgr. sales promotion, 1969; sr. staff asso. Sun Oil Co., Phila., 1970; mktg. research coordinator Cities Service Co., Tulsa, 1971-74, mgr. internal communications, 1974—. Drive coordinator Tulsa Area United Way, 1977; former chmn. Christian edn. Ascension Lutheran Ch. Recipient Editor of Year award Am. Petroleum Inst., 1979. Mem. Am. Mktg. Assn. (past pres. Tulsa chpt., citation for outstanding service), Tinker Soc. Profl. Engrs. and Scientists (cert. of appreciation). Editor Public Affairs News, 1977-79. Home: 10836 E 26th Pl Tulsa OK 74129 Office: PO Box 300 Tulsa OK 74101

PETERS, SID RALPH, assn. exec.; b. Cambridge, Md., Jan. 31, 1927; s. Ralph Hicks and Ruth Steele (Lowe) P.; B.S., Temple U., 1954, M.B.A., 1963; m. Patricia Reider, Dec. 14, 1957; children—Scott, Drew, John. Founder, Brandwine Coll., 1965, pres., 1965-75; pres. Martingham Real Estate Devel., St. Michaels, Md., 1969-76; exec. v.p. Nat. Assn. Indsl. and Office Parks, Arlington, Va., 1976—. Bd. dirs. Ams. for Competitive Free Enterprise System, Wilmington, Del., 1965-74; v.p. Delaware chpt. ARC, 1969-74; treas. Older Youth—Young Adult Research Project, Nat. Bd. Edn. of Methodist Ch., 1960-61. Served with USAAF, 1944-45. Decorated Air medal with oak leaf cluster. Mem. Eastern Bus. Tchrs. Assn. (dir. 1960-65), Little Acad. (charter), Adminstrv. Mgmt. Soc., United Bus. Schs. Assn., Delta Pi Epsilon (chpt. pres. 1953-54), Phi Delta Kappa. Club: Univ. (pres. 1966-67) (Wilmington). Author: (with Walter Brower) Supplies, Equipment and Facilities for Business Education, 1964; (with Jay W. Miller) Meetings Change in Technical Preparation for Business, 1965. Home: 5828 Upton St McLean VA 22101 Office: 1901 N Fort Myer Dr Arlington VA 22209

PETERS, STEVEN, architect; b. Houston, Feb. 18, 1948; s. Paul Stanley and Mary Elizabeth (Morris) P.; B.A. in Fine Arts, Rice U., 1972, B.Arch., 1972, M.C.E., 1974; m. Audrey Catherine Dillon, Jan. 2, 1970; 1 son, Johnson Dillon. With Pierce Goodwin Alexander, Houston, 1974—, partner, 1979—. Mem. AIA, Tau Beta Pi. Club: Houston Country. Home: 6154 Briar Rose St Houston TX 77057 Office: PO Box 13319 Houston TX 77019

PETERS, TED HOPKINS, ins. co. exec.; b. Greenville, Tex., Dec. 30, 1943; s. Joe Becton and Teddy Rose (Hopkins) P.; B.B.A., E. Tex. State U., 1965; postgrad., U. Tex., 1965-66; m. Fonda Lynn Carter, June 3, 1966; children—Amy Teigh, Andrew Lathen. Fire rate actuary, State Bd. Ins., Austin, Tex., 1966; agency dir., Union Security Life Ins. Co., Greenville, Tex., 1967-72, exec. v.p., dir., 1972—; sec., Greenville Hosp. Dist., 1975-78. Dir. East Tex. State U. Found., 1977-78; mem. exec. bd. North Central Tex. Council Govts., 1978—; foreman Hunt County Grand Jury, 1974; dir. Salvation Army advisory bd., sec., Greenville Indsl. Devel. Fund., 1966-70, pres., 1970—; mem. Nat. Eagle Scout Assn., mem. Nat. Genealogy Soc.; deacon, Central Christian Church, 1966—, treas., 1967—, tchr. Bible Study Class, 1974—; pres. Friends of Greenville Pub. Library, 1975—. Recipient Spl. Service award, Greenville United Fund, 1971. Mem. Tex. Assn. Life Ins. Ofcls. (pres., 1970-71), Life Ins. Advertisers Assn. Democrat. Club: Lambda Chi Alpha Author: Peters Family History, 1977. Home: 5401 Vale St Greenville TX 75401 Office: Union Security Life Bldg Box 1299 Greenville TX 75401

PETERS, VIVIAN JANET, savs. and loan assn. exec.; b. Martinsburg, W.Va., May 11, 1925; d. Thomas Norman and Gladys (Zimmerman) Wall; B.B.A., Fla. Internat. U., 1976; M.S. in Human Resource Mgmt., Nova U., 1978; m. Walton C. Peters, June 16, 1946. Adminstrv. asst. to dir. clin. research Johnson & Johnson, New Brunswick, N.J., 1961-67; adminstrv. asst. to mgr. Goodbody & Co., Miami, Fla., 1968-71; personnel and pub. relations dir. Larkin Gen. Hosp., Miami, Fla., 1971-72; personnel dir. So. region J. I. Kislak Morgage Corp., Miami, Fla., 1972-73; co-owner Mgmt. Guidance Techniques, Miami, Fla., 1973-79; instr. Miami-Dade Community Coll., 1977—. Cert. accredited personnel specialist. Mem. Am. Soc. Personnel Adminstrn., Personnel Assn. Greater Miami, Nova U. Alumni Assn. (dir.), Fla. Internat. U. Alumni Assn. (dir. 1979—), Phi Theta Kappa. Club: Everglades Bicycle (Miami). Home: 17800 SW 108th Ct Miami FL 33157

PETERSEN, BENTON LAURITZ, counselor; b. Salt Lake City, Jan. 1, 1942; s. Lauritz George and Arleane (Curtis) P.; A.A., Weber State Coll., 1966, B.A., 1968; M. Liberal Studies, U. Okla., 1980; m. Sharon Donnette Higgins, Sept. 20, 1974; children—Grant Lauritz, Tashya Eileen, Nicholas Robert. Radio announcer Sta. KVOG, Ogden, Utah, 1966-68; news dir. Sta. KWHO, Salt Lake City, 1969-71, Sta. KSOP, Salt Lake City, 1970-72, 74-76, Sta. KDXU, St. George, Utah, 1972-74; counselor Salvation Army, Midland, Tex., 1976—. Served with Army N.G., 1960-68. Mem. Am. Personnel and Guidance Assn., Am. Rehab. Counseling Assn., Assn. Mormon Counselors and Psychotherapists, Midland Health and Welfare Assn. Mormon. Home: 4505 Versailles St Midland TX 79703 Office: Salvation Army 300 S Baird St Midland TX 79702

PETERSEN, PAUL FREDERICK, educator; b. Harlan, Iowa, Apr. 10, 1941; s. Elmer Andrew and Signe Regina (Back) P.; B.B.A., So. Methodist. U., 1963; M.B.A., Clemson-Furman U., 1975; postgrad U. Ga., 19—; m. Ruth Anne Pendergrass, Apr. 8, 1967; children—Kendra Denice, Maren Christine. Sales engr. Am. Air Filter Co., Louisville, Ky., Charlotte, N.C. and Greenville, S.C., 1967-72; Sales rep. R.L. Bryan Co., Greenville, 1972-73; instr. dept. indsl. mgmt. Clemson U., 1974—; cons. in field. Served with U.S. Navy, 1963-66. Mem. Organizational Behavior Consortium Acad. Mgmt., Delta Sigma Pi. Author tng. manual. Home: 108 Albermarle Dr Clemson SC 29631 Office: Department of Industrial Management Sirrine Hall Clemson University Clemson SC 29631

PETERSON, ALAN CARL, banker; b. Tulsa, Okla., Sept. 11, 1951; s. Glen and Doreyn Elizabeth (Latimer) P.; B.A. in Econs. cum laude, Brigham Young U., 1975, M.B.A., 1977; grad. Nat. Comml. Lending Sch. Mem. mgmt. devel. program Bank of Okla., Tulsa, 1977-78, comml. banking officer, 1978-80, asst. v.p., 1980—; instr. econs. Tulsa Jr. Coll. Vol. missionary Ch. of Jesus Christ of Latter-Day Saints, Peru, S. Am., 1970-72. Mem. Am. Inst. Banking, Tulsa Credit and Fin. Mgmt. Assn., Nat. Assn. Credit Mgmt., Omicron Delta Epsilon, Phi Kappa Phi, Phi Eta Sigma. Republican. Home: 540 S 83 E Ave Tulsa OK 74112 Office: PO Box 2300 Tulsa OK 74192

PETERSON, ALDEN, educator; b. Chgo., Mar. 18, 1936; s. Carl Gustav Harry and Evangeline Joan (Anderson) P.; B.S. in Econ., Purdue U., 1958, postgrad. 1959; M.B.A., U. Toledo, 1967; D.Bus. Adminstrn. (fellow), Kent State U., 1975; m. Jeanne Nelson, June 26, 1959; children—Patricia, Kristine, John. Fin. acct. M.A. Hanna Co., Cleve., 1959-63; mgr. mktg. services White Products Div., Edward Lamb Industries, Toledo, Ohio, 1963-66; prof. bus. and econ. Ashland (Ohio) Coll., 1971-76; prof. bus. Meredith Coll., Raleigh, N.C., 1976-79; prof. mgmt. Appalachian State U., Boone, N.C., 1979—; condr. seminars for gen. and profl. bus. groups. Served with Ohio N.G., 1959. NSF Chautauqua Found. grantee, 1977-79. Mem. Am. Soc. Personnel Adminstrs., Am. Inst. Decision Scis., So. Mgmt. Assn., Omicron Delta Epsilon, Beta Gamma Sigma. Lutheran. Club: Vasa. Contbr. articles to profl. jours. Home: 625 Poplar Hill Dr Extension Boone NC 28607 Office: Dept Mgmt and Mktg Coll of Bus Adminstrn Appalachian State Univ Boone NC 28608

PETERSON, ALVIN OTIS, architect, specification writer; b. Coleman, Fla., July 31, 1925; s. Henry Turner and Trudy (Zipperer) P.; student Butler U., 1942-43; grad. Chgo. Tech. Coll., 1956; m. Alice Joyce McKay, Dec. 9, 1945; 1 son, David Eric. Design estimator Williams Devel. Co., Orlando, Fla., 1960-63; with Rogers, Lovelock & Fritz, Winter Park, Fla., 1963—, head specifications dept., 1971—. Bd. dirs. College Park Towers, 1976—; mem. Orlando Fire Prevention Code Bd. Appeals and Adjustments, 1980—. Served with USNR, 1942-45, 50-52. Mem. Nat. Fire Protection Assn. (bldg. constrn. com. 1973—, life safety code/detention and correctional occupancies subcom. 1976—), ASTM (fire hazards and fire tests com. 1974—), So. Bldg. Code Congress, Internat. Congress of Bldg. Ofcls., Constrn. Specifications Inst. Baptist (deacon 1959—, chmn. deacons 1977-78, ch. clk. 1959-60, Sunday sch. tchr. 1965—, ch. tng. dir. 1971-72, asso. Sunday sch. dir. 1961-62). Home: 1643 Crestwood Dr Orlando FL 32804 Office: 145 Lincoln Ave Winter Park FL 32789

PETERSON, BERNARD LEE, JR., educator; b. Richmond, Va., Dec. 4, 1926; s. Bernard Lee and Rosetta James (Bass) P.; A.B., Va. Union U., 1951; M.A., Atlanta U., 1953. High sch. tchr., 1953-55; adminstrv. asst. Ford Found. Fund for Republic, 1955-56; instr. English, dir. drama So. U., Baton Rouge, 1956-60, Benedict Coll., Columbia, S.C., 1960-62; instr. English, drama Elizabeth City (N.C.) State U., 1962-68, asst. prof. English and drama, 1968—, coordinator lang. arts workshop program, dept. modern langs., 1977-79. Served with AUS, 1945-49. Mem. NAACP, Rosicrucian Order, Alpha Psi Omega. Democrat. Baptist. Author articles, poems, biographies, bibliographies of Black Am. Playwrights. Home: 900 Parkview biographics Dr Elizabeth City NC 27909 Office: Box 93 Elizabeth City State Univ Elizabeth City NC 27909

PETERSON, DAVID BRUCE, educator; b. Camden, N.J., May 24, 1945; s. John William and Dorothy Emma (Smith) P.; B.A. in History, Tusculum Coll., Greeneville, Tenn., 1967; M.A. in Elementary Edn., E. Tenn. State U., 1969, Ed.D. in Ednl. Adminstrn., 1974. Tchr. elementary schs. in Tenn., 1967-70; tchr. edn. courses Walters State Community Coll., Morristown, Tenn., 1973-74; tchr. edn. courses, supr. student tchrs. Lincoln Meml. U., Harrogate, Tenn., 1974—, asst. prof. edn., 1974—; prin. Bear Sta. (Tenn.) Elem. Sch., 1979-80; tchr. intern Nat. Tchrs. Corps, 1967-69. Mem. Am. Assn. Sch. Adminstrs., Tenn. Profs. Ednl. Adminstrn., So. Regional Council Ednl. Adminstrs., Mid-South Ednl. Research Assn., Nat., Tenn. edn. assns., AAUP, Phi Kappa Phi, Phi Delta Kappa. Club: Moose. Address: Route 1 Box 44D Cumberland Gap TN 37724

PETERSON, DONALD ROBERT, mag. editor; b. Sandstone, Minn., Apr. 1, 1929; s. Martin Theodore and Margaret Mildred (Dezell) P.; student U. Minn., 1947-50; B.S., Gustavus Adolphus Coll., 1952; m. 2d, Edie Tannenbaum, Aug. 31, 1975; children—Wyatt A., Winston B., Whitney C., Westley D., Webster E. Asst. underwriter Prudential Ins. Co. Am., Mpls., 1953-64; chief health underwriter North Central Life, St. Paul, 1964-66; pres. First State Bank Murdock (Minn.), 1967-73; pres. EDON, Inc., Roswell, Ga., 1974—; editor Car Collector mag., Atlanta, 1977—; v.p., dir. Classic Pub. Inc., Atlanta, 1979—. Councilman City of Murdock, 1968-72, mayor, 1972-74; del. State Republican Conv., 1970-72; treas. Swift County Rep. Com., 1970-73. Served with U.S. Navy, 1946-47. Recipient Citation for Disting. Service, Classic Car Club Am., 1965. Mem. Internat. Soc. Philos. Enquiry, Mensa, Intertel, Soc. Automotive Historians, Milestone Car Soc., Torch. Clubs: Classic Car of America; Antique Automobile; Veteran Motor Car Am.; Packard. Home: 1400 Lake Ridge Ct Roswell GA 30076 Office: 5430 Jimmy Carter Blvd #108 Norcross GA 30093

PETERSON, DOUGLAS BRIAN, air force officer; b. Omaha, Jun. 26, 1935; s. Albert Rongen and Mary Helen (Underwood) P.; advanced fighter pilot tng. USAF, 1956; grad. Nat. War Coll., 1975; B.A., U. Tampa, 1976; m. Carlotta Ann Neal, Oct. 4, 1956; children—Michael Brian, Paula Marie, Douglas Neal. Served as enlisted man U.S. Air Force, 1954-56, commd. 2d lt., 1956, advanced through grades to col., 1977; pilot 36th Fighter Day Wing, Bitburg, Germany, 1957-60, 27th Tactical Fighter Wing, Cannon AFB, N.Mex., 1960-63; instr. 4453d Combat Crew Tng. Squadron, MacDill AFB, Fla., 1963-64; chief standardization, Eglin AFB, Fla., 1964-66; asst. ops. officer 433d Tactical Fighter Squadron, Ubon Air Base, Thailand, 1966; prisoner of war, North Vietnam, 1966-73; chief ops. plans Myrtle Beach AFB, S.C., 1975-76, dep. base comdr., 1976-78; base comdr. Seymour Johnson AFB, N.C., 1978—. Mem. patron com. Goldsboro (N.C.) City Schs.; bd. dirs. Goldsboro Salvation Army, Tuscarora Council Boy Scouts Am., Wayne County United Way. Decorated Silver Star (2), Legion of Merit, D.F.C., Bronze Star (3), Meritorious Service medal, Air medal (6), Purple Heart (2), Air Force Commendation medal. Mem. Air Force Assn., Red River Valley Pilots Assn., Vietnam-POW Assn., Goldsboro C. of C. (dir.), Am. Balloon Assn., Order of Daedalians, Mil. Order World Wars. Roman Catholic. Home: 304 Vandenberg Goldsboro NC 27530 Office: 4CSG/CC Seymour Johnson AFB NC 27531

PETERSON, EDGAR FULMER, educator; b. Jemison, Ala., Dec. 10, 1934; s. Julius Albert and Etta (Fulmer) P.; B.S., Auburn U., 1956, M.Ed., 1960; Ed.D., U. Ala., 1967; m. Ora Lee Bowen, June 3, 1961. Sci. tchr., Montgomery, Ala., 1959-62, Marietta, Ga., 1962-63; sch. prin., West Point, Ga., 1963-65; supr. student teaching U. Ala., Tuscaloosa, 1965-67; asso. prof. edn. Ga. Southwestern Coll., Americus, 1967—. Served with U.S. Army, 1957-59. NDEA sci. scholar, 1962, U. Ala. counseling scholar, 1961. Mem. NEA, Am. Assn. Higher Edn., Assn. Supervision and Curriculum, Ga. Assn. Educators (citations 1968-69, 76-77), Kappa Delta Pi, Phi Delta Kappa. Democrat. Baptist. Author: The Development of the County Superintendency in Alabama, 1967; The College Student's Perception of an Educated Person, 1972. Home: Route 4 Box 177 Americus GA 31709 Office: Ga Southwestern Coll Americus GA 31709

PETERSON, ELIZABETH BOWMAN, speech pathologist; b. Dallas, Dec. 22, 1937; d. Leonard Clifford and Aleene (Perry) Bowman; B.A. magna cum laude, So. Meth. U., 1961; M.A., U. So. Calif., 1964; m. Harold W. Peterson, June 14, 1969; 2 adopted children. With Houston Speech and Hearing Inst., 1963-68; with Houston Assos. in Psychiatry and Neurology, 1968-70; speech pathologist, resource tchr. Houston Ind. Sch. Dist., 1970—. Treas.,

Houston Council on Adoptable Children, 1979, pres., 1980; volunteer work in teaching English as second lang. Citizens for Animal Protection, 1976—. Named 1978 Tchr. of Yr., Houston Assn. for Children with Learning Disabilities. Mem. Am. Speech and Hearing Assn., Tex. Speech and Hearing Assn., Houston Assn. Communication Disorders, Houston Assn. of Children with Learning Disabilities. Episcopalian. Club: Civic Action Group. Office: 4535 Pine St Bellaire TX 77401

PETERSON, FONDA GILREATH, hosp. adminstr., nurse; b. Searcy, Ark., Feb. 14, 1933; d. Ruben Hillary and Ruby Mae (Holcomb) Gilreath; B.S.N., U. Tulsa, 1973; M.S., Tex. Woman's U., 1977; children—Manya Diane, John Ross. Nurse, St. Francis Hosp., Tulsa, 1973-75, 76-78; mem. faculty Oral Roberts U. Sch. Nursing, 1976-78; dir. ambulatory services Baptist Med. Center, Oklahoma City, 1978—; CPR instr. ARC; cons. in field. Mem. Am. Nurses Assn., Nat. League Nursing, Am. Assn. Critical Care Nurses, Emergency Dept. Nurses Assn., Gamma Epsilon Alpha. Home: 3116 NW Expy Apt 250 Oklahoma City OK 73112 Office: 3300 NW Expy Oklahoma City OK 73112

PETERSON, GARY WINSTON, educator; b. St. Paul, Sept. 23, 1940; s. Lawrence Burdette and Mildred Christine (Anderson) P.; B.A., Humboldt State Coll., 1963; M.A., Duke U., 1967, Ph.D., 1970; m. Carolyn Ann Boswell, July 18, 1976; children—Erik Edlund, Shawn Loren, Alan Gary. Peace Corps vol., Nigeria, 1963-65; counselor U. N.C., Charlotte, 1966-68; sr. counselor Duke U., Durham, N.C., 1970-72; research asso., asso. prof. Learning Systems Inst., human services and studies Coll. Edn. Fla. State U., Tallahassee, 1972—. Mem. Am. Edn. Research Assn., Am. Psychol. Assn., Phi Delta Kappa. Democrat. Presbyterian. Home: 305 Anton Dr Tallahassee FL 32303 Office: IA Tully Bldg Fla State U Tallahassee FL 32306

PETERSON, JOHN EDGAR, JR., ret. textile co. exec.; b. Radford, Va., Mar. 26, 1916; s. John Edgar and Mary Elizabeth (Dolan) P.; B.S. in Bus. Adminstrn., Va. Polytech. Inst., 1936; m. Mary Jane Crowell, May 8, 1943; children—John Edgar III, Mary Stuart Peterson Henegar, William Early. Jr. auditor Arthur Andersen & Co., N.Y.C. and Atlanta, 1937-39, sr. auditor, 1939-44; sec.-treas. Magnet Cove Barium Corp., Jamestown, Tenn. and Houston, 1944-46; asst. to controller Burlington Industries, Inc., Greensboro, N.C., 1946-47, sec.-treas. Burlington Mills Internat. Corp., 1947-48, co-div. mgr., 1948-49, div. controller, 1949-56, area controller, 1956-58, asst. corp. controller, 1958-70, asst. corp. v.p., from 1970, now ret.; dir. Custom Industries, Inc., Everetts' Lake Corp. Active ARC, United Fund, Greensboro, Boy Scouts Am., P.T.A.; mem. adv. com. Coll. Bus. Va. Polytech. Inst., 1969—. C.P.A., N.Y., Ga., Tenn., N.C.; certified internal auditor. Mem. Am. Inst. C.P.A.'s, N.C. Soc. C.P.A.'s., Inst. Internal Auditors. Presbyterian. Clubs: Starmount Forest Country, Three Lakes (dir.), Brush Creek Hunting (dir.), Masons. Home: 1001 Kemp Rd W Greensboro NC 27410 Office: 3330 W Friendly Ave Greensboro NC 27420

PETERSON, LARS PETER, psychologist; b. Blekinge, Sweden, Oct. 17, 1925; came to U.S., 1936, naturalized, 1945; s. T. Arthur and Ester (Jenson) P.; B.A., U. Wyo., 1950, M.A., 1951; Ed.D., U. Nebr., 1959; postgrad. U. Minn., 1964-65; m. Ardice L. Schwarting, Dec. 31, 1949; children—Kevin T., Barbara A., Jan M., Julie L. Instr., U. Wyo., 1952-53; asst. prof. Minn. State U., 1953-57; instr. U. Nebr., 1957-59; asst. prof. Cornell U., 1959-61; prof. St. Cloud U., 1961-66; asso. prof. St. John's U., 1966-68; asst. clin. prof. U. Minn., 1967-68; chief psychology service, coordinator research and devel., coordinator med. edn. VA Med. Center, Tuscaloosa, Ala., 1968—; adj. prof. U. Ala., 1968—; cons. various state and fed. hosps. and nursing homes; chmn. task force on mental health Ala. Health Planning. Served with USMCR, 1944-46. Mem. Am. Psychol. Assn., Southeastern Psychol. Assn., Ala. Psychol. Assn., Assn. Chiefs of Psychology, Ala. Acad. Neurology and Psychiatry, Sigma Xi, Psi Chi, Phi Delta Kappa, Chi Gamma Iota. Republican. Lutheran. Contbr. articles to profl. jours. Home: 12 Woodland Park Tuscaloosa AL 35404 Office: VA Med Center Tuscaloosa AL 35404

PETERSON, NEWTON CURTIS, JR., state senator, landscape architect; b. Lakeland, Fla., Aug. 23, 1922; s. Newton Curtis and Caroline Ellen (Smith) P.; student George Washington U., 1941-42, Fla. So. Coll., 1950-53; m. Ethel Lucille Schultz, Apr. 8, 1944; children—Newton Curtis III, Peter Karl. Landscape architect Peterson's Nurseries, Lakeland, Fla., 1953—, partner, 1958—; mem. Fla. Senate, 1972—; commr. Edn. Commn. States, 1974—; mem. Agrl. Advisory Council, Fla. Dept. Agr., 1961—, chmn., 1970-72; mem. plant industry tech. com. Div. Plant Industry Fla., 1961—; nursery industry rep. Fla. Agrl. Tax Council, 1962—, pres., 1967-70; mem. adv. com. Polk County Vocat. Tech. Sch., 1972—; chmn. Fla. Farm City Week, 1975. Mem. Polk County Dem. Exec. Com., chmn. campaign com.; del. Dem. Charter Conf., 1974; mem. Fla. Dem. Platform Com., 1977—; bd. dirs. Polk County Assn. Retarded Children, 1963—; bd. dirs. Agribus. Inst. Fla., 1971—, pres., 1977-79; bd. dirs. Fla. Sheriff's Girls Villa, 1972—; scoutmaster Boy Scouts Am., 1964-66; pres. Lakeland Conv. Bur., 1965-66. Served with USCGR, 1942-45. Named Fla. Nurseryman of Year, recipient Odenkirk Trophy, 1961; Distinguished Service award Fla. Agrl. Advisory Council, 1961-72; Senator of Year award Fla. Assn. Retarded Children, 1974; Outstanding Service award Polk County Assn. Retarded Children, 1974; Fla. Green Belt award Fla. Forest Festival, 1974; Merit awards Southland F. and A.M., 1975, Gamma Sigma Delta, 1976; Farm. Bur. Legislator of Year award, 1976; City of Lakeland Meritorious Civic Service award, 1976; Fla. Citrus Mut. Outstanding Service to Citrus and Agr. award, 1977; Allen Morris award as most effective in Senate com., 1977; Legis. Service award Fla. Assn. Community Colls., 1978 Outstanding Service to Public Edn. award Fla. Sch. Bds. Assn., 1978; Service award Agribus. Inst. Fla., 1978, White Hat award, 1979; Service award Fla. Poultry Fedn., Inc., 1978; Appreciation award Dairy Farmers, Inc., 1979; cert. of appreciation SHARE, 1979; Higher Edn. award Ft. Myers Campus, U. South Fla., 1979; award Fla. Coalition for Edn. Exceptional Students, 1979. Mem. Am. Assn. Nurseryman, So. Nurseryman's Assn., Fla. Nurseryman and Growers Assn. (past pres.), Sigma Nu. Democrat. Baptist. Home: 1504 Warren Ave Lakeland FL 33803 Office: 225 New Auburndale Rd Lakeland FL 33801 also 2034 S Combee Rd PO Box 180 Eaton Park FL 33840

PETERSON, PAMELA ANN, ins. co. exec.; b. Port Arthur, Tex., Sept. 21, 1946; d. Wesley M. and Dorothy (Huber) Dugan; B.S. in Elem. Edn., Lamar U., 1969; m. Philip C. Peterson, June 2, 1978. Elem. tchr. Port Arthur Sch. Dist., 1969-72, Houston Sch. Dist., 1972-73; travel agt. Kings World Travel, Hempstead, N.Y., 1973-74; asst. underwriter, mktg. rep., instr. INA, Buffalo, 1974-76, N.Y.C., 1976-77, Phila., 1977-78, tng. dir., Atlanta, 1978—. Mem. Am. Mgmt. Assn., Am. Soc. Tng. and Devel., Alpha Delta Pi. Office: 3340 Peachtree Rd NE Atlanta GA 30326

PETERSON, ROBERT EDWARD LEE, architect; b. Franklin, Va., Apr. 25, 1917; s. John Eure and Maggie Mae (Worrell) P.; student William and Mary Extension Coll., 1940-43, Internat. Corr. Schs., 1943; m. Louise Cherry Boyette, Jan. 1, 1942; 1 son, Robert Edward Lee. With U.S. Navy Bur. of Yards & Docks, Norfolk, Va., 1939-44; architect draftsman, designer C. C. Benton & Sons, Wilson, N.C., 1946-48; designer McMinn & Norfleet, Architects, Greensboro, N.C., 1948-55; architect, owner Robert E. L. Peterson, Architect, Greensboro, 1956—. Mem. bd. adjustments Greensboro, 1969-78, chmn., 1976-78. Served with USAAF, 1944-46. Mem. AIA. Democrat. Methodist. Clubs: Starmount Country, Kiwanis (dir. 1978-80), Jr. C. of C. Oldtimers (pres. 1977—), Masons (32 deg., Shriners). Home: 307 W Avondale St Greensboro NC 27403 Office: 414 Church St Greensboro NC 27402

PETKOFF, GEORGE SAMUEL, lawyer; b. Helena, Ark., Dec. 5, 1936; s. George and Florine Catherine (Saia) P.; B.S., Christians Bro. Coll., 1958; LL.B., Memphis State U., 1964; m. Ramona Jean Posey, Aug. 23, 1958; children—George Samuel, Douglas Andrew, Richard Joseph. Admitted to Tenn. bar, 1965; asso. firm Nelson, Norvell, Wilson, McRae, Ivy & Sevier, Memphis, 1965-70, partner, 1971-74; partner Udelshon, Turnage, Blaylock, Golden & Petkoff, Memphis, 1975-76; individual practice law, Memphis, 1976—; staff def. atty. City of Memphis, 1975—. Pres. sch. bd. Our Lady of Sorrows Parochial Sch., Memphis, 1975, pres. diocesan sch. bd., 1974. Mem. Am., Tenn., Shelby County, Memphis bar assns., Tenn. Def. Lawyers Assn., Lawyer Pilots Bar Assn., Fedn. Ins. Counsel. Clubs: K.C., Holly Hills Country. Contbr. articles to profl. jours. Home: 4004 Ridgedale St Memphis TN 38127 Office: 100 N Main St Suite 2429 Memphis TN 38103

PETRASH, LAWRENCE DEAN, ins. co. exec.; b. Ft. Monmouth, N.J., June 22, 1948; s. Edward B. and Mary R. (Mize) P.; A.A., Tyler Jr. Coll., 1968; B.B.A., Tex. A. and M. U., 1970, M.Ed., 1972; m. Paula Ann Benson, Aug. 10, 1968; children—Laura Diane, Jason William. Prodn. supr. Precision Mfg. Co., Plano, Tex., 1974-75; sales rep. Emloyers Casualty Co., Dallas, 1975-78, dist. sales mgr., San Antonio, 1978—. Served with U.S. Army, 1971-74, USAR, 1974—. Decorated Army Commendation medal, Army Res. medal, Nat. Def. Service medal. Mem. Sigma Iota Epsilon. Republican. Methodist. Club: Rotary. Home: 15703 Heimer Rd San Antonio TX 78232 Office: 9600 Data Point St San Antonio TX 78229

PETRONE, WILLIAM FRANCIS, microbiologist; b. Bklyn., Sept. 12, 1949; s. Arthur Carmen and Helen (Kenny) P.; B.A., U. Conn., 1972; M.S., U. Mass., 1974; Ph.D., U. R.I., 1978; m. Kathleen Anne Baron, Aug. 25, 1979. Research asso. Coll. Medicine, U. South Ala., Mobile, 1978—. Mem. Am. Soc. Microbiology, AAAS, N.Y. Acad. Scis., Sigma Xi. Roman Catholic. Contbr. articles on inflamation and white blood cell function to sci. jours. Office: Sch Medicine U South Ala Mobile AL 36688

PETROVSKA, MARIJA, French scholar, educator; b. Zagreb, Yugoslavia; d. Frantisek and Marija P.; B.A. in Drama, Conservatory Dramatic Arts, Prague, Czechoslovakia; diploma Institut Hautes Etudes d'Interpretariat, Milan, Italy, 1954; M.A. in French, U. Tenn., 1965; Ph.D. in French, U. Ky., 1972. Profl. actress, Czechoslovakia, 1946-50; free-lance translator, interpreter, journalist, Italy, 1950-63; instr. French and Italian, U. Tenn., Knoxville, 1963-72, asst. prof. French and Czech, 1972-76, asso. prof. French and comparative lit., 1976—. Fellow, Seminar in American Studies, Salzburg, Austria, 1960; Haggin grad. fellow, U. Ky., 1969-70. Mem. MLA, Czechoslovak Soc. Arts and Scis. in Am., AAUP. Author: Victor Hugo, l'écrivain engagé en Bohême, 1977; Prague Diptych, a novel, 1980; contbr. articles to scholarly jours. France and U.S. Home: 3617 Southwood Dr Knoxville TN 37920 Office: Univ Tennessee Knoxville TN 37916

PETRY, JOHN WRIGHT, lawyer; b. Laredo, Tex., Dec. 25, 1945; s. Herbert Charles and Josephine (White) P.; B.S., Trinity U., 1967; J.D., St. Mary's U., 1970; m. Jill Little, Aug. 10, 1968; children—Jana Lea, Jodi LaVerne. Admitted to Tex. bar, 1970; partner firm Petry & Petry, P.C., Carrizo Springs, Tex., 1970—; dir. P-K Investments, Inc., Carrizo Springs, Tri Motor Sales, Inc., Carrizo Springs, Union State Bank Carrizo Springs; mayor pro-tem City of Carrizo Springs, 1974-78. Served to capt., AUS Res. Mem. Dimmit County C. of C. (dir. 1971-78), Delta Theta Phi. Republican. Episcopalian. Lion (cabinet sec. dist. 1975—). Home: 200 S 20th St Carrizo Springs TX 78834 Office: PO Drawer 218 Carrizo Springs TX 78834

PETRY, THOMAS MERTON, civil engr.; b. San Pedro, Calif., Sept. 25, 1944; s. Oscar Henry and Evelyn Winifred (Grice) P.; B.S.C.E., U. Mo., Rolla, 1967; M.S.C.E., U. Mo., Columbia, 1968; Ph.D., Okla. State U., 1974; m. Susan Marie Nolte, Aug. 6, 1967; children—Karol Lynne, Kimberly Dawn, Benjamin Thomas. Engr., Parcher-Heiliger Haliburnton Found. Cons., Stillwater, Okla., 1972-74; asst. prof. geotechnical engring. U. Tex., Arlington, 1974—; cons. geotechnical engr., 1977—. Served with U.S. Army, 1969-71. Registered profl. engr., Tex. Mem. ASCE, Am. Soc. Engring. Edn., Transp. Research Bd., Tex. Soc. Profl. Engrs., Nat. Soc. Profl. Engrs., Sigma Xi, Tau Beta Pi, Chi Epsilon. Methodist. Office: PO Box 19309 Arlington TX 76019

PETTERSEN, ROBERT WINTON, petroleum exploration co. exec.; b. St. Paul, Jan. 9, 1921; s. John William and Winnefred Florence (Jones) P.; A.A., U. Minn. at Mpls., 1941, B.S. in Elec. Engring., 1948; m. Sybil Ethel Brown, May 10, 1945; children—Alan John, Barbara Lee, Gail Ann (Mrs. John Schoonover). Exploration geophysicist, also party chief, supr. throughout Western U.S., Geophys. Service, Inc., hdqrs. Dallas, 1948-56, mgr., supr., Sicily, 1956-58, mgr. North Africa, 1958-68; chief geophysicist Champlin Petroleum Co., Fort Worth, 1968-74, fgn. exploration mgr., 1974-75, asst. to exploration v.p., 1976-77, v.p. exploration Peru, Philippines, Indonesia, 1974-75; exec. v.p. Seiscom Delta, Inc., Houston, 1977-79; v.p. NORPAC Exploration, Inc., Denver, Houston, 1980—. Served with USAF, 1942-45. Decorated Air medal. Mem. Soc. Exploration Geophysicists, Houston Geophys. Soc., Res. Officers Assn., 2nd Air Div. 8th Air Force Assn., Fort Worth Geophys. Soc. (pres. 1974-75). Episcopalian. Mason. Home: 3638 Robinson Rd Missouri City TX 77459 Office: 7800 Bissonet St Suite 220 Houston TX 77074

PETTIGREW, EUNICE DAVIS, guidance counselor; b. Brinkley, Ark., Jan. 19, 1916; d. William Penn and Virginia (Manson) Davis; grad. Lydia Adams Sch. Beauty Cluture, Chgo., 1941; B.A. in Sociology, U. Ark., Pine Bluff, 1970, M.S. in Vocat. Edn., 1976; m. Alonzo Hardin Pettigrew, Feb. 8, 1937; children—Clarice, Carol, Alonzo Hardin, Paula, George, Robert. Rural sch. tchr., 1936-39; insp. Ark. Bd. Cosmetology, 1957-65; instr. cosmetology U. Ark., Pine Bluff, 1965-76, counselor, 1976—. Mem. Am. Personnel and Guidance Assn., Nat. Vocat. Guidance Assn., Ark. Beauticians Assn., Alpha Kappa Mu. Methodist. Home: 1908 Collegiate Dr Pine Bluff AR 71601 Office: Univ Ark Pine Bluff AR 71601

PETTIT, JOSEPH MORRIS, coll. adminstr.; b. Ellijay, Ga., Sept. 21, 1949; s. Morris and Laura (Waddell) P.; A.A., Freed-Hardeman Coll., Henderson, Tenn., 1969, cert. in Bible, 1970, B.A., 1977; m. Patsy Jane Wimpey, June 8, 1969; children—Mary Angela, Anna Lyn, Johnna Charicia, Christina Jo. Ordained minister Ch. of Christ, 1966, minister Junction City, Kans., 1970-71, Ellijay, Ga., 1971-73, Calhoun, Ga., 1973-76, Juno Ch. of Christ, Lexington, Tenn., 1976-78; asst. in devel. Freed-Hardeman Coll., 1976-78; dir. mktg. Am. Reading Acad., Jackson, Tenn., 1978-79; v.p. Edutrav Inc., Jackson, 1978-79; instr. Bible and preaching, dir. admissions Magnolia Bible Coll., Kosciusko, Miss., 1979—; dir. vacation Bible schs. Active Camaign for Christ in Albany, Rome and Blue Ridge, Ga., 1971-73; Bible tchr. N. Ga. Bible Camp, Inc., 1971-73, camp dir., 1973-76; instr. Bible N. Ga. Sch. Bible and Tchr. Tng., 1972-73. Regional editor The Ga. Good News, 1974-75. Home: 203 S Natchez Kosciusko MS 39090 Office: Magnolia Bible Coll PO Box 655 Kosciusko MS 39090

PETTY, ARTHUR VERNON, JR., ceramic engr.; b. Atlanta, May 2, 1947; s. Arthur Vernon and Anne Cochran (Bennett) P.; B.S., Ga. Inst. Tech., 1970, M.S., 1972; m. Susan Elizabeth McMullan, July 18, 1975; children—Roddy, Dina, Heather. Tchr., Ga. Inst. Tech., Atlanta, 1971-72; ceramic engr. Fed. Bur. Mines, Tuscaloosa, Ala., 1972—; cons. Recipient sci. award Bausch & Lomb, 1965; Glass Container Corp. grad research fellow, 1970-71. Mem. Am. Ceramic Soc., Nat. Inst. Ceramic Engrs., Keramos. Methodist. Research on high temperature ceramic materials based on zirconia, chem. strengthening of glass, devel. glass ceramic materials form wastes, devel. synthetic hwy. aggregates. Home: 4232 Hillsboro Dr Tuscaloosa AL 35401 Office: PO Box L University AL 35486

PETTY, ETALCAH CROCKETT, ret. county extension agt.; b. Eufaula, Ala., Mar. 24, 1915; d. Elliott A. and Pearl T. (Cunningham) Crockett; B.S., Prairie View A. and M. U., 1935; M.Ed., Colo. State U., Ft. Collins, 1953; m. Grayson Richard Petty, Jan. 3, 1946. Tchr. homemaking St. Paul High Sch., Greenville, Tex., 1935-42; county extension agt. Gregg County, Tex., 1942-76. Mem. E. Tex. Council on Alcohol and Drug Abuse, 1969—; sec. adv. com. E. Tex. Council Govts., 1974—. Recipient distinguished service award Tex. Agrl. Extension Service, 1962, award of superior service, 1974; community service award Friends of Gregg County, 1975. Mem. Nat., Tex. (pres. 1975-76) assns. extension home economists, Am. Home Econs. Assn., AAUW, Epsilon Sigma Phi, Phi Kappa Phi, Alpha Kappa Alpha. Baptist. Home: 2203 S Green St Longview TX 75601

PETTY, HAROLD MARTIN, motel chain exec.; b. Scottsboro, Ala., Dec. 25, 1940; s. Franklin G. and Pauline G. P.; m. Brenda Childress, Aug. 25, 1957; children—Karen Darlene, Harold Martin. Gen. mgr. Exec. Mgmt., Inc., Greensboro, N.C., 1974-76; regional mgr. John Yancey Mgmt. Inc., Newport News, Va., 1976-77, dir. adminstrn., 1978-79; dir. ops. Imperial 400 Nat. Inc., Arlington, Va., 1979—. Mem. Ch. of Christ. Home: 1404 Brethour Ct Apt 13 Sterling VA 22170 Office: Imperial 400 Nat Inc 1830 N Nash St Arlington VA 22209

PETTY, OLIVE SCOTT, geophys. engr.; b. Olive, Tex., Apr. 15, 1895; s. Van Alvin and Mary Cordelia (Dabney) P.; student Ga. Inst. Tech., 1913-14; B.S. in Civil Engring., U. Tex., 1917, C.E., 1920; m. Mary Edwina Harris, July 19, 1921; 1 son, Scott. Adj. prof. civil engring. U. Tex., 1920-23; structural engr. R.O. Jameson, Dallas, 1923-25; pres. Petty Geophys. Engring. Co., Petty Labs., Inc., San Antonio, 1925-52, chmn. bd., 1952-73; chmn. bd. Petty Geophys. Engring. Co. de Mex. S.A. de C.V., 1950-73; partner Petty Ranch Co., 1968—; ranching, minerals, timber and investment interests, 1937—. Patron, San Antonio Symphony Soc., McKay Art Inst.; sustaining mem. Gov. Clements Com.; sr. adv. council Young Ams. for Freedom; mem. exec. com., founding mem. chancellor's council U. Tex. System Austin, also founding mem., hon. life mem. Geology Found. Adv. Council. Served as lt. U.S. Army, 1917-18; AEF in France. Named hon. adm. Tex. Navy; recipient Disting. Grad. award U. Tex. Coll. Engring., Austin, 1962; registered profl. engr., Tex. Fellow Internat. Oceanographic Found (life), Tex. Acad. Sci. (hon. life); mem. San Antonio Livestock Assn. (life), Texas-Mid-Continent Oil and Gas Assn. (dir.), ASCE (hon. life; life Tex. sect.), AIME (Legion of Honor), Am. Assn. Petroleum Geologists, AAAS, Am. Petroleum Inst., Nat. Soc. Profl. Engrs. (life), Am. Geophys. Union, Houston Geophys. Soc., South Tex. Geol. Soc., Soc. Petroleum Engrs. (Legion of Honor), Am. Assn. Petroleum Geologists Trustee Assn., Soc. Am. Mil. Engrs., Soc. Expl. Geophysicists (hon. life), Newcomen Soc. N.Am., Soc. 1st Inf. Div. (founding), Tex. Heritage Found., Nat. Rifle Assn. (life), Tex. Ind. Producers and Royalty Owners Assn., La. Ind. Producers and Royalty Owners Assn., Tex. Soc. Profl. Engrs., Ind. Petroleum Assn. Am., Internat. Oil Scouts Assn., English Speaking Union, Ex-Students' Assn. U. Tex. (life), Dads' Assn. U. Tex. (life), Tex. Sheep and Goat Raisers Assn., Tex. Hort. Soc., Am. Forestry Assn., Tex. Forestry Assn., Tex. and Southwestern Cattle Raisers Assn., Nat. Pecan Growers Assn., Bandera Farm Bur., Tex. Pecan Growers Assn., Nat. Wildlife Fedn., Am. Mus. Natural History, San Antonio Mus. Assn., Nature Conservancy (life), Internat. Primate Protection League, Exotic Wildlife Assn., MZURI Safari Found., Wilderness Soc., Nat. Audubon Soc., Nat. Geog. Soc., San Antonio Zool. Gardens and Acuarium, Nat. Trust for Historic Preservation, Nat. Hist. Soc., Tex. Hist. Assn., Tex. Hist. Found., Smithsonian Assos. (charter), Am. Security Council (nat. adv. bd.), Inst. Am. Relations, Am. Cause, Citizens Com. for Right To Keep and Bear Arms., Tex. Energy Polit. Action Com., Nat. Tax Limitation Com., Explorers Club, Mil. Order World Wars (perpetual), VFW (life, nat. membership com. 1980), Am. Legion (life), Tex. Rifle Assn. (founding, life), Sewanee U. Assos., Trinity U. Assos., President's Assn. U. Tex. at Austin, President's Assn. U. Tex. at San Antonio, U. South Vice Chancellor's and Trustees Soc., Chi Epsilon (hon. life), Theta Xi, Tau Beta Pi. Baptist. Clubs: U.S. Senatorial; San Antonio Country, Argyle, St. Anthony (San Antonio). Author: Seismic Reflections, Recollections of the Formative Years of the Petroleum Exploration Industry, 1976; patentee geophys. methods, instruments, equipment. Home: 101 E Kings Hwy San Antonio TX 78212 Office: 711 Navarro St San Antonio TX 78205

PETTYJOHN, CHARLES STEPHENS, realtor; b. Denver, Aug. 30, 1910; s. Don C. and Myrtle (Stephens) P.; student Wis. Sch. Mines, 1929-33; B.S. Mich. Tech. Inst., 1934, postgrad., 1935; Petroleum Engr., Purdue U., 1937; postgrad. U. Chgo., 1940; m. Margaret A. Nekervis, July 26, 1937; children—Charles S. and Robert B. (twins). Research, inspection engr. Socony Vacuum Oil Co., East Chicago, Ill., 1936-47; engr., gen. mgmt. Standard Vacuum Petroleum, Mij, Palembang, Sumatera, 1947-58; sales finance Driggers Realty, Mount Dora, Fla., 1959-67; chmn. bd. Asso. Realty Services, Inc., Mount Dora, Tavares, and Leesburg, Fla., 1967—, Asso. Investmen Services Inc., 1978—. Commr. Planning and Zoning, Lake County, Fla., 1969—, chmn., 1971-78; bd. dirs. Central Fla. Planning and Zoning Assn., 1978—, Open Door Rehab. Center, 1977—; trustee Waterman Meml. Hosp., Eustis, Fla.; mem. E. Central Fla. Regional Land Use Planning Commn., 1977-78. Named Realtor of Year Lake County, 1970, 72. Certified real estate broker. Mem. Nat. Assn. Real Estate Bds., Nat. Inst. Real Estate Brokers, Lake County, Leesburg bds realtors, Mt. Dora (pres. 1970), Eustis (dir. 1974-75) chambers commerce. Kiwanian (past pres., lt. gov. 1974-75). Home: 8 Fairview Point Tavares FL 32778 Office: 237 Eustis-Mt Dora Hwy 19A Mount Dora FL 32757

PEUGH, TEAUPHUS, JR., retail co. exec.; b. Houston, May 19, 1939; s. Teauphus and Inez (Penrice) P.; B.S., Tex. So. U., 1963; m. Ruth Millard, July 24, 1965; children—Teauphus III, Talibah, Tobiah. Programmer, analyst Chrysler Corp., New Orleans, 1965-66, Lockheed Co., Houston, 1966-69, Am. Gen. Ins. Co., Houston, 1969-73, Superior Oil Co., Houston, 1973-74; mgr.

programming/analysis Foley's, Houston, 1974—. Served with USAF, 1963-65. Congregationalist. Home: 10309 Teneha St Houston TX 77033 Office: 1110 Main St Houston TX 77001

PEW, JOHN GLENN, ret. oil co. exec.; b. Beaumont, Tex., May 14, 1902; s. James Edgar and Martha (Layng) P.; student So. Methodist U., 1921, Northeastern U., Mass. Inst. Tech., 1923-24, Cornell U., 1922; m. Roberta Haughton, June 27, 1929; children—John Glenn, Jr., Richard Haughton. With Sun Oil Co., 1924-67, v.p. charge prodn., 1946-60, sr. v.p., 1960-67, dir., 1944-68; dir. Glenmede Trust Co. Bd. dirs. Boys Clubs Am., Southwestern Med. Found., Wadley Insts. Molecular Medicine, Dallas Hist. Soc., Internat. Oil and Gas Ednl. Center, Southwestern Legal Found.; dir. sci. and tech. So. Methodist U. Mem. Am. Petroleum Inst. (hon., v.p. div. prodn. 1953-54; certificate of appreciation 1954), Mid-Continent Oil and Gas Assn. (dir. 1936; distinguished service award Tex. 1942), Am. Inst. Mining, Metall. and Petroleum Engrs., Psi Upsilon. Republican. Presbyterian. Home: 3525 Turtle Creek Blvd Dallas TX 75219

PFAFF, GEORGE CHARLES, JR., aerospace co. exec.; b. Balt., Aug. 15, 1918; s. George Charles and Cecelia (Schmitt) P.; B.S., Mass. Inst. Tech., 1939; m. Mary Martha Beckwith, June 14, 1947; children—Carol Ann, Nancy Louise. Structural design engr. Glenn L. Martin Co., Balt., 1939-57; mgr. structures Martin-Orlando (Fla.), 1957-64; structures project engr. Martin-Marietta Corp., Denver, 1964-73, mgr. quality engring., New Orleans, 1973-79, mgr. interdivisional mx work, 1979—. Mem. Planning and Zoning Commn., Winter Park, Fla., 1960-64. Registered profl. engr., Colo. Fellow Am. Inst. Aero. and Astronautics (asso.); mem. Aerospace Industries Assn. (chmn. aerospace research and testing com. 1962-63), Nat. Acad. Sci. (material adv. bd. 1959-60), Sigma Nu. Club: MIT Alumni (chpt. pres. 1963-64) (Orlando, Fla.). Patentee in field. Home: 323 Landon Dr Slidell LA 70458 Office: PO Box 29304 New Orleans LA 70189

PFANNSTIEL, CURTIS ALTON, restaurant exec.; b. New Braunfels, Tex., Oct. 26, 1946; s. Benno Rudolph and Clara (Twiefel) P.; student U. Tex., summer 1967, Tex. Luth. Coll., 1965-69; B.A. in Speech, Drama and English; tchrs. cert. St. Mary's U., 1970. Tchr. drama, speech and English, Dept. Edn. V.I., St. Thomas, 1969-70; with Tower of the Ams., Magic Time Machines divs. Frontier Enterprises, 1970—, unit mgr., Austin, Tex., 1975-76, corp. dir. tng. and restaurant design, San Antonio, 1976—. Guest artist and dir. Community Actors Theatre, New Braunfels and Seguin, Tex., 1969—. Recipient Outstanding Young Am. award U.S. Jaycees, 1976. Mem. San Antonio Restaurant Assn. (dir.), Am. Soc. Tng. and Devel., Am. Mgmt. Assn., Internat. TV Assn., Nat. Restaurant Assn., Alpha Psi Omega (v.p. 1967-69), Omega Tau (pres. 1966-68). Lutheran. Home: 3819 Harry Wurzbach A-12 San Antonio TX 78209 Office: 8520 Crownhill Blvd San Antonio TX 78209

PFEIFFER, RICHARD JAMES, advt. agy. exec.; b. Highland Park, Mich., Oct. 1, 1924; s. Joseph and Mary Louise (Them) P.; student CCNY, 1943, Carnegie Inst. Tech., 1944; A.B. magna cum laude, U. Detroit, 1948; m. Betty L. Purcell, Sept. 11, 1948; children—Richard James, Kathryn M., Joseph F. Copy supr. Campbell-Ewald Advt. Agy., Detroit, 1958-70; v.p., asso. creative dir. Ketchum, MacLeod & Grove Ad Agy., Pitts., 1971-75; creative supr. McDonald & Little Advt. Agy., Atlanta, 1976; pvt. practice advt. counseling, Atlanta, 1977; creative dir. Case-Hoyt/Atlanta Mktg. Services, 1978—. Served with U.S. Army, 1943-45. Decorated Purple Heart; recipient Andy award Advt. Club N.Y., 1972; Am. Bus. Press Assn. award, 1965; Bravo award Art Dirs. Club Detroit, 1964-68; Deutsch and Shea award Grad. Sch. Rutgers U., 1972. Republican. Roman Catholic. Home: 8005 Monticello Dr Dunwoody GA 30338 Office: Case-Hoyt/Atlanta Mktg Services 53 Mangum St SW Atlanta GA 30313

PFEIL, WALTER JAMES MALONEY, ins. co. exec.; b. Buffalo, Sept. 20, 1945; s. Walter Fred and Mildred Agness (Maloney) P.; academia OAS, Quito, Ecuador, 1962; A.B. magna cum laude (George Catlin fellow), Union Coll., Schenectady, 1968; M.A. (NDEA fellow), U. Fla., 1969; m. Marie Horne Marshall, Mar. 26, 1980; children—Jennifer Jane, Jason Andrew; 1 stepdau., Jennifer Christine Marshall. Mgr., Walter F. Pfeil Wholesale Lumber Co., Williamsville, N.Y., 1964-65; chief liaison officer minority enterprise small bus. investment cos. Small Bus. Adminstrn., Dept. Commerce, Washington, 1969-70; research analyst Prudential Ins. Co. Am., Jacksonville, Fla., 1971-74, sr. research analyst, 1974-75, mgr. planning and analysis, 1975-80, gen. mgr. agys. adminstrn. and planning dept., 1980—. Pres., Help Them Learn Fund, Williamsville, N.Y.C., 1962-68. Mem. Am. Econ. Assn., U. Fla., Union Coll. alumni assns., Phi Beta Kappa, Beta Gamma Sigma, Phi Kappa Phi, Psi Upsilon. Republican. Episcopalian. Author: newspaper column Fire Facts, Clarence, N.Y., 1964-66. Home: 4642 Bluff Ave Jacksonville FL 32225 Office: PO Box 4579 Prudential Ins Co Jacksonville FL 32231

PFISTER, EDWARD JOSEPH, TV exec.; b. N.Y.C., June 9, 1934; s. Paul A. and Caroline P. (Safranck) P.; A.B., St. Peter's Coll., Jersey City, 1957; M.A., Seton Hall U., E. Orange, N.J., 1965; m. Kathryn M. Luchsinger, June 18, 1960; children—Edward Joseph, Therese, Anthony. Mgr. info. services Nat. Ednl. TV, N.Y.C., 1960-65; dir. Info. Services Agy. for Instructional TV, Bloomington, Ind., 1965-70; dir. public relations and info. services Nat. Assn. Ednl. Broadcasters, Washington, 1970-72, dir. to chmn.'s coordinating com., 1972-73; exec. asst. to chmn. bd. Public Broadcasting Service, 1973-76; pres. Public Communication Found. for N.Tex., 1976—. Mem. So. Ednl. Communications Assn. (chmn.), Nat. Assn. Ednl. Broadcasters. Author reports, articles in field. Home: 4818 Melissa Ln Dallas TX 75229 Office: 3000 Harry Hines Blvd Dallas TX 75201

PFLAUM, WILLIAM CHARLES, public relations, mktg. co. exec.; b. Dayton, Ohio, Aug. 11, 1941; s. Robert Henry and Mabel (Becker) P.; B.A., Ohio State U., 1964; m. Margaret Ellen Callanan, Aug. 30, 1968; children—Erin Kathleen, Eric Becker. Expediter, Columbia Gas of Ohio, 1960-64; dir. publicity Radow Advt. Agy., Columbus, Ohio, 1967; account exec. Daniel J. Edelman, Inc., Washington, 1968-70; founder, sole propr. William C. Pflaum Co., Washington, 1970-75; pres. William C. Pflaum Co. Inc., Reston, Va., 1975—. Bd. dirs. Greater Reston Arts Center, 1979—. Served to 1st lt., inf. U.S. Army, 1965-67; Vietnam. Mem. Am. Soc. Assn. Execs., Washington Soc. Assn. Execs., Public Relations Soc. Am., Packaging Inst., Sigma Chi. Club: Rotary. Home: 2025 Peppermint Ct Reston VA 22091 Office: William C Pflaum Co Inc Reston Internat Center 11800 Sunrise Valley Dr Reston VA 22091

PFLIEGER, KENNETH JOHN, architect; b. Washington, Feb. 20, 1952; s. Chester John and Madeline Virginia Pflieger; B.A., Clemson (S.C.) U., 1975, M.Arch., 1977; m. Katherine Colleran Greeves, Oct. 1, 1977. Urban design intern Md. Nat. Capital Park and Planning Commn., Silver Spring, 1974-75; designer E. Lonzo Greene & Assos., Greenville, S.C., 1975-76; health planning intern Greenville Hosp. System, 1976-77; project adminstr., designer, dir. health planning Clark Assos., Inc., Anderson, S.C., 1977—; mem. Anderson Hospice Com. Patron Anderson Community Theatre; mem. Anderson County Arts Council, Anderson Community Concert Assn. Mem. AIA (com. on architecture for health), Anderson Council Architects, Anderson C. of C., Tau Sigma Delta. Club: Cobb's Glen Golf and Racquet, Anderson Kiwanis (sec.-treas.). Home: 506 Walden Pkwy Anderson SC 29621 Office: 126 N McDuffie St Anderson SC 29621

PFOST, WILLIAM LOUIS, JR., fiber co. exec.; b. Orange, N.J., Oct. 13, 1936; s. William Louis and Dorothy May (Kustler) P.; student Fairleigh Dickinson U., 1958-65; B.S. in B.A., Widener Coll., 1970; m. Jane Ellen Berger, Apr. 6, 1957; children—William Louis, Penni, Patti, Ricky. With Thiokol Corp., Denville, N.J., summer 1955, draftsman, 1955-59, procedures analyst, 1959-62, employment rep., 1962-65, employee relations supr., Elkton, Md., 1965-66, personnel mgr., 1966-74, dir. indsl. relations, Waynesboro, Va., 1974-79; v.p. adminstrn., corp. sec. Wayn-Tex Inc., Waynesboro, 1979-80, v.p. ops., 1980—; mem. faculty Cecil Community Coll., 1973-74, Goldey Beacom Coll., 1973-74. Pres., United Way, Cecil County, 1970-71; chmn. adv. bd. Cecil County Bd. Edn., 1971-73; pres. Economic Devel. Council for Staunton, Waynesboro, Augusta County, Va., 1976-77. Mem. Elkton C. of C. (dir. 1972-73), Waynesboro-E. Augusta C. of C. (pres. 1977-78), Va. C. of C. (dir. 1979-80), Am. Soc. Personnel Adminstrn. Presbyn. Clubs: Masons, Kiwanis, Ruritan. Home: Route 1 PO Box 338 Waynesboro VA 22980 Office: 901 S Delphine Ave Waynesboro VA 22908

PFOUTS, RALPH WILLIAM, educator; b. Atchison, Kans., Sept. 9, 1920; s. Ralph Ulysses and Alice (Oldham) P.; B.A., U. Kans., 1942, M.A., 1947; Ph.D., U. N.C., 1952; m. Jane Hoyer, Jan. 31, 1945; children—James William, Susan Jane Pfouts Portman, Thomas Robert, Elizabeth Ann. Research asst., instr. econs. U. Kan., 1946-47, U. N.C., Chapel Hill, 1947-50, lectr. 1950-52, asso. prof., 1952-58, prof., 1958—, chmn. grad. studies dept. econs. Sch. Bus. Adminstrn., 1957-62, chmn. dept. econs., 1962-68. Social Sci. Research Council fellow U. Cambridge, 1953-54; Ford Found. faculty research fellow, 1962-63. Served as deck officer USNR antisubmarine duty, 1943-46. Mem. Am., N.C. (pres. 1951-52) statis. assns., Am., So. (pres. 1965-66) econ. assns., Population Assn. Am., Econometric Soc., AAAS, Atlantic Econ. Soc. (v.p. 1974-76, pres. 1977-78), Phi Beta Kappa, Pi Sigma Alpha, Alpha Kappa Psi, Omicron Delta Epsilon. Author: Elementary Economics: A Mathematical Approach, 1972. Editor So. Econ. Jour., 1955-75. Editor, contbr. Techniques of Urban Economic Analysis, 1960, Essays in Economics and Econometrics, 1960. Mem. editorial bd. Metroeconomica, 1961—, Atlantic Econ. Jour., 1973—, Quar. Jour. Ideology, 1976—. Contbr. articles to profl. jours. Home: 502 Ransom St Chapel Hill NC 27514

PHAM, QUANG HUU, state ofcl., engr.; b. Thanh Hoa, Viet Nam, Dec. 24, 1942; s. Ba Van and Oanh Thi (Le) P.; came to U.S., 1975; B.S. in C.E., U. Saigon, 1966; M.S. in C.E., U. Okla., 1971; m. Thanh Thi, Apr. 15, 1969; children—Tuyet, Tuan. Asst. chief bur. City of Saigon, Viet Nam, 1966-67, chief bur., 1969-70, asst. chief dept., 1972-75; instr. Engring. Sch. Corps. of Engrs., Viet Nam, 1967-68; dist. engr. Okla. State Health Dept., Oklahoma City, 1975-80, dir. public water supply engring., 1980—; lectr. U. Saigon, 1974-75. Sec.-gen., Vietnamese Buddhist Assn. Okla. Recipient awards City of Saigon, 1972-75; recipient AID scholarship, 1971-72. Registered profl. engr. Okla. Mem. Am. Pub. Works Assn. Buddist. Author: Proposal for Improving the Solid Waste System Management of Saigon City, 1971. Home: 6913 Greenway Dr Oklahoma City OK 73132 Office: NE 10th and Stonewall Sts Oklahoma City OK 73105

PHARES, CHARLES WILSON, mfg. co. exec.; b. Elkins, W.Va., Oct. 6, 1940; s. Charles Wilson and Virginia Lee (Carskadon) P.; B.A., Davis and Elkins Coll., 1962; m. JoAnn Letzkus, Nov. 9, 1963; children—Susan Marie, Charles Joseph. Tchr. public schs., Warren, Ohio, 1962-63; with Rubbermaid, Inc., Winchester, Va., 1963—, financial analyst, 1963-64, asst. credit mgr., 1965-66, corp. staff asst., 1967-68, credit mgr., 1968—. Vol. fund raising Boy Scouts Am. Mem. Nat. Assn. Credit Mgmt., Nat. Food Equipment Mfrs. Credit Group (nat. dir. 1979), Chgo.-Midwest Credit Mgmt. Assn., Tau Kappa Epsilon (chpt. pres. 1961-62). Republican. Club: Lions (pres. 1978-79) (Winchester). Home: 1221 Lewis Dr Winchester VA 22601 Office: 3124 Valley Ave Winchester VA 22601

PHARIS, RUTH MCCALISTER, banker; b. San Diego, Feb. 13, 1934; d. William L. and Mary Elizabeth (Beuk) McCalister; student Del Mar Coll., 1975-77; m. Elzy Edwin Pharis, Mar. 14, 1953; children—Beth, Tracey, Todd. Bookkeeper, Bank of Am., Oakland, Calif., 1952-56, Corpus Christi (Tex.) Nat. Bank, 1956; with Parkdale State Bank, Corpus Christi, 1957-79, bookkeeper, proof supr., head bookkeeper, personnel and ops. officer, v.p.; v.p., dir. personnel Cullen Bank, Houston, 1979—. Mem. Women's com. C. of C. Mem. Am. Soc. Personnel Adminstrs. (v.p.), Bank Adminstrn. Inst. (pres.), Nat. Assn. Bank Women, Am. Inst. Banking (instr., bank rep.). Republican. Baptist. Clubs: Order Eastern Star, Order Rainbow for Girls (mother advisor, 1970-75, grand visitor, Tex.). Home: 5102 Wightman Ct Houston TX 77069 Office: PO Box 1315 Houston TX 77001

PHELAN, JAMES HARRY, physician; b. Evanston, Ill., Feb. 2, 1949; s. Harry John and Victoria Christine (Jernberg) P.; B.S. with high honors, U. Ill., 1971; M.D., Baylor U., 1974. Resident in family practice Baylor Affiliated Hosps., Houston, 1974-77; program physician Inst. Clin. Toxicology, Houston, summer 1977; practice medicine, specializing in family practice, Humble, Tex., 1977—; clin. instr. Baylor Coll. Medicine, 1977—, U. Tex. Med. Br., Houston, 1977—; staff N.E. Med. Center Hosp., Humble, 1977—, chmn. emergency rm. com., 1978, vice chief of staff, 1980. Bd. dirs. Bayou City Fun Run, 1979—. Diplomate Am. Bd. Family Physicians. Fellow Am. Acad. Family Physicians; mem. Harris County Med. Soc., Tex. Med. Assn., Harris County Acad. Family Physicians, Tex. Acad. Family Physicians, Alpha Micro Users Soc. Contbr. articles to profl. jours. Office: 18953 Memorial Dr N Suite O Humble TX 77338

PHELAN, P. CAREN, psychologist; b. Forsyth, Ga., Nov. 9, 1927; d. William Thomas and Mary Grace (Rowland) Tyler; B.A., U. Md., 1967, M.Ed., 1968, Ph.D., 1973; postdoctoral U. Tex., Austin, 1977-78; m. Richard H. Phelan, Aug. 10, 1973; children—Michael L. Lipsie, William H. Lipsie, Caren Ann Betz. Rehab. counselor D.C. Dept. Rehab., Washington, 1968-70; supr. vocat. rehab. unit St. Elizabeths Hosp., Washington, 1970-72; instr. Acad. Health Sci., Fort Sam Houston, Tex., 1972-74; unit dir. San Antonio State Hosp., 1974-76; acting dep. commr. mental health Tex. Dept. Mental Health, Austin, 1976-78; asso. dir. mental health Div. Mental Health, Denver, 1978-79; chief psychology Austin State Hosp., 1979—. Chmn. Regional Alcohol Adv. Bd., San Antonio, 1975-76; mem. Citizens Adv. Com. on Alcohol Legis., 1977, Task Force on Autism, 1977; mem. profl. adv. com. Tex. Soc. for Autistic Citizens, 1977-78; mem. State Forum, White House Com. for Handicapped, 1977; bd. dirs. Coalition for Community Living. Cert. psychologist, Tex.; cert. rehab. counselor; lic. social psychotherapist. Mem. Am. Assn. Mental Deficiency, Am. Group Psychotherapy Assn., Am. Psychol. Assn., Am. Personnel and Guidance Assn., Assn. Advancement Behavioral Therapy, Orthopsychiat. Assn. Democrat. Home: Route 1 Box 168-WW San Marcos TX 78666 Office: Austin State Hosp 4110 Guadalupe St Austin TX 78751

PHELPS, ASHTON, newspaper exec., lawyer; b. New Orleans, Dec. 30, 1913; s. Esmond and Harriott K. (Barnwell) P.; grad. Woodberry Forest Sch., 1931; A.B., Tulane U., 1935, LL.B., 1937; student U. Mich. Law Sch., summer 1936; m. Jane C. George, Nov. 21, 1939 (dec. Feb. 1974); 1 son, Ashton. Admitted to La. bar, 1937, since practiced in New Orleans; mem. firm Phelps, Dunbar, Marks, Claverie & Sims, 1946-67; pres., pub. The Times-Picayune Pub. Corp., New Orleans, 1967—, also dir. Mem. bd. Christian edn. Presbyn. Ch. U.S., 1958-61, also mem. com. wills and bequests; pres. bd. New Orleans Community Health Assn., 1945-49, Howard Meml. Library Assn., from 1950; chmn. adv. bd. Female Orphan Soc. New Orleans, 1946-59; bd. visitors Tulane U., 1953-55, v.p. bd. adminstrs., 1955-72, adv. adminstr., from 1972; trustee Mountain Retreat Assn., 1958-67; bd. dirs. New Orleans Pub. Library, 1948-62, New Orleans YMCA, 1954—, New Orleans chpt. A.R.C., 1954-60. Oschner Found. Hosp. Mem. Bd. of Liquidation City Debt, Sewerage and Water Board. Served from ensign to lt. (s.g.). USNR, 1942-45. Mem. Am. (spl. com. anti trust sect. on revision rules FTC), La., New Orleans bar assns., Assn. Bar City N.Y., Am. Law Inst., Am. Newspaper Pubs. Assn. (dir.), Order of Coif, Phi Beta Kappa, Delta Tau Delta, Phi Delta Phi, Omicron Delta Kappa. Clubs: Boston, Louisiana, New Orleans Country; City (Baton Rouge). Presbyn. (elder, trustee). Office: 3800 Howard Ave New Orleans LA 70140*

PHELPS, EDWIN HARRIS, foundry exec.; b. Greenville, Ala., Dec. 18, 1919; s. Sam and Evilla (Perry) P.; A.B. in Bus. Adminstrn., Birmingham-So. Coll., 1942, B.S. in Chemistry, 1945; m. Helen E. Hughes, Feb. 2, 1943. Analyst, Chem. Lab., Am. Cast Iron Pipe Co., Birmingham, Ala., 1940-45, metall. researcher, 1945-47, spl. foundry researcher, 1947-50, with research dept., 1950-57, research supr., 1957—. Mem. Am. Foundrymen's Soc., Am. Ceramic Soc., Am. Soc. Metals, Soc. Plastics Engrs., Nat. Mgmt. Assn. Clubs: The Club, Green Valley Country. Patentee in field. Home: 3320 Winchester Rd Birmingham AL 35226 Office: 2930 N 16th St Birmingham AL 35202

PHELPS, WILLIAM RAY, psychologist; b. Hurricane, W.Va., Mar. 4, 1931; s. William Sansford and Zula Belle (Johnson) P.; A.B. in Psychology and Edn., Glenville State Coll., 1954; M.S. in Rehab. Counseling, W.Va. U., 1957; M.A. in Clin. Psychology, Marshall U., 1963; postgrad. U. Mo., 1959; m. Emma June Rice, Sept. 17, 1960. Caseworker, Putnam County Bd. Edn., Winfield, W.Va., 1954-55; instr. Poca (W.Va.) High Sch., 1955; rehab. counselor Div. Vocat. Rehab., Charleston, W. Va., 1955-59, state psychologist, 1959-61; asst. adminstr. W.Va. Rehab. Center, Institue, W.Va., 1961-62, project dir., 1962-65, asst. adminstr., 1965-66, adminstr., 1966-68; program dir. Regional Counselor Tng. Center, Charleston, 1968-73; chief of research and devel. Div. Vocat. Rehab., State Bd. Vocat. Edn., Charleston, 1973—; guest lectr. U. N.C., 1962-66; instr. W. Va. State Coll., 1970—; mem. W.Va. State Bd. Examiners of Psychologists, 1975—. Mem. Am., W.Va. (pres. 1977-78) psychol. assns., W.Va. Rehab. Assn. (dir. 1962-65), W.Va. Guidance Assn., Am. Personnel and Guidance Assn., W.Va., Nat. assns. retarded citizens, Nat., Am. rehab. counseling assns., Am. Assn. Mental Deficiency. Baptist. Club: Kiwanis. Contbr. numerous articles on vocat. rehab. and counseling to profl. publs. Home: 873 Observatory Dr Saint Albans WV 25177 Office: State Capital Bldg Charleston WV 25305

PHENICIE, MARLOND DEAN, mech. contractor; b. Champaign County, Ill., Mar. 11, 1930; s. Chester Leo and Gertrude Claudia (Steele) P.; ed. parochial schs., spl. courses; m. Blanche E. Seymour, July 6, 1953. Gen. foreman Colwell Pub. Co., 1952-55; sales mgr. Chief Heating & Air Conditioning Co., Urbana, Ill., 1956-60, pres., 1961-78; founder Woodland Village Devel. Co., Greens Ferry, Ark., 1978—. Served with AUS, 1949-51; Korea. Recipient tech. achievement award Carrier Corp., 1976, Select dealer award Janitrol Corp., 1962-70. Mem. Asso. Builders and Contractors. Republican. Home: Rural Route 1 Box 245 Edgemont AR 72044

PHILBECK, NORRIS RICHARD, optometrist; b. Forest City, N.C., June 11, 1947; s. Norris Ray and Margaret Clemmentine (Keeter) P.; student Western Carolina U., 1965-67; O.D., So. Coll. Optometry, 1971; m. Juliet Elizabeth Lipscomb, Dec. 28, 1968; children—Jason, Juliet, Jake. Pvt. practice optometry, Lancaster, S.C., 1973—. Bd. dirs. Lancaster Coounty (S.C.) Dept. Social Services, 1975—, chmn., 1976—; bd. dirs. Lancaster County Care Center, 1976—; plan devel. com. Three Rivers Health Systems Agy., 1976—; pres. Lancaster County chpt. Am. Cancer Soc., 1975-77); bd. dirs. Lancaster County Assn. for the Blind, 1975—. Served as capt. U.S. Army, 1971-73. Decorated Army Commendation Medal. Recipient Award for outstanding community leadership, Lancaster Jr. C. of C., 1976. Mem. Lancaster County C. of C., Lancaster Jr. C. of C. (dir. 1974-75), S.C. Optometric Assn., Am. Optometric Assn., So. Council Optometrists, Am. Legion. Baptist. Clubs: Sertoma, Moose, Masons (Shriner). Contbr. aticles in field to profl. jours. Home: 121 Rock Springs Rd Lancaster SC 29720 Office: 110 William St PO Box 905 Lancaster SC 29720

PHILBIN, TOBIAS RAPHAEL, III, govt. ofcl.; b. Balt., Feb. 19, 1949; s. Tobias Raphael and Anne (Scarborough) P.; B.A., La Salle Coll., Phila., 1970; Ph.D., King's Coll., U. London, 1975. Lectr. Soviet studies Va. Mil. Inst., Lexington, 1975-76, asst. prof. history, 1976-77; staff instr. history U.S. Naval War Coll., Newport, R.I., summer 1976; analyst Soviet Navy, U.S. Dept. Def., Washington, 1977—. Served with USN, 1970-71. Recipient Medal for naval history U. Pa., 1970. Mem. AAUP, Royal United Services Instn., Am. Hist. Assn., Soc. for Nautical Research, U.S. Naval Inst., Phi Alpha Theta. Home: 6202 Fort Hunt Rd Alexandria VA 22307

PHILEMON, ROY WILLIAM, JR., sch. adminstr.; b. Charlotte, N.C., Aug. 29, 1931; s. Roy William and Mary Emily (Caldwell) P.; B.A., Trevecca Nazarene Coll., 1954; M.A., Fla. State U., 1959; Ed.S., U. Fla., 1968; m. Iris Bennett Mays, June 9, 1951; children—Marilyn Faye, Linda Joyce, Roy William, Danny Ray. Band dir. Altha (Fla.) Pub. Sch., 1956-57, Blountstown (Fla.) Pub. Sch., 1957-60; prin. Crystal River (Fla.) Elementary Sch., 1960-61, W.E. Cherry Elementary Sch., Orange Park, Fla., 1961—; affiliated writer BMI. Minister of music Normandy Ch. of the Nazarene, Jacksonville, Fla., 1966-72, Oak Hill Ch. of the Nazarene, Jacksonville, 1972—. Served with AUS, 1954-56. U. Fla. Experienced Tchrs. Fellowship Program fellow, 1967-68. Mem. Ch. of the Nazarene (trustee 1972). Club: Lions (sec. 1958-60). Composer: A Joy That Will Last, 1974; The Light Shineth in Darkness, 1974 (songs); rec. album Because He Lives, 1973; single record A Truck Drivers Prayer, 1976. Home: 442 Brighton Ave Orange Park FL 32073 Office: 420 Edson Dr Orange Park FL 32073

PHILEN, OTIS DONALD, JR., soil scientist, mineralogist; b. Greenville, Ala., Sept. 26, 1935; s. Otis Donald and Mammie Essilene (Smith) P.; B.S., U. Ala., 1963; Ph.D., N.C. State U., 1972; m. Mary Ellen Kyle, Mar. 17, 1973; children—Donna Lynne, Charlotte Lee, Bradford Chapman. Research chemist TVA, Wilson Dam, Ala., 1963-67; research asso. dept. soil science N.C. State U., Raleigh, 1967-72; forensic soil scientist N.C. State Bur. Investigation, Raleigh, 1972-75; soil scientist N.C. Dept. Natural Resources and Community Devel., Raleigh, 1975—; cons. in field. Served with USAF, 1954-60. Mem. Am. Soc. Agronomy, Soil Sci. Soc. Am., Clay Minerals Soc., Mineral. Soc. Am., Am. Soc. Photogrametry, Soil Conservation Soc.

Am., Sigma Xi. Patentee fertilizer tech.; contbr. articles in field to sci. and profl. jours. Home: 5211 Asbury Circle Raleigh NC 27606 Office: PO Box 5073 Raleigh NC 27650

PHILION, JAMES ROBERT, car rental co. exec.; b. Glens Falls, N.Y., Jan. 3, 1944; s. Robert Francis and Margery Madeline (Streeter) P.; student Tex. A. and M. U., 1961-63, Arlington State U., 1963-64; m. Sharon Sue McGinness, Dec. 4, 1965; children—Robert Barton, Tami Renée. Ticket agt./sales rep. Central Airlines, Dallas, 1963-66; account exec. Hertz Corp., Houston, 1966-67; dist. sales mgr. Nat. Car Rental Systems, Inc., 1967-68, Los Angeles, 1968-69, regional sales mgr. western region, Los Angeles, 1969-70, nat. accounts mgr., Mpls., 1970-71, dir. sales, 1971, v.p. sales, 1971-78, corp. v.p., 1978-79; pres., chief exec. officer Airline Passengers Assn., 1979—. Mem. Nat. Passenger Traffic Assn. (Account Exec. of Year 1970), Traffic Clubs Internat., Am. Soc. Travel Agts., Sales and Mktg. Execs. Home: 2707 Shadow Wood Ct Arlington TX 76011 Office: 800 W Airport Freeway Irving TX

PHILIPPS, JOHN WILLIAM, pub. co. exec.; b. Whitestone, L.I., N.Y., Jan. 17, 1930; s. Albert E. and Agnes L. (Duffy) P.; A.B.A., U. Pa., 1960; m. Audrey D. Jones, Mar. 21, 1952; children—John William, Gail D., David A., Donald K., Terri A. Typesetter, Hartford (Conn.) Courant, 1954-56; statistician TV Guide, Radnor, Pa., 1956-60, advt. rep., Boston, 1960-62, regional mgr., Rochester, N.Y., 1962-75, Hollywood, Fla., 1975—. Mem. advt. adv. council U. Fla., 1978—. Served with USMC, 1948-52. Named Mgr. of Yr., TV Guide, 1978. Mem. Am. Advt. Fedn. (Club Pres. of Yr. 1978-79), Advt. Fedn. Greater Fort Lauderdale (pres. 1978-79), Rochester Advertisers (1st v.p. 1974-75). Home: 480 NE 37th St Boca Raton FL 33431 Office: TV Guide 2500 Hollywood Blvd Hollywood FL 33020

PHILIPS, WALLACE MERRITT, JR., ophthalmologist; b. Florence, S.C., Sept. 21, 1941; s. Wallace Merritt and Jane Elizabeth (Sumner) P.; B.S., Davidson Coll., 1963; M.D., Emory U., 1967; m. Carolee Osterholm, Aug. 24, 1963; children—Stephen Todd, Mark Wallace. Commd. ensign U.S. Navy, 1966, advanced through grades to lt. comdr., 1974; intern U.S. Naval Hosp., Portsmouth, Va., 1967-68; med. officer USS Shenandoah AD-26, 1968-69; dir. med. examinations U.S. Naval Hosp., Orlando, Fla., 1969-70; resident in ophthalmology U.S. Naval Hosp., Oakland, Calif., 1970-73; chief of ophthalmology U.S. Naval Hosp., Charleston, S.C., 1973-74; resigned, 1974; practice medicine specializing in ophthalmology, Orlando, 1974—; mem. staffs Orlando Regional Med. Center, Lucerne Gen. Fla., Winter Park Meml. hosps.; clin. instr. ophthalmology Med. Coll., U.S.C., Charleston, 1973-74; v.p. Magruder, Philips & Bates, M.D., P.A. Mem. Am. Acad. Ophthalmology and Otolaryngology, Am. Intra-ocular Implant Soc., Fla., Central Fla. socs. ophthalmology, Fla. Med. Assn., Orange County Med. Soc. (exec. com.), Alpha Omega Alpha. Republican. Episcopalian. Clubs: Med. Study (Orlando); Winter Park (Fla.) Racquet. Home: 452 Fletcher Pl Winter Park FL 32789 Office: 85 W Miller St Orlando FL 32806

PHILLIPS, A(NDREW) CRAIG, state ednl. adminstr.; b. Greensboro, N.C., Nov. 1, 1922; A.B., U. N.C., 1943, M.A., 1946, Ed.D. in Sch. Adminstrn., 1956; m. 1943; 4 children. Tchr., asst. supt. Winston-Salem (N.C.) City Schs., 1946-55, supt. schs., 1957-62; supt. Charlotte-Mecklenburg (N.C.) Schs., 1962-67; adminstrv. v.p. Richardson Found., 1967-68; supt. pub. instrn. State of N.C., Raleigh, 1969—. Mem. steering com. N.C. Gov.'s Com. To Study N.C. Pub. Sch. System, 1967-68; mem. So. Regional Edn. Bd.; mem. Council Chief State Sch. Officers, 1969—. Bd. visitors Duke Div. Sch. Mem. NEA, N.C. Assn. Edn., Am. Assn. Sch. Adminstrs. (exec. com. 1971—), Nat. Acad. Sch. Execs. (dir. 1969), So. Assn. Colls. and Schs. (trustee). Home: 2200 Barfield Ct Raleigh NC 27612 Office: State Dept Public Instruction State Capitol Raleigh NC 27612

PHILLIPS, BOBBYE JEAN, nurse; b. Talopoosa, Ga., June 22, 1931; d. Houston Loyd and Eron Ava (Taylor) Haywood; grad. Birmingham Bapt. Sch. of Nursing, 1969; B.S. in Nursing, U. Ala., 1976; m. Everett Arnton Phillips, July 17, 1951; children—Everett Anthony, Donald Keith, Kyle Haywood. Team leader med.-surg. nursing Bapt. Med. Center, Birmingham, Ala., 1969-72; coordinator-instr. continuing edn. N.W. Ala. State Jr. Coll., Phil Campbell, 1973-75; dir. inservice edn. Burdick-West Meml. Hosp., Haleyville, Ala., 1975—; instr. Sch. of Practical Nursing, S.W. Ala. State Tchrs. Coll., Hamilton, 1975—. Bd. dirs. N.W. Ala. Mental Health, Emergency Med. Services, Decatur, Ala., ARC; instr. advanced cardiac life support Ala. Heart Assn., 1970—, ARC, 1974—. R.N., Ala. Mem. Ala. State Nurses Assn., Am. Nurses Assn., Internat. Assn. Practitioners in Infection Control, Sigma Theta Tau. Baptist. Clubs: 20th Century Study (Haleyville, Ala.); Pilot. Home: Lakeview Rd Haleyville AL 35565 Office: Hwy 195 PO Box 780 Haleyville AL 35565

PHILLIPS, CECIL RANDOLPH, mgmt. cons.; b. Birmingham, Ala., July 30, 1933; s. Cecil Randolph and Alberta (Smith) P.; B.S., Ga. Inst. Tech., 1955, M.S., 1960; postgrad. Fed. Inst. Tech., Zurich, Switzerland, 1955-56; m. Sara Lee Kirby, Aug. 25, 1956 (div. Oct. 1978); children—Taylor Cy, Leslie Hope, Daniel Lee; m. 2d, Louise Bartlett Franklin, Feb. 1979. Tech. editor advt., sales promotion dept. Gen. Electric Co., Schnectady, 1956-58; project leader Operations Research, Inc., Silver Spring, Md., 1960-62, asst. tech. dir., Atlanta, 1962-63; exec. v.p. Mgmt. Sci. Atlanta, Inc., 1963-67; mgr. Kurt Salmon Assos., Inc., Atlanta, 1967-73, v.p., 1974; exec. dir. Ga. Conservancy, 1974-78; v.p. Kurt Salmon Assos., Atlanta, 1978—. Active Boy Scouts Am. Mem. Inst. Mgmt. Consultants (cert.), ANAK Soc., Ga. Conservancy (trustee), Sierra Club, Friends of the River, Omicron Delta Kappa, Alpha Tau Omega, Alpha Pi Mu. Club: Author: (with Joseph J. Moder) Project Management With CPM and PERT, 1964, 2d edit., 1970. Contbr. articles to profl. jours. Home: 10 Springlake Pl Atlanta GA 30318 Office: 400 Colony Sq Atlanta GA 30361

PHILLIPS, CHANEY LINDSEY, hosp. adminstr.; b. Baton Rouge, Dec. 27, 1949; s. Lawrence C. and Virginia C. (Calmes) P.; B.A. in Bus. Adminstrn., Southeastern La. U., 1974; m. Linda C. Guy, Apr. 17, 1978; children—Kimberly, Gregory, Ryan. Adminstr., St. Helena Parish Hosp., Greensburg, La., 1975—; bd. dirs. Mid-La. Health Systems Agy. Mem. adv. council Florida Parishes Vocat. Sch.; coordinator Am. Heart Assn. Fund Drive, 1977, 78, 79; pres. St. Helena Parish Civic Club, 1977, 78, 79. Served with U.S. Army, 1970-71. Cert. in child welfare State of La. Div. Family Services, 1975. Mem. Am. Legion. Baptist. Home: PO Box 212 Greensburg LA 70441 Office: PO Box 337 Greensburg LA 70441

PHILLIPS, CHARLES EDWARD, food co. exec.; b. Cullman, Ala., Oct. 15, 1943; s. Tandy Elmer and Thelma Elaine (Owens) P.; B.B.A., U. Houston, 1965; m. Nella Lou Pitts, Feb. 16, 1974; 1 dau., Penelope Victoria. Account rep., account exec. Pillsbury Co., Houston, Shreveport, La., 1965-71; regional sales mgr. Western nat. sales mgr. Anderson Clayton Foods, Dallas, 1971-76; sales mgr. Wilsey Foods, Inc., Fort Worth, 1976-78, asst. gen. mgr., 1979—. Mem. adv. council DAV. Served with U.S. Army, 1966-69. Mem. Nat. Restaurant Assn., Tex. Restaurant Assn., Dallas and Fort Worth Restaurant Assn., Am. Mgmt. Assn. Club: Canyon Creek Country. Office: 815 Grove St Fort Worth TX 76102

PHILLIPS, CLIFFORD CLAYTON, public schs. exec.; b. Winston-Salem, N.C., Aug. 28, 1929; s. Arthur Benbow and Essie Lee (Williams) P.; B.S.I.E., Va. Poly. Inst. and State U., 1953, B.S.E.E., 1957; postgrad. Wake Forest Coll., 1960, Duke U., 1962, N.C. State Coll., 1963, Greensboro Coll., 1964, Fla. Inst. Tech., 1966; m. Roberta George Stouch, June 10, 1956; children—Robert Benbow, Eric Erwin, Adam Joseph. Engr., Western Elec. Co., Winston-Salem, 1953-56; mem. tech. staff Bell Telephone Labs., Whippany, N.J., 1957-66; program mgr. overseas Radiation div. Harris Intertype, 1966-73; exec. mgr. Virginia County Public Schs., Manassas, Va., 1974-78; dir. phys. plant maintenance Fairfax County (Va.), 1978—; v.p. Bernard, Inc.; cons. Life Support Systems, Inc., Gen. Research Enterprises, Inc. Chmn. ch. council, synod rep. Lutheran Ch.; com. chmn., scoutmaster Boy Scouts Am., 1947—. Served with USAF, 1946-49. Recipient service award Prince William County, 1978. Mem. Am. Inst. Indsl. Engrs., IEEE, Fairfax C. of C., Alpha Phi Omega, Delta Kappa Epsilon. Clubs: Masons, Shriners.

PHILLIPS, GLYN RONALD, judge; b. nr. Clintwood, Va., Jan. 9, 1923; s. Robert A. and Rachel (Kiser) P.; A.B., Lincoln Meml. U., 1946, LL.D., 1973; student Carson Newman Coll., 1943, Northwestern U., 1944; LL.B., U. Va., 1948; postgrad. U. Nev., 1969; grad. Am. Acad. Jud. Edn., U. Ala., 1972, U. Colo., 1973; m. Rita Lambert, Oct. 7, 1950; children—Deborah Lee, Jennifer Lynn, Glyn Ronald. Admitted to Va. bar, 1948, practiced in Clintwood, 1948-56; atty. for Commonwealth of Va., 1956-60; judge 27th Jud. Circuit, Clintwood, 1967-75; chief judge 29th Jud. Circuit Va., 1975—. Vice pres. Wise (Va.) Appalachian Regional Hosp., 1968—, Cumberland Bank and Trust Co., Clintwood, 1972—. Mem. Va. Ho. of Dels., 1952-56; chmn. Dickenson County Democratic party, 1952-56. Bd. dirs. Johnston Meml. Hosp., Abingdon, Va. Served as lt. USNR, 1943-46: PTO. Mem. Am., Va. bar assns., Council on Ministries (chmn. 1969—). Methodist. Kiwanian (lt. gov. 1964). Address: Box 598 Clintwood VA 25228

PHILLIPS, HARRY, judge; b. Watertown, Tenn., July 28, 1909; s. Norman Cates and Bernice (Neal) P.; A.B., Cumberland U., 1932, LL.B., 1933, LL.D., 1951; m. Virginia Major, Nov. 26, 1936; children—Harriet (Mrs. Robert E. Scott), Rachel (Mrs. Sidney E. Eagles, Jr.), Caroline (Mrs. Robert M. Ligon), Martha (Mrs. James M. Robinson). Admitted to Tenn. bar, 1933; practiced in Watertown, 1933-37; mem. firm Phillips, Gullett & Steele and predecessor, Nashville, 1950-63; asst. atty. gen., Tenn., 1937-43, 46-50; exec. sec. Tenn. Code Commn., 1953-63; judge U.S. Ct. Appeals, 6th Circuit, 1963-69, chief judge, 1969-79, sr. judge, 1979—. Mem. Tenn. Legislature, 1935-37. Served to lt. comdr. JAG, USNR, 1943-46. Recipient award merit Bar Assn. Tenn., 1960. Fellow Am. Bar Found. (hon.); mem. Am. Bar Assn. (spl. com. on coordination fed. jud. improvements 1978—), SAR, Order Coif (hon.), Sigma Alpha Epsilon. Baptist. Clubs: University (Cin.); Cumberland, Exchange. Author: Phillips Family History, 1935; Phillips Prichard on Wills and Administration of Estates, 1955; (with others) History of Wilson County, Tennessee, 1962; co-author History of the Sixth Circuit, 1977. Home: 2809 Wimbledon Rd Nashville TN 37215 Office: US Ct House Nashville TN 37203 also US Ct House Cincinnati OH 45202

PHILLIPS, HOWARD OXFORD, retail grocery co. exec.; b. Thomasville, Ga., May 30, 1948; s. Francis M. and Edna Eugenia (Oxford) P.; A.A., magna cum laude, No. Fla. Jr. Coll., 1968; B.S. cum laude, Fla. State U., 1969; m. Patricia Panaway, Feb. 14, 1970; children—Jennifer, Katherine. Sr. auditor Coopers & Lybrand, Jacksonville, Fla., 1973-75; comptroller, office mgr. Miller Enterprises, Inc., Crescent City, Fla., 1975—. Chmn. fin. com. Howe Meml. United Meth. Ch., Crescent City, 1977—, chmn. long-range planning com., 1978—, chmn. fin. and promotions for bldg. com., 1979—. Served with USAF, 1970-73. Decorated Air Force Commendation medal. C.P.A. Mem. Nat. Assn. Retail Grocers U.S. (computer applications council 1979). Democrat. Home: 705 N Park St Crescent City FL 32012 Office: Miller Enterprises 331 Central Ave Crescent City FL 32012

PHILLIPS, JAMES WOODROE, educator; b. Fort Worth, Mar. 12, 1935; s. Woodroe Kelly and Leta (Allen) P.; B.A.A.S., Tarleton State U., 1977; m. Maureen Ann Lowe, Apr. 16, 1960; 1 son, Kelly. With Gen. Dynamics Co., Fort Worth, 1955-56, Ling Temco Vaught Co., Dallas, 1956; aircraft and engine mechanic Tex. Air N.G., Dallas, 1956-68, 69-70; aircraft and engine mechanic Braniff Air Lines, Dallas, 1968-69; aviation maintenance instr. Tex. State Tech. Inst., Waco, 1971—. Mem. N.G. Assn. Tex. Club: Masons. Home: Route 5 Box 1252 Waco TX 76705 Office: Tex State Tech Inst Bldg #8-2 Waco TX 76705

PHILLIPS, JIM R., broadcasting co. exec.; b. Dallas, Oct. 2, 1932; s. Hosea and Amerna Elizabeth (Guy) P.; B.S., Tex. Christian U., 1958; m. Nita Bentlay, Dec. 24, 1972; 1 son, Jimmy. Pres. Sta. KHWY, Inc., El Paso, 1979—; pres. Sta. KRMD, Inc., Shreveport, 1979—; v.p. Lone Star Broadcasting Co., 1979—. Pres El Paso County (Tex.) United Way. Served with USAF, 1950-54. Named El Paso Advt. Man of Yr., 1974. Mem. El Paso C. of C. (v.p.), Nat. Assn. Broadcasters, Tex. Assn. Broadcasters (pres.). Methodist. Office: 2419 N Piedras St El Paso TX 79930

PHILLIPS, LYLE RHINE, accountant; b. Stephens, Mo., Aug. 1, 1908; s. Elmer Vest and Atta Margaret (Lyle) P.; student So. Meth. U., 1943; B.C.S., Okla. Sch. Accountancy, 1953; postgrad. Tulsa U., 1952; m. Mary Frances Nichols, Jan. 2, 1931; children—Teddy Lyle, Veril LeRoy. From clk. to accountant C.E., U.S. Army, 1930-52, ret., 1952; owner, mgr. Harvard Furniture Co., Tulsa, 1952-62; pvt. practice accounting, Tulsa, 1952-62; bus. adminstr. First Christian Ch., Tulsa, 1962-75; pvt. practice accounting, part-time, Tulsa, 1975-77, real estate, part-time, Tulsa, 1975-77. Sec.-treas. Tulsa Met. Ministry, 1963-64; condr. Hotel Ministry, Adams Hotel, Tulsa, 1968-76, lay minister, Bible tchr., 1968-76. Licensed pub. accountant, Okla.; licensed real estate agt., Okla. Mem. Okla. Assn. Pub. Accountants, Met. Tulsa Bd. Realtors. Clubs: Toastmasters, Civitan (outstanding service award, 1967-68), Masons (32 deg.). Home: 5925 E 24th Pl Tulsa OK 74114 Office: 4528 S Sheridan Tulsa OK 74129

PHILLIPS, MARGARITA GOMEZ, microbiologist; b. Jerez, Zacatecas, Mexico, July 20, 1942; d. Jose Gomez Lozano and Guadalupe Lamas (de la Torre); came to U.S., 1964, naturalized, 1972; diploma Adult Tech. Sch., 1967; B.A. in Microbiology, U. South Fla., 1972; m. Perry Lineal Phillips, Jan. 13, 1962; 1 son, Jose. Med. lab. technician Manatee Meml. Hosp., Bradenton, Fla., 1967-68; med. technologist Community Hosp. of New Port Richey, Fla., 1973-74, head microbiology, 1974-75, asst. to mgr., 1975—. Mem. Am. Soc. Clin. Pathologists, Am. Soc. for Microbiology, Am. Soc. Med. Technologists, Fla. Assn. Blood Banks, Soc. Applied Anthropology, U. South Fla. Alumni Assn. Democrat. Roman Catholic. Home: 912 Linwood Terr Lutz FL 33549 Office: 205 High St New Port Richey FL 33352

PHILLIPS, MICHAEL LYNN, cellulose co. mgr.; b. Erwin, Tenn., June 18, 1952; s. M. L. and Margaret Virginia (Jones) P.; B.S.M.E. (Citizens Bank scholar), Tenn. Tech. U., 1976, M.A. in Bus. Adminstrn., 1978. Night clk. Clinchfield YMCA, Erwin, 1970; machine operator Crystal Ice Coal and Laundry, Erwin, 1970; engrng. aide. Union Carbide Corp., Oak Ridge, 1971-72, 73-74; salesman Southwestern Co., Nashville, 1975; report and instrns. manual writer Citizens Bank, Cookville, Tenn., 1977-78; area mgr. Buckeye Cellulose Corp., Memphis, 1978—. Youth chmn. Snodgrass for Gov. Tenn., 1970. Mem. ASME, Nat. Soc. Profl. Engrs., Order of Engrs., Theta Tau, Tau Beta Pi, Pi Tau Sigma, Kappa Mu Epsilon, Phi Kappa Phi, Omicron Delta Kappa. Republican. Baptist. Office: PO Box 3160 Huntsville AL 35810

PHILLIPS, OAIL ANDREW (BUM), football coach; b. Orange, Tex., Sept. 29, 1923; student Lamar Jr. Coll.; B.S., Stephen F. Austin State Coll., 1949. High sch. coach, 1950-56, 58-64; asst. coach football Tex. A. and M. U., 1957, U. Houston, 1965-66, San Diego Chargers, 1967-71, So. Meth. U., 1972, Okla. State U., 1973; asst. coach Houston Oilers, 1974, gen. mgr., head coach, 1975—. Office: Houston Oilers 6910 Fannin St Houston TX 77030*

PHILLIPS, RAYMOND FOY, oil and gas prodn. co. exec.; b. Vernon, Tex., July 26, 1935;; s. Robert Raymond and Margie Fay (Fowler) P.; B.S. in Chem. Engring., Tex. Tech. U., 1957; m. Maidie Bassett Baldwin, Aug. 28, 1960; children—Maidie Bland, Robert, Foy, Fowler Scott. Engaged in new product and new venture mktg. research Humble Oil and Refining Co., Baytown, Tex., Houston and N.Y.C., 1957-63; petroleum product mktg., advt. research Internat. Petroleum, Coral Gables, Fla. and Bogota, Colombia, 1963-65; chem. and environ. resource adviser Houston Research Inst., 1965-67; with Pennzoil Co., Houston, 1967-74, dir. land and water resources div., 1970, 71, with new products and new ventures, 1972-74; pres. Mondo Chem. & Supply Co., Houston, 1974-76, R. Foy Phillips & Assos., oil and gas prodn., Houston, 1977—. Mem. N.W. Harris County Public Safety Assn. (dir.), Chem. Mktg. Research Assn., S.W. Chem. Assn., Soc. Petroleum Engrs. Contbr. articles to profl. jours. Home: 13710 Hambleton Circle Houston TX 77069 Office: 3648 FM 1960 West Houston TX 77068

PHILLIPS, ROBERT WAYNE, ednl. counselor; b. Fort Benning, Ga., Dec. 24, 1942; s. Joseph Forrest and Margaret Magdelaine (Blissitt) P.; B.B.A., Ga. State U., 1971; M.S.Ed., U. So. Calif., 1976; M. Polit. Sci., U. Tex., El Paso, 1979; m. Jade Yonok, May 2, 1975; children—MeiLin, ShanLin. Tchr. overseas high sch. Korea br., St. Louis High Sch., Honolulu, 1975-76; edn. counselor, Army Edn. Center, Seoul, Korea, 1976-78; mem. staff tng. and devel. office Army Edn., Fort Bliss, Tex., 1978—; career and family guidance counselor Korea Fgn. Counseling Agy., 1975-77, cons., 1976—. Served with USAF, 1960-64, U.S. Army, 1971-75. Decorated Airmedal, Purple Heart; Vietnam Cross of Gallantry. Mem. Asian Counselors Assn. (v.p. 1976-77), Am. Personnel and Guidance Assn., Am. Sch. Counselors Assn., Nat. Vocational Counselors Assn., Fgn. Counselors Assn. Korea, Buddhist Counselors Assn., Am. Polit. Sci. Assn., Asian Edn. Fellow. Buddhist. Clubs: Rock Hound of Korea, Masons. Editor Orion Systems newsletter. Office: USAADS Fort Bliss TX 79916

PHILLIPS, SILAS BENT, JR., utilities exec.; b. Portland, Oreg., Feb. 3, 1915; s. Silas Bent and May (Stevenson) P.; B.S., Harvard, 1937; m. Frances May Rau, Jan. 17, 1943; children—Dabney Carr, Elizabeth May, Jane Rowland, William Stevenson. Dist. mgr. West Tex. Utilities Co., Marfa, 1953-57, adminstrv. asst., Abilene, 1957-60, v.p., 1960-64, pres., dir., also chief exec. officer, 1964-65; pres., dir. Central & S.W. Corp., Dallas (formerly Wilmington, Del.), 1965-76, chmn. bd., chief exec. officer, 1976—; pres., dir. Central and S.W. Services, Inc., Dallas, 1969-76, chmn. bd., chief exec. officer, 1976—. Served from pvt. to maj. USAAF, 1941-46. Home: 4711 N Lindhurst Dallas TX 75229 Office: 2700 One Main Pl Dallas TX 75250

PHILLIPS, THEODORE (TED) RAY, advt. agy. exec.; b. American Falls, Idaho, Oct. 27, 1948; s. Virn Elias and Jessie Nelean (Aldous) P.; B.A., Brigham Young U., 1972, M.A., 1974; m. Dianne Jacqulynne Walker, May 23, 1971; children—Scott Richard, Russell Glen, Stephen John. Asst. acct. exec. David W. Evans, Inc., 1972-73, acct. exec., 1973-75; dir. advt. DCE Advt. Co., Salt Lake City, 1975-78; sr. v.p., acct. supr. Evans/Lowe & Stevens, Inc., Atlanta, 1978-79, exec. v.p., mgr., 1979—; pres., chief exec. officer David W. Evans/Atlanta, Inc., 1980—. Mem. Town Council West Jordan, Utah, 1976; dir. public relations Western States Republican Conf., 1977; publicity dir. United Way Greater Salt Lake City, 1978. Recipient N.Y. Art Dirs. Club award, 1978. Mem. Am. Advt. Fedn. (recipient Addy award 1976, 77), Bus./Profl. Advt. Assn., Atlanta Advt. Fedn. Mormon. Club: W. Paces Racquet. Home: 1900 Branch Valley Dr Roswell GA 30076 Office: 550 Pharr Rd Atlanta GA 30305

PHILLIPS, TIMOTHY DUKES, educator; b. Jackson, Miss., Oct. 1, 1947; s. Robert C. and Mellie L. (Dukes) P.; B.S., Miss. State U., 1970; M.S., U. So. Miss., 1972, Ph.D., 1975; m. Pamela Marie Bodet, Oct. 10, 1970; children—Jennifer, Christina, Tracie. NDEA fellow, Dept. Chemistry, U. So. Miss., Hattiesburg, 1972-75; Welch fellow Baylor Coll. Medicine, Tex. Med. Center, Houston, 1975-76; sr. research asso. pharmacology and toxicology U. Miss. Med. Center, Jackson, 1976-79; asst. prof. Coll. Vet. Medicine, Pub. Health, Tex. A. and M. U., College Station, 1979—. Mem. Soc. Toxicology, Sigma Xi. Democrat. Methodist. Contbr. articles to profl. jours. Home: 2900 Pierre Pl College Station TX 77840 Office: Dept Vet Pub Health Tex A and M Univ College Station TX 77843

PHILLIPS, VIRGINIA GAIL, oil co. exec.; b. Phillipsburg, Kans., Feb. 1, 1952; d. Boyd D. and JoAnn (Larimore) Phillips; B.A. in Polit. Sci., Okla. State U., 1974; M.B.A., Phillips U., 1978; m. A. Calvin Johnson, Aug. 13, 1977 (div.). Social worker HEW, Enid (Okla.) State Sch., 1975-76, coordinator vol. services, 1976; office mgr. Phillips Oil Operating Co., Enid, 1976—; pres. Ra-Gale Ltd. Petroleum Investment Co., Enid, 1976—. Contact worker Christian Telephone Ministry, Enid, 1975; worker United Fund Dr., Enid, 1975; mem. aquatics com. YMCA, Enid, 1976. Selected as overseas student in Sweden, Phillips U., 1974, 1st female grad. of M.B.A. program, 1978; Mem. Nat. Polit. Sci Orgn., Desk and Derrick Nat. Women's Petroleum Industry Assn. (Enid chpt. membership chmn. 1978), Phillips U. Geol. Soc., Phillips U. Masters of Bus. Assn., Alpha Phi (v.p. 1972). Author: Requirements for Small Business Policy manual, 1978. Home: 2406 Sandpiper Enid OK 73701 Office: PO Box 706 Enid OK 73701

PHILLIPS, WALTER ELLIS, JR., microbiologist, educator; b. West Point, Miss., Mar. 7, 1947; s. Walter Ellis and Gloria Swanson (Shook) P.; B.S., Miss. State U., 1970, M.S., 1972; Ph.D., N.C. State U., 1975; m. Barbara Ann Taylor, Mar. 26, 1967; 1 dau., Stephanie Elizabeth. Research asso. in microbiology U. Ga., Athens, 1975; chief microbiologist Miss. Vet. Diagnostic Lab., Jackson, 1975—; adj. prof. microbiology Miss. State U., Mississippi State, Miss., 1976—; lectr., cons. in field. Research asst. Agrl. Found., N.C. State U., 1973; NSF/NASA, 1971-73 Dept. Interior Office of Water Resources grantee, 1970. Mem. Am. Soc. for Microbiology, Soc. for Indsl. Microbiology, Miss. Acad. Sci., Am. Assn. Vet. Lab. Diagnosticians, Assn. Vet. Microbiologists (past pres.), Sigma Xi, Phi Kappa Phi.

Baptist. Club: Masons. Contbr. articles to profl. publs. Home: 162 Crossover Dr Brandon MS 39042 Office: Miss Vet Diagnostic Lab 2531 N West St Jackson MS 39216

PHILLIPS, WILLIAM ERNEST, ednl. adminstr.; b. Philippi, W.Va., June 22, 1935; B.S. in Edn., Alderson-Broaddur Coll., Philippi, 1956; M.Ed. in Adminstrv. Supervision, Fla. Atlantic U., Boca Raton, 1966; postgrad. in Ednl. Media, So. Ill. U., Carbondale, 1968; married, 2 children. Tchr. Palm Beach County (Fla.) schs., West Palm Beach, 1958-65, supr., 1966-68, dir. learning resources, 1969-74; dir. curriculum and instrn. Barbour County (W.Va.) schs., Philippi, 1974-79, supt., 1979—. Sec. County Council PTA, 1972-74. Mem. W.Va. Assn. Sch. Adminstrn., Assn. Ednl. Communications and Tech. Club: Kiwanis (v.p. Philippi). Certified as adminstr., supr., Fla.; supr., W.Va.; specialist in instructional media. Home: PO Box 105 Philippi WV 26416 Office: 50 S Main St Philippi WV 26416

PHILLIPS, WILLIS PAUL, dentist; b. Hale Center, Tex., Oct. 7, 1927; s. Clyde C. and Ada Erma (Stutzman) P.; B.S., Tex. Tech. Coll., 1947; postgrad. Tex. A. and M. U., 1948, Wayland Coll., 1962, West Tex. State U., 1963; D.D.S., Baylor U., 1967; m. Grace Holden, Apr. 6, 1950; children—Charles Vincent, Barbara Camille, Brenda Karen. Instr., Knox County Vocational Sch., Munday, Tex., 1948-50, Hale County Vocat. Sch., Plainview, Tex., 1950-53; owner, operator dairy and farm, Hale Center, 1953-63; instr. Baylor U. Coll. Dentistry, Dallas, summer 1967; pvt. practice dentistry, Weatherford, Tex., 1967—; sec., dir. Preston Park Gas Coop., Hale Center, 1961-63. Mem. Planning and Zoning Bd., City of Weatherford, 1969-79, Water and Light Bd., 1979—. Mem. ADA, Tex. Dental Assn., Fort Worth Dist. Dental Soc., Am. Soc. Dentistry for Children. Methodist (lay leader 1968-71). Clubs: Masons, Rotary (dir. 1969-71, pres. 1970). Patentee in field. Home: 1302 Rona St Weatherford TX 76086 Office: 200 E Rentz St Weatherford TX 76086

PHILPOT, VAN BUREN, JR., pathologist; b. Houston, Miss., Mar. 3, 1923; s. Van Buren and Lois (Atkinson) P.; student Miss. Coll., 1942; M.D., Tulane U., 1950; children—Marjorie Gene, Eloise, James, Van Buren III, Rachel. Intern, Meth. Hosp., Bklyn., 1950-51; resident in pathology U. Wis., 1954-57; asst. prof. pathology U. Tenn., 1957-58; practice medicine specializing in pathology, Houston, Miss., 1964—; pathologist Gen. Hosps., Pvt. Lab., Houston, Miss., 1950—; mem. staff Gilmore Meml. Hosp., Amory, Miss., Union County Hosp., New Albany, Miss.; adj. asso. prof. biochemistry Tulane U. Med. Sch., 1974. Served with U.S. Army, 1944-46, 51-54. Decorated Bronze Star; USPHS grantee, 1958-61. Fellow Coll. Am. Pathologists; mem. NE Miss. Hist. Soc., Miss. Assn. Pathologists, AMA, Miss. Med. Assn., Royal Soc. Health. Democrat. Club: Exchange. Author: Battalion Medics, 1955; contbr. numerous articles to profl. jours. Office: PO Box 312 Houston MS 38851

PHILPOTT, ALBERT LEE, legislator, lawyer; b. Philpott, Va., July 29, 1919; s. John E. and Gertrude (Prillaman) P.; B.A., U. Richmond, 1941, LL.B., 1947, LL.D., 1978; m. Katherine Spencer, Aug. 7, 1941; children—Judy (Mrs. Philip Steward Marstiller), Albert Lee. Admitted to Va. bar, 1947; practiced in Bassett, 1947-52, 58—; partner firm Philpott & McGhee, Bassett, 1958—; commonwealth's atty. Henry County (Va.), 1952-57; mem. Va. Ho. of Dels., 1958—. Dir. 1st Nat. Bank, Bassett, Va. Bd. dirs. Patrick Henry Mental Health Clinic, Martinsville, Va. Served with USAAF, 1941-45. Recipient Distinguished Service award Am. Legion, 1977; Distinguished Alumni award U. Richmond, 1977; Va. Cultural Laureate award, 1977. Mem. Am., Va., Martinsville, Henry County bar assns., Am. Legion, Lambda Chi Alpha. K.P., Moose, Elk. Home: Route 4 Bassett VA 24055 Office: Main St Bassett VA 24055

PHILPOTT, JOHN EDWARDS, fin. cons.; b. Canton, Ohio, July 20, 1942; s. John Arthur and Margaret Louise (Edwards) P.; B.S., Purdue U., 1964, Ph.D., 1969; M. Real Estate, Am. Coll. Real Estate, 1974; m. Phyllis Jean Snyder, June 6, 1966; children—John Charles. Postdoctoral fellow Clark U. Worcester (Mass.) Found., 1969-70; staff scientist Southwest Found., San Antonio, 1970-72; founder, pres. Philpott Enterprises, San Antonio, 1972—; faculty Am. Coll. Real Estate, San Antonio, 1973-79; vis. prof. U. Tex., San Antonio, 1977; sr. instrs. Lowry/Nickerson Seminars, Reno, 1975—. NSF fellow, 1962-64; USPHS fellow, 1964-65; NIH fellow, 1965-69. Mem. Tex. Real Estate Tchrs. Assn. Club: Toastmasters (pres. 1974). Address: 20782 Tejas Trail E San Antonio TX 78257

PHIPPS, BENJAMIN KIMBALL, II, lawyer; b. Boston, Jan. 16, 1933; s. Benjamin Kimball and Bertha Elizabeth (Forsyth) P.; B.S. in Commerce, U. Va., 1955, LL.B., 1958; m. Phyllis Jarrett Anderson, Jan. 10, 1962; children—Lisa Jarrett, Christina Caroline. Admitted to Fla. bar, 1964; editor Municipal Code Corp., Tallahassee, 1964-65; practice law, Tallahassee, 1965—; counsel tax com. Fla. Ho. of Reps., 1966-70, counsel to speaker, 1972-74. Chmn. Historic Tallahassee Preservation Bd., 1970—; pres. Fla. Heritage Found., 1967. Trustee Maclay Sch.; adv. council WFSU-TV, chmn., 1978—. Served to capt., airborne arty. U.S. Army, 1958-64. Mem. Am. (tax sect.), Tallahassee bar assns., Fla. Bar (vice chmn. tax sect. 1978—, chmn. editorial bd. Jour./News 1979—), Jefferson Soc., Sigma Alpha Epsilon, Phi Alpha Delta, Phi Delta Epsilon. Clubs: Cosmos, Exchange, Tiger Bay (dir.), Economic, St. Andrews Soc. (pres. 1978-79), (Tallahassee). Contbr. articles in field. Home: Jubilee Thomasville Rd Tallahassee FL 32303 Office: PO Box 1351 Tallahassee FL 32302

PHLEGAR, CARL LESLIE, JR., electronics engr.; b. Springfield, Ohio, July 20, 1916; s. Carl Leslie and Beulah Emma (LaMarr) P.; student Anderson Coll., 1946-47, Valparaiso Tech. Inst., 1937-39, U. Iowa, 1960, Lake Mich. Coll., 1962; m. Thelma Virginia Morgan, Dec. 1, 1940; children—Kathy Lynn, Phillip Lee, Barbara Ann, Betty Jane. Engr., Radio Station WING, Dayton, Ohio, 1939-40, Allison Engring. Co., Indpls., 1940-44, Radio Station WHBU, Anderson, Ind., 1944-57; pres., dir. Micro-Lab. Industries, Anderson, 1951-58; chief engr. Rowe Industries, Toledo, 1958-59; sr. engr. Collins Radio Co., Cedar Rapids, Iowa, 1959-61, chief engr. Marine Products Health Co., St. Joseph, Mich., 1961-65; supr. Electronic Engring. Fed. Sign & Signal Corp., Blue Island, Ill., 1965-66; sr. engr. WABCO, Batesburg, S.C., 1966-68; quality information engr. Gen. Electric, Irmo, S.C., 1968-69; supr. antenna devel. Shakespeare Corp., Columbia, S.C., 1969-70; prof. electronic dept. Midlands Tech. Coll., Columbia, 1972—; pres., dir. GAR Electronics, Inc., Leesville, S.C., 1970—. Mem. AAUP, Am. Radio Relay League, IEEE. Baptist. Club: Ponderosa Country. Patentee fiberglass antenna. Home: 9 Turbeville Circle Leesville SC 29070

PHOENIX, GLORIA JONES, educator, univ. adminstr.; b. Norfolk, Va., June 19, 1941; d. Otis Ruppert and Carrie Allen (White) Jones; B.S., Va. Union U., 1963; postgrad. Miami U., 1963-64, U. Toledo, 1966-70, U. N.C., Chapel Hill, 1973-75; m. David Ducan Phoenix, Jr., Apr. 18, 1964; children—Diane Kimberley, Dayo Imani. Data analyst Lewis Research Center, NASA, Cleve., 1965-72; application programmer U. N.C., Chapel Hill, 1973-76, computer programmer lipid research program, dept. biostatistics, 1973-75; research asst. instl. research N.C. A & T State U., Greensboro, 1973, analyst programmer, 1976-77, planning asso., 1977-78, mgmt. info. systems coordinator, 1978—, instr. math., 1979—. Bd. dirs. Erwin Open Sch., Greensboro, 1978-80; treas. Black Women's Polit. Caucus, 1979-80. Recipient Cert. of Appreciation, Greensboro City Bd. Edn., 1979. Mem. Soc. Coll. and Univ. Planners, Assn. Computing Machinery, Digital Equipment Co. User Soc., N.C. Instl. Researchers, Delta Sigma Theta. Democrat. Baptist. Home: 2005 Acorn Rd Greensboro NC 27406 Office: 202 Noble Hall NC A&T State U Greensboro NC 27411

PIASTRA, ALAIN BERNARD, communications corp. exec.; b. Cusset, France, May 26, 1947; s. Henri D. and Marguerite M. (Lemasson) P.; M. in Data Processing, Coll. Arts and Scis., Paris, 1972; m. Margaret L. Tampke, Dec. 10, 1976. System-analyst INRA Biometric Lab., Nancy and Versailles, France, 1968-70; system engr., customer support mgr. Telsys, Paris, 1970-75, system network engr., Dallas, 1975-76, U.S. mgr., 1976—; cons. automation of banks, 1976-79; pres. ABP Assos., 1979—. Served with French Air Force, 1966-67. Mem. Internat. Fedn. Car Racing, French Fedn. Car Racing Assns., Alliance Francaise of Dallas (v.p. 1979-80). Home: 9420 Forestridge St Dallas TX 75238 Office: Telsys 8350 N Central Expressway Dallas TX 75206

PICKARD, BEN F. JONES, community coll. adminstr.; b. Memphis, Apr. 8, 1949; s. Lee Andrew and Betsy Jones (Shelton) P.; B.S.E., Ark. State U., 1971, M.S.E., 1974, Ed.S., 1980; m. Mary Anne Misenhimer, May 18, 1975. Counselor, Brinkley (Ark.) Public Schs., 1975-76; counselor spl. services program Miss. State U., Starkville, 1976-77; dir. spl. services program Three Rivers Community Coll., Poplar Bluff, Mo., 1977-78, East Ark. Community Coll., Forrest City, 1978—. Spl. Olympics coordinator Brinkley Public Schs., 1976. Mem. Am. Personnel and Guidance Assn., Am. Coll. Personnel Assn., Am. Assn. Higher Edn., So. Coll. Personnel Assn., S.W. Assn. Student Assistance Programs, Ark. Personnel and Guidance Assn., Ark. Coll. Personnel Assn., Ark. Assn. Student Assistance Programs, Sigma Pi (Outstanding Alumnus local chpt. 1975). Presbyterian. Club: Lions. Home: PO Box 1420 546 Calvert St Forrest City AR 72335 Office: East Arkansas Community College PO Box 4000 Forrest City AR 72335

PICKARD, JOSEPH LEE, clergyman, religious orgn. ofcl.; b. Charlotte, N.C., Mar. 17, 1937; s. James Bleecker and Helen Duffee (Tindal) P.; A.A., U. N.C., Charlotte, 1958; B.A., Presbyterian Coll., S.C., 1960; M.Div., Union Theol. Sem., Va., 1963; M. Christian Edn., Presbyn. Sch. of Christian Edn., Va., 1964; D.Min., McCormick Theol. Sem., Chgo., 1979; m. Annette Paige Gatlin, Jan. 25, 1963; 1 son, John Bleecker. Ordained to ministry Presbyterian Ch. in U.S., 1964; asst. minister First Presbyn. Ch., Greenville, N.C., 1964-68; asso. minister First Presbyn. Ch., Winston-Salem, N.C., 1968-74; asso. gen. presbyter for bus. affairs Presbytery of Concord, Presbyn. Ch. in U.S., Barium Springs, N.C., 1974—; adj. prof. fin. mgmt. McCormick Theol. Sem., Chgo., 1979—; mem. mission com. on stewardship edn. Presbyn. Synod of N.C., 1974-75, chairperson, 1974-75; commr. to 116th Gen. Assembly Presbyn. Ch. in U.S., 1976; cons. fin. mgmt. Presbyn. Ch. in U.S., 1977—. Mem. Mayor's Citizens Adv. Council, Greenville, N.C., 1965-67, chairperson, 1966-67. Mem. Am. Mgmt. Assn., Assn. of Presbyn. Ch. Educators, Presbyn. Ch. Bus. Adminstrs. Assn., Alpha Sigma Phi. Home: 905 Sherwood Ln Statesville NC 28677 Office: PO Drawer 129 Barium Springs NC 28010

PICKEL, CONRAD LAWRENZ, stained glass studio exec.; b. Neunburg, Germany, Feb. 10, 1906; s. Konrad and Katharina (Rauch) P.; came to U.S., 1927, naturalized; student Mayer Studios, Munich, Germany, Acad. Arts; m. Joan Friedlmaier, Dec. 1, 1933; children—Erma Pickel Obermayr, Robert Paul. Pres., owner Conrad Pickel Studio, Inc., New Berlin, Wis., 1945—, Fla., 1957—; owner, v.p. Gallery Fantasia, Boynton Beach, Fla., 1975—. Home: 500 SW 16th St Boynton Beach FL 33435 Office: 1000 S Federal Hwy Boynton Beach FL 33435 also 21415 W Greenfield Ave New Berlin WI 53151 also 7777 20th St Vero Beach FL 32960

PICKENS, JAMES CAIN, obstetrician, gynecologist; b. Atlanta, Feb. 1, 1938; s. John William and Cindia Althea (Cain) P.; student Emory U., 1955-57; B.S., U. Ga., 1959; M.D., Med. Coll. Ga., 1963; m. Barbara Ellen Spaulding, Dec. 10, 1964; children—Christopher James, John Carter, Kimberly Ann. Intern Macon (Ga.) Hosp., 1963-64; resident Columbia Hosp., George Washington U., Washington, 1964-67; practice medicine specializing in obstetrics and gynecology Permonente Med. Group, Hayward, Cal., 1969-71, Toccoa (Ga.) Clinic, 1971—; staff Permanente Hosp., Hayward, 1969-71; chief obstetrics and gynecology Stephens County Hosp., Toccoa, 1971—; faculty Toccoa Falls Inst., 1971—. Mem. state task force maternal and infant care, State Ga., 1974-75; regionalization sub-com., steering com. Health Service for N.E. Ga., 1974-75. Served with USAF, 1967-69. Diplomate Am. Bd. Obstetrics and Gynecology; cert. instrument flight instr. Fellow Am. Coll. Obstetrics and Gynecology, A.C.S.; mem. C. of C. U.S. Air Force Res. Assn., Mensa. Clubs: Elks, Rotary. Contbr. articles to profl. jours. Home: Route 3 Camp Mikell Rd Toccoa GA 30577 Office: 800 E Doyle St Toccoa GA 30577

PICKENS, WILLIAM DEAN, union ofcl.; b. Houston, Oct. 20, 1932; s. Thomas Conley and Artie (Maxwell) P.; ed. public schs., trade courses, spl. course U. Houston; m. Doris Ann Doss, June 3, 1971; children—Patricia Lou Cunningham, Doral Dean. Mem. United Assn. Nat. Journeymen and Apprentices of Plumbing and Pipe Fitting Industry U.S. and Can., 1956—, mem. local exec. bd., 1965-70, bus. agt., 1970-79, mem. tng. com. U.S. and Can., 1977—, pres. Gulf Coast Council Plumbers and Steamfitters, 1971—, bus. mgr. local 68, Houston, 1972—; adviser Plumbers Apprentice Com. of Houston; bd. trustees Plumbers Health and Welfare and Pension Plan; del. Harris County AFL-CIO and Tex. AFL-CIO; dir. com. polit activities. Served with USAF, 1951-55. Mem. Nat. Rifle Assn. (life), VFW. Democrat. Mem. Christian Ch. Home: 12702 Craigwood St Cypress TX 77429 Office: PO Box 8746 502 Link Rd Houston TX 77009

PICKENS, WILLIAM STEWART, cardiologist; b. Bentonville, Ark., Dec. 16, 1940; s. William Craig and Mary Elizabeth (McFarland) P.; B.S., U. Ark., Fayetteville, 1962; M.D., U. Ark., Little Rock, 1966; m. Patricia Dee Hughes, Nov. 8, 1975; children—Holly, Heather, Brian. Rotating intern Tampa (Fla.) Gen. Hosp., 1966-67; resident in radiology U. Fla. Med. Center, Gainesville, 1970-72; resident in internal medicine, then fellow in cardiology U. S. Fla. Med. Center, Tampa, 1972-75; fellow in cardiovascular radiology U. Fla. Med. Center, 1974; staff physician VA Hosp., Tampa, 1974-75; practice medicine specializing in cardiology, Pensacola, Fla., 1976—; mem. staff Baptist Hosp., Sacred Heart Hosp.; asst. prof. radiology and internal medicine U. Ark., Little Rock, 1975-76. Served as officer M.C., USAF, 1967-72; maj. Res. Rockefeller scholar, 1958-59; U. Ark. Alumni scholar, 1958-60; Edn. Found. scholar, 1958-62; Barton Found. scholar, 1965; C.V. Mosby scholar, 1966; diplomate Am. Bd. Internal Medicine. Mem. Sigma Xi (asso.), Alpha Omega Alpha, Phi Eta Sigma, Alpha Epsilon Delta. Republican. Episcopalian. Home: 6520 Scenic Hwy Pensacola FL 32504 Office: 1717 North E St Suite 503 Pensacola FL 32501

PICKERING, GEORGE ROSCOE, state legislator, farmer; b. Clarksville, Tenn., Aug. 12, 1912; s. George Roscoe and Annie Geneva (Nichols) P.; B.S. in Agr., Austin Peay State U.; m. Dorothy Heflin, Dec. 30, 1932; children—Bobby Dean, William Howard, Linda Gail. Engaged in farming, Adams, Tenn., 1940—; mem. Tenn. Ho. of Reps. from 68th Dist., 1967—, chmn. agr. com. Mem. Tenn. Livestock Assn., Montgomery County Farm Bur., Clarksville C. of C. Democrat. Mem. Ch. of Christ. Address: Route 1 Adams TN 37010

PICKETT, GEORGE BIBB, JR., ret. mil. officer; b. Montgomery, Ala., Mar. 20, 1918; s. George B. and Marie (Dow) P.; B.S., U.S. Mil. Acad., 1941; student Nat. War Coll., 1959-60; m. Beryl Arlene Robinson, Dec. 27, 1941; children—Barbara Pickett Harrell, James, Kathleen, Thomas. Commd. 2d. lt. U.S. Army, 1941, advanced through grades to maj. gen., 1966; instr. Inf. Sch., Fort Benning, Ga., 1947-50, instr. Armed Forces Staff Coll., Norfolk, Va., 1956-59; comdg. officer 2d Armored Cavalry Regiment, 1961-63; chief of staff Combat Devel. Command, 1963-66; comdg. gen. 2d. inf. div., Korea, 1966-67; ret., 1973; field rep. Nat. Rifle Assn., 1973—. Decorated Purple Heart with oak leaf cluster, D.S.M. with two oak leaf clusters, Bronze Star with two oak leaf clusters and V device, Silver Star, Legion of Merit with two oak leaf clusters, Commendation medal with two oak leaf clusters. Mem. SAR, Old South Hist. Assn., Ala. Assn. Engrs. and Land Surveyors, Am. Legion, VFW, Nat. Rifle Assn. (sr. rep. for Southeastern U.S.). Episcopalian. Club: Kiwanis (chmn. 1974—). Author: (with others) Joint and Combined Staff Officers Manual, 1959; contbr. articles on mil. affairs to profl. jours. Home: 3525 Flowers St Montgomery AL 36109 Office: PO Box 4 Montgomery AL 36101

PICKETT, JOSEPH C., govt. ofcl.; b. Dearborn, Mich., July 19, 1943; s. Orlie W. and Wilda D. (Pummill) P.; B.S., Troy State Coll., 1966, B.S. in Edn., 1969, Ed.S., 1979; M.A. C.T., Auburn U., 1971, M.P.A., 1979. Tchr., Lyman Ward Mil. Acad., Camp Hill, Ala., 1969-70; tchr. Goshen (Ala.) High Sch., 1971-72; teaching fellow in sociology Union Coll., Barbourville, Ky., 1972-73; social sci. coordinator, sr. faculty mem. social scis. Mohave Community Coll., Kingman, Ariz., 1973-77; grad. research asst. Center for Govt. and Pub. Affairs, Auburn U., Montgomery, Ala., 1978; program dir. arts adminstrn. Ala. Council on Arts and Humanities, Montgomery, 1978-79; Presdl. mgmt. intern, public adminstr., contract specialist NASA, Marshall Space Flight Center, Huntsville, Ala., 1979—; practicum Ala. Commn. Aging; Montgomery, 1977. Bd. dirs. Mohave Big Bros., 1973-76. Mem. Am. Assn. Higher Edn., Am. Soc. for Public Adminstrn., Pi Sigma Alpha, Kappa Delta Pi, Phi Delta Kappa, Delta Chi. Home: 1500 Sparkman Dr Apt 29J Huntsville AL 35805

PICKLE, JAMES JARRELL (JAKE), congressman; b. Roscoe, Tex., Oct. 11, 1913; s. J. B. and Mary P.; B.A., U. Tex.; m. Beryl Bolton McCarroll; children—Peggy Pickle Norris, Richard McCarroll and Graham McCarroll. Area dir. Nat. Youth Adminstrn., 1938-41; co-organizer Sta. KVET, Austin, Tex.; pub. relations and advt. bus.; dir. Tex. Democratic Exec. Com., 1957-60; mem. Tex. Employment Commn., 1961-63; mem. 88th-96th congresses 10th Dist. Tex. Served with USNR, World War II. Office: 242 Cannon House Office Bldg Washington DC 20515

PICO-SANTIAGO, GUILLERMO, ophthalmologist; b. Coamo, P.R., Dec. 9, 1915; s. Arturo and Maria-Teresa (Santiago) Pico; M.D., U. Md., 1940; m. Ivette Munoz, Jan. 1, 1970; children—Guillermo Mercedes, Carmencita, Guillermito, Jaime Arturo. Intern, Presbyn. Hosp., San Juan, P.R., 1940-41; resident ophthalmology St. Luke's Hosp., N.Y.C., 1945-46; asst. to Dr. Ramon Castroviejo, N.Y.C., 1946-48; practice medicine, specializing in ophthalmology, Santurce, P.R., 1948—; attending ophthalmologist, head dept. Ophthalmology San Juan Mcpl. Hosp., 1948-77, Univ. Hosp., San Juan, 1952-77, VA Hosp., San Juan, 1957-77; prof., head dept. ophthalmology Sch. Medicine, U. P.R., 1952-77, prof. emeritus dept ophthalmology, 1979—; dir. United Fed. Savs. Bank, San Juan. Chmn. Cancer League campaign, P.R., 1959. Bd. dirs. A.R.C., San Juan, 1958-63, chmn., 1958. Mem. AMA, Am. Ophthalmology Soc., A.C.S., P.R. Med. Assn. (pres. 1957), Am. Assn. Ophthalmology and Otolaryngology (3d v.p. 1970), Pan Am. Assn. Ophthalmology. Roman Catholic. Lion. Contbr. articles to profl. jours. Home: 2042 Jose Fidalgo Diaz-Rio Piedras PR 00927 Office: 1475 Wilson Ave Santurce PR 00907

PICOU, EDWARD BEAUREGARD, JR., paleontologist; b. Baton Rouge, Mar. 26, 1932; s. Edward Beauregard and Eugenia Violet (Babin) P.; B.S., La. State U., 1955. Paleontologist, Shell Oil Co., Baton Rouge, New Orleans, 1957-65, div. paleontologist, Lafayette, La., New Orleans, Houston, 1966-70, New Orleans, 1971-79, sr. staff paleontologist, div. paleontologist, New Orleans, 1979—. Served with U.S. Army, 1955-57. Mem. Soc. Econ. Paleontologists and Mineralogists (v.p.), AAAS, Am. Assn. Petroleum Geologists, Paleontological Soc., Paleontological Research Inst., New Orleans Geol. Soc., Houston Geol. Soc. Democrat. Roman Catholic. Contbr. articles to profl. jours. Home: 6771 Canal Blvd New Orleans LA 70124 Office: Shell Oil PO Box 60124 New Orleans LA 70160

PIEH, SAMUEL HINGHA, environ. health specialist; b. Sierra Leone, West Africa, July 9, 1948; came to U.S., 1968, naturalized, 1974; s. Peter and Nancy Pieh; student Grace Coll., 1968-69; B.A., Ind. Central U., 1972; postgrad. Butler U., 1972-73; M.P.H., U. Mich., 1975; m. Clara Denise Johnson, Mar. 25, 1978; 1 son, Samuel Hingha. Lab. asst. Ind. Central U., Indpls., 1970-72; asst. environ. microbiologist Indpls. Public Health Lab., 1972-74; asst. prof., coordinator environ. health Miss. Valley State U., Itta Bena, 1974—; mem. Miss. Gov.'s Steering Com. for Water and Waste water Initiative, 1979-80; cons. in field. Phelps-Stokes scholar Caribbean-Am. Exchange program, 1979; registered profl. environmentalist, Tenn. Mem. Nat. Environ. Health Assn., Miss. Assn. Santiarians, Miss. Public Health Assn. Democrat. Methodist. Home: 3793 Marty St Memphis TN 38109 Office: PO Box 8 Mississippi Valley State Univ Itta Bena MS 38941

PIEPER, PATRICIA R., artist, photographer; b. Paterson, N.J., Jan. 28, 1923; d. Francis William and Barbara Margareth (Ludwig) Farabaugh; student Baron von Palm, 1937-39, Deal (N.J.) Conservatory, summers 1939, 40, Utah State U., 1950-52; m. George F. Pieper, July 1, 1941; 1 dau., Patricia Lynn. One-woman shows: Charles Russell Mus., Great Falls, Mont., 1955, Fisher Gallery, Washington, 1966, Tampa City Library, 1977, 78, 79; exhibited in group shows: Davidson Art Gallery, Middletown, Conn., 1968, Helena (Mont.) Hist. Mus., 1955, Dept. Commerce Alaska Statehood Show, 1959, Joslyn Mus., Omaha, 1961, Denver Mus. Natural History, 1955; represented in pvt. collections. Pres., Bell Lake Assn., 1976-80; mem. Pasco County (Fla.) Water Adv. Council, 1978—, chmn., 1979-80. Recipient 2d and 6th pl. prizes Gen. Tel. All-Fla. Photo Competition, 1979. Mem. Nat. League Am. Pen Women (v.p. Tampa 1976-78, Woman of Year award 1977-78), Land O' Lakes C. of C. (dir. 1979-80; award), Fla. Geneal. Soc., Cambria County (Pa.) Geneal. Soc. Clubs: Lutz, Land O' Lakes Women's. Home and Studio: PO Box 15 Land O' Lakes FL 33539

PIERCE, CLARENCE ALBERT, JR., state legislator; b. Thornton, Miss., Oct. 1, 1928; s. Clarence Albert and Alice Vaiden (Herring) P.; B.A., U. Miss., 1950. Mem. Miss. Ho. of Reps., 1952—, chmn. interstate cooperation, 1957—, chmn. hwys. and hwy. financing com., 1972—. Mem. S.A.R., Miss. Gettysburg Meml. Commn., Carroll

County Farm Bur., Beta Theta Pi, Omicron Delta Kappa. Democrat. Episcopalian. Mason. Home: PO Box 277 Vaiden MS 39176

PIERCE, CLEVELAND CARROLL, banker; b. Opp, Ala., Jan. 3, 1921; s. Grover Cleveland and Georgia B. (Carroll) P.; student Marion Inst., 1935-39, La. State U. Sch. Banking, 1960-62; m. Kathryn Eloise Mathews, Dec. 9, 1939; children—Caroline (Mrs. Roger F. Etheridge), Louise (Mrs. Rowayne Harper), Rebecca (Mrs. Ronald McLeod), George C. With First Nat. Bank Opp, 1939—, asst. cashier, 1945-49, v.p., cashier, 1949-64, pres., dir., 1964—. Trustee Mizell Meml. Hosp., Opp, 1968—; bd. dirs. Lurleen B. Wallace Jr. Coll. Found.; bd. dirs. Opp Hist. Soc., Covington County Mental Health Assn. Served with Transport Service, AUS, 1943-46; ETO. Mem. Ala., Am., Independent bankers assns., Opp C. of C. (1st v.p. 1975-76, past pres., dir.). Methodist (trustee ch.). Mason (Shriner). Clubs: Civitan (dir. 1969-70), Country (Opp). Home: 203 E Ida Ave Opp AL 36467 Office: PO Drawer A Opp AL 36467

PIERCE, GEORGE FOSTER, JR., architect; b. Dallas, June 22, 1919; s. George Foster and Hallie Louise (Crutchfield) P.; student So. Methodist U., 1937-39; B.A., Rice U., 1942, B.S. in Architecture, 1943; diplome de architecture Ecole Des Beaux Arts, Fountainbleau, France, 1958; m. Betty Jean Reistle, Oct. 17, 1942; children—Ann Louis Pierce Arnett, George Foster III, Nancy Reistle. Founding partner Pierce, Goodwin, Alexander, Architects, Houston, 1947—. Trustee, Tex. Archtl. Found., 1960—, pres. 1974-75; trustee Mus. Nat. Sci., Houston; pres. Houston Contemporary Arts Mus., 1956-57, chmn. bd., 1957-58. Served as ensign AC, USNR, World War II. Named One of 5 Outstanding Young Texans, 1954. Fellow AIA (nat. chmn. com. on aesthetics 1963-64, nat. chmn. com. on chpt. affairs 1958-60), Sociedad Architectos Mexicanos (hon.); mem. Tex. Soc. Architects (pres. 1964), Houston C. of C. (chmn. future studies com. 1977-78). Methodist. Clubs: Houston Country, Petroleum of Houston, Rotary (Houston); Riverhill Country (Kerrville, Tex.). Architect: 4 prin. terminals and terminal area planning Houston Intercontinental Airport, Petroleum Club of Houston, Two Houston Center, Houston Mus. Natural Sci., 7 bldgs. Rice U., 2 bldgs. U. Houston. Office: PO Box 13319 Houston TX 77019

PIERCE, GERALD SWETNAM, business cons.; b. Sapulpa, Okla., Aug. 17, 1933; s. Harold Ellis and Mary Katherine (Snell) P.; student U. Tex. at Austin, 1953-54; A.B., Harvard, 1955; M.A. (Univ. fellow), U. Miss. at Oxford, 1956, Ph.D. (NDEA fellow), 1963; postgrad. U. N.M. at Albuquerque, 1956-57; m. Janis Fay Vaughn, May 27, 1956; children—Ann Elizabeth Swetnam, John Willard. Foreign Service officer U.S. Dept. State, Washington, also Rio de Janeiro, Brazil, 1957-60; asst. prof. history U. Miss. at Oxford, 1963-64; asst. prof. history Memphis State U., 1964-67, asso. prof., 1967-70, prof., 1970-80, also dir. internat. studies, 1974-75; pres. Consultants System Inc., 1975—; mem. firm Burleigh/Pierce, 1980—. Chmn., Tenn. Council on Internat. Edn., 1974-75; mem. Memphis Hist. Heritage Com., 1974-80, Forum for a Better Memphis; mem. Employee Benefits Council Memphis and Shelby County. Recipient Author's award for Tex., Theta Sigma Phi, 1969. Am. Philos. Soc. grantee, 1966-67. Mem. Am., So., Western, Mo., Okla. hist. assns., Orgn. Am. Historians, Inst. Soc., Ethics and Life Scis. (asso.), Internat. Assn. Fin. Planners, Phi Kappa Phi. Club: Harvard. Author: Texas Under Arms, 1969, Travels in the Republic of Texas, 1842, 1971. Gen. editor: Narratives of the American West, a series, 1971-77. Asso. editor Mil. History of Texas and the Southwest, a jour., 1969-77. Contbr. articles in field to profl. jours. Home: 4743 Park Ave Memphis TN 38117

PIERCE, JAMES ERIC, sociologist; b. St. Louis, Feb. 23, 1940; s. Eric F. and Virginia F. (Fears) P.; B.A., Miss. State U., 1961; B.D., Candler Sch. Theology, 1963; Ph.D., Emory U., 1977; m. Karen Marie Gregg, Oct. 7, 1977; children—Pamela, Heather. Asst. prof. sociology Lambuth Coll., Jackson, Tenn., 1969-71; coll. minister, dir. student activities Pfeiffer Coll., Misenheimer, N.C., 1972-78, asso. prof. sociology, 1978—; pres. Island Motels, Inc.; prin. Med. Cons. and Personnel Assos. Served with U.S. Army, 1964-69. Decorated Bronze Star, Purple Heart. Mem. So. Sociol. Soc., Alpha Kappa Delta, Phi Alpha Theta. Democrat. Methodist. Club: Rotary. Home: PO Box 595 Misenheimer NC 28109 Office: Pfeiffer Coll Misenheimer NC 28109

PIERCE, JANE ROSS, pharmacist; b. Monticello, Ark., Aug. 18, 1950; d. Joseph Mitchell and Corrinne (Shultz) Ross; student Ark. A&M Coll., 1968-70, Henderson State U., 1970; B.S., U. Ark. Med. Center, 1974; m. Jackson Erwin Pierce, Aug. 14, 1971; children—Jill Elaine, Jefferson Kendrick Allen. With Ross & Ross, Attys., Monticello, 1964-71; bookkeeper Treadway Electric, Little Rock, 1972; pharmacy clk. Consumers Pharmacy, Little Rock, Williamson Drug, North Little Rock, Ark., 1973, Rhea Drugs, Little Rock, 1973-74; pharmacist Monticello Drugs, 1974-76; chief pharmacist Drew Meml. Hosp., Monticello, 1977—; cons. pharmacist Leisure Lodge Nursing Home, 1978—; nursing home cons. Pharmacist Monticello Drug Abuse Campaign, 1974-75. Mem. Ark. Pharmacists Assn., Ark. Hosp. Pharmacists Assn., AAUW. Presbyterian. Club: Contract Bridge League. Office: Drew Meml Hosp Box 538 Monticello AR 71655

PIERCE, MARAH GAYLE, computer co. exec.; b. Franklinton, La., Apr. 1, 1938; d. Woodrow and Melba (Jenkins) Pierce; student Houston Conservatory Music, 1957-59, U. Houston, 1960-62, Thomas A. Edison Coll., 1977-78. Exec. sec. Gt. So. Life Ins. Co., Houston, 1958-62, computer programmer, 1962-64; programmer/analyst United Services Automobile Assn., San Antonio, 1964-69; research analyst computer div. RCA, Houston, 1969-70, project mgr., 1970, edn. mgr., 1970-71; systems mgr. Sperry Univac, Bellaire, Tex., 1972, So. ops. edn. mgr., 1972-75, sr. sales rep., 1975-77, account exec., 1977—. Bd. dirs. Houston Area Fed. Feminist Credit Union. Recipient Superior Systems Performance award RCA, 1969, Mktg. Achievement Club award, 1970, 71, Tiger Club award Univac SW region, 1972, Mktg. Quota Achievement Club award, 1976, 77, 78, 79; mem. Univac Million Dollar Club, 1976, 77, 78, 79. Mem. Data Processing Mgmt. Assn., Assn. Systems Mgrs., Life Office Mgmt. Assn., NOW, Tex. Women's Polit. Caucus. Methodist. Home: 5633 S Rice Ave Houston TX 77081 Office: 6700 W Loop S Suite 200 Bellaire TX 77401

PIERCE, MARY JANE, ednl. adminstr.; b. Batesville, Ark., Oct. 25, 1950; d. Nevyle G. and Bobbie M. (Hood) P.; A.B. magna cum laude, Ark. Coll., 1972; Ed.M., Memphis State U., 1975; M.A., Scarritt Coll., 1977. Land title abstractor Batesville Ins. & Abstract Co., 1972-73; youth dir. First United Meth. Ch., Beebe, Ark., 1975; grad. asst. Scarritt Coll., Nashville, 1976-77; dir. Christian edn. Univ. United Meth. Ch., Chapel Hill, N.C., 1977—; mem. adj. faculty Scarritt Coll., summer 1979. Trustee Scarritt Coll.; com. chairperson Heart Assn., Chapel Hill, 1979; UNICEF coordinator, Chapel Hill, 1979. Mem. N.C. Conf. Christian Educators Fellowship (sec.), Nat. Christian Educators Fellowship, Alpha Xi Delta. Democrat. United Methodist. Home: 20 Lanark Rd Chapel Hill NC 27514 Office: 150 E Franklin St Chapel Hill NC 27514

PIERCE, OPAL COLE, trade co. exec.; b. Bristol, Va., Nov. 26, 1926; d. Guy Marcus and Margret Elizabeth (Thomas) Cole; A.A., Bristol Community Coll., 1944; student fin. mgmt. Forsyth Tech. Inst., 1974, mgmt. devel. U. N.C., 1974; m. Oakley Cecil Pierce, July 5, 1947; 1 son, Michael Dean. Sec., Va. Dept. Hwys., Bristol, 1944-56; sec., J.W. Burress, Inc., Winstn-Salem, N.C., 1956-61, office mgr., 1961—. Sec. adminstrv. bd. Arcadia United Meth. Ch., Clemmons, N.C., 1967, treas., 1969—; sec. bd. dirs. Arcadia Fire Dept., 1975—. named woman of yr., 1976. Mem. Adminstrv. Mgmt. Soc. (sec. Va., N.C., S.C. area 1972—, pres. Winston-Salem chpt. 1973-74, Merit award 1972, Diamond Merit award 1974). Democrat. Home: Route 2 Clemmons NC 27012 Office: JW Burress Inc 3760 N Liberty St Winston-Salem NC 27105

PIERCE, ROBERT CARL, ins. agency exec.; b. Richton Park, Ill., June 19, 1933; s. Henry Harris and Eva Irene (Hanes) P.; student U. Ill., 1956-59; m. Sheryll Ann Wessels, Aug. 25, 1956; children—Robert Carl, Teresa Kaye, Timothy Allen, Deborah Jean. Mgr. circulation sales Chgo. Tribune, 1955-60; state mgr. Am. Mutual Ins. Co., 1960-65; owner Pierce Ins. Service, 1965-68; underwriting supr. Md. Casualty Co., Louisville, 1968; mktg. rep. Ins. Co. of N.Am., Louisville, 1968-72; v.p. Stewart G. Brown & Assos., Louisville, 1972-74; pres. Associated Agency Mgmt. Inc., Louisville, 1974—; dir. Mass Mktg. Inc. Served with U.S. Army, 1953-55. Mem. Ind. Ins. Agents Ky., Louisville Ins. Bd., Profl. Ins. Agents Ky., Ind. Ins. Agents Am. Republican. Mem. United Ch. of Christ. Clubs: Masons, Shriners. Home: 3500 Marlin Dr Jeffersontown KY 40299 Office: 141 N Sherrin Ave Louisville KY 40207

PIERCE, SHARON ELIZABETH, vocat. evaluator; b. Asheboro, N.C., July 3, 1954; d. John Wesley and Golda Melma (McKinnon) P.; B.A. in Psychology and Spl. Edn., Central Wesleyan Coll., S.C., 1976; M.Ed. in Guidance and Counseling, U. N.C., Greensboro, 1979. Spl. edn. tchr. Walhalla (S.C.) High Sch., 1976; vocat. evaluator, adult devel. activity program coordinator, Randolph Sheltered Workshop, Asheboro, 1976—. Sunday Sch. tchr. Rushwood Park Wesleyan Ch., Asheboro, 1976—. Mem. Am. Personnel and Guidance Assn., Nat. Rehab. Assn., Vocat. Evaluation and Work Adjustment Assn. Republican. Mem. Wesleyan Ch. Home: 1001 Sherwood Ave Asheboro NC 27203 Office: PO Box 1367 Asheboro NC 27203

PIERSON, BONNIE COLLINS, sch. counselor; b. Corsicana, Tex., Nov. 4, 1943; d. Bill and Reba (Edmundson) Collins; B.A., Sam Houston State U., 1965; M.Ed., U. Houston, 1968; m. E. Benjamin Pierson, Nov. 27, 1970; stepchildren—Ben, Kitty, Richard, Greg. Tchr. English and French, Cy-Fair High Sch., Cypress-Fairbanks Ind. Sch. Dist., Houston, 1965-68, counselor Dean Jr. High Sch., 1968-70; counselor Del Valle (Tex.) Mid-Sch., 1970—. Mem. Am. Assn. Retarded Citizens, NEA, Tex. Tchrs. Assn., Am. Personnel and Guidance Assn., Tex. Personnel and Guidance Assn. (lobbyist 1977—, pres.-elect. 1979-80), Am. Sch. Counselors Assn., Tex. Sch. Counselors Assn. (pres. 1978-79), Am. Assn. for Humanistic Edn. and Devel., Tex. Assn. for Humanistic Edn. and Devel., Tex. Career Guidance Assn., Tex. Assn. Non-White Concerns, Tex. Assn. Counselor Edn. and Supervision, Tex. Assn. Measurement and Evaluation in Guidance, Kappa Delta Pi, Alpha Chi Omega. Democrat. Presbyterian. Home: 10916 River Terr Austin TX 78746 Office: Del Valle Mid-School Del Valle TX 78617

PIGG, JOHN ORAN, metal mfg. co. exec.; b. Monroe, N.C., May 24, 1936; s. Oran A. and Annie (Helms) P.; B.S. in Edn., N.C. State U., 1958; mgmt. course Am. Mgmt. Assn., 1978; m. Margaret Flowers, Aug. 31, 1958; 1 son, Johnny Scott. Salesman to sales mgr. Teledyne Allvac, Monroe, N.C., 1965-71; mfg. mgr., v.p. Teledyne Titanium, Monroe, 1971-76, prodn. mgr., 1976—. Pres., Jr. C. of C., 1965-66, named Young Man of Yr., Marshville, 1967; dist. chmn. Central N.C. council Boy Scouts Am., 1978-79; co-chmn. Wingate Coll., 1977. Mem. Am. Soc. Metals. Republican. Methodist. Clubs: Civitan (pres., 1960-61), Rotary (treas., 1979). Home: Route 4 Box 220 Marshville NC 28103 Office: Teledyne Titanium PO Box 759 Monroe NC 28110

PIGG, WILLIAM HARVEY, sales exec.; b. Long Branch, N.J., May 10, 1924; s. Albert Milton and Emaline Celeste (Shead) P.; student Monmouth Jr. Coll., 1941-42, U. Va., 1942-44; A.B., So. Meth. U., 1949; m. Geraldine Beth Stroud, Apr. 17, 1949; children—Linda Jane, William Albert. Salesman Jefferson Standard Life Ins., Houston, 1946-48; salesman Radio City Distbg. Co., Dallas, 1949-55; factory rep. Gen. Electric Co., Louisville, 1955-57, advt. mgr., Indpls., 1957-65, mgr. sales tng., Dallas, 1965—. Active Boy Scouts Am. Served with U.S. Army, 1944-46, 50-53. Decorated Bronze Star medal with oak leaf cluster. Home: 3318 Lancelot Dr Dallas TX 75229 Office: Gen Electric Co 8401 Carpentar Freeway Dallas TX 75247

PILCHER, JAMES BROWNIE, lawyer; b. Shreveport, La., May 19, 1929; s. James Reese and Mattie (Brown) P.; B.A., La. State U., 1952; J.D. summa cum laude, John Marshall Law Sch., 1955; postgrad. Emory U.; m. Frances M. Pettit, Jan. 28, 1951; children—Lydia, Martha, Bradley. Admitted to Ga. bar, 1955, since practiced in Atlanta; legal counsel to speaker Ga. Ho. of Reps., 1961-64; asso. city atty. Atlanta, 1965-70; prof. law John Marshall Law Sch., 1955-59, 65—; pres. Trans-Atlanta Properties, Inc. Mem. Ga. Democratic Exec. Com., 1962-66, pres. Active Voters, 1966-69; pres. Young Dem. Club Fulton County, 1964-65, Ga., 1965-66; chmn. Fulton County Dem. Com., 1969-71. Bd. dirs. Whitehead Boys' Club. Served with USNR, 1946-48. Named Outstanding Young Man of Atlanta in Community Affairs, 1962, Ga., 1963. Mem. Am., Ga., Atlanta bar assns., Am. Trial Lawyers Assn., Atlanta Jaycees (pres. 1961-62). Baptist. Clubs: Kiwanis, West Paces Racquet. Home: 434 Brentwood Dr NE Atlanta GA 30305 Office: 63 14th St NE Atlanta GA 30309

PILCHER, JOE THOMAS, JR., lawyer; b. Selma, Ala., Oct. 11, 1929; s. Joe Thomas and Emmie Lundie (Sinclair) P.; B.S., Auburn U., 1951; LL.B., U. Ala., 1953; m. Anne E. Galt, Dec. 28, 1950; children—John Edward, Joseph Thomas, Mary Egleston, Emmie Sinclair. Admitted to Ala. bar, 1953; asso. firm Hill, Hill, Whiting, Harris, and Pilcher, Montgomery, Ala., 1955-58, firm Pilcher, Wright, Long and Booth, Montgomery, 1958-60; individual practice law, Selma, Ala., 1960—; prof. law, Jones Law Sch.; pres., dir. Asso. Builders, Inc., Associated Gulf Land Corp., Pilcher Land Corp., Pilcher Mortgage Co., Ala. Gulf Coast Devel. Corp., Ala. Point Properties, Inc.; dir. Capital Nat. Bank of Montgomery, Town-Country Nat. Bank, Mut. Savs. Life Ins. Co; Dallas County Dist. Atty., 1968-71. Dir. Waterworks and Sewer Bd., Selma, 1968—; dir., sec., treas. Craig Field Airport and Indsl. Authority, 1977—; v.p. Selma and Dallas County C. of C., 1977-78, pres., 1978—; atty. Dallas County Bd. Edn., 1966—; active Tukabatchee Area council Boy Scouts Am., 1955—; state pres. Young Democrats Ala., 1951-53. Served with staff Judge Adv. USAF, 1953-55. Recipient Farrah Order Jurisprudence, 1953. Mem. Am., Ala., Dallas County (pres.) Bar Assns., Ala. Trial Lawyers Assn., Ala. Defense Lawyers Assn., Am. Soc. Legal History, Am. Judicature Soc., Law-Sci. Acad. Am., Phi Alpha Delta. Democrat. Episcopalian. Clubs: Selma Country, Capitol City, Selma Hunting and Fishing, Elks, Pi Kappa Phi. Asso. editor Ala. Law Review, 1952-53. Home: 11 Chambliss Dr Selma AL 36701 Office: 28 Broad St Selma AL 36701

PILKO, GEORGE, chem./energy industry cons.; b. N.Y.C., Feb. 21, 1949; s. Peter J. and Martha (Tonti) P.; B.S.E. in Chem. Engring., U. Mich., 1971, M.B.A., 1973; m. Susan M. Wasvary, Apr. 28, 1973; 1 son, Brian George. Energy planner, project mgr., coal project Olin Chems., Stamford, Conn., 1973-75, sales rep., indsl. chems., Houston, 1975-77, coll. recruiter, 1974; chem. mktg. cons. Pace Cons. & Engrs., Houston, 1977-78, mgr. environ. mgmt. services, 1978-80; pres. Pilko & Assos., Inc., Houston, 1980—. Vice pres. Trailwood Village Community Assn., 1978-79 Recipient Branston prize U. Mich., 1968; Eiseman scholar, 1967-71. Mem. U. Mich. Alumni Club (dir. Houston chpt.). Contbr. articles to profl. jour. Home: 2215 Laurel Hill Kingwood TX 77339 Office: 9800 Northwest Freeway Suite 602 Houston TX 77092

PILLAR, HAROLD A., mgmt. engring. cons.; b. Aliquippa, Pa., June 28, 1941; s. James Walter and Jean Dixon (Byers) P.; B.S. in Indsl. Engring., Geneva Coll., 1966; M.B.A., U. Pitts., 1969; M.S.E., W.Va. U., 1972; m. Eileen Mary Fogarty, Oct. 14, 1967; children—David Dickson, Heather Anne. Project engr., Nabisco, Pitts., 1967; design engr. William Bailey Co., Pitts., 1968; asst. dir. engring. Emerson Electric Co., McKees Rocks, Pa., 1969-71; internal cons. Columbia Gas Co., Pitts., 1971-73; indsl. engr. J.H. Heinz Co., Pitts., 1973; mgr. mfg. engring. Badger Powhatan div. Am. LaFrance, Charlottesville, Va., 1974; pres. Harold A. Pillar Inc., Scottsville, Va., 1974—. Bd. dirs. Scottsville Mus. Served with USAF, 1963-69. Registered profl. engr., Pa., Md., Va., W.Va., Washington. Recipient grant HEW, 1972. Mem. Am. Inst. Indsl. Engrs., Nat., Va. socs. profl. engrs., Inst. Mgmt. Scis. Republican. Episcopalian. Home: Rt 1 Box 65C Scottsville VA 24590 Office: Larrah Lair Scottsville VA 24590

PILLOW, DORIS LATTA, nurse; b. Roxboro, N.C., May 28, 1932; d. Joseph Edward and Bertha Beatrice (Lloyd) Latta; R.N. diploma Watts Hosp. Sch. Nursing, Durham, N.C., 1955; m. Ernest Wilson Pillow, Oct. 15, 1955 (dec. Jan. 1976); children—Denise Leigh, Lynne Marie, Ernest Wilson, Deborah Kay. Head nurse surg. ward Leigh Meml. Hosp., Norfolk, Va., 1955-56, head nurse geriatrics, 1960; relief evening and night supr. Person County Meml. Hosp., Roxboro, 1957-58, emergency room supr., asst. dir. nurses, 1962—; asst. night supr. Eastern State Hosp., Williamsburg, Va., 1958-60; emergency med. technician examiner and tchr.; mobil intensive care nurse; tchr. CPR. Democrat. Methodist. Home: PO Box 1047 Roxboro NC 27573 Office: 615 Ridge Rd Roxboro NC 27573

PINCKNEY, LAWRENCE REID, audiovisual co. exec.; b. Orangeburg, S.C., Nov. 15, 1921; s. Samuel Marion and Lillian (Reid) P.; B.S., S.C. State Coll., 1943; M.S., Ind. U., 1956; M.S., Inst. Tech. U. So. Cal., 1973; D.Ed., Fla. State Christian U., 1973. Vocat. ednl. counselor U.S. Civil Service, Ft. Bragg, N.C., 1947-48; interior decorator, 1948-55; audiovisual dealer Signs Assos. Agy., Washington, 1955-60; audiovisual supr. Summerton (S.C.) Sch. Dist. 1, 1965-70, dir. instruction, 1970-72; dean learning, instructional materials center Denmark Tech. (S.C.), 1973-74; audiovisual edn. cons., owner Lawrence R. Pinckney & Assos., Orangeburg, 1974—; curator Pinckney Bros. Mus., 1978—. Active in adult edn., youth photo clubs, travel clubs. Served with AUS, 1942-47; ETO. Named Audiovisual Person of Year, Assn. Ednl. Communications and Technology S.C., 1969; recipient Outstanding Educator award Southeastern Businessmen Assos., 1973; certificates from seminars, workshops. Mem. NEA, S.C. Edn. Assn., Southeastern Regional Media Leadership Conf.. Southeastern Businessmen Assn., S.C. Tourist Assn., S.C. State Coll. Alumni. Clubs: Camera and Photo, Capital Press. Home: 1351 Monroe St Orangeburg SC 29115

PINDER, EDNA BOOTH, city ofcl.; b. Homestead, Mar. 23, 1922; d. William Joseph and Ruby Estelle (Albury) Booth; A.A. in Bus. Adminstrn., Miami-Dade Community Coll., 1974; m. Harry Lee Pinder, June 7, 1942 (div.); children—Michael Henry, Barry Edward. Dep. city clk. Homestead, 1951-66, city clk., 1966—. Mem. Internat. Inst. Mcpl. Clks., Fla. City Clks. Assn., Dade County Fin. Officers and Municipal Clks. Assn. Democrat. Home: 236 NE 9th St Homestead FL 33030 Office: 790 N Homestead Blvd Homestead FL 33030

PINE, DAVID ELLIS, air force officer; b. Visalia, Calif., May 10, 1945; s. Arthur and Ann Clara P.; B.A., San Diego State U., 1968; M.A., Tex. Christian U., 1978; m. Harriet Verna Hensen, Aug. 26, 1967; 1 dau., Amy Michelle. Commd. 2d lt. U.S. Air Force, 1968, advanced through grades to maj., 1978; pilot EC-121 aircraft, McClellan AFB, Calif., 1969-70, EC-47 aircraft, Vietnam, 1971; instr. pilot KC-135, Beale AFB, Calif., 1972-74, chief of safety, 1974-76; mgr. instructional systems Carswell AFB, Tex., 1976-79, Air Command and Staff Coll., Maxwell AFB, Ala., 1979—. Active, Boy Scouts Am., Am. Heart Assn. Decorated D.F.C., Air medal with 2 oak leaf clusters, Air Force Meritorious Service medal, Air Force Commendation medal with 1 oak leaf cluster; recipient Outstanding Young Man of Am. award U.S. Jaycees, 1979; Freedoms Found. Nat. Honor award, 1979. Mem. Air Force Assn., Order of Daedalians (vice flight capt. 1979—). Contbr. articles on nuclear safety to U.S. Air Force mags. Home: 3315 Old Dobbin Rd Montgomery AL 36116 Office: ACSC Maxwell AFB AL 36112

PINERO, ROSITA COSSIO, psychotherapist; b. Havana, Cuba, Dec. 9, 1940; came to U.S., 1964, naturalized, 1970; d. Alejo and Rosa (Miralles) Cossio del Pino; B.A., Coll. of Sacred Heart, P.R., 1974; M.S., U. Bridgeport, 1976; postgrad. U. Miami (Fla.), 1977-79; m. Emilio R. Pinero, Feb. 11, 1966; children—Luis Alejo, Luis Orlando, Mayra Arrondo, Eileen B. Psychotherapist, Mentally Retarded Inst. of P.R., 1976-77, Miami (Fla.) Mental Health Center, 1978, aftercare clincian and psychotherapist, hypnotechnician, 1979—, day treatment program coordinator, info. specialist, 1979-80; profl. cons., chmn. fin. com. Adaptación. Vice pres. Coll. Engrs., Architects and Surveyors, San Juan, P.R., 1968-76; mem. Dem. Com. of P.R. of Nat. Dem. Party, 1968-76; active Am. Cancer Soc., 1975—. Mem. Am. Mental Health Counselors Assn., Am. Personnel and Guidance Assn., Am. Assn. Counselors. Democrat. Roman Catholic. Club: Dorado Beach (PR.). Office: 2141 SW 1st St Miami FL 33142

PINES, JACK, real estate broker; b. Milw., July 9, 1925; s. Sidney and Mildred (Landfield) P.; B.S. in Chem. Engring., Mass. Inst. Tech., 1950; M.B.A., Harvard, 1952; m. Shirlee Jacobson, July 25, 1954; children—Margie, Anthony. Purchasing agt. Westinghouse Electric Co., Pitts., 1952-54 gen. mgr. Philip's Enterprises, Winter Haven, Fla., 1954—; realtor Jack Pines, Realtor, Winter Haven, 1956—; dir. Adams Packing Co., Auburndale, Fla.; 1970—. Vice pres. Lakeland YMCA, 1974—; bd dirs. Winter Haven and Lakeland United Way, 1973—; exec. com. chmn. Fla. Crusade Com., Am. Cancer Soc., 1976—; exec. com. Fla. Anti-Defamation League, 1975—. Mem. Am. Legion, Fla. Citrus Mut., Winter Haven Bd. Realtors, Internat. Council Shopping Centers. Clubs: Masons (Shriner), Elks, Kiwanis, Lakeland Yacht and Country. Home: 2345 Collins Ln Lakeland FL 33803 Office: PO Box 392 Winter Haven FL 33880

PINGREE, DIANNE, publisher, editor; b. Dallas; A.A., Richland Coll., 1974; B.F.A. magna cum laude, So. Meth. U., 1976; m. Harlan Pingree. Freelance writer, editor, 1973-76; editor-publisher Texas Woman mag., Dallas, 1977—, pres. Paragon III Assos., Inc., 1977—. Mem. Women in Communications (recipient Matrix award 1979),

Exec. Woman of Dallas, Sigma Delta Chi. Office: 5551 Yale Blvd Dallas TX 75206

PINION, RICHARD LEWIS, ins. co. exec.; b. Takoma Park, Md., Sept. 7, 1947; s. Jack Andrew and Eleanor Hampton (Whitacre) P.; A.A., Hagerstown Jr. Coll., 1968; B.S. in Bus. Adminstrn., Am. U., 1970, M.B.A., 1973; m. Maryruth Anne Chevalier, Feb. 23, 1976. Mgr. bank-agt. program First Nat. Bank of Washington, 1973-74; sponsored mktg. mgr. Aetna Life & Casualty. Arlington, Va., 1974—. Recipient Sales Mgmt. Forum award Aetna Life & Casualty, 1977. Mem. Am. Mktg. Assn., Assn. M.B.A.'s, Nat. Assn. Life Underwriters (Nat. Sales Achievement award 1977), Internat. Personnel Mgmt. Assn., Smithsonian Assos., Broyhill Park Civic Assn. Home: 3159 Norfolk Ln Falls Church VA 22042 Office: 1616 N Fort Myer Dr Suite 1420 Arlington VA 22209

PINKARD, LUTHER DWIGHT, civil engr.; b. Milltown, Ala., Feb. 23, 1927; s. Royal and Ezza (Stevens) P.; B.S., Auburn U., 1950; postgrad. U. Tenn., 1966-72; m. Laura Elizabeth Trantham, Oct. 31, 1952 (div. Jan. 1980); children—Robert, Susan, David, John, Roy. Materials engr. U.S. Bur. Reclamation, Lindsay, Cal., 1950; jr. engr. Tenn. Coal & Iron Co., Birmingham, Ala., 1951-52; asst. plant engr. Am. Bitumuls & Asphalt Co., Mobile, Ala., 1952-53; constrn. engr. Intrusion-Prepakt, Inc., Cleve., 1953-55; asst. dir. engring. So. Sash Sales & Supply Co., Sheffield, Ala., 1955-61; engr. TVA, Muscle Shoals, Ala., Knoxville, Tenn., 1961—. Served with USAAF, 1945-47. Registered profl. engr., Ala., Tenn. Mem. Nat. (chpt. pres. 1965), Tenn. socs. profl. engrs., Profl. Engrs. in Govt. (state sec.-treas. 1971-72, vice chmn. 1973), Lambda Chi Alpha, Phi Kappa Phi, Chi Epsilon. Home: 12527 Pony Express Dr Knoxville TN 37922 Office: 400 Commerce Ave Knoxville TN 37902

PINKENBURG, RONALD JOSEPH, ophthalmologist; b. Houston, Nov. 25, 1940; s. William Joseph and Winnie Vale (Downs) P.; B.A. cum laude, U. St. Thomas, 1963; M.D., Baylor U., 1967; m. Patricia Anne Regan, Oct. 21, 1967; children—Lisa, Anne Marie, Steven. Intern, U. Iowa, 1967-68; resident U. Okla., 1971-74, asst. clin. prof. ophthalmology, 1974—; gen. practitioner So. Calif. Permanente Med. Group-Kaiser Found. Hosp., Fontana, 1970-71; pvt. practice medicine specializing in ophthalmology, Tyler, Tex., 1974—; mem. staff Med. Center Hosp., Tyler, Mother Francis Hosp., Tyler. Served with USAF, 1968-70. Mem. Smith County Med. Soc., Tex. Med. Assn., AMA, Tex. Ophthalmology Assn., Am. Assn. Ophthalmology, Am. Intraocular Implant Soc. Roman Catholic. Office: 820 S Baxter St Tyler TX 75701

PINKSTAFF, CARLIN ADAM, anatomist, educator; b. Louisville, Ill., June 10, 1934; s. Lester D. and Helen Eva (Armstrong) P.; student Vincennes U., 1956-58; B.S. with honors, Eastern Ill. U., 1960; Ph.D., Emory U., 1964; m. Delores Aileen McCallum, Jan. 1, 1958; 1 dau., Cheryl Ann. Instr. anatomy U. Oreg. Dental Sch., Portland, 1964-65, asst. prof., 1965-67; asst. prof. anatomy W.Va. U. Sch. Medicine, Morgantown, 1967-70, asso. prof., 1970—; vis. external examiner in anatomy U. Ibadan (Nigeria), 1973; vis. scientist Yerkes Regional Primate Research Center, Atlanta, 1973; cons. in histochemistry FDA, Washington, 1978—. Served with USMC, 1954-56. Mem. Am. Assn. Anatomists. Histochem. Soc., Internat. Assn. Dental Research, Am. Assn. Dental Research, N.Y. Acad. Scis., AAAS, Am. Assn. Dental Schs., Sigma Xi, Psi Omega, Omicron Kappa Upsilon. Democrat. Contbr. articles to profl. jours. Home: 1200 Philip St Morgantown WV 26505 Office: WVa U Med Center Anatomy Dept Morgantown WV 26506

PINKSTAFF, RICHARD EUGENE, tng. and devel. cons. co. exec.; b. Flat Rock, Ill., Aug. 19, 1933; s. Samuel Earl and Grace Alice (Ford) P.; A.B. cum laude, McKendree Coll., 1958; M.B.A. with honors, U. Tulsa, 1959; m. Mildred Marlene Arthur, Sept. 2, 1955; children—Mark Richard, Jay Ralph. Manpower tng. specialist McDonnell Douglas Co., St. Louis, 1960-62; supr. manpower devel. N.Am. Rockwell Co., Tulsa, 1962-68; corp. dir. manpower tng. Nat. Gypsum Co., Buffalo, 1968-70; pres. Dick Pinkstaff Assos., Tulsa, 1970—. Chmn. Tulsa Area Manpower Authority, 1973-74; adv. bd. Sr. Ret. Vol. Program, 1973-76. Served with U.S. Army, 1953-55. Mem. Am. Soc. Tng. and Devel. (pres. Tulsa chpt. 1969), Nat. Mgmt. Assn. (dir. 1965-68). Methodist. Developer Appliskills Tng. System; co-author: Personal Skill Building for the Emerging Manager, 1979; presenter programs at numerous profl. clubs. Home: 4230 E 78th St Tulsa OK 74136 Office: 7030 S Yale St Suite 408 Tulsa OK 74136

PINKSTON, JOHN WILLIAM, JR., hosp. supt.; b. Valdosta, Ga., Aug. 11, 1924; s. John William and Fannie L. (Smith) P.; B.B.A., Emory U., 1946; m. Jane G. Grant, Nov. 12, 1959; children—Carol Grant, John William III. Trainee, Western Electric Co., 1947-48; with Grady Meml. Hosp., Atlanta, 1948—, exec. dir., 1964—; Sec. health and social service adv. council Atlanta Regional Commn., 1975; bd. dirs. North Central Ga. Health Systems Agy., 1976—. Served with C.E., AUS, 1944-46. Mem. Am. (chmn. pub. hosp. sect. 1976, mem. council on legis. 1975—), Ga. (treas. 1975, pres. 1977), hosp. assns., Assn. Am. Med. Colls. (mem. adminstrv. bd. council of teaching hosps. 1974-75). Home: 3176 Verdun Dr NW Atlanta GA 30305 Office: 80 Butler St SE Atlanta GA 30303

PINSON, JAMES RADFORD, interior designer; b. Hale Center, Tex.; s. James Roger and Jo Bailey (Maxey) P.; grad. Tex. Tech U.; student Fontainbleau Sch. Fine Arts, France. Owner, operator James Pinson Interiors, Lubbock, Tex. Served in inf. U.S. Army. Mem. Am. Soc. Interior Designers. Home: 3310 42d St Lubbock TX 79413 Office: 2023 Broadway Lubbock TX 79401

PINZON-CARRIZO, PABLO ANTONIO, obstetrician, gynecologist; b. Santiago, Panama, Jan. 4, 1942; s. Pablo Antonio and Luzmila Rita (Carrizo) P.; came to U.S., 1976; M.D., Universidad Autonoma de Guadalajara (Mex.), 1967; m. Anabel Pinzon, Feb. 18, 1978; 1 son, Pablo Antonio. Intern, Reddy Meml. Hosp., Montreal, Que., Can., 1967-68; resident Gorgas Hosp., C.Z., 1969-72; practice medicine specializing in ob-gyn, Oklahoma City, 1976—; mem. staff S. Community Hosp., 1976—, chief ob-gyn dept., 1978-80; mem. staff St. Anthony Hosp. Diplomate Am. Bd. Ob-Gyn. Fellow Am. Coll. Obstetricians and Gynecologists; mem. AMA, Oklahoma County Med. Soc., Ob-Gyn Soc. Oklahoma City, Sociedad Panamena de Ginecologia y Obstetricia, Med. Assn. Isthman C.Z. Roman Catholic. Home: 9408 S Walker St Oklahoma City OK 73139 Office: 4720 S Western St Oklahoma City OK 73109

PIPER, WILLIAM FRED, JR., acctg. co. exec.; b. Nashville, May 26, 1944; s. Willima Fred and Burnease (Towns) P.; B.S., U. Tenn., 1966; Asso. in Data Processing, Nashville State Tech., 1967; m. Juanita E. Hicks, Mar. 28, 1978; children—Deborah C., William F., Tiffany E., Keith B. Jr. accountant M.B. Cottle P.A., 1963-66; from jr. accountant to dir. prodn. control Phillips & Buttorff Corp., Nashville, 1966-76; mgr. prodn. control Tappan Appliance, Springfield, Tenn., 1976-77; owner, mgr., dir. Diversified Services of Nashville, 1977—; dir. ABC Bldg. & Maintenance Co., El Taco of Tenn., William F. Piper Acctg. and Tax Service. Mem. Nat. Soc. Public Accountants, Tenn. Soc. Public Accountants, Nat. Assn. Tax Consultors, Mcht. Brokers Exchange, Am. Prodn. and Inventory Control Soc. Jehovah Witness. Office: 4114 Gallatin Rd Box 4669 Nashville TN 37216

PIPES, STANLEY HOWARD, sugar co. exec.; b. Shreveport, La., Dec. 13, 1934; s. Luther Frank and Mary Sue (Stanley) P.; B.S., La. State U., 1966; m. Virginia Ann Ponder, July 9, 1953; children—Stanley Howard, Cynthia Ann. Sr. accountant Touche Ross & Co., New Orleans, 1966-71; v.p., treas. Sterling Sugars, Inc., Franklin, La., 1971—. Served with USN, 1962-63. C.P.A. La. Mem. Am. Inst. C.P.A.'s, La. Soc. C.P.A.'s. Club: Rotary. Home: Route 1 Box 159 Franklin LA 70538 Office: Sterling Sugars Inc PO Box 572 Franklin LA 70538

PIPPIN, JAMES LEE, data processor; b. Oklahoma City, Aug. 1, 1939; s. Robert A. and Ethel Emily (Gillmore) P.; student Okla. U., 1963, Oklahoma City U., 1964-65, Baylor U., Waco, Tex., 1968-69; m. Mary Zeola Logsdon, Dec. 27, 1963; children—Robert Gregory, Jennifer Denise. Programmer analyst Kerr McGee Oil Corp., Oklahoma City, 1963-66; systems and ednl. rep. Honeywell, Inc., 1966-67; asst. dir. data processing Baylor U., 1967-69; v.p. John Hawes Co., Waco, 1969-73; data processing officer First Nat. Bank, Waco, 1973-74; v.p. data processing Word, Inc., Waco, 1974—; cons. in field; vocat. tech. cons. data processing McLennan Community Coll., 1976—. Vol. worker McLennan County United Way. Served with AUS, 1961-67. Certified data processor. Mem. Data Processing Mgmt. Assn. (v.p. 1977, pres. elect 1978). Democrat. Methodist. Club: Masons (32 deg.), Scottish Rite. Home: Route 2 Box 204 McGregor TX 76657 Office: 4800 W Waco Dr Waco TX 76710

PIRKLE, DAVID EUGENE, mech. engr.; b. Atlanta, Aug. 8, 1927; s. David Ambrose and Eugenia (Bragg) P.; B.S., Ga. Inst. Tech., 1952; m. Mildred Ransie Edgens, Jan. 31, 1959. Mech. engr. Lockheed Aircraft Co., Marietta, Ga., 1952-59; individual engring. practice, Atlanta, 1959-63, 70—; mech. engr. Atlanta Army Depot, Forest Park, Ga., 1963-70. Recipient award Lockheed Mgmt. Club, 1954; award for outstanding performance in engring. Dept. Army, 1966, 69. Registered profl. engr., Ga. Address: 2203 Polar Rock Pl SW Atlanta GA 30315

PIRKLE, JOHN EUGENE, lawyer; b. El Paso, Sept. 12, 1949; s. Russell Lee and Eugenia (West) P.; B.B.A., U. Ga., 1971; J.D., Mercer U., 1974; 1 son, Jonathon M. Admitted to Ga. bar, 1974; individual practice law, Hinesville, 1974—. Trustee LeConte Woodmanston Gardens; co chmn. Liberty County Bicentennial, 1975-76. Mem. Jr. C. of C. (v.p. 1975), Hinesville, Ga., Am. bar assns., Atlantic Circuit Bar Assn. (treas. 1976-77), Ga. Trial Lawyers Assn., Assn. Trial Lawyers Am., Liberty County Hist. Soc. (pres. 1979-80). Democrat. Methodist. Club: Lions. Home: 507 Main St S Hinesville GA 31313 Office: 203 Court St E Hinesville GA 31313

PIRONE, THOMAS PASCAL, plant pathologist; b. Ithaca, N.Y., Jan. 3, 1936; s. Pascal Pompey and Loretta Muriel (Kelly) P.; B.S., Cornell U., 1957; Ph.D., U. Wis., 1960; m. Sherrill Sevier, Aug. 1, 1961; children—John Sevier, Catherine Sherrill. Asst. prof. La. State U., Baton Rouge, 1960-63, asso. prof., 1963-67; asso. prof. U. Ky., Lexington, 1967-71, prof., 1971—, chmn. plant pathology, 1978—. Sr. Fulbright Research fellow in U.K., 1974-75. Mem. Am. Phytopath. Soc., AAAS, Entomol. Soc. Am. Author or co-author numerous research publs. on plant virology; mem. editorial bd. Phytopathology, 1971-73, sr. editor, 1977-78; mem. editorial bd. Virology, 1974-76. Office: Dept Plant Pathology U Ky Lexington KY 40506

PIRRECA, MARCIA SKEEN, speech pathologist; b. Las Vegas, N.Mex., Nov. 15, 1948; d. Jerry L. and Phyllis M. (Cunningham) Skeen; B.A. (undergrad. trainee 1970-71, grad. fellow 1971-72), N.Mex. State U., 1972; M.A., Tex. Tech. U., 1968; m. Gene S. Pirreca, Aug. 16, 1969; 1 son, Andrew. Speech pathologist El Paso (Tex.) Rehab. Center, 1971-74; pvt. practice speech pathology and oral myology, El Paso, 1975—; exec. dir. El Paso Cleft Palate and Maxillofacial Abnormalities Clinic, 1975—; course developer, instr. El Paso Community Coll.; cons. in field. Mem. Am. Speech and Hearing Assn., Am. Cleft Palate Assn., Myofunctional Therapy Assn. Am. Roman Catholic. Office: 9398 Viscount St Bldg 1-F El Paso TX 79925

PIRTLE, CALEB JACKSON, III, writer; b. Kilgore, Tex., Dec. 30, 1941; s. Caleb Jackson, Jr., and Mary Eunice (Price) P.; A.A., Kilgore Coll., 1962; B.Journalism, U. Tex., Austin, 1964; m. Linda Greer, Aug. 31, 1963; 1 son, Joshua Jackson. Feature writer Ft. Worth Star Telegram, 1964-66; chief of media relations Tex. Tourist Devel. Agy., Austin, 1966-68; travel editor So. Living Mag., Birmingham, Ala., 1968-76; sr. writer So. Outdoors Mag., Waxahachie, Tex., 1977—; free-lance writer; author Callaway Gardens: The Unending Season, 1973; XIT: The American Cowboy, 1975; The Grandest Day, 1980; Southern Celebrities Outdoors, 1980; author movie: Hot Wire, 1979. Named Kilgore Coll. Alumnus of Year, 1976, So. Travel Dirs. Council Man of Year in Travel, 1974; recipient William Randolph Hearst award, 1964; Tex. AP award for feature writing, 1966. Mem. Soc. Am. Travel Writers, Phi Theta Kappa (alumnus of year 1975). Presbyterian. Home and Office: 401 E Marvin Waxahachie TX 75165

PIRTLE, GEORGE WILLIAM, geologist, petroleum cons.; b. Cecilia, Ky., Nov. 1, 1902; s. Thomas Louis and Laura (Shipley) P.; B.S., U. Ky., 1924, M.S., 1925; m. El Freda Taylor, July 16, 1928; 1 son, George William. Geologist, Ky. Geol. Survey, 1924-25; cons. geologist, partner Hudnall & Pirtle, Tyler, Tex., 1925-69; ind. petroleum cons., 1969—; dir. Peoples Nat. Bank. Past trustee Tyler Jr. Coll.; dir. South Central region Boy Scouts Am., mem. nat. exec. bd. Recipient Silver Beaver, Silver Antelope, Silver Buffalo awards Boy Scouts Am.; named Tyler's Outstanding Citizen, 1962. Mem. Tex. Acad. Sci., East Tex. C. of C. (past v.p.), Geol. Soc. Am., Am. Assn. Petroleum Geologists, Mich. Acad. Sci., Am. Inst. Mining, Metall. and Petroleum Engrs., Sigma Xi, Omicron Delta Kappa. Methodist. Endowed George W. Pirtle Tech. Center, Tyler Jr. Coll., 1979-79. Home: 115 E 2d St Tyler TX 75701 Office: 610 People Bank Bldg Tyler TX 75701

PIRTLE, IVYL LEORA FLEMING (MRS. J. MAX PIRTLE), librarian; b. nr. Ottumwa, Iowa, Jan. 11, 1906; d. Barton Earl and Lillie (Roberts) Fleming; student Iowa State Coll., 1931; B.A., U. Fla., 1944; M.A., Fla. State U., 1951; m. J. Max Pirtle, Sept. 17, 1938. Tchr. elementary schs., Iowa, 1924-39; tchr. Grace Stern Pvt. Sch., Miami Beach, Fla., 1939-40; tchr. elementary schs., Indiantown, 1940-43; tchr. primary grades, Stuart, 1943-50; demonstration tchr. Fla. State U., Tallahassee, summer 1949; tchr. Palmetto Sch., West Palm Beach, 1950-55; supr. elementary edn. Palm Beach County, 1955-65, dir. library services, 1965-70; mem. Fla. steering com. NDEA, 1958-68. Trustee Jr. Mus. Palm Beach County, 1960-63. Recipient certificate of appreciation Fla. Dept. Edn., 1969. Mem. Assn. Childhood Edn. Internat. (br. pres. 1953-55, primary edn. com. 1954-56), Fla. Assn. Sch. Librarians (area chmn. 1959-62), NEA, Fla. Edn. Assn. (state chmn. dept. suprs. 1959-60, dept. suprs. citation for meritorious service 1968), Assn. Supervision and Curriculum Devel., Delta Kappa Gamma (chpt. pres. 1955-59), Kappa Delta Pi, Phi Kappa Phi. Club: Zonta. Contbr. articles to profl. jours. Home: 340 Nottingham Blvd West Palm Beach FL 33405

PISACANO, NICHOLAS JOSEPH, physician, educator; b. Phila., June 6, 1924; s. Joseph Harry and Rafaella (Saquella) P.; B.A., Western Md. Coll., 1943, D.Sc. (hon.), 1980; M.D., Hahnemann Med. Sch., 1951; m. Virginia Leigh Burleson, May 8, 1978; children—Toni Ann, Nicki Rae, Dean Alan, Don Arlie, Lori Sue. Intern, Stamford, (Conn.) Hosp., 1951-52, resident, 1952-53; gen. practice medicine, South Royalton, Vt., 1953-55, Phila., 1955-62; med. dir. Am. Cancer Soc., 1958-62; dir. continuing med. edn. U. Ky., Lexington, 1962-69, asst. dean Coll. Arts and Scis., 1966-72, asst. to v.p. Med. Center, 1966-72, prof., chmn. dept. allied health edn. and research, 1975—, asso. dean Coll. Allied Health Professions, 1974—; prof. biology-medicine U. Ky. Med. Center; exec. dir., sec. Am. Bd. Family Practice, 1969—. Vice pres. Bluegrass Mental Health Assn. Served with U.S. Army, 1943-46. Recipient Disting. Teaching award U. Ky., 1967; Most Outstanding Alumnus of Yr. award Hahnemann Med. Coll., 1979. Mem. Am. Acad. Family Physicians (Thomas Johnson award 1977, Max Cheplove, M.D., award Erie County (N.Y.) chpt. 1977), Canadian Coll. Family Physicians (hon.), AMA, AAAS, Pan Am. Med. Assn. (v.p.), Assn. Am. Med. Colls., Soc. for Health and Human Values, Royal Soc. Health (Eng.), Soc. Tchrs. of Family Medicine, So. Med. Assn., N.Y. Acad. Scis., Ky. Med. Assn. Home: 395 Redding Rd Number 57 Lexington KY 40502 Office: 2228 Young Dr Lexington KY 40505

PISHEL, ROBERT GORDON, JR., psychologist; b. Tulsa, Dec. 20, 1942; s. Robert Gordon and Velma Myra P.; B.A., U. Okla., 1965, M.S., 1966, Ph.D., 1969. Dir. research and evaluation, HEW project obstetrics, gynecology and psychiatry U. Med. Center at Jackson, Miss., 1971-73; pres. Selindex, Tulsa., 1973—. Served to lt. USN, 1968-71. Mem. Am., South West pschol. assns. Republican. Home and office: 2404 University Club Tower Tulsa OK 74119 also 2300 E 14th St Suite 302 Tulsa OK 74114

PISHKIN, VLADIMIR, psychologist; b. Belgarde, Yugoslavia, Mar. 12, 1931; s. Vasili and Olga (Bartosh) P.; came to U.S., 1946, naturalized, 1951; B.A., Mont. State U., 1951, M.A., 1955, Ph.D., U. Utah, 1958; m. Dorothy Louise Martin, Sept. 12, 1953; children—Gayle Ann, Mark Vladimir. Dir. nueropsychiat. research labs. VA Hosp., Tomah, Wis., 1959-62; dir. Behavioral Scis. Lab., VA Med. Center, Oklahoma City, 1962—; prof. Coll. Medicine, U. Okla. Health Scis. Center, Oklahoma City, 1973—, chmn. research council, dept. psychiatry and behavioral scis. Coll. Medicine, 1972-75. Served in USAF, 1952-54. Recipient Distinguished Service award Jr. C. of C. Mem. Am., Southwestern (pres. 1973-74), Okla., Midwestern psychol. assns., AAAS. Clubs: Masons, Shriners. Author: (with Mathis and Pierce) Basic Psychiatry, rev. edit., 1972; editor-in-chief Jour. Clin. Psychology, 1974—; contbr. articles to profl. jours. Home: 3113 NW 62 Oklahoma City OK 73112 Office: VA Med Center (151A) 921 NE 13th St Oklahoma City OK 73104

PISTOR, CHARLES HERMAN, traffic cons.; b. St. Louis, Aug. 23, 1901; s. Charles F. and Augusta (Reh) P.; LL.B., Benton Coll., 1925, LL.M., 1926; student Washington U., 1927-28; m. Virginia Grace Brown, Jan. 18, 1929; children—Charles Herman, Walter Brown, Virginia Reh. Stenographer, clk. Mobile & Ohio R.R., St. Louis, 1918-24; commerce clk., chief rate clk. M.-K.-T. R.R., 1924-28; with T. & P. Ry., 1928-67, successively clk., chief clk., asst. gen. freight agt., gen. freight agt., asst. freight traffic mgr., freight traffic mgr., 1928-53, gen. freight traffic mgr., 1953-60, asst. v.p. mktg., 1960-67; cons. Western Traffic Cons., Dallas, 1967—. Life mem. Jr. C. of C. of St. Louis, former dir. Mem. Am. Soc. Traffic and Transp., Nat. Freight Traffic Assn., Assn. ICC Practitioners, Dallas Knights of the Round Table (pres. 1945), Transp. Club of Dallas. Presbyn. (elder). Club: Dallas Athletic. Address: 7038 Currin Dr Dallas TX 75230

PITCHER, LINDA RUTH TILLMAN, exec. and legal asst.; b. Orlando, Fla., June 3, 1943; d. Thomas John and Stella Frances (Block) Tillman; student Valencia Community Coll., Orlando, 1973-74, Fla. Jr. Coll., Jacksonville, 1976-77; m. Griffith Fontaine Pitcher, May 29, 1976; stepchildren—Virginia T., L. Brooke, William T.B., Margaret W. Exec. sec. to mgr. advance systems engring. Martin Marietta Aerospace Corp., Orlando, 1963-69; exec. sec. to pres., also office mgr., fashion coordinator and writer Act II Jewelry Inc., Orlando, 1969-76; legal asst., sec. Howell, Howell, Liles, Braddock & Milton, Jacksonville, Fla., 1976-78; exec. asst. to owners and developers Regency Sq. Shopping Center, Jacksonville, 1978-79; freelance exec. and legal asst., 1979—. Mem. Republican Nat. Com.; hospitality chmn., dir. Women of Jacksonville Art Mus., 1977-80; sec.-treas. No. Fla. chpt. Wine Investigation for Novices and Oenophiles. Mem. Jacksonville Bar Assn. Aux., Nat. Secs. Assn. (asst. treas. 1973-74, sec. 1974-75), LWV, Ladies Guild Cummer Gallery Art, Jacksonville Mus. Arts and Scis. Mem. Ch. Religious Sci. Club: Univ. (Jacksonville). Home: 951 Brookwood Rd Jacksonville FL 32207

PITCHFORD, HARRIET DAY, librarian; b. Canton, Miss.; d. Sterling G. and Lidie (Hunnicutt) Pitchford; B.S., Miss. So. U., 1935; M.A., George Peabody Coll., 1959; postgrad. Columbia U., summers 1961, 64, 66. Tchr. elementary sch., Miss., 1935-41; librarian Main Post Library, Camp Van Dorn, Miss., 1941-43, Camp Roberts, Calif., 1943-47, Camp Zama, Japan, 1947-49, Ft. Benning, Ga., 1949—, assigned Vietnam, 1970-71. Mem. AAUW, UN Assn. of Am. Clubs: Execs., Altrusa (pres. 1967-68) (Columbus, Ga.). Home: 115 Matheson Rd Columbus GA 31903 Office: PO Box 1972 Ft Benning GA 31905

PITT, ERNEST HAROLD, newspaper exec.; b. Greensboro, N.C., Dec. 19, 1945; s. Joseph and Lucille P.; B.A. in Journalism, U. N.C., Chapel Hill, 1974; m. Elaine Lynch, Oct. 21, 1977; 1 child, Khalilah. Journalism intern Durham (N.C.) Morning Herald, 1973-74; reporter Greensboro (N.C.) Daily News, 1974—; pub. Winston-Salem (N.C.) Chronicle, 1974—; mem. adv. bd. Southeastern Black Press Inst. Bd. dirs. Council on Drug Abuse, Big Bros., YMCA. Served with U.S. Army, 1964-67. Recipient Brotherhood award Winston-Salem Urban League Guild, 1979; cert. of appreciatoin United Negro Coll. Fund, 1979, Mid-west Piedmont Bus. Devel. Orgn., 1978; cert. of recognition Mid-Eastern Athletic Conf., 1978. Mem. N.C. Black Pubs. (co-chmn.), NAACP. Baptist. Home: 118 Mayfair Dr Winston-Salem NC 27105 Office: 516 N Trade St Winston-Salem NC 27102

PITT, THEOPHILUS HARPER, JR., savs. and loan assn. exec.; b. Rocky Mount, N.C., Apr. 5, 1936; s. Theophilus Harper and Mary Elizabeth (Whitaker) P.; B.A. in History, U. N.C., Chapel Hill, 1958; grad. Grad. Sch. Savs. and Loan, Ind. U., 1967; m. Molly Ray Browning, Oct. 23, 1965; children—Elizabeth Browning, David Harper. Spl. rep. Pilot Life Ins. Co., Rocky Mount, N.C., 1958-61; with Home Savs. & Loan Assn., Rocky Mount, 1961—, v.p., sr. operating officer, 1971-74, pres., chief exec. officer, 1974—; dir. Nat. Bd Cons., United Guaranty Corp; chmn. bd. trustees N.C. Savs. & Loan Acad. Pres., Rocky Mount Jaycees, 1963-64; v.p. N.C. Jaycees, 1964-65; nat. bd. dirs. U.S. Jaycees, 1966-67; bd. advs. Salvation Army, Rocky Mount, 1973; pres. Rocky Mount Family YMCA, 1975; pres. Rocky Mount C. of C., 1978; chmn. bd. Rocky Mount Central City Revitalization Corp. Named Boss of Yr., Rocky Mount Jaycees, 1977, Am. Bus. Women's Assn., 1978. Mem. Nat. Assn. Rev. Appraisers (cert.). Democrat. Baptist. Clubs: Benvenue Country,

Northgreen Country, Capitol City, Kiwanis (chpt. pres. 1974-75) (Rocky Mt.). Office: 224 S Franklin Rocky Mount NC 27801

PITTENGER, SALLY BRYANT, ins. co. exec.; b. Wichita, Kans., June 5, 1945; d. Howard S. and Harriet (Park) Bryant; student So. Meth. U., 1963; B.S., U. Tulsa, 1967. Copywriter, Rogers & Smith Advt., Dallas, 1967-68; mem. press br. Hemisfair, San Antonio, 1968; public relations writer Trinity U., San Antonio, 1968-69; public relations writer Community Service Bur., Dallas, 1970; with United Fidelity Life Ins. Co., Dallas, 1970—, v.p. communications, 1976—. Bd. dirs. Dallas Met. Ballet, 1976-78; v.p. Dallas Theater Center Assn., 1977-79; pres., bd. dirs. Dallas Big Sisters, Inc., 1976, Dallas Council World Affairs; bd. dirs. The 500, Inc., Girls Adventure Trails; public relations chmn., mem. scholarship com. Dallas Women's Council. Mem. Dallas Advt. League (dir.), Tex. Public Relations Assn. Republican. Presbyterian. Clubs: Press, Slipper, The Assemblage. Home: 4303 Emerson Dallas TX 75205 Office: 1025 Elm St Dallas TX 75202

PITTMAN, CHALMERS VAN ANGLEN, geophysicist; b. Trenton, N.J., July 25, 1904; s. Raymond Hill and Evanna Catherine (Van Anglen) P.; B.S., Haverford Coll., 1925; m. Margaret Ellen Hallett, Aug. 10, 1929; 1 dau., Janet McLellan. Geophysicist, Geophys. Research Corp., Houston, 1927-30, Geophys. Service, Inc., Dallas, 1930-42; exec. v.p., chmn. bd. Geochem. Surveys, Dallas, 1942-75, cons., 1975—. Bd. mgrs. Haverford Coll., 1971-74. Mem. Am. Assn. Petroleum Geologists, Soc. Exploration Geophysicists, Dallas Petroleum Club, SAR, Soc. Colonial Wars, Hereditary Order Descs. Colonial Govs., Corp. Haverford Coll., Nat. Huguenot Soc., Soc. Descs. Colonial Clergy. Mem. Soc. of Friends. Club: Dallas Country. Home: 3909 Miramar Ave Dallas TX 75205 Office: 2505 Turtle Creek Blvd Dallas TX 75219

PITTMAN, EDWIN LLOYD, sec. state Miss.; b. Hattiesburg, Miss., Jan. 2, 1935; s. Lloyd H. and Pauline M. Pittman; B.S., U. So. Miss.; J.D., U. Miss., 1960; m. Barbara Peel, Aug. 24, 1957; children—Melanie, Win, Jennifer. Admitted to Miss. bar, 1960; practiced in Hattiesburg, 1960-75; mem. Miss. Senate, 1964-72; treas. State of Miss., Jackson, 1976-80, sec. state, 1980—. Served to 2d lt. inf., U.S. Army; lt. col. Miss. N.G. Mem. Am. Bar Assn., South Central Miss. Bar Assn., U. So. Miss. Alumni Assn., U. Miss. Alumni Assn., Miss. Jaycees (past state dir.), Hattiesburg Jaycees (past pres.). Democrat. Baptist. Clubs: Lions, Masons. Office: PO Box 136 Jackson MS 39205

PITTMAN, JAMES ALLEN, JR., univ. dean, physician; b. Orlando, Fla., Apr. 12, 1927; s. James Allen and Jean C. (Garretson) P.; B.S., Davidson Coll., 1948; M.D., Harvard U., 1952; m. Constance Ming-Chung Shen, Feb. 19, 1955; children—James Clinton, John Merrill. Intern, asst. resident medicine Mass. Gen. Hosp., Boston, 1952-54; teaching fellow medicine Harvard U., 1953-54; clin. asso. NIH, Bethesda, Md., 1954-56; instr. medicine George Washington U., 1955-56; chief resident medicine U. Ala. Med. Center, Birmingham, 1956-58, instr. medicine, 1956-59, asst. prof., 1959-62, asso. prof., 1962-64, prof. medicine, 1964-71, dir. endocrinology and metabolism div., 1962-71, co-chmn. dept. medicine, 1969-71, also asso. prof. physiology and biophysics, 1966-71; asst. chief med. dir. research and edn. in medicine U.S. VA, 1971-73; prof. medicine Georgetown U. Med. Sch., Washington, 1971-73; exec. dean U. Ala. Sch. Medicine, 1973—; mem. pharmacology, endcrinology fellowships rev. commn. NIH, 1967-68, mem. endocrinology study sect., 1964-68; mem. drug research bd. Nat. Acad. Scis. Fellow A.C.P. (life); mem. Assn. Am. Physicians, Endocrine Soc. (council 1971-74), Am. Thyroid Assn. (v.p. 1972-73, dir. 1974-76), N.Y. Acad. Scis. (life), Soc. Nuclear Medicine, Am. Diabetes Assn., Am. Chem. Soc., Wilson Ornithol. Club, Am. Ornithologists Union, Am. Fedn. Clin. Research (pres. So. sect., mem. nat. council 1962-66), So. Soc. Clin. Investigation, Phi Beta Kappa, Alpha Omega Alpha, Omicron Delta Kappa. Author: Diagnosis and Treatment of Thyroid Diseases, 1963; contbr. articles in field to profl. jours. Home: 5 Ridge Dr Birmingham AL 35213

PITTMAN, SIDNEY EARL, hosp. exec.; b. Gulfport, Miss., Nov. 14, 1941; s. Adolph Arsene and Mary Elizabeth (Lyman) P.; A.S., Miss. Gulf Coast Jr. Coll., 1976; B.S., U. So. Miss., 1977; m. Carolyn Blalock, Oct. 7, 1964; 1 dau., Patrice Ann. Exec. housekeeper Meml. Hosp., Gulfport, Miss., 1964-67, Ochsner Med. Center, New Orleans, 1967-75; dir. environ. services W. Volousia Meml. Hosp., DeLand, Fla., 1976—; instr. hosp. housekeeping Miss. Gulf Coast Jr. Coll. Served with USMC, 1957-65. Mem. Nat. Exec. Housekeepers Assn. (certified, pres. Central Fla. chpt.), Southeastern Assn. Hosp. Housekeepers (pres. 1969, 76), Am. Hosp. Assn., Am. Assn. Contamination Control. Democrat. Roman Catholic. Club: Elks. Contbr. articles profl. jours. Home: 1855 Anchor Ave DeLand FL 32720 Office: PO Box 509 DeLand FL 32720

PITTMAN, VIRGIL, fed. judge; b. Enterprise, Ala., Mar. 28, 1916; s. Walter Oscar and Annie Lee (Logan) P.; B.S., U. Ala., 1939, LL.B., 1940; m. Floy Lasseter, 1944; children—Karen Pittman Gordy, Walter Lee. Admitted to Ala. bar, 1940; spl. agt. FBI, 1940-44; practiced law, Gadsden, Ala., 1946-51; judge Ala. Circuit Ct., Circuit 16, 1951-66; judge U.S. Dist. Ct. for Ala. So. Dist., 1966-71, chief judge, 1971—; lectr. in bus. law, econs. and polit. sci. U. Ala. Center at Gadsden, 1943-66. Mem. Ala. Bd. Edn., 1951; trustee Samford U., Birmingham, Ala. Served to lt., j.g., USNR, 1944-46. Mem. Ala. State Bar, Etowah County (Ala.) Bar Assn. (pres. 1949), Omicron Delta Kappa. Democrat. Baptist. Author: Circuit Court Proceedings in Acquisition of a Tract of Right of Way, 1959; A Judge Looks at Right of Way Condemnation Proceedings, 1960; Technical Pitfalls in Right of Way Proceedings, 1961. Office: 247 US Courthouse and Fed Bldg Mobile AL 36602

PITTMAN, VIRGIL LEE, JR., ins. co. exec.; b. Oil City, La., June 29, 1941; s. Virgil Lee and Nona M. (Byerley) P.; B.S., Northwestern La. State U., 1964; m. Diane Gates, Mar. 27, 1964; children—Philip Marc, Christy Lee, Jason B. Sr. asso. Planning Research Corp., Heidelberg, Germany, 1967-68, IBM Corp., Gaithersburg, Md., 1968-70; systems asst. dir. United Services Automobile Assn., San Antonio, 1970-75, systems dir., 1970-75, asst. v.p., 1974-75; sr. v.p. Equitable Gen. Ins. Co., Ft. Worth, Tex., 1975—. Served to lt. USN, 1964-67. Home: 7025 Falling Springs Rd Fort Worth TX 76116 Office: Equitable Gen Insurance Co Fort Worth TX 76151

PITTS, BEN ELLIS, librarian, educator; b. Pennington Gap, Va., Sept. 20, 1931; s. Ellis R. and Mary Kelly P.; B.S., Lincoln Meml. U., 1954; M.Ed., U. Ga., 1970, Ed.S., 1971, Ed.D., 1973; M.Div., Emory U., 1974; m. Gracie Scott, July 15, 1950; 1 son, Ben E. Tchr., prin. Lee County (Va.) Public Schs., 1950-54; ordained to ministry, United Meth. Ch., 1959; minister chs., 1955-67; media specialist Gwinnett County (Ga.) Public Schs., 1968-73; media specialist Rockdale County (Ga.) Public Schs., 1973-74; coordinator learning resource center Tenn. Tech. U., Cookeville, 1974-79; asso. prof. library/media Delta State U., Cleveland, Miss., 1979—; cons. Upper Cumberland Regional Library System, Tenn. Mem. Phi Kappa Phi, Kappa Delta Pi, Pi Delta Kappa. Club: Masons. Contbr. articles to profl. jours. Home: 263 Clover Dr Greenville MS 38701 Office: PO Box 3162 Delta State Univ Cleveland MS 38733

PITTS, MARGIE DELL, nursing edn. adminstr.; b. Thomaston, Ga., Aug. 23, 1930; d. John Hoke and Omie (Ellington) P.; diploma Nursing, Ga. Bapt. Hosp., 1951; B.S., Med. Coll. Ga., 1962, M.S., 1969. Operating room supr. Griffin Spaulding County Hosp., Griffin, Ga., 1956-60; head nurse Med. Coll. Ga., 1962-63, dir. in-service edn., 1963-65, dir. hosp. edn., 1965-68; dir. nursing Ga. Regional Hosp., Augusta, 1969-74, Univ. Hosp., Augusta, 1974-76; dir. tng. dept. human resources Ga. Regional Hosp., Augusta, 1976-78, tng. adminstr., 1978—; asst. prof. Augusta Coll. Nursing, 1977—; clin. prof. Med. Coll. Ga. Sch. Nursing, 1979—; instr.-trainer Ga. Heart Assn., 1977-79. Bd. dirs. Augusta Area Health Info. Resources, 1978-79. Mem. Am. Nurses Assn., Ga. Nurses Assn., Am. Assn. Transactional Analysis, 10th Dist. Nurses Assn. (dir. 1975-79), Sigma Theta Tau. Club: Goshen Country. Home: 1706 Goshen Rd Augusta GA 30906 Office: PO Box 5826 Augusta GA 30909

PITTS, MARVIN HOUSTON, JR., constn. and mining machinery sales exec.; b. Cookeville, Tenn., June 29, 1952; s. Marvin Houston and Klyda Moretta (Nairon) P.; student U. Tenn., 1970-74; m. Vicki Sue Tull, Sept. 8, 1973; 1 son, Jason Tull. Comml. credit analyst United Am. Bank, 1972-75; dir. Am. Properties, Inc., 1973-76; territorial mgr. Nixon Machinery Co., Knoxville, 1975—; dir. Eastern Distbg. Co., Inc. Active in polit. campaigns for Bill Brock, 1972, Winfield Dunn, 1972, Lamar Alexander, 1976. Mem. Am. Mgmt. Assn. Republican. Methodist. Clubs: Capital, Masons, Shriners. Home: 10705 Sallings Rd Concord TN 37720 Office: 6621 Wilbanks Rd Knoxville TN 37912

PITZNER, A(LWIN) FREDERICK, banker; b. Chgo., May 8, 1936; s. Alwin Frederick and Alice Rebecca (Girard) P.; B.A., Dartmouth Coll., 1958; m. Nancy Christine Gulin, Sept. 1, 1962; children—Christine Erika, Alexander Caldwell. Adminstrv. v.p. Am. Nat. Bank & Trust Co., Chgo., 1958-75; pres. Exchange Operating Services Corp., Tampa, Fla., 1975—, also dir.; corp. v.p. ops. Exchange Bancorp. Mem. Fla. Bankers Assn., Tampa C. of C., Com. of 100. Democrat. Clubs: Univ. of Tampa, Carrollwood Golf and Tennis. Home: 3118 Belmore Rd Tampa FL 33618 Office: PO Box 1809 Tampa FL 33601

PIVNIK, SHELDON IRWIN, transp. engr., lawyer; b. Bklyn., May 6, 1933; s. Saul Theodore and Lillian Hannah (Alperin) P.; A. Applied Sci., N.Y.C. Community Coll., 1953; B.B.A., U. Miami, 1973, J.D., 1977; m. Carole Lorraine Markowitz, Aug. 12, 1956; children—Jerome, Eric Ross. Asst. elec. engr. N.Y.C. Dept. Traffic, 1961-68, asst. chief bur. signals, communications and computer control, 1968-71; traffic engr. Travers Assos., cons. engrs., Clifton, N.J., 1968; head div. systems Dade County Dept. Traffic and Transp., Miami, Fla., 1971—; admitted to Fla. bar, 1977; of counsel firm Markus, Winter & Spitale P.A., Miami, 1977—. Pres., Matawan Twp. (N.J.) First Aid and Rescue Squad, 1967, S. Matawan Twp. First Aid Squad, 1971. Served with U.S. Army, 1954-56; Tokyo. Recipient award for journalistic excellence Internat. Mcpl. Signal Assn., 1977; Fed. Hwy. Adminstrn. Hwy. Transp. Research and Edn. fellow, 1976-77; registered profl. engr., N.Y., N.J., Pa., Fla. Fellow Inst. Transp. Engrs.; mem. Am. Bar Assn., Dade County Bar Assn., Assn. Trial Lawyers Am. Democrat. Home: 8300 SW 105th St Miami FL 33156 Office: 2251 SW 22d St Miami FL 33145 also 8675 NW 53d St Miami FL 33166

PIXLEY, JOHN SHERMAN, research co. exec.; b. Detroit, Aug. 24, 1929; s. Rex Arthur and Louise (Sherman) P.; B.A., U. Va., 1951; postgrad. Pa. State U., 1958-59; m. Peggy Marie Payne, Oct. 16, 1949; children—John Sherman, Steven, Lou Ann. Asst. cashier Old Dominion Bank, Arlington, Va., 1953-56; tech. dir. John I. Thompson & Co., research and engring. firm, Bellefonte, Pa., 1956-65; co-founder, exec. v.p. Potomac Research Inc., Alexandria, Va., 1965—. Mem. Fairfax County Republican Com., Annandale, Va., 1964-72; mem. fin. com. for U.S. Rep. Joel T. Broyhill, Republican, Va., 1970-72. Served to 1st lt. AUS, 1952-53; maj. Res. ret. Decorated Army Commendation medal. Mem. IEEE, Sleepy Hollow Woods Civic Assn. (v.p., pres. 1969-71). Presbyterian. Club: Quantico (Va.) Flying (charter mem.). Home: 3711 Sleepy Hollow Rd Falls Church VA 22041 Office: 1600 N Beauregard St Alexandria VA 22311

PIXLEY, SUZANNE LLOYD, lab. adminstr.; b. Columbus, Ohio, June 14, 1949; d. Park Hanning and Emily Ann (Carr) P.; B.A., Ohio Wesleyan U., 1971. Group leader gas chromatography Searle Diagnostic, Inc., Columbus, 1972-73, tech. communications supr., 1973-74, regulatory affairs mgr., 1974-75; lab. mgr. Interlab Assos., Inc., Miami, Fla., 1975—. Mem. Clin. Radioassay Soc. Republican. Home: 9411 Live Oak Pl Fort Lauderdale FL 33324 Office: 3236 N Miami Ave Miami FL 33137

PIZARRO LAGO, ANTONIA, health services adminstr.; b. Guayama, P.R., June 13, 1939; d. Alfonso Pizarro and Andrea Lago de Pizarro; B.A. in Secondary Edn., U. P.R., 1961, diploma in secretarial scis., 1962, M.S. in Health Services Adminstrn., 1970. Instr. in Spanish and social studies P.R. Jr. Coll., San Juan, 1961-64; tchr. Spanish, asst. dir. Facundo Bueso Sch., Santurce, P.R., 1964-65; exec. sec. mammography project dept. radiology I. Gonzalez Martinez Oncologic Hosp., San Juan, 1965-70, asst. adminstr., 1970-75; gen. adminstr. I. Gonzalez Martinez Oncologic Hosp. and P.R. League Against Cancer, P.R. Med. Center, San Juan, 1975-79; adminstr. P.R. chpt. ARC, San Juan, 1979—. Bd. dirs. Blue Cross P.R., 1978; active P.R. League Against Cancer; mem. spl. study com. on rehab. Ter. of P.R., 1977. Lic. tchr. and health services adminstr., P.R.; recipient awards Sociedad Venezolana de Radiologia, 1967, P.R. Assn. Hosp. Adminstrs., 1970, I. Gonzalez Martinez Hosp., 1976, 78, 79. Mem. Assn. Hosp. Adminstrs. P.R. (dir. 1971-78, Pres.'s prize 1971), Am. Public Health Assn., P.R. Public Health Assn., Assn. Hosps. P.R., Internat. Fedn. Hosps., Am. Soc. Law and Medicine, Health Fin. Mgmt. Assn., Am. Hosp. Assn. Roman Catholic. Home: Condominio Torremolinos Apt 701 Urb Torremolinos Guaynabo PR 00657 Office: Ponce de Leon Ave Stop 1 San Juan PR 00901

PLAMONDON, WILLIAM NELSON, JR., oil co. exec.; b. Chgo., Sept. 5, 1924; s. William Nelson and Elisabeth Cecile (Hauck) P.; B.Engring., M.E., Yale U., 1945; M.S. in Mgmt. Engring., N.J. Inst. Tech., 1954; m. Mary Elizabeth Heller, Aug. 17, 1946; children—William Nelson, Jeffrey, Donna Plamondon Scully, Mark. With Caltex Petroleum Corp., N.Y.C., 1951-55; with Continental-Emsco Co., N.Y.C. and Houston, 1956-73, mgr. sales-internat. div., 1967-73; mgr. mktg. Dixilyn Corp., Houston, 1973-76; v.p. sales and contracts Zapata Off-Shore Co., Houston, 1976-77; v.p. mktg. Dixilyn-Field Drilling Co., Houston, 1977—; lectr. marine offshore seminars Tex. A. and M. U., 1975, 76, 80. Served to lt. (j.g.) USN, 1943-46; PTO. Mem. Soc. Petroleum Engrs., Internat. Assn. Drilling Contractors (past chmn. Houston chpt.), Nomads. Republican. Roman Catholic. Clubs: Petroleum of Houston, Champions Golf. Contbr. articles to trade jours. Home: 629 Chadbourne Ct Houston TX 77079 Office: PO Box 4210 Houston TX 77210

PLANK, LAWRENCE ALLEN, credit services exec.; b. Ottumwa, Ia., Feb. 11, 1946; s. William Edward and Dorothy May (Ferguson) P.; B.S., Phillips U., 1968; m. Pauledde Caia Hester, Jan. 21, 1967; children—Bryan A., Amy L. Corporate sec., div. mgr. Credit Bur., Enid, Okla., 1966-69, 72; pres., gen. mgr. Stillwater (Okla.) Credit Bur., 1972—; dir., pres. Midwest Credit Services, Inc., Stillwater, 1977-79; treas. Indian-Meridian Vo-Tech., Stillwater, 1977-79; nat. adv. bd. mem. Credit Bur. Reports, Inc., 1976. Team capt., Stillwater United Fund, 1973, div. chmn. 1974, pub. chmn./dir., 1975, pres./dir., 1976, dir., 1977—; adminstrv. bd. First United Meth. Ch., Stillwater, 1976-77. Served with USAF, 1969-72. Recipient Certificate of Merit, Assoc. Credit Burs., Inc., 1974, 76; Okla. State Leadership award, Assoc. Credit Burs., Inc., 1976, Internat. Leadership award, 1975; certified credit bur. exec. Mem. C. of C., Assoc. Credit Burs., Med.-Dental-Hosp. Burs. Am., Am. Collectors Assn., Okla. Council Economic Edn., Internat. Consumer Credit Assn., Assoc. Credit Burs. Okla., Credit Women Internat. Methodist. Clubs: Rotary, Stillwater Golf and Country, Yost Lake Country, Elks. Home: 3111 N Monroe St Stillwater OK 74074 Office: PO Box 391 116 W 8th St Stillwater OK 74074

PLATONI, KATHERINE THERESA, counselor, therapist; b. Mt. Kisco, N.Y., Apr. 28, 1952; d. Eugene Joseph and Sydell (Greenberg) Platoni; B.S., Hobart and William Smith Coll., 1974; M.Ed. (grad. asst.), U. Miami, 1975; postgrad. in clin. psychology South Fla. Sch. Profl. Psychology, Miami. Intern counselor Univ. Family Services, Miami, Fla., 1975; resident aide Country House Sr. Citizens Home, Yorktown Heights, N.Y., 1976; behavior therapist Sunland Tng. Center, Fla. Dept. Health and Rehab. Services, Miami, 1976-77, retardation tng. specialist, 1977-78, behavior therapist Village South Intensive Treatment Unit, 1978-79; social worker Fellowship House, South Miami, Fla., 1979—. Mem. Am. Personnel and Guidance Assn., Am. Psychol. Assn., Am. Personnel Counselors Assn., Am. Assn. on Mental Deficiency. Contbr. articles on hypnosis to profl. jours. Home: 1876 S Miami Ave Miami FL 33129 Office: 5711 S Dixie Hwy South Miami FL 33143

PLATT, RICHARD LEROY, govt. adminstr.; b. Chewalla, Tenn., Oct. 10, 1930; s. John Ledbetter and Lurah Austin (Kimbrough) P.; B.S. in Public Affairs, Miss. State U., 1952; M.A. in Planning and Mgmt., Army Command and Gen. Staff Coll., 1965; M.S. in Public Adminstrn., George Washington U., 1972; postgrad. Va. Poly. and State U., 1974; m. Grace Ruth Perry, Feb. 18, 1960; children—Gayle Anne, Lurinda Ethel, Karen Richelle, Richard Edward Jonathan. Commd. 2d lt. U.S. Army, 1952; advanced through grades to lt. col., 1965; ops. officer, Japan and Korea, 1955-57, 63-64; comdg. office Air Def. Missile Units, Md., 1957-60; plans and policy officer U.S. Army Europe, 1960-63, ret., 1965; exec. dir. regional planning and devel. USAID, 1965-69; comptroller U.S. Army Engr. Center, 1969-72; dir. environ. services County of Arlington (Va.), 1972-74; dir. planning, community devel., public works and chmn. county staff County of St. Mary's (Md.), 1974-78; dir. planning, community devel. and public works City of Columbus (Miss.), 1978-79; exec. dir. Rapides Area Planning Commn., 1979—; pres. Alpha Omega Plums, Cons., Aberdeen, Miss., 1972—; tech. advisor to exec. bd. Golden Triangle Planning and Devel. Dist., 1978-79. Recipient Ministry of Home Affairs Republic of Korea Citation for Public Service, 1966; Kingdom of Thailand, Ministry of Interior Citation for Public Services, 1968; Nat. Assn. Counties Achievement Award for Excellence, 1977. Mem. Nat. Assn. Regional Councils, Nat. Utility Location and Coordination Council, Council for Internat. Urban Liaison, Am. Soc. Public Adminstrn., Am. Public Works Assn., Nat. Environ. Health Assn., Nat. Assn. Counties, Am. Planning Assn., Nat. Assn. Housing and Redevel. Ofcls., Nat. Trust for Historic Preservation, ASTM, Am. Mgmt. Assn., Bldg. Ofcl. and Code Adminstrs. Internat. Urban Land Inst., Nat. Assn. Counties, Nat. League Cities. Methodist. Club: Optimist. Contbr. articles to profl. jours. Home: 135 Camellia Heights Pineville LA 71360 Office: 818 Main St Pineville LA 71360 also 410 S Meridian St Aberdeen MS 39730

PLAXCO, JAMES CLARKE, architect, planner; b. Monroe, N.C., July 16, 1944; s. James McElwee and Rebecca Ann (Walton) P.; B.Arch., Clemson U., 1967. Archtl. draftsman Gutchow & Niesson, Hamburg, Germany, summer 1966; city planner City of Columbia (S.C.), 1968-71; architect, planner Sea Pines Co., Hilton Head Island, S.C., 1971-72, River Hills, S.C., 1972-73; v.p. planning and design Brandermill, Richmond, Va., 1973—; cons. Puerto Azul Resort, Manila, 1975-76. Asso. mem. Am. Inst. Planners, Tau Sigma Delta. Home: 605 N Davis St Apt 6 Richmond VA 23220 Office: Brandermill PO Box 287 Midlothian VA 23113

PLEASANT, GILBERT KAVANAUGH, univ. adminstr.; b. Lawrenceburg, Ky., Mar. 11, 1913; s. Phillip and Cora Lee P.; B.S., W.Va. State Coll., 1948; M.Ed., U. Cin., 1953; m. Harriette D., Nov. 26, 1941. Linotypist, Hemphill Press, Nashville, 1938-39, Louisville Leader, 1940, Atlanta Daily World, 1940-42; instr. W.Va. State Coll. 1948-53; asso. prof. indsl. technology Tenn. State U., 1953—, dir. printing services, 1953—. Chmn. bd. Gay-lea Christian Ch., Nashville. Served to capt. AC U.S. Army, 1943-46. Mem. Graphic Arts Edn. Assn., Tenn. Indsl. Arts Assn., Middle Tenn. In-Plant Printing Mgrs. Assn. (charter), Alpha Phi Alpha. Democrat. Club: Optimists (charter) (Nashville). Author: Elementary Printing, 1948. Home: 1007 39th Ave N Nashville TN 37209 Office: Tenn State U Nashville TN 37203

PLESE, CHARLES FRANCIS, JR., clin. chemist; b. Granite City, Ill., Mar. 5, 1947; s. Charles Francis Johanna (Bruncic) P.; M.S., Med. Coll. Ga., 1972; Ph.D., U. S.C., 1977; m. Patricia Ann Canonici, Aug. 16, 1974. Postdoctoral research asso. U. S.C., Columbia, 1977-79; clin. chemist, dir. esoteric testing Biomed. Reference Labs., Inc., Burlington, N.C., 1979—; instr. med. tech. trainee program and continuing edn. Am. Cancer Soc. research grantee, 1974. Mem. Am. Crystallographic Assn., Am. Fedn. Clin. Research, Sigma Xi. Condr. research devel. of clin. assays for cancer detection; contbr. articles in field to profl. publs. Home: 1318 Hanford Rd Graham NC 27253 Office: 1447 York Ct Burlington NC 27215

PLETCHER, RAYMOND EUGENE, indsl. engr., mfg. co. exec.; b. Ardmore, Okla., Apr. 18, 1937; s. Bruce Glesner and Winnie (Fondale) P.; B.S., Ill Inst. Tech., 1970; m. Donna Mae Maas, June 15, 1963; children—Kevin, Cheryl, Jason. Telegraph operator, wire chief, methods analyst C&NW Ry., Chgo., 1958-71; indsl. engr. Uniroyal Co., Ardmore, Okla., 1971-73; co. engr. Big Chief Roofing Co., Ardmore, 1973-74; v.p. prodn. SEM Corp., Springer, Okla., 1974—, sec. bd. dirs., 1974—. Served with U.S. Army, 1959-61. Registered profl. engr, Okla. Mem. Nat. Soc. Profl. Engrs., Okla. Soc. Profl. Engrs. Republican. Mem. Ch. Jesus Christ of Latter-Day Saints. Patentee in field. Home: 705 NW 5th St Wilson OK 73463 Office: SEM Corp PO Box 339 Springer OK 73458

PLITT, JEANNE GIVEN, librarian; b. Whitehall, N.Y., Aug. 27, 1927; d. Charles Russell and Anna Marie (Noyes) Given; student St. Lawrence U., 1945-47; A.B., U. Md., 1949; postgrad. Am. U., 1960-61; M.L.S., Cath. U. Am., 1968; m. Ferdinand Charles Plitt, Jr., Jan. 19, 1952; children—Christine, Marie, Charles Randolph. Library asst. Spl. Services div U.S. Army, 1949-51; tchr. secondary schs., Md. and Va.; reference librarian Alexandria (Va.) Library, 1967-68, asst. dir., 1968-70, dir., 1970—; chmn. librarians tech. com. Council Govts., Washington, 1971-72; chmn. Consortium No. Va. Library Networking Com., 1977—. Active Little Theatre Group, Alexandria. Recipient Alexandria Pub. Service award, 1964, 74. Mem. Va. Library

Assn., PTA, U. Md., Cath. U. alumni assns., Manuscript Soc., Alexandria Hist. Soc., Alexandria Assn., Urban League. Roman Catholic. Club: Zonta (sec. chpt. 1972-73, dir. 1973-74). Office: Alexandria Library 717 Queen St Alexandria VA 22314

PLOTT, ADAH ELIZABETH, cytotechnologist; b. Chatsworth, Ga., Nov. 2, 1938; d. Samuel Cole, Sr., and Elizabeth H. (Grahl) Plott; student LaGrange Coll., 1957-59, Emory U., 1960, Ga. State U., 1962. Trainee in cytotech., St. Joseph Infirmary, Atlanta, 1961-62; ednl. coordinator, Emory U., Cytotech. Sco., Atlanta, 1963-67; research cytotechnologist, Center for Disease Control, HEW, Atlanta, 1967—; instr. continuing edn. workshops, throughout U.S. Mem. So. Assn. Cytotechnologists (pres. 1971-72), Am., Ga. (editor newsletter) Socs. Cytology, Am. Soc. Med. Tech., Internat. Acad. Cytology (certified), Am. Soc. Clin. Pathologists (certified), Sigma Xi (asso.). Presbyterian. Speaker at profl. confs., workshops. Home: 969 Los Angeles Ave NE Atlanta GA 30306 Office: Pathology Div Bldg 1 Room 2301 1600 Clifton Rd NE Atlanta GA 30333

PLUMMER, A. Q., accountant; b. Moran, Tex., Dec. 23, 1921; s. John W. and Mittie (Gill) P.; B.B.A., U. Tex., 1947; m. Betty F. Cantrell, June 4, 1949; children—John Cantrell, Jim Mcclung, Betsy Beal. Accountant, The Tex. Co., Houston, 1947-55; tax accountant Tex. Gulf Producing Co., Houston, 1956-60, chief accountant, 1960-65, Libyan Am. Oil Co., Houston, 1960-65; sec.-treas. Barbers Hill Salt Water Co., Houston, 1960-65; pvt. practice C.P.A., Brenham, Tex., 1965—. Instr. accounting S. Tex. Coll., 1956-57; mem. Washington County Bluebonnet Trials Com., treas., 1961; mem. S.W. Houston Cub Scout pack Boy Scouts Am., Brazos Valley Estate Council. Bd. dirs. Bohne Hosp.; trustee St. Jude Hosp. Served with USAAF, 1943-45. C.P.A., Tex. Mem. Tex. Exec. Inst. (sec., treas. Houston), Tex. Soc. C.P.A.'s Washington County C. of C. Methodist (steward, auditor, sec. stewardship and fin. commn.). Lion (sec.). Home: Plum Hill Brenham TX 77833 Office: 201 W Main St Brenham TX 77833

PLUMMER, ADDISON WRENN, economist; b. Boston, Mar. 15, 1921; s. Charles Clarkson and Blanche Isabell (Wrenn) P.; B.B.A., U. Calif., Berkeley, 1947, B.A. in Slavic Langs., 1950; m. Sadie Salem, May 19, 1956; children—Elizabeth Wrenn, Susanna Clarkson. Accountant, Hood & Strong, San Francisco, 1948-49; economist Office Econ. Research, U.S. Govt., Langley, Va., 1952—. Served as officer, inf. U.S. Army, 1942-45. Recipient certificate of merit U.S. Govt., 1966. Mem. Alpha Mu Gamma, Potomac Rifle and Pistol Club, Nat. Rifle Assn. Home and office: 6802 Dean Dr McLean VA 22101

PLUMMER, ALAN LANE, physician; b. Ogallala, Nebr., Mar. 25, 1940; s. Virgil F. and Helen (Hultberg) P.; A.B., U. Nebr., 1962; M.D., Northwestern U., 1966; m. Virginia Pansing, June 13, 1964; children—Michael E., William L., Benjamin P., Patricia L. Intern, Passavant Hosp., Chgo., 1966-67; resident in internal medicine, fellow in pulmonary diseases Mayo Clinic, Rochester, Minn., 1967-71; staff physician Emory U. Clinic, Atlanta, 1971-73, partner, 1973—, med. dir. respiratory therapy dept. Emory U. Hosp., 1972—, med. dir. respiratory therapy technician program Emory U., 1975—, med. dir. programs in respiratory therapy, 1979—, asso. prof. medicine-pulmonary diseases, 1975—, asso. prof. allied health professions, 1978—, chief pulmonary disease subsect. Emory U. Clinic, 1971—; cons. pulmonary allergy and immunology adv. com. FDA. Mead Johnson scholar A.C.P., 1968-70. Fellow Am. Coll. Chest Physicians; mem. Ga. Thoracic Soc. (sec.-treas. 1976-78, pres. 1978—), Ga. Lung Assn., Atlanta Lung Assn., Am. Thoracic Soc., Am. Assn. Respiratory Therapy (bd. med. advisers), Nat. Assn. Med. Dirs. Respiratory Care, N.Y. Acad. Scis., Sigma Xi, Phi Beta Kappa, Alpha Omega Alpha. Episcopalian. Contbr. articles to profl. jours. Home: 663 Carriage Way NW Atlanta GA 30327 Office: 1365 Clifton Rd NE Atlanta GA 30322

PLUMMER, BENJAMIN FRANK, educator; b. Burlington Junction, Mo., Feb. 29, 1936; s. Marvin Ray and Lou Ella (Maier) P.; B.S., Iowa State U., 1958; Ph.D., Ohio State U., 1962; m. Gail Masterman, Mar. 25, 1961; children—Scott, Douglas, Suzanne, Jeffrey. Postdoctoral asso. Ga. Inst. Tech., 1962-63; asst. prof. chemistry S.D. State U., 1963-67; asst. prof. chemistry Trinity U., San Antonio, 1967-68, asso. prof., 1968-74, prof., 1974—, also chmn. dept.; project dir. NSF-Undergrad. Research Participation, 1970, 72. Robert A. Welch Found. grantee, 1967—. Mem. AAAS, Inter-Am. Photochem. Soc., Am. Chem. Soc., S.W. Sci. Forum, N.Y. Acad. Scis., AAUP. Presbyterian. Author: Selected Principles of Organic Chemistry, 1972; contbr. articles to profl. jours. Office: PO Box 52 Trinity U San Antonio TX 78284

PLUMMER, JACK MOORE, psychologist; b. Galveston, Tex., Apr. 19, 1940; s. Jack Moore and Sarah Carroll (Cochran) P.; B.A., St. Mary's U., 1962; M.S., Trinity U., 1968; Ph.D., Tex. Tech. U., 1969; A.A.S., Garland County Community Coll., 1978; m. Rose Marie Taylor, July 22, 1960; children—Cynthia Marie, Edward Moore, Elizabeth Anne, Sarah Lorraine, Jack Moore. Psychologist Okla. rehab. div. Okla. State Reformatory, Granite, 1968-69; dir. tng. Ark. Rehab. Research and Tng. Center, Hot Springs, 1970-71; pvt. practice psychology, Hot Springs, 1971—; psychol. cons. to Rehab. Services, Dept. Correction, Probation and Parole Div., also to physicians, attys., cts., law enforcement agys.; instr. Garland County Community Coll., Hot Springs, 1973—; cons. Parents Without Partners. Fellow Ark. Psychol. Assn.; mem. Am. Correctional Assn., Nat. Rehab. Assn., Nat. Rehab. Counseling Assn., Am. Psychol. Assn., Internat. Soc. for Study Symbols, Psychology-Law Soc. Democrat. Roman Catholic. Elk, Lion. Contbr. articles to profl. jours., chpt. in Handbook of Measurement and Evaluation in Rehabilitation. Home: 614 Ridgeview Dr Hot Springs AR 71901 Office: 600 W Grand St Hot Springs AR 71901

PLUMMER, STEPHEN RAY, furniture co. exec.; b. High Point, N.C., Oct. 18, 1952; s. Ray Craig and Rebecca Mae (Warden) P.; B.S., N.C. State U., 1974; m. June Pinson, Sept. 15, 1979. Prodn. control mgr. Marsh Furniture Co., High Point, N.C., 1974—. Mem. Adminstrv. Mgmt. Soc. (dir. 1979-80), Archdale-Trinity Jaycees (pres. 1978-79). Democrat. Home: Route 2 Hickory Trail Thomasville NC 27360 Office: PO Box 870 High Point NC 27261

PLUMMER, VIRGIL CLAGETT, JR., mech. engr.; b. North Jackson, Ohio, Feb. 18, 1931; s. Virgil C. and Lillian (Kimberly) P.; B.E., Youngstown U., 1960; m. Alma June Bartholomew, Feb. 10, 1951; children—Lawrence David, Laurel Susan, Ronald Allan, Neal Warren. Gen. foreman maintenance Corhart Refractories, Louisville, 1964-65; project engr. Procelain Metals Corp., Louisville, 1965-69, Carman Industries, Jeffersonville, Ind., 1969-70; project engr. Vibranetics, Inc., Louisville, 1970-76, sr. project engr., 1976-78, engring. mgr., 1978—; evening instr. Ind. U. S.E., New Albany, 1974-79. Served with U.S. Army, 1951-53. Registered profl. engr., Ohio, Ky. Patentee in field. Home: 4324 Foeburn Ln Louisville KY 40207 Office: 7310 Grade Ln Louisville KY 40219

PLUMMER, VIRGINIA STANLEY, newspaper exec.; b. Greenville, Ala., Dec. 11, 1920; d. John Glenn and Mary Louise (Beeland) Stanley; student Agnes Scott Coll., 1938-40, U. Ala., 1940-41, 42-43; m. McDonald Plummer, Oct. 15, 1946; children—McDonald, Virginia Beeland Plummer Nearing, Glenn Stanley Plummer Cooper. Receptionist, Eastern Air Lines, 1944; sec. Greenville (Ala.) Public Schs., 1951-58; society editor, columnist Greenville Advocate, 1960—, v.p., 1973—. Charter mem. local chpt. DAR, 1962; mem. Landmarks Found. Butler County, chmn. ann. Homes Tours, 1978, 79; mem. choir Presbyterian Ch. Mem. Ala. Press Assn., Ala. Hist. Assn., Butler County Hist. Soc. Clubs: Pride of Greenville Garden (pres., 1959-60), Am. Camellia Soc., Greenville Camellia Soc. (sec.), Delta Delta Delta. Contbr. feature story Camellia Jour., 1978. Home: 218 E Commerce St Greenville AL 36037 Office: 103 Hickory St PO Box 507 Greenville AL 36037

PLYLER, BOB LEE, ladder mfg. co. exec.; b. Batesville, Ark., Dec. 20, 1936; s. Lee Roy and Altha Cleo (McSpadden) P.; A.A., Arlington State Coll., 1955; B.A., Tex. A. and M. U., 1957; A.F.D. (hon.), London Inst., 1972; m. Paulette Durso; children—Vonda Lynn, Pamela Lee, Bobby Lee, Joseph Lane, Rick Todd. With Lone Star Ladder Co., 1957-66, plant mgr., 1966; founder, pres. Acme Ladders, Inc., Houston, 1966—. Pres., Gulf Meadows Civic Assn., 1962-67; former spl. adviser, master of ceremonies Consular Ball of Houston, 1964-75; former master of ceremonies Noches Americas Internat. Ball; v.p. Greater Houston Civic Found., 1965-67; mem. fund raising com. Nat. Jewish Hosp., Denver, 1968-74; protocol rep. to Office of Mayor, Houston Jaycees, 1966-73; chmn. Galveston County Drainage Dist. 3, 1973—; bd. dirs. Mayor's Houston Taipia Sister City Com., 1968-71. Served with USAF, 1955-56. Mem. C. of C. Baptist (v.p. 1969-70). Clubs: Masons, Shriners. Office: Box 26593 Houston TX 77207

PLYLER, CRANFORD OLIVER, JR., physician; b. Statesville, N.C., May 24, 1927; s. Cranford O. and Matie (Gray) P.; B.S., High Point Coll., 1948; certificate in medicine U. N.C., 1951; M.D., George Washington U., 1953; m. Ruth Hull, June 5, 1948; children—David Cranford, Michael Hull, Cranford Oliver, Rosemary Gray. Intern, Charlotte (N.C.) Meml. Hosp., 1953-54, resident in internal medicine, 1956-57; gen. practice medicine, Badin, N.C., 1954-56, Thomasville, N.C., 1956-76, Jacksonville, Fla., 1976—; chief of staff Community Gen. Hosp., Thomasville; asso. prof. U. Fla. Coll. Medicine, 1976—; dir. family practice residency program St. Vincent's Med. Center, Jacksonville, 1976—. Chmn. Thomasville Bd. Edn., 1960-64. Served with USAF, 1946-47. Diplomate Am. Bd. Family Practice. Mem. AMA, Royal Soc. Medicine, Am., Fla., N.C. (pres. 1975-76) acads. family physicians, Fla. Med. Assn. Methodist. Club: Lions (chpt. pres. 1964). Home: 3900 McGirts Blvd Jacksonville FL 32210 Office: 1824 King St Jacksonville FL 32204

PLYMALE, THOMAS WALTER, mfg. co. exec.; b. Bedford County, Va., Dec. 6, 1924; s. William B. and Virginia E. (Johnson) P.; B.S. in Civil Engring. with honors, Va. Poly. Inst. and State U., 1951; M.B.A., W.Va. U., 1964; m. Dorothy Irene Mitchell, Dec. 17, 1949; children—Wanda, Roger, Debra. With engring. div. Union Carbide Corp., South Charleston, W.Va., 1951—, mgr. constrn., domestic and fgn., 1974—. Chmn. Indsl. Div., United Fund Dr., Charleston, 1959. Served with U.S. Army, 1943-45. Mem. ASCE. Republican. Baptist. Home: 159 Oakwood Estate Scott Depot WV 25560 Office: Union Carbide Corp PO Box 8361 South Charleston WV 25303

POAG, GEORGE DANIEL, JR., realty co. exec.; b. Nashville, Apr. 4, 1941; s. George Daniel and Martha Roselle (Baker) P.; A.B. (Gooch Found. scholar 1959), Princeton U., 1963; postgrad. Columbia U., 1963-64; M.B.A. (Univ. Fellow), Emory U., 1965; m. Chloee Kasselberg, Nov. 27, 1965; children—Daniel Mark, Joshua Duncan, Jeremy Moseley. Vcie pres. APTCO, Chem. Mark SE, Atlanta, 1965-68, SE Beverage and Ice Equipment Co., Atlanta, 1968-70, Schumacher Mortgage Co., Memphis, 1970-73; gen. partner Land Ventures, Memphis, 1972—; pres. Equity Ventures, Inc., Memphis, 1973-75, Diversified Realty Mgmt. Co., Memphis, 1973-75, Poag Co., Memphis, 1975—. Chmn. play finding com. Theater Memphis, 1977-79, dir., 1976—, v.p., mem. exec. bd., 1977, pres., 1979-80; bd. dirs. Theatre Memphis Found., 1977—; team chmn. Am. Cancer Soc., 1974; dir. First Unitarian Church, 1975—, canvas dir., 1974-77. Cert. property mgr. Mem. Memphis Bd. Realtors, Tenn., Nat. assns. realtors, Inst. Real Estate Mgmt., Nat. Mktg. Inst. Republican. Clubs: Racquet of Memphis, Princeton Alumni Assn. (chmn. schs. com. 1975—). Home: 4275 Gwynne Rd Memphis TN 38117 Office: 4711 Poplar Ave Suite 210 Memphis TN 38117

POAGE, WALLER STAPLES, III, architect; b. Wythe County, Va., Apr. 25, 1936; s. Waller Staples and Mary Crockett (Simmerman) P.; B.Arch., Va. Poly. Inst. and State U., 1960; m. Elizabeth B., June 21, 1975; children—Mary Elizabeth, Mary Margaret. Asso., Dales Y. Foster, Inc., Architects, Dallas, 1974-76; pvt. practice Waller S. Poage & Asso., Architects, Planners, Houston, 1965—, Wytheville, Va., 1967-69, Arlington, Tex., 1973-76; owner, prin. Community Planners Inc. of Laredo, Tex., 1976—. Commr., Airport Zoning Bd., City of Laredo, 1979—; adv. to city council, Constrn. Industry Council, Houston, 1969-71. Recipient Award of Merit for residential design, House and Home Mag., 1968; Award of Merit, Constrn. Specifications Inst., 1971; registered architect, Tex., La., Va., Ark. Mem. AIA, Tex. Soc. Architects, Constrn. Specifications Inst. (ofcl. rep. and exec. v.p. 1970-72, 1st. v.p. 1972, dir. 1970-73), Laredo C. of C., Am. Inst. Planners. Republican. Episcopalian. Clubs: Rotary (dir. 1978—), Exchange (bd. dirs. 1967-68, pres. 1969). Archtl. works include Jim Hogg County Jail, Hebbronville, Tex., 1978, Webb County Jail, Laredo, Tex., 1978, Westgate Pl., 1977, Country Club Estates, 1978, The Quadrangle, 1978, The Century Bldg., Laredo, 1976, Wytheville (Va.) Community Hosp., 1969-70, Wythe County Vocational Sch., 1969-70, Steamboat Recreational Complex, 1971-73, additions to Alma Pierce Sch., Laredo, modifications McDonnell Sch., Laredo, others. Home: 701 Banyon Ct Laredo TX 78041 Office: Community Planners of Laredo Inc PO Box 2427 7080 San Bernardo St Laredo TX 78041

POARCH, JOHN THOMAS, II, state ofcl.; b. Richmond, Va., Dec. 22, 1947; s. John Thomas and Florence Gaynelle (Lee) P.; B.A. with distinction, U. Va., 1970, M.P.A., 1979. Personnel recruiter Va. Dept. Personnel and Tng., Richmond, 1971-73, personnel mgr. Div. Motor Vehicles, 1975, dir. personnel and tng., 1975-77, facilities dir., 1977-78; personnel dir. Va. Housing Devel. Authority, Richmond, 1979—. Served with U.S. Army Res., 1970-76. Mem. Am. Mgmt. Assn., Am. Soc. Tng. and Devel., Am. Soc. Personnel Adminstrn., Va. Coll. Placement Assn. (sec. 1975-76, Certificate of Appreciation 1976), Grad. Pub. Adminstrn. Assn. U. Va. (treas.), Va. Mus. (sponsoring mem.), Va. Municipal League, U. Va. Alumni Assn., Sigma Alpha Mu. Contbr. articles to profl. jours. Home: 4514 Patterson Ave Richmond VA 23221 Office: 13 S 13th St Richmond VA 23219

PODGORNY, GEORGE, emergency physician; b. Tehran, Iran, Mar. 17, 1934; s. Emanuel and Helen (Parsian) P.; came to U.S., 1954, naturalized, 1973; B.S., Maryville Coll., 1958; postgrad. Bowman Gray Sch. Medicine, 1958; M.D., Wake Forest U., 1962; m. Ernestine Koury, Oct. 20, 1962; children—Adele, Emanuel II, George, Gregory. Intern in surgery N.C. Bapt. Hosp., Winston-Salem, 1962-63, chief resident in gen. surgery, 1966-67, in cardio-thoracic surgery, 1967-69; sr. med. examiner Forsyth County, N.C., 1972—; dir. dept. emergency medicine Forsyth Meml. Hosp., Winston-Salem, 1974—; sec.-treas. Forsyth Emergency Services, Winston-Salem, 1970—; dir. Emergency Med. Services Project Region II of N.C., 1975—. founder Western Piedmont Emergency Med. Services Council, 1973; mem. N.C. Emergency Med. Services Adv. Council, 1976—; asso. prof. clin. surgery Bowman Gray Sch. Medicine, Wake Forest U., Winston-Salem, 1979—. Bd. dirs. Piedmont Health Systems Agy., 1975—; trustee Forsyth County Hosp., Authority, 1974-75; bd. dirs. N.C. Health Coordinating Council, 1975—. Fellow Internat. Coll. Surgeons, Internat. Coll. Angiology, Royal Soc. Health (Gt. Brit.), Southeastern Surg. Congress; mem. Am. Coll. Emergency Physicians (charter; pres. 1978-79), AMA, (sec. council of sect. emergency medicine 1976—), Am. Bd. Emergency Medicine (pres. 1976—). Contbr. articles to profl. publs. on trauma, snake bite and history of medicine. Home: 2115 Georgia Ave Winston-Salem NC 27104 Office: 3333 Silas Creek Pkwy Winston-Salem NC 27103

PODOLSKY, SAMUEL, mgmt. cons.; b. Mexico City, Dec. 20, 1945; s. Manuel and Miriam (Rapoport) P.; B.A., U. Nacional Autonoma, Mexico City, 1967; M.B.A., U. Pa., 1971; m. Paulette Levy, June 28, 1969; children—David, Daniel. Sr. auditor Alexander Grant & Co., Mexico City, 1967-69; adminstrv. mgr., cons. Booz, Allen & Hamilton, Mexico City, 1971-73; sr. v.p., gen. controller Sistema Bancos de Comercio, Mexico City, 1973-76; founder, partner Podolsky y Asociados, A.P., Mgmt. Cons., Mexico City, 1976—. Inst. Internat. Edn. grantee, 1969-71, U. Mex. grantee, 1969-71. Jewish. Club: Wharton (pres. Mexico City chpt. 1975-78). Author: PERT/CPM and the Audit of Financial Statements, 1969. Home: Sierra Madre 450 Mexico City 10 DF Mexico Office: Monte Pelvoux 110 Lomas Chapultepec Mexico City 10 DF Mexico

POE, WILLIE E., govt. ofcl.; b. Jackson, Tenn., Jan. 25, 1944; s. Ulridge and Warnett Poe; B.A.S., U. Richmond, 1977; M.B.A., L.I. U., 1979; J.D., Antioch Sch. Law, 1979; m. Angelyn Craft, Feb. 8, 1964; children—Steven, Marc. Pres., Media, Inc., 1971-72; exec. dir. Church Hill Econ. Devel. Corp., 1972-75; asst. dist. dir. minority small bus. SBA, Richmond, Va., 1975—. Recipient cert. of recognition SBA, 1978, cert. of commendation, 1979. Office: 400 N 8th St Richmond VA 23240

POFAHL, C.F. (SANDY), lawyer, ind. oil producer; b. Aberdeen, S.D., Oct. 7, 1941; s. Frederick Albert and Margaret Ruth (Draeger) P.; B.A., Stanford U., 1963, J.D., 1967; postgrad. Princeton U. Sem., 1963-64; children—Quinn, Kristi, Dusti, Brady. Admitted to Tex. bar, 1968; asst. to partner Lincoln Property Co., Dallas, 1967-69; pres. Commonwealth Devel. Co., Dallas, 1969-75; Asian investment coordinator Trammell Crow Co., Asia, S. Pacific, 1975-76; pres. Commonwealth Energy, Inc., Dallas, 1976—; investment property atty. Mem. Dallas Bar Assn., Tex. Ind. Producers and Royalty Owners Assn., Ind. Producers Assn. Am., Internat. Assn. Fin. Planners, Mid-Continent Oil and Gas Assn., Dallas-Fort Worth Stanford U. Alumni Assn. (pres. 1968-69). Republican. Presbyterian. Home: 4135 Buena Vista Dallas TX 75204 Office: 2301 N Akard Suite 204 Dallas TX 75201

POFANDT, WERNER PETER, mech. engr.; b. Dresden, Germany, Sept. 19, 1934; s. Erich and Ilse (Posselt) P.; ed. vocat. sch. Dresden, 1949-51; m. Sharon Lynne Planck, Nov. 22, 1975; 1 dau., Kelly Lynne. Machinist, Sachsenwerk Dresden, 1949-57, Joseph Meyer, Mohlin, Switzerland, 1958-65; engr. Opto Mechanik Inc., Melbourne, Fla., 1969—, asst. head engring. dept., 1976—. Served with Germany Army, 1952-55. Office: Opto Mechanik Inc PO Box 640 Melbourne FL 32901

POFFENBARGER, PHILLIP LYNN, physician; b. Lafayette, Ind., Oct. 13, 1937; A.B., Ind. U., Bloomington, 1959, M.S., Indpls., 1963, M.D., 1963; m. 1957; 6 children. Intern, U. Washington Hosp., Seattle, 1963-64, resident Affiliated Hosps., 1964-65; asst. prof. medicine U. Tex. Med. Br., Galveston, 1970-73, asst. prof. biochemistry, 1971-73, asso. prof. medicine, human biology chemistry and genetics, 1973—, dir. div. endocrinology and metabolism and Clin. Research Center, 1975—, now Raymond L. Gregory prof. in internal medicine, 1978—; NIH fellow U. Washington, 1965-66. Recipient Research and Devel. award Am. Diabetes Assn., 1968-69; NIH spl. fellow, 1969-70. Mem. AAS, Am. Fedn. Clin. Research, Endocrine Soc., Am. Diabetes Assn., Am. Soc. Clin. Investigation. Office: Clin Research Center U Tex Med Br Galveston TX 77550

POGUE, FORREST CARLISLE, historian; b. Eddyville, Ky., Sept. 17, 1912; s. Forrest Carlisle and Frances (Carter) P.; A.B., Murray State Coll., 1931, LL.D., 1970; M.A., U. Ky., 1932; Ph.D., Clark U., 1939, L.H.D., 1975; Am. Exchange fellow, Inst. des Hautes Etudes Internationales, U. Paris, 1937-38; Litt. D., Washington and Lee U., 1970; m. Christine Brown, Sept. 4, 1954. Instr., Western Ky. State Coll., 1933; from instr. to asso. prof. Murray (Ky.) State Coll., 1933-42, prof. history, 1954-56; mem. hist. sect. U.S. Forces, ETO, 1944-46; with Office Chief Mil. History, Dept. Army, 1946-52; ops. research analyst Ops. Research Office, Johns Hopkins, Heidelberg, Germany, 1952-54; dir. George C. Marshall Research Center, 1956-64, George C. Marshall Research Library, 1964-74, Dwight D. Eisenhower Inst. Hist. Research, Smithsonian Instn., Washington, 1974—; exec. dir. George C. Marshall Research Found., 1964-74, life mem. adv. com., 1974—; Mary Moody Northen vis. prof. history Va. Mil. Inst., 1972; mem. adv. com. Dir. Naval History, Dept. Navy, Air Force Hist. Office, Dept. Air Force; chmn. adv. com. Senate Hist. Office; trustee U.S. Commn. Mil. History, Am. Com. History World War II (former chmn.); mem. adv. com. publ. Eisenhower papers Johns Hopkins U.; mem. adv. com. Nat. Hist. Soc.; chmn. adv. com. coll. campus program Former Mems. of Congress Assn.; nat. adviser Ky. Bicentennial Oral History Commn.; former regent Omar N. Bradley Found.; trustee U.S. Capitol Hist. Soc.; bd. dirs. Harry S. Truman Library Inst. Served with AUS, 1942-45; ETO. Decorated Bronze Star; Croix de Guerre (France); recipient Distinguished Alumnus award Murray State Coll., 1964; Distinguished Alumnus Centennial award U. Ky., 1965. Fellow Am. Mil. Inst. (past pres.), Soc. Am. Historians; mem. Am., So. hist. assns., Orgn. Am. Historians, NEA, Oral History Assn. (past pres.), Am. Legion. Democrat. Presbyterian. Club: Cosmos. Author: The Supreme Command, 1954; George C. Marshall: Education of a General, vol. 1, 1963; George C. Marshall: Ordeal and Hope, 1939-42, vol. 2, 1966; George C. Marshall: Organizer of Victory, 1943-45, vol. 3, 1973; co-author: The Meaning of Yalta, 1956; contbr. to Command Decisions, 1960, Total War and Cold War, 1962, D-Day: The Normandy Invasion in Retrospect, 1971, Soldiers and Statesmen, 1973, The Continuing Revolution, 1975, Bicentennial History of the U.S., 1976; The War Lords, 1976. Address: 1111 Army-Navy Dr Arlington VA 22202

POHANI, BHAGWAN PITUMAL, chem. engr.; b. Karachi, Pakistan, Jan. 8, 1940; came to U.S., 1963, naturalized, 1976; s. Pitumal J. and Thakuri P. (Khatwani) P.; B.Chem. Engring., U. Bombay (India), 1963; M.S., U. Calif., Berkeley, 1964; postgrad. Columbia U., 1964-66; M.B.A., U. Houston, 1979; m. Asha N. Ramchandani, July 14, 1967; children—Celia Fiona, Rajesh Kumar. Vis. lectr. thermodynamics City U. N.Y., 1965-66; project mgr. Sci. Design Co. Inc., N.Y.C., 1966-77, mgr. fin. controls, Houston, 1977—. Du Pont fellow, 1964-65; registered profl. engr., Tex. Mem. Am. Inst. Chem. Engrs., Nat. Soc. Profl. Engrs. Hindu. Home: 3602

Oak Gardens Dr Kingwood TX 77339 Office: 6750 West Loop South Bellaire TX 77401

POHLKE, PHILIP AUGUSTUS, mech. engr.; b. Collingswood, N.J., July 24, 1908; s. Otto Henry and Emma Louise (Deiser) P.; B.S. in Mech. Engring., U. Pa., 1929; m. Elizabeth Fairfield Boothe, Oct. 4, 1952; 1 son, Fredric B. Engr., Publicker Comml. Alcohol Co., Gulf Oil Corp., Allen Sherman Hoff Co., 1929-38; designer, devel. engr., project engr. tech. specialist Hercules Inc., Wilmington, Del., 1938-39, 67-70, Brunswick, Ga., 1939-41, Hopewell, Va., 1941-58, 70—, Magna, Utah, 1958-67; pvt. practice mech. engring., Hopewell. Registered profl. engr., Va. Mem. ASME, AIAA, Nat. Soc. Profl. Engrs., Sigma Xi. Patron Air Force Assn. Home: Route 1 Box 96 Disputanta VA 23842

POILEY, JEFFREY EDWARD, physician; b. Balt., Mar. 21, 1941; s. Samuel Milton and Sarah (Levin) P.; B.A., Johns Hopkins U., 1961; M.D., U. Md., 1965; m. Shelby T. Weiner, June 6, 1971; children—Shawn M., Seth D. Intern, Jackson Meml. Hosp., Miami, 1965-66, resident in internal medicine, 1966-67; resident in internal medicine U. Miami, 1969-70, fellowship in rheumatology, 1970-72; gen. practice medicine and rheumatology, Orlando, Fla., 1972—. Served with USAF, 1967-69. Diplomate Am. Bd. Internal Medicine. Mem. Fla., Orange County med. assns., Am. Rehumatism Assn., Fla. Soc. Rheumatology. Contbr. articles in field to profl. jours. Office: 615 E Princeton St Orlando FL 32803

POINTER, ROBERT ANTHONY, fgn. employment service exec.; b. St. Louis, Apr. 20, 1943; s. Ralph Clinton and Florence Anna (Frahm) P.; Bus. degree U. Mo., St. Louis, 1967; m. Susan Louise Grim, Apr. 10, 1971; children—Bret, Ahren. Partner, Filter Queen of Chesapeake, Balt., 1967-71; field rep. Meridian Waterproofing Corp., Balt., 1971-73, S.W. Sunsites, Inc., Houston, 1973-74; pres. World Scan, Inc., Dallas, 1975-80; dir., cons. Maek-a-Wae, Inc., Dallas, 1976—. Served with USMC, 1961-64. Republican. Presybterian. Asst. editor, staff writer World Scan Press, 1976-80. Office: PO Box 1033 Plano TX 75074

POITEVINT, KATHERINE BROWN, speech pathologist; b. Eufaula, Ala., Oct. 5, 1949; d. John C. and Edna Louise (Campbell) Brown; student Agnes Scott Coll., 1968-69; B.A., U. South Ala., 1972; M.A., Auburn U., 1974; m. James William Poitevint, Nov. 29, 1975. Chief speech and lang. pathologist Auburn U. at Montgomery (Ala.) Mental Health Clinic, 1974-76; owner, operator Speech Therapy Services, Montgomery, 1977—; adj. instr. Auburn U., Montgomery, 1978—; cons. Montgomery Community Action, Head Start, nursing homes, U. Ala. Tng. Outreach Program for Sensory Impaired, 1978—, others. Mem. Jasmine Hills Arts Council, Montgomery, 1979-80. Mem. Ala. Speech and Hearing Assn. (exec. council 1980); Am. Speech and Hearing Assn. (cert. clin. competence), Am. Acad. Pvt. Practitioners in Speech Pathology and Audiology, Montgomery Speech and Hearing Assn., Phi Kappa Phi, Psi Chi. Clubs: Ashmolean Soc., Order of the Rogue, Montgomery Jr. Woman's. Home: 3233 Wilmington Rd Montgomery AL 36105 Office: 2900 McGehee Rd Montgomery AL 36111

POKLUDA, SANDRA JEAN, educator; b. Madisonville, Tex., Dec. 25, 1940; d. Reginald Marvin and Dorothy Mae (McCollum) Whearley; B.B.A., Sam Houston State U., 1963, M.Ed., 1975; m. James Alois Pokluda, June 7, 1963; children—Jamie Ann, Brian James. Tchr., LaMarque (Tex.) Ind. Sch. Dist., 1963-73, Mexia (Tex.) Ind. Sch. Dist., 1974-75; asst. team project dir. Mexia State Sch., 1976-77, edn. specialist quality assurance, 1977-78, coordinator alternate placement and follow-up, 1978—. Mem. Am. Assn. Mental Deficiency, Tex. Assn. Mental Deficiency, Tex. Public Employees Assn., Sam Houston State U. Alumni Assn. Democrat. Baptist. Office: PO Box 1132 Mexia TX 76667

POLACK, FRANK M., ophthalmologist; b. Lima, Peru, Apr. 28, 1929; came to U.S., 1955, naturalized, 1959; s. Enrique M. and Rosa (Ramirez) P.; B.S., Sch. Medicine San Marcos U., Lima, Peru, 1954, M.D., 1955; m. Patricia Garcia, May 31, 1956; children—Frank E., Peter J., William A. Lab. asst. dept. pathology and tropical medicine U. San Marcos, 1953-55, chief lab. neuropathology Sch. Medicine, 1953-55; asst. Eye Clinic, Hosp. St. Toribio, Lima, 1954-55; intern Charity Hosp., Lima, 1954-55; intern Grasslands Hosp., Valhalla, N.Y., 1956-57, resident in ophthalmology, 1957-60, attending ophthalmologist, 1962-67; resident in ophthalmology Inst. Neoplastic Diseases, Lima, 1955; resident in neurology and psychiatry N.J. State Hosp., Malboro and Princeton U. Postgrad. Sch., 1955-57; asst. attending ophthalmologist Vanderbilt Clinic, Columbia Presbyn. Hosp., N.Y.C., 1962-67; attending ophthalmologist St. Vincent's Hosp., N.Y.C., 1964-67, White Plains (N.Y.) Hosp. and St. Agnes's Hosp., White Plains, 1964-67; asso. prof. ophthalmology Coll. Medicine, U. Fla., Gainesville, 1967-74, prof., 1974—, chief corneal and external disease dept. ophthalmology, 1978—, mem. com. on disabled students, univ. senate, del. Sch. Medicine; cons. ophthalmology VA Hosp., Gainesville, 1969—; cons. U.S. Navy Hosp., Jacksonville, Fla., 1976—; med. dir., bd. dirs. N. Fla. Lions Eye Bank, 1970—; chief glaucoma clinic Shands Teaching Hosp., U. Fla., 1975—. Recipient Damon Runyon award Columbia U., 1960; Biennial Sci. prize Republic of Argentina, 1967; NIH spl. fellow Columbia U., 1960-64, Fla. collaboration grantee L. Godwin Inst. Cancer Research, 1967-68, mem. task force immunology, 1967. Fellow Am. Acad. Ophthalmology (honor award 1974), A.C.S.; mem. AMA, Assn. Research in Vision and Ophthalmology, Peruvian Ophthalmology Soc., Alachua Med. Soc., Fla. Soc. Ophthalmology, Castroviejo Soc. (sec.-treas.), Peruvian Am. Med. Soc., Société Française d'Oftalmologie, Société de Medicine Paris, Am. Soc. Contemporary Ophthalmology, Pan Am. Assn. Ophthalmology (vis. prof. Latin Am. 1973), Barraquer Inst. (Spain), AAUP, Am. Ophthalmol. Soc., Internat. Soc. Eye Research, Fundacion Malbran (Argentina) (advisor), Colombian Oftalmologica Soc. (hon.), French Soc. Arts, Scis. and Letters (hon.), Moacyr Alvaro Ophthalmol. Soc. (Sao Paulo, Brazil) (hon.). Roman Catholic. Author: Corneal Transplantation, 1977; editor Interam. Symposium on Corneal and External Diseases, 1972; editorial bds. profl. pubs., contbr. articles to refereed jours.; book reviewer. Office: Box J-284 JHMHC Gainesville FL 32610

POLAN, NANCY MOORE, artist; b. Newark, Ohio; d. William Tracy and Francis (Flesher) Moore; A.B., Marshall U., 1936; m. Lincoln Milton Polan, Mar. 28, 1934; children—Charles Edwin, William Joseph Marion. One-man shows Charleston Art Gallery, 1961, 67, 73, Greenbrier, 1963, Huntington Galleries, 1963, 66, 71, N.Y. World's Fair, 1965, W.Va. U., 1966, Carroll Reese Mus., 1967, Mountaineer Dinner Theatre, Winfield, W.Va., 1972; exhibited in group shows: Am. Watercolor Soc., Allied Artists of Am., Nat. Arts Club, 1968, 69, 70, 71, 72, 73, 74, 76, Pa. Acad. Fine Arts, Opening of Creative Arts Center W.Va. U., 1969, Internat. Platform Assn. Art Exhibit, 1968-69, 72, 73, Allied Artists W.Va., 1968-69, Joan Miro Graphic Exhbn., Barcelona, Spain, 1970, XXI Exhibit Contemporary Art, La Scala, Florence, Italy, 1971, Ressegna Internazionale d'Arte Grafica, Siena, Italy, 1973, Opening of Parkersburg (W.Va.) Art Center, 1975, traveling exhbn. Am. Watercolor Soc., 1972-73, Accademia Leonardo da Vinci, Rome, 1979, Nuevo Acropoli, Rome, 1979, numerous others. Mem. internat. com. Centro Studi e Scambi Internazionale, Rome, Italy, 1968, spl. rep., 1970, hon. v.p., 1979. Recipient Norton Meml. award 3d Nat. Jury Show Am. Art, Chautauqua, N.Y., 1960; purchase prize, Jurors award for Watercolor Huntington Galleries, 1960, 61; Gold medal Masters of Modern Art exhbn., La Scala Gallery, Florence, 1975; Grumbacher award Pen and Brush, 1978, many others. Mem. D.A.R., Allied Artists W.Va., Huntington Galleries, Internat. Platform Assn. (3d award 1977), Allied Artists Am. (asso.), Tri-State Arts Assn., Sunrise Found., Pen and Brush (hon. mention), Am. Watercolor Soc. (asso.), Am. Fedn. Arts, Nat. Arts Club (watercolor award 1969), Leonardo da Vinci Acad., Accademia Italia (Gold medal), Sigma Kappa. Episcopalian. Address: 2 Prospect Dr Huntington WV 25701 also 2106 Club Dr Vero Beach FL 32960

POLAND, THOMAS MITCHELL, writer; b. Augusta, Ga., Feb. 4, 1949; s. John Mitchell and Mary Ruth (Walker) P.; B.A. in Journalism, U. Ga., 1971, M.Ed. in Media, 1975; postgrad. U. S.C., 1977; m. Rebecca Jean Emanuel, Mar. 25, 1978; children—Elizabeth W., Rebecca A. Instr. media-journalism-edn. Columbia (S.C.) Coll., 1974-78; scriptwriter, cinematographer S.C. Wildlife, Columbia, 1978—; films include: The Magnificent Pelican, 1978; Sand Dunes, 1978; Triumph of the Wood Duck, 1979; Carolina Bays, 1979; Blackwater Rivers, 1980; contbg. writer/photographer: The Vanity Fair Lithographs: An Illustrated Checklist; The Vanity Fair Gallery: A Collector's Guide to the Caricatures. Recipient award superior media contbs. Assn. Ednl. Communications and Tech., 1978, Best Film for TV award Am. Assn. Conservation Info., 1979. Home: 14 Westchester Ct Columbia SC 29210

POLATTY, ROSE JACKSON, civic worker; b. Atlanta, Sept. 17, 1922; d. James Wilmot and Esther Ann (Sweeny) Jackson; A.B. in Journalism, U. Ga., 1943; postgrad. Oglethorpe U., 1962-63, Ga. State U., 1963; m. George Junius Polatty, Nov. 27, 1942; children—George Junius, Robert Wilmot, Rose Crystal, Richard James. Active U. Ga. Alumni Soc., pres. Class of 1943 Alumni, 1948-58, bd. mgrs., 1966-69, v.p., 1971-73, chmn. seminar, 1971; exec. sec. Atlanta Boy Choir, 1968-69; bd. dirs. Atlanta Arts Council, 1968-69; advisory com. Kennesaw Coll. on Wheels, 1974-78; bicentennial chmn., City of Roswell, Ga., 1975-76, sec. hist. preservation commn., 1978—; active Ga. Trust for Hist. Preservation, Ga. Conservancy, Roswell Hist. Soc., Women's Assn. Atlanta Symphony Orchestra; adminstrv. bd., chmn. altar guild, Roswell United Meth. Ch. Recipient recognition award Nat. 4-H Alumni, 1959, service award City of Roswell, 1976, community service award Roswell Optimist Club, 1977, Roswell Jaycee Leadership award, 1977, community service award Zion Bapt. Ch., 1977. Mem. Women in Communications, Colonial Dames XVII Century (v.p. chpt. 1980—), Delta Omicron, Phi Beta Kappa, Phi Kappa Phi, Kappa Delta Pi. Clubs: Kappa Delta, P.E.O. (chpt. AA, Ga., charter 1977), D.A.R. (Joseph Habersham chpt.), Roswell Women's (charter 1948, pres. 1966-68), Roswell Garden (charter 1951, pres. 1975-77), N. Fulton Council Garden Clubs (charter 1975, pres. 1975-77). Home: 889 Mimosa Blvd Roswell GA 30075

POLICHINO, JOSEPH ANTHONY, JR., wholesale co. exec.; b. Houston, Oct. 17, 1948; s. Joseph Anthony and Josephine Adeline P.; student Spring Hill Coll., 1966-67; A.A. cum laude, S. Tex. Jr. Coll., 1969; student U. Houston, 1969-71; m. Jean Elliott McDowell, Oct. 7, 1978. Sales posting clk. Jax Beer Co., Houston, 1971-72, route salesman asst., 1972; sales supr. Nat. Beverage Co., Houston, 1972-74, pres., 1974-76; owner, pres. Coors Northeast Distbg. Co., Houston, 1976—. Bd. dirs. Houston Livestock Show and Rodeo, 1978—, Houston Muscular Dystrophy Assn., 1977—, Bill Williams Capon Charity Dinner, 1977—. Mem. Sons of Bosses Internat. (regional v.p. 1974-75), Jesuit Coll. Prep. Alumni Assn. (pres. 1977-79), Houston Citizens C. of C. (dir. 1977—), Nat. Beer Wholesalers Assn., Wholesale Beer Distbrs. Tex., Houston Wholesale Beer Distbrs. Assn. Roman Catholic. Club: Toastmaster.

POLICY, JOSEPH JAMES, broadcasting exec.; b. Youngstown, Ohio, July 12, 1945; s. Vincent James Policy and Anna Marie (Berardi) Policy Bartone; A.B., Southeastern U., Washington, 1965; B.S., U. Md., 1968; m. Carole Ann Davis, May 10, 1969; children—Amy Annette, Holly Anne. Mgmt. trainee broadcast div. Triangle Pubs., Phila., 1968-69; asst. program dir. Sta. WFIL-TV, Phila., 1968-69; dir. spl. events Sta. WNCH-TV, New Haven, 1968-69; dir. advt. Sta. WQXI-TV, Atlanta, 1972-73, gen. mgr. prodn., 1973-74; v.p. Pace Corp., Atlanta, 1974-75; cons. Coca-Cola USA, Kearney Nat. Co., Atlanta, 1973—; dir. advt. and sales promotion Sta. WWL-TV, New Orleans, 1975-77; dir. mktg. Photo Electronics Corp., 1977—; dir. broadcast services Sta./WPEC-TV, West Palm Beach, Fla., 1977—; officer promotion adv. bd. ABC-TV. Served with U.S. Army, 1969-72. Named Collegiate Broadcaster of Yr., U. Md., 1967, J.R. Stram award, 1968; recipient award Ad Club Palm Beaches, 1978-79, Freedoms Found. award, 1969. Mem. Broadcast Promotion Assn. Office: WPEC-TV Fairfield Dr West Palm Beach FL 33407

POLING, WILLIAM OBED, real estate agt., ret. hosp. adminstr.; b. Belington, W.Va., July 13, 1910; s. Daniel Boyles and Rosa Esteline (Simon) P.; A.B., Glenville State Coll., 1934; A.M., W.Va. U., 1942; M.S. in Health Adminstrn., Northwestern U., 1949; m. Pauline Elizabeth Clutter, Aug. 30, 1974; children—Marian Sue, Janet Ruth Poling Toth. Tchr., prin. Barbour County Schs., Philippi, W.Va., 1929-36; asst. cashier state tax dept., Charleston, W.Va., 1936-39; supt. Barbour County Schs., 1939-44; field rep. U.S. Office Edn., 1946-47; adminstr. Myers Clinic Hosp., Philippi, 1949-54, Broaddus Hosp., Philippi, 1954-60, Union-Protestant Hosp., Clarksburg, W.Va., 1960-71; supt. Weston (W.Va.) State Hosp., 1971-77; with Goodwin Real Estate Agy., 1978—; lectr. Alderson-Broaddus Coll., Philippi, 1954-60. Chmn. bd. trustees Alderson-Broaddus Coll.; Bd. dirs. Central Dist. Mental Health Centers, Inc. Served with USN, 1944-46. Life fellow Am. Coll. Hosp. Adminstrs.; mem. W.Va. Hosp. Assn. (pres. 1954), Assn. Mental Health Adminstrs., Nat. League for Nursing, Mental Health Assn. Democrat. Baptist. Clubs: Kiwanis (dist. gov. 1968), Bridgeport Country, Barbour County Country, Masons, Shriners. Contbr. articles in field to profl. jours. Home: 317 Philadelphia Ave Bridgeport WV 26330 Office: Room 2B2 Schroath Bldg Clarksburg WV 26301

POLIZZI, NICHOLAS GERALD, constrn. co. exec.; b. Cleve., Dec. 3, 1935; s. Alfred M. and Philomena (Valentino) P.; B. Bldg. Constrn., U. Fla., 1957; m. Mary Ann Palmer, Aug. 4, 1974; children—Andrea W., Phillip A., Nicole A., Michael C. Vice pres., dir. Thompson-Polizzi Constrn. Co., Coral Gables, Fla., 1957-60; sec., treas., dir. Polizzi Constrn. Co., Coral Gables, 1960-76, pres., 1976—; sec., treas., dir. Nicholas G. Polizzi & Assos., constrn. cons., 1975—. Active Met. Dade County Unsafe Structures Housing Appeals Bd., 1966-70, Met. Dade County Planning Adv. Bd., 1974—; ann. mem. Dade County United Fund, Coral Gables, 1964—, div. chmn., 1967—; bd. dirs. Dade County March of Dimes, 1969-70, Internat. Found. Employee Benefit Fund, 1975; trustee Met. Mus. and Art Center, 1971—, sec. bd., 1977-78; mgmt. trustee various labor trust funds, 1969-75; pres. Progress for Dade County, 1973-79; chmn. bd. trustees Constrn. Industry Advancement Fund, 1961—. Served with USAF Res., 1958-62. Recipient Am. Service Honor medal, Citizens com. Army, Navy, Air Force, 1958. Mem. Asso. Gen. Contractors Am. (pres. 1971-72; chpt. dir. 1967—), State Council Am. Gen. Contractors (mem. com. 1966), Beta Theta Pi. Clubs: Palm Bay, University (Miami, Fla.); K.C. (trustee 1964-67). Home: 4980 San Amaro Dr Coral Gables FL 33146 Office: 298 Granello Ave Coral Gables FL 33146

POLK, CHARLES HENRY, coll. pres.; b. Lofkin, Tex., July 11, 1942; s. John and Eva Mae (Wilmon) P.; B.S. in Sociology, Stephen F. Austin State U., 1963, M.A., 1965; Ed.D., N.C. State U., 1970; m. Ann Paula Tricomi, Jan. 23, 1965; children—John, Anthony. Instr. sociology Odessa (Tex.) Coll., 1965-66, Sandhills Community Coll., Southern Pines, N.C., 1966-68; adminstrv. intern Wayne Community Coll., Goldsboro, N.C., 1958-70; dean adult and continuing edn. Wilkes Community Coll., Wilkesboro, N.C., 1970; asst. dean, then dean adult and continuing edn. Fla. Jr. Coll., Jacksonville, 1970-73, exec. dean downtown campus, 1973-74; pres. Daytona Beach (Fla.) Community Coll., 1974—. Mem. Nat. Coop Edn. Commn., 1976—; bd. govs. Daytona Beach Community Coll. Found., 1974—; bd. counselors Bethune-Cookman Coll., Daytona Beach, 1974—; bd. dirs. United Way, East Volusia. Mem. Am. Assn. Community and Jr. Colls., Assn. Community Coll. Trustees, Council Advancement and Support of Edn., Halifax Hist. Soc. Presbyterian. Clubs: Rotary, Masons (32 deg.). Contbr. articles on ednl. adminstrn. to profl. publs. Home: 885 Willow Run Ormond Beach FL 32074 Office: PO Box 1111 Daytona Beach 32015

POLK, JOHN DAVID, psychologist; b. Piedmont, Okla., Apr. 30, 1917; s. Granvil Jenkins and Rachel Aleta (Poage) P.; B.A., U. Corpus Christi (Tex.), 1956; M.Div., S.W. Bapt. Theol. Sem., 1960; Ed.D., N. Tex. State U., 1965; m. Margaret Morris, Jan. 1, 1977; children by previous marriage—Hazel, John. With S.W. Bell Telephone Co., 1937-42, 45-63; faculty S.W. Baptist Coll., 1963-74; unit dir. Rusk State Hosp., Tex., 1974-76, dir. staff devel., 1976-77, curriculum dir. employee tng., 1977—; vis. prof. Pa. State U. 1967-68; cons. Christian Civic Found.; adviser Greenview (Mo.) Nursing Home for Retarded Adults. Post adviser Explorer Scouts. Served with USN, 1942-45. Certified psychologist, Mo. Fellow Mo. Psychol. Assn.; mem. Am., S.W. psychol. assns. Democrat. Baptist. Club: Masons. Home: 1801 Daniels St Rusk TX 75785 Office: Box 318 Rusk TX 75785

POLK, LARRY DOUGLAS, wholesale grocery co. exec.; b. Charlotte, N.C., Sept. 10, 1945; s. James Buxton and Annie Ruth (Carpenter) P.; B.S. in Bus. Adminstrn., U. N.C., 1967; m. Linda Kay Blue, Nov. 23, 1966; 1 son, Larry James. Mgmt. trainee Thomas & Howard Co., Charlotte, 1967-69, dir. data processing for N.C. and Va., 1969-74, dir. ops., Fayetteville, N.C., 1974-78, sec., asst. gen. mgr., 1978-80, v.p., gen. mgr., dir., 1980—. Served with U.S. Army, 1967-69. Mem. Nat. Am. Wholesale Assn., N.C. Food Service and Lodging Assn. (dir.), N.C. Restaurant Assn. Democrat. Mem. Ch. of Christ. Club: Fayetteville Kiwanis. Home: 1739 St Augustine Fayetteville NC 28304 Office: Thomas & Howard Co Drawer C 315 Robeson St Fayetteville NC 28302

POLK, RONALD EDWARD, personnel exec.; b. Nashville, July 7, 1945; s. James Roland and Gloria Ann (Gadsey) P.; B.S., Middle Tenn. State U., 1973, M.S., 1979; m. Paula Gayle Russell, Mar. 19, 1977; children—Patti Lynn, Jennifer Leigh. Mgr. prodn. and personnel Vulcan Corp. Clarksville, Tenn., 1973-76; personnel mgr. Batesville Casket Co., Manchester, Tenn., 1976-80; mgr. employee and community relations Onan Corp., Huntsville, Ala., 1980—; faculty Tenn. Learning Center, Nashville, 1979-80. Vice pres. Coffee County United Givers Fund, 1979-80; mem. adv. bd. Motlow State Community Coll., 1977-80. Served with USAF, 1966-70. Mem. Tenn. Indsl. Personnel Conf., Am. Soc. Personnel Adminstrn., Am. Legion, Am. Vets., Epsilon Pi Tau. Republican. Methodist. Home: 104 Independence Dr Toney AL 35773 Office: PO Box 1800 West Sta Huntsville AL 35806

POLK, VICTOR HENRY, investment co. exec.; b. Chgo., Oct. 15, 1908; s. Victor H. and Evelyn (Bernson) P.; student Princeton U., 1925-27, Cambridge (Eng.) U., 1927-28; m. Dorothy Alden Smith, May 17, 1942 (div.); children—Elizabeth Alden, Douglas George, Anthony Everett, Victor Henry. Corr., Universal Service, London, 1928; pub. Elizabeth (N.J.) Times Herald, 1930-31; advt. rep. Hearst Newspapers, Detroit, 1932-34; propr. Marley Co., London and N.Y.C., 1938-40; sales rep. Ency. Brit., 1947; partner Wykoff, Parish, Polk, advt., Miami, Fla., 1948-50; pres. Polk Pools, Inc., Miami, 1951-65; pres., chmn. Mut. Funds Adv. and The Fundpack Group of Investment Cos., also Fundpack Mgmt., Inc., Coral Gables, Fla., 1965-79; dir. Narcissa Inst., Miami, 1979—. Mem. Speakers Bur., Dem. Nat. Com., 1940. Served to capt. U.S. Army, 1940-45. Mem. No Load Fund Assn. (bd. govs.). Unitarian. Clubs: Princeton of N.Y., Princeton of S. Fla., Coral Gables Country. Author: My Finger is on American Publishers, 1962; In Adolphus' New World, 1977; Narcissa, 1979. Home: 5219 SW 71st Pl Miami FL 33155

POLLARD, CAROLYN ROUTH, jour. editor; b. Waltham, Mass., Dec. 12, 1940; d. Leslie Kenney and Isabelle Carolyn (Ward) P.; student Smith Coll., 1959-61; B.A., U. Wis., Madison, 1964. Sec. to editor Intercollegiate Bibliography of Cases in Bus. Adminstrn., Grad. Sch. Bus. Adminstrn., Harvard U., Cambridge, Mass., 1964-65, editorial asst. Harvard Bus. Review, 1965-70; asst. editor Atlanta Econ. Review, Coll. Bus. Adminstrn., Ga. State U., Atlanta, 1970-72, asso. editor, 1972-75, editor, 1975-79; editor Business mag., 1979—; editorial cons. Financial Mgmt. jour., 1972-73; cons. in field for various articles, books; editor ACIV News, newsletter Atlanta Internat. Student Bur./Atlanta Council of Internat. Visitors, 1977-78. Recipient Recognition award Ga. State U. Found., 1975, 76, GABC award merit and IABC/Dist II awards, 1976, 77. Mem. Am. Mktg. Assn., Internat. Assn. Bus. Communicators (sec.-treas. Atlanta 1977, v.p. membership 1978), Smith Coll. Club Atlanta, Smith Coll. Alumnae Assn., Walnut Hill Sch. Alumnae Assn., Indsl. Relations Research Assn., Assn. U. Bus. and Econ. Research (v.p. editors' bd. 1974-75, mem. program and promotion coms. 1974-77, pres. 1975-76), Women in Communications. Contbr. author: Women and Management: An Expanding Role, 1977. Office: Business Mag Coll Bus Adminstrn Georgia State Univ Atlanta GA 30303

POLLARD, DEMPSEY, univ. adminstr.; b. Brantley, Ala., Jan. 5, 1945; s. Gerald F. and Katherine P.; B.S., Huntingdon Coll., 1969; postgrad. Auburn U., Montgomery, Ala., 1974-75; m. Sharon Berry, Aug. 28, 1966; children—Randy, Tony. Buyer, Gayfers Dept. Store, Montgomery, Ala., 1966-71; adminstrv. technician Gunter Air Force Sta., Ala., 1972-73; mgr. auxiliary services Auburn U., Montgomery, 1973—, bd. dirs. Fed. Credit Union, 1975-76. Team chmn. United Way campaign, 1970; sec.-treas. PTA, 1977-78. Served with U.S. Army Res., 1967—. Recipient Bookstore Mgr. of Year award Ala. Coll. Bookstores Assn., 1978. Mem. Nat. Assn. Coll. Store (field rep. Ala.), Nat. Com. Employer Support Guard and Reserve, Ala. Coll. Bookstore Assn. (pres. 1977-78), Jr. C. of C. Democrat. Baptist. Club: Dalraida Recreation. Home: 1213 Cedric Ct Montgomery AL 36109 Office: Auburn U Montgomery AL 36117

POLLARD, MARY KILIAN, educator; b. Chgo., July 12, 1926; d. William F. and Johanna Agnes (Cashman) P.; B.A., Clarke Coll., Dubuque, Iowa, 1948; M.A., Loyola U., Chgo., 1952, M.Ed., 1972. Joined Sisters of Charity, Roman Catholic Ch., 1949; tchr. schs. in Ill. and Tenn., 1948-49, 52-70, guidance counselor, vice prin. Memphis

Cath. High Sch., 1970—. Grantee NSF, summer 1965, Christian Bros. Coll., summer 1970; recipient Cath. Human Relations award, 1974. Mem. Am. Personnel and Guidance Assn., Am. Sch. Counselors Assn., Nat. Cath. Guidance Conf. Home: 584 E Trigg Ave Memphis TN 38106 Office: 61 N McLean Blvd Memphis TN 38104

POLLARD, WILLIAM ALBERT, lawyer; b. Nashville, July 7, 1946; s. Thomas Brown and Hilda Alexine (Jolly) P.; B.S., U. S.C., 1967, J.D., 1974. Admitted to S.C. bar, 1974; partner firm Nexsen, Pruet, Jacobs & Pollard, attys., Columbia, S.C., 1979—. Served with USN, 1968-71. Mem. Columbia C. of C., Alston Wilkes Soc., Am. Bar Assn., S.C. Bar Assn., Richland County Bar Assn., Am. Soc. Hosp. Attys., Am. Soc. Law and Medicine, Nat. Assn. Accts., Am. Legion, Phi Delta Phi, Omicron Delta Kappa. Methodist. Clubs: Summit, Sertoma. Home: 1350 Raintree Dr Columbia SC 29210 Office: 1200 First Nat Bldg Main at Washington Columbia SC 29201

POLLNOW, JAMES LESTER, nat. guard officer; b. Milw., Oct. 23, 1935; s. Lester Karl and Edna Caroline (Goll) P.; grad. Armed Forces Indsl. Coll., 1969, Air War Coll., 1977; m. Susan Elizabeth Mann, Dec. 15, 1961 (dec.); children—James Wesley, Viki Sue, Kelly Ann, Penny Marie. Builder, designer, Little Rock, 1958-68; pres., dir. Checkard Systems, Inc., Little Rock, 1970-76; dir. Nat. Guaranty Corp.; lic. minister World Ministry Fellowship. Pres., Abundant Life Kitchens, 1980—; bd. dirs. Bridge Ministries Inc., 1975-79, Life Unltd. Christian Fellowship, 1975-80. Served with U.S. Army, 1954-56, USAAF, 1968-70, 76-79; lt. col. Ark. Air N.G. Decorated Air Force Commendation medal; named Ark. Outstanding Unit Comdr., 1979. Mem. N.G. assns. U.S., Ark., Air Force Officers Assn. Patentee water pipe sleeve. Author, pub: My God, Why?, 1979. Address: 1310 Aldersgate Rd Little Rock AR 72205

POLLOCK, JOHN CHURCH, ret. assn. exec.; b. N.Y.C., July 26, 1913; s. A. John and Minnie (Church) P.; B.S., U.S. Naval Acad., 1937; postgrad. N.Y. U., 1941-42, Columbia U., 1946-48; m. May Brose Pollock, Sept. 16, 1944; children—Richard Brose, Barbara May, John Frederick. Personnel dir. Scandinavian Airlines, N.Y.C., 1946-52; merchandising dir. Am. Houses, Inc., Allentown, Pa., 1952-58; mktg. dir. Nat. Assn. Homebuilders, Washington, 1958-67, organizer, dir. Sales and Mktg. Council, 1958-67; mktg. cons. Bill Eliot & Assos., Paramus, N.J., 1967-68; exec. v.p. Nat. Insulation Contractors Assn., Silver Spring, Md., 1968-75, ret., 1975. Named Mktg. Man of Year, 1956, Sales Mgr. of Year, Tulsa, 1967; recipient Complete House marketing award Living mag., 1956, Am. Builder award, 1957. Mem. Am. Soc. Assn. Execs., U.S. Naval Acad. Alumni Assn. Editor Outlook, 1968-75, Insulator, 1968-75. Home:

POLLY, F(ELIX) WINSTON, III, lawyer; b. Asheville, N.C., Aug. 23, 1945; s. Felix Winston and Thelma (Waite) P.; B.A., N.C. Central U., 1967, J.D., 1971; postgrad. in law Georgetown Law Center, 1972; m. Linda Marie Moore, Dec. 30, 1967; children—Danell Annette, Duywuna Auiyete. Admitted to W.Va. bar, U.S. Dist. Ct. bar So. Dist. W.Va., No. Dist. W.Va.; staff atty. FTC, 1971-73; project dir., atty. W.Va. Human Rights Commn., 1973-74; sr. counsel, legal advisor W.Va. Workmen's Compensation Fund, 1975-76; individual practice law, Beckley, W.Va., 1976-78; asst. pros. atty. Raleigh County, W.Va., also part-time individual practice civil law, Beckley, 1978—. Pres. Greater Kanawha Valley Cystic Fibrosis Found., 1975-76; chairperson Quad Counties Opportunities Industrialization Center, 1976—; bd. dirs. Raleigh County YMCA, 1977—, City of Beckley Scholarship Com., 1979. Recipient Outstanding Service award Workmen's Compensation Fund, 1976. Mem. Mountain State Bar Assn. (sec. 1976-77), Nat. Bar Assn., Raleigh County Bar Assn., Omega Psi Phi, Gamma Theta Upsilon, Phi Alpha Delta. Editor in chief N.C. Central U. Law Jour., 1970-71. Home: 127 Grant St Beckley WV 25801 Office: 338 S Fayette St Beckley WV 25801

POLSTON, JAMES LIONEL, mfg. co. exec.; b. Atlanta, July 2, 1941; s. Lovic Lionel and Annie Maude (Redwine) P.; student Hancock Jr. Coll., 1965; m. Vera Frances Hughes, Sept. 7, 1963; children—Darrell Eugene, Randall Scott. With Edo Aire Mitchell Co., Mineral Wells, Tex., 1969—, prodn. mgr., 1973-78, prodn. control mgr., 1978-79, master planning scheduler, 1979—; pres. Liberty Enterprises, 1977—. Served with USAF, 1960-67; Vietnam. Democrat. Methodist. Home: 1501 NW 5th Ave Mineral Wells TX 76067 Office: PO Box 610 Mineral Wells TX 76067

PONCE, BLANCA NILDA RIVERA, librarian; b. Barceloneta, P.R., Oct. 3, 1930; d. Aurelio Rivera and Mariana Hernandez; B.A. in Edn., U. P.R., 1952, M.L.S., 1968, M.Sch. Supervision and Adminstrn., 1973; m. Jose A. Ponce, May 21, 1955; children—Nilda Maria, Omar Antonio. Tchr. elem. schs., 1951-68; librarian 1969-72; asst. prof. library sci. U. P.R., 1972-73; librarian in secondary sch., 1974, dir. library, 1974-77; library services supr. Interam. U., San Juan, 1975-77; dir. Spl. Edn. Sch., 1977-79; now dir. public libraries P.R. Dept. Edn., Hato Rey. Mem. Tchrs. Assn., P.R. Librarians Assn., ALA. Mem. New Progressive Party. Roman Catholic. Office: Public Libraries Services Dept Edn PO Box 759 Hato Rey PR 00919

PONCE, LUIS FELIPE, hotel bus. exec.; b. La Habana, Cuba, Nov. 11, 1936; came to U.S., 1960, naturalized, 1969; s. Jose F. and Rosa V. Ponce; B.B.A., Villanova U., 1958; m. Norma Leon, Oct. 7, 1960; children—Norma, Ana Margarita, Nereida, Rosa M., Beatris, Jose. Acct., Lincoln Hotel, Havana, Cuba, 1956-57; controller DeLuxe Hotel La Concha, P.R., 1960-65; exec. asst. mgr. Rock Resorts, Little Dix Bay, Brit. V.I., 1965-66; controller Caesars Palace, Las Vegas, Nev., 1969-70; v.p. Inns of the Americas Inc., Dallas, 1973-76, pres. Latin Am. div., 1976—; pres. Hotel Adminstrn. Inst., San Juan, P.R., 1962-64. Mem. Internat. Assn. Hospitality Accts., Internat. Council of Mgmt. Contracts, Am. Soc. Travel Agents. Roman Catholic. Home: Reforma #825 Mexico 10 DF Mexico Office: 4141 Blue Lake Circle Dallas TX 75234

POND, BART MERRILL, sales exec.; b. Detroit, Mar. 15, 1948; s. Elwyn and Kathryn Medcalf P.; B.S. in Math., Fla. Inst. Tech., 1971. Asst. mgr. quality control McDonough Power Equipment Co. (Ga.) div. Fuqua Industries, 1971-73; dist. sales mgr. Overhead Door Corp., Athens, Ga., 1973-79, div. sales mgr. Ga. div., 1979—. Sec., Young Republicans Club. Mem. Pi Kappa Alpha. Home: 705 Langford Ln NW Atlanta GA 30327 Office: PO Box 1683 Athens GA 30603

POND, HARRY SEARING, urologist; b. New Orleans, Jan. 22, 1939; s. Harry Searing and Elizabeth (Lewis) P.; student Tulane U., 1960; M.D., U. Tenn., 1963. Intern, Phila. Gen. Hosp., 1963-64; resident in urology Johns Hopkins Hosp., Balt., 1967-71; staff physician Ochsner Clinic, New Orleans, 1971-73; practice medicine, specializing in urology, Mobile (Ala.) Urology Group, 1973—; asso. prof. U. S. Ala., Mobile, 1973—. Bd. trustees St. Paul's Sch., Mobile, 1976-77; warden of vestry St. Paul's Episcopal Ch., 1978-79. Served with USPHS, 1964-66. Recipient First prize for research, Am. Urologic Assn., 1970; Med. Assn. of Ala. award for services to humanity, 1977. Mem. Am., So. med. assns., Am. Urologic Assn., Am. Bd. Urology, Ala. Med. Assn., Am. Assn. Clin. Urologists, A.C.S. Club: Country, Fairhope Yacht. Contbr. articles in field to med. jours. Home: 4 Kingsway St Mobile AL 36608 Office: 1720 Center St Mobile AL 36608

POND, JOHN ALLAN, investment counselor; b. Scarsdale, N.Y., Dec. 29, 1929; s. Harold Covington and Margaret Carlyle P.; B.A., Bowdoin Coll., 1952; M.B.A., Harvard U., 1956; m. Ruth Pifko, Oct. 27, 1973; children—Dwight A., Nancy C., Andrew C. Vice pres. Kidder, Peabody & Co., Inc., N.Y.C., 1956-69, partner, 1966-69; founder, pres. Castine Capital Co. Inc., Miami, Fla., 1969-73; partner, corp. sec. Willoughby, Holin, Pond, Inc. (formerly Landmark Investment Counsel, Inc.), Plantation, Fla., 1973—; indsl. fin. counseling Am. Coll. Investment com. United Way of Broward County. Served with Submarine Service USN, 1953-54. Mem. Fin. Analysis Soc., Bond Club of Ft. Lauderdale (pres. 1976-77), Harvard Bus. Sch. Assn. So. Fla. (pres. 1974-75), Harvard Club of Broward County (dir.). Republican. Episcopalian. Club: Indian Hammock Hunt and Riding (dir.) (Ft. Drum, Fla.). Contbr. freelance columns to mags. Home: 8090 NW 10th Court Margate FL 33063 Office: PO Box 17230 Plantation FL 33318

POND, MARGARET (PEGGY) MACE PINNER, public affairs dir.; b. Suffolk, Va., Aug. 30, 1931; d. Donald Colin and Anna Elizabeth (Hall) P.; student Greensboro (N.C.) Coll., 1949-51, Norfolk (Va.) Bus. Coll., 1951-52; m. Samuel Barber Pond, Mar. 24, 1951; children—Samuel Barber, Donna Margaret, Lee MacRae. Tchr., Suffolk (Va.) Sch. System, 1955, Princess Anne County (Va.) Sch. System, 1961-62; news editor Southside Va. News, McKenney, Va., 1962-63; editor Springfield Independent (Va.), 1965-67; asst. dir. pub. relations Fairfax Hosp., Falls Church, Va., 1967-72; dir. corporate community relations Fairfax Hosp. Assn., 1972—; tchr. creative writing Fairfax County YMCA; chmn. adv. bd. Family Savs. and Loan Co., Springfield, Va., 1978-79; sec. West Springfield Civic Assn., 1964-66. Mem. Va. Press Women (sec. 1974-76, 1st v.p. 1978-80, Press Woman of Yr. 1976), Nat. Fedn. Press Women (regional dir. 1969-71, Top Ten Writers award 1970), Va. Soc. for Hospital Public Relations (pres. 1974-75). Club: No. Va. Press (pres. 1972-73). Home: 7712 Harwood Pl Springfield VA 22152 Office: 3300 Gallows Rd Falls Church VA 22046

PONDER, HARRY GLENN, horticulturist, educator; b. Opelika, Ala., Oct. 28, 1948; s. Glenn Allen and Marie (Hornsby) P.; B.S., Auburn U., 1970, M.S., 1971; Ph.D., Mich. State U., 1974. Horticulturist, Met. Atlanta, on faculty U. Ga. Athens, 1974-78; asso. prof. ornamental horticulture Auburn (Ala.) U., 1978—; adv. Atlanta Bot. Garden, State of Ga. Active Methodist Ch. Named nurseryman of yr. Ga. Nurserymen's Assn., 1976; recipient educator of yr. award Ga. Comml. Flower Growers Assn., 1977, Disting. Service award Atlanta Nurserymen's Assn., 1977. Mem. Am. Soc. for Hort. Sci., Ga. Nurserymen's Assn., Ala. Nurserymen's Assn., Sigma Xi, Phi Kappa Phi, Gamma Sigma Delta. Participant in design, installation of landscape around Presdl. Visitors Center, Plains, Ga., 1977. Home: 600 DeKalb St Auburn AL 36830 Office: 106 Funchess Hall Horticulture Dept Auburn U Auburn AL 36830

PONDER, JAMES ALTON, clergyman, evangelist; b. Ft. Worth, Tex., Jan. 20, 1933; s. Leo A. and Mae Adele (Blair) P.; B.A., Baylor U., 1954; Ed.M., Southwestern Bapt. Theol. Sem., 1965; m. Joyce Marie Hutchison, Sept. 1, 1953; children—Keli, Ken. Ordained to ministry Bapt. Ch., 1953; pastor Calvary Bapt. Ch., Corsicana, Tex., 1953-57, First Bapt. Ch., Highlands, Tex., 1957-62, Ridglea West Bapt. Ch., Ft. Worth, 1963-66, First Bapt. Ch., Carmi, Ill., 1966-67; dir. evangelism Ill. Bapt. State Conv., 1968-70, Fla. Bapt. Conv., 1970—; fgn. mission bd. evangelist in various countries of Asia, Central Am., Middle East, 1960—; project dir. Korea Major Cities Evangelization Project, 1978-80; evangelist ch. revivals, area crusades and evangelism confs., 1951—; mem. faculty Billy Graham Schs. of Evangelism, 1970—; co-founder Church Growth Inst. of Fla., 1976; co-dir. Ch. Growth Crusades, 1978-79; sports announcer Sta. KIYS, Waco, Tex., 1950-54. Bd. dirs. N.Fla. chpt. Leukemia Soc. Am. Mem. Internat. Platform Assn., Fellowship of Christian Athletes, Smithsonian Inst. Democrat. Club: Kiwanis. Author: The Devotional Life, 1970; Evangelism Men...Motivating Laymen to Witness, 1975; Evangelism Men...Proclaiming the Doctrines of Salvation, 1976; Evangelism Men...Preaching for Decision, 1979; contbr. articles to religious publs. Home: 7907 Woodleigh Dr S Jacksonville FL 32211 Office: 1230 Hendricks Ave Jacksonville FL 32207

PONDER, LEONARD HAROLD, chemist; b. N.C., Aug. 11, 1939; s. Garfield Leonard and Oleta (McDevitt) P.; B.S., So. Missionary Coll., 1961; M.S., U. N.C., Cullowhee, 1978; m. Gloria Anne Crews, Aug. 20, 1961; children—Leigh, Brian, Lauren. Instr. chemistry Union Coll., Lincoln, Nebr., 1961-62; project engr. Carrier Corp., Syracuse, 1962-65; chemist, group leader Am. Enka Co., Akzona, Inc., Enka, N.C., 1965—; organizer symposia Nat. Computer Conf. Cert. profl. chemist. Fellow Am. Inst. Chemists; mem. Am. Chem. Soc., Am. Oil Chemists Soc. (organizer symposia), Chromatography Discussion Group London. Editorial bd. Liquid Chromatography Abstracts, 1974—, Gas Chromatography Abstracts, 1974—; contbr. articles on polymer and analytical chemistry to sci. jours. and tech. confs.; developer computer programs for analytical chemistry. Home: Route 1 Box 192 Candler NC 28715 Office: American Enka Co Enka NC 28728

PONDS, OTIS D., JR., psychotherapist; b. Gainesville, Fla., Sept. 18, 1936; s. Otis D. and Clara B. (Burton) Ponds; student Stetson U., Deland, Fla., 1959-60; B.S., U. Nebr., Lincoln, 1970-71; M.S.W., Fla. State U., Tallahassee, 1974; Dr.Pubic Adminstrn., Nova U.; m. Barbara Lou Brandriff, Mar. 15, 1973; children—Gregory A., Debora S. With Williams Plumbing, Clearwater, Fla., 1953-55, Howdeshell Plumbing, Largo, Fla., 1961-62; social worker Pasco Mental Health, Pasco County, Fla., 1971-72; social worker VA, Bay Pines, Fla., 1974; social worker, asso. dir. Emergency Mental Health, Pinellas County, Fla., 1975-76; pvt. practice Christian psychotherapy, Clearwater, Fla., 1976—; cons. home health services. Asso. dir. Emergency Mental Health, Clearwater, 1975-76. Served with U.S. Army, 1963-69. Decorated Bronze Star with 2 oak leaf cluster, Air Medal with 2 oak leaf clusters, Purple Heart. Mem. Fla. Assn. Health and Social Services, Nat. Assn. Christian Social Workers, Acad. Cert. Social Workers, Social Work. Clin. Registry. Baptist. Home: 2115 Poinciana Dr Clearwater FL 33521 Office: 217 Circle Blvd New Port Richey FL 33552

POODRY, JANIE GOOLSBY, artist, designer; b. Coldwater, Miss., Dec. 1, 1923; d. William Arthur and Nettie (Bramlitt) Goolsby; student Hans Hofmann, 1945-47; M.A. in Painting, Tex. Woman's U., 1948; m. Leonard Poodry, Apr. 21, 1950 (dec.); children—Deborah Walne, Andrew Bramlitt. Designer, Memphis Cotton Carnival, 1938-41, Binswanger Grass Co., 1943-44; asst. prof. art Stetson U., Deland, Fla., 1948-51; asso. prof. art Memphis State U., 1963—. developer plastics design program and complex, 1973-77; one woman shows: E.H. Little Gallery, Memphis, 1973, 77, Women's Exchange Club, Memphis, 1977; group shows include: Deland Watercolor Show, 1948, Williamsville (N.Y.) Art League, 1955, Goldsmith's Center, Memphis, 1973. Mem. Coll. Art Assn., Southeastern Coll. Art Assn., Woman's Caucus for Art, Nat., So. assns. sculptors, Women's Resources of Memphis. Episcopalian. Home: 1187 Central Ave Memphis TN 38104 Office: Dept Art Memphis State U Memphis TN 38152

POOL, MARILYN MYERS, theatre dir.; b. Fresno, Calif., Nov. 2, 1934; d. Laurence B. and Asa (Griggs) Myers; B.A., Stanford, 1955, postgrad., 1955-56; postgrad. U. Tex., 1957-60, W. Tex. State U. summers 1962, 63; m. Joseph Harold Pool, Dec. 28, 1955; children—Pamela Elizabeth, Victoria Anne, Catherine Marcia. Pvt. tchr. drama, speech, acting, directing, speech correction, Amarillo, Tex., 1960—; free-lance radio and TV actress; asst. mng. dir. Amarillo Little Theatre, 1964-66, mng. dir., 1966-68; mng. dir. Horseshoe Players, touring profl. theatre, 1969-73; actress, multi-media prodn. Palo Duro Canyon, 1971. Pres., Tex. Non-Profit Theatres, 1972-74, 75-77; 1st v.p. High Plains Center for Performing Arts, 1969-73; dir., toured children's play The Land of Zareba in all Amarillo Elem. Schs., 1977-78; play dir. Theatre Amarillo, 1980. Mem. adv. council U. Tex. Coll. Fine Arts, 1969-72; community adv. com. for women Amarillo Coll., 1975-79. Bd. dirs. Domestic Violence Council, 1979—, YMCA Motivation of People, March of Dimes, 1979—, Tex. Panhandle Heritage Found., 1964—; bd. dirs. Amarillo Found. Health and Sci. Edn., 1976—, v.p. for program, 1979—. Recipient certificate of appreciation Woman of Year, Amarillo Bus. and Profl. Women's Club, 1966; Best Actress award for Hedda Gabler role Amarillo Little Theatre 1965, Best Dir. award for Rashomon, 1967. Travel fellow AAUW, 1973, 78. Mem. Am. Community Theatre Assn. (dir. 1969-72), S.W. Theatre Conf. (dir. 1973-76), Tex. Theatre Council (dir. 1974—, exec. com., pres. 1975-76), AAUW, (br. pres. 1973-75, state chmn. cultural interests 1975-77, 1st v.p. Tex. div. 1977-79), D.A.R. (chpt. chaplain 1971-75, historian 1975-76), C. of C. (fine arts council), U.S. Judo Assn., Symphony Guild, Amarillo Art Assn., Amarillo Law Wives Club (pres. 1976-77). Disciples of Christ. Home: 2410 Teckla St Amarillo TX 79106 Office: Box 7563 Amarillo TX 79109

POOLE, ELIZABETH RUTH, mgmt. analyst; b. Natchez, Miss., Nov. 17, 1945; d. Thomas J. and Agnes E. (Wilson) Foster; B.S. in Mktg., N.E. La. U., 1968; M.B.A., Miss. Coll., 1976; grad. Realtors Inst., 1977; m. William Kendall Poole, Apr. 8, 1968; children—Kendall, Amanda. Market research asst. Miss. Research & Devel. Center, Jackson, 1970-75, acting mgr. market analysis br., 1978, new venture analyst, 1975—; instr. entrepreneur devel. workshops, 1978-79. Recipient Outstanding Performance award Miss. Research and Devel. Center, 1978; named to Outstanding Young Women Am., 1979. Mem. Am. Mgmt. Assn., Miss. Indsl. Devel. Council, D.A.R., Phi Mu. Author: Retail Trade Analysis, 1972; Developing a Business Plan, 1979. Home: 28 Westridge Dr Brandon MS 39042 Office: PO Drawer 2470 Jackson MS 39205

POOLE, PATRICIA HIGGINS, law firm adminstr.; b. Toledo, Apr. 15, 1942; d. Peter Henry and Mary Elizabeth (Bacon) Higgins; grad. in comml. art Tomlinson Vocat. High Sch., 1959; m. Avery Dawes Poole; children—Carey Samuel, Deborah Freda. Office mgr. Belair Fabrics and Decorators, Clearwater, Fla., 1969-71; bus. mgr. Clearwater Gardens Nursing Home, 1971-73; office mgr. Green-Freifeld Enterprises, St. Petersburg, Fla., 1973-76; legal adminstr. Pattillo, MacKay & McKeever, P.A. Attys. at Law, 1976—. Mother advisor Order of Rainbow for Girls, 1968-69. Mem. Nat. Assn. Female Execs., Assn. Legal Adminstrs., Marion County Home Builders Assn. Women's Aux. Republican. Club: Order Eastern Star. Home: 3117 SE 12th St Ocala FL 32670 Office: PO Box 1450 Ocala FL 32670

POOLE, RICHARD WILLIAM, educator; b. Oklahoma City, Dec. 4, 1927; s. William Robert and Lois (Spicer) P.; B.S., U. Okla., 1951, M.B.A., 1952; Ph.D., Okla. State U., 1960; m. Bertha Lynn Mehr, July 28, 1950; children—Richard William, Laura Lynne, Mark Stephen. Research analyst Okla. Gas & Electric Co., Oklahoma City, 1952-54; mgr. Sci. and Mfg. Devel. dept. Oklahoma City C. of C., 1954-57; asst. to pres. Frontiers of Sci. Found., 1956; mgr. Office of James E. Webb, Washington, 1957-58; instr. econs., asst. prof., asso. prof., prof., Okla. State U., 1960-65, dean Coll. of Bus., 1965-72, v.p. univ. relations and devel., 1972-74, v.p. Univ. relations, devel. and extension, 1974—; cons. NASA, Midwest Research Inst.; mem. Gov's gen. adv. com., tech. com. Statis. Standards, 1964-66; mem. adv. exec. com. Nat. Govs. Conf., 1965. Bd. dirs. Stillwater Indsl. Found., 1967-78, Stillwater YMCA, 1966, Mid-Continent Research and Devel. Council, 1965-78, chmn., 1969; bd. dirs. Okla. Council on Econ. Edn., 1965—, mem. exec. council, 1965—. Served from pvt. to 2d lt., AUS, 1946-48. Mem. Am., So. econ. assns., Okla. (dir. 1965—), Stillwater (dir. 1965-78, pres. 1968) chambers commerce, Am. Assembly Collegiate Schs. Bus. (dir. 1971-72), Southwestern Econ. Assn. (pres. 1968), Res. Officers Assn., Southwestern Bus. Adminstrn. Assn. (pres. 1973), Phi Eta Sigma, Beta Gamma Sigma, Pi Gamma Mu, Phi Kappa Phi, Omicron Delta Kappa. Contbr. articles to profl. jours. Home: 124 Georgia Ave Stillwater OK 74074

POOLE, SUE, reclamation services co. exec.; b. Clearfield, Pa., Oct. 31, 1952; d. Robert Thomas Poole and Mary B. (Edwards) (stepmother) and Patricia Alice (Coleman) (stepmother) P.; m. Charles Howard Cardwell, Nov. 24, 1979; 1 son, Jonathon Aaron. Clk.-typist Ky. Dept. Mines and Minerals, 1974; sr. reclamation insp. div. reclamation Ky. Dept. Natural Resources, Madisonville, 1974-77; pres. Reclamation Services Unltd., Inc., Madisonville, 1977—; chmn. West Ky. adv. group Office Surface Mining, Dept. Interior, 1979—; mem. Ky. Adv. Com. on Strip Mine Regulation, 1979—. Served with WAC, 1972-73. Mem. West Ky. Coal Operators Assn. (dir.), Mining and Reclamation Council Am. (chmn. reclamation subcom.), W.Va. Surface Mine Assn., Nat. Reclamation Assn. West Ky. contbg. editor Ky. Coal Jour. Home: Route 4 Central City KY 42330 Office: 54 W Lake St Madisonville KY 42431

POOLE, THOMAS CARL, JR., mfg. co. exec.; b. Leeds, Ala., Feb. 19, 1921; s. Thomas Carl and Grace (King) P.; B.S., Auburn U., 1948; postgrad. Coll. Advanced Traffic of Chgo. at Jacksonville State U., 1950-51; m. Mary Louise Miller, Oct. 7, 1960; children—Thomas Carl III, John Preston. Mgr. Traffic and shipping planning Dresser Mfg. div. Dresser Industries, Anniston, Ala., 1949—. Traffic cons. various firms, 1960—. Served with USAF, 1943. Mem. N.E. Ala. Traffic and Transp. Club (gov. 1960), Phi Kappa Tau. Home: Route 5 Box 567 Anniston AL 36201 Office: W 23d St Anniston AL 36201

POOLE, VAN B., ins. co. exec., state senator; b. Jackson, Tenn., July 5, 1935; s. Martin VanBuren and Louise (Paul) P.; B.S. in Philosophy and Psychology, Memphis State U., 1958; children—Cynthia Lynne, Kimberly Anne, Mark Devereaux, Katherine Kelley. Mem. mktg. mgmt. staff Exxon Corp.; with Krieg, Kostas, and Poole Ins., Inc., Hollywood, Fla., 1968—; mem. Fla. Ho. of Reps., 1970-78; mem. Fla. Senate, 1978—; dir. Sinniland Bank of Ft. Lauderdale. Pres. Broward YMCA. Served with U.S. Army, 1953-61. Recipient Outstanding New Jaycee for State Tenn., 1961; Cert. Appreciation for Legis. Efforst in Edn., Sch. Bd. of Broward County; Good Govt. award Ft. Lauderdale Jaycees, 1978. Mem. Holly Life Underwriters, Broward County Life Underwriters, Fla. Assn. Ins. Agts. Ind. Ins. Agts. Broward County, Inc. (dir.). Republican. Roman Catholic. Office: Suite 417 Bayview Bldg Fort Lauderdale FL 33304

POOR, CHARLES R., psychologist; b. Oklahoma City, Nov. 19, 1935; s. O.C. and Dorothy Elizabeth (Ragan) P.; B.A., Okla. Bapt. U., 1958; M.S., Okla. State U., 1961; m. Joanna Williams, Feb. 1, 1964; children—Philip Williams, Julianna. Counseling psychologist Rehab.

Inst., Kansas City, Mo., 1961-64; counselor Tex. Edn. Agy., 1964-66; dir. vocat. dept. Tex. Inst. Rehab. and Research, Houston, 1966; asst. prof. dept. rehab. Baylor Coll. Medicine, Houston, 1966—, dir. edn. and tng. Tex. Inst. Rehab. and Research, 1974—; cons. Social Security Adminstrn., 1962, HEW, 1968. Mem. Am. Congress Rehab. Medicine, Am. Psychol. Assn., Am. Soc. Health Manpower, Edn. and Tng. Home: 10619 Cranbrook St Houston TX 77042 Office: 1333 Moursund St Houston TX 77030

POOR, RICHARD LONGSTREET, ret. utilities exec., real estate salesman; b. Summit, N.J., Dec. 28, 1910; s. Charles Longstreet and Mary L. (Austin) P.; B.S., U.S. Naval Acad., 1933; m. Margaret Key English, July 12, 1934 (div. July 1940); children—Richard Longstreet, Austin E.; m. 2d, Elizabeth Louise Snavely, July 1942 (div. July 1962); 1 son, Earl S.; m. 3d, Elizabeth Maurey Salvesen, Oct. 17, 1963; stepchildren—Tina S., Jan S. Electric field supt. Beach Electric Co., Newark, 1946-48; electric insp. Fla. Power & Light Co., Miami, 1948-49, electric constrn. supt., 1949-50, asst. distbn. supr., 1950-52, comml. supr., 1952-53, asst. mgr. comml., 1953-55, asst. purchasing agt., 1955-60, asst. to v.p. operating, 1960-75, ret., 1975; mgmt. cons., 1975-76; real estate salesman, 1977—. Served with AC, U.S. Army, 1933-34; from ensign to comdr. USN, 1934-46; rear adm. Res. (ret.). Decorated D.F.C. and Gold star, Air medal; registered profl. engr., N.J., Fla. Mem. IEEE, Nat. Soc. Profl. Engrs., Fla. Engring. Soc., Soc. Am. Mil. Engrs., Miami Beach C. of C. (zoning, bldg. com. 1953-54), U.S. Naval Inst., Navy League, Greater Miami Aviation Assn., Mil. Order World Wars, Assn. Naval Aviators, Quiet Birdmen. Episcopalian. Club: Rotary. Home: 9011 N Bayshore Dr Miami FL 33138

POORE, KENNETH WAYNE, urban designer, planning cons.; b. Norfolk, Va., June 19, 1939; s. Millard Elbridge and Margaret Elizabeth (Blake) P.; B.Arch., Va. Poly. Inst., 1966, M. Urban and Regional Planning, 1966; m. Ann Hutchinson, Aug. 27, 1960; children—Anthony Kirk, Jonathan Blake, Ross Jennings. Designer, Md. Nat. Capital Park and Planning Commn., Silver Spring, 1965; partner Poore & Price Assos., Williamston, N.C., 1967; planning cons. Div. Community Planning, Dept. Conservation and Devel. State of N.C., Washington, N.C., 1966-67; urban-regional planner Harland Bartholomew & Assos., Richmond, Va., 1967-78; planning-design cons. K.W. Poore and Assos., Richmond, 1978—; cons. graphics and visual fine arts; vis. guest lectr. Va. Poly. Inst. and State U., 1979. Active Tuckahoe Little League, 1973-79; vis. guest artist Culpepper Art Fair, 1976. Recipient Distinguished Achievement award Prescriptions for Williamsburg Environment, 1975. Mem. Am. Planning Assn., Am. Inst. Cert. Planners, Windsor Park Land Assn. (pres. 1976). Democrat. Baptist. Club: Wimbly Swim and Racket. Award-winning artist. Home: 11301 Wimberly Dr Richmond VA 23233 Office: 8501 Patterson Ave Richmond VA 23229

POPADIC, JOSEPH STEPHEN, educator; b. Bridgeport, Conn., Nov. 6, 1945; s. Joseph Peter and Pauline Katherine (Vrabel) P.; B.Landscape Arch., SUNY, 1967, M.Landscape Arch., 1974; m. Mary K. Rountree, Dec. 16, 1978. Landscape architect New Haven Redevel. Agy., 1967-68; with Reimann & Buechner, Landscape Architects, Syracuse, N.Y., 1970-71, Moriece and Gary, Landscape Architects, Cambridge, Mass., 1974; prin. Haynes, Popadic, Abbey Asso., Landscape Architects, Baton Rouge, 1978—; asso. prof. Landscape Architecture, La. State U., Baton Rouge, 1972—, mem. faculty senate, 1977—. Served to 1st lt., U.S. Army, 1968-70, now capt. USAR. Mem. Am. Soc. Landscape Architects, La. Soc. Landscape Architects. Home: 1135 Highland Park Dr Baton Rouge LA 70808 Office: Dept Landscape Arch La State Univ Baton Rouge LA 70803

POPE, ANDREW JACKSON (JACK), JR., judge; b. Abilene, Tex., Apr. 18, 1913; s. A.J. and Ruth (Taylor) P.; B.A., Abilene Christian U., 1934; LL.B., U. Tex., 1937; m. Allene Nichols, June 11, 1938; children—Andrew Jackson, Walter Allen. Admitted to Tex. bar, 1937; began practice of law in Corpus Christi, Tex., 1937, mem. firm Pope & Pope, 1937-44, Cannon, Pittman & Pope, 1946; judge Dist. Ct., 94th Jud. Dist., 1946-50; justice Ct. Civil Appeals, 4th Jud. Dist., San Antonio, 1950-65; asso. justice Supreme Ct. Tex., Austin, 1965—; chmn. Tex. Jud. Sect., 1962, Tex. State Law Library Bd., 1971-75. Pres. San Antonio YMCA, 1957. Served with USNR, 1944-46. Recipient Silver Beaver award Boy Scouts Am.; Outstanding Alumnus award Abilene Christian Coll., 1965. Mem. Am. Judicature Soc., Am., Nueces County (pres. 1947), San Antonio, Travis County bar assns., State Bar Tex., Order of Coif, Phi Delta Phi, Alpha Chi. Mem. Ch. of Christ. Club: K.P. (grand chancellor Tex. 1948). Contbr. articles to profl. jours. Office: Supreme Ct Bldg Capitol Sta Box 12248 Austin TX 78711

POPE, KENNETH ELVIN, engring. co. exec.; b. Middletown, Ohio, June 17, 1925; s. George E. and Mable (Emrick) P.; student pub. schs., Germantown, Ohio; children—Sidney K., Stacie B., Anthony Dian. Tool designer Buckeye Aluminum Co., Wooster, Ohio, 1946-47; prodn. engr. Sandia Lab., U. Calif., Albuquerque, 1948-51; design engr. Hydro Aire Inc., Van Nuys, Calif., 1951-53; staff mem. research and devel. dept. Sandia Corp., Albuquerque, 1953-57; div. mgr., chief engr. research and devel. Integrated Dynamics Co. div. Globe Industries, Inc., Albuquerque, 1957-64; sr. staff engr. Unidynamics Co. div. UMC Industries, Phoenix, 1965-69; advanced products mgr. Computer Access Systems, Salem, N.H., 1969-70; pres., cons. engr. Concepts, Inc., Albuquerque, 1970-78; sr. devel. engr., research and devel. C-E Natco-Combustion Engring., Inc., 1978—; pres. Soma Systems Inc.; sr. design engr. large diameter drilling machine Fenix & Scisson Inc., 1979—; cons. Advance Tech. Cons., Washington. Served with USNR, 1943-46. Mem. Soc. Automotive Engrs., Soc. Astronautical Engrs. Patentee in field. Home: Route 3 Box 217 Wagoner OK 74467

POPE, ROBERT SCOTT, anatomist; b. Battle Creek, Mich., Aug. 20, 1946; s. George R. and Agnes P. (Hill) P.; B.S., Alma Coll., 1968; M.S., U. N.D., 1971, Ph.D., 1973; m. Marlene Rae Frazee, Aug. 24, 1968; children—Christopher Scott, Aimee Michelle, Geoffrey Rea. Instr. anatomy W.Va. U., Morgantown, 1973, asst. prof. anatomy, 1974-79, asso. prof., 1979—, adv. NSF honors research program, 1973—; regional resources cons. Alma (Mich.) Coll., 1976—. Mem. Monogalia County (W.Va.) Commn. Citizen's Adv. Bd., 1976—; pres. Pleasant Hills Homeowner's Assn., 1977-79, chmn. exec. com., 1978-79. NIH fellow, 1968-73; NIH grantee, 1974-75, 77-80. Mem. Am. Assn. Anatomists, So. Soc. Anatomists, AAAS, Sigma Xi. Presbyterian. Contbr. articles to sci. publs. Home: 12 Edwin St Morgantown WV 26505 Office: 4047 Basic Science Dept of Anatomy West Virginia Univ Medical Center Morgantown WV

POPE, WILLIAM ROBERT, lawyer, former state rep.; b. Mt. Mourne, N.C., Feb. 24, 1918; s. James Robert and Mary (Kelly) P.; grad. Brevard Jr. Coll., 1938; B.S., Davidson Coll., 1940; LL.B., U. N.C., 1948; m. Esther Maria Johnson, July 31, 1976; children—William Robert, James Shuford, Charles Vance, Elizabeth Barber, Deborah, Caroline Amelia. Admitted to N.C. bar, 1948; pvt. practice, Mooresville, 1948—; judge Mooresville Recorder's Ct. 1952-63; gen. counsel Crescent Electric Membership Corp. Dir. Cornelius Devel. Co., Inc.; atty. Town of Mooresville; pres. Braco, Inc.; bd. mgrs. Northwestern Bank. Mem. N.C. House of Reps., 1951-52, 63-64; chmn. adv. com. Iredell County Govtl. Complex; mem. Lowrance Hosp., Inc.; past pres. bd. regents Barium Springs Home for Children. Served to lt. USNR, 1940-46. Decorated D.F.C. Mem. Am., N.C., Iredell County bar assns., Phi Delta Phi. Democrat. Presbyterian. Clubs: Masons, Rotary. Home: US 21 Mooresville NC 28115 Office: PO Box 27 Mooresville NC 28115

POPLI, SHANKAR D., research pharmacist; b. India, Aug. 4, 1941; s. Parshotam D. and Kunwar B. Popli; D.Pharmacy, Med. Coll. India, 1959; B.Pharmacy, Panjab U., 1963, M.Pharmacy, 1965; Ph.D., U. Alta. (Can.), 1972; m. Uma K. Khatri, July 28, 1963; children—Krishan, Anand, Raaj. Pharmacist, Govt. Hosp., Panjab, India, 1959-60; jr. research fellow Panjab U., 1963-65; sr. research fellow, 1965-67; teaching asst. U. Alta., 1967-71; research asso. U. Mich., 1971-72; research asst. U. Conn., 1972-73; with A.H. Robins Co., Richmond, Va., 1973—, group mgr. biopharmaceutics, 1979—. Mem. Am. Pharm. Assn., Acad. Pharm. Scis., Sigma Xi. Contbr. articles to profl. jours. Home: 4902 Rodney Rd Richmond VA 23230 Office: 1211 Sherwood Ave Richmond VA 23220

POPOVICH, PAUL JOHN, radiologist; b. St. Louis, Jan. 26, 1928; s. John Thomas and Josephine Marie (How) P.; M.D., St. Louis U., 1951; m. Kathleen Mary Underwood, Nov. 26, 1955; children—Adria, Paul J., John, Conan, Megan. Intern, St. Louis County Hosp., Clayton, Mo., 1951-52; resident in radiology VA Hosp., St. Louis, 1952-54, 56-57; practice medicine specializing in radiology, Great Falls, Mont., 1957-60, Delray Beach, Fla., 1960-61; dir. dept. radiology Sacred Heart Hosp., Cumberland, Md., 1961-63, Brevard Hosp., Melbourne, Fla., 1963—; mem. Health Systems Agy. of East Central Fla. Pres. Brevard chpt. Am. Cancer Soc., 1970. Served with M.C., USAF, 1954-56. Mem. AMA, Radiol. Soc. N.Am., Soc. Nuclear Medicine, Am. Coll. Radiology (councillor from Fla.), Fla. Radiol. Soc. (pres. 1976), Fla. Med. Assn. (com. of 17, 1974, med. ins. com. 1975-77; del. to council med. specialties 1974-76), Brevard County Med. Soc. Am. Inst. Ultrasound in Medicine. Roman Catholic. Club: Rotary (pres. Melbourne 1974; chmn. devel. com. dist. 699 Rotary Found. 1977). Home: 150 Riverside Dr Melbourne FL 32951 Office: Brevard Hosp Melbourne FL 32901

POPP, DANIEL MCVAGH, linguist, humanist, educator; b. Ft. Wayne, Ind., Jan. 29, 1939; s. Milton Frederick and Alberta (Loop) P.; B.A., Yale U., 1960; M.A., U. Chgo., 1962, Ph.D., 1971; m. Barbara Ann Marsh, June 9, 1962; children—Randi Katherine, Kari Kristine. Asst. prof. Scandinavian langs. and lits. U. Kans., Lawrence, 1966-67, St. Olaf Coll., Northfield, Minn., 1967-70, Moorhead (Minn.) State U., 1970-73; asso. prof. Scandinavian langs. and lits. U. Fla., Gainesville, 1973—. Mem. Soc. for Advancement of Scandinavian Study (life), Norsk folkeminnelag (life), Landslaget for bygde- og byhistorie (life). Author: Asbjørnsen's Linguistic Reform. I. Orthography, 1977. Home: 1211 NW 36th St Gainesville FL 32605 Office: 143 ASB U Fla Gainesville FL 32611

POPP, JOHN WILLIAM, mfg. co. exec.; b. Clarksburg, W.Va., Sept. 29, 1943; s. George Arthur and Henrietta Helen (Gunkle) P.; B.S. in M.E., Purdue U., 1968; m. Judith Laree Conley, Nov. 8, 1969; children—Gretchen Elisabeth, Jason Christopher. Student engr. Carbon Products div. Union Carbide Corp., Clarksburg, Cleve. and Fostoria, Ohio, 1962-68; project and design engr., Fostoria, 1968-72, project engr., asst. chief engr., Yabucoa, P.R., 1973-76, project engr., staff engr. div. central engring., Clarksville, Tenn., 1976-79, supt. prodn., 1979—. Home: 526 Wingate St Clarksville TN 37040 Office: PO Box 903 Clarksville TN 37040

POPPELBAUM, MARTHA CLAIRE, rehab. counselor; b. Buenos Aires, Argentina, Jan. 22, 1936; d. Dewey James and Claire Marie (Gilday) Sabin; B.A., U. Okla., 1957; M.A., Colgate U., 1969; postgrad Syracuse U., 1968, CUNY, 1969; 1 dau., Claire. Employment/counseling human resources devel., dept. labor State of N.Y., 1964-72, vocat. rehab., 1972-77, also rehab. counselor, hosp. program coordinator; rehab. counselor Comprehensive Center, State of Tenn., Smyrna, 1977—. Mem. Am. Personnel and Guidance Assn., Am. Rehab. Counselors Assn. Office: Comprehensive Center Smyrna Industrial Park Smyrna TN 37167

PORTER, ALAN MILLER, condr., singer, educator; b. McKeesport, Pa., Feb. 28, 1933; s. William Bruce and Cornelia Boggs (Miller) P.; B.Music cum laude, Mt. Union Coll., 1961; M.Music with performance honors (tuition scholar), U. Ill., 1963; postgrad. Ball State U., summer 1977; m. Joyce Elaine Cahoon, June 17, 1961; children—Gregory Alan, David Leland. Singer-actor Civic Light Opera Co., Pitts., 1950, 51, 57, 58; dir. music Fayetteville (N.C.) Little Theater, 1966-74, 79—, Hay St. United Meth. Ch., Fayetteville, 1963—; asst. prof. music Meth. Coll., Fayetteville, 1963—; dir. music, singer, actor Ft. Bragg (N.C.) Playhouse; singer, recitalist, opera and oratorio soloist, musical comedy, 1950—. Bd. dirs. Fayetteville Civic Music Assn., 1964—; dist. music rep. Fayetteville Dist. United Meth. Ch., 1966-72; bd. dirs. Fayetteville Youth Symphony, 1977—; pres. bd. dirs. Dance Theater of Fayetteville, 1979—. Served with USAF, 1951-56. Recipient cert. of commendation U.S. Govt. as music dir. at Ft. Bragg, 1973. Mem. Nat. Assn. Tchrs. of Singing, Fellowship of United Meth. Musicians, Am. Guild English Hand Bell Ringers, Pi Kappa Lambda. Republican. Methodist. Researcher early music. Home: 5810 Arbutus Trail Fayetteville NC 28301 Office: Raleigh Rd Fayetteville NC 28301

PORTER, ANDREW THOMAS, personnel cons. co. exec.; b. Keyser, W.Va., Apr. 16, 1933; s. James Atkinson and Louise Jemiah (Gilpin) P.; A.A., Potomac State Jr. Coll., 1954; B.A., Shepherd Coll., 1959; postgrad. W.Va. U., until 1973. Tchr. various schs., 1959-73; personnel specialist pres. Ace Assos., Keyser, 1974—. Served with U.S. Army, 1955-57. Taft Found. fellow, 1971. Mem. Mineral County Fedn. Tchrs., Nat. Ret. Tchrs. Assn., DAV, Theta Sigma Chi. Republican. Presbyterian. Clubs: West End Social, Keyser Duplicate Bridge (v.p., 1966, 74, dir. 1967-79), Am. Contract Bridge League, Masons, Shriners, DeMolay. Home: Route 4 Box 128 Keyser WV 26726 Office: PO Box 121 Keyser WV 26726

PORTER, AUBREY L., lawyer; b. Mt. Pleasant, Tex., July 6, 1898; s. R. J. and Lavenia (Hall) P.; student E. Tex. Tchr's Coll., 1917-21; LL.B., Kent Coll. Law, Chgo., 1925; m. Hazel Harvey, Jan. 2, 1927 (dec. Dec. 1969); 1 son, Robert M. Admitted to Fla. bar, 1926; pros. atty. Wakulla County (Fla.), 1926-32; county judge, 1932-57; gen. law practice, 1957—; tree farming. Mem. Wakulla County Welfare Assn.; past chmn. adv. com. Tallahassee Jr. Coll. Mem. Am. Legion, 40 and 8, Fla. Bar, 2d Jud. Circuit Bar Assn. (past pres.), Wakulla County C. of C. (past pres.). Democrat. Methodist (ofcl. bd. mem., past chmn.). Club: Masons. Address: Crawfordville FL 32327

PORTER, CLYDE, mil. officer, architect; b. Galveston, Tex., May 14, 1944; s. Clarence and Vera Louise (Benefield) P.; B.S., Prairie View A&M U., 1967; m. Jean Taylor, Feb. 18, 1968; 1 son, Gregory Dwain. Engring. designer Dow Chem. Corp., Freeport, Tex., 1966-67; city planner, Corpus Christi, Tex., 1970; archtl. draftsman Harrel and Hamilton, Architects, 1970; archtl. draftsman Army and Air Force Exchange Service, Dallas, 1970-73, architect, 1973—. Served to capt., C.E., U.S. Army, 1967-70. Decorated Bronze Star, Air medal (2), Army Commendation medal. Mem. Soc. Am. Mil. Engrs., Am. Inst. for Design and Drafting, AIA (asso. nat. chpt.), Tex. Soc. Architects, Dallas chpt. AIA, Epsilon Pi Tau. Home: 6815 Woodwick Dr Dallas TX 75232 Office: Army and Air Force Exchange Service 3911 Walton Walker Blvd Dallas TX 75222

PORTER, GARY LYNN, state ofcl.; b. Bartlesville, Okla., Feb. 18, 1946; s. Leonard Edwin and Rosella Elizabeth Best (Smith) P.; B.S., Southwestern Okla. State U, 1969; M.B.A., Oklahoma City U., 1974; postgrad. U. Okla., 1975—; m. Mary Elizabeth Nicholson, Jan. 23, 1971; 1 son, Martin Edwin. Intern pharmacist VA Hosp., Oklahoma City, 1968; registered pharmacist Wright's Drug Store, Poteau, Okla., 1969-79; instr. pharmacy adminstrn. and pharmaceutics Southwestern State U., Weatherford, Okla., 1970-75, admission counselor, 1970-73, dir. continuing edn., 1973-75; preventive med. cons. Okla. State Dept. Health, Oklahoma City, 1974-75, pharmacy cons., 1975-78, dir. Okla. Poison Info. Center, 1975-78; dir., exec. com. mem. Pharmat, Inc., Lawrence, Kans., 1973-75; pres. RLM, Inc., 1978—, RLM Mgmt. Co.; adminstr. Hodges Nursing Home, Inc. Mem. adminstrv. bd. United Methodist Ch., Elk City; mem. Elk City C. of C. Ambassadors. Recipient Disting. Alumnus award Southwestern Pharmacy Alumni Assn., 1975. Fellow Am. Coll. Apothecaries; mem. Am. Pharm. Assn., Am. Soc. Hosp. Pharmacists, Nat. Assn. Retail Durggists, Okla. Pharm. Assn., Am. Assn. Colls. Pharmacy, Am. Assn. Poison Control Centers, Okla. County Pharm. Assn., Adult Edn. Assn. U.S.A., Higher Edn. Alumni Council Okla., Okla. Edn. Assn., Okla. Adult and Continuing Edn. Assn., C. of C., Phi Delta Chi. Democrat. Clubs: Elks; Weatherford Rotary (treas. 1974-75), Kiwanis (sec nw Oklahoma City 1975-76, pres. 1977-78). Home: PO Box 532 Elk City OK 73644 Office: 301 N Garrett St Elk City OK 73684

PORTER, GWENDOLYN HANKERSON, counselor; b. Lakeland, Fla., Aug. 24, 1942; d. Samuel and Daner (McTier) Hankerson; B.S. in Home Econs., Hampton Inst., 1964, M.A. in Home Econs., 1972, M.A. in Guidance and Counseling, 1975; children—Gerald Lynn, Vernon Cordell. Home economist N.C. Agrl. Extension Service, Jackson, 1964-69; dept. head support services RCA, Choanoke Area Devel. Assn., Rich Square, N.C., 1970, 71-73; counselor student spl. services Hampton (Va.) Inst., 1973-75, dir. student spl. services, 1976—; cons.; condr. workshops and tng. sessions; public speaker. Recipient Cert. of Merit, Hampton Bus. and Profl. Women's Club, 1977; named Outstanding Woman Mgr., RCA, 1973; named Personality Plus of Month, Project Times News, 1973. Mem. Am. Personnel and Guidance Assn., Assn. Humanistic Edn. and Devel., Va. Assn. Ednl. Opportunity Program Personnel (sec.), Kappa Delta Pi (pres. Iota Mu chpt.). Democrat. Office: Box 6064 Hampton Institute Hampton VA 23668

PORTER, H. LEONARD, III, hosp. ofcl.; b. Denver, July 12, 1945; s. Howard Leonard and Margaret Johnson P.; B.A., Monmouth (Ill.) Coll., 1967; M.S., U. Ill., Champaign, 1968; m. Mary Ellen Biciste, June 22, 1968; 1 son, Andrew James. Dir. public relations Monmouth Coll., 1968-69, 72-73, asst. dir. devel., 1972-73; dir. public relations Detroit Osteopathic Hosp. Corp., 1973-78; dir. public relations Greenville (S.C.) Hosp. System, 1978—; instr. Carl Sandburg Community Coll., Galesburg, Ill., 1973. Served with Med. Service Corps, USAF, 1969-72. Mem. Mich. Hosp. Public Relations Assn. (pres. 1978), Nat. Assn. for Hosp. Devel., Public Relations Soc. Am., Am. Soc. Hosp. Public Relations, Monmouth Coll. Alumni Bd., Carolina Hosp. Public Relations Assn., Greenville C. of C. Republican. Presbyterian. Contbr. articles to profl. pubIs. Home: 101 Merrifield Dr Greenville SC 29605 Office: Greenville Hosp System 701 Grove Rd Greenville SC 29605

PORTER, RICHARD CHARLES, JR., lawyer; b. Louisville, Nov. 11, 1939; s. Richard Charles and Ruth Hundley (Crutcher) P.; B.A., U. Louisville, 1961, J.D., 1967; m. Helen Marie Hodges, Dec. 22, 1962; children—Richard Charles, Beth, Andrew, Claire, Jason. With E. I. Dupont de Nemours & Co., Inc., Louisville, 1962-64, Potlatch Corp., Louisville, 1964-68; admitted to Ky. bar, 1968, Fla. bar, 1972, U.S. Supreme Ct. bar, 1971; individual practice law, Louisville, 1968—; lectr. bus. law Ky. Sch. Mortuary Sci., Louisville, 1970-73; asst. county atty. Jefferson County (Ky.), Louisville, 1969-70; lectr. Am. govt. Jefferson Community Coll., Louisville, 1977. Commr., chmn. Housing Authority Jefferson County, 1970-76; mem. Louisville-Jefferson County Republican exec. com., 1975—; trustee Jefferson County Law Library, 1978—. Mem. Am., Ky., Fla., Louisville bar assns., Rep. Attys. Assn. (pres. 1974), Phi Eta Sigma. Baptist (deacon 1970—, moderator congregation 1973-74). Home: 1531 Sylvan Way Louisville KY 40205 Office: 377 Starks Bldg Louisville KY 40202

PORTER, RICHARD DENSON, engr.; b. Houma, La., Apr. 15, 1952; s. Willis Denson and Christine P.; B.M.E., Ga. Tech. Inst., 1976. Process engr. Delta Air Lines, Atlanta, 1971-75; field engr. for No. Europe, Oceanic Contractors, 1976-78, project engr., Aberdeen, Scotland, 1978—. Mem. Am. Soc. Engrs. Home: 17 Alexandra Pl Fort Walton Beach FL 32548 Office: care Oceanic Contractors Inverlair House Aberdeen Scotland

PORTER, ROBERT WILSON, JR., social worker, govt. ofcl.; b. Birmingham, Ala., Sept. 22, 1944; s. Robert Wilson and Mary Leola (Chandler) P.; B.S., U. Ala., 1966, M.S.W., 1973; m. Nancy Marie Weeks, Nov. 7, 1970; children—Pamela Lynn, Paige Lea, Nancy Latrelle. Coordinator alcohol treatment unit Walla Walla (Wash.) VA Med. Center, 1977-78; chief social work service Muskogee VA Med. Center (Okla.), 1978—; asst. clin. prof. dept. psychiatry Tulsa Med. Coll., U. Okla., 1978—. Treas., bd. dirs. Walla Walla Community Alcohol program, 1977-78; pres., bd. dirs. WA-2 Fed. Credit Union, Walla Walla, 1977-78. Served to capt., USAF, 1966-70, 73-77. Decorated Air Force Commendation Medal; recipient Community Service award City of Tuscaloosa (Ala.), 1970; VA Grad. stipendee, 1973. Mem. Soc. for Hosp. Social Work Dirs., Acad. Cert. Social Workers, Delta Sigma Pi, Pi Kappa Alpha. Democrat. Baptist. Home: 2905 Augusta St Muskogee OK 74401 Office: Muskogee VA Med Center Honor Heights Dr Muskogee OK 74401

PORTER, ROY MALCOLM, JR., librarian; b. Henderson, Ky., Sept. 22, 1950; s. Roy Malcolm and Anna Jane (Warren) P.; B.A., U. Evansville, 1971; postgrad. Coll. Law, U. Ky., 1972-73, Coll. Architecture, 1975—; m. Julia Lynn Damron, Dec. 21, 1975. Librarian, U. Ky. Med. Center Library, Lexington, 1973-74; apprentice Margaret I. King Library Press, 1977; librarian Margaret I. King Library, U. Ky., Lexington, 1978—. Mem. Nat. Audubon Soc., Friends of Earth, Am. Hist. Assn., Friends of Pleasant Hill, Pi Gamma Mu. Episcopalian. Illustrator: The Confectionery of Monsieur Giron, 1979.

PORTER, WAYNE RANDOLPH, physician; b. Washington, Jan. 10, 1948; s. James Randolph and Betty Rose (Burgess) P.; B.S., MIT, 1970; M.D., Duke U., 1973. Intern, U. Miami Affiliated Hosps., 1973-74, resident in internal medicine U. Miami Sch. Medicine (Fla.), 1973-76, resident in dermatology, 1976-78, clin. instr. dermatology, 1978—; individual practice medicine specializing in dermatology, North Miami Beach, 1978—. Diplomate Am. Bd. Internal Medicine, Am. Bd. Dermatology. Fellow Am. Acad. Dermatology; mem. Dade County Med. Assn., Fla. Med. Assn., AMA, So. Med. Assn., Miami

Dermatol. Soc. Club: Kiwanis. Home: 11890 SW 72d Pl Miami FL 33156 Office: 909 N Miami Beach Blvd North Miami Beach FL 33162 also 11880 SW 40th St Miami FL 33175

PORTER, WILLIAM HOWARD, JR., physicist; b. Greenville, Tex., Dec. 25, 1941; s. William Howard and Anita Erdene (Kirby) P.; B.S., E. Tex. State U., 1965, M.S., 1968; m. Ryta Ann Bibby, Aug. 6, 1965; children—David, Darren. Instr. physics Hill Jr. Coll., Hillsboro, Tex., 1968—. NSF fellow, 1969, 71-73, 76; Energy Research and Devel. Adminstrn. Fellow, 1972,75. Mem. Am. Assn. Physics Tchrs., Am. Acad. Human Services, Tex. Jr. Coll. Tchrs. Assn. Democrat. Baptist. Home: 1045 Park Dr Hillsboro TX 76645 Office: PO Box 619 Hillsboro TX 76645

PORTMAN, BARNARD MARTIN, lawyer; b. Savannah, Ga., Sept. 29, 1942; s. Ben H. and Pearl P. (Maltinsky) P.; B.A., U. Fla., 1964; J.D., U. Va., 1967; m. Joanne Lynn Slavitt, Mar. 17, 1968; children—Daniel Frank, Stephanie Rae. Admitted to Ga. bar, 1966, U.S. Supreme Ct. bar, 1978; partner firm Portman, Marburger & Hughes, Savannah, 1967-79; prin. Diamond Mfg. Co., Inc., Savannah, 1973, sec., dir., 1975—; 5th dist. commr., Chatham County, Ga., 1979—. Pres., B'nai B'rith Jacob Synagogue Brotherhood, Savannah, 1971-73; bd. govs. Savannah Jewish Council, 1976—, 1st v.p., 1979—. Served with USCG, 1967-68. Recipient award for outstanding achievement United Jewish Appeal, 1977. Mem. Am. Bar Assn., Savannah Bar Assn., Savannah Plaintiff's Trial Lawyers Assn. Mem. editorial bd. Va. Law Rev., 1965-67. Home: 306 Stuart St Savannah GA 31405 Office: 31 Montgomery St Savannah GA 31401

PORTWAY, PATRICK STEPHEN, computer co. exec.; b. Chgo., June 18, 1939; s. Christopher L. and Cecila K. Portway; B.A., U. Cin., 1963; M.A., U. Md., 1972; m. Joanne E. Billups, June 10, 1961; children—Shawn, Pam, Victoria. With GSA, 1963-68; regional ADP coordinator Control Data Corp., 1968-69; mgr. strategic mktg. planning Xerox Corp., 1969-73; mgr., plans and programs System Devel. Corp., McLean, Va., 1974-78, Satellite Business Systems, 1978—; guest lectr. Va. Poly. Inst., George Washington U. Pres. Va. Citizens Consumer Council, 1976-78, Va. Citizens Consumer Found., 1976-78, Consumer Affairs in Banking and Ins., 1977—; presdl. elector, 1976; Democratic candidate Va. Ho. of Dels., 1971; consumer advocate in ins. and banking, 1975—; mem. Nat. Ins. Consumer Action Panel, 1975-78. Served to 1st. lt. U.S. Army, 1963-65. Named Outstanding Young Man Am., Dale City and Woodbridge Jaycees, 1973. Mem. Air Force Assn., Assn. U.S. Army, Def. Preparedness Assn., Soc. Consumer Affairs Profls., Nat. Consumers League, Chantilly Jaycees (pres. 1970; U.S. Jaycees Disting. Service award 1969, numerous regional awards). Club: Regency Racquet. Author: Action/In Action, 1971; editor, pub. Prince William mag., 1968-69. Home: 11014 Blue Roan Rd Oakton VA 22124 Office: 8003 Westpark Dr McLean VA 22101

PORTZ, ALEX THOMAS, mental health orgn. adminstr.; b. Sioux Falls, S.D., Apr. 15, 1922; s. Joseph Nicholas and Caroline Elizabeth (Noll) P.; B.A., St. John's U., 1945; M.A., Fordham U., 1951; Ph.D., U. Mich., 1964; m. Barbara June Ward, Dec. 4, 1966; children—William, Linda, Mark, Ward. Asst. prof. psychology St. John's U., Collegeville, Minn., 1950-59; psychologist Huron Valley Child Guidance Center, Ypsilanti, Mich., 1964-66; regional coordinator Mich. Dept. Mental Health, Lansing, 1966-68; exec. dir. Appalachian Mental Health Center, Elkins, W.Va., 1968—; mem. rural mental health task force U.S. Pres. Commn. Mental Health, 1977; mem. W.Va. Bd. Health, 1978—. Chmn. Randolph County United Way Campaign, 1978. Mem. Nat. Council Community Mental Health Centers (dir. 1970-71), W.Va. Psychol. Assn. (pres. 1973-74). Club: Rotary. Home: 102 Maryland Ave Elkins WV 26241 Office: Appalachian Mental Health Center Wilmoth and Yokum Sts Elkins WV 26241

POSEY, BRENDA KAYE, counselor; b. Winnsboro, La., Aug. 5, 1948; d. Earl Theo and Lucy Jewel (Williams) P.; B.S., N.E. La. U., 1970, specialist degree in counseling, 1980; M.Ed., Miss. U. for Women, 1974. Tchr., Morehouse Parish Sch. Bd., Bastrop, La., 1970-73, St. John Parish Sch. Bd., Reserve, La., 1974-76, Franklin Parish Sch. Bd., Winnsboro, La., 1976-79, Ouachita Parish Sch. Bd., Monroe, La., 1979—. Mem. Am. Personnel and Guidance Assn., Assn. Humanistic Edn. and Devel., Am. Sch. Counselor Assn., NEA, La. Edn. Assn., Assn. Classroom Tchrs., AAUW. Democrat. Baptist. Club: Monroe Pilot. Home: Route 2 Box 65 Winnsboro LA 71295

POSEY, KENNETH CLAYTON, SR., carpet co. exec.; b. Dalton, Ga., Feb. 5, 1931; s. William Henry and Jessie Frances (Sissom) P.; B.B.A., U. Ga., Atlanta, 1956; m. Hellen Deloris Kinsey, Mar. 6, 1955; children—Kenneth Clayton, William Stephen Griggs, Penelope Helen. Asst. personnel mgr. H.W. Lay & Co., Atlanta, 1957-61; personnel and advt. mgr. Paramount Dairies, Inc., Dalton, 1961-64; personnel mgr. Thomas Pride Mills Co., Calhoun, Ga., 1964-65, Star Finishing Co., Dalton, 1965-67, carpet div. Collins & Aikman Co., Dalton, 1967—; co-chmn. employees div. Whitfield County (Ga.) United Appeal, 1963—, publicity dir., 1964. Advisor Atlanta Jr. Achievement, 1959-60, sec., 1965-69, pres., dir. Dalton Jr. Achievement, 1969-70, dir., 1970-78; active Boy Scouts Am., Dalton, 1972—; deacon 1st Presbyn. Ch., Dalton, 1967-69, 75-77, sec. bd. deacons, 1969; bd. dirs. Dalton chpt. ARC, 1978—. Served with USAF, 1950-52. Mem. Am. Soc. for Personnel Adminstrn., Tufted Textile Mfg. Assn. (sec. indsl. relations club 1962-63, v.p., 1963-64, chmn., 1964-65), Carpet & Rug Inst. (chmn. indsl. relations club 1968-69), NW Ga. Personnel Assn. (v.p. 1972, pres. 1973, dir., 1974, Delta Sigma Pi. Presbyterian. Clubs: The Nine O'Clocks, Tut Skiers & Kite Flyers, Inc. (mem. bd. dirs.), Elks. Home: 1401 Braiden Rd Dalton GA 30720 Office: Smith Indsl Blvd Dalton GA 30720

POSEY-LOVE, LYNN ELIZABETH, pathologist; b. New Orleans, Oct. 13, 1951; d. Donald Phillip and Dora Grace (Volz) Posey; B.S. summa cum laude, La. State U., 1973, M.S., 1975, Ph.D., 1977, M.D., 1979; m. Ian Leslie Love, Dec. 29, 1979. Clin. instr. dept. med. tech. La. State U. Med. Center, New Orleans, 1973-74, clin. instr. pharmacology, 1977-79, fellow in surg. oncology and dir. Oncology Lab., 1979—, research cons. pharmacology, 1979—; fellow in surgery Tulane U., 1974-75; fellow in surgery Johns Hopkins Hosp., Balt., 1979. Recipient Ortho award in blood banking, 1973; La. State U. Decennial Honor award, 1969-73; lic. physician, La. Mem. Am. Soc. for Med. Tech., Am. Assn. for Cancer Research, Am. Chem. Soc., Am. Assn. for Clin. Chemists, Johns Hopkins Med. and Surg. Assn., Sigma Xi, Phi Kappa Phi. Democrat. Jewish. Contbr. articles to profl. jours. Home: 1000 Broadway New Orleans LA 70118 Office: 1430 Tulane Ave New Orleans LA 70112

POST, ALLEN, lawyer; b. Newnan, Ga., Dec. 3, 1906; s. William Glenn and Rosa Kate (Muse) P.; A.B. summa cum laude, U. Ga., 1927; B.A. with first honors in Jurisprudence (Rhodes scholar), Oxford U., 1929, B.C.L., 1930, M.A., 1933, Ph.D.; m. Mary Chastaine Cook, Dec. 27, 1934; 1 son, Allen W. Admitted to Ga. bar, 1930; spl. atty. gen. Ga., 1933, 1935; asst. atty. gen. assigned Ga. Pub. Service Commn., 1934; partner Moise, Post & Gardner, Atlanta, 1942-61, specializing in bus. and corp. law; partner Hansell, Post, Brandon & Dorsey, 1962—; dir., mem. exec. com. Atlanta Gas Light Co.; hon. dir. First Nat. Bank Atlanta, First Atlanta Co.; dir. Thomaston Mills, Am. Cast Iron Pipe Co.; dir. numerous other corps.; also lectr., writer on legal subjects. Chmn. Navy Day, Atlanta, 1937-39; pres. Atlanta Estate Planning Council, 1960; trustee W.N. Banks Found., Howell Fund, Ragan and King Found.; mem. State Democratic Exec. Com., mem. com. to rewrite election laws and revise primary rules of Ga., 1956; Dem. presdl. elector; mem. Gov's. staff; mem. State Com. to Revise Income Tax Laws of Ga., 1956; mem. Ga. Income Tax Study Commn. Served as lt. comdr., USNR World War II. Fellow Am. Coll. Trial Lawyers, Am. Coll. Probate Counsel; mem. Atlanta (exec. com., pres. 1956), Am., Ga. bar assns., Am. Judicature Soc., Atlanta Claims Assn., SAR, Navy League, Res. Officers Naval Services (1st pres. Atlanta chpt.), Mil. Order World Wars, Am. Legion (comdr.), Am. Assn. Rhodes Scholars, Gridiron, Sphinx, Phi Beta Kappa, Phi Kappa Phi, Phi Delta Phi, Kappa Alpha. Methodist (chmn. adminstrv. bd., trustee). Clubs: Rotary, Capital City, Piedmont Driving, Lawyers (Atlanta); Old War Horse Lawyers (pres. 1962); Commerce. Home: 620 Peachtree Batte Ave NW Atlanta GA 30327 Office: 1st Nat Bank Tower Atlanta GA 30303

POST, CHARLES WILLIAM, singer; b. Denver, Sept. 17, 1918; s. John Harvey and Anna Jane (Rist) P.; Mus.B., Colo. State U., 1942, B.S. in Chemistry, 1947; postgrad. U. Chgo., 1946, Lucien Muratore Ecole de Chant, Paris, 1950-51, U. Va., 1952, Manhattan Sch. Music, 1956; M.A., U. Denver, 1960; m. Trudi Adler, July 7, 1949; children—David Lucien, Luann Marcia. Profl. tenor in opera, concert, radio and TV, Europe, U.S.A., 1947-57; mem. music faculty Tex. Tech U., Lubbock, 1957—, prof. music, voice, 1976—, dir. cultural events for univ., 1972-75; music dir., cantor Congregation Shaareth Israel, Lubbock, 1960—. Bd. dirs. Community Concerts, 1959—; bd. dirs. Lubbock Civic Ballet, 1973-79, pres., 1975-77. Served with AUS, 1942-45; ETO. Recipient Tex. Tech. U. Spl. Services award, 1976. Mem. Nat. Assn. Tchrs. of Singing (lt. gov. N. Tex. S.W. region 1965-68, asst. gov. S.W. region 1968-73, state gov. N. Tex. Texoma region 1979—, editor French Art Song Listings 1969). Jewish. Home: 3812 54th St Lubbock TX 79413 Office: Dept Music Tex Tech U Lubbock TX 79409

POST, SHAWN ALLISON, counselor, ednl. adminstr.; b. Paterson, N.J., Mar. 10, 1953; d. Milton H. and Sally (Bergen) Kalish; B.Ed., U. Miami (Fla.), 1973, M.Ed., 1974, Ph.D., 1978; m. Charles M. Post, Mar. 24, 1977. Grad. asst. U. Miami (Fla.), 1975-78, diagnostician/clinician guidance center, 1977-79, lectr. ednl. psychology, 1978—, dir. psychoednl. support services Stamen Comprehensive Center, 1979—; cons. in field; spl. faculty Coll. of Bahamas, 1978. Mem. Am. Personnel and Guidance Assn., Internat. Reading Assn., Coll. Reading Assn., Assn. for Sch. Counselors, Phi Delta Kappa. Home: 10639 SW 113d Pl Miami FL 33176 Office: 6020 SW Bird Rd Miami FL 33155

POSTER, GERBRAND, III, sales exec.; b. New Rochelle, N.Y., Nov. 6, 1943; s. Gerbrand and Nellie (Baarslag) P.; student Clemson U., 1961-63; B.A. cum laude, U. South, 1965; M.A., Rice U., 1967; m. Mary Lee, Jan. 29, 1967; 1 son, Gerbrand, IV. Instr., U.S. Naval Acad., Annapolis, 1969-71, Clemson (S.C.) U., 1971-74; merchandising dir. The Great Escape, Greenville, S.C., 1974-75; publs. editor Liberty Life Ins., Greenville, 1975-77; tng. mgr. Bigelow-Sanford, Inc., Greenville, S.C., 1978-79, dir. merchandising, 1978—; advt./merchandising cons. AEGIS Assos., Greenville, 1975—. Served to lt. USN, 1967-71. Recipient Certs., Life Ins. Advertisers, 1976, Sperry and Hutchinson Inst. Mgmt., 1979, Cert. of Appreciation, City of Greenville, 1977, Addywards, Advt. Fedn. Greenville, 1977; Rice U. grad. study fellow, 1965-67. Mem. Am. Mgmt. Assn., South Atlantic Modern Lang. Assn., Mensa. Republican. Episcopalian. Club: Rotary. Author: The Great Escape-Bicyclist's Source Book, 1974; Product Profile Series, 1979; Designer: Speaking, 1971; Parish in the Heart of the City, 1977; editor: Colloguy, 1969-74, Leaders, 1975-77. Home: 102 W Mountain View Ave Greenville SC 29609 Office: Box 3089 Greenville SC 29602

POTENZA, DAISY MCKASKLE (MRS. JULIUS ORIAN POTENZA), newspaperwoman; b. Houston, Mar. 5, 1906; d. George Washington and Dora Amy (Crump) McKaskle; student Sinclair Bus. Coll., 1925, Massey's Bus. Coll., 1924-26, U. Houston; m. Julius Orian Potenza, Sept. 26, 1928; 1 dau., Marjorie Ann Potenza Hale (dec.). With Houston Chronicle, 1926—, adminstrv. asst. to editor-in-chief, 1930—. Exec. sec. Houston Endowment, Inc., 1968-69; mem. Bayou City Democratic Women's Club; bd. dirs. Pin Oak Charity Horse Show. Recipient certificate of award United Fund, 1967; named Outstanding Ticket Sales awardee Pin Oak Charity Horse Show, Tex. Children's Hosp., 1975-80. Mem. Nat., Tex. press women, Women in Communications, Press Club Houston (hon. life). Methodist. Club: Farm and Ranch. Home: 2405 San Felipe Rd Houston TX 77019 Office: 801 Texas Ave Houston TX 77002

POTNIS, KRISHNARAO SHRINIVAS, obstetrician and gynecologist; b. Vengurla, India, Apr. 16, 1934; s. Shrinivas Shantaram and Laxmi Vishnu (Chitnis) P.; came to U.S., 1963; B.A., U. Bombay (India), 1957, M.D., 1962. Intern, Bridgeport (Conn.) Hosp., 1964; resident in obstetrics and gynecology State U. N.Y. Hosp., Buffalo, 1965-69; instr. obstetrics and gynecology U. Miss. Sch. Medicine, Jackson, 1969-71, asst. prof., 1971—, asst. prof. family medicine, 1979—; chief dept. obstetrics and gynecology Kuhn Meml. State Hosp., Vicksburg, Miss., 1974—, med. dir., 1978—; cons. Jackson-Hinds Comprehensive Health Center, 1973-78; med. dir. Vicksburg div. Issaguena-Warren-Sharkey County Health Improvement Project, 1971-72; cons. Ob-Gyn programs dist. VII-B, Miss. Bd. Health, 1978—. Diplomate Am. Bd. Obstetrics and Gynecology. Fellow Am. Coll. Ob-Gyn.; mem. AMA, Miss. Med. Assn., West Miss. Med. Soc., AAAS, Miss. Obstet. and Gynecol. Assn. Hindu. Home: 1201 South St Vicksburg MS 39180 Office: Kuhn Meml State Hosp Vicksburg MS 39180

POTTER, BARBARA ANN, retail promotion exec.; b. Chgo., Apr. 19, 1945; d. John Francis and Mignonne Elinor (Huffman) Burke; student U. Chgo., summers 1964, 65; B.A. (Univ. scholar), Purdue U., 1967; postgrad. U. Ga., Athens, 1978—. Programmer, data processing Time, Inc., Chgo., 1967, interviewer, personnel dept., 1967-69, asst. employment mgr., personnel dept., 1969-70, dept. head, mag. subscriber relations, 1970-72, mem. adminstrv. staff, 1972-76; promotion exec. Paul Harris Stores, Inc., Indpls., 1976-79; production asst. WSB-TV, Atlanta, 1979—; mng. dir. Ron Nielsen Photography, Nielsen Communication Team, Four Quarters, Chgo., 1973—. Vol. worker Children's Meml. Hosp., 1969-72, Rehab. Inst. Chgo., 1973—. Mem. Women in Communications (2d v.p. membership 1974-75, chmn. hospitality com. 1973-74), Chgo. Press Club, Purdue Alumni Assn., Mortar Bd., Zeta Tau Alpha. Presbyterian. Clubs: Canyon, Indpls. Advt. Address: 268 Rumson Rd NE Atlanta GA 30305

POTTER, DOROTHY WILLIAMS, publisher; b. Chattanooga, Aug. 6, 1937; d. John Malcolm and Eva Lee (McWaters) Williams; m. John Leith Potter, Dec. 15, 1957; children—Stephen Leith, Dorothy Anne, Carol Jean. Owner, pub. DWP Publs., Tullahoma, Tenn., 1962—; cons., advisor, lectr. in field. Cited Tenn. Hist. Commn., 1973; recipient Spl. recognition award City of Tullahoma, 1976. Mem. Soc. Am. Archivists, N.C. Lit. and Hist. Assn., Nat. Archives Assn., New Eng. Hist. Geneal. Soc., Ky., Tenn. hist. socs., Nat. Trust Historic Preservation, Tenn. Anthrop. Assn., Tenn. Archaeol. Soc., Nat. Geneal. Soc., Coffee County Hist. Soc. (chmn. bd. 1972-74, editor quar. 1969-74), Tenn. Am. Revolution Bicentennial Commn., Tullahoma Bicentennial Commn. (chmn.), Soc. Descs. Washington's Army at Valley Forge, Nat. Soc. Colonial Dames XVII Century, Nat. Soc. Sons and Daus. Pilgrims, DAR, Nat. Soc. U.S. Daus. 1812. Author: Indian, Spanish and Other Land Passports for the Southeastern U.S., 1770-1823, 1978. Home: 804 Westwood Dr Tullahoma TN 37388

POTTER, JOHN MICHAEL, lawyer; b. Corpus Christi, Tex., Aug. 7, 1949; s. Christopher Burtt and Marion (Jenkins) P.; B.B.A., Baylor U., 1971, J.D., 1972. Admitted to Tex. bar, 1972, U.S. Supreme Ct. bar, 1976, U.S. Ct. Appeals for 5th circuit, 1976; asst. dist. atty. Nueces County (Tex.), Corpus Christi, 1972-75; research atty. Tex. Ct. Criminal Appeals, Austin, 1975-77; asst. U.S. atty. So. Dist. Tex., Houston, 1977—. Cert. in criminal law Tex. Bd. Legal Specialization. Mem. Am., Tex. bar assns., Harris County Young Lawyers, Nat. Dist. Attys. Assn., Tex. Criminal Def. Lawyers Assn., Tex. County and Dist. Attys. Assn. Baptist. Club: Kiwanis. Home: 10307 Sagegate Houston TX 77089 Office: US Attorneys Office Federal Bldg 515 Rusk St Houston TX 77002

POTTER, RICHARD CHARLES, librarian; b. Davenport, Iowa, Aug. 9, 1924; s. Clifford Joseph and Grace Marie (Ruth) P.; B.A., St. Ambrose Coll., Davenport, 1951; M.A., Fla. State U., 1957; m. Dolores Ann Pavao, Aug. 13, 1949; children—Michael H., Robert A., Richard B., Ann C., Caroline C., Patrick J., Mary T. Librarian, Escambia County (Fla.) Sch. System, 1958-76; librarian Pensacola (Fla.) Catholic High Sch., 1976—; instr. Naval Res. Officers Sch., Pensacola, 1958-64; cons. Pensacola News-Jour., 1959-70; historian-statistician Pensacola-PGA Golf Tournament, 1960—. Served with USMC, 1943-46, U.S. Navy, 1952-54. Democrat. Roman Catholic. Contbr. articles to profl. jours. Home: 404 Clairmont Dr Pensacola FL 32506 Office: 3043 W Scott St Pensacola FL 32505

POTTER, ROBERT ELLIS, librarian; b. Knoxville, Tenn., Mar. 16, 1937; s. Pollye Jack and Violet Belle (Walker) P.; B.S.J., U. Tenn., 1961; M.S. in L.S., U. Tenn., 1978; m. Rosemary Byrd Lee, Dec. 28, 1963; children—Robert Ellis and Kenyon David (twins). Student asst. U. Tenn. Libraries, 1959-61; copyreader The Knoxville News-Sentinel, 1961-62; library asst. U. Tenn. Libraries, 1962-63; library aide Los Angeles County Library System, El Monte, Calif., 1963-65; reference librarian, bus. and sci. collection City of Hialeah Library div. Hialeah John F. Kennedy Library (Fla.), 1966-73, head librarian bus., sci. and tech. dept., 1973—. Counselor, Trail Blazer's Camps, Inc., N.Y.C., 1958; chaplain's asst. U.S. Army Res., 1959-64; cubmaster Boy Scouts Am., 1976-77, asst. Webeloes leader, 1977-78, committeeman, 1978—. Served with AUS, 1959. Mem. Am., Southeastern, Tenn., Fla., Dade County (pres. 1970-71, historian 1976—, archivist 1975), library assns., Hialeah Library Div. Staff Assn. (pres. 1974-75, sec. 1976), U. Tenn. Century Club, U. Tenn. Nat. Alumni Assn. (bd. govs. Greater Miami chpt., v.p. 1973-74, pres. 1975-77), Hist. Assn. So. Fla., East Tenn. Hist. Soc., Sigma Delta Chi. Mem. United Ch. of Christ (treas. 1974-77, pres., 1977, chmn. ch. council 1977—, mem. mission council Dade-Monroe counties). Editor newsletter Dade County Library Assn., 1970-75, bull. SORT, ALA, 1971-74; contbr. articles to profl. jours. Home: 1441 Norwood Ave Clearwater FL 33516 Office: 190 W 49th St Hialeah FL 33012

POTTER, WALLACE DELIN, hosp. exec.; b. Salt Lake City, May 4, 1925; s. Wallace Edwin and Mary Viola (King) P.; B.S.E.(E., U. Utah, 1951; m. Naomi Harwood, Nov. 20, 1945; children—Linda Jean, Susan Carol, Patricia Ann. Field engr. Gen. Electric Co., 1951-59; product mktg. mgr. Tex. Instruments Co., Dallas, 1959-62; pres. Beta Instruments, Dallas, 1962-64; sales mgr. Sci. Control Corp., Dallas, 1964-68; pres. Remcom Systems, Dallas, 1968-72, Kessler Hosp., Inc., Dallas, 1972—, also dir.; dir. Gar Chem. Corp., Beta Instruments, Remcom Systems. Served with USN, 1942-46. Named Vet. of Year, Aerobics Activity Center, 1978. Mem. Tex. Hosp. Assn., Fedn. Am. Hosps., Hubbard Lake Hosp. Group. Republican. Mormon. Home: 15735 Kingscrest Circle Dallas TX 75248 Office: 201 E Colorado Blvd Dallas TX 75203

POTTINGER, DANN KIRKCONNELL, savs. and loan assn. exec.; b. Honduras, Aug. 14, 1947; s. Lewis Talbott and Alyce Fermina (Kirkconnell) P.; student Rollins Coll., Winter Park, Fla.; m. Mary Bartelle Carter, Feb. 2, 1973; children—Kathryn Elizabeth, Virginia Leigh. With Orlando Fed. Savs. and Loan Assn., 1971-76; v.p. Dade Fed. Savs. and Loan Assn., Orlando, 1976-78; pres., dir. 1st State Savs. and Loan Orlando, 1978—; dir. KYFLA Investments, Ocean Club North, Inc. Chmn. legis. action com. Winter Park C. of C., 1973-75; campaign leader local United Way; mem. fin. commn. Episc. Diocese Central Fla. Served with AUS, 1968-71. Named Ky. col., 1966. Mem. U.S. League Savs. Assn., Orlando-Winter Park, Orlando bds. realtors, Home Builders Central Fla., Fla. Assn. Realtors. Democrat. Episcopalian. Clubs: Citrus, N. Orlando Kiwanis, Cracker. Home: 1256 Wilkinson St Orlando FL 32803 Office: 730 N Magnolia St Orlando FL 32801

POTTS, NANCY NEEDHAM, marriage and family therapist; b. Houston, Dec. 21, 1947; d. Sidney Boyd and Katie Sue (McDonald) Needham; B.A., Baylor U., 1970; M.Ed., Sam Houston State U., 1974; Ed.D., U. Houston, 1979; m. Lloyd Lewroy Potts, Mar. 21, 1970. Tchr., Spring Branch (Tex.) Ind. Sch. Dist., 1971-74; counselor, program cons. South Main Bapt. Ch., Houston, 1974-75; therapist Center for Counseling, Houston, 1975-76; partner Bourne & Potts Marriage, Family and Divorce Cons., Houston; dir. Thunderbird, Inc., Stafford, Tex. Mem. AAUW, Womens Caucus (chmn. com. 1974), Am. Assn. Marriage and Family Therapists, Am. Orthopsychiat. Assn., Am., Tex. personnel and guidance assns., Am. Sch. Counselors Assn., Assn. Measurement and Evaluation in Guidance. Democrat. Baptist. Author: Beginning Again: Challenge of Formerly Married, 1976; Counseling Single Adults, 1978; Loneliness: Living Between the Times, 1978; contbr. articles to mags. in field. Home: 3111 West Creek Club Dr Missouri City TX 77459 Office: 8700 Commerce Park Dr Suite 139 Houston TX 77459

POTTS, RUSSELL, athletic adminstr.; b. Richmond, Va., Mar. 4, 1939; s. Harry Russell and Mary (Bruce) P.; B.S., U. Md., 1964; m. Emily Strite, Nov. 27, 1965; children—Kristi, Katie, Kelly. Sports editor Winchester (Va.) Evening Star, 1964-70; dir. sports promotions U. Md., College Park, 1970-73, asst. athletic dir., 1973-78; dir. athletics So. Meth. U., Dallas, 1978—; dir. Capital Bank, Dallas; mem. basketball com. Nat. Collegiate Athletics Assn.; mem. TV com. S.W. Conf. Served with U.S. Army Res., 1958-64. Recipient Big D award Shenandoah Apple Blossom Festival, Winchester, 1968-70, Golden Apple award, 1979. Methodist. Home: 9022 Meadowknoll Circle Dallas TX 75243 Office: PO Box 216 Dallas TX 75275

POULIS, KATHERINE MOFFAT, nurse; b. Turtle Creek, Pa., Aug. 25, 1918; d. Thomas McIntyre and Edith Margaretta (Friedel) Moffat; R.N., H.C. Frick Meml. Hosp., 1938; postgrad. Southwest Tex. State U., 1976-78; m. Byron Poulis, Aug. 10, 1940 (dec.); children—Byron Moffat, Nancy Jane Poulis Haley. Nursing service supr. Lutheran Gen. Hosp., San Antonio, 1959-63; dir. central service and respiratory therapy depts. Baptist Meml. Hosp., San Antonio, 1963—; nurse cons. 3M Co., 1976—. Republican. Lutheran. Club: Order Eastern Star

(Worthy Grand Matron of Tex. 1958-59, past Grand Matron of Tex.). Contbr. articles to Infection Control in Urol. Care, 1976-78. Home: 104 Chimney Rock Ln San Antonio TX 78231 Office: Baptist Memorial Hospital 111 Dallas St San Antonio TX 78286

POULSON, JERRY LEE, educator; b. Davenport, Iowa, Jan. 11, 1945; s. Lyle D. and Alice M. (Bushlow) P.; B.S.E. in Chemistry, Wayne State Coll., 1967; M.Ed., S.W. Tex. State U., 1979; m. Cynthia Clare Nystedt, May 10, 1969; children—Donalle Jercynda, Jerissa Althia. Sci. tchr., coach North Mahasku High Sch., New Sharon, Iowa, 1967-69, Papillion (Nebr.) Jr. High Sch., 1973-74; sci. tchr., athletic dir. Lockhart (Tex.) Jr. High Sch., 1974—. Served to 1st lt. C.E., U.S. Army, 1969-73. Mem. Assn. Tex. Educators, Tex. Sci. Tchrs. Assn. Republican. Methodist. Home: PO Box 1224 Lockhart TX 78644 Office: Lockhart Jr High Sch PO Box 120 Lockhart TX 78644

POUNDERS, KENNETH WAYNE, ednl. counselor; b. Golden, Miss., July 14, 1948; s. Wayne C. and Hazel A. (Hall) Hopkins; student N.E. Miss. Jr. Coll., 1966-68; B.S., Miss. State U., 1970, M.S., 1974; postgrad. Lamar U., 1973; m. Linda Farris Pounders, Jan. 23, 1969; children—Dustin, Kimberly. Drafting instr. Stephen F. Austin High, Port Arthur, Tex., 1970-74; drafting instr. West Point (Miss.) Vo-Tech Center, 1974-76, vocat. counselor, 1976—. Mem. Am. Vocat. Assn., Nat. Sch. Counselors Assn., Miss. Personnel and Guidance Assn. (regional treas. 1979), Miss. Vocat. Assn., Miss. Vocat. Counselors Assn. Baptist. Club: Luncheon Civitan (pres. elect 1979-80) (West Point). Home: Route 1 Box 47 West Point MS 39773 Office: PO Box 1136 West Point MS 39773

POWELL, ANICE CARPENTER (MRS. ROBERT WAINWRIGHT POWELL), librarian; b. Moorhead, Miss., Dec. 2, 1928; d. Horace Aubrey and Celeste (Brian) Carpenter; student Sunflower Jr. Coll., 1945-47, Miss. State Coll. Women, 1947-48; B.S., Delta State Coll., 1961, M.L.S., 1973; m. Robert Wainwright Powell, July 19, 1948; children—Penelope Elizabeth, Deborah Alma. Librarian, Sunflower (Miss.) Pub. Library, 1958-61; instr. English, Isola (Miss.) High Sch., 1961-62; dir. Sunflower County Library, 1962—; mem. adv. council State Instl. Library Services, 1967-71; participant Inst. Library Service to Disadvantaged, U. S. Fla., summer 1971; mem. adv. com. Miss. Gov.'s Conf. Libraries, 1978-79; mem. Library Services and Constrn. Act adv. com. Miss. Library Commn., 1978—. Chmn. Miss. Heart Assn., Sunflower, 1963-73; chmn. library category Sunflower County Merit Program, 1973; mem. Sunflower County Rural Area Devel. Com. Mem. ALA, Miss. Library Assn. (sect. chmn. 1965, treas. 1970, fed. relations coordinator 1973-74, chmn. intellectual freedom com. 1975, exec. dir. Nat. Library Week 1975, chmn. right to read com. 1976, mem. legis. com. 1973-77, mem. constn. by laws com. 1978, chmn. legis. com. 1979), Sunflower County Hist. Soc., Am., Southeastern library assns., Kappa Delta Pi. Methodist. Home: Box 387 Sunflower MS 38778 Office: 201 Cypress Dr Indianola MS 38751

POWELL, CHARLENE L., ednl. adminstr.; b. Marshall County, Ky., June 5, 1911; widowed. B.S. in Elementary Edn., Murray (Ky.) Coll., 1936, M.A. in Adminstrn., Supervision, 1960, postgrad. in adminstrn., supervision. Elem. tchr. Marshall County (Ky.) Public Schs., 1930-43; supervision chemist Ky. Ordnance Works, Paducah, Ky., 1943-46; prin. Farley Elem. Sch., Paducah, 1947—; adminstr., supr. Adult Basic Edn., Paducah, 1967—. Treas., Farley Vol. Fire Assn., 1955. Mem. PTA, Nat., Ky., McCracken County Edn. Assns., McCracken County Tchrs. Assn. (v.p. 1959, pres. 1960, legis. chmn. 1966-70), Murray Alumni Assn. Recipient certificate appreciation for outstanding service to youth Boy Scouts Am., 1966; Citizen of Year award Southside Kiwanis, Paducah, Ky., 1969; Cuchess of Paducah award, 1970; Certificate of Merit award, 1971; Honor award Soil Conservation Dist. Ky., 1974. Home: Route 3 Box 467 Paducah KY 42001

POWELL, DANIEL AUGUSTUS, JR., labor union ofcl.; b. Wilson, N.C., July 29, 1911; s. Daniel A. and Lillian L. (Warren) P.; student Presbyn. Jr. Coll., Maxton, N.C., 1930, U. N.C., 1930-31; m. Rachel Ola Staples, Dec. 26, 1945; children—Daniel A., Pamola Rachel. Advt. salesman Memphis Press-Scimitar, 1937-38; account exec. O'Callaghan Advt. Agy., Memphis, 1939-40; asst. info. dir. W. Tenn. Office Price Adminstrn., Memphis, 1945; so. dir. CIO Polit. Action Com., Memphis, 1945-55; dir. region 5, com. on polit. edn. AFL-CIO, Memphis, 1955—. A floor leader for presdl. candidate Estes Kefauver, Nat. Dem. Conv., 1952; mem. Tenn. adv. com. to U.S. Commn. on Civil Rights, 1965-77; bd. dirs. W. Tenn. ACLU, 1967—, v.p., 1977—; mem. Tenn. Com. for Humanities, 1975-78; cons./panelist div. pub. programs Nat. Endowment for Humanities; v.p. Tenn. Council on Human Relations, 1967-73; mem. adv. and review bd. Memphis Regional Med. Program, 1970-77; mem. Center for Study of Dem. Instns., 1966—; v.p. Memphis chpt. UN Assn., 1967-70; mem. selection com. Leadership Memphis, 1979—; active NAACP, Am. Vets. Com., Unitarian Universalist Fellowship of Memphis, Am. Humanist Assn. Served with USAAF, 1942-45. Recipient Bill of Rights award W. Tenn. ACLU, 1975, Peter Cooper Service awards Memphis Unitarian Universalist Fellowship, 1971, 74, Outstanding Service plaques Tenn. State AFL-CIO Labor Council, 1973, Fla. AFL-CIO Council, 1977. Mem. Am. Acad. Polit. and Social Sci., Acad. Polit. Sci. Club: W. Tenn. Hist. Soc. Author: The Program of Progress for State AFL-CIO Labor Councils, Ala., 1960, Ark., 1962, Miss., 1961, N.C., 1963, Tenn., 1961; contbr. sect. to Essays in Southern Labor History, 1977. Home and office: 5298 Revere Rd Memphis TN 38117

POWELL, DONALD ASHMORE, psychologist; b. Spartanburg, S.C., Oct. 29, 1938; s. Russell Kirmet and Mignon Kathleen (Cox) P.; B.S., U. S.C., 1960, M.S., 1962; Ph.D., Fla. State U., 1967; m. Palmyra Langston, July 5, 1961 (div.); children—Donald Langston, Donetta Palmyra, Ashley Preston, Stephanie Ann. Clin. intern VA Hosp., Coral Gables, Fla., 1966-67; postdoctoral fellow USPHS, U. Miami, Coral Gables, 1967-69; clin. research psychologist VA Med. Center, Columbia, S.C., 1969—; asst. prof. U. S.C., Columbia, 1969—. Mem. research and allocations com. S.C. Heart Assn. Mem. AAAS, Am., Southeastern psychol. assns., Psychonomics Assn., Soc. Neuroscience, Soc. Psychophysiol. Research, Geront. Soc. Democrat. Home: 619 S Ott Rd Columbia SC 29205 Office: VA Med Center Neurosci Lab Columbia SC 29201

POWELL, DUDLEY EVANS, safety engr.; b. Henderson, Ky., June 30, 1910; s. Elias Davis and Bertie Mae (Evans) P.; B.S. in Indsl. and Mech. Engring., U. Ky., 1934; postgrad. Tex. A&M U., 1943-44, Tex. Inst. Tech., 1951-52, Dept. Agr. Grad. Sch., 1958-60, U. Okla., Norman, 1961-62; m. Fae Freedman, Oct. 12, 1935; children—Jeanne Maude, Jay Michael, Carolyn Rudy, Ruthe Sara. Dist. engr. Traders & Gen. Co., Dallas and Lubbock, Tex., 1935-55; mgr. engring. dept. Nat. Surety Corp., Houston, 1955-61, Nat. Surety/Firemans Fund, Oklahoma City, 1961-66; safety dir. Hemis Fair, San Antonio, 1966-68; regional engring. mgr. Gulf Group, Kansas City, Mo., 1968-73, asst. mgr. exec. offices, 1973-77; cons. engr. Union Standard, Dallas, 1977—; mem. adj. faculty various schs. Pres. Men's Club Brotherhood B'nai Israel, Oklahoma City, 1961-64, mem. choir, 1965—; mem. adv. bd. Rainbow Girls, Order of DeMolay, Lubbock. Registered profl. engr., Calif. Mem. Am. Soc. Safety Engrs. (v.p. Region IV 1970-72, asst. adminstr. div. cons. 1978-79), Nat. Safety Mgmt. Soc. Clubs: Masons, Order Eastern Star. Contbr. tech. articles to co. publ., newspapers. Home: 10012 Regal Park Ln Apt 211 Dallas TX 75230

POWELL, FRANCES KAY VANNEST, ednl. adminstr.; b. Gilroy, Calif., Oct. 18, 1942; d. Orval Lee and Ruth Mae (Sills) Vannest; B.A. in English and Journalism, Central State U., Edmond, Okla., 1968, M.Ed. in English, 1971; postgrad. U. Guam, 1971-73, Okla. State U., Stillwater, 1975—; m. Bobby Dean Powell, June 3, 1961; children—Michael Dean, Jon David, Stefani Kay. Reporter, editor Daily Oklahoman and Oklahoma City Times, 1968-69; tchr. Oklahoma City schs., 1969-71, Guam public schs., 1971-75; dir. community relations Union Public Schs., Tulsa, 1975—; cons. to sch. supts. throughout Okla. Vol. worker Okla. ERA, 1978—. Mem. Nat. Sch. Public Relations Assn. (state coordinator), Okla. Sch. Public Relations Assn. (past pres.), Women in Communications (ERA liaison Tulsa chpt.), Ednl. Press Assn., Coop. Council of Okla. Sch. Adminstrs. (asso.), Phi Delta Kappa. Contbr. articles to profl. jours. Home: 22117 E 63d St Broken Arrow OK 74012 Office: 9134 E 46th St S Tulsa OK 74145

POWELL, JAMES BOBBITT, pathologist; b. Burlingotn, N.C., Aug. 28, 1938; s. Thomas Edward and Sophia Maude (Sharpe) P.; A.B., Va. Mil. Inst., 1960; M.D., Duke U., 1964; m. Pamela Oughton, Sept. 6, 1969 (div.); 1 dau., Daphne Oughton; m. 2d, Brent Atwater, Sept. 21, 1979. Intern, Duke U. Hosp., Durham, N.C., 1964-65; resident in pathology N.Y. Hosp., N.Y.C., 1965-67, Englewood (N.J.) Hosp., 1967-69; pres. Biomed. Reference Labs., Inc., Burlington; v.p. Granite Diagnostics, Inc., Burlington, 1972—; v.p. Carolina Biol. Supply Co., Burlington, 1972—; med. dir. med. lab. technician course Elon Coll., 1974—; dir. Wachovia Bank, Burlington. Bd. dirs. YMCA, Burlington, Elon Coll. Diplomate Am. Bd. Pathology. Mem. Am. Soc. Clin. Pathology, Coll. Am. Pathologists, Assn. Clin. Scientists, Am. Soc. Cytologists, AMA, N.C. Med. Soc., Am. Clin. Lab. Assn. (dir.). Republican. Contbr. sci. articles to profl. jours. Home: 2307 York Rd Burlington NC 27215 Office: 1447 York Ct Burlington NC 27215

POWELL, JAMES ORMOND, editor; b. Andalusia, Ala., Oct. 24, 1919; s. Abner Riley and Gertrude (Deer) P.; B.A., U. Fla., 1942; m. Ruth Hogan, June 27, 1951; children—James Ormond, Lee Riley. Reporter, Ala. Jour., Montgomery, 1940; reporter, state capitol corr. Tampa (Fla.) Tribune, 1946-54; state capitol corr. Miami (Fla.) Herald, 1955; adminstrv. asst. Senator George Smathers, Washington, 1955-56; editorial writer, asso. editor Tampa Tribune, 1956-59; editor editorial page Ark. Gazette, Little Rock, 1959-73, editorial dir., 1973—. Chmn. media group tour to People's Republic of China, China-Am. Relations Soc., 1973. Exec. com. Gov.'s Council Human Resources, 1967-70; pres. Community Concert Assn. Little Rock, 1968; bd. dirs. Ark. Opera Assn., 1961-63. Served with AUS, 1941-45. Poynter fellow Yale U., 1977. Recipient Mrs. David Terry award Little Rock Council on Human Relations, 1971. Mem. Am. Soc. Newspaper Editors, InterAm. Press Assn. (freedom of press commn. 1978—), Nat. Conf. Editorial Writers, NCCJ (dir. Ark. council 1964-65, recipient nat. editorial writing award 1969), Nat. Com. Support of Pub. Schs., Sigma Delta Chi (chpt. v.p. 1965), Sigma Nu. Democrat. Baptist. Home: 311 Schoolwood Ln Little Rock AR 72207 Office: Ark Gazette 112 S 3d St Little Rock AR 72201

POWELL, JO ANN, librarian; b. Morrilton, Ark.; d. Billie and Electra (Brewer) Lasater; B.S. in Elem. Edn., U. Central Ark., Conway, 1965, M.S. in Counselor Edn., 1970, postgrad. in Media Edn., 1979; m. Glenn Powell; children—Glenda, Janis, Steve. Credit mgr. Sears, Morrilton, Ark., 1958-59; tchr. Morrilton Pub. Schs., Dist. #32, 1965-67, librarian Morrilton High Sch., 1967—. Mem. Ark., Morrilton edn. assns., NEA, ALA, Ark. Library Assn., Ark. Audio-Visual Assn., Kappa Kappa Iota (sec. 1965-68), Delta Kappa Gamma. Home: Northview Subdivision Morrilton AR 72110 Office: 701 E Harding St Morrilton AR 72110

POWELL, JOHN GILBERT, printing co. exec.; b. Rocky Mount, N.C., Jan. 1, 1932; s. William Sidney and Ora Lee (Carter) P.; A.S., Chowan Coll., 1957; m. Ruth Joyce Rackley, June 10, 1956; children—Teresa Joyce, Johnna Lynn. With Parker Bros., Inc., Ahoskie, N.C., 1956—, supr. typesetting dept., 1958-65, mgr. comml. dept. printing, 1966—, asst. sec. bd. dirs., 1966, sec., 1977—. Served with USN, 1950-54. Mem. Jaycees. Democrat. Baptist. Club: Lions. Home: 513 Garrett St Ahoskie NC 27910 Office: 116 McGlohon St Ahoskie NC 27910

POWELL, JOSEPH HERBERT, hosp. adminstr.; b. Etowah, Tenn., Oct. 5, 1926; s. Newton Carter and Savannah (Smith) P.; B.S., U. Tenn., 1950; M.H.A., U. Minn., 1955; m. Ann Marie Lockeman, Mar. 10, 1956; children—Charlotte Marie, Margaret Annabelle, Susan Lea. Adminstrv. resident Bapt. Meml. Hosp., Memphis, 1954-55, adminstrv. asst., 1955-58, asst. adminstr., 1958-72, v.p., 1972-75, exec. v.p., adminstr., 1975-80, pres., 1980—; sec.-treas. West Tenn. Cancer Clinic, 1962-64; dir., mem. exec. com. Blue Cross and Blue Shield Memphis; mem. Tenn. Malpractice Rev. Bd., 1976—; trustee Tenn. Hosp. Edn. and Research Found.; asst. dir. Am. Indsl. Devel. Corp.; mem. adv. bd. Memphis Bank & Trust Co. Chmn. hosp. div. United Way, 1963, chmn. health services div., 1979. Served with U.S. Army, 1945-46, 51-53. Fellow Am. Coll. Hosp. Adminstrs. (regent for Tenn. 1978—); mem. Am. Hosp. Assn., Tenn. Hosp. Assn. (trustee, 1972-77, exec. com. 1973-77, chmn. 1975-76, speaker ho. of dels. 1976-78), Internat. Hosp. Fedn., Memphis Hosp. Council (pres. 1961-62), Presidents Club (Am. Mgmt. Assn.), Baptist. Club: Rotary (service to handicapped com. 1978) (Memphis). Home: 4341 Burgundy Rd Memphis TN 38111 Office: 899 Madison Ave Memphis TN 38146

POWELL, MANNIE STEVENS, ins. co. exec.; b. Texarkana, Ark., Nov. 17, 1934; s. Roy Silas and Arvilla (Stevens) P.; B.S. in Bus. Adminstrn., U. Ark., 1956; m. Diane Ford Thompson, Dec. 30, 1960; children—Priscilla Jane, Casey Stevens. Asst. agy. mgr. Travelers Co., Dallas, 1960-68; v.p. Southland Equity Sales Co., Inc., Dallas, 1968—, also dir.; v.p. Southland Life Ins. Co., Dallas, 1968—. Served to capt. USN, 1956-60. Robert P. Gatewood C.L.U. Inst. fellow, 1977. Mem. Am. Soc. C.L.U.'s (dir. Dallas chpt 1972-78, pres. 1976-77), Am. Coll. Life Underwriters (C.L.U.), Gen. Agts. and Mgrs. Assn., Dallas Assn. Life Underwriters, Estate Planning Council, Res. Officers Assn., Navy Res. Officers Assn. Clubs: Ins. of Dallas, Dallas Athletic, Chapparal. Office: PO Box 2220 Dallas TX 75221

POWELL, MARY LOUISE WELLS, psychologist, educator; b. Asheville, N.C., July 7, 1935; d. John Kendall and Beatrice (Rice) Wells; A.B., U. N.C., 1957, M.S., 1964, Ph.D., 1976; m. Elton George Powell, June 21, 1969. Tchr., Myers Park High Sch., Charlotte, N.C., 1957-58; editorial research asst. Time, Inc., N.Y.C., 1959-60; recreation and program dir. Spl. Services U.S. Forces Europe, Germany and France, 1960-62; resident adviser undergrad. women U. N.C. at Chapel Hill, 1963-64, research asso. and asst. to project coordinator State/Fed. Inst. for Profl. Devel., 1964-66; prof. organizational indsl. personnel psychology Appalachian State U., Boone, N.C., 1967—. NDEA fellow, 1966. Mem. Am., N.C., Southeastern psychol. assns., Am., N.C. personnel and guidance assns., Am. Soc. Tng. and Devel., Am. Soc. Personnel Adminstrn., Am., N.C. Coll. Personnel Assn., Nat., N.C. vocat. guidance assns., AAUP, AAUW, NOW, Pi Delta Phi. Home: 200 Anne Marie Dr Boone NC 28607 Office: 112-A Smith Wright Hall Appalachian State U Boone NC 28608

POWELL, ORRIN BERT, JR., ednl. counseling coordinator; b. Savannah, Ga., Sept. 16, 1916; s. Orrin Bert and Bessie (MacClenny) P.; B.S. in Social Sci., Fla. State U., 1952; M.S. in Psychology, 1953, Ed.D., 1963; m. Kathryn Avine Summers, June 4, 1939; children—Orrin B. III, Bettianne, Kathy, Vickery P. Asst. coordinator counseling Fla. State U., Tallahassee, 1961-75; dir. guidance, testing and placement Winthrop Coll., Rock Hill, 1975—, prof. and coordinator grad. program in counseling edn., 1975—; dir. project Woman Power. Served to 1st lt. F.A., U.S. Army, World War II. Decorated 4 Bronze Stars. Mem. Am. Psychol. Assn., Am. Personnel and Guidance Assn., Assn. of Counselor Edn. and Supervision (chmn. adminstrv. com. on curriculum). Presbyterian. Club: Towne. Author: Woman Power-Vocat. Direction for Mature Women, 1974. Home: 521 Meadowbrook Ln Rock Hill SC 29730 Office: School of Education Winthrop College Rock Hill SC 29733

POWELL, PHILLIP MORGAN, hosp. public relations dir.; b. Douglas, Ariz., July 2, 1932; s. James Custer and Mary Margaret (McCormack) P.; B.A. U. Tex., Austin, 1954; M.S. in Health Care Adminstrn., Trinity U, San Antonio, 1976; m. Patricia Kathleen McGuinness, Dec. 20, 1969. Tchr. high sch., Eagle, Colo. and Wheaton, Md., 1957-59; edn. specialist Dept. Navy, Washington, 1961-68; tchr. high sch. El Paso (Tex.) Ind. Sch. Dist., 1968-73; public relations dir., adminstrv. asst. Meml. Hosp., Lufkin, Tex., 1976—. Served with U.S. Army 1954-56. Mem. Tex. Hosp. Assn., Am. Hosp. Assn., Am. Soc. Hosp. Public Relations. Democrat. Roman Catholic. Home: 1522 Turtle Creek Lufkin TX 75901 Office: PO Box 1447 Lufkin TX 75901

POWELL, RAMON JESSE, lawyer, cons. water resources; b. Macon, Mo., Mar. 1, 1935; s. Robert Evan and Blanche Odella (Dry) P.; A.B in Econs. with distinction, U. Mo., 1957; postgrad. (Fulbright scholar), U. Brussels, 1957-58; J.D., Harvard U., 1965. Admitted to D.C. bar, 1966, Va. bar, 1975, U.S. Supreme Ct. bar, 1975; atty., advisor Office Gen. Counsel, Office Chief Engrs., Dept. Army, 1965-70; gen. counsel U.S. Water Resources Council, Washington, 1970-74; individual practice law, Washington, 1975-76; pres., gen. counsel Leman Powell Assos., Inc., Alexandria, 1976—. Served as officer USAF, 1958-62. Mem. D.C. Unified Bar, Bar Assn. D.C., Am., Fed. bar assns., Va. State Bar, Va. Trial Lawyers Assn., Nat. Lawyers Club, Beta Theta Pi, Phi Beta Kappa, Omicron Delta Kappa, Delta Sigma Rho. Office: Suite 303 Wythe Bldg 515 Wythe St Alexandria VA 22314

POWELL, ROBERT JACKSON, III, life ins. co. exec.; b. Durham, N.C., Dec. 30, 1947; s. Robert Jackson and Catherine Ravenel (Gant) P.; B.A., Davidson Coll., 1969; M.B.A., U. N.C., Chapel Hill, 1971; m. Clarine Gatling Pollock, June 13, 1970; children—Robert Jackson IV, Graham Pollock, John Gatling. Research analyst R.S. Dickson, Powerll, Kistler & Crawford, Charlotte, N.C., 1971-72; v.p. The Powell Group, Inc., Charlotte, 1972-75; v.p. Moroil Corp., Charlotte, 1975-76, dir., 1975—; agt. Equitable Life Assurance Soc., Greenville, N.C., 1976-78, dist. mgr., 1978—; dir. Glen Raven Mills, Inc. Div. chmn. Pitt County United Fund, 1977-78; young churchmen's adv. St. Paul's Episcopal Ch., 1977-79, mem. edn. and fin. coms., 1979—. Served with Field Arty., U.S. Army, 1971. Mem. Nat. Assn. Life Underwriters, N.C. Assn. Life Underwriters, Pitt County Assn. Life Underwriters, N.C. Officers Assn., Assn. U.S. Army, Jr. C. of C. Clubs: Greenville Sports, Greenville Golf and Country. Office: Equitable Life Assurance Soc PO Box 42 Greenville NC 27834

POWELL, ROLAND LADSON, chem. engr.; b. Greer, S.C., Aug. 23, 1950; s. Ladson James and Sara Jo (Jones) P.; B.S. in Chem. Engring., Clemson (S.C.) U., 1972; m. Deborah Lyre Fuller, Dec. 31, 1976; 1 dau., Christine Lyre. Project engr. Davis & Floyd Engrs., Inc., Greenwood, S.C., 1973-75, project mgr., 1975—. Registered profl. engr., S.C., La., Fla. Mem. Am. Inst. Chem. Engrs., Water and Pollution Control Assn. S.C., N.C. Water Pollution Control Assn. Home: 109 Orchard Dr Greenwood SC 29646 Office: PO Drawer 428 Greenwood SC 29646

POWELL, ROY JAMES, educator; b. Miami, Fla., Feb. 18, 1934; s. Ernest Everett and Edna Lodessa (Hand) P.; B.Ed., U. Miami, 1966; M.Ed., Fla. Atlantic U., 1967; Ph.D., U. Miami, 1971; m. Joyce Bridges Powell, June 28, 1979; 1 adopted son, Jon Cleighton. Broadcast engr. radio station WRUF, Gainesville, Fla., 1958-59; communications technician City Miami, Fla., 1959-60; electronics tech. Eastern Airlines, Miami, 1960-64; sci. instr. Youth Manpower Tng. Program, 1964; curriculum writer Dade County Pub. Schs., 1965; electronics instr. Miami Sr. High Sch., 1965-66; researcher Dade County Pub. Schs., 1966-67; grad. asst. tchr. corps tng. program U. Miami, Coral Gables, 1967-68; research asso., dir. bus. affairs Fla. Migratory Child Survey Center, 1968-69; chmn. dept. elec. engring. techs. Miami-Dade Community Coll., 1969-77, asso. prof., 1977—. Engring. cons. Gemini Marine Research, Hialeah, Fla., 1965, Inst. Applied Biology, Bay Harbor Islands, Fla., 1979-80; sound cons. Ferendino Grafton Spillis Candela, Architects, Engrs. and Planners, Inc., Miami, 1971-73; audio cons. pvt. indvls., Miami, Fla., 1963. Served with USAF, 1952-56. Mem. Fla. Assn. Community Colls., Med. Electronics and Data Soc., I.E.E.E., Phi Delta Kappa. Author: Electronics Instructor's Guides, 1965. Editor and contributor Radio and Television Servicing Instructor's Guide and Electricity Instructor's Guide, 1965. Contbr. to Migrant Children in Florida, 1969. Home: 13500 NW 97th Ave Hialeah Gardens FL 33010

POWELL, THOMAS EDWARD, JR., scientist, bus. exec.; b. Warrenton, N.C., July 6, 1899; s. Thomas Edward and Clara Morton (Bobbitt) P.; A.B., Elon Coll., 1919, D.Sc. (hon.), 1968; A.M., U. N.C., 1923; Ph.D. in Biology, Duke U., 1930; m. Sophia Maude Sharpe, 1922 (dec. 1944); children—Sophia Maude Powell Wolfe, Thomas Edward, John Sharpe, James Bobbitt; m. 2d, Annabelle Council, 1945; children—William Council, Joseph Eugene, Samuel Christopher, Annabelle Council. Instr. biology and geology Elon (N.C.) Coll., 1919-20, asst. prof., 1920-24, prof., 1924-36; founder Carolina Biol. Supply Co., Burlington, N.C., 1927, chief exec., 1936—; founder Waubun Labs., Inc., Schriver, La., 1945, Rana Labs., Brownsville, Tex., 1970; founder, chmn. Granite Diagnostics, Inc. subs. Carolina Biol. Supply Co., 1971—; dir. Wachovia Bank & Trust Co., Burlington. Mem. Alamance County Bd. Edn., 1934-61; pres. N.C. Sch. Bds. Assn., 1943-45; mem. N.C. Citizens Com. for Better Schs., 1958; life mem. parents council Va. Mil. Inst., co-chmn., 1961. Served to 2d lt. U.S. Army, 1918, to capt., inf., Res., 1923-35. Named a Paul Revere Patriot of Mass., 1965. Mem. AAAS, Newcomen Soc., Soc. Protozoologists, Am. Inst. Biol. Scis., Assn. Scientists and Industrialists. Clubs: Masons (master Elon 1924-25); Alamance Country (Burlington). Office: Carolina Biol Supply Co Burlington NC 27215

POWELL, WILBUR KINDRED, JR., financial cons.; b. Roanoke Rapids, N.C., Nov. 17, 1946; s. Wilbur Kindred and Julia Jordan (Woodard) P.; student Coll. of William and Mary, 1964-66; B.S. in Bus. Adminstrn. and Accounting, Campbell Coll., 1968; M.B.A.,

Emory U., 1971; m. Stephanie Annette Millican, Dec. 18, 1971. Vice pres. Day Mortgage Co., Inc., Atlanta, 1971-74; pres., owner Enterprise Financial Services, Inc., Atlanta, 1974—. Pres. Homeowners Assn., Sea Pines Plantation, Hilton Head Island, S.C., 1974-80; testified as expert on rural business before Joint Congl. Com. on Rural Devel., 1976. Served with USAR, 1968-74. Southern Baptist. Contbr. articles in field. Home: 135 Tamarisk Dr NE Atlanta GA 30342 Office: 5825 Glenridge Dr NE Atlanta GA 30328

POWELL, WILLIAM ARNOLD, JR., banker; b. Verbena, Ala., July 7, 1929; s. William Arnold and Frances (Baxter) P.; B.S. in Bus. Adminstrn., U. Ala., 1953; grad. Sch. of Banking, La. State U., 1966; m. Barbara Ann O'Donnell, June 16, 1956; children—William Arnold, Barbara Ann Powell McCaleb, Susan Frances, Patricia Baxter. With First Nat. Bank, Birmingham, Ala., 1953—, v.p., br. supr., 1968-71, sr. v.p., 1971-73, exec. v.p., 1973-79, pres., 1979—, also dir.; pres. Ala. Bancorp., Birmingham, 1979—, also dir.; dir. Engel Mortgage Co. Inc., Alabanc Fin., Inc.; instr. Banking Sch., La. State U., 1977-79. Chmn., Met. Devel. Bd., 1979; bd. dirs. Big Bros./Big Sisters of Greater Birmingham, 1975—, Ala. Banking Sch., 1976—, Warrior-Tombigbee Waterway Assn. Served to 1st lt. U.S. Army, 1954-56. Methodist. Clubs: Downtown, The Club, Green Valley Country, Riverchase Country, Birmingham Country, Kiwanis (pres. 1970). Home: 3309 Thornton Dr Birmingham AL 35226 Office: PO Box 11007 Birmingham AL 35288

POWELL, WILLIAM COUNCIL, mfg. co. exec.; b. Burlington, N.C., Nov. 5, 1948; s. Thomas Edward and Annabelle (Council) P.; B.S., Va. Mil. Inst., 1971; M.B.A., Wake Forest U., 1974; student Elon Coll., 1971, U.S.C., 1968-70; m. Jacqueline Garrison, July 3, 1976; 1 son, William Council. Vice pres. Bobbitt Labs., Burlington, N.C., 1974-77, pres., 1977—; chmn. bd. Home Entertainment & Decor Systems, Inc., Burlington, 1978—; v.p. Warren Land Co., 1978—; pres. Powell Leasing Co., 1979—. Served to capt. USAR, 1971-79. Real estate broker, N.C. Mem. Soc. Plastics Engrs., Nat. Assn. Mfrs. Democrat. Methodist. Home: 1616 Rockwood Ave Burlington NC 27215 Office: 1834 W Davis St Burlington NC 27215

POWER, JOHN DIETRICH, air force officer; b. Lynchburg, Va., Aug. 20, 1947; s. Thomas Yville and Rosamond (Brown) P.; B.S., Va. Mil. Inst., 1969; M.A., George Washington U., 1972; m. Kimberley Klein, Feb. 27, 1977. Commd. 2d lt. U.S. Air Force, 1972, advanced through grades to capt., 1974; adminstrv. asst. command surgeon Hdqrs. Command, Andrews AFB, Washington, 1972-74; presdl. social aide The White House, Washington, 1972-77; dir. Dept. Med. Edn. and Training, USAF Med. Center, Andrews AFB, 1974-76; mem. med. subcom. Armed Forces Inagural Com., 1976-77; clinic adminstr. USAF Clinic, San Vito, Italy, 1977—; instr. City Coll. Chgo., Troy State U., 1978—. Mem. Am. Hosp. Assn., Am. Coll. Hosp. Adminstrs., Air Force Assn. Home: 3101 Link Rd Lynchburg VA 24503

POWERS, DARDEN, physicist; b. Holly Springs, Miss., Nov. 15, 1932; s. Percy Harmon and Irene (Matthews) P.; B.S., Okla. U., 1955; M.S., Calif. Inst. Tech., 1957, Ph.D., 1961; m. Patricia Ann Walls, July 6, 1957; children—Susan, John, David, James (dec.), Peter. Asst. prof. physics Baylor U., 1961-63, asso. prof., 1963-67, prof., 1968—, dir. Van de Graaff Lab., 1964—, dir. grad. studies dept. physics, 1976—. Served with U.S. Army, 1951-53; Korea. NSF grantee, 1964-74; Robert A. Welch Found. grantee, 1968—. Mem. Am. Phys. Soc., Am. Assn. Physics Tchrs., Internat. Commn. on Radiation Units, Phi Beta Kappa, Sigma Xi, Sigma Pi Sigma. Baptist. Contbr. articles to phys. Rev. Home: 3217 Forrester Ln Waco TX 76708 Office: Baylor U Dept Physics Waco TX 76706

POWERS, GEORGIA M., state senator; b. Springfield, Ky., Oct. 29, 1923; d. Ben and Frances (Walker) Montgomery; ed. Louisville Municipal Coll., 1940-42; m. James L. Powers; 1 son from previous marriage, William F. Davis. Supr. IBM Data Processing div. U.S. Census Bur., 1959-62; asst. hosp. adminstr., Louisville, 1966; mem. Ky. State Senate, 1968—. Mem. Gov.'s Adv. Council on Mental Retardation, 1967-68. Dist. chmn. Jefferson County Democratic Exec. Com., 1964-66; chmn. Blume for Congress campaign, 1966; del. Dem. Nat. Conv., 1968. Bd. dirs. Louisville area chpt. A.R.C., 1970-72. Recipient Kennedy-King Meritorious award Ky. Young Dems., 1968; Achievement award Zion Bapt. Ch., 1968; certificate of appreciation Ky. Sch. Bds. Assn., 1968; Woman of Yr. award YWCA, 1978, Watson Meml. award, 1979. Mem. So. Christian Leadership Conf., N.A.A.C.P., Urban League. Address: 733 Cecil Ave Louisville KY 40211

POWERS, JOSEPH DUDLEY, physician; b. Upland, Calif., Apr. 13, 1927; s. Hardy Carrol and Ruby Mae (King) P.; B.S., So. Methodist U., 1952; D.D.S., Baylor U., 1956; M.D., U. Tex., 1962; m. Mary Joan Clester, June 8, 1951; children—Bradford Eric, Peter Kerry, Elizabeth Ann, Stephanie Sue. Mem. faculty Baylor U. Coll. Dentistry, 1956-58; intern Decatur-Macon County Hosp., Decatur, Ill., 1962-63; adminstr., med. dir. Nazarene Mission Hosp., Kudjip, Western Highlands, Papua, New Guinea, 1965-69; pvt. practice medicine specializing in family practice, Bethany, Okla., 1969—; mem. staff Bethany Med. Clinic Assos., 1969—, pres., 1977—; mem. staff Bethany Gen. Hosp., 1969—, trustee, 1970-79, chief of staff, 1977-78; mem. staff Deaconess Hosp., Bapt. Hosp., Oklahoma City; pres. Patient Care Inc. Lay mem. gen. bd. Ch. of the Nazarene, Internat. Hdqrs., Kansas City, Mo., 1972-80, chmn., 1978. Served with USN, 1945-46. Recipient Gold Headed Cane award U. Tex. Med. Br., 1962; diplomate Am. Bd. Family Practice. Fellow Am. Acad. Gen. Practice; mem. Am. Med. Assos., Oklahoma County Med. Assn., Okla. Med. Assn., Mu Delta. Republican. Club: Kiwanis. Home: 7401 NW 19th St Bethany OK 73008 Office: 6801 NW 39th Expressway Bethany OK 73008

POWERS, RICKMAN, accountant; b. Verona, Ky., Feb. 25, 1914; s. Omer Kirtley and Relda Ricketts (Roberts) P.; B.S., Eastern Ky. U., 1937; postgrad. Boston U., 1940-41, U. Cin., 1948-50; m. Barbara Ann Butler, Dec. 27, 1941; children—Perrin Sue Powers Shields, Robert R., Scott M., Jackson D. Accountant, Cotton & Eskew, C.P.A.'s, Louisville, 1937-40, Rohm & Haas Co., Phila., 1941-42; treas. The Stewart Iron Works Co., Covington, Ky., 1951-54; treas. Hickman, Williams & Co., Cin., 1954-64, sec., 1964-71, dir., sec., 1971-74, dir., v.p., sec., 1974—; lectr. in field; trustee City of Edgewood, Ky., 1949-51. Past bd. mem., treas. YMCA, Covington, Ky. Served to Capt. AUS, 1942-46. C.P.A. Ohio, 1951, Ky., 1953. Mem. Ohio Soc. C.P.A.'s (v.p., dir. Cin. chpt.), Am. Inst. C.P.A.'s, Alumni Assn. Republican. Presbyterian (elder, trustee). Clubs: Optimist of Covington (bd. mem., past pres.); Cincinnati (Ohio). Home: 143 Parkway Dr Fort Mitchell KY 41017 Office: 814 First National Bank Bldg PO Box 538 Cincinnati OH 45201

POYNOR, KENNETH J., realtor; b. Chelsea, Okla., July 3, 1916; s. James Madison and Nova K. (Aldridge) P.; B.S., Okla. State U., 1937; m. Dorothy O. Smith, May 24, 1937. With U.S. Dept. Agr., Stillwater, Okla., 1938-43; tchr. vocat. agr., Noble, Okla., 1943-44, Altus, Okla., 1944-45; owner, operator Ken Poynor Agy. real estate and ins., Norman, Okla., 1951—; owner, operator farms and ranches. Mem. Okla. Ho. of Reps., 1958-62. Named Norman Realtor of Year, 1969. Mem. Okla. Realtors (state chmn. legis. com. 1965-73, agrl. research and edn. com. 1965-73), Norman Bd. Realtors (pres. 1960-71), C. of C., Okla. U. Alumni Assn. (life). Clubs: Masons, Shriners, Kiwanis, Norman Golf and Country. Home: 1306 Melrose Dr Norman OK 73069 Office: 708 W Main St Norman OK 73069

POYNTER, MARION KNAUSS, journalist; b. Poughkeepsie, N.Y., Apr. 17, 1926; d. Louis Eugene and Rose Alvina (Arndt) Knauss; A.B., Vassar Coll., 1946; postgrad. Fla. State U., 1950, Am. U., 1960, U. S. Fla., 1971; m. Nelson Paul Poynter, May 4, 1970. Advt. sales rep. R.H. Donnelley Corp., 1946-47; researcher Time-Life, Inc., N.Y.C., 1948-49; researcher CIA, Washington, 1952-60; editorial writer, researcher St. Petersburg (Fla.) Times, 1961-70; contbg. editor Times Pub. Co., St. Petersburg, 1970—; dir. Times Pub. Co. Mem. Fla. Gulf Coast Symphony Bd., 1973-77; trustee St. Petersburg Mus. Fine Arts, 1978—; mem. Pres.' Roundtable Eckerd Coll., 1973—. Mem. Women in Communications, Fla. Press Club, Internat. Press Inst. Home: 900 Park St N Saint Petersburg FL 33710

POYTHRESS, DAVID BRYAN, state ofcl. Ga.; b. Macon, Ga., Oct. 24, 1943; s. John M. and Dorothy Randall (Bayne) P.; B.A., Emory U., 1964, J.D., 1967; m. Darla Chris Hilton, Aug. 19, 1972. Admitted to Ga. bar, 1967; asst. atty. gen. Ga., 1971-72; dep. revenue commr. Ga., Atlanta, 1972-79, sec. of state, 1979—. Faculty, U. Md., Far East Extension, DaNang, Republic of Vietnam, 1969-70; adj. faculty Golden Gate Coll., San Francisco, 1971, DeKalb Jr. Coll., DeKalb County, Ga., 1972. Served with JAG Dept., USAF, 1967-71. Decorated Air Force Commendation medal. Office: 214 State Capitol Atlanta GA 30334

PRADO, DANIEL HERRERA, fin. co. exec.; b. San Antonio, May 27, 1949; s. Domingo F. and Juanita H. (Herrera) P.; B.B.A., St. Mary U., 1971, M.B.A., 1974; m. Tamara Jean Little, May 30, 1970; children—Nicole Denise, Danielle Marie. Mktg. analyst Volkswagen of Am., San Antonio, 1971-72, advt. asst., 1972, asst. distbn. mgr., 1972-73, dist. sales mgr., 1973-76; pres. Las Cocinas, Inc., San Antonio, 1976—, Profl. Fin. Services, Inc., San Antonio; mem. bus. faculty San Antonio Coll., 1977—. Lic. real estate broker. Mem. Am. Mktg. Assn., Assn. M.B.A. Execs., Tex. Restaurant Assn., League United Latin-Am. Citizens, St. Mary U. Alumni Assn. Roman Catholic. Home: 90 Mossey Cup Ln San Antonio TX 78231 office: 830 NE Loop 410 Suite 303 San Antonio TX 78209

PRASSEL, FREDERICK FRANZ, constrn. co. exec.; b. San Antonio, Nov. 14, 1934; s. Victor, Sr. and Eda Marie (Groos) P.; student U. Tübingen (Ger.), Trinity U.; B.A., U. Tex., Austin, 1959; postgrad. Calif. Western U.; m. Barbara Fry, July 2, 1959; children—Charlotte, Victor B., Edie C. Owner, pres. Prassel Constrn. Co., San Antonio, 1959—; dir. Pras-Mel Corp.; pub. speaker. Bd. dirs. YMCA; deacon First Presbyterian Ch.; pres. Arthur Gray Jones Choir, 1978, 79; mem. Leadership San Antonio Program, 1979-80. Served with AUS, 1957-59. Mem. Am. Mgmt. Assn., Builders Exchange Tex., Internat. Platform Assn., YMCA, Jaycees (dir. 1961-62), Arts Council San Antonio, Ducks Unltd., San Antonio Mus. Assn. Clubs: Toastmasters (pres. 1976), Oak Hills Country, Beethoven Maennerchor, Rotary (sec. 1978-79, service chmn. 1979-80). Home: 116 Cardinal Ave San Antonio TX 78209 Office: 1000 S Comal St PO Box 526 San Antonio TX 78292

PRATER, JESSE WALLACE, dentist; b. Ocala, Fla., Mar. 23, 1932; s. Jesse A. and Helen (Jones) P.; D.M.D., U. Louisville, 1962; m. Bettye Beam, June 15, 1952 (div.); children—Jesse W., Suzanne Beam. Practice dentistry, Tampa, Fla., 1962—; pres. Stat Inc., 1969—, TRI ARC Prodns., 1970—(both Tampa); lectr. dental practice mgmt. and tech. dentistry; faculty adviser Fla. Coll. Med. and Dental Assts.; cons. The Practice Mgmt. Group, Fla. Dept. Health and Rehab. Services, Fla. Cripple Children's Soc. Served with AUS, 1953-55. Fellow Royal Soc. Health; mem. Lauritzen (chmn. 1968-69), Hillsboro County dental research groups, Am. Soc. Preventive Dentistry (v.p. Fla. chpt. 1972-73, pres. Fla. chpt. 1973-74), Fedn. Dentaire Internationale, ADA, Am. Prosthodontic Soc., Fla. W. Coast Dental Soc., Am. Acad. Craniomandibular Orthopedics, Am. Acad. Dental Practice Adminstrn., Hillsboro County Dental Soc., Pierre Fauchard Acad., So. Acad. Clin. Nutrition (charter), Am. Equilibration Soc., Internat. Platform Assn., Nat. Rifle Assn., Psi Omega, Alpha Epsilon Delta. Clubs: Masons (32 deg.), Shriners, Sertoma. Author: Book Ways to Better Days in Your Practice, 1970; cons. editor Dental mgmt. mag.; contbg. editor Dentalpractice mag. Home: 4409 Vieux Carre Circle Lutz FL 33549 Office: 2630 W Water Ave Tampa FL 33614

PRATER, REX JOE, speech pathologist, educator; b. Logan, Ohio, Jan. 18, 1948; s. Joe Ed and Sara Ellen (Oiler) P.; B.S., Ohio State U., 1970, M.A., 1972, Ph.D., 1975; m. Constance Charlene Stollar, Sept. 15, 1968; children—Trevor Christian Josef, Trent Joseph Edward. Speech pathologist Columbus (Ohio) public schs., 1968-76; asst. prof. speech pathology U. N.C., Greensboro, 1976—. Mem. Am. Speech, Hearing and Lang. Assn. (cert. of clin. competence), N.C. Speech Hearing and Lang. Assn. Home: 3 Amberhill Ct Greensboro NC 27405 Office: 1000 Spring Garden St Greensboro NC 27412

PRATHER, DUDLEY ALAN, hosp. adminstr.; b. Shreveport, La., Sept. 1, 1952; s. Dewey Harmon and Esta Lee (Young) P.; B.S. in Public Adminstrn., U. Ark., 1974; m. Mary Jane, June 14, 1975. Purchasing dir. City Hosp., Fayetteville, Ark., 1974-75, asst. adminstrn., 1976-77; asst. adminstr. Washington Regional Med. Center, Fayetteville, 1975-76; adminstr. Fayetteville City Hosp., 1977—. Mem. Local Govt. Com., Fayetteville. Mem. Am. Hosp. Assn., Ark. Hosp. Assn., Ark. Nursing Home Assn., Am. Coll. Nursing Home Adminstrs., N.W. Ark. Hosp. Adminstrs. Council, Ark. Young Adminstrs. Forum. Democrat. Methodist. Club: Exchange (dir. club). Home: 2545 Karyn St Fayetteville AR 72701 Office: 221 S School St Fayetteville AR 72701

PRATHER, HELEN THAXTON, ednl. adminstr.; b. Post, Tex., Mar. 4, 1932; d. Cecil Ragland and Loree (Dennis) Thaxton; student Abilene Christian Coll., 1948-50; B.B.A., U. Tex., 1952, M.B.A., 1959; Ed.D., U. Houston, 1974; m. Charles M. Prather, Sept. 11, 1954; children—John, Janet, Jim. Bus. tchr. Bellaire High Sch., Houston, 1960-67; instr. bus. Tarrant County Jr. Coll., Ft. Worth, 1967-68; chmn. bus. careers dept. Houston Community Coll., 1974-76; chmn. bus. services tech. dept. U. Houston, 1976—; cons. mgmt. and communications. Certified bus. educator. Mem. Nat. Bus. Edn. Assn., Assn. Records Mgrs., Tex. State Teachers Assn., Delta Pi Epsilon. Republican. Mem. Ch. of Christ. Club: River Oaks Bus. Women's Assn. Home: 412 E Gaywood St Houston TX 77079 Office: University of Houston 1 Main St Houston TX 77002

PRATHER, JOHN WILLIAM, JR., structural engr.; b. Spartanburg, S.C., Dec. 6, 1916; s. John William and Essie Iola (Nanney) P.; grad. high sch.; m. Ruth Montine Whitmire, Aug. 16, 1942; 1 son, John William III. With Duke Power Co., Charlotte, N.C., 1936-38; with Lockwood Greene Engrs., Inc., Spartanburg, 1938-58, head govt. dept. S.C. office, 1954-58; prin. Prather & Thomas, Spartanburg, 1958-66; sr. partner Prather, Thomas, Campbell & Assos., Spartanburg, 1966-72; sec.-treas. Prather Thomas Campbell Pridgeon, Inc., Spartanburg, 1972—. Mem. Spartanburg Planning Commn., 1964-66, 67-70, chmn., 1969. Named Young Man of Yr., Spartanburg Jaycees, 1947, 49; registered profl. engr., S.C., Ga. Mem. Nat. Soc. Profl. Engrs., Nat. Fire Protection Assn., Am. Concrete Inst. (pres. Carolinas chpt. 1978), ASTM, S.C. Soc. Engrs., S.C. Soc. Profl. Engrs. (pres. chpt. 1963), S.A.R., Magna Charta Barons. Methodist. Clubs: Country (pres. 1971, 72) (Spartanburg); Sertoma (past v.p.). Home: 533 Palmetto St Spartanburg SC 29302 Office: PO Box 3028 405 S Pine St Spartanburg SC 29304

PRATS, MANUEL L., banker; b. Aguada, P.R., June 15, 1934; s. Juan and Maria (Rivera) P.; B.A., St. Mary's U., 1957; B.B.A., U. P.R., 1961; m. Betty Vega, July 28, 1957; children—Manuel Ramon, Juan-Carlos, Alfredo-Gerardo. Vice pres. Banco Popular de P.R., San Juan, 1959-72; pres. Housing Bank, San Juan, 1972-73, dir., 1972—; partner Campo-Palou-Prats, Bayamon, P.R., 1973-75; pres. Banco Regional DeAhorro, Bayamon, 1976—; dir. Banco Regional, 1976—, Bayamon Fin. and Mortgage Corp., 1973-76. Pres., Boy Scouts Am., Rio Piedras, 1976-77, PTA, San Antonio Coll., 1973-76. Served with USAF, 1953-57. Mem. Am. Bankers Assn., Am. Inst. Banking, Mortgage Bankers Assn. Am. Republican. Roman Catholic. Club: Exchange. Home: Vermont St Suite 315 San Gerardo Urb San Gerardo Rio Piedras PR 00926 Office: PO Box 2813 Bayamon PR 00619

PRATT, JOHN LEE, lawyer; b. Shattuck, Okla., July 10, 1948; s. Ora Avery and Donna Vae (Blasingame) P.; B.S. in Psychology cum laude, N. Tex. State U., Denton, 1970; J.D., U. Tex., Austin, 1973; m. Kiona Helen Dugan, Aug. 14, 1966; children—Bret, Elizabeth. Admitted to Tex. bar, 1973; pvt. practice, Austin, 1973-74, Odessa, 1974—; partner firm Alexander, Lowe & Pratt, Odessa, 1974-76; 1st asst. county atty. Ector County, 1976-79. Mem. Tex. Bar Assn., Tex. Trial Lawyers Assn., Ector County Bar Assn., Ector County Young Lawyers Assn. (pres. 1979-80), Tex. Dist. and County Attys. Assn. Democrat. Methodist. Club: Odessa Downtown Rotary.

PREAS, JOHN EDWARD, educator; b. Toledo, Mar. 7, 1947; s. John and Frances (Moon) P.; B.A. in Communication Arts, Loyola U., Chgo., 1969; M.A. in Speech, Northeastern Ill. U., 1975; m. Marjorie Mary Mehigan, Sept. 6, 1969; children—Andrew Thomas, John David. Tchr. English and speech, dir. debate and forensics Loyola Acad., Wilmette, Ill., 1969-75; instr. English and public speaking Telshe Yeshiva Rabbinical Tng. Coll., Chgo., 1973-75; instr. speech, dir. speech activities Westark Community Coll., Ft. Smith, Ark., 1975—. Mem. Speech Communication Assn., Ark. Speech Communication Assn., Blue Key, Phi Delta Kappa. Mem. Christian Ch. Office: Box 3649 Fort Smith AR 72913

PRELLER, JOHN GEORGE, mgmt. cons.; b. Bklyn., Sept. 27, 1913; s. John Adam and Barbara (Thomas) P.; student John's U., 1928-29; m. Flavia V. Klarikaitus, Jan. 10, 1946; children—Carol Ann, Laura Virginia. Partner brokerage firm McGinnis, Bampton & Selger McGinnis & Co., N.Y.C., 1946-53; pres. Rent'Em, Inc., Watkinsville, Ga., 1955-79; mgmt. cons.; dir. Roper Lumber Co. Served with AUS, 1941-45. Decorated Bronze Star medal. Mem. Linen Supply Assn. Am. (dir. 1973-75), S.E. Textile Rental Assn., (pres. 1971), S.W. Linen and Indsl. Launderers Assn., Inst. Indsl. Launderers, Am. Legion, VFW. Republican. Roman Catholic. Clubs: Athens Country, Elks, Moose. Home and Office: 145 Riverhill Ct Athens GA 30606

PREMACK, IRWIN JOSEPH, mktg. research co. exec.; b. Chgo., June 2, 1927; s. Hyman Abraham and Bertha (Friedman) P.; B.S. in Psychology, Roosevelt U., 1948; m. Audrey Twersky, Dec. 19, 1948; children—Steven, Richard. Pres., Premack Research Corp., St. Petersburg, Fla., 1960—; columnist Miami Rev., Bergida Enterprises, 1971—; lectr. TV program Channel 13, Tampa, Fla., Channel 10, Miami, Channel 4, Miami, also producer 11 TV spls., 1971-74; public speaker Fla. Econs. Club, Am. Mktg. Assn., Fla. Public Relations Assn., Ft. Lauderdale, Miami, Tallahassee advt. fedns.; condr. TV election returns CBS-TV, 1976, 78, 80, 2 TV spls. for CBS, 78, 4 TV spls. for CBS, 1979; researcher for 28 U.S. Congressmen, 11 U.S. Senators, 9 govs. now in office; personal researcher for U.S. Pres.; cons. numerous clients on 5 continents. Bd. dirs. Gulf Coast Jewish Family Service. Served with AUS, 1945. Subject of 3 TV spls., 1973, 2 spls., 1976. Mem. Am. Assn. Polit. Consultants, Am. Mktg. Assn. (charter mem.), St. Petersburg (dir. mktg. com.), Orlando (environ. resources com.) chambers commerce. Republican (cons. Nat. Com.). Jewish. Club: Tiger Bay (Miami). Home: 717 Pruitt Dr Madeira Beach FL 33708 Office: 6727 1st Ave S Saint Petersburg FL 33707

PRENTICE, JOHN MICHAEL, ins. and investments exec.; b. Dyess, Ark., Oct. 16, 1950; s. Ruben and Elsie Juanita P.; student Ark. State U., 1970, Memphis State U., 1971; m. Marion O. Prentice, Oct. 3, 1975; 1 dau., Lisa Jean. Supr., Baron, Inc., Memphis, 1971; owner, operator Pride Bildors, Memphis, 1971-74, Anderton-Prentice & Assos., Memphis, 1974—; regional v.p. A.L. Williams and Assos., 1979—. Hon. dep. sheriff, Shelby County, Tenn., 1976; recipient Order of Golden Eagle, Nat. Home Life Assurance, 1979. Mem. Memphis Jaycees (chmn. crippled children's benefit 1976, 77), Nat. Assn. Term Life Underwriters. Republican. Baptist. Home: 1105 Hester Rd Memphis TN 38116 Office: 3000 Walnut Grove Memphis TN 38111

PRENTICE, PIERREPONT ISHAM, journalist; b. Newark, Sept. 10, 1899; s. Sartell and Lydia Beekman (Vanderpoel) P.; B.A. cum laude, Yale U., 1920; m. Mildred Belcher, Sept. 30, 1922; children—Mildred Barbara Prentice Kulesh, Carolyn Sumner Prentice, Falise; m. 2d. Janet McNeir Pflieger, Nov. 1, 1944. Reporter, N.Y. Tribune, 1921-24; editor, pub. Camden (N.J.) Post Telegram, 1924-26; mng. editor New Bedford (Mass.) Times, 1926-29; news editor Phila. Record, 1929-30; bus. mgr. Fortune mag., 1930-34; circulation dir. Time, Life and Fortune mags., 1934-41; v.p. Time, Inc., 1939-65, v.p. corp. affairs, 1945-49, prin. officer charge problems housing and urban affairs, 1949-65, cons., 1965—; pub. Time mag., 1941-45; editor, pub. Archtl. Forum, 1949-54; founder, editor, pub. Mag. of Housing, 1952-62; v.p., dir. Nat. Assn. Homebuilders Research Found., 1965—; cons. in housing mktg., 1965—; adv. com. Fed. Housing Adminstrn., 1954-56; founder, dir. Housing Industry President's Council, 1954-67; mem. housing fin. com. Com. Econ. Devel., 1966-67; property tax com. Nat. Tax Assn., 1976—; chmn. Nat. Council Property Tax Reform, 1976—. Bd. dirs. Lincoln Found., 1963-71; bd. dirs. Robert Schalkenbach Found., 1963—, pres., 1973—. Served to 2d lt. U.S. Army, 1918-19. Recipient Distinguished Service award Nat. Assn. Homebuilders, 1951, 58, named to Housing Hall of Fame, 1978; Jesse H. Neal editorial achievement award Asso. Bus. Publns., 1958-60, 62; F. Stuart Fitzpatrick Meml. award AIA, Nat. Assn. Homebuilders, Producers Council, Asso. Bldg. Contractors, and Bldg. Research Inst., 1963; award of honor Bldg. Research Advisory Bd., 1977, also awards for outstanding contbn. to housing progress, 1952-77; named Man of Year, Turntable Builders, 1976. Hon. mem. AIA (trustee found.); mem. U.S. C. of C. (mem. Task Force Economic Growth and Opportunity 1965-66, Urban and Regional Affairs Com. 1968-74). Presbyterian. Address: 220 Belleview Blvd Belleair FL 33516

PRENTNER, JAMES ROBERT, devel. co. exec.; b. Hamilton, Ohio, May 2, 1941; s. Joseph and Margaret Elizabeth (Clark) P.; ed. public schs.; m. Pamela Louise Windsor, Sept. 4, 1965; 1 dau., Dawn Venessa. Prodn. mgr. Hamilton Caster & Mfg. Co., Hamilton,

1965-69; v.p. purchasing/printing Lehigh Corp., Lehigh Acres, Fla., 1969—. Mem. Lehigh Acres Community Council, 1973-74. Served with U.S. Army, 1960-65. Mem. Lehigh Acres C. of C. (v.p. 1979-80), Lehigh Acres Pvt. Sch., Inc. (pres. 1978-79), Nat. Office Products Assn., Nat. Assn. Printers and Lithographers. Office: 230 E Joel Blvd Lehigh Acres FL 33936

PRESBITERO, JULIA VILLANUEVA, physician; b. Negros Occidental, Philippines, Apr. 27, 1922; d. Jacinto Villareal and Julita (Villanueva) Presbitero; came to U.S., 1971; A.A., U. Philippines, 1939, M.D., 1944, LL.B. cum laude, 1963. Intern, St. Catherine Hosp., East Chicago, Inc., 1946-47, resident, 1947-48; resident in anesthesia Evanston (Ill.) Hosp., 1948-49; resident in anesthesiology Ill. Research and Edn. Hosps., 1950; pvt. practice medicine specializing in anesthesia Philippine Gen. Hosp., 1950-71; asso. prof. anesthesia and med. jurisprudence Coll. Medicine, U. Philippines, 1950-72; professorial lectr. med. jurisprudence Coll. Law, U. Philippines, 1967-71; professorial lectr. legal medicine, and profl. ethics Philippine Women's U., 1968-70; fellow in anesthesiology Albert Einstein Coll. Medicine, 1971-72, attending in anesthesiology, 1972-73; attending in anesthesia Med. Center, Jersey City, N.J., 1973-75; asst. clin. prof. N.J. Coll. Medicine, 1973-75; asso. prof. anesthesiology U. Tex. Med. Sch., 1975—. Mem. Am., Philippine (sec.-treas. 1951-59) socs. anesthesiology, Philippine Med. Assn., Philippine Med. Women's Assn. (chmn. com. on legislation 1969-71, councilor 1970-71), U. Philippines Women's Lawyer's Circle. Author (with T. Quiazon) Law on Taxation, Income, Estate, Inheritance, and Gift Taxes, 1964. Contbr. articles to profl. jours. Home: 10322 Meadow Lake Houston TX 77042 Office: 6431 Fannin St Houston TX 77030

PRESCOTT, ETHELIND SOUTHERLAND, educator; b. Arcadia, Fla., Sept. 22, 1930; d. Frederick and Clara E. (Warlick) Southerland; B.S. magna cum laude in Edn., Fla. So. Coll., 1969; m. Bedford A. Prescott, Mar. 18, 1951; children—Linda G., Donald B. Classroom tchr., lang. arts tutorial tchr. Zolfo Elementary Sch., Zolfo Springs, Fla., 1969-74, tchr. lang. arts for migrant students of Hardee County, 1974—. Organist, New Hope Baptist. Ch., Wauchula, Fla., 1973—, mem. youth devel. com., 1974—, dir. youth and youth music, 1974-76. Mem. Fla., Hardee County (mem. math. devel. com. 1970-71) edn. assns. Club: Wauchula Jr. Woman's (sec. 1956-58). Home: PO Box 52 Wauchula FL 33873 Office: Zolfo Elementary Sch Zolfo Springs FL 33890

PRESNAL, BILL, state legislator; b. Bryan, Tex., Apr. 26, 1932; s. Will and Marjorie Lee (Marquart) P.; B.S., Tex. A. and M. U., 1953, M.S., 1960; m. Cecille D'Aun McCoy, June 6, 1954; children—James Scott, Stephen Earl, DeAnna Kay. Instr. West Tex. State U., 1953-54; farmer-rancher, 1957-62; counselor Tex. A. and M. U., 1962-68; mem. Tex. Ho. of Reps. from 28th Dist., 1969—. Served with USAF, 1954-56. Mem. Nat. Conf. State Legislatures (chmn. sci. and tech. com.). Democrat. Home: Route 1 Box 74 Bryan TX 77801 Office: PO Box 2910 Tex Ho of Reps Austin TX 78711

PRESSLER, HERMAN PAUL, III, judge; b. Houston, June 4, 1930; s. Herman Paul Jr. and Elsie Wildbahn (Townes) P.; A.B. cum laude, Princeton U., 1952; J.D., U. Tex., 1957; m. Nancy Avery, Feb. 28, 1959; children—Jean Townes, Anne Lyle, Herman Paul, IV. Admitted to Tex. bar, 1957; mem. Tex. Ho. of Reps. from Harris County, 1957-59; with firm Vinson & Elkins, Houston, 1958-70; judge 133d Jud. Dist. Ct. Tex., Houston, 1970-78; asso. justice 14th Ct. Civil Appeals, 1978—. Bd. dirs. Houston Christian Business Men's Found.; chmn. Evang. Christian Edn. Found.; deacon 1st Bapt. Ch., Houston; bd. dirs. Internat. Students, Inc. Served to lt. (j.g.) USNR, 1952-54. Recipient Distinguished Service award Houston Jr. C. of C., 1957, Faith in God award, 1976; Medal of Honor, DAR, 1976. Mem. Tex., Houston bar assns., Am. Judicature Soc. Clubs: Houston Country, Houston Allegro Soc. Home: 282 Bryn Mawr Circle Houston TX 77024 Office: 301 Fannin St Houston TX 77002

PRESSLY, WILLIAM LAURENS, headmaster; b. Louisville, Ga., July 24, 1908; s. Paul and Lois (Moffatt) P.; A.B., Princeton U., 1931; M.A., Harvard U., 1947; D.Litt., Washington and Lee U., Lexington, Va., 1949; LL.D. (hon.), Hangygang U. (Korea), 1978; m. Alice Fletcher McCallie, Aug. 28, 1940; children—Paul Moffatt, William Layrens. Co-headmaster, McCallie Sch., Chattanooga, 1936-51; founding pres., headmaster Westminster Schs., Atlanta, 1951-73; adminstr. Atlanta Hist. Soc., 1973—; past pres. Nat. Council Ind. Schs., So. Assn. Schs. and Colls., Headmasters Assn.; past trustee Coll. Entrance Exam. Bd., Ednl. Testing Service, Nat. Assn. Ind. Schs., Erskine Coll., Rabun-Gap Nacooche Sch.; chmn. President's Commn. Presdl. Scholar. Chmn. trustees Atlanta Coll. Art; life trustee Atlanta Arts Alliance; elder First Presbyn. Ch., Atlanta. Recipient Edward S. Noyes award Coll. Entrance Exam. Bd., 1976. Mem. Am. Assn. Museums, Nat. Trust Hist. Preservation. Home: 3770 Peachtree Rd Atlanta GA 30319 Office: 3099 Andrews Dr Atlanta GA 30305

PRESSON, CHARLES ARNOLD, ins. co. exec.; b. Jackson, Miss., Oct. 30, 1942; s. Ewart Knox and Mary Elizabeth (Mobley) P.; A.A., Itawamba Jr. Coll., 1960; B.S. in Bus., Miss. Coll., 1964; m. Norma Kay Storm, Nov. 11, 1967; children—Charles Anthony, Dawn Elizabeth. Cashier trainee Jefferson Standard Life Ins. Co., Jackson, 1965-66, officer mgr., Tulsa, 1966-67, San Antonio, 1967-77, sales service supr., Houston, 1977—. Served with USAF, 1964-65. Democrat. Baptist. Club: Masons (sr. warden 1976-77). Office: 8323 SW Freeway Suite 700 Houston TX 77074

PRESTON, CYNTHIA ANN, nurse; b. San Angelo, Tex., Sept. 30, 1943; d. David Crockett and Becky (Gault) Drake; 1964; m. Jerry Wayne Preston, Dec. 28, 1963; children—Shelley Kay, Michael Drake, Theresa Ann. Staff nurse operating room Breckenridge Hosp., Austin, Tex., 1964; staff nurse emergency room Meth. Hosp., Tex. Med. Center, Houston, 1965; with St. Luke's-Tex. Children's Hosp., Houston, 1966-75, supr. teaching service operating room, 1969-73, adminstrv. supr., 1974; dir. operating room Park Plaza Hosp., Houston, 1975—; mem. adv. bd. operating room technician program Houston Community Coll. Mem. Houston Assn. Dirs. Nursing, Nat. League Nurses, Nat. Assn. Female Execs., Assn. Operating Room Nurses. Episcopalian. Home: 9031 Grape St Houston TX 77036 Office: 1313 Hermann St Houston TX 77004

PRESTON, JOHN RICHARD, bank holding co. exec., lawyer; b. Cleve., July 1, 1945; s. Stanley Walter and Lillian H. (Nyland) P.; B.A., Bowling Green U., 1967; J.D., Case Western Res. U., 1970; m. Linda Kay Nelson, Aug. 12, 1967; 1 dau., Kate Nelson. Admitted to Ohio bar, 1971, Okla. bar, 1978; practiced law, Cleve., 1971-73; asst. counsel, asst. sec. Union Commerce Corp., Cleve., 1973-75; asst. v.p. Soc. Nat. Bank of Cleve., 1975-77; sr. v.p., gen. counsel, sec. First Okla. Bancorp., Inc. and First Nat. Bank & Trust Co., Oklahoma City, 1977—; dir. various privately held real estate, oil, gas and investment cos. Mem. Am. Bar Assn., Okla. Bar Assn., Oklahoma County Bar Assn., Ohio Bar Assn. Clubs: Beacon, Greens Golf and Racquet (Oklahoma City). Editor in chief: Case Western Res. Jour. Internat. Law, 1969-70. Office: 120 N Robinson St Oklahoma City OK 73102

PRESTON, LOYCE ELAINE, educator; b. Texarkana, Ark., Feb. 25, 1929; d. Harvey Martin and Florence (Whitlock) P.; student Texarkana Jr. Coll., 1946-47; B.S., Henderson State Tchrs. Coll., 1950; certificate in social work La. State U., 1952; M.S.W., Columbia U., 1956. Tchr. pub. schs., Dierks, Ark., 1950-51; child welfare worker Ark. Dept. Pub. Welfare, Clark and Hot Spring counties, 1951-56, child welfare cons., 1956-58; casework dir. Ruth Sch. Girls, Burien, Wash., 1958-60; asst. prof. spl. edn. La. Poly. Inst., Ruston, 1960-63; asst. prof. Northwestern State Coll., Shreveport, La., 1963-73; asst. prof. La. State U., Shreveport, 1973-79; ret., 1979. Chpt. sec. La. Assn. Mental Health, 1965-67, Gov's. adv. council, 1967-70; mem. Mayor's Com. for Community Improvement, 1972—. Mem. AAUW (dir. Shreveport br. 1963-69), Acad. Cert. Social Workers, Nat. Assn. Social Workers (del. 1964-65, pres. N. La. chpt., state-wide com. 1968-69), La Conf. Social Welfare, La. Fedn. Council Exceptional Children (pres. 1970-71), La. Tchrs. Assn. Home: 602 Pickwick Pl Shreveport LA 71108 Office: 8515 Youree Dr Shreveport LA 71105

PRESTON, ROBERT ANDREWS, univ. adminstr.; b. Richmond, Va., June 6, 1931; s. Joseph Martin and Mary Edythe (Andrews) P.; B.A., Belmont Abbey Coll., 1953; M.A., Cath. U., 1958, Ph.D., 1960; m. Frances Helen Solari, Sept. 6, 1958; children—Kathryn, Robert, Mary Frances, Margaret, James. Asst. prof. philosophy John Carrol U., 1960-63, St. Louis U., 1963-66; dean Bellarmine Coll., 1966-75; acad. v.p. Loyola U. of New Orleans, 1975—; cons. Belmont Abbey Coll., 1972-74, Spring Hill Coll., 1974-75. Bd. dirs. NCCJ, New Orleans. Served with U.S. Army, 1953-55. Mem. AAUP, Am. Council Edn., Am. Assn. Colls., Assn. Cath. Colls. and Univs. Roman Catholic. Home: 5420 La Cour Monique New Orleans LA 70114 Office: 6363 St Charles Ave New Orleans LA 70118

PRESTON, THOMAS LYTER, public relations agy. exec.; b. Carrollton, Ky., Sept. 25, 1934; s. Thomas Jefferson and Mary Lyter (Robertson) P.; A.B. in Journalism, U. Ky., 1956; postgrad. U. Wash., 1958; m. Carolyn Louise Points, June 1, 1957; 1 son, Matthew Thomas. Editor, Carrollton (Ky.) News-Democrat, 1956-57; owner, pub. Cynthiana (Ky.) Pub. Co., 1959-68; owner, prin. Thomas L. Preston Public Relations, Lexington, Ky., 1958—; sec. Preston & Assos. Cons. Engrs., 1960-70; pres. Standard Blueprint, Inc., Lexington, 1977-80; guest instr. dept. journalism U. Ky., Eastern Ky. U. Asso. dir. Ky. Better Rds. Council, 1965; mem. Ky. Council on Public Higher Edn., 1966-70; commr. Ky. Dept. Public Info., 1971-74; spl. asst. to Gov. Wendell H. Ford of Ky., 1971-75; adminstrv. asst. to U.S. Senator Wendell H. Ford, 1975. Served to 1st lt. U.S. Army, 1957-59, 61. Recipient citation of merit 6th U.S. Army, 1959, 101st Airborne Div., 1961; numerous journalistic and communications awards; named Outstanding Young Man of Ky., Jaycees, 1966. Mem. Public Relations Soc. Am. (accredited), Am. Soc. Bus. and Mgmt. Cons. (charter), Sigma Delta Chi, Phi Kappa Tau. Democrat. Presbyterian. Exec. editor Letterman mag., 1970-71. Home: Route 2 McCowans Ferry Pike Versailles KY 40383 Office: Suite 4 2134 Nicholasville Rd Lexington KY 40503

PRETSCH, FELIX HARRY, indsl. hygienist, librarian; b. Elkins, W.Va., Sept. 13, 1915; s. Felix and Minnie (Day) P.; B.S., Johns Hopkins U., 1945, postgrad. Johns Hopkins Sch. Hygiene and Public Health, 1946-48; M.S.L.S., U. Ky., 1970; postgrad. Auburn U., 1974-77; m. Anna Barrett, June, 1946 (dec. 1956); 1 son, Felix Day; m. 2d, Mary Frances Barnes, 1958 (div. 1967); 1 dau., Mary Catherine. Bacteriologist, Balt. City Health Dept., 1936, sanitarian, 1939-43, chief bur. of indsl. hygiene, 1943-45; chief indsl. hygiene engr. Md. State Health Dept., 1947-49; sr. asst. sanitarian USPHS, 1951-70; indsl. hygienist Humble Oil and Refining Co., Baytown, Tex., 1952-56; sr. research indsl. hygienist, cons. Esso Research and Engring. Co., Med. Research Div., Linden, N.J., 1956-59; chief indsl. hygiene services Arabian Am. Oil Co., Dhahran, Saudi Arabia, 1959-68; ops. mgr. Agatha Corp., Cin., 1968-70; gift and exchange librarian Auburn (Ala.) U., 1971, sci. and tech. librarian, 1971-73, librarian II, 1973—, adj. asst. prof. indsl. engring., 1973-78. Mem. Am. Acad. Indsl. Hygiene, AAUP, Brit. Occupational Hygiene Soc., Nat. Ret. Tchrs. Assn., Southeastern Library Assn., Beta Phi Mu, Phi Alpha Theta, Sigma Xi. Republican. Home: 400 2d Ave Opelika AL 36801 Office: Auburn Univ Auburn AL 36830

PRETZER, DWAYNE LEWIS, geophysicist; b. Clatonia, Nebr., Aug. 11, 1923; s. William Bernhart and Mary Viola (Cornelius) P.; B.S. in Civil Engring., U. Nebr., 1945; postgrad. Cornell U., 1945; m. Mildred Hopkins, Dec. 28, 1949; children—James Lewis, Donald Holmes. Trainee, Geophys. Services, Inc., Dallas, 1946; seismologist, party chief supr. Delta Exploration Co., Jackson, Miss., 1947-69; mgr. interpretation services Seiscom Delta, Inc., Houston, 1969-73; sr. geophysicist, group leader Conoco, Inc., Houston, 1973—; dir. Delta Exploration Co. Served with USN, 1944-46; PTO. Mem. Soc. Exploration Geophysicists, Am. Orchid Soc., Sigma Tau. Republican. Methodist. Club: Exchange (Jackson, Miss.). Home: 11303 Pecan Creek Houston TX 77043

PREUSS, ALAN CONRAD, mfg. co. ofcl.; b. McKeesport, Pa., Aug. 1, 1945; s. Fred Arthur and Lillian Ester (Carpenter) P.; A.S. in Electronic Tech., Broward Community Coll., 1976; m. Mary Ann Poff, Aug. 26, 1967; 1 son, Mathew Alan. Supr. broadcast engring. Sta. WMPT-AM-FM, 1963-68; supr. tech. tng. Bendix Avionics div. Bendix Corp., Ft. Lauderdale, Fla., 1968—. Bd. dirs. Christ Meth. Ch., Ft. Lauderdale. Radiotelephone lic. 1st class FCC; advanced amateur radio lic. Mem. Am. Radio Relay League (sr.), Soc. Broadcast Engrs., Gold Coast FM Assn. Author: Digital Devices Training Manual, 1976; Microprocessor Training Manual, 1979. Home: 370 SW 13th St Pompano Beach FL 33060 Office: Bendix Avionics 2100 NS 62d St Fort Lauderdale FL 33310

PREYER, L. RICHARDSON, congressman; b. Greensboro, N.C., Jan. 11, 1919; s. William Y. and Mary Norris (Richardson) P.; grad. Woodberry Forest Sch.; A.B., Princeton U., 1941; LL.B., Harvard U., 1949; LL.D. (hon.), Elon Coll., 1972, U. N.C., Greensboro, 1972, Davidson Coll., 1977, U. N.C., Chapel Hill, 1978; m. Emily Irving Harris, May 11, 1946; children—L. Richardson, Mary Norris, Britt Armfield, Jane Bethell, Emily Harris. Admitted to N.C. bar; mem. firm Preyer & Bynum, Greensboro, 1950-56; city judge, Greensboro, 1953-56; N.C. superior ct. judge, 1956-61; U.S. dist. judge 18th Dist. N.C., 1961-63; engaged in N.C. gubernatorial campaign, 1963-64; sr. v.p., trust officer N.C. Nat. Bank, Greensboro, 1964-66, exec., 1966-68; mem. 91st-96th Congresses from 6th Dist. N.C. Washington trustee Folger Shakespeare Library. Served with USNR, World War II. Decorated Bronze Star medal; named Greensboro's Outstanding Young Man, U.S. Jr. C. of C., 1954, Outstanding Leader, Inter-Club Council, 1968; recipient Disting. Service award U. N.C. Med. Sch., 1975. Mem. Newcomen Soc. Democrat. Home: 603 Sunset Dr Greensboro NC 27408 Office: Rayburn House Office Bldg Washington DC 20515

PREYSZ, LOUIS ROBERT FONSS, III, banker; b. Quantico, Va., Aug. 1, 1944; s. Louis Robert Fonss, Jr., and Lucille (Parks) P.; B.A., U. Wis., Madison, 1968; M.B.A., U. Utah, Salt Lake City, 1973; student Stonier Grad. Sch. Banking, Rutgers U., 1979—; m. Claudia Ann Karpowitz, Sept. 9, 1967; children—Louis Robert Fonss IV, Christine Elizabeth, Michael Anthony. Teaching and research asst. U. Utah, 1971-73; mktg. and personnel officer Security 1st Nat. Bank of Sheboygan (Wis.), 1973-76; mktg. dir. 1st Nat. Bank of Rock Island (Ill.), 1976-77; asst. v.p., mktg. sales mgr. 1st Nat. Bank of Birmingham (Ala.), 1977-78; v.p., mktg. mgr. Sun 1st Nat. Bank of Orlando (Fla.), 1978—; mem. part-time faculty U. Wis., 1973-76, Fla. Inst. Tech., 1976-77, St. Ambrose Coll., Davenport, Iowa, 1976-77. Mem. Indsl. Devel. Commn. Mid-Fla., Inc., Downtown Bus. Assn., Orlando Area Tourist and Trade Assn. Served to capt. U.S. Army, 1968-72. Mem. Bank Mktg. Assn., Sales and Mktg. Execs. Internat., Gen. Agts. and Mgrs. Assn., U. Wis. Alumni Assn., U. Utah Alumni Assn., Fla. Bankers Assn., Orlando Area C. of C., Phi Gamma Delta. Roman Catholic. Clubs: Citrus, Ft. Gatlin Swim and Tennis. Author: How to Introduce a New Service, 1976; contbg. editor: Target Market, an Instructional Approach to Bank Cross Selling of Services, New Accounts Training Manual, 1977; Tested Techniques in Bank Marketing, 1977; contbr. articles to mags. Home: 1338 Buckwood Dr Orlando FL 32806 Office: 200 S Orange Ave Orlando FL 32806

PRICE, DOROTHY MARION, ednl. adminstr.; b. Marshalltown, Iowa, May 3, 1927; d. John Patrick and Linnie Mae (Pool) McCarthy; student Marshalltown Jr. Coll., 1945-46; B.A., U. No. Iowa, 1949; M.A., Tex. Christian U., 1971; postgrad. Tex. Woman's U., 1977; m. David Virgil Price, Aug. 15, 1945; children—Mary Lynne, Margo Elaine, Peggy Ellen, Erin Colleen, Patrick David, Sean Stewart. Speech pathologist Albia (Iowa) schs., 1950-51, Chariton (Iowa) public schs., 1951-52, St. Joseph (Mo.) public schs., 1958-59, Ft. Worth (Tex.) Ind. Sch. Dist., 1965-68, Sch. Dist. 63, Niles-Glenview, Ill., 1968-70; speech pathologist Ft. Worth Ind. Sch. Dist., 1970-75, supr. speech, lang. and hearing services, 1975—; adj. faculty Tex. Christian U., Ft. Worth, 1976—. V.F.W. Aux. scholar, 1945-46, 46-47. Mem. Am. Speech and Hearing Assn., Tex. Speech and Hearing Assn., Speech and Hearing Assn. of N. Tex., Assn. for Children with Learning Disabilities, NEA, Tex. Tchrs. Assn., Tex. Elem. Prin. and Suprs. Assn., Assn. of Women Adminstrs. in Edn., Council of Suprs., Coordinators and Adminstrs. of Lang., Speech and Hearing Services, Tex. Council of Suprs. of Lang., Speech and Hearing, Deaf-Blind Multihandicapped Assn. of Tex., Delta Kappa Gamma. Mem. Christian Ch. Contbr. articles in field to profl. jours. Office: 5533 Whitman St Fort Worth TX 76133

PRICE, EDGAR HILLEARY, JR., citrus processing co. exec., ex-state senator; b. Jacksonville, Fla., Jan. 1, 1918; s. Edgar Hilleary and Mary (Phillips) P.; student U. Fla., 1937-38; m. Elise Ingram, May 24, 1947; 1 son, Jerald Steven. Gen. mgr. Terra Ceia Bay Farms, Inc., Palmetto, Fla., 1945-49; mgr. Fla. Gladiolus Growers Assn., Bradenton, 1949-55; exec. v.p. Tropicana Products, Inc., Bradenton, 1955-79, now dir., mem. exec. com.; chmn. bd., pres. Price Co., Inc., Bradenton, 1979—; dir. Indsl. Glass Co., Inc.; dir. Ellis First Nat. Bank of Bradenton, Fla. Power and Light Co., Gen. Telephone Co. Fla., 1st City Fed. Savs. and Loan Assn., Ellis Banking Corp., Bradenton; mem. Fla. Senate, 1958-66; adv. com. Fla. Citrus Mut.; dir. Fla. Citrus Expn., 1958—, Fla. Cypress Gardens, Inc.; chmn. Fla. Citrus Commn.; bus. and agrl. cons. Gov. of Fla., 1971—. Del. Democratic Nat. Conv., 1958-62; mem. gov.'s com. employment of physically handicapped, 1960; chmn. bd. trustees Manatee County Sch. Dist., 1956-57; chmn. Bradenton Housing Authority, 1951-57, commr., 1951—; bd. dirs. Salvation Army, Bradenton, 1954—; regional chmn. Crusade for Freedom, 1952-53; chmn. ARC, 1950; active Manatee County Crippled Children's Soc., Boys' Club, Blood Bank; commn. chmn. Census of 12th Jud. Circuit, 1957; mem. Fla. Bd. Control, 1957-58; mem. Fla. Plant Bd., 1957-58; chmn. Gov.'s Freeze Damage Survey Team, 1957-58; commr. Manatee County Indsl. Commn., 1956; trustee Univ. S. Fla. Found.; mem. Fla. Commn. Ethics, 1976—; mem. U.S. Circuit Judge Nominating Commn., 1977—. Served from pvt. to sgt., M.C., AUS, 1941-43, to 1st lt. USAAF, 1943-45. Decorated Air medal with 4 oak leaf clusters; named outstanding freshman senator Fla. Legislature, 1959; recipient Distinguished Service award U.S. Jr. C. of C., 1949; Fla. Man of Year in Agr. Progressive Farmer mag., 1961; Good Govt. award Jr. C. of C., 1961; Allen Morris award most valuable mem. Fla. Legislature, 1965; St. Petersburg Times award for most outstanding senator, 1965. Mem. Fla. (pres. 1970-71), Manatee County (pres. 1968) chambers of commerce, Com. of 100 (vice chmn.), Fla. State Fair Assn. (dir.), Future Farmers, Fla. Hort. Soc. (pres. 1967-68), Fla. Fruit and Vegetable Assn. (dir. 1968), NAM (dir. 1962-63, 71-73). Baptist (deacon, tchr. Sunday sch.). Club: Kiwanis (past pres. Bradenton). Home: 3009 Riverview Blvd W Bradenton FL 33505 Office: 9th St and 13th Ave W Bradenton FL 33505

PRICE, JAMES, govt. ofcl.; b. Sylvania, Ga., Oct. 13, 1948; s. Willie and Mary Ella P.; B.S., Savannah State Coll., 1970; M.Ed., U. Ga., 1971; Ed.S., U. S.C., 1976; postgrad. Atlanta U.; m. Dorothy Harrison, June 1, 1975; 1 child. Mental health counselor Uptight Crisis Center, Savannah, Ga., 1969-70; psychiat. social worker Moncrief Army Hosp., Ft. Jackson, S.C., 1972-74; psychologist S.C. Dept. Corrections, Columbia, 1974-75; edn. services specialist Edn. Center, Ft. McPherson, Ga., 1976-79; compliance specialist Office Civil Rights, HEW, Atlanta, 1979—. Served with U.S. Army, 1971-74. Ford Found. fellow, 1970-71. Mem. Am. Personnel and Guidance, Assn., So. Assn. Counselor Edn. and Supervision, Ga. Adult Edn. Assn., Am. Sch. Counselors Assn., Gresham Park Athletic Assn., Phi Delta Kappa. Methodist. Home: 4515 Riverwood Circle Decatur GA 30035 Office: HEW 101 Marietta Towers Suite 2700 Atlanta GA 30303

PRICE, JEROME T., acct.; b. Bronx, N.Y., June 27, 1942; s. Benjamin and Dora P.; B.A., Queens Coll., 1968; m. Iris Price, Dec. 24, 1968; children—Sharon, Steven. With Ernst & Ernst, N.Y.C., 1968-72, with Main LaFrentz & Co., Miami, Fla., 1973-77, partner, 1974—; partner Schechter Beame Pfeiffer & Burstein, Miami, 1977—. Served with U.S. Army, 1964-66. Mem. Am. Inst. C.P.A.'s, N.Y. State Soc. C.P.A.'s, Fla. Inst. C.P.A.'s, Nat. Assn. Accts. Democrat. Jewish. Office: 151 SW 1st St Miami FL 33130

PRICE, LARRY EDWARD, real estate devel. corp. exec.; b. Atlanta, May 20, 1949; s. Louis and Iola (Leslie) P.; B.A., Clark Coll., 1972; 1 dau., Tiffany. Sales rep. contract carpet sales Rollins Services, Atlanta, 1972-74; sales rep. Pitney Bowes Inc., Atlanta, 1974-76; mgmt. cons. Gilbert Lane Inc., Atlanta, 1976-78; co-founder, pres. L Properties, Inc. (parent co. Price Industries Inc.), Atlanta, 1978—; co-chmn. design com. Central Atlanta Progress, Inc. Hon. life mem. Boys Clubs Am. Mem. Atlanta C. of C., Nat. Honor Soc. Democrat. Methodist. Office: 66 Luckie St Atlanta GA 30303 also PO Box 1021 Atlanta GA 30301

PRICE, STERLING MARCUS, social worker; b. Henderson, Tex., July 21, 1943; s. Sterling Joseph and Hazel Jeraldine (Whitmarsh) P.; B.A., Baylor U., 1965; M.R.E., Southwestern Bapt. Theol. Sem., Ft. Worth, 1971; M.S.S.W., U. Tex., Arlington, 1971; m. Susan Snider, June 5, 1965; children—Christopher, Carrie, Colleen. With Home Mission Bd., So. Bapt. Conv., 1965-69, Meth. Children's Home of Waco (Tex.), 1971, 75; minister edn. Highland Bapt. Ch., Waco, 1971-74; social worker Schlesinger Geriatric Center, Beaumont, Tex., 1976-77, Buckner Children's Village, Beaumont, 1977-79; dir. social services Beaumont Neurol. Center, 1979—. Mem. Acad. Cert. Social Workers, Nat. Assn. Social Workers. Home: 996 W Lucas St Beaumont TX 77706 Office: Beaumont Neurol Center 3250 Fannin St Beaumont TX 77701

PRICE, WILLIAM DOW, JR., med. co. ofcl.; b. Shelbyville, Ky., Aug. 8, 1927; s. William Dow and Louise (Deakins) P.; B.A., Temple U., 1949; postgrad. U. Louisville, 1958-59; M.B.A., Wade Hampton Coll., 1961, D.B.A. (hon.), 1963; m. Carol J. Bramer, Feb. 20, 1971; children—Michelle Lynn, Kimberly Ann. Cost accountant Brown-Forman Distillers, Louisville, 1949-52; bus. mgr. Children's Hosp., Louisville, 1952-54, asst. adminstr., 1954-62; adminstr. Louisville Meml. Hosp., 1962-70; dir. welfare City of Louisville, 1962-70; adminstr. Community Hosp. South Broward, 1971-72; exec. dir. Parkway Med. Center, Louisville, 1972-74; adminstr. S.W. Jefferson Community Hosp., Louisville, 1974-78; regional rep. Charter Med. Corp., La Grange, Ky., 1978—; mem. adv. council State Sch. Practical Nursing, 1967-69; mem. Ky. Comprehensive Health Planning Council, 1975—. Mem. adv. council Community Coll. Louisville; councilman City of St. Regis Park (Ky.), 1979. Served with M.C., USN, 1944-47; with Transp. div. USNR, 1947-50. Recipient Outstanding Young Bus. Man award, 1961; Recognition awards City of Louisville, 1966-69; South Broward Hosp. Adminstrn. Achievement award, 1972; named Boss of Year, Louisville chpt. Nat. Secs. Assn., 1969. Fellow Am. Coll. Hosp. Adminstrs.; mem. Fedn. Am. Hosps., Am. Assn. Hosp. Accountants (v.p. 1956), Ky., Fla. hosp. assns., Nat. Assn. Cost Accountants (v.p. 1957-59), Adminstrv. Mgmt. Soc. (v.p. 1959-60, pres. 1961-62, nat. dir. secondary schs. 1959-61, membership dir. 1961-62, nat. functional dir. 1962-63, nat. area dir. 1967-69), Soc. Advancement Mgmt. (internat. v.p. 1969-70, pres. chpt. 1969-70), Am. Legion, AIM, Fla. League Hosps. Contbr. articles, papers to profl. jours. Home: 2426 Aintree Way Louisville KY 40220 Office: 507 Yager Ave La Grange KY 40031

PRICHARD, JOHN FRANKLIN, dentist; b. Lancaster, Tex., Apr. 16, 1907; s. John Allen and Lillie (Hood) P.; D.D.S., Baylor U., 1928; m. Edna Crabtree, Nov. 6, 1928; 1 dau., Catherine Prichard Kaplan. Pvt. practice dentistry, Lamesa, Tex., 1928-30, Ft. Worth, 1930—; sr. cons. periodontal dept. U. Wash., Seattle, 1950—; vis. lectr. periodontal dept. U. Pa., Phila., 1946—; bd. dirs. Dental Services Corp., 1967-74. Recipient Outstanding Alumnus award Baylor U. Coll. Dentistry, 1978; diplomate Am. Bd. Periodontology (vice chmn. bd. dirs. 1970-76). Fellow Tex. Dental Assn., Am. Acad. Periodontology, Am. Coll. Dentists, Am. Med. Writers Assn., S.W. Soc. Periodontology; mem. Am. Soc. Periodontists (pres. 1964-65), Am. Acad. Oral Roentgenology, Internat. Assn. Dental Research, Southwestern Soc. Dental Medicine (pres. 1940-41), Ft. Worth Dist. Dental Soc. (pres. 1942), Delta Sigma Delta, Omicron Kappa Upsilon. Baptist (deacon 1936-70). Author: Diagnosis and Treatment of Periodontal Disease, 1979, others; contbr. articles to profl. jours. Home: 5662 Westover Court Fort Worth TX 76107 Office: 3833 Camp Bowie Blvd Fort Worth TX 76107

PRICHARD, THORA INEZ, secretary; b. Miller County, Ark., Dec. 25, 1908; d. Andrew M. and Eliza Anne (Hendren) Sanders; grad. Bus. Adminstrn., Texarkana Bus. Coll., 1933; m. William C. Boone, Oct. 28, 1936; children—Billyeanne, Andrew Sanders; m. 2d, Cliff B. Prichard, Jan. 14, 1950. Chief, personnel and payroll Lone Star Ordinance, Texarkana, Tex., 1941-46; with Southwestern Transp., subsidiary Cotton Belt R.R., Texarkana, 1947-49, Phillips Petroleum Co., Bartlesville, Okla., 1949-50; sec. First Bapt. Ch., Bartlesville, 1958-74, Arnold Moore Funeral Service, part-time, Bartlesville, Dr. Wayne J. Boyd, M.D., Psychiatrist, Bartlesville, part-time 1975—; hostess Bartlesville Elks, part-time, 1978—. Pres., Am. Cancer Soc., Washington County Unit, Bartlesville, 1975—. Mem. Smithsonian Inst. Democrat. Baptist. Clubs: Hillcrest Country, Pilot, Sashay Singles Square Dance. Home: 100 SE Choctaw St Bartlesville OK 74003 Office: Lake Crace Shores Grand Lake of the Cherokees La Casa Del Lago Afton OK 74331

PRICKETT, GARY JAMES, paper products co. exec.; b. Paul's Valley, Okla., Oct. 21, 1950; s. Loy E. and Roberta (Wynn) P.; student Southwestern State U., 1968-69; B.A., So. Oreg. State Coll., 1973; m. Janet L. Haney, Sept. 21, 1971; 1 dau., Pamela Jean. Sales rep. Splevin's Music Corp., Los Angeles, 1973-74; asst. mgr. Thrifty Drug Stores, Inc., Los Angeles, 1974-75; store mgr., student store buyer UCLA, 1975-77; with Recycled Paper Products, Inc., Houston, 1977—, S.W. regional sales mgr., 1978—, dir., 1980—. Office: PO Box 53242 Houston TX 77052

PRIDGEN, GRADY CLIFTON, JR., television exec.; b. Rocky Mount, N.C., May 9, 1936; s. Grady Clifton and Olive Blanche (Crumpler) P.; A.B., U. N.C., 1958; postgrad. Yale U., 1959; m. Shirley Joy Carpenter, Mar. 23, 1957; children—Grady Clifton III, Alisa Joy, Cher Anita, Sean Carpenter, Christopher, Jonathan Paul, Melanie Rebekah. Sales rep. Sta. WBT, Charlotte, N.C., 1962-63; sales rep. Sta. WBTV, Charlotte, 1963-66, asst. sales mgr., 1966-68, sales mgr., 1969; gen. mgr. Sta. WWBT, Richmond, Va., 1969—, v.p., 1973—. Served with USAF, 1958-62. Mem. Advt. Club Richmond (sec. bd. dirs. 1970-71). Home: 11751 Rexmoor Dr Richmond VA 23235 Office: PO Box 12 Richmond VA 23235

PRIDMORE, CHERYL ANNE, psychologist, educator; b. Houston; d. James Arthur and Rosabelle (Ragin) P.; B.A. in Psychology, N. Tex. State U., 1969, M. Ed. in Clin. and Counseling Psychology, 1973. Unit psychologist San Angelo (Tex.) Center, 1973-76; psychologist, therapist Land Manor Halfway House, Beaumont, Tex., 1976-78; residential psychologist, dir. community tng. program, dir. behavior mgmt. program Beaumont State Center, 1976-78; founder Lafeyette (La.) Profl. Counseling Inst., 1979; chem. cons. Hunter Chems., Inc., Beaumont; lectr. in field. Recipient certificate achievement Tex. Research Inst. Mental Scis. Certified psychologist, Tex. Mem. Am., Tex. assns. mental deficiency, Am. Personnel and Guidance Assn., Am. Rehab. Counseling Assn., Tex. Rehab. Assn. (legis. com. 1976—), Zeta Tau Alpha. Methodist. Developed, dir. statewide pilot rehab. tng. program for mentally retarded adult, 1976-79. Home: 1630 Willow Bend Vidor TX 77662

PRIEBE, FLORENCE MCCLAIN, sch. adminstr.; b. Paris, Tex., Apr. 27, 1941; d. Ted E. and Emma Louise (Walker) McC.; B.A., So. Methodist U., 1963; M.A., Tulane U., 1971; m. Louis Victor Priebe, June 25, 1966; children—Allison Louise, Louis Bradley. Speech and lang. pathologist Houston Ind. Sch. Dist., 1963-66, Jefferson Parish Sch. Dist., New Orleans, 1969-70; speech and lang. pathologist Fairfax County (Va.) Public Schs., Fairfax, 1970-73, speech and lang. supr., 1973—. Recipient Community Leader award, New Orleans, 1969. Mem. Am. Speech and Hearing Assn., Fairfax Edn. Assn., NEA, Va. Edn. Assn., Kappa Alpha Theta. Republican. Episcopalian. Club: Fairfax Country. Home: 8115 Langbrook Rd Springfield VA 22152 Office: 10515 School St Fairfax VA 22030

PRIEBE, LESLIE ALEXANDER, elec. engr.; b. Okeene, Okla., Dec. 27, 1942; s. Leslie Alexander and Vera Lucerne (Gile) P.; B.S., Okla. State U., 1970; M.S., U. Tex., 1972, Ph.D., 1975; m. Virginia Ann MacDonald, Jan. 14, 1967; children—Kara Alexandra, Kelli Marie. Technician, RCA Internat. Service Co., Cocoa Beach, Fla., 1965-67; design engr. TRW, Inc., Redondo Beach, Calif., 1972-73; dir. laser research U. Tex., Austin, 1973-78, asst. prof. dept. elec. engring., 1976-78; systems engr. Tex. Instruments, Inc., Dallas, 1978—. Served with USMC, 1960-65. Mem. IEEE, Sigma Xi, Phi Kappa Phi, Eta Kappa Nu, Sigma Tau, Phi Eta Sigma. Republican. Baptist. Contbr. articles in field to profl. jours. Home: 1609 Papeete St Plano TX 75023 Office: Texas Instruments Inc PO Box 225012 Dallas TX 75265

PRIEBE, LOUIS VICTOR, public relations exec.; b. Enid, Okla., Nov. 11, 1941; s. Victor Hugo and Helen (Morell) P.; B.A. in Journalism, U. Okla., 1964; m. Florence Ann McClain, June 25, 1966; children—Allison Louise, Louis Bradley. Pub. relations asst. Atlanta Gas & Light Co., 1966-68; with Ins. Info. Inst., 1968-72, mgr. New Orleans dist., 1968-70, asst. mgr. relations, Washington, 1970-72; Washington pub. relations rep. Carl Byoir & Assos., 1972-74; dir. pub. relations dept. Am. Automobile Assn., Falls Church, Va., 1974-76; Washington mgr. pub. relations Motor Vehicle Mfrs. Assn., 1977-79; v.p. Daniel J. Edelman, Inc., public relations consultants, Washington, 1979—. Mem. La. Gov.'s Hurricane Task Force, 1970; v.p. fin. Okla. State Soc., gen. chmn. Okla. Bicentennial Ball, 1976; bd. dirs. YMCA Met. Washington, 1978-80. Served to lt. AUS, 1964-66. Mem. Pub. Relations Soc. Am. (accredited Silver Anvil award 1969, dir.; v.p. chpt., pres. Nat. Capital chpt. 1980), Okla. State Soc. Washington (membership v.p. 1979), Smithsonian Assos., Nat. Eagle Scout Assn., Beta Theta Pi. Episcopalian. Clubs: Toastmaster, Country of Fairfax (Va.); Nat. Press. Home: 8115 Langbrook Rd Springfield VA 22152 Office: 1730 Pennsylvania Ave NW Suite 460 Washington DC 20006

PRIESTMAN, BRIAN, conductor; b. Birmingham, Eng., Feb. 10, 1927; s. Miles and Margaret Ellen (Messer) P.; B.Mus., U. Birmingham, 1950, M.A., 1952; Dipl. Superieur de Direction, Conservatoire Royal Brussels, 1952; D.H.L., U. Colo., 1976; D.F.A., Regis Coll., Denver, 1972; m. Mary-Ford McClave, Mar. 2, 1972; 1 dau., Catherine Kelly. Mus. dir. Royal Shakespeare Theatre, 1960-62, Edmonton (Can.) Symphony, 1964-68; resident condr. Balt. Symphony, 1968-69; mus. dir. Denver Symhpony, 1970-78; prin. condr. N.Z. Nat. Orch., 1972-75; mus. dir., condr. Fla. Philharm., Miami, 1977. Office: 150 SE 2d Ave Miami FL 33131

PRIGMORE, CHARLES SAMUEL, educator; b. Lodge, Tenn., Mar. 21, 1919; s. Charles H. and Mary Lou (Raulston) P.; A.B., U. Chattanooga, 1939; M.S., U. Wis., 1947, Ph.D., 1961; m. Shirley Melaine Buuck, June 7, 1947; 1 son, Philip Brand. Social caseworker Children's Service Soc., Milw., 1947-48; social worker Wis. Sch. for Boys, Waukesha, 1948-51; supr. tng. Wis. Bur. Probation and Parole, Madison, 1951-56; supt. Tenn. Vocational Tng. Sch. for Boys, Nashville, 1956-59; asso. prof. La. State U., 1959-64; ednl. cons. Council Social Work Edn., N.Y., 1962-64; exec. dir. Joint Commn. Correctional Manpower & Tng., Washington, 1964-67; prof. Sch. Social Work, U. Ala., 1967—, chmn. com. on Korean relationships; Fulbright lectr., Iran, 1972-73; cons. Iranian Ministry Health and Welfare, 1976-78; part-time cons. with four research projects, 1959-76; part-time tchr. U. Md., 1965-67; frequent lectr. and workshop leader. Chmn. Ala. Citizens Environmental Action, 1971-72, Tuscaloosa Council Environmental Quality, 1970-72. Served to 2d lt. USAAF, 1940-45. Decorated Air medal with oak leaf cluster. Recipient Conservation award Woodmen of the World, 1971; Fulbright-Hays research fellow, Norway, 1979-80. Mem. Acad. Certified Social Workers, Am. Correctional Assn., AAUP, Am. Soc. Criminology, Am. Sociol. Assn., Council Social Work Edn., Nat. Assn. Social Workers, Nat. Council Crime and Delinquency, Royal Soc. Health, Tuscaloosa C. of C., Tuscaloosa Civitan Club, Alpha Kappa Delta, Beta Beta Beta. Club: Tuscaloosa County. Author: Textbook on Social Problems, 1971; Social Work in Iran Since the White Revolution, 1976; sr. author: Social Welfare Policy Analysis and Formulation, 1979; editor 2 books; contbr. articles to profl. jours. Home: 19 High Forest Tuscaloosa AL 35401 Office: Box 1935 University AL 35486

PRIGOGINE, ILYA, educator; b. Moscow, Jan. 25, 1917; s. Roman and Julie (Wichmann) P.; Ph.D., Free U. Brussels, 1941; hon. degrees: U. Newcastle, U. Poitiers, U. Chgo., U. Bordeaux, Uppsala U., U. Liege; m. Marina Prokopowicz, Feb. 25, 1961; children—Yves, Pascal. Prof., U. Brussels, 1947—; dir. Internat. Insts. Physics and Chemistry, Solvay, Belgium, 1959—; dir. Center for Statis. Mechanics and Thermodynamics, U. Tex., Austin, 1967—. Recipient Prix Francqui, 1955, Prix Solvay, 1965, Swante Arrhenius gold medal Royal Acad. Scis. (Sweden), 1969, Bourke medal Chem. Soc. (Gt. Britain), 1972, Rumford gold medal Royal Soc. (London), 1976, Nobel prize in chemistry, 1977. Fellow Am. Chem. Soc. (Am. Centennial fgn. fellow); mem. Royal Acad. Belgium, Am. Acad. Arts and Scis. (fgn. hon.), N.Y. Acad. Scis., Rumanian Acad. Sci., Royal Soc. Scis. Uppsala, Fgn. Assn. Nat. Acad. Scis. U.S.A., Soc. Royale des Scis. Liege (Belgium), (corr.), Acad. Gottingen, Deutscher Akademie der Naturforscher Leopoldine (Cothenius gold medal 1975), Oesterreishische Akademie der Wissenschafter (corr.), Chem. Soc. Poland (hon.). Author: (with R. Defay) Traite de Thermodynamique conformement aux methodes de Gibbs et de De Donder, 1944; Etude Thermodynamique des Phenomenes Irreversibles, 1947; Introduction to Thermodynamics of Irreversible Processes, 1962; (with A. Bellemans and V. Mathot) The Molecular Theory of Solutions, 1957; Non quilibrium Statistical Mechanics 1962; (with others) Non Equilibrium Thermodynamics, Variational Techniques and Stability, 1966; (with R. Herman) Kinetic Theory of Vehicular Traffic, 1971; (with P. Glansdorff) Thermodynamic Theory of Structure, Stability and Fluctuations, 1971; (with G. Nicolis) Self-Organization in Non Equilibrium Systems from Dissipative Structures to Order through Fluctuations; From Being to Becoming, 1980; La Nouvelle Alliance, 1980. Office: Center for Statis Mechanics and Thermodynamics U Tex UT Station Austin TX 78712 also 67 ave Fond Roy 1180 Brussels Belgium

PRINCE, BETTY, mfg. co. ofcl.; b. Sycamore, Ill., Nov. 28, 1942; d. Bertrand Bradford Prince and Margaret Hammond (Safford) Swanson; B.S. in Physics cum laude, U. N.Mex., 1964, M.S., 1965; divorced; children—David Patrick Phelan, Sharon Margaret Phelan. Instr. sci. Chgo. City Colls., 1966-68; sr. engr. Fairchild Semicondr. Co., Mountain View, Calif., 1973-76; mem. tech. staff solid state div. RCA Corp., Findley, Ohio, 1976-77; mktg. mgr. Motorola Inc., Austin, Tex., 1977—; exec. com. N.Mex. Acad. Sci., 1960-64. Chmn. Greater Richmond (Calif.) Interfaith Program, 1971-73; dist. dir. East Bay, United Meth. Ch., 1973-74. Ford Found. fellow, 1963-65; Albuquerque Realtor's Assn. scholar, 1960. Mem. Soc. Women Engrs. (v.p. Tex.), IEEE, Kappa Mu Epsilon, Phi Kappa Phi. Democrat. Home: 10401 Mourning Dove St Austin TX 78750 Office: 3501 Ed Bluestein Blvd Austin TX 78721

PRINCE, JOHN RANDOLPH, JR., univ. adminstr.; b. Shuqualak, Miss., Aug. 12, 1929; s. John Randolph and Carolyn (Boggess) P.; B.S.C.E., Miss. State U., 1951; M.B.A., Tulane U., 1968; postgrad. Am. U., 1969; grad. Command and Gen. Staff Coll., 1962, Armed Forces Staff Coll., 1965; m. Patricia Jane Adams, June 24, 1956; children—John Randolph III, Timothy Adams, Philip Bennett. With Internat. Paper Co., Natchez, Miss., 1951; commd. 2d lt., U.S. Army, 1951, advanced through grades to col., 1970; served with arty.; ret., 1972; dir. planning, budget, and personnel services Okla. Bapt. U., 1972—; lectr. in geography. Chmn. Pottawatomie County chpt. ARC, 1980; dist. chmn. Last Frontier council Boy Scouts Am., 1977-79; bd. dirs. Redland council Girl Scouts U.S.A., 1979-80. Decorated Legion of Merit, Bronze Star, Purple Heart, Army Commendation Medal with oak leaf cluster, Dept. of Def. Commendation Medal; recipient Vigil Order of Arrow, Silver Beaver awards Boy Scouts Am. Mem. Assn. Instnl. Research, Am. Soc. Personnel Adminstrn., Nat. Assn. Coll. and Univ. Bus. Officers, Okla. Affirmative Action Assn., Okla. Assn. Coll. and Univ. Personnel Adminstrn. Baptist. Clubs: Shawnee Kiwanis (pres. 1979), Elks. Home: 1841 N Pennsylvania St Shawnee OK 74801 Office: 500 W University St Shawnee OK 74801

PRINDLE, RICHARD A(LAN), public health adminstr.; b. Mansfield, Ohio, Dec. 28, 1925; s. Raymond and Georgia Anna (Richardson) P.; student Centenary Coll., La., 1942-44; M.D., Harvard U., 1948, M.P.H. cum laude, 1954; m. Susan Lee McLeod, Apr. 14, 1979; children—John, Michael, Noreen Grimsey; children by previous marriage—Mark R., Timothy E. Research fellow in epidemiology Harvard U. Med. Sch., Boston, 1948-51, research asso., 1951-54; commd. USPHS, 1951, med. dir.; asst. chief poliomyelitis investigations USPHS, 1951-53; asst. chief health and sanitation div. ICA, Haiti, 1954-57; epidemiologist air pollution program USPHS, 1954-60, dep. chief div. air pollution, 1960-63, chief div. public health methods Office Surgeon Gen., 1963-66, asst. surgeon gen., 1964-71, chief Bur. State Services, 1964-66, dir. Bur. Disease Prevention and Environ. Control, 1966-68, spl. asst. to surg. gen., 1968-70; vis. lectr. U. Pa., 1961-70; chief dept. Health and Population Dynamics, Pan Am. Health Orgn., 1970-77; dir. Thomas Jefferson Dist. Health Dept., 1977—; clin. prof. internal medicine U. Va., 1977—; mem. expert com. on air pollution WHO, 1963-70; cons. adv. com. health stats. Pan Am. Health Orgn., 1964-70. Bd. dirs. Phipps Inst., Phila., 1961-65; mem. adv. com. environ. scis. Nat. Colls. Art and Scis. Recipient Meritorious Service medal USPHS, 1963; Fed. Exec. fellow Center for Advanced Study, Brookings Instn.; diplomate Am. Bd. Public Health and Preventive Medicine. Fellow AAAS, Am. Coll. Preventive Medicine, Am. Public Health Assn.; mem. AMA, Royal Soc. Health, Assn. Tchrs. Preventive Medicine, Air Pollution Control Assn. (dir. 1962-63). Contbr. articles to profl. jours. Office: 1138 Rose Hill Dr Charlottesville VA 22901

PRINGLE, ROBERT DURRELL, savs. and loan exec.; b. Saginaw, Mich., Aug. 29, 1943; s. Durrell B. and Geraldine M. P.; B.S. in Bus. Adminstrn., Ferris State Coll., Big Rapids, Mich., 1966; children—Spencer Robert, Merideth Ellen. Acctg. supr. First Savs. & Loan, Saginaw, Mich., 1970-73; asst. controller First Fed. Savs. & Loan, Tarpon Springs, Fla., 1973-76; asst. v.p., asst. controller Guaranty Savs. & Loan, St. Petersburg, Fla., 1976-79, v.p., ops., 1979—. Served with USAF, 1967-70. Mem. Inst. Fin. Edn., Pinellas County Personnel Assn., Sunshine State Systems Users Group, Data Processing Mgmt. Assn., Soc. Br. Mgrs., Fin. Mgrs. Soc., Pi Kappa Alpha. Republican. Roman Catholic. Clubs: Sertoma, O.L.L. Booster, Gulf Coast Youth Soccer. Home: 2207 Bay Blvd Indian Rocks Beach FL 33535 Office: 2100 66th St Saint Petersburg FL 33710

PRINTUP, JOHN MONROE, ret. advt. and mktg. cons.; b. Oak Park, Ill., Oct. 14, 1919; s. John Monroe and Edna Mae (Hartman) P.; student No. Ill. U., No. Ill. Coll. Optometry; children—Michael, Bonnie, Richard, Susan. Owner-operator clothing store and bowling alley, Hampshire, Ill., 1947-51; So. mgr. Indsl. Publs., New Orleans, 1951-52; pres. John Printup & Assos., Miami, Fla., 1952-64, chmn. bd., Atlanta, 1965-77; cons. Cahners Pub. Co., Inc., Atlanta, 1977-79. Served with USAF, 1941-45. Recipient Eagle Scout award with bronze palm; Meritorious Service award USAF. Mem. Bus. and Profl. Advt. Assn. (chmn. edn. com. 1974—). Republican. Methodist. Clubs: Masons, Shriners. Contbr. articles to profl. jours. Home: 210 Worth Dr NW Atlanta GA 30327

PRIOR, WILLIAM ALLEN, electronics co. exec.; b. Benton Harbor, Mich., Jan. 14, 1927; s. Allen Ames and Madeline Isabel (Taylor) P.; A.B., Harvard U., 1950, M.B.A., 1954; m. Irmgard C.L. Becker-Ehmck, Oct. 30, 1971; children—Stephanie Sayles, Alexandra Taylor, Robert Eames, Eleanor Norton, Michael Becker-Ehmck, Jeffrey Renner. Salesman, IBM Corp., N.Y.C., 1950-52; sales engr. Lincoln Electric Co., Cleve., 1954-57; v.p., dir. Hammond, Kennedy & Co., Inc., N.Y.C., 1957-67; v.p. Singer Co., N.Y.C., 1967-68; pres., dir. Tansitor Electronics, Inc., Bennington, Vt., 1968-71; pres. Aerotron, Inc., Raleigh, N.C., 1971—; dir. Aerotron Barbados Ltd., Occidental Life Ins. Co. N.C., McM Corp., Waycom Internat. Ltd. Served with A.C., AUS, 1945-46. Mem. IEEE. Clubs: River, Harvard (N.Y.C.); Raleigh Racquet, North Ridge Country (Raleigh). Home: 6816 Rainwater Rd Raleigh NC 27609 Office: US Hwy 1 N Raleigh NC 27611

PRISANT, ROBERT STEPHEN, accountant; b. Albany, Ga., May 24, 1951; s. Bennie Martin and Zelma (Mozelle) P.; B.B.A., Albany State Coll., 1977; m. Mary Alice Branch, June 10, 1979; children—Ronald Warren Brown, Cath Mary Brown. Accountant, Sheraton Motor Inn Hotel div. Hick's and Assos., Albany, 1975-79; pres. Acctg. Consultants, Albany, 1979—; fin. cons. Sandhurst Corp., 1977-79. Mem. Am. Inst. C.P.A.'s (asso.). Jewish. Home: 2014 Melrose Dr Albany GA 31707 Office: 2809-G Old Dawson Rd Albany GA 31707

PRITCHETT, JOHN CHRISTOPHER, librarian; b. Mobile, Ala., May 17, 1945; s. John Christopher and Ruth Goodwyn (Jones) P.; B.A., Livingston U., 1968; M.A., U. Miss., 1969; M.L.S., U. Ala., 1974, Ed.S., 1979; postgrad U. N.C., Chapel Hill, 1974; m. Pamela Pace, Nov. 17, 1979. Instr. English, Troy (Ala.) State U., 1969-73; asst. to supr. extension dept. Mobile Public Library (Ala.), 1975-78; asst. to dir., 1979-80; reference librarian McLure Edn. Library, U. Ala., University, 1980—. Nat. Teaching fellow, 1969. Mem. ALA, Ala. Library Assn., Southeastern Library Assn., Ala. Hist. Assn., Nat. Soc. Historic Preservation, Sigma Tau Delta, Beta Phi Mu. Home: 1604 Lake Ave Tuscaloosa AL 35401 Office: Box S University AL 35486

PRITCHETT, MARK STOLL, univ. adminstr.; b. Morganfield, Ky., July 21, 1953; s. Charles Martin and Elizabeth Stoll (Haley) P.; B.A. with distinction, U. Ky., 1976, M.S., 1978; m. P. Dianne Bruce, May 15, 1976; 1 dau., Meredith Waller. Coordinator residence hall life U. Ky., Lexington, 1977—; cons. various state univs. concerning residence halls, 1978—. Volunteer counselor local cancer clinic, Lexington, 1977; active Big Bros. of Lexington, 1975—. Recipient Am. Legion Citizenship award, 1971; Jaycees Outstanding Young Man of Am. award, 1978. Mem. Am. Personnel and Guidance Assn., So. Coll. Personnel Assn., Nat. Assn. Student Personnel Adminstrs., U. Ky. Alumni Assn., Phi Sigma Gamma. Democrat. Episcopalian. Club: Lexington Tennis. Home: 666 Montclair Dr Lexington KY 40502 Office: 539 Patterson Office Tower Lexington KY 40506

PRITCHETT, WILLIAM NORMAN, oil co. exec.; b. Phila., Jan. 2, 1924; s. Loren Spence and Helen Blanche (Parvis) P.; student U. Ala., 1941-43; B.S. in Commerce, Ohio U., 1948; m. Dorothy J. Speaker, Aug. 20, 1949; children—William L., Robert B., Holly Ann. Sales rep. Mobil Oil Corp., Peoria, Ill., 1948-56, asst. dist. mgr., 1956-58, retail programs mgr., 1958-60; gen. sales mgr. Kerr-McGee Corp., Oklahoma City; 1960-78; v.p. mktg. Kerr-McGee Refining Corp., Oklahoma City, 1978—. Served with USAAF, 1943-46. Mem. Am. Petroleum Inst. (mem. gen. com. mktg. div. 1978—), Okla. Petroleum Council (dir. 1965—). Republican. Presbyterian. Club: Petroleum. Home: 3024 Chapel Hill Rd Oklahoma City OK 73120 Office: Kerr McGee Center Oklahoma City OK 73102

PROCTOR, BERNARD CARLSON, cons. engring. co. exec.; b. Newport News, Va., Dec. 3, 1948; s. William Bernard and Katherine (Palmer) P.; B.S. in Civil Engring., Va. Poly. Inst. and State U., 1970; M.B.A., Lynchburg (Va.) Coll., 1980; m. Jane Carter Feagans, July 24, 1971; 1 son, Andrew Feagans. Cons. engr. Whitman, Requardt and Assos., Balt., 1973-75; asst. county adminstr., county engr. County of Campbell, Va., 1976-78; asso. engr. James C. May and Assos., Lynchburg, Va., 1978—. Served with USMC, 1970-73. Registered profl. engr., Va. Mem. ASCE (pres. Lynchburg br. 1978), Internat. City Mgmt. Assn. Republican. Baptist. Home: 37 Mistletoe Dr Forest VA 24551 Office: PO Box 718 Lynchburg VA 24505

PROCTOR, JOHN HOWARD, mgmt. cons. co. exec.; b. Bronx, N.Y., June 3, 1931; s. John Carol and Carolyn Elizabeth (Slade) P.; B.S., Davidson Coll., 1953; M.S., Purdue U., 1954, Ph.D., 1958; m. Jayne Alexander, Dec. 28, 1956; children—Donna Lynn, Susan Carol, John Christopher, James Alexander. Cons. Humble Oil & Refining Co., 1957-58; dir. tng. and personnel research Bleached Bd. div. W.Va. Pulp and Paper Co., 1958-60; mem. tech. staff Mitre Corp., 1960-64; sr. project dir. Data Dynamics Inc., 1964-66; gen. mgr. Eastern ops. Mellonics div. Litton Systems Inc., Ft. Walton Beach, Fla., 1966-70; pres. Data Solutions Corp., Vienna, Va., 1970—, also chmn. bd. Mem. adv. com. on rights and responsibilities of women HEW, 1976; mem. Nat. Def. Exec. Res. Served with AUS, 1954-56. Diplomate Am. Bd. Profl. Psychology. Mem. AAAS, Am. Psychol. Assn., Soc. Gen. Systems Research, Soc. Engring. Psychologists, Acad. Mgmt., N.Y. Acad. Scis., Sigma Xi. Club: Masons (32 degree). Author: (with W.M. Thornton) Training: A Handbook for Line Managers, 1961; contbr. to Strategies for Public Health: Promoting Health and Preventing Disease; contbr. articles to profl. jours. Home: 505 Arnon Meadow Rd Great Falls VA 22066 Office: 2095 Chain Bridge Rd Vienna VA 22180

PROCTOR, MADREA JANE KALBAUGH, nurse; b. Cumberland, Md., Mar. 25, 1923; d. Elmore Porter and Hazel Luray (Zehrbach) Kalbaugh; B.S., Carson Newman Coll., 1945; B.S. in Nursing, Johns Hopkins U., 1948; M.S., Coll. of Edn., Fla. State U., 1975; m. Charles Lucious Proctor, Jan. 2, 1978; children—Cynthia Jane, Deborah Lynn. Pediatric supr., nursing educator St. Monica's Hosp., Phoenix, 1948-49; obstetrics nurse St. Mary's Hosp., also charge nurse Permanente Clinic, Long Beach, Calif., 1949-53; instr. vocat. nursing Harbour Jr. Coll., Wilmington, Calif., 1953-54; night head nurse nursery, night head nurse CCU, Glendale (Calif.) Adventist Hosp., 1964-67; asst. inservice dir. Glendale (Calif.) Community Hosp., 1967-68; instr. health edn. dept. Lively Vocat. Sch., Tallahassee, Fla., 1969-70; inservice instr. Tallahassee Meml. Regional Med. Center, 1972, inservice dir., 1972-78, dir. dept. edn., 1978—; mem. health edn. adv. com. Lively Vocat. Sch., 1974—, chmn., health edn. adv. com., 1979—; mem. Fla. State Task Force on Nursing Edn., 1979—, Fla. State Adv. Com. for Health and Public Service Edn. Community chmn. Girl Scouts U.S.A., Long Beach, Calif., 1957-59, leader, Long Beach, 1958-63, Glendale, 1963-65; adv. chmn. Leon County chpt. Am. Heart Assn., 1979, mem. Fla. bd. dirs., 1979; bd. dirs. Fla. Lung Assn., 1975-78. Recipient Outstanding Service award Fla. Lung Assn., 1975; Outstanding Service award Tallahassee chpt. Am. Heart Assn., 1976, Bronze Medallion award Fla. State Affiliate, 1977. Mem. Nat. League for Nursing, Am. Soc. Health Edn. and Tng., Fla. Soc. Health Edn. and Tng. (state dir.), Fla. Nurses Assn. (dist. pres. 1974-76), Sigma Theta Tau, Iota Lambda Sigma. Club: Order Eastern Star. Home: 104 W Meridianna Dr Tallahassee FL 32303 Office: Tallahassee Meml Regional Med Center Magnolia Dr and Miccosukee Rd Tallahassee FL 32304

PROCTOR, WILLIAM LEE, coll. pres.; b. Atlanta, Jan. 27, 1933; s. Samuel Cook and Rose Elizabeth (Nottingham) P.; B.S. in Edn., Fla. State U., 1956, M.S., 1964, Ph.D. (HEW fellow), 1968; m. Pamela Evans Duke, Mar. 16, 1958; children—Samuel Matthews, Priscilla Nottingham. Tchr. and athletic coach, public schs., Seminole and Orange counties, Fla., 1956-62; asst. football coach Fla. State U., Tallahassee, 1962-65, asst. dean men, 1965-67; supt. public schs. Dist. 3, Rock Hill, S.C., 1968-69; dean men Fla. Technol. U., Orlando, 1969-71; pres. Flagler Coll., St. Augustine, Fla., 1971—; dir. Atlantic Bank of St. Augustine, 1976—. Chmn. City Planning Commn., St. Augustine, 1975—; elder Flagler Meml. Presbyn. Ch., 1973—; mem. ministerial relations com. Presbytery of N.E. Fla., 1975—; trustee Flagler Hosp., 1977—. Served with inf., U.S. Army, 1957. Mem. Am. Assn. Presidents of Ind. Colls. and Univs., Ind. Colls. and Univs. of Fla. (past chmn.), Phi Delta Kappa, Kappa Delta Pi. Club: Rotary (past pres.). Home: 11 Nelmar Saint Augustine FL 32084 Office: PO Box 1027 Saint Augustine FL 32084

PRODAN, JAMES CHRISTIAN, educator; b. Columbus, Jan. 4, 1947; s. Nicholas Mackley and Muriel Eileen (Bennett) P.; B.S. in Edn., Ohio State U., 1969, D.M.A., 1976; Mus.M., Catholic U. Am., 1972; m. Sherry Jean Prodan, Nov. 17, 1974; children—Christopher Nicholas, Tana Jean. Tchr. music Otterbein Coll., Westerville, Ohio, 1972-74; grad. adminstrv. asso. to asst. dir. Sch. Music, Ohio State U. 1973-75; asst. prof. music U. Akron, 1975-79; asst. prof. music U. N.C., Greensboro, 1979—. Served with U.S. Army, 1969-72. Mem. Am. Fedn. Musicians, Am. Symphony Orch. League, Internat. Double Reed Soc., Nat. Assn. Music Instrument Technicians, Ohio Music Educators Assn., Music Educators Nat. Conf., Nat. Assn. Coll. Wind and Percussion Instrs., Kappa Kappa Psi, Phi Mu Alpha Sinfonia. Home: 4614 A Mercury Dr Greensboro NC 27410 Office: U NC Greensboro NC 27412

PROEHL, ROBERT FRANCIS, computer software co. exec.; b. LaSalle, Ill., May 19, 1945; s. Arthur Francis and Ethel Hannah (Manahan) P.; student U. Md., 1964-67, Tarrant County Jr. Coll., 1969-70; m. Kathy Nell Kinser, Sept. 28, 1964; children—Sammye, Robert Francis. Writer, Allied Research Assos., Balt., 1968-71; tech. writer LTV Aerospace Corp., Dallas, 1968-71; tech. writer Electronic Data Systems, Dallas, 1971-73; pres. Omnigraphix Advt. Co. subs. Electronic Data Systems, Dallas, 1973-76; mktg. support mgr. Equimatics div. Informatics Inc., Dallas, 1976-78, adminstrv. support mgr., 1978—. Area chmn. College Hills Fort Worth Republican Com., 1968. Served with USAF, 1963-67. Fellow Life Mgmt. Inst.; mem. CUEFS Fin. Systems User Group (sec.-treas.), LIFE-COMM User Group (sec.-treas.). Club: Manchester Soccer (sec.). Home: 916 Dunbarton St Richardson TX 75081 Office: 10300 N Central Expressway Dallas TX 75231

PROFFITT, RICHARD CANTRELL, govt. ofcl.; b. Richmond, Va., May 11, 1931; s. George Woodson and Sara Lois (Scruggs) P.; B.S. in Gen. Engring., U.S. Naval Acad., 1954; m. Joan Mary Tully, Mar. 1, 1956 (div. May 1977); children—Richard Cantrell, Stephanie Joan, Elaine Susan, Michelle Erika. Commd. 2d lt. USAF, 1954, advanced through grades to 1st lt., 1955; tactical missile ops. officer, 1955, resigned, 1958; engr. Martin Co., Orlando, Fla., 1958-62, Gen. Electric Co., Phila., 1962-63; staff engr., space div. Chrysler Corp., New Orleans, 1963-64; with Kennedy Space Center, NASA, Fla., 1964—, chief launch complex 39 spacecraft ops., 1969-76, chief environ. control and fuel cell systems br. (shuttle engring.), 1976—. Mem. Nat. Rifle Assn., Fla. State Smallbore Rifle Assn. (pres.), Missile, Space and Range Pioneers. Home: 2346 Middlecoff Ct Titusville FL 32780 Office: Mail Code VE-FSD-3 Kennedy Space Center FL 32899

PROHASKA, THEODORE, II, auto refinishing chain exec.; b. N.Y.C., Aug. 20, 1934; s. Theodore and Ruby (Sawyer) P.; LL.B., LaSalle U., 1962; m. Elisabeth Stutz, May 5, 1957; children—Christine, Theodore. Vice pres. Earl Scheib, Inc., Beverley Hills, Calif., 1960-74; dir. ops. Maaco Enterprises, King of Prussia, Pa., 1974-76; pres. Ted Prohaska, Inc., Dallas, 1976—. Chmn. Citizens Dist. Council, Pontiac, Mich., 1972-75; Citizens Crime Commn., 1972-73. Served with U.S. Army, 1954-56. Patentee thermo-viscous auto refinishing process. Home: 6940 Winterwood Ln Dallas TX 75240 Office: 11426 Garland Rd Dallas TX 75218

PROPES, CLARENCE DUANE, sch. adminstr.; b. Joinerville, Tex., Mar. 14, 1936; s. Cullen Augustus and Robbie (Husband) P.; A.A., Kilgore Coll., 1956; B.S., U. Houston, 1967; M.Ed., E. Tex. State U., 1978; m. Joan Carlisle, June 14, 1958; 1 son, Duane Carlisle. Engring. draftsman Hughes Tool Co., Houston, 1956-61; tchr. drafting Galena Park (Tex.) Ind. Sch. Dist., 1961-67, Longview (Tex.) Ind. Sch. Dist., 1967-69, Kilgore Coll., 1969-73; supr. vocat. indsl. edn. Longview Ind. Sch. Dist., 1973—. Bd. dirs., former chmn. Christian Bus. Men's Com.; mem. Republican Nat. Com. Mem. Am. Vocat. Assn., Nat. Council Loca, Adminstrs., Tex. Vocat. Tech. Assn., Tex. Assn. Vocat. Dirs. and Suprs. (pres. Area 3, state dir.), Am. Soc. Tng. and Devel. (chpt. sec.-treas.), Longview C. of C. Baptist. Home: 1402 Auburn Dr Longview TX 75601 Office: Box 3268 Longview TX 75601

PROSAPIO, RICHARD GREGORY, psychotherapist; b. Chgo., June 11, 1935; s. Anthony and Dorthea Sheele; B.A., U. Tex., El Paso, 1974; M.S.W., U. Houston, 1977; m. Ada Helen Avila, Apr. 7, 1979; children—Christy, Winter, Abel. Dir. TV prodn. Sta. KVIA-TV, El Paso, 1968-69; dir. media prodn. deBruyn Advt., El Paso, 1969-72; research asst. HumRRO, El Paso, 1974-75; dir. social services R.E. Thomason Gen. Hosp., El Paso, 1977—. Served with U.S. Army, 1954-56. Mem. Nat. Assn. Social Workers, Am. Assn. Behavior Therapy, Assn. for Advancement Ethical Hypnosis, Internat. Grapho Analysis Soc. Home: 244 Flynn St El Paso TX 79932 Office: R E Thomason General Hospital 4815 Alameda St El Paso TX 79905

PROTOPAPAS, PANAYOTIS (TAKO) ELIA, engring. co. exec.; b. Athens, Greece, June 4, 1945; came to U.S., 1969, naturalized, 1981; s. Elia Tako and Vasiliki Polyxeni (Giagiannos) P.; Engr's. degree in Mining Engring., Nat. Tech. U. Athens, Greece, 1968; B.S. in Metall. Engring., Carnegie-Mellon U., 1970; M.S. in Mineral Engring., Stanford U., 1972, Ph.D. in Applied Earth Scis., 1975, postgrad. in Chem. Engring., 1975—, postgrad. in Mgmt. and Adminstrn., 1972—. Pres. Fuel and Mineral Resources, Ltd., Athens, Greece, 1966-68; research asso. Nat. Tech. U., Athens, 1963-69; research and devel. metall. engr. Carnegie-Mellon Research Inst., Pitts., 1969-70; sr. research asso. Stanford U., Palo Alto, Calif., 1970-74; dir. earth scis. and tech. J.J. Davis Assos., Inc., McLean, Va., 1974-75; sr. phys. scientist TRW Systems Group, McLean, 1975-77; dir. fossil fuels and geotech. scis. Sci. Applications, Inc., McLean, 1977-79; dir. Washington ops. Ford, Bacon & Davis Utah, Inc., Arlington, Va., 1979; pres. Fuel & Mineral Resources, Inc., Reston, Va., 1979—; dir. JJDA and FMR corps.; expert cons. to U.S. Congressional Coms. on Environment, Fuel and Mineral Resources, Energy. Mem. AIME, Am. Soc. Metals, Brit. Iron and Steel Ins., Brit. Inst. for Metals, Can. Metall. Soc., Greek Chamber of Tech., Soc. Mineral. Engrs. (reviewing com. for publs.), Sigma Xi. Democrat. Greek Orthodox. Club: Nat. Dem. Lectr. profl. confs., U.S., France; contbr. articles to profl. publs. Office: PO Box 2790 Reston VA 22090

PROUDFOOT, WARREN HARDING, surgeon; b. Belington, W.Va., Jan. 9, 1921; s. Ervin Shafter and Sylvia Pearl (Foy) P.; student Harvard U., 1947, M.D., 1950; m. Winifred Marion Fogg, Feb. 21, 1946; children—Wendell, Martin, Richard, Glenn. Intern, USPHS Hosp., Boston, 1950-51; resident in surgery, fellow in orthopedics USPHS Hosp., S.I. N.Y., 1951-56; chief surgery Navaho Med. Center, Indian Health, Ft. Defiance, Ohio, 1956-58, Miners Meml. Hosp., Pikeville, Ky., 1958-63; practice medicine specializing in surgery, Morehead, Ky., 1963—; chief surgery St. Claire Med. Center, Morehead, 1963-76; asso. prof. surgery (vol.) U. Ky. Med. Center, Lexington. Mem. Rowan County Sch. Bd., 1971-79, chmn., 1975—. Served with USN, 1940-45, USPHS, 1950-58. Diplomate Am. Bd. Surgery. Mem. ACS, AMA, Rowan County Soc., Ky. Med. Assn., Ky. Sch. Bd. Assn. Democrat. Presbyterian. Home: 314 Cecil Dr Morehead KY 40351 Office: Cave Run Clinic Flemingsburg Rd Morehead KY 40351

PRUETT, HASKELL, educator; b. Mingus, Tex., June 16, 1897; s. Ozie D. and Minerva (Small) P.; B.S., Peabody Coll., 1926, M.A., 1930, Ph.D., 1933; M.S., U. Okla., 1930; m. Agnes Murray, July 28, 1920; children—Mildred, Dresslar. Sch. tchr., Greer County, Okla., 1917-20; county supt. schs. Greer County, 1920-23; rural sch. supr. State of Okla., 1923-26; dir. sch. bldgs. and transp. Okla. Dept. Edn., 1926-35; bus. mgr. Okla. State U., 1935-36, prof. edn., 1936-48, head dept. photography, 1948—. Pres., Old Greer County Mus. and Hall of Fame, 1972—. Mem. Photog. Soc. Am., Profl. Photographers Am., Phi Kappa Delta, Kappa Delta Pi. Baptist. Club: Masons (32 deg.). Author: The Pruett-Pruitt Family, 1975; also articles on edn. and photography. Home: 155 S Redwood Dr Stillwater OK 74074

PRUITT, DAVID WARD, utility co. exec.; b. Greenville, Tex., Jan. 18, 1946; s. Marion Manoah and Dorothy Nell (Ward) P.; B.S., Tex. A. and M. U., 1968; M.S., Tex. Tech. U., 1970; m. Patricia Ann Roach, Aug. 16, 1948; children—Jana Alison, John David. Mgr. area devel. Deaf Smith Electric Coop., Hereford, Tex., 1971-78; gen. mgr. Greenbelt Electric Coop., Wellington, Tex., 1978—. Trustee, Sch. Bd. Hereford, 1977-78; pres. United Way Deaf Smith County, 1977; chmn. Tex. First Program, 1975-76, Boy Scouts Am. fund dr., 1973-74; bd. dirs. Big-Bros./Big-Sisters, Deaf Smith County, 1973-75. Served as officer U.S. Army, 1970. Named Hereford Kiwanian of Month, 1977. Mem. Tex. Mem. Service Assn. Electric Coops (pres. 1974-75), Alpha Zeta, Gamma Sigma Delta, Omicron Delta Epsilon. Methodist. Club: Kiwanis. Office: PO Box 948 Wellington TX 79095

PRUITT, MILDRED ADELAIDE, counselor; b. Coopers, W.Va., June 3, 1937; d. James Elwood and Lida Louise (Johnson) Turner; A.B., Milligan (Tenn.) Coll., 1960; M.A., Ohio State U., Columbus, 1969; m. Carl Windsor Pruitt, Aug. 12, 1960; children—Jennifer, Carl Windsor II, James Turner. Tchr. English, Colerain Jr. High Sch., Cin., 1960-63; counselor Columbus public schs., 1972-75, Ky. Christian Coll., Grayson, 1975—; pvt. practice counseling, Grayson. Active local PTA; tchr. 1st Ch. of Christ, Grayson. Mem. Am. Coll. Personnel Assn., Am. Personnel and Guidance Assn. Republican. Club: Younger Woman's. Home: Route 1 Box 872 Grayson KY 41143 Office: Ky Christian Coll Grayson KY 41143

PRUITT, TOMMIE LEE, city ofcl.; b. Chattanooga, May 28, 1949; s. Alfred Erskin and Ethel Lee (Sanford) P.; B.A., Knoxville Coll., 1971; m. Janice Yvonne Woods, Apr. 27, 1973; children—Kelvin DeVon, Marcus Jeffrey, Tomyra Nicole. Counselor, Chattanooga Concentrated Employment program, 1972; project dir. Chattanooga Community Action program, 1973-74; vocat. counselor Chattanooga Human Services Dept., 1974-75; adminstrv. asst. Office of the Mayor, City of Chattanooga, 1975—. Bd. dirs. Big-Bros., Big-Sis. of Chattanooga, 1975—, Achievement Tng. Opportunities of Chattanooga, 1974—, 9th St. Devel. Corp., 1979—; organizer Nat. Urban League, Chattanooga br., 1979. Alfed P. Sloan fellow, 1966-67. Mem. Kappa Alpha Psi. Baptist. Home: 2403 LeAnn Circle Chattanooga TN 37406 Office: 100 E 11 St Chattanooga TN 37402

PRYOR, ALYCIA COLLEEN, fin. exec.; b. Sellersville, Pa., Dec. 28, 1946; d. George Herbert and Dorothy Louise (Jefferies) Datesman; student Palm Beach (Fla.) Jr. Coll., 1965; student Valparaiso U., 1969, Internat., Corr. Schs. 1 dau., Prudence Leigh. Receptionist, West Palm Beach, Fla., 1964-65; clk.-typist Valparaiso U., 1965, R.C.A., West Palm Beach, 1965; acct. clk. ITT Semicondrs., West Palm Beach, 1966-68; receptionist, sec. Lawyer's Title Service, West Palm Beach, 1969; with South Fla. Water Mgmt. Dist., West Palm Beach, 1969—, adminstrv. asst., 1974-77, acct., 1977-78, dir. fin., 1978—, controller, 1979—. Mem. Am. Legion Aux. Democrat. Lutheran. Home: 4724 Carver St Lake Worth FL 33463 Office: PO Box V West Palm Beach FL 33402

PRYOR, CHARLES WINGFIELD, JR., nuclear power generation co. ofcl.; b. Lynchburg, Va., Dec. 31, 1944; s. Charles Wingfield and Elizabeth (Baldock) P.; B.S. in Civil Engring. with honors, Va. Poly. Inst., 1966, M.S. in Structural Engring., 1968, Ph.D. in Civil Engring., 1970; grad. mgmt. devel. program Northeastern U.; m. Mary Jane Pryor; children—Charles Wingfield, Laurie K. Grad. instr. Va. Poly. Inst., Blacksburg, 1969-70; sr. engr. McDonnell Douglas, St. Louis, 1970-72; sr. engr. Babcock & Wilcox, nuclear power div., Lynchburg, Va., 1972-76, unit mgr., 1976-77, mgr. component engring. sect., 1977-80, mgr. project engring., 1980—. NSF fellow, 1967-69. Registered prof. engr. Va. Mem. ASCE, Sigma Xi (grad. award, Va. Poly. Inst., 1968), Phi Kappa Phi, Tau Beta Pi. Baptist. Clubs: Boonsboro Country (Lynchburg), Lynchburg Exchange, Babcock & Wilcox Employees (v.p., 1976, treas., 1975). Contbr. articles to profl. publs. in field. Home: 4744 John Scott Dr Lynchburg VA 24503 Office: PO Box 1260 Lynchburg VA 24505

PRYOR, DAVID H., congressman; b. Camden, Ark., Aug. 29, 1934; s. William Edgar and Susan (Newton) P.; B.A., U. Ark., 1957, LL.B., 1964; m. Barbara Lunsford, Nov. 28, 1957; children—David, Mark, Scott. Pub., editor Ouachita Citizen, Camden, 1957-61; admitted to Ark. bar, 1964; partner firm Pryor & Barnes, Camden, 1964-66; mem. Ark. Legislature, 1960-66; mem. 89th to 92d congresses from 4th Ark. dist.; mem. Appropriations Com., mem. D.C. Subcom., Ind. Offices and HUD Subcom.; gov. State of Ark., 1974-79; mem. U.S. Senate from Ark., 1979—. Mem. Sigma Alpha Epsilon. Democrat. Presbyterian. Office: Office of Gov State Capital Little Rock AR 72201

PRYOR, HAROLD S., coll. pres.; b. Livingston, Tenn., Oct. 3, 1920; s. Hubert S. and Ethel (Stockton) P.; B.S., Austin Peay State U., 1946; M.A., George Peabody Coll., 1947; Ed.D., U. Tenn., Knoxville, 1951; m. LaRue Vaughn, June 26, 1946. Dir. student teaching Austin Peay State U., 1951-52, head dept. edn. and psychology, 1952-56, dir. tchr. edn., 1956-68; pres. Columbia (Tenn.) State Community Coll., 1968—; dir. 1st Farmers & Mchts. Nat. Bank. Mem. Tenn. Edn. Assn., NEA, Tenn. Coll. Assn. (past pres.), Columbia-Mt. Pleasant C. of C. (dir.), Kappa Delta Pi, Phi Delta Kappa. Presbyterian. Club: Kiwanis. Office: PO Box 670 Columbia TN 38401

PRYOR, WALLACE CYRAL, oil and gas mfg. co. exec.; b. Concord, Ga., Sept. 16, 1922; s. Harry Gwyn and Maude Mae (Johnson) P.; student St. Olaf Coll., Northfield, Minn., 1946; m. Myrtle Nelsen, Nov. 2, 1946 (div. 1967); children—John Wallace, David Nelsen, Paul Richard, Mark Bernard, Peter Gwyn, Joel Phillip, Andrew George. Farmer, Pike County, Ga., 1946-54; civilian electrician Atlanta Army Depot, Forest Park, Ga., 1954-62; electrician and mechanic Spellman Engring., Orlando, Fla., 1962-64; vocat. instr. State of Ga., Atlanta, 1964-66; mechanic, electrician, Atlanta, 1966-68; 1969; pres. Pryor Oil Co. and Pryor Gasohol Co. Inc., Griffin, Ga., 1969—; v.p. U.S. Fuels, Inc., Griffin, Mid-Ga. Gasohol, Inc. Served with USNR, 1942-46. Mem. Ga. Oilmen's Assn., Ga. Ind. Oilmen's Assn., S.E. Gasohol Conf. (co-chmn. 1979), Am. Legion (past comdr.), Ga. Gasahol Commn. (pres. 1979—), DAV, Nat. Gasohol Commn. Democrat. Baptist. Clubs: Masons, Order Eastern Star (past worthy patron). Home: 715 N Poplar St Griffin GA 30223 Office: Pryor Oil Co 1234 W Taylor St Griffin GA 30223

PRYOR, WILLIAM LEE, educator; b. Lakeland, Fla., Oct. 29, 1926; s. Dahl and Lottie Mae (Merchant) P.; A.B., Fla. So. Coll., 1949; M.A., Fla. State U., 1950, Ph.D., 1959; postgrad. U. N.C., 1952-53; pvt. art study with Florence Wilde; pvt. voice study with Colin O'More and Anna Kaskas. Asst. prof. English, dir. drama Bridgewater Coll., 1950-52; vis. instr. English Fla. So. Coll., MacDill Army Air Base, summer 1951; grad. teaching fellow humanities Fla. State U., 1953-55, 57-58; instr. English, U. Houston, 1955-59, asst. prof., 1959-62, asso. prof., 1962-71, prof., 1971—, asso. editor Forum, 1967, editor, 1967—; vis. instr. English, Tex. So. U., 1961-63; vis. instr. humanities, govt. U. Tex. Dental Br., 1962-63; lectr. The Women's Inst., Houston, 1967-72; lectr. humanities series Jewish Community Center, 1972-73; originator, moderator weekly television and radio program The Arts in Houston on KUHT-TV and KUHF-FM, 1956-57, 58-63. Bd. dirs. Houston Shakespeare Soc., 1964-67; bd. dirs., program annotator Houston Chamber Orch. Soc., 1964—; bd. dirs., program annotator Music Guild, Houston, 1960-67, v.p., 1963-67, adv. bd. 1967-70; bd. dirs. Contemporary Music Soc., Houston, 1958-63; mem.-at-large bd. dirs. Houston Grand Opera Guild, 1966-67; mem. repertory com. Houston Grand Opera Assn. 1967-70; bd. dirs. Houston Grand Opera, 1970-75, adv. bd., 1978-79; mem. cultural adv. com. Jewish Community Center, 1960-66; bd. dirs. Houston Friends Pub Library, 1962-67, 73—, 1st v.p., 1963-67; adv. mem. cultural affairs com. Houston C. of C., 1972-75. Mem. Coll. English Assn., Modern Langs. Assn. L'Alliance Francaise, English-Speaking Union, Alumni Assn. Fla. State U., Am. Assn. U. Profs., S. Central Modern Lang. Assn., Coll. Conf. Tchrs. English, Am. Studies Assn., Phi Beta (patron), Phi Mu Alpha Sinfonia, Alpha Psi Omega, Pi Kappa Alpha, Sigma Tau Delta, Tau Kappa Alpha, Phi Kappa Phi. Episcopalian. Contbg. author: National Poetry Anthology, 1952; Panorama das Literaturas das Americas, 4 vols., 1958-60; contbr. articles to scholarly jours. Home: 2625 Arbuckle St Houston TX 77005 Office: 3801 Cullen Blvd Houston TX 77004

PSIHAS, GEORGE PETER, automotive co. exec.; b. Detroit, Mar. 3, 1927; s. Peter and Anastassia (Moskovus) P.; B.S., U.S. Mil. Acad., 1951; M.B.A., Ind. No. U., 1971, D.B.A., 1974; m. Bessie A. Annas, June 17, 1951; children—Pamela Renia, Xenia Ann. Commd. 2d lt. U.S. Army, 1951, advanced through grades to lt. col., 1972, ret., 1957; asst. mgr. planning and control Missile div. Chrysler Corp., Huntsville, Ala., 1957-61, mgr. govt. relations def. div., 1961-70, dir. mktg. def. group, 1970-76, mgr. adminstrn. electronics div., 1976-80, div. def. planning and adminstrn., 1980—; adj. prof. mgmt. and adminstrn. Ind. No. Profl. Sch. Mgmt., Marion; lectr. Southeastern Inst. Tech., Webster Coll., Detroit. Trustee Southeastern Inst. Tech., Huntsville. Decorated D.S.C., Purple Heart. Mem. Am. Def. Preparedness Assn. (past chmn. tank and automotive div.; bronze medallion for tech. chairmanship), Assn. U.S. Army (past adv. bd., past pres. Mich. chpt.), C. of C., West Point Soc. (Tenn. Valley chpt.), Legion of Valor. Democrat. Greek Orthodox. Clubs: Army-Navy Country (D.C.); Huntsville Country. Home: 11311 Mountaincrest SE Huntsville AL 35803 Office: 102 Wynn Dr Huntsville AL 38505

PTACEK, MAXINE GREEN, psychologist; b. Columbus, Miss., Sept. 15, 1929; d. Maxwell and Euline (Freeman) Green; B.S., Samford U., 1961; M.A., U. Ala., 1963; m. Robert A. Ptacek, Dec. 23, 1970. Tchr. Jefferson County (Ala.) Sch. System, 1957-60, guidance counselor, 1960-62; sch. psychologist State of Ala., 1963-65; dir. testing Jefferson State Jr. Coll., Birmingham, 1965-66; counseling psychologist VA, Roanoke, Va., 1966-70, Milw., 1970-72, San Antonio, 1972—; mem. faculty U. Va., 1967-70. NDEA fellow, 1964; certified rehab. counselor. Mem. Am. Psychol. Assn., Southwestern, Tex. psychol. assns., Am. Personnel and Guidance Assn., AAUW, Kappa Delta Pi. Presbyterian. Home: 210 Dawnridge St San Antonio TX 78213

PTASZKOWSKI, STANLEY EDWARD, JR., civil engr.; b. N.Y.C., June 11, 1943; s. Stanley Edward and Elsie Helena (Heihs) P.; Asso. Applied Sci., Acad. Aeros., 1967; B.S. in Civil Engring., U. Mo., 1975. Sr. draftsman to consultants and designers Grumman Aircraft, N.Y.C., 1965; engring. technician/design engr. McDonnell Douglas Astros., St. Louis, 1966-72; structural engr., asso. engr. Brown and Root, Inc., Houston, 1975-79; sr. structural engr. Marathon Marine Engring. Co., Houston, 1979—; asst. mgr. Montmartre Apts., Columbia, Mo., 1974-75. Mem. ASCE, Am. Inst. Aeros. and Astronautics. Lutheran. Home: 12916 Greenway Chase Ct Houston TX 77072 Office: Suite 1700 Marathon Bldg 600 Jefferson Houston TX 77002

PUCKETT, WILEY COLUMBUS, paving co. exec.; b. Barrow County, Ga., July 18, 1928; s. Wiley Hershel and Dozette Mozelle (McDougal) P.; ed. pub. schs., Gwinnett County, Ga.; m. Betty Ellen Cannon, Sept. 1, 1950; children—Linda Jewell, Michael Cannon, Laura Doris. With Gen. Motors, Doraville, Ga., 1949-60; founder, owner Puckett Constrn. Co., Lilburn, Ga., 1960—; dir. Young Refining Corp., Douglasville, Ga. Mem. Gwinnett County Airport Authority, 1972—. Served with 82d Airborn Div., AUS, 1946-47. Recipient B'nai B'rith citation for Outstanding Service, 1970. Mem. Ga. Asphalt Pavement Assn., Nat. Asphalt Pavement Assn., Gwinnett County C. of C. (dir. 1973). Mason. Home: Puckett Terr Lilburn GA 30247 Office: Puckett Constrn Co PO Box 668 Lilburn GA 30247

PUDDY, DONALD RAY, ofcl. NASA; b. Ponca City, Okla., May 31, 1937; s. Lester Andrew and Mildred Pearl (Olson) P.; B.S. in Mech. Engring., U. Okla., 1960; M.B.A., U. Houston, 1978; m. Dana Carol Timberlake, Sept. 8, 1956; children—Michael, Douglas, Glenn. With NASA, Johnson Space Center, Houston, 1964—, sect. head lunar module systems br., 1966-69, asst. chief br., 1969-72, asst. chief space sci. and tech. br., 1972-74, flight dir. Apollo 16, 1972, flight dir. Skylab, 1973-74, br. chief mission ops. br., 1974-76, chief flight dir., space shuttle approach and landing test, 1976-78, flight dir. manned spacecraft ops., 1978—. Asst. scoutmaster, membership chmn. Boy Scouts Am., Seabrook, Tex.; pres. Ed White Elem. P.T.A. Served with USAF, 1960-64. Recipient NASA Exceptional Service medal, 1973, 78, Presdl. Medal of Freedom group award, 1970. Mem. Order DeMolay, Pi Tau Sigma, Sigma Tau, Phi Kappa Phi, Phi Gamma Delta. Author: Space systems Operational Design Criteria Manual, 1972. Home: 221 Bayou View Dr Seabrook TX 77586 Office: NASA Johnson Spacecraft Center Houston TX 77058

PUGH, CHARLES WERNIS, SR., educator; b. Nashville, Nov. 25, 1931; s. Ernest Thomas and Madlyn (Abertnathy) P.; B.A., Tenn. State U., 1955, M.S., 1957; postgrad. U. Denver, 1960, 68, U. Tenn., 1960, 68, La. State U., 1979—; m. Amy Lea Brazier, June 7, 1960; children—Charles Wernis, Charmaine, Eric, Reginald. Instr. English, So. U., Baton Rouge, 1958-72, asst. prof., 1972—. Mem. sophomore com. Jack and Jill of Am.; res. sheriff East Baton Rouge Parish Res. Tng. Program, 1972—; mem. com. Black Poetry Festival. Served with AUS, 1952-54; lt. Res. Mem. Am. Fedn. Tchrs., AAUP, Phi Beta Sigma. Baptist. Life mem. Callaloo, Black Jour. Arts and Letters. Home: 2822 77th Ave Baton Rouge LA 70807 Office: So Univ Branch Post Office Baton Rouge LA 70807

PUGH, JULIAN FRANKLIN, constrn. co. exec.; b. Houston, Sept. 22, 1938; s. Jack Thomas and Lora Virginia (Smith) P.; student Abilene Christian U., 1962; m. Sharon D. Brasell, Dec. 16, 1966; children—Julian Franklin, II, Shawnna Diane, Steven Craig. Sales mgr. Superior Homes, Inc., Houston, 1962-67; pres. Am. Gen. Land Corp., Houston, 1967-68; pres. Land Investments Tex., Inc., Houston, 1968—; v.p. mktg. and pub. relations Superior Homes, Inc., Houston, 1974—. Mem. Greater Houston Builders Assn. (Mktg. Dir. of Yr. 1979), Tex. Assn. Builders, Nat. Assn. Homebuilders (One of Top 10 Mktg. Men in U.S.A. 1977, Sales and Mktg. Person of Yr. 1979, Disting. Achievement award 1978-79), Sales and Mktg. Council, Smithsonian Inst. Democrat. Ch. Christ. Club: Optimist Internat. (pres. 1971-73). Author: Guide to Real Estate Investment, 1970. Home: 26214 Hwy 75 Spring TX 77373 Office: PO Box 38290 Houston TX 77088

PUGH, ROBERT RALPH, counselor; b. West Point, N.Y., May 23, 1947; s. Ralph H. and Elizabeth G. P.; B.A., Stetson U., 1969, M.Ed. in Guidance, 1979; m. Mary Louise Sackett, Feb. 13, 1969; children—Mike, Carolyn, Steve, Jennifer. Mgr. retail div. Sears, Roebuck & Co., St. Petersburg, Fla., 1971-76; mgr. Auto Center, Meridian, Miss., 1976-77; counselor Miller Middle Sch., Crescent City, Fla., 1979—. Chmn., Sch. Adv. Com., 1978—. Served to 1st lt. USAR, 1970-71. Decorated Army Commendation medal. Mem. Am. Personnel and Guidance Assn., Am. Coll. Placement Assn., Am. Sch. Counselor Assn., Phi Delta Kappa. Republican. Baptist. Home: 118 Magnolia St Crescent City FL 32012 Office: PO Box 35 Crescent City FL 32012

PUGH, WILLIAM ED, banker; b. Ballard County, Ky., Dec. 31, 1913; s. Richard Lockhart and Della Mae (Gates) P.; ed. spl. courses in agr. and banking; m. Robbie Jeanette, Dec. 2, 1933; 1 dau., Eleanor Lynn Pugh Van Nuise. With Armour & Co., Louisville, 1937-59, Swift & Co., Nashville, 1959-68; agr. rep., security officer Citizens Bank & Trust Co., Glasgow, Ky., 1968—. Mem. Adv. bd. Future Farmers Am. Alumni. Served with U.S. Army, 1942-46. Mem. Ky. Bankers Assn., Future Farmers Am. Internat. (hon.), Glasgow C. of C. (Legion of Merit). Clubs: Glasgow Kiwanis (dist. chmn. 1975—, lt. gov. internat. 1973-74). Lions. Office: Box 419 Citizens Bank & Trust Co Glasgow KY 42141

PUJADAS, GUILLERMO MANUEL, orthopedic surgeon; b. Havana, Cuba, Dec. 9, 1922; s. Guillermo Felix and Manola (Lopez) P.; came to U.S., 1948, naturalized, 1954; B.Arts and Scis., Instituto Vedado, 1940; M.D., Havana U., 1948; m. Yolanda Esperanza de Moya, Nov. 13, 1948; children—William George, Thomas Edward. Intern, St. Bernard's Hosp., Chgo., 1949; resident in orthopedic surgery Northwestern U., Chgo., 1950-52; chief orthopedic and rehab. services VA Hosp., Lake City, Fla., 1953-55; practice medicine specializing in orthopedic surgery, Jacksonville, Fla., 1962—; mem. staff Hope Haven Hosp., Jacksonville, 1962—, pres. staff, 1969-70; mem. staff Baptist Meml., St. Luke's Riverside, St. Vincent's hosps.; clin. instr. orthopedics U. Fla.; chief orthopedics Meth. Hosp., Jacksonville, 1969—. Served to maj. USAF, 1955-60. Diplomate Am. Bd. Orthopedic Surgery. Mem. Am. Acad. Orthopedic Surgery, Internat. Coll. Surgeons, AMA, Fla. Orthopedic Assn., Fla. Med. Assn., Jacksonville Orthopedic Soc. (pres. 1971-72), Duval County Med. Soc. (James A. Deals award 1970). Roman Catholic. Clubs: San Jose Country, Ponte Vedra. Home: 2312 River Rd Jacksonville FL 32207 Office: 1300 Gary St Jacksonville FL 32207

PUJARI, BHASKER RAO, surgeon; b. Secunderabad, Andhra, India, Sept. 10, 1937; s. Kanniah and Krishna B. (Kasula) P.; M.B., B.S., Osmania U., India, 1960; m. Alice Jane Wood, July 24, 1965; children—Davina, Alison Jane, Kristen Barbara. Rotating intern Osmania U. Hosps., 1960; resident urology Queen's U. Hosps., Kingston, Ont., Can., also chief resident, research fellow; practice medicine, specializing in gen. surgery, Eng., 1962-70, Can., 1970-74; practice urology, Bluefield, W.Va., 1974—; staff urologist St. Luke's Hosp., also founder urology service; staff urologist Community Hosp., Princeton, W.Va., 1974—, Community Hosp., Bluefield, 1974—; cons. urologist Community Hosp., Tazewell, Va., 1975—. Diplomate Am. Bd. Urology. Fellow A.C.S., Royal Coll. Surgeons of Edinburgh; mem. Am. Urol. Assn., W.Va. Urol. Soc., W.Va. State Med. Soc., Mercer County Med. Soc., So. Med. Assn., Am. Cancer Soc. (dir. 1975—, chmn. profl. edn. com. 1977-79), Brit. Assn. Urol. Surgeons, Cadauceus Med. Club. Hindu. Clubs: Kiwanis, Masons. Contbr. articles to med. jours.

PULIZZANO, JOSEPH VINCENT, canning co. exec.; b. Chgo., Nov. 30, 1934; s. Henry and Catherine (Perniciaro) P.; asso. degree Pearl River Jr. Coll., 1956; B.S., U. Miss. So., 1958; M.B.A., Loyola U., New Orleans, 1971; m. Diane Elizabeth Feliu, Oct. 28, 1962; children—Joel Jacob, Jodee Elizabeth. Gen. acct. J. Ray McDermott & Co., New Orleans, 1961-62; budget and fiscal officer La. Civil Def. Agy., New Orleans, 1962-66; cost acct., fin. systems analyst Boeing Co., New Orleans, 1966-70; internal auditor, fiscal analyst U. New Orleans, 1970-76; controller, v.p. fin. Coastal Canning Enterprises, Inc., Reserve, La., 1976—, asst. sec.-treas., 1976—; asst. sec.-treas. C.M.&T. Asst. scoutmaster, troop treas. Boy Scouts Am., 1976-79. Served with U.S. Army, 1958-61. Mem. Nat. Assn. Accts. (Man of Yr. 1968, 69, past pres.), Paul C. Taylor Assn. (sec.) Am. Legion, Delta Sigma Pi. Democrat. Roman Catholic. Clubs: Spinning Squares (asst. treas.), SUWEV. Home: 705 Grand Dr Metairie LA 70003 Office: PO Drawer E Reserve LA 70084

PULLEN, HAROLD BAILEY, computer service exec.; b. French Camp, Miss., Oct. 27, 1935; s. Malcolm Henry and Dezree (Bailey) P.; student Miss. State U., 1954-55, U. Md., 1958-60; m. Anna Lewora, Feb. 11, 1961; children—Larry, Eric, David, Scotty. Programmer, analyst Riggs Nat. Bank, Washington, 1961-63; dir. data processing Kay Retail Stores, Washington, 1963-64; mgr. data processing NEA, Washington, 1964-71; pres. Asso. Computer Services, Inc., Springfield, Va., 1971—. Cubmaster Boy Scouts Am.; active Little League Baseball, recipient certificate of appreciation. Served with USNR, 1955-57. Mem. Data Processing Mgmt. Assn. (certified data processor), NEA (life). Home: 8609 Queen Elizabeth Blvd Annandale VA 22003 Office: 5406A Port Royal Rd Springfield VA 22151

PULLIAM, WALTER TILLMAN, pub., editor; b. Knoxville, Tenn., Nov. 5, 1913; s. James R. and Jennie Blanche (Badgett) P.; A.B., U. Tenn., 1936; m. Julia Brownlow; 1 dau., Mary Doffermyre. Copy editor Knoxville Jour., 1936; reporter Knoxville News-Sentinel, 1936-42, polit. writer, 1946; nat. affairs reporter, asst. city editor Washington Post, 1947-49; editor, pub. Harriman (Tenn.) Today's News, also pres., gen. mgr. Record Printing Co., Inc., 1949—; pres. La Follette Press Inc. (Tenn.), 1968—; pub. La Follette Press, Jellico (Tenn.) Advance-Sentinel, Lake City (Tenn.) Town Crier. Chmn., Indsl. Devel. Commn. Harriman; mem. Harriman Pub. Library Bd.; pres. Monteagle Sunday Sch. Assembly, 1979-80; trustee Tenn. Newspaper Found., Roane State Community Coll. Found., Monteagle Endowment Found., Tenn. Newspaper Hall of Fame. Served in inf. AUS, 1942-46; staff Mediterranean edit. Stars and Stripes. Mem. Tenn., Harriman businessmen's assns., Tenn. Press Assn. (past pres.), East Tenn. Hist. Soc. Presbyterian (elder). Clubs: City, Cherokee Country (Knoxville); Nat. Press (Washington); Rotary (dist. gov. 1972-73, internat. publs. com. 1979—); Emory Golf and Country. Author: Harriman-The Town That Temperance Built. Home: 413 Cumberland St Harriman TN 37748 Office: 512 Devonia St Harriman TN 37748

PULLIAMS, KENNETH ARNOLD coach, educator; b. San Antonio, Sept. 25, 1948; s. Charles A. and Dorothy M. (Brown) P.; B.S., Prairie View A.&M. U., 1970, M.S., 1971; postgrad. U. Tex., Austin, 1977, U. Tex. San Antonio, 1978, S.W. Tex. State U., 1978; m. Norma Jean Jasper, July 18, 1970; children—Christopher A., Kennetra A. Tchr., coach San Antonio Ind. Sch. Dist., 1970-73; field counselor Sanyo, San Antonio, 1973; asst. prof., head basketball coach St. Philips Coll., San Antonio, 1973. Summer youth counselor, athletic dir. Concerned Athletes in Action, 1978-80. Mem. Tex. Jr. Coll. Athletic Assn., Nat. Jr. Coll. Athletic Assn., Tex. Sr. Coll. Tchr. Assn., Omega Psi Phi. Baptist. Club: Masons.

PULLUM, ARTHUR ADAM, JR., health care adminstr.; b. Camp Shelby, Miss., Apr. 23, 1945; s. Arthur Adam and Anna Mae (Trotter) P.; student Fla. A&M U., Tallahassee, 1964-65; A.S. in Bus. Adminstrn., Mo. Southern U., 1971, B.S. in Mktg. and Mgmt., 1975; postgrad Miss. Coll., 1977, Jackson State U., 1980—; m. Elizabeth Ann Floyd, Nov. 29, 1975; children—Theresa, Glennis, Monica. Salesman, Sears Roebuck & Co., Hattiesburg, Miss., 1969; asst. mgr. Fred's Dollar Store, Shelby, Miss., 1971-72; jr. acct. Tougaloo (Miss.) Coll., 1972-73; dept. mgr. Gen. Cable Corp., Brandon, Miss., 1973-74; registered rep. Western Res. Fin. Services, Jackson, Miss., 1973-74; v.p. Robinson & Assos., 1974-75; asst. adminstr. Kidney Care, Inc., Jackson, Miss., 1976—. Participant, Govs. Conf. on Urban Devel. of Mo., 1970; mem. End-Stage Renal Disease Council, 1979—; adv. council Miss. Health Systems Agy., Inc., 1980—. Served with USAF, 1965-68. Recipient Freedom Found. award, 1970. Mem. Soc. Advancement of Mgmt., Am. Mgmt. Assn., NAACP, Afro-Am. Soc. (v.p. 1969-70), Omega Psi Phi. Home: 4734 Kirkley Dr Jackson MS 39206 Office: 3310 N State St Jackson MS 39216

PULSIFER, ROY, govt. offcl.; b. Schenectady, Oct. 20, 1931; s. Joseph R. and Marie (Phillips) P.; B.A., Columbia, 1953, M. Internat. Affairs, 1958, J.D., 1958; m. Maryann Foreman, Dec. 18, 1963. Admitted to N.Y. bar, 1958, U.S. Supreme Ct. bar; enforcement officer Internat. Air Transport Assn., N.Y.C., 1959-60; atty. adviser FAA, Washington, 1960-63; with CAB, Washington, 1963—, asst. chief, routes div., office gen. counsel, 1968-70, asst. dir. Bur. Operating Rights, 1970-78, asso. dir. for licensing programs and policy devel. Bur. Domestic Aviation, 1978—. Served with AUS, 1954-56. Recipient Meritorious Service award CAB, 1975. Mem. Am. Bar Assn., Am. Econ. Assn. Co-author govt. studies; contbr. articles to profl. jours. Home: 210 Lawton St Falls Church VA 22046 Office: Civil Aeronautics Board Washington DC 20428

PURCELL, JOE EDWARD, lt. gov. Ark.; b. Warren, Ark., July 29, 1923; s. Edward L. and Lynelle M. (Cunningham) P.; certificate Little Rock Jr. Coll., 1949; J.D., U. Ark., 1952; m. Helen C. Hale, Oct. 14, 1948; children—Lynelle Purcell Lehman, Ede Purcell Hogue. Admitted to Ark. bar, 1952, since practiced in Benton; city atty., Benton, 1955-59; municipal judge, Benton and Saline County, Ark., 1959-66; atty. gen. State of Ark., 1967-71, lt. gov., 1975—. Chmn., Ark. Democratic Party, 1970-72; nat. Dem. committeeman, 1972; chmn. Ark. March of Dimes, 1975—; Ark. chmn. Am. Bicentennial Revolution Commn., 1976. Served with AUS, 1943-45. Mem. Am., Ark. (state chmn. membership com. 1971-72) bar assns., Am. Judicature Soc., Delta Theta Phi (chancellor dist. 1971—, state chmn. Ark. 1975—). Methodist. Club: Lions. Office: 102 W Ashley St Benton AR 72015 also Office of Lt Gov State Capitol Little Rock AR 72201*

PURCELL, RENE, mfg. co. exec.; b. Penuelas, P.R., Feb. 28, 1923; s. Santiago and Leonor (Bauza) P.; dip. bus. mgmt. LaSalle Extension U., 1963-66; m. Adelaida Gatell, Mar. 1, 1945; children—Rene, Waldemar, Jorge. Owner, personnel mgr. Omark Caribbean, Bayamon, P.R., 1952-70; adminstrv. officer U.S. Dept. Interior, P.R., 1970. Counsellor, Jr. Achievement, Bayamon, P.R., 1977. Served with U.S. Army, 1943-45. Mem. Am. Soc. Personnel Adminstrn. (pres. 1978, pres. bd. dirs. 1979, Superior Merit award 1978), Am. Mgmt. Assn. New Progressive Party. Roman Catholic. Home: Apt 1207 Cobian's Plaza Condominium Santurce PR 00908 Office: 88-90 D St Minillas Industrial Pk Bayamon PR 00619

PURCELL, SHIRLEY ANN TEAGUE, army officer; b. Houston, June 10, 1942; d. Lloyd Dee and Harriett (Hammett) Teague; student (A. Jeanette Jones scholar) U. Houston, 1960-61; diploma Lillie Jolly Sch. Nursing, 1963; student Houston Bapt. Coll., 1964-65; B.S. in Nursing Lorretto Heights Coll., 1972; div.; 1 son, Timothy. Staff nurse, various hosps., Tex., 1963-66; commd. 2d lt. Nursing Corps, U.S. Army, 1966, advanced through grades to maj., 1975; staff, head nurse evacuation hosps., Vietnam, 1966-67, 68-69; supr. operating room Army Hosp., Wurzburg, Germany, 1972-73, head nurse med. surgery, 1973-74; head nurse med. ward, Fort McClellan, Ala., 1974-75, spl. projects officer, 1975-76; infection control nurse, supr. central material service Chief Nurse's Office, Womack Army Hosp., Fort Bragg, N.C., 1976-78; infection control nurse, chmn. infection control com. U.S. Army MEDDAC, Ft. Bragg, 1978-79; infection control nurse Brooke Army Med. Center, Ft. Sam Houston, Tex., 1979—. Vol. speaker Veitnam MEDCAP program, 1966-69. Decorated Cross of Gallantry with Palm, Nat. Def. medal (both Republic of Vietnam), Army Commendation medal with 2 oak leaf clusters, Nat. Def. Service medal, Meritorious Service medal with oak leaf. Mem. Am. Nurses Assn., Assn. U.S. Army, Assn. Practitioners Infection Control, Assn. Mil. Surgeons U.S., Res. Officers Assn., Am. Heart Assn. Home: 8210 Pioneer Hills Converse TX 78109 Office: Infectious Disease Service Brooke Army Med Center Beach Pavilion PO Box 543 Fort Sam Houston TX 78234

PURCIFULL, DAN ELWOOD, plant virologist; b. Woodland, Calif., July 1, 1935; s. Ernest Lee and Virginia Carolina (Margaroli) P.; BS., U. Calif., Davis, 1957, M.S., 1959, Ph.D., 1964; m. Marcia Ann Weatherby, Sept. 7, 1966; children—Scott, Douglas. Asst. prof. plant pathology U. Fla., Gainesville, 1964-69, asso. prof., 1969-75, prof., 1975—. Mem. Morningside Nature Center Commn., Gainesville, 1978—. Served with U.S. Army, 1957. Mem. AAAS, Am. Phytopath. Soc., Fla. Hort. Soc., Sigma Xi. Contbr. articles to profl. jours. Home: 3106 NW 1st Ave Gainesville FL 32607 Office: Dept Plant Pathology U Fla Gainesville FL 32601

PURDOM, RAY CALDWELL, physicist; b. Lebanon, Ky., Sept. 8, 1943; s. Claude Caldwell and Elizabeth (Ray) P.; B.S., Duke U., 1965; M.S., Purdue U., 1967, Ph.D. (Purdue Research Found. fellow 1967-70, NSF summer fellow 1967), 1970; m. Margaret Ellen Sommer, June 13, 1965; children—Elizabeth Sommer, John Kirkland, Clayton Caldwell. Asst. prof. physics Ky. Wesleyan Coll., 1970-75, asso. prof., 1975—; research fellow in med. physics U. Cin. Coll. Medicine, 1977-78. Mem. Am. Phys. Soc., Am. Assn. Physics Tchrs., AAUP. Democrat. Presbyterian. Club: Owensboro (Ky.) Tennis (pres. 1976-77). Contbr. articles to profl. jours. Office: Dept Physics and Math Ky Wesleyan Coll Owensboro KY 42301

PURDUM, RAYMOND LESLIE, acct.; b. Raymondville, Tex., Oct. 26, 1945; s. Leslie V. and Rosalia (Buffenbarger) P.; student Inst. Computer Systems, 1968-69; A.A., Claremore Jr. Coll., 1970; B.A., Okla. State U., 1972; m. Eldonna Lyda, Mar. 15, 1967; children—Leslie, Perry, William Mix. Office mgr. Floair, Inc., Wichita, Kans., 1967-69; acct., computer technician Cities Service Oil Co., Tulsa, 1972-74; acct. R. J. Ackerman Oil Co., Casper, Wyo., 1974-76; pvt. practice acctg. tax practitioner, Claremore, Okla., 1976—; instr. Claremore Jr. Coll., 1977—. Served with AUS, 1963-66. Mem. Okla. Soc. Ind. Pub. Accts. Clubs: Claremore Golf Assn., Claremore Jaycees, Ind. Order of Odd Fellows. Home: 1414 Danny Claremore OK 74017 Office: Surrey Profl Center 115 1/2 W Blue Starr Claremore OK 74017

PURDY, DON CHARLES, athletic dir.; b. Harrison, Ark., May 16, 1945; s. Lemuel M. and Dorothy B. Purdy; B.S. in Edn., Ouachita Baptist U., Arkadelphia, Ark., 1969; M.Ed.S., N.Tex. State U., Denton, 1972; m. Dora Ann King, July 13, 1968; 1 son, Alan Don. Tchr., coach Crowley (Tex.) Public Sch., 1968-74; asst. basketball coach, head baseball coach Ouachita Bapt. U., 1974-78; athletic dir., basketball coach Belmont Coll., Nashville, 1978—. Mem. Nat. Assn. Intercollegiate Athletics, Coachs Assn. Tenn. Secondary Athletics, Phi Delta Kappa. Republican. Baptist. Club: Lions (sec. local club 1975-78). Home: 197 Delvin Dr Antioch TN 37013 Office: Belmont Coll Belmont Blvd Nashville TN 37203

PURDY, HAROLD JOHN, clergyman; b. Newcomerston, Ohio, June 14, 1914; s. Earle Edson and Mabel (Wilson) P.; student Alderson-Broadus Coll., 1932-34, Salem Coll., 1934-36, A.B., 1946; D.D., So. Bapt. Theol. Sem., 1942, B.D., M.D.V., 1975; postgrad. Oxford (Eng.) U., 1965; m. Virginia Elisabeth Burdette, Apr. 23, 1935. Ordained to ministry Bapt. Ch., 1935; pastor 1st Ch., Madison W. Va., 1935-39, Northview Ch., Clarksburg, W. Va., 1933-35; asso. pastor Deer Park Ch., Louisville, 1939-41; pastor 1st Ch., Madisonville, Ky., 1941-46, 1st Ch., Bowling Green, Ky., 1946-50, Belmont Heights Ch., Nashville, 1950-64, 1st Bapt. Ch., Madisonville, Ky., 1964-80; trustee Bapt. Sunday Sch. Bd.; exec. bd. Ky. Bapt. Conv., 1964-73, mem. hosp. commn., 1964-73; mem. exec. com. So. Bapt. Conv., 1966-73; mem. faculty Boyce Sch., So. Bapt. Sem., 1974—; pres. Tenn. Bapt. Conv., 1963; moderator Nashville Bapt. Assn., 1962-63. Trustee Tenn. Bapt. Children's Home, 1951-63, Belmont Coll., 1953-64; bd. dirs. Western Recorder, 1974-79. Club: Kiwanis. Contbr. to ch. periodicals. Home: Greenville Pike Madisonville KY 42431 Office: 1st Baptist Ch 246 N Main St Madisonville KY 42431

PURTLE, JOHN INGRAM, state justice; b. Enola, Ark., Sept. 7, 1923; s. John Wesley and Edna Gertrude (Ingram) P.; student U. Central Ark., 1946-47; LL.B., then J.D., U. Ark., Fayetteville, 1950; m. Marian Ruth White, Dec. 31, 1951; children—Jeffrey, Lisa K. Admitted to Ark. bar, 1950, Fed. bar, 1950; individual practice law, Conway, Ark., 1950-53, Little Rock, 1953-78; mem. Ark. State Legislature, 1951-52, 69-70; asso. justice Ark. Supreme Ct., 1979—. Tchr., deacon Baptist Ch. Served with U.S. Army, 1940-45. Mem. Ark. Bar Assn., Am. Judicature Soc., Am. Bar Assn., Ark. Judicial Council. Democrat. Office: Justice Bldg Little Rock AR 72201

PURYEAR, JOHN WALTER, mech. engr.; b. Tulsa, Mar. 31, 1938; s. Cecil E. and Gerry R.; student Tex. A.&M. Coll., 1956-57, Alvin (Tex.) Jr. Coll., 1957-58, Tulsa Jr. Coll., 1977—; m. Patricia E. Martin, Sept. 20, 1958; children—Sandra, Valarie. Draftsman, P.G.A.C., Houston, 1957-59; quality control mgr. Zebco/Brunswick, Tulsa, 1959-74, sr. project engr., 1974-77, engrng. mgr. research and devel., 1977—. Mem. ASME, Adminstrv. Mgmt. Assn. Republican. Baptist. Club: Masons (32 deg.). Patentee crossbow trigger assembly, 8 fishing reel designs. Home: 7272 E 101st St S Tulsa OK 74133 Office: 2724 N Sheridan Tulsa OK 74101

PUTCHAT, NATHAN, environ. and planning engr.; b. Trenton, N.J., May 17, 1915; s. David and Bertha (Berkman) P.; B.C.E., U. N.D., 1938; postgrad. N.Y. U., 1944-45; J.D., Blackstone Sch. Law, 1975; m. Sally Silver, Aug. 27, 1939; 1 son, Bruce S. Pres., Gen. Builders, Inc., Gen. Home Builders, Inc., Thomas Conste Assos., 1952-57; exec. dir. Bucks County (Pa.) Water and Sewer Authority, 1964-68; v.p. Host Enterprises, 1969-70; now environ. adviser Martin County (Fla.) Bd. County Commrs.; numerous other engrng. positions; mem. constrn. industry panel Am. Arbitration Assn. Registered profl. engr., Pa., N.J., Del., Fla.; diplomate Am. Acad. Environ. Engrs. Mem. Nat. Assn. Profl. Engrs., Trenton Engrs. Club, Am. Concrete Inst., Am. Assn. Cost Engrs., Am. Water Works Assn., Water Pollution Control Fedn., Am. Pub. Works Assn., Inst. Municipal Engrs., Constrn. Surveyors Inst., St. Lucie River Power Squadron. Clubs: Lions, The Soundings Yacht and Tennis, Masons, Shriners. Home: 10393 SE Coconut Ln Hobe Sound FL 33455 Office: PO Box 965 Hobe Sound FL 33455

PUTNAM, JUDD LEE, elec. engr.; b. Centralia, Ill., July 24, 1945; s. George W. and Edna Aliene (Berkshire) P.; B.S. in Elec. Engring., U. Tex., El Paso, 1973; m. Betty Barbara Bomar, Sept. 2, 1967; children—John Eric, Phillip Andrew, Laura Leigh. With Dallas Power & Light Co., 1973—, design engr., 1973-78, distbn. engr., 1979—. Deacon Northminster United Presbyn. Ch., 1975-76; active YMCA fund drive, 1977. Served with USAF, 1967-70. Registered profl. engr., Tex. Mem. IEEE, Power Engring. Soc., Tau Beta Pi, Eta Kappa Nu, Alpha Chi. Club: Lake Highlands Square Dance (pres. 1976-77, del. 1977-78, historian 1978-79). Co-author report on thermal properties of elec. distbn. system. Office: 1506 Commerce St Dallas TX 75201

PUTNAM, RICHARD ROACH, psychologist; b. Terlton, Okla., July 18, 1945; s. Guy Alfonzo and Myrtle Ethel (Canary) P.; B.S., N. Tex. State U., 1972, M. Ed., 1973; postgrad. Tex. A&M U., 1979—; m. Carlyn Vance, Feb. 1978; children by former marriage—Brian Keith, Christopher Robert. Counselor, social worker Southwestern N.Mex. Services to Handicapped Children and Adults Inc., Silver City, 1973-74; dir. student services Frank Phillips Coll., Borger, Tex., 1974-75; asso. psychologist Dallas Ind. Sch. Dist., 1975-79; grad. asst. ednl. psychology dept. Tex. A&M U., College Station, 1979—. Chmn. mental health com. Area Human Resources Council, Silver City, 1974; bd. dirs. Planned Parenthood Silver City, 1974, Denton (Tex.) Unitarian Fellowship, 1976. Served with U.S. Army, 1963-66. Decorated Parachutists Combat Inf. Badge, Purple Heart. Mem. Tex. Psychol. Assn., Dallas Psychol. Assn. Democrat. Presbyterian. Clubs: Dallas Wildebeeste R.F.C. (sec.-treas. 1978-79), Tex. A&M Rugby, Masons. Home: 505 Nagle St Apt 1 College Station TX 77840 Office: Ednl Psychology Dept Tex A&M U College Station TX 77843

PUTNAM, VICTOR MONTELLE, JR., oil co. exec.; b. Memphis, May 15, 1943; s. Victor Montelle and Opal Juanita (Thrailkill) P.; B.S. in Chem. Engring., Miss. State U., 1965; m. Lynn Miller Putnam, Jan. 1, 1966; 1 dau., Mieke Erin. Chem. engr. refining dept. Texaco, Port Arthur, Tex., 1965-70, start-up engr. refinery Baton Rouge, 1966, staff engr. internat. refinery, N.Y.C., 1970-72, project engr. process dept. Port Arthur, 1972-73, asst. to supr. ops. refining dept., 1973-76, supr. ops. refining dept., 1976—. Treas., United Community Services, 1974; campaign worker Republican Congressional Elections, 1974. Mem. Am. Inst. Chem. Engrs., Port Arthur C. of C. (govtl. task force). Republican. Mem. Ch. of Jesus Christ of Latter-Day Saints. Home: 692 Meadowgreen Dr Port Neches TX 77651 Office: PO Box 712 Port Arthur TX 77640

PUTNEY, CHARLES WALKER, elec. engr.; b. Staunton, Va., June 10, 1936; s. Charles Walker and Louise (Gathright) P.; B.S., Va. Mil. Inst., 1957; M.S., San Jose State Coll., 1968; m. Karen Marie Albright, Jan. 12, 1957 (div. Dec. 1, 1977); children—Wainscott, Pamela, Sarah. Maintenance test engr. U.S. Steel, Munhall, Pa., 1957-60; test and evaluation engr. Polaris Fire Control and Guidance, Gen. Electric, Pittsfield, Mass., 1960-63; dynamics engr. Lockheed Missiles & Space Co., Sunnyvale, Calif., 1963-66; sr. hybrid computer simulation engr. Martin Marietta, Orlando, Fla., 1968-74; v.p., dir. Silvercrest Furnishings, Inc., Orlando, 1974-76; owner Putney Motor Coach Rentals, Winter Park, Fla. Mem. parents council Va. Mil. Inst., 1975-78. Served to 2d lt. USAF, 1957-58, capt. Res. Mem. I.E.E.E. Baptist. Home: 2233 Via Tuscany Winter Park FL 32789

PUYAU, FRANCIS ALBERT, physician; b. New Orleans, Dec. 1, 1928; s. Frank Albert and Rose Sue (Jones) P.; B.S. in Chemistry, Notre Dame U., 1948; M.D., La. State U., 1952; m. Geraldine Sally di Benedetto, June 6, 1951; children—Michael, Stephen, Jeanne Marie, Julie, Melissa. Intern, Charity Hsop., New Orleans, 1952-53; resident in pediatrics Charity Hosp., New Orleans, 1955-57, Dept. Diagnostic Radiology, 1968-70; practice medicine specializing in pediatrics and radiology, New Orleans, 1972—; instr. pediatrics La. State U. Sch. Medicine, New Orleans, 1957-59, asst. prof. pediatrics, 1959-61, clin. asso. prof. pediatrics, 1968-71, prof. radiology and pediatrics, 1971-74, acting head Dept. Radiology, 1971-72, head Dept. Radiology, 1972-74; prof. radiology, pediatrics and medicine Tulane U. Sch. Medicine, New Orleans, 1974—, acting chmn. Dept. Pediatrics, 1976-78; asst. prof. pediatrics Vanderbilt U., 1961-68; vis. physician Charity Hosp., New Orleans, 1955-61; vis. staff Touro Infirmary, New Orleans, 1958-61; staff Vanderbilt U. Hosp., Nashville, 1961-68; cons. Slidell Meml. Hosp., 1974-75, Mercy Hosp., New Orleans, 1971-76, VA Hosp., New Orleans, 1971-74; sr. vis. physician radiology La. State U. Div., Charity Hosp., New Orleans, 1971-74; cons. radiology New Orleans Pub. Health Service Hosp., 1975-76; cons. St. Tammany Hosp., Covingotn, La., 1968—; dir. cardiac catherization lab. Dept. Cardiology, Charity Hosp., New Orleans, 1979—; staff Hotel Dieu, New Orleans, 1973—; staff head X-Ray Dept., Children's Hosp. New Orleans, 1976—. Served with USPHS, 1953-55. Licensed physician, La., Tenn.; diplomate Am. Bd. Petiatrics, Am. Bd. Radiology, Fellow Am. Coll. Cardiology; mem. Orleans Parish Med. Soc., La. Pediatric Soc., Tenn. Pediatric Soc., Davidson County Pediatric Soc., So. Soc. for Pediatric Research, Am. Coll. Radiology, La. State Radiology Soc., New Orleans Radiology Soc., New Orleans Pediatric Soc., Radiol. Soc. N. Am., Am. Roentgen Ray Soc., Am. Assn. Univ. Radiologists, Alpha Omega Alpha. Roman Catholic. Clubs: So. Yacht, Pontchartrain Yacht. Contbr. articles in field to med. jours. Home: 2104 State St New Orleans LA 70118 Office: Dept Radiology Tulane Univ Med Center 1415 Tulane Ave New Orleans LA 70112

PUZAR, VINCENT DOMINIC, Realtor, mgmt. cons.; b. Grand Rapids, Mich., Mar. 30, 1928; s. Vincent Alexander and Anna Marion (Bajorinas) P.; Asso. Sci., Grand Rapids Jr. Coll., 1947; student U. Central Mich., 1957-58, U. Mich., 1959-62; m. Joan Eileen Thompson, Apr. 4, 1959; children—Barbara Jean, Brad Kendall, Nancy Ellen, Laurie Anne; m. 2d, Karin Treiber Blake, Sept. 16, 1978. Analyst, researcher Dow Chem. Co., Midland, Mich., 1949-56; owner Accordion Inst., Midland, 1956-59, Midland Real Estate Exchange, 1959-62; v.p. comml. sales and devel. Brantley Assos., Realtors, St. Petersburg, Fla., 1963-67; pres. Vince Puzar Assos., Realtors, Action Mgmt., Inc., Action Properties, Inc., St. Petersburg, 1967—. computer cons. Realtron Corp., Detroit, 1972—; dir. Gulf Beach-Seminole Bd. Realtors, 1969—, pres., 1971; mem. St. Petersburg Bd. Realtors, Clearwater Bd. Realtors; adj. prof. real estate U. Fla., Gainesville. Nat. and state judge classical accordion competitions; alt. del. Mich. Republican Conv., 1962; mem. fin. com. Little Ears, Inc., St. Petersburg. Recipient citation for articles on real estate exchanging Internat. Traders Club, 1964; named Realtor of Year, Gulf Beach-Seminole Bd. Realtors, 1971. Mem. Nat., Fla. assns. Realtors, Nat., Fla. assns. mortgage brokers, Fla. Assn. Real Estate Educators, Nat. Musicians Union. Club: Elks. Author: A Computerized Bookkeeping System-Plan A, 1973; Real-Tabs, A Computerized Real-Time Accounting and Business System, 1980. Composer: Rhapsodie Dramatique, 1958. Patentee in chem. engring. field. Home: 520 59th Ave Saint Petersburg Beach FL 33706 Office: 5905 Gulf Blvd Saint Petersburg Beach FL 33706

PYATT, EDWIN EUGENE, educator; b. Bloomington, Ill., May 13, 1929; s. Edwin Hulett and Florence (deVore) P.; B.S., Calif. Inst. Tech., 1951; M.S., U. Calif., Berkeley, 1953; D.Eng., Johns Hopkins U., 1959; m. Carol Jean Collar, Feb. 25, 1961; 1 son, Dale Hulett. San. engr. Pomeroy & Assos., Pasadena, Calif., 1955-56; instr. Johns Hopkins U., Balt., 1956-59; asst. prof. Northwestern U., Evanston, Ill., 1959-62; sr. research engr. Travelers Research Center, Hartford, Conn., 1962-65; prof. engring. U. Fla., Gainesville, 1965—, chmn. dept., 1970—; cons. U.S. Geol. Survey, EPA, City of Jacksonville (Fla.), AID, Bechtel Corp., World Bank. Served to 1st lt. USAF, 1953-55. Diplomate Am. Acad. Environ. Engrs.; registered profl. engr., Calif., Ill., Fla. Mem. Am. Soc. Profl. Engrs., ASCE, Am. Water Works Assn., AAAS, Am. Public Health Assn., Water Pollution Control Fedn., Am. Soc. Engring. Edn., Am. Water Resources Assn., Blue Key, Sigma Xi, Chi Epsilon, Tau Beta Pi, Sigma Tau, Phi Kappa Phi, Omicron Delta Kappa. Contbr. articles to profl. jours. Home: 3951 SW 6th Pl Gainesville FL 32607

PYKE, GEORGE ALBERT, physician; b. New Orleans, Sept. 24, 1948; s. George Norman and Una Gladys (Walsh) P.; A.A. (scholar), Palm Beach Jr. Coll., 1968; B.S., U. Fla., 1970; M.T., St. Mary's Hosp. Sch. Med. Tech., 1971; M.D., U. Miami. Resident in family medicine Fla. Hosp., Orlando, 1975-78; clin. asso. dept. family medicine U. S. Fla. Sch. Medicine, 1975—; practice medicine specializing in family medicine, Longwood, Fla., 1978—; team physician Union Park Jr. High Sch., Longwood, 1978—, Lake Brantley High Sch., Longwood, 1978—; mem. staff Altamonte Springs, Apopka, Orlando, Walker Meml. (Avon Park, Fla.) hosps. Diplomate Am. Bd. Family Medicine. Fellow Am. Acad. Family Practice; mem. AMA, Fla. Acad. Family Practice, Orange County Med. Soc., Lake Mary C. of C., Alpha Epsilon Delta. Club: Optimist of South Seminole County (v.p. external affairs 1979—). Home: 901 S Grant St Longwood FL 32750 Office: PO Box 3377 100 Lake Shore Dr Longwood FL 32750

PYLE, K. RICHARD, educator; b. Brazil, Ind., Jan. 26, 1939; s. Floye Evans and Matilda Adams (Chapman) P.; B.A., William Jewell Coll., 1961; M.S., Ill. State U., 1963; Ph.D., U. Fla., 1976; m. Betty Boyd, Nov. 26, 1965; children—Kimberly, Matthew, Melissa. Dir. guidance LeRoy High Sch., LeRoy, Ill., 1962-64; residence hall dir. DePauw U., Greencastle, Ind., 1964-66; resident dean U. Calif. at La Jolla, 1968-69; counseling psychologist-training center dir. Peace Corps Tng. Center, Ponce, P.R., 1969-73; asso. dean students Ga. Coll., Milledgeville, Ga., 1976—; vol. tchr. Peace Corps, Lucea, Jamaica, 1966-68. Chmn. work area on missions, Methodist. Ch. Mem. Am. Personnel and Guidance Assn., Nat. Assn. Student Personnel Adminstrs., Am., So. coll. personnel assns., Assn. for Counselor Edn. and Supervision, Phi Delta Kappa. Clubs: Milledgeville Tennis, Rotary. Contbr. articles in guidance to profl. jours. Home: Route 5 Box 339 Pearl Dr Milledgeville GA 31061 Office: Ga Coll Milledgeville GA 31061

PYLE, RAYMOND JAMES, JR., outdoor advt. exec.; b. Oak Park, Ill., Jan. 15, 1932; s. Raymond James and Bessie Inez (Osborn) P.; student U. Wis., 1951-56, U. Notre Dame, 1968; student mgmt. U. South Fla., 1972; m. Mabel Lee Freeman, June 28, 1952; children—Dale, David, Steven, Carol Lynn. Sales rep. Leader Dept. Store, 1955-57, London Wholesale Hardware, 1957-58, Martin Outdoor Advt., 1958-65; gen. mgr. Martin Outdoor Advt., 1965-66, v.p., 1966-69, pres., 1969-76; Fla. regional mgr., v.p. Foster & Kleiser div. Metromedia, Tampa, Fla., 1976—; bd. fellows, counselor U. Tampa, 1970-77. Former treas. Easter Seal Soc. Tampa, now bd. dirs.; bd. dirs. A.R.C. of Tampa; active Heart Fund, United Fund, Boy Scouts Am. Mem. Outdoor Advt. Assn. of Fla. (pres.), Inst. Outdoor Advt. S.E. U.S.A. (treas.), Tampa Advt. Fedn. (past pres., Advt. Man of Year 1969, Silver Medal award 1979-80), Sales and Mktg. Execs. Tampa (past pres., Sales and Mktg. Exec. of Year 1970), Pi Sigma Epsilon, Mchts. Assn. Tampa (past dir.). Democrat. Baptist. Clubs: Univ., Rotary (Tampa); Palma Ceia Golf and Tennis; Feather Sound Golf and Tennis; Masons. Home: 1206 S Suffolk Dr Tampa FL 33609 Office: 5555 Ulmerton Rd Clearwater FL 33520

PYLES, RODNEY ALLEN, archivist; b. Morgantown, W.Va., June 21, 1945; s. Melford John and Luci L. (Scarcella) P.; B.A., W.Va. U., 1967, M.A., 1972; m. Carol Louise Wrobleski, May 20, 1972; 1 dau., Janessa Louise. Teaching fellow polit. sci. W.Va. U., 1968-69; instr. polit. sci. Alderson-Broaddus Coll., Philippi, W.Va., 1969-71; asst. curator W.Va. U. Library, 1971-77; dir. archives and history div. W.Va. Dept. Culture and History, Charleston, 1977—. Mem. Morgantown Democratic Exec. Com., 1969-71; mem. Monongalia County Dem. Exec. Com., 1972-76. Mem. Soc. Am. Archivists, Am. Mus. Assn., Mid-Atlantic Regional Archivists Conf., Mid-West Archives Conf., Mid-West Mus. Conf., W.Va. Hist. Soc., W.Va. Hist. Assn., Nat. Assn. State Archives and Records Adminstrs., W.Va. Library Assn. Methodist. Mng. editor W.Va. History Quar., 1977—. Office: 5 Truslow St Charleston WV 25311

PYLES, STEVE, naval officer; b. Caswell County, N.C., July 31, 1948; s. Clarence O'Neil and Mary Jane (Long) P.; B.S., Va. Poly. Inst., 1970; M.B.A., Armstrong Savannah State Coll., 1978; m. Lufreda Williams, Mar. 12, 1977. Commd. ensign U.S. Navy, 1971, advanced through grades to lt., 1975; combat info. officer aboard ship, 1973-74, line div. officer, 1973-74, supply officer, 1974; jr. instr., adviser ROTC unit Savannah (Ga.) State Coll., 1974-77, asst. carrier air traffic control officer USS John F. Kennedy, 1978—. Coach Pee Wee Baseball, 1976. Decorated Air medal. Mem. Am. Phys. Soc., Phi Beta Lambda. Club: Shriners. Home: 441 Prince of Wales Dr Virginia Beach VA 23452 Office: ROTC Unit Savannah State Coll Savannah GA 31404

QADIR, SYED MUHAMMAD ABDUL, chemist; b. Bazid Pure, Bihar, India, July 12, 1943; s. Syed Muhammad Sajjad and Saghira Begum Abdul Rasheed; came to U.S., 1970, naturalized, 1978; B.Sc. with honors (Kolsum-Bai-Valika Merit scholar), Karachi (Pakistan) U., 1964, M.Sc. (Kolsum-Bai-Valika Merit scholar), 1965; m. Rafia Majeed, Jan. 2, 1970; 1 dau., Shabnum Sehar. Quality control chemist E. W. Saybolt Co., Kenilworth, N.J., 1971-73; prodn. chemist Gordon Terminal Service Co., Bayonne, N.J., 1973-77; analytical chemist chem. div. analytical research group PPG Industries, Lake Charles, La., 1977-80, research chemist, environ. research group, 1980—; cons. Assn. Cons. Geologists, Karachi, 1966-70. Fellow Am. Inst. Chemists; mem. Am. Chem. Soc., Sci. Soc. Pakistan, AAAS, Union Concerned Scientists. Developer corrosion inhibitors, gas chromatography method for evaluation of chlorinated hydrocarbons in liquid chlorine. Home: 4712 Green Field Circle Lake Charles LA 70605 Office: PPG Industries Chem Div Columbia Southern Rd Lake Charles LA 70602

QUACH, AHN, chem. engr.; b. Saigon, S. Vietnam, Mar. 24, 1943; s. Tich-Ky and Ngoc-Muci (Lam) Q.; came to U.S., 1966, naturalized, 1977; B.S., Nat. Taiwan U., 1966; M.S., Pa. State U., 1968; Ph.D., Case Western Res. U., 1971; m. Thuyanh To, July 6, 1966; children—James Trivinh, Karen Khailinh. Sr. research chemist PPG Industries, Pitts., 1971-74; scientist Motorola Inc., Phoenix, 1974-75; mem. research staff Xerox Corp., Dallas, 1975—. Am. Chem. Soc. Petroleum Research Fund fellow, 1968-71. Mem. Am. Chem. Soc., Sigma Xi, Phi Lambda Upsilon. Contbr. articles profl. publs. polymer physics, phys. chemistry rheology, scanning electron microscopy, coatings and electronics materials, 1971—. Office: Xerox Corp 1341 W Mockingbird Ln Dallas TX 75247

QUADER, MOHAMMED ANWARUL, orthopedic surgeon; b. Jhenidah, Bangladesh, Dec. 21, 1938; came to U.S., 1973; s. Ebadat Ali and Saleha (Khatoon) Malita; M.D., Dacca Med. Sch. (Bangladesh), 1962; m. Lisa Gaye, June 24, 1976. Intern, Dacca Med. Coll., 1963-67; resident Norfolk & Norwich Hosp., Norwich, Eng., Charing Cross Hosp., London and Royal S. Hants Hosp., Southampton, Eng., 1969-73; practice medicine, specializing in orthopaedic surgery, Madisonville, Ky., 1974-77, Owensboro, Ky., 1977—; staff Hopkins County Hosp., Madisonville, 1974-77, Owensboro-Daviess County Hosp., 1977—, Our Lady of Mercy Hosp., Owensboro, 1977—, Ohio County Hosp., Hartford, Ky., 1978—. Diplomate Am. Bd. Orthopedic Surgery. Fellow Royal Coll. Surgeons Edinburgh; mem. Royal Coll. Surgeons (London), AMA, Ky. Med. Assn., Daviess County Med. Soc., Ohio County Med. Soc. Republican. Islam. Home: 3854 S Griffith St Owensboro KY 42301 Office: 1700 Frederica St Owensboro KY 42301

QUAN, ALICE BROWNE, civic worker, clubwoman; b. Ft. Worth, Apr. 4, 1908; d. Virgil and Maimee Lee (Robinson) Browne; A.B., U. Okla., 1930, M.A. in History, 1939; m. Frank James Quan, Feb. 22, 1966; 1 son, Floyd Davis Raupe. Substitute tchr. history jr. and sr. high schs., Oklahoma City, 1941-45; Okla. state pres. Children Am. Revolution, 1941-45, hon. pres., 1945, nat. v.p., 1945-47, nat. librarian, curator 1947-51, editor yearbook 1941-45; organizing regent, hon. regent DAR, Paul's Valley, Okla., 1947, Okla. state chmn. bldg. fund, 1950-52, Okla. state membership chmn., 1946-50, rec. sec. Okla. state officers club, 1960; Okla. state women's com. chmn. savings bond civ. U.S. Treasury Dept., 1950-64; docent Bklyn. Children's Mus., 1940-41; mem. pres.'s council Sch. of the Ozarks, Mo., 1973—; mem. pres.'s council Oklahoma City, U., 1974—, also mem. adv. council; mem. women's com. Okla. Symphony Soc., chmn. 1950-52; v.p. Okla. Art Center, 1945-46; decoration chmn. Beaux Arts Ball, 1958; hospitality chmn. Town Hall, Oklahoma City, 1967-70; v.p. Civic Music Assn., 1974-75, 76—; adv. com. Oklahoma City Sch. Music, 1975—. Bd. dirs. Oklahoma City Opera, Southwestern Hospitality; mem. nat. council Met. Opera, 1977—. Recipient Outstanding Service award U.S. Treasury Dept. 1962; Spl. Service certificate ARC, 1942-46. Mem. Okla. Soc. Mayflower Descs., Soc. Old Plymouth Colony Descs., Soc. Descs. Knights of Order of Garter (life), Jr. League Oklahoma City (sustaining), Okla. Sci. and Arts Found., Sovereign Colonial Soc. Americans Royal Descent, Order of Washington, English Speaking Union (travel chmn. 1974-76, chmn. membership com. 1976-78), Colonial Order of Crown, Plantagenet Soc., Okla. Assn. Women Hwy. Leaders, Magna Carta Dames, Okla. Art League (pres. 1968-69), Gamma Phi Beta. Presbyterian. Clubs: Ladies Music (v.p. 1957-64), Redbud Women's (pres. 1968-69), Oklahoma City Golf and Country, The Beacon, The '75, Whitehall, Lotus, Mayfair, Embassy (charter), Aristophanian, Chandelle, Colonial Bridge (trophy 1935). Address: 1304 Huntington Ave Oklahoma City OK 73116

QUARLES, CHARLES C., dentist; b. Charleston, W.Va., Feb. 22, 1950; s. Curtis and Emma Lee (Whittington) Q.; B.A., W.Va. U., 1971, D.D.S., 1975. Instr. dept. operative dentistry W.Va. U. Sch. Dentistry, Morgantown, 1975-76; pvt. practice dentistry, Spindale, N.C., 1976—; corporate sec.-treas. Free Spirit Aviation, Inc., Rutherfordton, N.C. Licensed dentist, W.Va., N.C. Mem. ADA, Am. Acad. Gen. Dentistry, Isothermal Dental Soc., Omicron Kappa Upsilon, Xi Psi Phi. Home: 204 Reservation Dr Spindale NC 28160 Office: 204 Reservation Dr Spindale NC 28160

QUARLES, FREDERICK HUNDLEY, III, aircraft co. exec.; b. Charlottesville, Va., June 24, 1940; s. Frederick Hundley and Sara Louise (Hunter) Q., Jr.; m. Hollace Ellen Henkel, Apr. 12, 1969; children—Ashley Louise, Ellen Michelle. Real estate investor, 1965-70; pres. Mooney Mite Aircraft Corp., Charlottesville, Va., 1970-78; dir. Commonwealth Capital Corp., 1978—, D.F.F., Inc., Charlottesville; airline transport pilot, flight instr. in airplanes and instruments; Served with USNR, 1965-67. Mem. U. Va. Alumni Assn., Aircraft Owners and Pilots Assn., Mooney Mite Owners Assn. (exec. dir. 1965-78). Lutheran. Editor Mooney Mite Owners Assn. Bull., 1967—; patentee in field. Office: Box 3999 Charlottesville VA 22903

QUARLES, FREDERICK HUNDLEY, III, aircraft co. exec.; b. Charlottesville, Va., June 24, 1940; s. Frederick Hundley and Sara Louise (Hunter) Q., Jr.; m. Hollace Ellen Henkel, Apr. 12, 1969; children—Ashley Louise, Ellen Michelle. Real estate investor, 1965-70; pres. Mooney Mite Aircraft Corp., Charlottesville, Va., 1970-78; dir. Commonwealth Capital Corp., 1978—, D.F.F., Inc., Charlottesville; airline transport pilot, flight instr. in airplanes and instruments; Served with USNR, 1965-67. Mem. U. Va. Alumni Assn., Aircraft Owners and Pilots Assn., Mooney Mite Owners Assn. (exec. dir. 1965-78). Lutheran. Editor, Mooney Mite Owners Assn. Bull., 1967—; patentee in field. Office: Box 3999 Charlottesville VA 22903

QUATTLEBAUM, DOROTHY EVELYN CLEWIS (MRS. WALTER EMMETT QUATTLEBAUM, JR.), investment exec.; b. Unadilla, Ga., Nov. 1, 1924; d. Otis Clyde and Mabel (DuPree) Clewis; student Puttman Bus. Sch., 1953, Chipola Jr. Coll., 1962-64; m. Walter Emmett Quattlebaum, Jr., Oct. 19, 1946; children—Walter Emmett III, Amalia Ann. Sec.-treas. Sneads Telephone Co., 1948-55, Cottondale Telephone Co., 1954-55, Grand Ridge Telephone Co., 1954-55; sec.-treas., dir. Tri-County Telephone Co., Inc., Bonifay, Fla., 1955-62; asst. to stock analyst Quattlebaum Investments, Bonifay, 1962—. Methodist (pres. Wesleyan service guild 1957, 58). Address: PO Box 56 Bonifay FL 32425

QUATTLEBAUM, THOMAS WALTER, JR., accountant; b. Columbia, S.C., Mar. 23, 1942; s. Thomas Walter and Mabel (Hunt) Q.; B.S., U. S.C., 1965, M.B.A., 1967; m. Patricia Sims, June 18, 1966; children—Patrick Todd, Kelli Lynn. Sales rep. Va. Electric & Power, Clifton Forge, 1965-66, S.C. Electric & Gas, Columbia, 1967; asst. treas. Fed. Land Bank, Columbia, 1968—. Mem. citizens adv. council Campbell Pre-Release Center, 1978—; pres. Columbia FCE Fed. Credit Union, 1977-79; soccer coach YMCA, 1977—, dir., chmn. youth dept., 1978-79; dir., chmn. Contact Help, 1977—; dir., vice chmn. Palmetto Place, 1978-79; vol. Richland County Foster Parents Assn., 1977-79; mem. fin. com. and blood donor resources ARC, 1980. Mem. Nat. Assn. Accountants. Lutheran. Club: Optimist (gov. 1978-79). Home: 204 Valley Springs Rd Columbia SC 29204 Office: PO Box 1499 Columbia SC 29202

QUATTLEBAUM, WALTER EMMETT, JR., telephone co. exec.; b. Midville, Ga., Dec. 22, 1922; s. Walter Emmett and Eva (Bagley) Q.; student Murrey Vocat. Sch., 1941, U. Hawaii, 1943; m. Dorothy Evelyn Clewis, Oct. 19, 1946; children—Walter Emmett, Amalia Ann. Former owner Fla. Telephone Exchange, Sneads, Cottondale, Grand Ridge, Bonifay, Westville and Seagrove Beach; past pres., chmn. bd. dirs. Tri-County Telephone Co., Bonifay; v.p., dir. Seminole Telephone Co., Donalsonville, Ga.; now investment analyst. City councilman, Sneads, 1950-52, pres. City Council, 1953. Served with AUS, 1944-46. Mem. Fla. Telephone Assn. (dir.), Telephone Pioneers Am. Methodist. Address: Bonifay FL 32425

QUEEN, RICHARD KEITH, textile co. exec.; b. Sylva, N.C., Dec. 22, 1948; s. Edwin Wesley and Ollie (Brown) Q.; B.S. Engring., N.C. State U., 1971; M.B.A., U. N.C., 1978; m. Jane Wynette Hill, Apr. 17, 1976; children—Keith Council. Sr. engr. Newport News Shipbldg. (Va.), 1971-73; chief indsl. engr. Environ. Cons., Greensboro, N.C., 1973-74; sr. adminstr. Fairchild Industries, Winston-Salem, N.C., 1974-76; div. mgr. planning and control Hanes Knitwear, Winston-Salem, 1976—. Vice-pres. bd. dirs. Homeowners Assn., 1975-76. Mem. Am. Inst. Indsl. Engrs., Am. Mgmt. Assn., Soc. Mfg. Engrs., Assn. M.B.A. Execs., N.C. State U. Alumni Assn. Moravian. Club: Wolfpack.

QUEEN, RUBY GORDON, decorating service exec.; b. Glenhayes, W.Va., Nov. 7, 1914; s. Checker Stanley and Yorka May (Crum) Q.; student Morehead State Tchrs. Coll., 1933, U. N.M., 1948; m. Doris L. Lockhart, Sept. 5, 1964; children—Rodney G., Jenifer G. Asst. ednl. advisor Civilian Conservation Corps, Paintsville, Ky., 1932-35; owner, operator R.G. Queen Decoration Co., Charleston, S.C. 1969—; v.p., gen. mgr. Allied Engring. & Constrn. Corp., Huntington, W.Va., 1960-65. Served with AUS, 1942-45. Mem. Tug Sandy Central C. of C. (organizer, sec., mng. dir. 1961-62), VFW, Am. Legion. Club: Moose. Poet, portrait painter, sculptor, musician. Address: 615 End St Charleston SC 29407

QUEEN, VIRGINIA, educator; b. Dallas, Oct. 25, 1921; d. James Floyd and Idelia Virginia (Hartsfield) Q.; B.A., Ouachita Bapt. U., 1944, Mus.B., 1944; postgrad. Peabody Tchrs. Coll., summer 1945; Mus.M., Am. Conservatory, Chgo., 1949; postgrad. U. Colo., summer 1954, 56; student Norman Shetler, Vienna, 1967. Tchr. high sch. music, Prescott, Ark., 1944-45; tchr. piano, organ, theory Tenn. Coll. for Women, Murfreesboro, 1945-46; prof. piano, piano pedagogy, theory Ouachita Bapt. U., Arkadelphia, Ark., 1946—; organist First Baptist Ch., Arkadelphia, 1950-65, 69-75. Bd. dirs. Inspiration Point Fine Arts Colony, Eureka Springs, Ark., 1958-64. Mem. Music Tchrs. Nat. Assn. (certified), Ark. State Music Tchrs. Assn. (dir. 1963—, named Outstanding Coll. Piano Tchr. 1979), Nat. Fedn. Music Clubs, Sigma Alpha Iota. Home: 2806 Walnut St Arkadelphia AR 71923 Office: Ouachita Bapt U Box 701 Arkadelphia AR 71923

QUEEN, ZEPHIE RAY, ins. exec.; b. Logan, W.Va., June 21, 1926; s. Bee and Hassie Queen; C.L.U., Am. Coll., 1978; m. Ruby Emma, Mar. 17, 1951; 1 stepson, Kenneth R. Wilson. Clk. Appalchian Power Co., 1950-52; salesman, Nabisco, 1952-62; life underwriter Stonewall Jackson Co., 1962-63; life underwriter Northwestern Mut. Life Ins. Co., Logan, 1963—, spl. agt., 1971—. Mem. Logan City Council, 1970-72; bd. dirs., fund chmn. United Fund, 1979-80; elder First Presbyn. Ch., 1977—. Served with USN, 1944-46; PTO. Mem. VFW (comdr. 1958), Nat. Assn. Life Underwriters, Am. Soc. C.L.U. Republican. Home: 621 Stratton St Logan WV 25601 Office: Box 56 Logan WV 25601

QUENG, JOSEPH T., allergist; b. Fukien, China, Sept. 20, 1933; M.D. (cum laude), U. Santo Tomas, Philippines, 1958; m. Theresa P. Chan. Rotating intern, Kings County Hosp. Center, Bklyn., 1958-59; resident in pediatrics Beth-El Hosp., Bklyn., 1959-60; asst. in pediatrics Baylor Coll. Medicine, Houston, 1960-64, resident in pediatrics, 1960-62, fellow in pediatric allergy, 1962-64, clin. asst. prof. pediatrics, 1969-76, clin. asso. prof., 1977—; asst. prof. pediatrics Far Eastern U. Inst. Medicine, Manila, Philippines, 1965-67; clin. asso. prof. allergy, U. Tex. Grad. Sch. Bio-Med. Scis., Houston, 1970—; chief, pediatric allergy clinic Children's Med. Center, Quezon City, Philippines, 1964-67; St. Luke's Hosp., Quezon City, 1966-67; St. Joseph's Hosp., Houston, 1969—; now practice medicine specializing in allergies, Houston; mem. staff Tex. Children's Hosp., Hermann Hosp., Bayshore Gen. Hosp.; cons. in allergy Rosewood Gen. Hosp. Lectr. on allergies; mem. Sci. adv. council Tex. Allergy Research Found., Houston, 1977—; vice chmn. Children's Med. Center (Philippines) Foundin Am., 1978—. Recipient plaque of appreciation Children's Med. Center, Philippines, Inc., 1977; Mead Johnson Travel grant Am. Coll. Allergists, 1963. Diplomate Am. Bd. Pediatrics, Am. Bd. Allergy and Immunology. Fellow Am. Acad. Allergy, Am. Coll. Allergists, Am. Assn. Certified Allergists, Am. Acad. Pediatrics; mem. Internat. Corr. Soc. Allergists, AMA (physician's recognition award), Tex. Med. Assn., Harris County Med. Soc., So. Med. Assn. (cert. of appreciation 1974), Tex. Pediatric Soc., AAAS, Houston Allergy Soc. (charter), Tex. Assn. Philippine Physicians (gov. 1979—), Sigma Xi. Home: 5742 Reamer St Houston TX 77096 Office: McGovern Allergy Clin 6969 Brompton St Houston TX 77025

QUENTIN, ALBERT PETER, JR., elec. engr.; b. Kiating, Szechuan, China, Nov. 2, 1917; came to U.S., 1957; s. Albert Peter and Caroline Winnifred (Harris) Q.; B.A., U. Toronto, 1941, B.A. in Elec. Engring., 1945; m. Mary G. Matthews, May 4, 1946; children—Peter Trevor, Margaret Suzanne. With Union Carbide Corp., 1948—, mng. dir., Sao Paulo, Brazil, 1958-65, dir. consumer products, Hong Kong, 1969-72, prin. engr. agrl. products div., Jacksonville, Fla., 1977-79. Served with Can. Army, 1945. Profl. engr., Ont., Can. Mem. Can. Power Squadrons. Mem. United Ch. Canada. Home: 13939 Mandarin Oaks Ln Jacksonville FL 32223 Office: Union Carbide 7825 Bay Meadows Way Jacksonville FL 32216

QUESADA, SANDRA, psychologist; b. Miami, Fla., Oct. 9, 1948; d. Jesus Sejas and Dolores (Flores) Q.; B.A. in Psychology, U. South Fla., 1973; M.A. in Psychology, U. West Fla., 1974; postgrad. doctoral program Fla. State U. Cons. and liaison psychologist Child and Family Comprehensive Mental Health Inc., Pinellas County, Fla., 1974-77; adminstrv. psychologist Comprehensive Mental Health Services of Pinellas County, Clearwater, Fla., 1979—. Bd. dirs. Coconut Grove Cares—After School House, 1977-79. Mem. Am. Personnel and Guidance Assn., Am. Psychol. Assn. (asso.), Psi Chi. Office: Comprehensive Mental Health Services of Pinellas County PO Box 4516 Clearwater FL 33516

QUESEP, ADA, real estate broker; b. Guanabacoa, Havana, Cuba; d. Antonio and Amelia (Cancio) Q.; came to U.S., 1962, naturalized, 1973; Prof., Normal Sch. for Tchrs. (Cuba), 1937-41; Ph.D., U. Havana, 1958. Prof., Adult Edn. Center, Guanabacoa, Havana, 1945-62; sec. to asst. adminstr. Cuban Electric Co., Havana, 1947-59, adminstrv. asst., 1959-62; med. sec. Nat. Children's Cardiac Hosp., Miami, Fla., 1962-65; sec. to Dr. Agustin Castellanos, M.D., Miami, 1965-74; staff coordinator U. Miami Hosps. and Clinics, 1974-78, bus. office mgr., 1978—; real estate broker, Miami, 1976—. Lic. real estate broker, Fla. Mem. Miami Bd. Realtors, Miami Multiple Listing Service, Nat. Notary Assn. Roman Catholic. Club: U. Miami Faculty. Home: 3025 NW 4th St Miami FL 33125

QUEYJA, MICHAEL THOMAS, educator; b. Havana, Cuba, Apr. 1, 1926; s. Migual Q. Nunez and Arceli Alvarez (Degado) Queyja; came to U.S., 1948, naturalized, 1953; B.A., U. Miss., 1966, M.A., 1969; m. Mary Ida Morgan, Dec. 24, 1971; 1 son, Thomas Brian. Dir. modern langs. lab., U. Miss., 1966-72, instr. of Spanish, 1966—. Served with U.S. Army, 1952-53; Korea. Decorated Bronze Stars (3). Mem. Miss. Modern Lang. Assn., South Central Modern Langs. Assn., Am. Assn. Tchrs. of Spanish and Portuguese AAUP (v.p. local chpt. 1978), Sigma Delta Pi. Democrat. Roman Catholic. Home: PO Box 2913 University MS 38677 Office: Dept of Modern Languages University MS 38677

QUIGLEY, A. JOSEPH, JR., fin. service co. exec.; b. South Bend, Ind., Mar. 26, 1943; s. Arthur J. and Arlene Frances (Rose) Q.; B.A., St. Joseph's Coll., 1966. With Retail Credit Co. (now Equifax Services), 1966—, unit supr., Chgo., 1971-72, sales rep., Milw., 1972-75, first nat. account exec., Atlanta, 1976—. Named Salesman of Yr., Atlanta chpt. Sales and Mktg. Execs. Internat., 1977. Mem. Ga. Assn. Credit Mgmt. Home: 680 Darlington Circle Atlanta GA 30305 Office: PO Box 4180 Atlanta GA 30302

QUIGLEY, MARTIN MARK, obstetrician, gynecologist; b. N.Y.C., Apr. 18, 1947; s. Martin Scofield and Katherine Julia (Dunphy) Q.; B.S., Georgetown U., 1967, M.D., 1971; m. Jane Maureen Marrion, June 28, 1969; children—Martin Timothy, Patrick Griffin, Brendan Andrew. Rotating intern Naval Hosp., Nat. Naval Med. Center, Bethesda, Md., 1971-72, resident, 1972-75; fellow in reproductive endocrinology and infertility Duke U. Med. Center, Durham, N.C., 1978-80, asst. prof. Dept. Obstetrics and Gynecology, 1979-80; asst. prof., head sect. reproductive endocrinology and infertility, dept. Ob-Gyn, U. Tex. Health Sci. Center, Houston, 1980—. Served with M.C., USNR, 1970-78. Recipient Physician Recognition awards, AMA, 1973—; Merck Manual award, 1971; Research award N.C. United Way Fund, 1979-80. Fellow Am. Coll. Obstetricians and Gynecologists (Conn. sect. chmn. jr. fellows, dist. I, 1977-78); mem. Am. Fertility Soc., F. Bayard Carter Soc. Obstetricians and Gynecologists, Endocrine Soc., Soc. for Study Reproduction. Republican. Roman Catholic. Contbr. articles in field to profl. jours. Office: Dept Ob-Gyn U Tex Health Sci Center 6431 Fannin St Houston TX 77030

QUILLEN, HOWARD EUGENE, dentist; b. nr. Gate City, Va., July 16, 1920; s. Hobart McKinley and Cora Mae (Vermillion) Q.; B.A., Emory and Henry Coll., 1950; postgrad. E. Tenn. State U., 1951, 57-58; D.D.S., Med. Coll. Va., 1962; m. Grace Jacqueline Broadwater, Dec. 31, 1949; children—Jacqueline Ann, Howard Eugene (dec.). Coach, Washington County Sch. Bd., 1948-50, Scott County Sch. Bd., 1950-53, Tazewell County Sch. Bd., 1953-57; pvt. practice dentistry, Gate City, Va., 1962—. Mem. gen. adv. com. Scott County Vocat. Center, 1973—; mem. Scott County Sch. Bd.; bd. dirs. Mountain Empire Community Coll. Served with AUS, 1942-46. Recipient Deleware Valley Outstanding Student award Med. Coll. Va. Dental Sch., 1962. Mem. Acad. Gen. Dentistry, Am. Hist. Soc., Am., Va. State, S.W. Va. (peer rev. com.) dental assns., Smithsonian Assos., Am. Legion, Am. Heritage Soc., Nat. Hist. Soc., AAAS, VFW. Republican. Methodist (fin. com. 1971—). Club: Rotary. Home and Office: PO Box 482 Gate City VA 24251

QUILLEN, JAMES H(ENRY), congressman; b. Wayland, Va., Jan. 11, 1916; s. John A. and Hannah (Chapman) Q.; ed. high sch.; LL.D. (hon.), Steed Coll., Johnson City, Tenn., 1963, Milligan Coll., Tenn., 1978; m. Cecile Cox, Aug. 9, 1952. With Kingsport Press, 1934-35, Kingsport Times, 1935-36; founder, pub. Kingsport Mirror, 1936-39; founder, pub. Johnson City Times, 1939-44, converted to daily, 1940; mem. Tenn. Ho. of Reps., 1954-62, legis. council, 1957-59, 61; mem. 88th-96th Congresses from 1st Tenn. Dist., ranking minority mem. house rules com., mem. Republican leadership of house. Served to lt. USNR, 1942-46. Mem. Am. Legion, VFW, C. of C. Methodist. Clubs: Lions; Ridgefield Country (Kingsport); Capitol Hill (Washington). Home: 1601 Fairidge Pl Kingsport TN 37664 Office: 102 Cannon House Office Bldg Washington DC 20515

QUILLIAN, WARREN WILSON, II, pediatrician; b. Miami, Fla., Jan. 21, 1936; s. Warren Wilson and Rosabel (Brown) Q.; M.D., Emory U., 1961; m. Sallie Ruth Creel, July 26, 1958; children—Rutledge, Ruth, Warren C., Frances. Intern in pediatrics Vanderbilt U., Nashville, 1961-62; resident in pediatrics Children's Hosp. Med. Center, Boston, 1962-63; chief resident in pediatrics Grady Meml. Hosp., Atlanta, 1963-64; practice medicine specializing in pediatrics, Coral Gables, Fla., 1966—; mem. staffs Variety Children's Hosp., Doctor's Hosp., Jackson Meml. Hosp.; asso. clin. prof. pediatrics Sch. Medicine, U. Miami (Fla.); cons. Fla. Div. Med. Services. Bd. dirs. Dade County March of Dimes, 1968-76, Dade County Assn. Retarded Children, 1968-76. Served in M.C., U.S. Army, 1964-66. Diplomate Am. Bd. Pediatrics (bd. dirs., v.p., sec.-treas., pres.-elect). Fellow Am. Acad. Pediatrics; mem. AMA, So., Fla. med. assns., Dade County Med. Assn., So. Soc. for Pediatric Research, So. Perinatal Soc., Fla. Pediatric Soc., Miami Pediatric Soc. Democrat. Methodist. Club: Riviera Country. Contbr. articles to med. jours. Home: 6901 Camarin St Coral Gables FL 33146 Office: 140 Alhambra Circle Coral Gables FL 33134

QUIMBY, MYRON JAY, author; b. San Antonio, June 17, 1922; s. Myron Jay and Martha Eller (Dane) Q.; student U. Md., 1952. Joined U.S. Army, 1941, advanced through grades to 1st lt., 1959; served in Scotland, Eng. France, Luxembourg, Belgium, Germany, Austria, Czechoslovakia; tng. officer Radio Intelligence officer, Ethiopia, 1952-53; French interpreter NATO, Fountainbleau, France, 1957-59; ret. 1959; with Pinkerton's, Sanderson's Secret Service, Burns Internat. Security Service, St. Petersburg, Fla., 1972-78; lectr. pub. libraries Pinellas County, Fla., 1970-78; monthly columnist Evening Ind., St. Petersburg. Decorated Croix de Guerre with palm (France). Mem. St. Petersburg Writers Club (pres. 1972-73). Author: Scratch Ankle, U.S.A., 1969; The Devil's Emissaries, 1969, 4th edit., 1974; Twilight of the Gods, 1976; Cherokee Gold, 1977. Contbr. articles to profl. jours. Home: 1461 52d Ave N Saint Petersburg FL 33703 Office: PO Box 7351 Saint Petersburg FL 33734

QUINN, BARBARA ANN, athletic adminstr.; b. Freehold, N.J., Jan. 13, 1933; d. Walter Stanley and Mary (Craig) Harris; B.S. in Health and Phys. Edn., Ursinus Coll., 1955; M.A., Trenton State Coll., 1968. Dir. phys. edn. for girls Charles Ellis Sch., Newtown Square, Pa., 1956-60; instr. phys. edn. Pennsbury Schs., Yardley, Pa., 1960-63, Exeter Twp. High Sch., Reading, Pa., 1963-66, Hartwick Coll., Oneonta, N.Y., 1966-68; asst. prof. phys. and health edn. Madison Coll., Harrisonburg, Va., 1968-71; instr. phys. edn. Whitemarsh Jr. High Sch., Plymouth Meeting, Pa., 1971-74; dir. women's intercollegiate athletics U. Nev., Las Vegas, 1974-76; dir. women's intercollegiate athletics Simpson Coll., Indianola, Iowa, 1977-78; dir. women's athletics U. N.C., Asheville, 1978—; site dir. Western Region, Women's U.S. Olympic Basketball Trials, Las Vegas, 1976, U.S. Volleyball Assn. Coaches Clinic, Simpson Coll., 1977; chmn. selection com. Va. State Lacrosse Tournament, 1970-71; mem. selection com. So. Dist. Lacrosse Tournament, 1970-71; coach So. dist. team U.S. Women's Lacrosse Assn. Nat. Tournament, 1971; participant 5th Nat. Inst. Girls' Sports Advanced Basketball Coaching, 1969. Mem. AAHPER (sec. coll. div. N.Y. State chpt. 1967), Va. Women's Lacrosse Assn. (chmn. nominations com. 1970-71), Nat. Assn. Phys. Edn. Coll. Women, Nat. Assn. Coll. Athletic Dirs. Address: PO Box 522 26 Lakeshore Dr Weaverville NC 28787

QUINN, VIRGINIA NICHOLS, educator; b. N.Y.C., June 12, 1937; d. Henry Edward and Kathleen Veronica (Farrell) Nichols; B.A., Hunter Coll., 1957; Ed.M., Harvard U., 1960, postgrad., 1960-64; postgrad. U. Va., 1974; m. Paul G. Quinn, Nov. 25, 1964; children—Dana Phyllis, Stephen Nichols. Tchr. Sachem Central Schs., N.Y., 1957-59; research asst. Harvard U., Cambridge, Mass., 1960-63; tech. staff Mitre Corp., Bedford, Mass., 1962-64, Inst. Def. Analysis Weapon Systems Evaluation Group, Washington, 1964-66; dir. psychology Children's Seashore House, Atlantic City, 1969-73; prof. psychology No. Va. Community Coll., Loudoun Campus, Sterling, 1973—; speaker, cons. tchr. assns., PTA's. Mayor Town of Round Hill, Va., 1976-77, planning commr., 1975-76; mem. sch. bd. Pleasantville, N.J., 1972-73; bd. dirs. LWV, Atlantic County, N.J., 1968-71. No. Va. Community Coll. grantee, 1974-77. Mem. Am. Psychol. Assn., Am. Assn. Jr. Colls., Eastern Psychol. Assn. Roman Catholic. Clubs: Harvard (Washington); Hunter Coll. Alumni Assn., Loudoun Preservation Soc., Loudoun Golf and Country, Smithsonian Assos. Author: Psych Path: A Handbook of Instruction, 1979; student workbook for textbook in field, 1979. Home: Mulberry St Round Hill VA 22141 Office: 1000 Harry Flood Byrd Highway Sterling VA 22170

QUINNELLY, ROBERT MARSHALL, social worker; b. Meridian, Miss., Mar. 3, 1937; s. Horace Watkins and Mildred Elizabeth (Thomas) Q.; B.A., Miss. State U., 1959; M.S.W., Tulane U., 1963; m. Janice Gay Bolling, Sept. 21, 1958; children—Karen Elizabeth, Michael Andrew. Chief child welfare services Ga. Dept. Family and Children Services, Atlanta, 1968-70; chief community mental demonstration project Tuscaloosa (Ala.) VA Med. Center, 1970-75; chief social work service VA Center, Tuscaloosa, 1975—. Served with U.S. Army, 1960-61. Lic. cert. social worker, Ala. Mem. Acad. Cert. Social Workers, Nat. Assn. Social Workers (past state bd. Ala. chpt.). Methodist. Office: Loop Rd Tuscaloosa AL 35404

QUINONES, GILDA, rehab. counselor; b. N.Y.C., May 27, 1948; d. Jose and Hilda (Pereyo) Q.; B.A. in Sociology, Coll. Sacred Heart, Santurce, P.R., 1969; M.A. in Rehab. Counseling, U. P.R., 1973. Staff counselor Vocat. Rehab. Program, P.R., 1970—, vocat. rehab. counselor IV, Caguas, 1978—. Recipient award Ospri Acad., 1978; cert. rehab. counselor; lic. rehab. counselor, P.R. Mem. Am. Personnel and Guidance Assn., Am. Rehab. Assn., Nat. Rehab. Assn., Assn. Rehab. Counselors P.R. (treas. 1974-75). Roman Catholic. Author papers in field. Home: 35 Homero Alto Apolo Rio Piedras PR 00927 Office: PO Box 7319 Caguas PR 00625

QUIÑONES, INES MARIA, counselor; b. Vega Baja, P.R., Feb. 15, 1928; d. Eulogio and Reparado (Molina) Pabon; A.D. in Edn., U. P.R., 1947; B.A., Cath. U. P.R., 1966; M.A. InterAm. U., 1967; m. Glidden Quiñones, Dec. 25, 1947; children—Glidden, Erick. Tchr. elem. sch. Rio Piedras, P.R., 1948-57, secondary sch., Rio Piedras, 1957-63; counselor Ponce (P.R.) High Sch., 1964-69; dir. guidance program U. P.R. Ponce Regional Coll., 1970—, asst. prof. edn., 1972—, acting dean students, 1975-76; cons. Council Prevention Drug Abuse. Mem. Coll. Level Counselors Orgn. (founder, pres.), Tchrs. Local Assn. Penuelas (pres.), Tchrs. Assn. P.R., P.R. Personnel and Guidance Assn., Am. Personnel and Guidance Assn. Clubs: Rotary, Lions, Deportivo de Ponce. Home: 707 Dr Loyola St Penuelas PR 00724 Office: Univ Puerto Rico Ponce Regional Coll Box 7186 Ponce PR 00731

QUISENBERRY, GEORGE ROBERT, data processor; b. Richmond, Va., June 22, 1940; s. Robert Smith and Frances (Smethie) Q.; B.S. in Stats., Va. Tech. U., 1963; postgrad. U. Richmond, 1965-68; M.S. in Bus. Mgmt., Va. Commonwealth U., 1972; m. Susan Braemore Gunn, Dec. 20, 1969. Programmer, Va. Dept. Hwys., 1963-65; asst. dir. data processing Richmond public schs., 1965-71; data processing cons. The Computer Co., Richmond, 1971; mgr. systems and programming Miller-Morton Co., Richmond, 1976—. Vice pres., tournament chmn. Richmond Bridge Assn., 1965, 74, 75; chmn. data processing adv. bd. Richmond Tech. Center. Mem. Assn. for Systems Mgmt. (pres. Richmond chpt.), Va. Tech. Alumni Assn. (dir. chpt.). Baptist. Club: Westwood Racquet. Home: 2 Banbury Rd Richmond VA 23221 Office: AH Robins Inc 1407 Cummings Dr Richmond VA 23220

RAAB, SPENCER OLIVER, physician; b. Seattle, Feb. 22, 1926; s. John H. and Floy (Spencer) R.; B.A., U. Buffalo, 1950, M.D., 1954; m. Mary Lane Jerista, Oct. 10, 1970; children—Kelley, Stephen, Katie, Rachel, S. Matthew. Intern, Buffalo Gen. Hosp., 1954-55, asst. resident in medicine, 1955-57; clin. hematology fellow Salt Lake Gen. Hosp., 1957-59; chief clin. fellow Salt Lake County (Utah) Gen. Hosp., 1958-59; research fellow in hematology U. Utah Sch. Medicine, Salt Lake City, 1959-63; practice medicine specializing in hematology and oncology, Phila., N.Y.C., Little Rock; asst. physician Salt Lake County Gen. Hosp., 1958-63; attending physician Salt Lake VA Hosp., 1959-63; asst. chief Woman's Med. Coll. Med. Service, Phila. Gen. Hosp., 1963-66, cons. hematologist, 1963-67; attending physician Phila. VA Hosp., Bellevue Hosp., N.Y. U. Hosp., U. Ark. Med. Center; cons. in internal medicine and hematology VA Hosp., Little Rock, 1971—; asst. prof. medicine Woman's Med. Coll. Pa., Phila., 1963-64, asso. prof. medicine, 1964-67, dir. div. hematology, 1963-67; asst. prof. medicine N.Y. U. Sch. Medicine, 1970-71; asso. prof. medicine U. Ark. Med. Sch. Center, 1971-77; prof. East Carolina Sch. Medicine, Greenville, N.C., 1977—, also chief div. hematology and oncology; cons. hematologist Phila. VA Hosp., 1964-67, VA Hosp., Wilmington, Del., 1966-74; book reviewer Annals of Internal Medicine, 1963—, AMA Archives of Internal Medicine, 1963—; chief hematology div. Cath. Med. Center Bklyn. and Queens, 1967-71, acting dir. medicine, 1970-71. Served with U.S. Army, 1945-46. Diplomate Am. Bd. Internal Medicine, Nat. Bd. Med. Examiners. Mem. Am. Soc. Hematology, A.C.P., Internat. Soc. Hematology, AAUP, Am. Fedn. Clin. Research, Sigma Xi. Contbr. articles on hematology to med. jours. Home: 112 Cardinal Dr

Greenville NC 27834 Office: E Carolina U Sch Medicine Greenville NC 27834

RABIN, JACK MICHAEL, educator; b. Bklyn., Jan. 3, 1945; s. Saul and Etta R.; B.A., U. Miami (Fla.), 1965, M.A., 1967; Ph.D. (NSF fellow, NDEA fellow), U. Ga., 1972; m. Sandra Lynne Clar, Dec. 8, 1979. Instr. public adminstrn. Auburn U., Montgomery, Ala., 1971, asst. prof., 1972-76, asso. prof., 1976—; vis. asso. prof. U. Ga., 1978-79; cons. Exec. Office of Pres., 1972-75. Mem. Am. Soc. Public Adminstrn., So. Polit. Sci. Assn., So. Public Adminstrn. Edn. Found., Inc. (pres.). Editor, So. Rev. Public Adminstrn., 1977—, Jour. Health and Human Resources Adminstrn., 1978—, Internat. Jour. Public Adminstrn., 1979—, Annals Public Adminstrn., 1980—; gen. series editor: Public Administration and Public Policy Series, 1979—. Home: 807 Wesley Dr Montgomery AL 36111 Office: Dept Govt Auburn U Montgomery AL 36117

RABINOWITZ, GEORGE E., obstetrician and gynecologist; b. San Antonio, Feb. 16, 1918; s. Abraham and Sadie (Ladabaum) R.; B.S., St. Mary's U., 1937; M.D., U. Tex., 1942; m. Johanna Bass, June 17, 1947; children—A. Charles, Michael Leigh, Joan Elise. Intern, Mt. Sinai Gen. Hosp., Cleve., 1946-47; resident St. Ann's Hosp., Cleve., 1947-48, Wesley Hosp., Wichita, 1948-49; practice medicine specializing in obstetrics and gynecology, McAllen, Tex., 1949—; asso. prof. U. Tex., Med. Br., Galveston, 1965, U. Tex. Health Sci. Center, San Antonio, 1949-76; staff McAllen Gen. Hosp., Mission Mcpl. Hosp., Edinburgh Gen. Hosp. Chmn. Sub-standard Housing Com., City of McAllen, 1976-77, emergency ambulance vice chmn., 1978-79. Served with USAAF, 1943-46. Diplomate Am. Bd. Obstetrics and Gynecology. Fellow Am. Coll. Obstetricians and Gynecologists (founding fellow), A.C.S.; mem. Phi Delta Epsilon. Jewish. Office: 710 Laurel St McAllen TX 78501

RABOURN, WARREN JOSEPH, JR., chemist; b. Indpls., Nov. 12, 1921; s. Warren Joseph and Mary Olive (Rothenbush) R.; B.S., Purdue U., 1949, M.S., 1950, Ph.D., 1953; m. Hazel Lucille Laird, June 2, 1965; 1 son, Warren Jeffrey. Instr. U. Pitts., 1953-54; postdoctoral fellow, asst. prof. Purdue U., West Lafayette, Ind., 1954-57; chemist Upjohn Co., LaPorte, Tex., 1963—. Bd. dirs. East End YMCA, Houston, 1973—. Served with USNR, 1940-45. Decorated Purple Heart. Mem. A.A.A.S., N.Y. Acad. Sci., Am. Chem. Soc., Am. Legion (comdr. 1959-60), Sierra Club, Sigma Xi. Democrat. Unitarian-Universalist. Eagle. Contbr. articles to profl. jours. Home: 1202 E Princeton Ln Deer Park TX 77536 Office: Upjohn Co Battleground Rd LaPorte TX 77571

RABY, KENNETH NELSON, bank ofcl.; b. Knoxville, Tenn., June 28, 1922; s. Fred S. and Nettie O. (Rash) R.; B.S., U. Tenn., 1947; postgrad. FBI Acad., 1949; m. Mildred L. Epps, Mar. 26, 1943; children—Joanne, Jane, Marcia. Office mgr. Gray Iron Foundry, Knoxville, 1946-49; spl. agt. FBI, 1949-76, supr., 1953-59, asst. agt. in charge, 1959-61; v.p., dir. security United Am. Bank, Knoxville, 1976—; instr. Bank Adminstrn. Inst. Served to capt., inf. U.S. Army, 1943-46. Decorated Bronze Star, Purple Heart. Mem. Former FBI Agt. Soc. (pres. E. Tenn. chpt. 1979-80), Knoxville C. of C., 78th Div. Vet. Assn. (judge adv. 1976—), Knox County Banking Security Assn. (organizer), U. Tenn. Alumni Assn., Delta Sigma Pi. Presbyterian. Club: Rotary. Office: United Am Bank Plaza 800 Gay St Knoxville TN 37929

RACEY, FREDERICK WILLIAM, utility exec.; b. Asheville, N.C., June 9, 1947; s. Frederick Sibert and Mary Emily (Propest) R.; B.S., U. N.C., Chapel Hill, 1969; m. Martha Diane Blake, Aug. 24, 1968; children—Barbara Diane, Frederick William, Jr. Mktg. rep. Carolina Power & Light Co., Raleigh, 1973-74, instr. trainee, 1974-75, instr., 1975-76, tng. supr., 1976-77, mgr. tng., 1977—. Pres., Van Story Hills Homeowners Assn., 1977, chmn. dirs., 1978. Served with USAF, 1969-73. Mem. Am. Soc. Tng. and Devel. Democrat. Baptist. Office: PO Box 1551 Raleigh NC 27602

RACHEL, JAMES NOLAN, accountant; b. Texarkana, Tex., Sept. 5, 1945; s. Harmon H. and Doris E. Rachel; A.B.A., Texarkana Coll., 1966; B.B.A., U. Tex., Austin, 1968; m. Virginia Gayle Talbert, May 29, 1965; children—Susan Gayle, James Talbert. Commd. 2d lt. U.S. Army, 1968, advanced through grades to capt., 1968; served in Vietnam; ret., 1976; accountant Howard-Gibco, Inc., Texarkana, 1971-72; sec.-treas. Mid South Oil Co., Inc., Texarkana, 1972-76; chief fin. exec., controller Mister Twister, Inc., Minden, La., 1976—; partner Carpenter, Rachel & Co., C.P.A.'s, Shreveport, 1979—; exec. cons.; mgmt. cons. various corps. Decorated Bronze Star, Purple Heart, Air Medal with four oak leaf clusters. C.P.A., Tex., Ark., Okla., La. Mem. Am. Inst. C.P.A.'s, Tex. Soc. C.P.A.'s, La. Soc. C.P.A.'s, Tex. Ex-Student Assn. Mem. Ch. of Christ. Club: Lions Internat. Home: 1504 Eames St Minden LA 71055 Office: 3616 Youree Dr Shreveport LA 71105

RACHMEL, LEO, educator; b. N.Y.C., Aug. 31, 1919; s. Jack and Sarah (Winter) R.; B.B.A., Coll. City N.Y., 1940; M.S., U. Richmond, 1964; Ed.D., U. Sarasota, 1972; m. Carolyn Hentshel Miller, June 12, 1943; children—Lee Winter, Sandra Rae (Mrs. David Ellis Evans). Commd. 2d lt. U.S. Army, 1942, advanced through grades to lt. col., 1961; asst. prof. N.C. State U., 1949-53; instr. U.S. Army Logistics Mgmt. Center, Fort Lee, Va., 1962-67, logistics research analyst, 1967-69, chmn. research, devel., test and evaluation dept., 1969-71, dir. intern tng., 1971-74; asst. prof. Sch. Bus. Adminstrn. Va. State Coll., Petersburg, 1966-74, asso. prof., 1974—. Instr. econs. Richard Bland Coll., Petersburg, Va., 1965-66, Coll. William and Mary, Williamsburg, Va., 1965-68; chmn. combined fed. campaign U.S. Army Logistics Mgmt. Center, Ft. Lee, Va., 1971. Mem. Nat. Def. Exec. Res. Office Pres. U.S., 1972—. Bd. dirs. Tri-Cities YMCA, 1973—, pres., 1975-76; bd. dirs. Southside Va. Mental Health Assn., 1966-68. Decorated Army Commendation medal with oak leaf cluster, Bronze Star medal. Recipient Outstanding Performance award U.S. Civil Service, 1967, certificate contract mgmt. Nat. Contract Mgmt. Assn., 1969. Fellow Soc. Logistics Engrs. (chmn. nat. edn. com. 1966-68); mem. AAUP, Am., So. econs. assns., Amateur Athletic Union U.S. (bd. mgrs. Va. assn. 1960-62), Am. Mgmt. Assn., Am. Soc. for Personnel Adminstrn., Va. Bus. Edn. Assn., Am. Contract Bridge League. Home: 2123 Armistead Ave Petersburg VA 23803 Office: Bus Adminstrn Dept Sch Bus Adminstrn Va State Coll Petersburg VA 23803

RADABAUGH, JAMES BENTON, JR., heating, air-conditioning, and refrigeration contractor; b. Greensboro, N.C., May 3, 1939; s. James Benton and Frances Hackney (Ward) R.; student Guilford Coll., 1964-68, U. N.C., Greensboro, 1965-66; children—Christopher Benton, Lisa Gail. Shipping clk. Sears Roebuck and Co., Greensboro, 1964-66; prodn. coordinator Western Electric Co., Burlington, N.C., 1966-69; salesman Pilot Life Ins. Co., Greensboro, 1969-71; serviceman D & W Heating Co., Graham, N.C., 1971-73, Chisholm Service Co., Burlington, N.C., 1973-79; v.p., sec. Rahco, Inc., Burlington, 1979—. Served with USAF, 1957-64. Lic. refrigeration, heating, air-conditioning, and elec. contractor, N.C. Mem. Refrigeration Service Engrs. Soc., ASHRAE, Refrigerating Engrs. and Technicians Soc. Baptist. Club: Masons (Biaritz, France). Home: Route 1 Box 585 Graham NC 27253 Office: PO Box 1149 Burlington NC 27215

RADER, FRANK K., gas transmission co. exec.; b. 1919; B.A., So. Meth. U., 1941; LL.B., Harvard U., 1948; married. With Tex. Gas Transmission Corp., Owensboro, Ky., 1952—, v.p., 1957-61, sr. v.p. regulation, rates, sales, gas supply and corp. planning, 1961-67, exec. v.p., 1967-68, pres., 1968-76, vice chmn. bd., 1976—, also dir. Office: Tex Gas Transmission Corp 3800 Frederica St Box 1160 Owensboro KY 42301*

RADER, JAMES EDWARD, engring. exec.; b. Delaware, Ohio, Feb. 14, 1939; s. Lawrence Harold and Elizabeth Jane (Healy) R.; B.C.E., Ohio State U., 1962; m. Judith Mae Davis, June 10, 1961; children—Melissa Jo, Jill Suzanne, Mary Leigh. Sales engr. Armco Steel Corp., Houston, 1965-67; project engr. Brown & Root, Inc., Houston, 1967-69, Dannenbaum Engring. Corp., Houston, 1969-77; project dir. Mischer Corp., Houston, 1977-78; sr. engr. Putney, Moffatt and Easley, Houston, 1978—; lectr. U. Houston Sch. Real Estate. Mem. adminstrv. bd. Memorial Drive United Meth. Ch., 1978—; youth soccer coach St. Francis De Salle's Soccer Club, 1977, 78; active PTA. Registered profl. engr., Tex., Ohio. Mem. ASCE, Houston Engring. and Sci. Soc., Nat., Tex. socs. profl. engrs., Pi Kappa Alpha. Club: Shriners. Home: 8411 Leader St Houston TX 77036 Office: 908 Town and Country Blvd Houston TX 77024

RADFORD, LOREN EUGENE, physicist, educator; b. Randolph, Neb., Oct. 4, 1928; s. James Arthur and Lydia (Engel) R.; B.S. in Math., U. Wash., 1950; M.S. in Physics, U. Va., 1960, Ph.D. in Physics, 1962; postgrad. U.S. Army Command and Gen. Staff Coll., 1964-65, N.Y. U., 1972-73; m. Lorraine Margaret Morgan, June 9, 1950; 1 son, Loren Eugene. Commd. 2d lt. U.S. Army, 1950, advanced through grades to col., 1970; arty. officer, Europe, U.S., 1950-58; asst. prof. physics U.S. Mil. Acad., 1961-64, asso. prof., 1965-74, ret., 1974; prof. physics, chmn. div. sci. and math. W. Va. No. Community Coll., 1974—. Decorated Legion of Merit with oak leaf cluster. U.S. Army Research Office grantee, 1969-74. Mem. Am. Phys. Soc., Am. Assn. Physics Tchrs., W.Va. Acad. Scis., Phi Beta Kappa, Sigma Xi. Contbr. articles to profl. jours. Home: Shawnee Hills Wheeling WV 26003 Office: WVa No Community Coll Coll Sq Wheeling WV 26003

RADICE, PEARL ROSE, personnel adminstr.; b. Bklyn., Apr. 4, 1935; d. Gerald and Ida Gloria Rose; A.S. cum laude in Mgmt.-Devel., Miami-Dade Community Coll., 1975; B.S. in Marketing-Mgmt., Barry Coll., 1977, M.B.A., 1979; m. Gerard Allan Radice, July 30, 1952 (dec. 1970); children—Helen Marie Radice Dube, Patricia Anne Radice Petersen, Gerard Allen. Sec./bookkeeper Morton Sales Corp., Miami, 1963; sec. Am. Title Ins. Co., Miami, 1963-70, secretarial supr., 1970-74, purchasing agt., 1974-77, human resources officer, 1977—. Mem. Holy Family Sch. Bd., 1977-78; chmn. sec. Holy Family Stewardship Program, 1977-78; campaign coordinator United Way, 1974—; sec. Latin Affairs Com., North Miami Beach, Fla.; vol. ARC, Heart Fund, Community OutReach, Big Bros. and Big Sisters of Greater Miami. Mem. Am. Soc. Personnel Adminstrs., Am. Bus. Women's Assn., M.B.A. Assn., Phi Lambda Pi. Republican. Roman Catholic. Home: 1311 NE 154th St North Miami Beach FL 33162 Office: 1101 Brickell Ave Miami FL 33101

RADLE, A. W., JR., hosp. adminstr.; b. Lott, Tex., Nov. 28, 1937; s. A.W. and Cora Margaret (Tepe) R.; B.S., Sam Houston State Coll., 1961; M.B.A., George Washington U., 1967; m. Sharon Kay Lands, Dec. 11, 1975; 1 dau., Casey Colleen. With Galveston County Meml. Hosp., Texas City, Tex., 1965-69, Oak Cliff Med. and Surg. Hosp., Dallas, 1969-74, Park Cities Surg. Center, Dallas, 1974-75, Mesquite (Tex.) Meml. Hosp., 1975, Brandon (Fla.) Community Hosp., 1975-78; exec. dir. Peachford Hosp., Atlanta, 1978—. Bd. dirs. Health Systems Agy., Hillsborough County, Fla., 1978; mem. adv. bd. Hillsborough Community Mental Health Center, Tampa, Fla. Served with Med. Service Corps, U.S. Army, 1962-64. Mem. Am. Coll. Hosp. Adminstrs., Tex. Hosp. Assn., Assn. Mental Health Adminstrs., Brandon C. of C. (dir.). Roman Catholic. Home: 5009 Buckline Crossing Atlanta GA 30338 Office: Peachford Hosp 2151 Peachford Rd Atlanta GA 30338

RADMANN, WOLF DIETER, lawyer, educator; b. Bergen-Ruegen, Germany, Feb. 5, 1924; came to U.S., 1965; Doktor der Rechte, U. Berlin, 1958; assessor, Frankfurt/Main, 1959; referendar Sch. Law and Econs., U. Mainz, 1950. Cons., Am. Consulate Gen., Frankfurt/Main, W. Ger., 1951-52; asst. dir. internat. ins. dept. Anderson, Clayton & Co., Houston, 1954-57; admitted to German bar, 1959; dir. German C. of C. for Africa, Johannesburg, 1959-62; cons. German Parliamentary Com. Transnat. Corps., Frankfurt/Main, 1963-64; asso. firm Messrs. Moesner & Radmann, Frankfurt/Main, 1963—; asso. prof. internat. law Sch. Public Affairs, Tex. So. U., Houston, 1965—. Mem. Am. Fgn. Law Assn., Am. Soc. Internat. Law, African Studies Assn., Afrika Verein. Author articles in field, also treatise on liability. Home: PO Box 66696 Houston TX 77006 Office: Box 170 Tex Southern Univ Houston TX 77004

RADOMSKI, JACK LONDON, educator, scientist; b. Milw., Dec. 10, 1920; s. Joseph Elwood and Evelyn (Hansen) R.; B.S., U. Wis., 1942; Ph.D., George Washington U., 1950; m. Teresa Pascual, Feb. 19, 1971; children—Mark, Linda, Eric, Janet, Maria. Chemist, Gen. Aniline & Film Corp., Binghampton, N.Y., 1942-44; pharmacologist FDA, Washington, 1944-52, acting chief acute toxicity br., 1952-53; prof. pharmacology U. Miami, Coral Gables, Fla., 1953—. Cons. to WHO, Gen. Accounting Office, EPA, HEW. Recipient Spl. award Commr. FDA, 1952. Mem. Am. Soc. Pharmacology and Exptl. Therapeutics, Soc. Toxicology, Am. Assn. Cancer Research, Internat. Assn. Biochem. Pharmacology. Contbr. articles to profl. jours. Home: Box 311-D Route 3 Andalusia AL 36420 Office: Dept Pharmacology U Miami Med School PO Box 016189 Miami FL 33101

RADVANYI, JANOS, educator; b. Budapest, Hungary, Aug. 24, 1922; s. Geza and Erzsebet (Lanyi) R.; came to U.S., 1962; diploma Acad. Fgn. Affairs (Hungary), 1948, Grad. Sch. Diplomacy (Hungary), 1954; M.A., Stanford, 1969, Ph.D., 1971; m. Julianna Megyeri, Nov. 17, 1951; children—Julianna, Janos. With Hungarian Diplomatic Service, 1948-67, chief of mission, Washington, 1962-67; fellow Center for Internat. Studies, Stanford, 1968-70; prof. history Miss. State U., State College, 1971—. Ford Found. fellow, 1968-70; Rockefeller fellow, 1975-77. Author: Hungary and the Superpowers, 1972; Delusion and Reality, 1978; contbr. articles to profl. jours. Home: 300 Briarwick Dr Starkville MS 39759 Office: Dept History Miss State U State College MS 39762

RADWAY, DOROTHY JEANNE, nurse; b. Zanesville, Ohio, Nov. 29, 1918; d. Ralph Leo and Gladys (Burns) Paul; grad. Grant Hosp. Sch. Nursing, 1940; B.S., Athens Coll., 1972; m. George J. Radway, Mar. 21, 1941; children—George-Ann Radway Duffy, George J., Victoria Jeanne Radway Stora. Pvt. duty nurse, 1941-43; substitute sch. nurse, Fort Worth, 1956-58; substitute public health nurse, Athens, Ala., 1958-59; dir. nursing service Athens Limestone Hosp., 1959-60; practical nurse instr. State of Ala., Huntsville, 1961-72; coordinator practical nurse edn. J.F. Drake State Tech. Coll., Huntsville, 1972—; mem. State Planning Com. for Edn., 1974-75, State Steering Com. for Practical Nurse Edn., 1974-75. Mem. Ala. Edn. Assn., NEA, Ala. Vocat. Assn. (v.p. 1975-76, pres. 1976-77), Am. Vocat. Assn., Ala. Nurses Assn., Am. Nurses Assn. Democrat. Episcopalian. Club: Altrusa (pres.). Home: Route 1 Box 269 Huntland TN 37345 Office: 3421 Meridian St North Huntsville AL 35811

RADZEWICZ, ETHEL COLE, geologist; b. McComb, Miss., Nov. 12, 1929; d. Johnnie Page and Mary Ethel (Carter) Cole; B.S., Millsaps Coll., 1952, B.A., 1963; m. Paul Anthony Radzewicz, Sept. 15, 1949; children—Gene Anthony, Maureen Ethel. Tchr. pub. schs., Jackson, Miss., 1953-59; geologist with Paul Radzewicz, ind. oil producer, Jackson, 1966—; sec. treas. Radzewicz Operating Corp., 1974—; Starboard Oil Co., Jackson, 1963—, Petroc Corp., Natchez, Miss., 1976—. Licensed pvt. pilot. Mem. Miss. Geol. Soc., Gulf Coast, Am. assns. petroleum geologists. Republican. Baptist. Clubs: Ninety-Nine's, Inc., Jackson Yacht, Gulfport Yacht. Office: Suite 1829 Deposit Guaranty Bldg Jackson MS 39201

RADZEWICZ, PAUL ANTHONY, oil co. exec.; b. nr. Hudson County, N.J., Apr. 7, 1925; s. Anthony Radzewicz and Helen (Lewicki) R.; grad. Fort Trumble Maritime Acad., 1944; student Millsaps Coll., 1950-51; LL.B., Jackson Sch. Law, 1951; m. Ethel Odel Cole, Sept. 15, 1949; children—Gene Anthony, Maureen Ethel. Instr. nav. machinery USN, Pearl Harbor, Honolulu, Hawaii, 1941-43; organizing sec., chief engr. internat. S.S. Line, Long Beach, Calif., 1947-49; pres. Starboard Oil Co., Jackson, Miss., 1949—; pres. Anthony's Yachts Co., Jackson, 1968—, Radzewicz Operating Corp. Served with U.S. Maritime Service, 1943-46; PTO. Mem. Am. Petroleum Inst. (pres Miss. chpt. 1968), Jackson Power Squadrons, Ind. Petroleum Assn. Am., Internat. Oil Scouts Assn., Marine Engrs. Benefit Assn., Internat. Assn. Petroleum Landmen, Miss. Landmen's Assn. Clubs: Gulfport (Miss.) Yacht; Patio Jackson Yacht, Jackson Country, University, Capital City-Petroleum (Jackson). Home: 1802 Eastover Dr Jackson MS 39211 Office: Deposit Guaranty Nat Bank Bldg 200 E Capitol St Jackson MS 39201

RAETSCH, BARBARA MORRIS, educator; b. Wilmington, Del., Nov. 7, 1946; d. Robert P. and Frances S. (Prince) Morris; B.A., Winthrop Coll., 1968; M.Ed., U. Ga., 1971, Ed.D., 1973; m. Frederick Carl Raetsch, Aug. 21, 1971; 1 son, Frederick Carl II. Reading tchr. Sumter Sch. Dist. 17, S.C., 1968-70; teaching asst. U. Ga., 1970-72; asst. prof. reading No. Va. Community Coll., Annandale, 1972; asst. prof. edn. Clemson (S.C.) U., 1973—; vis. prof. U. Ga., 1974, Furman U., 1974. Leader Old 96 council Girl Scouts U.S.A., 1968-75. Clemson U. Faculty research grantee, 1974. Mem. Internat. Reading Assn., Coll. Reading Assn., AAUP, Phi Kappa Phi, Kappa Kappa Iota, Phi Delta Kappa, Kappa Delta Pi. Home: Route 4 Stone Creek Cove Anderson SC 29624 Office: Godfrey Hall Clemson Univ Clemson SC 29631

RAFALSKY, LLOYD ALVES, steel co. exec.; b. Alpine, Tex., Apr. 21, 1920; s. Paul William and Ann Mae (Alves) R.; B.S., Tex. A. and M. Coll., 1941; m. Marjorie Dieter, June 9, 1941; children—Lloyd Arthur, Lee Paul, Diane Lynn, Celeste Ann. Engr. trainee Truscon Steel Co., Youngstown, Ohio, 1946-48, dist. engr., Birmingham, Ala., 1948-56; chief engr. Connors Steel Div., Birmingham, 1956-62, sales mgr., 1962-64; pres., chmn. bd. L & L Steel Corp., Helena, Ala., 1964—; chmn. bd. Ironco Mfg. Co., Inc., Helena, 1970—; dir. Bank Pelham (Ala.), 1972—, mem. exec. com., 1974—. Mem. Nat. Fedn. Ind. Bus., Ala. Credit Execs., Nat. C. of C. Lion (pres. 1961-62). Home: 2212 Royal Crest Circle Vestavia AL 35216 Office: PO Box 304 Helena AL 35080

RAFFALOVICH, VICTOR ALAN, computer sales co. mgr.; b. Atlanta, Sept. 22, 1946; s. Alan Gergor and Alys Goulden R.; student Ga. Inst. Tech., 1964-69; B.S. in Bus. Mgmt., Troy State U., 1977; m. Rebecca Ann Manley, June 10, 1972. Zone mgr. Burroughs Corp., Montgomery, Ala., 1977—. Served with U.S. Army, 1968-76. Decorated Army Commendation medal; recipient Wall St. Jour. award, 1977. Mem. Center for Study of Presidency, Gamma Beta Phi. Episcopalian. Home: 201 White Dr Troy AL 36081 Office: Burroughs Corp 2401 Fairlane Dr Montgomery AL 36116

RAFFERTY, FRANK THOMAS, psychiatrist; b. Greenville, Miss., Jan. 28, 1925; s. Frank Thomas and Mary (Jordan) R.; B.S., St. Mary's Coll., Winona, Minn., 1948; M.D., St. Louis U., 1948; children—F. Thomas, Margaret, Gerard, Elizabeth, Anne, Jennifer, Christine. Intern, St. Louis City Hosp., 1948-49; resident Colo. Psychopathic Hosp. of U. Colo., 1948-53; dir. Utah Child Guidance Center, Salt Lake City, 1956-61; asst. prof. U. Utah, 1957-61; dir. div. child psychiatry Psychiat. Inst. U. Md., 1961-71; prof. U. Md., 1966-71; prof. U. Ill., 1971-79; dir. Inst. Juvenile Research, Chgo., 1971-79; med. dir. The Brown Schs., Austin, Tex., 1979—; vice chmn. State Mental Health Reps for Children and Youth, 1978—. Served with U.S. Army, 1949-55. Diplomate Am. Bd. Psychiatry and Neurology. Mem. Am. Psychiat. Assn., Am. Acad. Child Psychiatry, Soc. Profs. Child Psychiatry, Am. Soc. Adolescent Psychiatry, Am. Orthopsychiat. Assn., Am. Assn. Psychiat. Services for Children, Am. Assn. Residential Treatment Centers, Am. Assn. Dirs. Psychiat. Residency Tng. Contbr. articles in field to profl. jours. Home: 8130 Greenslope St Austin TX 78759 Office: 1110 E 32d St Austin TX 78722

RAGAN, ELIZABETH HOFFMAN (MRS. HERBERT TOMLINSON RAGAN), wholesale co. exec.; b. Albemarle, N.C., Nov. 11, 1916; d. Joseph Filson and Lilly Bassett (Carter) Hoffman; certificate bus. adminstrn. High Point Coll., 1937; m. Herbert Tomlinson Ragan, Oct. 14, 1939; 1 son, Herbert Tomlinson. Head bond dept. Sunflower Ordnance Works, Hercules Powder Co., DeSota, Kan., 1942-45; sec.-treas. Ragan-Carmichael, Inc., High Point, N.C., 1956-74, Staple Products, Inc., High Point, 1956-74, R & C Holding Co., Inc., High Point, 1956-74, sec. Ragan Hardware Co., Inc. (merger), High Point, 1974—; trustee Ragan-Carmichael, Inc. Profit Sharing Trust and Pension Trust. Cellist N.C. Symphony, 1932-35. Mem. adv. bd. Maryfield Nursing Home, 1975-79. Mem. High Point Hist. Soc. (dir. 1977—, pres. 1979-80). Democrat. Mem. Soc. of Friends (organist, choir dir.). Author, compiler: The Lineage of the Amos Ragan Family, 1976. Home: 201 Lake Dr E Thomasville NC 27360 Office: 1116 Ward St High Point NC 27261

RAGAN, SEABORN BRYANT TIMMONS, oil co. exec.; b. Augusta, Ga., Apr. 28, 1929; s. Alexander Timothy and Ela Lucille (Timmons) R.; student Emory U., 1946-49, U. Ga., 1952-53; A.B., Ga. State Coll., 1960; m. Sandra Glyn Farris, Sept. 5, 1958; children—Seaborn Bryant Timmons, Sandra Leigh. With Gulf Oil Co., various locations, 1957—, v.p. Korea Oil mktg. ops., Seoul, Korea, 1967-73, dist. mktg. mgr., Phila., 1973-76, project mgr. new products and new bus. devel., mktg. coordination, Houston, 1976-79, coordinator survey research, 1979—. Counselor, USO, Korea, 1972-73. Served with U.S. Army Res., 1948-60. Mem. alumni exec. com. Salisbury Sch., Conn., 1975-76, S.W. field rep., 1976—. Mem. SAR, Audubon Soc., Soc. Archtl. Historians, Nat. Trust for Historic Preservation, Early Am. Soc., Nat. Hist. Soc., Nat. Geog. Soc., Smithsonian Assos., Am. Mus. Natural History, Am. Enterprise Inst. for Pub. Policy Research, Nat. Archive Asso., Victorian Soc. in Am., Houston Bd. Realtors, Costeau Soc., Oceanic Soc., Am. Mktg. Assn. Republican. Episcopalian. Club: Wilchester. Home: 13502 Barryknoll St Houston TX 77079 Office: PO Box 2001 Houston TX 77001

RAGONE, STANLEY, utilities co. exec.; b. Norfolk, Va., May 7, 1925; s. Vincent George and Jennie (Gross) R.; B.S. in Mech. Engring., Va. Poly. Inst. and State U., 1947, M.S., 1948; m. Bertha Perlin, Sept. 5, 1954; children—Vernon George, Mitchell Floyd, Sharon. With Va. Electric and Power Co., 1948—, mgr. Richmond dist., 1965-66, mgr. electric ops., 1966-67, v.p. power, 1967-73, sr. v.p. power, 1973-77, exec. v.p., 1977-78, pres., chief operating officer, dir., 1978—; dir. United Va. Bank, Richmond, Dana Corp.; dir. Atomic Indsl. Forum, Am. Nuclear Energy Council; mem. Gov.'s Coal and Energy Study Commn. Served with USNR, 1944-46. Registered profl. engr., Va. Fellow ASME, Va. Acad. Sci. (trustee); mem. AAAS, Va. Sci. Mus. Found. (dir.). Jewish. Clubs: Oak Hill Golf, Masons, Shriners. Office: 1 James River Plaza PO Box 26666 Richmond VA 23261

RAGSDALE, CHALON LAND, educator; b. McLeansboro, Ill., June 27, 1952; s. Frank Darrell and Carol Jordan (Land) R.; B.S., Auburn U., 1973; M.Mus., East Carolina U., 1975; m. F. Dell Martin, Sept. 16, 1972; 1 son, Chalon Aaron. Dir. instrumental music Reeltown (Ala.) High Sch., 1973-74; grad. teaching asst. East Carolina U., Greenville, N.C., 1974-75; asso. prof. percussion, asst. band dir. U. Ark., Fayetteville, 1975—; percussion and band clinician; festival judge. Mem. Percussive Arts Soc., Nat. Assn. Coll. Wind and Percussion Instrs., Music Educators Nat. Conf., Ark. Sch. Band and Orch. Assn., Ark. Bandmasters Assn., Phi Beta Mu, Pi Kappa Lambda, Kappa Delta Pi. Home: 830 N Willow St Fayetteville AR 72701 Office: Band Bldg U Ark Fayetteville AR 72701

RAGSDALE, PAUL, state legislator; b. Jacksonville, Tex., Jan. 14, 1945; s. Emmittee Arnwine R.; B.A. in Sociology, U. Tex., Austin, 1966. Social scientist Tracor, Inc., Austin, 1966-68; chief planning and evaluation Crossroads Community Center, Dallas, 1968-72; mem. Tex. Ho. of Reps., 1973—; project dir. E. Tex. Project. Mem. NAACP. Democrat. Methodist. Home: 5206 Rocky Ridge St Dallas TX 75241 Office: 1209 E Red Bird Ln Dallas TX 75241

RAHALL, NICK JOE, II, Congressman; b. Beckley, W.Va., May 20, 1949; s. Nick Joe and Alice R.; A.B., Duke U., 1971; postgrad. George Washington U.; m. Helen McDaniel, Aug. 19, 1972; children—Rebecca Ashley, Nick Joe. Staff asst. U.S. Sen. Robert C. Byrd (D-W.Va.), 1971-74; sales rep. WWNR Radio, Beckley, 1974; pres. Mountaineer Travel, Inc., Beckley, 1975-77; mem. 95th-96th Congresses from 4th W.Va. Dist.; mem. Interior and Insular Affairs and Pub. Works and Transp. Coms. Ho. of Reps.; dir. Rahall Communications Corp. Del., Democratic Nat. Conv., 1972, 74, 76, 78. Named Outstanding Young Man in W.Va., 1977. Mem. Beckley Jr. C. of C. (Young Man of Year 1972). Presbyterian. Clubs: Masons, Shriners, Rotary, Elks, Moose. Office: 408 Cannon House Office Bldg Washington DC 20515

RAHE, FREDERICK ALBERT, audiologist; b. Chgo., Feb. 24, 1954; s. Harris Lee and Dorothy Irene (Nelson) R.; B.A., U. Fla., 1975, M.A., 1976. Audiologist, Plantation Ear, Nose and Throat Clinic (Fla.), 1977-78; audiologist, co-founder W. Broward Hearing Diagnostic Lab., Plantation, 1978—. Mem. Am. Speech-Lang.-Hearing Assn. (cert. clin. competence), Fla. Speech, Lang. and Hearing Assn. (chmn. audiology standards com. 1979—, chmn. audiology program 1980 conv.), So. Audiol. Soc., Soc. Med. Audiology, Am. Tinnitus Assn. Democrat. Club: Rotary. Home: 2330 NW 110th Terr Sunrise FL 33322 Office: W Broward Hearing Diagnostic Lab 4101 S Hospital Dr Suite 9 Plantation FL 33317

RAIFORD, DANIEL BURNLEY, computer programmer; b. Franklin, Va., Jan. 26, 1939; s. William Burnley and Pauline (Terrell) R.; B.S. (Dana scholar), Guilford Coll., 1963; M.A. (NASA grantee), Coll. William and Mary, 1965; m. Betty Elizabeth Pyrtle, Aug. 3, 1963; children—Laura Kristen, Matthew Jackson. Sr. devel. engr. Albemarle Paper Co., Roanoke Rapids, N.C., 1966-68; programmer analyst Space Radiation Effects Lab., Newport News, Va., 1968-72; systems analyst U. Wyo., Laramie, 1972-76; mgr. systems and programming Distributed Data Systems, Inc., Raleigh, N.C., 1976—. Served in USAF, 1956-60. Home: 6901 Oak Ridge Dr Raleigh NC 27612 Office: Box 18305 Raleigh NC 27609

RAIFORD, ERNEST LEE, former YMCA exec.; b. Greensboro, N.C., Feb. 16, 1905; s. Ernest Eugene and Nannie Lewis (Tillery) R.; B.S., Howard U., Washington, 1928; postgrad. U. Pa., U. Mich., U. So. Calif.; m. Blanche Marie Reynolds, June 15, 1931; children—Josephine Anne Raiford Hinton, Roger Lee, Linda Marie Raiford Fowler. Tchr., Dudley High Sch., Greensboro, 1930-41; founder Jesse Moorland YMCA, Greensboro, 1932; dir. USO, Tuskegee Inst., Ala., 1941-42, Augusta, Ga., 1943, at 12th St. YMCA, Washington, 1944-45; gen. dir. Raleigh (N.C.) YMCA, 1946-79; ret., 1979. Mem. Raleigh Community Action Council, 1974-77; exec. com. Wake County Democratic Club, 1974-77. Named Citizen of Year, Raleigh Community Relations Commn., 1972; recipient Meritorious Citizenship award St. Augustine's Coll., Raleigh, 1973. Mem. Nat. Assn. Profl. YMCA Dirs., Acad. Polit. and Social Scis., Nat. Task Force on Strengthening YMCA in Black Communities, Phi Beta Sigma. Methodist. Home: 1010 Benbow Rd Greensboro NC 27406

RAINBOW, EDWARD LOUIS, musician; b. Waterloo, Iowa, June 18, 1929; s. Everett W. and Bessie E. R.; B.A., No. Iowa U., 1955, M.A., 1956; Ph.D., U. Iowa, 1963; children—Pamela, Charles, James, Thomas. Profl. musician, 1947-51; tchr. pub. schs., Davenport, Iowa, 1956-60; instr. music U. Iowa, 1961, U. of Pacific, 1961-66; asso. prof. music N. Tex. State U., 1966-78, prof. music, 1978—; chmn. Music Edn. Research Council, 1976-78; mem. Ft. Worth Symphony Orch., 1966-80; rep. Internat. Seminar in Music Edn. Research, Gummersbach, Germany, 1972, Mexico City, 1974, Graz, Austria, 1976, Bloomington, Ind., 1978. Served with U.S. Army, 1951-53. Mem. Music Educators Nat. Conf., Internat. Music Educators, Am. Fedn. Musicians. Democrat. Contbr. articles to profl. jours. Home: Rt 1 Yacht Club Estates Frisco TX 75034 Office: Sch Music North Tex State U Denton TX 76203

RAINER, JACKSON PATTEN, music therapist; b. Tifton, Ga., Nov. 15, 1954; s. Joel Price and Helen Patten R.; Mus.B. in Music Therapy magna cum laude, Fla. State U., 1976; M.Ed. in Counseling Psychology, Ga. State U., 1980; m. Jimmie Karen Mitchell, Dec. 9, 1978. Activities therapist Goodwood Nursing Home, Tallahassee, 1975-76; mental health treatment coordinator, music therapist Kennestone Hosp., Marietta, Ga., 1977-78; sr. music therapist Ga. Mental Health Inst., Atlanta, 1978—; behavior modification specialist Metro Weight Control Clinic, Atlanta, 1977—; vol. faculty mem. Appalachian Primary Health Care Project; pvt. practice community arts cons. U.S. cultural rep. Internat. Trade Fair, Damascus, Syria, 1974. Registered music therapist. Mem. Nat. Assn. Music Therapy (v.p. southeastern conf.), Am. Personnel and Guidance Assn., Kappa Kappa Psi (life). Democrat. Presbyterian. Office: Ga Mental Health Inst 1256 Briarcliff Rd NE Unit Four Atlanta GA 30306

RAINES, EDWIN LEE, communications analyst; b. Seminole, Okla., Jan. 13, 1940; s. Forrest Lee and Ruth Virginia (Matthews) R.; B.A. in Liberal Arts, Rice U., 1961; m. Virginia Gail Anderson, June 4, 1961; 1 dau., Susan Leigh. Trainee, Southwestern Bell Telephone Co., Houston, 1965-66, wire chief, Marlin, Tex., 1966-68, supr., foreman, Houston, 1968-71; ops. mgr. Arcata Communications Co., 1971-72, western U.S. ops. mgr., 1972-74; mgr. voice communications Occidental Petroleum Corp., Houston, 1974-79; mgr. telecommunications ops. and planning div. Huessner Info. Systems, Houston, 1979—. Served with USN, 1961-65. Mem. Internat. Communications Assn., Petroleum Industry Elec. Assn., S. Tex. Communications Assn. (founder, 1st pres.), Rice Alumni Assn., Full Gospel Businessmen's Fellowship. Democrat. Office: 13934 Saint Mary's St Houston TX 77079

RAINES, JEFF, biomed. scientist, med. research dir.; b. N.Y.C., Sept. 5, 1943; s. Otis J. and Mildred C. (Wetzler) R.; B.S. in Mech. Engring., Clemson U., 1965; M. in Mech. Engring., U. Fla., 1967; Ph.D. in Biomed. Engring. (NIH fellow), M.I.T., 1972; m. Arnita Marlene Halyburton, July 1, 1978; 1 dau., Gretchen Christena. Mem. staff M.I.T., Cambridge, 1968-70; biophysicist dept. surgery Mass. Gen. Hosp., Boston, 1972-73, dir. Vascular Lab., 1972-77; instr. surgery Harvard Med. Sch., Boston, 1973-77; preceptor Harvard/M.I.T. Sch. Health Scis., 1976-77; research dir., dir. Vascular Lab., Miami (Fla.) Heart Inst., Miami Beach, 1977—; adj. asst. prof. bioengring. U. Miami, Coral Gables, 1977—; adj. prof. surgery U. Miami (Fla.) Sch. Medicine, 1977—; prin. investigator series drug studies NIH and pharm. firms, 1977—; Harvard Travelling fellow lectr. in Europe, 1975. Recipient Apollo Achievement award NASA, 1969. Fellow Am. Coll. Cardiology, Am. Assn. of Physicists in Medicine; mem. Biomed. Engring. Soc., Instrument Soc. Am., Am. Heart Assn., Internat. Cardiovascular Soc., Cardiovascular System Dynamics Soc. (founding mem.; editor 1976—), New Eng. Cardiovascular Soc., AAAS, ASME, Sigma Xi, Tau Beta Pi. Republican. Presbyterian. Clubs: Kiwanis; La Gorce Country; Harvard, M.I.T. Contbr. numerous articles on biomechanics, cardiovascular dynamics and instrumentation to sri. jours.; patentee med. devices; developer math. models of arterial hemodynamics and clin. use of autotransfusion. Office: 4701 N Meridian Ave Miami Beach FL 33140

RAINEY, DENNIS RODGERS, mortgage co. exec.; b. Cullman, Ala., Mar. 29, 1950; s. Dennis W. and Dorothy (Rodgers) R.; B.A., U. Ala., 1972. With Mortgage Corp. of South and predecessor firms, Birmingham, Ala., 1972-78, 79—, v.p., div. mgr. loan closing div., 1978, v.p. corp. adminstrn., 1979—; mgr. prodn. adminstrn. Arvida Mortgage Co., Miami, Fla., 1978-79. Mem. Birmingham Mortgage Assn. (chmn. 1975-76), Mortgage Bankers Assn. Am., Mortgage Bankers Assn. Ala. Home: 557 Shades Crest Rd Birmingham AL 35226 Office: 2119 6th Ave N Birmingham AL 35203

RAINEY, JOHNNIE MAE, educator; b. Atlanta, Ga., Dec. 12, 1937; d. John Webster and Izella (Knox) Upshaw; A.B., Clark Coll., 1960; M.A., Atlanta U., 1963, Ed.S., 1970; postgrad. Ga. State U., 1978—; m. James Rainey, Aug. 19, 1964; children—Jamesa Michelle, Jena Melissa. Tchr., Jefferson County (Ga.) Bd. Edn., 1960-61; tchr., counselor Paulding County (Ga.) Bd. Edn., 1961-62; counselor, instr. Clark Coll., Atlanta, Ga., 1963-66; counselor Atlanta Bd. Edn., 1966—; chmn. guidance dept. Northside High Sch., Atlanta, 1974-77; chmn. guidance dept. Grady High Sch., Atlanta, 1978—. Cons. YWCA Youth Workshop on Career Edn. undergrad. advisor Zeta Phi Beta, Clark Coll., 1963-66. Mem. steering com. YWCA; dir. edn., mem. service guild, mem. adminstrv. bd., council on ministries United Meth. Ch. Recipient Chi Mu Epsilon scholar, 1956; NDEA Guidance Inst. grantee, 1962-63. Mem. Am., Ga. personnel and guidance assns., Ga. Assn. of Educators, Nat., Atlanta edn. assns. Democrat. Home: 255 Carter Ave SE Atlanta GA 30317 Office: Grady High School 929 Charles Allen Dr NE Atlanta GA 30309

RAINEY, LUTRELLE DELANO, clergyman, coll. counselor, instr.; b. Newport News, Va., Dec. 28, 1945; s. Howard Harrison and Fannie (Davis) R.; A.B., Va. Union U., 1968; M.Div., Pitts. Theol. Sem., 1972; M.S.W., U. Pitts., 1972; postgrad. Union Theol. Sem., 1974—; Ed.S., U. Va., 1978; m. Alice Paulette Turner, Jan. 3, 1970; children—Lisa Dionne, Lutrelle Delano. Asst. dir. Urban Indsl. Ministries, Aliquippa, Pa., 1970-72; project dir. Richmond (Va.) Redevel. and Housing Authority, 1972; exec. dir. Charles City-New Kent CAA, Inc., Providence Forge, Va., 1973; ordained to ministry Baptist Ch., 1970; pastor First Bapt. Ch., Lexington, Va., 1973-74; asst. dean students Washington and Lee U., 1973-74; instr. sociology, coordinator Info. and Referral Center, Va. State Coll., Petersburg, 1974-75, dir. Coll. Counseling Center, 1975-77; instr. dept rehab. counseling Va. Commonwealth U., 1979—; pastor Shiloh Bapt. Ch., Chesterfield County, Va., 1975—. Mem. Gov.'s Manpower Service Council, 1975—; trustee, mem. exec. bd. Children's Home of Va. Bapt., Inc.; bd. dirs., v.p. Manpower Action Caucus of Richmond. Named Outstanding Young Man of Am., 1974; Gov.'s grantee U. Va., 1976—; registered social worker, Va. Mem. Nat. Personnel and Guidance Assn., Nat. Coll. Personnel Assn., NAACP, Va. Council on Social Welfare, Bapt. Gen. Conv. Va., Progressive Nat. Bapt. Conv., Goodwill Chorus of Petersburg and Vicinity, Bapt. Ministers Conf. Petersburg and Vicinity. Home: 104 Diagonal Rd Petersburg VA 23803 Office: 6711 Hickory Rd Petersburg VA 23803

RAINOSEK, JACKALYN, therapist, cons.; b. Iraan, Tex., Apr. 14, 1942; d. Emil Pete and Mary Claude (Norwood) R.; B.A., U. Tex., Austin, 1964; M.Ed., S.W. Tex. State U., 1971, postgrad. Tex. A. and M. U., 1972—. Tchr., Del Rio (Tex.) High Sch., 1966-68, Crockett High Sch., Austin, 1968-69; psychometrist Austin Ind. Sch. Dist., 1971-73; counselor, cons. Allen Jr. High Sch., Austin, 1973-74; teaching asst. Tex. A. and M. U., College Station, 1975-76; intern inpatient and outpatient therapy Brazos Valley Mental Health Center, Bryan, Tex., 1975-76; pvt. practice cons. and psychotherapy, specializing in working with chronic illness (Simmonton method), Houston, 1976—; profl. mem. Nat. Tng. Lab. Mem. Am. Psychol. Assn. (asso.), Am. Personnel and Guidance Assn., Assn. Humanistic Psychology, Internat. Assn. Applied Social Scientists, Internat. Acad. Cancer Counselors and Consultants (sec.-treas. 1979-80). Home: 15002 Elmont Dr Houston TX 77095 Office: 6100 Richmond St Suite 114B Houston TX 77057

RAINS, DALE OSBORN, educator; b. Natchitoches, La., Oct. 22, 1936; s. John Franklin and Vera Mae (Osborn) R.; B.A., Baylor U., 1958, M.A., 1963; Ph.D., La. State U., 1976. Tchr., Bay City (Tex.) High Sch., 1960-63, LaPorte (Tex.) High Sch., 1963-67; mem. faculty dept. speech and drama Presbyn. Coll., Clinton, S.C., 1967—, asso. prof., 1979—. Recipient Disting. Service citation Bay Area Fine Arts Assn., La Porte, 1967. Mem. Am. Theatre Assn., Southeastern Theatre Conf., S.C. Theatre Assn. (dir., v.p. 1978-79, pres. 1979—), Laurens County Arts Council, Mensa, AAUP. Democrat. Episcopalian. Home: PO Box 57 Clinton SC 29325 Office: Presbyterian Coll Clinton SC 29325

RAINS, THOMAS NELSON, real estate exec.; b. Atlanta, Apr. 15, 1941; s. Baxter Smith and Elinor (Nelson) R.; A.B., Washington and Lee U., 1963; m. Laura Whitner Dorsey, Dec. 10, 1963; children—Laura Whitner, Adair Baxter. Comml. officer 1st Nat. Bank Atlanta, 1964-69; account exec. Eastman, Dillon, Union Securities, Atlanta, 1969-71; pres. The Rains Co. and affiliates, Atlanta, 1971—. Bd. dirs. Big Bros. Assn. Atlanta, 1970-77; mem. Hosp. Authority Fulton County, 1978—. Served as 1st lt. U.S. Army, 1964-66. Mem. Atlanta Bd. Realtors (affiliate), Atlanta C. of C. (dir. 1976-79), Westminster Schs. Alumni Assn. (pres. 1977). Presbyterian. Club: Piedmont Driving (Atlanta). Home: 130 The Prado NE Atlanta GA 30309 Office: 2006 Peachtree Center-Cain Tower 229 Peachtree St NE Atlanta GA 30303

RAINS, WAYNE ALAN, land use specialist; b. Robinson, Ill., Nov. 2, 1944; s. Harry Emmitt and Annis Marjorie (Vinsel) R.; A.S., Wabash Valley Coll., 1969; B.S., So. Ill. U., 1971; m. Faye Louise Wiswall, June 28, 1969; children—Andrew Jason, Cynthia Alayne. Soil scientist Soil Conservation Service, Ashland, Ohio, 1971; land use specialist TVA, Paris, Tenn., 1971—. Bd. dirs. Cottage Grove (Tenn.) Vol. Fire Dept., 1975-76, chmn., 1976; mem. Henry County (Tenn.) Sch. Bd., 1977-78; mem. Tchr. Corps Community Council, 1978-79; bd. dirs. Little League, 1979; vol. fireman, 1975-79; pres. Henry County Helping Hand, 1979. Served with USMC, 1963-67. Pres. fellow So. Ill. U., 1971. Mem. Soc. Am. Foresters, Forest Farmers Assn., Am. Forestry Assn. Home: Box 270 Route 1 Cottage Grove TN 38224 Office: Box 280 W Blythe Paris TN 38242

RAINWATER-BRYANT, BRENDA JOY, educator; b. Laurel, Miss., May 24, 1951; d. Rush and Zeline Burgess R.; student Jones County Jr. Coll., Ellisville, Miss., 1969-70; B.S., U. So. Miss., 1973, M.Ed., 1976; postgrad. Jackson State U., 1977-79, Memphis State U., 1979—; m. Gregory W. Bryant. Tchr., dormitory staff Ellisville State Sch., 1973-74, head tchr. Satellite Center, 1974-75; coordinator homebound program for physically handicapped Miss. Crippled Children's Treatment and Tng. Center, Jackson, 1976-77, adminstrv. asst., 1977-78, acting dir., 1978-79; mem. part-time faculty U. So. Miss. Mem. Am. Assn. Mental Deficiency, Council Exceptional Children, Phi Kappa Phi, Kappa Delta Pi. Methodist. Home: 3596 Walker Apt 6 Memphis TN 38111

RAISIG, ARTHUR GEORGE, petroleum engr.; b. Wichita, Kans., Mar. 31, 1922; s. George Alexander and Katherine Elizabeth (Lochmann) R.; student U. Wichita, 1940-43; B.S., U. Okla., 1948; m. Betty Marie Osler, Oct. 14, 1943; children—Patricia Ann Raisig Siblo, Paul Arthur. Petroleum engr. Atlantic Refining Co., Dallas, 1948-52, regional reservoir engr., 1952-61, sr. engr., Tyler, Tex., 1961-70; dist. engr. Atlantic Richfield Co., Tyler, 1970—. Bus. capt. Dallas Heart Assn., 1960-61. Republican precinct chmn., Dallas, 1952. Served with USAAF, 1943-45. Decorated Bronze Star medal. Registered profl. engr., Tex. Mem. Soc. Petroleum Engrs. of Am. Inst. Mining, Metall. and Petroleum Engrs., (chpt. dir. 1972-73), Tau Beta Pi, Sigma Tau. Methodist (adminstrv. bd. 1968-76). Home: 3107 DeCharles St Tyler TX 75701 Office: PO Box 9000 Tyler TX 75711

RAIT, ROBERT ALEXANDER, petroleum co. exec.; b. Lincoln, Nebr., Mar. 10, 1911; s. Alexander Hamilton and Ida (Hoffman) R.; B.S. in Civil Engring., U. Nebr., 1933; m. Sybil Frances Smith, June 11, 1939; children—Rosemary (Mrs. David Sykes), Patricia (Mrs. Gary Middleton). With Exxon Co. U.S.A., Corpus Christi and Houston, Tex., 1944-76, tech. adviser design, constrn. gas facilities, 1973-76; prin. engr. Gulf Interstate Engring. Co., Houston, 1976-78; cons. engr., Houston, 1979—. Named Corpus Christi Area Distinguished Engr. of Year, 1976. Named to Order of Engr., Houston, 1979. Registered profl engr., Tex. Fellow ASCE (life mem., pres. Houston br. 1956, past chmn. exec. com. pipeline div.); mem. Tex., Nat. socs. profl. engrs., Am. Inst. Mining Engrs., Pi Mu Epsilon. Home: 10915 Meadow Lake Ln Houston TX 77042

RAKE, VIRGINIA JOAN, former retail co. exec.; b. Parkersburg, W.Va., Feb. 19, 1934; d. Denver Earl and Mabel Louisa (Patterson) Harbin; student Pitts. Art Inst., 1953; m. Ted Alan Rake, Mar. 5, 1956; children—Nathan (dec.), Christopher, Cassandra. With Dils Bros. & Co., Parkersburg, 1962—, advt. mgr., 1965-79. Recipient 2d award Direct Mail competition Direct Mktg. mag.-Nat. Retail Mchts. Assn., 1974, hon. mention, 1977. Mem. Internat. Platform Assn., Smithsonian Assos., Am. Mus. Natural History. Home: 1806 17th St Parkersburg WV 26101

RAKENTINE, LLOYD WILLIAM, engring. co. exec.; b. E. Rutherford, N.J., Jan. 26, 1915; s. William and Sarah (Niebling) R.; student Internat. Corr. Schs., 1946-47, Dallas Night Sch., 1951-55; m. Viola Ethel Varga, Sept. 11, 1942; 1 child, G. Ilona. Salesman, Crucible Steel Co. Am., N.Y.C., 1931-46; with purchasing dept. Celanese Corp. Am., N.Y.C., 1946-50; asst. sec.-treas., comptroller Tears Engrs. Inc., Dallas, 1950—; dir., comptroller Hunnicut Corp., 1958—; sec.-treas. Ford, Bacon & Davis Tex., Inc., 1966—; asst. sec.-treas. Ford, Bacon & Davis Utah, Inc., Salt Lake City, 1972—. Served with USAAF, 1942-45. Mem. Nat. Assn. Accountants, Am. Legion. Methodist. Republican. Home: 6624 Hialeah Dr Dallas TX 75214 Office: 2908 National Dr Garland TX 75040

RAKES, GANAS KAYE, educator; b. Floyd County, Va., May 2, 1938; s. Samuel Durward and Ocie Jane (Peters) R.; B.S., Va. Tech. Inst., 1960, M.S., 1965; D.B.A., Washington U., 1971; m. Mary Ann Simmons, Oct. 1, 1961; 1 dau., Sabrina Darrow. Instr., Roanoke Coll., Salem, Va., 1964-65; grad. asst. Washington U., St. Louis, 1965-68; asst. prof. McIntire Sch. Commerce, U. Va., Charlottesville, 1968-72, asso. prof., 1972—; cons. to fin. insts.; dir. Guaranty Savings and Loan Assn., Charlottesville, 1976—. Mem. Albermarle County Rep. Com., 1974—. Served with U.S. Army, 1961-63. Decorated Army Commendation Medal; NDEA fellow, 1966-68. Mem. Fin. Mgmt. Assn., Eastern Finance Assn., So. Case Research Assn., Va. Assn. Economists, Alpha Kappa Psi, Beta Gamma Sigma. Republican. Episcopalian. Clubs: Farmington Country, Colonnade, Rotary. Contbr. articles to profl. jours. Home: 2513 Smithfield Rd Charlottesville VA 22901 Office: Monroe Hall U Va Charlottesville VA 22903

RAKOUSKAS, MICHAEL GERARD, state ofcl.; b. Holyoke, Mass., Oct. 6, 1944; s. Adam and Germaine Marie (Geoffroy) R.; B.B.A., U. Mass., 1968; M.P.A., Cornell U., 1972; m. Elaine Corsi, June 8, 1968; children—Michael Gerard, Stephen. Budget analyst State of Wis., 1972-74; sect. chief, office of intergovernmental relations State of N.C., Raleigh, 1974-75; staff dir. econ. planning Dept. Natural and Econ. Resources, State of N.C., 1976-77; head econ. research for indsl. devel. State of N.C., 1977—. Served to lt. USN, 1968-70. Recipient N.C. Gov.'s commendation, 1978. Mem. So. Indsl. Devel. Council, N.C. Indsl. Developer's Assn., Beta Gamma Sigma. Roman Catholic. Clubs: North Hills Swim, Area Bridge. Home: 5600 Laniel Ct Raleigh NC 27612 Office: State of NC 430 N Salisbury St Raleigh NC 27611

RALL, LLOYD LOUIS, civil engr.; b. Galesville, Wis., Dec. 7, 1916; s. Louis A. and Anna L. (Kienzle) R.; student Gale Coll., Galesville, Wis., 1934-36; B.S. in Civil Engring., U. Wis., 1940; m. Mary M. Moller, July 12, 1952; children—Lauris, David, Christopher, Jonathan. Commd. 2d lt. U.S. Army C.E., 1940, advanced through grades to col., 1955; asst. dist. engr., Seattle, 1952-54; dep. engr. Communications Zone, France, 1954-56; dir. Geod. Intelligence and Mapping Research and Devel. Agy., Ft. Belvoir, Va., 1964-66; dir. def. mapping and charting, Washington, 1969-72; ret., 1972; dir. Washington office Optical Systems div. ITEK Corp., 1977—. Prof. mil. sci. U. Mo., Rolla, 1957-60. Decorated Legion of Merit with oak leaf cluster, Bronze Star medal. Registered profl. engr., Wis. Mem.

Am. Congress on Surveying and Mapping, AIAA, Nat. Space Club. Home: 301 Cloverway Alexandria VA 22314

RALLS, RAWLEIGH HAZEN, educator, cons.; b. Oklahoma City, Dec. 14, 1932; s. Rawleigh Hazen and Rosemary Thelma (Sprigg) R.; B.S., U.S. Mil. Acad., 1955; M.S., U.S. Naval Postgrad. Sch., 1964; D.B.A., George Washington U., 1971; m. Barbara Yates, May 24, 1975; children—Creighton Leigh, Yates Ralls, Rawleigh Hazen Yates Ralls; children by previous marriage—Elizabeth Anne, Devon Anne. Commd. 2d lt. arty. U.S. Army, 1955, advanced through grades to maj., 1965; various assignments, 1955-66, chief arty. systems group Office Army Chief of Staff, Washington, 1966-67, prof. ops. research U.S. Army Mgmt. Sch., Fort Belvoir, Va., 1967-68; asso. prof. quantitative mgmt. sci., also coordinator statistics Coll. Bus. Adminstrn., U. Ark., Fayetteville, 1968-76; adj. faculty Webster Coll., 1980. Gen. partner Edn. & Research Assos., Alexandria, Va., 1968; pvt. cons. mgmt. and decision sci., Fayetteville, 1969—; pres. Edn. and Research Assos., Inc., 1970—, Atty.'s Econ. Consultants, Inc., 1975; pres., chmn. bd. The Hazen Collection, Inc., 1975—; pres. Automated Computer Services Inc., 1977—. Fellow AAAS: mem. N.Y. Acad. Scis., Ops. Research Soc. Am., Am. Econ. Assn., Am. Inst. for Decision Sci., Mensa. Episcopalian. Home: 12901 Southridge Dr Little Rock AR 72212

RALSTON, CARL CONRAD, constrn. co. exec.; b. Owensboro, Ky., Nov. 1, 1927; s. Carl C. and Elizabeth (Little) R.; Asso. B.B.A., Ky. Bus. Coll., 1949; B.A., Ky. Wesleyan Coll., 1956; m. Patricia Warren, Nov. 12, 1971; children—Pamela Kay, Kelly Michelle. Pub. accountant, 1956; chief accountant, estimator Mills & Jones Inc., 1957-60, project mgr., 1960-65; v.p. Mills & Jones Constrn. Co., St. Petersburg, Fla., 1965—. Pres., Cross Bayou Little League, Seminole, Fla., 1959-61; treas. Seminole Lake Civic Assn., Seminole, 1959-62. Trustee Southeastern Ironworkers' Health and Welfare Fund. Served with USAAF, 1945-47. Mem. Am. Mgmt. Assn., Assn. Gen. Contractors (chpt. dir. 1969-70), Am. Inst. Constructors, Am. Soc. Profl. Estimators. Clubs: Seminole Lake Country (gov. 1964-67, chmn. bd. 1967-68); Bardmoor Country; Feather Sound Country; Masons, Elks. Home: 1451 Seagull Dr St Petersburg FL 33707 Office: 400 23d St S St Petersburg FL 33731

RALSTON, CLARICE MCDUFFIE, nurse; b. Tampa, Fla., Feb. 11, 1932; d. Welbourne Clifton and Louise Teresa (Sellers) McDuffie; R.N. diploma Gordon Keller Sch. Nursing, 1953; m. William Kent Ralston, Mar. 12, 1954; children—Diana Lynn (dec.), Stephen Kent. Staff nurse Jackson Meml. Hosp., Miami, Fla., 1953-54, New Braunfels (Tex.) Gen. Hosp., 1954-55; nurse supr. Wichita Falls (Tex.) State Hosp., 1971—. Mem. Am., Tex. (charter mem. continuing edn. program) nurses assns., Fla. State Student Nurses Assn. (charter), Tex. Pub. Employees Assn., Am. Legion Aux., Air Force Sgt. Assn. Aux. Democrat. Methodist. Club: Order Eastern Star. Research on hygiene for elderly patients. Home: 815 Preston St Burkburnett TX 76354 Office: Wichita Falls State Hosp PO Box 300 Wichita Falls TX 76307

RALSTON, JOHN ALLAN, mfrs. rep.; b. Dallas, Nov. 13, 1951; s. John C. and Edith (Kallus) R.; student Eastfield Coll., 1970-74, Abilene Christian Coll., 1977-78; m. Cheryl Lynne Gauntt, Apr. 7, 1972; children—Jennifer Lynne. Regional mgr. John C. Ralston Co., Dallas, 1970-76; dep. sheriff Dallas County Sheriff's Office, 1976-77; partner John C. Ralston Co. mfrs. reps., Dallas, 1977—, mgr. Houston office, 1978--. Mem. Southwest Tackle Reps. Assn., Tackle Reps. Assn. Internat., Abilene Christian Coll. Former Studies Assn. Republican. Roman Catholic. Home: 9119 Spellman Rd Houston TX 77031 Office: 9119 Spellman Rd Houston TX 77031

RAMAKRISHNAN, RAMASWAMI, civil engr.; b. Madras, India, May 16, 1938; s. C.S. Ramaswami and Ponnammal Krishnan; came to U.S., 1970; B. Engring., Madras (India) U., 1960; M.S. in Civil Engring., Villanova U., 1971; m. Ramani Ramakrishnan, Apr. 26, 1964; children—Ronnie, Raj. Engr., Richardson & Cruddas, Madras, 1960-63; chief of design and drafting Coromandel Steels, Madras, 1964-69; engr. W.S. Atkins & Partners, London, 1969-70; grad. asst. Villanova (Pa.) U., 1970-71; sr. engr. Big Bend Engring. Co., Tallahassee, 1971-72; v.p., chief engr. Mudano Assos., Clearwater, Fla., 1972-74; sr. engr. Bechtel Power Corp., Houston, 1974-78, engring. group supr., 1978—. Chartered structural engr., London: registered profl. engr., Tex. Mem. ASCE, Instn. Structural Engrs. London, Tau Beta Pi. Home: 661B Casablanca Dr Houston TX 77088 Office: Bechtel Power Corp 320 Briar Hollow Bldg 520 S Post Oak St Houston TX 77027

RAMDEEN, PATRICK EDWARD, process engr.; b. Trinidad, W.I., Feb. 27, 1936; came to U.S., 1961; s. Sonny and Joyce Marinetta (Deare) R.; B.B.A., Dallas State Coll., 1974; m. Louise S. Riley, June 23, 1964; 4 children. Sales mgr. Martins Mktg., Trinidad, W.I., 1960; with Nerlanger Blumgart Co., Inc., N.Y.C., 1961-67; credit union mgr. Owens Corning Fiberglas Corp., Aiken, S.C., 1967-70, process engr., 1979—. Chmn. United Way evaluating com., 1976; mem. Aiken Sch. Adv. Com., 1979—. Mem. S.C. Dept. Wildlife and Marine Resources. Democrat. Baptist. Clubs: Credit Union Founders, Pres.'s. Office: Owens Corning Fiberglas Corp Aiken SC 29801

RAMEY, DAVID THOMAS, steel mfg. co. exec.; b. Chattanooga, July 24, 1940; s. James Thomas and Undean (McHenry) R.; grad. Tenn. Military Inst., 1958; B.S., U. Chattanooga, 1961; m. Mary E. Pursley, May 8, 1965; 1 dau., Mary Elizabeth. Bookkeeper, Elder and Co., Chattanooga, 1962-64; salesman Vance Iron and Steel Co., Chattanooga, 1964; with O'Neal Steel, Inc., Birmingham, Ala., 1964—, industry mktg. mgr., 1977—. Active Boy Scouts Am.; bd. dirs. Franklin Acad., Birmingham. Mem. Anthrop. Assn. Can., Birmingham Audubon Soc. Republican. Baptist. Home: 513 Zinnia Ln Birmingham AL 35215 Office: 744 40th St N Birmingham AL 35202

RAMEY, JAMES RICHARD, III, orthopaedic surgeon; b. Middlesboro, Ky., July 2, 1939; s. James Richard and Juanita Virginia (Carr) R.; student Cumberland Bapt. Coll., 1958-59; B.S., U. Ky., 1962, postgrad., 1962-63; M.D., U. Louisville, 1967; m. Doris Jean Steedly, Sept. 15, 1961; children—James Christopher, Richard Brian. Intern, Pensacola (Fla.) Edn. Program, 1967-68; resident in orthopaedic surgery U. Ala., 1970-74, Georgetown U., 1975; practice medicine, specializing in orthopaedic surgery, Lexington, Ky., 197Home: 3575 Wiley Rd Montgomery AL 36106

RAMGOPAL, VADAKEPAT, physician; b. Kerala State, India, May 2, 1945; s. Gopala Kunnireth and Vadakepat (Malathi) Menon; came to U.S., 1970; M.B.B.S., Kilpauk Med. Coll., U. Madras, India, 1969; m. Lakshmi Ramgopal, Mar. 28, 1974. Intern, Govt. Gen. Hosp., Madras, India, 1969-70; med. intern, U. Ky., Lexington, 1970-71, jr. asst. resident in internal medicine, 1971-72, asst. resident in internal medicine, 1972-73, chief resident internal medicine, 1973-74; fellow in infectious diseases, U. Wis. Hosps., lMadison, 1974-75, 75-76, clin. instr. in medicine sect. infectious diseases, 1976, dir. clin. microbiology lab., 1976-77; pvt. practice medicine specializing in internal medicine and infectious diseases, Oklahoma City, 1977—; clin. asst. prof. medicine U. Okla., 1977—; cons. in internal medicine, VA Hosp., Madison. Recipient prizes in physiology, 1965, ophthalmology, 1966, pediatrics, 1967, Gold medal Kilpauk Med. Coll., U. Madras, 1967. Diplomate Am. Bd. Internal Medicine. Fellow Royal Coll. Physicians and Surgeons of Can. (certified); mem. Am. Soc. Internal Medicine (asso.), ACP, Am. Soc. Microbiology, Am. Coll. Emergency Physicians. Contbr. articles, reports to profl. publs. Home: 11204 N St Charles Oklahoma City OK 73132 Office: Doctors Med Bldg Bapt Meml Hosp 5700 NW Grand Blvd Oklahoma City OK 73112

RAMIREZ, JOSE RAMON, real estate cons.; b. Bayamon, P.R., Sept. 22, 1921; s. Abigail Ernesto and Maria Julia (Higuera) R.; B.B.A., U. P.R., 1943; m. Thelma Torres, Dec. 1, 1946; children—Maria Margarita Ramirez Angel, Thelma Katherine, Jose Ramon. Gen. mgr. J. Ramirez e Hijo, Wholesalers, Bayamon, 1943-59; chief dept. comml. devel. Econs. Devel. Adminstrn., San Juan, 1959-61; undersec. of commerce P.R. Dept. Commerce, San Juan, 1961-65, acting sec., 1965; pres. Ramirez, Spector & Assos., San Juan, 1965-67; v.p. Action Real Estate, Inc., San Juan, 1965-67; sr. asso. Jose Ramon Ramirez & Assos., San Juan, 1965—; v.p. Caribbean Wonderland, Inc., San Juan, 1970; prof. real estate Interam. U., 1978-80. Vice pres. Lions Eye Bank of P.R., San Juan, 1974-75; mem. Regional Exports Expansion Council for P.R., V.I., 1973; pres. devel. com. Bayamon Central U., 1973-74, trustee, 1978-80; sec. traffic sector Accident Prevention Council, 1974-75; mem. P.R. CARE Com., 1972-75; mem. Empty Plate Campaign, Washington, 1975. Bd. dirs. Todo-Bayamon, 1971-75. Served with AUS, 1943-45. Mem. Chamber of Wholesale Mchts. of P.R. (exec. dir. 1966), Orgn. Coops. of Am. (tech. adviser 1970-71), San Juan Bd. Realtors (pres. 1976), P.R. (pres. 1977-78), Nat. (dir. 1977-80) assns. realtors, Sales and Mktg. Execs. Internat., Am. Soc. Internat. Execs., Fedn. Latin Am. and Caribbean Exporters Assn., Internat. Trade Assn., P.R., Bayamon chambers commerce. Democrat. Roman Catholic. Lion (dist. gov. 1972-73). Contbr. articles to profl. jours. Home: Las Cumbres Garden Apt 211 La Cumbre Rio Piedras PR 00926 Office: GPO Box 2632 San Juan PR 00936

RAMIREZ, MANUEL JOSE, microbiologist; b. Managua, Nicaragua, Nov. 30, 1933; s. Manuel and Lily Adela (Fernandez) R.; came to U.S., 1950, naturalized, 1977; B.S., Tulane U., 1954; M.S., La. State U., 1962; postgrad. U. Ky., 1964; m. Blanca Erlinda Leets, Oct. 8, 1960; children—Carla Maria, Manuel Jose, Claudia Patricia. Chief lab. Nat. Inst. Social Security Polyclinic, Managua, Nicaragua, 1957-59; chief lab. Med. Center, Managua, Nicaragua, 1959-60, dir. labs., 1962-63; bacteriologist-in-charge Caylor Nickel Clinic Hosp., Bluffton, Ind., 1964-67; asso. clin. pathology Emory U. Sch. Medicine, Atlanta, 1967-69; bacteriologist-in-charge Ga. Bapt. Hosp., Atlanta, 1969-71; microbiologist, chief lab. Gen. Hosp., Managua, Nicaragua, 1971-73; microbiologist Ga. Bapt. Hosp., Atlanta, 1973—. Faculty Emory U. Sch. Med. Tech., Atlanta, 1967-69; lectr. microbiology Nat. U. Nicaragua, Managua, 1971-73; microbiology cons. Med. Center, Managua, Nicaragua, 1971-73, S.W. Community Hosp., Atlanta, 1973—. Co-v.p. Medlock Sch. P.T.A., Decatur, Ga., 1975-77. Mem. Am. Soc. Microbiology, Nat. Registry Microbiologists, N.Y. Acad. Sci. Roman Catholic. Contbr. articles to profl. jours. Home: 2396 Woodridge Dr Decatur GA 30033 Office: 300 Blvd NE Atlanta GA 30312

RAMIREZ, SISTER MERIDA, pharmacist; b. Lajas, P.R., Apr. 27, 1942; d. Victor and Merida R.; B.S. in Pharmacy, U. P.R., Rio Piedras, 1962. Joined Daus. of Charity of St. Vincent de Paul, Roman Catholic Ch., 1962; staff pharmacist DePaul Gen. Hosp., St. Louis, 1964-66, chief pharmacist, 1966; chief of pharmacy dept. USPHS Hosp., Carville, La., 1972—; counselor. Recipient award of merit U.S. Cath. Guild Pharmacists, 1975; named Woman of Yr., Carville, 1979; lic. pharmacist, Mo. Mem. Am. Soc. Hosp. Pharmacists, Nat. Guild Cath. Pharmacists, Am. Pharm. Assn., Internat. Fedn. Pharmacists. Democrat. Research on drug treatment of Hansen's disease. Home and Office: PO Box 128 Carville LA 70721

RAMIREZ, MIRIAM JEAN, physician; b. Caguas, P.R., June 24, 1941; d. Victor M. and Angela (Garcia) Ramirez; student Marymount Coll. br., Barcelona, Spain, 1958, U. Md. br., Munich, Ger., 1959; pre-med. degree, U. P.R., San Juan, 1960; M.D., U. Madrid (Spain), 1967; m. Tomas Ferrer, Sept. 6, 1974; 1 dau., Lissette. children by previous marriage—Miriam Jean, Tommy, David, Roberto. Intern, Caguas Municipal Hosp., 1968-69; resident in obstetrics and gynecology Caguas Sub-Regional Hosp., 1970-73; regional dir., Family Planning Agy., P.R. Dept. Health, Caguas, 1973-74; clin. obstetrician, gynecologist Med. Center, Mayaguez, P.R., 1974—. Chmn. Bush for Pres. for Western P.R., 1980. Mem. Assn. Planned Parenthood Physicians (dir. P.R. chpt.), P.R., Caguas (del.-at-large) med. assns., Med. Doctor's Wives Assn. Caguas (pres. 1973-74). Mem. Statehood Polit. Party. Roman Catholic. Club: Altrusa (pres. Caguas 1972-74, pres. Mayaguez 1975-76). Address: Ave Los Maestros 25 Urb Hostos Mayaguez PR 00708

RAMIREZ, RENATO F., colon and rectal surgeon; b. Cabanatuan City, Philippines, Dec. 31, 1935; s. Lucas S. and Encarnacion (Fajardo) R.; came to U.S., 1960, naturalized, 1971; B.S., U. of the Philippines, 1960, M.D., 1960; M.S. in Colon and Rectal Surgery, U. Minn., 1966; m. Elaine Farrell, June 22, 1963; children—Ray, Steven, Jill, Cindy, John, Julie. Intern, St. Peter's Hosp., Albany, N.Y., 1960-61, resident in gen. surgery, 1961-63; fellow, resident in colon and rectal surgery Mayo Clinic, Mayo Grad. Sch., U. Minn., Rochester, 1963-66; staff colon and rectal surgery Portsmouth Gen. Hosp., Maryview Hosp., Portsmouth, Va., 1967—. Bd. dirs. Community United Way Fund, 1976-77. Diplomate Am. Bd. Colon and Rectal Surgery. Fellow A.C.S., Am. Soc. Colon and Rectal Surgeons; mem. AMA. Roman Catholic. Contbr. articles to profl. jours. Home: 4237 Fletcher Ct Chesapeake VA 23321 Office: Olde Towne Med Center 620 London Blvd Portsmouth VA 23704

RAMIREZ, SALVADOR MANUEL, orthopaedic surgeon; b. N.Y.C., Mar. 17, 1936; s. Salvador H. and Providencia (Torres) R.; B.S., St. John's U., 1956; M.D., Chgo. Med. Sch., 1960; m. Janis Marie Tarpo, Nov. 26, 1960; children—Sally Ann, Robert Anthony, Elena Marie, Elizabeth Ann. Intern Kings County Hosp., Bklyn., 1960-61; resident in orthopaedic surgery Jewish Hosp., Bklyn., 1963-67; practice medicine specializing in orthopaedic surgery, Miami, Fla., 1967—. Served with USN, 1961-63. Diplomate Am. Bd. Orthopaedic Surgery. Fellow ACS, Internat. Coll. Surgeons, Am. Acad. Orthopaedic Surgeons; mem. Fla. Med. Assn., Dade County Med. Assn., Miami Orthopaedic Soc. Clubs: Palm Bay, Surf. Home: 4425 Banyan Ln Bay Point Miami FL 33137

RAMIREZ, SAMUEL AMADOR, geneticist, educator; b. El Paso, Tex., Apr. 28, 1936; s. Amador and Berta (Arivizu) R.; B.A., U. Tex., El Paso, 1958; M.S. (NSF fellow), Tex. Tech. U., 1966; Ph.D. (NIH trainee), Ind. U., 1974; m. Nora Ethel Fairchild, Sept. 7, 1957; children—Kenneth Thomas, Alice Elaine. Tchr. pub. high sch., El Paso, 1961-66; instr. U. Tex., El Paso, 1966-69; teaching asso. Ind. U., Bloomington, 1969-71; NIH research fellow Baylor Coll. Medicine, Houston, 1973-75; asst. prof. genetics U. Tex., San Antonio, 1975—, Affirmative Action-EEO officer, 1977—; research staff histopathology study S. Tex. outer continental shelf Bur. Land Mgmt., 1976—; cons. Eagle Pass High Sch.; co-investigator Minority Biomed. Support Program. Served with M.C., AUS, 1958-61. Fellow Nat. Assn. Chicanos in Higher Edn.; mem. Am. Inst. Biol. Scis., AAAS, Genetics Soc. of Am., Am. Genetic Assn., Am. Soc. for Cell Biology, N.Y. Acad. Scis., Am. Soc. Herpetologists and Icthyologists, Sigma Xi, Beta Beta Beta, Phi Sigma. Methodist. Contbr. articles to profl. jours. Home: 11915 Mesquite Mesa San Antonio TX 78249 Office: Div Allied Health and Life Sciences University of Texas San Antonio TX 78285

RAMIREZ-RIVERA, JOSÉ, physician; b. Mayaguez, P.R., June 26, 1929; s. Jesús Ramírez Quiles and Nieves Rivera; B.A., Johns Hopkins U., 1949; M.D., Yale U., 1953; m. Leila Suñer, May 14, 1971; 2 sons, 4 daus. Rotating intern U. Md. Hosp., 1953-54; asst. resident in internal medicine U. Hosp., Balt., 1954-55, fellow in hematology, 1958-59, asst. resident in internal medicine, 1959; staff physician VA Hosp., Balt., 1960-67, asso. chief of staff, 1962-68; asso. prof. medicine Duke U., Durham, N.C., 1968-70; dir. med. edn. and clin. investigation Western Region P.R., 1970; mem. staff chief of medicine Mayaguez Med. Center, 1971—; clin. prof. medicine U. P.R., San Juan, 1974—; mem. staffs Hosp. La. Concepcion, San Germán, Bella Vista Hosp.; dir. Rincón Rural Health Initiative Project, 1975; coordinator Western Consortium Med. Edn., 1976. Diplomate Nat. Bd. Med. Examiners, Am. Bd. Internal Medicine. Fellow ACP; mem. Royal Soc. Medicine, AMA, Am. Fedn. Clin. Research, Am. Thoracic Soc. Club: El Deportivo. Contbr. articles to profl. publs. Home: Andalucia 67 Res Sultana Mayaguez PR 00708 Office: Consorcio Educ Oeste-Centro e(cico Mayaguez PR 00708

RAMON, ADOLPH IGNACIO, educator; b. San Antonio, June 6, 1933; s. Ignacio T. and Mary F. (Garcia) R.; B.A., U. Tex. at Austin, 1956; B.S., Incarnate Word Coll., 1964; B.B.A., St. Mary's U., 1973; M.S., Trinity U., 1972. Librarian, Bus. Sci. Tech. dept. San Antonio Pub. Library, 1965-67; chief med. records librarian Santa Rosa Med. Center, San Antonio, 1967-69, dir. med. record and med. typing depts., 1969-73; chief med. record adminstr. Brooke Army Med. Center, Fort Sam Houston, Tex., 1974-78; asst. prof. health adminstrn. S.W. Tex. State U., San Marcos, 1978—, also chmn. dean's adv. council. Served with USN, 1956-58. Fellow Royal Soc. Health (Eng.); mem. Adminstv. Mgmt. Soc., Am. Acad. Med. Adminstrs., Am. Hosp. Assn., Am. Med. Record Assn., Am. Personnel and Guidance Assn., Am. Mental Health Counselors Assn., Am. Coll. Health Assn., Am. Pub Health Assn., Am. Soc. Hosp. Personnel Adminstrn., Am. Soc. Personnel Adminstrn., Assn. MBA Execs., Assn. Mental Health Adminstrs., Assn. Record Mgrs. and Adminstrs. Democrat. Roman Catholic. Home: 566 Donaldson Ave San Antonio TX 78201 Office: SW Tex State U San Marcos TX 78666

RAMOS, NANCY BITNER, nurse; b. Louisville, Oct. 14, 1944; d. Harry Dale and Dorothy Ida (Smith) Bitner; B.S. in Nursing, Med. Coll. Va., 1967; M.S. in Nursing, U. Md., 1970; m. Francisco E. Ramos, May 15, 1971. Staff nurse Med. Coll. Va. Hosp., Richmond, 1967-68; head nurse No. Va. Mental Health Inst., Falls Church, 1968-69; clin. coordinator psychiatric nursing St. Mary Hosp., Richmond, 1970-73; dir. nursing service Univ. Hosp., Pensacola, Fla., 1975—; adj. instr. nursing U. of West Fla., 1977-78. Mem. Escambia County Mental Health Assn. (pres. 1979-80), Mental Health Assn. Fla. (v.p. 1980), Dist. 1 Fla. Nurses Assn. (v.p. 1978-79). Democrat. Presbyterian. Home: 1627 Bulevar Menor Pensacola Beach FL 32561 Office: University Hospital 1200 W Leonard St Pensacola FL 32501

RAMPY, RITA ALIECE, nurse; b. Palestine, Tex., Nov. 12, 1949; d. Therel Hubert and Mary Elbertyne (Bayless) Rampy; student N. Tex. State U., 1966, Tex. Womans U., 1967, Stephen F. Austin State U., 1969; R.N. with honors, John Peter Smith Hosp. Sch. Nursing, 1971; B.S. in Nursing, Tex. Eastern U., Tyler, 1977. Surg. floor supr. Navarro County Meml. Hosp., Corsicana, Tex., 1971-75; pvt. duty nurse Homemakers-Upjohn, Dallas, 1975, service dir., Tyler, Tex., 1976-77; nurse hemodialysis unit Med. Center Hosp., Tyler, 1977—, supr., dept. head hemodialysis unit, 1978-79. Active ARC. Mem. Am. Nurses Assn., Nat. League Nursing (mem. council for diploma programs), Am. Assn. Nephrology Nurses and Technicians. Mem. Ch. of Christ. Home: 4202 Sherwood Forest Tyler TX 75703 Office: Hemodialysis Unit Med Center Hosp Tyler TX 75701

RAMQUIST, RAYMOND CARL, educator; b. Berwyn, Ill., Apr. 14, 1938; s. William and Leona (Hackbarth) R.; Ph.B., DePaul U., 1963; M.S.Ed., Ind. U., 1965, Ed.D., 1971; M.A., U. Minn., 1974; m. Joyce Sutton Luenstroth, Aug. 14, 1965; children—Thomas, David, Kevin. Dir. audiovisual DePaul U., Chgo., 1959-64; head audiovisual services U. Ill. at Chgo. Circle, 1965-67; instr. ednl. media U. Utah, Salt Lake City, 1969-70; asso. prof. info. media St. Cloud (Minn.) State U., 1970-75; head dept. library sci. and ednl. media James Madison U., Harrisonburg, Va., 1975—. Mem. ALA, S.E. Library Assn., Va. Library Assn., Va. Ednl. Media Assn., Assn. for Ednl. Communications and Tech., Phi Delta Kappa. Author: A Needs Study of School Library Centers in Virginia Schools K-12, 1979. Home: 1126 Rockingham Dr Harrisonburg VA 22801 Office: James Madison U Harrisonburg VA 22801

RAMSEL, DOUGLAS ALEXANDER, elec. engr.; b. Georgetown, Tex., July 11, 1922; s. Arthur August and Ann Evelyn (Phillips) R.; asso. degree in elec. engring. Center for Degree Studies, 1977; Asso. in Sci., SUNY, 1978; A.A., SUNY; m. Dorothy Virginia Pace, Mar. 5, 1944; children—Dorothy Virginia, Mary Ann. Joined U.S. Army Air Force, 1939. advanced through grades to maj. U.S. Air Force, ret., 1960; field engr. RCA, 1961-63; machine designer Cupples Co., Austin, Tex., 1964-70 elec. designer Engring. Inc., Austin, 1970-71; elec. designer Page-Southerland-Page, architects, engrs., Austin, 1971—, sr. asso., 1978—. Mem. IEEE, Soc. Mfg. Engrs., Illuminating Engring. Soc., Ret. Officers Assn. Clubs: Masons, Shriners. Home: 1308 Yorkshire Dr Austin TX 78723 Office: 606 W Ave Box 2004 Austin TX 78767

RAMSEY, GARY ROBERT, nurse; b. Maryville, Tenn., Oct. 12, 1949; s. Glenn Everett and Bobbie Joan (Coker) R.; student U. Tenn., 1967-69; B.S. in Nursing, E. Tenn. State U., 1972; M.S. in Nursing, Med. Coll. Ga., 1974; m. Glenda Charlene Horvath, Dec. 19, 1970; children—Christopher Matthew, Lori Ann. Staff nurse, charge nurse U. Tenn. Hosp., Knoxville, 1972-73, Univ. Hosp., Augusta, Ga., 1973-74; asst. prof. nursing E. Tenn. State U., Johnson City, 1974-79; chief nursing Lakeshore Mental Health Inst., Knoxville, 1979—. Vice pres. Forestview Condominium Assn., 1976-78; mem. vol. nursing team Spl. Olympics for Mentally Retarded, 1975-79. Med. Coll. Ga. grantee, 1973-74. Mem. Am. Nurses Assn., Tenn. Nurses Assn., Nat. League Nursing, Tenn. League Nursing, Mental Health Assn. Knox County, Tenn. Hosp. Assn., Sigma Theta Tau. Democrat. Baptist. Home: Route 4 Box 107 Louisville TN 37777 Office: 5908 Lyons View Dr Knoxville TN 37919

RAMSEY, JACKSON EUGENE, educator; b. Cin., Dec. 20, 1938; s. Leonard Pershing and Edna Willa (Blakeman) R.; B.S. in Metall. Engring., U. Cin., 1961; M.B.A., SUNY, Buffalo, 1969, Ph.D., 1975; m. Inez Mae Linn, Apr. 22, 1961; children—John Earl, James Leonard. Welding engr. Gen. Electric Co., Cin., 1961-62, Westinghouse-Bettis Lab., Pitts., 1962-66; prodn. control mgr. Columbus-McKinnon Corp., Buffalo, 1966-71; asst. prof. mgmt. SUNY, Buffalo, 1971-73; asso. prof. mgmt. James Madison U., Harrisonburg, Va., 1973—; cons. in field. Chmn. Harrisonburg Republican Party, 1978—, vice chmn., 1974-78. Served with

USMCR, 1956-62. Named Outstanding Young Scholar, Xerox Corp., 1976; registered profl. engr., Va., Ohio. Mem. Acad. of Mgmt., Am. Inst. for Decision Scis., Inst. of Mgmt. Sci., Am. Soc. for Metals, Nat. Soc. Profl. Engrs. Republican. Baptist. Author: R D Strategic Decision Criteria, 1978; contbr. articles to profl. jours. Home: 282 Franklin St Harrisonburg VA 22801 Office: Dept Mgmt and Mktg James Madison U Harrisonburg VA 22807*

RAMSEY, LEWIS ANDREW, petroleum co. exec.; b. Edinburg, Tex., Jan. 25, 1927; s. Leon and Victoria E. R.; B.S., U. Tex., 1950; grad. Advanced Mgmt. Program, Harvard U., 1974; m. Aurora Flores, Mar. 9, 1952; children—Laura Ann, Lynn Susan, Elizabeth, Nita Louise. Engr., Mene Grande Oil Co., Caracas, Venezuela, 1952-66; mgr. Bolivian Gulf Co., Bolivia, 1966-68; ops. mgr. Gulf Eastern, London, 1968-69; sr. v.p., pres. Iberian Gulf, Madrid, Spain, 1969-71; staff advisor Gulf Oil Corp., Pitts., 1971; v.p., pres. Mene Grande Oil Co., Caracas, 1971-75; exec. v.p. Gulf Oil-U.S., pres. Gulf Energy and Minerals Co., 1975-78; exec. v.p., chief operating officer Gulf Oil Exploration and Prodn. Co., Houston, 1978—; dir. Keydril Co., Key Internat. Drilling Co., Ltd., Gulf Oil (Nigeria), and others. Mem. U. Tex. Coll. Engring. Found. Adv. Bd. Served with USAAF, 1944-46. Decorated Francisco Miranda medal (Venezuela). Mem. Soc. Petroleum Engrs. Republican. Clubs: Houston, Petroleum, Meml. Drive Country. Office: 712 Main St Houston TX 77002

RAMSEY, LLOYD BRINKLEY, savs. and loan exec.; b. Somerset, Ky., May 29, 1918; s. William Harold and Mary Ella Ramsey; A.B., U. Ky., 1940; postgrad. Command and Gen. Staff Coll., 1950, Army War Coll., 1954, Harvard U., 1961; m. Glenda Burton, Feb. 22, 1941; children—Lloyd Ann Ramsey Wallace, Larry Burton, Judi Ramsey Derr. Commd. 2d lt., inf. U.S. Army, 1940, advanced through grades to maj. gen., 1968, ret., 1974; chmn. bd. McLean Savs. & Loan Assn. (Va.), 1974—. Baptist. Home: 6451 Drydon Dr McLean VA 22101 Office: McLean Savings and Loan Assn 1307 Dolley Madison Blvd McLean VA 22101

RAMSEY, ODESSA DILLARD, hosp. personnel exec.; b. Spartanburg, S.C., May 4, 1932; s. Lewis Coble and Clara Mae (Seay) R.; student Clemson U., 1950-51; m. Bettie Jo Smith, Jan. 27, 1954; children—Michael Keith, Frederick Lewis, Kevin Brian, Lisa Marlane. Served as enlisted man U.S. Navy, 1951-71, advanced through grades to chief petty officer, 1966; assigned Kwajalien Atoll, Marshall Island, 1952-53, NATO Hdqrs., Naples, Italy, 1953-56, Naval Weapons Sta., Yorktown, Va., 1956-60, San Francisco, 1960-63, Washington, 1963-67, Am. embassy, Santiago, Chile, 1967-71, ret., 1971; personnel mgr. Spartanburg (S.C.) Gen. Hosp., 1971-75; personnel dir. Mary Black Meml. Hosp., Spartanburg, 1975—. Mem. allocations panel, mem. United Services Council, United Way, 1978, 79. Decorated Joint Service Commendation medal. Mem. Am. Soc. Hosp. Personnel Adminstrn., Am. Soc. Personnel Adminstrn., S.C. Hosp. Soc. Personnel Dirs., Spartanburg Area Personnel Assn. (dir.). Baptist. Club: Masons. Home: 124 W Forest Dr Spartanburg SC 29301 Office: Mary Black Meml Hosp 1700 Skylyn Dr Spartanburg SC 29304

RAMSEY, RALPH HEYWARD, JR., lawyer; b. Wedgefield, S.C., Apr. 7, 1900; s. Ralph Heyward and Una Elizabeth (Wells) R.; B.S., U. S.C., 1921, M.A., 1923, LL.B., 1924; m. Mary Dick Alford, Aug. 27, 1926; children—Mary Ann, Ralph Heyward III, Gayle Edward, Sarah Martha. Admitted to S.C. bar, 1924, N.C. bar, 1926; mem. firm Purdy & Ramsey, Sumter, S.C., 1924-26; practice of law, Hendersonville, N.C., 1926, Brevard, N.C., 1926—; sr. mem. firm Ramsey, Smart, Ramsey & Hunt, P.A., and predecessor firms, 1961—. Mayor, Town of Brevard, 1931-33, city atty., 1933-53; county atty. Transylvania County, N.C., 1939-60, 64-72; state senator 32d dist. of N.C., 1935-37; dir., sec. Golf Club Estates, Inc., Round Hill Estates, Inc.; asst. sec. Sapphire Valley Devel. Corp., Connestee Falls Devel. Corp.; sec.-treas., dir. Evergreen Devel. Co. Mem. N.C. Sch. Commn., 1941-43, Commn. on Solicitorial and Jud. Dists., 1945-47, N.C. Gen. Statues Commn., 1946-49, N.C. Med. Care Commn., 1953-56, Western N.C. Regional Planning Commn., 1956-61, N.C. Jud. Council, 1975—. Trustee, past chmn. Transylvania Community Hosp.; trustee Mars Hill Coll., 1962-66, 68-71, 73—, vice chmn., 1965-66, chmn., 1970-71; chmn. Lyday Meml. Hosp., Brevard, 1933-40. Mem. C. of C. (dir. 1937-74), Am. Legion, Brevard Music Found. (mem. bd. trustees 1947-60). Am., 29th Jud. Dist. (pres. 1945), Transylvania County, N.C. bar assns., N.C. State Bar (council 1962-75, chmn. grievance com. 1968-71, 1st v.p. 1972-73, pres. 1973-74), Am. Judicature Soc., Nat. Conf. Bar Presidents, Internat. Platform Assn., Pi Kappa Phi. Democrat. Baptist. Clubs: Kiwanis (sec. 1928-30, pres. 1930, dir. 1931-48, lt. gov. 1st div. Carolinas 1965), Lake Toxaway Country. Author: (booklet) Economic and Social Survey of Sumter County, 1923; (articles) Indians of Sumter County, The Old Village of Manchester. Home: High Meadows Route 4 Box 196 Brevard NC 28712 Office: Legal Bldg Brevard NC 28712

RAMSEY, ROBERT RUSSELL, JR., ednl. cons.; b. Stewart County, Tenn., Apr. 22, 1929; s. Robert Russell and Bonnie Kate (Goforth) R.; B.A., Yale U., 1950; Ed.M., Harvard U., 1954, Ed.D., 1959; m. Susan Charlotte Randolph, June 30, 1962. Asst. to dir. admissions Harvard U. Law Sch., 1954-57; asst. in financial aid office, head proctor, mem. bd. freshman advisers Harvard Coll., 1957-59; asst. dean freshman year, asst. dir. Office Ednl. Research, Yale U., 1959-61, asst. master Branford Coll., 1960-63, univ. dir. admissions and freshman scholarships, 1961-66; asst. dir. program devel. Va. Council Higher Edn., 1966-68, asso. dir., 1968-69; dir. evaluation Commn. Instns. Higher Edn., New Eng. Assn. Schs. and Colls., 1969-76; sec. edn. Gov.'s Cabinet, Commonwealth of Va., 1976-78; Va. commr. Edn. Commn. States, 1976-78; ednl. cons., 1978—; chancellor W.Va. Bd. Regents, 1980—; cons., panelist div. edn. programs Nat. Endowment for Humanities, 1976—. Bd. dirs. Resources, Inc., 1978—. Served with AUS, 1950-53. Mem. Am. Psychol. Assn., Am. Sociol. Assn. (asso.). Home: 950 Kanawha Blvd E Charleston WV 25301

RAMSEY, WILLARD ALVIS, minister, elec. engr.; b. Franklin, Ky., May 9, 1930; s. Willard Leslie and Latona (Williams) R.; student U. of Tenn., 1955-57, U. of S. Miss., 1962-63, Bob Jones U., 1965-67; m. Juanita Minchey, May 29, 1954; children—Nikki Robyn, Prudence Jill, Shaun Edmand. Ordained minister, Baptist Ch., 1967; customer engr. IBM, Dayton, Ohio, 1954-55; chief engr. WOKE Radio Station, Oak Ridge, Tenn., 1955-57; developmental lab technician, RCA Missile Test Project, Cape Canaveral, 1957-60; field engr. Gen. Dynamics-Electronics, Keesler AFB, Miss., 1960-63; head research and development in apparel automation Her Majesty Industries, Mauldin, S.C., 1964-68, Stone Mfg. Co., Greenville, S.C., 1968-71; engr. research and devel. textiles machinery, Saco Lowell, Easley, S.C., 1971-76; pastor Hallmark Baptist Ch., Greenville, 1976—; bd. dirs. Ch. History Research and Archives, Lafayette, Tenn., 1975-78, pres., 1975-77. Served with USN, 1949-53. Mem. Creation Research Soc. Holder 11 patents in apparel mfg.; contbr. article and 3 books on religion. Home: Rt 3 Moore Rd Simpsonville SC 29681

RANDALL, GEOFFREY LANCE, ins. co. exec.; b. Far Rockaway, N.Y., Mar. 30, 1942; s. Henry George and Henrietta Rose (Gradinger) R.; B.A. (scholar), U. Miami, 1964; grad. Pension Sch., Purdue U., 1973; m. Lois Hanken, June 18, 1967; 1 son, Adam Clinton. Comml. account exec. Can. Life Assurance Co., Miami, Fla., 1967-71; pres. Randall-Dade Underwriters Ins. Agy., Inc., North Miami, Fla., 1971—; cons. in field. Named Miami Gen. Agent's and Mgrs. Assn. Man of Yr., 1967-69; Nat. Quality award, 1973; Nat. Sales Achievement award, 1973; Health Ins. Quality award, 1974. Mem. Miami Assn. Life Underwriters, Nat. Assn. Life Underwriters, Million Dollar Round Table, Top of the Table (charter), Greater Miami Jaycees (named Key Man of Yr. 1969). Home: 13305 Biscayne Island Terr Island 5 Keystone Point Miami FL 33181 Office: 901 NE 125th St North Miami FL 33161

RANDALL, PATRICIA ANN, utility exec.; b. Pensacola, Fla., July 29, 1951; d. Gene Tunny and Essie Mae (Tate) Owens; A.A., Pensacola Jr. Coll., 1978; postgrad. U. West Fla., 1979—. Advt. supr. G.C. Murphy Co., Pensacola, 1969-72; jr. mech. engr. Neptune Meter Co., Greenwood, S.C., 1972-73; with Gulf Power Co., Pensacola, 1974—, staff asst. system planning, 1978-79, sr. staff asst. system planning, 1979—, active speakers corp., 1979—. County council devotionalist, 4-H, 1966, pres., 1967, county council v.p., 1968, dir. girls in action, 1978. Democrat. Roman Catholic. Office: PO Box 1151 Pensacola FL 32520

RANDALL, ROBERT STANLEY, educator; b. Ferris, Tex., June 17, 1928; s. Robert F. and Gladys Loraine (Gressett) R.; B.A., Howard Payne Coll., 1957; postgrad. Sul Ross State Coll., 1958-59, Tex. Western Coll., 1959-60; Ph.D., U. Tex., 1964; m. Lucinda Prather, Aug. 1, 1974; children—Robert Stanley, Billy Michael, Rebekah Ann, Norma Sue, Cynthia Lee, Mel Gunther Knight. Heavy equipment operator Associated Pipe Line Construction, Fargo, N.D., 1952, crew chief, Helena, Mont., 1953; sales mgr. Century Metalcraft Corp., Dallas, 1954-56; tchr. math. Norton (Tex.) High Sch., 1957-58, also coach, 1957-58; prin. Fort Hancock (Tex.) High Sch., 1958-61; tchr. math. Allen Jr. High Sch., Austin, Tex., 1961-62; instr. math. U. Tex., Austin, 1963-64; asst. prof. ednl. psychology Tex. A&M U., College Station, 1964-67; dir. program devel. Southwest Ednl. Devel. Corp., Austin, 1966-67, dir. research and evaluation, 1967-70, sr. program dir., 1970-76; prof. edn. research and evaluation U. Houston, 1976—; cons. U.S. Office Edn., Washington, 1967-72; pres. Found. of Ednl. Adminstrn., Austin, 1964-65; pres., founder Tex. A&M Council for Tchrs. Math., 1965-66; vis. lectr. U. London (Eng.), 1972; pres., founder RanShaw, Inc., Houston, 1976. Precinct chmn. Democratic Com., Austin, 1971-72. Served with USN, 1945-46; PTO. Named Hon. Citizen of New Orleans, 1970. Mem. Am. Ednl. Research Assn., Phi Delta Kappa. Mem. Christian Ch. Club: Rotary. Home: 10302 Briar Dr Houston TX 77042 Office: Univ of Houston College of Education Houston TX 77004

RANDALL, WILLIAM MADISON, educator; b. Belleville, Mich., Aug. 16, 1899; s. Will M. and Emma Adele (Henry) R.; A.B., U. Mich., 1921, A.M., 1924; Ph.D. summa cum laude, Hartford Theol. Sem., 1929; Litt.D. (hon.), U. N.C., 1971; travelling fellow Gen. Edn. Bd., 1935, Am. Assn. Learned Socs. (Middle East), 1938; m. Myldred Randolph Cady, June 21, 1924; children—William David, Duncan Peter; m. 2d, Mary Johnson McGee, 1954. Asso. prof. library sci. U. Chgo., 1929, prof., 1931, asst. dean of students, 1938; v.p. Snead & Co., Orange, Va., 1946; dir. libraries, student affairs U. Ga., 1947; capt. U.S. Maritime Service; acad. dean U.S. Mcht. Marine Acad. 1948-51; dean Wilmington (N.C.) Coll., (name changed to U.N.C. at Wilmington 1969), 1951-58, pres., 1958-68, pres. emeritus, prof. modern langs., 1968-78. Pres. Wilmington chpt. N.C. Symphony Soc., 1957-60. Mng. editor Library Quarterly, 1931-42; cons. Carnegie Corp. of N.Y., 1929-32; active in ednl. survey work, Gen. Edn. Bd., Meth. Bd. Edn., N. Central Assn., 1929-39; dir. Nat. Conf. Christians and Jews; chmn. county chpt. Nat. Found. Infantile Paralysis. Mem. legislative com. So. Assn. Jr. Colls.; sec.-treas. N.C. Jr. Coll. Athletic Conf., 1955-63. Mem. commn. sent to reorganize Vatican library, Carnegie Endowment for Internat. Peace, 1928. Served from maj. to lt. col. USAF, 1942-45, with War Dept. Intelligence, stationed Cairo, Egypt, Casablanca, Morocco. Mem. N.C. State Community Coll. Com. 1952. Mem. A.L.A., N.E.A., Phi Sigma. Democrat. Episcopalian. Clubs: Rotary, Executives. Author: The College Library, 1932; (with F. L. D. Goodrich) Principles of College Library Administration, 1935, 38; Acquisition and Cataloging of Library Materials, 1941. Home: 4622 Mocking Bird Ln Wilmington NC 28403

RANDLE, WILLIAM MALCOLM, banker; b. Jacksonville, Fla., Dec. 22, 1939; s. William Yancy and Frances Romano (Goff) R.; A.A., Jacksonville U., 1959; B.S. in Bus. Adminstrn. (Schenley Found. scholar), U. Fla., 1962; M.B.A., Loyola U., New Orleans, 1969; m. Judy Mary Mroczek, Dec. 31, 1963; children—William Malcolm, Andrew F. With Atlantic Bancorp., Jacksonville, 1969—, mktg. officer, 1970-72, asst. v.p., 1972-73, v.p., dir. mktg., 1973—; conf. speaker. Chmn., Jacksonville Area C. of C. Nat. Advt. Task Force, 1977-79. Served with USN, 1962-69. Mem. Bank Mktg. Assn., Sales and Mktg. Execs. Jacksonville, Jacksonville Advt. Club, Jacksonville Research Assn. (pres. 1971-72), Beta Gamma Sigma. Democrat. Clubs: Ye Mystic Reveller, Univ. Office: 200 W Forsyth St Gen Mail Center Jacksonville FL 32231

RANDLETT, DAVID PAUL, ednl. adminstr.; b. Pitts., Sept. 2, 1938; s. Paul Norman and Lillian Ann (Saicoe) R.; B.Music, Eastern Nazarene Coll., 1963; M.Music Edn., George Peabody Coll. for Tchrs., 1968; m. Mildred Jane Harrison, May 21, 1963; children—Karen, Paul. Band dir. H.L. Ferguson High Sch., Newport News, Va., 1963-65; mem. faculty Free Will Baptist Coll., Nashville, 1965-73, adminstr., 1967-73; prof., coll. music adminstr. Liberty Bapt. Coll., Lynchburg, Va., 1973—; owner retail music store; producer, co-producer records, Nashville, 1967—, solo, group, choir albums; mus. dir. Old Time Gospel Hour, syndicated TV broadcast, 1974—; guest condr. choral/instrumental groups; adjudicator instrumental and choral contests. Mem. Music Educators Nat. Conf., Va. Music Educators, Nat. Ch. Music Fellowship, Nat. Assn. Music Merchants. Baptist. Home: 206 Dean St Lynchburg VA 24502 Office: Liberty Mountain Lynchburg VA 24502

RANDOLPH, JAMES BOLTON, secondary sch. prin.; b. Richland, La., July 23, 1923; s. Augustine and Emma (Hall) R.; B.A., Fla. A. and M. U., 1950; M.A. (Rockefeller Found. fellow), Western Res. U., 1951; postgrad. U. Miami, 1959, Barry Coll., 1969; m. Gloria D. Jackson, June 1, 1954; children—Gina Lynne, Cecily Karen, James Bolton. Asst. prof. drama Fla. A&M U., 1951-54; dir. Community Youth Center, Springfield, Mo., 1954-56; asst. prof. speech Prairie View (Tex.) A. and M. Coll., 1956-58; tchr. drama North Dade Jr. Sr. High Sch., Miami, 1958-66, S.W. Miami Sr. High Sch., 1966-69; writer coordinating com. on discipline Dade County (Fla.) Pub. Schs., summer 1967, writer com. to develop units on Negro history and culture, summer 1969; item writer Ednl. Testing Service, Princeton, N.J., 1969-70; asst. to the prin. Carol City Jr. High Sch., Miami, 1969-70, asst. prin. for adminstrn., 1970-73; prin. Westview Jr. High Sch., Miami, 1973-78, Madison Jr. High Sch., Miami, 1978—. Asst. dir. Fla. A. and M. U. Playmakers Guild, 1951-54, tech. dir. Creative Children's Theatre, 1951-54; dir. Community Center Players, Springfield, Mo., 1954-56; dir. Miami Actors Co., 1966-67; chmn. evaluation com. for English, Matthew Gilbert High Sch., Duval County, Fla., 1962; mem. com. on resolutions Secondary Sch. Theatre Conf., 1967. Bd. dirs. Secondary Sch. Theatre Conf., 1967-69. Served with Transp. Corps, AUS, World War II. Recipient Distinguished Service award North Dade High Sch., 1962-63, Outstanding Service award Deerfield Beach Elementary Sch., 1963, Drama award of excellence U. Miami, 1966. Mem. Nat., Fla. (mem. resolutions com. 1967) edn. assns., Am., Dade County Classroom (chmn. profl. problems 1967-68), Dade County Speech (pres. 1964-65, sec. 1966-67) tchrs. assns., Fla. Speech Assn., Nat. Assn. Dramatics and Speech Arts, Fla. Interscholastic Speech and Drama Assn. (pres. 1962-64), Am. Nat. Theatre and Acad., Internat. Thespian Soc., Phi Delta Kappa (pres. U. Miami chpt. 1979—), Omega Psi Phi (editor 1973-76). Mem. Congl. Ch. (vice chmn. ch. council 1973-75). Editor: Informer newsletter, 1954-56; contbr. articles to profl. jours. Home: 1030 NW 87th St Miami FL 33150 Office: 3400 NW 87th St Miami FL 33147

RANDOLPH, JAMES HARRISON, SR., realty co. exec.; b. Springfield, Tenn., Feb. 17, 1917; s. Bayless Jones and Effie Lee (Cummings) R.; B.S. in Bus. Adminstrn., U. Tenn., 1940; m. Millicent Roma Lincoln, Aug. 14, 1943; 1 son, James Harrison. Spl. agt., adminstrv. asst. to dir. FBI, Washington, 1942-52, also Bur. speaker, insp.; personnel dir. Dallas Housing Authority, 1952-54; real estate broker Bolanz & Bolanz, Dallas, 1954-58; real estate broker, investor Jim Randolph & Co., Realtors, Dallas, 1958—. Bd. govs. U. Tenn. Mem. Soc. Former Spl. Agts. of FBI (chmn. chpt. 1960), Soc. Indsl. Realtors, Dallas C. of C. (hon. life, vice-chmn. membership 1954-57), Scarabbean, Phi Sigma Kappa. Baptist. Club: Brookhaven Country (Dallas). Subject of articles in Nat. Real Estate Investor, July, 1961. Home: 11433 Lamplighter St Dallas TX 75229 Office: 211 N Ervay Bldg Dallas TX 75201

RANDOLPH, JENNINGS, U.S. Senator; b. Salem, W.Va., Mar. 8, 1902; s. Ernest and Idell (Bingman) R.; B.S. magna cum laude, Salem Coll., 1924, D.Aero. Sci. (hon.), 1943; LL.D., Davis and Elkins Coll., 1939, U. Pitts., 1965, Alderson-Broaddus Coll., 1966, Milton Coll., 1967, W.Va. U., 1967, Waynesburg Coll., 1967, W.Va. Wesleyan Coll., 1967, Oral Roberts U., 1972, Morris Harvey Coll., 1973, Pikeville Coll., 1973, Gallaudet Coll., 1976, Marshall U., 1978, Coll. of Steubenville, 1978; Litt.D., Southeastern U., 1940; D.Hum., W.Va. State Coll., 1964, Wheeling Coll., 1976; D.H.L., Maryville Coll., 1966, West Liberty State Coll., 1978; D.Pub. Service, Bethany Coll., 1970; m. Mary Katherine Babb, Feb. 1933; children—Jennings, Frank. Mem. editorial staff Clarksburg (W.Va.) Daily Telegram, 1924-25; asso. editor W.Va. Rev., 1925-26; former co-owner, asso. editor Randolph Enterprise-Rev., Elkins, W.Va.; prof. pub. speaking and journalism Davis and Elkins Coll., 1926-32, Southeastern U., 1935-43; dean Coll. Bus. and Fin. Adminstrn., 1952-58; asst. to pres., dir. pub. relations Capital Airlines, 1947-58; mem. 73d-79th congresses from 2d Dist. W.Va.; senator from W.Va., 1958—; chmn. Environment and Pub. Works Com.; mem. Human Resources Com., chmn. Handicapped Subcom., mem. Vets. Affairs Com. Mem. James Madison Meml. Commn., Nat. Commn. on Water Quality, Hwy. Beautification Commn.; mem. adv. bd. Nat. Council for Advancement of Small Colls.; mem. council advisers Careers Abroad Programs; mem. nat. adv. com. United Bus. Sch. Assns., Embry-Riddle Aero. Inst. Bd. dirs. Police Boys Club, Claude Worthington Benedum Found.; trustee Salem Coll., Woodward Sch. for Boys; trustee, chmn. adv. cabinet Southeastern U. Recipient N.Y. State Commn. for the Blind award, 1963, State of Israel Bonds award, 1965, Am. Humanics Found. award, 1966, Distinguished Service award NEA, 1968, Gold Medal of Merit, VFW, 1969, Vocat. Rehab. award, 1970, Nat. Service Recognition, Izaak Walton League Am., 1974, Belle Greve award Nat. Rehab. Assn., 1975, numerous others. Mem. W.Va. (dir.), Elkins (dir.) chambers commerce, Nat. Aero. Assn. (v.p.), First Flight Soc., Univ. Aviation Assn., Am. Rd. Builders Assn. (treas., pres. airport div.), Upper Monongahela Valley Assn., W.Va. Sportsmen Unltd., W.Va. Press Assn., Nat. Press Club, People to People, W.Va. Acad. Sci., W.Va. Soc. D.C., U.S. Capitol, W.Va., Randolph County hist. socs., Transp. Assn. Am. (hon.), Am. Assn. Airport Execs. (hon.). Democrat. Baptist. Clubs: Moose, Lions (gov. W.Va. clubs), Rotary (hon.), Kiwanis (hon.); Univ.; Congressional Flying (Washington). Author: Going to Make a Speech?; co-author Mr. Chairman, Ladies and Gentlemen; contbr. articles to nat. mags. Home: 4200 Cathedral Ave NW Washington DC 20016 Office: 3203 Dirksen Senate Office Bldg Washington DC 20510 also 328-29 Federal Bldg 300 3d St Elkins WV 26241

RANDOLPH, LESTER KENNETH, counselor; b. Jenning, Fla., Jan. 6, 1937; s. Jessie and Katie Mae Randolph; B.S., Edward Waters Coll., Fla., 1968; M.Ed., Fla. A&M U., 1971; Nat. Def. Loan Sci. grantee U. Fla., 1970-71; divorced; children—L.K., Rolando, Kevin, Valeria. Tchr., Duval County Schs., Jacksonville, Fla., 1968, 76; asst. chief therapist Jacksonville Drug Program, 1974-75; counselor U. North Fla., Jacksonville, 1976—. Served with USNR, 1956-59. Mem. Am. Personnel and Guidance Assn., Assn. Non-White Concerns, Kappa Alpha Psi. Democrat. Address: 3903 Notter St Jacksonville FL 32206

RANDOLPH, ROBERT MANICE, edn. and cons. firm exec.; b. N.Y.C., July 31, 1934; s. Robert S. and Peggy (Price) R.; B.B.A., U. Okla., 1956; M.B.A., Northwestern U., 1959; m. Valerie Jean Vandaveer, Oct. 20, 1956; children—Tamera M., Teresa M., Robin V. Dist. mgr. Gen. Am. Transp. Corp., Tulsa, 1959-61, asst. gen. mgr. container div., Chgo., 1961-65; asst. to exec. v.p. Joy Mfg. Co., Pitts., 1965-66; div. planning mgr. Marbon div. Borg-Warner Corp., Parkersburg, W.Va., 1966-68, group planning mgr., 1968-69; founder, pres., dir., also chief exec. officer Planagement Inc., Northbrook, Ill. 1969-72, Tulsa, 1972—. Faculty YMCA Coll., Chgo., 1969-71. Bd. dirs. Chgo. chpt. Cystic Fibrosis, 1971-72; mem. Dean's Council Bus. Coll. Tulsa U., 1973—. Served as lt. j.g. USNR, 1956-58. Mem. Am. Mgmt. Assn. (speaker 1968—, chmn. programs 1968), Nat. Council for Small Bus., Am. Marketing Assn., Adminstrv. Mgmt. Soc., Am. Soc. Tng. and Devel., Beta Gamma Sigma, Delta Sigma Pi, Delta Tau Delta. Author: Planagement—Moving Concept into Reality, 1975. Contbr. articles to profl. jours. Home: 6921 S Delaware Pl Tulsa OK 74136 Office: Planagement Inc 406 S Boulder Tulsa OK 74103

RANDOLPH, ROBERT RAY, JR., educator; b. Stillwater, Okla., Nov. 2, 1925; s. Robert Ray and Myrtle Nina (Stewart) B.; B.S., Okla. State U., 1949, M.S., 1955; m. Laura V. Hall, Nov. 11, 1945; children—Candace M., Robert Ray III, Enola Anne. Tchr. indsl. arts pub. schs., Atoka, Okla., 1949-50; tchr.-prin. pub. schs., Wanetta, Okla., 1952-54; tchr. indsl. arts Riverside Indian Sch., Bur. Indian Affairs, 1954-64, prin. Ft. Sill Indian Sch., 1964—. Served with U.S.

Army, 1943-45, 50-52; col. Res. Decorated Air medal with two oak leaf clusters, Bronze Star. Recipient Twenty Years Service Recognition award Bur. Indian Affairs, 1970. Mem. Res. Officers Assn., Nat. Assn. Secondary Sch. Prins. Mem. Christian Ch. (Disciples of Christ). Clubs: Lions (dist. gov., 1968-69; named Lion of Year, Anadarko club 1963-64, Lawton Moon club 1973-74), Masons, Order Eastern Star, K.T. Home: 2504 Austin Dr Lawton OK 73505 Office: Fort Sill Indian School Lawton OK 73501

RANELLE, HAROLD WILLIAM, osteo. physician; b. Ft. Worth, Jan. 24, 1943; s. Hugo John and Lee DeMarco R.; student U. Tex., 1961-64; D.O., Kansas City Coll. Osteo. Medicine, 1968; m. Linda Sue Clark, Aug. 31, 1963; children—Ann R., Michael. Intern, Ft. Worth Osteo. Hosp., 1968-69; resident in ophthalmology Okla. Osteo. Hosp., Tulsa, 1971-73; practice osteo. medicine specializing in ophthalmology, Ft. Worth, 1973—; mem. staffs Ft. Worth Osteo., Med. Plaza, Hurst Gen. hosps.; chmn. dept. ophthalmology Tex. Coll. Osteo. Medicine, Ft. Worth, 1973—; adv. Lions Eye Bank. Diplomate Am. Bd. Ophthalmology. Fellow Am. Osteo. Coll. Ophthalmology, Am. Acad. Ophthalmology and Otolaryngology; mem. Am. Osteo. Assn., Osteo. Coll. Ophthalmology and Otorhinolaryngology, Tex. Osteo. Med. Assn. Democrat. Roman Catholic. Editorial bd. Jour. Am. Osteo. Assn., 1977—; contbr. articles to profl. jours. Office: 3513 Mattison Ave Fort Worth TX 76107

RANEY, RICHARD BEVERLY, med. educator; b. Raleigh, N.C., July 21, 1906; s. Richard Beverly and Kate Whiting (Denson) R.; B.A., U. N.C., 1926; M.D., Harvard, 1930; m. Carolyn Haldane Fuller, Feb. 5, 1938; children—Richard Beverly III, Thomas Blount Fuller. Intern, Strong Meml. Hosp., Rochester, N.Y., 1930-31, resident, 1931-34; resident Duke Hosp., 1934-37; asso. instr. orthopaedic surgery Duke Hosp., 1937-48, asst. prof., 1948-52; prof., chmn. div. orthopedic surgery U. N.C., Chapel Hill, 1952-67, clin. prof. orthopaedic surgery, 1967-77. Hon. life trustee Wake County Library System 1970—. Trustee Olivia Raney Library, Raleigh, 1945—, N.C. Symphony Soc., 1970-72. Recipient N.C. Gov's., award as Physician of Year, 1964. Mem. Internat. Soc. Orthopaedic Surgery and Traumatology, Orthopaedic Research Soc., Am., So. med. assns., Am. Acad. Orthopaedic Surgery (v.p. 1961-62), Phi Beta Kappa, Alpha Omega Alpha, Alpha Tau Omega, Nu Sigma Nu. Author: Handbook of Orthopaedic Surgery, 9th edit., 1978; A Primer on the Prevention of Deformity in Childhood, 1941. Home: PO Box 2467 Chapel Hill NC 27514 Office: NC Meml Hosp Chapel Hill NC 27514

RANGEL, CARLOS ENRIQUE, mgmt. cons.; b. Bogota, Colombia, Jan. 18, 1928 (parents Venezuelan citizens); s. Nicolas and Carmen (Rodriguez) R.; came to U.S., 1968, naturalized, 1978; grad. indsl. elec. engr. Indsl. Tech. Sch., 1948; postgrad. Xavier U., 1977—; m. Maria Begonia Palacios, Apr. 23, 1958; children—Carlos Eduardo, Esmeralda, Roberto, Maria Teresa, Mike. Br. mgr. IBM Corp., Caracas, Venezuela, 1955-56, sales mgr., 1957-60, areas sales mgr. S.Am., Lima, Peru, 1960-64, div. mgr. S.Am., Montevideo, Uruguay, 1964-68, mfg. mgr. Latin Am., Lexington, Ky., 1968-72, country mgr., Venezuela, 1973-75; pres. Rangel Dynamics, Lexington, 1976—; lectr. Transylvania U., 1978—; mgmt. devel. tchr. banking, fast food and real estate bus., Lexington, 1977—. Bd. dirs. Caracas YMCA, 1958-60; pres. Christian Family Movement, Montevideo, 1965, Partners of Am., Venezuela-Tenn., 1974-75, Search Com. Sisters Cities, 1977—. Recipient awards IBM, 1952, 53, 57, 72. Mem. Am. Soc. Tng. and Devel., Sales and Mktg. Execs. Clubs: Optimists, Lafayette, Toastmasters. Home: 1523 Port Royal Lexington KY 40504 Office: 386 Waller Ave 2 Lexington KY 40504

RANGEL MEDINA, DAVID, lawyer; b. San Luis Potosi, Mex., Oct. 27, 1919; s. Antonio Rangel Ruiz de Esparza and Anastasia Medina Nunez; Lawyer, Nat. U. Mex., 1943, D. in Law, 1951; m. Consuelo Ortiz, June 1, 1950; children—David, Carlos, Horacio, Alfredo, Monica, Luis Xavier. Admitted to Mexican bar, 1945; sr. partner firm Basham, Ringe & Correa, Mexico City. Prof. adminstrv. law Iberoamericana U. Mex., 1965—; prof. indsl. property law Nat. U. Mex., 1974-79; lectr., Mexican del. internat. congresses on indsl. property, copyright and transfer of technology, Puerto Rico, France, Switzerland, Portugal, Australia, U.S.A., Hungary, Brazil, Philippines, Japan, Mex. Recipient Gt. Cross of Forensic Order of Honor, Mexican Bar and Nat. Lawyers Assn., 1971. Founder mem. Mexican Assn. Indsl. Property Agts. (pres. 1966), Inst. Pub. Adminstrn., Internat. Assn. for Protection of Indsl. Property (sec. Mexican group 1964-79); mem. Mexican Bar (dir.), Interam. Copyright Inst. (v.p. 1975-76), Inter-Am. Bar Assn., World Peace Through Law Center, Mexican Acad. Processal and Criminal Law, Interam. Assn. Indsl. Property (hon.), Bolivian Assn. Indsl. Property (corr.), Colombian Assn. Indsl. Property (corr.), League Internat. contre la Concurrence Deloyale (corr.). Author: Copyright and its Legal Protection in Mexico, 1944; Trademarks and its Compulsory Legende, 1958; Mexican Trademark Treatise, 1960; (with others) The Regime of the Industrial Property and the Economic Integration of the ALALC, 1969, World Patent Litigation, 1967, International Encyclopadia of Comparative Law, 1974, International Encyclopedia Unfair Competition, 1978. Editor, dir. Revista Mexide la Property Ind. y Artistica, 1973-79. Contbr. to publs. in field. Home: Cerrada de Xitle No 19 Jardines Pedregal de San Angel Mexico City 20 Mexico Office: 123 Liverpool St Mexico City 6 Mexico

RANK, SCOTT J., graphic designer; b. Riverside, Calif., Apr. 30, 1953; s. David J. and Eunice Ruth (Stepanek) R.; B.A. in Advt. Design, Iowa State U., 1975. Art dir. Sheppard Advt., Melbourne, Fla., 1975-76; graphic designer Harris Corp., Melbourne, 1977—. Recipient Chmn. award U.S. Jaycees, 1978; Sparkplug award Fla. Jaycees, 1978. Mem. West Melbourne Area Jaycees (state dir. 1977-78, sec. 1979—), Tau Sigma Delta, Sigma Phi Epsilon. Democrat. Mem. Ch. of Christ. Home: 101 Seminole Ave Apt 4 Melbourne FL 32901 Office: PO Box 37 Melbourne FL 32901

RANKEN, HOWARD BENEDICT, real estate exec.; b. Troy, N.Y., Sept. 14, 1898; s. William Hugh and Alma Florence (Eichholz) R.; student Rensselaer Poly. Inst., 1914-18; m. Edith May Manning, Mar. 5, 1920; children—Howard Benedict, William Allison, Doris Eleanor (Mrs. George M. Angleton). Design and devel. engr. Glens Falls (N.Y.) Machine Works, 1919-21, 1922-24; civil engr. W.C. Bliss, Miami, 1921-22, 1924-26; structural engr. M.H. Treadwell Co., N.Y.C., 1926-27; maintenance engr. Bklyn. Edison Co., 1927-28, The Tex. Co., Port Arthur, 1928-29; devel. engr. Smoot Engring. Co., N.Y.C., 1929-31; supervising engr., also asst. state supr. N.J. Geodetic Survey, Newark, 1933-40; marine devel. engr. Lidgerwood Mfg. Co., Elizabeth, N.J., 1941; ordnance engr. U.S. War Dept., N.Y.C., 1942-43; cons. engr. Cranford, N.J., 1944-45; cons. engr., also Realtor, New Smyrna Beach, Fla., 1945—. Councilman, City of Edgewater (Fla.), 1954-55; mem. Volusia County Democratic Exec. Com. Served with U.S. Army, 1918-19. Named Realtor of Year, S.E. Volusia County, 1972. Mem. Am. Soc. Mech. Engrs., Am. Def. Preparedness Assn., Soc. Am. Mil. Engrs., S.A.R., Am. Legion, New Smyrna Beach Bd. Realtors (pres. 1949-54, treas. 1966—). Democrat. Episcopalian. Rotarian. Home: Ranken Dr PO Box 202 Edgewater FL 32032 Office: 124 Canal St New Smyrna Beach FL 32069

RANKIN, HENRY HOLLIS, JR., lawyer; b. Mission, Tex., Jan. 11, 1915; s. Henry Hollis and Iva (Adams) R.; A.A., Edinburg Jr. Coll., 1933; LL.B., U. Tex. at Austin, 1936; m. Ann Lucille Chesnutt, July 24, 1939; children—Henry Hollis III, Robert Carlton, Deborah Ann (Mrs. Gary Paul Wagner). Admitted to Tex. bar, 1936; gen. practice law, Edinburg, Tex., 1936-58; partner firm Rankin, Kern & Layer, Inc., McAllen, Tex., 1958—; judge Hidalgo County Ct. at Law, 1951-53; dir. Tex. Hist. Commn., 1969-76. Trustee Mission Ind. Sch. Dist., 1963-69. Bd. dirs. Tex. Hist. Found., 1969-71, 80—, Tex. Law Enforcement Found., 1969. Cert. in civil trial law Tex. Bd. Legal Specialization. Fellow Tex. Bar Found. (life); mem. Am., Hidalgo County (dir. 1973-75, pres. 1976-77), Tex. (legal publs. com. 1972-77, com. on assistance to local bar assns. 1977—) bar assns., S.A.R., Tex. Assn. Def. Counsel, Phi Theta Kappa, Theta Xi. Democrat. Methodist. Clubs: McAllen Country, Tower. Home: 900 E Cedar St McAllen TX 78501 Office: 804 Pecan Ave PO Box 3744 McAllen TX 78501

RANSBURG, FRANK SCHELLER, univ. ofcl.; b. Keatchie, La., Jan. 29, 1943; s. Thomas Reed and Ella D. (McClure) R.; B.A., So. U., 1965; M.A., La. State U., 1970; m. Ivory Nell Bowie, Dec. 31, 1971; 1 dau., Ursula Tranell. Counselor, So. U., Baton Rouge, 1965-68, asst. dean men, 1968-69, dir. freshman affairs, 1969, dir. student activities, 1969-75, dir. student services, 1976—; counselor La. State U., 1969-73, asst. dir. high sch. relations, 1975-76; mem. lt. gov.'s staff La., 1973-74. Mem. Am., So. polit. sci. assns., A.A.U.P., N.A.A.C.P., Am. Personnel and Guidance Assn. Home: 6739 Willow Springs Ave Baton Rouge LA 70811 Office: Student Services Office 223 Student Union Bldg So Univ Baton Rouge LA 70813

RANSDELL, DONALD LEE, univ. adminstr.; b. Louisville, Sept. 8, 1937; s. Edward James and Anna Mae R.; B.A., Bellarmine Coll., 1960; postgrad. U. Louisville, 1966-67; m. Ann Quinn Leachman, Aug. 29, 1959; children—Leanne, Cheryl, Lee, Michael. Sr. buyer Rohm & Haas Chem. Co., 1965-69; purchasing agt. Kroger Co., Cin., 1969-73; mgr. comml. sales Knodel Tygrett Co., Cin., 1973-76; dir. purchasing No. Ky. U., Highland Heights, 1976—. Mem. Nat. Assn. Purchasing Mgrs., Nat. Assn. Coll. Aux. Services, Boone County Businessmen's Assn. (dir. 1979-80), Ky. Jaycees (regional v.p. 1974), Boone County Jaycees (pres. 1972-73). Democrat. Roman Catholic. Club: Rotary (pres. 1979-80) (Covington, Ky.). Home: 7029 Manderlay Dr Florence KY 41042 Office: Nunn Dr Highland Heights KY 41076

RANSOM, MARY ANN, bus. exec.; b. Sistersville, W.Va., Jan. 25, 1916; d. Lewis Velton and Florence Elizabeth (Clawson) R.; student Ohio U., 1941. Asso. with Parkersburg Office Supply Co., 1934—, sec.-treas., dir., 1947—; 1st violinist Marietta Coll. Symphony. W.Va. rep. nat. bd. Woman's Med. Coll. Pa., Phila.; v.p. Community Concert Assn.; trustee Alderson-Broaddus Coll. Member D.A.R., Nat. Soc. Arts and Letters, Parkersburg Art League, P.E.O. Baptist. Club: Parkersburg Country. Home: 601 Tenth and One Half St Parkersburg WV 26101 Office: 326 5th St Parkersburg WV 26101

RANSOM, RONALD EDWARD, city ofcl.; b. Atlanta, June 24, 1931; s. Claude Edward and Cassie Anne (Wood) R.; student Ga. State U., 1968-75; m. Marjorie Evelyn Bailey, Sept. 19, 1953; children—Ronald Edward, Scott Pierce. With City of Atlanta Parks and Recreation Dept., 1963-73, Six Flags Over Ga., Atlanta, 1973-75; dir. parks and recreation City of Marietta (Ga.), 1975—. Served with U.S. Army, 1953-55. Recipient Phoenix award City of Atlanta, 1971. Mem. Nat. Recreation and Park Assn., Ga. Recreation and Park Assn. Democrat. Baptist. Home: 265 Lucky Dr Marietta GA 30067 Office: City Hall PO Box 609 Marietta GA 30061

RANSON, KERWIN RALPH, II, drilling co. exec.; b. St. Albans, W.Va., Aug. 10, 1942; s. Kerwin Ralph and Aileen Virginia (Cunningham) R.; B.A., W.Va. Wesleyan Coll., 1964; m. Belva Anderson, Aug. 15, 1964; children—Robbie Anne, Mark Anderson, Michael Todd. With Union Drilling, Inc., 1964—, corporate sec., 1968—, also dir. Pres. Acad. PTA, 1975-77; pres. AB.-U. Intermediate Sch. Parent Tchr. Group, 1978—; rep. to bd. trustees W.Va. Wesleyan Coll., 1977—, chmn. president's athletic task force, 1979—; bd. dirs., fin. cons. Upshur County Art Center, 1976; trustee Ohio Valley Coll., Parkersburg, W.Va., 1978—. Mem. Am. Assn. Petroleum Landmen, Ind. Oil and Gas Assn. W.Va. (pres. 1979—), W.Va. Oil and Natural Gas Assn. Republican. Mem. Church of Christ. Club: Buckhannon Country. Home: 18 Allman Ave Buckhannon WV 26201 Office: PO Drawer 40 Buckhannon WV 26201

RANSONE, COLEMAN BERNARD, JR., polit. scientist, educator; b. Norfolk, Va., Jan. 27, 1920; s. Coleman Bernard and Natalie (Neblett) R.; A.B., Coll. William and Mary, 1941; M.Pub. Adminstrn., Harvard, 1947; Ph.D., 1950; m. Katherine May, Dec. 19, 1949; children—Natalie Gray. Kathleen Susan. Katherine Neblett. Instr. to asso. prof. polit. sci. U. Ala., 1947-57; prof. govt. Coll. William and Mary, 1957-58; prof. polit. sci. U. Ala., 1958—, ednl. dir. So. regional tng. program in pub. adminstrn., 1958—. Served to 1st lt. USAAF, 1943-46. Fund for Advancement Edn. faculty fellow, 1953-54. Mem. Am., So. (v.p. 1963) polit. sci. assns., Am. Soc. Pub. Adminstrn. (sr.), Nat. Assn. Schs. for Pub. Affairs and Adminstrn. (exec. com. 1962-65), Phi Beta Kappa (pres. Alpha of Ala. chpt. 1961-62, 74-75), Pi Sigma Alpha. Episcopalian (lay reader). Author: The Office of Governor in the South, 1951; The Office of Governor in the United States, 1956; Ethics in Alabama State Government, 1972; The Alabama Government Manual, 1977. Mem. editorial bd. Public Adminstrn. Rev., 1967-70, Internat. Jour. Public Adminstrn., 1979—. Home: 34 Ridgeland Tuscaloosa AL 35406 Office: Drawer I University AL 35486

RAPHAELI, AVI S., psychologist; b. Israel, Feb. 13, 1946; came to U.S., 1973; s. Mordecai and Haia Raphaeli; B.A., U. Tel Aviv, 1973; M.A., U. Houston, 1974, Ph.D., 1977; m. Miriam Barer, Mar. 17, 1970. Lectr., U. Houston, 1975—; practice psychology specializing in clin. and ednl. psychology, Houston, 1977—; mem. staff 4 area hosps. Mem. Am. Psychol. Assn., Tex. Psychol. Assn., Houston Psychol. Assn., Am. Ednl. Research Assn., Houston Behavioral Therapy Assn., Sigma Xi. Club: B'nai B'rith. Office: 2600 S Gessner Suite 501 Houston TX 77063

RAPHAEL IGLESIAS, LORENZO, cons. engr.; b. Santurce, P.R., Mar. 5, 1940; s. Lorenzo Silvester Iglesias-La Cruz and Carmen Velez-Paradis; B.S.M.E., U. P.R., 1963; postgrad. (scholar) U. So. Calif., 1966, U. P.R., 1957-63; m. Sylvia Garcia-Menendez, June 28, 1972; children—Robert, Lorena, Marisol, Roxana, Lourdes. External plant designer P.R. Telephone Co., 1962; transp. engr. Dept. Public Works, San Juan, P.R., 1965; chief air pollution control program Dept. Health, San Juan, 1965-71; asso. dir. for air and water Environ. Quality Bd., 1971-77; cons. environ. engr., Santurce, 1977—. Served with U.S. Army, 1963-65. Recipient commendation HEW, 1967, Nat. Air Pollution Control Adminstrn., HEW, 1968. Diplomate Am. Acad. Environ. Engrs. Mem. Inst. Engrs. and Surveyors of P.R. (treas. Carolina chpt. 1979—), ASME, Air Pollution Control Assn., Water Pollution Control Fedn., Soc. Am. Mil. Engrs., Nat. Soc. Profl. Engrs., Soc. Engrs. of P.R., Am. Water Resources Assn., Am. Conf. Govtl. Indsl. Hygienists. Developed, established, directed 1st air pollution control program for P.R.

RAPOPORT, BERNARD, ins. co. exec.; b. San Antonio, July 17, 1917; s. David and Riva (Feldman) R.; B.A., U. Tex., 1939; m. Audre Jean Newman, Feb. 15, 1942; 1 son, Ronald B. Credit mgr. Zales Jewelry, Austin, Tex., 1936-39, mgr., 1943; with Kruger Jewelry Co., 1939-40; partner Art's Jewelry Store, Waco, Tex., 1944-49; gen. agt. Pioneer Am. Life Ins. Co., Waco, 1950-51; with Am. Income Life Ins. Co., Waco, 1951—, chmn. bd., chief exec. officer, 1977—; dir. Citizens Nat. Bank. Trustee, Paul Quinn Coll., Waco, 1963—; bd. dirs. Mexican Am. Legal Def. and Ednl. Fund, 1976—; chmn. United Negro Coll. Fund, Waco, 1979—; mem. adv. bd. Am. Fedn. State, County and Mcpl. Employees, Washington, 1976—; bd. regents New Direction, Whitney, Pa., 1978—; mem. Nat. Council Crime and Delinquency, 1979—, Univ. Cancer Found., Houston, 1976—; mem. com. for establishment of Wayne Morse Chair of Law and Politics, U. Oreg., 1975—; mem. Democratic Nat. Fin. Com., 1976—, Tex. Dem. Party Fin. Council, Austin. 1975—, Dem. House and Senate Council, 1978—. Recipient award Am. Digestive Disease Soc., 1979; Disting. Spl. award Office and Prof. Employees Internat. Union, 1977; award for public service Oil, Chem. and Atomic Workers Internat. Union, 1979. Jewish. Club: B'nai B'rith. Office: 1200 Wooded Acres Waco TX 76710

RAPOPORT, MARTHA ANN, speech pathologist, audiologist; b. Norfolk, Va., Aug. 27, 1951; d. Herman Leonard and Phyllis Marilyn (Sperans) R.; student Beaver Coll., 1969-71; B.S. in Speech, Northwestern U., 1973; M.Ed. in Speech Pathology, U. Va., 1975, M.Ed. in Audiology, 1976 Chief audiologist Sharpstown Gen. Hosp., Houston, 1976-77; speech pathologist Vis. Nurse Assn., Houston, 1978-79; speech pathologist and audiologist Bellaire (Tex.) Speech and Hearing Cons.'s, 1979—; speech and hearing cons. Diagnostic Center Hosp., Houston, Neurorehab. Center Pasadena (Tex.), Mem. Learning Diagnostic Center, Houston, Rosewood Audiology Services, Houston, others. Counselor, dir. art program Offender Aid and Restoration, Charlottesville, 1974-76; recreation therapist ARC, Portsmouth, Va., summer 1973; fundraiser Com. of Responsibility, Phila., 1969-70; tutor underprivileged children, Portsmouth, 1968-69, Glenside, Pa., 1969-70. Fellowship grantee U. Va., 1975-76. Mem. Hear-Say, Houston Area Assn. for Communicative Disorders, Acoustical Soc. Am., Am. Inst. Physics, Am. Speech and Hearing Assn. (cert.), Speech and Hearing Assn. Tex. Home and Office: 3808 Stanford B Houston TX 77006

RAPP, JOANNA MAY, nurse; b. Youngsville, Pa., Nov. 22, 1920; d. Wade Hampton and Edith Blanche (Hodges) Brazee; R.N., City Hosp., 1941; B.S., Western Res. U., 1947; m. Ellsworth G. Rapp, Nov. 6, 1976; children by previous marriage—Sallie Patricia Bean, Susan Margaret Reynolds. Instr. nursing Warren (Pa.) State Hosp., 1963-70; Alford-field team nurse U.S. Bur. Occupational Health, Morgantown, W.Va., 1970-71; forensic instr. NIMH John Howard Pavilion, St. Elizabeth Hosp., Washington, 1971-72, supvr., 1976-78; adminstr. supr. Allentown (Pa.) State Hosp., 1972-73; supr. Hale Makua, Wailuku, Hawaii, 1973-76; quality assurance coordinator Harlingen State Mental Health Center, 1978-79; nursing supr. Upjohn Healthcare, Harlingen, 1979—. Mem. Am. Nursing Assn., Am. Legion. Served to 1st lt. Army Nurse Corps., 1944-45. Methodist. Home: 814 E Whitehouse Circle Harlingen TX 78550

RAPP, SANDU Z., architect; b. Targoviste, Rumania, Mar. 23, 1917; came to U.S., 1959, naturalized, 1965; s. Zissu Benjamin and Berthe (Loebel) R.; diploma in architecture Poly. Inst., Bucharest, Rumania, 1941; grad. Conservatory of Music, Bucharest, 1940; m. Katherine Gruenberg, Jan. 12, 1958. Pvt. practice architecture, Bucharest, Rumania, 1940-50, Tel Aviv, Israel, 1950-59; asso. P. Birnbaum, N.Y.C., 1959-65, Evans & Delehanty, Architects, N.Y.C., 1965-73; pvt. practice architecture Miami Beach, Fla., 1973—. Served as 2nd lt., Rumanian Army, 1940-41. Registered architect, Israel, N.Y., Fla. Mem. AIA. Democrat. Archtl. works include Palace of the Swedish Legation, Bucharest, 1941-43; composer various works for piano, orch., chamber music, songs. Address: 1865 79 St Causeway North Bay Village FL 33141

RAPPAPORT, HAROLD, civil engr.; b. Boston, Feb. 10, 1920; s. Louis Joshua and Rebecca (Rubinstein) R.; B.S. in Civil Engring. cum laude, Northeastern U., 1950; m. Bertha Bennett, Oct. 15, 1944; children—Paul Miles, Jill Allison. Draftsman, Mark Linenthal, cons. engr., Boston, 1944-50; structural designer, asso. Goldberg, LeMessurier & Assos., Inc., cons. engrs., Boston, 1950-67; specification writer, dir. Connell Metcalf & Eddy, Inc., architects and engrs., Miami, Fla., 1967-79; mgr. tech. services Greenleaf Telesca, Architects & Engrs., Miami, 1979—. Served with AUS, 1942-44. Recipient nat. award James F. Lincoln Arc Welding Found. Competition, 1966. Registered profl. engr., Mass. Mem. Constrn. Specifications Inst. (pres. Greater Miami chpt. 1975-76; cert.), Mensa. Prin. engring. works include: Blue Shield Bldg., Boston, Jewett Art, Theatre, Music bldg Wellesley (Mass.) Coll., Am. Airlines Hangar, Logan Internat. Airport, Boston, various NASA space exploration program structures at Cape Kennedy. Editor manuals of engring. office practice. Home: 8662 SW 154th Circle Pl Miami FL 33193 Office: 2650 SW 27 Ave Miami FL 33133

RAPPAPORT, MARTIN PAUL, physician; b. Bronx, N.Y., Apr. 25, 1935; s. Joseph and Anne (Kramer) R.; B.S., Tulane U., 1957, M.D., 1960; m. Sharon Ann Hayes, Sept. 9, 1976; children—Karen, Steven, Sheila. Intern, Charity Hosp. of La., New Orleans, 1960-61, resident in internal medicine, 1961-64; practice medicine specializing in internal medicine, Seabrook, Tex., 1968-72, Webster, Tex., 1972—; mem. courtesy staff Galveston County (Tex.) Meml. Hosp., 1968—, Bapt. Meml. System, 1969-72; mem. staff Clear Lake Hosp., 1972—; cons. staff St. Mary's Hosp., 1973-79; fellow in nephrology Northwestern U. Med. Sch., Chgo., 1968; clin. instr. in medicine and nephrology U. Tex., Galveston, 1969—; lectr. emergency med. technician course, 1974-76; adviser on respiratory therapy program Alvin (Tex.) Jr. Coll., 1976—; cons. nephrology USPHS, 1979-80. Served to capt. M.C., U.S. Army, 1961-67. Diplomate Am. Bd. Internal Medicine, Nat. Bd. Med. Examiners. Fellow Am. Coll. Chest Physicians; mem. A.C.P., Internat., Am. socs. nephrology, So. Med. Assn., Tex. Med. Assn., Am. Soc. Artificial Internal Organs, Am. Diabetes Assn., Tex. Acad. Internal Medicine, AAAS, Galveston County Med. Soc., Am. Diabetes Assn., Am. Geriatrics Soc., Bay

Area Heart Assn. (bd. govs. 1969-75), Clear Lake C. of C., Phi Delta Epsilon, Alpha Epsilon Pi, Tulane Alumni Assn. Jewish. Club: Rotary. Home: 16623 Abbeywood Dr Houston TX 77058 Office: Clear Lake Med Cons PA 400 Medical Center Blvd Suite 209C Webster TX 77598

RAPPAPORT, YVONNE KINDINGER, educator, lectr.; b. Crestline, Ohio, Feb. 15, 1928; d. Paul Theodore and Florence Iona (Cover) Kindinger; B.S. summa cum laude, Northwestern U., 1949; M.A., Va. Poly. Inst. and State U., 1973; C.A.G.S., 1979; Ph.D., 1980; m. Norman Lewis Rappaport; children—Michael, Laura, Hilary, Stephen, Jocelyn. Personnel officer, then cons. and mgmt. analyst USAF, 1953-63; cons. mgmt. analysis, personnel and pub. relations, 1963-67; cons. program devel., instr. U. Va., 1967-70, dir. continuing edn. for women, 1970-76, dir. continuing edn. for adults, 1976—; dir., performer theatre, children's theatre, radio and TV, 1953—; mem. editorial adv. bd. New Viewpoints div. Franklin Watts, Inc., pubs., 1979—; cons. in field. Mem. Va. Adv. Legis. Com. Continuing Edn., 1970-71, No. Va. Adv. Com. Ednl. Telecommunications, 1971—; bd. dirs. Home and Sch. Inst., Washington, 1971-79; mem. adv. bd. Service League Va., 1976-78. Recipient Meritorious Service award USAF, 1959. Mem. Nat. Assn. Women Deans, Adminstrs. and Counselors (S.E. regional coordinator 1973—), adult edn. assns. U.S. (Nat. Leadership award 1973, 74, 76, 77, 78; chmn. commn. status women in edn. 1972—, dir. 1973—, chmn. council affiliate orgns. 1974-75, chmn. pub. affairs, 1975-78, v.p. 1978-79), Va. (pres. 1971-73; Recognition of Merit award 1971-73), LWV (state dir. 1968-73, nat. pub. relations com. 1970—), AAUW, PTA, Am. Personnel and Guidance Assn., Nat. Univ. Extension Assn., Assn. Continuing Higher Edn., Am. Bus. Women Assn. (award 1960). Club: Order Eastern Star. Author handbooks and work books, also radio, TV scripts. Home: 3225 Atlanta St Fairfax VA 22030 Office: Sch Continuing Edn Univ Va Charlottesville VA 22903

RAPSTINE, FRANK, petroleum landman; b. Carson County, Tex., May 12, 1920; s. Henry William and Agnes Catherine (Gordzelik) R.; B.S. with honors, Tex. Tech. U., 1942; m. Frances Louise Schulze, May 1, 1943; children—Mary Elizabeth, Catherine Louise, Bonnie Breanne, Inge Frances, Greta Annett, Frank. Research chemist Phillips Petroleum Co., Bartelsville, Okla., 1946-48; owner, mgr. wholesale food co., Pampa, Tex., 1948-50, constrn. and land devel. co., Tex. and N.Mex., 1950-79; pres. Lufrank Corp., Amarillo, Tex., 1963—; gen. partner Morris-Higgins & Assos., Amarillo, 1967—, Paradox Petroleum Co., Amarillo, 1969-79; dir. Tex. Petroleum Fund, Teckla, Inc. Mem. Amarillo Zoning Bd., 1957-62, Panhandle Regional Planning Commn., 1969-76; bd. dirs. YMCA, Amarillo, Kidney Found.; state chmn. Builders for Johnson, 1964; area campaign chmn. Tex. Democratic candidate for U.S. Senate, 1964; area mgr. Dem. candidate for Pres., 1968; chmn. Community Devel. Commn., Amarillo; mem. Tex. Constl. Revision Com., 1973. Served with USN, 1942-45. Recipient citation Panhandle Regional Planning Commn., 1974, 75. Mem. Nat. Assn. Home Builders (life dir.), Intertel (life), Am. Geophys. Union, Mineral. Soc. Am., Panhandle Geol. Soc., Am. Assn. Petroleum Landmen, Nat. Assn. Securities Dealers, Panhandle Producers and Royalty Owners Assn. (dir.), Internat. Platform Assn., Mensa (Amarillo coordinator), Amarillo C. of C. Democrat. Roman Catholic. Clubs: McLean Country, K.C. Home: 2015 Teckla St Amarillo TX 79106 Office: 3721 Wolflin Ave Amarillo TX 79102

RAPTOULIS, ARTHUR STEVEN, pediatric cardiologist; b. N.Y.C., Jan. 4, 1943; s. Arthur and Evelyn (Pardales) R.; M.D., SUNY, Downstate Med. Center, 1971; m. Diane M. Castelanetta, June 12, 1971; children—Dana Lyn, Nicholas Arthur. Intern, N.Y. Hosp.-Cornell Med. Center, N.Y.C., 1971-72, resident, 1972-73; fellow in pedatric cardiology Cornell Med. Coll., 1973-75; head div. pediatric cardiology Orlando (Fla.) Regional Med. Center, 1977—; cons. in field. Diplomate Am. Bd. Pediatrics, sub-bd. pediatric cardiology. Mem. Central Fla. Heart Assn. (dir. 1977-79). Address: 1131 S Orange Ave Orlando FL 32806

RASBERRY, RONNIE DALE, dermatologist; b. Black Oak, Ark., Apr. 30, 1944; s. Dale Martin and Mable Lee (Watson) R.; B.S., Ark. State Coll., 1965; M.D., B.S. in Medicine, U. Ark., 1969; m. Michale Jane Rheinbolt, May 17, 1967; children—Richard Dwight, Martin Wesley. Intern, John Peter Smith Hosp., Ft. Worth, 1969-70; resident in dermatology Naval Regional Med. Center, San Diego, 1973-76; practice medicine in dermatology, owner Rasberry Dermatology Clinic, Searcy, Ark., 1977—; mem. staff Central Ark. Gen., White County Meml. hosps. Served with USN, 1970-77. Diplomate Am. Bd. Dermatology. Fellow Am. Acad. Dermatology; mem. AMA, Dermatology Found., Assn. Mil. Surgeons, Assn. Mil. Dermatologists, Internat. Soc. Tropical Dermatologists, Ark. Med. Soc., White County Med. Soc., Ark. Dermatology Soc., Ark. Oncology Soc. Mem. Ch. of Christ.

RASE, HOWARD FREDERICK, chem. engr.; b. Buffalo, Oct. 18, 1921; s. Henry Leonhard and Sophie Augusta (Braun) R.; B.S. in Chem. Engring., U. Tex., 1942; M.S. in Chem. Engring., U. Wis., 1950, Ph.D. in Chem. Engring., 1952; m. Beverly Wills Bonelli, June 12, 1954; children—Carolyn Victoria, Howard Frederick. Chem. engr. Dow Chem. Co., Freeport, Tex., 1942-44; process engr. Eastern States Petroleum Co., Houston, 1944; process and project engr. Foster Wheeler Corp., N.Y.C., 1944-49; asst. prof. chem. engring. U. Tex., Austin, 1952-56, asso. prof., 1956-61, prof., 1961-74, W. A. Cunningham prof., 1974—, chmn. dept. chem. engring., 1963-68; vis. prof. Tech. U. Denmark, 1957; cons. to industry. Del. Travis County and Tex. Republican. Convs., 1976; adviser Young Republicans, U. Tex.; bd. dirs. Kirby Hall Sch. Recipient Excellence in Teaching Gen. Dynamics award Coll. Engring., U. Tex., 1961, Distinguished Advisor award, 1967. Fellow Am. Inst. Chem. Engrs.; mem. Am. Chem. Soc., Tex. Fine Arts Assn., Sigma Xi, Tau Beta Pi, Omega Chi Epsilon (nat. treas. 1958-70), Phi Lambda Upsilon. Mem. United Ch. Author: (with M.H. Barrow) Project Engineering of Process Plants, 1957; Philosophy and Logic of Chemical Engineering, 1961; Piping Design for Process Plants, 1963; Chemical Reactor Design for Process Plants, 1977; contbr. numerous articles to profl. jours.; patentee in field. Home: 3700 River Rd Austin TX 78703 Office: Dept of Chem Engring U of Tex Austin TX 78712

RASHID, RICHARD CHARLES, ophthalmologist; b. Montgomery, W. Va., Nov. 22, 1937; s. Mitchell and Mosa Mary (Mettry) R.; M.D., Med. Coll. Va., 1962; m. Eleanor Mary Kousaie, Dec. 27, 1969; children—Richard Charles, Mitchell Nicholas, Nichole Mary, Paul Ferris. Intern Springfield (Ohio) Mercy Hosp., 1962-63; resident Case Western Res. U., and Lakeside Hosp., Cleve., 1965-68; practice medicine specializing in ophthalmology, Charleston, W. Va., 1968—; chief ophthalmology H.J. Thomas Meml. Hosp., 1969—; asso. clin. prof. ophthalmology and family practice W.Va. Med. Sch. Trustee, Sunrise Art Mus., Charleston, 1975—, mem. acquisitions com., 1977—; bd. dirs. W.Va. Opera Theatre, 1977-80, Physicians Edn. Network; patron Charleston Symphony Orch., 1969—, bd. dirs.; patron Kanawha Players, 1968—. Served with USN, 1963-65. Diplomate Am. Assn. Ophthalmology; mem. Am., W.Va. acads. ophthalmology and otolaryngology, Am. Intraocular Implant Soc., Am., W.Va. med. socs., Kanawha County Med. Soc. (past sec.-treas., council, del. state med. soc. 1970-77), Physicians Edn. Network (charter), Am. Assn. Contemporary Ophthalmology, Assn. Am. Physicians and Surgeons, Med. Coll. Va. Alumni (chpt. pres.). Republican. Roman Catholic. Home: 3 Burkewood Pl Charleston WV 25314 Office: 424 Division St South Charleston WV 25309

RASKIN, JEFFREY BARRY, physician; b. N.Y.C., July 30, 1940; s. James Miles and Devy (Hirsch) R.; student U. Miami, 1961, M.D., 1965; m. Bobbie Ann Campbell, July 17, 1965; children—Scott, Tracy, Lori. Intern, Jackson Meml. Hosp., Miami, Fla., 1965-66, resident in internal medicine and gastroenterology, 1968-72; asst. prof. medicine U. Miami Sch. Medicine, 1972-76, asso. prof., 1976—; chief diagnostic and therapeutic gastrointestinal endoscopy Jackson Meml. Hosp., 1972—; practice medicine specializing in gastroenterology, Miami, 1972—. Served to capt. USAF, 1966-68. Diplomate Am. Bd. Internal Medicine. Fellow ACP; mem. Am. Gastroenterol. Assn., Am. Soc. Gastrointestinal Endoscopy, Am. Soc. Internal Medicine, Am. Soc. Contemporary Medicine and Surgery, So. Med. Assn., Fla. Med. Assn., Dade County Med. Assn. Contbr. articles to profl. jours. Home: 13100 108th Pl SW Miami FL 33176 Office: Div Gastroenterology Jackson Memorial Hospital Miami FL 33136

RASMUSSEN, GORMAN LEONARD, social service adminstr.; b. Evanston, Ill., Nov. 27, 1931; s. Gorman and Julie (DuRack) R.; A.B., Culver Stockton Coll., 1959; M.S.W., U. Mo., 1961; m. Lois Bumgarner, Dec. 27, 1958; children—Gorman Leonard, Anne Marie. Psychiat. social worker U. Mo. Med. Center, 1961-62, Grant County Guidance Center, Lancaster, Wis., 1962-64, Racine County (Wis.) Mental Health Clinic, 1964-65; part-time project dir. Gateway House, Racine, 1965-66; dir. casework services Racine Family Service, 1965-68; supr. social worker, dir. dept. med. social work Kitchener-Waterloo (Ont.) Hosp., 1968-73; part-time field instr. Waterloo Luth. U.. 1968-71, lectr. sociology, 1968-69; part-time lectr. social work Conestoga Coll. Applied Arts and Scis., Kitchener, Ont., 1970-71; dir. profl. services Family Service of So. Lake County. Highland Park, Ill., 1973-74; dir. dept. social services, asst. prof. social work U. Ky. Coll. Medicine, 1974-76; dir. dept. social services M.D. Anderson Hosp. and Tumor Inst., Houston, 1976—; mem. health curriculum adv. com. U. Houston, 1976—. Mem. adv. council, research and demonstration project Lexington-Fayette County Health Dept., 1974-76; treas. Lexington-Fayette County Human Services Council, 1974-76; mem. health task force Ky. State Council, 1975-76; mem. Missouri City Planning Commn. Served with USAF, 1952-56. Fellow Ky. Soc. Clin. Social Work, Am. Orthopsychiat. Assn.; mem. Tex. Psychotherapy Assn., Nat. Assn. Social Workers, Tex. Soc. Hosp. Social Work Dirs., Acad. Certified Social Workers, Am. Group Psychotherapy Assn., Am. Assn. Marriage and Family Counselors (clin. mem.), Social Work Vocat. Bur., Soc. Hosp. Social Work Dirs. of Am. Hosp. Assn. Editorial bd. Cancer Nursing. Home: 3955 Point Clear Dr Missouri City TX 77459

RATANASIT, SOMSAK, radiologist; b. Thailand, Mar. 14, 1941; s. Manit and Fueng (Opaso) R.; came to U.S., 1970; M.D., Mahidhol U. (Thailand), 1966; m. Somtawin, Aug. 11, 1973; children—Dan, Arlene. With public health, Thailand, 1966-70; intern and resident Nassau (N.Y.) Hosp., 1970-75; radiologist Stonewall Jackson Hosp., Weston, W.Va., 1975-76, VA Med. Center, Tuskegee, Ala., 1976—. Mem. AMA, Am. Coll. Radiology. Buddhist. Home: 323 Seminole Dr Montgomery AL 36117 Office: VA Medical Center Tuskegee AL 36083

RATARD, RAOULT CLAUDE-BERNARD, physician; b. Santo, New Hebrides, Dec. 13, 1944; came to U.S., 1977; m. Aubert and Suzanne Marie-Louise (Lafforgue) R.; B.S., U. Paris, 1967, M.D., 1968; D.M.&I., Institut Pasteur, Paris, 1970; M.S., La. State U., 1976; M.P.H., Tulane U., 1976; m. Margaret S. Francez, Dec. 14, 1970; children—Laennec, Marceau, Paulin. Intern, Hosp. Vaugirard, Paris, 1968-69; chief med. officer Rural Health Services, Vila, New Hebrides, 1972-77; dep. dir. region 9, Tex. Dept. Health, Uvalde, 1977-79, leprosy cons., 1977-79; dir. Jefferson Parish Health Dept., Metairie, La., 1980—; leprosy cons. WHO, Suva, Fiji, 1979. WHO fellow, 1973, 75-76. Mem. Am. Public Health Assn., Tex. Public Health Assn., Tex. Med. Assn., Am. Soc. Tropical Medicine and Hygiene, Royal Soc. Tropical Medicine and Hygiene, Internat. Health Soc., Am. Coll. Preventive Medicine. Contbr. articles to profl. jours. Home: 4109 Cleveland Pl Metairie LA 70003 Office: 111 N Causeway Metairie LA 70003

RATCLIFF, RAYMOND FRANKLIN, investment co. exec.; b. Athens, Tex., Mar. 4, 1944; s. Raymond Franklin and Delia Grace (McGinnty) R.; children—Raymond, Bianca. Financial analyst 1st Nat. Bank Dallas, 1966-68; sr. v.p., gen. mgr. Robert S. Folsom Investments, Dallas, 1968-74; prin., chmn. bd. Raymond F. Ratcliff Investments, Inc., Dallas, 1974—; dir. Whiterock Nat. Bank, KERA TV/Radio Sta., Ramahal Corp., Kelley Co., Inc. Served with U.S. Army, 1966-69. Mem. Phi Delta Theta Alumni Assn. (dir., past pres.). Republican. Baptist. Clubs: Preston Trail Golf, Bent Tree Country, So. Meth. U. Mustang. Home: 6410 Beckwith Ct Dallas TX 75248 Office: 4949 Westgrove Dallas TX 75248

RATHER, HUGH HENRY, JR., architect; b. Holly Springs, Miss., May 29, 1916; s. Hugh Henry and Marie Nelms (Butler) R.; student U. Miss., 1934-36, Washington U., St. Louis, 1936-39; B.S. in Architecture with high honors, U. Ill., 1940; m. Dorothy Gretchen Wright, June 6, 1956; 1 son, Hugh Henry III. Draftsman, Furbringer & Ehrman, Architects, Memphis, 1940-42, Charles T. Main Constrn. Co., Boston, Camp McCain, Grenada, Miss., 1942-43; designer engring. dept. Goodyear Aircraft Co., Akron, Ohio, 1943, Furbringer & Ehrman, Architects, Memphis, 1945-47; archtl. designer, asso. architect N.W. Overstreet Architects and Engrs., Jackson, Miss., 1947-54; pvt. practice architecture, Jackson, 1955-56, Holly Springs, 1956—. Served with USN, 1944-45. Mem. AIA, U. Miss. Alumni Assn., Marshall County Hist. Soc. Episcopalian. Club: Rotary (Holly Springs). Prin. archtl. works include Henry High Sch. Gymnasium, Byhalia, Miss., Marshall County Library, Holly Springs, Marshall County Health Center, Holly Springs. Home: 515 Woodland Heights Holly Springs MS 38635 Office: 35 Alderson St Holly Springs MS 38635

RATLEDGE, EARL RICHARD, financial exec.; b. Friendsville, Tenn., Oct. 30, 1924; s. Wright Alexander and Eva Jane (Simerly) R.; student U. Tenn., 1948-52; m. Joan Sandberg, May 16, 1964; children—Carol Renee, Kristi Lynn, Earl Richard. Asst. mgr. Tenn. Valley Finance Corp., Knoxville, Tenn., 1952-58; pres. Holston Ins. Agy., Inc., Knoxville, 1958—; registered rep. Integrated Resources Equity Corp., Knoxville, 1969—; mem. exec. com., dir. Farmers Mutual Ins. Co., Knoxville, 1977—. Young boys basketball coach Knoxville YMCA, 1958-68, Service to Youth award, 1963. Served with U.S. Army, 1949-51. Decorated Bronze Star. Mem. Internat. Assn. Fin. Planners, Profl. Ins. Agts. Assn., Soc. Certified Ins. Counselors. Republican. Presbyterian. Home: 3533 Raines Ln Knoxville TN 37920 Office: 109 Northshore Dr Knoxville TN 37919

RATLIFF, BYRON ALLEN, engr.; b. Decatur, Ala., Feb. 13, 1938; s. George Malcolm and LaVerne Ann (Allen) R.; certificate Decatur Iron & Steel Co. Engring. and Drafting Sch., 1956; student U. Ala., 1965; certificate Barnard & Burk Power Plant Engring. Program, 1972; m. Stella Wanell Standridge, June 23, 1957; children—Angela Wanell, Scott Allen. draftsman Decatur Iron & Steel Co. (Ala.), 1956-57, draftsman, 1957-58; draftsman Thiokol Chem. Corp., Huntsville, Ala., 1958-62, sr. draftsman, 1962-64; designer Brown Engring. Co., Huntsville, 1964-66, sr. designer, 1966-68; sr. designer, project coordinator, sect. head Barnard & Burk Inc., Baton Rouge, 1968-77, chief engr. piping dept., 1977-80; mgr. engring. services div. Imes and Assos., Inc., Baton Rouge, 1980—. Vice pres. Barnard & Burk Recreation League, 1971-73, pres., 1974-76; dir. youth dept. Chapelwood Ch. of God, Baton Rouge, 1970—, chmn. bd. Christian edn., 1973, 74. Mem. Inst. for Certification Engring. Technicians. Democrat. Home: 9634 Glennsade Ave Baton Rouge LA 70814 Office: 11756 S Harrell's Ferry Rd Baton Rouge LA 70816

RATTIGAN, JACK MARTIN, broadcasting co. exec.; b. Shenandoah, Pa., Aug. 18, 1928; s. Martin Henry and Philomena Elizabeth (Monahan) R.; B.S. in Biology, Coll. Holy Cross, Worcester, Mass., 1950; m. Adelaide C. O'Hare, Sept. 24, 1955; children—Martin, Neil, Brendan, Maria, Adelaide, Jacqueline. Radio and TV personality NBC, Phila., 1958-65; dir. public affairs Sta. KYW, 1965-67; sales mgr. Sta. WMMR, Phila., 1967-71; broadcast exec. Rust Communications, Norfolk, Va., 1971-75; gen. mgr. Sta. WCHS/WBES, Charleston, W.Va., 1975-77; gen. mgr. Sta. WRAP, Norfolk, 1977—. Vice pres. parish council Ch. of Resurrection, Portsmouth, Va. Served with USAF, 1950-53. Mem. Tidewater Assn. Radio Broadcasters (pres.), Va. Assn. Broadcasters, Tidewater Ad Club. Office: 13 Downtown Plaza Norfolk VA 23501

RAUCH, JEANNE GIRARD (MRS. MARSHALL ARTHUR RAUCH), textile mill exec.; b. Gastonia, N.C., Sept. 15, 1923; d. Frank Henry and Ida Sadie (Paradies) Goldberg; student Duke, 1940-41; B.S., Syracuse U., 1944; m. Marshall Arthur Rauch, May 18, 1946; children—Ingrid, Marc, Peter, Stephanie, John. With Pyramid Mills, Bessemer City, N.C., 1959—, v.p., 1963—, also dir. Sec. Rauch Found., Inc., 1965-72. Bd. dirs., United Fund, Gaston, 1970, 71, 72; mem. county bd., Girl Scouts, 1950; arts commr. N.C. Museum Art, 1973—; mem. Gaston County Bicentennial Com., 1975; pres. Gaston Fine Arts Council, 1975-76, Gaston County Museum Art and History, 1975-77. Occupational adv. bd. Gaston Coll., 1971-73; bd. visitors Sacred Heart Coll., 1971-72. Mem. Sisterhood Hadassah (pres. 1954-57), Little Theater (1st sec. 1949, 50), Gaston Art Guild (1st pres. 1963, 65), Sir Walter Cabinet (v.p. 1969), Alpha Epsilon Phi, Alpha Epsilon Rho. Democrat. Home: 1121 Scotch Dr Gastonia NC 28052 Office: Box 755 Bessemer City NC 28016

RAUCH, MARSHALL ARTHUR, textile co. exec.; b. N.Y.C., Feb. 2, 1923; s. Nathan A. and Tillie (Wohl) R.; student Duke, 1940-43; m. Jeanne Girard, 1946; children—John, Ingrid, Marc, Peter, Stephanie. Chmn. bd., pres., dir. Rauch Industries, Inc., Gastonia, N.C.; chmn. bd., treas., dir. Pyramid Mills Co., Inc., Bessemer City, N.C., 1954-73, Pyramid Dye Corp., Bessemer City, 1956-73, Homeside Yarn, Inc., Bessemer City, 1960-71, Nile Star, Inc., Woodmere, N.Y., 1961—, Gastonia Dyeing Corp. (N.C.), 1968-73; treas., dir. E.P. Press, Inc., Gastonia, 1965—; dir. Ins. Financing Corp., Gastonia, Plastivac Corp., Charlotte, N.C.; mgr. Narco Molding Co., Bessemer City. Chmn. Gaston Jewish Welfare Fund, 1958-62, 68-70; 1st v.p. N.C. Assn. Jewish Men, 1966; mem. nat. council Am. Jewish Joint Distbn. Com., 1968-70; mem. Gov.'s Good Neighbor Council, 1963—; chmn. Gastonia Human Relations Com., 1964-67; chmn. N.C. Com. on Population and Family, 1968—; mem. N.C. Jail Study Commn., 1968; pres. Asso. Industries, 1964-65; chmn. Employ the Handicapped Com., 1964-65; mem. N.C. Citizens Com. for Dental Health, 1968; sr. adviser Gastonia Boys Club, 1947-63; mem. cons. commn. Pioneer council Girl Scouts U.S.A., 1968-69; pres. Gaston County YMCA, 1972. Mayor pro tem City of Gastonia, 1952-54, 61-63, mem. city council, 1952-54, 61-65; mem. N.C. State Senate, 1967-79. Bd. dirs., treas. Rauch Found.; bd. dirs. N.C. United Jewish Appeal Cabinet, 1968-70, Gaston Skills, 1964-66, Salvation Army Boys Club, 1963—, United Fund, 1963-67, Gaston Boys Club, 1964—, Carolina Amateur Athletics Union, 1951-53, Gaston Mus. Natural History, 1963-64, Holy Angels Nursery, Belmont, N.C., 1960—, Planned Parenthood and World Population, N.Y.C., 1968-69, Gaston Community Action, 1966, Gaston-Cleveland Tb Assn., 1968; bd. govs. N.C. Jewish Home for the Aged, 1968-70; mem. adv. council N.C. Com. for Children and Youth, 1968-69; bd. dirs. Gastonia YMCA, 1959-62, 67-69, v.p., 1968-70; v.p., bd. dirs. Community Concert Assn., 1960-61; mem. top mgmt. adv. com. Gaston County Indsl. Mgmt. Club, 1963-65; bd. advisers Gardner Webb Coll., 1969-70; trustee U. N.C., 1969-70; mem. adv. com. N.C. Vocational Textile Sch., 1970-71; trustee N.C. Land Conservancy, 1978; mem. Intangibles Tax Study Commn., 1978. Served with AUS, World War II; ETO. Decorated Combat Infantry Badge; recipient Nat. Recreation citation Nat. Recreation Assn., 1965; Brotherhood award Nat. Council Christians and Jews, 1969; named Man of Yr., Gastonia Jaycees, 1957, Gastonia Jr. Women's Club, 1964, Gaston County chpt. Omega Psi Phi, 1966, N.C. Health Dept., 1968, Gastonia Red Shield Boys Club, 1970. Mem. Duke Alumni Assn. (pres. Gaston chpt. 1961-62). Jewish religion (pres. temple 1962-64, tchr. Sunday sch. 1951-56). Mem. B'nai B'rith. Home: 1121 Scotch Dr Gastonia NC 28052

RAUH, J. RANDALL, obstetrician, gynecologist; b. Hardtner, Kans., June 30, 1947; s. John Harry and Dorothy Mae (Dimmick) R.; B.S., Northwestern State Coll., Alva, Okla., 1969; M.D., U. Okla., 1973; m. Janice Yvonne Weigand, July 1, 1967; children—Heather Elaine, Sarah Elaine, Travis Randall, Joshua Blaine. Resident in obstetrics and gynecology Tulsa Med. Edn. Found., 1973-76; pvt. practice medicine specializing in obstetrics and gynecology, Okmulgee, Okla., 1976-80, Stillwater, Okla., 1980—; preceptor U. Okla. Coll. Medicine; clin. instr. obstetrics and gynecology Tulsa Med. Coll. Diplomate Am. Bd. Obstetrics and Gynecology. Fellow Am. Coll. Obstetrics and Gynecology; mem. AMA, Okla. State Med. Assn., Tulsa County Obstetrics and Gynecology Soc., Am. Fertility Soc., U. Okla. Coll. Medicine Alumni Assn. (life), Am. Assn. Gynecol. Laparoscopists. Republican. Lutheran. Home: 1909 Iba Dr Stillwater OK 74074 Office: 1510 W 8th St Stillwater OK 74074

RAUSCH, THOMAS LOUIS, indsl. engr.; b. Lafayette, Ind., Nov. 13, 1944; s. Louis Charles and Alberta Justina (Brown) R.; B.S., Purdue U., 1972; m. Linda Louise Person; children—Lisa Louise, Jennifer Lynn. Indsl. engr. Ross Gear div. TRW, Lafayette, Ind., 1956-72, project engr., Lebanon, Tenn., 1972-73, mgr. systems and design, Greeneville, Tenn., 1973-76, personnel adminstr., 1976-79, mgr. engring. United Greenfield div. TRW, Augusta, Ga., 1979; mgr. indsl. engring. Cooper Industries, Houston, 1979—. Served with U.S. Army. Mem. Am. Inst. Indsl. Engrs., Am. Mgmt. Assn., Jaycees. Roman Catholic. Club: Moose (Greeneville).

RAVITZ, LEONARD J., physician; b. Cuyahoga County, Ohio, Apr. 17, 1925; s. Leonard R. and Esther Evelyn (Skerball) R.; B.S., Case Western Res. U., 1944; M.D., Wayne State U., 1946; M.S., Yale U., 1950. Asst., A.J. Derbyshire, Ph.D., EEG Dept., Harper Hosp., Detroit, 1943-46; trainee med. hypnosis, Milton H. Erickson, M.D., Wayne State U., 1945-46; faculty psychiatry and mental hygiene Yale U. Med. Sch., New Haven, 1947-49, research fellow, asso. H.L. Burr, Ph.D., dept. neuro-anatomy, 1949-50; instr., asso. in nueropsychiatry, asso. R.S. Lyman, M.D., Duke Hosp. and Med. Sch., Durham, N.C., 1950-53; asst. dir. profl. tng. VA Hosp., Downey, Ill., 1953-54; asso. in psychiatry Sch. Medicine, U. Pa., Phila., 1955-58; dir. tng. and research Eastern State Hosp., Williamsburg, Va., 1958-60, asst. spl. research project E. Cushing, M.D., 1958; practice neuropsychiatry, Norfolk, Va., 1961—; staff Norfolk Gen. Hosp., 1961—; cons. Div. Alcohol Studies and Rehab., VA Dept. Mental Hygiene and Hosps., 1961—, nutrition project Old Dominion U., Norfolk, 1978—, USPHS Hosp., Norfolk, 1979—. Vice pres. Willoughby Civic League, 1970—. Served to 1st lt. U.S. Army, 1942-46. Diplomate Am. Bd. Psychiatry and Neurology. Fellow N.Y. Acad. Sci., Am. Psychiat. Assn., AAAS, Am. Soc. Clin. Hypnosis, Royal Soc. Health (London); mem. Sigma Xi. Contbr. numerous articles to profl. jours.; research electromagnetic-field correlates of hypnosis, health and disease, psychiat. disorders, aging, other med. phenomena. Office: 807 Med Tower 400 Gresham Dr Norfolk VA 23507

RAVOIRA, JAMES, artist; b. Weirton, W.Va., Sept. 4, 1933; s. James and Josephine; B.A., W. Liberty State Coll., 1962; M.A., Kent State U., 1966, M.F.A., 1977; m. LaWanda Faye Pugh, Nov. 19, 1977. Asst. prof. Indian River Community Coll., Ft. Pierce, Fla., 1967-69; faculty Thornton Community Coll., Harvey, Ill., 1969-70; asst. prof. The Citadel, Charleston, S.C., 1971-74; prof. art U. S.C., Myrtle Beach, 1974—; one-man show Myrtle Beach Conv. Center, 1977, Lynn Kottler Galleries, N.Y.C., 1977, 78; exhibited in group show Artist/U.S.A., 1978-79; painting Dance, the Birth of Life represented in Artist/USA, 1977, The Experiment, 1978. Recipient Eleanor D. Caldwell award, Bethany (W.Va.) Coll., 1961, Carnegie Library award, 1961. Mem. Coll. Art Assn. Home: 35 Hasell St Apt C Charleston SC 29401

RAWE, STEPHEN E., neurosurgeon; b. New Martinsville, W.Va., Nov. 14, 1943; s. Elmer David and Geneva Joan (Calvert) R.; B.A., W.Va. U., 1965; M.D., U. Pa., 1969; m. Jill B. Tumpson, June 21, 1970; children—Stephen Kinsey, Julia Ann. Resident in neurol. surgery Yale U., 1971-75, instr., 1976; asst. prof. Med. U. S.C., 1976-79, asso. prof., 1979—. Mem. AMA, S.C. Med. Assn., Charleston County Med. Assn., Am. Assn. Neurol. Surgeons, So. Neurosurg. Soc., S.C. Neurol. Surgery Assn., Phi Beta Kappa. Contbr. articles to profl. jours. Home: 113 Norview Dr Charleston SC 29407 Office: 171 Ashley Ave Charleston SC 29403

RAWL, ALFRED ERASTUS, JR., radiologist; b. Charleston County, S.C., Mar. 13, 1921; s. Alfred Erastus and Juanita Gertrude (Armstrong) R.; B.S., Coll. of Charleston, 1941; M.D., Med. U. S.C., 1944; m. Mary Virginia Gasser, May 7, 1943; children—Alfred Victor, Angela Renee, Marshall Brian, Michael Bruce, Dana Anthony. Intern, James Walker Meml. Hosp., Wilmington, N.C., 1944-45; resident Med. Coll. Hosps., Charleston, 1955-58; gen. practice medicine, Charleston, 1946-53; radiologist St. Francis Xavier Hosp., Charleston, 1958-66; pres. Alfred E. Rawl, Jr. M.D., Charleston Heights, S.C., 1966—; cons. radiologist Coastal Center, Ladson, S.C., USPHS, Charleston; contract radiologist Naval Regional Med. Center. Served with USN, 1945-46, 53-54. Fellow Am. Coll. Radiology; mem. AMA, S.C., So., Charleston County med. assns., Radiol. Soc. of N. Am. Democrat. Methodist. Clubs: Country Club of Charleston, Seabrook Island, Retired Officers Assn. Home: PO Box 297 Johns Island SC 29455 Office: 2130 Arapahoe St Charleston Heights SC 29405

RAWLINGS, WILMA JEAN, purchasing exec.; b. Melbourne, Ark., Aug. 28, 1940; d. Delbert and Ednas Marie (Rhodes) Reynolds; children—Carol Jean, Crystal Ann. Exec. sec. Aerojet Ordnance & Mfg. Co., Batesville, Ark., 1964-74; purchasing agt. Gen. Tire & Rubber Co., Batesville, 1974—; mem. office occupations adv. bd. Gateway Vocat. Tech. Sch., 1976—. Mem. Am. Mgmt. Assn., Nat. Assn. Purchasing Mgmt., So. Rubber Group. Home: 904 Woodland St PO Box 119 Cave City AR 72521 Office: Hwy 167 N Batesville AR 72501

RAWLINS, CHARLES EDWARD, bus. services co. exec.; b. New Brighton, Pa., Jan. 3, 1941; s. Edward Fred and Dorothy Mae (Schramm) R.; ed. high sch.; m. Sandra R. Radford, June 25, 1977; children—Karen Staats, Tim Staats, Heidi. Asst. editor div. SWL, McLean, Va., 1979—. Served with USAF, 1958-78. Decorated Air Force Commendation medal, Meritorious Service medal, Joint Service medal with oak leaf cluster. Mem. VFW. Democrat. Lutheran. Home: 4425 Round Hill Rd Alexandria VA 22310 Office: SWL Suite 700 Park Pl 7926 Jones Branch Dr McLean VA 22101

RAWLINS, GEORGE SKEVINGTON, civil engr.; b. Geneva, N.Y., Oct. 18, 1904; s. Thomas H. and Elizabeth R. (Baxter) R.; C.E., Cornell U., 1925; s. Lois Cassidy, June 3, 1950; 1 son, Malcolm B. Instr. dept. civil engring. Drexel Inst., Phila., 1926; design engr. Water Bur. of Reading, Pa., 1926-28, asst. engr. design of Maiden Creek Filter Plant, 1932-36; engr. William H. Dechant & Sons, engrs. and architects, Reading, 1928-32; design engr. Chester Engrs., Pitts., 1936-37; engr. water works design and constrn. City of Charlotte, N.C., 1937-39; owner G.S. Rawlins, civil engr., Charlotte, 1939-41; partner J.N. Pease Assos., Charlotte, 1941-42, exec. v.p., 1942-73, pres., 1973-74, vice chmn. bd., 1974-75, cons., 1975—. Mem. engring. adv. council of U. N.C., Charlotte, 1972—; mem. N.C. Engrs. and Surveyors Joint Com. on Registration Law, 1972-76, chmn., 1973-75. Registered profl. engr., N.C., Fla. Mem. ASCE (pres. N.C. sect. 1961-62, named outstanding Civil Engr. in N.C., 1969), Nat. Soc. Profl. Engrs. (nat. dir. 1954-63, v.p. southeastern region 1964-65, chmn. ethics com. 1965-66), Profl. Engrs. N.C. (Outstanding Service award 1964, Meritorious Service award 1962, dir. 1951-52, pres. 1953-54), N.C. Sewage and Indsl. Waste Assn. (Arthur Sidney Bedell award 1958), Am. Water Works Assn. (dir. 1951-54, George Warren Fuller award 1955), Am. Acad. San. Engrs., Charlotte Engrs. Club (Distinguished Service award 1966, pres. 1950), N.C. Assn. of Professions, Water Pollution Control Fedn. (dir. 1946-48), Engrs. Council for Profl. Devel. (chmn. ethics com. 1966-75). Contbr. articles to profl. publs. Lutheran. Home: 101 Wrenwood Ln Charlotte NC 28211 Office: 2925 E Independence Blvd Charlotte NC 28205

RAWLS, CAROLINA DEMONTIGNE, pub. relations dir.; b. Oshkosh, Wis.; d. Arthur Joseph and Frances (Wever) DeMontigne; B.S., Fla. State U., 1935, postgrad. library sci.; m. Oscar Greison Rawls, July 16, 1936; 1 dau., Carolina DeMontigne. Librarian, Landon High Sch., Jacksonville, Fla., 1935-36; county supr. sch. libraries, Palo Pinto County, Tex., 1936-37; woman's commentator, radio sta. KARK, Little Rock, 1938-39; advt. layout and copy, editor house organ and serviceman's paper Cohen Bros. Dept. Store, Jacksonville, 1944-46; writer, producer 13 weeks series hist. programs, radio sta. WPDQ, Jacksonville, 1945; commentator radio sta. WOBS, Jacksonville, 1947; fashion commentary, coordination, prodn. (free lance), Jacksonville dept. stores and shops, including 2 fashion movies WMBR-TV, WJHP-TV and city-wide fashion show for C. of C., 1946—; compiler The Jacksonville Story, a history and pictorial record of city, C. of C., 1951; condr. programs WJHP-TV, 1955; asso. editor, feature writer Suntime mag., Jacksonville, 1952-56; pub. relations dir. Guild Players, Inc., 1955-71, bd. dirs., 1st woman trustee, 1956-71; instr. Jacksonville U. Dir., sec. Ednl. TV, Inc., 1953-56; mem. program planning com. Ednl. TV of Jacksonville, WJCT-TV, 1957-58; dir. Queens Contest, Gator Bowl Assn., 1955-60; pres. Jr. Cotillion of Jacksonville, 1955-56; treas. Sr. Cotillion, 1956-58; publicity dir., mem. bd. Little Theatre of Jacksonville, 1948-54; instr. self-improvement courses YWCA, 1957-58; sec. Jacksonville Council of the Arts, 1957-61; performance chmn. Citywide Arts Festival, 1966-67; coordinator Furchgott's Dept. Store 100th Anniversary Celebration, 1967; 1st v.p. Four Found., Inc., 1971-73, pres. 1973-76; mem. Jacksonville Bicentennial Commn., 1974-76; membership chmn. Jacksonville Children's Museum, 1974-75; bd. dirs. Girls Clubs; mem. Fine Arts Forum. Recipient Eve award Fla. Pub. Co., 1971. Mem. P.T.A., Friends of The Library, Friends of Jacksonville U. Library, Jacksonville, Fla. hist. socs., Fla. Fedn. Women's Clubs, Panhellenic, Mortar Bd., Garnet Key, Alpha Chi Omega (chmn. nat. pub. relations com., mem. nat. awards com.), Epsilon Sigma Omicron (chmn. state chpt. 1976—), Phi Kappa Phi, Kappa Delta Pi. Democrat. Episcopalian. Club: Woman's of Jacksonville (2d v.p., civic dir. 1968, 1st v.p., fine arts dir. 1969-71, pres. 1971-73). Home: 1357 Tiber Ave Jacksonville FL 32207

RAWLS, J. LEWIS, JR., lawyer, former state senator; b. Suffolk, Va., Dec. 7, 1923; s. J. Lewis and Azzie (Gatling) R.; student Va. Mil. Inst., 1942-43, Duke, 1943-44; LL.B., U. Va., 1950; m. Mary Helen Macklin, Oct. 4, 1947; children—John Lewis III, Rebecca Macklin (Mrs. Habel), Frank Macklin. Admitted to Va. bar, 1950; gen. counsel Taylor Cos., 1952-57; individual law practice, Suffolk, 1950-52, 57-63; partner firm Rawls & Bagnell, Suffolk, 1963-70, Rawls, Habel & Rawls, Suffolk, 1977—; mem. Va. Ho. of Dels., 1962-70, Va. Senate, 1976-80; pres., chief exec. Suffolk Oil Mill, Inc., 1969-76; dir., sec.-treas. Old Dominion Investors Trust, Suffolk, 1967—; mem. Suffolk bd. Va. Nat. Bank; sec., dir. Home Guaranty Ins. Corp., HGIC Corp. Pres., March of Dimes, Suffolk, 1951-52; sec. Suffolk Swimming Pool Corp., 1951-62. Served with USNR, 1943-46. Mem. Am., Va. bar assns. Mason, Elk, Rotarian. Home: 603 Dumville Ave Suffolk VA 23434 Office: PO Box 1458 Suffolk VA 23434

RAWLS, JOHN MELVIN, ednl. psychologist, counselor; b. Corrigan, Tex., July 7, 1939; s. Phillip and Minnie R.; B.S., N. Tex. State U., 1968; M.Ed., Prairie View A&M U., 1971; Ab.D., Baylor U., 1976; m. Barnell Butler, Nov. 27, 1969; 1 child. Biology tchr. Devereux Found., Victoria, Tex., 1968-69; asst. dir. Manpower Ednl. Tng. (CETA), Diboll, Tex., 1969-70; sr. counselor and rep./coordinator Career Ednl. and Vocat. Program in Vietnam, U.S. Office Edn./HEW, 1971-72, regional vets. coordinator, Kansas City, Mo., 1972-73; asst. prof. counselor edn. Prairie View A&M U., 1974-77; asst. prof. psychology Alcorn State U., Lorman, Miss., 1977-79; adj. asst. prof. psychology E. Tex. State U., Commerce, 1979; career edn. coordinator Wilmer Hutchin (Tex.) Ind. Sch. Dist., 1980—; with U.S. Dept. Labor (Health Programs), Wash. Pres., United Collegiate Scholarship for Minorities, 1978-80; dir. youth programs Baptist Ch., Corrigan, Tex., 1971-75, ordained to ministry, 1974. Served with USN, 1956-63. Recipient Office Edn./HEW award; EPDA leadership award HEW. Mem. Am. Personnel and Guidance Assn., AAUP, Am. Vocat. Assn., Phi Delta Kappa. Democrat. Home: Box 26006 S Magnolia St Corrigan TX 75939

RAWLS, MARTHA GROGAN (MOLLY), librarian; b. Winston-Salem, N.C., Feb. 18, 1949; d. Joseph Cherry and Angelia (Mackie) Grogan; B.A., U. N.C., 1971, M.S.L.S., 1972; m. Jeffrey D. Rawls, June 4, 1978. Mktg. research librarian R.J. Reynolds Tobacco Co., Winston-Salem, 1973-75, mgmt. info. librarian R.J. Reynolds Industries, Winston-Salem, 1976-79, mgr. mgmt. info. services, 1979—; former cons. Mandala Center, Inc., Winston-Salem. Mem. Spl. Libraries Assn., Nat. Micrographics Assn., Assn. Records Mgrs. and Administrs. Democrat. Baptist. Home: 4680 Forest Manor Winston-Salem NC 27103 Office: 401 N Main St Winston-Salem NC 27102

RAWLS, ROY HERMAN, hosp. engr.; b. Jasper, Tex., Jan. 27, 1908; s. Sebern Robert and Beulah Jeanette (May) R.; student U. Houston, 1931-32; m. Gertrude Florence Augsburger, Sept. 25, 1937; children—Alan Keith, Linda Jane, Beverly Kay. Surveyor seismograph research Amerado Petroleum Co., 1933-40; with layout and constrn. Lockwood Andrews Engring. of Houston, 1940-42; communication chief San Jacinto Ordnance Depot, U.S. Army, Channelview, Tex., 1942-60; chief engr. Tidelands Gen. Hosp., Channelview, 1960-80, cons., 1980—; instr. gen. plant ops. and maintenance. Active local sch. bd., 1944-52; co-founder Water Control Dist. #21, Channelview, 1956-57, chmn., sec. ofcl. bd., 1957-58; precinct chmn. Republican primary, 1952, county del. to Rep. party, 1952-68. Recipient service cert. ARC, 1961; various service awards Tidelands Hosp. Mem. Tex. Hosp. Engrs. Methodist. Clubs: Masons, Scottish Rite. Home: 1116 Redbud Rd Channelview TX 77530 Office: 15101 East Freeway Channelview TX 77530

RAWLS, WALTER CECIL, JR., scientist, lawyer, bus. exec.; b. Richmond, Va., Sept. 13, 1928; s. Walter Cecil and Ella (Freeman) R.; A.B., U. Mo., 1951; J.D., Washington U., St. Louis, 1958; D.Sc., Davis Coll., 1973; m. Sheila Daphne Kirsch; children—James David, Richard Wayne. Agt. for France, Am. Trust Life Ins. Co., Wichita Falls, Tex., 1953-54; admitted to Fla. bar, 1958, since practiced in Jacksonville; mem. firm Ragland, Kurz, Toole, 1958, Marks, Gray, Yates, Conroy, Gibbs, 1959; pvt. practice, 1960-63, 1969—; partner Thomas & Rawls, 1963-67, Ogier, Stubbs & Rawls, 1967-69, RAWB & Co.; pres. Biomagnetics Internat., Inc.; treas., dir. Ga.-Fla. Oil Co.; dir. F.I.D. Internat., Capitol Res. Ltd. Mem. adv. council Washington U. Law Sch., St. Louis. Served with AUS, 1951-53. Fellow Coll. Human Scis. mem. Internat., Am., Jacksonville bar assns., Fla. Bar, Am. Soc. Internat. Law, Am. Judicature Soc., Am. Legion, S.A.R., Sons Confederate Vets., English Speaking Union, Am. Trial Lawyers Assn., Am. Arbitration Assn. (arbitrator), AAAS, N.Y. Acad. Scis., Internat. Platform Assn., Am. Philatelic Soc., Com. of 100, Jacksonville C. of C., Fedn. Am. Scientists, Phi Delta Theta, Delta Theta Phi. Republican. Conglist. Clubs: Explorers; Capitol Hill (Washington); Republican, Metropolitan Dinner (officer, mem. orgn. com.) (Jacksonville, Fla.). Co-author: Magnetism and its Effects on the Living System, The Magnetic Effect, The Rainbow in Your Hands; A Blueprint of Life with Magnetism. Home: 3584 Beauclerc Rd Jacksonville FL 32217 Office: 2301 Park Ave Orange Park FL 32073

RAWSON, JOHN ELTON, physician; b. Okolona, Miss., Jan. 31, 1938; s. Elton P. and Marjorie Morgan (Jones) R.; B.S. in Chemistry, Millsaps Coll., 1960; M.D., U. Miss., 1965; m. Mary Asbury Crouch, June 24, 1962; children—Katherine Asbury, Edwin Lauderdale. Intern, Vanderbilt U. Hosp., Nashville, 1965-66, resident, 1966-67; chief resident pediatrics U. Miss. Hosp., Jackson, 1967-68; fellow in newborn medicine U. Miss., 1970-72, asst. prof. pediatrics, 1972-77, asso. prof., 1977—; dir. newborn service Hinds Gen. Hosp., Jackson. Bd. dirs. St. Andrews Sch.; state chmn. March of Dimes/Nat. Found., 1977—. Served with USAF, 1968-70. Diplomate Am. Bd. Pediatrics. Mem. Miss., Central Miss. med. assns., Central Miss. Pediatric Club, So., Nat., perinatal assns., Am. Acad. Pediatrics, Am. Assn. Respiratory Therapy. Episcopalian. Club: Rotary. Home: 5335 Kaywood Dr Jackson MS 39211 Office: 1850 Chadwick Dr Jackson MS 39204

RAY, ALICE TAYLOR, dietitian; b. Clay County, Tenn., Jan. 19, 1933; d. George Clemons and Clora (Cole) T.; B.S., Tenn. Technol. U., 1952; postgrad. U. Tenn., 1962-63; m. Bascom Ray, May 28, 1952; children—Barbara, Kenneth, Sylvia. Supr. food service Vanderbilt U. Hosp., Nashville, 1953-54; supr. spl. diet kitchen St. Thomas Hosp., Nashville, 1954-56; dietitian's asst. Sumner County Meml. Hosp., Nashville, 1962-63; chief dietitian Jesse H. Jones Hosp., Nashville, 1963-69; dir. dietetic services Middle Tenn. Mental Health Inst., Nashville, 1969—; cons. in field. Adv. com. Nashville Area Vocat.-Tech. Sch., 1975-75, Vol. State Community Coll., 1977—. Mem. Am. Dietetic Assn. (registered dietitian), Tenn. Dietetic Assn., Nashville Dist. Dietetic Assn., Am. Soc. Hosp. Food Service Adminstrs. (area rep. Tenn. chpt. 1974-75, chpt. pres. 1975-76), Hosp., Instn. and Ednl. Food Service Soc. (state adv. 1976—). Baptist. Home: Route 3 Box 315 Springfield TN 37172 Office: Middle Tenn Mental Health Inst 1501 Murfreesboro Rd Nashville TN 37217

RAY, CHARLES MITCHELL, educator; b. Sweeden, Ky., Nov. 19, 1938; s. Stanford Mitchell and Dorothy Lee (Kinser) R.; A.B., Bowling Green Coll. Commerce, 1960; M.S., Ind. U., 1962; Ed.D., U. Ky., 1968; m. Linda Louise Walsh, Aug. 27, 1966; children—Stanford Warren, Kyle Edward. Asst. prof. bus. edn. Morehead (Ky.) State U., 1962-69; prof. bus. and office adminstrn. Western Ky. U., Bowling Green, 1969—. Co-chmn. steering com. Free Enterprise Fair, 1979. Mem. Adminstrv. Mgmt. Soc. (past pres. Nashville chpt.), Nat. Bus. Edn. Assn., Am. Bus. Communication Assn., Ky. Bus. Edn. Assn. (past pres.), Delta Pi Epsilon. Contbr. articles to profl. jours. Home: 1635 Chestnut St Bowling Green KY 42101 Office: 514 Grise Hall Western Ky U Bowling Green KY 42101

RAY, EDWARD HUNT, physician; b. Sharpsburg, Miss., Jan. 14, 1899; s. Thomas Jackson and May Eliza (Allison) R.; B.S., U. Miss., 1920; M.D., Tulane U., 1922; m. Louise Duncan Moore, Jan. 5, 1926; children—Edward Hunt, Thomas Allison, Margaretta Duncan. Intern, Touro Infirmary, New Orleans, 1922-23; preceptor in gen. surgery under W. O. Bullock, Lexington, Ky., 1923-27; fellow in urology Mayo Clinic, Rochester, Minn., 1927-29; practice medicine specializing in urology, Lexington, 1929-80; mem. faculty, 1st prof., head urology U. Ky. Med. Center, 1963-69; mem. staff St. Joseph, Good Samaritan, Central Bapt., Univ. hosps. Served with AUS, 1942-46. Diplomate Am. Bd. Urology. Fellow A.C.S. (past pres. Ky. chpt.), So. Surg. Assn.; mem. Ky. Surg. Soc. (past pres.), AMA (sec. urology sect, chmn.), Am. Assn. Univ. Urologists, Excelsior Surg. Soc. Ky. Civil War Roundtable (hon. mem., 2d v.p.). Episcopalian. Clubs: Thoroughbred of Am., Iroquois Hunt, Idle Hour Country. Inventor Ray kidney stone forceps. Contbr. articles to profl. jours. Edward H. Ray sr. vis. professorship in urology established at U. Ky. Med. Center, 1973, also his portrait hangs there. Home: 1009 Turkey Foot Rd Lexington KY 40502

RAY, GEORGE WASHINGTON, III, educator; b. Binghamton, N.Y., Dec. 4, 1932; s. George Washington and Margaret (Nicholson) R.; A.B., Wesleyan U., 1954; grad. preceptor Colgate U., 1957-59; Ph.D., U. Rochester, 1966; m. Elizabeth DuPree Osborn, Dec. 29, 1956; children—Virginia, George, Melissa, Grace Elizabeth. Instr., U. Rochester (N.Y.), 1961-62, U. Va., Charlottesville, 1962-64; instr. Washington and Lee U., Lexington, Va., 1964-66, asst. prof., 1966-69, asso. prof., 1969-74, prof. English, 1974—; fellow cooperative program in humanities Duke U. and U. N.C., Chapel Hill, 1967-68; exchange fellow Univ. Coll., Oxford, 1980. Bd. dirs. Rockbridge Concert-Theatre Series, 1966—, Rockbridge Area Mental Health Assn., 1975-78. Served as 1st. lt. USMC, 1954-57. Mem. Va. Humanities Conf., Southeastern Renaissance Conf., Renaissance Soc. Am., Chi Psi. Democrat. Presbyterian. Author: Chapman's The Conspiracy and Tragedy of Charles, Duke of Byron, edited with a commentary and notes from the text of the 1608 quarto, 2 vols., 1979. Office: Washington and Lee U Lexington VA 24450

RAY, GERALD LEROY, indsl. engr.; b. Atlanta, Tex., Aug. 13, 1939; s. Frederick Leroy and Velma Annette (Paul) R.; B.S. in Agrl. Engring., La. Tech. U., 1962; M.S. in Agrl. Engring., La. State U., 1971, M.S. in Indsl. Engring., 1976; m. Betty Jean George, June 9, 1962; children—Gerald Leroy Jr., Brian Phillip. Instr., La. State U., Baton Rouge, 1966-68; methods engr. La. Dept. Hwys., 1968-74, asst. rd. maintenance engr., Baton Rouge, 1974-76, road maintenance engr., 1976-79; maintenance systems engr. Dept. Transp., 1979—; cons. agrl. and indsl. engring., 1972-74; council mem., multiple com. assignments Transp. Research Bd., Nat. Acad. Scis., 1970—, chmn. maintenance equipment com., 1979. Served from ensign to lt., submarine service, USN, 1962-66; comdr. Res. ret. Mem. La. Engring. Soc., Profl. Engrs. in Govt. (pres. 1977), Am. Soc. Agrl. Engrs. (pres. Baton Rouge chpt. 1972). Republican. Methodist. Contbr. articles on hwy. maintenance and equipment. Home: 1143 Oakley Dr Baton Rouge LA 70806 Office: PO Box 44245 Capitol Sta Baton Rouge LA 70804

RAY, HUGH EDWARD, assn. exec.; b. DeFuniak Springs, Fla., Feb. 3, 1940; s. Myles Warren and Zullemar Mae (Howell) R.; B.A. in Bus. Adminstrn., Fla. State U., 1965; m. Janet Lee Duncan, Aug. 9, 1963; children—Jana Kathrine, Christina Ann. Exec. asst. Fla. Dept. Gen. Services, Tallahassee, 1969-72; dir. staff commerce com., adviser to pres. Fla. Senate, Tallahassee, 1972-77; exec. dir. Fla. Assn. Domestic Ins. Cos., Inc., 1977-79, Fla. Assn. Life and Casualty Insurers, 1979—. Bd. dirs. Leon County Mental Health Soc.; exec. com., treas. Big Bend Health Planning Council. Served with Armed Forces, 1959-65. J. Edwin Larson ins. scholar, 1963-64. Mem. Fla. State U. Sch. Bus. Alumni Assn. (dir., past pres.), Soc. Pub. Adminstrs., Fla. Farm Bur. Democrat. Baptist (Sunday sch. tchr.). Club: Capital City Tiger Bay. Home: 415 Cloverdale Dr Tallahassee FL 32312

RAY, JACK LEROY, banker; b. Gadsden, Ala., Jan. 1, 1928; s. John L. and Mary Lou (Allday) R.; student Tenn. Mil. Inst., 1945; A.B., Duke, 1949; m. Lugenia Morgan, Feb. 17, 1949; children—John Richard, Harold Daniel, William Allen. Salesman, Dowd Press, Charlotte, N.C., 1949-50, Mut. Life Ins. Co. of N.Y., Protective Life, 1950-54; pres. Ray Constrn. Co., Gadsden, 1954—; chmn. bd. 1st State Bank, Altoona, Ala., 1959—; vice chmn. bd., dir. Exchange Bank, Attalla, Ala.; pres., dir. Gadsden Corp., Attalla Trust Co. Mem. Am., Ala., Ind. bankers assns., Home Builders Assn. Etowah County (pres. 1957), Beta Theta Pi. Baptist. Lion (pres. Gadsden 1958-59). Home: 2917 Scenic Hwy Gadsden AL 35901 Office: 1st State Bank Altoona AL 35952

RAY, JOHN M., ins. agt.; b. Gleason, Tenn., Nov. 13, 1938; s. John H. and Elsie L. (Kimbel) R.; student Lindsay Wilson Jr. Coll., 1962-63, U. Tenn., 1964-66; B.S., Trevecca Nazarene Coll., 1979; m. Phyllis J. Brown, Nov. 8, 1958; children—John F., Joanna P., Jacquelyn J. With accounting dept. Avco Corp., 1966-68; ins. agt. pvt. practice Nashville, 1968—. Pres. Gideon Camp, Nashville, 1971-72; chmn. bd. Ch. Nazarene, 1975—, adv. bd. Tenn. Dist., 1976—, spl. adv. com. Trevecca Nazarene Coll., 1977—. C.L.U. Mem. Nat. Assn. Life Underwriters (bd. dirs. 1978-80), Assn. C.L.U.'s (chmn. pub. relations 1977-78), Nashville Assn. Life Underwriters (edn. chmn.), Pres.'s Club State Farm Ins. (life). Home: 5305 Williamsburg Rd Brentwood TN 37027 Office: Suite 322 Two Maryland Farms Brentwood TN 37027

RAY, MARCELLO SALVADORE, furniture co. exec.; b. Houma, La., Aug. 26, 1923; s. Lucas Michael and Archangel (Thibodaux) M.; student La. State U., 1940-43, Soule Bus. Sch., 1946; m. Gloria Daigle,

Sept. 7, 1947; children—Bernadette Marcello Babin, Martha M. Boudreaux, Ursula M. Breaux, Ray Salvadore. Accountant, Quality Furniture House, Houma, 1947-68, pres., 1968—. City councilman, Houma, 1974-82. Served with USAAF, 1943-45. Decorated Air medal with two oak leaf clusters, Purple Heart. Recipient Service award City of Houma, 1978; Silver Beaver award Boy Scouts Am. Mem. Nat. League Cities, La. Mcpl. Assn., Houma Council Home Assn. (sec.-treas.), DAV, Am. Legion. Democrat. Roman Catholic. Clubs: K.C. (Knight of Yr. 1968), Terrier, Houma Golf. Home: 119 Leuron St Houma LA 70360 Office: 333 W Main St Houma LA 70360

RAY, MICHAEL NEIL, geophysicist; b. Stillwater, Okla., Dec. 11, 1948; s. Beverly N. and Helen M. (Matlock) R.; A.S., Okla. Mil. Acad., 1969; postgrad. U. Okla., 1969-70, U. Tex., 1973-75, U. Houston, 1978—; m. Sherry Sturgis Adams, Apr. 22, 1978. Inventory man Washington Inventory Service, Houston, 1972-74; asst. geophysicist Shell Oil Co., Houston, 1974—. Sec. Young Republicans, 1973. Served with C.E., U.S. Army, 1971-72. Mem. Soc. Am. Mil. Engrs., U.S. Naval Inst., U.S. Armor Assn., Field Artillery Assn., Assn. U.S. Army, Smithsonian Assos., Nat. Geog. Soc. Republican. Club: Demolay. Home: 1219 Banks St Houston TX 77006

RAY, PHILIP MONROE, mfg. co. exec.; b. Baxter, Tenn., Apr. 29, 1932; s. Whitney Leroy and Bessie K. (Kinnaird) R.; cert. in tool design Gen. Motors Inst., 1958; m. Ruby Muncrief, Dec. 4, 1954; children—Daniel, Virginia. With Fleetwood Cadillac, Detroit, 1952-62; product engr. Rockwell Internat., Russellville, Ark., 1964-73; sr. process engr. Timex, Little Rock, 1973-76; tool engrng. mgr. A.M.F., Little Rock, 1976—; cons. in field. Served with U.S. Army, 1952-54. Mem. Soc. Mfg. Engrs. Mem. Christian Ch. Club: Masons. Patentee field of parking meters. Home: Route 2 PO Box 1198 Royal AR 71968 Office: AMF 65 and Patterson Sts Little Rock AR 72209

RAY, RATHBURN APPLEGATE, real estate investment broker; b. Chattanooga, Apr. 17, 1908; s. George Lee and Mary Elizabeth (Thornton) R.; student Tenn. Wesleyan Coll., 1929; B.S. in Bus. Adminstrn., U. Tenn., 1931; postgrad. Vanderbilt U., 1935; m. Mary Margaret Prophater, Dec. 26, 1934; children—Margaret Suzanne (Mrs. William C. Stanton), Sandra Darlene (Mrs. Herbert R. Sherlin), Mary Elizabeth (Mrs. Frank W. Davis), Rathburn Applegate, Donna Virginia (Mrs. J.E. Moore, Jr.), Ann Carol (Mrs. Ronald H. Kersey), George Lee II, Laura Melissa. Rep. western area TVA, Knoxville, Tenn., 1935-43, supr. prodn. control center Tenn. Eastman Corp., Oak Ridge, 1943-46; owner Rathburn A. Ray Co., Athens, Tenn., 1946—. Chmn., McMinn County Indsl. Devel. Corp., 1955-56. Mem. Athens C. of C., Athens Bd. Realtors (pres. 1969-70, 71-72), Nat. Soc. Exchange Counselors, Nat. Assn. Real Estate Bds. (recipient Medal of Service 1957), Internat. Traders Club (nat. dir. 1962-63), Nat. Office Mgmt. Assn., Nat. Motel Brokers Assn. Am., Omega Tau Rho, Delta Sigma Pi, Phi Pi Phi. Methodist (trustee local ch. 1952-56). Clubs: Elks, Kiwanis, Springbrook Country. Research in real estate. Home: 413 Madison Ave NE Athens TN 37303 Office: 104 Washington Ave NE Athens TN 37303

RAYBURN, WENDELL GILBERT, ednl. adminstr.; b. Detroit, May 20, 1929; s. Charles Jefferson and Grace Victoria (Winston) R.; B.A., Eastern Mich. U., 1951; M.A., U. Mich., 1952; Ed.D., Wayne State U., 1972; m. Gloria Ann Myers, Aug. 19, 1962; children—Mark K., Rhonda Renee, Wendell Gilbert. Tchr., adminstr. Detroit Pub. Schs., 1955-68; asst. dir. office spl. projects U. Detroit, 1968-69, asso. dir., 1969-70, dir., 1970-72, asso. dean academic supportive programs, 1972-74; dean Univ. Coll., U. Louisville, 1974—, prof. liberal studies, 1976—; tchr. Wayne State U., 1972-74; cons. in field; dir. Louisville br. Fed. Res. Bank of St. Louis. Chmn. counseling and social services com. Metro United Way, 1976—; chmn. Louisville and Jefferson County Human Relations Commn., 1977—. Served with U.S. Army, 1952-54. Decorated Korean Service Ribbon with 2 bronze stars; recipient numerous awards and citations, including Keyman's award Optimist Club Central Detroit, 1974, citation Mich. Council on Edn. Opportunity Programs, 1974. Mem. Am. Assn. Higher Edn., Am. Personnel and Guidance Assn., Am. Coll. Personnel Assn., Assn. Counselor Educators and Suprs., Nat. Vocat. Guidance Assn., Nat. Univ. Extension Assn., Assn. Continuing Higher Edn., Wayne State U. Alumni Assn., Phi Delta Kappa, Phi Eta Sigma, Alpha Sigma Lambda. Author: (with George E. Leonard) Career Education: Disadvantaged Students, 1973. Contbr. articles to profl. jours. Home: 4009 Gingerwood Dr Louisville KY 40220 Office: Univ Coll U Louisville Strickler Hall Room 244 Louisville KY 40208

RAYES, JAMES GEORGE, orthodontist; b. Detroit, Feb. 21, 1931; s. George Hobala and Effie (Saliba) R.; B.S. U. Detroit, 1952; D.D.S., Northwestern U., 1956; M.S., U. Tenn., 1961. Pvt. practice dentistry, Key West, Fla., 1957-58; mem. dental staff Detroit Receiving Hosp., 1958-59; resident Harper Hosp., Detroit, 1959; pvt. practice orthodontics, Clearwater, Fla., 1961—. Cons., Sertoma Speech and Hearing Clinic, Sarasota, Fla., 1961-62, Morton Plant Hosp. Speech and Hearing Clinic, Clearwater, 1963—, Fla. Crippled Children's Commn., 1961—, Anclote Psychiat. Center, Tarpon Springs, Fla., 1974—. Served with USNR, 1954-67. Diplomate Am. Bd. Orthodontics. Fellow Royal Soc. Health (Howard Peterson Meml. award 1979); mem. Am., Fla. dental assns., Am. Assn. Orthodontists, Coll. Diplomates Am. Bd. Orthodontics, Gator Orthodontic Forum, Am. Inst. Hypnosis, N.Am. Begg Soc. Orthodontists, Mich. Soc. Psychosomatic Dentistry, Oral Health Research Assn. (pres.), European Orthodontic Soc., Ed Dart Sertoma Club (charter, life), Fedn. Dentaire Internationale, Upper Pinellas Dental Soc. (pres. 1973-74), Am. Soc. Dentistry for Children, Walter Reed Soc., Internat. Platform Assn., Fla. Cleft Palate Assn., Am. Soc. Clin. Hypnosis, European Begg Soc. Orthodontists, U. Tenn. Orthodontic Alumni Assn. (pres. 1970), Gulf Coast Dental Research Assn., Pan Am Med. Assn., Assn. Am. Dentists, Purinton Internat. Study Group, Xi Psi Phi. Republican. Roman Catholic. K.C. Contbr. articles to profl. jours. Home: 1880 S Cardinal Dr Clearwater FL 33520 Office: 1510-D Barry St Clearwater FL 33516

RAYMAKER, RUDOLPH LOUIS, physician; b. Brussels, Belgium, Sept. 24, 1938; s. Andre Joseph and Cecile (Evrard) R.; came to U.S., 1947, naturalized, 1952; B.A., U. Richmond, 1964; M.D., Med. Coll. Va., 1968; m. Patricia L. Weatherington, June 25, 1966; children—John, Brian, Catherine. Inter, Mercy Hosp., Springfield, Ohio, 1968-69; resident in internal medicine Med. Coll. Va., 1969-72; practice medicine specializing in internal medicine Nassawadox, Va., 1972-74; staff physician, dir. med. and coronary ICU, VA Hosp., Lake City, Fla., 1974—, asst. chief medicine, 1979—. Served in USAF, 1956-60. Diplomate Am. Bd. Internal Medicine. Mem. ACP. Roman Catholic. Home: Route 8 Box 93 Lake City FL 32055 Office: Lake City VA Hosp Lake City FL 32055

RAYMER, RICHARD TILLMAN, retail exec.; b. Mooresville, N.C., Apr. 7, 1946; s. John M. and Inez Monday R.; student U. N.C., Charlotte, 1965, King's Bus. Coll., 1965-67; m. Pauline Dianne Gaddy, Sept. 6, 1970; 1 son, Ryan Richard. Salesman, Andy Campbell Food Brokers, Charlotte, N.C., 1967-68; salesman Cooper Labs., Inc., Charlotte, N.C., 1970-75, key account mgr., 1975-77, dist. mgr., 1977-79, regional sales mgr., Atlanta, 1979—. Served with U.S. Army, 1968-70. Decorated Bronze Star. Mem. So. Pharm. Assn. Baptist. Club: MG Classic Car Club. Home and Office: 862 Countryside Ct Marietta GA 30067

RAYMOND, EDWARD LAUNITZ, fin. cons.; b. East Orange, N.J., July 13, 1904; s. William Albert and Emily (Launitz) Schwarzkopf; student N.J. State Coll. of Agr., 1922-23, Stewart Automobile Sch., 1924, N.Y. State Sch. Agr., 1925; m. Adrienne Bailey Dittman, June 4, 1960; children—Robert Edward, Margaret Emily. Milkplant operator Ash Grove Farms, Saratoga Springs, N.Y., 1932-34; mgr. Burlingame, Field, Pierce & Browne, Inc., N.Y.C., 1934-37; dairy herd mgr. Mt. Paul Farm, Gladstone, N.J., 1937-38; farm mgr. Ockanickon Farm, Jobstown, N.J., 1938-42; supr. lime and fertilizer dept. Burlington County (N.J.) Farmer's Co-op, Inc., 1942-45; gen. supt. Ferncliff Farm, Rhinebeck, N.Y., 1945-50; ins. salesman Investors Diversified Services, Inc., Palmetto, Fla., 1950-52; sales agt. King Merritt & Co., N.Y.C., 1952-60; founder, pres. Raymond & Associates, Inc., 1960, sr. v.p. Raymond, James & Associates, Inc., 1964-68; exec. dir. Charles & Myrtle Fillmore Found., Lee's Summit, Mo. Unity Sch. of Christianity, 1967-68; wholesale rep. for Franklin Distributors, Inc., southeastern U.S., 1968-69; registered rep. various cos., Sarasota, Fla., 1970-72; resident mgr. Anchor Nat. Fin. Services, Inc., Phoenix, after 1974; now fin. planner, Sarasota; Notary public, Fla. Mem. Internat. Assn. Fin. Planners. Republican. Clubs: Lions, Rotary, Kiwanis, Masons (32 deg.). Office: PO Box 15198 Sarasota FL 33579

RAYMOND, JOHN EDWARD, III, airline pub. relations exec.; b. Fitchburg, Mass., July 27, 1941; s. John Edward and Loretta Marion (Bolduc) R.; student liberal arts St. Michael's Coll., Journalism and Pub. relations Boston U.; m. Helen Rose Vitelli, Oct. 14, 1961; children—J. Robert, Kathleen J., John Edward, IV. Wire editor and reporter Fitchburg (Mass.) Sentinel, 1959-67; dir. pub. relations Nat. Mutual Ins. Co., Keene, N.H., 1967-69; pub. relations specialist Carrier Corp., Syracuse, N.Y., 1969-75; dir. pub. relations Am. Airlines, Inc., Dallas, 1975—. Recipient Med. Journalism award AMA, 1967; Spl. award investigative journalism Mass. Police Assn., 1963, 65, 66. Mem. Pub. Relations Soc. Am., Tex. Pub. Relations Assn., Internat. Assn. Bus. Communicators, Aviation, Space Writers' Assn., Am. Travel Writers' Assn. Republican. Roman Catholic. Home: 2015 Knollwood Ln Carrollton TX 75006 Office: Am Airlines Parkway Plaza Suite 5 East PO Box 61047 Dallas TX 75261

RAYMOND, MICHAEL JOHN, geologist; b. Cin., Aug. 30, 1950; s. John Arthur and Bernice Eleda (Larson) R.; B.S., La. State U., 1972, M.S., 1975, M.S. in Applied Stats., 1976. Cons. geologist Stress Analysis, Baton Rouge, 1971-72; exploration geologist Gulf Oil Corp., New Orleans, 1975-78, Oklahoma City, 1978-79, sr. geologist, 1979—; research asst. dept. stats. La. State U., 1973-75. NSF Pre-doctoral fellow, 1972-75. Mem. Am. Assn. Petroleum Geologists, Internat. Assn. Math. Geology, Am. Statis. Assn., Assn. Computing Machinery. Republican. Roman Catholic. Home: 6363 NW 63d St Apt 252 Oklahoma City OK 73132 Office: 324 N Robinson St Oklahoma City OK 73102

RAYMOND, RONALD GARY, indsl. supply co. exec.; b. Quincy, Ill., Feb. 14, 1946; s. Harold Leslie and Wilma Catherine (Lowe) R.; m. Karen A. Koenigs, Jan. 26, 1980; children—Anthony, Andrew, Ann. With The Kroger Co., Quincy, 1964-66, Gardner-Denver Co., St. Louis, 1966-70; sr. ter. mgr. CM Hoist div. Columbus McKinnon Corp., Tonnawanda, N.Y., 1970-76; pres., gen. mgr. J. G. Christopher Co., Jacksonville, Fla., 1976—. Pres., Woodlands Civic Assn., 1976, Montclair Parent Faculty Assn., 1978; precinct capt. Precinct 18, Clay County, Fla., 1978—. Mem. Purchasing Mgrs. Fla., Sales and Mktg. Execs. Jacksonville. Republican. Roman Catholic. Clubs: Elks, Dist. Edn. Am. (pres. 1965-66). Office: 5323 Highway Ave Jacksonville FL 32205

RAYMOND, WYNN RUSSELL, biochemist; b. Great Falls, Mont., Jan. 18, 1944; s. Russell Arden and Audrey Camille (Jeffries) R.; B.S., Wash. State U., 1966, M.S. in Food Sci., 1968, Ph.D. in Food Sci., 1971; m. Sharon Lee Duncan, June 5, 1966; children—Shawn Merlin, Corey Michael, Heather Marie. Postdoctoral research asso. U.S. Dept. Agr., Pasadena, Calif., 1971-73; sr. research chemist research and devel. Foods Div., Coca-Cola Co., Plymouth, Fla., 1973-76, sect. head chemistry, 1976—. Active Boy Scouts Am., 1976—. NDEA Title IV fellow, 1968-71. Mem. Am. Chem. Soc. (past chmn. Orlando (Fla.) subsect.), Inst. Food Technologists. Republican. Christian. Contbr. articles in field to profl. jours. Home: 126 Des Pinar Ln Longwood FL 32750 Office: PO Box 550 Plymouth FL 32768

RAZDAN, MAHARAJ KRISHAN, physician; b. Kashmir, India, June 10, 1940; came to U.S., 1971; s. Jagan Nath and Rupawati (Gadoo) Razdan (Hashia); M.B., B.S., Gandhi Med. Coll., Bhopal, 1962; M.D., All-India Inst. Med. Sci., New Delhi, 1967; m. Vijay Sadhu, Oct. 12, 1962; children—Ashutosh, Aurobindo. Instr. clin. pharmacology Med. Coll., Kashmir, 1963-66; sr. research fellow Council Sci. and Indsl. Research, India, 1967-70; teaching fellow in medicine and nephrology Case Western Res. U., Cleve., 1973-76; sr. instr. internal medicine, 1977-78; practice medicine specializing in internal medicine and nephrology, McAllen, Tex., 1978—; clin. asst. prof. U. Tex., McAllen, 1978—; cons. McAllen Gen. Hosp., Edinberg Gen. Hosp., Mission Mcpl. Hosp., Valley Community Hosp., Brownsville, Tex. Mem. AMA, Tex. Med. Assn., Am. Soc. Internal Medicine, Kidney Found. N.E. Ohio. Contbr. articles to profl. jours. Office: 816 S 12th St McAllen TX 78501

RE, JOHN JOSEPH, communications co. exec.; b. Bklyn., Jan. 22, 1952; ed. public schs., Bklyn. Asst. lithographic platemaker Arevian Corp., N.Y.C., 1969-71; exec. sec. Integral Yoga Inst., N.Y.C., 1971-73, instr., 1973, exec. sec. Dallas br., 1972-73; supr. customer service Budget Rent-A-Car, Dallas, 1973-74; salesman, asst. mgr. Fuller Brush Co., Bklyn., 1974-76; nat. accounts mgr. MCI-Telecommunications Corp., Dallas, 1976-78; v.p. mktg. and public relations John D. Laufman & Assos., Inc., Dallas, from 1978; major account rep. ITT, Dallas. Office: One Aviation Place Suite 3000 Dallas TX 75235

REA, JOHN WILLIAM, sch. supt.; b. Randolph, Miss., Apr. 24, 1909; s. James Thomas and Modena (Gardner) R.; B.S., Ark. State U., 1949; M.Ed., U. Miss., 1951; m. Zola Lucille Beshears, Jan. 11, 1937; children—Patricia (Mrs. Joe Ray Price), William L. Prin., Center Elementary Sch., Wynne, Ark., 1941-48, McCrory (Ark.) High Sch., 1948-55, Crawfordsville (Ark.) High Sch., 1955-56; supt. Gosnell Sch., Blytheville, Ark., 1956-77. State chmn. Impacted Area Schs. Information Service, 1969—, area chmn. region 6, 1970—. Mem. Ark Edn. Assn., Am., Ark. assns. sch. administrs., Nat. Sch. Bd. Assn. Methodist. Mason (Shriner); mem. Order Eastern Star; Kiwanian (bd. dirs.). Home: 904 N Franklin St Blytheville AR 72315

READ, DON ROBERT, surgeon; b. Ft. Worth, Jan. 17, 1942; s. Nathaniel Barksdale and Mary Evelyn (Hodges) R.; B.A., Austin (Tex.) Coll., 1964; M.D., U. Tex., Galveston, 1968; m. Roberta Colton Teeling, June 14, 1969; children—Sarah, Alison. Intern, Passavant Meml. Hosp., Chgo., 1968-69; resident in gen. surgery Northwestern U. Hosp., Chgo., 1971-73, Cook County Hosp., Chgo., 1973-76; resident in colon-rectal surgery Cook County Hosp., 1976-77; attending surgeon, dir. surg. edn. Cook County Hosp., also asst. prof. surgery Abraham Lincoln Med. Sch., U. Ill., Chgo., 1977-78; practice medicine specializing in colon and rectal surgery, Dallas, 1978—; mem. staff Med. City Dallas Hosp., Baylor Med. Center, Plano Gen. Hosp., Richardson Med. Center, Brookhaven Hosp.; clin. instr. U. Tex. Southwestern Med. Sch., Dallas. Served to lt. M.C., USNR, 1969-71; Vietnam. Decorated Bronze Star; recipient Ohio Valley Proctologic Soc. award, 1975. Asso. fellow Am. Soc. Colon and Rectal Surgery; mem. AMA, Assn. Acad. Surgery, Am. Soc. Gastrointestinal Endoscopy, Royal Soc. Medicine (affiliate), Midwest Surg. Assn., Tex. Med. Assn. Presbyterian. Home: 4440 Northhaven St Dallas TX 75229 Office: 7777 Forest Ln Suite 319 Dallas TX 75230

READ, DONALD LLOYD, univ. ofcl., family counselor; b. St. Louis, Jan. 11, 1926; s. Marshall Lloyd and Eveland B. R.; A.B., Washington U., St. Louis, 1949; Th.M., Dallas Theol. Sem., 1954; M.A. in Clin. Psychology, N. Tex. State U., 1971, Ph.D. in Higher Edn. Adminstrn., 1980; m. Fontaine Bridge, June 13, 1950; children—Helen C. Read Nelson, Donald M., John L. Research project dir. Sun Oil Co., Richardson, Tex., 1955-64; exec. dir. Sky Ranch Camps, Denton, Tex., 1964-71; asso. dean students Dallas Baptist Coll., 1972-75; v.p. U. Mary Hardin-Baylor, Belton, Tex., 1975—; dir. Christian Family Counseling Services, 1976—; ordained Baptist minister, counselor; v.p. Sky Ranches Inc., 1956-71; pres. bd. Meaningful Life Camps, 1972-75. Mem. Am. Personnel and Guidance Assn., Am. Assn. Univ. Adminstrs., Am. Psychol. Assn., Am. Coll. Personnel Assn., Am. Camping Assn. (certified camp dir.), Nat. Orgn. Legal Problems in Edn., Am. Assn. Higher Edn., Belton C. of C., Phi Delta Kappa. Club: Rotary (past pres. local chpt.). Home: 802 Estate Dr Belton TX 76513 Office: U Mary Hardin-Baylor Belton TX 76513

READY, ROBERT KNOWLES, educator; b. Wellington, Kans., Sept. 1, 1924; s. James Wendell and Leah Marie (Knowles) R.; B.A. in History, U. Kans., 1948; M.B.A., Harvard, 1950, D.C.S., 1955; m. Mildred Marks, Jan. 30, 1949 (dec. 1978); children—James M., John M., Scott F., Craig R.; m. 2d, Patricia Comeaux, Sept. 7, 1979. Asst. prof., asso. prof., prof. U. Western Ont., London, 1955-64; program adviser Ford Found., Cairo, Egypt, 1964-66, Colombia, 1966-68; internat. dir. NTL Inst. for Applied Behavioral Sci., Washington, 1968-70; prof., chmn. mgmt. U. West Fla., Pensacola, 1970-77, asso. provost orgn. studies and public policy, 1977-79; mgmt. cons. various cos. in U.S. and Can., UN, AID, Ford Found. and other internat. agys. in S.Am., Mexico, Africa, Middle East, India. Chmn. long range revenue study City of Pensacola, 1972-77. Served to 2d lt. USAAF, 1942-45. Recipient McKinsey Found. award for outstanding research in mgmt., 1967. Mem. Internat. Assn. for Applied Social Scientists, Acad. Mgmt., Am. Acad. Polit. and Social Sci., Am. Soc. Pub. Adminstrn., Soc. for Applied Anthropology, Am. Sociol. Assn., Soc. for Internat. Devel., Pensacola C. of C. (chmn. long range study 1975-76), Phi Beta Kappa, Omicron Delta Kappa, Phi Kappa Phi. Author: The Adminstrator's Job: Issues and Dilemmas, 1967. Home: Route 4 Box 128E Pensacola FL 32504

REAGAN, STUART ARTHUR, govt. ofcl.; b. Covington, Ky., Oct. 22, 1949; s. Harry Clement and Joan Mary (Gardner) R.; A.B. with high distinction, Eastern Ky. U., 1971, M.P.A., 1974; M.A., U. Ky., 1972; m. Cherilynn DeRonde, July 27, 1974. Adminstrv. intern Fayette County (Ky.) Dept. Fiscal Mgmt., 1973; tng. and personnel officer Ky. Dept. Transp., Frankfort, 1973-75; budget analyst and policy adv. on state budget Office for Policy and Mgmt., Ky. Dept. Fin., Frankfort, 1975—; mem. Ky. Sch. Bldg. Authority, 1979—. Chmn., Capital dist. and bd. dirs. Bluegrass council Boy Scouts Am., 1977-80. Named Outstanding Polit. Sci. Grad., Eastern Ky. U., 1971. Mem. Nat. Assn. State Budget Officers. Democrat. Presbyterian. Club: Kiwanis (pres. club 1978-79) (East Frankfort, Ky.). Home: 531 Menominee Tr Frankfort KY 40601 Office: 200 Capitol Annex Frankfort KY 40601

REAMES, JAMES MITCHELL, univ. librarian; b. Rembert, S.C., Aug. 31, 1920; s. James Alex and Carrie (James) R.; B.A., Furman U., 1941; B.L.S., U. N.C., 1942; M.L.S., U. Mich., 1954; m. Mary Beall Hall, July 24, 1948; 1 son, James Alan. Reference librarian Clemson U., 1946-52; asso. librarian, asso. prof. Northwestern State U. La., 1952-58; dir. U. S.C. Undergrad. Library, 1958-66, asso. dir. libraries, 1966-70; dir. James A. Rogers Library, prof. Francis Marion Coll., Florence, S.C., 1970—. Mem. evaluation com. So. Assn. Colls., 1962—; cons. library devel. Warren Wilson Coll., Erskine Coll., Lander Coll. Dir., mem. exec. com. Alston Wilkes Soc., 1968-73; mem. Gov.'s Mansion and Lace House Commn., 1970-71; bd. govs. Christian Action Council, 1968-72. Trustee Claflin Coll. Served with USNR, 1942-46. Mem. S.C. (pres. 1949, 70-71), Southeastern library assns., South Caroliniana Soc. Democrat. Methodist (del. S.C. ann. conf. 1974-79, mem. adminstrv. bd. 1971-79). Contbr. articles to ednl., religious periodicals. Home: 1905 Marsh Ave Florence SC 29501 Office: Francis Marion Coll Florence SC 29501

REAMS, GERALD BROCK, surgeon; b. Lexington, Ky., Sept. 17, 1929; s. George Elbert and Nelle (Brock) R.; B.S., U. Ky., 1948; M.D., Northwestern U., 1952; m. Karolyn Spillman, June 20, 1950; children—Jerry, Mary, Mark, Carol, Lynn. Intern, Charity Hosp., New Orleans, 1952-53; resident surgery U. Miami (Fla.) Sch. Medicine, 1953-S7; practice medicine specializing in surgery, Ashland, Ky., 1962—; med. officer Project Mercury, NASA, 1960-62; asso. clin. prof. surgery U. Ky., 1962—; asso. clin. prof. surgery Marshall U. Sch. Medicine, 1977—. Served to maj., M.C., USAF, 1957-62. Diplomate Am. Bd. Surgery. Mem. A.C.S., Am. Coll. Chest Physicians, Southeastern Surg. Congress, Transplantation Soc. (charter), Central Ky. Horse Assn. (exec. bd.). Kiwanian. Home: 940 Dysard Hill Ashland KY 41101 Office: 2301 Lexington Ave Ashland KY 41101

REASER, JOEL MONROE, research co. exec.; b. Altoona, Pa., June 23, 1940; s. Paul Louis and Hilda Jean (Gardner) R.; A.B., Gettysburg (Pa.) Coll., 1962; M.A., So. Ill. U., 1971, Ph.D., 1972; m. Susan Leigh Erickson, Sept. 12, 1970; children—Atticus John, Mason Paul. Sr. asso. programmer IBM, Poughkeepsie, N.Y., 1965-68; sr. staff scientist Human Resources Research Orgn., Alexandria, Va., 1972-76, dir. program applied social sci. research, 1974-76; pres. the Prosys Corp., research and cons., 1976-78, The EXCEL Corp., Reston, Va., 1978—; cons. ARC, Systems Devel. Corp., Nat. Inst. Community Devel.; prin. organizer Youth Dynamics Corp., McLean, Va., 1973. Mem. adv. council Nat. Capital Area ARC, 1975. Bd. dirs. Fairfax County (Va.) chpt. A.R.C., 1974—, 1st vice chmn., 1975, chmn., 1976. Served with AUS, 1963-65. Mem. Am., Va. psychol. assns., Assn. Computing Machinery, Human Factors Soc., Common Cause, ACLU. Home: 11424 Running Cedar Rd Reston VA 22091 Office: 11737 Bowman Green Dr Reston VA 22090

REAVES, (RUFUS) LEE, broadcasting co. exec.; b. Warren, Ark., Dec. 10, 1909; s. B. A. and Ellie (Martin) R.; A.B., Ark. A&M Coll., 1934; M.S., U. Ark., 1947; m. Glenda Pittman, Feb. 21, 1942; children—Glenda Anne, Robin Lee. Instr., Sch. for the Blind, Little Rock, 1931-32; tchr. schs., Warren, 1934-36; supt. schs., Hermitage, Ark., 1936-51; mem. Ark. State Senate, 1939-55, sec. of senate, 1961—; owner, operator Sta. KWRF, Warren, 1953-59; v.p. Ark. A&M Coll., 1959-63; dir. Ark. Ednl. TV Network, Conway, 1963—. Chmn. Bradley County (Ark.) Election Commn., 1951-59; mem. War Meml. Stadium Commn., Little Rock, 1948-63; chmn. Warren

Planning Bd., 1957-59; mem. Warren Sch. Bd., 1953-59, Bradley County Sch. Bd., 1957-59. Named Disting. Alumnus, U. Ark., Monticello, 1973. Methodist. Club: Rotary. Author: Rule Book for Arkansas Senate, 1943. Office: 305 Donaghey St Conway AR 72032

REAY, THOMAS MORGAN, newspaper exec.; b. Madison, Wis., Nov. 11, 1930; s. Thomas Morgan and Phyllis (Smith) R.; student U. Ill., 1949-50, 52, Wis. State Coll., 1951; m. Patricia Ann Curley, Sept. 10, 1955; children—Thomas, Timothy, Todd. Reporter, LaSalle (Ill.) News Tribune, 1948, Dixon (Ill.) Evening Telegraph, 1952, Champaign (Ill.) News-Gazette, 1950-51; reporter, city editor, mng. editor, exec. editor Rockford (Ill.) Morning Star and Register-Republic, 1952-76; editor, gen. mgr. Austin (Tex.) Citizen, 1976—. Pres., No. Ill. Council on Alcoholism; United Fund, Rockford; trustee United Way, Austin. Mem. Associated Press Mng. Editors (dir. 1971-73. Roman Catholic. Club: Headliners (Austin). Office: 621 W Saint John St Austin TX 78752

RECCORD, ROBERT EUGENE, clergyman; b. Norfolk, Va., Sept. 26, 1951; s. Estel and Ruth (Moye) R.; B.A. in Psychology, Ind. U., 1972; M.Div., Southwestern Bapt. Theol. Sem., 1975, D.Min., 1979; m. Cheryl Ann Burger, Dec. 16, 1972; children—Christina Joy, Bryan Christopher. Ordained to ministry Bapt. Ch., 1973; minister of youth Calvary Bapt. Ch., Evansville, Ind., 1970, Grove Level Bapt. Ch., Dalton, Ga., 1971; evangelist Collegiate Evang. Assn., Ind., 1971-72; minister youth edn. Fielder Rd. Bapt. Ch., Arlington, Tex., 1973-74; preacher crusade Joong Ang. Bapt. Ch., Seoul, Korea, 1974-77; dir. witness tng. Bapt. Home Mission Bd., Atlanta, 1977-79; dir. leadership tng. U.S.A. for Evangelism Explosion III Internat., Ft. Lauderdale, Fla., 1979—; speaker Tex. So. Bapt. Youth Evangelism Conf., 1978; participant Oxford (Eng.) Assn. Research in Revival and Evangelical Awakening, 1979. Author: The Minister of Evangelism, 1979. Research in Christian nominality. Home: 2868 NW 122d Ave Coral Springs FL 33065 Office: PO Box 23820 Fort Lauderdale FL 33307

RECE, STEPHEN CRAIG, trust co. exec.; b. Richmond, Va., Nov. 9, 1943; s. Donald Allen and Dorothy May (Stein) R.; B.S., Valdosta State Coll., 1970; postgrad. in bus. adminstrn. Mercer U.; m. Patsy Dianne Gordon, Dec. 21, 1969; children—Nicole Kathleen, Mandy Dianne. With So. Trust Ins. Co., 1970—, gen. mgr. subs. Camann Packaging Co., 1973-74, controller So. Trust Ins. Co., Macon, Ga., 1974-77, v.p., treas., 1977—. Chmn. bd. trustees Dixon United Meth. Ch., Macon. Served with USAF, 1963-67. Mem. Ins. Acctg. and Stats. Assn. Methodist. Office: PO Box 250 Macon GA 31202

RECIO, FRANCISCO HERNÁNDEZ, mgmt. cons.; b. Havana, Cuba, June 18, 1944; s. Francisco Hernández and Josefina (Madrazo) R.; came to U.S., 1960, naturalized, 1970; B.Engring., Rensselaer Poly. Inst., 1964, M.S., 1966; m. Irene Canosa, May 27, 1967; children—Irene María, Francisco Hernández, III, Ana María. Indsl. engr. Huyck Corp., Rensselaer, N.Y., 1966-68; mgmt. cons. Haskins & Sells, Miami, Fla., 1968-76, mgr., 1974-76; prin. in charge of Latin Am. mgmt. cons. Peat Marwick Mitchell & Co., Miami, 1976—; community prof. mgmt. Fla. Internat. U. Bd. dirs. Greater Miami Philharmonic Soc., 1976-77. Mem. Nat. Assn. Accountants, Am. Inst. Indsl. Engrs. (v.p. Miami chpt.), Fla. Inst. C.P.A.'s. (asso.) Clubs: La Gorce Country, American in Miami, Banker's. Home: 2615 Alhambra Circle Coral Gables FL 33134 Office: 1000 Brickell Ave Miami FL 33131

RECKER, GLENDA JUNE, remfg. co. exec.; b. Mountainair, N.Mex., June 7, 1941; d. Luther Clabourn and Viola Merle (McBee) Jones; grad. in cost acctg. Durham's Sch. Bus., 1964; m. Clifton Simon Recker, July 31, 1958; children—June Michelle Recker Johnson, Brett Steven, Monelle Kathryn, Brent Clifton. Bookkeeper, girl Friday, E & R Shannon, San Antonio, 1964-65; bookkeeper K. J. Smith & Sons, Inc., San Antonio, 1965-69; bookkeeper R & R Auto Parts Co. (name changed to R & R Auto Electric Rebuilders Inc. 1971), San Antonio, 1959-71, corp. sec.-treas., comptroller, 1971—; accounts receivable clk. Ace Brake Co., San Antonio, 1969-70. Pres., Wood Valley Acres Home Owners Assn., Adkins, Tex., 1974-76. Recipient numerous bowling awards and championships, including San Antonio Women's Bowling Assn. Local-All-Events Champion, 1975, 76; recipient appreciation trophy United Way, 1975, Girls Softball, 1975; cert. appreciation La Vernia Cystic Fibrosis Breath of Spring Bike-A-Thon, 1979; named Citizen of Month, Tex. Bank, 1976. Mem. S.E. Bus. and Profl. Women's Club (editor bull. 1977-78; state 2d pl. award 1978), Am. Bus. Women's Club, S.E. Devel. Found. (dir.), Greater San Antonio C. of C., La Vernia C. of C., Nat. Write Your Congressman Club, Women's Internat. Bowling Congress (del., tellers com. 1980), Tex. Women's Bowling Assn., San Antonio Women's Bowling Assn. (dir.), Nat. Ind. Businesspersons' Assn., 600 Bowling Club, Les Dames 700 Bowling Club, PTA, Tex. Farm Bur., Nat. Motor Club. Democrat. Mem. Assemblies of God Ch. Clubs: Order Foresters, Sons of Hermann, Moose Aux., Turner's Bowling, Highland Social. Editor ch. bull., 1969-73; editor periodic column Thinkin' Out Loud, La Vernia News, 1977—. Home: Route 2 Box 860 Adkins TX 78101 Office: 2750 Rigsby Ave San Antonio TX 78222

RECTOR, NORMAN KENNETH, cons. engr.; b. Newkirk, Okla., Oct. 14, 1902; s. Ira Clifford and Daisey (Farmer) R.; student Okla. State U., 1921-24; m. Mary Josephine Johnson, Nov. 24, 1927. Draftsman, Okla. State Hwy. Dept., 1925-26, Marland Oil Co., 1926-27, Oklahoma City Engring. Dept., 1927-28, jr. engr. Forrest E. Gilmore Co., Tulsa, 1928-30; design engr. Petroleum Engring., Inc., Tulsa, 1930-34; plant supt. Gregg-Tex Gasoline Co., Longview, Tex., 1934-36; with Petroleum Engring., Inc., 1936-51; ind. cons. engr., Houston, 1951-52, Tulsa, 1952—. Registered profl. engr., Okla., Tex. Mem. Engrs. Soc. Tulsa. Republican. Methodist. Patentee in field. Home and office: 1905 E 36th St Tulsa OK 74105

RECTOR, ROBERT LEE, businessman; b. Washington, June 16, 1943; s. Hilden LaVern and Lois Marie (Hickok) R.; B.S., Kent State U., 1965; M.S., State U. N.Y., Albany, 1968; m. Linda Martha Zuschlag, Dec. 19, 1964; children—Courtenay Marie, Drew Alan, Egan Alward. Systems analyst, programmer IBM Corp., Kingston, N.Y., 1965-68; div. mgr. systems Allied Chem. Co., N.Y.C., 1968-70; cons. Booz, Allen and Hamilton, N.Y.C., 1971; pres., founder, Rector's Lemon Tree, landscape firm and nursery, Tarpon Springs, Fla., 1971—; prin., founder Anson Lee Rector & Assos., Clearwater, 1975—; dir. Homes Internat., Inc., Exec. Tng. Inst.; seminar leader, speaker numerous colls. and univs. in U.S. and Can.; ordained minister, former pastor Christian Life Ch., Clearwater. Past mem. Bd. of Appeals and Adjustments, City of New Port Richey, Fla. Mem. Inst. Mgmt. Scientists, Indsl. Mgmt. Soc., Am. Mktg. Assn., Am. Inst. Profl. Cons., Acad. Mgmt., Nat. Soc. Public Accts., Clearwater, New Port Richey chambers of commerce. Republican. Author books, fin. tng. manuals, numerous mag. articles. Home: 1122 Jasmin Dr New Port Richey FL 33552 Office: 23 S Walton Ave Tarpon Springs FL 33589

REDDICK, W(ALKER) HOMER, social worker; b. River Junction, Fla., Mar. 26, 1922; s. Walker H. and Lillian (Anderson) R.; B.S., Fla. State U., 1951, M.S.W., 1957; m. Anne Elizabeth Hardwick, Sept. 7, 1947; children—Walker Homer, Andy Hardwick (dec.). Chief juvenile probation officer Muscogee County Juvenile Ct., Columbus, Ga., 1952-53; sr. child welfare worker Floyd County Dept. Pub. Welfare, Rome, Ga., 1955-56; chief social worker Montgomery County Dept. Pub. Health, Montgomery, Ala., 1957-59; dir. social services Ala. Bapt. Childrens Home, Troy, 1959-64; casework supr. Youth Devel. Center, Milledgeville, Ga., 1964-71; dir. Family Counseling Center, Macon, Ga., 1972—. Cons. Appleton Ch. Home for Girls Group Homes, Macon, 1974—; pres. Council Service Agys., Macon, 1975. Mem. Ala. State Adv. Com. on Children and Youth, 1961-64. Bd. dirs. Middle Ga. Drug Council. Served with AUS, 1940-43. Licensed marriage and family counselor, Ga. Fellow Royal Soc. Health; mem. Nat. Assn. Social Workers (bd. mem.-at-large Ga. chpt.), Acad. Cert. Social Workers, Am. Assn. Marriage and Family Therapists, Transactional Analysis Study Group of Macon (dir.). Episcopalian. Club: Masons. Contbr. articles to profl. jours. Address: 2485 Kingsley Dr Macon GA 31204

REDDIX, DOROTHY BROOKS, librarian; b. Meridian, Miss., Apr. 28, 1932; d. Joe C. and Arlena (Hopkins) Brooks; B.S. in Edn., Jackson (Miss.) State U., 1954; M.S. in L.S., Atlanta U., 1969; m. Joseph B. Reddix; children—Michael A., Carl M. Tchr., Marion County Schs., Columbia, Miss., 1956-57; librarian Columbia Municipal Sch. Dist., 1957-70; library coordinator Biloxi (Miss.) Sch. Dist., 1970—. Mem. Biloxi Edn. Assn., ALA, Miss. Tchrs. Assn. (sec. library sect. 1974-75), Miss., Sixth Dist. assns. media educators NAACP, Nat. Council Negro Women, Jackson State U. Alumni Assn. Recipient award for STAR Tchr., Miss Econ. Council. Home: 402 Debuys Rd Biloxi MS 39531 Office: PO Box 168 Biloxi MS 39533

REDFEARN, BEVERELY YVONNE, fin. and mgmt. cons.; b. Dallas, May 20, 1935; d. Raymond Joseph and Ocie Lee (Lamb) R.; ed. So. Meth. U. Accountant, Annuity Bd., So. Bapt. Conv., Dallas, 1959-67; bus. mgr. firm Akin, Vial, Hamilton, Koch & Tubb, Attys., Dallas, 1967-74; bus. mgr., legal adminstr. firm Rain, Harrell, Emery, Yong & Doke, Attys., Dallas, 1974-77; pres., prin. B. Redfearn & Assos., Fin. Mgmt. Cons., Dallas, 1977—; guest instr. law office mgmt. So. Meth. U. Sch. Law, 1976-77; adj. instr. paralegal program Dallas County Community Coll. Dist., 1977-78; mem. adv. com. sect. on econs. Am. Bar Assn., 1976-77. Mem. mid-mgmt. adv. com. Dallas County Community Coll. Dist., 1977-78, mem. legal asst. adv. com., 1978-79, 79-80. Real estate broker, Tex. Mem. Am. Mgmt. Soc., Nat. Assn. Legal Adminstrs., Dallas Assn. Legal Adminstrs. (pres. 1976-77), Am. Soc. Bus. and Mgmt. Cons. Republican. Baptist. Author book, seminar and fin. planning portfolio: How to Develop Your Dynamic Dollar Sense, 1979. Office: 8306 Londonderry Ln Dallas TX 75228

REDMAN, LYNN LOVELL, mech. engr.; b. St. Joseph, Mo., Oct. 17, 1944; s. Lovell Gibbins and Irene Elizabeth (Maltsberger) R.; B.S. in M.E., U. Mo., Columbia, 1967; postgrad. UCLA, 1967, U. So. Calif., 1969-74, U. Calif., Berkeley, 1975-76; m. Andrea Jacqueline Tweedle, Aug. 10, 1968; children—Patrick Tweedle, Joseph Lovell. Project engr. Shell Oil Co., Wilmington, Calif., 1967-71; chief draftsman Hunt-Wesson Foods, Inc., Fullerton, Calif., 1971-73, engring. adminstr., 1973, project engr., 1973-74; design supr. Sullivan Systems, Inc., Tiburon, Calif., 1974-75, project engr., 1975-77, mech. engr., 1977-78; sr. systems engr. Pullman Kellogg, Houston, 1978—; cons. in field. Recipient Ben L. Perry Writing award, 1960; Pi Tau Sigma Writing award, 1966. Registered profl. engr., Calif., Tex. Mem. ASME, Nat. Soc. Profl. Engrs. Club: Houston City. Developer low energy high vacuum process systems. Home: 12014 Sugar Springs Dr Houston TX 77077

REDMOND, JOHN DURHAM, ins. co. exec.; b. Columbus, Ga., June 5, 1948; s. Melvin Sims and Beebe (Durham) R.; A.S., Columbus Coll., 1968, B.S., 1970, M.B.A., 1977; M.B.A., Ga. State U., 1975; m. Patricia Ann Tate, Mar. 22, 1970; children—John Douglas, Brandi Leigh. Provider auditor Blue Cross-Blue Shield, Columbus, 1972-73, financial analyst, 1973, internal auditor, 1973-76, dir. internal audit and work measurement, 1976, dir. actuarial/underwriting, 1976—. Served with AUS, 1970-72. Cert. internal auditor; cert. in mgmt. acctg. Mem. Delta Sigma Pi (treas. chpt. 1969-70). Methodist (adminstrv. bd. 1973—, chmn. com. fin. 1975—, chmn. com. on stewardship 1978—, vice chmn. council on ministries 1980—). Home: 4008 Tifton Dr Columbus GA 31907 Office: PO Box 7368 Columbus GA 31908

REECE, BENNY RAMON, educator; b. Asheville, N.C., Dec. 7, 1930; s. Judson Jones and Ina Marie (Blalock) R.; B.A., Duke, 1953; M.A., U. N.C., 1954, Ph.D., 1957; postgrad. U. Munich, 1957-58; m. Ethel Patricia Van Dyke, June 4, 1960; 1 son, Judson Benjamin. Instr., U. N.C., 1954-57; asst. prof. Mercer U., 1957-60; asso. prof. classical langs. Furman U., Greenville, S.C., 1960—, chmn. dept. classical langs., 1960-72; vis. prof. U. N.C., 1968. Fulbright fellow, 1957-58; So. fellow, 1959; Am. Philos. Soc. fellow, 1967, 71. Mem. Am. Philol. Assn., Classical Assn. Middle West and South, Eta Sigma Phi, Alpha Phi Omega. Presbyn. Author: Documents Illustrating Cicero's Consular Campaign, 1967; Sermones Ratherii Episcopi Veronensis, 1969; Learning in the Tenth Century, 1972; A Bibliography of First Appearances of the Writings by A. Conan Doyle, 1975; The Role of the Centurion in Ancient Society, 1976; translator Plautus: Epidicus, 1967. Home: Route 7 Roe Ford Rd Greenville SC 29609

REECE, JANE VERNON, coll. adminstr.; b. Charlotte, N.C., Sept. 5, 1947; d. Vernon Lewis and May (Mitchell) R.; B.A., Presbyn. Coll., 1970; postgrad. Fla. State U., 1970-71; M.Ed., Western Carolina U., 1973. Head Start tchr. Opportunities Corp., Asheville, N.C., 1971-72; dir. residence hall Western Carolina U., Cullowhee, N.C., 1972-74; admissions counselor Spartanburg (S.C.) Tech. Coll., 1974-75, dir. counseling, 1975-77, dir. cognitive mapping research, 1977-78, dir. staff and program devel., 1978—. Sec., S.C. Career Info. Systems Steering Com., 1977; steering com. staff devel. S.C. Bd. Tech. and Comprehensive Edn., 1980—; task force S.C. Assn. Religious Values and Issues in Counseling. S.C. Vocat. Edn. grantee, 1977-78. Mem. Nat. Council Staff and Program Devel., Am. Personnel and Guidance Assn., Am. Ednl. Scientists Assn., S.C. Personnel and Guidance Assn., Carolina Soc. Tng. and Devel. Research and publs. on cognitive style mapping. Office: Spartanburg Tech Coll Spartanburg SC 29303

REECE, LINDA ELIZABETH CLEMONS, interior designer; b. Des Moines, Oct. 30, 1938; d. James Clifford and Agnes Simpson (Freeman) Clemons; student Simpson Coll., 1957-59; B.S., Iowa State U., 1961, M.A., 1972. Sales clk. Younkers Store for Homes, Des Moines, 1961-62; bookkeeper Fairbanks (Alaska) Pub. Co., 1962-63; advt. illustrator Fasmaster Products, Inc., Shenandoah, Iowa, 1963-66; tchr. art Orient (Iowa) Macksburg Community Schs., 1966-67; extension home economist Iowa State U. Co-op Extension Service, Winterset, 1967-70, grad. teaching asst., 1970-72; extension specialist coop. Extension Service, U. Minn., St. Paul, 1972-78; home furnishings extension specialist U. Ky. Co-op Service, Lexington, 1978—; cons. Minn. Consumer Bur., 1972-77; chpt. adv. Elec. Womens Round Table, Inc., 1978—, chpt. pres., 1976-78. Mem. Am. Soc. Interior Designers, Am. Home Econs. Assn. (issues chmn. art sect. 1976-77), Am. Assn. of Housing Educators, Nat. Home Fashions League (v.p. edn. 1977, nat. found. dir. 1978), Epsilon Sigma Phi. Home: 3440 Milam Ln Lexington KY 40502 Office: 206 Scovell Hall Univ of Ky Lexington KY 40546

REED, ADDISON WALKER, coll. adminstr., educator; b. Steubenville, Ohio, Apr. 22, 1929; s. Addison Benjamin and Ardessa Elizabeth (Miller) R.; A.B. Kent (O.) State U., 1951, M.A., 1953, B.S., 1957; Ph.D. (Ford fellow), U. N.C., 1973; 1 dau., Mary Elizabeth. Instr. music Booker High Sch., Sarasota, Fla., 1958-61; asst. prof. music St. Augustine's Coll., Raleigh, N.C., 1961-65, chmn. dept. music, 1969—, chmn. div. humanities, 1976—; asst. prof. Albany (Ga.) State Coll., 1965-69. Bd. dirs. N.C. Symphony Orch., Raleigh Chamber Music Guild. Served with AUS, 1954-56. Mem. Music Educators' Nat. Conf., Sonneck Soc., Am. Musicological Soc., Nat. Assn. Tchrs. Singing. Contbg. author: Grove's Dictionary, 1971, Black Perspective in Music, 1975, 79. Home: 207 Loft Ln Apt 53 Raleigh NC 27609

REED, BILLY JACK, acctg. exec.; b. San Angelo, Tex., June 10, 1949; s. Perry Wilson and Winnie Faye (Ray) R.; B.B.A. in Acctg., Tex. Tech. U., 1972; m. Janet Kay Phillips, July 26, 1969; children—Peter William, Adam Andrew. Dir. gen. acctg. T.I.M.E.-DC, Inc., Lubbock, Tex., 1969—. Mem. Am. Trucking Assn., Am. Acctg. and Fin. Council, Tex. Acctg. and Fin. Council (dir.), Nat. Acctg. Fin. Council. Methodist. Club: South Plains Toastmasters (ednl. v.p. 1978). Office: PO Box 2787 Lubbock TX 79408

REED, BOYD FREDERICK, mining co. exec.; b. Shamokin, Pa., Sept. 3, 1897; s. Daniel F. and Catherine (Reitz) R.; student Bliss Bus. Coll., 1913-14, LaSalle Extension U., 1916-17; m. Ruth Maurer, June 22, 1920; children—Alvin, Helen, David, Mariana, Phyllis. Chief clk. Trevorton Colliery (Pa.), 1914-1920; auditor Liggetts Creek Coal Co., Scranton, Pa., 1920-22; treas. J.P. Burton Co., Cleve., 1922-27; organizer, treas. Turner Elkhorn Mining Co., Drift, Ky., 1927-72, pres., 1972—; dir., chmn. bd. Floyd County Devel. Corp., Drift, 1979—; chmn. bd. First Guaranty Bank, Martin, Ky., 1950-80. Fin. chmn. Lonesome Pine council Boy Scouts Am., 1953, pres., 1954, recipient Silver Beaver award, 1954, Silver Antelope award, 1955; chmn. fund raising campaign Floyd County Bookmobile, 1953; elder Presbyterian Ch., Drift, 1947—; emeritus mem. bd. trustees Pikeville Coll., 1948-70; bd. regents Morehead (Ky.) State U., 1954-78. Recipient Public Service award Morehead State U., 1972; named Coal Man of Yr., Ky. Coal Assn., 1977. Mem. Big Sandy Elkhorn Coal Operators Assn. (founder, pres. 1947-52, dir. 1931-80), Nat. Coal Assn. (dir. 1964-77), Ky. Coal Assn. (dir. 1954—), Ky. C. of C. (dir. 1953-54). Clubs: Kiwanis, Masons. Home: PO Box 47 Drift KY 41619

REED, CHESTER RAY, archtl. engr.; b. Ponca City, Okla., Jan. 30, 1931; s. Paul Emery and Eva Cecelia (Eaton) R.; Asso. Sci., No. Okla. Jr. Coll., 1951; B.Archtl. Engring., Okla. State U., 1954; m. Ethel Cylvesta Adams, Mar. 15, 1957; children—Thomas Paul, Clayborn Ray. Engr.-in-tng. Roof Structures, Inc., St. Louis, 1954-55; engr.-in-tng. to profl. engr. Mullen & Powell Cons. Structural Engrs., Dallas, 1955-60; prin. C.R. Reed, structural engr., Dallas, 1960-69; pres. Chester R. Reed, Inc., 1969—, Probe Test Systems, Inc., Dallas, 1970—; owner, developer Panther Creek Pass, Mt. Vernon, Tex. Cons. structural engring. Pres. United Fund, Heart Fund. Registered profl. engr., Tex., Okla. Mem. Tex. Soc. Profl. Engrs., Am. Concrete Inst., Nat. Fedn. Independence Bus., Dallas, North Dallas chambers commerce, Sigma Tau, Chi Epsilon, Phi Kappa Phi. Mem. Christian Ch. (deacon 1957—). Principal works: Dallas Cowboy Football Stadium roof, Irving, Tex., 1971, 4th Nat. Bank Bldg., Tulsa, 1971, Preston Tower Apts., Dallas, 1963, others. Home: 4501 Arcady Ave Dallas TX 75205 Office: 3511 Cedar Springs Rd Dallas TX 75219

REED, DALE CHARLES, business exec.; b. Bethesda, Md., Aug. 22, 1948; s. Dale Calvin and Barbara Loraine (Thurman) R.; B.A. in Economics, Trinity Coll., Hartford, Conn., 1970; postgrad. Kent State U., 1971, Northwestern U., 1972-73, Bryant Coll., Smithfield, R.I., 1974-75, Ga. State U., 1978-79; m. Gayle Irene Ponto, Feb. 2, 1974; children—Dustin Christopher, Lindsey Diana. Fin. analyst of reinforced plastics operation Automotive Products Group, Rockwell Internat. Corp., Ashtabula, Ohio, 1970-71; accountant J & H Internat. Corp., Chgo., 1971-73; div. controller Fiberloys div. Rogers Corp. (Conn.), 1973-76, controller, adminstrv. mgr. Engineered Products Group, Lithonia, Ga., 1976—. Bd. dirs. Friends of Trinity Rowing. Mem. Am. Mgmt. Assn., Nat. Security Indsl. Assn., Nat. Assn. Amateur Oarsmen, Ga. Bus. and Industry Assn., Mensa, Alpha Chi Rho. Republican. Episcopalian. Home: 4015 Pineridge Dr Lilburn GA 30247 Office: 5259 Minola Dr Lithonia GA 30058

REED, DAVID BENSON, bishop; b. Tulsa, Feb. 16, 1927; s. Paul Spencer and Bonnie Francis (Taylor) R.; B.A., Harvard, 1948; M.Div., Va. Theol. Sem., 1951, D.D. (hon.), 1964; D.D. (hon.), U. of South; m. Susan Riggs, Oct. 30, 1954; children—Mary, Jennifer, David Benson, Sarah, Catherine. Ordained priest Episcopal Ch.; missionary priest, Colombia, 1951-58; asst. to dir. overseas dept. Nat. Council Episc. Ch., 1958-61; vicar St. Matthews Ch., Rapid City, S.D., 1961-63; consecrated bishop; bishop of Colombia, 1964-72, of Ecuador, 1964-70; bishop coadjutor Diocese of Ky., 1972-73; bishop of Ky., 1974—. Pres. Anglican Council Latin Am., 1969-71; mem. standing commn. on ecumenical relations Episc. Ch., 1974—. Trustee U. of South, 1971—, regent, 1977—; chmn. Louisville United Against Hunger, 1976-78. Served with USNR, 1945-46. Home: 1823 Ballard Mill Ln Louisville KY 40207 Office: 421 S 2d St Louisville KY 40202

REED, DONALD WAYNE, ins. co. exec.; b. Kingsport, Tenn., Feb. 9, 1938; s. H. Grady and Eulene (Young) R.; student U. Tenn., 1957-60, student E. Tenn. State, 1963-64; student La. State U., 1974; m. Suzanne Gannaway, Jan. 31, 1960; 1 dau., Rachel Love. Agent, Fidelity Union Life Ins. Co., Johnson City, Tenn., 1964-65, gen. agt., Johnson City, 1965-66; regional dir. Guaranty Ins. Co., Johnson City, 1966-69; mktg. dir. Shenandoah Life Ins. Co., Roanoke, Va., 1969-72, branch mgr., Greenville, S.C., 1972-77, gen. mgr., Greenville, 1977—; pres. Don Reed & Assos. Active Boy Scouts Am., 1968. Served with Army Security Agency 1960-63. Mem. Underwriters Assn. (v.p.), Greenville Sales and Mktg. Exec. Assn. (past pres.), Gen. Agents and Mgrs. Assn., Greenville C. of C. (group leader exec. Sales Club). Episcopalian. Elk. Clubs: Kiwanis, Lions, Rotary (Johnson City). Home: 10 Botany Rd Greenville SC 29607 Office: 15 Manly St Greenville SC 29601

REED, FRANCIS ALEXANDER, JR., physician; b. Miami Beach, Fla., Dec. 2, 1946; s. Francis A. and Rochelle (Fox) R.; A.B., Holy Cross Coll., 1968; M.D., Tulane U., 1972; m. Debra Hataway, Aug. 4, 1979. Intern, Ochsner Clinic, New Orleans, 1974; resident in internal medicine, 1972-75; practice medicine, specializing in internal medicine, Alexandria, La., 1976-78, Ft. Lauderdale, Fla., 1978—; physician Lauderdale Med. Group, 1978—; mem. staff North Ridge Gen. Hosp., Holy Cross Hosp., Ft. Lauderdale. Diplomate Am. Bd. Internal Medicine. Mem. Am. Soc. Internal Medicine, Broward County Med. Assn. Office: 3000 Bayview Dr Fort Lauderdale FL 33306

REED, GEORGE FRANCIS, architect; b. Miami, Fla., Sept. 25, 1928; s. George Francis and Lillian Lucille (Hellerman) R.; B.S. in Architecture, Ga. Inst. Tech., 1951, B.Arch., 1953. Draftsman-designer Rufus Nims, Architect, Miami, 1954-56; asso. architect Robert B. Browne, Architect, Miami, 1957-60; pvt. practice architecture, Miami, 1961—; chmn. Miami Design Rev. Bd., 1967,

Dade County (Fla.) HUD Adv. Bd., 1968—; pres. South Fla. Inter-Profl. Council, 1970-71; mem. Dade County Art in Public Bldgs. Adv. Bd., 1974-77, Dade County Community Devel. Adv. Bd., 1975—, Dade County Housing Planning Adv. Bd., 1977—. Pres. Coconut Grove Assn., Miami, 1972-73. Served as ensign USCGR, 1952. Recipient various awards for archtl. design and public service Soc. Am. Foresters, 1967, 70, 73, South Fla. Inter-Profl. Council, 1968, 69, 70, Met. Dade County, 1968, 77, 78, Housing Corp. Am., 1971. Fellow AIA (Fla. Assn. awards 1964, 67, 68, 69, 73, Fla. South chpt. award 1964, 66, 67, 68, 75, 78, pres. Fla. South chpt. 1967). Office: 3050 Bird Ave Coconut Grove Miami FL 33133

REED, GEORGE LINDMILLER, cons. civil engr.; b. Charlotte, N.C., Mar. 14, 1937; s. George Lindmiller and Lois Olive (Carrington) R.; B.S. in Civil Engring., N.C. State U., 1963, M.S. in Transp., 1965; m. Margaret Virginia Davis, Mar. 13, 1960; children—Candace Elizabeth, Angela Davis, Christina Louise. Project engr. Harland Bartholomew and Assos., Greenville, S.C., Memphis, South Bend, Ind., 1965-71; project mgr., v.p. William S. Pollard Cons.'s, Memphis, 1971-74; asso. and dir. transp. plan div. Harland Bartholomew & Assos., Inc., Memphis, 1974—; lectr. U. Notre Dame, 1968. Registered profl. engr., Ind., Mich., Tenn., N.C., Fla. Mem. ASCE (D.W. Mead award 1970), Inst. Transp. Engrs., Planners Club Memphis. Presbyterian (elder 1974-78). Contbr. articles to profl. jours. Home: 4653 Clearwater Dr Memphis TN 38128 Office: 188 Jefferson Ave Memphis TN 38103

REED, HARRY LOWE, corporate lawyer; b. Houston, Dec. 16, 1923; s. Ira Franklin and Geneva Dewey (Lowe) R.; B.A., U. Tex., Austin, 1943, J.D., 1948; m. Betty Anne Ghiselin, Dec. 10, 1949; children—Barry, Bruce, Christopher, Shirley. Admitted to Tex. bar, 1948; atty. Shell Oil Co., Houston, 1948-75, gen. atty., 1975—, pres. Shell Communications, Inc., 1971—; v.p. Butte Pipeline Co., Houston, 1971-75, Four Corners Pipeline Co., Houston, 1971-75; v.p. dir. Plaza Del Oro Corp., Houston, 1975-78; adj. prof. law South Tex. Coll. Law, Houston, 1952—. Councilman, City of Bellaire, Tex., 1953-56, mayor, 1956-57. Served with USNR, 1943-46. Mem. Am., Houston bar assns., State Bar Tex., Am. Judicature Soc. Methodist. Home: 5422 Dumfries St Houston TX 77096 Office: PO Box 2463 Houston TX 77001

REED, JERRY LEE, food operating co. exec.; b. Henryetta, Okla., Sept. 13, 1941; s. Hershell E. and Ethel Marie (Marler) R.; student U. Calif., Bakersfield, 1965-69; m. Linda Ann Prigge, May 10, 1975; 1 dau., Tami Leigh. Vice-pres. sales Golden West Homes, Porterville, Calif., 1966-67; salesman nat. accounts 3M Co., San Jose, Calif., 1967-69; dir. mktg. Data-Link Corp., San Diego, 1969—; pres., Century One, Inc.; pres. Solatrex Corp., operating co. for Jim's Hickory Smoked Products and Village Kitchen Foods, San Antonio, 1976—. Mem. Am. Mgmt. Assn. Republican. Unity Ch. Home: 11009 N Millbend St Woodlands TX 77380 Office: Solatrex Corp PO Box 20106 San Antonio TX 78220

REED, JESSE FRANCIS, business exec.; b. Federalsburg, Md., June 6, 1925; s. Homer F. and Lola Irene (Stevens) R.; B.A. in Fine Art, Montclair Coll., 1950; D.D., Gnostic Sem., 1968; m. Mary Grace Mayo, July 9, 1944; 1 son, Gary. Owner, Reed's Frozen Foods, Paterson, N.J., 1950-59; pres. A.E. Inc., N.Y.C., 1959-72, Intercontinental Bus. Research & Devel. Inc., San Francisco, 1959-72, Dallas and Washington, 1972—, Intercontinental Oil & Ore Inc., Carson City, Nev., 1972—; chmn. bd., pres. Cosmo U.S.A., Inc., Dallas and Washington, 1974—, Internat. Fine Art Inc., 1979—. Bd. dirs. Gnostic Ch. Served with USN, 1942-46. Recipient various Art Show awards in Tex., Calif., N.J., N.Y. Mem. Screen Writers Guild, Cattlemen's Assn. Inventor protein converter, system to translate all ednl. disciplines into their pictorial presentations. Home: 6071 Village Bend Dr Apt 505 Dallas TX 75206 Office: Box 12488 Dallas TX 75225

REED, JIMMY BURL, SR., auto supply co. exec.; b. Williamson, W.Va., June 30, 1924; s. William Sidney and Mary (Purdy) R.; B.S. in Bus. Adminstrn., U. Palm Beach, 1949; m. Lorene Helen Alderman, Oct. 11, 1947; children—Jimmy Burl, William Michael, Helen Lynn. Retail salesman Goodyear Tire & Rubber Co., Inc., West Palm Beach, Fla., 1949-51, retail store mgr., Miami, Fla., 1951-53, retail store mgr., Tampa, Fla., 1953-59, dist. truck tires sales mgr., Jacksonville, Fla., 1959-62, dist. petroleum sales mgr. State of Ala., 1962-65, regional petroleum sales mgr. So. region, 1965-67; propr., pres. Dublin Auto Supply Co. (Va.), 1967—, Leisure Living Homes, Inc., Dublin, 1973—. Pres. Dublin United Way, 1973-74; chmn. Pulaski County (Va.) United Way, 1975; mem. New River Community Coll. Adv. Bd., 1975—; bd. dirs. Pulaski County Lifesaving, 1974-75. Served with USN, 1943-46; PTO. Mem. Nat. Assn. of Ind. Bus., Pulaski County C. of C. (dir. 1976-77). Club: Lions (dir. 1974-76). Methodist. Home: 7th and Jordan Sts Radford VA 24141 Office: Dublin Auto Supply PO Box 1107 Dublin VA 24084

REED, JO ANNE WRIGHT, telephone co. exec.; b. Olton, Tex., June 22, 1931; d. Willis Eugene and Sally Sylvesta (Thetford) Wright; student N. Tex. State U., 1974, Tex. Christian U., 1978, U. Kans., 1978; children—James Dennis, Joni Rene. With Gen. Telephone Co. S.W., 1951—, area bus. office supr., Lewisville, Tex., 1973-74, div. mgr., Sulphur Springs, Tex., 1974-76, Denton, Tex., 1976-78, Garland, Tex., 1979—; dir. First Nat. Bank, Garland. Campaign chmn. Denton County Cancer Crusade; chmn. corp. div. United Way; mem. adv. bd. Salvation Army; bd. dirs. Garland Symphony, Greater Denton Industries and C. of C. Mem. Tex. Assn. Bus. (public relations chmn.), Bus. and Profl. Women's Club (dir.). Baptist. Club: Soroptimist (pres.)(Denton). Office: Gen Telephone Co of SW 3622 North Star St Garland TX 75040

REED, JOHN MARTIN, radiologist; b. Lexington, Ky., Dec. 4, 1930; s. Elmer Martin and Bertha Earl (Kemper) R.; B.S. (Margaret Voorhis Haggin scholar), U. Ky., 1953; M.D. (Rural scholar, Am. Heart Assn. grant), U. Louisville, 1960; m. Wilma Mae Donovan, July 1, 1949; children—Phillip Martin, Diane. Intern, St. Joseph Infirmary, Louisville, 1960-61; practice medicine specializing in family practice, Mayfield, Ky., 1961-66; resident in radiology U. Fla., Gainesville, 1966-69; practice medicine specializing in radiology, Jacksonville, Fla., 1969—; chmn. radiology dept. Meml. Hosp., Jacksonville, 1974—. Diplomate Am. Bd. Radiology. Mem. Radiol. Soc. N. Am., Soc. Nuclear Medicine, AMA. Baptist. Clubs: San Jose Country, Sawgrass Golf, Masons. Contbr. articles in field to profl. jours. Home: 2916 Caballero Ct Jacksonville FL 32217 Office: 3599 University Blvd S Jacksonville FL 32216

REED, JOSIAH FREDERICK, JR., physician; b. Harrisburg, Pa., Sept. 21, 1924; s. Josiah Frederick and Anna Duncan (Wills) R.; B.S., Va. Mil. Inst., 1951; M.D., U. Va., 1950; m. Tamara Eugenia Duffer, Oct. 18, 1958; children—John, Elizabeth. Intern, Union Meml. Hosp., Balt., 1950-51; resident Walter Reed Army Hosp., Washington, 1953-56; fellow in genitourinary pathology Armed Forces Inst. Pathology, 1954; pvt. practice medicine specializing in urology, Montgomery, Ala., 1971—; mem. active staff Harrisburg (Pa.) Polyclinic Hosp., 1959-71, cons. staff, 1971—, chief coordinator urology, 1966-71; asso. clin. prof. urology Hahnemann Med. Coll., 1970-71; chief urology service Holy Spirit Hosp., Camp Hill, Pa., 1963-68, cons. urology, 1968-71; cons. urology Hershey (Pa.) Hosp., 1959-71; cons. urology Milton S. Hershey Med. Center, 1968-71; mem. active staff Montgomery (Ala.) Bapt. Hosp., 1971—; mem. courtesy staff Jackson Hosp. & Clinic, Montgomery, 1971—, St. Margaret's Hosp., Montgomery, 1971—. Served with USAF, 1950-59; col. Res. Mem. Am. Urol. Assn., Urol. Assn. Pa. (founding sec.-treas. 1964-71), Am. Fertility Soc., Assn. Mil. Surgeons, Soc. Air Force Clin. Surgeons, A.C.S., Soc. Pediatric Urology, Internat. Coll. Surgeons, Am. Assn. Clin. Urologists, Pan Am. Med. Assn., Am., Pa. med. assns., Med. Assn. Ala., Montgomery County Med. Soc., Ala. Urol. Soc., Societe Internationale D'Urologie. Contbr. articles to profl. jours. Home: 3044 Boxwood Dr Montgomery AL 36111 Office: 1111 E South Blvd Montgomery AL 36111

REED, KATHLYN LOUISE, univ. adminstr.; b. Detroit, June 2, 1940; d. Herbert Curtis and Jessie Ruth (Krehbiel) R.; student U. Wis., 1958-61; B.S., U. Kans., 1964; M.A., Western Mich. U., 1966; Ph.D., U. Wash., 1973. Temporary supr., occupational therapist Vis. Nurse Assn., Beloit, Wis., 1964; staff occupational therapist Kans. U. Med. Center, Kansas City, 1964-65; instr. U. Wash., Seattle, 1967-70; research asso. Child Devel. Center, Seattle, 1972-73; prof., chmn. dept. occupational therapy U. Okla., Oklahoma City, 1973—; cons. HEW Pub. Health grant to Ohio State U., 1970-71, NIH grant to Am. Occupational Therapy Assn., 1972-73; acting instr. U. Puget Sound, Tacoma, Wash., 1971; cons. Devel. Disabilities Child Study Center, Oklahoma City, 1975-79; cons. Medicaid, nursing homes Okla. Dept. Health, 1976-77; cons. developmental disabilities Children's Convalescent Center, Oklahoma City, 1977—. Telephone worker, counselor Open Door Clinic, 1968-72; mem., co-chmn. citizen's bd. Seattle Mental Health Center, 1970-72, mem. exec. bd., 1971-72. Recipient Elmer H. Wilds award Western Mich. U., 1966, Traineeship HEW-Rehab. Services Adminstrn., 1970-72. Fellow Am. Occupational Therapy Assn. (chmn. nominating com. 1972, bylaws com. 1979—); mem. Am. Assn. Mental Deficiency, Council Exceptional Children (chpt. treas. 1970-72, v.p. 1976-78), Am. Pub. Health Assn., Okla. Coalition of Citizens with Disabilities, Okla. (practice chmn. 1973-74, pres. 1974-76, del. 1976-79), Wash. (del. 1968-73) occupational therapy assns., World Fedn. Occupational Therapists, Sigma Kappa, Pi Lambda Theta. Home: 8800 Rolling Green Oklahoma City OK 73132

REED, LEMUEL MORRIS TIPTON, state ofcl. Ky.; b. Clear Springs, Ky., Dec. 13, 1918; s. James Calvin and Vera Cruz (Hurt) R.; B.S., Murray State Coll., 1950; LL.D., J.D., U. Ky., 1954; m. Vivian Lee Waldrop, Oct. 1, 1943; children—Lemuel Morris Tipton, Thomas Jefferson Boyd, Ralph Shannon Lee. Admitted to Ky. bar, 1954; mem. Ky. Ho. of Reps., 1951-55; mem. firm Martin, Neely & Reed, Mayfield, Ky., 1955-59, Neely & Reed, Mayfield, 1959-69, Neely, Reed and Brien, Mayfield, 1969-75, Reed & Reed, Mayfield, 1976—; referee workmen's compensation Ky., 1955-59; commonwealth atty. 1st. Judicial Dist., Graves County, Ky., 1963—; mem. Ky. Gen. Assembly, 1951-56; pres. Lawpart Realty Co., Mayfield; cons. in field. Mem. Ky. Crime Commn., 1968—; mem. Ky. Gov.'s Adv. Commn., 1972—. Served to capt., A.C., U.S. Army, 1941-45. Mem. Commonwealth Attys. Assn. Ky. (pres. 1972-73), 52d Judicial Dist., 1st Judicial Dist., Ky., Am. bar assns., Regional Dist. Attys. Assn. Democrat. Methodist. Club: Mayfield Golf and Country. Home: 612 Pryor St Mayfield KY 42066 Office: 238 N 7th St Mayfield KY 42066

REED, MARY F. KURTS, educator; b. Parsons, Tenn., Sept. 28, 1935; d. Johnnie G. and Callie S. (Hays) Delashmit; B.S., Memphis State U., 1969, M.Ed., 1975; m. Thomas S. Reed, May 13, 1977; children—Susan L. Kurts, Linda C. Kurts Thomas, Lisa G. Kurts; stepchildren—Tammie M. Reed, Terrie J. Reed, Leah A. Reed, Richard W. Reed. Tchr. educatable mentally retarded Shelby County (Tenn.) Bd. Edn., 1969-71; mgr. printing dept. Memphis Jewish Community Center, 1971-72; tchr. trainable mentally retarded, instructional resource class Memphis Bd. Edn., 1972--. Mem. Nat., Tenn., Memphis (merit award) edn. assns., Assn. W. Tenn. Edn., Council Exceptional Children, Soc. Autistic Children. Democrat. Presbyterian. Home: 1012 Dillworth St Memphis TN 38122 Office: Westside Elementary Sch 3347 Dawn Dr Memphis TN 38127

REED, MURRAY ORVILLE, judge; b. Fulton, Miss., Jan. 27, 1899; s. Charles Nathaniel and Alma (Gregory) R.; student Ark. Law Sch.; bus. coll. diploma; m. Ellen Vineyard, Apr. 23, 1922; 1 dau., Meralen (Mrs. David A. Ruffin). Admitted to Ark. bar, 1920, U.S. Supreme Ct. bar, also Fed. Dist. Cts.; practiced in Little Rock, 1921-56; mem. Ark. Ho. of Reps., 1930-32; dep. pros. atty. 6th jud. dist., 1934, 42, 46; asst. bank commr. Ark., 1937-41; investigator War Regulation II, 1942; govt. appeal agt. Little Rock Draft Bd., 1941-45; chancery judge 2d Div., 1st Chancery Dist. Ark., 1948-49; gen. counsel Ark. Hwy Commn., 1949-52; municipal judge City of Little Rock, 1955-56; judge Chancery Ct. 1st Div., 1st Chancery Circuit Ark., 1957-79; ret., 1979. Atty. OPA, 1946; pres., Jud. Council Ark., 1969-70; del. Nat. Conf. State Trial Judges, 1972, 73. Pres. Little Rock Bd. Edn., 1940-41. Mem. Am., Ark., Pulaski County bar assns., Am. Judicature Soc. Democrat. Mem. Christian Ch. Kiwanian, Eagle, Elk. Home: 4920 Lakeview Rd North Little Rock AR 72116

REED, PATRICIA BRIDGES, clin. social worker; b. Dallas, Aug. 12, 1927; d. Murphy Foster and Bess Ethel (Jones) Bridges; B.S., La. State U., 1948; M.S.W., Tulane U., 1971; m. Warren Gardner Reed, Oct. 1, 1948 (div.); 1 dau., Tena Patricia. Social worker Caddo Parish Welfare Dept., Shreveport, La., 1965-70; psychiat. social worker Hill Crest Hosp., Birmingham, Ala., 1971—, dir. social services, 1974—; dir. social services Higdon Hill Sch. and Group Home, 1976—; cons. in field; part-time faculty U. Ala., Birmingham and Tuscaloosa, field supr., 1976—. Adv. bd. social work dept. U. Ala., Birmingham. Cert. social worker, Ala. Mem. Acad. Cert. Social Workers of Nat. Assn. Social Workers, Am. Group Psychotherapy Assn., Soc. Hosp. Social Work Dirs. of Am. Hosp. Assn., Ala. Soc. Hosp. Social Workers, Ala. Conf. Social Work, Central Neuropsychiat. Hosp. Assn., Med. Social Work Club, Mental Health Assn. Jefferson County (Ala.), Pi Beta Phi. Democrat. Episcopalian. Home: 4225 Warren Rd Birmingham AL 35213 Office: Hill Crest Hosp 6869 50th Ave S Birmingham AL 35213

REED, RAYMOND DERYL, architect, univ. adminstr.; b. Alturas, Calif., Mar. 29, 1930; s. Russell Jacob and Nita Ferne (Wilcox) R.; B.Arch., Tulane U., 1953; M.Arch., Harvard U., 1958; m. Patricia Reinerth, Apr. 30, 1954; children—Kathryn, Russell, Ann, Andrea. Chmn. dept. architecture U. So. La., Lafayette, 1958-64; head dept. architecture Iowa State U., 1964-70, dir. archtl. research, 1970-73; dean Coll. of Architecture and Environ. Design, Tex. A&M U., College Station, 1973—. Served with USNR, 1953-58. Mem. AIA, Tex. Soc. Architects, Internat. Council Fine Arts Deans, Assn. Collegiate Schs. Architecture. Home: 1601 Wolfpen Ln College Station TX 77840 Office: Coll of Architecture Tex A&M U College Station TX 77843

REED, RICHARD ALLEN, educator; b. Cleve., June 1, 1941; s. Marvin George and Ruth Marie R.; B.A., Stetson U., 1962; M.A. (NDEA fellow), Emory U., 1965, Ph.D., 1971; m. Margaret Ann Simpson, Mar. 3, 1979. Asst. prof. lit. U. N.C., Asheville, 1968-72, asso. prof., dir. humanities, 1972-75, prof., chmn. lit., 1976—, chmn. faculty senate, 1979—; cons. Nat. Endowment for Humanities, N.C. Humanities Com. Chmn. bd. Thomas Wolfe Meml., N.C. Dept. Cultural Resources, 1975—. Mem. S. Atlantic MLA. Episcopalian. Clubs: Edwards Creek, Order of Those. Home: 4 Twin Oaks Banbury Cross Asheville NC 28801 Office: Dept Lit U NC Asheville University Heights Asheville NC 28804

REED, ROBERT DEHART, chem. engr.; b. Bluffton, Ind., May 2, 1905; s. Robert Addison and Gertrude (DeHart) R.; student Okla. A. and M. Coll., 1924-27; Sc.D. (hon.), Embry Riddle Coll., 1971; m. Iva Leone Dodd, Dec. 3, 1939; children—Alyce Claire, Michael Dodd. With John Zink Co., Tulsa, 1936—, chief engr., 1942-57, v.p. engring., 1957—, also dir.; adj. prof. U. Tulsa. Named to Hall of Fame, U. Tulsa; named Inventor of Year, Okla. Bar Assn., 1977. Mem. Am. Inst. Chem. Engrs., Tau Beta Pi, Engrs. Club Tulsa. Republican. Presbyn. Club: Masons. Author: Furnace Operations. Contbr. articles to profl. jours.; patentee in field. Home: 4192 S Troost Pl Tulsa OK 74105 Office: PO Box 7388 Tulsa OK 74105

REED, ROBERT EDWARD, lawyer; b. Natchez, Miss., Nov. 15, 1941; s. Jack Thomas and Mary Magdeline (McDonald) R.; B.A., U. Houston, 1968, J.D., 1971; postgrad. Coll. William and Mary; m. Patricia E. Fleming. Admitted to Tex. bar, 1971; mem. firm Day & Zimmerman, Inc., Texarkana, Tex., 1971-72; pvt. practice law, Port Arthur, Tex., 1972—. Active Sunnyside Speech and Hearing Clinic, Port Arthur, 1973—, v.p., 1974-75, dir., 1973—. Served with USN, 1959-64. Recipient John B. Van Ness award U. Houston, 1974, Outstanding Service award, 1969, 1970. Mem. Am., Jefferson County, Port Arthur bar assns., State Bar Tex., Nat. Criminal Def. Lawyers Assn., Tex. Trial Lawyers Assn., U. Houston Alumni Assn. (dir. 1974—, pres. Golden Triangle chpt. 1972-75). Clubs: Masons, Scottish Rite, Rotary. Office: 2125 Jefferson Dr Port Arthur TX 77640

REED, RONALD LOUIS, research advisor; b. Long Beach, Calif., July 26, 1926; s. Louis Archibald and Ruth Sellers (Ferguson) R.; B.S.-Ch.E., Northwestern U., 1946; M.S. in Chem. Engring., U. Kans., 1948, Ph.D. in Math. Physics, 1954; m. Margaret Jane Chastain, Mar. 27, 1948; children—Ronald Christopher, Marianna, Michael Allen. Systems analyst Sandia Corp., Albuquerque, 1954-56; supr. new recovery processes Gulf Research & Devel. Co., Pitts., 1956-62; asso. prof. petroleum engring. U. Tex., Austin, 1962-64; prof. mech. engring. Drexel Inst. Tech., Phila., 1964-66; prof. chem. engring. U. Houston, 1966-70; supr. chem. recovery processes Exxon Prodn. Research Co., Houston, 1970-76; vice chmn. Gordon Conf. on Fluids in Permeable Media, Meridan, N.H., 1979. Youth baseball coach, 1972, 74. Served with USNR, 1943-46. Mem. Soc. Petroleum Engrs., Am. Petroleum Inst., Sigma Xi, Tau Beta Pi, Pi Mu Epsilon, Phi Eta Sigma, Pi Epsilon Tau. Republican. Presbyterian. Author tech. publs. Patentee oil recovery processes. Home: 12502 Winding Brook Houston TX 77024 Office: PO Box 2189 Houston TX 77001

REED, SCOTT, state supreme ct. justice; b. Lexington, Ky., July 3, 1921; s. Wilbur Scott and Florence (Young) R.; J.D., U. Ky., 1945; m. Charlotte Sue Charles, Oct. 12, 1946; 1 son, Geoffrey Scott. Admitted to Ky. bar, 1944, practice in Lexington, 1944-64; partner firm Wallace, Turner & Reed, 1954-64; atty., Fayette County, Ky., 1952; judge 1st div. Fayette Circuit Ct., 1964-69; justice Ct. Appeals Ky., Frankfort, after 1969; chief justice Ky. Supreme Ct., 1976-77; acting asso. prof. U. Ky. Law Sch., 1948-56. Recipient Algernon Sydney Sullivan medallion U. Ky., 1945. Nat. Coll. Judiciary fellow, 1965. Mem. Am., Ky., Fayette County bar assns., Am. Law Inst., Spindeltop Faculty Alumni Assn., Lexington Civil War Roundtable, Order of Coif, Phi Delta Phi. Mem. Disciples of Christ. Kiwanian. Club: Cricket (Lexington). Editor-in-chief Ky. Law Jour., 1944. Author prefaces. Home: 508 Spring Hill Dr Lexington KY 40503 Office: care Adminstrv Office Cts 1520 Louisville Rd Frankfort KY 40601

REED, THOMAS BEAVERS, JR., ret. banker; b. Iaeger, W.Va., Apr. 5, 1918; s. Thomas Beavers and Lexye Linda (Clifton) R.; student LaSalle Extension U., 1936-39; m. Grace E. Gullatt, June 1, 1940 (dec.); children—Linda (Mrs. John R. McNally), Dianne (Mrs. Neil V. Spillane), Vikki Reed Hayden, Thomas Beavers III, David; m. 2d, Carmen Kellam. Asst. treas. Comml. Credit Corp., Charleston, W.Va., 1939-44, Macon, Ga., 1945-53; mgr. finance Gen. Acceptance Corp., Atlanta, 1953-55; sr. v.p. Pan Am. Bank, Miami, Fla., 1955-59; v.p. Walter Heller Co., Chgo., 1959-60, also asst. to pres.; sr. v.p. Union Trust Nat. Bank, St. Petersburg, Fla., 1960-74; pres. Landmark Bank of Tarpon Springs (Fla.), 1974-76 pub. relations Fla. Div. Blind Services, also Fla. Soc. Prevention Blindness, 1976—. Tchr. consumer lending Am. Inst. Banking, 1955-58, mem. com. Boy Scouts Am., 1960-76; v.p. No. Fla. Eye Bank, 1970-71, pres. 1971-72. Bd. dirs. Fla. Lions Found. for Blind. Served with AUS, 1945. Mem. Consumer Bankers Assn. (bd. govs. 1972-74), Am. Bankers Assn. (mem. adv. bd. 1972-74), Fla. Bankers Assn. (chmn. credit div. 1970-71; chmn. installment credit com. 1969-70), Group IV Installment Bankers Assn., Am. Legion, 40 and 8. Lion (dist. gov. 1969-70, pres. 1965-66; chmn. council govs. Fla. 1969-70; mem. adv. council Div. Blind Services 1971-78, chmn. 1971-72), Mason, Lion. Address: 6404 Corona Ave Holiday FL 33590

REED, W. ALLEN, corrugated paper products mfg. co. exec.; b. Worchester, Mass., Oct. 16, 1925; s. Winthrop A. and Leona L. (Hickox) R.; B.S., N.Y. U., 1951; m. Jane Anita Winters, Aug. 8, 1947; children—Thomas Allen, William Andrew, Jo Anne, Joel Ernest. Package designer Hankins Container Co., Union, N.J., 1949-54; package designer, salesman Wachusett Corrugated Corp., Worchester, 1954-55; salesman Weyerheauser Corp., Malden, Mass., 1955-60; gen. mgr. Boxmakers div. Warner Packaging, The Rexham Corp., Pinetops, N.C., 1970-80; gen. mgr. Avon Corrugated Corp., Rocky Mount, N.C., 1980—. Mem. N.C. Gov.'s Energy Conservation Corp. Served with USAAF, 1943-46. Mem. Packaging Inst., Paper Bd. Packaging Council (chmn. So. area), Nat. Fedn. Ind. Bus. Unitarian. Club: Kiwanis. Home: 303 S 3d St Pinetops NC 27864 Office: Avon Corrugated Corp Rocky Mount NC

REED, WALTER, educator; b. Meridian, Miss., Sept. 20, 1933; s. Williams Bryant and Beatrice (Coleman) R.; B.S., Jackson State U., 1955; M.S., Ind. U., 1961; Ed.D., U. Miami, 1973; m. Martha Duckworth, Jan. 14, 1957; children—Clifton, Kathy Denise, Walter Anthony. Tchr., coach Newton County Schs., Lawrence, Miss., 1955-57; elem. prin. Newton (Miss.) Public Schs., 1957-65; baseball coach Jackson (Miss.) State U., 1965-66, asst. prof. health, phys. edn., 1974-77, athletic dir., 1977—; prin. N.H. Pilate High Sch., Newton, 1966-70; asst. supt. schs. Newton Public Schs., 1970-71; staff specialist Miss. State U., Starkville, 1974. Bd. dirs. Metro YMCA, 1978—, Valley N. YMCA, 1977—; mem. deacon bd. Mt. Helm Bapt. Ch., 1975—. Mem. Nat. Assn. Athletic Dirs., AAHPER, Jackson State U. Alumni Assn., Ind. U. Alumni Assn., Nat. Assn. Intercollegiate Athletics (dist. sec.-treas. 1977—). Democrat. Baptist. Club: Touchdown (dir. 1977—). Author: Book of Basketball Drills, 1959; Intramural Handbook, 1975. Home: 325 Post Oak Rd Jackson MS 39206 Office: PO Box 17118 Jackson MS 39217

REED, WILLIAM GUY, restaurant exec.; b. Richmond, Ky., Feb. 6, 1942; s. William S. and Nina (Kanatzar) R.; B.A., Eastern Ky. U., 1963; postgrad. Eastern Ky. U., 1963-64; m. Janice Woods, Feb. 28, 1974; children—Tommy, Guy, Dee Dee. Tchr. Richmond, Ky., 1963-64; asst. mgr. Jerry's Restaurants, Lexington, 1964-65; mgr., v.p.

Corbin Restaurant Inc., Lexington, 1965-68, pres., 1968—; pres. Middlesboro Restaurant Inc., Lexington, 1971—; v.p., London Restaurant Inc., Lexington, 1975—; sec.-treas. Sioux Empire Restaurant Inc., Lexington, 1975—. Mem. Corbin, London, Middlesboro (Ky.) chambers commerce, Ky. Cols. Ky. Restaurant Assn. Baptist. Masons, Shriners. Home: 909 Chinoe Rd Lexington KY 40502 Office: 152 E Reynolds Rd Lexington KY 40503

REED, WILLIAM HENRY, materials engr.; b. Fayette County, Ky., Feb. 21, 1947; s. Avery Henry and Alma Virginia (Collins) R.; B.S. in Metall. Engring., U. Tenn., 1970; M.S., U. Ky., 1972; m. Patsy Sue Chadwell, Aug. 30, 1968; children—Brian Matthew, Laurel Jane. Metall. engr. Office Products div. IBM Corp., Lexington, Ky., 1970-74, project engring. mgr., 1974-76, tech. asst. to dir. engring., 1976-77, materials engring. mgr., 1977—; cons. materials engr., 1972—; adj. prof. metall. engring. U. Ky., 1978—. Registered prof. engr., Ky. Mem. Am. Soc. for Metals (chmn. Bluegrass chpt. 1975-76), Sigma Xi, Tau Beta Pi. Republican. Methodist. Contbr. articles to profl. jours. Home: 771 Longwood Rd Lexington KY 40503

REED, WILLIAM THOMAS, III, publisher, real estate exec.; b. Richmond, Va., Jan. 3, 1934; s. William T. and Mary Ross (Scott) R.; B.S., Hampden-Sydney Coll., 1956; m. Helen Scott Townsend, June 14, 1966; children—William T., Laird Scott Townsend, Philip Winston. With Larus & Bros. Co.. Richmond, 1958-65; partner Reed Bros., real estate, Manakin-Sabot, Va., 1966—; owner, pub. The Gazettes Goochland, Powhatan and Midlothian Counties, 1971—; dir. 1st & Mchts. Nat. Bank. Pres., Conservation Council Va., 1971-72, treas., 1973-75; pres. Sheltering Armys Hosp., 1971-74; exec. com., dir. State Fair Va. Served with AUS, 1956-58. Episcopalian. Republican. Clubs: Goochland Ruritan (pres. 1968), Commonwealth, Country of Va., Deep Run Hunt; Fishers Island (N.Y.) Country. Home: Chastain Manakin-Sabot VA 23103 Office: PO Box 177 Manakin-Sabot VA 23103

REEDER, EUGENE MARION, JR., mfg. co. exec.; b. Springfield, Ill., Sept. 24, 1941; s. Eugene Marion and Anita Belle (Strobel) R.; B.B.A., U. Tex. at Austin, 1964, M.B.A., 1965; m. Charla Mae Ernst, Aug. 1, 1964; 1 dau., Cara Michele. Mgr. resistor sensistor products br. Tex. Instruments Co., Dallas, 1965-70; v.p. prodn. Woodward subs. Time, Inc., Austin, Tex., 1971-75; v.p. mfg. Accelerator, Inc., Austin, 1975-78; pres. T-F Electronics, Inc., Austin, 1978—; instr. U. Tex. at Austin extension Sch. Bus., 1976—. Bd. dirs. Austin Minority Econ. Devel. Corp., 1973-76, Austin Com. on Fgn. Relations, 1976—; pres. Tejas Found., 1976-77. Licensed real estate broker, 1974—. Mem. Tex. Assn. Bus. (dir. Tex. 1976—, chmn. Centex chpt. 1976—), Austin C. of C. (mem. internat. affairs com., industry recognition week 1975—). Lutheran. Home: 11127 Shady Hollow Austin TX 78748

REEDER, WILLIAM DEAN, consultant; b. Nashville, Dec. 18, 1921; s. Elmer Cannon and May (Tyndall) R.; student Command and Staff USAF Air U., 1951, Tenn. Realtors Inst., 1974; m. Winifred Davis, Apr. 29, 1943; children—Ruth Reeder Crouch, William Dean, Susan Reeder Bala, Judith Reeder Kerrigan. Commd. 2d lt. U.S. Air Force, 1943, advanced through grades to col., 1964; served as bombardment pilot, Eng., Africa, 1943-45, telecommunications officer, Fla., Caribbean, 1946-50, Washington, 1950-54, communications squadron comdr., Guam, 1954-56, insp. gen. hdqrs. Norton AFB, Calif., 1954-60, communications comdr., Greece/Eng., 1960-64, sr. staff officer Scott AFB, Ill., Langley AFB, Va., CINCPAC, Hawaii, 1964-72, ret., 1972; realtor, Clarksville, Tenn., 1973-79; cons. real estate projects, Clarksville, 1979—; adj. prof. Austin Peay State U., 1978-79. Active Clarksville-Montgomery (Tenn.) Airport Bd., 1975—, Clarksville Community Devel. Adv. Bd., 1974—, Clarksville Hist. Zoning Bd., 1976—, Montgomery County Hist. and Recreation Bd., 1977—; pres. Montgomery Hist. Soc., 1976. Decorated Legion of Merit, D.F.C. with 3 oak leaf clusters, Air medal with 3 oak leaf clusters, AF Commendation Medal with 2 oak leaf clusters, AF Meritorious Service Medal. Mem. Nat. Assn. Realtors, Tenn. Assn. Realtors, Clarksville Bd. Realtors (pres. 1977; hon.). Methodist. Club: Masons. Home: 301 Trahern Circle Clarksville TN 37040

REEDY, JOHN RILEY, hosp. adminstr.; b. Hattiesburg, Miss., Feb. 10, 1934; s. Charles A. and Louise (Davis) R.; B.S., U. So. Miss., 1956; M.B.A., Miss. State U., 1975; married; children—Lucretia Ann, Rene Michelle, Sabrina Leigh, Sean Marie. Asst. adminstr., bus. mgr. Forrest County Gen. Hosp., Hattiesburg, 1958-60; adminstr. Stone County Hosp., Wiggins, Miss., 1960-67; exec. dir. St. Joseph Community Hosp., Meridian, Miss., 1967-75; exec. dir. Riverside Hosp., Jackson, Miss., 1975—. Bd. dirs. Miss. Kidney Found., 1970-74; mem. Miss. Econ. Council, 1975—. Mem. Miss. Hosp. Assn. (chmn.-elect), Am. Coll. Hosp. Adminstrs., Hosp. Fin. Mgmt. Assn. (past pres. Miss. chpt.), Meridian Hosp. Council (past pres.), Jackson C. of C., Rankin County C. of C. Roman Catholic. Home: 28 Fox Glen Cove Brandon MS 39042 Office: E Lakeland Dr Jackson MS 39216

REEDY, RUTH MILDRED, librarian; b. Corsicana, Tex., July 22, 1915; d. John Edward and Emma (Jarman) Clark; B.A., La. Coll., 1935; B.S. in L.S., U. Ill., 1937; postgrad. La. State U., 1952, 56; m. John Francis Reedy, Aug. 21, 1952. Librarian, Rayville High Sch., Rayville, La., 1937-42, Lake Charles (La.) High Sch., 1942-61; materials center librarian McNeese State U., 1961-72, library dir., 1972—; exec. sec. Library Devel. Com. La.; vis. prof. La. State U.; La. dir. Nat. Library Week; mem. evaluation team So. Assn.; cons. to sch. libraries. Elder, Presbyterian Ch., Lake Charles, La. Mem. La. Library Assn. (pres. 1956-57, Modisette award 1954, Essae M. Culver award 1980), Southwestern Library Assn., ALA (councilor), NEA, Nat. Congress Parents and Tchrs. (hon. life), Delta Kappa Gamma (pres. 1966-67), Sigma Sigma Sigma. Democrat. Club: Rev. Contbr. articles to profl. jours. Office: McNeese State U Lake Charles LA 70609

REEMELIN, ANGELA NORVILLE, dietitian, hosp. food service dir.; b. Pitts., Apr. 28, 1945; d. Richard Gerow and Kathleen Taylor (Brannen) Norville; B.S., U. Tenn., Knoxville, 1967; m. Philip Barrows Reemelin, Nov. 17, 1973; 1 son, Richard Barrows. Dietetic intern Woodruff Med. Center, Emory U., Atlanta, 1967-68; adminstrv. dietitian Servomation of Atlanta, 1968-70; therapeutic dietitian DePaul Hosp., ARA Food Services, Norfolk, Va., 1970-72, chief therapeutic dietitian, 1972-73, food service dir., 1973—; cons. in field; lectr. Am. Heart Assn., 1970-73. Instr. water safety ARC, 1963—; active Cystic Fibrosis, Leukemia Soc. Mem. Am. Dietetic Assn., Tidewater Dietetic Assn. (treas. 1971-73, 77—, corr. sec. 1975-76; Outstanding Young Dietitian 1974-75), Am. Soc. Hosp. Food Service Adminstrs., U. Tenn. Alumni Virginia Bay Area, Alpha Xi Delta, Omicron Nu. Roman Catholic. Home: 1772 Nobel St Alcoa TN 37701 Office: DePaul Hosp 150 Kingsley Ln Norfolk VA 23505

REEP, ROBERT GREGG, city ofcl.; b. Warren, Ark., June 17, 1954; s. Robert Ellis and Eloise (Galloway) R.; B.A. in Polit. Sci., U. Ark., Monticello, 1976. Dir. community devel. City of Warren (Ark.). Bd. dirs. S.E. Ark. Housing Devel. Corp., 1978—, Bradley County Med. Clinic, Inc., 1979—; pres. Bradley County Young Democrats, 1977—; mem. Ark. State Dem. Com., 1977—. Baptist. Club: Lions (pres. 1977-78) (Warren). Office: City of Warren PO Box 352 Warren AR 71671

REES, JOHN, educator; b. Bangor, Wales, U.K., Mar. 25, 1948; s. Thomas Eirwyn and Kitty A. (Jones) R.; came to U.S., 1969; B.A. with honors, U. Wales, 1969; M.A., U. Cin., 1971; Ph.D., London Sch. Econs., 1977; m. Janet L. Siegrist, Dec. 28, 1971; children—David Wynn, Mark Eirwyn, Catherine May. Asst. prof. Calif. State U., Chico, 1973-75; asso. prof. geography and polit. economy U. Tex., Dallas, 1975—, acting dir. S.W. Center for Econ./Community Devel., 1978—; cons. Joint Econ. Com., U.S. Congress, 1978—, Rep. of Tex. Corp., 1979—, N. Tex. Commn., 1978—, HUD, 1979. Mem. coms. on econ. devel. City of Dallas, 1978-79; mem. Metroplex Econ. Adv. Council, 1979—, Interuniv. Council of N. Tex., 1978—. NSF grantee, 1976—. Mem. Assn. Am. Geographers, Am. Econ. Assn., Regional Sci. Assn., Regional Studies Assn. (U.K.), Internat. Geog. Union. Contbr. articles in field to profl. jours. Home: 2224 Flat Creek Richardson TX 75080 Office: Sch Social Science U Tex at Dallas Richardson TX 75080

REESE, BUENA WRIGHT, educator; b. Newport News, Va., Aug. 2, 1933; d. Rufus Benjamin and Ethel Mae (Riddick) Wright; B.S., Hampton Inst., 1951, M.A., 1964, postgrad., 1971; M.Ed., So. Meth. U., 1969; postgrad. in urban affairs Norfolk State U., 1975-79; children—Deborah Renee, Timothy David. Tchr. public schs., Newport News, 1956-59, reading specialist, 1969-70; asst. prof. Hampton (Va.) Inst. and prin. nongraded model lab. sch., 1970-72; asst. prof. reading Norfolk (Va.) State U., 1972—; lectr., reading cons.; dir. St. Paul A.M.E. Ch. Child Care Center, Newport News, 1973-76. Sec.-treas., bd. dirs. Peninsula Agy. on Aging, Newport News-Hampton, 1976—; mem. Hampton Bd. Bank Vol. Action Center. So. Meth. U. research fellow, 1968-69; recipient Mace Silver pin, Internat. Reading Assn., 1975. Mem. Internat. Reading Assn., Va. Reading Assn., Norfolk Reading Assn., Va. Adult Edn. Assn., AAUP, Delta Sigma Theta. Mem. A.M.E. Ch. (pres. ch. hist. soc.). Clubs: Order Eastern Star, Daus. of Isis. Contbr. articles profl. jours. Home: 1036 Randall Ct Hampton VA 23666 Office: Norfolk State Univ Norfolk VA 23504

REESE, DAVID JOHN, physician; b. Danville, Pa., May 16, 1940; s. Robert E. and Helen (Deppen) R.; A.B., Princeton U., 1962; M.D., U. N.C., 1968; m. Eleanor Jane Sullivan, Aug. 7, 1965. Intern, U. Va. Hosp., 1968-69, resident in pediatrics, 1968-71; practice medicine specializing in pediatrics, Arlington, Va., 1973—; dir. pediatric edn. Arlington Hosp., 1973—, chmn. dept. pediatrics, 1974—; asst. prof. pediatrics Georgetown U. Sch. Medicine, 1975—; mem. com. for hypothyroid screening program for infants, State of Va., 1977—; mem. tech. adv. panel on neonatal intensive care Health Systems Agy. of No. Va., 1977—. Mem. Juvenile Services Study Task Force, No. Va. Planning Dist. Commn., 1976—; pres. Arcturus Park Assn., 1975—; mem. community adv. bd. No. Va. Community Service League, 1976-78. Served to maj. M.C., U.S. Army, 1971-73. Recipient Tchr. of Yr. award Georgetown U. Dept. Pediatrics, 1976, Cert. of Recognition, Gov. Va., 1978; diplomate Am. Bd. Pediatrics. Mem. No. Va. Pediatric Soc., Arlington County Med. Soc. Home: 824 Arcturus on the Potomac Alexandria VA 22308 Office: 1701 N George Mason Dr Arlington VA 22205

REESE, DOROTHY HARMON, educator; b. Fowler, Kans., Feb. 1, 1930; d. Harry Hershel and Edith Clare (Miller) Harmon; B.S. in Secondary Edn., Auburn U., 1967; M.A. in Spl. Edn., U. South Fla., 1974; children by previous marriage—Edith (Mrs. Richard Piatt), Virginia (Mrs. Kent Emory Bryant), Patricia Lee. Dir. Happy House, Albany, Ga., 1963-66; tchr. Silver Sands Sch., Ft. Walton Beach, Fla., 1967-70; instr. Hillsborough County Sch., Tampa, Fla., 1970-78; tchr. multi-handicapped Savannah (Ga.)/Chatham Bd. Edn., 1978-79; cons. for multi-handicapped, tchr. mentally retarded Tift. County Bd. Edn., Tifton, Ga., 1979-80, resource for physically/multi-handicapped, 1980—. Dir. Okaloosa County (Fla.) Summer Recreation Program, 1969; chmn. profl. adv. bd. com., caseworker epilepsy services program Gulf Coast Epilepsy Found. Bd. dirs. Fla. Epilepsy Found., past sec; mem. Council for Exceptional Children (sec. 1969—); adv. council Gulf Coast Epilepsy Found.; mem. Developmental Disabilities Planning Council Fla. Author: (with B. Wiley, A. Jensen) Okaloosa County Curriculum Guide for Educable Mentally Retarded, 1969. Home: 621 Chestnut Ave Tifton GA 31794 Office: 207 N Ridge Tifton GA 31794

REESE, JOHN OLAN, switchboard corp. exec.; b. Detroit, Nov. 26, 1939; s. Olan Cecil and Thressie Ellen (Johnston) R.; B.S. in Elec. Tech., U. Houston, 1974; m. Kathryn Arlene Sisson, July 18, 1970; children—Rhonda Lynn, William Olan. Chief draftsman Engineered Elec. Equipment Corp., Houston, 1964-70; mgr. elec. engring. Hutchison-Hayes Internat., Houston, 1970-71; mgr. engring. Internat. Switchboard Corp. div. Stewart & Stevenson Co., Houston, 1971-77, sales engr., 1977-78, mgr. D.C. drive applications, 1978—, mgr. mfg., 1979—; instr. generator control Am. Petroleum Inst., U. Tex., Petroleum Extension Service, 1977—. Baptist. Home: 15615 Boulder Oaks Dr Houston TX 77084 Office: 7514 Azabonson Rd Houston TX 77088 also PO Box 40425 Houston TX 77040

REESE, LAWRENCE TUCK, ophthalmologist; b. Bklyn., Jan. 18, 1948; s. Samuel I. and Miriam B. (Bernstein) R.; B.A. in Chemistry, N.Y. U., 1969; M.D., Cornell U., 1973; m. Lois Carol Reinhardt, July 30, 1977. Intern, Bellevue Hosp., N.Y.C., 1973-74; resident, chief resident N.Y. Hosp.-Cornell Med. Center, N.Y.C., 1974-77; Nat. Eye Inst. fellow in macular and retinal diseases Bascom Palmer Eye Inst., U. Miami (Fla.) Sch. Medicine, 1977-78; practice medicine specializing in ophthalmology, North Miami Beach, Fla., 1979—; clin. instr. ophthalmology U. Miami Sch. Medicine, Bascom Palmer Eye Inst. Permanent panel Bur. Blind Services, dept. health and rehabilitative services State of Fla. Served to capt. N.Y. N.G., 1974-77, M.C., Fla. Army N.G., 1978—. Fellow Am. Acad. Ophthalmology; mem. AMA, Fla. Med. Assn., Dade County Med. Soc., Am. Assn. Ophthalmology, Bascom Palmer Eye Inst. Alumni Assn. Club: B'nai B'rith. Contbr. articles to profl. publs., presentations to profl. confs. Office: 16800 NW 2nd Ave North Miami Beach FL 33169

REESE, MILDRED SCOTT, business exec.; b. Hendersonville, N.C., Feb. 7, 1923; d. James Brown and Mary Lillian (Scott) Reese; student public schools, Henderson, N.C. Chief clk. SSS, Hendersonville, 1945-47; legal sec., 1948-49; payroll clk., order editor Cranston Print Works Co., 1950-51; sec., group head stenographic services, adminstrv. asst. Film div. Olin Corp., Pisgah Forest, N.C., 1951-77; records officer Ecusta paper and film group, 1978-80, office services mgr., 1980—. Presbyterian. Home: 2606 Haywood Rd Hendersonville NC 28739 Office: Olin Corp PO Box 200 Pisgah Forest NC 28768

REESE, SUE BRYSON, nurse, educator; b. Moundsville, W.Va., Oct. 6, 1931; d. Harry A. and Virginia Elizabeth (Moore) Bryson; B.S.N., Hartwick Coll., Oneonta, N.Y., 1955; postgrad. Syracuse U., 1967; M.S.N., Cath. U. Am., 1974; m. Charles David Reese, Dec. 7, 1957; children—Becki, Cyndi, Suzi. Clin. coordinator Wheeling (W.Va.) Hosp., 1955-57; instr. Monongalia Gen. Hosp., Morgantown, W.Va., 1958-61, staff nurse, 1962; staff nurse Indiana (Pa.) Hosp., 1963, instr., 1963-66; instr. Syracuse (N.Y.) U., 1966-67; coll. health nurse, instr. West Liberty (W.Va.) State Coll., 1968-71; inservice edn. and asst. dir. nursing service Greater S.E. Community Hosp., Washington, 1971-73; asso. prof. nursing, dir. nursing edn. Shepherd Coll., Shepherdstown W.Va., 1974—. Mem. Am. Nurses Assn., W.Va. Nurses Assn., W.Va. Health Systems Agy., Inc., W.Va. Heart Assn., W.Va. Lung Assn., W.Va. Acad. Sci., DAR (nat. defense chmn. Pack Horse Ford chpt.), Sigma Theta Tau, Zeta Tau Alpha. Republican. Methodist. Clubs: Order Eastern Star, Women's (health com.) (Shepherdstown, W.Va.). Home: PO Box 220 Shepherdstown WV 25443 Office: Shepherd Coll Shepherdstown WV 25443

REEVE, HAROLD RICHARD, nuclear engr.; b. Chgo., Sept. 20, 1937; s. Harold Bernard and Ann Jeanette (Zolner) R.; B.S. in Chem. Engring., Ill. Inst. Tech., 1959; M.S. in Nuclear Engring., Purdue U., 1968, Ph.D. in Nuclear Engring., 1969; m. Carol Ann Haubl, June 6, 1959; children—Scott Richard, Stephen Michael, Brett Robert, Susan Ann. Design engr. E.I. duPont Co. Savannah River Lab., Aiken, S.C., 1961-65, research physicist, 1969-71, process physicist, 1971-75, area supr., 1975-78, chief supr., 1978—; asso. prof. U. S.C., Aiken, 1974-76. Chmn. planning-evaluation com., exec. com., bd. dirs. Aiken County United Way of Am., 1977, Gold award, 1976; v.p. Dixie Youth Baseball, 1971; pres. St. Mary's Home Sch. Assn., 1973; chmn. St. Mary's Sch. Bd., 1976, St. Angela Sch. Bd., 1978—. Served with USNR, 1959-61, comdr. Res. AEC spl. fellow, 1966-69. Mem. Am. Nuclear Soc. (chmn. Savannah River sect. 1978, nat. local sect. com. 1979—), Naval Res. Assn., Sigma Xi. Roman Catholic. Club: Toastmasters. Home: 1212 Fernwood Ct Aiken SC 29801 Office: Savannah River Plant Aiken SC 29801

REEVE, JAMES KEY, museum dir.; b. Lewistown, Mont., Sept. 24, 1925; s. John Rumsey and Isabelle (Key) R.; B.A., U. Tulsa, 1950; M.A., N.Y. U., 1954; postgrad. U. London Courtauld Inst., 1961-63. Lectr. Toledo Mus. Art, 1954-58; curator Univ. Art Gallery, asst. prof. art history U. Notre Dame, 1958-61; curator Anglo-Am. Art Mus., asst. prof. La. State U., 1963-67; curator Am. art Toledo Mus. Art, 1967-71; curator Philbrook Art Center, Tulsa, 1972-74; art mus. cons., 1974-75; dir. Okla. Mus. Art, Oklahoma City, 1975—; lectr. USIS, Am. Embassy, London, 1962-63. Mem. Mayor's Spl. Com. on Archtl. Preservation, Toledo, 1968-71. Served with USCGR, 1943-46. Mem. Coll. Art Assn. Am., Soc. Archtl. Historians, Nat. Trust for Hist. Preservation, Am. Assn. Museums, Okla. Museums Assn. (governing council 1979—), Advocates for the Arts, Lambda Chi Alpha. Home: 1613 Carlisle Ct Oklahoma City OK 73120 Office: Okla Mus Art 7316 Nichols Rd Oklahoma City OK 73116

REEVES, BILL EUGENE, univ. ofcl.; b. Brownwood, Tex., Mar. 13, 1932; s. Lester M. and Tommie Jewel (Castleberry) R.; B.S., Midwestern U., 1954; Ed.M., Tex. Tech. U., 1958, Ed.D., 1965; m. Paula Mae Roos, Apr. 15, 1976; children—Katherine Rene, Leslie Carol, Robin Kaye. Secondary sch. tchr. Petersburg (Tex.) Ind. Sch. Dist. 1957-59, Olney (Tex.) Ind. Sch. Dist., 1959-61; high sch. prin. Lamesa (Tex.) Ind. Sch. Dist., 1961-64; research asst. dept. edn. Tex. Tech. U., 1964-65; supt. schs. Spearman (Tex.) Ind. Sch. Dist., 1965-68; consortium coordinator and dir. planning Edn. Service Center, Amarillo, Tex., 1968; state dir. tchr. edn. Tex. Edn. Agy., Austin, 1969-70; dean Sch. Edn. Pan Am. U., Edinburg, Tex., 1970—; cons. to Tex. Edn. Agy., 1970-76, numerous public schs. in Tex., 1968—. Served with U.S. Army, 1954-56. Mem. Tex. State Tchrs. Assn., Am. Assn. Colls Tchr. Edn., Tex. Assn. Sch. Adminstrs., Phi Delta Kappa. Democrat. Presbyterian. Club: Rotary. Home: PO Box 33 Edinburg TX 78539 Office: 1201 W University Edinburg TX 78539

REEVES, DENNIS EARL, accountant; b. Louisville, Nov. 1, 1944; s. Garland Emery and Rhea (Kitchens) R.; B.S. in Acountancy, Western Ky. U., 1967, B.A. in Bus. Mgmt., 1967. Internal auditor DuPont Co., 1967-74, mfg. supr., 1974-75, computer ops. supr., 1975-76, acctg. supr., Martinsville, Va., 1976—. Served with U.S. Army, 1967-70. Decorated Bronze Star. Mem. Martinsville-Henry County Fin. Mgrs. Assn., Jaycees (v.p. 1976-77, dir.), Alpha Kappa Psi, Alpha Phi Omega. Unitarian. Home: 615 Mulberry Rd Martinsville VA 24112 Office: PO Box 4831 Martinsville VA 24112

REEVES, DOUGLAS DALE, mfg. and mktg. co. exec.; b. Detroit, Nov. 10, 1947; s. Donald Earl and Alta Luella (Cochran) R.; student U. Oreg., 1966, East Central State U., Ada, Okla., 1974, U. Okla., 1979—; m. Carol Ann Melvin, June 20, 1970; 1 son, Donald Matthew. Owner, operator Republic Block & Supply Co., Pauls Valley, Okla., 1970-75; dist. sales mgr. Acme Brick Co., Oklahoma City, 1976-78, regional sales mgr., 1978—. Served with USMC, 1967-69. Republican. Presbyterian. Office: 2500 NW 10th St Oklahoma City OK 73124

REEVES, EARL JAMES, JR., educator; b. Muskogee, Okla., Mar. 16, 1933; s. Earl James and Berneice Elizabeth (Jordan); student Kans. State U., 1950-51, Friends U., 1951-52; B.A., Wichita State U., 1954, M.A., 1959; Ph.D., U. Kans., 1962; m. Wilma Gail Reece, Aug. 30, 1959; children—Barbara Gail, Gregory Alan, Carolyn Elaine. Faculty U. Kan., Lawrence, 1961-62, U. Omaha, 1962-64, U. Mo., St. Louis, 1964-70; faculty U. Tulsa, 1970—, dir. urban studies program, 1970—, prof., 1971—. Cons. Central Midwestern Regional Edn. Lab., 1966-68, Tulsa C. of C. Leadership Tulsa, 1973-76, Tulsa area Agy. on Aging, 1973-76. Vice pres. city council, Berkeley, Mo., 1966-70; mem. Tulsa Community Relations Commn.. 1971-76, chmn., 1975; mem. met. Tulsa Growth Strategy Com., 1975-76; bd. dirs. Indian Nations Council Govts., 1977—; mem. mission direction and priorities com. United Presbyn. Ch., U.S.A., 1977—. Served with USAF, 1954-58. Mem. Am. Polit. Sci. Assn., Am. Soc. Pub. Adminstrn., Council of Univ. Insts. for Urban Affairs. Presbyn. (chmn. planning com. 1974-75, mem. met. ministries bd. 1970-76). Kiwanian. Research editor, pres. editorial bd. Midwest Review of Pub. Adminstrn., 1974-76. Contbr. articles to profl. jours. Author: Approaches to the Study of Urbanization, 1963; The Cross and the Flag: Evangelical Christianity and Contemporary Politics, 1972; Protest and Politics: Christianity and Contemporary Affairs, 1968; Back Talk: Press Councils in America, 1972; Urban Community, 1978. Home: 5212 S 76th E Ave Tulsa OK 74145 Office: 600 S College St Tulsa OK 74104

REEVES, GEORGE PAUL, bishop, Episcopal Ch.; b. Roanoke, Va., Oct. 14, 1918; s. George Floyd and Harriett Faye (Foster) R.; B.A., Randolph-Macon Coll., 1940; B.D., Yale, 1943; D.D., U. of South, 1970, Nashotah House, 1970; m. Adele Beer, Dec. 18, 1943; children—Cynthia (Mrs. Karl Pond), George Floyd II. Ordained priest Episcopal Ch.; consecrated bishop, 1969; chaplain USN, 1943-47, Fla. State U., 1947-50; rector All Saints Ch., Winter Park, Fla., 1950-59, Ch. of Redeemer, Sarasota, Fla., 1959-65, St. Stephens Ch., Miami, Fla., 1965-69; bishop of Ga., Savannah, 1969—. Mem. Phi Beta Kappa. Home: 112 E 52d St Savannah GA 31405 Office: 611 E Bay St Savannah GA 31401

REEVES, HUBERT LISBON, economist; b. Little Rock, Sept. 30, 1904; s. Alfred Randolph and Jency (Hubert) R.; B.A., Morehouse Coll., 1924; postgrad. Northwestern U., 1926-28; M.A., Am. U., 1950; postgrad. N.Y. U., 1950-51; m. Stella Elizabeth Jones, Sept. 3, 1938. Economist, War Manpower Commn., Washington, 1942-45, U.S. Dept. Labor, Washington and N.Y.C., 1945-54; asso. internat. labor specialist U.S. Dept. Labor, Washington, 1955, economist, 1956-62, manpower devel. specialist, 1962-64, manpower research analyst, 1964-67; lectr. econs. Savannah State Coll., 1968-72; econ. cons. A.L.

Nellum & Assos., Washington, 1973-79. Bd. dirs. Bethle-Community Center, 1969-73; trustee 1st Congl. Ch. Recipient Superior Performance award Dept. Labor, 1966. Mem. Am. Econ. Assn., Internat. Assn. Personnel in Employment Security, Alpha Phi Alpha. Club: Pigskin (Washington). Contbr. articles to profl. jours. Home: 901 E 32d St Savannah GA 31401

REEVES, MARVIN COKE, business exec.; b. Mt. Airy, N.C., Dec. 29, 1911; s. Marvin Coke and Sarah Myrtle (Spaugh) R.; B.A., Westminster Coll., 1933; m. Rose Everitt, Feb. 29, 1976; children from previous marriage—Marvin Coke III, Mary Lynne, Sarah Elizabeth, Virginia Louise. Civil engr. So. Mapping & Engring. Co., Greensboro, N.C., 1941-44; partner Western Wood Products Co., Houston, 1947-50; pres. Bentex Pharm. Co., Houston, 1950-71; v.p. pharm. group ICN Pharms., Pasadena, Calif., 1971-73; owner Reeves of Tex., 1973—, Houston Consumer Center, 1979—; pres. Colo. Gold & Silver, Inc., 1980—. Served to lt. USNR, 1944-47. Mem. Mensa, Phi Delta Theta. Home and office: 3615 S Braeswood Blvd Houston TX 77025

REEVES, ODIS, JR., ins. co. exec.; b. Ocoee, Fla., Mar. 31, 1941; s. Odis and Carrie (Curenton) R.; student pub. schs., Ocoee, Winter Garden, Fla.; m. Sandra Ann Stack, Sept. 15, 1962; children—Timothy Blake, Odis Reeves. With Nat. Standard Life Ins. Co., Orlando, Fla., 1959-66, supr. computer operators and programmers, 1964-65, asst. mgr. data processing, 1965-66; programmer/analyst Orange County (Fla.) Data Center, 1966, data processing coordinator, 1968-70, mgr. computer tech. and research, 1971-72, acting dir., 1970-71; programmer/analyst Gen. Guaranty Mortgage & Ins. Co., Winter Park, 1966-68; sr. systems engr. Deering Millican Research Center, Spartanburg, S.C., 1972-74; systems analyst Blue Cross Blue Shield of Tenn., Chattanooga, 1974—; cons. electronic data processing. Chmn. troop com. Cherokee council Boy Scouts Am., 1975-78; chmn. civic com. Cross Timbers Community Club, Chattanooga, 1975-77. Home: 8417 Dunnhill Ln Chattanooga TN 37443 Office: 801 Pine St Chattanooga TN 37402

REEVES, REBECCA KEMP, speech pathologist; b. Delray Beach, Fla., Aug. 2, 1949; d. Vernon and Elizabeth W. K.; B.A., S.C. State Coll., 1971; M.A., U. Ill., Champaign-Urbana, 1972; m. Michael D. Reeves, Dec. 15, 1973. Speech clinician S.C. State Coll., Orangeburg, summer 1971, also 1972-73, clin. supr., instr. speech pathology, 1973-75; Nat. Teaching fellow speech pathology Allen U., Columbia, S.C., 1975-76; instr. English as 2d. lang., Indo-chinese Refugee Agy., Columbia, 1976; dir. speech and hearing Midlands Center, Columbia, 1976-77; instr. public speaking Midlands Tech. Coll., Columbia, 1976-77; asst. prof. speech pathology U. S.C., Columbia, 1974—, acting chmn. dept. communicative disorders, 1979—; pvt. practice speech pathology, Columbia, 1975—; cons. in field. Lic. speech pathologist, S.C.; cert. personnel mgmt. tng., S.C. Mem. Am. Speech-Lang-Hearing Assn. (legis. councillor, S.C. rep. 1979—)(cert. clin. competence), Council Exceptional Children, S.C. Speech and Hearing Assn. Democrat. Office: Room 605 William Brice Sch Nursing U SC Columbia SC 29208

REEVES, ROBERTA LEE, printing co. ofcl.; b. Hannibal, Mo., Dec. 16, 1936; d. Albert Leo and Sara Ruth (Venne) Love; grad. high sch.; div.; 1 son, Geneal Austin. Bookkeeper, NCO Club, Barksdale AFB, La., 1957; bookkeeper, credit mgr. Taube's Women's Apparel, Minot, N.D., 1961-63; bookkeeper, credit mgr. O'Neal Anderson, Houston, 1969-71; acctg. supr. D. Armstrong & Co. Inc., Houston, 1975—. Served with USAF, 1955-57. Baptist. Home: 1515 Pech #135 Houston TX 77055 Office: 2000 B Governor's Circle Houston TX 77092

REEVY, WILLIAM ROBERT, psychologist, govt. ofcl., educator; b. Dobsina, Czechoslovakia, Feb. 3, 1922; s. Stefan Jan and Maria (Soltis) Revay; B.A. in Econs. and Psychology, Stanford U., 1946; postgrad. N.Y. U., 1946-48; Ph.D. in Clin. Psychology, Pa. State U., 1954; m. Carole May Jones, June 18, 1960; children—Anthony William, Carolyn Upton and Gretchen Maria (twins). Psychology intern VA Mental Hygiene Clinic, Newark, 1948-49, Newington VA Hosp., Conn., 1949-50; teaching asst. in gen. psychology Pa. State U., University Park, 1952-53; asso. prof. psychology Richmond (Va.) Profl. Inst., Coll. of William and Mary, 1954-55; instr. DePaul U., Chgo., 1955, asst. prof., 1956-57; counselor Student Counseling Service, U. Ill., Chgo., 1959; asst. prof. psychology counselor, Sacramento (Calif.) State Coll., 1957-60; lectr. in psychology U. Conn., Storrs, 1960; asso. prof. psychology Tex. Technol. Coll., Lubbock, 1960-61; dir. of clin. studies No. Va. Mental Health Project, Falls Church, 1961-62; asso. chief psychologist D.C. Gen. Hosp., 1962-64; cons. Dept. of Mental Hygiene, State of N.Y., 1964-68; asst. prof. psychiatry Georgetown U. Med. Sch., Washington, 1962-64; asso. prof. psychology State U. N.Y., Cortland, 1964-68; mem. instructional staff Frederick A. Moran Meml. Inst. on Crime and Delinquency, St. Lawrence U., Canton, N.Y., 1967; panel psychologist div. vocat. rehab. N.Y. State Edn. Dept., 1967-68; asso. prof. psychology N.Mex. Inst. of Mining and Tech., Socorro, 1968-69, prof., 1969-73, head dept. psychology, 1968-71; mem. dean's council State of N.Mex., Dept. Edn., 1968-72; cons. in psychology N.Mex. State Hosp., Las Vegas, 1969-72; clin. psychologist Rensselaer County (N.Y.) Mental Health Center, Troy, 1973-75; staff psychologist Fed. Reformatory, Petersburg, Va., 1975-76; chief of psychology services Fed. Correctional Instn., Butner, N.C., 1976-77, unit psychologist, 1977—; mem. faculty Chapman Coll., Ft. Lee, Va., 1975-76; vis. prof. psychology State U. of N.Y., Oneonta, 1968. Certified psychologist N.Y., Calif. Fellow Soc. for Applied Anthropology, Soc. for the Sci. Study of Sex, Inst. for Rational Living; mem. Am. Soc. for Aesthetics, Acad. Polit. Sci., N.Y. Acad. of Scis., Soc. for Psychol. Study of Social Issues, Am. Assn. of Marriage and Family Therapy, Am. Psychol. Assn., Acad. of Psychologists in Marital and Family Therapy (pres.), Sigma Xi, Phi Beta Kappa, Psi Chi. Contbr. articles on marriage counseling and sex edn. to periodicals and profl. jours. Home: 730 Crestview Dr Durham NC 27712 Office: Federal Correctional Institution PO Box 1000 Butner NC 27509

REGA, JANE LOUISE, ednl. adminstr.; b. El Paso, Tex., Dec. 8, 1951; d. John A. and Mary G. (Palombo) R.; B.A., Spring Hill Coll., 1973; M.A., U. Ala., 1974, Ph.D., 1980. Counselor-coordinator N. Ala. Ednl. Opportunity Center, Huntsville, 1974-75; counseling coordinator div. instnl. plans and programs Spring Hill Coll., Mobile, Ala., 1975-77; grad. dir. univ. housing, U. Ala., 1977-79, grad. asst. counselor edn., 1979, asst. dir. Capstone summer honors program, 1979, counselor freshman counseling U. Ala., 1974, grad. intern, career planning and placement service, 1979—. Mem. Am. Personnel and Guidance Assn. (sec., conf. coordinator U. Ala. chpt. 1978-79), Ala. Coll. Personnel Assn., NOW, Am. Coll. Personnel Assn., Nat. Assn. Student Personnel Adminstrs., Kappa Delta Pi. Home: PO Box 357 University AL 35486

REGAN, CARROLL ROBERT, newspaper pub., editor; b. Beaumont, Tex., July 3, 1936; s. Alva Bates and Georgie (Johnson) R.; B.A. in Journalism, La. State U., 1959; m. Carol Adams, Nov. 26, 1959; children—William Bates, Robert Leo. Mgr., Gen. Adjustment Bur., Tallulah, La., Vicksburg, Miss., 1961-68; pub., editor Madison Jour., Tallulah, 1968—. Chmn. bd. trustees Madison Parish Hosp., 1973—. Served with USN, 1959-61. Recipient award of merit La. Assn. Planning and Devel. Dists., 1973. Mem. La. Press Assn. (pres.), Nat. Newspaper Assn., Nat. Editorial Found., Madison Parish C. of C. (pres. 1969-70). Democrat. Baptist. Club: Tallulah Rotary (pres. 1975-76). Home: 4 Caledonia St Tallulah LA 71282 Office: 119 N Chestnut St Tallulah LA 71282

REGGIA, FRANK, elec. engr.; b. Northumberland, Pa., Oct. 30, 1921; s. Nicola and Rachela (DiPhillips) R.; student George Washington U., 1949-53, U. Md., 1955-58; B.S. in E.E. cum laude, Bucknell U., 1970, M.S. in E.E., 1971; m. Betty Jo Patterson, Jan. 14, 1945; children—James Allen, Daniel Lee. Electronic scientist Nat. Bur. Standards, Washington, 1945-54; research electronic engr. (microwaves) Harry Diamond Labs., Dept. Army, Washington, 1954-78; cons. microwave devel. labs. Def. Dept., 1960-76, Radio Sta. W3LQJ. Pres., Chevy Chase (Md.) Coquelin Run Citizens Assn., 1960-61; scoutmaster, chmn. Bethesda-Chevy Chase council Boy Scouts Am., 1962-70. Served with USN, 1940-45; CBI, PTO. Decorated Purple Heart; recipient Engr. of Year award Washington Soc. Engrs., 1953; Superior Accomplishment awards Commerce Dept., 1954, Dept. Army, 1959; Dept. Army study fellow U. Md., 1956-57, Bucknell U., 1969-70; Dept. Army Research and Devel. Achievement award, 1975; Inventor of Yr. award Harry Diamond Labs., 1977; Outstanding Fed. Service award Nat. Assn. Ret. Fed. Employees, 1978. Fellow IEEE, Washington Acad. Sci., AAAS; mem. Soc. Preservation Barbershop Quartet Singing in Am., Am. Legion (dir. 1971-75), VFW, Nat. Rifle Assn., Nat. Engring. Honor Soc., Tau Beta Pi. Methodist (trustee 1975-78). Clubs: Military Officers (Washington). Patentee in microwave acoustics and ferrites. Contbr. numerous articles, tech. reports to profl. jours. Home: 5227 N Garden Ln Roanoke VA 24019

REGISTER, LEVON CALVIN, accountant; b. Vero Beach, Fla., Oct. 23, 1927; s. Abbott Drafus and Ivy Grace (Benton) R.; A.A., Emmanuel Coll., 1948; B.B.A, U. Ga., 1951, M.B.A., 1952; LL.B., Atlanta Law Sch., 1955; m. Elmaise Turnage, Oct. 10, 1948; children—Levon Calvin, Daniel W., Vicki L. Register Eldredge, Bette C. Register Rogers. With Arthur Andersen & Co., Atlanta, 1952-62, tax mgr., 1959-66, tax mgr., Chattanooga, 1962—, partner, 1966—. Teaching asst. U. Ga., Athens, 1951-52; tax cons. Mem. estate planning council Chattanooga, 1964—, pres., 1971-72; co-chmn. cancer drive, Chattanooga, 1971-73; chmn. accountants fund drive, Chattanooga, 1974-75; mem. Allied Arts Assn., Chattanooga. Bd. dirs. Am. Cancer Soc., Chattanooga, 1968—; organizer, bd. dirs. Must Share, Inc., Royston, Ga., 1972—; bd. dirs., exec. com., sec., finance com. chmn. Emmanuel Coll., 1963—; pres. cabinet mem. Oral Roberts U., 1965; pres. Register Found., 1979—. Served with USNR, 1945-48. Recipient Medal of Honor, Inst. Continuing Legal Edn. Ga., 1970. Mem. Houston Museum, Hunter Art Museum, Chattanooga C. of C., Am. Inst. C.P.A.'s, Nat. Assn. Accountants (pres. 1969-70), Ga. Soc. C.P.A.'s, Tenn. Soc. C.P.A.'s (mem. state taxation com. 1962-66). Lion. Clubs: Mountain City; Signal Mountain Golf and Country. Contbr. articles to profl. jours. Home: Franklin Springs GA 30639 Office: 734 Market St Chattanooga TN 37402

REGNIER, CLAIRE NEOMIE, assn. exec.; b. Fort Riley, Kans., May 2, 1939; d. Eugene Arthur and Claire Janet (Macfarlane) Regnier; B.S. cum laude in Journalism, Trinity U., San Antonio, 1961. Advt. cons., San Antonio, 1961-68; editor Paseo del Rio Showboat newspaper, San Antonio, 1968—; exec. dir. Paseo del Rio Assn., San Antonio, 1968—. Chmn., Centro 21 Downtown Revitalization Task Force, San Antonio; rep. San Antonio River Corridor Com.; mem. Fiesta San Antonio Commnd.; bd. dirs. San Antonio Area council Girl Scouts U.S.A.; mem. adv. bd. San Antonio Parks and Recreation Dept. Recipient awards of excellence for Showboat, Alamo Bus. Communicators, 1970, 71, 73, 74. Mem. Internat. Assn. Bus. Communicators, Women in Communications (Headliner for Public Endeavor, San Antonio chpt. 1980), Tex. Public Relations Assn., Alamo Bus. Communicators (Communicator of Yr. 1977), San Antonio Mus. Assn., San Antonio Conservation Soc. Home: 7772 Woodridge St San Antonio TX 78209 Office: 306 N Presa St San Antonio TX 78205

REHM, JOHN EDWIN, mfg. co. exec.; b. Bucyrus, Ohio, Oct. 20, 1924; s. Lester Carl and Mary O'Dale (Myers) R.; student Heidelberg U., 1942, U. Ala., 1943-44, Ohio State U., 1946-49. Asst. plant engr. Shunk Mfg. Co., Inc., Bucyrus, 1949-53, prodn. mgr., 1953-61, plant mgr., 1961-65, mgr. prodn. services, 1965-68, mgr. customer service dept., 1968-69, ops. mgr., 1969-70, v.p. ops., 1970-71; materials mgr. Oury Engring. Co., Marion, Ohio, 1971-73, W.W. Sly Mfg. Co., Cleve., 1973—; v.p., gen. mgr. Moody Mfg. Co., Inc., Maben, Miss., 1979—. Bd. dirs. Bucyrus United Community Fund, 1969-70. Served with AUS, 1943-46; PTO. Decorated Bronze Star (2). Mem. Am. Soc. Personnel Adminstrn., Bucyrus Area C. of C. (v.p. 1966, pres. 1967). Republican. Clubs: Elks, Rotary. Home: 48 Chickasaw St Starkville MS 39759

REHM, WALTER LEO, hospitality industry exec.; b. St. Louis, Sept. 30, 1943; s. Walter L. and Frances (Sucher) R.; B.S., U. Mo.-Columbia, 1966; m. Ruth Ann Lange, Dec. 27, 1970; 1 son, Charles Walter. Sales rep. Dietary Products div. Am. Hosp. Supply Corp., Knoxville, Tenn., 1970-72, product mgr., McGaw Park, Ill., 1972-74, ter. mgr., Atlanta, 1974-78; pres. Kearney-Baccus-Rehm & Assos., Lawrenceville, Ga., 1978—; speaker to indsl. related groups, 1971—. Served to 1st lt., Q.M.C., AUS, 1966-69. Named Top Nat. Rep., Dietary Products, 1974-77. Mem. Am. Dietetic Assn., Am. Soc. Hosp. Food Service Adminstrs., Trout Unltd., Ducks Unltd., Kappa Alpha Alumni. Republican. Roman Catholic. Office: Kearney-Baccus-Rehm & Assos 620 N E Pike St Lawrenceville GA 30245

REICHARDT, DELBERT DALE, real estate investment co. exec.; b. Chgo., Mar. 2, 1927; s. Arthur Christian and Kristine Neoline (Fulsaas) R.; B.A., Carroll Coll., Waukesha, Wis., 1949; M.B.A., Harvard, 1956; m. Ann Metaalf Sturgis, Mar. 25, 1972; children—Leslie Kirsten, Delbert Dale. Vice pres. Kidder, Peabody & Co., Inc., Boston, N.Y.C., 1956-68; fin. v.p. GAC Corp., Allentown, Pa., also Miami, Fla., 1968-72; exec. v.p. fin. and adminstrn. Gt. Am. Mgmt. & Investment Co. (formerly Gt. Am. Mortgage Investors), Atlanta, 1972-79; dir. Gt. Am. Mgmt. and Investment Inc., Atlanta, 1979—. Served to 1st lt. USAF, 1950-54. Mem. Fin. Execs. Inst. Clubs: Capital City, Harvard Bus. Sch. (Atlanta); Masons; Harvard (N.Y.C.). Contbg. author: Chief Executive's Handbook, 1976. Home: 2976 Nancy Creek Rd NW Atlanta GA 30327 Office: 5775D Peachtree Dunwoody Rd NE Atlanta GA 30342

REID, CHARLES MORROW, lawyer, mfrs. rep.; b. Ft. Worth, May 15, 1948; s. Wilbur Raymond and Majorie Francine (Morrow) R.; student U. Calif., Berkeley, 1969; B.A., U. Tex., Austin, 1970, J.D., 1974; m. Susan Keller Hyden, July 12, 1975. Admitted to Tex. bar, 1974; house counsel Foster Fin. Corp., Ft. Worth, 1974-75; individual practice law, Ft. Worth, 1975—; exec. v.p. Keller-Hyden, Inc., Ft. Worth, 1977—; pres. Cimmar Corp., 1979—; sec.-treas. Internat. Marketers, Inc., 1979—. Vice-chmn., Ft. Worth Public Transp. Adv. Com.; sec. Forum Ft. Worth, 1979-80; mem. budget rev. com. Tarrant County United Way. Mem. Tex. Bar Assn., Am. Bar Assn., Tarrant County Bar Assn., Young Lawyers Assn., Automotive Affiliated Reps. Democrat. Methodist. Clubs: Rivercrest Country, Ridglea Country, Steeplechase, Rotary. Home: 1809 Dakar Rd E Fort Worth TX 76116 Office: 2525 Ridgmar Blvd Suite 404 Fort Worth TX 76116

REID, FRANK SAM, mfg. co. exec.; b. Cumbid, Md., Oct. 26, 1920; s. Frank Ernest and Sarah Pierce (Tipton) R.; B.S., U. Md., 1942; m. Aug. 19, 1953. Salesman, Shell Chem. Corp., Balt., 1946-50; owner Quality Chem. Corp., Wilson, N.C., 1950-61; owner, pres. Agricraft Co., Inc., Wilson, 1961—. Served to 1st lt. U.S. Army, 1942-46. Mem. N.Y. Plant Food Assn., Pa. Plant Food Assn., N.J. Plant Food Assn., N.C. Plant Food Assn., S.C. Plant Food Assn., Md.-Del. Plant Food Assn., Va. Plant Food Assn. Republican. Methodist. Inventor bug catcher, 1956. Office: 1801 Baldree Rd Wilson NC 27893

REID, GERALD THOMAS, tobacco co. exec.; b. Phila., Jan. 28, 1950; s. Walton Scott and Lillian Evelyn Reid; B.B.A., U. Wis., Whitewater, 1971; M.B.A., U. Wis., Madison, 1972; m. Dorothy J. Vrastiak, Aug. 23, 1969; 1 dau., Jacqueline Chantal. Asst. brand mgr. Drackett Co., Cin., 1973, brand mgr., 1974-76; brand mgr. Brown & Williamson Tobacco Ct., Louisville, 1976-77, sr. brand mgr., 1978-79, group product mgr., 1979—. Served with U.S. Army. Mem. Beta Gamma Sigma. Republican. Office: 1600 W Hill St Louisville KY 40201

REID, LELIA, hosp. edn. adminstr.; b. Safford, Ala., Nov. 19, 1938; B.S. in Nursing, Berea Coll., 1961; M.Ed. in Adult Edn., Ala. A&M U., Normal, 1977; children—Mark, Kimberlie. Public health nurse Vis. Nurse Assn., Cleve., 1961-64; sch. nurse Cleve. Bd. Edn., 1965-67; nursing instr. Cleve. Met. Gen. Hosp., 1967-69, ambulatory care supr., 1969-71; nursing instr. Calhoun Community Coll., 1973-75, mem. adv. com. dept. nurses continuing edn., 1979—; inservice edn. dir. Decatur (Ala.) Gen. Hosp., 1977—. Mem. Am. Nurses' Assn., Adult Edn. Assn., Am. Heart Assn., Am. Soc. Health Manpower, Edn. and Tng., Ala. Nurses Assn., Eta Phi Beta, Phi Kappa Phi. Democrat. Roman Catholic. Club: Toastmistress (Athens, Ala.). Home: Route 9 Box 13-A Athens AL 35611

REID, MERRY LOU ARTHUR, bank holding co. exec.; b. Orlando, Fla., Aug. 26, 1935; d. Thomas Lee and Luna Lee (Hedick) Arthur; student Auburn U., 1952-54; B.A., U. North Ala., 1970; Mus.M. (fellow), Fla. State U., 1973, postgrad. (fellow), 1974-79; children—Jack, Mark, Jeanne. Mgr., Cherokee Bldg. Materials Co. (Ala.), 1962-67; instr., library adminstr. U. North Ala., Florence, 1970-73; instr. Samford U., Birmingham, Ala., 1973-74; instr. Fla. State U., Tallahassee, 1974-76; tng. and communications cons. Fla. Credit Union League, Tallahassee, 1976-78; with Central Bancshares of South, Birmingham, 1978—, officer, dir. tng. and mgmt. devel., 1979—. Founder, bd. dirs. Cherokee Public Library, 1964-67; mem. women's com. Ala. Symphony Orch. Named Outstanding Jayceette of Ala., 1963, 65. Mem. Am. Inst. Banking, Nat. Assn. Bank Women, Am. Soc. Tng. and Devel. (1st v.p. Ala. chpt.), Fla. Public Relations Assn., Birmingham Delta Zeta Alumni. Republican. Episcopalian. Club: Zonta. Author: Musical Axiologies of Antiquity, 1974. Office: Central Bancshares of the South 701 S 20th St Birmingham AL 35296

REID, RICHARD STETSON, JR., air force officer; b. Colorado Springs, Colo., Mar. 4, 1945; s. Richard S. and Jean Burns (Hartley) R.; B.S. in Bus. Adminstrn., Auburn U., 1968; M.S. in Logistics Mgmt., Air Force Inst. Tech., 1971; profl. mil. edn. certificate Air U., 1975. Commd. 2d lt. U.S. Air Force, 1968, advanced through grades to capt., 1970; assigned McConnell AFB, Kans., 1968-69, 69-70, Gila Bend Air Force Sta., Ariz., 1969; computer support officer and leader supply def. team DaNang Air Base, Vietnam, 1971-72; chief supply equipment mgmt. br., tech. rep. for contracting office Aviano Air Base, Italy, 1972-74, chief supplies mgmt. br., tech. rep. for contracting officer, 1974-76; chief data systems supply item acctg. sect. Gunter Air Force Sta., Ala., 1976-78, chief data systems supply mgmt. sect., 1978—; logistics cons. Data Systems Design Center. Coach YMCA Youth Soccer League, 1978-79; bd. advisers Gunter Air Force Sta. Teen Town, 1978-79. Decorated Air Force Commendation medal, Meritorious Service medal, Bronze Star. Mem. Soc. Logistics Engrs., Delta Sigma Pi, Delta Tau Delta, Sigma Iota Epsilon. Home: 4004 Camellia Dr Montgomery AL 36109 Office: AFDSDC/LGSM Gunter Air Force Station AL 36114

REIFF, GLEN EDWARD, educator; b. Ogallala, Nebr., May 1, 1935; s. Dennis Harold and Emma Elisa (Nacke) R.; Th.B. summa cum laude, God's Bible Sch. and Coll., Cin., 1957; M.Div., Luther Rice Sem., 1978, D.Min., 1979; m. Barbara Nell Thornton, Aug. 15, 1958; children—Darrell, Stanley, Duane. Missionary, Evangelistic Faith Missions, C.Am., 1955-76, mission coordinator, 1970-76, occupational missionary, Guatemala, 1972-76; chmn. missions dept. Hobe Sound (Fla.) Bible Coll., 1977—; Bible sch. dir., Jalapa, Guatemala, 1960-63. Methodist. Home: PO Box 1065 Hobe Sound FL 33455 Office: Hobe Sound Bible Coll Hobe Sound FL 33455

REIFF, MARTIN HACKMAN, JR., oil co. exec.; b. Gloucester, Mass., Feb. 25, 1947; s. Martin Hackman and Jennie (Ninfo) R.; B.S. in Math., The Citadel, 1969; postgrad. in computer sci. and mgmt. U. Tex., Dallas, 1976—; m. Elisabeth Hope Sandifer, June 1, 1969. Customer liason Electronic Data Systems Corp., N.Y.C., 1973, systems engr., Hartford, Conn., 1974-76, systems engr., edn. cons., Dallas, 1976-79; supr. human resources tech. devel. support Mobil Corp., Dallas, 1979—. Served to capt. U.S. Army, 1969-73; Vietnam. Decorated Air medal, Bronze Star; Vietnamese Gallantry cross and honor medal; Joseph D. Aiken scholar, 1965-69. Episcopalian. Office: PO Box 900 1201 Elm St Dallas TX 75221

REILAND, JOHN STEPHEN, oil and gas co. exec.; b. Houston, Nov. 5, 1949; s. Floyd J. and Sara Reiland; B.B.A., U. Houston, 1973; m. Rose Ann Deluke, Nov. 25, 1970; 1 dau., Rachel. Staff accountant, mgr. Price Waterhouse & Co., Houston, 1973-78; v.p. fin. Mid-Am. Oil & Gas Inc., Houston, 1978-80; chief fin. officer Tatham Corp., Houston, 1980—. Bd. dirs. Spring Creek Forest Assn. Served with USMC, 1968-69; Vietnam. Mem. Tex. Soc. C.P.A.'s, Am. Inst. C.P.A.'s. Roman Catholic. Home: 6710 Twin Leaf St Spring TX 77379 Office: 1200 Milam St Suite 3310 Houston TX 77002

REILLY, FRANK WARD, JR., mfg. and metal fabrication co. exec.; b. Chattanooga, Dec. 13, 1928; s. Frank Ward and Margaret Collins (White) R.; B. Indsl. Engring., Ga. Inst. Tech., 1953; m. Lenda Catherine Gay, Jan. 9, 1954; children—Frank Ward, III, Lenda Gay. With Sherman & Reilly, Inc., Chattanooga, 1954—, v.p. sales, 1960-67, pres., 1967—. Bd. dirs. Jr. Achievement of Chattanooga, Chattanooga Girls Club, Chattanooga C. of C. Aeros. Com. Bd. dirs. Ducks Unltd.-Chattanooga, recipient Conservation Service award, 1974. Served with USAF, 1953-54. Mem. IEEE, Power and Communication Contractors, Young Pres's. Orgn. Republican. Episcopalian. Clubs: Lookout Mountain Fairyland, Lookout Mountain Golf, Mountain City, Walden, Blue Springs Hunting Fishing; Kiwanis (Chattanooga). Office: PO Box 11267 Chattanooga TN 37401

REILLY, FRANK WENDELL, mgmt. cons. co. exec.; b. Youngstown, Ohio, Dec. 31, 1926; s. Frank Joseph and Coletta Elizabeth (Albaugh) R.; B.A., U. Calif. at Los Angeles, 1951; M.P.A. (Littauer fellow), Harvard U., 1959; m. Bettie Jean Randall, July 26,

1974; children by previous marriage—Patricia, Eric, Colleen, Kent, Brett, Bryan; 1 step-dau., Mari-Alice. Dir. mgmt. services U.S. Postal Service, Washington, 1961-64; v.p. Booz, Allen and Hamilton, Inc., Washington, 1964-68; pres. Med. Aid Tng. Schs., Silver Spring, Md., 1972-79; pres., co-founder Macro Systems, Inc., Silver Spring, 1969—; past pres., dir. Nat. Council Profl. Service Firms. Mem. exec. com. NAACP, Montgomery County, Md., 1959-68, Center for Christian Renewal, 1968-72; dir. Center for Handicapped, 1975—. Served with USN, 1944-46. Mem. Assn. Computing Machinery, Assn. Pub. Adminstrn., ACLU. Club: Univ. (Washington). Developed ZIP code, 1963; founder earth sci. (Geol. Survey) lab. for fed. govt., 1955. Home: Route 1 Box 84 Delaplane VA 22025 Office: 8630 Fenton St Silver Spring MD 20910

REILLY, KATHERINE LOUISE, counselor; b. Columbus, Ohio, Sept. 28, 1944; d. James Burnham and Marion Louise (Briley) R.; B.A., Brenau Coll., 1966; M.Ed., U. Va., 1972. Tchr. English, 1st Colonial High Sch., Virginia Beach, Va., 1966-69, 72-73, guidance counselor, 1973—. Mem. Am. Personnel and Guidance Assn., Va. Personnel and Guidance Assn., Hampton Roads Personnel and Guidance Assn., NEA, Va. Edn. Assn., Virginia Beach Edn. Assn., Potomac & Chesapeake Admissions Counselors Assn., Kappa Delta Pi. Republican. Roman Catholic. Home: 211B 85th St Virginia Beach VA 23451 Office: 1272 Mill Dam Rd Virginia Beach VA 23454

REIMOLD, ROBERT JAMES, ecologist, state ofcl.; b. Greenville, Pa., Nov. 15, 1941; s. Frank Ellis and Frances Lyle (Rickard) R.; B.A., Thiel Coll., 1963; M.A., U. Del., 1965, Ph.D., 1968; m. Mardith Harriet Osborne, June 15, 1963; children—Reid Elizabeth, Rae Katherine, Raymond Miles. Research asst. U. Del., 1966-68; postdoctoral fellow U. Ga., Sapelo Island, 1968-69, research asso. Marine Inst., 1969-74, adj. asst. prof. dept. zoology, 1970-74; asso. prof. Marine Resources Extension Center, U. Ga., Brunswick, 1974-75; dir. coastal resources div. Ga. Dept. Natural Resources, Brunswick, 1978—; vis. prof. Fairleigh Dickinson U.; partner Coastal Consultants; cons. COR Communications Ltd.; Coastal Zone ecol. cons.; prin. investigator research grants from AEC, NSF, EPA, U.S. Army C.E., pvt. industry. Mem. Ga. Gov.'s Coastal Zone Adv. Council, 1974—. Mem. Soc. Am. Mil. Engrs., Am. Fisheries Soc., Am. Soc. Limnology and Oceanography, A.A.A.S., Am. Inst. Biol. Scis., Ecol. Soc. Am., Estuarine Research Fedn. (pres.), Southeastern Estuarine Research Soc. (pres.), Brit. Ecol. Soc., Estuarine and Brackish Water Scis. Assn., Sigma Xi. Mason. Editor: Ecology of Halophytes, 1973. Contbr. articles profl. jours. Home: 140 Belle Point Pkwy Brunswick GA 31520 Office: 1200 Glynn Ave Brunswick GA 31520

REIN, HOWARD EDWARD, JR., ins. exec.; b. Phila., July 14, 1920; s. Howard Edward and Marietta (Caple) R.; student Pa. State U., 1938-40, Pensacola Jr. Coll., 1958-62, U. West Fla., 1979; m. Joyce Pohlmann, May 8, 1945; children—Karen, Lynn, Gail. With Western Electric Co., Phila., 1940-41, 46-48; supr. Rein's Formal Wear Inc., Pensacola, Fla., 1948—; pres. New Eng. Life Ins. Co., Pensacola, 1956—. Chmn. planning com. United Way, 1970-78; mem. City Council Pensacola, 1978—. Served with USN, 1941-46. Mem. Estate Planning Council N.W. Fla., Pensacola Assn. Life Underwriters, Am. Formal Wear Assn., Am. Soc. C.L.U.'s. Democrat. Lutheran. Club: Lions (past pres.). Home: 2101 E Cross St Pensacola FL 32503 Office: 335 Brent Bldg Pensacola FL 32501

REINARZ, GILBERT ROCHETTE, ins. agt.; b. New Braunfels, Tex., Sept. 25, 1921; s. Gilbert Otto and Lottie (Tolle) R.; B.S., Tex. A&M U., 1949; m. Bertha Tays, Sept. 4, 1948; children—Thomas H., Jack F. Owner, Rochette Reinarz Ins. Agy., New Braunfels, 1949-71; owner Comaltex Ins. Agy., Inc., New Braunfels, 1971—; pres. Risk Counseling Services, Inc., New Braunfels, 1977—; lectr. for profl. ins. agts. Dist. chmn. Guada Coma dist. Boy Scouts Am., 1977-79; active Little League. Served with inf. U.S. Army, 1942-46. Recipient Silver Beaver, Boy Scouts Am., 1971; President's award New Braunfels C. of C.; cert. ins. counselor. Mem. Profl. Inst. Agts., Ind. Ins. Agrs. Assn. Democrat. Mem. United Ch. of Christ. Club: Lions. Home: Route 5 Box 846D New Braunfels TX 78130 Office: 457 Landa St New Braunfels TX 78130

REINEL, ROLAND, painter, sculptor; b. Lausanne, Switzerland, Oct. 20, 1936; came to U.S., 1977; student of Casmir Reymond, Sch. Fine Art, Lausanne, 1952-54; student Florence, Italy, 1954-55, Geneva, Switzerland, 1959-60, Montreal, Que., Can., 1974; m. Erika Gaspar, Oct. 12, 1972; 1 son, Daniel R. Exhibitions include Art Center, Peru, 1966, Potterat Gallery, Lausanne, Switzerland, 1966, 67, Martal Gallery, Montreal, Que., Can., 1969, Orly Airport, Paris, France, 1971, Marlborough Gallery, N.Y.C., 1972, P.M. Gallery, San Francisco, 1974, Peace Gallery, Edgartown, Boston, 1976, Biennale de Gabrovo, Bulgaria, 1977, Harris Galleries, Houston, 1978, Elliott Mus., Stuart, Fla., 1979, various galleries Germany, U.S., Italy, Spain, 1966—; paintings, drawings, illustrations represented ofcl. collections Paris, Atlanta, Los Angeles, Dallas, Seattle, Phila., Montreal, Stuart, Switzerland, Bulgaria, Spain; illustrator 8 publs., author poetic text with illustrations 4 publs. Winner bronze medal Biennale de Gabrovo, Bulgaria, 1977. Home: The Citadel Tropical Farms PO Box 325 Stuart FL 33494

REINHARD, ERWIN ARTHUR, educator; b. Poth, Tex., Jan. 29, 1931; s. Erwin John and Agnes Pauline (Miculka) R.; student St. Marys U., 1952-53; B.S. (Schlumberger scholar), U. Tex., Austin, 1956, M.S. (Tex. Found. fellow), 1959, Ph.D. (NSF fellow, W. Alton Jones fellow), 1968; postgrad. U. Pitts., 1959-62; m. Irene Cecilia Salzman, Aug. 11, 1951; children—Nicolette (Mrs. Alan C. Cunningham), Lisa, Francis, Erwin, Tracie, Katherine. Nuclear research scientist Westinghouse Electric Corp., Bettis Atomic Power Lab., West Mifflin, Pa., 1959-63; prof. elec. engring. U. Ala., University, 1963—. Cons., Army Missile Command, Huntsville, Ala., NASA, Huntsville. Pres. Elementary P.T.A., 1963-66; active Warrior council Boy Scouts Am., 1968-70. Served with AUS, 1950-52. Named Outstanding Elec. Engring. Instr., 1971, 75; recipient U. Ala. Nat. Alumni Assn. Outstanding Commitment to Teaching award, 1978. Mem. Am. Soc. Engring. Edn., IEEE, Sigma Xi, Eta Kappa Nu, Tau Beta Pi. Democrat. Roman Catholic. Author: Basic Electric Circuits for Engineers, 1967; Basic Electronics for Engineers and Scientists, 1972. Contbr. articles profl. jours. Home: 276 Woodland Hills Tuscaloosa AL 35405 Office: PO Box 6169 University AL 35486

REINHARD, JACK EDWARD, civil engr.; b. Floresville, Tex., Nov. 25, 1947; s. Gilbert Edward and Dorothy Mae (Meyer) R.; B.S. Civil Engring., U. Tex., Austin, 1971; M.A. in Econs., U. Tex., Arlington, 1976; m. Shirley Ann Mzyk, Sept. 14, 1968; children—Renee Marie, Robin Michelle. Engr. trainee U.S. Army C.E., New Orleans, 1971, civil engr., Fort Worth, 1972-76; project mgr. Econ. Devel. Adminstrn., Austin, Tex., 19766-77; chief architecture and engring. div. Poth Corp., Austin, Tex., 1978—, also dir. Recipient commendations U.S. Army C.E., 1972, 73. Mem. Internat. Solar Energy Soc., Internat. Platform Assn., ASCE, Austin C. of C., Chi Epsilon. Roman Catholic. Club: Woods and Waters (Austin, Tex.). Home: 4710 Sagebrush Trail Austin TX 78745 Office: 315 Bowie St Austin TX 78703

REINHART, ELIZABETH, nurse, educator; b. Richville, Minn., Oct. 30, 1927; d. Oliver Mike and Merwyn Florence (Parsons) R.; B.S. with high distinction, U. Minn., 1955; M.S. in Counseling, St. Cloud State Coll., 1969; Ph.D. in Adult Edn., Kans. State U., 1976. Instr., head nurse, operating room supr., dir. nursing service St. Cloud (Minn.) Hosp., 1950-67; clin. specialist, psychiat. nursing VA Hosp., St. Cloud, 1969-70, asso. chief nursing service for edn., 1970-72; asso. chief nursing service for edn. VA Hosp., Topeka, 1972-76; asso. chief nursing service for edn. VA Med. Center, Augusta, Ga., 1976-79, asso. chief of staff for edn., 1979—; asso. clin. prof. Med. Coll. Ga., 1978—. Recipient Dir.'s commendation VA Hosp., Topeka, 1976. Mem. Am. Nurses Assn., Am. Soc. Tng. and Devel., Adult Edn. Assn., Cath. Hosp. Assn., Sigma Theta Tau. Roman Catholic. Home: 511 Ashland Dr Augusta GA 30909 Office: VA Med Center Augusta GA 30904

REINHOLD, WILLIAM ROBERT, II, utility exec.; b. Cleve., May 13, 1947; s. William Robert and Elizabeth (Charlton) R.; B.A., U. S. Fla., 1976; m. Jane Marie MacIntyre, Aug. 6, 1966; children—Christina Marie, Michelle Lynn, Alicia Leigh. Stone cutter Fairlawn Supply, Akron, Ohio, 1963-65; with UPS, Ft. Meyers, Fla., 1970; with Lee County Electric Coop. Inc., North Ft. Myers, Fla., 1970—, mgr. methods and procedures, 1978—. Served with USAF, 1966-70; Vietnam. Mem. Am. Mgmt. Assn., Data Processing Mgmt. Assn., Assn. Records Mgrs. and Adminstrs., Am. Public Power Assn. Republican. Roman Catholic.

REININGER, EDWARD JOSEPH, physiologist; b. Chgo., Dec. 30, 1929; s. David and Ida Edith (Behn) R.; B.S., U. Ill., 1950, M.S., 1952; Ph.D., Ohio State U., 1957; children—David Jay, Jonathan Terry. Research asso., instr. Ohio State U., 1957-58; lectr., then asst. prof. McGill U., Montreal, Que., Can., 1958-71; asso. prof. Ind. U., Terre Haute, 1971-74; prof. So. Ill. U., Springfield, 1974-76; prof. physiology U. Caribe Sch. Medicine, Cayey, P.R., 1977—, chmn. dept. physiology and pharmacology, 1977; physiologist St. Johns Hosp., Springfield, 1974-76; mem. med. adv. com. Coal Miners Respiratory Disease Program, Ill. Dept. Public Health, 1975, chmn., 1976. Chmn., Terre Haute Citizens Com. Flouridation, 1972-73; exec. com. Montreal br. Nat. Ballet Guild Can., 1968-71. Mem. Am. Physiol. Soc., Can. Physiol. Soc., Am. Thoracic Soc., AAUP, Animal Welfare Inst., Sigma Xi. Contbr. articles to profl. jours. Home: 2305 Laurel St Apt 807 Santurce PR 00913 Office: Box 935 Cayey PR 00633

REINKEN, MARY LOUISE, psychologist; b. Billings, Mont., Apr. 23, 1928; d. Harold Matheson and Violet Winnefred (Cantrell) Lindstrom; B.S., Syracuse U., 1951; M.A., Furman U., 1970; Ph.D., U. S.C., 1975-77; children—Louis Arthur III, Dirk Christian. High sch. English tchr., S.C., 1963-65; psychologist Community Mental Health Center, Anderson, S.C., 1969-75; S.C. Dept. Mental Health grantee, S.C. Mental Health Assn. scholar U. S.C., Columbia, 1975-77; coordinator consultation and Edn. Orangeburg (S.C.) Mental Health Center, 1977; dir. Bamberg County (S.C.) Mental Health Satellite. Mem. Am., S.C. psychol. assns., Am., S.C. personnel and guidance assns., Carolina Soc. Adolescent Psychiatry, AAUW, Bus. and Profl. Women, Am. Assn. for Counselor Edn. and Supervision, S.C. Acad. Profl. Psychologists, Delta Gamma. Episcopalian. Home: 204 Cannondale Rd Columbia SC 29210

REINMILLER, ELINOR CALMBACH, librarian; b. Oswego, Kans., Aug. 29, 1919; d. William Garfield and Clara Elinor (Bruns) Calmbach; B.A., U. Iowa, 1939; B.S. in L.S., North Tex. State U., 1947, M.A., 1954. Reference and acquisition librarian U. Tex. Health Sci. Center, Dallas, 1947—. Cons. uniformed services U. Health Scis., 1975. Mem. Spl. Libraries Assn., Am. Soc. Indexers, Med. library assns., Phi Alpha Theta, Alpha Delta Pi. Author: (with C.B. Chapman) The Physiology of Physical Stress, a Selective Bibliography, 1975. Home: 2033 W Oak St Denton TX 76201 Office: 5323 Harry Hines Blvd Dallas TX 75235

REISINGER, MARTHA JEAN, archtl. and engring. co. exec.; b. Houston, Aug. 6, 1933; d. Edwin Lee and Ruby Elizabeth (Davis) Michie; student Southwestern Bus. U., 1953; bus. cert. Wayland Baptist Coll., Plainview, Tex., 1959; diploma Ahrens SW Sch. Real Estate, Houston, 1972; m. Frank Albert Reisinger, Oct. 28, 1972; 1 son, Paul Warner Carlin. Various positions Koetter Tharp Cowell & Bartlett, Inc. (merged into Lockwood Andrews & Newnam 1978), 1968-78, v.p. adminstrn., 1974-78, head office services dept. Lockwood Andrews & Newnam, 1978—. Mem. Archtl. Secs. Assn. (charter mem. Houston chpt., treas. 1977-78, pres.-elect 1974), Tex. Soc. Architects, AIA, Am. Mgmt. Soc. Baptist. Home: 3002 Durban St Houston TX 77043 Office: Lockwood Andrews & Newnam 1900 Saint James Pl Houston TX 77056

REISMAN, FREDRICKA KAUFFMAN, educator; b. Rochester, N.Y., Sept. 22, 1930; d. Samuel Hopkins and Rosalind (Lessen) Kauffman; student Barnard Coll., 1951; B.A., Syracuse U., 1952, M.S., 1963, Ph.D., 1968; 1 dau., Lisa M. Lectr., Syracuse U., 1967-69; asst. prof. mathematics edn. U. Ga., Athens, 1969-74, asso. prof., 1974-79, prof., 1979—; vis. prof. U. Calif. at Riverside, Marianne Frostig Center Ednl. Therapy, Los Angeles; cons. in diagnostic teaching math. Mem. Nat. Council Tchrs. Math., Am., Psychol. Assn., Am. Edn. Research Assn., Council Exceptional Children, Pi Lambda Theta, Phi Delta Kappa. Author: Guide to the Diagnostic Teaching of Arithmetic, 1972, 2d edit., 1978; Diagnostic Teaching of Elementary School Mathematics: Methods and Content, 1977; co-author: Mathematics Instruction for Special Educational Needs, 1980. Home: 130 Cedar Circle Athens GA 30605 Office: 427 Aderhold U Ga Athens GA 30602

REISTLE, CARL ERNEST, JR., petroleum engr.; b. Denver, June 26, 1901; s. Carl E. and Leonara I. (McMaster) R.; B.S., U. Okla., 1922; student Harvard Sch. Bus. Adminstrn., 1948; D.Sc., U. Tulsa, 1966; m. Mattie A. Muldrow, June 23, 1922; children—Bette Jean (Mrs. Geo. F. Pierce), Mattie Ann, (Mrs. James Tracy Clark), Nancy L. (Mrs. Wilson Hayes Holliday), Carl Ernest III. Petroleum chemist U.S. Bur. Mines, 1922-29, petroleum engr., 1929-33; chmn. East Tex. Engring. Assn., 1933-36; with Humble Oil & Refining Co., 1933-66, successively engr. in charge, chief petroleum engr., gen. supt. prodn., mgr. prodn. dept., dir. mgr. prodn. dept., dir. charge prodn. dept., 1951-55, v.p. charge prodn. dept., 1955-57, exec. v.p., 1957-61, pres., 1961-63, chmn. bd. and chief exec. officer, 1963-66, cons., 1966—; former chmn. exec. com. Olinkraft, Inc.; dir. Eltra Corp. Trustee Houston Mus. Natural Sci. Recipient Anthony Lucas medal, 1958; Engr. of Year award Nat. Soc. Profl. Engrs., 1966. Mem. Mining and Metall. Soc. Am., Am. Petroleum Inst. (dir.), Am. Inst. Mining and Metall. Engrs. (pres. 1956), Sigma Xi, Tau Beta Pi, Sigma Tau, Alpha Chi Sigma. Clubs: Petroleum, Ramada, River Oaks Country, Anglers of N.Y. Contbr. tech. articles to profl. jours. Home: 3196 Chevy Chase Houston TX 77019 Office: 1100 Milam Bldg Suite 4601 Houston TX 77002

REISZ, ALOYSIUS IGNATIUS, JR., engring. co. exec.; b. Henderson County, Ky., Sept. 28, 1937; s. Aloysius Ignatius and Susan Elizabeth (Ward) R.; B.S., U. Ky., 1961; m. Franklin Jeanette Skinner, Apr. 19, 1969. Mech. engr. Martin-Marietta Corp., Denver, 1963-64; engr. Brown Engring. Co., Huntsville, Ala., 1964-65, Boeing Co., Huntsville, 1965-70; cons. engr., Huntsville, 1970-74; pres., chief engr. Reisz Engring. Co., Huntsville, 1974—; owner, mgr. farm, nr. Owensboro, Ky., 1970—. Cons. Research Inst., U. Ala., Huntsville, 1975—. Served to 2d lt. AUS, 1961-63. Registered profl. engr., Ky., Ala., Tenn. Mem. ASME (cir., chmn. North Ala. sect. 1975), Nat. (project named one of 10 outstanding engring. projects 1978), Ala. (dir., Outstanding Young Engr. award Huntsville chpt. 1973, pres. Huntsville chpt. 1979) socs. profl. engrs., Am. Soybean Assn. Home: 7313 Chadwell Rd Huntsville AL 35802 Office: PO Box 1349 Hwy 72W Huntsville AL 35807

REITER, DAVID EDWIN, printing exec.; b. Niagara Falls, N.Y., Apr. 25, 1938; s. Donald E. and Gladys Irene R.; B.A., U. Buffalo, 1960; m. Jane Ann, Jan. 17, 1959; children—David Francis, Alice Jane. Mem. planning dept. Moore Bus. Forms, 1960-69; plant mgr. Lewis Bus. Forms, 1969-74; v.p. Arnold Graphic Industries, Ashland, Va., 1974—; cons., tchr. Mem. Nat. Bus. Forms Assn., Printing Industries Am. Republican. Home: 2407 Jewett Dr Richmond VA 23228 Office: PO Box 2079 Ashland VA 23005

REITER, JACKIE READER, word processing exec.; b. Houston, July 13, 1936; d. Hymen and Hattie (Sandler) Reader; student Southwestern Bus. U., 1953-54, McMahan Sch. Ct. Reporting, 1971-72; m. Harris M. Hauser, Feb. 12, 1953 (div. 1970); children—Terri Lynn, Karen Louise, John Bradley, Ann Kathryn, Heather Joan; m. 2d, Bernard A. Reiter, Apr. 2, 1978. Founder, pres. Transcriber Corp., Houston, 1972—; guest lectr. Sch. Med. Record Scis., U. Houston at Clear Lake, Houston-Galveston Med. Records Assn. Del. Republican State Conv., 1964. Mem. Internat. Word Processing Assn. (dir. Houston chapt. 1978), Nat. Assn. Word Processing Specialists, Am. Mgmt. Assn., Internat. Platform Assn., Am., Tex., Houston-Galveston Area med. record assns. Republican. Jewish. Club: Houstonian. Home: Number 3 Pinewood Circle Houston TX 77024 Office: 2502 Robinhood St Houston TX 77005

RELFE, CHARLES PERRY, banker; b. Tallassee, Ala., Sept. 6, 1943; s. Julien Massey and Evelyn (Perry) R.; B.S., U. Ala., 1965; J.D., Samford U., 1975; children—Charles Perry, William Ashley. Sr. auditor Arthur Young & Co., Birmingham, Ala., 1969-71; sr. v.p., comptroller, chief adminstrn. div., mem. money mgmt. and systems planning coms. Birmingham Trust Nat. Bank (Ala.), 1971—; asst. treas. Jackson Co., 1975—; dir. Birmingham Trust Mobile Services Inc., 1978—; instr. Am. Inst. Banking; lectr. Ala. Bankers Assn. Bd. dirs., treas. Greater Birmingham Arts Alliance. Served to capt. USAF, 1965-69. Mem. Am. Bar Assn., Ala. Bar Assn., Am. Inst. C.P.A.'s, Ala. Soc. C.P.A.'s, Fin. Execs. Inst., Am. Inst. Banking, Bank Adminstrn. Inst., Phi Alpha Delta, Delta Sigma Phi, Kappa Alpha. Methodist. Office: PO Box 2554 Birmingham AL 35290

RELYEA, RICHARD DALE, oilfield equipment co. exec.; b. Waco, Tex., Feb. 7, 1947; s. Richard Russell and Frances Irene (Brooks) Relyea; B.S. in Mech. Engring., U. Tex., Austin, 1970; m. Rita Ann Brossett, Aug. 23, 1969; 1 dau., Elesha Ann. Engr., Marlin Drilling Co., Inc., Houston, 1970-71, project engr., 1972-73, mgr. internat. drilling and ops., 1974-75; mgr. engring. Tropic Drilling & Exploration Co., Houston, 1975-76; mgr. product engring. oilfield div. Stewart Stevenson Co., Houston, 1976; v.p. Ross Hill Controls Corp., Houston, 1977-78; mgr. research and devel. B.J. Hughes Co., Round Rock, Tex., 1978—; cons. in field. Certified engr.-in-tng., Tex.; registered profl. engr., Tex. Mem. Am. Soc. M.E., Soc. Petroleum Engrs. of Am. Inst. Mech. Engrs., Nat., Tex. socs. profl. engrs. Republican. Mem. Charismatic Assembly of God. Club: Spring Creek Civic Assn. (Spring, Tex.). Home: 7305 Grass Cove Austin TX 78759 Office: PO Box 398 Round Rock TX 78664

REMENCHIK, ALEXANDER PAVLOVICH, physician; b. Chgo., Sept. 13, 1922; s. Paul Samuelovich and Irina Alexandra (Babich) R.; B.S. in Physics, U. Chgo., 1943, M.D., 1951; m. Mary Margaret Mays, Apr. 19, 1947; children—Alex Kevin, Ellen Jean, Karen Ann, Margaret Lynn. Intern, Cook County Hosp., Chgo., 1951-52; resident U. Ill. Research and Ednl. Hosps., 1952-53, fellow, 1953-54; clin. investigator VA Hosp., Hines, Ill., 1960-62; practice medicine specializing in internal medicine, Chgo., 1953-72, Montclair, N.J., 1972-74, Houston, 1974—; asst. med. supt. Mcpl. Contagious Disease Hosp., Chgo., 1953-59; instr. medicine U. Ill., Chgo., 1954-59; asst. prof. medicine Stritch Sch. Medicine, Loyola U., Maywood, Ill., 1960-63, asso. prof., 1964-67, prof., 1967-72, pres. Faculty Collegium, 1970-71, asst. chmn. dept. medicine, 1964-70; dir. dept. nuclear medicine Loyola U. Hosp., 1969-71; attending physician Cook County Hosp., 1959-72; Mountainside Hosp., Montclair, 1972-74, dir. med. edn., 1972-74; attending mem. active staff Parkway Hosp., 1974-79, Citizens Gen. Hosp., 1974—, chief med. service, 1977, chief of staff, 1979—, mem. governing bd., 1977—; mem. staff Eastway Gen. Hosp., 1974—, chmn. dept. medicine, 1976-80; pres. East Loop Emergency Med. Clinic, Houston, 1979—, East Loop Cardio Pulmonary Center, Inc., 1979—. Mem. Zoning Commn. Oak Park (Ill.), 1969-72; trustee Unitarian-Universalist Ch. of Oak Park, 1969-70. Served to lt. (j.g.) USN, 1943-46. Diplomate Am. Bd. Internal Medicine. Fellow A.C.P.; mem. Tex. Soc. Internal Medicine, Houston Soc. Internal Medicine, Soc. Exptl. Biology and Medicine, Am. Fedn. Clin. Research, Harris County Med. Soc., AMA, Tex. Med. Assn., Am. Soc. Internal Medicine, Sigma Xi. Editor: (with P.J. Talso) Mechanisms of Disease, 1968; contbr. over 50 articles on internal medicine to profl. jours. Home: 9330 Oakford Ct Houston TX 77024 Office: 9343 N Loop East Houston TX 77029

REMSBURG, VERA BARON, educator; b. Eunice, W.Va., Sept. 4, 1920; d. Joe Joseph and Julie Ella (Barnard) Baron; B.S. in Edn., Longwood Coll., Farmville, Va., 1942; M.A. in Zoology, U. Va., 1952; m. Brent Remsburg, May 1952. Tchr., Martinsville (Va.) High Sch., 1942-46; instr., then asst. prof. biology Longwood Coll., 1946-52; chmn. sci. dept. Halifax County (Va.) High Sch., 1952-58, Herndon High Sch., Fairfax County 1959-72; tchr. biology, chmn. sci. dept. Patrick Henry High Sch., Emory, Va., 1975—. Named Tchr. of Yr., Am. Chem. Soc., 1958. Mem. Va. Acad. Sci. (pres. 1979-80; Tchr. of Yr. award 1946, 47, 48), Nat. Assn. Biology Tchrs. (Tchr. of Yr. for Va. award 1968), AAAS, AAUW, Nat. Sci. Tchrs. Assn., NEA, Va. Edn. Assn., Delta Kappa Gamma. Presbyterian. Club: Abingdon Women's. Home: PO Box 789 Abingdon VA 24210 Office: Patrick Henry High Sch Emory VA 24327

RENALDS, JUETTE OSBORNE, JR., business exec.; b. Front Royal, Va., May 24, 1917; A.B., Bridgewater (Va.) Coll., 1938; postgrad. U. Va.; LL.B., LaSalle Extension U., Chgo., 1953; m. Marie Terral Smith, Aug. 1942; children—Juette Osborne III, Catherine Allene Renalds Wittan Carol Marie. Salesman, sales dir. Continental Products, Inc., Staunton, Va., 1939-41; employer-employee relations counsellor Va. Employment Commn., Staunton, 1947-49; sales mgr. Sky-Line Sales Corp., Staunton, 1949-55; asst. prof. mil. sci. and tactics Fishburne Mil. Sch., Waynesboro, Va., 1955-59; pres. Fouress, Inc., Staunton, 1955—, A.I.D. Bus. Outfitters, Inc., Staunton, 1965—; pres., co-owner A.I.D. W&R Enterprises, 1964—; chmn. bd. Asso. Investment Developers, Inc., 1964—, Automated Intermarket Datamatrics, 1968—, Carole Ashley Gray div. Fouress, Inc., 1974—; pres., owner J.O. Renalds Direct Mail Services, 1965—, A.R.T.S. Rapid Print Service, 1969—; owner 303 Co., 1967—, Renalds Enterprises, 1969—; pres. Dunsmore Bus. Coll., 1971—; mng. dir. A.I.D. Market and Data Research Field Services, 1969—; exec. dir. Soc. Profl. Salesmen, 1965—. Mem. Gov. Va. Hwy. Safety Com.,

1948-50; active local Boy Scouts Am., 1929—; pres. Men's Bible class Hebron Presbyn. Ch., 1974, pres. Men of Ch., 1975; rep. Presbytery of Shenandoahs, Presbyn. Ch. of Synod of Va. Men in Mission, 1975-76, treas., 1976-80, v.p. Men in Mission, 1980—. Served to maj. AUS, 1941-47; ETO; col. Res. ret. Mem. Am. Mktg. Assn., Staunton Retail Mchts. Assn., A.I.M. (asso.), Am. Inst. Indsl. Engrs. (affiliate), Nat. Rifle Assn. (life), Inf. Museum Soc. (life), Mensa, Intertel, Assn. U.S. Army, VFW, Am. Legion, Res. Officers Assn. (past chpt. pres.), Nat. Sojourners, Travellers Protective Assn. (sec.-treas. post). Clubs: Shriners, Elks, Moose, Eagles, Exchange (pres. Staunton 1950, now sec.-treas. Staunton, div. dir. Va. dist., pres. Va. dist. 1978-79), Eagles; Direct Mktg. (Washington). Address: 113 Lake Ave Staunton VA 24401

RENDALL, DAVID SATYAPAL, telecommunications exec.; b. Rangoon, Burma, May 30, 1934; came to U.S., 1975, naturalized, 1979; s. Gnanamanickam Robert and Enid Mary (Dawson) R.; B.E., Birla Inst. Tech. and Sci., Pilani, India, 1959; M.Sc. in Engring., U. Poona, India, 1962; m. Suganthi Eleanor Pithavadian, Nov. 4, 1962; children—Shalini, Vaneetha. Asst. prof. elec. engring. Birla Inst. Tech. and Sci., 1962-65; staff engr. Asso. Elec. Industries, Woolwich, London, 1965-67; systems engr. No. Telecom, Montreal, 1967-71, mgr. systems engring., Toronto, 1971-73, mgr. mktg., Toronto, 1973-75, dir. tech., Boston, 1975-76, v.p. mktg., Raleigh, N.C., 1976-78, v.p. corp. staff, Raleigh, 1978—; internat. lectr. Elder Presbyterian Ch., 1979. Sr. teaching fellow Govt. of India, 1959-62. Mem. No. Telecom Council Engrs. (pres. 1970-71). Contbr. articles to communications mags. Instrumental in introducing digital switching to U.S. and Can. Home: 4809 Poland Pl Raleigh NC 27609 Office: 1000 Wade Ave Raleigh NC 27605

RENFRO, JOHN EDWIN, athletic dir.; b. Williamsburg, Ky., Sept. 25, 1929; s. Simon Leonard and Mary Renfro; B.S., Ga. So. Coll., 1951; M.S., U. Tenn., 1955, Ed.S. in Ednl. Adminstrn., 1965; Ed.S. in Health, U. Ala., 1970; m. Bernice Meadors, 1950; children—John Erwin, Rhonda Kay. Phys. dir. Boys Club, Knoxville, Tenn., 1952-53; head health, phys. edn. and athletics, basketball coach Bacon County High Sch., Alma, Ga., 1953-55; head health, phys. edn. and athletics, also basketball, baseball and golf coach Pikeville (Ky.) Coll., 1955-58; mem. athletic staff Cumberland Coll., Williamsburg, 1959—, dir. dept. health, athletic dir., 1970—; v.p. Renfro Supply Co., Williamsburg, 1959—. Brochure chmn. Cumberland Valley Resource Conservation and Tourist Devel. Com., 1974-76, 77-78; tourism chmn. Cumberland Valley Area Devel. Dist., 1974-76; chmn. matching funds regional com. Cumberland Valley, Ky. Dept. Public Info., 1974-76; chmn. Ky. Highlands Assn., 1976-78. Recipient Lifetime sports cert. achievement AAHPER, 1968; named Coach of Yr., Dist. 24 Nat. Intercollegiate Athletic Assn., 1968. Mem. AAHPER, Am. Sch. Health Assn., Ky. Assn. Health, Phys. Edn. and Recreation (past pres. athletic div.; editor jour. 1970-73; Disting. Service award 1974), Ky. Edn. Assn., Scientists and Engrs. for Appalachia. Methodist. Club: Optimists (internat. v.p. 1978). Address: PO Box 982 CC Station Williamsburg KY 40769

RENICK, CECIL OREN, JR., med. care found. exec.; b. Amarillo, Tex., Oct. 26, 1944; s. Cecil Oren and Mattie Lea (Bellue) R.; B.A., Miss. Coll., 1966, M.A., 1967; Th.M., New Orleans Bapt. Theol. Sem., 1970; M.P.H., Tulane U., 1974; postgrad. Miss. Coll. Sch. Law, 1975-78; m. Judy Angeline Smith, Dec. 18, 1966; children—Scott Oren, Lea Robin. Adminstr., La. Cancer Registry and Tumor Registrar Tng. Program, Charity Hosp. La., New Orleans, 1970-73; coordinator project devel. and community liaison La. Regional Med. Program, New Orleans, 1973-74; dir. div. quality assurance Miss. Found. Med. Care, Jackson, 1974-78; exec. dir. S.E. La. Med. Quality Rev. Found., New Orleans, 1979—; part-time faculty Miss. Coll. Sch. Bus. and Public Adminstrn., 1976—; clin. faculty Tulane U. Sch. Medicine, New Orleans, 1979—; dir. Sem. Extension Centers (Jackson, Miss. and New Orleans) of sems. of So. Bapt. Conv., 1978—; cons. Interqual, 1977, La. Regional Med. Program, 1974-75, Plaquemines Parish alcoholism and drug abuse program, 1973; ordained to ministry, Bapt. Ch., 1969; pastor Canal Blvd. Bapt. Ch., New Orleans, 1972-74. Recipient Am Jur awards Miss. Coll. Sch. Law, 1977, 78. Mem. Am. Acad. Health Adminstrn., Am. Acad. Polit. and Social Sci., Am. Coll. Hosp. Adminstrs., Am. Coll. Utilization Review Physicians, Am. Public Health Assn., Assn. Trial Lawyers Am., Omicron Delta Kappa. Democrat. Baptist. Clubs: Miss. Coll., Century. Contbr. articles to profl. jours. Home: 1229 Gardena Dr New Orleans LA 70122 Office: 3000 Magazine St Suite 200 New Orleans LA 70115

RENKEN, ROBERT KENNETH, SR., fin. co. exec.; b. Charleston, S.C., Oct. 29, 1927; s. Walter Albert and Azile Ermine (Hackemann) R.; A.B., The Citadel, 1948; m. Willie Mae Zetrouer, June 2, 1951; children—Robert Kenneth, Janice Lynn, Nancy Azile. Partner, Charleston Auto Credit Co., 1950-67; treas. Renken Boat Mfg. Co., Charleston, 1960-79, v.p. sales, 1979—; pres. Charleston Fun Bowl, Inc., 1965—, Renken Loan & Discount Co., Inc., Charleston Heights, S.C., 1967-79, Renken Fin. Co., Inc., Charleston, 1971-79; dir. Galaxy Boat Mfg. Co. Inc., Keela Co., Inc. Mem. Democratic Exec. Com. Charleston County and City of Charleston, 1974—; mem. Gov.'s Legis. Study Com. on Uniform Consumer Credit Code, 1972-73. Served with inf. U.S. Army, 1949-50. Mem. S.C. Consumer Fin. Assn. (dir., past pres.), Ind. Consumer Fin. Assn. S.C. (pres. 1978-80), Charleston C. of C., Charleston Air Force Assn. (past pres.), S.C. Hist. Soc., Preservation Soc. Lutheran. Clubs: Country of Charleston, Hibernian Soc., Arion Soc., Elks. Home: 11 Guerard Rd Charleston SC 29407 Office: 1750 Signal Point Rd Charleston SC 29412

RENNEKER, STANLEY LEON, coast guard officer, marine engr.; b. Hamilton, Ohio, Apr. 18, 1947; s. Donald M. and Lois Ann (Zimmer) R.; B.S., U.S. Coast Guard Acad., 1969; O.E. in Ocean Engring., M.S. in Naval Architecture and Marine Engring., M.I.T., 1974; M.B.A., Tulane U., 1977; postgrad. Loyola U. Law Sch., New Orleans, 1978—; m. Barbara Wood Minnick, May 6, 1972; 1 son, Karl Minnick. Commd. ensign U.S. Coast Guard, 1969, advanced through grades to lt., 1979; various engring. assignments U.S. Coast Guard Cutters, Viet Nam, 1970, Arctic Ocean, 1971; staff engr. U.S. Coast Guard Mcht. Marine Tech. Office, New Orleans, 1974-77; marine insp. U.S. Coast Guard Marine Inspection Office, New Orleans, 1977-78, supr. marine inspection, 1978-79, adminstrv. asst. to officer in charge, 1979—. Registered profl. engr., Ohio. Mem. Am. Soc. Naval Engrs., Nat. Soc. Profl. Engrs., La. Engring. Soc. (hon.), Soc. Naval Architects and Marine Engrs., Ohio Soc. Profl. Engrs., Beta Gamma Sigma, Beta Alpha Psi. Roman Catholic. Home: 2177 S Glencove Ln Gretna LA 70053 Office: Suite 2300 1440 Canal St New Orleans LA 70112

RENO, DONALD EDWIN, tool mfg. co. exec.; b. Shreveport, La., Sept. 7, 1932; s. Lester and Lovel (Foster) R.; student Sacramento Jr. Coll., 1952-54; m. Clara Jean, Dec. 17, 1959; children—Sharon Ann, Linda Jean, Donna Denise. With Yuba Sutter Scavenger Co., Marysville, Calif., 1954-57; with Simonds Cutting Tools, Shreveport, La., 1957—, sales mgr., 1977—. Served with USAF, 1950-54. Mem. Nat. Assn. Purchasing Mgmt., Tex. Forestry Assn., Miss. Forestry Assn., So. Saw Filers Assn., Shreveport C. of C., DAV, VFW. Democrat. Clubs: Lions, Elks. Patentee on investment cast tooth. Home: 9704 McLeod St Shreveport LA 71118 Office: Simonds Cutting Tools 1214 Hawn Ave Shreveport LA 71107

RENO, VINCENT CHARLES, educator; b. N.Y.C., June 8, 1911; s. Frank Joseph and Virginia (Colletti) R.; student N.Y. Inst. Tech., 1919-31; m. Dorothy M. Douglas, June 21, 1946; 1 dau., Gena M. Style dir. WACS, WAVES, World War II; mgr. Miami cosmetology salon, 1945-79, owner, 1945-76; instr. vocat. sch., Miami, 1965-70; mem. bd. examiners Fla. Bd. Cosmetology, 1976-78; mem. Dist. 5 Fla. Bd. Cosmetology, 1976-78; mem. Interstate Bds. Cosmetology, 1976-78; mem. adv. bd. Vocat. Sch. System Fla., Miami, 1965-70; vice chmn. Fla. Bd. Cosmetology, Miami, 1978—; instr. various high schs. Named hon. Ky. Col., hon. citizen City of Miami Beach. Democrat. Office: 1830 SW 92d Pl Miami FL 33165

RENSCH, EDWARD, JR., health facility adminstr.; b. East St. Louis, Ill., Aug. 16, 1927; s. Edward L. and Dorothy (Munson) R.; B.S., St. Louis U., 1955; M.H.A., Washington U., St. Louis, 1957; m. Marjorie Jill Maisel, June 6, 1956; children—Allison Rensch Grimes, Todd. Supt. central supply dept. St. Louis Childrens Hosp., 1954-55; adminstrv. resident VA Hosp., Houston, 1956-57; adminstr. Crete (Nebr.) Mcpl. Hosp., 1957-59; adminstr. Wabash Gen. Hosp., Mt. Carmel, Ill., 1959-63; asst. supt., adminstr. New Castle (Ind.) State Hosp., 1963-66; asst. adminstr. St. Vincent Infirmary, Little Rock, 1966-67; dir. Ark. Comprehensive Health Planning Program, Little Rock, 1967-70; asso. coordinator Ark. Regional Med. Program, Little Rock, 1970-73; exec. dir. Central Ark. Radiation Therapy Inst., Little Rock, 1973—; mem. Gov.'s Health Adv. Council, Gov.'s Med. Adv. Com. for Title XIX. Bd. dirs. Community Council Central Ark., 1974-77, pres. 1976-77; bd. dirs. Hospice of Ark., 1978—, pres., 1978; bd. dirs. Pulaski County unit Am. Cancer Soc.; mem. planning and research com. United Way of Pulaski County, Inc.; mem. adv. council Ark. Manpower Council; mem. Gov.'s Adv. Council on Children and Youth. Served with Hosp. Corps, USN, 1945-49, 51-52. Mem. Am. Coll. Hosp. Adminstrs., Am. Hosp. Assn., Ark. Assn. for Mental Health (mem. profl. adv. bd.), Assn. of Community Radiation Therapy Centers (pres. 1977-78), Nat. Assn. Accts. Club: Rotary (West Little Rock, Ark.). Home: 27 Inverness Circle Little Rock AR 72212 Office: PO Box 5668 Markham St and University St Little Rock AR 72215

RENTFRO, LARRY DEAN, hosp. adminstr.; b. Independence, Kans., Mar. 14, 1941; s. Floyd R. and Helen L. R.; B.S., Okla. State U., 1964; M.H.A., Washington U., St. Louis, 1972; m. Clariece Van Valkenburgh, Jan. 25, 1964; children—Donald Ray, Sheri Renee. Head basketball coach Edison High Sch., Tulsa, 1966-70; asst. adminstr. St. John's Hosp. and Sch. Nursing, Tulsa, 1972-76; asst. v.p. St. John's Med. Center, Joplin, Mo., 1976-78; asst. adminstr. Wadley Hosp., Texarkana, Tex., 1978—; mem. Emergency Med. Services Bd., 1978-80, Tri-State Shared Services Bd., 1978-80. Loaned exec. United Way, 1978; mem. bd. Texarkana Little League Baseball, 1978-79. Served with M.C., U.S. Army, 1964-66. Foster McGaw grantee, 1972. Mem. Am. Coll. Hosp. Adminstrs., Am. Hosp. Assn., Tex. Hosp. Assn. Republican. Methodist. Club: Oaklawn Rotary. Home: 5810 Wilshire St Texarkana TX 75503 Office: 1000 Pine St Texarkana TX 75501

RENTON, WILLIAM JAMES, aerospace co. exec.; b. Medina, N.Y., Dec. 4, 1941; s. William Basil and Marie Agnes R.; B.C.E., Rensselaer Poly. Inst., 1963; M.C.E., N.C. State U., 1965; D.A.S., U. Del., 1974; m. Patricia Ann Griessman, Sept. 3, 1966; children—Robyn Marie, Kristopher Benjamin. Stress engr. Lockheed Ga. Co., Marietta, Ga., 1965-68; research engr. Boeing Vertol Co., Phila., 1968-70; fellow U. Del., 1973-75; research scientist Advanced Technology Center, Grand Prairie, Tex., 1975-77; program mgr. advanced composites Vought Corp., Grand Prairie, 1977—; adj. prof. U. Del., 1973-75, Wilmington Coll., 1973, U. Tex., 1977—. Served with USMCR, 1962-68. Air Force Office of Sci. Research grantee, 1972-74; Air Force Materials Lab. grantee, 1976, NASA-Langley grantee, 1978, Naval Air Systems Command grantee, 1977-79. Mem. ASME, AIAA, Soc. Advancement of Material and Process Engring. Editor: Hybrid and Select Metal-Matrix Composites, 1978; contbr. articles in field to profl. jours. Office: 9314 W Jefferson St Grand Prairie TX 75211

RESCHLY, WILBUR ROY, physician; b. Henry County, Iowa, Dec. 23, 1945; s. Henry R. and Mable E. (Roth) R.; student Iowa State U., 1964-67; M.D., U. Iowa, 1971; m. Julianne Woodhouse, June 8, 1968; children—Maureen Kay, Matthew John, Karen Nicole. Intern, Hennepin County Hosp., Mpls., 1971-72; resident in dermatology Duke U. Med. Center, 1972-75; practice medicine specializing in dermatology, Lakeland, Fla., 1975—; chmn. dept. dermatology Lakeland Gen. Hosp., 1978. Gen. Motors Corp. Merit scholar, 1964-67; recipient Mosby Book award, 1971; diplomate Am. Bd. Dermatology. Mem. AMA, Fla. Med. Assn., Polk County Med. Assn., Phi Eta Sigma, Alpha Omega Alpha. Republican. Mennonite. Home: 3425 Myrtle Hill Dr Lakeland FL 33803 Office: 4316 Highland Park Blvd Lakeland FL 33803

RESLEY, GEORGE BOULTER, sales exec.; b. Ft. Stockton, Tex., Nov. 23, 1945; s. Horace Ernest and Annie Jane (Boulter) R.; B.B.A., Tex. A. and M. U., 1969; grad. Dale Carnegie Course, 1976; m. Virginia Beth Hopper, July 22, 1972. Sales rep. for 3-C Corp., Odessa, Tex., 1969-72; mid-continent sales rep. Vetco 3-C Corp., Tulsa, 1973-74; mid-continent sales mgr. Vetco Services, Inc., Tulsa, 1974-78; regional sales mgr. C-E Vetco Services, Tulsa, 1979—. Recipient 10 Yr. award C-E Vetco Services, 1979. Mem. Internat. Assn. Drilling Contractors, Nat. Assn. Corrosion Engrs., Soc. Petroleum Engrs., Tex. Muzzle Loading Rifle Assn., Osage Muzzle Loading Rifle Assn. Republican. Christian Scientist. Clubs: Tex. A. and M. Univ. Century, N. Am. Aerospace Rod and Gun, Westerners. Office: 4343 S 118th East Ave Tulsa OK 74145

RESO, ANTHONY, geologist; b. London, Eng., Aug. 10, 1934; s. Harry and Marion (Gerth) R.; came to U.S., 1940, naturalized, 1952; A.B., Columbia Coll., N.Y.C., 1954; M.A., Columbia U., 1955; postgrad. U. Cin., 1956-57; Ph.D. (fellow) Rice U., 1960; postgrad. Grad. Sch. Bus. U. Houston, 1964-68. Instr. geology Queens Coll., Flushing, N.Y., 1954; geologist Atlantic Richfield Corp., Midland, Tex., 1955-56; asst. prof. geology and curator invertebrate paleontology Pratt Mus., Amherst (Mass.) Coll., 1959-62; staff research geologist Tenneco Oil Co., Houston, 1962—. Cons. in geol. research Tenn. Gas and Oil Co., 1960-61; lectr. U. Houston, 1962-65; vis. prof. Rice U., 1980—; mem. bd. advisers Gulf Univs. Research Corp., Galveston, Tex., 1967-75, chmn., 1968-69. Mem. Houston Apt. Assn., 1970—; dir. Stewardship Properties, Houston, 1968—. Recipient research grants Am. Assn. Petroleum Geologists, 1958, 59, Geol. Soc. Am., 1958, Eastman Fund, 1962; NSF fellow, 1959. Fellow Geol. Soc. Am., A.A.A.S.; mem. Am. Assn. Petroleum Geologists (life, gen. chmn. nat. conv. 1979), Paleontol. Soc., Soc. Econ. Paleontologists and Mineralogists, Paleontol. Research Instn., Internat. Paleontol. Union, Marine Tech. Soc., Tex. Acad. Sci., Houston Geol. Soc. (v.p. 1973-75, pres. 1975-76), Houston Symphony Soc., English-Speaking Union U.S. (dir. Houston chpt. 1978—), Sigma Xi, Sigma Gamma Epsilon, Beta Theta Pi. Episcopalian. Club: Shadyside Tennis. Contbr. profl. jours. Home: 1801 Huldy Houston TX 77019 Office: Tenneco Oil Co PO Box 2511 Houston TX 77001

RESSLER, PARKE E(DWARD), lawyer, accountant; b. Lancaster, Pa., Aug. 21, 1916; s. Parke H. and Sadie (Weiser) R.; B.S., U. Pa., 1947; B.B.A., Baylor U., 1947, LL.B., 1952, J.D., 1969; M.B.A., U. Houston, 1949; m. Margaret B. Tucker, June 3, 1944; children—Nancy Parke, Margaret Anne. Agt. Internal Revenue Service, 1947-50; part time instr. Baylor U., 1950-65; admitted to Tex. bar, 1952, since practiced in Waco; asso. firm Edwin P. Horner. Mem. Am. Inst. C.P.A.'s, Tex. Soc. C.P.A.'s, Am., Tex., McLennan County bar assns., Am. Assn. Atty.-C.P.A.'s, Phi Alpha Delta, Delta Sigma Pi. Mem. Christian Ch. Rotarian. Clubs: Ridgewood Country, Hedonia, Ridgewood Yacht, Baylor Bear. Home: 2209 Arroyo Rd Waco TX 76710 Office: 4830 Lakewood Dr Waco TX 76710

RESTA, PETER PAUL, elec. engr.; b. Phila., May 16, 1924; s. Frank and Carolina (DiFiore) R.; B.S., Drexel U., 1963; M.S.E.E., So. Meth. U., 1971; children—Frank R., Craig M. Asst. prof. electronics Southeastern Okla. State U.; chmn. engring. tech. Nash Tech. Inst., Rocky Mount, N.C.; now with Boeing Airplane Co., Wichita. Served with USAAF, 1942-45, USAF, 1948-52. Mem. IEEE. Democrat. Roman Catholic. Home: 6111 Willowbend 804 Houston TX 77096 Office: Boeing Airplane Co 3800 S Oliver Wichita KS 67210

RETHERFORD, CHARLES WILLIAM, tax cons.; b. Amarillo, Tex., July 15, 1930; s. Charles Thomas and Dessie Isabel (Shackelford) R.; student W. Tex. State Coll., 1948-52; m. Exa Louise Long, Mar. 14, 1953; children—Ronald Ray, Carldene Sue, Clint William. Carpenter, Lewisville, Tex., 1958-60; truck driver, Lewisville, 1960-64; layout man Span Inc., Dallas, 1964-71; owner, mgr. Retherford Tax Services, Lewisville, 1971—; tchr. public schs., Mo., 1957-58. Mem. Nat. Assn. Tax Cons., Lewisville C. of C. Mem. Ch. of Christ. Address: 385 Crockett Dr Lewisville TX 75067

RETZKE, FRANKLIN ALBERT, chem. engr.; b. Venice, Ohio, Oct. 13, 1916; s. Frank Albert Carl and Laura Louise (Schoewe) R.; Chem. E., Ohio State U., 1950, M.S., 1950; m. Dorothy Viola Payne, Sept. 22, 1951; children—Melanie Jayne, Miriam Louise, David Franklin. Jr. chem. engr. Gen. Aniline and Film Corp., Linden, N.J., 1950-51; prin. chem. engr. Battelle Meml. Inst., Columbus, Ohio, 1951-55; research engr., asst. production mgr. Smith Agrl. Chem. Co., Columbus, 1955-59; production mgr. carbon dept. Barney-Cheney Co., Columbus, 1961; supr., mgr. research and devel. fertilizer, asst. prodn. mgr., tech. mgr. fertilizer sect. Smith-Douglass div. Borden Inc., Norfolk, Va., 1961—. Dir. Thalia Civic League, 1970—, pres., 1973-74. Served with U.S. Army, 1941-45. Decorated Bronze Star. Mem. Am. Inst. Chem. Engrs., Am. Chem. Soc. (chmn. div. fertilizer and soil chemistry 1976-77). Republican. Lutheran. Co-patentee in fertilizer industry; contbr. articles to profl. jours. Home: 3869 Thalia Dr Virginia Beach VA 23452 Office: PO Box 419 Norfolk VA 23501

REUBEN, EILEEN RUTH, speech pathologist; b. Chgo., May 8, 1949; d. Meyer Zelig and Rochelle (Suckman) Reuben; B.S. Edn., U. Mo., 1971: postgrad. U. Ga., 1971-74; M.Ed., Ga. State U., 1975. Speech and lang. pathologist DeKalb Home Health Services, Inc., Decatur, Ga., 1971—; supervising tchr., supr. spl. edn. program Atlanta Bur. Jewish Edn., 1971—; speech and lang. pathologist DeKalb County Bd. Edn., Atlanta, 1971-79; speech and lang. pathologist, Atlanta, 1974—; speech and lang. diagnostic and therapeutic pathologist Ga. Mental Health Inst., Atlanta, 1975. Vol., Am. Cancer Soc. Mamie Jo Jones scholar, 1971-75. Mem. Am. Speech and Hearing Assn., Ga. Speech and Hearing Assn., Atlanta Assn. Retarded Citizens, Acad. Aphasia, Greater Atlanta Voice Masters. Jewish. Home: 2583 Ashford Rd NE Atlanta GA 30319

REUL, GEORGE JOHN, JR., cardiovascular surgeon, educator; b. Milw., Apr. 19, 1937; s. George John and Ann Rose (Klune) R.; B.S., Marquette U., 1958, M.D. (Nat. Tobacco Inst. fellow, NIH fellow), 1962, M.S. (Allen Bradley Research Lab. fellow, Am. Cancer Soc. fellow), 1968; m. Kay Joan Ross, Mar. 3, 1962; children—George John III, Ross Michael, David Kevin, Darren Sean. Intern, U. Chgo. Clinics, 1962-63; resident Marquette Affiliated Hosps., Milw., 1963-66, 68-69, Baylor Coll. Medicine, Houston, 1969-71; clin. instr. surgery Marquette U., 1963-69; instr. surgery, Baylor U., 1971-72, asst. prof., 1972-73; asso. cardiovascular surgeon St. Luke's Episcopal Hosp., Houston, 1973—, Tex. Children's Hosp., Houston, 1973—, Tex. Heart Inst., Houston, 1973—. Fellow A.C.S., Am. Coll. Cardiology, Internat. Coll. Angiology, Am. Coll. Chest Physicians; mem. Am., Tex., Harris County (Tex.) med. assns., Am. Heart Assn., Internat. Cardiovascular Soc., Soc. Vascular Surgeons, Soc. Thoracic Surgery, Am. Assn. Thoracic Surgery, S.W., Western surg. congresses, Alpha Omega Alpha. Contbr. articles to profl. jours. Home: 11603 Applewood Ln Houston TX 77024 Office: PO Box 20345 Houston TX 77025

REVELEY, HUGH PRICE, physician; b. Little Rock, May 22, 1915; s. Samuel Lawson and Sarah Ozella (McCracken) R.; A.B., U. Tex., 1936; M.D., U. Tex., Galveston, 1942; m. Evelyn Elsa Woeltz, Nov. 19, 1942; children—Michael August, Marilyn. Intern, Santa Rosa Hosp., San Antonio, 1942-43; gen. practice medicine, San Antonio, 1943-48; resident in internal medicine Alexander Blain Hosp., Detroit, 1948-49; resident in internal medicine John Sealy Hosp., Galveston, Tex., 1949-51; practice medicine specializing in internal medicine, San Antonio, 1953-59; chief med. service VA Hosp., Kerrville, Tex., 1961-66; mem. psychiatry service VA Hosp., Temple, Tex., 1966—. Served in U.S. Army, 1951-53. Nat. Heart Inst. trainee, 1950-51. Mem. AMA, Tex. Med. Assn., Bell County Med. Soc. Methodist. Contbr. articles in field to med. jours. Home: 3810 Deer Trail Temple TX 76501 Office: Olin E Teague Vets Center Temple TX 76501

REVELS, THOMAS REX, hosp. adminstr.; b. Durham, N.C., Feb. 1, 1953; s. Rex Carlton and Mildred Thomas R.; B.S. in Bus. Adminstrn., U. N.C., Chapel Hill, 1975; M. Health Adminstrn., Duke U., 1977; m. Rhonda Powell, Aug. 11, 1973; 1 dau., Jennifer Leigh. Asst. chief support services John Umstead Hosp., Butner, N.C., 1978—; adminstr. Children's Psychiat. Inst., Butner, 1977-78. Angier B. Duke fellow, 1975-77. Mem. Hosp. Fin. Mgmt. Assn., Am. Coll. Hosp. Adminstrs., Assn. Mental Health Adminstrs., N.C. Hosp. Assn., N.C. Jaycees. Baptist. Office: John Umstead Hosp 12th St Butner NC 27509

REVIER, PAUL RAYMOND, geneticist, plant breeder; b. Lubbock, Tex., July 22, 1928; s. Frank Fancher and Minnie Louise (Tubbs) R.; B.S., Tex. Tech. U., 1952, M.S., 1958; m. Nell Rhodes, June 1, 1951; children—Charles Thomas, Robert Franklin, Paula Kim, David Lee, Alice Faye. Mgr., Sunnyview Seed Farms, Lubbock, 1952-53; seed analyst Tex. Dept. Agr., 1953-55; self-employed as farmer and seed producer, Lubbock, 1955-56; plant breeder J. W. Lindsey Seed Co., Lubbock, 1956-63, dir. research, 1963-65, v.p. research, 1965-67, dir., 1963-67; self-employed as agrl. cons., Lubbock, 1967-69; mgr. sorghum research Funk Bros. Seed Co., Lubbock, 1969-78, prin. research scientist, 1978—. Deacon, sec. bd. deacons Calvary Baptist Ch., 1978-79. Served with U.S. Army, 1946-47. Mem. Am. Soc. Agronomy, Crop Sci. Soc., Am. Genetic Assn., AAAS, Tex. Cert. Seed Producers (pres. 1963), Lubbock C. of C., Sigma Xi. Clubs: Masons, Shriners, Lions. Home: Route 8 Box 230 Lubbock TX 79407 Office: 719 26th St Lubbock TX 79404

REVIS, FRANCES W., ret. educator; b. Colbert, Okla., Dec. 10, 1910; d. Harvey R. and Ophelia (Dane) Williamson; B.S., Southeastern State Tchrs. Coll., 1931; M.A., Tex. State Coll. Women, 1950; Ed.D., Tex. Woman's U., 1958; m. Sidney M. Revis, Jan. 19, 1963. Tchr. home econs. Checotah (Okla.) High Sch., 1931-33; county dir. pub. welfare, Cotton, Logan, LeFlore counties, Okla., 1933-40; tchr. vocat. homemaking Colbert (Okla.) High Sch., 1940-57; faculty mem. Southeastern Okla. State U., Durant, 1958-76, asst. prof. home econs., 1958-65, asso. prof., 1965-69, prof., head home econs. dept., 1969-76, prof. emeritus, 1976—. Sec.-treas. western sect., So. Regional Conf. Coll. Food and Nutrition Tchrs., 1957-76. Named Outstanding Tchr., Southeastern State U., 1973-74. Mem. Am., Okla. home econs. assns., Okla. Edn. Assn., A.A.U.P., Higher Edn. Alumni Council Okla., N.E.A., A.A.U.W., Am., Okla. voca. assns., Am., Okla. sch. food service assns., Nat. Council Adminstrs. Home Econs., Soc. Nutrition Edn., Delta Kappa Gamma. Home: PO Box 70 Colbert OK 74733

REW, JAMES ALFRED, JR., radio sta. exec.; b. Nassawadox, Va., Jan. 24, 1945; s. James Alfred and Ethel Finney (Ames) R.; student U. Va., 1963-66; radio engring. certificate, Eastern Shore Community Coll., 1974; student Old Dominion Coll., 1969; student of Eugene List (piano), 1977—; Communications Arts degree SUNY, 1979; m. Irene Kaye Jenkins, Jan. 13, 1942; 1 dau., Jennifer Ames. With WESR Radio, Tasley, Va., 1966-68; with WEXM Radio, 1968-71, gen. mgr., Exmore, Va., 1972—; tchr. Eastern Shore Acad., Parksley, 1971-72. Performer piano UN cultural exchange program, 1967; radio sta. planning cons., 1973; piano coach, 1968—; piano concert tour including local radio, TV, stage performances, 1967. Bd. dirs. Eastern Shore Community Concert, Exmore, 1967. Recipient First Place Music award, Lions, 1959; Onancock Sci. award, 1963; Am. Cancer Soc. awards in appreciation for fund raising concert, 1967; Pub. Service Broadcasting awards, 1975. Clubs: Masons, Shriners, Nat. Beta. Composer ballads. Home: Box 282 Onley VA 23418 Office: Box 218-D Exmore VA 23350

REX, GERALD BARTLETT, ins. co. exec.; b. St. Louis, June 19, 1945; s. Clarence Bartlett and Vivian (Cowgill) R.; B.Mgmt. Engring., Rensselaer Poly. Inst., 1967, M.S., 1968; m. Judith Lanese, June 22, 1968; children—Traci, Bryan, Adam. Indsl. engr. Procter & Gamble, N.Y.C., 1968-69, Prepared Mix Dept. supr., 1969-71, packing mgr. Food Div. and product protection coordinator, 1971-75; agt. Conn. Gen. Life Ins. Co., Norfolk, Va., 1975—; lectr. estate planning. Vice chmn. Churchland Interfaith Council, 1978-79. Recipient Nat. Sales Achievement award Nat. Assn. Life Underwriters, 1977-79, Health Ins. Quality award, 1977-79. Mem. Churchland Jaycees (internal v.p. 1974), Norfolk Assn. Life Underwriters, Nat. Assn. Security Dealers. Roman Catholic. Club: Million Dollar Round Table. Home: 2936 Princess Ann Crescent Chesapeake VA 23321 Office: 1515 First Va Bank Tower Norfolk VA 23510

REY, WILLIAM KENNETH, engr., educator; b. N.Y.C., Aug. 11, 1925; s. William and Frances Sophia (Sauer) R.; B.S. in Aero. Engring., U. Ala., 1946, M.S. in Civil Engring., 1949; postgrad. U. Ariz., 1961; m. Ruth Jeanette Vickery, Nov. 27, 1946; children—Jeanette (Mrs. Felix Edward Todd), William Kenneth. Instr. math. U. Ala., University, 1946-47, instr. engring. mechanics, 1947-49, asst. prof. engring. mechanics, 1949-52, asso. prof. aero. engring., 1952-58, prof. aero. engring., 1958-60, prof. aerospace engring., 1960—, acting head dept., 1972, dir. high sch. relations, 1970—, asst. dean engring., 1976—; cons. research NACA, NASA, Army and Air Force depts. Recipient Dist. Scouter award Boy Scouts Am., 1970; registered profl. engr., Ala. Asso. fellow Am. Inst. Aeros. and Astronautics; mem. Nat. Soc. Profl. Engrs., Am. Soc. Engring. Edn., Air Force Assn., Capstone Engring. Soc. (exec. dir. 1976—), Theta Tau (grand regent, nat. pres. 1963-66, grand marshal 1968-72), Tau Beta Pi, Omicron Delta Kappa, Sigma Gamma Tau, Pi Mu Epsilon. Baptist (deacon). Clubs: Kiwanis (dir. Tuscaloosa, Ala., 1969-74 76—, 1st v.p. 1976-77, pres. elect 1977-78, pres. 1978-79, zone chmn. 1975-78), University (bd. govs. Tuscaloosa 1970-78, pres. 1976). Contbr. NACA and NASA reports, revs., lab manual. Home: 77 Woodland Hills Tuscaloosa AL 35405 Office: PO Box 1968 University AL 35486

REYER, RANDALL WILLIAM, anatomist; b. Chgo., Jan. 23, 1917; s. William Cleveland and Elsie Mary (Hardy) R.; A.B., Cornell U., 1939; M.A., 1942; Ph.D., Yale U., 1947; m. Carolyn Elizabeth Murray, June 12, 1943; children—Elizabeth Ann, Mary Louise. Instr. in Biology, Conn. Wesleyan U., 1946-47; instr. in Zoology, Yale U., 1947-50; asst. prof. Anatomy, U. Pitts., 1950-57; asso. prof. anatomy, W.Va., U., 1957-67, prof., 1967—, acting chmn. dept., 1977-78. Recipient research grants NIH, 1951-79. Mem. Am. Assn. Anatomists, Am. Soc. Zoologists, Internat. Soc. Developmental Biologists, Soc. for Developmental Biology, Assn. for Research in Vision and Ophthalmology, So. Soc. Anatomists, Am. Inst. Biol. Sci., Assn. Am. Med. Colls., Sigma Xi, Phi Beta Kappa, Phi Kappa Phi, Pi Kappa Alpha, Phi Rho Sigma. Presbyterian. Research on devel. and regeneration of lens in amphibian eye, 1948-79. Home: 1316 Fairfield Street Morgantown WV 26505 Office: Dept Anatomy Med Center W Va U Morgantown WV 26506

REYES, LONNIE CONTRERAS, clergyman; b. Lockhart, Tex., June 1, 1942; s. Jose M. and Angela (Contreras) R.; M.Th., St. Thomas U., Houston, 1969. Ordained priest Roman Catholic Ch., 1969, named monsignor, 1976; asso. pastor St. Louis Ch., Waco, Tex., 1969; mem. staff diocesan office Hispanic affairs, Austin, Tex., 1970—, chancellor Diocese of Austin, 1972—; adminstr. St. John's Ch., Luling, Tex., 1976, Cristo Reg Ch., Austin, 1978—. Mem. City of Austin Police and Fire Commn., 1976—; vice-chmn. Austin Civil Service Commn., 1978—; dir. East Austin Scholarship fund, 1979. Decorated Knight of Holy Sepulchre (Vatican). Mem. Nat. Assn. Ch. Personnel Adminstrs., Mex. Am. C. of C. Austin and Travis County, Austin Charro Assn. (hon.). Democrat. Home: 2109 E 2d St Austin TX 78702 Office: 1600 N Congress Ave PO Box 13327 Capitol Sta Austin TX 78711

REYMORE, HAROLD EUGENE, JR., chemist; b. Meadville, Pa., Mar. 30, 1937; s. Harold Eugene and Jean Louise (Ricci) Phelps; certificate Chinese, Yale U., 1955-58; B.S., U. New Haven, 1969; m. Roberta Ann Ward, Aug. 27, 1960; children—Gene Louise, Tracy Ann. Polymer chemist Carwin Chem. Co., N. Haven, Conn., 1961-62, Donald S. Gilmore Research Labs., Upjohn Co., N. Haven, 1962-67; patent agt. trainee Upjohn Co., N. Haven, 1967-69, asst. to dir. research, 1969-71, supr., head tech. services, 1971-72, mgr. isocynate applications, 1972-78; tech. dir. E.R. Carpenter Co., Richmond, Va., 1978—; lectr. in field. Commentator, Ch. of Resurrection Roman Cath. Ch., Wallingford, Conn. 1972—. Served with USAF, 1955-60. Recipient William E. Upjohn award, 1974; U. New Haven evening student scholar, 1965-69. Mem. Soc. Plastic Engrs. (sr.), Am. Chem. Soc., Wallingford Rod and Gun Club. Republican. Roman Catholic. K.C. (3 deg.). Contbr. articles on isocyanate polymer chemistry to profl. publs. Patentee U.S., abroad. Home: 1700 Turnmill Dr Richmond VA 23235 Office: 2400 Jefferson Davis Hwy Richmond VA 23261

REYNOLDS, CRAIG E., engring. co. exec.; b. Omaha, 1944; s. P.B. and T. U. R.; M.B.A., N. Tex. U., 1967; m. Karen Reynolds, Aug. 1965; children—Jean, Tracy, Paige. Acct., Coopers & Lybrand, Dallas, 1967-71; controller Brandt Engring. Co., Inc., Dallas, 1971-76, treas., 1976—. Mem. Am. Inst. C.P.A.'s, Tex. Soc. C.P.A.'s. Office: PO Box 29559 Dallas TX 75229

REYNOLDS, DAVID PARHAM, metal products mfg. co. exec.; b. Bristol, Tenn., June 16, 1915; s. Richard Samuel and Julia Louise (Parham) R.; student Princeton U., 1938; m. Margaret Harrison, Mar. 25, 1944; children—Margaret Allis, Julia Parham, Dorothy Harrison. With Reynolds Metals Co., 1937—, salesman, asst. mgr. aircraft parts, 1937-44, asst. v.p., 1944-46, v.p., 1946-57, exec. v.p., 1958-75, gen. mgr., 1969-75, vice chmn. bd., chmn. exec. com., 1975, now chmn., chief exec. officer; chmn. bd., dir. Robertshaw Controls Co., 1978—; dir. Reynolds Metals Co., United Va. Bankshares, Reynolds Aluminum Sales Co., Reynolds Internat., Inc., Reynolds Aluminum Co. Can., Eskimo Pie Corp., Reynolds Jamaica Mines, Ltd., Can. Reynolds Metals Co., Ltd.; mem. Prime Aluminum Products Industry Adv. Com., Fed. Govt., 1951—; chmn. Aluminum Assn., 1975-77. Trustee Lawrenceville Sch.; bd. dirs. Nat. Center for Resource Recovery. Home: 8905 Tresco Rd Richmond VA 23229 Office: 6601 Broad St Rd Richmond VA 23261

REYNOLDS, DONALD EUGENE, educator; b. Munday. Tex., July 20, 1931; s. William Erwin and Abbigail (Norman) R.; B.A., N. Tex. State U., 1957, M.A., 1958; Ph.D., Tulane U., 1966; m. Martha Ann Sawyer, Apr. 17, 1960; children—William Norman. Donald Wayne. Instr. history Decatur (Tex.) Bapt. Coll.. 1958-61; asst. prof. E. Tex. State U., Commerce, 1965-68. asso. prof., 1968-72, prof. history, 1972—. Served with USNR, 1951-55. Recipient Tex. Writers Roundup award of excellence, 1971; faculty award for distinguished achievement E. Tex. State U., 1973. Mem. Am., So., Tex. hist. assns. Democrat. Baptist. Lion. Author: Editors Make War: Southern Newspapers in the Secession Crisis, 1971. Contbr. articles to profl. jours. Home: 2805 Rix St Commerce TX 75428

REYNOLDS, DOREEN WATSON, nurse; b. Steamboat Springs, Colo., Mar. 15, 1941; d. Richard James and Martha Jane (Noyes) Watson; B.S. in Nursing, Tex. Woman's U., 1962; m. Jackie Dale Reynolds, Mar. 5, 1960; children—J.D., Laura Gail, Adrian Keith. Staff nurse Dallas County Hosp. Dist., Dallas, 1962-66, head nurse, 1966-69, asst. supr. operating rm., 1969-74, supr. operating rm., 1974—; clin. instr. hosp. nursing care U. Tex. Health Sci. Center, Dallas, 1974—. Mem. Assn. Operating Rm. Nurses (sec. 1978—). Presbyterian. Home: Route 4 Box 26 Quinlan TX 75474 Office: 5201 Harry Hines Blvd Dallas TX 75474

REYNOLDS, DOROTHY EDWINA, businesswoman; b. Annapolis, Md., Aug. 3, 1940; d. Charles Edward and Dorothy LaVohn (Overmiller) Harkins; B.S., U. Md., 1962; postgrad. No. Ill. U., 1965-67, U. Calif., Riverside, 1968-73; m. Gordon D. Reynolds, Oct. 24, 1964. Tchr. public schs., Bel Air, Md., 1962-65, Malta, Ill., 1966-68, Riverside, Calif., 1968-75; sec.-treas. Claude F. Reynolds & Son, Inc., Dallas, 1976—, v.p. mgmt., 1979—. Democrat. Episcopalian.

REYNOLDS, F(RANK) FISHER, ret. geophys. co. exec.; b. Ft. Worth, June 13, 1906; s. Frank Towner and Lavinia (Fisher) R.; B.S. in Elec. Engring., Rice U., 1928; m. Hazel Anderson, Oct. 16, 1930; children—Jane (Mrs. William Clyde Lindsey), Frank Fisher, Norman Towner, Richard Vining. Party chief Geophys. Research Corp., Houston, 1928-32; pres. Seismic Exploration, Inc. (firm sold 1962 to Mandrel Industries, Inc.), Houston, 1932-62, staff cons., 1962-70. Bd. govs. Rice U. Mem. Soc. Exploration Geophysicists, Am. Assn., Petroleum Geologists, AAAS, European Assn. Exploration Geophysicists. Club: River Oaks Country. Home: 3230 Chevy Chase Houston TX 77019

REYNOLDS, GERALD FRANCIS, computer services co. exec.; b. Worcester, Mass., July 19, 1939; s. Francis Aloysius and Phyllis May R. A.B. in English, Assumption Coll., 1962; postgrad. Suffolk Law Sch., 1969-72; m. Birgitta E. Andersson, Jan. 11, 1962; children—Christina Maria, Owen Francis, Elisabet Ellen. Sales rep. Procter & Gamble, Hartford, Conn., 1966-67, Varco, Inc., Boston, 1967-69, Automatic Data Processing, Boston, 1969-72, sales tng. mgr., 1972, regional v.p. sales, Pitts., 1972-75, gen. mgr., 1975-77, div. v.p., Nashville, 1977-79; pres. Computer Resources, Inc., Greenville, S.C., 1979—. Library commr., Shrewsbury, Mass., 1961-62; town meeting precinct rep., Shrewsbury, 1961-62; voter registrar, Boylston, Mass., 1969-72. Served to lt. U.S. Navy, 1962-66. Mem. Jaycees. Democrat. Clubs: K.C., Adelphi Council (lectr. 1969-70, pres., dir. 1970-72). Office: 400 S Pleasantburg Rd Greenville SC 29606

REYNOLDS, GRACE HOLLEY, educator; b. Galveston County, Tex., Dec. 14, 1932; d. Milton W. and Pauline E. (Krause) R.; B.S., U. Houston, 1963; M.S., Tex. Woman's U., 1967, Ph.D., 1971; m. Cecil L. Reynolds, Oct. 21, 1950; children—Johnny Sue, Milton Wayne. Tchr. homemaking Medina Valley Ind. Sch. Dist., Castroville, Tex., 1963-65, Harlandale Ind. Sch. Dist., San Antonio, 1965-68; faculty S.W. Tex. State U., San Marcos, 1968-71; asst. prof. Mary Hardin-Baylor U., Belton, Tex., 1971-73; asso. prof. Incarnate Word Coll., San Antonio, 1973—. Tour chmn. King William Assn., 1975-79, bd. dirs., 1973-76; active San Antonio Conservation Soc., Night in Old San Antonio, 1975-79. Recipient Franklin award U. Houston, 1962. Mem. Am. Home Econ. Assn., Tex. Home Econ. Assn., Dist. B. Home Econ. Assn., Am. Vocat. Assn., Tex. Tchrs. Assn., Vocat. Homemaking Tchrs. Tex., Vocat. Tchrs. Assn. Tex., Nat. Council Adminstrs. Home Econs., Kappa Lambda Kappa, Delta Kappa Gamma, Phi Upsilon Omicron. Baptist. Contbr. articles to profl. jours. Office: 4301 Broadway San Antonio TX 78209

REYNOLDS, HORACE GERALD, lawyer; b. Alexander City, Ala., July 16, 1940; s. James Horace and Melba Victoria (Scott) R.; student U. So. Miss., 1958-59; B.A., Auburn U., 1962; J.D., Samford U., 1965; m. Mary Alice McGiboney, Sept. 3, 1960; children—Mary C., Horace Gerald, Amy E., Richard J. Admitted to Ala. bar, 1965; pvt. practice law, Alexander City, Ala., 1965-67; judge Ct. Common Pleas, Alexander City, Ala., 1967; pvt. practice law, Alexander City, Ala., 1968-71; corporate counsel U.S. Pipe & Foundry Co., Birmingham, Ala., 1971-72; environmental counsel Jim Walter Corp., Tampa, Fla., 1972—. Mem. Ala. Constitutional Commn., 1970-75; mem. exec. com. Tallapoosa County (Ala.) Dem. Com., 1970-71; pres. South Brandon Little League, 1977-79; chmn. bd. trustees 1st Meth. Ch., Brandon, Fla. Mem. Am., Ala., Fla., Hillsborough County bar assns., Ala. (v.p. 1970-71, dir. govtl. affairs 1968-70), U.S. jaycees, Sigma Phi Epsilon, Sigma Delta Kappa, Omicron Delta Kappa, Blue Key. Democrat. Elk. Club: Brandon Swim and Tennis. Home: 2214 Village Ct Brandon FL 33511 Office: 1500 N Dale Mabry Tampa FL 33607

REYNOLDS, JERRY DANIEL, acct.; b. Ruston, La., May 30, 1949; s. Bennie and Bonnie Virginia (Bryant) R.; student La. State U., 1967-69; B.S. in Acctg., So. U., 1971; postgrad. E. Tex. State U., 1978—; m. Kathaleen Gipson, June 8, 1974; 1 son, Jerry Daniel. Jr. auditor Touche Ross and Co., Mpls., 1971-73; sr. auditor Laventhol and Horwarth, Dallas, 1973-75; spl. asst. to controller and treasury, asst. controller Am. Quasar Petroleum Co., Inc., Ft. Worth, Tex., 1975-76; sr. auditor, audit mgr. Anderson Clayton Foods, Dallas, 1976—. Bd. dirs. Dallas Opportunity Industrialization Center. Mem. Black Accts. Soc., C. of C., Am. Mgmt. Assn., Black C. of C., Omega Psi Phi. Democrat. Baptist. Home: 9420 County View Rd Dallas TX 75249 Office: PO Box 226165 Dallas TX 75266

REYNOLDS, JOHN ARCHIBALD SEABROOK, dentist; b. Lenoir, N.C., Feb. 16, 1933; s. Archibald Seabrook and Eva Mae (Craven) R.; student The Citadel, 1951-54; D.D.S., U. N.C., 1958; m. Jeanne Kathleen Fleming, July 5, 1958; children—Kathleen Fleming, Mary McLeod, Patricia Lynn. Pvt. practice dentistry, Charlotte, N.C., 1960—. Instr. dental interne program Charlotte Meml. Hosp., 1960—; cons. dental asst. program Community Coll., Charlotte, since 1962. Adviser, Explorer Scouts, 1968. Served with Dental Corps, USNR, 1958-60; now capt. Res. Mem. Am. Dental Assn., N.C. (ethics com. 1971-76, chmn. 1971-72, 75-76, chmn. ann. meeting), 2d Dist., Charlotte dental socs., Citadel Alumni Assn., Res. Officers Assn. U.S., Naval Res. Assn., Omicron Kappa Upsilon, Xi Psi Phi. Episcopalian (vestryman 1964-67, lay reader 1958—). Club: Myers Park Country (dir. 1974-77). Home: 2101 Coniston Pl Charlotte NC 28207 Office: 1944 Brunswick Ave Charlotte NC 28207

REYNOLDS, LARRY JOHN, educator; b. Springfield, Ohio, Dec. 5, 1942; s. William John and Stella Marie (Grauer) R.; B.S., U. Cin., 1966; M.A. in English, Ohio State U., 1971; Ph.D., Duke U., 1974; m. Carol Joan Gregersen, Aug. 28, 1965; children—Brian Christopher, Sean William, Robin Scott. Aerodynamics engr. N. Am. Rockwell, Columbus, Ohio, 1966-69; aeronautical research engr. Battelle Meml. Inst., Columbus, 1971; asst. prof. English, Tex. A&M U., College Station, 1974-79. asso. prof., 1979—; chmn. bd. PRW, Inc., Columbus, 1969-71 Duke U. grad. teaching fellow, 1972-74; Fed. Research grantee, 1974; Tex. A&M U. summer research grantee, 1975, 76, 78. Mem. AAUP, MLA, S. Central Modern Lang. Assn., Melville Soc., Hawthorne Soc., Theta Chi. Contbr. articles in field to profl. jours. Home: 1411 Lawyer St College Station TX 77840 Office: Dept English Tex A&M Univ College Station TX 77843

REYNOLDS, LESLIE B(OUSH), JR., physician; b. Lakeland, Fla., Aug. 16, 1923; s. Leslie Boush and Verna (Powell) R.; B.S., Randolph-Macon Coll., 1949 M.S., Ga. Inst. Tech., 1951; Ph.D., Med. Coll. S.C., 1941; M.D., Northwestern U., 1966; m. Alma Carter, Oct. 24, 1947; children—Alma Mary, Margaret Mary. Engr., E.I. du Pont de Nemours & Co., Inc., Kinston, N.C., 1951-53, group leader, 1954-55, lab. supr., 1956-57; asst. prof. physiology Northwestern U. Med. Sch., Chgo., 1961-64, research asso. medicine, 1964-66; intern St. Joseph Hosp., Chgo., 1966-67; practice medicine specializing in pulmonary disease, Memphis 1968-76, now Kingsport, Tenn.; mem. staff Holston Valley Community Hosp., Kingsport; asst. prof. medicine U. Tenn., 1967-71, asso. prof. medicine, 1971-76, asso. prof. physiology and biophysics, 1967-76, acting chmn. dept. physiology and biophysics, 1968-69; asso. prof. family practice E. Tenn. State U. Coll. Medicine, Kingsport, 1977-79, prof., 1979—, prof. physiology, 1977—, asst. dean, dir. med. edn., 1979—; dir. AL-Med Corp., Dresden, Tenn., 1976-77 Served with USNR, 1942-46. Mem. Am. Physiol. Soc., AMA, Am. Thoracic Soc., Am. Coll. Chest Physicians, Aerospace Med. Assn., Am. Acad. Family Practice, Am. Chem. Soc., Sigma Xi, Phi Lambda Upsilon. Research in respiratory reflexes, treatment of respiratory diseases. Home: Box 924 Kingsport TN 37662 Office: 202 Ravine Kingsport TN 37660

REYNOLDS, LESSIE PRATT MALLARD, educator; b. Beulaville, N.C., Dec. 28, 1923; d. Alvin Raymond and Lessie Mae (Bostic) Mallard; A.B., U. N.C., 1953, M.A., 1957; Ph.D. (Horace Rackham grad. fellowship), U. Mich., 1969; m. Leslie Ralph Casey, Nov. 30, 1941 (div.); children—Mary (Mrs. Jim Bazemore), Michael; m. 2d, Christopher Macdonald Reynolds, Sept. 20, 1957. Film asst. U. N.C. Communication Center, Chapel Hill, 1955-56; staff mem. WUNC-TV, Chapel Hill, N.C., 1956-57; faculty Winthrop Coll., Rock Hill, S.C., 1957—, asso. prof. English, drama, affirmative action adminstr., 1973—. Free-lance theatre and film acting; free-lance theatre writing and directing. Second v.p., bd. mem. S.C. Council for Human Rights, 1973. Mem. Univ. Film Assn., Soc. for Cinema Studies, Speech Communication Assn. (sec. mass communication div. 1973—), S.C. Council of Tchrs. of English (media com. 1972-73), Am. Theatre Assn., Southeastern Theatre Conf., South Atlantic Modern Lang. Assn., Phi Beta Kappa, Phi Kappa Phi, Zeta Phi Eta. Democrat. Home: 624 College Ave Rock Mill SC 29730

REYNOLDS, RANDALL O., state legislator, dentist; b. nr. Chatham, Va., Oct. 19, 1907; s. Booker J. and Rowena (Mahan) R.; student U. Richmond, 1925-26; D.D.S., Med. Coll. Va. Sch. Dentistry, 1930; m. Billie Jean Wheeler, 1963; children—Elizabeth, Mary, Jean; 1 dau. (by previous marriage), Jane Rowe (Mrs. John B. Murray). Practice dentistry, Chatham, 1930—; mem. Va. Ho. of Dels., 1956-66, 68-76. Former pres. Planters Bank & Trust Co., 1948-52, 72—, dir., 1938—; pres. Rex Motor Co., Inc., 1956—; pres. Gretna Finance Services, Inc., 1971—. Mayor, Chatham, 1948-50; mem. council Town of Chatham, 1938-48. Trustee Hargrave Mil. Acad., 1945—, sec. bd., 1950—. Mem. ADA, Va., Piedmont dental socs., Pierre Fauchard Dental Hon. Soc., Farm Bur., Farmers Union, Psi Omega. Baptist. Mason, Lion (past local pres.). Club: Cedars Country. Home: Peach St Chatham VA 24531 Office: Main St Chatham VA 24531

REYNOLDS, ROBERT LLOYD, banker; b. Clarksburg, W.Va., Mar. 10, 1952; s. William Edward and Juanita (Cutright) R.; B.S. in B.A., W.Va. U., 1974; m. Karen Ann Hummel, Feb. 5, 1977; 1 dau., Emily Katherine. Trust rep. Wheeling (W.Va.) Dollar Bank, 1974-76, asst. trust officer, 1976-77; asst. trust officer N.C. Nat. Bank, Hickory, 1977, trust officer, 1978, asst. v.p., trust officer, 1979—. Vice pres., then pres. Catawba Valley Estate Planning Council, 1978-80; bd. dirs., treas. Community Ridge Day Care Center, 1978-79; bd. dirs. United Way, 1976-77, Soc. for Crippled Children, 1975-77, Heart Fund, 1975-77, Am. Cancer Soc., 1975-77, Boy Scouts Am., 1975-77. Named Jr. C. of C. Man of the Year, 1976. Mem. Wheeling Jr. C. of C. (bd. dirs. 1975-77, v.p. 1976-77), C. of C., Nat. Assn. Estate Planning Councils. Republican. Methodist. Club: Kiwanis. Home: 1072 16 Ave NW Hickory NC 28601 Office: PO Box 2408 Hickory NC 28601

REYNOLDS, WILLIAM JENSEN, ch. musician, hymnologist, composer; b. Atlantic, Iowa, Apr. 2, 1920; s. George Washington and Ethel (Horn) R.; student Okla. Baptist U., 1937-39; A.B., Southwest Mo. State Coll., 1942; M.S.M., Southwestern Bapt. Theol. Sem., 1945; M.M., North Tex. State U., 1946; Ed.D., George Peabody Coll. Tchrs. 1961; m. Mary Lou Robertson, July 6, 1947; children—Timothy Jensen, Kirk Mallory. Minister of music First Bapt. Ch., Ardmore, Okla., 1946-47; minister of music First Bapt. Ch., Oklahoma City, 1947-55; music editor Ch. Music dept. Bapt. Sunday Sch. Bd., Nashville, 1955-62, dir. editorial services, 1962-67, supr. music publs., 1967-71, head ch. music dept., 1971-78, music dir. So. Bapt. Conv., Houston, 1958, Phila., 1972 Portland, Oreg., 1973, Dallas, 1974, Miami Beach, 1975, Norfolk, 1976, Kansas City, 1977, Atlanta, 1978, Houston, 1979, St. Louis, 1980; guest prof. Southwestern Bapt. Theol. Sem., Ft. Worth, 1980—; music dir. Bapt. World Alliance, Rio de Janeiro, 1960, Stockholm, 1975, Toronto, 1980; music dir. Bapt. World Youth Conf., Toronto, 1958, Beirut, 1963, Berne, 1968; nat.

cons. Center for Study of So. Culture, U. Miss.; mem. hymnal com. Baptist Hymnal, 1956; chmn. hymnal com., gen. editor Baptist Hymnal, 1975; gen. editor New Broadman Hymnal, 1977; composer: Ichthus, 1971; Reaching People, 1973; Share His Word, 1973; Bold Mission, 1977; numerous choral anthems, hymn tunes, songs, etc.; dir. Sacred Harp Pub. Co. Bd. dirs. John W. Work Meml. Found. Recipient B.B. McKinney Found. award, 1960; W. Hines Sims Achievement award, 1971; North Tex. State U. Sch. Music Alumni citation, 1972. Mem. Hymn Soc. Am. (pres. 1978-80), Ch. Music Pubs. Assn. (v.p. 1973-75), ASCAP, Nat. Acad. Rec. Arts and Scis., Gospel Music Assn., So. Bapt. Ch. Music Conf., Harpeth Valley Sacred Harp Singing Assn. (pres. 1966—). Author: A Survey of Christian Hymnody, 1963; Hymns of our Faith, 1964; Christ and the Carols, 1967; Congregational Singing, 1975; Companion to the Baptist Hymnal, 1976; co-author: A Joyful Song: Christian Hymnody, 1977; compiler: Building an Effective Music Ministry, 1980. Home: 2817 White Oak Dr Nashville TN 37215

REZAC, REGINALD NOLAN, educator; b. Breckenridge, Minn., Mar. 13, 1942; s. Edward and Sophie Adaline (Fosmark) R.; B.S., Jamestown (N.D.) Coll., 1964; M.S., U. N.D., 1965; Ph.D., U. No. Colo., 1974; m. Peggy Ann Askegaard, Nov. 25, 1966; children—Leslie Ann, Robert Nolan. Internal auditor Peavey Co., Mpls., 1965-66; asst. prof. acctg. St. Cloud (Minn.) State U., 1966-75; grad. asst. U. No. Colo., Greeley, 1972-74; asso. prof. acctg., acctg. coordinator Angelo State U., San Angelo, Tex., 1975—. Vice-pres. Trinity Lutheran Sch. Parent Tchr. League, 1978-79; team mgr. Little League Baseball, 1977-79, v.p., 1978; pres. Ch. Bowling League, 1978; mem. ch. council Calvary Luth. Ch., 1975-77; auditor Civic Theater, 1979. Served with U.S. Army, 1967. St. Cloud State U. grantee, 1972-74. Mem. Am. Acctg. Assn., Beta Alpha Psi, Alpha Sigma Upsilon, Delta Pi Epsilon. Mem. editorial bd. Prentice Hall Fed. Tax Course, 1980. Home: 3805 Ingelwood St San Angelo TX 76901 Office: Dept Bus Adminstrn Angelo State U San Angelo TX 76901

RHEIN, CHARLES LYONS, educator; b. Elmhurst, Ill., June 2, 1922; s. Charles H. and Gertrude (Miller) R.; student Canal Zone Jr. Coll., 1952-53; B.S., Hofstra U., 1956, M.S., 1957; postgrad. Adelphi U., 1957, N.Y. U., 1961; m. Phyllis Beardsley Brown, June 18, 1953; children—Deborah Lee, Pamela Cathleen. Began as IBM trainee, operator, systems planner, asst. supr. Bath Iron Works Corp. (Maine), 1944-48; police officer, photographer, investigator City of Bath, 1948-49; IBM asst. supr. U.S. VA, White River Junction, Vt., 1949-50; IBM equipment operator, accounting clk. Sperry Gyroscope Corp., Great Neck, N.Y., 1953-55; grad. asst. Hofstra U., 1955-56; tchr. Union Free Sch., Uniondale, N.Y., 1955-57; dir. census and transp. Central Sch. Dist., Plainview, N.Y., 1957-59; dir., owner Ednl. Data Processing Corp., Massapequa, N.Y., 1958-62, mgr., 1962-64; data processing mgr. Union Free Sch. Dist. 22, Farmingdale, N.Y., 1960-65; dir. research and data processing Bd. Coop. Ednl. Services, West Nyack, N.Y., 1965-76; asst. dir. Lower Hudson Regional Computer Center, Elmsford, N.Y., 1976-77; ret., 1977; cons. Rhein DA-PRO Cons., Kings Park, N.Y., 1963—; author, pub. bi-monthly newsletter Charlie's Random Happenings, 1979—. Served with USNR, 1942-43; with AUS, 1950-53. Mem. NEA, Am. Assn. Sch. Adminstrs., Data Processing Mgmt. Assn. (internat. dir. 1960—, div. chmn. 1966-67), Assn. for Ednl. Data Systems, Soc. for Automation in Bus. Edn., N.Y. State Tchrs. Assn., N.Y. State Assn. Sch. Bus. Ofcls., N.Y. State Attendance Tchrs. Assn., Am. Legion, Nat. Campers and Hikers Assn. Christian Scientist. Mason. Odd Fellow. Contbr. articles to profl. jours.; mem. manuscript rev. bd. Data Mgmt. mag. Home: 5016 Silk Oak Dr Sarasota FL 33582

RHEINSCHELD, JOHN HENRY, health care adminstr.; b. Logan, Ohio, Apr. 1, 1939; s. Harold Eugene and Charlotte Ernestine (Foltz) R.; student U. Md., 1957-60; A.B., Ohio U., 1963, M.A., 1967; M.P.A., U. So. Calif., 1977—; m. Mary Jo Stepp, Mar. 17, 1973. Enlisted, U.S. Air Force, 1957, resigned 1960, commd. 2nd lt., 1964, advanced through grades to maj., 1975; liaison officer Chelsea (Mass.) Naval Hosp., 1966-67; adminstr. USAF Hosp., Phan Rang, Viet Nam, 1967-68; asso. adminstr. USAF Hosp., London, 1968-70; asst. chief Tng. Ops. Div., Sch. Health Care Scis., Sheppard AFB, Wichita Falls, Tex., 1970-71; chief tng. div. (med.), Hdqrs. Air Tng. Command, Randolph AFB, San Antonio, 1971-72; dir. allied health programs Community Coll. of Air Force, 1973, exec. officer Med. Inspection div., 1973-75, comdr. med. squadron David Grant USAF Med. Center, Travis AFB, Calif., 1975-77, asso. adminstr., 1977-78; dir. health edn. and tng. Hdqrs. Air Tng. Command, Randolph AFB, Tex., 1978—; tng. fellow Ohio U., 1963-64, lectr., 1964-66. Decorated Bronze Star medal, Meritorious Service medal, Air Force Commendation medal. Mem. Am. Coll. Hosp. Adminstrs., Am. Hosp. Assn., Assn. Allied Health Professions, Am. Soc. Pub. Adminstrn., Am. Acad. Polit. and Social Sci. Democrat. Author: Systematic Development of Teaching Competency in the Health Professions; contbr. to Cases in Public Management, 1979. Home: 12831 Country Ridge San Antonio TX 78216 Office: Hdqrs Air Tng Command Randolph AFB TX 78148

RHENWRICK, LAFRANCE, mfg. ofcl.; b. Gary, Ind., Nov. 20, 1953; s. Allen Wesley and Mattie Camilla (Burrell) R.; B.S. in Indsl. Mgmt., Purdue U., 1974. Material handling mgr. Procter & Gamble, Albany, Ga., 1975-76, prodn. mgr., 1976-77, employee relations and orgnl. mgr., 1977—. Active Albany Urban League. Mem. Am. Mgmt. Assn., Kappa Alpha Psi. Home: 2206 Oxford St Albany GA 31707 Office: Route 19 Albany GA 31705

RHETT, HARRY MOORE, JR., pvt. investor; b. Huntsville, Ala., Mar. 3, 1912; s. Harry Moore and Marie Louise (Rison) R.; A.B., Washington and Lee U., 1935; postgrad. Harvard U., 1935-37; m. Sharon Barbour, June 14, 1952; children—Louise Rison, Harry Moore, William Warren Barbour, Leslie Carrere. Asst. underwriter, spl. agt. Accident & Casualty Ins. Co., N.Y.C., 1937-39, Los Angeles, 1939-41; asst. to pres. Rison Banking Co., Huntsville, 1946-48; pvt. investor, Huntsville, 1948—; dir. First Ala. Bank of Huntsville, First Ala. Bancshares, Inc., Montgomery, Gen. Computer Services, Huntsville, Huntsville Indsl. Assos. Pres., Huntsville-Madison County Indsl. Devel. Assn., 1959-61; chmn. Huntsville Hosp. Found., 1978—; trustee U. Ala.-Huntsville Found., 1970—; trustee, chmn. Randolph Sch., 1972—; mem. adv. com. Redstone Arsenal U.S. Army, 1955—; chmn. civilian adv. com. George C. Marshall Space Flight Center, 1960-73. Served with U.S. Army, 1941-46. Decorated Army Commendation medal with oak leaf cluster. Mem. Huntsville Madison County C. of C. (pres. 1952, Outstanding Citizen award 1973). Democrat. Episcopalian. Clubs: Huntsville Rotary (pres. 1952), Harvard, Chatham Beach and Tennis (pres. 1977—), Nat. Steeplechase and Hunt Assn., Masters of Foxhounds Assn., Byrd Spring Rod and Gun, Phi Delta Theta. Home: 603 Adams St SE Huntsville AL 35801 Office: 200 W Court Sq Huntsville AL 35801

RHODARMER, SUE HAYNES, psychologist; b. Waynesville, N.C., Feb. 25, 1924; d. Allen Thurman and Alice Marie (Hawkins) H.; M.A., Middle Tenn. State U., 1970; children—Ricki Rhodarmer Tigert, Nancy Rhodarmer Allen, William Kim Rhodarmer. Tchr., elementary schs. Guam, Marianas Island, 1950-51; supr. kindergarten, Westover AFB, Holyoke, Mass., 1952-53; supr. kindergarten, child care center Smyra (Tenn.) AFB, 1955-67; psychol. examiner Mental Health Center, San Angelo, Tex., 1971-72; asst. prof. psychology Cleve. State Community Coll. (Tenn.), 1972—. Mem. adv. bd. Bradley County Mental Health Center, Cleve.; counselor, Contact, Cleveland; dir. Girl Scouts Camps, Smyrna, Tenn., 1954-57; bd. dirs. Hiwassee Mental Health Center. Mem. Am., Tenn. psychol. assns., Am. Mgmt. Assn., NEA, Tenn., E. Tenn. edn. assns. Democrat. Methodist. Clubs: Order Eastern Star, Order Amaranth. Home: 2330 Timber Trace Pl Cleveland TN 37311 Office: Box 1205 Cleveland TN 37311

RHODES, BETTY JEAN, nurse; b. Fulton, Ky., June 30, 1935; d. Carl and Mary A. (Willis) Johnson; student Murray State U., 1954, U. Ky., 1955; A.A. in Nursing, U. Tenn., 1973, B.S. in Nursing, 1980; m. Bobby J. Rhodes, July 5, 1953; children—Melody, Barry. Staff nurse Obion County Gen. Hosp., Union City, Tenn., 1973-75, head nurse, 1975-78, supr., 1978-79; with Comprehensive Nursing Services, Inc., St. Louis, 1979—; lectr. on death and dying. Mem. Profl. Traveling Nurses Assn., Am., Tenn. nurses assns., Nurses Assn. of Am. Coll. Obstetricians and Gynecologists, Assn. Critical Care Nurses, Make Today Count. Democrat. Presbyterian. Home: Route 1 Water Valley KY 42085

RHODES, EDWIN FRANKLIN, mfg. co. exec.; b. Mishawaka, Ind., Oct. 24, 1921; s. Edward R. and Edna (Arnold) R.; B.S., N.C. State U., 1940; m. Helen Hickman, Sept. 29, 1952; children—Charles, Mary Lisa (dec.), Christopher, Thomas, Cynthia Rhodes Shutt, Priscilla, Eric, Stephanie. Installationist engr. Otis Elevator Co., 1940-41; tchr. pub. schs., Mishawaka, 1941-42, engr., tool engr., spl. project engr., specialist, purchasing agt. Dodge Mfg. Co. div. Reliance Electric, Mishawaka, 1942-58, mgr. purchases, 1958-69; mgr. ops. controls, spl. asst. to pres. Baldor Electric Co., Fort Smith, Ark., St. Louis, Columbus, Miss., Charleston, S.C., Westville, Okla., 1969-80; mng. dir. Southwestern Die Casting, Boehm Mfg. Mem. C. of C. Methodist. Mason (32 deg., Shriner). Home: 4112 S 35th St Fort Smith AR 72903 Died Jan. 16, 1980.

RHODES, ERIC FOSTER, editor, pub.; b. Luray, Va., Feb. 5, 1927; s. Wallace Keith and Bertha (Foster) R.; A.A., George Washington U., 1949, A.B., 1950, M.A., 1952, Ed.D., 1967; m. Barbara Ellen Henson, Oct. 19, 1946; children—Roxanne Jane, Laurel Lee; m. 2d, Lorraine Endresen, July 29, 1972. Tchr. high sch., Arlington, Va., 1950-52; counselor Washington Lee High Sch., Arlington, 1952-53, dir. publs., 1953-54, chmn. dept. English, 1954-55; exec. sec. Arlington Edn. Assn., 1952-53, Montgomery County (Md.) Edn. Assn., 1955-57; lectr. edn. George Washington U., 1955-60, professorial lectr., 1972—; salary cons. NEA, Washington, 1957-58, asst. dir. membership div., 1958-60, dir. N.Y. regional office, N.Y.C., 1960-64; ednl. cons. Ednl. Research Services, White Plains, N.Y., 1964-65; pres. Ednl. Service Bur., Inc., Arlington, 1965-72, chmn. bd., 1972—; pres. Negotiations Consultations Services, Inc., 1968-80, EFR Corp., 1972—; exec. dir. Nat. Assn. Edn. Negotiators, 1971—; cons. Va. Dept. Community Colls., 1965-78; lectr. edn. Frostburg (Md.) State Coll., 1967-68; vice chancellor Va. Community Coll. System, 1970-71. Mem. Civil Rights Commn. Franklin Twp. (N.J.), 1962-64, Franklin Twp. Bd. Edn., 1964-65; mem. adv. bd. Keep Am. Beautiful, 1964-75, nat. chmn., 1968. Served with U.S. Army, 1945-47. Mem. Am. Assn. Sch. Adminstrs., NEA, Edn. Press Assn., Phi Delta Kappa (chpt. pres. 1959-60). Fed. Schoolmen's Club, N.Y. Schoolmasters Club. Club: Lions. Author: Negotiating Salaries; editor: Adminstrv. Leadership, Salary and Merit. Home: 10803 N Oregon Circle Tampa FL 33612 Office: 1400 Massachusetts Ave New Port Richey FL 33552

RHODES, MERRILL JAY, JR., athletic dir.; b. Balt., Apr. 13, 1949; s. Merrill Jay and Anna Marie (Willoughby) R.; B.A. in Bus. Adminstrn., Towson State U., 1971; M.B.A., Winthrop Coll., 1976; m. Sandra Jean Bailey, Dec. 21, 1972; children—Jason C., Jonathan M. Coach, tchr. Gaffney (S.C.) Day Sch., 1971-72; coach, resident dir. Montreat (N.C.)-Anderson Coll., summers 1970-73, 75; counselor, asst. dir. dining service Camp Ridgecrest (N.C.) for Boys; dir. athletics, basketball coach, asso. dean students Limestone Coll., Gaffney, 1973—. Active Youth Fellowship, United Methodist Ch., Gaffney, 1973—. Mem. Nat. Assn. Intercoll. Athletics Basketball Coaches Assn., Nat. Assn. Intercoll. Athletics Athletic Dirs. Assn. Democrat. Address: Limestone Coll Gaffney SC 29340

RHODES, PATRICK L., counselor; b. Santa Barbara, Calif., Mar. 17, 1946; s. George and Edwina (Burruss) R.; B.A., Guilford Coll., 1972; M.S., Madison Coll., 1974. Dir. behavior modification Youth Rehab. Center, Roanoke, Va., 1972-73; asst. prof. Tidewater Coll., Portsmouth, Va., 1974-77; fellow U. So. Miss., Hattiesburg, 1977-78; with U. N.C., Greensboro, 1978—. Served with AUS, 1968-70. Mem. Va. Assn. Specialists in Group Work (exec. council), Profl. Counselors Assn., Mensa, Phi Delta Kappa, Psi Chi, Lambda Alpha Epsilon. Office: Box 5682 Tate St Sta Greensboro NC 27403

RHODES, PHILIP HAMILTON, JR., electronic funds transfer co. exec.; b. Norwood, Mass., Oct. 28, 1933; s. Philip Hamilton and Lillian Winn R.; B.S. in Elec. Engring., Ind. Inst. Tech., 1959; M.B.A., So. Meth. U., 1972; m. Tadako Takahashi, Mar. 10, 1955; children—Philip Hamilton III, Henry Winn. Project engr. Collins Radio Co., Dallas, 1959-69; mfg. program mgr. Recognition Equipment Co., Dallas, 1970-72, program mgr. Bell Helicopter/Textron, Hurst, Tex., 1972-79; corporate sec., dir. Nat. Transaction Network, Inc., Richardson, Tex., 1979—; mem. faculty Richland Jr. Coll.; bus. and fin. cons. Served with USAF, 1953-57. Mem. Am. Mgmt. Assn., Assn. Mfg. Engrs., Am. Radio Relay League, So. Meth. U. Alumni Assn., Ind. Inst. Tech. Alumni Assn., Beta Gamma Sigma. Republican. Congregationalist. Home: 610 LaSalle Dr Richardson TX 75081 Office: Nat Transaction Network Inc 725 S Central Expressway Richardson TX 75081

RHUDY, JOHN ROBERT, retail shoe chain exec.; b. Moscow, Idaho, Nov. 12, 1943; s. John Harvey and Jean Graham R.; B.A. in Bus. Adminstrn., Davidson (N.C.) Coll., 1966; m. Cynthia Adams Chambers, Aug. 29, 1965; children—Tanya, Crista, Ty. Inventory mgr. Hanes Knitwear, Winston-Salem, N.C., 1969-70; nat. dir. sales and distbn. Huntley of York, Ltd., York, S.C., 1970-71; gen. mgr. Distbn. Technology Inc., Charlotte, N.C., 1971-76; v.p. distbn. Pic N Pay Stores, Inc., Charlotte, 1977—. Served to capt. U.S. Army, 1966-69. Mem. Am. Inst. Indsl. Engrs., Volume Footwear Retailers Assn. (vice chmn. Footwear Traffic and Distbn. Council), Nat. Council Phys. Distbn. Mgmt., Charlotte Traffic Club, Delta Nu Alpha. Republican. Presbyterian. Home: 6351 Forest Way Dr Charlotte NC 28212 Office: PO Box 34000 Charlotte NC 28261

RHYS, DAVID HALL, educator; b. Galman, Argentina, Oct. 2, 1915; s. David Ivor and Edith Elizabeth (Hall) R.; came to U.S., 1964, naturalized, 1974; M.A. in Edn., Andrews U., 1965; Ph.D., U. Calif. at Riverside, 1976; m. Adela Chaij, July 11, 1938; children—Nidia Rhys Vyhmeister, Myrtha Rhys Pizarro, Carlos. Prin., Fla. Acad., Buenos Aires, Argentina, 1938-42; dean of men River Plate Coll., Puiggari, Argentina, 1943-45, dean of studies, 1945-54; prin. Uruguay Acad., Montevideo, 1955-59, Coll. Adventista de Chile, Chillán, 1960-64; instr. in Spanish, Andrews U., Berrien Springs, Mich., 1964-66; academic dean Coll. Union, Lima, Peru, 1966-71; tchr. asst. U. Calif. at Riverside, 1972-73; instr. San Bernardino Valley Coll., 1973-75; dir. dept. edn. InterAm. div., Coral Gables, Fla., 1975—; Trustee Montemorelos U., 1975—; bd. regents Gen. Conf., Washington, 1975—. Fed. grantee, 1973-74; OAS fellow, 1975. Mem. Argentine Astronomic Assn., Am. Assn. Geographers, Am. Soc. Photogrammetry, Nat. Geog. Soc. Home: 1371 SW 40th Ave Miami FL 33134

RICCI, FRED JOSEPH, elec. engr.; b. N.Y.C., July 1, 1939; s. Fred Q. and Mary (Vaccaro) R.; A.A.S., W. Community Coll., 1959; B.S., Mich. State U., 1962; M.S., Newark Coll., 1966; Ph.D., Cath. U. Am., 1973; m. Mary Jo Guadagno, June 5, 1965; children—Ferdinand, Dante. Tech. aid Bell Telephone Labs., N.Y.C., 1959-60, mem. tech. staff, 1962-63; cons. Electronic Assos., Inc., West Long Branch, N.J., 1963-69; asst. prof. depts. elec. engring. and physics Monmouth (N.J.) Coll., 1963-69; mem. tech. staff Mitre Corp., McLean, Va., 1969-71; staff engr. HRB-Singer, Inc., Reston, Va., 1971-72; with Def. Communications Agy., Reston, 1972-77; adv. engr., scientist Fed. Systems div. IBM, Arlington, Va., 1976—; chmn. Washington Bio-Med. Engring. Group; asso. prof. George Washington U., Washington, 1970—, Va. Poly. Inst. and State U., Blacksburg, 1970-77; cons. in field. Mem. community services bd. Fairfax-Falls Ch., 1979—; prin. Sunday sch. St. John's Ch., 1969-71; v.p. Navy PTA, 1974-76; bd. dirs. Reston Cath. Community, 1976-77; del. Dem. Party, 10th Dist., 1977—; del. USSR Popov Soc., 1976. NSF grantee, 1967-69. Mem. IEEE (sec. switching com.; editor Communications mag. 1979—), Am. Mgmt. Assn., Vale Home Demonstration Club (v.p. 1971—). Club: Internat. Town and Country (fin. com.). Contbr. articles to profl. jours.; editor IEEE Jour., 1978—; author: Analog/Logic Computer Programming, 1972. Home: 11421 Vale Rd Oakton VA 22124 Office: 1701 N Fort Myer Dr Arlington VA 22209

RICCI, SERAPHINE THERESA, nun, nurse; b. Rimini, Italy, Apr. 29, 1936; d. Oreste and Adele (Melucci) R.; student Incarnate Word Coll., San Antonio, 1968, Centenary Coll., Shreveport, La., 1968-69; R.N., Med. Center Nursing Sch., Shreveport, 1971; came to U.S., 1962, naturalized, 1969. Joined Sisters of O.L.S., 1953; dir. health care service, asst. adminstr. Holy Angels Sch. for Retarded Children, Shreveport, 1975—; superior Holy Angels O.L.S., Shreveport, 1977—. Roman Catholic. Home and Office: Holy Angels Sch Retarded Children 10450 Ellerbe Rd Shreveport LA 71106

RICE, CHARLES DREW, credit bur. ofcl.; b. Vero Beach, Fla., Dec. 9, 1953; s. Byronn and Rosa Ramona (Monroe) R.; student Albany (Ga.) Jr. Coll., 1971-73, Ga. State U., 1973-75. Mail clk. Dougherty County, Albany, 1971-73; with So. Bell Telephone Co., Atlanta, 1973-74; teleprocessing trainee Equifax Inc., Atlanta, 1974-75, asst. mgr. logistics, 1975-78, mgr. teleprocessing, 1978-79, mgr. telecommunications and logistics, 1979—; speaker on telecommunications, 1977—. Mem. Southeastern Telecommunications Assn., Telecomputer Applications Group (program chmn.), Pi Kappa Phi. Democrat. Methodist. Home: 4545 Northside Pkwy Apt 17-M Atlanta GA 30339 Office: 1600 Peachtree St Atlanta GA 30302

RICE, DANIEL WEBSTER, III, social worker; b. Bennettsville, S.C., Apr. 6, 1951; s. Daniel Webster and Mae Catherine (Pate) R.; B.S.W., East Carolina U., 1973; postgrad. U. N.C., 1979—; m. Johnnee Clarkin, Mar. 29, 1975; 1 son, Jonathan Daniel. Program supr. N.C. Dept. Corrections, Boone, 1973; youth coordinator Woodmen of World Life Ins. Soc. N.C., Kinston, 1974-76; social worker Bapt. Children's Homes of N.C., Inc., Kinston, 1976—. Deacon, Spilman Meml. Baptist Ch., 1975—, vice chmn. bd. deacons, 1977, tchr. Sunday sch., 1975—. supt. Sunday sch. dept., 1978-79, chmn. youth com., 1976, mem. pastor selection com., 1977, 79. Mem. Nat. Assn. Social Workers, E. Carolina U. Alumni Assn. Republican. Clubs: Lions (2d v.p. 1979-80, sec. 1977-79), Woodmen of World (chmn. bd. dirs. N.C. 1979—, chmn. Bright Belt dist. assn. 1978-80), Pirate. Home: 706 Parrott Ave Kinston NC 28501 Office: Bapt Children's Homes NC Inc Route 2 Box 48 Kinston NC 28501

RICE, DAVID FLEMING, state ofcl.; b. Hawkinsville, Ga., Aug. 30, 1907; s. Alexander John and Janie (Fleming) R.; B.S. in Civil Engring., Ga. Inst. Tech., 1929; m. Erlyne Lanier, July 22, 1934; children—David Lanier, Robert Fleming; m. 2d, Anagene P. Bartram, Jan. 29, 1966. Dept. head Sears Roebuck & Co., Atlanta, 1929-37; owner, operator Ellen Rice Restaurant, 1937-48, Town House Restaurant, 1948-54; apt. builder; officer various corps. Mem. Ga. Bd. Edn., Atlanta, 1961-76, vice chmn., 1970—; bd. regents Univ. System Ga., Atlanta, 1954-61. Mem. Am. Assn. Sch. Adminstrs. (mem. mission to study edn. in Soviet Union 1969—), Am. Vocat. Assn., N.E.A., Ga. Edn. Assn., Navy League U.S., Atlanta Restaurant Assn. (pres. 1945-46, 52), Internat. Platform Assn., Nat. Assn. State Bds. Edn. (v.p. 1966-67, 67-68), Pi Delta Epsilon, Sigma Nu. Episcopalian. Clubs: Rotary, Atlanta Athletic. Address: The Habersham Apt 813 3060 Pharr Court North NW Atlanta GA 30305

RICE, HOWARD GENE, bus. exec.; b. Arkansas City, Kans., June 6, 1928; s. Otho Paul and Harriet E. (Howard) R.; B.S., Okla. State U., 1953; m. Barbara June Kitterman, Oct. 30, 1948; children—Paula Joanne, Mark Alan. Vice pres. Goodner Van Co., Tulsa, 1947-57; owner Andy Jansen Co., Tulsa, 1957-60; chief engr. Gardner Hotel Supply Co., Dallas, 1960-67; owner, pres. H.G. Rice & Co., Inc., Irving, Tex., 1967—. Registered profl. engr., Okla., La., Tex. Mem. Am. Soc. Heating, Refrigeration and Air Conditioning Engrs., Food Service Consultants Soc. Internat. Methodist. Club: Masons. Patentee in field. Office: 114 E 2d St Irving TX 75060

RICE, IVAN GLENN, gas turbine engr.; b. Phoenix, July 24, 1924; s. Harvey Clifford and Charlotte Abegail (Burre) R.; student Phoenix Coll., 1946-47; B.S.M.E. with high distinction, U. Ariz., 1950; Carolyn Ruth Keyes, June 16, 1950; children—Thomas Glenn, Kathleen Elizabeth, James Nelson. With Gen. Electric Co., 1950-69, gas turbine application engr., for S.W. U.S.A., Houston, 1957-64, regional turbine engr. for U.S., Can. and Mexico, Houston, 1964-69; mgr. nat. and worldwide mktg. DeLaval Turbine Inc., Houston, 1969-74; cons. engr., Spring, Tex., 1974—. Mem. adv. com. Turbo-Machinery Symposium, Tex. A and M U., 1972—; mem. planning com. First Offshore Tech. Conf., Houston, 1969. Pres. Spring High Sch. P.T.A., 1972-73; mem.-at-large Sam Houston Area council Boy Scouts Am. Chmn. Harris County Republican Precinct 110, 1976-78. Served with Transp. Corps, AUS, 1943-46; ETO. Recipient Mgmt. awards Gen. Electric Co., 1955, 61, 66, Breakthrough 60 award Gen. Electric Co., 1960, Scouters award Boy Scouts Am., 1966. Fellow ASME (Meritorious Service award 1968, gas turbine div. commendation 1971, chmn. S. Tex. sect. 1975-76, chmn. div. gas turbine 1976-77, Council award 1977, 80, Centennial medallion 1980); mem. Nat., Tex. socs. profl. engrs., Soc. Petroleum Engrs., AAAS, Houston Engring. and Sci. Soc., Pi Mu Epsilon, Phi Kappa Phi, Tau Beta Pi, Pi Tau Sigma. Republican. Methodist (adminstrv. bd. 1975-76). Contbr. articles on gas turbines to profl. jours. Patentee gas turbine heat rate control. Home: 1007 Lynwood St Spring TX 77373 Office: PO Box 233 Spring TX 77373

RICE, MATILDE MCLAUGHLIN, nursing educator; b. Everett, Mass., Aug. 12, 1921; d. David James and Beatrice Ann (Scacciavillani) McLaughlin; grad. Mass. Meml. Hosp. Sch. Nursing, 1943; B.S.N.Ed., Boston U., 1948; M.Ed., U. N.C., Greensboro, 1970; m. Moses Edward Rice, Jr., Sept. 5, 1948; children—David, John

Carroll, James Newkirk, Mary Bea. Pvt. duty nurse New Eng. Bapt. Hosp., Mass. Meml. Hosp., Mass. Gen. Hosp., Boston, 1946-48; inservice educator Mass. Meml. Hosp., 1946-48; instr. med.-surg. nursing Med. Coll. Va., Richmond, 1949-53; instr. ARC, Mullins, S.C., 1953-60; relief office nurse pvt. physician's offices, Mullins, 1953-64; substitute tchr. sci. Mullins High Sch., 1960-65; instr. Spl. Tng. for Econ. Progress, State S.C., 1964-66; instr. med.-surg. nursing U. S.C. Sch. Gen. Studies, asso. degree program, Florence, 1966-68; instr. nursing and pharmacology Guilford Tech. Inst., Jamestown, N.C., 1968-73; instr. U. N.C. Sch. Nursing, Greensboro, 1972-74, 74—; nurse cons. Internat. Assn. Laryngectomies, 1977. Bd. dirs. Greensboro Cancer Soc., Cancer Expositions, 1975-77; bd. mem. Eastern Music Festival Aux. Served to 1st lt., Nurses Corps, U.S. Army, 1945-46. Am. Cancer Soc. grantee, 1978. Mem. Internat. Assn. Laryngectomies, Am. Speech and Hearing Assn., Am. Nurses Assn., AMA Aux., N.C. Nurses Assn., East West Acad. Healing Arts, Guilford County Med. Aux., Mass. Meml. Hosp. Nurses Assn., Boston U. Alumni Assn., U. N.C. Greensboro Alumni Assn., U. N.C. Greensboro Mus. Arts Guild, Greensboro Artists League, N.C. Watercolor Soc., Democrat. Clubs: Greensboro Tennis Assn., High Point Artists Guild. Home: 1703 W Market St Greensboro NC 27412 Office: 1000 Spring Garden Greensboro NC 27412

RICE, MAURICE RICHARDSON, mfg. co. exec.; b. Henrico County, Va., June 26, 1940; s. Clifford A. and Sarah Catherine (Moody) R.; B.Com., U. Richmond, 1971; postgrad. in bank adminstrn. U. Wis., 1973; m. Betty Ann Loving, Sept. 10, 1960; children—Patricia Nanette, Michael Scott. Staff acct. Reynolds Metal Co., Richmond, Va., 1963-67; gen. acctg. supr. David M. Lea & Co., Inc., Richmond, 1967-69; asst. controller, v.p., bank group controller, v.p. mgmt. acctg. United Va. Bankshares, Inc., Richmond, 1969-78; dir. adminstrn. Baker Equipment Engring. Co., Inc., Richmond, 1978—. Deacon, tchr. Sunday Sch., Bapt. Ch., 1975—. Served with USAF, 1963. Mem. Fin. Execs. Inst. (past v.p. Va.; sec., treas., dir.). Home: 1627 Westcastle Dr Richmond VA 23233 Office: 1700 Summit Ave Richmond VA 23260

RICE, RONALD JAMES, hosp. adminstr.; b. Springfield, Mo., Feb. 5, 1944; s. Glen Elwood and Alice Jeanett (Robinson) R.; B.S.B.A., Central Mo. State U., 1966, M.A.B.A., 1969, specialist degree, 1972; m. Paula Edde, June 3, 1974. Dir. personnel Methodist Hosp., Jacksonville, Fla., 1972-73, adminstrv. officer, 1973-74; asst. adminstr. Greater Orange Park (Fla.) Hosp., 1974-75, asso. exec. dir., 1975-76; adminstr. Cathedral Health and Rehab. Center, Jacksonville, 1977-79, Nassau Gen. Hosp., Fernandina Beach, Fla., 1980—; cons., tchr. in field. Served with U.S. Army, 1967-69, Decorated Army Commendation medal; lic. nursing home adminstr., Fla. Mem. Am. Coll. Hosp. Adminstrs., Am. Hosp. Assn., Am. Soc. Personnel Adminstrn., Fla. Hosp. Assn., Am. Mktg. Assn., Fedn. Am. Hosps., Fla. Assn. Rehab., Orange Park Jaycees (v.p. membership), Tau Kappa Epsilon. Democrat. Mem. Unity School of Christianity. Clubs: Sea Ray Boat (sec.), Rotary. Home: 1744 Horton Dr Orange Park FL 32073 Office: 1700 E Lime St Fernandina Beach FL 32034

RICE, STANLEY IRVING, JR., mgmt. co. exec.; b. Pittsfield, Mass., May 21 1930; s. Stanley Irving and Katrina (Davies) R.; B.A., U. Md., 1949. Vice pres. mktg. Allied Audio Assn., Washington, 1959-62; news dir. Star Broadcasting Co., Fredericksburg, Va., 1962-67; sales mgr. Morrison Industries, 1967-71, Marine div. Browning Arms Co., Ft. Walton Beach, Fla., 1971-73; pres. K.R. Stanick, Inc., Atlanta, 1974—. Served with AUS, 1946-59. Decorated Silver Star, Bronze Star with V, Purple Heart. Mem. Community Assn. Inst., Am. Legion. Club: Stafford (Va.) Lions (v.p.). Office: 6755 Peachtree Industrial Blvd Suite 209 Atlanta GA 30360

RICE, WILLIAM VAUGHN, JR., air force officer, educator; b. Hiawassee, Ga., Dec. 5, 1926; s. William Vaughn and Anne Julia (O'Quinn) R.; B.S., U.S. Mil. Acad., 1949; M.B.A., USAF Inst. Tech., 1958; Ph.D., La. State U., 1974; m. Claire L. Mikulin, Aug. 24, 1950; children—Michael D., William Vaughn III, Tamara Anne. Commd. 2d lt. USAF, 1949, advanced through grades to col., 1967; air crew mem. SAC, 1950-57; ednl. adviser Republic of Korea Air Acad., Seoul, 1958-59; asst. prof. aerospace studies La. State U., 1960-66; sr. instr. Acad. Instr. Sch., Air U., Montgomery, Ala., 1967-68, chief, labor-mgmt. relations div., 1969-75; instr. econs. Troy State U. Adult Edn. Program, 1966-75; asst. prof. econs. and mgmt. U. Houston at Clear Lake City, Tex., 1975-78, asso. prof., 1978—, also dir. Center for Econ. Edn. Mem. Am., So. econ. assns., Air Force Assn., Omicron Delta Epsilon. Mason. Author: Introduction to Air Force Labor Relations, Vol. I, 1971. Contbr. articles to profl. jours. Address: 2700 Bay Area Blvd Houston TX 77058

RICE, WILLIAM YNGVE, petroleum distbg. co. exec.; b. Tyler, Tex., June 22, 1930; s. John Herbert and Mamie Lucille (Horton) R.; B.B.A. in Mgmt., Baylor U., 1951; m. Rachel Gallenkemp, Jan. 26, 1952; children—William Yngve III, John Robin, Drew. With accounting dept. Tex. Eastman Co., 1951-58; partner in petroleum product sales co. for Cities Service Oil Co., 1958-70; pres., dir. Eastex Oil Co. Inc., Longview, Tex., 1970-79; v.p., dir. Magnum Corp., Longview, 1980—; chmn. bd., dirs. Town North Nat. Bank, Longview; dir. Southland Savs. Assn., Longview, Amectran, Inc., Dallas, Computer Funds Inc., Dallas. Commr. City of Longview, 1969—, mayor, 1970-71, 76-77; vice chmn. East Tex. Council Govts., 1970. Recipient Longview Outstanding Citizen of Yr. award, 1971; Community Achievement award Phillips Petroleum Co., 1975. Mem. Tex. Oil Marketers Assn., Nat. Oil Jobber Council, Longview C. of C., East Tex. C. of C. (dir.), Delta Sigma Pi. Clubs: Longview Rotary; Dallas-Caddo; Oak Forest Country; Baylor-Longview, Masons. Home: 1308 Inverness St Longview TX 75601 Office: PO Box 1406 Longview TX 75606

RICE, WINSTON EDWARD, lawyer; b. Shreveport, La., Feb. 22, 1946; s. Winston Churchill and Margaret (Coughlin) R.; student Centenary Coll. La., 1967; J.D., La. State U., 1971; m. Barbara Reily Gay, Apr. 16, 1977; 1 son, Andrew Hynes; children by previous marriage—Winston Hobson, Christian MacTaggart. Cons. geologist Crosby Mineral Co., Gulfport, Miss., 1968-70; admitted to La. bar; partner firm Phelps, Dunbar, Marks, Claverie & Sims, New Orleans, 1971—; instr. law La. State U., Baton Rouge, 1970-71. Com. worker Sta. WYES, pub. TV, New Orleans, 1975-77. Mem. Am. (vice-chmn. com. maritime ins. law 1979—), La., New Orleans bar assns., New Orleans Assn. Def. Counsel, Maritime Law Assn. U.S., Assn. Average Adjusters U.S., Order of Coif, Phi Delta Phi, Phi Kappa Phi, Kappa Alpha. Republican. Episcopalian. Clubs: Mariners (treas. 1974-75, 78-79, sec. 1975-76, v.p. 1976-77, pres. 1977-78), Boston, Stratford, New Orleans Lawn Tennis, Petroleum (New Orleans). Asso. editor La. Law Rev., 1970-71. Office: 1300 Hibernia Bank Bldg New Orleans LA 70112

RICH, FLOYD, software engr.; b. Union County, Ga., Oct. 26, 1932; s. Harry Benjamin and Mamie Lilian (Deaver) R.; A.A., Allan Handcock Jr. Coll., 1971; m. Annie Ruth Williams, Sept. 27, 1952; children—Deborrah Lynn, Michael Anthony. Enlisted U.S. Air Force, 1951, advanced through grades to master sgt., 1969; electronics technician and instr.; ret., 1971; field engr., software engr. Sperry Univac, Lompoc, Calif., 1971-79; software engr. Gen. Electric Co., Port Orange, Fla., 1979—; mem. internat. adv. panel Electronics Mag., 1976-77; instr., cons. USAF Satellite Tracking Center, 1966-71. Democrat. Baptist. Club: Kiwanis. (pres.). Home: 475 Spruceview St Port Orange FL 32019 Office: PO Box 2500 Daytona FL 32015

RICH, HELEN WALL (MRS. ARTHUR L. RICH), educator; b. Chester, S.C., May 4, 1912; d. George Addison and Georgia (Hardin) Wall; student Queen's Coll., 1930-32; B.S. summa cum laude, Catawba Coll., 1934 diploma in piano Juilliard Sch. Music, 1938; diplomas Christiansen Choral Sch., 1950, 51; m. Arthur Lowndes Rich, July 26, 1934; children—Arthur Lowndes, Ruth Anne. Instr. music Catawba Coll.; Salisbury, N.C., 1934-43; organist Mercer U., Macon, Ga., 1944-50, asst. prof. music, 1950-74, emeritus prof., 1974—; organ recitalist throughout Southeast; v.p. Tudor Apts., Atlanta, 1960-68; sec.-treas. Richelieu Apts., Macon, 1955-68. Mem. Federated Music Clubs (chmn. scholarship contest), Ga. Piano Tchrs. Guild, Nat. Assn. Schs. Music (asso.), Am. Coll. and U. Concert Mgrs. Assn. (asso.), Cardinal Key Soc. Mercer U. (hon.), Delta Omicron. Club: Morning Music (dir.) (Macon). Home: 369 Candler Dr Macon GA 31204

RICH, ISADORE ALEXANDER, educator; b. Montgomery, Ala., Nov. 22; s. Lydia Lois R.; B.S., Ala. State U., 1967, M.Ed., 1970; postgrad. U. Ga., 1971, Ky. State U., 1974-77. Tchr. pub. schs., Ga., 1967-69, Ala., 1971-72; counselor Stillman Coll., Tuscaloosa, Ala., 1970; counselor, instr. edn. dept. Kentucky State U., Frankfort, 1973—; counselor Upward Bound program, Frankfort, Ky., 1973-76. Recipient Service award Stillman Coll., 1972, State of Ky., 1973, 74, 75, 76, 77; named Tchr. of Yr. in Ga. State C. of C., 1969. Mem. NEA, Am. Personnel and Guidance Assn., Phi Delta Kappa, Alpha Phi Alpha, Alpha Phi Omega. Episcopalian. Home and Office: Ky State U PO Box 148 Frankfort KY 40601

RICH, ROBERT CARROLL, editor; b. Kincaid, Ill., Apr. 8, 1930; s. Charles Rice and Fannie Ruth (Shreve) R.; A.B., U. Chgo., 1953; M.A., So. Ill. U., 1957; m. Anne Beckman, June 12, 1950 (div. June 1970); children—Beckman, Stuart, Leah. Reporter, Springfield (Ill.) Register, 1953-54; coll. traveler Holt, Rinehart & Winston, N.Y.C., 1959-61; asso. editor Saturday Evening Post, Indpls., ance 1973-74; mng. editor Personnel and Guidance Jour., Washington, 1974-76; editor State Ct. Jour., Williamsburg, Va., 1977—. Mem. Soc. Scholarly Pubs., Am. Assn. Pubs. Contbr. articles to various publs. Office: 300 Newport Ave Williamsburg VA 23185

RICH, ROBERT REGIER, med. educator; b. Newton, Kans., Mar. 7, 1941; s. Eldon Stahly and Margaret Joy (Regier) R.; A.B., Oberlin Coll., 1962; M.D., U. Kans., 1966; m. Susan Jepsen Solliday, Mar. 22, 1974; children by previous marriage—Kenneth Eldon, Cathryn Louise. Intern, U. Wash., Seattle, 1966-67, resident internal medicine, 1967-68; clin. asso., sr. staff fellow, NIH, Bethesda, Md., 1968-71; NIH spl. research fellow Harvard Med. Sch., Boston, 1971-73; asst. prof. microbiology and immunology Baylor Coll. Medicine, Houston, 1973-75, asso. prof., 1975-78, prof., 1978—, asst. prof. medicine, 1973-75, asso. prof., 1975-79, prof., 1979—, head immunology sect., 1977—, chief clin. immunology, 1978—; investigator Howard Hughes Med. Inst., 1977—. Program dir. Gen. Clin. Research Center, Meth. Hosp., Houston, 1974-77; attending physician VA Hosp., Houston, 1973—; mem. immunobiology study sect. NIH, 1977—. Served with USPHS, 1968-70. Recipient Russell Haden Research award, 1964; Roche award U. Kan., 1966; USPHS Research Career Devel. award, 1975-77. Fellow A.C.P.; mem. Am. Assn. Immunologists, Am. Soc. for Clin. Investigation, So. Soc. Clin. Investigation, Am. Acad. Allergy, Am. Assn. Pathologists, Am. Fedn. Clin. Research, A.A.A.S., Harris County Med. Soc., Sigma Xi, Alpha Omega Alpha. Asso. editor Jour. Immunology; contbr. articles to profl. jours. Home: 3703 Underwood St Houston TX 77025 Office: 1200 Moursund St Houston TX 77030

RICH, STEPHEN RICHARD CARDON, chem. co. exec.; b. Logan, Utah, June 23, 1947; s. Russell Rogers and Margaret Roundy (Cardon) R.; B.S. in Acctg., Brigham Young U., 1971; M.Bus. in Taxation, U. So. Calif., 1976; m. Calva Rae Taylor, Mar. 21, 1969; children—Darrell, Austin, Erin Michelle, Amanda Kristine. Tax staff Arthur Anderson & Co., Los Angeles, 1971-75, tax mgr., 1975-77; dir. taxes Hooker Chem. Co., Houston, 1977—. C.P.A., Calif., Tex. Mem. Am. Inst. C.P.A.'s, Tax Execs. Inst., Tex. Soc. C.P.A.'s, Calif. Soc. C.P.A.'s. Republican. Mormon. Home: 1719 Briarmead St Houston TX 77057 Office: PO Box 4289 Houston TX 77210

RICHARD, ANTHONY GERARD, II, petroleum landman; b. Austin, Tex., July 2, 1945; s. Anthony Gerard Richard and Dorothy Nell (Shelton) Fournier; B.B.A., U. Tex., Austin, 1976; m. Janis Joann Sash, May 11, 1972; children—Anthony G., III, Melissa Shana, Jonathan Royal, Elizabeth Caron. Petroleum landman Alpar Resources, Perryton, Tex., 1976; petroleum landman, San Antonio, 1976-77; petroleum landman Continental Oil Co., Houston, Midland, Oklahoma City, 1977-78; landman Gen. Crude Oil Co., Houston, 1978-79; staff landman Sanchez O'Brien Minerals Corp., Laredo, Tex., 1979—. Served with USN, 1963-70. Mem. Am. Assn. Petroleum Landmen, Houston Petroleum Landmen, Corpus Christi Assn. Petroleum Landmen, Denver Assn. Petroleum Landmen, VFW, AM. Legion, Alpha Kappa Psi, Phi Theta Kappa. Roman Catholic. Home: care 1951 W Mistletoe St San Antonio TX 78201 Office: PO Box 2986 Laredo TX 78041

RICHARD, BECKIE SCHICK, mfg. co. exec.; b. Shreveport, La., Sept. 9, 1951; d. James Albert and Ellee Euniceteen (Simmons) Schick; student Draughon Bus. Coll., 1970-72; 1 dau. by previous marriage—Denise Marie. Office mgr., bookkeeper Cane Equipment Coop., Inc., Plaquemine, La., 1970-72; legal sec., office mgr. Raymond B. Gautreau, Atty., Donaldsonville, La., 1973-77; office mgr., bookkeeper Red Stick Gravel Co., Baton Rouge, 1978—; grad. asst. Dale Carnegie night classes. Mem. Am. Mgmt. Assn., Am. Legion (past pres. aux.). Baptist. Clubs: Bass and Gal Assn., Baton Rouge Health. Home: 11585 Harrells Ferry Apt 18-6 Baton Rouge LA 70816 Office: 3679 Florida Blvd Baton Rouge LA 70806

RICHARD, LYNN ALLAN, chem. engr.; b. Davenport, Iowa, Sept. 9, 1951; s. Cletus Martin and Rose Margaret (Curry) R.; B.S. in Chem. Engring., Iowa State U., 1973; M.S., La. State U., 1977; m. Christine Mary Louviere. Mech. engr. Army Weapons Command, Rock Island, Ill., 1973; computer applications engr. Celanese Chem. Corp., Clear Lake, Tex., 1975-77, process engr., 1977-78; project engr. Setpoint, Inc., Houston, 1978—. Lector, St. Paul Cath. Ch., Nassau Bay, Tex., 1976-77, St. Bernadette Cath. Ch., Clear Lake City, 1977-79, St. Cyril Cath. Ch., 1979—; pres. Chemlake Bowling League, 1977-78. Recipient certificate of commendation Dept. Army, 1970; registered profl. engr., La.; NSF fellow, 1973-75; Shell fellow, 1973-75. Mem. Am. Inst. Chem. Engrs. Club: Cath. Alumni of Houston (vp. 1976-77, 78, treas. S. Central conv. 1978). Office: 901 Threadneedle Suite 150 Houston TX 77079

RICHARD, WILMAR JOHN, JR., chem. mfg. co. exec.; b. New Orleans, Feb. 4, 1944; s. Wilmar J. and Nelva (Brignac) R.; B.A., Southeastern La. U., 1966; postgrad Loyola at New Orleans, 1966-68; m. Diane Cheryl Colliniatis, June 27, 1964; 1 son, Rene. Field examiner NLRB, 1966-69; mgr. indsl. relations Gulf Coast area, Witco Chem. Corp., Gretna, La., 1969-74; dir. ops. Malter Internat. Corp., New Orleans, 1974—; prin. Wil Richard & Assos.; instr. Delgado Coll. Republican candidate for constable, 1972; mem. Govs. Com. Analyze Labor Environment of La. Mem. Am. Soc. Personnel Adminstrs., Personnel Mgmt. Assn. New Orleans, Interat. Soc. Stress Analysis. Roman Catholic. Bd. mgrs. YMCA; instr. ARC. Club: Timberlane Country. Home 440 Fairfield Ave Gretna LA 70053 Office: Box 6099 New Orleans LA 70174

RICHARDS, BLAIR PATTON, ch. ofcl.; b. Scranton, Pa., July 18, 1940; s. William Arthur and Dorothy (Blair) R.; B.S., Union Coll., 1963; M.S. in Christian Edn., Emory U., 1965; 1 son, Troy Albert. Dir. Christian edn. Scottsdale (Ariz.) United Methodist Ch., 1966-68, Grace United Meth. Ch., Mesa, Ariz., 1968-69, 1st United Meth. Ch., San Pedro, Calif., 1969-70; supr. Quincy (Pa.) United Meth. Children's Home, 1970-71; dir. Christian edn. St. Luke United Meth. Ch., Columbus, Ga., 1971—. Bd. dirs. Columbus/Phenix City Christian Enrichment Sch., 1971—. Mem. Christian Educators Fellowship of United Meth. Ch., S. Ga. Christian Educators Fellowship, Union Coll. Alumni Assn. (dir. 1975—). Author: Come, Let Us Celebrate, 1976. Home: 3514 Edgewood Rd Columbus GA 31907 Office: St Luke United Methodist Church PO Box 867 Columbus GA 31902

RICHARDS, CHRISTINE PARHAM, psychologist, educator; b. Mt. Pleasant, Tex., Oct. 16, 1926; d. Austin C. and Edith M. Parham; B.S., E. Tex. State U., 1946; M.S., Utah State U., 1967; postgrad. in ednl. psychology U. Houston, 1976—, Sam Houston State U., 1976-77; m. Wilton M. Richards, Dec. 20, 1946; children—Randall Wilton, Martha Lynn, Larry Austin, Sharla Darlene. Sec. to pres. E. Tex. State U., Commerce, 1946-48; tchr. elem. sch. Chapel Hill Ind. Sch. Dist., Tyler, Tex., 1948-50, Leary Elem. Sch., New Boston, Tex., 1955-56; tchr. math. and bus. New Boston High Sch., 1956-59; tchr. math. Marshall (Tex.) Ind. Sch. Dist., 1959-61; tchr. bus. and math. Box Elder High Sch., Brigham City, Utah, 1961-63, counselor, 1963-69; tchr. math. South Houston High Sch., Pasadena, Tex., 1969-70; instr. psychology San Jacinto Coll., Pasadena, Tex., 1970—, adv. to student edn. assn., 1972—. Den mother Cub Scouts Am., Marshall, 1960-61; sec. Lakeview Elem. Sch. PTA, Brigham City, 1962-63. NSF scholar, 1961; cert. tchr., guidance counselor, Tex. Mem. Tex. Psychol. Assn., Southwestern Psychol. Assn., Tex. Jr. Coll. Tchrs. Assn., Delta Kappa Gamma, Bus. and Profl. Women's Club. Democrat. Mem. Ch. of Christ. Club: San Jacinto College. Home: 1013 X St Deer Park TX 77536 Office: 8060 Spencer Hwy Pasadena TX 77505

RICHARDS, EVERETT LYLE, research mech. engr.; b. Austin, Minn., Oct. 21, 1936; s. Lyle Earnest and LaVera Floy (Grems) R.; student U. Minn., 1957-58; B.M.E. with highest honor, Ga. Inst. Tech., 1964, M.S. in Mech. Engring., 1966, Ph.D., 1970; m. Cornelia Ann Vaughan, Nov. 4, 1960; children—Beth Ann, Amy Vaughan. Draftsman, Ga. State Hwy. Dept., Atlanta, 1960-61; design engr.-draftsman Ga. Inst. Tech. Expt. Sta., Atlanta, 1962-64; lectr., grad. asst. Ga. Inst. Tech., 1967-68; research mech. engr. Naval Coastal Systems Lab., Panama City, Fla., 1969—; parttime instr. Gulf Coast Jr. Coll., 1969. Served with AUS, 1958-60. NSF summer trainee, 1963. Mem. ASME, Am. Def. Preparedness Assn., Sigma Xi, Pi Tau Sigma, Tau Beta Pi. Methodist. Club: N.W. Fla. Anthrop. Soc. Home: 512 Illinois Ave Lynn Haven FL 32444 Office: Code 721 Naval Coastal Systems Center Panama City FL 32407

RICHARDS, GEORGE ROY, lawyer; b. Munising, Mich., Mar. 18, 1934; s. George Charles and Lucille Beverly (Morin) R.; B.S., U. Notre Dame, 1956; LL.B., M.B.A., U. Mich., 1959; m. Jacqueline Sue Brush, Sept. 13, 1958; children—Robin, Charles, Barton. Admitted to Mich. bar, 1959, U.S. Supreme Ct. bar, 1963, Fla. bar, 1967; atty. SEC, Washington, 1963-67; partner firm Myers, Kaplan, Levinson, Kenin & Richards, Miami, Fla., 1967—. Served with USNR, 1960-63. Mem. Fed., Am., Fla. (chmn. securities com. 1972-73), Dade County bar assns. Contbr. articles to profl. jours. Home: 10161 SW 53d Ave Miami FL 33156 Office: 1428 Brickell Ave Miami FL 33131

RICHARDS, LEORA FRANCES (BROOKS), corporate pilot, flight instr.; b. Louisville, Oct. 9, 1932; s. William Francis and Frances Mary (Nelson) Lucas; student U. Louisville, 1950-52, 79—; m. John L. Richards, 1952 (div. 1975); children—John L., Nancy Brooks, William Lucas, Jane McGowan. Flight instr. single and multi-engine planes, instruments Ky. Flying Service, Louisville, 1970—, charter pilot, 1972—; corporate pilot Luckett & Farley, Architects, 1977—; participant Powder Puff Derby, 1976, Angel Derby, 1977, Air Race Classic, 1977. Lic. airline transport, flight instr. Mem. Jr. League of Louisville, 1963-66; mem. ball group, charities com. Younger Women's Club, Louisville, 1962-68. Named Flight Instr. of Yr. in Ky., FAA, 1973. Mem. Air Craft Owners and Pilots Assn., Ninety Nines. Democrat. Episcopalian. Home: 577 Sunnyside Dr Louisville KY 40206

RICHARDS, STEPHEN MALONE, port terminal exec.; b. Columbus, Ga., Feb. 11, 1922; s. Stephen Malone and Jessie Juanita (Page) R.; B.E.E., Ga. Inst. Tech., 1948; m. Marjorie Gene Swartz, Dec. 15, 1951; children—Elfrida Gene, Kathleen, Robin. Engr., project engr., plant mgr. Texasgulf, Inc., 1948-53; chief engr. Pan Am. Sulphur Co., 1953-60; v.p. Pakbank Fla., Inc., Tampa, and predecessor firm, 1961-68, exec. v.p., 1968-71, pres., 1971—; pres. Brimstone Terminals, Inc., 1968—; dir. Sutherland Properties, Inc., Houston, Trend Publ., Inc., Tampa. Bd. dirs. Tenn. Tombigbee Waterway Devel. Authority, 1972-79. Served to capt. ordnance, AUS, 1943-46; ETO. Decorated Soldiers medal. Mem. Nat. Waterways Assn. (dir.), AIME (past chmn. Fla. sect. 1967), Port of Tampa Propeller Club (pres. 1968), Greater Tampa C. of C. (dir. 1975-78). Republican. Episcopalian. Clubs: Tampa Univ., Tampa Yacht and Country. Home: 943 S Sterling Ave Tampa FL 33609 Office: 4333 S 50th St Tampa FL 33619

RICHARDS, WILLIAM GEORGE, savs. and loan exec.; b. Lockhart, Tex., Feb. 20, 1920; s. Cyrus F. and Gussie (Baldridge) R.; LL.B., U. Tex., 1948; m. Winnifred Adams, Nov. 23, 1940 (dec. May 1969); children—Bettye Ann (Mrs. Rogers), Mark Andrew; m. 2d, Corrie Marsh, Mar. 29, 1972. Admitted to Tex. bar, 1948; practiced law with father, Lockhart, 1948-55; v.p., atty., dir. Lockhart Savs. & Loan Assn., 1948-55; exec. v.p. Benjamin Franklin Savs. & Loan Assn., 1955-64, pres., 1964-74, vice-chmn. bd., 1974-75; chmn. bd., chief exec. officer Surety Savs. Assn., Houston, 1977-79; trustee Savs. & Loan Found., Inc., 1957-59. Mem. Tex. Ho. of Reps., 1947-50; mayor of Lockhart, 1954-55. Mem. adv. com. Coll. Bus. Adminstrn. U. Houston, 1966-70. Served with USNR, 1942-45. Mem. Nat. League Insured Savs. Assns. (exec. com. 1962-66), Houston C. of C. (dir. 1966, 68-73), Tex. Savs. and Loan League (dir. 1953-63, 63-66; pres. 1967-68), Phi Delta Phi. Democrat. Episcopalian. Clubs: Onion Creek, The Citadel (Austin). Home: 11007 Pinehurst Dr Austin TX 78747

RICHARDSON, ANITA MARIE, guidance counselor; b. Lake Charles, La., Sept. 30, 1945; d. Curtis Leo and Lois Marie (Bailey) R.; student Asbury Coll., 1961-64; B.A., U. Ky., 1965; M.Ed., U. Va., 1972; postgrad. Old Dominion U., Radford U. Tchr., Highland-Biltmore Elementary Sch., Portsmouth, Va., 1965-68, Churchland Jr. High Sch., 1968-72, guidance counselor, 1972-77,

Churchland High Sch., 1977—. Mem. Am., Va., Hampton Roads personnel and guidance assns., Am. Sch. Counselor Assn., Alpha Delta Kappa (pres. chpt. 1976-78). Methodist. Home: 3124 Biscayne Dr Chesapeake VA 23321 Office: 5601 High St W Portsmouth VA 23703

RICHARDSON, BARBARA DRUMMOND, vocat. counselor; b. Winston-Salem, N.C., July 22, 1936; B.S., N.C. A&T State U., 1968; M.Ed., Clemson U., 1978; m. Franklin D. Richardson, Mar. 29, 1954; children—Franklin, DeNorris, Renwick. Adminstrv. asst. Concentrated Employment Program Center, Winston-Salem, 1968, dir. op. mainstream, 1969, dir. new careers, 1969-70; tchr. Greenville (S.C.) Tech. Coll., 1971; tchr. bus., distributive edn., coordinator Greenville County Schs., 1971-75; dir. CETA, Greenville County, Greenville, 1975—. Bd. regents Greenville County Council for Community Actions, Inc. Mem. Southeastern Employment and Tng. Assn. (chmn. nominating com.). Democrat. Baptist. Home: 120 Lynch Dr Greenville SC 29605 Office: Suite 210 300 University Ridge Greenville SC 29601

RICHARDSON, CHARLES RAY, editor; b. Gorman, Tex., Sept. 19, 1935; s. E. W. and Maxine (Loyd) R.; B.S., Howard Payne Coll., 1958; M.A., Hardin Simmons U., 1971; M.S., East Tex. State U., 1977; m. Karin Kay Dean, July 24, 1964; children—Timothy Clark, Zachary Charles. City editor Brown County Gazette, Bangs, Tex., 1957; reporter Brownwood (Tex.) Bull., 1957-58, 60; staff writer, state and Sunday editor, religion columnist Abilene (Tex.) Reporter-News, 1961, 62-65; news dir. Golden Gate Bapt. Theol. Sem., Mill Valley, Calif., 1961-62; dir. pub. info. Hardin-Simmons U., Abilene, 1965-67, 68-73; press. rep. Tex. Bapt. Exec. Bd., Dallas, 1967-68; asst. editor Bapt. Standard Pub. Co., Dallas, 1973-76; asst. editor Bibl. Recorder, Raleigh, N.C., 1976—. Instr. journalism Hardin Simmons U., fall 1966; pub. relations cons. Cisco Jr. Coll., summer 1965; publicity dir. Bapt. Assn. Abilene, 1971-73. Vice chmn. Abilene Citizens for Better Govt., 1972-73; v.p. bd. dirs. Abilene Mental Health Assn., 1971-73; interpreter state missions offering Bapt. State Conv., 1978. Served with AUS, 1958-60. Mem. Nat. Press Photographers Assn., So. Bapt. Press Assn., So. Bapt. Conv. Public Relations Assn. (pres. 1971-73), Tex. Bapt. Public Relations Assn., N.C. Christian Action League (trustee 1979—), Descs. William Oscar and Cynthia Effie Loyd (pres. 1975-77), Sigma Delta Chi. Baptist (deacon 1967—). Democrat. Kiwanian (bd. dirs. 1968-70). Contbr. to Rupert N. Richardson: The Man and His Works, 1971. Home: 3608 Octavia St Raleigh NC 27606 Office: Box 26568 Raleigh NC 27611

RICHARDSON, CLAY VANCE, hosiery mfg. exec., city ofcl.; b. nr. Star, N.C., Dec. 27, 1899; s. John W. and Mary Lou (Parks) R.; student pub. schs.; m. Elsie Presnell Richardson, May 22, 1922 (dec. 1943); children—Emma Louise (Mrs. Jack M. Hartley), Ann Marie (Mrs. C. C. Winstead, Jr.), Joseph E.; m. 3d, Lola Monroe, Dec. 27, 1944; children—Clay Vance, John Monroe. Retail furniture bus., 1924-31; pres. Clayson Knitting Co., Inc., 1931-65, Star Indsl. Corp.; owner, v.p. V. & M. Furniture Mfg. Corp., 1965—. Vice pres. Montgomery Meml. Hosp., Troy, N.C., 1950—, chmn. bd., 1950-65. Mayor Town of Star, N.C., 1963-65, 75—. Mem. co-founders club Sch. Medicine, U. N.C., Chapel Hill; mem. adv. bd. N.C. Zool. Soc.; bd. regents Oral Roberts U., Tulsa, 1973—. Methodist. Rotarian. Address: PO Box 39 Star NC 27356

RICHARDSON, DAISY ADELAIDE WATKINS (MRS. ROBERT WILLIAMS RICHARDSON, JR.), real estate developer; b. Swannanoa, N.C., Aug. 18, 1920; d. George Agustus and Kitty Sue (Wilson) Watkins; secretarial degree Asheville Bus. Coll., 1940; m. Robert Williams Richardson, Jr., Aug. 18, 1940; children—Catherine Gail (Mrs. Clark Gayle Crozer) Vicki Joan (Mrs. Peter Ashton Lyon), Robert Williams III. Real estate salesman Keystone Realty, Palm Beach, 1966-73, LeBaron Real Estate Corp., Palm Beach, 1973—; sec. Richardson Devel. Corp., Palm Beach, 1973—; v.p., sec. Nu-Lan Improvement Corp., Palm Beach, 1972—. Bd. dirs. Lake Dogwood Assos., Inc. Club: Sailfish (Palm Beach). Home: 111 Bradley Pl Palm Beach FL 33480 Office: Bradley House Arcade Palm Beach FL 33480

RICHARDSON, DONALD EDWARD, neurosurgeon; b. Vicksburg, Miss., Oct. 5, 1931; s. Edward K. and Anamae (Cooper) R.; B.S., Milsaps Coll., 1953; M.D., Tulane U., 1957. Intern, Charity Hosp., New Orleans, 1957-58; resident neurol. surgery Ochsner Found., New Orleans, 1958-60, VA Hosp., New Orleans, 1960-61, Charity Hosp., 1961-62; practice medicine, specializing in neurosurgery, New Orleans 1962—; attending neurosurgeon Charity Hosp., New Orleans, 1962-75, VA Hosp., New Orleans, 1962-75; cons. neurosurgeon U.S. Pub. Health Hosp., 1962-70; active staff neurosurgery Touro Infirmary, Bapt. Hosp., Meth. Hosp.; dir. pain rehab. unit Hotel Dieu Hosp. (all New Orleans); instr. Tulane U., New Orleans, 1962-64, asst. prof. surgery, 1964-67, asso. prof., 1967-74; asso. clin. prof. La. State U., New Orleans, 1974—. Diplomate Am. Bd. Neurol. Surgery. Fellow A.C.S.; mem. Am. Med. Assn., La., Orleans Parish med. socs., So. Med. Assn., La., New Orleans neurol. socs., Research Assn. Neurol. Surgeons, Am. Assn. Neurol. Surgeons, So. Neurosurgical Soc., Internat. Soc. for Functional and Stereotaxic Surgery, A.A.A.S., Assn. for Acad. Surgeons, N.Y. Acad. Scis., Royal Soc. Medicine (London), Internat. Neurosurgical Soc., Internat. Assn. for Study of Pain, Alpha Omega Alpha. Contr. articles to profl. jours. Home: 401 Atherton Dr Metairie LA 70005 Office: 2714 Canal St Suite 300 New Orleans LA 70119

RICHARDSON, DOUGLAS SCOTT, dermatologist; b. Rochester, N.Y., Apr. 2, 1945; s. Donald William and Marion Roat R.; A.B. in Chemistry, Bucknell U., 1967; M.D., SUNY, Buffalo, 1971; m. Nancy Horner, Aug. 8, 1970; children—Matthew Scott, Thomas William. Intern, D.C. Gen. Hosp., 1971-72; resident Naval Regional Med. Center, Phila., 1975-77, Nat. Naval Med. Center, Bethesda, Md., 1977-78; practice medicine specializing in dermatology, Leesburg, Va., 1979—; clin. faculty Georgetown U.; spl. lectr. George Washington U. Served with USN, 1972-79. Cert. Am. Bd. Dermatology. Fellow Am. Acad. Dermatology; asso. A.C.P.; mem. Va. Dermatol. Soc., Assn. Mil. Dermatologists, D.C. Dermatol. Soc., Am. Dermatology Found., No. Va. Dermatology Found., Loudoun County Med. Soc., AMA, Rd. Runners Club Am., D.C. Rd. Runners. Republican. Baptist. Home: 336 Club View Dr Great Falls VA 22066 Office: 310 E Market St Leesburg VA 22075

RICHARDSON, FRANCIS JOSEPH, III, banker, fin. analyst; b. New Orleans, Mar. 22, 1943; s. Francis J. and Stella M. (Schulze) R.; B.B.A., Tulane U., 1965, postgrad. Tax Insts., 1967-74; M.B.A., Loyola U., New Orleans, 1970; postgrad. Goethe Inst., W. Ger., summer 1966; cert. Am. Inst. Banking, 1972; m. Carolyn Mary Bienvenu, Apr. 17, 1971; children—Caroline LeGardeur, Edward Emile. Jr. mech. engr. Michoud plant, Saturn launch systems br. Boeing Aerospace, New Orleans, 1964-66; various positions IBM Computer Systems Engring., New Orleans, 1966-71; investment service rep. First Nat. Bank of Commerce, New Orleans, 1971-76, v.p. and mgr. trust investment dept., 1976-78, investment counsel, fin. analyst, 1978—; account exec., registered rep. William O'Neil & Co. Inc. of Los Angeles, New Orleans, 1978-79; account exec. retail/instl. Bache, Halsey, Stuart, Shields, New Orleans, 1979—. Mem. Republican State Central Com., 1st Rep. Dist., 1969-70; bd. dirs. Big Bros., 1973-74, Museums Com. Jeuness D'Orleans, 1974-75. Fellow Fin. Analysts Fedn.; mem. Fin. Analysts Soc. New Orleans, New Orleans C. of C. (del. 1974-75), Le Debut de Jeunnes Filles Novelle Orleans, Navy League, Am. Econ. Assn., Am. Mgmt. Assn., La. Soc. SAR (state treas. 1973-74), Mil. Order Fgn. Wars, Mil. and Hospitaller Order St. Lazarus of Jerusalem (So. del. editor), Thackeray Soc. New Orleans (founding dir.), Soc. War of 1812 New Orleans, Tulane Assn. Bus. Alumni, Phi Delta Phi (Cert. of Merit 1970), Young Men's Bus. Club Greater New Orleans (dir. 1965-68), Alpha Tau Omega. Roman Catholic. Clubs: Masons, So. Yacht; Calif. Yacht (Marina del Rey); New Orleans Country, New Orleans Athletic, Roundtable of New Orleans (sec. 1972-74); Wailers Ski (Los Angeles); Rotary. Home: 1765 Coliseum St Apt 201 New Orleans LA 70130 Office: 1228 Race St New Orleans LA 70118

RICHARDSON, FRANK WOODBURY, III, steel co. exec.; b. Portland, Maine, May 18, 1943; s. Frank W. and Lila (Thompson) R.; B.S. in Marine Engring., Maine Maritime Acad., 1965; m. Diane L. Lang, June 24, 1966; children—Frank Woodbury IV, Teresa L., Christy E. Marine engr., Texaco Inc., Port Arthur, Tex., 1965-69; ship supt. Bethlehem Steel Corp., Beaumont, Tex., 1969-72, night supt., 1972-74, asst. to gen. supt. Shipbldg., 1974-76, gen. foreman maintenance, 1976-77, asst. plant engr., 1977—. Mem. adminstrv. bd., chmn. bd. trustees, mem. fin. com. North End United Meth. Ch., Beaumont, Tex., 1975-78; mem. Neches River Oil Control Com., 1976. Served to comdr. USNR. Mem. Naval Res. Officers Assn., Res. Officers Assn. Am., Young Men's Bus. League Beaumont, Maine Maritime Alumni Assn., Beaumont PTA. Club: Masons. Home: 3430 Crestwood Dr Beaumont TX 77706 Office: PO Box 3031 Beaumont TX 77704

RICHARDSON, GARY LOWELL, oil co. exec.; b. Poplar Bluff, Mo., Sept. 5, 1937; s. Lowell Leonard and Esther Maurine (Foster) R.; B.S., La. Tech. U., 1960; postgrad. U. Tex., 1960-61; M.S., U. Alaska, 1964; Ph.D., N. Tex. State U., 1970; m. Gayle LaGrone, June 13, 1959; children—Teri Jean, Lisa Gayle, Rick Foster, Christ Danielle. Engr. Tex. Instruments, Dallas, 1964-68; prof. mgmt. sci. U. So. Fla., Tampa, 1970-73; spl. cons. to comptroller Def. Communications Agy., Washington, 1973-79; prof. bus., computing sci., operation mgmt. Tex. A and M. U., College Station, 1974-79; asst. to gen. mgr. data processing Texaco Inc., Houston, 1979—; cons. to various orgns. Served with USAF, 1960-64. Fed. Faculty fellow, 1974. Mem. So. Mgmt. Assn., Ops. Research Soc. Am., Am. Inst. Decision Scis., Data Processing Mgmt. Assn., Sigma Iota Epsilon, Delta Sigma Pi. Contbr. articles to profl. jours. Author: Problem Solving Using PL/C, 1975; Contemporary PL/I Using Structured Programming Techniques, 1980; A Primer on Structured Design, 1980. Home: 3602 Highgreen Kingwood TX

RICHARDSON, GILBERT P(AYTON), assn. exec.; b. Lawrenceburg, Tenn., Nov. 4, 1926; student Mexico City Coll., 1948; B.A. in History, Sociology and Bus. Adminstrn., David Lipscomb Coll., 1949; M.A. in U.S. Polit. History, Sociology, Edn. and Mgmt.-Labor Relations, George Peabody Coll., 1951; grad. U.S. Air U. Acad. and Allied Officers Sch., 1967; postgrad. in internat. relations Am. U., 1956-59; LL.D. (hon.), Sch. of Americas, Panama City, C. Am., 1970, Inter-Am. Air Force Acad., Panama City, 1970; m. Lee Ann Gillen; children—Amy, Gilbert P., Susan. Motion picture dir.-writer indsl. prodns. Tasco Motion Pictures Corp., Atlanta, 1952-53; dir. admissions Fla. So. Coll., 1953-56, instr. Western civilization, mgmt., labor relations, 1956-57, asst. prof. Latin Am. history, polit. sci., 1957-61, chmn. dept. Am. culture, 1955-56; pvt. researcher, lectr., profl. speech writer, including research and surveys in Argentina, Chile, Peru, and Panama, Soviet Union, 1962-64; asst. prof. history and polit. sci. Pepperdine Coll., 1964-66; asso. prof. internat. relations Grad. Sch., Def. Intelligence Agy., Washington, 1966-68, sr. prof., 1968-70; lectr., 1970-78; exec. dir. Am. Assn. for Study of U.S. in World Affairs, Annandale, Va., 1978—. Asso. exec. dir., editor Fla. Citizenship Clearinghouse, bd. dirs., 1957-61, del. Nat. Clearinghouse, 1957; mem. internat. relations com., faculty Grad. Sch., U.S. Dept. Agr., Washington, 1969-74; lectr. No. Va. Community Coll., Alexandria, 1973-76. Served with U.S. Army, 1945-47; ETO. Recipient citation Freedoms Found., 1956; Disting. Service award and named to Outstanding Young Men of 1960, U.S. Jr. C. of C. Mem. Am. Legion (chmn. Americanism in sch. affairs dept. Fla. 1955-57, vice-comdr. post 1954, 55), Am. Assn. for Study of U.S. in World Affairs (exec. dir. 1978—), U.S. in World Affairs Inst. (dean 1980—), Pi Gamma Mu, Sigma Tau Delta. Author: Our Rigorous Race With Russia, 1963, 2d edit., 1966; contbr. articles on Latin Am. to profl. jours.; subject of articles, interviews in various newspapers, TV; numerous travels, including top secret travels for U.S. Govt.

RICHARDSON, GORDON HENRY, JR., direct mail advt. co. exec.; b. Wheeler, Tex., Oct. 30, 1938; s. Gordon Henry and Mary Frances (Viles) R.; B.B.A., Tex. Tech. Coll., 1964; m. Maryln Jones, May 6, 1961; children—Brett, Leslie. Asso. buyer Foleys Dept. Store, Houston, 1967; buyer, then mdse. mgr. Dillards Dept. Store, San Antonio, 1968-77; pres. Ad-Mail San Antonio, 1978—; lectr. St. Mary's U., U. Tex. (both San Antonio). Home: 2167 NE Loop 410 Suite E-8 San Antonio TX 78217 Office: 318 E Nakoma St San Antonio TX 78216

RICHARDSON, HAROLD NELSON, army officer; b. Alma, Mich., Sept. 23, 1942; s. Harold Nelson and Harriett Agnes (Dunn) Abbott; B.S. in Chemistry, Central Mich. U., 1965; M.S. in Systems Mgmt., Fla. Inst. Tech., 1979; m. Park Chong Hoi, Jan. 21, 1967; children—Harold Nelson, Susanne. Commd. 2d lt. U.S. Army, 1965, advanced through grades to maj., 1975; staff officer Ordnance Group, South Korea, 1965-67; project officer Watervliet (N.Y.) Arsenal, 1967-68; sr. adv. Air Def. Arty. Brigade, Republic of Korea, 1969-71; exec. officer, comdg. officer Ordnance Missile Direct Support Unit, Ft. Riley, Kans., 1971-72, W. Ger., 1972-74; maintenance officer 32d Army Air Def. Command in Germany, 1974-76; project officer Developing Systems Tng. and Devices Directorate, U.S. Army Tng. Support Center, Ft. Eustis, Va., 1976—. Decorated Meritorious Service medal with oak leaf cluster. Mem. Am. Def. Preparedness Assn., Mil. Ops. Research Soc. Office: US Army Tng Support Center Fort Eustis VA 23604

RICHARDSON, HARRY VAN BUREN, clergyman, former sem. pres.; b. Jacksonville, Fla., June 27, 1901; s. Martin Van Buren and Bertha Isabelle (Witsell) R.; A.B., Western Res. U., 1925; S.T.B., Harvard U., 1932; Ph.D., Drew U., 1945; D.D., Wilberforce U., 1938, Bethune-Cookman Coll., 1976, Interdenomination Theol. Center, 1975; m. Selma Theodocia White, June 22, 1927. Ordained to ministry A.M.E. Ch., 1930; elder United Meth. Ch., Atlanta, 1949—; chaplain Tuskegee Inst. (Ala.), 1932-48; pres. Gammon Theol. Sem., Atlanta, 1948-59, Interdenominational Theol. Center, Atlanta, 1959-68, pres. emeritus, 1968—; del. from Meth. Ch. to 2d and 3d assemblies World Council Chs., 1954, 61; mem. Meth. Seminar on Theology, Oxford U. (Eng.), 1962; mem. Lacour Evangelistic Crusade to Japan, 1954. Exec. dir. United Negro Coll. Fund, 1969-70; mem. Citizens Adv. Com. for Urban Renewal of Atlanta, 1964-68; bd. dirs. Atlanta Community Chest, Family Service Soc., 1963-68, Ga. Council Alcohol Problems, Atlanta Tb Assn., Atlanta Urban League; mem. Mayor's Com. of Atlanta Coordinating Council, 1963-68. Recipient Liberty Bell award Atlanta Bar Assn., 1968, Pres.'s award Assn. Pvt. Colls. and Univs. in Ga., 1976, Martin Katzenstein award Harvard Div. Sch., 1979. Mem. Greater Atlanta Council Chs., Assn. Meth. Theol. Schs. (pres. 1955), Ga. Assn. Pastoral Care (dir. 1962-68), Council Evangelism of Meth. Ch., Nat. Council Chs. of Christ in U.S., So. Regional Council (dir. 1942—), Sigma Pi Phi. Democrat. Author: Dark Glory, 1947; Dark Salvation, 1976; contbr. numerous articles to religious mags. Home: 3127 Mangum Ln SW Atlanta GA 30311 Office: PO Box 42156 Atlanta GA 30311

RICHARDSON, JAMES ALBERT, restaurant chain exec.; b. Franklin, Ind., Jan. 10, 1939; s. Maynard Louis and Thelma May (Hendricks) R.; A.B., Ind. U., 1965, J.D., 1968. Account exec. Instn. Mag., Cahners Publs., Chgo., 1968-70; project dir. Harris, Kerr, Forster & Co., Chgo., 1970-71; dir. client devel. Amcon Internat., Memphis, Tenn., 1971-72; v.p. terminal lease devel. Dobbs Houses, Inc., Memphis, 1972—. Served with U.S. Army, 1961-64. Mem. Nat. Restaurant Assn., Am. Assn. Airport Execs., Airport Operators Council Internat. Home: 1276 Timberbrook Lane Memphis TN 38134 Office: Dobbs Houses Inc 5100 Poplar Ave Memphis TN 38137

RICHARDSON, JAMES E., hosp. adminstr.; b. Ruston, La., Mar. 23, 1949; s. James and Martha Evelyn (Rives) R.; B.S., La. Tech. U., 1972; postgrad. U. Ala., 1975-76; m. Paula Sue Frisby, May 19, 1973. Auditor, Blue Cross of La., 1972, sr. auditor, 1973; controller Savoy (La.) Meml. Hosp. Found., 1974-76, exec. dir., 1976—; pres. Health Care Fin. Mgmt., Inc., Mamou, 1976—; bd. dirs. Savoy Pharmacy; bd. dirs., sec.-treas. Aquarius Offshore Logistics, Inc. Vice pres. Acadian Acres Assn., 1976—. Mem. Hosp. Fin. Mgmt. Assn., Hosp. Mgmt. Systems Soc., Mid-La. Health Systems Agency. Democrat. Baptist. Clubs: Sertoma (dir.), Mamou Racquet and Aquatic (v.p.), Rotary (pres.). Home: PO Box 163 Mamou LA 70554 Office: 801 Poinciana Ave Mamou LA 70554

RICHARDSON, JAMES MILTON, clergyman; b. Sylvester, Ga., Jan. 8, 1913; s. James Milton and Pallie (Stewart) R.; A.B., U. Ga., 1934; B.D., Emory U., 1936, M.A., 1942; postgrad. Va. Theol. Sem., 1938, D.D., 1965; LL.D., John Marshall Law Sch., 1948; D.D., Episcopal Theol. Sem. Ky., 1960, U. South, 1961, Episc. Theol. Sem. S.W., 1976; m. Eugenia Preston Brooks, June 14, 1940; children—James Milton, Eugenia (Mrs. James R. Nash), Joan Stewart (Mrs. James R. Doty), Preston Brooks. Ordained to ministry Episc. Ch., 1938; rector St. Timothy's Ch., Atlanta, 1938-40; asst. rector St. Luke's Ch., Atlanta, 1940-43, rector, 1943-52; dean Christ Ch. Cathedral, Houston, 1952-65; bishop Episc. Diocese Tex., Houston, 1965—. Trustee Church Life Ins. Corp., Church Ins. Co., Church Hymnal Corp. Chmn. bd. trustees St. Stephen's Episc. Sch., 1965—, Episc. Theol. Sem. S.W., 1967—; pres. St. Luke's Episc. Hosp.; trustee Ch. Pension Fund, Episc. Radio-TV Found., U. South, Baylor Coll. Medicine. Mem. Blue Key, Phi Beta Kappa, Phi Kappa Phi, Omicron Delta Kappa, Alpha Tau Omega (worthy grand chaplain 1945-52, 56—, nat. pres. 1952-56). Home: 14 Shadowlawn Circle Houston TX 77005 Office: 520 San Jacinto St Houston TX 77002

RICHARDSON, JAMES ROBERT, JR., ins. exec.; b. Dallas, June 15, 1938; s. James Robert and Jonnie Francis (Bowden) R.; B.B.A., N. Tex. State U., 1961; m. Cynthia Gayle Roberts, Nov. 20, 1960; children—Pamela, Susan. Bond supr. Ins. Co. N. Am., Dallas, 1961-65, Oklahoma City, 1965-67; partner Grant & Co. Ins. Agy., Tulsa, 1967-72; v.p. Fred S. James & Co. of Okla., Tulsa, 1972—; mem. ins. adv. com. Tulsa Jr. Coll. Served with USMC, 1958-64. C.P.C.U. Mem. Ind. Agts. Greater Tulsa (pres. 1976-77), N.E. Okla. Soc. C.P.C.U.'s. Republican. Clubs: Shadow Mountain Racquet, Tulsa Tip (past pres.). Author: Contractors Bonding Guide, 1977. Home: 7345 Sleepy Hollow St Tulsa OK 74136 Office: 525 S Main St Tulsa OK 74103

RICHARDSON, JIMMY DELANO, accountant; b. Florence, Ala., Aug. 22, 1938; s. Robert Dee and Florrie Elizabeth (Calvert) R.; B.S., U. N. Ala., 1967; m. Mae Elizabeth Keel, Oct. 4, 1959; children—Della Faye, Ralph Dwight, Michael Layne. Gen. acctg. mgr. Kayser Roth, Haleyville, Ala., 1970-74; fin. analyst Kimberly Clark, Coosa Pines, Ala., 1974-76; pvt. practice as public accountant, Talladega, Ala., 1976—. Served with USAF, 1955-59. Mem. Nat. Soc. Public Accountants, Ala. Assn. Public Accountants. Home: 1012 Sedgefield Dr Sylacauga AL 35150 Office: 201 E Battle St Talladega AL 35160

RICHARDSON, JOSEPH THOMAS, dentist, educator; b. Mount Pleasant, Tenn., Oct. 20, 1926; s. Mark Schultz and Lillian (Brown) R.; D.D.S., Middle Tenn. State U., 1947-48; D.D.S., U. Tenn. Coll. Dentistry, 1948-51; M.A. in Teaching, The Citadel, 1972; m. 1950; children—Steve, David; m. 2d, Agnes Bailey Angell Richardson, Jan. 20, 1971; children—Earle Angell, Olivia Angell. Gen. practice dentistry, Columbia, Tenn., 1954-70; faculty crown and bridge dentistry Coll. Dental Medicine, Charleston, S.C., 1970-79, acting chmn. dept., 1975-78, chmn., 1978—, named outstanding clin. instr., 1972, 77; asso. dean student affairs U. Tex. Sch. Dentistry, San Antonio, 1979—; mem. dental staff Maury County (Tenn.) Hosp., 1954-70; resident dentist Tenn. Orphans Home, Spring Hill, 1958-70. Mem. Maury County Bd. Health, 1966-70, chmn., 1968-70. Served with U.S. Mcht. Marine, 1945-46, with USNR, 1952-54. Mem. 6th Dist. Dental Soc. (pres. 1962-63), Am. Acad. of Crown and Bridge Prosthodontics, Psi Omega, Omicron Kappa Upsilon. Contbr. articles to profl. jours. Home: 10714 Moss Bank San Antonio TX 78230 Office: 7703 Floyd Curl Dr San Antonio TX 78284

RICHARDSON, KENNETH MILLER, utility co. exec.; b. Manila, Ark., Apr. 5, 1927; s. Albert Lee and Beersheba Rebecca (Miller) R.; grad. in elec. engring. Internat. Corr. Schs., 1963; m. Myra Ann Neely, July 24, 1945; 1 dau., Karen Ann. Engr.'s helper Ark.-Mo. Power Co., Blytheville, Ark., 1948-51, sr. engring. clk., 1951-57, dist. constrn. supt., 1957-64, mgr. Monette (Ark.) area, 1964-75, asst. dist. supt. So. dist., 1975—; dir. Monette Indsl. Devel. Corp., sec.-treas. 1967—; owner Kenneth Richardson Realty, Monette, 1975—. Sec.-treas. N.E. Ark. Safety Council, 1959, chmn., 1960; active Eastern Ark. council Boy Scouts Am., 1948—, dist. commr., 1963-64, mem. exec. bd., 1960-66, recipient Silver Beaver award, 1960. Served with USNR, 1945-46. Mem. I.E.E.E. Democrat. Baptist (chmn. deacons 1972). Mason, Lion. Home: 301 Ball St Monette AR 72447 Office: 211 E Flager St Monette AR 72447

RICHARDSON, LAWRENCE OLIVER, elec. engr.; b. Clovis, N.Mex., July 15, 1944; s. Jesse M. and Dortha Fay (Stoddard) R.; B.S.E.E., N.Mex. State U., 1968; m. Fronnie Taz Bealer, June 2, 1967; 1 dau., Totie. Aerosystems engr. Gen. Dynamics Co., Ft. Worth, 1968-71; chief engr. antennas div. Tandy Corp., Ft. Worth, 1971-74; engring. supt. Cryovac div. W.R. Grace Co., Iowa Park, Tex., 1974-79; elec. engr. Surgikos, Inc. div. Johnson & Johnson, Arlington, Tex., 1979—; owner Richardson Engring.; instr. physics Midwestern State U., 1976-77, mem. electronics tech. advisory com., 1977-78; mem. Iowa Park Elec. Bd.; mem. advisory bd. Wichita Falls Tech. Tng. Center. Registered profl. engr., Tex. Mem. IEEE, Tex., Nat. socs. profl. engrs. Jehovah's Witness. Home: 3402 Killala Ct Arlington TX 76014 Office: 2500 Arbrook Blvd Arlington TX 76014

RICHARDSON, NEAL ANDERSON, computer specialist; b. Auburn, Ala., Jan. 14, 1945; s. Euell Calhoun and Annie Mae (Neal) R.; B.S. in Math., Auburn U., 1967; B.S. in Meteorology, Pa. State U., 1969. Commd. 2d lt. USAF, 1968, advanced through grades to capt., 1972; service in Korea; mathematician Air Force Data Services Center, Washington, 1973-77; computer specialist Air U. Data Automation, Maxwell AFB, Ala., 1977-78, Air Force Data Systems Design Center, Gunter AFS, Ala., 1978—. Home: 127 S DeBardeleben St Auburn AL 36830 Office: Software Transition AFDSDC Gunter AFS AL 36114

RICHARDSON, PENNY WAN, audiologist; b. Nashville, Dec. 27, 1953; d. Everett Edward and Wanda (Alessio) Templeton; B.S. in Speech and Hearing, Middle Tenn. State U., 1975; M.A. in Audiology, U. Tenn., Knoxville, 1976; m. Hugh McClain Richardson, III, May 27, 1977. Audiologist, Donelson, Tenn., 1977; audiologist, office mgr. Audiology Assos., Inc., Nashville, 1977—; student tchr. Indsl. Hearing Conservation Commn., Nashville League Hard Hearing. Mem. Am. Speech and Hearing Assn., Audiological Resource Assn., Gamma Beta Phi. Democrat. Roman Catholic. Home: 137 Carriage Dr Nashville TN 37221 Office: 1915 State St Nashville TN 37203

RICHARDSON, PHILO PARMER, dentist; b. Frederick, Okla., Jan. 8, 1919; s. Philo Parmer and Pearl May (McClelland) R.; D.D.S., Baylor U., 1950; m. Jane Hurst, Dec. 29, 1972; children by previous marriage—Thomas David, Mary Ann, Patricia Sue, James Parmer; 1 stepson, Christopher Marshall. Gen. practice dentistry, Dallas, 1952—. Served with USNR, 1941-45. Fellow Internat. Coll. Dentists, Acad. Gen. Dentistry (pres. Tex. 1978-79); mem. Am. Coll. Dentists, ADA, Tex. Dental Assn. (dir. 1979-80, v.p. N.E. div. 1980-81), Dallas County Dental Soc. (pres. 1977-78), Oak Cliff Dental Study Club (pres. 1965-66). Democrat. Methodist. Clubs: Masons, Oak Cliff Lions (pres. 1973-74, dep. dist. gov. 1974-76). Editor dental newspaper G.P., 1972-75. Home: 1326 Meadow Green Duncanville TX 75116 Office: 201 W 10th St Dallas TX 75208

RICHARDSON, RAYMOND THOMAS, JR., computer co. exec.; b. Long Branch N.J., Jan. 29, 1944; s. Raymond T. and Lois M. R.; B.S. in Acctg., Seton Hall U., 1969; postgrad. U. South Fla., 1979; m. Betty S. Hudson, Oct. 14, 1978; children by previous marriage—Gina, Joanna; stepchildren—DeNice, Jay. Staff acct. Samuel Klein & Co., C.P.A.'s, Newark, 1967-70, Brout, Isaacs & Co., C.P.A.'s, N.Y.C., 1970-71; controller Garden State Tire Corp., Lodi, N.J., 1971-75, BIA Ins. Assos., Naples, Fla., 1975-76, Stottlemyer & Shoemaker Lumber Co., Sarasota, Fla., 1976-79; pres. Dataline Corp., Maitland, Fla., 1979—; sec., treas., dir. Bldg. Supply Credit Asso., Inc., Sarasota, 1978-79; fin. cons. to bldg. materials trade. Mem. corporate coordinating com. United Appeal. Mem. Nat. Soc. Public Accts., Nat. Assn. Accts., Fla. Lumber and Bldg. Materials Dealers Assn., Nat. Lumber and Bldg. Materials Dealers Assn. Roman Catholic. Clubs: Sarasota Racquetball, Elks. Home: 2241 Shadow Oaks Rd Sarasota FL 33582 Office: 140 Circle Dr Maitland FL 32751

RICHARDSON, RICHARD JUDSON, educator; b. Poplar Bluff, Mo., Feb. 16, 1935; s. Jewell Judson and Naomi Fern (Watson) R.; B.S., Harding Coll., 1957; certificate (Rotary Internat. fellow) U. Dublin (Ireland), 1958; M.A. (Edgar Stern fellow), Tulane U., 1961, Ph.D., 1967; m. Sammie Sue Cullum, Dec. 29, 1961; children—Jon Mark, Anna Cecile, Ellen Elizabeth, Megan Leigh. Instr., Tulane U., New Orleans, 1962-64; asst. prof. Western Mich. U., Kalamazoo, 1964-67, asso. prof., 1968-69; vis. asso. prof. U. Hawaii, Honolulu, 1967-68; asso. prof. U. N.C., Chapel Hill, 1969-72, prof. polit. sci., asso. chmn. dept., 1973-75, chmn., 1975—, Burton Craige prof., 1977—; adj. prof. policy scis. Duke, Durham, N.C., 1971—. Cons. to Hawaii Senate, 1968-69, N.C. Gov.'s Com. on Law and Order, 1969-71, Adminstrv. Office of Cts., 1972-73, N.C. finance chmn. Oak Hills Home for Children, 1969; cub scout pack master Occoneechee council Boy Scouts Am., 1972-73; del. Inter-Ch. Council, Chapel Hill, 1973. Del. county conv. Democratic party, 1972. Recipient Tanner award for distinguished teaching U. N.C., 1972; named Granville Favorite Prof., 1978. Mem. Am. (Edward S. Corwin award 1967), So., N.C. (pres. 1979) polit. sci. assns. Author: (with Kenneth N. Vines) The Politics of Federal Courts, 1971; (with Darlene Walker) Perspectives on the Criminal Justice System, 1972. Home: 1701 Fountainridge Rd Chapel Hill NC 27514 Office: Dept of Political Science University of North Carolina Chapel Hill NC 27514

RICHARDSON, RUPERT NORVAL, educator; b. nr. Caddo, Tex., Apr. 28, 1891; s. Willie Baker and Nannie (Coon) R.; A.B., Hardin-Simmons U., Abilene, Tex., 1912; Ph.B., U. Chgo., 1914; A.M., U. Tex., 1922, Ph.D., 1928; m. Pauline Mayes, Dec. 28, 1915; 1 son, Rupert Norval. Prin. high sch., Cisco, Tex., 1914-16, Sweetwater, 1916-17; prof. history Hardin-Simmons U., 1917—, dean students, 1926-28, exec. v.p., 1928-38, exec. v.p., 1938-40, acting pres., 1943-45, pres., 1945-53, pres. emeritus, prof., 1953-67, Piper prof., 1963—, Distinguished prof., 1967—; asso. prof., prof. hist. U. Tex. 8 summers, also 1940-41. Mem. So. Bapt. Edn. Commn., 1952-55; mem. Tex. Hist. Survey Com., 1953-67, pres., 1961-63. Served 2d lt. U.S. Army, 1918. Recipient Cultural Achievement in Lit. award West Tex. C. of C., 1967; Ruth Lester award Tex. Hist. Commn., 1972; award of merit Nat. Assn. State and Local History, 1953, 76, 77; Leadership award Tex. State Hist. Assn., 1976; Citizen of Year award Abilene C. of C., 1975; citation of honor Tex. Soc. Architects, 1978. Fellow Tex. State Hist. Assn. (pres. 1969-70); mem. Tex. Philos. Soc. (pres. 1962-63). Baptist. Mason. Lion (past pres., dist. gov.). Author: The Comanche Barrier to the South Plains Settlement, 1933; (with C. C. Rister) The Greater Southwest, 1934; Texas: the Lone Star State, 1943; Adventuring with a Purpose, 1952; The Frontier of Northwest Texas, 1963; Colonel Edward M. House: The Texas Years, 1964; Famous Are The Halls: Hardwin-Simmons University as I Have Seen It, 1975; Caddo, Texas: The Biography of a Community, 1966; Along Texas Old Forts Trail, Abilene, 1972. Editor: West Tex. Hist. Assn. Yearbook, 1929—. Contbr. to hist., ednl. publs. Home: 2220 Simmons Ave Abilene TX 79601

RICHARDSON, SYLVIA OVERTON, nurse; b. Elizabeth City, N.C., Aug. 21, 1938; d. Anthony Ashley and Annie (Bell) Overton; B.S.N., N.C. Agrl. and Tech. State U., 1959; postgrad. N.C. Central U., 1960-63, 78-79; M.S.N., U. N.C., Chapel Hill, 1973; children—William, Rodney Dion. Dir. nursing edn., asst. dir. nursing Lincoln Hosp. Sch. Nursing, Durham, N.C., 1959-66; staff nurse VA Hosp., Durham, 1966-72, N.C. Meml. Hosp., Chapel Hill, 1971-73; vis. lectr. N.C. Central U., 1972-73, asst. prof. nursing, 1973—. Mem. Durham Com. on Affairs of Black People; mem. planning com. for women's center YWCA, Durham. Recipient Moses H. Cone award N.C. Agrl. and Tech. State U., 1957. Mem. N.C. State Nurses Assn., Am. Nurses Assn., N.C. League Nursing, Nat. League Nursing, Agrl. and Tech. State U. Alumni Assn., U. N.C. at Chapel Hill Alumni Assn., Women in Action for Prevention Violence and its Causes, Alpha Kappa Alpha, Chi Eta Phi. Mem. A.M.E. Ch. Home: 2901 Apex Rd Durham NC 27713 Office: NC Central U Fayetteville St Durham NC 27707

RICHERSON, ROBERT DELBERT, record producer, booking agt.; b. Searles, Tenn., July 13, 1936; s. Alexander and Lillie Pearl (Jernigan) R.; student pub. schs., Middleton, Tenn.; m. Belva Lucille Jorgensen, Feb. 17, 1957; children—Tammie Marie, Delbert Craig. Salesman Auto Fair, San Antonio, 1975; sales rep. John Kenagy Motor Co., New Braunfels, Tex., 1976; pres. Richerson Sales Co., Converse, Tex., 1976—, Richerson Enterprises, Converse, 1976—; talent dir. Wolf-Rich Pub. and Rec. Co., Converse, 1978—; partner The Delleon Agy., Converse, 1979—; newspaper columnist for the Valley News (column entitled Country Music Hotline), Universal City, Tex., 1978—. Served as m/sgt. USAF, 1954-74. Decorated Air Force Commendation medal. Mem. Greater Randolph Area C. of C. (Community Service award 1978, chmn. diplomate club 1978), San Antonio C. of C., Internat. Traders, Splty. Mdse. Assn., DAV, VFW, Am. Legion (comdr. 1974-75, 78-79, adj. Dept. of Tex., 1978—), Air Force Sgts. Assn. (pres. 1971, 74). Democrat. Baptist. Address: 521 Willow Dr Converse TX 78109

RICHEY, WILLIAM C., mktg. cons.; b. Lonoke, Ark., Mar. 29, 1925; s. W.C. and M.C. Richey; student various universities, including U. Ark., U. Syracuse, U. Houston; married, May 23, 1948; 2 children. Owner, operator So. Appliance Co., 1950-54; exec. sales dir. Interstate Engring. Corp., 1954-61; founder, pres. N.Am. Electronics Corp., 1961-75; founder, pres. Mktg. Cons. of Am., Memphis, 1976—. Served to 1st lt. USAAF, 1943-45. Mem. Am. Mgmt. Assn., Am. Mktg. Assn., Internat. Franchise Assn., Can. Franchise Assn., N.Am. Licensing Assn. Republican. Methodist. Author: Meetings—Their Planning, 1979; Site Locations, 1979. Office: Mktg Cons of Am 474 Perkins Extension Memphis TN 38117

RICHIE, R. K., corp. exec.; b. 1930; B.S., U. Louisville, 1953; married. Pres., Oceanic Contractors Inc. subs. J. Ray McDermott & Co. Inc., 1953-57, 64-77, with J. Ray McDermott subs., 1957-64, pres. parent co., New Orleans, 1977—, also dir. Office: J Ray McDermott & Co Inc 1010 Common St Box 60035 New Orleans LA 70160

RICHMOND, JOHN MELVYN, jewelry co. exec.; b. Chgo., Feb. 13, 1939; s. Harry and Clarice (Costulas) R.; student pub. schs., Chgo., Los Angeles; m. Ellen Gale Riley, Nov. 28, 1959; children—Kelly, Robyn, Shannan. Salesman Sarong Inc., div. Playtex, Dover, Del., 1964-66; key account coordinator Exquisite Form, Pelham Manor, N.Y., 1964-66; regional mgr., nat. trainer Benrus Corp., Ridgefield, Conn., 1966-70, regional mgr. Wells Inc., div. Benrus Corp., Attleboro, Mass., 1970-74, nat. sales mgr., 1974-75; v.p., nat. sales mgr. Imperial Pearl Syndicate, Chgo., 1975-76; nat. sales mgr., v.p. Gall Fashion Jewelry Co., Dallas, 1977—; pres. JMR Fine Jewelry, 1977—, Classique D'Or Inc., Dallas. Served with U.S. Army, 1958-61. Mem. Retail Jewelers of Am. Home: 14918 Hillcrest Rd Dallas TX 75248 Office: PO Box 5466 Richardson TX 75080

RICHMOND, MOSSIE JESSE, JR., univ. ofcl.; b. Wynne, Ark., Nov. 21, 1936; s. Mossie J. and Josephine (Wright) R.; B.A. in Music and Edn., Philander Smith Coll., 1960; postgrad. in Linguistics, Wichita State U., 1966; M.A. in Ednl. Adminstrn., Ball State U., 1970, Ph.D., 1973. Tchr. high sch., Star City, Ark., 1960-64; tchr. Lincoln High Sch., Wabbeseka, Ark., 1964-67, asst. prin., 1967-68, prin., 1968-69; tchr. sch., Wynne, Ark., 1969-71; asst. to systems coordinator for student affairs Ball State U., Muncie, Ind., 1971-72, adminstrv. asst. to adminstrv. asst. to v.p. student affairs, 1972-73; coordinator Univ. Coll. and asst. prof. edn. Ark. State U., State University, 1973-75, dean Univ. Coll., 1975—, prof. edn., 1973—; participant numerous confs. and workshops in edn.; manuscript reviewer Coll. Student Jour., 1975—. Bd. dirs. Northeastern Ark. Area council Boy Scouts Am., 1978—, treas. exec. council, 1979-80. Mem. Ark. Sch. Adminstrs. Assn., Ark. Deans Assn., So. Coll. Personnel Assn., Nat. Assn. Student Personnel Adminstrs., Ark. Assn. Colls. Tchr. Edn., Ark. Ednl. Research and Devel. Council, Phi Delta Kappa (treas. 1976-79), Kappa Delta Pi. Mem. Ch. of God in Christ. Author: Issues in Year-Round Education, 1977; contbr. articles on adminstrn. of higher edn. to profl. publs.; editorial bd. Jour. Edn., 1975—. Home: 1704 Loberg Ln Jonesboro AR 72401 Office: PO Drawer DDD State University AR 72467

RICHMOND, ROBERT LEE, fin. co. exec.; b. Rockland, Wis., Oct. 4, 1937; s. Clifford Lee and Bertha (Cumella) R.; A.A., Meridian Jr. Coll., 1976; B.S., Miss. State U., 1979; m. Peggy Jean Harvey, June 1, 1973; children—Timothy L., Brian E.; stepchildren—Vicki C. Palmer, Susan M. Palmer. Enlisted U.S. Air Force, 1955, advanced through grades to m/sgt., 1975; served in Okinawa, 1960-63, Vietnam, 1967, Thailand, 1967-68, ret., 1975; asso. mgr. United Co., Meridian, Miss., 1979—. Instr. electronics Lenoire (N.C.) Community Coll., 1974. Decorated Air medal with 3 clusters. Mem. VFW, Air Force Sgts. Assn., Miss. State U. Alumni Assn., Meridian Jr. Coll. Alumni Assn. Club: Masons. Home: Route 4 Box 110 Meridian MS 39301 Office: PO Box 5733 Meridian MS 39301

RICHSTEIN, ABRAHAM RICHARD, lawyer, govt. ofcl.; b. N.Y.C., Apr. 18, 1919; s. Morris and Ida (Stupp) R.; B.S. in Social Sci., Coll. City N.Y., 1939; LL.B., Fordham U., 1942; LL.M. in Internat. Law, N.Y. U., 1956; M.S. in Internat. Affairs, George Washington U., 1966, J.D., Fordham U., 1968; m. Rosalind Bauman, Nov. 29, 1942; children—Eric B., Jonathan W. Enlisted as pvt. U.S. Army, 1942, advanced through grades to col., 1966; admitted to N.Y. bar, 1942, U.S. Supreme Ct. bar, 1956, D.C. bar, 1977; faculty Nat. War Coll., Washington, 1966-68; joint staff planner Policy and Planning Directorate Joint Chiefs of Staff, Washington, 1968-69; ret., 1969; asst. gen. counsel AID, State Dept., 1969—. Decorated Bronze Star, Joint Ser. Commendation medal with oak leaf cluster, Army Commendation medal with 2 oak leaf clusters. Mem. Am. Soc. Internat. Law. Book rev. editor Fordham Law Rev., 1941-42; editorial bd. Mil. Law and Law of War Rev., 1960-63. Home: 8713 Mary Lee Ln Annandale VA 22003 Office: 21st and C Sts Washington DC 20523

RICHTER, CARL ARPAD, food industry cons.; b. Budapest, Hungary, Dec. 12, 1917; s. John and Irene (Mathes) R.; came to U.S., 1936, naturalized, 1942; student Trade Sch. for Cooks, Bucharest, Romania, 1931-34, U. Bucharest, 1935-36; m. Frances Regina Brady, Feb. 16, 1943. Chef Casino at Hecules Bad, 1934-35; pvt. chef to wife of Premier of Romania, 1935-36; with Racquet Club, Phila., also Strawbridge & Clothier and Slater System, Phila., 1936-41; with Slater System, Balt., 1946-49; v.p. food standards and research Servomation, Inc., Balt., 1950-72; with food service div. Green Giant Co., Miami, Fla., 1972-77; cons. chef; dir. spl. food seminars for chefs and mgrs.; judge culinary art shows; guest speaker; cons. food industry. Served with AUS, 1941-45. Recipient silver and gold medal Profl. Inst. Chefs of Am., 1966, gold medal Am. Acad. Chefs, Hon. Order Golden Toque, 1976; cert. exec. chef. Mem. Acad. Golden Togue (gold medal), Epicurean Club Greater Miami, Balt. Culinary Art Assn. (pres. 1964-66), Profl. Inst. Chefs (nat. v.p. 1964-65), Am. Culinary Fedn. (v.p. 1978-79). Home: 1901 SE Felton Ave Port Saint Lucie FL 33452

RICHTER, JAMES ARTHUR, hosp. adminstr.; b. Seattle, Oct. 19, 1943; s. John August and Leah Marie (Kilpatrick) R.; B.B.A., Stetson U., 1966; M.B.A., U. Fla., 1968; m. Gail Annetta Floyd, Aug. 14, 1965; children—Scott Andrew, Sean Arthur. Adminstrv. resident Warm Springs Found. Hosp., Warm Springs, Ga., 1967-68; asst. adminstr. Miss. County Hosps., Osceola, Ark., 1971-73; acting adminstr. Osceola (Ark.) Meml. Hosp., 1973-80. Mem. exec. bd. Osceola Meml. Hosp. Aux., 1972-80; cubmaster pack 221 Boy Scouts Am., 1979. Served to capt. Med. Service Corps, AUS, 1968-71; mem. Res. Decorated Bronze Star. Horace Moses Found. scholar, 1962-63. Mem. Am. Coll. Hosp. Adminstrs., Hosp. Fin. Mgmt. Assn. (advanced mem.), Ark. League for Nursing, Ark. Hosp. Assn., Ark. NE Hosp. Dist. (pres. 1976-77), Ark. Hosp. Adminstrs. Forum (treas. 1977), Ark. Young Adminstrs. Forum (charter, sec.-treas. 1978). Episcopalian (sr. warden 1973, 79, mem. vestry 1972-74, 77-79). Rotarian. Home: 716 W Arizona Ave DeLand FL 32720

RICKARD, JOSEPH CONWAY, psychologist; b. Weatherford, Tex., July 16, 1926; s. Joe Smith and Mattie Mae (Wright) R.; A.A., San Angelo Coll. 1948; Ph.D., U. Chgo., 1955; m. Dorothy June Wilson, May 29, 1948; children—Miles, Janis, Robert, Martha, Sarah. Instr. dept. psychology U. Tex., Austin, 1956-59, 60-62, 66-67, Temple (Tex.) Jr. Coll., 1965-66; asso. prof. Mary Hardin-Baylor Coll., Belton, Tex., 1966-74; clin. psychologist VA Center, Temple, 1955-60; chief psychology service Olin E. Teague VA Center, Temple, 1960—; cons. Bell County Rehab. Center, 1956-61, Temple Sch. System, 1965-79, Killeen (Tex.) Sch. System, 1971—, McGowan Stephens Sch., 1978—. Scoutmaster Heart O'Tex council Boy Scouts Am., 1964-68; bd. dirs. Bell County Crippled Children's Soc., 1955-62. Served with U.S. Army, 1945-46. Fellow Soc. Personality Assessment; mem. Southwestern Psychol. Assn., Tex. Psychol. Assn. (profl. standards com. 1972—), Bell County Psychol. Assn., Am. Psychol. Assn., Bell County Council Alcoholism, Sigma Xi. Episcopalian. Home: 3302 Oaklawn St Temple TX 76501 Office: Olin E Teague Veterans Center Temple TX 76501

RICKELTON, DAVID, cons. engr.; b. Glasgow, Scotland, Nov. 8, 1916; s. John and Catherine (Simpson) R.; student Bklyn. Poly. Inst., 1940, Pratt Inst., 1942; m. Virginia Thompson, Nov. 29, 1942 (dec.); children—David Kendall, John Thompson; m. 2d, Geneva Y. Brown, June 19, 1968. Came to U.S., 1923, naturalized, 1929. With Aeronca Inc. Environ. Control Group (formerly Buensod Stacey Corp.), Charlotte, N.C., 1940-77, successively draftsman, engr., cons., 1940-65, v.p., 1965-77, also gen. mgr.; cons. engr. in pvt. practice, 1977—. Served from pvt. to lt. AUS, 1942, served to capt., 1944-46. Registered profl. engr., N.C. Fellow Am. Soc. Heating, Refrigeration and Air Conditioning Engrs. (past pres.); mem. Nat. Soc. Profl. Engrs. Mem. Ch. of Christ (elder). Address; 3413 Highview Rd Charlotte NC 28210

RICKENBAKER, HUGH KELLEY, JR., ins. co. exec.; b. Pelham, Ga., Sept. 16, 1922; s. Hugh Kelley and Mary Annette (Bradford) R.; B.A. in Journalism, Emory U., 1947; m. Helen Scarlett Blanton, Dec. 15, 1951; children—Hugh Kelley, Alexander Blanton, Virginia Scarlett. Advt. copy writer Ga. Power Co., Atlanta, 1947-54; asso. dir. public relations Life Ins. Co. of Ga., Atlanta, 1954-65, asst. v.p. public relations, Atlanta, 1965-75, v.p., 1975-79, v.p. corp affairs, 1979—. Served with U.S. Army 1942-46. Mem. Life Ins. Advertisers Assn. (pres. 1972-73), Public Relations Soc. Am., Mktg. Communications Execs. Internat. (past pres. Atlanta chpt.), Better Bus. Bur. of Met. Atlanta (dir.), Sigma Delta Chi, Alpha Delta Sigma, Delta Tau Delta. Episcopalian. Home: 7120 Faunsworth Dr NW Atlanta GA 30328 Office: 600 W Peachtree St NW Atlanta GA 30308

RICKER, WILLIAM ELMER, assn. exec.; b. Carbondale, Pa., June 23, 1933; s. Elmer Joseph and Lillian (Deegan) R.; student U. Ala., 1958, 79; m. Frances Rose Leonard, Jan. 15, 1956; children—Laura, David, Gabrielle, Regina. Exec. sec. to Mayor of Birmingham (Ala.), 1967-70; exec. dir. Operation New Birmingham, 1970-73; planning dir. Jefferson County Community Chest/United Way, Birmingham, 1973—; mem. faculty U. Ala. Spl. Studies Inst, 1978. Active Birmingham Festival of Arts 1967-74, ARC, 1968—, Sertoma Center for Communicative Disorders, 1979; v.p. Birmingham Symphony Assn., 1979; mem. Birmingham Parole Bd., 1967-70; bd. dirs. Ala. Zool. Soc. Served with U.S. Army, 1952-54. Mem. Public Relations Soc. Am., Nat. Press Photographers Assn., Sigma Delta Chi, Sigma Chi. Clubs: Birmingham Press, Downtown, The Club, K.C. Photography work used to illustrate various publs. Home: 1514 Milner Crescent Birmingham AL 35205 Office: 3600 8th Ave S Birmingham AL 35222

RICKETTS, DIANE WILLS, mfg. co. mgr.; b. Chgo., Dec. 19, 1955; d. Lowell E. and Violet (Heery) Wills; B.Chemistry, Wheaton Coll., Mass., 1975; postgrad. Bus. Sch. Tulane U., 1977; m. Philip Malone Ricketts, June 26, 1976. With Procter & Gamble, 1975—, tech. brand asst., Cin., 1975, supr. manufacture synthetic granules package soap and detergent, Kansas City, Kans., 1976, supr. packing synthetic granules, 1977, prodn. planning mgr. Folger Coffee, New Orleans, 1978, warehouse and maintenance mgr. Folger Coffee, 1979—; sponsor summer engr. program, 1977. Bus. cons. Jr. Achievement project, 1976, 77; chmn. Wheaton Coll. recruiting, 1976—; pres. Wheaton Coll. New Orleans Alumnae Chpt., 1978-79; active French Branch Homeowners Alliance, 1978-79. Mem. Am. Chem. Soc., AAAS, AAUW. Republican. Presbyterian. Club: UDC. Home: 113 Rue Aries Slidell LA 70458

RICKETTS, FRED R., fin. co. exec.; b. Sayre, Okla., Mar. 30, 1924; s. Rayble L. and Ethel M. (Harris) R.; B.S., U. Tulsa, 1947; m. Sybil Marie Hunter, Dec. 27, 1941; children—Ronald, Allison. Exec. v.p. Automatic Radio Mfg. Co., Boston, 1959-61; pres. Vanguard Mfg. Co., Dallas, 1961-64; pres. First Main Capital Corp., Dallas, 1964—; chmn. bd., chief exec. officer Morton Foods, Dallas, 1976—; guest lectr. Am. Mgmt. Assn., So. Meth. U. Mem. Dallas Citizens Council. Served with USAAF, 1942-45. Decorated D.F.C., Air medal with eight oak leaf clusters. Hon citizen, New Orleans. Mem. Assn. for Corp. Growth (pres.), Dallas C. of C. Methodist. Clubs: City, Brookhollow Country, Quadrant Town. Author Series of Articles on Corporate Directorships for Financial Trend, 1976, Series of Articles on Corporate Merger Trends - Multiple Coverage, 1977. Home: 4057 Deep Valley Dr Dallas TX 75234 Office: 8700 King George Dr Dallas TX 75235

RICKS, JOHN ADDISON, educator, historian; b. Charlotte, N.C., Aug. 18, 1939; s. John Addison and Mamye Snow (Turner) R.; B.A., Davidson Coll., 1961; M.A., Tulane U., 1963; Ph.D., U. N.C., 1974; m. Nancy Elaine McLeod, Apr. 23, 1966; children—Elizabeth Anne, John Addison IV. Instr. history Montreat-Anderson Coll., Montreat, N.C., 1966-68; instr. history Valdosta (Ga.) State Coll., 1968-70, 73; research asst. U. N.C., Chapel Hill, 1970-72, teaching asst., 1972-73; asst. prof. history Valdosta State Coll., 1974-78, asso. prof. history, 1978—. Mem. Valdosta Bd. Edn., 1976—; chmn. Lowndes County Democratic Com., 1978-80, sec.-treas., 1976-78; mem. Ga. Dem. Exec. Com., 1975—; chmn Lowndes County Campaign Com. for Jimmy Carter, 1976; mem. adv. council Retired Sr. Vols. Program Lowndes County, 1977—; cubmaster Alapaha Area council Boy Scouts Am., 1977-80; mem. arrangements com. Ga.-Jefferson-Jackson Day Dinner, 1979; 2d Congressional Dist. coordinator Common Cause, 1975-76. Served as 1st lt. U.S. Army, 1963-65. Ford Found. fellow, 1967; Valdosta State Coll. Alumni Endowment grantee, 1976-77; Nat. Endowment for Humanities grantee, 1978. Mem. AAUP (dir.), Ga. Assn. Historians, So. Hist. Assn., Am. Hist. Assn., Ga. Sch. Bds. Assn., Valdosta-Lowndes County C. of C., Phi Alpha Theta. Presbyterian. Club: Kiwanis. Home:

104 Georgia Ave Valdosta GA 31601 Office: Patterson St Valdosta GA 31601

RIDDELL, MARY ELLEN, poet; b. Rochester, N.Y., Dec. 20, 1897; d. John Blackwell and Jennie (Jordan) Riddell; student Pa. State U. Extension, Columbia. Exec. legal sec. Furst, McCormick Muir, Lynn & Reeder, Williamsport, Pa., 1931-62; sec. to head bond dept. Lycoming Trust Co., 1931; sec. to exec. v.p. Susquehanna Trust Co., 1928-30; registered rep. Waddell & Reed, Inc., 1968-71; corporate sec., dir. Haven Securities Inc., 1971-73. Team capt. local fund drives United Fund, Heart Assn., A.R.C.; vol. worker Williamsport Hosp. Recipient Woman of Year award Susquehanna chpt. Am. Bus. Women's Assn., 1958, 1st prize for poetry Williamsport Community Arts Festival, 1961. Fellow Internat. Poetry Soc.; mem. Am. Bus. Women's Assn., D.A.R., Lycoming County Hist. Soc., Pa. Poetry Soc., Inc., Am. Legion Aux., Fla. State Poets Assn. (rec.-corr. sec. 1978). Presbyn. Author: Thoughts in the Night (poetry), 1965. Contbr. poetry to anthologies, poetry jours., mags. Home: 60-40 Sheoah Blvd Winter Springs FL 32707

RIDDICK, EDGAR KADER, JR., cons. engr.; b. Walnut Ridge, Ark., July 16, 1923; s. Edgar Kader and Eleanor Champion (Wilkes) R.; student Northwestern U., 1942-43, Hamilton Coll., 1943-44, U. Ariz., 1945-46; B.S. in Mech. Engring., U. Ark., 1948; m. June Dudney Runyan, Aug. 29, 1959; children—Ellen (Mrs. Harold H. Simpson, II), Leigh, Edgar Kader III; stepchildren—Cinde Bauer, Michael Bauer. Engr., Phillips Petroleum Co., Bartlesville, Okla., 1948-55; partner Blass, Riddick & Chilcote (formerly Erhart, Eichenbaum, Rauch, Blass), Architects, Little Rock, 1955—; cons. engr., Little Rock, 1968—; pres. Riddick Engring. Corp., 1978, Sunrise Aircraft Corp. Chmn. Goals for Central Ark., 1973—. Bd. dirs. Sr. Citizens Activities Today, 1974—. Served with AUS, 1943-46. Mem. Am. Soc. Heating, Refrigerating and Air Conditioning Engrs. (chmn. nat. energy conservation com. 1975-76), Ark. Soc. Profl. Engrs., Nat. Soc. Profl. Engrs.-Profl. Engrs. in Pvt. Practice, Am. Cons. Engrs. Council, Assn. Cooperation in Engring. (nat. chmn. coordinating com.). Clubs: Little Rock Country, Capitol, Little Rock. Patentee in field. Home: 7 Greenbrier Dr Little Rock AR 72202 Office: 2310 1st Nat Bank Bldg Broadway at Fifth Little Rock AR 72201

RIDDLE, ALTHAE SPEAR IRELAND, artist; b. Burlington, N.C.; d. John Alfred and Inez (Spear) Ireland; student Guilford Bus. Coll., 1923-24, Elon Coll., 1933; m. Norman William Riddle, Aug. 11, 1931 (dec. 1976); 1 son, Norman William. Executed coats of arms, 1948, owner bus., 1972-76; exhibited in numerous group shows in U.S. Co-chmn., flower show cons. Flower Show Schs., W.Va., 1963-67, master certificate as judge; past pres. Garden Lovers Club, Burlington, N.C., Cumberland Garden Club, Bluefield, W.Va., past dir. Dist. 5, N.C. Garden Clubs (life mem.). Mem. D.A.R. (registrar chpt., 1962-68, regent John Chapman chpt., mem. house com. Nat. Soc., resolutions com. 1970-72), Bluefield Fine Arts Soc., Internat. Platform Assn., U.D.C. (pres. Bluefield 1965-68, pub. cook book 1967, v.p. W.Va. div. 1968-69, pres. Charles F. Fisher chpt. 1970-73), Elon Coll. Rose Soc., Nat. Soc. Magna Charta Dames, C. of C. (chmn. hostess com. women's div. 1972-73, dir. 1973-76), Alamance County Arts Assn., Delphian Lit. Soc. (pres. Bluefield), Nat. Geneal. Soc., Internat. Soc. Heraldry and Family Trees, Dau. Am. Colonies, Colonial Dames XVII Century (sec. Earl of Shrewsbury chpt.), Sovereign Soc. Ams. Royal Descent. Episcopalian (pres. women of ch. 1958-60, dir. altar guild 1961-68). Clubs: Bluefield Woman's (past sec.), Altrusa (dir. 1972-73; pres. 1974-75, sec. 1976-77). Address: 1308 Sunset Dr Burlington NC 27215

RIDDLE, BRIAN LEE, hosp. adminstr.; b. Marshall, Tex., Aug. 20, 1948; s. Dexter Lee and Frances Audrey (Cone) R.; B.B.A., E. Tex. State U., 1970; student Baylor U., 1971; M.S., Trinity U., 1973; m. Jennifer Ann Fusilier, Dec. 28, 1976; children—Ashley Gayle, Hayley Brook. Night adminstr. Baptist Hosp. System, San Antonio, 1972-73; adminstrv. resident Medicare div. State Health Dept., Austin, Tex., 1974; asst. adminstr. Ville Platte (La.) Gen. Hosp., 1974-75; asso. adminstr. Doctor's Hosp. of Jackson (Miss.), 1975; adminstr. Ville Platte Gen. Hosp., 1975-77; exec. dir. Beaumont (Tex.) Med. Surg. Hosp., 1977—; dir. Indigent Care Clinic, Beaumont, Tex., 1979—. Mem. Am. Coll. Hosp. Adminstrs., Beaumont C. of C. Club: Rotary. Home: 6930 Westgate Beaumont TX 77706 Office: 3080 College St Beaumont TX 77702

RIDDLE, JESSE LEONARD, II, retail exec.; b. Coolidge, Tex., Apr. 10, 1921; s. Jesse Leonard and Bessie Zula (Herring) R.; student St. Olafs Coll., 1943, U. Ga., 1944; m. Dorothy M. Graves, Oct. 10, 1943; 1 son, John L. Store mgr. Montgomery Ward & Co., Kansas City, Mo., 1949-57, Godchaux's Clothing Co., New Orleans, 1960-73; sales mgr. men's and boys' apparel Gibson's Trade Show, Dallas, 1974—. Served with USN, 1941-45. Decorated DFC, Air medal (3); named Lion of Yr., 1970. Mem. Lakeside Mchts. Assn. (pres. 1968), Nat. Retail Mchts. Assn., Nat. Assn. Mens Sportswear Buyers. Clubs: Lions (pres. 1969-70), Elks. Home: 7448 Chesterfield St Dallas TX 75237 Office: 1266 E Ledbetter Dr Dallas TX 75216

RIDDLE, LINDSEY GRANT, ret. broadcasting co. exec., elec. engr.; b. Preston, Mo., Aug. 11, 1910; s. Joseph Grant and Jessie (Lindsey) R.; grad. pub. high sch.; m. Edwina Giles Barthe, Sept. 3, 1951; 1 dau., Martha Riddle Bankson. Studio supr. WHB Broadcasting Co., Kansas City, Mo., 1933-46; chief engr. Stephens Broadcasting Service, Inc. (name changed to WDSU Broadcasting Corp., 1950), New Orleans, 1946-48, chief engr., 1949-66, v.p., chief engring. Royal St. Corp., WDSU-TV Inc., New Orleans, from 1966, now ret. Mem. tech. adv. com. Delgado Coll., New Orleans, 1970—; chmn. services subcom. La. Industry Adv. Com., 1967—; mem. Lakewood Property Owners Assn. New Orleans, 1961—. Registered profl. engr., La.; recipient certificate of excellence U.S. Cath. Conf. Mem. Nat. Assn. Broadcasters (tech. com. 1969-71), Assn. Broadcast Engring. Standards (tech. com.), IEEE (sr. mem.), Assn. Fedn. Communications Cons. Engrs., Nat. Soc. Profl. Engrs., La. Engring. Soc., Armed Forces Radio Services, Nat. Ry. Hist. Soc., New Orleans Engring. Club, New Orleans C. of C., S. Central Modern Lang. Assn., Royal Radio Club (pres.), Delta DX Amateur Radio Club, New Orleans VHF Radio Club, Am. Radio Relay League, Broadcast Pioneers, Old Timers Club. Democrat. Methodist. Contbr. articles to profl. jours. Home: 5646 Bellaire Dr New Orleans LA 70124

RIDGE, DAVY-JO STRIBLING, librarian; b. Anderson, S.C., Jan. 16, 1932; d. David Warren and Thelma Josephine (Braselton) Stribling; B.A., Queens Coll., 1954; M. Librarianship, Emory U., 1955; certificate in Med. Librarianship, Med. Library Assn., 1957; m. George Ross Ridge, June 9, 1956 (div. Dec. 1964). Instr. cataloging U. Ga. Libraries, 1955-56; reference librarian DeKalb County Library System, Decatur, Ga., 1956-64; head, reference dept. U. S.C. Library, Columbia, 1965-72, asst. dir. libraries, 1973-75, asso. dir., 1975—. Patron, Friends of Emory U. Library, 1970—. Mem. A.L.A., Southeastern, S.C. (chmn. pub. relations com. 1972—, co-chmn. interlibrary loan com. 1973-74, chmn. legislation com. 1976, chmn. local arrangements 1976) library assns., South Caroliniana Soc. (hon. life), Nat. Columbia (dir.) Audubon socs., Queens Coll. Alumnae Assn. (Spl. Recognition), Emory U. Alumni Assn. (Spl. Recognition). Episcopalian. Clubs: Carolina Bird (S.C. and N.C.); Columbia Bird (pres. 1970), Palmetto Cat (sec. 1971, pres. 1977, entry clk. cat show 1972—) (Columbia) Editor: Rare Books in the McKissick Memorial Library of the University of South Carolina, 1966, A Checklist of Microforms in the University of South Carolina Libraries, 1971, Library Handbook, 1971. Contbr. articles to library jours. Home: 112 Carriage Hill Columbia SC 29206

RIDGEWAY, TILMAN LEON, mortician; b. Dover, Tenn., Aug. 3, 1939; s. John Tilman and Lillie Ruth (Call) R.; B.S., Union U., Jackson, Tenn., 1957; M.S., Dallas Inst. Mortuary Sci., 1959; m. Lanita Carol Wyatt, Aug. 7, 1965; children—Christopher Leon, Bradley Wyatt. With advt. and sales promotion dept. Memphis div. Kroger Food Stores, 1958; with Ridgeway Morticians, Paris, Tenn., 1959—, pres., owner, 1976—; pres. Rose Lawn Memory Garden & Mausoleum; mem. adv. bd. health occupations W.J. Neese Vocat. Sch.; tchr. indsl. 1st aid, lectr. death and dying. Chmn. Henry County chpt. ARC, 1963-69; bd. dirs. Paris Jaycees, 1964-67; exec. dir. Queen of Tenn. Valley Beauty Pageant, 1961-66; adv. bd. Henry County Distributive Edn. Club; nat. pres. Distributive Edn. Clubs Am., 1957-58. Named Ky. col., Tenn. col. Mem. Nat., Tenn. assns. funeral dirs., Tenn. Acad. Mortuary Sci. Coll. Grads., Am. Cemetery Assn., Cemetery Assn. Tenn., Henry County C. of C. Democrat. Baptist. Clubs: Rotary (sgt.-at-arms), Shriners (past pres.), Elks, Order Eastern Star (past patron) (Paris). Home: 206 Peachtree St Paris TN 38242 Office: PO Box 788 Paris TN 38242

RIDINGS, PAUL OVERTON, pub. relations agy. exec.; b. Meadville, Mo., May 3, 1917; s. Joseph Willard and Lilly May (Sayers) R.; B.A., Tex. Christian U., 1938; M.A., U. Mo., 1939; m. Freddie Williams, Oct. 21, 1939; children—Ruth Anne (Mrs. Robert D. Rayel), Paul Overton. Asst. sports editor Fort Worth Press, 1938; editor Ennis (Tex.) Daily News, 1939-40; dir. pub. relations, chmn. dept. journalism Midland Luth. Coll., Fremont, Neb., 1940-42; dir. pub. relations Ill. Inst. Tech. and affiliates, Armour Research Found., Inst. Gas Tech., Chgo., 1942-44; dir. pub. relations Mpls. office McCann-Ericson, Inc., 1944-45; pres., owner Ridings & Ferris, Inc., Chgo., 1945-48; dir. pub. relations, chmn. dept. journalism Tex. Christian U.. Fort Worth, 1948-50; co-owner, co-pres. Witherspoon & Ridings, Inc., Fort Worth, 1950-55; pres., owner Paul Ridings Pub. Relations, Ft. Worth, 1955—; dean, chief exec. officer Northwood Inst. Tex., Cedar Hill (on leave), 1974-75; founding dir. Granville Walker Ministerial Scholarship Found., 1969—. Recipient Most Valuable Alumnus award Tex. Christian U., 1954, Royal Purple award, 1971; Meritorious Service award Counselors sect. Pub. Relations Soc. Am., 1972; Quality Dealer Pub. Relations award Time mag., 1972; Golden Wheel award Overseas Motors Corp., 1974. Mem. Tex. Christian U. Alumni Assn. (nat. pres. 1953-54), Pub. Relations Soc. Am. (pres. Chgo. chpt. 1948, nat. dir. 1949, pres. North Tex. chpt. 1968, sec.-treas. S.W. dist. 1969, nat. exec. com. counselors sect. 1969-71, nat. sec.-treas. counselors sect. 1971), Publicity Club Chgo. (dir. 1943-44, 46-48), Kappa Phi Omega (nat. pres. 1937-40, 44-45), Delta Upsilon, Sigma Delta Chi, Pi Delta Epsilon (grand nat. councilman 1940-42, 43-44), Kappa Tau Alpha. Mem. Christian Ch. Mason (Shriner). Clubs: Colonial Country; Fort Worth. Home: 600 Green River Trail Fort Worth TX 76103 Office: 3467 West Freeway Fort Worth TX 76107

RIDLEY, CLARENCE HAVERTY, lawyer; b. Atlanta, June 3, 1942; s. Frank Morris and Clare Malone (Haverty) R.; B.A., Yale U., 1964; M.B.A., Harvard U., 1966; J.D., U. Va., 1971; m. Sarah Eleanor Horsey, Aug. 23, 1969; children—Augusta Morgan, Clare Haverty. Admitted to Ga. bar, 1971; partner firm King & Spalding, Atlanta, 1977—; dir. Haverty Furniture Cos., Inc., Scofield Properties, Inc., Southeastern Timber Co., Inc. Mem. Atlanta Citizens Adv. Council on Urban Devel., 1973-74; bd. dirs., mem. exec. com. Goodwill Industries Atlanta, Inc.; trustee St. Joseph's Village. Served to lt. U.S. Army, 1966-68. Mem. Atlanta Council Younger Lawyers (dir. 1974-75), Am., Atlanta bar assns., State Bar Ga., Am. Judicature Soc. Democrat. Roman Catholic. Clubs: Piedmont Driving, Commerce, Homosassa. Home: 2982 Habersham Rd Atlanta GA 30303 Office: 2500 Trust Co Tower Atlanta GA 30303

RIDLEY, GLENDA AMANDA, nurse; b. Tift County, Ga., Jan. 21, 1940; d. Jack and Hazel Amanda Griffin; B.S. in Nursing, Emory U., 1963; m. William Donald Ridley, Aug. 4, 1962; children—William Donald, Donna Amanda. Mem. nursing staff Central State Hosp., Milledgeville, Ga., 1964-73, nursing service adminstr., 1973-78, coordinator nursing and spl. services, 1978—; adv. council Ga. Coll. Sch. Nursing. Mem. Am. Nurses Assn., Ga. Nurses Assn., 14th Dist. Nurses Assn., Central Ga. Soc. Nursing Service Adminstrs., Eatonton Service League. Baptist. Home: Route 1 Box 169 B Eatonton GA 31024 Office: Powell Bldg Central State Hosp Milledgeville GA 31062

RIEDEL, PAUL SCHREITER, mobile homes co. ofcl.; b. Minden City, Mich., Oct. 8, 1911; s. Louis Herman and Anna (Schreiter) R.; student Mich. State U., 1928-31, Detroit Bus. U., 1932; m. Dorothy Artha Slack, Oct. 17, 1932; children—Daniel P., Andrea Lynn. Propr., L.H. Riedel Lumber Co., 1941-46, pres. L.H. Riedel Lumber Co., Inc., 1946-53; hon. chmn. Vindale Corp., mobile homes, Brookville, Ohio; dir. First Nat. Bank of Dayton. Presbyterian. Clubs: Racquet, Dayton Country, Bicycle (Dayton); Capitol Hill (Washington); Moorings Country (Naples, Fla.); Le Mirador Country (Mont Pelerin, Switzerland). Home: 4051 Gulf Shore Blvd N Naples FL 33940

RIEGER, SAM LEE, ins. co. exec.; b. Durango, Colo., May 14, 1946; s. Lee Roy and Ruth (Harris) R.; student U. Tex., 1964-68; m. Pamela J. Robinson, Apr. 7, 1973. Sales agt. Prudential Ins. Co., Dallas, 1970-72; sales supr. Great Am. Res. Inc. Co., San Antonio, 1972-74, dir. manpower devel., 1974-76, agy. mgr., Austin, Tex., 1974-76, S.W. Agy., San Antonio, 1976—. Served with U.S. Army, 1969. Recipient Nat. Mgmt. award Gen. Agts. and Mgrs. Conf., 1979, 80. Mem. Nat. Assn. Life Underwriters, San Antonio Assn. Life Underwriters, Gen. Agts. and Mgrs. Assn. Republican. Methodist. Clubs: Los Rios Country, Canyon Creek Country. Home: 14118 Oakland Mills San Antonio TX 78231 Office: 4414 Centerview St Suite 150 San Antonio TX 78228

RIES, EDWARD RICHARD, petroleum geologist, oil co. exec.; b. Freeman, S.D., Sept. 18, 1918; s. August and Mary F. (Graber) R.; student Freeman Jr. Coll., 1937-39; A.B. magna cum laude, U. S.D., 1941; M.S., U. Okla., 1943, Ph.D. (Warden-Humble fellow), 1951; postgrad. Harvard, 1946-47; m. Amelia D. Capshaw, Jan. 24, 1948 (div. Oct. 1956); children—Rosemary Melinda, Victoria Elise; m. 2d, Maria Wipfler, June 12, 1964. Asst. geologist Geol. Survey S.D., Vermillion, 1941; geophys. interpreter Robert Ray Inc., Oklahoma City, 1942; jr. geologist Carter Oil Co., Mont., Wyo., 1943-44, geologist Cutbank, Mont., 1944-49; sr. geologist Standard Vacuum Oil Co., India, 1951-53, sr. regional geologist, Indonesia, 1953-59, geol. adviser for Far East and Africa, White Plains, N.Y., 1959-62; geol. adviser Far East, Africa, Oceania, Mobil Petroleum Co., N.Y.C., N.Y., 1962-65; geol. adviser for Europe, Far East, Mobil Oil Corp., N.Y.C., 1965-71, sr. regional explorationist Far East, Dallas, 1971-73, Asia-Pacific, Dallas, 1973-76, sr. geol. advisor, 1976—. Grad. asst., teaching fellow U. Okla., 1941-43, Harvard, 1946-47. Served with AUS, 1944-46. Mem. N.Y. Acad. Scis., Am. Assn. Petroleum Geologists (asso. editor 1976—), Geol. Soc. Am., Am. Hort. Soc., Internat. Platform Assn., Am. Geol. Inst., A.A.A.S., Nat. Audubon Soc., Nat. Wildlife Fedn., Soc. Exploration Geophysicists, Wilderness Soc., Am. Legion, Phi Beta Kappa, Sigma Xi, Phi Sigma, Sigma Gamma Epsilon. Republican. Mennonite. Club: Harvard (Dallas). Contbr. articles to profl. jours. Home: 6009 Royal Crest Dr Dallas TX 75230 Office: 7200 N Stemmons Dallas TX 75247 also Mobil Oil Corp PO Box 900 Dallas TX 75221

RIESGO, VILMA MELBA, guidance counselor; b. Tampa, Fla., Nov. 23, 1942; d. Joseph and Esperanza (Ferreiro) Riesgo; B.A., U.S. Fla., Tampa, 1963, M.A., 1975; student Tulane U., 1964-67. Tchg. asst. Tulane U., 1964-67; tchr. English, French, Spanish Woodrow Wilson Jr. High Sch., Tampa, Fla., 1968-69, tchr. Spanish, Lakewood High Sch., St. Petersburg, Fla., 1969-76, guidance counselor, 1976—. Co-founder GUIDE. Mem. Pinellas County Guidance Assn., Fla., Am. personnel and guidance assns., Am. Sch. Counselors Assn. Democrat. Roman Catholic. Home: 4108 San Luis St Tampa FL 33609 Office: 1400 54th Ave S St Petersburg FL 33711

RIEWE, MARVIN EDMUND, agronomist; b. Pottsville, Tex., July 6, 1926; s. Edmund Fred and Henrietta (Wehmeyer) R.; B.S., Tex. A. and M. U., 1949, M.S., 1959; m. Fern Loraine Drees, Apr. 23, 1955; children—Brian Edmund, Paul William, Andrew Marvin. Jr. agronomist Agrl. Research Sta., Tex. A. and M. U., Angleton, 1949-55, asst. agronomist, 1955-61, asso. agronomist, 1961-67, asso. prof.-in-charge, 1967-74, prof.-in-charge, 1974—. Cons. in field V.I. Agrl. Expt. Sta., Kingshill, St. Croix, 1973, Instituto de Zootecnia, Sao Paulo, Brazil, 1974, Instituto Nacional de Investigaciones Agricolas, Torreón, Mexico, 1974—. Served with USNR, 1945-46. Named Profl. Conservationist of the Year, Waters Davis Soil Conservation Service Dist., 1973. Mem. Am. Soc. Agronomy, Crop Sci. Soc. Am., So. Pasture and Forage Crop Improvement Conf. (mem. exec. com. 1965-70, chmn. 1969). Lutheran. Lion. Contbr. numerous articles in field to profl. jours. Home: 717 Southside Dr Angleton TX 77515 Office: PO Box 728 Angleton TX 77515

RIFE, LOU GEHRIG, social worker; b. Huntington, W.Va., Aug. 18, 1945; s. Timothy Marvin and Lillian Vance (Gibson) R.; B.A. in Psychology, David Lipscomb Coll., 1969; m. Gwen Luna, Sept. 2, 1972. Psychotherapist, Genesee Psychiat. Clinic, Flint, Mich., 1971-72; counselor pre-sch. children Project OutReach, Crossville, Tenn., 1973-75; dir. social services Cumberland Med. Center, Crossville, 1975—. Bd. dirs. Plateau Mental Health Center, 1975, Kids, Inc., 1975—, Crossville Group Home, 1979—. Served with U.S. Army, 1969-71. Named Outstanding Young Man of Yr., Crossville Jaycees, 1976. Mem. Tenn. Soc. Health Care Social Workers (dir. 1976-77). Mem. Ch. of Christ. Club: Rotary (dir. 1978—). Home: Route 5 18 Bee Circle Crossville TN 38555 Office: Cumberland Med Center Box 667 Crossville TN 38555

RIFFE, LAVERN EDGAR, petroleum co. exec., banker; b. Hollister, Okla., Sept. 3, 1914; s. Oscar Hamilton and Dora Myrtle (Blair) R.; B.S. in Chemistry, Okla. State U., 1939; m. Alice Allene Rives, Sept. 17, 1939; children—Sandra Morris, Martha Atkinson, Regina Johnson, Susan Suliburk, Sarah Martin, Cynthia Kirsch. Asst. supt. refinery Allied Materials Corp., Oklahoma City, 1940-46; asst. to mgr. refining div. Kerr-McGee Oil Co., Oklahoma City, 1946-52; v.p. refined products mktg. Anchor Petroleum Co., Tulsa, 1952-57; pres. Riffe Petroleum Co., Tulsa, 1957—; chmn. bd. NuWay Emulsions; owner, chmn. bd. 1st State Bank, Ketchum, Okla. Bd. dirs. Okla. State U., Stillwater, 1965-79, pres. adv. bd., 1965-79; bd. dirs. St. Gregory's Coll., Shawnee, Okla., 1975-79, chmn. bd., 1976-79; bd. dirs. YMCA, Boy Scouts Am. Mem. Am. Petroleum Inst., Asphalt Technologists Assn., Asphalt Emulsion Mfrs. Assn., Twenty-five Yr. Club of Petroleum Industry, C. of C. Democrat. Roman Catholic. Clubs: So. Hills Country, Tulsa, Summit, Petroleum, Cherokee Yacht, Ocean Reef, Pinnacle Peak. Office: 1111 Philtower Bldg Tulsa OK 74103

RIFKINSON, NATHAN, neurosurgeon; b. Lithuania, May 23, 1912; s. Samuel and Sarah (Ginsburg) R.; came to U.S., 1917, naturalized, 1923; M.D., Emory U., 1936; m. Mae Persky, Aug. 6, 1940; children—Jan Stephen, Stephanie. Rotating intern Trinity Hosp., N.Y.C., 1936-38; sr. municipal physician St. Thomas (V.I.) Dept. Health, 1939-42, chief emergency med. service, 1941-42; resident in pathology Sch. Tropical Medicine, San Juan, P.R., 1942-43; pathologist, chief clin. labs. Bayamon Dist. Hosp. div. hosps. P.R. Dept. Health, 1943-45, neurosurgeon for div. hosps., 1948—; fellow and asst. in neurol. surgery Washington U., St. Louis, 1945-48; asst. prof. clin. neurology and neurol. surgery U. P.R., 1951-66, asso. prof. neurol. surgery, 1967-72, prof. neurol. surgery, dir. sect. neurol. surgery, 1973—, lectr. in pharmacology Sch. Medicine and Dentistry, 1959-63, lectr. in neurology Sch. Dentistry, 1959-69; chief neurol. surgery VA Hosp., San Juan, 1963—; mem. staff Affiliated Hosps. of P.R. Med. Center, Presbyn. Community, San Jorge, Doctors hosps. (all Santurce), Tchrs., Auxilio Mutuo hosps (both Hato Rey); neurosurgeon P.R. Ins. Fund, 1948—. Diplomate Am. Bd. Neurol. Surgery. Fellow ACS (pres. P.R. chpt. 1973); mem. Am. Assn. Neurol. Surgeons, P.R., Am. med. assns., Congress Neurol. Surgeons, Soc. Neurol. Surgeons, Caribbean Assn. Neurol. Surgeons, Internat. Assn. Study of Pain. Contbr. articles to med. jours.; editorial bd. Boletin, 1968—; editor Neurosurgery, U. P.R., 1975—. Home: 1351 Magdalena Ave Santurce PR 00907 Office: 309 Ashford Med Center Santurce PR 00907

RIGAU, JUAN JOSÉ, research chemist; b. Sabana Grande, P.R., Nov. 24, 1939; s. Juan and Irma (Sepúlveda) R.; B.Sc., U. P.R., 1960, M.Sc. in Organic Chemistry, 1965; Ph.D., Wayne State U., Detroit, 1969; m. Carmen Margarita Rozas, Dec. 22, 1962; children—Irma Margarita, Juan José, Alex Agustín, Adelle Marie. Research asst. radiochemistry, then research asst. div. organic chemistry P.R. Nuclear Center, 1960-65; research fellow Wayne State U., 1965-69; head organic chemistry div. P.R. Dept. Research and Devel., Econ. Devel. Adminstrn., 1969-73; dir. Office Petroleum Fuels Affairs, Office Gov. P.R., 1973-76; head fossil fuels research Center Energy and Environ. Research, U. P.R., 1977—; pres. Energy and Environ. Dynamics, Inc.; pres. Coll. Chemists P.R., 1974-75; lectr., adviser in field. Am. Syntex Steroids Research fellow, 1959-60. Mem. Am. Chem. Soc., Sigma Xi, Phi Lambda Upsilon. Roman Catholic. Contbr. articles to profl. jours. Home: A-10 Mirador de Borinquen Gardens Rio Piedras PR 00926 Office: Center for Energy and Environ Research Caparra Heights Station San Juan PR 00935

RIGBY, JERRY, carpet co. adminstr.; b. Alma, Ga., June 2, 1946; s. Luziner Bryan and Trudie (Stewart) R.; student South Ga. Coll., 1964-65, Univ. Off-campus, Waycross, Ga., 1966-68; B.A. in Mktg., U. Ga., 1971; m. Mary Olivia Johnson, Dec. 15, 1973. Terr. mgr. Milliken Carpets, Va. and N.C., 1971-75, Met. Washington, 1976-77, mgr. sales tng., LaGrange, Ga., 1977-78, corp. sales tng. dir., 1979—; speaker. Ky. col., 1979. Mem. Pine Mountain Orchid Soc. (v.p. 1979-80), Am. Mktg. Assn., U. Ga. Baptist Student Alumni Assn. (pres. 1975-77, trustee 1977—), Pi Sigma Epsilon. Republican. Baptist. Home: 322 Country Club Rd LaGrange GA 30240 Office: 1 Dallis St LaGrange GA 30240

RIGBY, RICHARD HILLMAN, educator; b. East Liverpool, Ohio, Apr. 25, 1926; s. Clarence Albert and Elsie Muriel (Hillman) R.; B.A., U. Tampa, 1970; M.A., U. South Fla., 1973; m. Betty Ruth Dixon, Apr. 21, 1951 (div. 1965); children—Jeffrey G., Richard D., Leslie G. Mfrs. med. rep. Schenley Labs., 1952-66; program coordinator retardation units H.A.R.C., Tampa, Fla., 1971-72; tchr., Sarasota, Fla., 1972—; owner TV sales and service co., Sarasota, 1975—. Active Boy Scouts Am. Served with USAAF, 1944-46. Mem. Am. Gerontol. Soc., V.F.W., Psi Chi. Mason (Shriner). Home: 2725 S Lockwood St Sarasota FL 33582 Office: 3949 Sawyer Rd Sarasota FL 33583

RIGGAN, WILSON BUTLER, agrl. economist; b. Waverly, Va., Sept. 15, 1914; s. Jesse Thomas and Ellie (Butler) R.; B.S. with honors, Va. Poly. Inst., 1950; Ph.D., N.C. State U., 1966; m. Edna Irene Downs Joyner, Aug. 8, 1953; children—Wilson Butler, Jesse Edmund. Asst. agrl. economist N.C. State Coll., 1955-57, instr., 1957-58; asst. prof. agrl. econs. and econometrics, grad. prof. U. Fla., 1958-64, supervisory statistician, biometry sect. ecol. research br., div. health effects research Nat. Air Pollution Control Adminstrn., Durham, N.C., 1964-66, chief biometry sect., 1966-67, asst. chief ecol. research br., 1967-71, asst. dir. for research operations, div. health effects research, 1971-73, research coordinator Human Studies Lab., 1973-74, health scientist (research) epidemiology br., 1974—. Served with U.S. Mcht. Marine, 1942-46. Mem. Am. Farm Econs. Assn., Am. Statis. Assn., Econometric Assn., Am. Econ. Assn., Am. Acad. Polit. and Social Sci., Biometric Assn., Am. Pub. Health Assn., Phi Kappa Phi, Alpha Zeta, Gamma Sigma Delta. Methodist. Home: 3609 Westover Rd Durham NC 27707 Office: Environmental Research Center Environmental Protection Agy Research Triangle Park NC 27711

RIGGEN, GAYLORD RAY, JR., systems analyst; b. San Luis Obispo, Calif., May 31, 1935; s. Gaylord Ray and Eleanor Mary (Jespersen) R.; student San Jose (Calif.) Community Coll., 1968-73; A.A., Claremore (Okla.) Jr. Coll., 1976; m. Donna Jane Lair, Aug. 18, 1956; children—Rod, Cindy, Steve. Office worker Guarantee Chevrolet, San Diego, Calif., 1956-57; accountant Royal Mcbee Corp., Palo Alto, Calif., 1957-61, United Stero Tapes, Sunnyvale, Calif., 1961-62; ins. salesman I.O.F., San Jose, 1962-63; sr. crew scheduler Am. Airlines, San Francisco, 1963-73, functional systems analyst, Tulsa, 1973—, now sr. systems analyst. Leader Rogers County 4-H, 1974—; supt. Rogers County Fair, 1976—; leader Boy Scouts Am., 1967-73; pres. Home Owners Assn., 1976. Served with USNR, 1953-56. Democrat. Home: Route 4 Box 457R Claremore OK 74017 Office: 3800 N Mingo Rd Tulsa OK 74151

RIGGINS, STEVEN CRANDAL, constrn. co. exec.; b. Waycross, Ga., Aug. 5, 1947; s. Henry Harry and Mary Winnefred (Thompson) R.; student U. Ga., 1965-66; B.S., Troy State U., 1977; m. Elaine Childs, Aug. 9, 1969; children—S. Christopher, Courtney Louise. With Daniel Constrn. Co., Dothan, Ala., 1971—, cost engr., 1975-78, services mgr., 1978—; tax cons., public acct. Served to capt. AUS, 1966-70. Mem. Ala. Sheriffs Assn., Am. Mgmt. Assn. Democrat. Methodist. Club: Masons. Home: Route 1 Box 198 Ozark AL 36360 Office: PO Box 417 Dothan AL 36301

RIGGS, BARRY LYNN, utility co. adminstr.; b. Martinsville, Va., Feb. 27, 1953; s. John Clyde and Mary Ruth (Biggs) R.; B.S., Va. Poly. Inst. and State U., 1975; M.B.A., Va. Commonwealth U., 1981. Indsl. engring. trainee Am. Safety Razor Co., Staunton, Va., 1971; co-op student, indsl. engring. trainee Westinghouse Nuclear Steam Turbine, Charlotte, N.C., 1972-74; asst. engr. Va. Electric & Power Co., Richmond, Va., 1975-77, asso. engr., 1977-78, inventory analyst, 1978-79, sr. analyst devel. and implementation of materials mgmt. system, 1979—. Mem. Nat. Soc. Profl. Engrs., Am. Inst. Indsl. Engrs. Baptist. Home: 3200 J Tanners Way Richmond VA 23224 Office: 4113 Castlewood Rd Richmond VA 23234

RIGGS, CECIL GRAHAM, communications co. exec.; b. Durham, N.C., Aug. 23, 1935; s. Otho Graham and Mildred Louise (Massey) R.; grad. Cleve. Inst. Electronics, 1962; grad. Advanced Mgmt. Program, Harvard, 1973; m. Carolyn Jean Wilson, Oct. 6, 1956; children—Sabrina, Janita. Electronic technician. Automatic Electric Co., 1956-69; v.p. Continental Communications Constrn. Co., Tampa, Fla., 1969-70, pres., chief exec. dir., 1971-73; pres. Concomco Can., Ltd., Montreal, 1971—; operating v.p. Arcata Installation Co., Tampa, 1972-73; v.p. Telephone Plant Constrn. Corp., 1972—; pres. Continental Communications Service Corp., Tampa, Fla., 1973—, Concomco Corp., Tampa, 1973—, Omega Internat. Corp., Tampa, 1974—. Asst. dir. Tampa Concentrated Employment Program, 1970—; industry rep. Nat. Alliance Businessmen Program, 1973—. Mem. Ind. Telephone Pioneers Assn. (dir. 1970—), Fla. Telephone Assn., Internat. Platform Assn., Tampa C. of C. Clubs: Tower, Commerce (Tampa); Buckhorn Golf and Country (Brandon, Fla.); Harvard Business School Fla. West Coast (dir. 1977-78). Home: 207 Wheeler Rd Seffner FL 33584 Office: PO Box 23727 Tampa FL 33622

RIGGS, JAMES CRAIG, state ofcl.; b. Bryan, Tex., Mar. 22, 1943; s. John K. and Alice W. R.; B.S. in Zoology, Tex. A&M U., 1966, M.S. in Biology, 1968. Tech. prodn. supr. stabilized pulp products group Johnson & Johnson Domestic Operating Co., Chgo., 1970-71, asso. research scientist, 1971-72; head statewide planning coordination and implementation sect., comprehensive outdoor recreation planning br. Tex. Parks and Wildlife Dept., Austin, 1972—; cons., advisor outdoor recreation planning and funding matters. Served to 1st. lt. U.S. Army, 1968-70. Mem. AAAS, Tex. Recreation and Parks Soc., Assn. Former Singing Cadets of Tex. A&M U., Sigma Xi. Presbyterian. Co-author state and regional summary vols. of Texas Outdoor Recreation Plan, 1975; contbr. articles in field to publs. Office: Comprehensive Planning Branch Texas Parks and Wildlife Dept 4200 Smith School Rd Austin TX 78744

RIGGS, VIRGINIA LOUISE HOLLOWAY (MRS. ARTHUR J. RIGGS), lectr., clubwoman; b. Conway, Ark.; d. Keith Leaming and Harriett (Bennett) Holloway; B.A., U. Ark.; m. Arthur J. Riggs, Oct. 15, 1942; children—Arthur James, Emily Adele (Mrs. John W. Freeman), Keith Holloway, George Bennett. Editor, Virginia's Kitchen. Park Cities North Dallas News, 1955-60; lectr. cooking, related topics, 1955—, hist. topics, 1960—. Pres., LeBonnet Bleu Garden Club, 1966-68, Seneca Rev. Club, 1967-68, Dallas Browning Club, 1970-72, S'Amuser Club, 1966-67, Jr. Matheon Club, 1971-72. Mem. Kappa Kappa Gamma. Club: Matheon. Home: 4116 Amherst St Dallas TX 75225

RIGNEY, ELEANOR, coll. adminstr.; b. Union Hill, N.J., June 22, 1923; d. Harry and Mae (Goode) R.; A.B. summa cum laude, U. N.C., 1950; M.A.T., Duke U., 1965; Ph.D. candidate Emory U., 1974—. Chmn. spl. ability and talented Charlotte-Mecklenburg (N.C.) Schs., 1961-69; asst. prin. Bartram Sch., Jacksonville, Fla., 1969-71; asst. prof. social sci. Brenau Coll., Gaineville, Ga., 1971—, dean student affairs, 1975—. Campaign dir. March of Dimes, 1979—. Served in WAVES, 1943-46. Coe Found. fellow, 1963, 69; Ga. Humanities grantee, 1973-75. Mem. So. Personnel Assn., Ga. Assn. Women Deans, Phi Beta Kappa, Delta Kappa Gamma. Episcopalian. Contbr. poem to jour.; author: Centennial History of Brenau College. Office: Brenau Coll Gainesville GA 30501

RIGSBEE, HERBERT KENNETH (KEN), JR., profl. engr.; b. Houston, June 23, 1943; s. Herbert K. and Myra B. (Kitchens) R.; B.S. in Archtl. Engring., U. Tex., 1967; m. Sharon S. Waters, Apr. 13, 1968; children—Heather Dawn, Scott Austin. Engring. trainee Phillips Petroleum Co., Bartlesville, Okla., 1966-68, constrn. engr., Raleigh, N.C., 1968-70, Kenai, Alaska, 1970-71, design engr., Bartlesville, 1967-68, mgmt. analyst, 1971-72, sr. projects analysis engr. gas and gas liquids dept., 1972-74, ednl. communications rep., 1974-76, ednl. relations coordinator, 1976-78, staff planning dir. natural resources group, 1978—. Sec. Osage County Water Dist. 1, 1979—; v.p. Bartlesville Bd. Edn., 1971-75; trustee NSPE Ednl. Found., Inc., 1978—. Named Outstanding Young Oklahoman, Okla. Jaycees, 1977, Okla. Young Engr. of Yr., 1978; recipient Disting. Service award Bartlesville Jaycees, 1976; registered profl. engr., Tex., Okla. Mem. Am. Soc. Engring. Edn., Nat. Soc. Profl. Engrs., Okla. Soc. Profl. Engrs., Engrs. Council for Profl. Devel., Bartlesville Engrs. Club, Bartlesville Area C. of C. Republican. Methodist. Club: Heelpoppers Square Dancing. Home: 809 Crestland Dr Bartlesville OK 74003 Office: 14 C1 Phillips Bldg Bartlesville OK 74004

RIKLIN, SAM JONATHAN, advt. agy. exec.; b. San Antonio, Aug. 22, 1921; s. Jacob J. and Tillie R.; B.A., U. Calif., 1948; postgrad Stanford U., 1948-50; m. Ann Riklin, July 2, 1955; children—Seth Jonathan, Alicia Beth, Leah Ann. With NBC, Los Angeles, 1952; account exec., creative dir. J. Walter Thompson, Los Angeles, 1953; gen. mgr. Tex. Printing and Pub. Co., San Antonio, 1954-57; creative dir. Pitluk Advt. Co., San Antonio, 1957-62; pres. Sta. KAPE, San Antonio, 1962; pres. Advt. and Mktg. Services, San Antonio, 1965—; adj. univ. lectr., 1965-75. Pres., Boysville, San Antonio, 1959; pres. Beautify San Antonio Assn., 1960-61; chmn. Heart Assn., San Antonio, 1961-64, 75. Served with USAF, 1942-46. Named Outstanding Citizen, City of San Antonio, 1955; recipient U.S. Navy Service award, 1966; Air Force award, 1977; Mem. San Antonio Advt. Assn. Clubs: Rotary, B'nai B'rith, Temple El Brotherhood (pres. 1957), Am. Legion (post comdr. 1970), San Antonio Tennis Assn. (pres. 1970). Home: 1000 Jackson Keller San Antonio TX 78212 Office: 3355 Cherryridge St San Antonio TX 78230

RILES, GEORGE GRIFFITH, stockbroker; b. Macon, Ga., Dec. 16, 1948; s. Frederick Emerson and Gladys Alice (Griffith) R.; B.S. in Indsl. Mgmt., Ga. Inst. Tech., 1970; M.B.A., Valdosta State Coll., 1977; m. Carolyn Victoria McGarity, Mar. 21, 1970; children—Robert Frederick, Katherine Victoria. Research asso. Fed. Res. Bank, Atlanta, 1970-71; v.p. Robinson-Humphrey Co., Inc., Albany, Ga., from 1973; now asst. v.p., mgr. Merrill Lynch Pierce Fenner & Smith Inc., Albany. Served to capt. U.S. Army, 1971-73. Mem. Albany Assn. for Retarded Children, YMCA, Ga. Inst. Tech. Alumni Assn. (v.p. 1977-78, pres. 1978-79), Phi Kappa Phi. Presbyterian. Clubs: Doublegate Country; Elks, Pine Forest Racquet (Albany). Home: 1709 Lowell Ln Albany GA 31707 Office: PO Box 1609 Albany GA 31702

RILEY, JOHN KILLIAN, mgmt. exec.; b. Indpls., Apr. 18, 1933; s. Walter R. and Virginia L. (George) R.; B.A., Wabash Coll., 1955; m. Virginia L. Vogel, July 2, 1955; children—Bruce, John, Jeffrey. Field rep. Retail Credit Co., Clarksville, Nashville, 1957-59; div. head home office staff, Atlanta, 1960-62, asst. mgr., Detroit, 1962-63, mgr., Saginaw, Mich., Lakewood, Ohio, Seattle, Wash., 1963-68, asst. v.p. employee relations and personnel, Atlanta, 1968-70, regional v.p. Equifax, Phila., 1970-74; pres. Hunnicutt & Assos., St. Petersburg, Fla., 1974-78; pres. Atwell-Vogel-Sterling, Atlanta, 1979—; dir. Equifax Affiliated Cos. Served with U.S. Army, 1955-57. Mem. Am. Mgmt. Assn., Beta Theta Pi. Methodist. Clubs: Kiwanis, Horseshoe Bend Country, Elks, Rotary. Home: 440 Sassafras Ln Roswell GA 30076 Office: 1875 Century Blvd NE Atlanta GA 30345

RILEY, RAY JOE, agronomist; b. Plainview, Tex., May 11, 1935; s. James Ray and Edna (Davis) R.; student Tex. A. and M. U., 1952-53; B.S. with high honors, Tex. Tech U., 1956, postgrad., 1956-57; m. Jo Eddy Scott, Oct. 7, 1961; children—Kevin Ray, Jodie Ed. Instr. agronomy, registered plant breeder Tex. Tech U., 1957; registered plant breeder Riley Farms, Hart, Tex., 1958-59; registered plant breeder, agronomist Riley Yieldmaster Seed Corp., 1960, exec. v.p., 1961—; v.p., dir. Trans Tex. Cattle Co., Bonham, Tex., 1965—; pres., dir. Estacado Industries Inc., Dimmitt, Tex. Chmn. U.S. Cotton Producers and Ginners del. to Universal Cotton Standards Confs. Dir. Running Water Soil and Water Conservation Dist., 1973; pres. bd. trustees Springlake Earth Ind. Sch. Dist., 1974-79; vice-chmn. High Plains Research Found. Served with AUS, 1958. Recipient Gerald W. Thomas Outstanding Agriculturalist award Tex. Tech. U., 1975; Man of Year in Tex. Agr. award Tex. County Argl. Agts. Assn., 1977. Mem. Plains Cotton Growers Inc. (pres. 1971-74, chmn. bd. 1974-75), Tex. Assn. Cotton Producer Orgns. (dir. 1971—), Tex. Certified Seed Producers Inc. (dir. 1966-68), Alpha Zeta, Phi Eta Sigma, Alpha Chi. Democrat. Mem. Ch. of Christ. Author (with Chester C. Jaynes and Coleman Y. Ward) A Laboratory Manual for Freshmen Agronomy Students, 1957. Patentee shelled corn-cottonseed animal feed, 1972. Home: Route 2 Hart TX 79043

RILEY, RICHARD WILSON, gov. of S.C.; b. Greenville, S.C., Jan. 2, 1933; s. Edward Patterson and Martha Elizabeth (Dixon) R.; B.A., Furman U., 1954; J.D., U. S.C., 1960; m. Ann Osteen Yarborough, Aug. 23, 1957; children—Richard Wilson, Anne Y., Hubert D., Theodore D. Admitted to S.C. bar, 1959; partner firm Riley & Riley, Greenville, 1959—; spl. asst. to subcom. U.S. Senate Jud. Com., 1960; mem. S.C. Ho. of Reps., 1963-66; mem. S.C. Senate from Greenville-Laurens Dist., 1966-76; gov. State of S.C., 1979—; mem. Pres. Carter's Adv. Commn. on Intergovtl. Relations, 1977. Vice pres. S.C. Young Democrats, 1968. Served to lt. (j.g.) USNR, 1954-56. Named Outstanding Young Man of Greenville and S.C., Jr. C. of C., 1965; named Outstanding Legislator, S.C. Young Democrats, 1976. Mem. S.C., Greenville bar assns., Furman U. Alumni Assn. (pres. 1968-69). Democrat. Rotarian. Office: Office of Gov State House Columbia SC 29211

RILEY, RONALD PATRICK, SR., chem. packaging co. exec.; b. Bridgeton, N.J., Mar. 17, 1948; s. Walter F. and Ethel F. (Homola) R.; B.B.A., Memphis State U., 1970; m. Virginia Anne Armstrong, June 7, 1968; children—Ronald Patrick, Michael Preston. Project mgr. W. M. Barr & Co., Memphis, 1976-77, dir. corp. devel., 1977—. Safety officer Memphis Sr. Squadron CAP, 1978—. Served to capt. USAF, 1971-76. Decorated Air medal, AF Commendation medal, Combat Readiness medal. Republican. Methodist. Home: 2090 Shenandoah Dr Memphis TN 38134 Office: PO Box 1879 Memphis TN 38101

RILEY, WILLIAM O., steel co. exec.; b. 1921; student Ga. Inst. Tech.; LL.B., Atlanta Law Sch.; married. With Atlantic Steel Co., Inc., Atlanta, 1940—, dir. indsl. reins., 1958-60, asst. sec., 1960-63, v.p. indsl. reins., 1963-68, v.p. indsl. and public reins., 1968-69, v.p. adminstrn., treas., 1969-71, sr. v.p., 1971-76, exec. v.p., 1976-78, pres., 1978—, also dir.; dir. Atlantic Bldg. Systems Inc. Office: Atlantic Steel Co Inc 1300 Mecaslin St NW Box 1714 Atlanta GA 30301*

RILING, EUGENE HAROLD, engr.; b. Spiro, Okla., Aug. 23, 1936; s. Lester and Eva Rowena (Clark) R.; B.S., Calif. State U., 1968; m. Irla Kay Hughey, May 6, 1960; children—Barton, Quentin. Engring. asst. E.B. Hall, 1960-62 br. mgr. Grant Oil Tool, Compton, Calif., 1962-65; prodn. engr. Thums Long Beach Co., Long Beach, Calif., 1965-71; sr. application engr. Byron Jackson Pump Co.-Centrilift, Midland, Tex., 1971-76; mgr. field service TRW Reda Pump, Bartlesville, Okla., 1976—. Mgr., Little League, 1969-70, 71-74; active YMCA. Section leader Republican party, 1968-69. Served with AUS, 1956-59. Mem. Am. Inst. Mining, Metall. and Petroleum Engrs., Am. Petroleum Inst., Am. Soc. Plant Engrs. Baptist. Club: Hillcrest Country. Author, illustrator: Handbook for Oilfield Subsurface Electrically Driven Pumps, 1975; Tee Up in the Oilpatch, 1976. Patentee in field. Cartoonist. Home: 934 Briarwood Dr Bartlesville OK 74003 Office: 4th and Dewey Bartlesville OK 74003

RIMBERT, SUZANNE BOITER, human resources cons.; b. Enid, Okla., Mar. 26, 1946; d. Ansel Luther and Mary Anna (Richardson) Boiter; student Furman U., 1964-66; B.A. in Sociology, Case Western Res. U., 1968; M.B.A. in Mgmt., Ga. State U., 1973, postgrad. in organizational behavior, 1979—; m. Philippe Pierre Rene Rimbert, Dec. 28, 1974; 1 dau. Stephanie Camille Françoise. Personnel counselor, asst. tng. dir. Rolco, Chgo., 1968-70; adminstr., head tchr. Purucker Sch., Atlanta, 1971; asst. corp. sec., mgr. personnel services Glasrock Products, Inc., Atlanta, 1971-73; personnel specialist Michelin Tire Corp., France and S.C., 1974; project mgr., internal cons. Rollins, Inc., Atlanta, 1976-80; v.p. Frantech Corp., Atlanta, 1980—. Sec.-treas. Nigerian Nat. Mus. Soc., 1975. Cert. employment cons. Nat. Employment Assn. Mem. Am. Soc. Tng. and Devel., Women's Forum (founding mem. Atlanta chpt.). Episcopalian. Editor, Fancy That newspaper Am. Women's Club, Nigeria, 1975; contbr. poems to various publs. Home: 1762 N Rock Springs Rd Atlanta GA 30324 Office: Frantech Corp 5891 New Peachtree Rd Suite 108 Doraville GA 30340

RIMEL, GEORGE WILLIAM, editor; b. West Chester, Pa., Oct. 5, 1944; s. George William and Barbara Joy (Burns) R.; B.A., Miami Dade Coll., 1964; m. Helen Charlene Redford, Mar. 17, 1978; children—George Jarrett, Christine Kimber. Account exec. Miami Herald, Miami, Hollywood, Fort Lauderdale, 1968-73; sales mgr. N. Dade Jour., Miami, 1973-74; display advt. mgr. Bradenton (Fla.) Herald, 1974-75, circulation dir., 1975-77; gen. mgr., mng. editor Community Reporter Mag., Miami, 1978—. Loan exec. United Fund, 1973, 74, 76; Cub Scout master Boy Scouts Am., 1978-79. Served with U.S. Army, 1965-68. Recipient award Kroehler Furniture, 1970, award United Fund, 1977, Addy award, 1977; Eagle Scout, 1956. Mem. Internat. Newspaper Advt. Execs., Savings and Loan Mktg. Execs., So. Circulation Mgrs. Democrat. Methodist. Clubs: Sertoma, Toastmasters. Home: 285 W 56th St Hialeah FL 33012 Office: 1515 NW 167th St Suite 110Y Miami FL 33169

RIMEL, MERWYN DELENOR, hosp. adminstr.; b. Coatesville, Pa., Mar. 16, 1941; s. Edward D. and Dorothea A. Rimel; student public schs., Downing Town, Pa.; children—Tracy, Richard, Tara. Painting contractor, South Hampton, Pa., 1969-73; storeroom mgr. Doctors Hosp., Lake Worth, Fla., 1973-74, purchasing agt., 1974-78, dir. materials mgmt., 1979—; owner, dir. Environ. Services, Boynton Beach, Fla., 1978—; active S. Fla. Shared Purchasing Program and Cost Containment. Mem. Am. Hosp. Assn., Fla. Hosp. Purchasing and Materials Mgmt. Assn. Office: Doctors Hospital of Lake Worth Box 1649 Lake Worth FL 33460

RIMER, LAURA PEEPLES, banker; b. Atlanta, Feb. 12, 1921; d. Ralph Woods and Clara Elizabeth (Smith) Peeples; student DeKalb Coll., 1965; postgrad. Sch. Bank Mktg., U. Colo., 1970-71; m. James Roland Rimer, Oct. 6, 1939; children—Ruthanne (Mrs. Donald Mulvihill), James Roland Laura (Mrs. Anthony M. Lanza). Woman's editor Decatur-DeKalb News, Decatur, Ga., 1958-65; asst. to woman's editor Lynchburg News (Va.), 1965-66; v.p., public relations officer Fidelity Am. Bank, N.A., Lynchburg, 1967—; public relations cons. Holiday Lake 4-H Ednl. Center, Westminster-Canterbury, Inc.; del. Va. Gov.'s Conf. on Libraries and Public Info., 1979. Bd. dirs., sec. Lynchburg Kaleidoscope, Inc., 1975-79; mem. public info. com. Central Lynchburg Renewal and Devel.; mem. adv. bd. on public info. Lynchburg Public Schs. bd. dirs. Lynchburg Hist. Found., Inc., Lynchburg Humane Soc. Inc., Jones Meml. Library, Lynchburg unit Am. Cancer Soc., 1975-79. Mem. Lynchburg Area Public Relations Assn. (treas., Douglas Southall Freeman Public Relations Profl. of Yr. award 1978), Nat. Assn. Bank Women, Advt. Club Lynchburg (sec. 1968, 69, 70), Va. Bankers Assn. (mem. com. on pub. info. and mktg. 1976-78). Episcopalian. Home: 81 N Princeton Circle Lynchburg VA 24503

RINEHART, LEILA MAE, bus. exec.; b. Chester County, Pa., July 16, 1938; d. Chester G. and Elsie Annie (Dahms) Kirkhoff; student Pierce Jr. Coll., Phila., 1955-57, LaSalle Extension U., 1963-64, Northwestern Sch. Taxidermy, Nebr., 1967-69. Exec. sec., Phila., 1957-64; plant security officer Penguin Industries Inc., Parkesburg, Pa., 1964-70; partner F.I. D'Imperio Sales & Internat. Trade Co., Exton, Pa., 1960-65; co-owner, bus. mgr. Rinehart's Inc., Nantmeal Village, Pa., 1967-75; v.p., adminstrv. asst. Woodcrest Mgmt. Corp./Andrew Devel. Corp./Fred Sternberg/Wynn Devel. Corp., Fort Lauderdale, Fla., 1972-78; v.p., corp. sec. Standard Mech. Contractors Inc., Pompano Beach, Fla., 1978—; owner, operator L.M. Rinehart Bus. Services Co., Pompano Beach, 1978—. Mem. Nat. Rifle Assn. (life), Am. Water Ski Assn. (affiliate). Contbr. articles to Popular Mechanics, World of Taxidermy. Home: Apt 110 Club House Cove 1100 Crystal Lake Dr Pompano Beach FL 33064

RINKER, GEORGE ERNEST, physician; b. Wichita, Kans., Oct. 17, 1939; s. John Robert and Minnie (McPherson) R.; B.A., Centre Coll. Ky., 1961; M.D. Wake Forest Coll., Winston-Salem, N.C., 1965; m. Barbara Ann Blackwelder, Aug. 29, 1964; children—Lillian Hamilton, Elizabeth Ann, Verne Blackwelder. Intern, N.C. Bapt. Hosp., Winston-Salem, 1965-66; resident in anatomic and clin. pathology Bowman Gray Sch. Medicine, N.C. Baptist Hosp., Winston-Salem, 1965-67, 68-70, resident internal medicine, 1967-68, 70-71; dir. anatomic pathology Biomed. Reference Labs., Burlington, N.C., 1976—. Diplomate Am. Bd. Pathology, Nat. Bd. Med. Examiners. Fellow Coll. Am. Pathologists, Am. Soc. Clin. Pathologists; mem. A.C.P., AMA, N.C., Alamance-Caswell County med. socs., Internat. Acad. Pathology, AAAS, N.C. Soc. Pathologists. Home: 817 Colonial Dr Burlington NC 27215 Office: 1308 Rainey St Burlington NC 27215

RINNE, AUSTIN DEAN, ins. co. exec.; b. Indpls., Aug. 14, 1919; s. Hermann H. and Marie (Knudsen) R.; student Ind. U., 1938-40; grad. ins. marketing Purdue U., 1947; m. Martha Jo Runyan, Dec. 29, 1941; children—Erik Knudsen, Barbara Jane. With Northwestern Mut. Life Milw., 1946—, dist. agt., Indpls., 1956-58, gen. agt. N. Tex., Dallas, 1958—; dir. Bank of Dallas. Guest lectr. Purdue U., 1956, So. Meth. U., 1961. Pres., Dallas Estate Planning Council, 1966-67; mem. adv. council ins. dept. North Tex. State U., 1975. Bd. dirs. Dallas Civic Opera Guild, Park Cities YMCA, Dallas. Served to capt. USAAF, 1941-45; ETO. Decorated Air medal with cluster, Purple Heart. Mem. Am. Legion (comdr. 1967-68), Nat. Assn. Barbed Wire Clubs (pres. 1947-48), Grad. Soc. Insts. Ins. Marketing (pres. 1949-50),

Dallas Gen. Agts. and Mgrs. Assn. (dir. 1962-63), Dallas Assn. Life Underwriters (dir. 1960-63), Dallas Sales and Mktg. Execs. (dir. 1973-74, 79-80), Mil. Order World Wars, Ind. U. Alumni Assn. Dallas-Ft. Worth (pres. 1966-67), Internat. Platform Assn., English Speaking Union (dir. Dallas chpt.), Phi Kappa Psi Alumni Assn. (pres. 1951-52), Phi Kappa Psi (exec. Council 1972-74). Clubs: City, Dallas Country, Northshore (Dallas); Sertoma (pres. 1967-68). Home: 4311 Bordeaux St Dallas TX 75205 Office: 3635 Lemmon Ave Dallas TX 75219

RIORDAN, ELISABETH GALLIGAN, counselor; b. New Bern, N.C., June 18, 1943; d. Edward P. and Nora G. (Williams) Galligan; B.S., Old Dominion U., 1964; M.A., George Washington U., 1970, now doctoral candidate; m. Barrett J. Riordan, Feb. 14, 1975; 1 son, Matthew B. Tchr., Chesapeake (Va.) City Sch. System, 1964-68; editor Chesepeake Mag., 1966-67; tchr. Fairfax County (Va.) Sch. System, 1968-70; counselor Prince Georges County (Md.) Schs., 1970-76; cons., Alexandria, Va., 1976—; adj. faculty George Washington U., 1979-80. mem. Fairfax County Environ. Quality Adv. Council, 1980—. Cert. counselor, Md. Mem. Am. Personnel and Guidance Assn., Assn. Measurement and Evaluation in Guidance, Alpha Xi Delta. Home and Office: 3803 Ivanhoe Ln Alexandria VA 22310

RIORDAN, MICHAEL E., nuclear engr., naval officer; b. Lansing, Mich., Aug. 19, 1949; s. Robert E. and Ruth (Madole) R.; B.S., U.S. Naval Acad., 1971; M.E., U. Va., 1972; m. Janet K. Bitzer, Aug. 12, 1978. Nuclear power trainee Bainbridge, Md. and West Milton, N.Y., 1972-73, commd. ensign U.S. Navy, 1971, advanced through grades to lt. comdr., 1977, main propulsion asst. U.S.S. Kamehameha, 1973-74, communications officer, 1975-76, engring. officer USS Sunfish, 1977—. Univ. fellow U. Va., 1971-72. Mem. Am. Nuclear Soc., AAAS, U.S. Naval Inst., ACLU, Tau Beta Pi. Club: Kiwanis. Home: 824 Warren St Pascagoula MS 39567 Office: US Navy USS Sunfish (SSN649) FPO New York City NY 09501

RIOS, LUIS MANUEL, plastic surgeon; b. Mexico City, Feb. 12, 1935; s. Manuel and Maria Luisa (Pastrana) R.; came to U.S., 1960, naturalized, 1977; B.S., Nat. U. Mex., 1952, M.D., 1960; m. Mary Ann Mungovan; June 23, 1962; children—Luis M., Daniel G., Edward X., Jennifer Ann. Intern, St. Mary of Nazareth Hosp., Chgo.; resident in gen. surgery Creighton U. Med. Sch., Omaha, 1963-66; resident in plastic surgery U. Tex. Med. Sch., San Antonio, 1969-71; practice medicine specializing in plastic and reconstructive surgery, McAllen, Tex., 1971—; mem. staffs McAllen Gen., Edinburg Gen., Mission Mcpl., Knapp Meml. Meth. hosps.; asso. clin. prof. U. Tex. Health Sci. Center, San Antonio; mem. adv. bd. Rio Grande Valley Cranio-Facial Anomalies Adv. Group. Diplomate Am. Bd. Plastic Surgery. Fellow Internat. Acad. Cosmetic Surgery, A.C.S.; mem. Am. Soc. Plastic and Reconstructive Surgeons, Internat. Soc. Clin. Plastic Surgeons, AMA (Physicians Recognition award), Tex. Med. Assn., Hidalgo-Starr County Med. Soc. Roman Catholic. Office: 1414 Galveston St McAllen TX 78501

RIPLEY, ROBERT KENYON, JR., newspaper editor; b. Virginia Beach, Va., Aug. 3, 1950; s. Robert Kenyon and Martha Phillips (Van Patten) R.; A.B. in Journalism, U. N.C., Chapel Hill, 1972; m. Vickie Louise Corbett, Aug. 5, 1972. Founder, editor The Branch, monthly publ. Inter-Varsity Christian Fellowship, U.S.A., Madison, Wis., 1972-75; editor, bus. mgr. Spring Hope (N.C.) Enterprise, 1975—; free-lance journalist, tchr. Trustee Spring Hope Library; chmn. Spring Hope Recreation Assn. Recipient 1st place feature writing award Charlotte (N.C.) Observer competition, 1971; 1st place column writing award Southeastern Coll. Newspaper competition, 1971; 3d pl. interpretive reporting nat. competition Hearst Found., 1971; 1st Place Editorial Writing award N.C. Press Assn., 1976, 3d Pl. Editorial Writing award, 1977; Public Service award Town of Middlesex, 1976. Mem. Am. Sci. Affiliation, N.C. Editorial Writers Assn. (exec. com.), N.C. Jaycees, Phi Beta Kappa, Sigma Delta Chi (named Most Outstanding Journalism Grad., U. N.C. 1972), Kappa Tau Alpha. Democrat. Episcopalian. Home: PO Box 185 Spring Hope NC 27882 Office: PO Box 399 Spring Hope NC 27882

RIPPLE, HELEN BERNICE, nurse; b. Plummer, Minn.; d. Alex C. and Mary R.; R.N., St. Elizabeth Hosp., Yakima, Wash., 1957; B.S. in Nursing, St. Louis U., 1971, M.S., 1974. Supr., head nurse John Cochran VA Hosp., St. Louis, 1970-73; cons. nursing St. Louis City Hosp., 1973, dir. nursing, 1973-75; dir. nursing, asso. adminstr. U. Va. Med. Center, Charlottesville, 1976—, asso. prof. Sch. Nursing, 1976—; vice chmn. subaera council Va. Health Service Area I, 1976—; mem. Jefferson Area Bd. Aging, 1977—. Mem. parish council St. Thomas Roman Catholic Ch., Charlottesville, 1976—. Served with Nurse Corps, USAF, 1965-70. Decorated Air Force Commendation medal. Mem. Am. Nurses Assn., Am. Cancer Soc., Aerospace Med. Assn., Nat. League Nursing, Am. Soc. Nursing Service Adminstrs. (dir., pres. Va. chpt. 1979). Home: Route 8 Box 155 Charlottesville VA 22901 Office: Univ Va Med Center Box 405 Charlottesville VA 22908

RISER, JIMMY ROBERT, mgmt. systems engr.; b. Saluda, S.C., June 24, 1937; s. Robert Karl and Eula Mae (Connelly) R.; ed. high sch.; m. Ethel Mae Rowe, Mar. 24, 1960; children—Hope Elizabeth, Faith Letitia, Zachary Robert. Engring. rate clk. Deering-Milliken Corp., Marietta, S.C., 1963-64, jr. indsl. engr., 1964-66, indsl. engr., 1966-67; asst. indsl. engr. Greenville (S.C.) Hosp. System, 1967-73; mgmt. systems engr. Humana Inc., Louisville, 1973—. Served with USAAF, 1956-59. Mem. Am. Inst. Indsl. Engrs., Hosp. Mgmt. Systems Soc., Am. Hosp. Assn. Democrat. Lutheran. Home: 9113 Cox Ct Louisville KY 40222 Office: 1 Riverfront Plaza Louisville KY 40202

RISER, MARY ELIZABETH, geneticist; b. Richland, Wash., Aug. 1, 1945; d. Manning Walker and Mary Virginia (Dillard) R.; B.S., Tulane U., 1967; M.S., U. Tex., 1970, Ph.D., 1973; m. Robert Donald Colligan, Sept. 1, 1978. NIH postdoctoral fellow Baylor Coll. Medicine, Houston, 1974-76, instr., 1976-77, asst. prof. dept. cell biology, 1977—. Rosalie B. Hite predoctoral fellow, 1970-73. Mem. Tissue Culture Assn. (pres. Tex. br.), Am. Soc. Cell Biology, Tex. Geneticists, U. Tex. Grad. Student Assn. (pres. 1972-73), Chi Omega. Methodist. Contbr. articles to sci. jours. Home: 10402 Woodwind St Houston TX 77025 Office: Dept Cell Biology Baylor Coll Medicine Houston TX 77030

RISINGER, PEGGY, hosp. adminstr.; b. Elmer, Okla., Mar. 23, 1931; d. Loyd J. and Iva B. (Williams) Briscoe; B.S., Southwestern Okla. State U., 1951; m. Johnnie Lee Risinger, May 29, 1952; children—Kris, Mark, Marilyn, Kelly. Bus. office mgr. Jackson County Meml. Hosp., Altus, Okla., 1957-65, asst. adminstr., 1965-67, chief exec. officer, 1967—; mem. task force Okla. Health Systems Agy.; bd. trustees Okla. Blue Cross/Blue Shield; mem. State Health Coordinating Council; mem. Gov.'s Task Force to Implement Public Law 93-641; mem. ops. com. S.W. Okla. Shared Services. Mem. Am. Coll. Hosp. Adminstrs., Okla. Hosp. Assn. (chmn. bd. trustees), Hosp. Fin. Mgmt. Assn., Am. Hosp. Assn. (polit. action com.), Okla. Emergency Med. Services (dir.). Democrat. Baptist. Home: 1041 E Liveoak St Altus OK 73521 Office: 1200 E Pecan St Altus OK 73521

RISTROPH, MARIE GIBBENS, planning and mgmt. cons.; b. Baton Rouge, Aug. 31, 1943; d Richard Thomas and Virgil Veronica (Bush) Gibbens; B.A., La. State U., 1967; m. Robert Michael Ristroph, June 3, 1972; children—Robert, Alice, Trygve, Einar. Urban planner New Orleans City Planning Commn., 1967-72; head ops. Houston City Planning Dept., 1972-74; chief comprehensive planning div. City of Houston, 1974-78; planning and mgmt. cons., 1978—; mem. adv. bd. Local Govt. Center, Santa Barbara, Calif., 1976—. Co-founder La. Libertarian Party, 1971; officer Harris County (Tex.) Libertarians, 1972-76; co-founder Assn. Rational Environ. Alternatives, 1974. Recipient resolution of commendation New Orleans City Planning Commn., 1972. Mem. Am. Inst. Planners (Outstanding Service award Gulf-S.W. 1972), Am. Soc. Planning Ofcls., As. Pub. Works Assn. Author: Getting the Most for Your Planning Dollar, 1978; contbr. articles in field to profl. jours. Home: 2320 Wordsworth St Houston TX 77030

RITCHEY, OZZIE KINCHEN, univ. adminstr.; b. Cordele, Ga., Oct. 31, 1936; d. Warren and Ozzie Bell (Stripling) Kinchen; A.A., Miami Dade Community Coll., 1972; B.S. (Coll. Scholar), Barry Coll., 1974; M.S., Fla. Internat. U., 1977; m. David Ritchey, May 30, 1955; children—Angela, Wanda, David, Dwight, Nicholas, Elliott, Alicia, Alfonso, Marianne. Dir. student devel. Fla. Internat. U., Miami, 1973, admission counselor, 1974, asst. v.p. for student affairs, 1974—; mem. faculty Miami Dade Community Coll., 1972—. Recipient Presdl. award Miami Dade Community Coll., 1972; Ford Found. scholar, 1973; Fla. Student Asst. grantee, 1973. Mem. AAUW, Nat. Identification Program for Advancement of Women. Democrat. Mem. Pentecostal Ch. Home: 3811 NW 174th St Miami FL 33055 Office: Fla Internat U Miami FL 33199 .

RITCHIE, ERIS ALTON, JR., retail exec.; b. Athens, Ala., Apr. 18, 1935; s. Eris Alton and Mary Ethel (Tackett) R.; B.S. cum laude, Abilene Christian U., 1957, M.Ed., 1961; m. Annita Hartsell, July 29, 1960; children—Matthew Eris, Robin Annette, Holly Hart, Michael Christopher. Band dir. Trent (Tex.) Pub. Schs., 1957-59, Cisco (Tex.) Pub. Schs., 1959-68; pub. relations dir., band dir. Cisco Jr. Coll., 1968-73, coordinator Band-Belles, 1973-77, one of 15 groups appearing in Macy's Thanksgiving Day Parade, N.Y.C., 1971, 73, 77, also nat. TV appearances Dir. Cisco Jr. Music Festival, 1960-77; owner women's and children's retail store, 1969-79, embroidered emblems mktg. dealership, 1975—; dir. summer camp clinics for baton twirlers, cheerleaders, drill teams, 1960—. Bd. dirs. Cisco Community Chest, West Tex. Fair, 1975—. Mem. Cisco Jr. C. of C., Cisco C. of C. (pres. 1970-71, Outstanding Young Citizen award 1964, Outstanding Citizen 1968). Mem. Ch. of Christ. Rotarian. Home: 1307 Park Dr Cisco TX 76437

RITSCH, JEANNETTE MCCLUNG, artist; b. Bremen, Ga., July 10, 1931; d. Troy E. and Doris Magdalen (Noles) McClung, Sr.; B.A. LaGrange Coll. 1953; M. of Art Edn., U. of Ga. 1955; postgrad. U. of Strasbourg, France 1957-58; m. Frederick Field Ritsch Jr., June 14, 1957; children—Frederick F., III, Lise Catharina. Art coordinator U. of Ga. Demonstration Sch., Athens, 1953-55; tchr. art Lane High Sch., Charlottesville, Va. 1955-57; art cons. Charlottesville Pub. Schs. 1955-60; lectr. art edn. Converse Coll., Spartanburg, S.C. 1962-73; art dir. Summer Arts Camp, Spartanburg Arts Council 1969; curator The Gallery, Spartanburg 1969-70; one person shows include: Aug. W. Smith Gallery, Spartanburg, 1969, 79, Spartanburg Arts Center, 1971; group shows include: High Mus., Atlanta, 1967, Art center, Tryon, N.C., 1970, Spartanburg Bank & Trust Ann., 1973, 74, 75, 77, Kennedy Center, Washington, 1976; represented in permanent collections: LaGrange Coll., Laurens, S.C., Palmetto Bank, S.C. Nat. Bank, Spartanburg Bank & Trust, Spartanburg Humanities Center, Converse Coll.; also numerous pvt. collections; paintings include: Virginia Countryside, 1968, Hunting Island, 1969, Snow Bank, 1969, Sun, Wind, and Surf, 1969, Tulip Fields, 1974, Studio Still Life, 1975, The Shuttered Window, 1977. Leader Cub Scout Troop, Boy Scouts of Am., Spartanburg, 1968-69. Recipient grad. assistantship U. of Ga., Athens 1953-54; recipient numerous place and purchase awards in juried art exhibitions. Mem. Artists Guild of Spartanburg (exhibition chmn. 1967-70, program chmn. 1970-72, pres. 1972-74), Arts Council of Spartanburg (advisory bd. 1972-75), Nat. League of Am. Penwomen (state art chmn. 1970-80, dir. 1975—, 2d v.p. 1978—, membership chmn. 1980—). Presbyterian. Clubs: Wed. Study, Book. Home: 663 Otis Blvd Spartanburg SC 29302

RITSON, SPENCER LEE, psychiat. technician; b. Los Angeles, Feb. 25, 1940; s. John William and Lula Mae (Murphy) R.; student Ventura Coll., 1959-72, Western Ky. U., 1974-75; m. Brenda Jane Taliaferro, Nov. 16, 1973. Psychiatric technician State of Calif., Mental Hygiene Dept., Camarillo, 1962-72; mental hygiene technician N. Central Comprehensive Care, Inc., Elizabethtown, Ky., 1973-76; psychiatric nursing asst. VA Hosp., Louisville, 1976—; notary pub., Ky., 1974—. Licensed psychiat. technician. Mem. Ky. Assn. Human Services Technologists (founder, exec. dir. 1975—), Nat. Assn. Human Services Technologies, Inc., Council for Exceptional Children, Ky. Health Systems Agy. W., Internat. Fancy Guppy Assn. Baptist. Address: 203 College St Hodgenville KY 42748

RITTER, HARLAN W., r.r. exec.; b. Hoisington, Kans., May 11, 1941; s. Ralph W. and Ida Marie R.; B.S. in Bus. Adminstrn., Ft. Hays Kans. State U., 1964; postgrad. Harvard U., 1974; m. Rita JoAnn Gutierrez, Aug. 1, 1964; 1 son, Darren Burnell. With Mo. Pacific R.R. Co., 1960-77, asst. gen. mgr., Houston, 1975-77, asst. to v.p., St. Louis, 1977; asst. gen. mgr. Houston Belt & Terminal Ry. Co., Houston, 1978—. Mem. Transp. Club Houston, Houston C. of C. Republican. Baptist. Home: 14127 Cleobrook St Houston TX 77070 Office: Houston Belt & Terminal Ry Co 501 Crawford St Houston TX 77002

RITTER, THOMAS EDWARD, mech. engr.; b. Union City, Okla., Feb. 8, 1932; s. Albert Frederick and Mary Katherine (Gatz) R.; B.S. (Okla. Pub. Co. scholar), Okla. State U., 1958; M.S., Chrysler Inst. Engring., 1960; m. Brenda Beatrice Adam, Sept. 3, 1960; children—Mary, Anne, Theresa, James, Jennifer, Amy, John, Amber. Devel. engr. Chrysler Corp., Detroit, 1958-62; lead design engr. Ling Temco Vaught, Dallas, 1962-65; project mgr. Gen. Motors Research Lab., Detroit, 1965-71; sr. research engr. S.W. Research Inst., San Antonio, 1971—. Treas., Tranchese Meml. Service Corp., 1975—; bd. dirs. Christian Family Movement, 1974—; bd. dirs. St. Elizabeth Ann Seton Ch., 1978—; mem. adv. bd. Apostolate of Laity, Archdiocese of San Antonio, 1975—, eucharistic minister, 1979—. Served with USAF, 1951-55. Registered profl. engr., Okla. Roman Catholic. Contbr. tech. articles to profl. jours. Patentee in field. Home: 28075 Aqueduct Ln Route 4 Box 4607 Boerne TX 78006 Office: 8500 Culebra Rd San Antonio TX 78284

RITTERMAN, SHAREN BRUNEAU, audiologist; b. Boston, May 1, 1949; d. Roger Joseph and Arlene Frances (Weisend) Bruneau; A.A., Manatee Jr. Coll., 1969; M.S., U. South Fla., 1972; m. Stuart I. Ritterman, Sept. 2, 1977. Audiologist, Hillsboro County Public Schs., Tampa, Fla., 1972-75; vis. instr., clin. supr. U. South Fla., Tampa, 1975; clin. audiologist/program dir. audiology Central Fla. Speech and Hearing Clinic, Lakeland, 1976-77; speech/lang. pathologist Pasco County Schs., Dade City, Fla., 1977—. Recipient cert. clin. compentence Am. Speech and Hearing Assn.; cert. of registration in audiology, Fla. Mem. Fla. Speech, Lang. and Hearing Assn., Am. Speech, Lang. and Hearing Assn. Roman Catholic. Address: 181 Ellerbee Rd Zephyrhills FL 33599

RITTERMAN, STUART I., speech pathologist, educator; b. Bklyn., May 21, 1937; s. Nathan and Ettie (Fried) R.; B.A., N.Y. U., 1959; postgrad Coll. City N.Y., 1962-64; Ph.D., Case Western Reserve U., 1968; 1 dau. by previous marriage, Moriah. Speech clinician Bklyn. Coll. Clinic, City Univ. N.Y., Bklyn., 1963, Bergan Pines County Hosp., Paramus, N.J., 1963-64; Vocational Rehab. Adminstrn. trainee Cleve. Hearing and Speech Center, 1964-66; speech clinician Benjamin Rose Hosp., Cleve., 1965-66; NIH career investigator trainee Case Western Res. U., Cleve., 1966-68, research asso. in dental edn., 1967-68; asst. prof. dept. communication disorders U. Okla. Med. Center, Oklahoma City, 1968-69, dir. diagnostic services in speech pathology, 1968-69; asst. prof. speech pathology and audiology inst. U. S. Fla., Tampa, 1969-71, asso. prof., 1972-76, prof., 1976—, dir. diagnostic services, 1969-71, dir. research in communicology, 1976—, acting dir. program in speech pathology and audiology Coll. Social and Behavioral Sci., 1971, dir., 1971—. Cons. in speech pathology Cleve. Soc. for Crippled Children, 1967-68, Dept. Health and Rehab. Services, Fla. Bur. for Crippled Children, Tampa, 1970—, U. Okla. Center, Oklahoma City, 1968-69, Tampa Gen. Hosp., 1970-71, Model Cities, Wolf Diagnostic Center, Tampa, 1970-74, Multiphasic Evaluation and Treatment-Community Coordinated Child Care Pilot Clinic, Tampa, 1971. Dept. Dept. Health Edn. and Welfare grantee, USPHS, 1971, Office Edn., 1971, Fla. Dept. Edn., 1971. Fellow Royal Soc. Health; mem. Am., Fla. speech and hearing assns., Am. (research com. 1972—), S.E. Am. (chmn. speech pathology and audiology sec. 1969-74, local arrangements chmn. ann. meeting 1971) assns. on mental deficiency, Southeastern Conf. on Linguistics, Fla. Acad. Sci. (program chmn. behavorial sci. 1975-76), Linguistic Soc. Am. Contbr. articles to profl. jours. Home: Route 8 Box 181 Zephyr Hills FL 33599 Office: U S Fla CBA 241 Tampa FL 33620

RIVAS, BERNARD TOWNELY, counselor; b. Phila., Sept. 28, 1941; s. Alfred M. and Mary Rose R.; B.S., U. Md., 1975; M.Ed., 1976; postgrad. Coll. William and Mary, 1978—; m. Devon Alexandra Douglas, Dec. 20, 1976. Joined USAF, 1959, advanced through grades to master sgt., 1975; chief publs. br., adminstrv. div., Ellsworth AFB, S.D.. 1970-72; asst. chief adminstrn. 376 Strategic Wing, Kadnea Air Base, Japan, 1970-72; spl. asst. to comdr. 313 Air Div., 1975-76; adminstr. Keystone Counseling Center, Okinawa, 1976-77; asst. dir. adminstrn. HQ Tac Comm Area, Hampton, Va., 1977-79; ret., 1979; dir. Counseling Clinic, Okinawa Prefecture, 1978—; lectr. human relations Thomas Nelson Community Coll., 1979—; mng. dir. Tucker Office Systems Group, Newport News, Va., 1979—. Chmn. U.S. community participation in World Youth Assembly of World Oceanic Exposition, 1975-76; mem. counseling bd. Contact Peninsula. Mem. Am. Personnel and Guidance Assn., Am. Mental Health Counselors Assn., Internat. Transactional Analysis Assn., Internat. World Processing Assn., Va. Foster Parents Assn. Home: 153 Bloxom Dr Newport News VA 23602

RIVENBARK, REMBERT REGINALD, shipbldg. exec.; b. St. Paul, S.C., Sept. 9, 1912; s. Reginald Vernon and Kathleen Frances (Fussell) R.; grad. Goldsboro (N.C.) High Sch.; m. Marie Barbour, July 20, 1932; children—Patricia (Mrs. Dewey H. Pate), Rembert Reginald, Herbert William Barbour. Foreman bottling dept. Coca Cola Bottling Co., New Bern, N.C., 1927-32; with Barbour Boat Works, New Bern, 1932—, successively bookkeeper, office mgr., gen. mgr., v.p., gen. mgr., 1945-57, pres., 1957-71, chmn. bd., 1957—; chmn. bd., pres. Marine Trading Corp., New Bern, 1948—; dir. Ocean Scallops, Inc. Bd. dirs. United Fund. Mem. Am. Boat Builders and Repairers Assn. (pres. 1963), Am. Boat Builders and Engine Mfrs. Assn., N.C. Med. Assn. (hon.), Am. Mgmt. Assn., U.S. C. of C., Am. Ordnance Assn., Crippled Childrens Assn. (life), N.C. Wildlife Assn., N.C. Fisheries Assn. (dir.). Methodist (ofcl. bd., chmn. commn. on stewardship and finance). Mason (Shriner), Elk, Rotarian. Club: East Carolina Yacht (charter). Home: Trent Shores Dr New Bern NC 28560 Office: 522-525 Tryon Palace Dr New Bern NC 28560

RIVES, JAMES ALLEN, civil engr.; b. Norfolk, Va., Dec. 16, 1914; s. James Allen and Catherine Holly (Drewry) R.; student Old Dominion U., 1934-36; B.S. in Civil Engring., Va. Poly. Inst., Blacksburg, 1938, M.S. In San. Engring., 1940; m. Ethel Maxine Burks, Sept. 6, 1947; children—James Allen, Frank Burks. Supt. constrn. R.R. Richardson & Assos., Norfolk, 1938-39, 41-42; san. engr. Kellogg Found., Allegan, Mich., 1940; asso. prof. civil and san. engring. Va. Poly. Inst., 1946-51, head dept. san. engring., 1949-51; v.p., cons. engr. McGaughy, Marshall & McMillan, Norfolk, 1951-76, sr. v.p.-in-charge, Houston, 1976—, project mgr., chief engr. King Abdulaziz Mil. Acad., Saudi Arabia. Past pres. Va. Bd. for Exam. and Certification Architects, Profl. Engrs. and Land Surveyors; past dir. N.E. Zone, Nat. Council State Bds. Engring. Examiners. Mem. Norfolk Democratic Exec. Com., 1966-75, Sec., 1969-73, chmn., 1973-75; co-chmn. dist. advisory Com. Dems. for Gov. Mills E. Godwin. Pres. Larchmont-Edgewater Civic League, 1968, Naval Base Little League, 1962-64. Served from ensign to comdr. CEC, USNR, 1942-46; ETO. Decorated Commendation medal. Fellow ASCE (past pres. Va. sect.); mem. Va. Soc. Profl. Engrs. (past pres., recipient certificate for outstanding service), Va. Water Pollution Control Assn. (past pres.), Am. Water Works Assn. (Old Dominion citation), Chi Epsilon, Alpha Phi Omega. Mem. Legion Honor, Order DeMolay. Kiwanian. Clubs: Va. Poly. Inst. University (pres. 1950); Engrs. of Hampton Roads (Va.); Cedar Point. Contbr. articles to profl. Jours. Home: 1706 Prism Ln Houston TX 77043 Office: 3100 Richmond Ave Houston TX 77098

RIVIERE, PAUL FRANKLIN, state govt. ofcl.; b. Drew County, Ark., July 17, 1947; s. Frank and Maybell (Barnett) R.; B.A., George Washington U., 1971; J.D., U. Ark., Little Rock, 1975; m. Carolyn Lee Moore, 1973; children—Mary Catherine, Rebecca Lee. Staff asst. to U.S. Senator John L. McClellan, 1968-71; adminstrv. asst. Ark. Jud. Dept., 1971-74; mem. Gov. Ark. Commn. Crime and Law Enforcement, 1974-76; legal asst. to sec. state State of Ark., 1977-78, sec. state, 1979—. Bd. dirs. Big Bros. Pulaski County, Ark. Am. Legion Boys State, 1975-77. Democrat. Mem. Bible Ch. Home: 1014 N Spruce St Little Rock AR 72205 Office: 256 State Capitol Little Rock AR 72201

RIZK, WADE SALEEM, physician; b. Jacksonville, Fla., Mar. 25, 1903; s. Saleem Kaleel and Wadeeha (Fisher) R.; B.S., Georgetown U., 1927, M.D., 1929; m. Lois Greiner, Nov. 3, 1933; children—Roger Wade, Norman Wade, Katherine Wade. Commd. lt. (j.g.) M.C., U.S. Navy, 1929, advanced through grades to comdr., 1943; intern U.S. Naval Hosp. Bklyn.. 1929; ret., 1945; resident radiology U. Pa., 1945-46, Louisville Gen. Hosp., 1946-47, Bellevue Hosp., N.Y.C., 1947-48; dir. dept. radiology St. Luke's Hosp., Jacksonville, 1950-60; practice medicine, specializing in radiology, Jacksonville, 1960—; mem. staff Univ. Hosp., Meth. Hosp., Bapt. Hosp., Meml. Hosp., Cathedral Health and Rehab. Center, Hope Haven Hosp. (all Jacksonville), Union County Hosp., Lake Butler, Fla., Bradford County Hosp., Starke, Fla. Dir. Joe Berg Sci. Seminars for High Sch. Students; pres. N.E. Fla. Regional Sci. Fairs, 1967-68. Diplomate Nat. Bd. Med. Examiners, Am. Bd. Radiology. Fellow Am.

Coll. Radiology; mem. Fla. Radiology Soc. (pres. 1969-70), Am. Radium Soc., Radiol. Soc. N.Am., AMA, Fla. Med. Assn., So. Med. Assn., Fla. Thoracic Soc., Duval County Med. Soc. (pres. 1966-67), A.A.A.S. Kiwanian (pres. 1959). Club: Ortega School Dad's (pres. 1956-57). Contbr. articles to profl. jours. Home: 3861 Ortega Blvd Jacksonville FL 32210 Office: 1471 San Marco Blvd Jacksonville FL 32207

RIZZOLO, EDWARD ANTHONY, physician; b. Belleville, N.J., Aug. 20, 1928; s. Edward Michael and Josephine (DiGeronemo) R.; B.S., Seton Hall Coll., 1950; M.D., Baylor U., 1956; m. Ruth Ann Helmers, Dec. 19, 1958; children—Cindye Arlene, Edward Michael, Beverly Lynette. Intern, St. Joseph Hosp., Houston, 1956-57; resident in obstetrics and gynecology U. Tex., Houston, 1957-60; pvt. practice medicine specializing in obstetrics and gynecology, Houston, 1960—; clin. instr. U. Tex. Med. Br., Houston, 1960—. Diplomate Am. Bd. Obstetrics and Gynecology. Fellow Am. Coll. Obstetrics and Gynecology; mem. Am., Tex. med. assns., Harris County Med. Soc., Houston Gynecol.-Obstet. Soc. Roman Catholic. Home: 2611 Green Tee Dr Pearland TX 77581 Office: 7620 Bellfort Blvd Houston TX 77061

ROACH, ALFRED PATRICK, mfg. co. exec.; b. Bklyn., Nov. 16, 1943; s. Alfred James and Dorothy Mary R.; B.A., Fairfield U., 1965; M.A., U. Notre Dame, 1971, postgrad., 1971-74; m. Silvia Turnes, Aug. 9, 1970; children—Alfred S., Michael P., Michele A. Teaching asst. U. Notre Dame, 1971-72; with T.I.I. Industries, Inc., Toa Alta, P.R., 1974—, exec. v.p., 1976—. Served with USAF, 1967-70. Mem. P.R. Mfrs. Assn., P.R. C. of C., Latin Am. Studies Assn., Am. Polit. Sci. Assn. Clubs: Caparra Country, K.C. Home: A-16 Sun Valley Garden Hills Guaynabo PR 00657 Office: PO Box 433 Toa Alta PR 00758

ROACH, EVELYN CLINE, social worker; b. Winston-Salem, N.C., Sept. 2, 1924; d. John and Kitty (Plott) Cline; B.A. in English, Duke U., 1944; m. Henry Herman Roach, Jr., Nov. 12, 1948; children—Frances Roach Sink, Nancy Kathryn, Elizabeth Cline. Office mgr., dir. Methodist youth fund N.C. Conf. Meth. Ch., Durham, 1945-50; social worker Davidson County Dept. Social Services, Lexington, N.C., 1963-68, Bapt. Children's Homes of N.C., Thomasville, 1968-70; social worker Davidson County Mental Health Center, 1970-75, social work supr., mental retardation specialist, 1975—, mem. bd. dirs., 1975—; cons. in field. Mem. adminstrv. bd. First United Methodist Ch., Lexington, N.C., 1954, tchr. ch. sch., 1955-75; chmn. Christian social involvement United Meth. Women, 1978-79, hon. life mem. Mem. Am. Assn. Mental Deficiency, N.C. Assn. Social Workers in Mental Health, Davidson County Assn. Retarded Citizens, Davidson County Mental Health Assn., AAUW, Alpha Chi Omega. Democrat. Clubs: Charity League, Lexington Music Study, Lexington Home and Garden. Home: 411 Fairview Dr Lexington NC 27292 Office: Davidson County Mental Health Center 205 Old Lexington Rd Thomasville NC 27360

ROACH, GEORGE STEPHEN, constrn. co. exec.; b. Commerce, Tex., Apr. 20, 1949; s. George Calvin and Mary Lynn (Bulls) R.; A.A., Odessa Jr. Coll., 1969; B.B.A. in Mktg., Tex. Tech. U., 1971; m. Mary Jane Harris, June 30, 1973. Market rep. Mobil Oil Corp., Oklahoma City, 1971-73; project office mgr. Area Builders of N.C., Durham, 1973-76; project office mgr. Area Builders, Inc., Pecos, Tex., 1976, project scheduler, Odessa, Tex., 1976-77, exec. asst., 1977—. Constrn. div. chmn. United Way of Odessa, 1977, 78; promotional speaker Odessa Cultural Council's Cultural Awareness Month, 1979. Recipient Odessa Mayor's award for United Way work, 1978. Mem. Associated Builders and Contractors. Baptist. Club: Lions. Home: 1713 Glenwood St Odessa TX 79761 Office: 1111 Pagewood St Odessa TX 79761

ROACH, HENRY HERMAN, JR., coll. adminstr.; b. Greenville, Ala., Aug. 24, 1923; s. Henry Herman and Kate Herbert (McGehee) R.; B.A., Duke U., 1947, Ed.D., 1976; M.S., N.C. State U., 1956; m. Evelyn Frances Cline, Nov. 12, 1948; children—Evelyn Frances, Nancy Kathryn, Elizabeth. Bus. mgr. Thomasville (N.C.) City Schs., 1951-53; dir. personnel and indsl. relations Siceloff Mfg. Co., Inc., Lexington, N.C., 1953-63; individual practice psychology Lexington, N.C., 1960-64; dean evening coll. Davidson County Community Coll., Lexington, 1963-65, dean of student affairs, 1965-78, v.p. student affairs, 1979—. Pres. Central Piedmont Safety Council (N.C.), 1956; v.p. Davidson County Mental Health Assn., 1960; v.p. Children's Center for the Handicapped, Inc. of Davidson County, 1958-60; pres. Lexington United Fund, 1962; sec. Lexington YMCA, 1959; mem. various evaluation coms. So. Assn. Colls. and Schs. N.C. State U. fellow, asst. in clin. psychology, 1950-51; recipient Jaycee Disting. Citizen award, 1958. Mem. N.C. Mental Health Assn. (dir. 1964), Student Services Personnel Assn. N.C. (pres. 1968), Am. Personnel and Guidance Assn., Student Services Personnel Assn. N.C., N.C. Assn. Educators, NEA, N.C. Lit. and Hist. Assn., Kappa Chi, Pi Kappa Alpha, Democrat. Methodist. Club: Lions. Author: Attitudes of Owners and Managers of N.C. Business and Industry Toward the Services of an Industrial Psychologist, 1956; Placement Test Scores and the Academic Achievements of Students at a Community College, 1976. Home: 411 Fairview Dr Lexington NC 27292 Office: Intersection I-85 and Old Greensboro Rd Lexington NC 27292

ROACH, JONES WILLIAMSON, elec. engr.; b. Richmond, Va., July 31, 1933; s. William Thomas and Mary Gertrude (Williamson) R.; B.S. in Elec. Engring., Va. Mil. Inst., 1955; M.A., U. Houston, Clear Lake, 1976; m. Sherry Ann Jessen, Nov. 1, 1957; children—Martha, Jones Williamson Jr. Sales engr. Linde Air Products, Pitts., 1955-56; engr. Va. Electric & Power Co., Richmond, 1959-61; mgr. tech. ops. NASA-Johnson Space Center, Houston, 1962—. High priest Reorganized Ch. Jesus Christ of Latter-day Saints. active Boy Scouts Am. Served as capt. USAF, 1956-59, 61-62. Recipient Exceptional Service medal NASA, 1972, Certificate of Commendation, 1969, 70, 71. Registered profl. engr., Tex. Asso. fellow AIAA; mem. Nat. Soc. Profl. Engrs., Tex. Soc. Profl. Engrs. Contbr. articles to profl. jours. Home: 4123 Manorfield Dr Seabrook TX 77586 Office: Johnson Space Center NASA Rd 1 Houston TX 77058

ROACH, WILLIAM LESTER, high sch. prin.; b. Ashland, Miss., Aug. 29, 1911; s. Julius P. and Nannie (Kidd) R.; B.S., George Peabody Tchrs. Coll., 1937; M.S., Miss. State Coll., 1945; M.E., U. Miss., 1953; postgrad. U. Tex., summer 1937, Miss. State U., summer 1970; m. Ethye D. Young, Nov. 21, 1945; children—William Lester, Ruby Nan. Tchr. sci., coach Egypt (Miss.) High Sch., 1937-38, Noxapater (Miss.) High Sch., 1938-41; prin. elementary sch., coach high sch., Carthage, Miss., 1941-42; prin. Columbia (Miss.) Grammar Sch., 1942-46; prin. Brookhaven (Miss.) High Sch., 1946-79, adminstrv. asst. to supt., 1979-81; Mem. Miss. Accrediting Commn., 1952-58, chmn., 1957-58; chmn. conf. steering com. Big Eight Athletic Conf., 1963-80; col. gov.'s staff, 1960-68; mem. Miss. Ednl. Finance Commn., 1972—; mem. supt.'s adv. com. Y-Teens and Hi-Y. Trustee Lincoln County Hosp., 1960—. Recipient Distinguished Profl. Service certificate Nat. Assn. Secondary Sch. Prins., 1957. Mem. Nat., Miss. (chmn. high sch. sect. 1953-54), Brookhaven edn. assns., Big Eight Prins. Orgn, (chmn. 1955-58), Nat., Miss. (chmn. 1957-58) assn. secondary sch. prins., Miss. Assn. Sch. Adminstrs., Miss. High Sch. Activities Assn. (sec. dist. 7, 1950—, mem. council 1966-68, 72-73, mem. exec. com. 1968-72, 73-80), Henry Boswell Soc. (trustee 1950—, pres. 1954-59), Red Red Rose, Phi Delta Kappa, Kappa Delta Pi. Baptist. Mason (Shriner), Lion (past sec.). Contbr. articles on discipline to profl. jours. Home: 505 Pine Dr Brookhaven MS 39601 Office: High Sch E Monticello St Brookhaven MS 39601

ROADEN, ARLISS LLOYD, univ. pres.; b. Corbin, Ky., Sept. 27, 1930; s. Johnie Samuel and Nora Ethel (Killian) R.; student (Am. Legion scholar) Cumberland Jr. Coll., 1949; A.B., Carson Newman Coll., 1951; M.S., U. Tenn., 1958, Ed.D., 1961; m. Mary Etta Mitchell, Sept. 1, 1951; children—Janice, Sharon. Tchr. elementary sch., 1949-50; staff asst. Univ. Relations div. Oak Ridge Inst. Nuclear Studies, 1957-59; asst. prof. Auburn U., 1961-62; asst. prof., dir. grad. studies Ohio State U., 1962-64, asso. prof., 1964-65, asst. dir. Coll. Edn., 1965, asso. dir., 1966, prof., 1967, asso. dean Coll. Edn., 1968, acting dean, 1969, vice provost for research, dean grad. sch., 1970-74; pres. Tenn. Technol. U., 1974—; vis. prof. Marshall U., summer 1961, Nat. Inst. for Study of Ednl. Change, Ind. U., summer 1967; dir. Am. Bank and Trust, Cookeville, Tenn.; cons. sch. systems, univs., ednl. instns., profl. groups. Chmn. bd. govs. Phi Delta Kappa Found. Served with AUS, 1951-53. Recipient Centennial medallion for Distinguished Faculty and Alumni, Coll. Edn., Ohio State U., 1970, Distinguished Alumnus award Cumberland Coll. Mem. Tenn. Coll. Assn. (pres. 1978), Nat. Assn. State Colls. and Land Grant Univs., Am. Assn. Higher Edn., Nat. Soc. for Study of Edn., AAAS, Am. Ednl. Research Assn., Nat. Acad. Polit. and Social Sci., Phi Delta Kappa (Distinguished Service award), Phi Kappa Phi, Kappa Phi Kappa, Kappa Delta Pi. Lion, Rotarian. Author: Problems of Schoolmen in Depressed Urban Centers, 1968; (with Blaine R. Worthen) The Research Assistantship, 1975. Contbr. numerous articles to profl. jours. Home: 1155 N Dixie Ave Cookeville TN 38501 Office: Box 5007 Tenn Technol U Cookeville TN 38501

ROAN, CHARLES THURSTON, mgmt. cons.; b. Atlanta, May 15, 1928; s. Augustus Morrow and Margaret Josephine (Zattau) R.; B.B.A., U. Ga., 1954; m. Tattie Mae Williams, Mar. 26, 1960; children—Ansley Josephine, Caroline Tabitha. With Lockheed Ga. Co., Marietta, Ga., 1951-73, mgr. materials systems, 1961-64, mgr. indsl. engring. systems, 1965-68, mfg. ops. systems adminstr., 1968-73; pres. Roan & Assos., mgmt. cons., Atlanta, 1974—; lectr., chmn. tng. and orientation seminars for various orgns. and computer mfg. cos. Served in U.S. Army, 1946-49. Certified in data processing Inst. for Certification of Computer Profls. Mem. Am. Mgmt. Assn., Adminstrv. Systems Assn., Am. Prodn. and Inventory Control Soc., Inst. Mgmt. Consultants (cert. mgmt. cons.), Assn. Mgmt. Consultants. Presbyterian. Home: 991 Oakdale Rd NE Atlanta GA 30307 Office: 1387 Oxford Rd NE Atlanta GA 30307

ROARK, FRANK HOLLYWORTH, JR., investment co. exec.; b. New Orleans, Mar. 12, 1922; s. Frank Hollyworth and Eunice (Foley) R.; student La. State U., 1946-49, Am. Coll., 1962; m. Norma Elizabeth Guillot, Jan. 15, 1950; children—Frank Hollyworth III, Mary Rebecca, Holly Elizabeth, Erin Patricia. Agency mgr. Mut. of N.Y., Orlando, Fla., 1954-69; pres. Planned Fin. Services, Inc., PFS Equities, Inc., Winter Park, Fla., 1970—; gen. partner Sand Fork Coals, Ltd., Glenville Coals, Ltd., Hickory Coals, Ltd., So. Mineral Resources; pres. Hickory Mining Co.; v.p. Morley Enterprises; charter v.p., dir. Bank of Central Fla.; dir. Ridge Coal Co.; faculty Central Fla. Soc. C.L.U., 1978—. Served with USAAF, 1942-45, USAF, 1950-52. Decorated D.F.C. with cluster, Air medal with 4 clusters. Mem. Am. Soc. C.L.U., Central Fla. Estate Planning Council. Clubs: Winter Park Sertoma (charter pres.), Univ. (Winter Park); Citrus (Orlando). Home: 816 Tuscarora Trail Maitland FL 32751 Office: 280 Canton Ave W Suite 300 Winter Park FL 32789

ROARK, HELEN JO, educator, guidance counselor; b. Allen, Okla., Apr. 7; d. Floyd and Anna Genevia (Maynord) Heddleson; B.S. cum laude in Behavioral Scis., Bartlesville (Okla.) Wesleyan Coll., 1976; M.T.A. in Social Scis., U. Tulsa, 1978; children—Eric Bryan, Regina Gayle. Women's swimming tchr. Bartlesville Wesleyan Coll., 1976; substitute tchr. Pawhuska (Okla.) Public Schs., also Wynona (Okla.) Public Schs., 1977-78, substitute tchr. Pawhuska Public Schs., 1978-79; part-time tchr. Bartlesville Wesleyan Coll. and full-time vocat. rehab. counselor Washington and Osage Counties, Bartlesville, 1979—. Program chmn. Osage County Mental Health Assn., 1973-76, Pawhuska PTA, 1966-68; children's choir dir. 1st Baptist Ch., 1976-79; ARC swimming instr. Osage County and Pawhuska, 1970-79. Mem. Okla. Edn. Assn., NEA, AAUW, Am. Personnel and Guidance Assn., Phi Alpha Theta, Pi Gamma Mu, Kappa Delta Pi. Club: Eastern Star. Home: 1319 Sunset Rd Pawhuska OK 74056 Office: 1824 SE Hillcrest Bartlesville OK 74003

ROARK, JAMES OLIVER, aerospace corp. engr.; b. Graham-Young County, Tex., Mar. 30, 1922; s. George Ross and Ola (McLemore) R.; B.A. in Math. and Chemistry, Howard Payne U., 1950; m. Betty Ruth Perkins, June 29, 1947; children—Carol Sue, Nancy Ann, Stephen Douglas, James Michael. Aircraft mechanic N.Am. Aviation, Inc., Englewood, Calif., 1941-43; flight test engr., structures engr., quality control engr. Gen. Dynamics Corp., Ft. Worth, 1950—; instr. engring. drawing U. Tex., Arlington, 1954; speaker Am. Soc. Quality Control, Hurst, Tex., 1965. Alderman, Benbrook, Tex., 1964-68, mayor City of Benbrook, 1968-70; mgr. Tex. Teenage Boys Baseball, Benbrook Recreation Assn., 1964-67; mgr. Boys Baseball Inc., Forest Hill (Tex.) Recreation Assn., 1973-75. Served with USAF, 1943-46. Recipient certificate of appreciation for pub. service City of Benbrook. Baptist. Club: Lions. Contbr. sports article Roark's Round-Up to Benbrook Banner, 1968. Home: Route 7 Box 150 Fort Worth TX 76119

ROATH, WALTER HERBERT, archtl. cons.; b. Harrisburg, Pa., May 20, 1915; s. Philip B. and Anna (Leach) R.; B.S., Columbia, 1938; m. Martha Jane Moore, Oct. 5, 1940; children—Margaret, Sharon (Mrs. John Davidson), Philip Charles. With Armstrong Cork Co., Dallas, 1939-77, archtl. rep., archtl. ceiling systems div., 1960-77; archtl. cons. Brown's Applied Vinyls, Dallas, 1977—. Precinct chmn. Republican party, 1952-65. Served with U.S. Mcht. Marine, World War II. Mem. Producers Council (pres. North Tex. chpt. 1954-55), Constrn. Specifications Inst. (sec.-treas. 1957-59), Beta Theta Pi. Club: Dallas Country. Home: 5310 Wenonah St Dallas TX 75209

ROBB, ARTHUR DALE, data processor; b. Alexandria, Va., Aug. 23, 1947; s. Dale Huntley and Louise Catherine (Camp) R.; ed. St. Mary's U., San Antonio, 1970; m. Ruby Irene Kuhlmann, Aug. 31, 1968. Programmer computer center St. Mary's U., 1966-69; pres., co-owner Computer Cons., San Antonio, 1968-72; data processing mgr. Central Bus. Office, San Antonio, 1972-73; sr. systems analyst San Antonio Housing Authority, 1973-77, adminstrv. mgr., 1977—. Mem. Data Processing Mgmt. Assn. (pres. 1977, internat. dir. 1978—). Home: 5226 LaPosita San Antonio TX 78233 Office: 1405 N Main Ave San Antonio TX 78212

ROBB, CHARLES SPITTAL, lt. gov. Va.; b. Phoenix, June 26, 1939; s. James Spittal and Francis Howard (Woolley) R.; student Cornell U., 1957-58; B.B.A., U. Wis., 1961; J.D., U. Va., 1973; m. Lynda Bird Johnson, Dec. 9, 1967; children—Lucinda Desha, Catherine Lewis, Jennifer Wickliffe. Admitted to Va. bar, 1973, U.S. Supreme Ct. bar, 1976; law clk. to John D. Butzner, Jr., U.S. Ct. Appeals, 1973-74; atty. Williams Connolly & Califano, 1974-77; lt. gov. Va., 1978—; v.p., dir. LBJ Co., 1971—; exec. v.p., dir. No. Va. Radio Co., 1978—. Mem. various bds. U. Va., 1974—, U. Richmond, 1974—, Hampton Inst. Tech., 1977—; mem. Nat. Capital Area exec. bd. Boy Scouts Am., 1976—, chmn. No. Va. Scout Expo, 1976, 77; mem. Fairfax County bd. Am. Cancer Soc., 1976—; profl. gifts chmn. United Way of Fairfax County, 1976; dep. gen. counsel, asst. parliamentarian Democratic Nat. Com. Platform Com., 1976; mem. Fairfax County Dem. Com., 1975—, Dem. State Central Com., 1976—. Served with USMC, 1961-70; co. comdr., aide to comdg. gen., 2d Marine Div.; social aide to White House, Washington; inf. co. comdr., Vietnam. Decorated Bronze Star, Vietnam Service medal with 4 Stars, Vietnamese Cross of Gallantry with Silver Star; recipient Raven award, 1973, Seven Socs. Orgn. award U. Va. Mem. Am., Va. bar assns., Va. Trial Lawyers Assn., Res. Officers Assn., USMC Res. Officers Assn., Am. Legion, Raven Soc., Omicron Delta Kappa. Episcopalian. Office: Office Lt Gov State Capitol Richmond VA 23219*

ROBB, WARREN DRAKE, univ. adminstr.; b. Louisville, Sept. 23, 1934; s. Deloss H. and Janet R.; B.S., Purdue U., 1956; M.B.A., U. Louisville, 1965; Ph.D., Ariz. State U., 1974; m. Zee Cora Engle, June 3, 1961; children—Eric Parker, Brian Kendall. Asst. personnel dir. Scottsdale (Ariz.) Schs., 1966-69; personnel dir. Madison Sch. Dist., 1971-75; asst. prof. Ariz. State U., Tempe, 1975-76; dir. counseling, testing and career placement U. Tex., Arlington, 1976—, instr. mgmt., 1977-78. Served with USAF, 1957-58. Danforth Found. asso., 1979. Mem. Adminstrv. Mgmt. Soc., Am. Soc. Personnel Adminstrn., Am. Mgmt. Assn., Am. Assn. Higher Edn., Am. Assn. Sch. Personnel Adminstrs., So. Coll. Placement Assn., S.W. Coll. Placement Assn., Western Coll. Placement Assn., Mid-Cities Personnel Assn. (pres.), Pi Kappa Phi. Club: Elks. Office: U Tex Arlington TX 76019

ROBB, WILLIAM BROWN, III, constrn. co. exec.; b. Ft. Riley, Kans., July 18, 1944; s. William Brown and Harriett Ann (Collard) R.; student Calif. Luth. Coll., 1962-63; B.S., Ariz. State U., 1965; m. Natalie Kathryn Kaiser, Aug. 21, 1965; 1 son, Christopher William. Credit mgr. Fashionette-Sportique Shops of Phoenix, 1962-67; v.p. sales Robb Constrn. Co. Inc., Del Rio, Tex., 1976—; asso. Realtor. Chmn. budget com., bd. dirs. United Fund of Del Rio, 1978, 1st v.p., pres.-elect, chmn. fund dr., 1979; pres. bd. dirs. Community Concert Series; bd. dirs. Amistad Navy, Amistad Lake, Tex. Served to capt. USAF, 1968-76. Mem. Del Rio C. of C. (asst. chmn. membership com. 1978), Del Rio Bd. Realtors, Tex. Assn. Realtors, Nat. Assn. Realtors, Nat. Home Builders Assn., Am. Mgmt. Assn. Republican. Lutheran. Club: Rotary. Home: 205 Far Hills Dr Del Rio TX 78840 Office: Robb Constrn Co 110 Foster St Del Rio TX 78840

ROBBIE, JOSEPH, lawyer, profl. football team exec.; b. S.D., July 7, 1916; s. Joseph Robbie and Jennie (Ready) R.; A.B., U. S.D., 1943, LL.B., 1946, LL.D. (hon.), 1979; LL.D. (hon.), Biscayne Coll., 1970; Ph.D. (hon.), Mt. Marty Coll., Yankton, S.D., 1979; m. Elizabeth Ann Lyle, Dec. 28, 1942. Admitted to S.D. bar, 1946, Minn. bar, 1951; practiced in Mitchell, S.D., 1946-53, Mpls., 1953—; founder, 1965, since pres., gen. mgr. Miami Dolphins, Ltd. Dep. state atty. Davison County, S.D., 1947-49; regional counsel, acting regional enforcement dir. Office Price Stblnz., Mpls., 1951-52, regional dir., 1952-53; author Minn. Municipal Commn. Act., 1959-60, 1st chmn. commn., 1959-65; charter mem., sec.-treas. Twin Cities Met. Planning Commn., 1957-67; spl. counsel com. for hearings to create Dept. Urban Affairs, U.S. Senate, 1961; exec. sec., legal counsel Commn. Municipal Annexation and Consol. Minn. Legislature, 1957-59, Commn. Municipal Laws Minn. Legislature, 1959-61; exec. dir. Minn. Candy and Tobacco Distbrs. Assn., 1959—; asst. prof. econs. Dakota Wesleyan U., 1946-48; spl. instr., debate coach Coll. St. Catherine, St. Paul, 1953-54. Vice pres., presiding officer Am. Lebanese Syrian Asso. Charities, 1966—; co-chmn. Notre Dame Summa Fund Raising Campaign, 1967; chmn. Biscayne Coll. Challenge Fund Raising Campaign, 1968-69; chmn. Miami Easter Seal Campaign, 1969; gen. chmn. Heart Fund Greater Miami. Chmn. Am. Football League Player Relations Com., 1969; exec. com. Nat. Football League Mgmt. Council, 1972-77; mem. S.D. Legislature, 1949-51, joint caucus leader; chmn. S.D. Democratic Party, 1948-50; candidate gov. S.D., 1948, U.S. Congress from Minn., 1956, 58; chmn. Minn. advisory com. Nat. Dem. Com., 1954-58; chmn. Dade County (Fla.) Dem. Exec. Com., 1972; campaign chmn. Humphrey for Pres., Charleston, W.Va., 1960. Bd. govs. St. Jude Children's Research Hosp., Memphis, 1959—; bd. dirs. Crippled Children's Soc., Miami, 1967—, Boys Town Fla., Variety Children's Hosp.; advisory bd. Fla. Meml. Coll., Miami, 1967—, Fla. Internat. U., 1972—; past bd. dirs. Operation South Help; bd. dirs., mem. exec. com. United Fund of Dade County; trustee Biscayne Coll., Dade Found., Dade County Community Relations Bd., Public Health Trust, Jackson Meml. Hosp., 1973-79; mem. Citizens Bd. U. Miami (Fla.); hon. chmn. Century of Service Fund Campaign, Yankton, 1978; bd. dirs. Jesuit Program for Living and Learning, 1978—; bd. dirs. Cath. Service Bur., Archdiocese of Miami, 1976—, chmn. bd. dirs., 1977—. Served with USNR, 1941-45. Decorated Bronze Star; recipient Nathan Burkan Meml. award for essay copyright law, 1946; J. Ernest O'Brien Commendation award Nat. Assn. Tobacco Distbrs., 1966; Horatio Alger award, 1979; named Nat. Football League Owner of Year, Minutemen of Mpls. and St. Paul, 1971; Profl. Football Exec. of Year, L.I. Athletic Club, 1972. Mem. Greater Miami C. of C. (gov. 1971—). Home: 339 W Elmwood Pl Minneapolis MN 55419 also 1301 NE 100th St Miami Shores FL 33138 Office: 330 Biscayne Blvd Miami FL 33132 also 710 Cargill Bldg Minneapolis MN 55402

ROBBINS, CLARK B., mgmt. cons.; b. N.Y.C., Sept. 19, 1941; s. James Henry and Bette (Demer) R.; B.B.A., N.Y. U., 1963; M.S. in Computer Sci., 1968; m. Jina R. Jones, May 26, 1979. Mgr. on-line systems Am. Airlines, N.Y.C., 1963-68; dir. info. systems and communications Singer Co., N.Y.C., 1968-77; dir. systems and communication LTV Corp., N.Y.C-, 1977-79; pres. Sunbelt Nat., Inc., Dallas, 1979—; chmn. tech. adv. com. U.S. Dept. Commerce, 1976-78. Radio officer U.S. C.G. Aux., 1974—; communications officer ARC radio facility, Dallas, 1976—. Mem. Data Processing Mgmt. Assn., Assn. Systems Mgmt., Am. Radio Relay League. Author: Computer/Communications Networks on a Community Wide Basis, 1976; Terminals, The Human Interface to Networks, 1977. Home: 704 Carriage Way Duncanville TX 75137 Office: Suite 242 2636 Walnut Hill Ln Dallas TX 75229

ROBBINS, EVELYN WALL (MRS. HOMER ERWIN ROBBINS, JR.), musician; b. Lake City, S.C., Oct. 21, 1914; d. Victor Sterling and Ella Lou (Able) Wall; A.B., Agnes Scott Coll., 1937; m. Homer Erwin Robbins, Jr. Mar. 4, 1950. Asst. voice dept. Agnes Scott Coll., 1937-40; organist, dir. Decatur (Ga.) 1st Bapt. Ch., 1937-40, Meth. Ch., Atlanta, 1940-42; minister music Peachtree Rd. Meth. Ch., Atlanta, 1947-50, organist Larchmont Av. Ch., N.Y.C., 1950, Summerfield Meth. Ch., Port Chester, N.Y., 1951-52, St. John's Meth. Ch., New Rochelle, N.Y., 1952-54; minister music Salem United Ch. of Christ, Allentown, Pa., 1954-67; organist-dir. music St. James Meth. Ch., Atlanta, 1967-71, Druid Hills United Meth. Ch., Atlanta, 1972-76, 1st Presbyn Ch., Marietta, Ga., 1976—; tchr. organ Cedar Crest Coll., Allentown, 1955-58. Mem. Am. Guild Organists (past dean Lehigh Valley chpt.), Meth. Musicians, Presbyn. Assn. Musicians. Home: 7362 Cardigan Circle NE Atlanta GA 30328

ROBBINS, JAMES TATE, mfrs. agt.; b. Washington, Feb. 12, 1945; s. Frank Mix and Margaret Elizabeth (Williams) R.; B.A. in Econs., U. N.C., 1967; postgrad. U. Md., 1969-70, U. Tenn., Chattannooga, 1970-71; grad. Tenn. Exec. Devel. Program, U. Tenn. at Knoxville, 1979; m. Martha Carol Walker, Sept. 2, 1972; children—John Walker, Margaret Elizabeth. Sales engr. Robbins & Bohr, Knoxville, 1970—, v.p., 1975—, also dir. Served to lt. U.S. Army, 1967-70. Mem. Park West Sertoma Club (bd. dirs. 1975-76), Am. Soc. Heating, Refrigeration and Air Conditioning Engrs., Am. Foundrymen's Soc. Republican. Methodist. Clubs: Mountain City, Concord Yacht; West Knoxville Sertoma. Home: 1708 Leavitt Dr Signal Mountain TN 37377 Office: 915 Pineville Rd Chattanooga TN 37405

ROBBINS, JERRY HAL, univ. ofcl.; b. De Queen, Ark., Feb. 28, 1939; s. James Hal and Barbara I. (Rogers) R.; B.A. in Math, Hendrix Coll., 1960; M.Ed., U. Ark., 1963, Ed.D., 1966. Tchr. math., music Clinton (Ark.) Pub. Schs., 1960-61; prin. Adrian (Mo.) High Sch., 1961-63; exec. sec. Ark. Sch. Study Council, Fayetteville, 1963-65; mem. faculty U. Miss., University, 1965-74, prof. ednl. adminstrn., 1970-74, chmn. dept. ednl. adminstrn., 1970-74; dean Coll. Edn., U. Ark., Little Rock, 1974-79; asso. v.p. for acad. affairs Ga. State U., Atlanta, 1979—. Mem. NEA, Am. Assn. Sch. Adminstrs., Nat. Assn. Secondary Sch. Prins., So. Regional Council Ednl. Adminstrn. (pres. 1970-71), Phi Delta Kappa, Kappa Delta Pi (v.p. chpt. devel. 1978—). Methodist. Author: (with S.B. Williams, Jr.) Student Activities in the Innovative School, 1969, School Custodian's Handbook, 1970, Administrator's Manual of School Plant Administration, 1970. Home: 90 Forrest Pl Atlanta GA 30328 Office: 132 Sparks Hall Ga State U Atlanta GA 30303

ROBBINS, KENNETH RANDALL, educator, playwright; b. Douglasville, Ga., Jan. 7, 1944; s. James Aubrey and Cornelia Inez (Graham) R.; A.A., Young Harris Jr. Coll., 1964; B.S. in Edn., Ga. So. Coll., 1966; M.F.A. in Theatre, U. Ga., 1969; grad. fellow So. Ill. U., 1978—. Tchr. speech, English, coach drama, speech Robert E. Lee Inst., Thomaston, Ga., 1966-67; tchr., drama coach Elbert County (Ga.) High Sch., Elberton, 1968-70; instr. Georgetown (Ky.) Coll., 1970-71; dir. theatre arts program, co-dir. summer theatre Minot (N.D.) State Coll., 1971-74; asst. prof. theatre arts Jacksonville (Fla.) U., 1974-77; asst. prof., dir. theatre Newberry (S.C.) Coll., 1977-80; founding dir. Pastime Players, Elberton, 1968-70, Jacksonville Summer Repertory Theatre, 1975—; adminstrv. asst., dir. Barter Theatre, summers 1978-80. Mem., soloist Minot Chamber Chorale, 1973-74. Mem. heritage com. Minot Bicentenniel Com., 1973-74. Bd. dirs. Area Council of Arts. Named Star Tchr., Elbert County Sch. System, 1970; recipient award Palo Alto Bicentennial Playwriting Contest, 1976, Fla. Theatre Conf. Playwriting Contest, 1977. Mem. Speech Communication Assn., Am. Theatre Assn., Dramatists Guild, Authors League, Southeastern Theatre Conf. Author plays Dallas File, Goober Peas, Molly's Rock, others. Home: Barter Theatre Abington VA 24210

ROBBINS, ORVILLE MONTIA, educator; b. Seminole County, Okla., Aug. 11, 1929; s. Clarence Allen and Olive (Kelso) R.; B.A., Tex. Christian U., 1957, M.A., 1958; postgrad. U. Tenn., 1960-65; m. Louise Stevens, Nov. 26, 1966; children—Patrick Booth, Gregory John. Job-office mgr. Farnsworth and Chambers Co., Houston, 1947-51; asst. br. mgr. Boehck Engring. Co., Inc., Beaumont, Tex., 1953; teaching fellow Tex Christian U., Fort Worth, 1957-58; instr. U. Houston, 1958-60; teaching asst. U. Tenn., 1960-65, instr., 1965-67; asst. prof. East Central U., Ada, Okla., 1967—. Mem. Ada Arts and Humanities Council, 1972-79, pres., 1976-77; chmn. Democratic precinct, 1972-79; mem. Ada Task Force on Community Needs, 1972-79. Served with U.S. Army, 1951-53. Mem. NEA, Okla. Edn. Assn., Sci. Fiction Research Assn. Roman Catholic. Home: 219 W 20th St Ada OK 74820 Office: Dept English East Central U Ada OK 74820

ROBBINS, VIOLA MAE, educator; b. Konawa, Okla., Jan. 14, 1914; d. Oscar Oliver and Alta Eliza (Hinton) W.; B.S., Abilene Christian U., 1954, M.S. summa cum laude, 1960, M.B.A., 1980; m. Woodard Robbins, Aug. 19, 1936; children—Kenneth Ray, Gail Ann. Office mgr., Furr Food Stores, Lubbock, Tex., 1932-36; asst. to fiscal agt. Abilene (Tex.) Christian U., 1954-60, mem. faculty dept. bus. adminstrn., 1960—, prof. acctg. Mem. text book com. Abilene Public Schs., 1970. Mem. Am. Acctg. Assn., AAUW (pres. chpt. 1970-72), Alpha Chi, Delta Kappa Gamma. Republican. Mem. Ch. of Christ. Home: 666 College Dr Abilene TX 79601 Office: Box 7129 Abilene TX 79699

ROBBINS, WAYNE LINDSEY, educator; b. Covington, Tenn., Jan. 8, 1936; s. J. L. and Arlena (Wortham) R.; B.S., Miss. State U., 1958; B.Div., Southwestern Baptist Theol. Sem., 1963, M.Div., 1973; M.Ed., U. Ark., 1967, Ed.D., 1975; m. Faye Elaine Wellborn, Nov. 3, 1961; 1 son, Wayne Lindsey. With Balt. Oriole baseball orgn., 1958; dean of men Bluefield (Va.) Coll., 1963-65; asst. to dean of arts and scis. U. Ark., Fayetteville, 1965-70, head baseball coach, 1965-70; press sec. to U.S. Senator Strom Thurmond, 1970-73; asst. to U.S. Rep. J. P. Hammerschmidt, 1973-74; press sec. to U.S. Senator Bill Brock, 1974; dir. fed. programs Tenn. Dept. Edn., 1975; v.p. Belmont Coll., Nashville, 1976—; radio and TV announcer, 1956-70. Lay minister Baptist Ch., 1956—; active Republican Party, 1970-76. Served to capt. Mil. Police, U.S. Army, 1958-59. Mem. Am. Assn. Coll. and Univ. Adminstrs., Nashville C. of C., Phi Delta Kappa. Club: Lions. Home: 500 Plantation Ct V-2 Nashville TN 37221 Office: Office of Vice President Belmont College Nashville TN 37203

ROBERDS, CAMMACK ALVIN, JR., accountant, real estate exec.; b. Mobile, Ala., Apr. 29, 1943; s. Cammack Alvin and Helen Rae (Threadgill) R.; B.S., Auburn U., 1965; postgrad. Ga. State U., 1975; m. Janice Elizabeth Starr, June 7, 1964; children—Shawn Elizabeth, Catherine Ann. C.P.A. Arthur Andersen & Co., Atlanta, 1965-66, 69-74; v.p. fin. Nash & Nagel, Inc., Atlanta, 1974-75; pres. So. Realty Mgmt., Inc., Atlanta, 1975—; dir. So. Realty Devel., Inc., Roberds Broadcasting, Inc. Served to capt. USAF, 1966-69. C.P.A., Ga. Mem. Am. Inst. C.P.A.'s, Ga. Soc. C.P.A.'s, Apt. Owners and Mgrs. Assn. Atlanta, Inc. Methodist. Clubs: Ansley Golf, West Paces Racket. Home: 2475 Greenglade Rd NE Atlanta GA 30345 Office: 1600 Tullie Circle S-146 Atlanta GA 30329

ROBERSON, DENNIS ARLEN, computer exec.; b. Coulee Dam, Wash., Jan. 12, 1949; s. William Sidney and Marian Florence (Sweiberg) R.; B.E.E. and B.S. in Physics, Wash. State U., 1971; M.E.E., Stanford U., 1974; m. Debra Lin Schroeder, Sept. 28, 1974; children—James Tyler, Joel Edward. Elec. technician U.S. Bur. Reclamation, Coulee Dam, Wash., 1968-70; sr. tech. asso. Bell Telephone Labs., Holmdel, N.J., 1970; research asst. Wash. State U., Pullman, 1970-71; from jr. engr. to project engring. mgr. IBM, Los Gatos, Calif. and Rochester, Minn., 1971-77, from devel. engring. mgr. to sr. engring. mgr., Boca Raton, Fla. 1977—; guest lectr. various schs. and profl. orgns. Leader Christian Service Brigade, Calif., Minn. and Fla., 1974—; elder Bibletown Community Ch., 1978—; mem. sch. bd. Boca Raton Christian Sch., 1978—. Recipient numerous coll. awards and Outstanding Contbn. award IBM Corp. Mem. IEEE, IEEE Computer Soc., Assn. Computing Machinery, Christian Businessmen's Com. Computer architect, lead engr. in devel. IBM portable computer; contbr. articles, speeches in field low-end computer architecture and tech. Home: 1901 Sharon St Boca Raton FL 33432 Office: PO Box 1328 - 26A/032-1 Boca Raton FL 33432

ROBERSON, FRANK DEREK, assn. exec.; b. Detroit, Feb. 24, 1935; s. Franklin F. and Dorothy M. (Prouse) R.; B.S., Mich. State U., 1966, M.S., 1967; m. Julia F. Ormsby, Aug. 15, 1959; children—Kimberly Jean, Vickie Lynn, Steven A. Mem. Garden City (Mich.) Police Dept., 1959-63; research analyst State of Ill., 1967-68; mgmt. cons. Internat. Assn. Chiefs Police, Gaithersburg, Md., 1969-74, dir. research div., 1975—; lectr. criminal justice Am. U. Served with Submarine Service, USN, 1955-57. Author papers in field. Home: 309 E Leesburg Pike Sterling VA 22170 Office: 11 First Field Rd Gaithersburg MD 20760

ROBERSON, JAMES HOUSTON, textile machinery co. exec.; b. Los Angeles, Aug. 12, 1938; s. John Houston and Fannie Belle (Larrene) R.; B.S. in Mech. Engring., Clemson U., 1963; m. Mary Louise Howard, Nov. 14, 1958; children—James Houston, John Howard. Sr. analytical engr. Pratt & Whitney Aircraft Corp., West Palm Beach, Fla., 1963-66; mgr. engring. Crompton & Knowles Corp., Mauldin, S.C., 1966-77; pres. Automation Technology Corp., Mauldin, 1977—. Pres. Laurel Creek Elementary Sch. PTA, Greenville, 1973; mem. budget com. Greenville County United Fund, 1970; cubmaster Blue Ridge council Cub Scouts Am., 1969-71. Served with U.S. Army, 1955-58. Mem. ASME, Tau Beta Pi. Patentee in mech., elec. and textile engring. fields. Home: Route 6 Ashwood Ave Greenville SC 29607 Office: PO Box 443 Mauldin SC 29662

ROBERSON, ROBERT STEPHEN, archtl. woodwork mfg. co. exec.; b. Mt. Kisco, N.Y., Nov. 30, 1942; s. Robert H. and Mercedes C. (Stack) R.; B.S., N.Y. U., 1964; M.B.A., Coll. William and Mary, 1973; m. Barbara Colbert Drane, Oct. 21, 1967; children—Elizabeth deV., Merritt B., Barbara D. Various positions in fin. and bldg. industries, 1964-67; with Weaver Bros., Inc., Newport News, Va., 1967—, now treas., exec. v.p., dir.; treas., dir. Drane Lumber Co., Inc., N.Y.C. Past bd. dirs. Peninsula unit Am. Cancer Soc. Va.; past bd. dirs. Heritage council Girl Scouts, Hampton; trustee Newport News Public Library; mem. Newport News Republican City Com. Mem. Newcomen Soc., St. Nicholas Soc. City of N.Y., Gen. Soc. Colonial Wars, Gen. Soc. S.R., Colonial Order of Acorn, Vet. Corps. Arty., Huguenot Soc. N.J., Sovereign Mil. Order Temple of Jerusalem, Assn. Ex-Mems. Squadron A, Blue Key. Episcopalian. Clubs: Rotary; Church, Union (N.Y.C.); Farmington Country (Charlottesville, Va.); James River Country, Hampton Rds. Cotillion (Newport News). Home: 58 James Landing Rd Newport News VA 23606 Office: 24th-26th Sts at Terminal Ave Newport News VA 23607

ROBERT, GUS JOHNNY, architect; b. Columbia, S.C., May 16, 1943; s. Guss and Amy (Hampton) R.; B.Arch., Hampton (Va.) Inst., 1967; M.Ed., S.C. State Coll., Orangeburg, 1979; m. Thomasine Cheryl Brazeal, Apr. 16, 1965; children—Tanya Marie, Stephan Augustas. Archtl. apprentice Reid Hearn & Assos., Architects, Columbia, 1965-68, architect, 1973-75; head dept. engring. Denmark (S.C.) Tech. Edn. Center, 1975-77; instr. pre-vocation Hopkins (S.C.) Jr. High Sch., 1977-80; asst. prof. engring. S.C. State Coll., 1978—; pres. ARCHIZIGN, Inc., Columbia, 1976—. Pres. John P. Thomas P.T.A., 1976-78; vice chmn. Lexington County Adv. Bd., 1975-77; active Mid-Carolina Council on Alcoholism, cert. of appreciation, 1975. Served with U.S. Army, 1968-73; Vietnam. Decorated Air medal, Army Commendation medal; registered architect, S.C. Mem. Columbia Council Architects (v.p. 1978), Am. Vocat. Assn., S.C. Vocat. Assn., NEA, S.C. Edn. Assn., Richland County Tchrs. Assn., Am. Fedn. Tchrs., S.C. Fedn. Tchrs., Hampton Inst. Alumni Assn., S.C. State Coll. Alumni Assn., Phi Beta Sigma. Episcopalian. Home: 221 Meadowbury Dr Columbia SC 29203 Office: 6701 Two Notch Rd Columbia SC 29204

ROBERTS, ARTHUR T., museum adminstr.; b. Ft. Knox, Ky., June, 13, 1948; s. Arthur Thatcher and Mary Katherine Roberts; B.S. in Social Sci., Va. Commonwealth U.; children—Jennifer Leigh, Brian Kendall. Registered rep. Travelers Ins. Co., Richmond, Va., 1971; showroom mgr. Best Products Co., Richmond, 1971-75, Value House, Inc., Lewiston, Maine, 1975-78; adminstr. Va. Mus. Fine Arts, Richmond, 1978—; cons. corp. sales improvement. Mem. combined legis. task force Conservation Council Va. Served with USMC, 1970-71. Mem. Am. Mgmt. Assn., Affirmative Action Assn. Am., Sierra Club. Office: Va Mus Fine Arts Boulevard at Grove Ave Richmond VA 23221

ROBERTS, CAROL LEE, otolaryngologist; b. N.Y.C., Feb. 16, 1946; d. William D. Roberts and Joan (Lazar) Kryger; B.A., Radcliffe Coll., 1968; M.D., U. Tex., San Antonio, 1974; m. John J. Mikos, June 23, 1972; children—David Roberts, Andrew Roberts. Resident in surgery Albert Einstein Coll. Medicine Hosps., N.Y.C., 1974-75, resident in otolaryngology, 1975-78; practice medicine specializing in otolaryngology, Brandon, Fla., 1978—. Mem. edn. com. Brandon Cultural Center, 1979—; mem. Brandon League Fine Arts, 1978—. Diplomate Am. Bd. Otolaryngology. Mem. Hillsborough County Med. Assn., Brandon C. of C. Jewish. Office: 250 Monarch Towers Dr Brandon FL 33511

ROBERTS, CLARKE, oilfield equipment rental co. exec.; b. New Orleans, Sept. 1, 1936; s. Henry Clay and Theresa Brunhilde (Gonzales) R.; student U. New Orleans; m. Doris Porche, July 12, 1976; children—Callie, Carla, Cristi, Maria, Michael, Oscar. Payroll clk., then billing clk. Canal Rental Tools, Inc., Harvey, La., 1957-60; from billing clk. to store mgr. Taylor Equipment Co., Harvey, 1960-68; store mgr. Oilfield Rental Service Co., Harvey, 1968-72; New Orleans area mgr., purchasing mgr. Prodn. Rentals, Inc., 1972—; past pres., owner Profl. Pipe Straighteners, Inc.; owner Oilfield Lease Trucks Co., 1975; owner, sec.-treas. InFilCo., 197S—. Mem. Am. Petroleum Inst. Democrat. Mem. Assembly of God Ch. Office: PO Box 158 Harvey LA 70059

ROBERTS, DONALD EARL, oil co. exec.; b. Edmond, Okla., Oct. 7, 1935; s. Wesley Lee and Lillibelle (Rogers) R.; student Central State U., 1956; m. Sally Ann McDowell, June 6, 1964; children by previous marriage—Robin, Rand. With Firestone Tire & Rubber Co., Akron, Ohio, 1956-69; owner, operator Roberts-Seales Oil Co., Stillwater, Okla., 1970—, Robco Quik-Draw Stores, Stillwater, 1973—, Roberts Retail Liquor, Stillwater, 1974—, Robco Safety Service, Stillwater, 1971—, Robco, Inc., Stillwater, 1973—; partner Perkins Rd. Devel., Stillwater, 1978—. Served with Okla. N.G., 1956-59. Mem. Okla. Oil Marketers. Home: 924 Westwood St Stillwater OK 74074 Office: 301 E 6 St Stillwater OK 74074

ROBERTS, DUANE FAY, office bldg. devel. co. exec.; b. Milford, Utah, Dec. 23, 1938; s. Duane J. and Hazel (Wilson) R.; student U. Nev., 1957-59, Howard U., 1962-63, U. Utah, 1964-66; m. Dian Campbell, July 15, 1961; children—Miles, Marny, Travis. Owner, operator Custom Constrn. Co., Salt Lake City, 1968-70; leasing and property mgr. Del E. Webb Realty & Mgmt. Co., Phoenix, 1970-74, v.p. leasing, Phoenix, 1974-78; v.p. mktg. Joseph C. Canizaro Interests, New Orleans, 1978—. Served with U.S. Army, 1959-62. Mem. Inst. Real Estate Mgmt. (cert. property mgr.; author cassette program 1977), Bldg. Owners and Mgrs. Assn. (dir. Ariz. chpt. 1975-77). Republican. Club: Plimsol. Author: Marketing and Leasing of Office Space, 1979. Home: 64 Yellowstone Dr New Orleans LA 70114 Office: 111 Rue Iberville New Orleans LA 70130

ROBERTS, ERNEST WILSON, bank exec.; b. Chipley, Fla., Feb. 6, 1938; s. Bert Ray and Jessie Maudie (Sconyers) R.; B.S., U. Fla., 1960; LL.B., LaSalle Extension U., 1966; postgrad. Sch. Bank Mktg., U. Colo., Grad. Sch. Banking, U. Wis.; m. Sally Cross Hunt, May 22, 1961; children—Richard Wilson, James Sheperd, Carolyn Amelia. Salesman, Herff-Jones Co., Miami, 1960-65; state mgr. Olan Mills Studios, Inc., Miami, 1965-68; pres. Andover Assos., Inc., Ins. and Investments, Miami, 1968-70; pres., dir. Donut Kastle, Inc., Atlanta, 1970-72; exec. v.p., dir. Nat. Savs. Ins. Co., Ardmore, Okla., 1972-75; exec. v.p., dir. Lincoln Financial Corp., Lincoln Bank and Lincoln Center Corp., Bank Holding Co., Ardmore, 1975—; dir. Nat. Savs. Ins. Co. Bd. dirs. Arbucle council Boy Scouts Am.; mem. Emergency Schs. Assistance Act Com., Ardmore. Served with AUS, 1961-63. Mem. Okla., Am. bankers assn., Ardmore C. of C. (dir.), Delta Sigma Pi. Republican. Methodist. Club: Dornick Hills Country. Author: How, When and Where to go Public with a Small Company, 1973. Home: 936 Osage Ardmore OK 73401 Office: 400 Lincoln Center Ardmore OK 73401

ROBERTS, GEOFFREY ARTHUR SEBRY, electronic mfg. co. exec., internat. trade exec.; b. London, Eng., Sept. 25, 1913; s. Arthur Bell and Elizabeth Kate (Sebry) R.; B.Sc. in Elec. Engring., London U. (Eng.), 1937; m. Clara Diana Meruelo, Jan. 22, 1954; children—Diane Elizabeth, Ian Geoffrey. Came to U.S., 1945, naturalized, 1952. With Marconi's Wireless Telegraph Co., London, Eng., 1937-40; spl. overseas rep. for Latin Am., RCA, 1945-59; founder OKI Electronics Am., Inc., Fort Lauderdale, Fla., 1959, chmn. bd., 1959—; founder, past chief exec. officer P.E.C. Industries Inc. subs. Reliance Electric Co., Ft. Lauderdale; founder, chief exec. officer Cosmopolitan Bus. Group Inc., Ft. Lauderdale. Past mem. Council 100, Broward Indsl. Bd., Ft. Lauderdale; bd. dirs. Opera Guild; chmn. bd. dirs. Fla. Oaks Sch., Ft. Lauderdale. Served with RAF, 1940-45. Recipient Key to Port Everglades, Fla., 1969. Mem. Aircraft Owners and Pilots Assn., Nat. Pilots Assn. (recipient Safe Pilot award 1970), Nat. Aero. Assn., Nat. Bus. Aircraft Assn., N.Am. Telephone Assn. (past dir.), Fla. C. of C., Silver Wings Frat. Republican. Roman Catholic. Clubs: Le Club Internat., Lauderdale Yacht, Tower (Ft. Lauderdale). Office: Cosmopolitan Bus Group Inc 1040 Bayview Dr Fort Lauderdale FL 33304

ROBERTS, GEORGE FRANKLIN, JR., psychotherapist; b. Alexandria, La., Mar. 25, 1935; s. George Franklin and Percy Ann (LeBlanc) R.; A.B., Centenary Coll., 1959; M.S.W., Tulane U., 1960; m. Bennie Henry, Nov. 22, 1956; children—Kim Capri, Ben Franklin. With Family Service Agy., Shreveport, La., 1960-65, casework supr., El Paso, 1965-67; dir. profl. services Family Guidance Center, Dallas, 1967-69; pvt. practice psychotherapy, marriage and family therapy, Dallas, 1969—; practicum instr. Sch. Social Welfare, La. State U., 1963-64; practicum worker Perkins Sch. Theology, 1967-69; trainer, staff aid Suicide Prevention, 1968—; instr. marriage and family courses LaTuna Fed. Prison, 1967-68; cons. dir. Cathedral Counseling Center, 1969-70; practicum instr., grad. program So. Meth. U., 1975—, also field work instr.; cons., therapist Tex. Guild Infant Survival, 1976—; condr. tng. seminars for clergy, community marriage enrichment seminars; producer weekly radio series on marriage and family, 1964-65, 66-67; mem. Nat. Council on Family Relations. Lic. lay reader Episcopal Ch.; warden for lay readers Ch. of the Resurrection, 1975-76, warden for ushers, 1976-77, also adv. com. and cons. to counseling program. Lic. psychotherapist, Tex. Mem. Am. (clinician, approved supr. and trainer), Tex. (screening com. 1974-75), Dallas County assns. marriage and family counselors, Tex. Psychotherapy Assn., Am. Personnel and Guidance Assn. Club: Optimists. Postgrad. trainer on utilization of research in social services: thesis advisor, dir. research projects. Office: 6060 N Central Expressway Suite 424 Dallas TX 75206

ROBERTS, GUSTAVE WILLIAM, psychologist; b. Berlin, N.H., Aug. 14, 1943; s. Rene and Arline (Forbes) R.; B.A. cum laude, Northeastern U., 1968; Ph.D., Tex. Tech. U., 1972; m. Stephanie Patricia Wallach, Aug. 21, 1965; children—Sherrin Frances, Nicole Renee. Chief psychologist Dist. V Mental Health Center/Dallas County Mental Health/Mental Retardation, Dallas, 1972, coordinator outpatient services, 1973, diagnostic and evaluation services, and alcoholism safety action treatment program, 1973-74, adminstrv. asst. to dir., 1974-75, asst. dir., 1975; chief clin. services Dallas Adult Mental Health Clinic, 1975-76, asst. dir., 1976-78, dir., 1978-79; acting dir. Beverly Hills Hosp., Dallas, 1978—; pvt. practice psychology, Dallas, 1975-79; pvt. practice psychology, Houston, 1979—; adj. faculty U. Tex. Sch. Allied Health Scis., Dallas, 1975. Chmn. subcom. program evaluation N. Central Tex. Council Govt.'s Regional Alcoholism and Drug Abuse Adv. Com.; pres. bd. dirs. Dallas Council Alcoholism; adv. com. Alcoholism Tng. Project program, Center for Urban and Environ. Studies, So. Methodist U. Recipient Lasting Contbn. award North Central Tex. Council Govts., 1977. Licensed psychologist, Tex. Mem. Dallas (pres. 1977-78), Tex., Southwestern, Am. psychol. assns. Home: 7722 Southmeadow Dr Houston TX 77071 Office: Raleigh Hills Med Clinic 6160 South Loop E Houston TX 77087

ROBERTS, HYMAN JACOB, physician; b. Boston, May 29, 1924; s. Benjamin and Eva (Sherman) R.; M.D. cum laude, Tufts U., 1947; m. Carol Antonia Klein, Aug. 9, 1953; children—David Barry, Jonathan Stuart, Mark Elliott, Stephen, Scott F., Pamela Beth. Intern Boston City Hosp., 1947-48, resident, 1948-49; resident Municipal Hosp., Washington, 1949-50; fellow in medicine Lahey Clinic, Boston, 1950-51; instr. in medicine, research fellow Tufts U. Med. Sch., Boston, 1948-49, Georgetown Med. Sch., Washington, 1949-50; pvt. practice medicine, West Palm Beach, Fla., 1955—; sr. attending staff St. Mary's Hosp., Good Samaritan Hosp.; 1st Eugene Dibble ann. lecture Tuskegee Inst., 1967; dir. Palm Beach Inst. for Med. Research, 1964—. Mem. Palm Beach Philanthropic Council; trustee Am. Physicians Fellowship for Israel Med. Assn.; pres. Jewish Community Day Sch. Palm Beaches, 1975-76; mem. SHARE (Spl. Help for Agrl. Research and Edn.) council; bd. dirs. Am. Jewish Com., Inst. for Jewish Policy Planning and Research, Synagogue Council Am.; mem. president's council U. Fla. Served from lt. (j.g.) to lt. USNR, 1943-45, 51-54. Recipient Fla.'s Outstanding Young Men award Jr. C. of C., 1959. Diplomate Am. Bd. Internal Medicine. Fellow Am. Coll. Angiology (Fla. gov.), Royal Soc. Health, Am. Coll. Chest Physicians; mem. Am. Fedn. Clin. Research, Endocrine Soc., Am. Assn. Study Headache, Am. Soc. Internal Medicine, N.Y. Acad. Scis., A.C.P., Am. (stroke council), Fla. heart assns., Am. Diabetes Assn., A.A.A.S., Internat. Assn. for Accident and Traffic Medicine, Am., So., Fla. med. assns., Internat. Acad. Metabology, Fla. Thoracic Soc., Physicians for Automotive Safety, Am. Assn. for Automotive Medicine, Alpha Omega Alpha. Mem. B'nai B'rith (v.p. 1958-59). Rotarian (charter mem., dir. 1956-58) (West Palm Beach, Fla.). Club: Millennium Tufts U. Sch. Medicine. Author: Difficult Diagnosis; A Guide To The Interpretation of Obscure Illness, 1958; The Causes, Ecology and Prevention of Traffic Accidents, 1971; Is Vasectomy Safe? Medical, Public Health and Legal Implications, 1979; also numerous sci.

papers; donor Hyman and Carol Roberts Med. Library to Tufts U. Coll. Medicine. Home: 6708 Pamela Ln West Palm Beach FL 33405 Office: 300 27th St West Palm Beach FL 33407

ROBERTS, JAMES ALLEN, educator; b. Beach, S.D., May 31, 1934; s. Earl Fernando and Maria Ellen (Johnson) R.; M.D., U. Chgo., 1959; m. Joan Terry, July 15, 1956; children—Jennifer Lou, Mary Ellen, Thomas J. Intern, U. Chgo. Clinics, 1960, resident, 1960-65; practice medicine, specializing in urology, New Orleans and Covington, La., 1967—; faculty Tulane U. Sch. Medicine, New Orleans, 1967—, prof. urology and head Dept. Urology, Tulane U. Delta Regional Primate Research Center, Covington, La., 1971—. Pres., St. Tammany Parish Hosp., Covington, 1977-78. NIH grantee, 1969-80. Diplomate Am. Bd. Urology. Fellow ACS; mem. St. Tammany Parish Med. Soc. (pres. 1979-80), Soc. Research on Calculous Kinetics, La. Med. Soc., La. Urol. Soc., Am. Urol. Assn., Soc. Univ. Urologists, Urodynamics Soc., AAAS, Assn. Am. Med. Colls., Nat. Kidney Found., Soc. Exptl. Biology and Medicine. Editorial bd. Jour. Club Urology, 1978-80; reviewer, Pediatrics, 1978-80, Investigative Urology, 1977-80, Jour. Med. Primatology, 1977-80; contbr. articles to profl. jours. Office: 1323 S Tyler St Covington LA 70433

ROBERTS, JAMES GORDON, dairy exec.; b. Lincoln, Nebr., July 20, 1909; s. James Russell and Clare (West) R.; A.B., U. Nebr., 1932; m. Dolly Wilson Anderson, Sept. 23, 1967; children—Diane Virga (Mrs. Frank Virga), Sheila Rae. Advt. mgr. Roberts Dairy Co., Omaha, 1932-39, exec. v.p., 1939-44, pres., 1944-70, chief exec. officer, 1970-72, chmn. bd., 1944-72; dir. Omaha Nat. Bank, 1964-72. Chmn Omaha com. Am. industry Nat. Fund for Med. Edn., 1957; mem. Pres. Eisenhower's Citizens Adv. Com. on Fitness of Youth, 1957-61; council mem. at large Boy Scouts Am., 1958; del., treas. Nebr. com. White House Conf. on Children and Youth, 1959-60; conferee White House Conf. Food, Nutrition and Health, 1969. Bd. dirs. Douglas County unit Am. Cancer Soc., 1962-65, Jr. Achievement, Omaha, 1962-70, Omaha-Douglas County ARC, 1962-64, YMCA, Omaha, 1958-63, Milk Industry Found., 1960-66, Big Brothers of Omaha, 1961-64; pres., chmn. bd. dirs. Nat. Boys Football Found., 1948-60, chpt. pres., 1962; adv. bd. Lutheran Hosp., Omaha, 1957-60; bd. regents Coll. St. Mary's, 1966-70; trustee Inst. Gen. Semantics, 1958—, Omaha Safety Council, 1958-70, Douglas County chpt. Nat. Multiple Sclerosis Soc., 1960-64, Brownell Hall, 1957-65, Met. Coll., Council Bluffs, Iowa, 1966-68. Recipient certificate of service U. Nebr., 1973, also numerous awards for civic and youth work. Mem. Nebr. Assn. Mental Health (pres. 1965), Dairy Soc. Internat. (dir. 1957-60), Omaha Zool. Soc. (dir. 1962-69), Nat. Independent Dairies Assn. (exec. com. 1969—), SAR (chpt. pres. 1963-65), U. Nebr. Alumni Assn., Phi Epsilon Kappa. Author: Cancer: How and Why It May Be Wiped Out, 1977. Contbr. articles to profl. publs. Home: 161 Flamingo Dr Clearwater FL 33516 Office: 238 Shaker Pl 10730 Pacific Omaha NE 68114

ROBERTS, JAMES OSCAR, electric co. exec.; b. Phenix City, Ala., Jan. 9, 1931; s. Arthur Allen and Aggie Lee R.; student Whirlpool Refrigeration Sch., Nashville, Carrier Sch. Refrigeration, New Orleans; m. Dorothy Carver, May 19, 1960; children—Katrina, Lisha, Glenn, Julie Ann. Elec. supr. Dixilyn Corp., Morgan City, La., 1960-68; v.p., then pres. Master Electric Service Co., Inc., 1968—, also dir.; pres., dir. Master Leasing Inc., Master Supplies, Inc.; dir., sec. Andot, Inc.; dir. La Gasahol Corp. Mem. St. Mary Indsl. Group, Elec. Apparatus Service Assn. Democrat. Baptist. Clubs: Rotary, Masons, Order Eastern Star. Office: PO Drawer M Morgan City LA 70380

ROBERTS, JERRY LYNN, evangelist; b. Lamesa, Tex., June 1, 1943; s. Hilburn Carter and Fern (Strickland) R.; grad. Sunset Sch. Preaching, Lubbock, Tex., 1970; m. Joyce Marie Huse, Nov. 16, 1961; children—Rhonda Lynn, Steven Ray. Farmer, Dawson County, Tex., 1959-63; utility serviceman Pioneer Natural Gas Co., Odessa, Tex., 1964-68; asso. minister Ch. of Christ, Muleshoe, Tex., 1971; evangelist Ch. of Christ, Waukesha, Wis., 1971-74, Sunset Ch. of Christ, Carlsbad, N.Mex., 1974-77; personal evangelism minister Broadway Ch. Christ, Lubbock, 1977-79; evangelist South Plains Ch. of Christ, 1979—. Office: 6802 Elkhart St Lubbock TX 79424

ROBERTS, JIMMY NEHEMIAH, physician; b. Albertville, Ala., Apr. 10, 1939; s. James Emory and Euverlia (Hedgepeth) R.; M.D., Med. U. S.C., 1974; m. Regina Eva Christa Gessert, July 19, 1958; children—Jimmy Nehemiah, Steven M., Regina A., Thomas C., Susan M. Intern, USAF Hosp., Keesler AFB, Miss., 1974-75; gen. practice medicine, Manning, S.C., 1977-79, Birmingham, Ala., 1979—; mem. staff East End Meml. Hosp. Served with USAF, 1961-65, 75-77. Diplomate Am. Bd. Family Practice, Am. Bd. Med. Examiners. Fellow Am. Acad. Family Practice; mem. AMA, Ala. Med. Assn., Jefferson County Med. Soc., Civil Aviation Med. Assn., Aerospace Med. Assn. Republican. Baptist. Office: 924 Montclair Rd Birmingham AL 35213

ROBERTS, JOE CLYDE, mathematician, computer scientist; b. Alice, Tex., Mar. 3, 1947; s. John M. and Alpha Inez (Young) R.; B.A., Rice U., 1969; M.S., U. Chgo., 1970, postgrad. 1970-73; postgrad. U. Ill., 1973-74; m. Mary Ethel Sparkman, Mar. 29, 1969; children—Julie Nicole, Joelle Elaine. Mathematician, information systems div. math. and computation dept. David Taylor Naval Ship Research and Devel. Center, Bethesda, Md., 1974-76; mem. tech. staff, project leader Computer Scis. Corp., Wallops Island, Va., 1976-77; software programmer analyst Tex. Instruments, Dallas, 1977-79; sr. software systems engr. Rockwell Internat., Dallas, 1979—; propr. Applicable Software Systems, Garland, Tex., 1978—; Organizer, mgr. Omega Food Coop., Chgo., 1971-73. Rockwell scholar, 1966-69; Ford Found. summer grantee, 1967; NSF trainee, 1969-73. Mem. Am. Math. Soc., Am. Sci. Affiliation, Math. Assn. Am., Assn. Computing Machinery, IEEE Computer Soc. Baptist (former chmn. bd. deacons). Home: 1529 Meadowcrest Garland TX 75042

ROBERTS, JOHN CARROLL, SR., state ofcl., civil engr.; b. Frankfort, Ky., Apr. 15, 1934; s. Bowen Henry and Mayme (Burchfield) R.; B.S. in Civil Engring., U. Ky., 1960; m. Roberta Bow Miller, Apr. 14, 1956; children—Kathryn Miller, John Carroll, Patricia Jane. Sales rep. Atlas Powder Co., Wilmington, Del., 1960-63; chief engr. Geoghegan & Mathis, Inc., Bardstown, Ky., 1963-69, v.p., 1967-69; v.p. Ky. Materials Co., Frankfort, 1963-67, pres., 1972-74; chief engr. Bush Contracting Co., 1969-71; pvt. practice civil engring., 1972-74; sec. Ky. Dept. Transp., Frankfort, 1975-77; Ky. highway commr., Frankfort, 1975-77; sec. Ky. Pub. Protection and Regulation Cabinet, 1977-78; v.p. Midwest ops. Vollmer Assos., Inc., Louisville, 1978-80; v.p. D.B. Grugin Oil Co., 1963—; chmn. Ky. Airport Zoning Commn., 1975-77; ex-officio mem. Ky. Energy Resources Commn., 1975-77; mem. Turnpike Authority of Ky., 1975-77; commr. Ky. Occupational Safety and Health Rev. Commn., 1977—; dir. State Nat. Bank, 1975—; chmn. Ky. State Bd. Registration for Profl. Engrs. and Land Surveyors, 1976—. Former chmn. Frankfort Municipal Sewer Bd.; former mem. Capital Plaza Authority, 1970-74; pres. Elkhorn Elementary PTA, 1969. Past bd. dirs. Franklin County chpt. A.R.C. Served with USNR, 1955-57. Registered profl. engr., Ky. Fellow ASCE; mem. Nat., Ky. socs. profl. engrs., Ky. Hist. Soc. (life), U. Ky. Alumni Assn. (life), Am. Road Builders Assn., Am. Pub. Works Assn. Ducks Unltd. (chmn. Wetherby chpt. 1978), Kappa Sigma. Democrat. Mem. Christian Ch. (deacon). Elk (past chmn. bd. govs.). Club: Frankfort Country (dir. 1972-75). Home: 300 Ute Trail Frankfort KY 40601 Office: 300 Ute Trail Frankfort KY 40601

ROBERTS, JOHN ELGIN, mag. editor; b. Shelby, N.C., Sept. 14, 1926; s. John Ellis and Annie (Spake) R.; diploma Gardner-Webb Jr. Coll., 1947-49; B.A., Furman U., 1951, LL.D., 1972; M.A., George Peabody Coll. Tchrs., 1952; D.Litt., Bapt. Coll. at Charleston, S.C., 1971; m. Helen E. Goodwin, Sept. 8, 1950; children—Wayne, Mark, Glenn, Jonna, Jill, Julie. Tchr. Gastonia (N.C.) City Schs., 1951-54; dir. pub. relations Gardner-Webb Coll., 1954-60; dir. pub. relations, editor Charity and Children Bapt. Children's Homes of N.C., Thomasville, 1960-65; editor, bus. mgr. The Bapt. Courier, Greenville, S.C., 1966—. Mem. So. Bapt. Editors Conf., So. Bapt. Inter-Agy. Council; bd. advisers New Orleans Bapt. Theol. Sem.; mem. Thomasville (N.C.) Bd. Edn., 1963-65; trustee So. Bapt. Radio and TV Commn., 1978—; pres. S.C. Bapt. Conv., 1980. Served with AUS, 1945-46. Mem. So. Bapt. Pub. Relations Assn. (pres. 1956—), Bapt. World Alliance Commn. on Communication. Baptist (deacon). Rotarian. Home: 106 Trinity Way Greenville SC 29609 Office: 100 Manly St Greenville SC 29602

ROBERTS, JOHN HAROLD, metall. engr.; b. Peoria, Ill., Feb. 24, 1943; s. John Gerald and Helen Ruth (Gauger) R.; B.S., U. Ill., 1965. Engr., Sundstrand Aviation, Rockford, Ill., 1965-69; engr. Tex. Instruments Co., Dallas, 1969-71; mgr. process engring. Consol. Casting Corp., Dallas, 1971-78, chief engr., 1978—. Registered profl. engr. Mem. ASME, Am. Soc. Metals, Investment Casting Inst., Mensa. Club: Mason. Home: 13677 Purple Sage Rd Dallas TX 75240 Office: 2425 Caroline St Dallas TX 75201

ROBERTS, JOSEPH BOXLEY, JR., educator, writer; b. Yazoo City, Miss., Feb. 13, 1918; s. Joseph Boxley and Sheila (Hill) R.; B.A., U. Ala., 1950; M.A. (Rockefeller Found. scholar), U. N.C., 1954; Ph.D., U. Denver, 1959; m. Enyd Turner, Nov. 19, 1945; children—Joseph Boxley III, Sheila Anne Roberts Tweed. Served as enlisted man U.S. Army Air Corps, 1942-43, commd. 2d lt. U.S. Air Force, 1951, advanced through grades to lt. col., 1966; asst. prof. English, U.S. Mil. Acad., West Point, N.Y., 1953-56; asso. prof. English, dep. head dept. U.S. Air Force Acad. (Colo.), 1956-63; dir. info. Office Aerospace Research, Washington, 1963-66; chief ops. Psychol. Ops. Directorate, Vietnam, 1966-67; head psychol. ops. civic action dept. Spl. Air Warfare Sch., Hurlburt Field, Fla., 1967-68; ret., 1968; instr. English, U. Ala., Huntsville, 1950; prof. English, Troy (Ala.) State U., 1968—, chmn. dept., 1968-71, dean Coll. Arts and Scis., 1971-72. Weekly newspaper columnist It Seems to Me, 1973-79, syndicated by Contemporary Features Syndicate, Inc., 1976-79. Decorated Bronze Star medal, Commendation medal. Mem. Modern Lang. Assn. Am., Nat. Council Tchrs. English, Conf. on Coll. Composition and Communication, South Atlantic Modern Lang. Assn., Troy C. of C. (chmn. edn. com. 1969-70), Air Force Assn., Ret. Officers Assn., Phi Beta Kappa. (pres. Troy Assn. 1969-70), Phi Eta Sigma, Phi Kappa Phi (pres. Troy State U. chpt. 1972-73), Sigma Tau Delta (adviser 1974-76). Episcopalian (vestryman 1974-77). Rotarian (dir. 1970-71). Author: Airway to India, 1945; Faint Voice Calling, 1945; Beginner's Handbook of Gold and Tropical Fish, 1947, rev. edit., 1952; Pet Shop Manual, 1953; Web of Our Life, 1957; The Sound of Wings, 1957; On Poetry and the Poetic Process, 1971; Of Time and Love, 1980. Home: 107 Richmond Ave Troy AL 36081 Office: Dept English Troy State U Troy AL 36081

ROBERTS, KENNETH LEWIS, banker; b. Dungannon, Va., Dec. 12, 1932; s. Clarence Eugene and Katherine (Osborne) R.; B.A., Vanderbilt U., 1954, LL.B., 1959; m. Anne Foster Cook, Sept. 10, 1955; children—Stephen Cook, Kenneth L., Patrick Foster. Admitted to Tenn. bar; asso. prof. law Vanderbilt U., 1959-60; asso. Waller, Lansden & Dortch, Nashville, 1960-66; exec. v.p. Commerce Union Bank, Nashville, 1966-71; pres., chief exec. officer, dir. Central Nat. Bank, Richmond, Va., 1971-76, First Am. Nat. Bank, Nashville, 1976—; dir. First Amtenn Corp., 1976—, vice chmn., 1976-77, chief exec. officer, 1977—, pres., 1977-80, chmn., 1980—; past pres., dir. Central Nat. Corp.; dir. A.H. Robins Co., Inc., Thalhimer Bros., Inc. Mem. regional adv. com. on banking policies and practices Comptroller of Currency, from 1974. Trustee Vanderbilt U.; bd. dirs. St. Thomas Devel. Found., Nashville Symphony, Tenn. Performing Arts Mgmt. Corp., Blair Sch. Music, Leadership Nashville; mem. exec. bd. Middle Tenn. council Boy Scouts Am. Served to lt., Chem. Corps, AUS, 1955-57. Mem. Am., Tenn., Nashville bar assns., Am., Va. (bank mgmt. com. from 1975) bankers assn., Assn. Res. City Bankers Young Pres.'s Orgn., Retail Mchts. Assn. Greater Richmond (dir. 1975—). Nashville C. of C. (treas.). Clubs: Cumberland, Rotary, Belle Meade Country. Office: First American Center Nashville TN 37237

ROBERTS, MICHAEL LEE, painter; b. Marion County, Ind., Jan. 30, 1945; s. Hershel Edison and Martha Mable (Baldwin) R.; student John Herron Inst. Art, 1962-66. Exhibited in one-man show Lorenzo Bergan Gallery, Houston, 1979; group shows: Ind. Prints Show, Indpls., 1965, Beach Show, Estero Beach, Fla., 1974, other; represented in permanent collections; works include: Stern's Observation (Marilyn Monroe), Daughter of Houston (Jaclyn Smith), Duke (John Wayne); nat. chmn. Nat. Cape Coral Ann. Art Exhbn. #9. Recipient awards and hon. mentions in various juried exhibits. Mem. Indpls. Art Dirs. Assn., S.W. Fla. Art Council, Art League Houston, Audubon Soc., Cousteau Soc.

ROBERTS, RAY, congressman; b. nr. McKinney, Tex., Mar. 28, 1913; s. Roy C. and Margaret (Burton) R.; student Tex. A. and M. Coll., 1930-31, North Tex. State Coll., 1931-32, U. Tex., 1933-35; m. Elizabeth Bush, Nov. 12, 1946; 1 dau., Kay (Mrs. Tom Murray II). Mem. staff Speaker Sam Rayburn, U.S. Ho. of Reps., 1940-42; mem. Tex. Senate from 9th Dist., 1955-62; elected 87th Congress to fill unexpired term of Speaker Rayburn, 1962; mem. 88th-96th Congresses from 4th Tex. Dist. Served to capt. USNR, World War II. Democrat. Office: 2184 Rayburn House Office Bldg Washington DC 20515

ROBERTS, RAY, congressman; b. nr. McKinney, Tex., Mar. 28, 1913; s. Roy C. and Margaret (Burton) R.; student Tex. A. and M. Coll., 1930-31, North Tex. State Coll., 1931-32, U. Tex., 1933-35; m. Elizabeth Bush, Nov. 12, 1946; 1 dau., Kay (Mrs. Tom Murray II). Mem. staff Speaker Sam Rayburn, U.S. Ho. of Reps., 1940-42; mem. Tex. Senate from 9th Dist., 1955-62; elected 87th Congress to fill unexpired term of Speaker Rayburn, 1962; mem. 88th-95th congresses from 4th Tex. Dist. Served to capt. USNR, World War II. Democrat. Home: 509 Tucker St McKinney TX 75069 Office: 2455 Rayburn House Office Bldg Washington DC 20515

ROBERTS, ROBERT, III, lawyer; b. Shreveport, La., July 22, 1930; s. Robert, Jr., and Mary Hodges (Marshall' R.; student Davidson Coll., 1947-49; B.A., La. State U., 1951, J.D., 1953; m. Susan Forrester, Mar. 16, 1974; children—Robert IV, Campbell Marshall, Francis T. Kalmbach, Jr., Ellen A. Kalmbach (Mrs. Howard Baker), Lewis F. Kalmbach, Samuel A. Kalmbach. Admitted to La. bar, 1953; partner Blanchard, Walker, O'Quin & Roberts, Shreveport, La., 1955—. Mem. citizens adv. com. Peabody Report on Caddo Parish Schs., 1968; dir. Caddo Bossier Legal Aid Soc., 1961-64; chmn. legal div. Caddo and Bossier Parishes United Fund, 1966; dir. Family Counseling and Children's Services, 1968-73, 1st v.p., 1971-72, pres., 1973. Trustee Southfield Sch., 1964-68, treas., 1965-67; bd. dirs. St. Mark's Day Sch., 1979—, vice chmn., 1980. Served to 1st lt. J.A.G.C., AUS, 1953-55. Mem. La. Bar Assn. (ho. 1960-63, gov. 1973-74), Shreveport Bar Assn. (pres.-elect 1980), La. Law Inst. (mem. council, mem. mineral law adv. com.), Shreveport Petroleum Club (dir. 1971-74, sec. 1972), Soc. Bartolus, Soc. Henri Capitant, Order of Coif, Phi Kappa Phi. Democrat. Episcopalian. Clubs: Shreveport, Shreveport Petroleum, Pierremont Oaks Tennis. Home: 4314 Richmond Ave Shreveport LA 71106 Office: PO Drawer 1126 Shreveport LA 71163

ROBERTS, ROY RAYMOND, urologist; b. Ned, Pa., Nov. 11, 1920; s. Sherl Levi and Sarah Bertha (Earnest) R.; B.S., Waynesburg Coll., 1942; M.D., Western Res. U., 1944; m. Gladys Ellen Heimerdinger, May 2, 1944; 1 son, Philip. Intern, Polyclinic Hosp., Harrisburg, Pa., 1944-45; resident in urology Aspinwall (Pa.) Hosp., 1948-52; practice medicine specializing in urology, Plainview, Tex., 1952—; mem. staff Nichols Hosp., 1952—, chief dept. urology, 1952—; mem. staff Central Plains Hosp., 1952—, chief dept. urology, 1952—. Served to capt. M.C., U.S. Army, 1946-48. Diplomate Am. Bd. Urology. Mem. AMA, A.C.S., Am. Urol. Assn., Tex. Med. Assn. Club: Masons. Home: 2404 Yonkers St Plainview TX 79072

ROBERTS, RYAN TERRETT, city ofcl.; b. Ekalaka, Mont., Apr. 7, 1947; s. Harry Thomas and Beverly Leone (Olsen) R.; A.A., Metro. State Coll., 1972, B.A., 1973; M.S. in Ed., U. So. Calif., 1976; M.P.A., Golden Gate U., 1980; m. Sheryl White, June 6, 1969. Tchr. adult edn. Pasco County (Fla.) pub. schs., 1976-77; tng. dir. City of Lakeland (Fla.), 1976—. Served with U.S. Army, 1973-76, USAR, 1976—. Mem. Am. Legion, Am. Soc. Tng. and Devel., DAV, Res. Officers Assn. Home: 1773 Rosewall Dr Land O'Lakes FL 33539 Office: 1000 E Parker St Lakeland FL 33802

ROBERTS, STEVEN MAURICE, psychologist; b. Dothan, Ala., Nov. 2, 1949; s. Huie, Jr. and Katherine (Hayes) R.; B.A. in Religious Studies, U. Ala., 1974; M.S. in Counseling and Guidance, Troy (Ala.) State U., 1977; m. Vicki Ann Johnston, June 2, 1973; 1 son, Joseph Dylan. Psychiat. aide, then asst. chaplain Bryce State Hosp., Tuscaloosa, 1972-74; outpatient counselor Wiregrass Mental Health Center, Dothan, 1974-77; clinic dir. Red River County Mental Health Clinic, Clarksville, Tex., 1977-78; unit dir. Tyler County outpatient clinic Deep E. Tex. Mental Health-Mental Retardation Center, Woodville, 1978—. Mem. Army N.G., 1970-76. Mem. Am. Personnel and Guidance Assn., Am. Mental Health Counselors Assn. Baptist. Clubs: Lions, Jaycees. Home: Route 1 Box 86-0-4 Woodville TX 75979 Office: 101A Pecan St Woodville TX 75979

ROBERTS, SUSAN C., educator; b. N.Y.C., June 20, 1945; d. Bruno and Ilse Grossman; B.A., Rollins Coll., 1966; M.A., U. South Fla., 1969; Ph.D. (fellow), U. Fla., 1972; m. Norman T. Roberts, Aug. 9, 1964. Tchr. retarded children, Brevard County, Fla., 1966-68, curriculum coordinator for exceptional children, 1968-70; asst. prof. edn. U. Miami, Coral Gables, 1972-73; asst. prof. edn. Barry Coll., Miami Shores, Fla., 1973-76, asso. prof. edn., 1976—; cons. Dade County (Fla.) Public Schs., 1972-73; cons. U. Miami, 1973. Mem. Council for Exceptional Children, Nat. Council Jewish Women (dir.), Am. Bus. Women's Assn. Phi Delta Kappa. Club: Hadassah. Contbr. articles to profl. jours. Office: 11300 NE 2d Ave Miami Shores FL 33161

ROBERTS, THOMAS G., research physicist; b. Ft. Smith, Ark., Apr. 27, 1929; s. Thomas Lawrence and Emma Lee (Stanley) R.; A.A., Armstrong Coll., Savannah, Ga., 1953; B.S., U. Ga., 1956, M.S. (Alumni fellow), 1957; postgrad. (Spl. Alumni fellow), 1958; Ph.D., N.C. State U., 1967; m. Alice Anne Harbin, Nov. 14, 1958; children—Lawrence Dewey, Regina Anne; foster child, Marcia Yvette Barber. Instr. physics U. Ga., 1956-57; research physicist U.S. Army Missile Command, Redstone Arsenal, Ala., 1958—; dir. Clark, Roberts and Co., Huntsville, Ala.; instr. physics U. Ala., Huntsville, evenings, 1960-61, 75-77, Athens (Ala.) Coll., eves., 1968-69; instr. physics Southeastern Inst. Tech., Huntsville, eves. 1976-79, physics coordinator, 1977-79. Served with USAF, 1948-52. Recipient Wheatley Physics award U. Ga., 1956, Sci. and Engring. Achievement award Dept. of Army and Army Missile Command, 1968, Research award U.S. Army, 1970. Mem. Am. Phys. Soc., Am. Rocket Soc., Assn. U.S. Army, Am. Optical Soc., I.E.E.E. (sr.), Toastmasters Internat. (exec. lt. gov. dist. 48, 1962-63), Phi Beta Kappa, Sigma Psi, Phi Kappa Phi, Sigma Pi Sigma, Pi Mu Epsilon. Episcopalian. Patents, publs. in field. Home: 2815 Bentley St SE Huntsville AL 35801 Office: US Army Missile Command DRDMI-HS RRP Redstone Arsenal AL 35809

ROBERTS, WALTER FREDERICK, JR., architect; b. Richmond, Va., Jan. 21, 1940; s. Walter Frederick and Audrey Marie (Grubbs) R.; B.Arch., Va. Poly. Inst. and State U., 1963; m. Patricia Ann Suddarth, July 29, 1978; children—Jefferson Frederick, Anne Marie. With J. Jansons Architect, Falls Church, Va., 1964-67; prin., designer Jansons & Roberts Architects, Falls Church, 1967-71, JRTA Assos., Reston, Va., 1971-76; individual practice architecture, Reston, 1976—; vis. prof. Grad. Sch., Coll. Architecture, Va. Poly. Inst. and State U., Blacksburg, 1975; works include Reston Cath. Ch., 1974, Scope Inc., 1967, Montrose Bapt. Ch., 1969. Recipient award 1st Passive Solar Home Competition, HUD, 1979. Registered architect, Va., Md., D.C., Pa. Mem. AIA (energy com.; numerous design awards), Internat. Solar Energy Soc., Underground Space Assn. Office: 1634 Chimney House Rd Reston VA 22090

ROBERTS, WILLIAM HENRY, JR., educator; b. Pine Bluff, Ark., Oct. 29, 1920; s. William H. and Iva M. (Hankins) R.; B.S., Ark. State Tchrs. Coll., 1943; M.A., U. Kans., 1948; B.Mus.Edn., U. Mich., 1955; M.Mus.Edn., U. Ark., 1964. Tchr., Star City (Ark.) High Sch., 1957-63; music dir. Lakeside Methodist Ch., Pine Bluff, Ark., 1957-65; tchr. Altheimer (Ark.) High Sch., 1963-66; dir. extension classes Pine Bluff (Ark.) A&M Coll., 1964-72; music dir. Central Presbyn. Ch., Pine Bluff, 1970—; asst. prof. U. Ark., Monticello, 1966—; substitute choir dir., organist various chs. Dir., actor, pres. Pine Bluff Little Theater, 1957-64. Served with Signal Corps., U.S. Army, 1943-46. Mem. NEA, Ark. Edn. Assn., Ark. Speech Tchrs., Nat. Council Tchrs. English, Jefferson County Audubon Soc., Am. Choral Dirs. Assn. Democrat. Presbyterian. Editor Ark. Tchrs. Coll. newspaper, 1942-43. Home: 920 W 35th St Pine Bluff AR 71603 Office: Univ of Ark Dept Communication Arts Monticello AR 71655

ROBERTS, WILLIAM LAWRENCE, appraiser, broker, realtor; b. Boston, Jan. 20, 1924; s. James Joseph and Mary Margaret (Galvin) R.; student Northeastern U., 1949-51, Rutgers U., 1952-54; LL.B., Blackstone Sch. Law, 1959; grad. Realtors Inst., 1975; m. Josephine Mary DeLeo, July 22, 1945; children—James Joseph, Linda Marie (Mrs. John Hamilton Glover), William Lawrence. With RCA, Camden, N.J., 1951-58, Midwest regional rep., 1955, N.E. regional rep., 1956; sr. mem. tech. staff Thompson Ramo Wooldridge Co., Redondo Beach, Calif., 1958-60, N.E. regional mgr., 1960-61; mgr.

marketing Sperry Rand Research Center, Sudbury, Mass., 1961-62; research and devel. marketing mgr. Litton Industries, Beverly Hills, Calif., 1962-65, dir. data systems, div. aero Service Corp., 1965-66; with Collins Radio Co., Dallas, 1966-74, venture analyst, mgr. sales service div., 1973-74; with Paula Stringer Realtors Inc., Plano, Tex., 1974—, v.p., 1977—. Chmn. cub scouts Fort Stanwix council Boy Scouts Am., 1956-57, asst. dist. commr., 1965-66; pres. Meadowbrook P.T.A., Pennsauken, N.J., 1953-54; capt. fund drive Plano YMCA, 1975. Campaign mgr. Kennedy/Johnson, Rome, N.Y., 1960. Served with USNR, 1942-45: PTO. Recipient Citizens award City Utica (N.Y.), 1963; cert. residential specialist, residential broker. Mem. I.E.E.E. (sr. mem., nat. exec. com. 1960-64), Am. Rocket Soc., Am. Inst. Aero. and Astronautics, Armed Forces Communications and Electronics Assn. (nat. dir. 1959-67), Am. Angus Assn., Nat. Mktg. Inst., Soc. Real Estate Appraisers (sr. residential appraiser), Collin County Bd. Realtors (v.p.). Author: (with Vernon Poehls) Naval Shipboard Communications Building Block Design Handbook, 1952; Test Agenda and Record of Performance of Shipboard Electronic Systems, 1953. Home: 3021 Princeton Dr Plano TX 75074 Office: 3100 Independence Pkwy Plano TX 75075

ROBERTSON, BRENT ERNEST, automotive corp. exec.; b. Indpls., Oct. 28, 1940; s. C.I. and Mary A. (Stevenson) R.; B.S. in Civil Engring., Rose-Hulman Inst., 1962; postgrad. George Washington U., 1966; M.B.A., U. Akron, 1970; m. Diane Lynn Bandy, Oct. 25, 1962; chidlren—Brent, David. With sales-mktg. B.F. Goodrich Co., Ohio, Tex., 1967-74; sales mgr. Tire & Battery Corp., Memphis, 1975—. Dist. troop officer Portage council Boy Scouts Am., 1967-72; ofcl. U.S. Soap Box Derby, 1969-72. Served to maj. C.E., AUS, 1962-67. Mem. Nat. Tire Dealer and Retread Assn., Automotive Parts Accessories Assn., Soc. Am. Mil. Engrs., ASCE, Alpha Tau Omega. Methodist. Office: Tire & Battery Corp Box 18342 4770 Hickory Hill Rd Memphis TN 38138

ROBERTSON, CARL LESTER, home furnishings mfg. co. exec.; b. Fort Smith, Ark., July 31, 1929; s. Nelson Mather and Rebecca (Harder) R.; student Fort Smith Jr. Coll. and Ark. Tech. Coll., 1947-50; m. Gweneth Crowe, Sept. 17, 1950; children—Carl Lester, Gregg, Stephen Brian. Vice pres. Standard Cycle & Hobbies Inc., Oklahoma City, 1955-63; v.p., gen. mgr. Novel Ideas subs. Newell Cos., Oklahoma City, 1963-76; pres. Robertson Home Products Corp., Oklahoma City, 1976—. Mem. Nat. Bath, Bed and Linen Assn. Republican. Methodist. Clubs: Rotary, Masons, Shriners. Home: 3104 Carlton Way Oklahoma City OK 73120 Office: PO Box 12647 Oklahoma City OK 73157

ROBERTSON, CLYDE WISE, JR., former trucking co. exec.; b. nr. Abilene, Tex., Aug. 27, 1917; s. Clyde Wise and Effie Beulah (Trantham) R.; grad. high sch.; m. Lena Ruth Harris, June 25, 1939; children—Bruce, Susan (Mrs. Stephen Elliott Davis), Jane (Mrs. Don Hall). With Am. Nat. Bank, Amarillo, Tex., 1940-44; office mgr. Hill Lines, Inc., Amarillo, 1944-46, gen. auditor, 1946-52, asst. gen. mgr., 1952-60; gen. mgr. H-M div. Ill.-Calif. Express, Inc., Amarillo, 1960-62, v.p., Amarillo and Dallas, 1962-70, pres., Denver, 1970-76, also dir.; pres. Strickland Transp. Co., Inc., Dallas, 1976-78; ret., 1978; pres., The Tattered Cover, Inc., also dir.; dir. Exchange Savs. and Loan Assn., Dallas. Bd. govs. Regular Common Carrier Conf. Mem. S.W. Operators Assn. (dir.), Western Hwy. Inst. Republican. Baptist. Clubs: Garden of the Gods (Colorado Springs); Las Colinas Country (Dallas). Home: 3727 Princess Ln Dallas TX 75229 Office: 3011 Gulden Ln Dallas TX 75212

ROBERTSON, CURTIS, JR., constrn. co. exec.; b. Bakersfield, Calif., Dec. 4, 1941; s. Curtis and Lorene (Ledford) R.; student Del Mar Tech. Inst., Corpus Christi, Tex., 1961-65; B.S.M.E., Carnegie Inst. Engring., 1970; m. Edith Louise Hennesay, June 23, 1959; children—James Randal, Ricky Ray, Rodney Vaughn. Constrn. worker, Corpus Christi, 1960-65; pres. Robertson Mech. Contractors, Aqua Pools Inc., Sinton, Tex., 1968-74, Trinity Valley, Inc., Houston 1975—. Asso. minister Kenifick Baptist Ch., Dayton, Tex., 1976—, outreach dir., 1976—. Mem. Nat. Radio Broadcasters Assn., Associated Gen. Contractors Assn., Full Gospel Businessmen's Fellowship (dir.). Republican. Club: Lions. Home: PO Box 1034 Dayton TX 77535 Office: 2425 Wadsworth St Houston TX 77015

ROBERTSON, FRANK LEWIS, bishop; b. Covington, Ga., Apr. 22, 1917; s. Herman William and Nell (Hutchins) R.; A.B., Emory U., 1940; M.Div., Yale, 1942; postgrad. Columbia; D.D., LaGrange Coll., 1961; L.H.D., Ky. Wesleyan Coll., 1973; LL.D., Union Coll., 1974; Litt.D., Lambuth Coll., 1976; m. LuReese Ann Watson, June 18, 1941; children—Jane (Mrs. Westerfield), Frank Lewis. Ordained to ministry United Methodist Ch., as deacon, 1942, elder, 1944; pastor, Baker Village Ch., Columbus, Ga., 1942-47, First Ch., Hawkinsville, Ga., 1947-51, First Ch., Douglas, Ga., 1951-55, St. Luke Ch., Columbus, Ga., 1955-60, Mulberry St. Ch., Macon, Ga., 1964-69, First Ch., Valdosta, Ga., 1969-72; dist. supt. Savannah, Ga., 1960-64; consecrated bishop, 1972; bishop Louisville area, 1972—. Trustee Lake Janaluska Assembly, N.C., Ky. Wesleyan Coll., Lindsey Wilson Coll., Ky., Union Coll., Barbourville, Ky. Kiwanian, Rotarian. Home: 800 S 4th St Louisville KY 40203 Office: 1115 S 4th St Louisville KY 40203

ROBERTSON, GERALD LESLIE, foundry co. exec.; b. St. Joseph, Mo., Aug. 8, 1934; s. James Leo and Laura Elizabeth R.; student Gen. Motors Inst., Flint, Mich., 1952-56; grad. Mgmt. Program Harvard, 1974; m. Joan Alice Brock, Aug. 16, 1956; children—Stephen, Christopher, Julianne, Scott. Supr., Central Foundry div. Gen. Motors, Defiance, Ohio, 1952-58; methods engr. Diamond Nat. Corp., Middleton, Ohio, 1958-60; indsl. engr. Mead Containers, Cin., 1960-62, mgr. dist. mfg., Durham, N.C., 1962-66, mgr. dist. mfg., Chgo., 1966-68; gen. mgr. Xenia Services, Zurich, Switzerland, 1968-72; v.p., gen. mgr. Soil pipe ops. Mead Corp. Anniston, Ala., 1972-74; exec. v.p. Mead Indsl. Products, Birmingham, 1974-75; pres. Lynchburg Foundry Co., (Va.), 1975—; dir. United Va. Bank/First Nat. Vice chmn. United Way Central Va., Lynchburg, 1975, chmn., 1976; pres., 1977—, dir., 1978—; bd. dirs. Jr. Achievement, 1978, pres., 1979; bd. dirs. United Way Central Va., 1978; chmn. S.E. region Foundry Edn. Found., 1977-78, trustee-at-large, 1978—; pres. council Randolph-Macon Woman's Coll., 1979-80. Mem. Am. Foundrymen's Soc., Foundry Edn. Found., Va. Mfrs. Assn. (dir. 1978), Iron Castings Soc., Am. Edn. Found., Va. Mfrs. Assn. (dir. 1978), Iron Castings Soc., Am. Mgmt. Assn., Lynchburg C. of C. (dir. 1978). Home: 3001 Sedgewick Dr Lynchburg VA 24503 Office: PO Box 411 Lynchburg VA 24505

ROBERTSON, IDA ROBERTS (MRS. SAMUEL THOMPSON ROBERTSON), home economist; b. Shawboro, N.C., Mar. 8, 1918; d. James M. and Ida C. (Perkins) Roberts; B.A., East Carolina U., 1939; postgrad. Woman's Coll., U. N.C. (now U. N.C. at Greensboro), 1948, 62; m. Samuel Thompson Robertson, June 30, 1949. Faculty pub. high sch., Kenansville, N.C., 1939-40; home mgmt. supr. county Farmer's Home Adminstrn., Raleigh, N.C., 1940-46; vocational home econs. tchr., high sch., Williamston, N.C., 1946-48; tchr. English high sch., Woodsdale, N.C., 1954-55; asst. dir. Dairy Council Richmond (Va.), 1957-62. Mem. Am. (life), Richmond (v.p. 1958-60, publicity chmn. 1960-62, membership chmn. 1963-66, treas. 1965-67), home econs. assns., Va. (chmn. ways and means com. 1959-61), Richmond home economists in bus., Currituck County Hist. Soc., East Carolina Alumni Assn. (life mem., sec.-treas. Richmond area 1963-70), Richmond Agrl. Grange, Phi Sigma Alpha (pres. 1967-68, named Woman of Year 1968, extension officer, 1971-73, publicity chmn. 1970-71, corr. sec. 1968-71, 73-75, v.p. 1977-78). Democrat. Methodist. Home: 5710 W Franklin St Richmond VA 23226

ROBERTSON, JACK CLARK, accountant, educator; b. Marlin, Tex., Apr. 27, 1943; s. Rupert Cook and Lois Lucille (Rose) R.; student Rice U., 1961-63; B.B.A., U. Tex., 1965, M.P.A., 1967; Ph.D. (Ernst & Ernst fellow), U. N.C., 1970; m. Caroline Susan Hughes, Oct. 23, 1965; children—Sarah, Elizabeth. Staff accountant Peat, Marwick, Mitchell & Co., Houston, 1965-66, Wade, Barton & Marsh, C.P.A.'s, Austin, Tex., 1966-67; mem. staff office mng. partner Coopers & Lybrand, N.Y.C., 1975-76; asst. prof. U. Tex., Austin, 1970-74, asso. prof., 1974-79, Price Waterhouse auditing prof., 1979—; instr. continuing profl. edn. courses sponsored by Nat. Assn. State Bds. Accountancy, Am. Inst. C.P.A.'s; speaker various profl. accounting meetings. Vestryman, treas., layreader St. Mathew Episcopal Ch., Austin. C.P.A., Tex. Mem. Am. Inst. C.P.A.'s, Am. Accounting Assn. Author: Cost Accounting for Small Manufacturers, 1971; Income Determination Through Use of Current Cost Accounting, 1977; Auditing, 1979. Home: 5804 Westslope Dr Austin TX 78731 Office: BEB 300 U Tex Austin TX 78712

ROBERTSON, MARY ELLA, ednl. adminstr., social worker; b. Lake Charles, La., Sept. 5, 1924; d. John and Mildred (Gardner) Robertson; B.A. summa cum laude, Xavier U., 1947; M.S.W., Atlanta U., 1949; advanced certificate in social work, Smith Coll., 1955; research fellow Adminstrv. Sci. Center, U. Pitts., 1959-60; D.Social Work, U. Pitts., 1962. Psychiat. social worker VA, Montrose, N.Y., 1949-53; supr. social services Family Service Assn., Ann Arbor, Mich., 1953-54; asst. prof. Case Western Res. U. Sch. Social Work, Cleve., 1955-57; exec. dir. Cleve. Guidance Center, 1957-59; asst. dean, asso. prof. U. Pitts. Grad. Sch. Social Work, 1962-66; vis. prof., asst. dean curriculum devel. U. Wis., Milw., 1966-67; dean, prof. Howard U. Sch. Social Work, Washington, 1967-69; prof. Boston Coll. Grad. Sch. Social Work, Chestnut Hills, Mass., 1969-72; prof. social service Ind. U.-Purdue U. at Indpls., 1972-74; v.p. for community services at Gov.'s State U., Park Forest South, Ill., 1974-77; prof. social policy Kent Sch. Social Work, U. Louisville, 1977—, dir. continuing edn. and community programs, 1977—; cons. social services various state and govt. agys. Mem. adminstrv. rev. panel child welfare policies Office of Children and Youth, Harrisburg, Pa., 1964-65; mem. com. on profl. edn. Comprehensive Mental Health Study Com. for Pa., 1964-66; mem. adv. com. to pres. Mt. Mercy Coll., Pitts., 1965-68; mem. adv. com. to sec. labor and industry Commonwealth of Pa., 1965-66; mem. adv. com. on population HEW, 1975—. Bd. dirs. Human Life Found., Washington, Parents and Childrens Services Children's Mission, Boston. Named Pitts. Woman of Year Mayor's Com. on Pub. Service, 1965; Outstanding Alumna, Atlanta U. Sch. Social Work, 1969; Dau. Commonwealth of Pa. Mem. Nat. Assn. Social Workers, Council on Social Work Edn. (past chmn. nat. com. on admissions, mem. dean's adv. com., mem. Ho. of Dels. 1967-70), Pitts. Commn. Cath. Charities (del. assembly), Kappa Gamma Pi, Alpha Kappa Mu. Contbr. articles to profl. jours. Home: 800 S 4th St Louisville KY 40203 Office: Kent Sch Social Work U Louisville Louisville KY 40208

ROBERTSON, SANDRA LEA, univ. adminstr.; b. Fort Hood, Tex., Sept. 20, 1946; d. Daniel and Robbie Jean (Walters) Martin; B.S.E., Ouachita Bapt. Coll., 1967; M.A., U. Ark., 1970; m. Charles D. Robertson, Sept. 2, 1973. Tchr. English high schs., Bismarck, Ark., 1967-68, Farmington, Ark., 1969-70, Mills High Sch., Pulaski County, Ark., 1970-76; tchr. reading public schs., Little Rock, 1976-79; learning lab. coordinator U. Ark., Little Rock, 1976—; sec. Ark. Consortium for Developmental Edn., 1978-79. Mem. Internat., Ark. reading assns., Ark., Am. coll. personnel assns., Am. Personnel and Guidance Assn., South West Assn. Student Assistance Programs, Ark. Assn. Student Assistance Programs (rep. to regional bd. 1979-80), LWV. Methodist. Home: 45 White Oak Ln Little Rock AR 72207 Office: Learning Lab Univ Ark Little Rock AR 72204

ROBESON, STUART HOGAN, lawyer; b. Mooresville, N.C., Apr. 26, 1909; s. James Bailey and Katie Stuart (Drew) R.; student Duke U., 1927-30; B.S., Ga. Inst. Tech., 1931; LL.B., George Washington U., Washington, 1935, M. Juridicial Sci., D. Juridicial Sci., 1938; m. Mary Elizabeth Leigh, Aug. 3, 1936; children—James Bailey, Stuart Hogan, Palmer E. Admitted to D.C. bar, 1937, Va. bar, 1940; practice law Washington, 1942-76; partner firm Robeson, Murphy & Robeson, Manassas, Va., founder, officer, dir. numerous corps., 1942—; lectr. in field. Chmn. bd. trustees Falls Ch. Presbyn. Ch. (Va.), 1941-44; pres. McLean (Va.) Citizens Assn., 1960; life mem. McLean Vol. Fire Dept. Served to lt., USNR, 1944-46; PTO. Mem. D.C., Va. bar assns. Democrat. Methodist. Clubs: Nat. Lawyers, Masons, Shriners. Home: 1222 Dolly Madison Blvd McLean VA 22101 Office: 9119 Church St PO Box 349 Manassas VA 22110

ROBEY, HARRY RUSSELL, coll. adminstr.; b. Buena Vista, Va., Sept. 30, 1895; s. William Thomas and Susan (Connor) R.; grad. Dunsmore Coll. Accounting, 1917; Washington and Lee U., 1918; m. Margaret Durham, Sept. 12, 1922. Cashier Kingsport Pulp Corp. (Va.), 1918-19; treas. Farmers & Mchts. Mills, Buena Vista, Va., 1920-22; treas., bus. mgr., partner So. Sem. and Jr. Coll., Buena Vista, Va., from 1922, now trustee emeritus. Mem. Buena Vista City Council, 1934-50; mem. Buena Vista Planning Commn., 1936-50; chmn. Buena Vista United Fund, 1968-72; organizer Buena Vista Health Dept., City Recreation Dept., City Planning Commn.; chmn. Buena Vista Bicentennial Commn.; head Va. Gov.'s Spruce Up Campaign; active various local hist. landmark restoration projects. Served with USNR, 1917-19. Mem. Nat. Trust for Historic Preservation (chmn.), Rockbridge Hist. Soc. Episcopalian (mem. exec. council 1970-72). Mason. Clubs: Farmington Country, Shenandoah, Tri-Brook Country, U.S. Senatorial (founder). Author: As I Remember It, 1977. Home: 2656 N Chestnut Ave Buena Vista VA 24416 Office: Southern Seminary & Jr Coll Buena Vista VA 24416

ROBIDEAU, ROBERT GORDON, accountant; b. Rayville, La., Oct. 2, 1933; s. George Gordon and Ida (Mayo) R.; B.S., Miss. State U., 1962; m. Irma Jeanette Robideau, Oct. 20, 1958; children—Michael Gordon, James Richard. Staff accountant Arthur Andersen & Co., 1962-65; partner Walborg, Lockett, Paul & Co., Houston, 1965-73; pvt. practice accounting, 1975—. Trustee, chmn. finance com. Leukemia Soc. Am., Houston., 1968-69. Served with USMCR, 1953-56. C.P.A., Tex., Miss. Mem. Am. Inst. C.P.A.'s, Tex., Miss. socs. C.P.A.'s, Nat. Assn. Accountants, Soc. for Advancement Mgmt., Beta Alpha Psi. Democrat. Baptist (deacon 1956—). Mason (Shriner). Home: 711 Longview Dr Sugarland TX 77478 Office: 1130 Tex Bank & Trust Tower Houston TX 77036

ROBIN, VINCENT JOSEPH, III, corp. exec.; b. Larose, La., Mar. 4, 1918; s. Vincent Joseph and Edverine (Savoie) R.; student Internat. Corp. Sch., 1943-45, Internat. Corr. Schs., 1965; Certificate in Mgmt. Tng., La. State U., New Orleans, 1965; m. Erline E. Chaisson, June 1, 1935 (div.); children—Joel P., Marian (Mrs. Russell DiMarco), Donald J., Vincent Joseph IV; m. 2d, Linda L. Rostran, Mar. 25, 1975; children—Alexandra Cristina, Victoria Elisa. Owner, exec. pres. Marian Ann, Inc., Robin Towing Corp., Robin Marine Supplies Ltd., Robin Realty, Inc., Harvey, La., 1947—; owner, mgr. Triple R Ranch, Foxworth, Miss., 1971—, Hacienda Robin S.A., coffee plantation, Managua, Nicaragua. Patron mem. Boy Scouts Am. Mem. New Orleans C. of C., Am. Security Council, A.I.M., Nat. Ocean Industries Assn., Am.-Internat. Charolais Assn., Harvey Canal Indsl. Assn., Propeller Club U.S. Rotarian, K.C. Clubs: Krewe of Bacchus, Krewe of Janus Carnival, Krewe of Alla, Young Man's Business (New Orleans). Home: 797 Marlene Dr Gretna LA 70053 Office: 440 Pailet St PO Box 526 Harvey LA 70059

ROBINER, RONALD ALAN, chiropractor; b. Detroit, Oct. 9, 1937; s. Myer and Betty (Burdick) R.; student Ferris State Coll., 1955-57, Wayne State U., 1957-58; D.C., Nat. Coll. Chiropractic, 1967; m. Carol Slotnick, June 13, 1965; children—Pamela, Mitchell, Todd. Head field test procedures Aerojet Gen. Corp., Azusa, Calif., 1962-64; dir. Brighton Chiropractic Clinic, 1967-74; pvt. practice chiropractic medicine, West Palm Beach, Fla., 1974—. Bd. dirs. Palm Beach County Health Planning Council, 1975—; mem. Royal Palm Beach Village Council, 1980—. Served with AUS, 1958-62. Mem. Am., Fla. (chmn. health planning) chiropractic assns., Palm Beach County Chiropractic Soc. Jewish. Clubs: K.P., Odd Fellows, Kiwanis (dir.), Lions. Home: 797 Lilac Dr Royal Palm Beach FL 33411 Office: 5818 S Dixie Hwy West Palm Beach FL 33405

ROBINETT, ELIZABETH ANN MCCLAIN, counselor; b. Keene, Tex., June 30, 1936; d. Ted Roy and Ida Mae (Hutson) McClain; B.A., Angelo State U., 1968; M.Ed., Tex. Tech. U., 1972, Ed.D., 1975; children—Lee Marshall, Lisa Marlene. Tchr. Central High Sch., San Angelo, 1968-69; edn. specialist Army Edn. Center, Fort Richardson, Alaska, 1969-71; student life adviser Tex. Tech. U., Lubbock, 1972-75; counselor Midland (Tex.) Coll., 1975—; practice psychotherapy; cons. Aptitude Inventory Measurement Service. Bd. dirs. Planned Parenthood, Midland, 1976—, Human Relations Council, 1977—. Mem. Am. Soc. Adlerian Psychology, Am. Psychol. Assn., Jr. Coll. Student Personnel Assn. Tex., Am. Personnel and Guidance Assn., Tex. Jr. Coll. Tchrs. Assn., Mayflower Soc. Mem. Christian Ch. (Disciples of Christ). Home: 2001 Community Ln Midland TX 79701 Office: 3600 Garfield St N Midland TX 79701

ROBINETTE, RONALD LEE, ins. agt.; b. Welch, W.Va., Mar. 11, 1947; s. Lacy Joseph and Myrtle Louise (Brewster) R.; B.A. magna cum laude in History, W.Va. U., 1973, postgrad., 1973; m. Linda Muncy, Aug. 17, 1974. Tchr., Berwind (W.Va.) Jr. High Sch., 1974-75; sales rep. Met. Life Ins. Co., Tazewell, Va., 1975-76, sales mgr., Beckley, W.Va., 1976-77, sales rep., Beckley, 1977—; instr. Life Underwriters Tng. Council. Deacon Meml. Baptist Ch., Beckley. Served with USAF, 1966-70. Mem. Nat. Assn. Life Underwriters, W.Va. U. Alumni Assn., Beckley Assn. Life Underwriters (pres. elect, sec.), Phi Beta Kappa. Democrat. Home: 105 Majestic Ct PO Box 1619 Beckley WV 25801 Office: Met Life Ins Co 21 Mallard Ct Suite C PO Box 1619 Beckley WV 25801

ROBINS, MIRIAM BLASBERG, clin. psychologist; b. Columbus, Ohio, Oct. 14, 1917; d. Henry Benjamin and Nettie (Tahl) Blasberg; B.S., U. Cin., 1939; M.A., U. Nebr., 1960; Ph.D., U. Houston, 1969; m. Thomas A Janes, III; 1 dau., Bonnie Robins Davis. Co-owner Robins' Jewelers, Tallahassee, 1946-50, Keith Jewelers, Gulfport, Miss., 1950-55; employment counselor Tex. Employment Agy., Dallas, 1959; diagnostic testing supr., then lectr. psychology U. Houston, 1964-67; cons. Model Cities, Houston, 1970; chief psychologist Hauser Clinic, Houston, 1970; mem. courtesy staff Meml. City Hosp., Houston, 1970-71 affiliate staff mem., 1979; human relationship specialist, Houston, 1970—; clin. instr. Baylor U. Coll. Medicine, 1971-75; clin. asso. M.D. Anderson Hosp., Houston, 1978-79. Mem. nat. alumni bd. U. Cin.; co-leader Houston Group Psychotherapy Soc., 1970. Houston VA Hosp. fellow, 1969; USPHS grantee, 1964-66. Mem. Am., Southwestern, Tex. (com. chmn. 1977), Houston psychol. assns., Tex. Psychotherapy Assn., Nat. Alliance Family Life, Assn. Advancement Psychology, Acad. Psychologists for Marital and Family Therapy, Assn. Humanistic Psychology, Internat. Platform Assn., Zool. Soc. Houston. Clubs: Meml. Forest; Baylor U. Coll. Medicine Women's Faculty. Author papers in field. Home: 301 Wilcrest Dr Apt 7601 Houston TX 77042 Office: 902 Frostwood St Suite 145B Houston TX 77024

ROBINSON, ADELBERT CARL, lawyer; b. Shawnee, Okla., Dec. 13, 1926; s. William H. and Mayme (Forston) R.; student Okla. Baptist U., 1944-47; LL.B., Okla. U., 1950, J.D., 1970; m. Marilyn Ruth Stubbs, Dec. 28, 1963; children—William, James, Schuyler, Donald, David, Nancy, Lauri. Admitted to Okla. bar, 1950; practiced in Muskogee, 1956—; with legal dept. Phillips Petroleum Co., 1950-51; adjuster U.S. Fidelity & Guaranty Co., 1951-54, atty., adjuster-in-charge, 1954-56; partner Fite & Robinson, 1956-62; partner Fite, Robinson & Summers, 1963-70, Robinson & Summers, 1970-72, Robinson, Summers & Locke, 1972-76, Robinson, Locke & Gage, 1976—; police judge, 1963-64; municipal judge, 1964-70. Pres., dir. Wall St. Bldg. Corp., 1969-78, Three Forks Devel. Corp., 1968-77, Robinson, Locke & Gage, 1976—, Rolo Leasing, Inc., 1971—, Suroya II, Inc., 1977—; sec., dir. P & H Supply, Inc., Weddles Food Stores, Wudlite, Inc., Broadway Theatres, Inc., Muskogee Tom's, Inc., Helmer Printing Co., Inc., Blue Ridge Corp., Harborcliff Corp. Chmn. Inter-Organizational Relations Com., 1960-63; chmn. Muskogee County Law Day, 1963; chmn. Muskogee Area Redevel. Authority, 1963; chmn. Muskogee County chpt. Am. Cancer Soc., 1956; chmn. Profl. Cooperation Com., 1965-69. Pres., bd. dirs. Muskogee Community Council; bd. dirs. Muskogee Community Concert Assn., Muskogee Tourist Information Bur., 1964-68; bd. dirs., gen. counsel United Cerebral Palsy Eastern Okla., 1964-68. Served with inf. AUS, 1945-46. Mem. Am., Okla. (chmn. uniform laws com. 1970-72, past regional chmn. grievance com.), Muskogee County (pres. 1971, mem. exec. council) bar assns., Okla. Assn. Def. Counsel (dir.), Okla. Assn. Municipal Judges (dir.), Muskogee C. of C., Delta Theta Phi. Methodist. Rotarian (pres. 1971-72). Home: 2800 Robin Ln Muskogee OK 74401 Office: 530 Court St PO Box 87 Muskogee OK 74401

ROBINSON, ARTHUR GROVE, univ. adminstr., painter, printmaker; b. Asheville, N.C., May 17, 1935; s. Whitfield Locke and Eula (Grove) R.; A.A., Mars Hill Coll., 1955; postgrad. U. N.C., Chapel Hill, 1955-56; B.F.A., Columbia U., 1958, M.F.A., 1960; m. Cynthia Randolph, June 26, 1965; 1 dau., Lexanne. Fulbright fellow, France, 1958-59; instr. art Meredith Coll., Raleigh, N.C., 1965-71; chmn., asso. prof. art Union U., Jackson, Tenn., 1971—; lectr. art history Memphis State U. Grad. Sch., 1979; v.p. visual arts Jackson Arts Council, 1972-74; mem. crafts adv. panel Tenn. Art Commn., 1972-76; represented in permanent collections: N.C. Mus. Art, Raleigh, Carroll Reece Mus., E. Tenn. State U., Johnson City; also pvt. collections. Recipient award N.C. Mus. Art, 1956, 61. Mem. So. Graphics Council, Tenn. Watercolor Soc. Democrat. Baptist. Club: W. Tenn. Radio Control Flyers. Home: 17 Laurel Ln Jackson TN 38301 Office: Union U Art Dept Jackson TN 38301

ROBINSON, BARBARA BATTLE, ret. dietitian; b. Mobile, Ala., Jan. 12, 1923; d. Charles Tecumseh and Leana Johnnie (Peters) Battle; B.S., Howard U., 1943; m. Wilbur Ronald Robinson, Nov. 23, 1949; children—Wilbur, John, Alfonso. With VA Med. Center, Tuskegee,

Ala., 1945-53, 54-80, 61-79, asst. chief dietetic service, 1961-63, chief dietetic service, 1963-80; dir. dietetics John A. Andrew Meml. Hosp., Tuskeegee (Ala.) Inst., 1953-54. Mem. Am. Dietetic Assn. (registered), AAUW, Delta Sigma Theta. Methodist. Clubs: The Links, Opti-Mrs. Home: 103 Alabama Ave Tuskegee Institute AL 36088

ROBINSON, CLIFTON HIGHT, JR., ind. landman; b. Shreveport, La., Sept. 15, 1927; s. Clifton Hight and Edna Viola (Norris) R.; student Centenary Coll., 1945, 47-48, 51-53; m. Cora Helen Baker, Dec. 27, 1947 (dec. Feb. 1973); children—John Clifton, Kathy Sue, Richard Alan; m. 2d, Billy Langdon, June 22, 1977; children—Steven Matheney, Michael L. Matheney. Clk., K.C.S. R.R., Shreveport, 1943-45; with Southwestern Gas & Electric Co., Shreveport, 1948-50; draftsman Phillips Petroleum Co., Shreveport, 1950-53, scout, Corpus Christi, 1953-62, leaseman, Houston, 1962-67, sr. titleman, 1967-69, sr. leaseman, 1969-75; landman Watson Oil Corp., Shreveport, 1975-77; Ind. landman, 1977—. Served with AUS, 1946-47. Mem. Am., Ark.-La.-Tex. assns. petroleum landmen, Ark.-La.-Tex. Gem. and Mineral Soc. (pres. 1970-71), Petroleum Club Shreveport. Baptist. Mason (Shriner). Club: University (Shreveport). Home: 1818 Old Oaks St Shreveport LA 71119 Office: 322 Johnson Bldg PO Box 148 Shreveport LA 71166

ROBINSON, DAVID FRANKLIN, JR., sch. dist. ofcl.; b. Birmingham, Ala., Apr. 5, 1921; s. David F. and Eula (McCartney) R.; student West Tex. State U., Tex. A. and M. U., Clarendon Jr. Coll., U. Tex.; m. JoLynn Williams, May 30, 1942; children—Linda Lynn Robinson Watson, Ocie Dale. County clk. Collingsworth County (Tex.), 1946-51; sch. bus. mgr. Lefors (Ind.) Sch. Dist., 1951-56; sch. tax adminstr. Andrews (Tex.) Ind. Sch. Dist., 1968—; property valuation appraiser and cons., 1958—. Chmn. Andrews County United Way, 1973-74. Served with aviation engrs. U.S. Army, 1942-45. Registered profl. assessor, Tex. Mem. Tex. Sch. Assessors Assn. (pres. 1977—, editor news bull. 1971—, dir. 1971-79), Internat. Assn. of Assessing Officers, Tex. Sch. Assessors Assn., Tex. Assn. of Assessing Officers (Achievement award 1973), Soc. of Real Estate Appraisers, Tex. Assn. of County Assessors, Andrews C. of C. Democrat. Baptist. Clubs: Lions, Masons. Contbr. articles on assessment to profl. publs. Home: 1302 NW 12th St Andrews TX 79714 Office: 405 NW 3d St Andrews TX 79714

ROBINSON, DEBRA MCREYNOLDS, speech pathologist; b. Dermott, Ark., Oct. 10, 1952; d. Walter Ford and Louise (Simons) McReynolds; B.A., U. Ark., Fayetteville, 1973, M.A., 1974; m. Howard Benjamin Robinson, Nov. 3, 1978; 1 stepson, Howard Benjamin, Jr. Speech pathologist Jenkins Meml. Children's Center, Pine Bluff, Ark., 1974-79; public sch. therapist Alma (Ark.) Public Schs., 1979—; asst. supr. practicum students in speech pathology. Mem. Am. Speech and Hearing Assn., Ark. Speech and Hearing Assn. Baptist. Home: 1310 S 22d St Fort Smith AR 72901 Office: Alma High Sch Alma AR

ROBINSON, DONALD, SR., community agy. exec.; b. Washington, La., Sept. 14, 1945; s. Thonis and Hinda Elizabeth (Savant) R.; B.A. in English, So. U. and A&M Coll., 1968; J.D., So. U. Sch. Law, 1972; m. Jacqueline Savoy, Dec. 29, 1969; children—Kevin Duane, Dona Inez, Donald, Hinda Rasheda. Asst. mgr. Krauss Co. Ltd., New Orleans, 1969; asst. mgr. Robinson's Family Soul Prodns., Inc., 1972, sec., 1972—; dir. planning Tri-Parish Progress, Inc., Crowley, La., 1974-75; exec. dir. St. Landry Parish Community Action Agy., Opelousas, La., 1975—. Sec. St. Landry Parish Bi-Racial Com., 1970-71; mem. Town of Washington Planning Com., 1974; mem. adv. com. Washington High Sch. and Courtableau Elem. Sch., 1979-80. Recipient cert. of merit Gov. Edwin W. Edwards, 1979; cert. awards Community Services Adminstrn., 1978, La. State Tng. Headstart, 1978, Dept. Urban and Community Affairs, 1978; Am. Legion award, 1968; Council on Legal Edn. Opportunity grantee, 1969-72. Mem. Nat. Headstart Assn., NAACP, Nat. Community Action Agy. Exec. Dirs. Assn., La. Assn. Community Action Agys. Democrat. Baptist. Club: Masons. Home: 716 Buhot St PO Box 264 Washington LA 70589 Office: St Landry Parish Community Action Agy Airport Rd PO Box 899 Opelousas LA 70570

ROBINSON, DONALD EDWIN, physician; b. Athens, Tenn., Oct. 7, 1949; s. Fred A. and Juanita Bell (Newman) R.; B.S., U. Tenn., Knoxville, 1970; M.D., U. Tenn., Memphis, 1974; m. Dawn Diane Rumbolt, Mar. 18, 1972; children—Amanda, J.B., Christopher. Intern straight medicine U. Tenn., Memphis, 1974-75; resident internal medicine, 1975-77; practice medicine specializing in internal medicine, Cleveland, 1977—; vice chief staff Cherokee Park Hosp., Cleveland, Tenn., 1978—, chief medicine, 1978—; chief medicine Bradley Meml. Hosp., Cleveland, 1979—. Diplomate Am. Bd. Internal Medicine. Mem. AMA, Am. Soc. Internal Medicine, Tenn. Med. Assn., Bradley County Med. Soc., Pi Kappa Phi, Phi Chi. Democrat. Methodist. Club: Rotary (Cleveland). Home: 1250 Summerfield Ave Cleveland TN 37311 Office: 2850 Westside Dr Suite 4 Cleveland TN 37311

ROBINSON, DORRIS REGINA, coll. adminstr.; b. Little Rock, Oct. 4, 1947; d. James and Eleise (Cox) Brown; B.S., Ark. Bapt. Coll., 1970; M.S.E., Ouachita Bapt. U., 1975; m. Preston D. Robinson, Oct. 2, 1966; 1 dau., Patrina Mechelle. Inspector, Timex, Inc., Little Rock, 1966-70; asst. to the registrar Ark. Bapt. Coll., Little Rock, 1970, bus. mgr., dir. fin. aid, 1970-79, dir. bus. and fiscal affairs, 1979—. Sec., Stephen Sch. P.T.A., Little Rock, 1979—; mem. bd. Christian edn. St. Mark Baptist Ch., 1979-80, chmn. benevolent com., 1978-80. Mem. Nat. Assn. Student Fin. Aid Adminstrs., Nat. Assn. Female Execs., Ark. Assn. Student Fin. Aid Adminstrs., Southwest Assn. Student Fin. Aid Adminstrs., So. Assn. Coll. and Univ. Bus. Officers, Ark. Student Personnel Assn., Urban League. Clubs: Order Eastern Star, Order Golden Circle. Home: 12563 Southridge Dr Little Rock AR 72212 Office: Arkansas Baptist College 1600 High St Little Rock AR 72202

ROBINSON, EMMETT EDWARD, educator; b. Ocala, Fla., Feb. 27, 1914; s. Emmett Edward and Lucille (McKowen) R.; B.S., Coll. Charleston, 1935, D.Litt., 1971; M.F.A., Yale U., 1941; m. Patricia Ann Colbert, June 30, 1950; children—Jennet Colbert, Alix Patricia. Dir. Footlight Players, Inc., Charleston, S.C., 1936-39, 41-77; lectr. Coll. Charleston, 1943-54, 67-70, prof. fine arts, 1972—; cons. WCSC-TV, WCSC, Inc., Charleston, 1955-58; lectr. Baptist Coll., Charleston, 1970-71. Exhibited sculptor works Columbia (S.C.) Art Mus., 1965; important works include All Saints Ch., Jacksonville, Fla., 1965, St. Luke and St. Paul's Chs., 1974; cons., designer Provost Mus., 1966-68, Charleston Mus., 1967, 69-71, Middleton Place Gardens, 1970, Charleston Jail Mus., 1975. Rockefeller Found. fellow, 1938; Julius Rosenwald Found. fellow, 1949. Mem. Am. Theatre Assn., S.C. Hist. Soc., Charleston Library Soc., Soc. for Preservation of Spirituals, Carolina Art Assn. Episcopalian. Home: 76 Ashley Ave Charleston SC 29401

ROBINSON, EVELYN BARRON, ins. co. exec.; b. Corsicana, Tex., Sept. 6, 1938; d. Leon Richard and Lessie Dolores (Hall) Barron; B.B.A., U. Tex., 1960; M.Ed., East Tex. State U., 1971, Ed.D., 1978; M.Liberal Arts, So. Meth. U., 1975; children—Gina Lynn, Timothy Edward. Tchr., Athens (Tex.) Ind. Sch. Dist., 1970-71; tchr. math. Greenhill Sch., Dallas, 1972-78; dir. co. tng. Members Ins. Co., Dallas, 1978—; cons. in math., 1976-78; instr. East Tex. State U., summer, 1978; mgmt. cons. Certified CPR, vol. Am. Heart Assn., 1979—; mem. Dallas Symphony Orch. League, 1979—; vol. Dallas Civic Opera, 1979—. Mem. Am. Soc. Tng. and Devel., Ins. Co. Ednl. Dirs. Soc., Ins. Women of Dallas. Contbr. articles to profl. jours.

ROBINSON, FLORENCE CLAIRE CRIM, educator; b. Carbondale, Ill., Oct. 26, 1932; d. Alonzo V. and Doddridge M. (Taylor) Crim; B.A., So. Ill. U., 1950, Ph.D., 1963; M.A., Denver U., 1956; postgrad. Northwestern U., 1950-51, U. Colo., 1960-62; m. Carl Robinson, Aug. 9, 1951 (div. 1970); children—Carl Emil, Joan Gayle. Tchr. music Denver pub. schs., 1953-62, coordinator music, 1962-65; asso. prof. music So. Ill. U., Carbondale, 1965-67; prof. music edn. Bishop Coll., Dallas, 1967-71, chmn. music dept., 1967-71; prof. music Clark Coll., Atlanta, 1971-76, chmn. dept., 1971—, chmn. div. arts and humanities, 1976—; vis. prof. Emory U., Atlanta, 1974, Fisk U., Nashville, 1969, 70, 71, U. Colo., Denver, 1963-65; guest prof. Atlanta U., 1972-79, Interdenominational Theol. Sem., 1972; also profl. piano accompanist; hostess Florence Robinson Radio Show, radio sta. WPLO, Atlanta, 1971-73, The Many Sides of Black Music, syndicated (recorded 1977), 1974—. Mem. adv. bd. John F. Kennedy Center. Mem. Human Relations Commn., Denver, 1965. Mem. N.E.A., Music Educators Nat. Conf., A.F.T.R.A., Kappa Delta Pi, Pi Delta Theta, Mu Phi Epsilon, Alpha Kappa Alpha, Phi Kappa Phi. Home: 2885 Pine Needle Dr Atlanta GA 30344 Office: Div Arts and Humanities Clark Coll Atlanta GA

ROBINSON, HEBB EASTERLING, hosp. adminstr.; b. Rowland, N.C., June 11, 1918; d. Edward Bogan and Ethel (Shadrick) Easterling; B.A., Flora Macdonal Coll., 1939; B.C.S., U. Ga., 1947; m. Lathan Cousar Robinson, Oct. 11, 1958. Tchr., Nashville (N.C.) public schs., Norwood (N.C.) public schs.; cost acct. U.S. Engrs., Charlotte, N.C., Atlanta; cost acct. Springs Mills, Inc., Lancaster, S.C., 1948-60; dir. purchasing Marion Sims Meml. Hosp., Lancaster, 1961-70; dir. purchasing and materials handling Elliott White Springs Meml. Hosp., Lancaster, 1970—; charter mem. mgmt. adv. com. Carolinas Group Purchasing Program. Mem. Am. Soc. Hosp. Purchasing and Materials Mgmt. (dir.), S.C. Soc. Hosp. Purchasing and Materials Mgmt. (past pres.), S.C. Hosp. Assn., Southeastern Hosp. Conf. of Purchasing Agents, Lancaster County Soc. Hist. Preservation. Presbyterian. Clubs: New Era Book, Evening Graden, Shrine Aux. Home: 401 N Main St Lancaster SC 29720 Office: 800 W Meeting St Lancaster SC 29720

ROBINSON, JAMES KENNETH, Congressman; b. nr. Winchester, Va., May 14, 1916; s. Ray and Ida Helen (Robinson) R.; B.S., Va. Poly. Inst., 1937; m. Kathryn Rankin, Mar. 28, 1946; children—James Kenneth (dec.), Patrick M., Keveney M., Helen Ray, James, J. Kelly, Sallie. Mem. 92d-96th congresses from 7th Dist. Va.; mem. Va. Senate, 1965-70. Bd. dirs. Apple Blossom Festival, Winchester Meml. Hosp. Served to maj., inf., AUS, World War II. Named Farmer of Year, Progressive Farmer mag., 1964. Mem. Va. Poly. Inst. Alumni Assn. (dir.), Am. Legion, Winchester Hist. Soc., Izaak Walton League. Republican. Mem. Soc. of Friends. Clubs: Rotary, Moose, Elks. Office: House Office Bldg Washington DC 20515*

ROBINSON, JOHN HAROLD, mech. engr.; b. Jackson, Tenn., Oct. 14, 1921; s. Charles Albert and Katie May (Reeder) R.; student State Tenn. Tchrs. Coll., 1941; B.S.M.E., Internat. Corr. Schs., 1964; postgrad. State Tech. Inst. Memphis; m. Virginia Elizabeth Marbury, Sept. 26, 1942; children—Sandra Elizabeth, Sharon Lane, Wanda Jane, John Herold. Chief engr. Claridge Hotel, Memphis, 1939-42, 45-47, Tenn. Tb Control, State of Tenn. Tb Hosps., 1948-57, Humko Products Co., Champaign, Ill., 1957-58; cons. engr. to Tb Bd. Fla., Fla. Tb Control, W.T. Edwards-Fla. State Hosp., 1958-61; engring. mgr., Cudahy Refining Co., Memphis, 1961-63; engring. mgr. Humko Sheffield Chem. div. Kraft Inc., Memphis, 1963—; pres. AME Assos. Inc.; mem. Memphis Elec. Code Adv. Bd. Active Chickasaw council Boy Scouts Am., 1970-78. Served to sgt. USAAF, 1942-45; ETO. Decorated Air medal with 3 oak leaf clusters, D.F.C.; recipient Scouters award Boy Scouts Am., 1974, 75, named Leader of Distinction, 1975; registered profl. engr., Tenn. Mem. Am. Inst. Plant Engrs. (cert. plant engr.; pres. local chpt. 1975-76), Engring. Joint Council, Am. Hosp. Assn. Hosp. Engrs., Refrigeration Engrs. and Technicians Assn. (pres. chpt. 1955-57). Presbyterian. Home: 3336 Chancellor St Memphis TN 38118 Office: 1231 Pope St Memphis TN 38108

ROBINSON, JOHN TINSLEY, actuary; b. Frederick, Okla., June 27, 1941; s. William Powell and Frances Lois (Baldwin) R.; B.S., U. Okla., 1963; M.S., Okla. State U., 1965; m. Nancy Ruth Lynn, Dec. 28, 1963; children—Thomas Alan, John Clark, Mary Frances. Actuarial asst. Nat. Life and Accident Ins. Co., Nashville, 1965-69; asst. actuary So. Farm Bur. Life Ins. Co., Jackson, Miss., 1973-78, v.p., chief actuary, 1978—. Fellow Soc. Actuaries; mem. Am. Acad. Actuaries, Southeastern Actuaries Club, Jackson Actuarial Club, Phi Eta Sigma, Mu Alpha Theta. Presbyterian (deacon 1974-76, treas. 1975). Office: 515 E Amite St Jackson MS 39205

ROBINSON, LAWRENCE PAUL, mfg. engr.; b. Fresno, Calif., Sept. 3, 1946; s. Donald J. and Hazlene Thelma (Davenport) R.; student Shawnee (Okla.) public schs.; m. Sharon Fay Mitchel, Nov. 26, 1966; children—Lacey Dee, Morgan Kyle. Tool room machinist Continental Industries, Tulsa, 1964-65; machinist Red River Research, Ardmore, Okla., 1965, Murphey's Machine Co., Ardmore, 1965-66; tool and electrode maker, customcutter, Tulsa, 1966-67; tool and die maker GT & E, Shawnee and Bangor, Maine, 1967-72; tool and die designer Westinghouse Elec. Corp., Norman, Okla., 1972-76; prodn. foreman Mercury Marine, Stillwater, Okla., 1976-77, chief mfg. engr., 1977—. Served with USNG, 1967. Recipient 1st place award in machine shop work, Okla. region Wilke Bros. Trade Contest, 1964. Mem. Soc. Mfg. Engrs. Republican. Office: 3003 N Perkins Rd Stillwater OK 74074

ROBINSON, LEONARD WALLACE, author, editor; b. Malden, Mass., Nov. 9, 1912; s. Henry Morton and Ellen Elizabeth (Flynn) R.; student Columbia U., 1931-35, New Sch. for Social Research, 1944-47; M.A., Instituto Allende de Guanajuato, 1975; m. Patricia Goedicke, June 3, 1971; 1 son by former marriage, Roderick Wallace. Successively exec. editor Henry Holt & Co., N.Y.C.; mng. editor Esquire Mag., N.Y.C.; writer, reporter The New Yorker mag., N.Y.C.; editor-in-chief fiction dept. Colliers mag., N.Y.C.; chmn. mag. dept. Grad. Sch. Journalism, Columbia U., N.Y.C., 1969-71; Spencer prof. U. Syracuse (N.Y.); writer-in-resident Kalamazoo Coll.; now lectr., vis. prof. U. Guanajuato, San Miguel Allende, Mexico. Recipient O Henry prize for short stories, 1950; Best Short Stories award, Foley Collection, 1965. Mem. Delta Psi. Democrat. Roman Catholic. Author: The Assassin, 1968; With Time Running Out, 1970; The Man Who Loved Beauty, 1976, 2nd edit. 1977; contbr. short stories to leading mags., including The New Yorker, Harpers, Sat. Evening Post, Mademoiselle, others. Address: Apdo 462 San Miguel Allende Guanajuato Mexico

ROBINSON, LUCY CLOUGH, coll. adminstr.; b. Athens, Ala., Dec. 4, 1922; d. Thomas Clough and Roberta Elise (McCall) R.; B.S., George Peabody Coll., 1945, M.A., 1947; postgrad. Ind. U., 1963; Ed.D., U. Tenn., 1976. Instr., Marietta (Ga.) High Sch., 1946-52; asso. prof. bus. edn. Ga. Coll., 1952-65; curriculum specialist for bus. edn. Fla. Dept. Edn., Tallahassee, 1965-69, asst. program adminstr., bus. edn., 1971-75, planning specialist div. vocat. edn., 1975-79; dir. adminstrv. services Brevard Community Coll., Cocoa, Fla., 1979—; grad. teaching asst. U. Tenn., 1970-71; pres. Ga. Bus. Edn. Assn., 1949-50; cons., panelist, speaker in field. Bd. dirs. Easter Seal Rehab. Center, Tallahasse, 1972-75, Big Bend chpt. March of Dimes, 1979—; mem. U.S. Pres.'s Adv. Council on Nat. Security, 1975-78. Recipient Disting. Service award Ga. Bus. Edn. Assn., 1950; Ford Found. fellow, 1963-64. Mem. Am. Vocat. Assn., Nat. Bus. Edn. Assn. (Ga. rep. 1950-52, Fla. chmn. bldg. fund 1977—), Internat. Soc. Bus. Edn., Adminstrv. Mgmt. Assn., Nat. Micrographics Assn., Am. Edn. Research Assn., Phi Delta Kappa, Delta Pi Epsilon Delta Kappa Gamma (award of merit 1958), Pi Gamma Mu. Democrat. Methodist. Editor sects. on shorthand and typewriting Bus. Edn. Forum, 1958-60, Nat. Bus. Edn. Quar., 1968-69; editor: A Guide for Business Education in Florida Schools, 1967; Career Development for Business Education, 1971; Business Education in Florida, 1972. Office: Brevard Community Coll Cocoa FL 32922

ROBINSON, LYNN BROWN, educator; b. Mobile, Ala., July 29, 1938; d. Samuel and Carolyn G. Brown; B.B.A., Emory U., 1960; M.B.A., U. Ala., Tuscaloosa, 1965, Ph.D., 1972; m. John Kenneth Robinson, Feb. 27, 1963; children—Jennifer Kay, John Kenneth. Mem. faculty U. South Ala., Mobile, 1968—, prof. mktg., 1979—, dir. grad. studies Coll. Bus. and Mgmt., 1977—; cons. mktg. and human resource mgmt. Pres. Women of Ch., Christ Episcopal Ch., Mobile, 1975; bd. dirs. St. Mary's Home for Children, 1979, Mobile chpt. Ala. Rehab., 1979; mem. adv. council Jr. League of Mobile, 1979. Mem. Am. Mktg. Assn., Internat. Transactional Analysis Assn., Sales and Mktg. Execs. Internat., Southwestern Mktg. Assn., So. Mktg. Assn., Beta Gamma Sigma. Office: Coll Bus and Mgmt U South Ala Mobile AL 36688

ROBINSON, MILDRED BLACKWELL, educator; b. Alachua, Fla., Feb. 20, 1917; d. John William and Sarah Frances (Harmon) Blackwell; B.S., Fla. Meml. Coll., 1960; M.A., Fisk U., 1967; Ph.D., Fla. State U., 1974; children—Mayme Riley, Edward D. Riley. Sec., Duval County Sch. Bd., Jacksonville, Fla., 1953-60, elem. tchr., curriculum asst. 1960-75; prof. edn. Edward Waters Coll., Jacksonville, 1975-78, chmn. Div. Edn., 1978—. Experienced Tchr. fellow, 1966-67; NDEA grantee, summer 1965. Mem. NAACP, Fla. Assn. Tchr. Educators, Fla. Assn. Colls. for Tchr. Edn., Phi Delta Kappa, Kappa Delta Pi. Baptist. Clubs: YWCA, Order of Eastern Star, Heroines of Jericho (sr. matron 1976—), Daus. of Isis Rabia (treas. 1968-72, high priestess 1976-79). Contbr. articles in field to profl. jours. Office: 1658 Kings Rd Jacksonville FL 32209

ROBINSON, NATHANIEL DAVID, physician; b. Providence, May 21, 1904; s. Harry and Lena (Chernick) R.; B.S., Tufts, 1928, M.D., 1931; postgrad. opthalmology N.Y. U., 1945-46; m. Dorothy Mae McLaughlin, Mar. 27, 1940; children—Nathaniel David Jr., Judith A., Nancy L. (Mrs. John Frederick Clayton). Intern, Gallinger Mcpl. Hosp., Washington, 1931-32; gen. practice medicine Providence, 1932-40; resident ophthalmology Bellevue Hosp., N.Y.C., 1946-49; practice medicine specializing in ophthalmology, Providence, 1949—; cons. staff R.I., Miriam, VA, Roger Williams, Chapin hosps., Providence, Meml. Hosp., Pawtucket, R.I. Served to capt. USNR, 1940-45: PTO. N.Y. Kiwanis Club grantee for ophthalmology. Named adm. Neb. Navy. Diplomate Am. Bd. Ophthalmology and Otolaryngology. Mem. R.I., Providence, Collier County med. socs., R.I., New Eng., Pan Am. ophthal. socs., A.M.A., Am. Acad. Ophthalmology and Otolaryngology, Pan Am. Med. Assn., Soc. Eye Surgeons, R.I. Hist. Soc., English Speaking Union, Audubon Soc., Narragansett Bay Power Squadron, Ret. Officers Assn., Mil. Order Fgn. Wars. Unitarian. Clubs: University, Moorings Country. Home: 2880 Gulf Shore Blvd N Apt 308 Naples FL 33940

ROBINSON, PETER CLARK, stone co. exec.; b. Brighton, Mass., Nov. 16, 1938; s. Richard and Mary Elizabeth (Cooper) R.; B.S. in Fgn. Service, Georgetown U., 1961; M.B.A., Babson Inst., 1963; m. Sylvia Phyllis Petschek, Aug. 26, 1961 (div. 1973); children—Marc Louis, Nicholas Daniel, Andrea Suzanne. Asst. supt. prodn. Mass. Broken Stone Co., Weston, 1961-62, night shift supt., 1962-65, v.p. operations, 1968, v.p. dir., 1969-75; gen. supt. Berlin Stone Co., 1965-67, v.p. operations, 1968, v.p., dir., 1969-75; v.p., dir Holden Trap Rock Co., to 1975; pres. J.P. Burroughs & Sons, Inc. aggregate div., subsidiary Blount, Inc., Saginaw, Mich., and Montgomery, Ala., 1975—, v.p. mktg. Blount, Inc., 1978-. Mem. Am. Mgmt. Assn., Am. Mktg. Assn., Engring. Soc. Detroit, Nat. Crushed Stone Assn. (dir.). Clubs: Economic (Detroit), Saginaw; Capital City, Montgomery Country. Home: PO Box 11561 Montgomery AL 36111 Office: PO Box 949 Montgomery AL 36102

ROBINSON, PREZELL RUSSELL, coll. pres.; b. Batesburg, S.C., Aug. 25, 1922; s. Clarence and Annie (Folks) R.; A.B. in Sociology, St. Augustine's Coll., 1946; M.A. in Social Sci. and Psychology, Cornell U., 1951, Ed.D. in Sociology-Ednl. Adminstrn., 1956; D.C.L. (hon.), U. of South, 1970; L.H.D. (hon.), Cutting U. Coll., Monrovia, W. Africa, 1976; D.C.L. (hon.), Bishop Coll., 1979; m. Lulu Harris, Apr. 9, 1950; 1 dau. Tchr. social sci., French Bettis Jr. Coll., Trenton, S.C., 1946-48; successively registrar, tchr., acting prin. high sch., acting dean jr. coll., instr., dir. adult edn. Voorhees Jr. Coll., Denmark, S.C., 1948-56; prof. sociology, dean coll. St. Augustine's Coll., Raleigh, N.C., 1956-64, exec. dean, 1964-68, acting pres., 1966-67, pres., 1967—; scholar-in-residence Nairobi (Kenya) U., 1973. Dir., Wachovia Bank & Trust Co. Mem. exec. com. N.C. Edn. Com. on Tchr. Edn.; mem. N.C. Bd. Edn.; chmn. bd. Assn. Episcopal Colls. Vice chmn. Wake County div. Occoneechee council Boy Scouts Am., 1959-67, chmn. Wake Occoneechee council, 1963-66, mem. exec. com., 1965—; vice chmn. Wake County chpt. ARC; chmn. edn. div. United Fund of Raleigh, mem. budget com., 1965—; mem. exec. com. Wake County Libraries; pres. United Negro Coll. Fund, 1978—; trustee Voorhees Coll.; chmn. United Bd. for Coll. Devel. Served with AUS, 1942. Recipient Distinguished Alumni award Voorhees Coll., 1967; decorated Star of Africa (Liberia). Fulbright fellow to India, summer 1965. Mem. AAAS, Am. Acad. Polit. and Social Sci., Am., N.C. (exec. com.) sociol. socs., So. Sociol. Assn., Am. Acad. Polit. Sci., Nat. Geog. Soc., N.C. Lit. and Hist. Soc., N.C. Hist. Soc., Phi Delta Kappa, Phi Kappa Phi, Alpha Kappa Mu, Phi Beta Lambda, Delta Mu Delta. Protestant Episcopalian (lay reader). Contbr. articles to profl. publs. Home: 821 Glascock St Raleigh NC 27604 Office: Saint Augustine's Coll Raleigh NC 27611

ROBINSON, RALPH CARLISLE, JR., lawyer; b. Columbia, S.C., Aug. 27, 1935; s. R. Carlisle and Anna Elizabeth (Hiller) R.; B.S., Univ. S.C., 1957, J.D., 1966; m. Sara Elyce Powell, Dec. 2, 1964; children—Ralph C., Heyward Elliot, Sara E. Admitted to S.C. bar, 1966; practice in Columbia, 1967—; law clk. U.S. Dist. judge Hemphill, Dist. S.C., Columbia, 1966-67; now mem. firm Robinson & Britt. Served with USAF, 1957-63. Mem. S.C. State Bar (mem. corp. law com., mem. splzn. com.), Fed., Am., S.C., Richland County bar assns., Am. Judicature Soc. Home: 312 Wateree Ave Columbia SC 29205 Office: 1247 Sumter St Columbia SC 29201

ROBINSON, RALPH ROLIN, physician; b. Nashville, Kan., July 7, 1913; s. Walter S. and Mary (Inslee) R.; B.S. in Indsl. Arts, Okla. A and M, 1935; M.D., U. Wash., 1951; m. Mona R. McGraw, Mar. 28, 1953; children—Kim, Mark, Nancy, Ralph Rolin II, Katherine. Engr., Vornado Corp., Stillwater, Okla., 1934-41, Boeing Co., Seattle, 1941-51; intern Okla. U. Hosp. 1951-52, resident, 1952-55; practice medicine, specializing in obstetrics and gynecology, Oklahoma City, 1951-55, Middlesboro, Ky., 1955—; pres. staff Miners Meml. Hosp., Middlesboro, 1958; asso. prof. U. Okla., 1955. Pres., Creative Ornament Co., Edmond, Okla.; v.p. R.K. Odor Research Co., Oklahoma City. Chmn. Safety Com. Okmulgee County, 1956. Fellow A.C.S.; mem. Am. Coll. Obstetrics and Gynecology, Am. Soc. Abdominal Surgery, Phi Kappa Phi. Author: Endocrine Therapy for Gynecology, 1957. Co-inventor Vornado airplane, 1935; inventor controceptor. Home: 322 Englewood Rd Middlesboro KY 40965 Office: 2024 Cumberland Ave Middlesboro KY 40965

ROBINSON, RICHARD FRANCIS, journalist; b. Passaic, N.J., June 13, 1941; s. Francis Ward and Evelyn (Burnett) R.; student Coll. of William and Mary, 1959-60; B.A. in Journalism, Mich. State U., East Lansing, 1964; m. Brenda Kay Moore, Feb. 6, 1970; 1 dau., Kelly. Regional reporter, columnist The Herald-News, Passaic, N.J., 1964-67; med. writer, columnist The Oakland Press, Pontiac, Mich., 1967-75; sci. writer The Nat. Enquirer, Lantana, Fla., 1975-79; bd. dirs. Krynova Enterprises, Inc., St. Petersburg, Fla., 1968—; cons. Mich. State Dept. Mental Health, 1973-74; free-lance writer, 1972—. Mem. Exec. bd. Mich. Fedn. Young Republicans, 1970; del. Mich. State Republican Conv., 1970; mem. county com. Republican Party of Oakland County (Mich.), 1971-72. Served with AUS, 1964-65. Recipient 1st newswriting place award AP, 1973, Certificate of Outstanding News Coverage, Mich. Heart Assn., 1974, 75; named finalist for Swope Meml. Newspaper Reporting award Newspaper Editorial Workshop Services, 1974; nominee for Pulitzer prize, 1975. Mem. Nat. Assn. Sci. Writers, Am. Med. Writers Assn., Mich. State U. Alumni Assn., Sigma Delta Chi. Republican. Episcopalian. Club: Lake Worth (Fla.) Racquet and Swim. Contbr. articles to newspapers and mags. Home and office: 213 Walton Heath Dr Atlantis FL 33462

ROBINSON, ROBERT OBIE, physician; b. Beaumont, Tex., Aug. 1, 1943; s. Haskell E. and Betty Welch; B.S., Lamar U., 1964; M.D., U. Tex., Galveston, 1968; m. Linda Fay Parent, Dec. 23, 1964; children—Craig, Blake, Alan. Intern, Hermann Hosp., Houston, 1968-69; resident in ophthalmology U. Tex., Galveston, 1971-74; practice medicine specializing in ophthalmology, Beaumont, 1974—; dir. The Eye Clinic, Beaumont Eye Assos., Beaumont; mem. staff Med. and Surg. Hosp., Bapt. Hosp., St. Elizabeth Hosp. Mem. fin. com. Trinity Meth. Ch.; del. Tex. Dem. Conv., 1978; bd. dirs. Am. Cancer Soc., 1977-79; trustee Beaumont Art Mus. Served with USPHS, 1969-71. Fellow Am. Acad. Ophthalmology; mem. Jefferson County Med. Soc., Tex. Med. Assn. (Texpac chmn.) Tex. Ophthalmol. Assn., Tex. Soc. Prevention Blindness, Tex. Soc. Ophthalmology and Otolaryngology Assn., Bus. and Profl. Men's Club, Smithsonian Assos., Am. Orchid Soc., Bromeliad Soc., Lamar U. Ex-Student Assn., Am. Intra-Ocular Implant Soc., Ducks Unltd., Phi Beta Pi. Club: Lions. Home: 6285 Gladys St Beaumont TX 77706 Office: 3195 Med Center Dr Beaumont TX 77701

ROBINSON, RONALD ALLEN, pub. relations exec.; b. Oklahoma City, Apr. 3, 1943; s. Edgar Fulton and Martha Corinna (Reid) R.; B.A. in Journalism, U. Ark., 1965; postgrad. Boston U., 1966; m. Mary Kay Stevens, June 11, 1966; 1 son, Reid Stevens. Sportswriter Ark. Gazette, Little Rock, 1960-63; v.p., dir. public relations, dir. Cranford-Johnson-Hunt & Assos., Little Rock, 1970—. Info. chmn. Ark. chpt. Arthritis Found., 1973-76, v.p., 1978—, nat. communications chmn., 1976-78, recipient bd. award, 1975. Served to capt. USAF, 1965-70. Decorated Bronze Star. Mem. Pub. Relations Soc. Am. (counselors sec.), Phi Delta Theta. Club: Pinnacle Stamp Ark. (pres. 1979—). Editor-in-chief Ark. Traveler, 1964-65. Home: 6626 Kavanaugh Pl Little Rock AR 72207 Office: 2200 First Nat Bldg Little Rock AR 72201

ROBINSON, RONALD JAMES, oil co. exec.; b. Pueblo, Colo., Mar. 10, 1946; s. James Claude and Doris Loraine Robinson; B.S. in Math. and Physics, So. Colo. State Coll., 1968; M.S. in Physics, Baylor U., Waco, Tex., 1971: Ph.D. in Petroleum Engring., Tex. A. and M. U., 1974; m. Bonnie Lynn Martin, Aug. 31, 1968; children—Kevin James, Kyle Bryant, Kurt David. With Getty Oil Co., 1973-78, dist. reservoir engr., Bakersfield, Calif., 1975-78; mgr. thermal recovery Grace Petroleum Corp., Oklahoma City, 1978-79; sr. cons. INTERCOMP Resource Devel. and Engring., Houston, 1979—. NASA fellow, 1968. Mem. Soc. Profl. Well Log Analysts, Soc. Petroleum Engrs. (dir.), Scientists Research Soc. N. Am., Sigma Xi. Club: Kiwanis. Author papers in field. Address: 614 Windsor Glen Dr Katy TX 77450

ROBINSON, THOMAS DONALD, hosp. adminstr.; b. Welch, W.Va., Aug. 18, 1941; s. George Will and Martha Mattie R.; B.B.A., Marshall U., 1964; M.H.A., Georgia State U., 1977; m. Bonnie Bennett, Apr. 11, 1970; children—Thomas Donald, Brooke DeAnna. Mem. dept. gen. acctg. Ashland Oil and Refining Co., 1965-68; mem. dept. cost acctg. R.J. Reynolds Industries, 1968-70; bus. devel. cons. Forsyth County Investment Corp., Winston-Salem, N.C., 1970-72; v.p. Winston Industries, Winston-Salem, 1970-72; exec. dir. High Point Devel. Corp. (N.C.), 1972-75; adminstr. Welch (W.Va.) Emergency Hosp., 1977—. Bd. dirs. McDowell County Health Action Council, Gary, W.Va.; co-chmn. McDowell County Cancer Crusade. Recipient Wally Clagg award, Winston-Salem Jaycees, 1969. Mem. Am. Coll. Hosp. Adminstrs., W.Va. Assn. Health Service Execs., W.Va. Public Health Assn., Kappa Alpha Psi. Episcopalian. Club: The Boule. Home: 126 Central Ave Welch WV 24801 Office: 454 McDowell St Welch WV 24801

ROBINSON, WILBURN VAUGHN, steel co. exec.; b. Whigham, Ga., Apr. 28, 1934; s. Rufus Hill and Martha Elaine (Vaughn) R.; B.B.A., U. Ga., 1962, M.B.A., 1963; m. Gayle Walden, Dec. 19, 1968; children—Michael, Richard, Kim. With Peat, Marwick, Mitchell & Co., Greenville, S.C., 1963-68; asst. dir. for fiscal affairs Spartanburg (S.C.) Gen. Hosp., 1968-69; dir. hosp. implementation Computer Communications Network, Inc., Nashville, 1969-70; with Georgetown (S.C.) Steel Corp., 1971-74, v.p., controller, 1972-74; v.p., controller Korf Industries, Inc., Charlotte, N.C., 1974-77; pres. Guilmont Devel. Co., High Point, N.C., 1974-78; v.p., controller Intercontinental Metals Corp., 1977—; treas., dir. Intercontinental Metals Can. Ltd., 1978—; pres., dir. Cardinal Steel Corp., 1979—; treas. Mountain Holding Co., 1979—; dir. Trammell Candy Co., Atlanta, 1970-73. Served with AUS, 1955-58. Recipient Haskins and Sells Found. award, 1962. C.P.A., Ga., S.C. Mem. Am. Inst. C.P.A.'s. Methodist. Home: 3000 Wamath Dr Charlotte NC 28210 Office: PO Box 220263 Charlotte NC 28222

ROBINSON, WILLIAM DICK, hosp. adminstr.; b. Oklahoma City, July 24, 1937; s. Charles Watson and Mary Beatrice (Sewell) R.; B.S., U. Okla., 1962; M.S., U. Miss., 1966; postgrad. Trinity U.; m. Marellie Allen, Nov. 21, 1973; children—Pamela Marie, Mari Alene, Mary Brice. Student pharmacist Taylor Pharmacy, Norman, Okla., 1958-62; instr. U. Miss., Oxford, 1964-66; owner, pharmacist T. Roy Barnes Pharmacy, Tulsa, 1966-71; asso. adminstr. Bartlett Meml. Med. Center, Sapulpa, Okla., 1971—. Bd. dirs. Center Pharmacy, Mannford, Okla., 1978—; adv. bd. Central Area Vo-Tech Tng. Sch., 1973—. Mem. Am. Soc. Hosp. Pharmacists, Okla. Soc. Hosp. Pharmacists, Tulsa Hosp. Council. Episcopalian. Club: Philcrest Hills Tennis. Home: Drawer 400 Jenks OK 74037 Office: Bartlett Memorial Medical Center 519 S Division Sapulpa OK 74066

ROBINSON, WILLIAM POWELL, ret. educator, author; b. Butler, Okla., Nov. 28, 1910; s. William Winfred and Annie (Simpson) R.; student Vanderbilt U., 1928-29; B.A., U. Okla., 1933; M.A., U. Chgo., 1938; m. Frances Lois Baldwin, July 23, 1928; children—Lamyra Robinson Stark, William B., John T. Tchr., prin. Purcell (Okla.) high Sch., 1933-39; tchr. Central High Sch., Tulsa, 1939-43, Western Mil. Acad., Alton, Ill., 1943-45; dir. pub. relations Tulsa schs., 1945-47; prin. Tulsa elementary schs., 1947-75. Spl. writer Tulsa schs., 1945-60; ghost writer, 1947—; lectr. 1955—. Vice chmn. Okla. Profl. Practices Commn., 1965-66, chmn., 1966-69, mem., 1970-72. Recipient Sequoyah Book award Okla. Sch. Librarians, 1964. Mem. Tulsa Elementary Prins. Assn. (pres.), Armed Forces Writers League (past mem. editors jury), N.E.A., Okla. Reading Council, Nat. Soc. Lit. and Arts, S.A.R., Phi Delta Kappa. Democrat. Presbyn. (ruling elder). Author: Where the Panther Screams, 1961; (with C. X. Dowler) Now, Wait A Minute, 1950.

ROBISON, CORWIN MILTON, II, ins. agy. exec.; b. Logan, W.Va., Sept. 3, 1950; s. Gerald Dean and Betty Lou (Clay) R.; B.A., U. S.C., 1972. With Richway div. Rich's Inc., Atlanta, 1972; ins. agt. State Farm Ins., Marietta, Ga., 1973-75; ind. contractor agt. State Farm Ins. Cos., Marietta, 1975—. Mem. Marietta Jr. C. of C. (dir. 1973-74, pres. 1978—), Am. Soc. Risk and Ins. Club: Civitan. Author: Vietnam: China's China, 1972. Home: 381 Keeler Woods Dr Marietta GA 30064 Office: 100 Cherokee St Suite 140 Marietta GA 30060

ROBISON, JOHN WILLIAM, TV news exec.; b. Grand Prairie, Tex., Mar. 16, 1951; s. William Edgar and Viola (White) R.; student U. Tex., Arlington, 1969-71; B.A. in Speech and Drama, North Tex. State U., 1973; m. Marjorie Attebery, Nov. 18, 1977. Retail control mgr. Safeway, Arlington, Tex., 1968-73; radio lab. instr. U. Tex., Arlington, 1971; news and program dir. stas. KWEL, KBAT, Midland, Tex., 1974; news dir. sta. KCTV, San Angelo, Tex., 1974—; also free-lance photographer. Mem. San Angelo Press Club (chmn. membership com.). Baptist. Home: 818 W Ave L San Angelo TX 76903 Office: KCTV 2800 Armstrong San Angelo TX 76901

ROBISON, MARY ELOISE, ednl. public relations and publicity rep.; b. Fyffe, Ala., July 22, 1914; d. Milford Grady and Belle (Bryant) Beaird; student U. Md., 1932-34; m. Jerome Talmadge Robison, Dec. 26, 1936; children—Ann, Sue, Jane. Free lance photographer, 1940-74, Camera Arts Studio, Gadsden, Ala., 1950-74; public relations and publicity rep. Gadsden (Ala.) State Jr. Coll. Community Services, 1977—; photography instr., 1955-65. Active Gadsden Concert Assn., Friends of Gadsden Public Library. Mem. NE Ala. Geneal. Soc., Ga. Geneal. Soc., Ala. Hist. Assn., Etowah Hist. Soc. Democrat. Baptist. Condr. research photography, profl. mags. in field, 1968-70. Home: 205 Chilton St Gadsden AL 35901 Office: Gadsden State Junior College George Wallace Dr Gadsden AL 35903

ROBISON, WILLIAM HARDEN, III, musician; b. Quantico, Va., Dec. 12, 1935; s. William Harden and Sadie Mae (Bentley) R.; B.S.Ed., U. Ga., 1957, M.Mus. Edn., 1960, Ed.S., 1963, Ed.D., 1970; m. Mary Eleanor Hale, June 16, 1957; children—William Harden IV, Sheilah Anne Robison Miller. Instr. music Clarke County Schs., Athens, Ga., 1958-67; asst. prof. music Ga. Coll., Milledgeville, 1968-69; supr. music Bibb County Schs., Macon, Ga., 1969-72; mem. faculty Berry Coll., Mount Berry, Ga., 1972—, asso. prof. music, 1972-74, prof., 1975—. Deacon, mem. choir 1st Christian Ch., Rome, Ga.; mem. Gov.'s Honors Program Staff, 1969-72. Mem. Ga. Music Educators Assn. (pres.), Music Educators Nat. Conf., Phi Mu Alpha, Phi Eta Sigma, Kappa Phi Kappa, Pi Kappa Lambda, Phi Beta Mu. Contbr. articles to Ga. Music News, Jour. Band Research, Nat. Student Musician. Home: PO Box 157 Mount Berry GA 30149 Office: Berry Coll Box 157 Mount Berry GA 30149

ROBY, RICHARD ELLIS, pub. relations counselor; b. Oklahoma City, May 9, 1939; s. Frank H. and Doris M. (Cross) R.; grad. Oklahoma City U.; m. Pauline Garner, June 13, 1959; children—Richard Ellis, Rhonda Kay, David. With sales dept. Lee Way Motor Freight, Inc., Oklahoma City, 1961-63, mgr. advt. and pub. relations, 1963-66; pres. Richard Roby Assos., Oklahoma City, 1966-76; cons. Pub. Relations Counselors, Inc., Oklahoma City, 1977—; adj. instr. in pub. relations Central State U., 1974, Okla. State U., 1976—; communications cons. Pres.'s Council on Youth Opportunity-Nat. Alliance Businessmen. Pres. Kidney Found. of Okla., 1973; bd. dirs. Deaconess Hosp., Oklahoma City, 1973—, Mercy Health Center, Oklahoma City, 1976—. Mem. Pub. Relations Soc. Am. (accredited; pres. Oklahoma City chpt. 1972), Oklahoma City C. of C. Methodist. Club: Lions (pres. Downtown club 1973-74) (Oklahoma City). Home: 6701 N Pendell St Oklahoma City OK 73116 Office: 3824 N Meridian St Suite 101 Oklahoma City OK 73112

ROCK, JOSEPH ADAM, JR., food co. exec.; b. Chgo., Aug. 16, 1943; s. Joseph Adam and Margaret R.; B.A., U. Ill., 1970, M.S., 1974; m. Virginia Forster, Nov. 19, 1971. Staff acct. Lybrand, Ross Bros. & Montgomery, Chgo., 1970-71; internal auditor U. Ill., Urbana, 1971-76; audit supr. Church's Fried Chicken, San Antonio, 1976-78, dept. head corporate internal audit, 1978—. Served with U.S. Army, 1962-67. C.P.A., Ill., Tex. Mem. Am. Inst. C.P.A.'s, Inst. Internal Auditors, Tex. Soc. C.P.A.'s, AAU. Club: San Antonio Road Runners. Office: Box BH001 San Antonio TX 78284

ROCKAFELLOW, HOWARD LEROY, newspaper exec.; b. Iowa City, Aug. 21, 1938; s. Lowell Sidney and Irene (Tharp) R.; student U. Iowa, 1956-57; m. Agnes Irene Kook, July 5, 1959; children—Theresa Irene, Michael Howard, Craig Andrew. With West Liberty Index, 1954-57, Ruthenberg Clothing Store, 1957-58; mgr. classified advt. Muscatine (Iowa) Jour., 1958-68; retail advt. salesman Odessa (Tex.) American, 1968-72, asst. advt. mgr., 1972-74, dir. advt., 1974—. Pres., Girls Club Odessa, Inc., 1976-77. Mem. Tex. Daily Newspaper Advt. Mgrs. Assn., Tex. Daily Newspaper Assn. (advt. adv. com.), Permian Basin Ad Club (past pres.). Methodist. Club: Breakfast Optimists. Home: 3301 Deering St Odessa TX 79763 Office: 222 E 4th St Odessa TX 79760

ROCKEFELLER, JOHN DAVISON, IV, gov. W.Va.; b. N.Y.C., June 18, 1937; s. John Davison III and Blanchette Ferry (Hooker) R.; A.B., Harvard U., 1961; student Japanese lang. Internat. Christian U., Tokyo, 1957; postgrad. in Chinese, Yale U. Inst. Far Eastern Langs.; m. Sharon Percy, Apr. 1, 1967; 3 sons, 1 dau. Mem. nat. adv. council Peace Corps, 1961, spl. asst. to dir. corps, 1962, ops. officer in charge work in Philippines, until 1963; desk officer for Indonesian affairs Bur. Far Eastern Affairs, Dept. State, 1963, later asst. to asst. sec. for Far Eastern affairs; cons. Pres.'s Commn. on Juvenile Delinquency and Youth Crime, 1964; field worker Action for Appalachian Youth program, from 1964; mem. W.Va. Ho. of Dels., 1966-68; sec. state W.Va., 1968-72; pres. W.Va. Wesleyan Coll., Buckhannon, 1973-77; gov. W.Va., 1977—. Trustee U. Chgo., 1967—, U. Notre Dame, 1974—. Contbr. articles to mags. including Life, N.Y. Times Sunday mag. Home: 1515 Barberry Ln South Hills Charleston WV 25314 Office: Office of Gov State Capitol Charleston WV 25305

ROCKWELL, ELIZABETH DENNIS, savs. and loan assn. exec.; b. Houston; d. Robert Richard and Nezzell Alderton (Christie) Dennis; student Rice U., 1939-40, U. Houston, 1938-39, 40-42; divorced. Asst. purchasing agt. Standard Oil Co. Tex., 1942-66; with Heights Savs. Assn., Houston, 1966—, asst. sec., 1967-70, asst. v.p., 1970-75, v.p., mgr. bus. services dept., 1975—; 2d v.p. Desk and Derrick Club Am., 1960-61; instr. Coll. of Mainland, Texas City, Tex.; instr. Downtown Coll. and Continuing Edn. Center, U. Houston, also mem. savs. and loan adv. com. Downtown Coll., mem. adv. com. Coll. Bus. Adminstrn. Named Outstanding Woman of Yr., YWCA. Mem. Am. Savs. and Loan League (state dir. 1973-76, chpt. pres. 1971-72; pres. S.W. regional conf. 1972-73; Leaders award 1972), Savs. Inst. Mktg. Soc. Am. (Key Person award 1974), Inst. Fin. Edn., Fin. Mgrs., Soc. Savs. Instns., U.S. Savs. League, Houston Heights Assn. (charter, dir. 1973-77), Houston North Assn. Author articles. Home: 3617 Yoakum Blvd Houston TX 77006 Office: PO Box 7483 Houston TX 77008

ROCKWELL, STANLEY BALDWIN, JR., psychologist; b. Farmville, Va., May 18, 1954; s. Stanley Baldwin and Marion Ann (Martin) R.; B.A., Coll. of William and Mary, 1976, M.Ed., 1977, postgrad. 1978—; m. Shelley Rae Rubenking, June 17, 1978. Grad. asst. TV services Coll. of William and Mary, Williamsburg, Va., 1975-77; technician Center for Excellence, Inc., Williamsburg, 1977-78; research and training asst. Social Skills Training Project, Eastern State Hosp., Williamsburg, 1978, research psychology asst., Dept. Tng. and Research, 1978—; volunteer tutor Adult Skills program, 1978; alcoholism counselor Eastern State Hosp., 1979—. Mem. Am. Personnel and Guidance Assn., Assn. Specialists in Group Work, Va. Mus., Am. Psychol. Assn. Methodist. Contbr. articles in field to profl. jours. Home: PO Box 2022 Williamsburg VA 23185 Office: Dept of Training and Research Eastern State Hosp Williamsburg VA 23185

RODAK, GEORGE, JR., mfg. co. exec.; b. Steubenville, Ohio, Aug. 3, 1945; s. George and Mary L. (Macey) R.; B.A., Coll. Steubenville, 1967; M.B.A., Wake Forest U.; m. Barbara Lynn Voytecek, May 17, 1975. Tchr., St. Paul's Sch., Weirton, W.Va., 1966-68; tchr., coach Weirton (W.Va.) High Sch., 1968-70, Warren Consol. High Sch., Tiltonsville, Ohio, 1970-71, Whitehall High Sch., Columbus, Ohio, 1971; head coach, gen. mgr. Cleve. Browns Farm Team, Youngstown (Ohio) Pro-Football, 1971-72; mgmt. cons. Alexander Proud Foot Co., Chgo., 1972-76; staff services mgr. Hanes Textiles, Ponce, P.R., 1976-78, ops. mgr., Winston Salem, N.C., 1978-80, dir. ops., 1980—. Mem. Am. Prodn. Inventory Control Soc., Am. Mgmt. Assn. Office: Hanes Knitwear PO Box 3019 Winston Salem NC 27102

RODGERS, HUGH IRMON, educator; b. Brewton, Ala., July 17, 1934; s. Henry Hilborn and Bessie Lee (Smith) R.; B.A., U. Ala., 1956, M.A., 1957; Ph.D., U. Tex., 1968; m. Sandra Elizabeth Lester, Aug. 14, 1966; 1 son, Barton Hugh. Asst. prof. history Andrew Coll., Cuthbert, Ga., 1960-64; asst. prof. Columbus Coll., 1967-69, asso. prof., 1969-74, prof., 1974—, acting chmn. dept. history, 1977—; adj. asso. prof. Ga. State U., 1972-73. Served with U.S. Army, 1958-60. German Academic Exchange Service grantee, 1979. Mem. AAUP, Am. Hist. Assn., So. Hist. Assn., Assn. Ga. Historians, Conf. Group Central European History, Phi Alpha Theta (recipient Best First Book award 1975). Episcopalian. Club: Ga. Conservancy. Author: Search for Security: A Study in Baltic Diplomacy, 1920-1934, 1975. Contbr. articles to profl. jours. Home: 4315 Cheshire Bridge Rd Columbus GA 31904 Office: Dept History Columbus College Columbus GA 31907

RODGERS, JOHN HASFORD, JR., biologist; b. Dillon, S.C., Feb. 1, 1950; s. John H. and Connie Marie (Turner) R.; B.S. in Botany, Clemson U., 1972, M.S., 1974; Ph.D. in Aquatic Ecology, Va. Poly. Inst. and State U., 1977; m. Martha Willis Robeson, Aug. 30, 1969; 1 son, Daniel Joseph. Research asso. Va. Poly. Inst. and State U., Blacksburg, 1977-78; asst. prof. East Tenn. State U., Johnson City, Tenn., 1978-79; research scientist N. Tex. State U., Denton, 1979—; cons. aquatic ecologist to Sch. Public Health, U. Tex., Houston, 1977—, Va. State Water Control Bd., Richmond, 1977, Center for Environ. Studies, Va. Poly. Inst. and State U., 1978-79, Tenn. Eastman Co., Kingsport, 1978—; guest lectr. plant ecology and environ. biology Clemson U., 1977. Served with USAF, 1976. Mem. Ecol. Soc. Am., Am. Inst. Biol. Scis., Am. Soc. Limnology and Oceanography, N. Am. Benthological Soc., Water Pollution Control Fedn., AAAS, Sigma Xi, Phi Sigma. Contbr. numerous articles on aquatic biology and plant ecology to sci. jours. Home: 2524 Freedom St Denton TX 76201 Office: Institute Applied Sciences NT Box 13078 North Texas State Univ Denton TX 76203

RODGERS, LAWRENCE RODNEY, educator, physician; b. Clovis, N.Mex., Mar. 9, 1920; s. Samuel Frank and Lillian (O'Connor) R.; B.S., W. Tex. State U., 1940; M.D., U. Tex., 1943; m. Ivy Lorna Piper, Aug. 6, 1943; children—Lawrence Rodney, Ivy Elizabeth (Mrs. James H. Walsh III), George Piper. Intern, Phila. Gen. Hosp., 1943-44, resident medicine, 1946-49; asso. internist Tumor Inst., U. Tex. M.D. Anderson Hosp., Houston, 1949—; chmn. dept. medicine Hermann Hosp., Houston, 1966-71; asso. prof. clin. medicine Baylor U., 1949—; prof. clin. medicine U. Tex., 1972—. Bd. dirs. Tex. Med. Found. Served to maj. M.C., AUS, 1944-46. Decorated Bronze Star with oak leaf cluster. Diplomate Am. Bd. internal Medicine. Fellow A.C.P. (gov. for Tex. (So.) 1979—); mem. AMA (alt. del.), Harris County Med. Soc. (exec. bd. 1978—), Am. Heart Assn., Houston Soc. Internal Medicine (pres. 1974). Editor: Harris County Physician, 1976—. Home: 5508 Briar Dr Houston TX 77056 Office: Hermann Profl Bldg Houston TX 77030

RODGERS, WILLIAM LEE, oil operator; b. Anna, Tex., Feb. 27, 1914; s. Forrest G. and Minnie E. (Coffey) R.; B.A., Baylor U., 1937; m. Francis Ann Harrell, Apr. 29, 1950; children—William Randolph, Francis Renee. With research and devel. dept. Gulf Oil Corp., Houston, 1937-42; ind. oil and gas operator, Ft. Worth, Tex., 1946—. Pres. bd. dirs. Lena Pope Children's Home, 1965-66; v.p. bd. dirs. Ft. Worth Mus. Sci. and History, 1962-73; bd. dirs. Tex. Bapt. Children's Home, 1957-61; trustee Ft. Worth Children's Hosp., 1962-65. Served with USNR, 1942-46. Mem. Am. Assn. Petroleum Landmen, Petroleum Club Ft. Worth. Baptist. Clubs: Ft. Worth, River Crest Country, Exchange. Home: 4604 Alta Dr Ft Worth TX 76107 Office: Ft Worth Nat Bank Bldg Ft Worth TX 76102

RODHOLM, ROSE MARIE, dietitian; b. Clare, Mich., Jan. 19, 1918; d. Lawrence William and Josephine Louise (Cour) Jackson; B.S. in Home Econs., Mich. State U., 1939; postgrad. U. Chgo.; m. Ansgar Kolhede Rodholm, June 21, 1941 (dec. 1951); children—Anne Marie, Patricia, Peter Jackson. Staff dietitian U. Chgo., 1940-41; dir. dietary dept. Driscoll Found. Children's Hosp., Corpus Christi, Tex., 1953—; clin. instr. Baylor U. Coll. Medicine, Houston, 1959-73; participant White House Conf. Food, Nutrition and Health, 1969. Recipient Ourstanding Service award Driscoll Found. Children's Hosp., 1973. Mem. Am. Dietetic Assn., Tex. Dietetic Assn., Tex. Soc. Hosp. Food

Service Dirs., Texans Asso. Nutrition Advance Assn., Tex. Hosp. Assn., Coastal Bend Diabetes Assn. (dir.), Corpus Christi Dietetic Assn. Roman Catholic. Home: 621 Indiana St Corpus Christi TX 78404 Office: 3533 S Alameda St Corpus Christi TX 78411

RODICK, RICHARD GLEN, automotive aftermarket exec.; b. Kansas City, Mo., Dec. 29, 1936; B.S.B.A. in Acctg., Central Mo. State U., 1959; m. Betty G. Clemens, June 2, 1956; children—Julie, Richard G., Jeffrey. Accountant, Thomas J. Lipton Inc., Kansas City, Mo., 1959-63; acctg. mgr. Thompson Hayward Chem. Co., Kansas City, Mo., 1963-66; with Union Carbide Corp., 1966-72, regional fin. dir. Union Carbide India, Ltd., New Delhi, 1970-71, asst. treas. Union Carbide Eastern, N.Y.C., 1971-72; div. v.p. STP Internat. Inc., Ft. Lauderdale, Fla., 1972—. Mem. Nat. Assn. Accountants, Singapore Mgmt. Assn. Democrat. Office: 1400 Commercial Blvd Fort Lauderdale FL 33310

RODINE, ROY WAYNE, edn. counselor; b. Smolan, Kans., Feb. 27, 1928; s. Roy Sanford and Edith Marie (Gustofson) R.; B.S., Bethany Coll., Lindsborg, Kans., 1952; M.S., Ft. Hays (Kans.) State U., 1965; m. Opal Eloise Lowe, Nov. 27, 1974; children—Dwayne, Cheryl, Cynthia, Denise, Kristin, Amanda, Kurtis. Sch. adminstr. Wichita (Kans.) Public Schs., 1952-68; edn. counselor U.S. Army, Ft. Riley, Kans., 1968-74, Ft. Polk, La., 1974—; public relations liaison. Recipient Outstanding Service award, U.S. Army, 1978, Sustained Superior Performance award, 1979. Mem. NEA, Am. Personnel and Guidance Assn. Clubs: Baptist Men's, Officers. Research on edn. needs of minorities. Home: PO Box 8189 Lumberton TX 77711 Office: Bldg 7801 Fort Polk LA 71459

RODMAN, PAUL KEITH, civil engr.; b. Marshall, Ark.. Feb. 12, 1945; s. Toy Keith and Kathaleen Myrtle (Cory) R.; B.S., Okla. State U., 1968, M.S., 1969; M.S., U. Wis., 1972; posigrad. Southwestern Bapt. Theol. Sem., 1969-71; m. Nancy Olivia Mock, Dec. 20, 1969; 1 son. John-Paul Jefferson. Undergrad. and grad. research asst. Okla. State U., Stillwater, 1966-69; hydraulic engr. U.S. C.E., Fort Worth, 1969—, chief urban hydrology unit, 1973—. Mem. U.S. Com. on Irrigation and Flood Control, 1973-77. Recipient Outstanding Engr. award Okla. State U., 1968. C.E. planning fellow, 1971-72. Registered profl. engr., Tex. Mem. ASCE, Am. Soc. Agrl. Engrs., Am. Water Research Assn., Phi Kappa Phi, Sigma Tau, Alpha Zeta, Farm House. Baptist (dir. recreation program 1970-71). Contbr. articles to profl. jours. Home: 2317 Arrowhead Ct Fort Worth TX 76103 Office: Box 17300 Room 3C17 Fort Worth TX 76102

RODRIGUEZ, ALEJANDRO JAVIER, diversified industry exec.; b. Monterrey, N.L., Mex., Apr. 19, 1939; s. Servando and Enriqueta (Miechielsen) R.; B.S. in Chem. Engring., Universidad de Nuevo Leon, Monterrey, 1960; postgrad. Notre Dame U., 1962; M.B.A., U. Pa., 1964; m. Carmen Bonetti de Rodriguez, Aug. 31, 1961; children—Alejandro, Carmen Teresa, Ivonne, Karla. High sch. prof. chemistry and math., 1957-58; plant operator Fierro Esponja, 1959, research and devel., 1960; procurement mgr. Empresas Industriales, 1960-62; asst. to metall. supt. Hojalata y Lamina, 1964-65, prodn. planning and control mgr., 1965-66, mktg. mgr., 1966-69; corp. planning dir. Valores Industriales, Monterrey, 1969-73; v.p. planning Alfa, 1973-75; pres. Nylon de Mexico, S.A., 1975—; pres. Fibras Quimicas, S.A., 1977—; exec. v.p. Alfa Industrias, 1979—, pres. consumer goods sector; tchr. engring. econs. State U., Nuevo Leon, 1964; tchr. adminstrn. grad. level U. N.L., 1965-69; mktg. mgmt., 1966-67. Mem. Am. Soc. Metals (v.p.), Am. Mktg. Assn., Instituto Mexicano de Ingenieros Quimicos. Clubs: Futbol Monterrey (pres.), Casino (Monterrey); Campestre; Sierra Madre Tennis; Valle Altq. Home: 220 Pte Danubio Monterrey NL Mexico Office: PO Box 5000 Monterrey NL Mexico

RODRIGUEZ, ANTONIO RUELAN, physician; b. Tabuelan, Cebu, Philippines, June 13, 1943; came to U.S., 1969; s. Teopisto Cometa and Loreto Suico (Ruelan) R.; A.A., U. San Carlos, 1963; M.D., Cebu Inst. Medicine, 1968; m. Belma Cabatingan, Apr. 7, 1972; children—Olga, Noreen, Antonio Ruelan. Intern, DePaul Hosp., Norfolk, Va., 1969-70; resident in internal medicine Med. Coll. Ohio, Toledo, 1970-73; fellow in hematology Med. Coll. Ga., Augusta, 1973-75, asst. prof. medicine, 1975—. Fellow Internat. Soc. Hematology; mem. AMA, Am. Soc. Hematology, Philippine Am. Med. Assn. Ga., A.C.P. Roman Catholic. Home: 152 Morehead Dr Martinez GA 30907 Office: Hematology Section Dept Medicine Medical College of Georgia Augusta GA 30912

RODRIGUEZ, BEATRIZ MARTA, educator, prin.; b. Havana, Cuba, Apr. 21, 1937; d. Pedro Manuel and Elena Caridad (Borras) R.; came to U.S., 1967, naturalized, 1973; student Orbon Conservatory Music, 1945-55, grad., 1959; student U. Havana, 1955-56; B.S.T., Regina Virginum Coll., 1965; B.S. in Edn. magna cum laude, Medaille Coll., 1972; M.S. in Counseling, Barry Coll., 1975; postgrad. U. Miami (Fla.), 1975—. Joined Sister Apostolate, Roman Catholic Ch., 1959-76; draftsman Mr. Gross Co., Havana, 1957-58; tchr. elementary sch. Lestonac Sch., Havana, 1958-59; tchr. Apostolado High Sch., Madrid, 1959-67; tchr. jr. high sch. St. Mary of Sorrows, Buffalo, 1967-68, 70-71, St. Matthew, Hallandale, Fla., 1968-70; religion coordinator Loyola Sch., Miami, Fla., 1971-72; prin. St. Monica Sch., Carol City, Fla., 1972-77; guidance counselor, dir. activities Curley High Sch., Miami, 1977—; part-time tchr. Miami Dade Community Coll.; coordinator Spanish Speaking Sisters of the Archdiocese, Miami, 1972-74; del. to Sisters' Council, Miami, 1972-74; mem. coordination of religion instruction team, Miami, 1974-75; mem. Archdiocesan Personnel Policy Planning Com., 1979—, also other coms.; very active with vol. work and as instr., coordinator, facilitator, speaker in areas of edn., religion and guidance. Recipient various honors in fields of music, theology, edn. and counseling while in sch. Mem. Am. Personnel and Guidance Assn., Kappa Delta Pi. Democrat. Roman Catholic. Pub. monthly religious bull., 1975-76; developer personality program for religious community; appears musical plays, recitals, TV, and radio performances. Home: 60 W 11th St Hialeah FL 33010 Office: 300 NE 50th St Miami FL 33137

RODRIGUEZ, CHARLES F., chemist; b. San Antonio, July 1, 1938; s. Leopoldo Fernando and Maria del Carmen Mellado R.; B.S. in Chemistry, St. Mary's U., 1961, postgrad., 1962-69; m. Karen Lee Vargo, Dec. 29, 1962; children—Miguel Luis, Felipe Xavier, Carlos David, Gregorio Alejandro. Technician, S.W. Research Inst., San Antonio, 1961, asst. chemist, 1961-64, research chemist, 1964-75, sr. research chemist, 1975—. Chmn. bd. Mexican Am. Programs in Housing, 1974-76; mem., officer St. Dominic's Ch. Council, 1968-74; mem. bond issue steering com. City of San Antonio, 1969; baseball coach Cath. Youth Orgn., 1971-75; mem. bd. edn. Teresian Schs. San Antonio, 1973-78, pres., 1973-75, v.p., 1976-78; adult leader Boy Scouts Am., 1975—. Mem. Am. Chem. Soc. (treas. 1970, program chmn. 1971, pres. 1972, mem. exec. bd. 1978-81), Soc. Applied Spectroscopy, Am. Soc. Mass. Spectrometry, Mexican Am. Republicans Tex. (sec. 1973-77), Delta Sigma Phi, Sigma Xi. Republican. Roman Catholic. Contbr. articles to profl. jours. Home: 5905 Deer Horn Dr San Antonio TX 78238 Office: 6220 Culebra Rd San Antonio TX 78284

RODRIGUEZ, CLEMENTINA, educator; b. Raymondville, Tex.; d. Wenceslao Sosa and Carmela (Espinoza) R.; B.S., Tex. Woman's U., 1963; M.A., Incarnate Word Coll., 1970; M.A., St. Mary's U., 1977. Tchr. biology Edgewood Ind. Sch. Dist., San Antonio, 1963-67; tchr. biology and chemistry Raymondville (Tex.) Ind. Sch. Dist., 1967-72; tchr. biology Northside Ind. Sch. Dist., San Antonio, 1972-77, counselor, 1977—; co-chmn. sci. and soc. workshop, Incarnate Word Coll., 1972-73. Named Tchr. of the Year, Raymondville High Sch., 1971-72; Tex. Tchr. of Conservation, 1975; Outstanding Biology Tchr. Tex., 1977; NSF grantee Howard U., 1965, Boston U., 1966, Boston Coll., 1969, Knox Coll., 1970, 71, 72. Mem. Am. Biology Tchrs. Assn., Sci. Tchrs. Assn. Tex., S. Tex. Assn. Guidance and Personnel, Am. Personnel and Guidance Assn., Northside Counselors Assn., Delta Kappa Gamma, Phi Delta Kappa. Roman Catholic. Home: 2408 W Woodlawn St San Antonio TX 78228 Office: 8000 Lobo Ln San Antonio TX 78240

RODRIGUEZ, DOLORES MARIE, counselor; b. Galveston, Tex., Jan. 23, 1947; d. Alfred and Hilda (Vidaurri) R.; B.S., Lamar U., 1969; M.Ed., Stephen F. Austin Coll., 1973; diploma Para-Legal Inst., Arlington, Va., 1978. Tchr. phys. sci. French High Sch., Beaumont, 1969-70, Ball High Sch., Galveston, 1970-72; counselor elementary schs., San Antonio, 1973-75; counselor Coke R. Stevenson Middle Sch., San Antonio, 1975-77; with Clk.'s Office, U.S. Supreme Ct., 1978; Cath. youth asst. coordinator City of Galveston, 1978—. Mem. Am., Tex., S.W. Tex. personnel and guidance assns., Am. Sch. Counselor Assn., Tex., Northside Ind. tchrs. assns. Roman Catholic. Home: 5218 Avenue R Galveston TX 77550

RODRIGUEZ, JOHNNY GOMEZ, accountant; b. Sinton, Tex., May 15, 1945; s. Gregorio E. and Josefa P. (Gomez) R.; A.A. (scholar), Del Mar Coll., 1965; B.B.A., Tex. A. and I. U., 1976. Owner, operator R & R Bookkeeping Service, Sinton, 1973-75; bus. mgr., fiscal officer S. Tex. Health Systems Agy., Kingsville, 1976-78, propr. Johnny Rodriguez Enterprises, 1979—. Served with USAF, 1969-71; Vietnam. Decorated Air Force Commendation medal. Mem. Ams. for Liberal Action, Accounting Soc. Tex., Notary Pubs. Assn., Am. Legion. Roman Catholic. Home: 612 Ave C Sinton TX 78387 Office: PO Box 272 Main Station Sinton TX 78387

RODRIGUEZ, JUAN GUADALUPE, entomologist, acarologist, educator; b. Espanola, N.Mex., Dec. 23, 1920; s. Manuel D. and Lugardita (Salazar) R.; B.S., N.Mex. State U., 1943; M.S., Ohio State U., 1946, Ph.D., 1949; m. Lorraine Ditzler, Apr. 17, 1948; children—Carmen, Teresa, Carla, Rosa. Asst. entomologist U. Ky., Lexington, 1949-55, asso. entomologist, 1955-61, prof. entomology, 1961—; adviser entomology Universidad de San Carlos, Guatemala, 1961; vis. scientist Warsaw U., Poland, 1971; del. Internat. Congress Entomology, Vienna, Austria, 1960, Moscow, 1968, 1st Internat. Conf. Insects and Diseases of Coffee, San Jose, Costa Rica, 1965; del. 1st Internat. Congress Acarology, Ft. Collins, Colo., 1963, 2d Internat. Congress, Nottingham, Eng., 1967, 3d Internat. Congress, Prague, Czechoslovakia, 1971, 4th Internat. Congress, Saalfelden, Austria, 1974, sec. V Internat. Congress; dir. pest mgmt. curriculum Coll. Agr. Bd. dirs. Lexington chpt. Nat. Conf. Christians and Jews. Served with inf. AUS, World War II. Recipient U. Ky. Alumni Assn. award for distinguished research, 1963; Thomas Poe Cooper award for distinguished achievement in research U. Ky. Coll. Agr., 1972. Mem. Am. Inst. Biol. Scis., Acarological Soc. Am. (gov. bd.), Ky. Acad. Sci., AAAS, entomol. socs. Can., Ont., Am. (br. sec.-treas. 1963-65; br. com. man-at-large 1968—), Hon. Order Ky. Cols., Sigma Xi, Gamma Alpha, Gamma Sigma Delta. Roman Catholic. Editor: Insect and Mite Nutrition, 1972; Recent Advances in Acarology, Vols. I and II, 1979; contbr. numerous sci. and tech. publs. Researcher nutritional ecology and physiology of insects and mites, axenic arthropoda. Home: 1550 Beacon Hill Rd Lexington KY 40504

RODRIGUEZ, JULIO RAMON, accountant; b. Havana, Cuba, Sept. 2, 1939; s. Julio Pastor and Obdulia (Abella) R.; came to U.S., 1961, naturalized, 1971; A.A., Miami-Dade Jr. Coll., 1970; B.B.A., U. Miami (Fla.), 1972; postgrad. Fla. Internat. U.; m. Osmilda Silva, Aug. 6, 1966; children—Linda Maria, Julio Ramon. Head accountant Canadian Gulf Line of Fla., Miami, 1968-72; pvt. practice pub. accounting and cons., Coral Gables, Fla., 1973—; exec. v.p. Gali Mfg. Corp. Mem. Interam. Assn. of Businessmen, Coral Gables C. of C. Clubs: Country (Coral Gables); Kiwanis (Miami); Latin Am. (sec. 1976-77, v.p. 1977-78, pres. 1978-79). Home: 1415 Lisbon St Coral Gables FL 33134 Office: 253 Minorca Ave Coral Gables FL 33134

RODRIGUEZ, MIGUEL ANGEL NIEVES, mercantile exec.; b. Penuelas, P.R., May 8, 1913; s. Vicente Cosme Nieves and Gertrudis Rodriguez; student U. P.R., 1967; m. Ana Maria Rodriguez, Dec. 10, 1934; children—Maria del Rosario, Miguel Angel, Ana Teresa, Carmen Luisa, Jose Randolph. Office mgr. Bosch Bros., Ponce, P.R., 1930; corr. El Imparcial newspaper, P.R., 1933; columnist various local newspapers, P.R., 1932-74; announcer, script writer Sta. WPRP, Ponce, P.R., 1934-47; founder Sucn. J. Serralles, Mercedita-Ponce, P.R., 1933-41; sales mgr. Colgate-Palmolive Co., San Juan, P.R., 1964; gen. mgr. and asst. v.p. Spanish Am. Trading, San Juan, P.R., 1966; exec. dir. Bd. Trade of P.R., San Juan, 1967—; 1st v.p. Inst. Psicopedagogico of P.R., 1957. Apptd. personal escort to rep. of Pope Paul VI, Mariologic Congress, Santo Domingo, Dominican Republic, 1964; bd. dirs. P.R. council Boy Scouts Am., 1963. Served with N.G., 1940. Recipient Merit award Bd. Trade of P.R., 1975, Merit award Broadcasters Associates of P.R., 1978. Mem. Am. Assn. of Mental Deficiency. Roman Catholic. Clubs: Penolano, K.C. (4 deg.).

RODRIGUEZ, PAUL HENRY, biologist, educator; b. Central, N.Mex., Nov. 27, 1937; s. Henry and Estella (Atencio) R.; B.S., Creighton U., 1960; M.S., U. N.Mex., 1963; Ph.D., U. R.I., 1970; m. Lottie Isabel Izaguirre, Dec. 19, 1964; children—Karl Andrew, Elena Patricia, Anna Isabel. Research technician VA Hosp., Albuquerque, 1962-63; vis. prof. biology U. Honduras, 1963-66; cons. biology BSCS/NSF/AID, San Jose, Costa Rica, 1966; research asso. U. Notre Dame, 1970-72; research biologist U. Tex., Houston, 1972-73; asst. prof. U. Tex., San Antonio, 1973-76, asso. prof. genetics, 1976— (on leave); program mgr. NSF, 1978-79; cons. NIH/MBS, 1972-75, Am. Inst. Research, 1975—, NSF, 1977—. Fulbright-Hays fellow to Honduras, 1963-66; NIH predoctoral fellow, 1966-70, postdoctoral fellow, 1970-72. Mem. Am. Genetics Assn., AAAS, Am. Mosquito Control Assn., Am. Soc. Parasitology, Genetics Soc. Am., Internat. Filariasis Assn., Environ. Mutagen Soc., Tex. Acad. Sci., Tex. Genetic Soc. Roman Catholic. Contbr. articles to profl. jours. Home: 5603 Charlie Chan San Antonio TX 78240 Office: U Texas San Antonio TX 78285

RODRIGUEZ, RAMON, anesthesiologist; b. Ponce, P.R., Sept. 8, 1943; s. Ramon and Dolores (Rivera) R.; B.S., Cath U. P.R., 1961; M.D., U. P.R., 1969; m. Mirta Toro, May 27, 1967; children—Juan Carlos, Diana, Jose Ramon. Intern, Univ. Dist. Hosp., San Juan, P.R., 1964-70, resident 1970-72; resident Mayo Clinic, Rochester, Minn., 1972; staff anesthesiologist P.R. Med. Center, San Juan, 1972-73; staff anesthesiologist, acting chief anesthesia sect. VA Hosp., San Juan, 1975-76, chief anesthesia sect., 1976—; asso. prof., chmn. anesthesiology U. P.R. Sch. Medicine, San Juan, 1977—; cons. in field. Served to maj., M.C., U.S. Army, 1973-75. Recipient AMA Physicians Recognition award, 1976-79. Diplomate Am. Bd. Anesthesiology. Fellow Am. Coll. Anesthesiologists, Am. Coll. Chest Physicians; mem. P.R. Heart Assn. (bd. dirs. 1977-79), P.R. Anesthesia Soc. (pres. 1977-79), Am. Soc. Anesthesiologists, Internat. Anesthesia Research Soc., AMA, P.R. Med. Assn., ACP, Pan Am. Med. Assn., Soc. Acad. Anesthesia. Roman Catholic. Home: E-1 Alamo Dr Guaynbo PR 00657 Office: U PR Med Sch GPO Box 5067 San Juan PR 00936

RODRIGUEZ, VICTOR MANUEL, obstetrician, gynecologist; b. Ponce, P.R., May 17, 1945; s. Antonio and Juana (Torres) R.; B.S. magna cum laude, Mayaguez (P.R.) A&M U., 1968; M.D., U. P.R., 1972, M.P.H., 1975; m. Mildred Díaz, Aug. 8, 1965; children—Victor M., Gil A., Mildred, Velma M. Lectr. zoology Interam. U., San Juan, P.R., 1964; intern Univ. Dist. Hosp., San Juan, 1972-73, resident in Ob-Gyn, 1973-76; obstetrician/gynecologist, dir. Lighthouse Teenager's Clinic, Montgomery, Ala., 1978; practice medicine specializing in ob-gyn, El Dorado, Ark., 1979—. Served to maj., M.C., USAF, 1976-79. Diplomate Am. Assn. Gynecologic Laparoscopists. Recipient Charles Darwin award Mayaguez A&M U., 1968. Mem. Am. Coll. Ob-Gyn, So. Med. Assn., P.R. Med. Assn., Assn. Mil. Surgeons, Soc. Air Force Clin. Surgeons, Am. Public Health Assn. Roman Catholic. Home: 123 Woodland St El Dorado AR 71730 Office: 700 W Faulkner St El Dorado AR 71730

RODRIGUEZ, WALDEMER VENTURA, JR., distbn. co. exec.; b. San Juan, P.R., Nov. 24, 1953; s. Waldemar Ventura and Nilda Milagros (Santiago) R. B.B.A. in Acctg., U. P.R., 1974; M.B.A. in Mktg., Interam. U., Santurce, P.R., 1978; m. Yolanda Maria Suarez, Aug. 7, 1976. Auditor, Peat, Marwick & Mitchell & Co., C.P.A.'s, San Juan, 1974-75; adminstrv. mgr. Ventura Rodriguez & Sons, San Juan, 1975-78, gen. mgr., chief exec. officer, 1978—; chmn. bd. H.R. Muxo, Inc., Cadierno Corp. Adv., P.R. Jr. Achievement, 1979—. Mem. Am. Mgmt. Assn., Fin. Execs. Inst., Fin. Analysts Assn., Sales and Mktg. Execs. Assn., Spanish C. of C. (dir.), C. of C. P.R., Fedn. Equestrian Sports, Centro Ecuestre P.R. Author articles in field. Home: 1359 Luchetti St Apt 4 Condado PR 00907 Office: PO Box 3471 San Juan PR 00904

RODRÍGUEZ-ESTRADA, MARCOS ANTONIO, judge; b. Rio Piedras, P.R., Sept. 8, 193[illegible]; s. Marcos and Julia (Estrada-Saldana) Rodríguez-Saldaña; B.B.A. in Accounting, U. P.R., 1959, J.D., 1963; postgrad. So. Methodist U., 1969, Harvard Law Sch., 1970, Nat. Coll. State Judiciary, U. Nev., 1976; m. Ana Rodríguez, Apr. 7, 1972; children—Marcos Jesús, Rosa Julia. Admitted to P.R. bar, 1963; with Office of Gov. of P.R.; with P.R. Planning Bd.; dir. Office Legal Services, San Juan, P.R., 1963-74; judge P.R. Superior Ct., San Juan, 1974—. Chief accountant Dept. Pub. Works, Govt. of P.R., San Juan, 1952-63. Served with AUS, 1952. Mem. Am., P.R., Inter-Am. bar assns., Am. Accounting Assn., P.R. Planning Assn., U. P.R. Alumni Assn. Roman Catholic. Home: 920 Fordham St University Gardens Rio Piedras PR 00927 Office: Judicial Center Call Box CJ Hato Rey PR 00919

RODRIGUEZ-HERNANDEZ, JESUS M., hosp. adminstr.; b. Quebradillas, P.R., Apr. 25, 1930; s. Jesus Maria and Maria Luisa (Hernandez) Rodriguez; B.S., U. P.R., 1952; M.S., Columbia U., 1957; m. Maria Teresa Estevez, May 1, 1954; children—Jesus M., Maria Teresa. Hosp. adminstr. Humacao (P.R.) Health Center and Hosp., 1954-55; asst. exec. dir. Ponce (P.R.) Dist. Hosp., 1957-58, Arecibo (P.R.) Dist. Hosp., 1958-59 asst. dir. adminstrv. services No. health area Dept. Health, 1959-69; adminstr. San Juan (P.R.) Municipal Hosp., 1969-71, Presbyn. Community Hosp., San Juan, 1971-76, Guadalupe Gen. Hosp., Hato Rey, P.R., 1976—; pres. Compañia Cientifica Internacional; cons. Hyat Mgmt. Med. Services P.R. and S. Am. Dist. chmn. Boy Scouts Am., 1958-60, ARC campaign, 1960; dist. supr. Cancer campaign, 1959; mem. Indsl. Com. Arecibo; mem. P.R. Health Com., 1959—; mem. Com. to Study and Establish Universal Health Plan 1973—; dep. regent Dist. 1 (P.R.); bd. examiners for health adminstrs. State Dept., San Juan; bd. govs. Girl Scouts Am.; bd. dirs. Nat. Assn. Crippled Children and Adults, Blue Cross of P.R., Employees City of Arecibo; trustee Dept. Health Coop., P.R., 1959-61; pres. fin. com. San Antonio Abad Coll., 1972. Served as lt. AUS, 1952-54. Named Exec. of Year, Secs. Assn. San Juan Municipal Hosp., 1970, Presbyn. Community Hosp., San Juan, 1972, Presbyn. Community Hosp. Employees, 1975; Community Hosp. Leader, Broadcasters Assn. P.R., 1975. Mem. Am. Hosp. Assn. (trustee P.R. chpt. 1960-61, com. mem. health care for disadvantaged), Am. Coll. Hosp. Adminstrs., Royal Soc. Health, Latin Am. Hosp. Fedn. (founder, 2d v.p.), Tb Assn., Navy League U.S., Hosp. Adminstrs. Assn. P.R., P.R. Hosp. Assn. (dir., pres.), P.R. Hosp. Adminstr. Assn (dir.), Internat. Fedn. Hosps. (del. 20th congress), Fin. Health Mgmt. Assn. (pres. P.R. chpt.), Chamber of Arecibo (v.p. Key Mem. Year), Phi Eta Mu (pres. supreme council 1961). Roman Catholic. Clubs: K.C., Garden Hills Lions, Rotary, Arecibo Country. Home: 559 Independencia St Baldrich Hato Rey PR 00919 Office: Guadalupe Gen Hosp 435 Ponce de Leon Ave Hato Rey PR 00917

RODRIGUEZ-NIETO, RAFAEL, research engr.; b. Cerritos, Mex., Oct. 24, 1940; s. Juan Rodriguez and Petra Nieto; B.S., Universidad Nacional de Mex., 1967; M.S., U. Tulsa, 1969; m. Hortensia Gloria de la Torre, Nov. 18, 1967; children—Adriana Guadalupe, Mabel, Ileana. Research engr. Ingeniero "D", Sepanal, Mexico City, 1964-66; investigator, Instituto Mexicano Del Petroleo, Mexico City, 1966—. Tchr., U. Mex., 1970—. Mem. Am. Inst. Mining, Metall. and Petroleum Engrs., Colegio de Ingenieros Petroleros de Mexico, Colegio de Profesores de Mathematicas, Escuela Nacional Estudios Professionales Cuautitlan. Home: 63 Fray Juan Perez Colon Echegaray Mexico Office: 152 Av de Los 100 Metros Mexico City 14 Mexico also Faculty Engring Div Earth Scis Mexico 20 DF Mexico

RODRIGUEZ-TELLAHECHE, JUAN ANTONIO, architect; b. Havan, Cuba, Dec. 20, 1948; s. Juan Antonio Rodriguez and Blanca R. Tellaheche; came to U.S., 1961, naturalized, 1978; B.A. in Architecture, U. Fla., 1974. Draftsman, designer archtl. firms in Coral Gables and Tavernier, Fla., 1969-75; partner Alvarez, Cazo, Rodriguez & Assos., Coral Gables, 1975-77; owner Rodriguez-Tellaheche, A.I.A. & Assos., Miami, 1977—; adv. elderly housing matters Useful Aged Assn.; mem. Community Devel. Housing Task Force; dir. Dadeland Broadcasting Inc. Mem. policy com. Minority Bus. Enterprise. Recipient various certs. appreciation. Mem. AIA, Fla. Council Aging, Greater Miami Latin Fedn. (pres. 1977—), Fla. Jaycees (past pres. dist. 19), Latin Am. Jaycees Miami (past pres.), Latin C. of C. (dir.) Democrat. Roman Catholic. Author articles in field. Miami FL 33134 Office: 8384 Bird Rd Miami FL 33155

ROE, BURTON JAMES, petroleum co. exec.; b. White Plains, N.Y., Nov. 1, 1922; s. Henry Thurston and Marian Lura (West) R.; B.S. in Chem. Engring., Pa. State U., 1943; m. May Belle McGarvey, Feb. 26, 1944; 1 dau., Virginia. Process engr. Mobil Oil Co., Paulsboro, N.J., 1946-51; sr. process engr. Catalytic Constrn. Co., Phila., 1951-55, mgr. process engring., Sarnia, Ont., Can., 1955-56; mgr. process plant engring. Walter Kidde Constructors, N.Y.C., 1956-60; mgr. diversification plants Nc. Natural Gas Co., Omaha, 1960-66; asst. to exec. v.p. Union Tex. Petroleum div. Allied Chem. Corp., Houston, 1966-71, asst. to pres., 1971-73, dir. planning and engring., 1973-75, dir. engring. and petrochems., 1975-79, gen. mgr. mfg., 1979—; cons. Weinrich & Assos.. Washington, 1960. Chmn. indsl. sect. United Fund, Omaha, 1964. Served to lt. (j.g.) USNR, 1943-46. Mem. Am. Inst. Chem. Engrs. (vice chmn. petrogroup 1972-73), Houston Gas Men's Assn., Gas Processors Assn. (govt. relations com.), Am. Arab C. of C. Republican. Presbyn. (deacon 1963-72). Club: Warwick, Champions Country. Home: 13615 Appletree Rd Houston TX 77079 Office: One Riverway PO Box 2120 Houston TX 77001

ROE, CHARLES WILLIAM, hosp. adminstr.; b. DeKalb County, Ala., Sept. 29, 1930; s. John M. and Velma O. (Ragsdale) R.; B.S. in Pharmacy, Samford U., 1957; M.B.A., Jacksonville State U., 1972; m. Faynell E. Latham, Aug. 24, 1952; 1 dau., Joy Denise. Chief pharmacist Baptist Meml. Hosp., Gadsden, Ala., 1957-65, purchasing agt., 1962-65, asst. adminstr., 1966-67, asso. adminstr., 1967-69, v.p., 1969-71, sr. v.p., 1971-76, exec. v.p., 1976-77, adminstr. and exec. v.p., 1977—. Div. chmn. for hosps. ann. fund drive United Givers Fund of Etowah County, 1970-75; deacon Twelfth St. Bapt. Ch., Gadsen, 1960—, Sunday sch. tchr., 1957—; bd. dirs. Gadsden Concert Assn., 1973—, ARC, Etowah County, 1977—. Served with USAF, 1951-53. Fellow Am. Coll. Hosp. Adminstrs.; mem. Am. Hosp. Assn., Ala. Hosp. Assn., Bapt. Hosp. Assn., Northeast Ala. Hosp. Council (pres. 1970-71), Southeastern Soc. Hosp. Pharmacists, Birmingham Regional Hosp. Council (mem. codes and regulations com. 1975-79), Ala. Soc. for Crippled Children and Adults (dir. Etowah county chpt. 1970-75), Gadsden Metro C. of C. (mem. com. on health care and planning 1976-77). Club: Civitan. Home: 1425 Monte Vista Dr Gadsden AL 35901 Office: 1007 Goodyear Ave Gadsden AL 35999

ROE, DONALD WINSTON, chemist, educator; b. Catlettsburg, Ky., Jan. 22, 1932; s. Lorenzo Dow and Myrtle Elizabeth (Rowland) R.; student Duke, 1949-51; B.S., Marshall U., 1955, M.S., 1956; postgrad. (AEC fellow), U. Tenn., 1956-57; Ph.D. (NSF fellow), W.Va. U., 1961; m. Betty Jo Bailey, Dec. 31, 1960; children—Sara Nell, Daniel Winston. Control chemist C. & O. Ry., Huntington, W.Va., 1955-56; research chemist Nat. Steel Corp., Weirton, W.Va., 1960-62; engr. RCA, Lancaster, Pa., 1962-68; asst. prof. chemistry U. Tampa (Fla.), 1968-70, chmn. chemistry dept., 1969-72, asso. prof., 1970-72; part time instr. So. W.Va. Community Coll., Pineville, 1977—; cons. in field. Fellow Am. Inst. Chemists; mem. Am. Chem. Soc., NEA, Sigma Xi, Phi Lambda Upsilon. Methodist. Contbr. articles to profl. publs. Research in microwave spectra, semiconducting glasses, preparation and studies thin films for electronic devices. Patentee in field. Home and office: Route 1 PO Box 428 Princeton WV 24740

ROEHL, LINDA ANNE, ednl. adminstr.; b. Beaumont, Tex., July 20, 1942; d. Charles Fredrick and Geraldine Esther (Doll) Hanser; A.A., Del Mar Coll., 1962; B.S., Tex. A. and I. U., Kingsville, 1964; postgrad. U. Ala., 1977-79, Corpus Christi State U., 1976-79; m. Steven Carl Roehl, Dec. 9, 1978; children—Laura Anne, Tracy Elizabeth, Kenton Gregory. Tchr. art, spl. edn. Corpus Christi (Tex.) Ind. Sch. Dist., 1965-66, tchr./ counselor Behavioral Guidance Center, 1974-76; dir. vol. services, public info. officer Corpus Christi State Sch., 1976—. Mem. Internat. Visitors Com., 1979; campaign mgr. Councilman Dr. Jack Best, 1979; bd. dirs. Art Mus. S. Tex., Speech and Hearing and Lang. Center, Goodwill Industries; active Jr. League. Mem. Assn. Retarded Citizens, Tex. Assn. Mental Deficiencies. Episcopalian. Mem. editorial staff Tides Mag., 1976-79. Office: 902 Airport Rd PO Box 9297 Corpus Christi TX 78408

ROELING, GERARD HENRY, investment co. exec.; b. New Orleans, July 11, 1939; s. William Henry and Gladys Nathalie (Pavlovich) R.; B.A., U. Mich., 1960, M.B.A. with honors, 1961; m. Bette Ann Bichet, Jan. 30, 1960; children—Gerard Patrick, Stewart VanWay, William Jeffrey. Chemist, La. FDA, New Orleans, 1957-59; mem. div. and corp. fin. and mktg. staff Ford Motor Co., Dearborn, Mich., 1961-66; mem. mktg. staff Exxon Corp., Houston, 1966-69; dir. research and planning Asso. Credit Burs., Inc., exec. v.p. Credit Services Internat., Inc., Houston, 1969-72; pres., chmn. bd. Am. Forum Corp., Houston, 1972—. Mem. econ. adv. com. to staff Pres. Nixon, 1970-72. Pres., Brookwood Estates Assn., Livonia, Mich., 1964-66; 1st v.p. Livonia Fedn. Civic Assn., 1965, pres., 1966; chmn. Livonia Civic Affairs Com., 1965, Outstanding Young Man award, 1965; mem. Citizens Adv. Com., 1964-66; pres. Houston Museum Am. History, 1974-77; mem. Capital Improvement and Long Range Planning Com., 1964-66, Sch. Bd. Adv. Com., 1965-66, United Fund, 1966-67, Houston Grand Opera, 1975, Houston Symphony, 1976—, Houston Advanced Urban Analysis Com., 1968, Meml. Glen Assn., 1968, 69, Inst. Internat. Edn., 1972—; mem. exec. com. Houston chpt. Nat. Found., 1975-78; bd. dirs. Mus. Am. Architecture and Decorative Arts, Houston chpt. March of Dimes. Named Southener of Distinction, 1978. Mem. Am. Mktg. Assn., Nat. Assn. Real Estate Bds., Am. Inst. Profl. Consultants, Mktg. Research Assn., C. of C., Phi Kappa Phi, Alpha Kappa Psi. Author articles. Home: 11910 Clarendon Ln Houston TX 77024 Office: 6300 Richmond Ave Houston TX 77057

ROETSCHKE, RONALD CLAY, oil pipe co. exec.; b. Clifton, Tex., Mar. 18, 1934; s. August, Jr., and Susana M. (Seljos) R.; B.S., Tex. A. and M. U., 1955; postgrad. Okla. State U., 1957-59; m. Elizabeth Ann McGowen, Aug. 19, 1972; children—Martha Rice, Ramona Lindsey, Drucilla Morren. Range conservationist Soil Conservation Service, U.S. Dept. Agr., Colorado City, Tex., 1955; chemist Phillips Petroleum Co., Pasadena, Tex. and Bartlesville, Okla., 1955-61, office mgr., Pasadena, Calif., Akron, Ohio and Detroit, 1961-66, tech. sales and devel. engr., Atlanta, 1966-68; owner, pres. Coastal Pipe Co. and Coastal Pipe and Supply, Inc., Houston and Midland, Tex., 1968—. Worker Nat. Republican Congl. Com. Mem. Soc. Plastics Engrs., Am. Security Council (nat. adv. bd.). Lutheran. Clubs: Midland A. and M., Century A. and M., Tex. A. and M. Home: 1609 N Garfield St Midland TX 79701 Office: PO Box 4813 Midland TX 79701

ROEVER, FREDERICK HENRY, physician; b. Phila., June 9, 1940; s. Henry Frederick and Irma Suzanna (Lux) R.; B.S., Haverford Coll., 1962; M.D., Hahnemann Med. Coll., 1966; m. Patricia Anne Ayars, Sept. 4, 1965; 1 son, Christopher Paul. Chief med. resident Mercy Catholic Med. Center, Phila., 1972; dir. med. edn. Tarpon Springs (Fla.) Hosp., 1973—, chief dept. medicine, 1976—, also mem. staff; practice medicine, specializing in internal medicine, Tarpon Springs. Served to capt., inf., U.S. Army, 1968-69; Vietnam. Decorated Bronze Star, Air medal, Vietnamese Honor medal 1st class. Diplomate Am. Bd. Internal Medicine. Fellow A.C.P.; mem. AMA (student teaching award 1976), Undersea Med. Soc., Christian Med. Soc., Am. Soc. Internal Medicine, Assn. U.S. Army, VFW, Am. Legion. Democrat. Lutheran. Office: 1 E Valencia Dr New Port Richey FL 33552

ROGERS, CAMILLA CATHERINE, clin. psychologist; b. Anderson, S.C., Aug. 2, 1949; d. Robert Lincoln and Marguerite (Witherspoon) R.; B.S., E. Carolina U., 1971, M.A. in Edn., 1972; postgrad. U. Va., 1976—; m. William Alfred Cothren Jr., Aug. 24, 1968 (div. Jan. 1978). Tchr. home econs. Martin County Schs., Williamston, N.C., 1971; counselor Wayne Community Coll., Goldsboro, N.C., 1972-76; clin. psychology intern VA Med. Center, New Orleans, 1979—; lectr., cons. in field; vol. crisis intervention. DuPont fellow, 1977-78. Cert. tchr., counselor N.C. Mem. Am. Psychol. Assn. (student), Am. Assn. Marriage and Family Therapists (student), Am. Personnel and Guidance Assn., Phi Upsilon Omicron. Home: 1225 Burgundy St New Orleans LA 70116 Office: VA Med Center 1601 Perdido St New Orleans LA 70146

ROGERS, CLARENCE DIAL, state ofcl.; b. Lynn County, Tex., Dec. 14, 1935; s. Robert Dial and Nellie Vivian (Baker) R.; student Tex. Technol. U., 1954-58; m. Iris Grace Dial, Nov. 26, 1958; children—Samuel Dial, Clarissa Grace. With Tex. Dept. Hwys. and Public Transp., Lubbock, 1957—, adminstrv. technician, safety coordinator, 1971—; co-owner D&R Rentals, 1968—, D&R Laundries, 1959-68. Bd. dirs. S. Plains Fed. Credit Union. Mem. Tex. Public Employees Assn. (pres. 1965, 76), Aircraft Owners and Pilots Assn. Methodist. Home: 5408 47th St Lubbock TX 79414 Office: Tex Dept Hwys and Public Transp 606 Slaton Rd Lubbock TX 79404

ROGERS, COLONEL HOYT, agrl. cons.; b. Mullins, S.C., Jan. 6, 1906; s. Colonel Cross and Mary (Page) R.; B.S., Clemson Coll., 1926; M.S. (Research fellow), U. Ky., 1927; Ph.D. in Plant Physiology (Teaching research fellow), Rutgers U., 1930; m. Justine Frances Harris, Sept. 27, 1927; children—James H., Richard L. Instr. biology Ark. State Coll., Jonesboro, 1927-28; instr. botany Rutgers U., New Brunswick, N.J., 1928-29, asst. research plant physiology, 1929-31; plant pathologist Tex. A. and M. U., Temple, 1931-42; plant pathologist tobacco and cotton research Coker's Pedigreed Seed Co., Hartsville, S.C., 1942-60, v.p., 1960-72, cons. U.S. and fgn. agr., 1972—; mem. bd. rev. tobacco N.C. State U. Mem. faculty adv. com. plant pathology and physiology and bd. visitors Clemson U., 1972-74. Named Man of Year, Progressive Farmer, 1969, Man of Year, Farmer Coops., 1972, Man of Year, Mullins (S.C.) C. of C., 1977, Man of Year in Agr., N.C. State U., 1976; recipient Distinguished Service award S.C. Tobacco Warehouse Assn., 1969, N.C. State U., 1976. Contbr. sci. and popular articles in field to profl. jours. Developer 21 varieties tobacco; leader tobacco breeding program in Italy. Address: Route 4 Box 532 Mullins SC 29574

ROGERS, DECATUR BRAXTON, mech. engr., educator; b. Starkville, Miss., June 28, 1942; s. Theodis Henry and Vernice Rogers; Asso. Applied Sci., N.Y. State U., Farmingdale, 1963; B.S., Tenn. State U., Nashville, 1968; M.S., Vanderbilt U., 1968, 72, Ph.D., 1975; children—Michelle Lisa, Nichole Monique. Tool designer Grumman Aerospace Corp., Bethpage, N.Y., 1963-65, thermal control engr., 1968-69; asst. prof. mech. engring., also dir. planning Tenn. State U., Nashville, 1969-76, asso. prof. mech. engring., 1979—; asso. prof. mech. engring., v.p. phys. plant Prairie View (Tex.) A&M U., 1977-79; cons. in field. Sec., Organized Citizens for Community Devel. of 21st Dist., Nashville, 1976—. Danforth fellow, 1968-69, 72-75. Registered profl. engr., Tex. Mem. ASME (asso.), AAAS, Omega Psi Phi. Contbr. articles to profl. publs. Home: 3258 Brick Church Pike Apt A-14 Nashville TN 37207

ROGERS, DON BIRDSONG, paper corp. exec.; b. Meridian, Miss., Jan. 17, 1947; s. Malcolm Randolph and Leatha (Birdsong) R.; B.S., La. State U., 1973; m. Kathryn Elizabeth Smith, Oct. 15, 1966; children—John Mark, Benjamin Charles, Jennifer Paige. Chemist, Ga. Pacific Corp., Port Hudson, La., 1973-76; refining supt. Olin Corp., Pisgah Forest, N.C., 1976—. Charter mem. Roseland Terr. Civic Assn., Baton Rouge, 1975. Mem. TAPPI. Democrat. Lutheran. Office: Olin Corp PO Box 200 Pisgah Forest NC 28768

ROGERS, DONALD LEE, indsl. equipment mfg. co. exec.; b. Dallas, Jan. 28, 1930; s. John Ernest and Maude Kathleen (McCool) R.; B.S. in Elec. Engring., Tex. A. and M. U., 1951; M.B.A., Harvard, 1957; children—Lance H., Celia I., Donna L. With Comet Rice Mills, Dallas, 1953-71, v.p., 1957-66, pres., 1966-68, chmn. bd., 1968-71; chmn. Country Cupboard, Inc., Dallas, 1970-71; pres., chmn. bd. Burgess Industries Inc., Dallas, 1971—. Served to 1st lt. Signal Corps, AUS, 1951-53. Mem. Young Pres.'s Orgn. Republican. Methodist. Clubs: Dallas Country, Dallas Petroleum. Office: 8101 Carpenter Freeway Dallas TX 75247

ROGERS, DONALD ONIS, educator; b. Springfield, Mo., Oct. 9, 1938; s. Onis Lee and Wilma (Gideon) R.; B.S., S.W. Mo. State U., 1961; M.A., La. State U., 1968; Ph.D., U. Southwestern La., 1979; m. Mora Jeannine, Aug. 19, 1961; children—Donald Scott, Anne Margaret. Lang. coordinator Ralls County Pub. Schs., Ralls County, Mo., 1961-66; grad. teaching asst. La. State U., Baton Rouge, 1966-68; asst. prof. La. State U., Eunice, 1968-74, asso. prof., 1974-79, head Div. Liberal Arts, dir. Acad. Affairs, 1973-78, prof. English, dir. acad. affairs and services, 1979—. Bd. dirs. Bayouland Library System, 1974-78. Served with USNR, 1957-59. Mem. Ralls County Tchrs. Assn. (pres. 1965-66), Coll. English Assn., La. Council Tchrs. English, S.W. Regional Conf. English in 2-Yr. Colls., Mod. Lang. Assn., South Central Mod. Lang. Assn. Democrat. Mem. Ch. of Christ. Contbr. articles to profl. jours. Home: PO Box 301 Cheneyville LA 71325 Office: PO Box 1129 Eunice LA 70535

ROGERS, E. ALLEN, oil co. exec.; b. Muskogee, Okla., July 29, 1945; s. E. J. and G. A. Rogers; B.S. in Math., Northeastern Okla. State U., 1967; m. Loretta I. Sherman, Aug. 5, 1967; children—Bret, Christopher. With Conoco, Inc., 1969—, supervising analyst, Stamford, Conn., 1974-77, dir., adminstr., crude oil trading-internat., Houston, 1977—; tchr. math. Okla. Mil. Acad., 1967-68. Bd. dirs., treas. Kingwood (Tex.) Area Emergency Med. Service, 1978—. Cert. Emergency Med. Technician, Tex. Mem. Planning Execs. Inst., Alpha Chi. Methodist. Club: Kingwood Country. Home: 2027 Willow Point Dr Kingwood TX 77339 Office: PO Box 2197 Houston TX 77001

ROGERS, ELMER A., lawyer; b. N.Y.C., Dec. 9, 1900; s. Joseph and Louisa (Weis) R.; ed. Coll. City N.Y., N.Y. U.; LL.B., N.Y. Law Sch., 1922; m. Berenice Feltenstein. Admitted to N.Y. bar, 1927, So. Dist. N.Y., 1929, Eastern Dist., 1932, Tax Ct. of U.S., 1948, U.S. Supreme Ct. bar, 1949, U.S. Customs Ct., 1950, FCC, 1950; asst. to Supreme Ct. Justice Henry L. Sherman, N.Y. state senatorial contest, 1928; spl. dep. asst. atty. gen., 1931-32; counsel to spl. com. of Washington Heights Taxpayers Assn. to investigate pub. utility cos., 1933; mem. panel arbitrators Am. Arbitration Assn., 1939—. Asst. sec. City Title Ins. Co., 1941; pres. First Nat. Bank of Ardsley, 1943; investment adviser, gen. counsel Securus Corp. Am., Sunrise Equities Corp. Nev. adv. bd. Franklin Nat. Bank. Patron N.Y. U. Bellevue Med. Center. Bd. dirs. U.S. Com. Sports for Israel; mgr. U.S. crew competing in Internat. Boat Races, Lucerne, Switzerland. Mil. instr., 1st lt. World War I; served with USCGR, 1944-45. Mem. George Washington Bicentennial Commn., 1932; mem. com. Citizens Reconstrn. Orgn., 1932; dir. purchasing dept. Greater N.Y. Civilian Def. Vol. Office, 1943; mem. adv. planning bd., N.Y.C. Planning Commn., 1946-51; mem. Mayor's Com. Celebration Golden Anniversary N.Y.C., 1948. Decorated knight officer Greek Order St. Dennis of Zante; named Hon. citizen of Mesolongi, Greece; col. gov.'s staff, also hon. atty. gen. State of La.; recipient diploma and medal Inst. for Amelioration of Wealth-Producing Sources of Greece; silver medal City of Paris; gold medal Legion des Volontaires du Sang; War Cross of Royal Yugoslav Army; Cross of Merit, Greek Am. Legion; La Croix de Merite de La Croix-Rouge (Japan); Grand Cross Republic of Haiti. Diplomate Acad. Arts, Letters, Sci. and Culture (Rome). Mem. N.Y. County Lawyers Assn. (past mem. com. on membership, com. profl. econs.), Fed. Bar Assn. of N.Y., N.J. and Conn. (past mem. OPA com., past chmn. com. on unlawful practice of the law), Detectives Endowment Assn. (hon.), Grand Street Boys Assn., Acad. Polit. Sci., N.Y. Soc. City N.Y. (pres. 1953-56, chmn. exec. com. 1956-57), Tammany Soc. or Columbian Order, Army and Navy Union of U.S.A. (nat. judge adv. 1955-56), Am. Legion (comdr. local post, 1952, past chmn. com. on sch. awards for Americanism, chmn. war meml. com.), 40 and 8, Soc. Am. Mil. Engrs. (mil.), Navy League U.S., Amateur Athletic Union. Mason; mem. Improved Order Red Man (dep. grand sachem, 1931-37, chmn. nat. com. Americanism 1933). Club: N.Y. University Faculty. Author: All-Purpose Real Estate Contract, 1941; Improved Form of Direct-reduction Mortgage, 1941; Embezzlement Has Its Tax Problems, Too, 1948; How the Federal Income Tax Applies to Illegal and Unlawful Gains, 1949; Comprehensive Mortgage, 1954; many legal forms. Home: 500 Ocean Dr Juno Beach FL 33408

ROGERS, GERALD WAYNE, psychiat. social worker; b. Amarillo, Tex., Oct. 20, 1948; s. Howard March and Juanita Ruth (Shelton) R.; B.S., West Tex. State U., 1972, M.A., 1973; M.S.W., Our Lady of the Lake U., San Antonio, 1977; m. Bonnie Heath, Apr. 26, 1969; children—Leslie Dawn, Cody Heath. Dir. drug program Amarillo Hosp. Dist., 1972-74; dir. residential treatment, staff psychologist Central Counties Mental Health-Mental Retardation, Temple, Tex., 1974-78; exec. dir. Temple Coordinated Child Care Council, 1978-79; social worker psychiat. dept. Tex. Dept. Health, Canyon, Tex., 1979—; part-time pvt. practice psychiat. social worker, Amarillo, 1979—; cons. Dept. Human Resources. Served with USMCR, 1967-72. Licensed child care adminstr. Mem. Nat. Assn. Social Workers, Psi Chi. Presbyterian. Home: 5812 Radiant St Amarillo TX 79109 Office: Box 161 West Tex Sta Canyon TX 79016

ROGERS, HERBERT FRANCIS, clergyman, educator; b. Morse, Kans., Mar. 12, 1911; s. Edwin Joseph and Evelyn Frances (Schettenhelm) R.; B.A., U. So. Calif., 1946, M.Th., 1949, Ph.D. (univ. fellow), 1951; m. Mary Louise Rhoton, Mar. 1, 1945; children—Karen Michele Rogers Daniel, Janine Adele Rogers Harris. Supr., Firestone Tire & Rubber Co., Los Angeles, 1928-42; ordained to ministry Methodist Ch., 1949; minister So. Calif., Ariz. Conf., Meth. Ch., Los Angeles, 1942-55; prof. religion and philosophy, chmn. dept. Clark Coll., Atlanta, 1955—. Mem. AAUP, Nat. Assn. Bibl. Instrs., Phi Beta Kappa, Phi Chi Phi, Phi Kappa Phi. Clubs: Optimist (chaplain 1947-74), Masons. Author: Pre Exilic Hebrew Kingship, 1951; Isaiah's Philosophy of Government, 1950. Home: 756 Havenridge Dr Conyers GA 30207 Office: Box 258 240 Chestnut St SW Atlanta GA 30314

ROGERS, JAMES EDWIN, govt. ofcl.; b. Waco, Tex., Feb. 24, 1929; s. Charles Watson and Jimmie (Harp) R.; student Rice U., 1947-49, Baylor U., 1953; B.S., U. Tex., 1955, M.A., 1961; m. Margaret Anna Louise Bruchmann, Oct. 10, 1957; 1 son, James Frederick. With U.S. Geol. Survey, 1956—, supervisory hydrologist, Alexandria, La., 1963—. Scoutmaster, Boy Scouts Am., Alexandria, 1971-72. Served with AUS, 1950-52. Fellow Geol. Soc. Am.; mem. Gem, Mineral and Lapidary Soc. Central La. Phi Beta Kappa, Sigma Gamma Epsilon. Baptist. Home: 4008 Innis Dr Alexandria LA 71301 Office: 3717 Government St Alexandria LA 71301

ROGERS, JAMES GAMBLE, II, archtl. engring. co. exec.; b. Chgo., Jan. 24, 1901; s. John A. and Elizabeth (Baird) R.; student Dartmouth, 1921-24; m. Evelyn Claire Smith, Sept. 28, 1929; children—James Gamble IV, John Hopewell. Established archtl. engring. firm Rogers, Lovelock & Fritz (formerly Jas. Gamble Rogers, II), Winter Park, Fla., 1935—; adv. com. Orlando div. Dade Fed. Savs., Miami, Fla.; cons. and authority on jail design. Mem. Fla. Assn. Architects, 1935—. Named Architect of the Year, Bldg. Stone Inst., 1963; recipient certificates of appreciation, Sec. Army, 1959, Chief of Engrs., 1959. Mem. Fla. Bd. Architecture 1935-44, pres., 1940-44. Mem. AIA (pres. central chpt. 1938-42, chmn. Fla. regional judiciary com. 1963), Archtl. League N.Y., Soc. Am. Mil. Engrs., Am. Hosp. Assn., Ch. Archtl. Guild Am., Nat. Jail Assn., Orlando Art Assn., Hispanic Inst. Presbyn. Clubs: University, Racquet (Winter Park). Contbr. articles to profl. jours., popular mags. Executed Fla. Supreme Ct. Bldg., Tallahassee, 1949; county courthouse Orlando, 1958, courthouse Fort Pierce, Fla., 1960; mil. work in U.S. and fgn. countries including launching platforms at Cape Canaveral (Fla.), guidance towers Kennedy Space Center and Antigua Island; hosp. Fla. A and M. Coll., Tallahassee, 1949, hosp. MacDill AFB, Tampa, 1971, student union Stetson U., Deland, 1956; academic bldgs. Fla. State U., Tallahassee, 1959-62, Orlando Jr. Coll., 1954-65, Rollins Coll., Winter Park, 1951-68, addition Hillis Miller Health Center, Gainesville, Bush Sci. Center, Rollins Coll., 1969, Naval Regional Med. Center, Orlando, 1979, First United Meth. Ch. Complex, Winter Park, Fla., 1979. Home: PO Drawer 730 Winter Park FL 32790 Office: 145 Lincoln Ave Winter Park FL 32789

ROGERS, JOHN RICHARD, lawyer; b. Ashburn, Ga., June 30, 1924; s. Edwin A. and Ella Mae (Evans) R.; LL.D., U. Ga., 1949; m. Reginald Ann Cox, Aug. 6, 1953; children—Sylvia, Starr. Admitted to Ga. bar, 1949; gen. practice, Ashburn, 1949—. Pres. Monroe Mall Corp., 1965—; pres. First Fed. Savs. & Loan Assn. of Turner County. Served to 1st lt. AUS, 1944-46. Mem. Turner County C. of C. (pres., past dir.), Am., Tifton Circuit bar assns., Am. Trial Lawyers Assn., Am. Judicature Soc., Phi Eta Sigma, Sigma Chi, Phi Alpha Delta. Home: Madison Ave Ashburn GA 31714 Office: Rogers Plaza Ashburn GA 31714

ROGERS, JON GUY, clin. psychologist, educator; b. Kansas City, Kans., Jan. 17, 1938; A.B., Emporia State U., 1960; M.A., U. Ark., 1963; Ph.D. (NDEA fellow 1965-67), U. N.Mex., 1967; m. Kathryn Frances Counts, June 29, 1962; children—Laura Lea, Todd Matthew. Instr., U.S. Air Force, 1962-63; vis. faculty mem. Ark. State Tchrs. Coll., summer 1965; asst. prof. Hendrix Coll., 1962-65; mem. human factors staff Sandia Corp., summer 1966; research psychologist NASA, 1967-68; asst. prof. psychology U. Ala., Huntsville, 1968-70, asso. prof., 1970-74, prof., 1975—, dean Sch. of Humanities and Behavioral Scis., 1972—; cons. vocat. rehab. services. Mem. Am. Psychol. Assn., N.Y. Acad. Sci., Human Factors Soc., Nat. Rehab. Assn., Sigma Xi. Recipient profl. award Ala. Gov.'s Com. on Employment of the Handicapped, 1976. Methodist. Club: Rotary. Contbr. articles to profl. jours. Home: 2702 Churchill Dr Huntsville AL 35801 Office: PO Box 1247 Huntsville AL 35807

ROGERS, JOSEPH BROWN, ret. physician; b. New Albany, Miss., Oct. 18, 1911; s. Joe L. S. and Effie (Brown) R.; Ph.C., U. Miss., 1932, B.S., 1941; M.D., Northwestern Med. Sch., 1944; m. Carolyn McMillan, June 23, 1937; children—Joseph B., Warren K. Intern, Johns Hopkins Hosp., 1944, resident, 1944-45; resident Balt. City Hosp., 1945-46; practice medicine specializing in ophthalmology, Oxford, Miss., 1948-75; mem. staff Howard Meml. Hosp., Biloxi, Miss., Gulf Coast Community Hosp., Biloxi, Garden Park Community Hosp., Gulfport, Miss.; clin. prof. ophthalmology U. Miss. Med. Sch. from 1948, now ret.; dir. Miss. Blue-Cross-Blue Shield, 1954-72. Mem. exec. com. Adv. Health Planning Council for Comprehensive Health Planning, Miss., 1968-69. Served to capt. AUS, 1946-48. Diplomate Am. Bd. Ophthalmology. Fellow La.-Miss. Ophthal. and Otolaryn. Soc. (past pres.), Am. Acad. Opthalmology and Otolaryngology, Pan-Am. Ophthal. Soc., Soc. Cyro-Ophthalmology, Wilmer Resident's Assn., Johns Hopkins Med.

and Surg. Soc.; mem. North Miss. Med. Soc. (pres. 1964-65), AMA (alternate del. 1969-72, del. 1972—), Miss. (pres. 1968-69), So. med. assns., Kappa Psi, Phi Chi. Methodist (steward 1953—, trustee). Rotarian. Clubs: Oxford Country; Broadwater Country (Biloxi, Miss.). Home: 220 Southern Circle Gulfport MS 39501

ROGERS, KING WALTER, JR., grocery stores exec.; b. Dyersburg, Tenn., Aug. 19, 1912; s. King Walter and Essie (Martin) R.; B.A., U. Tenn., 1934; postgrad. Harvard Bus. Sch., 1934-36; m. Mildred Hampton Moss, May 23, 1943; children—King Walter III, Robert Moss. Exec., Pennel-Edenton Wholesale Grocery, Dyersburg, 1936-39; with K.W. Rogers & Son, Inc., Dyersburg, 1939—, pres., dir., 1943—; pres. Nehi Bottling Co., Dyersburg, Ardmore Tel. Co. (Tenn.); dir. Holiday Inns, Dyersburg, United Tel. Co., Chapel Hills, Tenn., Crockett Tel. Co., Friendship, Tenn., First Citizens Nat. Bank, Dyersburg; pres. Tipton County Utilities Inc., Dyersburg. Chmn., U. Tenn. Devel. Council, 1969-70; mem. Tenn. Planning Commn., 1970; mem. exec. com. Hosp. for Crippled Adults, Memphis, 1961-70, also Obion-Forked Deer Basin Authority. Bd. dirs. West Tenn. Area council Boy Scouts Am.; bd. mgrs. Meth. Hosp., Memphis, 1972-79, pres. bd. trustees, 1975-79. Served with AUS, 1942-45. Recipient Boy Scouts Silver Beaver award, Humanitarian award Dyersburg Jaycees, 1974; named Outstanding Businessman, Dyersburg C. of C., 1972. Mem. Tenn. Retail Mchts. Council (pres. 1967), Nat. Piggly Wiggly Operators Assn. (pres. 1964-65). Methodist (trustee Memphis conf. 1953-56). Rotarian (dist. gov. 1960-61). Home: 950 Troy Ave Dyersburg TN 38024 Office: 408 W Court St Dyersburg TN 38024

ROGERS, LEONARD GILBERT, corporate exec.; b. N.Y.C., July 11, 1929; s. Arthur and Julia (Gilbert) R.; student Westminster Coll., 1947-48, Syracuse U., 1948-49; m. Adelle Maureen McClendon, Mar. 21, 1959; children—Julia Lynn, Douglas Arthur, Laura Elizabeth. Pres., Rogers Inc., N.Y.C., 1951-69; v.p. allied products Consol. Cigar Corp., N.Y.C., 1969-70, v.p. internat. and corporate devel., 1970-71, v.p. internat. ops. and devel., 1972-73; sr. v.p. consumer products div. Gulf & Western Industries, 1973-74; chmn. bd. Todhunter Internat. Inc., West Palm Beach, Fla., 1974—; chmn. bd. trustees, pres. Wespac Investors Trust, 1975—. Mem. N.Y.C. Mayor's Com. for Youth, 1962. Mem. Nat. Assn. Tobacco Distbrs. (exec. mgmt. div.), Assn. Corporate Growth, Sigma Nu. Clubs: N.Y. Athletic; Beach (Palm Beach). Home: PO Drawer 0 West Palm Beach FL 33402 Office: 203-207 Commerce Bldg 324 Datura St PO Drawer O West Palm Beach FL 33401

ROGERS, LEWIS FRANK, educator; b. Meridian, Miss., May 31, 1939; s. Marion Dewitt and Birdie Mae (Dement) R.; A.A., Meridian Jr. Coll., 1959; B.S., U. So. Miss., 1961; Ph.D., U. Ga., 1979; m. Betty Martha Carlisle, Feb. 14, 1970; children—Kellie Elizabeth, Sean Lewis. Tchr., coach Jackson (Miss.) Public Schs., 1966-67; instr. sci. and electronics Meridian (Miss.) Jr. Coll., 1967-70; instr. U. Ga., Athens, 1970-74; asso. prof. geology and physics Gainesville (Ga.) Coll., 1974—. Served to lt. col. USMC, 1961-67. Decorated Air medal (7). Mem. Nat. Sci. Tchrs. Assn., Clay Mineral Soc., Marine Corps Res. Officers Assn., Res. Officers Assn., Marine Corps Aviation Assn., Phi Kappa Phi, Phi Delta Kappa, Am. Legion. Methodist. Home: Route 9 Box 286-A Gainesville GA 30501 Office: Gainesville College Gainesville GA 30501

ROGERS, LEWIS HENRY, environ. cons.; b. De Funiak Springs, Fla., Oct. 1, 1910; s. Henry J. and Ruby (Rose) R.; B.S. in Chem. Engring., U. Fla., 1932, M.A., 1934; Ph.D., Cornell U., 1941; m. Lucille Ellenberg, June 2, 1934; children—Mary Frances Rogers Rasmus, James Lewis. Faculty, U. Fla., Gainesville, 1934-48, prof., 1939-48; research supr. Union Carbide Nuclear, Oak Ridge, 1948-52; leader analytical div. Kraftco Corp., Research Lab., Oakdale, N.Y., 1952-54; sr. chemist Air Pollution Found., Los Angeles, 1954-58; with Automation Industries, West Orange (N.J.) Research Lab., 1958-69, dir., 1965-69, corp. dir. research and devel., Los Angeles, 1969-71; exec. v.p. Air Pollution Control Assn., Pitts., 1971-78; environ. cons. Gainesville, 1978—; sr. cons. Environ. Sci. and Engring., Gainesville, 1978—. Mem. tech. adv. com. Los Angeles County Air Pollution Control Dept., 1955-58; mem. sch. bd. Chatham Twp., N.J., 1960-63, pres., 1963; adv. com. Allegheny County Bur. Air Pollution Control, 1971-78. Served to maj. USAAF, 1942-46. Gen. Edn. Bd. fellow (Rockefeller Found.), Cornell U., 1940-41. Mem. Air Pollution Control Assn., Am. Chem. Soc., AAAS. Democrat. Club: Rotary. Contbr. articles to profl. jours. Home: 2607 NW 22d Ave Gainesville FL 32605 Office: PO Box 13454 Univ Sta Gainesville FL 32604

ROGERS, LOIS IRBY (MRS. RALPH WILLETT CARR), civic worker; b. Knoxville, Tenn.; d. James Harrison and Jane Rachel (Bolinger) Rogers; grad. Harriet Gregg's Pvt. Bus. Sch., 1940; m. Ralph Willett Carr, June 25, 1936; 1 dau., Sylvia Sue (Mrs. George Richard Gettys). Sec., TVA, Knoxville, 1938-63. Pres., Fountain City Grammar Sch. P.T.A., Knoxville, 1946-48, Chi-Omega Mothers Club, U. Tenn., Knoxville, 1957-58, Dixie Hwy. Garden Club, Knoxville, 1952-54, 65-67; state historian Tenn. Fedn. Garden Clubs, 1951-53, rec. sec., 1969-71, dir. IV, 1975-77, dist. membership chmn., 1971-73, ways and means chmn., mem. exec. com. Knox County council, 1971-72, gov. Racheff Park and Gardens, 1975—, life state mem., state parliamentarian, 1977-79; pres. Clionian Club, Lenoir City, Tenn., 1969-70; mem. women's com. Dulin Gallery Art, Knoxville, 1969—; chmn. all area chmn. East Tenn., 1964, membership chmn., Lenoir City, 1965-69; chmn. Dulin Dogwood Arts Festival and Auction, Knoxville, 1970-71; chmn. Knox County Hist. Zoning Com., Knoxville, 1973-74; treas. Knoxville chpt. Assn. for Preservation Tenn. Antiquities, 1966-68, membership co-chmn., 1969-70, pres., 1972-74, dir., 1975—; mem. Blount Mansion Assn., Knoxville, 1965—, Nat. Trust for Historic Preservation, 1972—; mem. Women's Guild Knoxville Symphony Soc., 1955—, area chmn. women's guild, 1966-67; area chmn. for Lenoir City for Met. Opera Co. and John F. Kennedy Performing Arts, 1967; bd. govs. Knoxville Civic Opera Co., 1979—. Asst. Teen Bd. Knoxville from Lenoir City, 1965—. Mem. Knoxville Heritage, Tenn. Bot. Gardens and Fine Arts Center. Club: Tuesday (pres. 1975) (Lenoir City). Address: Aquarell Beals Chapel Rd Lenoir City TN 37771

ROGERS, LON B(ROWN), lawyer; b. Pikeville, Ky., Sept. 5, 1905; s. Fon and Ida (Brown) R.; B.S., U. Ky., 1928, LL.B., 1932; L.H.D. (hon.), 1979; m. Mary Evelyn Walton, Dec. 17, 1938; children—Marylon Walton, Martha Brown, Fon II. Admitted to Ky. bar, 1932; practiced law in Lexington, 1932-38, Pikeville, 1939—. Dir. East Ky. Beverage Co., Pikeville, Pikeville Nat. Bank & Trust Co. Mem. Pikeville City Council, 1951; mem. local bd. SSS, 1958-69; mem. Breaks Interstate Park Commn., Ky.-Va., 1960-68, chmn., 1960-62, 64-66, vice chmn., 1966-68; chmn. Community Services Commn., Pikeville Model Cities, 1969-71; mem. Ky. Arts Commn., 1965-72, Ky. Travel Council, 1967-70, 73-75; pres. Ky. Mountain Laurel Festival Assn., 1971-72. Chmn. bd. trustees Presbytery Ebenezer, U.S.A., 1950-71; chmn. bd. trustees Pikeville Coll., 1951-72, 73-79, trustee emeritus, 1979—; sec. bd. trustees Presbytery of Transylvania, 1971—; mem. bd. nat. missions United Presbyn. Ch. Am., 1954-66; trustee Appalachian Regional Hosps., Inc., 1963-67, Ky. Ind. Coll. Found., 1973—; bd. dirs. Meth. Hosp. of Ky., 1966—. Mem. Ky. C. of C. (regional v.p. 1962-64, 69-74), Ky. Hist. Soc., S.A.R., Sigma Alpha Epsilon, Phi Delta Phi. Republican. Presbyn. (elder). Clubs: Kiwanis (past lt. gov.); Filson, Green Meadow Country, LaFayette, Blue Grass Automobile (pres. 1971-74, dir.). Home: 501 5th St Pikeville KY 41501 Office: PO Box 181 Rogers Bldg Pikeville KY 41501

ROGERS, LORENE LANE (MRS. BURL GORDON ROGERS), ret. univ. pres.; b. Prosper, Tex., Apr. 3, 1914; d. Mort M. and Jessie L. (Luster) Lane; B.A., N.Tex. State Coll., 1934; M.A. (Parke, Davis fellow), U. Tex., 1946, Ph.D., 1948; D.Sc., Oakland U., 1972; LL.D., Austin Coll., 1977; m. Burl Gordon Rogers, Aug. 23, 1935 (dec. June 1941). Prof. chemistry Sam Houston State Coll., Huntsville, Tex., 1947-49; research scientist Clayton Found. Biochem. Inst., U. Tex., Austin, 1950-64, asst. dir. 1957-64, prof. nutrition, 1962—, asso. dean Grad. Sch., 1964-71, v.p. univ., 1971-74, pres. ad interim, 1974-75, pres., 1975-79, mem. dean's adv. com. grad. fellowship program, 1966-71. Vis. scientist, lectr., cons. NSF, 1959-62; cons. S.W. Research Inst., San Antonio, 1959-62; mem. Grad. Record Exams. Bd., 1972-76; adv. com. Internat. Tel. & Tel. Corp. Internat. Fellowship, 1973—. Eli Lilly fellow, 1949-50. Recipient U. Tex. Students Assn. Teaching Excellence award, 1963; Distinguished Alumnus award N. Tex. State U., 1972, U. Tex., 1976; Outstanding Woman of Austin award, 1971; named to Austin's Outstanding Women, 1975. Fellow Am. Inst. Chemists; mem. AAAS, Am. Chem. Soc. (sec. 1954-56), Am. Inst. Nutrition, Am. Soc. Human Genetics, Assn. Grad. Schs. (internat. edn. com. 1967-71), Sigma Xi, Alpha Lambda Delta, Omicron Delta Kappa, Phi Kappa Phi, Iota Sigma Pi. Research in hydantoin synthesis, intermediary metabolism, biochem. and nutritional aspects of alcoholism, mental retardation, congenital malformations. Home: 4 Nob Hill Circle Austin TX 78746 Office: U Tex Academic Center 400 Austin TX 78712

ROGERS, MADELEINE BECK, banker; b. Piennes, France, Aug. 16, 1943; d. Pierre and Reine (Mangrolles) B.; came to U.S., 1963; A.A., San Jacinto Coll., 1974; B.S., U. Houston, 1978; m. Barry Rogers, Dec. 12, 1963. Tchr. French, Berlitz Sch. Langs., 1964; title clk., office mgr. Lou Ehlers Cadillac, Beverly Hills, Calif., 1965-67; v.p., cashier League City Bank & Trust Co. (Tex.), 1968—; instr. banking Alvin Jr. Coll., 1979. C.P.A., Tex. Mem. Am. Inst. Bankers, (chmn.), Nat. Assn. Bank Women, Am. Inst. C.P.A.'s, Tex. Soc. C.P.A.'s. Home: 16374 Larkfield St Houston TX 77059 Office: PO Box 759 League City TX 77573

ROGERS, MARY-JANE REGINA, librarian, educator; b. Pawtucket, R.I., Sept. 13, 1914; d. James L. and Amelia Marie (Barnes) Joels; A.B., Washington Square Coll., 1959; M.L.S., St. John's U., N.Y., 1961; m. Willis N. Rogers, July 4, 1952. Sec., U.S. Dept. Navy, Washington and Bklyn., 1938-55; asst. children's librarian then children's librarian Queens Borough Pub. Library, Jamaica, N.Y., 1961-64; librarian, tchr. Linden Jr. High Sch., St. Albans, N.Y., 1964-67, St. Andrew Sch., Orlando, Fla., 1968—. Mem. Catholic Library Assn. Club: Ret. Officers' Wives. Home: 559 The Villages Altamonte Springs FL 32701 Office: 877 Hastings Dr Orlando FL 32808

ROGERS, NATHANIEL SIMS, banker; b. New Albany, Miss., Nov. 17, 1919; s. Arthur L. and Elizabeth (Bouton) R.; A.B., Millsaps Coll., 1941; M.B.A., Harvard, 1947; m. Helen Elizabeth Ricks, July 3, 1942; children—Alice, John, Lewis. With Deposit Guaranty Bank and Trust Co., Jackson, Miss., 1947-69, 1st v.p., 1957-58, pres., dir., 1958-69, chmn. bd. dirs. 1st City Nat. Bank Houston, 1969—; pres. 1st City Bancorp. Tex. Inc.; dir. Standard Life Ins. Co., Lomas & Nettleton Fin. Corp., Gt. So. Life Ins. Co., Houston br. Chmn. Jackson United Givers Fund, 1957, pres., 1959, bd. dirs., 1958-61; pres. Andrew Jackson area council Boy Scouts Am., 1962; trustee Miss. Found. Ind. Colls., 1959-69; past pres., trustee Millsaps Coll.; trustee Methodist Hosp., Houston. Served to lt. (s.g.) USNR, 1942-46. Named Outstanding Young Man of Year, Jackson Jr. C. of C., 1955. Mem. Am. (pres. 1969-70), Miss. (pres. jr. banker sect. 1952-53; pres. 1964-65) bankers assns., Robert Morris Assos. (pres. S.E. chpt. 1954-55, nat. dir. 1959-62), Assn. Res. City Bankers, Jackson C. of C. (pres. 1962), Houston C. of C. (chmn. 1979-80), Young Pres.'s Orgn., Millsaps Coll. Alumni Assn. (pres. 1955-56), Newcomen Soc., Omicron Delta Kappa, Kappa Alpha. Methodist (chmn. ofcl. bd.). Home: 3631 Meadow Lake Ln Houston TX 77027 Office: PO Box 2557 Houston TX 77001

ROGERS, OMAR GERALD, guidance counselor; b. Watonga, Okla., Feb. 15, 1944; s. Omar Jesse and Katie Maxine (Bowman) R.; B.S.E., Emporia State U., 1969, M.S.E., 1972; m. Sharon Kay Morrow, Feb. 2, 1967; children—Odette Kilynn, Omar Gerald II. Tchr., Martin West Elem. Sch., Atchison, Kans., 1969-70; dorm supr. Wingate High Sch., Ft. Wingate, N.Mex., 1970-73; counselor Sherman Indian High Sch., Riverside, Calif., 1973-74, Tuba City (Ariz.) High Sch., 1974-78, Great Onyx Job Corps, Ky., 1978-79; head counselor Pine Knot (Ky.) Job Corps, 1979—; EEO counselor, 1974-78. Mem. Nat. Council Bur. Indian Affairs Employees Tchrs. Assn. (pres. 1976), NAACP, Am. Personnel and Guidance Assn., AWARE, Omega Psi Phi. Baptist. Club: Lions (pres. Tuba City 1976-77). Home: PO Box 758 Pine Knot KY 42635 Office: Pine Knot Job Corps Pine Knot KY 42635

ROGERS, PAUL (GRANT), lawyer, former congressman; b. Ocilla, Ga., June 4, 1921; s. Dwight L. and Florence (Roberts) R.; B.A., U. Fla., 1942, J.D., 1948; hon. degrees Albany Med. Coll., N.Y. Med. Coll., George Washington U., U. Miami, U. Md., Fla. Atlantic U., Nova U.; m. Rebecca Bell, Dec. 15, 1962; 1 dau., Rebecca Laing. Admitted to Fla. bar, 1948, U.S. Supreme Ct. bar, 1953, D.C. bar, 1978; mem. 84th-95th congresses from 11th Fla. Dist.; partner firm Hogan & Hartson, Washington, 1979—; mem. adv. com. on civil rules Jud. Conf. U.S. Mem. Pres.'s Commn. for Nat. Agenda for Eighties; mem. Inst. Medicine, Nat. Acad. Scis. Served to maj., F.A., AUS, 1942-45; ETO. Mem. Phi Delta Phi, Phi Delta Theta. Methodist. Club: Kiwanis. Home: 2800 N Flagler Dr West Palm Beach FL 33407 Office: 815 Connecticut Ave NW Washington DC 20006 also West Palm Beach FL

ROGERS, RALPH LACEY, hosp. adminstr.; b. Aiken, S.C., June 19, 1929; s. Lacy Badger and Bertha Ola (Kennedy) R.; B.A., Wofford Coll., 1952; m. Jeannette F. Tippins, June 5, 1955; children—William Michael, Mary-Lynn, Ralph Lee, Susan Jeanette. Hosp. adminstrv. intern McLeod Regional Hosp., Florence, S.C., 1953-56; bus. mgr. Onslow Meml. Hosp., Jacksonville, N.C., 1956; adminstr. Pender Meml. Hosp., Burgaw, N.C., 1957-62, Wallace Thomson Hosp., Union, S.C., 1962-68, Columbus County Hosp., Whiteville, N.C., 1968—. County chmn. Cancer Crusade, 1958-60; dir. Pender County Fair Assn., 1961-62; chmn. Union County ARC blood program, 1963-68; chmn. Cape Fear Health Four County Council, 1971-74; adv. com. Area Health Edn. Center, Wilmington, N.C., 1972—. Mem. N.C. Hosp. Assn. (Dist. V vice chmn. 1962), S.C. Hosp. Assn., N.C. State Hosp. Assn. (bd. dirs. 1979—), Am. Hosp. Assn. Democrat. Baptist. Clubs: Rotary, Lions (bd. dirs.). Home: 115 Jefferson St Whiteville NC 28472 Office: Columbus County Hosp Whiteville NC 28472

ROGERS, RICHARD LEHN, financial exec.; b. Decatur, Ill., Sept. 28, 1940; s. Ralph and Helen (Lehn) R.; B.S., Millikin U., 1961; B.S. in Mech. Engring., U. Ill., 1963; m. Kathleen Marie Marsh, Aug. 12, 1967; children—Erin Courtney, Julie Marie, Ronald Lehn. Aerospace engr. Boeing Co., Seattle, 1963-68; engr. and engring. mgr. aerospace div. Gen. Electric Co., King of Prussia, Pa., 1968-73; v.p. fin. counseling Consumer Econ. Services, Inc., Houston, 1973-78, pres., chmn. bd., 1978—. Republican. Methodist. Home: 5730 Wigton St Houston TX 77096

ROGERS, ROBERT JULIAN, banker; b. Tampa, Fla., Jan. 24, 1950; s. Robert Jackson and Lelia B. (Oxford) R.; B.A., U. S. Fla., 1972. Examiner, Fed. Home Loan Bank Bd., Atlanta, 1972-76; v.p. corporate planning First Fed. Savs. and Loan Assn. of Miami, 1976-77; sr. v.p. fin. and service corps. Orlando div. Am. First Fed. Savs. and Loan Assn., (Fla.), 1977—; exec. v.p. Am. Group One, Inc., Orlando, 1977—. Home: 1630 Lasbury Ave Winter Park FL 32789 Office: 455 S Orange Ave Orlando FL 32802

ROGERS, ROBERT LEE, oil and gas producer; b. Enid, Okla., Nov. 28, 1932; s. Truman Clifford and Bessie Laverl (Stienert) R.; B.A., Phillips U., 1954; m. Dorothy June Galyon, June 16, 1951; children—Janet Sue, Robert Galyon. Geologist, Sampson & Moore Oil Co., Wichita, 1954-55; cons. geologist, Garber, Okla., 1955-57; partner Sampson & Rogers Oil Co., Wichita, 1958-64; ind. oil producer, Enid, 1965—; dir. Central Nat. Bank & Trust Co. Enid. Mem. adv. bd. Salvation Army, Enid. Mem. Oklahoma City Geol. Assn., Okla. Ind. Producers Assn. Republican. Mem. Disciples of Christ. Club: Lions (pres.).

ROGERS, RODNEY PAUL, paper distbn. co. exec.; b. Mullins, S.C., Aug. 9, 1940; s. Robert Howard and Josephine (Rogers) R.; B.S., Clemson U., 1963; M.B.A., U. S.C., 1970; m. Mary LeVan Collins, Feb. 2, 1963; children—Angela René, Rodney Paul. Tchr. chemistry Bennettsville (S.C.) High Sch., 1963; with Package Products, Inc., Charlotte, N.C., 1965-68, prodn. control div. mgr., 1967-68; mktg. analyst Ethyl Corp., Richmond, Va., 1970-74; v.p., gen. mgr. Dillard Paper Co., Winston-Salem, N.C., 1974—; bus. advisor Forsyth Tech. Inst., 1975-79. Coach, referee Optimist Soccer League, 1976-79; bus. group campaign com. U. Richmond, 1974. Served to 1st lt. U.S. Army, 1963-65. Mem. Adminstrv. Mgmt. Soc., Winston-Salem C. of C., Beta Gamma Sigma. Methodist. Clubs: Symphony Guild, Little Theatre. Home: 100 Prestwould Dr Lewisville NC 27023 Office: PO Box 10519 Salem Sta Winston-Salem NC 27108

ROGERS, ROWENA ELIZABETH, nursing service adminstr.; b. Johnson City, Tenn., Oct. 22, 1925; d. Roy Monroe and Carrilee Mildred (Dyer) Rumley; B.S., U. Mid-Fla., 1972; m. Herbert L. Rogers, Apr. 21, 1946; children—Teresa Ann, Patricia Lee, Herbert L. Sec., Office Chief of Chaplains, U.S. Army, 1943, Doolittle Tractor Co., Jacksonville, Fla., 1946-47, Milam Acctg. Services, Jacksonville, 1948; unit mgr. Stanley Products, New Orleans, 1949-59; asst. adminstr., dir. nursing services Lake Highlands Retirement and Nursing Home, Lake Minnehaha, Clermont, Fla., 1959—; vol. nursing cons. Am. Cancer Soc.; mem. Bd. Examiners Nursing Home Adminstrn., 1978—. Mem. adv. bd. Lake Vo-Tech Sch., 1977—; pres. Fla. Council on Aging, 1973-74, Clermont Welfare League, 1970-71. Recipient Better Life award Fla. Nursing Home Assn., 1976; Diana award Epsilon Sigma Alpha, 1971; other awards Fla. Health Care Assn. Fellow Am. Coll. Nursing Home Adminstrs.; mem. Am. Nurses Assn., Fla. Nurses Assn., Assn. Seventh-day Adventists Nurses, Council Nursing Service Adminstrs., Council Nursing Home Nurses. Democrat. Seventh-day Adventists. Editorial bd. Jour. Geriatric Nursing, 1977—, Aging and Leisure Living, 1979—; contbr. articles to profl. jours. Address: 151 E Minnehaha Ave Clermont FL 32711

ROGERS, STANLEY FRANCIS, JR., physician; b. Houston, Nov. 9, 1920; s. Stanley Francis and Ledia (Monceaux) R.; B.A., U. of Houston, 1945; M.D., U. of Tex., Galveston, 1945; m. Marjorie Wiggs, Jan. 8, 1949; children—Deborah Rogers Carroll, Patrice Rogers Frank, Richard Stanley. Intern USN Hosp., Shoemaker, Calif., 1945-46; resident St. Joseph's maternity, Houston, 1948-49, Presbyn. Chgo., 1949-50, Free Hosp. for Women, Brookline, Mass., 1950-51; clin. prof. Baylor Coll. Medicine Houston, 1951-53; individual practice medicine specializing in Gynecology, Houston, 1953—; pres., founder Obstetrical and Gynecological Asso., Houston, 1953—; asst. chief gynecological services Methodist Hosp., 1955-75, chief gynecology audit com., 1960-72; clin. prof. Baylor Coll., Houston; founder, chief surg. services The Woman's Hosp. of Tex., Houston, 1975-77, chmn. of bd., 1975. Served as lt. with USN, 1945-52. Diplomate Am. Bd. Obstetrics and Gynecology. Mem. AMA, Tex. med. assns., Harris County Med. Soc., Am. Fertility Soc., Tex. Assn. of Obstetrics and Gynecology, Am. Assn. Gynecologists Laparoscopists and Microsurgeons, Houston Gynecological Obstetrical Soc., Houston Surg. Soc. Clubs: Sugar Creek Country, The University, The Doctor's. Contbr. numerous articles in field to profl. jours.; designer Rogers hysterectomy surg. clamps. Cons. films on surgical technique, advances in gynecology, infertility. Home: 25 Charleston Square N Sugar Land TX 77478 Office: 7550 Fannin St Houston TX 77054

ROGERS, THEODORE COURTNEY, diversified mfg. and fin. services co. exec.; b. Lorain, Ohio, Aug. 25, 1934; s. William Theodore and Leona Ruth (Gerhart) R.; B.S. in Social Sci., Miami U., Oxford Ohio, 1956; postgrad. Johns Hopkins U., 1957; M.B.A. summa cum laude, Marquette U., 1965; m. Adele Lee Woods, June 15, 1957; children—Pamela Anne, Theodore Courtney. With Armco Inc., Middletown, Ohio, 1958, gen. mgr. indsl. products group, 1973; pres. Olympic Fastening Systems, Downey, Calif., 1969, Bathey Mfg. Co., Plymouth, Mich., 1970, group v.p. Hitco, Irvine, Calif., 1970-73; exec. v.p. Nat. Supply Co., Houston, 1974-76, pres., 1976—, v.p. parent co., 1976—; group v.p. Armco Inc., 1979; pres., chief operating officer NL Industries, 1980—; dir. Parsons Corp., Bank of the Southwest. Div. chmn. United Fund, 1980, Houston, 77-79; gen. campaign chmn. Tex. Gulf Coast United Way, 1980; bd. dirs. Houston Met. YMCA, 1977-79; fin. chmn. Houston Explorer Scouting Program, 1977-78; bd. dirs. nat. bd. Palmer Drug Abuse Program, 1978, 79; bd. dirs. U. Tex. Health Center Devel. Bd., 1978-80, bd. dirs. Fisher Inst., Houston Ballet Soc., Houston chpt. Am. Heart Assn.; chmn. Houston Heart Fund, 1980. Served with USN, 1956-58. Mem. Petroleum Equipment Suppliers Assn. (bd. dirs.), Am. Petroleum Inst., Nat. Def. Preparedness Assn., Young Pres.'s Orgn., Nat. Ocean Industries Assn. (dir.), Kappa Phi Kappa, Beta Gamma Sigma. Clubs: Univ. (chmn. bd. govs. 1977-79),

Lakeside Country, Ramada, Sigma Chi Alumni, Miami U. Alumni (dir.). Home: 206 Millbrook St Houston TX 77024 Office: 1455 W Loop S Houston TX 77027

ROGERS, W.D., JR., broadcasting exec., former mayor; b. Waco, Tex.; ed. Baylor U.; m. Edith Tighe; children—Kerry Rogers Caddell, Kay Rogers Salem, Karol Rogers McMillan. Founder sta. KEYL-TV (now sta. KENS-TV), San Antonio, 1949, operator, 1949-51; founder Tex. Telecasting, Inc., 1951; founder sta. KDUB-TV, Lubbock, Tex., 1952; established West Tex. TV Network, 1956, operator, 1956-61; now pres. Rogers Broadcasting Co., Lubbock, Tremont Corp., Lubbock; mayor, Lubbock, 1966-70. Co-founder, past chmn. bd. TV Bur. Advt., N.Y.C., now chmn. emeritus; founder TV Stas., Inc., N.Y.C. organizer Automatic Program Logging for TV stas. to IBM. Mem. Tex. Council Higher Edn.; mem. adv. bd. Tex. Tourist Devel. Council; past chmn. Lubbock Auditorium-Coliseum and Civic Center, Inc.; past chmn. Citizens Adv. Com. City of Lubbock. Past. bd. dirs. Salvation Army, Lubbock, Tex. United Fund, Lubbock United Fund, Caprock council Girl Scouts Am.; past mem. adv. bd. Lubbock Christian Coll.; past trustee, chmn. pub. relations and devel. com. Meth. Hosp., Lubbock. Decorated Order Republic of Chad; named to Am. Hall of Fame, 1969; recipient Legion of Honor Order DeMolay, Outstanding Community Salesman award, 1970. Mem. Nat. Assn. Broadcasters (founder predecessor TV Assn. Broadcasters; past chmn. bd.), Soc. TV Pioneers (pres. 1957—), Assn. Broadcasting Execs. Tex., Young Pres. Orgn., Lubbock C. of C. (past pres.; past chmn. indsl. and econ. devel. com.), So. Plains Assn. Govts., Tex. Assn. Mayors, Councilmen and Commrs., Sales Execs. Club, Kappa Kappa Psi, Alpha Delta Sigma. Mem. Christian Ch. (deacon, chmn. ofcl. bd. 1974-75). Lion (mem. League for Crippled Children). Address: 6 First Fed Plaza PO Box 1475 Lubbock TX 79408

ROGGINGER, RONALD JOSEPH, advt. agy. exec.; b. Chgo., Mar. 19, 1932; s. John Charles and Florence Agnes (Cichy) R.; student U. Ill., Chgo., 1950-51, North Park Coll., 1954; B.S., Northwestern U., 1960; m. Dorothy Ellen Werner, July 15, 1977; 1 son, Richard Carl. With Import Motors of Chgo., 1960-65, advt. mgr., 1965; advt. mgr. N. Am. Van Lines, 1965-67; advt. mgr. Volkswagen Southeastern Distbr., 1967-69, pub. relations mgr., 1970-72; advt. mgr. Volkswagen of Am., Inc., 1969-70; gen. sales mgr. Porsche Audi at O'Hare, Elk Grove Village, Ill., 1972-73; account exec. Doyle Dane Bernbach, Inc., Jacksonville, Fla., 1973—. Bd. dirs. United Cerebral Palsy, Jacksonville, 1971. Served with USNR, 1953-55. Mem. Sports Car Club Am., Porsche Club Am. Home: 1260 Montego Rd E Jacksonville FL 32216 Office: Doyle Dane Bernbach Inc 2121 Corporate Square Blvd Jacksonville FL 32216

ROGILLIO, CARLYLE ALONZO, author, investor, pilot, oil co. exec.; b. Alexandria, La., Feb. 14, 1926; s. Alonzo Carlyle and Minnie Mae (Musgrove) R.; B.S., La. State U., 1950; m. Irene Marie Greco, Aug. 31, 1949; children—Carlyle Alonzo III, Clifford. Profl. writer, invester; comml. multi-engine land and sea plane pilot; various domestic and fgn. positions with major oil co. Flight ops. officer CAP, 1971-74; mem. vestry bd. Episcopal Ch., 1968-76; mem. Jefferson Parish Aviation Adv. Com., 1979—. Served with USAAF, 1943-45. Mem. Am. Petroleum Inst., Internat. Assn. Drilling Contractors, Pilots Internat. Assn., Nat. Pilots Assn., Smithsonian Assos. Home: 4913 Dreyfous Ave Metairie LA 70002 Office: PO Box 7 Harvey LA 70058

ROHE, JAMIE MARIUS, architect; b. Pasadena, Tex., Jan. 3, 1945; s. James Marshall and Billy Jean (Fields) R.; B.Arch., Tex. A&M U., 1968, M.Architecture in Interior Space Design, 1972; m. Vickie L. Nesom, Nov. 23, 1966 (dec. May 1979). Draftsman, Mies Van Der Rohe, Chgo., 1966; interiors draftsman Oglesby Group, architects, Dallas, 1972-73; head interiors Greener & Summner, architects, Dallas, 1973; prin. Rohe & Assos., Dallas, 1973-76, Concept Cons., Inc., architects, Dallas, 1976—; prin. works include Carl Barnett residence, Dallas, 1976, Nat. Mortgage Corp. Am. hdqrs., Dallas, 1978, Fitz & Floyd showroom, Dallas, 1979, J.P. Stevens Carpet Showroom, Dallas, 1979, Holly Corp. Offices, Dallas, 1980. Served with USNR, 1968-71. Recipient award Reynolds Aluminum Co. competition, 1968, Nat. Passive Solar Design award, 1978. Mem. AIA, Urban Rehab. League, Big Bros. Dallas, Childrens Arts and Ideas Found. Presbyterian. Home: 6863 Gaston Ave Dallas TX 75214 Office: 2911 Lemmon Ave E Dallas TX 75204

ROHLFING, DENNIS LEE, internal mgmt. cons.; b. Chester, Ill., Nov. 3, 1939; s. Albert and Esther C. (Meyer) R.; B.S., So. Ill. U., Carbondale, 1961; m. Alberta M. Hapke, May 3, 1958; children—Steven C., Richard D., Lauren K. With Phillips Petroleum Co., Bartlesville, Okla., 1961—, beginning as sales trainee, St. Louis, successively real estate rep., dist. rep., Jacksonville, Ill., city mgr., Peoria, Ill., mktg. asst., Bartlesville, asst. mgr. prices and supply, San Mateo, Calif., mgmt. adviser, Bartlesville, 1961-76, mgmt. advisor Phillips Chem. Co., Bartlesville, 1976-78, dir. mgmt. services, 1978—; guest lectr. indsl. engring. U. Okla. Mem. Okla. Govt. Reorgn. Commn., 1975; project leader Bur. Indian Affairs Mgmt. Study, Am. Indian Policy Rev. Commn., 1976. Recipient Service award State of Okla., 1975, Am. Indian Policy Rev. Commn., 1976. Mem. Am. Inst. Indsl. Engrs., Assn. Internal Mgmt. Consultants. Methodist. Clubs: Masons, Elks. Home: 2315 Chapel Hill Rd Bartlesville OK 74003 Office: Phillips Petroleum Co 16AIPB Bartlesville OK 74004

ROHR, ARTHUR WADE, stockbroker; b. Masontown, W.Va., Dec. 18, 1916; s. George W. and Minnie (Spiker) R.; student Cin. Conservatory, 1939; B.Mus.Ed., Shenandoah Conservatory Music, 1940; m. Julia Wynnyk, June 5, 1940; 1 dau., Julie Ann. Music supr., Pub. Schs., Kannapolis, N.C., 1939-50; South East sales rep. Targ & Dinner Chgo., 1950-54; mgr. Arthur Smith Music Co., Sarasota, 1954-69; founder, condr. Sarasota Concert Band, 1954—. Served with AUS, 1944-45. Named Nat. Music Mcht. of Year Nat. Assn. Music Mchts., 1962, (wife Julia Rohr) Sarasota County Patriot of 1976, Bicentennial Commn. Fla., 1976. Mem. Sarasota C. of C., Am. Fedn. Musicians, Am. Bandmasters Assn., Nat. Band Assn., Democrat. Presbyterian. Clubs: Kiwanis, Elks, Masons, Shriners, K.T. Home: 318 E Lake Dr Sarasota FL 33582 Office: PO Box 2780 Sarasota FL 33578

ROISMAN, JOSEPH, apparel mfg. co. exec.; b. Havana, Cuba, May 22, 1946; came to U.S., 1968, naturalized, 1973; s. Yudka and Sonia (Gibes) R.; grad. Orgn. for Rehab. and Tng. Vocat. Sch., Netanya, Israel, 1964; m. Aida Lubin, Jan. 4, 1970; children—Maurice, Regan, Michael. Asst. sales mgr. and southeastern rep. Carol Shoe Corp., Miami, Fla., 1969-70; salesman Supreme Internat. Corp., Miami, 1970-72, sales mgr., 1973-77, v.p. in charge of purchases and sales, 1977—. Served to sgt. Israeli Def. Army, 1967. Mem. Greater Miami Jewish Fedn., Cuban Hebrew Congregation. Jewish. Home: 6519 SW 113th Ave Miami FL 33173 Office: 7495 NW 48th St Miami FL 33166

ROLAND, CLARENCE NELSON, graphic arts exec.; b. York, Pa., Feb. 4, 1926; s. Clarence William and Alene Elizabeth (Seitz) R.; A.A., Rittenhouse Coll. 1948; B.S., Temple U., 1950, M.A., 1951; m. Mary Allyene McKinley, Sept. 30, 1947; children—Rhonda Allene, Rochel Mary, Randel William. Supt. Jackson Twp. (Ohio) Pub. Schs., 1951-52; librarian, head English dept. Imlay City (Mich.) High Sch., 1952-54; nat. sales mgr. Follett Pub. Co., Chgo., 1954-56, v.p., 1964-69; sales mgr. Simon & Shuster Pub. Co., N.Y.C., 1957-59; pres. R&R Sales Corp., Ridgewood, N.J., 1960-64; exec. v.p. Phillips Corp., Spring Grove, Ill., 1969-71; exec. v.p. J.Ruzicka-South Inc., Greensboro, N.C. 1972-77, pres. 1977—; cons. mgmt.; instr. mgmt. courses, 1957-71. Bd. dirs. Gen. Greene council Boy Scouts Am., Greensboro, 1975—, v.p., 1975-77, 79—; mem. Gov.'s Citizens' Adv. Com., Raleigh, 1978; mem. Nat. UN Day Com., 1979; mem. Carolina Theatre Commn. Served with USN, 1943-44. Recipient Recognition award Am. Library Assn. Exhibits Roundtable, 1967; Outstanding Service award Greensboro C. of C., 1974. Mem. ALA, Library Binding Inst., Nat. Assn. Businessmen (dir. 1976-77), Greensboro C. of C. (hon. life mem.; v.p. 1976), Temple U. Alumni Assn. (life). Democrat. Christian Scientist. Club: Moose. Home: 709 Westminster Dr Greensboro NC 27410 Office: 911 Northridge St Greensboro NC 27420

ROLING, RICHARD KEITH, pub. relations specialist; b. Troy, Ala., June 14, 1953; s. C. Freeman and Ellen (Miller) R.; student Stamford U., 1971-72; B.A., Troy State U., 1975. Reporter, Troy Messenger, 1970-72; mgr. Riverside Clothiers, Troy, 1972-75; dir. univ. relations Troy State U., 1975-78, dir. public affairs, 1978—; exec. asst. Dothan-Houston County C. of C., 1977-79. Pres. Dothan (Ala.) Community Concert Assn., 1977—. Mem. Council for Advancement and Support of Edn., Lambda Chi Alpha, Lambda Alpha Epsilon, Alpha Phi Omega. Baptist. Clubs: Dothan Advt. Fedn., Jaycees (bd. dirs. 1977—, state regional dir. 1978), Dothan Interclub Council (pres. 1979). Club: Rotary (internat. group study exchange to Australia 1979). Home: PO Box 1721 Dothan AL 36301 Office: PO Box 6947 Dothan AL 36301

ROLLINS, ALAN CHARLES, human services adminstrn., community social worker; b. Pittsfield, Mass., May 2, 1945; s. Charles and Mildred E. (Hayden) Warren; student Rockland Community Coll., 1964-65, McConnell Airline Sch., 1965, Daytona Beach Community Coll., 1969-71, Fla. Technol. U., 1971-72, U. Miami (Fla.), 1973, U. Ga., 1976, Fla. State U., 1979, Eckerd Coll., 1979; m. Sue Kathryn Curry, Dec. 28, 1968; 1 dau., Mariah. Community organizer Vista Vol., Ga., 1966-68; counselor Reality House, Daytona Beach, Fla., 1972-73, asst. dir., 1973-74; substance abuse counselor Human Resources Center, Daytona Beach, 1974-75; program planner and coordinator Mental Health Bd. Daytona Beach, 1975-76; exec. dir. Community Out-Reach Services, Inc., DeLand, Fla., 1977—. Chmn. City of Holly Hill (Fla.) Charter Rev. Commn., 1978-79; mem. Planning Bd. City of Holly Hill, 1977-78; pres. Young Democrats of Volusia County, 1978-79; bd. dirs. Wiser Women's Center, Daytona Beach, 1977-78, Miss Daytona Beach Pageant, 1979-80, Jr. Athletic Championship, 1978-79. Served with USN, 1962-63. Mem. Fla. Assn. for Health and Social Services (exec. bd. 1977-78), State Assn. Alcoholism Coordinators (sec.-treas. 1976-77), Fla. Assn. of Halfway Houses (dir. 1978), Am. Soc. Criminology, Nat. Assn. for Alcoholism Treatment Programs, Deland C. of C., Daytona Beach Jaycees (Man of the Year nominee award 1979), DAV, Alcohol and Drug Problems Assn. N.Am. Mem. Unity Ch. Home: 828 N Ridgewood Ave Ormond Beach FL 32074 Office: 442 E New York Ave DeLand FL 32720

ROLLINS, ALBERT WILLIAMSON, cons. engr.; b. Dallas, July 31, 1930; s. Andrew Peach and Mary (Williamson) R.; B.S. in Civil Engring., Tex. A. and M. U., 1951, M.S. in Civil Engring., 1956; m. Martha Ann James, Dec. 28, 1954; children—Elizabeth Ann, Mark Martin. Engring. asst. Tex. Hwy. Dept., Dallas, 1953-55; dir. pub. works City of Arlington (Tex.), 1956-63, city mgr., 1963-67; partner Schrickel, Rollins & Assos., land planners-engrs., Arlington, 1967—. Mem. Gov.'s Energy Adv. Council; chmn. Tex. Mass Transp. Commn.; bd. dirs. Tex. Turnpike Authority. Served as 1st lt. AUS, 1951-53. Registered profl. engr., Tex., La., Okla. Mem. Internat. City Mgmt. Assn., Nat. Soc. Profl. Engrs., ASCE, Am. Water Works Assn., Water Pollution Control Fedn., Sigma Xi, Phi Eta Sigma, Tau Beta Pi, Phi Kappa Phi, Chi Epsilon. Contbr. articles to profl. jours. Home: 3004 Yellowstone Dr Arlington TX 76013 Office: 604 Ave H East Arlington TX 76011

ROLLINS, CARL PADGETT, lawyer; b. Tallahassee, Fla., July 8, 1943; s. Mack A. and Perdita P. (Padgett) R.; A.B., Mercer U., 1964, LL.B., 1966; m. Carole Wyatt, Aug. 30, 1969; children—Henderson Wyatt, Elizabeth Padgett. Admitted to Ga. bar, 1966; law clk. Harris, Russell & Watkins, Macon, Ga., 1964-66; asso. firm McCamy, Minor, Phillips & Tuggle, Dalton, Ga., 1968-70, partner, 1970—. Bd. dirs. Big Bros. Assn. Dalton, 1968-76, pres., 1974; dist. com. Boy Scouts Am., 1969-72, dist. commr., 1970-72; bd. dirs. United Way of Whitfield County, 1971-73, v.p., 1972-73; chmn. Whitfield Health Planning Council, 1971-76; bd. dirs. Looper Speech and Hearing Clinic, 1972-74; bd. deacons 1st Presbyn. Ch. of Dalton, 1973-75, 77-79, chmn., 1975. Served to 1st lt., M.P., U.S. Army, 1966-68. Mem. Am., Conasauga Circuit bar assns., State Bar Ga., Cherokee Area Estate Planning Council (sec. 1977), Mercer U. Alumni Assn. (exec. com. 1976—, v.p.). Democrat. Clubs: Dalton Exchange (sec. 1970, pres. 1971), Dalton Golf and Country (sec. 1976, pres. 1977), Dalton Rotary (dir.). Home: 1602 Southmont Dr Dalton GA 30720 Office: 411 W Crawford St Dalton GA 30720

ROLLINS, SAMMIE LEE, systems analyst; b. Walls, Miss., May 26, 1951; s. Mattie L. Martin; student Reed Coll., 1969-71, U. Tenn., Knoxville, 1971-73; m. Janice Elaine O'Neal, July 7, 1979. Teaching asst. U. Tenn., Knoxville, 1971-73; customer engr., programming systems rep. IBM Corp., Louisville, 1973-76; systems cons. Mammoth Life Ins. Co., Louisville, 1976-77; systems analyst NCR Corp., Atlanta, 1977—, now telecommunications coordinator, project leader; lectr. Ind. U., Clarksville. Canvasser, voter registration. Mem. NCR Employees Assn. (pres.), IBM Club (past pres.), Ky. Cols., Am. Mgmt. Assn. Democrat. Methodist. Home: 1474 Dodson Dr SW Atlanta GA 30311 Office: 1587 NE Expressway Suite 100 Atlanta GA 30329

ROMAN, JESSE, nematologist; b. Cabo Rojo, P.R., June 18, 1931; s. Ramon and Adoracion (Toro) R.; B.S., U. P.R., Mayaguez, 1956; M.S., Auburn U., 1959; Ph.D., N.C. State U., Raleigh, 1968; m. Zaida Rodriquez, Dec. 26, 1956; 1 son, Jesse. Nematologist, Agrl. Expt. Sta., U. P.R., Rio Piedras, 1956—, acting asso. dir. Agr. Expt. Sta., 1979—. Mem. Soc. Nematologists, Orgn. Tropical Am. Nematologists (pres. 1971), Am. Soc. Agrl. Scis. (pres. 1974). Author: Fitonematologia Tropical, 1978; contbr. articles to profl. jours. Home: 242 Hortensia St Round Hill Rio Piedras PR 00928 Office: Dept Entomology Agrl Experiment Station U PR Rio Piedras PR 00928

ROMAN DE JESUS, JOSE COSME, anesthesiologist; b. Cabo Rojo, P.R., Dec. 22, 1934; s. Jose Roman Rios and Candida Rosa de Jesus; B.S., Universidad Autonoma, Guadalajara, Mex., 1952; M.D., Universidad de Madrid, 1958; m. Elizabeth Carlo, Sept. 29, 1957; children—Jose, Rosa, Carlos, Maria, Ernesto. Intern, Hospital de Damas, Ponce, P.R., 1958-59, resident in anesthesiology, 1960-62; resident in surgery Hosp. Auxilio Mutuo, Hato Rey, P.R., 1959-60; practice medicine specializing in anesthesiology, San German, P.R., 1962—; chief dept. anesthesia Hospital Concepcion, 1962-74; mem. Servicios Medicos de Anestesia, 1974—; sec. Importadora Mexicana, Inc.; v.p. Clinica de Cirugia Ambulatoria, Inc. Mem. Am. Soc. Anesthesiologists, Internat. Research Soc. in Anesthesia, Centro Medico de Mayaguez (hon.). Puerto Rican Socialist. Club: Deportivo del Oeste. Author: Glomectomy and Pulmonary Function Tests, 1964; Intravenous Regional Anesthesia, 1966; Postural Headache and Spinal Anesthesia, 1967; Ketamine: Clinical Experience, 1972; Pain: New Concepts, 1979. Home: 22 K St San German PR 00753 Office: Sol Esq Victoria San German PR 00753 also De Diego 52 E Mayaguez PR

ROMANIK, ROBERT JOHN, ins. co. exec.; b. Chgo., Feb. 24, 1946; s. Peter Anthony and Bernice Agnes (Rathnow) R.; B.A., DePaul U., 1968; m. Nancy Quintarelli, Nov. 27, 1971; children—Gina Elena, Robert John, Nicholas Peter. Prodn. supr. Ford Motor Co., East Chicago Heights, Ill., 1968-69; comml. lines underwriting supr. Kemper Ins. Group, Long Grove, Ill., 1969-74; v.p., asst. sec. Am. Bankers Ins. Group, Miami, Fla., 1974—. Mem. Am. Mgmt. Assn. Home: 8420 SW 142d Miami FL 33183 Office: 600 Brickell Ave Miami FL 33131

ROMANO, SAMUEL ANDREW, surgeon; b. Vicksburg, Miss., Nov. 25, 1906; s. Samuel Andrew and Mary Elizabeth (Dohler) R.; B.S., U. Notre Dame, 1928; M.D., Johns Hopkins U., 1932; m. Alice Josephine Colgate, Apr. 8, 1933; children—Samuel Andrew, Carole Colgate. Intern, Johns Hopkins Hosp., Balt., 1932-33; asst. in gynecology Tulane U., New Orleans, 1933-34; mem. staff Charity Hosp. La. at New Orleans, Touro Infirmary; teaching fellow surgery U. Minn., Mpls., 1934-35; instr. surgery La. State U. Sch. Medicine, New Orleans, 1935-38, asst. prof., 1943-50, clin. prof., 1950-77, clin. prof. emeritus, 1977—; cons. surgery VA Hosp., Biloxi, Miss., 1949-65. Diplomate Am. Bd. Surgery. Fellow A.C.S.; mem. AMA, La. State, Orleans Parish med. socs., New Orleans, James D. Rives surg. socs. Contbr. articles to med., surg. jours. Home: 1507 Dufossat St New Orleans LA 70115 Office: 1001B Pere Marquette Bldg New Orleans LA 70112

ROMANOWSKI, SONJA BILGER, social worker; b. Dallas, Nov. 23, 1940; d. Raymond Ernest and Elma Bettina (Bilger) Romanowski; B.A., H. Sophie Newcomb Coll., Tulane U., 1962; M.S.W., Tulane U., 1964. Social worker Hope Cottage-Children's Bur., Inc., Dallas, 1964-71, dir. intake, 1971-74, staff supr., 1974-78, supr. adminstrn., 1978—; field instr. U. Tex. at Austin, 1968, 69, Arlington, Tex., 1969-71, Tex. Women's U., Denton, 1972. Mem. Nat. Assn. Social Workers (treas. local chpt. 1970-72; chmn. Whitney Young meml. scholarship com. 1971-72, sec. 1973-75, state dir. 1979—; gen. co-chmn. 3d ann. state conv. 1978; Social Worker of Year Dallas 1979), Acad. Certified Social Workers, Nat. Register Clin. Social Workers, Mental Health Assn. (chmn. foster parent edn. task force 1980), Internat., Nat. confs. social welfare, Tex. Assn. Services to Children (sec. North Tex. chpt. 1972-73), Dallas Mus. Fine Arts Dallas Shakespeare Festival, The 500, Inc., Friends of Dallas Symphony League, Dallas Civic Music Assn., Delta Zeta (pres. Beta Upsilon chpt. 1961-62). Home: 5904 Sandhurst Ln No 147 Dallas TX 75206 Office: 4209 McKinney Ave Dallas TX 75205

ROMBOUGH, CHARLES THOMAS, nuclear engr.; b. San Rafael, Calif., Nov. 25, 1947; s. Kenneth Earl and Veronica Louise (Petkovsek) R.; B.S., U. Tex., 1969, M.S., 1970, Ph.D., 1975; m. Jane Ellen Stevenson, July 12, 1969; children—James Steven, Charles David. Physicist, Esso Prodn. and Research Co., Houston, 1969; sr. engr. Babcock & Wilcox, Lynchburg, Va., 1974-77, supervisory engr., 1977—, lead engr. devel. new on-line computer software, 1974—. Lay leader Marsh Meml. United Meth. Ch., 1977—; pres. Christian Workers' Sch., Lynchburg, 1977—. Served with U.S. Army, 1970-72. Registered profl. engr. Va. AEC fellow, 1969-70, 72-74. Mem. Nat. Soc. Profl. Engrs., Am. Nuclear Soc., Phi Beta Kappa, Sigma Pi Sigma, Phi Kappa Phi, Republican. Clubs: Am. Contract Bridge League, Am. Legion. Contbr. articles to profl. publs. Home: 108 Bonneville Pl Lynchburg VA 24501 Office: PO Box 1260 Lynchburg VA 24505

ROMERO, ORLANDO, mfg. co. exec.; b. Calexico, Calif., June 22, 1937; s. Jose Leopoldo and Marina (Flores) R.; B.S. in Commerce and Econs., U. Vt., 1962; M.A., U. of Americas, 1965; m. Lucy Tuna Eaton, Sept. 21, 1963; children—Veronica Yvonne, Orlando Rollie, Roberto Robbie. Market devel. mgr. Cyanamid Co., Wayne, N.J., 1963-65; mgr. mktg. and gen. sales House of Fuller, Mexico City, Mex., 1966-71; dir. mktg. and sales Premier Co., The Hague, Holland, 1971-74; v.p. Automotive Castings, Panama City, Panama, 1974-76; v.p. internat. div. N-S-W Corp., Houston, 1976-78; pres. Internat. Devel. Inc., 1978—. Served with U.S. Navy, 1962-63. Mem. Am. Welding Soc. Democrat. Roman Catholic. Club: K of C. Home: 2419 Meadow Way Missouri City TX 77459 Office: PO Box 686 Stafford TX 77477

ROMERO, RICHARD MICHAEL, coal co. exec.; b. Pensacola, Fla., Jan. 17, 1948; s. Richard and Anna Elizabeth (McLaughlin) R.; student Catholic U., Washington, U. Mo.; m. Toni Diane Harrison, Nov. 23, 1974; children—Michael, Christian, Paige, Erin. Bookkeeper, ACR Electronics Co., Westbury, N.Y., 1969-70; corp. staff Peabody Coal Co., St. Louis, 1970-75, mem. underground ops. services staff, Evansville, Ind., 1975-77, adminstrv. supr. underground ops. East div., Greenville, Ky., 1977-79; dir. adminstrn. and fin. Pyro Mining Co., 1979—. Republican. Roman Catholic. Mem. Lancer Yacht Assn., U.S. Yacht Racing Union. Home: 1121 Scherm Rd Owensboro KY 42301 Office: PO Box 267 Sturgis KY 42459

ROMERO-BARCELÓ, CARLOS, gov. P.R.; b. San Juan, P.R., Sept. 4, 1932; s. Antonio Romero and Josefina Barcelo; grad. Phillips Exeter Acad., Exeter, N.H., 1949; B.A., Yale, 1953; LL.B., U. P.R., 1956; m. Kathleen Donnelly, Jan. 2, 1966; children—Carlos, Andres, Juan Carlos, Melinda. Admitted to P.R. bar, 1956, thereafter practiced in San Juan; asso. firm Rivera Zayas, Rivera Cestero & Rua, 1958-62, partner, 1962-63; mem. firm Segurola, Romero & Toledo, 1963-68; mayor, San Juan, 1969-77; gov. P.R., 1977—. Pres., Citizens for State 51, 1965-67; a founder United Statehooders Group; a founder New Progressive Party, 1967, v.p., 1967, 1st v.p., 1971-74, pres., 1974—; mem. exec. com. Nat. League Cities, 1969-74, 2d v.p., 1974, pres., 1975; mem. exec. com. U.S. Conf. Mayors, 1970-74, adv. council 1974-77; mem. Nat. Adv. Council on Edn. Disadvantaged Children, 1976. Named Young Man of Yr., Jaycees, 1968. Mem. Nat. Govs. Assn., So. Govs. Assn. (vice chmn. 1979—). Office: Office of Governor San Juan PR 00901

ROMICK, MORRIS, data processing exec.; b. Ennis, Tex., Mar. 9, 1935; s. Harry B. and Sadie (Towb) R.; B.B.A., So. Meth. U., 1967, M.B.A., 1970; m. Lynn E. Sparks, Aug. 7, 1960; children—David, Mark, Jeffrey, Staci. Quality control supr., systems analyst/programmer Tex. Instruments, Dallas, 1965-67; data control supr., configuration control mgr., operating systems designer, cons. Collins Radio Co., Dallas, 1967-73; systems designer, software support mgr. Action Communications Systems, Dallas, 1973-75; tech. services mgr. Tex. Internat. Co., Oklahoma City, 1976-77; tech. services mgr., dir. systems planning ENSERCH Corp., Dallas, 1977-79; dir. computer services Lone Star Gas Co., Dallas, 1979—. Cons. United Fund; adult leader Boy Scouts Am., 1973—. Served with AUS, 1958-61. Mem. Temple Shalom Brotherhood (pres. 1973-74). Home: 7819 Briaridge St Dallas TX 75248 Office: 301 S Harwood St Dallas TX 75201

ROMINE, THOMAS BEESON, JR., cons. engring. firm exec.; b. Billings, Mont., Nov. 16, 1925; s. Thomas Beeson and Elizabeth Marjorie (Tschudy) R.; student Rice Inst., 1943-44; B.S. in Mech. Engring., U. Tex. at Austin, 1948; m. Rosemary Pearl Melancon, Aug. 14, 1948; children—Thomas Beeson III, Richard Alexander, Robert Harold. Jr. engr. Gen. Engring. Co., Ft. Worth, 1948-50; design engr. Wyatt C. Hedrick, architect/engr., Ft. Worth, 1950-54, chief mech. engr., 1954-56; pres., chief mech. engr. Thomas B. Romine, Jr., cons. engr. (now Romine, Romine & Burgess, Inc., cons. engrs.), Ft. Worth, 1956—. Mem. Plan Commn., City of Ft. Worth, 1958-62; mem. Supervisory Bd. Plumbers, City of Ft. Worth, 1963-71, chmn., 1970-71, chmn. Plumbing Code Review Com., 1968-69; mem. Mech. Bd., City of Ft. Worth, 1974—, chmn., 1976—; chmn. plumbing code bd. North Central Tex. Council Govts., Ft. Worth, 1971-75. Bd. mgrs. Tex. Christian U.-South Side YMCA, Ft. Worth, 1969-74; trustee Ft. Worth Symphony Orch., 1968—; v.p. Orch. Hall, 1975—. Served with USNR, 1943-45. Registered profl. engr., Tex., Okla., La., Ga. Fellow Am. Soc. Heating, Refrigeration and Air Conditioning Engrs. (pres. Ft. Worth chpt. 1958, nat. committeeman 1974—), Automated Procedures Engring. Cons. (trustee 1970-71, 75, 1st v.p. 1972-73, internat. pres. 1974), Am. Cons. Engrs. Council; mem. Nat., Tex. (dir. 1956, treas. 1967) socs. profl. engrs., Cons. Engrs. Council of Tex. (pres. North Tex. chpt., also v.p. state orgn. 1965, dir. state orgn. 1967), Starfish Class Assn. (nat. pres. 1970-73, nat. champion 1976), Delta Tau Delta, Pi Tau Sigma. Episcopalian. Rotarian. Club: Colonial Country. Author numerous computer programs in energy analysis and heating and air conditioning field. Contbr. articles to profl. jours. Home: 3232 Preston Hollow St Fort Worth TX 76109 Office: 300 S Greenleaf St Fort Worth TX 76107

ROMINGER, DONALD WILLIAM, JR., educator, coll. adminstr.; b. Shawnee, Okla., Feb. 27, 1940; s. Donald William and Winnie Anna (Townsend) R.; B.S., Okla. Baptist U., 1962; M.A., U. Okla., 1967; Ph.D. in History, Okla. State U., 1976; m. Janelle Morgan, July 14, 1974; children—Leslie Leigh, Anne Elizabeth, Robert Morgan. Tchr. public schs., Pottawatomie County, Okla., 1961-62; tchr., coach high sch., Commerce, Okla., 1962-65, Miami, Okla., 1965-66, Minco, Okla., 1966-68; instr., coach Northeastern Okla. A&M Coll., 1968-71; prof., coach McPherson (Kans.) Coll., 1973-78, athletic dir., 1977-79; dir. student devel. U. Sci. and Arts, Chickasha, Okla., 1979—. Mem. N.Am. Soc. Sport History. Republican. Baptist. Home: 139 Orchard Dr Chickasha OK 73018 Office: USAO PO Box 2598 Chickasha OK

RONCAGLIONE, CARL JAMES, orthopedic surgeon; b. Oak Hill, W.Va., Feb. 25, 1923; s. Louis R. and Hazel Jean (Burgess) R.; B.A., Emory & Henry Coll., 1943; M.D., Med. Coll. Va., 1951; m. Tommie Ballard McCoy, June 25, 1949; children—Tommie Sue, Margaret Kathleen, Carl James. Intern, Med. Coll. Va., 1951-52, resident in orthopedic surgery, 1952-56; practice medicine specializing in orthopedic surgery, Charleston, W.Va., 1956—; mem. staff Charleston Area Med. Center, 1956—, chmn. dept. orthopedics, 1976-77; mem. staff Thomas Meml. Hosp., chief orthopedic surgeon, 1963—; mem. staff St. Francis Hosp., 1956-70, mem. cons. staff, 1970—. Mem. W.Va. Bd. Edn., 1974—, sec., 1976, v.p., 1977, pres., 1978. Served to lt. USN, 1942-46. Diplomate Am. Bd. Orthopedic Surgery. Fellow A.C.S., Am. Acad. Orthopedic Surgeons; mem. W.Va. Med. Assn. (exec. council 1976-80), So. Med. Assn., Kanawha Med. Soc. (life, sec. 1977, v.p. 1978, pres. 1979), Eastern Orthopedic Assn. (sec. 1973-76), Tri-State Orthopedic Soc. (pres. 1976, 79), Southeastern Surg Congress, Pan Am. Med. Assn., Alpha Omega Alpha, Sigma Zeta. Republican. Baptist. Clubs: Masons, Shriners, Exchange. Contbr. articles to med. jours. Office: 414 Division St S Charleston WV 25309

RONDEAU, CHARLES FRANK, vocat. educator; b. Cable, Wis., May 16, 1941; s. Charles J. and Bernice K. R.; B.A., U. South Fla., 1974; m. Donna Sue Jeffery, Dec. 21, 1965; children—Kelly Sue, Leslie Marie. Contractor, Waterloo, Iowa, 1957-70; instr. Hawkeye Inst. Tech., Waterloo, 1970-71; cons. Jamaica Tourist Bd., Kingston, 1971-73; sales mgr. Green Giant Corp., Mpls., 1973-74; indsl. edn. coordinator Pinellas Vocat. Tech. Inst., Clearwater, Fla., 1974—. Mem. Am. Vocat. Assn., Fla. Vocat. Assn., Fla. Assn. Trade and Indsl. Edn., Kappa Delta Pi. Home: 2776 Terrace Dr Clearwater FL 33516 Office: 6100 154th Ave Clearwater FL 33320

RONDEAU, CLEMENT ROBERT, petroleum geologist; b. Ironwood, Mich., July 6, 1928; s. Clement Matthew and Beatrice Ida (Johnson) R.; B.S., Tulane U., 1955; m. Irmtraut Juliana Gretler, Aug. 7, 1949; children—Robert M., Stephen R., Paul H. (dec.), Charles R. Geol. supr. Texaco Inc., New Orleans, 1955-63; area mgr. Pubco Petroleum Corp., New Orleans, 1963-69; cons. petroleum geologist, Harahan, La., 1969—; owner Natural Gas Exploration Co., 1977—. Served with AUS, 1946-49, 50-51. Mem. Am. Assn. Petroleum Geologists, Soc. Exploration Geophysicists, New Orleans Geol. Soc., AAAS, Explorers Club, Ind. Petroleum Assn., N.Y. Acad. Sci., Internat. Platform Assn., Phi Beta Kappa, Sigma Gamma Epsilon. Democrat. Roman Catholic. Club: New Orleans Athletic. Home: 632 Stratford Dr Harahan LA 70123 Office: 958 Hickory Suite A Harahan LA 70123

RONDEAU, EDMOND PAUL, architect; b. Brockton, Mass., Dec. 7, 1945; s. Edmund Lewis and Helga (Johannsdoitter) R.; diploma archtl. drafting Chgo. Tech. Coll., 1964; B.Arch., Ga. Inst. Tech., 1969; m. Sarah F. Davenport, Apr. 15, 1972. Job capt., project architect Tomberlin Assos., Atlanta, 1973-75, Ferending/Grafton/Spillis/Candella, Architects, Atlanta, 1975; architect, partner Team Concept Design, Architects and Planners, Inc., Atlanta, 1975-76; architect Ladner & Co., Mobile, Ala., 1976-77; staff architect Auburn (Ala.) U., Office of Univ. Architect, 1977-80; constrn. mgr. Coca-Cola Co., Atlanta, 1980—. Served to 1st lt., C.E., U.S. Army, 1969-71. Registered architect, Ala., Ga., S.C. Mem. AIA (treas. Auburn chpt. 1979, v.p. 1980), Atlanta C. of C., Constrn. Specifications Inst., Soc. Campus and Univ. Planning, Inst. Urban Design, Tau Sigma Delta. Methodist. Club: Trinity Meth. Softball Team. Home: 1500 Scott St Opelika AL 36801 Office: PO Drawer 1734 Atlanta GA 30301

ROOD, RALPH EDWARD, lawyer; b. Washington, Ga., Nov. 7, 1943; s. Arthur Edward and L. Amelia (Golucke) R., Jr.; B.B.A., U. Ga., 1965; J.D., U. Miss., 1972; m. Cynthia Merriman Hooper, June 9, 1966; children—Virginia Hooper, Amelia Gordon. Admitted to Miss. bar, 1972, U.S. Supreme Ct. bar, 1977; mem. firm Gholson, Hicks & Nichols, Columbus, Miss., 1971—. Mem. E. Miss. Council, 1972—. Served to lt. USNR, 1966-69. Mem. Am., Miss. State Bar assns., Maritime Law Assn. U.S., Miss. Def. Lawyers Assn., Duck's Unltd., Columbus-Lowndes Hist. Soc., Columbus-Lowndes C. of C. (chmn. legis. Affairs com. 1974), Sigma Chi, Phi Delta Phi. Republican. Episcopalian (vestryman). Clubs: Columbus Country, Magowah Gun and Country. Editor: Miss. Law Jour., 1971. Home: 2801 Niles Rd Columbus MS 39701 Office: 605 2nd Ave N Columbus MS 39701

ROOKER, ROY LEE, JR., fin. exec.; b. Siloam Springs, Ark., Sept. 5, 1948; s. Roy Lee and Mary Elizabeth (Douglas) R.; B.B.A., Midwestern U., 1970; m. Lindal Kay Newby, Jan. 16, 1970; children—Denna Beth, Kimberlee Dawn. Staff acct. Montgomery & Hart, C.P.A., Graham, Tex., 1970-72; asst. corporate controller, group controller Stange Co., Chgo., 1972-74; asst. controller, supr. ops. analysis Gardner-Denver Co., Dallas, 1974-78; fin. v.p. Media Graphics, Inc., Dallas, 1978—; fin. and system cons. Served to 2nd lt., U.S. Army, 1970. Mem. Jr. C. of C. (treas. 1970-72), Delta Sigma Pi. Democrat. Methodist. Home: 2204 Parkhaven St Plano TX 75075 Office: 2175 Brangus Dr Irving TX 75062

ROOKER, RUBY JOYCE, librarian; b. Memphis, June 16, 1942; d. James Forrest and Ruby Neal (Williams) R.; student Itawamba Jr. Coll., 1963-65, Miss. State Coll. for Women, 1966-67, U. Houston, 1969, downtown campus, 1977—. Asst. to dir. Lee County Library, Tupelo, Miss., 1960-66; reference librarian Fort Worth Pub. Library, 1967-68; head librarian Pace Companies, Houston, 1969-77; mgr. tech. info. services Jacobs Engring. Group, Houston, 1977—. Mem. Spl. Libraries Assn., Assn. Record Mgrs. and Adminstrs. Office: PO Box 53495 Houston TX 77052

ROOS, EDWARD WILLIAM, ret. chem. co. exec.; b. Newark, June 20, 1910; s. John Peter and Katherine (Treffinger) R.; B.S. in Chemistry; m. Mildred J. Seagren, July 20, 1934; 1 dau., Judith D. With indsl. chem. div. Pitts. Plate Glass Industries, N.Y.C., 1943-75, mktg. (sales) account exec., 1954-75. Dir. pub. safety City of West Orange (N.J.), 1952-62; pres. West Orange Town Council, 1962-68; vice chmn. Essex County Republican Com., 1960, 62; chmn. bd. trustees W.O. Sr. Citizen Housing, West Orange, 1970-73; trustee Essex County Cerebral Palsey Assn., Camp Nejda Camp for Diabetic Children, First Presbyterian Ch. of East Hanover; mem. East Hanover Planning Bd.; pres. East Hanover Rep. Club; trustee 1st Presbyn. Ch. of East Hanover. Named Citizen of Year, Pitts. Plate Glass Industries, 1973. Mem. Essex County Police Adminstrs. (pres. 1961-62), Essex County League Municipalities (founder), Elected Ofcls. Essex County Assn. (pres. 1959-62). Republican. Mason (Shriner). Home: 2011 Castille Dr Spanish Pines Palm Harbor FL 33563

ROOSEVELT, GLENN ALLAN, clergyman, psychotherapist; b. Austin, Tex., Jan. 20, 1943; s. Douglas Vernon and Evelyn Ruth (Lowther) R.; B.A., U. Tex., Austin, 1966; M.Div., So. Bapt. Theol. Sem., 1971; M.S.S.W., U. Louisville, 1971; D.Min., Louisville Presbyn. Theol. Sem., 1978; m. Levitia Ann McLemore, July 28, 1968. Ordained to ministry Presbyterian Ch., 19—; chaplain, psychotherapist So. Ind. Mental Health and Guidance Center, Jeffersonville, Ind., 1971—, also co-dir., clin. dir., co-founder Louisville Poetry Therapy Inst., 1976—; poet, 1974—; contbr. to The Christian Century, Ky. Poetry Rev. Cert. Acad. Cert. Social Workers. Mem. Assn. Poetry Therapy (v.p. Ky. and Ind.), Nat. Assn. Social Workers, Fellowship of Reconciliation, Phi Kappa Phi. Democrat. Home: 608 Upland Rd Louisville KY 40206 Office: 207 W 13th St Jeffersonville IN 47130

ROOT, PAUL JOHN, cons. petroleum engr.; b. Pitts., Apr. 1, 1929; s. Eugene Robert and Hilda Amelia (Schmoker) R.; B.S., Pa. State U., 1952, M.S., 1954; Ph.D., U. Tex., 1961; m. Rosemary Clare Short, June 16, 1956; children—Christopher Robert, Paula Rose, Amy Jean, Marybeth. Natural gas engr. Consol. Gas Supply Corp., Pitts., 1953-55; instr. Pa. State U., 1955-56; asst. prof. U. Tex. at Austin, 1956-61; sr. research engr. Gulf Research and Devel. Co., Harmarville, Pa., 1961-65; asso. prof. U. Okla., 1965-70, prof., 1973-75; tech. dir. Nat. Gas Survey, FPC, 1970-73; dir. ednl. programs H. Zinder & Assos., Inc., Norman, Okla., 1975-77; pres. Petroleum and Geol. Engring. Inc., Norman, 1977—. Republican precinct chmn., 1970, rep. state party convs., 1967, 69. Served with AUS, 1946-48. Mem. Soc. Petroleum Engrs., ASME, Am. Soc. Engring. Edn., AAAS, Tau Beta Pi, Sigma Xi, Sigma Gamma Epsilon, Pi Epsilon Tau. Republican. Roman Catholic. Clubs: Univ. Univ. Okla. Patentee polymer injection process. Home and Office: 1839 Rolling Hills Norman OK 73069

ROPER, JOHN LONSDALE, 3D, shipyard exec.; b. Norfolk, Va., Jan. 19, 1927; s. John Lonsdale and Sarah (Dryfoos) R.; B.S. in Mech. Engring., U. Va., 1949; B.S. in Naval Architecture and Marine Engring., M.I.T., 1951; m. Jane Preston Harman, Sept. 29, 1951; children—Susan Roper Fuller, John Lonsdale IV, Sarah Preston, Jane Harman, Katherine Hayward. With Norfolk Shipbldg. & Drydock Corp., 1946—, now pres., chief exec. officer, dir.; pres., dir. Lonsdale Bldg. Corp., Marepcon Corp.-Internat.; v.p., sec. Schooner Point, Inc.; dir. John L. Roper Corp., Botetourt Bldg. Corp., Cruise Internat., Inc., Dominion Nat. Bank Tidewater, Maritime Terminals, Inc., Desert Am. Ins. Co. Dir. Tidewater (Va.) Devel. Council. Mem. adv. council Inst. Mgmt., mem. pres.'s council Old Dominion U.; mem. Norfolk Community Hosp. Commn.; bd. dirs. Norfolk State Coll. Found., Greater Norfolk Corp., United Communities Fund, Norfolk YMCA, Med. Center Hosps.; founding mem. Naval War Coll. Found. Served with USCG, 1945-46. Mem. Nat. Maritime Council (gov.), Am. Bur. Shipping (dir.), NAM (dir. So. div.), Shipbuilders Council Am. (dir.), Nat. Propeller Club U.S. (dir.), Soc. Naval Architects and Marine Engrs., Am. Soc. Naval Engrs., Chiselers Club N.Y., Am. Legion (trustee, past post comdr.). Episcopalian. Clubs: Virginia, Princess Anne Country, Norfolk Yacht and Country, Harbor of Norfolk, Norfolk Assembly, Cedar Point Country, Norfolk German. Home: 8005 Blanford Rd Norfolk VA 23501 Office: PO Box 2100 Norfolk VA 23505

ROPP, GUS ANDERSON, educator, chemist; b. Columbia, S.C., July 31, 1918; s. Gus Anderson and Dolores (Eargle) R.; B.S. in Chemistry, U. S.C., 1940; Ph.D. in Organic Chemistry, U. Tenn., 1949; m. Nancy Young, Dec. 19, 1966. Research scientist Union Carbide Corp., Oak Ridge, 1948-64; prof. chemistry Coker Coll., Hartsville, S.C., 1965—. USPHS-NIH Sr. Postdoctoral fellow Oxford (Eng.) U., 1955-56. Mem. Am. Chem. Soc., Am. Inst. Chemists, AAUP, Sigma Xi. Club: Toastmasters. Author: (with V.F. Raaen and H.P. Raaen) Carbon-14, 1968. Contbr. articles to profl. jours. Home: 301 Park Ave Hartsville SC 29550

ROQUE, JOHN LOPEZ, physician; b. Malaga, Spain, Jan. 22, 1941; s. Antonio L. and Luisa F. (Hildago) R.; came to U.S., 1966, naturalized, 1971; B.S., I.S. Isidoro, Spain, 1959; M.D. summa cum laude, U. Sevilla, 1965; m. Dora Kuwilsky, Jan. 29, 1966; children—Anthony, Victor. Intern Greater Balt. Med. Center, 1966-67; resident in internal medicine Sinai Hosp., Balt., 1967-69, chief med. resident, 1969-70, clin. fellow, 1970-71; research fellow endocrinology Johns Hopkins Med. Sch., 1971-72, chief div. endocrinology Univ. Hosp., Jacksonville, Fla., 1973—; asst. prof. med. U. Fla. Med. Sch., 1972-78, asso. prof., 1978—, acting chief dept., 1975. Served with Spanish Army, 1965. Diplomate Am. Bd. Internal Medicine. Mem. A.C.P., Am., Fla. med. assns., Duval County Med. Soc., Fla. Endocrine Soc. (v.p.), Jacksonville Internists Soc. (chmn. sci. programs 1974-75). Republican. Roman Catholic. Home: 3741 Cathedral Oaks N Jacksonville FL 32217 Office: Univ Hosp Jacksonville FL 32209

ROSADO, JOSE FRANCISCO, investment banker; b. Havana, Cuba, Nov. 27, 1948; came to U.S., 1960, naturalized, 1971; s. Jose Jesus and Maria Luisa (Blanco) R.; B.A., U. Miami (Fla.), 1970; M.B.A. summa cum laude, Fla. Internat. U., 1976; m. Cristina Falcon, Dec. 29, 1972; children—Victor Francisco, Javier Jose. Vice pres. acquisitions Fla. Atlantic Investments, Inc., Miami, 1976-78; pres. Shearson Properties Internat., Inc., Miami, 1978—; dir. Totalbank, Miami. Mem. Miami Bd. Realtors. Home: 7600 SW 72d Ct Miami FL 33143 Office: 2720 Coral Way Suite 400 Miami FL 33145

ROSAS-GUYON, LUIS ISIDRO, JR., mfg. co. exec.; b. Havana, Cuba, Dec. 18, 1947; s. Luis Isidro and Blanca Rosa (Pineiro) R.-G.; came to U.S., 1961, naturalized, 1970; B.S. in Elec. Engring., U. Miami, 1969; m. Elena Carmen DeVilliers, Dec. 27, 1969; children—Louis, Margaret. Engr., Bendix Corp., Fort Lauderdale, Fla., 1969-70; v.p. Instant Forms Ops., Inc., Miami, 1970-71; pres. Wattron Elec. Engring., Inc., Medley, Fla., 1971—; dir. Real Estate Devel. Co. Am., Discount Parts Corp. Mem. Dade County (Fla.) Zoning Appeals Bd., 1976—; chmn. adminstrv. com. Faith Methodist Ch., 1977—. Registered profl. engr., Fla. Mem. Am. Mgmt. Assn., IEEE, Fla. Engring. Soc. Democrat. Home: 7425 SW 127th Ct Miami FL 33183 Office: 10900 NW South River Dr Medley FL 33178

ROSE, BOBBY LEE, leather craftsman, store owner; b. Tazewell, Va., Mar. 29, 1944; s. Charlie Sam and Hazel F. (Bowling) Rose; ed. trade sch.; m. Lillian Rose; 1 stepson, Keith. Leather craftsman, Bland, Va., 1966—; owner, operator Leather Shop, Bland, 1966—. Home: Route 1 Box 366 Cedar Bluff VA 24609 101164 Route 2 BCC Bland VA 24315

ROSE, CHARLES GRANDISON, III, Congressman; b. Fayetteville, N.C., Aug. 10, 1939; s. Charles Grandison, Jr. and Anna Frances (Duckworth) R.; A.B., Davidson Coll., 1961; LL.B., U. N.C., 1964; m. Sara Louise Richardson, June 30, 1962; children—Charles Grandison IV, Sara Louise. Admitted to N.C. bar, 1964; chief prosecutor Dist. Ct., 12th Jud. Dist., 1967-70; mem. 93d-96th congresses from 7th N.C. Dist. Pres., N.C. Young Democrats, 1968. Presbyn. Office: 2435 Rayburn House Office Bldg Washington DC 20515*

ROSE, CHARLES HENRY, JR., steel co. exec.; b. Ft. Worth, June 8, 1919; s. Charles Henry and Maybelle Neal (Connor) R.; student Centenary Coll., 1937-40; B.B.A., U. Tex., 1949; m. Leatha Louise Hogan, Apr. 19, 1942; children—Dianne Louise (Mrs. Lawrence K. McCollum), Donna (Mrs. Edwin Lowe Gouedy, Jr.). Estimator, Indsl. Steel Products Co., Shreveport, La., 1949-56, sales engr., 1956-69, v.p., 1969—. Served to maj. USAAF, 1940-45. Mem. Constrn. Specifications Inst. (treas. local chpt. 1974-75), Am. Legion, U.S., Shreveport (Outstanding Achievement award 1973) chambers of commerce. Republican. Methodist (ofcl. bd.). Rotarian. Home: 702 Ontario St Shreveport LA 71106 Office: 3440 McWillie St Shreveport LA 71103

ROSE, CHARLES ROBERT FLETCHER, fin. co. exec.; b. Richmond, Va., Sept. 7, 1938; s. Charles and Aline Priscilla (Lindsey) R.; student U. Va., 1956-58; cert. Smithdeal Massey Bus. Coll., 1959; cert. acctg. U. Richmond, 1965, B.C., 1969; m. Joanne Simmons Hartman, June 25, 1960; 1 son, Charles Douglas. Bookkeeper The Furniture Studio, Inc., Richmond, 1959; acct. Via Co. & Via Constrn. Co., Richmond, 1959-60, sec., treas. 1960-61; acct. Albemarle Paper Mfg. Co., Richmond, 1961-62, asst. cost acct., 1963, cost acctg. supr., 1964-65, budget acct., 1965, chief budget acct., 1965-66, budget dir., 1966-68, mgr. systems and data processing, 1968-69, corp. controller and asst. sec.-treas., 1969-72; mill controller and asst. corp. sec. Hoerner Waldorf Corp., St. Paul, 1969-72; asst. corp. controller Chesapeake Corp. of Va., 1972-74, corp. controller, 1974—. Treas., Roanoke Rapids ARC, 1971-72; treas. Roanoke Rapids area United Givers Fund, 1971-72; pres. West Point (Va.) Ecumenical Choir, 1974-75; treas. United Meth. Ch., West Point, 1977—; sec. Roanoke Rapids Diamond Jubilee, Va., 1972. Served with Va. N.G., 1962-68. Mem. Planning Execs. Inst. (pres. Richmond chpt. 1969), West Point Country Club Estates Assn. (dir. 1975-78), Cross Keys (pres. 1967). Club: West Point Country. Home: 607 Mocking Bird Ct West Point VA 23181 Office: The Chesapeake Corp of Va PO Box 311 West Point VA 23181

ROSE, ELIZABETH, educator; b. Aiken County, S.C., Dec. 20, 1927; d. Elvin and Julia (Williams) McMillan; B.S., Claflin Coll., 1950; M.A., N.Y. U., 1959; postgrad. S.C. State U., 1958, 61, Ind. U., 1968; m. Arthur Rose, Aug. 31, 1948; children—Patricia Rose Frasier, Arthur, Bernard, Marcia. Tchr., Brewer High Sch., Greenwood, S.C., 1950-51; mem. faculty Claflin Coll., Orangeburg, S.C., 1954-66, 68—, asst. prof. 1969—, dir. phys. edn., 1972—; data processing traffic research Ind. U., summer 1967; dir. inservice recreational program, recreation dir. Upward Bound. First aid instr. Orangeburg County chpt. ARC. Mem. Nat. Alliance Health, Phys. Edn. and Recreation, S.C. Assn. Health, Phys. Edn. and Recreation, Daus. of Isis, Zeta Phi Beta (asso. dir. 1969-72). Methodist. Home: 385 Boulevard NE Orangeburg SC 29115 Office: College Ave Orangeburg SC 29115

ROSE, JACQUELINE CAROLE, architect; b. Phila., Apr. 2, 1942; d. David Morris and Betty Lorraine (Gelb) R.; student Rensselaer Poly. Inst., 1963-64; B.Arch., U. Okla., 1978, B.S. in Environ. Design, 1978; B.S. in Liberal Studies, SUNY, 1978. Pvt. practice architecture, Kansas City, Mo., 1971-73; planner/designer URS/Hewitt & Royer, Inc., Architects-Engrs.-Planners, Kansas City, 1973-75; cons./chief planner Sci. Mus. of Va., Richmond, 1976-77; cons. in arch. research, Alexandria, Va., 1978-79; architect Office of Sec. for Facilities Engring., HEW, Washington, 1980—; dir. Broadway-Westport Neighborhood Devel. Corp., Kansas City, 1973-75; vis. lectr. Cornell U. Sch. Architecture, Ithaca, N.Y., 1977, 78, Washington, 1979, U. Va., 1977, U. Mo. Sch. Law, 1974, U. Kans. Sch. Law, 1974, Va. Commonwealth U., 1977. Mem. Mo. Adv. Council on Hist. Preservation, 1974-75; mem. Landmarks Commn., Kansas City, 1970-75; mem. total transp. policy com., citizens adv. bd. Mid-Am. Regional Council of Govts., 1973-75, transp. tech. review com., 1975. Registered architect, Mo. Mem. AIA (nat. com. hist. resources 1975-78, nat. com. regional devel. and natural resources 1978—), Nelson/Atkins Gallery of Art, Soc. of Fellows. Home: 6491 Frenchmens Dr Apt 101 Alexandria VA 22312 Office: 330 Independence Ave SW Washington DC 20201

ROSE, MARK STEPHEN, petroleum engr.; b. San Francisco, Apr. 22, 1949; s. Rudolph Nicholas and Alberta (Spell) R.; B.S., La. State U., 1971; m. Mary Ashleigh Mingee, Dec. 22, 1970; children—Katherine Ashleigh, Rebecca Julia. Asso. petroleum engr. Gulf Oil Co., Lafayette, La., 1971-72, petroleum engr. Jackson, Miss., 1972-73, Houston, 1973-75, sr. petroleum engr., Morgan City, La., 1976, area engr., Morgan City, 1977, tech. mgr. Cabinda Gulf Oil Co., Angola, 1977-78, chief utilization engr., New Orleans, 1978—; rep. U.S. Prodn. Dept. to Gulf Faculty Forum, 1975; speaker Gulf Vital Source Program, 1975—. Counselor, Jr. Achievement program, Houston, 1973-75. Mem Am. Petroleum Inst., Am. Inst. Mining, Metall. and Petroleum Engrs., Pi Kappa Phi. Republican. Methodist. Home: 810 Freedom Ln Slidell LA 70458 Office: Gulf Oil Co E & P PO Box 61590 New Orleans LA 70161

ROSE, RUPERT HUGHES, ry. exec.; b. Smithfield, N.C., Sept. 17, 1926; s. Garland Mills and Eunice (Creech) R.; B.A., King's Bus. Coll., Raleigh, N.C., 1947; m. Julia Anne Perry, June 24, 1950; children—Rupert Hughes, Patricia Anne. Staff traffic dept. So. Ry., Raleigh, N.C., 1947-50; dist. sales mgr. Seaboard Air Line R.R., Jacksonville, Fla., 1951-68; gen. mgr. traffic Richmond,

Fredericksburg & Potomac R.R. Co., Richmond, Va., 1968—. Served with U.S. Army, 1952-54. Mem. Nat. Freight Transp. Assn., Nat. Def. Transp. Assn. Republican. Baptist. Clubs: Pinnacle (N.Y.C.), Willow Oaks Country (Richmond). Home: 8627 Chippenham Rd Richmond VA 23235 Office: Richmond Fredericksburg & Potomac RR Co 2134 W Laburnum Ave Richmond VA 23227

ROSE, SHIRLEY ELIZABETH, ednl. adminstr.; b. Miss., Apr. 8, 1936; d. Earl William and Gladys Dora (Patterson) Corley; B.S., U. Houston, 1960, M.Ed., 1968, Ed.D., 1973; m. Donald Malcolm Rose, Nov. 24, 1959. Secondary tchr. Houston Ind. Sch. Dist., 1960-63; Clear Creek Ind. Sch. Dist., League City, Tex., 1963-64, Austin (Tex.) Ind. Sch. Dist., 1964-67; dir. instructional services Harris County (Tex.) Dept. Edn., 1973-78, asst. county sch. supt., 1978—; mem. undergrad. studies com. U. Houston, 1977-79; mem. community adv. bd. for gifted and talented programs Houston Ind. Sch. Dist.; mem. adv. bd. Law Enforcement and Criminal Justice Magnet Sch., Houston Ind. Sch. Dist. Mem. edn. adv. com. Houston Clean Cities Commn., 1979. Mem. Am. Assn Sch. Adminstrs., Tex. Assn. Sch. Adminstrs., Assn. Supervision and Curriculum Devel., Tex. Assn. Supervision and Curriculum Devel., Nat. Council Social Studies, Tex. Council Social Studies, Kappa Delta Pi, Phi Delta Kappa. Contbr. articles to profl. jours. Office: 6515 Irvington Houston TX 77022

ROSE, WILLIAM LOUIS, bus. cons.; b. Michigan City, Ind., Oct. 10, 1925; s. Sylvan Meyer and Mary Kathern (Deets) R.; B.S. in Elec. Engring., Purdue U., 1950; m. Eileen Margaret Meyn, June 18, 1947; children—Karin S., Kim E., Jeffrey W., Mark G. Project mgr. Cape Kennedy, 1950-55; exec. v.p., founder Milgo Electric Corp., Miami, Fla., 1955-67, dir., 1955-67; pres. Sunair Electric Corp., Ft. Lauderdale, Fla., 1967-71, dir., 1967-71; founder, pres. Rose Internat., Inc., Miami, 1971-76, dir., 1971-76; pvt. practice bus. cons., Plantation, Fla., 1977—; chmn. bd. William L. Rose & Assos., 1978—, Precision Electronics & Instruments, Delray Beach, Fla., 1978—. City councilman City of Eau Gallie (Fla.), 1954-55; dir. Channel 2, ETV, Miami, 1962-66; mem. Tax Rev. Bd. Dade County, 1964; scout master Boy Scouts Am., 1965-75; mem. Policy Advisory Committee Fla., 1975-76; sr. warden Episcopal Ch. Served in USNR, 1943-46; PTO. Named Young Man of Yr., Jr. C. of C., 1954. Mem. Am. Mgmt. Assn., Asso. Industries Fla., Am. Ordnance Assn., Inst. Asso. Industries. Republican. Clubs: Kiwanis, Lions. Home and Office: 531 N University Dr Plantation FL 33324

ROSEBERRY, CHARLENE GRACE, buyer; b. Dunsar, W.Va., Oct. 16, 1927; d. Leonard Everett and Elva Mae (Stover) Hughes; children—Debra Ann, Karen Sue, Joe Robert. Asst. bookkeeper, office mgr. Dominion Oil & Gas Assn., 1962-63; with Columbia Gas Transp. Corp., Charleston, W.Va., 1963—, buyer, 1974—. Mem. Tri-State Purchasing Mgmt. Assn. Baptist. Home: 710 Oaks St South Charleston WV 25302 Office: 1700 McCorkle Ave Charleston WV 25304

ROSEKRANS, CHARLES STETSON, conductor; b. San Francisco, Aug. 4, 1934; s. John Newton and Alma Emma (Spreckels) R.; B.A., U. Calif., Berkeley, 1956; postgrad. Mannes Sch. Music, 1958. Prin. conductor, music dir. Houston Grand Opera, 1958-75; founder, conductor Houston Chamber Orch., 1964-76; conductor Houston Ballet, 1972-78; music dir., conductor Charlotte (N.C.) Opera, 1968—; conductor Theatre Under the Stars, Houston, 1974—, N.C. Opera, 1979—, Dallas Ballet, 1979—; conductor Brevard Music Center, 1965-72, Chautauqua Opera, 1961-64, San Francisco Spring Opera, 1963-66; guest conductor opera, symphonic music, ballet, operetta and mus. comedy with orchs. throughout U.S. Served with U.S. Army, 1957. Office: 110 E 7th St Charlotte NC 28202

ROSELAND, PAUL LUTHER, interior designer, artist; b. Viroqua, Wis., May 11, 1917; s. Luther M. and Alida B. (Anderson) R.; student Augsburg Coll., 1935-37; B.A., U. Minn., 1941; M.F.A., U. So. Calif., 1960; postgrad. U. Mexico, 1937, U. Cal. at Los Angeles, 1959; m. Evelyn Marie Sandberg, Aug. 30, 1942; children—Nancy Lynn, Paul Luther. Exhibited one-man show at Tex. Woman's U., 1962; exhibited two man show at U. So. Calif., 1960; exhibited group shows at Ball State Coll., 1961, Beaumont Art Mus., 1961, S.W. Am. Painting and Sculpture, Okla., 1962; represented in permanent collections at City of Los Angeles, also pvt. collections; regional mgr. Knoll Internat., N.Y.C., 1945-49; mgr. Western states Herman Miller Inc., Zeeland, Mich., 1949-59; asso. prof. art Tex. Womens U., 1961-67; prof. art Tex. Technol. U., Lubbock, 1968-71; mgr. ion div. Am. Desk Mfg. Co., Temple, Tex., 1972-74; propr. Roseland Orgns., Temple, 1975-78; with Corps Engrs., Ft. Worth, 1978—; vis. prof. design Ohio U., 1967-68. Served from ensign to lt., USNR, 1942-45. Mem. Am. Soc. Interior Designers. Lutheran. Address: 3119 Camp Bowie Blvd Suite 76 Fort Worth TX 76107

ROSENBAUM, MARCOS, physicist; b. Mexico City, Feb. 26, 1935; s. Gerson and Fanny (Pitluck) R.; B.S., U. Mexico, 1957; M.S. in Engring., U. Mich., 1959, Ph.D., 1963; m. Meryem Emir, Aug. 18, 1965; 1 dau., Tamara. Research asst. U. Mich., 1961-63, research asso., 1963-64; mem. research staff Gen. Elec. Tempo Center for Advanced Studies, Santa Barbara, Calif., 1964-71; research prof., dir. center for nuclear studies U. Mexico, Mexico City, 1976—; cons. Nat. Inst. for Nuclear Energy. Mem. Mexican Acad. Sci., Am. Phys. Soc., AAAS, Sociedad Mexicana de Fisica, Sigma Xi. Jewish. Contbr. articles to sci. jours.; co-author: Mathematics and Reality, 1970. Home: Manantial 128 Mexico 20 DF Mexico Office: Centro de Estudios Nucleares UNAM Circuito Exterior CU Mexico 20 DF Mexico

ROSENBERG, DENNIS MELVILLE LEO, surgeon; b. Johannesburg, South Africa, Jan. 27, 1921; s. Nathan and Dorothy (Lee) R.; B.Sc. with honors, U. Witwatersrand, South Africa, 1941, M.B., B.Ch., 1945; m. Jeanna Van der Kar, Jan. 1947. Came to U.S., 1946, naturalized, 1953. Intern Johanesburg Gen. Hosp., 1946; resident in surgery Tulane U. Ochsner Found. Hosp., New Orleans, 1947-51, Childrens Hosp., Johannesburg, 1952; asst. thoracic surgeon Biggs Hosp., Ithaca, N.Y., 1953-54; practice medicine, specializing in cardiovascular and thoracic surgery, New Orleans, 1955—; sr. surgeon Touro Infirmary, New Orleans, 1955—, chief dept. cardiovascular and thoracic surgery, 1972—; surgeon East Jefferson Gen. Hosp., Metairie, La., 1970—, St. Charles Gen. Hosp., New Orleans, 1972—; sr. vis. surgeon Charity Hosp., New Orleans, 1962—; sr. investigator Touro Research Inst., 1964—. Served with M.C., S. African Army, 1940-45. Fellow A.C.S., Am. Coll. Chest Physicians; mem. Am. Coll. Cardiology, AMA, Am. Heart Assn., Am. Assn. Thoracic Surgery, So. Thoracic Surg. Assn., Internat. Cardiovascular Soc., Am. Thoracic Soc., Soc. Thoracic Surgeons, Soc. Vascular Surgery, Soc. Internationale de Chirugie, So. Assn. Vascular Soc. Home: 3115 Prytania St New Orleans LA 70115 Office: 3600 Prytania St New Orleans LA 70115

ROSENBERG, LEON JOSEPH, educator; b. Atlanta, Oct. 9, 1918; s. Harry Manville and Gertrude Dora (Hassenbusch) R.; B.S. in Indsl. Mgmt., Ga. Inst. Tech., 1939; M.S. (univ. scholar), Columbia U., 1940; Ph.D., N.Y. U., 1967; m. Phylis Jane Israel, Feb. 6, 1943; children—Joanne (Mrs. Donald W. Wilson), Paul Harvey; m. 2d, Louise M. Nachman, Oct. 15, 1977. Sr. research analyst Federated Dept. Stores, Inc., Cin., 1949-52; research dir. Sanger Bros. Dept. Store, Dallas, 1952-56; gen. supt. Sanger-Harris Dept. Store, Dallas, 1956-67; asso. prof. Coll. Bus. Adminstrn., U. Ark., Fayetteville, 1967-74, prof., 1975—; bus. cons. Pres., Dal-Worth Shippers Assn., 1964-66, Jewish Family Service, Dallas, 1960-62. Served to capt. USAAF, 1940-46. Mem. Am. Mktg. Assn., Nat. Council Phys. Distbn. Mgmt., Jewish Welfare Fedn. (exec. com. Dallas chpt. 1963-67), Alpha Phi Omega (adviser 1970-72), Beta Gamma Sigma, Alpha Kappa Psi. Jewish. Clubs: Masons, B'nai B'rith. Author: Sangers' Pioneer Texas Merchants, 1978; contbr. articles to profl. jours. Home: 1124 Lakefront Dr Fayetteville AR 72701

ROSENBERG, RAYMOND, chem. co. exec.; b. Chgo., June 19, 1921; s. William and Sophia (Rothman) R.; B.S. in Chem. Engring., Tex. A. and M. U., 1947; m. Florence Rose Corenblith, Dec. 5, 1948; children—Barbara Elaine, Marsha Yvonne, William Harry. Research and devel. engr. Tin Processing Co., Texas City, Tex., 1947-52; process engr. Monsanto Co., Texas City, 1952-55, sr. process engr., 1955-57, ops. supr., 1957-66, mfg. supt., 1966-78; dir. tech., engring. and mfg. Chem. div. Alscondel SA/Monsanto-Iberica, Barcelona, Spain, 1978—. Mem. adv. bd. Coll. Mainland Theatre, 1973-78. Served to capt. AUS Chem. Warfare Service, 1943-46; ETO. Decorated Bronze Star medals. Registered profl. engr. Mem. Am. Inst. Chem. Engrs. Patentee in field. Home: 1406 19th Ave N Texas City TX 77590 Office: 800 N Lindbergh Blvd 5370 Saint Louis MO 63166

ROSENBLUM, HAROLD, elec. engr.; b. Paterson, N.J., Mar. 30, 1918; s. Joseph and Sadie (Rozman) R.; B.Ch.E., Cooper Union, 1943; M.E.E., N.Y. U., 1951; m. Hannah B. Wrubel, June 15, 1941; children—Lawrence, Susan Rosenblum Shevitz, Ira. Head radar systems sect. N.Y. Naval Shipyard, Bklyn., 1947-54; head flight trainers br. Naval Tng. Equipment Center, Orlando, Fla., 1954-57, head air tactics br., 1957-60, strike-air def. systems trainers dept., 1960-65, aerospace systems trainers dept., 1965-67, asst. tech. dir., 1967-69, dep. dir. engring., 1969-74; cons. mgmt. engring., Orlando, 1974-77; dir. tech. mktg. Applied Devices Corp., 1977-79; mgr. tng. systems Advanced Tech., Inc., 1979-80; prin. staff cons. Singer-Link div., 1980—. Bd. dirs. Congregation Ohev Shalom, Orlando, 1969-77, Marathon Jewish Community Center, Douglaston, N.Y., 1960-64, Temple Israel, Orlando, 1966-69; dir. sci. projects North Shore Hebrew Acad., Gt. Neck, N.Y., 1958-61; bd. govs. Solomon Schechter Sch. Queens, Rego Park, N.Y., 1962-65; pres. Jr. High Sch. 172 PTA, Queens, N.Y., 1956-57; chmn. Orlando Cath./Jewish Dialogue, 1977-78. Served with USN, 1945-46. Recipient Superior Accomplishment award U.S. Navy, 1960, 63, 64. Mem. IEEE (sr.), N.Y. Acad. Scis., Sci. Research Soc. Am., Sigma Xi. Club: Toastmasters (pres. 1966-67) (Orlando). Home: 1310 Webster St Orlando FL 32804

ROSENBLUTH, MORTON, periodontist; b. N.Y.C., Sept. 28, 1924; s. Jacob and Eva (Bigeleissen) R.; B.A., N.Y.U., 1943, grad. program in periodontia, oral medicine, D.D.S., 1946; m. Sylvia Fradin, July 2, 1946; children—Cheryl Bonnie, Hal Glen. Intern, Bellevue Hosp. N.Y.C., 1946-47, resident, 1947; individual practice dentistry, N.Y.C., 1947-59; individual practice periodontia, North Miami Beach, Fla., 1960—; periodontist Mt. Sinai Hosp., N.Y., Polyclinic Hosp. and Med. Sch. N.Y., Mt. Sinai Hosp., Miami Beach, Fla., Parkway Gen. Hosp.; chief dental dept. North Miami Gen. Hosp.; chmn. periodontia sect. Dade County Research Center; lectr. throughout U.S.A., Israel, Mexico, Rome, Teheran, Bangkok, Hong Kong, Tokyo, Honolulu, Jamaica, Paris, London, Sicily, Budapest, Berlin, Luxembourg, South Africa, and others; vis. lectr. U. Tenn. Dental Coll., N.Y.U. Dental Coll.; cons. VA Hosp., Miami. Mem. adv. bd. U. Fla. Coll. Dentistry; mem. profl. adv. bd. North Dade Childrens Center, Hope Sch. for Mentally Retarded Children; mem. sci. adv. com. United Health Found. Chmn. Dental div. United Fund of Dade County, Combined Jewish Appeal; nat. chmn. Hebrew U. Sch. Dental Medicine; bd. dirs. Health Planning Council S. Fla. Served with AUS, 1943-44, as capt. USAF, 1951-52. Recipient Maimonides award State of Israel, 1979; diplomate Am. Bd. Periodontology. Fellow Am. Coll. Dentists, Internat. Coll. Dentists; mem. Am. Acad. Periodontology, Am., Fla. socs. periodontists, Am. Assn. Hosp. Dental Chiefs, Am. Acad. Dental Medicine, Am. Soc. Advancement Gen. Anesthesia in Dentistry, ADA, Assn., Northeastern Soc. Periodontists, Fla. (chmn. council on legislation), Miami, Miami Beach, East Coast (sec.-treas. 1968, pres. 1971-72), North Dade (pres. 1963-64) dental socs., Fedn. Dentaire Internationale, Fla. Acad. Dental Practice Adminstrn., Alpha Omega (pres. 1967-68, internat. regent 1973-75, internat. editor 1975-77, internat. pres. elect 1977-78, internat. pres. 1979). Jewish (trustee congregation 1961-64). K.P., Mason, Kiwanian (dir. 1965). Clubs: Nocoma (pres. 1958-60), N.Y.U. Century (local chmn.). Contbr. articles to profl. jours. Home: 2030 NE 197th Terr North Miami Beach FL 33179 Office: Profl Center 1100 NE 163d St North Miami Beach FL 33162

ROSENBUSH, MARY LOUISE, furniture co. exec.; b. Batesville, Miss., May 27, 1933; d. Albert Burns and Myrtle Essie (Milam) Bell; B.A., U. Miss., 1954, M.Ed., 1957; M. Religious Edn., Southwestern Theol. Sem., 1960; certificate in interior design N.Y. Sch. Interior Design, 1979; m. Bert Julius Rosenbush Jr., June 7, 1971. Public sch. tchr., Miss., Tex. and Ala., 1955-66; asst. dean of students, dir. women's univ. housing, dir. residence halls U. Ala., University, 1966-71; sec., treas. Rosenbush Furniture Co., Demopolis, Ala., 1971—. Mem. Ala. Hist. Assn., AAUW, Marengo County Hist. Soc., Music Study Club, Study Club of Demopolis, Zeta Tau Alpha, Kappa Delta Pi. Baptist. Clubs: Demopolis Country; Debonaires. Home: Route 1 Box 158 Lake Miriam Demopolis AL 36732 Office: Rosenbush Furniture Co 101 N Walnut St PO Drawer R Demopolis AL 36732

ROSENFELD, LOUIS, surgeon; b. Nashville, June 18, 1911; s. David and Minnie (Lowenstein) R.; B.A., Vanderbilt U., 1933, M.D., 1936; m. Helen Werthan, Mar. 7, 1949; 1 son, Robert Louis; 1 foster son, Roger Werthan Cohn. Intern, Vanderbilt Hosp., 1936-37, asst. resident, resident surgeon, 1939-42; resident surgeon Beth Israel Hosp., Boston, 1937-39; gen. practice surgery, Nashville, 1946—; cons. Thayer VA Hosp., Nashville, 1947—; prof. clin. surgery Vanderbilt Med. Sch., 1963—. Pres. Davidson County unit Am. Cancer Soc., 1965—. Served to maj. AUS, 1942-45. Decorated Bronze Star Medal. Diplomate Am. Bd. Surgery. Fellow A.C.S.; mem. Nashville Surg. Soc. (past pres.), Nashville Acad. Medicine (pres. 1969), Soc. Univ. Surgeons, Soc. Head and Neck Surgeons, Southeastern Surg. Congress, So. Surg. Assn., So. Med. Assn., Alpha Omega Alpha. Contbr. articles in field to med. jours. Home: 4434 Tyne Blvd Nashville TN 37215 Office: 1211 21st Ave S Suite 422 Nashville TN 37212

ROSENGARTEN, FREDERIC, JR., author, spice prodn. exec.; b. Phila., Oct. 4, 1916; s. Frederic and E. Marion (Sims) R.; A.B., Princeton, 1938; m. Miriam B. Osterhoust, June 18, 1941; children—Miriam Suydam (Mrs. Gerrit Lansing), Clara (Mrs. Eric Urbahn), Lynn, Joan Davison. Mgr. v.p. Exptl. Plantations, Inc. (subsidiary Merck & Co.), C.A., 1940-43, in charge of quinine plantations in Guatemala and Costa Rica, 1940-43; self-employed producer coffee, spices, essential oils in Guatemala, 1947-58; pres. Monte de Oro, S.A., Guatemala Corp., Guatemala City, Guatemala, 1958-72. Pres., Found. U. Valley of Guatemala; trustee Escuela Agricola Panamericana, El Zamorano, Honduras, Pacific Tropical Bot. Garden. Served to 1st lt., AUS, 1944-46. Decorated Order of the Quetzal (Guatemala). Hon. research fellow econ. botany Harvard. Fellow Linnean Soc. London. Episcopalian. Clubs: Guatemala Country (pres. 1957); Seminole Golf (Palm Beach, Fla.); Racquet (Phila.). Developer of Guatemalan cardomon. Author: The Book of Spices, 1969; Freebooters Must Die!, 1976. Home: 247 Jungle Rd Palm Beach FL 33480

ROSENSTEIN, DAVID H., EDP auditor; b. Cin., Feb. 20, 1945; s. Jerome David and Betty Jean R.; cert. in mgmt. info. systems Fla. Internat. U., 1976; cert. in programming Control Data Inst., 1970; student Bank Adminstrn. Inst., 1978; m. Robin Virginia Smotrick, Dec. 10, 1966; children—Deena Beth, Carrie Jill. Programmer, analyst S.E. Banking Corp., Miami, Fla., 1970-72, sr. auditing officer EDP, 1972—; adj. lectr. Fla. Internat. U., Miami, 1978-79. Served with USAF, 1966-68. Mem. EDP Auditors Assn. (dir. S. Fla. chpt.), Bank Adminstrn. Inst. (chmn. EDP audit com., mem. audit commn.), Inst. Internal Auditors. Author: Auditing the Systems Development Life Cycle, 1979. Home: 13005 SW 115th Ct Miami FL 33176 Office: 100 S Biscayne Blvd Miami FL 33131

ROSENSTEIN, ROBERT NATHAN, optometrist; b. Durham, N.C., Apr. 16, 1947; s. Abraham and Wilma Lee (Craig) R.; student Louisburg Coll., 1965-69, U. N.C., 1969-70; B.S. in Optometry, Mass. Coll. Optometry, 1974, O.D., 1974; m. Deborah Broadwell, July 20, 1970; children—Allison, Nicole. Pvt. practice optometry, Durham, 1974-79; dir. Planters Nat. Bank & Trust Co.; v.p. Family Investment and Real Estate Co. Bd. dirs. Durham-Chapel Hill Fedn. Jewish Charities, 1976, Beth-El Synagogue, 1975-77, N.C. Vis. Israel Scholar Program, Durham YMCA; Durham County bd. dirs. NCCJ. Recipient citations Gov. Hunt of N.C. Mem. Eastern Dist. N.C. Optometric Soc., N.C. Optometric Soc., Am. Optometric Assn., Am. Acad. Optometry. Clubs: Durham Kiwanis, B'nai B'rith (pres. 1976, outstanding lodge pres. N.C., N.C. pres. 1978-79, recipient Gov.'s award). Home: 2201 Wilshire Dr Durham NC 27707 Office: PO Box 8 323 W Main St Durham NC 27702

ROSENSTIEL, BLANKA ALDONA, civic worker, sculptress; b. Warsaw, Poland, July 9; d. Waclaw and Karaszewska Irenea (Karaszewska de Antoniewski) Wdowiak; came to U.S., 1956, naturalized, 1962; student Ecole des Arts et Metiers, Brussels, Gimnazium Helena Rzeszotarska, Warsaw; D. Honoris Causa, Internat. Fine Arts Coll., Miami, Fla., 1976, Alliance Coll., Cambridge Springs, Pa., 1978; m. Harry King Tucker, 1956 (dec.); m. 2d, Joseph Konwiser, 1960 (div.); m. 3d, Lewis Solon Rosenstiel, 1967 (dec.). Founder, pres. Am. Inst. Polish Culture, Miami, Fla., 1972—, Chopin Found. Am., Miami, 1977; pres. Rosenstiel Found. N.Y.; trustee U. Miami (Fla.); bd. dirs. Am. Council Polish Cultural Clubs, Washington, Miami Philharmonic Soc., Opera Guild, Miami, Kosciuszko Found., N.Y.C., Council Internat. Visitors, Miami, Internat. Chopin Soc., Mus. of Sci., Miami, Met. Mus., Miami Art Center, Papanicolaou Cancer Research Inst., Fla. Internat. U. Found., Miami. Sculpture represented in permanent collections. Home: 1350 W 29th St Miami Beach FL 33140 Office: 1000 Brickell Ave Miami FL 33131

ROSENTHAL, HARVE O., motel exec.; b. Chgo., Apr. 23, 1943; B.S., Upper Iowa U., 1962; m. Sept. 2, 1968; children—Brent, Richard, Mark. With Holiday Inn, 1973—, gen. mgr., Birmingham, Ala., 1976—. Mem. Birmingham Hotel and Motel Assn. (pres. 1978-79). Club: Sertoma. Address: 1548 Montgomery St Birmingham AL 35216

ROSENTHAL, MORRIS WILLIAM, pediatrician; b. Houston, July 1, 1926; s. Louis Isaac and Della (Stramer) R.; student Tex. Tech. U., 1944, Tex. A. and M. U., 1945, U. Houston, 1946-47; M.D., U. Tex., 1951; m. Julien Bliss Epstein, Sept. 11, 1949; children—Laura Ann, Lee Stephen, Sara Jan, Louis Isaac, Martha Bliss. Intern, Jefferson Davis Hosp., Houston, 1951-52; resident in pediatrics Baylor Coll. Medicine-Tex. Children's Hosp., Houston, 1953-55; practice medicine specializing in pediatrics, Houston, 1955—; a founder Spring Branch Meml. Hosp., 1958; mem. staffs Spring Branch Meml., Tex. Children's, St. Luke's, Meml. City Gen., Meth. and Rosewood hosps.; clin. asso. prof. pediatrics Baylor Coll. Medicine. Served with U.S. Army, 1944-46. Diplomate Am. Bd. Pediatrics. Fellow Am. Acad. Pediatrics; mem. AMA, Tex., Houston pediatric socs., Tex.; Harris County med. socs. Home: 11330 Somerland St Houston TX 77024 Office: 8830 Long Point Rd Houston TX 77055 also 14730 Barryknoll Houston TX 77079

ROSENTHAL, SAMUEL GERSON, plastic surgeon; b. N.Y.C., May 28, 1939; s. Benjamin Daniel and Rachael (Osofsky) R.; B.A., Yeshiva U., 1960, B.Hebrew Letters, 1960; M.D., State U. N.Y., Syracuse, 1964; m. Elaine Rosen, June 24, 1962; children—Caryn Beth, Bradley David, Pamela Jill. Intern, Kings County Hosp., Bklyn., 1964-65, resident, 1965-71, pres. house staff, 1968-70; chmn. dept. plastic surgery Jacksonville (Fla.) Gen. Hosp., 1974—, vice chief staff, 1976—; chief div. plastic surgery Orange Park (Fla.) Hosp., Community 1975—; instr. surgery U. Fla., 1972-77, clin. asst. prof. surgery (plastic), 1977—; cons. in plastic surgery Naval Regional Med. Center, Jacksonville, 1977—; pres. Com. Interns and Residents of N.Y., 1969-70. Diplomate Am. Bd. Surgery, Am. Bd. Plastic Surgery. Fellow A.C.S.; mem. Am., N.E. Fla. (pres. 1976-77) socs. plastic and reconstructive surgeons, Fla., Southeastern socs. plastic surgery, Am. Soc. for Aesthetic Plastic Surgery, Am. Assn. Cosmetic Surgeons. Jewish. Clubs: Beaucherc Country, Ponte Vedra, Sawgrass Country. Contbr. articles to med. jours. Office: 3599 University Blvd S Jacksonville FL 32216

ROSENZWEIG, MARGARET CLAGHORN, speech pathologist; b. Buenos Aires, Argentina, Nov. 19, 1940; came to U.S., naturalized, 1959; B.A., U. Houston, 1962, M.A., 1970; m. Joel Rosenzweig, July 21, 1974; 1 son, Richard. Tchr. presch. hard of hearing Lions Lighthouse of Galveston County, 1962-63; public sch. clinician Aldine Sch. Dist., 1963-68, tchr. learning disabled, 1968-69; dir. dept. communication disorders Cerebral Palsy Treatment Center, Houston, 1970-78; speech pathologist for orthopedically handicapped Spring Br. Ind. Sch. Dist., Houston, 1978—; cons. sch. dists; guest lectr., supervising clinician for grad. students U. Houston, 1970-78. Bd. dirs. Jewish Marriage Encounter, ORT. Mem. Am. Speech and Hearing Assn., Tex. Speech, Hearing and Lang. Assn., Houston Area Assn. Communication Disorders (founding mem.), NEA, Tex. State Tchrs. Assn., Spring Br. Edn. Assn. Jewish. Club: B'nai B'rith (dir.). Home: 1611 Stone Lake Dr Missouri City TX 77459

ROSHKIND, DAVID MICHAEL, dentist; b. N.Y.C., June 10, 1950; s. Stanley and Marian (Weill) R.; B.A., Cornell U., 1972; D.M.D., U. Pa., 1975, M.B.A., 1976; m. Robin Bogen, June 25, 1972. Practice dentistry, Phila., 1975-76, W. Palm Beach, Fla., 1976—; bd. dirs. Health Planning Council, Palm Beach County. Pres., Health Planning Council. Recipient Community Service award Am. Legion, 1968. Mem. Am. Soc. Dentistry Children (award of merit 1976), ADA, Fla. Dental Assn., Acad. Gen. Dentistry, Assn. M.B.A. Execs., Am. Coll. Hosp. Adminstrs., Palm Beach C. of C., Omicron Kappa Upsilon. Clubs: Palm Beach Polo and Country; Bonnette Hunting and Fishing. Office: 2407 N Flagler Dr West Palm Beach FL 33405

ROSIER, ROBERT PETER, pathologist; b. Lynbrook, N.Y., Oct. 30, 1941; s. Alfred M. and Roslyn (Brous) R.; student, Dartmouth Coll., 1962, M.D., State U. N.Y., Downstate, 1966; m. Patricia Delman, Mar. 31, 1963; children—Elizabeth Roslyn, Jacob Charles. Intern USPHS Hosp., Staten Island, N.Y., 1966-67, resident in pathology, 1967-69; resident in pathology Duke U., 1969-71; instr. pathology, research fellow in electron microscopy in surg. pathology, 1971; pathologist Baptist Hosp., Birmingham, Ala., 1972; instr. pathology U. Ala., Birmingham, 1972-73; pathologist Lee Meml. Hosp., 1973—, Lehigh Acres Gen. Hosp., Fort Myers, Fla., 1973-79, dir. labs. and blood bank, 1974—; pathologist Cape Coral Hosp., 1977—; asst. med. dir. SW Fla. Regional Labs., Fort Myers, 1976-78; pres. Drs. Rosier and Lefer. Chmn. bd. dirs. Lee County Jr. Mus. and Planetarium, 1974; bd. dirs. Ft. Myers Symphony Orch., 1979, 2d flutist, 1979—; asst. dir. Project Bike Paths, Lee County, 1973. Served with USPHS, 1966-69. Recipient Physician Recognition award, AMA, 1974—; continuing Edn. award. Am. Soc. for Clin. Pathology and Coll. Am. Pathologists, 1974—. Fellow Am. Soc. Clin. Pathology, Coll. Am. Pathology, Internat. Coll. Surgeons; mem. Am. Assn. Blood Banks, Fla. Assn. Blood Banks, AAAS, N.Y. Acad. Science, Lee County Med. Soc., Fla. Med. Assn., Fla. Assn. Pathologists, South Fla. Soc. Pathologists, Fla. Soc. Dermatology, Am. Soc. Dermopathology, Lepidopterists Soc., Audubon Soc., Lee County Orchid Soc. Clubs: Yacht (Fort Myers), Rangoon, Fort Myers Swim, Fort Myers Racquet. Contbr. articles to med. jours. Office: PO Box 1625 Fort Myers FL 33902

ROSIN, CHARLES ALAN, clin. psychologist; b. Coleman, Tex., July 9, 1949; s. Morris and Ethel (Rosenberg) R.; B.A., U. Tex., Austin, 1971; M.S., St. Louis U., 1974, Ph.D., 1976. Clin. psychology intern Western Mo. Mental Health Center, Kansas City, Mo., 1974-75; staff psychologist Terrell (Tex.) State Hosp., 1975-77; clin. psychologist Richardson (Tex.) Med. Center, 1977-78; pvt. practice psychotherapy, Dallas, 1978—. Cert. psychologist, Tex. Mem. Nat. Register Health Service Providers (council), Acad. Psychologists in Marital and Family Therapy, Am., Tex., Dallas psychol. assns., Soc. Clin. and Exptl. Hypnosis Assn., Assn. Advancement Behavior Therapy, Southwestern Group Psychotherapy Soc., Dallas Group Psychotherapy Soc., Am. Group Psychotherapy Assn.

ROSIN, MORRIS, mfg. co. exec.; b. San Antonio, Feb. 21, 1924; s. Berco and Leia (Dupchansky) R.; student Tex. A. and M. U., 1942, St. Mary's U., 1941, 45-47; m. Ethel Rosenberg, Dec. 15, 1965; children—Susan, Charles, Lindsay. Sec.-treas. Bimbi Mfg. Co., 1949-67; pres. Bimbi Shoe Co. div. Athlone Industries, San Antonio, 1970-72; v.p. Athlone Industries, Parsippany, N.J., 1967-72; pres. Ardo Pro, San Antonio, 1966-74, Yoakum Bend Corp., San Antonio, 1968—; sec.-treas. R & R Corp., San Antonio, 1970-72. Served with USAAF, 1942-45. Mason (32 deg., Shriner). Home: 6325 B Bandera Dallas TX 75225 Office: PO Box 12625 Dallas TX 75225

ROSKELLY, MICHAEL, health ins. co. exec.; b. Brisbane, Australia, Dec. 12, 1946; s. Ralph and Joan Marcia (Flanagan) R.; student Upsala Coll., 1964-66; B.A., Murray State U., 1969; postgrad. U. Louisville, 1970, U. N.C., 1971-73; m. Hepzibah Effie Crawford, June 6, 1970; children—John Nicholas, Hepzibah Kathleen. Tchr., Louisville Public Schs., 1970-71; tng. coordinator Blue Cross and Blue Shield Ky., Louisville, 1973-75, mgr. employment and corp. tng., 1975—; adj. faculty Sullivan Bus. Coll., 1977. Mem. Am. Soc. Tng. and Devel., Cherokee Rd. Runners. Democrat. Baptist. Home: 272 Claremont Ave Louisville KY 40206 Office: Blue Cross and Blue Shield Ky 9901 Linn Station Rd Louisville KY 40223

ROSLER, VIRGINIA SEGAL, reporter, communications and mktg. exec.; b. Chgo., July 24, 1942; d. Jack M. and Myra Martha (Ro-ville) Segal; B.S. in Communications, U. Wis., 1964. Advt. copywriter, copy supr. Montgomery Ward & Co., Chgo., 1965-67; account exec. Cooper & Golin, Inc., Chgo., 1967-68, Fuller & Smith & Ross Inc., Chgo., 1968-70; pres. V.S. Rosler Assos., Chgo., 1970-74; pub. relations dir. Hume-Smith-Mickelberry, Inc., Miami, Fla., 1976-78; pres. Picaza & Rosler Inc., communications and mktg., Miami, 1978—; host radio service program Virginia and Friends, Sta. WWWL, Miami, 1976-78, The Virginia Rosler Show, Sta. WNWS, Miami, 1978; Sta. WKAT, 1979—; Latin Am. feature reporter Sta. WNWS, 1978-79. Bd. dirs. Profl. Women for Brain Research, Chgo., 1967-71; mem. MACH-1 vol. orgn. Miami Met. Mus. and Art Center; auctioneer Sta. WPBT, 1977—, named Auctioneer of Yr., 1978; mem. ball com. Internat. Yr. of Child, 1980. Home: 920 Sevilla Ave Coral Gables FL 33134 Office: 1100 Brickell Ave Suites 430/435 Miami FL 33131

ROSLOW, SYDNEY, psychologist; b. N.Y.C., July 29, 1910; s. Joseph and Anna (Lipman) R.; B.S., N.Y. U., 1931, M.A., 1932, Ph.D., 1935; m. Irma Sternberg, Oct. 21, 1932; children—Richard Jay, Susan Jane, Peter Dirk. Research asst. in market, indsl., personnel research Psychol. Corp., 1931-41; sch. psychologist, mem. bd. edn., Hastings on Hudson, N.Y., 1937-48; pub. opinion research program surveys div. Dept. Agr., 1939-43; founder Pulse, Inc., market and audience research in radio, television, advt. industries, N.Y.C., 1941-78; adj. asso. prof. Baruch Coll. City U. N.Y., 1967-75; asso. prof. dept. mktg. and environ. Fla. Internat. U., 1976—. Mem. Am. Psychol. Assn., Am. Mktg. Assn. (pres.-elect Miami chpt. 1979-80), Market Research Council, Radio-Television Research Council (past pres.) Radio and Television Execs. Soc., Phi Beta Kappa. Contbr. articles to profl. jours. Home: 601 Three Islands Blvd Hallandale FL 33009

ROSNER, EDMOND, surgeon; b. Bucharest, Romania, Nov. 14, 1925; s. Isaak and Jenny (Ekstein) R.; came to U.S., 1960, naturalized, 1965; M.D. magna cum laude, U. Bucharest, 1949; m. Lucia C. Cergau, Oct. 3, 1951. Intern, 1st Surg. Clinic, U. Bucharest, 1949-50; 1st surgeon U. Bucharest Surg. Clin., 1950-59; vis. surgeon U. Vienna (Austria) Med. Sch., 1959-60; chief of surgery Central State Hosp., Petersburg, Va., 1961-64; practice medicine specializing in surgery, Colonial Beach, Va., 1964—; mem. staff Tidewater Meml. Hosp. Founder, pres., bd. dirs. Historyland Playground Inc., 1965—. Fellow Am. Soc. Abdominal Surgeons; mem. Am. Med. Soc. of Vienna (life), Colonial Beach C. of C. (pres. 1966-68, dir.), Republican. Roman Catholic. Clubs: Lions, Moose. Contbr. articles to med. jours. Home: 2525 Riverview Dr Colonial Beach VA 22443 Office: 35 Colonial Ave Colonial Beach VA 22443

ROSNER, PHILLIP ERNEST, psychologist; b. Chgo., Aug. 13, 1943; s. Samuel Roy and Mildred (Pasternak) R.; B.A., Ind. U., 1966; M.A., Ga. State U., 1971, Ph.D., 1972; m. Carla Cenker, Aug. 8, 1971; children—Seth Louis, Alicia Rose. Cons. psychologist Rohrer, Hibler and Roplogle, Inc., Atlanta, 1972-76; pres. Human Resource Devel., Inc., Atlanta, 1976—; dir. Hayes Data Systems, Inc., Achievement Motivation Tng. Inst. Corporate dir. Not For Dels. Only, Inc., Atlanta. Mem. Am. Psychol. Assn., Southeastern Psychol. Assn., Ga. Psychol. Assn., Nat. Register of Health Service Providers in Psychology, Orgn. Devel. Inst., Internat. Registry of Orgn. Devel. Profls., Phi Epsilon Pi, Psi Chi, Alpha Phi Omega. Home: 1850 Alderbrook Rd NE Atlanta GA 30345 Office: Suite 104 3781 NE Expressway Atlanta GA 30340

ROSS, BARRY, accountant; b. Phila., Aug. 11, 1942; s. Myron L. and Pearl S. (Layton) Rosenbleeth; B.S. in Bus. Adminstrn., U. Fla., 1964; m. Elaine Chausky, June 19, 1965; children—Sheri, Marc. Accountant S.D. Leidesdorf & Co., N.Y.C., 1964-65; sr. accountant Rashba & Pokart, N.Y.C., 1965-66; auditor Ernst & Ernst, Miami, Fla., 1966-68; with Cavanagh Communities Corp., Miami, 1968-73, chief adminstrv. and fin. officer, 1969, then sr. v.p., treas., dir., mem. exec. com.; sr. partner Barry Ross & Co., C.P.A.'s, Miami, 1973—; instr. U. Miami, 1969. Asso. nat. chmn. young leadership cabinet United Jewish Appeal; bd. dirs. Congregation Beth David, Greater Miami Jewish Fedn. Recipient Stanley Meyers leadership award; C.P.A., N.Y., Fla. Mem. Am. Inst. C.P.A.'s, Fla. Inst. C.P.A.'s, N.Y. State Soc. C.P.A.'s, Miami Jr. C. of C., Nat. Assn. Accountants, Alpha Chi Sigma, Beta Alpha Psi, Tau Epsilon Phi. Clubs: Kings Bay Country, Standard (Miami); Masons, B'nai B'rith. Home: 9602 SW 69th Pl Miami FL 33156 Office: 1401 Brickell Ave Miami FL 33131

ROSS, EDWIN STUART, VI, hosp. adminstr.; b. New Brunswick, N.J., Apr. 22, 1943; s. Edwin Stuart and Mary Christine (Hickey) R.; B.S., U. Dayton (Ohio), 1965; M.S., U. So. Calif., 1976; m. Pamela Lee Snyder, Feb. 5, 1966; children—Edwin Stuart VII, Stephen Eric, Sarah Johanna. Commd. 2d. lt., U.S. Army, 1965, advanced through grades to maj., 1977, med. adminstrv. officer, Med. Service Corps, Atlanta, 1965-66, asst. chief med. supply and service, Darnall Army Hosp., Ft. Hood, Tex., 1969-72, procurement officer FitzSimmons Gen. Hosp., Denver, 1972-73, chief med. supply U.S. Army Hosp., Okinawa, Japan, 1973-76, asst. dir. logistics Acad. Health Scis., San Antonio, 1976-77, ret., 1977; dir. sterile processing and central supply U. Tex. Med. Br. Hosp., Galveston, 1977—; lectr., cons. in field. Decorated Bronze Star, Meritorious Service Medal, Army Commendation Medal. Registered referee, U.S. Soccer Fedn. Mem. Material Mgmt. Assn. Health Care Facilities (chmn. bd. govs. 1978—), Houston Soc. for Central Service Personnel (chmn. bd. govs. 1979—), Am. Hosp. Assn. Soc. for Central Service Personnel (dir. 1978—), Tex. Hosp. Assn. for Central Service Personnel (dir. 1979—), Nat. Assn. Hosp. Purchasing Agts. and Material Mgrs. Contbr. articles to profl. publs. Home: Dickinson TX 77539 Office: U Tex Med Br Hosp 8th and Mechanic Sts Galveston TX 77550

ROSS, JAMES STUART, automotive components co. exec.; b. Detroit, Aug. 12, 1920; s. Stuart Alexander and Grace Margaret (Townley) R.; B.S., U. Va., 1947; M.B.A., Harvard U., 1949; m. Ruth Forest Hartman, Dec. 20, 1948; children—Russell S., Laurie P. With Chrysler Corp., 1949-61, dir. for Latin Am., Havana, Cuba, 1960-62; pres. Auto Parts Internat., 1963-65; gen. mgr. Fed. Mogul de Mex co, 1965-69; pres., gen. mgr. Argentine Subs. of ITT, 1970-71; staff asst., office of ITT pres., ITT, N.Y.C.; v.p., gen. mgr. Rockwell Internat., N.Y.C., 1971-74, pres. internat. group, 1975-77, v.p. internat. bus. devel. Rockwell Internat. Automotive ops., 1978—; dir. Rubery Owen Rockwell (Eng.), NIH-Rockwell Co. Ltd. (Japan), Rockwell de Venezuela, Dina Rockwell Nacional S.A. (Mexico). Chmn. adv. council Henry Ford Hosp. Troy Center, 1978, chmn., 1979. Served with AUS, 1942-46. Decorated Purple Heart, Bronze star. Mem. Soc. Automotive Engrs. (co-chmn. internat. truck com.), Nat. Council for US-China Trade (chmn. transp. com.). Republican. Episcopalian. Clubs: Detroit Athletic, Oakland Hills Country; Farmington Country (Charlottesville, Va.). Office: 2135 W Maple Rd Troy MI 48084

ROSS, JO ANN ROPER, artist, educator; b. Greenville, S.C., Jan. 22, 1936; d. Walter Andrew and Bessie (Wilson) Roper; degree in Comml. Art, Ringling Sch. Art, Sarasota, Fla., 1957; student various artists; m. Wallace Edward Ross, Sept. 3, 1955; children—W. Craig, Marty J., E. Andy. Comml. artist Greenville New-Piedmont, 1957-58; artist Ivey's of Greenville, 1958-62; owner pvt. bus., Greenville, 1962-68; instr. N. Greenville Jr. Coll., 1973; tchr. drawing and painting. Greenville Tech. Coll., 1974—; free lance artist various businesses, ann. sales Greenville Mus. Active Locate Ad Club, 1957; contbr. art work Little Theatre, 1959, Miss S.C., 1979. Mem. So. Watercolor Soc., Internat. Soc. Artists, Found. Advancement of Artists, S.C. Watercolor Soc., Greenville Artist Guild, Guild S.C. Artists, Blue Ridge Invitational Art Festival Clemson (purchase award 1977), Tempo Gallery. Designer logo French Room Ivey's Dept. Store, 1960; contbr. article to Popular Ceramic. Home: Route 11 Box 220 Greenville SC 29611

ROSS, JOSEPH COMER, physician, educator; b. Tompkinsville, Ky., June 16, 1927; s. Joseph M. and Annie (Pinckley) R.; B.S., U. Ky., 1950; M.D., Vanderbilt U., 1954; m. Isabelle Nevins, June 15, 1952; children—Laura Ann, Sharon Lynn, Jennifer Jo, Mary Martha, Jefferson Arthur. Intern, Vanderbilt U. Hosp., Nashville, 1954-55; asst. resident in medicine Duke U. Hosp., Durham, N.C., 1955-57, research fellow, 1957-58; instr. medicine Ind. U. Sch. Medicine, Indpls., 1958-60, asst. prof., 1960-62, asso. prof., 1962-66, prof., 1966-70; prof. medicine, chmn. dept. medicine Med. U. S.C., Charleston, 1970—; staff physician VA Hosp., Indpls., 1958-60; cons. staff St. Francis Xavier Hosp., 1976—; mem. cardiovascular study sect. NIH, 1966-70, program project com., 1971-75; mem. ad hoc coms. Nat. Acad. Sci., 1966, 67; mem. Pres.'s Nat. Adv. Panel on Heart Disease, 1972; mem. merit rev. bd. in respiration VA, 1972-76, chmn., 1974-76. Served with U.S. Army, 1945-47. Diplomate Am. Bd. Internal Medicine (mem. subsplty. bd. on pulmonary diseases 1972-78, bd. govs. 1975—); lic. physician, S.C., Tenn. Fellow Am. Coll. Cardiology, Am. Coll. Chest Physicians (S.C. gov. 1970-76, chmn. bd. govs. 1975-76, pres. 1978), A.C.P.; mem. Am. Fedn. Clin. Research (chmn. Midwest sect. 1968-69), Am. Heart Assn. (exec. com. cardiopulmonary council 1973-75), AMA, Am. Thoracic Soc., Ind. Thoracic Soc. (pres.-elect 1970), Ind. Tuberculosis and Respiratory Disease Assn., Marion County Tb and Respiratory Disease Assn. (dir. 1965-70, exec. com. 1969-70), S.C. Heart Assn., S.C. Lung Assn. (dir. 1971-76, exec. com. 1974-75, v.p. 1974-75), S.C. Lung Assn. (coastal br. dir. 1972-76, pres. 1975-76), S.C. Med. Soc., Am. Physiol. Soc., Am. Soc. Clin. Investigation, Am. Soc. Internal Medicine, Assn. Am. Physicians, Assn. Profs. Medicine, Central Soc. Clin. Research, Charleston County Med. Soc., Coastal Lung Assn., So. Soc. Clin. Research, Sigma Xi, Phi Beta Kappa, Alpha Omega Alpha, Alpha Epsilon Delta. Mem. Ch. of Christ. Contbr. articles in field to profl. jours.; mem. editorial bd. Jour. Lab. Clin. Medicine, 1964-70, Chest, 1968-73, Jour. Applied Physiology, 1968-73, Archives of Internal Medicine, 1976—, Heart and Lung, 1977—. Office: Dept Medicine Med Univ of SC Charleston SC 29403

ROSS, LEONARD EDWARD, energy co. exec.; b. Jacksboro, Tex., Aug. 5, 1920; s. Lewis Alvin and Iva Lea (Doss) R.; student Bentley Draughon Sch., 1938; m. Lula Mae Graves, June 8, 1941; children—Richard E., Gloria J., Brenda G., Terry W. With Curtis Candy Co., Graham, Tex., 1942-48; salesman Gen. Foods, Lubbock, Tex., 1949-50; commn. agt. Texaco, Inc., Quanah, Tex., 1950-77; oil jobber Ross Energy, Dist. Texaco Products, Quanah, 1977-79, pres., 1979—. Mem. Quanah City Council, 1960-72; mem. Vol. Fire Dept., Quanah, 1958-79; bd. dirs. Am. Cancer Soc., 1961-79, speech tchr., 1961-79, life mem. bd. dirs., 1979—. Served with USAAF, 1942-46. Am. Cancer Soc. grantee, 1961. Mem. Nat. Assn. Texaco Wholesalers. Baptist. Clubs: Masons (Shriner), Lions (pres. 1963-64). Home: 904 Eddy St Quanah TX 79252 Office: East 2nd St Box 678 Quanah TX 79252

ROSS, PATTI JAYNE, physician; b. Brookfield, Ohio, Nov. 17, 1946; d. James J. and Mary (Nicastro) R.; B.A. in Zoology with honors, DePauw U., 1968; M.D., Tulane U., 1972; m. Allan R. Katz, May 23, 1976. Intern in ob-gyn Johns Hopkins Hosp., Balt., 1972-73; resident in ob-gyn Jackson Meml. Hosp., Miami, Fla., 1973-75, chief resident, 1975-76; asst. prof. dept. ob-gyn U. Tex. Med. Sch., Houston, 1977—, dir. adolescent unit, 1977—. Active Houston Orgn. for Parent Edn. Diplomate Am. Coll. Ob-Gyn. Mem. AMA, Am. Women's Med. Assn., Tex. Med. Assn., Harris County Med. Soc., Am. Fertility Soc., Tex. Assn. Obstetricians and Gynecologists, Houston Obstet. and Gynecol. Soc., So. Perinatal Assn., Sigma Xi, Beta Beta Beta. Roman Catholic. Contbr. articles to profl. jours. Home: 9449 Briar Forest Houston TX 77063 Office: 6431 Fannin Houston TX 77030

ROSS, ROBERT HARTSEL, concrete equipment co. exec.; b. Gorman, Tex., Aug. 30, 1920; s. Reuben B. and Madena E. Ross; student Tarleton State Coll., Stephenville, Tex., 1941; B.G.S., Howard Payne U.; m. Joy McAuley, Feb. 14, 1975; children—Bruce M., DiAnn Ross Wristen, Vicki L. Mng. partner Ross & Sons Constrn. Co., Brownwood, Tex. 1946-67; founder, pres., chief exec. officer Ross Co., Brownwood, 1956—; owner, operator cattle ranch Lake Brownwood, Tex., 1960—; pres. Comml. Janitorial Supplies, Brownwood, 1980—; chmn. bd. Century Machinery Co., Phoenix, 1979—; adv. dir. Dublin Nat. Bank (Tex.); dir. Citizens Nat. Bank Brownwood. Mem. Brownwood Pub. Sch. Bd., 1952-56; finance chmn. finance com. Coggin Ave. Baptist Ch. Brownwood, 1968—; trustee Howard Payne U., Brownwood, 1958—; mem. adv. commn. Tex. Rangers, 1972—. Served to lt. col. USAAF, 1940-45. Named SBA Small Businessman of Year Tex., 1973, Outstanding Soil Conservationist Brown County, 1970; life mem. Tex. Rangers Hall of Fame, 1976; certified law enforcement officer Tex. Mem. Am. Concrete Paving Assn. (dir. 1972—), Nat. Ready Mix Concrete Assn. (dir. 1972—), Concrete Plant Mfrs. Bur. (chmn. 1970-72), Nat. Asso. Equipment Distbrs. Assn. (nat. industry round table com. 1974—), Tex. Ready Mixed Concrete Assn., W. Tex. Fair Assn. (v.p. Abilene 1971-73), Baptist. Clubs: Rotary (chmn. internat. info. and contact com. 1975-76, pres. 1980-81), Mason (Shriner). Home: Route 1 PO Box 265R Lake Brownwood TX 76801 Office: PO Box 70 911 E Commerce St Brownwood TX 76801

ROSS, ROBERT ROY, JR., urologic surgeon; b. Dearborn, Mich., May 25, 1936; s. Robert Roy and Elizabeth A. (Austin) R.; A.S., Henry Ford Coll., Dearborn, 1956; B.S., U. Mich. at Ann Arbor, 1958; M.D., Wayne State U., Detroit, 1962; m. Antoinette Juozunas, June 29, 1963; children—Robert Roy III, Karen E., Tracey A. Intern, Detroit Meml. Hosp., 1962-63; resident urologic surgery Wayne State U. Hosp., 1966-70; practice medicine specializing in urologic surgery, Venice, Fla., 1972—; chief surgery sect. Venice Hosp., 1975—, chief staff, 1978—; instr. surgery Wayne State U. Sch. Medicine, Detroit, 1969-70, asst. prof. urology, 1971-72. Served with USAF, 1963-66. Fellow A.C.S.: mem. Am., Southeastern Sect. urol. assns., Fla. Urol. Soc., Fla. Med. Assn., Sarasota County (Fla.) Med. Soc. Kiwanian. Contbr. articles in field to profl. jours. Home: #3 The Anchorage Nokomis FL 33555 Office: 219 Palermo Pl Venice FL 33595

ROSS, SAMUEL MORGAN, athletic dir.; b. Buckhannon, W.Va., Dec. 30, 1930; s. Cecil Byron and Mary (Morgan) R.; B.S., W.Va. Wesleyan Coll., Buckhannon, 1952; M.S., W.Va. U., 1958; m. Mary Buffington, Aug. 7, 1955; children—Jane Alice, Nancy B. Coach, dean students W.Va. Wesleyan U., 1973, athletic dir., 1973—. Served with USN, 1952-54. Recipient Alumni award W.Va. Wesleyan U., 1972. Mem. AAHPER, Nat. Assn. Intercollegiate Athletic Dirs., Nat. Assn. Athletic Dirs., W.Va. Intercollegiate Athletic Assn., Omicron Delta Kappa. Club: Lions. Home: 23 Victory St Buckhannon WV 26201 Office: WVa Wesleyan Coll Buckhannon WV 26201

ROSS, STANLEY ROBERT, historian; b. N.Y.C., Aug. 8, 1921; s. Max George and Ethel (Aks) R.; A.B. (scholar), Queens Coll., 1942; M.A., Columbia, 1943, Ph.D. (Schiff fellow), 1951; m. Leonore Jacobson, Oct. 7, 1945 (dv. 1975); children—Steven David, Alicia Ellen, Janet Irene; m. 2d, Geraldine D. Gagliano, Dec. 18, 1977. Instr. history Queens Coll., 1946-48, Bklyn. Coll., 1948; from instr. to prof. history U. Nebr., 1948-62; prof. history, chmn. dept. State U. N.Y. at Stony Brook, 1962-66, acting dean Coll. Arts and Scis., 1963-66, dean, 1966-68; prof. history, dir. Inst. Latin Am. Studies, U. Tex., Austin, 1968-71, provost arts and scis., 1971-72, provost, 1972-73, v.p., provost, 1973-76, prof. history, dir. Border research program, 1976—; lectr. CCNY, 1946, Columbia, 1960, U. Colo., 1962; chmn. Conf. Latin Am. History, 1968; U.S. nat. mem. commn. on history Pan Am. Inst. Geography and History, 1969-73; mem. joint com. Latin-Am. studies Am. Council Learned Socs.-Social Sci. Research Council, 1968-71. Vice chmn. Suffolk County (N.Y.) Com. to Study Sch. Redistricting, 1965; chmn. Three Village Council Edn., 1966-67. Served to 1st lt. USAAF, 1943-46. Travel grantee State Dept., 1947-48; Doherty Found. fellow, 1952-53; U. Nebr. grantee, 1955; Rockefeller Found. grantee, 1958-59, 61, 68-69; U. Nebr. fellow, 1961. Mem. Conf. Latin Am. History (chmn. Bolton Prize com. 1965), Am. Hist. Assn., Assn. Am. Historians, Latin Am. Studies Assn. (chmn. com. govt. relations 1968-69), AAUP, Acad. Am. Franciscan History (corr.), Instituto Mexicano de Cultura (corr.). Author: Francisco I. Madero, Apostle of Mexican Democracy, 1955, rev. edit., 1977; co-author, co-editor: Historia Documental de Mexico, 1964. Editor: Is the Mexican Revolution Dead?, 1965, 75 (Spanish edit. 1972, rev. 1978, Japanese edit. 1976); Fuentes de la Historia Contemporanea de Mexico: Periodicos y Revistas, 2 vols., 1966-67; Latin America in Transition, 1970; (with Paul Kennedy) The Middle Beat, 1971; co-editor Criticas Constructivas del Sistema Politico Mexicano, 1973; Views Across the Border: The United States and Mexico, 1978; adv. editor The Americas, 1956-70; contbg. editor The Handbook of Latin American Studies, 1960-70; mng. editor Hispanic Am. Hist. Rev., 1970-75; editorial bd. Hispanic Am. Hist. Rev., 1960-66. Home: 102 Canyon Rim Dr Austin TX 78746 Office: Sid Richardson Hall U Texas Austin TX 78705

ROSS, THOMAS HOWARD, dermatologist; b. Bridgeport, Conn., Apr. 19, 1946; s. Michael Maurice and Goldie (Friedman) R.; B.A., U. Conn., 1968; M.D. with honors, Meharry Med. Coll., 1973; m. Betty Zyskind, Nov. 25, 1972; 1 son, David Lee. Intern, U. Miami (Fla.) Affiliated Hosps., 1973-74; resident in dermatology Hosp. U. Pa., Phila., 1974-77; practice medicine specializing in dermatology, West Palm Beach, Fla., 1977—; mem. staff Doctors Hosp., Lake Worth, Fla., John F. Kennedy Meml. Hosp., Atlantis, Fla., Good Samaritan Hosp., West Palm Beach. Diplomate Am. Bd. Dermatology. Fellow Am. Acad. Dermatology; mem. Soc. Investigative Dermatology, AMA, Dermatology Found., Palm Beach County Med. Soc., Fla. Med. Assn., Alpha Omega Alpha. Jewish. Contbr. articles to med. jours. Office: 1825 Forest Hill Blvd Suite 101 West Palm Beach FL 33406

ROSSANO, MARCELLO JOSEPH, coll. ofcl.; b. Bklyn., Sept. 30, 1920; s. Emilio J. and Julia (Olivieri) R.; student Bklyn. Coll., 1938-40; B.A., Trinity U., 1954; postgrad. U. Md., 1955-57; M.B.A., Syracuse U., 1958; Ph.D., U. Tex., 1975; grad. Air Command and Staff Coll., 1951; m. Mary Ozelle Edgar, Dec. 23, 1943; children—Mary Lynn, Mark Joseph. Enlisted U.S. Air Force, 1941, commd. 2d lt., advanced through grades to col., 1965; various air combat crew assignments, 1943-50; dep. dir. personnel U.S. Air Force Security Service, 1950-53, Nat. Security Agy., Washington, 1954-57; dep. chief of staff for personnel 17th Air Force, 1958-59; manpower resources planner Air Force Personnel Systems Devel. Office, 1960-64; manpower resources planner Office of the Joint Chiefs of Staff, Washington, 1964-67; manpower and orgn. planner Supreme Hdqrs., Allied Powers Europe, 1967-70; asst. dep. chief staff for personnel U.S. Air Force Security Services, 1970-72, ret., 1972; dean fin. and adminstrv. services Alvin (Tex.) Community Coll., 1974—; adj. instr. U. Md., 1958-59, U. Houston 1977. Vestryman Grace Episcopal Ch., Alvin, Tex., 1977-80; bd. dirs. Alvin Museum Soc., 1978-80. Decorated Legion of Merit with cluster, Air medal with seven clusters, D.F.C. Mem. Am. Assn. Community and Jr. Colls., Am. Assn. Higher Edn., Nat. Assn. Univ. and Coll. Bus. Officers, Tex. Assn. Coll. Bus. Officers, AAUP, Alvin C. of C., Ret. Officers Assn., Air Force Assn., Navy League, Houston Area Ret. Officers Assn. (treas. 1977), Phi Delta Kappa, Beta Gamma Sigma, Kappa Delta Pi, Sigma Iota Epsilon. Episcopalian. Clubs: Masons, Shriners, Rotary. Office: 3110 Mustang Rd Alvin TX 77511

ROSSEN, ROBERT HENRY, chem. engr.; b. Chgo., Apr. 14, 1947; s. Henry Randall and Betty June (Cantzler) R.; B.S. (Stauffer scholar), U. Ill., 1968; M.A. (NSF fellow), Princeton, 1969, Ph.D. (NSF fellow), 1972. With Sinclair Research Co., Harvey, Ill., summers 1966, 67; with Exxon Prodn. Research Corp., Houston, 1972—, supr. spl. projects, 1979—. Recipient Agnes Sloan Larson award, 1966, Rodebush award, 1968, Am. Inst. Chem. Engrs. Jr. award, 1967, Cedric Ferguson award, 1976; Churchill fellow, 1968. Mem. Am. Inst. Chem. Engrs., Soc. Petroleum Engrs. (tech. info. com.), Am. Inst. Mining Engrs., Phi Beta Kappa, Tau Beta Pi, Phi Kappa Phi, Sigma Tau, Phi Lambda Upsilon. Contbr. articles to profl. jours. Home: 922 Daria Dr Houston TX 77079 Office: Exxon Production Research Co PO Box 2189 Houston TX 77001

ROSSER, ROY HASLE, clin. social worker; b. LaGrange, Ga., July 21, 1948; s. Roy Whatley and Martha Judson (Torbert) R.; B.A., Mercer U., 1970; M.A., New Orleans Bapt. Theol. Sem., 1971; M.S.W., Tulane U., 1972; m. Jacklyn Hill, May 19, 1973. Cons. social worker Plantation Nursing Home, New Orleans, 1972-73; psychiat. social worker McKinney Halfway House, New Orleans, 1972-73; coordinator La. Assn. Mental Health, New Orleans, 1972-73; clin. social worker VA Med. Center Psychiatry Service, New Orleans, 1972—, coordinator inpatient psychiatry service, 1979—; mem. faculty Tulane U. Mem. Health Edn. Authority La., 1975-76; coordinator Crisis Line City of New Orleans; mem. continuing edn. com. Tulane U., 1978; mem. Mayor's Task Force on Human Service Needs, 1979. Recipient VA outstanding performance award, 1976; cert. social worker, La.; cert. Acad. Cert. Social Workers. Mem. Mental Health Assn., La. Health Council, Acad. Family Therapists, Nat. Assn. Social Workers, Nat. Inst. Am. Psychotherapists, New Orleans Mus. Art, New Orleans Symphony Assn., Tulane Alumni Assn. Democrat. Roman Catholic. Research on origins of schizophrenia, reasons for recividism of mentally ill. Address: 2031 Pine St New Orleans LA 70118

ROSSI, DON A., golf found. exec.; b. Detroit, June 2, 1918; s. Isaia and Maria (Notrianni) R.; B.S., Mich. State U., 1940, M.A., 1950; student U. Mich., So. Meth. U.; m., May 31, 1941; children—Gayle Ann, Mary Donn, Elizabeth Noel, Michael Joseph. Asst. football coach Mich. State U., 1940; football coach Tex. Mil. Inst., San Antonio, 1947; coach Jesuit High Sch., Dallas, 1948-50; Western promotion mgr. A.G. Spalding & Bros., 1951-52, 56-58; gen. mgr. Dallas Texans Football Club, 1958-60; v.p. John T. Riddell Inc., 1961-68; exec. dir. Nat. Golf Found., North Palm Beach, Fla., 1968—. Served with USAAF, 1942-46, USAF, 1952-56. Named Football Ofcl. of Yr., Knute Rockne Club, Kansas City, Mo., 1960. Mem. Internat. Assn. Golf Adminstrs., World Wide Conf. Golf Facility Devel. (permanent chmn.), Nat. Golf Fund, U.S. Golf Assn. (Bob Jones award com.), Nat. Assn. Golf Course Owners (exec. dir. pro tem), Allied Assns. in Golf (founder), Nat. Assn. Public Golf Course Owners (founder). Roman Catholic. Clubs: J.D.M. Country, Frenchman's Creek Country (Palm Beach Gardens, Fla.). Office: 200 Castlewood North Palm Beach FL 33408

ROSSI, ROBERT JOHN, newspaper mgmt. cons.; b. Pitts., Jan. 5, 1928; s. John Baptist and Carmella Marie (Pastore) R.; B.A., Denison U., 1950; postgrad. 1963; m. Mary Kathryn Rust, June 30, 1951; children—Shannon Elizabeth, Claudia Irene. With advt. dept. Willoughby (Ohio) News-Herald, 1953-60; advt. dir. Elgin (Ill.) Courier-News, 1960-64; editor and pub. New Albany (Ind.) Tribune and Sunday Ledger, 1964-71; mgmt. cons. Thomson Newspapers, Inc., Chgo., 1971, gen. mgr. So. div., Tampa, Fla., 1972-73; v.p. ops. Park Newspapers, Inc., 1974-79; dir. No. N.Y. Pub. Co., Manassas Journal, Warner Robins Daily Sun, Plymouth (Ind.) Pilot-News, Norwich (N.Y.) Evening Sun, Bremen Enquirer, Nappanee Advance-News, Lockport Union Sun Jour., Brooksville Sun Jour., Nebr. City News-Press Bd. dirs. Ky. Opera Assn., Ky.-Ind. Comprehensive Health Planning Council. Served with U.S. Army, 1946. Mem. Am., So. newspaper pubs. assns. Club: Filson. Republican. Methodist. Home and Office: Turnip Creek Farm Rural Route 1 Box 227-B Brookneal VA 24528

ROSSIE, RAOUL LAZARO, truck sales and services co. exec.; b. Havana, Cuba, Jan. 3, 1943; s. Raoul and Ofelia (Palacio) R.; came to U.S., 1960, naturalized, 1965; student LaSalle U., 1963-65; B.B.A., Baruch Coll., 1974; m. Antonia Caputo, June 20, 1964; children—Angela Maria, Patricia. Certified pub. accountant Denis & Nodar, Havana, Cuba, 1959-60; accountant Schraffts, N.Y.C., 1960-62; mgr. fleet maintenance Branch Motor Exchange, N.Y.C., 1963-74; v.p., gen. mgr. Comml. Vehicle Service, Tampa, Fla., 1974-78; pres. R & R Transp. Service Inc., Tampa, 1978—. Served with U.S. Army, 1962-63. Mem. Am. Mgmt. Assn., K.C. Republican. Roman Catholic. Home: 3804 Treadway Dr Valrico FL 33594 Office: 1905 N 43d St Tampa FL 33605

ROSSMAN, SALLY JO, med. technologist, writer, editor; b. N.Y.C., July 7; d. Norman A. and Sadye (Kooperman) R.; student U. Fla., 1953-54, Davis. Inst. Med. Tech., 1954-55. Supr., Cardiology Dept., Mt. Sinai Med. Center, Miami Beach, Fla., 1956-69; lectr. in field. Named Technician of Year, Miami chpt. Am. Cardiology Technologists Assn., 1975; recipient Disting. Achievement award Am. Med. Technologists, 1978; named Technologist of Year, Fla. State Soc. of Am. Med. Technologists, 1978. Mem. Nat. Soc. Cardiology Technologists (founding mem. 1976, sec. 1976-80, editor newsletter Hearticles), Fla. Soc. Med. Technologists (exec. com. 1978-79, editor publ. Electrolyte 1979—), Am. Cardiology Technicians (sec. Miami chpt. 1974-76). Author: (text) Cardiology Technology Review, 1979; contbr. articles to med. and sci. jours.; editor, Fla. Jour. Med. Technologists, 1978—. Address: 909 W 47 St Miami Beach FL 33140

ROSSON, BARRY A., psychiatrist, neurologist; b. Memphis, Aug. 16, 1946; s. Walter E. and Eleanor (Arbetter) R.; student Rice U., 1964-67; M.D., U. Tex. at Dallas, 1971. Resident, Menninger Sch. Psychiatry, 1971-74; resident in neurology U. Tex. Southwestern Med. Sch., 1974-76; practice medicine, specializing in psychiatry and neurology, Dallas, 1974—; instr. dept. neurology U. Tex. Southwestern Med. Sch., 1977—. Diplomate Am. Bd. Psychiatry and Neurology. Mem. Am. Psychiat. Assn., Am. Acad. Neurology, Tex. Med. Assn., Dallas County Med. Soc. Home: 9316 Chimney Corner Dallas TX 75231 Office: 4210 Walnut Hill Ln Suite 410 Dallas TX 75231

ROSTAN, STEPHEN EDWIN, dermatologist; b. Toluca, N.C., Sept. 19, 1944; s. Stephen and Hattie Jane (Reynolds) R.; B.S., Davidson (N.C.) Coll., 1966; M.D., Vanderbilt U., 1970; m. Barbara Ann Hay, July 6, 1968; children—Robert, Scott. Intern, gen. med. officer, then resident in dermatology Brooke Army Med. Center, San Antonio, 1970-75; practice medicine specializing in dermatology, Pinehurst, N.C., 1976—; mem. staff Moore Meml. Hosp.; cons. McLain Hosp. Mem. So. Pines (N.C.) Bd. Adjustment, 1978—. Served to maj. M.C., USAR, 1970-76. Diplomate Am. Bd. Dermatology. Fellow Am. Acad. Dermatology, Am. Coll. Cryosurgery; mem. AMA, N.C. Med. Soc. Democrat. Episcopalian. Clubs: Pinehurst Country; Elks, Rotary (dir.) (So. Pines). Home: 115 James Creek Southern Pines NC 28387 Office: Box 699 Pinehurst NC 28374

ROSVOLL, RANDI VEIE, pathologist; b. Trondheim, Norway, Apr. 26, 1928; came to U.S., 1949, naturalized, 1960; s. Alv and Margit (Ness) Veie R.; B.S., Am. U., 1953; M.D., George Washington U., 1957. Rotating intern, Washington Hosp. Center, 1957-58, resident in anatomic pathology, 1958-59; resident in anatomic pathology New Eng. Deaconess Hosp., Boston, 1959-60, resident in clin. pathology, 1960-61; chief resident in pathology George Washington U. Hosp., Washington, 1961-62; fellow Meml. Hosp., Sloan Kettering Center for Cancer, N.Y.C., 1962-63; pathologist Grady Meml. Hosp., Atlanta, 1963-70; dir. clin. labs. Emory U. Hosp., Atlanta, 1964-70, dir. Blood Bank Tng. Center, 1967-70; dir. Emory U. Sch. Med. Tech., Atlanta, 1964-70; dir. blood bank New Eng. Deaconess and New Eng. Bapt. Hosps., Boston, 1970-76, asst. chief clin. pathologist, 1974-76; pathologist Crawford W. Long Meml. Hosp., Atlanta, 1972—, Drs. Meml. Hosp., Atlanta, 1972—, Peachtree Labs., Atlanta, 1972—; dir. clin. pathology Crawford W. Long Meml. Hosp. and Drs. Meml. Hosp., 1976—; dir. Crawford W. Long Meml. Hosp. Sch. Med. Tech., 1972—; cons. VA Hosp., 1963-70, Ga. Mental Health Inst., 1966-70, Arabian Am. Oil Co., Dhahran Health Center, 1975-76, Pathologists Service P.A., 1977—; asst. prof. pathology Emory U. Sch. Medicine, Atlanta, 1963-67, asso. prof. pathology, 1967-70; asst. prof. pathology Harvard Med. Sch., Boston, 1971-76; clin. prof. Allied Health, Ga. State U., Atlanta, 1976—; mem. sci. adv. bd. Geometric Data, 1979—. Recipient Physicians Recognition award, AMA/Coll. Am. Pathologists, 1973-76, 74-77, 78—; lic. physician, D.C., N.Y., Ga., Mass. Diplomate Am. Bd. Pathology, Nat. Bd. Med. Examiners. Mem. Am. Assn. Blood Banks, Am. Soc. Clin. Pathology (fellow), Coll. Am. Pathologists (fellow), AMA, Soc. Surg. Oncology, Am. Thyroid Assn. (treas. 1973-76), Med. Assn. Atlanta, Med. Assn. Ga., Ga. Soc. Pathologists, Soc. Med. Oncologists, World Assn. Pathology Socs., Alpha Omega Alpha. Contbr. articles to profl. jours. Home: 1473 Rainier Falls Dr Atlanta GA 30329 Office: 35 Linden Ave Atlanta GA 30308

ROSZELL, CALVERT THEODORE, JR., lawyer; b. Lexington, Ky., Mar. 30, 1924; s. Calvert Theodore and Besse Myrtle (Byrd) R.; LL.B., U. Ky., 1948; m. Nancy Jane Bradford, June 21, 1952; children—Calvert Theodore, Stephen R., Kathryn Ann. Admitted to Ky. bar, 1948, since practiced in Lexington; adj. prof. law U. Ky. Coll. Law, 1956-71; judge pro-tem Fayette County Ct., 1959-62. Pres. Blue Grass council Boy Scouts Am., 1970-71; chpt. chmn. ARC, 1961; pres. United Community Services, 1956. Served with AUS, 1943-45. Decorated Bronze Star medal. Mem. Am., Ky., Fayette County bar assns., Phi Delta Theta, Phi Delta Phi. Democrat. Methodist. Clubs: Masons, Rotary (pres. 1962-63) (Lexington). Home: 1840 Blairmore Ct Lexington KY 40502 Office: 156 Market St Lexington KY 40501

ROTH, ALEXANDER DUNBAR, lawyer; b. New Orleans, Apr. 22, 1946; s. Richard James and Shirley Adele R.; B.A., Stanford U., 1968; J.D., U. Mich., 1975; m. Wendy Nordvik, Sept. 4, 1971; children—Elsa Lynne, Justin Alexander. Programmer, systems engr. IBM Corp., Washington, 1968-72; asst. dir. law sch. computer facility U. Mich., 1973-74, dir., 1974-75; admitted to Ill. bar, 1975, Va. bar, 1979; atty. Swift & Co., Chgo., 1975-78; dir. Washington office Am. Fedn. of Info. Processing Soc., Arlington, Va., 1978—. Mem. Am. Bar Assn., Fed. Bar Assn. Exec. editor Am. Fedn. Info. Processing Soc. Washington Report, 1978—. Office: 1815 N Lynn St Arlington VA 22209

ROTH, J(OHN) REECE, educator, cons.; b. Washington, Pa., Sept. 19, 1937; s. John Meyer and Ruth E. (Iams) R.; B.S. in Physics, M.I.T., 1959; Ph.D. in Engring. Physics, Cornell U., 1963; m. Helen Marie DeCrane, Jan. 14, 1972; children—Nancy Ann, John Alexander. Aerospace research scientist NASA Lewis Research Center, Cleve., 1963-78; mem. faculty dept. elec. engring. U. Tenn., Knoxville, 1978—; cons. Mem. IEEE (sr.; asso. editor Transactions on Plasma Sci. 1973—), AAAS (life), Am. Phys. Soc., Am. Nuclear Soc., Archaeol. Inst. Am., AIAA, Sigma Xi. Contbr. articles to profl. jours.; discovered continuity-equation plasma oscillation, geometric mean plasma frequency. Home: 5120 Stonewood Dr Knoxville TN 37921 Office: U Tenn Knoxville TN 37916

ROTH, JACK, broadcasting co. exec.; b. San Antonio, July 17, 1926; s. Eugene J. and Dorothy (Schaffer) R.; B.S., Trinity U., 1952; m. LaVerne Whitehead, Dec. 14, 1948; children—John, Nancy, Lee, Julie. Pres., Mission Broadcasting Co., San Antonio, 1959—; pres., owner Mission Central Co., stas. KONO and KITY-FM, San Antonio, 1967—; pres. Mission Broadcasting Co., Nev., 1967—, Mission Advt. Co., San Antonio, 1960—, Mission Denver Co., Sta. KERE, 1971—. Bd. dirs. A.R.C. Served with USNR, 1944-46. Mem. Tex. Assn. Broadcasters (pres. 1963), San Antonio Zool. Soc. (dir.). Office: PO Box 2338 San Antonio TX 78298

ROTH, JOHN AUSTIN, chem. engr.; b. Louisville, May 14, 1934; s. Horace H. and Suzanna Lydia (Paslick) R.; B.Chem. Engring., U. Louisville, 1956, M.Chem. Engring., 1957, Ph.D. in Chem. Engring., 1961; m. Alene Burns, Dec. 18, 1959; children—Suzan, John. Faculty, Vanderbilt U., Nashville, 1962—, asst. prof., then asso. prof. chem. engring., 1962-70, prof., 1970—, asst. dean, 1968-70, asso. dean, 1970-72, chmn. div. chem., fluid and thermal scis., 1972-75; commr. Bur. Environ. Protection, Dept. Natural Resources and Environ. Protection, State of Ky., 1977-78. Bd. dirs. Dede Wallace Mental Health Center, 1975-77. Served with USAF, 1960-62. Registered profl. engr., Ky., Tenn. Mem. Am. Inst. Chem. Engrs., Am. Chem. Soc., Nat. Soc. Profl. Engrs., Am. Soc. Engring. Edn., Water Pollution Control Fedn. (Ky.-Tenn.), Internat. Ozone Assn., Sigma Xi, Tau Beta Pi. Episcopalian. Contbr. articles to profl. publs. Home: 840 Highland Crest Dr Nashville TN 37235 Office: Box 1574 Station B Nashville TN 37235

ROTH, OLIVER RALPH, radiologist; b. Cumberland, Md., Nov. 30, 1921; s. DeCoursey Andrew and Mabel (Lathrum) R.; B.S., Frostburg (Md.) State Coll., 1942; M.D., U. Md., 1950; m. Virginia McBride, June 2, 1943; 1 dau., Sheila Diane. Resident, Johns Hopkins Hosp., Balt., 1954-57; cancer research fellow Middlesex Hosp., London, 1957-58; founder dept. radiation oncology Presbyterian Hosp., Charlotte, N.C., 1958-62; attending radiologist King's Daus. Hosp., Ashland, Ky., 1962—; mem. adv. com. Ky. Cancer Commn., 1978; Bd. dirs. Boyd County chpt. Am. Cancer Soc., 1978. Served in USN, 1942-45. Diplomate Am. Bd. Radiology. Commanded to Buckingham Palace, June 17, 1958; recipient Disting. Alumni award Frostburg State Coll., 1979. Mem. AMA, Am. Coll. Radiology, Radiol. Soc. N. Am., Am. Radium Soc., Royal Faculty Radiology, Brit. Inst. Radiology. Democrat. Lutheran. Club: Shriners (Cumberland, Md.). Book reviewer Radiology, 1954-55. Home: 2912 Cogan St Ashland KY 41101 Office: 1200 Bath Ave Ashland KY 41101

ROTH, WILLIAM STANLEY, hosp. found. exec.; b. N.Y.C., Jan. 12, 1929; s. Sam Irving and Louise Caroline (Martin) R.; A.A., Asheville-Biltmore Jr. Coll., 1948; B.S., U. N.C., 1950; m. Hazel Adcock, May 6, 1963; children—R. Charles, W. Stanley. Dep. regional exec. Nat. council Boy Scouts Am., 1953-65; exec. v.p. Am. Humanics Found., 1965-67; dir. devel. Bethany Med. Center, Kansas City, Kans., 1967-74; exec. v.p. Geisinger Med. Center Found., Danville, Pa., 1974-78; exec. v.p. Found., Baptist Med. Centers, Birmingham, Ala., 1978—. Mem.-at-large Nat. council Boy Scouts Am., 1972-79; ruling elder John Knox Kirk, Kansas City, Mo., Grove Presbyn. Ch., Danville, Pa. Recipient Silver award United Methodist Ch., 1970, Mid-West Health Congress, 1971. Fellow Nat. Assn. Hosp. Devel. (nat. pres. 1975-76); mem. Nat. Soc. Fund Raisers (pres. Kansas City, Mo., chpt. 1972-73), Am. Hosp. Assn., Mid-Am.Hosp. Devel. Assn. (pres. 1973-74), Mid-West Health Congress (devel. chmn. 1972-74), Alpha Phi Omega (nat. pres. 1958-62, dir. 1950-80, Nat. Disting. Service award 1962), Delta Upsilon (pres. N.C. Alumni 1963-65). Clubs: Rotary (pres. club 1976-77), Relay House, Green Valley, Elks, Order Holy Grail, Order Golden Fleece, Order of The Arrow (Nat. Disting. Service award 1958). Editor Torch and Trefoil, 1960-61. Home: 341 Laredo Dr Birmingham AL 35225 Office: 3201 Fourth Ave S Birmingham AL 35222

ROTHE, ERNST, paper mfg. co. exec.; b. N.Y.C., Feb. 19, 1941; s. Tyge Ernst and Delight Dawson (Hall) R.; A.B. in Econs., Brown U., 1963; m. Nancy Louise Eberhart, Feb. 28, 1976; children—Ernst, Alden Augustus. Salesman, S.D. Warren Products Co., Geneva, Switzerland, 1967-69; asst. v.p. for Latin Am., Moller & Rothe Inc., N.Y.C., 1969-76; sales mgr. Caribbean Forest Products Co., Arecibo, P.R., 1977-78; project mgr. McLean Securities Inc., N.Y.C., 1979—; computer cons. Fish and Neave. Served to lt. U.S. Navy, 1963-67. Club: Badminton of N.Y. Home: Calle Taft No 1 Santurce PR 00911

ROTHEL, DAVID DELBERT, ednl. adminstr.; b. Berea, Ohio, Dec. 23, 1936; s. Bert Irvin and Kate (Rogers) R.; B.S., Ashland Coll., 1959; postgrad. Kent State U., 1960-65; m. Nancy Chandler, Dec. 18, 1966; children by previous marriage—David Michael, Loren Christopher; 1 dau., Laura Lynne. Tchr. drama and speech, Avon and North Royalton, Ohio, 1959-65; Fulbright tchr., Akureyri, Iceland, 1965-66; tchr. drama and speech Sarasota (Fla.) High Sch., 1966-68; producer, dir. The Players Theatre of Sarasota, 1968-71; creator, producer, dir. Sarasota Drug Edn. Program, 1972-79; dir. Sarasota Visual and Performing Arts Center, Sarasota County Schs., 1979—. Author: Who Was That Masked Man?: The Story of the Lone Ranger, 1976; The Singing Cowbuys, 1978; The Gre

ROTHENBERG, IRWIN Z., med. technologist; b. Bklyn., Feb. 17, 1944; s. Alex and Tillie (Rothstein) R.; B.S., Bklyn. Coll., City U. N.Y., 1965; M.S., Colo. State U., 1969; M.T., Good Samaritan Sch. Med. Tech., 1973. Staff techologist in microbiology Carl Hayden Community Hosp., Tucson, 1974; adminstrv. technologist McKee Med. Center, Loveland, Colo., 1974-79; lab. mgr. Crittenden Meml. Hosp., West Memphis, Ark., 1979—; lab. mgmt. cons. Performance Improvement Cons., Inc., 1979; state med. technologist rep. to Colo. PSRO, 1977-78. NSF exchange scientist, Antarctica, 1967-68. Mem. Am. Soc. Clin. Pathology, Am. Soc. Med. Tech., Clin. Lab. Mgmt. Assn., Sigma Xi, Phi Kappa Phi. Jewish. Home: 99 N Main St Apt 1810 Memphis TN 38103 Office: 200 Tyler St West Memphis AR 72301

ROTHGEB, RICHARD PRICE, hosp. personnel adminstr.; b. Richmond, Va., Nov. 21, 1941; s. Clark Martin and Jenetta (Price) R.; A.C., U. Richmond, 1973, B.C., 1974, M.B.A., 1977; m. Susan McCarn, Aug. 2, 1968; children—Joseph Wall, Michael Price. Staff acct. Brenco Inc., Petersburg, Va., 1972-73; chief acct. Retreat Hosp., Richmond, 1973-74, dir. personnel, 1974—; lectr. in field. Served with U.S. Army, 1963-64. Shotzberger scholar, 1970. Mem. Am. Soc. Hosp. Personnel Adminstrn., Va. Assn. Hosp. Personnel Adminstrn. (treas. 1978-79), Am. Soc. Personnel Adminstrn., Midlothian Jaycees (treas. 1975). Methodist. Home: 1710 Winfore Ct Midlothian VA 23113 Office: 2621 Grove Ave Richmond VA 23220

ROTHROCK, THOMAS BURTON, property mgmt. exec.; b. Halifax, N.C., Nov. 21, 1946; s. Kenneth Peddycord and Catherine P. (Williamson) R.; B.S. in Polit. Sci. and History, Appalachian State U., 1973; m. Alice Marie Lyons, Sept. 6, 1975. Gen. mgr. Land of Oz Theme Park, Banner Elk, N.C., 1973; salesman Moore Bus. Forms, Winston-Salem, N.C., 1974; v.p. Forsyth Mgmt., Inc., Myrtle Beach, S.C., 1975-78; gen. mgr. South Wind Assos., Myrtle Beach, 1978—; exec. v.p. Southwind Property Mgmt., Inc., 1979—. Active United Way, Cancer Fund. Served with U.S. Army, 1970-72. Mem. Myrtle Beach Hotel-Motel Assn. (pres. 1977-78, chmn. bd. 1978-80), Grand Strand C. of C. Democrat. Methodist. Club: Grand Strand Sertoma. Home: 1 Landing Rd PO Box 2269 Myrtle Beach SC 29577 Office: 5310 N Ocean Blvd Myrtle Beach SC 29577

ROTHSCHILD, BERNHARD ANDREW, JR., steel co. exec.; b. DeQuincy, La., July 18, 1914; s. Bernhard A. and Esther (Glasson) R.; student Centenary Coll., 1930-32; m. Dorothy Hoskins, May 5, 1942. Field supt. erection Rothschild Boiler & Tank Works, Shreveport, La., 1935-40, v.p. mfg. and constrn., 1945-59, pres., 1959-69, pres., chmn. bd., 1965—; dir. La. Bank; pres. Leets Corp. Pres. Shreveport Indsl. Council, 1960; chmn. Salvation Army, 1969; chmn. Shreveport Boys Club, 1968-69. Trustee Gulf South Research Inst. Served with AUS, 1941-46. Mem. Am. Welding Soc., Shreveport C. of C. (dir. 1955-62), Miss. Valley Assn. (dir. 1965-71, v.p. 1972-75), Red River Valley Assn. (dir. 1960-80). Episcopalian (sr. warden, mem. finance com. Diocese of La.). Mason (Shriner). Home: 815 Crescent Rd Shreveport LA 71107 Office: PO Box 1663 Shreveport LA 71165

ROTHWELL, PAUL DAVID, physician; b. Boston, Feb. 21, 1948; s. Mel-Thomas and Helen (Francis) R.; B.S., Bethany Nazarene Coll., 1969; M.D., U. Okla., 1974; m. Jan Shearer, Mar. 15, 1969; children—David, Timmy, Katie. Intern, Baptist Med. Center of Okla., 1974-75; practice medicine specializing in family practice, Bethany, Okla., 1975—; clin. faculty U. Okla. Coll. Medicine, Dept. Family Practice, 1977—; lectr. Keystone Profl. Inst. (Colo.), 1980—; chief of staff Bethany Gen. Hosp., 1979-80. Mem. ch. bd. Nazarene Ch., Bethany, 1978—. Diplomate Am. Acad. Family Physicians. Fellow Am. Acad. Family Physicians; mem. AMA, Okla. County Med. Soc., Okla. Med. Soc. Republican. Club: Oak Tree Golf. Home: 2100 Briarcliff St Bethany OK 73008 Office: 7530 NW 23rd St Bethany OK 73008

ROUBEY, LESTER WALTER, clergyman, educator; b. Balt., Feb. 11, 1915; s. Abraham and Sara (Cordish) R.; A.M., Johns Hopkins, 1936, Ph.D., 1938; M.H.L. and Rabbi, Hebrew Union Coll., 1947, D.D. (hon.), 1972; m. Charlotte Helen Stern, June 1, 1947; 1 son, Robert Arthur Stern. Rabbi, 1947; rabbi, Lancaster, Pa., 1947-53, Reading, Pa., 1954-64, East Orange, N.J., 1964-66, Baton Rouge, 1966—; adj. prof. religion Franklin and Marshall Coll., Lancaster, 1951-53; asso. prof. Romance langs. Kutztown (Pa.) State Coll., 1961-64; lectr. Romance langs. La. State U., Baton Rouge, 1966-70, asso. prof., 1970—. Mem. civic com., Lancaster, 1950-53; mem. adv. bd. Baton Rouge Gen. Hosp., 1967—, trustee, 1972—; mem. religious com. Reading round table NCCJ; chmn. Reading com. Am. Jewish Tercentenary, 1954-55; bd. dirs. ARC, 1968-71. Mem. Central Conf. Am. Rabbis, Hebrew Union Coll.-Jewish Inst. Religion Alumni Assn. (trustee 1953-56), Am. Assn. Tchrs. French, Am. Assn. Tchrs. Italian, AAUP, Modern Lang. Assn., Am. Council Teaching Fgn. Langs., South Central Modern Lang. Assn. (chmn. Italian sect. 1969), Phi Sigma Iota. Mason (32 deg., Shriner), Rotarian. Club: Baton Rouge Country. Producer, conductor series of TV worship programs, Lancaster, 1951-53. Office: 3354 Kleinert Ave Baton Rouge LA 70806 also Dept Fgn Langs La State U Baton Rouge LA 70803

ROUBY, RALPH ANTHONY, constrn. co. exec.; b. Kinston, N.C., Nov. 30, 1944; s. Anthony and Mildred Christine (Redd) R.; student U. N.C., Wilmington, 1967; m. Eunice Jeanette Sims, Mar. 31, 1973; children—Anthony Brian, Kevin Michael, Ralph Andrew. Sr. Acct., then cost acct. IBM, 1967-72; fin. analyst, then project acct. Daniel Constrn. Co., Greenville, S.C., 1972-73; mgr. acctg. W.H. Weaver Constrn. Co., Greensboro, N.C., 1976; treas. Davis Mech. Contractors, Inc., Greenville, 1976—. Office: Davis Mech Contractors Inc PO Box 1847 Greenville SC 29602

ROUECHE, JOHN EDWARD, II, educator; b. Statesville, N.C., Sept. 3, 1938; s. John Edward and Mary (Harris) R.; B.A., Lenoir Rhyne Coll., Hickory, N.C., 1960; M.A., Appalachian Coll., Boone, N.C., 1961; Ph.D., Fla. State U., 1964; m. Suanne Davis; children by previous marriage—Michelle Renee, John Edward, III. Dean coll. Gaston Coll., Gastonia, N.C., 1964-67; asso. research educator U. Calif., Los Angeles, 1967-69; dir. jr. coll. div. Nat. Lab. Higher Edn., 1968-71, also asso. prof. edn. Duke U.; prof. edn., dir. community coll. leadership program U. Tex., Austin, 1971—; community coll. editor Jessey-Bass Publishers, 1971—. Pres. Doss Sch. PTA, 1974-75; chmn. bd. Northwest Hills United Methodist Ch., 1973-76. Recipient Distinguished Service award A.M.E. Ch., 1971, Outstanding Research award Council of Univs. and Colls., 1978; Outstanding Alumnus award Appalachian State U., 1979; named lifetime ambassador for N.C., 1978, Ky. col., 1979; Kellogg fellow, 1962-64. Mem. Am. Assn. Community and Jr. Colls., Am. Assn. Higher Edn., Council Univs. and Colls. (dir.), Phi Beta Kappa, Phi Delta Kappa. Author books, articles, monographs. Editorial bd. profl. jours. Home: 6804 Edgefield Dr Austin TX 78731 Office: EDB 348 Univ Tex Austin TX 78712

ROULSTON, CHARLES ROBERT, educator; b. Balt., May 27, 1930; s. William Andrew and Mildred (Wright) R.; B.A., U. Md., College Park, 1954, Ph.D., 1965; M.A., Ind. U., 1957; m. Helen Hoglund, Jan. 11, 1939; 1 dau., Katherine Elizabeth. Instr. English, U. N.D., Grand Forks, 1957-60, U. Md., College Park, 1960-64; prof. English, Murray (Ky.) State U., 1964—. Mem. Modern Lang. Assn., AAUP, Ky. Philol. Assn. Home: 1706 College Farm Rd Murray KY 42071

ROUNDTREE, GEORGE ALEXANDER, educator; b. Vicksburg, Miss., Feb. 14, 1930; s. Raymond Ernest and Margaret Mary (Wright) R.; B.S., La. State U., 1968, M.S.W., 1970, Ed.D., 1976; m. Nellie Font, July 19, 1950; children—George Aaron, Jonathan Arlen. Analyst, La. Dept. Hwys., Baton Rouge, 1949-53; quality control chemist Kaiser Aluminum & Chem. Co., Baton Rouge, 1953-70; health planner, asst. dir. La. Capital Area Health Planning Council, Baton Rouge, 1970-71, exec. dir., 1971-73; asst. chmn. corrections specialization La. State U., Baton Rouge, 1973-78, dir. social work extension and continuing edn., 1978—, asso. prof., 1979—, acting chmn. of correction specialization, 1978-79; expert witness E. Baton Rouge Parish Family Ct., 1979; cons. Manpower Adv. Council, 1974. Mem. exec. com. Baton Rouge Alcohol and Drug Abuse, 1979—; mem. Eden Park Adv. Council, 1979—, pres., 1979; mem. com. La. Health Planning Council, 1978; reserve dep. sheriff Iberville, Orleans and E. Baton Rouge Parishes, 1979—; advisor Baker City Ct., 1979. Served with U.S. Army, 1948-49. Recipient E. Baton Rouge Parish Family Ct. Plaque of Appreciation for Service, 1977; La. Dept. Corrections Cert. of Award, 1976; NIMH fellow, 1968-69. Mem. Acad. Cert. Social Workers, Nat. Assn. Social Workers Clin. Registry, Am. Public Health Assn., Am. Correctional Assn., Correctional Edn. Assn., Nat. Council on Crime and Delinquency, La. Public Health Assn., La. Assn. of Criminal Justice Social Workers (treas. 1976-77), La. Council on Criminal Justice (sec. 1977-78). Democrat. Baptist. Clubs: Optimists, Kiwanis, Masons, Gideons. Author: Self Esteem and Social Adjustment - The Minerva Associates, 1979; contbr. articles in field to profl. jours. Home: Route 9 PO Box 696 Denham Springs LA 70726 Office: Sch Social Welfare La State Univ Baton Rouge LA 70803

ROUNTREE, HORACE GENE, retail trade co. exec., religious orgn. ofcl.; b. Pelican, La., Oct. 19, 1931; s. Perry and Ada M. (DeSoto) R.; B.S., Southwest Mo. State Coll., 1959; Ed.M., U. Okla., 1964; postgrad. Washington U., St. Louis, 1966, U. Ark., 1970-75; m. Carol J. Thompson, June 23, 1962; children—William Hunter, Clare Marguerite. Tchr. Johnson Jr. High Sch., Cheyenne, Wyo., 1962-63, Centennial High Sch., Pueblo, Colo., 1959-61; instr. English and reading Meramec Community Coll., St. Louis, 1965-66; counselor Hamsher High Sch., Webster Grove, Mo., 1965-66; personnel and mktg. dir. west central div. Ralston Purina Co., Rogers, Ark., 1966-71; v.p. pub. relations Wal-Mart Stores, Inc., Bentonville, Ark., 1972—. Cons. human behavior and communications, Bentonville, Ark., 1971—. Chmn. Gov.'s Commn. on Employment of Handicapped, 1967—; mem. Pres.'s Com. on Employment Handicapped, 1967—; dist. chmn. Beaver Lake Dist. council Boy Scouts Am., 1970-72, v.p. Westark council, 1971-72; mem. Mo. Liturg. Council, Roman Catholic Archdiocese of St. Louis, 1966; extraordinary minister of eucharist, St. Vincent DePaul Cath. Ch., Rogers, Ark., 1976—; leader Rotary group study exchange team, India, 1976. Bd. dirs. Ozark Guidance Center, pres., 1973-77; bd. dirs. Nat. Council of Catholic Laity, 1971—, pres., 1971-73; bd. dirs. Easter Seal Soc., 1968-75; mem. task force study com. on vocat. edn. U. Mo., Columbia, 1978. Recipient Distinguished Service award Jr. C. of C., 1969, Nat. citation Muscular Dystrophy Assn. Am., 1959. Mem. Ark. Free Enterprise Assn. (pres. 1969-70), Am. Mgmt. Assn., Am. Soc. Personnel Adminstrs., Mass Retailing Inst. (personnel exec. com. 1974-76), Rogers (dir. 1967-70, mayor's citizens com. 1967-69), U.S. (pub. affairs com. 1974—) chambers commerce, Ark. and Mo. Retail Mchts. Assn. (dir. 1976—), Ark. Found of Asso. Colls. (trustee 1975—), Phi Delta Kappa, Alpha Psi Omega. Roman Catholic. Rotarian (pres. 1969-70, dist. gov. 1980-81, American Citizens award 1970), K.C. Author: Thy Will Be Done in All Things, 1962. Editor: Eight Hundred Colleges Face the Future (Danforth Found. Commn.), 1966; Church Sponsored Higher Education in the United States (M. Patillo, J. McKenzie). Contbr. articles on personnel counseling and edn. to profl. publs. Home: 905 S 15th St Rogers AR 72756 Office: PO Box 116 702 SW 8th St Bentonville AR 72712

ROUP, SUSAN WADE, nurse; b. Waynesboro, Va., Aug. 18, 1942; d. Robert Joseph and Frances (Blackwell) Wade; diploma Lynchburg (Va.) Gen. Hosp., 1964; 1 dau., Robin Renee. Nurse, Waynesboro Community Hosp., 1964-67; staff nurses operating room Stuart Circle Hosp., Richmond, Va., 1967-70; operating room supr. St. Mary's Hosp., Richmond, Va., 1970-73, dir. operating room-recovery room services, 1973-80; dir. operating room services Palmyra Park Hosp., Albany, Ga., 1980—. Mem. Assn. Operating Room Nurses. Baptist. Club: Tuckahoe Village Recreational Assn. Home: 1906 Chatham Dr Albany GA 31702 Office: Palmyra Park Hosp PO Box 1908 Albany GA 31702

ROUS, STEPHEN NORMAN, physician, educator; b. N.Y.C., Nov. 1, 1931; s. David H. and Luba (Margulies) R.; A.B., Amherst Coll., 1952; M.D., N.Y. Med. Coll., 1956; M.S., U. Minn., 1963; m. Margot Woolfolk, Nov. 12, 1966; children—Benjamin, David. Intern, Phila. Gen. Hosp., 1956-57, resident, 1959-60; resident Flower-Fifth Ave. and Met. Hosp., N.Y.C., 1957-59, Mayo Clinic, Rochester, Minn., 1960-63; practice medicine specializing in urology, San Francisco, 1963-68; asso. prof. urology N.Y. Med. Coll., N.Y.C., 1968-72, asso. dean, 1970-72; prof. surgery, chief div. urology Mich. State U., East Lansing, 1972-75; prof., chmn. dept. urology Med. U. S.C., Charleston, 1975—; urologist-in-chief Med. U. S.C. and County hosps., Charleston, 1975—; cons. urologist Saginaw VA Hosp., 1972-75, Charleston VA Hosp., 1975—. Mem. East Lansing Planning Commn., 1974-75; Vestryman, jr. warden Episcopal Ch., 1974-75, layreader, mem. diocesan com. continuing edn., 1975—; vestryman St. Michael's Episc. Ch., 1979—, chmn. every mem. canvass, 1979, 80; del. Diocesan Conv., 1978. Diplomate Am. Bd. Urology. Fellow A.C.S., Am. Acad. Pediatrics mem. Soc. Univ. Urologists, Internat. Soc. Urology, Am. Urol. Assn., AMA, Nat. Urologic Forum. Soc. Pediatric Urology, Mayo Alumni Assn. (v.p., chmn. devel. com. 1979—). Republican. Club: Seabrook Island. Author: Understanding Urology, 1973; Urology in Primary Care, 1976. Contbr. articles to profl. jours. Home: 43 Legare St Charleston SC 29401 Office: Dept Urology Med Univ South Carolina 171 Ashley Ave Charleston SC 29403

ROUSAKIS, JOHN PAUL, mayor; b. Savannah, Ga., Jan. 14, 1929; s. Paul V. and Antigone (Alexopoulos) R.; B.B.A., U. Ga.; LL.D., John Marshall U.; m. Irene Fotopoulos, Sept. 5, 1953; children—Rhonda, Paul, Thea, Tina. Ins. broker; mayor, Savannah, 1970—; mem. Adv. Council Intergovtl. Relations. Mem. Ga. Motion Picture and TV Adv. Com. Mem. Chatham County (Ga.) Commrs., 1965-70, vice-chmn. commn., 1969-70. Served with CIC, AUS, Named Outstanding Young Man Savannah, 1962, Outstanding Young Man of Ga. Mem. Nat. League Cities (2d v.p., past pres., dir.), U.S. Conf. Mayors (adv. com.), Ga. Mcpl. Assn. (past pres.), Sertoma, Ahepa, Am. Legion. Elk, Mason (Shriner). Home: 1905 Colonial Dr Savannah GA 31406 Office: City Hall PO Box 1027 Savannah GA 31042

ROUSE, ERNEST PHILIP, entomologist; b. Bridgeport, Nebr., Aug. 5, 1913; s. Ernest Grant and Mary Arminda :Stevens) R.; student John Brown Coll., 1930-31; B.S.A., U. Ark., 1948, M.S. in Entomology, 1958; m. Marie May Shaffer, June 21, 1940; children—George Ernest, Joe Philip. Def. worker Denver Ordnance Plant, 1941-43, Pine Bluff (Ark.) Arsenal. 1944-45; county agrl. agt., agrl. extension service U. Ark.. Ozark and Mountain Home, 1948-52, curator Entomol. Mus. dept. entomology, Fayetteville, 1955—; field rep. Cameron Feed Mills, Little Rock, 1952-53; owner operator Gold Nugget Mill Co., Flippin, Ark., 1953-54; tchr. sci., high sch., Cotter, Ark., 1954-55. Served with USN, 1936-40. Mem. Entomol. Soc. Am., Kans. Entomol. Soc.. Am. Registry Profl. Entomologists, SAR, Alpha Lambda Tau, Gamma Sigma Delta. Democrat. Presbyn. Mason, Rotarian, Lion. Contbr. articles to profl. jours. Home: 849 Kelly St Fayetteville AR 72701

ROUSEY, JOHN SHELTON, computer co. exec.; b. Swifton, Ark., Apr. 9, 1943; s. John Walter and Violet Emogene (Louks) R.; B.S. in Math., Ark. State Coll., 1965; M.A. in Math., U. Ala., 1969; m. Joyce Kirby, Jan. 28, 1963; children—John David, Robert Edward. Lead programmer Boeing Co., Huntsville, Ala., 1965-69; with Univ. Computing Co., Dallas, 1969—, mgr. systems programming, 1973-76, mgr. tech. services, 1976-78, dir. 370 service center, 1978—. Del. Democratic Senatorial Dist. Conv., 1975. Mem. Assemblies of God. Ch. Office: 1930 Hiline Dr Dallas TX 75207

ROUSON, WILLIE ERVIN, coll. adminstr.; b. Elizabeth City, N.C., Dec. 31, 1928; s. Willie Winston and Helen (Hill) R.; B.S., Xavier U. La., 1951; M.A., N.C. Central U., 1958; Ph.D., Fla. State U., 1972; m. Vivian Reissland, June 22, 1953; children—Lizette, Darryl, Brigette, Janine, Damian. Tchr., coach St. Lucy High Sch., La., 1955-57; librarian asst. N.C. Central U., 1957-58; dir. student personnel and guidance Gibbs Jr. Coll., St. Petersburg, Fla., 1958-65; counselor, dir. counseling St. Petersburg Jr. Coll., 1965-70, dir. counseling, 1972-74, dir. student campus life, 1976-78; v.p. student affairs Palm Beach Jr. Coll., 1978-79; faculty adviser Fla. State U., Tallahassee, 1970-72; dean coll. Roxbury Community Coll. Boston, 1974-76; cons. in field. Chmn. sch. bd. Immaculate Conception Day Care Center, 1970-74; mem. Coll. Scholarship Adv. Bd. Pinellas County, 1976—; bd. dirs. St. Paul's Sch., 1977—, Family Counseling Center Pinellas County, 1976—. Named Mr. Wonderful, Delta Sigma Theta, Omega Speaker of Yr., 1978; recipient Community Service award NAACP, 1978; Omega scholar, 1947-49; N.C. Central U. Grad fellow, 1957-58. Mem. Am. Coll. Personnel Assn., Nat. Vocat. Guidance Assn., Am., Fla., Suncoast personnel and guidance assns., Mass. Coll. Personnel Assn. (co-founder), S.C. Personnel Assn., Nat. Assn. Student Personnel Adminstrs., Nat. Student Devel. Council, NEA, Fla. Teaching Profession, Omega Psi Phi, Phi Delta Kappa. Democrat. Roman Catholic. Clubs: K.C., Optimists. Home: 5415 Fox Valley Trail Lake Worth FL 33463

ROUSSEL, HERBERT JOSEPH, JR., engring. co. exec.; b. New Orleans, July 13, 1931; s. Herbert Joseph and Dorothy (Moll) R.; B.S. in Civil Engring., Tulane U., 1961, M.S. in Civil Engring., 1964, D.Eng., 1979; m. Joyce Ellen Freeling, Aug. 4, 1956; children—Herbert Joseph III, Karen Elizabeth. Engr., Shell Oil Co., Norco, La., 1961-62, J. Ray McDermott & Co., New Orleans, 1962-64, Avondale Shipyards Inc., New Orleans, 1964, Boeing Co., New Orleans, 1964-65; asso. N.P. Jeffrey, New Orleans, 1965-68; pres. Roussel Engring., Inc., Kenner, La., 1968—; adj. prof. civil engring. Tulane U., 1964—. Served with AUS, 1952-54. Recipient La. Hwy. Engr. Assn. award, 1961; W.F. Thompkin's award Tulane U., 1961, Alumni award, 1969; registered profl. engr., Tex., La., Miss., Ala., N.J. Mem. Am. Concrete Inst., Am. Soc. C.E., Soc. Tulane Engrs., La. Engring. Soc., Nat. Soc. Profl. Engrs., Am. Soc. for Testing and Materials, Am. Welding Soc., Soc. Petroleum Engrs., Sigma Xi, Tau Beta Pi, Alpha Sigma Lambda. Home: 1901 Cleary Ave Metairie LA 70001 Office: PO Box 1369 Kenner LA 70063

ROUSSELL, NORWARD, supt. schs.; b. New Orleans, July 11, 1934; B.A., Dillard U., 1960; M.A. in Sci. Edn., Fisk U., 1965; Ed.D., Wayne State U., 1973; married, 3 children. Prin., James Derham Jr. High Sch., New Orleans; dir. secondary edn. New Orleans Public Schs., 1973-74, supt. dist. IV, 1979—; program officer C.S. Mott Found., Flint, Mich., 1975-79. Bd. dirs. Nat. Center Community Edn., Flint, 1972-73, Urban League Flint, 1976-79, Flint Bus. Devel. Corp., 1977-79, Urban Coalition of Greater Flint, 1978-79; mem. New Orleans Met. Area Manpower Com., 1973-75; adv. council Greater New Orleans Urban League Street Acad., 1973-75; mem. adminstrv. bd. Genesee County Community Action Agy., 1976; chmn. Flint area appeal United Negro Coll. Fund, 1976-79. Mem. Am. Assn. Sch. Adminstrs., Assn. Supervision and Curriculum Devel., Assn. Black Found. Execs., Nat. Alliance Black Sch. Educators, Nat. Assn. Secondary Sch. Prins., Nat. Council for Yr.-Round Edn., Nat. Community Edn. Assn., Mich. Community Edn. Assn., Phi Delta Kappa Omega Phi Psi, Lion. Home: 7552 Briarheath New Orleans LA 70128 Office: 2440 Mirabeau Ave New Orleans LA 70122

ROUX, KERMIT LOUIS, JR., anesthesiologist; b. New Orleans, Mar. 18, 1941; s. Kermit Louis and Elmire Louise (Escobedo) R.; M.S., Tulane U., 1964, M.D., 1964; m. Kathryn Mary Felt, Apr. 21, 1967; children—Kermit Louis III, Kristin. Intern, U. Minn. Hosps., Mpls., 1965-67, resident in anesthesiology, 1965-67; mem. staff Charity Hosp., New Orleans, 1971—; chief anesthesiologist East Jefferson Gen. Hosp., Metairie, La., 1971—; asst. prof. surgery Tulane Med. Sch., 1971—; dir. Comml. Bank, Metairie. Diplomate Am. Bd. Anesthesiology. Fellow Am. Coll. Anesthesiology; mem. Am. Soc. Anesthesiology, La. Soc. Anesthesiology (pres. 1977), La. Med. Soc., Jefferson Parish Med. Soc., So. Med. Assn., Nat. Rifle Assn. (life), Internat. Wine and Food Soc., La. Hist. Soc. Clubs: Game Conservation Internat., Safari Internat. Contbr. articles to sci. jours. Home: 5200 Purdue Dr Metairie LA 70003 Office: 4200 Houma Blvd Metairie LA 70002

ROVENSTINE, WENDELL OTIS, clergyman, coll. adminstr.; b. Colorado Springs, Colo., Mar. 7, 1938; s. John Monson and Aleda C. (Warmerdam) R.; B.A., Bartlesville Wesleyan Coll., 1960; m. Esther L. Schendel, May 29, 1959; children—Allen D., J. Nathan, M. Kurtis, Mick, Dalene. Ordained to ministry, Wesleyan Ch.; pastor Wesleyan Ch., Iola, Kans., 1959-61, Winona (Kans.) Wesleyan Ch., 1961-66, Salina (Kans.) Wesleyan Ch., 1966-76; dir. public affairs/recuitment Bartlesville (Okla.) Wesleyan Coll., 1976—. Exec. sec. Bill Glass Crusade, Salina; pres. PTA, Hageman Grade Sch., Salina, 1974-75; v.p. Kans. Wesleyan Youth, 1963-72. Mem. Okla. Coll. Public Relations Assn. Republican. Home: 1906 S Dewey St Bartlesville OK 74003 Office: 2201 Silverlake Rd Bartlesville OK 74003

ROWAN, JOHN ROBERT, med. services adminstr.; b. Joliet, Ill., Aug. 19, 1919; s. Hugh Hamilton and Elizabeth Margaret (Maloney) R.; student Butler U., 1952-53, Ind. U., 1953-54; m. Ruth Elaine Boyle, June 17, 1944; 1 son, Robert J. Personnel specialist VA br. office, Chgo., 1946; personnel officer VA Hosp., Ft. Benjamin Harrison, Ind., 1946-51, VA Hosp., Indpls., 1951-56; asst. mgr. VA Hosp., Iron Mountain, Mich., 1956-60, asst. dir., 1960-67; hosp. adminstrn. specialist VA Central Office, Washington, 1967-69; dir. VA Hosp., Manchester, N.H., 1969-71, VA Hosp., Buffalo, 1971-72; dir. VA Med. Center, Lexington, Ky., 1972—, VA Med. Dist. 11, 1975—; mem. Ohio Valley Regional Med. Programs, Regional Adv. Council, 1972-76, Ky. Comprehensive Health Planning Council, 1972—. Bd. dirs. Broadripple Ind. Civic League, 1952-56, pres., 1952, 54; bd. dirs. Am. Cancer Soc., Ind. div., 1966-67, United Way of the Blue Grass, 1976—, East Ky. Health Systems Agy., 1976—. Served with USAAF, 1942-46. Decorated Bronze Star; recipient Merit citation DAV, 1964, 1970, 1975, Outstanding Performance award VA, 1974, Meritorious Service award Am. Legion of Ky., 1975, Citation of Merit, Mil. Order of the Cooties Supreme Pup Tent, 1970. Fellow Am. Coll. Hosp. Adminstrs.; mem. Am. Hosp. Assn., Ky. Hosp. Assn. (trustee 1979—, v.p. Blue Grass dist. 1979—), Lexington Hosp. Council, Ky. Fed. Exec. Assn. (pres. 1975-76), Assn. of Mil. Surgeons, Fed. Hosp. Inst. Alumni Assn. Roman Catholic. Home: Quarters 8 Veterans Administration Med Center Lexington KY 40507 Office: Veterans Adminstration Med Center Lexington KY 40507

ROWE, BONNIE GORDON, music co. exec.; b. Buford, Ga., May 3, 1922; s. Bonnie Gordon and Alma (Poole) R.; student Ga. Evening Coll., 1939-41, U. Wichita, 1948-49, Ga. State Coll., 1949-52; m. Mary Wilburta Shidler; 1 dau., Sharon Lynn; m. 2d, Gloria Lucille Fairfax, Feb. 17, 1962 (div.); 1 dau., Susan Rebecca. Traffic mgr. Bonanza Air Lines, Las Vegas, 1946-48; music tchr. 1948-52; owner Rowe Accordion Distbg. Co., Rowe Accordion Center, Atlanta, 1952-56, Atlanta Music Pub. Co., 1956—, B. Rowe Music Co., Atlanta, 1957—; pres.-treas. B.C.R. Corp. Served to lt. col. USAAF, World War II; ETO. Decorated Air medals with three oak leaf clusters. Mem. Southeastern Accordion Assn. (past pres.), Nat. Assn. Music Mchts., Atlanta Fedn. Musicians, Travelers Protective Assn., Atlanta C. of C. Res. Officers Assn., Internat. Platform Assn., Gamma Delta Phi. Elk. Clubs Sandtown Civitan (past pres.; v.p. Met. Atlanta chpt., lt. gov. Ga. dist. North), Dobbins AFB Officers. Composer: Accordionique, 1953 Vivolet, 1956, More and More and More, 1964, Dedication, 1964, All I Really See Is You, 1965, I Love Only You, 1965, Predudio Reminisci, 1969. Home: 5085 Erin Rd SW Atlanta GA 30331

ROWE, CHARLES SPURGEON, editor; b. Fredericksburg, Va., May 28, 1925; s. Josiah Pollard and Genevieve Sinclair (Bailey) R.; A.B., Washington & Lee U., 1947, postgrad. in law, 1947-49; m. Mary Ann Else Huntsman, May 1, 1970; children by previous marriage—Ashley K. Rowe Gould, Charles S., Timothy D.; stepchildren—Laura Huntsman, Kathleen Huntsman. Editor, co-publisher The Free Lance Star, Fredericksburg, 1949—; mng. editor, 1949-76; pres. The Free Lance Star Publishing Co., 1949—; pres. Star Broadcasting Corp., Fredericksburg, 1957—; dir. AP, 1976—, Fredericksburg Savings and Loan Assn. Chmn. bd. trustees Central Rappahannock Regional Library, Fredericksburg, 1969-75. Served with USNR, 1943-46. Recipient George Mason award, 1974; named Fredericksburg Jaycees Outstanding Young Man, 1958. Mem. Associated Press Mng. Editors Assn. (pres. 1969), Am. Soc. Newspaper Editors (dir. 1971-77, 79—), Am. Newspaper Publishers Assn., So. Newspaper Publishers Assn., Va. Press Assn. (dir. 1977—), Va. Freedom Info. Council (chmn. 1977-79), Phi Beta Kappa, Omicron Delta Kappa, Phi Delta Phi, Delta Tau Delta, Soc. Profl. Journalists, Sigma Delta Chi. Episcopalian. Home: 501 Hanover St Fredericksburg VA 22401 Office: 616 Amelia St PO Box 617 Fredericksburg VA 22401

ROWE, RICHARD THOMAS, mfg. co. exec.; b. Champaign, Ill., Mar. 17, 1930; s. John Clifford and Margaret (Moore) R.; A.A., Joplin Jr. Coll.; indsl. supervision cert. Internat. Corr. Schs.; m. Norma Darlene Kellenberger, Aug. 19, 1955; children—Margaret Lynn, Thomas Mark, Stacy Rene. With Hilti Mfg. Co., Inc., Tulsa, 1979—, mfg. engr., 1979—. Mem. Soc. Mfg. Engrs., Am. Inst. Indsl. Engrs. Republican. Mem. Christian Ch. Club: Masons. Home: 5155 E 27th Place Tulsa OK 74114 Office: Hilti Mfg Co Inc 5404 S 122nd E Ave Box 35408 Tulsa OK 74145

ROWE, ROBERT LAIRD, petroleum co. exec.; b. Chgo., Oct. 24, 1924; s. Charles Laird and Margaret Park (Jaques) R.; A.B., Columbia U., 1948; postgrad. in bus. N.Y. U., 1949-51; m. Alma Jean Beers, Oct. 2, 1948; children—Barbara Anne, George Allen. With Shell Oil Co., including subs. and associated cos., 1948—, various positions in treasury and services, now mgr. communication services. Founder, dir. treas. Fairlawn (N.J.) Mental Health Center, 1960-71; mem. Citizen's Sch. Com., Fairlawn, 1962-68; com. chmn. Boy Scouts Am., Fairlawn, 1967-69. Mem. United Ch. of Christ (pres. ch. 1977—). Home: 6226 Elmgrove Rd Spring TX 77379 Office: Shell Oil Co PO Box 2463 Houston TX 77001

ROWLAND, BOBBIE HAYNES, educator; b. Cherryville, N.C.; d. Andrel Hall and Ethel Estelle (Ritch) Haynes; A.B., U. N.C., 1951, M.S., 1968, Ph.D., 1974; m. Walter A. Carnes, Jr., Sept. 1, 1951 (dec.); children—Linda Carole Carnes Queen, Laura Leslie; m. 2d, Ralph C. Rowland, Jr., Dec. 21, 1966. Dir. children's work 1st United Methodist Ch., Gastonia, N.C., 1957-67; asso. prof. human devel. and learning U. N.C., Charlotte, 1969—. Bd. trustees Gaston Coll., 1971-79; mem. Gaston County Sch. Bd., 1969-73. Mem. Assn. Supervision and Curriculum Devel., Nat. Assn. Edn. of Young Children, Assn. Childhood Edn. Internat., Christian Educators Fellowship, N.C. Kindergarten Assn. (pres. 1969). Methodist. Author: (with Nancy White) Creative Activities, 1972. Home: 317 Rosemary Ln Gastonia NC 28052 Office: College of Human Development University of North Carolina Charlotte NC 28223

ROWLAND, CLYDE RAYMOND, JR., mobile home sales co. exec.; b. Richmond, Ind., Feb. 5, 1949; s. Clyde Raymond and Nellie Mae (Hughes) R.; student Pasco-Hernando Community Coll., 1979—; m. Jo-Ann Louisette Roy, Jan. 27, 1976. Sec.-treas. Rowland Motor Co. Inc., Brooksville, Fla., 1966-72; owner, operator Bushnell Mobile Home Sales (Fla.), 1973, Village Mobile Home Sales, Brooksville, 1973-78, Aire-King of Brooksville (Fla.), 1977—; owner, pres. Village Mobile Homes Sales Inc. Brooksville, 1978—. Mem. Nat. Fedn. Ind. Businesses (mem. actional council 1979—), Hernando County C. of C., Suncoast Better Bus. Bur. Democrat. Home: PO Box 1540 Brooksville FL 33512 Office: Village Mobile Homes Sales Inc 709 US Hwy 98 N Brooksville FL 33512

ROWLAND, DAVID JACK, coll. adminstr.; b. Columbus, Ohio, June 17, 1921; s. David Henry and Ethel Ryan R.; B.S., Ohio U., 1949; M.A., U. Ala., 1951; Litt.D. (hon.), Athens Coll., 1963; LL.D. (hon.) Jacksonville U., 1967; m. Mary Ellen Stinson, Apr. 8, 1944; children—David Allen, Ryan Stinson, Sue Ellen. With Gen. Electric Co., Zanesville, Ohio, 1946-49; prin. Warrior High Sch., Birmingham, Ala., 1949-56; pres. Walker Coll., Jasper, Ala., 1956—; dir. 1st Nat. Bank, Jasper. Chmn., Ala. Surface Mining Commn., 1976—; pres. Jefferson Health Found.; mem. Indsl. Devel. Bd., 1970—; pres. Black Warrior council Boy Scouts Am., 1967. Served with U.S. Army, 1942-46. Decorated Legion of Merit, Army Commendation medal; recipient Silver Beaver award Boy Scouts Am. Mem. Res. Officers Assn., Jasper C. of C. (past pres.), Kappa Phi Kappa. Methodist. Clubs: Rotary (past pres.), Relay House. Home: 1005 Valley Rd Jasper AL 35501 Office: Walker Coll Jasper AL 35501

ROWLAND, JAY MILLER, JR., container co. exec.; b. Boulder, Colo., Feb. 15, 1921; s. Jay Miller and Maude Louise (Eckel) R.; student Tulane U., 1940-43, Kans. State Tchrs. Coll., 1943; LL.B., Tulane U., 1948, J.D., 1969; postgrad. in Bus. Adminstrn., Houston U., 1964; m. Leonora Schwartz, Dec. 9, 1943; 1 son, Jay Miller. Staff adjuster, storm loss supr., br. claims mgr. Gen. Adjustment Bur., Inc., Colo., Wyo., N.Mex., 1948-54; claim examiner, dist. claim office mgr., claim analyst Allstate Ins. Co., Miss. and Ark., 1954-58; home office claims mgr. Delta Fire and Casualty Co., Baton Rouge, La., 1958-59; claims dept. mgr. Pioneer Mut. Casualty Co., Columbus, Ohio, 1959-61; supt. claims, claims sec., asst. v.p. Preferred Ins. Co. of Grand Rapids (Mich.), 1961-62, v.p. subs. S.W. Indemnity Co. of Dallas, 1961-62; investigator-negotiator, asst. dir. indsl. relations Ala. Dry Dock and Shipbldg. Co., Mobile, 1962-67; dist. claim mgr., div. claim tng. adminstr. Am. Mut. Ins. Cos., Bryn Mawr, Pa., 1967-69; personnel dir., mgr. personnel relations U. S.Ala., Med. Center, Mobile, 1969-75; mgr. indsl. relations The Lerio Corp., Mobile, 1975—; part-time freelance photojournalist. Mem. port devel. and legis. coms. C. of C., 1964-67; past mem. bd. dirs. Mobile County Assn. Mental Health, C.A.N. Rehab. Found., 1974-79; mem. Pres.'s Com. Employment Handicapped; mem. project rev. com. S.W. Health Systems Agy. Served with USAF, 1942-46; U.S.N.G., 1953-54. Recipient Certificate of Appreciation, Vocat. Rehab. and Crippled Children Services, 1970; Citation for Meritorious Service, Pres. Com. on Employment of the Handicapped, 1972; Outstanding Service award Mobile County Assn. Mental Health, 1973; Certificate of award Internat. Assn. Personnel in Employment Security, 1975; Outstanding Service award Ala. Assn. Mental Health, 1976; cert. appreciation U. South Ala. Med. Center, 1975, Mobile County chpt. Nat. Assn. for Mental Health, 1979; recipient prizes and awards for photography. Mem. Am. Soc. Personnel Adminstrn. Personnel Accreditation Inst. (accredited exec.), Mobile Personnel Assn. (past dir.), Am. Arbitration Assn., Nat. Panel Consumer Arbitrators, Asso. Industries of Ala., Mobile Press Club, Camera South of Mobile (v.p.), Amateur Trapshooting Assn., Bur. of Nat. Affairs, Inc. (personnel policies forum 1977-78). Presbyterian. Clubs: Lake Forest Yacht and Country (dir. 1965-67), Hole in One, Tulane Alumni T, Masons. Numerous photos and articles published in newspapers and mags. Home: PO Box 113 Spanish Fort AL 36527 Office: PO Box 2084 Mobile AL 36601

ROWLAND, THOMAS CLIFFORD, JR., physician; b. Dawson, Ga., Aug. 23, 1934; s. Thomas Clifford and Ethel (Cunningham) R.; student U. S.C., 1952-55; M.D., Med. Coll. S.C., 1959; m. Isabelle Hall, Aug. 3, 1957; children—Thomas C., Mary Hall, Elliott Holmes, Lewis Cunningham. Intern, Greenville (S.C.) Gen. Hosp., 1959-60; resident Nat. Naval Med. Center, Bethesda, Md., 1962-65; commd. lt. M.C., U.S. Navy, 1959, advanced through grades to lt. comdr., 1965; ret., 1968; practice medicine specializing in obstetrics and gynecology, Columbia, S.C., 1968—; chief obstetrics and gynecology S.C. Baptist Hosp., 1971-72, chief staff, 1978—; chief obstetrics and gynecology Richland Meml. Hosp., 1973-74; asso. clin. prof. dept. obstetrics and gynecology U. S.C. Sch. Medicine; dir. Citizens & So. Nat. Bank S.C. Bd. dirs. S.C. Cancer Soc.; bd. dirs. Central S.C. council Boy Scouts Am.; trustee Heathwood Hall Episcopal Sch. Diplomate Am. Bd. Obstetrics and Gynecology. Mem. Richland County Med. Soc., S.C. Med. Assn., Am. Coll. Obstetrics and Gynecology, AMA, So. Gynecol. Soc., Am. Fertility Soc., Am. Assn. Gynecologic Laparoscopists. Presbyterian. Clubs: Summit, Forest Lake. Home: 19 Cedarwood Ln Columbia SC 29204 Office: 1333 Taylor St Columbia SC 29201

ROWLES, EDWARD WALTER, marine co. exec.; b. Boise, Idaho, Nov. 27, 1937; s. Edward Behle and Donna (Klossner) R.; B.S.B.A., U. Fla., 1976; postgrad. U. N. Fla., 1977-78. Served as non-commd. officer U.S. Navy, 1955-74, ret., 1974; personnel mgr. CDI Marine Co., Jacksonville, Fla., 1976-77, adminstrn. div. mgr., 1978, mgr. adminstrn., 1979—; v.p. Skyline Mortgage and Investment, Inc., 1979. Mem. Democratic county exec. com., 1980. Notary public; lic. mortgage broker. Mem. Fleet Res. Assn. Home: 8090 Atlantic Blvd G84 Jacksonville FL 32211 Office: 9951 Atlantic Blvd Bldg 2 Jacksonville FL 32211

ROWLETT, OLEN MERLE, conservationist; b. Ft. Cobb, Okla., Dec. 13, 1921; s. Joseph Benjamin and Gladys Mae (Combest) R.; student Okla. State U., 1941-43, 46-47; student Ark. A. and M. Coll., 1943; m. Norma Irene Wesner, Dec. 26, 1966; children—Kathy Ann (Mrs. Thomas Missen), Kristy Jean. Sr. instr. Vets. Agr. Tng. Program, Ft. Cobb (Okla.) schs., 1947-54; soil conservationist, Hollis, Okla., 1954-55, Alva, Okla., 1955; dist. conservationist U.S. Dept. Agr., Blackwell, Okla., 1955-58, Cordell, Okla., 1958-66, area conservationist, Clinton, Okla., 1966—. Served with USMCR, 1942-46. Recipient cert. of merit U.S. Dept. Agr., 1962, 79, letter of commendation, 1963, Superior Service award, 1965, 76, certificate Merit, 1970, Outstanding Rating award, 1972. Mem. Soc. Range Mgmt. (mem. Council 1970, pres. 1971-72), Soil Conservation Soc. Am. Democrat. Presbyn. (elder 1968-73). Rotarian (pres. Cordell club 1962-63). Home: 631 S 19th St Clinton OK 73601 Office: 517 E Prairie Chief St Clinton OK 73601

ROWNTREE, ROBERT JAMES, II, physician; b. Amarillo, Tex., Jan. 19, 1948; s. Robert James and Audrey Mae (Estopinal) R.; B.A., W. Tex. State U., 1970; M.D., U. Tex., Galveston, 1974; m. Carol Ann Nussbaum, June 2, 1972; 1 dau., Emily Rebecca. Intern, U. Tex., Galveston, 1974, resident in internal medicine, 1974-77; practice medicine specializing in internal medicine, Longview, Tex., 1977—; mem. staff Good Shepherd Hosp. Diplomate Am. Bd. Internal Medicine. Mem. Gregg County Med. Soc., A.C.P., Tex. Med. Assn., Tex. Soc. Internal Medicine. Roman Catholic. Office: 801 N 4th St Longview TX 75601

ROY, CHARLES WILLIAM, JR., steel co. exec.; b. Hope, Ark., Apr. 2, 1926; s. Charles W. and Helen G. R.; B.S. in Bus., La. Tech. U., 1950; postgrad. Centenary Coll. of La., 1958; m. Doris Johnston, Sept. 1, 1947; children—Mark R., Charles Bryan, James Brandon. Jr. acct. Tex. Eastern Corp., Shreveport, La., 1950-53, acct., 1953-58, sr. acct., 1958-66; adminstrv. asst. Fabsteel div. Universal Oil Products, Waskom, Tex., 1966-68, adminstrv. mgr., 1968-72; corp. sec. Fabsteel Co., Waskom, 1972—, v.p. adminstrn., 1975—; dir., sec. Mesker Steel Inc.; sec.-treas. Par Excellence, Ltd., Fabsteel Co. La.; sec.-treas., dir. Fabsteel Galvanizing Co. Served with USAAF, 1943-46. Mem. Shreveport C. of C. (indsl. relations com.), Assn. Records Adminstrs., Am. Mgmt. Assn., Soc. Safety Engrs. Democrat. Baptist. Home: 6225 Santa Monica Shreveport LA 71119 Office: 210 Travis Pl Shreveport LA 71101

ROY, ELSIJANE TRIMBLE (MRS. JAMES M. ROY), justice Ark. Supreme Ct.; b. Lonoke, Ark., Apr. 2, 1916; d. Thomas Clark and Elsie Jane (Walls) Trimble; J.D., U. Ark., 1939, LL.D. (hon.), 1978; m. James M. Roy, Nov. 23, 1943; 1 son, James Morrison. Admitted to Ark. bar, 1939; mem. firm Reid, Evrard & Roy, Blytheville, Ark., 1947-54, Roy & Roy, Blytheville, 1954-63; atty. Ark. Revenue Dept., Little Rock, 1939-64; law clk. Ark. Supreme Ct., Little Rock, 1963-65; judge Pulaski County Circuit Ct., Little Rock, 1966; asst. atty. gen. State of Ark. Little Rock, 1967; sr. law clk. U.S. Dist. Ct., Little Rock and Ft. Smith, 1968-74; asso. justice Ark. Supreme Ct., Little Rock, 1975—. Mem. med. adv. com. U. Ark. Med. Center, 1952-54; mem. chmn. com. Ark. Constnl. Commn., 1967-68. Committeewoman Democratic party 16th Jud. Dist., 1940-42; vice-chmn. Ark. Dem. State Com., 1946-48. Mem. Nat. Assn. Women Lawyers, Ark. Bar Assn., Am. Assn. U. Women, Little Rock Women Lawyers (pres. 1939, 42), U. Ark. Alumni Assn. (dir. 1946-48), Ark. Women Lawyers (pres. 1940-1941), Mortar Bd., P.E.O., Chi Omega. Home: 1101 Riviera Apts Little Rock AR 72207 Office: Supreme Ct of Ark Justice Bldg Little Rock AR 72201

ROY, FRANCIS CHARLES, elec. co. exec.; b. Iota, La., Nov. 28, 1926; s. Fernan A. and Gussie M. (Matte) R.; B.S. in Elec. Engring., La. State U., 1949; M.S., U. Tex., Austin, 1958; m. Pauline Bertha Dischler, June 4, 1949; children—Mary Monica, Michael Anthony, Richard Regan (dec.). Engr., Allis Chalmers Mfg. Co., 1949-51; instr. Jeff Davis Vocational Tech. Sch., Jennings, La., 1951-55; asso. prof. engring. La. Tech. U., 1955-65; engr., exec. v.p. Indsl. Supply Co. La., Inc., Lake Charles, 1965-79, Indsl. Equipment & Engring., Inc., Lake Charles, 1979—; computer specialist, program engring. tchr. NSF, summers 1961-62; cons. United Gas Co. research labs., summer 1965. Served with USAAF, 1944-46. Registered profl. engr., La. Sr. mem. IEEE (past sect. pres.); mem. La. Engring. Soc. (pres. Lake Charles chpt. 1973-74, state dir. 1974-76, state sec.-treas. 1976-77, state 2d v.p. 1977-78, state 1st v.p., pres. elect 1978-79, state pres. 1979-80), Tau Beta Pi, Eta Kappa Nu. Home: 216 Park Ave Lake Charles LA 70601 Office: PO Box 1663 Lake Charles LA 70602

ROY, JOHNNY BERNARD, urologist; b. Baghdad, Iraq, Jan. 21, 1938; s. Bernard Benedict and Regina V. (Saka) R.; came to U.S., 1965, naturalized, 1976; M.D., U. Baghdad, 1962; m. Sandy L. Gaede, Sept. 23, 1978; 1 dau., Jennifer Ann. Chief resident in urology U. Ky. Hosp., 1969-70; NIH research fellow U. Okla. Med. Center, 1970-71; chief urology Kaiser Found. Hosps. Hawaii, 1972-75; chief urology VA Med. Center, Oklahoma City, also asst. prof. urology U. Okla. Med. Center, 1975—. Diplomate Am. Bd. Urology. Mem. AMA (Physicians Recognition award 1970—), Am. Urol. Assn., A.C.S., Internat. Coll. Surgeons, Am. Fertility Soc., Soc. Univ. Urologists, So. Med. Assn., Okla. Med. Assn., Okla. County Med. Assn., Okla. Kidney Found. (pres. 1979—), Okla. Urol. Assn. (exec. sec., pres.-elect 1979—). Republican. Roman Catholic. Contbr. articles to med. jours. Home: 11400 N Barnes St Oklahoma City OK 73120 Office: 800 NE 13th St Oklahoma City OK 73190

ROY, SYLVIA RAY, real estate broker; b. Meridian, Miss., Mar. 19, 1936; d. Charles Adrian and Martha (Singley) Ray; B.A., Sophie Newcomb Coll., 1957; M.Ed., Tulane U., 1968; m. John Overton Roy, Jr., Dec. 26, 1959; children—Charles Overton, John Parker. Tchr. secondary schs., New Orleans, 1957-67; with Trade-Mark Realty, New Orleans, 1968-75; broker, pres. Sylvia Roy Properties, Ltd., New Orleans, 1975—; asst. prof. Loyola U. of the South, New Orleans, 1979—. Mem. Nat. Assn. Realtors, La. Realtors Assn., Real Estate Bd. New Orleans, Women's Council Realtors, Grad. Realtors Inst., Farm and Land Inst. Republican. Clubs: Orleans, D.A.R. Home: 70 Audubon Blvd New Orleans LA 70118 Office: 1836 Valence St New Orleans LA 70115

ROYAL, FREDDIE EUGENE, city ofcl.; b. Greenville, Tex., Mar. 11, 1946; s. Lorenzo and Edith (Morris) R.; student E. Tex. State U., 1973-74, Richland Coll., 1974-76, U. Tex., 1976—; m. Peggy McCleveland, Feb. 5, 1965; children—Edith, Stephanie, Freddie, Valerie, Ericka Royal. With City of Garland (Tex.) Water Dept., 1970—, acting asst. water supt., 1974-75, water operation supt., 1975—. Vice-pres. City of Garland Employees Credit Union, 1976-79; mem. Garland City Safety Bd., 1974-77; mem. mid-mgmt. advisory com. Richland Coll., 1975-77. Served with USN, 1964-69. Mem. Apollo Water Utility Assn. Home: 1014 Tensley St Garland TX 75040 Office: 2343 Forest St Garland TX 75040

ROYAL, JACK LEE, physician; b. Earle, Ark., Feb. 10. 1938; s. Joe B. and Vera C. (Roachell) R.; B.S.Medicine, U. Ark., 1962, M.D., 1962; m. Dimple Elaine Burks, Aug. 21, 1962; children—Jennifer, Janice, Jack Lee. Intern, Baptist Meml. Hosp., Memphis, 1962-63; post surgeon U.S. Army Depot, Ingrandes, France, 1963-66; gen. practice medicine, Hope, Ark., 1966-70; chief staff Hempstead County Meml. Hosp., 1969-70; resident in radiology U. Ark. for Med. Scis., Little Rock, 1970-73; radiologist So. Clinic, Texarkana, Ark., 1973—, chief dept. radiology; mem. staff St. Michael Hosp. Diplomate Am. Bd. Radiology. Mem. AMA, Am. Coll. Radiology, Tex., So. med. assns., Ark., Miller County (pres. 1978) med. socs., Ark.-La.-Tex. Radiol. Soc. Club: Masons. Methodist. Home: 16 Lambeth Rd Texarkana TX 75503 Office: 300 E 6th St Texarkana AR 75502

ROYALS, HOMER EARL, chemist; b. Atlanta, Sept. 8, 1945; s. E. Earl and M. Edith R.; student Pensacola Jr. Coll., 1964-66; B.S., U. Fla., 1969, M.S., 1970; m. Marilyn Diane Best, June 24, 1966; children—Beverly, Carolyn. Chemist, Fla. Game and Fresh Water Fish Commn., Eustis, 1972—; cons. Lake County Sch. System. Chmn. Planning and Zoning Bd., City of Eustis, 1974-77, vice mayor, commr., 1978—. Served with U.S. Army, 1971-72. Mem. Eustis C. of C. (dir. 1979). Democrat. Baptist. Club: Kiwanis (pres. Eustis). Home: 1507 Tyringham St Eustis FL 32726 Office: Fla Game and Fresh Water Fish Commn PO Box 1903 Eustis FL 32726

ROYDS, RICHARD ALLAN, lawyer; b. Dayton, Ohio, Jan. 13, 1938; s. Charles Nuttal and Mary (Ousey) R.; A.B., Stanford U., 1960; LL.B., Harvard U., 1963; m. Ellin Pear, Aug. 26, 1961; children—Richard Allan, Charles Bradley, Carleton Wesley. Admitted to Tex. bar, 1963; asso. firm Bracewell & Patterson, Houston, 1963-68, partner, 1968—; officer, dir. Finomic Research Assos. Inc., Houston; dir. Med. Center Bank, Houston, Pasadena Nat. Bank (Tex.), Rosenberg Bank & Trust (Tex.), United Bancshares, Inc. Mem. Am. Bar Assn., Tex. Bar Assn., Houston Bar Assn., Houston C. of C., Phi Beta Kappa. Club: Rotary. Home: 10607 Twelve Oaks St Houston TX 77024 Office: 2900 S Tower Pennzoil Pl Houston TX 77002

ROYER, ROBERT L., utility co. exec.; b. 1928; B.S. in Elec. Engring., Rose Poly. Inst., 1949; married. With Louisville Gas and Electric Co., Inc., 1949—, v.p., gen. supt., 1964-69, v.p. ops., 1969-78, exec. v.p., from 1978, now pres., chief exec. officer, dir. Served in Armed Forces, 1953-55. Office: Louisville Gas and Electric Co Inc 311 W Chestnut St Louisville KY 40232

ROZELLE, JOE DAVID, vol. services adminstr.; b. Rusk, Tex., Jan. 6, 1948; s. Ralph Smith and Sibyl R.; A.A., Tyler Jr. Coll., 1968; B.B.A., Stephen F. Austin State U., 1970; M.S., So. Ill. U., Carbondale, 1973; m. Christine Sue Conant, Dec. 22, 1973. Asst. coordinator vol. services Rusk (Tex.) State Hosp., 1970-71, coordinator vol. services, 1972—. Bd. dirs., campaign chmn. United Way, 1975, pres., 1976. Mem. Assn. for Vol. Adminstrn. (v.p. 1980-81), Rusk C. of C. (dir., pres. elect 1980). Methodist. Club: Kiwanis (pres. 1975) (Rusk). Home: PO Box 254 Rusk TX 75785 Office: Rusk State Hosp US Hwy 69 N Rusk TX 75785

RUA, MILTON FRANCISCO, lawyer; b. San German, P.R., Dec. 8, 1919; s. Urbano F. and Josefa A. (Gonzalez-Ferrer) R.; B.A. cum laude, U. P.R., 1941, LL.B., 1943; m. Marina Cabrer, Mar. 31, 1945; children—Milton J., Jaime L. Admitted to P.R. bar, 1943; legal counsel Dept. Finance of P.R., 1943-46; sr. partner Rivera-Zayas, Rivera-Cestero & Rua, San Juan, P.R., 1950-73; founder, sr. partner Rúa, Mercado & Gonzalez, Hato Rey, P.R., 1973—; founder, counsellor Banco Mercantil de P.R., Rio Piedras, 1966—, chmn. bd. dirs., 1975—; founder Asso. Ins. Agencies, Inc., San Juan, 1972, Fajardo Fed. Savs. & Loan Assn. (P.R.), 1972—; pres., dir. Lincoln Fin. Mortgagees, Inc., San Juan. Mem. bar exam. com. Supreme Ct. P.R., 1955-56; spl. counsel com. natural resources and beautification P.R. Ho. of Reps., 1967-68; mem. citizens com. nuclear plants Environ. Quality Bd. of P.R., 1972; chmn. Electoral Reform Commn., 1973—; mem. organizing com. First Latin Am. Biennal Graphic Arts, P.R., 1970; bd. dirs. Casa el Libro, chmn., 1960-70; bd. dirs. Inst. of Culture of P.R., 1968-79, Students Art League of San Juan, Mus. P.R. Mem. Found. Bar Assn. P.R. (hon. pres. 1976-78), Bar Assn. P.R., Am., Inter-Am. bar assns., Iberoamerican Inst. Aero. Law. Clubs: Bankers, Union League (N.Y.C.), Elks. Home: Condominio del Mar 1401 Delcasse St Condado PR 00907 Office: 1 Mercantile Plaza Hato Rey PR 00919

RUBANO, ROBERT, mfg. co. exec.; b. N.Y.C., Oct. 30, 1946; s. Pat and Frances Mary (Catinella) R.; B.S.E.E., Fla. Atlantic U., 1977; m. Rebecca Lynn Steinat, Sept. 2, 1977; 1 son, Robert Michael. With Bendix Corp., Ft. Lauderdale, Fla., 1971—, supr. computer facilities, 1975—. Served with USAF, 1966-70. Lic. pvt. pilot. Mem. Soc. Profl. Engrs., Bendix Avionics Employees Flying Club (pres. 1978-79). Christian. Home: 7350 NW 75th St Fort Lauderdale FL 33319 Office: 2100 NW 62d St Fort Lauderdale FL 33310

RUBASH, JOYCE NEWBORN, univ. adminstr.; b. Liberty, Tex., Nov. 10, 1930; d. Jacob Andrew and Adenisa (Vincent) Newborn; B.S., U. Houston, 1966; m. James Joseph Rubash, Mar. 14, 1950; children—John Mark, Bradley Andrew. Unit dietitian Coll. Food Service, Rice U., Houston, 1966-68, prodn. mgr., 1968-72, coll. food dir., 1972—; instr. coordinated vocat. acad. and edn., U. Houston, 1975-78; adj. clin. prof. dept. nutrition U. Tex. Sch. Allied Health Sci., Houston, 1977—; metric coordinator Nat. Assn. Coll. and Univ. Food Services, 1976—; lectr. in field. Del., State Dem. Conv., Dallas, 1970; Sunday sch. tchr. Bapt. Ch., Houston, 1961-73; active Little League, Houston, 1962-76. Mem. Am. Dietetic Assn., Nat. Assn. Coll. and Univ. Food Services (citation for meritorious service 1977), South Tex. Dietetic Assn., Tex. Dietetic Assn., Tex. Restaurant Assn., Internat. Assn. Milk, Food and Environ. Protection, Nat. Conf. Weights and Measures, Phi Upsilon Omicron. Democrat. Baptist. Home: 6610 Flamingo St Houston TX 77087 Office: PO Box 1892 Houston TX 77001

RUBIN, BRUCE STUART, pub. relations counselor; b. Miami, Fla., June 28, 1947; s. Earl Myron and Claire Malbin R.; student U. Fla., 1965-67; B.A. in Journalism, U. Miami, 1969; m. Brenda Blumin, June 5, 1970. Vice pres. Ronald Levitt Assos., Pub. Relations, Coral Gables, Fla., 1969-75; pres., prin. Bruce Rubin Assos., Inc., Public Relations Counselors, S. Miami, Fla., 1975—; cons. to pub. info. unit Dade County Pub. Safety Dept.; guest lectr. in field various colls. and univs. Recipient Service award Big Bros. Miami, 1973. Mem. Public Relations Soc. Am. (past pres. Miami chpt.), U. Miami Alumni Assn. (past dir.), Miami C. of C. (tourism action com.), Alpha Delta Sigma, Alpha Epsilon Pi. Office: Bruce Rubin Assos Inc 7600 SW 57th Ave Suite 104 South Miami FL 33143

RUBIN, HOWARD STANTON, cardiologist; b. Houston, Sept. 19, 1949; s. Alfred Lewis and Mildred Elaine (Solomon) R.; student Tulane U., 1967-70; M.D. magna cum laude, U. Tex., Galveston, 1974; m. Rozanne Halfant, July 30, 1972; children—Alissa Brett, Stacey Elaine. Intern, U. Tex. Southwestern Med. Sch., Dallas, 1974-75, resident, 1975-77, fellow in cardiology, 1977-79; practice medicine specializing in cardiovascular diseases, Houston, 1979—; mem. staffs Meth. Hosp., Meml. System Affiliated Hosps. Diplomate Am. Bd. Internal Medicine. Fellow Am. Coll. Cardiology, A.C.P.; mem. Tex. Med. Assn., Harris County Med. Soc., Houston Soc. Internal Medicine, Houston Soc. Cardiology, AMA, Alpha Omega Alpha. Jewish. Home: 7518 Coachwood St Houston TX 77071 Office: 6560 Fannin St Suite 1554 Houston TX 77030

RUBIN, MARVIN ALEXANDER, motel exec.; b. San Antonio, Oct. 17, 1921; s. Frank and Gussie (Finesilver) R.; B.S. in Civil Engring., Ind. Inst. Tech., 1956; postgrad. So. Meth. U., 1957; m. Edith Solomon, Sept. 27, 1947; children—Glenda Rubin Kane, Jan Rubin Newland. Asst. to v.p. engring. Mo., Kans. & Tex. R.R., 1952-57; dynamics engr. Chance Vought Aircraft Co., Dallas, 1957-58; partner Frank Rubin & Son, San Antonio, 1958-69; v.p., prin. Travis-Braun & Assos., Cons. Engrs., San Antonio, 1973—; v.p. project devel. LaQuinta Motor Inns, Inc., San Antonio; cons. energy conservation, modular bldg. Served with USMC, 1942-45, 50-51; Decorated Purple Heart. Mem. Am. Assn. Cost Engrs., Tex. Soc. Solar Engrs., Internat. Soc. Solar Engrs., Precast Concrete Inst., Constrn. Specifications Inst. Jewish. Designer, developer solar energy project for motor inns. Home: 1321 Grey Oak St San Antonio TX 78213 Office: PO Box 32064 San Antonio TX 78216

RUBIN, RICHARD MARK, physicist; b. Pensacola, Fla., July 26, 1937; s. Nathan Samuel and Betty (Rubin) R.; B.S.E., U. Mich., 1959; M.Nuclear Engring., U. Okla., 1961; Ph.D., Kan. State U., 1970; m. Rose Mohr, June 22, 1963; children—Mark, Debra. Asst. prof. nuclear engring. Miss. State U., 1970-77; project physicist Radiation Research Assoc., Ft. Worth, Tex., 1977—. Sec., Civitan Club Starkville, 1976-77; vice pres. Congregation Bnai Israel, Columbus, Miss., 1975-77. Registered profl. engr., Miss., Tex. Mem. Am. Nuclear Soc. (chmn. Miss. sec. 1975-77, public info. chmn. 1977-78, vice chmn. North Tex. sect. 1978-79), Sigma Xi. Home: 4309 Sarita Dr Fort Worth TX 76109 Office: 3550 Hulen St Fort Worth TX 76107

RUBIN, RICHARD STEVENS, architect, planner, developer; b. St. Louis, May 8, 1945; s. Philip Charles and Sarah (Nieman) R.; B.S., Washington U., 1968; M.S., Miami U., 1975; m. Carolyn Sanguinet, July 20, 1968; children—Jason Philip, Stefan Arnold. Architect, Peckham Guyton, Architect, St. Louis, 1969-71; planner PBS & J Post, Buckley, Schuh & Jernigan, Miami, Fla., 1972-74; dir. community devel. City of Tamarac (Fla.), 1975-78; dir. planning Craven & Thompson, Ft. Lauderdale, Fla., 1978; pres. Homeland Enterprise, Inc., land mgmt. and devel., Ft. Lauderdale, 1979—. Bd. dirs. South Fla. Regional Burn Center, 1978-79; weekly instr. Tamarac Elem. Sch. - 5th Grade Gifted Class, 1976—; chmn. Broward County Tech. Adv. Com. for Comprehensive Planning, 1977-78; mem. Broward County Community Devel. Com., 1977-79. Mem. Broward Planners Assn. (pres. 1978-79), Am. Planning Assn., AIA, Builders Assn. S. Fla. Club: Kiwanis (bd. dirs. 1978-79). Contbg. author: Broward County Zoning Glossary, 1977; designer West End Restaurant in Sunrise Mus. Theatre, 1977; architect, developer Edgewater Village, Tamarac, Fla. Home: 7424 NW 75 St Tamarac FL 33319 Office: 1150 N Fed Hwy Suite 630 Fort Lauderdale FL 33304

RUBIN, SAMUEL SOLOMON, psychologist, educator; b. N.Y.C., Apr. 21, 1931; s. George and Matilda R.; B.S. magna cum laude, Columbia U., 1953, M.A., 1956, Ph.D., 1962; grad. Advanced Inst. Analytic Psychotherapy, 1973. Adj. prof. psychology Queens Coll., City U. N.Y., 1965-75; supervising psychologist Advanced Center Psychotherapy, Forest Hills, N.Y., 1967-79; faculty Advanced Inst. Analytic Psychotherapy, N.Y.C., 1971-79; asso. dept. human behavior Columbia U. Dental Sch., 1977-78; dir. N.Y. Workshop Living Learning, 1977-79; practice clin. psychology, Bon Air, Va., 1979—. Cert. psychologist, Va., N.Y. Mem. Nat. Accreditation Assn. Psychoanalysis (certified), Council Nat. Register Health Service Providers Psychology (certified), N.Y. Soc. Clin. Psychologists, Am., Eastern psychol. assns., Phi Beta Kappa. Jewish. Contbr. articles to psychol. jours. Home: 3060 Visa Point Rd Midlothian VA 23113

RUBINOFF, IRA, research inst. adminstr.; b. N.Y.C., Dec. 21, 1938; s. Jacob and Bessie (Rose) R.; B.S., Queens Coll., 1959; A.M., Harvard U., 1960, Ph.D., 1964; m. Anabella Guardia, Feb. 10, 1978; children—Jason, Andres. Research fellow Harvard U., 1964, asso. in icththyology Museum Comparative Geology, 1965; biologist Smithsonian Instn., Washington, 1965-66, asst. dir. Smithsonian Tropical Research Inst., C.Z., 1967-73, dir., 1974—; chmn. bd. fellowships and grants Smithsonian Instn.; courtesy prof. Fla. State U. Trustee Rare Animal Relief Effort, 1976—; bd. dirs. Charles Darwin Found. for Galapagos Islands. Woods Hole Oceanographic Inst. fellow, 1960. Fellow Linnean Soc. London; mem. Am. Soc. Naturalists, Soc. Study Evolution, Ecol. Soc. Am., N.Y. Acad. Scis., Sigma Xi. Clubs: Cosmos (Washington); Balboa Yacht. Contbr. articles to profl. jours. Office: PO Box 2072 Balboa Republic of Panama

RUBOTTOM, DONALD JULIAN, investment and mgmt. co. exec.; b. Tulsa, Sept. 29, 1926; s. George William and Nellie D. (Core) R.; B.S., Okla. State U., 1951; M.S., Tulsa U.; m. Wanda Mae Stockton, Apr. 29, 1951; children—Rinda Louise, Joy Lynn, Donald Jay, Jill Anna. Registered rep. Smith Barney Harris Upham & Co., Tulsa, 1950-51; v.p. First Nat. Bank, Tulsa, 1955-66; exec. v.p., dir. F&M Bank & Trust Co., Tulsa, 1966-68; pres. Rubottom & Assos., Inc., Tulsa 1968—; dir. Air Cargo Equipment Corp. Mem. adv. bd. Salvation Army, 1975—; mem. bd. stewards Boston Ave. United Methodist Ch. Served with inf. U.S. Army, 1945-46. Mem. Inst. Chartered Fin. Analysts, Fin. Analysts Fedn., Inst. Cert. Mgmt. Cons. Club: Tulsa, Tulsa Ski, Rotary. Office: Rubottom & Assos 1920 First Place Tulsa OK 74103

RUBY, RALPH, JR., educator; b. Newburgh, N.Y., Apr. 11, 1944; s. Ralph and Justine (Wilson) R.; B.S., U. Tenn., 1969, M.S., 1972; Ed.D., U. Mo., Columbia, 1975; m. Dorothy Nelle Privette, Apr. 28, 1969; children—Laconya Dannet, Ralph III, Vanessa Rae. Tchr., Valley Central High Sch., Montgomery, N.Y., 1969-75; asst. prof. vocat. edn. U. Ark., Fayetteville, 1975-79; asst. prof. bus. edn. Ark. State U., State University, 1979—. Served with USNR, 1961-67. EPDA fellow, 1973-75. Mem. Am. Vocat. Assn. (life), Nat. Bus. Edn. Assn., Nat. Assn. Tchr. Edn. for Bus. and Office Edn. (life), So. Bus. Edn. Assn., Ark. Bus. Edn. Assn., Ark. Vocat. Bus. Edn. Assn., Antique Auto Club Am., Oldsmobile Club Am., Phi Beta Lambda, Delta Pi Epsilon, Kappa Delta Pi, Phi Delta Kappa. Baptist. Author: Business Law Quizzes, 1976; Proofreading, 1978; Merchandising, 1978. Office: Coll Bus Edn Ark State U Box 2534 State University AR 72467

RUCINSKI, CAROLE ANN, food co. exec.; b. Moundsville, W.Va., Sept. 6, 1942; d. Harold William and Annabelle (Heflin) Brown; student Capitol U. Without Walls, 1978-79; m. Kenneth J. Rucinski, July 20, 1963. Sec., Richman Bros. Co., Cleve., 1960-68; exec. sec. Columbia Gas System, Charleston, W.Va., Columbus, Ohio, 1969-72; with McDonald's Corp., Columbus, 1972-78, zone licensing mgr., Atlanta, 1978—; owner, operator Big Red Q Quickprint Center, Atlanta, 1979—, Shaklee Products, Atlanta, 1979—. Mem. Am. Soc. Profl. and Exec. Women, Nat. Assn. Female Execs., Cobb County C. of C. Roman Catholic. Clubs: Providence Corners Civic Assn., Providence Corners Swim and Tennis, Fairfield Country. Home: 1140 Gray Squirrel Crossing Marietta GA 30062 Office: 5775 Peachtree Dunwood Rd Suite 200A Atlanta GA 30342

RUCKART, JOHN LEONARD, JR., real estate co. exec.; b. Richmond, Va., Feb. 1, 1939; s. John Leonard and Pearl Moon (Johnson) R.; B.S., Va. Poly. Inst. and State U., 1961; m. Brenda Louise Butler, Mar. 25, 1960; children—Sherry, Laurie, Kathy, Amy, Mitzi, April, Jennifer. Indsl. engr. Newport News Shipbldg. and Dry Dock Co. (Va.), 1961-63; mfg. supr. DuPont, Richmond, 1963-65, indsl. engr., 1966-68; mfrs. rep. D.W. Larsen Co., Richmond, 1965-66; sales rep. Howard & Underwood Realtors, Richmond, 1968-70, Robert M. Goodman, Richmond, 1970-73; owner, pres. Property Cons., Inc., Richmond, 1973—. Pres. Richmond (Va.) Stake, Ch. of Jesus Christ of Latter-day Saints, 1978—. Mem. Nat. Bd. Realtors, Va. Bd. Realtors, Richmond Bd. Realtors. Home: 5611 Jamson Rd Richmond VA 23234 Office: Property Consultants Inc 4222 Bonniebank Rd Richmond VA 23234

RUCKEL, JOHN MARVIN, ins. agt.; b. Galveston, Tex., July 27, 1948; s. Peter E. and Sybil V. R.; B.B.A. in Mgmt., Stephen F. Austin U., 1970; m. Deborah Laros, Aug. 31, 1968; children—John Damon, Kendall Grant. Life agt. Am. Gen. Life Ins. Co., Nacogdoches, Tex., 1969—, agy. mgr., 1975-78. County chmn. Phil Gram U.S. senatorial campaign, 1976; county co-chmn. John Tower U.S. senatorial campaign, 1978; Republican candidate for Tex. Ho. of Reps., 1978; county chmn., mem. state steering com. John Connally presdl. campaign, 1979-80; active fund drives various local charitable orgns. Mem. Tex. Assn. Life Underwriters, Pineywood Assn. Life Underwriters (past pres., past dir.), Million Dollar Round Table. Mem. Ch. of Christ. Home: 2303 Twin Oaks St Nacogdoches TX 75961 Office: 414 Pillar St Nacogdoches TX 75961 also Am Gen Life Ins Co PO Drawer 1762 Nacogdoches TX 75961

RUCKER, DAVID RAY, clergyman; b. Abilene, Tex., July 2, 1950; s. John Morris and Wanda Maude (Partain) R.; B.A. cum laude, McMurry Coll., 1972; M.Th., So. Meth. U., 1976; m. Elizabeth Marie Camille Cook, Aug. 17, 1974. Ordained to ministry, United Meth. Ch., 1977; youth dir. Forrest Heights United Meth. Ch., Lubbock, Tex., 1972; asso. pastor Tyler St. United Meth. Ch., Dallas, 1976—; mem. faculty Tyler Street Christian Acad., 1974-76. Mem. N. Tex. Evang. Fellowship, Nat. Assn. Dirs. Christian Edn. Office: 927 W 10th Dallas TX 75208

RUCKER, HAROLD JAMES, lawyer; b. Paducah, Ky., Dec. 8, 1921; s. Morton Val Dean and Birdie (Flora) R.; A.B., U. Ky., 1947, J.D., 1949; m. Robbie Boggess; children—Carol Jane, Morton Val Dean, Douglas McCauley, Helen Lynne Louise. Admitted to Ky. bar, 1949, Tex. bar, 1950; mem. staff land dept. Shell Oil Co., Midland, Tex., 1949-50; practiced in Midland, 1950—; mem. firm Perkins, German, Mims & Bell, 1951-54, Perkins & Bezoni, 1955-56, Rucker & Rassman, 1958-60. Dir. Chancellor Chair Co., Optic Boutique, Inc. Past pres., bd. dirs. Am. Cancer Soc., Midland, 1960-61; mem. Midland YMCA, 1961-68, pres., bd. dirs., 1962-68, chmn. endowment com., 1964-65, chmn. Century Club, 1965-66, pres., bd. dirs. S.W. Area Council, 1962-66, mem. program com., chmn. workshop area council meeting, Dallas, 1963; past bd. dirs. Midland County Child Welfare Unit, 1957-58; pres., bd. dirs. Midland Diagnostic Cancer Clinic, 1961-62; pres. bd. trustees Trinity Sch., Midland; trustee St. Andrew's (Tenn.) Sch., Sch. Bd. of Diocese of N.W. Tex. (Episcopal). Served to 1st lt. AUS, 1942-46. Named Boss of Year, Legal Secs. Assn., Midland, 1963; named Ky. col., 1974. Mem. Am., Midland County, Ky. bar assns., State Bar Tex., Am. Judicature Soc., Phi Alpha Delta, Sigma Chi. Episcopalian (vestryman). Kiwanian (pres., dir. 1955-57). Clubs: Petroleum, Racquet (dir. 1962) (Midland). Office: 716 First Nat Bank Bldg Midland TX 79701

RUCKER, ISRAEL L., clergyman; b. Edwards, Miss., Mar. 10, 1927; s. Whitney E. and Luberta J. Rucker; A.B., Rust Coll., 1950; B.D., Gammon Theol. Sem., 1956; M.Div., Interdenominational Theol. Center, 1973; D.Div., Rust Coll., 1973; m. Velma B. Brandon, Sept. 12, 1950; children—Edward Earl, Debra A. Ordained to ministry United Methodist Ch., 1950; pastor, Pickens, Miss., 1950-53, Asbury Ch., Holly Springs, Miss., 1956-60; chaplain Rust Coll., Holly Springs, 1956-60; dir. food stamp program Wesley United Meth. Ch., Greenwood, Miss., 1960-68, dist. supt. Starkville (Miss.) Dist., 1968-73; dir. mission and ethnic concerns United Meth. Ch., Atlanta, 1973—. Chmn. Greenwood Freedom Movement, 1960-68; chmn. Starkville Bi-Racial Com., 1970-72; chmn. Starkville Separate Sch. Dist. Bd. Edn., 1972-73. Served with U.S. Army, 1944-46; ETO. Recipient Man of Yr. award Greenwood, 1966; Disting. Service award Starkville City Sch. Bd., 1973, others. Mem. Internat. Assn. Investigators and Spl. Police, Nat. Assn. Coll. Chaplains. Club: Masons. Author: The How To of A Hungry Action/Community Economic Development Program, 1977; Town and Country Workbook, 1976. Home: 2541 Elkhorn Dr Decatur GA 30034 Office: 159 Forrest Ave Atlanta GA 30308

RUCKER, NORMAN HENRY, physician; b. Washburn, Tenn., Feb. 26, 1918; s. John Thomas and Doris (Clark) R.; M.D., U. Tenn., 1940; postgrad. Columbia, 1949; m. Katharan Gladys Bradley, 1944; children—Patricia (Mrs. Jack Walker), Ann (Mrs. Jesse Lynn), John, Bradley. Intern Knoxville (Tenn.) Gen. Hosp., 1940-41; resident Manhattan St., Columbia Presbyn. Hosp., 1945-48; practice medicine specializing in psychoanalysis, New Orleans, 1949-72, Knoxville, 1972—; mem. staff Charity Hosp.; asst. prof. psychiatry Tulane U., 1949-51; clin. prof. psychiatry La. State U. 1967-72; tng. and supervision analyst New Orleans Psychoanalytic Inst., 1954-72; staff physician St. Mary's Hosp., Knoxville, 1972—; cons. Childrens Bur., VA Hosp. Sec., Green Acres Civic Assn. Bd. dirs. Family Service Soc. Served to maj. AUS, 1942-45. Mem. A.M.A., Am. Psychiat. Assn., Am. Psychoanalytic Assn., Phi Rho Sigma. Democrat. Baptist. Home: 5121 Malibu Dr Knoxville TN 37918 Office: 701 Magdalon Clarke Towers Knoxville TN 37917

RUCKER, VERNON BRUCE, city ofcl.; b. Coleman, Tex., Mar. 30, 1917; s. Henry Franklin and Lee Ola (Berry) R.; student pub. schs., Coleman, Tex.; m. Aug. 22, 1937; children—Francis Elaine, Marilyn Bernice. Operator skating rink, 1934-51, operator paint and hardware store, 1947-78; mem. Vol. Fire Dept., 1941-79, fire chief, 1951-79; fire chief City of Killeen Fire Dept., 1957-79; Bell County fire marshall and civil def. coordinator, Belton, Tex., 1980—; instr. Fire Sch., Tex. A. and M. U., 1953-79. Mem. city council, Killeen, 1947-51. Served with USNR, 1945-46. Mem. Nat. Fire Protection Assn., Internat. Assn. Fire Chiefs (pres. S.W. div. 1974), State Firemen's and Fire Marshal's Assn. Tex. (pres. 1962), Central Tex. Firemen's Assn. (pres. 1953). Democrat. Baptist. Clubs: Kiwanis (pres. 1965), Masons, Shriners. Home: 1015 Carrie St Killeen TX 76541 Office: Box 749 Bell County Belton TX 76513

RUCKER, WALTER CLIFFORD, area manpower rep.; b. Atlanta, Apr. 23, 1936; s. Unk and Fannie Mae (Young) R.; A.B.A., John Marshall U., 1973; B.A., Shaw U., 1975; J.D., John Marshall Law Sch., 1975; children—Wakita, Walter Clifford. Distbg. clk., accounting clk., personnel clk. U.S. Postal Service, 1959-70; area rep. Human Resources Devel. Inst., AFL-CIO, Atlanta, 1970—; labor liaison Nat. Alliance Businessmen; mem. arbitration panel Better Bus. Bur.; mem. Atlanta Employment and Tng. Adv. Council, 1972—, Ga. Employment and Tng. Council, DeKalb Manpower Adv. Council; chmn. DeKalb County Youth Council, 1979—; chmn. Atlanta's Youth Employment and Tng. Council, 1978—, PIC-Atlanta, Inc., 1979—, Urban Enterprises for Youth Devel. Atlanta, Inc., 1979—; mem. DeKalb County Overall Econ. Devel. Planning Com.; mem. adv. bd. Project M.O.V.E.; mem. Atlanta regional commn. Planning Process and Participation Task Force, 1978—; mem. Fulton County CETA Planning Council, 1979. Sec. bd. mgrs. East Central br. YMCA, 1972-74; mem. exec. com. Atlanta Region Open Housing Coalition, 1972—. Vice pres. Atlanta chpt. A. Philip Randolph Inst., 1974—. Served with AUS, 1954-56, mem. Res., 1956—. Mem. Postal Press Assn., Indsl. Relations Research Assn., Nu Beta Epsilon. Democrat. Baptist. Clubs: Villa (treas.), Masons. Editor of Atlanta Metro Report of Am. Postal Workers Union, 1968—. Office: 250 10th St N E Atlanta GA 30309

RUCKMAN, FRANELIN DAVID, ednl. adminstr.; b. East Rainelle, W.Va., Sept. 30, 1944; s. David Andrew and Violet Harvey (Ruckman; B.S., Trevecca Nazarene Coll., 1970; M.Ed., Middle Tenn. State U., 1974 m. Sylvia Corinne Jamison, Dec. 17, 1967; children—Franklin David, John Andrew. Sch. bus. driver Metro Nashville Bd. Edn., 1967-69, phys. edn. tchr., 1969; coach girls basketball and boys football, phys. edn. tchr. Sumner County (Tenn.) Bd. Edn., 1970—; asst. prin. Gallatin (Tenn.) Jr. High Sch., 1973-76; prin. Westmoreland (Tenn.) High Sch., 1976—. Mem. NEA, Nat. Assn. Secondary Sch. Prins., Tenn. Edn. Assn., Tenn. Assn. Secondary Sch. Prins., Sumner County Edn. Assn., Sumner County Secondary Prins. Assn. (past pres.). Mem. Ch. of the Nazarene. Clubs: Gideons (zone leader), Westmoreland Lions, Westmoreland Athletic. Office: PO Box 719 Westmoreland TN 37186

RUDDER, INA BELL, nurse; b. Greenville, Tex., Dec. 2, 1928: d. John Paul and Ruby Florence (Cravens) Kuykendall: R.N. diploma Parkland Hosp. Sch. Nursing, Dallas, 1951; B.S. in Health Edn., Oklahoma City U., 1977; B.S. in Health Care Adminstrn., Okla. Baptist U., 1978; postgrad. Okla. U. Sch. Public Health, 1979—; children by previous marriage—Dave Alan, Rebecca Lynn. Evening supr. Beverly Hills Sanitarium, Dallas, 1951-53; head nurse, staff nurse Parkland Meml. Hosp., Dallas, 1953-61; supr., dir. nurses Dallas Osteo. Hosp., 1961-66; adminstr. McLean (Tex.) Hosp., 1966-67; supr., dir. nursing service, asst. adminstr. Willow View Hosp., Oklahoma City, 1967—; Lic. nursing home adminstr., Okla. Mem. Am. Nurses Assn., Okla State Nurses Assn., Am. Soc. Nursing Service Adminstrs., Okla. Soc. Nursing Service Adminstrs., Okla. Hosp. Personnel Assn., Oklahoma City Area Hosp. Council (dir. nursing service sect.). Baptist. Club: Order Eastern Star. Home: 109 W Lilac Ct Midwest City OK 73110 Office: PO Box 11137 Oklahoma City OK 73136

RUDE, JOE CHRISTOPHER, III, radiologist; b. Memphis, Feb. 1, 1944; s. Joseph Christopher, Jr. and Eleanora (Wallenfels) R.; B.A., U. Tex. at Austin, 1966; M D., U. Tex. Southwestern Med. Sch., 1970. Intern, Meml. Med. Center, Corpus Christi, Tex., 1970-71; resident Emory Affiliated Hosps., Atlanta, 1973-76, radiology spl. procedures vascular fellow, 1976-77; practice medicine, specializing in radiology, Atlanta, 1977—. Served with USAF, 1971-73. Decorated Air medal with 2 oak leaf clusters. Mem. AMA, Aerospace Med. Assn., Radiol. Soc. N.Am., Ga., Atlanta radiol. socs., Am. Coll. Med. Imaging, Ga. Med. Assn., Cobb County Med. Soc., Southeastern Angiographic Soc., Profl. Photographers Am., U.S. Judo Fedn. (2 deg. black belt). Tex. State Judo champion, 1963. Home: 1050 Riverbend Club Dr Atlanta GA 30339 Office: 3865 Story Dr SW Marietta GA 30060

RUDENBERG, F(RANK) HERMANN, physiologist, environmentalist, educator; b. Berlin, Germany, Dec. 4, 1927; s. Reinhold Gunther and Lily (Minkowski) R.; brought to U.S., 1938, naturalized, 1944; B.S. cum laude, Harvard, 1949; M.S. (Univ. scholar, AEC fellow), U. Chgo., 1951, Ph.D., 1954; m. Jean Colladay, Feb. 28, 1952 (div. July 1973); children—George Montgomery, Eric Charles, Peter David, Karen Suzanne; m. 2d, Mary Helen Ryder Toombs, Jan. 9, 1979; stepchildren—Barry Lee, Ronny Martin. AEC fellow Marine Biol. Lab., Woods Hole, Mass., 1949; teaching asst. U. Chgo., 1952-53; instr. dept. physiology and pharmacology Mich. State U., East Lansing, 1954-58, asst. prof., 1958; asst. prof. dept. physiology and biophysics U. Tex. Med. Br., Galveston, 1958-62, asso. prof., 1962—, adj. asso. prof. Sch. Allied Health Scis., 1976, asso. prof., 1977—; cons. S.W. Research Inst., San Antonio, 1967-74; evaluator NASA-Nat. Sci. Tchrs. Assn. Youth Sci. Congress, Region VII, 1971, 72; evaluator for sci. for citizens program NSF; judge sci. fairs, 1976—; mem. Barrier Island observers com. Tex. Coastal and Marine Council, 1976—. Mem. Mayor's Anti-litter Com., Galveston, 1971-72; mem. Oil and Gas Master Plan Com., Galveston, vice chmn., 1977-78; mem. Galveston Marine Affairs Council, 1978, chmn. beach and dune erosion subcom.; bd. dirs. Science, Inc., 1976—, vice chmn. exec. com., 1977—; mem. Friends of Rosenberg Library, Galveston, Galveston County Cultural Arts Council, Galveston Hist. Found. Fellow Tex. Acad. Scis.; mem. AAAS, AAUP, Am. Inst. Biol. Scis., Assn. for Advancement Med. Instrumentation (mem. aerospace tech. com. 1971-76), Biophys. Soc. (charter), Neuroelectric Soc., N.Y. Acad. Scis., Tex. Soc. for Electron Microscopy, Soc. for Neurosci., Sierra Club (chmn. conservation Galveston regional group 1973-75, mem. exec. com. 1973—, chmn. 1975-77, treas. 1977—), exec. com. Lone Star chpt. 1977—, vice chmn. 1978, coastal affairs chmn. 1978—), U. Chgo. Alumni Assn. (chmn. Galveston County chpt.), S.W. Sci. Forum (charter), LWV, Audubon Soc., Nat. Wildlife Fedn., Sigma Xi (treas. Galveston chpt. 1965). Research in central nervous system trauma, cellular physiology and electron microscopy, med. instrumentation, med. edn. Home: 3327 Ave Q 1/2 Galveston TX 77550

RUDOLPH, ANDREW HENRY, dermatologist; b. Detroit, Jan. 30, 1943; s. John J. and Mary M. (Mizesko) R.; M.D. cum laude (Regent's scholar), U. Mich., 1966; m. Mary Martha Fox, Aug. 17, 1963; children—Kristen Ann, Kevin Andrew. Intern, Univ. Hosp., U. Mich. Med. Center, Ann Arbor, 1966-67, resident dept. dermatology, 1967-70; asst. prof. dermatology Baylor Coll. Medicine, Houston, 1972-75, asso. prof., 1975—; chief dermatology service VA Hosp., Houston, 1977—; mem. adv. panel number 6 U.S. Pharmacopeia; mem. adv. com. on dermatology VA Central Office; mem. staff Ben Taub Gen. Hosp., Jefferson Davis Hosp., Meth. Hosp., Tex. Children's Hosp., St. Luke's Episcopal Hosp., Hermann Hosp., Tex. Inst. for Rehab. and Research. Served as surgeon USPHS, 1970-72. Diplomate Am. Bd. Dermatology. Fellow Am. Acad. Dermatology; mem. AMA, So. Med. Assn., Tex. Med. Assn., Harris County Med. Soc., Houston Dermatol. Soc. (pres.), Tex. Dermatol. Soc., Am. Geriatric Soc., Assn. Mil. Dermatologists, Internat. Soc. Tropical Dermatology, Royal Soc. Health, Am. Venereal Disease Assn. (pres.), Am. Public Health Assn., Assn. Mil. Surgeons U.S., Am. Soc. for Dermatol. Surgery, Soc. for Investigative Dermatology, S. Central Dermatologic Congress, Mich. Alumni Assn. (life), Alpha Omega Alpha, Phi Kappa Phi, Phi Rho Sigma, Theta Xi. Mem. editorial bd. Jour. of Sexually Transmitted Diseases, 1977—. Contbr. to med. jours., periodicals and textbooks. Office: 1200 Moursund Ave Houston TX 77030

RUDOLPH, GUILFORD GEORGE, educator; b. Kiowa, Kans., Jan. 2, 1918; s. Esmond Francis and Marian (Richardson) R.; B.A., U. Colo., 1940; M.S., Wayne State U., 1942; Ph.D., U. Utah, 1948; m. Catharine Griffin, Sept. 28, 1944; children—Esmond Francis II, Martha Jane, Paul Norwood. Teaching fellow Wayne State U., Detroit, 1940-42; instr. U. Utah, Salt Lake City, 1946-48; research assoc. U. Chgo., 1948-49; asst. prof. Vanderbilt U., Nashville, 1949-57, asso. prof., dir. Clin. Chemistry Lab., 1960-67; asso. prof. U. Md., College Park, 1957-60; asst. dean basic scis. La. State U. Sch.

Medicine, Shreveport, 1967-73, prof., head, dept. biochemistry, 1967—. Served with USN, 1942-45. Diplomate Am. Bd. Clin. Chemistry. Fellow AAAS, Am. Inst. Chemists; mem. Am. Physiol. Soc., Am. Assn. for Clin. Chemistry, Am. Chem. Soc. Home: 550 Dunmoreland St Shreveport LA 71106 Office: Louisiana State University 1501 Kings Hwy Shreveport LA 71130

RUDY, JANE HUNTER, audiologist; b. Akron, Ohio, Mar. 9, 1951; d. Robert Moore and Maxine (Hulse-Evans) Hunter; B.S., Miami U. (Ohio), 1973; M.A. with distinction, U. Md., 1974; m. James William Rudy, Apr. 26, 1975. Cin. audiologist VA Hosp., Columbia, S.C., 1975-76, Shreveport, La., 1976; clin. audiologist dir. hearing aid dispensary Dr. Pou, Quinn, Watkins & Thornton, Shreveport, 1976—; clin. practicum La. State U. Med. Sch., Shreveport, med. sch. supr., 1979—; clin. supr. Am. Speech and Hearing Assn., 1978-79. Edn. chmn. Am. Heart Assn., 1978, pub. relations chmn., 1979. Recipient Cert. of Clin. Compentence, Am. Speech and Hearing Assn., 1977. Mem. Am. Speech and Hearing Assn., Am. Auditory Soc., La. Speech and Hearing Assn., La. Hearing Aid Soc., Northwestern La. Rehab. Assn., Pi Beta Phi. Methodist. Clubs: Jr. League of Shreveport, Am. Strokers (cons. 1977-79). Office: 2121 Line Ave Shreveport LA 71104

RUDY, RICHARD ALAN, real estate broker; b. Houston, Apr. 30, 1936; s. Israel and Edna S. (Soloman) R.; student U. Tex., 1954-56; m. Janice Abramson, Dec. 30, 1956; children—Keith, Kenneth, Kirk, Kerry. Pvt. real estate broker, Houston, 1963-65; partner Columbia Properties, Houston, 1965—; pres. Columbia Communities, Inc., Houston, 1969—; dir. Security Nat. Bank, Houston, First Fidelity Life Ins. Co., Houston. Pres. Jewish Fedn. Met. Houston, 1977-78. Licensed real estate broker, Tex. Mem. Harris County Flood Control Task Force, 1974-75; mem. mayor's commn. for better housing, 1969-71. Mem. Houston Apt. Assn., Houston Bd. Realtors, Greater Houston Builders Assn. Home: 9151 Briar Forest Dr Houston TX 77024 Office: 6009 Richmond St Suite 100 Houston TX 77057

RUDY, STEVEN JAY, real estate redevel. exec.; b. Houston, Dec. 17, 1945; s. Israel and Edna Solomon R.; student Ga. Inst. Tech., 1963-65; m. Sandra Roberson, July 27, 1974. Pres., SJR Designs, Inc., Houston, 1970; dir. property mgmt. Gulf Mgmt. Co., Houston, 1971-72; founder, pres. Creative Restoration, Inc., Houston, 1972—; pres. Restored Realty, Inc., Houston, 1973—; mng. partner various real estate redevel. investment partnerships; instr. continuing edn. U. St. Thomas, U. Houston. Mem. exec. com. Mainstreet Festival of Arts, 1972-76. Served with USN, 1968-69; Viet Nam. Recipient Environ. Contbn. award Mcpl. Arts Commn. and Houston chpt. AIA, 1977. Mem. Houston Apt. Assn., Houston C. of C. Jewish. Office: Creative Restoration Inc 330 Fairview St Houston TX 77006

RUEDA, JORGE EUGENIO, obstetrician and gynecologist; b. Bogota, Colombia, Jan. 7, 1938; came to U.S., 1963; s. Jorge and Margarita (Gomez) R.; M.D., Universidad Javeriana, Bogota, 1963; m. Mary Elizabeth Nicoll, Dec. 1, 1964; children—Teresa, Jorge E. Intern, Meml. Hosp., Savannah, Ga., 1964-65, resident in obstetrics and gynecology, 1965-66; resident in obstetrics and gynecology Mayo Clinic, Rochester, Minn., 1966-67, Jackson Meml. Hosp., Miami, Fla., 1967-70; instr. obstetrics and gynecology U. Miami Sch. Medicine, 1970-71, asst. prof., 1971-75, clin. asst. prof., 1975—; practice medicine, specializing in obstetrics and gynecology, Miami, 1972—; mem. staff North Shore Hosp., Jackson Meml. Hosp. Diplomate Am. Bd. Obstetrics and Gynecology. Fellow Am. Coll. Obstetricians and Gynecologists, Am. Fertility Soc.; mem. Fla. Med. Assn., Dade County Med. Assn. Roman Catholic. Office: 13733 NW 7th Ave Miami FL 33168

RUELLE, RICHARD, fishery biologist; b. Vermillion, S.D., July 6, 1934; s. Robert R. and Madge (Kuze) R.; B.S., S.D. State U., 1961, M.S., 1963; m. Janice F. Andersen, Aug. 7, 1960; 1 son, Scott R. Research asso. U. Idaho, Moscow, 1963-65; fishery biologist U.S. Fish and Wildlife Service, Grand Island, Nebr., 1965-68, Yankton, S.D., 1968-73, Clemson, S.C., 1973-78, Lafayette, La., 1978—; pres. S.C. Fishery Workers, 1977-78. Webelo leader, cub master Boy Scouts Am., Yankton, 1971-72. Served with U.S. Army, 1954-57. Recipient Key Man cert. Jaycees, 1966. Mem. Am. Fisheries Soc. (cert.), Am. Inst. Fishery Research Biologists, Sigma Xi, Xi Sigma Pi, Gamma Sigma Delta. Lutheran. Clubs: Elks, Masons. Contbr. articles to profl. jours.

RUEVE, RONALD KEITH, acctg. ofcl.; b. Louisville, Sept. 11, 1948; s. Robert Lee and Ruth Hazel (Hutcheson) R.; B.A. in Acctg., Bellarmine Coll., 1970; m. Jane Ellyn Bader, Apr. 22, 1972; children—Ronald Benjamin, Mary Katherine. Sr. tax acct. Ernst & Ernst, Louisville, 1970-72; tax mgr. Glenmore Distillery Co., Louisville, 1972-73; asst. tax dir. Humana, Inc., Louisville, 1973—. Served with USAR, 1970-76. Mem. Tax Execs. Inst. (treas. 1979-80). Democrat. Roman Catholic. Club: Ky. Lions. Home: 4113 Pomeroy Ct Louisville KY 40218 Office: PO Box 1438 1 Riverfront Plaza Louisville KY 40201

RUF, HENRY LAWRENCE, philosopher, educator; b. Wausau, Wis., June 28, 1932; s. Fred and Emma Lydia (Zyburski) R.; B.A., Macalester Coll., 1958; M.A., Emory U., 1960, Ph.D., 1964; m. Takeko Minami, Dec. 30, 1953; children—Debra, Phyllis, Christopher, Beverly, George. Asst. prof. Boston U., 1964-70; asso. prof., chmn. dept. philosophy State U. N.Y. at Oswego, 1970-75; prof., chmn. dept. philosophy W.Va. U., Morgantown, 1975—, dir. debate and forensics, 1977—. Served with USAF, 1950-54. Mem. Am. Philos. Assn. Author: Moral Investigations, 1978. Home: 380 Dorsey Ave Morgantown WV 26505 Office: Dept Philosophy West Virginia State U Morgantown WV 26506

RUF, PATRICIA KAYE, metallurgist; b. McCook, Nebr., May 6, 1949; d. Manuel LeRoy and Margalee Alice (Lyons) Ruf; B.S., U. Nebr., 1971; M.S., Mich. Tech. U., 1973; postgrad. U. Calif., 1973-74. Metall. scientist U. Calif., Berkeley and Livermore, 1973-74; metallurgist Bechtel Corp., San Francisco, 1974-75, welding engr. on Alaska Pipeline, Fairbanks, 1975-78; metallurgist Eagleton Engring. Co., Houston, 1978-80; metallurgist, owner R&B Cons., Houston, 1980—; chmn., speaker workshops. Recipient Disting. Alumna award U. Nebr., 1978; sci. fellow Alpha Sigma Mu, 1972; grantee AEC, 1970, 73. Registered profl. engr., Calif., Tex., La., Alaska, Ohio, Mich., Nebr. Mem. Am. Soc. Metals, Am. Soc. Quality Control, Am. Welding Soc., Soc. Women Engrs. Contbr. articles to profl. jours. Home: 6305 Westward St Apt 187 Houston TX 77081 Office: 6427 Hillcroft Suite 1010 Houston TX 77081

RUFFIN, DARLENE WISE, nursing adminstr.; b. Dallas, Dec. 3, 1940; cert. Palestine Sch. Nursing, 1962; cert. Baylor U. Med. Center, 1963; A.A., R.N., El Centro Coll., 1967; B.S., LaVerne Coll., 1971; married; 1 son, Eric; children by previous marriage—Harolyn, Shermaine, Cedric. Staff nurse Palestine (Tex.) Meml. Hosp., 1962-63, Baylor U. Med. Center, Dallas, 1963-69; dir. sch. health services Dallas Ind. Sch. Dist., 1969-70; dir. nursing services Forest Ave. Hosp., Dallas, 1970-73; clin. coordinator critical care area Methodist Hosp., Dallas, 1973-75; instr. Oak Cliff Community Hosp., Dallas, 1973-75; asst. adminstr. nursing services Southwest Community Hosp., Atlanta, 1975-78; coordinator med. nursing Grady Meml. Hosp., Atlanta, 1978—; instr. Am. Tng. Inst., Dallas, 1970-71; founder Minority Devel. Found., Dallas, 1973, exec. dir., 1972-75. Mem. adv. bd. El Centro Coll., div. nursing, 1974—; bd. dirs. Dallas Brotherhood Crusade, 1973-75, chmn., 1973-75. Named Tex. Nurse of the Year, Tex. Nurses Assn., 1972, Citizen of the Year, Dunbar Neighborhood Council, 1974; recipient Sickle Cell Anemia award, 1975. Mem. Am. Nurses Assn., Ga. Nursing Assn., Nat. Black Nurses Assn. (dir. 1977—), Atlanta Black Nurses Assn. (pres. 1978—), NAACP, Ga. Soc. for Hosp. and Nursing Service Adminstrs., Tex. Assn. of Sickle Cell Anemia (dir. 1973-74). Home: 2156 Shancey Ln College Park GA 30349 Office: 80 Butler St Atlanta GA 30301

RUFFIN, JAMES HAWES, geologist; b. Greensboro, N.C., July 23, 1931; s. Albert Leslie and Julie Ernestine (West) R.; B.S., U. S.C., 1954; postgrad. U. Colo., 1955-58; M.S., U. Okla., 1962; m. Janet Beatrice Hull, Jan. 31, 1970; 1 dau., Leslie Hawes. Research geologist Pan Am. Oil Co., Tulsa, 1958-59, Texaco Oil Co., Houston, 1960-64; sr. geol. specialist Tenneco Oil Co., Houston, 1964—; instr. U. St. Thomas, Houston, part-time 1964-76. Served to 1st lt. USAF, 1954-56. NSF grantee, 1960. Mem. Houston Geol. Soc., Am. Assn. Petroleum Geologists, Am. Inst. Profl. Geologists, Am. Assn. Stratigraphic Palynologists, Sigma Xi. Office: PO Box 2511 Houston TX 77001

RUFFNER, CHARLES LOUIS, lawyer, accountant; b. Cin., Nov. 7, 1936; s. Joseph H. and Edith Louise (Solomon) F.; B.S. in Bus. Adminstrn., U. Fla., 1958; LL.B. cum laude, U. Miami (Fla.), 1964; m. Mary Ann Kaufman, Jan. 30, 1966; children—Robin Sue, David Robert. IRS agt., Miami, 1959-64; admitted to Fla. bar, 1964, U.S. Supreme Ct. bar, 1966; trial atty. tax div. U.S. Dept. Justice, Washington, 1964-67; pres. Ruffner, Hagen & Rifkin, P.A., Miami, 1975—; lectr. tax law Fla. Internat. U., 1977—; guest speaker on taxation and profl. service corps. to various profl. groups throughout U.S., Mex., Europe, Caribbean, 1969—; tax columnist Miami Rev., newspaper. Mem. Am., Fed., Dade County bar assns., Fla. Bar (exec. council tax sect. 1967—), Greater Miami Tax Inst., Greater Miami Estate Planning Council, Phi Kappa Phi, Phi Alpha Delta, Pi Lambda Phi. Jewish. Clubs: Masons, Shriners, Scottish Rite, B'nai B'rith (pres. Scopus lodge 1977). Contbr. articles to legal jours.; editorial bd. U. Miami Law Rev., 1963-64. Home: 6250 SW 135th St Miami FL 33156 Office: Suite 800 Rivergate Plaza Bldg 444 Brickell Ave Miami FL 33131

RUGG, FREDERIC WALDO, II, real estate broker; b. Brookline, Mass., Nov. 28, 1923; s. Robert Billings and Margaret Josephine (Hurley) R.; student Wesleyan U., 1943; student Georgetown U., 1944; A.B., Harvard, 1948; postgrad. U. Fla., 1967, 68, Tulne U., 1970, U. Tampa, 1971, U. Ga., 1969; m. Virginia Bell Reiter, Mar. 28, 1947; children—Linda Lee, Frederic Waldo III. Vice pres. Hammons-Rugg & Assos., Daytona Beach, Fla., 1957-63; partner, developer Ocean Grove Terr. Subdiv., Ormond Beach, Fla., 1965-70; owner, broker Ted Rugg & Assos., Ormond Beach, 1963—; sales agt., broker, Aquarius Oceanfront Condominium Complex, Ormond Beach, 1971-73; pres., developer Regency Manor Estates, Ormond Beach, 1965-70; sec. North Penn, Inc., Ormond Beach, 1960—. Mem. Daytona Area Bd. Realtors (by-laws com. 1974-76). Clubs: Oceanside Country (pres. 1963-64, dir. 1964-66, 71-73), Quarterback. Home: 946 John Anderson Dr Ormond Beach FL 32074 Office: 54 E Granada Blvd Ormond Beach FL 32074

RUIZ, RICHARD STRANAHAN, ophthalmologist; b. Houston, Tex., July 12, 1932; s. John J. and Luz (Stranahan) R.; student Tex. A. and M. U., 1951-53; M.D., U. Tex., 1957; m. Yvonne Mosher, June 11, 1955; children—Roseanna, Raymond and Robert (twins), Kathleen, Cindy. Intern, Hermann Hosp., Houston, 1957-58; resident City of Detroit Receiving Hosp. and Wayne State U., 1958-61, Kresge Eye Inst., Detroit, 1961-62; Retina Found. fellow, Mass. Eye and Ear Infirmary, Harvard Med. Sch., Boston, 1961-62; practice medicine specializing in ophthalmology, Houston, 1962-80; clin. prof. U. Tex. Med. Sch., Houston, 1971—, chmn. dept. ophthalmology, 1971—; chief of ophthalmology service St. Anthony Center, Houston, 1971-80; mem. staff Hermann Hosp., 1962-80, chief ophthalmology service, 1967-80; acad. chief ophthalmology St. Joseph Hosp., 1965-76, mem. med. research com., 1967-80. Diplomate Am. Bd. Ophthalmology. Fellow Am. Acad. Ophthalmology and Otolaryngology; mem. A.C.S., Pan Am. Assn. Ophthalmology, Retina Soc., Assn. Research in Vision and Ophthalmology, Soc. Eye Surgeons, Tex. Soc. Ophthalmology and Otolaryngology, Harris County Med. Soc., Tex. Med. Assn., AMA, Tex. Soc. Prevention Blindness (chmn. of state med. adv. com. 1975-76), Eye Study Club, Research to Prevent Blindness, Inc. (ad hoc com. 1970-80). Contbr. numerous articles on ophthalmology to profl. jours. and periodicals. Home: 4634 Bryn Mawr Ln Houston TX 77027 Office: Hermann Eye Center 1203 Ross Sterling Ave Houston TX 77030

RULIFFSON, SCOTT HARMON, ins. co. exec.; b. Cleve., Sept. 25, 1950; s. Harmon Leslie and Florence Topinka R.; student Tyler Jr. Coll., 1968-69; B.B.A., N. Tex. State U., 1973; m. Dayna Jan Broughton, May 22, 1971; children—Jessica, Jon-Christopher. Claims adjuster Liberty Mut. Ins. Co., 1974-75; with Evans Cooperage Co., Harvey, La., 1976—, reconditioning plant mgr., 1979; underwriter, claims mgr. Underwriters Marine Services, Inc., New Orleans, 1979—; instr. Delgado Jr. Coll. Mem. Am. Mgmt. Assn., Delta Safety Soc., Nat. Safety Council. Republican. Episcopalian. Club: Mariners (New Orleans). Home: 8523 Sycamore Pl New Orleans LA 70125 Office: 1516 One Shell Plaza New Orleans LA

RULLAN, ANTONIO, otolaryngologist, educator; b. Yauco, P.R., Jan. 22, 1918; s. Pedro and Teresa (Rodriguez' R.; B.S., St. John's U., 1939; M.D., N.Y. U., 1943, M.Sc. in Otolaryngology, 1954; m. Jane B. Hryhorczuk, Aug. 3. 1946; children—Anthony J., Jane T. (Mrs. Frankie Viejo), Pedro P., John V. Intern, Kings County Hosp., Bklyn., 1943; resident Bellevue Hosp., N.Y.C., 1950-52; practice medicine specializing in otolaryngology, San Juan, 1952—; dir. otolaryngology Univ. Hosp., San Juan, 1974-78; head dept. otolaryngology San Juan City Hosp., 1974-78; mem. faculty U. P.R. Sch. Medicine, San Juan, 1952—, prof., 1974—, chief otolaryngology, 1974-78; part-time attending otolaryngologist VA Hosp., San Juan, 1978—; dir. Blue Cross Plan P.R., 1954-60, Blue Shield Plan P.R., 1974—. Served to capt. M.C., AUS, 1945-46. Named Distinguished Alumnus N.Y. U., 1968. Diplomate Am. Bd. Otolaryngology. Fellow A.C.S. (pres. P.R. chpt. 1965), Am. Triological Soc., Am. Broncho-Esophagology Assn., Am. Acad. Otolaryngology; mem. N.Y. U. Alumni Club P.R. (pres. 1955-56). Rotarian. Contbr. articles to profl. jours. Home: 4 Green Hill St Garden Hills Guaynabo PR 00657 Office: Ashford Medical Center San Juan PR 00907

RUMAGE, JOSEPH PAUL, physician; b. Newark, N.J., Nov. 29, 1927; s. William T. and Veronica (McGuiness) R.; B.A., Columbia U., 1946; M.D., N.Y. U., 1950; m. Nancy Simms, June 15, 1955; children—Sarah, Paul, William. Intern, Charity Hosp. of La., New Orleans, 1950-51; resident Tulane U., Eye, Ear, Nose & Throat Hosp., New Orleans, 1953-56; practice medicine specializing in ophthalmology, New Orleans, 1956—; asso. clin. prof. ophthalmology Tulane U. Sch. Medicine, New Orleans, 1956—; founder, bd. dirs., Ednl. Research & Treatment Center, New Orleans; cons. in ophthalmology Ochsner Hosp., Jefferson, La., Belle Chasse (La.) State Sch., Div. for the Blind, La. Dept. Vocat. Rehab.; mem. staff Eye, Ear, Nose & Throat Hosp., New Orleans; vis. staff Charity Hosp. at New Orleans, Methodist Hosp., New Orleans, W. Jefferson Gen. Hosp., Marrero, La., St. Bernard Gen. Hosp., Jo Ellen Smith Hosp., New Orleans; dir. Low Vision Clinic, Eye Center, La. State U. Med. Sch. Served with M.C., U.S. Army Reserve, 1951-53. Diplomate Am. Bd. Ophthalmology. Fellow Am. Acad. Ophthalmology; mem. New Orleans Acad. Ophthalmology, La. Miss. Ophthalmol. Assn., Orleans Parish Med. Soc. Contbr. articles to profl. jours. Office: 705 Audubon Bldg New Orleans LA 70112 also Pratt St and Westbank Expressway Gretna LA 70053

RUMAGGI, LOUIS JACOB, ret. army officer, cons.; b. Memphis, Dec. 3, 1900; s. Louis and Garnet (Huntsbarger) R.; student Miami U., Oxford, Ohio, 1917-18; B.S., U.S. Mil. Acad., 1922; B.S. in Civil Engring., U. Calif. at Berkeley, 1927; m. Miriam Louise Tuggle, Mar. 30, 1950; 1 dau., Louise Herron (Mrs. Alan Lyndal Reed). Commd. 2d lt. C.E., U.S. Army 1922, advanced through grades to maj. gen., 1953; acting chief engr. Army Forces, S.W. Pacific, 1945-46; engr. 8th U.S. Army, Korea, 1952-53; dep. chief engrs. U.S. Army, 1954-55; chief staff 6th U.S. Army, 1955-57; div. engr. North Central div., Corps Engrs., 1957-59; asso. Tex. Instruments, Inc., 1959-62. Decorated Legion of Merit with oak leaf cluster, D.S.M.; Ulchi medal (Korea). Fellow ASCE; mem. Mil. Order World Wars, SAR (nat. trustee Tex. soc.), Soc. Am. Mil. Engrs., Am. Legion. Clubs: Rotary; Army and Navy (Washington). Home: 6337 Diamond Head Circle Dallas TX 75225

RUMMELL, CLARENCE SMITH, occupational safety and health cons.; b. Lewistown, Pa., Jan. 21, 1924; s. Edward Everett and Margaret Ann (McCracken) R.; B.S., Temple U., 1949; M.S. in Biochemistry, Yale U., 1957; m. Christina Kathleen Clancy, June 9, 1955; children—Patricia Ann, Dean Edward, Kathleen Marie, Margaret Ann, Edward E., Mary M. Spectrograph operator, chemist Aleghany Ludlum Steel, Phoenix, 1957-62; spl. project engr. Union Carbide Corp., Torrence, Calif., 1962-66, Florence, S.C., 1966-74; spl. asst. to city engr. City of Florence, 1974-77; mgr., safety engr. Palmetto Safety Cons., Inc., Columbia, S.C., 1977—; engring. mgr. IPS Inc., Columbia, 1977—. Served with USN, 1942-54. Decorated Silver Star, Purple Heart, Navy Cross. Mem. Soc. Mfg. Engrs. (cert.), Am. Soc. Safety Engrs. Republican. Presbyterian. Contbr. articles to profl. jours. Office: 2719 Middleburgh Dr Suite 101 Columbia SC 29204

RUMMERFIELD, BENJAMIN FRANKLIN, geophysicist; b. Denver, May 25, 1917; s. Lawrence L. and Helen A. (Roper) R.; Engr. Geology, Colo. Sch. Mines, 1940; grad. Harvard Advanced Mgmt. Program, 1947, Indsl. Coll. Armed Forces, 1963, Aspen Inst. Humanistic Studies, 1958; m. Mary Merchant, Feb. 16, 1979; children—Ann S., Michael J., Benjamin F., Mary Susan, Lila, Sonya, Karim. Asst. mgr. Seismograph Service Corp., Mexico City, Mexico, 1947-50, Caracas, Venezuela, and Colombia, 1945-47; exec. v.p. Century Geophys. Corp., Tulsa, 1950-60, also dir.; pres. GeoData Corp., Tulsa, 1960—, Gulf Coast GeoData, Houston, 1962—; dir. Rockall GeoData, Internat. of London (Eng.), Permian Exploration, Custom Data Services; cons. Petroleos Mexicanos. Bd. dirs. YMCA, Tulsa, 1955—, pres., 1956-59. Recipient Outstanding Service award YMCA, Tulsa, 1958, 63, Disting. Achievement medal Colo. Sch. Mines, 1978, hon. mention for painting Philbrook Art Mus., 1961. Mem. Tulsa Geol. Soc., Colo. Sch. Mines Alumni Assn. (pres. 1953), Asociacion Mexicana de Geologos Petroleos, Am. Assn. Petroleum Geologists, Soc. Exploration Geophysicists (nat. v.p. 1958), Sigma Gamma Epsilon. Clubs: Tulsa, Harvard (Tulsa). Contbr. numerous articles to profl. jours. Home: 6787 Timberlane Dr Tulsa OK 74105 Office: GeoData Bldg Box 3476 Tulsa OK 74101

RUMPF, WILLIAM JOSEPH, acct.; b. Auburn, N.Y., Nov. 1, 1946; s. Donald Joseph and Rose Mary (Blowers) R.; ed. U. South Fla., Tampa, 1971; m. Elaine Marie LaPorte, Dec. 12, 1969; children—Bryan, Thomas, Sheryl. Acct., Tornwall, Lang & Lee, C.P.A.'s, St. Petersburg, Fla., 1969-75, Tornwall, Kearney & Wintz, C.P.A.'s, St. Petersburg, 1975-76; tax dir. Cherry, Bekaert & Holland, C.P.A.'s, St. Petersburg, 1976; cons. taxes; guest tchr. U. Ala. (Birmingham); discussion leader nat. tax courses; lectr. profl. groups and civic clubs. Mem. Com. of 100 of Pinellas County. Served with USNR, 1965-69. Mem. Fla. Inst. C.P.A.'s (asso.), St. Petersburg C. of C. Republican. Roman Catholic. Clubs: Breakfast Optimist (dir. 1979-80), St. Petersburg Yacht. Home: 240 57th Ave S Saint Petersburg FL 33705 Office: PO Box 300 Saint Petersburg FL 33731

RUMPFF, CORNELIS JAN, brewery exec.; b. Groningen, Netherlands, Feb. 20, 1946; came to U.S., 1976; D. in Econs., Erasmus U., Rotterdam, Netherlands, 1972; m. Barbara Bryant, May 15, 1976; 1 son, Ronald. Corp. planner, Schuitema, Netherlands, 1972-74; mktg. mgr. Spar Orgn., Gieten, Netherlands, 1974-76; v.p. fin. Grolsch Importers, N.Y.C., 1976-78, Atlanta, 1978, pres., 1978—. Recipient Vivo award, 1973. Mem. Nat. Assn. Beverage Importers, Assn. Distbn. Economists Netherlands. Clubs: Sleepy Hollow Country (Briarcliff Manor, N.Y.); Horseshoe Bend (Roswell, Ga.). Author: (in Dutch) The Development of the Systems Approach in the Retailing Industry, 1973. Office: 1775 The Exchange #550 Atlanta GA 30339

RUNDELL, BOB RAY, educator; b. Evansville, Ind., Apr. 27, 1933; s. Robert W. and Helen Eloise (Meyer) R.; B.S. in Bus. Adminstrn., U. Evansville, 1955; M.S. in Urban Affairs, U. Tex., Arlington, 1977; m. Cynthia Denise Poston, Apr. 20, 1979; children—Scott Edward, Shannon Lynn. Exec. dir. Evansville Boys Club, 1957-60, Evansville Assn. for Retarded Citizens, 1962-66; asst. dir. United Funds of Evansville, 1966-68; exec. dir. Ky. Assn. for Retarded Citizens, 1968-70; regional rep. Nat. Assn. for Retarded Citizens, 1970-75; project dir. Human Resource Center, Grad. Sch. Social Work, U. Tex., Arlington, 1975—. Bd. dirs. Arlington YMCA, 1972-74, pres., 1973; bd. dirs. Ft. Worth State Sch. for Mentally Retarded, 1977-80, pres. bd., 1979-80, chmn. adv. council, 1979-80. Recipient citation Govt. of Ark., 1972, Nat. Youth Assn. for Retarded Citizens, 1972, Gov. of Okla., 1973; award Ft. Worth Mid-Cities chpt. Am. Soc. Tng. and Devel., 1978. Mem. Nat. Assn. Retarded Citizens, Tex. Assn. Retarded Children, Arlington Assn. Retarded Citizens (dir.), Conf. of Execs. of Assns. Retarded Citizens (pres. 1969-70), Am. Soc. Tng. and Devel. (pres. 1978, dir. 1977-80). Home: 2706 Hollywood Dr Arlington TX 76013 Office: Human Resource Center Grad Sch Social Work U Tex Arlington TX 76019

RUNDELL, MALCOLM RAY, chemist, univ. adminstr.; b. Monroe, La., Oct. 9, 1935; s. Charles Edward and Bertha E. (Stout) R.; B.S., La. Tech. U., 1957; M.S., Northwestern U. La., 1963; Ed.D., U. Houston, 1975; m. Barbara Anne Ball, Aug. 23, 1957; children—Teresa Ann, David Glen. Tchr. chemistry Bossier City (La.) High Sch., 1957-62, Pasadena (Tex.) High Sch., 1962-64, Sam Rayburn High Sch., Pasadena, 1964-65; instr. chemistry San Jacinto Coll., Pasadena, Tex., 1965-75, chmn. dept., 1975-79, acad. dean, registrar San Jacinto Coll. S., Houston, 1979—. Mem. Tex. Jr. Coll. Tchrs. Assn., Phi Delta Kappa. Baptist. Office: 13735 Beamer Houston TX 77089

RUNKLE, FREDERICK STEPHEN, engr., engring. exec.; b. Elkhart, Ind., Aug. 2, 1940; s. Leroy William and Marcella Mae (Christler) R.; student Tri-State Coll., 1960-63; m. Patricia Ann Moore, July 14, 1963; children—Stephen Dale, Susan Lynn. Prodn. engr. CTS Corp., Elkhart, Ind., 1959-66; test engr. Collins Radio, Dallas, 1966-73; sr. project engr. Martin Marietta, Orlando, Fla., 1973-74; supr. engring. dept. Scientific-Atlanta, Atlanta, 1974—. Com. mem. Boy Scouts Am., Atlanta, 1975—; mem. Scientific-Atlanta Amateur Radio Club, 1975-77, pres., 1975-76. Served with U.S. Army, 1963-64. Mem. Am. Radio Relay League, N.G. Assn. Tex. Methodist. Home: 25 Stonehedge Dr Buford GA 30518 Office: 3845 Pleasantdale Rd Atlanta GA 30340

RUNKLE, LOWE WINFIELD, advt. agy. exec.; b. El Reno, Okla., June 22, 1908; s. Ralph Evans and Clara Leslie (Lowe) R.; B.A., U. Okla., 1930; m. Alice Escoe, Dec. 15, 1937; children—Ralph Layton, Kent Evans. Copywriter, Ray K. Glenn Advt., Oklahoma City, 1934-39, v.p., Oklahoma City, 1940-46, Dallas, 1940-46; founder, pres. Lowe Runkle Co., Oklahoma City, 1946-72, chmn. bd., chief exec. officer, 1972—; dir. Union Bank & Trust Co., Oklahoma City. Chmn. Okla. Jud. Nominating Commn., 1967-73, Oklahoma City Zoo Trust; nat. bd. govs. Oklahoma Christian Coll. Served with USAAF, 1944-45. Recipient Disting. Service award Oklahoma City Advt. Club, 1952; Silver medal award Advt. Fedn. Am., 1965; Outstanding Layman award Okla. Bar Assn., 1970; Liberty Bell award Oklahoma County Bar Assn., 1972; Herbert Lincoln Harley award Am. Judicature Soc., 1973. Mem. Am. Judicature Soc., Advt. and Mktg. Internat., Okla. Heritage Assn. (v.p.), Oklahoma City C. of C. (dir.), Alpha Delta Sigma, Alpha Tau Omega. Democrat. Presbyterian. Clubs: Petroleum, Beacon (Oklahoma City); Men's Dinner, Okla. Econ. Home: 412 NW 39th St Oklahoma City OK 73118 Office: Lowe Runkle Co 6801 N Broadway Oklahoma City OK 73114

RUNNELS, THOMAS RAY, banker; b. West Point, N.Y., Apr. 28, 1952; s. William R. and Mary M. R.; B.S., Miss. State U., 1974. Mgmt. trainee 1st. Nat. Bank, Birmingham, Ala., 1975-76, asst. br. mgr., 1976-77, adminstrv. asst./br. adminstrn., 1977, asst. cashier, 1977, br. mgr., 1977, mgr. corp. services, 1977—, now asst. v.p. Active Jr. Achievement; adv. com. Sid McDonald for Gov. State of Ala. Adv. Com., 1978. Mem. Am. Inst. Banking (cert.), Ala. Automated Clearing House Ops. Com., Bank Adminstrn. Inst. Home: 919 Valley Ridge Dr Apt 212 Birmingham AL 35209 Office: 1st Nat Bank Birmingham PO Box 11007 Birmingham AL 35288

RUNNING, JOSEPH M(ARTIN), JR., respiratory therapist; b. Mpls., Aug. 7, 1945; s. Joseph Martin and Jeanne Louise (Eastmn) R.; student Centenary Coll. La., 1964, E. Central Okla U., 1966-68, Ottawa U., 1978-79; cert. respiratory therapy U. Okla. Health Sci. Center, 1971; m. Sherry Corliss Kolb, Aug. 1, 1964; children—Joseph Martin, Sandra Jean, Melanie June. Staff therapist Valley View Hosp., Ada, Okla., 1967-68, U. Okla. Health Sci. Center, Oklahoma City, 1968-70; dir. dept. respiratory therapy Grandway Gen. Hosp., Oklahoma City, 1970-71, Muskogee (Okla.) Gen. Hosp., 1971-74; coordinator respiratory therapy program Tulsa Jr. Coll., 1974—; trustee Nat. Bd. Respiratory Therapy, 1979—. Bd. dirs. Green County affiliate Okla. Lung Assn., 1973. Registered respiratory therapist. Mem. Am. Assn. Respiratory Therapy (dir. 1974-78), Okla. Assn. Respiratory Therapy (Presdl. award 1979, Okla. Thoracic Soc., Am. Philatelic Soc., other philatelic socs. Republican. Episcopalian. Home: 14004 E 26 St Tulsa OK 74134 Office: Tulsa Jr Coll 10th and Boston Sts Tulsa OK 74119

RUNNINGER, JACK, optometrist; b. Aurora, Ill., July 16, 1923; s. Guy M. and Gladys (Grossman) R.; student (Rector scholar) De Pauw U., 1941-44; Dr. Optometry So. Coll. Optometry, 1948; m. Mary Gibson, July 31, 1945; children—Nancy (Mrs. Joe Watson), Star, Janet. Practice optometry, Rome, Ga., 1948—. Treas. YMCA, 1963-66; pres. Rome Inter Club Council, 1954. Mem. Gov.'s Comprehensive Health Planning Council, 1970-73. Served to lt. (j.g.) USNR, 1943-46. Recipient Distinguished Service in Journalism award Am. Optometric Assn., 1971. Mem. Ga. Optometric Assn. (pres. 1953), So. Council Optometrists (pres. 1961), Am. Acad. Optometry (pres. Ga. chpt. 1962), Rome Jaycees (pres. 1952). Methodist (steward 1949—). Lion (pres. 1957). Club: Rome Exec. (pres. 1959). Author: (with Nick Powers) Junior Samples Jokebook and Favorite Jokes of Mountain Folks in Boogar Hollow, 1971; editor: So. Jour. Optometry, 1973—; cons. editor Optometric Mgmt. mag., Eye Talk mag.; contbr. articles to popular mags. and profl. jours. Home: 1 Pine Valley Rd Rome GA 30161 Office: 206 E Third St Rome GA 30161

RUNYAN, CAROLYN BUCHANAN, county pub. health adminstr.; b. Athens, Tenn., Jan. 15, 1933; d. Carter Ewing and Mary Lee (Moulton) Buchanan; student E. Tenn. State Coll., 1951-52; m. Robert H. Runyan, Mar. 8, 1955; children—Robert Carter, Sarah Melanie. Typist, Meigs County (Tenn.) Health Dept., 1952-56; typist McMinn County (Tenn.) Health Dept., 1958-60, 63-72, office mgr. and clerical supr., 1972—; receptionist, switchbd. operator Mayfield Dairy, Inc., Athens, 1960-61; interviewer Tenn. Dept. Employment Security, 1962. Recipient 20 Yrs'. Service award State of Tenn., 1977. Mem. Tenn. Pub. Health Assn., Tenn. Assn. Pub. Health Secs. (pres. 1979—), Tenn. State Employees Assn. (pres. Hiwassee chpt.). Democrat. Home: 123 Keith Ln Athens TN 37303 Office: PO Box 665 Athens TN 37303

RUPEL, LAWRENCE MICHAEL, clergyman, psychotherapist; b. South Bend, Ind., Sept. 5, 1948; s. Maurice Eugene and Mary Elizabeth (Tamplen) R.; B.A., U. Tex., Austin, 1971; M.Div., Josephinum Sch. Theology, 1975. Ordained priest Roman Catholic Ch., 1975; mem. staff Marriage Tribunal Diocese Corpus Christi, 1975—; chaplain Incarnate Word Sisters, 1975-76; asso. pastor Our Lady of Guadalupe Ch., Corpus Christi, 1976-77; asso. pastor St. Paul Cath. Ch., Corpus Christi, 1977-79; asso. pastor St. Elizabeth Cath. Ch., Alice, Tex., 1979—; chmn. dept. measurement and evaluation Office Cath. Schs., 1976-78; alcoholism and drug abuse counseling, 1979. HEW grantee. Mem. Am. Personnel and Guidance Assn., Canon Law Soc. Am., Nat. Cath. Guidance Assn., Am. Measurement and Evaluation in Guidance, Tex. Psychotherapy Assn. Democrat. Office: PO Box 1009 Alice TX 78332

RUSCO, CLARK DAVID, civil engr.; b. Great Bend, Kans., Nov. 17, 1949; s. Clarence Comfort and Esther Caroline (Jaerger) R.; student Fort Hays State U., 1967-69; B.S., Kans. State U., 1971; m. Donna Marie Schenk, Aug. 22, 1970. Civil engr. bridge design Kans. Dept. Transp., Topeka, 1971-74, facilities engring. div., Fort Riley, Kans., 1974-78; civil engr. Mideast div. U.S. Army C.E., Winchester, Va., 1978-80; city engr. Great Bend (Kans.), 1980—. Registered profl. engr., land surveyor, Kans. Mem. ASCE, Soc. Am. Mil. Engrs. Methodist. Home: 3016 Broadway Great Bend KS 67530 Office: 1209 Williams St Great Bend KS 67530

RUSE, GARY ALAN, author; b. Miami, Fla., Aug. 24, 1946; s. Layton Newman and Virginia Mae (Singer) R.; B.A., U. Miami, 1968. Book illustrator William Morrow & Co., N.Y.C., 1969; painter, graphic artist; author: Houndstooth, 1975; A Game of Titans, 1976. Served as reporter C.E., AUS, 1969-70; Vietnam. Mem. Sci. Fiction Writers Am., Mystery Writers Am., Authors Guild. Methodist.

RUSH, DAVID CHARLES, geophysicist; b. Cin., May 26, 1943; s. Charles Arthur and Eleanor Marian (Coulthard) R.; B.S. in Geology, Ohio State U., 1966; M.S. in Applied Geophysics, U. Houston, 1971; m. Sandy Ann Williams, Feb. 4, 1967; children—Julianne, Christina. Seismologist, Ray Geophys. div. Mandrel Industries, Inc., Houston, 1969-71; supr. geophysics Conoco, Houston, 1972-75; offshore geophysicist Anadarko Prodn. Co., Houston, 1975-76; div. dir. exploratory projects Conoco, Oklahoma City, 1977—. Served to 1st lt. AUS, 1967-69. Mem. Soc. Exploration Geophysicists, Am. Assn. Petroleum Geologists, Sigma Gamma Epsilon. Home: 6409 W Kensington Rd Oklahoma City OK 73132 Office: 3525 NW 56th Oklahoma City OK 73112

RUSH, GEORGE EDWARD, religious adminstr.; b. Satartia, Miss., June 26, 1905; s. Charles Edwin and Julia Elizabeth (Roberts) R.; student U. Ark., 1926-27; LL.B., U. Memphis, 1934, Memphis State U., 1963; m. Opal Palmer, Feb. 25, 1928; children—Evelyn Marie Rush Leslie, Dorothy Ann Rush Black, Martha Nell Rush Pearson. Asst. credit mgr. mail order Sears Roebuck & Co., Memphis, 1928-44; asst. credit mgr. Plough Inc., Memphis, 1944-48; office mgr. Miller-Wohl Co., Memphis, 1949-54; gen. mgr. House of Hale Furniture Mfg. Co., Memphis, 1954-55; mgr. internat. hdqrs. office Gideons Internat. Co., Chgo., 1956-57; bus. adminstr. Bellevue Baptist Ch., Memphis, 1958-71, 1st. Assembly of God Ch., Memphis, 1971—; cons. in field. Chmn. bd. deacons, LaBelle Baptist Ch., Memphis, 1938, Bellevue Baptist Ch., 1947, 52, 57; pres. camp Gideons Internat., Memphis, 1945-46, Tenn. state pres., 1946-49; bd. dirs. Mid-South Bible Coll., Memphis, 1947-56; treas. Teen Challenge of Memphis, 1972—. Admitted to Tenn. bar, 1934. Cert. fellow in ch. bus. adminstrn., 1964. Mem. Nat. Assn. Ch. Bus. Adminstrs. (pres. Tenn. Chpt. 1970, pres. Five Star chpt. 1971, nat. dir. 1974-75), Delta Theta Phi. Editor Bellevue Messenger, 1960-71. Home: 4131 Hilldale Ave Memphis TN 38117 Office: 1st Assembly of God Ch 255 N Highland St Memphis TN 38111

RUSH, HENRY LESTER, JR., systems mgr.; b. Shreveport, La., May 22, 1951; s. Henry Lester and Katherine (Wilkins) R.; B.S. magna cum laude, La. Tech. U., 1973. Mgr. data base support Tex. Eastern Corp., Houston, 1973—. Mem. Am. Mgmt. Assn., Assn. Computing Machinery, Honeywell Large Systems Users Assn. (chmn. data mgmt. subcom. 1978—), Omicron Delta Kappa. Democrat. Home: 12682 Briar Patch Houston TX 77077 Office: PO Box 2521 Houston TX 77077

RUSH, MICHAEL E., endocrinologist; b. St. Louis, Nov. 9, 1947; s. Merrill and Eleanor (Ikin) R.; student U. Mo., Columbia, 1965-67; B.A., U. Mass., Amherst, 1969; M.S., Boston U., 1972; Ph.D., Fla. State U., Tallahassee, 1978; m. Carol Rae King, July 29, 1979; 1 stepson, Jeffrey William Archibald. Postdoctoral fellow dept. anatomy U. Nebr. Med. Center, Omaha 1978-80; with dept. anatomy U. Ky. Med. Center, Lexington, 1980—; lectr. med. schs. Served alt. mil. duty Beth Israel Hosp., Boston, 1970-72. Mem. Soc. Study Reprodn. (Hon. mention Young Investigator of Yr. award), AAAS, Sigma Xi (grantee-in-aid 1978-79). Democrat. Jewish. Office: Dept Anatomy U Ky MN 220 Med Center Lexington KY 40536

RUSH, ROSE LEE ZEIGLER, health care exec.; b. Orangeburg, S.C., Sept. 6, 1914; d. Walter and Daisy Graves (Oliver) Zeigler; B.S. in Home Econs., S.C. State Coll., 1939; M.S., Columbia U., 1950, postgrad. 1951-54; m. Clay Connor Rush, June 7, 1941; children—Clay Connor, Ella Andra and Daisy Andrea (twins), Rose Mary. Tchr. public schs. and jr. colls., S.C., 1939-60, U. S.C., 1968, 72, Clemson U., 1972; pres., adminstr. State Eureka Sunshine Meml. Manor, Inc., Orangeburg, S.C., 1967—; pres., dir. State Eureka Inc. & Trust, Orangeburg, 1976—. Mem. Am. Judicature Soc., Nat. Hist. Soc., Am. Forestry Assn., Am. Security Council, Nat. Wildlife Fedn., Fed. Bar Assn., Am. Hosp. Assn., Am. Public Health Assn., S.C. Public Health Assn., Smithsonian Soc., Am. Heritage Assn., Zeta Phi Beta. Roman Catholic. Club: Holy Trinity Women's. Address: PO Box 220 Orangeburg SC 29115

RUSHFELDT, JAMES LEONARD, freight co. exec.; b. St. Paul, Sept. 9, 1948; s. Victor Lee Roy and Catherine R.; B.S., U.S. Mil. Acad., 1970. Pres., Jim Rushfeldt, Inc., refrigerated trucking, Miami, Fla., 1976—. Served to capt. U.S. Army, 1970-75. Home and Office: 540 NW 113th St Miami FL 33168

RUSHING, BARNIE ELMER, JR., retail co. exec.; b. Plainview, Tex., Oct. 27, 1916; s. Barnie Elmer and Zelma A. (Flake) R.; student Tex. Technol. Coll., 1933-35, U.S. Coast Guard Acad., 1944; m. Dorothy Ann York, Feb. 11, 1939; 1 son, Robert York. With Hemphill-Wells Co., Lubbock, Tex., 1934—, v.p., sec., 1952—. Pres., United Fund, Lubbock, 1959-60; former dir. Tex. United Fund; organizational chmn. Lubbock Council Chs., 1960; chmn. devel. commn. Civic Center, Library. Bd. dirs. Tex. Found. Mental Health and Mental Retardation, 1970—, Tex. Tech. U. Med. Sch. Found., 1970—, Tex. Tech U. Found., 1970—; vice chmn. bd. dirs. Textile Research Found., Tex. Tech U., 1969-75; chmn. bd. mgrs. Lubbock County Hosp. Dist., 1969-75; trustee, vice-chmn. Tex. Bd. Mental Health and Mental Retardation, 1970-73; trustee Spencer A. Wells Found., 1958—, Mary Baker Rumsey-Hemphill-Wells Found., 1963—; chmn. Support Unlimited, 1962—; bd. dirs. West Tex. Health Planning Systems, Methodist Hosp., Salvation Army, Tex. Tourist Council. Served with USCG, 1941-45. Recipient Distinguished Salesman's award for community service, 1965. Mem. Retail Mchts. Assn. Tex. (past exec. com.), Nat. Better Bus. Bur. (past gov.), Lubbock Better Bus. Bur. (past pres.), Tex. Retail Assn. (dir.), Red Raider Club (past pres.), Kappa Sigma, Delta Sigma Pi. Mem. Christian Ch. (past chmn. ofcl. bd. 1954, past chmn. bd. elders 1956). Mason (Shriner), Kiwanian. Clubs: Lubbock Country, Lubbock, University City. Home: 4510 W 17th St Lubbock TX 79416 Office: PO Box 981 1212 Ave J Lubbock TX 79408

RUSHING, JOE B., coll. chancellor; b. Zephyr, Tex., May 23, 1921; s. Cordie M. and Vallie (Parson) R.; B.A., Howard Payne Coll., 1946; M.A., East Tex. State Coll., 1949; Ph.D., U. Tex., 1952; postdoctoral study U. Mich., 1959; m. Elaine Whitis, Dec. 21, 1946; children—Anita Sherron, Cynthia Ann, Robert Scott. Tchr. sci., adminstr. Levelland (Tex.) High Sch., then Mt. Pleasant (Tex.) High Sch., 1946-50; teaching fellow U. Tex., 1950-52; dir. adult edn. Wharton Jr. Coll., 1952-54; dean grad. div. Howard Payne Coll., 1954-58, adminstrv. v.p., 1956-60; pres. Jr. Coll. of Broward County. Ft. Lauderdale, Fla., 1960-65; pres. Tarrant County Jr. Coll. Dist., Ft. Worth, 1965-69, chancellor, 1969—. Mem. Nat. Endowment for Humanities Com., 1976—. Served with U.S. Army, 1942-46. Recipient Carl Bredt award U. Tex., 1977; Paul Harris fellow, 1972; named Educator of Year, Press Club Ft. Worth, 1974; Disting. Alumnus Howard Payne U., 1976, E. Tex. State U., 1979; Boss of Year Nat. Secs., 1971. Mem. Nat. Council on Humanities, Pi Sigma Alpha, Phi Delta Kappa, Kappa Delta Pi. Baptist. Address: 1400 Electric Service Bldg Fort Worth TX 76102

RUSHING, KAREN CLINARD, speech pathologist; b. Nashville, Apr. 21, 1950; d. Robert Bell and Dorothy Dorris C.; B.S., George Peabody Coll. for Tchrs., 1971; M.S., Vanderbilt U., 1973; m. John Bryant Rushing, Aug. 16, 1971; children—Susan Elizabeth, Shannon Lee. Speech pathologist Rockdale County (Ga.) Bd. Edn., 1973-76, Davison Sch. Inc., Atlanta, 1972-73, 1977—. Tchr. Sunday Sch., Presbyn. Ch., Stone Mountain, Ga., 1978—. George Peabody Coll. for Tchrs. scholar, 1968-71; Vanderbilt U. fellow, 1971-73. Mem. Am. Speech-Lang.-Hearing Assn. Home: 718 13th Ct Pleasant Grove AL 35127

RUSHING, ROY EUGENE, banker; b. San Antonio, May 21, 1943; s. Ellison Dumas and Dorothy Jean (Wager) R.; B.B.A., Southwestern U., Georgetown, Tex., 1968; grad. Southwestern Grad. Sch. Banking, So. Meth. U., 1977; m. Ruthann Bray, Sept. 3, 1965; children—Deirdre, Alicia. Various positions Tex. State Bank, Austin, 1964-68; mgmt. trainee Capital Nat. Bank, Austin, 1968-70, asst. mgr. credit dept., 1971, mgr., 1972-73, mgr. exec. and profl. lending, 1973-77; v.p., mgr. profl services center Am. Nat. Bank, Austin, 1977—. Bd. dirs. Balcones council Campfire Girls, 1973-79, pres., 1978-79. Served with Tex. Nat. Guard, 1965-71. Mem. Young Men's Bus. League (dir. 1973, 75), Am. Inst. Banking, Robert Morris Assos., Los Amigos, Phi Gamma Delta (pres. grad. chpt. 1974). Republican. Presbyn. Home: 1702 Michael St Austin TX 78704 Office: 221 W 6th St Austin TX 78701

RUSHLOW, BONNIE MILLER, bus. woman; b. Detroit, Feb. 21, 1929; d. Robert Ellsworth and Linda (Lynam) Miller; M.A., Mich. State U., 1959; m. Philip L. Rushlow, June 25, 1945; children—Philip Lee, David Robert. Program exec. ednl. television, Lansing, Mich., 1959-61, corporate officer Azure Internat. Corp., Lansing and Ft. Lauderdale, Fla., 1961-64; corporate officer, chief designer Fashion Industries, Miami, Fla., 1964-68; owner, mgr. Bonnie Rushlow, Inc., retail outlets, Bal Harbour, Ft. Lauderdale and Miami, 1968-73; sec.-treas. Group Three Advt. Corp., Inc., Fort Lauderdale, 1973—, also dir.; officer, dir. Rushlow, Philips and David Corp., Pompano Beach, Fla.; dir. Richelieu Assos., Inc. Office: 2600 NE 14th St Causeway Pompano Beach FL 33062

RUSHTON, WILLIAM JAMES, life ins. exec.; b. Birmingham, Ala., July 10, 1900; s. James Franklin and Willis (Roberts) R.; B.S., Washington & Lee U., Lexington, Va., 1921; H.H.D., Southwestern at Memphis, 1959; m. Elizabeth Perry, November 24, 1926 (dec. 1972); children—William James III, James. Asst. mgr. Birmingham Ice & Cold Storage Co., 1922-27, v.p., 1927-32, pres., 1932-38, vice chmn. bd., sec., 1938-57; pres. Protective Life Ins. Co., 1937-67, chmn. bd. dirs., 1967-76, chmn. bd. emeritus, 1976—, dir., 1927—; mem. adv. bd. Investment Co. of Am. (Calif.); chmn. bd. Franklin Coal Mining Co., 1927-42; past dir. First Nat. Bank of Birmingham, Alabama Power Co., Gulf, Mobile & Ohio R.R. Co., Moore-Handley Hardware Co., Ill. Central Gulf R.R. Chief, Birmingham Ordnance Dist., U.S. Army, 1946-61. Vice chmn., trustee So. Research Inst.; pres. Birmingham Boy Scout Council, 1927-30 (dir. 1925-55); mem. nat. citizens com. United Community Campaigns Am., 1961; dir. Birmingham Community Chest, 1937—, v.p., 1942-43, 48-52, pres., 1954, mem. exec. com., 1945—; dir., trustee Birmingham Mus. Art; local dir. Salvation Army, Y.M.C.A.; trustee Children's Hosp., Agnes Scott Coll., Decatur, Ga., 1935-45. Served to col. U.S. AUS Army, World War II. Decorated Legion of Merit. Mem. Am. Ordnance Assn. (past v.p.), Nat. Assn. Ice Industries (dir. 1928—, pres. 1936-37), Nat. Assn. Refrigerated Warehouses (pres. 1933-35; mem. Nat. Code Authority), Am. Warehousemen's Assn. (pres. 1935-36), Life Ins. Assn. of Am. (dir. 1955-61), Health Ins. Assn. Am. (dir. 1964-67), Am. Life Conv. (Ala. v.p.), Inst. Life Ins. (dir. 1963-69), Asso. Industries Ala. (dir 1956-63), Beta Gamma Sigma, Beta Theta Pi, Omicron Delta Kappa, Delta Sigma Rho. Presbyn. (mem. bd. deacons, chmn. bd. trustees, elder, mem. bd. annuities and relief Presbyn. Ch. in U.S. 1959—). Mason (32 deg., Shriner). Rotarian (chpt. pres. 1952-53) Clubs: Mountain Brook, Country, Downtown, The Club, Relay House (Birmingham); Chaparal (Dallas). Home: 2848 Balmoral Rd Birmingham AL 35223 Office: Protective Life Ins Co Birmingham AL 35202

RUSHTON, WILLIAM JAMES, III, ins. co. exec.; b. Birmingham, Ala., Apr. 23, 1929; s. William James and Elizabeth (Perry) R.; B.A. magna cum laude in Mathematics, Princeton U., 1951; m. LaVona Price, Aug. 19, 1955; children—William James IV, Deakins Ford, Tunstall Perry. Asso. actuary, Protective Life Ins. Co., Birmingham, 1954-59, dir., 1956—, agt., 1959-62, v.p., 1962-63, agy. v.p., 1963-67, pres., 1967—, chief exec. officer, 1969—; dir. Ala. Power Co., 1970—, The So. Co., 1971—, First Nat. Bank of Birmingham, 1973—, The Economy Co. of Okla., 1974—, Avondale Mills, 1977—, Ala. Bancorp., 1979—, Birmingham Fire Ins. Co., 1956-62, Moore-Handley Hardware Co., 1956-62. Mem. advisory bd. Samford U. Sch. of Bus., 1971—; mem. bd. of visitors Coll. of Commerce and Bus. Adminstrn., U. Ala., 1972—; chmn. United Way Campaign, 1977; deacon First Presbyn. Ch., Birmingham; trustee Highland Day Sch., 1975, So. Research Inst., 1973—, Children's Hosp., 1964—, Birmingham-So. Coll., 1977—, Baptist Hosp. Found., 1967—. Served to capt., arty., U.S. Army, Korean War. Decorated Bronze Star; named to Million Dollar Round Table, 1962, Ala. Acad. Honor, 1979. Fellow Soc. of Actuaries; mem. Am. Life Ins. Assn. (state v.p. 1975 Ala.), Am. Council Life Ins. (dir. 1977-80), Birmingham C. of C. (dir. 1975), Birmingham Council of Soc. Agys. Clubs: Rotary (dir. 1973-74), Mountain Brook Country, Birmingham Country. Home: 2900 Cherokee Rd Birmingham AL 35223 Office: Protective Life Insurance Co PO Box 2606 Birmingham AL 35202

RUSKELL, DOUGLASS MCFERRIN, educator; b. Mt. Pleasant, Tenn., Dec. 28, 1925; d. James Abston and Annie Hall (Acuff) McFerrin; student Huntingdon Coll., 1943-45; B.A., U. Tenn., 1947; M.A., George Peabody Coll., 1964; m. G.C. Ruskell; children—Virginia Ann, Julia Ruskell, George Channing, Elizabeth McFerrin; m. 2d, William Rudkoff, June 11, 1979. Tchr., Maury County Schs., Columbia, Tenn., 1960-62, Franklin County, Sullivan, Mo., 1962-65; mem. faculty Reinhardt Coll., Waleska, Ga., 1965-78, prof. English, 1965-78, chmn. humanities div., 1973-78; head dept. English Tri-County Community Coll., Murphy, N.C., 1978—. Pres., Clay County Hist. and Arts Council, 1979-80; pres. Council on Ministries, United Meth. Ch., 1977-78. Mem. Nat. Council Tchrs. English, AAUW (chairperson cultural affairs 1979-80), N.C. Assn. Tchrs. English. Home: Rt 1 Box 143E Brasstown NC 28902 Office: Tri County Community Coll Box 40 Murphy NC 28906

RUSSEK, HENRY IRVING, cardiologist; b. N.Y.C., Aug. 30, 1911; s. Louis and Henrietta (Rosenthal) Rosuck; student Coll. City N.Y., 1938-41; M.D. Royal Coll. Physicians and Surgeons, Edinburgh, Scotland, 1936; postgrad. Harvard U., 1939, 40; m. Elayne Corak, Dec. 24, 1946; children—Linda, Karen, Shelley. Intern USPHS Hosp., S.I., N.Y., 1938-39, resident, 1939-41; practice medicine specializing in cardiology, S.I., 1941—; chief, cons. cardiovascular disease USPHS Hosp., S.I., 1941-54; cons. cardiologist St. Barnabas Hosp., N.Y.C., 1966—; vis. prof. cardiovascular disease Hahnemann Med. Coll. and Hosp., Phila., 1966—; clin. prof. cardiovascular research N.Y. Med. Coll., N.Y.C., 1973—. Pres. Russek Found., Inc., 1962—. Served with USPHS, 1938-46. Recipient Cummings Humanitarian award U.S. Dept. State, 1964, 66, 67, 73. Fellow A.C.P., Am. Heart Assn., Am. Coll. Cardiology (pres. 1963-65, trustee 1965-70), Am. Coll. Chest Physicians (regent 1967-70), Royal Soc. London, Internat. Coll. Angiology; mem. AMA, N.Y. State, Richmond County med. socs., Am. Fedn. Clin. Research, Harvey Soc., Am. Soc. Clin. Pharmacology and Therapeutics, Am. Geriatrics

Soc., B'nai B'rith. Club: Masons. Editor: Coronary Heart Disease, 1971; Changing Concepts in Cardiovascular Disease, 1972; New Horizons in Cardiovascular Practice, 1973; Cardiovascular Disease: New Concepts in Diagnosis and Therapy, 1974; The Paul D. White Symposium on Cardiovascular Disease, 1976; Cardiovascular Problems: Perspectives and Progress, 1976; Cardiovascular Therapy: The Art and the Science, 1976; contbr. articles in field to med. jours. Home: 600 S Ocean Blvd Boca Raton FL 33432 Office: One N Ocean Blvd Boca Raton FL 33432

RUSSELL, CHARLES RAYFIELD, mgmt. scientist, educator; b. West Palm Beach, Fla., Mar. 22, 1931; s. Charles Edward and Alma Ernestine (Johnson) R.; B.S., Fla. A&M U., 1952; M.S., Ind. U., 1962; Ph.D., Fla. State U., 1972; m. Nancy Ellen Mosley, Dec. 8, 1953; children—Tamara Verline, Leslie Ann, Gail Trinise, Carla Raye, Charles Rayfield. Tchr. jr. high sch., Palm Beach County, Fla., 1956-68; specialist labor relations Fla. Edn. Assn., Tallahassee, 1968-69; grad. asst. mgmt. systems Fla. State U., Tallahassee, 1970; adminstrv. asst. Fed. Higher Edn. Programs, Fla. Dept. Edn., Tallahassee, 1971-72; registrar Fla. A&M U., Tallahassee, 1972-76, asst. prof. mgmt. sci., 1976—, acting dir. div. mgmt. sci., 1978-79; cons. mgmt. systems, planning and budgets. Bd. dirs. Tallahassee chpt. NAACP; chmn. bd. dirs. Palm Beach County (Fla.) Community Action Council, 1964-65. Served to 1st lt. U.S. Army, 1952-55; Korea; maj. Res. ret. Mem. Am. Mgmt. Assn., Res. Officers Assn., Alpha Phi Alpha. Democrat. Baptist. Clubs: Charmers; Jack and Jill Am. Home: 433 Mercury Dr Tallahassee FL 32301 Office: 301 Lee Hall Fla A&M U Tallahassee FL 32307

RUSSELL, DAVID EMERSON, cons. mech. engr.; b. Jacksonville, Fla., Dec. 20, 1922; s. David Herbert and Wilhelmina (Ash) R.; B.Mech. Engring., U. Fla., 1948; postgrad. Oxford (Eng.) U. Mech. engr. United Fruit Co., N.Y.C., 1948-50, U.S. Army C.E., Jacksonville, 1950-54, Aramco, Saudi Arabia, 1954-55; v.p. Beiswenger Hoch and Assos., Inc., Jacksonville, 1955-57; owner, operator David E. Russell and Assos., cons. engrs., Jacksonville, 1957—. Chmn. Jacksonville Water Quality Control Bd., 1969-73; mem. Jacksonville Bicentennial Commn., 1973—. Served to 2d lt. AUS, 1943-46. Recipient Outstanding Service award City of Jacksonville, 1974. Registered profl. engr., Fla., Ga. Mem. ASME (chmn. N.E. Fla. 1967-68), Nat. Soc. Profl. Engrs., ASHRAE, Am. Soc. Inventors, Fla. Engring. Soc. Episcopalian. Club: University (Jacksonville). Contbr. articles to profl. jours. Patentee in field. Home: 1606 King St Jacksonville FL 32204 Office: 110 Riverside Ave Jacksonville FL 32202

RUSSELL, ELBERT WINSLOW, psychologist, health service scientist; b. Las Vegas, N.M., June 4, 1929; s. Josiah Cox and Ruth Annus (Winslow) R.; B.A., Earlham Coll., 1951; M.A., U. Ill., 1953; M.S., Pa. State U., 1958; Ph.D., U. Kan., 1968; m. Susan Hadfield, Mar. 31, 1962; children—Gwendolyn Marie, Franklin Winslow, Kirsten Nash, Jonathan Nash. Clin. psychologist Warnersville (Pa.) State Hosp., 1959-61; neuropsychologist VA Hosp., Cin., 1968-71; dir. neuropsychology lab. VA Hosp., Miami, Fla., 1971—. Mem. Am. Psychol. Assn., Internat. Neuropsychology Soc., Sigma Xi. Democrat. Mem. Soc. of Friends. Author: (with Charles Neuringer and Gerald Goldstein) Assessment of Brain Damage. Contbr. articles on neuropsychology, peace research, religion and anthropology to profl. jours. Home: 7951 SW 120th St Miami FL 33156 Office: VA Hospital 1201 NW 16th St Miami FL 33125

RUSSELL, EUGENE, III, chemist, univ. ofcl.; b. Juniper, Ga., Feb. 23, 1944; s. Eugene and Viola S. Russell, Jr.; B.S., Albany State Coll., 1966; M.S.M.T., Ga. State U., 1980; m. Betty Jean Ousley, Mar. 25, 1967; children—Chandra Patriece, Tania Cherie, Eugene IV. Tchr. sci. Fulton County Sch. Systems, College Park, Ga., 1979-72; technologist S.W. Community Hosp., Atlanta, 1972-74; asst. supr. Ga. Bapt. Hosp., Atlanta, 1974—; chief technologist dept. medicine Emory U., Atlanta, 1975—, vol. faculty Med. Lab. for Primary Health Care Centers, 1978—. Served with U.S. Army, 1966-69; Korea. Recipient cert. of appreciation Ga. Dept. Human Resources, 1979. Mem. Am. Soc. Clin. Pathologists (cert. chemist), Am. Public Health Assn., Clin. Lab. Mgmt. Assn., Alpha Phi Alpha. Democrat. Baptist. Club: Masons. Home: 3470 Old Fairburn Rd Atlanta GA 30331 Office: 191 Edgewood Ave SE Atlanta GA 30303

RUSSELL, GEORGE ERWIN, JR., environmental horticulture exec.; b. Miami, Fla., Oct. 27, 1925; s. George E. and Flossie M. (Key) R.; student U. Miami, 1953-54; m. Jacquline J. Thayer, Sept. 24, 1948; children—Joyce Ann, George Lee, Garry Eugene, Glenn Edward. Foreman, Farens Tree Surgeons, Miami, 1942-49; owner Russell Tree Maintenance, Miami, 1949-56; pres. Russell, Inc., Miami, 1956—. Mem. stewardship com. Miami Bapt. Assn. Served in U.S. Army, 1944-47. Mem. Am. Assn. Nurserymen, Am. Inst. Landscape Architects, So. Nurserymen, Fla. Nurserymen and Growers Assn. (state pres. 1975-76, Butler Odenkirk award 1974; Outstanding chpt. pres. award 1971, Dick Pope award 1979), Greater Miami Landscape and Nursery Assn. (pres.). Democrat. Home: 13334 NW 21st Ave Miami FL 33167 Office: 13050 NW 30th Ave Opa Locka FL 33054

RUSSELL, HAROLD GILMORE, ret. aerospace co. financial exec.; b. Humbird, Wis., July 8, 1919; s. Walter Hugh and Inga (Goplin) R.; student Wis. State Coll., 1938-39; Ohio State U., 1949-50; B.S. in Elec. Engring., Air Force Inst. Tech., 1951; M.B.A., U. Chgo., 1956; m. Florence Theresa Peters, Apr. 21, 1965; children—John Hugh, Janet Elaine (Mrs. James Williams), James Michael, Kathleen Dahly (Mrs. Roger Wechter). Enlisted as pvt. USAAF, 1941, advanced through grades to col. USAF, 1967; exptl. test pilot, 1951-55; dir. Dyna-Soar Test Force, X-15 Research Airplane Test Program, Edwards AFB, Cal., 1957-60; comdr. 6555th Aerospace Test Wing, Cape Canaveral, Fla., 1961-64; dir. Saturn IB/Centaur Program NASA, Washington, 1964-65; asst. dir. Apollo Program NASA, Washington, 1966-67; ret., 1967; mgr. plans and control dept. LTV Aerospace Corp., Dallas, 1968-72, chief accounting systems, 1973-77. Bd. dirs. East Cedar Creek Fresh Water Supply Dist., 1979—. Decorated Air medal, Purple Heart; recipient Apollo Achievement award NASA, 1969. Mem. Air Force Assn., Ret. Officers' Assn. Democrat. Lutheran. Mason. Author govt. papers. Home: 118 Lakeshore Dr Harbor Point Route 3 Mabank TX 75147

RUSSELL, JERRY LEWIS, public relations counselor, polit. cons.; b. Little Rock, July 21, 1933; s. Jerry Lewis and Frances (Lieb) R.; B.A. in Journalism, U. Ark., 1958; children (by previous marriage)—Jerry L. III, Susan Frances; m. 2d, Alice Anne Cason, Feb. 14, 1969; children—Leigh Anne, Andrew J. III. Pub. relations dir. Little Rock C. of C., 1958; editor, pub. The Visitor, Little Rock, 1959-60; sec.-mgr. Ark. Press Assn., Little Rock, 1960-61; account exec. Brandon Agy., Little Rock, 1961-65; founder, pres. Guide Advt. (now part of River City Enterprises, Inc.), also River City Pubs., Little Rock 1965-70, 72—; pres. River City Enterprises, Inc.; dir. pub. relations services S.M. Brooks Agy., Little Rock, 1970-72; founder, pres. Campaign Cons., Inc., 1974—; pub., editor Campaign Insight newsletter, 1979—. Served with AUS, 1953-56. Mem. Ark. Advt. Fedn. (pres. 1967-68), Pub. Relations Soc. Am. (pres. Ark. chpt. 1974), Am. Assn. Polit. Consultants, Orgn. Am. Historians, Western Hist. Assn., Little Big Horn Assos., Ark., Pulaski County hist. socs., Civil War Round Table Ark. (charter pres. 1964-65), Civil War Round Table Assos. (founder 1968, nat. chmn.), Order Indian Wars (founder, nat. chmn.), Circus Fans Assn. Am., Westerners Internat. (charter pres. Little Rock corral 1974—). Home: 9 Lefever Ln Little Rock AR 72207

RUSSELL, JOHN FRANCIS, librarian; b. Mt. Carmel, Ind., Apr. 30, 1929; s. David Freeman and Bertha (Major) R.; B.A., DePauw U., 1951; postgrad. Ind. U., 1951-52; M.A., Johns Hopkins U., 1954; student Cath. U. Am., summer 1955; M.S., Grad. Sch. Library Sci. Drexel U., 1977; m. Edith Raymond Hyde, June 27, 1953; 1 dau., Anne Marie. Tchr. English, Park Sch. Balt., 1954-75, chmn. dept., 1957-75; tchr. speech, dir. Ira Aldridge Players Morgan State Coll., fall 1965-66; tchr. drama Loyola Coll., 1964, 66. Pres. Tchrs.' Assn. Ind. Sch. Balt. Area, 1960-62, advisory bd., 1966-67, chmn. com. on English, 1966-68; exec. com. Assn. Ind. Md. Sch., 1967-68. Dir., costumer Johns Hopkins U. Playshop, 1963-64; lectr. Lecture Group, Woman's Club Roland Park, others, 1964—. Bd. dirs. Balt. area council World Federalists U.S.A., 1961-67, vice chmn., 1964-67, nat. exec. council, 1963-65; bd. dirs. Center Stage, 1964-77; dir., v.p. Pasadena Little Theatre. Recipient Nat. Citation of Merit Am. Shakespeare Festival, 1961. Mem. Harris County Heritage Soc., Am. Film Inst., Nat. Film Soc., Am. Theatre Assn. (v.p. Mid-Atlantic dist. 1967-68, pres. 1968-69, nat. dir. 1970-73, Mid-Atlantic chpt. award for achievement and contbn. to theatre 1973), Secondary Sch. Theatre Assn. (v.p. devel. 1974-75), Religion and Theatre Council, Religious Drama Soc. Gt. Britain, Tex. Non-Profit Theatre, Nat. (bd. dirs. 1969), Md. (pres. 1969-70) councils tchrs. English, Capital Area Media Educators Orgn. (exec. com. 1970-73, screening chmn. 1971-73), ALA, Southwestern Library Assn., Tex. Library Assn., Assn. for Ednl. Communication and Tech., Phi Beta Kappa, Phi Eta Sigma, Beta Phi Mu. Editor: The Secondary School Theatre, 1972-74. Home: 7817 Grove Ridge Houston TX 77061 Office: Bracewell Br Houston Public Library Kleckley Dr Houston TX 77075

RUSSELL, LAO (MRS. WALTER RUSSELL), philosopher, author, educator; b. Ivinghoe, Buckinghamshire, Eng.; d. Alfred William and Florence (Hills) Cook; naturalized, 1947; ed. pvt. tutors; m. Walter Russell, July 29, 1948. Founder, Walter Russell Found. (now known as U. Sci. and Philosophy), Waynesboro, Va., 1948, mng. dir., 1948—, pres., 1949—; founded Shrine of Beauty known as Swannanoa Palace and Sculpture Gardens, 1948. Founder Man-Woman Equalization League, 1955, Age of Character Clubs, 1966. Author: God Will Work With You But Not For You (named 1 of 6 best books of year N.Y. Herald Tribune 1955), 1955; An Eternal Message of Light and Love, 1964; Love-A Scientific and Living Philosophy of Love and Sex, 1966; Why You Cannot Die! The Continuity of Life-Reincarnation Explained, 1972; (with Walter Russell) Home Study Course in Universal Law, Natural Science and Living Philosophy, 1950, Scientific Answer to Human Relations, 1951, Atomic Suicide?, 1957, The World Crisis-Its Explanation and Solution, 1958, The One-World Purpose, 1960. Executed statue (with husband) The Christ of the Blue Ridge, 1948, also colossal model, 1950. Address: Univ Science and Philosophy Swannanoa Waynesboro VA 22980

RUSSELL, MAY HILL, county ofcl.; b. Key West, Fla., May 1, 1909; d. Oak Preston and Ethel C. (Watkins) Hill; student U. Fla. Extension, 1930-34; m. Orion A. Russell, Dec. 24, 1936 (dec. 1970); 1 dau., Virginia Russell Mosley. Tchr. public schs. of Monroe County, Key West, Fla., 1928-43; bus. adminstr. Monroe County (Fla.) Library System, 1962—, public relations dir., 1962—; commr. Fla. Keys Meml. Hosp., 1967—. Founder, Old Island Restoration Found., Fla., 1960, dir., 1960-70; mem. adminstrv. bd. First United Meth. Ch., Key West, 1970-76, mem. hist. records com., 1970-76, trustee, 1972-74. Recipient Award of Merit, Monroe County Library System, 1966; named Outstanding Woman of Yr., Bus. and Profl. Woman's Club, 1970, One of 5 Outstanding Women in Monroe County, 1976; recipient Cert., Betsy Ross Soc., 1973. Mem. Fla. Library Assn., Hist. Assn. of So. Fla., Smithsonian Assos. Democrat. Methodist. Clubs: Key West Woman's (Named Outstanding Woman 1961), Key West Garden. Contbr. articles to local newspapers; also booklets. Home: 1409 White St Key West FL 33040 Office: 700 Fleming St Key West FL 33040

RUSSELL, PEGGY TAYLOR, soprano, educator; b. Newton, N.C., Apr. 5, 1927; d. William G. and Sue B. (Cordell) Taylor; Mus.B. in Voice, Salem Coll., 1948; Mus.M., Columbia U., 1950; postgrad. U. N.C., Greensboro, 1977; student Am. Inst. Mus. Studies, Austria, 1972, 78; student of Clifford Bair, Nell Starr, Salem Coll., Winston-Salem, N.C., Edgar Schofield, Chloe Owen, N.Y.C.; student opera-dramatics Boris Goldovsky, U. N.C., Greensboro, Ande Andersen, Max Lehner, Graz, Austria; m. John B. Russell, Feb. 23, 1952; children—John Spotswood, Susan Bryce. Mem. faculty dept. voice Guilford Coll., Greensboro, 1952-53, Greensboro Coll., 1971-72; pvt. tchr. voice, Greensboro, 1963—; vis. instr. in voice U. N.C., Chapel Hill, 1973-77; debut in light opera as Gretchen in The Red Mill, Winston-Salem Opera Assn., 1947; debuts include: Rosalinda in Die Fledermaus, Piedmont Festival Opera Assn., 1949, Lola in Cavalleria Rusticana, Greensboro Opera Assn., 1951, Violetta in La Traviata, Greensboro Opera Assn., 1953, Fiordiligi in Cosi fan tutte, Piedmont Opera Co., 1956; appeared as Marguerite in Faust, Brevard Music Center Resident Opera Co., 1967, First Lady in The Magic Flute, Am. Inst. Mus. Studies, Graz, Austria, 1972; mem. Greensboro Oratorio Soc., 1955-59, soprano soloist in The Messiah, 1952, 58, The Creation, 1955, Solomon, 1958; soprano soloist Presbyterian Ch. of the Covenant, Greensboro, 1958-71; guest appearances Sta. WFMY-TV, Greensboro, 1958-62; soprano soloist with Greensboro Symphony Orch., 1964, 80, Eastern Music Festival Orch. 1965; soloist in numerous recitals including: Wesleyan Coll., 1964, Roanoke Symphony Guild, 1967, Am. Inst. Mus. Studies, Austria, 1972, 78, U. N.C., Chapel Hill, 1974, 75, 76, 77, N.C. Mus. of Art, 1980. Bd. dirs. Music Theater Assos., Greensboro Friends of Music, N.C. Lyric Opera. Mem. Nat. Assn. Tchrs. of Singing (state gov. 1976—), N.C. Fedn. Music Clubs (dir. 1956-58), Music Educators Nat. Conf., Greensboro Music Tchrs. Assn. (pres. 1966-67), Symphony Guild (dir. 1977-78), Broadway Theater League (chmn. 1961-63), Civic Music Assn. (chmn. 1963-64). Presbyterian. Home: 3012 W Cornwallis Dr Greensboro NC 27408

RUSSELL, RALPH ERNEST, librarian; b. Bradenton, Fla., Jan. 25, 1938; s. Wilbur Lee and Beatrice (Parrish) R.; B.A., Fla. State U., 1960, M.S., 1961, Ph.D. (Univ. System of Fla. Bd. Regents fellow), 1973; M.A., N.Y. U., 1962; m. Linda Dee Sherman, June 16, 1962; 1 dau., Lauren Susan. Reference librarian Queens Borough (N.Y.) Pub. Library, 1961-62; circulation and acquisition librarian U. So. Calif., 1964-66; head librarian Fla. Jr. Coll., Jacksonville, 1966-68; sci. librarian U. Ga., 1968-71; dir. library services East Carolina U., 1973-75; univ. librarian Ga. State U., 1975—; cons. in field; chmn. bd. dirs. Southeastern Library Network. Mem. membership com. Downtown Atlanta YMCA. Served with USN, 1962-64. Higher Edn. Act of 1965 II-B fellow, 1972-73; Council Library Resources Library Services Enhancement Program grantee, 1977-78. Mem. Am., Southeastern, Ga. library assns., Assn. Coll. and Research Libraries (acad. status com.), AAUP, Presbyterian. Columnist: Southeastern Librarian, 1977—. Home: 96 Springlake Pl NW Atlanta GA 30318 Office: 100 Decatur St SE Atlanta GA 30303

RUSSELL, RICHARD OLNEY, JR., physician, educator; b. Birmingham, Ala., July 9, 1932; s. Richard Olney and Louise (Taylor) R.; A.B., Vanderbilt U., 1953, M.D., 1956; m. Phyllis Hutchinson, June 15, 1963; children—Scott Richard, Katherine Hutchinson, Meredith Cooper, Stephen Wilbon. Intern, Peter Bent Brigham Hosp., Boston, 1956-57, resident, 1959-60, 63-64; fellow in cardiology Med. Coll. Ala., Birmingham, 1960-62, instr., 1962-63; instr. medicine U. Ala., Birmingham, 1964-65, asst. prof., 1965-70, asso. prof., 1970-73, prof., 1973—. Served to capt. AUS, M.C., 1957-59. Decorated Commendation medal. NIH Research fellow, 1966-67. Diplomate Am. Bd. Internal Medicine, Am. Bd. Cardiovascular Diseases. Fellow, Am. Coll. Physicians, Am. Coll. Cardiology, Council Clin. Cardiology, Am. Heart Assn. (pres. Ala. affiliate 1975-76), Am. Coll. Chest Physicians. Author: (with Charles Edward Rackley) Hemodynamic Monitoring in a Coronary Intensive Care Unit, 1974, Coronary Artery Disease—Recognition and Management, 1979; (with Benigno Soto and Roger E. Moraski) Radiographic Anatomy of the Coronary Arteries—An Atlas, 1976. Home: 4408 Kennesaw Dr Birmingham AL 35213 Office: University Sta Birmingham AL 35294

RUSSELL, ROBERT LEONARD, assn. exec.; b. Mt. Vernon, Ill., July 18, 1916; s. Charles Arthur and Edna Mabel (Yearwood) R.; student St. Petersburg Jr. Coll., 1971-72; B.Sc., U. Mid-Fla., 1973, M.S., 1974; m. Jeanne Lucille Tackenberg, May 21, 1942. Reporter, Peoria (Ill.) Jour., 1939-42, 46-47, Chgo. Daily News, 1947-57; asst. exec. dir. Profl. Golfers Assn., Dunedin, Fla., 1957-65; exec. dir. United Vol. Services, San Mateo, Calif., 1965-66; reporter St. Petersburg (Fla.) Evening Ind., 1967-70; exec. v.p. Fla. Health Care Assn. (formerly Fla. Nursing Home Assn.), Orlando, 1970-77; exec. v.p. Mortgage Bankers Assn. Fla., Orlando, 1977—, Mortgage Bankers Assn. Central Fla., Orlando, 1978—; adminstr. Fla. Health Care Self Insurers Fund, 1972-78; sec.-treas. Mortgage Bankers Fla. Polit. Action Com., 1977—; pres. Profl. Assn. Services, Inc., 1977—. Pres., Aldrich & Assos., 1967-70. Elder, Park Lake Presbyn. Ch., Orlando, 1979—. Served with USAAF, 1942-46. Mem. Am. (certified), Fla., Central Fla. socs. assn. execs., Am. Coll. Nursing Home Adminstrs. (hon.), Fla. Sheriffs Assn. (hon.), U.S. Basketball Writers Assn. (pres. 1956-57), Football Writers Assn. Am. (dir. 1955-57). Republican. Presbyterian. Editor: Profl. Golfer mag., 1957-65; Nat. Golfer mag., 1965-66; communicator, 1977—; exec. editor Rx Sports and Travel mag., 1966-67. Home: 6586 Kreidt Dr Orlando FL 32808 Office: PO Box 3586 Orlando FL 32802

RUSSELL, ROGER ALLEN, psychologist, educator; b. Brownsville, Tex., July 23, 1952; s. C.W. and Ola Faye (White) R.; B.A., S.W. Tex. State U., 1974, M.Ed., 1975; postgrad. in counseling psychology Tex. A&M U., 1979—. Asso. sch. psychologist Killeen (Tex.) Ind. Sch. Dist., 1975-77; asso. sch. psychologist Abilene (Tex.) Ind. Sch. Dist., 1977-79; mem. adv. bd. West Tex. Services for Deaf, 1977-79. Mem. Am. Personnel and Guidance Assn., Tex. Psychol. Assn., NEA, Tex. State Tchrs. Assn., Tex. Sch. Psychol. Affiliates, Alpha Chi, Pi Gamma Mu, Alpha Kappa Delta (pres. chpt. 1974-75). Home: 100 Jersey Apt 30 College Station TX 77840 Office: Dean's Office Coll Edn Tex A&M U College Station TX 77843

RUSSELL, SAMUEL E., educator; b. Jacksonville, Fla., June 20, 1920; s. Samuel and Gladys Russell; B.S., Fla. A.&M. U., 1950, M.S., 1952; Ed.D. (fellow So. Fellowship Fund 1959-60), U. Pa., 1966; m. Careta Rose Lotson, Apr. 5, 1953; children—Kenneth, Kathryn, John. Asst. dir. Baghdad (Iraq) Tech. Inst., 1953-57; prof., asst. dir. vocat. edn. Fla. A. and M. Tech. Inst., Tallahassee, 1957-70; prof., chmn. vocat. dept. Fla. A&M U., 1976-71; chmn. vocat. edn. U. N.Fla., Jacksonville, 1971—; cons. in field. Bd. dirs. Jacksonville Urban League, 1979—. Served with AUS, 1941-45. Recipient Silver plaque Iraqi Ministry Edn., 1955. Mem. Am. Vocat. Edn. Research Assn., Fla. Vocat. Assn., Fla. Assn. Vocat. Tchr. Educators (pres. 1977-79), Phi Delta Kappa, Iota Sigma Sigma, Alpha Phi Alpha. Democrat. Baptist. Author: Test Items in Industrial Education, 1965; also monograph. Home: 2201 Ribault Dr Jacksonville FL 32208 Office: Box 17074 Univ North Fla Jacksonville FL 32216

RUSSELL, TED C., distbg. co. exec.; b. Forest, Miss., Jan. 16, 1943; s. T.W. Russell and Jean (Adams) Barger; student San Diego U., 1961; m. Norma Rials, Feb. 29, 1976; children—Melissa Kay, Jason Scott. Sales rep. Western Auto Co., 1974-75; asst. mgr. Republic Personnel Service, Jackson, Miss., 1975; parts mgr. Carrier Distbg. Co., Jackson, 1975-78; sales mgr. AC Distbrs., Jackson, 1978—. Served with AUS, 1960-68. Mem. Am. Legion, VFW. Home: Route 2 Box 76A Crystal Springs MS 39059 Office: AC Distbrs 3984 Terry Rd Jackson MS 39212

RUSSELL, WILLIAM LAWSON, geneticist; b. Newhaven, Eng., Aug. 19, 1910; s. Robert Lawson and Ellen Frances (Frost) R.; B.A., Oxford (Eng.) U., 1932; Ph.D., U. Chgo., 1937; m. Elizabeth B. Shull, Aug. 29, 1936; children—Richard L., John S., James J., Ellen M.; m. 2d, Liane R. Brauch, Sept. 23, 1947; children—David L., Evelyn R. Came to U.S., 1932. Sherman Pratt fellow Amherst Coll., 1932-33; fellow U. Chgo., 1933-34, asst. 1934-36; research asso. Roscoe B. Jackson Meml. Lab., Bar Harbor, Maine, 1937-47; prin. geneticist Oak Ridge Nat. Lab., 1947-77, chief mammalian genetics sect., 1953-68, scientific dir. mammalian genetics sect., 1969-77, cons. 1977—; spl. work genetic effects of radiation and chemicals in mice; mem. U.S. del. Geneva confs. Peaceful Uses Atomic Energy, 1955, 58, 71; mem. com. biol. effects atomic radiation, com. biol. effects ionizing radiations Nat. Acad. Sci., 1955—; adviser U.S. del. to UN Sci. Com. on Effects of Atomic Radiation, 1962—; adv. com. Fed. Radiation Council, 1964-70. Dir. Tenn. Citizens for Wilderness Planning, 1969-70, 74—, pres., 1971-73; dir. Tenn. Scenic Rivers Assn., 1969-70. Mem. bd. Nat. Council Radiation Protection and Measurements, 1965—. Recipient Roentgen Medal Internat. award, 1973; Disting. Service award Health Physics Soc., 1976; Fermi award, 1977. Mem. Nat. Acad. Scis., Genetics Soc. Am. (pres. 1965), Radiation Research Soc. (asso. editor 1958-59), Environ. Mutagen Soc., Wilderness Soc., Sierra Club, Nat. Audubon Soc. Editorial bd. Mutation Research. Home: 130 Tabor Rd Oak Ridge TN 37830 Office: Biology Div Oak Ridge Nat Lab PO Box Y Oak Ridge TN 37830

RUSSELL, WILSON LEE, indsl. cons.; b. Grimes County, Tex., Jan. 26, 1913; s. Carl Andrew and Frankie Catherine (Wilson) R.; student Sam Houston State Tchrs. Coll., 1929-32, Am. Sch. Law, Chgo., 1934-35, Howard Payne Coll., 1938, Internat. Corr. Schs., 1943-46; certificate in plant mgmt. U. Tex., 1957; m. Ernestine Elizabeth Pool, Nov. 30, 1935; children—Wilsa Rose, Mada Ernestine, Johan Yvonne, John Lynn. Tchr., 1932-38; rancher, 1934-39; with Baytown (Tex.) Ordnance Depot, 1940, San Jacinto (Tex.) Ordnance 1941; with Shell Oil & Chem. Co., 1942-64, process supr. City of Deer Park (Tex.), 1952-64; ind. cons., 1965—; prin. Wilson Russell, Inc., Center Point, Tex., 1965—; exec. com. Oil Workers Internat. Union Local 367, 1945-46, 1st v.p., 1950-52, supr. mfg. process, 1952-64, cons. new chem. plant, 1965—. Alderman, City of Shoreacres (Tex.), 1949, fire marshall, 1950-52; del. Democratic County Conv., 1946-64, 76, state and nat. convs., 1952. Mem. Am. Ordnance Assn. (life), Am. Def. Preparedness Assn., Nat. Rifles and Firearm Dealers Assn., Hon. Brotherhood Oilworkers, Shell Old Timers and Gun Owners Am., Am. Security Council (nat. adv. bd.), Coalition for Peace through

Strength. Baptist. Clubs: Petroleum, Lions (past officer). Home: PO Box 232 Center Point TX 78010

RUSSOTTO, JOHN CARMEN, social worker; b. N.Y.C., July 16, 1948; s. John Vincent and Margaret Ann (Sarli) R.; B.A., Memphis State U., 1970; M.S. in Social Work, U. Tenn., 1975. Tchr., vice prin. Little Flower Sch., Memphis, 1970-73; family counselor Memphis House, Inc., 1975-76; family services supr. Memphis Housing Authority, 1976; marriage and family counselor Family Service Memphis, 1976-79; clin. social worker U. Tenn. Med. Center Hosp., Memphis, also clin. instr. dept. psychiatry; pvt. practice. Mem. Acad. Cert. Social Workers, Nat. Assn. Social Workers, Gerontol. Soc., Nat. Council on Aging, Alpha Kappa Delta. Editor Memphis br. newsletter Nat. Assn. Social Workers. Home: 3512 Boxdale St Apt 7 Memphis TN 38118 Office: 842 Jefferson St Memphis TN 38103

RUTA, THEODORE RALPH, retail automotive co. exec.; b. Norwalk, Conn., Nov. 19, 1940; s. Ralph Robert and Josephine Ann (Angerio) R.; B.S. in Math., Fla. State U., 1962, B.S. in Stats., 1962; postgrad. in acctg. Stetson U., 1970; m. Charlotte Mae Sims, Aug. 13, 1960; children—Ralph Steven, Debra Jovonne, Michelle Christine, Theodore Scott. Fin. analyst TRW, Inc., Kennedy Space Center, 1966-71; comptroller McCotter Motors, Inc., Titusville, Fla., 1971-75, v.p., 1976—; treas. T & R Motor Parts Inc. Chmn. North Brevard (county, Fla.) Park and Recreation Commn., 1979. Served with USAF, 1962-65. Mem. Arnold Air Soc., Mid-Coast Ofcls. Assn. (pres. 1973-74), So. Coaches and Ofcls. Assn., So. Ind. Collegiate Ofcls. Assn., Amateur Softball Assn., Fla. Recreation Softball Assn. (umpire in chief 1977-78), Fla. High Sch. Activities Assn. Club: Rotary (dir.). Office: PO Box 6446 Titusville FL 32780

RUTEN, STEPHEN CHARLES, bldg. constrn. co. exec.; b. Aurora, Ill., Dec. 30, 1947; s. Leo C.L., Jr. and Shirley Elaine (Dudgeon) R.; student Tex. Tech. U., 1967-71; m. Ella Ann Hill, Nov. 11, 1967; children—Michelle Elaine, Christopher Stephen Leo. Carpenter H.A. Padgett Constrn., Lubbock, Tex., 1971-73; estimator, project mgr. Page & Wirtz Constrn., Lubbock, 1973-76; constrn. mgr., chief estimator Furr's Inc., Gen. Contractors, Lubbock, 1976-78; v.p., gen. mgr. Furr's Constrn. Co., Inc., Lubbock, 1978-79, pres., 1979—; dir. Solortech Inc. Served with USAF, 1966-69. Lic. contractor N.Mex. Mem. Asso. Gen. Contractors, Profl. Estimators Soc., Constrn. Specifications Inst. (local chpt. industry dir.), Am. Radio Relay League, Aircraft Owners and Pilots Assn., Jaycees. Republican. Baptist. Clubs: Lubbock Amateur Radio, Lubbock Computors, Masons (32 deg.), Scottish Rite. Home: 3513 57th St Lubbock TX 79413 Office: 2202 Avenue E Lubbock TX 79408

RUTENBERG-ROSENBERG, SHARON LESLIE, journalist; b. Chgo., May 23, 1951; d. Arthur and Bernice (Berman) R.; student Harvard U. Summer Sch., 1972; B.A., Northwestern U., 1973, M.S.J., Medill Grad. Sch. Journalism, 1975; m. Michael J. Rosenberg, Feb. 3, 1980. Bus. mgr. Northwestern U. Yearbook, 1971-72; reporter-photographer Lerner Home Newspapers, Chgo., 1973-74; corr. Medill News Service, Washington, 1975; reporter-newsperson UPI, Chgo., 1975—; mem. exec. bd. Northwestern U. Student Adv. Council, 1972-73. Vol. worker Chgo.-Read Mental Health Center. Cert. student pilot, cert. scuba diver. Mem. Hadassah, Sigma Delta Chi, Sigma Delta Tau. Exclusive interviews include White House interview with former chief of staff Donald Rumsfeld, with nation's only mother and son on death row. Address: 18 S Pine Circle Clearwater FL 33516

RUTH, LESTER RUFUS, JR., coll. adminstr.; b. Alliance, O., Aug. 5, 1924; s. Lester Rufus and Lola Mary (Buchanan) R.; B.A., Emory U., 1949, M.A., 1950; Ed.S., U. Fla., 1976; Ed.D., Fla. State U., 1979; m. Teresa Ellen Miller, Dec. 19, 1948; children—Lola Ruth Cox, Teresa (Mrs. Jerry Carter), Charles, Douglas. Instr., Truett-McConnell Jr. Coll., Cleveland, Ga., 1950-51; tchr. Jackson (S.C.) High Sch., 1956-57, Acad. Richmond County, Augusta, Ga., 1957-60; asst. prof. Newberry (S.C.) Coll., 1960-62; instr. langs and philosophy Lake-Sumter Community Coll., Leesburg, Fla., 1962-73, coordinator planning, programming, budgeting systems, 1973-75, dir. planning and research, 1975—. Served with AUS, 1943-46. Mem. Fla. Assn. Community Colls., Fla. Assn. Staff and Program Devel., Fla. Assn. Resource Devel. Democrat. Methodist. Kiwanian. Home: 1319 Riviera Dr Leesburg FL 32748 Office: Lake-Sumter Community College Leesburg FL 32748

RUTH, ROBERT DOUGLAS, sociologist, educator; b. Lockport, N.Y., Dec. 6. 1943; s. Robert Adam and Elizabeth Gertrude (Dobbins) R.; B.A. (N.Y. State Regent's scholar), State U. N.Y. at Buffalo, 1966; M.A. (N.D.E.A. fellow), Duke U., 1968, Ph.D. (NIMH trainee), 1975; 1 son, Robert Joseph. Sr. research asso. Center for Community Research, N.Y.C., 1970-71; instr. dept. sociology Davidson (N.C.) Coll., 1971-74, asst. prof., 1974—, acting chmn., 1977-79, chmn., 1979—; lectr. Hofstra U., 1970, Rutgers U., Newark, 1971; vis. prof. sociology U. N.C. at Chapel Hill, summers 1976, 77; vis. lectr. criminal justice U. N.C., Charlotte, fall 1978, summer 1979; cons. N.C. Ednl. Computation Service, 1973, Mecklenburg County (N.C.) Dept. Social Services, 1972, Campus Research Assos., N.Y.C., 1970-71, Can. Penitentiary Service, 1975-76; vis. scholar Hoover Inst. of Stanford U., 1975. Mem. N.C. Dept. Corrections grievance com., South Piedmont Region, 1975-76. Research grantee HEW, 1970-75, Can. Ministry Def., Donner Found. and Duke U., 1975, 78, NSF, 1971, Davidson Coll., 1973-76, Can. Penitentiary Service Staff Coll., 1976. Mem. Am., N.C. (chmn. nominations com. 1974) sociol. assns., Eastern, So. sociol. socs., So. Regional Demographic Group. Presbyterian. Club: Davidson Lions (pres. 1979-80). Contbr. articles to profl. jours. Home: PO Box 2134 Davidson NC 28036 Office: Dept Sociology Davidson Coll Davidson NC 28036

RUTH, WILLIAM AMES, lawyer; b. Newark, Nov. 26, 1942; s. Wilbur Amos and Vera (Spies) R.; B.S., Davidson Coll., 1964; J.D., U. Fla., 1971; LL.M., N.Y. U., 1972; m. Kathleen Ann Hunter, Oct. 7, 1967; children—Mary Beth Christine, Natasha McKeran, Amie Hunter. Admitted to Fla. bar, 1971, S.C. bar, 1973, D.C. bar, 1978; mem. firm Dowling, Sanders, Dukes, Novit & Svalina, Hilton Head Island, S.C., 1972—. Chmn. Hilton Head Island United Way, 1977; pres. Hilton Head Heart Assn., 1976—; mem. exec. com. Hilton Head Govt. Commn., 1974—; chmn. bd. trustees Sea Pines Acad., 1975—; trustee Hilton Head Charitable Found., 1975—, Hilton Head Island Inst. for Arts, 1975—. Served as lt. USNR, 1966-69. Mem. Hilton Head Bar Assn. (co-founder, past chmn.), Hilton Head Island C. of C. (dir., v.p., pres. 1975), Hilton Head Island Jaycees, Am., S.C. bar assns., Beaufort County Estate Planning Council. Home: 34 Gloucester Rd Hilton Head Island SC 29928 Office: PO Drawer 5706 Hilton Head Island SC 29928

RUTH, WILLIAM AUGUSTUS, III, illustrator; b. Albany, N.Y., Oct. 16, 1925; s. William Augustus and Loretta Mary (Kilmade) R.; student George Peabody Tchrs. Coll., 1943, U. Pa., 1946-48. Illustrator U.S. Army Engr. Sch., Ft. Belvoir, Va., 1956—; painter in oils and acrylics. Served in USAAF, 1943-46, U.S. Army, 1950-53. Mem. Indsl. Graphics Internat. Roman Catholic. Club: K.C. Home: 10317 Burke Lake Rd Fairfax Station VA 22039

RUTHERFORD, SHELLEY HOWE, educator; b. Houston, Feb. 19, 1918; d. Julius Holland and Rose Taylor (Knasel) Howe; B.A., U. Okla., 1940; M.A. in English, Northwestern U., 1942; D.Ed., Okla. State U., 1969; divorced; children—Shelley Howe Rutherford Zuhdi. Instr. English, ASTP, U. Ill., Champaign, 1943; mem. faculty Sterling (Colo.) Jr. Coll., 1944-46, Okla. State U., Stillwater, 1955-70; mem. faculty Central State U., Edmond, Okla., 1970—, asso. prof. English, 1976—. Mem. South Central Modern Lang. Assn., Nat., Okla. (dist. chmn. lang. arts 1976) edn. assns., AAUW, D.A.R. (past regent), UDC, Higher Edn. Assn. Republican. Methodist. Author papers in field. Home: 310 N 7th St Ponca City OK 74601 Office: Liberal Arts Bldg 204 Central State Univ Edmond OK 73034

RUTHERFORD, WARREN LOYD, hosp. adminstr.; b. Omaha, May 22, 1936; s. Loyd Aldewin and Veola Agda Theresia (Magnusson) R.; student Northwestern U., 1954-56; B.B.A., U. Minn., 1958, M.H.A., 1961. Asst. to comptroller Abbott Hosp., Mpls., 1957-59; adminstrv. resident St. Barnabas Hosp., Mpls., 1960-61; asst. adminstr. The U. Tex. M.D. Anderson Hosp. and Tumor Inst., Houston, 1961-69, asso. adminstr., 1969-76; adminstr. The U. Tex. System Cancer Center, M.D. Anderson Hosp. and Tumor Inst., Houston, 1976—, dir. hosp.-clinic, 1979—; dir. Greater Houston Hosp. Service Corp., 1974-76, sec., 1976-77, chmn., 1979-80. Adminstrv. bd. First United Meth. Ch., Houston, 1978—; pres. Unitex Credit Union, 1968. Recipient Am. Surg. Trade Assn. award for highest scholastic standing in program in hosp. adminstrn. at U. Minn., 1961. Mem. Am. Coll. Hosp. Adminstrs., Houston C. of C., Tex. Hosp. Assn. (vice chmn. Houston div. 1978-80), Greater Houston Hosp. Council (sec. 1978-79, v.p. 1979-80, dir. 1977—), Am. Hosp. Assn., Am. Mgmt. Assn., Alumni Assn. U. Minn., Delta Sigma Pi. Methodist. Club: Masons (Shriner). Contbr. articles in field to profl. jours. Home: 3703 Roseland St Houston TX 77006 Office: 6723 Bertner Ave Houston TX 77030

RUTLEDGE, ERVIN EDGAR, computer technologist; b. Charleston, W.Va., Sept. 5, 1939; s. Ervin Edgar and Gertrude May (Davis) R.; B.S. magna cum laude, Steed Coll., Johnson City, Tenn., 1978; m. Nancy Mitchell, Dec. 19, 1959; children—Sharron Lynn, Allan Edward. Apprentice technician RTR Sales and Service, Charleston, W.Va., 1957-60; field service technician Sperry Univac Co., Bristol, Tenn., 1968-74, asst. supr., 1974—. Pres. Johnson City Band Boosters, 1978-79. active Boy Scouts Am., Girl Scouts U.S. Served with USAF, 1960-68. Cert. engring. technician. Mem. Phi Theta Pi (pres. alumni chpt.). Delta Gamma. Democrat. Methodist. Clubs: Masons, K.T. Home: 1905 Club Dr Johnson City TN 37601 Office: Sperry Univac Co Univac Rd Bristol TN 37620

RUTLEDGE, PAUL RICHARD, regional shopping center exec.; b. Johnstown, Pa., Mar. 13, 1953; s. Robert G. and Jeanne M. R.; B.A. in Mass Communications, U. South Fla., 1975; m. Donna Pieschel, Aug. 27, 1977. Sales rep. retail advt. Tampa (Fla.) Tribune & Times, 1974-75; retail advt. rep. Sun Sentinel/Ft. Lauderdale (Fla.) News, 1975-76; gen. mgr. Palm Beach Mall, Edward J. DeBartolo Corp., West Palm Beach, Fla., 1976-79; gen. mgr., leasing cons. Oakbrook Sq. and Harbour Bay Plaza, 1979—; cons. in field. Active United Way, West Palm Beach, Cystic Fibrosis, West Palm Beach, Sheriff's Boys Ranch. Recipient Nat. Research Bur. Retail Mktg. award, 1979; Fla. Newspaper Advt. Execs. Award, 1979. Mem. Advt. Fedn. Palm Beach. Lutheran. Clubs: West Palm Beach Rotary, Palm Beach Runners. Home: 1830 San Juan Dr #23-D CB-0 Delray Beach FL 33445 Office: 1801 Palm Beach Lakes Blvd West Palm Beach FL 33401

RUTLEDGE, ROGER KENT, psychiat. social worker; b. Atlanta, Feb. 27, 1943; s. Talmadge Dewitt and Eva Lou (Stokes) R.; B.A. in Sociology, U. S.C., 1966; M.A. in Social Work, U. Chgo., 1968; m. Judy Elaine Conrad, Aug. 8, 1964 (div. Sept. 1974); 1 son, Bryan Kent; m. 2d, Catherine Lee Dowdey, Jan. 23, 1976; 1 stepson, Mark Hampton Hood. Psychiat. social worker Sumter (S.C.) Mental Health Clinic, 1968-72; instr. sociology Clemson U., Sumter, 1969-70; med. social worker S.C. Dept. Social Services, 1972-73; pvt. practice psychiat. social work, mem. Columbia Psychiat. Assos., 1973—; social service cons. to 12 nursing homes, 1969—; cons. Columbia Sch. Autistic Children. Recipient stipend S.C. Dept. Mental Health, 1966-68; registered social worker, S.C.; cert. instr. parent effectiveness tng. Mem. Nat. Assn. Social Workers, Carolina Soc. Adolescent Psychiatry. Lutheran. Clubs: North Lakes Sertoma (sec.), Masons. Home: 113 Mine Head Rd Irmo SC 29063 Office: 1401 Laurel St Columbia SC 29201

RUWITCH, LEE, publisher; b. Escanaba, Mich., Nov. 21, 1913; s. Harry and Ida (Carroll) R.; B.B.A., U. Minn., 1939; m. Francien Chaney, Aug. 18, 1958; 1 son, Roby. Exec. v.p., gen. mgr. Sta. WTVJ, Miami, Fla., 1948-64; pub., owner Miami Rev., Broward Rev., Ft. Lauderdale, Fla., Law Rev. of Palme Beach County; owner Review Fin. Printers, Inc.; sec.-treas. Sta. WMMB, Melbourne, Fla.; pres. Channel 2, Ednl. TV, Miami, 1968-69. Mem. bd. exec. advisors U. Miami Sch. Bus. Adminstrn. Served with USNR, 1942-45. Recipient award of merit for disting. service to legal profession Fla. Bar, 1967. Mem. Assn. Area Bus. Publs., Fla. Press Assn., Am. Ct. and Comml. Newspaper Assn. (past pres.). Office: 100 NE 7th St Miami FL 33101

RYAN, COLLEEN ANNE, psychologist; b. Joplin, Mo., July 7, 1943; d. Edwin Eugene and Charlotte (Maib) R.; B.S., U. Kans., 1965, M.S., 1967; Ph.D. in Psychology, Ohio State U., 1973. Research asso. U. Kans., 1965-67; teaching fellow Ohio State U., 69-71; dir. children's ednl. unit Western Mo. Mental Health, Kansas City, 1966-68; dir. ednl. program Children's Mental Health, Columbus, Ohio, 1968-69; teaching asst. psychology Ohio State U., 1969-71; mem. field faculty U. Miami (Fla.) Sch. Medicine, 1971-74; founding faculty, 1971, then instr. dept. psychol. ednl. services Fla. Internat. U., 1971-73, asst. prof., 1973-75, asso. prof., 1975—. Bd. dirs., mem. profl. adv. bd. Mental Health Assn.; chmn. Woman's Concerns Council; mem. Miami Commn. on Status of Women; mem. profl. adv. bd. Vanguard Sch.; adv. bd. Finding Place. NDEA fellow, 1964-66; HEW fellow, 1968-70. Mem. Am. Psychol. Assn., Council for Exceptional Children, Am. Assn. Mental Deficiency, Assn. for Supervision and Curriculum Devel., Phi Delta Kappa. Office: Dept Psycho-Ednl Services Fla Internat Univ 151 Biscayne St North Miami FL 33181

RYAN, DANIEL BRUNO, banker; b. New Orleans, Aug. 18, 1922; s. Cornelius J., Jr., and Viola M. (Havswald) R.; student Niagara U., 1943-44; m. Joyce A. Johnson, Oct. 6, 1961; children—Maureen, Daniel, Donna, Joseph. Chief clk. E.I. duPont de Nemours & Co., 1945-55; teller to exec. v.p., cashier and dir. Nat. Bank of Commerce, Jefferson, La., 1955—. Served with inf. U.S. Army, 1942-45. Decorated Purple Heart. Mem. Bank Adminstrn. Inst. (past pres. New Orleans chpt.), La. Bankers Assn. (past chmn. So. regional clearinghouse), La. Ind. Bankers Assn. (bd. dirs.). Democrat. Roman Catholic. Club: Colonial Golf and Country. Office: 2400 Jefferson Hwy Jefferson LA 70121

RYAN, JAMES WALTER, biomed. scientist, educator; b. Amarillo, Tex., June 8, 1935; s. Lee Walter and Emma Elizabeth (Haddox) R.; A.B., Dartmouth Coll., 1957; M.D., Cornell U., 1961; Ph.D., Oxford U., 1967; m. Una Harriet Scully, June 17, 1973; children—James P.A., Alexandra L.E., Amy J.S. Asst. resident medicine Montreal (Que., Can.) Gen. Hosp., 1962-63; research asso. NIMH, NIH, Bethesda, Md., 1963-65; guest investigator Rockefeller U., N.Y.C., 1967-68, asst. prof. biochemistry, 1968; investigator Howard Hughes Med. Inst., Miami, Fla., 1968-71; asso. prof. medicine U. Miami (Fla.) Sch. Medicine, 1968-79, prof. medicine, 1979—; hon. med. officer to Regius prof. medicine Oxford U., 1965-67; vis. prof. Clin. Research Inst. Montreal, 1974; vis. faculty Mayo Clinic, 1974; sr. scientist Papanicolaou Cancer Research Inst., Miami, 1972-77; speaker 500th Anniversay U. Uppsala (Sweden), 1977. Served to lt. comdr. USPHS, 1963-65, now comdr. inactive res. Recipient William Mecklenberg Polk Research prize, 1961; Travel award Rockefeller Found., 1962; Research prize Montreal Clin. Soc., 1963; William Waldorf Astor travelling fellow, 1966; USPHS Career Devel. award, 1968; Pfizer travelling fellow, 1972. Mem. AAAS, Biochem. Soc., So. Soc. Clin. Investigation, N.Y. Acad. Sci., Am. Inst. Chemists (fellow), Am. Soc. Biol. Chemists, Am. Chem. Soc., Microcirc. Soc., Am. Heart Assn., Council on Cardiopulmonary Disease of Am. Heart Assn. (med. advisory bd. Council High Blood Pressure Research), Sigma Xi. Baptist. Contbr. articles to profl. jours.; patentee in field. Office: 1399 NW 17 Ave Rm 207 Miami FL 33125

RYAN, MICHAEL PHILLIP, univ. adminstr.; b. Chgo., Mar. 23, 1942; s. Phillip Walter and Estelle Frances (Zicosky) R.; B.A., U. Tex., El Paso, 1962; M.A., U. Okla., 1971; m. Della Jill Holmes, May 28, 1968; children—John Kevin, Sean Phillip. Tchr. journalism and publs. adv. Irvin High Sch., El Paso, 1964-66; dir. public relations, instr. journalism Odessa (Tex.) Coll., 1966-70; head dept. journalism Angelo State U., San Angelo, Tex., 1971-73, dir. news and info., 1973-76, asst. to pres., 1976—. Mem. public relations com. Tom Green County United Way, 1975-78; vol. Concho Valley Home for Girls, 1975-77; active Boy Scouts Am., 1977—. Mem. Council for the Support and Advancement of Edn., Sigma Delta Chi, Lambda Chi Alpha. Episcopalian. Home: 3402 Cumberland Ct San Angelo TX 76901 Office: 2601 W Ave N San Angelo TX 76901

RYAN, WILLIAM JOSEPH, broadcasting co. exec.; b. Nyack, N.Y., Apr. 14, 1932; s. William Joseph and Elizabeth Mary (Langley) R.; B.A., U. Notre Dame, 1954; m. Jane Householder, June 27, 1970; children—Ashley Allison, William Joseph III. Mem. staff WSBT-WSBT-TV, South Bend, Ind., 1953-55; producer Jules Power Prodns., Chgo., 1955-56; pres., gen. mgr. Radio Naples Inc. (WNOG-WNFM), Naples, Fla., 1956-69; v.p. and gen. mgr. Radio Naples div. Palmer Communications Inc., 1969—, v.p., gen. mgr. Palmer Cablevision div., 1972—; dir. 1st Nat. Bank & Trust Co., Naples. Pres., Collier County unit Am. Cancer Soc., 1972-74; mem. for Collier County, Republican State Com., 1971-72; bd. dirs. Naples Community Hosp. Served with AUS, 1958-67. Mem. Fla. (pres. 1974-76, chmn. 1976-79), So. (pres. 1978-79) cable TV assns., Fla. Assn. Broadcasters (chmn. Fla. State Industry Adv. com. 1963—, pres. 1970-71), Naples Area C. of C. (pres. 1969-70), Naples Council Navy League (pres. 1971-72). Kiwanian (pres. 1966-67), Cable Pioneers, Broadcast Pioneers. Clubs: K.C. (grand knight), Elks, Royal Poinciana Golf and Country, Naples Bath and Tennis, Naples Athletic, Tower. Home: 1312 Murex Dr Naples FL 33940 Office: 333 8th St S Naples FL 33940

RYANT, CARL GEORGE, historian, educator; b. Cleve., June 28, 1942; s. George Charles and Lolita Margaret (Burwell) R.; B.A., Case-Western Res. U., 1964, M.A. (Wis. Alumni Research Found. fellow), U. Wis., 1965, Ph.D. (Univ. fellow, Knapp fellow), 1968; m. Mary Louise Neville, Aug. 5, 1970. Asst. prof. history U. Louisville, 1968-72, asso. prof., 1972—, dir. Oral History Center, 1971—. Mem. exec. bd. Louisville Civil Liberties Union, Ky. Civil Liberties Union. Mem. Am., So. hist. assns., Orgn. Am. Historians, Oral History Assn., Oral History Soc., Soc. Historians Am. Fgn. Relations. Filson Club. Democrat. Contbr. articles to profl. jours. Home: 1839 Roanoke Ave Louisville KY 40205 Office: Dept History U Louisville Louisville KY 40292

RYBOLT, STEPHEN BALLARD, human resources cons.; b. Highland Park, Ill., Oct. 29, 1930; s. Myron Carson and Helen (Lamb) R.; B.A., U. Mo., 1952; B.D., Eden Theol. Sem., 1956; A.B.D., Union Theol. Sem., 1962; M.A., St. Louis U., 1974; m. Mary Elizabeth; children—Kathryn Jo, Gayle J. Parent, Stephen A., Mary R., Peter. Ordained to ministry Presbyn. Ch., 1956; pastor various chs., N.Y. and Mo., 1957-61; pastor Westminster Presbyn. Ch., St. Louis, 1962-69; personnel supr. Monsanto Co., St. Louis, 1969-71; asso. planner Greater St. Louis Health Systems Agy., 1971-75; cons. alcoholism treatment programs, employee assistance programs, 1975—; lectr. in field. Pres., West St. Louis (Mo.) Ecumenical Parish, 1967-68; moderator Presbytery of St. Louis, 1968. Served as chaplain, comdr., USNR, 1954-72. Mem. Nat. Assn. Alcoholism Counselors (cert. alcoholism counselor), Nat. Council Alcoholism, Alcohol and Drug Problems Assn., Alliance of Labor Mgmt. Cons.'s on Alcoholism, Alcohol and Drug Abuse Assn. Democrat. Presbyterian. Contbr. articles to profl. jours. Home: 4820 Westgrove St Dallas TX 75248

RYBURN, FRANK COMPERE, automobile co. exec.; b. Rison, Ark., Apr. 22, 1922; s. Lewis Frank and Josephine Ione (Compere) R.; student Ark. A. and M. U., 1941; B.S., Tex. Christian U., 1943; m. Dixie Wood; 1 dau., Salli Josephine. Adminstrv. asst. to Congressman Oren Harris, Washington 1962-64; v.p., Bank Dallas, 1964-67; exec. v.p. Ryburn Ford Sales Inc., Jonesboro, Ark., 1967-70; pres. Frank Ryburn Ford Inc., Millington, Tenn., 1970—; chmn. Ford Dealer Council Memphis Dist., 1972-73. Chmn. Personnel Appeals Bd. Millington City Council, 1973—; commr. City of Millington Housing Authority, 1973—. Bd. dirs. pres. USO, Memphis; bd. dirs. Salvation Army, Shelby County Econ. Devel. Council; mem. exec. bd. dirs. Chickasaw council Boy Scouts Am. Served to lt. USNR, 1942-46. Recipient Mil. Outstanding Civilian award Memphis Area C. of C., 1978. Mem. SAR, Navy League (pres. Memphis council 1978). Democrat. Episcopalian. Clubs: Mil. Order World Wars (comdr. Memphis chpt. 1977—), Summitt, Petroleum; Lions (pres. Millington 1972-73). Home: 4769 Hallbrook Dr Millington TN 38053 Office: 4701 Navy Rd Millington TN 38053

RYLE, JACK LAVERN, state ofcl.; b. Wichita Falls, Tex., Sept. 28, 1930; s. Raymond L. and Aylene O. (Fisher) R.; B.S., Hardin-Simmons U., 1968; postgrad. S.W. Tex. State U., 1971-74; m. Kathryn Elizabeth Lennington, Oct. 19, 1952; children—Deborah, Steven, Richard, Timothy, Mark. Mcpl. police officer, McAllen and Abilene, Tex., 1954-68; tchr. pub. schs., Abilene, 1968-70; instr. Hardin-Simmons U., Abilene, 1969-70; ednl. cons. Tex. Commn. Law Enforcement Officer Standards and Edn., Austin, 1970-73; dir. cert. and staff services Tex. Commn. on Law Enforcement, Austin, 1973—. Served with USMC, 1950-54; Korea. Decorated Bronze Star. Mem. Internat. Assn. Chiefs of Police, Nat. Assn. State Dirs. Law Enforcement Tng., Tex. Police Assn., Am. Mgmt. Assn. Methodist. Club: Masons. Home: 5800 Whitebrook St Austin TX 78723 Office: 1106 Clayton Ln Suite 220-E Austin TX 78724

RYMER, FREDERICK ROSCOE, state ofcl.; b. Traverse City, Mich., Dec. 21, 1917; s. Albert Edward and Daisey Lillian (Easterwood) R.; A.A., Temple (Tex.) Jr. Coll., 1937; B.A., U. Tex., Austin, 1940, postgrad., 1940, 49; m. Minerva Inez Reese, May 14, 1948; 1 dau., Sandra Kathleen. Asst. firearms and document examiner

Sci. Crime Lab., Tex. Dept. Pub. Safety, Austin, 1941-43, supr. ballistics sect., 1943—; instr. crime investigation procedures law schs. U. Tex., U. Okla., U. Kan., Denver U., Tex. A. and M. U. Recipient Dept. Pub. Safety award, 1958. Fellow Am. Acad. Forensic Scis.; mem. Internat. Assn. Identification (past pres.), Am. Firearms and Tool Mark Examiners, Nat. Rifle Assn., Am. Def. Preparedness Assn., Tex. Police Assn., Tex. Pub. Employees Assn. (pres. Dept. Pub. Safety chpt., 1963-64). Democrat. Club: K.P. Home: 1314 Ridgemont Dr Austin TX 78723 Office: 5805 N Lamar Blvd Austin TX 78765

RYON, THOMAS S(HIPLEY), tobacco co. exec.; b. Washington, May 29, 1917; s. Norman Eugene and Mary (Shipley) R.; A.B., Duke U., 1938; m. Ruth Elizabeth Green, Apr. 12, 1940; children—Thomas Shipley, David Osmond. Travel and study in Europe and Africa, 1938; real estate and income tax specialist, Washington, 1939; mgr. A.C. Monk Enterprises, 1940-43; accountant A.C. Monk & Co., Inc., Farmville, N.C., 1943-45, asst. sec., 1945-54, sec., 1954—, v.p., 1971—; v.p. Dixon Hamilton Tobacco Suppliers, 1968—; sec., dir. Eastern Tobacco Co.; sr. v.p., dir. First Fed. Savs. & Loan Pitt County, 1972—; v.p. Molenco Corp., Wendell, N.C., 1976—. Pres. Farmville Tobacco Bd. Trade, 1966-68. Chmn. Farmville Fed. Housing Authority, 1974—. Chmn. Farmville com. Boy Scouts Am., 1957-63; dir. Farmville Little League, Farmville Community Chest, Farmville United Fund; vice chmn. Farmville Sch. Bd., 1957, chmn. 1958-63. Treas., Jones for Congress Com., 1967—. Mem. N.C. World Trade Assn. (dir.), Farmville C. of C. (dir.). Democrat. Episcopalian. Clubs: Wilson Coin; Farmville Coin, Farmville Country (past sec.-treas.). Home: 1007 Fountain Hwy Farmville NC 27828 Office: West Marlboro Rd Farmville NC 27828

RYSKIEWICH, DANIEL PAUL, chemist; b. Pawtucket, R.I., June 30, 1931; s. Stanley J. and Stella H. (Trocki) R.; B.S., Providence Coll., 1951; Ph.D. (Geigy Corp. grantee), N.Y. U., 1957; m. Lillian Ann Siuzdak, Oct. 15, 1955; children—Paul D., Cheryl A., Thomas S. With Geigy Corp., Providence, 1951-71, supr., 1957-62, group leader, 1962-71; group leader, metabolism support CIBA-Geigy Corp., Greensboro, N.C., 1971—; speaker at local colls. Mem. adv. bd. Blessed Sacrament Roman Catholic Ch., Burlington, N.C., 1977-78, chmn. fin. com. 1978. Recipient Founders Day award N.Y. U., 1957. Mem. Am. Chem. Soc. (course adminstr.), Sigma Xi, Phi Lambda Upsilon. Clubs: Burlington (N.C.) Cotillion (v.p. 1978), Moose. Contbr. articles to profl. jours. Home: 1034 Briarcliff Rd Burlington NC 27215 Office: 410 Swing Rd Greensboro NC 27409

SAADY, JOSEPH JOHN, toxicologist; b. Richmond, Va., Mar. 24, 1947; s. Joseph Paul and Madelyn Mary (Lewis) S.; B.S. in Chemistry, U. Richmond, 1969; M.S. in Pharmacology, Va. Commonwealth U.-Med. Coll. Va., 1977; m. Diane Marie Fahed, July 12, 1969; children—Matthew, Dawn. Analytical chemist Va. Div. Consol. Lab. Services, Richmond, 1970-73, Med. Coll. Va.; toxicologist Med. Coll. Va., Richmond, 1973—. Served with USAF, 1970. Mem. Am. Chem. Soc. Maronite Catholic. Author: Tace Elemental Survey of Ancient Samples, 1977. Office: MCV Station Box 597 Richmond VA 23298

SAARINEN, ARTHUR WILLIAM, JR., civil engr.; b. West Palm Beach, Fla., Dec. 9, 1927; s. Arthur William and Elsie (Gillespie) S.; student Ga. Inst. Tech., 1944-45; B.C.E., U. Fla., 1950; m. Mary Jane Emig, June 30, 1950; children—Mary Louise, Linda Jane (div. May 1973); m. Jacqueline René Smith, Mar. 1, 1974 (div. Mar. 1979); 1 son, Justin; m. 2d, Phyllis Park Weiner, Apr. 21, 1979. With Fla. Bd. of Health, 1950, Broward County Bd. County Commrs., 1951; staff engr. J.H. Philpott, engrs., 1953-54, v.p., 1954-67, pres., 1967—; exec. Ross, Saarinen, Bolton & Wilder, Ft. Lauderdale, Fla.; dir., sr. v.p. environ. engring. div. and internat. div. Camp Dresser & McKee, Inc., Boston, Century Nat. Bank of Broward, Inc., Ft. Lauderdale; cons. to Govt. of Bahama Islands for water supply, 1966-72. Chmn. Broward County Water Resources Adv. Bd., 1964-77; v.p. Fla. Atlantic U. Found., 1971-73; mem. exec. council South Fla. council Boy Scouts Am. Hon. trustee Broward Community Coll. Served with AUS, 1946-47. Diplomate Am. Acad. Environmental Engrs. Fellow ASCE; mem. Fla. Inst. Cons. Engrs. (pres. 1962-63), Am. Cons. Engrs. Council (dir. 1971-72), Am. Water Works Assn., Fla. Pollution Control Assn. (sec.-treas. 1977-78, v.p. 1978-79, pres. 1979-80), Sigma Chi. Methodist. Club: University Fla. Alumni (dist. v.p. 1966). Home: 2167 NE 21st Dr Fort Lauderdale FL 33308 Office: 2001 NW 62d St Fort Lauderdale FL 33309

SABATELLA, JOSEPH JOHN, univ. adminstr.; b. Chgo., May 5, 1931; s. John Joseph and Mary Rose (Genovese) S.; B.F.A., U. Ill., 1954, M.F.A., 1958; m. Ruth Anne Bernacki, Aug. 16, 1952; children—John J., Steven L., Michael J., Joseph P., Philip A., Thomas F., Mary K., Clarissa L. Mgr., Elenhank Designers, Inc., Riverside, Ill., 1958-59; instr. architecture U. Fla., Gainesville, 1959-66, asst. dean Coll. Architecture and Fine Arts, 1966-75, prof. art, 1975—, dean Coll. Fine Arts, 1975—. Bd. dirs. United Way of Alachua County (Fla.), 1976-79. Served with U.S. Army, 1954-56. Mem. Internat. Council Fine Arts Deans, Acad. Affairs Adminstrs., Nat. Assn. Land Grant Colls. and Univs. (mem. fine arts commn.). Roman Catholic. Office: Coll Fine Arts U Fla Gainesville FL 32611

SABATER, SOCRATES SILVANO, architect; b. Bayamo, Cuba, Feb. 20, 1930; came to U.S., 1961, naturalized, 1967; s. Socrates Diego and Micaela Ernestina (Fonseca) S.; B.S. summa cum laude, LaSalle Sch., 1947; M.Arch. summa cum laude, U. Havana, 1953; postgrad. (scholar), Beaux Arts Ecole, Paris, 1954-55; m. Olga Gomez, Dec. 17, 1960. Partner, Sabater-Salman-Sanchez, architects, Cuba, 1953-61; asso. Bianculli & Palm, Architects, Chattanooga, Tenn., 1961-63, Frank Gibson Architect, Chattanooga, 1963-65; asso. architect Selmon T. Franklin Asso. Architects Inc., Chattanooga, 1965-73; pres. Socrates S. Sabater, Planning Assos. Inc., architects, Chattanooga, 1973—. Mem. AIA, Tenn. Soc. Architects, Chattanooga C. of C. Roman Catholic. Clubs: Kiwanis, Walden. Home: 2928 Folts Circle Chattanooga TN 37415 Office: Socrates S Sabatgr Planning Assos Inc 1112B McCallie Ave Chattanooga TN 37404

SABISTON, DAVID COSTON, JR., educator, surgeon; b. Onslow County, N.C., Oct. 4, 1924; s. David Coston and Marie (Jackson) S.; B.S., U. N.C., 1943; M.D., Johns Hopkins, 1947; m. Agnes Barden, Sept. 24, 1955; children—Anne Sabiston Leggett, Agnes Foy, Sarah Coston. Successively intern, asst. resident, chief resident surgery Johns Hopkins Hosp., 1947-53; successively asst. prof., asso. prof., prof. surgery Johns Hopkins Med. Sch., 1955-64, Howard Hughes investigator, 1955-60; Fulbright research scholar U. Oxford (Eng.), 1960; research asso. Hosp. Sick Children, U. London (Eng.), 1961; James B. Duke prof. surgery, chmn. dept. Duke U. Med. Sch., 1964—. Served to capt. M.C., AUS, 1953-55. Recipient Career Research award NIH, 1962-64. Fellow A.C.S. (chmn. bd. govs. 1974-75, bd. regents 1975—); mem. Soc. Univ. Surgeons (pres. 1968-69), Am. (pres. 1977-78), So. (pres. 1973-74) surg. assns., Am. Assn. Thoracic Surgery, Soc. Clin. Surgery, Internat. Soc. Cardiovascular Surgery, Soc. Vascular Surgery, Halsted Soc., Surg. Biology Club II, Soc. Thoracic Surgery, Soc. Surgery Alimentary Tract, Soc. Thoracic Surgeons Great Britain and Ireland, Phi Beta Kappa, Alpha Omega Alpha. Co-editor: Gibbon's Surgery of the Chest; editor: Davis-Christopher Textbook of Surgery; chmn. editorial bd. Annals Surgery, 1974—, Jour. Cardiovascular and Thoracic Surgery, Circulation, World Jour. Surgery. Home: 1528 Pinecrest Rd Durham NC 27705

SACHAU, WILLIAM HENRY, diversified energy co. ofcl.; b. Ridgewood, N.Y., Feb. 6, 1924; s. Hans Richard Koenig and Christine H. (Betke) S.; B.S. in Bus. Adminstrn., Duquesne U.. 1950; M.B.A., U. Denver, 1953; m. Dorothy Jean Fjone, Nov. 1, 1952; children—Christy Jean. Susan Melinda, William Eric. X-ray technician Presbyn. Hosps. Med. Center. N.Y.C. and Pitts., 1946-50; staff mem. Ralph B. Mayo & Co., C.P.A.'s, Denver. 1951-54; auditor Ford Motor Co.. Dearborn, Mich.. 1954-59; auditor Collins Radio Co., Dallas, 1959-60, supr. operations control, 1960-62, mgr. auditing and procedures. 1962-71, mgr. accounting and consolidations, 1971-74; mgr. auditing Cities Service Co., Tulsa, 1974—. Instr., So. Methodist U.; lectr., mem. adv. bd. North Tex. U. Mem. Dallas United Fund, 1968-72; active Boy Scouts Am.; judge, timer Pard Swim Team, Richardson, Tex., 1966-73. Bd. dirs. Richardson Credit Union, 1971-76. Served with Armored Div., AUS, 1943-45, ETO; 1951-52, Korea; capt. Res. (ret.). Decorated Bronze Star, Commendation medal, Purple Heart; named Outstanding Mem., Inst. Internal Auditors of Dallas, 1964-65; cert. internal auditor. Mem. Inst. Internal Auditors (internat. dir. 1966-67, regional dir. 1967-70, research com. mem. 1970-77), Am. Accounting Assn., Nat. Assn. Accountants, Am. Assn. Cost Engrs., Am. Inst. C.P.A.'s (com. on internal acctg. control). Republican. Lutheran (council 1955-68, 75-79). Contbr. articles to profl. jours. Home: 4123 E 85th St Tulsa OK 74136 Office: 521 S Boston St Box 37 Tulsa OK 74102

SACHER, CHARLES PHILIP, lawyer; b. Bklyn., Sept. 5, 1939; s. Hans Philip and Mary Carmel (O'Reilly) S.; B.B.A. in Accounting magna cum laude, U. Notre Dame, 1961; LL.B.. 1964; m. Dorothy Anne Cronin, June 16, 1962; children—Charles Stephen, John Michael, Richard James. Admitted to Fla. bar, 1964; practice in Ft. Lauderdale, i966-67, Miami, 1968—; pres. Charles P. Sacher, P.A.; partner firm Walton, Lantaff, Schroeder & Carson. Trustee Fairchild Tropical Garden, 1973—. Served to capt. AUS, 1964-66. Mem. Am., Dade County (chmn. taxation com. 1969-77) bar assns., Greater Miami Tax Inst. Republican. Roman Catholic. Club: Notre Dame of Greater Miami. Contbr. articles to legal jours. Home: 7341 SW 162d St Miami FL 33157 Office: 900 Alfred I duPont Bldg Miami FL 33131

SACKETT, KAREN MAUREEN, lang. pathologist; b. Marshalltown, Iowa, Oct. 26, 1943; d. William Louis and Elnora Muriel (Lucas) S.; B.S., U. Tulsa, 1967; M.S., Fla. State U., 1974. Speech clinician, Brevard County, Fla., 1968-76; pre-sch. lang. pathologist, Seminole County, Fla., Sanford, 1976—. Mem. Am. Speech and Hearing Assn. Democrat. Roman Catholic.

SACKETT, RICHARD DAVID, advt. exec.; b. New Orleans, Mar. 6, 1947; s. Mark William and Pearl F. S.; student Tulane U., 1965-67; B.A. in Communications, Loyola U., New Orleans, 1970. Program dir. Sta. WWOM, 1967-68; v.p. Max Fetty Advt. Co., New Orleans, 1969-70; pres. Custom Media Inc., New Orleans, 1970-72; v.p. Ladas Advt. Co., New Orleans, 1973; pres. Sackett and Assos. Advt., New Orleans, 1974—; host talk show You Call the Shots, New Orleans, 1978; cons. USCG, 1970-74. Served with USCG, 1968-69. Mem. Homebuilder Assn. St. Tammany Parish. Clubs: New Orleans Yacht, Jefferson Racquet, Colonial County, Westbank Petroleum. Contbr. articles to profl. jours. Office: 8600 Pontchartain Blvd Suite 213 New Orleans LA 70124

SACKETT, WALTER WALLACE, JR., physician, surgeon, state legislator; b. Bridgeport, Conn., Nov. 20, 1905; s. Walter Wallace and Hermine Marie (Archambault) S.; student Harvard, 1922-23; A.B., U. Miami, (Fla.), 1932; M.D., Rush Med. Coll., Chgo., 1938; m. Sophie Georgeff, Nov. 22, 1972; children by previous marriage—Monica Ann, Walter Wallace III; 1 stepson, Charles A. Dunn; 1 adopted son, John A. (dec.). Instr. anatomy U. Ala. Med. Sch., 1934-36, instr. obstetrics, student health physician, 1939-40; prof. anatomy Coll. Mortuary Sci., St. Louis, 1936-37; intern Berwyn (Ill.) Hosp., 1937-38, St. Luke's Hosp., St. Louis, 1938-39; resident Charity Hosp., Natchez, Miss., 1940-41; pvt. gen. practice, Miami, Fla., 1941—; mem. staff Doctors, Jackson Meml., Variety Children's, Coral Gables, Dade County (sec. 1962-66), Bapt. hosps.; mem. Med. Research Found., U. Miami, 1950-53; mem. Fla. Ho. of Reps. from 110th Dist., 1966—; dir. Physicians & Surgeons Underwriters Corp.; adv. com. poliomyelitis to surgeon gen. U.S., 1960-61; cons. diabetes and arthritis USPHS, 1961-62; pioneer oral polio vaccine in new borns, 1960-61. Trustee, U. Miami, 1961-63. Recipient Outstanding Alumni award U. Miami, 1957. Mem. Am. (v.p. 1963-64), Fla. (founder-mem., pres. 1965), Dade County (pres. 1951-52) acads. gen. practice, Assn. Am. Physicians and Surgeons (chmn. Fla. membership), Am., World, Pan Am. (chmn. N. Am. sect. 1962—), So. (sec. vice chmn. then chmn. gen. practice sect. 1955-58), Fla., Dade County (sec. 1953, pres. 1957, chmn. trustees, 1960-61) med. assns., Am. Cancer Soc., Am. Soc. Abdominal Surgeons, Coral Gables C. of C., U. Miami Alumni Assn. (pres. 1959), Sigma Xi, Phi Chi. Roman Catholic. Clubs: Moose, Elks. Author: Bringing up Babies, 1962. Contbr. articles to profl. jours. Home: 333 University Dr Coral Gables FL 33134 Office: 2500 Coral Way Miami FL 33145 also State Capitol Tallahassee FL 32304

SADJADI, FIROOZ AHMADI, elec. engr.; b. Tehran, Iran, Mar. 18, 1949; came to U.S., 1968; s. Ali Akbar Ahmadi and Fakhri (Mohsen) S.; B.S.E.E., Purdue U., 1972, M.S.E.E., 1974; E.E.E., U. So. Calif., 1976; postgrad. U. Tenn., 1977—. Grad. research asst. Image Processing Inst., dept. elec. engring. U. So. Calif., Los Angeles, 1974-77; grad. researcher dept. elec. engring. U. Tenn., Knoxville, 1977—; cons. image processing and pattern recognition. Mem. IEEE, AAAS, Soc. Photo-optical instrumentation engrs., Sigma Xi. Contbr. articles to profl. jours. Home: 3500 Sutherland Ave C-222 Knoxville TN 37919 Office: Box 16272 University Center Knoxville TN 37916

SADLER, GUY ALBERT, architect; b. Norfolk, Va., Sept. 6, 1933; s. Robert Dewey and Dorothy Lovisa (Diggs) S.; B.Arch., Va. Poly. Inst., 1960; m. Orpha Ann Quesenberry, Apr. 22, 1961; 1 dau., Pamela. Intern archtl. firms, Washington, 1960-64; architect, Beery & Rio, architects, Annandale, Va., 1964-67; self-employed as architect and land planner, Falls Church, Va., 1967—. Served with USAF, 1951-55. Mem. A.I.A. (mem. design awards com. Va. chpt. 1977-78). Methodist. Prin. archtl. works include Adeson Residence, Village Square Townhouse Wheystone Court Townhouse Project, Franconia Village Townhouse Project, Fairfax County, Va., United Methodist Ch., Fredericktown, Ohio, Gilligan Residence, Fairfax County, Oak Cluster Townhouse Project, Alexandria. Home: 11301 Fieldstone Ln Reston VA 22091

SAEIDI, FABIAN E., restauranteur; b. Abadan, Persie, Jan. 31, 1947; came to U.S., 1965, naturalized, 1973; s. Zinal and Joan S.; A.A.S., Navarro Jr. Coll., 1970; B.B.A., East Tex. State U., 1972; M.B.A., Central Mich. U., 1976; postgrad. Catholic U. Am. Asst. office mgr., bookkeeper Alexandria (Va.) Seafood & Poultry Co., 1973-75; acct. Potomac Butter & Egg Co., Washington, 1975-77; gen. mgr., comptroller Potomac Food Distbrs., Alexandria, Va., 1977-79; propr. restaurant, Leesburg, Va., 1979—; tchr. No. Va. Community Coll. Mem. Am. Logistic Assn., Am. Mgmt. Assn., Soc. Advancement Mgmt., Leesburg C. of C., Delta Chi. Home: 2545 Herrell Ct Falls Church VA 22042 Office: 15 S King St Leesburg VA 22075

SAENZ, MICHAEL, coll. adminstr.; b. Laredo, Tex., Oct. 25, 1925; s. C. A. and Pola R. S.; B.S. with honors in Accounting, Tex. Christian U., 1949, M.Ed., 1952; Ph.D. in Econs., U. Pa., 1961; m. Nancy Elizabeth King; children—Michael King, Cynthia Elizabeth. Dep. collector IRS, Ft. Worth, Dallas, 1949-52; adminstr. United Christian Missionary Soc., Bayamon, P.R., 1954-57, 59-65, exec. sec., Indpls., 1965-71; acad. dean Laredo Jr. Coll., 1971-74; pres. N.W. campus Tarrant County Jr. Coll., 1975—; trustee Tex. Christian U., Brite Div. Sch. Bd. dirs. Civic Ballet of Laredo (Tex.), Ft. Worth chpt. NCCJ, Juliette Fowler Homes, Dallas; chmn. Aztec Dist., dir. Gulf Coast council Boy Scouts Am., 1971-75; gov. Career Devel. Center, Arlington, Tex.; chmn. Laredo's Bicentennial Com., 1973-76; trustee, bd. dirs. United Way Ft. Worth, 1979-82. Mem. Tex. Jr. Coll. Tchrs. Assn., Tex. Assn. Jr. Coll. Instructional Adminstrs., Am. Acad. Polit. and Social Scis., Urban Ministries in Higher Edn, Civic Music Assn. Laredo, N. Ft. Worth C. of C. (dir. 1978—). Mem. Christian Ch. (Disciples of Christ). Club: Rotary (North Ft. Worth). Home: 4201 Westmont Ct Fort Worth TX 76109

SAENZ, NANCY ELIZABETH KING (MRS. MICHAEL SAENZ), civic worker; b. Greenville, Tex., Jan. 28, 1930; d. Henry M. and Vallie (Wheatley) King; A.B. with honors, Tex. Christian U., 1950, B.S. magna cum laude, 1952; postgrad. Hartford Sem. Found., 1952-53, Escuele de Idiomas, 1953; Lexington Theol. Sem., 1953; m. Michael Saenz, July 28, 1950; children—Michael King, Cynthia Elizabeth. Missionary, United Christian Missionary Soc., Indpls., serving in P.R., 1954-65; bd. dirs. Adminstrv. Bd. Christians Chs., P.R., 1950-65; counsellor and tchr. State Christian Youth Fellowship Conf., P.R., 1954-57; chmn. dept. Christian edn. Christian Chs., P.R., 1962-64, sec., 1959-61, state dir., 1963; dept. Christian edn. P.R. Council Chs., 1959-64, sec., 1959-60; sec. and counsellor State Christian Women Fellowship of Christian Chs., P.R., 1955-57, 59-63, dist. chmn., Indpls., 1968-71; pres. elect Christian Ch. in S.W., 1974-76, pres., 1976—; mem. gen. bd. Christian Ch. in U.S. and Can., 1974—. Sec., Disciples of Christ Acad. P.T.A., Bayamon, P.R., 1962-63; mem. state com. Home for Aged, United Ch. Women, P.R., 1963; women's com. Ind. State Symphony Soc., 1967—; women's com. Internat. Christian U. Japan, 1962-64, 65—, pres. Indpls. chpt. 1967-68; mem. exec. bd. Indpls. council P.T.A., 1967-70; mem. vocat.-tech. adv. council Laredo Ind. Sch. Dist., 1971—; vol. coordinator Am. Bible Soc., 1974—; mem. Laredo Mercy Hosp. Aux., 1973-75, pres.-elect, 1974-75; dist. cons., mem. adminstrv. com. Christian Women's Fellowship in Tex., 1972-75; mem. nominating com. Internat. Christian Women's Fellowship, 1974—; mem. Tarrant County Vol. Center Com., 1975—, vice chmn., 1978-79, chmn., 1980—. Bd. dirs. Greater Indpls. Fedn. Chs., 1970-71; pres.-elect Tarrant Area Community of Chs., 1980—; bd. sponsors Laredo Civic Ballet Soc., 1971-75; bd. dirs. Laredo Planned Parenthood Assn., 1972-75, v.p., 1973-74, pres.-elect, 1974-75; bd. dirs. Ruthe B. Cowle Rehab. Center, 1974-75; bd. dirs. Ft. Worth Area Council Chs., exec. interim dir., 1979; mem. adv. council Vols. in Pub. Schs., Ft. Worth, 1977—; bd. dirs., mem. ch. fin. council Christian Ch., Disciples of Christ, 1978—. Mem. Irvington Union of Clubs (exec. bd. 1966—, 2d v.p. 1968-70), Young Mothers Club Irvington (v.p. 1965, pres. 1967), Marion County Guardian Home Guild (pres. 1968-70), Art Assn. Indpls., Thistle Hill Docent Guild, Art League, Irvington, AAUW, Laredo and Ft. Worth Table II, Ch. Women United (pres. 1980), Pan Am. Roundtable, Alpha Chi, Phi Sigma Iota. Clubs: Rotary Anns, Women's College (P.R.); Tex. Christian U. Women Execs. (Fort Worth); Irvington Women's; Laredo Tuesday Music and Lit. (pres. 1973); Women's City. Author: Winds of Change, 1968. Home: 4201 Westmont Ct Fort Worth TX 76109

SAENZ, RAY, psychotherapist; b. Brownsville, Tex., May 6, 1948; s. Felix C. and Maria del Carmen (Larrasquitu) S.; B.A., Tex. A&I U., 1971; M.A., U. Chgo., 1975; m. Victorine Marie Lies, Oct. 25, 1969; 1 dau., Kara Christine. Dir. outreach and moblzn. dept. Nueces County Mental Health/Mental Retardation Community Center, Corpus Christi, Tex., 1971-73; psychotherapist, cons. to local agys., Corpus Christi, 1975—; therapist Family Counseling Service, Corpus Christi, 1976-77; instr. psychology Del Mar Coll., Corpus Christi, 1977—, mem. scholarship com., 1979-80. Bd. dirs. Inst. Hispanic Culture, 1978—, mem. cultural activities com., 1978—; bd. dirs. Vol. Action Center, 1978—, v.p. bd., mem. exec. com., nominating com., exec. dir. selection com., 1979—; mem. Nueces County Grand Jury, 1977. Mem. Nat. Assn. Social Workers, Acad. Cert. Social Workers, Nat. Register Clin. Social Workers, Tex. Jr. Coll. Tchrs. Assn., N.Y. Acad. Scis., Am. Group Psychotherapy Assn., Del Mar Edn. Assn. (chmn. legis. com. 1979-80). Home: 4214 Patrick Dr Corpus Christi TX 78413 Office: 1718 Santa Fe Ave Corpus Christi TX 78404

SAFFAN, BENJAMIN DAVID, physician; b. Bklyn., July 4, 1928; s. David Eli and Rose (Angel) S.; M.D., Emory U., 1953; m. Marie Rousso, Dec. 27, 1953; children—David, Rose. Intern, Grady Meml. Hosp., Atlanta, 1953-54, resident in internal medicine, 1954-56; fellow in internal medicine and endocrinology Emory U., Atlanta, 1958-60; practice specializing in internal medicine, Atlanta, 1960—; v.p. staff Crawford W. Long Meml. Hosp., Grady Meml. Hosp., St. Josephs Infirmary; clin. asst. prof. medicine Emory U. Sch. Medicine; pres. Diabetes Assn. Atlanta, 1975; sec. Ga. affiliate Am. Diabetes Assn., 1979. Served as capt. M.C., AUS, 1955-57. Diplomate Am. Bd. Internal Medicine. Mem. AMA, Med. Assn. Ga., Med. Assn. Atlanta. Jewish. Home: 2529 Greenglade Rd NE Atlanta GA 30345 Office: 401 Peachtree St NE Atlanta GA 30308

SAFFIR, HERBERT SEYMOUR, cons. civil engr.; b. N.Y.C., Mar. 29, 1917; s. A.L. and Gertrude (Samuels) S.; B.S. in Civil Engring. cum laude, Ga. Inst. Tech., 1940; m. Sarah Young, May 9, 1941; children—Richard Young, Barbara Joan. Civil engr. TVA, Chattanooga, 1940, NACA, Langley Field, Va., 1940-41; structural engr. Ebasco Services, N.Y.C., 1941-43, York & Sawyer & Fred Severud, N.Y.C., 1945; engr. Waddell & Hardesty, Cons. Engrs., N.Y.C., 1945-47; asst. county engr. Dade County, Miami, Fla., 1947-59; cons. engr. Herbert S. Saffir, Coral Gables, Fla., 1959—. Adj. lectr. civil engring. Coll. Engring., U. Miami, 1964—; adviser on civil engring. Fla. Internat. U., 1975—; cons. Govt. Bahamas on bldg. codes; cons. on engring. in housing to UN, govt. and industry; mem. Nat. Adv. Group on Glass Design. Served with AUS, 1943-44. Recipient Outstanding Service award Fla. Profl. Engrs., 1954, NOAA Pub. Service award, 1975; named Miami Engr. of Yr., 1978. Registered profl. engr., Fla., N.Y., Tex., P.R., Miss. Fellow ASCE (sect. past pres.), Fla. Engring. Soc. (award for outstanding tech. achievement 1973); mem. Soc. Am. Mil. Engrs., Am. Concrete Inst., ASTM (com. on performance bldg. constrn.), Prestressed Concrete Inst., Colegio de Ingenieros P.R., Am. Meteorol. Soc., Am. Nat. Standards Inst. (com. bldg. design loads), Nat. Panel Arbitrators, Am. Arbitration Assn., Miami, Coral Gables (pres.-elect) chambers commerce, Tau Beta Pi. Author: Housing Construction in Hurricane Prone Areas, 1971; Nature and Extent of Damage by Hurricane Camille, 1972; also papers presented at seminars, articles in profl. jours., chpts. to books. Designer Saffir/Simpson hurricane scale. Home: 4818 Alhambra Circle Coral Gables FL 33146 Office: 255 University Dr Coral Gables FL 33134

SAFLEY, CHARYL TAYLOR, editor; b. Geneva, N.Y., Mar. 27, 1953; d. Charles Edmond and Margery Ann (Rupp) Taylor; B.S. in Communications, U. Tenn., Knoxville, 1975; M.S. in Edn., Okla. State U., 1978; m. Charles Daniel Safley, July 5, 1975. Intern, Faller, Klenk & Quinlan, advt., Buffalo, 1973-74; dir. traffic and promotions Sta. KOSU-FM, Stillwater, Okla., 1976; asst. info. officer div. engring., tech. and architecture Okla. State U., Stillwater, 1976-79; asst. editor Internat. Fire Service Tng. Assn., Stillwater, 1979—. Jessie Pulcipher scholar, 1974. Mem. Am. Personnel and Guidance Assn., Am. Coll. Personnel Assn., Mortar Board (chpt. pres. 1979), Sigma Delta Chi, Kappa Delta Pi, Alpha Xi Delta (chpt. public relations officer 1976—). Episcopalian. Office: IFSTA Okla State Univ Stillwater OK 74074

SAFRIET, MARIAN LAMBETH, hosp. exec.; b. Fayetteville, N.C., Dec. 14, 1923; d. Alva Sherwood and Nell (Wilson) Lambeth; B.S. in Acctg. and Fin., Fla. State U., Tallahassee, 1945; postgrad. Columbia U., U. N.C., Chapel Hill; m. Hubert Wilson Safriet, July 26, 1951; children—Nancy Lambeth, Philip Wilson; 1 stepdau., Barbara S. Carpenter. Instr. acctg. Fla. State U., 1946-47, Queens Coll., Charlotte, N.C., 1948-50, Kings Coll., Charlotte, 1950-51, Crofts Bus. Coll., Concord, N.C., 1955-61, Crofts Bus. Coll., Greensboro, N.C., 1963-69; dir. fin. services Annie Penn Meml. Hosp., Reidsville, N.C., 1971—. Mem. Hosp. Fin. Mgmt. Assn. (chmn. ednl. council N.C. chpt. 1977-78, v.p. 1979), DAR (regent 1973). Democrat. Episcopalian. Club: Woman's (pres. 1954). Home: 1017 Sherwood Dr Reidsville NC 27320 Office: Annie Penn Meml Hosp S Main St Reidsville NC 27320

SAGE, EARL RICHARD, educator; b. Cardington, Ohio, Feb. 19, 1926; s. Walter J. and Lulu Inez (Caris) S.; B.Sc., Ohio State U., 1949; M.B.A., Harvard U., 1960; Ph.D., Ohio State U., 1973; m. Dorotha Ann Dufford, Apr. 12, 1958; children—Anne Leslie, Bradley James, Audrey Lynn. Buyer, Hydraulic Press Mfg. Co., Mt. Gilead, Ohio, 1949-53; traffic rep. No. Consol. Airlines, Fairbanks, Alaska, 1953-54; buyer, mng. buyer Radio Corp. Am., Findlay, Ohio, 1954-58, budget mgr., adminstr. standards and cost estimating, Mountaintop, Pa., 1960-63; research asso., course dir. chmn. Dept. Mgmt. and Quantitative Techniques Ohio State U., Columbus, 1963-73; asst. prof. U. N.C., Charlotte, 1973, dir. mgmt. devel. programs, 1973-76, asso. prof., 1976—. Served with USN, 1943-46. Sarnoff fellow, 1958-60. Mem. Acad. Mgmt., Beta Gamma Sigma. Republican. Methodist. Club: Metrolina World Trade. Home: 4414 Barwick Rd Charlotte NC 28211 Office: Coll of Bus Univ of NC Charlotte NC 28223

SAGE, RUSSELL RICHARD, lawyer; b. Omaha, Aug. 27, 1931; s. James Russell and Claire (Frank) S.; B.S. in Law, U. Minn., 1953, LL.B., 1955; m. Arleta Marie Jons, Feb. 10, 1952; children—Robert Richard, James Russell, Vickie Ann. Admitted to Minn. bar, 1955, D.C. bar, 1962, Va. bar, 1968; atty. ICC, Washington, 1957-62; practice law, Washington, 1962—; mem. firm Turney, Major and Sage, 1963-67, Major, Sage & King, 1968—. Served with AUS, 1955-57. Mem. D.C., Minn., Va. bar assns., Assn. ICC Practitioners, Motor Carrier Lawyers Assn. Democrat. Presbyn. Home: 4807 Manion St Annandale VA 22003 Office: 6121 Lincolnia Rd Alexandria VA 22312

SAHAI, HARDEO, statistician, educator; b. India, Jan. 10, 1942; B.Sc. in Math., Stats. and Physics, Lucknow (India) U., 1962; M.Sc. in Math., Banaras Hindu U., Varanasi, India, 1964; M.S. in Stats., U. Chgo., 1968; Ph.D. in Stats., U. Ky., 1971. Lectr. math. and stats. Banaras Hindu U., 1964-65; asst. statis. officer Durgapur (India) Steel Plant, 1965; statistician research and planning div. Blue Cross Assn., Chgo., 1966; statis. programmer Cleft Palate Center, U. Ill., Chgo., 1967, Chgo. Health Research Found., 1968; teaching asst. dept. stats. U. Ky., Lexington, 1968-69, research asst., 1969-71; mgmt. scientist Burroughs Corp., Detroit, 1972; asst. prof. dept. math. U. P.R., Mayaguez, 1972-76, asso. prof., 1976—; vis. research prof. Fed. U. Ceará (Brazil), 1978-79; cons. P.R. U. Cons. Corp., P.R. Driving Safety Evaluation Project, Water Resources Research Inst., Mayaguez, Transp. Research Inst., Mayaguez. Govt. of India merit scholar; Council Sci. and Indsl. Research fellow. Mem. Inst. Math. Stats., Bernoulli Soc. Math. Stats. and Probability, Biometrics Soc., Indian Statis. Assn., Am. Statis. Assn. Referee, Biometrics, Can. Jour. Stats.; reviewer Math. Revs., Internat. Statis. Rev. Address: Dept Math U Puerto Rico Mayaguez PR

SAHR, AARON EMMANUEL, clin. psychologist; b. Detroit, Dec. 11, 1942; s. William Robert and Alice Drusilla (Wohl) S.; B.A., Adams State Coll., 1968; M.A., Central Mich. U., 1970, Specialists Degree in Psychol. services, 1971; m. Mary Moore Bryant, Dec. 27, 1975; 1 stepson, Kelly Bryant. Clin. psychologist Monadnock Children's Spl. Services Center, Keene, N.H., 1970-71, Mental Health Services Roanoke Valley, Roanoke, Va., 1972—. Served with U.S. Army, 1960-62. Mem. Va. Personnel and Guidance Assn., Am. Psychol. Assn. Home: 1836 Westchester Ave SW Roanoke VA 24018 Office: Liberty and Williamson Rds Roanoke VA 24012

SAILORS, BILLY MATHIS, catalog showroom exec.; b. Athens, Ga., June 16, 1931; s. Wilburn Travis and Sybil Edna (Coile) S.; student Athens public schs.; m. Patsy Jane Thompson, June 21, 1957; children—David Mathis, Rhonda Kay, Vicki Lynn. With Athens Hardware Co., 1950-72, buyer, 1960-72; gen. mgr., personnel dir., buyer J.B. Alexander, Inc., Athens, 1972—, v.p., 1972—. Bd. dirs. Green Acres Community Assn.; co-organizer, bd. dirs. Athens Youth Orgn.; co-organizer, bd. dirs. Internat. Little League, also coach minor, little and sr. league teams; high sch. basketball and football ofcl.; mem. Tax Equalization Bd. Clarke County; chmn. bd. Athens Gen. Hosp. Authority. Served with AUS, 1954-56. Recipient numerous service awards. Mem. PTA, N.E. Ga. Ofcls. Assn. (pres. 1966-72). Democrat. Baptist. Club: East Athens Civitan (charter, dir.). Home: 485 Greencrest Dr Athens GA 30605 Office: 880 Barber St Athens GA 30601

SAIN, HELEN CARPENTER, real estate co. exec.; b. Lincoln County, N.C., Nov. 9, 1929; d. Kelly Victory and Odessa (Gantt) Carpenter; student Gaston Coll., 1965; m. Paul Samuel Sain, Feb. 14, 1949; children—Rita Sain Childs, Timothy Paul. Bookkeeper, Seth Lumber Co., Lincolnton, N.C., 1970-72; office mgr. Boger City Lumber Co., Lincolnton, 1972-75; with Craig P. Gates, Inc., Lincolnton, 1975—, Sales mgr., Realtor, 1979—. Mem. Nat. Bd. Realtors, N.C. Bd. Realtors, Bus. and Women's Profl. Club: Republican. Baptist. Home: Box 544 Route 7 Lincolnton NC 28092 Office: Craig P Gates Inc Box 941-C Route 4 Lincolnton NC 28092

SAINE, LEONARD WATSON, contractor; b. Acworth, Ga., July 1, 1894; s. James Paty and Elizabeth (Watson) S.; student civil engring. Ga. Sch. Tech., 1911-14; student law U. Mich., 1915; LL.B., Atlanta Law Sch., 1916; m. Mary Ruth Hudson, Apr. 17, 1918; 1 dau., Mary Elizabeth (Mrs. Robert Reynolds). Engr., constrn. supt. J.B. McCrary Co., Atlanta, 1917-27, salesman, sales mgr., dir. Central Foundry Co., N.Y.C., 1927-33, sales engr. Walworth Co., N.Y.C., 1935-40; pres., dir. Saine Co., Inc., gen. contractors, 1942—; owner Leonard W. Saine Registered Dealers, municipal and utility supply co., Orlando. Served with C.E. Corps, USN, 1918-19. Registered profl. engr. Mem. Nat. Soc. Profl. Engrs., Fla. Engring Soc., Beta Theta Pi. Mason. Home: 1555 W Fairbanks Ave Winter Park FL 32789

ST AMANT, ROBERT PARKER, physician; b. Baton Rouge, Mar. 13, 1949; s. Parker Haile and Edna Geneviva (Torres) St A.; B.S., U. Southwestern La., 1971; M.D., La. State U., New Orleans, 1975; m. Claudette Marie LeBlanc, June 16, 1973; children—Brandon Scott, Lindsay Anne. Intern, Earl K. Long Hosp., Baton Rouge, 1975-76, resident in family medicine, 1975-78; practice family medicine Baton Rouge Family Med. Center, 1978—; mem. staff Our Lady of Lake Med. Center, Woman's Hosp., Baton Rouge Gen. Hosp., Earl K. Long Hosp.; instr. La. State U. Med. Center, 1978—; team physician Lee High Sch., Baton Rouge, 1978—; lectr. chem. dependency unit Baton Rouge, 1978—. Diplomate Am. Bd. Family Practice. Fellow Am. Acad. Family Physicians; mem. AMA, La. Med. Soc., La. Acad. Family Physicians, 6th Dist. Postgrad. Study Group, East Baton Rouge Parish Med. Soc., Baton Rouge Bromeliad Soc. Republican. Roman Catholic. Home: 2522 Lancelot St Baton Rouge LA 70816 Office: 6010 Perkins Rd Baton Rouge LA 70808

ST. ANGELO, DOUGLAS GENE, educator; b. Huntingburg, Ind., Apr. 6, 1931; s. George A. and Lillian M. (Salat) St. A.; B.A., North Central Coll., 1953; M.A., U. Chgo., 1957, Ph.D., 1960; m. Patricia Jean Schneller, June 4, 1953; children—Scott, Jill. Asst. prof. polit. sci. St. Olaf Coll., 1959-63, acting chmn. dept., 1961-63; asst. prof. polit. sci. Fla. State U., 1963-66, asso. prof., 1966-75, dir. Polit. Research Inst., 1966-69, prof., 1975—; cons. Fla. Dem. Party, 1970, Fla. House Com. on Elections, 1971, Fla. House Com. Govtl. Operations, 1969. Congl. campaign mgr., Minn., 1960; financial dir. Minn. Gubernatorial Dem. Farm-Labor Campaign, 1962; mem. state central com. Minn. Dem. Farm-Labor Party, 1960-63. Dir. Tallahassee Urban League, 1969-71, Human Relations Council Tallahassee, 1964-65; Tallahassee-Leon Community Action Program, 1967-69. Served with AUS, 1953-55. LaVerne Noyes Found. scholar, 1956; Ford Found. Federalism Project fellow, 1957-59. Mem. Am., So. polit. sci. assns., Midwest Conf. Polit. Scientists, United Faculty of Fla. Author: (with A.M. Hartsfield and H. Goldstein) State Library Policy: Its Legislative and Environmental Context, 1971; (with Daniel Elazar, Robert Carroll and E. Lester Levine) Cooperation and Conflict: the Dynamics of American Federalism, 1969; (with A.M. Hartsfield and H. Goldstein) Study of State Library Legislation, 1970. Contbr. articles to profl. jours. Home: 1310 Parga St Tallahassee FL 32304

ST. CLAIR, HAL KAY, elec. engr.; b. Los Angeles, Oct. 11, 1925; s. Millard T. and Ruth (McGrew) St. C.; student U. So. Calif., 1943-44; B.S., U. Calif., Berkeley, 1946, M.S., 1948; m. Jane Creely, June 24, 1949; children—Gregory, Russell, Elizabeth. Research engr. Marchant Calculators, Emeryville, Calif., 1948-52; project engr. RCA, Camden, N.J., 1953-54; program mgr. IBM, San Jose, Calif., 1954-69, tech. staff, Boca Raton, Fla., 1969-72, mgr. input/output devel., 1972-75, mgr. gen. lab. devel., 1975—; instr. U. Calif. Extension Div., 1951-52. Tech. adv. U.S. Nat. Com. Internat. Electrotechnical Commn., 1967-69. Mem. Republican Central Com. of Calif., 1962-66. Served to lt. (j.g.) USNR, 1943-46. Mem. IEEE, SAR, Mensa, Phi Beta Kappa, Sigma Xi, Tau Beta Pi, Eta Kappa Nu. Home: 875 Oleander St Boca Raton FL 33432 Office: 2000 NW 51st St Boca Raton FL 33432

ST. CYR, CORDELL JOSEPH, engr.; b. Opelousas, La., Aug. 22, 1939; s. Harvey A. and Jennie Lee (Richard) St. C.; B.S.C.E., La. State U., 1967; m. Lora Ann Lefler, July 18, 1959; children—Cynthia, Jacqueline, Christopher, Randall, Brian. Pipeline systems analyst, designer, project mgr. Monterey Pipeline Co., New Orleans, 1967-71; with gen. services dept., office bldgs. architecture and engring. sect. Exxon Co., U.S.A., 1971—. Served with U.S. Army, 1961-64. Mem. Assn. Energy Engrs. (v.p. Houston chpt.), Am. Soc. Heating, Ventilating and Air Conditioning Engrs. Republican. Roman Catholic. Home: 11518 Mullins Dr Houston TX 77035 Office: PO Box 2180 800 Bell Ave Houston TX 77001

ST. JOHN, HENRY SEWELL, JR., utility co. exec.; b. Birmingham, Ala., Aug. 18, 1938; s. H. Sewell and Carrie M. (Bond) St. J.; student David Lipscomb Coll., 1956-58, U. Tenn., 1958-59, U. Ala., 1962-64; m. J. Ann Morris, Mar. 9, 1959; children—Sherri Ann, Brian Lee, Teresa Lynn, Cynthia Faye. Engring. aide Ala. Power Co., Enterprise, 1960-62, Birmingham, 1962-66; asst. chief engr. Riviera Utilities, Foley, 1966-71, sec.-treas., gen. mgr., 1971—; bd. dirs. AGAPE of Mobile, 1977—. Zone v.p. Baldwin County unit Am. Cancer Soc., 1976, chmn. bd. dirs., 1977; bd. dirs. South Baldwin Civic Chorus, 1979—. Mem. IEEE, South Ala. Power Distbrs. Assn. (chmn. 1973-74), Ala. Consumer-Owned Power Distbrs. Assn. (chmn. 1974-75), Municipal Electric Utility Assn. Ala. (mem. exec. com., dir. 1971—), South Baldwin C. of C. (pres. 1974). Mem. Ch. of Christ (deacon). Rotarian. Club: Gulf Shores Golf (dir. 1975). Home: PO Box 818 Foley AL 36535 Office: PO Box 550 Foley AL 36535

ST. JOHN, WYLLY FOLK, journalist, author; b. nr. Ehrhardt, S.C., Oct. 20, 1908; d. William Obed and Annie Claire (Mattox) Folk; A.B.J. summa cum laude, U. Ga., 1930; m. Thomas F. St. John, Jan. 1, 1930; 1 dau., Anne (Mrs. Neil D. Pratt). Staff writer Atlanta Jour. and Constn. mag., 1941-75; free lance writer. Bd. dirs. Sr. Citizens Council, Walton County, Ga. Named Ga. Author of Year, 1968, Ga. Author of Year in Fiction, 1973, Ga. Merit Mother, 1974. recipient spl. award as Edgar nominee Mystery Writers Am., 1973, 74; McGarity Citizenship award Walton County, 1977. Mem. Authors League, Authors Guild, Mystery Writers Am., Atlanta Press Club, Heritage Rose Group, Phi Beta Kappa, Phi Kappa Phi, Theta Sigma Phi (Brenda award for outstanding contbn. to journalism 1970). Clubs: Atlanta Plot, Social Circle Garden. Author: The Secrets of Hidden Creek, 1966; The Secrets of The Pirate Inn, 1967; The Mystery of The Gingerbread House, 1968; The Christmas Tree Mystery, 1969; The Mystery of The Other Girl, 1971; The Ghost Next Door, 1971; Uncle Robert's Secret, 1972; The Secret of the Seven Crows, 1973; The Mystery Book Mystery, 1976. Contbr. stories and articles to numerous mags. Home: 198 Dogwood Ave Social Circle GA 30279

ST. JULIAN, CURTIS LEIN, engring. co. exec.; b. Dayton, Tex., July 10, 1938; s. Dalton and Lillie (Nichols) St. J.; student pub. schs., Baytown, Tex.; b. LaVerne Marie Barrett, Aug. 6, 1960; children—Curtis Bryan, Kimberly Marie, Dwain Allan, Jennifer Yvette. Electronics technician United Tech. Center, Sunnyvale, Calif., 1965, Electromec Design & Devel. Co., Santa Clara, Calif., 1965-66; data technician Brown & Root-Northrup, Houston, 1966-67; with Fed. Electric Corp., Lompoc, Calif., 1967-69; instrumentation technician Exxon Research & Engring., Baytown, Tex., 1976—. Mem. Barrett Sta. Civic League, Crosby, Tex., 1966-79, v.p. 1974-75; trustee-asst. sec. Crosby Ind. Sch. Dist., 1976—. Served with USAF, 1956-65. Mem. Instrumentation Soc. Am. Democrat. Roman Catholic. Clubs: Loyal Assistance Orgn. Charity (v.p. 1972-79), Knights of St. Peter Claver (dep. grand knight 1972-79). Address: 12805 Crosby-Lynchburg Rd Crosby TX 77532

ST. MARTIN, ALLEN H., JR., univ. adminstr.; b. Lafayette, La., Sept. 22, 1932; s. Allen H. and Norma (Landry) St. M.; B.S., U. Southwestern La., 1953, M.Ed., 1960; Ed.D., U. Houston, 1974; m. Mary Alice Kidder, June 7, 1954; children—Sherrie Lynn Sanborn, Dwain Penn, Craig Allen, Lisa Kay, Julie Marie. Tchr. math., LaGrange Jr. High Sch., Lake Charles, La., 1955-59; tchr. LaGrange Sr. High Sch., 1959-63; prin. F.K. White Jr. High Sch., Lake Charles, 1963-64; math. supr. Calcasieu Parish Sch. System, Lake Charles, 1964-68; prin. S.J. Welsh Jr. High Sch., 1968-69; dean student services U. Southwestern La., Lafayette, 1969-74, dean of community and sch. services, 1974—. Bd. dirs. Bayou council Girl Scouts U.S., 1974-76. Served with USNR, 1949-74. Mem. La. Edn. Research Assn. (pres.), La. Assn High Sch. Relations Personnel (past pres.), Gulf Regional Interstate Collegiate Consortium (exec. bd.), La. State Rally Assn. (exec. bd.), Sigma Xi, Phi Kappa Phi, Phi Delta Kappa, Theta Xi (nat. dir.). Democrat. Roman Catholic. Club: Kiwanis. Home: 729 Brentwood Blvd Lafayette LA 70503 Office: PO Box 4-4548 Lafayette LA 70504

SAIONTZ, HENRY ALLEN, surgeon; b. Balt., May 25, 1940; s. Carl Benjamin and Cecilia (Friedman) S.; student Johns Hopkins U., 1957-61; M.D., U. Md., 1965; m. Sharon R. Rosenblatt, Dec. 25, 1965; children—Cindy, Marc and Gregory (twins). Intern, U. Md., Balt., 1965-66; resident in neurosurgery Albert Einstein Med. Sch., 1967-73; practice medicine specializing in neurosurgery, West Palm Beach, Fla., 1973—; mem. staff Good Samaritan Hosp., St. Mary's Hosp., Community Hosp. of Palm Beach-West Palm Beach, J.F. Kennedy Hosp., Doctor's Hosp., Lake Worth, Fla., Palm Beach Gardens (Fla.) Hosp.; cons. Childrens Med. Services. Diplomate Am. Bd. Neurosurgery. Fellow A.C.S.; mem. Congress Neurol. Surgeons, Fla. Med. Assn., AMA Am. Assn. Neurol. Surgeons. Jewish. Office: 2247 Palm Beach Lakes Blvd Suite 108 West Palm Beach FL 33409

SAKSEN, LOUIS CARL, architect; b. Washington, Dec. 30, 1946; s. Louis Karl and Sara Flower (Farr) S.; B.Arch., Cath. U. Am., 1969; M.Arch., Va. Poly. Inst., 1974; M.S. in Psychology, Old Dominion U., 1975; m. Elizabeth Helen Wilson, June 24, 1972; children—Alexander Wilson, Katherine Kennedy. Planner, asst. prof. Va. Commonwealth U., Richmond, 1975-79, dir. facilities planning and constrn., 1978—; designer, planner, draftsman Glave Newman Anderson, Richmond, 1976; cons., designer Hardwicke Assos., Richmond, 1977. Served with USN, 1971-74. Mem. AIA (chpt. dir. 1977-79, pres.-elect 1980), Am. Inst. Planners, Assn. Univ. Architects, Soc. Coll. and Univ. Planning. Republican. Roman Catholic. Clubs: Engrs., Rotary. Home: 600 W 33rd St Richmond VA 23225 Office: 327 W Main St Richmond VA 23284

SALA, LUIS FRANCISCO, surgeon; b. N.Y.C., Dec. 13, 1919; s. Luis and Josefina (Goenaga) S.; B.S. cum laude, Georgetown U., 1939, M.D., 1943; M.Med. Sci., U. Pa., 1951; m. Judith Colon, June 5, 1943; children—Luis E., Francisco A., Jorge P., Jose M. Chief resident Grad. Hosp., U. Pa., 1947-51, instr. surgery, 1950-51; clin. asst. surgery Med. Coll. Pa., 1950-51; pvt. practice surgery Ponce, P.R., 1951—; pres. staff Damas Hosp., 1959, chmn. dept. surgery, 1955—, dir. surg. edn., 1957—; prof. surgery U. P.R. Sch. Medicine, 1972—. Dir. Ponce Broadcasting Corp., 1956-77, chmn. bd., 1970—; dir. Banco de Ponce. Pres. P.R. Bd. Health, 1968-73. A founder Statehood Party, 1967. Bd. dirs. Ponce YMCA, 1954-56, Boys Home, Ponce, 1966—; successively chmn., dist. com. health. dist. chmn.. bd. dirs., v.p. local Boy Scouts Am. 1955-74, recipient Silver Beaver award, 1963; chmn. bd. Sala Found.; bd. regents Catholic U. P.R., 1970—, mem. exec. com., 1972-77, pres. planning and devel. com., 1974-77, pres. student affairs, 1977—. Decorated knight Order Holy Sepulchre. Diplomate Am. Bd. Surgery. Fellow A.C.S. (gov. 1965-74, internat. relations com. 1974—, exec. com. 1975—, pres. P.R. chpt. 1978); mem. P.R. Med. Assn. (pres. 1965-66), Internat. Soc. Surgeons, Am. Legion, Assn. de Profesionales. K.C. Contbg. author: Surgery of the Ambulatory Patient, 1974. Home: 6 Almenas Alhambra Ponce PR 00731 Office: 43 Concordia St Ponce PR 00731

SALA, PEDRO ALFONSO, elec. engr.; b. Mexico City, Mexico, Oct. 30, 1933; s. Pedro and Concepcion (Venzor) S.; B.S., Milw. Sch. Engring., 1959; m. Gerda Brigitte Alisch, Oct. 14, 1967; children—Ricardo, Kristina. With Gen. Electric de Mexico, S.A., Mexico City, 1959-76, chief engr., 1964-68, mgr. mfg. and engring., 1968-76; tech. dir. Philco S.A., Mexico City, 1976—. Mem. Electronics Mfrs. Chamber Mexico (v.p., 1973, 77, 78), IEEE. Author: Television a Colores, Teoria y Aplicacion, 1967. Home: Lomas de Tarango 250 Mexico 19 DF Mexico Office: Clavel 157 Mexico 4 DF Mexico

SALAS, MARIO MARCEL, community organizer; b. San Antonio, July 30, 1949; s. Peter John and Delores (Aboullah-Dull) S.; student engring. tech. San Antonio Coll., 1968-70. Community orgn. specialist Ella Austin Community Center, San Antonio, 1971-72; public info. dir. Orgns. United for Eastside Devel., 1979-80; voter rights edn. specialist SW Voter Registration Edn. Project, San Antonio, 1979—; founder 1st Black student union in San Antonio at San Antonio Coll., 1969, organizer 5 Black Student unions, San Antonio, 1969-74; field sec. SNCC, 1969-72; pres. Black Coalition Mass Media, 1974-79; internat. news editor Inner City Jour., San Antonio, 1978-79; internat. news analyst; owner Afro-Am. Bookstore. Mem. NAACP, San Antonio Movement in Solidarity with African Liberation, Intra-City Urban Communications Coalition, Orgns. United for Eastside Devel., San Antonio Coalition against Racism. Home: PO Box 893 San Antonio TX 78293

SALATICH, JOHN SMYTH, physician; b. New Orleans, Nov. 28, 1926; s. Peter B. and Gladys (Malter) S.; B.S. cum laude, Loyola U., New Orleans, 1946; M.D., La. State U., 1950; m. Patricia L. Mattison, Sept. 26, 1959; children—John Smyth, Elizabeth, Allison, Stephanie. Intern Charity Hosp., New Orleans, 1950-51, resident, 1951-54, dir. emergency rooms and satellite clinics; practice medicine, specializing in cardiology and internal medicine, New Orleans, 1954—; dir. EKG dept. Southeastern La. Hosp., Mandeville, La., Fairview Hosp., Bayou Vista, La., Lakewood Hosp., Morgan City, La.; asst. prof. clin. medicine La. State U. mem. staff Touro Infirmary, St. Charles Gen. Hosp.; chmn. dept. medicine Hotel Dieu. Pres., New Orleans Emergency Room Corp.; adv. bd. Bank La. Bd. dirs. La. Regional Med. Program, 1972. Served to capt. M.C., AUS, 1954-56; Korea. Decorated Medallion of Greek Army. Diplomate Am. Bd. Internal Medicine. Fellow Am. Coll. Chest Physicians, A.C.P.; mem. Am. Coll. Emergency Room Physicians, Am., La. (dir.) heart assns., New Orleans Acad. Internal Medicine, La. Thoracic Soc., La. Soc. Internal Medicine, A.M.A., La., Orleans Parish med. socs., Theta Beta, Alpha Sigma Nu, Delta Epsilon Sigma. Club: New Orleans Country. Contbr. articles to profl. and bus. jours. Home: 433 Country Club Dr New Orleans LA 70124 Office: Maison Blanche Bldg New Orleans LA 70112

SALAZAR, JAMES MICHAEL, mktg. exec.; b. Tooele, Utah, Nov. 5, 1952; s. James Robert and Dolores M. Salazar; B.B.A., N.Mex. State U., 1975; m. Yolanda Ann Padilla, May 14, 1954. Mktg. trainee IBM, Midland, Tex., 1975, systems engr., 1976, mktg. rep., San Angelo, Tex., 1977-79; v.p. L. C. Buchanan and Assos., Inc., San Angelo, 1979—. Mem. Am. Mgmt. Assn. Democrat. Roman Catholic. Club: Paul Thorpe's. Office: 2819 Loop 306 Suite 104 San Angelo TX 76901

SALCH, STEVEN CHARLES, lawyer; b. Palm Beach, Fla., Oct. 25, 1943; s. Charles Henry and Helen Louise (Alverson) S.; B.B.A., So. Methodist U., 1965, J.D., 1968; m. Mary Ann Prim, Oct. 7, 1967; children—Susan Elizabeth, Stuart Trenton. Admitted to Tex. bar, 1968, since practiced in Houston; partner firm Fulbright & Jaworski,

1975—; moot ct. instr. So. Meth. U. Law Sch., 1967-68. Treas. Tex. Intercollegiate Students Assn., 1964-65. Mem. Am. (chmn. subcom. trial and pre-trial matters, taxation sect. 1972-73; chmn. com. ct. procedure 1975-77, spl. adv. 1977-79; chmn. subcom. current devels. 1970-72), Houston bar assns., Internat. Fiscal Assn., State Bar Tex., Harris County Heritage Soc., Order of Coif, Phi Eta Sigma, Beta Alpha Psi, Phi Delta Phi. Clubs: Briar, Westside Tennis (Houston). Contbr. articles to legal jours. Mng. editor Southwestern Law Jour., 1967-68; asso. editor Tax Lawyer, 1970-71-73-75. Home: 342 Tamerlaine Houston TX 77024 Office: 600 Bank of Southwest Bldg Houston TX 77002

SALE, TOM S., III, fin. economist, educator; b. Haynesville, La., July 27, 1942; s. Thomas and Mary Belle (Fagg) S.; B.A., Tulane U., 1964; M.A., Duke, 1965; Ph.D., La. State U., 1972; m. Liza Spivey, July 13, 1966; children—Thomas Sanderson IV, Jennifer Elizabeth, Sarah Elaine. Mem. faculty La. Tech. U., Ruston, 1965—, prof. econs., 1975—, head dept. econs. and fin., 1974—. Bd. dirs. La. Council for Econ. Edn., 1974—. Mem. Am., So. econ. assns., Am. Fin. Assn., Dallas Assn. Fin. Analysts, Omicron Delta Kappa, Omicron Delta Epsilon. Episcopalian. Contbr. articles to profl. jours. Home: 2203 Winchester Ruston LA 71270 Office: Louisiana Tech U Ruston LA 71272

SALERNO, CHARLES ANTHONY, assn. exec.; b. N.Y.C., Nov. 10, 1934; s. Ignatius Charles and Lena Fortunato S.; LL.B., LaSalle Extension U., 1966; B.A., Fla. Internat. U., 1977; m. Jan. 19, 1955; children—Kathi, Donna, Charles, Christine. Police officer City of Miami (Fla.), 1956-77; exec. sec. Fla. lodge Fraternal Order of Police, Tallahassee, 1977—; lectr. Fla. A. and M. U., Fla. Internat. U. Mem. Indsl. Relations Research Assn., Miami Fraternal Order of Police. Democrat. Roman Catholic. Club: Elks. Home: Route 3 Box 579C Tallahassee FL 32308 Office: Fraternal Order of Police 107 E Call St Tallahassee FL 32301

SALET, EUGENE ALBERT, ret. army officer, coll. adminstr.; b. Standish, Calif., May 25, 1911; s. August and Marie (Irigary) S.; B.A., U. Nev., 1934, LL.D. (hon.), 1968; LL.D. (hon.), Dickinson Law Sch., 1966; m. Irene Taylor, June 13, 1936; children—Suzette Taylor Salet Cook, Eugene Michael. Commd. 2d lt. U.S. Army, 1934, advanced through grades to maj. gen., 1963, ret., 1970; trust devel. officer 1st Nat. Bank & Trust Co., Augusta, Ga., 1970-73; pres. Ga. Mil. Coll., Milledgeville, 1973—. Decorated D.S.M., Silver Star, Legion of Merit with 3 oak leaf clusters, Bronze Star with 2 oak leaf clusters; Mil. Valor Cross (Italy), Croix de Guerre (France), Fourragere (France). Mem. Internat. Platform Assn., So. Assn. Colls. and Schs., 3d Inf. Div. Assn., VFW, Ret. Officers Assn., Nat. Assn. Uniformed Services, C. of C. Republican. Roman Catholic. Clubs: Kiwanis; Harvard (Atlanta). Home: Route 1 Box 104-75 Eatonton GA 31024 Office: 201 E Greene St Milledgeville GA 31061

SALINAS, CYNTHIA MARIE, home economist; b. Laredo, Tex., June 18, 1948; d. Frank T. and Hortencia (Zamora) S.; B.S., Southwest Tex. State U., 1970. Home economist Central Power & Light Co., Laredo, Tex., public affairs rep., Corpus Christi, Tex.; now consumer cons., San Benito, Tex. Mem. Am. Home Econs. Assn., Tex. Home Econs. Assn., Home Economists in Bus., Elec. Women's Roundtable. Roman Catholic. Home: 1608 Sam Houston St Apt F-10 Harlingen TX 78550 Office: Box 1991 San Benito TX 78586

SALINAS, ROMEO, JR., info. specialist; b. Alice, Tex., Apr. 13, 1943; s. Romeo and Maria S.; A.A., DelMar Coll., 1964; B.B.A., Tex. A. and I. U., 1969; m. Maria G. Corpus, Nov. 15, 1969; 1 son, Jesus Javier. Salesman, Sears Roebuck & Co., Corpus Christi, Tex., 1969-71; mgr. Circle K Corp., Corpus Christi, 1971-72; info. specialist Groce Wearden Co., Victoria, Tex., 1972—. Democrat. Roman Catholic. Home: 303 E Brazos Victoria TX 77901 Office: 204 N Brownson Victoria TX 77901

SALISBURY, BRIAN GREGORY, physician; b. Phila., Apr. 12, 1944; s. Gregory Bonderenko and Arden Rose (Auerbach) S.; B.A. magna cum laude, Haverford Coll., 1966; M.D., U. Pa., 1970; m. Susan Vilma Nielsen, Feb. 20, 1972; 1 son, David Byron. Intern, U. Miami Med. Center, 1970-71, resident, 1971-72; pulmonary fellowship U. Pa., 1972-74; practice internal medicine, specializing in pulmonary disease, Clearwater, Fla., 1976—; med. dir. respiratory therapy dept. Morton F. Plant Hosp., Clearwater, 1976—; clin. asst. prof. medicine U. South Fla., Tampa, 1977-78. Served with USAF, 1974-76. Diplomate Am. Bd. Internal Medicine, Am. Bd. Pulmonary Disease. Fellow Am. Coll. Chest Physicians; mem. A.C.P., Am. Thoracic Soc., Phi Beta Kappa. Jewish. Home: 2390 Kent Pl Clearwater FL 33516 Office: 1013 Lotus Path Clearwater FL 33516

SALK, GARY CLIVE, psychologist; b. Detroit, Mar. 6, 1944; s. Alvin Henry and Dorothy Eileen (Collins) S.; B.S., Mich. State U., 1966; M.A., U. Iowa, 1969; Ph.D., U. Louisville, 1975; m. Martha Louise Scheer, Feb. 4, 1967; 1 son, Carl Frederick. Psychologist, Diagnostic and Detention Center, Louisville, 1972-73; psychol. intern Wichita (Kans.) VA Hosp., 1973-74; staff psychologist Wernersville (Pa.) State Hosp., 1974-75; pvt. practice clin. psychology, Oak Ridge, 1976—; cons. Community Services for Exceptional Children, Oak Ridge. Bd. dirs. Five County Mental Health Assn., 1975—, Tenn. Mental Health Assn., Oak Ridge Civic Music Assn., 1976—, Oak Ridge Arts Council. Lic. clin. psychologist, Tenn. Mem. Am., Tenn. psychol. assns., AAAS, Assn. Advancement Behavior Therapy. Quaker. Home: 117 Lancaster Rd Oak Ridge TN 37830 Office: 14-3 Ten-kuki Bldg Oak Ridge TN 37830

SALMON, FINNIS LARRY, lawyer; b. Rome, Ga., Mar. 29, 1938; s. Finnis Cartwright and Bonnie (Smith) S.; student Ga. Inst. Tech., 1956-57; B.B.A., U. Ga., 1962, J.D., 1963; grad. Nat. Coll. D.A.'s, 1973; m. Sally Frances Meroney, July 23, 1961; children—Stacy Leigh, Finnis Kevin. Admitted to Ga. bar, 1962; with Legal Aid Dept., Athens, Ga., 1962-63; practice law, Rome, 1963-69; asst. solicitor gen., Rome, 1966-69; dist. atty. Rome Judicial Circuit, 1969—. Vice chmn. Pros. Atty.'s Council of Ga., 1975-76, chmn., 1979; mem. Ga. Jud. Planning Com., Ga. Crime Commn. Mem. exec. com. Floyd County Democratic Assn., 1973; pres. Young Democrats of Floyd County, 1967; treas. Young Democrats Ga., 1967; chmn. Ga. delegation Nat. Conv. Young Democrats Am., 1968, Southeastern region dir., 1968-69. Recipient young Democrat of year award Young Democrats of Floyd County, 1968. Mem. Am., Rome bar assns., State Bar Ga. (chmn. criminal law sect. 1973-74), Nat., Ga. (mem. exec. com. 1973, pres. 1976, Disting. Service award 1979) dist. attys. assns., Floyd-Polk County Young Lawyers Sect. (pres. 1973-74), Am. Judicature Soc., Rome Area, Rome Jr. chambers commerce, Phi Delta Phi, Alpha Tau Omega. Baptist. Elk, Optimist. Club: Floyd Ruritan. Home: Route 1 Rome GA 30161 Office: Floyd County Courthouse Rome GA 30161

SALOOM, KALISTE JOSEPH, JR., judge; b. Lafayette, La., May 15, 1918; s. Kaliste and Asma (Boustany) S.; B.A. with high distinction, Southwestern La. U., 1939; J.D., Tulane U., 1942; m. Yvonne Adele Nassar, Oct. 19, 1958; children—Kaliste Joseph III, Douglas, Leanne, Gregory John. Admitted La. bar, 1942; pvt. practice, 1942—; city atty. Lafayette, 1948-52, city judge, 1953—. Mem. judicial council La. Supreme Court. Chmn. La. Parish Draft Bd., 1950-71; mem. La. Youth Commn., 1958-72, chmn., 1970-72; mem. com. cts., codes and laws La. Hwy. Safety Commn.; mem. Nat. Com. on Uniform Traffic Laws, Washington, 1975—; mem. La. Pub. Affairs Research Council; chief U.S. del. World Congress Christian Bros. Sch. Alumni, Spain, 1964, Can., 1967; del. White House Conf. on Children and Youth, 1960; invitee 1st Nat. Conf. on Bail and Criminal Justice, Dept. Justice, Washington, 1963; chmn. com. on traffic law revision Jud. Council of La. Supreme Ct.; mem. U.S. Dept. Transp. Nat. Hwy. Safety Adv. Com., 1977—; Am. Bar Assn. rep. to adv. com. model non-resident violators compact Council State Govts., 1977. Dir. La. Gulf Coast Oil Expn.; exec. bd. Evangeline area council Boy Scouts Am.; mem. bd. dirs. United Givers Fund, S.W. La. Mardi Gras Assn., United Democrates La., 1957-59; trustee Am. Lebanon-Syrian Asso. Charities, 1957-65; founder Lafayette Area Safety Council, 1961; mem. bd. Lafayette Mental Health Assn.; bd. dirs. Nat. Center for State Cts., Williamsburg, Va., 1977—, Lafayette Diocese Cath. Youth Orgn. Served as spl. agt. CIC, U.S. Army, 1942-45. Recipient Alumni award U. Southwestern La., 1939, grant-in-aid Esso Safety Found., Traffic Safety Conf., 1958, award traffic safety program Am. Bar Assn., 1958, 59, 61, 63, 64, Lafayette Civic Cup award, 1965; named Man of Year, Salvation Army, 1966. Fellow Law-Science Acad. Am.; mem. Am. (lectr. traffic ct. advance seminars, mem. traffic ct. program, standards of criminal justice, automobile law coms. 1975—, mem. asso. and adv. com., recipient Outstanding Traffic Ct. judge award 1969), Lafayette (pres. 1955-56) bar assns., Am. Judicature Soc., Nat., La. (pres. 1963-64) councils juvenile court judges, N.Am. (bd. govs. 1969—), Am. (bd. govs. 1973—), La. City judges assns. (past pres.), La. Law Inst. (adv. com.), Am. Legion (judge adv. La. 1953-56), La. Conf. Social Welfare (dir. 1961), Nat. Inst. Municipal Law Officers, World Assn. Judges, S.W. La. Univ. Alumni Assn. (pres. 1959—), Nat. Council on Crime and Delinquency, Nat. Council Spl. Ct. Judges (chmn. traffic ct. com. 1975—), Nat. Council Municipal Judges, La. Hist. Soc., Council for Devel. of French in La. (pres. Lafayette Parish chpt. 1975), Blue Key, Order Coif, Kappa Sigma, Pi Gamma Mu, Pi Kappa Delta, Alpha Phi Omega, Phi Alpha Theta, Phi Kappa Phi. Clubs: Knife and Fork (dir.), Lafayette Town House (dir.), Rotary. Author: Traffic Court Judge's Check List, 1965; also articles. Home: 502 Marguerite Blvd Lafayette LA 70501 Office: 211 W Main St Lafayette LA 70501

SALT, ALBERT ALEXANDER, wood products co. exec.; b. Corona, N.Y., July 14, 1920; s. Albert Edward and Elizabeth (Glass) S.; B.S., U. Ga., 1942; M.F., Yale, 1947; m. Gertrude Essig, June 19, 1947; children—Gary Craig, Alger Dean. Apprentice, children—Atticus John, Mason Paul. Co., 1947, lab. technician, 1947-49, dir. quality control, 1952-54; v.p., mgr. Cape Fear Wood Preserving, Inc., Fayetteville, N.C., 1954-57; pres., mgr. Salt Wood Products, Inc., Cove City, N.C., 1957—; dir. Br. Banking & Trust Co., Trenton, N.C. 4-H adult leader, Cove City and Craven County, N.C., 1959—; organizer Ruritan and Vol. Fire Dept., Cove City, 1959-60; mem. steering com. Craven Tech. Inst., 1960. Served to capt. AUS, 1943-46; ETO. Decorated Bronze Star. Mem. Forest Products preservers assns., Forest Products Research Soc., Asso. Gen. Contractors Am., Soc. Am. Foresters, Quality Wood Preservers Soc., Am., N.C. (pres. 1972-73) wood preservers assns., U. Ga., Yale alumni assns., 2d Cav. Assn. (life), Blue Key, Xi Sigma Pi, Alpha Zeta. Mason; mem. Order Eastern Star. Club: Quaker Neck Golf and Country (membership and finance com. 1966—'. Office: PO Box 68 Cove City NC 28523

SALTER, ADELE SARAH BODKER (MRS. ROGER NOBLE SALTER), librarian; b. Ponchatoula, La., Mar. 9, 1915; d. Albert John and Sarah Caroline (Bendix) Bodker; B.A., Newcomb Coll., 1936; B.S. in L.S., La. State U., 1952; m. Roger Noble Salter, Jan. 9, 1971. Tchr., Ponchatoula (La.) High Sch., 1936-39; asst. Ponchatoula br. Tangipahoa Parish Library, 1949-53, librarian Tangipahoa Parish Library, Amite, La., 1953-79. Mem. S.W., La. (chmn. pub. library sec. 1961) library assns., Beta Phi Mu. Democrat. Presbyn. Home: Box 236 Ponchatoula LA 70454

SALTER, METHVIN THOMSON, educator; b. Atlanta, Nov. 27, 1925; s. Freeman Daniel and Nell Miller (Lovelace) S.; student Emory U., 1943-44; B.F.A., U. Ga., 1948, M.F.A., 1950, Ed.S., 1970. Tchr., Wardlaw Jr. High Sch., Columbia, S.C., 1950-52, LaGrange (Ga.) High Sch., 1952-53, S.W. High Sch., Atlanta, 1953-63; resource tchr. Atlanta Public Schs., 1963-65, coordinator art, 1965-66; asst. prof. Kennesaw Coll., Marietta, Ga., 1966-75, asso. prof. art, 1975—; tchr. Chapman Coll. World Campus Afloat, 1966; one-man shows LaGrange Coll., 1953, Oglethorp Coll., 1962, Artists Assos. Gallery, Atlanta, 1963, 77, Valdosta State Coll., 1965-70, 77, West Ga. Coll., 1969, West Ga. Regional Library, 1969, 78, Marietta Fine Arts Center, 1978, Kennesaw Coll., 1967, 72, 79. Served with U.S. Army, 1944-46. Fulbright grantee Italy, 1970. Mem. AAUP, Coll. Art Assn., Southeastern Arts Assn., Ga. Art Edn. Assn. (pres. 1950), Assn. Ga. Artists, Atlanta Art Assn., Marietta Fine Arts Club. Methodist. Home: 3197 Tower View Dr Atlanta GA 30324 Office: Kennesaw Coll Marietta GA 30061

SALTZ, MARK LAWRENCE, architect; b. Bklyn., Aug. 11, 1949; s. Isaac Harry and Sidel (Jurofsky) S.; B. Arch., CCNY, 1972; m. Gail Pons, June 4, 1972; children—Lisa, Jennifer. Sr. draftsman Rudolph L. Melk, Architect, Valley Stream, N.Y., 1972-73; job capt., Sandrow Assos., Miami, 1973-74; project architect, office mgr. James M. Hartley, Architect, Hollywood, Fla., 1974-77; propr. Mark L. Saltz, Architect, Hollywood, 1978—. Registered architect Fla., cert. gen. contractor Fla.; cert. Nat. Council Archtl. Registration Bds. Mem. AIA (corp.; chpt. Honor award 1979), South Broward Bus. Council, Constrn. Specifications Inst. Democrat. Club: Odd Fellows (Bklyn.). Office: 5900 Johnson St Hollywood FL 33021

SALTZBERG, BERNARD, biomed. engr., biomathematician; b. Chgo., Apr. 21, 1919; s. David and Pearl (Weiss) S.; B.S., Ill. Inst. Tech., 1952, M.S., 1953; Ph.D., Marquette U., 1973; m. Evalyn Freidin, Oct. 17, 1942; children—Steven, Larry, Dale, Eugene, Gwen. Research engr. Am. Television Co., Chgo., 1946-53, Am. Machine & Foundry Corp., Chgo., 1953-56; mem. sr. sci. staff Ramo-Wooldridge Space Tech. Lab., Los Angeles, 1956-60; sr. scientist Bissett-Berman Corp., Santa Monica, Calif., 1960-65; dir. div. of med. computing scis., Sch. of Medicine, Tulane U., New Orleans, 1967-69, prof. biomath. dept. psychiatry and neurology, 1965-76; head info. analysis sect. Tex. Research Inst. Mental Scis., Houston, 1976—; prof. U. Tex. Med. Sch., Houston, Baylor Coll. Medicine; adj. prof. biomed. engring. Rice U.; adj. prof. psychophysiology U. Houston; prin. investigator Air Force EEG research contract Aeromed. Lab., Wright-Patterson AFB, Dayton, Ohio, 1954-56. Recipient Schleider Scholar award, 1963. Registered profl. engr., Ill. Mem. Am. EEG Soc., Neuroelectric Soc., Soc. of Biol. Psychiatry, AAAS, IEEE, Computer and Biomath. Scis., Biomed. Engring. Soc., Soc. for Neurosci. Contbr. numerous articles on biophysics, brain research, and encephalography to profl. jours. Patentee in field. Home: 7449 Brompton Rd Houston TX 77025 Office: 1300 Moursund St Houston TX 77030

SALTZMAN, BENJAMIN NATHAN, physician; b. Ansonia, Conn., Apr. 24, 1914; s. Joseph N. and Frances (Levine) S.; A.B., U. Oreg., 1935, M.A., 1936, M.D., 1940; m. Ruth Elizabeth Bohan, Dec. 19, 1941; children—Sue Ann, John Joseph, Mark Stephen. Intern Gorgas Hosp., Ancon, C.Z., 1941, resident, 1942; pvt. practice, Mountain Home, Ark., 1946-74; past mem. staffs Mountain Home, Ark., Boone County Hosp., Harrison, Ark., Marion County Hosp., Yellville, Ark.; past chief of staff Baxter Gen. Hosp.; pres. Saltzman-Guenthner Clinic Ltd.; preceptor Sch. Medicine, U. Ark., Little Rock, also asso. clin. prof., 1972-74, prof., chmn. dept. family and community medicine Med. Center, 1974-76, dir. rural med. devel. programs, 1976—, coordinating dir. family practice programs Coll. Medicine, 1977-78; mem. staff Univ. Hosp., St. Vincent Hosp., Ark. Bapt. Med. Center, Ark. Children's Hosp., Little Rock VA Hosp. (all Little Rock). Mem. Ark. Bd. Health, 1972-80, pres., 1976-77; mem. Gov.'s Health Council Ark.; mem. rev. com. Community Health Services, Washington, 1965-67; mem. Gov.'s Com. on Mental Retardation, Ark., 1962-66, Ark. Comprehensive Health Planning Council, 1967-70, Gov.'s Adv. Council Developmental Disabilities, 1970—, Gov.'s Adv. Council on Community Mental Health Centers; Baxter County health officer, Mountain Home, 1948-74. Pres. Ark. Tb Assn., 1958-63, nat. rep. dir., pres. So. Tb Conf., 1969-70; past pres., dir. Tri-States Assn. for Cripples, 1959-60; pres. bd. Ozark Regional Mental Center, 1970-74; mem. bd. Baxter County Day Service Center; bd. dirs. Ark. Health Systems Found., 1974-76, Ark. Regional Med. Program, 1969-76; alderman Mountain Home City Council, 1947-52; bd. dirs. First Ark. Devel. Finance Corp, Hosp. Crippled Adults, Memphis, 1969—; bd. dirs., regional v.p. Nat. Assn. Retarded Citizens; pres. Ark. div. Am. Cancer Soc., 1970-71, Ark. Assn. Retarded Children, 1971-73; pres. Ark. Endowment for Humanities, 1979-80. Served from lt. to capt. AUS, 1942-46; lt. col. USAF Res. ret. Named Man of Year, Ark. Conf. Tb Workers, 1960, Ark. Democrat, 1975; recipient outstanding award Nat. Tb Assn., 1961, Will Ross medal Am. Lung Assn., 1979. Diplomate Am. Bd. Family Practice. Fellow Am. Acad. Family Physicians; mem. Ark. Acad. Gen. Practice (pres. 1954-55), Ark. Med. Soc. (pres. 1974-75), World, Am. (chmn. council rural health), So. Ark. (treas.), Baxter County (past pres., sec.), Pulaski County med. assns., Am., Ark. thoracic socs., Am., Ark. (Tom T. Ross award 1975; outstanding achievement award) pub. health assns., Am. Sch. Health Assn. (com. mem.), Aeromed. Assn., Assn. Mil. Surgeons, Ark. Heart Assn. (dir. 1972-76, 79—), Ark. Soc. for Clin. Hypnosis (pres. 1978-80), Ark. Gerontol. Soc. (dir. 1971-75), Res. Officers Assn., Am. Legion (former comdr.), Flying Physicians Assn. (nat. v.p.), Mountain Home C. of C. (pres. 1954-56, 65-67), V.F.W., Sigma Xi. Democrat. Unitarian. Mason (Shriner), Elk (pres. Ark.), Rotarian (dist. gov. 1952-54, pres. Mountain Home, 1949, internat. dir. 1961-63, trustee Internat. Found. 1965-67; Paul Harris award 1973, internat. chmn. health, hunger and humanity com. 1978-80). Home: PO Box 823 Mountain Home AR 72653 Office: 4301 W Markham St Slot 592 Little Rock AR 72205

SALTZMAN, HERMAN, lawyer; b. New Haven, Jan. 29, 1916; s. Joseph N. and Frances (Levin) S.; A.B., U. Fla., 1940; J.D., John B. Stetson U., 1950; m. Irene P. Cameron, Mar. 21, 1946; children—Martin Howard (dec.), Arlene Norma. Enlisted USAAF, 1941, commd., 1942, advanced through grades to lt. col., 1962; served PTO and CBI, 1943-45, Germany and Morocco, 1953-56; former staff judge adv. Moody AFB, Ga.; staff judge adv., Kadena AFB, Okinawa, 1962-63; chief mil. justice div. Amarillo Tech. Tng. Center, Texas, 1963-66; ret., 1966; practice law, Jacksonville, Fla., 1966—. Fellow Internat. Biog. Assn.; mem. Am., Jacksonville bar assns., Trial Lawyers Assn., Fla. Bar, Am. Judicature Soc., Judge Adv. Assn. Mason (Shriner). Home: 2701 Ocean Dr S Jacksonville Beach FL 32250 Office: Saltzman Bldg Jacksonville FL 32202

SALTZMAN, JACK DAVID, elec. co. exec.; b. N.Y.C., Aug. 4, 1920; s. Morris and Regina (Bauch) S.; B.S. in Elec. Engring., N.Y.U., 1940; m. Margaret Decker, Nov. 4, 1960; children—Mark David, Lisa Rachel, Ira Robert. Engr., Fischbach & Moore, Inc., 1940-48, chief engr., project mgr., 1948; chmn. bd. Tujax Industries, Inc., Artcraft Elec. Supply Del., Artcraft Elec. Supply Md., Consol. Elec. Supply Co., Orlando, Fla., Consol. Elec. Supply, Bradenton, Consol. Elec. Supply Co., Miami, Consol. Elec. Supply, Ft. Lauderdale, Bradenton, and Ft. Myers, Fla., Major Elec. Supply, Ft. Pierce, Stuart, Fla.; treas. Mid Eastern Funding, Union, Seigler Assos., East Orange, N.J., Mansion Assos., N.Y.C.; v.p. Hwy. Leasing Corp., Jersey City, Hwy. Terminal Corp., Jersey City, Mid-Eastern Funding, East Orange; pres. M.R. Saltzman, Deal. Chmn., Israel Bond Dr., Deal. Hon. chmn. bd. Hillel Sch., N.J., Monmouth County YW-YMHA; hon. chmn. bd., v.p. Jewish Hosp. and Rehab. Center N.J.; bd. dirs. Kingsbrook Jewish Med. Center, Bklyn., Hillel Community Day Sch., Miami, Jewish Fedn., Salvation Army, Jersey City, Fight for Sight; a founder Technion Inst. Israel; trustee, prin. Saltzman Found. Home: 5210 N 35th St Hollywood FL 33021

SALYER, KENNETH EVERETT, plastic surgeon; b. Kansas City, Kans., Aug. 18, 1936; s. Everett A. and Laurene S.; B.S., U. Mo. at Kansas City, 1958; M.D., U. Kans., 1962; m. Shaaron K. Steeby, Aug. 27, 1958; children—Kenneth Everett, Amy Leigh. Intern Parkland Meml. Hosp., Dallas, 1962-63, resident in surgery, 1963-67; prof., chmn. div. plastic surgery U. Tex. Health Sci. Center, Dallas, 1969-78; practice medicine specializing in plastic surgery, Dallas, 1978—; chmn. Plastic Surgery Research Council and Sr. Residents Conf., 1978-79. Fellow A.C.S.; mem. Am. Cleft Palate Assn., Am. Soc. Plastic and Reconstructive Surgeons, Am. Assn. Plastic Surgeons, Plastic Surgery Research Council, AMA (Hektoen Gold medal 1977). Editor: (with Mustarde, Tessier and Callahan) Plastic Surgery in the Orbital Region, 1976. Office: 3600 Gaston St Suite 1157 Dallas TX 75246

SALYER, PAUL HUDSON, coal co. exec.; b. Royalton, Ky., Nov. 29, 1930; s. Ollie and Fannie (Adams) S.; student pub. schs., Salyersville, Ky.; m. Marcella K. Hensley, Aug. 7, 1971; children—Donald P., Joe A. Owner, mgr. Gulf Service Sta., Salyersville, 1957-67, Salyer Excavating Co., 1965-73, Salyer Coal Co., 1974—; pres., owner Coastline Coal Corp., Salyersville, 1973—. Mem. city council City of Salyersville, 1963, mayor, 1964-65. Democrat. Baptist. Clubs: Kiwanis, Sportsman, Shriners. Home: PO Box 433 Salyersville KY 41465

SAMAHA, FRANCIS JOSEPH, periodontist; b. Washington, Apr. 16, 1928; s. Toufig Nickolas and Edna (George) S.; D.D.S., Georgetown U., 1951; m. Lili Ann Sheahin, July 4, 1951; children—Jeffrey F., Gary M., Lisa M., Richard G.; m. 2d, Gina A. Rota, Sept. 15, 1973; 1 dau., Nina M. Commd. 2d lt. USAF, 1950, advanced through grades to col., 1968; intern Fitzsimmons Army Hosp., Denver, 1951-52; assigned Bergstrom AFB, Tex., 1952-56; resident Tufts U., Boston, 1956-58; assigned Ramey AFB, P.R., 1958-61, Andrews AFB, Md., 1961-69, Clark Air Base, Philippines, 1969-70; ret., 1970; practice dentistry, 1970—; asso. prof., dir. grad. periodontics Georgetown U., Washington, 1970-72, U. Md., 1972-73. Cons. to surgeon gen. USAF, 1961-69; nat., internat. lectr. in field. Pres., Holy Name Soc., Bergstrom AFB, 1955-56; coach, mgr. Little League Baseball, Andrews AFB, 1961-64. Bd. dirs. Prince Georges County Boys Club, 1965-67. Decorated Legion of Merit, Commendation medal; diplomate Am. Bd. Periodontology. Fellow Am. Coll. Dentists, Am. Acad. Occlusodontia; mem. Am. Dental Assn., Am. Acad. Oral Medicine, Am. Acad. Periodontology, Am. Acad. Oral Pathology, Greater Washington Soc. Periodontology (sec. 1964-66, pres.-elect 1966-67, pres. 1967-68), Va. Dental Assn. (del. 1977—), Omicron Kappa Upsilon. Melkite Catholic. Home: 1551 Dunterry Pl McLean VA 22101 Office: 6845 Elm St Suite 607 McLean VA 22101

SAMANIE, DONALD PAUL, JR., oilfield equipment mfg. co.; b. Big Spring, Tex., Mar. 11, 1944; s. Donald Paul and Marie (Long) S.; B.A. (football scholarship 1962-66), Harding Coll., Searcy, Ark., 1966; M.A. (Dept. Labor fellow manpower tng. 1966-68), Okla. State U., 1968; m. Linda Carol Johnson, Sept. 6, 1966; children—Julie Rene, Tracie Marie. Plant mgr. Gearhart-Owen Industries, Inc., Scranton, Pa., 1973-76; chmn. bd., v.p. subs. GOEX, Inc., Scranton, 1976-77, chmn. bd., 1978—; chmn. bd. Gen. Tex. Corp., also dir.; v.p. Pengo Industries Inc., Ft. Worth, 1978—; dir. Peck-o-Matic Inc. Served to capt. USAF, 1968-73; Vietnam. Mem. Am. Mgmt. Assn. Republican. Mem. Ch. of Christ. Home: 712 Portofino St Arlington TX 76012 Office: Pengo Industries Inc 1400 Everman Pkwy Fort Worth TX 76140

SAMARITAN, GEORGETTE ASEFF, health edn. ofcl.; b. Atlanta, Nov. 13, 1948; d. George Vincent and Bettie (Mansour) A.; B.S., Ga. Inst. Tech., 1971; R.N., Ga. State U., 1973, B.S.N., 1975; m. Louis Anthony Samaritan, Nov. 4, 1978. Staff nurse intensive care Med. Service, Grady Meml. Hosp., Atlanta, 1973-75; patient/consumer health edn. coordinator DeKalb Gen. Hosp., Decatur, Ga., 1975—; cons. in field. Active anti-smoking clinics Am. Cancer Soc. Recipient award Ga. Hosp. Public Relations Soc., 1979. Mem. Ga. Heart Assn., Am. Assn. Diabetes Educators, Ga. Nurses Assn. 5th. Dist., Mortar Bd., Sigma Theta Tau (sec.-historian chpt. 1976—, newsletter editor 1978—). Roman Catholic. Club: Cath. Alumni (pres. Atlanta chpt. 1977-78). Author booklets for patients: Chemotherapy, 1978; Rehabilitation After Stroke, 1979; developer audiovisual program for post-mastectomy patients, 1977. Office: DeKalb Gen Hosp 2701 N Decatur Rd Decatur GA 30033

SAMFORD, FRANK PARK, JR., life ins. co. exec.; b. Montgomery, Ala., Jan. 29, 1921; s. Frank Park and Hattie (Noland) S.; student Auburn U., 1937-38; B.A., Yale, 1942; LL.B., U. Ala., 1947; m. Virginia Carolyn Suydam, May 27, 1942; children—Frank Park III, Laura Alice, John Singleton Pitts, Mae Virginia. With Liberty Nat. Life Ins. Co., Birmingham, Ala., 1947—, v.p., 1955-60, pres., 1960-73, chmn. bd., 1973—, also dir.; dir. Golden Enterprises, S. Central Bell Telephone Co., Ala. Great So. R.R. Co., So. Co., Saunders Leasing System, Inc. Pres. Ala. Safety Council, 1968-70. Past exec. com. Am. Life Conv.; past chmn. Life Insurers. Conf., 1970; chmn. Jefferson County United Appeal, 1963. Bd. dirs. Jefferson County Community Chest pres., 1965-66; bd. govs. Indian Springs Sch., Helena, Ala.; trustee Auburn U. Served to lt. (s.g.) USNR, 1942-45. Mem. Assn. C.L.U.'s, Ala. Assn. Ind. Colls. and Univs. (gov.), Alpha Tau Omega, Phi Delta Phi, Berzelius. Presbyterian. Clubs: Rotary, Birmingham Country, Mountain Brook Country (Birmingham). Office: 2001 Third Ave S Birmingham AL 35202

SAMFORD, MAURYCE STACY, architect; b. Denison, Tex., Dec. 11, 1922; s. Ocie Lee and Lucy Jane (Willig) S.; student Austin Coll., 1947-49; B.S., U. Houston, 1951; m. Betty June Rich, Oct. 5, 1946; children—Gregory Mark, Jeffrey Dale, Todd Stacy. Architect firm Charles Oliver, Architect, Houston, 1950-51; architect U.S. Corp. of Engrs., Galveston, Tex., 1951-52; architect firm Thomas M. Price, Architect, Galveston, 1963-66; resident architect U. Tex. Med. Br., Galveston, 1952-63, 1966—; practice architecture, Galveston, 1967—; res. instr. architecture and engring. Galveston Coll., 1976—. Mem. Elementary Study Com. Galveston Indep. Sch. Dist., 1972—. Served with USAF, 1943-46. Mem. AIA, Tex. Soc. Architects. Baptist (deacon ch. 1957—). Home: 2506 Pine St Galveston TX 77551 Office: The University of Texas Medical Branch Galveston TX 77553

SAMFORD, WILLIAM JAMES, JR., lawyer; b. Opelika, Ala., Feb. 4, 1950; s. William James and Evlyn (Barnett) S.; B.A., Auburn U., 1972; J.D., U. Ala., 1978. Intern fed. dist. judge, Birmingham, Ala., 1977; admitted to Ala. bar, 1978; atty. litigation sect. FDIC, Washington, 1978-80; pres. Ala. Public Service Commn., 1980—; guest lectr. bus. law Brewer State Jr. Coll., Tuscaloosa, Ala., 1977-78. Senator, U. Ala. Sch. Law, 1975-77, senator student govt., 1977-78. Served with USAF, 1972-75. Mem. Am. Bar Assn., Ala. Bar Assn., Am. Trial Lawyers Assn., Ala. Trial Lawyers Assn., Am. Judicature Soc., Arnold Air Soc., Moot Court Bd., Scabbard and Blade, Bench and Bar. Democrat. Methodist. Home: 311 N 9 St Opelika AL 36801

SAMPLE, CHESTER E., athletic dir.; b. Athens, Tex., May 31, 1946; s. William E. and Bessie Sample; B.A., Wayland Coll.; M.S., Sul Ross (Tex.) State U.; Ed.D. (basketball teaching fellow 1973-75), E. Tex. State U.; m. Belinda Kay Sample, June 21, 1969; children—Michael, Denise. Asst. basketball coach Wayland Coll., Sul Ross State U., E. Tex. State U.; head basketball coach Freer High Sch.; chmn. phys. edn. dept. Langston U.; asst. prof. phys. edn., dir. phys. edn. and athletics Sul Ross State U. Served with U.S. Army, 1969-71. Named Coach of Year, TIAA Conf., 1978. Mem. Nat. Assn. Intercollegiate Athletics, AAHPER, Nat. Safety Council, Tex. Assn. Health, Phys. Edn. and Recreation (sec. coll. div.), Tex. Assn. Coll. Tchrs. Methodist. Address: Box C17 Alpine TX 79830

SAMPLE, DOROTHY EATON, state legislator, civic worker; b. Nyack, N.Y., May 1, 1911; d. Samuel Edward and Olive Bowers (Eddy) Eaton; B.A., Duke U., 1933, postgrad. Law Sch.; m. Richard Lardner Sample, Dec. 28, 1939. Admitted to N.C. bar, 1933; sec., firm Edwards & Leatherwood, Bryson City, N.C., 1933-34; atty. Home Owners Loan Corp., Salisbury, N.C.; sec. and atty. firm Whitlock, Dockery & Shaw, Charlotte, N.C.; mem. Fla. Ho. of Reps., 1976—. Pres. Save Our Bays, PTA, Pasadena Property Owners Assn., Band Boosters; v.p., regional dir. Fla. Wildlife Fedn.; v.p. West St. Petersburg Property Owners Assn.; chmn. Gerontology Council; VIP chmn. Mothers March of Dimes; chmn. Coastal Coordinating Council; founder Alliance for Conservation of Natural Resources; sponsor Jr. Coll. Service Club; legis. chmn. League Women Voters; bd. dirs. Gulf Coast and Fla. Tb Assn., Council Neighborhood Assns., Community Welfare Council, St. Petersburg Hist. Soc., Suncoast Active Vols. for Ecology. Recipient Outstanding Conservationist award Rod and Gun Club, 1967, Ecology award Suncoast Gem and Mineral Soc., 1973, Outstanding Service to Mankind award Sertoma Club, 1974, Spl. Service award Fla. Wildlife Fedn., 1977. Mem. Duke U. Alumni Assn. (chmn.), AAUW (legis. chmn.), Pan Hellenic Assn., Chi Phi, Delta Phi Rho Alpha. Republican. Episcopalian. Club: Sinawik (pres.). Home: 200 Sunset Dr S Saint Petersburg FL 33707 Office: 3110 1st Ave N Saint Petersburg FL 33713

SAMPLE, JACK BRUCE, city ofcl.; b. Chattanooga, Mar. 21, 1945; s. Bruce Dodson and Lillie Marie Sample; B.S. in Personnel Mgmt., U. Tenn., 1967, M.S., 1969; m. Carol Ann Abele, July 28, 1967; children—Anne Marie, David. Mgr. employee relations Champion Internat., Roxbury Inc., Chattanooga, 1972-74; personnel dir. Jackson Mfg. Co., Chattanooga, 1974-75; mgr. personnel and purchasing Phelps Dodge Mocassin Bronze Co., Chattanooga, 1975-77; asst. personnel dir. Electric Power Bd., Chattanooga, 1977—; asst. prof. Cleveland (Tenn.) State Community Coll., 1970—. Mem. Am. Soc. Personnel Adminstrn. (accredited personnel mgr.), Am. Compensation Assn., Chattanooga Indsl. Personnel Club (pres. 1975-78), Tenn. Valley Public Power Assn. (sec. personnel sect. 1980), Tenn. Indsl. Personnel Assn. Home: 2619 Maromede Ln Chattanooga TN 37421 Office: 537 Cherry St Chattanooga TN 37402

SAMPLES, JOHN CHARLES, music educator; b. Kilgore, Tex., May 4, 1941; s. John T. and Flossie Mae Samples; B.S., Jarvis Christian Coll., 1963; M.A., U. Okla., 1975; m. Mary L. Austin, Sept. 7, 1963; children—Cynthia Michelle, John Charles. Band dir. St. Paul Indsl. Tng. Sch., Malakoff, Tex., 1963-64, Mexia Dunbar High Sch., Mexia, Tex., 1964-66, Dunbar High Sch., Okmulgee, Okla., 1966-70; asst. band dir. Okmulgee High Sch., 1970-73, band dir., 1973—; supr. music Okmulgee Public Schs., 1973—. Named Outstanding Young Man of Am., U.S. Jaycees, 1971. Mem. NEA, Nat. Band Assn., Okla. Band Masters Assn. (pres. 1978-79), Okla. Music Educators, Okla. Educators Assn., Phi Beta Mu (pres. 1980-81), Alpha Phi Alpha. Democrat. Baptist. Club: Masons. Home: 908 E 3rd St Okmulgee OK 74447 Office: Okmulgee High School 3rd and Alabama Okmulgee OK 74447

SAMPSON, DOROTHY VERMELLE, lawyer, social worker; b. Sumter, S.C., Aug. 4, 1920; d. William B. and Bessie Vermelle (Moore) Sampson; B.S. in Edn., Hampton Inst., 1941; M.S.W., Atlanta U., 1952; J.D., N.C. Central U., 1963. Tchr. Durham (N.C.) pub. schs., 1950-52; social worker Ill. Pub. Aid Commn., Chgo.; social worker VA Hosp., Tomah, Wis., 1955-56; admitted to S.C. bar, 1964, U.S. Supreme Ct. bar, 1967; practiced in Sumter; partner firm Sampson & Sampson, Sumter. Mem. S.C. Pub. Welfare Services, Columbia, S.C. Candidate for S.C. Senate, 1968; mem. Sumter Black Caucus. Bd. dirs. YMCA, Sumter. Recipient United Fund award, 1968. Mem. Am. Bar Assn., N.A.A.C.P. Democrat. Club: Progressive Federated. Address: 39 S Washington St Sumter SC 29150

SAMPSON, LARRY LEROY, phys. therapist; b. Harrisonburg, Va., Jan. 13, 1941; s. Emory and Agnes Mearilla (Lam) S.; B.A., U.Va., 1963; cert. in phys. therapy U. Pa., 1964; M.S. in Phys. Therapy, Emory U., 1972; m. Marie Antoinette Weaver, Dec. 13, 1978. Phys. therapist U. Va. Hosp., 1964; pvt. practice phys. therapy, Columbus, Ga., 1967-70; asst. prof., clin. coordinator U. Vt., 1972-77; dir. phys. therapy dept. U. Ala., Birmingham, Ala., 1977—. Served with U.S. Army, 1965-67. Mem. Am. Phys. Therapy Assn., U. Va. Alumni Assn., Nat. Rifle Assn., Am. Bowling Assn. Methodist. Home: 4748 Wine Ridge Ln Birmingham AL 35244 Office: 1717 6th Ave S Birmingham AL 35233

SAMRA, NICHOLAS, career cons. co. exec.; b. Bklyn., May 6, 1917; s. Nicholas and Mary (Reehan) S.; B.A., N.Y. U., 1938; m. Virginia Baroody, Aug. 14, 1942; 1 son, Nicholas Alexander. With Sears, Roebuck & Co., 1939-55, mdse. mgr., N.C. and S.C., 1940-55; store mgr. Charles Stores, Greensboro, N.C., 1955-59; owner-operator Pied Piper Children's Shop, Greensboro, 1959-66; mgr. Zayre Dept. Stores, 1966-67, dist. mgr., 1967-68, mdse. mgr., Riverdale, Ga., 1969-79; v.p. Howard Corp. Exec. Search Firm, Atlanta, 1979—. Served with USAAF, 1942-45. Decorated Bronze Star medal, D.F.C. with 4 oak leaf clusters. Mem. Nat. Assn. Exec. Search Firms, Nat. Retail Mchts. Assn., Am. Legion, VFW, C. of C. Republican. Episcopalian. Home: 6809 Collier Way Riverdale GA 30296 Office: 4151 Memorial Dr Decatur GA 30032

SAMS, DORIS LAVERNE, coll. counselor; b. Youngwood, Pa., Apr. 26, 1926; d. Benjamin F. and Lucinda (Myers) S.; B.A., Seton Hill Coll., Greensburg, Pa., 1950; M.Ed., U. Pitts., 1959. Psychol. intern Inst. Living, Hartford, Conn., 1951; employment interviewer Conn. Employment Service, Thompsonville, 1952; ednl. therapist, grad. asst. U. Pitts., 1964-65; sch. psychologist, spl. edn. tchr. Hempfield Area, Greensburg, Pa., 1953-66; counselor, tchr., psychologist Broward Community Coll., Ft. Lauderdale, Fla., 1966—; leader human potential seminars. Frick scholar, 1956. Mem. Am. Personnel and Guidance Assn., Am. Coll. Personnel Assn., Broward County Psychol. Assn., Ft. Lauderdale Dog Club, Samoyed Club Am. Republican. Home: 1400 SW 19th St Fort Lauderdale FL 33315 Office: Broward Community Coll Fort Lauderdale FL 33314

SAMSELL, L(EWIS) PATRICK, auditor; b. Morgantown, W.Va., Feb. 20, 1943; s. Lewis Hildreth and Harriet Elizabeth (Gidley) S.; B.S. with honors in bus. adminstrn., W.Va. U., 1970; M.B.A., George Washington U., 1975; m. Linda Joyce Hewitt, July 19, 1967. Supervisory auditor U.S. Gen. Accounting Office, Washington, 1971-79; auditor U.S. Dept. Interior, Office of Comptroller for V.I., St. Thomas, 1979—; instr. bus. Prince George's Community Coll., Largo, Md., 1974-77. Mem. SCORE, 1979—; mem. resident camping com. Potomac Area council Camp Fire Girls, 1971-79; bd. dirs. Applewalk Condominium, Laurel, Md., 1975-79. Served with USN, 1964-67. Cert. mgmt. acct. Mem. Nat. Assn. Accountants (dir. Washington and Montgomery-Prince Georges; mem. nat. com. edn. 1980—), Assn. Govt. Accountants, Municipal Fin. Officers Assn., Am. Accounting Assn., Inst. Mgmt. Accounting, Am. Mgmt. Assn., Soc. for Advancement Mgmt., Navy League, W.Va. Soc. of Washington. Episcopalian. Home and Office: PO Box 7730 Saint Thomas VI 00801

SAMUEL, CHARLES (LARRY), lawyer; b. New Orleans, Dec. 27, 1950; s. Charles M. and Suzanne Weil S.; B.A., Transylvania U., 1971; J.D., Loyola U., 1977. Admitted to La. bar, 1977; mem. staff Mayor's Office of Consumer Affairs, New Orleans, 1972-74; law clk. Office of the Dist. Atty., Jefferson Parish, 1975-76; asso. firm Nelson, Nelson & Lombard, New Orleans, 1977—. Pres., La. Consumers League, 1977—; mem. La. Supreme Ct. Jud. Planning Subcom. on Small Claims Cts.; area coordinator Alliance for Good Govt.; mem. New Orleans Coalition. Mem. La. State Bar Assn., La. Trial Lawyers Assn. Office: 144 Elk Pl Suite 1202 New Orleans LA 70112

SAMUEL, CLARENCE RICHARD, educator; b. Magnolia, Ark., Apr. 26, 1919; s. William Edward and Lorene (Roper) S.; B.S.E., So. State Coll., 1953; M. Ednl. Adminstrn., U. Ark., 1958; postgrad. in bus. adminstrn. U. Okla., U. Wyo.; m. Helen Paula Smith, May 14, 1941; children—Linda Kay Samuel Martindale, Martha Ann Samuel Black. Tchr., coach Taylor (Ark.) High Sch., 1939-41; clk., checker Internat. Paper Co., Spring Hill, La., 1941-42; coordinator vocat. studies and vets. tng. Magnolia (Ark.) High Sch., 1946-50; bus. mgr. Magnolia Sch. Dist., 1950-51; instr. mktg. So. Ark. U., Magnolia, 1951-57, asst. prof., 1960-67, asso. prof., 1967—, also mgr. bookstore, 1952-57. Mem. McNeil (Ark.) Town Council, 1946. Served in U.S. Army, 1942-45; ETO. Decorated Bronze Star (2). Mem. Council Distributive Edn., Acad. Mgmt. (SW div.), Southwestern Mktg. Assn., Am. Legion (comdr. McNeil), Phi Delta Kappa. Democrat. Baptist. Office: So Ark U Box 1265 Magnolia AR 71753

SAMUEL, VALIYAVEETIL THOMAS, sociologist; b. India, May 15, 1939; s. Cherian V. and Rachel Thomas; M.Div., Andover Newton Theol. Sch., 1967; S.T.M., Yale U., 1968; Ph.D., Hartford Sem. Found., 1973; m. June 7, 1969; children—Rachel, Thomas, James. Lectr. anthropology Central Conn. State Coll., 1970-71; research asso. So. Asian Inst., Columbia U., 1973-74; asst. prof. sociology and anthropology Grambling (La.) State U., 1974—; ordained minister Christian Meth. Episcopal Ch., 1979. Indian Council Social Sci. Research grantee, 1975. Fellow Am. Anthropol. Assn.; mem. Nat. Assn. Interdisciplinary Ethnic Studies, Nat. Council Family Relations, Southwestern Social Sci. Assn., S.W. Soc. on Aging (charter mem.), Mid-South Sociol. Assn. Author: One Caste, One Religion and One God for Man: A Study of Sree Narayana Guru, 1977. Office: PO Box 491 Grambling LA 71245

SAMUELS, SEYMOUR, JR., lawyer; b. Nashville, Oct. 23, 1912; s. Seymour and Maude Stella (Rosenfeld) S.; B.A., Vanderbilt U., 1933, LL.B., J.D., 1935; m. Essie Schoen Wenar, July 7, 1937; children—Seymour III, Charles Wenar. Admitted to Tenn. bar, 1935, admitted to practice before U.S. Supreme Ct., Supreme Ct. Tenn., U.S. Ct. Appeals 6th Circuit, U.S Dist. Ct. and Trial Cts. Tenn.; practicing atty., 1935-40; partner Samuels & Allen, 1940-42; area rent atty., dep. rent dir. OPA, 1942-43; partner Nashville Bag & Burlap Co., 1946-62; dep. dir. law Met. Govt. of Nashville, 1963-67; with Hooker & Willis, 1967; partner Hooker, Hooker, Willis & Samuels, 1968, Farris, Evans & Evans, 1969-71, Farris, Warfield & Samuels, Nashville, 1972-74; affiliate Schulman, Pride & LeRoy, and predecessor firms, Nashville, 1975—; lectr., met. govt Malone Coll. Mem. Met. Traffic and Parking Commn., 1967-70; chmn. Davidson County Dem. Campaign Com., 1968; mem. Met. Govt. Charter Revision Com.; mem. Tenn. Bot. Gardens and Fine Arts Center, Nashville Symphony Assn., The Temple. Served with USNR, 1943-46. Mem. Am., Tenn., Nashville bar assns., Am. Judicature Soc., Order of Coif, Artus Club, Phi Beta Kappa. Club: Nashville City. Home: 4225 Harding Rd Nashville TN 37205 Office: 501 Union St Nashville TN 37219

SAMUELSON, FRED BINDER, artist, educator; b. Harvey, Ill., Nov. 29, 1925; s. Frederick Gustav and Theresa Marie (Binder) S.; student U. Chgo., 1947-53; B.F.A., Art Inst. Chgo., 1951, M.F.A., 1953; m. Sylvia C. DeBaca, Sept. 22, 1951; children—Fredric Michael, Lisa Maria. Adult edn. Chgo. Park Recreational Program, 1951-53; head lithography dept. Instituto Allende, San Miguel Allende, Guanajuato Mexico, 1955-63, head grad. studies, 1964—; faculty chmn. San Antonio Art Inst., 1963-64; condr. seminars Laredo Art Assn., 1964, 71, 78 Hill Country Art Found., Ingram, Tex., 1967—, Brownsville, Beaumont, Lamesa art leagues, Lubbock Art Assn., San Antonio Watercolor Soc., Laguna Gloria Mus., Austin, Tex.; represented in permanent collection Galeria Moderna, Banjaluka, Yugoslavia; guest lectr. Art League Houston, Art League, Laredo, Tex., Laguna Gloria Art Mus., Austin, Tex.; executed mural for Conv. Center, Hemisfair, 1968. Served with USAAF, 1943-45. Recipient numerous hon. mentions, purchase prizes, 1953—, including Denver Art Mus., Joslyn Art Mus., Omaha, Mulvane Art Mus., Topeka, Okla. Art Center, Hertzberg Gallery, San Antonio, Witte Mus., San Antonio, Ohio U., Athens. Home: 17 Fuentes Apdo 70 San Miguel de Allende Guanajuato Mexico

SANBORN, CHARLES EVAN, chem. engr.; b. Mankato, Minn., July 11, 1919; s. Walter A. and Gertrude Egryn (Evans) S.; student Mankato State Coll., 1935-37; B. Chem. Engr., U. Minn., 1941, Ph.D. (Allied Chem. fellow), 1949; m. Jane Martin McClanahan, June 24, 1941; children—Charles Evan, James Martin, Jane Ann Sanborn Russell, Rachel Elizabeth; m. 2d, Norma L. Young, Mar. 15, 1980. Engr., Shell Devel. Co., Emeryville, Calif., 1949-72, Shell Research N.V., Amsterdam, 1972-73 staff research engr. Shell Devel. Co., Houston, 1973—; mem. faculty U. Calif. Engring. Extension, 1950-55. Served to capt. AUS, 1941-45. Mem. Am. Inst. Chem. Engrs., AAAS, Sigma Xi. Contbr. articles on heat transfer and thermal stability of hydrogen peroxide to profl. jours. Patentee in field. Home: 13706 Chelwood Pl Houston TX 77069 Office: PO Box 1380 Houston TX 77001

SANCHEZ, ALBERTO E., cosmetic plastic surgeon; b. N.Y.C., Sept. 8, 1929; s. Alberto E. and Julia M. (Quinones) S.; B.S., U. P.R., 1950, M.D., 1950; m. Carmen R. Nogueras, Dec. 30, 1968; children—Michelle, Alberto. Intern, Valley Forge Army Hosp., Phoenixville, Pa., 1954-55; resident plastic surgery Baylor U. Med. Center, Houston, 1960-52; pvt. practice plastic surgery, San Juan, P.R., 1962—; dir. Inst. Cosmetic Surgery, Met. Hosp., Rio Piedras, 1971—; attending plastic surgeon Presbyn. Hosp., Santurce. Served with M.C., AUS, 1954-57. Diplomate Am. Bd. Plastic Surgery. Fellow A.C.S.; mem. Am. Soc. Plastic and Reconstructive Surgeons, Am. Soc. Aesthetic Plastic Surgery, Am. Cleft Palate Assn., Puerto Rican Med. Assn. Home: A-22 Harding St Guaynabo PR 00657 Office: Metropolitan Hosp Box EH San Juan PR 00922

SANCHEZ, CANDIDO, mathematician, educator; b. Artemisa, Cuba, Jan. 21, 1938; came to U.S., 1958, naturalized, 1969; s. Adolfo and Lydia M. (Sanchez) S.; A.A., Southwest Bapt. Coll., 1960; B.S., U. Miami, Fla., 1962; Ed.M., U. Md., 1969; M.S. in Math., Notre Dame U., 1972; m. Maria Alonso, Dec. 30, 1966; children—Lydia Maria, Paul Kevin. Tchr. math. High Point High Sch., Beltsville, Md., 1963-72; instr. math. Fla. Internat. U., 1972-76, adj. prof., 1976—; asso. prof. math. Miami Dade Community Coll., Miami, Fla., 1976—, math. instr. bilingual program, New World Campus, 1976-79; guest lectr. M.B.A. program, Ajijic, Mexico, 1979, Boca del Rio, Venezuela, 1977, 78. Choir dir. First Spanish Bapt. Ch., Coral Park, Miami, Fla., 1972-77. Mem. Math. Assn. Am., Nat. Council Tchrs. Math., Fla. Assn. Community Colls. Baptist. Reviewer chpts. in books Dickenson Pub. Co., 1977, Wadsworth Pub. Co., 1978. Home: 11411 SW 2nd St Miami FL 33174 Office: Miami Dade Community College New World Center Miami FL 33132

SANCHEZ, CARMEN MARIA, nurse; b. Manati, P.R., Mar. 21, 1936; d. Jesus and Maria Sanchez; m. Oct. 10, 1962; children—Jorge Torres, Rafael Torres. Gen. duty nurse Arecibo Dist. Hosp., 1958-60, instr. nursing, 1960-62, delivery room supr., 1964-65; nurse midwife Maternal & Child Health Rio Piedras, P.R., 1965-66, asst. dir. nursing services, 1966-70, instr. nursing, 1974-77, dir. nursing dept., 1977—. Mem. Colegio de Profesionales de la Enfermeria de P.R., Public Health Assn. Roman Catholic. Home: E-32 2 Lagos de Plata Catano PR 00632 Office: University Hospital Medical Center Rio Piedras PR 00935

SANCHEZ, FEDERICO FIDENCIO, real estate exec.; b. Havana, Cuba, June 4, 1941; s. Federico P. and Esther C. (Febles) S.; came to U.S., 1958, naturalized, 1963; B.C.E., Rensselaer Poly. Inst., 1962; M.B.A., Harvard, 1968; m. Elisa Ortiz-Brunet, Dec. 19, 1964; children—Federico, Ricardo, Elimari. Civil engr., project mgr. Chgo. Bridge & Iron Co., 1962-66; pres., v.p. various real estate devel. cos., Puerto Rico, 1968-73; pres. Federico F. Sanchez & Co., Villa Clarita Devel. Corp., Ure Corp.; gen. partner Mayaguez Ltd.; pres. FFS Assos., Inc., 1977—; prof. mgmt. U. P.R., 1969-71. Rep. Harvard Bus. Sch.; bd. govs. United Way. Mem. ASCE, Urban Land Inst., Nat. Assn. Realtors, Nat. Assn. Homebuilders (treas., dir.), P.R. Mfrs. Assn. (edn. com.). Roman Catholic. Clubs: Palmas Del Mar, Harvard Bus. Sch. of So. Fla.; Caparra Country; Rotary. Home: Surfide #5 Palmas Del Mar Box 2009 Humacao PR 00661 Office: Suite 1820 Banco Popular Center Hato Rey PR 00918

SÁNCHEZ, GILBERT, educator; b. Carrizo Springs, Tex., Jan. 13, 1945; s. Frank and Eusebia (Peña) S.; A.A., S.W. Tex. Jr. Coll., 1965; B.A., St. Mary's U., San Antonio, 1967; M.A., U. Tex. at San Antonio, 1977. Tchr. elementary sch. San Antonio Ind. Sch. Dist., 1967-68; tchr. English and Spanish West Orange Cove Consol. Ind. Sch. Dist., Orange, Tex., 1968-69 tchr. Spanish, Judson Ind. Sch. Dist., Converse, Tex., 1969-79 Riverside (Calif.) Unified Sch. Dist., 1979; counselor San Antonio Neighborhood Youth Orgn., 1972-73, summers, 1972-75; youth specialist Econ. Opportunities Devel. Corp., San Antonio, 1974-75; advisor Tex. Future Tchrs. Am., San Antonio, 1969-72, dist. co-advisor to officers, 1971-72. Recipient certificates of appreciation chpt. Future Tchrs. Am., 1970, 71, 72, award of Honor,

Pi Sigma Rho, 1970, 71; named Hon. Admiral Tex. Navy, 1971. Mem. Judson (1st v.p. 1972, certificates of appreciation 1971, 72), Tex. (co-chmn. dist. conv. div. future tchrs. sponsors 1970, 71) tchrs. assns., Tex. Classroom Tchrs. Assn., N.E.A., Fgn. Lang. Tchrs. Assn., Kirby Jr. High P.T.A. Home: 2160 Austin Hwy San Antonio TX 78218 Office: 5441 Seguin Rd San Antonio TX 78109

SANCHEZ, GREGORY VALDEZ, engring. technician; b. Weatherford, Tex., Mar. 9, 1942; s. Pete E. and Carmen (Valdez) S.; student Trimble Tech. High Sch.; m. Virginia Rodriquez, Jan. 29, 1965; children—Greg, Ray, Vera, Vivian. With Freese Nichols, Engrs., Fort Worth, 1966-68, Freese, Nichols & Rady & Assos., Fort Worth, 1968-72; civil engr. technician Carter & Burgess, Engr., Fort Worth, 1972-77, U.S. Army C.E., Fort Worth, 1977—. Mem. League United Latin Am. Citizens, Mexican Am. Govt. Employees, Am. Soc. Cert. Engring. Technicians (dir. Fort Worth chpt.). Roman Catholic. Club: Swingers Golf (pres.). Home: 2607 NW 25th St Fort Worth TX 76106 Office: 819 Taylor St Fort Worth TX 76102

SANCHEZ, JORGE ERNESTO, psychiatrist; b. Havana, Cuba, Nov. 7, 1919; s. Jorge J. and Isabel G. (Berriz) S.; B.Sci. and Art, Havana Inst., 1941; M.D. Havana U., 1947; m. Nereida Brito, Sept. 29, 1946; children—Jorge Alfredo, Ernesto Jorge, Nereyda. Intern Univ. Hosp., Havana, 1947-49; pvt. practice, Havana, 1948-61; gen. practice medicine and pediatrics Lawton Clinic. Havana, 1955-61; gen. practice Quinta Dependientes, Havana, 1956-61; staff physician Terrell (Tex.) State Hosp., 1964-67; resident psychiatry Southwestern Med. Sch., Dallas, 1967-70; chief psychiat. unit Terrell State Hosp., 1970-71, clin. dir., 1971—. Mem. Am. Psychiat. Assn., AMA, Tex. Med. Assn., Kaufman County Med. Soc. Roman Catholic. Address: Box 70 Terrell TX 75160

SANCHEZ, MARIA ANNA, nursing adminstr.; b. Corpus Christi, Tex., Sept. 22, 1934; d. Antonio and Angelina (Saenz) Ruiz: A.A., Del Mar Coll., 1974; also postgrad.; m. Faraon Sanchez, May 15, 1954; children—John, Rose, Sharon, Cynthia, Michael. Staff nurse Spohn Hosp., Corpus Christi, 1971-74; staff nurse Meml. Med. Center, Corpus Christi, asst. head nurse coronary care unit, 1976-78, nursing service supr., since 1978. Mem. Am. Nurses Assn., Am. Heart Assn. Home: 1726 Tarlton St Corpus Christi TX 78415

SANCHEZ, ROY, JR., govt. ofcl.; b. Corpus Christi, Tex., Oct. 24, 1933; s. Roy and Matilde (Trujillo) S.; A.A., Del Mar Coll., 1960; B.S., U. Corpus Christi, 1962; A.A.S. in Data Processing, Del Mar Coll., 1973; M.B.A., U. Houston at Clear Lake City, 1977; m. Elvia Ramirez, Aug. 28, 1955; children—Roy C., Elizabeth, Ronald. Supervisory accountant Kelly AFB, Tex., 1962-65; internal revenue agt. Internal Revenue Service, Houston, 1965-76, mgr. field audit group, 1976-79, CEP case mgr., 1979—; instr. adult edn. Del Mar Coll., Corpus Christi, 1972-74, Coll. of Mainland, Texas City, 1977-78, San Jacinto Coll., Pasadena, 1978—. Served with USAF, 1952-56. C.P.A., Tex. Mem. Tex. Soc. C.P.A.s

SANDER, WILLIAM AUGUST, III, electronic engr.; b. Charleston, S.C., May 11, 1942; s. William August, Jr., and Mary Lois (Riddle) S.; B.S.E.E., Clemson U., 1964; M.S.E.E., Duke U., 1967, Ph.D., 1973; m. Helen Rhyne Childress, June 3, 1967; children—Todd Rutledge, Kathryn Elizabeth. Electronic engr. AF Logistics Command, Robins AFB, Ga., 1964; engr. test methodology U.S. Army Airborne Communications and Electronics Bd., Ft. Bragg, N.C., 1972-75, elec. engr. facilities engrs., 1975; elec. engr. U.S. Army Research Office, Research Triangle Park, N.C., 1975—; instr. physics Fayetteville (N.C.) State U., 1974-75. Served with AUS, 1970-72. Decorated Army Commendation medal; recipient W.M. Riggs award, 1964; NASA trainee, 1964-67. Mem. IEEE, Sigma Xi, Tau Beta Pi, Phi Kappa Phi. Club: Kiwanis. Research and publs. on solid-state elec. power conditioning. Home: 3001 Downs Ct Raleigh NC 27612 Office: US Army Research Office PO Box 12211 Research Triangle Park NC 27709

SANDERLIN, CHRISTINA FAUST, indsl. trainer; b. Atlanta, Oct. 29, 1950; d. Henry Charles and Shirley Faye (Birdwell) Faust; B.A., Spring Hill Coll., 1973; postgrad. Ga. State U., 1974—; m. John G. Sanderlin, Sept. 6, 1975. Trainer, Fed. Res. Bank, Atlanta, 1973-77; project mgr., tng. dept. Coca Cola U.S.A., Atlanta, 1977—. Mem. Am. Soc. Tng. and Devel. Roman Catholic. Office: PO Drawer 1734 Atlanta GA 30301

SANDERS, AARON PERRY, educator; b. Phoenix, Jan. 12, 1924; s. DeWitt and Ruth (Perry) S.; B.S., U. Tex. at El Paso, 1950; M.S. (AEC fellow), U. Rochester, 1952; Ph.D., U. N.C., 1964; m. Betty Mae Gelein, Aug. 11, 1944 (div.); children—Merle Sanders Ireland Julie Ruth Sanders Jacome, James DeWitt; m. 2d, Georgia Anne Bullock, Nov. 26, 1972; 1 dau., Kai Marie. With Greyhound Bus. Lines, Phoenix, 1942, dispatcher, ticket agt., El Paso, 1946-50; asso. health physicist Brookhaven Nat. Lab., Upton, L.I., N.Y., 1951-53; instr. physics, radiol. safety officer N.C. State Coll., 1953; instr. radiology Duke Med. Center, Durham, N.C., 1953-56, dir. radioisotope lab., 1953-65, asso. radiology, 1956-57, asst. prof., 1957-64, asso. prof., 1964-65, asso. prof., dir. div. radiobiology, 1965-70, prof., dir. div. radiobiology, 1970—; Fulbright lectr. health physics, Argentina, 1958-59; cons. N.C. Bd. Health, 1961-76; mem. N.C. Radiation Protection Commn., 1976—, chmn., 1978—. Served with USNR, 1942-45. Diplomate Am. Bd. Health Physics. Mem. AAAS, Am. Assn. Physicists in Medicine Soc. Exptl. Biology and Medicine, Health Physics Soc., Soc. Nuclear Medicine, Biophys. Soc., Radiation Research Soc., Undersea Med. Soc., Sigma Xi, Sigma Pi Sigma. Contbr. articles to profl. jours. Address: Box 3164 Duke U Med Center Durham NC 27710

SANDERS, BOBBY RAY, broadcasting co. exec.; b. Ft. Worth, Apr. 2, 1947; s. James McKinley and Edith Mildred (Johnson) S.; B.A. in Journalism, N. Tex. State U., 1969. Reporter, writer Ft. Worth Star-Telegram, 1969-72; producer, reporter Sta. KERA-TV, Dallas, 1972-77; gen. mgr. Sta. KERA-FM, Dallas, Ft. Worth, 1977—. Bd. dirs. Ft. Worth Opera Assn.; v.p. Jr. Black Acad. Arts and Letters, Dallas/Ft. Worth. Recipient Am. Bar Assn. Cert. Merit, 1971; Tex. Gridiron Best TV Documentary award, 1972, Best TV Feature award, 1973, Documentary, 1974; Dallas Press Club Best TV awards, 1974-77; Chgo. Internat. Film Festival Cert. Merit, 1977. Mem. Press Club Ft. Worth (past pres.), Soc. Profl. Journalist (dir. 1974-76), Blacks in the Mass Media. Author plays: A Time to Build, 1976; Blues on 125th Street, 1978. Office: 3000 Harry Hines Blvd Dallas TX 75201

SANDERS, DON FLOYD, detective agy. exec.; b. Hot Springs, Ark., Nov. 15, 1930; s. George James and Fannie Beatrice (Grantstaff) S.; grad. Ark. State Fire Coll., 1965, Smith-Wesson Acad., 1976; m. Frances Lou Jarrell, Dec. 2, 1950; 1 son, Don. Patrolman, St. Louis Police Dept., 1954-55; owner, operator Sanders Detective & Security Agy., Hot Springs, Ark., 1959—. Served with U.S. Army, 1948-49. Lic. pvt. detective, Ark. Mem. Ark. Pvt. Investigators (pres. 1970-71), World Assn. Detectives, Nat. Sheriff Assn., Internat. Acad. Criminology. Democrat. Pentecostal Ch. Club: Masons. Home: 206 Rubys Dr Hot Springs AR 71901 Office: PO Box 962 Hot Springs AR 71901

SANDERS, GEORGE BENTON, surgeon; b. Kingston, Jamaica, Brit. W.I., Dec. 28, 1910; came to U.S., 1910, naturalized, 1911; s. George Crittenden and Eleanora Jane (Georges) S.; B.A., Cornell U., 1932, M.D., 1935; m. Elizabeth Shwab, Apr. 25, 1958; children—Ann C., George Benton. Intern, Barnes Hosp., St. Louis, 1935-36, resident, 1936-39; Harrison fellow in research surgery U. Pa., Phila., 1939-41; instr. surgery U. Louisville Sch. Medicine, 1946, asso. prof., 1947, asst. prof., 1947-49, prof. clin. surgery, 1950—; practice medicine specializing in gen. surgery, Louisville, 1946—; mem. staff Norton-Children's, Meth. Evang. hosps. Pres., Ky. div. Am. Cancer Soc., 1977. Served from capt. to lt. col., M.C., AUS, 1942-46. Recipient award for outstanding contbns. to control of cancer Am. Cancer Soc., 1977. Mem. A.C.S. (chmn. Ky. cancer liaison program), So. Surgeons Club, N.Y. Acad. Scis. Episcopalian. Clubs: Louisville Country, Wynn-Stay, River Valley (Louisville); Hillsboro (Pompano Beach, Fla.). Contbr. articles to med. and surg. jours. Home: 20 Stonebridge Rd Louisville KY 40207 Office: 558 Med Towers South Louisville KY 40202

SANDERS, HAROLD LEON, surgeon; b. Greenville, S.C., Jan. 8, 1925; s. John Lewis and Pearl Miriam (Matthews) S.; B.S., The Citadel, 1947; M.D., Emory U., 1947; m. Susanne Farley, Sept. 29, 1956; children—Lisa, Harold Farley. Intern, Greenville (S.C.) Gen. Hosp., 1947; intern Emory U. Hosp., 1947-48, resident in surgery, 1948-49; resident in gen. surgery U.S. Naval Hosp., Oakland, Calif., 1951-52; asst. resident in gen. surgery Meml. Center for Cancer and Allied Diseases, N.Y.C., 1953, sr. resident in gen. surgery, 1954-56, fellow in radioisotopes and radiation therapy, 1956-57; practice medicine specializing in surgery, Greenville, 1952, oncology and gen. surgery, Tampa, Fla., 1957—; mem. attending staff St. Joseph's Hosp., Tampa Gen. Hosp., vice-chief of surgery, 1963-65, chief surgery, 1966-68; mem. cons. staff Centro-Asturiano Hosp., chief of surgery, 1964-65; mem. attending staff Meml. Hosp., Tampa, chief surgery, 1979—; cons. staff VA Hosp.; dir. Tumor Clinic, Hillsboro County, 1961-74; clin. prof. surgery U. South Fla. Med. Sch., Tampa, 1972—, clin. prof. obstetrics and gynecology, 1973—. Served to lt., M.C., USN, 1949-52. Diplomate Am. Bd. Surgery, Am. Bd. Abdominal Surgery. Mem. A.C.S., Fla. Assn. Gen. Surgeons, Fla., So. med. assns., AMA, James Ewing Soc., Soc. Head and Neck Surgeons, Southeastern Surg. Soc., Fla. Assn. Tumor Clinics (sec. 1964-66, chmn. 1966-69). Episcopalian. Contbr. articles in field to med. jours. Home: 2804 Parkland Blvd Tampa FL 33609 Office: 2919 Swann Ave Tampa FL 33609

SANDERS, JAMES HERBERT, govt. ofcl.; b. St. Louis, Jan. 23, 1949; s. James Raymond and Laura (Brandhorst) S.; B.A., Park Coll., Parkville, Mo., 1975; m. Patricia Lingenfelter, May 8, 1971; children—Robert, Alan. Teller, Landmark North County Bank, St. Louis, 1967-71, 75; agt. IRS, Poplar Bluff, Mo., 1975-78; auditor USAF, Little Rock AFB, 1978—; instr. Three River Community Coll., Poplar Bluff. Pres. Butler County Foster Parents Assn., Poplar Bluff, 1978. Served with USAF, 1971-75. Mem. Butler County Jaycees, Greater N. Pulaski County Jaycees. Home: #75 Cardinal Valley Dr North Little Rock AR 72116 Office: Air Force Audit Agy Det 342 Little Rock AFB AR 72076

SANDERS, JAY WILLIAM, educator; b. Balt., July 26, 1924. s. Jay Will and May Magdalene (Fisher) S.; A.A., Louisburg Jr. Coll., 1948; B.A., U. N.C., 1950; M.A., Columbia, 1951; Ph.D., U. Mo., 1957; postgrad. (NIH fellow) Northwestern U., 1962-64; m. Mary Elizabeth St. John, Aug. 27, 1950; children—Mary Jean, John Jay, Elizabeth Ann. Instr. speech U. Mo., Columbia, 1952-57; asst. prof. speech Trenton State Coll., 1957-59, asso. prof., 1959-62; asst. prof. audiology Vanderbilt U., Nashville, 1964-65, asso. prof., 1965-71, prof. audiology, 1971—, research audiologist Bill Wilkerson Hearing and Speech Center, 1964—. Cons. in indsl. hearing conservation, 1968—. Served as pilot USNR, 1943-45. Fellow Am. Speech and Hearing Assn.; mem. Tenn. Speech and Hearing Assn. Asso. editor Jour. Speech and Hearing Research, 1967-70; editorial cons. Jour. Speech and Hearing Disorders, 1974-76; sect. editor Jour. Am. Audiology Soc., 1976—. Contbr. articles to profl. jours. Home: 5518 Vanderbilt Rd Old Hickory TN 37138 Office: Vanderbilt University Nashville TN 37232

SANDERS, JOHN DIXON, physician; b. Southport, N.C., Apr. 18, 1939; s. Michael Rudolph and Julia (Dixon) S.; student N.C. State U., 1957-58; B.S. in Pharmacy, U. S.C., 1966; M.D., Med. U. S.C., 1973; m. Linda Sue Morgan, Aug. 14, 1958; 1 dau., Linda Kathryn. Pharmacist, Clink Scales Drugs, Belton, S.C., 1966-68, Southcenter Drugs, Hendersonville, N.C., 1968-69; intern Med. U. S.C., Charleston, 1973-74, resident in internal medicine, 1974-76; practice medicine specializing in internal medicine, Charleston, S.C., 1976—; mem. staff North Trident Regional Hosp., Charleston; mem. adv. bd. Big Bros., Big Sisters. Served with 82d Airborne div. AUS, 1959-62. Mem. Dorchester County Med. Soc. (sec. treas. 1978-79), Coastal Med. Soc., Summerville Preservation Soc. Presbyterian. Club: Rotary. Home: 205 Sumter Ave Summerville SC 29483 Office: 9304 Medical Plaza Dr Charleston SC 29405

SANDERS, KENNETH ALTON, coll. adminstr.; b. Miami, Fla., Aug. 29, 1944; s. Thomas Bradford and Mary Louise (Carpenter) S.; B.A., Piedmont Coll., 1967; M.Ed., U. Ga., 1976; m. Helen JoAnn Damron, June 5, 1967; children—Christi Elise, Kendra Allison. Tchr., coach Dalton (Ga.) public schs., 1967-72, Toccoa Falls (Ga.) Acad., 1972-76; dean students, athletic dir., head basketball coach Toccoa Falls Coll., 1976—, also mem. adminstrv. bd. Recipient cert. appreciation City of Dalton; named Tri-State Asst. Coach of Year, 1968. Mem. Assn. Christian Deans Men (regional dir. 1976-78), So. Highlands Christian Conf. (sec., treas.). Baptist. Club: Kiwanis (dir. Tocco Falls 1975-77). Home: 114 Green Forest Dr Toccoa GA 30577 Office: PO Box 176 Toccoa Falls Coll Toccoa Falls GA 30577

SANDERS, KENNETH JOE, steel mfg. corp. controller; b. Laurens, S.C., Sept. 16, 1937; s. Paul William and Julia P. S.; student in bus. and acctg. Columbia (S.C.) Comml. Coll., 1969; m. Clara M. Thornhill, Dec. 30, 1960; children—Jean, Sharon, Stacey, Paul. Mgr. Public Fin. Co., Columbia, 1959-64; credit mgr. Friedman's Jewelers, Columbia, 1964-68; acct. Derrick, Stubbs & Stith, C.P.A.'s, Columbia, 1968-74; controller Kline Iron & Steel Co., Inc., Columbia, 1974—. Served with USAF, 1955-59. Mem. Am. Inst. C.P.A.'s, S.C. Assn C.P.A.'s (treas. Central chpt., continuing edn. com.). Presbyterian. Club: Coldstream Country. Home: 112 Lloydwood Dr West Columbia SC 29169 Office: PO Box 1013 Columbia SC 29202

SANDERS, KENNETH LEIGH, physician; b. Monmouth, N.J., July 4, 1944; s. Edward Hirsch and Billi (Davis) S.; B.A., Queens Coll., 1965; B.S., U. Miami (Fla.), 1969; M.D., Universidad Autónoma de Guadelajara (Mex.), 1973; m. Barbara Ellen Milberg, Mar. 30, 1974; children—Robert Simpson, Geoffrey Bradford. Clin. clerkship Maimonides Med. Center, Bklyn., 1973-74, intern, 1974-75, jr. and sr. resident in internal medicine, 1975-77; fellow in infectious diseases U. N.C., Chapel Hill, 1977-79; practice medicine specializing in internal medicine and infectious diseases, Fort Myers, Fla., 1979—; mem. infections control com. Lee Meml. Hosp., Fort Myers Community Hosp. Served with U.S. Army, 1966-68. Recipient William Dressler award in cardiology Maimonides Med. Center, 1975; diplomate Am. Bd. Internal Medicine. Mem. AMA, Am. Soc. Microbiology, AAAS, Assn. Practitioners in Infection Control, Am. Philatelic Soc. Office: 3677 Central Ave Suite H Fort Myers FL 33901

SANDERS, KINNEY LEE, ins. co. exec.; b. Commerce, Ga., Jan. 2, 1934; s. Robert L. and Carolyn L. (Kinney) S.; B.S., U. Miami, 1954; m. Altann T. Vinton, June 28, 1958; children—Anthony L., Lisa Marie, Lori Ann. Agt., asst. mgr. Prudential Ins. Co., Miami, Fla., 1959-61; regional sales dir. Franklin Life Ins. Co., Orlando, Fla., 1961-70; gen. mgr. Phoenix Mut. Ins. Co., Atlanta, 1970—. Served to lt. (j.g.) USNR, 1955-58. C.L.U. Mem. C.L.U. Soc., Gen. Agts. and Mgrs. Assn. (pres. Orlando 1970-71), Life Underwriters Assn. (dir. Orlando 1968-70). Republican. Methodist. Clubs: Atlanta Athletic; Bay Hill (Orlando). Home: 1000 The 16th Fairway Atlanta GA 30338 Office: 223 Perimeter Center Pkwy Suite 100 Atlanta GA 30346

SANDERS, LAWRENCE DOW, IV, system cons., ins. co. exec.; b. San Antonio, Mar. 29, 1939; s. Lawrence Dow and Margaret Helen (Lincecum) S.; B.A. in Math., U. Tex., Austin, 1963; m. Judith Elizabeth Carrabba, Aug. 8, 1971; children—Holly Vincele, Robin Elizabeth. Actuarial asst. Gt. So. Life Ins. Co., Houston, 1965-69; sr. programmer analyst Blue Cross-Blue Shield Tex., Dallas, 1969-71; mgr. actuarial systems TCC, Inc., Austin, 1971-73; project mgr. Am. Nat. Ins. Co., Galveston, Tex., 1973-75, sr. staff analyst, 1976-79, system cons. and mgr. systems planning and coordination, 1979—; data processing cons.; developer generalized computer software. Served with U.S. Army, 1963-65. Mem. Ins. Accounting and Statis. Assn., Life Office Mgmt. Assn., Data Processing Mgmt. Assn. Home: 1018 Montour St Houston TX 77062 Office: 1 Moody Plaza Galveston TX 77550

SANDERS, MARGUERITE DEES, b. Many, La., Sept. 1, 1914; d. W.E. and Mary J. (White) Dees; B.A. in Edn., Mathematics and Physics, La. State Normal Coll., Natchitoches, La., 1934; M.Ed. in Secondary Edn., Stephen F. Austin U., Nacogdoches, Tex., 1955; postgrad. U. Colo., Stephen F. Austin U., Baylor U., Northwestern U., 1959-69; m. Horace I. Sanders (dec.); 1 dau., Dorothy Sanders Tidwell. Mathematics coordinator, N. La. Supplemental Edn. Center, Natchitoches, La., 1967-69; curriculum coordinator Title 1, Sabine Parish Sch. Bd., Many, La., 1970-73, dir. Title I, 1973-74, dir. federal programs, 1974-76, asst. supt. Sabine Parish Schs., 1976—. Mem. NEA, La. Tchrs. Assn., La. Assn. Sch. Adminstrs. (federally assisted programs), La. Unit Assn. Sch. Curriculum Developers, La. Suprs. Assn., La. Sci. Tchrs. Assn. (pres., sec.), La. Mathematics Assn., Delta Kappa Gamma (Psi chpt.), Kappa Delta Pi. Recipient La. Sci. Tchrs. Honor Award, 1963. Home: Route 1 Box 55 Many LA 71449 Office: PO Box 1153 Sabine Parish Sch Bd Many LA 71449

SANDERS, MELVIN DOYLE, engring. co. exec.; b. Houston, Dec. 20, 1946; s. Chester Worthy and Dorothy Mae (Hawks) S.; B.S. Civil Engring., Tex. A. and M. U., 1969; children—Kyle Andrew, Virginia Lynn. Project engr. Continental Pipeline Co., Wichita Falls, Tex. and Ponca City, Okla., 1970-72; project engr. Williams Bros. Engring. Co., Tulsa, 1972-74, Williams Bros. Offshore Ltd., Newcastle Upon Tyne, Eng., 1974-75; pres. Sovereign Engring. Inc., Houston, 1975—, also dir. Served with C.E., AUS, 1971, capt. Res. Registered profl. engr., Tex., La., Okla., Miss., Ala., Calif. Mem. Nat. Soc. Profl. Engrs., ASCE, Tex. Soc. Profl. Engrs., Profl. Engrs. in Pvt. Practice, Houston Engring. and Sci. Soc. Home: 361 N Post Oak Ln Apt 237 Houston TX 77024 Office: 8584 Katy Freeway Suite 406 Houston TX 77024

SANDERS, RALPH WAID, orgn. exec.; b. Ft. Smith, Ark., Feb. 15, 1937; s. Floyd Hall and Ruth (Cooper) S.; A.A., Ft. Smith Jr. Coll., 1957; B.A., U. Tulsa, 1959; m. Roberta Hood, Apr. 2, 1960; children—Ralph Terrell, Mary Anne, Timothy Waid. Freelance writer, photographer, 1955-56; journalist KOTV News, Tulsa, 1957-60; dir. pub. relations U.S. Jr. C. of C., Tulsa, 1960-63; exec. v.p., chief operating officer World Neighbors, Oklahoma City, 1963—. Mem. Pub. Relations Soc. Am., Am. Mgmt. Assn., Am. Soc. Assn. Execs., Sigma Delta Chi. Home: 11312 Greystone Ave Oklahoma City OK 73120 Office: 5116 N Portland Ave Oklahoma City OK 73112

SANDERS, RAYMOND ABNEY, mfg. co. exec.; b. San Antonio, Nov. 23, 1941; s. Walter Cowart and Margaret (Abney) S.; student N.Mex. Military Inst., 1959-61; B.S., U.S. Naval Acad., 1965; m. Carolin Shands, June 19, 1965; children—John, Christopher, Robert. Mgmt. trainee Temple Industries, 1970-72, asst. to mgr. fiber products op., Diboll, Tex., 1972-76, plant mgr. Temple Eastex, 1976—. Served with U.S. Army, 1965-70. Decorated 2 Silver stars, 4 Bronze stars. Mem. Am. Hardboard Assn. (bd. dirs.), Tex. Forestry Assn. Home: 706 Lazy Ln Lufkin TX 75901 Office: 600 A St Diboll TX 75941

SANDERS, STEVEN GILL, telephone co. exec.; b. Chgo., Aug. 23, 1936; s. Raymond E. and Mildred (Gostow) S.; B.S., M.I.T., 1958; postgrad. Rutgers U., 1960-61; Ph.D. (NDEA fellow) in Physics, U. S.C., 1965; m. Gretchen Griffith, Jan. 15, 1959; children—Steven Gill, Meghan Griffith. Instr. mechanics U. S.C., Columbia, 1964-65; asst. prof. physics So. Ill. U., Edwardsville, 1965-67, chmn. dept. physics, 1967-71, asso. prof., 1969-75, prof., 1975-79; resident research asso. Argonne Nat. Lab., 1971-72; pres., gen. mgr. No. Ark. Telephone Co., Flippin, 1977—; referee Energy Research and Devel. Agy., 1974-76; cons. Ill. Office of Edn., 1970; dir. Citizens Bank and Trust Co., Flippin. NSF fellow, 1971. Mem. Am. Phys. Soc., Am. Assn. Physics Tchrs., Nat. Sci. Tchrs. Assn., IEEE, Ark. Acad. Sci., N.Y. Acad. Sci., Am. Mgmt. Assn., Ill. Sci. Tchrs. Assn. (dir. 1975-76), Sigma Xi, Sigma Pi Sigma. Club: Lions. Contbr. articles on physics to sci. publs. Home: PO Box 178 Bull Shoals AR 72619 Office: 301 E Main Flippin AR 72634

SANDERS, WALTER MCDONALD, III, govt. ofcl.; b. Bluefield, W.Va., Dec. 5, 1930; s. Walter McDonald II and Mary Minerva (Easley) S.; B.S. in Civil Engring., Va. Mil. Inst., 1953; M.S. in San. Engring., Johns Hopkins, 1956, Ph.D., 1964; m. Emily Joyce, Aug. 4, 1956; children—Emily Graham, Walter McDonald IV, Albert Brian, Stephen Craig. San. engr. Greeley & Hansen Engrs., Richmond, Va., 1953; san. engring. cons. ICA, USOM, Belo Horizonte, Brazil, 1956-58; asst. chief water supply sect., div. water supply and pollution control USPHS, Wasington, 1958-60, chief ecol. energetics sect. region IV, Clemson U., 1962-65; chief freshwater ecosystems br. S.E. Environmental Research Lab., EPA, Athens, Ga., 1965-75. asso. dir. water quality research Environmental Research Lab., 1975—; adj. prof., lectr. div. interdisciplinary studies Clemson U., 1962—; research asso.. prof. pollution ecology Inst. Ecology, U. Ga., Athens, 1967—; mem. Joint U.S.-USSR Sci. Del. for Research on Agrl. Chems. in Environment, Tech. Adv. Commn. for Chesapeake Bay Studies; U.S. project officer River Nile and Lake Nasser Studies. Served with USAF, 1953-55; commn. officer USPHS, 1956-66. Recipient commendations from USPHS, Boy Scouts Am., Izaac Walton League, Am. Water Works Assn. Mem. ASCE, AAAS, Am. Orchid Soc., Sigma Xi. Presbyn. (elder). Rotarian (pres. Athens West 1977-78). Club: Athens Men's Garden. Contbr. articles to profl. jours. Home: 195 Xavier Dr Athens GA 30606 Office: Environmental Research Lab EPA Athens GA 30605

SANDERS, WILLIAM BEAUREGARDE, broadcasting co. exec.; b. Durham, N.C., Apr. 11, 1948; s. Albert Neely and Elizabeth (Barron) S.; B.A. in Journalism cum laude, U. S.C., 1970, M. Mass

Communications, 1974. Announcer, WEAB-AM, Greer, S.C., 1966-67, WQOK-AM, Greenville, S.C., 1967-74, WCAY-AM, 1974-75; v.p., gen. mgr. WJAY-AM, WCIG-FM, Mullins, S.C., 1975-77; gen. mgr. WSSC-AM, Sumter, S.C., 1977—; pres., gen. mgr. Mid Carolina Communications, Inc., Sumter, 1978—; broadcast curriculum adviser, instr. Sumter Tech. Edn. Coll. Served with USNR, 1970-72. Named Boss of Year, Sumter Jaycees, 1978. Mem. S.C. Broadcasters Assn. (chmn. edn. com., chmn. summer and winter conv. com. 1980, dir.), Sumter Mchts. Assn. (dir.), Columbia Ad Club, Nat. Assn. Broadcasters, Radio Advt. Bur., Omicron Delta Kappa, Alpha Epsilon Rho, Sigma Delta Chi, Kappa Tau Alpha. Clubs: Pocalla Springs Country, Woodmen of World, Rotary. Home: PO Box 83 Sumter SC 29150 Office: PO Box 1468 Sumter SC 29150

SANDERSON, DONALD HILLER, chemist; b. Meriden, Conn., Oct. 21, 1942; s. Leroy and Mary Barbara (Hiller) S.; B.S., Central Conn. Coll., 1965; M.S., Purdue U., 1970, Ph.D., 1972. Asst. v.p. Licensing & Devel. Div., Pfizer, Inc., N.Y.C., 1972-76; devel. mgr. inorganic bromines sect. Great Lakes Chem., West Lafayette, Ind., 1976-78; mgr. workover/completion fluids dept. Magcobar Div., Dresser Industries, Houston, 1978-79; tech. mktg. mgr., workover/completion fluids div., Mobley Co., Inc., Kilgore, Tex., 1979—. Mem. Am. Chem. Soc., Am. Petroleum Inst. Contbr. articles to profl. jours. Home: 8241 Purdue St Tyler TX 75703 Office: PO Box 1640 Kilgore TX 75662

SANDERSON, GEORGE NELSON, bath accessories mfg. co. exec.; b. Morristown, Tenn., Aug. 31, 1941; s. George William and Margaret Clarice (Nelson) S.; B.S. in Acctg., Miss. State U., 1963; postgrad. U. Ala., 1965; m. Sandra Brook, Aug. 28, 1965. Auditor, Haskins & Sells, Birmingham, Ala., 1965-69; asst. controller Beneke Corp., Columbus, Miss., 1969-72, exec. asst. to pres., 1972-74, exec. v.p., 1974-75, pres., chief exec. officer, 1975—; dir. Beneke Industries, Ltd., Beneke GmbH. Bd. dirs. Columbus United Way; mem. president's council Miss. U. for Women; chmn. Bus. Week 79, Free Enterprise Edn. Project. Served with U.S. Army, 1965-66. Mem. President's Assn. of Am. Mgmt. Assn., Nat. Assn. Mfrs., Soc. Advancement Mgmt., Nat. Assn. Accountants, Columbus-Lowndes C. of C., Sigma Alpha Epsilon, Delta Sigma Pi. Republican. Episcopalian. Club: Kiwanis (Columbus). Home: 1711 Bramblewood Dr Columbus MS 39701 Office: Box 1367 Columbus MS 39701

SANDERSON, ROBERT MILTON, employee security planning exec.; b. Harvest, Ala., Oct. 22, 1922; s. Luther Earl and Mary Vain (Pitts) S.; B.S., U. Tenn., 1950; m. Louise Carleton, May 9, 1942. Spl. agt. Am. Mut. Liability Ins. Co., 1946-56; pres., chmn. bd. Sanderson Ins. Agy., Inc., Nashville, 1956-66; pres. Sanderson & Co. Ltd., Nashville, 1966-69; pres. Employee Security Planning, Inc., Nashville, 1970—; ordained to ministry Baptist Ch., 1972; chaplain Univ. Nursing Home, Nashville, 1972-75. Served with USAF, 1943-46; ETO. Democrat. Baptist. Clubs: Lions, Kiwanis, Masons, Shriners. Home: 2315 Woodmont Blvd Nashville TN 37215 Office: Exec Suite 7B 2500 21st Ave Nashville TN 37212

SANDERSON, TERRY ALLEN, surgeon: b. Houston, Apr. 7, 1938; s. Thomas Arnold and Gladys Adel (Kischel) S.; student Tex. Christian U., 1956-58, U. Houston, 1958-59; M.D., U. Tex., Galveston, 1963; m. Pamela Annette Levy, Dec. 12, 1971; children—Monti Louise, Joyce Allyn. Intern, then resident surgery Hermann Hosp., Houston, 1963-68; sr. fellow surgery M.D. Anderson Hosp., Houston, 1968-69; pvt. practice surgery, Houston, 1969—; chief surgery Westbury Hosp., 1973-79, chief of staff, 1976, vice chmn. governing bd., 1977; vice chief staff Sharpstown Hosp., 1980; clin. asso. in surgery U. Tex. Med. Sch., Houston, 1971—. Pres. Greater Houston unit Am. Cancer Soc., bd. dirs. Tex. div., 1978—. Recipient George Waldron Surg. award Hermann Hosp., 1968. Diplomate Am. Bd. Surgery. Fellow A.C.S.; mem. Tex. Med. Assn., Houston Surg. Soc., Harris County Med. Soc., Southwestern Surg. Congress, Alpha Kappa Kappa, Sigma Alpha Epsilon. Home: 10 Briar Hollow Number 17 Houston TX 77027 Office: 6601 Tarnef St Suite 104 Houston TX 77074

SANDHU, JOGINDER SINGH, educator; b. India, Aug. 1, 1929; s. Fauja Singh and Bachan Kaur (Singh) S.; came to U.S., 1959, naturalized, 1973; B.A., Punjab U., 1949, B.T., 1952; M.A., Delhi U., 1957; Ed.D., Peabody Coll., Nashville, 1961, Ph.D., 1965; m. Usha Sherma, June 6, 1970; children—Nisha, Amrita. Tchr., Khalsa High Sch., Tarsikka, Punjab, 1950-51, Hindu High Sch., Sonepat, Punjab, 1952-53; higher secondary tchr. Delhi Govt. Sch. System, 1953-58; editor asso. The Upper Room, Nashville, 1960-66; prof. English, chmn. dept. Limestone Coll., Gaffney, S.C., 1966—, vice chmn. humanities div., 1970—. Sec. Indo-Am. Friendship Assn., Nashville, 1963-66; pres. India Assn., Nashville, 1962-66. India Govt. fellow, 1948-49, 51-52. Mem. Modern Lang. Assn., S. Atlantic Modern Lang. Assn., Tenn. Folklore Soc., Kappa Delta Pi. Democrat. Sikh and Methodist. Kiwanian. Author articles. Home: 113 Crestview Dr Gaffney SC 29340

SANDIFER, ROBERT LOWRY, govt. ofcl.; b. Florence, S.C., Aug. 9, 1935; s. Charles Hightower and Lena Irene (Zehe) S.; B.S., Clemson U., 1957; m. Sherry Ann Jones, July 11, 1959; children—Steven Lowry, Jodie Irene, Robert Paul. Statistician statis. reporting service Dept. Agr., Columbia, S.C., Alexandria, La., Athens, Ga., 1958-67, economist soil conservation service, Columbia, 1967-70, pub. info. officer, 1970—. Dist. dir. S.C. Football Ofcls., 1977—; mem. Citizens for Advancement Phys. Handicapped; instr. Inst. Environ. Studies Clemson U., U. S.C., The Citadel, 1973-77. Served to lt. F.A. AUS, 1957-58. Recipient Certificate of Merit award Soil Conservation Service Dept. Agr., 1974, Outstanding Performance rating, 1976. Mem. Soil Conservation Soc. Am. (pres. S.C. chpt. 1970, southeastern regional councilman 1978—), S.C. Assn. Conservation Dists. (contbg.), Nat. Conservation Edn. Assn., S.C. Environ. Edn. Assn., S.C. Wildlife Fedn., Orgn. Profl. Employees U.S. Dept. Agr. Presbyterian. Club: Masons. Home: 7816 Loch Ln Columbia SC 29206

SANDLER, STEVEN NED, systems analyst; b. Balt., Feb. 3, 1951; s. Abraham and Leila (Kaplan) S.; B.S. in Info. Systems Mgmt., U. Md., 1972; m. Beth Lynn Schweriner, Nov. 19, 1972; children—Jeffrey Scott, Lisa Michelle. Computer programmer U. Md., College Park, 1971-72; computer specialist Office of Revenue Sharing, U.S. Dept. Treasury, Washington, 1972-78; systems analyst Lee County Electric Coop., Inc., North Fort Myers, Fla., 1978—. Recipient cert. of appreciation Office Sec. Treasury, 1974; letter of commendation U.S. Ho. of Reps., 1977. Jewish. Office: PO Box 3455 North Fort Myers FL 33903

SANDLIN, DOROTHY SOUTHERLAND, pianist, educator; b. Rose Hill, N.C., June 8, 1927; d. Hugh Stewart and Ethel (Southerland) Johnson; B.S. in Music Edn., E. Carolina U., Greenville, N.C., 1956; postgrad. Julliard Sch. Music, 1956-57, 58, St. Louis Inst. Music, summer 1965, Westminster Choir Coll., Princeton, N.J., summers 1969, 70, Orff Inst. Mozarteum, Salzburg, Austria, summer 1971; pupil of Clarence Adler, Joseph Kelsall, Stuart Bellows, Lorean Hodapp; m. James Delacy Sandlin, Jr., Apr. 14, 1945 (dec.); 1 son, James Delacy, III. Elementary sch. vocal tchr., E. Windsor Twp., Highstown, N.J., 1957-58, Monroe Twp., Prospect Plains, N.J., 1966-69, Manalapan-Englishtown Twp., Englishtown, N.J., 1969-71; pvt. piano tchr., Cranbury, N.J., 1958-64, Princeton, 1964-68, 71-75, also part-time pub. sch. tchr.; adjudicator Nat. Piano Guild; dir. music summer camps; organist, dir. First Presbyn. Ch., Plainsboro, N.J., 1961-66; interim dir. First Presbyn. Ch., Trenton, 1973-74; organist Bethel Lutheran Ch., Trenton, 1975; organist, pvt. tchr. piano, organ, voice and theory, Wilmington, N.C., 1975—; part-time piano tchr. Harrells (N.C.) Christian Acad. Recitalist Carnegie Hall, 1961, Paderewski Found. benefit, N.Y.C., 1972, 73, also at colls. Mem. Piano Guild (Gold medal Austin, Tex. 1960), AAUW (chpt. corr. sec.), Duplin County Hist. Soc. (charter sec. 1948), Wilmington Piano Tchrs. Guild (pres. 1978-79). Club: Thursday Morning Music. Author curriculum guide. Address: 310 Early Dr Wilmington NC 28403

SANDLIN, GEORGE WILSON, real estate broker, mortgage banker; b. Glen Rose, Tex., May 13, 1912; s. Walter Algie and Margaret (Parks) S.; student pub. schs., also Schreiner Inst.; m. Ruth Ina Zollinger, Sept. 21, 1941 (dec. Feb. 27, 1975); children—George Walter Raoul, Carole Ruth, Sarah Louise, Margaret Ina. Field rep. HOLC, San Antonio, 1934-36; pres. Sandlin Mortgage Corp., Austin, Tex.; owner Sandlin & Co., 1936—; chmn. bd., pres. Internat. Creations, Inc.; pres., dir. Trans-Pacific Resorts, Inc.; pres. Profl. Arts, Inc.; ind. fee appraiser. Chmn., Tex. Real Estate Commn., 1949-55. Mem. Austin City Planning Commn., 1947-52, chmn., 1951-52. Chmn. Tex. Dem. Exec. Com., 1954-56. Pres. chmn. bd. Tex. Found., 1955—. Served as lt. comdr. USNR, World War II; PTO. Recipient silver citizenship medal Vets. Fgn. Wars, 1957. Mem. Tex. Assn. Realtors (pres. 1979), Austin Real Estate Bd. (past pres.), Inst. Real Estate Mgmt., Mortgage Bankers Assn., Nat. Assn. Realtors (dir.), Am. Legion, V.F.W. Episcopalian. Clubs: Austin Country, Headliners. Home: 1801 Lavaca St Apt 7L Austin TX 78701 Office: 308 W 15th St Austin TX 78701

SANDOZ, LOUIS ANTHONY, III, data processing exec.; b. New Orleans, Feb. 5, 1945; s. Louis Anthony and Alice Mary (Loescher) S.; B.S. in E.E., La. State U., 1968; m. Barbara Jean Berthelot, Aug. 13, 1966; children—Thomas, Jeffrey. Guidance systems engr. IBM, Kennedy Space Center, 1968-69, digital interface engr., Owego, N.Y., 1969-70, application programmer, 1970-71; radar system hardware/software liaison engr. (IBM) Bell Labs., Whippany, N.J., 1971-73; data processing div. systems engr. IBM, New Orleans, 1973-76; data processing mgr. J. Ray McDermott, New Orleans, 1976—; cons. in field. Recipient Systems Engring. Symposium award IBM, 1976. Mem. IEEE. Roman Catholic. Home: 1415 Velma St Metairie LA 70001 Office: 1010 Common St New Orleans LA 70160

SANDRAPATY, RAMACHANDRA RAO, mech. engr., educator; b. Eluru, India, Feb. 15, 1942; s. Venkata Subbarao and Annapoornamma Sandrapaty; came to U.S., 1969; M.S. in Mech. Engring., U. S.C., 1971, Ph.D., 1974; m. Koppuravuri Kalyani Kumari, Apr. 7, 1966; children—Ravichandra Kumar, Kiran Kumar. Post-matriculation merit scholar Govt. of India, 1957-63; jr. research fellow Council Sci. and Indsl. Research, India, 1963-65, sr. research fellow, 1966-67; grad. research asst. U. S.C., 1969-73; prof. mech. engring. tech. S.C. State Coll., Orangeburg, 1973—; project engr. IBM, Research Triangle Park, N.C., summer 1974, Applied Engring. Co., Orangeburg, summer 1978, Western Electric Co., Chgo., summer 1979; mem. adj. staff S.C. Energy Research Inst. Registered profl. engr. Mem. ASME, Am. Soc. for Engring. Edn., Air Pollution Control Assn. Club: Indo-Am. (U. S.C.) (v.p. 1972-73). Research on combustion generated air pollution, energy and environ. engring. Home: 2688 Lakeside Dr NE Orangeburg SC 29115 Office: Box 1735 SC State College Orangeburg SC 29117

SANDS, LU ALICE, librarian; b. Montgomery County, Tenn., Dec. 30, 1926; d. Bailey Gay and Betty Marable (Minor) Lyle; B.A., George Peabody Coll., 1947; M.A., Fla. State U., 1961; postgrad. Emory U., 1967; m. John Earl Sands, Nov. 25, 1947; 1 son, Alan Minor. Head children's services S. Ga. Regional Library, Valdosta, 1956-59; dir. library and learning resources N. Fla. Jr. Coll., Madison, 1960—; cons. in field. Trustee Suwannee River Regional Library, Live Oak, Fla., 1972-74. Mem. Fla., Southeastern library assns. Democrat. Methodist. Author: Basic Materials for Junior College Libraries: Books: Philosophy, Religion, Art, and Music, 1963. Editor: Fla. Libraries, 1971-72. Home: 115 Hancock St SE Madison FL 32340 Office: North Florida Jr Coll Madison FL 32340

SANDS, ROBERT KENNETH, lawyer; b. Worcester, Mass., Aug. 25, 1926; s. John M. and Edith (Hammarlund) S.; B.A. cum laude with distinction in Polit. Sci., Ohio State U., 1949; J.D., Yale, 1952. Admitted to Tex. bar, 1952, U.S. Supreme Ct. bar, 1971; practiced in Dallas, 1952—; asso. firm Leachman, Matthews and Gardere, 1952-54, Matthews, Shelton and Fisher, 1954-55, Matthews, Shelton, Fisher and Budd, 1955-56, Matthews, Fisher, Budd and Stroud, 1956-60; mem. firm Matthews, Fisher, Budd and Sands, 1960-61, Matthews, Payne, Sands and Benners, 1961-67, Matthews, Sands and Tyler, 1967-69, Sands, Tyler Trimble and Jones, 1969-70; pres. Sands, Tyler and Trimble, 1970-73; pres. Sands & Tyler, 1973—. Trustee, Timberlawn Psychiat. Research Found., 1974—; bd. dirs. Yale Law Sch. Fund, 1974—. Served with USNR, 1944-46. Mem. Am., Tex., Dallas bar assns., Yale Law Sch. Assn. of Dallas (pres. 1966—), Yale Law Sch. Assn. (exec. com. 1977—), Confrerie des Chevaliers du Tastevin, Phi Beta Kappa. Clubs: Dallas, Inwood Racquet. Home: 2912 Hood Apt A Dallas TX 75219 Office: 2030 Republic National Bank Tower Dallas TX 75201

SANDVIG, WILLIAM WARD, trade co. adminstr.; b. Mpls., May 24, 1950; s. William Evans and Norma Jean (Hrebal) S.; B.S., U.S. Naval Acad., 1972; m. Mary Frances Younger, Sept. 22, 1973; 1 son, William Joseph. Regional engr. Airco Indsl. Gases Co., New Orleans, 1977-79, dist. sales mgr., Houston, 1979—; pastor children's ch. 1st Baptist Ch., Kenner, 1978-79. Served with submarines, USN, 1972-77. Mem. S.W. Meat Packers Assn. (asso.), Tex. Softdrink Assn., Okla. Bottlers of Carbonated Beverage Assn., Houston Jaycees. Republican. Office: Airco Indsl Gases Co 7950 Blankenship Dr Houston TX 77055

SANFORD, HAROLD WOODLIFF, JR., radiologist; b. Columbia, S.C., Sept. 12, 1939; s. Harold Woodliff and Leila Belle (Barton) S.; B.S., The Citadel, 1961; M.D., U. S.C., 1965; m. Catherine Knox Rigby, Mar. 6, 1965; children—George Woodliff, Julia Barton. Intern, U.S. Naval Hosp., San Diego, 1965-66; resident U.S. Naval Hosp., Phila., 1968-71; commd. ensign U.S. Navy, 1961, advanced through grades to comdr., 1973; staff radiologist U.S. Naval Hosp., Portsmouth, Va., 1971-73, ret., 1973; asst. prof. radiology Med. U. S.C.; staff radiologist VA Hosp., Charleston, S.C., 1973-74; asso. radiologist X-ray clinic Spartanburg, S.C., 1974—. Diplomate Am. Bd. Radiology. Mem. AMA (Physicians award in continuing med. edn. 1972, 76, 78), Am. Coll. Radiology, Radiol. Soc. N. Am., S.C. Radiol. Assn., S.C. Med. Assn., Spartanburg County Med. Soc., Assn. Citadel Men, U. S.C. Alumni Assn. Presbyterian. Clubs: Spartanburg Citadel. Home: 611 Perrin Dr Spartanburg SC 29302 Office: 157 Catawba St Spartanburg SC 29303

SANFORD, J(AMES) KENNETH, univ. ofcl.; b. Clyde, N.C., Jan. 23, 1932; s. James Edward and Bernice (Crawford) S.; A.A., Mars Hill Coll., 1952; A.B., U. N.C., 1954, M.A., 1958; m. Alice Pearl Reavis, Sept. 22, 1957; children—Timothy Edward, Scott Vernon, Jeannette LuAnn. Pub. relations officer United Appeal of Asheville and Buncombe County, Asheville, N.C., 1954; reporter, 2d copy editor Winston-Salem Jour. and Sentinel, 1957-59, asst. state editor, 1959-61, news editor, 1961-63, editorial writer, 1963-64; dir. information U. N.C., Charlotte, 1964—. Vice pres. Briarwood Sch. P.T.A.; mem. citizen adv. com., communication dept. Charlotte-Mecklenburg Schs., 1974—; asst. dist. chmn. Council for Advancement and Support of Edn., 1975—; editor dist. III newsletter. Served with AUS, 1954-56. Mem. Pub. Relations Soc. Am. (accredited; dir. N.C. chpt. 1975—, pres. 1978), Charlotte Pub. Relations Soc. (treas. 1971, sec. 1972, v.p. 1973, pres. 1974), Coll. News Assn. of Carolinas (chmn. 1967), Charlotte C. of C. (pub. relations com. 1971, communications action council 1973), Kappa Tau Alpha. Baptist (chmn. bd. asso. deacons 1967). Home: 1216 Braeburn Rd Charlotte NC 28211

SANFORD, JOHN CLAUDE, graphic cons.; b. Austin, Tex., June 18, 1947; s. John Harry and Marjorie Durham (Kidder) S.; m. Patricia Ann Horn, Dec. 30, 1970; 1 son, John Thomas. Communication technician Austin (Tex.) Police Dept., 1969-71; purchasing agent Von Boeckmann-Jones Co., Austin, 1971-73; mgr. graphics dept. Austin Nat. Bank, 1973-79; cons. various printing cos. Pres. Austin Litho Club, 1974; precinct chmn. Travis County Republican Com., Austin, 1970-78. Served with U.S. Army, 1967-68. Decorated officer service award. Republican. Home: 7205 Antoine Circle Austin TX 78744 Office: Austin Nat Bank Tower PO Box 95 Austin TX 78776

SANG, HERB A., supt. schs; b. Van Buren, Mo., Nov. 11, 1929; s. Charles Elbert and Omah (Turley) S.; m. Alice Jean Coleman, Aug. 3, 1952; children—Julie Anne, Allen Coleman. With Burstein Applebee Electronics Corp., Kansas City, Mo., 1957-64; asst. supt. charge adminstrn. services Kansas City (Mo.) public schs., 1964-70; asso. supt. charge personnel. chief negotiator Affirmative Action Office, Duval County (Fla.) public schs., Jacksonville, 1970-75, supt. schs., 1975—. Served with AUS, 1947-49. Mem. Am. Assn. Sch. Adminstrs., Fla. Assn. Dist. Sch. Supts., Phi Delta Kappa. Democrat. Baptist. Club: Rotary. Author ednl. materials. Home: 3851 Timucua Trail Jacksonville FL 32211 Office: 1325 San Marco Blvd Jacksonville FL 32207

SANTELMANN, PAUL WILLIAM, educator; b. Ann Arbor, Mich., Oct. 18, 1926; s. Alfred William and Frances Hazel (Eppens) S.; B.S., U. Md., 1950; M.S., Mich State U., 1952; Ph.D., Ohio State U., 1954; m. Susanna Porter, Dec. 28, 1950; children—Patricia Santelmann Emerick, Steven, Douglas, Barbara. Asst. prof. agronomy U. Md., 1954-61, asso. prof., 1961-62; asso. prof. agronomy Okla. State U., Stillwater, 1962-65, prof. agronomy, 1965-74, Regents prof. agronomy, 1974—, head dept. agronomy, 1977—; mem. adv. group on pest mgmt. and research President's Council on Environmental Quality, 1971-72, mem. USSR pest mgmt. research rev. team, 1974; mem. herbicide study group of adv. com. on hazardous materials EPA, 1972-73; mem. pest control team Nat. Acad. Scis., 1973-74; mem. integrated pest mgmt. rev. team U.S. Dept. Agr., 1976; mem. organizing and policy com. IX Internat. Congress Plant Protection, 1979. Served with AUS, 1944-46. Fellow Weed Sci. Soc. Am. (pres. 1978-79, editor newsletter 1972-75, named outstanding tchr. 1972), Am. Soc. Agronomy; mem. Am. Inst. Biol. Sci. (governing bd. 1979—), Council for Agrl. Sci. and Tech. (dir. 1975-78), So. Weed Sci. Soc. (pres. 1975-76), Intersoc. Consortium for Plant Protection (exec. bd. 1977—). Methodist (treas. ch. 1967—). Contbr. articles to sci. jours. Home: 1101 Lakeridge Dr Stillwater OK 74074

SANTIAGO, EUGENIO MARDONIO, civil engr.; b. Placetas, Cuba, Aug. 7, 1944; s. Mardonio Rodrigo and Aleida Estela (Retana) S.; came to U.S., 1961; B.S., U. Miami, 1972; m. Pury Lopez; children—Patricia Cristina, Amy. Draftsman, chief draftsman, structural engr. Crain & Crouse Engrs., Miami, Fla., 1968-69; structural engr. Planas, Franyie & Santiago, Inc., Miami, 1969-70, head structural dept., 1970-76, v.p., 1976; v.p., br. mgr. Mich. Testing Engrs. of Fla., Inc., Miami, 1976-79; v.p., head structural dept. Profl. Asso. Cons. Engrs., Coral Gables, Fla., 1979—. Registered profl. engr., Fla. Mem. Am. Concrete Inst. (v.p. South Fla. chpt.), Portland Cement Assn., Prestressed Concrete Inst., Am. Welding Soc., Am. Soc. Nondestructive Testing (sec. Fla. chpt.), Film Soc. Miami (founder, pres., program dir. Cine-Club film series). Home: 9460 SW 31st Terr Miami FL 33165 Office: 207 Santillane Coral Gables FL 33134

SANTIAGO-DELPIN, EDUARDO, surgeon; b. Santurce, P.R., Sept. 18, 1941; s. Carlos A. and Carmen M. (Delpin) S.; B.S., U. P.R., 1961, M.D., 1965; M.S., U. Minn., 1972; m. Zorayda Muñoz Fletcher, May 30, 1963; children—Eduardo, Yolanda, Zorayda, Julieta. Intern, Univ. Hosp., Rio Piedras, P.R., 1965-66, resident, 1966-70; practice medicine specializing in surgery, San Juan, P.R., 1966-70, 73—, Mpls., 1970-72; mem. staff San Juan VA, Univ., San Juan City, Auxilio Mutuo, Drs., Maestro hosps., transplant fellow U. Minn., 1971-72; asst. prof. surgery U. P.R., San Juan, 1973-76, asso. prof., 1976—, asso. research prof. dept. pathology, 1977—, chief of surg. research labs., 1972-77, coordinator cancer immunology Comprehensive Cancer Center, 1973-76; chief transplant service San Juan VA Hosp., 1973—. Recipient Lange Med. Publ. award, 1965, Gold medal award Southeastern Surg. Congress, 1975, 76; NIH fellow, 1971-72, Am. Cancer Soc. fellow, 1968-69; Davis and Geck Research grantee, 1969, Upjohn Co. grantee, 1973, 74, 75, 76, Ehret Found. grantee, 1974, 75. Diplomate Am. Bd. Surgery. Fellow A.C.S. (award 1965); mem. P.R. Med. Soc., Latin Am., Internat. socs. nephrology, Am. Fedn. Clin. Research, Assn. Academic Surgery, Am. Soc. Artificial Internal Organs, AAAS, Transplantation Soc., Am. Soc. Transplant Surgeons, AMA, Sociedad de Medicos Graduados de la Universidad de P.R., Soc. Exptl. Biology and Medicine, European Dialysis and Transplant Surgeons, Assn. Hemodialysis Technicians P.R. (hon.), N.Y. Acad. Scis., Soc. Univ. Surgeons, Alpha Omega Alpha, Phi Chi. Roman Catholic. Contbr. numerous articles on nephrology, transplant surgery and exptl. medicine to profl. jours.; editor: Manual for the Care of Surgical Patients, 1976. Home: 755 Gema La Alameda Rio Piedras PR 00926 Office: Dept Surgery San Juan VA Hosp San Juan PR 00936

SANTIBANEZ, TANIA AMELIA, educator; b. Hialeah, Fla., Cuba, Jan. 6, 1949; d. Eugenio and Zenaida S.; came to U.S., 1955, naturalized, 1967; student Brigham Young U., 1966-69, Fla. Internat. U., 1977-78, Nova U., 1979—. Tchr., Roosevelt Indian Reservation, Utah, 1968; tchr. head start N.Y.C. schs., 1969-74; tchr. Marian Center Sch., Opalocka, Fla., 1975; tchr. mentally retarded pre-schoolers Dade Assn. Retarded Citizens, Hialeah, 1976-77; home/hosp. tchr. profoundly retarded-multiply handicapped, Dade County, Fla. Mem. Council Exceptional Children, Am. Assn. Profoundly/Multiply Handicapped, Dade Assn. Retarded Citizens, Parents of Down's Syndrome, Am. Assn. Mental Deficiency. Democrat. Roman Catholic. Home: 525 W 69th St #105 Hialeah FL 33014

SANTORA, ALBERT VINCENT, graphic arts machinery mfg. co. exec.; b. Jersey City, Aug. 18, 1921; s. Daniel C. and Rose M. (Basso)

S.; B.S. in Indsl. Engring., Yale U., 1950; m. Rose M. Gardi; children—William Joseph, Guy Albert. Mgr. materials and mfg. Revere Corp. Am., Wallingford, Conn., 1952-57; dir. materials Kollsman Instrument Co., Elmhurst, N.Y., 1957-62; v.p. K.W. Tunnell Co. Inc., Phila., 1962-75; v.p. ops. Visual Graphics Corp., Tamarac, Fla., 1975—; materials and production control mgmt. cons., U.S.A., Europe, P.R.; guest lectr. mfg. controls U. Wis. Mem. advisory bd. Am. Productivity Center, Houston. Served with Signal Corps, U.S. Army, 1943-46. Cert. mfg. engr. Mem. Am. Inst. Indsl. Engrs., Am. Production and Inventory Control Soc. Ethical Humanist. Contbr. articles to profl. jours. and textbooks. Home: 1849 NW 82d Ave Coral Springs FL 33165

SANTOS-DEL VALLE, RAFAEL, lawyer, educator; b. Rio Piedras, P.R., Jan. 7, 1942; s. Rafael Santos Vazquez and Abelarda Del Valle; B.A. Econs. magna cum laude, U. P.R., 1964, LL.B. cum laude, 1967; LL.M., Yale, 1968, Ford Found. scholar urban law, 1970-71; married; children—Rafael, Diana, Luis. Admitted to P.R. bar, 1967; vis. prof. Grad. Sch. Planning, U. P.R., 1969-70, asso. prof. Law Sch., 1971-73, 77-78; individual practice law, 1978—; asst. sec. P.R. Dept. Justice, 1973; sec. P.R. Dept. Addiction Services, 1973-76; coordinator for P.R., Nat. Fedn. Drug Addiction Workers, 1973-76; counsel P.R. Mental Health Commn., 1973-76; bd. dirs. P.R. Med. Center, 1974-76, P.R. Crime Commn. Cons., 1974-76, Inst. Urban Law, U. P.R., 1968-70; mem. P.R. Mining Commn., 1971-72; P.R. rep. Assn. Caribbean Univs. and Research Insts., 1974—. Named one of most outstanding young men P.R. C. of C., 1974. Mem. Am., P.R. (bd. dirs. Law Rev. 1971-72) bar assns., Law and Society Assn., Yale Alumni Assn., Ateneo Puertorriqueno, Omicron Delta Epsilon. Mem. Popular Democratic Party. Roman Cath. Contbr. profl. jours. Asso. dir. U. P.R. Law Rev., 1966-67. Home: Box 21306 U PR Sta Rio Piedras PR 00931 Office: Chase Manhattan Bank 14th Floor Suite 1412 Hato Rey PR 00918

SANTRA, NITYANANDA, surgeon; b. India, Oct. 31, 1941; s. Krishna Chandra and Saraswati (Pattanayak) S.; came to U.S., 1967, naturalized, 1976; M.B.B.S., Calcutta U., 1966; 1 son, Robin. Intern, Christ Community Hosp., Oaklawn, Ill., 1967-68; resident in surgery Hosp. of Med. Coll. of Pa., Phila., 1968-72, fellow in surgery, 1972-73; surg. staff Davis Meml. Hosp., Elkins, W.Va., 1973—; asso. prof. clin. medicine W.Va. Sch. of Osteo. Medicine, Lewisburg, W.Va. Diplomate Am. Bd. Surgery. Fellow ACS; mem. AMA. Club: Elks. Home: 1720 S Davis Ave Elkins WV 26241 Office: 909 Gorman Ave Elkins WV 26241

SANYAL, MRINAL KANTI, physiologist; b. Faridpur, Bengal, India, Mar. 9, 1939; came to U.S., 1966, naturalized, 1979; B.S. with honors, U. Delhi, India, 1958, M.S., 1960, Ph.D., 1964; m. Margaret Ann Jacobson, June 29, 1970. Post-doctoral trainee Endocrinology-Reproductive Biology program U. Wis., Madison, 1966-68; research fellow dept. biochemistry Harvard U., 1968-70, research asso. dept. obstetrics and gynecology, 1970-72, prin. research asso., 1972-75; reproductive physiologist Nat. Inst. Environ. Health Scis. NIH, Research Triangle Park, N.C., 1976—. NIH grantee, 1971-75. Mem. The Endocrine Soc., Soc. Study Reprodn., AAAS, Sigma Xi. Contbr. articles to profl. jours. Home: 3326 Pinafore Dr Durham NC 27705 Office: PO Box 12233 Research Triangle Park NC 27709

SAPOZNIKOFF, JOHN BARRY, psychiatrist; b. Phila., Dec. 19, 1939; s. John and Mary Helen S.; A.B., Temple U., 1961; M.D., Hahnemann Med. Coll., Phila., 1965; m. Jane E. Pakenas, Nov. 17, 1962; children—Susan Jane, Barri Lynn. Intern William Beaumont Gen. Hosp., El Paso, Tex., 1965-66; psychiat. resident Letterman Gen. Hosp., San Francisco, 1966-69; chief neuropsychiatry dept. Ireland Army Hosp., Ft. Knox, Ky., 1969-71; dir. mental health unit Bay Meml. Hosp., Panama City, Fla., 1971-73; pvt. practice, Panama City, 1973—; cons. Northwest Fla. Mental Health Center, Panama City, 1973—. Served to maj. M.C., AUS, 1965-71. Decorated Army Commendation medal. Diplomate Am. Bd. Psychiatry and Neurology. Mem. Am., Fla. psychiat. assns., Am., So., Fla. med. assns., Am. Soc. Clin. Hypnosis, Internat. Soc. Hypnosis, Am. Soc. Psychiatry and Law. Home: 2409 Pretty Bayou Island Dr Panama City FL 32401 Office: 622 N Bonita Ave Panama City FL 32401

SAPP, PHYLLIS WOODRUFF (MRS. J.D. SAPP), author, lectr.; b. Oklahoma City, Oct. 21, 1908; d. John A. and Maude (Laws) Woodruff; student Oklahoma City U., 1926-27; B.A., Okla. U., 1930; m. J.D. Sapp, June 5, 1930; children—Kathryn (Mrs. Karl Malthaner), John Davis, Phillip Woodruff. Organizer, dir. Okla. City's first children's theatre, 1930-35; dir. Okla. City Theatre Guild, 1940-42; jr. high sch. tchr. drama Okla. City pub. schs., 1946-49; part-time instr. Sapp Inst. Real Estate; Real estate broker Sapp Realty Co. Exec. bd., 1st v.p. Okla. City YWCA, pres., 1977-79; bd. dirs. nat. YWCA, 1979—, v.p. Mid-States Region. Recipient $4,000 first prize Zondervan's Christian Fiction Contest, 1957. Mem. Okla. Heritage Assn. (exec. bd.), Internat. Platform Assn., Nat. League Am. Pen Women (br. v.p. 1963-65, pres. local br. 1968-70, 75-76, nat. 4th v.p. 1970-72, chmn. nat. letters bd. 1972-74, nat. chaplain 1974-76, pres. Okla. City br. 1976-78), Mortar Bd., Alpha Phi, (Distinguished Alumnus award honor 1972), Pi Kappa Delta. Baptist. Author: Accidental Hero (3-act play), 1949; The Ice Cutter, 1948; Whisper Out of the Dust, 1951; For Such a Time, 1954; The Long Bridge, 1957; God of All the Earth, 1960; Gifts from God, 1962; Small Giant, 1957; Life at Its Best, 1963; Living for Jesus, 1961; Working Together in Our Church, 1963; Lighthouse on the Corner, 1964; Creative Teaching in the Church Sch., 1967; 59 Programs for Pre-Teens, 1969; (juvenile) Who Am I?, 1972, Jeff the Baptist, 1973, Very Best Friend, 1976; Real Estate Workbook, 1973; Baptists in California, 1978; Whose Plan is This?, 1978; There's a Light on the Hill, 1980; contbr. to Sunday sch. quarterlies So. Bapt. Sunday Sch. Bd. Address: 7100 S Kentucky St Oklahoma City OK 73159

SARABIA, FERMIN, psychiatrist; b. Santiago de Cuba, Oriente, Cuba, Aug. 9, 1931; s. Enrique and Dulce Maria (Ramos) S.; M.D., U. Havana (Cuba), 1959; m. Perla L. Perez de Castro, Apr. 29, 1961; children—Anthony, Perla Maria, Lilliam Maria, Patricia. Came to U.S., 1961, naturalized, 1967. Rotating intern, Orange Meml. Hosp., Orlando, Fla., 1962-63; resident in psychiatry, Central State Griffin Meml. Hosp., Norman, Okla., 1963-66; staff psychiatrist San Antonio (Tex.) State Hosp., 1966-67, clin. dir., 1967-69; practice medicine, specializing in psychiatry, San Antonio, 1969—; clin. asst. prof. psychiatry U. Tex. at San Antonio Health Scis. Center, 1977—; staff Santa Rosa Med. Center, Bapt. Meml. Hosp., San Antonio. Bd. dirs. Halfway House of San Antonio, 1969—, pres. 1973. Recipient Am. Med. Assn. Physicians Recognition award, 1973-76, 79-82. Diplomate Am. Bd. Psychiatry and Neurology. Mem. AMA, Tex. Med. Assn., Bexar County Med. Soc., Am. Psychiatric Assn. (sec.-treas. 1979—), Sociedad Medica Hispano-Americana de Tex. Republican. Roman Catholic. Clubs: The Plaza, Turtle Creek Country, Club Sembradores de Amistad (pres. 1978-79). Contbr. articles to profl. jours. Office: 343 W Houston St Suite 412 San Antonio TX 78205

SARAFOGLU, THEODORE, neurosurgeon; b. Cavala, Greece, July 12, 1933; s. Serafim and Eugenia (Zahariades) S.; came to U.S., 1961, naturalized, 1970; M.D., U. Salonica, 1956; m. Margaret McBrayer, May 1, 1965; children—Constantine, Alexander. Intern, Mercy Hosp., Canton, Ohio, 1961-62, resident in gen. surgery, 1962-63; resident in neurosurgery U. Miami (Fla.) Sch. Medicine, 1963-67; instr. neurosurgery U. Miss., Jackson, 1967-70; chief neurosurgery VA Hosp., Jackson, 1967-70; practice medicine specializing in neurosurgery, Miami, 1971—; asst. prof. neurosurgery U. Miami Sch. Medicine, 1971—. Served with M.C., Greek Armed Forces, 1956-59. Diplomate Am. Bd. Neurol. Surgery. Mem. Dade County, Am. med. assns., Am. Assn. Neurol. Surgeons, Congress of Neurol. Surgeons, Greater Miami Neurosurg. Soc. Mem. Greek Orthodox Ch. Contbr. articles in field to profl. jours. Office: 8740 N Kendall Dr Suite 110 Miami FL 33176

SARGENT, BRENDA HARMON, fin. analyst; b. Richmond, Va., Mar. 10, 1947; d. Holt Richardson and Clara Wagner) Harmon; B.A., Coll. William and Mary, 1969; M.B.A., U. Denver, 1977. Asso. editor med. jour. Va. Commonwealth U., Richmond, 1969-71; public affairs and public relations staff N.C. Electric Membership Corp., Raleigh, 1971-75; staff fin. analyst Gulf Oil Exploration and Prodn. Co. Internat., Houston, 1977—. Republican. Editor: Carolina Country, 1971-75. Office: PO Box 2100 Gulf Bldg Houston TX 77001

SARGENT, FLORENCE BURGLY, dietitian; d. George A. and Dorothy (Trefry) Burgly; B.S. in Instn. Mgmt., Pratt Inst., 1958; M.S. in Dietetics, Emory U., 1973; dietetic intern Walter Reed Army Med. Center, 1959; m. Charles F. Sargent, Apr. 20, 1963; stepchildren—Ross M., Wayne S. Commd. 2d lt., Med. Specialist Corps, U.S. Army, 1958, advanced through grades to lt. col., 1978; assignments in Md., N.C., Ga., Washington, and Germany; ret., 1978; chief clin. dietitian Moore Meml. Hosp., Pinehurst, N.C., 1978-79; food service dir. Meml. Hosp. of Alamance County, Burlington, N.C., 1979—; cons. dietitian to hosp., nursing home. Decorated Meritorious Service medal with 2 oak leaf clusters. Mem. Am. Dietetic Assn., Am. Soc. Hosp. Food Service Adminstrs.

SARGENT, GARY LEE, oil co. exec.; b. Flint, Mich., Mar. 20, 1942; s. William W. and Mary S.; B.S. in Elec. Engring., Mich. State U., 1965; m. June 1965; children—Kelly, Jill. Mech. engr., Shell Oil Co., Midland, Tex., 1965-69, sr. mech. engr., Houston, 1970-71, New Orleans, 1972-73, Denver, 1973, Houston, 1974-77; div. ops. engr. Superior Oil Co., Conroe, Tex., 1977—. Pres., Spring Creek Forest Utility Dist., 1975-79. Mem. Am. Assn. Cost Engrs., Am. Mgmt. Assn. Republican. Mem. Ch. Assembly of God. Office: Woodlands TX 77380

SARGENT, RICHARD DAVID, educator; b. Gainesville, Ga., Nov. 28, 1945; s. Bennett William and Lula May S.; A.A., Truett McConnell Coll., 1966; B.B.A., U. Ga., 1969; M.Ed., Brenau Coll., 1978; m. Sarah Helen West, Oct. 9, 1971; children—Richard, Lisa. Econ. devel. specialist City of Gainesville (Ga.), 1969-71; human resources planner Assos. in Planning and Devel. Cons., Inc., Gainesville, 1971-72; employer relations rep. Ga. Dept. Labor, Gainesville, 1972-73; health adminstr., dist. planner Ga. Dept. Human Resources, Gainesville, 1973-76, tng. dir. dist. 2, 1974-76; dir. career and profl. devel., office of continuing edn. Gainesville Jr. Coll., 1976—. Mem. adminstrv. bd. St. Paul United Methodist Ch.; trustee Christian Edn. Center; chmn. Mayor's Com. on Employment of Handicapped. Mem. Am. Mgmt. Assn., Ga. Adult Edn. Assn., United Comml. Travelers of Am. (sr. counselor 1975-76). Democrat. Club: Lions (pres. Gainesville 1975-76, dist. gov. 1978-79, named Outstanding Dist. Gov. 1979). Home: Route 12 167 C Gainesville GA 30501 Office: Gainesville Jr Coll PO Box 1358 Gainesville GA 30501

SARGENT, WILLIAM EARL, ednl. adminstr.; b. Balt., Aug. 2, 1919; s. Edward Brown and Lucy Edna (Simms) S.; B.A. in History, Am. U., 1953, M.Ed. in Adminstrn. and Supervision, 1963; postgrad. Va. Poly. Inst. and State U., 1976—. Dir., Burgundy Farm Country Day Sch., Alexandria, Va., 1960-63; elem. classroom tchr., Arlington County, Va., 1954-60, 67-70, 77-78, tchr. seminar for gifted elem. students, 1963-67, sch. social worker, 1970-72, child devel. cons., 1972-76, elem. sci. tchr., 1976-77, tchr. English as 2d lang., 1978-79; team leader, asst. to dir. Arlington-Trinity Tchr. Corps Project in Bilingual and Multicultural Edn., 1979—; vol. Spanish Speaking Com. Va. Mem. Fairfax County Dem. Com., 1970; mem. Greenbelt Consumer Services Inc., 1979—. Served with USN, 1942-46; PTO. Mem. Am. Orthopsychiat. Assn., Am. Personnel and Guidance Assn., Am. Sch. Counselors Assn., Nat. Assn. for Bilingual Edn., United Teaching Profession, Clan Fraser Soc. N. Am., Clan Stewart Soc. in Am., Sims-Simms Family Geneal. and Meml. Soc. Unitarian. Clubs: Leabhar (Isle of Lewis, Scotland), Comunn na Canain Albannaich (Isle of Lewis, Scotland). Home: 902 Myers Circle SW Vienna VA 22180 Office: 200 S Carlin Springs Rd Arlington VA 22204

SARGENT, WILLIAM LEON, educator; b. Cordova, Ala., Mar. 29, 1939; s. William Washington and Ida Lee (Estill) S.; student Walker Coll, 1959-60; B.S., U. Ala., 1962, M.A., 1965, A.A., 1969; postgrad U. Ky., 1963, U. Calif., Davis, 1973, 77, U. Ala., 1979; profl. cert. Samford U., 1974. Tchr. history Minor High Sch., Birmingham, Ala., 1962-70; instr. history Walker Coll., Jasper, Ala., 1970-79. Nat. Endowment Humanities fellow, 1973 77 summers; Gen. Electric fellow, 1963. Mem. Ala. Hist. Assn. Address: Rt 1 Box 14 Cordova AL 35550

SARKIS, MUNIR FUAD, counselor; b. Cairo, Egypt, Dec. 12, 1935; s. Fuad Sarkis and Josephine HIlda (Sarkis) Salama; B.S., Mont. State U., 1964; Ph.D., U. Ala., 1977; m. Monica Sandström, June 14, 1970; children—Louisa Magdalena, Eric William. Chmn. dept. fgn. langs. Am. Community Sch., Addis Ababa, Ethiopia, 1965-71; asst. headmaster Am. Sch. Bilbao, Spain, 1971-75; dir. counseling Daytona Beach (Fla.) Community Coll., 1977—. Served with USAR-ROTC, 1960-62. Mem. U. Ala. Alumni Assn., Am. Personnel and Guidance Assn., Phi Delta Kappa, Kappa Delta Phi. Home: 930 Old Mill Run Ormond Beach FL 32074 Office: PO Box 111 Daytona Beach FL 32017

SARKISSIAN, KAREN MITCHELL, educator; b. Logan, W.Va., Aug. 25, 1940; d. Lacy Avinell and Dorothy Eunice (Tabor) Mitchell; B.S., W.Va. U., 1962, M.S. in Genetics and Biochemistry, 1966; postgrad. Tex. A&M U., 1977-79; m. Igor V. Sarkissian, Aug. 23, 1966 (dec.); children—Steven, Gregory, Lisa Michele. Research biochemist Campbell Soup Co., Riverton, N.J., 1966; 8th grade sci. tchr. Bryan (Tex.) Ind. Sch. System, 1967-68; prof. biology Blinn Coll., Bryan, 1975—. Mem. AAAS, Sigma Xi. Episcopalian. Club: Order Eastern Star. Home: Route 3 Box 504 Bryan TX 77801 Office: 307 S Main St Bryan TX 77801

SARLES, KEN LEON, historian, theologian; b. Highland Park, Mich., Sept. 22, 1948; s. Hugh Edward and Virginia Carroll (Batchelor) S.; Ph.B. with honor, Wayne State U., 1971; Th.M., Dallas Theol. Sem., with high honor, 1978, postgrad., 1978—; m. Elizabeth Ann Caldwell, May 18, 1974. Campus dir. Campus Crusade for Christ, Houston, 1971-74; instr. hist. theology Dallas Theol. Sem., 1978—. Mem. Am. Hist. Assn., Am. Soc. Ch. History, Orgn. Am. Historians. Home: 2122 Millmar St Dallas TX 75228 Office: Dallas Theol Sem 3909 Swiss Ave Dallas TX 75204

SARTAIN, ROBERT LEE, mathematician; b. Borger, Tex., Sept. 1, 1939; s. Lee Aston and Naomi Gertrude (Landreth) S.; B.S., Wayland Bapt. Coll., 1961; M.S., U. Iowa, 1963; Ph.D., Tex. Tech U., 1972; m. Janet Carol Butler, July 18, 1960; children—Timothy Lee, David William, Melissa Carol. Teaching asst. U. Iowa, 1961-63; pastor Downey Bapt. Ch., West Branch, Iowa, 1963-64; asst. prof. Howard Payne U., Brownwood, Tex., 1964-67, prof. math., 1972—, head dept. math., 1971—; instr. Tex. Tech. U., Lubbock, 1967-71; minister of music Woodland Heights Bapt. Ch., Brownwood, Tex., 1966-67, 73-76, First Bapt. Ch., Santa Anna, Tex., 1977-79, First Bapt. Ch., Coleman, Tex., 1979—. Recipient Timothy award Wayland Bapt. Coll., Plainview, Tex., 1961; Tex. Bapt. Faculty fellow, 1967-69. Mem. Math. Assn. Am., Am. Math. Soc., Soc. Indsl. and Applied Math. Home: 2406 14th St Brownwood TX 76801 Office: Howard Payne U Box 426 Brownwood TX 76801

SARTOR, BARBARA JEAN, chemist; b. Balt., June 20, 1947; d. Frank Arthur and Fannie (Lyles) Sartor; B.S., Morgan State U., 1976; M.S., Rensselaer Poly. Inst., 1978; M.B.A., Loyola Coll., 1981. Instr. chemistry Morgan State U., Balt., 1976-77; research chemist Gen. Electric Research and Devel. Center, Schenectady, 1976-78; info. analyst Philip Morris Research Center, Richmond, Va., 1978—. Mem. Am. Chem. Soc., Soc. Plastic Engrs., Delta Sigma Theta. Home: 2706 Sutters Mill Ct Midlothian VA 23113 Office: Philip Morris Research Center PO Box 26583 Richmond VA 23261

SARTOR, DANIEL RYAN, JR., lawyer; b. Vicksburg, Miss., June 2, 1932; s. Daniel Ryan and Lucy Leigh (Hubbs) S.; B.A., Tulane U., 1952, LL.B., 1955; m. Olive Guthrie Moss, Oct. 12, 1957; children—Clara Moss, Daniel Ryan III, Walter Moss. Admitted to La. bar, 1955; instr. law Tulane U., New Orleans, 1955-56, asst. prof., 1956-57; pvt. practice law, Monroe, La., 1957—; mem. law firm Snellings, Breard, Sartor, Inabnett & Trascher, Monroe, 1957—, partner, 1960—. Bd. visitors Tulane U., 1974—, mem. adv. bd. Law Sch., 1970—; chmn. bd. trustees St. Paul's United Meth. Ch., 1971-77. Fellow Am. Bar Found.; mem. La. State Law Inst. (mem. council 1969—, sec. civil law sect. 1969—), La. State Bar Assn. (chmn. sect. of trust, probate and immovable property law 1973-74, mem. bd. govs. 1974-75), Tulane U. Alumni Assn. (treas. 1974-75, sec. 1975-76, pres. 1979-80), Order of Coif, Phi Beta Kappa, Omicron Delta Kappa, Sigma Alpha Epsilon. Editor-in-chief Tulane Law Rev., 1954-55, mem. adv. bd. editors, 1970—. Home: 2405 Pargoud Blvd Monroe LA 71201 Office: 1503 N 19th St Monroe LA 71201

SARVAIDEO, ROBERT JOSEPH, air force officer; b. Mt. Vernon, N.Y.; A.A., Orange County Community Coll., 1968; B.S. in Biology, SUNY, New Paltz, 1971; M.S. in Environ. Health Scis., N.Y. U., 1974; m. Lynne Scarola, Nov. 21, 1971. Library aide Orange County Community Coll., Middletown, N.Y., 1965-68, biology lab. asst., 1968; library aide SUNY, New Paltz, 1968-70; inhalation/cancer researcher A.J. Lanza Research Labs., Inst. Environ. Medicine, N.Y. U. Med. Center, Tuxedo, 1970-79; commd. capt. USAF, 1979; cons. Environ. Sci., Occupational and Environ. Health Lab., Biomed. Scis. Corps, Brooks AFB, Tex., 1979—. Sec.-treas. Sterling Forest Indsl. Softball League, Tuxedo, 1978-79; dep. warden Sterling Forest Fish and Game Dept., Tuxedo, 1972-79; 2d lt. Sterling Forest Vol. Fire Co., Tuxedo, 1973-79. Office: USAF Occupational and Environ Health Lab Brooks Air Force Base TX 78235

SARVIS, ALVA TAYLOR, art educator; b. Nanking, China, Nov. 27, 1924 (parents Am. citizens); s. Guy Walter and Pearl Maude (Taylor) S.; B.F.A., Calif. Coll. Arts and Crafts, 1952; M.A., U. N.Mex., 1954; m. Doris Mae Crabtree, Aug. 14, 1956; children—Clancy, William, Mary. Art supr. Sch. Dist. #70, Winnebago County, Ill., 1959-60; instr. U. N.D., Grand Forks, 1960-63; asst. prof. art San Diego State Coll., 1963-65, Western Carolina Coll., Cullowhee, N.C., 1965-70; asst. prof. art. Va. Poly. Inst. and State U., Blacksburg, 1970-73, asso. prof., 1974—; numerous one-man shows nationally, 1960—. Served with USN, 1941-46. Mem. SE Coll. Art Conf., Coll. Art Assn. Contbr. articles in field to profl. jours. Home: 110 Orchard View Ln Blacksburg VA 24060 Office: Dept Art Va Polytech Inst & State U Blacksburg VA 24061

SASMOR, JAMES CECIL, pubs. rep.; b. N.Y.C., July 29, 1920; s. Louis and Cecilia (Mockler) S.; B.S., Columbia U., 1942; M.B.A., Calif. Western U., 1977, Ph.D., 1979; m. Jeannette L. Fuchs, May 30, 1965; 1 dau., Elizabeth Lynn. Advt. exec. N.Y. World Telegram, 1946-48, Chain Store Age, 1948-50, Am. Girl mag., 1950-59; registered rep. Nat. Assn. Security Dealers, 1956-57; founder, owner J.C. Sasmor Assos. Pub.'s Reps., N.Y.C., 1959—; co-founder, pres. dir. adminstrn. Continuing Edn. Cons.'s, Inc., Tampa, 1976—; pub. cons., 1959—. Team tchr. childbirth edn. Am. Soc. Childbirth Educators; bd. dirs. Tampa chpt. ARC, also chmn. instructional com. on nursing and health; county nursing ednl. cons. ARC. Served with USN, 1942-46. Recipient cert. of appreciation ARC, 1979; cert. sex educator Am. Assn. Sex Educators, Counselors and Therapists; cert. econs. tchr. Mem. Assn. Pubs. Reps. (pres. 1965-66), Am. Soc. Psychoprophylaxis in Obstetrics (dir. 1970-71), Am. Assn. Childbirth Educators (co-founder, dir. 1972—), Nurses Assn. of Am. Coll. Obstetricians and Gynecologists (asso.), Health Edn. Media Assn., Nursing Educators Assn. Tampa. Contbr. chpt.: Childbirth Education: A Nursing Perspective, 1979. Home: 7113 Lynnwood Dr Tampa FL 33617 Office: PO Box 16159 Tampa FL 33687

SASSER, DOROTHY PILLEY (MRS. JOHN T. SASSER), educator; b. Pantego, N.C., Aug. 15, 1926; d. Leonard R. and Mattie (Winfield) Pilley; B.S. in Secretarial Adminstrn., Woman's Coll. U. N.C., 1947; postgrad. U. Tenn., 1952; m. John T. Sasser, Dec. 30, 1951 children—Sandra, Sabrina. Co-owner, dir. Myrtle Beach (S.C.) Bus. Coll., 1952; owner Quality Mimeograph Shop, Whiteville, N.C., 1953—; tchr. pub. schs., Clarkton, N.C., 1953-57; tchr. Hallsboro (N.C.) Sch., 1957-59, Elizabethtown (N.C.) Sch., 1959, Alexander Graham Jr. High Sch., Fayetteville, N.C., 1960; chmn. bus. edn. dept. Terry Sanford Sr. High Sch., Fayetteville, 1961-78; ret., 1978. Mem. N.C. Edn. Assn., Bus. and Profl. Woman (corr. sec. 1958), Delta Kappa Gamma. Democrat. Presbyn. Clubs: Evening Garden (sec. 1957-58), Executives, Merrymakers (Elizabethtown). Home: 906 Emeline Ave Fayetteville NC 28303

SASSER, JAMES RALPH, U.S. Senator; b. Memphis, Sept. 30, 1936; s. Joseph Ralph and Mary Nell (Gray) S.; B.A., U. Tenn., 1955; LL.B., Vanderbilt U., 1961; m. Mary Gorman, Aug. 18, 1962; children—Gray, Elizabeth. Admitted to Tenn. bar, 1961; mem. firm Goodpasture, Carpenter, Woods & Sasser, Nashville, 1961-76; mem. U.S. Senate from Tenn., 1977—. Chmn. Tenn. Dem. Exec. Com., 1973-76; so. vice chmn. Assn. Dem. State Chairmen, 1975-76. Mem. Am. Bar Assn., Am. Judicature Soc., NCCJ (bd. mem. Nashville chpt.), Nashville Com. Fgn. Relations. Office: 2104 Dirksen Senate Office Building Washington DC 20510*

SASSER, JIMMY FRANCIS, credit union exec.; b. Geary, Okla., July 31, 1933; s. Floyd Edward and Mary Frances (Dyer) S.; B.A., Pan Am. U., 1955; student S.W. Credit Union Nat. Assn. Sch., U. Houston, 1977; m. Genene Elizabeth Serviere, Sept. 25, 1953; children—Cathy Genene, Carole Cay, Corine Lee. Elem. tchr. Edinburg (Tex.) Consol. Ind. Sch. Dist., 1955-57; mgr. Brumley's Store for Men, Edinburg, 1957-72; pres. Edinburg Tchrs. Credit Union, 1972—; chmn. Tex. Credit Union League Services, Inc.; dir. Mems. Ins. Cos., Credit Union Trust Co., CU Bank Shares, Inc. Commr. City of Edinburg, 1968-70; deacon 1st Baptist Ch. of Edinburg. Mem. Tex. Credit Union League (2d vice chmn., dir.), Credit Union Nat. Assn. (dir.). Club: Edinburg Lions (pres. 1967-68). Home: 1108 S 13th St Edinburg TX 78539 Office: 312 W University Dr Edinburg TX 78539

SASSER, JOHN THOMAS, sch. adminstr.; b. Wilson, N.C., Apr. 6, 1923; s. James Tonkin and Bettie (Howell) S.; A.A., Mars Hill Coll., 1942; B.A., Wake Forest Coll., 1944, M.A., 1948; postgrad. U. N.C., 1950-51; m. Dorothy Pilley, Dec. 30, 1951; children—Sandra, Sabrina. Researcher Library of Congress, 1944; prin. Topsail Pub. Sch., Hampstead, N.C., 1944-47, Leaksville-Spray High Sch., Leaksville, N.C., 1947-51; pres. Myrtle Beach Bus. Coll., 1951-53; prin. Whiteville High Sch., Whiteville, N.C., 1953-59, Elizabethtown (N.C.) Pub. Schs., 1959-60, Terry Sanford Sr. High Sch., Fayetteville, 1960—. Mem. Nat. Assn. Secondary Sch. Prins., N.C. Prins. Assn., Nat. (life), N.C. (pres. Whiteville unit 1954-55) edn. assns., Horace Mann League Am. Presbyn. Rotarian (pres. 1957-58). Home: 906 Emeline Ave Fayetteville NC 28303 Office: Fort Bragg Rd Fayetteville NC 28303

SASSER, LYLE BLAINE, animal nutritionist; b. Tremonton, Utah, Feb. 20, 1939; s. Luther Blaine and Ardeena (Nalder) S.; B.S., U. Idaho, 1961; M.S., Colo. State U., 1965; Ph.D., Colo. State U., 1968; m. Sonja Nelson, June 12, 1963; children—Bruce Lyle, Kyla, Kirt Nelson, Jenise. Instr. animal sci. Fresno (Calif.) State U., 1967; research scientist U. Tenn. Agrl. Research Lab., Oak Ridge, 1968-73, sr. research scientist, 1973-77; asso. prof. Comparative Animal Research Lab., 1977—. Served with U.S. Navy, 1961-63. Mem. Am. Assn. Vet. Nutritionists, Am. Inst. Nutrition, Am. Soc. Animal Sci., Soc. Exptl. Biology and Medicine, Soc. Environ. Geochemistry and Health. Mormon. Home: Route 2 Early Dr Powell TN 37849 Office: 1299 Bethel Valley Rd Oak Ridge TN 37830

SASSER, MARY HELLER, business ofcl.; b. Dallas, July 10, 1950; d. Frank Henry and Jacquelyn (Morphis) Heller; A.A. summa cum laude, Mt. Vernon Coll., 1970; B.F.A. magna cum laude, So. Meth. U., 1972, M.F.A. summa cum laude, 1973; m. Thomas Benjamin Sasser, Aug. 30, 1974. Gen. mgr. Dallas Ballet Co. and Dallas Civic Ballet Co., 1973-76; dir. regional services, asst. to pres. and dir. mktg. Dallas Symphony Orch. Assn., 1977-79; mktg. exec., mgr. nat. retail distbn., club mgr. Inovision of Electronic Data Systems, Dallas, 1979—, tchr. ballet Krassovska Sch. Ballet, 1977-78, Kirby Dance Studio, 1978—; critic Park Cities News, 1977-78; tchr. classical ballet Dallas Ballet Acad., 1973-76; mgmt. cons. for arts, 1978—. Mem. Dallas Mus. Fine Arts League, Dallas Symphony League, Dallas Summer Musicals Guild, Young Women for Arts, Am. Bus. Women's Assn., Dallas Council World Affairs, Interlude Study Club, Holy Trinity Council Cath. Women. Roman Catholic. Clubs: Colony, 500 Inc. Home: 4236 Bordeaux St Dallas TX 75205 Office: 14580 Midway Rd Dallas TX 75234

SASTRE, CESAR JULIO, urologist; b. Bogota, Colombia, Oct. 25, 1930; s. Julio Cesar and Lilia (Sanchez) S.; came to U.S., 1958, naturalized, 1965; B.S., Xaveriana U., Bogota, 1955, M.D., 1958; m. Karin Graser, June 10. 1962; children—Cesar A., Greta A., Michael A. Intern St. Vincent's Hosp., Jacksonville. Fla., 1958-59; resident gen. surgery St. Luke's Hosp., Jacksonville, 1959-60; resident urology Bellevue Hosp., N.Y.C., 1960-62, Washington Hosp. Center, 1962-63; pvt. practice urology, Miami, Fla., 1965—; mem. staff North Shore, Palmetto Gen., Hialeah hosps. Bd. dirs. Palmetto Gen. Hosp., Miami. Diplomate Am. Bd. Urology. Fellow Am.. Internat. colls. surgeons; mem. Am.. Fla., Dade County med. assns., Am. Urol. Assn. Rotarian. Home: 1125 NE 92d St Miami Shores FL 33138 Office: 8340 NE 2d Ave Miami FL 33138

SATO, SHIGEKO (SHIGEKO SATO WALTON), ceramic sculptor; b. Tokyo; came to U.S., 1964, naturalized, 1972; d. Fukue and Masako Sato; Master of Tea Ceremony, Tokyo, 1960; M. Flower Arrangement, Ikenobo Sch., Tokyo, 1960; student Meiji Gakuen U., Tokyo, 1962-64; B.A. summa cum laude, San Jose State Coll., 1967; M.A., U. Calif., Berkeley, 1968; M.F.A., U. Ga., 1972; student sculpture, Cortona, Italy, 1972; postgrad. U. Fla., 1974-76; m. Nyle K. Walton, Sept. 28, 1967. Prof. flower arrangement and tea ceremony, Tokyo, 1960-64; teaching asst. U. Ga., Athens, 1971-72; instr. ceramics design and constn. Valdosta (Ga.) State Coll., 1972-73; instr. glass blowing, sculpture and ceramics Southwestern Coll., Americus, Ga., 1973-74; instr. ceramics, jewelry and metalwork U. Fla., Gainesville, 1974—; one-man shows of ceramics include: Yen-Yen of Malaya, San Francisco, 1968, U. Calif., Berkeley, 1968, Banks Haley Art Gallery, Albany, Ga., 1970, U. Ga. Law Library, 1972, Valdosta State Coll., 1973, Savannah (Ga.) Art Assn., 1976, Henri Gallery, Washington, 1979, Artist Market Gallery, Clearwater, Fla., 1979; numerous group shows, latest being: Fla. State U., Tallahassee, 1975-76, Lowe Mus. Art, U. Miami, Coral Gables, Fla., 1976, Telfair Mus., Savannah, 1976, Gallery X, U. Fla., Gainesville, 1976, 79, Harmon Gallery, Naples, Fla., 1977, Thomas Center, Gainesville, 1977, Southeastern Center for Contemporary Art, Winston-Salem, N.C., 1977, Lighthouse Gallery, Palm Beach, Fla., 1977, LeMoyne Art Found., Tallahassee, 1978, Mint Mus. Art, Charlotte, N.C., 1978, Grove House, Miami, Fla., 1978, Cummer Mus. Art, Jacksonville, Fla., 1978, Henri Gallery, 1979, Makers Gallery, N.Y.C., 1979, Kitchen Show, Micanopy, Fla., 1979, LeMoyne Art Found., Tallahassee, 1979, 80, Grove House, Coconut Grove, Fla., 1979, Fla. Invitational Exhibit, Jacksonville, 1979, Fla. Internat. U., Miami, 1979, Salisbury (Md.) State Coll., 1979; represented in permanent collections: St. John River Community Coll., Barnett Bank, Jacksonville. Recipient numerous best in show and category awards; Fine Arts Council Fla. grantee, 1979-80. Fellow Italian Cultural Soc.; mem. Fla. Craftsmen, Coll. Art Assn. Am., Am. Crafts Council, Nat. Council Edn. for Ceramic Art, Japan Scholar's Assn. Home: 3008 W University Ave Gainesville FL 32607

SATTER, ABDUS, petroleum engr.; b. Birbhum, West Bengal, India, Mar. 1, 1932; came to U.S., 1955, naturalized, 1966; s. Enayet Hossain and Aklima Khatun (Choudhury) Mollick; B.Sc.M.E., U. Dacca, 1954; Petroleum Engr., Colo. Sch. Mines, 1958, M.S., 1959; Ph.D., U. Okla., 1963; children—Muneer A., R. Shereen, Rabi H. Lectr. mech. engring. Ahsanullah Engring. Coll., Dacca, Bangladesh, 1954-55; sr. research engr. Amoco, Tulsa, 1962-67; asst. prof. engring. sci. U. Western Ont. (Can.), London, 1967-68; research petroleum engr. Texaco Inc., Bellaire, Tex., 1968-69, 70-74, sr. research petroleum engr, 1974-79, technologist, 1979—; sr. cons. engr. Frank W. Cole Engring., Dallas, 1969-70. Bd. dirs. Undercroft Montessori Sch., Tulsa, 1964-66; active Boy Scouts Am., 1973-78. Govt. of Pakistan-Colo. Sch. Mines scholar, 1955-59; Colo. Sch. Mines grad. fellow, 1957-59; Socony Mobil fellow, 1959-62. Registered profl. engr., Okla. Mem. Soc. Petroleum Engrs. of AIME (editorial com. 1977-78), Sigma Xi, Pi Epsilon Tau. Club: Toastmasters. Contbr. articles to profl. publs. Patentee in field.

SATTERFIELD, DAVID EDWARD, III, congressman; b. Richmond, Va., Dec. 2, 1920; s. David Edward, Jr. and Blanche (Kidd) S.; student U. Richmond, 1939-42; LL.B., U. Va., 1948; m. Anne Elizabeth Powell, Dec. 27, 1943; children—David Edward IV, John Bacon. Admitted to Va. bar, 1948, since practiced in Richmond; partner firm Satterfield, Haw, Anderson, Parkerson & Beazley; asst. U.S. atty. Eastern Dist. Va., 1950-53; councilman City Richmond, 1954-56; mem. Va. Gen. Assembly from Richmond City, 1960-64; mem. 89th-96th congresses from 3d Dist. Va. Past. sec.-treas., dir. Richmond Baseball, Inc., The Virginians, A.A.A. baseball club of Internat. League. Served to lt., pilot, USNR, World War II; PTO; capt. Res. Decorated Purple Heart. Mem. Phi Gamma Delta, Phi Alpha Delta. Democrat. Mason (32 deg., Shriner). Office: Federal Bldg Richmond VA 23290 also 2348 Rayburn House Office Bldg Washington DC 20515*

SATTERFIELD, GEORGE HOWARD, JR., obstetrician and gynecologist; b. Raleigh, N.C., Feb. 29, 1932; s. George Howard and Alleece (Sapp) Satterfield; B.S. in Agrl. and Biol. Chemistry, N.C. State U., 1954; M.D., Duke, 1957; m. Joyce Satterfield; children—Karen Joyce, Debra Kay, George Howard III, Lisa Ann, Diane Lynn. Intern Med. Coll. Va. Hosp., 1957; resident obstetrics and gynecology Duke Hosp., 1958-60, 62-63; pvt. practice obstetrics and gynecology, Raleigh, 1962-70, Greenville, N.C., 1971—; mem. attending staff Pitt County Meml. Hosp., 1971—; clin. instr. U. N.C. Sch. Medicine, 1970-71; vis. instr. Sch. Nursing, East Carolina U., 1971—, clin. asst. prof. obstetrics and gynecology med. Sch.; cons. Pitt County Health Dept. obstetrics and gynecology clinic, also cancer clinic Pitt County Health Dept., 1973—. Served to capt. USAF, 1960-61. Mem. A.C.S.. Am. Coll. Obstetricians and Gynecologists, Am. Fertility Soc.. Bayard-Carter Obstet. and Gynecol. Soc., Royal Soc. Medicine, Am. Assn. Gynecologic Laparoscopists, Pan Am. Med. Assn., N.C., Pitt County med. socs., Soc. Agrl. Chemists, Phi Kappa Phi, Phi Eta Sigma, Lambda Sigma Epsilon. Sigma Chi. Home: 315 Kenilworth Dr Greenville NC 27834 Office: Bldg 5 Doctors Park Greenville NC 27834

SATTERFIELD, MARY (YARBROUGH) MC ADEN, ret. educator, civic worker; b. Semora, N.C., Mar. 15, 1911; d. John H. and Ella T. (Yarbrough) McAden; A.B., Meredith Coll., 1931; postgrad. N.C. State U., 1965, U. Va. Extension, 1965, U. N.C., summer, 1963, Appalachian State U., 1932; m. Lynn Banks Satterfield, Nov. 29, 1933; children—Lynn Banks, John De Berniere. Tchr. Caswell County (N.C.) elementary schs., 1931-34; tchr. sci. Caswell County high schs., 1934-36; postmaster U.S. Post Office, Milton, N.C., 1936-41; tchr. elementary grades Caswell County pub. schs., 1962-71. Clk., Town of Milton, 1959-61, sec. bd. of elections, 1976, registrar, 1979-80. Mem. N.C., Caswell County (pres. 1962-64, sec. 1977—) hist assns., N.C. Assn. Educators, Nat. Ret. Tchrs. Assn., N.C. Lit. and Hist. Assn., Museum of History Assos., UDC, Semora Extension Homemakers Assn. Democrat. Baptist. Clubs: Milton Woman's (pres. 1961-62, v.p. 1962-64, sec. 1965—), Milton Community (sec. 1937-44, pres. 1965-67), Order Eastern Star. Home: PO Box 75 Milton NC 27305

SATTLER, JON INMAN, plastic surgeon; b. Miami Beach, Fla., Mar. 4, 1944; s. Charles and Margaret Sattler; B.A., Fla. State U., 1966; M.D., U. Fla., 1970; children—Airlie, Jon. Intern, U. Chgo., 1970-71; resident in gen. surgery U. Miami (Fla.), 1971-72, Emory U., Atlanta, 1972-75; resident in plastic surgery Med. Coll. Ohio, Toledo, 1975-77; practice medicine, specializing in plastic surgery, Columbia, S.C., 1977—; staff Lexington County Hosp., Bapt. Hosp., Providence Hosp. Mem. S.C. Plastic Surgery Soc., Southeastern Plastic Surgery Soc., Assn. Plastic and Reconstructive Surgeons, Burn Assn., Columbia Med. Assn., Lexington County Med. Assn., S.C. Med. Assn., AMA, S.C. Polit. Action Com., Am. Med. Polit. Action Com. Address: 3321 Medical Park Rd Columbia SC 29203

SATULOFF, BARTH, accountant; b. Buffalo, Dec. 13, 1945; s. Bernard and Annette (Lurie) S.; B.B.A., U. Miami, 1967, M.B.A., 1969; m. Marsha Steiner, May 25. 1974. Staff accountant Price Waterhouse & Co., C.P.A.'s, Miami, 1969-71; tax staff Laventhol & Horwath, C.P.A.'s, Miami, 1973-74; self-employed as C.P.A., Miami, 1974—; pres. Satuloff Bros., Inc., Buffalo; pres. Chartered Investment Research Corp., Miami, 1979—. Mem. Estate Planning Council Greater Miami, 1974—. Mem. endowment fund com. U. Miami. Served with Fla. N.G., 1970-76. C.P.A., Fla., N.Y., Ill., La. Mem. Am. Accounting Assn., Am. Taxation Assn., Am., Fla. insts. C.P.A.'s, N.Y. State, Ill., La. socs. C.P.A.'s, Econ. Soc. South Fla., Accounting Research Assn., Fin. Accounting Found. (asso. mem.), R. Warner Ring Ednl. Found. Home: 9614 SW 134th Ct Miami FL 33186 Office: 8024 SW 81st Dr Miami FL 33143

SATURLEY, DAVID WAYNE, corp. data processing mgr.; b. Louisville, Nov. 18, 1941; s. David Gaither and Opal Pearl (Cathcart) S.; student Bethel Coll., 1960; m. Martha Ann Lanham, Jan. 7, 1978; children—Faith Renae, David Todd, Gant Gaither. Prodn. control analyst Thomas Industries, Inc., Hopkinsville, 1960-64, computer programmer, 1964-66, systems programming mgr., 1966-67, data processing mgr., 1967-69, dir. data processing, 1969-78, corp. data processing mgr., Louisville, 1978—. Sec. Hopkinsville Little League Baseball Assn., 1970-74; chmn. Hopkinsville-Christian County Recreation Commn., 1975—. Mem. Data Processing Mgmt. Assn. (internat. bd. dirs.). Democrat. Baptist. Clubs: Masons, Shriners. Home: 408 Highwood Dr Louisville KY 40206 Office: 207 E Broadway Louisville KY 40202

SAUCIER, GENE DUANE, univ. ofcl.; b. Dallas, Sept. 25, 1931; s. Albert L. and Myrtle (West) S.; B.S. in Agronomy, Miss. State U., 1953; M.S. in Counseling, U. So. Miss., 1970, Ed.D., 1977; m. Marilyn Cox, Dec. 27, 1952; children—Alan, Steve, Renee. Builder and developer, City of Hattiesburg, Miss., 1956-70; dir. admissions U. So. Miss., Hattiesburg, 1970-72, dir. admissions and records, 1972-74, dean spl. acad. services, 1974—; ordained deacon Baptist Ch., 1971. Scoutmaster, Pine Burr area council Boy Scouts Am., 1960-72, mem. exec. council, 1970-72. Served to 1st. lt. USAF, 1953-56. Mem. Am. Assn. of Collegiate Registrars and Admissions Officers, So. Assn. of Collegiate Registrars and Admissions Officers, Miss. Assn. of Collegiate Registrars and Admissions Officers, Phi Delta Kappa, Omicron Delta Kappa Home: 3310 Arlington Loop Hattiesburg MS 39401 Office: U So Miss Southern Sta Box 5011 Hattiesburg MS 39401

SAUCIER, RANDOLPH JOSEPH, petroleum engr.; b. Houma, La., Apr. 24, 1939; s. Robert Finley and Inez Marie (Brunet) S.; B.S. in Mech. Engring., La. State U., 1962; M.S., Tulane U., 1965; m. Patricia Ann Amonc, Jan. 27, 1962; children—Randall, Cheli, Rebecca. Prodn. engr. Shell Devel. Co., Houston, 1964-69; sr. prodn. engr. ops. Shell Oil Co., New Orleans, 1969-72; sr. research engr. Shell Devel. Co., 1972-77; staff research engr. Shell Devel. Co., 1977—. Chmn. troop com. Boy Scouts Am. Served to capt. C.E., AUS, 1965-67. NDEA fellow, 1962-64. Mem. Soc. Petroleum Engrs. (mem. coms.), Tau Beta Pi, Pi Tau Sigma. Contbr. articles to profl. jours. Patentee in field Home: 10906 Ashcroft St Houston TX 77096 Office: PO Box 481 Houston TX 77001

SAUDER, A. LELAND, petroleum co. exec.; b. Madison, Kans., Jan. 17, 1925; s. Aaron Leland and Bessie (Wiggins) S.; B.S. in Petroleum Engring., U. Kans., 1950; m. Johnnie Marie Waggoner, Nov. 17, 1951; children—Alane Marie, John Waggoner, Suzanne. With Gulf Oil Co., 1950-51; ind. oil operator, Wichita Falls, Tex., 1951—; dir. Moran Drilling Co.; dir. profit sharing trust Sauder Mgmt. Co.; cons. in field; cattle rancher, Wichita and Wise counties. Mem. adv. bd. Geology Assos., U. Kans. Served to ensign USNR, 1944-46. Mem. Am. Assn. Petroleum Geologists (del.), North Tex. Geol. Soc., Ind. Petroleum Assn. Am., Tex. Ind. Producers and Royalty Assn., North Tex. Oil and Gas Assn. (dir.), Kappa Sigma, Tau Beta Pi. Clubs: Wichita, Wichita Falls Country Chaparral. Home: 2300 Irving Pl Wichita Falls TX 76308 Office: 202 Hamilton Bldg Wichita Falls TX 76301

SAUER, ENNO THIEME, chem. engr.; b. Michigan City, Ind., June 6, 1915; s. Oscar Adelbert and Beata (Thieme) S.; B.S. in Chemistry, U. Richmond, 1935; M.S. in Chem. Engring., Mass. Inst. Tech., 1937; m. Marie Rach, Sept. 20, 1941; children—James D., Kenneth A., Thomas J. Supr. pilot plant Rohm & Haas Co., Phila., 1937-47, process mgr. prodn. dept. 1947-52, supr. new plant. Toronto, Ont., Can., 1954-55, supr. of production control, Phila., 1953-60, asst. plant mgr., Knoxville, Ky., 1960-62; pres. Rohm and Haas Ky. Inc., Louisville, 1962—; dir. Asso. Industries of Ky., 1973-76. Chmn. mfg. div. of Metro United Way, Louisville, 1975; mem. Ky. Environ. Quality Commn., 1973—; gen. chmn. Cedar Lake Lodge Fund Raising Campaign, 1973-74; mem. Gov.'s Econ. Devel. Commn., 1975, Ky. Gov.'s Commn. on Hazardous Waste Mgmt., 1979—; bd. dirs. Concordia Pub. House, Luth. Ch., Mo. Synod, 1972—, Old Ky. Home Council of Boy Scouts, 1977—, Action Now, Inc., 1977—, Ohio River Valley Safety Council, 1966—, pres., 1969. Registered profl. engr., Pa., Ky. Mem. Am. Inst. Chem. Engrs., AAAS, Ky. C. of C. (dir. 1971-74), Louisville C. of C. (v.p. 1973, dir. 1971-73). Democrat. Lutheran Club: Rotary (dir. 1976—). Home: 2317 Clarkwood Rd Louisville KY 40207 Office: PO Box 32260 Louisville KY 40232

SAUER, JOE DEAN, chemist; b. Thomas, Okla., May 31, 1948; s. Daniel William and Juanita (Likes) S.; B.S. cum laude, Southwestern State Coll., 1970; Ph.D., La. State U., 1976; m. Carolyn Beth Haggard, June 1, 1969; children—Daniel Denell, Anne Marie. Data processor, teletype operator Kellwood Co., Clinton, Okla., 1968-70; teaching asst. La. State U., Baton Rouge, 1970-73, departmental sabbatical leave replacement, 1974, research asst., 1973-74, instr. Chemistry Dept., 1975-77, acting research supr., 1977; applications chemist Ethyl Corp., Baton Rouge, 1977—; faculty freshman chemistry, night sch. La. State U., 1978, 79. Named Outstanding Organic Grad. Student of the Year, La. State U., 1976; Coates Found. Meml. award, 1976; DuPont Teaching award, 1973; NSF-URP participant, 1968, 70; Pres.'s scholar, 1966. Mem. Am. Chem. Soc. (sect. sec. 1978), La. Acad. Sci., Sigma Xi. Republican. Methodist. Contbr. articles to profl. jours. Home: 166S 10515 Airline Hwy Baton Rouge LA 70816 Office: PO Box 341 Baton Rouge LA 70821

SAUER, RAY NEAL, corp. exec.; b. Houston, July 30, 1934; s. Ray George and Anna Maria (Johnson) S.; A.B. in Chem. Engring., Rice U., 1956; M.S. in Chem. Engring., U. Tex., 1958; m. Bettie Marian Hickman, Oct. 22, 1969; children—Steven N., Lynn H., Nancy L. Research engr., Marathon Oil Co., Littleton, Colo., 1958-59; sr. systems engr., product mktg. rep., mgr. data acquisition and control systems, IBM Corp., Houston and Los Angeles, 1959-69; staff mgr., Transamerica Corp., Los Angeles, 1970-72; region mgr., Cin. Milacron, Houston, 1972-76; pres., AccuraTech, Inc., Houston, 1976—. Usher St. Luke's Methodist Church, 1973—. Served to lt. U.S. Army, 1957. Recipient IBM Outstanding Contribution award, 1964; registered profl. engr., Tex. Mem. Project Mgmt. Inst., Tau Beta Pi, Sigma Tau, Omega Chi Epsilon, Phi Lambda Upsilon. Developer LESS/TIME and TIMETABLE, computer software for project mgmt. Home: 5422 Chevy Chase Dr Houston TX 77056

SAUGEY, CHARLES RAGLE, health center adminstr.; b. Alexander, Ark., Dec. 2, 1915; s. Henry and Ethel Claire (Corbin) S.; student U. Ark., Fayetteville, 1934-37; m. Frances Padgett, Jan. 17, 1942; children—Steve, Carol, Gene. Prodn. foreman Maumelle (Ark.) Ordnance Cities Service, 1942-45; with Cutter Labs., Berkeley, Calif., 1945-58, regional mgr., 1948-54, gen. sales mgr., 1954-58; regional mgr. McGaw Labs. div. Am. Hosp. Supply Corp., Dallas, 1958-71; dir. materials mgmt. St. Vincent Infirmary, Little Rock, 1971—; speaker on cost containment. Tchr., youth tchr. various chs., 1960—; mem. fund raising com. Aldersgate, Methodist Ch. camp, Little Rock; co-chmn. St. Vincent Infirmary United Fund. Mem. Am. Hosp. Assn., Ark. Hosp. Assn., Ark. Shared Purchasing Assn.(founder 1975, pres. and chmn. 1975-79), Soc. Hosp. Purchasing and Materials Mgmt. (pres. local chpt. 1973-74), Central Ark. Health Systems Agy. Methodist. Home: Route 3 Box 389E Little Rock AR 72211 Office: Saint Vincent Infirmary Markham at University Sts Little Rock AR 72201

SAUL, ROBERTA JUNE, indsl. devel. co. exec.; b. Atlanta, Oct. 17, 1947; d. Robert Miles and Eunice (O'Neal) S.; B.B.A. (Ga. Educators Assn. fellow), Ga. State U., 1970, M.Profl. Acctg. and Bus. Info. Sci. (Univ. fellow), 1978. Sr. acct. textile ops. Oxford Industries, Inc., Atlanta, 1969-71; acct. U.S. Dept. Treasury, Atlanta, 1971-76; fin. dir. Conway Pubs., Inc. Conway Research, Inc., Atlanta, 1976—; mem. adult edn. faculty U. Ga., 1972-76; cons. in field. Mem. Asso. Info. Mgrs., Info. Industry Assn., Am. Info. Sci. Assn., Ga. State U. Alumni Assn. Co-author: Industrial Park Growth, 1979; New Industries of the Seventies, 1978, 2nd edit. 1979; Composite Case History of New

Facility Location-Utility Services, 1978. Home: 3030 Oakdale Rd Hapeville GA 30354 Office: 1954 Airport Rd Atlanta GA 30341

SAULS, CHARLES WADE, educator; b. Tylertown, Miss., Oct. 8, 1932; s. Charlie Wood and Rubye Lee (Andrews) S.; B.A., Southeastern La. Coll., 1953; M.Ed., La. State U., 1959, Ph.D., 1971; m. Eldora Jenkins, Mar. 5, 1954; 1 son, David Preston. Tchr., E. Baton Rouge Sch. System, 1953-54, 56-63; sixth grade supr. La. State U. Lab. Sch., Baton Rouge, 1963-66; asso. prof. dept. curriculum and instruction La. State U., Baton Rouge, 1966—; elem. mathematics cons. Served with U.S. Army, 1954-56. Mem. Nat. Council Tchrs. English, Nat. Council Tchrs. Mathematics, Phi Kappa Phi, Phi Delta Kappa, Kappa Delta Pi. Baptist. Contbr. articles in field to profl. jours. Home: 732 Louray St Baton Rouge LA 70808 Office: Dept Curriculum and Instruction La State Univ Baton Rouge LA 70803

SAUNDERS, CHARLES DOLEAN, educator; b. Selma, N.C., Nov. 17, 1909; s. Charlie Hugh and Ardelia (Ferrell) S.; A.B., Shaw U., 1956; postgrad. SUNY at Oneonta, Albany, 1958-61, N.Y. U., 1961, 69, 70; M.Ed., Pa. State U., 1961; Ed.D., U. Sarasota, 1978; m. Eula Mae Smith, Dec. 23, 1955. Tchr. jr. high sch. Canaan, (N.Y.) Dist., 1956-63, chmn. social studies, 1963-64; supr. Project Uplift, N.Y. Urban League, N.Y.C., summer 1964; tchr. mentally retarded Bd. Edn. of City N.Y., 1965-66, Public Sch. 93K, 1966-70, tchr. spl. edn. Public Sch. 40K, 1970-74; pvt. practice tutoring mentally retarded, Selma, 1974-79; cons. spl. edn., 1979—. Mem. Town of Selma Recreation Com., 1976—. Mem. Council Exceptional Children, Am. Assn. Mental Deficiency, Nat. Council Social Studies, Shaw U. Alumni Assn., U. Sarasota Alumni Assn. Democrat. Baptist. Home and Office: 704 W Noble St Selma NC 27576

SAUNDERS, DEWEY SAMUEL, JR., educator; b. Newnan, Ga., June 27, 1931; s. Dewey Samuel and Grace (Knox) S.; B.S., Morris Brown Coll., Atlanta, 1952; M.A., Fisk U., Nashville, 1961; m. Jewell Terrill, May 2, 1979; children—Duahanne, Dewey Samuel, III, Daphne, Johnny. Tchr., Cleve. public schs., 1958-65, supr. sci., 1966-78; spacemobile rep. NASA, 1965-66; planetarium dir. Supplementary Edn. Center, Cleve., 1966-78; intermediate sci. curriculum study tchr. Dunwoody (Ga.) High Sch., 1978—. Served to capt., navigator, USAF, 1952-58. Mem. Nat. Sci. Tchrs. Assn., Ga. Sci. Tchrs. Assn., Ohio and Cleve. Sci. Tchrs. Assn., Gt. Lakes Planetarium Assn., Phi Beta Sigma (past chpt. pres.). Republican. Methodist. Home: 1133 Village St Stone Mountain GA 30088 Office: 5034 Vermack Rd Dunwoody GA 30338

SAUNDERS, DONALD MCFERREN, coll. dean; b. New Castle, Pa., Dec. 17, 1938; s. Donald Franklin and Ruth Lee (McFerren) S.; B.A., Westminster Coll., 1968; M.A., Carnegie Mellon U., 1973; m. Anita M. Palmer, Apr. 18, 1958; children—Julie Ann, Jay Justin. Dir. ednl. affairs World Affairs Council Pitts., 1968-73; dir. mgmt. devel. Mellon Bank, N.A., Pitts., 1973-77: asst. dean, dir. career counseling and placement Grad. Sch. Bus. Adminstrn. Duke U., Durham, N.C., 1977—; mem. adv. bd. Sch. Bus. and Mgmt., Morgan State U., 1977—. Served with AUS, 1958-61. Carthage Found. fellow, 1973-74. Mem. So. Conf. Placement Assn., Coll. Placement Council, Middle Atlantic Placement Assn., N.C. Placement Assn. Clubs: Rotary, Masons. Office: 138 Social Sci Bldg Durham NC 27706

SAUNDERS, JEAN ARLENE, educator; b. Buffalo, June 29, 1928; d. Fred Hobson and Alma Jenny (Hanes) Brown; diploma with honors Moody Bible Inst., 1956; B.S. with honors, U. Ill., 1962; M.A. with honors, Northeastern Ill. U., 1970; postgrad. U. Va., Union Grad. Sch. Tchr. spl. edn., Champaign, Skokie and Deerfield, Ill., also Mpls. and Robbinsdale, Minn., 1962-69; ednl. dir. (Stone Found. grantee) The Lambs facility for mentally handicapped young adults, Libertyville, Ill., 1969-70; instr. spl. edn. Trinity Coll., Deerfield, Ill., 1967-70; asst. prof. edn. State U. Coll. N.Y., Buffalo, 1970-71, Houghton (N.Y.) Coll., 1971-74; learning counselor East Aurora (N.Y.) High Sch., 1974-76; pres. Career Growth Assos., Inc., Richmond, Va., 1976—; vocat. counselor Charlottesville (Va.) High Sch., 1976-78; asst. prof. Med. Coll. Va., Richmond, 1978—; dir. Christian Assn. Psychol. Studies, Grand Rapids, Mich., 1972-77, Niagara Frontier Christian Counseling Service, Buffalo, 1972-76; mem. various profl. research and devel. teams; coordinator workshops in field. Mem. Am. Personnel and Guidance Assn., Assn. Specialists in Group Work, Council Exceptional Children, Am. Mental Health Counselors Assn., Kappa Delta Pi. Contbr. articles to profl. jours. Home: 1517 Front Royal Dr Richmond VA 23228 Office: Career Growth Assos Inc 1900 Hickstead Rd Richmond VA 23235 also Med Coll VA Sch Medicine MCV Sta Box 565 Richmond VA 23298

SAUNDERS, JOHN RUDOLPH, physician; b. Lewiston, N.C., Apr. 27, 1904; s. John B. and Annie (Bazemore) S.; B.A., Wake Forest Coll., 1924; M.D., Emory U., 1926; m. Vera Lee Coxwell, Mar. 2, 1929; children—Barbara (Mrs. Robert L. Brown), Janice (Mrs. Ned D. Hemric), John R. Asst. physician Fla. State Hosp., Chattahoochee, 1926-30, State Hosp., Morganton, N.C., 1930-33; gen. practice medicine, Lewiston, 1933-38; asst. supt. State Hosp., Morganton, 1938-42, supt., 1942-45; mem. med. staff Westbrook Psychiat. Hosp., Richmond, Va., 1945-60, med. dir., 1960—; asso. clin. prof. psychiatry Med. Coll. Va., Richmond, 1947—. Diplomate Am. Bd. Psychiatry and Neurology. Fellow Am. Psychiat. Assn. (past speaker assembly dist. brs.; area V trustee 1972-75); mem. Neuropsychiat. Soc. Va. (past pres.), Med. Soc. Va. (chmn. mental health com. 1963—), Am. Coll. Psychiatrists, Am. Psychiat. Assn. (past v.p.), Nat. Assn. Pvt. Psychiat. Hosps. (chmn. membership com. 1972—, past pres.), Alumni Assn. Wake Forest Coll. (past pres.). Author articles. Home: 8201 Tyndale Rd Richmond VA 23227 Office: 1500 Westbrook Ave Richmond VA 23227

SAUNDERS, MACKEY RILEY, architect; b. Eastman, Ga., Feb. 10, 1945; s. Chester and Martha (Mackey) S.; student U. Fla., 1963-64, Middle Ga. Jr. Coll., 1964-65; B.Bldg. Constrn., Auburn U., 1969; m. Diane Louise Diez, Dec. 9, 1972; 1 son, Bertrand Mackey. Specification writer Harry A. MacEwen, Architect, Tampa, Fla., 1969, specifications and constrn. adminstr., 1970, br. office mgr., Albany, Ga., 1972; gen. practice architecture, Simeon E. Fallis, Architect, Albany, 1973-77; pvt. practice architecture, Albany, 1977—. Served with Army N.G., 1968-69. Mem. AIA, NCARB (cert.), Hist. Soc. (archtl. rev. bd. 1979-80). Clubs: Sertoma, S.W. Ga. Art Assn., Thronateeska Heritage Found. Address: 1104 W 1st Ave Albany GA 31707

SAUNDERS, WILLIAM ARTHUR, chem. co. exec.; b. Ottawa, Ont., Can., Oct. 13, 1930; came to U.S., 1970; s. Arthur M. and Irene Saunders; B.Sc. in Biochemistry, McGill U. (Can.), 1954; M.B.A. in Econs. and Fin., U. Western Ont. (Can.), 1956; M.Comm. in Econs. and Mktg., U. Toronto (Can.), 1960; m. Barbara Card, May 5, 1956. Econ. analyst Imperial Oil Ltd., Toronto, 1956-63; supr. distbn. Polysar Ltd., Sarnia, Ont., 1963-69; venture mgr. Polysar Plastics Inc., Westport, Conn., 1969-77; advisor strategy devel. Gulf Oils Chems. Co., Houston, 1977—. Mem. Assn. for Corp. Growth, Comml. Devel. Assn. Congregationalist. Home: 4011 Levonshire Dr Houston TX 77025 Office: PO Box 3766 Houston TX 77001

SAVAGE, WILLIAM WOODROW, educator; b. Onley, Va., Jan. 9, 1914; s. Frank Howard and Florence Elmira (Twyford) S.; A.B., Coll., William and Mary, 1937; M.A., U. Chgo., 1946, Ph.D., 1955; student U. Va., summer 1951; m. Margaret Jane Clarke; children—Earl R., William W. Research editor, div. rural research Fed. Emergency Relief Adminstrn., Richmond, Va., 1935-36; div. mgr. Montgomery Ward & Co., Newport News, Va., 1937-38; statis. worker WPA, Richmond, 1938-39; counselor Va. Consultation Service, Richmond, 1939-42, acting dir., 1942-45; asst. state supr. guidance and consultation services Va. Dept. Edn., 1946-47; dean Longwood Coll., Farmville, Va., 1947-52; project coordinator, asso. dir. Midwest Adminstrn. Center, U. Chgo., 1952-56; dean Coll. Edn., U. S.C., 1956-65, prof. edn., 1956-79, curator mus. of edn., 1973—. Mem. visitation and appraisal com. Nat. Council Accreditation Tchr. Edn., 1964-67. Mem. S.C. Assn. Sch. Adminstrs., Palmetto State Tchrs. Assn., Phi Delta Kappa. Methodist. Club: Wardlaw (pres. 1974-75). Co-author: Readings in American Education, 1963. Author: Interpersonal and Group Relations in Educational Administration, 1968. Editor: Work and Training, monthly Va. Bd. Edn., 1941-47, Administrator's Notebook, monthly Midwest Adminstrn. Center, 1954-56, U. S.C. Edn. Report, 1957—; adv. com. Sch. Rev., 1954-56. Contbr. articles to various jours. Home: 6316 Eastshore Rd Columbia SC 29206

SAVAS, CHARLES RICHARD, mechan. engr.; b. Huntsville, Ala., Oct. 1, 1939; s. Theodore Charles and Margaret Kathleen (McKelvey) S.; student U. of Ala. in Huntsville, 1968—; m. Linda Kay Pylant; children—Jill Hampton, Holly Elizabeth. Draftsman, The Boeing Co., Huntsville, 1965; engring. designer, Sperry-Rand Co., Huntsville, 1965-66, Teledyne-Brown Engring., Huntsville, 1966-68; project engr. Sewart Seacraft, Berwick, La., 1968; mfg. engr. GTE Automatic Elec., Huntsville, 1969-74; project mgr. Cutler-Hammer, Arab, Ala., 1974—. Jaycees, 1967—. Served with USN, 1958-61. Decorated commendation; recipient patent award GTE Automatic Elec., 1974. Mem. Soc. Plastic Engrs., Huntsville Automatic Clubs, Inc. (bd. dirs., 1971-73, pres. 1973-74), Soc. for Advancement of Mgmt. Democrat. Methodist. Home: 204 Curtis Circle SE Huntsville AL 35803 Office: 8th Ave SE Arab AL 35016

SAVERANCE, CLIFTON R., ret. supt. schs.; b. Bethune, S.C., Sept. 16, 1913; s. Junius Edwin and Beulah I. (Carter) S.; B.S., Clemson U., 1938; M.Ed., U. S.C., 1955; m. Martha Augusta Godbold, June 16, 1939; children—Clifton R., Robert Edwin. Tchr., Williamsburg County Schs., Hemingway, S.C., 1938-42; tchr. Lamar (S.C.) Schs., 1946-50, prin., 1953-57; supt. Hemingway Area Schs., 1957-68, Lamar (S.C.) Schs., 1968-77. Served to maj., inf. AUS, 1942-46; PTO; 1950-52. Mem. S.C., Am. assns. sch. adminstrs., Nat. Acad. Sch. Execs. (state chmn.), S.C., Darlington County, Williamsburg County edn. assns., Internat. Platform Assn., Forty and Eight, Am. Legion, Alpha Tau Alpha. Presbyterian. Clubs: Masons, Civitan (Lamar). Home: Box 603 Lamar SC 29069

SAVINI, DORIS DIANA, educator; b. Sherburne, N.Y., Feb. 16, 1922; d. Volney Delos and Dora (Follett) Goodrich; B.A., Roberts Wesleyan Coll., 1958; m. Howard James Savini, July 12, 1952 (dec.); children—Sharon Ann, Sylvia Dawn. Primary tchr. Lakeland (Fla.) Christian Sch., 1960-63; tchr. exceptional child edn. Polk County (Fla.) Bd. Edn., 1963-65, Martin County (Fla.) Bd. Edn., 1965-66, Palm Beach County (Fla.) Bd. Edn., 1966-80, Westward Community Sch., West Palm Beach, Fla., 1973-80; social worker Fla. Dept. Pub. Welfare, 1959-60. Counselor, Hobe Sound Crusader Club Mission, 1977-79. Named Tchr. of Year, Jupiter Schs. of Fla., 1970; U. Fla. grantee, 1964. Mem. Nat., Fla. edn. assns., Classroom Tchrs. Assn., Fla. Assn. for Supervision and Curriculum Devel. Republican. Methodist. Developer elementary workshop for mentally and emotionally handicapped intermediate children in pub. schs. Home: 9048 SE Pine Cone Ln Hobe Sound FL 33455

SAVITZ, ALAN DAVID, wholesale import-export co. exec.; b. Wilkes Barres, Pa., Dec. 19, 1937; s. Abe and Sylvia Shirley (Strauss) S.; B.B.A., U. Miami (Fla.), 1960; m. Lucille Mona Kahn, Feb. 25, 1961; children—Lisa Ann, David Alan, Michael Charles. Vice pres., dir. Am. Star Co., Miami, 1961-65; chmn. bd., pres., dir. Universal Home Products, Inc., Miami, 1965—. Served as 2d lt. USAR. Mem. Nat. Assn. Retail Dealers, Nat. Assn. Installment Cos., Nat. Assn. Textile Apparel Wholesalers, Res. Officers Assn., U. Miami Alumni Assn. Jewish. Clubs: U.S. Power Squadron, Masons, Shriners. Home: 11094 Paradela St Coral Gables FL 33156 Office: 1920 N Miami Ave Miami FL 33136

SAVOCA, ANTHONY FRANCIS, psychologist; b. New Orleans, July 21, 1922; s. Frank and Carrie (Munsch) S.; B.S., Tulane U., 1949; M.Ed., Loyola U., New Orleans, 1954; Ph.D., La. State U., 1965; m. June Ida Ross, Dec. 8, 1957; children—Emily, Christopher. Counselor, tchr. New Orleans pub. schs., 1950-57; lectr. Loyola U., 1956—; chief psychologist New Orleans Mental Health Center, 1962—; cons. psychologist, New Orleans, 1966—. Mem. Mayor New Orleans Youth Council, 1966-68. Served as officer USAAC, 1942-45; mem. Air N.G., 1953-69. Decorated Air medal; Ford Found. fellow, 1956. Mem. Am., La. psychol. assns., Nat. Rehab. Assn., Cross Keys. Club: Aurora Country. Author research papers. Home: 5877 MacArthur Blvd New Orleans LA 70114 Office: 3100 General DeGaulle Blvd New Orleans LA 70114

SAWYER, JAMES EDWARD, accountant; b. San Antonio, May 4, 1943; s. James Eldren and Freida Loyce (Pannill) S.; B.B.A., Tex. Christian U., 1967; m. R. Eileen Massey, Dec. 27, 1967; children—Bryan Lynn, Yolonda Lynn. Sr. accountant Arthur Young & Co., Ft. Worth, 1967-70, Bogota, Colombia, 1970-71; bus. mgr. Johnson Chevrolet, Dallas, 1971-73: sr. tax accountant First Nat. Bank, Dallas, 1973; controller Malouf Co., Dallas, 1973-75; partner Ellis, Martin & Sawyer, C.P.A.'s, Lawton, Okla., 1976-79; owner, prin. James E. Sawyer, C.P.A., Lawton, 1979-80; pres. James Sawyer & Co., Inc., C.P.A.'s, Lawton, 1980—. Co-chmn. drive Arts for All Lawton, 1978, bd. dirs., 1978— pres., 1978-79; bd. dirs. Lawton Philharmonic Orch., 1978—, v.p., 1979; chmn. Redcoat-Ambassadors of Lawton C. of C., 1978-79; mem. high council Lawton Stake Ch. Jesus Christ of Latter-day Saints, 1976-79. C.P.A., Tex., Okla. Mem. Am. Inst. C.P.A.'s, Am., Okla. (pres. S.W. chpt. and state dir. 1977-79), Tex. socs. C.P.A.'s, Lawton C. of C., Beta Alpha Psi, Beta Gamma Sigma. Republican. Mormon. Club: Kiwanis (dir. 1979—). Home: 1205 Maple Ave Lawton OK 73501 Office: PO Box 2276 208 SW 3d St Lawton OK 73502

SAWYER, MARY ELLEN, speech pathologist; b. Lewiston, Maine, Mar. 30, 1951; d. Malcolm P. and Carol May (Conner) S.; B.A., Baylor U., 1973, M.S., 1975. Asst. arts and crafts Pine Tree Camp for Crippled Children, Rome, Maine, 1970, 71, 72; speech therapist Minot-Poland-Mechanic Falls Sch. System, Mechanic Falls, Maine, 1973, Yoakum (Tex.) Ind. Sch. Dist., 1975—. Mem. Am. Speech, Lang. and Hearing Assn. (cert. clin. competence), Tex. Speech, Lang. and Hearing Assn., NEA, Tex. Edn. Assn., Yoakum Educators Assn. (sec. 1979-80). Lutheran. Home: 306 Nieman St Yoakum TX 77995

SAWYER, RALPH EDWARD, chemist; b. Palestine, Tex., Aug. 10, 1945; s. Ralph Edward and Esther Adell (Whitaker) S.; B.S. in Chemistry, U. Tex., 1967; M.B.A., St. Edwards U., 1976; m. Karolynn Kadera, Sept. 17, 1977. Scientist, Radian Corp., Austin, Tex., 1972-77, staff scientist, Phys. Chemistry Dept., 1977—. Pres., Radian Employees Fed. Credit Union, 1979-80. Served to capt. USAF, 1967-72. Mem. Am. Chem. Soc., Delta Mu Delta. Episcopalian. Contbr. articles to profl. jours. Home: 1501 Woodgreen Dr Round Rock TX 78664 Office: 8500 Shoal Creek Blvd Austin TX 78766

SAWYERS, JOHN LAZELLE, physician; b. Centerville, Iowa, July 26, 1925; s. Francis Lazelle and Almira (Baker) S.; A.B., U. Rochester, 1946; M.D., Johns Hopkins, 1949; m. Julia Edwards, May 25, 1957; children—Charles Lazelle, Al Baker, Julia Edwards. House officer surgery Johns Hopkins Hosp., Balt., 1949-50; asst. resident, resident in surgery Vanderbilt U. Hosp., Nashville, 1953-58; practice medicine specializing in surgery, Nashville, 1958—; surgeon Edwards-Eve Clinic, 1958-60; chief surg. service Nashville Gen. Hosp., 1960-77; surgeon-in-chief St. Thomas Hosp., Nashville, 1977—; prof. surgery Vanderbilt U. Bd. dirs. Davidson County unit Am. Cancer Soc. Served from lt. (j.g.) to lt. M.C., USNR, 1950-52. Diplomate Am. Bd. Surgery, Am. Bd. Thoracic Surgery. Fellow A.C.S.; mem. Am. Surg. Assn. Home: 403 Ellendale Dr Nashville TN 37205 Office: St Thomas Hosp PO Box 380 Nashville TN 37202

SAXENA, DHIRENDRA SWARUP, engring. testing co. exec.; b. Allahabad, India, June 11, 1940; s. Mahesh Swarup and Omwati (Verma) S.; B.S., U. Allahabad, 1958; B.Tech. (honors), Indian Inst. Tech. (Kharagpur), 1962; M.Engring. in Civil Engring. (NRC Can. grantee 1966-67), Nova Scotia Tech. Coll. (Halifax, Can.), 1968; m. Urmila Saxena, Feb. 4, 1964; children—Anupam, Jayant. Came to U.S., 1969. Civil engr. Heavy Engring. Corp. Ltd., Ranchi, India, 1962-66; soils engr. firm Dames & Moore, Toronto, Ont., Can., 1967-69; sr. soils engr. Internat. Minerals & Chem. Corp., Bartow, Fla., 1969-70; sr. engr. Woodward-ETCO & Assos., Houston, 1970-73; v.p. geotech. div. Harlan Engring. Labs. Inc., Lakeland, Fla., 1973-78, pres., 1978—. Registered profl. engr., Fla., Tenn., Tex. Mem. ASCE (nat. soil dynamics com. 1972-76, chpt. pres. 1974-75), Nat. (membership com. 1971-72), Tex. (named outstanding engr. year 1972) socs. profl. engrs., Am. Soc. Mining Engrs., ASTM, Fla. Engring. Soc. (chpt. pres. 1976-77; Outstanding Engr. of Yr. 1975). Lion. Home: 1068 Sugartree Dr S Lakeland FL 33803 Office: PO Box 5050 Lakeland FL 33803

SAXON, PAUL DAVID, computer usage co. exec.; b. Springfield, Tenn., Feb. 27, 1941; s. John Davis and Sarah William (Connor) S.; student Perkinston Jr. Coll., 1962-63, Electronic Computer Programming Inst., 1966; m. Patsy Ruth Mercer, June 15, 1974. Mgmt. trainee Community Loan, Albany, Ga., 1963-65; sales corr. Scripto, Inc., Atlanta, 1966; from programmer trainee to sr. programmer/analyst Oxford Industries, Inc., Atlanta, 1967-70; programmer/analyst III, First Nat. Bank of Atlanta, 1970-71; systems analyst Computer Usage Co. (formerly Scidata, Inc.), Atlanta, 1971-74, mgr. systems software devel. Atlanta Product Mktg. Devel. Center, 1974—. Served with USMC, 1958-62. Republican. Mem. Ch. of the Nazarene. Office: 6433 Warren Dr Norcross GA 30093

SAYEGH, ISAAC, stockbroker; b. Beirut, Apr. 4, 1948; came to U.S., 1976; s. Gamil and Renee (Turquieh) S.; B.A. in Econs. and Bus. Adminstrn.; m. Teri L. Burman, Dec. 23, 1973; children—Noam, Gabriel. Trust officer, overseas rep. Trade Devel. Bank, Geneva, 1975-76; stockbroker Merrill Lynch, Houston, 1977—. Mem. Houston C. of C. Researcher fgn. currencies in controlled markets, N. African community in France. Office: Merrill Lynch Suite 600 1st City Bank Bldg 1021 Main St Houston TX 77002

SAYFIE, EUGENE JOSEPH, internist; b. Charleston, W.Va., Sept. 13, 1934; s. Snow and Selma (Zakaib) S.; B.S. magna cum laude, W.Va. U., 1956; M.D., Washington U., St. Louis, 1960; m. Suzanne Morin, Feb. 22, 1969; children—Stephanie, Nicole, Lisa, Amy Jo. Practice medicine specializing in internal medicine and cardiology, Miami, Fla.; mem. staff Miami Heart Inst., chief med. staff, 1978-80, former chief of medicine; cons. staff physician Jackson Meml. Hosp., Miami; clin. asso. prof. Sch. Medicine, U. Miami. Recipient Silver Meritorious award Miami Heart Inst., 1977. Fellow ACP, Am. Coll. Cardiology, Am. Coll. Angiology, Am. Coll. Chest Physicians; mem. AMA, Am., Fla., Greater Miami (dir.) heart assns., Fla., Dade County med. assns. Mem. Eastern Orthodox Ch. Clubs: LaGorce Country, Palm Bay, Bath, Jockey. Office: 550 Brickell Ave Miami FL 33131

SAYRE, JOHN LESLIE, clergyman, educator; b. Hannibal, Mo., Mar. 28, 1924; s. John Leslie and Clara (Haden) S.; student U. Okla., 1942-43; A.B., Phillips U., 1947; B.D. cum laude, Yale, 1950; M.L.S., U. Tex. at Austin, 1963; postgrad. Union Theol. Sem., 1955; Ph.D., U. Tex. at Austin, 1973; m. Herwanna Lee Harrouff, June 18, 1948; children—Barbara Ann, John Richard, Alan Douglas, Melody Lyn Sayre Hildebrand. Ordained to ministry Christian Ch. (Disciples of Christ) 1946; asso. minister Christian chs., Enid, Okla., 1945-47, minister, Stillwater, Okla., 1950-57, Austin, Tex., 1957-62; instr. Phillips U., 1954-55, asso. prof. theol. bibliography, 1962—, sem. librarian, 1962-71, dir. univ. libraries, 1971—; instr. Okla. State U., 1950-57; sometimes lectr. Mem. Am. Theol. Library Assn., Am., Okla., S.W. library assns., Beta Phi Mu, Theta Phi, Phi Kappa Phi. Democrat. Author: A History of Disciples Student Work, 1950; A Manual of Forms for Term Papers and Thesis, 1966; An Index to Festschriften in Religion, 1971; An Illustrated Guide to the Anglo-American Cataloging Rules, 1971; Tools for Theological Research, 1972; An Illustrated Guide to the International Standard Bibliographic Description for Monographs, 1972. Address: Box 2212 University Sta Enid OK 73701

SAYRE, ROBERT DUANE, engring. firm exec.; b. Canton, S.D., Oct. 20, 1928; s. Lawrence Carl and Edith Lydia (Doolittle) S.; B.S. in Civil Engring., S.D. Sch. Mines and Tech., 1950; M. Civil Engring., U. Va., 1952; m. Margaret Estelle Mann (dec. 1977); children—Robert Duane, David Mann. Area engr. E.I. DuPont de Nemours, Savannah River Project, S.C., 1952-53; chief engring. lab. Corps of Engrs., Washington, 1953-56; materials engr. Parsons, Brinckerhoff, Quade and Douglas, Richmond, Va., 1956-58; chief engr., also corporate sec. Froehling and Robertson, Inc., Richmond, 1958-68; pres. Sayre and Assos., Cons. Engrs., Richmond, 1968—; dir. Terra Ins. Ltd., Ayers & Ayres, Inc. Fellow ASCE; mem. Va. Soc. Profl. Engrs. (recipient Outstanding Service award 1968, Distinguished Service award 1973; pres. 1972-73), Cons. Engrs. Council Va. (pres. 1980—), Va. Assn. Professions, Internat. Soc. Soil Mechanics and Found. Engring., Engrs. Club Richmond (pres. 1970). Presbyn. (ruling elder). Mason. Home: 6604 W Franklin St Richmond VA 23226 Office: PO Box 9532 5407 Lakeside Ave Richmond VA 23228

SCAFE, JOSEPH BRUCE, television producer/dir., media cons.; b. Aurora, Ill., Sept. 11, 1942; s. Dennis Verne and Anna (Martine) S.; B.S. in Music Edn., U. Ill., Urbana, 1964, M.S. in Radio-Television, 1966; m. Kathleen Scafe, July 30, 1966 (div. Apr. 1979); children—Paula Kathleen, Sara Elizabeth. Television producer/dir. WSIU-TV, So. Ill. U., Carbondale, 1970-73; television prodn. crew chief WFAA-TV, Dallas, 1973-74; television producer/dir. KLRN-TV, Austin, Tex., 1974-77; dir. ednl. media prodn. Tex. Dept. Human Resources, Austin, 1977—; producer, dir. The Session, 1973; dir. Carrascolendas, 1974, Austin City Limits, 1976-77, Every Tub On

Its Own Bottom, 1978. Recipient Outstanding Merit award for network television Chgo. Film Festival and cert. of recognition Nat. Assn. Ednl. Broadcasters (both for Austin City Limits), 1977. Home: 1120-A Gillespie Pl Austin TX 78704 Office: Media Services Div Dept Human Resources Box 2960 Austin TX 78769

SCALERA, PHILIP VAN ETTEN, architect; b. Somerville, N.J., Dec. 15, 1937; s. Mario and Mildred (Newkirk) S.; B.A., Lehigh U., 1960; B.Arch., R.I. Sch. Design, 1964; m. Martha Ruth Worth, May 4, 1968; children—Jonathan Worth, Marisa Newkirk, Philip Clarkson. Asso. various archtl. firms, 1964-75; owner, prin. firm. Philip V. Scalera, Architect, Tampa, Fla., 1976—; archtl. cons. 1st Fla. Banks, Inc. Bd. dirs. Golf Land Civic Assn. Served with U.S. Army, 1966-68. Registered architect, Fla.; cert. Nat. Council Archtl. Registration Bd. Mem. AIA, Central Fla. chpt. AIA. Republican. Presbyterian. Prin. works include: 1st Nat. Bank Fla.: Interbay, Brandon, N. Tampa, Carroll Wood offices; Intercity Nat. Bank: West Bradenton office; 1st Nat. Bank Kissimmee: St. Cloud office; 1st Am. Bank Pensacola: Garden St. office; 1st Nat. Bank Lakeland: S. Lakeland office. Home: 11534 Forest Hills Dr Tampa FL 33612

SCANDALIOS, JOHN GEORGE, geneticist; b. Nisyros Isle, Greece, Nov. 1, 1934; s. George John and Calliope (Broujos) S.; came to U.S., 1946; B.A., U. Va., 1957; M.S., Adelphi U., 1962; Ph.D., U. Hawaii, 1965; m. Penelope Anne Lawrence, Jan. 18, 1961; children—Artemis Christina, Melissa Joan, Nikki Eleni. Asso. in bacterial genetics Cold Spring Harbor Labs., 1960-62; NIH postdoctoral fellow U. Hawaii Med. Sch., 1965; asst. prof. Mich. State U., East Lansing, 1965-60, asso. prof., 1970-72; prof., head dept. biology U. S.C., Columbia, 1973-75; prof., head dept. genetics N.C. State U., Raleigh, 1975—; vis. prof. genetics U. Calif., Davis, 1969; vis. prof. OAS, Argentina, Chile and Brazil, 1972. Served with USAF, 1957. Alexander von Humboldt travel fellow, 1976; mem. exchange program NAS, US/USSR. Mem. Genetics Soc. Am., Am. Soc. Human Genetics, Am. Genetic Assn., AAAS, Soc. Devel. Biology, Sigma Xi. Greek Orthodox. Author: Physiological Genetics, 1979; editor: Developmental Genetics Jour.; co-editor: Isozymes, 4 vols., 1975; Monographs in Developmental Biology, 1968—. Office: PO Box 5487 Raleigh NC 27650

SCANZONI, LETHA DAWSON, writer, lectr.; b. Pitts., Oct. 9, 1935; d. James Jackson and Hildegard Elizabeth-Emma (Koch) Dawson; student Eastman Sch. Music, Rochester, N.Y., 1952-54; Moody Bible Inst., Chgo., 1954-56; A.B. with high distinction, Ind. U., 1972; m. John H. Scanzoni, July 7, 1956; children—Stephen James, David John. Rural religious worker Village Missions Southwestern Oreg., 1958-61; freelance writer, lectr. religion, social issues, 1961—; weekly columnist Sunday Sch. Times, Phila., 1964-67; editorial asso. The Other Side, Phila., 1975—, columnist, 1978; contbg. editor Radix, Berkeley, Calif., 1976— nat. officer, 1980 program chair Evang. Women's caucus; a sponsor Religious Leaders' Consultation, UN Decade for Women World Conf., Washington, 1980. Mem. NOW, Phi Beta Kappa. Democrat. Presbyterian. Author: Youth Looks at Love, 1964; Why Am I Here? Where Am I Going?, 1966; Sex and the Single Eye, 1968; Sex Is a Parent Affair, 1973; (with Nancy Hardesty) All We're Meant To Be, 1974; (with John Scanzoni) Men, Women, and Change: A Sociology of Marriage and Family, 1976, 2d edit., 1980; (with Virginia Ramey Mollenkott) Is the Homosexual My Neighbor? 1978. Home and Office: 4512 Grendel Rd Greensboro NC 27410

SCARBOROUGH, CLAUDE MOOD, JR., lawyer; b. Columbia, S.C., Dec. 7, 1929; s. Claude M. and Gelene (Stallworth) S.; student U. of South, 1947-49; A.B., U.S.C., 1951, LL.B., 1952; m. Sarah Carpenter, June 30, 1955; children—Sarah Catherine, Elizabeth Ann, Claude M. III, Gelene Bivins. Admitted to S.C. bar, 1952, U.S. Dist. Ct., 1956; U.S. Ct. Appeals, 1957; asso. firm Nelson, Mullins & Grier, Columbia, S.C., 1955-61, partner Nelson, Mullins, Grier & Scarborough, 1961—. Spl. hearing officer U.S. Dept. Justice, 1962-68. Trustee Legal Aid Soc. Richland Co., 1960-67, pres., 1960-64; mem. Gov.'s Com. to Study Police and Community Relations, 1975-76; mem. indsl. adv. bd. S.C. Dept. Corrections, 1974-76. Served to 1st lt. AUS, 1952-55. Mem. Internat. Assn. Ins. Counsel, Am., S.C. (treas. 1968-72, exec. com. 1972-74, chmn. exec. com. 1973-74, pres. 1975-76), Richland County bar assns., S.C. Bar Found. (dir. 1976—, chmn. bd. 1977-80), U.S. 4th Circuit Jud. Conf. (permanent mem.), S.C. Def. Attys. Assn., Def. Research Inst., Am. Judicature Soc. (Herbert Harley award 1976), Phi Delta Phi. Episcopalian (lay reader, vestryman, warden). Clubs: Palmetto, Summit, Wildewood, Forest Lake Country, Kiwanis. Home: 1514 Tanglewood Rd Columbia SC 29205 Office: 3d Floor Keenan Bldg Columbia SC 29201

SCARBOROUGH, ELIZABETH BARTLETT, educator; b. Atlanta, Dec. 24, 1928; d. Ruben I. and Hassie (Powell) Bartlett; B.B.A. in Law, U. Ga., Athens, 1951, edn. specialist in adminstrn. and supervision, 1974; M.Ed. in English, Mercer U., Macon, Ga., 1966 postgrad. Ga. State U.; m. John C. Scarborough, Jr. (dec.); children—Richard Wilson, Teresa S. Nalls (Mrs. A. Craig). Legal sec. Sinclair Refining Co., Atlanta Ga. 1957-58; tchr. Crawford County (Ga.) Bd. Edn., Roberta, 1960-68, dir. curriculum, then asst. supt. instrn., 1968—. Chmn. Crawford County Democratic Com., 1970—. Mem. NEA, Crawford County Edn. Assn., Assn. Supervision Curriculum Devel., Phi Delta Kappa, Delta Kappa Gamma Phi Kappa Phi. Contbr. article. Home: PO Box 337 Roberta GA 31078 Office: PO Box 8 Roberta GA 31078

SCARBOROUGH, WILLIAM KAUFFMAN, historian, educator; b. Balt., Jan. 17, 1933; s. James Blaine and Julia Irene (Kauffman) S.; A.B. in History, U. N.C., Chapel Hill, 1954, Ph.D., 1962; M.A., Cornell U., 1957; m. Patricia Estelle Carruthers, Jan. 16, 1954; children—Catherine Lee, William Bradley. Asst. prof. history Millsaps Coll., Jackson, Miss., 1961-63, NE La. U., Monroe, 1963-64; asso. prof. history U. So. Miss., Hattiesburg, 1964-76, prof., 1976—; cons. Nat. Endowment for Humanities div. public programs, La. State U. Press, U. Press of Miss., U. Ill. Press, U. Del. Press, Jour. Southern History. Served with USN, 1954-56. Nat. Endowment for Humanities summer stipend, 1967. Mem. Am. Hist. Assn., So. Hist. Assn., Orgn. Am. Historians, Agrl. History Soc., Miss. Hist. Soc. (pres.), Phi Beta Kappa. Author: The Overseer: Plantation Management in the Old South, 1966; editor: The Diary of Edmund Ruffin, vol. 1, 1972, vol. 2, 1977. Home: 1120 Estelle St Hattiesburg MS 39401 Office: Department of History University of Southern Mississippi Southern Station Box 8371 Hattiesburg MS 39401

SCARBROUGH, CHARLIE WADE, JR., broadcasting announcer; b. Pine Bluff, Ark., Oct. 28. 1942; s. Charlie Wade and Doris (Mobley) S.; student U. Ark. at Fayetteville, 1961-63. Program dir. sta. WTUP, Tupelo, Miss., 1963; sports dir. sta. KALO, Little Rock, 1964-66; asst. program dir. sta. KAAY, Little Rock, 1967-68; sports and music dir. sta. KMYO, Little Rock, 1969-71; announcer radio, TV commls. sta. KARN, Little Rock, 1972-75; freelance comml. announcer, 1975—. Announcer on TV auctions, telethons, radiothons for numerous civic causes, including multiple sclerosis, muscular dystrophy, St. Judes' Hosp.. cystic fibrosis, Toys for Tots. Justice of Peace, Pulaski County, Ark., 1968-70. Recipient local and regional Addy awards for radio and TV commls. Mem. Ark. Advt. Fedn., Tau Kappa Epsilon. Address: 1201 N Pierce St Suite 62 Little Rock AR 72207

SCARBROUGH, GEORGE ADDISON, educator; b. Benton, Tenn.. Oct. 20, 1915; s. William Oscar and Louise Anabel (McDowell) S.; student (lit. fellow) U. of South, 1941-43; B.A., Lincoln Meml. U., Harrogate, Tenn., 1947; M.A., U. Tenn., Knoxville, 1954; studies in English, Writers Workshop Iowa State U., 1957. Tchr. English in secondary schs. and colls., 1943-68; book reviewer Chattanooga Times, 1940—, Sewanee Rev., 1943-65, Appalachian Jour., 1975—, reader and lectr. Mem. Friends of Oak Ridge Pub. Library. Recipient Borestone Mountain award, 1961; Mary Rugeley Fergueson Poetry award Sewanee Rev., 1964; Lincoln award Lincoln Meml. U.. Harrogate, Tenn., 1947, Actors' award, 1947; Gov.'s Outstanding Tennessean award, 1978; Albanese award Spirit mag., 1979; Carnegie Fund grantee, 1975; Am. br. PEN grantee, 1975; Author's League Fund grantee, 1975. Mem. Poetry Soc. Am., Nat. Wildlife Fedn. Unitarian. Author: (poems) Tellico Blue, 1949; The Course is Upward, 1951; Summer So-Called, 1956; George Scarbrough: New and Selected Poems, 1977; Hymns from the Home County (editor Phyllis Tickle), 1979, also on cassette; also articles; poems in numerous anthologies; donor books to Tenn. Wesleyan Coll., Athens, Cherokee (N.C.) Community Library, Oliver Springs (Tenn.) High Sch. Library. Address: 100 Darwin Ln Oak Ridge TN 37830

SCARINGELLI, FRANK PHILIP, chemist; b. Hartford, Conn., Jan. 18, 1921; s. Gaetano Carl and Maria C. (Lea) S.; B.S., Bklyn. Coll., 1948, postgrad., 1948-54; postgrad. U. N.C., 1975-76; m. Vincenza B. DiBuono, Dec. 7, 1946; children—Frank Philip, Carl J., Janet R., Sally M., Mark A. Analytical chemist U.S. Ordnance Dept., Raritan (N.J.) Arsenal, 1948-50; sr. analytical organic chemist U.S. Treasury Dept., N.Y.C., 1950-64; chief lab. method research HEW, Cin., 1964-70; sr. scientist EPA, Research Triangle Park, N.C., 1970-76; research asso. N.C. State U., Raleigh, 1977—. Pres., Willowbrook Homeowners Assn., 1963-64; coach jr. basketball and baseball teams, Cary, N.C., 1973-77. Served with USAAF, 1942-46; ETO. Recipient Research Paper of Yr. award Am. Indsl. Hygiene Assn., 1967; Spl. Service award U.S. Treasury, 1962. Mem. ASTM, Am. Chem. Soc., Assn. Ofcl. Analytical Chemists, Am. Men and Women of Sci., Sigma Xi. Clubs: K.C. (dist. officer 1957-60) Kings Castle (bd. dirs. 1957-64). Contbr. articles to profl. jours. Home: 1002 Manchester Dr Cary NC 27514 Office: 3102 Biltmore Hall NC State U Box 5488 Raleigh NC 27650

SCARMINACH, CHARLES ANTHONY, lawyer; b. Syracuse, N.Y., Feb. 19, 1944; s. John Louis and Lucy Antoinette (Egnoto) S.; B.A., U. Buffalo, 1965; student Sch. Law St. John's U., 1965-66; J.D., Syracuse U., 1968; m. Anne Marie Ventre, Aug. 19, 1967; children—John Francis, Catherine Anne. Admitted to N.Y. State bar, 1968, S.C. bar, 1974; with Sea Pines Co., Hilton Head Island, S.C., 1973—, sec., asso. corp. counsel, 1974-75, corp. counsel, sec., 1976-78; individual practice law, Hilton Head Island, 1978—. Served with AUS, 1968-73, Res., 1973—. Mem. Am., N.Y. State S.C. bar assns., Hilton Head Island Bar Assn., Res. Officers Assn. U.S., Phi Delta Phi, Jr. C. of C. Roman Catholic. Lion. Home: 55 Stoney Creek Hilton Head Island SC 29928 Office: Exec Office Bldg PO Box 5962 Hilton Head Island SC 29948

SCHAAF, WILLIAM EDWARD, statistician; b. Martins Ferry, Ohio, Aug. 9, 1938; s. Weldon Elmer and Vera Vivian (Peterson) S.; B.S., Duke, 1961; M.A., U. N.C., 1963; Ph.D., U. Mich., 1972; m. Helen Patricia Biggers, Mar. 17, 1961; children—Elizabeth Anne, William Edward, Katherine Lynn. Research asst. physiology Duke Med. Sch., 1956-61; statistician Nat. Heart Inst., NIH, Bethesda, Md., 1963-66; biometrician Inst. Fisheries Research, Mich. Dept. Natural Resources, Ann Arbor, 1966-69, Beaufort (N.C.) Lab., Nat. Marine Fisheries Service, 1969-75, 76—; with Internat. Commn. for Conservation Atlantic Tunas, Madrid, 1975-76. Woodrow Wilson scholar, 1956; USPHS trainee, 1969; NSF fellow, 1973. Mem. Am. Statis. Assn., AAAS, Am. Fisheries Soc. Home: PO Box 54 Gloucester NC 28528 Office: Nat Marine Fisheries Service Beaufort NC 28516

SCHACHAR, RONALD A., physician; b. Bklyn., Dec. 28, 1941; s. David and Doris (Friedman) S.; B.S., City Coll. N.Y., 1963; M.D., Downstate Med. Center, 1967; Ph.D., U. Chgo., 1975. Intern, Sinai Hosp. of Balt., 1967-68; jr. asst. resident, USPHS trainee ophthalmology, U. Chgo., 1970-71, sr. asst. resident, USPHS trainee, 1971-72, resident and USPHS trainee, 1972-73, chief resident, USPHS trainee, 1973-74, asst. prof. ophthalmology, 1974-76; practice medicine specializing in ophthalmology, 1974—; adj. asst. prof. dept. biophysics and physiology U. Tex. Health Sci. Center, Dallas, 1975-78; adj. prof. depts. life scis. and physics Bishop Coll., Dallas, 1978—; adj. prof. physics U. Tex., Arlington, 1979—; chmn. Infectious Disease Control, Meml. Hosp. of Denison, 1976; mem. utilization com. Madonna Hosp., 1976; mem. staff, continuing edn. com. Texoma Med. Center, 1978. Pres., founder Diabetic Retinopathy Found.; founder, sec. Keratorefractive Soc. Served with MC AUS, 1968-70. Diplomate Am. Bd. Ophthalmology, Nat. Bd. Med. Examiners. Fellow Am. Coll. Surgeons; mem. Ill. Ophthalmol. Soc., AAAS, Assn. Research in Vision and Ophthalmology, Chgo. Ophthalmol. Soc., Am. Acad. Ophthalmology and Otolaryngology, Am. Intraocular Lens Soc., Grayson County Med. Soc., Dallas Ophthalmol. Soc., Am. Assn. Ophthalmology, Phi Beta Kappa, Sigma Xi. Author: Intraocular Lenses, 1979. Patentee horizontally mounted intraocular lens and the method of implantation thereof. Contbr. numerous articles to med. jours. Office: Texoma Eye Inst 1020 N Hwy H 75 PO Box 145 Denison TX 75020

SCHAD, ROGER PERRY, savs. and loan co. exec.; b. Norfolk, Va., Feb. 8, 1930; s. Harry Clinton and Octavie Elizabeth (Lamkin) S.; B.S., Auburn U., 1947-51; M.S., U. Richmond, 1961; postgrad. U. Wis., 1961-63; m. Virginia Elizabeth Alston, Feb. 25, 1961; 1 dau., Tavie Lee. Asst. gen. auditor Fed. Res. Bank, Richmond, Va., 1953-66; v.p. N.C. Nat. Bank, Charlotte, 1966-75; exec. v.p. First Fed. of Broward, Fort Lauderdale, Fla., 1975—; dir. Oceanside Communities, Inc. Bd. dirs. Early Childhood Devel. Assn. Broward County. Served with U.S. Army, 1951-53. Mem. Assn. Systems Mgmt. (chpt. pres. 1973-74), Planning Execs. Inst. (chmn. bd. dirs. 1979-80), Inst. Internal Auditors (chpt. pres. 1967-68). Home: 710 NW 70th Terr Plantation FL 33317 Office: First Federal of Broward 301 E Las Olas Blvd Fort Lauderdale FL 33301

SCHAD, THEODORE GEORGE, JR., food co. exec.; b. N.Y.C., Mar. 4, 1927; s. Theodore George and Helen (Tennyson) S.; B.S. in Bus. and Econs., Ill. Inst. Tech., 1950, M.S., 1951; m. Karma Rose Cundell, Mar. 21, 1957 (dec. June 1978); children—Roberta, Theodore George III, Olive (Mrs. Richard L. Smith), Peter. Vice pres. mktg. Gt. Western Savs., Los Angeles, 1961-63; prin., nat. dir. mktg., and econs. Peat, Marwick, Mitchell & Co., C.P.A.'s, Los Angeles and N.Y.C., 1964-71; chmn. bd., pres., chief exec. officer Lou Ana Industries, Inc., Lou Ana Foods, Inc., Opelousas, 1971—, Lou Ana Industries Internat., Inc., Opelousas. Pres. Mamaroneck (N.Y.) Parents of Retarded Children. 1970-71; bd. dirs., dir. U.S. Indsl. Council, 1978—; trustee Va. Mil. Inst. Found., 1978—. Served as 2d lt. C.E., AUS, World War II; ETO, PTO. Mem. Am. Mktg. Assn. (pres. So. Calif. chpt. 1961-62, dir. 1962-63), Greater Opelousas C. of C. (pres. 1972-73). Republican. Methodist. Clubs: Indian Hills Country (Opelousas); Internat. House (New Orleans). Brentwood (Calif.) Sertoma (founding pres. 1963). Contbr. articles on mktg. and econs. to profl. jours. Home: 1155 Prudhomme Ln Opelousas LA 70570 Office: 731 N Railroad Ave Opelousas LA 70570

SCHADEL, LEES MALCOLM, JR., gynecologist; b. Phila., Jan. 23, 1915; s. Lees Malcolm and Minna Elizabeth (Wilde) S.; A.B., Gettysburg Coll., 1937; M.D., Hahnemann Med. Coll., Phila., 1941; M.Sc. in Medicine, U. Pa., 1947; m. Betty B. Whiteman, Aug. 5, 1940; children—Lees Malcolm 3d, Betty (Mrs. Kenneth Steil), William Alan. Intern Hahnemann Hosp., 1941-42; teaching fellow Hahnemann Med. Coll., 1944-46, mem. faculty, 1946-54, asso. obstetrics and gynecology, 1947, chief obstetrics, out-patient dept., 1947-54; pvt. practice gynecology, Ft. Lauderdale, Fla., 1954—; mem. staff Broward Gen. Med. Center, N. Beach Med. Center, Ft. Lauderdale Hosp. Diplomate Am. Bd. Obstetrics and Gynecology. Fellow A.C.S., Am. Coll. Obstetricians and Gynecologists, (founding), Internat. Coll. Surgeons; mem. N.Y. Acad. Scis., Confrerie de la Chaine des Rotisseurs (bailli Fort Lauderdale chpt.). Mason (32 deg., Shriner). Club: Palm Beach (Fla.) Gun. Home: 415 SE 17th Ave Fort Lauderdale FL 33301 Office: 303 SE 17th St Suite 404 Fort Lauderdale FL 33316

SCHAEFFER, RICHARD FRANKLIN, educator; b. Phila., July 6, 1941; s. Herman and Henrietta (Shulik) S.; B.A., Temple U., 1962, M.A. (U.S. Senatorial scholar), 1964; Ph.D. (USPHS fellow), Fla. State U., 1968; m. Sandra Ann Kaufman, Nov. 15, 1968; children—Craig, Heidi Rachel. Intern, U.S. Naval Hosp., Bethesda, Md., 1967-68; psychologist U.S. Navy Dispensary, Washington, 1968-69; pvt. practice clin. psychology, Salisbury, Md., 1970-72; asst. prof. psychology Salisbury State Coll., 1970-72; faculty behavioral scis. dept. Barry Coll., Miami Shores, Fla., 1972—, prof. psychology, 1977—, dir. psychology program, 1976—; pvt. practice clin. psychology, Miami, Fla., 1972—; adj. prof. psychology Fla. Internat. U., Miami, 1973, St. Vincent De Paul Sem., Boynton Beach, Fla., 1973-74; cons. mental health clinics, pvt. schs., govt. agencies; expert legal witness; tchr. S. Phila. High Sch., 1963-64. Served to 1st lt. USN, 1967-69. Mem. Am., Southeastern Dade County, Broward County psychol. assns., Dade County Mental Health Assn., Psi Chi. Jewish. Contbr. articles in field to profl. jours. Home: 14921 NE 5th Ave Miami FL 33161 Office: 2020 NE 163rd St Suite 208 North Miami Beach FL 33162

SCHAEZLER, CHRIS HAROLD, mfg. exec.; b. San Antonio, Mar. 15, 1942; s. Chris Bernhardt and Adele Louise (Kutschenrenter) S.; B.B.A., Tex. A&M U., 1964; M.B.A., U. Dallas, 1969; m. Anita Louise Preston, July 2, 1965; children—Brian, Scott. Salesman, Frigiking div. Cummins Engine Co., 1967-69, sales planning mgr., 1969-72, prodn. and inventory control mgr., 1972-73, product mgr., 1973-74, gen. mktg. mgr., 1974-76; dir. mktg. services Atlas Powder Co., Dallas, 1976-78, dir. corp. planning and devel., 1978-79; pres. Kinepak, Inc., 1979—. Served with AUS, 1965-67. Decorated Bronze Star. Mem. Am. Mktg. Assn., Am. Mgmt. Assn. Republican. Methodist. Office: 1000 Kinepak Rd PO Box 1155 Lewisville TX 75067

SCHAFER, DOUGLAS EUGENE, electronics mfg. co. ofcl.; b. Gainesville, Tex., Jan. 8, 1932; s. Harry Wright and Alma Edith (McBride) S.; student bus. mgmt. Gainesville Jr. Coll., 1956-61, N. Tex. State U., 1961-66; m. Margaret E. Schafer, July 3, 1953; children—Rick Gary Kim, Wendy (dec.), Scotty. Locomotive engr. Atchison, Topeka and Santa Fe Ry., Gainesville, Tex., 1952-62; technician Tex. Instruments Co., Dallas, 1962-65, supr., 1965-66, quality control infrared, 1966-70, glass expert, 1970-76, incoming supr. quality control flat glass, 1971—; lectr. in field. Served with U.S. Army. Mem. Nat. Rifle Assn., Brotherhood Locomotive Engrs. and Trainmen Santa Fe. Democrat. Baptist. Home: 1114 Drexel Dr Plano TX 75075 Office: 13500 NC Expressway Dallas TX 75022

SCHAFER, JOHN BOYLE, diversified industry exec.; b. Cheyenne, Wyo., Apr. 6, 1933; s. Edward Daniel and Martha Mary S.; B.S., Regis Coll., 1955; M.B.A., Harvard U., 1962; m. Maxine Lee Mohrbacher, Aug. 24, 1963; children—Stacey Ann, Thomas John. Mktg. exec. Dresser Indsl. Valve and Inst. div. Dresser Industries, Stratford, Conn., 1966-70, mktg. dir. Dresser Mfg. div., Bradford, Pa., 1970-74, gen. mgr. Dresser Measurement div., Houston, 1974-75, v.p. indsl. spl. products div., Brussels, 1975-78, dir. bus. devel. Dresser Power Systems Group, Houston, 1978—; mem. adv. bd. Nat. Fire Protection Assn. Chmn., United Fund, Bradford, 1973; pres. Briarforest Civic Assn., Houston, 1974 Served with USMC, 1955-59. Mem. Internat. Mgmt. Assn., Sales Promotion Execs. Assn. Internat., Air Pollution Control Assn., Am. Mgmt. Assn. Clubs: Briarwood Club, N.Y. Athletic, Brown Palace. Home: 12011 Riverview Dr Houston TX 77077 Office: 601 Jefferson St Houston TX 77002

SCHAFER, LOTHAR, chemist, educator; b. Dusseldorf, West Germany, May 5, 1939; s. Ernst Rudolf and Sybilla (Nolden) S.; diploma in chemistry U. Munich (Germany), 1962, Ph.D. in Chemistry, 1965; m. Gabriele Maria Brand, Apr. 9, 1965; children—Nicole, Nathalie. Came to U.S., 1967, naturalized, 1978. Research asso. Ind. U., 1967-68; asst. prof. dept. chemistry U. Ark., Fayetteville, 1968-72, asso. prof., 1972-75, prof., 1975—; vis. prof. Yukawa Hall, U. Kyot. (Japan), 1976. Recipient Distinguished Faculty award U. Ark. Alumni Assn., 1977. NATO postdoctoral fellow U. Oslo (Norway), 1965-67. Dreyfus Found. grantee, 1971. Mem. Am. Chem. Soc., Chem. Soc. Eng., AAUP. Contbr. articles on chemistry to sci. jours. Home: 828 Skyline Dr Fayetteville AR 72701

SCHAFFER, RONALD LEE, clergyman; b. Kansas City, Kans., Aug. 8, 1937; s. Roland Doyle and Ethel (Eckoff) S.; Th.G., Bapt. Bible Coll., 1960; B.A., Bapt. Christian Coll., 1976, LL.D. (hon.), 1978; M.A., Sacramento Bapt. Coll., 1978; Ph.D., Bapt. Christian U., 1978; D.D. (hon.), Hyles Anderson Coll., 1973; m. Martha Ann Raines, Mar. 31, 1957; children—Daniel Doyle, Jesse Glen, Alfred Wayne, Rebecca Joy. Ordained to ministry Baptist Ch., 1959; pastor Grace Bapt. Ch., Rogersville, Mo., 1958-59, Bible Bapt. Ch., Plattsburgh, N.Y., 1960-64, Bethany Bapt. Ch., Melbourne, Fla., 1964-69; pres., founder Brevard Christian Schs., Melbourne, Fla., 1966-69; founder, pres. Fla. Children's Home, Melbourne, 1968—; pastor First Bapt. Ch. Temple Heights, Tampa, Fla., 1969—; pres. Temple Heights Christian Schs., Tampa, 1969—; founder, pres. Faith Children's Home, Tampa, 1970—. Served with USN, 1954-56. Named Outstanding Young Religious Leader, Temple Terrace Jr. C. of C., 1973-74. Baptist. Home: 5305 Rosecrest Circle Tampa FL 33617 Office: 8406 46th St Tampa FL 33617

SCHAFFSTALL, ELEONOR DUBIEL, acctg. firm exec.; b. Buffalo, Feb. 22, 1933; d. Louis J. and Helen S. Dubiel; B.S., U. Buffalo, 1954; m. Eugene Schaffstall, May 1, 1954; children—Debora, Thomas, Carol. Payroll supr. City of Kansas City, Mo., 1963-64; asst. controller Berry World Travel, Kansas City, Mo., 1964-65; staff accountant Kenneth Chandler, C.P.A., Kansas City, 1965-66; asst. controller Advance Indsl. Security, Atlanta, 1967-69; partner DeLoach & Co., Atlanta, 1969-79; owner Schaffstall & Co., C.P.A.'s, Atlanta, 1979—. Treas., John L. Blandford campaign for Superior Ct. judge DeKalb County, Ga., 1976. C.P.A. Mem. Am. Inst. C.P.A.'s, Am. Woman's Soc. C.P.A.'s, Am. Soc. Women Accts. (pres. Atlanta chpt. 1977-78), Ga. Soc. C.P.A.'s (treas. DeKalb chpt. 1976-77), Women Bus. Owners (dir., membership chmn.), Atlanta Women's Network, Pres.'s

Council. Home: 1724 Granger Ct Chamblee GA 30341 Office: 30 Perimeter Park Atlanta GA 30341

SCHALLY, ANDREW VICTOR, med. research scientist; b. Europe. Nov. 30, 1926; s. Casimir Peter and Maria (Lacka) S.; B.Sc., McGill U. (Can.), 1955, Ph.D. in Biochemistry, 1957; m., Ana Maria Comaru, Aug. 12, 1976. Came to U.S., 1957. Research asst. biochemistry Nat. Inst. Med. Research, London, 1949-52, dept. psychiatry. McGill U., Montreal, Que., 1952-57; research asso., asst. prof. physiology and biochemistry Coll. Medicine. Baylor U., Houston, 1957-62; chief endocrine and polypeptide labs. VA Hosp., New Orleans, 1962—; asso. prof. Sch. Medicine, Tulane U., New Orleans, 1962-67, prof., 1967—. Recipient Dir.'s award for outstanding med. research VA Hosp., New Orleans, 1968. Van Meter prize Am. Thyroid Assn., 1969. Ayerst-Squibb award Endocrine Soc., 1970, William S. Middletown award VA, 1970, Ch. Mickle award U. Toronto, 1974, Gairdner Internat. award, 1974; Albert Lasker Basic Med. Research award, 1975; Nobel Prize in Physiology and Medicine, 1977; USPHS sr. research fellow, 1961-62; sr. med. investigator VA, 1973. Mem. Endocrine Soc., Am. Physiol. Soc., Soc. Biol. Chemists, Am. Chem. Soc., AAAS, N.Y. Acad. Scis., Soc. Exptl. Biol. Medicine, Internat. Soc. Research Biology Reprodn., Soc. Study Reprodn., Soc. Internat. Brain Research Orgn., Mexican Acad. Medicine, Am. Soc. Animal Sci., Endocrine Soc. Madrid, Sigma Xi, others. Contbr. articles to profl. jours. Home: 5025 Kawanee St Metairie LA 70002 Office: 1601 Perdido St New Orleans LA 70146

SCHANBACHER, EUGENE MURRY, educator; b. Carmen, Okla., Aug. 26, 1929; s. Murry Guy and Edna May (Wade) S.; B.S., Northwestern Okla. State U., 1952; M.A., U. No. Colo., 1953; Ed.D., U. Mo., 1961; m. Priscilla Rae Green, June 21, 1956; children—Gregory Wade, Lori Anne. Instr. engring. U. Mo., Columbia, 1958; tchr. pub. schs., Wichita, Kans., 1953-57, University City, Mo., 1959-61; vis. prof. Eastern Wash. State Coll., Chenny, summer 1965; edn. advisor, prof. Haile Sallassie I U., Ethiopia, 1968-70; faculty Murray (Ky.) State U., 1961-68, 70—, prof. industry and tech., 1974—; rep. for indsl. arts, speaker Treaty of Metre Conf., Nat. Bur. Standards, 1975; lectr. in field; tech. cons. Served with USAF, 1953-55. NSF grantee, 1978-80; U.S. Office Edn. grantee, 1977-78; Bur. Vocation Edn. grantee, 1974. Mem. Am. Indsl. Arts Assn., Am. Vocational Assn., Ky. Indsl. Edn. Assn. (dir. 1972-76), Am. Council on Indsl. Arts Tchr. Edn., Nat. Assn. Indsl. and Tech. Tchr. Edn., U.S. Metric Assn., Ky. Council Internat. Edn. (v.p. 1976—), Phi Delta Kappa, Epsilon Pi Tau. Democrat. Methodist. Clubs: Rotary (pres. Murray 1980—), Murray, Meth. Men's (pres. 1979—). Contbr. articles to profl. jours. Home: 1314 Farris Ave Murray KY 42071 Office: Murray State Univ Murray KY 42071

SCHANDL, EMIL KÁROLY, biochemist; b. Budapest, Hungary, Oct. 16, 1937; s. Emil and Anna (Koplik) S.; A.A., Allan Hancock Coll., 1963; B.A., U. Calif., Santa Barbara, 1965; M.S., San Diego State U., 1967; Ph.D., Fla. State U., 1970; m. Mara M. Piland, Dec. 26, 1963; children—E. Kenneth, Cynthia Anna. Postdoctoral fellow U. Laval, Que., Can., 1970-71; asst. prof. biochemistry Nova U., Ft. Lauderdale, Fla., 1971-73; asst. lab. supr., chief clin. chemist Community Hosp. South Broward, Hollywood, Fla., 1973-76; chief clin. and nutritional biochemistry and radioimmunoassay Am. Biomed Corp. and Nat. Health Labs., Miami, Fla., 1976-79; dir. Center for Metabolic Disorders and Lab., Dania, Fla., 1977—; adj. prof., mem. staff Community Hosp. South Broward; pres. Research Enterprises, Fort Lauderdale, 1976—; v.p. Ultranutrition Inst., Inc., Miami, 1979—. Recipient grants Am. Cancer Soc., NRC Can. Mem. Am. Assn. Clin. Chemistry, Sigma Xi. Republican. Club: Cooper City Davie Soccer (founder). Composer nutritional biochemistry screening profile and cancer biochem. profile; contbr. articles to profl. jours. Home: 5030 SW 90th Way Fort Lauderdale FL 33328 Office: 599 S Federal Hwy Dania FL 33004

SCHANK, STANLEY COX, cytogeneticist; b. Fallon, Nev., Oct. 31, 1932; s. LeRoy Christian and Prudence Verona (Cox) S.; B.S., Utah State U., Logan, 1954; Ph.D., U. Calif., Davis, 1961; m. Sandra Richards, Mar. 12, 1954; children—Colleen Schank McGrath, David S., Gary S., Linda, Rodney W. Mem. faculty U. Fla., Gainesville, 1961—, prof. genetics and plant breeding, 1972—; cons. IRI Research Inst., IICA, Brazil, 1966, 79; vis. prof., scientist Commonwealth Scientific and Indsl. Research Orgn., Brisbane, Australia, 1971, 78; vis. research prof. Empressa Brasileira de Pesquisa Agropecuaria, Brazil, 1973-75; co-dir., investigator AID grants. Adult leader N. Fla. council Boy Scouts Am., 1975-77. Served with AUS, 1955-57. Mem. Am. Soc. Agronomy, Crop Sci. Soc. Am., Canadian Genetics Soc., Fla. Soil and Crop Sci. Soc., Am. Genetic Assn., Gamma Sigma Delta, Phi Kappa Phi, Phi Sigma. Author articles, monograph. Home: 60 NW 44th St Gainesville FL 32607 Office: 2189 McCarty Hall Dept Agronomy Univ Fla Gainesville FL 32611

SCHANSBERG, DAVID ARTHUR, publisher; b. New Albany, Ind., Aug. 24, 1939; s. Alden J. and Jessey Marie S.; A.A., Mayo Tech. Sch., 1959; m. Sandra Weller, Jan. 10, 1963; children—David Eric, Christopher Regan, Cathlynn Marie. Printer, Voice of St. Matthews, Inc., 1957-59; bus. mgr. The Voice of St. Matthews, Louisville, 1962-65; gen. mgr. Voice Newspapers, Louisville, 1965-68, co-pub., v.p., 1968-73; gen. mgr. Dardanell Publs., Pitts., 1973; pub., editor Malone (N.Y.) Evening Telegram, 1973-78 pub. Fairfax (Va.) Globe and Rockville (Md.) Advertisers, 1978—. Trustee Sta. WCFE-TV, Ednl. TV Northeastern N.Y., 1978—; chmn. United Way Franklin County, 1976-78; sec. Franklin County Rehab. Program, 1976-77; pres. Franklin County Indsl. Devel., 1977-78; bd. dirs. Fairfax County YMCA. Served with USMCR, 1960-66. Mem. Nat. Newspaper Assn., N.Y. State Pubs. Assn., Fairfax City C. of C. (dir., exec. com.), Advt. Club Washington (dir. 1979—), Sigma Delta Chi (past chpt. dir.). Baptist. Club: Kiwanis. Home: 5242 Richardson Dr Apt 1 Fairfax VA 22030 Office: 3847 Pickett Rd Fairfax VA 22030

SCHANTZ, IRA JULIUS, educator; b. Roby, Tex., Aug. 11, 1922; s. Gus Leonard and Sena (Gruben) S.; Mus.B., N. Tex. State U., 1950, postgrad., 1951-64. Instr. music Tex. Tech. U., 1950-57, Howard County Jr. Coll., 1957-64; asso. prof. voice Tex. Christian U., Fort Worth, 1964—; profl. singer, N.Y.C., 1953-55; mem. Robert Shaw Chorale, N.Y.C., 1953-55; soloist symphony orchs., opera cos., univ. and coll. choirs and orchestras, choral socs., U.S., Europe, 1950-79. Served with U.S. Army, 1942-46; PTO. Mem. AAUP, Nat. Assn. Tchrs. Singing, Am. Philatelic Soc. Republican. Baptist. Home: 6221 S Hulen St Fort Worth TX 76133 Office: Sch Fine Arts Tex Christian U Fort Worth TX 76129

SCHAPPELL, LOLA IRENE, educator; b. Rochester, N.Y., Feb. 17, 1940; d. Harrison and Bertha Hill; m. Robert N. Schappell; children by previous marriage—Yvonne Washburn, Valerie Washburn; B.S. in Elementary Edn., State U. N.Y. at Brockport, 1962; M.S. in Ednl. Research and Ednl. Psychology, Purdue U., Lafayette, Ind., 1969; Ed.D. in Tchr. Edn. and Early Childhood Edn., U. Mass., Amherst, 1972. Tchr., Attica (N.Y.) Central Sch., 1962-63; reading coordinator Mexico (N.Y.) Central Sch., 1973-75; asst. prof. edn. Fed. City Coll., Washington, 1975-76; dir. reading Charlotte-Mecklenburg Schs., Charlotte, N.C., from 1976, now curriculum coordinator; adj. instr. Johnson C. Smith U. Treas., Am. Field Service, 1962-67; bd. dirs. Charlotte-Mecklenburg Literacy Council. Mem. NEA, Internat. Reading Assn., Am. Assn. Sch. Adminstrs., Nat. Assn. Edn. Young Children. Home: 2421 Inverness Rd Charlotte NC 28209 Office: Charlotte-Mecklenburg Schs Harding/Olympic Area Office 1501 Euclid Ave Charlotte NC 28203

SCHARFF, ARTHUR BERNARD, educator; b. Memphis, May 18, 1911; s. Abraham and Eva Kathleen (Clark) S.; student Washington and Lee U., 1930-31; B.A., Ohio State U., 1932; M.A., Columbia, 1933; certificates Sorbonne U. Paris (France), 1936, U. Rome (Italy), 1937, U. Jena (Germany), 1939, U. Milan (Italy), 1969, Georgetown U., 1976; 1 dau., Kathleen Clark. Statis. analyst U.S. Dept. Agr., Washington, 1940-43; budget analyst U.S. Dept. State, Washington, 1946-47, budget officer, Paris, 1947-52, asst. adminstrv. officer, Manila, Philippines, 1952-54; travel mgr. br. Am. Express Co., Cin., 1955-64; instr. U. Va., 1964-65, Miami U., Oxford, Ohio, 1965-66, Wright State U., 1966-67; asso. prof. Romance langs. and comparative lit. Washington and Lee U., 1967-76; ret., 1976; now pvt. tutor, recorder for blind. Served with AUS, 1942-46; NATOUSA, ETO. Mem. Modern Lang. Assn. Am., Am. Assn. Tchrs. French, Alliance Francaise, A.A.U.P., Modern Fgn. Lang. Assn. Va., Phi Kappa Sigma, Phi Mu Alpha. Episcopalian. Club: Cincinnati. Contbr. articles to profl. jours. Home: 45 Woodlake Dr Charlottesville VA 22901

SCHARLE, JUDITH ALLEN, educator; b. Fairmont, W.Va., Feb. 26, 1944; d. Arthur Ray and Eleanor Estelle (Pugh) A.; A.B., Fairmont State Coll., 1962; M.S., Va. Poly Inst. and State U., 1977, postgrad., 1977—; m. Joseph Martin Scharle II, July 5, 1969 (div. Nov. 1978); 1 dau., Jennifer Anne. Tchr., Wood County Schs., Parkersburg, W.Va., 1966-68, Dept. Def. Overseas Schs., Goose High Sch., Goose Bay, Labrador, Can., 1968-69, Kempsville Jr. High Sch., Virginia Beach, Va., 1969-70, Kellam High Sch., Virginia Beach, 1970-73, Norfolk (Va.) Tech. Vocat. Center, 1973-78; adult edn. specialist Norfolk Public Schs., 1978—; lectr., cons. in field. Active polit. campaigns, Arthritis Found., Cancer Soc., Cystic Fibrosis Assn. Mem. Va. Bus. Edn. Assn. (corr. sec. 1976-78), Am. Vocat. Assn., Va. Vocat. Assn., Nat. Bus. Edn. Assn., Delta Pi Epsilon (v.p. chpt. 1979—). Republican. Methodist. Author: Office Reprographics, 1979; Progressive Filing, 1980, others; editorial rev. bd. Va. Bus. Edn. Jour. Home: 4100 Birch Ct Virginia Beach VA 23462 Office: Norfolk Public Schs 800 E City Hall Ave Norfolk VA 23510

SCHECHTER, ROBERT SAMUEL, educator; b. Houston, Feb. 26, 1929; s. Morris S. and Helen Ruth (Brilling) S.; B.S., Tex. A. and M. U., 1950; Ph.D., U. Minn., 1956; m. Mary Ethel Rosenberg, Feb. 15, 1953; children—Richard Martin, Alan Lawrence, Geoffrey Louis. Mem. faculty U. Tex. at Austin, 1956—, prof. chem. engring., 1961—, chmn. dept., 1970-73, E.J. Cockrell, Jr. prof. chem. and petroleum engring., 1975—, chmn. dept. petroleum engring., 1975-78, adminstrv. dir. Center Statis. Mechanics and Thermodynamics, 1968-72; vis. prof. U. Edinburgh, 1965-66, U. Brussels, 1969; distinguished vis. prof. U. Kans., spring 1968. Served with AUS, 1951-53. Mem. Profl. Engrs. Tex., Am. Chem. Soc., Soc. Petroleum Engrs., Nat. Acad. Engring., Am. Inst. Chem. Engrs., Am. Inst. Mining Engrs., Sigma Xi. Author: Variational Method in Engineering, 1967; Optimization: Theory and Practice, 1970. Developer method to measure surface viscosity and ultra low inter-facial tensions; discoverer instability of thermal diffusion. Home: 4700 Ridge Oak Dr Austin TX 78731 Office: Dept Petroleum Engineering Univ Texas Austin TX 78712

SCHECTER, GEORGE, physicist, research exec.; b. Phila., Jan. 14, 1917; s. Abraham and Anna (Tilishevsky) S.; B.S., Temple U., 1947; m. Ina Shain Polin, Nov. 18, 1972; children—Ellen L., Peter M. Research adviser, supervisory physicist, dir. plans and analysis U.S. Army Frankford Arsenal, Phila., 1941-71; v.p. Technalysis Inc., Phila., 1949-53; sr. asso. Ketron Inc., Arlington, Va., 1971-75; asst. to pres. Analytics Inc., McLean, Va., 1975-79, McLean Research Center, 1979—; lectr. in field; cons. Sandia Corp., AEC, mem. naval research advisory com. Naval Surface Weapons Bd., Marine Corps Panel, 1975—. Mem. Mil. Ops. Research Soc. (dir. 1974-77), Internat. Inst. for Strategic Studies, Am. Phys. Soc., Research Soc. Am. (pres. 1958), Smithsonian Inst. (asso.), AAAS, Sigma Xi. Club: Masons. Author: Information Retrieval, 1967; contbr. articles in field to profl. jours.; patentee in field. Home: 7306 Stafford Rd Alexandria VA 22307 Office: 6870 Elm St McLean VA 22101

SCHEERER, WILLIAM WOODROW, ret. coll. phys. edn. dir.; b. Chattanooga, May 17, 1913; s. Henry and Bonnie Lou (Deakins) S.; B.S., Memphis State U., 1935; M.A., Columbia, 1946; D.Sk., French-Swiss Coll., Boone, N.C., 1972; m. Mildred Louise Holder, July 19, 1936; children—Warren Devereaux, Raymond Henry, Beverly Jean. High sch. tchr. history and phys. edn., coach Edison, Ga., 1935-40, Ft. Lauderdale, Fla., 1940-42; dir. phys. edn. Middle Ga. Coll., 1946-47; dir., prof. phys. edn. Wofford Coll., 1947-77, prof. phys. edn. emeritus, 1977—. Camp dir. Bar-H, Hendersonville, N.C., summers 1940-41, 47-48; supr. city recreation, Ft. Lauderdale, 1941; baseball scout Atlanta Braves, 1947-58; cons. S.C. Bd. Edn., 1955—; participant White House Conf. on Phys. Fitness, 1968; S.C. Gov's. officer, 1971—. Instr. first aid A.R.C., Spartanburg, 1949-71. Bd. dirs. Multiple Sclerosis, Lung Assn. Served with USN, 1942-45. Recipient certificate of spl. recognition City of Spartanburg. Carnegie grantee, 1952; Romill Found. Western Europe grantee, 1963; Wofford Coll. Eastern Europe grantee, 1975. Mem. Am., S.C. (pres's. award 1964) assns. health, phys. edn. and recreation. Ret. Officers Assn., U.S. Golf Assn. (charter asso.), Spartanburg Gun Club. Baptist. Clubs: Lions, Elks, Huntington Hills Country. Author golf handicapping system for U.S. Golf Assn. and Nat. Golf Found., 1972-75. Contbr. articles to profl. jours. Inventor games. Home: 109 Pineville Rd Spartanburg SC 29302

SCHEFFLER, FRAN FRANKLIN, artist; b. Shreveport, La., Sept. 23, 1934; d. Andrew and Violet (Bewley) Franklin; student Jack Hopkins, Miami, Fla., 1961, Sandy Marchetti, Broward Community Coll., Fla., 1972; m. John J. Scheffler Jr., Dec. 14, 1968; 1 son, Edward Lee Parker. Owner, operator studio and gallery, Lauderdale-By-the-Sea, Fla., 1970—; group shows; Hollywood (Fla.) Art Mus., 1976, 79, Alley Gallery, 1975, Grove House, 1977, The Abstractionists, 1976, Broward County Bicentennial Exhbt., 1976. Mem. Artist Equity Assn. (dir. Broward County chpt.), Nat. League Am. Pen Women (2d v.p. Ft. Lauderdale br. 1980—). Clubs: Ocean Reef, Country of Coral Gables, Jockey. Home: 4025 N Federal Hwy Fort Lauderdale FL 33308 Office: 4344A Seagrape Dr Lauderdale-By-The-Sea FL 33308

SCHEIDER, JAMES PRINGLE, JR., real estate exec.; b. Savannah, Ga., Jan. 9, 1943; s. James Pringle and Mary Roberta (Bythewood) S.; A.B. in Polit. Sci., U. S.C., 1970; m. Lynn Jarrell, Sept. 9, 1972. Pres., James P. Scheider Real Estate, Inc., Hilton Head Island, S.C., 1973-76; tchr. local history, botany Sea Pines Acad., Hilton Head Island; mem. Hilton Head Island Bd. Realtors. Dir. S.C. Environ. Action; past pres. Hilton Head Island Community Assn.; organized course S.C. Low Country for local schs.; commr. Boy Scouts Am. Served with USMCR, 1962-63. Named among Outstanding Young Men Am., Hilton Head Island Jaycees, 1974; Realtor of Yr., Hilton Head Island Bd. Realtors, 1976. Republican. Home: PO Box 5058 Hilton Head Island SC 29928

SCHEINER, JAMES JOSEPH, orthopaedic surgeon; b. Cleve., May 4, 1936; s. Nathan and Lillian (Kronenberg) S.; B.S. summa cum laude, U. Cin., 1957, M.D., 1961; m. Marcia Wolosin, May 6, 1964; children—Marc, Michael, David, Alan. Intern, San Francisco Gen. Hosp., 1961-62; resident in orthopaedic surgery Tex. Med. Center, 1962-64, VA Hosp., Houston, 1966-68; practice medicine specializing in orthopaedic surgery, No. Va., 1968—; instr. Georgetown U. Coll. Medicine, 1968-69; founder Profls. Financial Corp.; organizer, dir. 1st Women's Nat. Bank, Washington. Served to capt. USAF, 1964-66. Recipient numerous grants from pharm. cos.; diplomate Am. Acad. Orthopaedic Surgery. Mem. AMA, So., Va., Arlington, Pan Am. med. socs., Eastern Orthopaedic Soc., Va. Orthopaedic Soc., Internat. Soc. Cardiovascular Surgery, Mil. Med. Soc., Phi Beta Kappa, Alpha Omega Alpha. Clubs: Nat. Press, Masons. Contbr. research articles to med. jours. Home: 11200 Braddock Rd Fairfax VA 22030 Office: 4600 King St Alexandria VA 22302

SCHELL, TERRY LEE, performing arts adminstr.; b. Richland Center, Wis., Nov. 5, 1945; s. Roy R. and Izetta Doris (Miller) S.; B.S., U. Wis., Platteville, 1968; m. Diane Ellen Young, Dec. 22, 1968; 1 son, Aaron Gilbert. Asst. dir. U. Wis. Platteville Student Union, 1968-70; salesman Lincoln Nat. Life Ins. Co., 1970-71, Kopper-Powers Ford, Dubuque, Iowa, 1971; asso. dir. Student Union, campus program dir., cultural arts coordinator Bemidji (Minn.) State U., 1971-74; dir. Chester Fritz Auditorium, U. N.D., Grand Forks, 1974-77, dir. Tulsa Performing Arts Center, 1977—. Vice pres. citizens bd. Greater Grand Forks Symphony, 1977. Mem. Nat. Entertainment and Collegiate Activities Assn., Internat. Assn. Auditorium Mgrs., Assn. Coll., Univ. and Community Arts Adminstrs., Grand Forks C. of C. Home: 1000 W Madison Ave Broken Arrow OK 74012 Office: Tulsa Performing Arts Center Tulsa OK

SCHELL, WILLIAM AZOR, III, process engr., geologist; b. Jacksonville, Fla., Mar. 3, 1951; s. William Azor Schell, Jr. and Nadia (Lamb) Schell Mead; B.S. in Geology, New Mex. Inst. Mining and Tech., 1973; M.B.A., U. N. Fla., 1977. Owner, mgr. Bill's Motocycles, Socorro, N. Mex., 1972-73; process engr. Fla. Wire & Cable Co., 1973; process engr. Humphreys Mining Co., Folkston, Ga., 1973-78; process engr., geologist Humphreys Engring. Co., Denver, 1978-79; metallurgist Zellars-Williams, Inc., Lakeland, Fla., 1979—. Mem. Geol. Soc. Am., Am. Welding Soc., Am. Mgmt. Assn., Soc. Mining Engrs. Episcopalian. Clubs: Fla. Yacht, Bigtree Racquet. Home: 5114 Forestgreen Dr W Lakeland FL 33803 also 7401 Greenway Dr Jacksonville FL 32210 Office: 4222 S Florida Ave Lakeland FL 33803

SCHELLER, ZBIGNIEW, pathologist; b. Gniezno, Poland, Apr. 7, 1941; s. Zygfryd and Helena (Zbytniewska) S.; came to U.S., 1972, naturalized, 1977; M.D., U. Gdansk (Poland), 1966; m. Anna Maria Michalowicz, Aug. 26, 1966. Intern, Copernicus U. Hosp., U. Gdansk, 1966-68; resident U. B.C., Vancouver, 1969-72, Sinai Hosp., Balt., 1972-73; clin. asso. dept. pathology U. South Fla., Tampa, 1973-74; asso. dir. labs. Palm Beach Gardens (Fla.) Community Hosp., 1974-75, dir. labs., chief pathology, 1975—, chief spl. services, 1978-79; med. dir. Diagnostic Lab. Inc., North Palm Beach, Fla., 1976—. Mem. AMA (award 1974), Am. Soc. Clin. Pathologists (Continuing Edn. award 1975-77), Coll. Am. Pathologists, Am. Soc. Cytology, Fla. Med. Assn., Palm Beach County Med. Soc. Club: Old Port Cove Tennis. Home: 11874 Lake Shore Pl North Palm Beach FL 33408 Office: 3360 Burns Rd Palm Beach Gardens FL 33410 also 1220 US Hwy 1 North Palm Beach FL 33408

SCHELLSTEDE, ELOISE JEANNETTE, artist; b. Tulsa, Sept. 11, 1918; d. Delmer Robert and Carrol (Rouse) Rees; B.A., Tulsa U., 1939; m. John E. Schellstede, Nov. 30, 1940 (dec. 1973); children—John Robert, Richard Lee. Owner Schellstede Gallery Fine Arts/Green Country Art Center; instr. art, 1939—; exhibited numerous one-man shows including University Club, YMCA, various chs., clubs, 1963—; exhibited group shows including Mayo Hotel, Nat. Bank Tulsa, Merc. Bank & Trust Co., Camelot Inn, Tulsa, Coll. Union, Tahlequah, Okla., Shangri-la Lodge on Grand Lake, Afton, Okla., Kerr Mus., Poteau, Okla.; owner Gallery of Fine Art, Tulsa, 1970—; represented in Kerr Mus., Cherokee Archives Mus., Ft. Gibson, Selco Corp. collection, other permanent and pvt. collections; dir. Internat. Petroleum Exhbn., Tulsa, 1976; specializing in oil portraits and landscapes of S.W., sculptor, instr. sculpturing. Founder Green Country Art Assn., Green Country Art Found., Green Country Sch. Art; founder, artist in residence Green Country Art Center; Green County chmn. Okla. Bicentennial Fine Arts Shows, 1976. Mem. Nat. Art Materials Trade Assn., Profl. Ins. Agts., DAR, Kappa Delta. Presbyn. Home: 1825 E 15th St Tulsa OK 74104

SCHENCK, ARTHUR CARL, constrn. mgr., cons. engr.; b. Phila., July 31, 1910; s. Rev. Dr. A. Clarence and Hattie Olive (Ritter) S.; B.S., U. Ala., 1934; m. Eloise Elena Williams, July 6, 1934; children—Nancy Elizabeth (Mrs. Robert Edward Smith), Jean Gray (Mrs. Richard George Rice). Field and resident engr. Stone & Webster Engring. Corp., 1934, 1936-42; engr. Stone & Webster Engring. Corp., 1934, 1936-42; insp. U.S. C.E., Phila., 1935-36; v.p. Carpenter Constrn. Co., Inc., Norfolk, Va., 1942-63; prin., A. Carl Schenck & Assos., constrn. mgmt. & engring. cons., 1963—. Mem. Bd. Review Real Estate Assessments, 1955—; mem. Va. Airports Authority, 1958—. Mem. Engring. Com. Devel. Council, U. Ala., 1958-62. Exec. council Tidewater chpt. Boy Scouts Am., 1958—; mem. lay adv. bd. DePaul Hosp., 1962—, chmn., 1971-72; mem. Citizens Adv. Com. Norfolk, 1965-68; mem. adv. council Norfolk Area Med. Center Authority, 1970-77; mem. grad. med. edn. com. of bd. commrs. Eastern Va. Med. Authority. Mem. Va. Soc. Profl. Engrs. (pres. Norfolk chpt. 1958-59), Asso. Gen. Contractors Am. (pres. Va. br. 1962), Builders and Contractors Exchange (dir. 1960-62), Am. Arbitration Assn., Tau Beta Pi, Theta Tau, Chi Beta Phi. Lutheran. Clubs: Engineers (Hampton Roads); Kiwanis (pres. 1966), Virginia (Norfolk); Harbor; Cedar Point Country. Home: 5601 Huntington Pl Norfolk VA 23509 Office: PO Box 7097 Norfolk VA 23509

SCHERER, CLARENCE HENRY, city ofcl.; b. Timber Lake, S.D., Apr. 21, 1926; s. Clement and Anna (Kamperschroer) S.; B.S., St. John's U. (Collegeville, Minn.), 1950; M.S., Trinity U., 1953; m. Eoline G. Jordan, Dec. 2, 1947; children—Andrew, Bonnie (Mrs. Harrel Alcorn), Mary (Mrs. Phillip Risner), Susan (Mrs. Joseph Velasquez), David, Theresa. Chemist, City San Antonio, 1950; dir. research Tex. Health Dept., Donna, 1951-52; research scientist U. Tex., Austin, 1953; supt. water supply treatment and reclamation City Amarillo, Tex., 1954—. Owner, cons. water and wastewater Chemlab. Service of Amarillo, 1960—; partner, exec. dir. Water and Environ. Tech., subengring. in water and wastewater. Vice chmn. environmental com. Panhandle Regional Planning Commn., 1970-74; chmn. water quality monitoring com. Canadian River Water Authority, 1969-74; vice chmn. Tex. Bd. Water and Waste Water Certification, 1972—; pres. Assn. Bds. Certification for Water and Wastewater Utility Operators U.S., 1979—. Served with AUS, 1945-47. Mem. Tex. Water Utilities Assn. (past pres.), Water Pollution Control Fedn. (George B. Gascoigne award 1953, 71, William D. Hatfield award 1970), Am. Water Works Assn., Am. Pub. Works Assn. Republican. Roman Catholic. K.C. Author: (with others) Manual for Sewage Plant Operators, 1964; (with others) Manual for

Wastewater Operations, 1971. Home: 1012 Melody Ln Amarillo TX 79108 Office: PO Box 1971 Amarillo TX 79186

SCHERER, LEE RICHARD, JR., govt. ofcl.; b. Charleston, S.C., Sept. 20, 1919; s. Lee Richard and Sara Mae (Getsinger) S.; B.S. in Elec. Engring., Naval Acad., 1942: B.S. in Aero. Engring., U.S. Naval Postgrad. Sch., 1949; M.S. in Aero. Engring., Calif. Inst. Tech., 1950; D.Engring. Sci., U. Central Fla., 1979; m. Betty Jean Hemsky, Feb. 21, 1944; children—Candace Scherer Hunt, William, Michael, Tracy. Commd. ensign U.S. Navy, 1942, advanced through grades to capt., 1962; program mgr. lunar orbiter NASA Hdqrs., Washington, 1962-67, dir. Apollo Lunar Exploration Office, 1967-71; dir. Flight Research Center, Edwards, Calif., 1971-74; dir. John F. Kennedy Space Center, Fla., 1974—. Recipient Exceptional Service award NASA, 1967, Exceptional Sci. Achievement award, 1969, Lunar Orbiter Group Achievement award, 1967, Surveyor Group Achievement award, 1968, Apollo Group Achievement award, 1969, Distinguished Service award, 1974. Mem. Sigma Xi, Tau Beta Pi. Office: John F Kennedy Space Center NASA Kennedy Space Center FL 32899

SCHERER, PAUL CLARENCE, lawyer; b. Evansville, Ind., Mar. 5, 1926; s. Paul Carl and Mildred (Rowe) S.; B.B.A., U. Tex., 1949, LL.B., 1949; m. LaNoe Fenner, July 28, 1949; children—Michael, Leta, Jane. Admitted to Tex. bar, 1948; asso. firm Peareson & Peareson, Richmond, 1949-51; partner firm Scherer, Roberts, Slone, Gresham & Lytle, and prodecessor firms, Richmond, Tex., 1952—; pres. Peareson Fort Bend Abstract Co.; dir. Sugar Land State Bank (Tex.); atty. City of Richmond, 1949—. Trustee Lamar Consol. Sch. Dist., 1955-76. Served with USAAC, 1944-45. Fellow Am. Coll. Probate Counsel; mem. Mem. Am., Tex., Fort Bend County bar assns., Phi Delta Phi., Am. Legion. Methodist (trustee). Rotarian. Home: 915 Foster St Richmond TX 77469 Office: 210 3d St Richmond TX 77469

SCHERMERHORN, JOHN WATSON, univ. dean; b. Englewood, N.J., Sept. 1, 1920; s. George William and Edna Rose (McAuley) S.; B.S., Coll. Pharmacy, Rutgers U., 1942; Ph.D. in Pharm. Chemistry, U. Minn., 1949; m. Lois M. Schilke, July 14, 1945; children—Susan, Nancy, John, James. Asst. prof. pharm. chemistry George Washington U., 1949-52, asso. prof., 1952-53; asst. prof. Mass. Coll. Pharmacy, 1953-57, asso. prof., 1957-63, prof., 1963-66, chmn. dept. pharmacy, 1964-66; prof. Northeastern U., Boston, 1966-69, dean div. allied health scis., 1969-71; dean Sch. Allied Health Scis., U. Tex., Dallas, 1971—; cons. allied health edn.; mem. task force on health magnet high sch. Dallas Ind. Sch. Dist. Served to 1st lt. U.S. Army, 1942-43, 43-46. Lic. pharmacist, D.C., N.Y., Mass. Fellow AAAS; mem. Am. Pharm. Assn. (life), Am. Soc. Allied Health Professions, Sigma Xi. Author Monographs I through VIII, The Lynn Index, A Bibliography of Phytochemistry, 1957-74. Office: 5323 Harry Hines Blvd Dallas TX 75235

SCHERMERHORN, WILLIAM LYNN, soft drink co. exec.; b. Salinas, Calif., June 28, 1942; s. Lynn George and Irma Genevive (Farnsworth) S.; B.S., U. S.D., 1966; m. Lynda Rae Cowley, Jan. 21, 1967; 1 son, Jonathan Tyler. Asso. product mgr. A.E. Staley Mfg. Co., Decatur, Ill., 1968-72; product mgr. Gen. Foods Corp., White Plains, N.Y., 1972-74; sr. product mgr. tobacco products Brown and Williamson Tobacco Corp., Louisville, 1974-77; nat. advt. mgr. Dr. Pepper Co., Dallas, 1977—. Served with U.S. Army, 1966-68. Mem. Am. Mktg. Assn., Assn. Nat. Advertisers, Delta Tau Delta. Republican. Roman Catholic. Clubs: Dallas Athletic Country, Hunting Creek Country. Home: 6707 Rolling Vista Dr Dallas TX 75248 Office: 5523 E Mockingbird Ln Dallas TX 75222

SCHEXNAYDER, GLENN DAVID, physician; b. New Orleans, Dec. 6, 1950; s. Earl Alfred and Vera Marie (Derbes) S.; B.S., La. State U., 1972, M.D., 1975; m. Shirley L. Hebert, Aug. 12, 1972; children—Glenn David, Brett Robert. Intern, Earl K. Long Hosp., Baton Rouge, 1975-78, resident in family medicine, 1975-78; practice medicine specializing in family medicine Schexnayder, Savoie, Hirsch & Schexnayder, Donaldsonville, La., 1979—; vice chief staff Prevost Meml. Hosp., 1979. Recipient Upjohn Achievement award, 1975. Fellow Am. Acad. Family Physicians; mem. Ascension Parish Med. Soc. (sec. treas. 1979), La. Med. Soc., Alpha Omega Alpha. Roman Catholic. Home: 107 Belle Alliance Dr Donaldsonville LA 70346 Office: 214 Clinic Dr Donaldsonville LA 70346

SCHIFF, LEON, physician, educator; b. Riga, Latvia, May 1, 1901; s. Mordecai and Esther (Liebschutz) S.; came to U.S., 1906, naturalized, 1913; B.S., U. Cin., 1922, M.D., 1924, M.S., 1927, Ph.D., 1929; m. Augusta Miller, June 9, 1925; children—Herbert Nolan (dec.), Gilbert Martin, Eugene Roger. Intern, then resident Cin. Gen. Hosp., 1924-27, 28-30; fellow medicine U. Munich and U. Leipiz (Germany), 1927-28; mem. faculty U. Cin. Med. Sch., 1930-70; prof., clin. prof. medicine U. Miami Med. Sch., Miami, Fla., 1970—; cons. gastroenterology and liver diseases. Recipient award Nat. Commn. Digestive Diseases, 1977. Master A.C.P.; mem. Am. Soc. Clin. Investigation, AAAS, Am. Fedn. Clin. Research, Central Soc. Clin. Research, Am. Gastroenterol. Assn. (Friedenwald medal 1973), Am. Soc. Gastroent. Endoscopy, Am. Assn. Study Liver Disease (past pres.), N.Y. Acad. Scis., Internat. Assn. Study Liver, Am. Med. Writers Assn., Royal Soc. Medicine (affiliate). Author: Differential Diagnosis of Jaundice, 1946; Clinical Approach to Jaundice, 1954. Editor: Diseases of the Liver, 4th edit., 1975; co-editor: Bile Salt Metabolism, 1969. Home: 625 Biltmore Way Coral Gables FL 33134

SCHIFFMAN, YALE MARVIN, environ. system scientist; b. Boston, July 31, 1938; s. Benjamin and Sara (Reznick) S.; B.L.S., Boston U., 1972, M.S., 1974; m. Nancy Elizabeth Perry, June 23, 1974. Tech. project specialist Gen. Electric Co., Weisbaden, Germany, 1962-66; program mgr. Raytheon Co., Bedford, Mass., 1966-75; prin. investigator Stone & Webster Engring. Corp., Boston, 1975-78; tech. coordinator Camp Dresser McKee, Boston, 1978; environ. systems scientist metrek div. Mitre Corp., McLean, Va., 1978—; teaching fellow Harvard U. Grad. Sch. Design, 1978—. Served with USAF, 1957-61. Recipient Raytheon Authors award, 1975. Mem. Council of Environ. Design Orgns. (co-chmn. bd. dirs.), Am. Planning Assn. (pres. energy div.), Am. Acad. Polit. and Social Scis., Met. Assn. Urban Designers and Environ. Planners, Boston U. Alumni Assn. (past dir.). Democrat. Jewish. Home: 7406 Forest Hunt Ct Springfield VA 22153 Office: 1820 Dolley Madison Blvd McLean VA 22102

SCHIFFRIN, MILTON JULIUS, physiologist; b. Rochester, N.Y., Mar. 23, 1914; s. William and Lillian (Harris) S.; A.B., U. Rochester, 1937, M.S., 1939; Ph.D. cum laude, McGill U., 1941; m. Dorothy Euphemia Wharry, Oct. 10, 1942; children—David Wharry, Hilary Ann. Instr. physiology Northwestern U. Med. Sch., 1941-45; lectr. pharmacology U. Ill. Med. Sch., 1947-57, clin. asst. prof. anesthesiology, 1957-61; with Hoffmann-La Roche, Inc., Nutley, N.J., 1946-79, dir. drug regulatory affairs, 1964-71, asst. v.p., 1971-79; pres. Wharry Research Assn., Port St. Lucie, Fla., 1979—. Served from 2d lt. to capt. USAAF, 1942-46. Mem. Am. Med. Writers Assn. (dir. 1967—; pres. N.Y. chpt. 1967-68; pres. 1972-73), Am. Physiol. Soc., Internat. Coll. Surgeons, Am. Therapeutic Soc., Coll. Clin. Pharmacology and Therapeutics, Am. Chem. Soc. Author: (with E.G. Gross) Clinical Analgetics, 1955. Editor: Management of Pain in Cancer, 1957. Office: 1430 Sans Souci Ln Port Saint Lucie FL 33452

SCHILDER, STEPHEN Z., child and adolescent psychiatrist; b. Bklyn., Oct. 28, 1937; s. Benjamin and Ida (Meltzer) S.; B.S., Bklyn. Coll., 1959; M.D., Upstate N.Y. Coll. Medicine, Syracuse, 1964; m. Sandra Ann Tutweiler, Dec. 31, 1972; children—Robert Monroe, Scott Matthew, Jason Harris. Resident child-adolescent and gen. psychiatry McAuley Neuropsychiat. Inst., St. Mary's Hosp., San Francisco, 1964-69; child-adolescent psychiatrist Michas, Schilder and Gill Psychiat. Assos., Ft. Walton Beach, Fla., 1971—; cons. Okaloosa County Sch. Dist. Served to maj. M.C., USAF, 1969-71. Decorated Commendation medal. Mem. Am. Psychiat. Assn., Am. Group Psychotherapy Assn., Am., Fla. med. assns., Okaloosa County Med. Soc. (pres. 1975), Gulf Coast Neuropsychiat. Soc., Fla. Psychiat. Soc., N.Y. Acad. Scis., Ft. Walton Beach C. of C. Jewish. Home: 299 Briarwood Circle Fort Walton Beach FL 32548 Office: W Circle Dr Fort Walton Beach FL 32548

SCHILLING, EDWIN CARLYLE, JR., lawyer; b. Greensburg, La., Sept. 25, 1921; s. Edwin Carlyle and Myrtle (Holland) S.; J.D., La. State U., 1948; m. Ann LeTard, Feb. 7, 1942; 1 son, Edwin Carlyle III. Admitted to La. bar, 1948, since practiced in Amite; individual practice law, 1948-62; mem. firm Schilling & Reid and predecessor firms, 1963—; v.p. 1st Savs. & Loan Assn., Hammond and Amite, La. Mem. adv. council La. Moral and Civic Found.; mem. exec. com. La. Bapt. Conv. Trustee La. Coll., Pineville, Pub. Affairs Research Council. Served with AUS, 1943-46. Mem. Am., La., Twenty First Jud. Dist. bar assns., Amite C. of C. (past pres.). Baptist (deacon). Rotarian (past pres.). Home: 305 Cedar St Amite LA 70422 Office: 109 N Bay St Amite LA 70422

SCHILLING, LOUIS ROBERT, JR., chem. co. exec.; b. Hackensack, N.J., Nov. 24, 1931; s. Louis Robert and Frances Elizabeth (Loehwing) S.; B.S., Villanova U., 1954; m. Joan Patricia Coughlin, Apr. 21, 1956; children—Louis Robert III, Lynn Patricia. Staff accountant Shell Chem. Corp., N.Y.C., 1958-61; cost mgr. I.T. & T., Paramus, N.J., 1962-65; accounting mgr. Gen. Foods Corp., White Plains, N.Y., 1965-67; fin. mgr. R.J.R. Foods, Inc., N.Y.C., 1967-69; controller, sec. Henkel Inc. (formerly Standard Chem. Products), Teaneck, N.J., 1969-73; fin. officer Polyester div. W.R. Grace Co., 1973-74; pres. L.R. Schilling & Assos., Montvale, N.J., 1974-76; budget mgr. govt. products div. Pratt and Whitney Aircraft Group United Technologies Corp., 1976—. Served with USNR, 1954-58, 61-62. Mem. Financial Execs. Inst., Assn. Systems Mgmt., N.Am. Yacht Racing Union. Club: Englewood (N.J.) Yacht. Home: 745 Dogwood Rd North Palm Beach FL 33408 Office: PO Box 2691 West Palm Beach FL 33402

SCHILLING, RALPH FRANKLIN, univ. pres.; b. Morris, Okla., July 5, 1921; s. R.F. and Mattie E. (Crume) S.; B.A., Oklahoma City U., 1948; M.Ed., Okla. U., 1950; Ed.D., Tex. Tech. Coll., 1957; m. Mary Katherine Brooks, Jan. 19, 1942; 1 son, Ralph Franklin. Instr., asst. coach Oklahoma City U., 1947-50; high sch. prin., Crosbyton, Tex., 1950-52, Littlefield, Tex., 1952-54; supt. schs., Littlefield, 1954-60; pres. Pan Am. U., Edinburg, Tex., 1960—. Chmn. adv. bd. Littlefield Salvation Army, 1959. Named Littlefield Man of Year, 1958. Mem. N.E.A. (life), Am. Assn. Sch. Adminstrs., Tex. Tchrs. Assn., Tex. Adminstrs. Assn. Methodist (past chmn. stewards, lay leader). Rotarian (pres. Littlefield 1959-60), Mason (32 deg.). Home: Box 232 Edinburg TX 78539

SCHINDLER, CHARLES ALVIN, educator; b. Boston, Dec. 27, 1924; s. Edward Esau and Esther (Weisman) S.; B.S. in Biology, Rensselaer Poly. Ins., 1950; M.A., U. Tex. at Austin, 1955, Ph.D., 1961; m. Barbara Jean Francois, Jan. 29, 1955; children—Esther M., Susan E., Neal L. Commd. 2d lt. U.S. Air Force, 1951, advanced through grades to maj., 1964; research scientist various armed forces research labs., including Armed Forces Inst. Pathology, Washington, 1961-67, USAF Armament Lab, Elgin AFB, Fla., 1967-68; ret., 1968; asst. prof. dept. microbiology U. Okla., Norman, 1968-72; asst. prof. natural sci. Flagler Coll., St. Augustine, Fla., 1972-73. Cons. Mead Johnson Research Center, 1961-67. Chmn. Cleve. County precinct Norman Democratic Com., 1973—; mem. Norman City Council, 1976—. Served with USAAF, 1943-46. Charles E. Lewis fellow, 1958; NSF grantee, 1971. Mem. Am. Soc. Microbiologists (exec. sec. Mo. Valley br. 1969-71), Am. Chem. Soc., N.Y. Acad. Scis., Soc. Gen. Microbiology (Gt. Britain), Sigma Xi. Patentee in field. Contbr. articles to profl. jours. Home: 2000 Morgan Dr Norman OK 73069

SCHJAASTAD, DOLORES FAY, writer; b. LaSalle County, Ill., Dec. 26, 1920; d. John B. and Anna M. (Schneider) S.; B.S. in Bus. Adminstrn. cum laude, U. Tampa, 1949; postgrad. Nashville Sch. Social Work of Vanderbilt, Peabody and Scarritt (now U. Tenn.), 1950-51, Nat. Cath. Sch. of Social Service, Cath. U. Am., 1951-52. With Hillsborough County Welfare Dept., Tampa, Fla., 1940-44, Family Service Assn., Tampa, 1949-50; free-lance writer, Tampa, 1958—; public relations worker Sigma Sigma Sigma. Mem. naval and mcht. marine subcom. of acad. adv. and selection com. of Rep. Sam M. Gibbons, 7th Congl. Dist. Fla., 1978-79. Served with USCGR, 1944-46, to lt. USNR, 1951-58. Recipient Triangle award Sigma Sigma Sigma, 1972, Hon. mention, 1973. Fellow Internat. Biog. Inst., Am. Biog. Inst.; mem. Res. Officers Assn. U.S. (dir. pub. relations Tampa chpt. 1977-78), Ret. Officers Assn., Internat. Platform Assn., U. Tampa Nat. Alumni Assn., Beta Sigma Phi, Sigma Sigma Sigma. Methodist. Home: 10014 Hyacinth Ave Tampa FL 33612 Office: PO Box 17841 Tampa FL 33682

SCHLABS, DAVID PATRICK, mfg. co. exec.; b. Dallas, Oct. 19, 1943; s. Henry Joseph and Freida Marie (Donoho) S.; B.B.A., Midwestern U., 1968; m. Carolyn Irene Connolly, Aug. 27, 1964; children—Craig and Chris (twins). Materials mgr. United Electric Co., Wichita Falls, Tex., 1965-68, mgr. systems and data processing, 1968-74; mgr. systems and data processing Allis-Chalmers Co., Wichita Falls, 1974-77, materials mgr., 1977—; v.p. Wichita Falls Chpt. Credit Unions. Scuba instr. YMCA; mem. advisory com. municipal info. system project Wichita Falls City Council. Recipient City Mgr.'s award, Wichita Falls, 1976; Pres.'s award Midwestern State U., 1976. Mem. Data Processing Mgmt. Assn. (pres. Wichita Falls chpt.), Am. Production and Inventory Control Soc., Houston Eleven Thirty User Group, Kappa Alpha Order. Republican. Roman Catholic. Club: K.C. Home: 1534 Southwinds St Wichita Falls TX 76302

SCHLAGETER, ROBERT WILLIAM, museum adminstr.; b. Streator, Ill., May 10, 1925; B.A., U. Ill., 1950, M.F.A., 1955; postgrad. U. Heidelberg (Ger.), 1949-50, U. Chgo., 1956, Harvard U., 1957. Asst. prof. art history U. Tenn., 1952-58; dir. Mint Mus. Art, Charlotte, N.C., 1958-66; asso. dir. Downtown Gallery, N.Y.C., 1967, Ackland Art Center at U. N.C., Chapel Hill, 1967-76; dir. Cummer Gallery Art, Jacksonville, Fla., 1976—. Office: 829 Riverside Ave Jacksonville FL 32204

SCHLEGEL, DWIGHT EARLE, distbn. co. exec.; b. Summit, N.J., Mar. 31, 1946; s. Augustus Earle and Colette Rose-Marie (Moore) S.; B.A. in Polit. Sci., Rutgers U., 1969; m. Barbara Marie Swinicki, Sept. 1, 1968; children—Melissa Marie, Erika Ann, Tracy Lee, Karey Elizabeth. Dist. mgr. Home News Co., N. Brunswick, N.J., 1968-69; adjuster Liberty Mut. Co., N. Brunswick, 1969-71; claims mgr. Reliance Ins. Co., Jacksonville, Fla., 1971-72; sales rep. Lloyd & Lee, Inc., Jacksonville, 1972-73; sales rep. LD Brinkman, Jacksonville, 1973-75, territorial sales mgr., 1975, gen. sales mgr., Jacksonville, 1975-79, Raleigh, N.C., 1979—. Mem. Greater Jacksonville Floor Covering Assn. (exec. com. 1974—). Roman Catholic. Home: 822 Manchester Dr Raleigh NC 27609 Office: 500 Departure Dr Raleigh NC

SCHLIESTETT, GEORGE VAN, aerospace engr.; b. Cedartown, Ga., Mar. 20, 1911; s. Thomas Walter and Chattie Ann (Ledbetter) S.; B.S., Ga. Inst. Tech., 1932, M.S., 1934; postgrad. M.I.T., 1935-36, Calif. Tech. U., 1949-50; m. Patsy Rhinehardt Cook, Dec. 3, 1977; children by previous marriage—Georgia Lynn, Debra Kay, James Alan, Thomas Van. Research asst. M.I.T., 1937-39; engr., div. head, Dept. Navy, 1939-55; exec. with several small engring. cos., 1955-59; aerospace staff engr. and project mgr. systems and energy TRW, Redondo Beach, Calif., 1958-70; ret., 1970. Served with USN, 1942-46. Mem. Am. Inst. Aeronautics Astronautics, Am. Def. Preparedness Assn., Sigma Xi, Tau Beta Pi. Clubs: Congressional (Bethesda, Md.); Indian Creek (Miami Beach). Contbr. articles to profl. jours.

SCHLINKMAN, BOB, phys. testing equipment mfg. co. sales rep.; b. Amarillo, Tex., June 5, 1949; s. Robert George and Geraldine Ruth (Hess) S.; B.S. in Phys. Edn., Tex. Tech. U., 1971, M.Edn., 1973. Order dept. supr. Wilson Sporting Goods Co., Dallas, 1972-73; pro golf and tennis sales rep. for SW and Central Tex., 1973-80; sales rep. Cybex Co., Dallas, 1980—. Mem. SW Profl. Golf Salesman's Assn., U.S. Golf Assn. (asso.). Club: So. Meth. U. Mustang. Contbr. article on heart rate study to mag. Home: 12363 Abrams Rd Dallas TX 75243 Office: Dallas TX

SCHLOTZ, RANDY CRAIG, oil co. engring. supr.; b. Perryton, Tex., Apr. 12, 1947; s. Samuel LeRoy and Leila Christina S.; A.S., Okla. State U., 1967, B.S. in Aero. Engring., 1970; postgrad. Okla. U., 1973, U. Tex. of Permian Basin, 1977-78, Hardin-Simmons U., 1978; m. Sandra K. Griffin, Nov. 27, 1970; children—John William, Leigh Anne. Sr. field supr. Ensearch Exploration, Inc., Midland, Tex., 1970-71, Jackson, Miss., 1971-73, Ashtabula, Ohio, 1973-73, petroleum engr., Oklahoma City, 1973-74, Dallas, 1974-75, Midland, 1975-76; sr. reservoir engr. Tex. Pacific Oil Co., Inc., 1976-78, reservoir engring. supr., Abilene, Tex., 1978—. Mem. Soc. Petroleum Engrs. of AIME, Soc. Petroleum Well Log Analysts. Home: 5002 Robertson St Abilene TX 79506 Office: 1290 S Willis St Abilene TX 79605

SCHMALFELD, ROBERT GEORGE, ednl. adminstr.; b. Chgo., Oct. 2, 1930; s. Harry Holger and Eva Doris (Hall) S.; B.A., Knox Coll., 1952; M.A., Northwestern U., 1957, postgrad., 1957-59; children—Mark Robert, Deborah Lee. Grad. research asst., head resident Northwestern U., Evanston, Ill., 1956-57; asst. dean men, instr. English and edn. Heidelberg Coll., Tiffin, Ohio, 1957-59, dean of men, 1959-63; asst. dean of men U. Ariz., Tucson, 1963-66; dean of students, prof. psychology Lea Coll., Albert Lea, Minn., 1966-68; dean student affairs Okla. State U., Stillwater, 1968—; part-time lectr. Northwestern U., Ind. U. Bd. dirs. YMCA, Stillwater; mem. Mayor's Commn. on Human Relations; mem. vestry Trinity Episcopal Ch. Served with USN, 1953-56. Mem. Am., Okla. coll. personnel assns., Nat., S.W. assns. student personnel adminstrs., Am. Assn. Higher Edn., Nat. Vocat. Guidance Assn., Okla. Personnel and Guidance Assn., Phi Eta Sigma, Phi Delta Kappa. Democrat. Home: 1000 N Star Dr 3 Stillwater OK 74074 Office: 369 Student Union Okla State Univ Stillwater OK 74074

SCHMAUSS, DAVID C., med. center exec.; b. St. Paul, Mar. 21, 1931; s. John Henry and Catherine Ann (Caulfield) S.; B.A., U. Minn., 1955, M. Hosp. Adminstrn., 1962: m. Judy Ann Buckbee, Oct. 8, 1955; children—Mark, Edward, Jennifer. Adminstr., Sister Elizabeth Kenny Rehab. Inst., Mpls., 1963-66; exec. sec. Cath. Hosp. Assn. Service Bur., Washington, 1966-68; adminstr. Appalachian Regional Hosp., Beckley, W.Va. 1968-74; asst. v.p. Appalachian Regional Hosps., Lexington, Ky, 1973-74; v.p., gen. dir. No. div. Albert Einstein Med. Center, Phila., 1974-78, bd. dirs., 1976-78; exec. dir. U. Hosp. and Clinics, Lexington, Ky., 1978—; bd. dirs. Internat. Assn. Rehab. Facilities; preceptor Xavier U.; mem. field faculty Meharry Med. Coll.; chmn. Raleigh County (W.Va.) Health Council. Bd. mgrs. Mpls. YMCA, 1966-68; area vice chmn. Mpls. United Fund, 1967. Served with USMCR, 1948-58. Fellow Am. Pub. Health Assn., Am. Coll. Hosp. Adminstrs.; mem. Assn. Am. Med. Colls., Nat. League Nursing. Home: 342 Weller Ave Lexington KY 40536 Office: U Hosp U Ky 800 Rose St Lexington KY 40536

SCHMELING, GARETH LON, educator; b. Algoma, Wis., May 28, 1940; s. Walter Charles and Tabea (Braem) S.; B.A., Northwestern Coll., 1963; M.A., U. Wis., 1964, Ph.D., 1968; m. Karen Eileen Weiss, Dec. 21, 1963. Asst. prof. U. Va., Charlottesville, 1968-70; asso. prof. classics U. Fla., Gainesville, 1970-75, prof., chmn. dept. classics, 1975—, dir. Center for Studies in Humanities, 1978—. Mem. Library Com., Gainesville, 1974-76. Am. Philos. Soc. grantee, 1970, 71, 72, 77-78; Nat. Endowment for Humanities fellow, 1973-74; Am. Council Learned Socs. grantee, 1974; recipient Prix de Rome, 1977-78. Mem. AAUP, Am. Philol. Assn., Classical Assn., Am. Classical League, Am. Acad. in Rome. Democrat. Lutheran. Author: Cornelius Nepos: Lives of Famous Men, 1971 Chariton and the Rise of Ancient Fiction, 1974; A Bibliography of Petronius, 1977; Xenophon of Ephesus, 1980. Home: 320 NW 30th St Gainesville FL 32607 Office: Dept Classics U Fla Gainesville FL 32611

SCHMELZ, GARY WILLIAM, nature center dir.; b. Jersey City, July 24, 1939; s. Henry and Katherine (Tibbatts) S.; B.S., Farleigh Dickinson U., 1961; M.S. in Zoology, U. Del., 1964, Ph.D. (Univ. fellow), 1970; m. Bernice A. Davies, Nov. 4, 1965. Research asso. U. Del., 1970-71; chief acuatic ecologist Deltona Corp., Marco Island, Fla., 1971; naturalist Big Cypress Nature Center, Naples, Fla., 1971-73, dir., 1973—. Instr. Edison Community Coll., 1972—. Served with USNR, 1964-66. Mem. Nat. Wildlife Fedn., A.A.A.S., Nat. Audubon Soc. Home: 1224 Hilltop Dr Naples FL 33940 Office: 1890 Goodlette Rd Naples FL 33940

SCHMIDGALL, ROBERT LEE, chemist; b. Peoria, Ill., Mar. 28, 1943; s. William Henry and Cleona Elizabeth (Ackerly) S.; B.A., Bradley U., 1965; Ph.D., Ind. U., 1969. Chemist, USDA, Peoria, 1963-65; instr. chemistry U. Ark., Fayetteville, 1969-70; mem. faculty Henderson State U., Arkadelphia, 1970—, asso. prof., 1972-77, prof., 1978—. Mem. Am. Chem. Soc., Sigma Xi. Home: 314 S 23d St Arkadelphia AR 71923 Office: Dept Chemistry Henderson State U Arkadelphia AR 71923

SCHMIDT, CHRISTINE SUE, neuropsychology technician; b. Greenfield, Iowa, Sept. 17, 1952; d. LaVerne Eugene and Leila (Mitchell) S.; B.S., Iowa State U., 1974; M.S., Old Dominion U., 1979. Mental health worker Portsmouth (Va.) Psychiat. Center, 1975, team coordinator, 1975-76; neuropsychology technician Center Psychiatrists, Portsmouth, 1976—. Cert. tech. asst., Va. Mem. Am. Mental Health Counselors Assn., Va. Mental Health Counselors

Assn., Am. Personnel and Guidance Assn., Old Dominion U. Personnel and Guidance Assn., Iowa State U. Alumni Assn., Old Dominion U. Alumni Assn., Alpha Delta Pi. Club: Norfolk Central YMCA Young Businesswomen's. Home: 521 Graydon Ave Norfolk VA 23507 Office: Center Psychiatrists Crawford Pkwy at Fort Ln Portsmouth VA 23704

SCHMIDT, HAROLD EUGENE, civil engr., land co. exec.; b. Cedar Rapids, Iowa, Oct. 12, 1925; s. Alfons W. and Lillie (Schlegel) S.; B.S., U. Iowa, 1949; M.S., Mass. Inst. Tech., 1953; m. Lucy Hermann, Apr. 13, 1957; children—Harold, Sandra. Research, devel. engr. Chgo. Pump Co., 1949-51; engr. A.B. Kononoff, Engrs., Miami, Fla., 1956-58; with Gen. Devel. Corp., Miami, 1958—, v.p. utilities, 1966-67, corporate officer, asst. v.p., 1967-72; pres. Gen. Devel. Utilities, Inc., 1972, v.p. community div., 1973—; dir. Port Charlotte Bank (Fla.). Served to capt. Med. Service Corps, USAF, 1951-56. Mem. Am. Water Works Assn., Water Pollution Control Fedn., Sigma Xi, Chi Epsilon. Home: 641 W 53d St Hialeah FL 33012 Office: 1111 S Bayshore Dr Miami FL 33131

SCHMIDT, JOHN VICTOR, retailer; b. Palestine, Tex., June 19, 1947; s. Victor Louis and Anita Elizabeth (Fendley) S.; student Wharton County Jr. Coll., 1966-67; Sam Houston State U., 1968-70; m. Molly Ann Richman, Mar. 12, 1970. Rep. Allied Fin. Co., Freeport, Tex., 1970-71; supr. asso. Bldg. Services, Houston, 1972-73; safety insp. Crane Splty. Co., Bay City, Tex., 1973-75; owner, mgr. Schmidt Furniture Co., Freeport, 1976—; advisor distributive edn. Brazosport Ind. Sch. Dist., Freeport, 1977—. Mem. Freeport Bus. and Profl. Assn. (sec. 1977—), Nat. Fedn. Ind. Businesses, Nat. Home Furnishings Assn., Freeport Jaycees, Brazosport C. of C. (President's Club 1979). Presbyterian. Home: 126 N Bow Dr Route 1 Freeport TX 77541 Office: 404 W 2d St Freeport TX 77541

SCHMIDT, LAWRENCE GEORGE, applied technologist, educator; b. South Charleston, W.Va., Feb. 29, 1932; s. Lawrence John and Angele Augusta (Bougamont) S.; B.A., W.Va. State Coll., 1978; m. Carolyn Jane Hutchinson, Dec. 20, 1954; children—Lawrence George II, James Franklin, Timothy John. Tchr., Sissonville (W.Va.) High Sch., 1963-70, Ben Franklin Vocat.-Tech. Center, Dunbar, W.Va., 1971-73; faculty Parkersburg (W.Va.) Community Coll., 1973—, chmn. div. applied tech., 1974—, coordinator air conditioning, refrigeration and heating, 1973—. Mem. City of South Charleston City Council, 1970-74; mem. Buckskin Council, exec. com., Boy Scouts Am., 1970. Silver Beaver award, 1964. Served with U.S. Army, 1951-53. Mem. W.Va. Edn. Assn., Am. Vocat. Assn. Democrat. Roman Catholic. Home: 256 Kenna Dr South Charleston WV 25303 Office: Dept Air Conditioning Refrigeration and Heating Parkersburg Community Coll Route 5 Box 167-A Parkersburg WV 26101

SCHMIDT, MARJORIE BELL, civic worker; b. Council Hill, Okla., Apr. 11, 1910; d. Homer Edwin and Anna Mariah (Neibling) Bell; pvt. edn.; m. Irvin Emil Schmidt, June 12, 1932; children—John Homer, Donald Irvin, David Michael. Treas., Republican Women's Club, Oklahoma City, 1954-58, del. Rep. conv., 1956, courtesy hostess polit. activities; state dir. edn. dept. Ladies Music Club, 1965-69; initiated ann. art scholarship, 1963; active art workshops, exhibits. Recipient hon. Okla. Gov., 1952, other awards. Mem. Internat. Platform Assn., Arts and Humanities Council, Am. Security Council, Gt. Plains Museum Hist. Assn., WCTU, Oklahoma City Opera Assn., Philharmonic Assn., Community Concert Assn., Nat. Trust for Historic Preservation. Clubs: Nat. Federated Women's, Rotary Ann, Book and Play Review, Exchangettes. Home: PO Box 2273 Panama City FL 32401

SCHMIDT, PATRICIA LOIS, educator; b. York, Pa., Nov. 8, 1942; d. Wesley and Hilda Louise (Gruver) Schmidt; B.A., Pa. State U., 1964, M.A., 1968, Ph.D., 1973. Instr. speech communications U. Del., Newark, 1968-71, also dir. debate; asst. prof. behavioral studies, speech communications U. Fla., 1973-76, asso. prof., 1976—, asst. dean Univ. Coll., 1976—, dir. integrative studies, 1976—, asst. dir. sponsored research, asso. dean for research, chmn. dept. behavioral studies, 1978—; co-investigator Fla. Endowment for the Humanities, 1976; cons. HUD. U. Fla. Humanities Council grantee, 1977. Mem. Speech Communication Assn. Am., Eastern States Communication Assn., Modern Lang. Assn., Internat. Soc. History of Rhetoric. Home: 2515 NW 38th St Gainesville FL 32608 Office: 219 Grinter Hall University of Florida Gainesville FL 32601

SCHMIDT, RICHARD LEE, land devel. co. exec.; b. North Little Rock, Ark., Apr. 14, 1931; s. Otto Herman and Winnie Fair (Whitfield) S.; B.S. in Chemistry, U. Ark., 1955; m. Shirley Faye Tucker, Dec. 19, 1957; 1 dau., Lisa Ann. With alumina research div. Reynolds Metal Co., Bauxite, Ark., 1955-59; pres., chief exec. officer S & S Art Glass Co., Benton, Ark., Eastwood Inc., land devel. co. Mem. Am. Chem. Soc. (sr.), Am. Inst. Chem. Engrs. (sr.), Am. Ceramic Soc. Lutheran. Patentee in field. Home: 1610 Lynnwood Dr Benton AR 72015 Office: PO Box 97 Bauzite AR 72011

SCHMIDT, SANDRA ESTRELLA SALGUERO, educator; b. Somerville, N.J., Oct. 15, 1949; d. Alejandro and Estrella (Roura) S.; B.A. magna cum laude, U. P.R., 1971; M.A., Central Mich. U., 1973; postgrad. U. Ill., Urbana, 1979—; m. Kenneth P. Schmidt, Aug. 14, 1971; children—Kenneth Alexander, Veronica Estelle. Grad. asst. in English, Central Mich. U., 1971-73; instr. English Colegio Universitario del Turabo, Caguas, P.R., 1973—; voice-over for Coco the Squirrel, TV Series, 1977; writer script, dir. ednl. film Shopping Day, 1979; writer script 2 ednl. programs in English for local public TV channel, 1979. Mem. Assn. Ednl. Communication and Tech., Tesol of P.R., Tchrs. Assn. P.R. Evangel., Wesleyan Ladies Fellowship (v.p. 1979). Contbr. article to profl. jour. Home: V22 Juan Ramos Urb Sta Paula Guaynabo PR 00657 Office: Dept English Colegio Universitario del Turabo Caguas PR 00625

SCHMIDTKE, RICHARD ALLEN, aerospace co. exec.; b. Benton Harbor, Mich., July 27, 1925; s. Albert Herman and Lillian May (Morlock) S.; B.S., U. Mich., 1948, M.S., 1949; Ph.D., Ill. Inst. Tech., 1953; m. Marjorie Erikson, Apr. 2, 1971; children—Terry, John, Joni, David, Nina. Asst. prof. Ill. Inst. Tech., Chgo., 1949-53; project engr., asst. to v.p. Melpar, Inc., Falls Church, Va., 1953-60; dir. applied research Pratt & Whitney Aircraft, West Palm Beach, Fla., 1960-70, sr. program mgr., 1970-76, v.p., 1976—; mem. Engrs.' Joint Council Accreditations Vis. Com., 1967-73, vis. com. Mech. Engring. Dept. U. Fla., 1964-67. Served with U.S. Army, 1944-46. Mem. ASME (engr. of yr. Palm Beach sect., 1976), Am. Astron. Soc., AIAA, Tau Beta Pi, Phi Kappa Phi, Sigma Xi, Pi Tau Sigma. Club: Elks. Patentee explosive joining device. Home: 372 Fairway N Tequesta FL 33458 Office: Pratt & Whitney Aircraft Government Products Division PO Box 2691 West Palm Beach FL 33402

SCHMITT, CHARLES RUDOLPH, chem. co. scientist; b. Bklyn., Mar. 31, 1920; s. Charles Joseph and Mary Catherine (Gerlinger) S.; B.S., Queens Coll., 1942; m. Alma Jean Peters, Nov. 10, 1945; children—Charles Jeffrey, Katherine Anne. Supr. TNT prodn. Plum Brook Ordnance Works, Sandusky, O., 1942-43; devel. engr. K-25 gaseous diffusion plant nuclear div. Union Carbide Corp., Oak Ridge, 1945-56, devel. chemist y-12 plant, 1956-65, sr. research chemist, 1965-68, devel. supr., 1968—. Cons. Rust Engring. Co. Served with AUS, 1944-45. Recipient Manhattan Dist. Spl. award U.S. War Dept., 1945. Registered profl. engr., Tenn. Mem. Am. Chem. Soc., Tenn. Acad. Sci., Nat., Tenn. socs. profl. engrs., Tenn. Wastewater Assn. Republican. Lutheran (trustee 1960-70). Author: Pyrophoricity, 1973. Contbr. articles to profl. jours. Home: 110 Adelphi Rd Oak Ridge TN 37830 Office: PO Box P Oak Ridge TN 37830

SCHMITT, ELBERT WILLIAM, physician; b. Jacksonville, Fla., Mar. 2, 1937; s. Elbert William and Elynor E. (Clay) S.; A.B., Emory U., 1957, M.D., 1962; m. Yvonne R. Walker, Jan. 14, 1963; children—Evie, Will, Rebecca. Intern, Grady Meml. Hosp., Atlanta, 1962-63; resident in orthopedic surgery Harvard U., 1965-68; practice medicine specializing in pediatric orthopedics, Atlanta, 1970—; asst. prof. orthopedic surgery Emory U., Atlanta, 1970—. Served with USNR, 1968-70. Diplomate Am. Bd. Orthopedic Surgery. Mem. Am. Acad. Pediatrics (chmn. sect. orthopedics), Atlanta Orthopedic Soc. (pres.-elect), Pediatric Orthopedic Study Group, Pediatric Orthopedic Soc., Am. Acad. Cerebral Palsy and Developmental Medicine, Scoliosis Research Soc., Am. Acad. Orthopedic Surgeons. Author: (with Nan E. Hilt) Pediatric Orthopaedic Nursing, 1975. Office: 1365 Clifton Rd NE Atlanta GA 30322

SCHMITT, GILBERT EUGENE, utility exec.; b. Seguin, Tex., Aug. 27, 1906; s. Lorenz and Mathilde (Glaeser) S.; B.S. in Elec. Engring., U. Tex., 1928; m. Maudine Hampton, Dec. 25, 1930; 1 dau., Patricia Nadine (Mrs. Henry A. Bunting III). Engr. substa. design and constrn. Central Power & Light Co., Corpus Christi, Tex., 1928-32, resident engr., 1929, gen. engr. design and constrn. changes, 1933-38; transmission supt. operations, engring. cons. Lower Colorado River Authority, Austin, Tex., 1939-40, chief engr., 1941-43, asst. gen. mgr., chief engr., 1944-73; cons. energy resources, 1974—. Fellow I.E.E.E. (past v.p.); mem. Tex. Soc. Profl. Engrs. (past pres.), Austin C. of C. (past v.p.), Ramshorn Club, Eta Kappa Nu. Mem. Ch. of Christ. Kiwanian. Home and office: 2804 Greenlee Dr Austin TX 78703

SCHMITT, HAROLD WILLIAM, environ. services and products co. exec.; b. Seguin, Tex., Aug. 11, 1928; s. Ben E. and Gertrude L. (Thiele) S.; student So. Methodist U., 1945-47; B.A., U. Tex., 1948, M.S., 1952, Ph.D., 1954; m. Jonell Britsch, May 4, 1952; children—Carol Emily, Ann Laine, Joy Diane. Research asso. Los Alamos Sci. Lab., 1952-54; research physicist Oak Ridge Nat. Lab., 1954-73, leader physics of fission group, 1960-73; pres. Environ. Systems Corp., Knoxville, Tenn., 1973—, also dir.; pres. ORTEC, Inc., 1960-61, chmn., 1960-64; pres. Pic-Air, Inc., 1968, chmn., 1968—. Bd. dirs. Oak Ridge Civic Music Assn., 1973-76. Fellow Am. Phys. Soc.; mem. ASTM, Am. Chem. Soc., Am. Mgmt. Assn., AAAS, Air Pollution Control Assn., Sigma Xi. Mem. editorial bd. Nuclear Data Tables, 1971-73; contbr. to books and ency.; contbr. articles in field to profl. jours. Home: 121 Canterbury Rd Oak Ridge TN 37830 Office: PO Box 2525 Knoxville TN 37901

SCHMITZ, CHARLES EDISON, clergyman; b. Mendota, Ill., July 18, 1919; s. Charles Francis and Lucetta M. (Foulk) Schmitz Kaufmann; student Wheaton Coll., 1936-37, summer 1937, 38, 39; A.B., Wartburg Coll., Waverly, Iowa, 1940; B.D., Wartburg Theol. Sem., Dubuque, Iowa, 1942, M.Div., 1977; m. Eunice M. Ewy, June 1, 1942; children—Charles Elwood, Jon Lee. Home mission developer and parish pastor Am. Luth. Ch., 1942-65, 73—, serving as founding pastor 10 parishes including Ascension (Los Angeles), Am. Evang. Luth. Phoenix, others in Prescott, Glendale, Ariz., Scottsdale, Ariz., Portales, N.Mex., Sebastian, Fla.; founder and prin. parochial schs. in Los Angeles and Phoenix; synodical Bible evangelist Am. Luth. Ch., 1965-73; dir. Intermountain Missions, 1948-60; dir. parish mission builder program; pastor Peace Luth. Ch., Palm Bay, Fla., 1973—. Former chmn., bd. mem. Ariz. Christian Conf., Christian Instnl. Ministry, Camelback Girls Residence, Ariz. Alcohol and Narcotics Edn. Assn., Phoenix Council Chs., Evang. Ministers Assn.; pres. Intermountain Conf., 1954-65; vice chmn. Nat. Worship and Ch. Music Commn., 1961-65; chmn. Billy Graham Ariz. Crusade, 1964, Nat. Luth. Social Welfare Conf., 1944-70. Mem. Ariz. Conf. Crime and Delinquency Control, 1957-65; referee Maricopa County Juvenile Ct., 1959-61; mem. Gov.'s Com. Marriage and Divorce Problems, 1962-64; chief chaplain Maricopa County Civilian Def., 1961-65; mem. Palm Bay Planning Commn. Recipient Distinguished Alumni award Wartburg Coll., 1959; City of Palm Bay Citizen of Yr. award, 1979. Mem. South Brevard Ministerial Assn. (chmn.). Lion (founding sec. and bd. mem. North Phoenix 1952-65, founding officer Palm Bay 1975—). Co-editor: The ABC's of Life; editor: Body of Christ-Evangelism for the Seventies. Contbg. editor Good News mag., 1965-71. Home: 301 SE Port Malabar Blvd Palm Bay FL 32905

SCHMITZ, RALPH KARL, life ins. co. exec.; b. Frankfurt, Germany, Jan. 29, 1932; s. Peter A. and Edith J. (Widder) S.; came to U.S., 1954, naturalized, 1959; student Inst. Lang., Darmstadt, Germany, 1950, Tex. Christian U., 1957; grad. Life Office Mgmt. Inst., 1960; m. Marianne Panzer, Oct. 29, 1953; children—Wilfried P., Keith J., Edith Maria, Peter Lynn. With World Service Life Ins. Co., Ft. Worth, 1954-74, v.p., dir. ordinary agencies, 1968-74; pres. Schmitz & Co., life ins. mktg., Ft. Worth, 1974—, Internat. Mktg. Cons., Inc., 1977—. Adviser, Jr. Achievement. Mem. Life Underwriters Assn., USAF Assn. Roman Catholic. Clubs: Petroleum, K.C., Optimist, Colonial Country (Ft. Worth). Home: 5001 Stacey Ave Fort Worth TX 76132

SCHMITZ, TERRY R., accountant; b. Colt, Ark., Aug. 22, 1936; s. Garland L. and Sue (Gilbert) S.; B.B.A., Memphis State U., 1962; m. Ruth Schmitz; children—Lee, John, Morgan. Staff accountant Harris, Kerr, Forster & Co., Memphis, 1962-63, Minor & Moore, C.P.A.'s, Memphis, 1963-65; audit supr. James Talcott, Inc., Atlanta, 1965-66, Ernst & Ernst, Jackson, Miss., 1966-70; individual practice accounting, Jackson, 1970—, subsequently at Forrest City, Ark.; audit mgr. Touche Ross & Co., 1972—. Served with USAF, 1954-58. C.P.A., Tenn., Miss., Ark. Mem. Am. Soc. C.P.A.'s, Nat. Assn. Accountants, Miss. Art Assn., Memphis Jr. C. of C., Am. Legion, Delta Sigma Pi (life). Republican. Clubs: Country of Jackson; Rotary, Forrest City Country. Home and Office: Suite 203 US Post Office Bldg PO Box 893 Forrest City AR 72335

SCHMOOK, JOHN EMMETT, real estate appraiser; b. Cherokee, Okla., Dec. 14, 1928; s. John Anthony and Cora Faye (Keiffer) S.; B.S., Okla. State U., 1960; postgrad. real estate Kans. State U., 1961, Dury Coll., 1963, U. Okla., 1965; m. Mary Luella Merrell, Oct. 9. 1948; chiloren—J. Lynn, Alan Merrell, Helen Faye (Mrs. Samuel Wylie). Farmer, rancher, Alfalfa County, Okla., 1949-59; appraiser farm real estate mortgages Met. Life Ins. Co., Newton. Kans., 1959-61; appraiser Kansas City (Mo.) Dist. U.S. Army C.E., 1961-65; reviewing appraiser U.S. Bur. Pub. Roads. Oklahoma City, 1965-67; fee real estate appraiser and cons. Schmook Appraisal Co., Oklahoma City, 1967—; pres. Alpha/Omega Homes, Inc., Red Carpet Real Estate, J and L Enterprise. Cons. appraiser for financial instns., Okla. Mem. Am. Instn. Real Estate Appraisers, Future Farmers Am. (hon. chpt. farmer), Okla. Farmhouse Frat. Alumni (pres. 1974). Sigma Delta Chi (Newsmaker of Year Okla. 1968). Mem. Full Gospel Businessmen's Assn. (dir., v.p. Oklahoma City West chpt.). Mason (32 deg.), Lion, Kiwanian. Home: 3121 Goshen Dr Oklahoma City OK 73120 Office: 4271 NW 63d St Oklahoma City OK 73116

SCHMUCKLER, EUGENE, indsl. psychologist; b. Bklyn., June 16, 1939; s. Morris and Sheva (Ewashkowsky) S.; B.S., Bklyn. Coll., 1960; M.A., La. State U., 1964, Ph.D., 1966; m. Sandra Faith Wieden, June 24, 1961; children—Raina Jill, Amie Robin, Marla Sue, Lisanne. Sr. research psychologist Electric Boat div. Gen. Dynamics Corp., Groton, Conn., 1966-67; asst. prof. psychology, dir. univ. research and testing U. West Fla., Pensacola, 1967-69; cons. indsl. psychologist Byron Harless & Assos., Tampa, Fla., 1969-73; pres. Perspectives Inc., Schmuckler, Moore and Assos., Tampa, 1973—; lectr. Tampa Police Acad.; adj. prof. psychology U. South Fla. Bd. dirs., vice chmn. Suncoast Goodwill Industries, 1970—; chmn. personnel com. Mental Health Assn., Hillsborough County, 1970-77, pres. bd. dirs., 1975; chmn. Mayors Com. to Revise Prostitution Statutes. Recipient Pres.'s award Greater Tampa C. of C., 1973, Community Leadership award, 1970, 71, 72. Mem. Am., Southeastern, Fla. psychol. assns., Nat. Rehab. Assn., Nat. Rehab. Counseling Assn., Acad. Mgmt., Am. Psychology Law Soc. Jewish. Clubs: Toastmasters (pres. 1974), Sertoma (Service to Mankind award 1980). Contbr. articles to profl. jours.; author: Age Differences In Biog. Inventories-A Factor Analytic Study, 1966. Feature editor WQSA radio. Home: 10509 Homestead Dr Tampa FL 33618 Office: 4600 W Cypress St Suite 405 Tampa FL 33607

SCHNECK, HERMINIA MALARET, guidance counselor; b. Preston, Cuba, July 6, 1925; d. Pedro Salvador and Herminia (Ponce de Leon) Malaret; B.A., Bryn Mawr Coll., 1946, M.A., 1948; m. George W. Schneck, Sept. 17, 1949 (div. June 1978); children—Karen Elizabeth, Laura Isabel. Psychometrician, Johnson O'Connor's Human Engring. Lab., Phila., 1947-48; research worker U. Pa. Press, Phila., 1948-50; translator Sharp & Dohme, Inc., Phila., 1950-52; tchr. St. John Sch., San Juan, P.R., 1958-62; prof. English Catholic U., Bayamon, P.R., 1966-68; English tchr. Academia del Perpetuo Socorro, Miramar, P.R., 1968-69, guidance coordinator, 1969-80; counselor St. John's Sch., 1980—; mem. Middle States regional council Coll. Bd., 1980—. Mem. adv. com. Title IV Dept. Edn., chmn. coordinating com. Cath. Schs. Guidance Services, 1976-77. Mem. Am. Personnel and Guidance Assn., Caribbean Counselors Assn. (pres. 1976-78). Mem. Partido Nuevo Progresista (Statehood Party). Home: Box 3957 Bayamon Gardens Sta PR 00620 Office: Marti & Central Sts Miramar Santurce PR 00907

SCHNEE, AMANDA MERYL MACNAB, physician; b. North Berwick, Scotland, Dec. 3, 1945; came to U.S., 1975; d. Hamish Stuart Duncan and Marjorie Daphne Croal (McDonald) M.; M.B., Ch.B., St. Andrews U., Scotland, 1968; m. Mark Schnee, Oct. 21, 1967; children—Samantha Joanne, Jicky Miranda, Pippa Meryl. Intern, Ballochmyle Hosp., Mauchline, Ayrshire, Scotland, 1968-69; resident in family practice Ayrshire Central Hosp., Irvine, Ayrshire, 1969-71; gen. practice medicine, Glasgow, Scotland, 1971-75; physician USAF, Omaha, 1975-77; mem. faculty U. Tex. Med. Sch., Houston, 1977—, asst. prof. dept. family practice, 1979—. Diplomate Am. Bd. Family Practice. Mem. Am. Acad. Family Practice. Home: 6313 Meredith Dr Bellaire TX 77401 Office: 208 Herman Profl Bldg 6410 Fannin St Houston TX 77030

SCHNEIDER, ALAN NEIL, mortgage banker; b. Louisville. Sept. 6, 1916; s. Samuel Joseph and Jennie S.; A.B., DePauw U., Greencastle, Ind., 1938; J.D., Harvard, 1942; m. Mabel M. Pedersen, July 4, 1950; 1 dau.. Karen Elizabeth. Admitted to Ky. bar, 1947; pub. relations dir. City of Louisville, 1947-48, adminstrv. asst. mayor. also spl. counsel, 1948-49; asst. city atty., 1950-59; pres.. chmn. bd. King's Way Mortgage Co., Coral Gables, Fla., 1960—, Veritas Ins. Agy., 1960—, Omega Title Corp., 1960—, Alpha Inc., 1960—; dir. Greenacre, Inc.; chief counsel Security Finance Agy., Inc., Southeastern Mortgage Co. Pres. Ky. Library Assn., 1957, pres. Am. Assn. Library Trustees. 1958-59, named Outstanding Trustee, 1959. Trustee Louisville Free Pub. Library, Red Cross Hosp., Louisville, Race Found.; bd. dirs. Fla. Soc. Prevention Blindness. Served to lt. comdr. USNR, 1941-45. Certified rev. appraiser. Mem. Assn. Former Intelligence Officers, Law Enforcement Officers Assn., Am., Ky., Louisville, Internat. bar assns., Mortgage Bankers Am., Phi Beta Kappa, Sigma Chi (Balfour award 1938). Presbyn. Clubs: Coral Gables Athletic. Coral Gables Country; Bankers, Harvard (Miami); Spl. Forces (London). Office: 265 Sevilla Ave PO Box 158 Coral Gables FL 33134

SCHNEIDER, DONALD JACOB, hotel exec.; b. Columbus, Ohio, Apr. 24, 1924; s. Herbert Uhlrich and Gladys (Davis) S.; student Jones Bus. Coll., 1952-54, U. Fla., 1954-55; Asso. Sci., Fla. Jr. Coll., 1978, A.A., 1979; student U. North Fla., 1979—; m. Ruth Louise Higginbotham, Sept. 3, 1949; children—Donald Jacob, Patricia Michele, Nancy Ann. Asst. sales mgr. Culligan Soft Water Co., Jacksonville Beach, Fla., 1947-49; with Ponte Vedra Club, Ponte Vedra Beach, Fla., 1949—, asst. mgr. reservations, 1963-66, v.p. hotel ops., 1966-77, v.p. facilities, 1977—; v.p., dir. Ponte Vedra Corp., 1977—. Pres., P.T.A. Ponte Vedra-Palm Valley Elementary Sch., 1971; mem. exec. com. Coquina council Boy Scouts Am., 1962—; chmn. adv. com. hotel curriculum Fla. Jr. Coll., 1970—; coach-player Jacksonville Beach Dolphins basketball team, 1953-58, baseball teams, 1963-65. Chmn. bus. sect. Ponte Vedra Beach United Fund, 1975. Bd. dirs. Tourist and Conv. Bur., Jacksonville, 1973—; bd. dirs., chmn. safety com. Jacksonville chpt. ARC, 1975-78. Served with inf. AUS, 1943-46; ETO. Decorated Bronze Star medal with oak leaf cluster; Croix de Guerre (France). Mem. Fla. Hotel and Motel Assn. (bd. dir., sec.-treas.), Jacksonville Beach C. of C. (dir. 1970-75), Ponte Vedra Men's Tennis & Golf Assn., Phi Theta Kappa. Democrat. Baptist. Clubs: Rotary (dir. 1974-76), Quarterback (dir. Jacksonville Beach 1973-76). Home: 194 San Juan Dr Ponte Vedra Beach FL 32082 Office: Ponte Vedra Blvd Ponte Vedra Beach FL 32082

SCHNEIDER, HARVEY IRA, metamorphic petrologist, educator; b. N.Y.C., July 19, 1952; s. Eugene and Helen Gertrude (Singer) S.; B.S. in Geology and Chemistry, State Coll. Fredonia (N.Y.), 1973; M.S. in Geology, U. Kans., 1976; Ph.D., Fla. State U., 1980. Research asst. Lake Erie Environ. Survey, Fredonia, N.Y., 1971-73, U. Kans., Lawrence, 1973-75; teaching asst. Fla. State U., Tallahassee, 1975-79; asst. geologist stratigrapher dept. natural resources, Fla. Geol. Survey, Tallahassee, 1979-80. Mem. Geol. Soc. Am., Geochem. Soc., Mineral. Soc. Am., Fla. Acad. Sci., Ga. Geol. Soc., Sigma Xi. Jewish. Contbr. articles to profl. publs. Office: Dept Geology Florida State University Tallahassee FL 32306

SCHNEIDER, LOUIS IRVIN, JR., exploration co. exec.; b. Houston, May 16, 1936; s. Louis Irvin and Olive (Bartine) S.; B.S. in Geology, U. Tex., 1960; m. Catherine Ann Bynum, June 26, 1965; 1 dau., Karen Suzanne. With Teledyne Exploration Co., Houston, 1963—, v.p., div. mgr. Marine div., 1970—. Scoutmaster, Buffalo Trail council Boy Scouts Am., 1964-67; adviser Key Club, 1964-71, divisional chmn., 1965-66. Served with USAF, 1961. Mem. Permian Basin (1st-2d v.p. 1967-68), Houston (sec. 1977-78) geophys. socs., Soc. Exploration Geophysicists. Presbyn. (pres. ch. bd. deacons 1972-74, elder, clk. session 1978—). Kiwanian. Club: Houston Petroleum. Home: 11418 Long Pine St Houston TX 77077 Office: Box 36269 Houston TX 77036

SCHNEIDER, ROBERT CARL, chem. engr.; b. Woodbury, N.J., Feb. 12, 1932; s. Edward Albert and Viola (Blittersdorf) S.; B.S. in Chem. Engring., Drexel U., 1954; m. Marie Eleanor Mellet, Aug. 18,

1956; children—Stephen Carl, Brian Robert. With Hercules, Inc., 1954—, devel. and research engr. Hercules Research Center, Wilmington, Del., 1954-58, supr. paper size and Tall Oil distillation ops., Savannah, Ga., 1958-67, supr. Tall Oil Startup, Hattiesburg, Miss., 1967-71, hydrogenation supr., 1971-72, plant safety supr., 1972-73, operating supt., 1973—; speaker in field Joe Berg Sci. Seminar Series; participant career guidance program Rotary Club. Bd. dirs. S. Central Miss. chpt. ARC, 1974—. Mem. Am. Chem. Soc., Miss. Acad. Scis. Lutheran. Club: Hub City Kiwanis (dir. 1971-74, pres. 1972-73). Home: 207 Mandalay Dr Hattiesburg MS 39401 Office: Hercules Inc 7th St Hattiesburg MS 39401

SCHNEIDER, SANDRA LEE, immunohematologist; b. Pueblo, Colo., July 10, 1944; d. Joseph A. and Evelyn (Strovas) S.; B.S., (Belle Bonfils scholar), So. Colo. State Coll., 1966; Med. Tech., U. Colo., 1966; B.B. (Red Cross Blood Bank scholar), Los Angeles Red Cross Sch. Blood Bank Tech., 1972; m. Raymond Costello, Dec. 14, 1973. Teaching asst. So. Colo. State Coll., 1964-65, U. Colo. Med. Sch., 1966-67, U. Kans. Med. Sch., 1969-70, Los Angeles Red Cross, 1971-72, U. So. Calif. Med. Sch., 1972; med. technologist, research asst. Belle Bonfils Meml. Blood Center, Denver, 1966-67; supr. blood bank East Tenn. Bapt. Hosp., Knoxville, 1968-69; med. technologist II, supr. instr. U. Kans. Med. Center, 1969-70; med. technologist, research asst. Knoxville Blood Center, Knoxville Blood Reagents, 1970-71; research scientist in microbiology and infectious disease, immunology and environ. scis. S.W. Found. Research and Edn., San Antonio, 1973—. Councilman, City of Grey Forest (Tex.), 1978-80. Recipient prize Regional Pfizer Antibody Contest, 1972. Mem. Am. Soc. Clin. Pathologists, Am. Assn. Blood Banks, Am. Soc. Med. Technologist, Calif. Assn. Med. Lic. Technologists, Am. Soc. Microbiology, AAUW, Am. Soc. Primatologists. Democrat. Club: Canyon Creek Country. Contbr. articles to profl. jours. Home: 288 Scenic Loop Dr Grey Forest TX 78023 Office: PO Box 28147 San Antonio TX 78228

SCHNEIDER, SANDRA LYNN, speech pathologist, childfind specialist; b. South Bend, Ind., Sept. 11, 1951; d. Gordon Roy and Marie Imogene (Skinner) S.; B.S., Western Mich. U., 1973; M.S., Vanderbilt U., 1975. Speech pathologist Exceptional Student Edn., Sarasota (Fla.) County Schs., 1975-77, diagnostician speech and lang., 1977-78, childfind specialist, 1978—; adj. prof. speech pathology Manatee Jr. Coll., 1979—; guest lectr. in field. Bd. dirs. W. Coast chpt. Nat. Found./March of Dimes, 1979—; area chmn. living endowment com. Vanderbilt U. Mem. Am. Speech and Lang. and Hearing Assn., Fla. Lang., Speech and Hearing Assn., Council for Exceptional Children. Baptist. Home: 5621 15th Ave W Bradenton FL 33505 Office: 3550 Wilkinson Rd Sarasota FL 33581

SCHNEIDER, VALERIE LOIS, educator; b. Chgo., Feb. 12, 1941; d. Ralph Joseph and Gertrude Blanche (Gaffron) Schneider; B.A., Carroll Coll., 1963; M.A., U. Wis., 1966; Ph.D., U. Fla., 1969. Tchr. English and history Montello (Wis.) High Sch., 1963-64, dir. forensics and drama, 1963-64; instr. speech U. Fla., Gainesville, 1966-68, asst. prof. speech, 1969-70; asst. prof. speech Edinboro (Pa.) State Coll., 1970-71; asso. prof. speech East Tenn. State U., Johnson City, 1971-76, prof., 1976—; author newspaper course Persuasion: The Art of Influencing Others, Johnson City Press-Chronicle, 1979. Chmn. AAUW Mass Media Study Group Com., Johnson City, 1973-74. Recipient Creative Writing award VA. Highlands Arts Festival, 1973. Danforth asso., 1977. Mem. Speech Communication Assn. (Tenn. rep. to states adv. council 1974-76), So., Tenn. (exec. bd., nominating com. 1974-76, v.p. 1976, pres. 1977) speech communication assns., Religious Speech Communication Assn. (Best Article award 1976), AAUW (pres. chpt. 1975-76), Fla. Speech Assn., Western Coll. Reading Assn., Tenn. Intercollegiate Forensics Assn., Bus. and Profl. Women's Club (chpt. v.p. 1976-77), Mensa, Delta Kappa Gamma, Phi Delta Kappa, Delta Sigma Rho-Tau Kappa Alpha. Presbyn. Asso. editor Homiletic, Jour. Tenn. Speech Communication Assn., 1974-76. Contbr. articles on speech to profl. jours. Home: C-5 Greenwood Apts 1409 Colony Park Dr Johnson City TN 37601

SCHNEIDER, WILLIAM JAMES, plastic surgeon; b. Miami, Fla., Dec. 19, 1943; s. James William and Reva Mae (Gross) S.; B.S., Stetson U., 1966; M.D., Vanderbilt U., 1970; m. Rebecca Jo Phillips, June 10, 1967; children—James Carter, Jason Christopher, Brian Phillips. Intern, resident in gen. surgery U. Fla., 1970-72; resident in gen. and plastic surgery Emory U., 1972-77; practice medicine specializing in plastic and reconstructive surgery, Knoxville, Tenn., 1977—; mem. staff E. Tenn. Bapt. Hosp., E. Tenn. Children's Hosp., Park West Hosp., Ft. Sanders Presbyn. Hosp. Justin Potter Merit scholar, 1966-70. Fellow A.C.S.; mem. Am. Soc. Plastic and Reconstructive Surgeons, Southeastern Soc. Plastic and Reconstructive Surgeons, Tenn. Soc. Plastic and Reconstructive Surgeons, Tenn. Med. Assn., So. Med. Assn., Knoxville Surg. Soc., Knoxville Acad. Medicine. Methodist. Clubs: Cedar Bluff Racquet, Deane Hill Country. Contbr. articles to med. jours. Home: 323 Forest Oak Dr Knoxville TN 37919 Office: 703 Blount Profl Bldg Knoxville TN 37920

SCHNELL, ALICE MARGUERITE, fin. researcher; b. Okeene, Okla., Feb. 12, 1918; d. Jacob Earl and Roxie Pearl (Herod) Baker; student public schs., Okeene; m. Oct. 16, 1938 (dec.); children—Kaye Lynn Schnell Evers, D.K., Mary K. Schnell Thomas, Jackie Schnell Wheeler, Earl Wade. Acct., Joe Preston Agy., Stillwater, Okla., 1961-63; news typist for Future Farmers Am., Vocat. Edn., Stillwater, 1963-65; research, fin. asst. Okla. State U., 1965—. Mem. Okla. Edn. Assn., Am. Bus. Women's Assn. Democrat. Home: 2134 W Sherwood Stillwater OK 74074 Office: Okla State U Monroe St Stillwater OK 74074

SCHNELLER, RAYMOND JOHN, ret. environ. engr.; b. Corona, L.I., N.Y., Nov. 10, 1916; s. Frederick Raymond and Louise Mary (Fritz) S.; B.S. in Mech. Engring., U. Ala., 1939; m. Helen Catherine Passineau, Aug. 17, 1946; children—John Frederick, Mary Lou (Mrs. Randall Angelle), George Ross. Livestock farmer, Royal, Ark., 1947-55; sr. civilian civil engr. U.S. Air Force, Columbus AFB, Miss., 1956-60; chief Civil Engring. div. McNutt-Schneller, Inc., cons. engrs., Little Rock, 1960-66; dir. Planning Commn., City of Hot Springs (Ark.), 1965-72, city engr., 1969-71; cons. engr. Albert Switzer & Assos., Inc., Baton Rouge, 1972-76; dir. environ. planning West Central Ark. Planning and Devel. Dist., Hot Springs, 1976-79, ret., 1979. Served with Corps Engrs., U.S. Army, 1939-41, 42-46; ETO. Registered profl. engr., Ala., Ark., Miss., Okla., Tex. Fellow ASCE; mem. Soc. Am. Mil. Engrs., Nat., Ark. socs. profl. engrs., Am. Inst. Planners, D.A.V. (Nat. Service award 1970). Democrat. Roman Catholic. Elk. Club: Sertoma. Home: 875 Wilson's Lake Ln Hot Springs AR 71901 Office: PO Box 1364 Hot Springs AR 71901

SCHNICK, JOHN CRUSE, physician; b. Beaumont, Tex., June 13, 1946; s. William Burl and LaDonna (Cruse) S.; B.S., Lamar U., 1968; M.D., U. Tex., 1973. Intern, Med. Center Hosp., Columbus, Ga., 1973-74, resident in family practice, 1974-76; emergency room physician Sharpstown Gen. Hosp., Houston, 1976-77, active staff, 1977—; practice medicine, specializing in family practice, Houston, 1977—; clin. instr. Dept. Community Medicine, Family Practice Div., Baylor Coll. Medicine, 1978—. Diplomate Am. Bd. Family Practice. Mem. AMA, Am. Acad. Family Physicians, Tex. Med. Assn., Tex. Acad. Family Physicians, Harris County Med. Soc., Harris County Acad. Family Physicians. Methodist. Office: 6630 De Moss St Houston TX 77074

SCHNITZLER, ROBERT NEIL, physician; b. Bklyn., Dec. 12, 1940; s. Jack and Mildred (Spero) S.; B.A., N.Y. U., 1961; M.D., State U. N.Y., 1965; m. Laura Lynn Schwartz, Dec. 12, 1965; children—Barbara Sue, Amy Joan. Intern, Kings County (N.Y.) Downstate Med. Center, 1965-66, resident, 1966-67; resident N.Y. Hosp.-Cornell Med. Center, N.Y.C., 1967-68; trainee U. Rochester (N.Y.) Med. Center, 1968-69, fellow, 1968-70; practice medicine specializing in cardiovascular diseases, San Antonio; asst. physician Strong Meml. Hosp., Rochester, N.Y., 1968-69; instr. in medicine U. Rochester, 1969-70; asso. attending physician St. Vincent's Hosp., S.I., N.Y., 1971-72; cons. in cardiology Doctors Hosp., S.I., 1971-72; asst. prof. medicine U. Tex. Health Sci. Center, San Antonio, 1972-76, clin. asso. prof., 1977—; dir. med. intensive care units Bexar County (Tex.) Hosp., 1973-76, Audie L. Murphy Meml. VA Hosp., 1973-76; asso. med. dir. Emergency Med. Service System, San Antonio, 1975-77; attending physician Meth., Luth., Community, Bapt. hosps.; chief cardiology St. Lukes Luth. Hosp., 1978, 80, Meth. Hosp., 1980; cons. to Met. Hosp., San Antonio, 1976; reviewer Med. Instrumentation Jour., 1975—. Bd. dirs. Solomon Schechter Day Sch., 1975-78, B'nai B'rith, 1975-78. Served with USPHS, 1970-72. D Diplomate Am. Bd. Internal Medicine. Fellow A.C.P., Am. Coll. Cardiology, Am. Coll. Chest Physicians; mem. N.Am. Soc. Pacing and Electrophysiology (founding), Am. Fedn. Clin. Research, Assn. Advancement Med. Instrumentation (chmn. com. on pacemakers 1977—), Emergency Med. Service Council, Am. Heart Assn. (fellow council clin. cardiology, pres. San Antonio chpt.), Tex. (research rev. com. 1974-76), N.Y. heart assns., N.Y. Acad. Scis., Cardiac Pacemaker Soc. (pres. 1971-78), San Antonio Club Internal Medicine (pres. 1977), Alpha Omega Alpha. Contbr. articles on cardiology to med. jours. Home: 5424 Lancashire San Antonio TX 78284 Office: 7711 Louis Pasteur Dr San Antonio TX 78229

SCHNUR, SIDNEY, physician; b. Bklyn., June 23, 1910; s. Joseph and Sadie (Broadman) S.; B.S., Coll. City of N.Y., 1930, M.S., 1931; M.D., N.Y. U., 1935; m. Wilma Adalene Boyce, Mar. 23, 1944; 1 stepson, Joseph Parnell. Intern, Morrisania City Hosp., N.Y.C., 1935-37; resident internal medicine Kings County Hosp., Bklyn., 1937-39; practice medicine, specializing in cardiology, Houston, 1939—; chief of staff, chmn. Dept. Medicine, St. Joseph Hosp., Houston, 1963-65, med. dir. electrocardiography, 1954—; emeritus clin. prof. medicine Baylor Coll. Med., Houston, 1977—, U. Tex. Med. Sch., Houston, 1977—; mem. hosp. licensing advisory council State of Tex., 1975—. Bd. trustees, exec. com. Houston Mus. Natural Sci., 1970—. Served to lt. col., M.C., USAAF, 1940-45. Decorated Bronze Star medal; recipient awards, Houston Heart Assn., 1975, Tex. Heart Assn., 1975; diplomate Am. Bd. Internal Medicine. Fellow ACP, Am. Coll. Chest Physicians, Am. Coll. Cardiology, Am. Heart Assn. (v.p. 1976); mem. Harris County Med. Soc. (pres. 1972), Houston Heart Assn. (pres. 1964), Tex. Heart Assn. (pres. 1972), Houston Soc. Internal Medicine (pres. 1965). Contbr. articles in field to med. jours. Home: 2139 Sunset Blvd Houston TX 77005 Office: 1525 St Joseph Profl Bldg Houston TX 77002

SCHOEFFLER, RONALD WILLIAM, council ofcl.; b. Gloversville, N.Y., July 4, 1949; s. William Charles and Helena Bertha (Bruse) S.; A.A., Fulton-Montgomery Community Coll., 1969; B.S., High Point Coll., 1971; M.Ed., U. N.C. at Greensboro, 1973; Ed.D., U. Ga., 1979; m. Vada Susan Cheshire, Aug. 25, 1974; children—Bryan Hall Brewster, John Howard, Rachel Helena. Resident hall mgr. High Point (N.C.) Coll., 1969-71; grad. residence hall counselor U. N.C., Greensboro, 1971-73; dist. scout exec. Boy Scouts Am., Tifton, Ga., 1973-75; family housing resident mgr. U. Ga., Athens, 1976-79; asst. dir. Athens Community Council on Aging, Inc., 1980—. Program dir. Boy Scouts Am., Camp Osborn, Albany, Ga., 1974, camp dir., 1975; leadership devel. cons. U. Ga. Student Devel. Lab., 1976-78; exec. officer U. Ga. Family Housing Council, 1976-79; cons. and sml. group facilitator Program of Edn. and Career Exploration, Div. Vocational Edn., Ga. Dept. Edn., 1977-78; facilitator or co-facilitator various workshops on student devel., leadership devel, 1975—; mem. ch. council St. Anne's Episcopal Ch., Tifton, Ga., 1975; mem. Tift County Bicentennial Com., 1974-75; mem. outreach com. Emmanuel Episcopal Ch., Athens, 1980—; patron Ga. Democratic Com., 1980—. Recipient Scouter's Training award, Boy Scouts Am., 1970, Pro Deo Et Patria Religious award, 1964. Mem. U. Ga. Student Personnel Assn., Ga. Coll. Personnel Assn., Am. Coll. Personnel Assn. (presenter convs. 1978, 79), Am. Personnel and Guidance Assn., Nat. Eagle Scout Assn., Nat. Service Fraternity Alpha Phi Omega. Asso. editor The Viewpoint, 1976-77; contbr. articles to profl. jours. Home: 505 Club Dr Athens GA 30607 Office: Athens Community Council on Aging Inc 230 S Hull St Athens GA 30605

SCHOENEWOLF, CARL DOUGLAS, hosp. adminstr.; b. Gatesville, Tex., Oct. 10, 1944; s. Carl William and Elfrieda (Apel) S.; B.A., Howard Payne U., 1972, B.S., 1973; student Trinity U., 1973; m. Stella Ann Holder, Sept. 26, 1970; children—Tamara Karen, Christi, Carla. Adminstr. resident Columbus Hosp., Chgo., 1974; asst. adminstr. Permian Gen. Hosp., Andrews, Tex., 1975, asso. adminstr., 1976, adminstr., 1977; v.p. patient services Driscoll Found. Children's Hosp., Corpus Christi, Tex., 1978-79; adminstr. Meml. Hosp., Kermit, Tex., 1979—. Pres., Andrews County chpt. Am. Cancer Soc., 1977. Served with USNR, 1965-68. Mem. Tex. Hosp. Assn., Am. Hosp. Assn. Democrat. Baptist. Club: Lions. Office: 821 Jeffee Dr Kermit TX 79745

SCHOENFELDT, CHARLES MARTIN, utility exec.; b. Independence, Kans., Feb. 3, 1929; s. Edward Herman and Leora (Charles) S.; B.S., Okla. State U., 1950; postgrad. U. Tulsa, 1954-56; m. Marilyn Jane Cleveland, Sept. 29, 1950; children—Michael C., Patrick C. With Okla. Natural Gas Co., Tulsa, 1950—, asst. to pres., 1969-71, v.p. energy systems and devel., 1971—. Instr. evening div. U. Tulsa, 1956, Okla. Bapt. U., 1962. Mem. Hist. and Ednl. Found. Bd. dirs. West of Main, Tulsa, Devel. Found., Okla. State U., Stillwater, Hurricane Club, U. Tulsa; trustee Children's Med. Center, Tulsa. Served to capt. USAF, 1951-53. Mem. Tulsa C. of C., Am., So. gas assns., Sigma Phi Epsilon. Presbyn. (elder, deacon). Republican. Clubs: Petroleum, Tulsa Country, Exchange (pres. Tulsa 1965-66). Home: 5374 E 21st St Tulsa OK 74114 Office: 624 S Boston St Tulsa OK 74102

SCHOFIELD, MIRIAM NORBERY, nurse, counselor; b. Uxbridge, Mass., July 17, 1923; d. Ralph William and Ida May (Lee) Norbery; S.B., R.N., Brown U./R.I. Hosp. Sch. Nursing, 1945; M.A. in Guidance Counseling, U. Ala., 1978; m. Albert Richardson Schofield, Jan. 6, 1951; children—Albert R., Christopher Norbery, Sarah Lee. Instr. nursing R.I. Hosp. Sch., 1945-59; staff nurse N.Y. Hosp., 1949-50; med. clin. instr. Hosp. U. Pa., 1954-56; instr. Wusasa Hosp., Zaria, Nigeria, 1962-63; nurse Teheran Am. Sch., Teheran, Iran, 1973-78, guidance counselor, 1978-79; nurse Perrine Dist. Schs., Miami, 1979—. Mem. Am. Personnel and Guidance Assn., Am. Nurses Assn., Am. League Nursing Edn. Unitarian. Club: Internat. Women's (Kaduna, Nigeria 1963). Home: 8025 SW 62d Ct Miami FL 33143 Office: 9970 SW 178th St Miami FL 33157

SCHOLIN, ALLAN RICHARD, journalist; b. Chgo., July 16, 1915; s. Lars Eric and Olga Richardina (Moberg) S.; A.B. in Communications, Am. U., Washington, 1959; postgrad. Air War Coll., Maxwell AFB, Ala., 1972; m. Mary Virginia Burke, Mar. 29, 1941; children—Allan Richard, Blain Taylor, Michael Bruce. Reporter, Bloomington (Ill.) Pantagraph, 1937; jr. writer U.S. Office Edn., Washington, 1940-42; commd. 2d lt. USAF, 1942, advanced through grades to col., 1968; ret., 1973; sr. info. specialist Hdqrs. USAF, 1946-58; asst. chief, pub. affairs N.G. Bur., Washington, 1958-62; asso. editor Air Force mag., Washington, 1962-68; spl. asst. to pub. affairs officer Hdqrs. U.S. Readiness Command, MacDill AFB, Fla., 1968-75; free lance writer non-fiction, Tampa, Fla., 1975—; staff officer U.S. Air N.G., Pa., 1946-48, D.C., 1948-53, 55-68, Mo., 1953-55; mil. editor Air Progress mag., 1963-75; res. dir. info. Hdqrs. Air U., Maxwell AFB, Ala., 1968-73. Decorated Meritorious Service medal; recipient Meritorious Civilian Service medal U.S. Govt., 1975, Lewis H. Brereton award Fla. Air Force Assn., 1980. Mem. Nat. Press Club, Aviation/Space Writers Assn. (award for best article on aviation subject 1969, 75), Soc. Profl. Journalists-Sigma Delta Chi (pres. student chpt. Am. U. 1952), Air Force Assn. (pres. Tampa 1970-71, 77-78). Clubs: Army-Navy Country (Arlington, Va.); Tampa Yacht and Country. Home and office: 8703 Bay Crest Ln Tampa FL 33615

SCHOLZ, HONEY BLANTON, advt. agy. exec.; b. Albuquerque, Apr. 24, 1934; d. Henry N. and Wilma N. (Meeks) D.; student U. N.Mex., 1954-56; m. Raymond Vincent Scholz, Dec. 30, 1967; children—Johanna Sue Marshall Gaddy, Richard Wayne Marshall, Ferrell Marshall. Media dir. Glenn, Bozell & Jacobs Advt. Co., San Antonio and Houston, 1968-70, Pitluk Group, San Antonio, 1970-74, Clunie & Ciaccio Advt. Co., San Antonio and Dallas, 1974-76; pres. Media Directions Inc., San Antonio, 1977—. Mem. San Antonio Advt. Fedn. (dir. 1978—), San Antonio Radio Advt. Broadcast Execs. (dir. 1979—), San Antonio C. of C. Republican. Presbyterian. Home: 205 Shavano Dr San Antonio TX 78231 Office: Media Directions Inc 1938 NE Loop 410 Suite 255 San Antonio TX 78217

SCHOLZ, LEO CHARLES, oil co. exec.; b. Marshall, Tex., Oct. 1, 1937; s. Leo and Madelyn Emma (Blackburn) S.; B.B.A., St. Mary's U., San Antonio, 1960; m. Sally Ann Enloe, July 15, 1961; children—Ann Marie, Diane Elaine. Landman, Exxon Co. U.S., New Orleans, 1967-68, with exploration dept., 1968-69; div. landman Samedan Oil Corp., Houston, 1969-74; mgr. land dept. Home Petroleum Corp., Houston, 1974—. Served to capt. Arty. U.S. Army, 1960-62. Mem. Houston Assn. Petroleum Landmen (dir.), St. Mary's U. Alumni Assn. (dir.), SVC. Roman Catholic. Clubs: Univ., Pine Forest Country, Denver Petroleum, K.C. Home: 12466 Kingsride St Houston TX 77024 Office: 2600 North Loop W Houston TX 77092

SCHOOLS, CHARLES HUGHLETTE, banker, bus. exec., lawyer; b. Lansing, Mich., May 24, 1929; s. Robert Thomas and Lillian Pearl (Lawson) S.; B.S., Am. U., 1952, M.A., 1958; J.D., Washington Coll. of Law, 1963; LL.D., Bethune-Cookman U., 1973; m. Rosemarie Sanchez, Nov. 22, 1952; children—Charles, Michael. Dir. phys. plant Am. U., 1952-66; owner, Gen. Maintenance Service Co., Washington, 1957—, Gen. Security Co., Washington, 1969—; pres., chmn. bd. McLean Bank (Va.) 1974—, Community Assn. Services Va.; dir. Computer Data Systems Inc., DAC Devel. Ltd., Am. Indsl. Devel. Corp., Intercoastal of Iran; mem. Met. Bd. Trades. Pres. McLean Boys' Club; bd. dirs. D.C. Spl. Olympics, Nat. Kidney Found., Washington; trustee Bethune Cookman Coll., Western Md. Coll. Served with USAAF, 1946-47, USAF, 1947-48. Mem. Va. C. of C., Profl. Businessman's Orgn. Democrat. Clubs: Touchdown of Washington, Univ. of Washington, Washington Golf and Country, Pisces (Washington); Halifax (Daytona Beach, Fla.); Masons. Home: 1320 Darnall Dr McLean VA 22101 Office: The McLean Bank PO Box 309 McLean VA 22101

SCHOOLS, GEORGE STRAUGHAN, physician; b. Richmond, Va., May 9, 1930; s. Percy Everett and Maude Evelyn (Mallory) S.; B.S., Coll. of William and Mary, 1949; M.D., U. Va., 1953; children—Jennifer Leigh, George S., Jonathan Andrew. Intern, Tripler Army Hosp., Honolulu, Hawaii, 1953-54; resident U. Mich. Med. Center, Ann Arbor, 1956-59; staff physician Pulmonary Disease sect. VA Hosp., Richmond, Va., 1959-61; asst. prof. internal medicine U. Tex., 1961-62; clin. asst. prof., 1962—; practice medicine specializing in pulmonary disease, Dallas, 1962—; established Pulmonary Lab., Baylor U. Med. Center, Dallas, 1963, med. dir., 1963-65; med. dir. Pulmonary Lab. & Respiratory Therapy Presbyterian Hosp., 1966-73; cons. Muscular Dystrophy Assn., Dallas. Bd. dirs. Am. Lung Assn., Dallas, 1976—. Served with U.S. Army, 1953-56. Diplomate Am. Bd. Internal Medicine. Fellow Am. Coll. Chest Physicians; mem. AMA, Am. Thoracic Soc., Tex., Dallas County med. assns. Democrat. Presbyterian. Contbr. articles in field to profl. jours. Home: 8522 Park Ln Apt 9 Dallas TX 75231 Office: Dallas Med and Surg Clinic Assn 4105 Live Oak Dallas TX 75204

SCHOONOVER, JACK RONALD, circuit judge; b. Winona, Minn., July 23, 1934; s. Richard M. and Elizabeth A. (Hargeisheimer) S.; student Winona State Coll., 1956-58; LL.B., U. Fla., 1962; m. Ann Marie Kroez, June 18, 1965; 1 son, Jack Ronald. Admitted to Fla. bar, 1962; since practiced in Charlotte County; atty. Charlotte County Sch. Bd., 1969-75; asst. state's atty., 1970-72; city judge, Punta Gorda, Fla., 1973-74; judge Fla. Circuit Ct., 1975—. Served with USAF, 1952-56. Mem. Am. Legion. Home: 1263 Laloosa Dr Fort Myers FL 33901 Office: Lee County Courthouse Fort Myers FL 33902

SCHOPPE, CONRAD JOSEPH, gas pipeline co. exec.; b. Childress, Tex., Nov. 13, 1921; s. Conrad Michael and Ada Louise (Mitchel) S.; B.S., U. Houston, 1943, postgrad., 1956; m. Ellen Patricia Condon, Aug. 24, 1946; children—Patricia, Gerald, Lorene, Charlotte, Janice, Michael. Engring. draftsman United Gas Pipeline Co., Houston, 1939-40; engring. draftsman Hunt Tool Co., Houston, 1940-41; engr. Houston Pipe and Steel Co., 1941-42, chief engr., 1942-44; v.p. Connect-A-Tube, Inc., Houston, 1943-44; engr. Tenn. Gas Pipeline Co., Houston, 1946-56, research div. supr., 1956—; cons. in field. Served with U.S. Army 1944-46. Recipient Cert. Appreciation, So. Gas Assn., 1978. Mem. Am. Soc. Metals (cert. appreciation 1966), Am. Welding Soc., Am. Petroleum Assn., Am. Gas Assn., Soc. Nondestructive Testing. Roman Catholic. Clubs: K.C., Tennwood Country. Contbr. articles to profl. jours. Home: 8111 Rampert St Houston TX 77081 Office: 5510 S Rice St Houston TX 77081

SCHOPPMEYER, MARTIN WILLIAM, educator; b. Weehawken, N.J., Sept. 15, 1929; s. William G. and Madeline (Haas) S.; B.S., Fordham U., 1950; Ed.M., U. Fla., 1955, Ed.D., 1962; m. Marilyn M. Myers, Aug. 8, 1958; children—Susan Ann, Martin William. Tchr., Fla. public schs., 1955-59; instr. U. Fla., Gainsville, 1960-62, asst. prof., 1962-63; asso. prof. Fla. Atlantic U., Boca Raton, 1963-65, prof., 1965-68, dir. continuing edn., 1965-67; asso. prof. U. Ark., Fayetteville, 1968-71, prof., 1971—; mem. nat. adv. council on Edn. Professions Devel., 1973-76; exec. sec. Ark. Sch. Study Council, 1976—; evaluator instr. tng. program, Nat. Tng. Fund, 1978. Bd. dirs. Womans Ednl. and Devel. Inst., Little Rock, Ark., 1977—. Served with U.S. Army, 1951-53; Korea. Mem. NEA, Ark. Edn. Assn., Ark. Assn. of Ednl. Adminstrs., Phi Delta Kappa. Roman Catholic. Clubs: Rotary, K.C. Author: (with VanPatten, Belok and Roucek) Conflict, Permanency, Change and Education, 1976; asso. editor Jour. of

Thought, 1974-80, La. Ednl. Research Jour., 1976-80; also articles, chpts. in books. Home: 2950 Sheryl Ave Fayetteville AR 72701 Office: 244 Graduate Education Bldg University of Arkansas Fayetteville AR 72701

SCHOR, ALLEN GEORGE, mental health center exec.; b. N.Y.C., Nov. 24, 1942; s. Herman and Frances Schor; B.A. in Biology, N.Y. U., 1964; M.A. in Psychology, U. R.I., 1972, Ph.D., 1974. Psychologist, Newport County (R.I.) Mental Health Clinic, 1973-74; dir. Tri-County (Md.) Youth Services Bur., 1974-75; center dir. N.W. Center for Community Mental Health, Reston, Va., 1975—; mem. task force NIMH, 1978, Va. Dept. Mental Health and Mental Retardation, 1979; state chmn. Nat. Council of Community Mental Health Centers 1976—. Mem. Va. Assn. Mental Health Providers (pres. 1979—), Am. Psychol. Assn., Assn. of Mental Health Adminstrs., Md. Psychol. Assn., Va. Psychol. Assn., Washington Psychol. Assn. Home: 12216 Bennett Rd Herndon VA 22070 Office: 11420 Isaac Newton Sq Reston VA 22090

SCHORNO, KARL STANLEY, petroleum co. chemist; b. Berkeley, Calif., Nov. 28, 1939; s. Werner Domonic and Margot Ann (Schreier) S.; B.A. in Chemistry, U. Calif., Berkeley, 1962; Ph.D., Okla. State U., 1967, postgrad. fellow, 1967-68; postgrad. U. Kans., 1968-69; m. Karen Sue Baker, May 27, 1966; children—Kistine Sue, Kevin Karl. Sr. research scientist geochemistry br. Phillips Petroleum Co., Bartlesville, Okla., 1969—. Mem. Am. Chem. Soc., N.Y. Acad. Sci., A.A.A.S., Nat. Wildlife Soc., Sigma Xi. Presbyn. (jr. high sch. advisor 1971—). Contbr. articles to profl. jours. Home: 1724 S Osage St Bartlesville OK 74003 Office: 225 RB 1 Bartlesville OK 74003

SCHOULTZ, A. C., III, savs. and loan assn. exec.; b. Tex., Feb. 29, 1940; s. A. C., Jr. and Juanita Louise (Otto) S.; B.B.A., U. Miami, 1963; M.B.A., Emory U., 1964; postgrad. exec. devel. course U. Ga., 1970, Harvard U., 1971; m. Linda Louise Dean, Dec. 1960; children—Frederick Harold, Scott Anthony. Dept. mar. Dadeland, asst. buyer Biscayne (Fla.) store Jordan Marsh-Fla., 1964-68; with Chase Fed. Savs. & Loan Assn., Dadeland and Miami Beach, 1968-75, asst. v.p. savs., 1970-72, v.p. mktg., 1972-75; asst. v.p., personnel dir. Washington Fed. Savs. & Loan Assn., Miami Beach, Fla., 1976-77, v.p. adminstrv. services dept., 1977—; mem. faculty Inst. Fin. Edn., Miami/Dade Community Coll. Bd. dirs. South Miami Hosp. Assos., 1977—, Kiwanis Youthland, Inc., 1977—; mem. Mayor's Milestone Com. on Rapid Transit, 1974-75; adviser Jr. Achievement Greater Miami, 1967-68. Mem. Inst. Fin. Edn. (pres. Fla. Greater Miami chpt. 29, 1979), South Dade C. of C., Greater Miami C. of C. (project leader 1973-75). Club: Perrine-Cutler Ridge Kiwanis (pres. 1977). Home: 7710 SW 127th Dr Miami FL 33183 Office: 1701 Meridian Ave Miami Beach FL 33139

SCHOULTZ, TURE WILLIAM, neurophysiologist; b. Alhambra, Calif., June 6, 1940; s. Ture William and Bernice Margaret (Bowie) S.; B.S., Colo. State U., 1965; M.A., U. Colo., 1967, Ph.D., 1971; children—Kristan, Jennifer, Karin. Instr., N.Y. U. Coll. Medicine, 1971-72; asst. prof. neurophysiology U. Ark. Coll. Medicine, 1972—, asst. dean Coll. Medicine, 1977—. Bd. dirs. Pulaski County Audubon Soc. Recipient Golden Apple award Student AMA, 1973. Author articles on spinal cord trauma. Home: 8301 Evergreen Dr Little Rock AR 72207 Office: Coll Medicine Univ Ark Medical Scis Campus Little Rock AR 72201

SCHRAM, RICHARD WEAVER, naval officer; b. Niles, Mich., Aug. 4, 1940; s. Richard Arney and Marjorie (Weaver) S.; B.S., Purdue U., 1963; grad. Armed Forces Staff Coll., 1975; m. Sharon R. Frost, June 16, 1970. Commd. ensign U.S. Navy, 1964, advanced through grades to comdr., 1979; student naval flight officer, Pensacola, Fla., Corpus Christi, 1963-64; bombardier, navigator, flight test officer VA-65, 1964-68; pub. affairs officer, narrator Blue Angels, Pensacola, 1969-71; bombardier, navigator, maintenance officer VA-75, 1972-74; asst. fleet ops. officer to comdr.-in-chief U.S. Atlantic Fleet, Norfolk, Va., 1975-77; strike ops. officer U.S.S. Independence (CV-62), 1978-80. Decorated D.F.C. (3), Air medals (26). Mem. Order Daedalians, Am. Inst. Aeros. and Astronautics, Aviation Space Writers Assn., Nat. Aero. Assn., Am. Def. Preparedness Assn., Aerobatic Club Am., Red River Valley Fighter Pilots Assn., Tailhook Assn., Combat Pilots Assn., Am. Aviation Hist. Soc., Exptl. Aircraft Assn., Air Force Assn., U.S. Naval Inst., Internat. Fighter Pilots Assn., Assn. Naval Aviation. Club: Nat. Press. Home: 3732 Redwood Farm Dr Virginia Beach VA 23452 Office: USS Independence (CV-62) FPO New York NY 09501

SCHRAMM, TEXAS E., football club ofcl.; b. Los Angeles, June 20, 1920. Publicity dir., then gen. mgr. Los Angeles Rams, 1947-57; asst. dir. sports CBS, 1957-60; gen. mgr. Dallas Cowboys, 1960—, pres., 1966—. Office: Dallas Cowboys 6116 N Central Expressway Dallas TX 75206*

SCHRANK, JOEL PALMER, cardiologist; b. Akron, Ohio, June 16, 1935; s. Harry P. and Rachel Schrank; student Cornell U., 1953-56; B.S., U. Akron, 1960; M.D., Case-Western Res. U., 1964; children—Julie, Paul, Beth, Allison. Intern, Harvard Med. Service, Boston City Hosp., 1964-65, resident, 1965-67; teaching fellow Harvard Med. Sch., 1967; asst. prof. internal medicine U. Va. Sch. Medicine, Charlottesville, 1969-75, asso. prof., 1975, dir. Adult Cardiac Catheterization Lab., 1969-75; asso. prof. internal medicine U. Ala. Sch. Medicine, Birmingham, 1975-79; dir. CCU, VA Hosp., Birmingham, 1975-79; dir. Heart Center, Bapt. Med. Center, Jacksonville, Fla., 1979—; cons., lectr. Internat. Med. Ednl. Corp., Englewood, Colo., 1972—. Served with U.S. Army, 1958-60. Diplomate Am. Bd. Internal Medicine, Am. Bd. Med. Examiners. Fellow A.C.P., Am. Coll. Cardiology; mem. AMA, Am. Heart Assn. (fellow council on clin. cardiology), Am. Fedn. Clin. Research, Am. Inst. Ultrasound in Medicine, Alpha Omega Alpha, Phi Sigma. Contbr. articles to med. jours. Home: 4034 Barcelona Ave Jacksonville FL 32207 Office: 800 Prudential Dr Jacksonville FL 32207

SCHRECK, MICHAEL H., painter, sculptor; b. Austria (father Am. citizen). One-man shows include Dominion Gallery, Montreal, 1950, 52, Selected Artists Gallery, N.Y.C., 1961, Collectors Gallery, L.I., N.Y., 1968, Roslyn Gallery, L.I., 1968, Gloria Luria Gallery, Miami, Fla., 1973, 76, Palm Beach (Fla.) Galleries, 1974, 77; exhibited in group shows, Vienna, 1932-38, London, 1938-48, Montreal and Paris, France, 1948-66, N.Y.C., 1966-76, Sculptors of Fla., 1975, Met. Mus. and Art Center, Miami, 1975; represented in permanent collections Mus. Fine Arts. Lausanne, Switzerland, Ft. Lauderdale Mus. of Arts, Mus. Modern Art, Haifa, Israel, Heckscher Mus., Huntington, N.Y., N.Y. U., Mus. Palm Beaches, Met. Mus., Miami, Tel Aviv (Israel) Mus., Jacksonville (Fla.) Art Mus. Recipient numerous awards and prizes. Life fellow Royal Soc. Arts (Eng.); mem. Artists Equity Assn., Am. Fedn. Arts, Sculptors of Fla., Smithsonian Instn. Address: 3111 N Ocean Dr Hollywood FL 33019

SCHREIBER, EDWIN DANIEL, city govt. ofcl.; b. Augusta, Ga., May 19, 1904; s. Herman Victor and Henrietta (Ramaker) S.; B.S., Peabody Coll., Nashville, 1932, M.A., 1938; postgrad. N.Y. U.; m. Johnnie Jean Varner, Sept. 4, 1931; children—Edwin Daniel, Barbara Jean. Mem. staff Boys YMCA, Washington, 1925-26; tchr., then prin. schs. in Tenn. and Ariz., 1929-45; mem. adminstrs. dept. Nashville city schs., 1945-46; counselor Tenn. Div. Vocat. Rehab., 1946-49; exec. dir. Tenn. Easter Seal Soc., 1949-50; community planner Tenn. Planning Commn., 1956-74; asst. city mgt., Oak Hill, Tenn., 1978—; sec. Tenn. Citizens Planning Assn., Mid Tenn. Conservancy Council, Tenn. Conservation League, Tenn. Environ. Council, SNAG Club for Planners. Active local Boy Scouts Am., A.R.C.; elder, clk. session, tchr. Bible classes Hillsboro United Presbyn. Ch., Nashville. Mem. Tenn. N.G., World War II. Fellow Peabody Coll., summers 1935-38; research fellow N.Y. U., 1939-40; recipient various service awards. Mem. Am. Soc. Public Adminstrn., Am. Planners Assn., Tenn. Ornithol. Soc. (past chpt. pres., state sec.), Am. Hort. Soc. Democrat. Club: Elks. Home: 3518 Pleasant Valley Rd Nashville TN 37204

SCHREIBER, JOSEPH PHILIP, retail sales co. exec.; b. Madison, Wis., Mar. 3, 1917; s. Cecil E. and Harriet Leone (Spoor) S.; B.A., U. Wis., 1940; m. Ruth Helen Lassen, Mar. 9, 1957; 1 son, Barry Alan. Staff auditor Arthur Andersen & Co., Chgo., 1940-42; comptroller T.C. Esser Co., Milw., 1946-60; v.p., treas., dir. Advance Distbrs. Inc., Advance Publishers, Inc., Adon, Inc., Mid-Fla. Collection Service, Inc. (all Orlando, Fla.), 1960-72; cons. to pres. Panning Lumber Co., Orlando, 1972—. Treas. Polit. Action Assn., Central Fla., 1965-66. Served to lt. Supply Corps, USNR, 1943-46; PTO. Mem. Nat. Assn. Accountants. Presbyn. Elk. Clubs: Central Florida Executives, Orlando NTC Officers. Club: Winter Park University. Home: 2123 Chippewa Trail Maitland FL 32751 Office: 5018 Colonial Dr Orlando FL 32808

SCHREYER, JAMES MARLIN, chemist; b. Asheville, N.C. Dec. 26, 1915; s. Roy and Vinnetta (McIntyre) S.; A.B.. U. N.C., 1938; Ph.D., Ore. State U.. 1948; m. Ethyl Huse, June 9, 1951; children—David Smith, Phillip, Janet (Mrs. Warren Koplowitz). Tchr., Asheboro (N.C.) High Sch., 1938-41; explosives insp. War Dept., Radford, Va., 1941-42; explosives engr. War Dept., Badger Ordnance Works, 1942-43; engr. U.S. Rubber Co., Charlotte, N.C., 1943-46; prof. chemistry U. Ky.. Lexington, 1948-51; chemist Oak Ridge Nat. Lab.. 1951-55; supt. chemistry devel. dept. Oak Ridge Y-12 plant Union Carbide Nuclear Co., 1955-77; sr. tech. adviser Nuclear div. Union Carbide Corp., Oak Ridge, 1977—; lectr. on clean homes and health, solar energy, corrosion. Named Most Popular Prof., U. Ky., 1951. Mem. Am. Chem. Soc., Internat. Platform Assn., Sigma Xi. Contbr. articles to profl. jours. Home: 9100 Burchfield Dr Oak Ridge TN 37830 Office: Bldg 9202 Y-12 Plant Oak Ridge TN 37830

SCHREYER-THOMSON, CAMELLA JOY, artist, editor; b. Lawrence, Kans., July 17, 1949; d. George Maurice and Camella Inez (Burnett) Schreyer; B.A. cum laude, Pfeiffer Coll., 1971; M.A., East Carolina U., 1974; research studies Europe and Gt. Britain; m. Douglas Arthur Thomson, May 6, 1973. One-man shows: Allas Art Galleries, Charlotte, N.C., 1971, Pfeiffer Coll. Gallery, 1975; group shows include: Durham (N.C.) Art Guild, Fayetteville (N.C.) Mus. Art, Shooren's, Rockport, Mass., East Carolina U.; represented in permanent collection Pfeiffer Coll., also pvt. collections; editor-in-chief Hist. Preservations Am. subs. Internat. Biog. Center, Raleigh, N.C., 1973—; class agt. Pfeiffer Coll. Alumni Assn., 1976—. Certified tchr. kindergarten through 9th grades, N.C. Mem. Am. Fedn. Arts, Nat. League Am. Pen Women, Stanly County Art Guild, Durham Arts Council, Phi Delta Sigma. Democrat. Methodist. Contbr. poems to lit. jours.; art editor The Phoenix of Pfeiffer Coll., also various annuals. Home: 302-4006 Twickenham Ct Raleigh NC 27612

SCHROEDER, ELAINE, speech and lang. pathologist; b. Corpus Christi, Tex., Aug. 30, 1948; d. Oscar William and Hilda (Vogel) S.; student Del Mar Jr. Coll., Corpus Christi, Tex., 1966-68; B.S. in Speech Pathology and Audiology, U. Tex., Austin, 1971; postgrad. A. and I.U., Kingsville, Tex., 1971; M.A. in Communication Disorders, Our Lady of the Lake U., San Antonio, Tex., 1976. Choral dir. jr. choir Christi Lutheran Ch., Corpus Christi, 1967-69; choral dir. adult choir Christ Lutheran Ch., Corpus Christi, 1970-72; speech/lang. pathologist Corpus Christi Independent Sch. Dist., 1971—; pvt. practice speech and lang. pathology, Corpus Christi, 1976—; sec. Speech/Lang. Pathology Mt. Olive Lutheran Pre-Sch., 1978—; Sec. Corpus Christi Chorale, 1976-77, v.p. 1977-78, pres., 1978-79, chmn. publicity, 1978-79; bd. dirs. Performing Players, Inc., Corpus Christi, 1978—, producer, 1979. Mem. Am. Speech and Hearing Assn. (cert. clin. competence), Tex. Speech and Hearing Assn., Coastal Bend Speech, Lang. and Hearing Assn. (pres. 1978-79), Council Exceptional Children, Am. Fedn. Tchrs., Corpus Christi Chorale. Lutheran. Home: 3630 Austin St Corpus Christi TX 78411 Office: 3130 Highland St Corpus Christi TX 78405

SCHROEDER, HERMAN MARCEL, lawyer; b. New Orleans, July 16, 1922; s. Herman A. and Marie (Cauhape) S.; LL.B., Loyola U., 1953; m. Ann Fleming, Nov. 16, 1963. Admitted to La. bar, 1953; partner firm Schroeder, Kuntz & Miranne, and predecessor firm, New Orleans, 1953—. Served to 2d lt. USAAF, World War II. Decorated Air Medal. Mem. La. Trial Lawyers Assn. Democrat. Roman Catholic. Lion. Home: 6127 Perlita St New Orleans LA 70112 Office: Richards Bldg New Orleans LA 70112

SCHROEDER, JOSE FEDERICO, hosp. adminstr.; b. San Juan, P.R., Aug. 1, 1946; s. Jose F. and Myriam (Griffo) S.; B.A. in Edn., U. P.R., 1968, M. Health Services Adminstrn., 1972; m. Maria Mercedes Suro, May 25, 1968; children—Maria Mercedes, Jose Federico, Fernando Manuel. Hosp. adminstr., Medicare surveyor Dept. Health, P.R., 1972-74; asst. adminstr. Teachers Hosp., Hato Rey, P.R., 1974-76; hosp. adminstr. Charter Med. of P.R., San Pablo Hosp., Bayamon, 1976—. Advisory com. on hosp. cost to consumer affairs commn. P.R. Chamber of Reps. Mem. Hosp. Fin. Mgmt., P.R. Hosp. Adminstrs. Assn. (dir. 1978-79), P.R. Hosp. Assn. (pres.). Roman Catholic. Club: Lions (asst. treas. Boriquen Baldrich chpt.). Home: 212 Rossy St Baldrich Hato Rey PR 00918 Office: Domenech Final Ave Hato Rey PR 00918

SCHROEDER, MARVIN KLOPSCH, pharmacist, hosp. ofcl.; b. Michigan City, Ind., Sept. 26, 1915; s. William Albert and Martha Johanna (Klopsch) S.; B.S., Purdue U., 1936; m. Jean Hirsch, Feb. 16, 1946; children—Charles William, Raymond Ernest. Owner, mgr. Schroeder Pharmacy, 1938-42, 46-47; dir. pharmacy South Bend (Ind.) Meml. Hosp., 1947-50; hosp. med. service rep. Parke, Davis & Co., Chgo., 1950-72; staff pharmacist Winter Haven (Fla.) Hosp., 1972-74; dir. pharmacy Lake Wales (Fla.) Hosp., 1974—; lectr. in field, cons. CD. Pres., Y's Men, LaGrange (Ill.) YMCA, 1953-54. Served with U.S. Army, 1942-45. Decorated Bronze Star. Registered pharmacist Ind., Ill., Fla. Mem. Am. Pharm. Assn. (life), Am. Soc. Hosp. Pharmacists, Fla. Pharmacy Assn., Fla. Soc. Hosp. Pharmacists, Ill. Pharmacists Assn., Am. Legion. Club: Am. Legion. Office: Lake Wales Hosp Box 391 410 S 11th St Lake Wales FL 33853

SCHROEDER, STEPHEN EDWIN, utilities exec.; b. Yorktown, Tex., Aug. 16, 1932; s. Edwin Otto and Ella (Kruse) S.; A.A., Tex. Luth. Coll., 1951; m. Billie Juanell Hutchins, June 14, 1953; children—Stephen Michael, Susan Michelle, Sondra Meliss. Apprentice lineman Central Power & Light Co., Kenedy, Tex., 1953-59, serviceman, Runge, Kenedy, Tex., 1959-62, mgr. Goliad, Berclair, Tex., 1962-69, mgr., Cotulla, Dilley and Millett, Tex., 1969—, conf. leader, 1960-62. Chmn. fund drive Boy Scouts Am., 1964, Girl Scouts, 1973-74; pres. Cotulla P.T.A., 1974-75. Election judge, precinct LaSalle County, 1974—. Chmn. nominating com., bd. dirs. Coastal Bend Respiratory Assn., 1969; bd. dirs. Goliad County Fair Assn. Served with AUS, 1954-56. Recipient pres.'s plaque for outstanding mgr. in marketing program Guadalupe Dist. Central Power & Light Co., 1967, S. Tex. C. of C. plaque for outstanding service, 1967. Mem. Goliad County (dir., past pres.), S. Tex. (dir. 1973-74), Cotulla (pres. 1970-71, 74-75) chambers commerce. Lutheran (lay reader). Lion (dir. Cotulla 1973-74, v.p. 1975-76). Home: 1008 Carizzo St Cotulla TX 78014 Office: 113 Center St Cotulla TX 78014

SCHROTER, ROBERT WILLIAM, supermarket chain exec.; b. Bklyn., Aug. 16, 1926; s. Robert Henry and Florence (Hass) S.; B.S.B.A., U. Fla., 1949; children—Linda Kaye, Donna Jean (dec.), William Shannon, Francie Ballou. With Publix Super Markets, Inc., 1949—, advt. dir., 1955-72, v.p., 1972-78, v.p. advt. and mktg., Lakeland, Fla., 1978—. Chmn. advt. and publicity bd. City of Lakeland. Served with U.S. Army, 1943-46. Mem. Greater Lakeland C. of C. (pres. 1964-65), Advt. Club of Polk County (past pres.), Food Mktg. Inst. Democrat. Episcopalian. Office: PO Box 407 Lakeland FL 33802

SCHUCK, MARJORIE BRACKENRIDGE MASSEY, publisher, editor, lectr.; b. Winchester, Va., Oct. 9, 1921; d. Carl Frederick and Margaret Harriet (Parmele) Massey; student U. Minn., 1941-43, Sch., N.Y.C., 1948, N.Y.U., 1952, 54-55; m. Ernest George Metcalfe, Dec. 2, 1943 (div. Oct. 1949); m. Franz Schuck, Nov. 11, 1953 (dec. Jan. 1958). Mem. editorial bd. St. Petersburg (Fla.) Poetry Assn., 1967-68; co-editor, pub. Poetry Venture Mag., St. Petersburg, Fla., 1968-69, editor, pub., 1968-74; founder, owner, pres. Valkyrie Press, Inc., St. Petersburg, 1972—, MS Records, Inc., 1974-79, Majorie Schuck Pub., Inc., 1974-79; co-dir., lectr., chmn. poetry Fla. Suncoast Writers' Confs. Assn. U. South Fla., 1973—; lectr. in field. Founder Valkyrie Press Round Table Writers' Workshop and Forum, 1975—, Valkyrie Press Reference Library for Writers and Poets, 1976—. Corr.-rec. sec. Women's Aux. Hosp. for Spl. Surgery, N.Y.C., 1947-59; active St. Petersburg Mus. Fine Arts (charter), St. Petersburg Sister City Com., St. Petersburg Arts Center Assn.; chmn. Pinellas County Arts Council, 1977-78, mem., 1977-79; lectr., mem. Friends of Library St. Petersburg; mem. Com. of 100 of Pinellas County; mem. adminstrv. bd. Suncoast Mgmt. Inst., 1977-78, chmn. women in mgmt. confs., 1977-78; bd. dirs., pub. relations chmn. Soc. for Prevention Cruelty to Animals 1968-71. Named One of 76 Fla. Patriots, Fla. Bicentennial Commn., 1976. Mem. Com. Small Mag. Editors and Pubs., Nat. Fedn. Am. Press Women, Coordinating Council Lit. Mags., Acad. Am. Poets, Fla. Poets Assn., Pinellas Suncoast C. of C., Pi Beta Phi. Democrat. Episcopalian. Author: Speeches and Writings for Cause of Freedom, 1973. Contbr. poetry to profl. jours. Home: 8245 26th Ave N Saint Petersburg FL 33710 Office: 2135-2139-2145-2149 1st Ave S Saint Petersburg FL 33712

SCHUDER, RAYMOND FRANCIS, lawyer; b. Wickford, R.I., Dec. 27, 1926; s. Rollie Milton and Selma (Ball) S.; A.B., Emory U., 1949, J.D., 1951; m. Betty Jo Williams, Mar. 14, 1948; children—Gregg Williams, Glen Arva. Admitted to Ga. bar, 1951; with Trust Co., Ga., Atlanta, 1951-54; asso. firm Wheeler, Robinson & Thurmond, Gainesville, Ga., 1954-59; pvt. law practice, Gainesville, 1959-70, 76—; partner firm Schuder & Brown, Gainesville, 1971-76; dir. Lanier Securities, Inc. Municipal ct. judge, Gainesville, 1956-60, 73-75; supr. Upper Chattahoochee Soil and Water Conservation Dist., 1971-74. Bd. dirs. Charles Thompson Estes Found., Inc., Gainesville. Served to cpl. USMCR, 1944-50; 1st lt. USA Res. (ret.). Mem. Gainesville-Northeastern (pres. 1969-70) Bar Assn., State Bar Ga. (gov. 1966-70), Am. Legion, V.F.W., Phi Alpha Delta. Methodist. Clubs: Chattahoochee Country, Elks. Home: 2224 Riverside Dr NE Gainesville GA 30501 Office: Lanier Bldg 500 Spring St Gainesville GA 30501

SCHUETT, STEPHEN THAXTON, advt. art dir.; b. Boston, Oct. 20, 1941; s. Norman H. and Timmie Jean (Nunnally) S.; B.V.A., Ga. State U., 1968; m. Linda Traver, Jan. 17, 1970. Sr. art dir. Leslie Advt., 1970-75; creative dir. Keys Printing, 1976-79; exec. art dir. Advt., Inc., Greenville, S.C., 1979-80; pres. Adgroup, Inc., Greenville, 1980—. Recipient over 75 design awards. Mem. Communicating Arts Soc. Episcopalian. Home: 116 Argonne Dr Greenville SC 29605 Office: PO Box 8479 Greenville SC 29606

SCHUETTE, GARY LYNN, textile co. exec.; b. Lafayette, Ind., July 27, 1946; s. Earl Raymond and Janice Arlene (Weishaar) S.; B.A. in Govt., Norwich U., 1968; m. Rebecca Elizabeth Boswell, July 30, 1970; children—Jennifer Elizabeth, Jeffrey Daniel. Salesman, Procter & Gamble, Atlanta, 1973-76; regional br. mgr. LaFrance Industries div. Riegel Textile Corp., Chgo., 1976-77, nat. dir. sales tng., 1977-79, controller LaFrance Fabrics div., Anderson, S.C., 1979, div. project mgr., 1979-80, sales mgr. Eastern region Convenience Products div., 1980—. Served with Mil. Intelligence, U.S. Army, 1968-73. Decorated D.F.C., Bronze Star, Air medal (26). Mem. Nat. Soc. Tng. Dirs., S.C. Soc. Tng. Dirs. Republican. Methodist. Office: Convenience Products Div Riegel Textile Corp PO Box 1903 Anderson SC 29622

SCHUFLETOWSKI, FRANK WALTER, govt. ofcl.; b. Havre, Mont., Jan. 24, 1940; s. Stephen Vincent and Florence Vera (Whipple) S.; B.A., S.W. Christian Sem., 1960, Th.M., 1961; M.A., Ariz. State U., 1962; Ph.D., Wash. State U., 1966; m. Sharon Joyce Paradis. Aug. 11, 1960; children—Lorelei, Suzanne, Drew. Tchr., pub. schs., Ariz., Wash., 1961-64; instr. Wash. State U., Pullman, 1964-65; asst. prof. edn. Idaho State U. Pocatello, 1966; asst. prof. U. Kans., Lawrence, 1966-70; sr. research asso.. acting dep. dir. U.S. Armed Forces Inst., Madison, Wis., 1970-72; instructional systems adviser. chief naval air tng. Naval Air Sta., Corpus Christi, Tex., 1972-75, prin. civilian adviser to chief naval air tg., 1975-79; tech. dir. for tng. systems devel. Air Tng. Command, Randolph AFB, Tex., 1979—; lectr. U. Wis. at Madison, 1970-72. Recipient Excellence of Instrn. award Am. Council Edn., 1967. Mem. Soc. Profs. Edn., Am. Ednl. Research Assn., Phi Delta Kappa. Author: (with D.C. Orlich) Introduction to Education: a Student Guide, 1966. Home: 1243 Cibolo Trail Universal City TX 78148 Office: XPTD Hdqrs Air Tng Command Randolph AFB TX 78148

SCHUH, LLOYD EVERETT, JR., ednl. adminstr.; b. Little Rock, Aug. 11, 1939; s. Lloyd and Norma Elenor (Parott) S.; B.A., Okla. State U., 1961; m. Shirlene Howard, Aug. 20, 1966; children—Todd Alan, Christopher Howard. Info. supr. Ark. Power and Light Co., Little Rock, 1963-66; v.p. Lioyd Schuh Advt. Co., Little Rock, 1966-70; dir. info. Baptist Med. Center System, Little Rock, 1970-71; exec. dir. Educare Centers, Ft. Smith, Ark., 1971—; pres. Childhood Products Corp.; cons. early childhood programs State of Ark. Mem. Ark. Child Care Facilities Rev. Bd., 1977—; mem. Govs Early Childhood Edn. advisory com. Mem. Am. Assn. Ednl. Adminstrs., Nat. Assn. for Edn. Young Children, Nat. Assn. for Child Devel. and Edn. (exec. v.p. 1977-78, 1st v.p. 1979-80), Ark. Profl. Child Care Assn. (pres. 1976—), Ark. Assn. on Children Under Six (pres. 1976-77). Presbyn. Clubs: Kiwanis, Little Rock, Town. Home: 10716

Hunters Point Fort Smith AR 72903 Office: PO Box 2750 Fort Smith AR 72913

SCHULER, ARNOLD LOUIS, pianist, organist; b. Friona, Tex., Feb. 22, 1933; s. Robert H. and Anna S. (Gallmeir) S.; B.S., U. Tex., 1958; M.M., N. Tex. State U., 1961, postgrad.; Organist, dir. music Trinity and Our Redeemer Lutheran chs., Dallas, 1958-63; instr. choral music Dallas Ind. Sch. Dist., 1959-62; instr. organ Hammond Organ Studios, Dallas, 1962-64; organist, dir. music Holy Cross Luth. Ch., Dallas, 1965-75; pres. Profl. Studio of Piano and Organ, Richardson, Tex., 1955—; numerous concert appearances throughout U.S., 1948—; chmn. state theory exams. Music Tchrs. Nat. Assn. Served with U.S. Army, 1953-55. Young Artist Piano Competition winner, 1949; cited with highest awards for outstanding musical achievement St. Johns Coll., 1951. Mem. Music Tchrs. Nat. Assn., Tex., Dallas, Richardson music tchrs. assns., Am. Guild Organists, Am. Coll. Musicians, Nat. Guild Piano Tchrs., Phi Mu Alpha. Home: 624 Winchester Dr Richardson TX 75080

SCHULER, GEORGE ALBERT, JR., food scientist; b. Altoona, Pa., Sept. 21, 1933; s. George Albert and Elizabeth (Deily) S.; B.S. in Poultry Sci., Pa. State U., 1959; M.S., U. Tenn., 1966; Ph.D. in Food Sci., Va. Poly. Inst. and State U., 1969; m. Barbara Jean Beichler, Jan. 7, 1961; children—Linda Lee, Karen Elizabeth, Beth Ann. Tchr., Madisonville (Tenn.) High Sch., 1964-66; research asst. Va. Poly. Inst. and State U., Blacksburg, 1966-70; extension food scientist U. Ga., Athens, 1970—. Owner, Pa. Poultry Service, Altoona, 1959-61. Served with U.S. Army, 1953-55; Korea. Dept. Commerce sea grantee, 1973. Mem. Catfish Farmers Ga. (exec. sec.), Ga. Poultry Fedn., World Poultry Sci. Soc. (life mem.), Sigma Xi, Phi Sigma. Author various extension booklets including Food Hands and Bacteria, 1971, Don't Send Your Profits to the Offal Room, 1978, Effect of Maladjusted Equipment on Yield in Poultry Processing Plants; producer film Food Handlers Sanitation, 1975. Home: 222 Holmes Ave Athens GA 30601 Office: Extension Food Sci Dept Coop Extension Service Univ Ga Athens GA 30601

SCHULER, THEODORE ANTHONY, civil engr.; b. Louisville, July 1, 1934; s. Henry R. and Virginia (Meisner) S.; B.C.E., U. Louisville, 1957, M.Engring., 1973; m. Jane A. Bandy, July 29, 1979; children—Marc, Elizabeth. Design, constrn. engr. Brighton Engring. Co., Frankfort, Ky., 1960-65; design engr. Hensley-Schmidt Inc., Chattanooga, 1965-68, asso. mem., 1969-73, sr. asso. mem., 1973-75, prin., asst. v.p., head Knoxville office, 1975—. Served to lt. (j.g.) USNR, 1957-60. Registered profl. engr., Ky., Tenn., Ga., N.C.; registered land surveyor, Ky. Mem. Nat., Tenn. socs. profl. engrs., ASCE. Clubs: Concord Yacht; West Knoxville Toastmasters (pres. 1979). Home: 5907 Adelia Dr Knoxville TN 37920 Office: Suite 1525 United Am Plaza Knoxville TN 37929

SCHULTE, HENRY CLYDE, furniture co. exec.; b. Jackson County, Mo., Nov. 8, 1921; s. Rudolph William and Mary Agnes (Fitzharris) S.; B.A., Kansas City Tchrs. Coll., 1940; M.A., S.W. Coll., 1942; postgrad. Kansas City U., 1945-47; m. Virginia M. Miller, Feb. 14, 1948; children—Stephen K., William D., also 2 foster sons. Vice pres. Coca Cola, Coin Changer Div., Kansas City, Mo., 1946-48; pres., owner Market Research Consumers Survey, Kansas City, Mo., 1948-51; v.p. Boy's Ranch, Amarillo, Tex., 1951-53; v.p. Turner Coffield Co., Waco, Tex., 1953-58; pres., chmn. bd. Donie Chair Co., Inc., Brownsville, Tex., 1958—; feature writer Colo. Skyline Rev., Denver, 1946-52; editor N. Kansas City News, 1948-49; chmn. bd. Mo. Bank & Trust, Platte County, Mo., 1949. Pres., World Youth Fund, 1946-52, Mexia Centenial, 1964; bd. dirs. Tex. State Tech. Inst., 1969-73; chmn. Million Dollar Fund Dr., Waco, 1952-56. Served with USAAF, 1942-46. Decorated Purple Heart with 2 oak leaf clusters. Named Man of Year, C. of C. Tex., 1963; recipient Service to Mankind award Nat. Sertoma Clubs, 1949. Mem. C. of C. (pres. 1959-62), E. Tex. C. of C. (v.p. 1963), Nat. Furniture Mfg. Assn., S.W. Furniture Mfrs. Roman Catholic. Clubs: Tex. Appaloosa Horse, Nat. Appaloosa Horse, K.C., Elks, Rotary (pres. 1953), Sertoma (v.p. and exec. sec. 1948-52). Home: Fountain Valley Ranch PO Box 1871 Brownsville TX 78520 Office: Brownsville Compress Bldg 3 PO Box 1871 Brownsville TX 78520

SCHULTZ, CLARENCE CARVEN, JR., educator, sociologist; b. Temple, Tex., Oct. 31, 1924; s. Clarence Carven and Beatrice (Newton) S.; B.S., S.W. Tex. State U.. San Marcos. 1948, M.A., 1949; Ph.D., U. Tex., Austin, 1970; m. Margie Frances Beran, Oct. 29, 1943; children—Timothy Wayne, Theresa Bea. Asst. mgr. McClellan Stores, Laredo and McAllen, Tex., 1946-47; instr. sociology and history S.W. Tex. State U., 1949-52; teaching fellow U. Tex., Austin, 1952-53; mem. social sci. faculty Lee Coll., Baytown, Tex., 1953-65, chmn. div., 1961-65; mem. faculty S.W. Tex. State U., 1965—, prof. sociology, 1973—, chmn. dept. sociology and anthropology, 1971-76; acting dean Sch. Liberal Arts, 1977-78, recipient Pedagog Teaching Excellence award, 1973, 74; social sci. cons., textbook editorial cons. Mem. adv. council Scheib Opportunity Center, San Marcos. Served to ensign USNR, 1943-46. Recipient Minnie Stevens Piper Prof. Teaching award S.W. Tex. State U., 1976, Distinguished Teaching award S.W. State Tex. U. Alumni Assn., 1976. Research grantee Tex. Traffic Safety Adminstrn., 1971-72. Mem. Am., Southwestern, Mid-South, So. sociol. assns., Tex. Jr. Coll. Tchrs. Assn. (dir. 1955-57), Southwestern Social Sci. Assn., Nat. Council Family Relations, Tex. Assn. Coll. Tchrs., Alpha Kappa Delta, Alpha Chi. Kiwanian (dir. San Marcos 1974-76). Author: Practical Probation: Handbook for Probation Workers, 1972. Editor: Family Perspective: A Sociological Reader, 1975. Home: 604 Franklin Dr San Marcos TX 78666

SCHULTZ, DONALD O., educator; b. Mt. Vernon, N.Y., Oct. 25, 1939; s. Emil Herman and Lillian (Schalm) S.; B.S., Calif. State U. at Long Beach, 1963; M.Pub. Adminstrn., U. So., Calif., 1967; m. Patricia Gail Omilak, Dec. 27, 1969; children—Donald O., Christopher Paul. Police officer Orange (Calif.) Police Dept., 1962-67; asst. prof. dept. law enforcement U. Neb., 1968-69; instr. police sci. Broward Community Coll., Fort Lauderdale, 1970—. Lutheran. Mason (Shriner). Author: (with Loren A. Norton) Police Operational Intelligence, 1968; Special Problems in Law Enforcement, 1971; (with William J. Bopp) A Short History of American Law Enforcement, 1972, Principles of American Law Enforcement and Criminal Justice, 1972; Police Unarmed Defense Tactics, 1973; The Subversive, 1974; Critical Issues in Criminal Justice, 1974; Police Traffic Enforcement, 1975; Crime Scene Investigation, 1977; Principles of Physical Security, 1978; Criminal Investigation Techniques, 1978; The Complete College Guide, 1979; Modern Police Administration, 1979; Police Pursuit Driving Handbook, 1979. Home: 11851 NW 24th St Coral Springs FL 33065 Office: Criminal Justice Inst Broward Community Coll Davie Rd Fort Lauderdale FL 33314

SCHULTZ, FREDERICK JOHN, chemist; b. Davenport, Iowa, Oct. 12, 1929; s. August William and Alma Calkins S.; student U. Ill., 1949-51; B.A., Augustana Coll., 1952; M.A., DePauw U., 1956; Ph.D., State U. Iowa, 1960; m. Donna Hansen Schultz, July 30, 1955; children—Laurie, Julie, David, James. With Lorillard div. Loew's Theatres, Inc., 1959—, sr. research chemist, Greensboro, N.C., 1962-65, product devel. mgr., 1965-68, research mgr., 1968-75, dir. research and devel., 1975-79, v.p. research and devel., 1979—. Served with C.E., U.S. Army, 1953-55. Mem. Am. Chem. Soc., Am. Inst. Chemists, AAAS, N.C. Acad. Scis., N.Y. Acad. Sci., Sigma Xi. Republican. Lutheran. Home: 815 Plummer Dr Greensboro NC 27410 Office: 420 English Greensboro NC 27420

SCHULTZ, FREDERICK JOHN, JR., mech. design engr.; b. Albany, N.Y., Mar. 13, 1942; s. Frederick John and Jennie Frances (Srednicki) S.; B.S. in Mech. Engring., Clemson Coll., 1962; postgrad. Carrier Air Conditioning Engrs. Design Sch., 1968, U. Tenn., 1975; m. Mary Emily Parnell, Aug. 29, 1964. Tech. devel. engr. DuPont Inc., Florence, S.C., 1962; distbn. engr. Ala. Power Co., Montgomery, 1966-67; mech. design engr. Maxwell AFB, Ala., 1967-70; sr. mech. design engr. Eglin AFB, Fla., 1970—; participant workshops U.S. Bur. Mines, 1970, Am. Gas. Assn., 1974. Mem. Air Univ. Boiler Plant Operators Licensing Bd., 1970. Active Maxwell AFB United Appeal, 1969, 70. Served to 1st lt. USAF, 1962-66. Recipient Chgo. Tribune Gold Medal award, 1962. Registered profl. engr., Fla. Mem. ASME (Service and Leadership award 1975, coll. student paper award 1962, sect. chmn. award 1969-70, group vice chmn. 1968-69, regional devel. com. 1970-72), ASHRAE, Assn. Energy Engrs. (asso.), Nat., Fla. socs. Profl. Engrs., Am. Soc. Plumbing Engrs. Democrat. Methodist. Home: 660 Golf Course Dr Fort Walton Beach FL 32548 Office: AD/DEEE Engineering Design Branch Eglin AFB FL 32542

SCHULTZ, JOEL SIDNEY, architect; b. Buffalo, Feb. 3, 1945; s. Raymond Abraham and Emilia Mimi (Citron) S.; B.Arch., Kans. State U., 1970; m. Betty Krul, Aug. 18, 1968; children—Andrea, Jennifer. Designer, draftsman John Highland Asso., Buffalo, 1970-71, Cannon Partnership, Buffalo, 1971-72, Connell Asso., Miami, Fla., 1972-73, Charles McAlpine, Architect, Ft. Lauderdale, 1973-75; pres. Summit Tech. Archtl. Group, Coral Springs, Fla., 1975—; faculty arch. Broward Community Coll., Ft. Lauderdale, 1972-73. Moeller Archtl. scholar, Kans. State U., 1965-70. Mem. AIA, Nat. Assn. Home Builders. Office: 11510 W Sample Rd Coral Springs FL 33065

SCHULTZ, JOHN CARL, JR., real estate cons., appraising firm exec.; b. Savannah, Ga., Oct. 27, 1939; s. John Carl and Adele (Helmly) S.; B.B.A. in Real Estate, U. Ga., Athens, 1963; m. Margaret Bellinger Johnson, Sept. 1, 1962; children—John Carl III, Angela Porcher, Druella Helmly. Appraiser, Stewart Wight Co., Atlanta, 1963-68; partner Wight, Couch & Schultz, Atlanta, 1968-72; v.p. Landauer Assos. of N.Y. subsidiary Marsh & McLennan, Atlanta, 1972-76; v.p., sec. Albritton, Schultz & Assos., Atlanta, 1976—. Mng. partner Campbellton Plaza Joint Venture, Atlanta, 1972-76; tchr. appraisal courses Am. Inst. Real Estate Appraisers, Soc. Real Estate Appraisers, Atlanta Area Tech. Sch., Atlanta Multiple Listing Service, Atlanta Bd. Realtors. Chmn., Property Comm., Cath. Archdiocese of Atlanta, 1974-76. Named Distinguished lectr., practitioner, Coll. Bus. Adminstrn., U. Ga. at Athens, 1975. Mem. Am. Inst. Real Estate Appraisers (pres. Ga. chpt. 1980, profl. recognition award 1976-81), Soc. Real Estate Appraisers (sr. real estate analyst; pres. Atlanta chpt. 8 1973-74, young men's council 1976-77, v.p. 1977), Atlanta Bd. Realtors (treas. 1979, dir. 1980—, Realtor of Yr. award 1978), Nat., Ga. (dir. 1974—) assns. realtors, Nat. Inst. Farm and Land Brokers, Jaycees (conv. com. nat. conv. 1971), Rho Epsilon (nat. pres. 1974-76). Roman Catholic. K.C., Elk. Home: 383 Springdale Dr NE Atlanta GA 30305 Office: 229 Peachtree St NE Suite 1515 Atlanta GA 30303

SCHULTZ, JULIUS, biochemist; b. Rochester, N.Y., May 7, 1914; s. Benjamin and Ann (Duran) S.; student Cornell, 1932-34; B.S., U. Mich., 1936, Ph.D., 1940; postdoctoral studies U. Pa. Sch. Medicine, 1939-46; m. Betty Jane Splane, Oct. 14, 1942. Asst. prof. biochemistry Temple U. Sch. Medicine, 1951-57; asso. prof. Hahnemann Med. Sch., 1957-62, prof., 1962; dir. Papanicolaou Cancer Research Inst. Miami, Fla., 1968-72, presdl. dir., 1972—. Adj. prof. biochemistry U. Miami Med. Sch.; mem. com. on enzymes Nat. Acad. Sci., 1966-70. Fellow A.A.A.S.; mem. Am., English biochem. socs., Am. Chem. Soc. (sec. div. biochemistry), Am. Assn. Cancer Research, Recticulo-Endothialal Soc., Am. Soc. Biol. Chemists, Southeast Cancer Research Assn. (pres. 1973—). Adv. bd. Cancer Biochemistry Biophysics, 1974—. Home: 240 W San Marino Dr Miami Beach FL 33139 Office: 1155 NW 14th St Box 6188 Miami FL 33101

SCHULTZ, KARL FREDERICK, gen. contractor; b. Phila., Aug. 19, 1938; s. Charles Frederick and Clara Anna (Fuhrmann) S.; B.A. in Chemistry, Lafayette Coll., 1960; m. Dorothy Anne Greene, Dec. 20, 1974; children—Kristina L., Karl Frederick, Christine A. Sales rep. Atlas Chem. Co., Chgo. and N.Y.C., 1962-67; sales mgr. Alcolac Chem. Co., Balt., 1968; account mgr. Givaudan Co., N.Y.C., 1969-71; owner Karl F. Schultz Gen. Contractor, Tarpon Springs, Fla., 1971—; cons. to cosmetic industry, 1970-71, to constrn. industry, 1972—. Mem. Twp. Com., 1969-70; dir. Econ. Devel. Com., 1976—. Served with USMCR, 1958-64. Recipient Energy Saver New Home award Fla. Power Co., 1977; certified Class A. gen. contractor, Fla.; named Ky. col. Mem. Am. Pharm. Assn., Soc. Cosmetic Chemists, Phi Delta Theta. Republican. Lutheran. Clubs: Innisbrook Country, Shriners, Masons, K.T., Scottish Rite, Moose, Elks, Tarpon Springs Sertoma (named Sertoman of year 1975, pres. 1976). Home and office: 1387 Ventnor Ave Tarpon Springs FL 33589

SCHULTZ, MARVIN HAROLD, surgeon; b. Cedar Rapids, Iowa, Feb. 4, 1922; s. Julius and Lena (Simon) S.; student Iowa State Tchrs. Coll., 1940-42; M.D., U. Iowa, 1946; m. Ethel I. Wedgle, Sept. 6, 1953; children—Dean, Vicki, Barry. Intern, St. Vincent's Hosp., Bridgeport, Conn., 1946-47; gen. practice medicine, Waterloo, Iowa, 1947-51; ear, nose, throat resident U. Iowa, Iowa City, 1953-56; practice medicine specializing in ear, nose and throat, Marquette, Mich., 1956-62, Fort Lauderdale, Fla., 1962—; chief surgery Holy Cross Hosp., Fort Lauderdale, 1978-79. Served to capt. M.C., USAF, 1951-53. Diplomate Am. Bd. Otolaryngology. Fellow A.C.S.; mem. AMA, Fla. Med. Assn., Broward County Med. Assn., Fla. Soc. Otolaryngology, Am. Acad. Otolaryngology. Clubs: Masons, Shriners. Office: 1940 NE 47th St Fort Lauderdale FL 33308

SCHULTZ, RONALD CARL, banker; b. Henderson, Tex., Nov. 15, 1939; s. Carl Milton and Mary Ann (DeGeurin) S.; B.S., Rice U., 1962; M.B.A., U. Tex., 1967; m. JoAnna Murray, June 3, 1961; children—Ronald Carl, William Randall. Investment officer Tex. Tchr. Retirement System, Austin, 1967-68; sr. v.p., investment officer City Nat. Bank of Austin, 1968-73; exec. v.p., investment officer, dir. Tex. State Bank of Austin, 1973-75; pres., dir. Univ. State Bank, Austin, 1975-76, cons., adv. dir., 1976—. Cons., Tex. County and Dist. Retirement System, 1972—. Treas. Austin YMCA, 1971, bd. dirs., 1971—; trustee Murray Found., 1965—; chmn. bd. Tarrytown Meth. Ch. Served to capt. USMCR, 1962-65. Mem. Austin Investment Assn. (dir. 1970—, pres. 1972), Austin, San Antonio Soc. Fin. Analysts (treas. 1973, pres. 1976-77), Young Men's Bus. League (dir. 1969—), Financial Analyst Fedn., Tex. Ind. Producers and Royalty Owners Assn., Marine Corps Res. Officers Assn., R Assn. Rice Univ. Home: 3105 Scenic St Austin TX 78703 Office: University State Bank Bldg PO Box 1788 Austin TX 78767

SCHULZ, HARRY JOHN, lawyer; b. Falls City, Tex., Mar. 27, 1913; s. John G. and Catherine (Sheehy) S.; student St. Mary's U., 1930-32; LL.B., U. Tex., 1935; m. Virginia Swett, Dec. 21, 1938; children—Mary Virginia (Mrs. Jack Johnson), Harriet Ann (Mrs. Lewis Robinson), Harry J., Betty (Mrs. Edward Schadle), Peggy (Mrs. Leo Saenz). Admitted to Tex. bar, 1935, since practiced in Three Rivers; county atty. Live Oak County, Tex., 1936-40; city atty. Three Rivers, 1945—. Pres., dir. Schulz Live Stock Co., Three Rivers, 1942-49, Spur S Ranch, Inc., Three Rivers, 1965—; dir. 1st State Bank, Three Rivers. Dir. Nueces River Authority, 1964—, pres., 1979—; mem. state exec. com. Democratic party, 1964-66; trustee Three Rivers Ind. Sch. Dist., 1956-75, pres., 1966-75; bd. dirs. Coastal Bend Council of Govts., Corpus Christi, Tex., 1966—, chmn., 1979-80. Mem. Am. Bar Assn., Tex. Bar Found., State Bar Tex. (dir. 1975-78), Three Rivers C. of C. Roman Catholic (Papal Knight, Order of St. Gregory, knight Equestrian Order Holy Sepulchre). K.C. Rotarian. Home: 101 Hazel St Three Rivers TX 78071 Office: 623 Harborth St Three Rivers TX 78071

SCHULZ, LUCILLE T. ALTHOFF, nurse; b. McGirk, Mo., Oct. 28, 1917; d. Edward and Carrie (Glenn) Althoff; diploma Sch. of Nursing, West Tex. Hosp. Lubbock, 1941; B.S. in Nursing, Incarnate Word Coll., San Antonio, 1945; m. Kenneth E. Schulz, Oct. 18, 1947; children—Richard Lee, Eda Carol. Head nurse West Tex. Hosp., Lubbock, 1946-49, supr., 1947-50, instr., 1951-54, nursing dir.dir., 1955-69; instr. Meth Hosp. Sch. of Nursing, Lubbock, 1970-62; nursing service dir. Meth. Hosp., Lubbock, 1973—. Mem. Adv. Bd. for Vocat. Nursing in Tex.; sec. PTA. Recipient Boss of Yr. award Caprock chpt. Nat. Secs. Assn., 1977; R.N., Tex. Mem. Am. Nurses Assn., Tex. Soc. for Hosps., Nursing Service Adminstrs., Local Council of Nursing Service Dirs., Nat. League of Nursing Edn., Dist. Nurses Assn. (past pres.), Bus. and Profl. Women's Club. Methodist. Club: Hobby. Home: 2718 58th St Lubbock TX 79413 Office: Meth Hosp 3615 19th St Lubbock TX 79410

SCHULZ, RAYMOND ANDREW, elec. engr.; b. Kane, Pa., Mar. 1, 1935; s. Raymond Andrew and Dorothy Henrietta (Luce) S.; B.S.E.E., Pa. State U., 1957; M.E.E., Syracuse U., 1963; m. Barbara Ann Linder, May 23, 1959; children—Kenneth Robert, Susan Lee. With IBM Corp., Owego, N.Y., 1957-74, asso. engr., 1959-61, sr. asso. engr., 1961-63, advisory engr., 1966-74, gen. systems div., Boca Raton, Fla., 1974—, sr. engr., 1977—. Mem. IEEE. Baptist. Holder U.S. patents in field. Home: 1057 NW 6th Dr Boca Raton FL 33432 Office: PO Box 1328 Boca Raton FL 33432

SCHUMACHER, WILLIAM CHARLES, transp. co. exec.; b. Erie, Pa., Sept. 27, 1918; s. Harry Leslie and Louise Catrinka (Scherman) S.; student Muskingum Coll., 1937-39; B.S., Grove City Coll., 1941; m. Dorothy Joan Dempsey, Mar. 24, 1944; children—William Charles, Robert David, Jean Louise. Auditor, asst. treas., various companies, Pa., Fla., 1946-57; sr. staff acct. Wells, Laney, Ehrlich & Baer, C.P.A.'s, Orlando, Fla., 1957-59; asst. treas. Hubbard Constrn. Co., Orlando, Fla., 1959-57; sec. treas. Kerrville Bus. Co. Inc., (Tex.), 1970—, Painter Bus Lines, Inc., 1970—, also Kerrville Tours, Inc., Union Bus Center of San Angelo, Inc. Served with USMCR, 1942-50. Mem. Nat. Assn. Accts. (treas. 1962-67), Adminstrv. Mgmt. Soc. (pres. 1967). Lutheran. Club: Mason. Home: PO Box 1441 Kerrville TX 78028 Office: PO Box 712 Kerrville TX 78028

SCHUMANN, AL, govt. archtl. engr., interior designer; b. Southampton, Eng., June 5, 1925; s. Irving and Ray (Friend) S.; came to U.S., 1926, naturalized, 1934; B.S. in Archtl. Engring., U. Tex., Austin, 1949; m. Shirley Breger, June 13, 1946; children—Alan, Paul, Marla Schumann Shivers. Archtl., structural designer Jack Corgan, Architect, Dallas, 1954-57; constrn. mgmt. engr. Gen. Services Adminstrn., Dallas, 1957-63; archtl. engr., also design coordinator of various computerized service centers IRS, Washington, 1963-65, interior designer, archtl. engr., Dallas, 1970—; archtl. designer Army and Air Force Exchange Service, Dallas, 1966-70; lectr. Office Landscape Users Group, 1977-79; speaker in field. Bd. dirs. Temple Emanu-el Brotherhood, Dallas, 1974—. Served as flight officer Air Corps, AUS, 1944-45. Recipient Office Design Honorable Mention award Adminstrv. Mgmt. Mag., 1976, Office of the Year award, 1975. Registered profl. engr., Tex. Mem. Inst. Bus. Designers (profl. mem.), Nat. (profl. mem.), Tex. (profl. mem.) socs. profl. engrs., Tex. Soc. Architects (profl. affiliate), AIA (Dallas chpt. profl. affiliate). Developer, tchr. tng. course for govt. employees on office space planning and design; designed worksta. for certain IRS employees. Office: 7839 Churchill Way LB-70 Dallas TX 75251

SCHUPP, JAMES CURRY, JR., laundry exec.; b. Wilmington, N.C., Oct. 31, 1951; s. James Curry and Edna (Dillon) S.; grad. Exec. Mgmt. Inst., Inst. of Indsl. Laundries, 1979; student U. S.C., 1979—; m. Peggy Hines, Apr. 23, 1970; 1 dau., Carrie Michelle. With Textilease Corp., Wilmington, 1970—, customer care dir., 1974, br. mgr., Sumter, S.C., 1975—; instr. route engring. Inst. Indsl. Laundries, Washington, 1979-80. Republican. Baptist. Clubs: Pocalla Springs Country, Belvedere Country. Home: 1055 Nottingham St Sumter SC 29150 Office: 60 S Shaw St Sumter SC 29150

SCHUSSLER, IRWIN, child psychiatrist; b. Bklyn., Nov. 14, 1943; s. Jack and Fannie Yetta (Blank) S.; B.S., Bklyn. Coll., 1964; D.O., Chgo. Coll. Osteo. Medicine, 1968; m. Myra Yvette Paget, June 26, 1966; children—Jeffrey Mitchell, Doreen Robyn, Kimberly Beth. Intern, Interboro Gen. Hosp., Bklyn., 1968-69; resident in gen. psychiatry U. Fla. Coll. Medicine, Gainesville, 1972-74, fellow in child and adolescent psychiatry, 1974-76; fellow in human sexual medicine U. Pa., Phila., 1975; practice medicine, specializing in child, adolescent and adult psychiatry, Ft. Worth, 1977—; clin. asso. prof. psychiatry N. Tex. State U. Health Sci. Center, Tex. Coll. Osteo. Medicine, 1979—; asst. prof. psychiatry and asst. prof. pediatrics U. Fla. Coll. Medicine, 1976-77; dir. impatient psychotherapy, 1976-77. Cert. sexual educator, sexual therapist; diplomate Am. Bd. Psychiatry and Neurology, Am. Osteo. Bd. Psychiatry and Neurology. Mem. Am. Psychiat. Assn., Am. Acad. Child Psychiatrists, Am. Acad. Adolescent Psychiatrists, Am. Assn. Acad. Psychiatrists, Am. Coll. Neuropsychiatrists, Am. Assn. Sex Educators and Therapists, Am. Osteo. Assn., Tex. Osteo. Med. Assn., Fla. Osteo. Med. Assn., Masters and Johnson Found. Jewish. Contbr. articles to profl. jours. Home: 3712 Myrtle Springs Rd Fort Worth TX 76116 Office: 3704 Mattison Ave Fort Worth TX 76107

SCHUST, RALPH HENRY, mktg. sales cons.; b. Saginaw, Mich., May 27, 1904; s. Edward and Della (Edelmann) S.; grad. Culver Mil. Acad., 1923; m. Hannah L. Sovereign, Jan. 27, 1932 (dec. Jan. 7, 1973); children—Penelope Schust Merrill, Deborah Schust Harding, Antonia Schust Zegras; m. 2d, Juliana Everist Haire, 1974. Sales mgr. Schust Co., Saginaw, 1928-37; asst. gen. mgr., sales mgr. Schust Bakery, Loose-Wiles, Kans., 1937-42; mgr. sales Loose Wiles Biscuit Co., 1942-43; v.p. Sunshine Biscuit Inc., N.Y.C., 1943-60; v.p., dir. sales, dir. Sunshine Biscuit Inc. subs. Am. Brands Co., N.Y.C., 1947-69; v.p. sales, dir. Office Price Emergency Preparedness, Washington, 1970-71; cons. mktg. sales, 1971—. Clubs: Saginaw; Detroit Athletic; Creek (Locust Valley, N.Y.); Union League (N.Y.C.); Ponte Vedra (Fla.); Balboa (Mazatlan, Mex.). Home: 7810 Westmoreland Dr Sarasota FL 33580 also Quogue NY 11959

SCHUSTER, CITA (SARAH ELIZABETH) FLETCHER, fine art appraiser, dealer, painter; b. El Paso, Tex., Sept. 12, 1929; d. Frank Barron and Mildred (Sullivan) Fletcher; A.B., Vassar Coll., 1950; postgrad. U. Tex., El Paso, 1976-78; m. Frank P. Schuster, Jr., May

17, 1972; children by previous marriage—Susan B. Platt Smith, Anne C. Platt Haddad, Jack Fletcher Platt. Owner, dir. Two Twenty Two Gallery, El Paso, 1963—; fine art appraiser, El Paso, 1965—; designer, partner La Cita Needlepoint Design, El Paso, 1969-73; exhibited in one man shows U. Tex., El Paso, 1975, 78; group shows Internat. Designer Craftsmen, El Paso Mus. Art, 1973, La. Watercolor Soc. 5th Internat., Baton Rouge, 1974, Internat. Women's Art Slide Festival, N.Y.C., 1976, 19th Annual Sun Carnival Art Exhibit, El Paso Mus. Art, 1976-77, El Paso Designer Craftsmen Invitational, 1979, Ark. Art Center, 1979. Vice pres. El Paso Sun Carnival Assn., 1961; sustaining mem. El Paso Mus. Art; mem. women's dept. El Paso Symphony, women's dept. El Paso C. of C.; bd. dirs. Planned Parenthood, El Paso, 1977—. Mem. Appraiser Assn. Am., Am. Soc. Appraisers (asso.), Valuors Consortium Houston (founding), Visual Artists and Galleries Assn. (charter), La. Water Color Soc., Am. Psychiat. Assn. Aux. (pres. Tex. dist. br. 1980). Episcopalian. Club: Jr. League El Paso (sustaining). Author: (with Frank P. Schuster, Jr.) The Status Game, 1973. Home and office: 6109 Pinehurst St El Paso TX 79912

SCHUSTER, H. FREDERICK ERNEST, III, educator; b. Athens, Ga., Aug. 10, 1936; s. H. Frederick Ernest and Julia Katherine (Taylor) S.; B.A. cum laude, Harvard Coll., 1958; M.S., U. Ga., 1960; D.B.A., Harvard Grad. Sch. Bus., 1969; m. Elizabeth Fegley, Aug. 21, 1965; children—Fritz, Hilary. Indsl. relations research asso. Ford Motor Co., 1961-63; mgmt. personnel mgr. Lockheed Aircraft Co., 1963-65; sr. asso. Cresap, McCormack & Paget, N.Y.C., 1967-69; prof. mgmt. Fla. Atlantic U., Boca Raton, Fla., 1969—. Ford Found. fellow, 1965-67; Stanford U. fellow, 1960-61. Mem. Acad. Mgmt., Am. Soc. Personnel Adminstrn. Roman Catholic. Clubs: Harvard (N.Y.C.), Ocean, Harvard Bus. Sch. of South Fla. Author: Human Resources Management: A Behavioral Systems Approach, 1978; Contemporary Issues in Human Resources Mgmt., 1980. Home: 7 Sabal Island Ocean Ridge FL 33435 Office: Dept Mgmt Coll of Bus Fla Atlantic Univ Boca Raton FL 33432

SCHUSTER, KENNETH HOWARD, wholesale distbn. co. exec.; b. Rockville Center, N.Y., Sept. 6, 1943; s. Howard E. and Edna A. (Henne) S.; B.S., Clarion State Coll., 1965; m. Sylvia D. Martin; children—Howard I., Dwayne M. Pres. ops. Kyle Enterprises, Inc., Greensboro, N.C., 1972-74, gen. mgr. System Staff div., Atlanta, 1974-77; dist. mgr. R.J. Carroll Co., Atlanta, 1977-78; dir. mgmt. resources Senco Southeast, Inc., Decatur, Ga., 1978—, also adviser to bd. dirs.; dir. Senpak, Inc., GM subs. Served with inf. U.S. Army, 1967-69. Mem. Ga. Assn. Temporary Services (pres. 1972), Alpha Phi Gamma. Club: Pinetree Country. Office: Senco Southeast Inc 5280 Panola Industrial Blvd Decatur GA 30035

SCHUSTER, LOUIS DANIEL, govt. exec.; b. Allentown, Pa., Oct. 10, 1936; s. Louis Aloysious and Cathrine Cecelia (Shine) S.; B.S., U. Utah, 1959; M.S., U. Pa., 1961; m. Norma Arcenas, Sept. 4, 1973; children by previous marriage—Diana R., Lisa C., Desiree C. With U.S. Navy, various locations, 1966—, adminstrv. officer Public Works Center, Subic Bay, Philippines, 1968-73, with def. attache office Am. embassy, Saigon, 1973-75, dir. resources Naval Regional Data Automation Center, Pensacola, 1975—. Regional coordinator Nat. Taxpayers Union, 1979-80. Served with USN, 1961-65. Recipient Disting. Service commendation evacuation Saigon, 1975. Mem. Nat. Assn. Fed. Mgrs., Saigon Mission Assn., Nat. Rifle Assn., Pensacola Chess Club, Pensacola Duplicate Bridge Club. Club: Toastmasters. Home: USAG Camp Humphreys HHD APO San Francisco CA 96271

SCHWAB, ELMO, lawyer; b. Gonzales, Tex., Jan. 17, 1937; s. Elmo S. and Mary Doris (Reimenschneider) S.; B.A. cum laude, U. Tex. at Austin, 1959, J.D., 1962; m. Claudette Taylor, Sept. 19, 1960; children—Mary Suzanne, Taylor Townsend. Admitted to Tex. bar, 1962, U.S. Supreme Ct., 1968; mem. firm Barker, Lain, Smith & Schwab, Galveston, Tex., 1967—. Dir. Galveston East Beach, Inc. Bd. dirs. Galveston Cultural Arts Council, 1971-73, Friends Rosenberg Library, 1970-72. Mem. Am. Bar Assn., Am. Judicature Soc., Am. Assn. Trial Lawyers, World Peace Through Law Conf., S.A.R., Sons Republic Tex., Sons Confederate Vets. Kiwanian. Home: 2618 Gerol Ct Galveston TX 77550 Office: 2200 Market St Suite 500 Galveston TX 77550

SCHWAB, KARL WOLF, geol. cons.; b. Toronto, Ont., Can., Apr. 27, 1938; s. Theodore J. and Frances Mary (Forsey) S.; came to U.S., 1943, naturalized, 1958; B.S., Ariz. State U., 1961; M.S. (Maxwell E. Short scholar), U. Ariz., 1963, postgrad., 1966-69; m. Dorothy P. Whigham, Nov. 28, 1964; children—Karl David, Theresa Ann. Geologist, Humble Oil & Refining Co., Houston and Tyler, Tex., 1963-66; research scientist Continental Oil Co., Houston, New Orleans, Ponca City, Okla., 1969-75; mgr. biostratigraphy GeoChem Labs., Inc., Houston, 1975-77; pres. Geo-Strat, Inc., 1977—; v.p. Discovery Exploration, Inc., 1979—. Mem. Am. Assn. Stratigraphic Palynologists, Am. Assn. Petroleum Geologists (certified petroleum geologist). Methodist. Contbr. articles to profl. jours. Home and Office: 1718 Triway Ln Houston TX 77043

SCHWAN, CARL CHRISTIAN, fin. co. exec.; b. Buffalo, Apr. 3, 1937; s. Carl Christian Herbert and Christine Virginia (Spencer) S.; B.A., Union Coll., 1959, B.M.E., 1959; M.B.A. with high distinction, Cornell U., 1964; postgrad. Vanderbilt U., 1964-66, Ohio State U., 1969-70; m. Joy McElroy, Aug. 26, 1961; children—Amber Michelle, Scott Edward. Instr. bus. adminstrn. Vanderbilt U., Nashville, 1964-66; v.p., controller Indsl. Nucleonics Corp., Columbus, Ohio, 1966-76; treas., chief fin. officer Jersey Miniere Zinc Co., Nashville, 1976-78; controller Gulf & Western Natural Resources Group, Nashville, 1978-79; v.p. fin. and adminstrn., sec. Hazleton Labs. Corp., Vienna, Va., 1979—. Served to capt. USAF, 1959-62. Recipient Wall St. Jour. Student Achievement award, 1964; Cornell Aero. Lab. fellow, 1963-64; C.P.A., Ohio. Mem. Fin. Execs. Inst., Am. Inst. C.P.A.'s, Phi Kappa Phi. Contbr. articles to profl. publs. Office: 9200 Leesburg Turnpike Vienna VA 22180

SCHWARTZ, AARON ROBERT, lawyer, state senator; b. Galveston, Tex., July 17, 1926; s. Joe and Clara (Bulbe) S.; student Tex. A. and M. Coll., 1944-47; LL.B., U. Tex., 1951; m. Marilyn Cohn, July 14, 1951; children—Robert Allen, Richard Austin, John Reed, Thomas Lee. Admitted to Tex. bar, 1951; practiced in Galveston, 1951—; asst. county atty., Galveston, 1951-53; mem. Tex. Ho. of Reps., 1954-58; mem. Tex. Senate, 1959—, now sr. mem., pres. pro tem., 1965-66. Vice pres. Harbor Broadcasting Co., Galveston. Chmn. southwestern regional bd. Anti Defamation League of B'nai B'rith, 1961-65, mem. nat. commn. of league, 1966; chmn. Tex. Council Coastal and Marine Affairs. Served with USNR, 1944-46. Mem. Coastal States Orgn. (chmn. 1974—). Home: 10 S Shore Dr Galveston TX 77550

SCHWARTZ, EDWARD MALCOLM, office furniture sales co. exec.; b. Woodmere, N.Y., Aug. 3, 1928; s. Mannie E. and Ruth (Nickeli) Helfat S.; B.A., U. Cin., 1949; m. Shirley Marie Drennan, Dec. 14, 1955; children—Adam Louis, Joseph Michael, Andrew David, Robert Stephen. With Davison-Paxon Co., Atlanta, 1953-54; buyer, mdse. mgr. Boylan Pearce Co., Raleigh, N.C., 1954-55; gen. mdse. mgr. The Fahy Store, Rome, Ga., 1955-56; v.p. The Fashion, Lafayette, Ind., 1956-57; pvt. practice mfg. rep., Atlanta, 1957-58; S.E. regional sales mgr. Herman Miller, Inc., Atlanta, 1958-75; pres. Haworth/Atlanta, Inc., 1975-79; pvt. practice mfg. rep. Southeast Eddie Schwartz & Assos., 1979—; guest lectr. U. Ga., 1974, U. Fla., 1971, Ga. Inst. Tech., 1968, Clemson U., 1969, Fla. State U., 1973. Served with USNR, 1951-53. Mem. Nat. Office Products Assn. Contbr. articles in field to profl. jours. Home: 6080 River Chase Circle NW Atlanta GA 30328

SCHWARTZ, GERALD, pub. relations, advt. firm exec.; b. N.Y.C., June 22, 1927; s. George and Martha (Friedman) S.; student N.C. State U., 1944-45, A.B., U. Miami, 1949, B.S., 1950; m. Felice Pred, June 25, 1950; children—Gary Robert, Gregg Richard, Wendy Lee. Staff writer Miami (Fla.) Herald, 1941-44; publicity dir. 3d Army, U.S. Constabulary in Europe, War Dept., 1946-48; sports editor Miami Beach Daily Sun, 1949; pub. relations dir. in Fla. for State of Israel Bonds, 1951-52, midwest mgr., 1958-59; owner pub. relations, fund raising firm, 1952-58; press sec. Gov. Nebr., 1959-60; exec. v.p. Bar-Ilan U., Israel, 1960-61; regional dir. Am. Friends Hebrew U., 1961-63; owner pub. relations, advt. and fund raising agy., Miami Beach, 1963—; chmn. bd. Nova Canaveral Corp. Mem. City Miami Beach Planning Bd., 1953-56, City Miami Beach Pub. Relations Bd., 1960-70; pres. Greater Miami Forge, 1952-54, S. Fla. Zionist Fedn., 1967-69; chmn. Miami Beach Hurricane Def. Com., 1979—; dep. chmn. Democratic Midwest Conf., 1958-60; Dem. candidate U.S. Congress, 1960; pres. Fla. Pres.'s council Zionist Orgn. Am., 1978-80; bd. dirs. Papanicolaou Cancer Research Inst., Miami, Urban League Greater Miami, 1979—; nat. bd. dirs. Am. Zionist Fedn. Served with inf. AUS, 1944-46. Recipient Gift of Life and Mission of Mercy awards Am. Red Magen David for Israel, Jerusalem Reunited award State of Israel Bonds, Shalom award Govt. of Israel Tourist Office. Mem. Am. Pub. Relations Assn., Pub. Relations Soc. Am. (treas. Fla. chpt. 1955-S7), Nat. Soc. Fund Raisers (v.p. 1975-79), Am. Soc. Bus. and Mgmt. Consultants, Internat. Assn. Bus. Communicators, Am. Mktg. Assn., Advt. Club Greater Miami, Miami Beach C. of C. (v.p. 1978-80, hon. life trustee 1979), Greater Miami C. of C., Alpha Delta Sigma, Omicron Delta Kappa, Theta Omicron Pi, Zeta Beta Tau. Jewish (dir. temple). Club: B'nai B'rith (past pres. Miami Beach lodge). Home: 7320 SW 123d St Miami FL 33156 Office: 420 Lincoln Rd Bldg Miami Beach FL 33139

SCHWARTZ, HENRY, II, lawyer; b. Chattanooga, May 15, 1919; s. Herman Loveman and Willie Frances (Marshall) S.; student U. Miami (Fla.), 1941; A.B., U. Tenn. at Chattanooga, 1946; J.D., U. Va., 1948; m. Margaret Frances MacMillian, May 26, 1951; 1 dau., Peigi Marshall. Dep. register Hamilton County, Chattanooga, 1939-46; admitted to Tenn., Va. bars, 1948, Tex. bar, 1957; pub. counsel Office Gen. Counsel, CAB, Washington, 1948-50; legal adviser U.S. Tax Ct., Washington, 1950-53, sr. legal adviser, 1953-56; with firm Ramey, Calhoun, Brelsford, Hull & Flock, Tyler, Tex., 1956-59; pvt. practice, Tyler, 1959—. Participant, patron Tyler Civic Theatre. Organizer, charter trustee Endowment Fund of Christ Episcopal Ch., Tyler, vice chmn. bd., 1960-62, hon. trustee, permanent chancellor, 1962—; trustee ex officio Joseph and Helen Davidson Charitable Found., 1967-71. Served to capt. USAAF, 1940-46; lt. col. USAF Res. (ret.). Mem. Tex., Va., Smith County bar assns., East Tex. Estate Council (charter mem., sec. 1960-61, dir. 1960-62, 68-71, pres. 1969-70), Southwestern Legal Found., Tyler C. of C., U. Va. (life), U. Tenn. at Chattanooga alumni assns. Episcopalian (vestryman 1959-61, chief usher 1958-77, lic. lay reader 1958-79). Clubs: Elks; Tyler Petroleum; Lookout Mountain (Tenn.) Fairyland. Author: Tax Consequences of the Payment of Substitute Royalties, 1958. Contbr. articles to profl. jours. Home: 608 E 3d St Tyler TX 75701 Office: 810 Peoples Nat Bank Bldg Tyler TX 75702

SCHWARTZ, HERBERT TOBIAS, lawyer; b. Miami, Fla., Sept. 13, 1936; s. Leo A. and Rosaline (Peretzman) S.; B.A. in Polit. Sci., U. Fla., 1959; M.S., Wichita State U., 1966; J.D., U. Fla., 1966; LL.M., U. Ill., 1968; m. Joanne Schwartz; children—Edwin A.D., Ashly H. Admitted to Fla. bar, 1967, also fed. cts.; asst. prof. law U. Ill. Law Sch., 1967-68; part-time asst. prof. social sci. U. Fla., 1968-71; practiced in Gainesville, Fla., Tallahassee, 1968—; dep. atty. gen. Fla., 1971-72, spl. asst. atty. gen., 1972—. Bd. dirs. Alachua County Mental Health Assn., Regional Blood Center, Gainesville YMCA, Boys Club. Served to capt. USAF, 1959-64, lt. col. Res. Mem. Am., Fla. bar assns., Am. Acad. Trial Lawyers, Acad. Fla. Trial Lawyers, Nat. Assn. Criminal Def. Lawyers, Air Force Assn., Lawyers-Pilots Assn. Democrat. Moose. Club: Civitan. Contbr. articles to legal jours. Office: 711 NW 23d Ave Suite 4 PO Box 1292 Gainesville FL 32602

SCHWARTZ, MARK EDWARD, diversified mfg. co. exec.; b. Dodge City, Kans., May 9, 1953; s. Eugene Wilbur and Margaret (Allen) S.; B.A., U. Kans., 1975; M.B.A., So. Meth. U., 1976. Fin. analyst Ft. Worth Nat. Bank, 1976, sr. fin. analyst, 1977, corr. bank rep., 1977, corr. bank officer, 1978, corr. bank officer II, 1978-79; mgr. ops. Synthetic Web Sling div. Wire Rope Corp. of Am., Ft. Worth, 1979—; lectr. in field; tchr. fin. planning for small bus. Ft. Worth Nat. Bank, 1978. Tchr. project bus. Jr. Achievement, Ft. Worth, 1977; bd. dirs. Ft. Worth Westside YMCA, 1978-79, basketball coach, 1978-79. Recipient Victor award Sales and Mktg. Execs. of Ft. Worth, 1979. Republican. Roman Catholic. Home: 1713 Carl St Fort Worth TX 76103 Office: 7725 Sand St Fort Worth TX 76118

SCHWARTZ, MORRIS FRANK, III, architect; b. Nashville, Apr. 10, 1952; s. Morris Frank, Jr., and Betty Jo (Patten) S.; B.Arch., U. Tenn., 1976, postgrad. in Engring., 1976—. Architect-designer, Taiwan Vice Ministry Edn., Taipei, 1974; designer-trainee Yearwood & Johnson, Architects, Nashville, 1975; architect-researcher Vice-Ministry Urban Planning, Govt. of Nicaragua, Managua, 1975-76; architect Gresham & Smith, Nashville, 1976-80; architect med. facilities Yearwood & Johnson, Architects & Space Planners, Nashville, 1980—; cons. in field. Mem. Constrn. Specifications Inst., AIA (asso. Middle Tenn. chpt.), Tenn. Soc. Architects (asso.), Tenn. Solar Energy Assn., Internat. Solar Energy Soc., Am. Heart Assn. (bldg. profl. div.). Democrat. Jewish. Architect highrise apts. for elderly, Gallatin, Tenn., Oak Ridge, Fayetteville, N.C., 1978, H.H. Raulerson Jr. Meml. Hosp., Okeechobee, Fla., 1977—, additions and renovations Forsyth County Hosp., Cumming, Ga., 1979, renovations Hermitage Hotel, Nashville, 1980, Moreland's earth-sheltered residence, Franklin, Tenn., 1980, others. Home: Route 5 Box 109 Sawyer Rd Franklin TN 37064 Office: 55 Music Sq W Nashville TN 37203

SCHWARTZ, SEYMOUR (SY), univ. dean;. b. N.Y.C., Mar. 15, 1919; s. Irving and Ida S.; B.A., U. Mich., 1940; m. Margaret M. Spellman, Sept. 8, 1946; 1 son, Karl B. Joined U.S. Army Air Force, 1942; commd. 2d lt., 1943, advanced through grades to coll., 1964-68; ret., 1968; asst. to dean Coll. Bus. Adminstrn., U. Tex., Austin, 1968-71, asst. dean Grad. Sch. Bus., 1971—. Med. evacuation specialist NATO, Paris, 1960-61. Decorated Bronze Star medal. Mobil Oil Found. Small Bus. grantee, 1972—; S.B.A. grantee, 1972—. Mem. Internat. Council Small Bus., Small Bus. Inst. Dirs. Assn., S.W. Fedn. Adminstrn. Disciplines, Ret. Officers Assn. Home: 1813 Polo Rd Austin TX 78703 Office: GSB 1-104 U Tex Austin TX 78712

SCHWARTZ, SOLOMON LEON, indsl. psychologist; b. Phila., Oct. 3, 1928; s. Max and Esther (Sadoff) S.; B.A., Temple U., 1951, M.A., 1953, Ph.D., 1957; m. Sydelle Miriam Unger, Dec. 23, 1956; children—Elizabeth Susan, Marjorie Ruth. Vice pres., dir. Psychometric Labs., Miami, Fla., 1957-61; pres. Search Assos., Inc., Miami, 1961—, also dir.; dir. Nat. Partitions, Inc., Loraine Corp. Mem. North Bay Village (Fla.) Citizens Adv. Council, 1969-71; chmn. North Bay Village Bicentennial Commn., 1975-76; co-chmn. North Bay Village Charter Rev. Bd., 1976-78. Served with AUS, 1946-48. Mem. Am. Mgmt. Assn., Am., Fla. psychol. assns. Author supervisory index test, mgmt. aptitude test. Contbr. articles to profl. jours. Home: 7621 Miami View Dr North Bay Village FL 33141 Office: 9999 NE 2nd Ave Miami Shores FL 33138

SCHWARTZOTT, FRANKLIN FREDERICK, JR., cons. co. exec.; b. Buffalo, N.Y., June 26, 1949; s. Franklin F. and Jean Mildred (Snyder) S.; Asso. in Applied Sci., Erie County Tech. Inst., 1969; B.S. in Bus. Adminstrn., SUNY, Buffalo, 1972, postgrad. in indsl. engring., 1975-76; postgrad. in indsl. engring., U. Okla., 1977-80; m. Darlene Gordon, Aug. 29, 1969. Methods analyst Twin Industries Corp., Cheektowaga, N.Y., 1969-70; standards analyst Marine Midland Bank, Buffalo, 1971-72; mgr. Cost acctg. dept. M & T Bank, Buffalo, 1972-76; dir. cost acctg. dept. Fidelity Bank, Oklahoma City, 1976-79; prin. Schwartzott Cons., Yukon, Okla., 1979—; guest lectr. U. Okla., 1979. Recipient Cert. Commendation, Bd. Regents of SUNY, 1972. Mem. Am. Assn. Cost Engrs. (sr. mem., v.p. community affairs 1979-80), Am. Inst. Indsl. Engrs. Republican. Mem. Christian Ch. Club: Westbury Golf and Country. Home and Office: 10316 Bonnycastle Dr Yukon OK 73099

SCHWARZBART, GÜNTER, surgeon; b. Berlin, Germany, Feb. 3, 1932; s. Sam and Harriet (Bernstein) S.; emigrated to Uruguay, 1939-46, came to U.S., 1946, naturalized, 1953; B.S. in Chemistry cum laude, Syracuse U., 1953; M.D., Basel (Switzerland) U., 1959; m. Rita Klara Sonderegger, Dec. 2, 1954; children—Vivienne E., Sheila D. Intern, Mt. Sinai Hosp., Miami Beach, Fla., 1959-60, resident, 1960-61; resident in surgery Coral Gables (Fla.) VA Hosp., 1961-64; practice medicine specializing in surgery, Miami, Fla., 1964-65, Miami Beach, 1965-75; asso. attending surgeon univ.-affiliated Mt. Sinai Hosp. Med. Center; staff St. Francis, South Shore hosps., Miami Heart Inst., North Miami Gen. Hosp.; staff surgeon, chief grade VA Hosp., Clarksburg, W.Va., 1975-79; ret., 1979; clin. asso. prof. gen. surgery U. W.Va., Morgantown, 1975—; tchr. various hosps. Diplomate Am. Bd. Surgery. Fellow A.C.S., Internat. Coll. Surgeons, Am. Soc. Abdominal Surgeons. Contbr. articles to profl. jours. Home: Del Prado-on-the-Bay 18061 Biscayne Blvd Apt 1601 North Miami Beach FL 33160

SCHWARZE, ESTELLA GERALDINE, social work adminstr.; b. New Orleans; d. William J. and Mary (Reynolds) Schwarze; B.S. in Social Sci., Loyola U., New Orleans, 1957, postgrad., 1958-59, 61-62; M.S.W., Tulane U., 1962; postgrad. U. New Orleans, 1973—, Loyola U. With Asso. Cath. Charities, 1946-59; exec. dir. Assn. for Retarded Children, 1956-57; with social service dept. Charity Hosp. of La., New Orleans, 1958-79, supr., 1965-79, also mem. adv. bd., vol. dept.; sect. head social service dept. La. Rehab. Inst., New Orleans, 1979—; field work instr. Atlanta U. Grad. Sch. Social Work, 1967—; cons. in social work Treme Neighborhood Improvement Assn.; curriculum cons., organizer, coordinator social studies symposia Rummel High Sch., New Orleans, 1973-74; lectr. community medicine La. State U., Tulane U.; lectr. social welfare So. U., New Orleans; field work instr. Worden Grad. Sch. of Social Work, San Antonio, Tulane Sch. Social Work. Founder, charter mem. Irish Channel Action Found., New Orleans, 1964; organizer Parent's Inst., New Orleans, 1962; organizer, originator Projects Aquarius; del. White House Conf. on Children and Youth, 1970, White House Conf. on Aging, 1971; mem. New Orleans Mayor's Task Force Aging. Mem. adv. bd., cons. health consumer edn. program New Orleans Urban League. Certified social worker, La. Mem. Nat. Assn. Social Workers (Social Worker of Yr. award S.E. La. chpt. 1965), La. Soc. Clin. Social Work, Am. Pub. Health Assn., Mercy Acad. Alumnae (pres. 1956-58), League Women Voters, Bus. and Profl. Womens Club. Democrat. Home: 915 Jefferson Ave New Orleans LA 70115 Office: Social Service Dept Charity Hosp of La 1542 Tulane Ave New Orleans LA 70130

SCHWARZENBACH, JOHN REED, physician; b. Big Spring, Tex., Sept. 25, 1944; s. Howard Frances and Marguerite (Reed) S.; B.S. in Zoology, Tex. A&M U., 1966; M.D., U. Tex. Med. Br., Galveston, 1971; m. Carol Ann, July 9, 1969; children—Nicholas, Loyd, David William, Frances Alison, Angela Christine. Intern, Touro Infirmary, New Orleans, 1971-72; resident in internal medicine Bexar County Hosp. Dist., San Antonio, 1972-74; practice medicine specializing in internal medicine, partner Valley Diagnostic Clinic, Harlingen, Tex., 1974—. Bd. dirs. S. Tex. Br. Arthritis Found., mem. adv. com., 1974-76. Diplomate Am. Bd. Internal Medicine. Mem. AMA, Tex. Med. Assn., So. Med. Assn., A.C.P., Cameron-Willacy County Med. Soc., Am. Soc. Internal Medicine. Republican. Episcopalian. Home: Route 3 Box 248 Harlingen TX 78550 Office: 2121 Pease St Suite 1-A Harlingen TX 78550

SCHWEHM, JERRY KENNETH, lawyer; b. New Orleans, May 6, 1948; s. James P. and Thelma C. (Tarantino) S.; B.A., La. State U., 1971, J.D., 1974; m. Nancy Stanley, June 16, 1972; 1 son, Jonathan. Admitted to La. bar, 1974; probation officer Orleans Parish Juvenile Ct., 1971; research asst. to mem. faculty La. State U. Law Sch., 1973; chief asst. dist. atty. of child support enforcement div., New Orleans, 1974-79; mem. faculty Nat. Coll. Dist. Attys. Child Support Enforcement Tng. seminars, 1975. Mem. exec. com. Met. New Orleans chpt. Nat. Found. March of Dimes, 1975-79, vice chmn., 1976-78, chmn., 1978-79; bd. dirs. Children's Bur. of New Orleans, 1975-78. Recipient Distinguished Faculty award Nat. Dist. Attys. Assn., 1975, Am. Jurisprudence award, 1974. Mem. Am. Bar Assn., Nat. Dist. Attys. Assn., La. Trial Lawyers Assn., La. Dist. Attys. Assn., La. Bar Assn., La. Child Support Enforcement Assn. (mem. exec. com. 1975-79). Home: 200 Lake Tahoe Dr Slidell LA 70458 Office: 1338 Gause Blvd Slidell LA 70458

SCHWEIKHARDT, WILLIAM, lawyer; b. E. Orange, N.J., June 22, 1942; s. Clarence J. and Angeline E. (Beifus) S.; B.S. in Bus. Adminstrn., Georgetown U., 1964, J.D., 1967; m. Kathleen Blaney, Dec. 28, 1972; children—Katherine, Ann. Admitted to N.J. bar, 1968, Fla. bar, 1968; with firm Adams & Peck, N.Y.C., 1969-70; pros. atty. Collier County, Fla., 1972-73; asst. states atty. 20th Jud. Circuit Fla., 1973-74; individual practice, Naples, Fla., 1970—; tchr. Collier County schs., 1977-79. Bd. dirs. Collier County YMCA, 1970-73; commr. Alligator dist. Boy Scouts Am., 1974-75; mem. Collier County Charter Commn., 1974-75; bd. dirs. Naples Blood Bank, 1973-77; bd. dirs. Naples Cath. Service Bur., 1975—, pres., 1980. Served with U.S. Army, 1967. Named Ky. col., 1976. Mem. Am. Bar Assn., Fla. Bar. Clubs: Toastmasters (pres. 1975), Rotary (dir. 1978-80, pres. 1980) (Naples). Home: 677 Fountainhead Ln Naples FL 33940 Office: 900 6th Ave S Naples FL 33940

SCHWEITZER, JEROME WILLIAM, educator; b. Tuscaloosa, Ala., Dec. 28, 1908; s. Abraham and Mary (Spiro) S.; A.B., U. Ala., 1930, M.A., 1932; Ph.D., Johns Hopkins, 1940; postgrad. U. Mexico, 1946; m. Anne Rachael Stoler, Oct. 1, 1931. Reporter, Tuscaloosa

News, 1928-30; dir. News Bur., U. Ala., Tuscaloosa, 1930-37; instr. romance langs. U. Ala., University, 1931-40, asst. prof., 1940-47, asso. prof., 1947-51, prof., 1951-76, prof. emeritus, 1976—; v.p. Schweitzer's, Inc., 1978—. Served with AUS, 1942-45; lt. col. Res. (ret.). U. Ala. research grantee, 1961-65. Mem. Modern Lang. Assn. Am., South Atlantic Modern Lang. Assn., Am. Assn. Tchrs. Spanish and Portuguese, The Comediantes, Ala. Edn. Assn., Nat. Ret. Tchrs. Assn., Ala. Ret. Tchrs. Assn., Société des Amis de Tristan L'Hermite (hon.), Société des études du dix-septième siècle, Phi Beta Kappa. Jewish. Author: (with C.B. Wicks) The Parisian Stage, 1961; Almahide, 1939, 73. Editorial bd. Revista De Estudios Hispánicos, 1967-75; co-editor: Théâtre Complet de Tristan l'Hermite, 1975. Home: 14 Arcadia Dr Tuscaloosa AL 35404 Office: Box 3195 Eastside Sta Tuscaloosa AL 35403

SCHWERING, BRUCE PAUL, mfg. co. exec.; b. Fort Dodge, Iowa, Oct. 3, 1946; s. Paul John and Evelyn Faye (Hasty) S.; B.S. in Bus. Adminstrn., Creighton U., 1968; m. Mary Ann Cahill, June 7, 1969; children—Timothy, Amy. Staff acct. Arthur Andersen Co., Omaha, 1968-73; controller Soo Tractor Sweeprake, Sioux City, Iowa, 1973-74; mgr. Arthur Andersen Co., Dallas, 1974-76; v.p. adminstrn. Austin Products Co., Dallas, 1976—. Served with AUS, 1969-71. C.P.A., Tex. Mem. Am. Inst. C.P.A.'s, Tex. Soc. C.P.A.'s. Home: 336 Squirebrook DeSoto TX 75115 Office: 1000 Singleton Blvd Dallas TX 75222

SCHWING, CHARLES EDWARD, architect; b. Plaquemine, La., Nov. 21, 1929; s. Calvin Kendrick and Mary Howard (Slack) S.; student La. State U., 1947-51; B.S., Ga. Inst. Tech., 1953, B.Architecture, 1954; 3e Assessit d'Architecture, Ecole des Beaux-Arts; m. Cynthia Benjamin, June 14, 1952 (div. 1967); children—Calvin Kendrick III, Therra Cynthia; m. 2d, Geraldine Fleniken Hofmann, Dec. 27, 1969; 1 stepson, Steven Blake. Field insp. Bodman, Murrell and Smith, Baton Rouge, 1954-55; asso. architect Post & Harelson, Baton Rouge, 1955-59; partner Hughes and Schwing, Baton Rouge, 1959-61; owner Charles E. Schwing, Baton Rouge, 1961-69, Charles E. Schwing & Assos., Baton Rouge, 1969—; v.p. Schwing Inc. Fellow AIA (treas., exec. com., dir., planning com., chmn. fin. com. 1976-77, 1st v.p. 1979, pres. 1980; treas., exec. com., dir., fin. com. AIA Research Corp. 1976-77; treas., dir. AIA Found. 1976-77, v.p. 1978, pres.-elect 1979); mem. La. Architect Assn. (sec.-treas. 1971, v.p. 1972, pres. 1973), C. of C., La. State U. Alumni Fedn., Ga. Tech. Alumni Club, Sigma Alpha Epsilon. Episcopalian. Clubs: Baton Rouge Country, City. Home: 8635 Jefferson Hwy No 12 Stone's Throw Baton Rouge LA 70809 Office: 721 Government St Baton Rouge LA 70802

SCIACCA, WILLIAM WAYNE, hosp. adminstr.; b. New Orleans, June 20, 1945; s. Thomas John and Pauline Louise Sciacca; B.A., La. State U., 1967; m. Priscilla Dianne Neal, Aug. 13, 1966; children—William, Deborah, Mark. Asst. mgr. Brennan's Restaurant, New Orleans, 1971-73; dir. dietary Hotel Dieu Hosp., New Orleans, 1973-76; dir. food service Tulane Med. Center Hosp. and Clinic, New Orleans, 1976—; cons. in field. CPR instr. Am. Heart Assn., New Orleans. Served to capt. U.S. Army, 1967-71. Decorated Bronze Star. Mem. Am. Soc. Hosp. Food Service Adminstrs., La. Restaurant Assn., Res. Officers Assn., Theta Xi. Democrat. Roman Catholic. Clubs: Lions, Confederation Mondiale des Activites Subquatiques. Home: 4236 Walmsley Ave New Orleans LA 70125 Office: 1415 Tulane Ave New Orleans LA 70112

SCIFRES, ROBERT EUGENE, gypsum co. exec.; b. Lafayette, Ind., Dec. 5, 1917; s. Clarence Edgar and Bertha Mae (McCord) S.; B.S. in Elec. Engring., Purdue U., 1938; M.B.A. (Sloan fellow 1950), M.I.T., 1950; m. Claire O'Brien, Sept. 12, 1969; children—Linda, Caryl, Cynthia, Dianne, Robert, Michael. With Nat. Gypsum Co., 1942—, corp. group v.p., 1972-77, vice chmn. bd., 1977, chmn. bd., chief exec. officer, Dallas, 1977—, also dir.; dir. Republic Nat. Bank, Dallas. Mem. Conf. Bd., NAM, Tex. Research League (dir.), Tex. Assn. Bus., Dallas Citizens Council, Dallas C. of C. Home: 7103 Spanky Branch Dallas TX 75248 Office: 4100 First Internat Bldg Dallas TX 75270

SCISSON, SIDNEY EUGENE, engring. co. exec.; b. Danville, Ark., Feb. 4, 1917; s. Eugene and Arvie (Keathley) S.; student Ark. Tech. U., 1934-36; B.S. in Gen. Engring., Okla. State U., 1939; m. Betti Shumaker, Sept. 8, 1942; children—Jane E., Judith A. Civil engr. U.S. Corps Engrs., Tulsa, 1939-42; civil engr. Pate Engring. Co., Tulsa, 1945-48; pres. Fenix & Scisson, Inc., Tulsa, 1948—; dir. Bank of Okla., Atlas Life Ins. Co. Treas., pres. Tulsa Civic Ballet, 1965-68. Served with USNR, 1942-45. Registered profl. engr., Ill., Ky., Ohio, Okla., R.I. Mem. Nat. Acad. Engring., Am. Inst. Mining, Metall. and Petroleum Engrs., Am., Okla. soc. civil engrs., Nat., Okla. socs. profl. engrs., Am. Gas Assn., Nat. Gas Processors Assn., Asso. Gen. Contractors Am. Clubs: So. Hills Country, Tulsa, Summit. Home: 2835 E 58th St Tulsa OK 74105 Office: 1401 S Boulder Tulsa OK 74119

SCOBEY, ELLIS HURLBUT, geologist; b. Kelso, Wash., Sept. 15, 1911; s. Guy Hurlbut and Bessie Merwin (Barrett) S.; B.A., Cornell Coll., Mt. Vernon, Iowa, 1933; M.S., U. Iowa, 1935, Ph.D., 1938; m. Dorothy June Wilson, Aug. 5, 1935; children—John, Margaret Scobey Putnam, Michael, Rosalind. Geologist, Gulf Oil Corp., Mattoon, Ill., 1938-44, Bay Petroleum Corp., Midland, Tex., 1944-47; dist. geologist So. Minerals Corp., Midland, 1947-51; chief geologist Guy Mabee Drilling Co., Midland, 1951-65; chief geologist Mabee Petroleum Corp., Midland, 1965-76; partner McFarland & Scobey, Inc., Midland, 1976—. Mem. Am. Assn. Petroleum Geologists, Sigma Xi. Home: 2 Chatham Ct Midland TX 79701 Office: Box 8048 Midland TX 79703

SCOGGIN, JAMES FRANKLIN, JR., educator; b. Laurel, Miss., Aug. 3, 1921; s. James Franklin and Berenice (Phares) S.; B.S., Miss. State U., 1941; B.S., U.S. Mil. Acad., 1944; M.A., Johns Hopkins U., 1951; Ph.D., U. Va., 1957; m. Madeline Eve Lannelle, Mar. 1, 1948; children—Tracy, Beryl, James Franklin III. Commd. 2d lt., U.S. Army, 1944, advanced through grades to col., 1966; ret., 1968; asso. prof. The Citadel, 1968-75, prof., 1975—. Recipient Outstanding Teaching award The Citadel, 1971. Registered profl. engr., S.C. Mem. Am. Phys. Soc., ASME, IEEE (chmn. Coastal S.C. sect. 1972), Am. Nuclear Soc., Radio Club Am., Sigma Xi, Tau Beta Pi. Presbyn.

SCOGGINS, JAMES MONTGOMERY, health systems planner; b. Little Rock, Sept. 16, 1942; s. Julian Albert and Mona Mae (Parks) Hawkins; B.A. in Sociology, U. Houston, 1969; M.A. in Sociology of Medicine and Health Systems, Case Western Res. U., 1971; M.H.A., Trinity U.; children—Christopher James, Sarah Elizabeth. Research asst. Tex. Research Inst. Mental Scis., Houston, 1966-69; asst. epidemiologist U. Tex. Sch. Pub. Health, Houston, 1969; dir. family health planning City of Cleve., USPHS, 1970-72; dir. planning and health maintenance orgn. devel. Bexar County Hosp. Dist., San Antonio, 1972-75; pres. S.W. Med. Plan, Inc., San Antonio, 1975—; chmn. bd. Gulf Coast Health Plan, Inc., Corpus Christi, Tex., 1979—; adj. asst. prof. div. environ. studies U. Tex., 1977. Served with USNR, 1961-65. NDEA fellow, 1969-71. Mem. Tex. Health Maintenance Orgns. Assn. (pres. 1975-76), Group Health Assn. Am. Home: 4940 Arbor Ridge San Antonio TX 78228 Office: Suite 470 6061 NW Expressway San Antonio TX 78224

SCOTT, ALTHA LILLIAN, hosp. food service supr.; b. Stephens County, Tex., Aug. 27, 1917; d. William Franklin and Lillian Nancy Ramsay; grad. high sch.; m. Paul W. Scott, Jan. 27, 1934; children—Ann Scott Holland, William Derrel, Vanda Scott Townsend, Connie Scott Smith. Staff, Yoakum County Hosp., Denver City, Tex., 1951—, now dietary supr. Mem. Phi Sigma Alpha. Baptist. Home: 401 W 5th St Denver City TX 79323 Office: Yoakum County Hosp 612 W 4th St Denver City TX 79323

SCOTT, ATHERIA CARTER, speech pathologist; b. Midland, Ga., Nov. 21, 1953; d. Willie Manuel and Dorothy Mae (Layfield) Carter; student Columbus Coll., 1972-73; B.S. in Edn., U. Ga., 1975, M.Ed., 1976; m. David Scott II, June 25, 1977. Speech pathologist Houston County Pub. Schs., Perry, Ga., 1976, Dekalb County Pub. Schs., Decatur, Ga., 1976-77, Jefferson Parish Pub. Schs., Gretna, La., 1977—. Cert. speech pathologist, La., Ga. Mem. Am. Speech and Hearing Assn. (cert. clin. competence), La. Speech and Hearing Assn., Alpha Kappa Alpha. Baptist. Home: 1040 E Mary Poppins Dr Apt 1206 Harvey LA 70058 Office: 1450 Jefferson St Gretna LA 70053

SCOTT, AVONNE SHORT, adminstr. health facility; b. Alberta, Va., Aug. 21, 1935; d. William Allen and Charlotte Lee (Graves Short) Murchison; B.S. in Nursing, Med. Coll. Va., 1957; m. Luther Thomas, Aug. 29, 1965; children—Luther Thomas, William Herbert. Staff nurse St. Philip Hosp., Richmond, Va., 1957-60; staff nurse, head nurse, nurse supr. Central State Hosp., Petersburg, Va., 1960-65; instr. nursing aides Va. Dept. Vocat. Rehab., Petersburg, 1966; asso. dir. nursing Central State Hosp., Petersburg, 1966-71; asst. dir. nursing Southside Va. Tng. Center, Petersburg, 1971-75, unit dir., 1975—. Sec., PTA Petersburg; officer Methodist Ch., Petersburg. Mem. Va. Govtl. Employees Assn., Am. Assn. Mental Deficiency, Nat. Rehab. Assn., Mental Health and Mental Retardation Soc. Va. Democrat. Home: 18 School Ct Petersburg VA 23803 Office: PO Box 4110 Petersburg VA 23803

SCOTT, BARBARA JEAN, nursing adminstr.; b. New Brighton, Pa., Apr. 5, 1929; d. Harold Courtney and Marie Teressa (Geisler) Clark; B.S., Mt. Union Coll., 1952; diploma St. Luke's Hosp. Sch. Nursing, Cleve., 1951; B.S.N., Case-Western Res. U., 1964; M.A., U. Iowa, 1970; m. Albert Scott, Sept. 2, 1972. With St. Luke's Hosp., Cleve., 1952-55, 56-72, mem. faculty, 1956-62, dir. staff devel., 1962-72; sch. nurse Beaver Falls (Pa.) Bd. Edn., 1955-56; asst. dir. nursing Meml. Hosp., Hollywood, Fla., 1973; dir. nursing Boca Raton (Fla.) Community Hosp., 1974-78; dir. nursing service adminstrn. L.W. Blake Meml. Hosp., Bradenton, Fla., 1979—. Recipient Yearbook dedication Sch. Nursing St. Luke's Hosp., 1962. Mem. Am. Nurses' Assn., Fla. Nurses' Assn., Dist. 21 Assn., Council Nursing Service Adminstrs., Fla. Soc. Hosp. Nursing Service Adminstrn. (dir.), Am. Hosp. Assn. Nursing Service Adminstrs., Sigma Theta Tau. Republican. Presbyterian. Author: The Process of Staff Development, 1974. Home: 4644 La Jolla Dr Bradenton FL 33507 Office: 2020 59th St W Bradenton FL 33505

SCOTT, BEVERLY G., personnel cons. co. exec.; b. Pecos, Tex., June 15, 1939; d. S. A. and Ethel S.; B.S., Hardin-Simmons U., 1961, postgrad., 1967; postgrad. N.Y. U., 1973. Tchr., Tex. and Iowa, 1961-70; pres., owner Career Woman Personnel Cons., Inc., Dallas, 1970—. Mem. Nat. Assn. Personnel Cons. (dir.), Am. Soc. Tng. and Devel., Tex. Assn. Personnel Cons. (dir.), Sales and Marketing Execs. Dallas (dir.), Dallas Personnel Assn., Dallas Assn. Personnel Cons. (past pres), Bus. and Profl. Women Dallas, Inc. Office: 1525 Elm St Suite 2030 Dallas TX 75201

SCOTT, CHARLES LEE, univ. adminstr.; b. Norman, Okla., Feb. 23, 1930; s. Lee L. and Olyva M. (Coppers) S.; B.S.B.A., U. Tulsa, 1952; M.B.A., UCLA, 1957; m. Virginia Carroll, Apr. 3, 1960; children—Stephen Windsor, Darren Christopher, Alicia Carroll. Mktg. research adminstr. Gen. Telephone Co. Calif., Los Angeles, 1957-62; mktg. research and planning adminstr. Gen. Telephone and Electronics Corp., N.Y.C., 1962-66; coordinator mktg. research Tuloma Gas Products Co. div. Standard Oil of Indiana, Tulsa, 1966-68; mgr. market devel. Williams Bros. Pipeline Co., Tulsa, 1968; coordinator mktg./econs. studies Skelly Oil Co., Tulsa, 1968-73; v.p. Leslie Brooks & Assos., Inc., Tulsa, 1973-74; dir. Mgmt. Devel. Center, U. Tulsa, 1974—; cons. in field. Served with USAF, 1952-56. Recipient Merit award Nat. Visual Presentation Assn., 1965, Appreciation award Am. Mgmt. Assn., 1963. Mem. Am. Mktg. Assn. (Nat. Recognition award), Am. Soc. Personnel Adminstrn., Am. Soc. Tng. and Devel., Nat. Univ. Extension Assn. Methodist. Author: Effective Time Management for Managers, 1978; Effective Time Management for Executive Secretaries and Administrative Assistants, 1979. Office: U Tulsa 600 S College Ave Tulsa OK 74104

SCOTT, CHARLES WATSON, counseling psychologist; b. Brookhaven, Miss., Apr. 25, 1909; s. Thom and Helen Gaines (Carden) S.; B.S., U. So. Miss., 1931; M.A., La. State U., 1948; Ed.D., U. Miss., 1957; m. Katrhyn Jane Butler, June 2, 1936; 1 dau., Kathryn Watson Scoper. Head bus. dept. Lexington (Miss.) Pub. Schs., 1934-36; dir. vocat. edn. and guidance Gulfport (Miss.) City Schs., 1936-43; asst. supr. edn. Convair Aircraft Corp., New Orleans, 1943-44; counseling psychologist VA, 1944-45; chief VA Center, La. State U., Baton Rouge, 1945-49; prof. edn. Miss. Coll., Clinton, 1949-79, dean students, 1949-74, dir. admissions, 1949-56, dir. counseling and career devel. center, 1974-79; vocat. cons. U.S. Social Security Adminstrn., 1978—; cons. Miss. Council on Aging, 1980—. Mem. career edn. council Miss. Dept. Edn. Tchr. Sunday sch., deacon, dir. brotherhood Baptist Ch. Recipient Meritorious Service award Miss. Coll., 1979, also coll. counseling center dedicated in honor Charles and Kathryn Scott; recipient Outstanding Service award Brotherhood Dept., Miss. Bapt. Conv. Bd., 1979; Resolution of Commendation, City of Clinton, also Miss. Legislature. Mem. Miss. (Distinguished Career award 1972, Spl. Service award 1977; pres. 1960-62, chmn. legis. com. 1972-76), Am. (del. to senate 1960-69), Capital Area (Disting. Service award 1979) personnel and guidance assns., Miss. Edn. Assn., Miss. Assn. Sch. Adminstrs., Am. Coll. Personnel Adminstrn., Am. Assn. Counselor Educators, So. Assn. Counselor Educators, Miss. Career Edn. Assn. (organizer; pres. 1978—), Miss. Gerontol. Soc., Phi Delta Kappa (Disting. Service award 1979), Kappa Delta Pi, Omicron Delta Kappa. Clubs: Live Oaks Country, Lions (charter mem., pres. Gulfport, sec. Clinton); Knife and Fork Dinner Internat. Contbr. articles to profl. jours. Home: 807 Leake St E Clinton MS 39056 Office: Mississippi Coll Clinton MS 39058

SCOTT, CURTIS PAUL, educator; b. Collins, Ga., Aug. 17, 1937; s. Curtis McGee and Virginia (Collins) S.; B.S. in Edn., Ga. So. Coll., 1959, M.Ed., 1964; Ed.S., Ga. State U., 1972, Ph.D., 1976; m. Bobbie Reynolds, Nov. 20, 1976; children—Colin Paul, Stuart Mack. Tchr. Butler High Sch., 1959-60; tchr., counselor Toombs Central High Sch., 1960-63, Irwin County High Sch., 1963-66; coordinator student personnel services Walker County Area Vocat.-Tech. Sch., Rock Spring, Ga., 1966-70; div. dir., dir. occupational research Ga. Dept. Edn., Atlanta, 1970-76; asst. prof. vocat. edn. U. Ga., Athens, 1976—, program dir., 1976—; mem. research com. So. Assn. Colls. and Schs.; bd. dirs. Vocat.-Tech. Consortium of States; mem. com. U.S. Office Edn. Chmn. Irwin County Heart Fund Drive; supt. Sunday sch., ruling elder Presbyterian Ch. Served with Army N.G., 1962. Recipient cert. Heart Fund, 1962, U.S. Air Force, 1963, Atlanta Pub. Schs., 1972, Interstate Consortium, 1976; U.S. Office Edn. grantee, 1972-77; Ga. Dept. Edn. grantee, 1976-79. Mem. Am. Personnel and Guidance Assn., Am. Vocat. Assn., Am. Vocat. Edn. Research Assn., Ga. Vocat. Assn., Nat. Vocat. Guidance Assn., Assn. for Supervision and Curriculum Devel., Phi Delta Kappa. Democrat. Contbr. articles to profl. jours., Am. Vocat. Assn. Yearbooks, 1976, 79. Home: 580 Forest Rd Athens GA 30605 Office: Aderhold Hall U Ga Athens GA 30602

SCOTT, DIANA LYN, shopping center exec.; b. Ladysmith, Wis., Oct. 22, 1951; d. Donald Arthur and Mae Ellen Zimmerman; B.S., Tex. Tech. U., 1972; m. William D. Scott, Jan. 6, 1973. Design asst. Johnston, Inc., Wylie, Dallas, Tex., 1973-74, asst. designer, 1974-76; asst. promotion dir. the Galleria, Houston, 1976-77, dir. mktg. and public relations, 1977—; asso. dir. the Galleria Center Assn. Mem. Fashion Group, Inc., Houston Livestock Assn., Houston Motion Picture Council, Internat. Council Shopping Centers, Gamma Phi Beta. Fashion designer. Office: Suite 3255 Galleria 5015 Westheimer St Houston TX 77056

SCOTT, DONALD LEE, clergyman; b. Pulaski, Va., Aug. 7, 1929; s. John Preston and Hallie Jewell (Swain) S.; B.A., Lynchburg Coll., 1951; B.D., Lexington Theol. Sem., 1959; M.A., Hartford Sem. Found., 1963; m. Clementeyne Hardy, Aug. 27, 1955; children—Lucinda Lee, Margaret Cardell (Mrs. Paul West). Ordained to ministry Christian Ch., 1951; dir. children's work Christian Ch. for Ky., Lexington, 1953-57; minister Christian edn. Woodland Christian Ch., Lexington, 1957-62, Gordon St. Christian Ch., Kinston, N.C., 1963-67; asso. minister First Christian Ch., Richmond, Ky., 1967—. Sec., Ky. Commn. United Ministries in Higher Edn., 1971-72; 2d v.p. Christian Ch. Ky.; ch. sch. curriculum writer. Youth chmn. Lexington-Fayette County Council on Family Relations. Bd. dirs. Richmond Opportunity for Wider Tutorial Help, Open Concern, Community Center. Mem. Madison County Assn. for Retarded Children (dir.), Pi Tau Chi. Kiwanian. Home: Route 8 Box 110 Old Irving Rd Richmond KY 40475 Office: First Christian Ch Main at Lancaster Richmond KY 40475

SCOTT, DOROTHY CARTER, ednl. counselor; b. Mansfield, La., July 19, 1948; d. James and Rever Mae (West) Carter; B.S., Southern U., 1970, M.Ed., 1972; Ed.S., U. Southwest La., 1976; m. Wilfred James Scott, Dec. 23, 1972; 1 son, Jon-Stephen Carter. Tchr. lang. arts Franklin (La.) Jr. High Sch., 1970-72, Morgan City (La.) Jr. High Sch., 1972-74; tchr. English and guidance counselor Carencro High Sch., Lafayette, La., 1974-76, guidance counselor, 1976—; workshop cons. Bur. Student Services, La. Dept. Edn.; lectr. various orgns. Vol. worker ARC, Lafayette. Mem. NEA, La. Personnel and Guidance Assn., Am. Personnel and Guidance Assn., Am. Sch. Counselors Assn., La. Counselors Assn. (treas. 1978-79), La. Assn. Edn. (del. 1978, 79), Lafayette Parish Counselors Assn. (sec. 1977-78), Lafayette Assn. Educators (exec. council, lobbyist 1980—), Acadiana Guidance Assn., Alpha Kappa Alpha (fundraising chmn. Eta Omega chpt. 1978-79, publicity chmn. 1978-80), Phi Lambda Pi. Democrat. Roman Catholic. Author articles on counseling. Home: 128 Carolyn Dr Lafayette LA 70508 Office: Route 2 Box 55-C-2 Lafayette LA 70507

SCOTT, ELIZABETH SPENCER, high sch. counselor; b. Guerrant, Ky., May 6, 1923; d. A.H. and May B. Spencer; B.A. in Edn., U. Ky., Lexington, 1961, M.A. in Guidance and Counseling, 1963; m. Frank L. Scott; 1 son, Fletcher L. Tchr., Paris (Ky.) city schs., 1957-62, high sch. counselor, 1962—. Mem. Ky., Central Ky. personnel and guidance assns., Ky. Sch. Counselors Assn., Ky., Paris edn. assns., Alpha Delta Kappa, Kappa Delta Pi. Home: 1427 Cypress St Paris KY 40361 Office: 7th St Paris KY 40561

SCOTT, ELLIS LAVERNE, educator; b. Casey, Iowa, June 11, 1915; s. Alexander Catell and Cora (Tilman) S.; B.S. in Edn. summa cum laude, Ohio State U., 1947, Ph.D. in Sociology, 1953; m. Florence Louise Green, Sept. 7, 1950; children—Susan Eileen, Katherine Ellen, Robert Tilman. Teaching asst., research asso. Ohio State U., 1946-53; asst. prof. U. N.Mex., 1953-56; asso. social scientist Rand Corp., 1957; human factors scientist System Devel. Corp., 1957-64; prof. mgmt. U. Ga., Athens, 1964—. Pres., Center for Study of Automation and Soc., 1969-73; chmn. com on social implications of automation Internat. Fedn. of Automatic Control, 1972; chmn. automation com. Am. Automatic Control Council, 1970-71, 74—, vice chmn., 1972-74; mem. Ga. Gov.'s Sci. Adv. Council, 1972-75; mem. sci. and mgmt. adv. com. U.S. Army Computer Systems Command, 1972-74; participant numerous sci. cons. Pres. Beechwood Hills Community Assn., 1971-72. Served with AUS, 1942-46. Mem. Am. Sociol. Assn. (chmn. sect. applied sociology), Am. Acad. Mgmt., So. Mgmt. Assn., World Future Soc., Phi Kappa Phi, Delta Chi, Sigma Iota Epsilon, Beta Gamma Sigma, Alpha Kappa Delta. Co-editor: EDP Systems for Public Management, 1968; Automation and Society, 1969; Automation Management, 1970. Contbr. numerous articles to profl. jours. Home: 124 Colonial Dr Athens GA 30601

SCOTT, GEORGE GALLMANN, public acct.; b. Hattiesburg, Miss., July 8, 1928; s. John Havers and Rebecca Evelyn (Gallmann) S.; B.S., Millsaps Coll., 1949; m. Patsy T. Womack, June 27, 1953; 1 son, George Gallmann. Clk., Spanish Trail Transport, Mobile, Ala., 1949-50, asst. auditor, 1953-55; bookkeeper Met. Engraving & Electrotype Co., Richmond, Va., 1952-53; chief clk. Central Truck Lines of Tampa, Fla., Mobile, 1955-56; gen. auditor M.R.&R. Trucking Co., Crestview, Fla., 1956-66, sec.-treas., 1967-77; public acct. enrolled to represent taxpayers before IRS, 1977—. Mem. data processing adv. com. Okaloosa-Walton Jr. Coll., Niceville, Fla., 1965-66, 72-73; mem. Okaloosa County Gen. Advisory Com. for Devel. Vocat. Edn., 1973, 79. Served with U.S. Army, 1950-52. Mem. Am. Trucking Assn. (nat. acctg. and fin. council 1956-77), Southeastern Acctg. and Fin. Council (dir. 1974-77), Greater Crestview C. of C. (chmn. bus. ethics com. 1973-74), Fla. Accts. Assn. (gov. 1979-80, pres. N.W. Fla. chpt. 1979-80), Pi Kappa Alpha. Methodist (choir dir. 1966—, chmn. ofcl. bd. 1971-73, chmn. fin. com. 1974-75, chmn. audit com. 1977—). Kiwanian. Home: 244 Seminole Trail NW Crestview FL 32536

SCOTT, HAROLD GEORGE, med. entomologist; b. Williams, Ariz., Aug. 20, 1925; s. Milton Raymond and Lucile Crosby S.; B.S., U. N.Mex., 1950, M.S., 1953, Ph.D., 1957; m. Bettie T. Scott, Aug. 6, 1948; children—Jasmine, Lorelei, Rodger, Clifford, Curtis, Conrad, Dolores. Commd. 1st lt. USPHS, 1955, advanced through grades to col., 1968—; ret., 1972; prof. tropical medicine Tulane U., 1971-76, lectr. community medicine, 1958—; cons. scientist, New Orleans, 1976—. Served with U.S. Army, 1943-51, USAF, 1951-55. Mem. Soc. Systematic Zoology, Entomol. Soc. Am., Ret. Officers Assn., Commd. Officers Assn. USPHS, Assn. Mil. Surgeons U.S., Sigma Xi, Delta Omega. Author books in field. Cons. editor Jour. Environ. Health, 1963—. Home: 8137 River Rd Waggaman LA 70094 Office: Box 4243 New Orleans LA 70178

SCOTT, HERBERT ANDREW, chem. engr.; b. Marion, Va., Mar. 29, 1924; s. Charles W. and Carolyn Enid (Snyder) S.; B.S., Va. Poly. Inst., 1944, M.S., 1947; m. Sarah Oneida Covington, Oct. 18, 1947; children—Mark Andrew, Paul Ethan. Chem. engr. Tenn. Eastman Co., Kingsport, 1947—, supt. Polymers div., 1964-66; plant mgr. Holston Def. Corp., Kingsport, Tenn., 1967-70; supt. engring. div. Tenn. Eastman Co., Kingsport, 1971—. Commr., Bays Mountain Nature Interpretive Park, Kingsport, 1971—. Served with AUS, 1944-46. Mem. Am. Inst. Chem. Engrs., Am. Mgmt. Assn., Nat. Soc. Profl. Engrs., Sigma Xi. Lutheran. Clubs: Kiwanis, Elks, Moose. Home: 4512 Chickasaw Rd Kingsport TN 37664 Office: Tenn Eastman Co PO Box 511 Kingsport TN 37664

SCOTT, HUGH LENOX, II, furniture conservator; b. Fort Leavenworth, Kans., June 2, 1909; s. David Hunter and Marguerite (McLellan) S.; B.A., Rice U., 1934; m. Celeste McAshan, Dec. 19, 1953; 1 son, Hugh Lenox III. With United Gas Co., various locations, 1934-46; oil operator Houston Drilling, Tex. and La., 1955-64; owner Regent's, 1955-64; asso. dir. Rice U. Alumni Assn., Houston, 1964-66; cabinetmaker, conservator, lectr. appraiser antique furniture, Houston, 1940—; instr. Houston Community Coll., 1975—. Mem. Am. Soc. Appraisers (sr.). Home: 401 Emerson St Houston TX 77006

SCOTT, JACK CRANSTON, controller; b. Jasper, Tex., Jan. 27, 1935; s. Euel C. and Mozel (Watkins) S.; B.B.A., Lamar Coll., 1963; m. Evelyn L. Vaughan, June 16, 1953; children—Patricia Gail Scott Boggs, Brenda Kay Scott Schwarz. IBM dept. operator Stedman Co., Beaumont, Tex., 1952-53; cost accountant Oil City Brass Works, Beaumont, 1960-62; sec.-treas., dir. L.C. Russell Co., Beaumont, 1962—; dir. Russco Paint Mfg. Co., Beaumont; chmn. bd., pres. Sabine Steel & Construction Co., Inc., Internat. Tank Co., Inc., 1968—, Capacity of Tex. Inc., 1977—; dir. First Bank & Trust. Served with U.S. Army, 1953-57. Mem. C. of C. Home: 5885 Pinkstaff St Beaumont TX 77706 Office: Hwy 365 Fannett TX 77705

SCOTT, JACK LEWIS, architect, engr.; b. Oklahoma City, Oct. 20, 1921; s. Lewis Henry and Iza Evelyn (Thompson) S.; B.S., Okla. State U., 1948; m. Betty Doreen Page, July 9, 1945 (div. 1965); children—John Lewis, Dorothy Jane; m. 2d, Donna Maude Ogden, Aug. 19, 1966; 1 son, Jeremiah Mark. Pres., Empire Builders, 1964; treas. concrete advisory bd. Oklahoma City, 1968-72; mem. Bldg. Code Commn., 1967-73. Pvt. practice architecture, Oklahoma City and Dallas, 1950—; owner Jack L. Scott & Assos., Architects-Engrs.; pres. A.E.C. Internat., Inc., project designers in Iran. Served from pvt. to capt. U.S. Army, 1943-46. Decorated Purple Heart. Mem. A.I.A., Nat. Soc. Profl. Engrs., N.W. C. of C. Oklahoma City (sec. bd. 1957-58), Internat. Assn. Shell Structures, Internat. Assn. Arts and Letters (pres. 1969), Am. Concrete Inst., Ambucs, Kappa Sigma. Mem. Christina Ch. Home: PO Box 442 Route 4 Guthrie OK 73044 Office: 1821 Classen Blvd Oklahoma City OK 73106 also 3131 Stemmons Dallas TX 75247

SCOTT, JAMES LEE, rehab. counselor for deaf; b. Sullivan, Ind., Oct. 3, 1931; s. Charles Cecil and Esther Jaunita (Dix) S.; student Terre Haute Comml. Coll., 1950; A.B., Johnson Bible Coll., 1954; postgrad. U. N.C., 1973, Gallaudet Coll., 1975—; m. Norma Jean Richeson, Sept. 5. 1953; children—Dora Jean, David Wayne, Daniel Lee. Ordained to ministry Ch. of Christ, 1951; minister Pine Grove Ch. of Christ, Bluefield, W. Va., 1954-58; minister, counselor Ardmore Ch. of Christ, Winston-Salem, N.C., also faculty Winston-Salem Bible Coll., 1958-60; minister, counselor to deaf Rich Acres Christian ch., Martinsville, Va., 1960-68; minister, counselor to deaf Alleghany Ch. of Christ, Christiansburg, Va., 1968-72; rehab. counselor for deaf Va. Dept. Vocat. Rehab., Alexandria, Va., 1972—; pub. speaker numerous states; radio-TV programmer, 1958-72. Bd. dirs. Piedmont Christian Service Camp, Patrick Springs Assembly Blue Ridge Youth Camp, 1958-72; founder, dir. Rich Acres Inst.; dir. Cap-Tel Gallaudet Coll., 1970-74, Va. Poly. Inst. and State U.; 2d v.p. Va. Registry of Interpreters for Deaf, 1974-76, 1st v.p., 1977-78. Bd. trustees Winston-Salem Bible Coll., 1960-68; bd. dirs. C.Y. Kim Korean Mission Orphanage, 1970-76; mem. Arlington County Mental Health-Mental Retardation Developmental Planning Council, 1974—. Recipient Am. Legion Citizenship award, 1954. Mem. Nat., Va. (bd. dirs. 1979) rehab. counselor assns., Nat. Rehab. Assn., Am. Deafness and Rehab. Assn., Nat., Va. assns. of deaf, Registry Interpreters for Deaf, No. Va. Speech and Hearing Profls., Internat. Platform Assn. Club: Lions (Alexandria, Va.). Home: 9425 Lee Hwy Fairfax VA 22031 Office: 901 N Washington Alexandria VA 22314

SCOTT, JAMES WALTER, oil co. exec.; b. Bethany, Mo., May 23, 1951; s. Edwin L. and Helena F. (Dowell) S.; A.A., Independence Community Jr. Coll., 1971; B.S., Okla. State U., 1973; m. Carol Lee Jay, July 23, 1977; children—Crystal Alieen, Sharon Elizabeth, Edie Ann. Pvt. piano tuner/technician, Independence, Kans., 1971-73; dist. sales rep. Conoco, Inc., Denver, 1974, acct., Ponca City, Okla., 1974-77, acctg. systems analyst, 1977-79; chmn. bd. K.E.G., Inc., Independence, Kans., 1974-79. Vol., Helpline, Ponca City, 1978-79; chmn. adv. com. Coveil Homer E Barkley chpt. Order of DeMolay, 1979. Mem. Beta Alpha Psi, Delta Psi Omega. Democrat. Methodist. Clubs: Toastmasters, Masons (32 deg.), K.T. Office: 1000 S Pine St Ponca City OK 74601

SCOTT, JERRY, judge; b. Nashville, Nov. 11, 1941; B.S., Austin Peay State U., 1962; J.D., Vanderbilt U., 1965; m. Ann Kathryn Brian, Apr. 21, 1974; 1 dau., Susan. Admitted to Tenn. bar, 1965, practiced in Waynesboro, 1968-73; mem. firm Keaton, Haggard, Turner and Scott, 1968-73; judge 11th Jud. Circuit, Waynesboro, 1973-79, Tenn. Ct. Criminal Appeals, 1979—; instr. Columbia (Tenn.) State Community Coll., 1970—, trustee Found., 1971-77. Wayne County campaign mgr. for U.S. Senator. Served to capt. Judge Adv. Gen. Dept., USAF, 1965-68; maj. Res. Mem. Am., Fed., Tenn., Decatur-Hickman-Lewis-Perry-Wayne Counties (v.p. 1969-70, sec. treas. 1970-72) bar assns., Tenn. Jud. Conf. (sec. 1976-77), Tenn. (v.p. 1972-73), Waynesboro (treas. 1969-70, pres. 1970-71, Distinguished Service award 1971, 72) jaycees, Am. Judges Assn. Am. Judicature Soc., Christian Legal Soc. Baptist. Moose, Lion (pres. 1971-72). Home and office: PO Box 431 Waynesboro TN 38485

SCOTT, JERRY DEAMUS, educator; b. Greeneville, Tenn., June 20, 1936; s. Deamus Elmus and Della Sue (Campbell) S.; B.S., U. Tenn., 1958, M.S. (Ednl. Profl. Devel. fellow 1974-75), 1975, Ed.D., 1977; M.Ed. (Experienced Tchr. fellow 1969-70), Miss. State U., 1970; m. Wilma Lee Clouse, Feb. 9, 1962; children—Eric, Karla, Stephanie, Celesta. Tchr. vocat. agr. Greene County schs., Greeneville, 1961-69; curriculum cons. Ga. Dept. Edn., 1970-72; dir. vocat. edn. Unico. County Schs., Erwin, Tenn., 1972-74, Oak Ridge City Schs., 1975—; cons. in field. Served with AUS, 1958-60. Mem. NEA, Nat. Council Local Adminstrs., Am. Soc. Curriculum Devel., Am. Vocat. Assn., Tenn. Edn. Assn., Tenn. Vocat. Agr. Tchrs. Assn., Tenn. Council Local Dirs. Vocat.-Tech. Edn., Tenn. Soc. Curriculum Devel., E. Tenn. Edn. Assn., Oak Ridge Edn. Assn., Am. Soc. Tng. and Devel., Phi Kappa Phi, Phi Delta Kappa, Omicron Tau Theta, Iota Lambda Sigma. Baptist. Club: Century Lions (sec. 1978-79, v.p. 1979-80, pres. 1980-81) (Oak Ridge). Home: 7801 Cranley Rd Powell TN 37849 Office: Oak Ridge City Schs Providence Rd Oak Ridge TN 37830

SCOTT, JESSE HOBSON, JR., paper mill exec.; b. Franklin, Va., Aug. 30, 1939; s. Jesse H. and Dorothy (Hunnings) S.; B.S., N.C. State U., 1960; m. Nancy Fisher, Nov. 23, 1974; children by previous marriage—Jesse Hobson, Chris E.; stepchildren—Penny Sue, Pamela Ann. With Mead Corp., Chillicothe, Ohio, 1960-64; paper mill supt. Remis Co., Inc., Peoria, Ill., 1964-67; asst. to prodn. mgr. Southland Paper Mills, Inc., 1967-74; cons. staff engr. Ford Bacon Davis, Monroe, La., 1979—. Served with U.S. Army to 1st lt., 1960-62. Mem. TAPPI, La. Engring. Soc. Contbr. articles to profl. jours. Home: 809 Erin St Monroe LA 71201 Office: PO Box 1762 Monroe LA 71201

SCOTT, JIMMIE DOW, health facility mgmt. exec.; b. Milo, Okla., Jan. 1, 1930; s. Preston William and Elnora Mae (Hancock) S.; B. Liberal Studies, U. Okla., 1974, M.P.A., 1976; m. Wanda Mae Tippit, Oct. 5, 1952; children—Jimmie Dow, Dwain Dawson. Seaman recruit U.S. Navy, 1948, advanced through grades to lt. comdr., 1968; asst. adminstr. patient affairs, security and edn. U.S. Naval Hosp., Pensacola, Fla., 1959-63; asst. adminstr. Yokosuka (Japan) Naval Hosp., 1963-67; chief patient relations br. Bur. Medicine and Surgery, Washington, 1967-71; ret., 1971; exec. asst. for adminstrn. Univ. Hosp. and Clinics, Oklahoma City, 1975—; Mem. Am. Acad. Med. Adminstrs., Am. Soc. Public Adminstrs., Acad. Polit. Sci., Am. Acad. Polit. and Social Sci. Republican. Baptist. Home: 2107 Fox Ave Moore OK 73160 Office: 800 NE 13th St Univ Hosp and Clinics Oklahoma City OK 73125

SCOTT, JOHN EDWARD, librarian; b. Washington, Ga., Aug. 12, 1920; s. John Edward and Martha Heard (Williams) S.; A.B., Morehouse Coll., 1948; B.S. in L.S., Atlanta U., 1949; M.S. in L.S., U. Ill., 1955; m. Dorris Louise, Webb, Jan. 28, 1948; children—Patricia Louise, Clifford Allen, Martha Ellen. Librarian, Kans. Tech. Inst., Topeka, 1949-55; circulation librarian Va. State Coll., Petersburg, 1955-56; asst. reference librarian U. Kans., 1956-57; head librarian W.Va. State Coll., Institute, 1957-74, dir. library resources, 1974—. Served with USNR, 1942-46. Mem. Am. (councilor), W.Va. (chmn. coll. library sect. 1958-60, pres. 1961-62, fed. relations coordinator 1962-64), Southeastern library assns., Assn. Coll. and Research Libraries (chmn. coll. libraries sect. 1969-70), AAUP, NEA, W.Va. Edn. Assn., Kappa Delta Pi, Beta Phi Mu, Alpha Phi Alpha. Home: PO Box 303 Institute WV 25112

SCOTT, KENNETH MUNRO, physician; b. Tsingtao, China, Mar. 22, 1916; s. Charles Ernest and Clara Emily (Heywood) S.; A.B., Davidson Coll., 1937; M.D., U. Pa. Sch. Medicine, 1941; m. Anna Marion Bicksler, July 11, 1942; children—Kenneth Munro, Charles Francis, Elisabeth Alden. Intern, Presbyn. Hosp., Phila., 1941-42; resident Grad. Hosp. U. Pa., Phila., 1947-49, Episcopal Hosp., Phila., 1949-50; supt., chief of surgery Presbyn. Hosp., Taegu, Korea, 1952-57; prof. surgery Yonsei U. Coll. Medicine, Seoul, Korea, 1958-63; dir. Korea Church World Service Tuberculosis Control Project, 1960-63; dir. Christian Med. Coll. and Hosp., Ludhiana, Punjab, India, 1963-74; staff physician Western N.C. Hosp., Black Mountain, N.C., 1974-80; med. dir. Highland Farms Health Care Center, Black Mountain, N.C., 1977—; mem. adv. med. com. State N.C. Indsl. Commn., 1975-80, Tb control officer, 1980—. Served with MC U.S. Army, 1942-46. Recipient Algernon Sidney Sullivan award, 1937. Diplomate Am. Bd. Surgery. Fellow Am. Coll. Surgeons; mem. Christian Med. Soc., Phi Beta Kappa. Presbyn. Rotarian. Home: 542 Warren Wilson Rd Swannanoa NC 28778 Office: Div Health Services Tb Control Unit Black Mountain NC 28711

SCOTT, LEE ALLEN, employee benefit cons.; b. Daniels, W.Va., Oct. 28, 1940; s. Minor Lee and Margaret Allen (Kay) S.; B.S. in Bus.Adminstrn., U. W.Va., 1962; M.B.A., U. Ky., 1967; m. Myrah Lou Erickson, July 15, 1962; children—Elizabeth Ashley, Stephanie Erickson, Lee Allen. Mgmt. trainee Gen. Telephone & Electronics, Lexington, Ky., 1965-66; regional group mgr. Prudential Ins. Co., Louisville, 1967-72, Cleve., 1972-76; ins. cons., pres. Scott & Assos., Inc., Parkersburg, W.Va., 1976—. Bd. dirs. YMCA, Parkersburg, 1979-80, Wood County Devel. Authority, 1980-83, United Fund, 1980-82. Served with U.S. Army, 1963-65. Decorated Army Commendation medal. CLU. Mem. Estate Planning Council, Am. Soc. CLU (continuing edn. chmn. Mid-Ohio Valley chpt. 1979-80), Nat. Assn. Life Underwriters, Am. Mgmt. Assn., Internat. Assn. Fin. Planners, Health Ins. Assn. Am. (chmn. W.Va healthcare com. 1979-80), C. of C. Methodist. Clubs: Parkersburg Country, Glade Springs Country, Elks. Home: 141 N Hills Dr Parkersburg WV 26101 Office: 410 1/2 Market St Parkersburg WV 26101

SCOTT, LEONARD WAYNE, lawyer, educator, writer; b. San Marcos, Tex., Nov. 12, 1938; s. Leonard Walter and Bonnie (Hinkle) S.; B.A., S.W. Tex. State Coll., 1961; J.D., U. Tex., 1962; M.A., Baylor U., 1971; postgrad. N.Y. U., summers 1972-74; m. Patricia Louise Pond, Aug. 27, 1960 (died Oct. 9, 1977); children—Kelly Lynn, Leonard Wade, Bradford Glenn. Admitted to Tex. bar, 1962; briefing atty. Ct. Criminal Appeals Tex., Austin, 1962-63, Supreme Ct. Tex., 1963-64; asso. mem. firm Sheehy, Cureton, Westbrook, Lovelace & Nielsen, Waco, Tex., 1964-69, partner, 1969-71; lectr. Sch. Law, Baylor U., Waco, 1968-71; asso. prof. law St. Mary's U., San Antonio, 1971-77, prof. law, 1977—; alternate U.S. commr. Waco div. U.S. Dist. Ct. for Western Tex., 1967-71. Bd. dirs. Campfire Girls, Waco. Mem. Waco-McLennan County (dir., v.p.), Tex. (mem. 11th dist. grievance com. 1969-71, mem. local bar services com.), Am. (publs. vice chmn., ins., negligance and compensation sect., vice chmn. legal edn. gen. practice sect.), Fed. bar assns., Am. Judicature Soc., Tex. Criminal Def. Attys. Assn. (charter mem.), Am. Assn. Criminal Def. Attys. Co-editor Tex. Lawyers' Weekly Letter, 1971—. Home: 1016 Mt Rainier St San Antonio TX 78213

SCOTT, LINDA, radio sta. exec.: b. Cleve., May 19, 1943; d. Roy and Sylvia B. (Brondfield) S.; student Ohio State U., 1961-62, Cooper Sch. Art, 1964, Cleve. Inst., Art, 1965. Adminstrv. asst. Alcan Aluminum Corp., Cleve., 1965-69; promotion dir. Sta. WERE, Cleve., 1969; promotion, publicity dir. Stas. WIXY/WDOK, Cleve., 1969-71; on-air-promotion supr., producer Sta. WKYC-TV, Cleve., 1971-72; acct. exec. Sta. WMYQ-FM, Miami, Fla., 1972-73, Sta. WIOD-AM, Miami, 1973-74; acct. exec. Sta. WLYF-FM, Miami, 1974-78, sales mgr., 1978—. Office: WLYF-FM 710 Brickell Ave Miami FL 33131

SCOTT, MARY ELOIS, educator; b. Faxon, Okla., Nov. 23, 1916; d. Claude Andrew and Nettie Lavinia (Park) Woods; B.S., SW Tex. U., 1952, M.Ed., 1960; m. Rush Norris Ewing, 1936 (div. 1961); children—Andrew Norris Ewing, Mary Jane Ewing Farmer, Ralph Woods Ewing, Charles Burgess Ewing; m. 2d, Russell Everett Scott, 1962 (dec. 1968). Spl. edn. tchr. San Marcos (Tex.) Ind. Sch. Dist., 1955-60, Midland (Tex.) Ind. Sch. Dist., 1961-68; resource tchr. Trinity Episcopal Sch., Midland, Tex., 1968-72, Freeman Elementary Sch., Garland (Tex.) Ind. Sch. Dist., 1973—. Active San Marcos Lung Assn., 1954-60, Mental Health-Mental Retardation Center, Midland, 1969-72. Mem. Tex. Assn. Tchrs., NEA, Garland Ednl. Assn., Garland Assn. for Retarded Citizens, Tex. Assn. for Children with Learning Disabilities, Alpha Chi, Kappa Delta Pi. Mem. Christian Ch. Club: Sons of Hermann (San Antonio). Contbr. articles to profl. jours. Home: 1839 Glenbrook Dr Apt 11 Garland TX 75040 Office: Freeman Elementary School 1220 W Walnut St Garland TX 75040

SCOTT, MYRON STOCKBRIDGE, accountant; b. Lake Charles, La., Nov. 8, 1952; s. Everett Rayburn and Zilpan (Connella) S.; student La. Tech. U., 1970-73, McNeese State U., 1973; B.S., La. State U., 1975; m. Rebecca Jane Eagle, Nov. 25, 1977; 1 dau., Chavanne. Accounts receivable clk. Our Lady of Lake Hosp., Baton Rouge, La., 1974; field auditor La. Legis. Auditor's staff, Baton Rouge, 1975; staff acct. Hollins & Comeaux, C.P.A.'s, Lake Charles, La., 1975-77; asst. treas. La. Savs. Assn., Lake Charles, 1977—; v.p., treas. Iris Realty Inc., Lake Charles, 1978—; tchr. Inst. Fin. Edn., 1977-78. Treas. Calcasieu Parish Com. to elect Bubba Henry Gov. La., 1980. Recipient Scholarship, La. Tech. U., 1970, Service award Jr. Achievement, 1979, Service award, Boys Clubs Greater Lake Charles, 1977. C.P.A., La. Mem. Am. Inst. C.P.A.'s, Soc. La. C.P.A.'s, Soc. S.W. La. C.P.A.'s, La. C.P.A. Polit. Action Com., La. State U. Alumni Assn., Sigma Alpha Epsilon Alumni Assn. Republican. Presbyterian. Club: Kiwanis (treas., 1978, Service award 1978) (Lake Charles, La.). Home: 916 9th St Lake Charles LA 70601 Office: PO Box 1448 Lake Charles LA 70602

SCOTT, NAUMAN S., fed. judge; b. New Roads, La., June 15, 1916; s. Nauman Steele and Sidonie (Provosty) S.; B.A., Amherst Coll., 1938; LL.B., Tulane U., 1941; m. Blanche Hammond, Jan. 8, 1942; children—Ashley Scott Smith, Nauman S., III, John W., Arthur Hammond. Admitted to La. bar, 1942; practiced law, Alexandria, 1942-70; chief judge U.S. Dist. Ct. for La. Western Dist., 1970—; mem. Jud. Council La. Supreme Ct., 1961-70. Chmn. United Fund, Alexandria, ARC, Alexandria; bd. dirs. La. Assn. Mental Health, Vocat. and Rehab. Center, YMCA, YWCA. Mem. Alexandria (pres. 1965-66), La. State, Am. bar assns., Alexandria C. of C., Young Men's Bus. Assn. Roman Catholic. Club: Kiwanis. Office: US Dist Ct PO Box 312 Alexandria LA 71301*

SCOTT, NORMA LINN (MRS. JOHN MITCHELL SCOTT), ret. educator, club woman; b. Wharton, Tex., Oct. 13, 1894; d. John Edward and Elizabeth Frances (Bolton) Linn; student Hollins Coll., 1913-14; B.S. in Edn., U. Tex., 1943, M.A., 1949; m. John Mitchell Scott, July 22, 1914; children—John Linn, Norma Elizabeth (Mrs. John R. Johnson), Lawrence Evans, Virginia Randolph (Mrs. N.B. Dismukes), Patricia Ruth (Mrs. Louis Meade Burton). Tchr. history, govt. and English in high schs. of Tex., 1918-65; with McCallum High Sch. Austin, until 1965, now ret.; asst. dept. govt. U. Tex., 1946-49; prin. Mullin (Tex.) High Sch., 1925-33, Buffalo (Tex.) High Sch., 1945-47. Leon County chmn. Jr. Red Cross, 1943-47; chmn. Buffalo (Tex.) chpt. A.R.C., 1945-46; v.p. YWCA, Austin, 1968-70, pres., 1970-72; active Infantile Paralysis, War Bond, United Fund, Community Chest drives; active Capital Area chpt. Am. Diabetes Assn.; mem. Travis County and Austin Community Council; mem. Bicentennial Com. Historic Preservation and Hist. Publs.; tchr. Sunday sch. Tarrytown Bapt. Ch. Recipient Kellog Found. scholarship U. Tex., 1944. Mem. A.A.U.W. (br. parliamentarian 1960—; pres. Austin 1962-64), Austin Classroom Tchrs. Assn. (pres. 1958-60), Heritage Soc. Austin, Tex. Geneal. Soc., U.D.C. (state pres. 1968-70, 70-72, chmn. Norma Linn Scott scholarship 1961-75), Tex. Tchrs. Assn. (pres. English sect. dist. X 1956—, mem. ho. dels. 1956—), Austin Ret. Tchrs. Assn., Daus. Republic Tex. (pres. 1975-77), Delta Kappa Gamma (pres. local chpt.), Alpha Epsilon, Gamma Psi. Baptist. Club: Austin Women's (exec. council). Home: 3001 Beverly Rd Austin TX 78703

SCOTT, PHILIP LAWLER, JR., architect; b. San Antonio, Dec. 21, 1948; s. Philip Lawler and Alyce Virginia (Lay) S.; B.Arch., Tex. Tech. U., 1973; m. Janice Elaine Alder, May 21, 1971; 1 dau., Rachel Susan. Designer, Brasher, Goyette & Rapier, Lubbock, Tex., 1971-74, dir. design br. office, Austin, Tex., 1974-77; dir. mktg. Holt & Fatter, Inc., Austin, 1977-78; v.p. mktg. and bus. devel. Holt, Fatter & Scott, Inc., Austin, 1978—, also dir. Registered architect, Tex. Mem. AIA, Tex. Soc. Architects (mem. architecture for justice com.), Profl. Services Mgmt. Assn., Soc. for Mktg. Profl. Services, Am. Mgmt. Assn., Am. Arbitration Assn. Office: 2525 Wallingwood Suite 501 Austin TX 78746

SCOTT, RANDALL LEE, furniture rental co. exec.; b. San Angelo, Tex., Jan. 5, 1952; s. Bob F. and Dorothe (Mann) S.; student N. Tex. State U., 1970-71, Tex. Christian U , 1971-74, Tex., U. 1974-77; m. Colon Elizabeth Smith, Mar. 1, 1980. With Finger Furniture Rental Co. of Dallas, Inc., 1976—, mgr., Ft. Worth, 1976—. Recipient Outstanding Service award, Apt. Assn. of Tarrant County, 1978. Mem. Apt. Assn. Tarrant County (dir. 1977—, 2d v.p. 1979—, product ser. chmn. 1979—), Tex. Apt. Assn. (dir. 1978—), Sales and Mktg. Execs. of Ft. Worth (Victor trophy 1980), Republican. Baptist. Club: Lions. Home: 2528 Ridgmar Blvd Fort Worth TX 76116 Office: 7917 Weatherford Hwy Fort Worth TX 76116

SCOTT, ROBERT CHARLES, educator; b. Wolf Lake, Ind., July 23, 1935; s. Robert Hudson and Madeline (Fowler) S.; Mus.B. Edn., Knox Coll., i957; M.A., Tex. A. and I. U., 1963; D.M.A., U. Tex., 1973; m. Patricia Darlene Long, June 6, 1959; children—Martin Leo, Michael Lee. Mem. St. Louis Municipal Opera, 1955; tchr. pub. schs., Salem, Ark., 1957-58, Port Aransas, Tex., 1958-60; chmn. dept. music Tex. A. and I. U., Kingsville, 1960—, asso. prof., 1975—, dir. univ. opera workshop, 1960—, research grantee. 1975. Recitalist, 1960—; clinician area high sch. music activities, 1960—; judge Mid-west Met. Opera Auditions, Tulsa, 1973; mus. dir. Corpus Christi Little Theater, 1972—. Festival dir. Kingsville Bi-Centennial Com., 1974—. Served to 1st lt., AUS, 1958-60. Mem. Central Opera Assn.. Tex. Choral Dirs. Assn., Actors Equity, Paton, Phi Mu Alpha, Kappa Kappa Psi, Delta Omicron. Presbyn. Condr.. dir. Tex. opera premieres Help, Help, The Globolinks (Menotti), 1970; The Good Soldier Schweik (Kurka), 1972. Home: 500 College Pl Kingsville TX 78363

SCOTT, ROBERT HUNTER, JR., wire rope co. exec.; b. Hackensack, N.J., Oct. 12, 1940; s. Robert Hunter and Peronne (Whitaker) S.; B.S. in Fin., U. Houston, 1977; m. Sally Sullivan, June 14, 1963; children—Sheryl, Bonny, Kimberly. Acct., Fairbanks, Morse & Co., Fairlawn, N.J., 1963-65; plant controller Gen. Cable Corp., Hackensack, N.J., 1965-68; police officer Pike County (Pa.) Sheriffs Office, 1968-75; sec.-treas. Gulf Coast Wire Rope, Inc., Pasadena, Tex., 1975—, also dir. Served with U.S. Army, 1959-62. Mem. Am. Mgmt. Assn. Club: Rotary. Home: 4522 Ponca St Pasadena TX 77504 Office: PO Box 1111 Pasadena TX 77501

SCOTT, ROBERT LEE, ednl. adminstr.; b. Richland County, S.C., Oct. 22, 1935; s. Charlie L. and Mary A. (Sinkler) S.; grad. Blayton's Bus. Coll., 1955; B.S., Benedict Coll., 1969; M.B.A. (scholar 1969-70), Atlanta U., 1970; Ed.D., U. S.C., 1980; m. Juanita Simons, Aug. 22, 1959; children—Robert Vincent, Felicia Cassandra, Julian Constinee. Phys. clk., counselor YMCA, Atlanta, 1954-58; personnel clk. U.S. Army, Ft. Belvoir, Va., 1959-61; phys. clk., counselor YMCA, Atlanta, 1961-62, process controller on adminstrv. staff Allied Chem., Irmo, S.C., 1962-66; dir. personnel and purchasing Benedict Coll., Columbia, S.C., 1969-70, adminstrv. asst. to pres., dir. personnel, 1970—, dir. safety and security, affirmative action officer, 1972—. Agy. co-chmn. Lexington-Richland United Way, 1973-76; chmn. bd. trustees Meth. Episcopal Zion (African) Ch., 1974—; pres., founder Benedict Coll. Fed. Credit Union, 1974--; del. Richland County Dem. Conv., 1975. Mem. Nat. Coll. and Univ. Personnel Assn. (coll. rep. 1973—), Am. Mktg. Assn., Phi Beta Sigma, Delta Mu Delta.

Democrat. Club: Masons. Home: 2217 Lorick Ave Columbia SC 29203 Office: Harden and Blanding Sts Columbia SC 29204

SCOTT, ROBERT LEE, JR., govt. personnel exec.; b. Marion, S.C., Dec. 15, 1944; s. Robert Lee and Miriam Louise (Ivey) S.; B.S. in Sociology, Va. Commonwealth U., 1970; postgrad. Central Mich. U., Va. State Coll., 1977-80; m. Delores Dean Rich, Sept. 4, 1965; 1 dau., Kimberly Dean. Personnel mgmt. specialist Def. Gen. Supply Center, Dept. Def., Richmond, Va., 1970-77, employee devel. specialist, 1971-77, sr. employee devel. specialist, 1977—. Vol. music dir. Meadowood Ch. of God, Richmond, 1967—; mem. Va. Ch. of God Laymen's Bd., 1974-75; adv., tchr. Richmond Adult Edn. Program. Served with U.S. Army, 1965-67; Vietnam. Named An Outstanding Young Man in Am., U.S. C. of C., 1974; recipient Outstanding Performance Rating, Def. Gen. Supply Center, 1976, cert. achievement, 1975, Commendable Service cert., 1972. Mem. Am. Soc. Tng. and Devel., Bellwood Mgmt. Assn. Home: 3909 Grizzard Dr Chesterfield VA 23832 Office: Office Civilian Personnel Def Gen Supply Center Richmond VA 23297

SCOTT, RONALD CHARLES, lawyer; b. Greenville, S.C., Jan. 8, 1948; s. Robert Claude, Jr. and Louise Helen (Tinsley) S.; B.B.A. (Univ. scholar), The Citadel, 1970; M.B.A. (Univ. fellow), U. S.C., 1972, J.D., 1976, M.Accounting, 1976; m. Debra Whaley, Aug. 11, 1973. Dir. legal residency U. S.C., Columbia, 1971-73; admitted to S.C. bar, 1976, U.S. Tax Ct. bar, 1977; pres. R.C. Scott and Assos., real estate devel., Columbia, 1974—; dir. research and adminstrn. S.C. Senate, Columbia, 1975-76; partner firm Scott & Matthews, P.A., Columbia, 1976—; lectr., instr. tax law U. S.C., 1976—; cons. Master Planning, Ltd., 1976—. Vol. fin. com. Nat. Democratic party; active Am. Cancer Soc., ARC, Easter Seal Soc., Heart Assn. S.C., Muscular Dystrophy Assn., United Way Midlands. Served to capt. U.S. Army, 1973. Mem. Am., S.C., Richland County bar assns., S.C. Bd. Realtors, Assn. Citadel Men, Am. Mgmt. Assn., S.C. Lawyer Referral Assn., Assn. U. S.C. Alumni, Assn. M.B.A. Alumni, Pi Sigma Epsilon. Clubs: Palmetto, Quail Racquet and Swim, Summit. Home: 4846 Quail Ln Columbia SC 29206 Office: 903 Calhoun St Columbia SC 29201

SCOTT, ROYCE MURLYN, chem. engr.; b. Cape Girardeau, Mo., Oct. 5, 1936; s. Royce Murlyn and Polly (Fink) S.; B.S. in Chem. Engring., U. Mo. at Rolla, 1958; m. Suzanne Rommelman, June 28, 1958; children—Deborah Suzanne, Kevin Robert. With Monsanto Co., 1958—, asst. engr. Sauget, Ill., 1958-59, engr., 1960-61, production supr., 1961-62, sr. engr., 1962-63, engring. supr., 1964-65, St. Louis, 1965-66, engring. specialist St. Louis, 1966-67, plantwide group leader, St. Louis, 1967-68, gen. mfg. supt. Nitro, W.Va., 1968-75, plant mgr., Nitro, 1975—. Served with U.S. Army, 1954-60. Registered profl. engr., Mo. Mem. Am. Inst. Chem. Engrs. Presbyterian. Clubs: Masons. Home: 2320 S Walnut Dr St Albans WV 25177 Office: Monsanto Co Nitro WV 25143

SCOTT, STANLEY TINNIS, appliance distbr.; b. Portsmouth, Ohio, May 2, 1927; s. Edward Dewey and Effie (Edmonson) S.; B.S., Wilmington (Ohio) Coll., 1960; m. Hope Scott; children—Michele Dian, Kevin Alan. With Frigidaire div. Gen. Motors Corp., 1950-71, sales mgr. Frigidaire Sales Corp., Detroit, 1965-68, zone mgr., Houston, 1968-71, Phila., 1971; v.p., gen. mgr. Straus-Frank Co., San Antonio, 1971—. Chmn. Film Industry Com., 1974-80. Served with USNR, 1945-46. Mem. Greater San Antonio C. of C., Gen. Motors Exec. Club (past pres. Houston), San Antonio Advt. Fedn., San Antonio Appliance Assn. Office: 1970 S Alamo St San Antonio TX 78292

SCOTT, SUSAN CARTER, speech pathologist; b. Macon, Ga., Jan. 18, 1954; d. Yancey Franklin III and Jean (Tucker) Carter; B.S., So. Methodist U., 1976, M.S. (Bur. Edn. Handicapped), 1977; m. Michael Devan Scott, June 24, 1978. Speech pathologist Plano (Tex.) Ind. Schs., 1977-79; speech pathologist dept. phys. medicine and rehab. Parkland Meml. Hosp., Dallas, 1979—, also cons. depts. oral surgery and ear, nose and throat; lectr. speech pathology Southwestern Med. Sch. Recipient McCord award for excellence in field of communication disorders, 1976. Cert. tchr., Tex. Mem. Am. Speech and Hearing Assn. (cert. clin. competence), Tex. Speech and Hearing Assn., Tex. Tchrs. Assn., Zeta Phi Eta.

SCOTT, THOMAS BRUCE, drugstore exec.; b. Caldwell, Tex., Nov. 26, 1925; s. Thomas Gilley and Alice (Inez) S.; B.S. in Pharmacy, U. Tex. at Austin, 1949; m. Mildred Louise Dill, Sept. 2, 1950; children—Philip Bruce II, Jon Eric. Owner, Scott Pharmacy. Conroe, Tex., 1951—. Bruce Scott Med. Center, Conroe, 1965—; v.p. Utilities Constrn. Inc., Conroe, 1973—; pres. Bruce Scott Pharmacy Inc., Wharton, Tex., 1957—; dir. Am. Bank. Pres. Montgomery County Am. Cancer Soc.. 1961-62, 63-64; pres. Montgomery County Am. Heart Assn., 1964-65; mem. Montgomery County Airport Bd., 1961-75, chmn., 1972-73; councilman City of Conroe, 1966-69; active United Fund; bd. dirs. YMCA Conroe, 1965, Montgomery County Found. for Performing Arts. Served with USNR, 1944-45. Recipient Man of Yr. award, 1979. Mem. Sam Houston (pres. 1967-68), Tex. pharm. assns., Assn. Ind. Pharmacies (treas. 1972-74), Conroe C. of C. (pres. 1977), Democrat. Methodist (trustee). Mason, Rotarian (pres. Conroe 1978). Clubs: Balladine Dance, Panarama Country (dir. 1976.) Home: 100 W Pauline St Conroe TX 77301 Office: 302 N Main St Conroe TX 77301

SCOTT, THOMAS RYALS, state senator; b. Clopton, Ala., Mar. 3, 1940; s. Angus McCallister and Mavis (Ryals) S.; B.B.A., Ga. State U., 1971; m. Jacqueline Bott, Aug. 30, 1969; children—Susannah Elizabeth, John-Thomas, Christopher Bott. With So. Ry. Systems, Atlanta, 1969—, now systems analyst; mem. Ga. State Senate, 1977—. Served with U.S. Army, 1958-62. Democrat. Baptist. Club: Elks. Office: 125 Spring St Atlanta GA 30303

SCOTT, VERNON PARKINSON, educator; b. Rexburg, Idaho, June 22, 1937; s. George Vernon and Ann Doney (Parkinson) S.; B.S., Brigham Young U., 1963; M.A. in Teaching, Ind. U., 1966; Ph.D., U. Utah, 1975; m. DeeAnne Perry, June 1, 1962; children—DeVern Perry, VerDean Perry, Kanda Perry. Tchr., Bonneville High Sch., Idaho Falls, Idaho, 1961-65; instr. Mesa Coll., Grand Junction, Colo., 1966-71; tchr. earth sci. Madison Jr. High Sch., Rexburg, 1972-78; asst. prof. W. Ga. Coll., Carrollton, 1978—; cons. geology, 1966—. NSF fellow, 65-66. Mem. Geol. Soc. Am., Nat. Assn. Sci. Tchrs., Internat. Solar Energy Soc., Am. Solar Energy Soc., Ga. Solar Energy Assn., Nat. Assn. Geology Tchrs., NEA, AAUP (chpt. pres. 1970-71). Author: Geology Laboratory Manual, 1968; Adaptive Theory-Educational Implications and an Exemplary Earth Science Curriculum, 1975; Idaho Solar Science, 1977. Office: W Ga Coll Carrollton GA 30118

SCOTT, VICTOR PINKSTON, steel co. exec., archtl. engr.; b. Sedalia, Mo., Sept. 30, 1932; s. Victor Estes and Virginia Bernice (Pinkston) S.; m. Dorothy Jean Cook, Aug. 21, 1954; children—Stephanie Ann Scott Bell, Victor Sheldon, Stuart Andrew. Design engr. Macomber, Inc., Canton, Ohio, 1959-64, dir. research and devel., 1964-69; exec. v.p., gen. mgr. Owen Joist Corp., Cayce, S.C., 1969—; exec. v.p. Owen Joist of Fla., Starke. Served with arty. AUS, 1954-56. Mem. Nat. Soc. Profl. Engrs., ASTM, ASCE, Am. Soc. for Metals, Steel Joist Inst. (pres. 1979—), Execs. Club. Home: 100 Loch Dr Columbia SC 29210 Office: 100 Foster PO Box 3 Cayce SC 29033

SCOTT, WALLACE REID, JR., marketing/sales exec.; b. Kansas City, Mo., Mar. 4, 1945; s. Wallace Reid and Rosemary (Shrewsbury) S.; B.S., U. Kans., 1968; M.S., Ga. Tech. U., 1973; M.B.A., Rider Coll., 1976; m. Marguerite Elizabeth Davis, Apr. 1, 1967; 1 dau., Christine Elizabeth. Project mgr. Gen. Physics Corp., Columbia, Md., 1973, mgr. tech. services, 1974; new ventures mgr.-utilities, mgr. spray cooling systems Intersoll Rand Co., Princeton and Phillipsburg, N.J., 1974-76; new products coordinator, dist. sales mgr., product mgr. Keystone Valve, Houston, 1976-80; v.p. sales AMRI Inc., 1980—. Served with USN, 1968-72. Mem. ASME, Am. Mgmt. Assn., Scabbard and Blade, Alpha Kappa Lambda, Sigma Tau. Presbyterian. Author, editor: (with others) Practical Nuclear Power Plant Technology, 1974. Home: 9014 Tami Renee St Houston TX 77040 Office: 9700 W Gulf Bank Houston TX 77040

SCOTT, WILDER PATTILLO, educator; b. Atlanta, Feb. 7, 1935; s. Ralph Wilder and Avis Sophronia (Pattillo) S.; B.A. in Romance Langs., Emory U., 1957, M.A. in Romance Langs., 1958; Ph.D. in Romance Langs., U. Ga., 1968; m. Shelley Mason Woodcock, Aug. 20, 1960; 1 son, Evan Wilder. Asst. prof. fgn. langs. Ga. State U., 1961-64; grad. teaching asst. Romance langs. U. Ga., 1964-67, instr., 1967-68, asst. prof., 1968—, dir. Univ. System of Ga. Study Abroad Program at U. Valencia (Spain), summers 1971, 75, Ibero-Am. U., Mexico City, summer 1977. Served with Adj. Gen. Corps, AUS, 1958-59, Psychol. Warfare, 1962. Mem. Modern Lang. Assn. Am., Southeastern Conf. Latin Am. Studies, Am. Assn. Tchrs. Spanish and Portuguese, Latin Am. Studies Assn., Gridiron Secret Soc., Phi Kappa Phi, Phi Sigma Iota, Kappa Phi Kappa, Pi Delta Phi, Sigma Delta Pi, Chi Phi. Democrat. Methodist. Translator: Mexico in the Theater (Rodolfo Usigli), 1976. Contbr. numerous articles to Romance Notes, South Atlantic Bull. Home: 310 Greencrest Dr Athens GA 30605 Office: Dept Romance Langs U Ga Athens GA 30602

SCOTT, WILLARD PHILIP, lawyer; b. Columbus, Ohio, Jan. 8, 1909; s. Wirt Stanley and Mabel Lynne (Rond) S.; A.B. with honors, Ohio State U., 1930; LL.B (Deans Scholar), Columbia, 1933; m. Lucille Westrom, June 27, 1936; children—Robert W., David W., Anne L. Admitted to N.Y. bar, 1934, D.C. bar, 1934, Okla. bar, 1969; partner Oliver & Donnally, N.Y.C., 1938-66; dir. Am. Potash & Chem. Corp., 1951-70; v.p., 1955-68, vice chmn. bd. dirs., 1968—; v.p., gen. counsel Kerr-McGee Corp., 1968-73, v.p. finance, 1973, sr. v.p., 1973—; counsel for bondholders com. in various railroad reorganizations, 1936-54; gen. counsel Savs. Bank Assn. N.Y.; dir. 1st Nat. Bank & Trust Co. Oklahoma City. Mem. bd. of appeals, 1957-68, mayor, Scarsdale, 1955-57, trustee, 1951-55, police commr., 1953-55, acting mayor, 1953-55. Bd. dirs. Oklahoma City Symphony Soc., Okla. Arts and Sci. Found. Fellow Am. Bar Found., Southwestern Legal Found.; mem. Am. Judicature Soc., Internat. Am. (chmn. sect. corp. banking and bus. law 1960-61, chmn. com. corp. laws 1964-70, editor Bus. Lawyer, 1958-59); N.Y., Okla., D.C. bar assns., Am. Law Inst., Assn. Bar City N.Y., Phi Beta Kappa, Phi Kappa Sigma, Phi Delta Phi, Phi Alpha Theta, Pi Sigma Alpha. Republican. Presbyn. (elder). Clubs: Union League, Madison Square Garden (N.Y.C.); Metropolitan (Washington); Oklahoma City Golf and Country, Whitehall, Beacon (Oklahoma City); Scarsdale Golf. Author: various articles on corporate law. Home: 1812 Drury Ln Oklahoma City OK 73116 Office: Kerr-McGee Center Oklahoma City OK 73102

SCOURTON, LILLIE RENFRO, educator; b. Devers, Tex., Mar. 11, 1924; d. Oliver James and Sisley Ann (Perkins) Renfro; B.A. cum laude, Huston-Tillotson Coll., 1952; student U. So. Calif., 1952, Tex. So. U., 1953, Lamar U., 1964-74, Tex. Women's U., 1967, Sam Houston U., 1971, U. Houston, 1972; M.Ed., U. Tex., 1960; m. Walter Lee Scourton, Sept. 20, 1952; 1 dau., Pamela Gail. Instr. cosmetology and sci. Tex. State Sch. for Blind, Deaf, and Orphans, Austin, 1947-56; tchr. deaf edn. South Park Pub. Schs., Beaumont, Tex., 1957-65, speech pathologist, 1965-70, ednl. diagnostician, 1971, material specialist, 1972-74, supr. spl. edn., 1974—. Chmn., Beaumont Art Mus., 1972; pres. Golden Tiangle Links chpt. Links, Inc., 1975-77, chmn. Western Area, 1979—. Benevolent Trust scholar First Security Nat. Bank, Beaumont, 1964; recipient award United Appeals Campaign Com., 1976. Mem. NEA, Am. Speech and Hearing Assn., Tex. State Tchrs. Assn., Council Exceptional Children, Council Ednl. Diagnostic Services, Council Adminstrs. Spl. Edn., Alpha Kappa Alpha (chpt. v.p. 1950—). Democrat. Methodist. Home: 2320 Cartwright St Beaumont TX 77701 Office: 1025 Woodrow St Beaumont TX 77705

SCRAGG, GEORGE HENRY, JR., aircraft co. exec.; b. Westchester, N.Y., Sept. 13, 1934; s. George Henry and Blanche (Hudson) S.; B.A., Princeton U., 1956; m. Sept., 1960; children—Caroline Eells, Marion Elizabeth, Laura Hudson. Exec. trainee Midland-Ross Corp., 1960-62; with Harris Corp., 1962-76, v.p., gen. mgr. Harris Intertype (Can.) Ltd., Toronto, 1971-73, v.p. sales Sheet Fed. Press div., Cleve., 1973-76; v.p. mktg. Mitsubishi Aircraft Internat. Inc., Dallas, 1976—. Served with USAF, 1956-59. Mem. Quiet Birdmen. Republican. Episcopalian. Clubs: Kirkland Country, Tavern, T Bar M Racquet. Pub., Q B Beam, 1968—. Office: 12700 Park Central Pl Dallas TX 75251

SCRANTOM, ELBERT LIPPIATT, ret. chem. engr., clergyman; b. Rochester, N.Y., May 5, 1916; s. Isaac Elbert and Mattie Mae Archer) S.; A.B., U. Rochester, 1938; LL.B., Am. Extension Sch. of Law, 1952; m. Margaretta Williamson Steele, July 27, 1942; children—Deborah Scrantom Resch, Julie Scrantom Kesterson, Elbert Steele. Chemist Eastman Kodak Co., Rochester, N.Y., 1936-41, 46-49; chem. engr. Tenn. Eastman Co., Kinsport, 1949-60, sr. chem. engr., 1960-76; ret., 1976; ordained to ministry Protestant Episcopal Ch. as deacon, 1969, priest, 1973; priest-in-charge St. Thomas Episcopal Ch., Elizabethton, Tenn., 1974—. Magistrate Sullivan County (Tenn.) Ct., 1966-70; chmn. Sullivan County Republican Orgn., 1957-59. Bd. dirs. Kingsport Mental Health Assn., 1972-75. Served with AUS, 1941-46. Mem. Am. Inst. Chem. Engrs., VFW, Am. Legion (post chaplain 1970-79, dist. chaplain 1975-76, 78—, state chaplain 1976-77, post comdr. 1979-80), Sigma Chi. Moose. Home: 1572 Greefield Ave Kingsport TN 37664 Office: St Thomas' Episcopal Ch PO Box 528 Elizabethton TN 37643

SCRIBNER, LOWELL EDWARD, retail store exec.; b. Chandler, Okla., Feb. 24, 1941; s. Claud Jackson and Neva Pearl (Smith) S.; B.A., Phillips U., 1963. Asst. mgr., then mgr. State Theatres, Inc., Oklahoma City, until 1966; mgr. Halpern's Fabrics, Baton Rouge, and Beaumont, Tex., 1967-68; mgr. Palais Royal, Orange, Tex., 1969—; tchr. Lamar U., Orange, Tex. Mem. mid-mgmt. adv. com. Lamar U.; bd. dirs. Orange Community Players. Recipient certificate of appreciation Home Econs. Coop. Edn. Program, Vidor, Tex., 1973, Orange County Career Edn., 1975; outstanding service award West Orange-Stark High Sch., 1978. Contbr. weekly theatre column to local newspapers. Home: 2541 Calder St Beaumont TX 77702 Office: Palais Royal 2642 W MacArthur Dr Orange TX 77630

SCROGGIN, CHARLES REECE, civil engr.; b. Cin., Dec. 1, 1946; s. Frederick Reece and Marilyn Jane (Wiegman) Scroggin; B.S. in Civil Engring., U. Ky., 1970, M.S. in Civil Engring., 1972; m. Ann Macdonald Stewart, Aug. 22, 1968. Staff engr. Hayes, Seay, Mattern & Mattern Engrs., Roanoke, Va., 1972-73, project engr. G. Reynolds Watkins Cons. Engrs., Inc., Lexington, Ky., 1974-75; v.p. Proctor, Davis, Ray, Cons. Engrs. Inc., Lexington, 1975—; instr. Dale Carnegie course, Lexington, Ky. Recipient U. Ky. Engring. Alumni award. Fed. Water Quality Adminstrn. grantee, 1971-72. Mem. Nat. Soc. Profl. Engrs., Ky. Soc. Profl. Engrs., ASCE, Water Pollution Control Fedn., Nat. Wildlife Fedn., League Ky. Sportsmen, Ky. Colonel, Sigma Alpha Epsilon. Home: 620 Cromwell Way Lexington KY 40503 Office: 210 Malabu Lexington KY 40502

SCROGGINS, DANNY LEE, human relations cons.; b. Atoka, Okla., Dec. 29, 1946; s. George L. and Ella Jane (Green) S.; B.A. in Sociology, Southeastern Okla. State Coll., 1970; postgrad. U. Okla., 1972; M. in Counseling Psychology, Southeastern Okla. State U., 1975; m. Ellen Janyce Barrett, Aug. 20, 1977. Dir. spl. ops. Thompson Communications Co., Atoka, Okla., 1970-73; dir. counseling services Bryan-Atoka Youth Services, Inc., 1973-77; spl. projects coordinator Kay County Juvenile Services, Inc., Ponca City, Okla., 1977-78; adj. instr. social sci. No. Okla. Coll., 1977-78; workshop instr. U. Okla. Student Devel. Assn., 1978—; human relations cons., Norman, Okla., 1978—; adj. instr. psychology and edn. Southeastern Okla. State U., 1977; behavioral cons. Indian Nations Community Action Agy. Edn. Program, 1976-77. Mem. Mcpl. Authority Commn. Atoka, 1973-75, city councilman, 1973-75; pres. Atoka Recreation Assn., 1972-73; mem. Atoka Parks and Recreation Com., 1973-75. Recipient Cert. of Commendation Kay County Juvenile Found., 1978; Okla. Crime Commn. grantee, 1975. Mem. Am. Personnel and Guidance Assn., Okla. Psychol. Assn., Internat. Transactional Analysis Assn., Assn. Specialists in Group Work, Okla. Assn. Youth Services (public relations com. 1977-78), Jr. C. of C. Democrat. Editor Youth Services Newsletter, 1977-78. Address: Apt 211 2900 Chautauqua Norman OK 73069

SCRUGGS, C.G., editor; b. McGregor, Tex., Nov. 4, 1923; s. John Fleming and Adeline (Hering) S.; B.S., Tex. A. and M. U., 1947; m. Miriam June Wigley, July 5, 1947; children—John Mark, Miriam Jan. Asso. editor Prog. Farmer, Dallas, 1947-61, editor, 1962—, v.p., 1964—, exec. editor, 1972, editorial dir., 1973—; pres. Torado Land & Cattle Co. Pres., Tex. Comml. Agr. Council, 1953-54; sec. 1960—. Mem. Gov.'s Com. for Agr., 1950, Tex. Animal Health Council, 1955-61; chmn. So. Brucellosis Com., 1956; pres. Tex. Rural Safety Com., 1957-59; mem. farm conf. Nat. Safety Council, 1958-70; chmn. Nat. Brucellosis Com., 1958-59, 71-72; del. World Food Congress, 1963; pub. mem. U.S. del. 17th Biennial Conf. of FAO, UN, Rome, 1973; chmn. Joint Senate-House Interim Com. Natural Fibers Tex. Legislature, 1971. Mem. coordinating bd. Tex. Coll. and U. System, 1965-69; bd. regents Tex. Tech. U., 1971—. Pres. S.W. Animal Health Research Found., 1961-63, trustee, 1961—; bd. govs. Nat. Agrl. Hall of Fame. Served to lt. col. U.S. Army; Res., ret. Recipient Southwestern Cattle Raisers award, 1962; Am. Seed Trade Assn. award, 1963; award of honor Am. Agrl. Editors Assn., 1964; Reuben Brigham award Am. Assn. Agrl. Coll. Editors, 1965; Distinguished Service award Tex. Farm Bur., 1966; Journalistic Achievement award Nat. Plant Food Assn., 1967. Mem. Am. Agrl. Editors Assn. (pres. 1963), Am. Soc. Mag. Editors, Tex. Agrl. Workers Assn., Tex. Assn. Future Farmers Am. (pres. 1940-41), Dallas Agrl. Club (pres. 1951), Nat. Livestock Confedn. Mexico (hon.), Alpha Zeta, Sigma Delta Chi. Author: The Peaceful Atom and the Deadly Fly, 1975. Office: 820 Shades Creek Pkwy Box 2581 Birmingham AL 35202

SCRUGGS, JIMMIE, ret. air force officer, educator; b. Humboldt, Tenn., Feb. 29, 1932; s. Sam Alexander and Annie Lois (Stokes) S.; B.S., S.W. Tex. State U., 1974, M.Ed., 1978; Adminstrv. Cert., Trinity U., San Antonio, 1979 m. Katherine Bragg, June 24, 1954; children—Michael, Angela. Commd. 2d lt. U.S. Air Force, 1954, advanced through grades to lt. col., 1970; maintenance control officer Camh Ranh Bay AFB, Vietnam, 1969-70; insp. gen. Randolph AFB, Tex., 1970-72; ret., 1972; tchr., coordinator Alamo Hts. High Sch., San Antonio, 1974—. Mem. Alamo Hts. Tchrs. Assn., Tex. State Tchrs. Assn., NEA, Tex. Indsl. Vocat. Assn., Tex. Vocat. Tech. Assn., Am. Vocat. Assn., Iota Lambda Sigma. Baptist (deacon). Home: 10410 Monte Sereno San Antonio TX 78213 Office: 6900 Broadway San Antonio TX 78209

SCRUGGS, PAUL CECIL (BUDDY), state legislator, business exec.; b. Knoxville, Tenn., Dec. 17, 1937; s. Paul C. and Alice M. (Bryson) S.; ed. U. Tenn.; m. Marilyn Lou Childress, July 5, 1959; children—Paul Delmas, Gina Luann, Jennifer Leigh. Asst. sales mgr. Commonwealth Life Ins. Co., 1961-68; group specialist Am. Fidelity Assurance Co., 1968-70; pres. Servicemaster Profl. Bldg. Maintenance, 1970-78, Profl. Bldg. Maintenance, Inc., Nashville, 1978—; now asso. agt. Ins. Service & Assos.; mem. Tenn. Ho. of Reps., 1976—. Mem. bd. mgmt. YMCA. Mem. Nat. Assn. State Legislators, Christian Freedom Found., Nat. Assn. Republican. Legislators, Am. Legion. Baptist. Clubs: Optimists, Masons. Office: 206 War Meml Bldg Nashville TN 37219

SCRUGGS, RICHARD TURNER, aluminum co. exec.; b. Birmingham, Ala., Apr. 4, 1915; s. Josiah Hubert and Willye (Turner) S.; student Birmingham So. Coll., 1933-34, U. Ala., 1934-36; m. Marilyn Perkins Bade, Sept. 7, 1938; children—Marilyn Craig (Mrs. Charles L. Tucker), Margaret Sarah (Mrs. Jarrel Estes), Richard Turner, John Hubert. Salesman, So. Culvert Co., Birmingham, Ala., 1936-38, v.p., 1938-42; asst. chief aircraft insp. Bechtel-McCone Corp., Birmingham, 1942-46; co-founder Vulcan Metal Products, Inc., Birmingham, 1946, pres., 1956—; pres. Scruggs Investment Co., Inc. Mem. adv. council Salvation Army; chmn. gen. council Lee Assos. Washington and Lee U., Lexington, Va., 1976-77. Recipient Silver Circle award Alpha Tau Omega, 1959, hon. award Washington and Lee U. chpt. Omicron Delta Kappa, 1973. Mem. Screen Mfrs. Assn. (dir.), C. of C., S.A.R., Birmingham-Jefferson Hist. Soc., Sales Exec. Club, Newcomen Soc., Delta Sigma Pi. Methodist (steward). Clubs: Rotary, Shoal Creek Country, Birmingham Country, Downtown, The Club. Home: 3524 Victoria Rd Birmingham AL 35223 Office: PO Box 6788 Birmingham AL 35210

SCRUGGS, ROBERT GORDON, state ofcl.; b. Asheville, N.C., Aug. 7, 1947; s. Robert Wade and Sue Belle (Bishop) S.; A.A.S., A.B. Tech. Inst., 1972; B.S., Mars Hill Coll., 1974. Rehab. placement specialist Employment Security Commn., Hendersonville, N.C., 1977-78; loan asst. Farmers Home Adminstrn., Asheville, N.C., 1978-79; housing officer div. community housing ARC, Raleigh, N.C., 1979—. Mem. Mayor's Com. on the Handicapped, Hendersonville, 1977-79; vice chmn. Regional Manpower Adv. Council, 1977-78. Served with USAF, 1966-70. Recipient Nat. Membership Recruitment award, Am. Legion, 1976. Mem. Am. Mgmt. Assn., Am. Legion (1st vice comdr. 1973-75, dist. comdr. 1976-77), VFW (dist. comdr. 1977-78, post comdr. 1978-79), DAV (dist. comdr. 1976-80, State Award for Membership, 1979), Amvets (vice chmn. 1976-77), Air Force Sgts. Assn. Democrat. Baptist. Clubs: Trout Unltd. (pres. 1978), Mil. Order of the Cootie, 40 and 8. Home: PO Box 18-626 Raleigh NC 27619 Office: PO Box 27687 Raleigh NC 27687

SCRUGGS, WILLIAM CLARENCE, JR., ednl. adminstr.; b. Hattiesburg, Miss., Jan. 19, 1942; s. William Clarence and Marie (Harper) S.; student U. So. Miss., 1960-62, B.S., 1966; m. Mary Ann

Bolton, July 29, 1965; children—Kimberly, Monica, Christina. Math. analyst Space div. Chrysler Corp., Slidell, La., 1966-68; systems mgr. W.E. Walker Stores, Inc., Columbia, Miss., 1968-71; dir. computing center U. So. Miss., Hattiesburg, 1971—; partner mgmt. info. cons. firm. Served with U.S. Army, 1963. Mem. Assn. for Instl. Research. Democrat. Presbyterian. Club: Civitan (sec.-treas. 1975-76). Home: 2900 Williamsburg Rd Hattiesburg MS 39401 Office: 304 Forrest County Hall So Sta Box 5171 U So Miss Hattiesburg MS 39401

SCULL, BERTON JAMES, geologist; b. Ft. Sill, Okla., Nov. 26, 1923; s. Orville Edward and Mary Jane (Dennis) S.; B.S. in Geology, U. Okla., 1946, M.S., 1947, Ph.D., 1956; m. Marjorie Ruth James, Feb. 25, 1945; children—Catherine Lee, Margaret Mary, Sara Anne. Field asst., jr. geologist Carter Oil Co., 1943, 44, 45; grad asst. U. Okla., 1945-47; field geologist Honolulu Oil Co., San Francisco, 1948; teaching fellow mineralogy Stanford U., 1947-49; instr. geology U. Nev., 1949-51; exploration geologist Continental Oil Co., Ardmore and Oklahoma City, Okla., 1951-53; econ. geologist Ark. Geol. and Conservation Commn., Little Rock, 1953-54; research geologist to sr. sect. mgr. Sun Oil Co., Richardson, Tex., 1955-69, profl. exploration geologist, sr. exploration geologist, Denver and Dallas, 1970-72, mgr. new opportunities, Dallas, 1973-74; advisor petroleum geology Norwegian Petroleum Directorate, Stavanger, 1974-77; sr. cons. geologist H.J. Gruy and Assos., Dallas and Stavanger, Norway, 1977-78; chief geologist Tipperary Corp., Midland, Tex., 1978—. Fellow AAAS; mem. Am. Inst. Profl. Geologists, Am. Assn. Petroleum Geologists, Internat. Assn. Sedimentologists, Soc. Econ. Paleontologists and Mineralogists, Soc. Petroleum Engrs., Norwegian Petroleum Soc., Dallas Geol. Soc., West Tex. Geol. Soc., Sigma Xi, Sigma Gamma Epsilon. Contbr. articles to profl. jours. Home: 1204 Princeton St Midland TX 79701 Office: 500 W Illinois St Midland TX 79701

SCULLY, DAVID MICHAEL, landscape architect; b. Columbus, Ohio, July 26, 1945; s. Robert M. and Lucille (Williams) S.; B. Landscape Architecture, U. Fla., 1969; m. Susan Margaret Knoll, June 21, 1968; 1 son, David M. Landscape architect, roadside devel. State of W.Va., Charleston, 1969; St. Thomas (V.I.) Gardens, 1970-71; Dade County (Fla.) Parks and Recreation Dept., Miami, 1971-74; prin. David M. Scully & Assocs., South Miami, Fla., 1974-79, Henderson-Rosenberg-Scully & Assos., South Miami, 1979—. Vis. design critic U. Miami, 1973. Vice chmn. Environ. Preservation Review Bd., City of Miami, 1975-76, chmn., 1976-77, mem., 1977—; mem. Environ. Bd. Dade County. Recipient Fla. Nurseryman and Growers Assn. State awards for design excellence, 1975, 76, 77, chpt. awards, 1975-76, City of Miami Com. on Ecology and Beautification awards, 1976, 77. Mem. Am. Soc. Landscape Architects (mem. exec. com.), Fla. Nurseryman and Growers Assn., Delta Tau Delta, Gargoyle. Democrat. Roman Catholic. Contbr. articles in field to profl. jours. Home: 12101 Pine Needle Ln Miami FL 33156 Office: 6333 Sunset Dr South Miami FL 33143

SCZEKAN, MARJORIE EVELYN, nurse, sociologist, educator; b. Mountain View, Calif.; d. Donald Edward and Pearl Ivy (Hoyt) Davenport; B.S., U. Colo., 1967, M.S., 1967; M.A., U. Tenn., Knoxville, 1971, Ph.D., 1976; m. Frank Sczekan, Dec. 3, 1950; children—Michael, Steven, Bernard. Staff nurse miscellaneous hosps., indsl. cos., Calif., Colo., Tenn., 1949-65; asst. prof. nursing So. Missionary Coll., Collegedale, Tenn., 1967-68, part-time instr. sociology, 1970-72; asso. prof., chmn. dept. nursing Dalton (Ga.) Jr. Coll., 1971-75; prof., dean Sch. Nursing, U. Tenn., Chattanooga, 1975—; cons. in field, lectr. health-related issues to profl. orgns. HEW long term nurse trainee, 1965-67, predoctoral fellow, 1969-71. Mem. Am. Nurses Assn., So. Sociol. Soc., Nat. League Nursing, Tenn. Nurses Assn. Office: Sch Nursing U Tenn 615 McCallie Ave Chattanooga TN 37402

SEABURY, GLEN NATHAN, JR., investment counselor: b. Fort Eustis, Va., Nov. 27, 1945; s. Glen Nathan and Mary Louise (Sharits) S.; student Harvard Coll., 1964-66; B.A., Brigham Young U., 1971; postgrad. U. Utah, 1972-73, U. Tenn., 1976: m. Lea Diane Newland, Sept. 13, 1969; children—Angela, Jared, Ryan. Instr., Latter-day Saints Sem., Salt Lake City, 1971-74; area dir. ch. edn. system Ch. Jesus Christ Latter-day Saints, East Tenn. and Ky., Knoxville, 1974-77; adminstrv. asst. to v.p. Aronov Realty Co., Inc., Montgomery, Ala., 1977-78, investment counselor, 1978—; real estate cons. Latter-day Saints Ch., bishop, 1977-78, missionary, Italy, Switzerland, U.S., 1966-69; active Boy Scouts Am., 1971-72, 74-75, 77-78; exec. Montgomery area United Way, 1979. Mem. Montgomery Bd. Realtors, Ala. Assn. Realtors, Nat. Assn. Realtors, Realtors Nat. Mktg. Inst., Realtors Securities and Syndication Inst., Mensa, SAR. Democrat. Home: 4263 Delmar Dr Montgomery AL 36109 Office: 520 S Court St Montgomery AL 36104

SEACAT, WALTER LOWELL, educator; b. Princeton, Ind., May 22, 1917; s. John Monroe and Etta Frances (Keim) S.; student U. Evansville (Ind.), 1936-40, Johns Hopkins U., 1956-57; A.A., Orlando (Fla.) Jr. Coll., 1962; B.S., Rollins Coll., Winter Park, Fla., 1963, M.B.A., 1966; Ed.D., Nova U., 1978; m. Stella Mae Camp, Nov. 20, 1940; children—Patricia Ann (Mrs. Richard C. Milnes II), Scott Alan. Engr., WGBF radio sta., Evansville, Ind., 1937-41, WISH radio sta., Indpls., 1941-52, WFBM radio and TV sta., Indpls., 1952-56; electronics test, evaluation engr. Martin Marietta Corp., Balt., 1956-57, Orlando, Fla., 1957-75; instr. math. and statistics Fla. So. Coll., McCoy AFB, Orlando, 1966-78, chmn. math. dept., 1976-78, asst. dir. for experiental learning, 1979—, coordinator faculty and ednl. research, 1979—; adj. asst. prof. physics U. Central Fla., Orlando, 1980—; tutor coll. math.; cons., lectr. in field. Pres., Warren Central High Sch. P.T.A., Indpls., 1952-53; mem. Quail Hollow Civic Assn., Winter Park, Fla., 1974—. Served with USNR, 1944-46. Named Man of the Year, Fla. chpt. Inst. Environ. Scis., 1972-73. Mem. Inst. Environ. Scis. (treas. 1969-71'. Mgmt. Club of Martin Marietta Corp., Phi Zeta chpt. Lambda Chi Alpha. Methodist (usher 1957—), elder 1960-64). Mason (Shriner); mem. Order of Eastern Star. Club: Miramar (Indpls.). Home: 432 Pointer Pl Winter Park FL 32789 Office: 8578 Ave C Orlando FL 32812

SEAFORD, NANCY IRVIN, speech and lang. pathologist; b. Mooresville, N.C., Nov. 29, 1950; d. Boyce Wayne and Mary Louise (Smith) Irvin; B.S., Appalachian State U., 1972, M.A., 1973; m. David Curtis Seaford, July 14, 1974; 1 son, David Curtis. Speech therapist Lenoir (N.C.) City Schs., 1973-74; learning abilities devel. coordinator Cabarrus County Schs., Concord, N.C., 1974-75, itinerant speech and lang. therapist, 1975-78; speech and lang. pathologist and cons. Cabarrus County Health Dept., Concord, 1976-78; pres., treas. Cabarrus Speech, Hearing Lang. Services, Inc., Concord, 1978—. Lic. speech/lang. pathologist, N.C. Mem. Am. Speech, Lang. and Hearing Assn. (cert. of clin. competence in speech/lang. pathology), N.C. Speech, Hearing and Lang. Assn., Council for Exceptional Children (chpt. pres. 1977-78). Presbyterian. Home and Office: Route 2 Box 551-A Rankin Rd Concord NC 28025

SEAL, JOAN LINDA, educator; b. West Palm Beach, Fla., May 27, 1946; d. Raymond Willis and Anna Maria (Van Ackooy) Seal; student Eckerd Coll., 1964-66; B.S., Fla. Atlantic U., 1971, M.Ed., 1975. Tchr., Boca Raton (Fla.) Middle Sch., 1971-72, Twin Lakes High Sch., West Palm Beach, 1972—. Crisis Line vol., 1975—; cardio-pulmonary resuscitation instr. Heart Assn., 1976—. Mem. Am., Fla., Palm Beach County assns. tchrs. math., Palm Beach County Council Tchrs. Math. (treas. 1978—), Am. Personnel and Guidance Assn., Am. Sch. Counselors Assn., NEA, Fla. Teaching Profession, Palm Beach County Classroom Tchrs. Assn. Democrat. Mem. Christian Ch. Home: 411 Monroe Dr West Palm Beach FL 33405 Office: Georgia and Hibiscus Sts West Palm Beach FL 33401

SEALE, MARGARET RUTH, music educator, bus. exec.; b. Knoxville, Ala., Apr. 20, 1915; d. James Andrew and Edna Lee (Phillips) Lamb; student Tulane U., 1958-59; B.Ch.Music, New Orleans Baptist Theol. Sem., 1960, M.Ch. Music, 1962; m. Clifton Carter Seale, Nov. 9, 1941 (dec. May 20, 1977); children—Clifton Carter, Joy Ruth, Robert Hamilton. Soloist, chorister New Orleans Opera Co., 1943-53; ch. soloist, concerts in New Orleans, Mobile, Ala., Meridian, Miss., others, 1944-70; contract tchr., voice and piano New Orleans Bapt. Theol. Sem., 1945-62; music therapist Willowwood Home for Ret., 1972-74; owner, operator Marsile Music Co., New Orleans, 1974—; pres. Big Parade Corp., 1975—; pres. Marsile Music Pub. Co. Mem. adv. bd. Delta Festival Ballet Co. Music Therapy Fund, 1950—; active League Women Voters, 1972—. Recipient New Orleans Mayor's awards, 1971, 75. Mem. La. Council for Music and Performing Arts, Nat., La., New Orleans (exec. bd.) music tchrs. assns., Nat. Music Council (bicentennial coordinator), Nat. (bicentennial coordinator), La. (New Orleans dist. coordinator 1964-74, v.p. 1972-74, pres. 1974-76) fedns. music clubs, Gottschalk Soc., Greater New Orleans Music Club, Jr. Philharmonic Soc., New Orleans C. of C. Aux., Gamma Xi, Mu Phi Epsilon. Author: (musical) Lil' Ol' Looziana; (songs) Welcome to New Orleans, Get-A-Goin', Lil' Ol' Looziana, Welcome to Louisiana, The Big Parade, Lovesong; (record) In The Now, 1975; (anthems) He Is Risen, Allelujah, Return To Me, It's So Wonderful; (solos) Oh that Men Would Praise the Lord, Unworthy As I Am; author, composer piano teaching series Fun for (Student's Name) and Friend. Home and office: 4674 Franklin Ave New Orleans LA 70122

SEALE, RICHARD, banker; b. Eunice, La., Jan. 21, 1931; s. Lemuel George and Alma (Fontenot) S.; B.S., Tex. A. and M. U., 1957; m. Julia Ann Stagg, Jan. 26, 1957; children—Richard Mannie, Martha Amanda, Susan Marie. Agrl. rep. First Nat. Bank Edna (Tex.), 1957-59, v.p., 1959-65; v.p., sr. loan officer First Nat. Bank Angleton (Tex.), 1965-66; exec. v.p. First Nat. Bank Crowley (La.), 1966-68, pres., 1968—, also dir.; chmn. bd. dirs. Bank of Lafayette (La.). Mem. adv. council Small Bus. Adminstrn., La., 1969-71; chmn. La. Warehouse Commn., 1972—; vice chmn. La. Devel. Authority for Housing Finance, 1972—. Chmn., City of Crowley BiRacial Com. Bd. dirs. Greater Crowley Indsl. Devel. Corp. Served with USNR, 1951-53. Mem. La. Bankers Assn. (legislative com.), Southwestern Clearing House Assn. (pres. 1969—), Greater Crowley C. of C. (ambassador 1969—, pres. 1970-71), Acadia Parish Cattlemen's Assn. Rotarian. Club: Crowley Town (pres. 1971-72, dir.). Home: 529 W 14th St Crowley LA 70526 Office: PO Box 267 Crowley LA 70526

SEALEY, JOHN CHARLES, petroleum co. exec.; b. Ottawa, Kans., Jan. 16, 1925; s. John H. and Ruth Bell (Toms) S.; B.S.M.E., U. Calif., Berkeley, 1947, B.A. in Bus. Adminstrn., 1947; m. Daphne Brown, June 29, 1947; children—Dana Sealey Latham, Janet Sealey Johnston. With Shell's Mktg. Orgn., 1947-67; mktg. mgr. northeastern U.S., Shell Oil Co., 1967-69; charge automotive div. Shell Internat. Petroleum Co., Inc., London, 1969-71; gen. mgr. mktg. econs. and distbn. Shell Oil Co., Houston, 1971, gen. mgr. retail mktg., 1971-73, gen. mgr. bus. services, 1973-75, gen. mgr. corp. real estate, 1975—. Served as ensign USN, 1943-46. Mem. South Main Center Assn. (exec. com.), West Houston Assn. (exec. com.). Clubs: Brae-Burn Country, Plaza. Home: 12422 Boheme St Houston TX 77024 Office: PO Box 2099 Houston TX 77001

SEALS, JAMES MADISON, educator; b. Gilmer, Tex., Nov. 2, 1935; s. William D. and Nadine M. (Morris) S.; Ph.D., E. Tex. State U., 1968; m. Caryl Neman, Mar. 19, 1960; children—Ann, James N. Counselor Tex. pub. schs., 1960-65; mem. faculty Okla. State U., Stillwater, 1968—, prof. applied behavioral studies, 1969—; cons. to schs. and community agys. Recipient Outstanding Tchr. award Okla. State U., 1975. HEW grantee, 1974-75. Mem. Am. Psychol. Assn., Am. Personnel and Guidance Assn., S.W. Psychol. Assn. Democrat. Christian. Author: Elementary School Career Education, 1975; Career Guidance Systems, 1976. Contbr. articles in field to profl. jours. Home: Box 64 Stillwater OK 74074 Office: Okla State U 315 N Murray Hall Stillwater OK 74074

SEALY, GLENN MICHAEL, utility ofcl.; b. Dallas, Aug. 17, 1950; s. Glenn Easterling and Evelyne Marie (Davis) S.; B.A., Brazosport Coll., 1971; B.B.A. with honors, U. Tex., Austin, 1973; m. Sharon Kay West, Aug. 6, 1971; children—Jared Michael, Shane Christopher. With Gulf States Utilities Co., 1973—, internal auditor, Beaumont, Tex., 1973-74, labor relations rep., 1974-76, coordinator employee benefits. 1977-78, div. personnel rep., Conroe, Tex., 1978-79, supr. indsl. relations, 1979—. Baptist. Office: PO Box 158 Conroe TX 77301

SEAMAN, EUGENE JOHN, ins. co. adminstr.; b. Pigeon, Mich., Apr. 11, 1930; s. John and Anna S.; M.S., Am. Coll., 1977; m. Ellen V. Brauer, Dec. 1, 1951; children—John A., Alana J. Seaman Martin, Eric L., Rand H., Timothy G. Agt., Prudential Ins. Co., Corpus Christi, Tex., 1956-63, div. mgr., 1958-63; gen. mgr. Mut. of N.Y., Corpus Christi, 1963—; dir. Merc. Nat. Bank. Pres., Harbor Playhouse Community Theatre, 1970-76; bd. dirs. Corpus Christi Symphony, 1970-78. Served to capt. AUS, 1952-56. Mem. Corpus Christi Estate Planning Council, Gen. Agts. and Mgrs. Assn. (past pres.), Nat. Assn. Life Underwriters, Am. Soc. Life Underwriters. Home: 5141 Ocean Dr Corpus Christi TX 78412 Office: 525 S Shoreline St Corpus Christi TX 78401

SEAMAN, JOHN GATES, lawyer; b. Galveston, Tex., Mar. 9, 1919; s. Harry Milton and Bera (Gates) S.; student U. Houston, summers 1938, 39; B.A., U. Tex., 1940, LL.B., 1942; m. Henri Etta Rester, Mar. 7, 1946; children—John G., Stephen H., Sandra Jane. Admitted to Tex. bar, 1942; practiced in Houston, 1946-51, Corpus Christi, Tex., 1951—; mem. firm Neel and Seaman, 1951-65, Keys, Russel, Watson and Seaman, 1965—. Served to lt. USNR, 1942-46. Named adm. Tex. Navy. Mem. State Bar Tex., Am., Nueces County bar assns., Am. Judicature Soc., Am., Corpus Christi assns. petroleum landmen, Navy League, Phi Beta Kappa, Phi Delta Phi, Alpha Tau Omega. Democrat. Episcopalian. Kiwanian. Clubs: Petroleum; Corpus Christi Town. Home: 618 Santa Monica St Corpus Christi TX 78411 Office: Bank and Trust Tower Corpus Christi TX 78401

SEAMAN, JOSEPH CARRYL, III, banker; b. Ferriday, La., Oct. 23, 1945; s. Joseph Carryl and Martha F. (Lancaster) S.; B.S., Miss. State U., 1968; m. Mary Ann Crosby, Jan. 10, 1976. With Am. Express Co., 1971-72; with First Tenn. Nat. Corp., Memphis, 1972-75, mgr. data services systems group, 1975, asst. mgr. systems devel., 1975-76; v.p. data processing Lubbock Nat. Bank (Tex.), 1976—; Mem. info. systems adv. panel South Plains Coll. Mem. Soc. for Computer Programmers (pres. 1975), Data Processing Mgmt. Assn. (sec.-treas. 1978-79), Bank Adminstrn. Inst., Am. Bankers Assn., Pi Sigma Epsilon, Pi Kappa Alpha. Methodist. Home: 5230 18th St Lubbock TX 79416 Office: PO Box 421 Lubbock TX 79408

SEAMON, JESSE LEE, JR., restaurant exec.; b. Morehead City, N.C., July 9, 1936; s. Jesse Lee and Lillie Belle (Whealton) S.; student U. N.C., 1956. Accountant, Shumaker, C.P.A., 1956-57; partner, gen. mgr. Sanitary Fish Market & Restaurant, Morehead City, 1967—. Environmental cons. Long Constrn. Co. Active in scouting; del. from N.C. to Nat. Rivers and Harbors Congress, 1966-74; mem. N.C. Nuclear Environmental Resources Com., 1968-69; mem. nat. adv. bd. Am. Security Council, 1969-74; mem. N.C. Marine Sci. Council, 1966-72, N.C. Emergency Med. Task bar 1969-72, N.C. Emergency Med. Services Council, 1972—; founder Carteret County Marine Sci. Council, 1968; dir. N.C. Travel Council, 1968-70; gen. chmn. N.C. Tribute to USCG, 1970; mem. adv. com. Hampton Mariners Mus. Mem. Internat. Oceanographic Found. Served with AUS, 1959-61. Recipient Distinguished Service award Jaycees, 1969, award from Gov. Dan Moore for contbn. to devel. N.C., 1969, award for contbns. in marine scis. U.S. Navy, 1971. Mem. N.C. Restaurant Assn. (dir.), Carteret County C. of C. (dir. 1960-64, 75-76). Baptist. Mason (Shriner). Home: Coral Bay Morehead City NC 28557 Office: 500 Evans St Morehead City NC 28557

SEARCY, PATRICK LAMBERT, lawyer; b. San Antonio, Apr. 21, 1938; s. Tyson Morey and Catherine Elizabeth (Wood) S.; B.S., Trinity U., San Antonio, 1963; J.D., St. Mary's U., San Antonio, 1969; m. Lois Jean Medlin, Aug. 16, 1972; children—Scarlette, Robyn, Tomye, Bryan, Tyson, Patrick Lambert. Exec. trainee Allied Stores, 1963-64, dept. mgr. Joskes of Tex., San Antonio, 1964-65; estate and tax planner Conn. Gen. Life Ins. Co., San Antonio, 1965-66; admitted to Tex. bar, 1969; asst. dist. atty. Bexar County, Tex., 1970-71; individual practice law, San Antonio, 1971-76; pres. Nautilus Fitness Center, Inc., 1974-76, Tex. Cardio-Diagnostic Center, Inc., 1974-76; motion picture and TV producer, San Antonio, 1976—; oil and gas producer, San Antonio, 1976—; adv. counsel to several law firms, since 1976—. Mem. del. selection com. for Pres. Ford, 1976; mem. Nat. Right To Work Com.; mem. Republican Nat. Com. Served with U.S. Army, 1957-58. Recipient spl. recognition award Center for Internat. Security Studies, Georgetown U., 1979; cert. of appreciation Rep. Nat. Com., 1977, 78, Senator John Tower, 1978. Mem. Am. Bar Assn., Tex. Bar Assn., San Antonio Bar Assn., Am. Film Inst., Internat. Entrepreneurs Assn., Aircraft Owners and Pilots Assn., Nat. Rifle Assn. (life), Confederate Air Force, Tex. Rifle Assn., Am. Security Council (nat. adv. bd.), Order of Alamo, Kappa Sigma. Roman Catholic. Clubs: San Antonio Christmas Cotillion, San Antonio Country. Home and Office: 418 Country Ln San Antonio TX 78209

SEARLE, RICHARD HENRY, business systems analyst; b. Rochester, N.Y., Nov. 27, 1930; s. Henry H. and Ina Searle; B.B.A., Tex. A&I U., 1975; m. Maureen Donovan, Mar. 8, 1952; children—Richard H., Robin D. Joined U.S. Marine Corps, 1948, commd. 2d lt., 1952, advanced through grades to lt. col.; ret., 1971; real estate broker, Kingsville, Tex., 1972-77; dir. mgmt. info. systems Mercy Hosp. of Laredo (Tex.), 1977—. Active Boy Scouts Am. Decorated Navy Commendation medal, Purple Heart. Mem. Tex. Hosp. Info. Systems Soc., Tex. Hosp. Assn. Clubs: Masons, Rotary. Home: 808 Eden Ln Laredo TX 78041 Office: 1515 Logan St Laredo TX 78040

SEARLES, ANNA MAE HOWARD, educator, civic worker; b. Osage Nation Indian Terr., Okla., Nov. 22, 1906; d. Frank David and Clara (Bowman) Howard; A.A., Odessa (Tex.) Coll., 1961; B.A., U. Ark., 1964; M.Ed., 1970; postgrad. (Herman L. Donovan fellow), U. Ky., 1972—; m. Isaac Adams Searles, May 26, 1933; 1 dau., Mary Ann Rogers (Mrs. Herman Lloyd Hoppe). Compiler news, broadcaster sta. KJBC, 1950-60; corr. Tulsa Daily World, 1961-64; tchr. Rogers (Ark.) High Sch., 1964-72; tchr. adult class rapid reading, 1965-76; tchr. Rogers extension North Ark. Community Coll.; tchr. adult edn. Learning Center Benton County (Ark.), Bentonville, 1973-77, supr., 1977-79. Sec. Tulsa Safety Council, 1935-37; leader, bd. dirs. Kilgore council Girl Scouts U.S.A., 1941-44, leader, Midland, Tex., 1944-52, counselor, 1950-61; exec. sec. Midland Community Chest, 1955-60; gray lady Midland A.R.C., 1958-59; organizer Midland YMCA, Salvation Army; dir. women's div. Savings Bond Program, Midland; mem. citizens com. Rogers (Ark.) Hough Meml. Library, women's aux. Rogers Meml. Hosp.; sec. Beaver Lake Literacy Council, Rogers, 1973-80; bd. dirs. Globe Theatre, Odessa, Tex., Midland Community Theatre, Tri-County Foster Home, Guadalupe, Midland youth centers, DeZavala Day Nursery, P.T.A., Adult Devel. Center; sec. Little Flock Planning Commn.; publicity chmn. South Central region Nat. Affiliation for Literacy Advance, 1977-78. Recipient Thanks badge Midland Girl Scout Assn., 1948. Mem. N.E.A. (del. conv. 1965), P.T.A. (life), Future Homemakers Am. (life), Ark. Assn. Public Continuing and Adult Edn. (state pres. 1980), Delta Kappa Gamma. Episcopalian. Clubs: Altrusa (pres.), Apple Spur Community (both Rogers). Home: Route 2 Rogers AR 72756

SEARS, EARL WAYNE, commodity orgn. exec.; b. Brownfield, Tex., June 29, 1927; s. Kelly and Era (McLeroy) S.; B.S., Tex. Tech U., 1948; m. Gwendolyn Y. Moon, June 28, 1949; children—Cathy Gwen, Robert E., David D., Krisitie Ann. Head Dept. Vocat. Agr., Lamesa, Tex., 1948-52; field rep. Nat. Cotton Council, Lubbock, Tex., 1952-54, supr. S.W. area, Dallas, 1954-65; product mgr. Hesston Corp. (Kans.), 1965-68, mktg. mgr., 1969-71; asst. to exec. v.p. Nat. Cotton Council, Memphis, 1971-75, adminstrv. v.p., 1975-77, exec. v.p., 1978—. Mem. Memphis Soc. Assn. Execs., Am. Soc. Assn. Execs., Am. Inst. Mgmt. Baptist. Home: 2174 Thornwood Memphis TN 38117 Office: PO Box 12285 1918 N Parkway Memphis TN 38112

SEARS, GERALD ALDEN, fin. exec.; b. Houston, July 18, 1938; s. Hubert Oscar and Francis Mariee (Kellogg) S.; B.S., U. Kans., 1967; postgrad. U. Tex., San Antonio, 1976-77; m. Bonnie Jo Comfort; children—Bonnie Jerilyn Cavia, Mary Annette, Joanna Mariee Sears Felts. Controller, Mid-Tex. Communications Systems, Inc., San Antonio, 1968-70; v.p., treas. Stanley Smith Security Inc., San Antonio, 1970-76; v.p. fin., sec.-treas. Anderson, Greenwood & Co., Houston, 1976—, also dir.; dir. Bellanca Aircraft Corp., AG Underwriters Ltd. (Cayman), Aries Underwriters Ltd. (Cayman), 1979—. Served with U.S. Army, 1957-60. Mem. Nat. Assn. Accts., Inst. Mgmt. Acctg., Am. Mgmt. Assn. Republican. Episcopalian. Club: Houstonian. Home: 11703 Wallaby Ct Houston TX 77477 Office: 5425 S Rice Ave Houston TX 77081

SEARS, PATRICIA ANN, ins. co. exec.; b. Maryville, Tenn., Jan. 7, 1936; d. Otto Francis and Margaret (Bond) Turner; B.A., Sherwood Music Conservatory, 1957; postgrad. Portland State U., 1968; m. Wayne Richard Sears, Mar. 15, 1968; 1 son, Martin Richard. Bookkeeper, office mgr., Portland, Oreg., 1957-65; sr. programmer Consol. Freightways, Portland, 1965-69; sr. systems analyst Standard Ins. Co., Portland, 1969-73; sr. systems analyst Lipmans, Portland, 1973-75; mgr. data processing Am. Nat. Ins. Co., Galveston, Tex., 1975-78; mgr. data processing Parkland Meml. Hosp., Dallas, 1978—; instr. data processing in-house tng. programs, 1968-72. Adviser accounting curriculum Beaverton Schs., 1973-74. Certified in data processing Data Processing Mgmt. Assn. Fellow Life Mgmt. Inst.; mem. Assn. Systems Mgmt. (past pres.), League Women Voters. Republican. Episcopalian. Club: Order Eastern Star. Home: 1605 Westridge Ct Hurst TX 76053 Office: 5201 Harry Hines Blvd Dept 11107 Dallas TX 75235

SEAWELL, HARRY DAVID, communications exec.; b. McAllen, Tex., Oct. 30, 1930; s. Harry H. and Mattie Laura (Johnston) S.; ed. high sch.; m. Randyl Elizabeth Kirwan, Aug. 20, 1977; 1 son, Donald Gardner; children by previous marriage—Harry David II, Matthew Blake, Logan Scott. Photographer, Parkersburg (W.Va.) News, 1953-55; partner Schaefer and Seawell, Parkersburg, 1955-70; pres. Harry Seawell Communications, Parkersburg, 1970-75, Seawell Multimedia Corp., Parkersburg, 1975—. Served as staff sgt. USMC, 1948-51; PTO. Exhibited in Parkersburg Art Center, 1962, Charleston Art Center, 1962, W.Va. Centennial Train, 1963, various one-man art and photography shows. Recipient sports photography award Look mag., 1954, news pictures of year award, 1955. Mem. Mid-Ohio Valley Communicators, Am. Soc. Mag. Photographers. Publisher: West Virginia in Color, 1963; West Virginia USA, 1976; film producer: A West Virginia Renaissance, 1980. Office: Seawell Multimedia Corp 1623 Washington Ave Parkersburg WV 26101

SEAWRIGHT, HAROLD SANDERS, newspaper exec.; b. Anderson, S.C., July 26, 1947; b. John Harold and Dena (Hardin) S.; B.A., U. N.C., Charlotte, 1970; student Wake Forest U., 1965-67. With Cargill, Wilson & Acree Advt. Agy., Charlotte, 1969-70; from copywriter to asst. promotion dir. Charlotte Observer and Charlotte News, 1970-73, book reviewer, 1970-75; public service/promotion dir. Nashville Banner, 1973-79, book reviewer, 1973—; promotion dir. Nashville Banner and The Tennessean, 1979—; instr. basic newspaper promotion Internat. Newspaper Promotion Assn., Mexico City, 1975, Atlanta, 1977, Washington, 1977, Va. Press Assn., 1978, Tenn. Press. Assn., 1979. Bd. dirs. Charlotte-Mecklenburg NCCJ, 1972-73; allocations rev. bd. mem. Nashville United Way, 1979. Served with USAR, 1968-74. Recipient various awards Tenn. Press Assn., Editor and Pub. mag. Mem. Internat. Newspaper Promotion Assn. Democrat. Methodist. Contbg. editor Contemporary Art/Southeast, 1977—; Nashville Area art critic Art Voices/South, 1978—. Home: 5651 Kendall Dr Nashville TN 37209 Office: Nashville Banner 1100 Broadway Nashville TN 37202

SEAY, C(HARLES) FRANK, JR., univ. adminstr.; b. Dallas, Dec. 27, 1913; s. Charles Frank and Hazel (Hinckley) S.; B.A. in Physics, U. Tex., 1934; m. Emily Ann Moore, Oct. 5, 1946; children—Charles Frank III, Carolyn Emily. Seismologist, Humble Oil & Refining Co., 1935; demonstration engr. Gen. Motors Corp., 1936; tutor U. Tex. at Austin, 1937, research fellow, 1941, research scientist Def. Research Lab., 1945-52; clk. Magnolia Petroleum Co., Dallas, 1938-40; research scientist Underwater Sound Lab., Harvard, 1941-45; head co. information center Collins Radio Co., Dallas, 1952-58; mgr. tech. information center Tex. Instruments, Inc., Dallas, 1958-61; asst. to pres. Grad. Research Center of S.W., Dallas, 1961-64; asst. to v.p. So. Meth. U., Dallas, 1964-66, dir. govt. relations, 1966-67, asst. to pres., 1967-71, exec. asst. to pres., 1971—. Cons. in acoustics, 1946—. Recipient U.S. Naval Ordnance Devel. award, 1945. Mem. Acoustical Soc. Am., I.E.E.E. (chmn. Dallas sect. I.R.E. 1957-58, dir. S.W. regional conf. 1963), Dallas Council Sci. Socs. (pres. 1961-62), Met. Philos. Soc., Am. Guild Organists, Inst. Noise Control Engring., Phi Beta Kappa, Sigma Xi, Sigma Pi Sigma, Phi Eta Sigma. Presbyn. (deacon 1949-52, elder 1956-65). Club: Brookhaven Country (Dallas). Home: 6939 Joyce Way Dallas TX 75225

SEAY, MAURICE SHEPARD, mfg. co. cons., ret. exec.; b. Vicksburg, Miss., Oct. 9, 1905; s. Charles B. and Rosa (Mackey) S.; student LaSalle Extension U., 1927-29, Miss. Coll., 1942-44, Alexander Hamilton Inst. Bus., 1952-73; m. Sylvia Roseberry, Dec. 18, 1929 (dec.); children—Maureen S. (Mrs. Richard T. Smart), William H., Donald W., Connie M. (Mrs. Cono Anthony Caranna II); m. 2d, M. Wanna Edward, Jan. 28, 1967. Personnel mgr. Marathon LeTourneau Co., Vicksburg, 1945-74, cons., 1974-75; ret., 1975. Pres., Junius Ward Johnson Meml. YMCA. Bd. dirs. Miss. Econ. Council. Mem. Am. Soc. Personnel Adminstrn. (past chpt. pres.), Central Miss. Personnel Mgmt. Assn. (past pres.), Miss. Mfrs. Assn. (dir.), Vicksburg Warren County C. of C. (dir.), Indsl. Mgmt. Club (past pres.), Foremans Club (past pres.). Methodist. Clubs: Vicksburg Y's Men's (past pres.), River Town, Optimist (past pres.). Home: 1456 Parkside Dr Vicksburg MS 39180 Office: LeTourneau Rural Sta Vicksburg MS 39180

SEBASTIAN, EDWARD JOHN, banker; b. Lebanon, Pa., Sept. 2, 1946; s. Stephen George and Helen Agnes (Smith) S.; B.S., Pa. State U., 1968; m. Susan Renee Snypes, May 3, 1969; children—Rosalind, Ashley. Sr. accountant Price Waterhouse & Co., N.Y.C., 1968-73, Charlotte, N.C., 1973, acting mgr., Columbia, S.C., 1973-74; controller Bankers Trust of S.C., Columbia, 1974—, v.p., 1974-77, sr. v.p., 1977—, asst. sec. to bd. dirs., 1978—, sec., treas. B.T. Bldg. Corp. subs., 1978—, mem. exec. com. Aiken Speir Inc. mortgage banking subs., 1978—, pres., chief exec. officer, 1979—; tchr. Price Waterhouse Accountant's Continuing Edn. courses Central Piedmont Community Coll., Charlotte, 1973. Chmn., Price Waterhouse United Fund, 1973; past trustee, treas., vice chmn. Wildewood Sch., Columbia. C.P.A., S.C.; cert. review appraiser. Mem. Nat. Assn. Accts., Am. Inst. C.P.A.'s, Am. Acctg. Assn., Am. Taxation Assn., Bank Adminstrn. Inst. (past dir. Columbia chpt.), Inst. Mgmt. Sci., Am. Inst. Indsl. Engrs., Am. Enterprise Inst. for Policy Research, Nat. Assn. Rev. Appraisers (sr.), Internat. Platform Assn., Pa. State U. Alumni Assn., Phi Kappa Psi. Democrat. Roman Catholic. Home: 6137 Hampton Ridge Rd Columbia SC 29209 Office: Bankers Trust of South Carolina Bankers Trust Tower Columbia SC 29202

SEBO, KATHERINE ANN HAGEN, govt. ofcl., former state senator; b. Mpls., July 9, 1944; d. Kristofer and Bertha Elvira (Johanson) Hagen; B.A., Oberlin Coll., 1965; M.A., Am. U., 1968, Ph.D., 1973; m. Paul C. Sebo, June 10, 1967 (div. Nov. 1977). Instr. polit. sci. Wake Forest U., Winston-Salem, N.C., 1967-68; instr. polit. sci. Guilford Coll., Greensboro, N.C., 1968-72, asst. prof., 1972-78; White House fellow Office Personnel Mgmt., Washington, 1979-80. Mem. N.C. tech. adv. com. Community-Based Alternatives to Tng. Sch., 1975-78; mem. N.C. State Senate, 1974-78. Chmn. Greensboro Mayor's Com. on Status of Women, 1972-73; mem. N.C. Non-Pub. Edn. Adv. Council; mem. legis. adv. council So. Regional Edn. Bd., 1977—; bd. dirs. nat. and state units ACLU, 1973-78, mem. adv. panel Z. Smith Reynolds Found., 1977—. Named Woman of Year Greensboro YWCA, 1975. Mem. Am., So. polit. sci. assns., AAUP (govtl. relations com.). Democrat. Methodist. Contbr. articles to profl. publs. on Equal Rights Amendment, Internat. Women's Yr., women in India. Home: 907 McGee St Greensboro NC 27403 Office: 1900 E St NW Washington DC 20415

SECREST, EVERETT LEIGH, educator; b. Tioga, Tex., Jan. 5, 1928; s. Walter Everett and Annie Jewell (Holloway) S.: B.S., N. Tex. State U., 1947, M.S., 1948; Ph.D., Mass. Inst. Tech., 1951; m. Bettye Jo Porter, June 4, 1948; children—Robert M., Charles H. Asso. prof. physics N. Tex. State U., 1951-54; chief nuclear physics Convair-Ft. Worth div. Gen. Dynamics, Ft. Worth, 1954-57; asst. mgr. physics and math. Babcock & Wilcox Co., Lynchburg, Va., 1957-59; chief scientist Gen. Dynamics, Ft. Worth, 1959-64; asso. dean engring. U. Okla., 1964-65; grad. dean Tex. Christian U., 1965-68, vice-chancellor for advanced studies and research, 1968-72, pres. TCU Research Found., 1965-77, Continental Nat. Bank prof. mgmt. sci., 1972—, vice chancellor, dean univ., 1978—; guest lectr. Mass. Inst. Tech., 1972. Bd. dirs. Trinity Valley Sch., Ft. Worth. Mem. Gulf Univs. Research Consortium (trustee, sec. 1969-71), Met. Philos. Soc. (pres. 1970-71), Assn. Tex. Grad. Schs., Am. Phys. Soc., Am. Nuclear Soc., Am. Soc. Engring. Edn., Soc. for Computer Simulation, Nat. Council U. Research Adminstrs., Phi Beta Kappa, Sigma Xi (pres. Tex. Christian U. br. 1967-68), Alpha Chi (pres. N. Tex. State U. chpt. 1945-46), Sigma Pi Sigma, Pi Mu Epsilon. Contbr. articles to sci. jours. Contbr. papers to profl. soc. meetings. Home: 2415 Wabash Ave Fort Worth TX 76109 Office: Tex Christian U Fort Worth TX 76129

SECRIST, LOIS JEAN, coll. adminstr.; b. Milw., Aug. 5, 1929; d. Harry Paulus and Alice Louise (Shaw) S.; A.A., Tenn. Wesleyan Coll., 1949; B.S. in Bus. Adminstrn., U. Tenn., 1959. Project leader Union Carbide Corp., Oak Ridge, 1953-68; systems design mgr. The First Ch. of Christ Scientist, Boston, 1968-71; computer services mgr. Ga. State U., Atlanta, 1971—. Cert. data processor. Mem. Data Processing Mgmt. Assn. (past pres. Knoxville, past dir. Atlanta, recipient Outstanding Performance awards 1976, 78), Assn. Computing Machinery. Democrat. Home: 3206-N Post Woods Dr NW Atlanta GA 30339 Office: Ga State U Computer Center University Plaza Atlanta GA 30303

SEE, JAMES MARVIN, chem. engr.; b. Piketon, Ohio, Dec. 13, 1943; s. James Elwood and Genevieve (Trimble) S.; student Ohio State U., 1961-62, U. Md., 1964; B.S. in Chem. Engring., Lafette Coll., Internat. Corr. Schs., 1975; m. Betty Kathryn Burns, Sept. 27, 1978; children by previous marriage—Shawn, Leanna Woods, Michael Woods. Performance engr. Ky. Power Co., Louisa, 1966-79, environ. staff engr., Ashland, Ky., 1979—; audiometric technician; cons. water treatment and distbn. systems, opacity monitor, environ. research tech. Served with U.S. Army, 1963-66; Korea. Cert. audiometric technician. Mem. Chem. Engrs. Assn. Democrat. Baptist. Home: Box 192 Louisa KY 41230 Office: Ky Power Co Box 1423 15th St and Canter Ave Ashland KY 41101

SEE, MARION JACK, lawyer; b. Saltpeter, W. Va., Sept. 15, 1904; s. Charles Frederick and Elizabeth (Goff) S.; student Cumberland Coll., 1926; A.A., U. Ky., 1929, A.B., 1929; m. Dorothy Elizabeth Heston, Dec. 26, 1933; children—Marion Jack, Charles Frederick III. Admitted to Ky. bar, 1937; editor Lawrence County Recorder, Louisa, Ky., 1926-27; instr. Staunton (Va.) Mil. Acad., 1927-28, Louisa High Sch., 1931-40; prin. Louisa Consol. Sch., 1931-40; partner firm C.F. See, Jr. (merger See & See), 1940—; atty. Lawrence County, 1940-42, Louisa City, 1942-44, 46-52, 63; asst. atty. gen. revenue and tax Govt. of Guam, 1957-59; atty. gen. Trust Ter. Pacific Islands, 1959-61; spl. judge Circuit Ct., Eastern Ky. dists., 1956-62. Mem. Am., Ky., Lawrence County (past pres., sec.) bar assns. Baptist. Clubs: Masons, Order Eastern Star, Rotary (pres. 1941), Nat. Lawyers. Home: 607 N Lock Ave Louisa KY 41230 Office: Recorder Bldg Louisa KY 41230

SEEDIG, LARRY RICHARD, savs. and loan exec.; b. Lone Grove, Okla., Apr. 30, 1947; s. Henry Erich and Leola Lorretta (Schlegel) S.; B.B.A., N. Tex. State U., 1970; m. Linda Kay Evans, Dec. 27, 1969; children—Lyle Richard, Landry Evan. With First Tex. Savs. Assn., 1972—, pres., Cleburne (Tex.) Region, 1979—. Mem. Inst. Fin. Edn. (state dir. 1978—), N. Tex. State U. Alumni Assn., Kappa Sigma. Democrat. Lutheran. Home: 3904 W Greenhills Ct Irving TX 75062 Office: First Texas Savings Assn 6060 N Central Expressway Dallas TX 75206

SEEGER, C(HARLES) RONALD, geologist, educator; b. Columbus, Ohio, Jan. 31, 1931; s. Karl Elder and Ethel Turney (Jones) S.; B.Sc., Ohio State U., 1953; M.S., George Washington U., 1958; Ph.D., U. Pitts., 1966; m. Barbara Ann Ashley, July 29, 1961; children—Leslie Ethel, Julie Ann. Engring. geologist Photronix, Columbus, 1958; ops. analyst Inst. for Def. Analyses, The Pentagon, Washington, 1958-60; earth scis. analyst Office of Naval Intelligence, Sci. and Tech. Intelligence Center, Washington, 1960-63. Asst. prof. Western Ky. U., Bowling Green, 1968-69, asso. prof., 1969-76, prof., 1977—; resident research asso. Goddard Space Flight Center, NASA, Greenbelt, Md., 1966-68; research fellow NASA-Johnson Space Center, Houston, summer 1977, 78. Served to lt. (j.g.) USNR, 1953-57. Mem. AAAS, Am. Geophys. Union, AAUP (chpt. pres. 1971-72), Geol. Soc. Am., Ky. Acad. Sci. (geol. sec. 1976-77, pres. 1977-78), Meteoritical Soc., Sigma Xi. Author 2 books. Contbr. articles on planetology, geology and geophysics to sci. jours. Home: 630 Ironwood Dr Bowling Green KY 42101

SEEGMILLER, WILLIAM EDWARD, city ofcl.; b. St. George, Utah, Sept. 9, 1941; s. William Wendell and Ida Mary (Mickleson) S.; B.A., Brigham Young U., 1968, M.P.A., 1970; m. Sheriene Campbell, Aug. 13, 1966; children—Rachelle, Jeremy, Jayson, Jared. Asst. to city mgr. City of Wichita Falls (Tex.), 1970-72; city mgr. City of Waxahachie (Tex.), 1972-75, Sherman, Tex., 1975-79, Abilene, Tex., 1979—. Mem. Am. Soc. Public Adminstrn., Mcpl. Fin. Assn., Internat. City Mgmt. Assn., Tex. City Mgmt. Assn. Mormon. Club: Rotary. Office: PO Box 60 Abilene TX 79605

SEELY, CHARLES WAYNE, oil co. exec.; b. Rockwall, Tex., Aug. 22, 1934; s. Wayne J. and Hallie L. (Moore) S.; B.S., Tex. A. and M. U., 1955; m. Ina Lea Bobbitt, June 11, 1955; children—Lea Anne, Linda Sheryl, Charles W., Jr. Petroleum engr. Mobil Oil Co., Wichita Falls, Tex., 1955-62; chief engr. Newmont Oil Co., Ft. Worth, Houston, 1962-65; prodn. mgr. Armer Oil Co., Ft. Worth, 1965—, pres., 1973-76; pres. Tamoco Prodn. Co., 1976-78, Seely Oil Co., Ft. Worth, 1978—; pres., dir. Metro Custom Plastics, Inc., Arlington, Tex. Served with U.S. Army, 1956-58. Mem. Soc. Petroleum Engrs. (chmn. Ft. Worth sect. 1971-72), Am. Assn. Petroleum Landmen, Tex. Mid-Continent, West Central Tex. oil and gas assns., Ind. Producers Assn. Am., Ft. Worth Wildcatters, Nat. Fedn. Ind. Businessmen, Former Students Tex. A. and M. U. (v.p. bd. dirs.). Baptist. Mason. Clubs: Petroleum (dir. 1973-78, pres. 1976-77), Century II, Colonial Country, Ft. Worth Boat, Ft. Worth (Ft. Worth). Home: 3417 Acorn Run Fort Worth TX 76109 Office: 1902 Ft Worth Nat Bank Bldg Fort Worth TX 76102

SEEMAN, SANDRA OLDHAM, nurse; b. Denver, Sept. 3, 1946; d. Hershel B. and Agnes Belle W. Oldham; B.S.N., U. Ark., 1968; m. John S. Seeman, Jr., Aug. 27, 1966; 1 dau., Shelley Brooke. Staff nurse Helena (Ark.) Hosp., 1968, VA Hosp., Fayetteville, Ark., 1968-71; with Memphis VA Hosp., 1971—, head nurse operating room/recovery room, 1975-76, supr. operating room/recovery room, 1976-79, supr. operating room/recovery room/ICU, 1979—. Mem. Assn. Operating Room Nurses (sec. Memphis chpt. 1978—, alt. nat. del. 1979), Operating Room Research Inst. Panel. Democrat. Lutheran. Office: VA Med Center 1030 Jefferson St Memphis TN 38104

SEFCIK, ROBERT EUGENE, soft drink bottling co. exec.; b. San Antonio, Oct. 18, 1937; s. Emil Joseph and Julia Catherine (Kostelnik) S.; B.B.A., St. Marys U., 1959; m. Ann Marie Jaeckle, Apr. 30, 1960; children—Joan Lynn, Julie Ann. Budget mgr. retail store 4, Goodyear Tire & Rubber Co., San Antonio, 1959-60; route mgr. Coca-Cola Bottling Co. San Antonio, 1961-63, adminstrv. asst. to v.p. and gen. sales mgr., 1964-65, sales rep., 1966-68, sales mgr. home market, 1968-70, asst. gen. sales mgr., 1971-74, v.p., 1975-78, div. mgr., 1975—, sr. v.p., 1978—. Vice chmn. Baptist Meml. Hosp. System Bd., 1976-78, chmn., 1978—, chmn. credit union, 1974—; city councilman City of Windcrest (Tex.), 1971-77; mayor pro tem City of Windcrest, 1977—. Mem. Am. Mktg. Assn. (dir. San Antonio chpt. 1974-77), Better Bus. Bur. San Antonio (dir. 1970-73), St. Mary's U. Alumni Assn. (dir. 1976—), San Antonio Livestock Assn., Northside C. of C. Roman Catholic. Clubs: Plaza (San Antonio), Woodlake, Order of Alhambra. Office: Coca-Cola Bottling Co of San Antonio 162 Exposition Dr San Antonio TX 78220

SEFTON, NORMAN HAROLD, univ. telecommunications exec.; b. Providence, June 11, 1934; s. Edwin and Mary Mildred S.; B.S. in Econs., U. R.I., 1956; m. Elizabeth Buening, Apr. 12, 1958; children—Lynn, Keith Karen. Purchasing buyer Applied Physic Lab., Johns Hopkins U., Laurel. Md., 1959-61, asst. to adminstrv. mgr., 1961-63, communications coordinator, 1963-67; dir. facilities and services Communications Satellite Corp., Washington, 1967-70; telephone systems engr. U. N.C., Chapel Hill, 1970-76; dir. univ. and med. center telecommunications Duke U., Durham, N.C., 1976-79, asst. bus. mgr.-communications, 1980—; communications cons. N.C. Gov.'s Task Force on Telecommunications, 1979--. Served to capt. AUS, 1956-58. Mem. Am. Assn. Coll. and Univ. Telecommunication (regional dir. 1972—, Outstanding Regional Dir. award 1978), N.C. Telecommunication Assn., Southeastern Telecommunications Assn., Internat. Communications Assn., Telmax Users Assn. (v.p. 1979-80, pres. 1980), S.W. Durham Athletic Assn. Democrat. Clubs: Duke Mgmt., Exchange Swim. Home: 5618 Woodberry Rd Durham NC 27707 Office: Duke U - Med Center 114-A Tel-Com Bldg Duke U Durham NC 27706

SEGAL, JERRY, shoe co. exec.; b. Wadesboro, N.C., Nov. 30, 1943; s. Albert Gerson and Dorothy Ann (Levine) S.; student East Carolina U., 1962-64, 1970-71; m. Linda Carole Angel, Nov. 24, 1974; children—Leslie Michelle, Barbara Paige. Store mgr. Pic'n Pay Stores, Matthews, N.C., 1964-65, accessory buyer, 1965-66, ladies buyer, 1966-70, supr., 1971-72, real estate mgr., v.p., 1972-76, exec. v.p., dir. real estate, 1976—, also dir. Mem. Internat. Council Shopping Centers. Home: 5807-B Sharon Rd Charlotte NC 28010 Office: PO Box 745 Matthews NC 28105

SEGAL, ROBERT MILTON, educator; b. Newark, Aug. 29, 1925; B.A., U. Wis., 1950; M.S.W., U. Pitts., 1952; Ph.D., Brandeis U., 1969; m. Beverly E. Gechman, June 21, 1953; children—Alicia, Paula, Beth. Caseworker, Family Service Bur., Chgo., 1952-55; psychiat. social worker VA Mental Hygiene Clinic, San Diego, 1955-57; casework supr. Child and Family Service, New Brunswick, N.J., 1957-58; caseworker Jewish Family and Children Service, Miami, Fla., 1959-62; planning cons. Welfare Planning Council of Dade County, Miami, 1962-66; program dir. social work Inst. for Study of Mental Retardation, U. Mich., Ann Arbor, 1969-78, asso. prof. Sch. Social Work, 1969-78; prof. Grad. Sch. Social Work, U. Houston, 1978—; cons. to various govt. agys. and schs., 1970—. Bd. dirs. Cresthaven Nursing Center, Austin, Tex., 1977-79. Mem. Nat. Assn. Social Workers (dir. 1966-68, chmn. social action com. Huron Valley chpt. 1969-71), Am. Assn. Mental Deficiency (vice-chmn. bd. social work sect. 1971-73). Contbr. articles to jours. in field.

SEGAL, SIMON, real estate exec.; b. Havana, Cuba, Apr. 16, 1941; s. Govsey and Julia (Getzug) S.; brought to U.S., 1955, naturalized, 1970; B.C.E., Cornell U., 1965. Owner, Simon Segal Constrn. Co., Miami Beach, 1971—; pres. Investex Realty Corp., Miami, Fla., 1973-75, S.S. Investments, Inc., Miami, 1975—. Recipient Key to City of Miami, 1974, Key to City of South Miami, 1975. Registered profl. engr., Fla.; registered real estate and mortgage broker, Fla. Mem. Fla. Engring. Soc., Nat. Soc. Profl. Engrs., ASCE (sec. 1970), Cornell Soc. Engrs., Greater Miami, Cuban Am. (founder, pres. 1971), Internat. (senator) jr. chambers commerce, Soc. Am. Mil. Engrs., Cornell U., Peekskill Mil. Acad. alumni assns. Club: Bankers (Miami). Home: 208 Meridian Ave Miami Beach FL 33139 Office: Ingraham Bldg Miami FL 33131

SEGEL, THOMAS DONALD, newspaper editor and pub.; b. Tacoma, June 11, 1931; s Nathan R. and Vesta Mae (Stater) S.; student San Diego State U., 1952-53, U. Tokyo, 1963-64; B.A., Arlington State U., 1961; m. Pattie Beatrice Hood, Dec. 30, 1950; 1 son, Jason Barry. Enlisted USMC, 1948, advanced through grades to master gunnery sgt., 1971; station mgr. Armed Forces TV, Okinawa, 1966-69; cmdr. Am. Forces Radio & TV, TuyHoa, Vietnam, 1970; ops. dir. Am. Forces Network, Saigon, 1971; sta. mgr. network opns. officer, Far East Network, Tokyo, 1971-74; ret., 1974; dir. pub. affairs Marine Mil. Acad., Harlingen, Tex., 1974-80; editor-in-chief, co-pub. Valley Citizen, newspaper, 1978—, MMA Jour., mag., 1978—. Pres. Rebel Days Inc., 1974-77; pres. PTA; mem. Republican Town Com. Decorated Bronze Star, Purple Heart (3), Cross of Gallantry. Recipient Thomas Jefferson award for journalistic excellence Army/Navy Times Found., 1974, Combat Corr. distinguished Service award, 1973, Combat Corr. Best Radio Prodn. award, 1972. Mem. Writers Guild, Mil. Writers League, Christian Writers Assn., Combat Corr. Assn., Nat. Broadcasters Assn., Fleet Res. Assn., VFW, Am. Legion, DAV, Marine Corp League, 1st Marine Div. Assn., Confederate Air Force Assn. Presbyn. (elder). Clubs: Elks, Lions (publicity dir. Harlingen 1978—), Arroyo Boat (commodore). Author: (with Dimitri Vail) Dateline Vietnam, 1967; Men in Space, 1976; Shadow of Honor, 1979. Home: 1629 Clarke St Harlingen TX 78550 Office: 310 E Jackson Harlingen TX 78550

SEGER, EDWIN CONRAD, psychologist; b. Bklyn., July 4, 1932; s. Ludwig Edwin and Anna Louise (Menninger) S.; B.S., Syracuse U., 1957; M.A., Ariz. State U., 1960, Ph.D., 1963; m. Patricia Roberta Martin, Oct. 1, 1976. Clin. psychologist Ariz. State Indsl. Sch. for Boys, Ft. Grant, Ariz., 1962-66; probation officer County of San Diego, San Diego, Calif., 1966-69; field assessment officer Peace Corps, Bogota, Columbia, S. Am., 1969-71; clin. psychologist U. Tex. Med. br., Galveston, 1971-72; clin. chief of psychology Bryce Hosp., Tuscaloosa, Ala., 1973—. Served with U.S. Army, 1952-54. Diplomate in clin. psychology Am. Bd. Profl. Psychology. Mem. Am., Canadian, Ala. (chmn. ethics com. 1976-77), Tuscaloosa (chmn. 1974-77) psychol. assns. Home: 43L Northwood Lake Northport AL 35476 Office: Bryce Hospital Tuscaloosa AL 35401

SEGREST, HERMAN BRAZILL, sports scientist, educator; b. Hico, Tex., Jan. 14, 1914; s. Ollie Reuben and Mattie Lee (Brazill) S.; B.S., N. Tex. State U., 1937, M.S., 1946; M. Ed., Tex. A&M U., 1955; Ed.D., Baylor U., 1962; m. Nettie Faye Baccus, Aug. 17, 1937; children—David, Connie, Gene. Dir. health and phys. edn. Monahans (Tex.) Public Schs., 1937-42; dir. required phys. edn. Tex. A&M U., College Station, 1945-63; coordinator phys. edn. service program Tex. Tech. U., Lubbock, 1963—. Active youth league baseball and football. Served from pvt. to capt. A.C., 1942-45. Mem. Tex. Assn. Health,

Phys. Edn. and Recreation (state honor award 1967), AAHPER, S.W. Football Ofcls. Assn., Assn. Phys. Edn. in Higher Edn. Methodist. Club: Masons. Author handbook of phys. activities for men, 1969. Home: 5203 17th St Lubbock TX 79416

SEGREST, JERE PALMER, biochem. pathologist; b. Dothan, Ala., Aug. 16, 1940; s. Jere Palmer and Grace (Hudgins) S.; B.A. in Chemistry, Vanderbilt U., 1962, M.D., 1967, Ph.D. in Biochemistry, 1969; m. Susan Clapp Freeman, Sept. 3, 1966; children—Jere Stuart, Charles Austin, Susan Chamberlain. Intern, resident in pathology Vanderbilt U. Hosp., Nashville, 1968-70; resident in pathology George Washington U. Sch. Medicine, Washington, 1974; asso. prof. pathology, biochemistry and microbiology, U. Ala., Birmingham, 1975—, scientist Comprehensive Cancer Center, Inst. Dental Research, Diabetes Research and Tng. Center; mem. molecular cytology study sect. NIH. Served with USPHS, 1970-74. NIH grantee; NSF grantee; diplomate Am. Bd. Pathology. Mem. AAAS, Am. Assn. Pathologists and Bacteriologists, Am. Chem. Soc. (com. on profl. tng.), Am. Soc. Exptl. Pathology, Am. Soc. Biol. Chemists, Biophys. Soc. (biopolymer and membrane biophysics subgroups), Fedn. Am. Scientists, N.Y. Acad. Scis., Am. Soc. for Cell Biology, Phi Beta Kappa, Sigma Xi. Mem. editorial bd. Membrane Biochemistry; contbr. articles to profl. jours. Home: 3709 Forest Run Rd Mountain Brook AL 35233 Office: G-019 Volker Hall U Ala Birmingham AL 35294

SEGROVES, KENNETH LEE, outdoor equipment co. exec.; b. Detroit, May 8, 1938; s. Melvin Norris and Ethel Fern (Anderson) S.; B.S., Eastern Mich. U., 1961; M.A., U. Mo., 1963; Ph.D. (scholar), U. Western Australia, 1968. Asst. prof. biol. scis. U. Conn., Storrs, 1967-70; research scientist sr. grade Amoco Prodn. Co., Tulsa, 1970-72; pres., owner The Wilderness Adventurer, Inc., Tulsa, 1972—. Mem. A.A.A.S., Bot. Soc. Am., Geol. Soc. Am., Am. Assn. Stratigraphic Palynologists. Contbr. articles to profl. jours. Home: Route 3 Box 732A Broken Arrow OK 74012 Office: 6508 E 51st St Tulsa OK 74145

SEGURA, PEARL MARY, ret. librarian, educator; b. Lafayette, La., June 12, 1909; d. Joseph Sidney and Celestine (Gutierrez) Segura; B.A., U. Southwestern La., 1930, postgrad. summer 1932, 42-43, 46-48, 51-52; B.S. in L.S., La. State U., 1941; postgrad. summers, Tulane U., 1931, Columbia, 1939, U. Ill., 1948, U. Houston, 1954. Tchr., librarian Indian Bayou (La.) High Sch., 1930-31; tchr. Maurice (La.) High Sch., 1931-33, tchr., librarian, 1933-41; asst. circulation librarian Stephens Meml. Library U. Southwestern La., Lafayette, 1941-44, acting reference librarian, 1944-46, reference librarian, 1946-62, librarian Jefferson Caffery La. room Dupre Library, 1962-75, asso. prof. library sci., 1953-75. Mem. La. Library Assn., AAUW, Nat. Trust for Historic Preservation, La., Attakapas hist. assns., La. Geneal. and Hist. Soc., La. Folklore Soc., Met. Opera Guild, Lafayette Community Concerts Assn., Lafayette Art Assn., Am. Camellia Soc., La. State U., U. Southwestern La. alumni assns., D.A.R. (1st chpt. vice regent 1968-71, state chmn. U.S.A. bicentennial com. 1967-71, chpt. chmn. 1969-77), U.D.C., U.S. Daus. of 1812, Cath. Daus. Am., Am. Iris Soc., S.W. La. Poetry Soc., France Amerique de la Louisiane Acadienne (sec. 1964—), Phi Kappa Phi, Beta Phi Mu, Delta Kappa Gamma (pres. chpt. 1947-49), Kappa Kappa Iota (state handbook chmn. 1960-61, pres. Lambda conclave 1957-60). Democrat. Roman Catholic. Author: Acadians in Fact and Fiction: A Classified Bibliography, 1955. Contbr. articles to profl. jours. Home: 140 S Magnolia St Lafayette LA 70501

SEHDEVA, JAGJIT SINGH, cardio-vascular surgeon; b. Patiala, India, Aug. 20, 1939; came to U.S., 1963; naturalized, 1976; B.S., Punjab U., India, 1957, M.D., 1962; m. Parkash K. Sodhi, Jan. 1968; 1 child—Pauljit. Intern, St. Luke's-Children's Med. Center, Phila., 1963-64; resident Mercy Douglass Hosp., Phila., 1964-67, Emory U., Atlanta, 1967-69; postdoctoral fellow Cardiovascular Center, Norfolk (Va.) Gen. Hosp., 1969-70, Baylor U. Med. Center, Dallas, 1970; practice medicine specializing in cardio-vascular and thoracic surgery, 1970—; asst. prof. surgery Med. Center, La. State U., New Orleans, 1970-72, clin. asst. prof., 1972—; mem. staffs Dixon Meml. Hosp., Denham Springs, La., West Feliciana Parish Hosp., St. Francisville, La., Women's Hosp., Baton Rouge, La., Baton Rouge Gen. Hosp., Pointe Coupee Gen. Hosp., New Roads, La., EKL Hosp., Baton Rouge. Chmn. bd. govs. La. Inst. Med. Scis., Inst. of All Nations. Fellow A.C.S., Am. Coll. Cardiology, Am. Coll. Chest Physicians; mem. Assn. for Academic Surgery, Am. Heart Assn., Soc. Thoracic Surgeons, So. Thoracic Surg. Assn., East Baton Rouge Parish Med. Soc., Surg. Soc. Baton Rouge, 6th Dist. Med. Soc., La. Surg. Soc., James D. Rives Surg. Soc., Osler Abbott Resident Soc., Southeastern Surg. Congress. Club: Rotary Internat. Contbr. articles to med. jours. Home: 2598 Dalrymple Baton Rouge LA 70808 Office: 2744 Florida Blvd Baton Rouge LA 70802

SEIDEL, EDMUND OTTO, civil and structural engring. cons.; b. New Braunfels, Tex., Dec. 5, 1922; s. Otto Georg and Johanna (Schmidt) S.; B.S., U. Tex., 1944, M.S., 1948; m. Mary Frances Steele, July 30, 1946; children—Georg Martin, Gretchen Ann, Helen Frances. Instr. civil engring. U. Tex., Austin, 1946-48; field engr. E.M. Freeman & Assos., Shreveport, La., 1948-50; structural designer, draftsman Austin Co., Freeport, Tex., 1950-52; structural designer Lummus Co., Houston, 1952; structural group leader Brown & Root, Inc., Lake Charles, La., 1952-54; structural engr. Frank T. Drought, Cons. Engrs., San Antonio. 1954-60; cons. engr. Edmund O. Seidel, San Antonio, 1960-67; partner Seidel & Livesay Cons. Engrs., Inc., 1967-71, Seidel, Livesay & Davis, cons. Engrs., Inc., 1971-74, Seidel & Davis Cons. Engrs., Inc., 1974-77; owner Edmund O. Seidel & Assos., Cons. Engrs., Inc., San Antonio, 1977—. Asst. scout master Boy Scouts Am., 1952-62, 64, scout master, 1962-63. Bd. dirs. Beethoven Maenerchor, pres., 1973—. Served with USNR, 1944-46. Fellow ASCE (br. pres. 1969-70, state dir. 1971-74, v.p. for ednl. affairs Tex. sect. 1979), Tex. Soc. Profl. Engrs. (chpt. pres. 1974-75, dir. 1968-69), San Antonio C. of C. (adv. mem. bd. dirs. 1974-75), Chi Epsilon. Home: 9507 Valley View San Antonio TX 78217 Office: 2735 Nacogdoches Rd San Antonio TX 78217

SEIDENBERG, BERNARD, surgeon; b. Jersey City, N.J., Sept. 5, 1922; s. Joseph and Yetta (Blankfein) S.; B.A., N.Y. U., 1944, M.D., 1947; m. Nina Nelson, Aug. 16, 1972; children—Wayne, Rhona, Beth, Lisa, Debra, Dorothy. Intern Queens (N.Y.) Gen. Hosp., 1947-49; resident surgery Montefiore (N.Y.) Hosp., 1950-52, 54-55; practice medicine specializing in gen. and vascular surgery, N.Y.C.. 1955-71, Miami, Fla., 1971—; asso. clin. prof. surgery Montefiore Hosp., Albert Einstein Med. Sch., N.Y.C., 1964-71; asso. clin. prof. surgery U. Miami Med. Sch., Coral Gables, Fla.. 1971—. Served with AUS, 1943-46, USAF, 1952-54. Diplomate Am. Bd. Surgery. Fellow A.C.S.; mem. Internat. Cardiovascular Soc., New York Soc. Cardiovascular Surgery, Soc. Surgery of Alimentary Tract, N.Y. Surg. Soc., Am., Fla., Dade County med. assns. Contbr. articles to med. jours. Home: 2200 NE 199th St N Miami FL 33180 Office: 1100 NE 163d St N Miami Beach FL 33162

SEIDL, FRANK JOSEPH, physician; b. Chgo., Nov. 12, 1932; s. Otto F. and Elizabeth (Fleishman) S.; M.D., Tulane U., 1964; m. Sylvia F. Firnandez, June 4, 1962; children—Elizabeth, Frank, Stephanie, Kristen. Intern, Tampa (Fla.) Gen. Hosp., 1964-65; resident Michael Reese Hosp. and Med. Center, Chgo., 1972-75; pvt. practice medicine, Clearwater, Fla., 1968—; clin. asso. prof. ophthalmology U. South Fla. Med. Sch., 1977—; mem. staff Morton F. Plant Hosp., Clearwater Community Hosp., Largo Med. Center. Served with USAF, 1954-57. Diplomate Am. Bd. Ophthalmology. Fellow A.C.S.; mem. Am. Assn. Ophthalmology. Roman Catholic. Office: 909 S Fort Harrison St Clearwater FL 33516

SEIDLE, DECIMA DAVIS, ednl. adminstr.; b. Copan, Okla., Mar. 12, 1915; d. George Leonard and Stella Bell (Brown) Davis; B.S., Okla. State U., 1958, M.S., 1966; m. Jack C. Seidle, July 29, 1932; children—Jack I., Jill Seidle Jennings. Accountant-clk., Phillips Petroleum Co., Bartlesville, Okla., 1942-52, librarian Phillips Chem. Co., 1955-56; tchr. Bartlesville City Schs., 1958-67, Caney (Kans.) Pub. Schs., 1967-69, Dewey (Okla.) Public Schs., 1969-71; sch. counselor, adminstrv. asst. Dewey Pub. Schs., 1971—. Certified tchr., sch. counselor, adminstr. Okla. Mem. Am., Okla. personnel and guidance assns., Nat., Okla. edn. assns., Am. Sch. Counselor Assn. Home: Stone Oak Ridge Route 1 Copan OK 74022 Office: 324 E 12th St Dewey OK 74029

SEIGLER, AUBREY BELMONT, labor relations exec.; b. Hawthorne, Fla., Oct. 16, 1921; s. James Gardnier and Bertha Mable (Davis) S.; student mil. sch. Locomotive engr. Seaboard Railroad, Wildwood, Fla., 1941; with Seaboard Air Line Ry., 1941—, chmn. legis. bd., 1969—; vice chmn. bd. appeals Brotherhood of Locomotive Engrs., Cleve., from 1971, now chmn. bd. appeals. Served with AUS, 1942-45; CBI. Named Ky. Col., Ark. Traveler, Lt. Col., Ala. State Militia. Mem. S.E. Assn. Locomotive Engrs., Southeastern Meeting Assn. Democrat. Baptist. Mason (Shriner, 32 deg.), Elk. Home and Office: 616 Powell St Wildwood FL 32785

SEILER, GARY DARRELL, educator, counselor; b. Evansville, Ind., July 5, 1942; s. William Russell and Dolores Margarite (Baker) S.; student U. Evansville, 1960-62; B.A. in Edn., U. Ky., 1964, M.A. in Edn., 1966; Ed.D., U. Mass., 1972; NIMH/USPHS fellow, U. Fla., 1973-74; m. Victoria Joy Wolske, Aug. 13, 1971. Tchr., Leestown Jr. High Sch., Lexington, Ky., 1964-65; instr. Fla. Atlantic U., Boca Raton, 1966-70; pvt. practice mental health counseling, Ft. Lauderdale, Fla., 1971-72; dir. community mental health programs Ariz. Dept. Health, Phoenix, 1974; asst. prof. counselor edn. U. Fla., Gainesville, 1974—; pres. Mental Health Counseling and Consultation Center; v.p. Malibu Corp., Luxury Homes, Inc. Mem. gen. assembly Nat. Council for Internat. Health, 1979-80; del. at large U.S. Com. for WHO, 1979-80; bd. dirs. UN Assn. Recipient Best Prof. award Fla. Atlantic U., 1969. Cert. clin. mental health counselor. Mem. Am. Personnel and Guidance Assn., Assn. for Counselor Edn. and Supervision, Am. Mental Health Counselor Assn., Nat. Assn. Sch. Psychologists, Phi Delta Kappa. Contbr. articles to profl. jours. Home: 2901 SE 24th Pl Gainesville FL 32601 Office: 1216 Norman Hall U Fla Gainesville FL 32611

SEILER, ROBERT E., accountant, educator; b. Fort Worth, Oct. 12, 1925; s. Ralph G. and Willie B. (Smith) S.; B.C.S., Tex. Christian U., 1949, M.B.A., 1951; Ph.D., U. Ala., 1953; m. Norma A. Allen, Aug. 30, 1948; children—Suzanne, Robert, Glenn, Richard. Asst. prof. accounting Miami U., Oxford, Ohio, 1953-55; asso. prof. U. Tex., 1955-65; prof. Stanford U. (Calif.), 1965-67; prof. U. Houston, 1967—, chmn. dept. accounting, 1975-77. Served in USN, 1942-46. C.P.A., Tex.; recipient Thurston award Inst. Internal Auditors, 1959, Pool award, 1972; Ford Found. fellow, 1963. Mem. Am. Inst. C.P.A.'s, Tex. Soc. C.P.A.'s, Fin. Execs. Inst., Am. Accounting Assn., Beta Gamma Sigma, Beta Alpha Psi. Author: Managerial Accounting, 1967, 2d edit., 1973; Administration of Research and Development, 1963; Elementary Accounting, 1963, 3d edit., 1979; also articles. Home: 134 Plantation St Houston TX 77024 Office: 210B Heyne U Houston Houston TX 77004

SEINSHELMER, J(OSEPH) F(ELLMAN), JR., ins. exec.; b. Galveston, Tex., Aug. 25, 1913; s. J.F. and Irma (Kraus) S.; grad. Mercersburg Acad., 1932; B.B.A., Tulane U., 1936; m. Jessie Lee Gould, July 19, 1938; children—Joseph Fellman III, Virginia Lee, Robert Louis. Salesman, Seinsheimer Ins. Agy., 1936-41; with Am. Indemnity Group, 1941—, successively agy. mgr., asst. sec., sec., v.p., 1941-51, pres. dir., 1951—; pres., dir. Am. Indemnity Co., Am. Fire & Indemnity Co., Am. Computing Co., Tex. Gen. Indemnity Co., Am. Finance Co., Galveston, U.S. Securities Corp., Am. Indemnity Financial Corp.; dir., v.p. Galveston Corp., Tex. Fiberglass Products, Inc., U.S. Nat. Bank, U.S. Nat. Bancshares, Inc. Clubs: Artillery, Galveston. Home: 4809 Woodrow St Galveston TX 77550 Office: One Am Indemnity Plaza Galveston TX 77550

SEIPOS, ANDREW GEORGE, SR., mfg. co. exec.; b. Easton, Pa., Feb. 6, 1918; s. Andrew and Theresa V. (Kovacs) Sipos; student Sch. Architecture, N.Y. U., 1938, Cooper Union, 1940; m. Mary Ann Doutrich, June 30, 1973; children by previous marriage—Lee Brooke, Andrew George, Thomas J. Vice pres., gen. mgr. Dixie Inc., Miami, Fla., 1952-56; asst. chief engr. Panelfab Inc., Miami, 1956-60; engring. designer Charles Payne & Assos., Inc., Miami, 1960-62; mgr. product engring. Wollard Aircraft Inc., Miami, 1962-72; mgr. product devel. Automated Building Components, Miami, 1972—; cons. to patent attys. Mem. Council on Furniture Engring. and Research (dir.), Nat. Assn. Furniture Mfrs., Nat. Wooden Pallet and Container Assn., Nat. Assn. Bedding Mfrs., Internat. Solar Energy Soc. Republican. Presbyterian. Patentee. Home: 661 Cardium St Sanibel Island FL 33957

SEITER, EVE VICTORIA CUSHMAN (MRS. KENNETH SEITER), writer, broadcaster, lectr.; b. Richwood, Ohio June 17, 1906; d. David Clyde and Grace (Watson) Cushman; student Miami U., Oxford, Ohio, 1924-25, Wooster Coll., 1947-57; m. Kenneth David Seiter, Sept. 5, 1925; children—Patricia Jeanne Seiter Burkholder, Richard David. Lectr. lit., civic, religious groups, convs., bus. meetings, libraries broadcaster lit. and religious programs throughout U.S., 1940—, lay preacher; life ins. agt. Prudential of Am., 1944-46. Pub. relations chmn. United Ch. Women of Licking County and South Central Ohio Region, 1949-57; edl. Bible study leader Nat. Presbyn. Women's Convocation, 1958; pres. Zanesville Presbyterial of Presbyn. Ch., 1954-56; ofcl. del. Licking County Council Chs., 1954-58; local spiritual life chmn. Presbyn. Ch., 1963-65; chmn. bd. Knox Library, Westminister Presbyn. Ch., Steubenville, Ohio; ruling elder Jekyil Island Community Presbyn. Ch., 1977, also liaison to Am. Bible Soc.; mem. leadership trust group nurture div. Savannah Presbytery, Presbyn. Ch. U.S., also mem. pulpit supply com.; mem. city council, Wintersville, Ohio, 1962-66; Republican candidate for mayor, Wintersville, 1965. Recipient Appreciation award Kiwanis clubs, Newark, Ohio, Lorain, Ohio, 1957, Steubenville, Ohio, 1960. Mem. Nat. League Am. Pen Women (2 1st awards 1964, W.Va. sec. 1964-65, chpt. pres. 1970-72), Jekyll Island Arts Assn., Chi Omega. Club: Soroptimist (pres. 1958-59); Wierton Womans (W.Va.); Jekyll Island Garden (chaplain). Contbg. author: Inklings, 1974; contbr. to speech jours., devotional guides, newspapers, mags. Address: 778 S Beachview Dr Jekyll Island GA 31520

SEITH, ROBERT THEODORE, mgmt. cons.; b. Racine, Wis., Aug. 12, 1926; s. Theodore Lewis and Ruth (Cleaver) S.; B.S. in Chem. Engring., Purdue U., 1949; m. Ruth Marilyn Sievert, Oct. 12, 1946; children—Michael Robert, Deborah Lynn, Elizabeth Jane. With Mosinee Paper Mills Co. (Wis.), 1949-69, successively research chemist, dir. product devel., sales mgr., 1957-61, v.p. marketing, 1961-69, exec. v.p. Celluponic System, Inc., 1962-69; v.p. marketing, paper div. Gulf States Paper Corp., 1969-77; mgmt. cons., 1977—; dir. Bag West Paper Co., 1965-69; dir. Shuld Mfg. Co. Active Children's Service Soc. Wis., Wis. Assn. for Mental Health. Co-chmn. Republican party Marathon County, 1953. Served with AUS, 1944-46. Mem. Def. Supply Assn. (dir., past pres. Midwest), Salesmens Assn. Paper Industry (v.p. Wis. div. 1962-63, nat. pres. 1966—), Am. Paper Inst. (bd. govs.), Am. Legion, Bleached Converting Assn. (dir.), Kraft Paper Assn. (exec. com. 1960, mem. research and devel. com.), Ala. World Trade Assn., Am. Legion, Sigma Phi Epsilon. Lutheran. Mason, Lion (pres. 1953-54). Author various articles profl. jours. Patentee in field. Home: 808 Indian Hills Dr Tuscaloosa AL 35401

SEITZ, THOMAS WILLARD, paint mfg. co. exec.; b. Lakewood, Ohio, Nov. 30, 1948; s. Francis Willard and Norma Edith (Wulf) S.; B.A., Case Inst. Tech., 1970; M.B.A., U. Chgo., 1974; postgrad. U. Tex., 1978; m. Nancy Ann Phelps, Dec. 29, 1971; children—Jonathan Willard, Jeremy Phelps. With Sherwin Williams Co., 1970—, sr. applications engr., Pontiac, Ill., 1974-76, sr. process engr., Garland, Tex., 1976-77, mgr. prodn. planning and scheduling, 1977-78, supt. paint prodn., Morrow, Ga., 1978—. Mem. Fedn. Socs. for Coatings Tech., Soc. Mfg. Engrs., Nat. Paint and Coatings Assn., Clayton County C. of C. Home: 8321 Yale Jonesboro GA 30236 Office: 6785 Main St Morrow GA 30260

SEITZ, WILLIAM ALFRED, educator; b. Waltham, Mass., Dec. 27, 1948; s. Alfred George and Ingeborg (Lohse) S.; B.A., Rice U., 1970; Ph.D., U. Tex., 1973; m. Patricia Ann Kennedy, May 19, 1971. Instr., postdoctoral fellow in chemistry U. Tex., Austin, 1973-74; postdoctoral fellow in physics Rice U., Houston, 1974-75, asst. prof. chemistry, 1975-76, 77—. Welch Found. fellow, 1976-77; Woodrow Wilson fellow, 1970; NSF trainee, 1970-73. Mem. Am. Chem. Soc. Episcopalian. Home: 1422 25th St Galveston TX 77550 Office: Dept Marine Sci Moody Coll Galveston TX 77553

SEKADLO, ROGER GEORGE, airport mgr.; b. Two Rivers, Wis., Dec. 14, 1924; s. George Frank and Linda Marie (Arneman) S.; student U. Wis., 1946-48; B.S., Purdue U., 1951; m. Rosalyn Louise Deau, Feb. 28, 1948; children—Steven, Penny, Nancy. Pilot, Purdue Aeros. Corp., West Lafayette, Ind., 1951; mgr. Municipal Airport Authority, Erie, Pa., 1951-57; airport dir. Milwaukee County, Wis., 1957-61; aviation dir. City Fort Worth, 1961-67; exec. dir., mgr. Greensboro-High Point Airport Authority, Greensboro, N.C., 1967—. Instr. airport mgmt. Guilford Tech. Inst., Jamestown, N.C., 1971-72. Served as pilot USAAF, 1943-46. Decorated Bronze Star. Mem. Airport Operators Council Internat. (dir. 1971-75), Am. Assn. Airport Execs. (dir. 1966-69, 73-78, pres. 1978-79). Lutheran. Elk, Rotarian (dir. 1976-79). Home: 3107 Robinhood Dr Greensboro NC 27408 Office: Box 8113 Greensboro NC 27410

SELBY, GREGORY VINCENT, aerospace engr.; b. Townsend, Del., Feb. 4, 1949; s. Hilbert Clifton and Hattie Regina (Nottingham) S.; B.S., U. Va., 1971; M.S., U. Del., 1979; m. Barbara Jean Grimes, June 15, 1969; 1 son, Gregory V. With NASA, 1971—, aerospace engr. NASA Lewis Research Center, Cleve., 1975-76, Wallops Flight Center, Va., 1976—. Mem. AIAA, ASME. Mem. Ch. of Christ. Home: PO Box 106 Wallops Island VA 23337 Office: NASA Wallops Flight Center Wallops Island VA 23337

SELBY, JOHN HORACE, surgeon; b. Springfield, Mass., Nov. 11, 1919; s. Howard Williams and Ethel (Wagg) S.; A.B., Dartmouth Coll., 1941; M.D., Boston U., 1944; postgrad. U. Pa., 1948; children (by previous marriage) John H., Susan, Sherrill, Lucinda; m. 2d, Carolyn Symes, Feb. 14, 1970. Intern Mary Hitchcock Meml. Hosp., Hanover, N.H., 1944-45; resident New Eng. Deaconess Hosp., 1945-46, Mass. Meml. Hosp., 1949-50, Boston City Hosp., 1950-51 (all Boston), practice medicine, specializing in thoracic surgery, Lubbock, Tex., 1952—; chief thoracic surgery Meth. Hosp., Lubbock, 1964-73, 77-79, chief surgery, 1954-56, 64-65; chief of staff St. Mary's Hosp., Lubbock, 1973, chief surgery, 1970; chief surgery Univ. Hosp., 1973; active staff Meth. Hosp., St. Mary's, Health Scis. Center; courtesy staff Highland Hosp.; cons. staff W. Tex., Univ., Lea County, Lovington, N.Mex., Meml., Seminole, Mercy, Slaton, Cook Meml., Levelland hosps.; chmn. bd. South Plains Health Systems, 1975—; mem. Statewide Health Coordinating Council, 1977—, exec. com., 1979; clin. prof. surgery Tex. Tech. Med. Sch.; mem. adv. com. Lubbock County Hosp. Dist. Bd., 1979—; trustee, med. dir. All Am. Security Life Ins. Co., 1954-55. Bd. dirs. Tex. Tb Assn., pres., 1967-68; bd. dirs. Lubbock Community Planning Council, 1954-56; chmn. adv. bd. Salvation Army, 1956-57; bd. dirs. Inst. for Internat. Research and Devel. Diplomate Am. Bd. Thoracic Surgery, Am. Bd. Surgery. Fellow A.C.S., Am. Coll. Chest Physicians, Internat. Coll. Surgeons, Internat. Acad. Medicine, Southwestern Surg. Coll.; mem. So. Thoracic Surgery Assn., S.W. Surg. Conf., Am. Thoracic Soc., Tex. Trudeau Soc. (pres. 1959-60), Lubbock-Crosby County Med. Soc., Panhandle S-Plains Med. Soc., Tex. Med. Assn. (ho. of dels. 1979—, com. on health planning 1979—), AMA, Am. Cancer Soc. (dir. Tex. div.), S. Plains Heart Assn. (pres. 1957), Lubbock County Tb Assn. (pres. 1959-60). Home: Altura Towers 1617 27th St Lubbock TX 79405 Office: Med-Profl Bldg 3801 19th St Lubbock TX 79410

SELBY, ROY SADLER, health planning agy. exec.; b. Belhaven, N.C., Oct. 16, 1940; s. Daniel Ottis and Edna Jane (Sadler) S.; B.S.P., East Carolina U., Greenville, N.C., 1973; m. Letha Daniels Selby, Dec. 27, 1967; children—Paul Douglas, Reggie Earl, Lisa Gay, Michael Scott. Trimmer operator Weyerhaeuser Co., Plymouth, N.C., 1965-69; collections mgr. GAC Fin. Corp., 1963-65; dir. HEW Comprehensive Health Planning, Washington, N.C., 1973-76; exec. dir. Eastern Carolina Health Systems Agy., Greenville, 1976—. Served with U.S. Army, 1959-62. Mem. Am. Health Planning Assn. Democrat. Methodist. Clubs: Masons, Shriners. Home: 1304 Red Banks Rd Greenville SC 27834 Office: PO Box 7306 Greenville NC 27834

SELCER, ROBERT RAYMOND, veterinarian, educator; b. Corpus Christi, Oct. 30, 1948; s. Fred and Elizabeth Kathern (Urbanovsky) S.; student Wharton County Jr. Coll., 1966-67; B.S., Tex. A&M U., 1970, D.V.M., 1971; M.S., Purdue U., 1974; m. Barbara Arnold, Nov. 24, 1973. Temporary instr. vet. sci., also intern U. Ga., Athens, 1971-72; resident, also grad. instr. small animal clinics Purdue U., Lafayette, Ind., 1972-74; asst. prof. vet. sci. U. Calif., Davis, 1974-77; asso. prof. vet. sci. U. Tenn., Knoxville, 1977—. Named faculty mem. of yr. U. Calif., Davis, 1976-77. Diplomate Am. Bd. Vet. Internal Medicine. Mem. Am. Vet. Neurology Assn. (pres.-elect 1979), Am. Vet. Med. Assn., Am. Animal Hosp. Assn., Am. Assn. Vet. Clinicians, Sigma Xi, Phi Kappa Phi, Phi Zeta. Contbr. articles to profl. publs. Home: Rural Route 1 Box 1266 Heiskell TN 37754 Office: PO Box 1071 U Tenn Knoxville TN 37901

SELETSKY, JUDY, speech therapist; b. Bronx, N.Y., Sept. 28, 1941; d. Robert and Esther (Reingold) Lindenfeld; B.S., Syracuse U., 1963, M.S., 1964; m. May 1, 1965; children—Greg, Todd, Kim. Tchr. of deaf Jr. High Sch. 47, N.Y.C., 1964-67, tchr. multiple handicapped deaf children, 1970-73; pvt. practice speech therapy and tutoring of deaf children in acad. subjects, Ormond Beach, Fla., 1973-78; substitute tchr. Broward County (Fla.) Public Schs., 1978-79, speech therapist, 1979—; speech therapist Stranahan High Sch., Ft. Lauderdale, Fla., Seminole Middle Sch., Plantation, Fla., 1979: co-chmn. Hearing and Eye Screening Program, Osceola Elem. Sch., Ormond Beach; participant Picture-Lady Program sponsored by Nat. Council Jewish Women, Daytona Beach, Fla. Vice pres., bd. dirs. Nat. Council Jewish Women. Recipient State cert. in deaf edn. and speech therapy, N.Y., Fla. Mem. Am. Speech and Hearing Assn., Council on Edn. of Deaf (profl. tchr. cert.). Home: 239 NW 84th Way Coral Springs FL 33065

SELF, CLARK, JR., mcht., land developer; b. Slaton, Tex., July 10, 1933; s. Clark and Mary Irene (Kost) S.; student Abilene Christian U., 1950-51; B.B.A. in Mktg., Tex. Tech. U., 1954; m. Jean Sargent, June 13, 1964; children—Leslie, Todd, Charles, Michael, Juli. Sales rep. Self Furniture Co., Slaton, 1954-66; v.p. Citizens State Bank, Slaton, 1966-68, dir., 1968—; owner, mgr. Self's Home Furnishings, Slaton, 1968—. Former bd. trustees Slaton Ind. Sch. Dist; mem. Slaton Bd. City Devel., 1969; former mem. Slaton City Commn.; bd. trustees Lubbock Christian Coll. Mem. S.W. Home Furnishings Assn. (past dir.), Slaton C. of C. (pres. 1961). Republican. Mem. Ch. of Christ. Club: Rotary. Home: 5527 79th St Lubbock TX 79424 Office: 235 W Garza St Slaton TX 79364

SELF, DWIGHT MITCHELL, broadcasting corp. exec.; b. Haleyville, Ala., May 28, 1936; s. James Wesley and Carmen Levesta (Hyatt) S.; student Radio Operational Engring. Sch., Burbank, Calif., 1954; M.Broadcast Mgmt., Broadcasters Coll., 1957; M.B.A., Coll. Pacific, 1978; m. Elizabeth Lynne Welch, May 25, 1957; children—Robert, Dwight, Michael, Timothy, Michelle. Staff announcer Sta. WJBB, Haleyville, 1952-54, Sta. WAJF, Decatur, Ala., 1954-55; sales mgr. Sta. WSUH, Oxford, Miss., 1955-59; pres., gen. mgr. Sta. WTRO, Dyersburg, Tenn., 1959-61; sales mgr. Sta. WLAY, Sheffield, Ala., 1961-71, pres., gen. mgr., 1971—; dir. First Nat. Bank, Tuscumbia, Ala. Chmn. Utilities Bd., Muscle Shoals, Ala., 1964—. Bd. dirs. Colbert County (Ala.) United Fund. Mem. Ala. Broadcasters' Assn. (dir.), Civitan Club, Muscle Shoals Bus., Profl. Club. Baptist (bd. deacons). Mason (Shriner). Home: 906 E Highland Ave Muscle Shoals AL 35660 Office: PO Box 220 Sheffield AL 35660

SELF, GLENDON DANNA, indsl. engr.; b. Waveland, Ark., Jan. 1, 1938; s. Charlie William and Alma (Vinesette) S.; Asso. Sci., Ark. Tech., 1956; B.S., U. Ark., 1958, M.S., 1959; Ph.D., Okla. State U., 1963; J.D., U. Tex., 1979; m. Sharon Darlene Glenn, June 4, 1960. Statis. quality control engr. Sandia Corp., Albuquerque, 1959-63; project analyst Gen. Dynamics, Ft. Worth, 1963-65; asst. prof. Tex. A. and M. U., College Station, 1965-66, 66-68, asso. prof., 1968-69; research specialist Boeing Co., Renton, Wash., 1966; mem. tech. staff Center for Naval Analyses, Arlington, Va., 1968; mgr. operations research Electronic Data Systems, Dallas, 1969-71, v.p. Dallas, 1971—; adj. prof. math. Tex. Christian U., 1964-65. Cons. in field. Mem. Operations Research Soc. Am., Inst. Mgmt. Sci., Am. Statis. Assn., Am. Soc. for Engring. Edn., Student Bar Assn. U. Tex., Sigma Xi, Tau Beta Pi, Alpha Pi Mu. Baptist. Contbr. articles to profl. jours. Home: 8903 Maple Glen Dr Dallas TX 75231 Office: 7171 Forest Ln Dallas TX 75230

SELF, JOHN GREGORY, aircraft leasing co. mktg. exec.; b. Houston, May 6, 1950; s. Johnnie Lloyd and Nadine (Jackson) S.; student Tyler Jr. Coll., 1968-70; B.S., E.Tex. State U., 1973; m. Glenda J. Gates, Sept. 10, 1977. Reporter Tyler (Tex.) Courier-Times Telegraph, 1970-72; news editor Lubbock (Tex.) Avalanche-Jour., 1973-74; news editor, crime reporter Houston Post, 1974-76; dir. public relations/flight ops. Hermann Hosp., Houston, 1976-77; v.p. mktg. Aviation Med. Services, Inc., Houston, 1977-79; v.p. Emergency Transport Systems, Inc., Houston, 1979—. Worker United Fund, Heart Fund Drive. Mem. Sigma Delta Chi (treas. East Tex. State U., 1972). Roman Catholic. Recognized in helicopter industry for pioneering hosp. concept. Office: 5662-D Birchmont St Houston TX 77091

SELF, PEGGY JOYCE, acct.; b. Anson, Tex., Oct. 3, 1938; d. C. Ernest and Ollie Bea (Morton) Glazner; B.S., Hardin-Simmons U., Abilene, Tex., 1960; M.B. in Edn. (grad. intern), Stephen F. Austin State U., Nacogdoches, Tex., 1974; postgrad. Tex. Christian U., Southwestern Bapt. Theol. Sem.; m. Jerry M. Self, June 11, 1960; children—Jay Mark, Angela. Various positions, 1960-70; instr. acctg. Stephen F. Austin State U., 1973-78; mgr. acctg. dept. Bapt. Sunday Sch. Bd., Nashville, 1978—; mem. adj. faculty Tenn. State U. Sec.-treas. Tex. Ministers Wives, 1973-74; mem. library bd. Nacogdoches City Commn., 1975-77. C.P.A., Tex. Mem. Nat. Acctg. Assn., Tenn. Soc. C.P.A.'s, CABLE, Beta Alpha Psi, Phi Chi Theta (hon.). Baptist. Home: 1223 Parker Pl Brentwood TN 37027 Office: 127 9th Ave N Nashville TN 37234

SELF, TIMOTHY HERBERT, clin. pharmacist; b. Nashville, June 1, 1948; s. Leslie O. and Elizabeth B. (Williams) S.; student David Lipscomb Coll., 1966-68; B.Sc., U. Tenn., 1971, Pharm.D., 1972; m. Melissa Matlock, June 14, 1975. Asst. prof. U. Tenn. Coll. Pharmacy, Memphis, 1972-77, asso. prof. dept. pharmacy practice, 1977—. Mem. Am. Soc. Hosp. Pharmacists, Am. Assn. Colls. Pharmacy. Mem. Ch. of Christ. Author: Systematic Approach to Patient Medication Profile Review, 1977; Systematic Review of Patient Medication Records for Nurses, 1980; also 25 articles in med. and pharm. jours. Office: Dept Pharmacy Practice U Tenn Memphis TN 38163

SELKINGHAUS, WALTER EUGENE, educator, nuclear engr., public relations officer; b. N.Y.C., Sept. 11, 1911; s. George William and Louisa (Rebscher) S.; B.S., Newark Coll. Engring., 1933; M.M.E., N.C. State U., 1940; student Oak Ridge Sch. Reactor Tech., 1960; m. Jeanne Douglas MacGregor, June 7, 1936; children—George Clifford, Charles William, Christine Louise, Bonnie Jeanne. Test engr. Wright Aeronautical Corp., Paterson, N.J., 1940-41; metallurgist Titeflex Corp., Newark, N.J., 1941-43; asso. prof. thermodynamics N.C State U., Raleigh, 1935-40, 1943-51; power plant superintendent Carolina Power & Light Co., Raleigh, 1951-67, dir. visitors centers, public relations officer, 1967-76. Counselor Boy Scouts Am., Hartsville, S.C., 1968-70; mem. Brunswick County Library Bd., 1979—. Registered profl. engr., N.J. Mem. Am. Nuclear Soc., Pi Tau Sigma. Clubs: Lion (pres. 1952-53, 79-80), Brunswick County Art Assn. (treas. 1976-77, pres. 1977-79), Rosicrucian. Co-author: Mechanical Engring. Lab, 1948. Home: PO Box 9 Supply NC 28462 Office: PO Box 488 Southport NC 28461

SELLERS, CLARENCE BLANCO, JR., speech pathologist, clin. audiologist; b. Tabor City, N.C., Jan. 8, 1945; s. Clarence Blanco and Lizzie Mae (Long) S.; B.A. (Escheats scholar), U. N.C., Chapel Hill, 1967; M.A., U. N.C., Greensboro, 1974, 75. Clin. audiologist Whitaker Regional Rehab. Center and Forsyth Hosp., Winston-Salem, N.C., 1974; cons. Goodwill Deafness Project, Winston-Salem, 1975; speech-lang. pathologist Forsyth Hosp., also Reynolds Hosp., Winston-Salem, 1975-76; instr. Rowan Tech. Inst., Salisbury, N.C., 1976—; pvt. practice speech and hearing Cabarrus Home Health Agy., Concord, N.C., 1976—; speech and hearing pathologist Stonewall Jackson Tng. Sch., Concord, 1976—, chmn. research and evaluation, 1976-79. Charter mem. Piedmont Residential Devel. Center, Concord, 1977. Mem. N.C. Assn. Educators, NEA, N.C. Speech and Hearing Assn., Am. Speech and Hearing Assn. (cert.). Methodist. Home: Route 5 Box 432 Concord NC 28025 Office: 1484 Old Charlotte Rd Concord NC 28025

SELLERS, GENE MARION HERRICK (MRS. MATTHEW BACON SELLERS), civic worker; b. Salt Lake City, Nov. 10, 1922; d. Harold Lewis and Marion (Wheelon) Herrick; student Traphagen Sch. Fashion, 1941-42; m. Matthew Bacon Sellers, June 1, 1946; children—Wendy (Mrs. Henry Medford Howell), Tracy (Mrs. Iftikhar Ali). Bd. mem. Friends of Fort Lauderdale (Fla.) Mus. Arts, 1969. Committeewoman Broward County Republican Exec. Com., 1967-73. Mem. DAR, Nat. Soc. Daus. Utah Pioneers. Club: Coral Ridge Yacht (Ft. Lauderdale). Home: 3030 NE 40th Ct Fort Lauderdale FL 33308

SELLERS, HAYWOOD CONRAD, banker; b. Greenville, N.C., Sept. 29, 1927; s. Robert Earl and Annie Ives (Andrews) S.; student East Carolina U., 1947-49; B.A., Wake Forest U., 1956; postgrad. Duke U., 1956-57; m. Betsy Anne Clarke, June 23, 1962; children—Mark Conrad, Jo Anne. Mgr. LPG div. Esso Standard Oil Co., Raleigh, N.C., 1957-58; agt. Pilot Life Ins. Co., Raleigh, 1958-60; account exec. A.B. Chance Co., Centralia, Mo., 1961-65; v.p., trust officer 1st Union Nat. Bank of N.C., Charlotte, 1966-76; head trust new bus. dept., v.p., trust officer So. Nat. Bank of N.C., Charlotte, 1976—; instr. Am. Inst. Banking; prof. bus. Central Piedmont Community Coll. Bd. dirs., pres. Carolinas Carrousel; advisor Meredith Coll.; former dir., v.p. Am. Cancer Soc.; founder, bd. dirs. Big Bros. of Charlotte; former deacon Sardis Presbyterian Ch. of Charlotte. Served with USN, 1945-47, to 1st lt. U.S. Army, 1949-53. Mem. Charlotte Sales and Mktg. Execs. (dir.), Charlotte Estate Planning Council, Charlotte C. of C., Assn. of Professions. Clubs: Masons (32 deg.), Shriners. Home: 2435 Valencia Terr Charlotte NC 28211 Office: 200 S College St Charlotte NC 28202

SELLERS, JACKIE, elec. distbn. mgr., educator; b. Murphy, N.C., Dec. 30, 1943; s. Carl Jack and Catherine Lola (McClure) S.; B.S.A. with honors, U. Ga., 1967, M.B.A., 1970, Ph.D., 1972; NDEA fellow Tex. A&M U., 1967-68; m. Brenda Howell, Mar. 20, 1965; 1 dau., Mary Katherine. Asso. prof. mgmt. Western Carolina U., 1972-77; dept. head mgmt. and mktg., asso. dir. Inst. Natural Resources, U. Ga., 1977—; mgr. Blue Ridge Elec. Membership Corp., 1979—; dir. local health services Clay County, N.C., 1978; cons. Mem. Am. Mgmt. Assn., So. Econ. Assn., Internat. Water Resources Assn. Methodist. Contbr. articles on natural resources to profl. jours. Office: PO Box 8 Young Harris GA 30582

SELLERS, JOSEPH AMOS, tire co. exec.; b. Abbeville, La., Aug. 27, 1929; s. Emile and Ematile (Lemaire) S.; student public schs.; m. Irene Dugas Sellers, Aug. 29, 1953; children—Karl Steven, Janet Claire. Rice farmer, 1947-48; asst. party chief U.S. Coast & Geodetic Surveys, 1948-53; high pressure pump operator Freeport Sulphur Co., 1953-54; owner Sellers Texaco Service, 1954-66; now mgr. tire center B.F. Goodrich Tire Co., Lafayette, La. Served with USAF, 1945-47. Mem. Greater Lafayette C. of C. Democrat. Roman Catholic. Office: 2802 Johnston St Lafayette LA 70503

SELLERS, MATTHEW BACON, land developer; b. N.Y.C., Nov. 13, 1919; s. Matthew Bacon and Ethel (Clark) S.; student Lehigh U., 1937-39; B.S., Franklin and Marshall Coll., 1941; m. Gene Herrick, June 1, 1946; children—Wendy (Mrs. H. Medford Howell), Tracy (Mrs. Iftikhar Ali). Dist. and br. mgr. Snow Crop Frozen Foods, Cin., 1946-52; v.p., gen. mgr. Urban Laundry Co., Balt., 1952-55; v.p., sec. Filterite Corp., Balt., 1955-60; land developer Broward and Palm Beach Counties, Fla., 1960—. Pres., Taxpayers League of Broward County, 1968-70; mem. Community Services and Facilities Bd., Ft. Lauderdale, Fla., 1970. Treas., Republican Exec. Com., 1966-67. Bd. dirs. Broward County Heart Assn., 1969-70, Fla. Heart Assn., 1970. Served to comdr. USNR, 1941-45. Mem. Nat. Soc. SAR (past pres. gen.), Soc. of Cincinnati, S.R., Soc. Colonial Wars, Washington Family Descs., Navy League U.S., Hon. Order Ky. Cols., Mil. Order of the Crusades, Ams. of Royal Descent, others, Phi Sigma Kappa. Club: Coral Ridge Yacht (past commodore). Home: 3030 NE 40th Ct Fort Lauderdale FL 33308

SELLERS, ROBERT VERNON, oil co. exec.; b. Bartlesville, Okla., Mar. 26, 1927; s. C. Vernon and Helen (Weeks) S.; B.M.E., U. Kans., 1948; grad. Advanced Mgmt. Program, Harvard; m. Anna Marie Hughes, Feb. 11, 1950; children—Barbara S. Bredemeier, Patricia S. Wheeler, Scott, John. Service engr. Dowell, Inc., 1949-50; various positions in transp., supply, corporate planning, fin. Cities Service Co., 1951-69, v.p. fin., 1969-71, dir., mem. exec. com., 1969—, vice chmn. bd., 1971-72, chmn. bd., chief exec. officer, chmn. exec. com., 1972—, chmn. fin. com., 1973—; dir. John Hancock Mut. Life Ins. Co. Asst. to dir. prodn. div. Petroleum Adminstrn. for Def., 1951-52. Bd. dirs., mem. exec. com. Am. Petroleum Inst.; mem. nat. advisory council Salvation Army; mem. advisory bd. U. Kans. Sch. Bus.; trustee Com. Econ. Devel., U. Tulsa, U. Kans. Endowment Assn.; bd. dirs. So. Growth Policies Bd. Served with USNR, 1945-46. Mem. Fin. Execs. Inst., Nat. Petroleum Council, Conf. Bd., Internat. (trustee U.S. council), Met. Tulsa (dir.) chambers commerce, Council on Fgn. Relations, Sigma Chi, Tau Beta Pi. Clubs: Nat. Golf Links Am., Board Room, Econ. (N.Y.C.); Summit, Tulsa, So. Hills Country (Tulsa); Internat. (Washington); Pipe Liners. Home: 2131 E 29th St Tulsa OK 74114 Office: Box 300 Tulsa OK 74102

SELLMEYER, RALPH LOUIS, educator; b. Osawatomie, Kans., Sept. 23, 1924; s. Albert George and Ethel Evelyn (Garretts) S.; student Baker U., 1946-48; B.J., U. Mo. at Columbia, 1949; M.A. in Ednl. Adminstrn., U. Mo. at Kansas City, 1950; m. Mildred Lucille Dahlstrom, Sept. 2, 1949; children—Melissa (Mrs. Don Glenn McCoy), Debra (Mrs. Richard Solomon), Sheri, Alison. Reporter Independence (Kan.) Daily Reporter, 1952; reporter, photographer, Kansas City (Mo.) Daily Drovers Telegram, 1953-54; sales mgr. Hot Coffee Caterers, Inc., Kansas City, Mo., 1954-57; editor Baldwin (Kans.) Ledger, 1957-60; prof., asso. chmn. mass communications dept. Tex. Tech U., Lubbock, 1960—. Served with USNR, 1942-46, 50-52. Mem. Nat. Profl. Advt. Soc. (nat. pres. 1970-73), Tex. Pub. Relations Assn. (1st v.p.), Sigma Delta Chi (pres. 1967—). Mason. Author: Professional Approach to Journalistic Photography, 1967, Publications: A Guidebook, 1974; Fifty Years of Red Raider Football, 1978. Editor Photolith Mag., 1973-78, Linage Mag., 1970-73, Sigma Phi Epsilon Jour., 1972-75. Home: 2326 55th St Lubbock TX 79412

SELLS, JAMES WILLIAM, ret. clergyman; b. Atchison, Kan., June 27, 1897; s. James LeGrande and Clara (Hull) S.; A.B., Millsaps Coll., 1929; LL.D., LaGrange Coll., 1955; D.D., Emory U., 1964; m. Vera Maude Britt, Jan. 13, 1921; 1 dau., Shirley Jeanne (Mrs. J. Robert Adams) (dec.). Licensed to ministry Methodist Ch., 1916; ordained deacon Miss. Ann. Conf., 1927, elder, 1929; supply pastor Taylorsville (Miss.) Meth Ch., 1920-21, Georgetown (Miss.) Meth. Ch., 1921-23; supply pastor Meth. Ch., Pascagoula, Miss., 1925, pastor, 1925-29; pastor Meth. chs., Summit, Miss., 1929-30, Ocean Springs, Miss., 1930-32, Forest, Miss., 1932-36, Hattiesburg, Miss., 1936-40, Crystal Springs, Miss., 1940-44; field sec. Whitworth-Millsaps Coll., 1930; exec. sec. Seashore Meth. Assembly, Biloxi, Miss., 1930-32; producer Meth. series The Protestant Hour, Atlanta, 1945-72, Southeastern Jurisdictional Council, 1945-72; dir. Joint Radio Com., 1945-72; pres. Spiritual Life Publishers, Inc., Atlanta, 1966—, Communicative Arts, Inc., 1970—; rural ch. editor Progressive Farmer, 1944-67, exec. dir. Inst. Communicative Arts, Inc., 1960-69, pres., 1969—; vis. prof. Candler Sch. Theol., Emory U., 1964. Bd. dirs. Protestant Radio and Tv Center, Atlanta, Hinton Rural Life Center, Hayesville, N.C., Paine Coll., Augusta, Ga.; pres. Spiritual Life Research Found. Served with USN, 1917-19. Recipient Rural Minister of the Year award, 1965. Mem. Nat. Meth. Rural Life Conf. (sec. 1947), Miss. Rural Life Council (sec. 1944-45). Author: How God Can Change Your Life; Effective Communication—the Person to Person Process; Partners with the Living Lord, 1974. Home: 457 Burlington Rd NE Atlanta GA 30307 Died Oct. 3, 1979.

SELMAN, MAGGIE BRUNE, sch. prin.; b. Austin County, Tex.; d. Erwin and Emmie Brune; B.S. in Edn. and English, Sam Houston Tchr. Coll., Huntsville, Tex., 1941; M.Ed. in Elementary Edn., U. Houston, 1951; m. John R. Selman. Tchr., Hacienda Sch., Sealy, Tex., 1937-42; tchr. Sealy Elementary Sch., 1942-47, prin., 1947—; mem. exec. bd., chmn. adv. com. Edn. Service Center, Region 6. Vol. activities dir. Sealy Nursing Home, Inc., 1965—; sec. Sealy Med. Center Found. Mem. Tex. State Tchrs. Assn. (state exec. com., past pres. local and dist. unit), Tex. Elementary Prins. and Suprs. Assn. (dist. pres.), Tex. PTA (life), Delta Kappa Gamma. Club: Order Eastern Star. Office: 901 West St Sealy TX 77474

SELMONOSKY, CARLOS ALBERTO, surgeon; b. Santa Fe, Argentina, Dec. 16, 1931; s. Manuel Luis and Rosa (Melman) S.; came to U.S., 1957, naturalized, 1968; B.A., Ward Coll., Buenos Aires, Argentina, 1948; M.D., U. Buenos Aires, 1956; m. Sonia Raquel Korob, Jan. 7, 1958; children—Daniel, Deborah, Arlene, Monica. Intern Lebanon Hosp., N.Y.C., 1957-58; asst. surg. resident Bronx Municipal Hosp., N.Y., 1958-59, surg. resident, 1959-60; surg. research fellow Albert Einstein Coll. Medicine, N.Y.C., 1960-61, asst. instr. surgery, 1962-63, sr. resident Bronx Municipal Hosp. Center, 1962-63; surgeon Karolinska Hosp., Stockholm, Sweden, 1963-64; clin. asst. dept. surgery Postgrad. Med. Sch. London Hammersmith Hosp., 1964, surg. registrar, 1964-65; instr. surgery, div. cardiovascular and thoracic surgery U. Iowa Hosps., Iowa City, 1966-67, asso. in surgery, 1967-68; asst. prof. thoracic surgery Med. Coll. Ga., Augusta, 1968-71, practice medicine specializing in thoracic and cardiovascular surgery, Austell, Ga., 1971—; chief of surgery Cobb Gen. Hosp., Austell, 1974-75. Diplomate Am. Bd. Surgery, Am. Bd. Thoracic Surgery. Fellow A.C.S., Am. Coll. Chest Physicians, Am. Coll. Cardiology; mem. Am. Thoracic Soc., So. Thoracic Surg. Assn., Soc. Thoracic Surgeons, Internat. Cardiovascular Soc., Fulton County, Cobb County med. socs., Ga. Thoracic Soc. Contbr. articles to med. jours. Home: 4275 Fawnlane Smyrna GA 30080 Office: 1678 Mulkey Rd Austell GA 30001

SELOVER, JOHN CHARLES, ret. r.r. exec.; b. Pueblo, Colo., Feb. 13, 1911; s. Alpheus Olin and Mary (Robertson) S.; B.A., U. Kans., 1932; m. Mary Elizabeth Livingston, Nov. 4, 1939 (dec. Oct. 1973); children—Paul Nicholas, Stephanie Lynne (Mrs. Maurice Wilson), Timothy Lee, Andrea Marie (Mrs. Darrel Aldrich), Robin Livingston; m. 2d, Tommie Francis Smart, July 1977. With M.P. R.R., 1936-74, asst. to v.p. traffic, St. Louis, 1962-63, traffic mgr. Western region, Kansas City, Mo., 1963-63, v.p. Tex. dist., Dallas, 1968-74; past pres., dir. Mchts. Cold Storage Co., Eagle Ford Land & Indsl. Co.; past dir. Abilene & So. Ry., Ft. Worth Belt Ry. Co., Gt. S.W. R.R., Inc., Tex.-N.M. Ry. Co., Weatherford-Mineral Wells & Northwestern Ry. Mem. Transp. Club Dallas, Dallas Camellia Soc. (pres.). Democrat. Presbyn. Clubs: Dallas City, Dallas Athletic. Home: 640 Beechwood Dr Tyler TX 75701

SELPH, WILLIAM KENNETH, computer services co. exec.; b. Palisade, Nebr., Mar. 29, 1942; s. Elmo Joseph and Mary B. (Jeffers) S.; B.A., DePaul U., 1969; m. Sharon-Ann Dorey, Feb. 24, 1965; children—Shane Nicole, Shannon Danielle. Dir. mgmt. scis. Greyhound Corp., Chgo., 1965-70; pres. Computer Resources, Inc., Austin, Tex., 1970-74; internat. accounts mgr. On-Line Systems, Inc., Dallas, 1974—; dir. Computer Resources, Inc., Austin, 1969-74. Pres., Valley Homeowners Assn., Denton County, Tex., 1972-74; campaign mgr. City Council, Denton County (Tex.), 1974. Served with USAF, 1961-65. Recipient Meritorious Service award Valley Homeowners Assn., 1974. Mem. Internat. Communications Assn., Project Mgmt. Inst., Data Processing Mgmt. Assn., Internat. Timesharing Users Assn., Am. Mgmt. Assn. Methodist. Home: 1002 Grove Dr Lewisville TX 75067 Office: 2525 Stemmons St Dallas TX 75207

SEMIDEI-FRANCESCHI, JULIO IRVING, advt. agy. exec.; b. Arecibo, P.R., May 24, 1945; s. Julio I. Semidei-Negroni and Rosita Franceschi-Semidei; student U. P.R., 1963-67. Cultural and press attache French Consulate in P.R., 1967-69; with Badillo/Compton, Inc., San Juan, P.R., 1969—, account exec., research dir., 1971-76, mktg. dir., 1976-77, sr. v.p., mktg. dir., mgmt. supr., 1977—; chmn. Inter-agy. Com. to Evaluate TV Audience Measurement Services; guest speaker Inter-Am. U. Bd. dirs. Opera de P.R., Inc., 1974—. Home: 128-C Paris Floral Park Hato Rey PR 00917 Office: Badillo/Compton Inc 1504 F D Roosevelt Ave San Juan PR 00922

SEMMER, JOHN RICHARD, physician; b. Nanticoke, Pa., Nov. 7, 1943; s. Frederick Lewis and Betty Romayne (Thomas) S.; B.A., U. of South, 1965; M.D., U. Tenn., 1968; m. Glenna Butler McMahan, Aug. 20, 1966; 1 dau., Johnna Blythe. Intern U. Tenn. Meml. Hosp., Knoxville, 1969-70, resident obstetrics and gynecology, 1970-73; commd. 1st lt. USAF, 1969, advanced to maj., 1973; chief obstetrics and gynecology, Base Hosp., Blytheville AFB, Ark., 1973-75; pvt. practice medicine specializing in obstetrics and gynecology, Knoxville, 1975-78; asso. clin. prof. Clin. Edn. Center, U. Tenn. Center for Health Scis., Knoxville, 1975-78, asst. prof. ob-gyn, dir. E. Tenn. regional perinatal program Coll. Medicine. 1978—; mem. med. adv. com. Planned Parenthood Assn. of Knox County. Bd. dirs. Florence Crittenton Agy. of Knoxville. Diplomate Am. Bd. Obstetrics and Gynecology. Fellow Am. Coll. Obstetrics and Gynecology; mem. A.M.A., Tenn. Med. Assn., So. Obstet. and Gynecol. Seminar Inc., East Tenn. Obstet. and Gynecol. Soc., Knoxville Acad. Medicine, U. Tenn. Alumni Assn., U. of South Asso. Alumni, Knoxville Track Club, Beta Theta Pi. Methodist. Contbr. articles to profl. jours. Home: 8625 Wimbledon Dr Knoxville TN 37923 Office: Ob-Gyn Dept U Tenn Center for Health Scis 1924 Alcoa Hwy Knoxville TN 37920

SEMOS, CHRIS VICTOR, state legislator; b. Dallas, June 2, 1936; s. Victor H. and Evelyn (Tassos) S.; B.B.A., So. Methodist U., 1962; m. Anastasia Tasie, Feb. 25, 1967; children—Mary Katherine, Victoria Evelyn. Owner, operator The Torch Restaurant, Dallas, 1962—, Semos Coffee and Tea Co., Dallas, 1967—; mem. Tex. Ho. of Reps. from 33d Dist. 1966-, chmn. bus. and industry com., 1975—, chmn. Dallas County legis. del., 1973-75, 75—. Chmn., Tex. Sesquicentennial Commn. 1980—; trustee Dallas Alliance; bd. dirs., v.p. Dallas Council World Affairs; bd. dirs., co-chmn. Dallas chpt. NCCJ; bd. dirs. Oak Cliff Cancer Soc.; pres. elect Dallas Assembly; nat. pres. Greek Orthodox Youth Am., 1961-62; mem. bd. diocese council Greek Orthodox Ch. N. and S. Am., archon depoutatos

Ecumenical Patriarch, 1980. Recipient Brotherhood award NCCJ, 1980. Mem. Nat. Soc. State Legislators, Nat., Tex., Dallas (dir.) restaurant assns. Democrat. Clubs: Westcliff Lions (Lion of Year 1968); Quorum 50 (Oak Cliff); Masons, Shrine. Home: 1939 W Colorado Blvd Dallas TX 75208 Office: 3620 W Davis St Dallas TX 75211

SEMRAU, LOUIS PHILLIP, JR., educator; b. Buffalo, N.Y., Mar. 13, 1938; s. Louis Phillip and Jane Erma (Austin) S.; B.S. in Edn., State U. N.Y., Buffalo, 1960; M.A. (NIMH fellow), George Peabody Coll., 1965; Ph.D. (U.S. Office Edn. fellow), U. Oreg., 1972; m. Barbara L. Wagner, Jan. 30, 1960; children—Lita Anne, Anthony James. Tchr., Starpoint Central Sch., Lockport, N.Y., 1960-62; vol. Peach Corps, Republic of Philippines, 1962-64, sci. edn. trainer San Jose State Coll., 1965; curriculum supr., program dir. Cumberland House Re-edn. Center, Nashville, 1965-67; dir. Tenn. Re-Edn. Center, Chattanooga, 1967-69; research asst. Oreg. Research Inst., Eugene, 1971-72; asst. prof. psychology in psychiatry Sch. Medicine, also asst. prof. spl. edn. Sch. Edn., U. N.C., Chapel Hill, 1972-77, dir. tng. Div. TEACCH, 1972-77; asso. prof. spl. edn./speech pathology Ark. State U., Jonesboro, 1977—, chmn. dept. spl. edn./speech pathology, 1977—; cons. in field. Bd. dirs. Assn. Retarded Citizens, Jonesboro; adv. Ark. Assn. Student Council Exceptional Children, 1977-80. U.S. Office Edn. Bur. For Edn. of Handicapped grantee, 1977-81. Mem. Council Exceptional Children, Am. Edn. Research Assn., Assn. Mental Deficiency, Am. Assn. Edn. Severly/Profoundly Handicapped, Nat. Soc. Autistic Children, Assn. Retarded Citizens, Ark. Fedn. Council Exceptional Children (v.p. 1978-79, pres.-elect 1980). Democrat. Unitarian-Universalist. Contbr. articles to profl. jours. Home: Route 6 Box 362 Jonesboro AR 72401 Office: PO Box 776 State University AR 72467

SEMTNER, ROY HERMAN, lawyer; b. Oklahoma City, Apr. 13, 1924; s. Otto William and Jennie Bob (Fullbright) S.; A.B., St. Benedicts Coll., 1946; J.D., U. Okla., 1948; m. Patricia Ann Schooling, Dec. 27, 1946; children—Karl Bernard, Christopher Benedict, Nicholas Otto, Roy Herman, Thomas Russell. Admitted to Okla. bar, 1948; pvt. practice law, Oklahoma City, 1948—; asst. county atty., Oklahoma County, 1949-53; municipal judge, Oklahoma City, 1956-58, asst. municipal counselor, 1958-61, municipal counselor, 1961-73. Trustee Oklahoma City Municipal Improvement Authority, 1961-73; bd. dirs. Okla. Safety Council, legal counsel, 1976—; mem. adv. bd. Municipal Studies Center, Coalition for Transp. Choices of Oklahoma City, 1976—; mem. citizens adv. com. on transp. system for Oklahoma City, 1977; mem. adv. bd. SW Legal Found., vice chmn., 1976—. Research fellow SW Legal Found., 1977—. Mem. Okla. (mem. com. legal internship 1968—), Am. (chmn. council local govt. 1973, mem. nat. com. on housing and urban devel. 1973-79, vice chmn. coordinating com. for a model procurement code 1973—, editor Newsletter 1968-69, chmn. adv. bd. to editor The Urban Lawyer 1969—), Oklahoma County (dir. 1968-71) bar assns., Bar ICC, Cath. Lawyers Soc. (v.p. 1960), Oklahoma City Soc. Title Attys. (pres. 1971), Oklahoma City Title Attys. Assn. (pres. 1972), Attys. Title Security Orgn. (trustee 1973-75), Okla. Assn. County Attys. (pres. 1952), Okla. Assn. Municipal Attys. (pres. 1963-64), Nat. Inst. Municipal Law Officers (regional v.p. 1966-73, state chmn. 1965-66, chmn. annexation com. 1966-73), Oklahoma City (pres. 1960, dir. 1961), Nat. (dir. 1960) alumni assns. St. Benedicts Coll., Okla. Diocesan Confraternity Christian Doctrine (pres., dir. 1960), C. of C., Phi Delta Phi. Roman Catholic. K.C. (4 deg., grand knight 1953-55, state dep. 1961-63), Lion. Clubs: Gibbons Dinner (pres. 1957), Serra (v.p. 1959) (Oklahoma City). Home: 324 NW 41st St Oklahoma City OK 73118 Office: 600 Fidelity Plaza Oklahoma City OK 73102

SENA, DEAN RICHARD, business broker; b. Rahway, N.J., June 15, 1945; s. Dominic Richard and Dorothy (Parsons) S.; student Miami Dade Jr. Coll., 1964-66; student U. Miami (Fla.), 1966-68; m. Cheryl Joyce Barfield, June 9, 1973; 1 son, Derek Richard. Owner Tropical Printing Co., South Miami, Fla., 1967-69; owner Sena Printing, Miami, 1966—; pres. Sena Enterprises and World Bus. Brokers, Inc., South Miami, 1969—; real estate salesman Marple Realty, Miami, 1972—. Adviser, cons. social activities Homestead Manor, 1963—. Mem. Am. Mktg. Assn., Nat. Assn. Bus. Brokers (pres.), Civitan Club. Club: Coral Gables (Fla.) Country. Inventor navigational plotters and dispensing equipment. Home: 6201 Riviera Dr Coral Gables FL 33143 Office: 9516 S Dixie Hwy Miami FL 33156

SENFT, WILLIAM BROCK, Salvation Army officer; b. Lexington, Miss., Aug. 28, 1952; s. William Davis and Effie Marie (Brock) S.; student Wallace Jr. Coll., 1976; grad. Salvation Army Sch. Officers' Tng., 1973; m. Joanne Marie Leavens, Apr. 12, 1975; 1 son, William Brock. Asst. officer, Anniston, Ala., 1973; comdg. officer, New Iberia, La., 1973-76, Dothan, Ala., 1976-78, on edn. leave U. Ala., University, 1978—. Mem. Christian Holiness Assn., Jaycees (named Outstanding Young Man 1976, Outstanding Young Religious Leader 1977), Beta Alpha Psi. Clubs: Masons, Order Eastern Star, Kiwanis. Office: PO Box 4033 University AL 35486

SENNEMA, DAVID CARL, mus. adminstr.; b. Grand Rapids, Mich., July 6, 1934; s. Carl Edward and Alice Bertha (Bieri) S.; B.A., Albion Coll., 1956; m. Martha Amanda Dixon, Feb. 22, 1958; children—Daniel Ross, Julia Kathryn, Alice Dixon. Mgr. Columbia Music Festival Assn., 1964-67; exec. dir. S.C. Arts Commn., Columbia, 1967-70; asso. dir. Federal-State Partnership and Spl. Projects programs Nat. Endowment for the Arts, Washington, 1971-73; prof. arts adminstrn., dir. community arts mgmt. program Sangamon State U., Springfield, Ill., 1973-76; dir. S.C. Mus. Commn., Columbia, 1976—; cons. in field. Mem. adv. panel Nat. Endowment for the Arts Music, 1968-70. Chmn. Springfield Arts Commn., 1975-76. Served with U.S. Army, 1957-58. Mem. Am. Assn. Mus., Am. Assn. State and Local History, Southeastern Mus. Conf., S.C. Fedn. Mus. Club: Rotary (chmn. cultural affairs com. 1978-80). Office: PO Box 11296 Columbia SC 29211

SENSABAUGH, LEONIDAS FRANKLIN, historian; b. Dublin, Tex., Oct. 9, 1903; s. Leonidas Franklin and Rosa Effie (Frank) S.; student Oklahoma City U., 1921-22; A.B., Vanderbilt U., 1925; Ph.D., Johns Hopkins U., 1928; m. Mary Holmes Greer, July 26, 1928; 1 dau., Frances Holmes. Head dept. history Oklahoma City U., 1929-36; asst. prof. history Birmingham-So. Coll., 1928-29, asso. prof. history, 1936-43, prof., chmn. div. social scis., 1943-56; dean Washington and Lee U., Lexington, Va., 1956-60, prof. history, 1960-74, prof., dean emeritus, 1974—. Chmn. Rockbridge Community Bicentennial Commn., 1974-76; mem. Lexington City Council, 1974-78. Rosenwald fellow to Brazil, 1941-42; fellow in humanities Duke U.-U. N.C., 1964-65. Mem. So. Hist. Assn., Phi Beta Kappa, Omicron Delta Kappa, Chi Phi. Methodist. Home: PO Box 685 Lexington VA 24450

SENSALE, CHARLES JOSEPH, elec. engr., engring. co. exec.; b. Paterson, N.J., Jan. 3, 1925; s. Charles George and Mary Ann (Heintjes) S.; B.A., Montclair State Coll., 1949, M.A., 1950; B.S. in Elec. Engring., N.J. Inst. Tech., 1961; m. Audrey Ada Jensen, June 28, 1952; children—Audrey Lynn, Alix Diane. Devel. engr. ITT, Nutley, N.J., 1957-60; sr. engr. Bendix Corp., Teterboro, N.J., 1961-62, Burroughs Corp., Paoli, Pa., 1963-64; mem. tech. staff TRW, Washington, 1965-66; sr. engr. IBM Co., Gaithersburg, Md., 1966-67; pres. Tensor Industries, Inc., Fairfax, Va., 1967—; cons. Ferranti Packard, Ltd., Toronto, Ont., Can., 1964, KLI, Inc., Ivyland, Pa., 1976-77. Served with USMC, 1943-46. Decorated Purple Heart. Mem. IEEE, Am. Inst. Aeros. and Astronautics, Nat. Fedn. of Ind. Bus., Naval Research Inst., Nat. Contract Mgmt. Assn., Naval Helicopter Assn., Assn. of Old Crows, No. Va. Power Squadron. Club: Westwood Country. Home: 903 Country Club Dr Vienna VA 22180 Office: 8415 Arlington Blvd Fairfax VA 22030

SENTELL, GILBERT LEVIRGIL, civil engr.; b. Reform, Ala., Dec. 12, 1943; s. Tommie Levirgil and Lizzie Ovella (Martin) S.; B.S., U. Ala., 1970; m. Suzanne Harrison, Aug. 23, 1969; 1 son, Christopher Gilbert. Draftsman Mitchell Engring. Co., Columbus, Miss., 1963-65; asst. engr. Alsey C. Parker and Sons, Engrs., Tuscaloosa, Ala., 1967-69; engr. Almon and Assos., Inc., Tuscaloosa, 1970-77, also v.p., bd. dirs.; chmn. bd. dirs., pres. Sentell, Morin and Bass, Inc., cons. engrs., Tuscaloosa, 1977—. Served with AUS, 1964-66. Registered profl. engr., Ala., Fla., Ga., Miss., Tenn.; registered land surveyor, Ala., Miss. Mem. ASCE, Nat., Ala. socs. profl. engrs., Ala. Soc. Profl. Land Surveyors, Am. Water Works Assn., Water Pollution Control Fedn., Am. Pub. Works Assn., Tuscaloosa Homebuilders Assn. Tuscaloosa C. of C. Baptist. Clubs: Civitan, Woodland Forrest Country. Home: 55 Woodland Forest 4 Tuscaloosa AL 35405 Office: PO Box 2682 1020 15th St Tuscaloosa AL 35403

SENTER, WILLIAM ROBERT, III, clergyman, social service worker; b. Chattanooga, Sept. 18, 1935; s. William R. and Virginia (Mack) S.; B.S. in Biology, U. of the South, 1957; postgrad. U. Tenn., 1957; B.D., Div. Sch., Kenyon Coll., Ohio, 1961; M.Div., Colgate-Rochester Theol. Sem., 1973; m. Linda Anne Howard, Feb. 9, 1963; children—Lydia Elizabeth, Matthew Mack. Tchr., East Lake Jr. High Sch., Chattanooga, 1958; summer field work St. Peter's Ch., N.Y.C., 1959; ordained deacon Episcopal Ch., 1961, priest, 1962; priest-in-charge St. Columba's Ch., Bristol, Tenn., 1963-68; clergy adviser for young ch. persons of upper east Tenn., 1964-67; camp staff clergy adviser for various age groups Diocese of Tenn., 1962, 64, 65, 73; priest-in-charge Epiphany Episcopal Ch., Lebanon, Tenn., 1968—; camp dir. for 5th and 6th graders Diocese of Tenn., 1974, 75; pres., treas. Senter Sch., Chattanooga, 1972-77; personnel and mgmt. cons. Cracker Barrel Old Country Stores, Inc., Lebanon, 1974-76; chaplain Camp Alleghany for Girls, Lewisburg, W.Va., 1976; chaplain for the day U.S. Senate, 1976; participant numerous workshops and confs. on mental health, marriage counselling, alcoholism and drug abuse, 1972—.Founder, chmn. Project Help, Lebanon, 1969-73; co-founder and mem. Lebanon-Wilson County (Tenn.) Alcohol and Drug Abuse Commn., 1969-71; pub. relations chmn. Nat. Found./March of Dimes, Sullivan County, Tenn., 1965-68, chmn., Wilson County, Tenn., 1968-71; mem. Wilson County Welfare Adv. Bd., 1974—; mem. exec. com. Wilson County Bicentennial Commn., 1974-78; mem. Gov.'s Adv. Commn. on Alcohol and Drug Abuse, 1972-78, vice chmn., 1975-78; bd. dirs. Lebanon YMCA, 1973-78. Cert. substance abuse counsellor, Tenn. Mem. Chaplains Assn. and Bristol Council Chs., Am. Assn. Arts and Scis., SAR, Profl. Assn. Alcohol and Drug Counselors Tenn., Nat. Model R.R. Assn., Tenn. Ornithol. Soc. (pres. Lebanon chpt. 1971-73), Ministerial Assn. (v.p. 1967, 76), Delta Tau Delta. Club: Lebanon Golf and Country. Author: Lent—How to Keep It for Your Soul's Health; contbr. book revs. to local newspapers and religious publs. Address: Route 10 Box 1-A Lebanon TN 37087

SEO, CHUNG WOON, food scientist, educator; b. Seoul, Korea, June 15, 1935; came to U.S., 1964; B.S. in Agrl. Chemistry, Korea U., Seoul, 1960, M.S. in Food and Nutrition, 1961; Ph.D. in Food and Nutrition, Fla. State U., 1971; m. YuJung Min, Dec. 28, 1969; children—Susan, David, Benjamin. Food research chemist Korea Army Research and Testing Lab., Seoul, 1960-64; prof. dept. home econs./food sci. N.C. A&T State U., Greensboro, 1969—. Soccer coach Greensboro Youth Soccer Assn. and City Recreation Dept., 1978—; active Cub Scouts, Boy Scouts Am. Served in inf. Korean Army, 1957-58. U.S. Dept. Agr. grantee. Mem. Inst. Food Technologists, Am. Dietetic Assn., Nutrition Today Soc., N.C. Council Food and Nutrition. Baptist. Contbr. articles to profl. jours. Office: NC A&T State U Greensboro NC 27411

SEPTIMUS, EDWARD JOEL, physician; b. N.Y.C., Feb. 21, 1947; s. Lewis Ira and Helen (Grapel) S.; B.S., Ohio State U., 1968; M.D., Baylor U., 1972; m. Susan Carol Stekin, Mar. 21, 1970; children—Joshua David, Daniel Adam. Intern, Baylor Affiliated Hosps., Houston, 1972-73, resident in internal medicine, 1973-75; fellow in infectious diseases Baylor Coll. Medicine, Houston, 1975-76, instr. medicine, 1976-77, clin. asst. prof. medicine, 1977—; clin. asst. prof. medicine U. Tex. Health Sci. Center, Houston, 1978—; practice medicine specializing in infectious diseases, Houston, 1977—; mem. staff Meml. Hosp., 1977—, chief infectious diseases, 1978—; mem. staff Sharpstown. Recipient Pres.'s Scholarship award, 1972; diplomate Am. Bd. Internal Medicine. Fellow A.C.P.; mem. Infectious Diseases Soc. Am., Am. Fedn. Clin. Research, Am. Soc. Microbiology, Am. Thoracic Soc., Houston Infectious Disease Soc., Tex. Med. Soc., Harris County Med. Soc. Jewish. Home: 8011 Candle Ln Houston TX 77071 Office: 7777 Southwest Freeway Suite 740 Houston TX 77074

SERAFINI, ALDO NICOLA, physician; b. Johannesburg, S. Africa, May 2, 1940; s. Anthony and Mary (Damiani) S.; came to U.S., 1967, naturalized, 1977; M.B., B.Chir., U. Witwatersrand, Johannesburg, 1966; m. Lani DeBeer, Sept. 1, 1967; children—Anton, Andre. Intern, Baragwanath Hosp., S. Africa, 1967; intern Jackson (Fla.) Meml. Hosp., 1967-68, resident in internal medicine, 1968-70, resident in nuclear medicine, 1970-72, mem. staff, 1972—; fellow in nuclear medicine Mt. Sinai Med. Center, Miami Beach, Fla., 1971-72; practice medicine specializing in internal medicine, Miami Beach, 1972—; mem. attending staff Mt. Sinai Med. Center, Miami Beach, asst. dir. div. nuclear medicine, 1974—, co-dir. div. of ultrasound, 1974—, asst. dir. Baumritter Inst. Nuclear Medicine, 1975-77, mem. research com., 1973—; dir. nuclear medicine U. Miami Hosps. and Clinics, Jackson Meml. Med. Center; instr. U. Miami Sch. Medicine, 1972-73, asso. prof., 1974—. NIH grantee, 1972-73; Am. Cancer Soc. grantee, 1973. Diplomate Am. Bd. Internal Medicine, Am. Bd. Nuclear Medicine. Mem. Soc. Nuclear Medicine, Fla., Dade County med. assns., Am. Inst. Ultrasound in Medicine. Roman Catholic. Club: Key Biscayne Yacht. Author: (with W. Smoak, A.J. Gilson) Nuclear Cardiology, 1976; contbr. chpts. on nuclear medicine to med. texts and articles in field to profl. jours.; editor Progress in Nuclear Medicine, 1977—; research in nuclear cardiology and ultrasound techniques in imaging. Office: Nuclear Medicine Dept U Miami PO Box 016960 Miami FL 33101

SERAPIGLIA, LOUIS ALFRED, JR., trucking co. exec.; b. Louisville, July 30, 1946; s. Louis Alfred and Ruby Emma (Yaeger) S.; B.E.E., U. Louisville, 1969; m. Mary Catherine Jenne, June 6, 1970; 1 son, Steven L. Electronics engr. Naval Ordnance Sta., Louisville, 1967-69, 69-71; pres. C&L Trucking Co., Inc., Louisville, 1971—, also pres., mgr. C&L Services Industries, Louisville; electronic and hydraulic system designer. Ky. Col. Mem. IEEE. Democrat. Roman Catholic. Home: 5411 Old Heady Rd Louisville KY 40299 Office: 733 Grade Ln Louisville KY 40213

SERNA, SUE H., motel exec.; b. Shreveport, La., Feb. 17, 1931; d. Sam and Ollie Gertrude (Estes) Collins; student U. Tex., El Paso, 1969. With Genpart, Inc., 1965—, mgr. Ramada Inn, Longview, Tex., 1970-72, asst. mgr., pub. relations dir. Rodeway Inn, El Paso, 1972-79, gen. mgr., 1979—; instr. El Paso Community Coll., 1980—. Vice pres. Discover El Paso. Mem. Am. Bus. Women in Am., Tex. Press Women (dist. pres. 1979), Cousteau Soc. Am., Pub. Relations Soc. Am. Office: 6201 Gateway W El Paso TX 79925

SERRINS, ALAN JACK, otolaryngologist, allergist; b. Buffalo, Aug. 31, 1930; s. Edward Louis and Naomi (Eloskey) S.; B.A., Emory U., 1952; M.D., U. Miami, 1957; m. Susan Jane Levinson, Sept. 4, 1960; children—Cathy Ellen, Robert Edward, Nancy Ann, Corey Alan. Intern Charity Hosp., New Orleans, 1957-58; resident surgery Jackson Meml. Hosp., Miami, Fla., 1960-61, resident otolaryngology, 1961-64; practice medicine specializing in otolaryngology, Coral Gables, Fla., 1964-73, Miami, 1973—; clin. instr. otolaryngology U. Miami Sch. Medicine, 1964-78, clin. asst. prof., 1979—, attending dept. otolaryngology ENT-Allergy Clinic, 1978-79; pres. Dadeland Allergy-Ear, Nose and Throat Assos., P.A., Miami; v.p. Audiology and Vestibular Center, Kendall, Inc., Miami. Served with AUS. 1958-60. Diplomate Am. Bd. Otolaryngology. Fellow A.C.S., Internat. Coll. Surgeons, Am. Acad. Ophthalmology and Otolaryngology, Am. Acad. Facial Plastic and Reconstructive Surgery, Am. Soc. Ophthalmologic and Otolaryngologic Allergy, Am. Coll. Allergists, Am. Assn. for Clin. Immunology and Allergy, Am. Acad. Allergy; mem. Fla., Dade County, So. med. assns., Fla. Soc. Allergy, S.E. Allergy Assn. Clubs: Ocean Reef Yacht and Country (Miami); Briar Bay. Contbr. articles to med. jours. Home: 9471 SW 97th St Miami FL 33176 Office: 7400 N Kendall Dr Miami FL 33156

SESSIONS, LARRY MICHAEL, civil engr.; b. Birmingham, Ala., July 4, 1945; s. Doyle Brough and Eula Fae (Putman) S.; B.S. in Civil Engring., U. Ala., 1969; M.Engring., U. Fla., 1975; m. Anne Moore Faircloth, May 17, 1969; children—Wade Manning, Elise Putman. Projects engr. U.S. Gypsum Co., Greenville, Miss., 1969-70; with Fla. Dept. Transp., Tallahassee, 1971-77, engr. III, 1972-73, profl. structural engr. I, 1973-76, profl. asst. state value engr., 1976-77; structural engring. div. dir. Johnson Engring. Inc., Ft. Myers, Fla., 1977—. Registered profl. engr., Ala., Fla. Mem. ASCE (sec.-treas. chpt. 1974), Fla. Engring. Soc., Theta Tau. Republican. Episcopalian. Club: U. Ala. Alumni (v.p. 1974). Home: 4700 Santa Del Rae Ave Fort Myers FL 33901 Office: 2158 Johnson St Fort Myers FL 33902

SESSIONS, WILLIAM LAD, philosopher, educator; b. Somerville, N.J., Dec. 3, 1943; s. William George and Alice Edna (Billhardt) S.; B.A., U. Colo., 1965; M.A., Union Theol. Sem./Columbia U., 1967; postgrad. Mansfield Coll., Oxford U., 1967-68; Ph.D., Yale U., 1971; m. Vicki Darlene Thompson, Aug. 28, 1965; children—Allistair Lee, Laura Anne. Asst. prof. philosophy Washington and Lee U., Lexington, Va., 1971-77, asso. prof., 1977—. Grantee Babcock Found. Nat. Endowment for Humanities, 1977. Mem. Am., Va. philos. assns., Center for Process Studies, Soc. for Philosophy of Religion. Democrat. Presbyterian. Contbg. author Two Process Philosophers, 1973. Home: 5 Lampe Circle Lexington VA 24450 Office: Dept Philosophy Washington and Lee U Lexington VA 24450

SESSUMS, THOMAS TERRELL, lawyer; b. Daytona Beach, Fla., June 11, 1930; s. Thomas L. and Dorothy (Cornwall) S.; B.A., U. Fla., 1952, J.D., 1958; LL.D. (hon.), Fla. So. Coll., 1973; Dr. Pub. Adminstrn. (hon.), Rollins Coll., 1974; m. Neva Ann Steeves, Aug. 16, 1958; children—Thomas T., Richard H., Sandra Lynn. Admitted to Fla. bar, 1958; asso. firm Hardee & Ott, Tampa, 1958-60; partner firm Albritton, Sessums & McCall, Tampa, 1961—; gen. counsel Tampa Port Authority, 1974—. Dir. S.E. Bank of Tampa, 1973, Blue Cross of Fla., 1977-78; adj. prof. polit. sci. U. South Fla., 1974-75, mem. council advisers, 1975-79. Mem. Fla. Gov.'s Citizens Com. on Edn., 1972-73; trustee U. Tampa, 1978—; mem. So. Regional Edn. Bd., 1972-75, Fla. Bd. Regents; mem. Fla. Ho. of Reps., 1963-74, 79—, speaker pro tem, 1968-70, chmn. edn. com., 1970-72, speaker, 1972-74; dist. lay leader Tampa dist. United Meth. Ch., 1977—. Served to capt. USAF, 1954-56. Mem. Greater Tampa C. of C. (gov., com. 100, gen. counsel 1978—), Am. Bar Assn., Fla. Bar. Kiwanian. Clubs: Palma Ceia Golf and Country, Tampa Yacht and Country, University. Home: 1113 Dunbar Ave Tampa FL 33609 Office: 100 Madison St Tampa FL 33602

SETO, JANE MEI-CHUN WONG, physician; b. China, May 15, 1927; d. Jee Kwun and Shee (Li) Wong; M.D., Kwang-Hwa Med. Coll., China, 1951; postgrad. Queen's U., Ireland, 1952-57, Tulane U., 1961-63; m. Yeb Jo Seto, Feb. 14, 1958; children—Samuel, Susanna. Intern, Regina (Sask.) Grey Nun's Hosp., 1957-58; resident Providence Hosp., Seattle, 1958-59; phsyician U. Wash. Health Center, 1959-61, Austin (Tex.) State Sch., 1961-62; research asst. M.D. Anderson Hosp., U. Tex., 1964-66; serologist State Bd. Health, New Orleans, 1967-69; instr. medicine Tulane U., 1969-70, research asso. electrosci. and biophysics research group, 1969—. Active Beverly Hill Civic Club (Metairie, La.). Fellow Royal Soc. Health; mem. A.M.A., Am. Pub. Health Assn., Am. Women in Medicine. Contbr. articles to profl. jours. Home: 4824 Purdue St Metairie LA 70003 Office: Tulane University New Orleans LA 70118

SETTLES, CARL EDMOND, psychologist; b. Houston, July 23, 1948; s. Paul Silas and Lena (Epps) S.; B.S., Prairie View A. & M. U., 1970, M.Ed., 1971; Ph.D., U. Tex. at Austin, 1976; m. Carol Ann Hadnot, July 3, 1967; children—Carl Edmond, Corey Tremayne. Intermediate teacher Waller (Tex.) Ind. Sch. Dist., 1970-71, Austin (Tex.) Ind. Sch. Dist., 1971-73; social sci. research asso. U. Tex. at Austin, summer 1974, teaching asst. Dept. Ednl. Psychology, 1973-75; research and counseling intern Tex. Youth Council, Austin, 1975; acting asst. to dir. Counseling Center, Prairie View A. & M. U., 1975-76, asso. dir. Counseling Services, 1976—; counseling-clin. intern VA Hosp., Houston, 1975-76. Recipient Henderson Found. fellowship, 1974-75; U. Tex. fellowship, 1974-75, Nat. Fellowship for Black Ams., 1975-76. Mem. Am. Psychol. Assn., Am. Personnel and Guidance Assn., Tex. Psychol. Assn., Tex. Acad. Sci. Assn., Southwestern Social Sci. Assn., Southwestern Sociol. Assn., Kappa Alpha Psi, Phi Delta Kappa (past pres. local chpt.). Mem. Church of Christ. Club: Hempstead-Prairie View Lions. Home: PO Box 2148 Prairie View TX 77445 Office: Counseling Services Prairie View A & M U Prairie View TX 77445

SEVERANCE, FREDERICK DOUGLAS, elec. products mfg. co. exec.; b. Asheville, N.C., Apr. 19, 1927; s. Frederick Duncan and Jane (Fleming) S.; B.S. in Elec. Engring., The Citadel, 1950; postgrad. U. Mich., 1950-51; m. Daphne Aina Johnson, July 26, 1958; children—Alisa, Carl, Sharon, Susan, Craig. Test design engr. Western Electric Co., Burlington, N.C., 1951-54; field engr. Oerlikon Tool & Arms Corp., Asheville, 1954-58; mfrs. rep. Bivins & Caldwell, Inc., High Point, N.C. and Orlando, Fla., 1958-62; organizer BCS Assos. Inc., mfrs. rep., Orlando, 1962-70, Huntsville, Ala., 1970-78, v.p., treas., 1962-78, br. mgr., 1970-78, also trustee profit sharing plan, dir.; sr. sales engr. John Fluke Mfg. Co. Inc., Huntsville, 1978—; dir. So. Bus. Communications, Inc., Orlando. Served with AUS, 1945-48. Mem. I.E.E.E. (past pres.), Instrument Soc. Am. (sec. Huntsville chpt.). Republican. Methodist. Club: Yacht (The Citadel). Home: 405

Sherwood Dr SE Huntsville AL 35802 Office: 3322 S Meml Pkwy Huntsville AL 35802

SEVERINO, ALEXANDRINO EUSEBIO, educator; b. Olhao, Portugal, July 17, 1931; s. Eusebio Joaquim and Maria Alexandrina (Rato) S.; came to U.S., 1946, naturalized, 1946; B.A., U. R.I., 1958; Ph.D., U. Sao Paulo (Brazil), 1966; m. Dorothea Regel Bresslau, Jan. 7, 1961; children—Alexander, Cornelia, Roger, Katherine. Prof., Faculdade de Marilia (Brazil), 1960-66; asso. prof. U. Tex., Austin, 1966-69; prof. Spanish and Portuguese, chmn. dept. Spanish and Portuguese, Vanderbilt U., 1969—. Served with U.S. Army, 1952-54. Mem. Modern Lang. Assn., Am. Assn. Tchrs. Spanish and Portuguese. Author: Fernando Pessoa na Africa do Sul, vol. 1, 1969, vol. II, 1970; editor: (with Enrique Pupo-Walker) Studies in Short Fiction: Contemporary Latin America, 1971; contbg. editor: Handbook for Latin American Studies. Home: 6708 Rodney Ct Nashville TN 32705 Office: PO Box 1640 St B Vanderbilt U Nashville TN 37235*

SEVERO, ARMANDO, computer systems cons., realtor; b. Buffalo, June 18, 1935; s. John Anthony and Marietta (Antonelli) S.; B.A. in Math., U. Buffalo, 1957; m. Roberta Edwards, Aug. 13, 1977. Research asso. Rensselaer Poly. Inst., 1957-59; coordinator computer systems Nat. Cancer Inst., Washington, 1959-61; computer systems analyst RCA, Washington, 1961-65; computer systems cons. Nat. Bur. Standards, Washington, 1965-73; cons. on computer systems, 1973—; lectr. Automatic Data Processing. Instr. skiing, Eastern U.S., 1968—; cons. ski programs and activities. Mem. Assn. for Computing Machinery, Eastern Ski Assn. (rep.), Nat. Bd. Realtors. Club: Ski of Washington (pres. 1972-73). Home: 3912 Pineland St Fairfax VA 22030

SEVERSON, HARRY LORUN, economist; b. Larchwood, Iowa, Feb. 27, 1901; s. Jacob B. and Annie (Johnson) S.; B.S., U. Minn., 1924; M.S., U. Chgo., 1931. Asst. prof. commerce Miss. A. and M. Coll. (now Miss. State U.), Starkville, 1925-26, asso. prof. finance, 1926-30; asst. prof. commerce St. Thomas Coll., St. Paul, 1930-31; acting asst. prof. econs. Ind. U., Bloomington, 1931-32, extension lectr. econs., accounting East Chicago div., 1932-35; asso. prof. econs. U. Omaha, 1935-37; head securities unit FDIC, Washington, 1937-44, asst. chief div. research and statistics, 1944-46; Washington rep. Bankers Trust Co., N.Y.C., 1946-47; cons. economist Municipal Service div. Dun and Bradstreet, N.Y.C., 1947-49; economist HHFA, Washington, 1949-51, OPS, Washington, 1951-52; spl. asst. to asso. dir. DPA, 1952-53; cons. economist, N.Y.C., 1953-64, Mobile, Ala., 1964—. Mem. Am. Econ. Assn., Am. Finance Assn., Lambda Alpha. Author: Severson Projections of Construction Expenditure of State and Local Governments and New Bond Offerings of State and Local Governments, 1957. Contbr. articles to profl. publs. Address: 315 S Monterey St Mobile AL 36604

SEVERYNSE, JOHN THOMAS, programmer; b. Bklyn., Mar. 12, 1937; s. William and Alice (Radcliff) S.; B.A., U. West Fla., 1976; M.S., Troy State U., 1979; m. Hazel Lipham, July 4, 1957; children—John William, Trevor Wesley. With Grumman Aircraft & Engring., Co., 1964-66, Independent Life and Accident Ins. Co., 1966-72, U.S. Army C.E., 1972-74; prescriptive programmer Sunland Tng. Center, Marianna, Fla., 1976—. Served with USAF, 1955-64. Mem. Am. Assn. on Mental Deficiency, Gamma Beta Phi. Democrat. Baptist. Home: 1001 Pennsylvania Ave Lynn Haven FL 32444 Office: Sunland Tng Center Marianna FL 32446

SEWARD, TROILEN GAINEY, sch. psychologist; b. Petersburg, Va., Nov. 26, 1941; d. Troy Leonidas and Mary Anna (Nester) Gainey; A.B., Coll. William and Mary, 1963, postgrad., 1977—; M.Ed., Va. Commonwealth U., 1977; m. William E. Seward, June 29, 1963; children—Susan, Bill. Tchr., Petersburg Public Schs., 1963-67; tchr., counselor Surry Acad., 1967-77; headmistress Tidewater Acad. Lower Sch., 1977-79; psychologist intern Franklin (Va.) Public Schs., 1979—. Trustee, Ritchie Meml. Episcopal Ch. Mem. Nat. Sch. Psychologists Assn., Am. Personnel and Guidance Assn., Am. Sch. Counselors Assn., Va. Personnel and Guidance Assn., Phi Kappa Phi, Delta Kappa Gamma. Club: Surry Jr. Woman's (pres. 1968). Home: PO Box 266 Claremont VA 23899

SEWELL, BARBARA JEAN SCOTT, educator; b. Chrisman, Ill., May 15, 1929; d. R. Otho and Ruth (Morris) Scott; B.S., Ind. State U., 1951; M.A., Western Carolina U., 1967; div.; children—Russell Earl, Barbara Jean. Asst. home adviser Vermillion County Extension, U. Ill., 1951; tchr. vocational home econs. various schs., Ill., 1951-63, Fla., 1963-67; guidance counselor jr. class Manatee High Sch., Brandenton, 1967-69, guidance counselor sr. class, 1969-71; asst. dir.-registrar and admissions Fla. So. Coll., Lakeland, 1970-71; sch. psychologist Community Mental Health, Winter Haven, Fla., 1971-72, Polk County (Fla.) Sch. Bd., Bartow, 1972—. Mem. textbook com. Fla. Dept. Edn., 1967-69, chmn. textbook selection com., 1968-69. Recipient awards including certificate of appreciation Fla. Dept. Edn., 1969. Mem. N.E.A., Fla., Manatee County edn. assns., Am., Fla. (mem. state workshop com. 1969-70) personnel and guidance assns., Fla. Sch. Counselors Assn. (mem. research com. 1968-69), Manatee Counselors Assn. (constn. com. mem. 1969), Fla. Assn. Sch. Psychologists, Delta Gamma Alumni. Episcopalian (Christian vocations com. 1968-70). Home: 1015 E George St Bartow FL 33830 Office: Polk County Sch Bd PO Box 391 Bartow FL 33830

SEWELL, MILTON EARL, travel agency exec.; b. Deberry, Tex., Nov. 3, 1947; s. Levi and Beaulah (Langley) S.; B.A., So. U., 1970-73; postgrad. 1973-74. Dir. student services, Gourmet Services, Baton Rouge, La., 1973-74, asst. dir. food services, Marshall, Tex., 1974-75; dir. adminstrv. services Henderson Travel Service, Inc., Atlanta, 1975-79; gen. mgr. Gavin-Robinson Travel Service, Inc., Jackson, Miss., 1979—. Dir. Young People for Christ, 1971. Served with USAF, 1966-70. Mem. Nat. Mgmt. Assn., Phi Beta Sigma, Epsilon Chi Phi. Democrat. Baptist. Contbr. article to coll. jour. Home: 536 Claiborne Ave Jackson MS 39209 Office: 414 W Pascagoula St Jackson MS 39203

SEXTON, HARLEY H., hosp. adminstr.; b. Clarksville, Ark.. May 4. 1913; s. William Jacob and Dena H. Hudson) S.; attended Henderson State Coll., Arkadelphia, Ark.; m. Nettie Little, June 22, 1940; Co-owner, sec.-treas. wholesale grocery co., Hot Springs, Ark., 1937-57; accountant, Hot Springs, 1958-62; asst. dir. Ark. Div. Legis. Audit, Little Rock, 1963-67; chief accountant Henderson State Coll., Arkadelphia, Ark., 1968-69; fiscal adminstr. St. Joseph's Hosp., Hot Springs, 1969—. C.P.A. Mem. Ark. Hosp. Assn., Hosp. Financial Mgmt. Assn., Am. Inst. C.P.A.'s, Ark. Soc. C.P.A.'s, C. of C. Methodist (bd. dirs.). Mason, Lions. Home: 265 Terry Hot Springs AR 71901 Office: 100 Whittington Hot Springs AR 71901

SEXTON, JAMES DAVID, educator; b. Lenoir City, Tenn., May 20, 1948; s. James Earl and Mary Nell S.; B.S., U. Tenn., Knoxville, 1970, M.S., 1974, Ph.D., 1980. Tchr., S.C. Dept. Mental Retardation, Whitten Center, Clinton, S.C., 1974-75, dir. early childhood edn., 1975-78, dir. alt. program devel., 1978-79, acting dir. ednl. services, 1970-80; asst. prof. rehab. and spl. edn. Auburn (Ala.) U., 1980—. Served with U.S. Army, 1970-72. Mem. Am. Assn. Mental Deficiency, Am. Home Econs. Assn., Southeastern Council Family Relations, S.C. Home Econs. Assn., Council for Exceptional Children. Contbr. articles to profl. jours. Home: 1139 Rudd Ave Auburn AL 36380 Office: 1230 Haley Center Auburn U Auburn AL 36380

SEXTON, JAMES TIMOTHY, bank exec.; b. Bristol, Va., Aug. 21, 1941; s. John Everett and Viola (Thompson) S.; B.S. in Bus. Adminstrn., Va. Poly. Inst., 1963; m. Betty Rose Townsend, Aug. 16, 1969; children—Helen Thompson, John Timothy. Examiner, Fed. Res. Bank of Richmond (Va.), 1963-72; asst. v.p. Va. Trust Co., Richmond, 1972-73 (name changed to Va. Nat. Bank 1976), v.p., 1972—; dir. Watkins-Cottrell, Inc. Bd. dirs. Va. Home for Boys, 1977—; membership com. Central Richmond Assn., 1973. Served with USAR, 1965. Mem. Robert Morris Assos. (dir. Carolina-Virginias chpt.). Baptist. Club: Downtown (Richmond). Home: 8808 Sierra Rd Richmond VA 23229 Office: 707 E Main St Richmond VA 23219

SEXTON, OSWELL STANTON, sch. adminstr.; b. Oneida, Tenn., Mar. 21, 1908; s. Caswell and Rachel R. (Cecil) S.; B.S., Tenn. Technol. U., 1937; M.S., U. Tenn., 1951; m. Rema Jeffers, Aug. 17, 1929; children—O. Sibley, Curtis, Donna Kay (Mrs. Robert L. Tallent), Ray Owen, Dwight David, Ella Rachel (Mrs. Danny Williams). Tchr., prin., elementary schs. Scott County, Tenn., 1927-37; coach Robins (Tenn.) High Sch., 1937, prin., 1937-46; edn. supr. Scott County (Tenn.) Schs., 1946; prin. Huntsville (Tenn.) High Sch., 1946-55, Madisonville (Tenn.) High Sch., 1955-64, Cohutta (Ga.) Elementary Sch., 1964-73; instr. Hercules Powder Co., Chattanooga, 1942. Chmn. war fund A.R.C., Scott County, 1943-44; dir. Sabin-Polio Clinic; dir. Monroe County Heart Assn.; chmn. ednl. dept. United Appeal Fund Drive, Whitfield County, 1968; mem. town council Town Cohutta, Ga., 1969-73; deacon 1st Bapt. Ch., Madisonville, 1972-80. Life mem. NEA; hon. life mem. Tenn. Edn. Assn.; mem. Ga. Edn. Assn., Ga. Elementary Principals Assn., Nat. Assn. Secondary Sch. Prins., Monroe County Ednl. Assn. (pres. 1959-60), Whitfield County Adminstrs. Ednl. Assn. (pres. 1968), Monroe County Assn. Ret. Tchrs. (v.p. 1974-78, pres. 1978-79), Phi Delta Kappa. Mason; mem. Order Eastern Star. Clubs: Senior Citizens, Lions (pres. Madisonville 1960, dir. 1979-80); Ruritan (dir.) (Cohutta, Ga.). Home: 512 US Hwy 411 Madisonville TN 37354

SEYDEL, SCOTT O'SULLIVAN, chem. co. exec.; b. Atlanta, Mar. 29, 1940; s. John Rutherford and Jane (Reynolds) S.; student Ga. Inst. Tech., 1959-62, Textile Engr.; student U. Ga. Sch. Journalism, 1962-63; student bus. adminstrn. North Tex. State U., 1963; m. Rosina Marie Bairstow, July 2, 1963; children—John Rutherford II, Rosina Marie, Lael Elizabeth, Scott O'Sullivan. With Tex. Textile Mills, Inc., McKinney, 1963-64; personnel dir. 1925 Corp., AZS Corp., Atlanta, 1965, pub. relations dir., 1966, asst. v.p., 1967, asst. exec. v.p., 1968, corporate dir., 1968—, v.p. diversification, dir. internat. activities, 1969-70; pres. Seydel Cos., Atlanta, 1970—; v.p., dir. SICHEM, Ghent, Belgium, 1975—, SICO South Africa, Durben, South Africa, 1975—, SIVEN, S.A., Caracas, Venezuela, 1971—, Quatic So., Inc., Atlanta, 1978—; dir. Quimicas de CentroAmerica, Guatemala, Sifin Oy, Aanakoski, Finland, Atlanta Trucks Co., Inc., Anilinas Argentinas div. SEYCO, Buenos Aires, Inpal, S.A. Rio de Janeiro, Atlanta Overseas Services, Inc., Seydel Peruana, Lima, Quimica Seydel de Mexico, Mexico, D.F. Bd. dirs. Coll. Internat. Bus., Ga. State U. Fellow Am. Assn. Textile Chemists and Colorists; mem. Internat. Council for Textile Technologists (dir. 1957—, sec. 1971—), So. Textile Assn., Atlanta Assn. Internat. Edn. (dir.), U.S. C. of C. (exec. res. com., export council), Atlanta Benedicts (v.p. 1972, dir. 1971—), Chi Phi. Rotarian. Clubs: Atlanta Commerce, Piedmont Driving (Atlanta). Contbr. articles to profl. jours. Home: 2700 Peachtree Rd NW Atlanta GA 30305 Office: 80 Broad St Atlanta GA 30325

SEYDELL, MILDRED, writer, lectr., traveler; b. Atlanta; d. Vasser and Elizabeth Cobb (Rutherford) Woolley; ed. Washington Sem., Atlanta, The Lucy Cobb Inst., Athens, Ga., and Sorbonne, Paris; m. Paul Bernard Seydel (dec.); children—Paul Vasser, John Rutherford; m. 2d, Max Seydel (dec.). Columnist Charleston (W.Va.) Gazette, 1921; rep. Hearst Crime Commn., in Europe, 1926, collecting data for series of articles and interviews; traveled in Belgium and Ireland, 1927, in Balkan States, Hungary, Turkey and Greece, 1929, Sweden, Germany and France, 1931; contributed Talks with Celebrities; made spl. study of liquor regulation in Sweden; traveled through Africa from Capetown to Cairo and into Palestine, 1934; made spl. study of history of diamonds and gold in S. Africa and native customs of Belgian Congo, investigation of activity of Jews in Palestine; adventure in friendship to South Sea Islands, New Zealand and Australia, 1937; Internat. News Service rep. in Germany and Czechoslovakia, 1938, Finland, 1939; corr. U.S. papers; adventures in Europe, 1955, Eng., Wales, 1956; pres. Mildred Seydell Pub. Co. Belgian dir. World Poetry Day. Mem. Ga. Mothers Com.; v.p. Meml. Day Com. Decorated knight Order Leopold (Belgium); recipient 1st Book of Golden Deeds award Roswell Exchange Club, 1978. Mem. Nat, League Am. Pen Women, Internat. Periodic Press (dir. poetry Belgian sect.), Friends of Emory U. Library (hon.), A.G. Rhodes Home (hon.), Beta Sigma Phi (hon.). Clubs: Peony Garden (hon.); American Women's (Brussels). Author: Secret Fathers, 1930; Then I Saw North Carolina, 1936; Chins Up, 1939; Come Along to Belgium, 1969. Editor: Poetry Profile of Belgium, 1960. Publisher: Silent Singing (poems); Essays Wise and Otherwise. Mem. adv. bd. Sunshine Mag., Fellowship in Prayer mag. Home: 9530 Scott Rd Route 2 Roswell GA 30075

SEYMOUR, CLIFFORD THEODORE, educator; b. Pueblo, Colo., Feb. 23, 1915; s. Matthew Otto and Mattie Aldridge S.; A.A., Pueblo Jr. Coll., 1939; B.S., Va. Union U., 1943; M.S., Ind. U., 1951, Ed.D., 1952; m. Anna Florine McDonnell, July 23, 1948; 1 son, Clifford T. Grad. asst. Ind. U., 1951-53; instr. Grambling Coll., 1952-55; mem. faculty dept. leisure sci. Southern U., Baton Rouge, 1955—, chmn. dept., 1955-79; cons. in field. Chmn. Greater Baton Rouge Council on Aging, 1975-77; mem. adv. com. Nat. Park Service; bd. dirs. Capitol Area Agy.; bd. dirs. Girl Scouts Am. Served with U.S. Army, 1943-46. Recipient Silver Beaver award Boy Scouts Am., 1976; Disting. Alumnus award Ind. U. Mem. AAHPER (v.p. recreation So. dist. 1978, dist. Honor award), La. State AAHPER (v.p. recreation sect.), Nat. Parks and Recreation Assn., Nat. Recreation Therapeutic Assn., Soc. Parks and Recreation Educators. Presbyterian. Office: Dept Leisure Services Southern Univ Baton Rouge LA 70813

SEYMOUR, JAMES MICHAEL, pub. co. exec.; b. Tulsa, Jan. 3, 1950; s. Winburn Woodrow and Theda (Callas) S.; B.B.A., U. Okla., 1973. Dir. advt. Parks Apparel Co., Oklahoma City, 1972-74; mktg. asst. Blue Cross/Blue Shield, Oklahoma City, 1974-76; dir. advt. and public relations The Economy Co., Oklahoma City, 1976-79, dir. spl. projects, 1979—; advt. cons. Jaegar Corp., 1973-75. Mem. Oklahoma City Arts Festival Com.; mem. Oklahoma City Ballet Com. Mem. Oklahoma Postal Customer Council, U. Okla. Alumni Assn., Mercedes Benz Club Am. Democrat. Methodist. Home: 1107 Glenwood St Oklahoma City OK 73116 Office: 1901 N Walnut St Oklahoma City OK 73125

SEYMOUR, JOHN MICHAEL, III, civil engr.; b. Selma, Ala., Jan. 5, 1946; s. John Michael and Flora Louise (O'Flinn) S., Jr.; Asso. Sci., Marion Inst., 1966; B.S. in Civil Engring., Auburn U., 1969; m. Brenda Sue Bailey, Sept. 6, 1968; children—John Michael IV, Christopher Scott. Engr. asst. Ala. Hwy. Dept., Montgomery, 1964-69, engr., 1969-70; engr. firm Gilbreath, Foster & Brooks, Tuscaloosa, Ala., 1973; sr. engr. So. Natural Gas Co., Birmingham, Ala., 1973—. Adviser, Jr. Achievement of Birmingham, 1973—. Served with C.E., AUS, 1970-73. Registered profl. engr., Ala., Ga., La., Miss., S.C., Fla., Tenn., Tex. Mem. ASCE, Nat. Soc. Profl. Engrs. Republican. Mem. Ch. of Christ. Clubs: Neckar Rod and Gun (chmn. bd. Nellingen, Germany chpt. 1970-72), Civitan (pres. Vestavia Hills 1978—). Home: 2725 Southview Dr Birmingham AL 35216 Office: First National Southern Natural Bldg 1900 5th Ave N Birmingham AL 35202

SEYMOUR, RAYMOND BENEDICT, educator, cons., chem. engr.; b. Boston, July 26, 1912; s. Walter A. and Marie E. (Doherty) S.; B.S., U. N.H., 1933, M.S., 1935; Ph.D., State U. Iowa, 1937; postdoctoral Rensselaer Poly. Inst., 1963, U. Utah, 1964; m. Frances B. Horan, Sept. 16, 1936; children—David Ray, Susan (Mrs. Howard Smith), Peter, Phillip Alan. Instr. chemistry U. N.H., 1933-35, U. Iowa, 1935-37; research chemist Goodyear Tire & Rubber Co., Akron, Ohio, 1937-39; chief chemist Atlas Mineral Products div. Electric Storage Battery Co., Mertztown, Pa., 1939-41, exec. v.p., gen. mgr., tech. dir., 1949-54, pres., dir., 1954-55; research group leader Monsanto Co., Dayton, Ohio, 1941-45; dir. research, U. Chattanooga, 1945-48; dir. research Johnson & Johnson, New Brunswick, N.J., 1948-49; pres., tech. dir. Loven Chem. of Calif., 1955-58; pres. Corrosion Resistant Products, Inc., 1956-57; pres., chmn. bd. Alcylite Plastics & Chem. Corp., 1958-60; prof. chemistry, chmn. sci. div. Sul Ross State U., 1959-64, asso. chmn. chemistry dept. U. Houston. 1964-66, coordinator polymer chemistry, 1964-76, asso. prof. chemistry, 1964-69, prof., 1969-76, prof. emeritus, 1976—, asso. dir. research, 1966-68; adj. prof. polymer sci. U. So. Miss., Hattiesburg, 1974-76, distinguished prof., 1976—; cons. edn. AID, U.S. Dept. State, East Pakistan, 1963; mem. execs. res. Dept. Def.; dir. NSF Inst., 1965; Nat. Acad. Scis. vis. prof., Yugoslavia, 1976, Australia, 1977, USSR, 1978, China, 1979. Recipient Western Plastics award, 1960; Teaching Excellence award U. Houston, 1975; Catalyst Excellence in Teaching award. Registered profl. engr., Tex., Ohio. Fellow AAAS, Am. Inst. Chemists, Tex. Acad. Sci.; mem. Am. Inst. Chem. Engrs., Am. Chem. Soc. (Southeastern Tex. Ann. award 1972), Soc. Plastics Industry, Nat. Assn. Corrosion Engrs., Am. Soc. Oceanography, AAUP, Soc. Plastic Engrs., Plastics Pioneers Assn., Miss. Acad. Sci., Sigma Xi, Phi Kappa Phi, Alpha Chi Sigma, Gamma Sigma Epsilon. Rotarian. Club: Hattiesburg Country. Author: National Paint Dictionary, 3d edit., 1948; Plastics for Corrosion Resistant Applications; 1955; Hot Organic Coatings, 1959; Introduction to Polymer Chemistry, 1971; General Organic Chemistry, 1971; Experimental Organic Chemistry, 1971; Modern Plastics Technology, 1974; Chemistry and You, 1974; Structure-Solubility Relationships in Polymers, 1977; Polymer Chemistry, 1977; Additives for Plastics, Vol. I and II, 1977; Introduction to Polymer Chemistry, 1979; Plastic Mortars, Sealants, and Caulking Compounds, 1979; Polymer Chemistry, 1980; Introduction to Polymer Chemistry (audio course), 1980; Plastics vs. Corrosives, 1980; Ann. Plastic Review 1948—; also articles. Patentee in field. Home: 111 Lakeshore Dr Hattiesburg MS 39401

SHAARA, MICHAEL JOSEPH, JR., author, educator; Jersey City, N.J., June 23, 1929; s. Michael Joseph and Florence Alleene (Maxwell) S.; B.S., Rutgers U., 1951 postgrad. Columbia U., 1952, U. Vt., 1953-54; m. Helen Elizabeth Krumwiede, Sept. 16, 1950; children—Jeffrey, Lila. Asso. prof. English, Fla. State U., Tallahassee, 1961-73; writer, producer, performer courses ednl. TV, 1961-65. Served with AUS, 1946-47. Recipient award for excellence in med. journalism AMA, 1966; Coyle Moore award for classroom excellence, 1967; Pulitzer Prize for fiction, 1975. Mem. AAUP, Writers Guild, Internat. Platform Assn., Gold Key Honor Soc., Theta Chi, Omicron Delta Kappa. Author: The Broken Place, 1968; The Killer Angels, 1974. Contbr. short stories, articles to Am., fgn. mags. Home and office: 3019 Thomasville Rd Tallahassee FL 32312

SHABEL, RONALD JOHN, audio visual communications mgr.; b. Chgo., May 21, 1938; s. John Frank and Ann Laura (Layky) S.; B.S. in Speech, Northwestern U., 1960; m. Margaret Patricia Scanlan, Aug. 29, 1964; children—Jeanne Idella, Kenneth Philip. Staging services coordinator NBC, Chgo., 1958-60; broadcast prodn. supr. Leo Burnett Advt., Chgo. 1964-69; creative dept. adminstr. Henderson Advt. Agy., Inc., Greenville, S.C., 1969-72; asst. dir. communications Liberty Corp., Greenville, 1972—; instr. Greenville County Mus. Art. Bd. trustees Phyllis Wheatley Center, 1978-79. Served with U.S. Army, 1961-64. Decorated Army Commendation Medal; recipient cert. of merit Life Advertisers Assn., 1975. Mem. Greenville Advt. Fedn. (dir. 1973-76), Greenville C. of C., Am. Advt. Fedn., Indsl. Audio Visual Assn. (cert.), Indsl. TV Assn., Greenville Public Relations Assn. Episcopalian. Home: 2 Whaling Way Greenville SC 29615 Office: PO Box 789 Greenville SC 29602

SHACHTMAN, RICHARD HYMAN, educator, cons.; b. Winston-Salem, N.C., Aug. 14, 1941; s. Hyman and Josephine (Cohn) S.; B.S. cum laude, N.C. State U., 1963; M.A., U. Md., 1967, Ph.D., 1968; m. Ann Mirvis, July 4, 1965; children—Marc Howard, Susan Lisa. Asst. prof. stats. and ops. research/system analysis U. N.C., Chapel Hill, 1969-73, asst. prof. biostats., 1973-75, asso. prof. biostats. and ops. research, 1975-79, prof., 1980—; research asso. health services research center, Carolina Population Center; cons. Carolina Population Center, 1972, 74, EPA, 1975, Instituto Universitario de Estudios Superiores de Aministracion, Caracas, Venezuela, 1974—, Population Council Mex., 1976, Duke U. and Indian Health Service, 1977—, Nat. Center for Health Services Research, Washington, 1978—, bus. firms, 1972—; legal cons. judge, pvt. and govt. legal orgns; pres., dir. Sumarc Electronics, Inc., 1975—; treas. Stereo Sound Acoustics, Inc., 1974—. Recipient various grants. Mem. Am. Public Health Assn. (chmn. sessions 1976-78), Am. Statis Assn., Biometric Soc., Ops. Research Soc. Am. (chmn. health applications sect. 1979—, Best Paper of Yr. award 1977, chmn. coms. and conf. sessions 1976—, jour. health and care and welfare editor 1978—), Inst. Mgmt. Scis., Population Assn. Am., Sigma Xi. Referee tech. articles Jours. Ops. Research, 1969—; contbr. articles to profl. publs. Office: 304 University Square 143 W Franklin St Chapel Hill NC 27514

SHADE, LESLIE NEAL, JR., lawyer; b. Washington, Jan. 31, 1924; s. Leslie N. and Mary R. (Hamilton) S.; B.S., U.S. Mil. Acad., 1946; J.D., Emory U., 1972; m. Bobbie Miriam Reaves, Feb. 2, 1952; children—Leslie N. III, Sharon A., Cynthia M. Commd. 2d lt. U.S. Army, 1946, advanced through grades to lt. col., 1964; service in Korea, Saudi Arabia; chief operational plans Hdqrs. 3d Army, Ft. McPherson, Ga., 1965-66, ret., 1966; investigator Fulton County Dist. Attys. Office, Atlanta, 1969-72; admitted to Fla. bar, Ga. bar, U.S. Supreme Ct. bar; practiced law, Atlanta, 1973-78; asst. public defender Hillsborough County, 13th Jud. Circuit, Tampa, Fla., 1979—; legal adv. Pre-trial Intervention Project for Young Adults, Atlanta, 1973-78. Decorated Bronze Star medal, Purple Heart; recipient Am. Jurisprudence award for criminal law Emory U., 1969. Mem. Am. Bar Assn., Ga. Bar, Fla. Bar. Republican. Roman Catholic. Office: PO Box 2048 Tampa FL 33601

SHADID, ERNEST GEORGE, psychiatrist, hosp. adminstr.; b. Elk City, Okla., Dec. 26, 1929; s. George O. and Nerose (Adwon) S.; B.A., U. Okla., 1950, M.D., 1955; m. Joyce N. Cohlmia, Aug. 9, 1953; children—Larry G., David L., Diane L., Gregory E. Intern, St. Francis Hosp., Wichita, Kan., 1955-56; resident psychiatry Menninger Sch. Psychiatry, Topeka, 1956-57; resident psychiatry Central State Griffin Meml. Hosp., Norman, Okla., 1959-61, dir. outpatient dept., 1961-62, clin. dir., 1962-66, asst. supr., 1966—; asst. clin. prof. psychiatry, neurology and behavioral scis. U. Okla. Sch. Medicine, 1968—; cons. psychiatry Okla. State Penitentiary, Okla. Dept. Pub. Welfare. Mem. exec. com. Okla. Council Juvenile Delinquency Planning, 1969; v.p. Okla. Health Planning Agy., 1973; mem. Okla. Mental Health Planning Com., 1963—; mem. St. Joseph Sch. Bd., Norman, Okla., 1964-66; mem., lectr. Nat. Drug Edn. Center Adv. Com., U. Okla., 1970—. Served to capt. USAF, 1957-59. Diplomate Am. Bd. Psychiatry and Neurology. Fellow Am. Psychiat Assn. (pres. Okla. 1969-70), Am. Coll. Psychiatrists; mem. Am. Orthopsychiat. Assn., AMA, Mid-Continent Psychiat. Assn., Acad. Religion and Mental Health, Okla. Health and Welfare Assn., Okla. Med. Assn., Cleveland-McClain County Med. Soc. (pres. 1971-72). Home: 2601 Smoking Oak Rd Norman OK 73069 Office: PO Box 151 Norman OK 73069

SHAFFER, REBA SIMPSON, personnel exec.; b. Hindsville, Ark., Feb. 14, 1931; d. Frank Sherman and Ida (Cannaday) Simpson; student Westark Community Coll., 1953; B.S. in B.A., U. Ark., 1975. Exec. sec. Okla.-Gas & Electric Co., Ft. Smith, Ark., 1954-62, Ark. Best Corp., Ft. Smith, 1962-64, 69-72; ADP coordinator Dept. Army, Aberdeen, Md., 1965-69; personnel dir. First Fed. Savings & Loan, Ft. Smith, 1976—. Recipient Certificate of Achievement, Dept. Army, 1969. Mem. LWV (sec. 1962-63), Am. Soc. Personnel Adminstrn., Inst. Fin. Edn., Chi Sigma (nat. pres. 1968). Episcopalian. Home: 2016 Garner Ln Fort Smith AR 72901 Office: 6th and Garrison St Fort Smith AR 72901

SHAFFER, SHELDON, drug center adminstr.; b. Mpls., Sept. 11, 1927; s. Benjamin and Martha (Miller) S.; B.S., Ohio State U., 1949; postgrad. U. Miami, 1973, Moreno Sch. Psychodrama, 1973; D.D., Ch. Universal Brotherhood, 1974; m. Dianne Hyman, Oct. 11, 1953; children—Steven, Benjamin, Susan. Distbr. Anatole Robbins Cosmetics, Ohio, 1948; zone mgr. Investors Diversified Services, Inc., Mansfield, Ohio, 1949; asst. advt. mgr. Dominion Elec. Corp., Mansfield, 1949-53, advt. mgr., 1953-59, exec. v.p., 1959-68, pres., 1968-70; asst. dir. The Starting Place, Ft. Lauderdale, then Hollywood, Fla., 1970-71, exec. dir., 1972—; dir. Samson-Dominion Ltd., Pan Western Ins. Co., Dominion Elec. Corp., The Shaffer Corp. Chmn. Mayor's Com. Pub. Affairs, Mansfield, 1963—. Bd. dirs. Ashland Coll., United Jewish Appeal, 1959, Jewish Community Centers of S. Fla., 1975. Served with USNR, 1945-46, 50-52. Mem. Am. Assn. Concerned Drug Abuse Workers, Fla. Assn. Drug Centers, Ohio State U. Assn., Am. Mgmt. Assn. Mason (Shriner). Author: Children, Parents and Drugs—A Survival Handbook, 1975. Home: 1000 N North Lake Dr Hollywood FL 33019 Office: 2057 Coolidge St Hollywood FL 33020

SHAFFER, SHIRLEY JEAN ANDERSON, mfg. co. exec.; b. Chgo., Sept. 23, 1925; d. Edwin W. and Marie G. (Nelson) A.; student Pan Am. U., 1943; gen. bus. diploma Durhams Jr. Bus. Coll., 1944; student Northwestern U., 1946-49; m. Lester E. Shaffer, Nov. 5, 1949 (div. 1964); children—Bonnie, Larry, Steven, Scott, Leslie. Owner, operator Grefan Kennels, Norridge, Ill., 1955-64; editorial asst. Peacock Bus. Press, Park Ridge, Ill., 1963-67; sales/service coordinator Goodyear Chem. div. Goodyear Co., Elk Grove, Ill., 1967-68; dir. sales rep., various companies, 1968-73; v.p. Mid Am. Investments, Dallas, 1973-74; credit and collection mgr. Hycel, Inc., Houston, 1974—. Mem. Nat. Conservative Polit. Action Com., The Conservative Caucus; mem. state adv. bd. Presdl. candidate Congressman Phillip M. Crane, 1979—. Mem. Nat. Assn. Credit Mgmt., Houston Assn. Credit Mgmt., Am. Kennel Club, Phi Gamma Nu. Republican. Methodist. Home: 8006 Edgemoor St Houston TX 77036 Office: 7920 Westpark St PO Box 36329 Houston TX 77036

SHAH, JITENDRA JIVANLAL, research scientist; b. Kathlal, Gujarat, India, Feb. 4, 1944; s. Jivanlal C. and Savitaben J. (Shah) S.; came to U.S., 1969, naturalized, 1977; B.Sc., P. B. Sci. Coll., Gujarat, India, 1965; M.Sc., Gujarat U., 1968; M.S., Memphis State U., 1971; m. Ramila J. Shah, May 4, 1967; children—Dipti, Nimisha, Balmukund. Tutor chemistry P. B. Sci. Coll., Kapadwanj, Gujarat, India, 1965-69; grad. teaching asst. Memphis (Tenn.) State U., 1969-70; research asso. dept. biochemistry U. Tenn., Memphis, 1971; dir. research and devel., research scientist Woodson-Tenent Labs., Inc., Memphis, Tenn., 1971—. Fellow Am. Inst. Chemists (profl. chemist); mem. Am. Chem. Soc., Assn. Vitamins Chemists, Inst. Food Technologists, Assn. Ofcl. Analytical Chemists (asso. referee 1973—), AAAS. Home: 4860 Brentdale Memphis TN 38118 Office: 345 Adams St Memphis TN 38101

SHAH, NANDKUMAR SHANKARLAL, pharmacologist; b. Nandurbar, India, May 6, 1928; s. Shankarlal Hirabhai and Parvatiben (Shankarlal) S.; came to U.S., 1961, naturalized, 1977; B.S. Gen., Poona (India) U., 1953, B.S. with honors, 1954, M.Sc., 1955; Ph.D., U. Fla., 1965; m. Kamla Davi (NeetaN.) Gupta, Feb. 23, 1961; 1 dau., Anita. Research fellow Poona U., 1955-56; research asst. Indian Council Med. Research, Rewa, 1957-58; demonstrator in biochemistry M.A. Med. Coll., New Delhi, 1958-60; research asst. AEC, Bombay, India, 1960-61, Coll. Medicine U. Fla., Gainesville, 1961-65; med. research asso. III, Galesburg (Ill.) State Research Hosp., 1965-67; research officer dept. pharmacology Indian Council Med. Research, Med. Coll., Baroda, 1968-70; chief Ensor Research Lab., William S. Hall Psychiat. Inst., Columbia, S.C., 1970—; adj. distinguished prof. Coll. Pharmacy, U. S.C., 1970—, asso. prof. neuropsychiatry Sch. Medicine, 1976-78, research prof. neuropsychiatry, adj. prof. pharmacology, 1978—; session chmn. developmental pharmacology Fedn. Am. Socs. Exptl. Biology, 1974. Pres. India Students Assn., U. Fla., 1963-65. Mem. Am. Soc. Pharmacology and Exptl. Therapeutics (Travel award to 6th Internat. Congress Pharmacology, Helsinki 1975), Internat., Am. socs. neurochemistry, Soc. Biol. Psychiatry, Assn. Physiologists and Pharmacologists of India. Hindu. Contbr. articles in field to profl. jours. Home: 2600 Quail Hollow Ln West Columbia SC 29169 Office: William S Hall Psychiat Inst Columbia SC 29202

SHAH, RAVINDRA HIRALAL, elec. engr.; b. Ahmedabad, India, Mar. 1, 1945; s. Hiralal Jethalal and Ramangouri (Hiralal) S.; B.S. in Mech. Engring., Gujarat U., Ahmedabad, 1966, B.S. in Elec. Engring., 1967; B.S. in Elec. Engring., U. South Fla., 1968, M.S., 1969; M.B.A., Rollins Coll., 1977. Test equipment design engr. Honeywell Info. Systems, Tampa, 1969-71; sr. group engr. Martin Marietta Aerospace Co., Orlando, 1971-78, prin. engr. Harris Corp., Melbourne, Fla., 1978—. Vol., Youth Programs, Inc.; v.p. India Assn. Mem. IEEE, Computer Soc., U. South Fla. Alumni Assn., Tau Beta Pi. Home: 225 Pennsylvania St Melbourne FL 32901 Office: Harris Corp PO Box 37 Melbourne FL 32901

SHAH, ZAFAR ALI, surgeon; b. Hoshiarpur, India, May 5, 1937; s. Bashir Ali and Habib Begum Shah; came to U.S., 1962; F.Sc. Med., Govt. Coll., Lahore, Pakistan, 1955; M.B., B.S., King Edward Med. Coll., Lahore, 1960; m. Jane Kathryn Reed, Sept. 19, 1970; children—Ruth Ann, Omar Jameel, Naseem Faye. Med. officer Dispensary No. 1, Peshawar, Pakistan, 1960-61; instr. physiology King Edward Med. Coll., 1961-62; intern Riverside Hosp., Toledo, 1962-63; resident in pathology and surgery Maumee Valley Hosp., Toledo, 1963-66; chief resident in surgery McLaren Gen. Hosp., Flint, Mich., 1966-67; asst. resident, then chief resident in surgery Ohio Valley Gen. Hosp., Wheeling, W.Va., 1967-69; resident in cardiothoracic surgery Victoria Hosp., U. Western Ont., London, 1970-71; practice medicine specializing in thoracic surgery, Guelph, Ont., Can., 1971-77, Paris, Tex., 1977—; mem. staff McCuiston Regional Med. Center. Diplomate Am. Bd. Surgery. Fellow Royal Coll. Surgeons Can., A.C.S.; mem. Pakistan Med. Assn., Tex. Thoracic Soc. Home: 3145 Mahaffey Ln Paris TX 75460 Office: 2850 Lewis Ln Paris TX 75460

SHAHAN, OTIS WALTER, JR., former educator; b. Morgantown, W.Va., Dec. 19, 1917; s. Otis Walter and Sarah Maude (Cool) S.; B.A., W.Va. U., 1961, M.A., 1966; M.A.T., U. Fla., 1971; m. Dorothy Mae Morris, Dec. 28, 1939; 1 son, Otis Walter. Enlisted U.S. Navy as apprentice seaman, 1935, advanced through ranks to lt., 1957; tchr. Morgantown (W.Va.) High Sch., 1961-66; instr. history and geography St. Johns River Jr. Coll., Palatka, Fla., 1967-79. Mem. Library Bd., Morgantown, 1966-67; city commr., Morgantown, 1966-67; v.p. Putnam County Tchrs. Credit Union, 1970-79. Mem. Assn. Am. Geographers, So. Hist. Assn., VFW, Phi Alpha Theta, Gamma Theta Upsilon. Club: Grafton Kiwanis. Home: 301 Valley St Grafton WV 26354

SHAHEEN, SHOUKY AZEEZ, real estate developer; b. Chgo., July 17, 1929; s. Azeez and Saleemeh (Balluteen) S.; B.A., U. Chgo., 1950, M.B.A., 1952; m. Doris Ann Bradshaw, May 28, 1961; children—William, Mary Gay. Treas., Katherine Rug Mills, Inc., Dalton, Ga., 1952-59; pres., Standard Textile Mills, Inc., Cartersville, Ga., 1959-64; owner Shaheen & Co., Atlanta, 1964—. Mem. bd. sponsors Atlanta Symphony Orch., 1971-75. Home: 3792 Dumbarton Rd NW Atlanta GA 30327 Office: 32 Peachtree St NW Atlanta GA 30303

SHAHROKHI, FEREYDOUN, physician, educator; b. Gorgan, Iran, May 5, 1942; came to U.S., 1970; s. Hossein and Sakineh (Mirkareemi) S.; M.D., Tehran (Iran) U., 1968; m. Kathleen Korzenowski, June 19, 1976. Intern, Morristown (N.J.) Meml. Hosp., 1971-72; resident in pathology Boston U., 1972; resident in neurology N.Y. U. Med. Sch., 1972-75; researcher Milbank Research Labs., 1973-75; clin. and research fellow Mass. Gen. Hosp., Harvard U., 1975-76; instr. dept. neurology La. State U., 1976-77, asst. prof., 1977—, staff neurologist Med. Center, 1976—; staff neurologist VA Med. Center, Shreveport, La., 1976—. Served with Iranian Health Corps., 1968-70. Diplomate Am. Bd. Psychiatry and Neurology. Mem. Am. Acad. Neurology, Am. Electroencephalographic Soc., Am. Epilspsy Soc., Eastern Soc. Electroencephalographers. Home: 3500 Milam St Apt 201 Shreveport LA 71109 Office: Dept Neurology La State U Med Center PO Box 33932 Shreveport LA 71130

SHAIA, HARRY, JR., lawyer; b. Richmond, Va., Aug. 29, 1930; s. Harry and Zackia S.; student U. Va., 1948-50; LL.B., U. Richmond, 1953; m. Margaret Ann Gibrall, Aug. 29, 1959; children—Anthony J., Gregory J., John J., Christopher J., Anne-Marie, Harry J. Admitted to Va. bar, 1953; practiced in Richmond, 1953—; mem. firms Blanton, Lumpkin & Shaia, 1960-70, Blanton, Shaia & Kelly, 1970-72, Shaia, Stout & Markow, 1974—. Served with AUS, 1953-55. Roman Catholic (chmn. ch. councils 1972-74). Club: Downtown (Richmond). Home: 300 DeSota Dr Richmond VA 23229 Office: 700 Bldg 7th and Main Sts Richmond VA 23219

SHAIKH, MUHAMMAD ASHRAF, shipyard exec.; b. Kasur, Pakistan, Jan. 14, 1940; came to U.S., 1966, naturalized, 1977; s. Fazal Elahi and Gulam Batool (Bakhash) Chawla; B.Sc., U. Punjab (Pakistan), 1959; LL.B., U. Kavachi (Pakistan), 1965; M.B.A., Northwestern U., 1970; m. Dec. 21, 1969. Officer trainee Bankers Tng. Inst., Karachi, 1960-62: officer class II State Bank of Pakistan, Karachi, 1962-66; systems analyst and corp. systems mgr. Essex Internat., Ft. Wayne, Ind., 1970-74; asst. to pres. Jacksonville (Fla.) Shipyards, Inc., 1974—; mem. faculty mgmt. acctg. Ind. U., Ft. Wayne, 1971-74. C.P.A., Fla. Mem. Nat. Assn. Accts., Am. Inst. C.P.A.'s, Fla. Inst. C.P.A.'s, Assn. Systems Mgmt., Data Processing Mgmt. Assn. Muslim. Club: Baymeadows Racquet. Home: 8439 Allerton Ln Jacksonville FL 32216 Office: 750 E Bay St Jacksonville FL 32203

SHAIVITZ, STEPHEN ADLER, neurologist; b. Balt., May 4, 1939; s. Sylvan B. and Rita (Adler) S.; A.B. cum laude, Columbia U., 1961; M.D., U. Mich., 1965; m. Patricia Miller, June 16, 1968; children—Eli M., Adam A. Intern, Phila. Gen. Hosp., 1965-66; resident in neurology Albert Einstein Coll. Medicine, Bronx, N.Y., 1966-69; asst. chief neurology St. Elizabeths Hosp., Washington, 1969-71; practice medicine specializing in neurology, West Palm Beach, Fla., 1971—; mem. staff Good Samaritan Hosp., West Palm Beach; mem. advisor Gold Coast chpt. Nat. Multiple Sclerosis Soc.; chmn. Gov.'s Drug Abuse Adv. Com., 1974-76. Mem. Am. Acad. Neurology, Am. EEG Soc., Am. Assn. Study Headache, Fla. Soc. Neurology, Fla. Med. Assn., Blockley Med. Soc. Office: 3701 Broadway West Palm Beach FL 33407

SHALLOWAY, ARTHUR MELVIN, electronic engr.; b. Atlanta, Mar. 20, 1922; s. David and Jeanne (Gordon) S.; B.S., Ga. Inst. Tech., 1943, M.S., 1951; postgrad. Cornell U., 1953-55; m. Johanna Elfriede Latta, June 12, 1955; children—David Glenn, Heidi Jeanne. Electronic engr. Signal Corps Lab., Red Bank, N.J., 1951-52, Convair Missile div., Pomona, Calif., 1952-53, Westinghouse Tube div., Elmira, N.Y., 1955-56; prin. engr. Stromberg Carlson Electronics div., Rochester, N.Y., 1956-59, Honeywell Inertial Guidance div., St. Petersburg, Fla., 1959-62; electronic engr. Nat. Radio Astronomy Obs., Charlottesville, Va., 1962—; instr. Cornell U., 1953-54; cons. Max Planck Inst. Radio Astronomie, 1969-71, Nat. Research Council of Can., 1977-79; dir. cons. firm Advanced Devel. Assos., Charlottesville, 1979—. Served to 1st lt. USAAF, 1943-46. Mem. I.E.E.E., Internat. Union Radio Sci. Patentee in field. Home: 201 Westminster Rd Charlottesville VA 22901 Office: Nat Radio Astronomy Observatory 2015 Ivy Rd Charlottesville VA 22903

SHAMBLIN, JAMES ROSCOE, JR., surgeon; b. Tuscaloosa, Ala., Mar. 19, 1933; s. James Roscoe and Martha Charlotte (Avery) S.; B.S., U. Ala., 19S4; M.D., Tulane U., 1958; m. Patricia Ann Terry, Apr. 1, 1967; children—Anne, Scott. Intern, U. Hosp., Birmingham, 1958-59; fellow in gen. surgery Mayo Clinic, Rochester, Minn., 1959-63; practice medicine specializing in gen. surgery, Tuscaloosa, Ala., 1965-73, Marion County, Winfield, Ala., 1973-78; chief surg. service Druid City Hosp., Tuscaloosa, Ala., 1973; chief gen. surgery Rankin Fite Hosp., Winfield, Ala., 1973-78, chief of staff, 1975-76; chief surgery Cherokee County Hosp., Centre, Ala., 1978—; cons. surgeon Guin (Ala.) Hosp., 1973-78, Lister Hill Hosp., Hamilton, Ala., 1973-78. Served with AUS, 1963-65. Paul Harris fellow, 1973. Fellow A.C.S.; mem. Am. Bd. Surgery, A.M.A., Southeastern Surg. Congress, Med. Assn. State Ala., Marion County Med. Soc. (pres. 1978). Republican. Methodist. Rotarian, Kiwanian. Home and office: PO Drawer R Centre AL 35960

SHAMBURGER, (ALICE) PAGE, author; b. Aberdeen, N.C.; d. Frank Dudley and Alice (Page) Shamburger; grad. St. Mary's Sch. and Jr. Coll., 1945, Marjorie Webster Coll., 1947. Roving editor Am. Aviation Mag., 1949-51; script writer radio sta. WHUC, 1951-53; Eastern editor Cross Country News, 1954-67, contbg. editor Air Progress, 1966-74; editor So. Aviation Times, 1975-76; mem. Woman's Adv. Com. on Aviation, 1964-68; mem. aviation div. N.C. Emergency Transp. Task Force, 1966-67; pres., co-owner Page Travel Agy., Inc. Sec., Mid-South Horse Show Assn.; asst. sec. Moore County Hounds. Recipient commendations N.C. Gov., 1967-68, USAF Tactical Command, 1966; Doris Mullen Meml. Scholarship for helicopter tng., 1969, Lady Hay Drummond-Hay award, 1971. Mem. Aviation/Space Writers Assn., 99s-Internat. Orgn. Licensed Woman Pilots, Aircraft Owners and Pilots Assn., Wingfoot Lighter-than-air Soc., Southeastern Aviation Trades Assn., 99's (gov. S.E. sect. and mem. exec. bd. 1969-70, 71, curator mus. 1969-76), Univ. Aviation Assn. (dir.), Nat. Intercoll. Flying Assn. (adv. bd.), Whirly-Girl 142. Democrat. Methodist. Author: Tracks Across The Sky, 1964; Classic Monoplanes, 1966; co-author: Command the Horizon, 1968; World War I Aces and Planes, 1968; Summon the Stars (named best non-fiction aviation book 1970 Aviation Space Writers Assn.), 1970; The Curtiss Hawks, 1972. Contbr. articles to profl. publs. Address: 500 Carolina St Aberdeen NC 28315

SHANBHAG, GAJANAN RAMNATH, gen., thoracic, cardiovascular surgeon; b. Bhatkal, Mysore, India, Nov. 26, 1938; s. Ramnath Vaman and Shevantu (Ramnath) S.; B.Int.Sc., Kanara Coll., Mysore, India, 1960; B.S., M.B., S.G.S. Med. Coll., Bombay, India, 1960; M.S. in Gen. Surgery, U. Bombay, 1965; m. Pramila Subrao Prabhu, May 6, 1961; children—Jyoti, Ashish, Nitin. Intern, K.E.M. Hosp., Parel, Bombay, 1960-61, resident in neurosurgery, gen. surgery, thoracic and cardiovascular surgery, 1961-66; surg. resident St. Joseph's Infirmary, Louisville, 1966-67, Oschner Found. Hosp., New Orleans, 1967-69; resident, fellow in thoracic and cardiovascular surgery Tex. Heart Inst., Houston, 1969-70; chief surgery resident Meml. Med. Center, Savannah, Ga., 1970-71; sr. resident St. Vincent Charity Hosp., Cleve., 1971-72, instr. in thoracic and cardiovascular surgery, 1972-73; practice medicine specializing in gen., thoracic and cardiovascular surgery, Woodruff, S.C., 1973—; attending thoracic and cardiovascular surgeon, Spartanburg Gen. Hosp.; attending gen. thoracic and cardiovascular surgeon, Workman Meml. Hosp., Woodruff. Mem. Spartanburg Bd. Mental Health. Diplomate Am. Bd. Surgery. Clubs: Woodruff Rotary, Greenville V.I.P. Home: 520 Hawthorne Ave Woodruff SC 29388 Office: PO Box 596 206 E Georgia St Woodruff SC 29388

SHANDS, RODNEY EDWARD, lawyer; b. New Albany, Miss., May 5, 1947; s. Robert Eugene and Margaret (White) S.; B.A., U. Miss., 1969, J.D., 1972; m. Mary Virginia Ginger Moore, Mar. 3, 1973; children—Katherine Ray, Leslie Elizabeth, Nancy Brett. Admitted to Miss. bar, 1972; asso. firm Talmadge D. Littlejohn, New Albany, 1972—; county pros. atty. Union County (Miss.), New Albany, 1972—; dir. Yonah Realty Co., United Inc., United Funeral Home Inc., United Funeral Service Inc. Bd. dirs. Leadership Miss. Alumni Assn. Named Outstanding Young Man Union County, 1974. Mem. Am., Miss. bar assns., Miss. Prosecutors Assn. Presbyterian. Club: Rotary (pres. New Albany 1976-77). Home: 260 Reeves St New Albany MS 38652 Office: PO Box 892 Main St New Albany MS 38652

SHANE, JOHN MARDER, obstetrician, gynecologist; b. Kansas City, Mo., Oct. 5, 1942; s. Henry K. and Ruth B. (Marder) S.; M.D., Okla. Med. Coll., 1967; m. Eileen Goodart, Sept. 2, 1967; children—Robert, Edward. Intern, Michael Reese Hosp., Chgo., 1967-68; resident Beth Israel Hosp., Boston, 1970-73; fellow in endocrinology Boston Hosp. for Women, 1973-75; asst. prof. Ob-Gyn, Harvard Med. Sch., Boston, 1975-77; dir. div. reproductive endocrinology and infertility Beth Israel Hosp., Boston, 1975-77; practice medicine specializing in reproductive endocrinology, infertility and gynecology, Tulsa, 1977—; mem. staffs St. Francis Hosp., St. John's Hosp., Hillcrest Hosp. Mem. Central Assn. Obstetricians and Gynecologists, Tulsa Ob-Gyn Soc., AMA, Endocrine Soc., Am. Soc. Andrology, Am. Fertility Soc., Am. Coll. Obstetricians and Gynecologists. Contbr. articles in field to med. jours., chpts. to books. Office: 6465 S Yale St Suite 304 Tulsa OK 74177

SHANK, LLOYD DEWITT, JR., elec. engr.; b. Newton, N.C., Oct. 21, 1946; s. Lloyd DeWitt and Jessie (Ervin) S.; B.S. in Elec. Engring. with honors, N.C. State U., Raleigh, 1972; m. Leslie Marie Cornman, Aug. 1, 1970; children—Brian Dewitt, Karlyn Sloan. With Duke Power Co., 1972-75; with City of Washington (N.C.), 1975—, dir. elec. utilities, 1975—; condr. seminars, cons. in field. Chmn. Miss Beaufort County Beauty Pageant, 1978. Served with USAF, 1964-68. Registered profl. engr., N.C. Mem. N.C. Assn. Mcpl. Elec. Systems (pres., dir. 1977-78), East Carolina Engrs. Assn., Washington Jaycees (past dir.). Methodist. Home: 105 Palmer St Washington NC 27889 Office: PO Box 850 N Market St Washington NC 27889

SHANK, MARIA THERESA, Realtor; b. Paterson, N.J., July 2, 1931; d. Josef and Anna (Falb) Totzauer; B. Mus. Edn., Oberlin Coll., 1953; M.A. in Edn., E. Carolina U., 1978; children—Michael B., Mark J., Timothy M. Tchr. music, pub. schs., Cleve., 1953-54, Birmingham, Ala., 1959-62, Hicksville, N.Y., 1954-55, Walpole, Mass., 1956-58; violinist Birmingham Symphony, 1959-62; realtor Aldridge and Southerland Agy., Greenville, N.C., 1970—; dir. coop. edn. and placement Pitt Community Coll., 1978—. Dir. Greenville Bd. Realtors, 1975-76; mem. adv. com. Pitt County Tech. Inst., 1975-78; mem. Greenville City Sch. Bd., 1972—, chmn., 1978-79; bd. dirs. League Women Voters Greenville, 1971, Pitt County Mental Health Assn., 1978—. Mem. NOW, N.C. Sch. Bd. Assn., N.C., Am. assns. realtors, Adult Edn. Assn. U.S., Kappa Delta Pi. Home: 1215 Drexel Ln Greenville NC 27834 Office: PO Drawer 7007 Greenville NC 27834

SHANKAR, K. H., mech. engr.; b. Coimbatore, India, June 16, 1940; came to U.S., 1966, naturalized, 1972; s. K. S. and K. S. (Rukmani) Harihar; Machineshop Engr., City and Guilds of London, 1960-64; B.S. in M.E., Howard U., Washington, 1972; m. Rajeswari Krishnan, Aug. 26, 1970; children—Ravi, Rajni. Instr. Kymore Tech. Inst., India, 1964-66; tech. asst. Rodana Research Corp., Bethesda, Md., 1968-69; supr. Fairfax Opportunities Unltd., Fairfax, Va., 1972-74; staff engr. Washington Gas Light Co., Springfield, Va., 1974—. Active Program for Enrichment of Gifted; tech. adviser Jr. Achievement, 1974—. Mem. ASME (v.p. 1969-70, sec. 1970-71), Am. Gas Engrs. Assn., Mgmt. Speakers Bur., Mid Atlantic Numismatic Soc., Am. Philatelic Assn., Tau Beta Pi (sec. 1971-72). Hindu. Contbr. articles to profl. jours. Home: 13326 Kirkdale Ct Woodbridge VA 22193 Office: 6801 Industrial Rd Springfield VA 22151

SHANKER, KASTURI GIRIJA, urologist; b. Madras, India, Jan. 20, 1939; came to U.S., 1971, naturalized, 1973; s. Kasturi Seshagiri and Kasturi Rukmini Rao; M.D., Madras Med. Coll., 1960; m. Kandukuri Uma, Mar. 6, 1968; children—Babu, Anita. Intern, Providence Hosp.,

Washington, 1971-72; resident in surgery Charleston (W.Va.) Med. Center, 1972-73; resident in urology Jefferson Med. Coll., Phila., 1973-76; practice medicine specializing in urology, Roanoke Rapids, N.C., 1976—. Diplomate Am. Bd. Urology. Mem. AMA, N.C. Med. Soc. Home: 801 Quail Ct Roanoke Rapids NC 27870 Office: 117 W 7th St Roanoke Rapids NC 27870

SHANKLIN, DEBRA KAY, music pub. and recording exec.; b. Nashville, Sept. 14, 1954; d. Joe H. and Beverly (Thompson) S.; B.B.A., Belmont Coll., 1976. With Paragon Assos., Inc., Nashville, 1976—, mgr. royalty and copyright dept., 1978—. Mem. Am. Mgmt. Assn., Gospel Music Assn., Ch. Music Pub. Assn., Nat. Music Pub. Assn. Baptist. Home: Route 5 Box 139A Franklin TN 37064 Office: Box 23618 Nashville TN 37202

SHANKLIN, DOUGLAS RADFORD, physician, marine biologist; b. Camden, N.J., Nov. 25, 1930; s. John F. and Muriel M. Shanklin; A.B. in Chemistry, Syracuse U., 1952; M.D., SUNY, Syracuse, 1955; m. Virginia A. McClure, Apr. 7, 1956 (div. 1976); children—Elizabeth, Leigh, Lois Virginia, John Carter, Eleanor; m. 2d, Jean C. Anderson, Jan. 1, 1977. Intern, Duke U., Durham, N.C., 1955-56; tng. in Ob-Gyn, SUNY, Syracuse, 1956-60, Coll. Medicine, U. Fla., 1960-67; prof. Ob-Gyn, U. Chgo., 1967-78; exec. dir. Santa Fe Found., Gainesville, Fla., 1978—. Mem. adv. panel U.S. Dept. Agr. Women-Infants-Children Nutritional Program, Research Triangle Park, N.C., 1979—. Served with M.C., USN, 1956-58. Recipient Physicians Recognition award AMA, 1969, 72, 75; named Best Basic Sci. Tchr., U. Fla. Coll. Medicine, 1967; diplomate Am. Bd. Pathology. Mem. Am. Assn. Pathologists, Soc. Pediatric Research, AAAS, N.Y. Acad. Scis., So. Soc. Pediatric Research, So. Med. Assn., Am. Acad. Reproductive Medicine (sec. 1969-74), Internat. Acad. Pathology, Pediatric Pathology Club (sec. 1970-75, pres. elect 1980-81), Am. Coll. Obstetricians and Gynecologists, Council Biology Editors, Internat. Soc. Gynecol. Pathologists, Am. Soc. for Law and Medicine, Sigma Xi. Democrat. Episcopalian. Clubs: Quadrangle, Hugo's Companions (Chgo.). Contbr. chpts. to books, articles to profl. jours. Home: 1238 NW 18th Terr Gainesville FL 32605 Office: 1212 NW 12th Ave Bldg C Suite 1 Gainesville FL 32601

SHANKLIN, JAMES GORDON, lawyer; b. Elkton, Ky., Dec. 10, 1909; s. William S. and Eva (Jones) S.; B.A., Vanderbilt U., 1932, LL.B., 1934; m. Emily Shacklett, July 15, 1933; children—Elizabeth Eve, William Samuel. Agt. FBI, W.Va., 1943-44, N.Y.C., 1944-46, supr., 1946-47, hdqrs. Washington, 1947-51, asst. spl. agt. in charge Mobile, Ala., 1951-53, spl. agt. in charge, 1953-55, Pitts., 1955-56, insp. hdqrs., Washington, 1956-58, spl. agt. in charge El Paso, Tex., 1958-59, Honolulu, 1959-63, Dallas, 1963-75; admitted to Tex. bar, 1975; mem. firm Johnson, Shanklin, Billings, Kelton & Porter, Dallas, 1975—; lectr. police acads.; admitted to Tenn. bar, 1934. Mem. Tenn., Fed., Tex., Dallas bar assns., E. Tex. Police Assn., Soc. Former Spl. Agts. FBI, Kappa Sigma. Baptist. Clubs: Chaparral, Insurance, Imperial, Masons. Home: 6023 Del Norte St Dallas TX 75225 Office: 1410 Republic Nat Bank Bldg Dallas TX 75201

SHANKS, HOMER KUYKENDALL, JR., assn. exec.; b. Abilene, Tex., July 17, 1936; s. Homer Kuykendall and Ora Nell (Hughes) S.; B.A. in English, Tex. A&M U., 1958; postgrad. U. Tex., El Paso, 1962-67; m. Mickey Anne McKee, Dec. 22, 1962; children—Eleanor McKee, Rebecca Pauline, Barbara Anne. High sch. math. tchr. El Paso Ind. Sch. Dist., 1963-67; sci. programmer BDM Corp., El Paso, 1967-71; bus. programmer Farah Mfg., El Paso, 1971-74; computer programmer analyst United Services Automobile Assn., San Antonio, 1974—. Served with U.S. Army, 1958-63. Mem. U.S. Naval Inst., Air Force Assn., Nat. Def. Preparedness Assn., Smithsonian Assos., Mus. Natural History (asso.), Soc. for Encouragement of Barber Shop Quartet Singing in Am., Mensa, Internat. Plastic Modelers Soc. Baptist. Club: Toastmasters (pres. club 1979, able toastmaster 1978, editor Top Ten bull. 1976), El Paso Scale Modeler Soc. (charter pres. 1971, founding editor bull. 1968-72). Founder, editor El Paso Council Math. Tchrs. Newsletter, 1963-67. Home: Box 32834 San Antonio TX 78216 Office: 9800 Fredricksburg Rd San Antonio TX 78288

SHANNON, DONALD SUTHERLIN, educator; b. Tacoma Park, Md., Dec. 28, 1935; s. Raymond Corbett and Elnora Pettit (Sutherlin) S.; B.A., Duke, 1957; M.B.A., U. Chgo., 1964; Ph.D., U. N.C., 1972; m. Virginia Ann Lloyd, June 24, 1961 (div.); children—Stacey Eileen, Gail Allison, Michael Corbett; m. 2d, Kay Powe, Dec. 30, 1977; stepchildren—Christopher, Bonnie Bertelson. Mem. auditing staff Price Waterhouse & Co., N.Y.C., 1957-61; sr. accountant Price Waterhouse, Chgo., 1964-65; instr. Duke U., Durham, N.C., 1964-69; asst. prof. bus. adminstrn. U. Ky., Lexington, 1969-76, asso. prof., 1976—. Served with AUS, 1958-59, 61-62. Mem. Ky. Soc. C.P.A.'s, Am. Inst. C.P.A.'s, Western Finance Assn., Am. Finance Assn., Beta Gamma Sigma. Home: 1351 Fontaine Rd Lexington KY 40502

SHANNON, LARRY ROLAND, ednl. adminstr.; b. Palmetto, Fla., June 29, 1933; s. Sam and Roberta Elnora (Gayle) S.; B.S., Fla. A&M U., 1959; M.A., Atlanta U., 1969; Ph.D., Iowa State U., 1974; m. Velma Charles, June 14, 1969; children—Herbert Norris, Larry Roland. Instr. biology and math., dept. chmn. Lincoln Meml. High Sch., Palmetto, 1959-65; instr. phys. sci., dept. chmn. Booker High Sch., Sarasota, Fla., 1966-67; instr. biology Brown High Sch., Atlanta, 1967-69, Lincoln U. (Mo.), 1969-71; asst. to dean Grad. Coll., Iowa State U., 1974-76; dir. planning and advancement affairs, asso. prof. biology Livingstone Coll., Salisbury, N.C., 1976—; cons. environ. scis., acad. planning. Organizer and scoutmaster troop #41, Sunniland council Boy Scouts Am., 1962-64; mayor Iowa State U. Married Community, 1973-74; chmn. Precinct Polls, Ames, Iowa. Served with U.S. Army, 1953-55. Named Tchr. of Yr., Manatee County (Fla.), 1965, Omega Man of Yr., Eta Alpha chpt., 1971; NSF fellow, summers 1962-64, acad. yr., 1965-66. Mem. Soc. Coll. and Univ. Planners, Am. Fisheries Soc., AAAS, Sigma Xi, Gamma Sigma Delta. Democrat. Presbyterian. Club: Masons. Contbr. articles to profl. jours. Home: 17-E Covey Ln Greensboro NC 27406 Office: 701 W Monroe St Salisbury NC 28144

SHANNON, RAY, cons. engr.; b. Taylor, Tex., Aug. 17, 1923; s. James Frank and Ethel Inez (Weeks) S.; B.S. in Mech. Engring., U. Tex., Austin, 1949; m. Wilma Deanna Singleton, July 17, 1945; children—Michael, Marilyn. Engr., Mobil Oil Corp., Beaumont, Tex., 1949-54; editor Hydrocarbon Processing mag., Houston, 1954-55; project engr. O'Donnell Engrs., cons., Beaumont, 1955-58; partner Deevy and Shannon, cons. engrs., Beaumont, 1958-74; exec. v.p. Devvy & Shannon, Inc., cons. engrs., Beaumont, 1975—. Served with USAAF, 1942-45. Registered profl. engr., Tex. Mem. ASME, Tex. Soc. Profl. Engrs., Instrument Soc. Am. Methodist. Club: Beaumont Lions. Home: Route 2 Box 154 Vidor TX 77662 Office: 1130 Petroleum Bldg Beaumont TX 77701

SHANNON, ROBERT FUDGE, psychiatrist; b. Melbourne, Ark., Apr. 15, 1933; s. Karr and Ollie Ellen (Fudge) S.; student U. Ark., Little Rock, 1950-52, U. Central Ark., 1952-53; B.S., U. Ark., 1957, M.D., 1957; children—Shawn, Scott; m. 2d, Lyra Carolyn Fugler; stepchildren—Jeff Conaway, Tim Conaway. Fellow psychiatry U. Ark. Med. Center, Little Rock, 1958-61; intern, Baptist Med. Center, Little Rock, 1957-58, now staff; resident in neurology-psychiatry U. Ark. Med. Center, 1958-59, in psychiatry, 1959-61; practice medicine specializing in psychiatry, Little Rock, 1965-71, now staff; faculty, U. Ark. Sch. Medicine, Little Rock, 1963—, asso. prof. psychiatry, dir. residency tng., coordinator jr. clerkship, 1971-76, now prof., head div. adult psychiatry; pres. Ark. Psychiat. Clinic, Little Rock, 1965-71; mem. staff Children's Hosp., 1963-67, St. Vincent's Infirmary; cons., Ark. Girls Tng. Sch., Alexander, 1963-65, Family Service Agy., Little Rock, 1965-66, Ark. Cleft Palate Clinic, Little Rock, 1964-67, Little Rock VA Hosp., 1971—. Mem. Health and Welfare Council, 1963-70. Bd. dirs. Elizabeth Mitchell Guidance Center, 1965-71, Gaines House, 1968-73. Served to capt. AUS, 1961-63. Diplomate Am. Bd. Psychiatry and Neurology. Fellow Am. Psychiat. Assn.; mem. Ark. Psychiat. Soc. (pres. 1970-71), A.M.A., Ark., Pulaski County med. socs. Home: 1611 Mountain Dr Little Rock AR 72207 Office: 4301 Markham St Little Rock AR 72205

SHANNON, ROBERT MCDONALD, architect, planner; b. Bristol, Va., Oct. 2, 1917; s. Robert McDonald and Helen Izetta (Coyner) S.; B.S., Va. Poly. Inst. and State U., 1939, M.S., 1940; postgrad. Woodrow Wilson Sch., Princeton U., 1949-50, Ohio State U., 1954-56; m. Anne MacGowan, June 20, 1953 (div. May 1964); children—Christopher, Alexandra, Nicholas. With U.S. Army C.E., 1940-61, comdg. officer 109th Engr. Bn., Mannheim, Germany; adviser Chinese Chief of Engrs., Taiwan; engr. N.Y. Engr. Dist.; dir. community shelter planning Hays, Saay, Mattern & Mattern, Roanoke, Va., 1961-63; dir. Roanoke Valley Regional Planning Commn., Roanoke, 1964-68; exec. dir. Fifth Planning Dist. Commonwealth of Va., 1969-72; asst. planning and constrn. Va. Commonwealth U., Richmond, 1973-; asst. prof. Ohio State U., 1953-56; instr. U. Md. Far East, 1958, U. Va. Roanoke Center, 1962-65. Mem. Arts Com. City of Roanoke, 1970-73; mem. com. Roanoke Valley Museum, 1970-73; U.S. observer UN Interregional Seminar, Madrid, Spain, 1972. Bd. dirs. Va. Citizens Planning Assn. Decorated Bronze Star. Registered architect, Va. Mem. AIA, Am. Planning Assn., Tau Beta Pi. Author met. area planning studies. Home: 58 Garden Dr Alexandria VA 22304 Office: PO Box 9062 Alexandria VA 22304

SHAPER, STEPHEN JAY, mfg. co. exec.; b. Houston, Oct. 7, 1936; s. Charles and Ruth Shaper; B.A., Rice U., 1958; M.B.A., Harvard U., 1960; m. Sue Zigenbein, June 6, 1959; children—Peter, Park, Page, Penn. Mfg. engr. Tex. Instruments, 1960; with El Pato Products and affiliated companies, 1962—, pres., dir. El Pato Products Corp., 1963—, Sun/Am. Corp., 1974—, Gen. Investment and Trust Corp., 1963—; v.p., dir. CDP Corp., 1975—, Trussway, Inc., 1972—, Trussway Central, 1978—, Trussway-Barns, 1979—, Seville Industries, 1978—; v.p., sec., dir. Dark's Silk Flowers, Inc., 1978—; dir. Cal-Tex Metals, Houston Check Service, Inc. Served with U.S. Army, 1961. Mem. Barbecue Industry Assn., Young Pres.'s Orgn., Houston Entrepreneurial Council, Rice U. Alumni Assn. (dir.), Principia Alumni Assn. Christian Scientist. Clubs: Kiwanis, Breakfast. Home: 325 Ripple Creek Houston TX 77024 Office: PO Box 125 Houston TX 77001

SHAPIRO, DAVID HOWARD, surgeon; b. Newark, Apr. 20, 1939; s. Nathan and Theresa Marie (Brown) S.; B.A., Williams Coll., 1961; M.D., Tufts U., 1965; 1 son, Seth Mark. Intern, Boston City Hosp., 1965-67; resident to chief resident Yale-New Haven Hosp., 1967-71; practice medicine specializing in gen. and vascular surgery, Belleair, Fla., 1974—; mem. staff, chief sect. gen. surgery Morton Plant Hosp., Clearwater, Fla., 1978; active staff, chief dept. surgery Med. Center Hosp., Largo, 1978-79; cons. attending Tampa (Fla.) VA Hosp.; instr. Yale Sch. Medicine, 1970-71; asst. clin. prof. surgery U.S. Fla. Sch. Medicine, Tampa, 1973—. Pres., bd. dirs. Pasco Subdiv. Regional Health Planning Commn., 1973-74; v.p. trustees Fla. West Coast Regional Health Planning Commn., 1973-74; bd. dirs. Pinellas Subdiv. Regional Health Planning Commn., 1974-75; med. adviser, chmn. profl. edn. com. Pasco unit Am. Cancer Soc., 1973-75, bd. dirs., 1976—, mem. profl. edn. com. Fla. div. and subcom. for cancer centers and tumor registries in Fla., 1974—, bd. dirs., chmn. profl. edn. com. Pinellas County, bd. dirs. Fla. div., mem. div. research com.; mem. Tampa Bay alumni acad. com. Williams Coll. Served to maj., M.C., AUS, 1971-73. Recipient William Dameshek award Tufts U. Sch. Medicine, 1965. Fellow S.E. Surg. Congress, A.C.S.; mem. AMA, Fla. Assn. Gen. Surgeons, Fla., Pinellas County med. assns., Tampa Surg. Soc. Club: Countryside Country. Home: 106 Poinciana Ln Largo FL 33540 Office: 1016 Ponce de Leon Blvd Belleair FL 33516

SHAPIRO, EDWARD MURAY, dermatologist; b. Denver, Oct. 6, 1924; s. Isador Benjamin and Sara (Berezin) S.; student U. Colo., 1941-43; A.B. with honors, U. Tex., 1948, M.D., 1952; m. Ruth Young, Oct. 14, 1944; children—Adrian Michael, Stefanie Ann. Intern, Jefferson Coll. Medicine Hosp., Phila., 1952-53; resident in dermatology U. Tex. Med. Br., Galveston, 1953-55; resident in dermatology Henry Ford Hosp., Detroit, 1955-56, asso. in dermatology div. dermatology, 1956-57; clin. instr. dermatology Baylor U. Coll. Medicine, Houston, 1957-68, asst. clin. prof., 1968—; staff Jefferson Davis Hosp., Houston, 1958—; attending staff Pasadena (Tex.) Gen. Hosp., 1958—, Pasadena Bayshore Hosp., 1962—, Southmore Hosp., Pasadena, 1958—. Served with USAAF, 1943-46. Henry J. N. Taub research grantee, 1958-60; diplomate Am. Bd. Dermatology. Fellow Am. Acad. Dermatology; mem. AMA, Tex. Med. Assn., Harris County Med. Assn. (dir. 1968-69), S.E. Br. Med. Assn., Houston Dermatology Assn., Houston Art League, Gulf Coast Art Soc., Am. Physicians Art Assn. Jewish. Clubs: B'nai B'rith, Rotary. Contbr. articles in field to med. jours. Home: 2101 S Houston Rd Pasadena TX 77502 Office: 1020 S Tatar St Pasadena TX 77506

SHAPIRO, LEONARD, former air force officer, bus. exec., govt. ofcl.; b. Rochester, N.Y., Feb. 1, 1917; s. Sam and Rose (Tomkin) S.; B.A., U. Ill., 1939; M.A., Georgetown U., 1948, Ph.D., 1949; m. Judith Torruella, Aug. 16, 1947; 1 son, John L. Commd. 2d lt., advanced through grades to col. USAF, 1951, chief ops. Missile Test Center, 1959-61, Congo, 1961-62, tech. tng., Amarillo, Tex., 1962-65, ret.; dir. Internat. Bus. Devel., Northrop Corp., Beverly Hills, Cal., 1965-69; asst. adminstr. Econ. Devel. Adminstrn., Govt. P.R., 1970—. Bd. govs. Georgetown U. Decorated Legion of Merit D.F.C., Air medal with 13 oak leaf clusters. Mem. Navy League (dir.). Roman Catholic. Club: Wings (N.Y.C.). Author: Soviet Treaty Series, 2 vols., 1949, 52. Home: 860 Ashford Ave Apt 9 A Santurce PR 00907 Office: Econ Devel Adminstrn GPO Box 2350 San Juan PR 00936

SHAPIRO, MYRON (MIKE) FREDERICK, communications co. exec.; b. Mpls., Dec. 16, 1918; s. Leo and Miriam (Levin) S.; student Duluth Jr. Coll., 1937-38, U. Minn., 1939; m. Conway Helen King, Oct. 24, 1942; 1 dau., Lynne Carole (Mrs. Duke Covert). Mgr. KTXL-Radio, San Angelo, Tex., KECK-Radio, Odessa, Tex., 1945-52; sales rep. WFAA-TV, Dallas, 1952-53; comml. mgr. KDUB, Lubbock, Tex., 1953-54; account exec. Avery Knodel, Chgo., 1954-55; v.p., mng. dir. Griffin Telecasting Properties, Tulsa and Little Rock, 1956-58; mgr. sta. WFAA-TV, 1958-60, gen. mgr., 1960-74; pres., dir. Belo Broadcasting Corp., Dallas, 1974—; mem. CBS Radio Adv. Affiliate Bd., 1975-78; dir. A.H. Belo Corp. Chmn. Dallas March of Dimes, 1970-71; mem. devel. bd. Jacksonville Lon Morris Coll., Jacksonville, Tex., 1971—, mem. bd. Communications Sch., U. Tex. at Austin, 1969-79. Bd. dirs. Family Guidance Center, 1967-69; bd. dirs. Am. Cancer Soc., 1965—, chmn. Dallas Crusade, 1975-76, chmn. bd. Dallas chpt., 1977-78. Served with A.C., AUS, 1941-45. Recipient Outstanding Broadcaster award Assn. Broadcast Execs. Tex., 1962. Mem. Nat. Assn. Broadcasters (chmn. bd. dirs. TV 1965-66, TV bd. mem. 1975-79), ABC-TV Affiliates Assn. (chmn. bd. govs. 1963), Assn. Broadcast Execs. Tex. (pres. 1959-60), Dallas Ad Club (bd. dirs. 1968-69), Dallas Ad League (bd. dirs. 1968-69), Better Bus. Bur. (bd. dirs. 1965—), Salesmanship Club (officer, dir.). Initiated weekly TV show pub. service Let Me Speak To The Manager (name Inside Television 1975), 1961—. Home: 13825 Hughes Dallas TX 75240 Office: Belo Broadcasting Corp Communications Center Dallas TX 75202

SHAPIRO, WILLIAM, cardiologist; b. Newark, N.J., Dec. 8, 1927; s. Aaron and Celia (Rossman) S.; B.A., Duke Univ., 1947, M.A., 1948, M.D., 1954; m. Olive May Derry, Sept. 22, 1951; children—Gordon Marc, Joan Celia, Robin Derry. Intern, Mt. Sinai Hosp., N.Y.C., 1954-55; resident Duke Hosp., Durham, N.C., 1955-58; instr. Med. Coll. Va., Richmond, 1960-62, asst. prof., 1962-65, SW Med. Sch., Dallas, 1965-68, asso. prof., 1968-79, prof., 1979—; chief Cardiovascular Sect., Med. Service, Dallas VA Hosp., 1968—. Served with M.C., USN, 1958-60. Diplomate Nat. Bd. Med. Examiners, Am. Bd. Internal Medicine. Fellow Am. Coll. Cardiology, Council Clin. Cardiology, A.C.P., Alpha Omega Alpha. Contbr. articles in field to profl. jours. Home: 5216 Palomar Ln Dallas TX 75229 Office: 4500 S Lancaster Dallas TX 75216

SHARBEL, HERBERT JAMES, auditor; b. Nashville, Mar. 26, 1947; s. Kelly Matthew and Margaret Elizabeth (Johnson) S.; student Tenn. Tech. U., 1965-66, 70; B.S. in Acctg., U. Tenn., Nashville, 1973; m. Elizabeth Mary Griffith, Sept. 2, 1972. Sports copy boy Nashville Banner, 1970-71; account clk. Dept. Employment Security, Nashville, 1971-73; auditor Div. State Audit, Nashville, 1973-74; accountant Clin. Labs. Nashville 1974; accountant, auditor U.S. Army C.E., Nashville, 1974—; budget technician Tenn. Air N.G., 1974—. Served with USMC, 1967-69. Mem. Assn. Govt. Accountants (research committeeman), Air Force Sgts. Assn. Roman Catholic. Clubs: Cedars, K.C. Home: 111 Donelsonwood Dr Nashville TN 37214

SHARIF, ALBERT MATTHEW, retail stores exec.; b. N.Y.C., Apr. 4, 1949; B.A., Adelphi U., 1972; M.B.A., Harvard U., 1976; m. Lois Anne Newman, Sept. 5, 1976. Mgmt. auditor GAO, N.Y.C., 1973-74; with Laurinburg Oil Co. (N.C.), 1976-78; v.p., owner, Almarks, Inc., Charlotte, N.C., 1978—. Served with USAF, 1969-70. Home: 5705 C Electra Ln Charlotte NC 28212 Office: 5237 Albemarle Rd Charlotte NC 28212

SHARMA, MUTYAM VENKATESWARE, physician; b. Bellary, India, Aug. 9, 1930; s. Mutyam Sitaram and Etur (Saraswathi) S.; came to U.S., 1972; M.B.B.S., Madras Med. Coll., 1954; m. Regina Michael Ann, Apr. 28, 1964. Rotating intern Govt. Gen. Hosp., Madras, India, 1954-55; house surgeon gen. surgery and urology Royal Infirmary, Bolton (Lancs), Eng., 1955; sr. house surgeon Bury and Rossendale Gen. Hosp., Lancs, Eng., 1956-57; sr. casualty officer emergency and trauma Bury (Lancs, Eng.) Gen. Hosp., 1957; house surgeon Hammersmith Hosp. and Postgrad. Med. Sch., London, Eng., 1958; sr. house surgeon emergency and trauma West London (Eng.) Hosp., 1958; registrar gen. surgery, chief resident Bury and Rossendale Group of Hosps., Bury (Lancs), Eng., 1959-61; registrar thoracic surgery, chief resident Victoria Hosp., Blackpool, Lancs, Eng., 1961-62; cons. surgeon, div. med. officer Indian Rwys. Hosp.. Hubli, 1962-65; sr. house surgeon thoracic surgery Frenchay Hosp., Bristol, Eng., 1965-66 physician, Santa Fe Drilling Co. (Eng.) Ltd., Tripoli, Libya, 1966-68; cons. surgeon. div. med. officer Indian Rwys. Hosp., Secunderabad. 1968-72; physician, Am. Peace Corps, Mysorec, Andkrapradesh, India, 1968-72; resident surgery St. Joseph Infirmary, Louisville, 1972-73, emergency physician, 1975-78, staff gen. surgery and emergency medicine, 1976-78; staff physician Ky. Bapt. Hosp., Bapt. Hosp. East, Louisville, 1973—; staff gen. surgery and emergency medicine Meth. Evang. Hosp., Louisville, 1979—. Fellow Royal Coll. Surgeons Eng., Royal Coll. Surgeon Edinburgh. Internat. Coll. Surgeons; mem. Am. Coll. Emergency Physicians. Mason. Home: 816 Melford Ave Louisville KY 40217 Office: 810 Barret Av Louisville KY 40217

SHARMA, SUNIL KUMAR, mgmt. engr.; b. Bikaner, India, Mar. 14, 1946; came to U.S., 1970, naturalized, 1975; B.E. in M.E., U. Indore, 1969; M.S. in Indsl. Engring., Miss. State U., 1974; postgrad La. State U., 1974-76; M.B.A., U. Houston, 1978; m. Rashmi Malviya, June 26, 1977. Supr. machine shop Indian Smelting and Refining Co., Bombay, 1969-70; sales mgr. Thomas Nelson Co., Nashville, 1972-76; mgmt. engr. St. Joseph Hosp., Houston, 1976-78; dir. mgmt. engring. St. Luke's Hosp., Tex. Children's Hosps., Tex. Heart Inst., Houston, 1978—; teaching asst. Miss. State U. Rep. So. region Nat. Assn. Fgn. Students Affairs. Mem. Am. Inst. Indsl. Engrs., Hosp. Mgmt. Systems Soc., Greater Houston Hosp. Mgmt. Systems Soc. (dir. 1977-79, sec. 1980, chmn. membership 1976-79), Alpha Pi Mu. Home: 15331 E Westwood St Houston TX 77071 Office: PO Box 20269 Houston TX 77025

SHARMA, TARA CHAND, surgeon; b. Hoshiarpur, India, Oct. 15, 1938; s. Gujjar Ram and Durga (Devi) S.; came to U.S., 1963; B. Chir., M.B., Med. Coll. Amritsar, India, 1960; M.B.B.S., Panjab U., 1960; m. Indu Vable, Apr. 17, 1968; children—Charunidhi, Sandeep. Intern, V.J. Hosp., Panjab, India, 1960-61; resident house officer in surgery Irwin Hosp., New Delhi, 1961, resident house officer in gen. medicine, 1962, registrar in clin. pathology, 1962; surg. intern Washington Hosp., 1963-64, resident in gen. surgery, 1964-65, resident in urology, 1965-68; chief resident in pediatric urology Children's Hosp., Washington, 1966; spl. fellow in urol. oncology Meml. Hosp. Cancer and Allied Diseases, N.Y.C., 1968-70; practice medicine specializing in urology, Huntington, W.Va.; attending urologist Huntington Hosp., St. Mary's Hosp., Cabell-Huntington Hosp., chmn. dept. urology, 1976—; cons. attending urologist Guthrie Hosp., VA Hosp.; clin. asst. prof. dept. surgery, div. urology Marshall U. Sch. Medicine, 1977—, also clin. asst. prof. dept. pediatrics; pres. med. staff Drs. Meml. Hosp., 1972-73; attending urologist Family Care Out Patient Center, Huntington, 1971—. Recipient Outstanding Young Man of Year award Huntington Jaycees, 1974, Outstanding W. Virginian award W.Va. Jaycees, 1974; Ernest Alva Gould award for excellence in surgery Washington Hosp. Centre, 1967-68. Diplomate Am. Bd. Urology. Fellow Internat. Coll. Surgeons, ACS, Royal Soc. Health, Southeastern Surg. Congress; mem. Am. Cancer Soc. (v.p. Cabell-Wayne chpt. 1972-73, pres. Cabell-Wayne chpt. 1973-74, dir. 1974), Cabell County Med. Soc., Cabell County Jr. Med. Soc., Am. Fertility Soc., AMA (Physicians Recognition award 1969, 72), W.Va. Urol. Assn., Assn. Mil. Surgeons U.S. (hon. mem.), Pan-Pacific Surg. Assn., Am. Geriatric Soc., Kidney Found. Club: Lions. Contbr. numerous articles on genitourinary pathology and diagnosis to med. jours. Home: 36 LynnMar Dr Huntington WV 25705 Office: PO Box 2507 Huntington WV 25725

SHARMAN, GEORGE ALBERT, dentist; b. Houston, July 13, 1917; s. George Robert and Cora Jane (Duke) S.; student U. Houston, 1935; D.D.S., Tex. Dental Coll., 1940; postgrad. Am. Sch. Applied Hypnotherapy, Hypnoanesthesia, 1952; m. Margie Eloise Worsham, June 22, 1940; 1 son, Robert Wayne. Practice dentistry, Houston, 1940—. Served to capt USAAF, 1942-46. Fellow Royal Soc. Health;

mem. Am. Endodontic Soc., Am. Soc. Clin. Research Dental Materials, Houston Dist., Tex., Am. dental assns., Hon. Order Good Fellow, Psi Omega. Home and Office: 2110 Airline Dr Houston TX 77009

SHARP, PAUL FREDERICK, educator, former univ. pres.; b. Kirksville, Mo., Jan. 19, 1918; s. Frederick J. and L. Blanche (Phares) S.; A.B., Phillips U., 1939; Ph.D., U. Minn., 1947; LL.D. (hon.), Tex. Christian U., 1961; L.H.D. Buena Vista Coll., 1967; Litt.D., Limestone Coll., 1971; m. Rosella Ann Anderson, June 19, 1939; children—William, Kathryn, Paul Trevor. Instr. U. Minn., 1942, 46-47, vis. lectr., 1948; asso. prof. Am. history, chmn. Am. Instns. program U. Wis., 1954-57, vis. lectr., 1953; vis. lectr. San Francisco State Coll., 1950, U. Ore. 1955; Fulbright lectr. Am. Instns., univs. Melborne and Sydney, Australia, 1952; pres. Hiram Coll., 1957-64; chancellor U. N.C., Chapel Hill, 1964-66; pres. Drake U., Des Moines 1966-71; pres. U. Okla., 1971-78, pres. emeritus, Regents prof., 1978—; dir. Sterndent Corp., Equitable of Iowa Co.; mem. exec. com. N. Central Assn. Commn. on Instns. Higher Edn.; chmn. bd. trustees Ednl. Testing Service, Princeton, N.J.; adv. council pres.'s Assn. Governing Bds.; chmn. Assn. Am. Colls.; chmn. commn. leadership devel. in higher edn. Am. Council Edn. Served from ensign to lt. (s.g.), USNR, 1943-46; naval liaison officer Royal Australian Navy, 1944-45. Research grants Minn. Hist. Soc., 1947, 48, Social Sci. Research Council, 1949, 51; Iowa State U. Alumni Fund award, 1952; Fulbright award to Australia, 1952; Ford Faculty fellow, 1954; recipient award of merit Am. Assn. State and Local History, 1955; Silver Spur award Western Writers Am., 1955; Outstanding Achievement award U. Minn., 1975; Guggenheim fellow, 1957. Mem. Phi Beta Kappa, Phi Kappa Phi, Pi Gamma Mu, Phi Alpha Theta, Phi Delta Kappa, Alpha Kappa Psi, Omicron Delta Kappa. Mem. Disciples of Christ Church. Author of Agrarian Revolt in Western Canada, 1948; Story of an Iowa Boyhood, 1952; Whoop-Up Country; Canadian American West, 1955. Editor: Old Orchard Farm, 1952; Documents of Freedom, 1957. Cons. author: Heritage of Midwest, 1958; regional editor Montana mag., editorial cons. Americana Press, 1955—. Contbr. articles profl. jours. Home: 701 Mockingbird Ln Norman OK 73071 Office: 630 Parrington Oval Room 105 Norman OK 73019

SHARP, SUSIE MARSHALL, judge; b. Rocky Mount, N.C., July 7, 1907; d. James Merritt and Annie (Blackwell) Sharp; LL.B., U. N.C., 1929; LL.D., Woman's Coll., U. N.C., 1950, Queens Coll., 1962, Elon Coll., 1963; L.H.D., Pfeiffer Coll., 1960; LL.D., Wake Forest Coll., 1965, Duke U., 1965, Catawba Coll., 1970, U. N.C., 1970, U. N.C., Wilmington, 1977, Atlantic Christian Coll., 1980. Admitted to N.C. bar, 1928; gen. law practice with father Sharp & Sharp, Attys., 1929-49; city atty. Reidsville, N.C., 1939-49; spl. judge Superior Ct. of N.C., 1949-62; asso. justice Supreme Ct. of N.C., 1962-75, chief justice, 1975-79; ret., 1979. Recipient Leadership and Service award N.C. State Grange, 1975; Alumni Service award U. N.C. at Greensboro, 1975; Spl. award for outstanding legal achievement N.Y. Women's Bar Assn., 1976; Distinguished Alumnus award U. N.C. at Chapel Hill, 1977; citation for disting. public service N.C. Citizens Assn., 1980. Mem. Am., N.C. bar assns., Order of Valkyries, Order of Coif, Phi Beta Kappa. Delta Kappa Gamma. Democrat. Methodist. Clubs: Soroptimist (hon.); Altrusa (hon.). Home: 629 Lindsey St Reidsville NC 27320 also 521 Wade Ave Raleigh NC 27605

SHARP, THOMAS SIMPSON, businessman; b. Hammond, La., Nov. 30, 1944; s. Wiley Howard and Melanie Louise (Ledet) S.; B.S., La. State U., 1967; B.M.E., S. La. U., 1971, M.Ed., 1973. Tchr., Holy Ghost Cath. Sch., 1968-70, 71-72; owner Lafayette Electronics, 1973-79; treas. Musike Squire Ltd., Hammond, 1979—; mgr. Columbia Theatre, Hammond, 1979; mng. exec. Cutting-Pike Investment Corp., 1979—. Choir dir. 1st Christian Ch., Hammond, 1972-79; pres. Columbia Theatre Players, 1976-78, exec. bd., 1978—, bd. dirs., 1978-80; mem. Hammond Arts Council, 1978-79. Mem. Am. Guild Organists, Am. Film Inst., Downtown Mchts. Assn., Hammond Hist. Dist. Assn., Miklos Rozsa Soc., Max Sternei Soc., Film Music Collection, Phi Mu Alpha Sinfonia, Delta Tau Delta (v.p. So. div. 1977-79, chpt. adv.). Republican. Roman Catholic. Clubs: Rotary (Hammond); Empire (New Orleans). Home: 23 Darrell Dr Hammond LA 70401 Office: PO Box 1672 Hammond LA 70404

SHARP, VAL, real estate broker, mental health counselor; b. San Augustine, Tex., Apr. 10, 1923; s. Val Henry and Thelma (Harris) S.; B.B.A., Stephen F. Austin U., 1949; M.L.A., So. Methodist U., 1973; M.S., E. Tex. U., 1978; m. Lucy Lane, Nov. 3, 1945; children—Lane, Valerie, James Gregory. Supr., Sun Oil Co., Beaumont, Tex., 1949-58; export supt. Venezuelan Sun Oil Co., Maracaibo, 1958-63; systems analyst Sun Co., Inc., Beaumont and Dallas, 1963-75; bus. mgr. Sun Info. Services Co., Dallas, 1975-80; real estate broker, mental health counselor, Plano, Tex., 1977—. Served with USNR, 1942-47. Mem. Nat. Assn. Realtors, Tex. Assn. Realtors, Greater Dallas Bd. Realtors, Collin County Bd. Realtors, Mental Health Assn. Tex., Mental Health Assn. Dallas County, Nat. Mental Health Assn., Am. Mental Health Counselors Assn., Alpha Chi. Presbyterian. Club: Plano Lions. Home: 1800 Ports O'Call Plano TX 75075 Office: 704 E 15th St Plano TX 75074

SHARP, WILLIAM HARRY, univ. ofcl.; b. Moorestown, N.J., Apr. 20, 1930; s. Alvin L. and Anna L. (Stiles) S.; B.A., Denison U., 1952; M.A., Ohio U., 1954; Ph.D., Ohio State U., 1959; m. Margaret Brown Wiltshire, Aug. 16, 1952; children—William Timothy, Margaret Joyce, Brian Wiltshire, Julie Anna. Dir. counseling and testing U. Wyo., Laramie, 1965-70, mem. adv. bd. Common Campus Ministry, 1968, mem. faculty dept. psychology, 1959-73, asst. prof., 1959-61, asso. prof., 1961-68, prof., 1968-73, dean of students, 1970-73; vice-chancellor and dean of students U. Houston, 1973—; cons. Wyo. Div. Vocat. Rehab., 1965-68, S.E. Wyo. Mental Health Center, Cheyenne, 1967-69, St. Joseph's Home for Children, Torrington, Wyo., 1969-70; vocat. cons. Bur. Hearings and Appeals, Social Security Adminstrn., HEW, 1965-73; mem. legis. subcom. Gov.'s Commn. on Mental Health Planning, 1965-66. Certified psychologist, Tex. Mem. Am. Psychol. Assn. (profl. affairs com. 1971), Am. Coll. Personnel Assn. (chmn. counseling commn. 1970-72, exec. com. 1971-74), So. Coll. Personnel Assn., Tex. Assn. Coll. and Univ. Student Personnel Adminstrs., Omicron Delta Kappa, Psi Chi, Lambda Chi Alpha. Presbyterian. Home: 13018 Taylorcrest St Houston TX 77079 Office: Dean of Students U Houston Houston TX 77004

SHARPE, ROBERT FAY, publishing cons.; b. Florence, Ala., Sept. 8, 1926; s. Thomas and Lida Mae (Gammill) S.; B.S. in Bus. Adminstrn. Memphis State U., 1957; m. Jane Allen, Dec. 28, 1948; children—Susan Sharpe Hedge, Robert Fay, Paul Allen, Timothy David. Life ins. agent Crown Life & Pilot Life, 1950-53, supr., 1953-54, gen. agent, 1954-59; exec. sec. Good News Broadcasting Assn., Lincoln, Nebr., 1959-63; exec. dir. Reformed Presbyn. Found., St. Louis, 1963-65; pres. Robert F. Sharpe, Inc., Memphis, 1965—; founder, dir. Nat. Planned Giving Inst., 1967—; pub. Give and Take, monthly newsletter; cons. not-for-profit inst. Served with USN, 1944-47. Recipient Distinguished Service award Memphis State U. 1978. Mem. Nat. Cath. Devel. Conf., Nat. Assn. Ch. Bus. Mgrs., Nat. Soc. Fund Raising Execs. Republican. Presbyterian. Club: Summit. Author: 27 Ways to Increase Giving to Your Church, 1977; The Planned Giving Idea Book, 1978; Before You Give Another Dime, 1979; producer filmstrips The State Has Made Your Will, Andy Average Plans His Estate; producer 36 cassette series Planned Giving on Cassette; contbr. articles to profl. and religious publs.; also numerous monographs on fin. devel. Home: 2289 Kirby Rd Memphis TN 38138 also 521 Mediterranean Dr Dunedin FL 33528 Office: 1222 White Station Tower Memphis TN 38157

SHARRY, JOHN JOSEPH, univ. dean; b. Somerville, Mass., Feb. 11, 1925; s. Thomas Martin and Mary (Murphy) S.; B.S., Tufts U., 1945, D.M.D., 1949; m. Rachel Thompson, Jan. 30, 1952; children—Paul, Ann, Thomas. Asst. prof. clin. dentistry Sch. Dentistry, U. Ala., 1953-56, asso. prof., 1956-60, prof. and chmn. prosthetic dentistry, 1960-68; dir. Ala. Office Learning Resources, 1968-71; dean Dental Sch., Med. U. S.C., 1971-75, dir. postdoctoral program in prosthetic dentistry, 1975-78; dean U. Tex. Dental Sch., San Antonio, 1978—; dir. cleft palate program State of Ala., 1957-59; cons. to VA, 1958—; mem. spl. grants rev. com. Nat. Inst. Dental Research; Kellogg prof. to Brazil, 1963; vis. prof. U. Ill., 1965. Trustee, Birmingham (Ala.) Symphony Orch., 1966-70, Charleston (S.C.) Symphony Orch., 1973-78; mem. exec. com. Jefferson County (Ala.) Com. Econ. Opportunity, 1968-71. Decorated U.S. Army Outstanding Civilian Service medal; NIH fellow, Malmo, Sweden, 1959-60. Mem. Am. Coll. Prosthodontists (pres. 1975-76). Club: Rotary. Author: Complete Denture Prosthodontics, 1962; contbr. numerous articles to profl. jours.; editor: Symposium on Complete Dentures, 1964; (with H.L. Holley, C.K. Meador, Sarah C. Brown) Rare Books and Collections of the Reynolds Historical Library: A Bibliography, 1968. Office: 7703 Floyd Curl Dr San Antonio TX 78284

SHARWELL, GEORGE ROBERT, educator, lawyer, social worker; b. Vineland, N.J., Jan. 2, 1937; s. Truman Parker and Agnes May (Shaud) S.; B.A., Allegheny Coll., 1960; M.S., Va. Commonwealth U., 1964; J.D., U. S.C., 1974; children—Brad Alan, Erin Elizabeth. Social worker Child Care Service of Chester County (Pa.), 1960-61; family counselor Jewish Family Service of Phila., 1964-65; chief social services Phila. Anti-Poverty Action Com., 1965-67; exec. dir. So. Md. Community Action Agy., 1967-69; asst. prof. Coll. Social Work, U. S.C., 1969-71, teaching asso., 1971-74, asso. prof., 1974—; admitted to S.C. bar, 1975; dir., chmn. S.C. Child Protection Adv. Bd., 1977—. Served with USAF, 1955-59. Mem. Acad. Certified Social Workers, Am. Bar Assn., S.C. Bar Assn., Nat. Assn. Social Workers (pres. S.C. chpt. 1978—), AAUP, Council Social Work Edn., Nat. Council Family Relations, Trial Lawyers Assn. Am., S.C. Social Welfare Forum (dir.). Methodist. Contbr. articles to profl. jours.; mem. editorial bd. Social Work Jour., 1976-78, cons. editor, 1978—; mng. editor Arete, 1970—. Home: 3523 Wilmot St Columbia SC 29205 Office: Coll Social Work U of SC Columbia SC 29208

SHAUGHNESSY, MARY ETHEL, hosp. dietetics adminstr.; b. Louisville, Feb. 6, 1918; d. Edward Michael and Carolyn Minnie (Jecker) S.; B.S. in Dietetics, Our Lady of Cin. (now Edgecliff Coll.), 1946; postgrad. St. Louis U., 1946-47. Joined Sisters of Mercy, 1938; dir. dietetics Our Lady of Mercy Hosp., Cin., 1948-55, Mercy Hosp., Hamilton, Ohio, 1955-65, St. Mary's Med. Center, Knoxville, 1965—, edn. coordinator U. Tenn. affiliation tng. program for registered dietitians, 1974—. Named Outstanding Dietitian, State of Tenn., 1971. Mem. Am. Soc. Hosp. Food Service Adminstrs., Am. Dietetic Assn., Tenn. Dietetic Assn. (chmn. food adminstrn. sect. 1967-68, pres. 1969-70, 70-71), Knoxville Dist. Dietetic Assn. (pres. 1969-70). Contbr. articles to profl. jours. Home and Office: Saint Mary's Medical Center Oakhill Ave Knoxville TN 37917

SHAVER, JAMES LEVESQUE, JR., lawyer; b. Wynne, Ark., Nov. 23, 1927; s. James Levesque and Louise (Davis) S.; J.D., U. Ark., 1951; m. Bonnie Wood, July 17, 1949; children—James Levesque III (dec.), Bonnie Sue Shaver Huff. Admitted to Ark. bar, 1951, since practiced in Wynne; partner firm Shaver, Shaver & Smith, 1951—. Dir. First Nat. Bank, Wynne; atty. St. Francis Levee Dist., 1970—; mem. Ark. Ho. of Reps., 1955—, speaker, 1977, chmn. judiciary com., 1969—, mem. rules com., 1967—. Mem. E. Ark. Devel. Com., 1967—. Served with USNR, 1945-46. Named Outstanding Mem. Ark. Ho. of Reps. for 1975 Session. Mem. Am., Ark., E. Ark. (treas. 1965—, pres. 1974-75) bar assns., Cross County Bar. Rotarian. Home: 568 N Killough Rd Wynne AR 72396 Office: 210 Merriman Ave Shaver Bldg Wynne AR 72396

SHAVER, THOMAS AUSTIN, educator; b. Healdton, Okla., July 9, 1928; s. Austin Wesley and Tessie Jewell (Hodges) S.; B.A., Abilene Christian U., 1949; M.A., So. Methodist U., 1952; M.R.E., Southwestern Baptist Theol. Seminary, 1965, D.R.E., 1967; m. Waunette Fitzgerald, Aug. 9, 1949; children—Sharla Denise, Guy Marcus. Ordained to ministry Ch. of Christ, 1944; minister Garland (Tex.) Ch. of Christ, 1949-53, Richardson (Tex.) Ch. of Christ, 1953-54, Lawton (Okla.) Ch. of Christ, 1954-55; with Abilene Christian U., 1955—, pres. bible and religious edn., 1955—; minister Westgate Ch. of Christ, Abilene, 1979—. Mem. Soc. Bibl. Lit., Soc. Bibl. Archeology, Religious Edn. Assn., Nat. Assn. Profs. Clubs: Lions (v.p. 1953-54), Rotary, Kiwanis, Civitan. Author: The Christian Home, 1960; Genesis-Esther, 1977; Personal Evangelism, 1979. Home: 801 Harrison St Abilene TX 79601 Office: Station ACU Box 8233 Abilene TX 79699

SHAVER, WILLIAM JOSEPH LOVELL, govt. ofcl.; b. Graham, Ky., Jan. 16, 1918; s. Cecil Park and Willie Mae (Lovell) S.; ed. high sch., Central City, Ky.; m. Winifred Marie Haworth, May 14, 1944 (dec.); 1 dau., Margaret Haden Shaver Verble. With U.S. Govt., various locations, 1945—, chief financing div. SBA, Nashville Dist. Office, 1964-74, dist. dir., 1974—; lectr. in field. Ofcl. bd. Glendale Meth. Ch., Nashville, Tenn., 1955—, chmn. adminstrv. bd. Served from pvt. to 1st. lt., U.S. Army, 1941-45. Mem. Nashville C. of C., DAV, Am. Legion. Republican. Club: Elks. Home: 6317 Rosewood Ct Route 2 Brentwood TN 37027 Office: 1012 Pkwy Towers 404 James Robinson Pkwy Nashville TN 37219

SHAW, BOBBY GENE, truck line exec.; b. Fayetteville, Ark., Jan. 11, 1940; s. Willis Dane and Helen Lorene (Dodd) S.; B.A., Hendrix Coll., 1962; M.Th., Perkin Sch. Theology, 1965; J.D., U. Ark., 1968; m. Diane DeWese, Dec. 27, 1961; children—Sherri, Brian. Admitted to Ark. bar, 1968; atty., A. Alvis Layne Law Offices, Washington, 1968; atty., treas. Willis Shaw Express, Elm Springs, Ark., 1968-70, v.p., 1970-72, pres., 1972—. Trustee, St. Paul Sch. Theology. Served with U.S. Army, 1957-58. Mem. Am. Trucking Assn. (dir. 1972—), Ark. Bus and Truck Assn. (mem. exec. com. 1975-78), Nat. Frozen Food Assn. (adv. dir. 1976-79), Nat. Perishable Traffic Assn., ICC Practitioners Assn., Motor Carrier Lawyers Assn., Am. Bar Assn., Ark. Bar Assn., Washington County Bar Assn., Springdale C. of C. (dir.), Ark. State C. of C. (dir.). Methodist (tchr. ch. sch.). Home: Rural Route 1 Springdale AR 72764 Office: Box 188 Elm Springs AR 72728

SHAW, CLYDE EDWARD, pediatrician; b. Decatur, Tex., Oct. 13, 1949; s. Forrest Clyde and Reba Mae (Gentry) S.; B.S., Southwestern U., Georgetown, Tex., 1971; M.D., U. Tex., Galveston, 1974; m. Barbara Anne Turner, July 5, 1975. Intern, John Sealy Hosp., 1974-75, resident in pediatrics, 1975-77; practice pediatrics Pediatrics Assos. Sherman (Tex.), 1977—; mem. staff Wilson N. Jones Meml., Med. Plaza hosps. Chmn. med. adv. com. March of Dimes chpt., 1978, Eastern Seals Crippled Children's Div., Sherman, 1979. Jesse Jones Houston Endowment scholar, 1967; Southwestern U. scholar, 1967-70. Fellow Am. Acad. Pediatrics; mem. Tex. Med. Assn., Grayson County Med. Soc. Episcopalian. Home: 1118 S Travis St Sherman TX 75090 Office: 600 N Highland St Sherman TX 75090

SHAW, FREDERICK CLYDE, dentist; b. Iredell County, N.C., Mar. 15, 1923; s. Robert Clyde and Annie Laura (Wright) S.; A.A., Phiffer Jr. Coll., 1948; B.S., Catawba Coll., 1949; D.D.S., Med. Coll. Va., 1953; m. Geraldine Efird, Aug. 3, 1945; children—Frederick Efird, Martha Rebecca. Pvt. practice dentistry, Lenoir, N.C., 1953—; staff, cons. Caldwell Meml. Hosp., Lenoir, N.C., 1953—, Blackwelder Hosp., Lenoir, 1953—. Ambassador, Oasis Temple, Lenoir, 1977—; bd. dirs. Patterson Sch., 1973-79. Recipient Pres. Award, Foothill Shrine Club, 1975; named Optimist of Year, Optimist Club, 1970; licensed dentist, Va., N.C. Mem. N.C., Western Piedmont (pres. 1958) dental socs., U.S. C. of C., ADA. Lutheran. Clubs: Optimist, Masons (Shriners), Cedar Rock Country. Home: 409 Hibriten Ave SW PO Box 693 Lenoir NC 28645 Office: 341 Harper Ave SW Lenoir NC 28645

SHAW, GEORGE HENRY, ins. co. exec.; b. McComb, Miss., Feb. 9, 1948; s. George Fletcher and Francis Dorothy (Klingman) S.; B.S., Brigham Young U., 1970; A.A., S.W. Miss. Jr. Coll., 1968; M. DeEtte Hanks, June 1, 1971; children—Christie Lynn, Kimberly, Douglas Fletcher, David Phillip. With Kemper Ins. Cos., 1970—, comml. lines underwriter, Jackson, Miss., 1970-73, underwriting supr., Orlando, Fla., 1973-75, underwriting mgr., 1975-77, underwriting mgr., Dallas, 1977-79, project leader, Atlanta, 1979—. James S. Kemper scholar, 1968-70. Mem. Ins. Inst. Am., Phi Theta Kappa. Mem. Ch. Jesus Christ of Latter Day Saints. Home: 2411 Prince Howard Trail Marietta GA 30062 Office: 1401 Peachtree St NE Atlanta GA 30309

SHAW, HOWARD BERNARD, telecommunications cons.; b. Phila., Apr. 12, 1918; s. I. and Marie (Bernard) S.; A.B. in Polit. Sci. and Econs., DePauw U., 1939; M.S. in Bus. Adminstrn., N.Y. U., 1940; m. Esther Wefald, Dec. 15, 1961; children—Bonnie, Teri. Advt. account exec., copywriter advt. agys., N.Y.C., Milw. and Miami, Fla., 1947-57; advt. and sales promotion mgr. Sci. & Mechanics Mag., Chgo., 1958-59; intercommunication specialist ITT/Terryphone Corp., Chgo., 1960-63; indsl. sales mgr. Boom Communications, Inc., 1964-66; advt. mgr. parts and service Motorola Co., Chgo., 1966-68; Upper Middle West regional mgr. Ampex Corp., Elk Grove Village, Ill., 1968-72; Southeastern regional mgr. Dictograph Telephone Co., Miami, 1972-73; v.p. U.S. Telephone Co., Miami, 1973-75; pres. Shaw Communications Cons., Miami, 1975—. Exec. committeeman Dade County (Fla.) Republican Party, Dist. 4, 1973—; founder, chmn. Sunny Isles Civic Assn. Served to lt. col. U.S. Army, 1941-46. Recipient Michael Schaap award N.Y. U., 1940. Mem. Internat. Soc. Telecommunications Cons. (charter; former nat. dir.), C. of C. of North Miami Beach, Winston Towers Condominium Assn. (past chmn. election com.), Alpha Delta Sigma. Methodist. Contbr. articles on job resumes to mags., 1955-59. Home and Office: 20341 NE 30th Ave North Miami Beach FL 33180

SHAW, JACK BRISLEY, research co. exec.; b. Vancouver, Can., Feb. 23, 1926; s. Archibald Ernest and Ruska Elise (Tobler) S.; came to U.S., 1942, naturalized, 1948; A.A., San Francisco City Coll., 1949; M.B.A., U. Chgo., 1959; m. Carol Jane Cann, Aug. 28, 1948; children—Caren Faye, Susan April, Brian Lee. Commd. 2d lt. USAF, 1950, advanced through grades to col., 1971; dep. div. chief, concepts doctrine and objectives directorate hdqrs. USAF, Washington, 1971-73; dep. for spl. projects, OSD historian Office Sec. Def., Washington, 1974-77; dir. survey systems and support Arbitron, Beltsville, Md., 1979—. Decorated Legion of Merit, D.F.C., Bronze Star, Air medal with 6 oak leaf clusters, Air Force Commendation medal. Mem. Air Force Assn., Air Force Acad. Athletic Assn. Republican. Episcopalian. Club: Bolling Air Force Base Officers. Author: Pilot Training Programs, 1969; Tactical Airlift Force Requirements, 1969; Air Force Tactical Forces, 2 vols., 1970; Strategic Arms Competition Chronology, 3 vols., 1974. Home: 1910 Diplomat Ct Falls Church VA 22043 Office: 4320 Ammendale Rd Beltsville MD 20705

SHAW, JAMES, computer programmer; b. Salt Lake City, June 26, 1944; s. James Irvin and Cleo Lea (Bell) S.; student San Antonio Coll., 1962-64; B.A., St. Mary's U., 1966. Tchr. history McCollum High Sch., San Antonio, 1966-67; computer operator VA Data Processing Center, Austin, Tex., 1967-74, computer programmer, 1974—. Mem. Am. Mgmt. Assn. Home: 206 W 38th St 111 Austin TX 78705 Office: 1615 E Woodward St Austin TX 78772

SHAW, JOHN ANDERSON, energy co. exec.; b. Odessa, Tex., Aug. 12, 1945; s. Charles A. and Ruth H. Shaw; B.B.A., Tex. Tech U., 1967; M.B.A., Angelo State U., 1976; m. Carolyn Glenn, May 24, 1970; children—Jimmy, Michael. Internal auditor Gen. Telephone Co. of S.W. San Angelo, Tex., 1970-72, area budget analyst, 1972-73, toll revenue accountant, 1973-76; sec., asst. treas. Southwestern Investment Co., Amarillo, Tex., 1976-79; asst. treas. Pioneer Corp., Amarillo, 1979—. Served to capt. Signal Corps, U.S. Army, 1967-70; Vietnam. Decorated Bronze Star, Army Commendation medal. Republican. Presbyterian. Club: Kiwanis. Home: 3719 Rutson St Amarillo TX 79109 Office: Pioneer Corp PO Box 511 Amarillo TX 79163

SHAW, MILTON EUGENE, engring. co. exec.; b. Macy, Ind., Dec. 2, 1925; s. Bernard Oliver and Mabel Marie (Dawald) S.; B.S. with distinction, Manchester Coll., 1949; M.B.A., Ind. U., 1950, D.B.A., 1969; m. Martha Lou Madeford, May 15, 1948; 1 dau., Valerie Elaine Shaw Brown. Prof. econs. Iowa Wesleyan Coll., Mt. Pleasant, 1950-51; asst. chief accountant Mason & Hanger-Silas Mason Co., Inc., Burlington, Iowa, 1951-54, fiscal mgr., Amarillo, Tex., 1956-63, fiscal staff asst., Lexington, Ky., 1964, asst. sec., 1964-73, v.p. adminstrn., 1973—, also dir. Mem. Am. Def. Preparedness Assn., Blue Grass Personnel Assn., Beta Gamma Sigma, Delta Pi Epsilon, Phi Delta Kappa. Home: 101 S Hanover Lexington KY 40502 Office: 200 W Vine Suite 7-A Lexington KY 40507

SHAW, RICHARD GORDON, state ofcl.; b. Clemson, S.C., July 25, 1943; s. Lewis H. and Grace W. Shaw; B.S., S.C. State Coll., 1964; m. Patricia A. Friday, Feb. 26, 1966; children—Sylvia G., Richard M., Raphael. Adminstrv. asst. Charles B. Lifflander & Co., N.Y.C., 1964-65; supt. controllers dept. Aetna Life & Casualty Co., Washington, 1968-73; controller Aetna Life & Casualty Co., Wheeling, W.Va., 1973-77; ins. commr. State W.Va., Charleston, 1977—; ex-officio mem. W.Va. State Bd. Ins. Vol., Wheeling Crisis Hotline Center; adv. com. W.Va. Inst. Tech.; ex-officio mem. State Tchr. Retirement Bd.; bd. dirs. Civitan Sheltered Workshop, Wheeling Area Transp. Authority, United Way. Served with USAF, 1965-68; Vietnam. Mem. NAACP (mem. exec. com. Wheeling-Ohio County), Am. Mgmt. Assn., Nat. Assn. Ins. Commrs. (chmn. credit ins. sub-com.). Home: 303 Marion Circle Charleston WV 25304 Office: 1800 Washington St E Charleston WV 25305

SHAW, ROBERT, music condr.; b. Red Bluff, Calif., Apr. 30, 1916; s. Shirley Richard and Nelle Mae (Lawson) S.; A.B., Pomona Coll., 1938, Mus.D. (hon.), 1953; Mus.D. (hon,), Coll. Wooster, 1951, St. Lawrence U., 1955, Mich. State U., 1960, Cleve. Inst. Music, 1966, Western Res. U,, 1966, Emory U., 1967, Fla. State U., 1968, Morehouse Coll., 1977; D.F.A. (hon.), U. Alaska, 1963; L.H.D., Kenyon Coll., 1963, U. Akron, 1976; H.H.D., Westminster Choir Coll., 1975, Oglethorpe U., 1977; m. Maxine Farley, Oct. 15, 1939; children—Johanna, Peter Thain, John Thaddeus; m. 2d, Caroline Sauls Hitz, Dec. 19, 1973; 1 son, Thomas Lawson. Dir. Fred Waring Glee Clubs, 1938-45; choral dir. Aquacades, 1942-43, Carmen Jones, 1943, Seven Lively Arts, 1944, My Darlin Aida, 1953; guest condr. CBS Symphony series, 1944-45, ABC Symphony series, 1945, NBC Symphony, 1946, N.Y.C. Symphony, 1946, Boston Symphony Orch., 1958, N.Y. Philharmonic, 1970, Nat. Symphony Orch., 1959, Chgo. Symphony Orch., 1960, Houston Symphony, 1970, 75, Dallas Symphony, 1969, 77, Minn. Orch., 1972, Richmond (Va.) Symphony, 1971, Pitts. Symphony, Ambler Festival, 1973-74, 76, Los Angeles Master Chorale and Sinfonia Orch., 1974-75, Mostly Mozart Festival, N.Y.C., 1974-75, 77, Cin. Symphony, 1974-75, Ives Festival, New Haven, 1974, Kansas City Philharmonic, 1974, Hamilton (Ont., Can.) Philharmonic, 1974, San Antonio Symphony, 1974, Buffalo Symphony, 1975, Los Angeles Philharmonic, 1976, Memphis Symphony, 1976; also numerous coll. and univ. orchs. and choruses; dir. choral music Berkshire Music Center, 1946-49; dir. choral activities Juilliard School Music, 1946-49; condr. San Diego Summer Symphony, 1953-58; asso, condr. Cleve. Orch., 1956-67; music dir., condr. Atlanta Symphony Orch., 1967—; artistic dir. Alaska Festival of Music, 1956-73; dir. Meadow Brook Sch. Music, 1965-67, Blossom Festival Sch., Cleve. Orch.-Kent (O.) State U., 1968-72, Brevard (N.C.) Music Festival, 1972-74. Founder, dir. Robert Shaw Chorale, which has made ann. tours of U.S., 1948-66, Middle East and Europe, 1956, USSR, 1962, S.Am., 1964; founder-dir. The Collegiate Chorale, 1941. Mem. Ga. Art Commn., 1967-71. Recipient Nat. Assn. Am. Composers and Condrs. award for outstanding Am. born condr., 1943, Alice M. Kitson award for service to Am. music Columbia, 1955, Gov.'s award in arts State of Ga., 1973; Distinguished Service award Ga. Coll., 1973, State U. N.Y. at Potsdam, 1975, Morehouse Coll., 1973, Atlanta Boys Clubs, 1975; Nat. Fedn. Music Clubs award, 1975; Ga. Gov.'s award for distinguished service, 1975; ASCAP award for service to contemporary music, 1976; Emory U. Barkley Forum award, 1977; Guggenheim fellow, 1944. Address: 3707 Randall Mill Rd Atlanta GA 30327

SHAW, SHARRILYN WHITING, brewing co. exec.; b. Mobile, Ala., Oct. 6, 1946; d. James Allen and Virginia Gordon (Hearn) Whiting; student U. Ala., 1965-68, U. So. Ala., 1968-69; m. Edwin P. Shaw, Jr., Oct. 20, 1976; 1 child, Ivey. Reporter, Mobile Press Register, 1968-69; writer Nashville Tennessean, 1969-70; account exec. Pitluk Group, San Antonio, 1975-77; advt./promotion mgr. KSAT-TV, San Antonio, 1977-79; advt. mgr. Lone Star Brewing Co., San Antonio, 1979—. Former chairperson network promotion adv. bd. ABC-TV; v.p. Children's Hosp. Found., San Antonio; bd. dirs. Tex. Soc. Prevention of Blindness; mem. steering com. Leadership San Antonio Alumni. Recipient Writing award, A.P. of Ala., 1969; Addy awards San Antonio Ad Fedn., 1977, 78. Mem. Tex. Public Relations Assn., Am. Mktg. Assn., Monte Vista Hist. Assn., Women in Communications (v.p. 1978-80). Clubs: St. Anthony, Bright Shawl, Mills County Hunting and Fishing. Office: 600 Lone Star Blvd San Antonio TX 78298

SHAY, FRANK THOMAS, II, mfg. co. exec.; b. Ft. Smith, Ark., Sept. 18, 1952; s. Frank Thomas and Evelyn Shirley (Brown) S.; student Hendrix Coll., 1970-71; A.A. in Acctg., Manatee Jr. Coll., 1975; m. Marilyn J. Shay, Dec. 3, 1976; 1 dau., Amanda Camille. Dir. youth activities, St. Paul United Meth. Ch., 1971; asst. mgr. A.J. August Menswear, Ft. Smith, Ark., 1971-72; advt. and merchandising mgr. Holiday Dept. Stores, Inc., Sarasota, Fla., 1972-80; founder, designer Razorbackers, Sarasota, 1977—. Pledge center coordinator Muscular Dystrophy Assn.; chmn. adv. bd. Riverview High Sch. Distributive Edn. Bd., 1978-79. Mem. Gulf Gate Mall Mchts. Assn. (pres. 1975-76). Methodist. Home: 3917 Sawyerwood Rd Sarasota FL 33583 Office: 350 Gulf Gate Mall Sarasota FL 33581

SHEA, JAMES DARRELL, orthopaedic surgeon; b. Corning, N.Y., July 10, 1932; s. James Basil and Louise (Clark) S.; B.A., Colgate U., 1954; M.S., U. Rochester, 1957, M.D., 1960; m. Ann Lisabeth McKalg, Sept. 10, 1955; children—Kimberly Ann, Todd Andrew, Melanie Lyn, James Randall. Intern, Strong Meml. Hosp., Rochester, N.Y., 1960-61; resident in orthopaedic surgery U. Pitts. Health Center Hosp., 1964-67; instr. orthopaedic surgery U. Pitts. Med. Sch., 1968-69; asst. prof. orthopaedic surgery and rehab. U. Miami Sch. Medicine, 1969-72; med. dir. Lucerne Spinal Injury Center, Orlando, Fla., 1974—; fellow Nuffield Orthopaedic Center, Oxford (Eng.) U., 1967. Served with USAF, 1962-64. Diplomate Am. Bd. Orthopaedic Surgery. Fellow A.C.S.; mem. AMA, Am. Acad. Orthopaedic Surgeons, Am. Spinal Injury Assn. (sec.-treas., dir.), So. Med. Assn., A.C.S. Presbyterian. Clubs: Country, University (Orlando). Contbr. articles to med. jours. Home: 1205 Windsong Rd Orlando FL 32809 Office: 1809 Bellvue Ave Orlando FL 32806

SHEA, M. COYLE, JR., physician; b. Memphis, Dec. 24, 1929; s. Martin Coyle and Ethel Marie (Fredette) S.; B.S., U. Tenn., 1952, M.D., 1952; m. Trina Key McKeithen, Dec. 29, 1972; children—Marc, Melinda (dec.), Madeline, Alison, Rachel, Jeff, Erin, Neil. Intern, U.S. Naval Hosp., Oakland, Calif., 1953; resident gen. surgery U.S. Naval Hosp., Bethesda, Md., 1955-57, resident otolaryngology, 1957-59; head dept. otolaryngology U.S. Naval Hosp., Memphis, 1959-62; otologist Memphis Otologic Clinic, 1962-67, Shea Otologic Group, Memphis, 1967—, also pres.; asso. prof. otolaryngology U. Tenn.; cons. U.S. Naval, Vets. hosps.; mem. staff Bapt. Meml. Hosp. Served to lt. comdr. M.C., USNR, 1952-62. Diplomate Am. Bd. Otolaryngology. Fellow ACS; mem. Memphis and Shelby County Med. Soc., A.M.A., Triological Soc., Am. Acad. Ophthalmology and Otolaryngology, Am. Council Otolaryngology, So., Tenn., Pan Am. med. assns., Tenn. Acad. Otolaryngology, Pan. Am., Memphis socs. otolaryngology, Am. Otological, Rhinological and Laryngological Soc., Flying Physicians Assn., Alpha Omega Alpha. Research on chronic ear disease. Home: 6009 Wood Trail Memphis TN 38138 Office: 1215 Poplar Ave Memphis TN 38104

SHEALY, DAVID LEE, physicist, educator; b. Newberry, S.C., Sept. 16, 1944; s. William Elmer and Elizabeth (Plaxico) Shealy; B.S., U. Ga., 1966, Ph.D., 1973; m. Elaine Wohlford, June 12, 1969. Systems analyst U. Ga., Athens, 1973; asst. prof. physics U. Ala., Birmingham, 1973-76, asso. prof., 1976—. Mem. Optical Soc. Am., Acoustical Soc. Am., Am. Assn. Physics Tchrs., Am. Phys. Soc., N.Y. Acad. Scis., Am. Inst. Aeros. and Astronautics, Soc. Photo-Optical Instrumentation Engrs., Phi Beta Kappa, Phi Kappa Phi. Contbr. articles to profl. jours. Home: 2521 Brookwater Circle Birmingham AL 35243 Office: Dept Physics U Alabama in Birmingham University Station Birmingham AL 35294

SHEALY, DOUGLAS WARD, bus. cons.; b. Columbia, S.C., Oct. 12, 1940; s. David Ward and Lila Helen (Frick) S.; cert. Columbia Sch. of Automation, 1963; m. Jane Lynette Davis, Aug. 23, 1964; children—Tracy Lynn, Karen Marie. IBM machine operator Charleston Naval Shipyard (S.C.), 1963-64; clk. U.S. Postal Service, Lexington, S.C., 1964-68, rural letter carrier, 1968—; pres. Shealy Enterprizes, bus. cons., Lexington, 1976—. Mem. ch. council St. Stephen's Lutheran Ch., v.p. Luth. Churchmen. Served with U.S. Army, 1959-60. Club: Masons (Lexington). Home and Office: 200 Wood Dale Dr Lexington SC 29072

SHEARER, CHARLES EDWARD, JR., lawyer, financial planner; b. Kokomo, Ind., Sept. 2, 1922; s. Charles Edward and Helen Lorene (Kidder) S.; A.S., Kokomo Jr. Coll., 1943; A.B., Ind. U., 1947, J.D., 1953; m. Ruth Mae Nicholson, June 26, 1948; children—Kay Ellen, Beth Ann. Indsl. relations cons. Internat. Harvester Co., Indpls., 1947-51; employee relations dir. Indpls. Rys., 1951-53; mgr. Shelbyville (Ind.) C. of C., 1953-55; partner firm Fink & Shearer Attys., Shelbyville, 1955-57; agy. supr. L. W. McDougall & Assos., Cleve., 1958-63; div. sales mgr. Coll. Life Ins., Indpls., also prin. Charles E. Shearer, Jr. & Assos. Life Ins. Agy., Indpls., 1964-70; sr. v.p. planning and export expansion Export-Import Bank U.S., Washington, 1970-72; v.p. Nat. Funding Analysts, Inc., Washington, 1972—; individual practice law, Washington, 1972—; dir. life and bus. benefits div. Cook, Treadwell & Harry, Springfield, Va. Vice pres. Met. Washington YMCA; chmn. bd. trustees U.S. Jaycee Found., Tulsa. Served with inf. U.S. Army, 1943-46. Named 1 of 3 Outstanding Young Men of Ind., Ind. Jaycees, 1957. Mem. Fed., Indpls., D.C. bar assns., Nat. Assn. Life Underwriters, C.L.U.'s. of D.C., Am. Legion, Sigma Pi, Phi Delta Phi. Republican. Episcopalian. Home: 4839 Yorktown Blvd Arlington VA 22207 Office: 1700 Pennsylvania Ave NW Suite 270 Washington DC 20006 also 6501 Loisdale Ct Springfield VA 22207

SHEARER, CHARLES LIVINGSTON, coll. adminstr.; b. Louisville, Nov. 23, 1942; s. Guy Cooper and Kathryn (Aufenkamp) S.; B.S., U. Ky., 1964, M.A. (Grad. fellow), 1967; M.A., Mich. State U., 1974; m. Susan M. Pulling, Nov. 30, 1968; children—Todd, Mark, Scott. Instr. econs., head basketball coach Henderson (Ky.) Community Coll., 1967-69; asst. prof. econs. Ferris State Coll., Big Rapids, Mich., 1969-71; grad. asst. Mich. State U., 1971-73; dir. liberal arts program in profl. mgmt., then dir. ops. Albion (Mich.) Coll., 1973-79, asst. sec. bd. trustees, 1976-79; v.p. fin. Transylvania U., Lexington, Ky., 1979—; exec. com. of bd. Homestead Savs. & Loan Assn., Albion, 1977-79. Vestryman, St. James Episcopal Ch., Albion, 1973-76. Served with USAR, 1967-68. Mem. Am. Mgmt. Assn., Nat. Assn. Coll. and Univ. Bus. Officers, Am. Econs. Assn. Club: Rotary. Author: Compensatory Financing of Export Fluctuations in Underdeveloped Countries, 1967. Home: 805 Glendover Rd Lexington KY 40502 Office: Transylvania Univ Lexington KY 40508

SHEARER, CLARENCE MAYNARD, JR., coll. choral dir.; b. Eufala, Okla., Oct. 24, 1940; s. Clarence Maynard and Mary Lorene (Ryan) S.; B.M.E., N. Tex. State U., 1962, M.M., 1967; D.Mus. Arts, U. Colo., 1976; m. Barbara Jeanne Clark, Jan. 27, 1963; children—Deborah Gail, Christopher Mark. High sch. choral dir., McAllen, Brownsville, Plainview and Edinburg, Tex., 1962-70; dir. choirs Del Mar Coll., Corpus Christi, Tex., 1970—; dir. choral activities Tex. Agrl. Indsl. U., and Corpus Christi State U., Corpus Christi, 1973—. Dir. ch. music, Tex., 1962-74; music dir., prodns. Little Theatre, Corpus Christi; tchr. chorus Mexico Nat. Symphony Orch., Corpus Christi Symphony Orch.; organizer all-state choir, Tex., 1968-69. Mem. Am. Choral Dirs. Assn., Tex. Choral Dirs. Assn. (sec. treas. 1966-68), Am. Choral Found., Music Educators Nat. Conv., Tex. Music Educators Assn. (clinician lectr. 1969, 70), Pi Kappa Lambda, Phi Mu Alpha. Contbr. articles on choral music to mus. jours. Composer choral works. Home: 1014 Dolphin St Corpus Christi TX 78411

SHEARER, JAMES OSTRANDER, accountant; b. Memphis, Dec. 10, 1912; s. Charles English and Annette (Ostrander) S.; student Purdue U., 1930-32; B.B.A., Memphis State U., 1965; m. Nelly Jane Galloway, May 13, 1972. With J.R. Watkins Co., 1932-33, Civil Works Adminstrn., 1933-34, Tenn. Hwy. Dept., 1934-35, U.S. Forest Service, 1935-37, Memphis dist. C.E., 1937-44, James A. Matthews & Co., C.P.A.'s, Memphis, 1944-46, Tri-State Constrn. Co., Memphis, 1946-51, Fordice Constrn. Co., Memphis, 1951-54; prin. James O. Shearer, C.P.A., Memphis, 1954-71; partner Shearer & Galloway Co., C.P.A.'s, Memphis, 1971—; faculty Memphis State U., 1965—. C.P.A., Tenn., 1950, Miss., 1963, Ark., 1963. Mem. Am. Inst. C.P.A.'s, Nat. Assn. Accountants, Tenn. Soc. C.P.A.'s (state v.p. 1956, state council 1954—), Tenn. State Bd. Accountancy (sec. 1976-79). Clubs: Optimist, Big Ten. Home: 1570 Linden Ave Memphis TN 38104 Office: 2161 Madison Ave Memphis TN 38104

SHEARER, JOHN BENTLEY, engring. cons.; b. Chgo., May 25, 1925; s. John Bentley and Eloise (McDoniell) S.; B.S. in Indsl. Engring., U. Ala., 1955; postgrad. Springhill Coll., 1962, Ala. A&M U., 1971-72; m. Mary Lou Lyles, Nov. 5, 1949; children—John Lyles, Joan Marie, James McDoniell. Indsl. engr. Stone Container Corp. Mobile, Ala., 1955-57; with Brookley AFB, Mobile, Ala., 1957-62, sr. staff indsl. engr., to 1962; tech. mgmt. and flight systems test engr. NASA Marshall Space Flight Center, Huntsville, Ala., 1962-75; prin. J.B. Shearer Engring., engring. cons., San Angelo, Tex., 1977—. Served with U.S. Army, 1944-46, 50-54. Registered profl. engr., Ala., Tex. Mem. Nat. Soc. Profl. Engrs., Am. Inst. Indsl. Engrs. (pres. Mobile chpt. 1961-62). Club: Masons. Home and Office: 5301 Meadow Dr San Angelo TX 76901

SHEARER, RUTH EASTER MANSBERGER (MRS. RICHARD E. SHEARER), educator; b. Turtle Creek, Pa., Apr. 3, 1920; d. Arlie Roland and Mary Mildred (Smith) Mansberger; B.A. summa cum laude, Western Md. Coll., 1941; M.Ed., U. Pitts., 1943; Ed.D. (Benedum scholar), Tchrs. Coll., Columbia, 1963; m. Richard E. Shearer, June 16, 1944; children—Patricia (Mrs. Richard F. Wilson), Suzanne (Mrs. Terry Lynn Jones), Richard Judson. Tchr. jr. high sch. Weirton, W.Va., 1941-42, sr. high sch., 1942-44, Rumson (N.J.) Country Day Sch., 1944-46; dean women Alderson Broaddus Coll., Philippi, W.Va., 1951-56, prof. edn., 1956—, supr. student internships in pub. schs., 1956—. Named W.Va. Mother of Yr., 1974. Danforth fellow Colo. Coll., 1963, Stephens Coll., 1965. Mem. AAUW, Assn. Higher Edn., NEA, AAUP, Am. Personnel and Guidance Assn., Am. Assn. Colls. for Tchr. Edn., P.E.O., Delta Kappa Gamma, Pi Lambda Theta, Kappa Delta Pi. Republican. Baptist. Club: College. Contbr. articles to jours. Home: Broaddus Knolls Philippi WV 26416

SHEEDER, WILLIAM BENJAMIN, univ. dean; b. Elmira, N.Y., Jan. 21, 1938; s. Fred and Amy Sheeder; A.B. in Philosophy, Ottawa (Kans.) U., 1960; M.A. in Human Relations, Ohio U., Athens, 1966; children—Lynn, Traci. Mem. faculty Ohio U., 1961-65, asso. dir. Baker U. Center, 1962-64, asst. to dean Coll. Arts and Scis., 1964-66; mem. adminstrn. U. Miami, Coral Gables, Fla., 1966—, dir. student activities Student Union, 1968-73, v.p., sec. Univ. Rathskeller, Inc., 1972—, asst. v.p. student affairs, 1973—, dean students, 1976—. Active Dade County Wesley Found., treas., 1971-73, chmn. bd. dirs., 1973-77; mem. work area higher edn. and campus ministry Fla. conf. Council Ministries, United Methodist. Ch., 1976-80. Mem. Assn. Coll. Unions (enrichment chmn. 1975), Nat. Assn. Student Personnel Adminstrs., Nat. Orientation Dirs. Assn., Am. Assn. Higher Edn., Am. Personnel and Guidance Assn., Am. Coll. Personnel Assn., Sigma Alpha, Omicron Delta Kappa, Phi Delta Kappa, Phi Kappa Epsilon, Omega, Phi Mu Alpha, Zeta Beta Tau (adj. brother 1971—). Author articles. Address: Office Dean Students Univ Miami Coral Gables FL 33124

SHEEHAN, EDWARD JAMES, former Dept. Army ofcl., tech. cons.; b. Johnstown, Pa., Dec. 31, 1935; s. Louis A. and Ethel F. (Schaefer) S.; B.S. in Physics, St. Francis Coll., 1959; M.S. (Sloan fellow), Mass. Inst. Tech., 1972; m. Florence Ann Hartnett, June 17, 1958; children—Edward, James, John, William, Mary. Project engr. Electronics Command, Dept. Army, 1959-61, project team leader electro-optic equipment for tanks, 1961-63, project team leader electro-optic equipment for infantry, 1963-65, tech. area dir. electro-optic/night vision equipment, 1965-73, asso. lab. dir. for devel. engring., 1973-76, lab. dir. Night Vision Lab., Fort Belvoir, Va., 1976—; pres. Sheehan Assos. Inc. Recipient numerous awards including Meritorious Civilian Service award Dept. Army. Home: 8502 Crestview Dr Fairfax VA 22030 Office: Sheehan Assos Inc 611 Cameron St Alexandria VA 22314

SHEEHAN, ELLA EAGER, physician; b. Stillwater, Okla., Dec. 2, 1924; d. Sherman Wesley and Ernestine Marie (Forester) Eager; B.S., Okla. State U., 1944; M.D., U. Okla., 1949; m. William Luther Sheehan, Aug. 4, 1951; children—William Luther II, Suzanne Patricia. Intern, Jersey City Med. Center, 1949-50; resident in pathology D.C. Gen. Hosp., Washington, 1953-54, Baylor U. Coll. Medicine Affiliated Residency Program, Houston, 1955-58; staff pathologist VA Hosp., Houston, 1958-63; pathologist, dir. labs. Med. Arts Hosp., Houston, 1963—; clin. asst. prof. Baylor U., 1960—. Diplomate Am. Bd. Pathology. Mem. Harris County Med. Soc., Tex., So., Women's med. assns., Houston Soc. Clin. Pathologists, Tex. Pathology Assn. Roman Catholic. Home: 104 Davis Rd League City TX 77573 Office: 1215 Walker St Houston TX 77002

SHEEHAN, JOHN GEORGE, publisher; b. Balt., Jan. 17, 1924; s. Francis Bernard and Julia Ann (Walker) S.; student Calvert Hall Coll.; m. Shirley Anita Bohn, June 14, 1969; 1 dau., Suzanne Marie. With Riss & Co., Balt., 1945-56; gen. mgr. Labor Pool, Inc., Balt., 1956-61; founder, pres. Personnel Pool, Inc., Washington, 1961-75, Medical Personnel Pool, Washington, 1969-73, Maid in America, Inc., Fairfax, Va., 1971-74; pres., founder, editor and pub. JGS, Inc., Merrifield, Va., 1975—. Mem. Nat. Assn. Newsletter Publishers, Nat. Mail Order Assn. Home: Reston VA Office: PO Box 525 Merrifield VA 22116

SHEEHY, LEO JOSEPH, JR., mfg. co. exec.; b. Washington, Apr. 9, 1928; s. Leo Joseph and Ruth Elizabeth (Freisheim) S.; B.A., Bellview Coll., Omaha, 1968; m. Maria Elisa Cosimi, Feb. 11, 1958; children—Mary Barbara, Catherine Ann, Lisa Marie. Commd. 2d lt. U.S. Air Force, advanced through grades to maj., 1968; dir. communication ops. U.S. Air Force, Korea, 1972-73, Warner Robins AFB, Ga., 1973-74; ret., 1974; mgr. product support Driltech, Inc., Gainesville, Fla., 1974—. Mem. Armed Forces Communications Electronics Assn. Roman Catholic. Home: 1322 NW 48th Terr Gainesville FL 32605 Office: Driltech Inc Alachua FL 32615

SHEETS, JOHN HOWARD, physician; b. Chillicothe, Ohio, May 20, 1928; s. John Anton and Lottie C. (Kiedrowski) S.; B.S., Ohio State U., 1949; M.D., Western Res. U., 1953; m. Angela Raquel Hinojos, June 27, 1975; children—Robin, Leslie, Nicky, Kimberli, Marty, Lauri. Intern, Jackson Meml. Hosp., Miami, Fla., 1953-54; resident ophthalmology Univ. Hosps., Columbus, Ohio, 1956-57; preceptorship Martin ... Cook, Springfield, Ohio, 1957-59; practice medicine specializing in ophthalmology, Odessa, Tex., 1960—; chief of staff Med. Center Hosp., Odessa, 1974-75; asso. clin. prof. U. Tex., Dallas, 1976-77, Tex. Tech. U., Lubbock, 1976-77; lectr. in field. Trustee Ector County Pub. Schs., 1967-70; bd. dirs. Globe Theater, Odessa, 1968-72, YMCA, Odessa, 1975. Served with USAF, 1953-56. Diplomate Am. Bd. Ophthalmology. Fellow Am. Acad. Ophthalmology and Otolaryngology, Internat. Eye Found. Soc. Surgeons; mem. Am., Pan Am. med. assns., Am. Assn. Ophthalmology, Tex. Ophthalmic Assn., Soc. Cryo Ophthalmology, Am. Intra-Ocular Implant Soc., Inst. Glaucoma Research Inc. Republican. Author manuals on lens implantation: Bridge Over Troubled Waters, 1975, Covered Bridge, 1977; designer sheets lens glide. Home: 2525 Palo Verde Odessa TX 79763 Office: Route 1 Box 210 Odessa TX 79763

SHEFFIELD, PAUL JAMES, physiologist; b. Brewster, Fla., Mar. 26, 1940; s. Lyman and Litha (Cooley) S.; B.S., U. Fla., 1962; M.S., U. So. Calif., 1971, Ph.D., 1972; m. June C. Campbell, Apr. 28, 1961; children—James Campbell, Robert Brian. Commd. 2d lt. USAF, 1962, advanced through grades to lt. col., 1979; hosp. adminstr. 4500 USAF Hosp., Langley AFB, Va., 1962-65; aerospace physiologist 4500 Physiol. Tng. Flight, Langley AFB, 1965-69; aerospace physiologist USAF Sch. Aerospace Medicine, Brooks AFB, Tex., 1971-74, hyperbaric physiologist, 1974—; lectr. and cons. hyperbaric physiology, 1971-79. Decorated Air Force Commendation medal, Meritorious Service medal (2). Fellow Aerospace Med. Assn. (asso.); mem. Aerospace Physiology Soc. (parliamentarian 1973-76, pres. 1978, gov. 1979, Paul Bert award 1979), Undersea Med. Soc., Survival and Flying Equipment Assn., Air Force Assn. (Tex. Scientist of Yr. award 1978), Phi Kappa Phi (life). Contbr. articles to profl. jours. Home: 5107 Round Table San Antonio TX 78218

SHEFFIELD, PAUL ROBINSON, govt. ofcl.; b. Pittsboro, Miss., Aug. 9, 1917; s. Hiram Clifton and Ida Mabel (Powell) S.; B.S. in Chemistry, Millsaps Coll., Jackson, Miss., 1939; grad. various U.S. Army schs.; m. Carolyn Kelly Buck, Nov. 23, 1940; children—Sandra (Mrs. James L. Crook), Paul Robinson, Carolyn Buck. Boy Scout exec., Jonesboro, Ark., 1940; enlisted in U.S. Army, 1935, warrant officer, 1940, commd. 1942, advanced through grades to col.; ret., 1970; now port dir. City of Memphis and Shelby County Port Commn.; pres. Inland River Ports and Terminals; mem. com. NRC, Transp. Research Bd.; mem. adv. bd. Multi-State Transp. System; dir. Nat. Waterways Conf. Pres. Gt. Plains council Boy Scouts Am., 1959, exec. bd. Chickasaw council. Decorated Army Commendation medal with oak leaf cluster, Legion of Merit with oak leaf cluster. Recipient Silver Beaver award Boy Scouts Am., 1959, Jack Carley award, 1974; named Boss of Year, Vicksburg (Miss.) chpt. Nat. Secs. Assn., 1970; named to U.S. Army Engr. Sch. Hall of Fame. Registered profl. engr., N.D., Miss., La. Fellow Soc. Am. Mil. Engrs. (pres. P.R. chpt. 1961, C.Z. chpt. 1963, dir. Memphis 1974); mem. Nat., Tenn. socs. profl. engrs., Memphis Area C. of C., Water Resources Congress (dir.), Am. Water Coalition, Assn. Preservation Tenn. Antiquities (dir. Memphis chpt.), Pi Kappa Alpha. Presbyn. (deacon). Mason (Shriner, 32 deg.), Rotarian. Clubs: Engineers, Propeller, World Trade (dir.) (Memphis). Author paper. Home: 296 Belle Meade Ln Memphis TN 38117 Office: PO Box 13142 Memphis TN 38113

SHEFFIELD, WALTER LINCOLN, JR., sales exec.; b. Wilmington, N.C., Apr. 27, 1920; s. Walter Lincoln and Eliza Catherine (Hayes) S.; B.S. in Commerce, U. N.C., 1941; m. Ruth Maxyne Smith, Jan. 25, 1947; children—Walter Lincoln, Douglas Calhoun. Sales agent Continental Can Co., Wilmington, N.C., 1945-66, southeastern regional mgr., 1967-71, nat. accounts mgr., 1972-73, cons. 1974-75; pres. Sheffield Products Co., Inc., Atlanta, 1973—; chmn. The Islander, Inc., Wrightsville Beach, N.C., 1977-78.

Finance chmn. Cape Fear area Council, Boy Scouts Am., Wilmington, 1963-65, pres. council, 1966-67, recipient Silver Beaver award; bd. dirs. United Fund, Wilmington, 1962-66. Served with USAF, 1941-45. Decorated Air Medal, D.F.C. Mem. U. N.C. Alumni Assn. (area pres. 1963-65), N.C., S.C., Ga. soft drink assns. Democrat. Presbyterian. Clubs: Carolina Yacht, Cape Fear Country, Cherokee Town and Country. Home: 21 Iron Bound Pl NW Atlanta GA 30318 Office: PO Box 52897 Atlanta GA 30355 also 3110 Maple Dr NE Atlanta GA 30305

SHELBURNE, C. DANIEL, banker; b. Green Bay, Va., Mar. 31, 1915; s. Thomas Pettus and Mabel (Daniel) S.; B.S., Hampden-Sydney Coll., 1936; M.B.A., U. Pa., 1939-40; postgrad. Stonier Grad. Sch. Banking, Rutgers U., 1946-49; m. Edith McDanel, Dec. 27, 1941; children—John Daniel, Edward McDanel, Thomas Maynard. Bank examiner Fed. Res. Bank, Richmond, Va., 1945-48, sr. bank examiner, 1949-50; with Wachovia Bank & Trust Co., N.A., Winston-Salem, N.C. and Raleigh, N.C., 1950—, v.p. in charge loan adminstrn. dept., Raleigh, 1955-69, sr. v.p., 1969—, in charge central region corp. loan adminstrn. dept., 1972—. Dir. Bus. Devel. Corp. N.C., 1974—. Instr., Grad. Sch. Consumer Banking, U. Va., 1961-77, trustee, 1972-75. Pres., Occoneechee council Boy Scouts Am., 1977-78; past pres. adv. bd. Wake County Salvation Army; past pres. Mental Health Bd. Wake County. Bd. dirs. Wake Tech. Inst. Found., 1971—, v.p., 1973-77; bd. dirs. N.C. Episcopal Ch. Found., 1973—; trustee, Hampden-Sydney Coll., 1979—. Served with Supply Corps, USNR, 1941-45; lt. comdr., ret. Recipient Silver Beaver award Boy Scouts Am., 1969. Mem. C. of C., Robert Morris Assos. (life, past pres. Carolinas-Va. chpt.), Sigma Chi. Episcopalian. Clubs: Carolina Country, Executives (Raleigh). Home: 2551 Wake Dr Raleigh NC 27608 Office: PO Box 27886 Raleigh NC 27611

SHELBY, BILLY LEE, engring. exec.; b. Memphis, Feb. 2, 1936; s. John Earven and Mary Erlyne (Gregory) S.; B.S. in Computer Sci., Memphis State U., 1977; m. LaVada Joy Maples, Oct. 16, 1963; children—John Marc, Terry Lynn, RaMona Gay, Eric Malcolm. Mgr. elec. engring. ITT Am. Elec. Co., Southaven, Miss., 1968-75, dir. engring., 1975—; participant profl. seminars. Served with USN, 1954-56. Mem. Illuminating Engring. Soc., Roadway Lighting Com. (chmn. standard practice subcom. 1977—), IEEE, Soc. Die Casting Engrs., Am. Nat. Standards Inst. (chmn. subcoms. 1975—). Mem. Ch. of God (councilman, Sunday Sch. supt., adult Bible tchr., pres. Men's Fellowship 1976). Contbr. articles to profl. jours. Home: 1304 Hickory Ridge Dr Memphis TN 38116 Office: PO Box 100 Southaven MS 38671

SHELBY, GLORIA DEAN, educator; b. Ruston, La., June 19, 1936; d. Brooks Harris and Alva Dean (Williams) Bryant; B.S., La. Tech U., 1957; M.B.A., Ind. U., 1958; postgrad. La. Tech. U., 1964, 68, La. State U., 1977; m. Harold Wayne Shelby, Aug. 16, 1958; children—Tracy Wayne, Gordon Bryant. Grad. asst. Ind. U., Bloomington, 1957-58; sec., recorder Sch. Bus. Adminstrn., La. Tech. U., Ruston, 1958-63; asst. prof. bus. adminstrn. La. State U., Alexandria, 1963—. Mem. La. Bus. Edn. Assn., So. Bus. Edn. Assn., Nat. Bus. Edn. Assn., Nat. Secs. Assn., AAUW, Rapides Parish Assn. for Gifted and Talented Edn., La. Assn. for Gifted and Talented Edn., Delta Pi Epsilon, Phi Kappa Phi, Beta Sigma Phi. Democrat. Baptist. Home: 5607 Skye St Alexandria LA 71301 Office: La State U Alexandria LA 71301

SHELBY, JAMES STANFORD, cardiovascular surgeon; b. Ringgold, La., June 15, 1934; s. Jesse Audrey and Mable (Martin) S.; student La. Tech. U., 1952-54; M.D., La. State U., 1958; m. Susan Rainey, July 15, 1967; children—Bryan Christian, Christopher Linden. Intern, Charity Hosp. La., New Orleans, 1958-59, resident surgery and thoracic surgery, 1959-65; fellow cardiovascular surgery Baylor U. Coll. Medicine, Houston, 1965-66; practice medicine specializing in cardiovascular surgery, Shreveport, La., 1967—; mem. staff Schumpert Med. Center, Highland Hosp.; asso. prof. surgery La. State U. Sch. Medicine, Shreveport, 1967—. Served with M.C., AUS, 1961-62. Diplomate Am. Bd. Surgery, Am. Bd. Thoracic Surgery. Mem. Am. Coll. Cardiology, AMA, Soc. Thoracic Surgeons, Am. Heart Assn., Southeastern Surg. Congress, So. Thoracic Surg. Assn. Home: 6209 Creswell Rd Shreveport LA 71106 Office: 865 Margaret Rd Shreveport LA 71101

SHELBY, MARTHA JANICE, educator; b. Austin, Tex., Mar. 26, 1920; d. Lemuel Evart and Mabel Clair (Wright) Shelby; B.A. magna cum laude, U. Tex., 1942, Ph.D. (Nat. Def. scholar), 1971; M.A., Sul Ross State Coll., 1947. Ednl. adminstr. Meth. Mission Schs., India, 1949-61; faculty Huston-Tillotson Coll., Austin, Tex., 1963-64, 67—, asso. prof. social scis., 1970-74, prof., 1974—; prof., head history dept. Butimba Coll., Mwanza, Tanzania, E. Africa, 1964-66. Served with WAC, 1942-45. Recipient Ford Found. grant, 1963-64. Mem. Am. Acad. Polit. and Social Scis., Sierra Club, Phi Beta Kappa, Kappa Tau Alpha, Phi Kappa Phi, Audubon Soc. Democrat. Contbr. articles in field to profl. jours. Home: PO Box 1261 Austin TX 78767

SHELBY, RICHARD CRAIG, Congressman; b. Birmingham, Ala., May 6, 1934; s. O.H. and Alice L. (Skinner) S.; A.B., U. Ala., 1957, LL.B., 1963; m. Annette Nevin, June 11, 1960; children—Richard Craig, Claude Nevin. Admitted to Ala. bar, 1961; law clk. Supreme Ct. Ala., 1961-62; practiced law, Tuscaloosa, Ala., 1963-79; mem. 96th Congress from 7th Dist. Ala.; mem. Ala. Senate, 1970-78; prosecutor City of Tuscaloosa, 1964-70; spl. asst. atty. gen. State of Ala., 1969-70; U.S. magistrate No. Dist. Ala., Western div., 1966-70. Pres., Tuscaloosa County Mental Health Assn. Mem. Am. Bar Assn., Ala. Bar Assn., D.C. Bar Assn., Tuscaloosa County Bar Assn. Democrat. Presbyterian. Club: Exchange (Tuscaloosa). Office: 1408 Longworth Bldg Washington DC 20515

SHELBY, THOMAS HALL, III, actuary; b. Gilmer, Tex., Dec. 24, 1935; s. Thomas Hall and Dorothy (Shepperd) S.; student Tyler Jr. Coll., 1954-55; B.A., U. Tex., 1959; postgrad. Northeastern U., 1967; M.R.E., Southwestern Bapt. Theol. Sem., 1974; m. Thyrza Christine White, Sept. 4, 1959; children—Atlantis Yvonne, Patricia Farrai, David Norton. Actuarial clk. Geo. Van Fleet, Austin, 1958-59; actuarial clk/programmer Am. Nat. Ins. Co., Galveston, Tex., 1959-60; statistician Occidental Life Ins. Co., Los Angeles, 1960-61; v.p., actuary Fidelity Union Life Ins. Co., Dallas, 1962-72; cons. actuary, Dallas, 1972-77; v.p., dir. Great Midwest Life Ins. Co., Dallas, 1977—; pres., dir. H. Raymond Strong & Co., Dallas, 1977—; instr. actuarial math. U. Tex., Arlington, 1977-78. Pres., dir. Dallas Girls Chorus, 1974-77. Mem. Am. Acad. Actuaries, Actuaries Club SW, Soc. Actuaries. Baptist. Home: 13619 Peyton Dr Dallas TX 75240 Office: 5440 Harvest Hill Rd Suite 236 Dallas TX 75230

SHELDON, ANSON HOISINGTON, polit. worker, bus. exec., farmer; b. Nehawka, Nebr., June 5, 1905; s. George Lawson and Rose (Higgins) S.; student pub. schs.; m. Beatrice Everett, Feb. 5, 1939; children—Patricia Ann Sheldon Strauss, Anson Hoisington, Lawson Everett. Various positions to service sta. mgr. Standard Oil Co. of Ky., 1921-22; dealer Internat. Harvester Co., 1924-26, road engr., sales southeastern U.S., 1926-29; sales Allis Chalmers Mfg. Co., Memphis br., 1930-36; distbr. Miss. and Ark., Massey Harris Co., 1938-39; dirt contractor and heavy equipment rentals, 1945-50; mfrs. agt. Baker Plow Co., 1957-67; factory rep. Howard Rotavator Co., 1961-68; Miss. state real estate broker, 1968—; chmn. bd. Machinery, Inc., 1968—; distbr. Grove Mfg. Co., 1962-66; farmer, 1923—. Commr. Washington County Soil Conservation Dist., 1947—. Mem. legis. com. Delta Council Water Resources Com., 1964-65; col. staff Gov. Cliff Finch, 1976. Mem. exec. com. Miss. Republican Com., 1944-64, state chmn., 1948-52, vice chmn., 1952-60; del Rep. Nat. Conv., 1956, 60. Mem. Miss. Soil Conservation Commrs. Episcopalian. Elk. Address: Keystone Plantation Avon MS 38723

SHELDON, ARTHUR KEITH, photojournalist; b. Providence, Feb. 1, 1928; s. Arthur Vincent and Louise Baron (Lovewell) S.; B.S. in Journalism, Boston U., 1957; m. Joyce Smith, July 24, 1954; children—Arthur Keith, Bruce Clayton. Photographer, reporter Woonsocket (R.I.) Call, 1956, Ft. Scott (Kans.) Tribune, 1957-59, Miami (Fla.) Herald, 1960, Lakeland (Fla.) Ledger, 1960-63; chief photographer Fla. Dept. Citrus, Lakeland, 1963—. Cubmaster, Gulf Ridge Council Boy Scouts Am., 1969-70. Served with USCG, 1945-46; USN, 1950-51. Mem. Res. Officers Assn. U.S., Nat. Writers Club, Lakeland Camera Club (pres. 1962-63). Editor, Polk Progress Newsletter, 1977-78. Numerous mag. cover photos. Home: 541 Palencia Pl Lakeland FL 33803 Office: PO Box 148 Lakeland FL 33802

SHELDON, BEATRICE EVERETT (MRS. ANSON H. SHELDON), polit. worker; b. Gunn, Miss., May 16, 1915; d. John Broadus and Pency Ann (Wooley) Everett; R.N., Dr. Willis Walley Sch. Nursing, Jackson, Miss., 1937; m. Anson H. Sheldon, Feb. 5, 1939; children—Patricia Ann Sheldon Strauss, Anson H., Lawson. Nurse, Kings Daus. Hosp., Canton, Miss., 1937, Greenville, Miss., 1937, Helena (Ark.) Hosp., 1938-39; sec.-treas. Machinery, Inc., 1966—. Mem. county com. Miss. Republican Party, 1944-60; alternate del. to Rep. State Conv., 1948, 52, 56, 60. Chmn. bd. trustees South Washington County Hosp., 1978-80. Mem. Miss. Registered Nurse Assn., Miss. Fedn. Women's Clubs, Longwood Community Culture Club (pres. 1975-78). Episcopalian. Home: Keystone Plantation Avon MS 38723

SHELINE, DARREL WAYNE, food co. exec.; b. Dowaglac, Mich., May 14, 1929; s. Vergil Melvin and Lela (Kesler) S.; student pub. schs.; m. Beverly May Smith, June 6, 1948 (div.); 1 dau., Rebecca Lynn; m. 2d, Lois Jean DeQuasie, Apr. 24, 1971 (div.); m. 3d, Anita L. Olcott, Nov. 24, 1977. Founder, pres. Advance, Inc., Belpre, Ohio, Parkersburg, W.Va., 1964—; v.p. Tusco Grocers, Inc., Urichville, Ohio, 1966-72; pres. Darrel's Inc., Parkersburg, 1972—; pres. Asso. Grocers, Urichville; treas., dir. Grand Central Mall, Parkersburg. Mem. Mayflower Soc., Sons and Daus. Pioneer Rivermen, Internat. Platform Assn. Club: Elks. Home: 208 North Hills Dr Parkersburg WV 26101 Office: Grand Central Mall Parkersburg WV 26101

SHELL, LOUIS CALVIN, lawyer; b. DeWitt, Va., Dec. 8, 1925; s. Roger LaFayette and Susie (Hill) S.; B.A., U. Va., 1946, LL.B., 1947; m. Barbara Marie Pamplin, Aug. 5, 1950; children—Pamela Temple, Patricia Ann. Admitted to Va. bar, 1947; asso. White, Hamilton, Wyche & Shell, Petersburg, Va., 1948-51, partner, 1951—, chief trial counsel, 1960—. Pres., Petersburg (Va.) Tb Assn., 1951; pres., Am. Cancer Soc., Petersburg, Va. chpt., 1952. Vice-mayor, City of Petersburg, Va., 1959-60, mem. council, 1957-60; campaign chmn. Senator William B. Spong, Petersburg, Va., 1966, 72; chmn. City Electoral Bd., 1952-55. Recipient award Jr. C. of C., 1956. Mem. Am. Coll. Trial Lawyers, Am. Judicature Soc., Am., Petersburg (pres. 1963) bar assns., Va. State Bar (mem. council 1972-75). Democrat. Methodist. (trustee 1968—). Kiwanian. Home: 1612 E Tuckahoe St Petersburg VA 23803 Office: 20 E Tabb St Petersburg VA 23803

SHELL, ROBERT NEILL, data processing exec.; b. Miami, Fla., Nov. 13, 1947; s. Edward Cleveland and Nora (Cole) S.; B.S. in Engring. with high honors, N.C. State U., 1969; M.B.A. in Fin., U. N.C., 1971; m. Teresa Elaine Haynes, Apr. 17, 1976; children—Robert Neill, Jr., Brian William. Staff analyst Arthur Andersen & Co., Charlotte, N.C., 1971-72; bus. analyst Tultex, Martinville, Va., 1972-76; supr. systems and programming Gravely div. Clarke Gravely, Clemmons, N.C., 1977, mgr. data processing and bus. planning, 1977—. Mem. Am. Mgmt. Assn., Am. Prodn. and Inventory Control Soc., N.Am. Soc. for Corp. Planning. Methodist. Home: 107 Charlotte Pl Advance NC 27006 Office: No 1 Gravely Ln Clemmons NC 27012

SHELLEY, WILLIAM PAUL, JR., lawyer; b. Telogia, Liberty County, Fla., Dec. 3, 1914; s. William Paul and Pauline (Lavender) S.; B.S. in Bus. Adminstrn., U. Fla., 1937, J.D., 1939; m. Erin Clark, Nov. 23, 1948. Admitted to Fla. bar, 1939; practiced in Tallahassee, 1939-42, 53—; adminstrv. asst. U.S. Senator Spessard L. Holland, Washington, 1946-53; pres., Shelley Properties, Inc., Tallahassee, 1959—. Glenn Realty Co., Tallahassee, 1959—. Mem., sec. Fla. State Racing Commn., 1941-42. Served with AUS, 1942-46; PTO; lt. col. Reserve ret. Decorated Bronze Star medal. Recipient Distinguished Alumnus award U. Fla., 1973. Mem. Am. Judicature Soc., Am. Legion, Am., Tallahassee bar assns., Reserve Officers Assn., Fla. Bar, Fla. Forestry Assn., U. Fla. Alumni Assn. (mem. exec. council 1953—, pres. 1957-58), Tallahassee Area C. of C. (pres. 1964), Phi Delta Phi, Alpha Tau Omega, Blue Key. Democrat. Methodist. Elk, Kiwanian. Clubs: Capital City Country, Killearn Golf and Country, U. Fla. Gator Boosters, Fla. State Seminole Boosters. Home: 506 S Ride Tallahassee FL 32303 Office: PO Box 1136 Tallahassee FL 32302

SHELLHASE, LESLIE JOHN, educator; b. Hardy, Nebr., Jan. 12, 1924; s. John Clayton and Sanna Belle (Muth) S.; A.B., Midland Coll., 1947; M.S.W., U. Nebr., 1950; D.Social Work, Cath. U. Am., 1961; m. Fern Eleanor Kleckner, June 6, 1948; children—Jeremy Clayton, Joel Kleckner. Parole supr. Child Welfare, Omaha, 1948-49; psychiat. social work intern Letterman Gen. Hosp., San Francisco, 1950-51; commd. 2d lt. U.S. Army, 1949, advanced through grades to lt. col., 1966; chief social worker 6th Infantry Div., Fort Ord, Calif., 1952-55; chief med. social worker Walter Reed Gen. Hosp., Washington, 1955-57; research investigator Walter Reed Inst. Research, Washington, 1957-63; head social work faculty Med. Field Service Sch., Ft. Sam Houston, Tex., 1963-66; chief sociologist U.S. Army, Pentagon, Washington, 1966-68; prof. Sch. Social Work, U. Ala., University, 1968—. Cons., Am. Vets. Com., 1962-71, Family Service Assn. Am., 1969—. Bd. dirs. Crisis Intervention Center; bd. dirs., chmn. Soc. for Crippled Children and Adults. Decorated Legion of Merit, Bronze Star, Purple Heart. Recipient Letters of Commendation, The Pres., 1968, Surgeon Gen., 1961. Fellow Am. Sociol. Assn.; mem. Nat. Assn. Social Workers (dir. 1963-66), Council Social Work Edn., Nat. Conf. Social Welfare, Acad. Certified Social Workers. ACLU, Am. Vets. Com., Ret. Officers Assn., So. Sociol. Soc. Democrat. Lutheran. Author: The Group Life of the Schizophrenic Patient, 1961; Bibliography of Army Social Work, 1962. Contbr. articles to nat. and internat. profl. jours. Home: 148 Woodland Hills Tuscaloosa AL 35405 Office: Box 1935 University AL 35486

SHELLNUT, THOMAS COCHRAN, banker; b. Baldwyn, Miss., Oct. 10, 1940; s. Elisha Andrew and Hettiemae Alice (Cochran) S.; B.B.A., U. Miss., 1962; M.B.A., N.Y. U., 1964; m. Sandra Kay Johnson, May 16, 1964; children—Susannah Ferrell, Kathryn Blair. Investment officer Brown Bros. Harriman & Co., N.Y.C., 1966-71; v.p. investments 1st Nat. Bank Commerce, New Orleans, 1971-76; pres. 1st Investors Mgmt. Corp., New Orleans, 1973-76; v.p., investment officer Hancock Bank, Gulfport, Miss., 1976—; instr. Miss. Gulfcoast Jr. Coll., Am. Inst. Banking. Sec. bd. dirs. Christ Episcopal Sch., 1979; dir. Episc. Services for the Aging, 1978-79; vestryman Trinity Ch., 1978. Served to lt., AUS, 1964-66. Mem. Fin. Analysts of New Orleans, Investment Assn. N.Y., Pass Christian Hist. Soc. (pres. 1978-79), Miss. Bankers Assn. Clubs: Pass Christian Yacht (treas. 1979), Pendennis, New Orleans Lawn Tennis. Office: Hancock Bank Gulfport MS 39501

SHELTON, BESSIE ELIZABETH, educator; b. Lynchburg, Va.; d. Robert and Bessie Ann (Plenty) Shelton; B.A. (scholar), W.Va. State Coll., 1958; student Northwestern U., 1953-55, Ind. U., 1956; M.S., State U. N.Y., 1960; diploma Nashville Sch. Songwriting, 1975. Young adult librarian Bklyn. Pub. Library, 1960-62; asst. head central reference div. Queens Borough Pub. Library, Jamaica, N.Y., 1962-65; instructional media specialist Lynchburg (Va.) Bd. Edn., 1966—, Bd. Edn. Allegany County, Cumberland, Md., 1977—; ednl. research specialist, 1974-77. Guest singer radio sta. WLVA, 1966—, WLVA-TV Christmas concerts, 1966—; cons. music and market research. Mem. YWCA, Lynchburg, 1966—, Fine Arts Center, Lynchburg, 1966—. Grantee Colegio Internacional, 1975. Mem. NEA, Allegany County Tchrs. Assn., Md. Tchrs. Assn., Internat. Entertainers Guild, Music City Songwriters Assn., Vocal Artists Am., Internat. Clover Poetry Assn., World Mail Dealers Assn., North Am. Mailers Exchange, Pi Delta Phi, Sigma Delta Pi. Contbr. poems to various publs. Democrat. Baptist. Clubs: National Travel. Gulf Travel. Home: PO Box 1357 Lynchburg VA 24505

SHELTON, CHARLES RICHARD, mgmt. cons.; b. Hugo, Okla., Aug. 1, 1937; s. Ralph McKinney and Minnie Eleanor (Grafford) S.; B.A. in Math, U. Tex., Austin, 1963; A.A. in Frank Phillips Jr. Coll., 1958; m. Marvine Troupe, Nov. 26, 1966; children—Lyle Elizabeth, Charles Colin. Mgr. sci. programming U. Tex., Dallas, 1964-69; mktg. and systems devel. mgmt. staff Univ. Computing Co., Dallas, 1969-79; mgmt. cons., Dallas, 1979—. Mem. Am. Mgmt. Assn., Project Mgmt. Inst., Assn. Computer Users, NRA, Phi Theta Kappa. Republican. Club: Am. Sportsman. Address: 2703 Lakewood Ln Carrollton TX 75006

SHELTON, GAYLE COCHRANE, JR., govt. ofcl.; b. Clarksdale, Miss., Aug. 11, 1918; s. Gayle Cochrane and Marguerite Perryman (Brown) S.; B.A., La. State U., 1940; LL.B., Georgetown U., 1942. Spl. agt. FBI, 1940-47; pres. Pacific Wholesale Corp., Agana, Guam, 1947-62, also Am. Overseas Sales Corp., San Francisco, 1957-62; dir. dist. office U.S. Dept. Commerce, Birmingham, Ala., 1962-78, area dir., 1978—; Southeastern regional export mktg. mgr. Office Field Ops., Domestic and Internat. Bus. Adminstrn., Washington, 1972, acting asst. dir., 1973-74, spl. asst. to dir. Office Bus. Services, Washington, 1971. Guest lectr. OFO Inst., U.S. Dept. Commerce, 1973-74, U. Ala., Birmingham, 1965; speaker U.S. Fgn. Service Comml. Officers Conf., 1978; exec. sec. Southwestern area Nat. Def. Exec. Res., 1964-74; dir. U.S. Trade Mission on Water Pollution, Belgium and Luxembourg, 1976; dir. U.S. Trade Mission on Mining and Mining Related Equipment, Greece and Turkey, 1977; exec. sec. Ala.-Miss. Dist. Export Council, 1971—. Vice pres. Birmingham Festival of Arts, 1972. Named Ala. World Trade man of year, 1972; recipient medals and awards for achievement U.S. Dept. Commerce, 1967—. Mem. Assn. Internationale des Etudiants on Sciences Economiques et Commerciales, Birmingham Area C. of C., Ala. World Trade Assn. (pres. 1974-77), Am. Mgmt. Assn., Am. Soc. Internat. Execs. Club: Relay House (Birmingham). Contbr. articles to trade and profl. jours. Home: 3308 Cliff Rd Birmingham AL 35205 Office: Suite 200 908 S 20th St Birmingham AL 35205

SHELTON, JANICE CAROLE, educator; b. Danville, Ky., Feb. 12, 1944; d. R. G. and Helen Virginia (Wright) S.; B.S., Georgetown Coll., 1966; M.A., U. Ky., 1968; Ed.D., U. N.C., 1979. Coach, instr. Georgetown (Ky.) Coll., 1966-67; tchr. phys. edn. public schs., Lexington, Ky., 1967-68; basketball coach, instr. East Tenn. State U., Johnson City, 1968-73, asst. prof. phys. edn., asst. athletic dir., 1974—. Mem. AAHPER, NEA, Tenn. Edn. Assn., Nat. Assn. Girls and Women's Sports (chairperson Upper East Tenn. bd. ofcls.). Democrat. Baptist. Home: 1607 Crystal Springs Johnson City TN 37601 Office: PO Box 21340-A East Tenn State Univ Johnson City TN 37601

SHELTON, JUNE BROOKS, speech and lang. pathologist; b. Sapulpa, Okla., Aug. 24, 1920; d. James Wilson and June Aileen (Mavity) Brooks; B.S. in Spl. Edn., U. Okla., 1958, Ph.D., 1965; m. D. Westbrook Shelton, Aug. 24, 1969; children—Toni Ford Wilkerson, Kay W. Ford, John M. Ford, Keri Ford Saling. Tchr. Lab. Sch., U. Okla., Norman, 1958-59, learning specialist Child Study Center, Oklahoma City, 1962-65; tchr. Norman Public Schs., 1959-60; dir. day study unit Scottish Rite Hosp. for Crippled Children, Dallas, 1965-67; asso. prof. Tex. Woman's U., Denton, 1967-70; exec. dir. Dean Meml. Learning Center, Dallas, 1970-76; exec. dir. June Shelton Sch. and Evaluation Center, Dallas, 1976—, also bd. dirs., sec. Nat. Def. Edn. fellow, 1962-65. Mem. Am. Speech, Lang. and Hearing Assn., Am. Psychol. Assn., Am. Montessori Soc., Assn. Montessori Internat., Assn. Children with Learning Disabilities, The Orton Soc. (dir. Dallas br.). Home: 628 Mimosa St Denton TX 76201 Office: 11722 Cromwell St Dallas TX 75229

SHELTON, LEWIS SAMUEL, mus. adminstr.; b. Jacksonville, Fla., Nov. 19, 1933; s. Lewis Samuel and Mattie (Wansley) S.; B.S., U. Ga., 1955, M.A., 1963, Ed.D. (NSF fellow 1964-65), 1965; m. Patricia Clarke Rae, Aug. 20, 1955; children—Barbara, Catherine, Jeffrey; m. 2d, Bernice Jordan Shelton, Nov. 13, 1979. Prof. dept. biology DeKalb Coll. and Oglethorpe U., Atlanta, 1964-66; dir. Fernbank Sci. Center, Atlanta, 1966—. Pres., Druid Hills Civic Assn., 1973-77; bd. dirs., pres. Druid Hills Civitan Club; bd. dirs. Planned Parenthood, Inc., 1973—; mem. cabinet Met. Ga. Heart Assn. Mem. Nat. Sci. Tchrs. Assn., Am. Mgmt. Assn. Home: 1177 Springdale Rd NE Atlanta GA 30306 Office: 156 Heaton Park Dr NE Atlanta GA 30307

SHELTON, ROBERT DEAN, communications co. exec.; b. State Center, Iowa, June 6, 1944; s. Donald Carl and Carylon (Davis) S.; Asso. in Electronics Technology, Northwestern Electronics Inst., 1973; B.A.S. in Telecommunications, U. Minn., 1974; m. Teruko Kuriwa, July 7, 1969; 1 son, Jerry Yoitchi. Communications watch officer Kentron LTV, Kwajalien Islands, Pacific, 1967-69; automatic supr. Western Union, Mpls., 1969-71; telecommunications tech. analyst Cargill Inc., Mpls., 1973-75; specialist network facilities Gen. Electric Credit Corp., Stamford, Conn., 1975-77; mgr. network integration Martin Marietta Data Systems, Orlando, Fla., 1977—. Served with USN, 1963-67. Decorated Air medal. Mem. AIAA, Am. Security Council, ARRL, VFW. Republican. Presbyterian. Home: 4000 Seabridge Dr Orlando FL 32809 Office: PO Box 13990 Orlando FL 32859

SHELTON, STEPHEN PAUL, civil engr., educator; b. Memphis, Feb. 26, 1948; s. John Paul and Jean (Dowbiggin) S.; B.S., U. Tenn., 1970, M.S., 1972, Ph.D., 1974; m. Cynthia C. Thomas, Aug. 29, 1970; 1 dau., Paige Stefany. Prof. engring. U. S.C., Columbia, 1974-77; asso. SCS Engrs., Long Beach, Calif., 1977—, Booz-Allen & Hamilton, Bethesda, Md., 1978—; cons. in field. Served to capt., USAF,

1974-77. Recipient Best Paper award, Am. Water Works Assn., 1974. Mem. ASCE, Am. Water Works Assn., Water Pollution Control Fedn., Assn. of Environ. Engring. Profs., Sigma Xi, Chi Epsilon, Omicron Delta Kappa, Pi Kappa Alpha Alumni Assn. of Central S.C. Republican. Methodist. Contbr. articles in field to profl. jours. Home: 117 Otter Trail West Columbia SC 29169 Office: Coll of Engring Univ of SC Columbia SC 29208

SHELTON, THOMAS CLEVELAND, II, civil engr.; b. Vicksburg, Miss., Feb. 28, 1953; s. Thomas Fyke and Helen Elizabeth (Gray) S.; B.S. in C.E., Miss. State U., 1975; m. Donna Jean Tennant, May 19, 1979. Supervisory civil engr. Vicksburg (Miss.) Dist., U.S. Corps of Engrs., 1975-80, project engr. Lake Chicot Pumping Plant, 1980—. Mem. Chi Epsilon. Methodist. Clubs: Miss. State U. Alumni, Miss. State U. Bulldog. Home: 255 Valley View Ln Vicksburg MS 39180 Office: PO Box 60 Vicksburg MS 39180

SHEMWELL, RONALD EUGENE, obstetrician, gynecologist; b. Shreveport, La., Nov. 2, 1935; s. Joseph Carlton and Mildred Elizabeth (Stoddard) S.; B.S., Centenary Coll., 1957; M.D., La. State U., 1962; m. Virginia Catherine Cage, Nov. 23, 1960; children—Melanie Catherine, Ronald Eugene, David Clayton, Margaret Claire. Intern, Confederate Meml. Hosp., Shreveport, 1962-63; gen. practice resident E. A. Conway Hosp., Monroe, La., 1965-66; fellow obstetrics-gynecology Ochsner Clinic, New Orleans, 1966-69, staff physician, 1969-71; practice medicine specializing in obstetrics-gynecology, Monroe, La., 1971—; head residency tng. dept. obstetrics-gynecology E. A. Conway Meml. Hosp., Monroe, La., 1971-79, acting chief Ob-gyn, 1979—; clin. asso. prof. La. State U. Sch. Medicine, Shreveport, 1979—. Served with M.C., AUS, 1963-65. Diplomate Am. Bd. Obstetrics and Gynecology. Mem. AMA, Am. Coll. Obstetricians and Gynecologists, A.C.S., Southeastern Gynecol. Soc., So., La. State med. assns., Ouachita Parish Med. Soc., Central Assn. Obstetricians and Gynecologists, Am. Assn. Gynecologic Laparoscopists. Contbr. articles to profl. jours. Home: 1919 Pargoud Blvd Monroe LA 71201 Office: 313 Wood St Monroe LA 71201

SHENKMAN, GERALD, ins. exec.; b. Miami, Fla., Nov. 25, 1930; s. Mack H. and Sara (Greenberg) S.; B.S. in Bus. Adminstrn., U. Fla., 1953; m. Elsa Celensac, Feb. 28, 1952; children—Michael David, Curtis Lauren. Field underwriter Gen. Accident Group, Phila., 1953-55, Atlanta, 1956-57; owner, prin. Shenkman Ins. Agy., Coral Gables, Fla., 1957—; tchr. courses in field. Served with Signal Corps, U.S. Army, 1953-54. C.L.U. Mem. Greater Miami Ins. Bd. (dir.), Assn. Chartered Property and Casualty Underwriters (pres. S. Fla. chpt., chartered property and casualty underwriter), Greater Miami Ins. Edn. Council (pres.), Nat. Assn. Watch Collectors, Am. Motorcycle Assn., Aircraft Owners and Pilots Assn., Nat. Rifle Assn. Clubs: Tamiami Sportsmen, K.P. Office: Shenkman Ins Agy 3081 Salzedo St Suite 305 Coral Gables FL 33134

SHENTON, ALTON O'NEIL, clergyman; b. Cambridge, Md., Mar. 6, 1935; s. Anthony William and Aline (Brown) S.; B.A., Western Ky. U., 1964; B.D., Emory U., 1967, M.Div., 1972; m. Nina Pauline Felts, Apr. 4, 1961; children—Paula Michelle, Gregory O'Neil. Ordained to ministry Meth. Ch., 1965; pastor, Bowling Green, Ky., 1960-64, Douglasville, Ga., 1964-67, Sonora, Ky., 1967-69, Kenwood United Meth. Ch., Louisville, 1969-77, 1st United Meth. Ch., Greenville, Ky., 1977-79, St. Mark United Meth. Ch., Louisville, 1979—; mem. Bd. Social Concerns, Louisville Conf., 1968-72, mem. Bd. Discipleship, 1973-80. Sec. bd. trustees Josephine Rudy Smith Scholarship Fund, 1974-80. Served with USN, 1955-59. Named Louisville Minister of Week, 1972. Mem. S.A.R. Optimist (Pres.'s Golden Circle award 1968). Clubs: A.M. Stickles History (Western Ky. Univ., Bowling Green); NATO Sportsman's (Naples, Italy). Address: 4605 Lowe Rd Louisville KY 40220

SHEPARD, ROBERT DEEMS, radiologist; b. Kidder, Mo., Aug. 31, 1915; s. Melvin Arthur and Letha Mary (Deems) S.; B.A., U. Nebr., 1937, M.D., 1941; m. Frances Marie Neil, Aug. 12, 1939; children—Neil T., Mitchell D. Intern St. Joseph Hosp., Kansas City, 1941-42; resident in pathology St. Joseph Hosp., 1946-47, radiology City Hosp. St. Louis, 1947-50; practice medicine specializing in radiology, 1950—; chief dep. radiology Good Samaritan Hosp., Lexington, Ky.; cons. Shriners Crippled Children's Hosp., Lexington, Cardinal Hill Crippled Children's Hosp., Lexington, John Graves Forde Meml. Hosp., Georgetown, Ky., Beres (Ky.) Hosp.; asst. clin. prof. radiology U. Ky., 1961—. V.p. bd. dirs. Lexington Y.M.C.A., 1962-63. Served with U.S. Army, 1941-47. Decorated Bronze Star. Fellow Am. Coll. Radiology (pres. Ky. chpt. 1967-68); mem. Am., Ky. med. assns., Fayette County, Madison County (hon.) med. socs. Republican. Methodist. Club: Lexington Kiwanis (pres. 1963). Office: 310 S Limestone Lexington KY 40508

SHEPHERD, CORNELIOUS ALSTON, JR., (NEIL), univ. ofcl.; b. Birmingham, Ala., Mar. 30, 1923; s. Cornelious Alston and Reba (Webb) S.; B.S., Howard Coll., 1948; J.D., Samford U., 1966; L.H.D. (hon.), Judson Coll., 1979; m. Betty Sue Garner; children—Susanne Elizabeth, Jacqueline Yvonne. Dir. alumni affairs Samford U., Birmingham, Ala. Chmn., Samford U. United Way Drive, 1975-76, 77, 78; deacon Ruhama Bapt. Ch., Vestavia Hills Bapt. Ch., 1978-79, also Sunday Sch. dir., chmn. bd. trustees. Served to 1st lt. USAAF, World War II. Decorated Air medal, D.F.C. Mem. Am. Assn. Univ. Adminstrs., Ala. Public Relations Assn., Ala. Archeol. Soc., Soc. Colonial Wars (sec. Ala. chpt. 1979—), SAR (v.p. Birmingham chpt. 1977-78), Birmingham Genealogical Soc. (v.p. 1979—), Nat. Genealogical Soc., Air Force Assn., Ala. Heart Assn., Ala. Real Estate Bd., Birmingham Real Estate Bd., 14th Air Force Assn., Sloss Furnace Assn., Mil. Order of World Wars (comdr. 1977-78), SCV, Newcomen Soc. N.Am., Nat. Soc. Magna Charta Barons, Nat. Rifle Assn., Council for Advancement and Support of Edn., Ala. Numismatic Soc., Aircraft Owners and Pilots Assn., Religious Heritage Am., Execs. Club of Birmingham (pres. 1979—), Sigma Delta Kappa, Pi Gamma Mu, Tau Kappa Alpha, Kappa Phi Kappa, Kappa Delta Pi, Pi Kappa Alpha (pres.). Clubs: Rotary (treas. 1977-78), Masons. Home: 909 Southridge Dr Birmingham AL 35216 Office: Samford U 800 Lakeshore Dr Birmingham AL 35209

SHEPHERD, HILTON JOHN, mgmt. cons.; b. Ft. Worth, Dec. 10, 1946; s. Hilton Daniel and Kathryn M. Shepherd; B.B.A., Tex. Christian U., 1969, M.B.A., 1970; M.S., East Tex. State U., 1974; Ph.D. in Psychology, 1976; m. Teresa Brown, Feb. 14, 1974; 1 stepson, Dustin Terrell Collins. Counselor, Tarrant County (Tex.) Juvenile Probation Dept., 1970-71; asst. sec.-treas. Hilton Shepherd Co., Inc., Ft. Worth, 1974-75, pres., 1975—; instr. Tex. Christian U.; mem. Tex. Bd. Examiners in Social Psychotherapy, 1979—. Bd. dirs. Big Bros. Tarrant County. Licensed social psychotherapist, Tex. Mem. Am. Psychol. Assn., MENSA, Beta Gamma Sigma, Omicron Delta Epsilon. Home: 4817 Inwood Rd Fort Worth TX 76109 Office: 3475 West Freeway Fort Worth TX 76107

SHEPHERD, JOHN DAVID, counselor; b. Salt Lake City, July 10, 1943; s. John Morgan and Genevieve (Mitchell) S.; B.S., Brigham Young U., 1967; M.A., Ariz. State U., 1970; postgrad. U. Redlands, 1968, U. So. Calif., 1975, Pepperdine U., 1972; m. Bonnie Jean Allen, Mar. 16, 1968; children—Todd, Tyler, Amy, John Adam, Jay Dee. Speech and voice tchr. Brigham Young U., 1967-68; tchr., counselor Fontana (Calif.) High Sch., 1968-70; speech tchr. Alta Loma (Calif.) Jr. Coll., 1969-70; area dir. Latter-day Saints Ch. Edn. System, No. area Va., 1976-79; profl. counselor, cons., Vienna, Va., 1975—; pres. Career Devel. Systems Inc.; cons. execs. in major corps., Washington area. Coach Alexandria (Va.) Youth Soccer Assn., 1976-77, Ft. Hunt Youth League, 1977-79; lectr. YW/YMCA groups on motivation and mental health; arranged speech competitions for Lions and Toastmasters groups; cons. campaign workers of Democratic and Republican candidates. Served with USAF, 1968-69. Mem. Am. Assn. Marriage and Family Counselors, Am. Personnel and Guidance Assn., Va. Personnel and Guidance Assn., Calif. Assn. Marriage and Family Counselors. Mormon. Home: 1095 Fairbank St Great Falls VA 22066 Office: 8144 Electric Ave Vienna VA 22180

SHEPHERD, MARK, JR., electronics co. exec.; b. Dallas, Jan. 18, 1923; s. Mark and Louisa Florence (Daniell) S.; B.S. in Elec. Engring., So. Meth. U., 1942; M.S. in Elec. Engring., U. Ill. at Urbana, 1947; m. Mary Alice Murchland, Dec. 21, 1945; children—Debra Aline (Mrs. Rowland K. Robinson), MaryKay Theresa, Marc Blaine. With Gen. Electric Co., 1942-43, Farnsworth TV and Radio Corp., 1947-48; with Tex. Instruments Inc., Dallas, 1948—, v.p., gen. mgr. semicondr.-components div., 1955-61, exec. v.p. co., 1961-66, pres., 1967-76, chief exec. officer, 1969—, chmn. bd., 1976—; dir. Republic Nat. Bank Dallas, Republic of Tex. Corp., U.S. Steel Corp.; mem. Internat. council Morgan Guaranty Trust Co. Mem. Adv. Council on Japan-U.S. Econ. Relations; nat. bd. Com. on Present Danger; mem. Trilateral Commn.; adv. council Am. Ditchley Found.; bd. govs., trustee So. Meth. U.; co-chmn. bd. trustees Conf. Bd.; trustee Com. for Econ. Devel., Am. Enterprise Inst. Pub. Policy Research; bd. dirs. Found. for Sci. and Engring. So. Meth. U. Served to lt. (j.g.) USNR, 1943-46. Registered profl. engr., Tex. Fellow IEEE; mem. Soc. Exploration Geophysicists, Newcomen Soc., Council on Fgn. Relations, Internat. C. of C. (trustee U.S. council), Bus. Council, Center for Strategic and Internat. Studies, Internat. Council on Future of Bus., Dallas Citizens Council, European Community-U.S. Businessmen's Council, Nat. Acad. Engring., Sigma Xi, Eta Kappa Nu. Home: 5006 Middlegate Rd Dallas TX 75229 Office: 13500 N Central Expressway PO Box 225474 Dallas TX 75265

SHEPHERD, RICHARD BUTLER HOOKE, civil engr.; b. Pond, Miss., Feb. 10, 1905; s. Arthur Merson and Louise Maria (Hider) S.; student Cornell U., 1922-23, Miss. State U., 1924, U. Mo., 1925-27, U. Tenn., 1945. Insp. C.E., Vicksburg, Miss., 1928-31, Memphis, 1931-32, civil engr., Memphis, 1932-47; geod. engr. 29th Engring. Ba. Base Topo, Manila, P.I., 1948-54; cartographer U.S. Army Map Service, Far East, Tokyo, Japan, 1954-60; ret. 1960; vol. ednl. therapy VA Hosp., Memhis, 1961-63, 69—; registered rep. White & Co., Memphis, 1964-69. Extension instr. U. Tenn., 1942-46, U. Ark., 1944. Vice pres. Travellers Aid. Fellow ASCE (life), Am. Congress on Surveying and Mapping (life); mem. Memphis Engrs. Club (life), Soc. Am. Mil. Engrs. (life), Cornell Soc. Engrs., SAR, Pi Tau Sigma. Episcopalian. Clubs: Memphis University; Tokyo Lawn Tennis, Memphis Civitan. Home: 1380 Lamar Ave Apt 707 Memphis TN 38104

SHEPHERD, ROBERT ASHLAND, lawyer; b. Huntsville, Tex., July 7, 1894; s. James L. and Julia (Josey) S.; grad. Sam Houston State U., 1914; student U. Tex. at Austin, 1916-17; m. Opal Powell, July 8, 1922; children—Robert Ashland, William Leftwich. Admitted to Tex. bar, 1921; with James L. Shepherd, Cisco, Tex., 1921; with Vinson, Elkins, Searls, Connally & Smith, Houston, 1921-70, partner, 1929—, mng. partner, 1951-59; v.p., dir. Duval Corp., 1947-70. Bd. dirs. Tex. Med. Center, Methodist Hosp., Houston; trustee Tex. Methodist Found., Austin, Lon Morris Coll., Jacksonville, Tex. Served as 2d lt., F.A. and aviation, U.S. Army, World War I. Mem. Am., Tex., Houston bar assns., SAR, Sons Republic Tex. Democrat. Methodist (trustee). Mason (Shriner, K.T.). Home: 2136 Inwood Dr Houston TX 77019 Office: First City Nat Bank Bldg Houston TX 77002

SHEPHERD, ROBERT LENWARD, TV exec.; b. Atlanta, Aug. 21, 1933; s. Earl Lenward and Linda (Grubbs) S.; A.B., U. Ala., 1959; m. Beverly Joyce Crowell, Oct. 1, 1960; children—Nancy Lynn, Scott Lenward and Susan Leigh (twins). Dir., announcer U. Ala. Broadcasting Services, Tuscaloosa, 1958; producer, dir. WEDU-TV, Tampa, Fla., 1959; prodn. mgr. St. Petersburg, Fla., 1959-63; program prodn. mgr. WDCN-TV, Nashville, Tenn., 1963-65; gen. mgr., 1965—; exec. v.p. Nashville Pub. TV Council, Inc., 1971—. Dir. summer lab workshops in ednl. TV, Belmont Coll., Nashville, 1966-67; coordinator Vanderbilt U. M.A. in Teaching Seminars, Nashville, 1966-74. Bd. dirs. Middle Tenn. Radio and TV Council, 1965-67; bd. dirs., pub. edn. dir. Pinellas County Unit, Am. Cancer Soc., St. Petersburg, Fla., 1962-63; bd. mgrs. Pub. Broadcasting Service, 1972-76, bd. dirs., 1980—. Served with CIC, AUS, 1955-57; PTO. Recipient George Washington Honor Medal awards Freedom Found., Valley Forge, 1964, 66. Mem. Nat. Assn. Ednl. Broadcasters, So. Ednl. Communications Assn. (dir. 1973—, treas. 1975-76, vice chmn. 1976-77, chmn. 1977-78), Pi Kappa Phi (pres. 1958, treas. 1957). Club: Nashville Civitan. Home: 713 Georgetown Dr Nashville TN 37205 Office: Box 120609 161 Rains Ave Nashville TN 37212

SHEPPARD, ALBERT EDWARD, architect; b. Mexico City, Mexico, Sept. 21, 1910; s. William Henry and Lillian Bedell (Endweiss) S.; came to U.S., 1919, naturalized, 1942; student San Antonio Jr. Coll., 1929-30; B.A., U. Tex., 1935; m. Reba May Masterson, Mar. 30, 1940; children—Albert Edward, Anthony Dallam, Michael Masterson. Draftsman, City Water Bd., San Antonio, 1930-33, U. Tex. Extension, Austin, 1933-35, Houston Ind. Sch., 1935-36; architect State Bd. Control, Houston, 1936-37; landscape architect Fleming & Sheppard, Houston, 1937-42; architect Brown Shipbldg., Houston, 1942-46; architect Brown & Root, Houston, 1946-56, mng. architect, 1956-75, cons. 1975-79. Mem. Sch. Architecture Found. adv. council U. Tex., 1974-76, chmn. dean's council, 1974-76. Mem. A.I.A., Tex. Soc. Architects. Clubs: Racquet, YMCA Health (Houston). Prin. archtl. works include Manned Spacecraft Center, Houston, Margaret Root Brown Coll., Rice U., Herman Brown Cardiovascular Research Center, Houston, Goodwill Industries Oeland Meml. Chapel, Houston, Brown & Root Internat. Hdqrs. Complex, Houston. Home: 306 W Cowan St Houston TX 77007 Office: 4100 Clinton Dr Houston TX 77001

SHEPPARD, ALBERT PARKER, JR., educator, univ. ofcl.; b. Griffin, Ga., June 6, 1936; s. Albert Parker and Cornelia F. (Cooper) S.; B.S. summa cum laude, Oglethorpe Coll., 1958; M.S. (Woodrow Wilson fellow), Emory U., 1959; Ph.D., Duke, 1965; m. Eleanor Davis, Feb. 8, 1978; children—Albert Parker III, Frank Philip. Sr. engr. Orlando (Fla.) research div. Martin Marietta Co., 1960-63; physicist U.S. Army Research Office, Durham, N.C., 1963-65; prin. research engr., also head spl. techniques br. electronics div. Ga. Inst. Tech., Atlanta, 1965-71, chief chem. scis. and materials div., 1971-72, asso. dean engring., 1972-74, asso. v.p. research, 1974—, prof. elec. engring., 1972—; faculty DeKalb Coll., Clarkston, Ga., 1967-71; chmn. bd., sec.-treas. Microwave Cons., Atlanta, 1969—. Recipient Distinguished Alumni award Oglethorpe U., 1974. Mem. IEEE (sr.), Am. Soc. Engring. Edn., Engring. Research Council (chmn. com. on research adminstrn. 1975-79, dir. 1976-78, com. on industry/univ. relations 1979—), Internat. Microwave Power Inst., Internat. Solar Energy Soc., Sigma Xi, Sigma Pi Sigma. Club: Ansley Golf (Atlanta). Contbr. articles to sci. jours. Home: 3591 Norwich Dr Tucker GA 30084 Office: Georgia Institute of Technology 225 North Ave Atlanta GA 30332

SHEPPARD, NAOMI KATE, nurse, educator; b. Portsmouth, Ohio, Aug. 12, 1929; d. Harold Wolf and Thelma Marie (Copas) Taylor; A.A., Temple Jr. Coll., 1955; B.A., U. Mary Hardin Baylor, 1966; M.S.N., U. Tex., Austin, 1973; postgrad. N. Tex. U., 1979, Tex. Woman's U., 1978; m. William Hill Sheppard, Sept. 4, 1948; children—Molly Renee, Julie Kay, Amy Lou. Registered nurse Scott and White Hosp., Temple, Tex., 1955-71, inservice dir., supr., 1966-71; mem. faculty dept. nursing Mary Hardin Coll., Baylor U., Belton, Tex., 1972—, asso. prof. psychiat. nursing, 1979—. Menninger Found. fellow, 1979. Mem. Tex. Nurses Assn., Am. Nurses Assn., Nat. League Nurses, Am. Orthopsychiat. Assn. Office: Box 287 University of Mary Hardin Baylor Belton TX 76513

SHEREMATA, WILLIAM ANTHONY, physician, neurologist; b. Westlock, Alta., Can., Sept. 25, 1934; s. Anthony and Gwendolyn Ruth (Payne) S.; B.S. U. Alta., 1955, M.D. 1959; m. Leah George Magel, Sept. 20, 1975; children—Shelley Ruth, Summer Leah. Intern, St. Paul's Hosp., Vancouver, B.C., Can., 1959-60; resident Naden Naval Hosp., Esqui-Mault, B.C., 1960-61, Sunnybrook Hosp., Toronto, Ont., Can., 1961-62, Queens U., Kingston, Ont., 1966-67, Lahey Clinic Asso. Hosps., 1967-68, Boston VA Hosp. and Boston City Hosp., 1968-71; research fellow Harvard U., Cambridge, Mass. 1970-71; lectr. neurology McGill U., Montreal, Que., Can., 1971-74, asst. prof. 1974-77; assoc. prof. neurology U. of Miami, Fla. 1977—, dir. Multiple Sclerosis Clinic and labs. 1977—; mem. med. advisory bd. Myesthenia Gravis Found., N.Y.C., 1977—, Multiple Sclerosis Soc. of Am., N.Y.C. 1977—. Served with Canadian Forces, NW Europe, 1962-66. Recipient Alta. Govt. bursary, 1956-57; prize in psychiatry U. Alta., 1959; ROTP scholarship U. of Alberta 1958-60; establishment grantee Med. Research Council of Quebec, Can. 1971; Med. Research Council of Can. 1972-77; Multiple Sclerosis Soc. of Can. 1973-77; of U.S. 1978—; St. Mary's Found. 1971-77. Fellow Royal Coll. of Physicians and Surgeons of Can., Royal Soc. Medicine, Am. Acad. of Neurology; mem. Canadian Neurological Soc., Neurosci. Soc. Contbr. various articles in field to profl. jours. Home: 7720 182nd St Miami FL 33151 Office: Dept Neurology Faculty of Medicine U of Miami PO Box 520875 Miami FL 33152

SHERERTZ, ROBERT FRANCIS, architect; b. Roanoke, Va., Oct. 4, 1926; s. Frank Jackson and Mary Edmonds (Williamson) S.; student Duke, 1944-45, U. N.C., 1945; B.S. in Architecture, U. Va., 1948; m. Nell Vann Cole, Sept. 6, 1947; children—Lawrence Collins, Lynn Sherertz Genheimer, Luanne Cole. Archtl. designer firm Eubank & Caldwell, Inc., Roanoke, 1948-55; architect firm Williams & Tazewell, Norfolk, 1955-56; partner firm. Eubank, Caldwell & Assos., Roanoke, 1956-70; partner firm Sherertz & Franklin (name changed to Sherertz, Franklin & Shaffner), Roanoke, 1970—. Mem. pub. adv. panel on archtl. services Gen. Services Adminstrn., 1971. Served with USN, 1944-45. Mem. A.I.A. (past pres. S.W. sect. Va. chpt., dir. Va. Soc.), Va. Assn. Professions, U.S., Va., Roanoke chambers commerce, Scarab, Raven Soc., Pi Kappa Alpha. Methodist (trustee). Club: Roanoke Rotary (dir. 1979—). Home: 2235 East View Dr SW Roanoke VA 24018 Office: 612 1st Fed Bldg Roanoke VA 24011

SHERIDAN, ROBERT HOWARD, JR., investment banker; b. Mpls., July 17, 1933; s. Robert Howard and Nora L. (McIntyre) S.; B.A., Rice U., 1954; postgrad. U. Tex., 1954-55; grad. Investment Bankers Assn. course Wharton Sch. Finance U. Pa., 1968; m. Mary Ellen Woodruff, Jan. 27, 1962 (div. Nov. 1971); children—Robert Howard III, Phillip Douglas. Vice pres. investments Tex. Nat. Bank, Houston, 1955-64; sr. v.p., dir. Moroney, Beissner & Co., Inc., Houston, 1964-74, Moroney, Beissner Mortgage Co., 1966-74; sr. v.p., dir. Rotan Mosle Mortgage Co., 1974-77; v.p. Rotan Mosle, Inc., 1974-78, 1st v.p., dir., 1978—; dir. Rotan Mosle Realty Inc., 1976—. Mem. Houston Soc. Financial Analysts, Nat. Assn. Securities Dealers, Securities Industry Assn., Phi Delta Theta. Clubs: River Oaks Country, Houston, Plaza (Houston). Home: 4944 Woodway Houston TX 77056 Office: 1500 South Tower Pennzoil Pl Houston TX 77002

SHERIDAN, ROGER WILLIAMS, civil engr.; b. Dallas, Jan. 26, 1921; s. Lawrence V. and Grace E. (Emmel) S.; student Purdue U., 1940-42, U.S. Mil. Acad., 1942, U. Utah, 1946-50; B.S. in Civil Engring., Westminster Coll., 1955; m. Shirley Parsons, June 12, 1944; children—Kathleen, Richard Parsons, Margaret Grace (Mrs. Duane Woody), Susan Fisher, Sherrie Ann (Mrs. Charles Vaughn), Charles Lawrence. Field engr. L.V. Sheridan, Los Alamos, 1948-52; pres., dir. Met. Engrs., Inc., 1952-56; gen. supt. Utah Constrn. Co. (Peru), project mgr. Kaiser Engrs., Volta River Project (Ghana), 1959-61; v.p. constrn. Homesmith, Inc., 1963-64; dir. engring. Khuzestan Water & Power, 1964-67; mgr. constrn. S.-E. Asia, Philco-Ford, 1967-68; asst. v.p., project mgr. Boise-Cascade Corp., 1968-70; v.p. Realtec, Inc., 1970-72; exec. v.p. Mesa Surveying & Engring. Co., 1972-73; v.p. gen. mgr. Eastern Pa. Marine Properties, Inc.; exec. v.p. Drums, Inc.; v.p. Lake of Four Seasons, Inc., Acqua Constrn. Co., 1973-74; regional mgr. Envirotech Systems Inc., 1974-75; dir. project ops. Grumman Ecosystems Corp., Bethpage, N.Y., 1975, also Archirodon Group, Athens, Greece; cons. civil engring. Served to capt. C.E., AUS, World War II; ETO. Decorated Purple Heart, Bronze Star medal. Registered profl. engr., Ga., Ala., N.C., S.C., Fla., Pa., Utah, N.J., Tex., Ind., Ariz., Colo., Wyo., Nev., Okla., Cal. Fellow Am. Soc. C.E., Beavers. Episcopalian. Elk. Address: Route 4 Deerfield Covington GA 30209

SHERIDAN, SUSAN JANE, educator; b. San Francisco, Dec. 6, 1941; d. William John and Mathilda Barbara (Zech) Warner; B.S., U. Oreg., 1963, M.Ed., 1964; Ed.D. (Univ. fellow), U. Houston, 1974; m. Jack Michael Sheridan, Jan. 11, 1964; children—Jane Margaret, Lisl Warner, Scott Michael. Tchr., Pearl Buck Sch., Eugene, Oreg., 1962-64; founder, tchr. Nellie Burke Sch., Ellensburg, Wash., 1967; supr. spl. edn. Galena Park (Tex.) Ind. Sch. Dist., 1973-75; asst. prof. diagnostic edn. U. Houston, Clear Lake City, Tex., 1975-78, adj. prof., 1978—; ednl. cons. Harris County (Tex.) Dept. Edn., 1978—; bd. dirs. Magnificat Half Way Houses, Inc., Spring Br. Acad., Sch. for Learning Disabled and Emotionally Disturbed Students. Recipient Spl. Recognition award Kiwanis, 1966; named an Outstanding Young Woman of Am., Ofelia Service club, 1966; U. Houston, Clear Lake City grantee, 1977-78. Mem. Am. Assn. Mental Deficiency, Council Exceptional Children, Houston Met. Ednl. Diagnosticians, Phi Delta Kappa. Author devel. learning materials. Home: 2736 Quenby St Houston TX 77005 Office: 6208 Irvington Blvd Houston TX 77022

SHERIFF, JIMMY DON, educator; b. Greenville, S.C., Dec. 8, 1940; s. James Donald and Gladys Ellie (Chapman) S.; B.A., Central Wesleyan Coll., 1964; M.B.A., U. Ga., 1970, Ph.D., 1976; m. Gwen Anne Campbell, Aug. 31, 1969. Accountant, Maremont Corp., Greenville, 1965-68; instr. U. Ga., Athens, 1970-73; asst. prof. Presbyn. Coll., Clinton, S.C., 1973-74; asso. prof. Clemson (S.C.) U., 1974—. Served as 1st lt. U.S. Army, 1964. Mem. Nat. Assn. Accts. (Most Valuable Mem. 1978, dir. 1975—, pres. Anderson area 1979-80), Am. Acctg. Assn. (doctoral consortium fellow 1972), Acad. Sci., Acad. Acctg. Historians, Nat. Council Govtl. Accounting,

AAUP, S.C. Assn. Acctg. Instrs. (pres. 1974-75), Central Wesleyan Coll. Alumni Assn. (pres. 1970-72), Beta Gamma Sigma, Beta Alpha Psi, Sigma Iota Epsilon. Baptist. Clubs: Lions (v.p.), Masons, Shriners. Author: Attitudes Toward Current Values, 1976. Home: Route 3 Box 335 Old Pendleton Rd Central SC 29630 Office: Dept Accounting and Finance Sirrine Hall Clemson U Clemson SC 29631

SHERIN, EDWIN ELI, credit card/fin. co. exec.; b. Elmira, N.Y., July 11, 1938; s. Arthur and Carrie Ardaline (Arnold) S.; B.S., Rutgers U., 1961; children—Barry, Troy, Derek. With Am. Express Co., 1968—, v.p. Eastern region, 1977-80, v.p. So. region, Ft. Lauderdale, Fla., 1980—. Bd. dirs. United Way of Broward County (Fla.); trustee Ft. Lauderdale Mus. Art; mem. S. Fla. Coordinating Com. Served to capt. Intelligence Corps, U.S. Army, 1961-68; ETO. Mem. N.Y. Met. Credit Grantors Assn. (dir.). Office: 777 American Expressway Fort Lauderdale FL 33317

SHERIN, ROBERT MORRIS, computer co. exec.; b. Boston, Apr. 17, 1939; s. Marcus Leon and Sarah (Burwen) S.; student Johns Hopkins, 1958-60, Emerson Coll., 1960-62; children—David Daniel, Susan Jenifer. Copywriter, announcer radio sta. WNBP, Newburyport, Mass., 1960-62; planneranalyst Eastern Airline, Inc., Miami, Fla., 1965-68; pres. Nova Computing Services, Inc., Miami, 1968—, Western Data Corp., 1976—; cons. software sales and service for numerous cos.; speaker state taxation of data processing. Served with AUS, 1962-65. Mem. Data Processing Mgmt. Assn. (newsletter editor 1971-72, publicity chmn. 1975, non-jud. legis. adv. 1977—), Assn. Data Processing Service Orgns. Contbr. articles on data processing to profl. publs. Home and office: 15805 SW 101 Ave Miami FL 33157

SHERMAN, ALICE MARGARET, mfg. co. exec.; b. Manchester, Ohio, Jan. 26, 1930; d. Otha Robert and Ruth Irene (Tuach) Prichard; student U. Cin., 1949-50; m. Robert Coolidge Sherman, Feb. 14, 1953; children—Kathryn Ann, Leslie Ann, Robert Russell, Brett Roderick, Kelly Ann. Costume designer Dorothee LaVelle, Inc., Cin., 1948-54; mem. trust dept. Central Trust Co., Cin., 1954-57; purchasing agt. Automated Industries Inc., Oak Ridge, Tenn., 1970-79, sec., treas., 1978-79; dir. ORBAC Consulting Activities. Active Boys Club Am., Oak Ridge. Mem. Nat. Assn. Purchasing Agts. Republican. Club: Ladies of Elks. Office: 108 Flint Rd PO Box 403 Oak Ridge TN 37830

SHERMAN, EDWIN BERNARD, mfrs. rep., lighting sales agy. exec.; b. Daytona Beach, Fla., Aug. 18, 1938; s. Al A. and Montelle (Epstein) S.; B.S. in Bus. Adminstrn., U. Fla., 1961, student law, 1961; children—Montelle, Allen. With Gen. Devel. Corp., Miami, Fla., 1961-62, Pillsbury Co., 1962-65, Thomas Industries, 1965-67; pres. E.B. Sherman Co., Inc., Miami, Fla., 1967—. Pres. Golden Shores Condominium Assn. Recipient sales awards. Mem. Illuminating Engring. Soc. (1st place lighting competition 1967, 2d place SE regional lighting competition 1967), Nat. Elec. Mfrs. Rep. Assn., Am. Home Lighting Reps. Assn., Am. Art Pottery Assn. (founding dir.), Alpha Epsilon Pi. (life). Democrat. Jewish. Clubs: Elks, Miami Ski. Home: 9037 SW 62d Terr Miami FL 33173 Office: PO Box 650126 Miami FL 33165

SHERMAN, FRANCES BUCK, artist; b. Santo Domingo, Jan. 30; d. Harry Catlett and Elizabeth (F.) Buck; student Sophie Newcombe Coll., 1936-37, St. Mary's Coll., 1937, New Orleans Acad. Art, 1947-48, Atlanta Sch. Art, 1967-68, Jacksonville Mus. Art, 1975-76; m. Walter Scott Sherman, Jr., Nov. 9, 1950; children by previous marriage—Thomas M. Frasier, Harry Buck Frasier; children—Gregory Scott, Frances Carolyn. Pvt. practice art instruction, New Orleans, 1947; free-lance model, New Orleans, 1948; staff model Burdines Dept. Store, Miami, Fla., 1949-50, asst. fashion coordinator, 1951-52; fashion cons. Coronet Sch. Modeling, Miami, 1953-54; art instr. Tampa Realistic Artist Gallery (Fla.), 1969-70; free-lance artist and photographer, Jacksonville, Fla., 1976—; art demonstrator Festival of Arts, Artists Gallery, Museum Arts and Scis., Arts Assembly, Jacksonville; art exhibit judge Jacksonville Women's Club; poetry contest judge Ind. Life Ins. Co., Jacksonville. Active Republican campaign hdqrs., 1976; hostess Jacksonville Arts Assembly, 1977. Named Outstanding Patriot, Patriots of Am. Bicentennial, 1976; recipient certificate of recognition Bicentennial Commn. Jacksonville, 1976. Fellow Intercontinental Biog. Assn.; mem. Am. Artists Profl. League, Nat. League Am. Pen Women (pres. Jacksonville br. and v.p. state assn. 1974-76), Fla. Poetry Soc., Arts Assembly Jacksonville, Jacksonville Art Museum, Nat. Writers Club, Artists Gallery (Jacksonville). Episcopalian. Poems included in various periodicals. Home: 4331 San Jose Ln Jacksonville FL 32207

SHERMAN, JAMES OWEN, psychologist; b. Iron Mountain, Mich., June 29, 1942; s. James W. and Gwendolyn S.; B.S., Trinity U., 1965, M.S., 1966; Ph.D., U.S. Internat. U., 1975; m. Marcia Anne Butler, June 3, 1963; children—Katherine Layne, Kelly Anne. Psychometrist, Trinity U. Counseling Center, San Antonio, 1965-66; lectr. U. Guelph (Ont., Can.), 1967-68; therapist Ont. Dept. Correctional Services, Galt, 1968-69; instr. Our Lady of the Lake U., San Antonio, 1969-73; child psychologist Bexar County (Tex.), San Antonio, 1975—; adj. asst. prof. Trinity U., 1977—; pvt. practice, 1976—. Presbyn. Gen. scholar, 1963-65. Mem. Assn. Humanistic Psychology, Am., Southwestern, Rocky Mountain psychol. assns. Home: 118 Bryker St San Antonio TX 78209 Office: 203 Nueva St W San Antonio TX 78209

SHERMAN, JEROME KALMAN, anatomist, cryobiologist; b. Bklyn., Aug. 14, 1925; s. Murray and Beatrice (Freilich) S.; A.B., Brown U., 1947; M.S., Western Res. U., 1949; Ph.D., State U. Iowa, 1954; m. Hildegard Schroeder, Dec. 26, 1952; children—Karen Sherman Vesole, Marc, Keith. Research asso. U. Iowa, 1952-54; Am. Found. Biol. Research, Madison, Wis., 1954-58; mem. faculty U. Ark. for Med. Scis. Med. Coll., Little Rock, 1958—, prof. anatomy, 1967—; spl. prof. chair of cryobiology, Chung Hsin U., Taiwan, 1973-74, cons. human male fertility, human semen cryobanking. Active local Boy Scouts Am., also Explorer Scouts; mem. bd. Temple B'nai Israel, Little Rock; adv. bd. Day Care Center, Little Rock. Served with USN, 1943-46. Recipient Lederle Med. Faculty award, 1961-64; Fulbright Sr. research award, Germany, 1965-66; Taiwan Nat. Sci. Council award, 1974. Club: Lions. Author articles in field. Home: 3012 N Grant St Little Rock AR 72207 Office: UAMS Dept Anatomy 4301 W Markham St Little Rock AR 72205

SHERMAN, JOHN FRANCIS, fin. exec.; b. N.Y.C., Apr. 3, 1933; s. Joseph Patrick and Anne Marie (McKenna) S.; B.B.A., St. Johns U., 1958; M.B.A., North Tex. State U., 1976; A.B.D., 1979; m. Jacqueline Ann Duncan, Sept. 10, 1960; children—Kara Elizabeth, Patrick Duncan, Cindy Marie. Sr. accountant Haskins & Sells, C.P.A.'s, N.Y.C., Dallas, 1958-65; controller Investment Bankers Inc., Dallas, 1965-67; chief fin. officer Nardis of Dallas, Inc., 1967—, also dir.; lectr. U. Tex., Dallas, 1978—, North Tex. State U., 1978—. Served with U.S. Army, 1952-54. C.P.A., Tex. Mem. Am. Inst. C.P.A.'s, Tex. Soc. C.P.A.'s, Nat. Assn. Accts., Am. Acctg. Assn., Fin. Execs. Inst. Roman Catholic. Office: 1300 Corinth St Dallas TX 75215

SHERMAN, KEITH, restaurant owner; b. Shreveport, La., Sept. 26, 1942; s. Keith Edward and Mercedes Sheplee S.; B.S. in Elec. Engring., Tex. A&M U., 1969; m. George Ann Love, July 3, 1964; children—Kevin Wade, Kerri Lynn. Mission engr. Remote Sensing, Inc., Houston, 1969-72; cons. to remote sensing industry, Houston, 1972-73; pres. The Jalapeño Tree, Inc., Webster, Tex., 1973—, chmn. bd., 1976—. Bd. dirs. Clear Lake Area Little League, 1975-76, pres., 1977. Served with U.S. Army, 1963-65. Decorated Bronze Star, Purple Heart, Army Commendation medal. Mem. Nat. Restaurant Assn., Tex. Restaurant Assn., Webster Bus. Assn. (v.p. 1979, dir.). Republican. Club: Rotary. Home: 3111 Lazy Pine Ln LaPorte TX 77571 Office: The Jalapeño Tree Inc 403 NASA Blvd Webster TX 77598

SHERMAN, LOUIS LEROY, educator; b. Leona, Kans., Oct. 22, 1932; s. Louis Arthur and Alma Lorene (Blum) S.; Mus.B., Bethany (Kans.) Coll., 1954; M.S., Kans. State U., 1962; Ph.D., U. Wis., Madison, 1976; m. Mildred Mozelle Clark, Aug. 14, 1954; children—Clark Michael, Gayla Dawn. Music tchr., Topeka, 1954-55, Norton, Kans., 1957-60; teaching asst. Kans. State U., 1960-62, instr. music, 1962-66; teaching asst. U. Wis., Madison, 1966-70, asst. coordinator student teaching, 1970-73; prof. music Howard Payne U., Brownwood, Tex., 1973—; adjudicator, clinician; ch. musician, recitalist, opera, oratorio and musical theatre; singer various polit. convs., also USO concerts. Served with U.S. Army, 1955-57. Elected to Ft. Kobbe (C.Z.) Hall of Fame, 1957; Bapt. Gen. Conv. Tex. Christian Edn. Coordinating Bd. grantee, 1978, 79. Mem. Nat. Assn. Tchrs. of Singing, Music Educators Nat. Conf., Tex. Music Educators Conf., Tex. Music Educators Assn., Am. Choral Dirs. Assn., Tex. Choral Dirs. Assn., Adult Edn. Assn. U.S.A., Aircraft Owners and Pilots Assn., Phi Mu Alpha Sinfonia (Orpheus award), Phi Delta Kappa, Pi Lambda Theta. Baptist. Club: Masons (Norton, Kans. and Brownwood). Home: 1705 Southgate Dr Brownwood TX 76801 Office: Howard Payne U Brownwood TX 76801

SHERMAN, RICHARD LAWRENCE, chiropractor; b. N.Y.C., July 15, 1944; s. Hyman and Natalie (Rubenstein) S.; B.S. in Life Scis., N.Y. Inst. Tech., 1975; D.C., Columbia Inst. Chiropractic, 1967; m. Carol Rebecca Bruno, Nov. 28, 1974; 1 son by previous marriage, Ryan Scott. Practice chiropractic medicine, Bronx, N.Y., 1967-74, Scarsdale, N.Y., 1974—; dir. Tremont Health Group, Bronx, 1970; dir. chiropractic Second Ave. Health Group, 1971—; dir. chiropractic Unity Health Care, Bronx, 1975—; dir. chiropractic Shakespeare Med. and Morris Heights Med., 1976—; health cons. City of Sunrise, 1979-80; practice chiropractic and acupuncture, Ft. Lauderdale, Fla.; cons. in field. Exec. chmn. fund raising campaign Sunrise United Way, 1979. Recipient merit award Columbia Inst. Chiropractic, 1967; award for service City of Sunrise, 1980; diplomate Nat. Bd. Chiropractic Examiners; cert. in acupuncture. Mem. Am. (council of diagnosis and internal disorders 1980), N.Y. State, Fla. chiropractic assns., Broward County Chiropractic Soc., Sci. Civil Rights and Research Found., Parker Research Found., Empire State Chiropractic Assn., Beta Omega Chi. Club: Elks. Office: 2133 NE 26th St Fort Lauderdale FL 33306

SHERMAN, ROBERT FREDERICK, property mgmt. exec.; b. Bridgeport, Conn., Dec. 28, 1942; s. Clifford Gould and Katherine Marie (Zumstag) S.; B.S., Bates Coll., 1964; M.B.A., Columbia U., 1967; m. Carolyn Harmon Kinney, Sept. 24, 1966; children—Jeffrey, Jonathan. Systems analyst First Nat. City Bank, N.Y.C., 1972; sec., dir. Rohdie-Schneider Assos., Upper Montclair, N.J., 1973-74; exec. v.p., dir. Schneider & Sherman Assos., Clifton, N.J. and Dallas, 1974—; pres., dir. S & S Properties, Inc., Dallas, 1975—. Tex. rep. alumni in admissions Bates Coll. Served in USNR, 1968-72. Mem. Nat. Assn. Securities Dealers, Tex. (dir.), Dallas apt. assns., North Dallas C. of C., N.J. Bates Coll. Alumni Assn. (sec.-treas. 1975-76). Episcopalian.

SHERMAN, RUTH TODD, marriage counselor; b. Memphis, July 3, 1924; d. Robbie M. and Lillie M. (Shreve) Todd; B.S., Memphis State U., 1972, M.Ed., 1975. With supply mgmt. dept. Def. Gen. Supply Center, Richmond, Va., 1979—; pvt. practice marriage, family and divorce counseling, Richmond, 1979—. Youth leader, dir. Assembly of God Chs., Memphis, 1962-66; drug counselor Teen Challenge Girls Home, Memphis, 1973-74; counselor Harbor House div. Alcoholics Anonymous, Memphis, 1974, Planned Parenthood, Memphis, 1974-77. Mem. Am. Assn. Marriage and Family Counselors, Am. Personnel and Guidance Assn. Democrat. Mem. Assemblies of God Ch. Home and office: 401 Westover Hills Apt B Richmond VA 23225

SHERMAN, WILLIAM EURASTI, lawyer; b. Tampa, Fla., Apr. 28, 1927; s. William Eurasti and Maryetta (Abbott) S.; B.A., U. Fla., 1950, J.D., 1953; m. Frances Rogers, 1950 (div. 1973); children—William Eurasti III, Valerie Ann; m. 2d, Vicki Lynn Peterson, June 9, 1974. Admitted to Fla. bar, 1953; spl. asst. to Atty. Gen. Fla., Tallahassee, 1953; asso. Francis P. Whitehair, DeLand, Fla., 1954-57; practiced in DeLand, 1958—; mem. firm Hall, Sweeney & Godbee, 1958-59, Hull, Landis, Graham & French, 1960-66, Landis, Graham, French, Husfeld and Sherman, 1966-69, Landis, Graham, French, Husfeld, Sherman & Ford, Profl. Assn., 1969—. Mem. Volusia County Charter Study Commn., 1969-71, Volusia County Charter Rev. Commn., 1975; mem. nominating commn. 5th Dist. Ct. Appeals, 1979. Bd. dirs. Internat. Music Festivals, Inc., 1969-71, Montreat (N.C.)-Anderson Coll., 1961-71, Mountain Retreat Assn., 1961-71. Served with Signal Corps, AUS, World War II. Mem. Fla. Bar (gov. 1970—, chmn. legislative com. 1973-76, exec. com. real property probate and trust sect., mem. Uniform Probate Code Study Commn.), Am., Volusia County (pres. 1969-70) bar assns., DeLand C. of C. (v.p. 1970-71), Phi Delta Phi, Pi Kappa Alpha, Alpha Delta Sigma. Democrat. Presbyn. (elder). Rotarian. Club: Halifax. Home: 810 Eastover Circle PO Box 329 DeLand FL 32720 Office: 110 W Indiana Ave DeLand FL 32720 also 412 N Wild Olive Daytona FL 32018

SHERMAN, WILLIAM FARRAR, state legislator; b. Little Rock, Sept. 12, 1937; s. Lincoln Farrar and Nancy Irene (Lowe) S.; B.A. in History and Govt., U. Ark., 1960; LL.B., U. Va., 1964; m. Carole Lynn Williams, Sept. 2, 1967; children—John F., Anna Katherine, Lucy. Admitted to Ark. bar, 1964, since practiced in Little Rock; partner firm Jacoway & Sherman, 1971—; asst. U.S. atty. Eastern Dist. Ark., 1966-69; commr. Ark. Securities Commn., 1969-71; mem. Ark. Ho. of Reps., 1974—; del. Ark. Constl. Conv., 1979. Bd. dirs. Little Rock Better Bus. Bur., Mental Health Assn. Ark., United Cerebral Palsy Assn. Ark.; bd. stewards First United Methodist Ch., Little Rock; committeeman Pulaski County Democratic Party, 1972-74; Dem. Presdl. campaign coordinator Pulaski County, 1972. Served with AUS, 1960-61. Fellow Ark. Bar Found.; mem. Am., Ark., Pulaski County bar assns. Home: 450 Midland St Little Rock AR 72205 Office: 504 Pyramid Life Bldg Little Rock AR 72201

SHERRARD, DAVID GIBSON, III, mktg. exec.; b. San Antonio, Nov. 10, 1942; s. David Gibson and Mercedes (Montesinos) S.; student N.C. State U., 1961-64; B.B.A. in Mgmt., Baylor U., 1974, B.B.A. in Acctg., 1975. Claims examiner VA, Waco, Tex., 1973-74; methods analyst Ga. Power Co., Atlanta, 1976-78; mktg. dir. Infoservices, Inc., Atlanta, 1978—. mktg. dir. Young Careers, Atlanta, 1979—. Served with U.S. Army, 1964-72. Decorated Bronze Star medal (3), Army Commendation medal, Air medal (15), Purple Heart; recipient Public Service commendations State of Ga., 1975, 76. Mem. Assn. U.S. Army, N.G. Assn. U.S., Alpha Phi Omega. Roman Catholic. Clubs: Atlanta Ski, Navy Flying, Sports Car Am., Holiday Marina. Home: 409X Lonesome Pine Ln Atlanta GA 30339 Office: Suite 22 1728 Montreal Circle Tucker GA 30084

SHERRATT, THOMAS ARCHIBALD, sch. psychologist; b. Raleigh, N.C., July 25, 1947; s. William Archibald and Evelyn Edward (McCullers) S.; A.A., Louisburg Coll., 1969; B.A., U. N.C., 1975; M.A., Pepperdine U., 1978. Mental health worker W. H. Trentman Mental Health Clinic, Raleigh, N.C., 1973-74; postulant Soc. of St. Francis, Mt. Sinai, L.I., 1975; spl. training instr. Self-Injurious Behaviour Program, Murdoch Center for the Retarded, Butner, N.C., 1975-76, ednl. specialist Developmental Skills Div., 1976-79; sch. psychologist continuing edn. program Drug Action Wake County, Raleigh, 1979—. Founding mem. U.S. chpt. 63 Amnesty Internat., 1979. Mem. Am. Assn. on Mental Deficiency (asso.), Am. Psychol. Assn. (asso.), N.C. Assn. for Drug Abuse Prevention, Audubon Soc., Nature Conservancy, Fortune Soc., Sierra Club, Order of the First Families of Va., Colonial Order of the Crown. Roman Catholic. Home: 1010 Virgie St Durham NC 27705 Office: Drug Action Wake County PO Box 12021 Raleigh NC 27605

SHERRELL, MARVIN EDWARD, petrochem. co. exec.; b. Mablevale, Ark., July 1, 1923; s. Mittleton Miller and Barbara Ellen (Lewis) S.; m. Carlene Ruth Rice Castleberry, Sept. 7, 1947; 1 dau., Vicky Lynn; 1 stepdau., Beverly Ann Castleberry Phelps. Operator, Neches Butane Co., Port Neches, Tex., 1947-56; tng. supt. ARCO Chem. Co., Channelview, Tex., 1956—. Served with U.S. Army, 1943-45. Decorated Purple Heart. Mem. Am. Petroleum Inst. (chmn. dist. 3 com. tng. and devel.), Am. Soc. Tng. and Devel. Baptist. Club: Masons. Home: 1310 Locklaine Pasadena TX 77502 Office: PO Box 777 Channelview TX 77530

SHERRILL, DONALD GENE, research planner; b. Youngstown, Ohio, May 22, 1944; s. G. D. and Caroline (Ribble) S.; student Iowa State U., 1962-63; B.A. in Sociology and Psychology, Mankato (Minn.) State U., 1967; M.C.P., Ga. Inst. Tech., 1973; m. Brenda Harris, June 4, 1972; 1 son, David Andrew. Community organizer AAY-CD, Inc., Charleston, W.Va., 1967-68; quality assurance mgr. Singer-Gen. Precision, Inc., Silver Springs, Md., 1970; planning intern S.C. State Planning and Grants Office, Columbia, 1970-71; research scientist Battelle So. Ops., Atlanta and New Orleans, 1973-79; research scientist Ga. Inst. Tech. Expt. Sta., 1979—; La. del. Am. Inst. Planners Policy Confs., Dallas and Washington, 1976-77. Co-chmn. spl. projects com. Ga. chpt. World Future Soc., 1979—. Served with USNR, 1967-69. Mem. Am. Planning Assn., Am. Inst. Cert. Planners. Author research studies C.E. and govtl. groups. Home: 1789 Eastgate Dr Stone Mountain GA 30087 Office: Ga Inst Tech Engring Expt Sta Atlanta GA 30332

SHERRILL, JAMES FENTON, mfg. co. exec.; b. Columbus, Miss., Dec. 19, 1924; s. Leon T. and Bertha E. (Geer) S.; student engring. U. Ala., 1946-54; LL.B., LaSalle Extension U., 1966; m. Hazel Joyce Kilgore, July 30, 1949; children—James Fenton, William Lynn, Julia LuAnn. Prodn. and material control mgr. Butler Mfg. Co., Birmingham, Ala., 1951-62; prodn. specialist Chrysler Corp., Huntsville, Ala., 1962-69; div. plant mgr. Thomas Industries, Inc., Johnson City, Tenn., 1969-70; v.p. mfg. Mor-Flo Industries, Inc., Johnson City and Cleve., 1970—; also dir.; gen. mgr. Tenn. Tank Co., Johnson City. Served with USNR, 1943-46, 50-51. Mem. Am. Prodn. and Inventory Control Soc., Civitan Internat. (program dir. 1960-62), Exchange Club (dir. 1968-69). Baptist. Club: Johnson City Country. Home: 1900 Sinking Creek Rd Johnson City TN 37601 Office: PO Box 1378 Johnson City TN 37601

SHERRILL, VANITA LOUISE LYTLE, educator; b. Nashville, Feb. 23, 1945; d. Erskine W., Jr., and Vanita Belle (Dismukes) Lytle; B.A., Fisk U., 1966, M.A., 1971: postgrad. Vanderbilt U., 1980—; 1 son, Jason Erskine Lytle Sherrill. Asst. project adminstr. child devel. clinic Meharry Med. Coll., Nashville, 1966-69; research asst. Tenn. State Planning Commn., Nashville, 1970-71; social worker cons. Metro Health Dept., Nashville, 1971-72; coordinator vocat. diagnostic component Nashville Concentrated Employment Program, 1973; instr., field supr. Vol. State Community Coll., Gallatin, Tenn., 1973—; edn. intern U. Tenn., 1977; instr. Gerontology Inst. Tenn. State U., 1977. Bd. dirs. Alive, Inc.; sec. bd. dirs. Samaritan Center; pres. Dede Wallace N.E. Br.; bd. dirs. Dede Wallace Center, Council of Community Services, Centry III Commn., Leadership Nashville, Hendersonville Chpt. Links, Inc., Jack and Jill, Inc., Alliance for Black Social Welfare, Dem. Women's Club of Davidson County; pres. info. and referral adv. com. Council Community Services. Phelps-Stokes Fund grantee for study in W. Africa, 1979. Mem. Vanderbilt U. Comm. for Behavioral Scis. of Instl. Review Bd., Am. Psychol. Assn., Am. Personnel and Guidance Assn., Nat. Assn. Black Social Workers, Delta Sigma Theta. Baptist. Home: 3503 Albion St Nashville TN 37209 Office: Nashville Pike Volunteer State Community College Gallatin TN 37066

SHERRINGTON, BRIAN THOMAS, pediatrician; b. Glasgow, Scotland, May 29, 1947; came to U.S., 1957, naturalized, 1969; s. Thomas Baldwin and Janet Barr (McLaughlin) S.; B.S., UCLA, 1969; M.D., U. Fla., 1973; m. Jeanette Cope, Apr. 14, 1973; children—Sheena Elaine, Laura Lynn. Intern, Pensacola (Fla.) Ednl. Program, 1973-74, resident in pediatrics, 1974-76; practice medicine specializing in pediatrics, Southern Pines, N.C., 1976—; mem. staff Moore Meml. Hosp., Pinehurst, N.C. Diplomate Am. Bd. Pediatrics. Fellow Am. Acad. Pediatrics; mem. AMA, N.C. Pediatric Soc. Roman Catholic. Home: 920 N Saylor St Southern Pines NC 28387 Office: Town Center Bldg Broad St Southern Pines NC 28387

SHERROD, HILTON HOWARD, brokerage firm exec., health care co. exec.; b. Waco, Tex., June 28, 1931; s. Marvin Ray and Tennie Louise (Davis) S.; B.S., Abilene Christian U., 1954; m. Reba D. Jenson, Sept. 3, 1954; children—Stephen K., Mitchell D., Jim N. Salesman, Upjohn co., Big Spring, Tex., 1954-61; stockbroker Goodbody & Co., Lubbock and Austin, Tex., 1962-70, br. mgr. Goodbody, Rotan & Mosle, Austin, 1970-72; pres. Homemakers of Austin, 1973—; br. mgr. Dean, Witter & Reynolds, Austin, Temple, 1978—; co-founder, dir. HomeHelp Care, 1974—. Bd. dirs. Hensel Meml. Camp, 1973—, pres., 1974-78. Served with USNR, 1946-51. Mem. Greater West Tex. Healthcare Assn. (dir. 1976--), Am. Opinion Speakers Bur. Mem. Ch. of Christ. Office: Homemakers of Austin Inc 611 Rio Grande Austin TX 78701

SHERWOOD, CHARLES FREDERICK, educator; b. Kalkaska, Mich., May 21, 1932; s. Elmer Creigh and Mabel Alta (Washburn) S.; B.A., Western Mich. U., 1954; M.A., Eastern Mich. U., 1959, Sp.A. in Reading, 1967; Ed.D., U. Miami (Fla.), 1972; m. Jeanne Marilyn Adams, June 13, 1953; children—Geoffrey, Randon, Stuart. Tchr. English, South Redford and Allen Park, Mich., 1956-60, counselor South Redford, 1960-65, dir. reading, 1965-68; specialist reading Miami, 1968-70; asst. prof. edn. Barry Coll., Miami, 1970-73; asso. prof., coordinator reading clinic U. Miss., University, 1973-77, asso. prof. elem. edn., coordinator reading edn., 1977—; cons. reading Ala., Ark., Miss. Served with U.S. Army, 1954-56. Mem. Internat. Reading

Assn. (state coordinator 1978—), Assn. for Supervision and Curriculum Devel., Miss. Reading Assn., Ole Miss Reading Council, Phi Delta Kappa, Kappa Delta Pi. Editor Mich. Reading Jour., 1966-68, Miss. Reading Jour., 1976—. Contbr. articles to profl. jours. Office: Reading Center U Miss University MS 38677

SHETLER, WILLIAM ALAN, social work adminstr.; b. Akron, Ohio, Mar. 25, 1947; s. Leonard Franklin and Harriet Helen S.; B.A., Miami U., Oxford, Ohio, 1969; M.S.W., U. Denver, 1976; m. Katherine Beaver, Nov. 4, 1972. Protective services worker Fla. Div. Family Services, St. Augustine, 1971-74; clin. social worker Tri-County Mental Health Services, St. Augustine, 1976-78; residence supr. Children's Home Soc., Jacksonville, Fla., 1978—. Mem. Nat. Assn. Social Workers, Acad. Cert. Social Workers. Office: Childrens Home Society PO Box 10097 Jacksonville FL 32207

SHETLEY, JACK HUBERT, accountant; b. Cocke County, Tenn., Apr. 15, 1912; s. William Henry ano Ethel Diane (Hunnicutt) S.; B.S. in Commerce, Wade Hampton Coll., 1960, D.Humanities, 1962; m. Willie Edith Lee, July 3, 1937; children—Mignon Harriet (Mrs. Stan Davis), Edith Elaine. Self employed pub. accountant, Greenville, S.C., 1945—. Sec., S.C. State Bd. Nursing. Served with inf. AUS, 1942-45. Mem. Nat., S.C. assns. pub. accountants, Am. Legion. Mason (Shriner), Moose, Elk, Toastmaster (dist. gov. 1969-70). Clubs: Touchdown, Tipoff. Home: 19 Cureton St Greenville SC 29605 Office: 209 E Stone Ave Greenville SC 29601

SHETTY, SHASHINDRA PADMA, physician; b. Udupi, India, Sept. 15, 1945; came to U.S., 1971; s. Padma S. and Sundari P. S.; student K.C. Coll., Bombay, India, 1965; M.B.B.S., Seth G. S. Med. Coll., Bombay, 1971; m. Deepika Shetty, Feb. 4, 1976; 1 son, Vilaas S. Rotating intern Meth. Hosp., Gary, Ind., 1972; resident in internal medicine, fellow in endocrinology VA Hosp., Northport, N.Y., 1973-76, chief resident, 1976-77; practice medicine specializing in internal medicine and endocrinology, Shawnee, Okla., 1977—. Diplomate Am. Bd. Internal Medicine. Mem. A.C.P., AMA, Am. Soc. Internal Medicine, Okla. State Med. Assn., Pottawatomie County Med. Assn. Office: 1902 G Cooper Dr Shawnee OK 74801

SHIELD, CHARLES FRANKLIN, JR., computer corp. exec.; b. Ontario, Cal., Apr. 2, 1919; s. Charles Franklin and Esther Amelia (Liller) S.; B.S. in Engring., UCLA, 1950; m. Annabelle Wingo, Dec. 12, 1944; children—Charles Franklin III, Linda Kay (Mrs. James Wells), Anita Louise (Mrs. Douglas Lee), James Floyd, Terra Lea. With IBM Corp., 1950—, tech. asst., Los Angeles and Endicott, N.Y., 1950-56, tech. engr., 1956-60, Owego, N.Y., 1960-62, staff engr., Oklahoma City, 1962-63, staff engr., Huntsville, Ala., 1963-65, project engr., 1965-69, staff engr., 1969-72, staff program evaluation analyst, 1972-76, program mgmt. solar energy studies, 1976—; tchr. summer course Samford U., USAF, IBM Corp. Active Boy Scout Am. Served to lt. col USAAF, 1941-46; mem. Res. (ret.). Decorated D.F.C., Air medal with 7 oak leaf clusters. Mem. IEEE (sr.), Air Force Assn. (state sect.-treas. 1966), Res. Officers Assn. (life mem.; pres. Ala. dept. 1966, nat. membership dir., state membership chmn. 1971—). Co-author: Computer Program Model for Job Resource Allocation, 1971. Comml. pilot. Home: 5611 Woodridge St Huntsville AL 35802 Office: 150 Sparkman Dr Huntsville AL 35805

SHIELDS, CHARLIE DEWITT, savs. and loan exec.; b. Center, Miss., Mar. 26, 1909; s. Charlie Walter and Mary Natie (Price) S.; grad. So. Bus. Coll., Vicksburg, Miss., 1929; law degree, Am. Law Sch., Chgo., 1930; m. Beatrice Williams, Sept. 2, 1934; children—Camille (Mrs. Lloyd Stakes), Sharlynn (Mrs. A.P. Baltzell). Admitted to Miss. bar, 1930, since practiced in Meridian; ins. agt. So. Guaranty Ins. Co., Meridian; founder, pres. First Savs. & Loan Assn., Meridian 1952-69; pres. Bankers Trust Savs. & Loan Assn. (merger First Savs. & Loan Assn. 1969), Jackson, Miss., 1969-76; individual practice law Jones, Shields & Woodall, 1976—; dir. So. Guaranty Ins. Co., Montgomery, Ala. City councilman, Meridian, 1956-60; chmn. Meridian Selective Service Draft Bd., 1952-72; chmn., sec. Lauderdale County Democratic exec. com., 1938-78. Former mem. bd. dirs. Meridian area Salvation Army; former trustee Clarke Coll., Newton, Miss., also pvt. founds. Served with U.S. Army, 1927-28. Mem. Miss. State Bar, Lauderdale County Bar Assn., Miss. Savs. and Loan Inst. Baptist (deacon). Mason (Shriner), Lion (pres. 1969-70). Home: 2715 28th St Meridian MS 39301 Office: 102 Shields Bldg Meridian MS 39301

SHIELDS, RICHARD HINTON, feed mill exec.; b. Lexington, Ky., Aug. 12, 1949; s. J. Paul and Frances Margaret (Hinton) S.; student U. Ky., 1968-70; m. Cordelia Douglas Strange, May 9, 1970; children—Carrie Ann, Amy Douglas. Owner, mgr. Beef Back Grounding Feed Lot, 1970-73; salesman Moorman Mfg., 1973-74; owner, operator Bourbon Feed Sale, Inc., Paris, Ky., 1974-77; gen. mgr. Custom Feed Mill, Morganfield, Ky., 1977-79, pres., 1979—. Republican. Presbyterian. Home: 419 S Morgan St Morganfield KY 42437 Office: 630 N Hughes St Morganfield KY 42437

SHIELDS, ROBERT JOSEPH, educator; b. Jacksonville, Ill., Aug. 14, 1938; s. Robert Lee and Theresa Catherine (Conroy) S.; student Ill. State U., Normal, 1956-58. Unit mgr. ABC, N.Y.C., 1959, CBS, N.Y.C., 1960; clinic coordinator Nat. Cheerleaders Assn., Dallas, 1960-71; dir., founder World Cheerleader Council, Dallas, 1971—. Served with U.S. Army, 1962-64. Mem. Nat. Assn. Student Councils, Nat. Assn. Workshop Dirs. Republican. Methodist. Author: Cheers & Chants, vol. 1, 1973, vol. 2, 1974, vol. 3, 1975, vol. 4, 1977, vol. 5, 1979; Cheers & Poms, yearly, 1973-79. Address: PO Box 7328 Dallas TX 75209

SHIELDS, STEPHEN JOHN, constrn. co. exec.; b. Dallas, Aug. 21, 1952; s. John Ellis and Billie Jean (Terry) S.; student Sam Houston U., 1970-72, U. Houston, 1972-73; m. Janet Kay White, June 14, 1974. Estimator, W. H. Branson Co., Houston, 1970-78; partner Shields & Shields Co., Houston, 1978-79; pres. Shields Constructors, Inc., Houston, 1979—; cons. in field. Mem. Houston Sheet Metal Contractors Assn., Sheet Metal and Air Conditioning Contractors Nat. Assn., Nat. Roofing Contractors Assn. Republican. Roman Catholic. Office: 9003 Opelika St Houston TX 77080

SHIELS, JAMES HENRY, JR., advt. and indsl. art. co. exec.; b. Dallas, Feb. 19, 1930; s. James Henry and Mary (Robbins) S.; B.A., So. Methodist U., 1957; m. Gay Nell Steelmen, June 28, 1957; 1 son, James Henry, III. Staff artist, sales rep., 1956-58; owner, art dir. Henry Shiels Indsl. and Advt. Art Studio, Dallas, 1958—. Vice pres., vice chmn. bd. Mary Shiels Hosp., 1966-74, chmn. bd. dirs., 1974—. Served to 1st lt. USAF, 1952-56; capt. USAF Res., 1960-65. Mem. Nat. Soc. Art Dirs., Dallas-Ft. Worth Art Dirs. Club, Dallas-Ft. Worth Soc. Visual Communications (dir.). Presbyn. Home: 2905 Purdue Dallas TX 75225 Office: Suite 216 Four Lemmon Park E Dallas TX 75204

SHIH, JASON CHANG-CHUAN, engr., architect, educator; b. Formosa, Sept. 19, 1940; came to U.S., 1964, naturalized, 1972; M.S., Va. Poly. Inst., 1966; Ph.D., Duke U., 1970; m. Janet Chin, May 20, 1971; children—Jennifer April, Jeffrey Allan. Sr. structural engr. Hakar-Best Assos., Inc., Chapel Hill, N.C., 1968-71; chief engr., v.p. John D. Latimer and Assos., Durham, N.C. and Taunton, Mass., 1971-76; asso. prof., dir. office bldg. research Sch. Architecture, La. State U., Baton Rouge, 1976—. Co-winner N.C. honor awards AIA, 1974, 75, 76; grantee U.S. Community Service Adminstrn., 1978-79, Dept. Energy, 1978, La. State Govt., 1977, 78, 79; lic. profl. engr., La., N.C., Va., Mass., Tex., Calif. Mem. Nat. Soc. Profl. Engrs. (chmn. bldg. code com. Central Carolina chpt. 1976), ASCE, Nat. Inst. Bldg. Sci. (nat. consultative mem.), Internat. Solar Soc. Invited speaker housing conf., Baton Rouge, 1977; invited program cons. conf., 1977-78, panel mem., 1977; chmn. structural div. Nat. Conf. on Earth Covered Settlements, 1978, co-editor Conf. Proc., 1979; contbr. sect. to book, reports, papers to profl. publs. in field. Home: 7703 Amesbury Circle Baton Rouge LA 70808 Office: Dept Architecture La State Univ Baton Rouge LA 70803

SHIH, SUN-FU, educator, engr.; b. Taoyuan, Taiwan, Mar. 2, 1935; s. Tung-Chi and Tsang-Wan S.; B.S., Nat. Taiwan U., 1959; M.S., N.C. State U., 19—, Ph.D., 1969; m. Wen-Fu Shih, Sept. 14, 1965; 1 child, Heidi Wen. Asst. engr. Taiwan Water Conservancy Bur., Taipei, 1961-64; grad. research asst. dept. agr. and biol. engring. N.C. State U., Raleigh, 1964-68, research asso., 1968-72; systems engr. II, S. Fla. Water Mgmt. Dist., West Palm Beach, Fla., 1972-76; asso. prof. Inst. Food and Agrl. Scis., Agrl. Research and Edn. Center, U. Fla., Belle Glade, 1976—. Mem. Am. Soc. Agrl. Engrs., ASCE, Am. Geophys. Union, Am. Water Resource Assn., Internat. Water Resource Assn., Am. Soc. Agronomy, Soil Conservation Soc. Am. Contbr. articles to profl. jours. Home: 1000 NW 39th St Gainesville FL 32605 Office: Univ of Fla PO Drawer A Belle Glade FL 33430

SHIH, WEN-FU PENG, statistician; b. Tokyo, Japan, Sept. 10, 1938; d. Yu-Tung and Chu-Mei Peng; came to U.S., 1965, naturalized, 1974; B.S., Nat. Taiwan U., 1961; M.S., N.C. State U., 1968; m. Sun-Fu Shih, Sept. 14, 1965; 1 dau., Heidi Wen. Tchr. math. Tarlung High Sch., Taiwan, 1961-65; research asst. dept. statistics N.C. State U., Raleigh, 1965-72; research asso. Inst. Behavioral Research, Fla. Atlantic U., Boca Raton, 1972-79; survey research dir. Bur. Econ. and Bus. Research, U. Fla., Gainesville, 1979—. Mem. Am. Statis. Assn., Biometric Soc., Am. Sociol. Soc., Technometric. Home: 1000 NW 39th St Gainesville FL 32605 Office: Bur Econ and Bus Research U Fla Gainesville FL 32611

SHIHATA, FIKRY KAMEL, anesthesiologist; b. Cairo, Egypt, Mar. 1, 1939; came to U.S., 1970, naturalized, 1975; s. Kamel Abdel Malak and Nargis Botrus (Gergis) S.; B.S., Ain-Shams Faculty of Sci., 1956, M.B. B.Ch., Sch. Med., 1962; m. Nahed Fakhry Francis; children—Nivin C., Jacqueline A. Intern, Muhlenberg Med. Center, 1970-71; resident Royal Albert Edward Infirmary, Eng., 1967-70, N.Y. Hosp., N.Y.C., 1971-73; instr. anesthesiology Cornell Med. Center, 1971-73; staff anesthesiologist Geisinger (Pa.) Med. Center, 1973-75, also med. dir. Sch. of Nurse Anesthetists; chief dept. anesthesiology Hamilton Meml. Hosp., Dalton, Ga., 1975—. Diplomate Am. Bd. Anesthesiology. Fellow Am. Coll. Anesthesiologists; mem. Am. Soc. Anesthesiologists, Ga. Soc. Anesthesiologists, AMA, Manchester Med. Soc. Club: Elks. Home: 1708 Southmont Dr Dalton GA 30720 Office: Hamilton Memorial Hospital Dalton GA 30720

SHILESKY, DONALD MARK, environ. engr.; b. Akron, Ohio, July 4, 1942; s. Ben Fred and Rose (Pollock) S.; B.S. in Biology, U. Cin., 1964, M.S. in Environ. Engring., 1966; D.Sc. (fellow), Washington U., 1973; m. Eileen Theresa Nevole, Jan. 25, 1969; children—David Mark, Michael S. Research asst., applied sci. div. Litton Industries, Mpls., 1969-70, mem. sr. tech. staff, Camarillo, Calif., 1970-71; program dir. East-West Gateway Coordinating Council, St. Louis, 1971-73; tech. coordinator Browning-Ferris Industries, Inc., Houston, 1973-75; dir. civil systems Waste Mgmt. Inc., Oak Brook, Ill., 1975-76; mgr. environ. studies Engring. Science, McLean, Va., 1976-77; v.p. SCS Engrs., Reston, Va., 1977—. Recipient Project of the Year award Camarillo Jaycees, 1970; USPHS grantee, 1966-67. Mem. ASCE (solid waste mgmt. com. 1975—, chmn. profl. coordinating com. 1978—), Nat. Solid Wastes Mgmt. (chmn. chem. waste com. 1974-76), Sigma Xi. Mem. editorial adv. bd. Sludge mag.; contbr. articles on solid waste mgmt. and hazardous waste mgmt. to profl. jours. Home: 10403 Pearl St Fairfax VA 22032 Office: 11800 Sunrise Valley Dr Reston VA 22091

SHIMP, ERNEST MORGAN, educator; b. Salem, N.J., Oct. 4, 1928; s. Samuel Kline and Leona Nellie (Ingersoll) S.; student Internat. Corr. Schs., 1958, High Point Tech. Sch., Largo, Fla., 1965-68; m. Fern Margaret Hamlin, May 23, 1953; children—Samuel, Shelly, Sterling. Dairy farmer nr. Cato, N.Y., 1950-60; heating, refrigeration and air-conditioning contractor, Syracuse, N.Y., 1960-65; service technician, troubleshooter Sears, Roebuck and Co., St. Petersburg, Fla., 1965-69; owner, operator refrigeration and air-conditioning service, St. Petersburg, Fla., 1969-72, Knippa, Tex., 1972-74; instr. refrigeration and air-conditioning S.W. Tex. Jr. Coll. Uvalde, 1974—. Tchr. adult Sunday sch., pres. elder's quorum Ch. of Jesus Christ of Latter-day Saints. Office: Dept Air Conditioning SW Tex Jr Coll Uvalde TX 78801

SHINGLER, WILLIAM H., cons. civil, mining, mech. engr.; b. Kenton, Mich., Aug. 8, 1909; s. William and Ednah (Lewis) S.; B.S., Mich. Tech. U., 1933; postgrad. naval staff officer tng. Princeton U., 1944; m. 2d, Virginia Q. Shingler, July 14, 1972; children by previous marriage—James W., Anne R. Field constrn. engr. U.S. Forest Service, 1934-37; civil engr. Bethlehem Steel Corp., Venezuela, 1937-39, mining metal. engr., Bethlehem, Pa., Cuba, Venezuela, 1939-43, constrn. engr., Venezuela, 1949-52, mgr. to v.p., Venezuela, 1952-74; owner, mgr. Industrias Marino, Plantation, Fla., 1975—. Served with USNR, 1943-46. Registered profl. engr., Mich. Mem. Plantation C. of C., Am. Assn. Ret. Persons (pres. 1979), U.S. Soc. Am. Mil. Engrs., Soc. Mining Engrs., AIME, Am. Security Council, Res. Officers Assn., Soc. Commd. Officers. Mem. Republican Nat. Com. Methodist. Clubs: Mich. Tech. U. Varsity Alumni; Rotary (Venezuela). Address: 1690 SW 59th Ave Plantation FL 33317

SHINGLETON, MABYN KEAN, advt. exec.; b. Baton Rouge, Mar. 15, 1952; d. Frank Hugh and Emily Lou (Mathews) Kean; B.S., La. State U., 1976; m. Patrick S. Shingleton, Feb. 17, 1979. Creative dir. Patt West Advt., 1976; pres. One Unltd. Inc., The Mabyn Kean Agy., Baton Rouge, 1977—. Recipient advt. awards Nat. Assn. Investment Clubs, 1978, 79, Advt. Club Baton Rouge, 1978. Mem. Advt. Club Baton Rouge, Baton Rouge C. of C., Public Relations Assn. La., Zeta Tau Alpha. Republican. Episcopalian. Home: 2044 Lake Hills Pkwy Baton Rouge LA 70808 Office: 619 Jefferson Hwy Suite 1G Baton Rouge LA 70806

SHINGLETON, ROYCE GORDON, educator, writer; b. Stantonsburg, N.C., Oct. 25, 1935; s. Wiley Thomas and Lossie Ellen (Vick) S.; B.S., East Carolina U., 1958; M.A., Appalachian State U., 1964; Ph.D., Fla. State U., 1971; m. Ruth Bennett, June 10, 1962; children—Royce Gordon, Justin Thomas. History tchr. Dinwiddie (Va.) High Sch., 1960-61; social studies tchr. Greene Central High Sch., Snow Hill, N.C., 1961-63; dean of men Lees-McRae Coll., Banner Elk, N.C., 1964-65; instr. history Ga. State U., Atlanta, 1968-73; vis. prof. Oglethorpe U., 1973-77; asst. prof. history Albany (Ga.) Jr. Coll., 1977—. Served with AUS, 1958-60. Mem. So. Hist. Assn., Ga. Assn. Historians, Albany Civil War Roundtable, Thronateeska Heritage Found., Pi Gamma Mu, Phi Alpha Theta, Theta Chi. Author: John Taylor Wood: Sea Coast of the Confederacy, 1979; editor: America in the Making, 1969. Contbr. articles to hist. jours. Home: 2323 Pheasant Dr Albany GA 31707 Office: Social Sci Div Albany Jr Coll Albany GA 31707

SHINGLETON, WILLIAM E., state legislator, banker; b. Fairmont, W.Va., Dec. 26, 1923; s. Loxley Oliver and Florence (Snodgrass) S.; B.S. in Bus. Adminstrn., W.Va. U., 1947; m. Willa J. Jenkins, July 16, 1949; children—Robert E., Sally Ann. Appraiser, Prudential Ins. Co., 1947-49; treas. Shingleton Bros., Clarksburg, W.Va., 1949-56; v.p. Henry & Hardesty, Inc., ins., Fairmont, 1956-62, pres., 1962—; pres. Marion Realty Co., also First Nat. Bank Fairmont; mem. W.Va. Ho. of Dels. from 26th Dist., 1971—, chmn. legis. rule making rev. com.; mem. exec. bd. Conf. Ins. Legislators. Past pres. Fairmont Community Council. Served with AUS, 1943-46. Mem. Fairmont C. of C. (past pres.). Presbyterian. Club: Fairmont Kiwanis (past pres.). Home: 803 Henry Dr Fairmont WV 26554 Office: 517 Fairmont Ave Fairmont WV 26554

SHINKLE, THOMAS HALE, real estate broker; b. Louiseville, Aug. 21, 1920; s. Alva Hale and Robert Ellen (McCaughey) S.; grad. mil. acad., Culver, Ind.; m. Priscilla Dana Young, Oct. 28, 1944; children—Thomas Hale, Mary Robert Shinkle Schuster. Leaf trainee P. Lorillard Co. (name now Loews Corp.), Louisville, 1940-42, supr. leaf processing and mfg., 1946-50, asst. mgr. leaf dept., Lexington, Ky., 1950-55, mgr. leaf processing and warehousing 1955-70; pres. Exec. Mgmt. & Realty Corp., Danville, Va., 1975-76; property mgr. Nat. Corp. for Housing Partnerships, 1975-76; asso. broker Routh Robbins Realtors, Alexandria, Va., 1976—. Deacon, First Presbyn. Ch., Danville, 1968-75; trustee 2d Presbyn. Ch., Lexington, 1957-62. Served to 1st lt. U.S. Army, 1942-46. Mem. Inst. Real Estate Mgmt. (cert. property mgr.). Home: 1307 Gatewood Dr Alexandria VA 22307 Office: 400 N Washington St Alexandria VA 23414

SHIPMAN, HAROLD LEO, JR., accountant; b. Abilene, Tex., Mar. 17, 1940; s. Harold Leo and Katherine Mercedes (Gavin) S.; student Rice U., 1957-58, Pan Am. Coll., 1959; B.B.A., U. Tex. at Austin, 1962; M.B.A. (teaching fellow), N. Tex. State U., 1964; m. Diane Roberts, June 1, 1962; children—Harold, Christopher. With Arthur Young & Co., Dallas and Houston, 1964-73, 79—, tax mgr., Dallas, 1969-71, Houston, 1971-73, tax prin., 1979—; controller Joe A. McDermott Inc., Houston, 1973-74; partner Davis & Shipman, C.P.A.'s, Houston, 1974-79. Mem. Am. Inst. C.P.A.'s, Tex. Soc. C.P.A.'s, A.C.L.U. Democrat. Unitarian. Home: 3510 Sunset St Houston TX 77005 Office: 2500 Pennzoil Pl South Tower 711 Louisiana Houston TX 77002

SHIPMAN, JACK HEWITT, banker; b. Robinson, Ill., Jan. 3, 1937; s. Emmitt Ira and Flo Sylvia (Holt) S.; B.S., Fla. So. Coll., 1958; student Stetson U., 1954-56; m. Jayne H. Lutz, Oct. 10, 1963; children—Kathryn Ann Bradley Joseph, Suzianne Marie. Vice pres., mgr. Shoppers Charge Service, Louisville, 1960-69; with Liberty Nat. Bank, Louisville, 1969—, exec. v.p. retail banking, 1980—. Bd. dirs. ACCEPT, Inc., 1977—. Served with U.S. Army, 1958-60. Mem. Adminstrv. Mgmt. Soc. Consumer Credit Execs. Assn. Republican. Methodist. Home: 8225 Hwy 329 Crastwood KY 40014 Office: 416 W Jefferson St Louisville KY 40202

SHIPP, MICHAEL DAVIS, corp. sales mgr.; b. Louisville, July 7, 1946; s. Warren Cloyd and Jane (Davis) S.; B.M.E., Ga. Inst. Tech., 1969. With Buckeye Cellulose Corp., Memphis, 1969—, various positions engring., mfg. and sales, now mgr. cellulose chem. sales. Account exec. United Way Greater Memphis, 1976, 77. Served to capt. U.S. Army, 1969-73. Mem. Mid-South Exporters Roundtable, Engrs. Club Memphis. Presbyterian. Home: 2501 Lovitt Dr Memphis TN 38138 Office: PO Box 8407 Memphis TN 38108

SHIPP, VICTORY RAY, ret. corp. exec.; b. Oklahoma City, Nov. 22, 1921; s. Ray and Pauline (Ballensky) S.; student public schs., Oklahoma City; m. Wilma Fay Scott, Sept. 27, 1948; children—Donald Ray, Mrs. Gerhardt A. Kratschmann, Mrs. James M. Butler, Jr. Owner, founder Star Printing Co., Oklahoma City, to 1942, Victor R. Shipp Co., 1945-49; sales engr. Am. Type Founders, Inc., 1949; prodn. engr. So. Calif. Newspaper Prodn. Com., to 1954; gen. mgr. Southwestern Press, Ft. Smith, Ark., 1954-59; mgmt. cons. engr., Greenville, S.C., 1959, then in Wichita Falls, Tex.; founder, chief operating officer Vic Shipp Typography, Inc., Oklahoma City, 1961-73; former sec. Creative Printers Am.; pub. Ad Galley newsletter, 10 years; profl. model; charter airline pilot. Mem. nat. adv. bd. Am. Security Council. Served to capt. USAAF, 1942-45; with Res., to 1963. Decorated D.F.C., Air medal; recipient awards in field. Republican. Club: U.S. Senatorial. Home: 625 NW 19 St Oklahoma City OK 73103

SHIPPEY, ORRLINE ELLIS (MRS. WOODROW W. SHIPPEY), librarian; b. Italy, Tex.; d. Forest Pierce and Mary Ella (Orr) Ellis; B.A., Trinity U., 1936; B.L.S., Tex. Woman's U., 1938; postgrad. George Peabody Coll., summer 1941; m. Woodrow W. Shippey, Oct. 21, 1945. Librarian pub. schs., Jefferson, Tex., 1936-39, White Oak Pub. Schs., Longview, Tex., 1939-58; cataloger Engring. Library, Tex. A. and M. Coll., College Station, summer 1942; dir. Nicholson Meml. Pub. Library, Longview, 1958—. Mem. AAUW, ALA, Tex. Library Assn. (chmn sch. div. 1944-45, chmn. children's div. 1950-51, dist. chmn. 1968). Methodist. Contbr. articles to profl. jours. Home: PO Box 1311 Longview TX 75606 Office: 400 S Green St Longview TX 75601

SHIRCLIFF, JAMES VANDERBURGH, broadcasting exec.; b. Vincennes, Ind., Dec. 11, 1938; s. Thomas Maxwell and Martha Bayard (Somes) S.; A.B., Brown U., 1961; postgrad. U. Va., 1963-64; m. Sally Anne Hoing, June 20, 1964; children—Thomas, Susan, Anne, Catherine, Caroline. Asst. gen. mgr. Pepsi Cola Allied Bottlers, Inc., Lynchburg, Va., 1964-65; gen. mgr. First Colony Canners, Inc., Lynchburg, 1965-66; v.p., divisional coordinator Pepsi Cola Allied Bottlers, Inc., Lynchburg, 1966-68, v.p., dir. personnel, 1968-70; v.p., gen. mgr. GCC Beverages, Inc., Lynchburg, 1970-74, group v.p. Va., 1974-75; corporate v.p. Gen. Cinema Corp., Beverage Div., Lynchburg, 1976-77; owner/mgr. WLLL-AM, WGOL-FM, Lynchburg, 1977—; pres. Jamarbo Corp., 1977— presdl. interchange exec., 1975-76; exec. dir. Nat. Indsl. Energy Council, Dept. Commerce, Washington, 1975-76; dir. Bank of Va., Lynchburg, 1971-75. Vice pres. JOBS, Lynchburg, 1970; dir. Central Va. Health Planning Council, 1974-75; mem. Govs. Indsl. Energy Adv. Council, 1976—; dir. Piedmont council, Boy Scouts Am., 1972-73; mem. City of Lynchburg Keep Lynchburg Beautiful Commn., 1974-75, chmn. emergency planning bd., 1974-75, chmn. overall econ. planning council, 1977—; bd. dirs. Lynchburg Broadway Theatre, 1973-75, Acad. Music, 1973-74, United Fund, Lynchburg, 1966-67, Central Va. Industries, 1971-72, United Way; chmn. Citizens for a clean Lynchburg. Served to lt. (j.g.), USN, 1961-63. Recipient Cloyd Meml. award for outstanding service, Greater Lynchburg C. of C., 1975; Va. Soft Drink Assn. citation, 1970, 73, 74; Abe Lincoln award So. Baptist Radio-TV Commn. Mem. Va. C. of C. (dir. 1976—), Greater Lynchburg C. of C. (dir. 1973-74, chmn. community appearance task force 1977—), Va. Soft Drink Assn. (pres. 1973-74), Va. Pepsi Cola Bottlers Assn. (pres. 1970-73), Nat., Va. (dir.) assns. broadcasters,

Lynchburg Advt. Club (v.p.), Va. AP Broadcasters Assn. (treas.), Lynchburg Fine Arts Center (pres.). Roman Catholic. Clubs: Mensa (N.Y.); Commonwealth (Richmond, Va.); Farmington Country (Charlottesville, Va.); Army-Navy (Washington); Oakwood Country (Lynchburg); Piedmont (Lynchburg); Navy League, Galliard, Rotary (pres. Lynchburg club). Home: 3525 Otterview Pl Lynchburg VA 24503

SHIRCLIFF, ROBERT THOMAS, bus. cons. co. exec.; b. Vincennes, Ind., May 20, 1928; s. Thomas Maxwell and Martha (Somes) S.; B.S., Ind. U., 1950; m. Carol Reed, May 9, 1953; children—Laura Howell, Elizabeth Somes. Vice pres., gen. mgr. Pepsi-Cola Bottling Co., Bloomington, Ind., 1950-55, v.p., treas., Charleston, W. Va., 1955-63; pres. Pepsi-Cola Allied Bottlers, Inc., Jacksonville, Fla., 1963-73; pres. Robert T. Shircliff & Assos., 1973—; dir. General Cinema Corp., Boston, 1968-73, Atlantic Nat. Bank, Jefferds & Moore, Inc., Shoney's Big Boy Enterprises, Inc. Chmn. bd. Duval County chpt. ARC, 1972, YMCA, United Fund; trustee Jacksonville U.; pres. Speech and Hearing Clinic, Jacksonville, 1972-73. Mem. Nat. Pepsi-Cola Bottlers Assn. (pres. 1971-72), Jacksonville C. of C. (pres.), Order of Malta, Sigma Alpha Epsilon. Rotarian (dir., pres. 1969-70, dist. gov. 1975-76). Clubs: River (pres.), Timuquana Country, University (Jacksonville). Home: 4918 Prince Edward Rd Jacksonville FL 32210 Office: 2529 Gulf Life Tower Jacksonville FL 32207

SHIREK, JOHN RICHARD, savs. and loan exec.; b. Bismarck, N.D., Feb. 5, 1926; s. James Max and Anna Agatha (Lala) S.; student U. Minn., 1944-46; B.S. with honors, Rollins Coll., 1978; m. Ruth Martha Lietz, Sept. 22, 1950; children—Barbara Jo Shirek Fowler, Jon Richard, Kenneth Edward. Sports editor Bismarck Tribune, 1943-44; with Gate City Savs. and Loan Assn., Fargo, N.D., 1947-65, v.p., dir., 1960-65; exec. v.p., dir. 1st Fed. Savs. and Loan Assn., Melbourne, Fla., 1966-70; pres., dir. 1st Fed. Savs. and Loan Assn., Cocoa, Fla., 1970—. Chmn., dir. United Fund, Fargo, 1962-65; dir., exec. bd. mem. Boy Scouts Am., 1960-70; bd. assos. Fla. Inst. Tech., pres., 1968; moderator St. Johns Presbytery, 1979. Served to lt. (j.g.) USNR, World War II. Mem. Fla. Savs. and Loan League (past dir.), Fla. Savs. and Loan Services (dir.), Savs. and Loan Found. (state membership chmn. 1976), Fla. Savs. and Loan Polit. Action Com. (dir. 1976—), U.S. Savs. and Loan League (chmn. advt. and pub. relations com. 1969-70), Downtown Melbourne Assn. (past pres.), Beta Theta Pi, Omicron Delta Epsilon. Republican. Clubs: Citrus (Orlando, Fla.), Masons, Shriners, Elks, Cocoa Rotary (pres. 1979); Suntree Country. Office: 505 Brevard Ave Cocoa FL 32922

SHIRES, WILLIAM ARCHER, univ. adminstr.; b. Jackson, Tenn., Mar. 1, 1926; s. William Monroe and Frances Ruth (Archer) S.; B.A., Lambuth Coll., 1947; postgrad. N.C. State U., 1955-57, E. Carolina U., 1974-77; m. Katherine Myers, Oct. 5, 1947; children—Kenneth Michael, Elizabeth Archer, Richard Paul; m. 2d, Mary Faye Martin, Apr. 14, 1971. With Memphis Comml. Appeal, 1945-47; with UPI, Atlanta, 1947-48, Richmond, Va., 1948-52, Raleigh, N.C., 1952-62, So. div. night news mgr., Atlanta, 1958-61; mgr. N.C. Assn. Afternoon Dailies, Inc., Raleigh, 1962-70, also columnist, chief corr.; dir. news bur. public relations East Carolina U., Greenville, N.C., 1970—. Chmn. N.C. Comml. and Sports Fisheries Adv. Bd., 1967-69. Recipient citation N.C. Travel Council, 1963. Mem. Am. Hist. Assn., Coll. News Assn. of Carolinas, Sigma Delta Chi, Phi Alpha Theta. Lutheran. Home: 1041 E Rock Spring Rd Greenville NC 27834

SHIREY, BRUCE EUGENE, petroleum technician; b. Dewey, Okla., July 29, 1933; s. Kenneth Eugene and Elizabeth Jean (Shira) S.; student Northeastern State Coll., Tahlequah, Okla., 1951-54; B.B.A., Okla. State U., 1957; m. Gloria Julene Hughey, Jan. 26, 1957; children—Tamitha Anne, Brent Eugene, Stacy Elizabeth, Sara Evangeline. Land trainee Phillips Petroleum Co., Bartlesville, Okla., 1957-58, div. order analyst, 1958-60, titleman, 1961-64, oil scout, 1964-67, leaseman, 1967-68, minerals landsman, 1969-70; ind. landman, Bartlesville, 1970—. Mem. Am., Tulsa assns. petroleum landmen. Address: 345 Robin Ave Bartlesville OK 74003

SHIRLEY, ELIZABETH SNIDER, social worker, hosp. supr.; b. Franklin, Ky., May 2, 1945; d. Douglas Brundage and Pearl (Steele) Snider; B.A., Western Ky. U., 1968; m. James Kelly Shirley, Nov. 29, 1968; children—Ellen Douglas, Keith Radford. Social worker So. Ky. Comprehensive Care Center, mental retardation-mental health facility, Bowling Green, Ky., 1968-70, Manassas (Va.) Manor Nursing Home, 1970-71; social worker adult services Fauquier County Welfare Dept., Warrenton, Va., 1971-74; dir. social service Fauquier Hosp., Warrenton, 1974—; cons. in field. Mem. home health utilization rev. com. Fauquier Health Dept., 1974-79; chmn. adult service adv. com. Fauquier Welfare Dept., 1975-78; sec. bd. dirs. Marshall Townhouse Homeowners Assn., 1978-79: Va. task force on families in developmental change, Va. Conf. on Families, for White House Conf. on Families, 1980. Mem. Nat. Assn. Social Workers, Nat. Soc. for Hosp. Social Work Dirs. Baptist. Home: 100 Pellam Ct Marshall VA 22115 Office: Fauquier Hosp 330 Hospital Dr Warrenton VA 22186

SHIRLEY, ERNEST MIDDLETON, JR., environ. engr.; b. Ruston, La., Jan. 21, 1936; s. Ernest Middleton and Eva Henderson S.; B.S. in Microbiology, La. Poly. U., 1961; m. Janell Hyde, July 6, 1957; children—Paul William, Lola Gale. With So. Research Inst., Birmingham, Ala., 1961-65, State of Fla. Bur. San. Engring., Apalachicola, Fla., 1965-67, St. Joe Paper Co., Port St. Joe, Fla., 1967-69; with ITT Rayonier, Fernandina Beach, Fla., 1969—, asst. tech. supt., 1980—; chmn., mem. bd. dirs. Rayonier Credit Union. Chmn. Nassau County Sch. Bd., 1974—. Mem. Nat. Air Pollution Control Assn., TAPPI, Nat. Council for Air and Stream Improvement, Fla. Pollution Control Assn., Fla. Air Pollution Control Assn., Fla. Assn. Water Quality Control. Democrat. Baptist. Club: Atlantic Flying (chmn. 1970-72). Home: 503 Stanley Dr Fernandina Beach FL 32034 Office: PO Box 2002 Fernandina Beach FL 32034

SHIRLEY, GEORGE, city ofcl.; b. Tompkinsville, Ky., July 3, 1939; s. Wick and Olene (Pipkins) S.; A.A., SouthWestern Christian Coll., 1962; B.A., Okla. Christian Coll., 1966; postgrad. Okla. U., 1975—; m. Della Winston, Oct. 28, 1966; children—Elender, Lashanda. Community program worker Community Action, Oklahoma City, 1966-68; personnel analyst City of Oklahoma City, 1968-77; dir. personnel City of Norman (Okla.), 1977—. Mem. Adminstrv. Mgmt. Soc., Internat. City Mgmt. Assn., Internat. Personnel Mgmt. Assn. Mem. Chs. of Christ. Home: 22 NE 64th St Oklahoma City OK 73105 Office: 201 W Gray St Norman OK 73070

SHIRLEY, PRESTON, lawyer; b. Fort Worth, Nov. 14, 1912; s. James Preston and Nevra (Boykin) S.; student Tex. Christian U., 1928-30; LL.B., U. Tex., 1933; m. Elizabeth Hodgson, Nov. 13, 1936; children—Susan (Mrs. John Eckel), Carolyn (Mrs. Bryan Wimberly), Sarah. Admitted to Tex. bar. 1933; partner firm Boykin, Ray & Shirley, Fort Worth, 1933-36; asso. prof. law U. Tex., Austin, 1936-40; partner firm Kelley & Looney, Edinburg, Tex., 1940-41, Holloway, Hudson & Shirley, Fort Worth, 1945-47, Mills, Shirley, McMicken & Eckel, Galveston, Tex., 1947—. Dir. First Hutchings-Sealy Nat. Bank, Galveston, mem. exec. com., 1967—, chmn. bd., 1974—; dir. Am. Indemnity Financial Corp., Galveston, Am. Indemnity Co., Am. Fire & Indemnity Co., Tex. Gen. Indemnity Co., Galveston Corp. Mem. U. Tex. Devel. Bd., Austin, chmn., 1965-66, 66-67; mem. devel. bd. U. Tex. Med. Br., Galveston, 1967—; pres. First Bapt. Found., Galveston. Chmn. Galveston Charter Rev. Commn., 1968, 72, mem., 74, 1970; mem. Planning Commn. City of Galveston, 1961-69; mem. Tex. Constl. Revision Commn., 1973—. Bd. dirs., exec. v.p. Sealy & Smith Found. for John-Sealy Hosp., Galveston; bd. dirs. U. Tex. Found., Pres., 1970-72; trustee U. Tex. Law Sch. Found., Mary Hardin Baylor Coll., Belton, Tex., 1974-78. Served from 2d lt. to lt. col. AUS, 1942-45; CBI. Fellow Am. Coll. Trial Lawyers, Am. Coll. Probate Counsel, Am., Tex. bar founds.; mem. Tex. Assn. Def. Counsel (pres. 1963-64), Galveston County (pres. 1954-55), Am. bar assns., State Bar Tex. (com. adminstrn. justice 1952-72), Internat. Assn. Ins. Counsel, Assn. Ins. Attys., Order of Coif, Phi Delta Phi, Phi Kappa Psi. Club: Galveston Artillery. Author: Texas Pattern Jury Charges, vols. 1 and 2, 1969. Home: 4602 Sherman Blvd Galveston TX 77550 Office: First Hutchings-Sealy National Bank Bldg Galveston TX 77550

SHIRLEY, TIMOTHY ROGER, accountant; b. Tuscaloosa, Ala., Oct. 21, 1955; s. Burley Hobson and Mary Emertha (Pounders) S.; B.S. summa cum laude in Acctg., U. Ala., 1976, M.A. (Grad. Council fellow), 1977. Salesman, Bill's, Inc., Huntsville, Ala., 1973; edit control clk. First Ala. Bank of Huntsville, 1973-75; balance clk. (part-time) First Nat. Bank of Tuscaloosa (Ala.), 1975-76; audit staff acct. Ernst & Ernst, San Antonio, 1977-78, sr. acct., 1979—. C.P.A. Mem. Nat. Assn. Accts. (dir. Houston chpt. 1979-80, San Antonio chpt. 1980—), Tex. Soc. C.P.A.'s, Am. Inst. C.P.A.'s Ala. Acctg. Soc., Beta Gamma Sigma, Beta Alpha Psi, Chi Phi. Contbr. articles to profl. and legal jours. Office: 1900 Frost Bank Tower San Antonio TX 78205

SHIVERS, ALLAN, JR., investment exec.; b. San Antonio, Jan. 21, 1946; s. Allan and Marialice (Shary) S.; grad. Lawrenceville (N.J.) Sch., 1964; diploma U. Tex. at Austin, 1964-68. Self-employed in investments, Austin, 1969—; dir. Am. Nat. Bank Austin, Thermal Systems Inc. Bd. dirs., v.p. Easter Seal Soc. for Crippled Children and Adults in Tex.; bd. dirs. Tex. Inst. Rehab. and Research. Served with USCG, 1968-69. Mem. Sigma Alpha Epsilon. Home: 1200 Gaston Ave Austin TX 78703 Office: 1600 W 38th St Suite 301 Austin TX 78731

SHIVLER, JAMES FLETCHER, JR., civil engr.; b. Clearwater, Fla., Feb. 17, 1918; s. James Fletcher and Estelle (Adams) S.; B.S. in Civil Engring., U. Fla., 1938, M.S. in Engring., 1940; m. Katherine Lucille Howlett, Feb. 2, 1946; children—James Fletcher III, Susan (Mrs. William J. Schilling). Mem. engring. faculty U. Fla., 1940-41; with Reynolds, Smith & Hills, Architects-Engrs.-Planners, Inc. (formerly Reynolds, Smith & Hills, architects and engrs.), Jacksonville, Fla., 1941—, partner, 1950—, pres., 1970—; partner Lewis-Eaton Partnership, Archi- tects-Engrs. & Planners, Jackson, Miss., 1969—; dir. Environmental Sci. & Engring., Inc., Gainesville, Fla. Mem. Fla. Bd. Engr. Examiners, 1964-70, v.p., 1964-65, pres., 1965-70. Served as lt. j.g., Civil Engr. Corps, USNR, 1943-46; PTO. Recipient Outstanding Service award Fla. Engring. Soc., 1971, Distinguished Alumnus award U. Fla., 1972, citation for service to constrn. industry Engring. News Record, 1973. Registered profl. engr., Fla., Ga., N.C. Fellow ASCE (pres. Fla. sect. 1952), Fla. Engring. Soc. (pres. 1960-61); mem. Nat. Soc. Profl. Engrs. (pres. 1972-73), Am. Cons. Engrs. Council, Fla. State (dir.-at-large 1971—), Jacksonville Area chambers commerce, Tau Beta Pi. Presbyn. Clubs: Jacksonville Exchange, University, River, Deerwood, Florida Yacht, Jacksonville Power Squadron. Home: 8191 Hollyridge Rd Jacksonville FL 32216 Office: PO Box 4850 Jacksonville FL 32201

SHOCKEY, THOMAS EDWARD, real estate exec., archtl. engr.; b. San Antonio, Aug. 17, 1926; s. Verlie Draper and Margaret Ruth (Shuford) S.; B.S., (Davidson fellow Tau Beta Pi) Tex. A. and M. Coll., 1950; postgrad. St. Mary's U., 1964, San Antonio Coll., 1972; m. Jacqueline McPherson. June 4. 1949; children—Cheryl Ann, Jocelyn Marie, Valerie Jean. With Petty Geophys. Survey, summers 1947-49, J.E. Ingram Equipment Co., 1950-51; co-owner, archtl. engr., realtor Moffett Lumber Co., Inc., San Antonio, 1952-76; cons. gen. contracting, gen. real estate, 1944—, retailer wholesale bldg. material, 1951—, v.p., 1959—; real estate counselor, appraiser, 1972—; real estate appraiser Gill Appraisal Service, San Antonio, 1977—; comml. loan appraiser, underwriter, analyst Gill Savs. Assn., Gill Cos., San Antonio, 1979. Served with inf. Signal Corps, U.S. Army, i944-46; ETO. Mem. San Antonio C. of C., Nat. Lumber Dealers, Nat. Home Builders, Nat. Real Estate Bd.. Nat. Inst. Real Estate Brokers, Internat. Soc. Real Estate Appraisers. Home: Rural Delivery Mico TX 78056 Office: Gill Companies PO Box 599 San Antonio TX 78292 also Gill Savs Assn PO Box 467 Hondo TX 78861

SHOCKLEE, JOHN WARREN, educator; b. Corsicana, Tex., Jan. 13, 1932; s. David Uvell and Alice (Kirkpatrick) S.; diploma Dallas Inst. Mortuary Sci., 1959; B.S., Bethany Nazarene Coll., 1964; M.Ed., Va. State Coll., 1975; postgrad. Va. Poly. Inst. and State U., 1977-78; m. Shirley Ann Statzer, Sept. 6, 1958; children—J. Mark, David Randol, Brian Clark. Apprentice funeral dir. Paul A. Rix Funeral Home, Odessa, Tex., 1960-62; funeral dir. Rhoton-Weiland-Merritt Funeral Home, Dallas, 1962-64; instr. Dallas Inst. Mortuary Sci., Dallas, 1964-69, dean, 1969-71; dir. funeral service program John Tyler Community Coll., Chester, Va., 1971—; mem. accreditation com., mem. standards and criteria com. Am. Bd. Funeral Service Edn. Served with USMC, 1951-54; Korea. Nazarene. Home: 3660 Applewood Rd Richmond VA 23234

SHOCKLEY, DORMAN, gas co. exec.; b. Anton, Tex., Apr. 23, 1927; s. William Ishum and Myrtice (Jones) S.; B.S., Tex. Tech. U., 1949; m. Shirley Jane Doan; children—Suzanne Renee, Houston Doan. Geologist, Sinclair Oil & Gas Co., Corpus Christi, Tex., 1956-63, Lafayette, La., 1963-64; geologist DeGolyer & MacNaughton, Dallas, 1964-69; geologist Inexco Oil Co., Houston, 1969-72; pres. Natural Gas Mgmt. Co., Houston, 1972—. Lectr. U. Corpus Christi (Tex.), 1957-63. Mem. Yule Toy Bd., Corpus Christi, Tex., 1960-63. Served with U.S. Maritime Service, 1945-46. Mem. Am. Assn. Petroleum Geologists, Ind. Petroleum Assn. Am., Am. Inst. Mining, Metall. and Petroleum Engrs., Houston, Corpus Christi geol. socs. Episcopalian (sr. warden 1979-80). Clubs: Sertoma (v.p. 1963-64) (Lafayette, La.); Dallas Petroleum; Petroleum (Houston). Home: 3003 Chevy Chase St Houston TX 77019 Office: 2001 Kirby Dr No 502 Houston TX 77019

SHOCKLEY, URIAH BURTON, JR., food corp. exec.; b. Bishops Head, Md., Sept. 18, 1925; s. Uriah B. and Berneice E. (Pritchett) S.; student U. Md., 1942-43, Eckles Coll. Sci., 1947-48; m. Jane E. Wills, May 4, 1950; children—Raynette, Uriah B. III. With Quaker Oats Corp., 1953-66, sales mgr. Flako Products, 1956-57, advt. mgr. Corn Goods, Flako, 1957-59, Puss N'Boots/Ken-L Ration, 1959-66, sales mgr., v.p. mktg. subs. firm Wolf Brand Products, Inc., Corsicana, Tex., 1966-76, pres., 1976—; v.p., sec. Magic Pan of Tex., Inc., Dallas, 1976—; guest speaker consumer econ. forums, 1975—. Advt. dir. United Fund, 1970-72. Served to 2d officer U.S. Mcht. Marine, 1944-47. Mem. Nat. Meat Canners Assn., Nat. Food Processors Assn. Republican. Methodist. Clubs: City of Dallas, Chaparral, Elks. Home: 821 Dobbins Rd Corsicana TX 75110 Office: Wolf Brand Products Inc PO Box 617 Corsicana TX 75110

SHOCKLEY, WILLIE M. JOHNSON, home economist, educator; b. Little Rock, Dec. 5, 1912; d. Wade Hampton and Nancy (Ware) Johnson; B.S., Philander Smith Coll., 1945; M.S. in Clothing and Textiles, Kans. State U., 1949; postgrad. Okla. State U., summer 1968, State Coll. Ark., 1971-72, U. Ark., summer 1973; diploma in interior decoration LaSalle Extension U., 1972. Asso. registrar Philander Smith Coll., Little Rock, 1945-64, asst. prof. home econs., 1946-64, 64-75, asst. prof., research specialist, 1975-77, asso. prof., research specialist, 1977-78, dir. home mgmt. residence, 1964-78, asso. prof., alumni coordinator, 1978-79, alumni coordinator, 1979-80, dir. alumni relations, 1980—, nat. dir. alumni affairs, 1970—. Recipient cert. of award for outstanding service to Philander Smith Coll., 1969, 72, 75, 79; cert. for meritorious service to higher edn. in Ark., Dept. Higher Edn., Ark. Edn. Assn., 1972, numerous others. Mem. Am. Home Econs. Assn., Ark. Home Econs. Assn., AAUW (pres. Little Rock br. 1979—), Philander Smith Coll. Alumni Assn., Nat. Council Negro Women, Urban League of Greater Little Rock, Federated Women's Club, Alpha Kappa Mu (nat. dir. alumni affairs), Beta Kappa Chi, Alpha Kappa Alpha. Methodist.

SHOEMAKER, JAMES MARSHALL, JR., lawyer; b. LaJolla, Calif., Aug. 25, 1932; s. James Marshall and Frances (Little) S.; B.A., U. Va., 1955, J.D., 1965; m. Mary Hunter Sloan, Jan. 3, 1959; children—James Marshall III, Edward Sloan, Jonathan Evans. Fgn. service officer U.S. Dept. State, Bur. Cultural Affairs, Washington, 1958-60, vice consul Am. Embassy, Tokyo, Japan, 1960-62; admitted to S.C. bar, 1965; mem. firm Wyche, Burgess, Freeman & Parham, Greenville, 1965—; dir. Engineered Custom Plastics Corp., Perception, Inc., Palmetto Spinning Corp. Pres., Family and Children Service, Greenville County, S.C., 1968-69; mem. Little Theatre Council, 1967-71; chmn. United Fund div., 1969-70; mem. Greenville City Council, 1971-73; mem. Greenville CSC, 1973—, chmn., 1978—; bd. dirs. Greenville Urban League, 1980—, Greater Greenville YMCA, 1980—. Served to maj. USMCR, 1955-58. Mem. Am., S.C., Greenville County bar assns., Greenville C. of C. (dir. 1970-71, 76-80, pres. 1979). Republican. Episcopalian. Kiwanian (dir. 1970-73, 76-77). Clubs: Greenville Country, Cotillion, Poinsett. Home: 109 Pine Forest Dr Greenville SC 29601 Office: 44 E Camperdown Way Greenville SC 29603

SHOEMAKER, LEONARD WILEY, cons. engr.; b. Long Beach, Cal., Nov. 11, 1937; s. Leonard Miller and Josephine (Berry) S.; B.S., Tex. A. and M. Coll., 1961; m. Bobby Jean Foster, June 1, 1958; 1 dau., Sharon Dawn. Civil engr. U.S. Forest Service, Lufkin, Tex., 1961-64, supervisory civil engr., Cleve., 1964-66; asso., v.p. Dannenbaum Engring. Corp., Houston, 1966-69; prin. R.G. Miller Engrs., Houston, 1969-70; pres. Leonard W. Shoemaker & Assos., Inc., Houston, 1970—. Bd. dirs. Houston Hunter-Jumper Charity Horse Show, 1977—, v.p., 1979. Mem. Nat., Tex. (pres. Sam Houston chpt. 1970-71, Outstanding Young Engr. 1969) socs. profl. engrs., ASCE, Greater Houston Builders Assn. (community developers council, FHA-VA steering com.), Nat. Home Builders Assn., Assn. Cons. Mcpl. Engrs., Tex. Hunter and Jumper Assn., Harris County Heritage and Conservation Soc. Presbyn. (elder, deacon). Clubs: Meml. Morning Optimist (v.p. 1969-70), Century, Tex. A&M Former Students, Pine Forest Country, Dad's (YMCA). Home: 22715 Hegar Rd PO Box 215 Hockley TX 77447 Office: 9235 Katy Freeway Houston TX 77024

SHOEMAKER, RALPH JOSEPH, library cons., author; b. East Lansdowne, Pa., July 13, 1906; s. Frank W. and Harriet (Mathews) S.; m. Elsie M. DeGraff, Dec. 9, 1951. Asst. librarian Phila. Pub. Ledger, 1920-34; asso. librarian Phila. Evening Ledger, 1934-42; chief librarian Courier-Jour. and Louisville Times, 1947-63; now library cons. and author. Vice chmn. of Phila. Library Council, 1933-34. Served from pvt. to capt., AUS, 1942-46. Named Ky. col., 1963; recipient gold award U. Mo. Columns Club, 1973, silver award, 1977. Mem. Ky. Library Assn. (pres. 1955-56), Spl. Libraries Assn. (chmn. newspaper div. 1935-36, Hall of Fame newspaper div. 1978), Louisville Library Club (pres. 1950-51), Friends of U. Mo. Library (life). Author: Memorial Tribute to Joseph F. Kwapil, 1934; The Presidents Words, vols. 1-7, 1954-61; Subject Classifications for Clipping and Picture Files, 1958; Newspaper Library Filing Systems, 1962; East Lansdowne: Early Facts and Fond Recollections, 1969; In the Classics series, part I, 1970, part II, 1973; High Glory: No Return, 1978; Uncle Ralph Jokes, 1978; contbr. articles and book revs. to mags., newspapers. Address: 5136 28th Ave N Saint Petersburg FL 33710

SHOENIGHT, PAULINE ALOISE SOUERS, author; b. Bridgeport, Ill., Nov. 20, 1914; d. William Fitch and Carrie (Milhouse) Souers; B.Ed., Eastern Ill. U., 1937; m. James Richard Tracy, Sept. 18, 1946 (dec. Aug. 1972); m. 2d, Hurley F. Shoenight, June 25, 1976. Mem. P.E.O. Sisterhood, Am. Poets Fellowship Soc. (hon.), Performing Arts Assn., Eastern Ill. Alumni, Ill. (charter), Ala. State poetry socs., Foley Extension Homemakers Club, Am. Poetry League, Nat. Audubon Soc., Pensters, Nat. Geog. Soc., Bird Friends Soc., Nat. Ret. Tchrs. Assn. Republican. Baptist. Club: Pleasure Island Sr. Citizens (charter). Author: His Handiwork, 1954; Memory is a Poet; The Silken Web, 1965; A Merry Heart, 1966; In Two or Three Tomorrows, 1968; All Flesh is Grass, 1971; Beyond the Edge, 1973. Address: Route 3 Box 1107 Foley AL 36535

SHOFFNER, ARTHUR RAY, real estate exec.; b. Hodgenville, Ky., May 14, 1895; s. William Henry and Sarah Janie (Morris) S.; m. Nellie Tate, Apr. 25, 1917 (dec. 1967); children—Roy Morris, Nellie (Mrs. William French), Irene (Mrs. Courtwright), Mary J.; m. 2d, Frances T. Newman; children—Thomas R., Jean F. Real estate broker, also auctioneer, Crestview, Fla., 1945—; founder, pres. A.R. Shoffner & Co., Frankfort, Ky. and Crestview, 1922—; founder, pres. Lincoln Lumber & Mfg. Co., Hodgenville and Crestview, 1936—; founder, pres. Farmers Union Oil & Royalty Co., Hodgenville and Crestview, 1930—; founder, pres. Morris Realty Co., Inc., Henderson, Ky.; founder, pres., also chmn. bd. Opportunities, Inc., Crestview, 1943—; founder, pres. Nat. Real Estate & Bus. Jour., Huntsville, Ala., 1950—; founder, pres. Shoffner Printing & Pub. Co., Inc., Crestview, 1954—; founder, builder Shoffner City (Fla.); developer Fla. Land Holdings. Ky. col. Address: Route 1 Box 280 Crestview FL 32536

SHOFFNER, CLARENCE LORENZO, dentist; b. Greensboro, N.C., Dec. 13, 1921; s. Ira Benjamin and Lelia Bernice (Harriston) S.; B.S., A. and T. U., Greensboro, 1942; D.D.S., Howard U., 1951; postgrad. U. Pa., 1946-47; m. Carrie Tena Carter, Nov. 13, 1943; children—Selia Lorene, Annah Yvonne. With div. oral hygiene N.C. Dept. Health, Raliegh, 1951-52; practice gen. dentistry, Weldon, N.C., 1952—; dep. dental examiner N.C. Bd. Dental Examiners; pres. Hillcrest Realty Subdiv., Roanoke Rapids, N.C. Mem. N.C. Human Relations Commn., 1970-75, Halifax County Selective Service Bd., 1969—. Bd. dirs. Weldon Bus. Bur., Rheasville Vol. Fire Dept.; trustee Halifax Community Coll. Served with USAAF, 1942-45. Recipient Howard U. Coll. Dentistry Alumni award, 1974. Fellow Acad. Gen. Dentistry, Acad. Dentistry Internat.; mem. ADA, N.C., Old North State (award) dental socs., Eastern Carolina Med., Dental and Pharm. Soc., Rocky Mount Acad. Medicine, Roanoke Rapids C. of C., Nat. Negro Golf Assn., Fla. Guardsman Inc., Basilius Omega Psi Phi. Democrat. Roman Catholic. Clubs: Masons, K.C., Meadowbrook

Country (life). Home: PO Box 266 Weldon NC 27890 Office: 100 Elm St Weldon NC 27890

SHOFFNER, ROY MORRIS, editor; b. Hodgenville, Ky., Jan. 25, 1918; s. Arthur Ray and Nellie (Tate) S.; student Ft. Worth Sch. Photography, 1948, Enterprise (Ala.) State Jr. Coll., 1964; m. Patricia Ogburn, Aug. 10, 1949; 1 son, James William. Vice pres. Opportunities, Inc., Crestview, Fla., 1945—; owner Shoffner Photo Studio, Crestview, 1948-50; editor-pub. Tenn. Valley News-Arab Enterprise, Huntsville, Ala., 1950; dir. Tng. Film Library, Camp Rucker, Ala., 1950-54; mng. editor Enterprise Daily Ledger, 1954-77, pub., editor, 1977—. Mem. Enterprise Planning Commn., 1966-72, State Bd. Edn. Ethics and Morals Commn., 1973-74, Enterprise Bicentennial Commn., 1973-76. City councilman, Enterprise, 1964-72. Pres. Pea River Hist. and Geneol. Soc., 1972-75, 76-77; bd. dirs. Soc. for Prevention Tb. in Wiregrass, Ala. Tb. Assn. Served with AUS, 1940-45. Decorated Purple Heart; recipient George Washington Honor medal Freedoms Found., 1965, Ala. Baptist Religious Journalism award, 1964, Extension Service Leadership award, 1974; named Enterprise Man of Year, 1965. Ky. col. Mem. Am. Legion, VFW (dist. comdr. 1957-58), DAV, Assn. U.S. Army, Boys Ranch, Ala. Hist. Assn. Lion (dist. gov. 1967-68). Home: 406 Doster St Enterprise AL 36330 Office: PO Box 1140 Enterprise AL 36330

SHOFSTAHL, ROBERT MAXWELL, savs. and loan exec.; b. New Orleans, Feb. 8, 1942; s. Maxwell Fredrick and Ellen Anna (Falkenstein) S.; B.A. cum laude, Tulane U., 1964, postgrad, in law, 1966; m. Lois Alice Berrigan, June 6, 1964; children—Tyson Brahm, Elisia Ellette, Christian Aric. Traffic supr. South Central Bell Telephone Co., New Orleans, 1964-67, traffic mgr., Baton Rouge, 1967-69, traffic mgr., Shreveport, La., 1969-71; asst. to pres. Pelican Homestead & Savs. Assn., New Orleans, 1971, v.p., 1971-73, sec., also exec. v.p., 1973-77, pres., 1978—, dir., 1973—. Mem. Inter-Industry Flood Ins. Com., 1973—; bd. dirs. Neighborhood Housing Services, 1978, treas., 1979. Mem. League Savs. and Loan-Homestead Assns. Greater New Orleans (pres. 1973-74), U.S. League Savs. Assns. (vice chmn. ad hoc flood ins. com. 1974-78, vice chmn. ins. and protective com. 1977-78, chmn. 1978-80), La. Savs. and Loan League (ins. com. 1974-76, exec. com. 1978—), Home Builders Assns. Greater New Orleans (asso.), Internat. House, New Orleans C. of C., Phi Beta Kappa, Phi Eta Sigma, Eta Sigma Phi. Episcopalian. Club: Metairie Country. Contbr. articles to profl. jours. Home: 336 Homestead Ave Metairie LA 70005 Office: Pelican Homestead & Savings Assn 344 Carondelet St New Orleans LA 70130

SHOJI, HIROMU, surgeon; b. Chiba-Ken, Japan; grad. Coll. Gen. Edn., 1959, U. Tokyo, grad. Faculty of Medicine, 1964. Intern, U. Tokyo Hosp., 1964-65, resident in surgery, 1965-67; resident in surgery Bklyn. Cumberland Med. Center, 1967-68, N.Y. U. Med. Center, 1968-69; bone tumor clinic fellow Meml. Sloan-Kettering Med. Center, N.Y.C., 1969-70; orthopedic fellow Hosp. for Spl. Surgery, N.Y.C., 1971-72; resident orthopedic surgery Bowman Gray Med. Sch., Winston-Salem, N.C., 1973-74; practice medicine specializing in orthopedic surgery, New Orleans, 1976—; mem. staff Charity Hosp., Hotel Dieu Hosp., Children's Hosp., Jo Ellem Smith Meml. Hosp., Mercy Hosp.; asso. prof. dept. orthopedic surgery La. State U. Med. Center, 1976—; asst. prof. dept. orthopedic surgery U. Calif., Davis, 1974-76; civilian cons. David Grant Meml. Hosp., Travis AFB, Calif., 1974-76. Diplomate Am. Bd. Orthopedic Surgery. Mem. Am. Acad. Orthopedic Surgeons, Japanese Orthopedic Assn., Orthopedic Research Soc., Japanese Soc. for Connective Tissue Research, Japanese Rehab. Assn., La. State Med. Soc., La. Orthopedic Assn., So. Med. Assn., AMA, Nat. Acad. Sci., Am. Rheumatism Assn. Contbr. numerous articles on orthopedic surgery to med. jours.; patentee orthopedic devices. Office: 1542 Tulane Ave New Orleans LA 70112

SHOMO, GLEN KELLER, III, elec. engr.; b. Harrisonburg, Va., Aug. 22, 1950; s. Glen Keller and Rosemary Eleanor (Burkett) S.; B.S. in Elec. Engring., Va. Poly. and State U., 1972; m. Nancy Marie Jiunta, June 17, 1972. Project engr., ComSonics Inc., Harrisonburg, Va., 1972-76, asst. dir. research and devel., 1976—; engr. Warren L. Braun Cons. Engrs., Harrisonburg, 1977—. Registered profl. engr., Va. Mem. Harrisonburg, Jr. C. of C. (dir. 1973-74), IEEE. Baptist. Patentee cable TV device. Office: PO Box 1106 Harrisonburg VA 22801

SHOOK, CHARLES EDWARD, engr.; b. Dekalb, Tex., Aug. 29, 1930; s. Paul J. and Cecile (Braswell) S.; B.S., Tex. Tech. Coll., 1959, M.B.A., 1968; m. Delores Garrett, Mar. 28, 1948; children—Joseph Thomas, Cheri Ann, Paul Edward, Yvonne Tracy, Yvette Stacy. Instrument technician Aero Instrument Supply, Dallas, 1956; test analyst Gen. Dynamics, Fort Worth, 1957; project engr. Campbell Steel Co./Mosher Steel Co., San Antonio, 1958-62; operations coordinator Lubbock Mfg. Co. (Tex.), 1963-68; prodn. engr. Binkley Co., Warrenton, Mo., 1968-69, prodn. mgr., Highland, Ill., 1969-74; pres. C. Shook, Inc., Greenville, S.C., 1974—. Active Boy Scouts Am. Served with USAF, 1950-54. Registered profl. engr., Tex. Mem. Am. Inst. Indsl. Engrs. (dir. 1966-68), Tex. Soc. Profl. Engrs., St. Louis Engrs. Club. Baptist. Mason (Shriner). Home: 103 Mill Estate Rd Taylor SC 29687 Office: 3404C Rutherford Rd Taylors SC 29687

SHOOK, DIANNE LEE, Realtor; b. Duluth, Minn., Dec. 21, 1936; d. Joseph Frank and Melville Elaine (Munslow) Proff; student Southeastern State U., Durant, Okla., 1958-59, Nat. Assn. Realtors, Comml. Real Estate, 1975; grad. Real Estate Inst.; 1976; m. Wendell E. Shook, Nov. 27, 1954; children—Warren Edward, Aimee Michaelle, Jonathan Everett, Lisa Dianne. Loan processor Durant (Okla.) Bank and Trust Co., 1968-71; real estate agt., mgr. comml. real estate div. Pride Real Estate, Oklahoma City, 1971-76; owner, pres. Century 21, Dianne Shook Co., Oklahoma City, 1976—. Vestry mem., ch. treas. St. James Episcopal Ch., Oklahoma City, 1976-77, mem. bishop's growth com. Episcopal Diocese Okla. Cert. real estate broker, cert. residential specialist. Mem. Oklahoma City Metro Bd. Realtors, Women's Council Realtors (dir.), S. Oklahoma City Bd. Realtors (sec., dir. 1977), Oklahoma City Sales and Mktg. Execs. Club, Oklahoma City Met., S. Oklahoma City chambers commerce. Republican. Clubs: Capitol Hill Bus. and Profl. Women's, Beta Sigma Phi (sec. Eta Xi chpt.). Home: 6300 S Broadway Dr Oklahoma City OK 73139 Office: 222 SW 74 St Oklahoma City OK 73159

SHOOK, GEORG ELZY, artist; b. Miss., May 24, 1932; s. David B. and Blanche (Denley) S.; student U. Fla., 1952-56; spl. student Ringling Inst. Art, Fla., 1956-58; m. Jean T. McNulty, Nov. 10, 1951; children—Lorna J. (Mrs. H. Deason), Jon E. One-man shows Great Expectations Gallery, Memphis, 1968, 70, Brooks Meml. Art Gallery, Memphis, 1971, Bruce Internat. Art Gallery, Memphis, 1972, Jason's Golden Fleece Art Gallery, Memphis, 1974; exhibited in group shows Tenn. All State Artists Exhbns., 1969-76, 78, Memphis Watercolor Soc. Touring Exhbns., 1971, 72, Central South Exhbn., 1970, 72, 73, Am. Watercolor Soc., N.Y.C., 1972, 73, 76, 77, Rocky Mountain Nat. Watermedia Exhbn., Golden, Colo., 1974, 76, 61st Ann. Allied Artists Am. Exhbn., N.Y.C., 1974, Watercolor U.S.A., 1970, 71, 72, 73, 76, Mainstreams, 1973, Tenn. Watercolor Soc., 1972-80, Franklin Mint Gallery of Am. Art, 1973-74, Southeastern Realist Invitational, Winston-Salem, N.C., 1974, Distinguished Artists Collectors Invitational, Little Rock, 1974-75, Nat. Small Printing Exhbn., Halley, Pa., 1974, Parthenon Galleries, Nashville, 1973, Brooks Meml. Art Gallery, Memphis, 1971, So. Watercolor Soc., 1977-80, also group invitationals, El Paso, 1974, Denver, 1974-75, Tulsa and Oklahoma City, 1973-74, Kalamazoo, 1975; represented in permanent collections Ark. Fine Arts Center, Pine Bluff, Springfield (Mo.) Art Mus., Hunter Mus. Art, Chattanooga, Rock City-Lookout Mountain, Inc., Chattanooga, Nat. Bank Commerce, Memphis, Tenn. Union Planters Nat. Bank, Memphis, 2d Nat. Bank, Jackson, Tenn., Hamilton Nat. Bank, Knoxville, No. Bank and Trust, Little Rock, Charlie Vergos Rendezvous, Memphis; art dir. Memphis Pub. Co., 1961—; mem. visual arts adv. panel Tenn. Arts Commn., 1973—; adv. bd. Shelby State Community Coll. Served with AUS, 1949-52. Recipient Carl F. Sahlin award Am. Watercolor Soc., 1973; Lloyd O. Angell award Rocky Mountain Nat. Watermedia Exhbn., 1974; Ark. Traveler award, 1975; Ellen J. Martin award; Thomas Hart Benton award. Mem. So. (v.p. 1975-77, pres. 1977—, 4 awards), Tenn. (pres. 1972-73, 8 awards), Memphis (co-founder 1969), Mid-So., Am. watercolor socs., Allied Artists Am., Art Dirs. Club Memphis (pres. 1970-72), Whiskey Painters of Am. Address: 1239 Cherrydale Cove Memphis TN 38111 Studio: 41 Union Ave #3 Memphis TN 38103

SHOOK, HAROLD GRAHAM, career cons.: b. Portland, Oreg., Apr. 25, 1920; s. Harold Edgar and Nellie Blanche (Graham) S.; A.A., San Francisco Jr. Coll., 1940; B.A., U. Calif., Berkeley, 1955; M.A. in Internat. Affairs, George Washington U., 1967: m. Rae B. Mayfield, Feb. 13, 1943 (dec. Apr. 1972); children—Stephen J., Michael G., David C., William M.; m. 2d, Marilyn J. Berger, Nov. 11, 1972. Commd. 2d lt. U.S. Air Force, 1941, advanced through grades to col., 1956; comdr. fighter squadrons, group Wing and Air Div., 1944-66; combat tour, Europe, 1944, Korea, 1953-54; commdr. USAF Instrument Instr. Pilot Sch., 1949-52; staff officer USAF Hdqrs. and Joint Chiefs of Staff, 1957-60; ret., 1968; asso., research dir. Internat. Research Inst., McLean, Va., 1968-78; v.p. Crystal Mgmt. Services, McLean, 1968-76; pres. Life Mgmt. Services, Inc., McLean, 1976—; cons. to govt. and bus. Decorated Legion of Merit, D.F.C., Air Medal with 18 oak leaf clusters (U.S.); Fouragierre (Belgium); Croix de Guerre (France). Mem. Am. Soc. Tng. and Devel., Am. Personnel and Guidance Assn., Air Force Assn., Am. Mgmt. Assn. Republican (mem. Nat. Com.). Episcopalian. Club: Masons. Home: McLean House Apt 1020 6800 Fleetwood Rd McLean VA 22101 Office: 6825 Redmond Dr McLean VA 22101

SHOOP, ROBERT ALAN, furniture co. exec.; b. Pitts., Sept. 4, 1917; s. Grant Sidney and Mary Isabel (DeYarman) S.; student Birmingham-So. Coll., 1934-37; B.S., Ga. Inst. Tech., 1941; postgrad. U. Tex., 1963; m. Lucy M. Justus, July 24, 1943; children—Robert Alan, Laura DeYarman. Asst. personnel dir. R.G. LeTourneau Inc., Toccoa, Ga., 1941-43; gen. mgr. Toccoa Casket Co., 1947-51; pres. Capitol Casket Co., Austin, Tex., 1951-67; v.p., dir. sales and mktg. Texwood Furniture Corp., Austin, 1967—; pres. Capitol Industries, Austin, 1969—. Served to 1st lt. U.S. Army, 1944-47. Mem. Nat. Sch. Supply and Equipment Assn. (dir.), Nat. Office Products Assn., Sigma Iota Epsilon, Tau Kappa Alpha. Republican. Episcopalian. Clubs: Kiwanis, Elk. Office: 3508 E 1st St Austin TX 78701

SHOPE, JAMES TERRY, transp. co. exec.; b. Little Rock, June 30, 1953; s. Charles Stelle and Christie Ann (Armstrong) S.; B.A. in Econs., U. Ark., 1974; M.B.A., U. Dallas, 1979; m. Sherry Lynn Clayton, Feb. 14, 1976. With Steere Tank Lines, Inc., Dallas, 1975—, asst. v.p., 1976-77, asst. v.p., treas., 1977-79, v.p., asst. treas., 1979—. Sustaining mem. Republican Nat. Com., 1979-80; mem. founders circle Fellowship of Christian Athletes. Mem. Nat. Fedn. Ind. Bus., N.Mex. Motor Carriers Assn. (dir.), Tex. Motor Carriers Assn. (dir.), Tex. Bulk Carriers Assn. (pres. 1980-81), Tex. Motor Transp. Assn., Tex. Acctg. and Fin. Council, Dallas Battle, U. Ark. Alumni Assn. Home: 10242 Deermont Trail Dallas TX 75243 Office: 2727 Turtle Creek Box 220998 Dallas TX 75222

SHOQUIST, THOMAS LEE, surface acoustic wave engr.; b. Stambaugh, Mich., Oct. 1, 1946; s. Lloyd Wallace and Betty Jean S.; student Mich. Tech. U., 1964-65, No. Mich. U., 1965-66; A.A., Richland Coll., 1975; B.A. in Physics, U. Tex., Dallas, 1978; m. Vicki Lynne Ellis, July 6, 1968; children—Laurie Ann, Paul Wayne. Microwave electronics specialist U.S. Air Force, Oklahoma City, 1971-72; sr. research asst. Tex. Instruments Inc., corporate research lab., 1972-76, surface acoustic wave design engr., 1976-78; surface acoustic wave fitter design engr. Sawtek Inc., Orlando, Fla., 1979—. Served with USAF, 1966-70. Mem. IEEE. Home: 340 W Wekiva Trail Longwood FL 32750 Office: 2541 Shader Rd Orlando FL 32804

SHORE, SHERMAN, journalist, ret. army officer; b. Yadkinville, N.C., Aug. 28, 1909; s. Sexton Denny and Minnie (Haire) S.; A.B., U. N.C., 1932; m. Patricia Patterson, Apr. 12, 1947 (div. Sept. 1970); 1 son, Mark Jeffrey. Reporter, feature writer Greensboro (N.C.) Daily News, 1932-35; with Winston-Salem (N.C.) Jour. and Sentinel, 1939-70, city editor, 1946-57, Sunday feature editor, 1957-70, lit. critic, 1957-70; instr. Army Command Gen. Staff Coll., 1961-64. Dir. warden service br. CD Orgn., Forsyth County, N.C., 1957-62. Served with AUS, 1942-45; to col. USAR, 1948-69. Mem. Am. Assn. Sunday and Feature Editors, Res. Officers Assn. (pres. Winston-Salem br. 1960), Asso. Artists Winston-Salem (past pres.), Delta Upsilon. Democrat. Methodist.

SHORT, CARL WINFRED, city ofcl.; b. Covington, Tenn., July 27, 1924; s. Martin Wise and Ora Myrtle (Proctor) S.; B.B.A. in Profl. Acctg., So. Meth. U., 1949; m. Alice Ward Letherman, July 7, 1964; children—Beverly Ann, Nancy June, Carl Martin, Martha Jane, Alice Marie. Served as enlisted man U.S. Navy, 1943-46; commd. ensign Supply Corps, U.S. Navy, 1950, advanced through grades to comdr., 1966, ret., 1971; mgr. Hammock Shop, Pawleys Island, S.C., 1971-76, Ginnie Thompson Originals, Pawleys Island, 1977-78; fin. dir. Consultant Systems, Inc., North Charleston, S.C., 1979, City of Georgetown (S.C.), 1979—. Mem. Ret. Officers Assn., Supply Corps Assn. Democrat. Clubs: Rotary (sec. 1978-79), Masons (Pawleys Island). Home: Hickory Dr Pawleys Island SC 29585 Office: City Hall Georgetown SC 29440

SHORT, JOHN EDWARD, architect; b. Lufkin, Tex., July 10, 1947; s. John Vernon and Luprell (Keller) S.; B.Arch. cum laude, Tex. A. and M. U., 1970; m. Janice Morgan, Jan. 2, 1971; children—Jeremy Collin, Matthew Bryant, Melissa Joy. Project architect Knowlton-Ratliff-English-Flowers, Bedford, Tex., 1974-76; v.p. TCB Architects, Bedford, 1976-78; with Lovett Sellars McSpedden Gober & Assos., Architects, Planners, Hurst, Tex., 1978—, asso., 1979—. Nat. Endowment Arts grantee, 1969-70; recipient H.E. Duff Meml. award Tex. A. and M. U., 1969. Mem. Mid Cities Bible Ch. Author, photographer: East Texas: A Visual Biography, 1969. Office: One Park Pl Suite 100 Hurst TX 76118

SHORT, JOHN PATRICK, mfg. co. exec.; b. Chgo., Jan. 4, 1937; s. Clifton Westly and Corinne Elizabeth S.; B.A., St. Ambrose Coll., 1958; m. Alice Greener, Dec. 28, 1957; children—Cheryl, Kevin, Deanne, Douglas, Steven. With Eagle Signal Corp., Austin, Tex., 1958—, application engr., 1959-63, sales engr., 1963-66, asst. sales mgr., 1966-69, gen. sales mgr., 1969-73, product mgr., 1973-74, systems mgr., 1974-77, customer service mgr., 1977-78, mktg. mgr., 1978—. Mem. Transp. Research Bd., Inst. Transp. Engrs., Internat. Mcpl. Signal Assn. Roman Catholic. Club: Kiwanis. Home: 3912 Greystone Austin TX 78731 Office: 8004 Cameron St Austin TX 78753

SHORT, LUCILLE DOUGHTON, educator, poet, lectr.; b. Bryan, Ohio, July 23, 1903; d. F.L. and Lamenta Campbell (Bayes) Doughton; A.B., Ohio Wesleyan U., 1926; A.M., Boston U., 1927, B.S. in Edn., 1943; postgrad. Tex. Woman's U., 1958, U. Chgo., 1962; m. Edward Preston Short, June 26, 1952. Instr. English and speech, Kenton, Ohio, 1929-39, Vt. Coll., 1944-46, Margaret Hall Sch. for Girls, Versailles, Ky., 1946-49, Radford Sch. for Girls, El Paso, Tex., 1949-50, Midway Jr. Coll., Lexington, Ky., summer 1947, St. Marys-on-the-Mountain Sch., Sewanee, Tenn., 1950-54, Germantown Sch., Memphis, 1954-68. Hostess radio program, Montpelier, Vt., 1944-45; writer Guidelines for fgn. lang. teaching Tchrs. of Shelby County, Tenn., 1959. Mem. Internat. (London), World (Madres, India), Tenn. (pres. 1965-66, program dir.) poetry socs., Nat. League Am. Pen Women (membership com. br. 1974-76), AAUW, Latin Tchrs. in West Tenn. (pres.), Am. Assn. Tchrs. Spanish and Portuguese (life). Liga Panamericana, Am. Classical Assn., Speech Assn., English Assn., New York Browning Soc., Acad. Am. Poets, Nat. Fedn. Press Women, Athenaeum Lit. Club, Alpha Delta Kappa (life). Episcopalian. Club: Tenn. Woman's Press and Authors (chaplain 1974-76). Contbr. poems to profl. publs., articles to mags. Home: 207 S Marne St Memphis TN 38111

SHORT, RODNEY DALE, tobacco machinery mfg. co. exec.; b. Richmond, Va., Oct. 12, 1954; s. Henry Lucien and Vera Ruth (Melton) S.; student Mars Hill Coll., 1973-76, Southeastern Bapt. Theol. Sem., 1976; m. Brenda Kay Spencer, Aug. 5, 1979. Youth dir. N.C. State Bapt. Conv., Rolesville, 1976; mgr. Best Products Co., Inc., Richmond, Va., 1977-79; customer service rep., U.S. customs expert Hauni Richmond, Inc., 1979—; freelance photographer. Counselor, Huguenot House Coffee House, Richmond, 1977—. Co-editor Fisherman's Jour., 1972-73. Home: PO Box 13430 Richmond VA 23225 Office: 5100 Charles City Rd Richmond VA 23231

SHORT, WILLIAM GEORGE, physician; b. Mullens, W.Va., Aug. 19, 1948; s. William George and Garnet (Mullens) S.; B.S., Marshall U., 1970; M.D., W.Va. U., 1974. Intern, Jacksonville (Fla.) Health Ednl. Program, Univ. Hosp. Jacksonville, 1974-75, resident, 1975-77, fellow in cardiovascular disease, 1977-79; practice medicine specializing in cardiology, Jacksonville, 1979—; asst. prof. medicine Jacksonville Health Ednl. Program, 1979—; mem. staffs Univ., Meth. hosps. Diplomate Am. Bd. Internal Medicine. Fellow Am. Coll. Cardiology; mem. A.C.P., Fla. Med. Assn., Duval County Med. Soc., N.E. Fla. Heart Assn. Democrat. Club: Jacksonville Racquetball. Home: 5885 Edenfield Rd Apt M-21 Jacksonville FL 32211 Office: 655 W 8th St Jacksonville FL 32209

SHORTALL, JOHN WILLIAM, III, naval architect; b. Chgo., Apr. 18, 1926; s. John William and Marie (Wolford) S.; B.S., Northwestern U., 1950; postgrad. U. Cal. at Los Angeles, 1950-52, U. N.M., 1950-52; grad. diploma Yacht Design Inst., 1975; m. Carole Mann, Dec. 16, 1978; children—Star V. Shortall Hickman, Thomas C.; stepchildren—William T. Bowley, H. Cameron Haight, Carron Haight. Physicist Los Alamos Sci. Lab., 1950-52; physicist Livermore (Cal.) Sci. Lab., 1952-54; physicist Lockheed Aircraft, Burbank, Cal., 1954-55; civilian scientist U.S. Air Force, Wiesbaden, Germany, 1955-59, 1959-62; scientist Fund for Peaceful Atomic Devel., Rome, 1962-65; scientist Gen. Electric Research Lab., Hong Kong, 1965-67; physicist Gen. Electric Tempo, Washington, 1967-70; pres. yacht research and design firm Caribbean Marine, Inc., Tarpon Springs, Fla., 1970—; adj. lectr. U. So. Fla., 1980—. Pres. Los Alamos Town Council, 1951-52; adult leader Boy Scouts Am., 1962-68. Served with U.S. Maritime Service, 1943-47. Mem. Soc. Naval Architects and Marine Engrs., Soc. Small Craft Designers, Am. Phys. Soc., Am. Yacht Research Soc. (editor Americas 1976-77), Exptl. Yacht Soc. (editor 1977-79), German, Italian, Hong Kong (past sec.) phys. socs., U.S. Yacht Racing Union, Am. Nuclear Soc., U.S. Power Squadron. Republican. Episcopalian. Clubs: Royal Hong Kong Yacht; Tarpon Springs Yacht. Author: Atomic Handbook V.I., Europe, 1965; (with Claire Shortall) Artichokes, Apartments and Aristocats - Live in Italy and Like It, 1966. Contbr. articles to profl. jours. Home and office: PO Box 1205 Tarpon Springs FL 33589

SHORTER, EDWARD SWIFT, artist, museum dir. emeritus; b. Columbus, Ga., July 2, 1902; s. Dr. James Hargraves and Elizabeth (Swift) S.; A.B., Mercer U., 1924; student Corcoran Sch. Art, 1924-28, Boston Museum Sch., 1925, Fontainebleau (France), with Andre Lhote (Paris), Wayman Adams, Hugh Breckenridge; LL.D., Mercer U., 1971; m. Mildred Watts, Oct. 3, 1953. Mem. staff Corcoran Sch. Art, 1930; exec. dir., also instr. art Columbus Mus. Arts and Crafts, 1952-70; now cons. in the arts Columbus Mus. and Hist. Columbus Found.; past lectr. U. Ga. Extension; represented in museums in cities throughout U.S., including: Atlanta, Montgomery, Macon, Columbus, Savannah (all Ga.), N.Y.C., Washington, New Orleans, Waco (Tex.), Ft. Hays (Kans.). Former trustee Boys' Club, Shorter Coll.; trustee Symphony Orch., Ga. Mus. Art (Athens), Ga. Hist. and Fine Arts Commn.; former bd. dirs. Atlanta Art Inst., Columbus Symphony, Brookstone Sch.; bd. dirs. Historic Columbus Found. Corcoran Art scholar, Paris, 1931; recipient Algenon Sydney Sullivan award Mercer U., Distinguished Alumnus award, 1977; Gari Melchers medal Artists Fellowship Inc. Mem. Shorter Coll. Hall of Fame. Mem. S.E. Art Mus. Dirs. Assn. (past dir.). Assn. Am. Museums (trustee), Am. Fedn. Arts, Ga. Hist. Soc., Artists Equity Assn., Am. Artists Profl. League, Nat. Art Club, Nat. Audubon Soc., Sigma Alpha Epsilon. Baptist. Clubs: Green Island Country, Big Eddy, Candun; Salamagundi (N.Y.C.). Home: 6001 Green Island Dr Columbus GA 31904 Office: 1251 Wynnton Rd Columbus GA 31906

SHORTT, HUBERT LAFAYETTE, electronic engr.; b. Damascus, Va., Jan. 18, 1910; s. Americus deLafayette and Ada Josephine (Salmon) S.; B.S. in Elec. Engring., U. Cin., 1930; m. Rosemary Gerard Viggiano, Feb. 22, 1958; children—Barbara Joan, Richard Alexander. Engr., Crosley Radio Corp., Cin., 1930-31, RCA, Camden, N.J., 1931-33; chief engr. Lafayette Radio Corp., N.Y.C., 1933-36; pres., chief engr. Transformer Corp. Am., N.Y.C., 1936-38, Wire Broadcasting Corp. Am. (now Muzak), N.Y.C., 1938-42; v.p. charge mil. electronic prodn. Airadio, Inc., Stamford, Conn., 1942-46; founder, pres. Polytron Corp., White Plains, N.Y., 1946-51; pres. Technograph, Inc., patent licensing all Eisler U.S. printed circuits patents, Winston-Salem, N.C., 1951—. Cons. in field. Fellow Radio Club Am.; mem. I.E.E.E. (sr.), Licensing Execs. Soc. Home: 3018 Cambridge Rd Winston-Salem NC 27104 Office: 920 Northwest Blvd Winston-Salem NC 27103

SHOTWELL, THOMAS KNIGHT, agrl. cons.; b. Hillsboro, Tex., May 31, 1934; s. James Douglas and Bonnie Maurine (Knight) S.; B.S., Tex. A. and M. U., 1955, M.Ed., 1962; Ph.D., La. State U., 1965; m. Shirley Imogene Plunkett, Dec. 29, 1955; 1 dau., Sharon Kay. Asst. county extension agt. Van Zandt County, Tex., 1955-56; head dept. biol. scis. Allen Acad. and Jr. Coll., 1958-62, 63-65; tchr. vocat. agr., pub. schs., Charleston, Mo. 1965-66; regulatory mgr. Salsbury Labs., Charles City, Iowa, 1966-70; dir. regulatory affairs Zoecon Industries,

Dallas, 1970-73; cons. research planning on drugs, pesticides, Dallas, 1973—; pres. Ronwell Corp., Dallas, 1976-77; v.p. Pace Internat., Dallas, 1979—. Served with arty. U.S. Army, 1956-58. Mem. Am. Soc. Agrl. Cons. (pres.-elect), AAAS, Am. Assn. Ind. Vets., N.Y. Acad. Sci., Mind Assn. Author: Laboratory Guide to The World of Plants; The Ecology of Antibiotic Usage; Guidelines and Policies for Veterinary Drugs; (with Paul W. Carr) Compendium of Veterinary Drug Efficiency; (with Paul W. Carr) New Animal Drug Applications; contbr. articles to profl. jours.; author agrl. newspaper column, 1965-66 (Best Agrl. Newspaper Column in State Mo. Sch. Journalism U. Mo. 1966). Home: 13243 Glenside Dr Dallas TX 75234 Office: Suite 175 2655 Villa Creek Dallas TX 75234

SHOULDERS, JOHN FRANCIS, agronomist; b. Horner, W.Va., Jan. 12, 1920; s. Charles Jesse and Martha Aeleta (van Tromp) S.; B.S., W.Va. U., 1943; M.S. in Agronomy, Pa. State U., 1951; m. Mary Ruth Shaffer, May 31, 1942; children—Mary Lea, John Francis, Susan Jane, Robert Edward. Asst. county agt. Mason County (W.Va.), 1946; county agt. Lincoln County (W.Va.), 1946-52; grad. asst. soils Pa. State U., 1949-50; asso. prof. agronomy, Va. Poly. Inst. and State U., 1952-76, prof., 1976-80, prof. emeritus, 1980—, asso. extension agronomist forage and turf, 1952-66, extension turfgrass specialist, 1966-80. Served with USMC, 1943-46; PTO. Recipient Disting. Service award Nat. Assn. County Agrl. Agts., 1973, Outstanding Service to Turfgrass Industry award Va. Turfgrass Council, 1973. Fellow Am. Soc. Agronomy; mem. Crop Sci. Soc. Am. (dir. 1973-76, chmn. turfgrass div. 1975), Internat. Turfgrass Soc. (conf. local arrangements chmn. 1973, Service award 1973), Va. Extension Service Assn. Presbyterian. Club: Lions. Author numerous extension publs.; contbr. articles to popular publs. Home: 509 Monte Vista Blacksburg VA 24060

SHOUP, TERRY EMERSON, mech. engr.; b. Troy, Ohio, July 20, 1944; s. Dale Emerson and Betty Jean (Spoon) S.; B.M.E., Ohio State U., 1966, M.S., 1967, Ph.D., 1969; m. Betsy Dinsmore, Dec. 18, 1966; children—Jennifer, Matthew. Asst. prof. mech. engring. Rutgers U., 1969-73, asso. prof., 1973-75; asso. prof. mech. engring. U. Houston, 1975-79, prof., 1979—; engring. cons. Recipient W.T. Kittinger teaching excellence award U. Houston, 1976-77; NDEA fellow, 1967-69. Mem. ASME, Am. Soc. Engring. Edn. (Dow Outstanding Young Faculty award 1974), U.S. Council for Theory of Machines and Mechanisms, Sigma Xi, Pi Tau Sigma. Author: (with L.S. Fletcher) Introduction to Engineering Including FORTRAN Programming, 1978; A Practical Guide to Computer Methods for Engineers, 1979; editor-in-chief, Mechanism and Machine Theory Jour., 1977—; contbr. tech. articles to profl. jours. Home: 9206 Portal Dr Houston TX 77031 Office: Mech Engring Dept U Houston Houston TX 77004

SHOURTS, JOHN LOUIS, educator; b. Clinton, Miss., May 26, 1929; s. Louis and Janie S. (Robinson) S.; B.S., Jackson State U., 1955; M.A., N.Y. U., 1959; Ph.D., So. Ill. U., 1975; m. Bessie Bailey, Dec. 13, 1953; children—Wanda Faye, John Louis. Tchr., Jackson (Miss.) pub. schs., 1955-64; teaching asst. So. Ill. U., Carbondale, 1973-75; faculty Jackson (Miss.) State U., 1964—, asso. prof. secondary edn., 1972—, coordinator Sophomore Career Decision program in tchr. edn.; cons. in career edn. Pres., Grove Park-Delta Dr. Community Neighborhood Assn., 1978—. Served with U.S. Army, 1951-53. Recipient Nat. Fellowship award So. Fellowship Found., 1973-75. Mem. Miss. Assn. Educators, NEA, Miss. Assn. Higher Edn., Am. Assn. Colls. Tchr. Edn., Phi Delta Kappa. Democrat. Baptist. Author: Sophomore Career Prospective Teachers, 1976. Home: PO Box 11221 Jackson MS 39213 Office: Jackson State Univ Lynch St Jackson MS 39217

SHOWS, CLARENCE OLIVER, dentist; b. nr. Brantley, Ala., Oct. 17, 1920; s. John Oliver and Cora (Nichols) S.; student Wis. State Coll., 1946-47; D.D.S., Northwestern U., 1951; m. Rachel LaRene Price, July 24, 1943; children—Toni Cherie (Mrs. Theodore Banks Kelly), Kristin Clare (Mrs. James Roger Ball), Bradley Scott, Gregory Norman, Jeffery Ryan. Individual practice dentistry, Valparaiso, Fla., 1951-53, Pensacola, 1953—. Mem. Pensacola Art Assn.; past pres. Escambia County Unit Am. Cancer Soc., now bd. dirs. Fla. unit, also hon. life mem.; mem. Eagle Scout Bd. Rev., Escambia County. Served with USCG, 1939-46. Fellow Royal Soc. Health, Internat. Coll. Dentists, Internat. Acad. Gen. Dentistry; mem. Am. Acad. Gen. Dentistry (master, past pres. Fla. unit), Internat. Orthodontic Assn., Internat. Acad. Preventive Medicine, Am. Orthodontic Soc., Gulf Breeze C. of C. (past pres.), Fla. Soc. Dentistry for Children (past pres.), Acad. Gen. Dentistry, ADA, AAAS, Am. Profl. Practice Assn., L.D. Pankey Dental Found., Fedn. Dental Internat., Am. Assn. Clin. Hypnosis, Northwestern U. Alumni Assn., Navy League (life), G.V. Black Soc. (life), Pensacola Jr. Coll. Found. (life), Psi Omega. Democrat. Presbyn. (elder). Mason (Shriner, Jester), Elks. Clubs: Pensacola, Exchange. Home: 516 Navy Cove Blvd Gulf Breeze FL 32561 Office: 3090 Navy Blvd Pensacola FL 32505

SHOWS, ROBERT JAMES, air force officer; b. North Island, Calif., Sept. 19, 1949; s. James Conley and Elizabeth Jean (Findley) S.; B.S. in Indsl. Engring., Tex. A&M U., 1972; m. Sharon Ann Morris, May 19, 1973; 1 dau., Gwendolyn Dawn. Commd. 2d lt. U.S. Air Force, 1972, advanced through grades to capt., 1976; assigned 33d Tactical Fighter Wing, Eglin AFB, Fla., 1974-75; pilot F-4, 57th Fighter Interceptor Squadron, Keflevik, Iceland, 1975-76; F-15 demonstration pilot, exec. officer 1st Tactical Fighter Wing, Langley AFB, Va., 1976-79, spl. asst. to wing comdr., 1978-79, asst. chief standardization/evaluation, 1979—, operational F-15 Eagle pilot, 1977—. Decorated Air Force Commendation medal. Mem. Air Force Assn. Mem. Churches of Christ. Office: 1st Tactical Fighter Wing Langley Air Force Base VA 23665

SHRADER, CHARLES WILLIAM, biologist; b. Martinsburg, W.Va., Dec. 24, 1917; s. Edward Franklyn and Mary Edith (Blake) S.; B.S., Randolph Macon Coll., 1947; B.A., Shepherd Coll., 1949; M.Ed., Western Md. Coll., 1960; m. Peggy Nelson McClung, Aug. 30, 1947; children—Gretchen Shrader, Steven Wyck. Lab. analyst Standard Lime & Stone Co., Martinsburg, 1940-47; biologist Am. Viscose Corp, Front Royal, Va., 1949-57; tchr. biology Baltimore County (Md.) Schs., 1957-61; asso. prof. biology Shenandoah Coll. Conservatory Music, Winchester, Va., 1961—. Served with USN, 1944-46. NSF grantee, 1961, 63, 64; HEW grantee, 1968. Mem. Preserve Historic Winchester, Va. Acad. Sci., AAAS, AAUP, Am. Legion, Phi Delta Theta, Alpha Phi Omega. Democrat. Episcopalian. Club: Odd Fellows. Home: 351 Jefferson St Winchester VA 22601 Office: Shenandoah Coll Conservatory Winchester VA 22601

SHRAUDER, PAUL ALFRED, forester; b. Enhaut, Pa., Dec. 10, 1927; s. Paul Winfield and Leona (Putt) S.; B.S., Pa. State U., 1953, M.S., 1954; m. Dorothy Louise Waltz, Aug. 25, 1951; children—David Earl, Michael Paul, Pauline Mary. Forester, Va. Forestry Commn., Waverly, 1954; forest ranger Ohio Div. Forestry, Zaleski State Forest, 1955-56; wildlife biologist S.C. Wildlife Resources Dept., McCormick, 1956-60; wildlife biologist, forester U.S. Forest Service, Jefferson Nat. Forest, Roanoke, Va., 1960-66; wildlife biologist, forester U.S. Forest Service, Regional Office, Atlanta, 1966-72; wildlife and range resources and info. and edn. staff officer Jefferson Nat. Forest, 1972-76, range, timber and wildlife staff officer, 1976—. Chmn. Va. Resource Use Council, 1974-76; dir. Emerald Estates Recreation Orgn., Decatur, Ga., 1970-72. Served with USAAF, 1946-49. Recipient Certificate of Merit, U.S. Forest Service, 1970. Mem. Nat. Wildlife Soc. (Va. state rep. 1972—), Nat. Wild Turkey Fedn. (dir. 1973—), Va. Herpetological Soc. Methodist (adminstrv. bd. 1962—). Mason (Shriner). Club: Olympic Recreation. Contbr. articles to profl. jours. Home: 3006 Fleetwood Ave SW Roanoke VA 24015 Office: US Forest Service Jefferson Nat Forest Poff Fed Bldg Franklin Rd Roanoke VA 24011

SHREVES, MELVIN LANKFORD, JR., coll. athletic ofcl.; b. Nassawadox, Va., May 30, 1942; s. Melvin Lankford and Nancy Virginia (Odom) S.; A.B., Elon (N.C.) Coll., 1966; postgrad., U. Va.; m. Peggy Jewel Hill, May 27, 1966; children—Michael David, Christopher Melvin. Tchr. Pittsylvania County (Va.) schs., 1966-68; bus. mgr., sports editor Star-Tribune, Chatham, Va., 1968-70; dir. news bur. Elon Coll., 1970-77, coordinator athletics, 1977-79, asso. athletic dir., 1979—. Recipient Ike Pearson Sports Info. Dir. award, 1977. Mem. Sports Info. Dirs. Assn. of Nat. Assn. Intercollegiate Athletes (pres. 1978; award of merit 1979), Athletic Dirs. Assn. of Nat. Assn. Intercollegiate Athletes, Coll. Sports Info. Dirs. Assn., Hargrave Mil. Acad. Alumni Assn. (pres. 1966-67), NAIA (dist. 26 chmn. 1979—). Democrat. Baptist. Club: Gibsonville Rotary (pres. 1977-78). Home: PO Box 801 Gibsonville NC 27249 Office: PO Box 2189 Elon College NC 27244

SHRIER, DONAGENE TEEGARDIN, designer; b. Norman, Okla., Feb. 4, 1928; d. Roy W. and Lula Rebecca (Meder) Teegardin; B.S. in Archtl. Engring., U. Okla., 1951; m. Donald Delos Shrier, Aug. 8, 1950; children—Donald Dee, John Roy Kimberly, Lewis Brent. Draftsman, U. Okla. Phys. Plant. 1948-49; designer, color coordinator, draftsman James & Durant, Architects, Sumter, S.C., 1952-53; designer Dixon Furlow Custom Builders, Richardson, Tex., 1965-67; designer custom homes Reynolds Constrn. Co., Richardson, 1967-71; prin. Dona Shrier, designer fine homes, landscaping, passive solar energy, cons., Richardson, 1971—; dir. Don-Rich Inc. Pres., PTA, 1964-65; den mother Cub Scouts, 1959-65, recipient awards; sec. bd. 1st Christian Ch., 1966-67, chmn. deaconess, 1978—, property chmn., 1979; bd. dirs. Teen Power, 1968-69. Mem. Home and Apt. Builders Assn. Met. Dallas. Clubs: Richardson Garden, Soroptomist. Home and Office: 825 Northlake Dr Richardson TX 75080

SHRINER, ROBERT DALE, economist, mgmt. cons.; b. Hobart, Okla., Nov. 28, 1937; s. William Dale and Mildred Ellen (Goodson) S.; B.A., U. Okla., 1965, M.A., 1967; Ph.D., Ind. U., 1974; m. Nancy Lee Thompson, June 6, 1961; 1 dau., Leslie Annette. Asst. chief ops. Gen. Dynamics-Astronautics, Altus, Okla., 1961-63; dir. Wyo. Tech. Assistance Program, Laramie, 1966-69; research asso. Bur. Bus. Research, Ind. U., Bloomington, 1969-71, dir. Aerospace Research Applications Center, 1972-76, mem. faculty Sch. Pub. and Environ. Affairs, 1972-77; asso. dir. Resource Devel. Internship Program, Council of State Govts., 1971-72; mng. asso., sr. economist Booz, Allen & Hamilton, Inc., Washington, 1977-79; dir. D.C. ops. Chase Econometrics, Washington, 1979—; cons. U.S. Catholic Conf., Dept. Commerce, EPA, Nat. Endowment for Arts, Inst. for Scrap Iron & Steel, Nat. Commn. Social Security, Ind. Tax Commn., Audubon Soc.; sci. adv. to gov. Wyo., 1969. Chmn. Rocky Mt. Tech. Services Council, 1968-69; bd. dirs. Fairfax County YMCA, 1978—. Served with USAF, 1957-61. Mem. Am. Econ. Assn., Nat. Assn. Bus. Economists, Nat. Economists Club, AAAS, Am. Soc. Pub. Admnstrn., Am. Pub. Works Assn., Midwest Regional Sci. Assn., Omicron Delta Epsilon, Beta Gamma Sigma. Club: Rotary (pres. Bloomington N. chpt., 1976-77). Editor, pub. Managing Tech. and Change mag., 1973-75; contbr. articles, reports in field. Home: 6432 Quincy Pl Falls Church VA 22042 Office: 900 17 St NW Washington DC 20006

SHRIVER, BRUCE DOUGLAS, SR., educator; b. Buffalo, Oct. 18, 1940; s. Millard D. and Arlene J. (Schalk) S.; B.S., Calif. State Polytechnic U., 1963; M.S., West Coast U., 1968; Ph.D., State U. N.Y., Buffalo, 1971; m. Beverly R. Connell, Aug. 17, 1963; children—Bruce Douglas, Mark D., Elizabeth A., Matthew C. Vis. sr. staff mem. U. Aarhus (Denmark), 1971-73; prof. computer sci. U. Southwestern La., Lafayette, 1973—. Grantee NATO, NSF, Danish Research Council, U.S. Army C.E. Mem. Assn. Computing Machinery (dir., editor newsletter spl. interest group on microprogramming), Am. Math. Soc., Soc. Indsl. and Applied Math., AAUP, Computer Soc. Contbr. profl. publns. Home: 402 Harwell Dr Lafayette LA 70503 Office: Dept Computer Sci PO Box 4-4330 Lafayette LA 70504

SHRIVER, DORIS (MRS. ELLSWORTH H. SHRIVER II), librarian; b. Cleve., Mar. 10, 1921; d. Harry A. and Vada M. (Custer) Ludasher; B.S., Ohio State U., 1943; m. Ellsworth Harold Shriver, II, Feb. 24, 1944; children—Deborah Lane, Ellsworth Harold, III, Keith Robinson. Wage adminstr. Thompson Products Co., Cleve., 1943-44; instr. Miss. So. Coll., 1944; reporter Hattiesburg (Miss.) Am. Newspaper, 1944-45; lab. technician Western Condensing Co., Appleton, Wis., 1945-48; pub. relations Shillito Kenwood Mall Store, Cin., 1966-68; music librarian Jacksonville (Fla.) U., 1971-76; mem. staff Cin. Suburban Newspapers, Inc., 1966; music librarian U. N.Fla. Audio-Visual-Music Library, 1976-79, dir. Media Resources Center, 1979—. Dir., instr. ARC swimming program Ross County Council Girl Scouts U.S., 1954-62; Ohio promotion chmn. Inter-League Survey Com. Ohio River Basin, 1964-66; mem. Gov. Ohio Com. UN Week, 1964-66; sec. Cin. Joint Com. UN Info., 1965-67; sec. League Women Voters, Chillicothe, 1955-57, 59-60, pres., 1960-63; Ohio Tri-Y adviser YWCA, Chillicothe, 1950-54, dir. Ross County, 1956-57; chmn. pub. relations Chilicothe Garden Club, 1961, pres., 1963-64; sec. Ross County PTA, 1956-58; chmn. pub. relations Flagler Coll. Beaux Arts Festival, St. Augustine, Fla., 1970. Mem. AAUW (pres. Jacksonville 1975-76), Ross County Hist. Soc., Am. Assn. UN (sec. Ohio 1962-64), Ohio State U. Alumni Assn. (county treas. 1955, county sec. 1956), Chioana Library Assn. (publicity chmn. 1968), Cin. Ceramic Guild (treas. 1967-68), Fla. Craftsman Guild, Delta Delta Delta (alumnae pres. 1949-50, 76-77), Phi Beta Psi. Christian Scientist. Clubs: Four Season Yacht; Century (Chillicothe); Beaches Woman's (editor 1969-70, 2d v.p. 1970-71); Compass Rose Internat. Toastmistress (sec. council sect. 1977—). Home: 13919 Shipwreck Circle N Jacksonville FL 32224 Office: PO Box 17074 Jacksonville FL 32216

SHRIVER, EDGAR LOUIS, psychologist, scientist; b. Canton, Ohio, Apr. 1, 1927; s. Elmer George and Clara (Kellogg) S.; B.A., Washington and Jefferson Coll., 1950; M.A., U. Rochester, 1951; Ph.D., U. Pitts., 1953; m. Beatrice Melrowin, 1951 (div. 1961); 1 son, John Adam; m. 2d, Sara Baker Eden, Aug. 15, 1961; children—Katherine Louise, Craig Edgar, Paul Kellogg. Research psychologist Am. Inst. for Research, Pitts., 1951-52; sr. staff scientist Human Resources Research Office, Washington, 1953-68; v.p., dir. Matrix Corp., Alexandria, Va.; pres. Tech. Tng. Corp., Washington, 1961-73; pres. Alexandria Community Sch., 1972-73; pres., chmn. bd. Kinton Inc., 1973—; cons. Westinghouse Corp., Am. Tel & Tel. Served with USNR, 1945-46. Fellow Am. Psychol. Assn.; mem. A.A.A.S., Eastern, D.C. psychol. assns., Phi Kappa Sigma. Presbyn. Home: 100 Prince St Alexandria VA 22314 Office: Suite 205 1500 N Beauregard Alexandria VA 22311

SHRIVER, JAMES GORDON, accountant; b. Escondido, Calif., Aug. 23, 1926; s. John Eastman and Evangeline R. S.; B.S. with honors in Acctg., San Diego State U., 1956; m. G. Aurora Romero, Apr. 3, 1959; children—John, James R. With Arthur Andersen Co., Houston, 1956—, partner, 1967—. Served with USMC, 1944-45, 52. Decorated Purple Heart with gold star; C.P.A., Calif., Tex., La. Mem. Calif. Soc. C.P.A.'s, Tex. Soc. C.P.A.'s. Club: Pine Forest Country (Houston). Office: Arthur Andersen Co 711 Louisiana St Houston TX 77002

SHUCK, LOWELL ZANE, educator; b. Bluefield, W.Va., Oct. 23, 1936; s. Carl Otis and Notre Dame S.; B.S. in Mech. Engring., W.Va. Inst. Tech., 1958; M.S. in Mech. Engring., W.Va. U., 1965, Ph.D. in Theoretical and Applied Mechanics, 1970; m. Annette Ulsh, Aug. 26, 1974; 1 dau., Kirsten Annette. Sales engr. W.Va. Armature Co., Bluefield, 1958-59; instr. mech. engring. dept. W.Va. Inst. Tech., Montgomery, 1959-65, asst. prof., acting chmn. dept., 1965-67, asso. prof., chmn. dept., 1967-68; NSF sci. faculty fellow, research engr., theoretical and applied mechanics dept. W.Va. U., Morgantown, 1968-70, asso. dir. engring. experiment sta., prof. mech. engring. and mechanics dept., 1976—; mech. engr. Morgantown Energy Research Center, ERDA, 1970-72, mech. engr., projects leader, 1972-74, supervisory mech. engr. and projects mgr., 1974-77; cons. Dept. Energy, 1976—; sci. adviser to W.Va. gov.; mem. W.Va. Coal and Energy Research Adv. Com.; sci. and tech. coordinator W.Va. Legislature, 1979-80. Registered profl. engr., W.Va.; cert. Nat. Council Engring. Examiners. Mem. ASME (chmn. emerging energy tech. com. 1979—, asso. editor trans.), AIME, Sigma Xi. Methodist. Club: Touchdown. Mem. editorial bd. In Situ Jour., 1977—; contbr. numerous articles to profl. jours.; patentee; producer tech. films. Office: Engring Experiment Sta WVa U Morgantown WV 26506

SHUCKER, HARRY BATDORFF, ednl. adminstr.; b. Lebanon, Pa., Apr. 20, 1942; s. Harry Swalm and Helen Emma (Batdorff) S.; B.A., Furman U., 1966; M.Ed., U. Ga., 1972; m. Pamela Ann Burgess, June 13, 1969; children—Harry Burgess, Cherington Love. Asst. dir. admissions Furman U., Greenville, S.C., 1968-71, dir. fin. aid, 1972-74, dir. residential living, 1974—; mem. S.C. Tuition Grant Advisory Com., 1973-74. Served with U.S. Army, 1966-68. Mem. Assn. Coll. and Univ. Housing Officers, So. Coll. Personnel Assn., Am. Personnel and Guidance Assn., Phi Kappa Phi, Kappa Delta Pi. Democrat. Baptist. Home: 200 Bromsgrove Dr Greenville SC 29609 Office: Furman Univ Greenville SC 29613

SHUEY, THEODORE GEORGE, JR., ednl. adminstr., cabinet co. exec.; b. Roanoke, Va., July 4, 1947; s. Theodore George and Mary Ellen (Long) S.; B.A. in History, Bridgewater Coll., 1969; M.Ed. (tuition grant), U. Va., 1974; m. Judith Hazel Lewis, June 21, 1969; children—Ellen Lewis, Theodore George. Tchr., New Hope (Va.) Elementary Sch., 1969-73; asst. prin. Hugh Cassell Elementary Sch., Waynesboro, Va., 1973-74; asst. prin., tchr. New Hope Elementary Sch., 1974-77; pres. Cabinet Craft of Va., Inc., Staunton, 1978—, Shenandoah Bldg. & Remodeling, Inc., 1979—, Ted Shuey Enterprises, Inc., 1978—. Reserve policeman City of Staunton, Va., 1969-75. Served with USNG, 1970—. Decorated Bronze Star, Army Commendation medal. Mem. Augusta County, Va., Nat. edn. assns., N.C. Exec. Dirs. Assn., Nat. Security Council, Va. N.G. Assn. (pres., ins. adminstr. 1979—, Meritorious Service citation, Past President's award) N.G. Assn. U.S., Am. Defense Preparedness Assn., Phi Delta Kappa. Republican. Lutheran. Home: 511 Willoughby Ln Staunton VA 24401 Office: 2203 N Augusta St Staunton VA 24401

SHUFF, SHELDON GARY, exploration geologist; b. Bklyn., Oct. 20, 1949; s. Harry Isadore and Etta Lee Shuff; B.A., SUNY, Buffalo, 1971; M.S., Miami U., Oxford, Ohio, 1974; M.B.A. with honors, Oklahoma City U., 1977. Geologist prodn. dept. Gulf Oil Corp., Oklahoma City, 1974-77; exploration geologist Tenneco Oil Co., Houston, 1977-80; with Phillips Petroleum Europe-Africa, 1980—; teaching and research asst. Miami U., 1971-73. Mem. Am. Assn. Petroleum Geologists, Soc. Econ. Paleontologists and Mineralogists, Houston Geol. Soc., Sigma Gamma Epsilon. Home: 5630-C Birchmont Houston TX 77091 Office: care Phillips Petroleum Europe-Africa 1702 Phillips Bldg Bartlesville OK 74003

SHUFFLEBARGER, DAVID TAYLOR, univ. ofcl.; b. Hampton, Va., Feb. 26, 1944; s. Charles Cosby and Emily (Taylor) S.; B.A. (Baker scholar, McElwee scholar) in Polit. Sci., Washington and Lee U., 1969; m. Patricia Grace Delk, June 8, 1968; children—Christopher Scott, Timothy Todd. Sports writer Daily Press, Newport News, Va., 1961-65; copy editor Virginian Pilot, Norfolk, 1965-67; dir. athletic publicity Va. Mil. Inst., Lexington, 1968; sch. tchr. Fairfield Sch., Lexington, 1969, also pastor; dir. pub. relations Va. Employment Commn., Richmond, 1969-70; v.p. for univ. relations Old Dominion U., Norfolk, 1970—. Dir. Communications Virginians for Constn., Richmond, 1970; campaign mgr. for candidate in Dem. primary for U.S. Senate, Richmond, 1970. Bd. dirs. Tidewater council Boy Scouts Am. Div. fellow, Duke, 1969, Univ. fellow, Yale, 1969. Mem. Pub. Relations Soc. Am., Am. Acad. Polit. Sci., Edn. Writers Assn., AAUP, Am. Soc. Pub. Adminstrn., Council for Advancement and Support of Edn. Office: 6200 Monroe Pl Norfolk VA 23508

SHUFFLEBARGER, FRANK ALBERT, accountant; b. Happy, Ky., July 18, 1921; s. Henry A. and Goldia Mae (Parsons) S.; student Alice Lloyd Jr. Coll., 1939-41, U. Minn., 1942-43, Cornell U., 1943-44; B.S. in Bus. Adminstrn., Berea Coll., 1948; postgrad. U. Ky., 1948-49; m. Janet J. Justice, Feb. 27, 1965. Tchr., McDowell (Ky.) High Sch., 1950-51; accountant Gen. Motors Corp., Hamilton, Ohio, 1951-53; sales engr. U.S. Radiator Co., Louisville, 1953-56; sr. accountant Heffner & Cecil, C.P.A.'s, Louisville, 1956-58; controller Ky. Telephone Co., London, 1958-63; pvt. practice accounting, Glasgow, Ky., 1963—; dir. Charles W. Knight & Sons, Louisville. Investment adviser to bus. firms; adviser to Fountain Run (Ky.) and Marrowbone (Ky.) water dists., 1970—. Pres. McDowell PTA, 1950. Served with USNR, 1942-46. Decorated Navy Commendation medal. C.P.A., Ky. Mem. Ky. Soc. C.P.A.'s, Am. Inst. C.P.A.'s, VFW. Democrat. Baptist. Mem. Hon. Soc. Ky. Mountain Men. Home: PO Box 203 Glasgow KY 42141 Office: 1028 W Main St Glasgow KY 42141

SHUFORD, PAUL MASON, lawyer; b. Richmond, Va., July 2, 1922; s. Jesse Franklin and Lois (Wright) S.; B.S., Washington and Lee U., 1943, J.D., 1948; m. Mary Campbell Gant, June 7, 1947; children—David Gant, Mark Campbell. Admitted to Va. bar, 1948; partner firm Wicker, Baker & Shuford, Richmond, 1948-60, Wallerstein, Goode, Dobbins & Shuford, Richmond, 1960-72; sr. v.p., sr. trust officer Central Nat. Bank of Richmond, 1973; corporate v.p., gen. counsel Central Nat. Corp., Richmond, 1974; individual practice law, Richmond, 1974—; instr. Washington and Lee U., 1948; instr. Richmond Coll. Law, 1950-54; lectr. bus. law U. Richmond, 1975-78. Vice-chmn. Richmond Area Community Council, 1956-59; chmn. Vol. Service Bur., 1954-56; dir., counsel Nat. Tobacco Festival, 1949-78. Trustee The Collegiate Schs., 1975-79. Served with USAAF, 1943-45. Decorated D.F.C. with cluster, Air medal with two oak leaf clusters, Purple Heart. Mem. Washington and Lee Alumni Inc. (dir., nat. pres. 1960-61), Am., Va., Richmond (pres. 1972) bar assns., Am. Judicature Soc., Phi Beta Kappa, Order Coif, Phi Delta Phi, Phi Kappa Sigma. Independent. Mem. Christian Ch. (moderator 1970-72, trustee 1966—, elder 1964—). Clubs: Commonwealth, Hermitage Country.

Author weekly editorial column Letter on the Law Richmond News, 1958-60. Home: 8 Glenbrooke Circle W Richmond VA 23229 Office: Mutual Bldg Suite 605 Richmond VA 23219

SHULA, DON FRANCIS, profl. football coach; b. Grand River, Ohio, Jan. 4, 1930; s. Dan and Mary (Miller) S.; B.S., John Carroll U., Cleve., 1951; M.A., Western Res. U., 1953; m. Dorothy Bartish, July 19, 1958; children—David, Donna, Sharon, Anne, Michael. Profl. football player Cleve. Browns, 1951-52, Balt. Colts, 1953-56, Washington Redskins, 1957; asst. coach U. Va., 1958, U. Ky., 1959, Detroit Lions, 1960-62; head coach Balt. Colts, 1963-70; head coach, v.p., part owner Miami Dolphins (winner Super Bowl 1972, 73), 1970—. Served with Ohio N.G., 1952. Recipient Coach of Yr. award, 1964, 67, 68, 70, 71, 72, 73. Roman Catholic. Address: Miami Dolphins-Biscayne Coll 330 Biscayne Blvd Bldg Miami FL 33132*

SHULER, CECIL WOODROW, ednl. adminstr.; b. Elloree, S.C., May 24, 1918; s. Millard Fillmore and Corrie Anne (Harley) S.; B.A., The Citadel, 1939; M.A., George Washington U., 1968; m. Katherine Dos Passos, July 5, 1941; children—Linda, Jane, Martha. Commd. 2d lt. U.S. Marine Corps, 1939, advanced through grades to col., ret., 1965; adminstrv. officer No. Va. Community Coll., Annandale, 1965—, dean fin. and adminstrv. services, 1968—, acting pres., 1979—; cons. adminstrn. of 2 year coll. Pres., Condominium Assn., 1972—; chmn. Memco Charitable and Scholarship Bd., Fairfax, Va., 1973—. Decorated Legion of Merit (2). Mem. Nat. Assn. Coll. and Univ. Bus. Officers, So. Assn. Coll. and Univ. Bus. Officers. Club: Army Navy Country (Arlington, Va.). Home: 7802 Dassett Ct #101 Annandale VA 22003 Office: 8333 Little River Turnpike Annandale VA 22003

SHULER, JANIS SMITH, speech pathologist; b. Robeline, La., Feb. 10, 1927; d. Zannie Leo and Lora Lena (Huling) Smith; B.A., Northwestern La. State U., 1953, M.A. (Univ. fellow 1966), 1967; m. Samuel Jackson Shuler, Oct. 17, 1946; children—Janet, Judith, Eric Van. Classroom tchr. public schs., La., 1945-46, 49-51, 53-67; speech pathologist Caddo Parish Sch. Exceptional Children, Shreveport, 1967—; part-time pvt. practice speech pathology, 1967-79; condr. workshops, guest lectr. in field. Recipient Outstanding Service awards NEA, 1964, 65. Mem. Am. Speech and Hearing Assn., Council Exceptional Children, Assn. Children with Learning Disabilities, La. Speech and Hearing Assn., Shreveport Speech and Hearing Assn., Hoover Watercolor Soc. Republican. Episcopalian. Club: Shreveport Art. Contbr. articles to profl. jours. Home: 9478 Blom Blvd Shreveport LA 71118 Office: 3202 Williams St Shreveport LA 71103

SHULMAN, ARNOLD, judge; b. Phila., Apr. 12, 1914; s. Edward Nathaniel and Anna (Leshner) S.; student Emory U., 1931; J.D., U. Ga., 1936; m. Mary Frances Johnson, Nov. 26, 1943; children—Diane Lifshey, Warren Scott, Amy Lynn Haney. Admitted to Ga. bar, 1937; judge Ct. of Appeals, State of Ga. tchr. Atlanta Law Sch., 1964—. Chmn. DeKalb County (Ga.) Sch. Study Commn., 1962-64, DeKalb County Sch. Salary Commn., 1960-62; mem. Fulton County-Atlanta Ct. Study Commn., 1961-62. Served to capt. AUS, 1941-46. Mem. Am., Atlanta bar assns., Ga. State Bar. Club: Lawyers (Atlanta). Author: (with Wiley H. Davis) Georgia Practice and Procedure, 1948, 3d edit., 1968, 4th edit. (with Warren S. Shulman), 1975. Contbr. articles to legal jours. Home: 1420 Stephens Dr NE Atlanta GA 30329 Office: 408 State Judicial Bldg Atlanta GA 30334

SHUMAKE, ROBERT SAMUEL, SR., govt. ofcl.; b. Detroit, Nov. 11, 1937; s. Homer Mecury and Mary Madgeline (Farley) S.; B.G.S. in Energy Tech., Wayne State U., 1978; M.A. in Bus. Mgmt., Central Mich. U., 1979; m. Deborah L. Fletcher, Oct. 7, 1967; children—Robert Samuel, Nikita, Norflette, Nehru. Energy conservation cons. Mich. Consol. Gas Co., Detroit, 1966-79; pres. Fuel Finders Internat., Inc., Detroit, 1973-75; asst. dir. New Detroit, Inc., 1974-76; energy conservation program specialist Dept. Energy, Dallas, 1979—. Asst. pastor Christian Temple Baptist Ch., Detroit, 1967-77; minister Good Street Bapt. Ch., Dallas, 1979—. Served with U.S. Army, 1959-62, USAF, 1962-66. Home: PO Box 1983 Dallas TX 75221 Office: Dept Energy 2626 W Mockingbird St Dallas TX 75235

SHUMAKER, FRANK GARRETT, JR., social worker; b. Princeton, W.Va., July 3, 1942; s. Frank Garrett and Mary Ellen (Harris) S.; A.B., Concord Coll., Athens, W.Va., 1964; M.S.W., U. Pitts., 1968; m. Linda Carol Campbell, Sept. 6, 1969; children—Frank Garrett III, Charles Alexander. Child welfare worker, juvenile probation officer W.Va. Dept. Welfare, Charleston, 1964-67, child welfare specialist juvenile delinquency services, 1968-74, dir. youth services, 1974—; instr. Morris Harvey Coll., 1973-79; cons. Nat. Center Juvenile Justice. Mem. Nat. Assn. Social Workers, Nat. Council Crime and Delinquency. Baptist. Club: Elks. Home: 608 Granada Way Charleston WV 25304 Office: 1900 Washington St E Charleston WV 25305

SHUMAKER, GEORGE CARROLL, elec. engr.; b. Vicksburg, Miss., July 10, 1943; s. David Jesse and Catherine Edna (May) S.; A.A., Hinds Jr. Coll., 1963; B.S., Miss. State U., 1967, postgrad., 1975-77; m. Peggy Ruth White, Mar. 6, 1965; children—Lynda Carol, David Carl. Lab. asst. elec. engring. Miss. State U., 1966-67; radar systems engr. Vitro Services, Eglin AFB, Fla., 1967-69, digital and timing systems engr., 1969-73; project engr. systems ops. and constrn. dept. Miss. Power & Light Co., Jackson, 1973-77; sales engr., accounts mgr. for So. Miss., GTE Sylvania Elec. Equipment Products, Jackson, 1977—; cons. in field. Mem. Miss. Democratic State Exec. Com., 1976—; vice chmn. Rankin County Dem. Exec. Com., 1976—; del. Dem. State Conv., 1976; adminstrv. bd. Brandon United Methodist Ch., 1974—, chmn. Council Ministries, 1978-79. Registered profl. engr., Miss.; licensed 1st class coml. radio-telephone operator, pvt. pilot. Mem. IEEE (vice chmn. Miss. sect. 1977-78, chmn. 1978-79). Club: High Noon Toastmasters of Jackson (pres. 1977). Home: 802 Louis Wilson Dr Brandon MS 39042 Office: 855 S Plaza Dr Jackson MS 39204

SHUMAN, IVY LEE, JR., physician; b. Savannah, Ga., Aug. 23, 1942; s. Ivy Lee and Elise Howard (Aldrich) S.; B.S. in Chemistry, Ga. So. Coll., 1965; M.S. in Nuclear Engring., Ga. Inst. Tech., 1971; M.D., Med. Coll. Ga., 1974; m. Sharon Kay Bohler, Oct. 20, 1972; children—Lisa, Leigh, Mandy, Christopher, Meredith. Intern, Meml. Med. Center, Savannah, 1974-75; practice family medicine, Sylvania, Ga., 1975—; med. dir. Sylview Nursing Home, 1976—; asst. clin. prof. Med. Coll. Ga., 1979—. Diplomate Am. Bd. Family Practice. Fellow Am. Acad. Family Practice; mem. AMA (physicians recognition awards, 1978, 79), Med. Assn. Ga., Am. Acad. Pediatrics (candidate), Ga. Nursing Home Med. Dirs. Assn. (sec.), Screven County C. of C. (dir.). Methodist. Home: Route 1 Sylvania GA 30467 Office: 211 Mims Rd Sylvania GA 30467

SHUMWAY, CHARLES LAKIN, real estate devel. co. exec.; b. Rochester, N.Y., July 8, 1936; s. Frank Ritter and Hettie (Lakin) S.; B.A., Brown U., 1958, M.A., 1966; m. Ann Osler Bent, June 18, 1977; children—Elizabeth, Stephanie, Charles Lakin, Hilary. Instr., Emory U., Atlanta, 1966-67; admissions officer Brown U., Providence, 1967-69; pres. Noteh Brook Co., Stowe, Vt., 1969-74; mng. partner Wilderness Country Club Partnership, Ltd., Naples, Fla., 1974-79; with 1st Plaza Corp., Naples, 1979—; gen. partner Meridian Partnership, Ltd., Naples, 1979-80. Trustee, Tougaloo Coll., 1979—. Mem. Am. Land Devel. Assn. Republican. Presbyterian. Clubs: N.Y. Yacht, Rochester Yacht. Home: 102 Tall Pine Ln Dr #3108 Naples FL 33942 Office: 1st Plaza Corp 3401 N Tamiami Trail Naples FL 33942

SHUPACK, SIDNEY IRVING, investment banker; b. Detroit, May 4, 1935; s. Harold Lawrence and Anne (Cahn) S.; B.B.A., U. Okla., 1958; postgrad. U. Tulsa, 1959-61; m. Jacque Elaine Lair, Dec. 31, 1967; children—Sheri Diane, Laura Elaine. Broker, Walston & Co., Tulsa, 1959-62; broker-adviser A.G. Edwards & Sons, Tulsa, 1962-66, Merrill, Lynch, Pierce, Fenner & Smith, Inc., Tulsa, 1966-72; pres., chmn. bd. First State Financial, Inc., Tulsa, 1972—; pres. First State Capital Fund, Inc., Tulsa; pres., chmn. bd. First State Banshares, Inc. Vice chmn. Bonds for Israel, 1974—; bd. dirs. YMCA, Tulsa, 1972—; chmn. bd. Thorton Family YMCA, 1978—; mem., financial adviser Handicapped Children of Tulsa. 1960—; active United Jewish Appeal, Tulsa Psychiat. Found. Served with USAF, 1958-59. Mem. Tulsa Soc. Investment Advisers, Petroleum Club Tulsa, Midwest Stock Exchange, Okla. Racquetball Assn. (chmn., pres., dir.). Mem. B'nai B'rith :past pres.). Club: Benien Racquetball. Author: Credit in the Stock Market, 1961; 12 Best Stocks for the Year. 1964-66; Marketing Bonds and Bank Securities. Home: 2707 E 67th Pl Tulsa OK 74136 Office: 5507 S Lewis St Tulsa OK 74105

SHURAYM, GEORGE PHILIP, office equipment mfg. exec.; b. Fakeha, Lebanon, Nov. 27, 1940; s. Philip and Nabiha (Murad) S.; came to U.S., 1962, naturalized, 1972; B.S. in Elec. Engring., Am. U. of Beirut, 1962; M.S. in Elec. Engring., Northwestern U., Evanston, Ill., 1963, Ph.D. in Elec. Engring., 1965; m. Souad Gellad, July 16, 1972; children—Mark, Maria-Christina, Ryan Philip. Middle East office mgr. Tex. Instruments, Inc., 1972-75; mng. dir. Gen. Systems S.A.R.L., Beirut, Lebanon, 1975-76; br. mgr. Tex. Instruments, Inc., Dallas, 1976-77; v.p., sec.-treas., dir. Contitronix, Inc., Garland, Tex., 1977—; vis. indsl. prof. So. Meth. U., 1966-69; asst. prof. elec. engring. Am. U. of Beirut, 1971-72. Mem. Bishop's Guild, Diocese of Dallas. Recipient nat. award for outstanding young elec. engr. Eta Kappa Nu, 1971, 72. Mem. Smithsonian Assos. Internat. Word Processing Assn., Dallas Exec. Assn. Roman Catholic. Club: St. Patrick's Men's. Contbr. articles tech. jours. Office: 3848 Marquis St Garland TX 75042

SHURICK, EDWARD PALMES, TV exec., rancher; b. Duluth, Minn., Dec. 15, 1912; s. Edward P. and Vera (Wheaton) S.; student U. Minn., 1932-33; B.A. in Econs., U. Mo., 1946; m. F(lossie) Dolores Pipes, Aug. 1, 1933; children—Patricia Annette (Mrs. Robert Dube), Sandra Sue (Mrs. Dean Hackley), Linda Jean (Mrs. James McBride), Edward P. III. Gen. sales mgr. Intermountain Network, Salt Lake City, 1937-41; advt. mgr. KMBC, Kansas City, Mo., 1941-47; research mgr. Free & Peters, N.Y.C., 1947-49; v.p. CBS Television, N.Y.C., 1949-57; exec. v.p. Blair Television, N.Y.C., 1957-62; pres., vice chmn., treas. H-R Television, N.Y.C., 1965-74, chmn. bd., chief exec. officer, 1975-77, dir., 1969—; pres. Nutmeg Farms, Charlottesville, Va., 1959-77, S & S Ranch Corp., Aspen, Colo., 1965—, Shurick Research Found., Bridgewater, 1959-72; v.p. Internat. Radio and TV Found., N.Y.C., 1964-74; dir. Broadcast Data Base, N.Y.C.; owner Sta. KXXX-AM-FM, Colby, Kans. Decorated Order du Merit (France), Ordre du Charolais Francais (Vichy, France); recipient Alumnus award U. Mo. at Kansas City, 1968. Mem. Wine and Food Soc., Internat. Radio and Television Soc. N.Y. (pres. 1967-69), Am. Internat. Charolais Assn. (pres. 1968-69), Colonial Charolais Breeders (dir. 1967-71), Internat. Livestock Exposition (dir. 1972-76), Broadcast Pioneers, Am. Nat. Cattleman's Assn. (tax com. 1968-76), World Fedn. Charolais (pres. 1973-74). Episcopalian (lay reader). Mason (32 deg. Shriner). Clubs: Farmington (Charlottesville, Va.); Windemere (Eleuthora Bahamas). Author: First Quarter-Century of American Broadcasting, 1946. Home: Box 29 Hickory Ridge Earlysville VA 22936 also Pompano Beach FL 33060

SHURLEY, JAY TALMADGE, psychiatrist; b. Eldorado, Tex., Dec. 20, 1917; s. Ira Lawrence and Jewell LaMarguerite (Choate) S.; B.A. in Zoology, U. Tex., 1940, M.D., 1942; m. Emily Webb Alexander Jackson, Jan. 4, 1964; children—Ronald Gene Jackson, Tom Henry, Guy Gibbs, Philip S., John Alexander. Intern, Ind. U. Med. Center, Indpls., 1943; Rockefeller fellow in neuropsychiatry Inst. of Pa. Hosp., Phila., 1944-47; practice medicine specializing in psychiatry, Phila., 1947-51, Austin, Tex., 1951-52, Oklahoma City, 1957—; acting chief Adult Psychiatry Br., NIMH, NIH, HEW, Bethesda, Md., 1955-57; chief psychiat. service VA Hosp., Oklahoma City, 1957-61; sr. med. investigator (psychiatry) VA, 1961-76; prof. psychiatry and behavioral scis. Coll. Medicine, U. Okla., Oklahoma City, from 1957, adj. prof. human ecology Coll. of Health, 1972—; med. dir. outpatient psychiatry Univ. Clinics, 1979—; vis. lectr. on human adaptation to polar zones Acad. Scis., Moscow, USSR, 1972; U.S. mem. of working group on human biology and medicine Scientific Com. Polar Research, Internat. Council Scientific Unions, Cambridge, Eng., 1972; dir. Behavioral Scis. Labs., VA Hosp. Oklahoma City and Oklahoma U. Coll. of Medicine, Oklahoma City, 1962-79; U.S. rep. working group on biology, Sci. Com. on Antarctic Research, Internat. Council on Sci. Unions, Canberra, Australia, 1970-72; vis. prof. of psychiatry U. Otago, Dunedin, New Zealand, 1975. Served to capt., M.C., U.S. Army, 1952-54. Recipient Distinguished Service award Okla. Psychol. Assn., 1974, Antarctic Service medal NSF, 1969; diplomate Am. Bd. Psychiatry. Fellow AMA, Am. Psychiat. Assn. (pres. Okla. dist. br. 1967-68), Am. Coll. of Psychiatry, Royal Coll. Psychiatry; mem. Phila. Assn. Psychoanalysis Aerospace Med. Assn., Internat. Soc. Chronobiology, Univs. Space Research Assn. (council large space structures 1977-78). Episcopalian. Co-author: Relating Environment to Mental Health and Illness: The Ecopsychiatric Data Base and Bibliography, 1979; contbr. articles on insulin therapy, sensory and social deprivation, human adaptation to exotic environments such as polar regions and space to sci. jours.; the Shurley Ridge of Pensacola mountains in Antarctica named in his honor. Home: 900 NW 41st St Oklahoma City OK 73118 Office: 400E Univ Clinics U Okla Health Scis Center PO Box 26901 Oklahoma City OK 73190

SHURN, PETER JOSEPH, III, lawyer; b. Queens, N.Y., Aug. 30, 1946; s. Peter J. and Vivienne (Tagliarino) S.; B.S. in Elec. Engring. magna cum laude, Poly. Inst. Bklyn., 1974; J.D. magna cum laude, New Eng. Sch. Law, 1977; m. Mary Ann Tantillo, Oct. 12, 1968; children—Steven Douglas, Vanessa Leigh. Admitted to N.C. bar, 1977, Va. bar, 1979; asso. firm Burns, Doane, Swecker & Mathis, Alexandria, Va., 1978—; individual practice law, Raleigh, N.C., 1977-78. Served with AUS, 1966-68. Mem. IEEE, AAAS, N.Y. Acad. Scis., Am. Bar Assn., N.C. Bar Assn., N.C. State Bar, Va. Bar Assn., Va. State Bar, N.C. Acad. Trial Lawyers, Assn. Trial Lawyers Am., Am. Patent Law Assn., Sigma Xi. Tech. editor New Eng. Law Rev., 1975-77. Home: 3326 Conquistador Ct Annandale VA 22003 Office: Burns Doane Swecker & Mathis George Mason Bldg Washington and Price Sts Alexandria VA 22313

SHURTZ, MARGARET CRAIG, former broadcasting exec.; b. Joliet, Ill., June 4, 1910; d. Herbert Walker and Winifred Grace (Dakin) Craig; B.S., U. Ill., 1932; m. Wendell Foster Shurtz, June 4, 1933; 1 dau., Barbara Shurtz Gilliam. Asst. dance dept. U. Ill., 1933-35; Welcome Wagon hostess, Johnson City, Tenn., 1944-75; hostess talk show Sta. WJCW, Johnson City, 1948-75, 50-75, program dir., 1951—; chmn. Mrs. America contest, Johnson City, also state judge, 1951; founder, dir. Johnson City Newcomers Club, 1945-75, hon. mem.; del. Nat. Housing Conf., 1958. Girl Scout leader, 1942-52; bd. dirs. Sister Cities Internat., 1969-77, hon. mem.; charter mem. women's div. Johnson City C. of C. Recipient Sterling award Movie Mirror mag., 1971, Spl. Community Service award, women's div. Johnson City C. of C., 1978. Mem. Internat. Platform Assn., D.A.R., Colonial Dames XVIII Century, Nat. Fedn. Press Women, Delta Zeta. Clubs: Tenn. Press and Authors, Monday, Music, Johnson City Country (Women's Golf champion, 1954). Address: 39 Forest Ln Tavares FL 32778

SHUSTER, CARL NATHANIEL, educator; b. Frenchtown, N.J., Feb. 16, 1890; s. Nathaniel Rittenhouse and Catharine (Draucker) S.; diploma Normal Sch., 1913; B.S., Tchrs. Coll. Columbia, 1915, A.M., 1918; Ph.D., Columbia, 1940; m. Edith Gilman, June 5, 1918; children—Carl Nathaniel, John Gilman, Jean S. Wessner. Head math. dept. Clark Sch., 1918-20, Orange High Sch., 1920-29; instr. Bowling Green U., summer 1920, 21, Pa. State U., summer 1925; instr. Columbia, 1926-52, prof., head dept. math. N.J. State Coll., Trenton, 1929-56; head dept. math. Pennington Sch., 1956-57; tchr. Sch. Indsl. Arts, Trenton, 1956-57; vis. prof. Yeshiva U., 1953-57; head math. dept. U. Tampa (Fla). 1957-60; prof. emeritus No. 1 Trenton State Coll.; head math. dept., dir. Adirondack So. Sch., St. Petersburg, Fla.; vis. prof. Coll. Advanced Sci., N.H. summer 1962, U. Fla., summer 1963, numerous others; lectr. against modern math., 1965—; sr. sci. editor U.S. Civil Service. Served with USNRF, 1917-18. Recipient alumni citation Trenton State Coll., 1961. Fellow AAAS, Fla. Council Sci.; mem. Fla. Acad. Sci., Assn. Math. Tchrs. N.J. (council 1926, permanent mem. 1955—, pres. 1952), Nat. Council Tchrs. Math. (charter mem., dir. 1946-48, pres. 1948-49), Am. Math. Soc., Math. Assn. Am., Columbia Press Assn. (charter, Gold Key), SAR, Phi Delta Kappa. Mason, Lion. Club: Torch (pres., exec. com.). Author: How to Use the Sextant, 1934; How to Use the Hypsometer and Clinometer, 1934; Field Work in Mathematics, 1936; Real Life Mathematics, Grades 3-8, 1938; Problems in Teaching the Slide Rule, 1940; Computation with Approximate Data, 1948; Plane Geometry, 1955; The Scribner Arithmetics, Grade 7-8, 1955; Functional Mathematics, Grades 7-12, 1956; author or co-author over 60 other texts; editorial bd. Mathematics Mag., 1946-60. Contbr. over 400 articles to jours. and mags. Research in sci. plant breeding; originated project method, 1907, field work in math., 1910, computation with approximate data, 1918, also numerous instruments and teaching devices. Home: 2035 26th Ave N Saint Petersburg FL 33713

SHUTT, ELIZABETH ANNE, speech and lang. pathologist; b. Richmond, Va., Nov. 9, 1951; d. William Henry and Mary Virginia (Seal) Gill; B.S., Radford Coll., 1973; M.Ed., U. Va., 1978; m. Bernard Ray Shutt, Aug. 11, 1973; children—Christopher Ray, Kelley Virginia. Tchr. hearing impaired Chesterfield County (Va.) Public Schs., 1973-74; speech pathologist Hanover County (Va.) Public Schs., 1974-76; speech/lang. pathologist Richmond (Va.) Cerebral Palsy Center, 1978—; mem. staff Tutoring Cons., Inc., 1976—. Mem. Speech and Hearing Assn. Va., Am. Speech-Lang.-Hearing Assn., Council Exceptional Children, Children With Communication Disorders. Roman Catholic. Home: 9327 Becton Rd Glen Allen VA 23060 Office: 1308 Sherwood Ave Richmond VA 23220

SHYLLON, PRINCE EMANUEL NATHANIEL, educator, lawyer; b. Freetown, Sierra Leone, Nov. 3, 1943; came to U.S., 1968; s. Henry and Lois (Johnson) S.; B.A., Shaw U., 1972; J.D., N.C. Central U., 1975; m. Millicent Boutchway, June 8, 1974; children—Nicky, Amaechi. Admitted to N.C. bar, 1977; partner firm Shabica, Shyllon & Shyllon, Raleigh, N.C., 1977-79, Shyllon, Shyllon & Ratliff, Raleigh, 1979—; asst. prof. bus. St. Augustine's Coll., Raleigh, 1976—. Bd. dirs. Wake County Credit Union. Recipient Award of Merit, N.C. Central Law Sch., 1975. Mem. Student Bar Assn. of N.C. Central U. (exec. body 1975-76), N.C. Assn. Black Lawyers, N.C. Sheriff's Assn., N.C. Bar Assn., Am. Bar Assn. Home: 1101 Athens Dr Raleigh NC 27606 Office: Suite 2045 Center Plaza Bldg Raleigh NC 27602

SIBLEY, JAMES ASHLEY, JR., educator; b. Shreveport, La., Oct. 21, 1916; s. James Ashley and Lucian Katherine (Hammond) S.; B.A., Centenary Coll., 1940, postgrad., 1941-53; M.Ed., La. State U., 1963; m. Anna May Switzer, Feb. 1, 1963 (dec. Mar. 1975). Asst. mgr. Sibley's Hardware and Variety Stores, 1935-41; farmer, Shreveport, 1941-45; tchr. sci., phys. edn. supr. Lab. Sch., Centenary Coll., Shreveport, 1941-42; tchr. pub. schs., Shreveport, 1942-44, Baton Rouge, 1958-71; dir. VITAL Career Information Center, La. Dept. Edn., Baton Rouge, 1971-76; dir. Grindstone Bluff Mus. and Environ. Edn. Center, La. Landmark, Shreveport, 1976—; ednl. cons., 1976—; personnel technician, examiner La. Civil Service Dept., Baton Rouge, 1944-48; employment counselor, test technician La. Employment Service, Shreveport, 1948-57; ednl. cons. Gulf S. Research Inst.; coordinator cultural resources Unit Project for humanities East Baton Rouge Parish Sch. Bd.; coordinator La. Arts and Sci. Center Planning Project, East Baton Rouge Parish Schs. Mem. econ. council East Baton Rouge Parish Sch. Bd., 1963-64; cons. sect. elementary sci. and social studies Assn. Childhood Edn. Internat., 1963-64; exec. asst. region 7, La. Jr. Acad. Scis., 1963-64, La. Social Studies Fair, 1972-76; adviser La. Indian edn. sect. Nat. Conf. on Employment Am. Indian; cons. La. Indian Cultural Heritage Ednl. Enrichment Program, 1975. Past mem. bd. dirs. Found for Hist. La. Co-founder, sponsor Jr. Archeol. Soc., Inc., Meml. Mus. and Library Fund. Recipient Merit award for outstanding service to pub. La. chpt. Internat. Assn. Personnel in Employment Security, 1952; La. Historic Preservation award. Mem. Nat. Social Studies Council (pres. East Baton Rouge Parish chpt. 1964-65), Assn. Supervision and Curriculum Devel., La. Hist. Soc., La. Geneal. and Hist. Soc., Am., La. (exec. com., bd. 1972-73) personnel and guidance assns., Nat. Vocat. Guidance Assn., (del.), La. Guidance Assn., Nat. Sci. Tchrs. Assn., Archeol. Inst. Am., Soc. for Am. Archeology, La. Acad. Scis., La. Tchrs. Assn., La. Sch. Counselors Assn., Soc. Hist. Archaeology, La., La. Sci. tchrs. assns., Am. Assn. Museums, La. Vocat. Guidance Assn. (pres. 1971-73), Nat. Trust for Hist. Preservation, Am. Anthrop. Assn., Nat., La. ret. tchrs. assns., La., No. La. (charter, past pres.) hist. assns., Ark., Okla., La. (past dir.), Tex. archeol. socs., Historic Preservation Shreveport, Am. Mus. Natural History, Am. Folklore Soc., Smithsonian Assos., Nat., La. wildlife fedns., Nat., La. recreation and park assns., Phi Delta Kappa, Psi Chi (charter mem. L.S.U. chpt.). Episcopalian (past treas. and vestryman). Author: Louisiana's Ancients of Man, 1967; The Junior Archeological Society, 1967; Geology of Baton Rouge and Surrounding S.E. La. Area, 1972; Grindstone Bluff, Sibleyshire, La. Landmark, 1975, others. Editor: Cultural Heritage of East Baton Rouge Parish, 1969; Handbook of Vital Career Information Center; The Development and Use of Behavioral Objectives, 1970; Cultural Heritage of Old Revenue Plantation, Carville, La., 1975. Contbr. articles to profl. publs. Address: PO Box 7965 Shreveport LA 71107

SICKEL, GEORGE WILLIAM, pathologist; b. Chester, Pa., Feb. 21, 1926; s. George Benson and Nelle Ione (Bittinger) S.; A.B., Dartmouth Coll., 1950; M.D., Temple U., 1954; m. Ruth Evelyn Bell, Sept. 29, 1956; 1 dau., Evelyn Ann. Intern, Chester Hosp., 1954-56, resident in pathology, 1956-58; resident in pathology, Wilmington, Del., 1958-59, Phila., 1959-61; dir. labs. Stanly County Hosp., Albemarle, N.C., 1961-63, Springfield (Ohio) Community Hosp.,

1963-66, John Peter Smith Hosp., Ft. Worth, 1966-76; mem. firm Severance & Assos., San Antonio, 1976-77; asso. pathologist Mercy Health Center, Oklahoma City, 1977-79; asst. clin. prof. pathology Southwestern Med. Sch., Dallas, 1966-76; pres. G. William Sickel & Assos., 1974-75; asso. Pathology and Nuclear Med. Assos., Baton Rouge, 1979—. Vestryman, fin. com. Episcopal Parish, Ft. Worth. Served with USNR, 1943-46; PTO. Diplomate Am. Bd. Pathology. Fellow Am. Soc. Clin. Pathologists, Coll. Am. Pathologists; mem. AMA (Physicians Recognition award), So. Med. Assn., Am. Assn. Blood Banks, La., East Baton Rouge Parish med. socs. Home: 12047 Oakhaven Way Baton Rouge LA 70810 Office: 5000 Hennessey Blvd Baton Rouge LA 70809

SICOTTE, ANDREW RONALD, rehab. worker; b. Flint, Mich., Aug. 17, 1946; s. Octave Lucien and Pauline (Rudnicki) S.; B.A. in Psychology, U. South Fla., 1973; M.S. in Rehab., U. Ariz., 1976. Psychol. technician Bay Front Med. Center, St. Petersburg, Fla., 1973; counselor Schumaker Elementary Sch., Tucson, 1975-76; rehab. counselor for deaf Tex. Rehab. Commn., San Antonio, 1976—. Served with U.S. Army, 1966-67; Vietnam. Mem. Am. Personnel and Guidance Assn., Am. Deafness and Rehab. Assn. (pres. Tex. chpt. 1978-80), Nat. Rehab. Assn., San Antonio Registry of Interpreters for Deaf. Home: 1211 Santa Monica San Antonio TX 78201 Office: 1015 Jackson-Keller Rd San Antonio TX 78213

SIDDONS, JAMES DEWITT, musicologist; b. Narsarssuaq, Greenland, Nov. 1, 1948; s. James Claudius and Willie Belle (Durham) S. (parents U.S. citizens); Mus.B., North Tex. State U., 1970; Mus.M., King's Coll., U. London, 1971; research student Tokyo U. of Arts, 1973-74; m. Joyce Lorraine Garbee, July 2, 1977. Asst. prof. music Liberty Baptist Coll., 1976-79, asso. prof., 1979—; co-owner, tchr. Siddons Sch. Music, Lynchburg, Va.; participant Nat. Endowment for Humanities Summer Seminar for Coll. Tchrs., 1978. Mem. Am. Musicol. Soc., Internat. Musicol. Soc., Music Library Assn. Am., Soc. Asian Music, Assn. Asian Studies, Soc. Ethnomusicology. Contbr. articles, revs. to profl. pubs.; editor Musical Analysis, 1972-74. Home: 210 Alta Ln Lynchburg VA 24502 Office: Liberty Bapt Coll Lynchburg VA 24506

SIDELNIK, MARY CROW, med. records adminstr.; b. Bonne Terre, Mo., Apr. 6, 1948; d. Wayman Detring and Barbara Elizabeth (Conrad) Crow; A.A., Mineral Area Coll., 1968; B.S., St. Louis U., 1970; m. Richard D. Sidelnik, Dec. 27, 1974. Asst. dir. med. record dept. St. Johns Med. Center, Joplin, Mo., 1970-71; dir. med. record dept. Hahnemann Hosp., San Francisco, 1971; dir. med. record dept. St. Joseph Hosp., Bloomington, Ill., 1971-74; med. record cons. Bailey Square Surg. Center, Austin, Tex., 1978—; chief med. record specialist Bur. Long Term Care, Tex. Dept. Health, Austin, 1975—. Mem. Am. Med. Record Assn., Tex. Med. Record Assn., Tex. Assn. Mental Defieciency, Am. Record Mgrs. Assn., Tex. Public Health Assn., Intergovtl. Tng. Council. Methodist. Office: Profl Services Div 1100 W 49th St Austin TX 78756

SIDES, JACK DAVIS, JR., lawyer; b. Dallas, Sept. 18, 1939; s. Jack Davis and Edith Eugenia (Lowrie) S.; B.B.A., U. Tex., 1962, J.D. with honors, 1963; children—Mary Katharine, Jack Davis III. Admitted to Tex. bar, 1963; mem. firm Jackson, Walker, Winstead, Cantwell & Miller, Dallas, 1963-68, White, McElroy, White & Sides, 1968-77; individual practice, 1978—. Active crusade Am. Cancer Soc., 1966-72; judge of moot ct. competition So. Meth. U., 1968-71. Cert. civil trial specialist Tex. Bd. Legal Specialization. Mem. Am., Tex., Dallas (ethics com. 1972-77, subcom. of grievance com. 1980—) bar assns., Dallas Def. Assn. (sec. 1972-73), Tex. Assn. Def. Counsel, Tex. Law Rev. Assn., Phi Gamma Delta, Phi Delta Phi. Club: Brook Hollow Golf. Home: 4552 Lorraine Ave Dallas TX 75205 Office: 2001 Bryan Tower Suite 2065 Dallas TX 75201

SIDES, KERMIT FRANKLIN, furniture mfg. co. exec.; b. Lee County, Miss., Feb. 13, 1932; s. Robert Franklin and Francis Jet (Cox) S.; grad. high sch., Wheeler, Miss.; m. Edna E. Heavener, Aug. 1, 1953; children—Connie Ann, Timothy Franklin. Mfg. supr. Futorian Mfg. Co., New Albany and Okolona, Miss., 1953-69; v.p. mfg., gen. mgr. Action Industries, Verona and Pontotoc, Miss., 1969-79; exec. v.p., sec., treas. PeopLounger Inc., Nettleton, Miss., 1979—, also dir. Indsl. chmn. Lee United Neighbors div. United Way, Tupelo, Miss., 1969-73. Baptist. Home: 2618 Pemberton St Tupelo MS 38801 Office: PO Drawer J Nettleton MS 38858

SIDES, LARRY EUGENE, advt./public relations exec.; b. Albany, Ga., Nov. 14, 1946; s. Robert N. and Florine Stewart S.; B.A., U. Southwestern La., 1970, M.S., 1975. Television newsman Sta. KATC-TV, ABC affiliate, Lafayette, La., 1969-71; account exec. Herbert Benjamin Assos., Lafayette, 1972-76; pres., gen. mgr. Sides & Assos., Lafayette, 1976—. Bd. dirs. Krewe of Bastille, ARC, Beaver Club Lafayette (Man of Yr. award 1976); v.p. Krewe of Triton; communications head, publicity chmn. United Givers Fund ann. drive. Recipient Disting. Service award Jaycees, 1977. Mem. Am. Soc. Hosp. Public Relations, Ad Club Acadiana, Polit. Campaign Inst., Ozark Soc., Lafayette C. of C. (local affairs chmn. 1978). Methodist. Home: 102 Quail Dr Lafayette LA 70508 Office: 404 Eraste Landry Rd Lafayette LA 70501

SIDLINGER, BRUCE CHESTER, mgmt. cons.; b. Cedar Rapids, Iowa, Dec. 10, 1927; s. Paul E. and Ruth (Wilson) S.; student U. Iowa, 1948, U. Ill., 1949-51; m. Joanne Leonard, May 16, 1956; 1 son, Bruce Douglas. Mgmt. cons. Sidlinger Products Co., Inc., Garland, Tex., 1948—; profl. trampolinist, 1951-67; appeared at Radio City Music Hall, 1955, Gary Moore Show, 1957, Paul Winchell Show, 1957. Served with AUS, 1946-48. Mem. Theta Xi. Patentee in field. Home: 2810 Country Club Rd Garland TX 75043 Office: 208-214 International Rd Garland TX 75042

SIDLINGER, JOANNE, mgmt. cons.; b. Dallas, Aug. 4, 1937; d. Richard Douglas and Joan (Frank) Leonard; student Christian Coll. of S.W., 1967; m. Bruce Chester Sidlinger, May 16, 1956; 1 son, Bruce Douglas. Profl. trampolinist, 1956-60; v.p. Sidlinger Products Co., Inc., Garland, Tex., 1957-76, corporate dir., mgmt. cons., 1976—; chief pilot Sidlinger Products Co., Inc., 1962-76. Candidate for Garland City Council, 1964. Mem. Nat. Sporting Goods Assn., ASTM, Internat. Platform Assn., Nat. Wildlife Fedn., Kiamichi Conservation Soc. (dir.). Republican. Club: Eastern Hills Country. Author: Instructional Manual for Trampolining, 1974. Home: 2810 Country Club Rd Garland TX 75043 Office: 202-214 International Rd Garland TX 75042

SIEBENTHALL, CURTIS ALAN, guidance counselor; b. Odessa, Tex., June 30, 1929; s. Curtis Arnold and Norma T. (Henry) S.; B.S., Midwestern State U., 1951, M.Ed., 1955; Ed.D., N.Tex. State U., 1972; m. Hazel Jane Madden, July 26, 1958; children—Rebecca Ann and David Alan. Chemist, Phillips (Tex.) Petroleum Co., 1953; tchr. Wichita Falls (Tex.) Ind. Sch. Dist., 1953-55, counselor, 1955-65, dir. counseling and testing, 1965-69; counselor Denton (Tex.) Ind. Sch. Dist., 1970-72; counselor, prof. psychology Tarrant County (Tex.) Jr. Coll., Fort Worth, 1972—; pvt. practice psychotherapy, Hurst, 1977—. Certified elementary and secondary sch. counselor, Tex.; licensed social psychotherapist, Tex. Mem. Tex. State Tchrs. Assn., Am., Tex. personnel and guidance assns., Am. Psychol. Assn. Office: 5301 Campus Dr Fort Worth TX 76119 also 1050 W Pipeline Rd Suite 202 Hurst TX 76053

SIEBERT, JAMES DAVID, savs. and loan exec.; b. Memphis, Tenn., Sept. 27, 1947; s. William Turner and Gladys Ruth (Taylor) S.; B.B.A. cum laude, Memphis State U., 1969; m. Charlotte Marie Zoccola, July 9, 1971; children—Lauren Marie, Karen Louise, Matthew David. Project leader Mo.-Pacific/Tex. and Pacific Ry. Cos., Fort Worth, 1971-75; inventory systems coordinator Miller Brewing Co., Fort Worth, 1975-76; asst. v.p. Leader Fed. Savs. and Loan Assn., Memphis, 1976—. Republican. Methodist. Home: 3086 Altruria Rd Bartlett TN 38134 Office: 158 Madison Ave PO Box 3410 Memphis TN 38103

SIEBLER, RONALD LEE, legal adminstr.; b. Wichita Falls, Tex., May 3, 1952; s. Harold A. and Norma Lee S.; student Midwestern State U., 1970-71, N. Tex. State U., 1978. Field rep. Wadley Central Blood Bank of Dallas, 1973-74; dir. planning and devel. Westgate Hosp., Denton, Tex., 1974-76; asst. adminstr. Med. Center Hosp. of Garland (Tex.), 1977; legal adminstr., adminstrv. cons. Foster and George, Attys., Denton, 1977—. Mem. adv. bd. Ann's Haven of Denton County; exec. dir. Health Sers. Assn. N. Central Tex.; chmn. Denton County Republican Party, 1976; vice chmn. Denton County Sub-Area Health Planning Council, 1979. Mem. Tex. Hosp. Assn. Methodist. Home: 1812 Westminster #10 Denton TX 76201 Office: 900 I-35 E Denton TX 76201

SIEGAL, FRANK ALAN, auto parts distbg. co. exec.; b. Birmingham, Ala., June 15, 1951; s. Irvin Fred and Rosalyn (Rittenbaum) S.; B.S., U. Ala., 1973. Ops. mgr. Automotive Hdqrs., Inc., Birmingham, 1973-78, v.p. ops., 1978—. Mem. adv. com., safety coordinating com. Ala. Senate, 1977; solicitor Birmingham Jewish Fedn.; bd. dirs. Temple Emanuel Synagogue. Mem. Auto Service Industry Assn. (vice-chmn. young execs. forum), Auto Warehouse Distbrs. Assn. (asso.), Distbrs. Inst. Home: 4344 Warren Rd Birmingham AL 35213 Office: 607 N 31st St Birmingham AL 35203

SIEGAL, FRED DON, lawyer; b. Tuscaloosa, Ala.. Nov. 11, 1941; s. Ed and Esther (Light) S.; B.S., U. Ala., 1964, LL.B., 1967; m. Barbara Solomon, Sept. 7, 1963; children—Rachelle Carole, Brian David. Admitted to Ala. bar, 1967; law clk. Tuscaloosa, Ala. 5th Circuit Ct. Appeals, 1967-68; practiced in Birmingham, Ala., 1968—; partner Berkowitz, Lefkovits & Patrick, 1968-76, Leitman, Siegal & Payne, Profl. Assn., 1976—; lectr., Practising Law Inst., San Francisco, N.Y.C., 1974; tchr., Ala. Bar Review Course, Inc., 1970—; mem. Ala. Continuing Legal Edn. Com., 1971-73. Chmn. State Ala., Anti-Defamation League, 1974-75. Bd. dirs. Jewish Community Center, Birmingham Jewish Fedn. Recipient Morrisette award of Constnl. Law U. Ala., 1967. Mem. Am., Ala., Birmingham bar assns., Jason's Soc. (pres. 1967), Farrah Law Soc. (dir. 1972), Shades Valley Jaycees (pres. 1971), Phi Beta Kappa, Phi Delta Theta, Alpha Epsilon Pi. Clubs: Pine Tree Country. The Relay House. Author: Rights and Liability of Automobile Owner-Bailor Under Owner Liability Statutes, 1966; The Corporate Law of Alabama, 1973; The Gift Tax Consequences of Political Contributions, 1973; Severing Joint Ownership, 1974; Planning a Lifetime Gift Program, 1979. Home: 3595 Rockhill Rd Birmingham AL 35223 Office: 425 1st Ala Bank Bldg Birmingham AL 35203

SIEGEL, BARRY D., savs. and loan exec.; b. Newark, N.J., Feb. 17, 1931; s. Herman H. and Sue (Nutes) S.; B.A., Bowling Green U., 1952; postgrad. Rutgers U., 1953; m. Nancy Dreskin, Aug. 4, 1955; children—Abby, John. Exec. dir. Zeta Beta Tau Found., N.Y.C., 1960-71; v.p. mktg. Am. Savs. & Loan Assn., Miami, Fla., 1971—; instr. Inst. Fin. Edn., 1971, v.p., 1977-78; v.p. Orgn. for Rehab. through Tng., 1978-79. Pres., Civic League of Miami Beach (Fla.), 1978; bd. dirs. B'nai B'rith, 1977-78, United Cerebral Palsy Assn., 1978, Am. Jewish Com., 1976, Mt. Sinai Med. Center, 1976. Served with Signal Corps, U.S. Army, 1953-55. Recipient various achievement awards community and civic orgns. Mem. Public Relations Soc. Am., Am. Mktg. Assn. (v.p. collegiate affairs 1977-78), Savs. and Loan Mktg. Soc. Fla. (pres. 1977-79), Sales and Mktg. Execs., Fla. Savs. and Loan League (chmn. mktg. com. 1977-78), Miami Beach C. of C. (dir. 1977-78, v.p. 1978-79), Miami Advt. Club (treas. 1976-79), Ft. Lauderdale Ad Club (dir. 1978-79), Palm Beach Advt. Club, Savs. Instns. Mktg. Soc. Am. Democrat. Jewish. Club: Kiwanis (dir. 1978-79). Home: 1831 W 23rd St Sunset Island 3 Miami Beach FL 33140 Office: Washington Ave at Lincoln Rd Miami Beach FL 33139

SIEGEL, JEROME SEYMOUR, physician; b. Memphis, Oct. 2, 1937; s. Max and Sophie Rebecca (Rosen) S.; student U. Pa., 1955-57, Southwestern Coll. Memphis, 1957-58; M.D., U. Tenn., 1961; m. Gloria Beryl Shubow, Dec. 22, 1957; children—David Alan, Karen Lynn. Rotating intern U. Chgo., 1961-62; gen. med. officer Barksdale AFB, La., 1962-64; resident internal medicine Wilford Hall USAF Hosp., Lackland AFB, Tex., 1964-67; chief internal medicine sect. USAF Hosp., Tackikawn AB, Japan, 1967-70; practice medicine specializing in internal medicine and cardiology, Memphis, 1970—; active staff Wm. F. Bowld, City Memphis hosps.; jr. staff Meth. Hosp.; cons. staff St. Joseph's Hosp., Memphis. Clin. instr. medicine U. Tenn. Coll. Medicine, 1970—; mem. teaching and active staff Bapt. Meml. Hosp., Memphis. Served to lt. col. USAF, 1962-70. Diplomate Am. Bd. Internal Medicine. Fellow Memphis Acad. Internal Medicine, A.C.P.; mem. Am. Soc. Internal Medicine, Memphis, Shelby County med. socs., So., Mid South med. assns., Tenn. Med. Soc., Tenn. Soc. Internal Medicine, Nat. Assn. Residents and Interns, AMA, Am., Memphis heart assns., Am. Coll. Cardiology, Phi Delta Epsilon. Republican. Jewish. Contbr. articles to med. jours. Home: 6624 Westminster Rd Memphis TN 38138 Office: 6025 Walnut Grove Rd Suite 607 Memphis TN 38138

SIEGEL, LAWRENCE IVER, real estate devel. co. exec.; b. Cleve., Aug. 19, 1925; s. Edward I. and Mary (Mentz) S.; B.B.A., Western Res. U., 1949, LL.B., 1952; m. Joyce Reske, Nov. 4, 1950; children—Leslie, Diane, Frederic, Edward. Pres., Lawrence I. Siegel Co., Baton Rouge, 1980—. Bd. dirs. Tara High Sch. Backers, Baton Rouge, Community Concerts Assn., New Orleans. Served with inf. U.S. Army, 1943-46; ETO, PTO. Named hon. col. on staff Gov. Edwin Edwards, 1974. Mem. Internat. Council Shopping Centers, Mortgage Bankers Assn. Am., Am. Bankers Assn. Club: Kiwanis. Office: 10455 Jefferson Baton Rouge LA 70809

SIEGEL, MARVIN IRA, biochemist; b. Bklyn., July 11, 1946; s. Morris and Ray Norma (Goldman) S.; B.S., Lafayette Coll., 1967; M.A., Columbia U., 1968; Ph.D., Johns Hopkins U., 1973; m. Frances Lea Greenstein, Nov. 20, 1970; 1 dau., Deborah Genevieve. Postdoctoral fellow dept. pharmacology and exptl. therapeutics Johns Hopkins U. Sch. Medicine, 1973-75; sr. staff scientist Wellcome Research Labs., Burroughs Wellcome Co., Research Triangle Park, N.C., 1975—; adj. asst. prof. biochemistry U. N.C. Sch. Medicine, 1975—. Mem. Am. Chem. Soc., Am. Inst. Chemists, AAAS, N.Y. Acad. Sci., Am. Soc. Pharmacology and Exptl. Therapeutics, Phi Beta Kappa, Sigma Xi. Contbr. articles to sci. jours. Office: Wellcome Research Labs 3030 Cornwallis Rd Research Triangle Park NC 27709

SIEGENDORF, ARDEN MICHAEL, judge; b. 1967-68, Beach, Fla., Oct. 13, 1938; s. N. James and Audrey Belle (Cutler) S.; student U. Fla., 1956-57; B.B.A., U. Miami, 1960, J.D., 1963; m. Rebecca Lyle; children—Stacey, James Michael. Admitted to Fla. bar, 1963; spl. asst. atty. gen. Fla. Legislature, Miami, 1963; research aide Fla. 3d Dist. Ct. Appeal, Miami, 1963-64; legal counsel Dade County Ho. of Dels. to Fla. Legislature, Miami, 1965-67; asst. atty. gen. Fla., Miami, 1965-71; city commr. Miami, 1971; judge Dade County Ct., Miami, 1971-74; circuit ct. judge 11th Jud. Circuit, Miami, 1974—; adminstrv. judge Appellate Div.; mem. Fla. Bd. Bar Examiners, 1971; mem. jud. com. Fla. Bicentennial Celebration, 1975-76; chmn. adv. bd. Comprehensive Offender Rehab. Program, 1975; chmn. Judges Speakers Bur., 1977; chmn. Bench-Media Relations Com., 1978. Pres. Young Democratic Club, Dade County, Fla., 1967[68, Young Dem. Clubs Fla., 1969-70. Named Outstanding Young Man Miami, 1973. Mem. U. Miami Alumni Assn. (pres. 1971-72, dir. 1972-76), Iron Arrow, Wig and Robe, Omicron Delta Kappa. Clubs: Elks, Optimist (pres. 1966); Tiger Bay (v.p. 1970). Home: 10300 SW 134th Ave Miami FL 33186 Office: 73 W Flagler St Miami FL 33130

SIEGENTHALER, CARL EDWARD, social worker; b. Buffalo, Dec. 11, 1923; s. Gottlieb and Agatha (LeBlanc) S.; A.B., Franklin and Marshall Coll., 1944; B.D., Yale U., 1946; M.S.W., Washington U., St. Louis, 1957; m. Eva Louise Beck, Dec. 26, 1950; children—Kathryn, Margaret, David, Susan, Theresa, Heidi. Researcher, N.Y.C. Mission Soc., 1946-48; pastor-supr. Caroline Mission, St. Louis, 1948-59; asso. for community program Synod of Calif., United Presbyterian Ch., Los Angeles, 1959-62; asso. dir. Welfare Planning Council., Los Angeles, 1962-64; dir. project devel. Urban Tng. Center, Chgo., 1964-74; dir. United Urban Council, Austin, 1974—; adj. prof. community ministy Austin Presbyn. Theol. Sem., 1974—; ordained to ministry Presbyterian Ch., 1948; ordained teaching elder U.P. Ch. and Presbyterian Ch. U.S. Mem. Nat. Assn. Social Workers, Acad. Cert. Social Workers, Am. Acad. Polit. and Social Sci., Nat. Presbyn. Health and Welfare Assn., Witherspoon Soc., IMPACT. Home: 1905 Greenbrook Pkwy Austin TX 78723 Office: 100 E 27th St Austin TX 78705

SIEGFRIED, CHARLES GEORGE, elec. engr.; b. Newark, July 31, 1929; s. George Phillip and Margaret Catherine (Brassell) S.; B.S.E.E., Newark Coll. Engring., 1961, postgrad., 1962-64; m. Iola Anne Orgeron, Sept. 7, 1952; children—Catherine Siegfried Kraft, Eric (dec.), Kurt, Carl. Asst. to asso. engr. Pub. Service Elec. and Gas Testing Lab., Maplewood, N.J., 1948-67; supervising engr. Ebasco Services, Inc., Houston, 1967—; instr. Newark Coll. Engring., 1962-63, U. Tex. Pipeline Sch., Houston, 1974-76, Kilgore Coll. Mem. Cranford (N.J.) Twp. Com., 1963-67, Cranford Planning Bd., 1965-70. Served with USAF, 1950-54. Certified corrosion engr. Mem. IEEE (sr.), Nat. Assn. Corrosion Engrs., Nat., Tex. socs. profl. engrs., Houston Engring. Soc. Republican. Roman Catholic. Clubs: Willowisp (Tex.) Country; Univ. Faculty (Houston). Presented numerous papers and lectures to engring. socs., instns. higher learning. Home: 5910 Burning Tree St Houston TX 77036 Office: 3731 Briar Park Dr Houston TX 77042

SIEGLER, HOWARD MATTHEW, physician; b. N.Y.C., May 26, 1932; s. Samuel Lewis and Shirley Kendall (Matthews) S.; B.S. in Biochemistry, Hofstra U., 1952; postgrad. Yale U., 1954; M.B., Ch.B., St. Andrews U., 1958; M.D., N.Y. Med. Coll., 1965; m. Toinette Andrau, Dec. 1, 1953; children—Samuel Lewis, Karel Lynn, Jacqueline Andrau, Todd Bradford. Intern, N.Y. U. Med. Center, N.Y.C., 1965, New Rochelle (N.Y.) Hosp., 1966-67; asst. to dean U. Tex. Southwestern Med. Sch., Dallas, 1967-68; sr. fellow dept. phys. medicine Baylor Coll. Medicine, Houston, 1968-69; resident family practice program Meml. Baptist Hosp., 1971; gen. practice medicine, Houston, 1971, 72—; clin. fellow in obstetrics and gynecology St. Lukes Episcopal Hosp., Houston, 1971-72; mem. staff Tex. Children's, St. Joseph, Center Pavilion, St. Luke's Episc. hosps., St. Anthony's Med. Center (all Houston); co-chmn. Muscular Dystrophy Soc., 1964-65; cons. div. disability determination Tex. Rehab. Commn., 1973. Active Assn. to Help Retarded Children; chmn. sr. div. Protestant Charities N.Y., 1964-65; trustee Huston-Tillotson Coll., Spencer Home for Boys; Rice asso. Rice U.; bd. mem. Benjy F. Brooks Found. for Children, Inc.; patron Houston Symphony, Houston Grand Opera, Houston Ballet, Mus. Fine Arts, Friends of Med. Center Library; asso. trustee The Kinkaid Sch.; col., a.d.c. Gov.'s staff, Tenn., Miss., La., 1971; lt. col., a.d.c. Gov.'s staff Ala., 1971. Appointed adm. Tex. Navy, 1973. Served to maj. 36th Airborne Battery, Tex. Air N.G.; to maj. USAR. Fellow Royal Soc. Health, Royal Soc. Medicine; mem. Am. Fertility Soc., Am. Geriatric Soc., AAAS, N.Y. Acad. Scis. (life), Australasian Coll. Biomed. Scientists, Am. Diabetes Assn., Internat. Soc. Cardiology (citation 1978), Am. Social Health Assn., S.W. Sci. Forum, Am. Soc. Bariatrics, Christian Med. Soc., Tex. Med. Assn., So. Med. Assn., Harris County Med. Soc., Am. Med. Soc. Alcoholism, Am. Assn. Gynecol. Laparoscopists, Am. Soc. Contemporary Medicine and Surgery, Tex. Acad. Family Physicians, Alumni Assn. Bellevue-N.Y. U. Med. Center (charter), Denton A. Cooley Cardiovascular Surg. Soc., Internat. Acad. Preventive Medicine, Tex. Assn. Disability Examiners, AMA, Internat. Platform Assn., Phi Chi (chancellor 1963). Episcopalian. Home: 1 Longfellow Ln Houston TX 77005 Office: Suite 1020 Hermann Profl Bldg 6410 Fannin St Houston TX 77025

SIENKIEWICZ, BERNARD ANTHONY, assn. exec.; b. Scranton, Pa., May 20, 1930; s. Bernard and Celia (Yerke) S.; B.S. in Acctg., LaSalle U., 1959; m. Josephine Evelyn Ofcharsky, May 17, 1952; children—Richard A., Nancy J. Statistician, Navy Dept., Washington, 1950-53; acct. Air-Conditioning and Refrigeration Inst., Arlington, Va., 1953-57, gen. mgr., 1976—. Precinct capt., mem. Fairfax County Central Republican Com., 1961-65. Served with U.S. Army, 1948-50. Mem. Am. Mktg. Assn. (pres. D.C. chpt. 1963-64), Nat. Assn. Execs. Club (dir. 1971-73), Nat. Indsl. Council (chmn. 1976). Home: 5723 Ash Dr Springfield VA 22150 Office: Air Conditioning and Refrigeration Inst 1815 N Fort Myer Dr Arlington VA 22209

SIENKNECHT, CHARLES WILLSON, physician; b. Abilene, Tex., Aug. 24, 1942; s. Charles and Margaret Wellman (Willson) S.; B.S., U. Tenn., Knoxville, 1964; M.D., U. Tenn., Memphis, 1967; m. Nancy Twist, Dec. 27, 1973; children—Stephen Eric and Jason Kurt (twins). Rotating intern Phila. Gen. Hosp., 1968-69; resident in internal medicine City of Memphis Hosp., U. Tenn., 1969-70; fellow in infectious disease U. Tenn., Memphis, 1972-73; fellow in rheumatology U. Toronto, rheumatic disease unit Wellesley Hosp., Ont., Can., 1974-75; asst. clin. prof. medicine U. Tenn. Coll. Medicine, Clin. Edn. Center, Chattanooga, 1975—; asst. project dir. Appalachian Regional Arthritis Center Found., 1975, 76; practice medicine specializing in rheumatology, Chattanooga, 1975—; mem. staff Baroness Erlanger Hosp., and Meml. Hosp., Chattanooga, Cumberland Med. Center, Crossville, Tenn., Cherokee Park Hosp., Cleveland, Tenn., Hamilton Meml. Hosp., Dalton, Ga. Served to maj. M.C., U.S. Army, 1970-72. Diplomate Am. Bd. Internal Medicine, Am. Bd. Rheumatology. Fellow ACP; mem. AMA, Am. Rheumatism Assn., Am. Assn. Med. Assistants (adv. 1978), Hamilton County Med. Soc. Contbr. articles in field to profl. jours. Office: Suite 223 Doctors Bldg 744 McCallie Ave Chattanooga TN 37402

SIERAKOWSKI, ROBERT LEON, aero. engr.; b. Vernon, Conn., Apr. 11, 1937; s. Stanley F. and Amelia C. (Misiaszek) S.; B.S. in Engring., Brown U., 1958; M.S., Yale U., 1960, Ph.D., 1964; m. Nina A. Shopa, May 3, 1975; children—Steven R., Sandra Marie. Engr., United Techs Corp., East Hartford, Conn., 1958-60, research engr., 1963-67; research asst. Yale U., 1960-63; vis. asst. prof. engring. mechanics U. Fla., 1967-68, asso. prof., 1968-72, prof., 1972—. Mem. Vernon Bd. Edn., 1965-67; mem. Vernon City Commn., 1967; mem. Gainesville (Fla.) Citizens Advisory Council for Elementary Schs., 1973-75. NRC sr. research fellow, 1972-73. Fellow Am. Inst. Aeros. and Astronautics (asso.); mem. ASME, Soc. Exptl. Stress Analysis, Soc. Engring. Sci. (editor procs. 1978), Soc. Materials Process Engrs., Am. Soc. Engring. Edn., Yale Engring. Assn., Sigma Xi, Sigma Tau, Tau Beta Pi, Phi Kappa Phi. Roman Catholic. Club: K.C. Contbr. numerous articles, revs. to profl. publs. Home: 1502 NW 52d Terr Gainesville FL 32605 Office: U Fla Dept Engring Gainesville FL 32601

SIERGIEJ, EDWARD STANLEY, aerospace co. exec.; b. Nanticoke, Pa., Jan. 14, 1928; s. John and Stasia (Filar) S.; B.E.E., U. Colo., 1958; B.S. in Communication Engring., U.S. Naval Post Grad. Sch., 1960; M.A. in Internat. Affairs, George Washington U., 1963; M.B.A., U. Dallas, 1977; m. Mary Olwen Vaughan, Sept. 16, 1952; children—Nancy Jean, E. David, Wendy Ann. Commd. ensign USN, 1948, advanced through grades to comdr., 1964; planning specialist LTV Electrosystems, Greenville, Tex., 1968-71; requirement coordinator Greenville div. E-Systems, Inc., 1971-77, gen. supr. requirements services, 1977-80, mgr. mktg. research, 1980—. Mem. Citizens Transp. Com., Greenville, 1970-71. Mem. U.S. Naval Inst., Ret. Officer's Assn., Assn. Old Crows, Am. Security Council, Navy League, Air Force Assn., Sigma Iota Epsilon, Eta Kappa Nu, Sigma Tau. Home: 108 Oak Glen Dr Greenville TX 75401 Office: Box 1056 Greenville TX 75401

SIERRA, MARIO SÁNCHEZ, export exec.; b. Tampa, Fla., June 10, 1938; s. Mario Pérez Sierra and María Luisa deSoto Sánchez; grad. in bus. Hillsboro Jr. Coll., 1970; m. Elizabeth Ann Wiley, Nov. 18, 1958; children—Mario, Ana María, Margarita, María Theresa, Daniel, David, Marilinda. Successively office mgr., sales mgr., Metalsource Co., Miami, Fla., 1965—, now mgr. internat. div. Mem. Am. Mgmt. Assn., Nat. Credit and Mgmt. Assn., Purchasing and Mgmt. Assn. Democrat. Roman Catholic. Clubs: Sertoma, Philatelic, Portuguese, Italian, Spanish. Home: 4881 NW 192d St Miami FL 33055 Office: Metalsource Co 6300 NW 35th Ave Miami FL 33147

SIGEL, MARSHALL ELLIOT, financial cons.; b. Hartford, Conn., Nov. 25, 1941; s. Paul and Bessie (Somer) S.; B.S., U. Pa., 1963. Exec. v.p. Advo-System, Inc., Hartford, 1963-69; pres. Ad-Lists, Inc., Hartford, 1963-69, Ad-Type Corp., Hartford, 1962-69, Advo-System div. KMS Industries, Inc., Hartford, 1969-72. Bd. dirs. Yeshiva of Hartford, Marshall E. Sigel Found., Hebrew Home For Aged. Mem. Young Pres.'s Orgn., U. Pa. Alumni Assn. (pres. class). Club: Standard. Home: 600 NE 36th St Apt 922 Miami FL 33137

SIGELMAN, CAROL KIMBALL, psychologist, educator; b. Montreal, Que., Can., Jan. 16, 1946; d. Ralph W. and Elaine (Painter) Kimball; B.A. magna cum laude, Carleton Coll., 1967; M.A., George Peabody Coll. for Tchrs., 1968, Ph.D., 1972; m. Lee Philip Sigelman, Sept. 6, 1969. Cons. English-lang. arts, bldg. coordinator, student tchr. trainee Tchr. Edn. Alliance for Metro, Nashville, 1970-72; research asso. Inst. on Sch. Learning, Peabody Coll., Nashville, 1970-72; research scientist Research and Tng. Center in Mental Retardation, Tex. Tech. U., Lubbock, 1972-73, dir. research at center, asst. prof. psychology at univ., 1974-79; asst. prof. psychology Eastern Ky. U., Richmond, 1979—; cons. in field. NDEA fellow, 1967-70. Mem. Am. Assn. on Mental Deficiency (chairperson psychology div. Region V 1976-78), Nat. Council on Rehab. Edn., Nat. Assn. Rehab. Research and Tng. Centers, Phi Beta Kappa. Co-author: Psychology: A scientific study of human behavior, 5th edit., 1979; contbr. articles on rehab. of adult mentally retarded. Office: Eastern Ky U Richmond KY 40475

SIGLE, ERICH HERMANN, social worker; b. Esslingen, Germany, May 10, 1934; came to U.S., 1953, naturalized, 1958; s. Hermann David and Maria Anna (Hill) S.; grad. in interior design Tech. Inst. of Esslingen, 1953; B.S. in Social Work, U. N. Ala., 1975; postgrad. U. Ala., 1979—; m. Gabriele Bauerle, July 25, 1959; 1 dau., Andrea R. With Hermann's Interiors, Esslingen, W. Ger., 1948-53; interior decorator, Florence, Ala., 1953-64; chief work adjustment supr. N.W. Ala. Rehab. Center, Florence, 1964-75; dir. Colbert-Lauderdale Attention Home, Inc., Florence, 1975—. Served with U.S. Army, 1957-59. Recipient Service to Mankind award, Muscle Shoals Sertoma Club, 1977; cert. rehab. counselor. Mem. Ala. Council on Crime and Delinquency, So. States Correctional Assn., Am. Personnel and Guidance Assn., 82D Airborn Div. Assn. Episcopalian. Clubs: Exchange, Am. Legion. Home: Route 4 Lingerlost Box 300 Killen AL 35645 Office: PO Box 742 Florence AL 35630

SIKORA, EUGENE STANLEY, profl. engr.; b. Duquesne, Pa., July 21, 1924; s. Adam Joseph and Helen (Pietrowska) S.; student Okla. Bapt. U., 1943-44; B.S. in Indsl. Engring., U. Pitts., 1949; C.E., Carnegie Inst. Tech., 1951; m. Corinne Mary Coliane, Sept. 7, 1946; children—Karyn Ann, Leslie Ann. Bridge design engr. Gannett, Fleming, Corddry & Carpenter, Pitts., 1949-50; structural designer Rust Engring. Co., Pitts., 1950-51, chief field engr., 1951-52, asst. project engr.; project engr. Frank E. Murphy & Assos., Bartow, Fla., 1952-55; v.p. Wellman-Lord Engring. Co., Lakeland, Fla., 1955-61; pres. Gulf Design Co., Lakeland, 1961-74, Sebco Resources Corp., Reno, 1975—; v.p. chmn. Continental Coke and Chem. Corp., Pitts., 1974—, Smiths Creek Sand Co. (Mich.), 1974—, Lakeland Constrn., 1974—; dir. Eldorado Resources Corp., Reno, Pine Lake Chems., Lakeland, Am. Bank of Lakeland. Bd. dirs. Polk County Mus. Badger Co. Inc., Cambridge, Mass., 1968-75; Served with USAAF, 1943-45. Mem. Nat. Soc. Profl. Engrs., Am. Inst. Mining, Metall. and Petroleum Engrs., Am. Mgmt. Assn., Am. Inst. Chem. Engrs., Am. Inst. Indsl. Engrs., Fla. Engring. Soc., Lakeland C. of C. (dir.). Democrat. Roman Catholic. Home: 1400 Seville Pl Lakeland FL 33803 Office: One Lone Palm Pl Lakeland FL 33801

SILBERMAN, DONALD JARED, pediatric psychiatrist; b. Birmingham, Ala., June 4, 1915; s. Louis and Dora (Gingold) S.; B.A., Samford U., 1934; M.D., U. Md., 1938; m. Anne Copeland, Dec. 6, 1959; children—Claire, Connie. Intern, Ill. Masonic Hosp., Chgo., 1938-39, Hillman Hosp., Birmingham, Ala., 1939-40; resident Hillman Hosp., 1940-41, Univ. Hosp., Birmingham, 1946-47; practice medicine specializing in pediatrics, Birmingham, 1947-64, specializing in gen. and pediatric psychiatry, Birmingham, 1964—; pres. med. staff Childrens Hosp., 1963-64, Hill Crest Hosp., 1970-71; clin. prof. pediatrics U. Ala., Birmingham, 1955—, clin. asso. prof. psychiatry, 1968—; mem. exec. com., sec. Jefferson-Blount-St. Clair Tri-County Mental Health Authority, 1977—. Served from 1st lt. to maj. AUS, 1941-46; col. Res. ret. Decorated Bronze Star medal, Meritorious Service medal; NIMH fellow in psychiatry, 1964-68. Diplomate Am. Bd. Pediatrics. Fellow Am. Acad. Pediatrics, Am. Psychiat. Assn. (pres. Ala. dist. br. 1973-74, mem. exec. com. 1971—, rep. to Assembly dist. brs., editor Ala. Dist. br. Newsletter 1971—), So. Psychiat. Assn.; mem. Ala. Med. Assn. (rep. to intersplty. council), Jefferson County Med. Soc. (chmn. athletic com. 1970—), Ala. Acad. Neurology and Psychiatry (trustee, pres.-elect), Birmingham Acad. Medicine, Birmingham Area C. of C. (chmn. football com. 1955-62). Clubs: The Club, Pinetree Golf and Country (Birmingham). Home: 3773 Locksley Dr Birmingham AL 35223 Office: 1717 11th Ave Birmingham AL 35205

SILK, DOLORES HAM, credit union exec.; b. Memphis, Dec. 4, 1943; d. James Asa and Mable (Turnage) Ham; student Memphis State U., U. Tenn., Memphis, 1965-66, Credit Union Sch. U. Ga., 1974-76; m. A. Evans Silk, May 6, 1972. Sec., Harland Bartholomew & Assos., Engrs., Memphis, 1961-62; clk. typist Civil Service Memphis Def. Depot, 1962-63; sec. Arms Control and Disarmament sect. Dept. State, Washington, 1964-65; sec. E.I. duPont Co., Memphis, 1965-71; mgr. Memphis Works Employees Credit Union, DuPont, 1971—; coordinator Memphis Area Mgrs. Assn. Mem. Credit Union Execs. Soc. (treas. Memphis area chpt. 1978-79). Home: 5587 Gates Cove Memphis TN 38118 Office: 2571 Fite Rd PO Box 27321 Memphis TN 38127

SILK, WILLIAM HENRY, architect, planner; b. Oklahoma City, Jan. 8, 1947; s. Henry Thomas and Betty Carrol (Angle) S.; B.Arch., Okla. State U., 1971. Intern architect various firms, Denver, 1971-73; project architect, Oklahoma City, 1973-79; pvt. practice architecture, Oklahoma City, 1979—. Bd. dirs. Celebrations Presch., Oklahoma City, 1979. Mem. AIA, Corridor Neighborhood Assn., Okla. County Hist. Soc. (chmn. sites and mus. com.). Presbyterian. Office: 3801 Classen Blvd Suite 300 Oklahoma City OK 73118

SILL, CYNTHIA SUE, social services adminstr.; b. Ft. Worth, June 25, 1948; d. Albert Lee and Nadine Pearl (Skipworth) Baker; A.A., Mountain View Coll., 1973; B.S., E. Tex. State U., 1974, M.S., 1976; 1 son, Paul Eric. Dir. community edn. services Mental Health Mental Retardation Regional Center of East Tex., Tyler, 1976-78, dir. cons. and edn., 1978—; cons. mental health; dir. Listening Ear (Crisis Intervention Center), 1975-76, tng. and screening vol. counselors, 1974-75, E. Tex. State U., Commerce. Com. mem. task force on community care for aged, blind and disabled Tex. Dept. Human Resources. Certified human potential group facilitator. Mem. Am., Tex. personnel and guidance assns., Am. Mental Health Counselors Assn. (co-chmn. Tex.), Tex. Mental Health Counselors Assn., Assn. for Humanistic Edn. and Devel., NOW. Democrat. Baptist. Home: 1008 W 7th St Tyler TX 75701 Office: 305 S Broadway 10th Floor Tyler TX 75702

SILL, GERALD DE SCHRENCK, hotel corp. exec.; b. Czechoslovakia, Dec. 11, 1917; s. Edward and Margaret (Baroness von Schrenck-Notzing) S.; B.S., Budapest Tech. U., 1942; m. Maria Countess Draskovich, May 11, 1946; children—Susan, Gabrielle. Came to U.S., 1948, naturalized, 1953. With econs. div. U.S. Hdqrs., Vienna, Austria, 1945-48; exec. hotel positions N.Y.C., 1948-52; managerial positions with Hilton Hotel Corp., 1953-61; exec. v.p. Houston Internat. Hotels, Inc., 1961-72, pres., chief exec. officer, 1972—; chmn. fgn. relations com. Preferred Hotels Assn. U.S., Can., Western Europe and S. Am.; v.p. Warwick Hotels, Inc.; dir. Tex. Commerce Med. Bank, Houston. Clubs: Warwick (pres.), River Oaks Country (Houston); Marco Polo (N.Y.C.). Home: 2227 Pelham Dr Houston TX 77019 Office: The Warwick 5701 Main St Houston TX 77005

SILLS, ROY KENNETH, indsl. engr.; b. Grand Rivers, Ky., Feb. 17, 1941; s. Roy Glen and Edna Marie (Kirk) S.; student Chgo. Tech. Coll., 1959-62; m. Sandra R. Watson, Oct. 3, 1959; children—Letitia Ken, Felicia Ken. Insp., group leader, prodn. technician Potter & Brumfield, Marion, Ky., 1960-68; supr. tool room and press room, indsl. engring. Arvin Industries, Princeton, Ky., 1968—. Certified pre-determine time analyst Ky. Mem. Am. Inst. Indsl. Engrs. Baptist. Club: Crittenden County Bass. Designer, developer, institutor machines, methods miter-fold speaker prodn., 1972—. Home: Route 2 Box 16 Marion KY 42064 Office: Arvin Industries Princeton KY 42445

SILVER, ERNEST GERARD, physicist; b. Munich, Germany, Dec. 26, 1929; came to U.S., 1941, naturalized, 1946; s. Fred and Ella (Gundersheimer) S.; B.A. summa cum laude, Boston U., 1952; M.A., Harvard U., 1954; Diploma, Oak Ridge Sch. Reactor Tech., 1955; Ph.D., U. Tenn., 1965; m. Frances Levine, June 20, 1954; 1 dau., Carolyn. Research physicist Oak Ridge Nat. Lab., 1954-74, asst. to dir. Breeder Reactor Program, 1977-78, asst. dir. Nuclear Standards Mgmt. Center, 1978—; exec. officer Inst. for Energy Analysis, Oak Ridge Asso. Univs., 1974-77. Chmn., Oak Ridge Charter Commn., 1972-73; chmn. Oak Ridge Expo-82 Com., 1979; mem. Knoxville Internat. Exposition Bd., 1978-80. Mem. Am. Phys. Soc., AAAS, Am. Nuclear Soc. (nat. program com., chmn. forum com., Meritorious Service award 1975). Jewish. Contbr. articles to profl. jours. Home: 107 Lehigh Ln Oak Ridge TN 37830 Office: Oak Ridge Nat Lab Bldg 9204-1 Y-12 PO Box Y Oak Ridge TN 37830

SILVER, FRANCIS, 5TH, environ. engr.; b. Martinsburg, W.Va., Jan. 4, 1916; s. Gray and Kate (Bishop) S.; student Va. Military Inst., 1933-34; B.E. in Gas Engring., Johns Hopkins U., 1937; m. J. Nevelyne Wyndham, Dec. 31, 1965 (dec.). With Standard Lime & Stone Co., Millville, W.Va., 1937-42; plant engr., Fairchild Aircraft, Hagerstown, Md., 1951-57, Boeing Aircraft, Renton, Wash., 1957; cons. environ. engr., boundary surveyor, Martinsburg, 1960—. Surveyor of lands, Berkeley County, 1964—; dir. Berkeley County Hist. Soc., 1967—; bd. trustees City Hosp., 1971—, pres., 1977-78. Served with U.S. Army, 1942-46. Registered profl. engr. W.Va. Fellow Royal Soc. Health; mem. AAAS, Am. Chem. Soc., ASME, Nat. Soc. Profl. Engrs., Air Pollution Control Assn., Am. Pub. Health Assn., Am. Acad. Environ. Engrs., Soc. Clin. Ecology, Am. Congress on Surveying and Mapping, W.Va. Assn. Land Surveyors, (pres. 1973-75), Sigma Xi. Democrat. Presbyterian. Contbr. chpts. to books. Home: 203 E Burke St Martinsburg WV 25401 Office: Berkeley County Ct House Martinsburg WV 25401

SILVERMAN, JACQUES BERNARD, cons. engr.; b. Los Angeles, Aug. 29, 1899; s. Michael Gabriel and Miriam (Silverman) Solomon; E.E., U. Cin., 1923; m. Helen Josephine Hughes, Dec. 15, 1929; 1 dau., Viola Miriam Silverman Clayton. Engr., Cin., Newport & Covington Ry. Co., Covington, Ky., 1932-37; layout engr. elec. projects Louisville Gas and Elec. Co., 1937-46; chief elec. engr. Chanaberry Engring. Co., Inc., Louisville, 1946-52; individual practice as cons. engr., Louisville, 1952—. Mem. Bd. Elec. Control, City Louisville and Jefferson County, 1955-60. Served with U.S. Army, 1918. Mem. Internat. Assn. Elec. Insps., Ky. Soc. Profl. Engrs., IEEE. Methodist (ofcl. bd. 1948-51). Club: Masons. Responsible for outdoor lighting of Baha-i House of Worship, Wilmette, Ill., 1952. Home and Office: 428 Southern Heights W Louisville KY 40214

SILVERMAN, MARVIN, child guidance specialist; b. Bklyn., July 21, 1949; s. Hyman and Betty (Cohen) S.; B.A., St. John's U., 1971; M.S., L.I. U., 1972; Ed.D., Nova U., 1980. Elem. sch. counselor, Monroe County, Fla., 1973-74; co-host Baby Jane Show, WKID-TV., Ft. Lauderdale, Fla., 1976; lectr. psychology Barry Coll., Miami Shores, Fla., 1978-79; elem. sch. counselor, Miami, Fla., 1974—; adj. prof. edn. Nova U., Ft. Lauderdale, 1977-78. Recipient Fla. Little Red Sch. House award, 1974. Mem. Am. Personnel and Guidance Assn., Fla. Personnel and Guidance Assn. Jewish. Author: (with others) State of Florida Elementary School Guidance Handbook, 1978, Elementary Guidance Outlook, 1975; contbr. articles to profl. jours. Home: 15700 NW 2d Ave Miami FL 33169 Office: 2020 NE 163d St Suite 111 Miami FL 33162

SILVERMAN, SEYMOUR, ins. agy. exec.; b. N.Y.C., Aug. 19, 1924; s. Harry and Ray S.; B.B.A., CCNY, 1949; B.Ed., U. Miami, 1951, M.Ed., 1953; m. Anita J. Silverman, Sept. 11, 1960; children—Barbara Lynn, Michael J., Richard Alan. Tchr., Dade County Bd. Public Instrn., 1949-51, supr. placement, registration and guidance, 1951-55; staff mgr. Prudential Ins. Co. Am., 1955-61; partner Sy Silverman C.L.U. & Assos. and predecessor firm, Hollywood, Fla., 1961—; pres. Abacus Pension Cons., 1968—; exec. v.p. Asso. Health Services, 1976—; prof. human relations Miami Dade Community Coll., part-time, 1970-76, Am. Coll. Life Underwriters. Vice pres., mem. exec. com. Hollywood Hills Baseball Inc., 1974-77, commr., 1978-79. Served with USAAF, 1943-45; ETO. Mem. Am. Soc. Pension Actuaries, Am. Personnel and Guidance Assn., Am. Inst. Hypnosis, Am. Psychol. Assn. (asso.), Nat. Assn. Life Underwriters, Hollywood Underwriters Assn. (dir. 1977), Million Dollar Round Table. Jewish. Office: Sy Silverman CLU & Assos 5848 Johnson St Hollywood FL 33021

SILVERMAN, SHERLEY SHER, artist; b. Maywood, Ill., Jan. 20, 1909; d. Adam and Elizabeth (Portnoy) Sher; student U. Ill., 1927-28, Chgo. Acad. Fine Arts, 1932-35, pvt. studies; m. I.J. Silverman, Oct. 27, 1928; 1 son, Bernard W. Exhibited in one-man shows in Thor Gallery, Louisville, 1967, Covenant Club, Chgo., 1968, B'nai B'rith Exhbn. Hall, Washington, 1969; exhibited in group shows Salon Internat. de Charleroi, Belgium, 1968, Dibuix Premi Internat. Joan Miro, Barcelona, Spain, 1970-73, Galleria D'Arte La Scala, Di Firenze, 1971, Gallery Benhur Sanchez, Bogota, Colombia, Barry Cleaving, New Zealand; represented in permanent collection B'nai B'rith Hdqrs., Washington, pvt. collections. Recipient Internat. medal Honor, Internat. Centro Studi E. Scambi, 1971; Acad. Internat. Leonardo Da Vinci, 1971; Honoris Causa Silver medal Acad. Internat., Campanella, 1972; Gold medal Recognition and Bronze plaque La Scala Gallery, Florence, Italy, 1972; certificate Merit Internat. Dictionary, 1973. Mem. N. Shore Art League, Internat. Arts Guild (comdr. 1965—), Suburban Fine Art League, Com. Gold Coast Art Fair, U.S. Com. Internat. Centro Studi E. Scambi, Acad. Internat. Leonardo De Vinci, Mid-Am. Art Assn. (pres. 1969-71, recipient award Recognition), Acad. Internat. Home: 9240 W Bay Harbor Dr Bay Harbor Island FL 33154 Studio: 1035 NE 125th St North Miami FL 33161

SILVEY, THOMAS JESSE, former supt. schs.; b. Roston, Ark., June 21, 1912; s. Jesse B. and Viola S. (Bailey) S.; B.S., U. Ark., 1937, M. Ednl. Adminstrn., 1963; m. Bobbie Nell Martin, June 5, 1938; 1 dau., Fredrica Nell. High sch. tchr., basketball coach, Patmos, Ark., 1933-35; adminstrv. officer Agr. Adj. Adminstrs. Office, Faulkner County, Ark., 1937; asst. county agt. Washington County, supr. U. Ark. Agr. Srs. majoring in agrl. extension, 1938, county agrl. agt., 1939-42; tchr. vets. on farm tng., 1945-51; high sch. prin., 1952-53; supt. Bodcaw Schs., 1953-64, Calico Rock (Ark.) Schs., 1964-75; operator farm, 1945-64. Co-organizer, pres. U. Ark. Boys 4-H House, 1936, v.p. Agr. Day Assn. U. Ark., 1937; chmn. Joint State Adv. Council on Sch. Health 1959-61; dist. commr., mem. exec. com. Boy Scouts Am., 1958-63; mem. Calico Rock City Planning Commn., 1969. Mem. Ark. Senate, 1949-52. Pres. bd. dirs. White River Planning and Devel. Dist. Served with USNR, 1942-45. Recipient State Community Devel. Leadership award, 1968. Mem. NEA, Ark. Edn. Assn., Supts. Assn., Am., Ark. sch. adminstrs. assns., Ark. Sch. Bds. Assn., Assn. Sch. Curriculum Devel., Ark. Activities Assn. (exec. com., parliamentarian), Am. Legion (past post comdr.), 40 and 8, S.W. Ark. Schoolmasters Club, S.W. Ark. Poultry Producers Assn. (past pres.), U.S. Poultry and Egg Producers Assn. (past nat. v.p.), Izard County Tchrs. Assn. (past pres.), Calico Rock C. of C. (past pres.). Baptist (deacon). Lion. Home: Karla St Calico Rock AR 72519

SILVIOUS, OWEN FRANKLIN, music pub., record mfg. and mail order co. exec.; b. Luray, Va., Jan. 15, 1939; s. Omey F. and Effie (Jewell) S.; student pub. schs.; m. Nancy A. Gochenour, Aug. 12, 1961 (div.); children—Owen F., Eugene F. Pres., Luray Music Co., 1966—, Frankie Record Co., Luray, 1966—; songwriter Broadcast Music, Inc., N.Y.C. and Nashville, 1967—; mng. dir. World Real Estate Investment Fund Ltd., Bahamas, 1971—, Worldwide Investment Bank Ltd., B.W.I., 1977—, Diamonds Investment Fund Ltd., Bahamas, 1971—; Worldwild Trading Co., Luray, Va., 1977—. Served with AUS, 1956-65. Mem. Nat. Songwriters Guild. Home: Luray VA 22835 Office: PO Box 52 Luray VA 22835

SIMARD, HOUSTON HERBERT, mfg. co. exec.; b. Fort Smith, Ark., Aug. 27, 1930; s. Joseph George and Vera Beatrice (Jackson) S.; student Ark. Poly. Inst., Russellville, 1948; m. Linda Marie Speer, Aug. 19, 1970; children—Rodney Joe, Timothy Vick. Vice-pres. Jackson's Furniture, Inc., Fort Smith, 1947-65; salesman Pratt & Lambert, Inc., Kansas City, Mo., 1965-69; sales mgr. Belwood div. U.S. Industries, Ackerman, Miss., 1969-70, v.p. mktg., 1970-72, exec. v.p., 1972-74, pres., 1974—. Served with AUS, 1947-48, 50-51. Republican. Lutheran. Home: 510 E College St Louisville MS 39339 Office: Belwood Div US Industries Inc PO Drawer A Hwy 15 S Ackerman MS 39735

SIMEL, PAUL JOSEPH, ophthalmic surgeon; b. N.Y.C., Mar. 7, 1930; s. Abraham and Esta (Schwartz) S.; A.B., Dartmouth Coll., 1951; M.D., Boston U., 1955; postgrad. Yale, 1959; m. Faye Ruth Holland, Apr. 14, 1968; children—David, Bruce, Mark, Dana. Intern, Boston City Hosp., 1955-56; resident, Yale-New Haven Med. Center, 1956-59; practice medicine specializing in ophthalmology, Greensboro, N.C., 1961—; instr. ophthalmologic surgery Yale U., 1959. Served to capt. M.C., AUS, 1959-61. Fellow Am. Acad. Ophthalmology and Otolaryngology, A.C.S.; mem. Am. Intraocular Implant Soc., N.C. Med. Soc. (mem. eye care com. 1963-68). Clubs: Starmount Forest Country, Pinetop Tennis. Home: 16C Fountain Manor Dr Greensboro NC 27405 Office: 111 W Wendover Ave Greensboro NC 27401

SIMES, FRANK JAMES, educator; b. Brockport, N.Y., Jan. 18, 1916; s. James A. and Janet L. (Hummel); B.A., U. Mich., 1938; M.A., State U. N.Y., Albany, 1948; Ed.D., Pa. State U., 1951; m. Mary Alice Stever, Apr. 16, 1949; 1 dau., Amy Caroline. Prodn. expediter Trico Products Corp., Buffalo, 1939-41, asst. prodn. mgr., 1946-47; tchr. social studies, guidance counselor Honeoye Falls (N.Y.) High Sch., 1946-50; dir. resident counseling Pa. State U., University Park, 1950-52, dean of men, 1952-67; v.p., acad. dean Hampden-Sydney (Va.) Coll., 1967-75, prof. psychology, 1975—. Served as capt. U.S. Army, 1941-46. Lic. prof. counselor. Mem. Am. Personnel and Guidance Assn., Assn Counselor Edn. and Supervision, Pa. Soc., Omicron Delta Kappa, Phi Kappa Sigma, Psi Chi, Phi Delta Kappa. Republican. Presbyterian. Club: Masons. Office: Hampden-Sydney Coll Hampden-Sydney VA 23943

SIMMONS, CARL HENRY, mathematician; b. Jackson, Tenn., May 25, 1934; s. William Henry and Hortense Florence (Bogle) S.; B.S., Union U., Jackson, Tenn., 1958; M.A., W.Va. U., 1961. Tchr. math. Greenbriar Mil. Sch., Lewisburg, W.Va., 1958-63; mem. faculty Chowan Coll., Murfreesboro, N.C., 1963—; prof. math., 1963—, chmn. dept., 1970—. Grantee NSF, 1969, 71, 70. Mem. N.C. Acad. Sci. (past sec. math. sect.). Baptist. Club: Murfreesboro Exchange (past pres., past dist. dir.; Dist. Dir. Achievement award 1976). Home: 103 E High St Murfreesboro NC 27855 Office: Chowan Coll Murfreesboro NC 27855

SIMMONS, GEORGE BENTON, educator; b. Nashville, Aug. 3, 1931; s. Avery Benton and Alice (Burnley) S.; B.A., U. Louisville, 1953; M.B.A., Ind. U., 1957, D.B.A., 1961; m. Mira Wilkins, June 15, 1968. Asst. prof. mktg. adminstrn. U. Tex., 1961; cons. AID, Mex., 1962; asst. prof. bus. Columbia, 1962-66; dir. Center for Bus. and Econ. Research, also asso. prof. bus. adminstrn. U. Mass., Amherst, 1966-68, prof., chmn. dept. mgmt., 1967-73; dean Sch. Bus. and Organizational Scis. Fla. Internat. U., 1974-79, Disting. Univ. Prof. internat bus., 1979—. Chmn. Fla. Adv. Com. on Greyhound Racing, 1975-77. Served to lt. (j.g.) USNR, 1953-56. Mem. Am. Inst. Decision Scis., Acad. of Mgmt., Acad. Internat. Bus., Beta Gamma Sigma, Kappa Alpha. Author: A Bibliography of International Business, 1964. Home: 40 Prospect Dr Coral Gables FL 33133 Office: Dept Fin and Internat Bus Fla Internat U Tamiami Trail Miami FL 33199

SIMMONS, GILBERT LARRY, dentist; b. Orange, Tex., Nov. 25, 1936; s. Raford Gilbert and Linadine (Smith) S.; B.S., Baylor U., 1959, D.D.S., 1962; m. Mary Sue Dillard, Aug. 31, 1957; children—Stanley A., Steven R., Wade A. Pvt. practice gen. dentistry, Denton, Tex., 1964—. Chmn. planning zoning commn. City of Argyle (Tex.), 1975-78. Licensed dentist, Tex. Mem. Denton County Dental Soc. (pres. 1971-72), Am., Tex. dental assns., Am. Soc. for Preventive Dentistry, Am. Acad. Gen. Dentistry, Denton C. of C. (dir. 1969-70), Am. Heart Assn. (dir. 1967-69). Baptist (deacon). Clubs: Denton Rotary (dir. 1970-71), Masons, Scottish Rite. Home: Route 2 Box 84 Argyle TX 76226 Office: 1002 N Elm St Denton TX 76201

SIMMONS, H. LARRY, sales exec.; b. Lamesa, Tex., June 7, 1948; s. Herbert Lewis and Sarah Elizabeth S.; student Odessa (Tex.) Coll., 1966-68; B.S. in Math., U. Tex., Arlington, 1971; m. Nancy McDaniel, Aug. 25, 1966; children—Stewart Clayton, Jeffrey Cole. Jr. exec. trainee Sanger Harris, Dallas, 1971-73; div. sales mgr. Communications Engring. Co., Dallas, 1973—. Served with USAFR, 1971-77. Recipient cert. of Merit U.S. Jaycees, 1975; cert. of Accomplishment Xerox Learning Systems, 1975; cert. of Achievement Wilson Learning Corp., 1978. Mem. Petroleum Electric Supply Assn., Am. Mgmt. Assn., Sales and Mktg. Execs. Internat., Sales and Mktg. Execs. Dallas. Republican. Baptist.

SIMMONS, HOWARD HELMUTH, educator; b. N.Y.C., June 26, 1915; s. Frederick Herbert and Marie Martha (Winkler) Simon; cert. in Commerce and Acctg., U. San Francisco, 1941; A.B. in Govt., George Washington U., 1949; M.B.A., Stanford U., 1951; m. Ruthellen Barnett, Dec. 27, 1941; children—Maria Jeanne Simmons Impink, Howard Keith. Commd. 2d lt. U.S. Army, 1937, advanced through grades to col., 1958; comptroller 7th Army, 1953-54; mem. Joint Staff, Joint Chiefs of Staff, 1959-61; pres. Fin. Corps Bd., 1963-64; dir. acctg., comptroller of Army, 1965-66; ret., 1966; chmn. dept. fin. adminstrn., adj. prof. Southeastern U., Washington, 1965-66; chmn. social scis. div. No. Va. Community Coll., Annandale, 1966, dean student services, 1967-71, prof. bus. mgmt., 1971—; pres. Anglo-Am. Schs., Athens, Greece, 1952-53. Active N. Ridge Citizens Assn. Decorated Legion of Merit with oak leaf cluster, medal of Honor first class for Vietnamese Merit; recipient outstanding award Fed. Govt. Accts. Assn., 1965, author award, Army Finance Jour., 1965. Mem. Am. Acctg. Assn., Alpha Phi Omega. Democrat. Lutheran. Contbr. articles to Army Finance Jour. Home: 3202 Old Dominion Blvd Alexandria VA 22305 Office: 8333 Little River Turnpike Annandale VA 22003

SIMMONS, JAMES HAROLD, JR., physician; b. Davenport, Iowa, Dec. 24, 1945; s. James Harold and Gladys Evelyn (Barstow) S.; student Augustana Coll., 1963-65; M.D., U. Iowa, 1972; m. Ann Marie Greenwood, June 20, 1970; children—John Pascal, Harold Lloyd. Intern, Bronson Meth. Hosp., Kalamazoo, 1972-73; resident in family practice Spartanburg (S.C.) Gen. Hosp., 1973-75, chief resident, 1975; practice medicine, specializing in family practice, Taylorsville, N.C., 1975—. Diplomate Am. Acad. Family Practice. Presbyterian. Club: Rotary. Office: 3d Ave SW Taylorsville NC 28681

SIMMONS, JIMMIE DALE, physician; b. Mt. Airy, N.C., May 26, 1933; s. Alpha Omega and Eva Elizabeth (Caudle) S.; B.S. in Medicine, Wake Forest U., 1954; M.D., Bowman Gray Sch. Medicine, 1957; m. Bette Lea Hickox, June 18, 1960; children—Deann Louise, David Lowell. Intern, City Meml. Hosp., Winston Salem, N.C., 1957-58; resident Naval Sch. Aviation Medicine, Pensacola, Fla., 1958; gen. practice medicine, Mt. Airy, 1961—; now pres. Mt. Airy Med. Assos., P.A., chief of staff No. Hosp. Surry County (N.C.); sec. Trail Inn, Inc.; pres. Southworth Corp. Pres., Greater United Mt. Airy Fund, 1966; dir., sec. Comprehensive Health Planning Region G, N.C., 1974-77; pres. regional bd. dirs. Surry-Yadkin Mental Health Assn.; pres. Surry County (N.C.) Bicentennial Commn.; trustee Wake Forest U. Served with U.S. Navy, 1958-61. Mem. AMA, N.C. Med. Soc., Surry Yadkin Med. Soc. Democrat. Baptist. Home: Shangri-La Mount Airy NC 27030 Office: 819 Rockford St Mount Airy NC 27030

SIMMONS, RICHARD ROSSON, cons.; b. Bayou LaBatre, Ala., Jan. 28, 1921; s. Robert Clifton and Elizabeth Delphine (Rosson) S.; B.S., U. Ala., 1956, M.S., 1968; m. Nellie Merle Hays, June 16, 1942; children—Sharon Elizabeth, Richard Rosson. Joined USAF, 1939; commd. 2d lt., 1944, advanced through grades to lt. col., 1958, ret., 1964; coordinator adult continuing edn., instr. indsl. relations U. Ala., Birmingham, 1964-69; founder, pres. Simmons Personnel Cons., Inc., Birmingham, 1970—. Chmn. bd. deacons Vestavia Hills (Ala.) Baptist Ch., 1971-72, deacon, 1949—, adult sunday sch. tchr., 1946—. Mem. Eastwood Rotary (dir. 1974—), Nat. Employment Assn., Ala. Employment Assn., Commerce Exec. Soc., Am. Inst. Profl. Cons., Alpha Kappa Psi. Home: 1912 Old Orchard Rd Vestavia Hills AL 35216 Office: 7710 Eastwood Mall Birmingham AL 35210

SIMMONS, ROBERT BURNS, educator; b. Gadsden, Ala., Dec. 27, 1937; s. Bruns Hunter and Grace Barbara (Armstrong) S.; B.S. in Chemistry, U. Ala., 1961; B.A. in Biology and History (Woodrow Wilson fellow), Athens State Coll., 1968, M.A. in Teaching, 1969; Ed.S. (Coll. Scholar), George Peabody Coll., 1976; M.A.S., U. Ala., 1978; m. Eleanor Conner, Nov. 11, 1959 (dec.); children—Kathleen D., Mary Ellen. Quality control chem. lab. supr. Goodyear Tire & Rubber Co., Gadsden, Ala., 1961-65; sect. leader, research and devel. chem. labs. Thiokel Chem. Corp., Redstone Arsenal, Huntsville, Ala., 1966-69; prof. history, polit. sci. and mgmt. John C. Calhoun State Community Coll., Decatur, Ala., 1969—; asst. acad. dean Vol. State Community Coll., Gallatin, Tenn., 1974. Chmn. coms. Decatur Band Boosters; program com. coordinator Congressman James Martin of Ala. U.S. Office Edn. grantee, 1970-71. Mem. Am. Hist. Assn., So. Hist. Assn., Ala. Hist. Assn., Am. Assn. Higher Edn., Ala. Edn. Assn., Am. Chem. Soc., Decatur C. of C., Beta Beta Beta, Phi Delta Kappa. Republican. Baptist. Club: Burningtree Country. Patentee missile propellants. Home: 2307 Burningtree Dr Decatur AL 35603 Office: Harris Bldg Calhoun Community Coll PO Box 2216 Decatur AL 35602

SIMMONS, ROBERT HOMER, tool co. exec.; b. McBride, Miss., Mar. 25, 1916; s. Homer Hirman and Nonnye Armildia (Cobb) S.; Asso. Sci. with honors, Copiah Lincoln Coll., 1936; B.S., La. State U., 1938, postgrad. bus. adminstrn., 1939. With Hunt Tool Co., Houston, 1939-75, dir., sec., 1960, sec.-treas., 1961, v.p., sec.-treas., 1972-75; sec.-treas. Hunt Engine & Equipment Co., Houston, 1958-75, also dir.; sec.-treas. Reagan Tool Co., Morgan City, La., 1963-64, also dir.; v.p., sec.-treas. Internat. Tool Co., Inc., Houston, 1963-75, pres., chmn. bd., sec.-treas., 1975—, also dir.; v.p. Clegg & Hunt, Inc., Houston, 1965-75, Geosource, Inc., Houston, 1975. Mem. Tenn. Walking Horse Breeders Assn., Sigma Nu, Kappa Mu Epsilon. Clubs: Cleveland (Miss.) Country; Houston Turn-Verein, Warwick, Univ. (Houston). Home: Rancho Verde 32402 Hwy 49 (Decker Prairie) Pinehurst TX Office: PO Box 803 Houston TX 77001

SIMMONS, RUBY KELLY, speech pathologist; b. Carteret County, N.C., Sept. 11, 1912; d. Rubin McKiney and Jessie Dama (Bell) Kelly; B.A., E. Carolina U., 1936: M.A., Western Carolina U., 1967; m. Y.Z. Simmons, June 1, 1937; 1 son, Leland McKinley. Tchr. home econs., sci., high schs., N.C., 1936-63, Beaufort (N.C.) High Sch., 1942-45, Newport (N.C.) High Sch., 1948-63; speech pathologist Carteret County Public Schs., Beaufort, 1963-73; pvt. practice speech pathology, Newport, 1973—, also nursing homes; a founder Speech and Hearing Clinic. Named Woman of Yr., Newport Bus. and Profl. Women's Club, 1979; lic. speech and lang. pathologist, N.C. Mem. Nat. Bus. and Profl. Women's Club (1st v.p. 1974-75, 2d v.p. 1975-76), NEA, N.C. Assn. Educators, Nat. Ret. Tchrs. Assn., Am. Speech and Hearing Assn., N.C. Speech and Hearing Assn., Carteret County Ret. Sch. Personnel (pres. 1978-80). Baptist. Home: Route 3 Box 147 Newport News NC 28570

SIMMONS, SAMUEL WILLIAM, ret. govt. ofcl.; b. Benton County, Miss., June 5, 1907; s. Britt L. and Ida E. (Pegram) S.; B.Sc. with honors, Miss. State U., 1931; A.M., George Washington U., 1934; Ph.D., Iowa State U., 1938; m. Lois Grantham, Aug. 5, 1928; children—Samuel William, Grant P. With U.S. Dept. Agr., Bur. Entomology, 1931-44; with USPHS, 1944-71, dir. Carter Meml. Lab., 1944-47, chief tech. devel. br., 1947-53, chief tech. br. communicable disease center 1953-66; chief pesticides program Nat. Communicable Disease Center, Atlanta, 1966-68; dir. div. pesticide community studies FDA, 1968-71; dir. div. pesticide community studies EPA, 1971-72, ret.; vis. lectr. tropical pub. health Harvard U., 1952-67; asso. preventive medicine and community health Emory U., 1957-72; USPHS rep. Fed. Com. on Pest Control. Recipient Alumni Achievement award George Washington U., 1946, Alumni Centennial Citation award Iowa State U., 1958, Distinguished Service medal USPHS, 1965, William Crawford Gorgas medal Assn. Mil. Surgeons U.S., 1968, Distinguished Career award EPA, 1972. Hon. cons. Army Med. Library, 1940-53; adv. bd. Inst. Agrl. Medicine, U. Iowa Sch. Medicine, U.S.-Japan Com. on Sci. Cooperation. Diplomate Am. Bd. Microbiology. Fellow Am. Soc. Tropical Medicine and Hygiene (councilor 1953), Chem. Spltys. Mfrs. Assns. (interdpl. com. pest control, subcom. vector control inter-agy. com. water resources, chmn. 1964-66), U.S.-Mex. Border Health Assn., WHO (chmn. com. on pesticides 1951, 56, 57), AMA (com. on insecticides 1950-59, com. on toxicology 1960), Research Soc. Am., Entomol. Soc. Am., Nat. Malaria Soc. (sec.-treas. 1951), Nat. Environ. Health Assn., Agrl. Research Inst., Horological Soc., Am. Mosquito Control Assn., Armed Forces Pest Control Bd., Nat. Research Council, Nat. Assn. Watch and Clock Collectors (nat. dir. 1979—), Sigma Xi, Phi Kappa Phi, Gamma Sigma Delta, Los Hidalgos. Contbr. articles to profl. jours.; editor and co-author: The Insecticide DDT and Its Significance, vol. II; contbr. to Human and Veterinary Medicine, 1959. Home: 2050 Blackfox Dr NE Atlanta GA 30345

SIMMONS, VIRGINIA MAY BARBER, psychologist; b. Kissimmee, Fla., Apr. 11, 1913; d. William Isaac and May Belle (Patterson) Barber; B.S. in Mathematics, Fla. State U., 1934; postgrad. Duke U., 1936; M.A., State U. Iowa, 1937, Ph.D., 1939; m. Haryl C. Simmons, Feb. 8, 1942; 1 son, William Haryl. Dir. child study service Davenport (Iowa) Schs., 1939-41; chief psychologist Iowa Div. Child Welfare, 1941-42; personnel mgr. Simmons Engring. Co., Davenport, 1943-45; sec.-treas., pres. Gopher Grinders, Inc., Anoka, Minn., 1949-68; cons. Minn. Sch. Dists., 1956-68; pvt. practice clin. psychology, Anoka, Minn., 1954-68, Orlando, Fla., 1970—; research psychologist Gateway Sch., Orlando, 1968-70. Lic. psychologist, Fla., Minn. Mem. Am., Fla., Southeastern psychol. assns., Am. Soc. Clin. Hypnosis, Central Fla. Assn. Profl. Psychologists, AAUW, League Women Voters (pres. local chpt. 1950-51), Phi Beta Kappa, Sigma Xi, Phi Kappa Phi. Republican. Presbyterian. Home: 11 Glendale Dr Kissimmee FL 32741 Office: 2111 E Michigan Ave Orlando FL 32806

SIMMONS, WILLIAM ISAAC, dentist; b. Waco, Tex., Feb. 14, 1924; s. Jared Claude and Blanche (Schwarz) S.; D.D.S., Loyola U., New Orleans, 1946; certificate in orthodontics U. Pa., 1950; m. Evelyn Kottle, June 11, 1967; children—Jared Claude, Walter Neil, Gina Denise, Nancy Dayan, Dylan Sara. Tchr., U. Tex. Dental Sch., 1951; individual practice dentistry, specializing in orthodontics, Shreveport, La., 1951—. Served with USAF, 1946-48. Mem. ADA (v.p. 4th Dist.), Am. Orthodontic Soc., Royal Soc. Health. Jewish. Clubs: Masons, Pieremont Oaks Tennis, Petroleum (Shreveport); Barksdale Air Force Officers. Office: 2042 Line Ave Shreveport LA 71104 also 3019 Old Minden Rd Bossier City LA 71112

SIMMS, JOAN RUTHERFORD, nurse; b. Lewisburg, W.Va., Apr. 25, 1943; d. Ira Jackson and Amie Monstella (Quick) Rutherford; R.N., Chesapeake and Ohio Hosp., 1965; m. Bernard Hale Simms, Sept. 1, 1965. Staff nurse C and O Hosp., 1965-66; staff nurse, Hercules, Inc., Covington, Va., 1967-74, head nurse, 1974-80, supervising nurse, 1980—. Mem. Am., Va. assns. occupational health nurses. Home: Route 1 Box 162ii Covington VA 24426

SIMMS, JOSEPH A., broadcasting co. exec.; b. Kansas City, Mo., June 4, 1950; s. Joseph A. and Juanita Jane (Reagan) S.; student U. Mo., Kansas City, 1969; grad. Career Acad. Broadcasting, Kansas City, 1970; m. Elizabeth Anne Morhart, Aug. 21, 1970; children—Eric, Christian. News dir. Sta. KUPK-TV, Garden City, Kans., 1970-71; dir. traffic and sports Sta. KTVC, Ensign, Kans., 1971-73; ops. mgr., program dir., weatherman Sta. KUHI-TV, Joplin, Mo., 1973-75; sales mgr. Sta. KFPW-TV, Ft. Smith, Ark., 1975-77; gen. mgr. Sta. WBOY-TV, Clarksburg, W.Va., 1977—, v.p., 1979—. Mem. exec. com. Kappa Sigma Pi Children's Home, 1977—; mem. exec. com. Harrison County (W.Va.) United Way, 1978—, gen. campaign chmn., 1979; bd. dirs. ARC, Salvation Army. Mem. Nat. Assn. Broadcasters. Roman Catholic. Club: Rotary. Home: 302 W Olive St Bridgeport WV 26330 Office: Sta WBOY-TV 912 W Pike St Clarksburg WV 26301

SIMMS, RICHARD HENRY, animal scientist; b. Urbana, Ill., June 24, 1932; s. Henry Allen and Lillian Ethel (Gill) S.; B.S., U. Ill., 1955; M.S., Purdue U., 1958, Ph.D., 1963; m. Vivian Ruth York, June 17, 1956; children—Katherine Ann, Karen Rae, Kaye Dianne, Kenneth Richard. Instr., animal sci. dept. Purdue U., Lafayette, Ind., 1955-62; livestock specialist U. Ill. Area Extension Center, Macomb, 1962-72; agrl. mgmt.-livestock cons. service, 1973-74; transp. cons. Ford Motor Co., Macomb, 1974-76; real estate sales Four Seasons Realty of Macomb, 1971-79. extension swine specialist U. Tenn., Nashville, 1979—. Ofcl. livestock judge Internat. Livestock Expn., 1967-70, Nat. Inter-Collegiate Livestock Judging Contest, 1967-69; ofcl. livestock judge Am. Royal Livestock Show, 1969-70, numerous Midwestern, So., Eastern state fairs, 1957-73; leader in agr. McDonough County 4-H Club, 1969-71. Mem. Macomb-Adair Unit Sch. Bd., 1967-74; adv. bd. Spoon River Jr. Coll., 1970-73; mem. Macomb Area Jr. Coll. Task Force Com., 1973-74. Recipient Community Leader of Am. award, 1969; named Tchr. of Month, Sch. Agr., Purdue U., Oct. 1962; Million Dollar Sales Club, Lamoine Valley, 1978. Mem. Am. Soc. Animal Sci., Soc. for Study Reprodn. and Fertility, U. Ill. Agr. Alumni Assn. (dir. 1967-73), Gamma Sigma Delta, Epsilon Sigma Phi. Methodist. Mason, Lion. Mem. rev. com. physiology sect. Jour. Animal Sci., 1970-72. Contbr. articles to profl. jours. Address: PO Box 11019 Nashville TN 37211

SIMMS, RUSSELL KEITH, mgmt. cons.; b. Beaman, Iowa, Feb. 24, 1913; s. Thomas William and Dolly Ellen (Oliver) S.; B.A., State U. Iowa, 1935; postgrad. Okla. State U., 1935-36; m. Ida May Wilson, Aug. 16, 1937. Apprentice engr. Phillips Petroleum Co., 1936; dist. engr. natural gas and gasoline dept., Borger, Tex., 1941-45, cons. chem. engr. patent div., Bartlesville, Okla., 1945-50; chief process engr. Phillips Chem. Co., 1950-63, br. mgr. engring. dept., Bartlesville, Okla., 1963-67; dir. corp. engring. Phillips Fibers Corp., Greenville, S.C., 1967-76; cons. to tech. mgmt., 1976—. Registered profl. engr., Okla. Mem. Am. Inst. Chem. Engrs. Mason. Home: 9 Pimlico Dr Bella Vista AR 72712

SIMMS, STEWART BROADUS, clergyman; b. Raleigh, N.C., Apr. 9, 1921; s. Robert Nirwana ano Virginia Adelaide (Egerton) S.; B.A., Wake Forest Coll., 1942; B.D., S.W. Bapt. Theol. Sem., Fort Worth, 1947; D.D., Furman U., 1973; m. Mary Ann Canaday, Jan. 2, 1943; children—Stewart Broadus, Robert Franklin, Carol Ann. Ordained to ministry Bapt. Ch., 1940; pastor Bailey (N.C.) Ch., 1939-40, Calvary Ch., Raleigh, N.C., 1940-42, First Ch., Grandview, Tex., 1943-45, Ridglea Ch., Fort Worth, 1945-48, Meml. Ch., Williamston, N.C., 1948-51, Woodland Heights Ch., Richmond, Va., 1951-61, 1st Ch., Greer, S.C., 1961—; moderator Roanoke Bapt. Assn., 1950-51; exec. com. Richmond Bapt. Assn., 1954-61; pres. Richmond Bapt. Pastors Conf., 1960; v.p. Bapt. Gen. Assn. Va., 1961; mem. Va. Bapt. Gen. Bd. Bapt. Extension Bd. Va., 1959-61; exec. com. So. Bapt. Conv., 1967-74, chmn., 1972-74, 1st v.p. conv., 1975; parliamentarian S.C. Bapt. Conv., 1970, 77-79, 1st v.p., 1971, pres., 1972. Mem. Greer Bi-Racial Com.; trustee S.C. Bapt. Hosps., 1963-67, 69-73; bd. dirs. Greer Relief Agy. Club: Kiwanis (Greer). Home: 308 W Poinsett St Greer SC 29651 Office: First Bapt Ch PO Box 531 Greer SC 29651

SIMON, DAVID RICHARD, physician; b. Chgo., Nov. 17, 1942; s. Hyman Leon and Betty S.; certificat de Francais Usuel Sorbonne, U. Paris, 1964; B.S., U. Miami, 1966, M.S. in Anatomy, 1967, Ph.D. in Anatomy, 1971, M.D., 1971; m. Andrea Loretta Carlo, June 4, 1967; children—Geoffrey, Elizabeth, Michelle, Stephanie. Intern, U. Miami Affiliated Hosps., 1971-72; resident in opthalmology Bascom Palmer Eye Inst., Miami, 1972-75; practice medicine specializing in ophthalmology, Plantation, Fla., 1977—; clin. asso. prof. anatomy U. Miami, 1977—; guest scientist Naval Med. Research Inst., Bethesda, Md.; cons. in field. Served to comdr. M.C., USN, 1975-77. Diplomate Am. Bd. Ophthalmology. Fellow Am. Acad. Ophthalmology and Otolaryngology. Recipient Kappa Delta award Am. Coll. Orthopedic Surgeons, 1975. Mem. AAUP, AMA, Broward County Med. Assn., Am. Soc. Cell Biology, Assn. Research in Vision and Ophthalmology, Sigma Xi. Contbr. articles to profl. jours. Office: Suite 106 201 N University Dr Plantation FL 33324

SIMON, DEAN THOMAS, coll. adminstr.; b. Woods County, Okla., Sept. 22, 1915; s. Clyde Augustus and Augusta Marie (Kaminska) S.; B.S., Northwestern State Coll. (Okla.), 1937; M.Ed., W.Tex. State U., 1954; m. Clara Marguerite Munkres, July 21, 1940. High sch. tchr., coach, Alva (Okla.) public schs., 1937-42, 46-51; tech. instr. U.S. Army Air Force, 1942-46; edn. specialist U.S. Air Force, Amarillo (Tex.) AFB, 1951-70; supr. adult vocat. edn. Amarillo Coll., 1970-72, dean Sch. Continuing Edn., 1972—. Mem. Tex. Panhandle Employment and Tng. Planning Council, 1972—. Mem. Tex. Assn. for Community Service and Continuing Edn., Tex. Assn. for Continuing Edn. Adminstrs. (bd. dirs.), Tex. Assn. Occupational Edn. Adminstrs. Home: 8604 Valley View Amarillo TX 79110 Office: Amarillo Coll PO Box 447 Amarillo TX 79178

SIMON, DONALD THOMAS, dietitian, nutritionist; b. St. Paul, Mar.26, 1937; s. Joseph John and Anna Edna (Werneke) S.; B.S., U. Minn., 1959; M.H.A., U. Philippines, 1977, M.P.H., 1979; m. Gloria Odi Bawaan, Aug. 26, 1967; children—Christina Maria, Angela Maria, Julienne Marie, Donald Thomas. Dietetic intern Colo. State Hosp., Pueblo, 1960-61; commd. 2d. lt. U.S. Air Force, 1962, advanced through grades to capt., 1966; dietitian various assignments, U.S., Philippines, 1962-74, nutrition cons. Med. Civic Action program, Philippines, 1973-76, ret. 1976; commd. lt. comdr. USPHS, 1977, advanced through grades to comdr., 1979, nutrition cons., dietitian USPHS Indian Hosp., Lawton, Okla., 1977—. Mem. Am. Dietetic Assn., Soc. Nutrition Edn., Res. Officers Assn. U.S., USPHS Commd. Officers Assn., Am. Public Health Assn., Dietetic Assn. Philippines. Roman Catholic. Office: USPHS Indian Hosp Lawton OK 73501

SIMON, ERIC, chem. industry cons.; b. Egelsbach, Germany, Jan. 8, 1920; came to U.S., 1937, naturalized, 1944; m. Isaac and Dina (Lehmann) S.; B.Ch.E., CCNY, 1945; m. June 23, 1951; children—Walker, Leslie, Clift. Prodn. foreman Harmon Colours, Kearney, N.J., 1945-49; group leader research Sun Chem. Co., N.Y.C., 1949-53; tech. dir., prodn. chief Pigmentos y Oxidos, Monterrey, Mex., 1954-74; tech. cons., 1974—; lectr. in field. Mem. Am. Chem. Soc., Assn. Cons. Chemists and Chem. Engrs. Contbr. articles to profl. jours.; patentee. Home: 15 Charleston Park Apt 904 Houston TX 77025

SIMON, H(UEY) PAUL, lawyer; b. Lafayette, La., Oct. 19, 1923; s. Jules and Ida (Rogers) S.; B.S., U. Southwestern La., 1943; J.D., Tulane U., 1947; m. Carolyn Perkins, Aug. 6, 1949; 1 son, John Clark. Admitted to La. bar, 1947, since practiced in New Orleans; asst. prof. advanced accounting U. Southwestern La., 1944-45; principal in C.P.A. firm Haskins & Sells, New Orleans, 1945-57; sr. partner law firm Deutsch, Kerrigan & Stiles, New Orleans, 1957-79; sr. partner firm Brian, Simon, Peragine, Smith & Redfearn, 1979—. Mem. Met. Crime Commn. C.P.A., La., Miss. Mem. Am. Judicature Soc., Internat. (com. on securities issues and trading 1970—), Inter-Am., Am. (com. ct. procedure and bar activities 1958—), La. (com. legislation and adminstrv. practice 1966—), New Orleans bar assns., Am. Inst. C.P.A.'s, New Orleans Assn. Notaries, Soc. La. C.P.A.'s, C. of C. (council 1952-66), Met. Area Com., Council for a Better La.,

Tulane Tax Inst. (program com 1960—), La. Tax Conf. (program com. 1968-72), N.Y. U. Tax Conf.-New Orleans (co-chmn. 1976), Bur. Govtl. Research, Am. Assn. Atty.-C.P.A.'s, Tulane Alumni Assn., Phi Delta Phi (past pres. New Orleans chpt.), Sigma Pi Alpha. Roman Catholic. Clubs: Young Men's Business (legislation com.), Lamplighter, Press, Toastmasters Internat., New Orleans Country, Petroleum (New Orleans); Internat. House (dir. 1976—); Paul Morphy Chess, Pendennis. Author: Louisiana Income Tax Law, 1956; Changes Effected by the Louisiana Trust Code, 1965; Gifts to Minors And the Parent's Obligation of Support, 1968; Deductions—Business or Hobby, 1975; Role of Attorney in IRS Tax Return Examination, 1978; asso. editor La. C.P.A., 1956-60; mem. bd. editors Tulane Law Rev., 1945-46. Home: 6075 Canal Blvd New Orleans LA 70124 Office: One Shell Sq Suite 4300 New Orleans LA 70139

SIMON, JUDITH CANFIELD, educator; b. Tulsa, Nov. 2, 1939; d. Ira and Billie (Reed) Canfield; B.S., Okla. State U., 1961, Ed.D., 1976; M.B.A., W. Tex. State U., 1969; m. Eugene John Simon, July 19, 1975; 1 son, Gregory. Sec., Cabot Corp., Pampa, Tex., 1961-67; tchr. Pampa High Sch., 1967-74, dept. chmn., 1971-74; instr. Okla. State U., Stillwater, 1974-75; asst. prof. Memphis State U., 1975—. Mem. NEA, Nat. Bus. Edn. Assn., Am. Bus. Communication Assn., Nat. Assn. Tchr. Educators for Bus. and Office Edn., Tenn. Edn. Assn., Tenn. Bus. Edn. Assn., United Teaching Profession (sec. Memphis state unit), Tex. State Tchrs. Assn., Pampa Classroom Tchrs. Assn. (pres.), Delta Pi Epsilon. Methodist. Contbr. articles to profl. jours. Home: 2525 Hacks Cross Germantown TN 38138 Office: Dept Office Adminstrn Memphis TN 38152

SIMON, LILLIE BELLE, nurse; b. Tunica County, Miss., Feb. 28, 1916; d. Joseph Ceily and Nannie Mae (Huskison) S.; R.N., Bapt. Meml. Hosp., Memphis, 1938; B.S., Siena Coll., 1959. Dir. nurses Oakville Meml. Sanatorium, Memphis, 1946-48, W. Tenn. Chest Disease Hosp., Memphis, 1948-69; staff nurse, coronary intensive care unit Meml. Hosp., Gulfport, Miss., 1969-73, asst. adminstr. nursing, 1973—. Named Nurse of Yr., Tenn. Nurses Assn., Dist. 5, Memphis, 1962; R.N., Tenn., Miss. Mem. Am. Nurses Assn., Am. Mgmt. Assn., Soc. Nursing Service Adminstrs. Methodist. Clubs: Met. Dinner, Altrusa (pres.) (Gulfport). Home: 120 Edmund Dr Long Beach MS 39560 Office: PO Box 1810 Broad Ave Gulfport MS 39501

SIMON, LORENA COTTS (MRS. SAMUEL C. SIMON), music tchr., poet; b. Sherman, Tex., Jan. 16, 1897; d. George Godfrey and Willie (Jones) Cotts; student Am. Conservatory, summer 1938, Julliard Music Sch., summer 1939; diploma Sherwood Music Sch., 1941; D. Lit. Leadership, Internat. Acad. Leadership, Philippines, 1967; Mus.D., St. Olav's Acad., Sweden, 1969; L.H.D., Nother Pontifical Acad.; m. Samuel C. Simon, Nov. 6, 1918 (dec.). Tchr. violin, piano, theory and harmony, Port Arthur, Tex., 1919—; organizer, dir. Schubert's Violin Choir, Port Arthur, 1919-55; judge Internat. Poetry Peace Award Contest, 1965; works of poetry in Internat. Poetry Archives, Manchester Central Library, Eng., 1965. Named Poet Laureate of Tex., 1961; Poet Laureate of Magnolia Dist., 1962-64; Poet Laureate of Port Arthur, 1962—; recipient gold plaque Tex. Fedn. Women's Club, 1962, spl. award 1st place in poetry and music Tex. heritage dept., 1963, spl. award in music and fine arts and outstanding service awards, 1965; 1st place in poetry, 1966; Medal of Honor and Diploma of Merit, Centro Studi Scambi Internat., Rome, 1965, Silver, Gold medals of merit, 1967, diploma of merit, 1966, 67; Hon. Poet Laureate-Musician, United Poets Laureate Internat., 1966, Karte of award, 1968, Hon. Internat. Catholic Poet Laureate, 1968, also Silver Laurel Health; Contemporary Internat. Poet Hall of Fame, 1968; honored by Tex. Senate and Ho. of Reps., 1967; named Cath. Lady of Humanity. Mem. Internat. Platform Assn., Nat., Tex. press women's assns., Nat. Council Cath. Women, Nat. Guild Piano Tchrs. (charter mem.; adjudicator), Am. Coll. Musicians (adjudicator), Am. Poetry League, Poets Soc. Tex. (counselor 1967—, critic judge), Am. Poets Fellowship Soc. Corp., U.S., UN Assn.-U.S.A., Alpha Delta Kappa. Clubs: Writers' (pres. 1963-64), Symphony. Author: The Golden Key, 1958; From My Heart (1st place award Ann. Poetry Writers Contest of Tex. Press Women's Assn. 1961), 1959; Children's Story Hour (1st place award Nat. Fedn. Press Women's Ann. Writers' Contest 1962), 1960; In Music Land, 1965; That Blessed Night, 1966. Songs pub. include Live Expectantly, 1962, In Search for Growth, 1963, Freedom's Light, 1963, What Can I Do for Jesus, 1963. Donor funds for constrn. of 8 churches in Africa including Holy Cross Ch., Imaculate Conception Ch., Sacred Heart Ch., Christ the King Ch. Address: 411 5th Ave Port Arthur TX 77640

SIMON, SISTER MARY ALVERA, hosp. adminstr.; b. Chandler, Okla., Nov. 9, 1927; s. John A. and Edna Lee S.; grad. Mercy Hosp. Sch. Nursing, Oklahoma City, 1951; B.S., St. Mary Coll., Xavier, Kans., 1955; M.H.A., St. Louis U., 1967. Joined Sisters of Mercy, Roman Cath. Ch., 1945; adminstr. Mercy Hosp., Oklahoma City, 1968-71, v.p., 1971-75; asso. adminstr. Mercy Hosp. of New Orleans, 1975-78; pres. Mercy Health Center, Oklahoma City, 1978—. Mem. Am. Coll. Hosp. Adminstrs., Nat. League Nursing, Okla. Conf. Cath. Hosps. (pres.-elect. 1979), Oklahoma City Area Hosp. Council (v.p. 1979), C. of C., Nat. Joint Practice Commn., Okla. Heritage Assn. Home: 4400 W Memorial Rd Oklahoma City OK 73120 Office: 4300 W Memorial Rd Oklahoma City OK 73120

SIMON, WILLIAM LEE, hosp. adminstr.; b. N.C., Dec. 8, 1923; s. John L. and Lela (Goodwin) S.; A.B., Duke U., 1949, cert. in hosp. adminstrn., 1951; m. Carolyn C. Campbell, Oct. 16, 1965; children—William, Jon, Douglas, Karen. Asst. dir. Hubbard Hosp., Meharry Med. Coll., 1951-52, exec. dir., 1952-54; adminstr. E. Tenn. Bapt. Hosp, Knoxville, 1954-66, N. Miami (Fla.) Gen. Hosp., 1966-71; adminstr. Am. Hosp., Miami, Fla., 1971-76, exec. dir., 1976—; exec. dir. N. Ridge Gen. Hosp., Ft. Lauderdale, Fla., 1977—; exec. v.p. Am. Hosp. Mgmt. Corp., Miami, 1971—. Trustee, deacon, personnel com. First Baptist Ch. of S. Miami. Fellow Am. Coll. Hosp. Adminstrs.; mem. Fla. Hosp. Trust Fund (chmn. bd. trustees), S. Fla. Hosp. Assn. (pres. 1968, 76, dir. 1966-71, 74-77), Am. Hosp. Assn., Tenn. Hosp. Assn. (v.p. 1965-66), Fla. Hosp. Assn. (dir. 1969-70, 76-78). Club: Rotary (pres. local chpt. 1963-64). Home: 7305 SW 146th Ct Miami FL 33183 Office: 11750 Bird Rd Miami FL 33175

SIMONDS, J. CLIFTON, hosp. adminstr.; b. Rochester, N.H., Aug. 26, 1921; s. Jesse Clifton and Arline May (Sinclair) S.; student Fla. So. Coll., 1948-52; m. Joann K. Simonds; children—Jesse Clifton, Sharon, Mary Ellen Simonds Smith, Karen A. Devlin. Asst. adminstr. Lakeland (Fla.) Gen. Hosp., 1953-57, So. Fla. Bapt. Hosp., Plant City, 1957-58; adminstr. Everglades Meml. Hosp., Pahokee, Fla., 1963-67, Rand Meml. Hosp., Freeport, Grand Bahama Islands, 1967-69, Calhoun Meml. Hosp. and Nursing Home, Arlington, Ga., 1969-72, Med. Center Kissimmee (Fla.), 1972—; adminstr. Emergency Med. Service Osceola County, 1974—; mem. adv. council trauma nursing Fla. Regional Med. Program, 1974—. Served to 1st lt. USAF, 1942-45; lt. col. Res. ret. Clubs: Masons, Lions, Elks. Office: 320 N Mitchell St Kissimmee FL 32741

SIMONDS, TROY WAYNE, labor relations specialist; b. Murphy, N.C., July 6, 1931; s. Henry Waldo and Anna Mae (Satterfield) S.; student Berry Coll., 1949-51, Internat. Corr. Sch., 1953-54; m. Billie Ruth Ricks, Nov. 16, 1951; 1 dau., Janet Leigh. Engring. office clk. Tenn. Copper Co., Copperhill, Tenn., 1953-60, field office clk. Tenn. Copper Co. and Cities Service Power, 1960-71, generation shift foreman Cities Service Power, Copperhill, 1971-72, generation asst. ops. supr., 1972-75, power generation ops. supr., 1975-77, labor relations specialist, 1977—. Blood chmn. Polk-Fannin Counties chpt. Ga. Red Cross, 1978; pres. Wolf Creek (N.C.), Cherokee County (N.C.) Community Devel. Councils, 1962-63. Served with U.S. Army, 1952-53. Mem. Tenn. Indsl. Personnel Conf., Am. Mgmt. Assn. Club: Cowanee. Home: Box 145 Route 6 Murphy NC 28906 Office: Cities Service Co Copperhill TN 37317

SIMONEAUX, FRANK PAUL, state legislator; b. Napoleonville, La., Oct. 30, 1933; s. Henry C. and Ann C. (Simoneaux) S.; student Nicholls State Coll., Thibodaux, La., 1954-56; B.A., La. State U., 1956, LL.B., (Superior Oil scholar), 1961; m. Marie M. Lancaster, June 21, 1961; children—Mignonne, Paul, Michelle, Rainier, Denis. Admitted to La. bar, 1961; atty. La. Dept. Revenue, Baton Rouge, 1961; law clk. Judge Albert Tate, 3d Circuit Ct. Appeals, Lake Charels, La., 1961; practiced in Baton Rouge, 1962—; partner firm Breazeale, Sachse & Wilson, Baton Rouge, 1967—; mem. La. Ho. of Reps., 1972—. Chmn. social order and responsibility com. Baton Rouge Goals Congress, 1970-71; pres. Inter-Civic Club Council, 1973; legal researcher Council for a Better La., 1964-70; dir. Campfire Girls, 1969-72. Served to capt. AUS, 1956-58, 61-62; col. JAGC, state judge adv. La. N.G. T.H. Harris scholar, 1954-56. Mem. Am., La., Baton Rouge (dir. 1967—) bar assns., La. State U. Alumni Fedn., Baton Rouge C. of C. (chmn. law enforcement com. 1970-71), Res. Officers Assn., Nat., La. N.G. assns., Scabbard and Blade, Omicron Delta Kappa, Phi Delta Phi, Pi Gamma Mu. Roman Catholic. Lion (pres. Lakeshore club 1969-70), K.C. (council 1963—). Clubs: Camelot, Bocage Racquet (dir. 1965-67) (Baton Rouge). Home: 5921 Forsythia Av Baton Rouge LA 70808 Office: PO Box 3197 Baton Rouge LA 70808

SIMONS, JAMES HOLMES, acct.; b. Florence, Ala., July 20, 1943; s. James Holmes and Doris (Mabry) S.; B.S., U. Ala., 1969; 1 son, Alan Brooks. Sr. acct. Price Waterhouse & Co., Nashville and Miami, Fla., 1969-72; controller Tellus Corp., Miami, 1973, Furniture Corp. Am., Miami, 1974; owner Simons & Snay, P.A., C.P.A.'s, Miami, 1974—, Condo Mgmt. and Realty, Inc., Miami, 1978—; adj. faculty U. Miami, 1974-76. Bd. dirs. Concept House, Inc., drug rehab. program, 1974—, treas., 1976-78, pres., 1978—. C.P.A., Fla. Mem. Am. Inst. C.P.A.'s, Fla. Inst. C.P.A.'s, Commerce Execs. Soc. of U. Ala. Republican. Club: Kiwanis. Home: 9505 SW 87th Ave Miami FL 33176 Office: 10651 SW 88th St Miami FL 33176

SIMONS, MICHAEL BRUCE, advt. agy. exec.; b. Phila., Aug. 7, 1947; s. Norman Howard and Helen (Greenfield) S.; B.A. in Oral Communications, Salem Coll., 1969; m. Cynthia Ochitell, Nov. 6, 1975; 1 son, Scott David; 1 dau. by previous marriage, Lori Michelle. Announcer, Sta. WHAR, Clarksburg, W.Va., 1967-69; press sec. Sam Huff Congressional campaign, 1st congressional dist. W.Va., 1969; local news dir. Sta. WBOY-TV, Clarksburg, 1969-72; mem. public relations dept. Jud-Lee Prodns., Los Angeles, 1972; mgr. ops. Sta. WRGT-FM, Clarksburg, 1973, Sta. WFGM-FM, Fairmont, W.Va., 1975; partner Berman and Simons Advt., Clarksburg, W.Va., 1974—; lectr. in field. Bd. dirs., chmn. drama dept. Clarksburg Art Center, 1977—; mem. spl. promotion com. Clarksburg Area Redevel. Task Force. Jewish. Home: 118 Westwood Ave Bridgeport WV 26330 Office: 120 S 3d St Suite 222 Clarksburg WV 26301

SIMPKINS, IRBY CLIFFORD, publishing co. exec.; b. Nashville, Mar. 17, 1944; s. Irby Clifford and Dorothy Joyce (Stockett) S.; B.S. in Civil Engring., Vanderbilt U., 1967; m. July 31, 1965; children—Elizabeth Paige, Irby Clifford. Founder, pres. Irby Simpkins Investments, Houston, 1969—; owner, chmn. bd. C.B.&T. Bancshares, 1976—, ICSI Constrn. Co., Houston, 1969; pres., chmn. exec. com. Harpeth Nat. Bank, Franklin, Tenn., 1977-79; pres. Nashville Banner Pub. Co., 1979—; dir. Lakeside Commerce Bank, Houston. Vice chmn. bd. Harpeth Acad., Franklin; co chmn. Republican gubernatorial campaign, 1978; mem. chancellors council Vanderbilt U.; mem. Higher Edn. Commn. Tenn., 1979—; trustee Meharry Med. Coll., 1980—. Served with USMC, 1962-68. Episcopalian. Clubs: River Oaks Country (Houston); Cumberland, Nashville City. Home: Route 11 Moran Rd Franklin TN 37064 Office: 1100 Broadway Nashville TN 37202

SIMPKINS, NANCY GRAY, ednl. career planning counselor; b. Nashville, Sept. 10, 1955; d. William Orinn and Doreene Dickey S.; B.A., Randolph-Macon Coll., 1977; M.Ed., U. Va., 1978. Paraprofl. counselor Randolph-Macon Coll., Ashland, Va., 1978; career planning counselor Vanderbilt U., Nashville, 1978—. Action Auction vol., Nashville, 1979; career planning com. Belle Meade United Meth. Ch., Nashville, counselor youth fellowship. Mem. Am. Personnel and Guidance Assn., Am. Coll. Personnel Assn., Tenn. Assn. Student Personnel Adminstrs., John T. Wightman Found. Clubs: Brentwood Acad. Alumni Assn., Randolph-Macon Alumni Assn., U. Va. Alumni Assn., Nashville Club. Home: 5764 Brentwood Trace Brentwood TN 37027 Office: Career Planning and Placement Service Vanderbilt 110 Alumni Hall Nashville TN 37240

SIMPKINS, PHILIP DOWLEN, trust co. exec., pension cons.; b. Houston, Oct. 7, 1943; s. Buford Douglas and Martha (Dowlen) S.; B.B.A., Tex. Technol. U., 1965; student U. San Carlos of Guatemala, 1976; children—Pauline Ellen, Philip Dowlen, Susan Elizabeth. Investment broker, Merrill Lynch, Dallas, 1969-76; v.p. Trust Co., Dallas, 1976-78; pres., co-founder First Benefit Trust Co. of Tex., Dallas, 1978—; lectr. in field. Mem. Internat. Assn. Fin. Planners. Republican. Presbyterian. Home: 418 Tall Oaks St Richardson TX 75081 Office: First Benefit Trust Co of Tex 1720 One Dallas Centre Dallas TX 75201

SIMPSON, CARLTON SKINNER, air force officer; b. Trenton, Tenn., July 19, 1941; s. Curry Otha and Nell (Davis) S.; B.S., USAF Acad., 1963; grad. Air Command Staff Coll., 1972, Indsl. Coll. Armed Forces, 1975; M.B.A., Trinity U., 1979; m. Dee Ann Clifford, Apr. 6, 1968; children—Bart T., Britt D., Brad C. Commd. 2d lt. U.S. Air Force, 1963, advanced through grades to lt. col., 1979; interceptor pilot, USAF, Ventura, Calif., 1964-65; forward air controller, air liaison officer 101st Airborne Div. and 5th Spl. Forces Group, Vietnam, 1966; instr. pilot Acad. Inst., Valdosta, Ga., 1967-69; intercollegiate football coach USAF Acad., Colo., 1969-72; flight command USAF Instr. Pilot Sch., Randolph AFB, Tex., 1973; mil. adviser Chinese Air Force Acad., Republic of China, 1974-75; mgmt. cons. Air Tng. Command Insp. Gen., San Antonio, 1976-78; dir. plans and programs div. Air Tng. Command, Randolph AFB, 1979—. Leader Cub Scouts; coach various youth athletics. Decorated D.F.C. with 2 oak leaf clusters, Bronze Star, Air medal with 14 oak leaf clusters, Meritorious Service medal with oak leaf clusters, Joint Service Commendation medal; Cross of Gallantry (Vietnam). Mem. Air Force Assn., Order of Daedalians. Republican. Baptist. Clubs: San Antonio Country, Plaza (San Antonio). Home: 150 Park Hill Dr San Antonio TX 78212 Office: Programs Div Hdqrs Air Tng Command Randolph AFB TX 78148

SIMPSON, CAROLYN F. SPARKS, speech pathologist; b. Little Rock, Dec. 31, 1941; d. Albert Reuel and Ruth Jane (Criglow) Sparks; B.A. in Speech Therapy, U. So. Miss., 1964, M.S. in Audiology (HEW fellow), 1965; postgrad. U. N. Fla., 1973-74; m. Carl David Simpson, Feb. 27, 1965; children—Carl David, Stephen Reuel, Edmond Scott. Speech pathologist S. Allen Smith Clinic, P.A., Jacksonville, Fla., 1971-73; tchr. deaf, hearing resource tchr. Duval County Bd. Public Instrn., Jacksonville, 1973-78; spl. edn. tchr. Stuttgart (Ark.) public schs., 1978-79, speech pathologist, 1979—. Mem. Am. Speech and Hearing Assn., Assn. Children with Learning Disabilities. Baptist. Home: 1203 Oliver St Stuttgart AR 72160 Office: Northside Elem Sch 119 E Superior St Stuttgart AR 72160

SIMPSON, DENNIS DWAYNE, educator, social scientist; b. Lubbock, Tex., Nov. 9, 1943; s. Homer A. and Georgie Lee (Barrett) S.; student Sul Ross State U., 1962-63; B.A., U. Tex., 1966; Ph.D., Tex. Christian U., 1970; m. Sherry Ann Johnson, Aug. 20, 1965; children—Jason Renn, Jeffrey Todd. Asst. prof. Inst. Behavioral Research, Tex. Christian U., Fort Worth, 1970-74, asso. prof., 1974-79, prof., 1979—. Mem. Evaluation Research Soc., Am., Southwestern psychol. assns., Sigma Xi, Psy Chi. Contbr. articles to profl. jours. Home: 3605 Winifred Dr Fort Worth TX 76133 Office: Tex Christian U Inst Behavioral Research Fort Worth TX 76129

SIMPSON, ERVIN PETER YOUNG, clergyman, historian; b. Mangere, N.Z., May 13, 1911; s. Thomas and Clara Glass (McEwen) S.; came to U.S., 1949, naturalized, 1974; Dip.Theol., N.Z. Baptist Theol. Coll., 1936; B.A., U. N.Z., 1948, M.A., 1949; B.D., Berkeley Bapt. Div. Sch., 1950, Th.M., 1950, Th.D., 1952; m. Lillian Eileen Andrew, June 30, 1937; children—Donald McEwen, John Martin. Sec., YMCA, Christchurch, N.Z., 1929-33; ordained to ministry Baptist Ch., 1936; parish minister, N.Z., 1937-49; asso. minister Lakeshore Ave. Bapt. Ch. Oakland, Calif., 1949-52; mem. faculty Berkeley (Calif.) Bapt. Div. Sch., 1949-67, prof. ch. history, 1955-67; prof. ch. history Grad. Theol. Union, Berkeley, 1962-67; sr. lectr. history Massey U., Palmerston North, N.Z., 1967-69; C. Shirley Donnelly chair of history Alderson-Broaddus Coll., Philippi, W.Va., 1969-77; ret., 1977; interim v.p. Bacone Coll., Muskegee, Okla., 1979-80. Served as chaplain N.Z. Army, 1939-45. Fulbright fellow, 1949-50. Fellow Royal Anthrop. Inst. Gt. Britain, Soc. Antiquarians of Scotland; mem. Am. Soc. Ch. History (past v.p.), Am. Baptist Hist. Soc. (dir.), Brit. Hist. Assn. Republican. Clubs: Kiwanis, Masons. Author: How the Church Got There, 1948; Ordination and Christian Unity, 1966; History of the New Zealand Baptist Missionary Soc., 1949; cons. editor Foundations, 1958-67. Home: Box 82 Alderson-Broaddus Coll Philippi WV 26416

SIMPSON, HAROLD BROWN, ret. air force officer, educator; b. Hindsboro, Ill., Apr. 3, 1917; s. Harry Leon and Louise (Brown) S.; B.S., U. Ill., 1940, A.M., 1950, M.S., 1950; Ph.D., Tex. Christian U., 1969; m. Vera Di Lendro, Sept. 6, 1977; children by previous marriage—Jeffrey, Harold Brown, Gregory, Georganna, Deborah. Commd. 2d lt., USAF (formerly USAAF), 1941, advanced through grades to col., 1954; intelligence analyst Directorate of Intelligence Hdqrs., 1950-54; dir. stats. services Hdqrs. USAFE, 1955-58; comptroller 12th Air Force, 1959-63; ret., 1963; chmn. dept. social sci. Hill Jr. Coll., Hillsboro, Tex., 1963—; adj. prof. history Tex. Christian U., 1970—. Decorated Commendation medal with oak leaf cluster. Fellow Co. Mil. Historians, Tex. Hist. Soc.; mem. Air Force Assn., Tex. Hist. Assn., Pi Kappa Phi, Alpha Phi Theta. Author: Brawling Brass North and South, 1960; Gaines' Mill to Appomattox, 1963; Texas In The War, 1861-1865, 1965; Red Granite For Gray Heroes, 1968; Hood's Texas Brigade In Poetry and Song, 1969; Hood's Texas Brigade: Lee's Grenadier Guard, 1970; Hood's Texas Brigade in Reunion and Memory, 1974; Audie Murphy: American Soldier, 1975; Hood's Texas Brigade: A Compendium, 1977; Cry Comanche, 1979. Home: 1411 Alford Dr Hillsboro TX 76645 Office: Hill Jr Coll Hillsboro TX 76645

SIMPSON, HASSELL ALGERNON, educator; b. Barksdale, S.C., May 8, 1930; s. John Algernon and Jewel (Boroughs) S.; B.S., Clemson U., 1952; M.A., Fla. State U., 1957, Ph.D., 1962; m. Grace Pinson Pow, June 6, 1953; children—David Steadman, John Algernon II, William Gavin. Instr. English, Fla. State U., 1958-59, Auburn U., 1959-62; asso. prof. English, Hampden-Sydney (Va.) Coll., 1962-65, prof., 1965—, chmn. dept. English, 1968-76, chmn. div. humanities, 1970-73; cons. So. Assn. Colls. and Schs. Served with inf. U.S. Army, 1952-54. Cottrell grantee, 1965; Shell grantee, 1969, 72, 73, 76. Mem. AAUP, MLA, Soc. for Study of So. Lit. Presbyterian. Author: Rumer Godden, 1973; contbr. articles to various periodicals. Home: Converse House Hampden-Sydney VA 23943 Office: Hampden-Sydney Coll Hampden-Sydney VA 23943

SIMPSON, JACK BENJAMIN, med. technologist, mng. exec.; b. Tompkinsville, Ky., Oct. 30, 1937; s. Benjamin Harrison and Verda Mae (Woods) S.; student Western Ky. U., 1954-57; grad. Norton Infirmary Sch. Med. Tech., 1958; m. Winona Clara Walden, Mar. 21, 1957; children—Janet Lazann, Richard Benjamin, Randall Walden, Angela Elizabeth. Asst. chief med. technologist Jackson County Hosp., Seymour, Ind., 1958-61; chief med. technologist, bus. mgr. Mershon Med. Labs., Indpls., 1962-66; founder, dir., officer Am. Monitor Corp., Indpls., 1966—; mng. partner Astroland Enterprises, Indpls., 1968—, 106th St. Assos., Indpls., 1969-72, Keystone Asso., Ltd., Indpls., 1972—, Delray Rd. Asso., Ltd., Indpls., 1970-71, Allisonville Asso., Ltd., Indpls., 1972—, Rucker Asso., Ltd., Indpls., 1974—; mng. partner Raintree Assos., Ltd., Indpls., 1979—, Westgate Assos., Ltd., Indpls., 1978—; dir. Topps Constrn. Co., Bradenton, Fla., Indpls. Broadcasting, Inc. Mem. Am. Soc. Med. Technologists (cert.), Indpls. Soc. Med. Technologists, Ind. Soc. Med. Technologists, Am. Soc. Clin. Pathologists, Royal Soc. of Health (London). Republican. Baptist. Clubs: Columbia of Indpls., Harbor Beach Surf, Fishing of Am., Elks. Home: 68 Isla Bahia Dr Fort Lauderdale FL 33316 Office: 7729 Rucker Rd Indianapolis IN 46250

SIMPSON, JAMES HARRISON, social worker; b. Stanford, Ky., June 14, 1934; s. William B. and Anna Mae (Logan) S.; B.A., Ky. State U., 1960; M.S.W., U. Louisville, 1965. With Ky. Dept. Child Welfare, Frankfort, 1961—, mgr. juvenile services br. Ky. Dept. Human Resources Bur. Social Servs., 1979—. Served with U.S. Army, 1954-56. Mem. Am. Public Welfare Assn., Am. Correctional Assn., So. States Correctional Assn., Ky. Welfare Assn., Child Welfare League Am. Democrat. Home: 490 Lima Dr Lexington KY 40505 Office: Kentucky Dept Human Resources 275 E Main St Frankfort KY 40621

SIMPSON, JAMES LEE, banker; b. Rehoboth, N.Mex., Aug. 28, 1936; s. Lester and Ozella (Wofford) S.; B.G.S. in History and Polit. Sci., U. Nebr., 1973; m. Karen Allene Smith, Sept. 1, 1956; children—Janet Allene, Alan Dale, James Austin. Enlisted man U.S. Air Force, 1953-61; commd. 2d lt., 1961, advanced through grades to maj., 1973; trained in electronic warfare; flew 215 missions in S.E. Asia; ret., 1974; sales mgr. Ek Products, 1974-76; pres. N.Am. Model Enterprises, Inc., Ft. Worth, 1977-79; asst. v.p. mktg. Citizens Nat. Bank, Denton, Tex., 1979—. Active fund drives United Fund, AF Aid Soc., U.S. Savs. Bonds. Decorated D.F.C., Air Medal with 7 oak leaf clusters. Mem. Acad. Model Aeros. (certified adminstrv. leader), Soaring Soc. Am., Nat. Soaring Soc., League Silent Flight, Fedn. Aeronautique Internationale Southwest Modelers Show (bd. dirs.). Mormon. Columnist, asso. editor RC Modeler Mag., 1966-77; columnist RC Sportsman, 1977—; Miniature aircraft designer;

designed remote controlled weather research air vehicle for Sch. Atmospheric Research. Home: 206 Diane Sanger TX 76266

SIMPSON, JANET YVONNE, hosp. exec.; b. Birmingham, Ala., Apr. 12, 1950; d. Melvin Ray and Nellie Eloise (Bradford) S.; B.Social Welfare, U. Ala., 1972, M.S.W., 1978. Welfare worker United Meth. Children's Home, Selma, Ala., 1972-73; med. social worker Univ. and Diabetes Hosp., Birmingham, 1973-77; public relations staff Title Books Co., Birmingham, 1978-79; coordinator social services Brookwood Med. Center, Birmingham, 1979—; cons. Mid-South Home Health Care. Vol., ARC, 1979, Am. Cancer Soc., 1976-77, Am. Heart Assn., 1976-77. Recipient stipend Center for Devel. and Learning Disorders, 1977-78. Mem. Soc. Hosp. Social Work Dirs., Ala. Soc. Hosp. Social Workers, Med. Social Service Orgn., Mu Phi Epsilon. Baptist. Clubs: Rising Tide, Gentle Spirit. Home: 1717 H Vestawood Ct Birmingham AL 35216 Office: 2010 Medical Center Dr Birmingham AL 35209

SIMPSON, JOHN DAVID, oil co. exec.; b. Houston, Aug. 19, 1951; s. Hubert Lyle and Elizabeth Jane (Feagin) S.; B.A. in Econs., U. Tex., 1973, M.B.A., 1976. Stockbroker, Underwood Neuhaus & Co., Inc., Houston, 1973-74; instr. corp. fin. U. Tex., Austin, 1975-76; sr. fin. analyst Shell Chem. Co., Houston, 1977-78; mgr. planning support Corp. div. Houston Oil and Minerals Corp., 1978-79, mgr. planning and adminstrn. Offshore div., 1979-80, mgr. planning and adminstrn. Offshore div., 1980—. Mem. N.Am. Soc. Corp. Planners, Planners League (founding dir.), Interactive Fin. Planning Assn. (v.p. 1978-79, pres. 1979-80). Office: 1100 Louisiana St Houston TX 77002

SIMPSON, JOHN NOEL, hosp. adminstr.; b. Durham, N.C., Feb. 27, 1936; s. William Hays and Lucile (McNab) S.; B.A., Duke U., 1957; M.H.A., Med. Coll. Va., 1959; m. Virginia Marshall, June 27, 1959; children—John Noel, William Marshall. Asso. adminstr. Riverside Hosp., Newport News, 1962-70; asso. adminstr. Richmond (Va.) Meml.Hosp., 1970-74, sr. v.p. and adminstr., 1974-77, exec. v.p., 1977—; chmn. Va. Hosp. Ins. Reciprocal, 1977-79. Served with M.S.C., U.S. Army, 1959-62. Recipient Edgar C. Hayhow award, Am. Coll. Hosp. Adminstrs., 1976. Fellow Am. Coll. Hosp. Adminstrs. (regent state of Va. 1976-80), Va. Hosp. Assn. (dir. 1974-80). Republican. Presbyterian. Club: Rotary (v.p. 1969-70). Contbr. articles in field to profl. jours. Home: 1503 Willingham Rd Richmond VA 23233 Office: 1300 Westwood Ave Richmond VA 23227

SIMPSON, RHYNE, JR., manufactured housing exec.; b. Dallas, Oct. 7, 1937; s. Rhyne and Avis L. (Miller) S.; B.A., U. Tex., 1959; M.B.A., Harvard U., 1964; children—Michael Rhyne, Martha Katherine, Zachary Booth. Vice pres. Republic Housing Corp., Dallas, 1964-68, pres., 1968-73; pres. Simpson & Company, Avinger, Tex., 1973—, also chmn. bd. Democrat. Presbyn. Clubs: Willow Bend Polo and Hunt (Dallas); Harvard (N.Y.C.). Address: PO Box 336 Avinger TX 75630

SIMPSON, RICHARD WILDER, automobile dealer; b. Battle Creek, Mich., Jan. 23, 1921; s. Nathan Duncombe and Louise Anthony (Lepper) S.; B.A., Mich. State Coll., 1946; m. Frances Adelaide Blake, Apr. 3, 1948; children—Virginia Kathleen, Barbara Ann, Martha Louise, Richard Nathan. With Fletcher Motors, Orlando, Fla., 1947; with Simpson Motors, Inc., Orlando, Fla., 1952—, owner, pres., 1960—; dir. Sun Bank, East Orlando; mem. bd. Chrysler Corp. Dealer Council. Pres., Optimist Little League Assn.; pres. Orlando Utilities Commn., 1972, 76; bd. dirs. Orlando Parking Commn., 1958-64, Orlando YMCA. Served as pilot USAAF, 1942-46. Decorated Air medals (3); recipient Quality Dealer award Chrysler Corp., 1956. Mem. Orlando Automobile Dealers Assn. (past pres.), Plymouth Advt. Assn. (past pres.), Orlando C. of C. (dir.). Methodist. Clubs: Orlando Optimist (dir., Internat. Appreciation award 1970), Orlando Athletic Assn. (dir.). Home: 1107 Seville Pl Orlando FL 32804 Office: 1020 N Orange Ave Orlando FL 32801

SIMPSON, ROBERT, state legislator; b. Amarillo, Tex., Dec. 8, 1943; s. Joshua Marion and Mattie Lou (Harrison) S.; B.S., U. Tex., Austin, 1966; J.D., 1970; m. Linda Lee Andrick, Jan. 29, 1969; children—Robert Andrick, J.M. Lee. Admitted to Tex. bar, 1969, since practiced in Amarillo; mem. Tex. Ho. of Reps. from 65th Dist., 1975—, chmn. ins. com. Mem. Am., Tex., Amarillo bar assns. Democrat. Methodist. Home: 3209 Parker St Amarillo TX 79109 Office: 2711 Paramount Amarillo TX 79109

SIMPSON, ROBERT EARL, hosp. adminstr.; b. Birmingham, Ala., May 2, 1943; s. Robert Zimmerman and Nannie Ray (Judge) S.; student U. Jacksonville, 1962-65; m. Brenda Littlejohn, Aug. 21, 1965; children—Robert Earl II, Shannon Nicole. Operating room unit mgr. Providance Hosp., Mobile, Ala., 1971-74; operating room adminstrv. coordinator Med. Center, Columbus, Ga., 1974-76; coordinator central supply Bapt. Montclair Hosp., Birmingham, Ala., 1976—. Served with USCG, 1966-71. Mem. Ala. Assn. Centra l Supply (pres.). Roman Catholic. Home: 2015 Outwood Rd Fultondale AL 35068 Office: 800 Montclair Rd Birmingham AL

SIMPSON, ROBERT TENNENT, IV, state ofcl.; b. Florence, Ala., Dec. 8, 1919; s. Robert Tennent and Emily (Ford) S.; B.S., U. Md., 1958; M.A., Troy State U., 1976; m. Gloria Page, Dec. 1, 1947; children—Emily, Robert T. V., John T., Mary Shea. Commd. 2d lt. U.S. Air Force, 1941, advanced through grades to col., 1964; various assignments as pilot, World War II, Korea, Vietnam; comdr. 834th Air div., Vietnam, 1966, ret., 1967; dir. customer relations Boeing Co., Phila., 1967-71; mem. cabinet State of Ala., Montgomery, 1971-74; mem. dept. ct. mgmt. Supreme Ct. Ala., Montgomery, 1974—; v.p. Nat. Congress Govs. Hwy. Safety Reps., 1974. Decorated Legion of Merit, D.F.C., Air medal with 11 oak leaf clusters; Croix de Guerre with silver star (France). Mem. Air Force Assn., DAV (life), VFW, SAR, Marion Mil. Inst. Alumni Assn. (nat. pres. 1975-76). Presbyterian. Club: Maxwell AFB Officers. Home: 1121 Felder Ave Montgomery AL 36106 Office: PO Box 644 Montgomery AL 36101

SIMPSON, WADE BLAND, oil co. exec.; b. Big Spring, Tex., Sept. 11, 1937; s. James Bland Simpson and Clara Modesta Stokes; B.A., Tex. Christian U., 1959, B.S., 1959; student U. Tex., 1964-66. Pres. Regalos, Inc., Austin, Tex., 1965-72; asso. Taylor Realtors, Austin, 1972-74; partner Simpson-Mann Oil Producers, San Angelo, Tex., 1974—; v.p. Modesta's Inc., Big Spring, 1962-77; sr. partner MWA Oil and Gas Co., San Angelo, Tex., 1975-77. Trustee Episcopalian Diocese, Amarillo, 1977; mem. bd. devel. Tex. Christian U., 1962. Served with USAF, 1960. Mem. Tex. Ind. Producers and Royalty Owners Assn., W. Tex. Geol. Soc., San Angelo Geol. Soc., Ind. Landman's Assn. Episcopalian. Home: 2604 Nasworthy San Angelo TX 76902 Office: PO Box 289 San Angelo TX 76902

SIMS, BENNETT JONES, clergyman; b. Greenfield, Mass., Aug. 9, 1920; s. Lewis Raymond and Sarah Cosette (Jones) S.; A.B., Baker U., 1943; postgrad. Princeton Theol. Sem., 1946-47; B.D., Va. Theol. Sem., 1949, D.D., 1966; postgrad. Cath. U., 1969-71; D.D., U. of South, 1972; m. Beatrice May Wimberly, Sept. 25, 1943; children—Laura (Mrs. John P. Boucher), Grayson, David. Ordained to ministry Protestant Episcopal Ch. as deacon, 1949, priest, 1950; recotr Ch. of Redeemer, Balt., 1951-64; dir. continuing edn. Va. Theol. Sem., 1966-72; bishop, Atlanta, 1972—; priest-in-charge St. Alban's Ch., Tokyo, 1962; spl. lectr. Diocesan Confs., U.S., overseas, 1969. Trustee U. of South. Served with USNR, 1943-46. Named Young Man of Year, Balt. C. of C., 1953, Distinguished Alumnus of Year, Baker U., 1972. Merrill fellow Harvard, 1964-65. Office: 2744 Peachtree Rd NW Atlanta GA 30305

SIMS, EDITH MARIE, librarian; b. Baton Rouge, Jan. 27, 1928; d. Lyle Wood and Thelma Kathleen (Tillman) Sims; B.S., La. State U., 1949, B.L.S., 1951. Tchr. pub. schs., Haynesville, La., 1949-50; newspaper librarian La. State U. Library, Baton Rouge, 1949-56, geology librarian, 1956-57, govt. documents librarian, 1957-68, asso. librarian, head social sci. div., 1968-77, asso. librarian central reference dept., 1978—, also vis. asso. prof. Sch. Library Sci. Sec., Baton Rouge chpt. La. Mental Health Assn., 1962; mem. Baton Rouge Symphony Aux., 1968—. Mem. Am., La. library assns., Spl. Libraries Assn., La. Hist. Assn., Geosci. Info. Soc., Phi Alpha Theta. Baptist. Home: 1475 W Chimes St Baton Rouge LA 70802

SIMS, ERNEST THEODORE, JR., horticulturist; b. Atlanta, Aug. 29, 1932; s. Ernest Theodore and Louise (Miller) S.; B.S.A., U. Ga., 1954; M.Sc., Ohio State U., 1959, Ph.D., 1962; grad. basic research course Oak Ridge Inst. Nuclear Studies, 1965; m. Margaret Elizabeth Richter, Dec. 28, 1963; children—Ernest Theodore, III, John Christopher Richter. Pomologist, Sims Fruit Farms, Conyers, Ga., 1956-57; grad. research asst. Ohio State U., 1957-62; asst. prof. horticulture Clemson (S.C.) U., 1962-67, asso. prof. horticulture, postharvest physiologist, 1967-72, prof., 1972—, mem. grad. faculty, 1968—, faculty senate, 1969-71. Troop committeeman Boy Scouts Am., 1967-69, 78-79. Served with AUS, 1954-56. Mem. Res. Officers Assn. U.S., Am. Soc. Hort. Sci. (S.C. reporter nat. jour. 1966—, recipient Carroll R. Miller award 1975), Am. Soc. Plant Physiologists, Internat. Soc. Hort. Sci., Sigma Xi, Phi Kappa Phi, Alpha Zeta, Gamma Sigma Delta. Presbyterian. Club: Lions. Contbr. articles to profl. jours. Home: 117 Poole Ln Clemson SC 29631

SIMS, JESSE BAXTER, auditor; b. Brandenburg, Ky., Sept. 12, 1924; s. Roma Allen and Grace Valera (Freeman) S.; student U. Ky., 1948-49; m. Mary Shelly Hager, Sept. 4, 1948; children—Paul Alan, Joseph Terry, Mary Susan, John Burke, Celia Anne. Various positions as farmer, bakery employee, 1951-53; with U.S. Dept. Agr., Meade County, Ky., 1954-66; with Gates Rubber Co., Elizabethton, Ky., 1966—, auditor, 1972—. Served with U.S. Army, 1943-47. Recipient certificates of achievement Soil Conservation Service, Nat. Mgmt. Assn. Mem. Nat. Mgmt. Assn., Modern Woodmen Am. (past sec., treas.). Democrat. Roman Catholic. Home: Route 2 Box 170 Vine Grove KY 40175

SIMS, KAREN LOUISE, med. counselor; b. Washington, Aug. 13, 1951; d. William Pierce and Doris Jane (Hannigan) S.; B.S., Emory U., 1973; M.Ed., U. Ariz., 1975. Clin. counselor dept. behavioral medicine Hilton Head Hosp., Hilton Head Island, S.C., 1976-79; dir behavior modification Diabetes Research and Tng. Center, Birmingham, Ala., 1979—; cons. in field. Mem. Am. Psychol. Assn., Am. Personnel and Guidance Assn., Am. Assn. Diabetes Educators, Am. Diabetes Assn. Home: 3216 Overton Manor Dr Birmingham AL 35243 Office: 1808 7th Ave S University Station Birmingham AL 35294

SIMS, MELVIN THOMAS, JR., lawyer; b. Hattiesburg, Miss., Nov. 27, 1933; s. Melvin Thomas and Ina Beryl (Mixon) S.; B.A., Miss. Coll., 1954; B.S., Southwestern Bapt. theol. Sem., 1957; J.D., U. Miss., 1975; m. Linda Faye Mattox, Dec. 28, 1953; children—Charles Mattox, Zoe Ann, Melinda Jean. Ordained to ministry Bapt. Ch., 1951; pastor Central Bapt. Ch., Port Neches, Tex., 1957-60, 1st Bapt. Ch., Lambert, Miss., 1963-65; admitted to Miss. bar, 1975; mem. firm Fortenberry & Sims, New Augusta and Hattiesburg, Miss., 1975-76, Sims & Perkins, Beaumont and Richton, Miss., 1977-79. pros.atty. Perry County, Miss., 1976—. Bd. dirs. South-Central Miss. chpt. ARC, SE Miss. Community Action Agy.; mem. Criminal Justice Planning Commn., State of Miss. Served as chaplain USAF, 1960-63, 65-73. Mem. VFW (nat. legal com.), Am. Bar Assn., Miss. Bar Assn., South-Central Miss. Bar Assn., Miss. Prosecutors Assn., Nat. Dist. Attys. Assn. Democrat. Baptist. Club: Rotary. Home: Hickory Dr Richton MS 39476 Office: 1 Federal Bldg Richton MS 39476

SIMS, RUSSELL ADRON, recreation adminstr., educator; b. Batesville, Ark., July 2, 1933; s. Adron A. and Mattie Bell (Roberts) S.; A.A., So. Bapt. Coll., 1953; B.A., Ouachita Bapt. Coll., 1956; Ed.M., U. Ark., 1970, Ed.D., 1974; children—Lisa Jo Sims Vickers, Russell Scott. Athletic dir. and head coach, Heber Springs (Ark.) High Sch., 1963-65, Mountain Home (Ark.) High Sch., 1965-69; head resident housing U. Ark., Fayetteville, 1969-72; dir. recreation Fairfield Communities Land Co., Fairfield Glade, Tenn., 1972-73; asst. prof. Ark. Tech. U., Russellville, Ark., 1973-79; pres. Internat. Recreation Consultants, 1979—; prin. adminstrv. asst. Arabian Bechtel Co., Ltd., Saudi Arabia, 1979—; v.p. Recreation and Park Systems Co., 1974-76. Mem. AAHPER, Ark. Assn. Health, Phys. Edn. and Recreation (pres. 1971-72, v.p. recreation div. 1978-79), Ark. Ofcls. Assn., Ky. Ofcls. Assn., Phi Delta Kappa. Baptist. Club: Optimist (pres. 1964). Office: Recreation Dept Western Ky U Bowling Green KY 42101

SIMS, SAM PIERCE, III, controller; b. Kosciusko, Miss., Aug. 4, 1935; s. Sam Pierce, Jr., and Helon Caroline (Magee) S.; B.S., U. So. Miss., 1962; m. Martha Lynn Holcomb, Aug. 27, 1960; children—Paul Edward, Douglas Carroll. Staff acct. Emerson & Emerson, C.P.A.'s, Hattiesburg, Miss., 1962-64; cost acct. Scott Paper Co., Mobile, Ala., 1964-67; controller MacMillan Bloedel, Inc., Pine Hill, Ala., 1967—. Treas. bd. Thomasville Hosp., 1978-79. Served with USMC, 1954-57. Mem. Nat. Assn. Accts. Democrat. Baptist. Club: Pineview Country (dir., pres. 1977). Home: 93 Kimbrough Ct Thomasville AL 36784 Office: MacMillan Bloedel Inc Pine Hill AL 36769

SIMS, WILLIAM ARTHUR, orthopedic surgeon; b. Jefferson City, Tenn., Mar. 2, 1936; s. William Finley and Madge Evelyn (Cates) S.; M.D., U. Tenn., 1961; m. Betty Anne Brandon, June 20, 1959; children—Libby, Sheri, Bill, Lisa. Intern, City of Memphis Hosps., 1961; resident in surgery Bapt. Meml. Hosp., Memphis, 1962; resident in orthopedic surgery Campbell Clinic, Memphis, 1963-67; pvt. practice orthopedic surgery, Decatur, Ala., 1967—; past chief of staff Decatur Gen. Hosp. Served with U.S. Army, 1963-69. Diplomate Am. Bd. Orthopedic Surgery. Mem. Am. Acad. Orthopedic Surgeons, Ala. Orthopedic Soc. (past pres.), Am. Orthopedic Soc. for Sports Medicine, Clin. Orthopedic Soc., AMA, So. Med. Assn., Morgan County Med. Soc. (past pres.). Presbyterian (elder). Club: Willis Campbell. Home: Route 4 Indian Hills Rd Decatur AL 35603 Office: 1103 16th Ave Decatur AL 35601

SIMSTEIN, NEIL LELAND, surgeon; b. N.Y.C., Nov. 16, 1942; s. Irving Jay and Rose (Spitzer) S.; B.S., Wake Forest U., 1964; M.D., N.Y. Med. Coll., 1970; m. Beverly Ann Stott, Nov. 24, 1971; children—Jessica, Julia, Rebecca. Intern, Baylor Affiliated Hosps., Houston, 1970-71; resident in surgery Naval Hosp., Portsmouth, Va., 1973-77; practice medicine specializing in surgery, Winston-Salem, N.C., 1978—; mem. staff Forsyth Meml. Hosp., Winston-Salem; clin. instr. surgery Bowman Gray Sch. Medicine, 1978—. Served with USN, 1971-78; Vietnam. Fellow Internat. Coll. Surgeons, Southeastern Surg. Soc., Michael E. DeBakey Surg. Soc.; mem. Assn. Mil. Surgeons U.S. Diplomate Am. Bd. Surgery. Republican. Jewish. Contbr. articles to profl. jours. Home: 265 Gloucestershire St Winston Salem NC 27104 Office: 112 Forsyth Med Park Winston Salem NC 27103

SINCLAIR, COLBY, food service co. exec.; b. Syracuse, N.Y., May 29, 1921; student U. Fla., 1940-41, U. Sheffield, 1945, Stetson U., 1947-49; 1 son by former marriage—Robert C. Mgr. Greyhound Post Houses, Daytona Beach, Fla., 1950-53; sales institutional food Jefferies, Monarch Foods, Fla., 1954-62; sales mgr. City Provisioners, Daytona Beach, 1963-69; exec. v.p. Holiday House Restaurants, Deland, Fla., also v.p. Holiday Supply Corp., Deland, 1969—, also dir.; v.p. 100% Real Estate, Inc., Winter Park, Fla., 1977—; owner Celebrity Reps., 1974—, Consol. Sales, Winter Park, Fla., 1975—; entertainment columnist Orlando (Fla.) Sentinel, 1967-74. Pres., Daytona Playhouse, 1961; 4th v.p. Fla. Theatre Conf., 1962; bd. dirs. Central Fla. Civic Theatre, 1978-80. Served with U.S. Army, 1941-46, 48. Mem. Food Ser. Execs. Assn., Nat. Assn. Corp. Real Estate Execs., Nat. Restaurant Assn., Nat.-Am. Wholesale Grocers Assn., Fla. Theatre Conf. Office: 100% Real Estate Inc 1881 Lee Rd Winter Park FL 32789

SINCLAIR, STANLEY REID, counseling psychologist; b. Rutherfordton, N.C., Aug. 17, 1947; s. James Reid and Mary Pearl (Jones) S.; B.S., Western Carolina U., 1969, M.A. in Edn., 1974; m. Theresa Maria Rossi, May 15, 1971; 1 son, Seth Benjamin. Edn. counselor, Ft. Bragg, N.C., 1975-76; edn. coordinator Dept. Army, Nashville, 1976; counseling psychologist VA, Winston-Salem, N.C., 1976—; human relations tng. instr. Served with USAF, 1969-73. Recipient Outstanding Achievement award U.S. CSC, 1976, Superior Performance award, 1979. Mem. Am. Personnel and Guidance Assn., Nat. Vocat. Guidance Assn., Assn. Measurement and Evaluation in Guidance, Phi Kappa Phi, Winston-Salem Jr. C. of C. Democrat. Roman Catholic. Club: Ind. Order Foresters. Home: 5921 Castillo Rd Winston-Salem NC 27106 Office: 251 N Main St Winston-Salem NC 27102

SINGER, CHARLES GREGG, educator; b. Phila.; s. Arthur Gregg and Edith Elizabeth (Good) S.; A.B., Haverford Coll., 1933; A.M., U. Pa., 1935, Ph.D., 1940; m. Marjorie Pouder, Sept. 6, 1939; children—Marjorie Jean, Richard Gregg, Terri Elizabeth, Robert Adams. Chmn. dept. history Wheaton Coll., 1944-48, Salem Coll., 1948-54; v.p. coll., chmn. history dept. Belhaven Coll., Jackson, Miss., 1954-58; chmn. dept. history Catawba Coll., Salisbury, N.C., 1958-77; prof. theology and ch. history Atlanta Sch. Bibl. Studies, 1977—. Mem. Am. Hist. Assn., Mediaeval Acad. Presbyterian. Club: Kiwanis. Author: A Theological Interpretation of American History, 1964; Toynbee, A Critical Study, 1965; John Calvin: His Roots and Fruits; The Unholy Alliance, 1976; From Rationalism to Irrationality, 1979. Home: 319 Wake Dr Salisbury NC 28144 Office: Atlanta Sch Bibl Studies 1924 Clairmont Rd Atlanta GA 30033

SINGER, JACK NORMAN, psychologist; b. Hartford, Conn., Mar. 27, 1943; s. William and Rose S.; B.A., U. Mass., 1965; M.A., Bowling Green State U., 1967; Ph.D., Colo. State U., 1975; m. Sharon F. Cohen, June 25, 1972; children—Amie Joy, Allison Jayne, Stacey Lynn. Commd. 2d lt. U.S. Air Force, 1967, discharged, 1971, recommd. maj., 1973; resident in psychology Wilford Hall Med. Center, San Antonio, 1975; psychologist, instr. Def. Race Relations Inst., Patrick AFB, Fla., 1976-78, base clin. psychologist, 1978-79, discharged, 1979; pvt. practice clin. and indsl. psychology, Plantation, Fla., 1979—; mem. faculty, Fla. Inst. Tech., Rollins Coll., Brevard Community Coll. Decorated Joint Services Commendation medal, Air Force Commendation medal with oak leaf cluster, Meritorious Service medal; Dept. Labor grantee, 1974; IRS grantee, 1975; lic. psychologist, Fla. Mem. Am. Psychol. Assn., Internat. Assn. Applied Psychology, Southeastern Psychol. Assn. Democrat. Jewish. Club: B'nai Brith. Office: 4100 S Hospital Dr Suite 200 Plantation FL 33317

SINGER, MARK LEE, psychologist; b. Colorado Springs, Colo., July 1, 1953; s. Lee M. and Betty L. S.; B.S., Vanderbilt U., 1976; M.A., U. Ala., 1978, postgrad., 1978—. Counselor Nat. Allergy Rehab. Found., Camp Bronco Junction, W.Va., 1976; histology technician in surg. pathology Vanderbilt U. Med. Center, Nashville, 1977; counselor new student orientation U. Ala., Tuscaloosa, 1979; resident counseling-psychologist W. Ala. Comprehensive Services for Substantially Handicapped Children and Adults, Tuscaloosa, 1978—; teaching cons. spl. edn. U. Ala.; instr. United Cerebral Palsy Inst., 1979, 80; cons. parent intervention program Rural Infant Stimulation Environ. U. Ala. Cert. psychometrist, Ala. Mem. Am. Personnel and Guidance Assn., Ala. Personnel and Guidance Assn., Student Orgn. of Profl. Counselors in Behavioral Studies U. Ala., Kappa Delta Pi. Episcopalian. Researcher in perceptual psychology. Home: 1909 Cedar Ridge Rd Huntsville AL 35801 Office: 14 Thomas Circle Tuscaloosa AL 35405

SINGER, RAYMOND, restaurateur; b. N.Y.C., Sept. 16, 1936; s. Richard and Herta Wilhelmina (Manske) S.; B.S., Fla. State U., 1961; m. June Kile, Mar. 19, 1971; children—Debrah, Katherine; step-children—Steven, James. Asst. mgr. Morrison's Food Service, Fla. State U., Tallahassee, 1959-61, mgr. Morrison's Cafeterias, Greenville, S.C., 1961-62, Spartanburg, S.C., 1962-63, Jacksonville, Fla., 1963-66; owner, operator Flaming Fountain Restaurant, Naples, Fla., 1966-76; cons. food service Naples and Miami, 1976-77; gen. partner and mgr. Everglades City Club (Fla.), doing bus. as Capt.'s Table, 1977—; cons. in field. Mem. food rev. bd. Collier County (Fla.), 1975-79, active Mental Health Bd., 1978-79. Mem. Naples C. of C., Fla. Restaurant Assn. (pres. 1973), Collier County Restaurant Assn. (pres. 1971, 72), Nat. Restaurant Assn. (outstanding restaurateur State of Fla. 1975), U.S. Ski Assn., Naples Bath and Tennis Club, Naples Snow Seekers. Home: 710 Willowhead Dr Naples FL 33940 Office: Capt's Table Restaurant Everglades City Club Ltd 102 Collier Blvd Everglades City FL 33929

SINGER, ROBERT NORMAN, educator; b. Bklyn., Sept. 27, 1936; s. Abraham and Ann (Norman) Singer; B.S., Bklyn. Coll., 1961; M.S., Pa. State U., 1962; Ph.D., Ohio State U., 1964; children—Richard, Bonni Jill. Instr. phys. edn. Ohio State U., Columbus, 1963-64, asst. prof., 1964-65; asst. prof. Ill. State U., Normal, 1965-67, dir. motor learning lab., 1965-69, asso. prof., 1968-69, asst. dean. Coll. Applied Sci. and Tech., 1967-69; dir. motor learning lab., asso. prof. Mich. State U., East Lansing, 1969-70; prof. Fla. State U., Tallahassee, 1970—, dir. motor learning lab., 1970-72, dir. div. human performance, 1972-75, dir. Motor Behavior Center, 1975—; cons. editor Holt, Rinehart and Winston, N.Y.C., 1971-77; lectr. U.S., Asia and Europe; cons. in field. Coordinator sport psychology, sports medicine council U.S. Olympic Com. Served with U.S. Army, 1955-58. Mem. Am. Ednl. Research Assn., AAHPER, N.Am. Soc. Sport Psychology and Phys. Activity. Author: Motor Learning and Human Performance, 1968, 75; Coaching, Athletics, and Psychology, 1972; Physical Education, 1972; Teaching Physical Education, 1974; Laboratory and Field Experiments in Motor Learning, 1975; Myths and Truths in Sports Psychology, 1975; editor: Readings in Motor Learning, 1972; The Psychomotor Domain, 1972; Foundations of Physical Education, 1976; editor Completed Research in Health,

Phys. Edn., and Recreation, 1968-74; mem. editorial bd. Research Quar., 1968—, Jour. Motor Behavior, 1968—, Jour. Sport Psychology, 1979—; contbr. articles to anthologies and profl. jours. Home: Route 1 Box 3155 Havana FL 32333 Office: 106 Montgomery Gym Fla State U Tallahassee FL 32306

SINGH, DHARMDEO NARAYAN, med. geneticist; b. Dumari, Sitamarhi, Bihar, India, July 2, 1932; came to U.S., 1966, naturalized, 1978; B.S., Agra (India) U., 1951; M.S., Patna (India) U., 1953; Ph.D., London U., 1961; m. Reva Kumari, June 2, 1955; children—Heramb Kumar, Madhurendra Kumar, Vinayek Kumar. Asst. prof. botany Patna U., 1953-66; Sessel fellow Yale U., 1966, research asso. dept. biology, 1966-68; prof. Claflin U., 1968-71; dir. devel. human genetics lab. S.C. Dept. Mental Retardation, Charleston, 1971-74; asst. clin. prof. pediatrics and pathology Med. U.S.C., Charleston, 1971-74; prof. pediatrics Meharry Med. Coll., 1974—; dir. Diagnostic and Tng. Lab. in Mental Retardation, Nashville, 1975—. Mem. Am. Soc. Human Genetics, Am. Genetics Assn., Am. Genetics Soc., Am. Inst. Biol. Scis., Indian Soc. Human Genetics (life,), Nat. Acad. Scis. I India (life), Internat. Dermatoglyphics Assn., Nat. Assn. Scis. India, S.C. Acad. Scis., Sigma Xi, Alpha Omega Alpha. Hindu. Research, numerous publs. on genetic and cytogenetic aspects of humans, animals and plants. Home: 519 Colice Jeanne Rd Nashville TN 37221 Office: Dept Pediatrics Meharry Med Coll Nashville TN 37208

SINGH, HARINDER S., computer co. cons.; b. Patiala, India, Dec. 23, 1941; s. Nihal and Lajwanti (Devi) S.; came to U.S., 1960, naturalized, 1968; B.A. with honors, Punjab U., 1959; M.S., U. N.C., 1962; Ph.D., St. Louis U., 1965; m. Harriet Mae Varnum, Dec. 31, 1963; children—Sarita, Sushila. Research geophysicist Digital Seismic Corp., 1965-69; dir. research and devel., dir. tng. Digital Resources Corp., 1969-70; sr. cons., educator Vought Corp., Dallas, 1970—; tchr. Tulane U., 1962-63, Tex. Christian U., 1971-73, U. Tex., Arlington, 1974—. Vol. fireman, Pantego, Tex., 1972—. Air Force Office Sci. Research grantee, 1963. Certified Geol. Scientist. Mem. Soc. Exploration Geophysicists, Am. Geophys. Union, World Affairs Council, Jr. C. of C. Club: Rotary. Home: 3400 Peachtree St Arlington TX 76013 Office: 8500 N Stemmons St Suite 308 Dallas TX 75247

SINGH, RAJENDRA PRATAP, surgeon; b. Allahabad, India, Sept. 16, 1939; s. Akbal Bahadur and Kamala (Devi) S.; B.Sc., Banaras U., India, 1958; M.B.B.S., Agra, India, 1963, M.S. in Surgery, 1966; M.A.M.S. in Surgery, Indian Acad. Med. Scis., New Delhi, 1971; m. Sushma Singh, Jan. 16, 1971; children—Sonia, Jay Pal. House surgeon S. N. Hosp., Agra, 1963-64; postgrad. in surgery Med. Coll., Agra, 1964-67; casualty officer Stockport Infirmary, Stockport, Eng., 1967; registrar in surgery Southmead Hosp., Bristol, Eng., 1968, Weston-Supermare Gen. Hosp., 1968-69, Northampton (Eng.) Gen. Hosp., 1969-70; registrar in thoracic surgery Nottingham (Eng.) City Hosp., 1972-73; surg. resident Bronx Lebanon Hosp., N.Y.C., 1973-74; sr. and chief surg. resident Appalachian Regional Hosp., Beckley, W.Va., 1974-76, attending staff, 1976—; attending surgeon VA Med. Center, Raleigh Gen. Hosp., Beckley Hosp., 1976—; asst. prof. surgery Marshall U. Med. Sch., Huntington, W.Va., 1978—. Diplomate Am. Bd. Surgery. Fellow Royal Coll. Surgeons (Edinburgh), Royal Coll. Surgeons (Eng.): mem. Raleigh County Med. Soc., W.Va. Med. Assn., Am. Fedn. Clin. Research. Contbr. numerous articles to med. jours. Office: Woodland Med Park Beckley WV 25801

SINGH, RAMCHANDRA SITARAM, civil engr., educator; b. Jabalpur, India, Mar. 24, 1934; s. Sitaram and Bhagwan (Pyari) S.; came to U.S., 1969; B.Sc., Nagpur U., India, 1954; B.E. with honors, Jabalpur U., 1958; M.E., Roorkee U., 1963; M.S., U. Ill. at Urbana, 1971; Ph.D., U. Wis., 1973; m. Sushila Katiyar, Dec. 12, 1964; children—Rajiv, Sanjay. Jr., asst. engr. irrigation Madhya Pradesh Pub. Works Dept., India, 1959-62; lectr. civil engring. Jabalpur Engring. Coll., 1964-67; lectr. Indian Inst. Tech., Kanpur, 1967-68; research asst., U. Ill., 1969-71, U. Wis., 1971-73; mem. faculty Madison Area Tech. Coll., 1973-74; data retrieval specialist NASA-Technicolor Co., Houston, summer 1974, 77; asst. prof. civil engring. McNeese U., 1974-77, Lamar U., Beaumont, Tex., 1977—. Recipient Bausch & Lomb Photogrammetric award hon. mention Am. Soc. Photogrammetry, 1969; Cubic Electrotape Fellowship award Am. Congress on Surveying and Mapping, 1969. Mem. Am. Soc. Photogrammetry, Am. Congress Surveying and Mapping. Developed cataloging system for remote sensing data. Home: 4801 Orleans St Lake Charles LA 70605 Office: Civil Engring Dept PO Box 10024 Lamra U Beaumont TX 77710

SINGH, TARA, environ. engr., cons.; b. Sanghol, India, Sept. 3, 1937; s. Santa and Bhagwant Kaur (Rehal) S.; came to U.S., 1963, naturalized, 1972; B.S. in Civil Engring., Ohio U., 1965; M.S. in Sanitary Engring., U. Mo., 1966; Ph.D. in Environ. Engring., Ill. Inst. Tech., 1972; m. Pritam K. Ubee, Jan. 5, 1968; children—Robert Paul, Prit Paul. Water resources engr. Pub. Works Dept., India, 1957-62; sr. research and devel. scientist Nalco Chem. Co., Chgo., 1966-68; project engr. Consoer, Townsend & Assos., Chgo., 1968-70; mgr. environ. engring. Harry O. Hefter Assos., Inc., Chgo., 1971-72; asso., chief environ. engring. div. H.D. Nottingham and Assos. div. Lyon Assos., Inc., McLean, Va., 1973-79; pres. Resource Applications, Inc., Herndon, Va., 1979—. Registered profl. engr., Va., Ill., N.C., N.J. Mem. Am. Acad. Environ. Engrs., Am. Water Works Assn., AAAS, Water Pollution Control Fedn., ASCE, Nat. Solid Waste Mgmt. Assn. Contbr. articles to profl. jours. Home: 1502 Gingerwood Ct Vienna VA 22180 Office: 808 Mosby Hollow Dr Herndon VA 22070

SINGH, VIJAY PAL, civil engr., educator; b. Agra, India, July 15, 1946; s. Gurdayal and Bhagwaan (Kumari) S.; B.S., U. P. Agrl. U., 1967; M.S., U. Guelph, 1970; Ph.D., Colo. State U., 1974; m. Anita Singh, Jan. 15, 1976; 1 child, Vinay. Came to U.S., 1970. Engr., mem. tech. staff Rockefeller Found., New Delhi, 1967-68; postdoctoral fellow in civil engring. Colo. State U., Ft. Collins, 1974; asst. prof. hydrology N.Mex. Inst. Mining and Tech., Socorro, 1974-77; asso. research prof. civil engring. George Washington U., Washington, 1977-78; asso. prof. civil engring. Miss. State U., Mississippi State, 1978—. Sr. judge N.Mex. Sci. and Engring. Fair, 1974-76; judge Md. Sci. and Engring. Fair, 1978. Research grantee NSF. Mem. Am. Geo-phys. Union, ASCE, Am. Water Resources Assn., Internat. Water Resources Assn., Instn. Engrs., Indian Assn. Hydrologists, Indian Soc. Agrl. Engrs., Colo. State U. Alumni Assn., U. Guelph Alumni Assn., Sigma Xi. Contbr. articles to profl. publs. Home: 29 Colonial Circle Starkville MS 39759

SINGLE, JOHN LEE, hosp. adminstr.; b. Akron, Dec. 16, 1942; s. John L. and Elouise S.; A.A., Jackson Jr. Coll., 1964; B.S., Western Mich. U., 1967; B.A., Lewis Coll., 1970; M.B.A., Loyola U., Chgo., 1971. Exec. dir. materials mgmt. St. Joseph Hosp., Houston, 1975-77, asst. adminstr. human resources, 1977-78, asst. adminstr. planning and ops. research, 1978—, also dir.; adj. instr. Houston Community Coll.; pres. John L. Single & Assos. Eagle Scout. Mem. Adminstrv. Mgmt. Soc. (dir. Houston chpt. 1979-80), Assn. M.B.A. Execs., Am. Soc. Personnel Adminstrn., Am. Inst. Indsl. Engring., Am. Coll. Hosp. Adminstrs. Home: 12932 Leader St Houston TX 77072 Office: 1919 LaBranch Houston TX 77002

SINGLETARY, HARRY KTHAW, JR., correctional adminstr.; b. Tarpon Springs, Fla., Mar. 6, 1946; s. Harry Kthaw and Kinnie (Fason) S.; B.A. in Sociology, Fla. Presbyn. Coll., 1968; M.A. in Social Work, U. Chgo., 1971; m. Jocelyn Pinckney Davis, Aug. 24, 1969; 1 child, Taiwo Yemaya. Youth conselor dept. corrections juvenile div., Reception and Diagnostic Center, Ill. Youth Center, Joliet, 1968-70, correctional counselor spl. services unit, 1970-72, supt., Kankakee, 1972-75, regional adminstr. Chgo. Cook County Region, 1975-77, correctional supt. St. Charles, 1977-79; regional dir. Region V, Fla. Dept. Corrections, Tampa, 1979—. Instr. corrections courses Loyola U., Chgo., 1975-77, Chgo. State U., 1975-76. Bd. dirs. Woodson-Delaney Ednl. Found., 1978—. Certified social worker, Ill. Mem. Am. Correctional Assn. Home: 2400 Granada Circle E Saint Petersburg FL 33712 Office: 5422-101 Bay Center Dr Tampa FL 33609

SINGLETARY, OTIS ARNOLD, JR., univ. pres.; b. Gulfport, Miss., Oct. 31, 1921; s. Otis Arnold and May Charlotte (Walker) S.; B.A., Millsaps Coll., 1947; M.A., La. State U., 1949, Ph.D., 1954; m. Gloria Walton, June 6, 1944; children—Bonnie, Scot, Kendall Ann. Mem. faculty U. Tex., 1954-61, prof. history, 1960-61, asso. dean arts and scis., 1956-59, asst. to pres., 1960-61; chancellor U. N.C. at Greensboro, 1961-66; v.p. Am. Council on Edn., Washington, 1966-68; dir. Job Corps, Office Econ. Opportunity, Washington, 1964-65; exec. vice chancellor acad. affairs U. Tex. System, 1968-69; pres. U. Ky., Lexington, 1969—. Dir. Anchor Hocking Corp., Dana Corp., Howell Corp. Regional chmn. Woodrow Wilson Nat. Fellowship Found., 1959-61; chmn. N.C. Rhodes Scholarship Com., 1964-66, chmn. Ky. com., 1970-72, 77; chmn. hist. adv. com. Dept. of Army, 1972—. Bd. dirs. Am. Assn. Higher Edn., 1969-72, Ednl. Change Inc., 1968—, Inst. Services to Edn., 1969—, So. Regional Edn. Bd., 1970—, bd. visitors Air U. MAFB, 1973-76. Served with USNR, 1943-46, 51-54; comdr. Res. Recipient Scarborough Teaching Excellence award U. Tex., 1958, Students Assn. Teaching Excellence award, 1958, 59; Grantee Carnegie Corp., 1961. Mem. Am., So. hist. assns., Am. Mil. Inst. (Moncado Book Fund award 1954), Phi Beta Kappa (mem. senate 1977—), Phi Alpha Theta, Omicron Delta Kappa, Pi Kappa Alpha. Democrat. Methodist. Author: Negro Militia and the Reconstruction, 1957; The Mexican War, 1960; American Universities and Colleges, 1968. Office: U Ky Lexington KY 40506

SINGLETON, ANNA CONVERSE EVANS, sociologist, cosmetologist; b. Napoleonville, La., Dec. 20, 1941; d. James and Velma (Joseph) Converse; B.A., So. U., 1970; M.A., Howard U., 1973; m. James V. Singleton, Mar. 13, 1976. Cosmetician, Magee's Beauty Salon, New Orleans, 1962-78; sec., counselor Howard U. Dept. Sociology, Washington, 1971-73; sociologist So. U., Baton Rouge, 1974-77; instr. cosmetology B.T. Washington Sr. High Sch., New Orleans, 1977—; public housing instr. and cons.; planning and operations specialist. Served with AUS, 1977. Cert. in vocat. edn, cosmetic therapy for tchrs; recipient Commendation Medal, La. N.G. Mem. AAUP, Alpha Kappa Delta. Democrat. Baptist. Author: Behavioral Perspective of Housing Management, 1976; Human Relations: A Study of the Socio-Psychological Effects of Occupancy Patterns of Four New Orleans Housing Projects, 1975. Home: 7225 Chef Ment Hwy New Orleans LA 70126 Office: 1201 S Roman St New Orleans LA 70125

SINGLETON, EMMETT FOYE, JR., bus. exec.; b. Lumpkin, Ga., Nov. 29, 1935; s. Emmett Foye and Louise (Williams) S.; B.S. magna cum laude, U. W. Fla., 1973, M.B.A., 1974; m. Wilda Ray Butler, Mar. 18, 1955; children—Kenneth Mark, Keith Alan, Emmett Foye III. Sr. systems analyst Potomac Research, Pensacola, Fla., 1975-76; systems analyst Tex. Instruments, Dallas, 1974-75; mgr. systems and data processing ITT Thompson Industries, Valdosta, Ga., 1963-70, mgr. systems and procedures, 1976-79; controller Hygroponics, Inc., Panama City, Fla., 1979—. Served with USAF, 1955-59. Republican. Mem. Assembly of God Ch. Home: 431 Beulah Ave Panama City FL 32401 Office: 3935 N Palo Alto Ave Panama City FL 32405

SINGLETON, NAN CHACHERE, educator, ednl. adminstr.; b. Prescott, Ark., July 2, 1930; d. Otis A. and Olivia D. Wells; B.S., La. Tech. U., 1950; M.A., U. Southwestern La., 1962; Ph.D., La. State U., 1974; m. Howard Singleton, June 28, 1971; children—Larry Chachere, Barbara Chachere Martin, Jon Scott Chachere. Home econs. tchr. Arnaudville High Sch., Grand Prairie High Sch., Opelousas High Sch., St. Landry Parish, La., 1950-74; asso. prof. home econs., asso. dean. Univ. Coll., La. State U., Baton Rouge, 1974—; home economist for pre-schs.; asst. in reading workshop. Nutrition Edn. and Tng. grantee, 1979, 80—. Mem. Am. Dietetic Assn., La. Dietetic Assn., Am. Home Econs. Assn., La. Home Econs. Assn., Soc. Nutrition Edn., NEA, Phi Delta Kappa, Omicron Nu, Delta Kappa Gamma, Gamma Sigma Delta. Democrat. Episcopalian. Club: Bus. and Profl. Women. Author booklet: Discovering Vegetable Treasures, 1977; contbr. articles to profl. jours. Office: Sch Home Economica La State U Baton Rouge LA 70803

SINGLETON, RAYMOND LEVON, office supply co. exec.; b. Rosedale, Okla., Oct. 26, 1927; s. James William and Ruby Mae (Robison) S.; student Okla. A&M U., 1946; m. Anna Lou Bates, Apr. 2, 1946; children—Sherrie Lurea, Gayla Jean. Dist. mgr. sales Okla. Office and Bank Supply Co., Shawnee, 1948-51; partner Nat. Office & Bank Supply Co., Enid, Okla., 1951-53; with Southwestern Stationery and Bank Supply, Inc., Lawton, Okla., 1954—, now v.p., sales mgr. Served with USN, 1946-47. Mem. C. of C., VFW, Am. Legion. Democrat. Mem. Ch. of Christ. Club: Lawton Country (pres.). Home: 2115 Atlanta St Lawton OK 73505 Office: Southwestern Stationery and Bank Supply Inc 309 SW 11th St Lawton OK 73502

SINGLETON, WILLIAM BRIGHTMAN, cons. urban planning; b. Washington, N.C., June 15, 1915; s. William Brightman and Addie Mae (Freeman) S.; student Davidson Coll., 1932-34; B.S., Ga. Inst. Tech., 1938; postgrad. Mass. Inst. Tech.. 1938-40; m. Elizabeth Jayne Miller, May 27. 1947. Field rep. Harland Bartholomew & Assos., St. Louis. 1945-49; planning dir. City-Parish Baton Rouge, 1949-51; planning dir. Brown & Butler Bodman & Murrell, Baton Rouge, 1951-52; mng. partner, owner City & Indsl. Planners, Baton Rouge, 1952—; treas. Five Ten Reymond, Inc., 1971—; owner, mgr. Forest Hill Tree Farm, 1979—; mng. partner Singleton Farms, 1970-78. Mem. Baton Rouge Goals Congress, 1963-65, La. Trails Council, 1975; bd. dirs. Fish, 1973-78, chmn., 1977; mem. Baton Rouge Hist. Dist. Preservation Commn., 1979; life mem. La. League Crippled Children; former vestryman, lay reader, Sunday sch. supt. St. James Episcopal Ch. Served with AUS, 1943-45. Mem. Am. Inst. Cert. Planners, Am. Planning Assn. (chpt. pres., 1968-70, Leadership citation 1970), AIA (affiliate), La. Architects Assn., Baton Rouge Bd. Realtors (asso.), Baton Rouge C. of C., SAR (La. dir. 1974-75, 79, chpt. dir. 1973—, chpt. v.p. 1977—). Clubs: Lions (dist. cabinet 1977), Bocage Racquet. Home: 2685 Edward Ave Baton Rouge LA 70808 Office: 3337 Convention St Baton Rouge LA 70806

SINHA, BRAJENDRA KUMAR, petroleum engr.; b. Patna, India, Nov. 9, 1939; s. Kapildeo and Sugandhi Prasad; came to U.S., 1961, naturalized, 1969; B.Sc. with honors, Indian Sch. Mines, 1961; M.S., U. Tulsa, 1963; Ph.D., Tex. A.&M. U., 1967; m. Rita Prasad, Mar. 9, 1971; children—Anita Rama, Sidhartha Ranjit, Sangita Rama. With Imco Services, Houston, 1967-71; with Halliburton Services, Duncan, Okla., 1971—, sr. research engr., 1972—. Recipient Distinguished Alumni award Ind. Sch. Mines, 1978. Mem. Soc. Petroleum Engrs., Am. Petroleum Inst. (chmn. S.W. Okla. chpt. 1976-77), Sigma Xi. Club: Toastmasters. Home: 2409 Randall Dr Duncan OK 73533 Office: Box 1431 Duncan OK 75533

SINHA, RANJIT, psychiatrist; b. Bihar, India, Nov. 9, 1931; s. B.B. and Dhana (Saran) S.; M.B.B.S., Patna U., India, 1956; m. Anita Prasad, May 30, 1957; children—Vinita, Sujit. Med. officer Patna Med. Coll. Hosp., India, 1956-57, State Dispensary Bengabad Hazaribragh, Bihar, 1958-60, Infectious Diseases Hosp., Patna, 1960-62; demonstrator in physiology Ranchi Med. Coll., Bihar, 1962-64; intern Meml. Hosp., Morristown, N.J., 1965, resident in psychiatry, 1966; resident in psychiatry N.J. State Hosp., Ancora Hammonton, 1967-69, Dalhousie U., Halifax, N.S., Can., 1970; staff psychiatrist Nova Scotia Hosp., Dartmouth, 1971-73; cons. psychiatrist Halifax County Hosp., Cole Harbor, 1972-73; med. dir. Cave Run Comprehensive Care Center, Morehead, Ky., 1973—; mem. med. staff St. Claire Med. Center, Morehead, 1974—, Mary Chiles Hosp., Mt. Sterling, Ky., Eastern State Hosp., Lexington, Ky. Diplomate Am. Bd. Psychiatry and Neurology. Fellow Royal Coll. Physicians and Surgeons Can.; mem. Am., Can., Ky. psychiat. assns., AMA, Ky., Rowan County med. socs. Home: Route 1 Lakeview Heights Morehead KY 40351 Office: 325 E Main St Morehead KY 40351

SINK, DAVID WILLIAM, JR., coll. dean; b. Lexington, N.C., Jan. 4, 1947; s. David William and Frances (Yow) S.; A.B., U. N.C., 1969, M.Ed., 1973; Ed.D., Va. Poly. Inst. and State U., 1980; m. Donna Tally, Dec. 26, 1969; children—Christine Alison, Matthew Wilson, Andrew David. Dean, Davidson Community Coll., Lexington, N.C., 1973-77, dean evening coll., 1979—; research asst. Va. Tech. U., Blacksburg, 1977-79; cons. in field. Active YMCA, 1976-77, United Way Fund drives, 1976-77; asst. scoutmaster Boy Scouts Am., Lexington, 1973—. Served with U.S. Army, 1969-71. Mem. Am. Personnel and Guidance Assn., Va. Personnel and Guidance Assn., Am. Sch. Counselor Assn., Am. Community and Jr. Coll. Assn., Sigma Phi Epsilon Alumni Bd. Democrat. Presbyterian. Contbr. articles in field to profl. jours. Home: 7 Grimes Circle Lexington NC 27292 Office: PO Box 1287 Lexington NC 27292

SINK, JAMES MARTIN, architect, planner; b. Little Rock, May 29, 1929; s. George Madison and Ellen Virginia (Kennedy) S.; student Washington U., St. Louis, 1948-49; B.Arch., U. So. Calif., 1953; m. Susan Ann Wald, July 25, 1959; children—John Martin, Katherine Jean. Project planner, architect, asso. Pereira & Luckman, Los Angeles, 1956-59; founder, dir. projects, sr. v.p., partner-in-charge, regional dir. and vice-chmn. mgmt. com. William L. Pereira Assos., Irvine, Calif. and Houston, 1959-73; founder, chmn., pres. James M. Sink Assos., Inc., Houston, 1973—; chmn. Horizon Unltd., Am. Marine Trade Systems, Inc.; dir. Operadora Akumal, S.A. Bd. dirs. U. So. Calif. Alumni Fund, 1977—; mem. internat. adv. council Fla. Internat. U., 1977—; mem. constrn. adv. com. FEA, 1976-78. Served with USN, 1953-56. Recipient Creative Programming award Nat. Univ. Extension Assn., 1968. Mem. AIA, Am. Planning Assn., Urban Land Inst., Internat. Inst. Edn., Soc. Am. Mil. Engrs., Navy League, Sigma Chi. Republican. Presbyterian. Clubs: Houston, Balboa Bay, SAR. Dir. design and planning of numerous archtl. projects, including: U. Calif., Irvine, 1965, Houston Center, 1973, Sci. and Math. Center, Riyadh, Saudi Arabia, 1977, Camp Pendleton (Calif.) Navy Hosp., 1973, Hotel Club Akumal Sur, Quintana Roo, Mex., 1979. Home: 3127 Avalon Pl Houston TX 77019 Office: 921 Main St Houston TX 77002

SINKAR, SURESH, chem. engr.; b. Bombay, India, Sept. 15, 1933; came to U.S., 1954, naturalized, 1964; s. V. B. and K. I. (Patkar) S.; B.Sc. with honors, U. Bombay, 1954; M.S. in Chem. Engring., U. Tulsa, 1960; postgrad. student Okla. State U., 1960-64; m. Rebecca M. Rice, Dec. 14, 1956; children—Nathan, Aaron, Kamal, Raj. Process engr. Phillips Petroleum Co., Bartlesville, Okla., 1960-65; process and design engr. Esso Research & Engring. Co., Florham Park, N.J., 1965-67; sr. process engr Conoco, Ponca City, Okla., 1967-71; project mgr. Pullman Kellogg, Houston, 1971—; adj. prof. dept. chem. engring. U. Houston, 1976—. Vice-pres. Sharpstown Jr. High Sch. PTA, Houston, 1973-74, pres., 1974-75; cubmaster Will Rogers council Boy Scouts Am., 1968-70. Mem. Am. Inst. Chem. Engrs., Sigma Chi. Unitarian (pres. fellowship 1968-69). Home: 8927 Troulon Houston TX 77036 Office: Greenway Plaza Houston TX 77046

SINKKING, ANDREA LYNN, speech pathologist; b. Burbank, Calif., May 2, 1951; d. John William and Virginia Irene (Rowland) S.; B.A. with honors, U. LaVerne, 1973; M.S., U. of Redlands, 1975; postgrad. U. Tex., 1979—. Speech therapist Colton Unified Sch. Dist. (Calif.), 1975; audiologist's asst. Tex. Sch. for Deaf, Austin, 1975-76; speech/lang. therapist Austin Ind. Sch. Dist., 1976-79; coordinator speech pathology Austin State Hosp., 1979—. Rec. sec. City of La Verne (Calif.), 1971-72, 73; active Republican party campaigns Calif. Ernest Carl Meml. scholar, 1971-72; Tuition scholar U. Redlands, 1974-75. Mem. Am. Speech, Lang. and Hearing Assn., Tex. Speech, Lang. and Hearing Assn. Home: 205 E Skyview Rd Austin TX 78752

SINNINGER, DWIGHT VIRGIL, research engr.; b. Bourbon, Ind., Dec. 29, 1901; s. Norman E. and Myra (Huff) S.; student Armour Inst., 1928, U. Chgo., 1942, Northwestern, 1943; m. Coyla Annetta Annis, Mar. 1, 1929. Electronics research engr. Johnson Labs., Chgo., 1935-42; chief engr. Pathfinder Radio Corp., 1943-44, Rowe Engring. Corp., 1945-48; Hupp Electronics Co. div. Hupp Corp., 1948-61; dir. research Pioneer Electric & Research Corp., Forest Park, Ill., 1961-65, Senn Custom, Inc., Forest Park and San Antonio, 1967—; dir. Rowe Engring. Corp. Registered profl. engr., Ill. Mem. IEEE, Instrument Soc. Am., Armed Forces Communications Assn. Holder several U.S. patents. Address: PO Box 40113 San Antonio TX 78229

SIPPERLY, DAVID WILLIAM, geologist, lawyer; b. Chico, Calif., Jan. 30, 1943; s. William and Marie Rose (Cassard) S.; B.A., Franklin and Marshall Coll., 1965; M.A., U. Tex., 1967, J.D., 1973; m. Judy Ann Kattawar, Oct. 11 1974; children—Jason Adam, William David, Suzanne Yvonne. Geologist, Dow Chem. Co., Coahuila, Mex., 1966-67, Dept. Environ. Conservation, State of N.Y., Albany, 1971; admitted to Tex. bar, 1974; atty. Coastal State Gas Prodn. Co., Corpus Christi, 1972; landman Atlantic Richfield Co., Lafayette, La. and Midland, Tex., 1973-75, dist. landman, Tulsa, 1976-77, mgr. exploration and land, Midland, 1978—. Pilot CAP, Midland, 1979. Served with USMC, 1967-70; mem. Res. Decorated Bronze Star, Purple Heart. Mem. Am. Bar Assn., Am. Assn. Petroleum Geologists, Am. Assn. Petroleum Landmen, Am. Petroleum Inst., State Bar Tex., Tex. Mid-Continent Oil and Gas Assn., N.Mex. Oil and Gas Assn. Roman Catholic. Home: 2809 Emerson Ln Midland TX 79701 Office: Atlantic Richfield Co PO Box 1610 Midland TX 79702

SIRCAR, ANIL KUMER, research chemist; b. Calcutta, India, Jan. 1, 1928; s. Aswini Kumer and Provabati (Sen) S.; came to U.S., 1965; B.Sc., Dacca U., 1948, M.Sc., 1949; D.Phil., Calcutta U., 1955; m. Smriti Palit, Aug. 7, 1951; children—Tamali, Manash, Tapash. Chemist, Sindri Fertilizers & Chems. Ltd. (India), 1951-52; research officer Indian Assn. Cultivation of Sci., Calcutta, 1952-57, 58-59; research fellow U. Minn., Mpls., 1958; sr. sci. officer Indian Rubber

Mfrs. Research Assn., Poona, 1960; mgr. lab. Nat. Rubber Mfrs. Ltd., Calcutta, 1960-65; research asso. So. Regional Research Lab., New Orleans, 1965-67; research chemist J.M. Huber Corp., Borger, Tex., 1967—; hon. lectr. in rubber chemistry and examiner in polymer chemistry U. Calcutta, 1962-65. Named Outstanding Toastmaster Dist. 44 Toastmasters Internat., 1973. Mem. Am. Chem. Soc. (sec. Panhandle Plains sect. 1971, program chmn. 1972, pres. 1973), N.Am. Thermal Analysis Soc. Club: Toastmasters (ednl. v.p. Club 218 1972, pres. 1972, area gov. area VI dist. 44 1973—, lt. gov. N. div. dist. 44, 1976-77). Contbr. articles to sci. jours. Home: 304 Houston St Borger TX 79007 Office: PO Box 2831 Borger TX 79007

SIRCHIA, RAYMOND JOSEPH, health services adminstr.; b. Bklyn., Feb. 4, 1941; s. Joseph and Mary A. (Burruso) S.; student N.Y. U., 1965, So. Meth. U., 1969-70; diploma Elkins Inst., 1971; student El Centro Coll., 1971-73; m. Carol Ann Kohler, Apr. 22, 1961; children—Linda Marie, Gary Thomas, Michelle Leigh. Sr. draftsman Pan Am. Airways, Jamaica, N.Y., 1962-65; contract aerospace designer Boeing Aircraft, Seattle, Gen. Dynamics, Ft. Worth, Grumman Aircraft, Bethpage, N.Y., 1965-67; environ. test engr. Grumman Aircraft, Bethpage, 1967-68; design engr. L.T.V. Corp., Grand Prairie, Tex., 1968, Aquatronics, Inc., Dallas, 1968-69, project engr., mgr., 1969-70; dir. ops., 1970-73; gen. partner Titan Internat. Co., Dallas, 1973-74; designer Collins Radio Group, Richardson, Tex., 1974-75; dir. environ. services Service Master Industries, Inc., Longview, Tex., 1975-79, regional ops. mgr. SW div., 1979—; owner Drafting and Design Service, 1977—. Chmn., Longview United Fund Campaign, 1977-78; coach Longview YMCA soccer team. Served with USAF, 1958-62. Recipient Excellence award Service Master Industries, 1976, 78; Leadership award Longview United Fund, 1978. Mem. Am. Soc. Hosp. Engrs., Nat. Fire Protection Assn. Baptist. Home: 2501 N Eastman Rd Longview TX 75601 Office: Service Master Industries 4255 LBJ & Midway Dallas TX 75234

SISCO, CHARLES PAUL, physician; b. San Antonio, Aug. 22, 1942; s. Friedman and Helen Lucielle (Vierheller) S.; B.S., U. Ark., 1963, M.D., 1967; div.; children—David William, Carol Ann. Intern, St. John's Med. Center, Tulsa, 1967-68; resident in internal medicine St. Louis U., 1968-70; fellow in allergy and immunology Nat. Jewish Hosp., Denver, 1970-72; practice medicine, specializing in internal medicine and allergy, Springdale, Ark., 1974—; chief pulmonary service Springdale Meml. Hosp. Served with USAF, 1972-74. Fellow Am. Coll. Chest Physicians; mem. AMA, Am. Acad. Allergy, A.C.P. Republican. Lutheran. Clubs: Rotary, Elks. Office: 100 S Shilo St Springdale AR 72764

SISEMORE, NORMA F., educator; b. Clyde, Tex., Feb. 3, 1943; d. Jesse J. and Loretta M. (Hester) Gabbert: B.A.A.S., Tarleton State U., 1976; m. Dyton David Sisemore, Apr. 30, 1961; children—David Duane, Dana Lynn, Danny Ray. Newspaper layout and designer Taylor (Tex.) Daily News, 1967-68; supr. Centralized Printing, Inc., Waco, Tex., 1968-70; reprodn. equipment supr. Tex. State Tech. Inst., Waco, 1970-73, asst. prof. printing tech., 1973—. Recipient Innovative Teaching award Tex. State Tech. Inst., 1975. Mem. Nat. Composition Assn., Printing Industries Am., Graphic Arts Tech. Found., In-Plant Printing Mgmt. Home: Route 1 Box 122 Axtell TX 76624 Office: Tex State Tech Inst Bldg 16-1 Waco TX 76705

SISK, GEORGE TERRY, real estate devel. co. exec.; b. Ft. Worth, July 23, 1942; s. George Toliver and Mary Elizabeth (McCorstin) S.; B.B.A., Tex. Wesleyan Coll., 1968; M.B.A., U. Dallas, 1975; m. Jeanie Gail Traister, Sept. 11, 1975. Auditor, Ft. Worth Nat. Bank, 1969-70; br. mgr. Fleet Rall Mortgage Co., Ft. Worth, 1970-73; v.p. devel. Hill Equity Corp., Dallas, 1973-75; gen. mgr. Richland Enterprises, Ft. Worth, 1975—; asso. prof. bus. extended studies div. Columbia (Mo.) Coll., 1979; dir. Rico Pronto, Inc., United Equity Investors, Inc., P.H.S. Constrn. Co. Served with USAF, 1961-65. Mem. Nat. Assn. Home Builders, Soc. Real Estate Appraisers, Tex. Assn. Builders, Colleyville C. of C. (publs. chmn. 1978), Ft. Worth Jr. C. of C. (named Most Outstanding 1st-Yr. Jaycee 1977, activation dir. 1977-78, adminstrv. dir. 1978-79). Republican. Baptist. Club: Rotary (Ft. Worth). Home: 7616 Overland Trail Colleyville TX 76034 Office: Richland Enterprises 5133 Davis Blvd Fort Worth TX 76118

SISK, JOHN KELLY, communications exec.; b. Cookeville, Tenn., Mar. 3, 1913; s. Thurman Kelly and Martha Jane (Sewell) S.; B.S., U. Ala., 1934; m. Isbell Lane, Sept. 30, 1936; children—John Kelly, Isbell Lane Sisk Irick. Pres., chief exec. officer Multimedia Inc., 1968-73, chmn., 1973—; chmn., pub. Greenville News-Piedmont Co. (S.C.); dir. S.C. Nat. Bank, Liberty Life Ins. Co., Dan River Inc. Past bd. dirs. YMCA; past chmn. Greenville County Planning and Devel. Bd.; past chmn. Greenville County chpt. ARC; trustee Converse Coll., Duke Endowment; adv. trustee Furman U.; past chmn. bd. trustees Greenville Gen. Hosp. C.P.A., N.Y., S.C. Mem. Downtown Greenville Assn. (dir. 1957), Am., So. (chmn. bd. 1964) newspaper pubs. assns., S.C. Press Assn. (pres. 1962), Nat. Press Club, Greater Greenville C. of C. (pres. 1953), Phi Gamma Delta. Methodist. Clubs: Poinsett, Greenville Country, Green Valley Country, Cotillion (Greenville); Biltmore (N.C.) Forest Country; Mountain City (Asheville, N.C.); Plantation (Hilton Head, S.C.). Home: 20 Southland Ave Greenville SC 29601 Office: 305 S Main St Greenville SC 29601

SISK, KATHERN IVOUS, radio broadcasting co. exec.; b. Guin, Ala., Nov. 18, 1936; d. Herman D. and Minnie L. (Sizemore) Thompson; B.S. in Art, Florence State U., 1959, B.S. in Home Econs., 1959; m. Olvie Eugene Sisk, Sept. 11, 1960. Extension home agt. Co-op Extension Service, U.S. Dept. Agr., Auburn (Ala.) U., 1959-67; co-propr. Sta. WVSA, Vernon, Ala., 1967—, Sta. WFTO, Fulton, Miss., 1968—, Sta. WEPA, Eupora, Miss., 1975—, Sta. WKNG, Tallapoosa, Ga., 1975—, Sta. WEXA, Europa, 1978—, Sta. WKEA, Scottsboro, Ala., 1978—, Sta. WPYK, Dora, Ala., 1978—, also Sta. WFTA, Fulton. Bd. dirs. Itawamba County Cancer Crusade, 1976-77, Itawamba County Fair Assn., 1970—, Itawamba County Bicentennial, Gospel Music Assn., Nat. Gospel Music Hall of Fame. Recipient Vol. Activist award State of Miss., 1977; Pres.'s Report award Miss. Federated Women's Clubs, 1977. Mem. Itawamba County Arts Council, Itawamba County Retardation Assn. (v.p. 1975-76), Am. Legion Aux., Miss. Federated Women's Clubs (dist. pres. 1978-80), Dist. III Club Woman of Yr. 1978), Florence State U. Alumni Assn. Mem. Ch. of Christ (Sunday sch. tchr. 1968—). Clubs: South Fulton Homemakers (pres. 1973-75), Fulton Civic (pres. 1976-77). Home: Hwy 25 South Fulton MS 38843 Office: PO Box 587 Fulton MS 38843

SISLER, HARRY HALL, chemist, author, educator; b. Ironton, Ohio, Mar. 13, 1917; s. Harry Chester and Minta Ann Sisler; B.Sc. with distinction, Ohio State U., 1936; M.S. in Chemistry, U. Ill., 1937, Ph.D. (fellow), 1939; Dr. h.c., U. Poznan (Poland), 1977; m. Helen Elizabeth Shaver, June 29, 1940; children—Elizabeth Ann Sisler Rider, David Franklin, Raymond Keith, Susan Carolyn; m. 2d, Hannelore L. Wass, Apr. 13, 1978. Instr. phys. sci. Chgo. City Colls., 1939-41; instr. chemistry U. Kans., Lawrence, 1941-42, asst. prof., 1942-45, asso. prof., 1945-46; asst. prof. chemistry Ohio State U., 1946-48, asso. prof., 1948-55, prof., 1955-56; head prof. chemistry U. Fla., Gainesville, 1955-64, chmn. dept. chemistry, 1964-68, dir. div. phys. scis. and math., 1964-68, dean arts and scis., 1968-70, exec. v.p., 1970-73, dean grad. sch., 1973-79, distinguished service prof. chemistry, 1979—; Arthur and Ruth Sloan vis. prof. Harvard U., 1962-63; vis. scientist cons. to various colls. and univs. in U.S., 1948; cons. to W.R. Grace & Co., 1951-73, U.S. Air Force Acad., 1958, Koppers Co., 1956-59, Batelle Meml. Inst., 1964-67, TVA, 1967, Dowden & Hutchinson, Inc., 1970-76, Naval Ordnance Lab., 1974-76; cons. editor phys. and inorganic series coll. texts Reinhold Pub. Corp., 1957-70; mem. exec. com. chemistry adv. panel, NSF, 1959-62. Recipient Centennial Achievement award Ohio State U., 1970; decorated Royal Order of North Star, King of Sweden, 1973 recipient James Flack Norris award Am. Chem. Soc., 1979. Mem. Am. Chem. Soc. (nat. chmn. div. chem. edn. 1957-58, award 1960, 69), Fla. Acad. Sci., AAAS, Sigma Xi, Phi Lambda Upsilon, Phi Eta Sigma, Kappa Phi Kappa, Kappa Delta Pi, Gamma Sigma Epsilon, Phi Kappa Phi. Methodist. Author 18 textbooks and reference books in field, latest being: Chemistry, A Systematic Approach, 1980; Chloramination Reactions, 1977; College Chemistry, 3d edit., 1967; Electronic Structure, Properties and the Periodic Law, 1973; (book poetry) Starlight, 1976; contbr. numerous articles on chemistry to sci. jours.; editorial bd. Jour. Chem. Edn., 1955-58. Home: 6014 NW 54th Way Gainesville FL 32601 Office: Room 201 Chem Research Bldg Univ Florida Gainesville FL 32611

SISSELMAN, MURRAY, educator, union exec.; b. N.Y.C., Jan. 10, 1930; B.E., U. Miami; M.S., Ed.S., Nova U.; children—David, Helen. Classroom tchr., Dade County, Fla., 1955—; v.p. Fla. Am. Fedn. Tchrs. AFL-CIO, 1974, pres. United Tchrs. Dade local, 1974, AFL-CIO, 1975—; v.p. Fla. Edn. Assn./United Tchrs. Dade, 1975-79, pres., 1979—; mem. exec. bd. S. Fla., AFL-CIO, 1977-78. Mem. Dade Democratic exec. com., 1971-74; patron Hist. Assn. So. Fla.; mem. com. juvenile health needs Mental Health Bd. Dade County; mem. com. on edn. Third Century U.S.A.; mem. nat. exec. bd. Jewish Labor Com., 1977-79; mem. rules com. Dem. exec. com. Fla.; mem. citizens adv. com. Fla. Dept. Health and Rehab. Services; mem. Dade County Bd. Rules and Appeals, 1975-77, Dade County Zoning Appeals Bd.; trustee City of Hope Pilot Med. Center, 1979—; ednl. dir. Temple Sinai of North Dade, 1966-71; religious sch. prin. Temple Emanu-El, Ft. Lauderdale, Fla., 1971-72. Served with U.S. Army, 1954-56; Korea. Recipient Personal Service award C. of C. North Miami Beach (Fla.); Cert. of Appreciation, Nat. Police Officers Assn., City of North Miami Beach, Am. Judges Assn., Fla. Edn. Assn./United. Mem. Nat. Congress Parents and Tchrs. (hon. life), Fla. Congress Parents and Tchrs. (hon. life), VFW (citation), Dade County Classroom Tchrs. Assn. (acting pres.), Fla. Edn. Assn. (dir., chmn. legis. com.), Nat. Hist. Soc. (founding asso.), Nat. Assn. Temple Educators, USS Constitution Museum Found. (charter), Alpha Phi Omega (past officer), Sigma Alpha Mu (past pres.), Pi Sigma Rho, Phi Delta Kappa, Kappa Delta Pi. Clubs: Elks, Masons. Home: 2316 NE 173d St #4 North Miami Beach FL 33162 Office: 2929 SW 3d Ave Miami FL 33129

SITES, JOHN WILBUR, horticulturist, ret. univ. dean.; b. Syracuse, N.Y., July 11, 1912; s. John Milton and Kathryn McKee (Hillery) S.; B.S., Ohio State U., 1935, M.S., 1940, Ph.D., 1950; m. Peggy Hunter, July 11, 1936; children—John Edward, Sharon Eleanor (Mrs. Joseph Pesek III), Kathryn Hunter (Mrs. Robert T. Shewey). Jr. horticulturist Dept. Agr., Zanesville, Ohio, 1935-36, asst. horticulturist, 1936-42; asso. horticulturist U. Fla. Agrl. Expt. Stas., Lake Alfred, 1942-45, horticulturist, 1946-55, Gainesville, 1955-67, asst. dir., 1955-57, head fruit crops dept., 1957-60, asso. dir., 1960-67, dir., dean for research, 1967-76, dean emeritus, 1977—. Pres., Winter Haven Pops (Fla.) Orch. Assn., 1954. Recipient Agrl. award for meritorious service Charles H. DuPont Found., 1970. Fellow Am. Soc. Hort. Sci.; mem. Am. Soc. Hort. Sci. (Gourley award for pomol. research 1951), Fla. Hort. Soc. (Krome Meml. Inst. award 1962, pres. 1976—), Soil and Plant Soc. Fla., Nat. Research Inst., Internat. Platform Assn., Sigma Xi, Alpha Gamma Rho, Gamma Sigma Delta, Pi Alpha Xi. Episcopalian (vestryman 1968—). Kiwanian (pres. Winter Haven 1950). Club: University of Fla. Faculty (pres. 1963-64). Home: 1819 SW 35th Ave Gainesville FL 32608

SITTLER, EDWIN CONRAD, mgmt. co. exec.; b. Keokuk, Iowa, Apr. 12, 1907; s. Joseph and Katherine (Wirtz) S.; B.S., U. Iowa, 1929; m. Lois Monks, Feb. 3, 1973; children by previous marriage—Susan, Edwin, Virginia, Penelope. Research engr. Frigidaire div. Gen. Motors Corp., Dayton, Ohio, 1929-36; research engr., asst. sales mgr. Liebel Flers Heim, Cin., 1936-42; supt. Chgo. Intensive Treatment Center, 1942-45; asst. sanitarian USPHS assigned to Chgo. Bd. Health, 1942-45; treas. Sittler Corp., pres. Sittler Sales Engring. Corp. (both Chgo.), 1945—; dir. DuPage Trust Co., Glen Ellyn, Ill. Mem. Triangle, Scabbard and Blade, Tau Beta Pi. Conglist. Clubs: Glen Oak Country (Glen Ellyn). Contbr. articles to profl. jours. Patentee in field. Home: 3 Woodvine Ln Clover SC 29710 Office: 18 N Ada St Chicago IL 60607

SIZEMORE, EARLEEN WILKERSON, state legislator; b. Worth County, Ga., July 29, 1938; d. Joseph Earl and Mamie Eloise (Roberts) W.; B.S., Ga. So. U., 1959; M.Ed., Ga. Coll., Milledgeville, 1965; postgrad. spl. edn. U. Ga., 1970; m. C.B. Sizemore, Aug. 8, 1957; children—Vicki Eloise, Staci, Robert. Tchr. Worth County Bd. Edn., 1959—; mem. Ga. Ho. of Reps., 1975—. Home: Route 3 Sylvester GA 31791

SIZEMORE, HIRAM, JR., psychiatrist; b. Mullens, W.Va., Mar. 27, 1924; s. Hiram and Ruby Alice (Trent) S.; B.S., U. Mo., 1947; M.D., Washington U., 1949; m. Gisela Walter, Dec. 13, 1952; 1 dau., Angelika. Intern, Walter Reed Gen. Hosp., Washington, 1949-50; county health officer Boone County (W.Va.), 1956-57; practice medicine, Shepherdstown, W.Va., 1958-68; resident in psychiatry U. Va. Hosp., Charlottesville, 1968-71; practice medicine specializing in psychiatry, Shepherdstown, 1971—; cons. psychiatrist Allegheny County Health Dept., Brooke Lake Psychiat. Center, Hagerstown, Md., VA Center, Martinsburg, W.Va. Mem. City Council Shepherdstown, 1963-65. Served with USMCR, 1950-52. Diplomate Am. Bd. Psychiatry and Neurology. Mem. AMA, W.Va. Med. Assn., Am. Psychiat. Assn., Va. Neuropsychiat. Assn., Eastern Panhandle Med. Soc. W.Va. (pres. 1971-75). Lutheran. Home and Office: Route 11 Shepherdstown WV 25443

SIZEMORE, MICHAEL MAYNARD, architect, energy planner; b. Detroit, July 20, 1943; s. Arthur Logan and Evelyn (Willer) S.; B.Arch., Ga. Inst. Tech., 1966; M. Arch., Carnegie-Mellon U., 1968; m. Christine Lazear Wick, June 1, 1968; children—Christine Corsaut, James Gawne. Project architect Heery & Heery, Architects & Engrs., Atlanta, 1970-71, Jova, Daniels & Busby, Architects, Atlanta, 1971-73; partner Sizemore & Assos., Atlanta, 1974-78; dir. Sizemore/CRS, Atlanta, also v.p. CRS Inc., Atlanta and Houston, 1978-79; partner Sizemore & Floyd, 1979—; cons., lectr. in field. Mem. AIA, Brookwood Hills Swim and Tennis Club. Presbyterian. Author: (with Henry O. Clark and William S. Ostrander) Energy Planning for Buildings, 1979. Office: Sizemore & Floyd 1900 Emery St NW Suite 200 Atlanta GA 30318

SIZER, PHILLIP SPELMAN, oil field service co. exec.; b. Whittier, Calif., Apr. 11, 1926; s. Frank Milton and Helen Louise (Saylor) S.; B.M.E., So. Meth. U., 1948; m. Evelyn Sue Jones, Aug. 16, 1952; children—Phillip Spelman, Ves Warner. With Otis Engring. Corp., Dallas, 1948—, project engr., 1958-62, chief devel. engr., 1962-70, v.p. research and devel., 1970-73, v.p. engring. and research, 1973-76, sr. v.p.-tech. dir., 1977—, dir., 1975—. Registered profl. engr., Tex., Okla., Alta. (Can.). Fellow ASME (Engr. of Year N. Tex. sect. 1971, chmn. exec. com. petroleum div. 1974-75); mem. Assn. Well Head Equipment Mfrs. (pres. 1976), Offshore Tech. Conf. (exec. com. 1976—), Soc. Petroleum Engrs., Nomads, Kappa Sigma, Kappa Mu Epsilon, Tau Beta Pi, Petroleum Engrs. Club Dallas. Patentee in field. Home: 14127 Tanglewood Dr Dallas TX 75234 Office: PO Box 34380 Dallas TX 75234

SKAGGS, FRED RANDALL, clergyman; b. Jonesville, Va., Nov. 16, 1933; s. Jesse Milton and Osalene (Spurrier) S.; B.A., U. Richmond, 1955; M.Div., Southwestern Bapt. Theol. Sem., 1963, M.R.E., 1965; D.Min., Union Theol. Sem., 1974; certificate clin. pastoral edn. Va. Commonwealth U., 1974; m. Julia Jane Brugos, Sept. 12, 1953; children—Debra Jane, Fred Randall, Angela Ruth, Cynthia Lou, John Milton. Ordained to ministry Bapt. Ch., 1962; asso. pastor Calvary Bapt. Ch., Richmond, Va., 1951-52; supply pastor, Warsaw and Montross, Va., 1952-54; pastor Wardville (Okla.) Bapt. Ch., 1963, 1st Bapt. Ch., Atoka, Okla., 1964-66, Skipwith Bapt. Ch., Richmond, 1966-73, Walnut Grove Bapt. Ch., Mechanicsville, Va., 1974—; mem. faculty U. Richmond Sch. Christian Edn.; radio and TV work. Mem. community action com. Fed. Headstart Program, 1966; chmn. bd. Lee-Davis Med. Center, 1979—; pres. Laurel Athletic Assn., 1969; pres., founder Skipwith Football Assn., Inc., 1971; chmn. bd. Met. Youth Football League, 1972. Fellow Acad. Parish Clergy (pres. 1978-79, dir.); mem. Am. Sci. Affiliation (asso.), Assn. Clin. Pastoral Edn., Am. Assn. Pastoral Counselors. Author: (with R.J. Pacciocco) The Sound of Falling Chains, 1972; Colors of the Mind, 1978; asso. editor The Bapt. Rev., 1973-75; contbg. editor Jour. Academic Parish Clergy, 1972-75; contbr. articles to religious periodicals. Home: 6308 Walnut Grove Ct Mechanicsville VA 23111 Office: PO Box 428 Mechanicsville VA 23111

SKANDALAKIS, MARIA JOHN, health services facility adminstr.; b. Atlanta, Mar. 28, 1952; d. John Peter and Eva (Pamfilis) S.; A.A., Emory U., 1972; B.S., Ga. Inst. Tech., 1975; Ed.S., Ga. State U., 1977; postgrad Va. Tech. U. Psychometrist, Griffin (Ga.) Coop. Service Agy., 1976-77; psychologist Lynchburg (Va.) Tng. Sch. and Hosp., 1977-79, center dir. health services, 1979—; grad. teaching asst. Va. Inst. Tech., 1979-80. Mem. Am. Assn. Mental Deficiency, Ga. Assn. Sch. Psychologists, Council for Exceptional Children. Greek Orthodox.

SKARUPA, JACK A., hosp. adminstr.; b. Torrington, Conn., Apr. 21, 1928; s. Michael John and Veronica Skarupa; B.S. in Econs., U. Conn., 1951; postgrad. Grad Program in Health Adminstrn., Duke U., 1954; m. Barbara Larmett, Apr. 19, 1952; children—Karen, Michael, Laurie. Adminstrv. resident Greenville (S.C.) Gen. Hosp., 1951-53, asst. adminstr., 1953-65; dir. ops. Greenville Hosp. System, 1965-71, exec. dir., 1971-78, pres., 1978—; mem. adv. bd. Bankers Trust of S.C., 1977—. Bd. dirs. Urban League of Greenville, 1978-79, United Way, 1979—. Served with U.S. Navy, 1945-47. Recipient Merit award S.C. Hosp. Assn., 1978. Mem. Carolinas-Va. Hosps. Conf. (pres. 1965-66), Am. Hosp. Assn. (trustee 1977—), S.C. Hosp. Assn. (pres. 1966), Am. Coll. Hosp. Adminstrs. Roman Catholic. Clubs: Green Valley Country, Poinsett (Greenville); Sea Pines (Hilton Head, S.C.). Home: 27 Alpine Way Greenville SC 29609 Office: 701 Grove Rd Greenville SC 29605

SKEAN, CHARLES THOMAS, clin. social worker; b. Kenova, W.Va., Apr. 15, 1937; s. Thomas Joseph and Ada Jewell (Money) S.; B.A. in History and Polit. Sci., Berea (Ky.) Coll., 1960; M.S.S.W., U. Louisville, 1971; m. Lynne Jane Meritt, June 12, 1961; children—Jerrol, Janette. Instr., Boyd County Bd. Edn., Catlettsburg, Ky., 1963-66; caseworker W.Va. Dept. Welfare, Wayne, 1966-70, staff tng. supr., 1970-72; clin. social worker Lansdowne Mental Health Center, Ashland, Ky., 1972-77, sr. clin. social worker children's services, 1977—. Served with M.P., U.S. Army, 1960-63. Lic. social worker and clin. social worker, Ky. Mem. Acad. Cert. Social Workers, Nat. Assn. Social Workers. Home: 202 8th St Kenova WV 25530 Office: PO Box 790 Lansdowne Mental Health Center Ashland KY 41101

SKEES, WILLIAM DALY, cons. co. exec.; b. Princeton, Ky., Mar. 27, 1939; s. Raymond Joseph and Barbara Allan (Boyd) S.; student Fordham U., 1957-58; A.B. cum laude, St. Benedict's Coll., 1961; postgrad. Am. U., 1961-62, Cath. U. Am., 1962-63; M.S., U. Ill., 1964, U. Wis., 1964-65, U. Ky., 1965-66, Am. U., 1968; m. Glenda Kay DeSpain, June 3, 1961; children—Shannon Marie, William Edward; m. 2d, Carol Ann Nanzer, Dec. 23, 1976; 1 son, John Daniel. Mathematician-programmer U.S. Naval Weapons Lab., Dahlgren, Va., 1961-62; project leader AC Electronics, Milw., 1964-65; mgr. operating systems U. Ky. Computer Center, Lexington, 1965-67; mgr. time sharing systems devel. C-E-I-R/Control Data Corp., Washington, 1967-69; asso. dir. Computer Sci. div. Ops. Research Inc., Silver Spring, Md., 1969-74; pres. Skees Assos., Inc., Alexandria, Va., 1974—; cons. in field; guest lectr. Indsl. Coll. Armed Forces, 1973-76. Pres., PTA, Georgetown Hill Elementary Sch., Potomac, Md., 1972-73. Recipient Am. Legion Citizenship award, 1957; Nat. Merit scholarship Certificate of Merit, 1957; St. Benedicts Coll. tuition scholar, 1958-61; George Peabody Coll. for Tchrs. fellow, 1962; USPHS stipend, 1962-63. Mem. Am. Psychol. Assn., Assn. Computing Machinery, Pi Mu Epsilon, So. Md. Sailing Assn. Democrat. Roman Catholic. Club: Regency Estates Swim. Contbr. articles in field to profl. jours. Home: 531 S Fairfax St Alexandria VA 22314

SKELTON, DOROTHY GENEVA SIMMONS (MRS. JOHN WILLIAM SKELTON), artist, educator; b. Woodland, Calif.; d. Jack Elijah and Helen Anna (Siebe) Simmons; B.A., U. Calif., 1940, M.A., 1943; m. John William Skelton, July 16, 1941. Sr. research analyst War Dept., Gen. Staff, M.I. Div. G-2, Washington, 1944-45; vol. researcher, monuments, fine arts and archives sect. Restitution Br., Office Mil. Govt. for Hesse, Wiesbaden, Germany, 1947-48; vol. art tchr. German children, Bad Nauheim, Germany, 1947-48; art educator, lectr. Dayton (Ohio) Art Inst., 1955; art educator Lincoln Sch., Dayton, 1956-60; art edn. instr. U. Va. Sch. Continuing Edn., Charlottesville, 1962-75; researcher in genealogy; exhibited in group shows, Calif., Colo., Ohio, Washington and Va.; represented in permanent collections: Madison Hall, Charlottesville, Madison Center (Va.). Mem. Nat. League Am. Pen Women, Am. Assn. Museums, Coll. Art Assn. Am., Nat. Soc. Arts and Letters, Inst. Study of Art in Edn., Dayton Soc. Painters and Sculptors, Va. Mus. Fine Arts, Calif. Alumni Assn., AAUW. Republican. Methodist. Clubs: Army Navy Country, Air Force Officers Wives, Lake of the Woods (Va.) Golf and Country. Address: Lotos Lakes Brightwood VA 22715

SKELTON, HOWARD CLIFTON, marketing exec.; b. Birmingham, Ala., Mar. 6, 1932; s. Howard C. and Sarah Ethel (Holmes) S.; B.S., Auburn U., 1955; m. Winifred Harriet Karger, May 19, 1962; 1 dau., Susan Lynn. Copywriter, Rich's, Inc., Atlanta, 1955-59, Ga. Power Co., Atlanta, 1959-61; dir. advt. and sales promotion Callaway Mills, Inc., LaGrange, Ga., 1961-65, Thomasville Furniture Industries (N.C.), 1965-66; v.p. in charge fashion and textiles Gaynor & Ducas, N.Y.C., 1966-70; dir. communications Collins & Aikman, N.Y.C.,

1970-73; exec. v.p. Marketplace, Inc., Atlanta, 1973-74; v.p. mktg. and communications Internat. City Corp., Atlanta, 1974-75; pres. Howard Skelton Assos., Atlanta, 1976—. Served with Signal Corps, AUS, 1956-58. Recipient Danforth Found. award, 1950. Mem. Atlanta Ad Club, Atlanta Press Club, Atlanta C. of C., Atlanta Conv. and Visitors Bur., Omicron Delta Kappa, Lambda Chi Alpha, Sigma Delta Chi. Home: 500 Windsor Pkwy NE Atlanta GA 30342 Office: 130 W Wieuca Rd NE Atlanta GA 30342

SKELTON, IRA STEVEN, food products industry researcher; b. Greenville, S.C., Mar. 18, 1949; s. Ira Gordon and Jennie Louise (Campbell) S.; B.A. in English, U. S.C., 1972, postgrad. in Social Work, 1978; D.Div., Universal Life Ch., 1979. Caseworker, Richland County (S.C.) Dept. Social Services, 1973-74; youth counselor John G. Richards Sch. for Boys, Columbia, S.C., 1974; clin. counselor Pee Dee Mental Health Center, Florence, S.C., 1974-76; grad. asst. coop. inservice tng. program Univ. Affiliated Facilities, U. S.C., 1976-77; mental health asso. Richland Meml. Hosp., Columbia, 1977-78; research technician, research and devel. Teepak, Inc., Columbia, 1978—; instr. Florence-Darlington Tech. Coll., 1975-76. Sec.-treas. Florence Human Services Assn., 1975-76. Chmn. religious edn. com., trustee Unitarian-Universalist Fellowship, Columbia, 1978-79; ordained minister Universal Life and All Faiths Chs., 1976. Mem. AAAS, Am. State Assn., Mensa (local sec., mem. exec. com. central S.C. 1978-79). Editorial asst. Fitzgerald/Hemingway Ann., 1971, 72; editor Univ. Affiliated Facilities Tng. Manual, 1977. Office: PO Box 11925 Columbia SC 29211

SKELTON, JAMES EDWARD, architect; b. Linden, Tex., Jan. 12, 1934; s. Lone Calep and Lena Belle (Kasling) S.; B.Arch., U. Tex., 1958; m. Margaret Morgan, July 30, 1960; children—Jeffrey Lone, Peter Daniel. With Carroll & Daeuble, Architects, El Paso, Tex., 1960-64, Middleton & Staten, Architects, El Paso, 1964-69, Carroll, Daeuble, Dusang & Rand, Architects, El Paso, 1970-77, George Staten & Asso., Architects, El Paso, 1977; owner James E. Skelton, Architects, El Paso, 1978—. Active, Boy Scouts Am., El Paso, 1975-78. Mem. AIA, Tex. Soc. Architects. Presbyterian. Home and Office: 4219 Santa Rita St El Paso TX 79902

SKELTON, JEAN WATSON, guidance counselor; b. Ithaca, N.Y., Sept. 8, 1947; d. William Epes and Margaret Ann (Groseclose) Skelton; B.A. in English and Spanish, Va. Poly. Inst. and State U., 1969; M.Ed., Va. Commonwealth U., 1971. Field dir. Commonwealth council Girl Scouts U.S.A., Richmond, Va., 1969-70; grad. asst., counselor dept. edn. Va. Commonwealth U., Richmond, 1970-71; tchr. English and Spanish, Salem Ch. Jr. High Sch., Richmond, 1971-73, guidance counselor, 1973-79; guidance coordinator Swift Creek Middle Sch., Midlothian, Va., 1979—. Cert. tchr. English, Spanish and Guidance secondary schs. Mem. Am., Va., Richmond personnel and guidance assns., Va. Vocat. Guidance Assn., Am. Sch. Counselor Assn., Nat. Assn. Women Deans, Adminstrs. and Counselors, Va. Poly. Inst. and State U. Alumni Assn., Phi Kappa Phi. Club: Westwood Jr. Women's (2d v.p. 1979-80). Home: 10302 Redbridge Ct Richmond VA 23235 Office: 3700 Old Hundred Rd Midlothian VA 23113

SKELTON, JESSE DANIEL, petroleum co. exec.; b. Wichita, Kans., Apr. 24, 1923; s. Jesse Albert and Anne (Goodman) S.; B.E.E., Kans. State U., 1948; M.E.E., Okla. State U., 1954; m. Gloria F. Mulcahy, May 21, 1944; children—Janet Sue Skelton Wood, Linda Kae Skelton Clark, Karen Ann Skelton Mai. Research engr. Carter Oil Co., Tulsa, 1948; div. mgr. Jersey Prodn. Research, Tulsa, 1958-64; dir., v.p. exploration research Esso Prodn. Research, Houston, 1964-67; asst. div. exploration mgr. Humble Oil & Refining Co., Houston, 1967-69; exploration data processing mgr. Exxon Co., U.S.A., Houston, 1969—. Mem. U.S. Nat. Commn. on Geology. Served to 1st lt. USAAC, 1943-46. Mem. Am. Assn. Petroleum Geologists, Assn. Profl. Geol. Scientists, Soc. Exploration Geophysicists (v.p. 1973-75, pres. 1975), Am. Geol. Inst. (v.p. 1975, pres. 1976), European Assn. Exploration Geophysicists, Sigma Tau, Eta Kappa Nu, Phi Kappa Phi. Republican. Baptist (deacon 1955-79, Sunday sch. tchr. 1960-79). Home: 13902 Pinerock Ln Houston TX 77079 Office: PO Box 2180 Houston TX 77001

SKELTON, LOUIS WAYNE, librarian; b. Greenwood, Miss., June 14, 1954; s. John Louis and Mary Lee (Daves) S.; B.S. in Library Sci. Edn., Miss. State U., 1974; M.S. in Library Info. Sci., Fla. State U., 1975; m. Mary Jean Bowen, Aug. 6, 1972; children—Jennifer Tracy, Kristina Chase. Dir., Greenwood-Leflore Pub. Library, Greenwood, 1975—; cons. Pres., Cottonlandia Mus. Mem. ALA, Southeast Library Assn., Miss. Library Assn., Miss. Museums Assn., C. of C. (dir.). Baptist. Club: Kiwanis. Office: Greenwood-Leflore Public Library 405 W Washington St Greenwood MS 38930

SKIBINE, MARJORIE LOUISE TALLCHIEF (MRS. GEORGE SKIBINE), ballerina; b. Denver; d. Alexander and Ruth (Porter) Tallchief; ballet tng. with Bronislava Nijinska, David Lichine. Became soloist Am. Ballet Theater while in 'teens; became ballerina Grand Ballet du Marquid de Cuevas, at age 19; later 1st American to become premiere danseuse etoile Paris Opera, 1st American to star at Bolshoi Theater, Moscow; now artistic dir. Dallas Civic Ballet Soc.; dir. Dallas Ballet Acad. Decorated chevalier du Nisham Iftikar for artistic achievement (Tunisia). Home: 7260 Kenny Ln Dallas TX 75230

SKIDMORE, LAWRENCE MICHAEL, county ofcl.; b. Tampa, Fla., Jan. 9, 1946; s. Joseph Soule and Helen S.; A.A., Manatee Jr. Coll., Bradenton, Fla., 1970; B.S. in Criminology, Fla. State U., 1972; M. Criminal Justice, Rollins Coll., Winter Park, Fla., 1977. Juvenile counselor Div. Youth Services State of Fla., Lakeland, 1970-72; criminal justice planner Central Fla. Regional Planning Council, Bartow, 1974-78; criminal justice coordinator Bd. County Commrs. County of Polk, Bartow, 1978—. Bd. dirs. Polk County Mental Health Assn. Served with USAF, 1964-67; Vietnam. Recipient cert. Appreciation, First Step, Inc., Polk County, 1976, Cert. Achievement Rollins Coll., 1977. Mem. Polk County Criminal Justice Task Force, Fla. Council on Crime and Deliquency. Club: Imperial Radio Control. Office: PO Box 60 Bartow FL 33830

SKINNER, CHARLES GORDON, chemist, educator; b. Dallas, Apr. 23, 1923; s. Charles Grady and Benona Pricilla (Skiles) S.; B.S., N. Tex. State U., 1943, M.S., 1947; Ph.D., U. Tex., Austin, 1953; m. Lilly Ruth Brown, Apr. 4, 1944; children—Robert Gordon, Gary Wayne. Eli Lilly postdoctoral fellow, 1953; chemist Clayton Found. Biochemistry Inst., Austin, 1954-64; prof. chemistry N. Tex. State U., Denton, 1964—, chmn. dept., 1969-75, asst. dean basic scis. Tex. Coll. Osteopathic Medicine, 1975—. Bd. dirs. Denton Diabetic Assn., 1969—. Served with U.S. Army, 1944-46. Recipient numerous NIH grants, NSF grants. Mem. Am. Chem. Soc. (councilor Dallas-Ft Worth sect.), Am. Soc. Biol. Chemistry, Am. Inst. Chemists, Am. Soc. Plant Physiology, Tex. Osteopathic Med. Assn., Tex. Acad. Sci., Sigma Xi, Alpha Chi Sigma, Phi Lambda Upsilon. Contbr. articles to profl. jours; patentee in field. Home: 5006 N T Station Denton TX 76203 Office: Tex Coll Osteopathic Medicine Fort Worth TX 76107

SKINNER, DAVID LYNN, statis. analyst, cost acct.; b. Paducah, Ky., Feb. 23, 1954; s. Marion James and Minnie Elisie (Martin) S.; privately educated. Bookkeeper, Fence builder, 1970-72; project designer electronic control devices, 1972-74; cost analyst agrl. commodities and projects design, Bismark, Ark., 1974-76; sr. acct. Fin. Analysis Services, Port Allen, La., 1976—; v.p. Skinner Electronics, Inc., R & D.; mgr. Skinner Farms; dir. Lendaire, Inc., Farmers Pecan Harvesters, Inc., Skinner-Hawkins, Inc. Mem. Nat. Assn. Public Accts. (del. at large 1978), Accts. Assn. La. (1st v.p. Baton Rouge chpt. 1979). Jehovah's Witness. Office: 159 N Jefferson Ave Suites 1 and 3 Port Allen LA 70767

SKINNER, GWENDOLYNNE WILLETTE, nurse; b. Clayton, N.Mex., July 5, 1935; d. Frank and Sadie Love (Harris) Means; B.S.N., Baylor U., 1956; M.A., U. No. Colo., 1974; postgrad. U. Tex., 1977—; m. Jerry Ponder Skinner, Aug. 3, 1956; children—Webby, Denise. Public health nurse Hidalgo County Health Dept., Edinburg, Tex., 1956-63; charge nurse Westland Manor Nursing Home, Lakewood, Colo., 1969-71; nursing instr. Presbyn. Med. Center, Denver, 1971-75; asso. prof. nursing Pan Am. U., Edinburg, 1975—. Bd. dirs. Rainbow for Girls, 1975—, Am. Field Service, 1978—. Area Health Edn. Center grantee for nurses, 1978. Mem. Nat. League for Nursing of Tex. Republican. Baptist. Club: Order Eastern Star (worthy matron, pres. dist. officers 1979-80). Home: 514 E Boone St Pharr TX 78577 Office: Dept Nursing Edn Pan Am U E University Dr Edinburg TX 78539

SKINNER, MERTON BYRON, surgeon; b. Joliet, Ill., May 29, 1903; s. James D. and Margaret Wilson (Boyd) S.; D.D.S., Chgo. Coll. Dental Surgery, 1933; B.S., Loyola U., Chgo., 1934; M.D., Loyola Med. Coll., Chgo., 1939. Resident oral surgery Cook County Hosp., Chgo., 1933-34, asso. staff, 1934-46; pvt. practice oral surgery, Chgo., 1934-39; intern Mercy Hosp., 1939-40; resident Ill. Eye and Ear Infirmary, 1940-42; practice medicine specializing in otolaryngology, Chgo., 1946-50; chief ear, nose and throat sect. VA Hosp., Lake City, Fla., 1950-59, VA Hosp., Columbia, S.C., 1959-68; mem. staff Armed Forces Entrance and Examination Sta., Fort Jackson, S.C. Served to lt. col. U.S. Army, 1942-46. Diplomate Am. Bd. Otolaryngology. Mem. AMA, Am. Acad. Ophthalmology and Otolaryngology, Blue Key, Omicron Kappa Upsilon. Presbyterian. Clubs: Spring Valley Country (Columbia, S.C.); Ponte Vedra (Fla.). Home and Office: 812 Brandon Ave Columbia SC 29209

SKINNER, ROBERT LEE, plastic products co. exec.; b. Pueblo, Colo., Jan. 29, 1944; s. Harold and Thelma (Baxter) S.; B.S. in Chem. Engring., U. Okla., 1967; M.B.A., U. Colo., 1975; m. Beverly J. Letukas, June 26, 1965; children—Michelle Ann, Steven Eric. Asst. prof. engring. U. Colo., 1972-75; corp. ops. control specialist Phillips Products Co., Hopkinsville, Ky., 1975-77, mgr. bus. services, 1977—. Served with USN, 1967-75. Holloway scholar, 1962-67. Mem. Nat. Rifle Assn., Ky. Cols. Clubs: Elks, Tenn. Squires. Home: 203 Browning Pl Hopkinsville KY 42240 Office: 1857 Calvin Dr Hopkinsville KY 42240

SKINNER, STANLEY ALAN, archaeologist, educator; b. Summit, N.J., Dec. 4, 1942; s. Robert Stanley and Helen Mildred S.; B.A., U. N.Mex., 1965; postgrad. U. Ariz., 1966-67; M.A., So. Meth. U., 1972, Ph.D., 1974; m. Nina Montgomery Runyon, May 14, 1965; children—Tara Maria, Rebecca Anne, Joshua Alan. Fellow in archaeology Mus. No. Ariz., Flagstaff, 1965-66; research archaeologist So. Meth. U., Dallas, 1968-72, dir. archaeology research program 1972-79, instr. anthropology, 1972-74, asst. prof., 1974-80; dir. anthropology Environ. Cons.'s, Inc., 1980—; dir. Archaeology Resource Cons.'s; pres., Tex. Archaeol. Found. Inc., 1976—. Mem. Soc. Am. Archaeology, Am. Soc. Conservation Archaeology, Tex. Archeol. Soc. (pres. 1976), Dallas Archeol. Soc. (pres. 1974-75). Democrat. Episcopalian. Contbr. articles to nat. and regional trade publs. Home: 6620 Pimlico Dr Dallas TX 75214

SKINNER, THOMAS COBB, agrl. engr.; b. Archer, Fla., Sept. 28, 1921; s. Isham Wilkins and Lucile (Cobb) S.; B.S. Agrl. Engring., U. Fla., 1946, M.A. Agrl. Engring., 1947; m. Maxine Randall, Feb. 18, 1944; 1 son, Wayne Randall. Instr., Vets. on the Farm Tng. Program, 1947; asst. prof. dept. agrl. engring. U. Fla., Gainesville, 1947-53, asso. prof., 1953-65, prof., 1965—; cons. V.I. Coop. Extension Service, 1968, Sunbeam Plastics Corp., Evansville, Ind., 1970-72, Babson Bros. Co., Oak Brook, Ill., 1970, Henegar Land & Cattle Co., Bloomington, Ind., 1974-75, Suwanee River Camp Ground, Dixie County, Fla., 1974-75. Served with USAF, 1942-45. Decorated Air medal with oak leaf clusters; recipient Superior Service award Fla. Dept. Agr., Div. State Farmers Markets, 1966, Appreciation award Fla. County Agt.'s Assn., 1975; registered profl. engr., Fla. Mem. Am. Soc. Agrl. Engrs. (mem. family housing and agr. structures code coms. 1972-76, Outstanding Service award 1964), Nat. Soc. Profl. Engrs., Soil Conservation Soc. Am. (dir. Fla. chpt. 1961-64, 72-75), Fla. Engring. Soc. (pres. N. Central chpt. 1971-72), Epsilon Sigma Phi (state disting. service award 1978), Gamma Sigma Delta. Democrat. Clubs: Exchange (dir. 1969), Kiwanis (Gainesville, Fla.). Contbr. articles to profl. jours. Home: 4210 SW 2d Ave Gainesville FL 32607 Office: 101 Rogers Hall U Fla Gainesville FL 32611

SKINNER, WALTER NATHANIEL, physician; b. Dallas, Oct. 23, 1933; s. Walter Nathaniel and Nina Naomi (Burns) S.; B.S., So. Meth. U., 1955; student Baylor U., 1955-57; M.D., Southwestern Med. Sch., 1959; m. Judith Ann Payne, Sept. 9, 1967; 1 son, Walter N. Intern Parkland Meml. Hosp., Dallas, 1959-60, resident in internal medicine, 1961-64; practice medicine specializing in internal medicine, Dallas, 1964—; dir. med. edn., asst. chief internal medicine Presbyn. Hosp., Dallas, 1967-69; asso. clin. prof. medicine Southwestern Med. Sch., Dallas, 1965—; dir. 1st Security Nat. Bank, Dallas. Diplomate Am. Bd. Internal Medicine. Fellow A.C.P.; mem. AMA, Dallas County Med. Soc., Tex. Med. Assn., N.Y. Acad. Scis., Alpha Omega Alpha. Republican. Presbyterian. Clubs: City, Bent Tree Country. Home: 4400 Belclaire Ave Dallas TX 75205 Office: 8210 Walnut Hill Ln Dallas TX 75231

SKINNER, WALTER WINSTON, educator; b. Donaldsonville, Ga., Sept. 6, 1934; s. George Washington and Golden (Zorn) S.; B.S., West Ga. Coll., 1963; M.Ed. (NDEA scholar), U. Ga., 1965, Ed.D., 1971; m. Sara Jane Trammell, Aug. 10, 1957; children—Walter Winston, Robert Young, George Rhodes. Tchr. social studies North Clayton High Sch., College Park, Ga., 1963-64; counselor Athens (Ga.) High Sch., 1965-66; dean students Brunswick (Ga.) Jr. Coll., 1966-69; faculty Ga. State U., Atlanta, 1971—, asso. prof. ednl. psychology, 1971—; cons. U.S. Army Inf. Sch., local sch. systems, various industries. Councilman, City of Waverly Hall (Ga.), 1972-76; mem. Harris County (Ga.) Democratic Exec. Com., 1972-76. Served to capt. USAR. Mem. Am., Ga. psychol. assns., Am. Personnel and Guidance Assn., NEA, Phi Delta Kappa. Baptist. Club: Masons. Author: Adolescent Development: A Book of Readings, 1977. Home: Route 1 Moreland GA 30259 Office: Box 1998 Fort Benning GA 31905

SKIPPER, ROBERT VERNON, psychologist; b. Ft. Lewis, Wash., Mar. 26, 1948; s. Norman Edwin and Anne Margaret (Phillips) S.; A.A., Freed-Hardeman Coll., Henderson, Tenn., 1972; B.A., David Lipscomb Coll., Nashville, 1974; M.A., U. N. Ala., 1979; m. Jo Ann Walker, June 15, 1967; children—Lani, Suzy, Tracy. Psychiat. technician Central State Psychiat. Hosp., Nashville, 1972-74; dir. Easter Seal Center Handicapped Children, Nashville, 1974-75, dir. ops. Goodwill Industries, Nashville, 1975-76; dir. patient activities psychiat. unit Eliza Coffee Meml. Hosp., Florence, Ala., 1977—; pvt. practice counseling, 1978—. Served with USCG, 1967-69. Mem. Am. Personnel and Guidance Assn., Psi Chi. Democrat. Mem. Chs. of Christ. Club: Elks. Home: 1504 Old Memphis Pike Tuscumbia AL 35674 Office: Eliza Coffee Meml Hosp Marengo St Florence AL 35630

SKODLAR, TONY VICTOR, energy co. exec.; b. Pittsburg, Kans., July 28, 1920; s. Anton and Louise (Setina) S.; B.A., U. Colo., 1942; m. Barbara A. Vanatta, June 16, 1951; children—Pamela Ann Skodlar Moyers, Patricia Susan Skodlar Fry. Cost acct. Holly Sugar Corp., Colorado Springs, Colo., 1946-51; chief acct. Platte Pipeline Co., Kansas City, Mo., 1951-60; controller Mapco Inc., Tulsa, 1960—. Served with USAAF, 1942-44, AUS, 1944-46. Decorated Bronze Star. Mem. Nat. Assn. Accts., Assn. Oil Pipelines. Club: Oaks Country. Home: 7528 E 53d Pl Tulsa OK 74145 Office: 1800 S Baltimore St Tulsa OK 74119

SKRIPAK, RICHARD ALVA, oral surgeon; b. Port Jefferson, N.Y., May 7, 1940; s. Robert Charles and Alva Theresa (Schiesser) S.; A.B., Colgate U., 1962; D.D.S., N.Y. U., 1966; children—Danielle Lorraine, Jocelyn Helene. Intern oral surgery Bellevue Hosp., N.Y.C., 1966-67; resident in oral surgery Nassau County Med. Center, East Meadow, N.Y., 1968-69; chief resident oral surgery Bellevue Hosp., N.Y.C., 1969-70; practice dentistry specializing in oral and maxillofacial surgery, Ft. Pierce, Fla., 1970—, Vero Beach, Fla., 1974—. Pres. St. Lucie County (Fla.) unit Am. Cancer Soc., 1974-76. Diplomate Am. Bd. Oral and Maxillofacial Surgery. Mem. Ft. Pierce St. Lucie County C. of C. (dir. 1971-74), Ft. Pierce Jaycees (pres. 1974), Tri County Dental Soc. (pres. 1977—), Am. Soc. Oral and Maxillofacial Surgeons. Home: 1639 Thumb Point Dr Fort Pierce FL 33450

SLACK, JOHN M., Congressman; b. Charleston, W.Va., Mar. 18, 1915; s. John M. and Jennie (Gilchrist) S.; ed. Va. Mil. Acad.; m. Frances J. Reid; 1 son. Mem. 86th-87th Congresses from 6th W.Va. dist., 88th-95th Congresses from 3d W.Va. dist.; mem. Appropriations Com., mem. Pub. Works Subcom., Treasury and Post Office Subcom.; chmn. State, Justice, Commerce, Judiciary Subcom. Mem. Kanawha County (W.Va.) Ct., 1948-52; assessor Kanawha County, 1952-58. Mem. S.A.R. Democrat. Presbyterian (treas., deacon). Mason (Shriner), Elk. Club: Exchange. Office: 1536 Longworth House Office Bldg Washington DC 20515

SLACK, LARRY DON, automotive co. exec.; b. Bowie, Tex., June 30, 1948; s. Claude Lawrence and Wanda LaRue (Dillard) S.; B.B.A., Midwestern State U., 1970; m. Virginia Kay Williams, July 3, 1970; children—Lesli Leigh, Brian Coleman. Accountant, Wichita Falls (Tex.) Times Pub., 1968-71; office mgr. United Electric Co., Wichita Falls, 1971-72; gen. mgr. Whitney Ford Co., Wichita Falls, 1972-79; owner Larry Slack Ford-Mercury, 1979—. Deacon, First Christian Ch., Wichita Falls, 1977-79. Recipient Award for Excellence in Bus. Mgmt., Ford Motor Co., 1973, 74, 75. Mem. Midwestern State U. Alumni Assn. (bd. dirs. 1977-79), Wichita Falls New Car Dealers Assn. Club: Optimist (v.p., dir. 1977-79). Home: 1101 Sessions Bowie TX 76230 Office: PO Box 1360 Bowie TX 76230

SLACK, LYLE HOWARD, ceramic engr., educator; b. Wellsville, N.Y., Jan. 6, 1937; s. Merle Bishop and Lillian (Bixby) S.; B.S. in Ceramic Engring., Alfred U., 1958, Ph.D., 1964; m. Mary Elizabeth Jacox, June 20, 1959; children—Bryan, Aaron, Vaughn, Rebecca. Mem. tech. staff Bell Telephone Lab., Murray Hill, N.J., 1964-67; research engr. Lexington Lab., Inc., Cambridge, Mass., 1960-61; research engr. The O Hommel Co., Pitts., 1958-60; asso. prof. materials engring. Va. Poly. Inst. and State U., Blacksburg, 1967—; cons. Naval Research Lab. Chmn. com. Blue Ridge council Boy Scouts Am., Blacksburg, 1977. Recipient J. Shelton-Horsley Research award, Va. Acad. Scis., 1971. Fellow Am. Ceramic Soc.; mem. Ceramic Ednl. Council, Electrochemical Soc., Am. Soc. Engring. Edn., Nat. Inst. Ceramic Engrs., Keramos, Alpha Sigma Mu. Republican. Baptist. Contbr. articles in field to profl. jours. Home: 702 Crestwood Dr SE Blacksburg VA 24060 Office: 310 Holden Hall Virginia Polytechnic Institute and State University Blacksburg VA 24061

SLACK, MARY KNOX PULLIAM (MRS. RICHARD JOHN SLACK), librarian; b. San Angelo, Tex., Oct. 1, 1912; d. Mark Bell and Mary Knox (Powell) Pulliam; student So. Meth. U., 1929-30; B.J., U. Mo., 1933; postgrad. Shorter Coll., 1968; M. Librarianship, Emory U., 1970; m. Richard John Slack, Aug. 19, 1935; children—Ann Knox (Mrs. Richard R. Lorelle), Mary Susan (Mrs. Robert Wycliffe Cheatham, Jr.). Corr., Dallas Jour., 1934-35; copywriter Robert E. Martin Co., Atlanta, 1943-44; serials librarian Shorter Coll., Rome, Ga., 1968-70, reference, serials librarian, 1970-72, asst. prof. ednl. media, 1971-72; founder, head bus. library Tri-County Regional Library, Rome, 1972-74; med. librarian N.W. Ga. Regional Hosp., Rome, 1974-78. Founder, Floyd Hosp. Sch. Nursing Library, Rome, 1968, cons., 1968—. Vol. ARC, 1957-67; mem. citizens adv. council Coosa Valley Community Mental Health Center, 1980—. Mem. ALA (regional audiovisual rev. com. Booklist 1970-73), Southeastern, Ga. (2d v.p. 1973-75), library assns., Spl. Libraries Assn. (new projects chmn. South Atlantic chpt. 1974-77), Am. Assn. Higher Edn., Ga. Assn. Educators, NEA Med. Library Assn., D.A.R., Gamma Alpha Chi, Delta Gamma. Democrat. Episcopalian. Editor: Directory of Special Libraries in the Georgia-South Carolina Area, 1975. Home: 2 Tabernacle St PO Box 1112 Cartersville GA 30120

SLACK, MICHAEL LEWIS, aerospace engr.; b. Refugio, Tex., June 17, 1951; s. Jack Lewis and Frances Alleene (Boone) S.; B.S., Tex. A. and M. U., 1973, M.S., 1974. Research asst. Tex. Research Found. Tex. A. and M. U. Hypervelocity Lab., 1973-74; aerospace engr. structures and mechanics div. NASA Johnson Space Center, Houston, 1974—. Mem. AIAA, Houston Engring. and Sci. Soc., Phi Kappa Phi, Sigma Gamma Tau, Tau Beta Pi, Phi Eta Sigma. Methodist. Home: 2404 Yorktown 145 Houston TX 77056 Office: Mail Code ES2 NASA Johnson Space Center Houston TX 77058

SLAMA, RONALD EUGENE, personnel employment co. exec.; b. Marysville, Kans., Apr. 5, 1941; s. Joseph Albert and Noreen Lucille S.; B.A., Phillips U., 1963; M.A., U. Tex., 1965. With Electronic Data Systems, Dallas, 1970-75; owner, pres. Secretary Recruiters, Computer Recruiters, Recruiters of Dallas, 1975—. Served with USN, 1965-70. Mem. Dallas Ind. Agencies Orgn. Home: Red Oaks Farms Route 1 Aubrey TX 76227 Office: Recruiters of Dallas 13101 Preston Rd Suite 300 Dallas TX 75240

SLATER, BETTY CAROL MONTGOMERY, nurse; b. Garrard County, Ky., Sept. 13, 1934; d. Walker Dudley and Peachie Mae (Hurt) Montgomery; diploma Good Samaritan Hosp. Sch. Nursing, Lexington, Ky., 1957; postgrad U. Ky., 1957-63, St. Josephs Coll., Windham, Maine, 1978—; m. Jack D. Slater, Aug. 17, 1974; children by previous marriage—Tracy Allen Stone, Sandra Carol Stone, William Dudley Stone. Staff nurse med-surg. Good Samaritan Hosp., Lexington, 1957; staff nurse psychiat. VA Hosp., Lexington, 1959-62; div. charge nurse Ob-Gyn, Univ. Hosp., Lexington, 1962-68; evening charge nurse VA Hosp., Lexington, 1968-70; drug abuse rehab.

counselor NIMH Clin. Research Center, Lexington, 1970-74; clin. dir. psychiatry and rehab. Meml. Med. Center, Savannah, Ga., 1974-77, coordinator psychiat. services, 1977—. Sec., Women's Aux. of Ritualistic Divan Alee Temple Shrine, Savannah, 1978—; patron Little Theatre of Savannah. Mem. SE Ga. Health Systems Agy., Am. Nurses Assn., Ga. Nurses Assn. (pres. 1st dist. 1979—), Am. Soc. Nursing Service Adminstrs. (council of assos. 1976—), Republican. Home: 9231 Garland Dr Savannah GA 31406 Office: 4700 Waters Ave Savannah GA 31405

SLATER, CALVIN DALE, acct.; b. Houston, June 2, 1954; s. Alton Ray and Jeannette (Robinson) S.; B.A., Rice U., 1976. With Ernst & Ernst, Houston, 1976-79; partner Davidson & Slater, C.P.A.'s, Houston, 1979—. C.P.A., Tex. Home: 5005 Georgi St Apt 56 Houston TX 77092 Office: 3272 Westheimer Suite 2 Houston TX 77098

SLATER, CONSTANCE, educator; b. Plymouth, Mass., Sept. 13, 1931; d. George Lewiston and Dorothy Mae (Darby) Finch; student Broward Community Coll., 1968-73; B.A., Shaw U., 1975; postgrad. Fla. Atlantic U., 1975-77; m. Fred Carl Slater, Nov. 22, 1952; children—Steven, Scott, Stacey Slater Owens, Sherrill. Office mgr. Comml. Union Assurance Co., Indpls., 1950, Family and Child Service Agy., San Bernardino, Calif., 1951, Gate City Sash and Door Co., Fort Lauderdale, Fla., 1952-54; tchr. aide Sundial Sch. for Retarded, Ft. Lauderdale, 1963-68; tchr. asst. Broward County Schs., Ft. Lauderdale, 1968-77, tchr. Wingate Oaks Center for Retarded, Ft. Lauderdale, 1977—; owner-dir. Tall Pine Camp for Exceptional Citizens, Coker Creek, Tenn., 1971—. Sec., Parents and Friends of Sunland Tng. Center, 1961-68; vice-chmn. Dist. 10, Fla. Human Rights Advocacy Com. on Mental Retardation, 1978—; tchr. rep. to N. Central Adv. Com., 1978-79, Supt. Schs. Dist. Adv. Com., 1979; bd. dirs. Broward County Assn. for Retarded Citizens. Vocat. Edn. for Handicapped fellow Fla. Internat. U., 1979-80. Mem. Council for Exceptional Citizens, Nat. Assn. for Retarded Citizens, Am. Assn. on Mental Deficiency. Democrat. Home: 6221 NW 17th St Fort Lauderdale FL 33313 Office: Wingate Oaks Center for Retarded Broward County Schs 1211 NW 33d Terr Fort Lauderdale FL 33311

SLATER, FRANK MICHAEL, bus. exec.; b. N.Y.C., Aug. 12, 1940; s. S. Frank and Mary E. (Fay) S.; B.S., Fordham U., 1965; M.B.A., Xavier U., 1977; m. Patricia Carter; children—Frank, Jeanne, Daniel, Susan, Erik. With IBM, 1960—, adminstrv. ops. mgr., 1967-68, methods and procedures analyst, 1969, systems analyst, 1970, word processing mgmt. devel., 1971, fin. analyst, 1972, mgr. adminstrn. and ops., 1973-74, bus. controls adminstr., 1975-76, mgr. bus. controls, 1976-78, fin. project mgr. adminstrv. acctg., 1978—. Mem. Assn. M.B.A. Execs. Office: IBM 740 New Circle Rd Lexington KY 40511

SLATER, LYNN WILLIS, boat mfg. co. exec.; b. Candler County, Ga., Feb. 26, 1952; d. Raymond and Martha Lanell (Phillips) Willis; student Swainsboro Tech.; m. James Curtis Slater, Jan. 27, 1968. Machiner operator Swainsboro Sportswear Inc. (Ga.), 1968-76; secretarial positions Custom Fiberglass Mfg., Inc., Metter, Ga., 1976—; office mgr. Swine Specialties, Metter, 1976—. Methodist. Office: 25 S Terrell St Metter GA 30439

SLATON, ROGER DAVID, bank exec.; b. Dawson County, Ga., May 25, 1941; s. Charles H. and Kathleen S. S.; B.B.A., U. Ga., 1963; postgrad Nat. Comml. Lending Sch., U. Okla., 1977; m. Loretta F. Cantrell, June 11, 1961; children—Barry Edward, Charles Fredrick, Julie Lynn. Personnel mgr. Lockheed Aircraft Corp., Marietta, Ga., 1965-69; v.p. Home Fed. Savings & Loan Assn., Gainesville, Ga., 1969-74; v.p. Gainesville Nat. Bank, 1974—. Vice chmn. Dawson County Sch. Bd.; regional dir. Am. Cancer Soc., Dawsonville, Ga.; dist. dir. Ga. Sch. Bd. Assn. Mem. Independent Bankers Assn. Baptist. Club: Dawson County High Sch. Booster. Home: Route 4 Dawsonville GA 30534 Office: PO Drawer 978 Gainesville GA 30503

SLATON, WYOMA BERTHA, nurse, hosp. ofcl.; b. Houstonia, Mo., July 5, 1919; d. Harry Louis and Minnie Weily (Brownfield) S.; R.N., Ark. Med. Center; postgrad. in mgmt. Baylor Med. Center, Dallas. Staff, Gaston Episcopal Hosp., Dallas, 1961—, supr. operating room, 1961—. Mem. Dallas Operating Room Nurses Assn., Tex. Nurses Assn. Republican. Baptist. Office: Gaston Episcopal Hosp 3505 Gaston Ave Dallas TX 75246

SLATTERY, JOSEPH EMMETT, camera co. exec.; b. Newark, Mar. 10, 1925; s. Robert Emmett and Agnes Theresa (Cummings) S.; student U. Chattanooga, 1943-44, Monmouth Jr. Coll., 1947, Spadea Sch. Criminology, 1948-49, LaSalle Extension U., 1953-55; married, Mar. 11, 1951; children—Caryn, Jean, Debra, Robert, Catherine, Ginger. Div. mgr. Willmark Service Systems, Inc., N.Y.C., 1949-58, field supr., Newark, 1949-50, asst. office mgr., Phila., 1950-51, mgr. Houston office, 1951-52, Washington office, 1952-58, pres. Filmdex, Inc., Centreville, Va., 1958—; dir., chmn. bd. Landmark Investment Corp., 1973—. Pres., Catharpin (Va.) Farms Estates Homeowners Assn., 1977-79. Served with U.S. Army, 1943-45; ETO. Mem. Am. Soc. Indsl. Security, Fairfax County C. of C. Republican. Roman Catholic. Club: Pochahontas Gun. Developer photographic charging systems for public library use, various photographic cameras for security applications. Home: 5209 Sudley Rd Manassas VA 22110 Office: 15500 Lee Hwy Centreville VA 22020

SLAUGHTER, ELMER CUNNINGHAM, mfg. exec.; b. Houston, Sept. 12, 1920; s. Elmer Carlton and Margaret (Cunningham) S.; student N. Tex. State U., 1936-37; E.E., U. Cin., 1942; m. Jeannette Kearney, June 27, 1942; children—Jean Slaughter Johnson, Susan Slaughter Sachs, Dorothy Slaughter Ashmead, Edward, Mary Slaughter McGraw, John, Richard, Michael, Doris, Rebecca, Nancy, Janet. Established test lab. Lear, Inc., Piqua, Ohio, 1942-45, chief design engr., 1945-46, chief engr., Grand Rapids, Mich., 1946-47; chief engr. Piqua Machine & Mfg. Co., 1948-54; pres. E-M Corp., Fletcher, Ohio, 1947-48, Slaughter Co., Ardmore, Okla., 1954—; cons. Lear, Inc., Grand Rapids, 1947-48, Polo Pump Co., Ill., 1947-49, Safa Alarm Co., Orrville, Ohio, 1948-50; chmn. Mayor's Indsl. Adv. Com., 1971-72. Commr., Piqua Boys' Baseball Assn., 1958-61; chmn. Ardmore Edn. Council, 1970-74; pres. Ardmore Sch. Bd., 1977; pres. bd. dirs. Ardmore Sheltered Workshop, 1970-72. Mem. IEEE, AAAS, Ardmore C. of C. (pres., dir. 1972-75, named Outstanding Citizen 1975), Tau Beta Pi, Eta Kappa Nu, Sigma Xi. Office: Moore and Hailey Sts Ardmore OK 73401

SLAUGHTER, FREEMAN CLUFF, dentist; b. Estes, Miss., Dec. 30, 1926; s. William Cluff and Vay (Fox) S.; student Wake Forest Coll., 1944; student Emory U., 1946-47, D.D.S., 1951; m. Genevieve Anne Parks, July 30, 1948; children—Mary Anne, Thomas Freeman, James Hugh. Practice gen. dentistry, Kannapolis, N.C., 1951—; mem. N.C. Bd. Dental Examiners, 1966-75, pres., 1968-69, sec.-treas., 1971-74; chief dental staff Cabarrus Meml. Hosp., Concord, N.C., 1965-66, 75; mem. N.C. Adv. Com. for Edn. Dental Aux. Personnel-N.C. State Bd. Edn., 1967-70; adviser dental asst. program Rowan Tech. Inst., 1973—. Trustee N.C. Symphony Soc., 1962-68, pres. Kannapolis chpt., 1961; mem. Cabarrus County Bd. Health, 1977—; active Boy Scouts Am., Eagle scout with silver palm. Served with USNR, 1944-46; ETO, MTO. Lic. real estate broker. Fellow Am. Coll. Dentists; mem. Am. Legion, Kannapolis Jr. C. of C. (v.p. 1952), Toastmasters Internat. (pres. Kannapolis 1963-64), ADA, Am. Assn. Dental Examiners (Dentist Citizen of Year 1975; v.p. 1977-79), So. Conf. Dental Deans and Examiners (v.p. 1969), N.C. Dental Soc. (resolution of commendation 1975), N.C. Dental Soc. Anesthesiology (pres. 1964), Southeastern Acad. Prosthodontics, So. Acad. Oral Surgery, Am. Soc. Dentistry for Children (pres. N.C. unit 1957), Internat. Assn. Dental Research, Cabarrus County Dental Soc. (pres. 1953-54, 63-64, 69), N.C. Assn. Professions (dir. 1976—), Omicron Kappa Upsilon, Alpha Epsilon Upsilon. Clubs: Masons, Shriners, Kannapolis Music (pres. 1962-63), Rotary (dir. 1977—). Home: 506 Dawn St Kannapolis NC 28081 Office: Professional Bldg Kannapolis NC 28081

SLAUGHTER, LURLINE EDDY, artist; b. Heidelberg, Miss., June 19, 1919; d. Gilbert Emmings and Lurline Elizabeth (Heidelberg) Eddy; B.S., Miss. U. for Women, 1939; m. James Fant Slaughter, Jan. 27, 1946; children—Beverly Slaughter Lowery, Anne Lumbley. Tchr. high sch., 1939-40; with VA, Washington, 1941; one-woman shows N.Y.C., Miss., Ark., Tenn.; exhibited in group shows: Brooks Art Mus., Memphis, 1970, Meridian (Miss.) Mus. Art, 1973, Delta State U., 1966, Miss. State U., 1967, Miss. U. for Women, 1969, others; represented in permanent collections: Miss. U. for Women, Miss. State U., Southeast La. U., Pine Bluff Art Mus., U. of the South. Bd. dirs. Miss. Art Colony, 1965—. Served as lt. (s.g.) USNR, 1942-45. Recipient numerous awards including Best in Show Arts Festival, McComb, Miss., 1967, 75, 76, Most Outstanding Artist award Arts Registry, N.Y.C., 1972, First prize Miss. Art Colony Traveling Exhbn., 1973. Mem. Miss. Art Assn. Methodist. Club: Humphreys County Country. Home: Seldom Seen Plantation Silver City MS 39166

SLAUGHTER, ROBERT LOUIS, ednl. adminstr.; b. Laredo, Tex., Jan. 4, 1942; s. Julian Louis and Pilar Feliz (Macias) S.; B.A., St. Edward's U., 1964; m. Judy Johnson, Dec. 22, 1973; 1 dau., Michelle Meredith. Head coach middle sch. Trinity Valley Sch., Ft. Worth, 1965-70, dir. testing, 1966-67, dir. admissions and testing, 1967-79, dir. summer sch., 1968-70, 73-78, head lower sch., 1968-70, athletic dir., 1970-71, 75-76, head middle sch. baseball coach, 1966-70, head middle sch. track coach, 1968-70, head varsity basketball coach, 1970-71, head varsity football coach, 1970-72, head middle sch. basketball coach, 1965-70, 71-77, head middle sch. football coach, 1966-70, 72-73, 77-78, coordinator middle sch. athletic facilities, transp. dir., 1970-80, mem. headmaster's council, 1968—, audio-visuals dir., 1970-78, dir. ops., bus. mgr., 1979—; sec. Tex. Ind. Schs. Conf., 1969-70. Instr., Confrat. Christian Doctrine, 1964-65. Named Tchr. of Year St. Edwards U., 1964. Republican. Roman Catholic. Clubs: Central Cath. (Fort Worth); Press, Internat.-Latin Am., Tex. (Austin). Home: 5716 Wales Ave Fort Worth TX 76133 Office: 6101 McCart Ave Fort Worth TX 76133

SLAVIN, RICHARD KENNETH, hosp. adminstr.; b. N.Y.C., Aug. 16, 1933; s. Jack and Lillian (Kulman) S.; B.S. in Pharmacy, Fordham U., 1956; postgrad. Rutgers U., 1965; M.B.A., Rensselaer Poly. Inst., 1975; m. June Lippman, Aug. 16, 1954; children—Mindy, Susan. Asso. dir. pharmacy Lenox Hill Hosp., N.Y.C., 1960-62; dir. pharmacy Mt. Sinai Hosp., N.Y.C., 1962-64, asst. dir. adminstrn., 1964-69, asso. dir., 1969-75; pres. Palmetto Gen. Hosp., Hialeah, Fla., 1975—; adj. asso. prof. Rensselaer Poly. Inst.; lectr. Mt. Sinai Sch. Medicine, City U. N.Y.; instr. in health care adminstrn. Fla. Internat. U.; mem. exec. com., bd. dirs. Health Systems Agy. So. Fla., 1977—; dir. Community Blood Bank, 1978—. Served with U.S. Army, 1956-58. Mem. Fla. Hosp. Assn., Fla. Med. Assn., Am. Hosp. Assn., Am. Coll. Hosp. Adminstrs., Fla. League Hosps. (treas. 1978-80), Hialeah Area C. of C. (dir. 1975—). Office: 2001 W 68th St Hialeah FL 33010

SLAVSKY, DAVID BRUCE, astronomer; b. Newark, Sept. 18, 1951; s. Max and Lillian S.; Sc.B., Brown U., 1973; S.M., Harvard U., 1975; postgrad. U. Tex., 1975—. Teaching fellow Harvard U., 1974-75; researcher dept. astronomy U. Tex., Austin, 1975-79, instr. astronomy, 1979—; sci. editor Star Date and McDonald Obs. News; resource person for spl. sci. reports Sta.-KLRJ, 1978-80. Tchr. English and math. to Chinese immigrant children, 1974-75. Recipient German award Brown U., 1969-70; Harvard U. fellow, 1973-74. Mem. Am. Astron. Soc., AAAS, Sigma Xi. Jewish. Research on rotation periods of Uranus and Neptune, 1978-80. Office: Dept Astronomy U Tex Austin TX 78212

SLAWSON, BOBBY JOE, restaurant exec.; b. Jacksonville, Tex., Apr. 19, 1939; s. Harvey E. and Eva (Hammonds) S.; student Baylor U., 1958-59; A.A., Lon Morris Coll., 1960; B.B.A., Sam Houston State U., 1962; M.B.A., So. Meth. U., 1971; m. Harriet N. Whigham, Sept. 1, 1961; children—Steven Edward, Susan Eleanor. Fin., cost, budget and acctg. mgr. Tex. Instruments, Dallas, 1965-71; controller Taylor Pub. Co., Dallas, 1971-76; chief fin. officer Bonanza Internat., Inc., Dallas, 1976-78; pres., chief exec. officer Steaks Renowned, Inc., 1978—. Served to lt. USAF, 1965-68. C.P.A., Tex. Mem. Am. Inst. C.P.A.'s, Tex. Soc. C.P.A.'s. Home: 1914 Shari Ln Garland TX 75043 Office: 1000 Campbell Centre 8350 N Central Expy Dallas TX 75206

SLAYDEN, KAY WILSON, mfg. co. exec.; b. Lyons, Ga., Dec. 1, 1934; s. Herbert L. and Marion S. (Lilliott) S.; B.S. in Engring., Auburn (Ala.) U., 1956; m. Nancy Murray, Aug. 11, 1957; children—Kevin, Stephen. Vice pres. ops. Teledyne Brown Engring. Co., Huntsville, Ala., 1960-70; v.p. ops. Fuqua Industries, Inc., Atlanta, 1970-73, later exec. v.p., now pres., chief operating officer; pres. McDonough Power Equipment Co. (Ga.), 1973-75; dir. Norell Corp., Atlanta. Served to capt. USAF, 1957-60. Registered profl. engr., Ga. Baptist. Office: 3800 First National Tower Bldg Atlanta GA 30303*

SLEADD, LORI SUE, sch. prin.; b. N.Y.C., July 20, 1944; d. Samuel J. and Elaine P. (Kaplan) Simon; B.A., Am. U., 1966; M.A., Western Ky. U., 1970, postgrad., 1975. Tchr. pub. schs., N.Y.C., Bowling Green and Louisville, Ky., 1966-74; counselor pub. schs., Louisville, 1974-79; prin. Roosevelt Elem. Sch., Louisville, 1979—. Recipient award for outstanding elem. guidance program Jefferson County, 1978. Mem. Am. Personnel and Guidance Assn., Ky. Personnel and Guidance Assn., Nat. Assn. Elem. Sch. Prins., Ky. Assn. Elem. Sch. Prins., Ky. Elem. Sch. Counselors Assn. (pres. 1978), Am. Sch. Counselors Assn., Ky. Sch. Counselors Assn., Ky. Assn. Sch. Adminstrs., Jefferson County Assn. Sch. Adminstrs. Home: 104 Old Bond Ct Louisville KY 40222 Office: 222 N 17th St Louisville KY 40203

SLEDGE, BARNETT JENKINS, JR., real estate exec.; b. Memphis, Nov. 3, 1942; s. Barnett Jenkins and Rachael Pauline (Davis) S.; B.S.M.E., U. Tenn., 1965. Engr., McDonnell Douglas Corp., St. Louis, 1965-67; partner Bond-Sledge Bldg. Contractors, Aspen, Colo., 1968; v.p., dir. Pyramid Properties Corp., Dallas, 1969-70, Pyramid Corp., Dallas, 1970-72; pres. Lakecroft, San Antonio, 1973—. Mem. Kappa Sigma, Pi Tau Sigma. Episcopalian. Office: 8500 Village Dr San Antonio TX 78217

SLEDGE, JOHN FREDERICK DOUGLASS, banker; b. Winston-Salem, N.C., Dec. 12, 1942; s. Frederick Douglass and Lucille Jacquelyn Sledge; B.S. in Math., Howard U., 1964; M.B.A., Babson Coll., 1970; m. Elizabeth Delores Walker, June 30, 1964; children—Russell B., Cassaundra L., Olivia J. Grad. asst. depts. mktg., acctg. and mgmt. Babson Coll., Wellesley, Mass., 1969-70; mgmt. asso. Marine Midland Bank, Buffalo, 1970-71, adminstrv. asst., 1971-72, asst. indsl. financing officer, 1972-74, indsl. financing officer, 1974; comml. loan officer N.C. Nat. Bank, Winston-Salem, 1974-75, asst. v.p., 1975-80, v.p., 1980—; pres., chief exec. officer, chmn. Basic Internat. Co., Inc., Winston-Salem, 1977—; rep. young mgmt. Marine Midland Inst. Banking, Rochester, N.Y., 1971; guest lectr. econs. and fin. SUNY, Buffalo, 1971, Winston-Salem State U., 1977, 78, 79. Coach Little League, Winston-Salem, 1976-78; mem. bd. advs. SUNY, Buffalo, 1971-73, Erie Community Coll., Buffalo, 1971-73; commr. Forsyth County (N.C.) Indsl. Facilities and Pollution Control Financing Authority, 1978—; alumni adv. Babson Coll., 1970-80; bd. dirs. Winston-Salem/Forsyth County YMCA's, 1974—, Vol. Action Center, Winston-Salem, 1977—. Served to capt. USAF, 1964-68. Mem. Winston-Salem C. of C., Howard U. Alumni Assn. (pres.). Democrat. Methodist. Club: Masons. Home: 2691 Nantucket Dr Winston-Salem NC 27103 Office: 102 W 3rd St Winston Salem NC 27101

SLEEMAN, WILLIAM CLIFFORD, JR., aerospace technologist; b. Birmingham, Ala., June 29, 1923; s. William Clifford and Olive Mae (Watson) S.; student Birmingham-So. Coll., 1940-42; B.S. in Aero. Engring., U. Ala., 1944; m. Mary Frances Mikell, Apr. 12, 1947; children—William Clifford III, Richard McDonald, Melanie Frances. Aero. engr. NACA/NASA Langley Research Center, Hampton, Va., 1944-52, aero. research engr., 1952-62, aerospace engr., 1962-67, aerospace technologist, 1967—, head flexible wing sect., 1967-73. Singer in prin. roles, chorus Peninsula Civic Opera Co., Newport News, Va. 1955-65. Choir dir. Hidenwood Presbyterian Ch., Newport News, 1956—, elder, 1967-75. Recipient Achievements awards NASA, 1968-70. Asso. fellow Am. Inst. Aeros. and Astronautics; mem. Engrs.' Club of Va. Peninsula (treas. 1963-64). Club: Warwick Yacht and Country (Newport News). Contbr. articles to profl. jours. Home: 207 Mistletoe Dr Newport News VA 23606 Office: NASA Langley Research Center Hampton VA 23665

SLENKER, NORMAN FREDERICK, lawyer; b. Washington, Pa., Oct. 12, 1929; s. Fred William and Esther Lenore (Lamp) S.; A.B., Ohio Wesleyan U., 1951; J.D., George Washington U., 1955; certificate Seminar for Lawyers, Med. Coll. Va., 1959; m. Berta King Ray, Sept. 20, 1952; children—Susan G., Donald P., Martha B. Ins. investigator-adjuster Kemper Ins. Co., Ins. Co. N.Am. and an ind. firm, Washington, 1951-56; admitted to Va. bar, 1956; since practiced in Arlington, partner firm Russell & Hulvey, 1956-59; trial atty. Jesse, Phillips, Kendrick others, 1960-62; partner firm Duff & Slenker, 1962-72, Slenker, Brandt & Jennings, 1972—; instr. U. Va. Extension, Arlington, 1956-57; instr. legal considerations of health care U. Va.; tchr. history and govt. Arlington Pub. Sch. System Night Sch., 1957-59. Fellow Am Coll. Trial Lawyers; mem. Am., Va. Arlington County bar assns., Am. Judicature Soc., Va. Trial Lawyers Assn., internat. Soc. Barristers, Delta Theta Phi, Beta Theta Pi. Home: 3861 N Ridgeview Rd Arlington VA 22207 Office: 1012 N Utah St Arlington VA 22201

SLESINSKI, THERESA MARION, tng. and orgn. devel. specialist; b. N.Y.C., July 10, 1944; d. Anthony Raymond and Antonina (Wnorowski) S.; B.A., Hunter Coll., 1973, M.S. in Edn., 1976. With CBS, Inc., N.Y.C., 1963-71; adminstrv. asst. to chmn. bd. New York Yankees, 1971-72; adminstrv. asst. Cowen & Co., N.Y.C., 1974-75; v.p., dir. Cornerstone for Change in Edn., Inc., N.Y.C., 1976-78; personnel devel. specialist Exxon Co., U.S.A., Houston, 1977—. Cert. in counseling, N.Y. Mem. Am. Soc. Trainers and Developers, Am. Personnel and Guidance Assn., Sigma Tau Delta, Alpha Kappa Delta. Home: April Point South #95 Montgomery TX 77356 Office: Exxon Co USA PO Box 2180 Houston TX 77001

SLIDER, JOHN ROBERT, optometrist; b. Gorman, Tex., Nov. 11, 1941; s. William Hardie and Eula (Clarke) S.; student Austin Coll., 1960-62; B.S., U. Houston, 1965, O.D., 1966; m. Betty Jo Suddith, Aug. 31, 1968. Partner with D.W. Leach, optometric practice, Odessa, Tex., 1968—. Bd. dirs. Odessa Council for the Blind, 1969, Ector County Cancer Assn., YMCA. Served to capt. AUS, 1966-68. Mem. Tex. (bd. dirs. 1978-79), Am. optometric assns., S.W. Contact Lens Soc., W. Tex. Optometric Soc. (pres. 1969, 70, 73), Jr. C. of C. Presbyn. (elder). Lion. Home: 3003 Eastover St Odessa TX 79762 Office: 415 N Sam Houston St Odessa TX 79761

SLIFER, KENNETH BENJAMIN, psychologist; b. Preble County, Ohio, Apr. 5, 1915; s. Omar William and Zola Fern (Early) S.; A.B., Trevecca Coll., Nashville, 1950; M.Div., Vanderbilt U., 1953; M.A., Austin Peay State U., 1965; Ed.D., Auburn U., 1973; m. Thelma Richards, Nov. 21, 1940; children—Marita Sue Slifer Smith. Sales and service positions, 1936-46; minister Ch. of Nazarene, Tenn., 1947-65; dir. evening sch. and adult program Gadsden (Ala.) Jr. Coll., 1968-69; dean instrn. Motlow State Community Coll., Tullahoma, Tenn., 1969-70; prof. psychology Trevecca Nazarene Coll., Nashville, 1970—. Mem. Tenn., Middle Tenn. psychol. assns., Phi Delta Kappa. Home: 3239 Doverside Dr Nashville TN 37207 Office: Trevecca Nazarene Coll Nashville TN 37210

SLIGER, BERNARD FRANCIS, univ. adminstr., economist; b. Sept. 30, 1924; B.A., Mich. State U., 1949, M.A., 1950, Ph.D., 1955; m. 1945; children—Nan, Paul, Greta, Sten. Tchr., Interior Twp. (Mich.) High Sch., 1947-48; asst. prof. econs. La. State U., 1953-56; asso. prof., 1956-61, prof., 1961-69, head dept. econs., 1961-65, dean acad. affairs, 1965-68, vice-chancellor, 1968-69; exec. dir. La. Coordinating Council for Higher Edn., Baton Rouge, 1969-72; prof. econs. Fla. State U., 1972—, exec. v.p., 1972-73, exec. v.p., chief acad. officer, 1973-76, exec. v.p., interim pres., 1976-77, pres., 1977—; vis. asst. prof. Mich. State U., 1955, vis. prof., 1961, vis. lectr., 1961; fellow U. Minn., 1962; mem., chief cons. to Gov. La.'s Tax Study Com., 1968; commr. of adminstrn., chief budget officer State of La., 1968-69. Served with U.S. Army, 1943-46. Mem. Am. Econs. Assn., Nat. Tax Assn., Omicron Delta Kappa, Phi Kappa Phi, Alpha Kappa Psi. Author: (with Ansel M. Sharp) Public Finance, 1970. Office: Office of Pres Fla State U Tallahassee FL 32306

SLINKER, JON JACOB, mfg. engr.; b. Lamar, Mo., Feb. 28, 1949; s. Robert K. and Ruth Pauline S.; B.S. in Engring., U. Nev., 1975; postgrad. U. No. Iowa, 1979—; m. Janice C. Osborne, Aug. 18, 1973; children—Erica Anne, Jon Jacob II. With Waterloo (Iowa) tractor works John Deere, 1976-79, mfg. project engr., drive train assembly layout and devel., 1979; sr. process engr., capital resources mgr. spl. projects Unit Rig & Equipment Co., Tulsa, 1979—. Served with USAF, 1968-72. Registered engr.-in-tng., Nev. Mem. Nat. Soc. Profl. Engrs., Engring. Soc. Okla., Soc. Mfg. Engrs. Office: Unit Rig & Equipment Co PO Box 3107 Tulsa OK 74101

SLINKER, PANDORA, speech and lang. therapist; b. Glasgow, Ky., Nov. 26, 1950; b. Leamon Sylvester and Creola Maldren (Morrison) S.; B.A. in Speech, Western Ky. U., 1972, M.A. in Speech Pathology, 1977. Speech therapist Metcalfe County Sch. System, Edmonton (Ky.) Elem. Sch., 1977—. Mem. Am. Speech and Hearing Assn., NEA, Ky. Speech and Hearing Assn., Ky. Edn. Assn., Metcalfe County Edn. Assn., Glasgow Bus. and Profl. Women's Club (sec.

1975, treas. 1976). Home: S Public Sq Glasgow KY 42141 Office: Edmonton Elem Sch Edmonton KY 42129

SLIWAK, FRANK RICHARD, mgmt. cons.; b. Bklyn., June 11, 1923; s. Frank Xavier and Mary (Maciag) S.; B.B.A., Pace Coll., 1952; M.B.A., Hofstra Coll., 1953; m. Corrinne A. Kozlowski, Apr. 23, 1949; children—Irene, Frank Jr. Quality control engr. Fairchild Engine Co., Farmingdale, N.Y., 1952-54, Grumman Aircraft Engring. Corp., Beth Page, N.Y., 1954-55; quality control mgr. Fairchild Camera Corp., Syosset, N.Y., 1955-57, Airborne Instruments Corp., Deer Park, N.Y., 1957-59, Martin-Marietta Corp., Orlando, 1960-68, McDonnell Douglas Corp., Titusville, Fla., 1969-79; mgmt. cons., 1979—; tchr. mgmt. and quality control Rollins Coll., Winter Park, Fla., 1962-69, Seminole Community Coll., Lake Mary, Fla., 1969-75. Served with USAAF, 1943-45, USAF, 1949-52. Registered profl. engr., Calif. Mem. Am. Soc. Quality Control (sr. mem., cert. reliability engr., nat. chmn.-elect aerospace and def. div.). Roman Catholic. Mem. editorial adv. bd. Quality Mag., 1973—. Home: Casselberry FL 32707

SLOAN, JAMES EUGENE, lawyer; b. Jonesboro, Ark., Mar. 25, 1923; s. Eugene and Beatrice Margaret (Lynch) S.; B.S. in Pub. Adminstrn., U. Ark., 1945; postgrad. Georgetown U., 1945-46; J.D., Vanderbilt U., 1948; m. Betty Carroll Teeter, Sept. 6, 1946; children—John Teeter, James Eugene, Kitty Clay, Cynthia R., Charles A., Mary E. Admitted to Ark. bar, 1948; partner firm Sloan & Sloan, Jonesboro, 1950—; individual practice law, Jonesboro, 1948-50; chmn. Ark. Bd. Rev., Employment Security Div., Little Rock, 1952-54; chmn. Flintrol, Inc., Jonesboro; pres. Elm Grove, Inc.; dir. Mercantile Bank; v.p., dir. E. Sloan Farms, Inc., Bay Gin Co.; sec., dir. Sloan-Jeter Devel. Co.; investor. Del., Ark. Constl. Conv., 1978, 79; bd. dirs. E. Ark. Area council Boy Scouts Am., 1963—, v.p., 1968-76, commr., 1977; bd. dirs., sec. E.Ark. Resource, Conservation and Devel. Project, 1972—; bd. dirs. E.Ark. Planning and Devel. Dist., 1967—, pres., 1976-77. Recipient Fund Dr. award United Way, 1954, Girl Scouts U.S.A., 1965; Silver Beaver award Boy Scouts Am., 1979. Mem. Ark. Farm Bur. Fedn. (dir. 1969—), Ark. Bar Assn., NE Ark. Estate Council. Democrat. Roman Catholic. Clubs: Rotary (pres. local club 1967-68), K.C. Died Nov. 8, 1979. Home: 1415 S Main St Jonesboro AR 72401 Office: PO Box 267 Jonesboro AR 72401

SLOAN, JAMES PARK, educator; b. Clinton, S.C., Oct. 2, 1916; s. Eugene Blakely and Janie Pressly (Lindsay) S.; B.A., Erskine Coll., 1937; M.A., Tulane U., 1938; m. Alice Catherine Gaines, June 26, 1941; children—James Park, Edwin Gaines. Tchr. econs., govt., sociology and English, Ga. Mil. Acad., College Park, 1938-39; tchr. history, govt. Clinton (S.C.) High Sch., 1939-41; asst. to chmn. S.C. Def. Council, Clinton, 1941-42; paymaster Joanna Mills Co. (S.C.), 1942, personnel dir., 1946-58, dir. indsl. pub. relations, 1958-64; editor co. monthly mag. The Joanna Way, 1950-64; asst. prof. polit. sci. Coll. of Charleston (S.C.), 1964-67; instr. polit. sci. Spartanburg regional campus U. S.C., 1967-70, 73—, asst. prof., 1970-79, asst. prof. emeritus, 1978—, dir. academic affairs, 1970-73. Mem. adv. council S.C. Employment Security Commn., 1955—; mem. planning bd. S.C. Accident Prevention Conf., 1954-57; mem. edn. task force Model Cities Program, City of Spartanburg, 1971-72; mem. long-range planning com. City of Spartanburg, 1970-73; vice chmn. Laurens County S.C. Heart Assn., 1953-64; mem. Laurens County Tri-Centennial Com., 1970; vice chmn. Laurens County chpt. Am. Cancer Soc., 1956-64, exec. dir. Joanna Community Chest, 1950-64; mem. standing com. on communications Asso. Reformed Presbyn. Synod, 1970-72, chmn. standing com. on publs., 1973-75, mem. standing com. on hist. concerns, 1979—; mem. Laurens County Bd. Election Commrs., 1970—, now chmn.; mem. adv. council S.C. dist. SBA, 1974—; del. Current Strategy Forum, U.S. Naval War Coll., Newport, R.I., 1975; chmn. Clinton City Am. Revolution Bicentennial Com., 1975-76; mem. S.C. Ho. of Reps., 1940-42; mem. Clinton City Council, 1954-60, mayor pro tem, 1958-60; mem. Clinton City Employee Appeal Bd., 1973—, Clinton City Mgr. Adv. Com., 1973—; del. Nat. Dem. Conv., 1956; del. S.C. Dem. Conv., 1942, 46, 48, 52, 54, 56, 60; mem. Laurens County Dem. Exec. Com., 1950-60, chmn., 1948-50; county chmn. S. Carolinians for Ind. Electors, 1956; del. S.C. Republican Conv., 1968, 70, 72, 74, 78, 80; chmn. Laurens County Rep. Conv., 1972; trustee Erskine Coll., 1949-53, Joanna Found., 1955-66; trustee John de la Howe Sch., 1975—, sec., 1976—; bd. dirs. Clinton-Newberry Natural Gas Authority, 1954-60. Served from apprentice seaman to lt. USNR, 1942-46; ETO, PTO. Recipient George Washington Honor medal Freedoms Found., 1963; named Distinguished Tchr. of Year, U. S.C. at Spartanburg, 1975, hon. mem. Student Govt. Assn., 1977, hon. crewman USS Mount Baker. Mem. South Caroliniana Soc., Am. Assn. Indsl. Editors (dir. 1950, 58-60, pres. 1960-61), So., S.C. polit. sci. assns., U.S. Naval Inst., Internat. Platform Assn., Laurens County Hist. Soc. (charter), Omicron Delta Kappa. Mem. Asso. Ref. Presbyn. Ch. (ruling elder, 1947-70, life ruling elder 1971, trustee 1974—, supt. Sunday sch. 1939-60, now tchr. men's class). Club: Piedmont (Spartanburg, S.C.). Author: A History of the Providence Associate Reformed Presbyterian Church, 1977. Contbr. articles to trade jours., religious and hist. publs. Home: 103 W Maple St Clinton SC 29325 Office: U SC Spartanburg SC 29303

SLOAN, ROBERT SIDNEY, city ofcl.; b. Decatur, Ga., Mar. 20, 1940; s. Robert Sidney and Fannie Lou (Love) S.; B.A., Tex. A & M. Coll., 1962; m. Martha Pollock, Oct. 10, 1968. Reporter, Dallas Times Herald, 1964-68; asst. city sec. City of Dallas, 1968-76, city sec., 1976—. Served with U.S. Navy, 1962-64. Mem. Assn. Records Mgrs. and Adminstrs., Nat. Micrographics Assn., Internat. Inst. Mcpl. Clks., Soc. Southwest Archivists. Home: 9306 Clearwater Dr Dallas TX 75243 Office: City Hall Dallas TX 75201

SLOAN, SHARON BAIRD, ednl. adminstr.; b. Houston, June 3, 1946; d. Lewis Phillip and Mary Privott Baird; B.A., U. Tex., Austin, 1968; 1 son, Aaron Baird. Sec. to Rep. Atwell, Tex. Ho. of Reps., Austin, 1965; adminstrv. asst. to pres. Guidance Testing Assos., Austin, 1965-70; adminstrv. asst. to chmn. Spanish-Portuguese dept. U. Tex., Austin, 1970-75, adminstrv. asst. to dean div. of continuing edn., 1977-79, adminstrv. asst. to dir. Performing Arts Center, 1979—. Mem. U.S. Lawn Tennis Assn. (ranked 7th in mixed doubles, Tex., 1977), Capitol Area Tennis Assn., City Women's Soccer League, Delta Gamma, Sigma Delta Pi. Club: Courtyard Tennis. Home: 404 W 32d St Austin TX 78705 Office: Coll of Fine Arts Performing Arts Center U Tex Austin TX 78712

SLOANE, HARVEY, mayor Louisville. Office: Office of the Mayor City Hall 6th and Jefferson Sts Louisville KY 40202*

SLOOP, EDGAR WAYNE, clin. psychologist; b. Mooresville, N.C., Nov. 10, 1942; s. Edgar Brown and Sara Elizabeth S.; A.B. in Psychology, U. N.C., 1965; M.S., Fla. State U., 1967, Ph.D., 1969; m. Sharon Millard, June 17, 1962; 1 dau., Stephanie Leigh. Asst. prof. psychology Winthrop Coll., 1969-70; asst. prof. dept. behavioral medicine and psychiatry W.Va. U., 1970-73; dir. residential services Lynchburg (Va.) Tng. Sch. and Hosp., 1977-78; pvt. practice clin. psychology, Lynchburg, 1978—; cons. Old Dominion Job Corps Center, 1979. Bd. dirs. Info. and Referral Center, 1973-76, Big Bros. and Sisters of Central Va., 1979. Mem. Am. Psychol. Assn., Assn. Advancement of Behavior Therapy, Am. Assn. Mental Deficiency (pres. Va. chpt. 1979). Democrat. Methodist. Club: Hill City Exchange. Mem. editorial bd. Jour. Behavioral Medicine, 1978-79. Home: Route 2 Box 103 Forest VA 24551 Office: 9102 Timberlake Rd Lynchburg VA 24502

SLOUGH, WILLIAM FRED, mgmt. cons.; b. Kingsport, Tenn., Oct. 15, 1944; s. Fred William and Mary Dixie (Greer) S.; B.S. in Polit. Sci., East Tenn. State U., 1966, M. City Mgmt., 1972; m. Sandra O. Phibbs, June 27, 1970. Adminstrv. asst. City of Johnson City (Tenn.), 1971-73; city mgr. Brevard, N.C., 1973-74; mgmt. cons. S.C. Appalachian Council of Govts., Greenville, 1974-78, dir. services, 1978—. Asso. mem. Internat. City Mgmt. Assn. Club: Optimist (dir. 1972-73, v.p. 1973-74) (Brevard, N.C.). Author: Merger Feasibility in Sullivan County, Tennessee, 1970; Water Department Management in City X, 1972. Home: 105 Forest Hill Dr Taylors SC 29687 Office: Piedmont East Bldg Greenville SC 29687

SLOWIK, RICHARD ANDREW, air force officer; b. Detroit, Sept. 9, 1939; s. Louis Stanley and Mary Jean (Zaucha) S.; B.S., U.S. Air Force Acad., 1963; B.S. in Bus. Adminstrn., No. Mich. U., 1968; LL.B., LaSalle Extension U., 1969; M.B.A., Fla. Technol. U., 1972; M.S. in Adminstrn., Ga. Coll., 1979. Commd. 1st lt. U.S. Air Force, 1963, advanced through grades to lt. col.; pilot Craig AFB, Ala., 1963-64, Sawyer AFB, Mich., 1964-68; forward air controller Pacific Air Forces, South Vietnam, 1968-69; pilot SAC, McCoy AFB, Fla., 1969-71; asst. prof. aerospace studies Va. Poly. Inst. and State U., Blacksburg, 1972-76; br. chief current ops. br. Robins AFB, Ga., 1976—. Group ops. officer CAP, Marquette, Mich., 1967-68, Orlando, Fla., 1970-72. Decorated Air medal with 9 oak leaf clusters, Commendation Medal. Mem. Acad. of Mgmt., Assn. of M.B.A. Execs., Air Force Assn., Am. Def. Preparedness Assn., Am. Security Council, Order of Daedalians. Roman Catholic. Home: 108 Meriwood Dr Warner Robins GA 31093 Office: 19 Bombardment wing/Current Ops Br Robins Air Force Base GA 31093

SMALL, HYMAN JULIUS, mfg. co. exec.; b. Camden, N.J., Mar. 14, 1946; s. Samuel and Bertha (Bascove) S.; B.S., Temple U., 1969; M.A., Sam Houston State U., 1976; m. Catherine Claytor Rose, Dec. 3, 1977; children—William Marvin, Hudson Holmes. Tchr., Cherry Hill (N.J.) Sch. Bd. Edn., 1969-71; staff therapist Operation Concern, Cherry Hill, 1972; state project dir. Alston Wilkes Soc., S.C., 1974-76; divisional dir. human resource devel. J.P. Stevens, Stuart, Va., 1977—; cons. in field; condr. seminars. Mem. Am. Mgmt. Assn., Carolina Soc. Tng. and Devel., Am. Soc. Tng. and Devel. Contbr. articles to profl. jours. Home: 812 Corn Tassel Trail Martinsville VA 24112 Office: PO Box 519 Stuart VA 24171

SMALL, MELVIN D., physician, educator; b. Somerville, Mass., May 22, 1925; s. Sidney J. and Ida (Gelbsman) S.; student Boston U., 1942, U. Colo., 1942-43, Ga. Tchrs. Coll., 1943, U. N.H., 1943, State U. Ia., 1943-44, Boston Coll., 1950; A.B., U. Wis., 1950; postgrad. U. Vt., 1950-51, U. Lausanne, 1954-56, Harvard, 1958; M.D., Duke U., 1959; m. Judith Nogee, Dec. 23, 1962; children—Michael Dorian, Michele. Fellowship in gastrointestinal research with F. Ingelfinger, Mass. Meml. Hosp., Boston, 1951-53, with N. Zamcheck, Boston City Hosp., 1953-59; research asst. Boston U. Sch. Medicine, 1956-57; intern Georgetown U. Hosp., 1959-60, resident in medicine, 1960-61, chief gastrointestinal research, 1961-64; chief gastroenterology service Georgetown div. D.C. Gen. Hosp., 1964-68; pres. Gastroenterology Assos. Corp.; chmn. continuing edn. com. Alexandria (Va.) Hosp., also chmn. dept. medicine, 1974-77; instr. Georgetown U., 1961-67, clin. asst. prof. medicine, 1967—; bd. dirs. Jefferson Meml. Hosp., 1965-71. Witness, U.S. Senate Small Bus. Subcom. on Drug Pricing; chmn. Internat. Faculty for Postgrad. Med. Edn., No. Va. Consortium Continuing Med. Edn.; chmn. Nat. Council State Coms. on Continuing Med. Edn., 1975-79; mem. exec. com. and adv. bd. Found. for Continuing Med. Edn.; chmn. colorectal cancer project No. Va. chpt. Am. Cancer Soc. Served with AUS, 1943-45. Fellow Royal Soc. Medicine (London), Internat. Acad. Proctology; mem. Am. Physiol. Soc., Am. Inst. Nutrition, AAAS, AMA, Alexandria Med. Soc. (v.p. 1978-79), Am. Coll. Gastroenterology, A.C.P., Am. Gastroent. Assn., Am. Fedn. for Clin. Research, Am. Soc. Internal Medicine, Med. Soc. Va. (chmn. commn. continuing edn. 1975-78), Am., D.C. Met. (pres.) socs. gastrointestinal endoscopy. Contbr. articles to profl. jours. Home: 7648 Burford Dr McLean VA 22101 Office: 4600 King St Alexandria VA 22302 also 2616 Sherwood Hall Ln Alexandria VA 22306

SMALL, RONALD HUGH, hosp. pharmacist; b. Alamance County, N.C., Sept. 8, 1942; s. W.H. and Annabelle H. Small; B.S., U. N.C., 1966; m. Pamela Jo Beroth, Mar. 6, 1976; children—Ronald Gregory, Kimberly D. Staff, N.C. Bapt. Hosp., Winston-Salem, 1966-71, dir. pharmacy, 1975—; dir. pharmacy Med. Park Hosp., Winston-Salem, N.C., 1971-75; lectr. class for med. students Bowman Gray Sch. Medicine. Bd. dirs. Forsyth Health Planning Council, 1972-76. Mem. Am. Soc. Hosp. Pharmacists, Am. Pharm. Assn., N.C. Pharm. Assn., N.C. Soc. Hosp. Pharmacists, N.C. Acad. Pharmacy, N.C. Pharm. Polit. Action Com., Forsyth Pharm. Soc. (past pres.). Democrat. Baptist. Office: N C Bapt Hosp 300 S Hawthorne Rd Winston-Salem NC 27103

SMALL, SUSAN MANSFIELD, univ. exec.; b. Bar Harbor, Maine, Nov. 7, 1947; d. Kenneth Hambleton and Margaret Elizabeth (Bennett) Mansfield; student Colby Coll., 1965-67, U. New Haven, 1967-71; B.S., U. Maine, 1976; children by previous marriage—Mark M., Barbara E. Personnel specialist, coordinator EEO, Office Chancellor U. Maine, Bangor, 1974-77; payroll, personnel officer Tenn. Tech. U., Cookeville, 1977—. Mem. Employer Adv. Com. State of Tenn., 1979—, state steering com., 1980—; chmn. employer adv. com. Tenn. Job Service Improvement Program, Putman, White, Cumberland, Smith Counties, 1979—. Bus. and Profl. Women career advancement scholar, 1975-76; mem. Am. Soc. Personnel Adminstrn. (nat. com. equal employment opportunity, pres. Upper Cumberland chpt.), Coll. and Univ. Personnel Assn., Nat. Council EEO, Beta Gamma Sigma, Beta Sigma Phi (pres. Cookeville chpt.). Club: Parents without Partners (treas.). Home: 1124 Meadow Rd Cookeville TN 38501 Office: Box 5037 Tenn Tech U Cookeville TN 38501

SMALLEY, ARTHUR LOUIS, JR., engring. and constrn. co. exec.; b. Houston, Jan. 25, 1921; s. Arthur Louis and Ebby (Curry) S.; B.S. in Chem. Engring., U. Tex., 1942; m. Ruth Evelyn Britton, Mar. 18, 1948; children—Arthur Louis, III, Tom E. Dir. engring. Celanese Chem. Co., 1945-70; sales exec. Fish Engring. & Constrn. Co., 1970-72; pres., dir. Matthew Hall, Inc., Houston, 1972—; dir. Matthew Hall Internat., Ltd. Recipient Silver Beaver award Boy Scouts Am., 1963; registered profl. engr., Tex. Mem. Am. Soc. Chem. Engrs., Am. Petroleum Inst. Republican. Episcopalian. Clubs: Houston Rotary, Petroleum, Houston (Houston); Les Ambassadeurs, Oriental (London); Chemists (N.Y.C.). Internat. adv. bd. Ency. Chem. Processing and Design, 1975—. Home: 438 Hunterwood Dr Houston TX 77024 Office: 3428 Entex Bldg 1200 Milam St Houston TX 77002

SMALLEY, WILLIAM GENE, chem. co. exec.; b. Fox Lake, Ill., May 25, 1931; s. George Frederick and Gertrude Edith (Schmidt) S.; B.S. in Econs., Kans. State U., 1953; M.B.A. in Finance, Rollins Coll., Winter Park, Fla., 1970; m. Darlene Joy Schissler, Apr. 4, 1953; children—Kimberly Ann, Roxanne Joy. With Martin Marietta Corp., Orlando, Fla., 1956-70, finance mgr./controller, 1966-70; corp. tax and securities analyst Purisch, Levine, et al, C.P.A.'s, Miami, Fla., 1970-73; v.p. finance and adminstrn. Jim Jackson Contractor, Little Rock, Ark., 1973-76; dir. finance and adminstrn. Arkla Equipment Co., Shreveport, 1976-78; dir. fin. and adminstrn. Thiokol Chem. Corp., Shreveport, 1978—. Vice chmn. United Appeal and Cancer Soc. Served to capt. USMC, 1953-56. Recipient Distinguished Service award S.E. Blood Bank, 1970. Mem. Am. Inst. C.P.A.'s, Am. Mgmt. Assn., N.La. Mgmt. Assn. (treas.), Sales and Mktg. Execs. Assn., Little Rock Execs. Assn., ASME. Lutheran. Club: Masons. Author papers. Home: 918 Capt Shreve Dr Shreveport LA 71105 Office: PO Box 30058 Shreveport LA 71130

SMALLING, CLAUDE WILLIAM, III, chem. engr.; b. El Dorado, Ark., Aug. 7, 1946; s. Claude William and Carolyn (Reeves) S.; B.S. in Chem. Engring., U. Tex., 1970; m. Deborah Lynne Roach, Nov. 16, 1970; children—William Reeves, Michael Charles. Process engr. Reynolds Metals Co., Gregory, Tex., 1970-72; engr. Tex. Air Control Bd., Corpus Christi, 1972-78, sect. chief, Austin, 1978—, chief emissions standards and engring. sect., 1978—. Registered profl. engr., Tex. Mem. Air Pollution Control Assn. (chpt. chmn. 1977-78), Am. Inst. Chem. Engrs Home: Office: 6330 Hwy 290 E Austin TX 78723

SMALLY, DONALD JAY, cons. engr.; b. Cleve., Aug. 12, 1922; s. Daniel James and Alice (Rohrheimer) S.; B.M.E., U. Cin., 1949; m. Ruth Janet Glasser, July 8, 1944; children—Alan Jon, Leonard Arthur. Prodn. engr. N. Pensohoff, Inc., Cin., 1949-50; chief engr. Mosby Engring. Assos., Sarasota, Fla., 1952-55; prin. Smally, Wellford & Nalven, Inc., Sarasota, 1956—; partner Ardaman & Assos., Engring. Testing Labs., Sarasota, 1962-68. Mem. Manatee Jr. Coll. tech. adv. com., 1965—; v.p. YMCA, Sarasota, 1968-71; mem. adv. com. Vocat.-Tech. High Sch., Sarasota, 1968—; chmn. Vol. Talent Pool, 1973-76; sec.-treas. Civitan Found., 1965-79; bd. dirs. Suncoast Heart Assn., 1976. Served with AUS, 1942-45; ETO. Recipient Good Citizenship medal S.A.R., 1975; named Citizen of Year Sarasota Civitan Club, 1975, Engr. of Year, Sarasota-Manatee Engrs. Soc., 1976. Fellow Am. Cons. Engrs. Council, Fla. Engring. Soc. (pres., mem. Sarasota County C. of C. (dir. 1962-65, 70-73), Cons. Engrs. Council, Fla. Cons. Engrs. Council (pres. 1968), Fla. Soc. Profl. Land Surveyors (pres. Manasota chpt. 1973), Am. Water Resources Assn., Sarasota Manatee Engring. Soc. Home: 3986 Overlook Bend Sarasota FL 33580 Office: 133 S McIntosh Sarasota FL 33582

SMART, CLIFTON MURRAY, JR., architect, univ. adminstr.; b. Blytheville, Ark., Aug. 8, 1933; s. Clifton Murray and Elizabeth Haley S.; B.Arch., Tulane U., 1976; M.S., U. Ill., 1960; m. Carolyn Jo Jones, Aug. 22, 1959; children—Clifton Murray, John David. Instr. dept. city planning U. Ill., 1959-50; asso. Uzzell S. Branson, Blytheville, Ark., 1960-66; mem. faculty Sch. Architecture, U. Ark., Fayetteville, 1966—, dean, prof., 1977— Deacon 1st Baptist Ch., 1970—. Served with U.S. Army, 1957-59 Mem. AIA, Soc. Archtl. Historians, Fayetteville C. of C., Omicron Delta Kappa, Tau Sigma Delta, Sigma Alpha Epsilon. Democrat. Author: (with C. Carnes) City Appearance and the Law, 1972. Home: 858 Woodlawn Fayetteville AR 72701 Office: Walker Hall 209 U Ark Fayetteville AR 72701

SMART, WILLIAM EDWARD, JR., arts adminstr., educator; b. Jefferson City, Mo., Feb. 28, 1933; s. William Edward and May Ferne (Whiteside) S.; A.B., Kenyon Coll., 1955; M.A., U. Conn., 1960; postgrad. U. Birmingham (Eng.), 1964-66; m. Marymartha Kistenmacher, Aug. 27, 1955 (div. 1975); children—Paul, David, Anne Fern; m. 2d, Juliana Frosch, Dec. 26, 1976; 1 dau., Sarah. Instr. English, U. Conn., Storrs, 1955-56, 58-60; field rep. Harcourt, Brace & Co., 1956-57; instr Skidmore Coll., Saratoga Springs, N.Y., 1960-64; asso. prof. English Sweet Briar (Va.) Coll., 1966—; dir. Va. Center for Creative Arts, Sweet Briar, 1975—; mem. adv. panel Va. Com. for Arts, 1977-80; cons. Bravo Arts. Fulbright grantee, 1964-66. Club: 13. Author: Eight Modern Essayists, 1965, 3d edit., 1980; Women & Men/Men & Women, 1975; contbr. stories, poems and essays to The Reporter, The Carleton Miscellany, The Kenyon Rev., The New Republic, others; adv. editor New Va. Rev., 1979—. Address: Mount San Angelo Sweet Briar VA 24595

SMARTT, JOHN MADISON, lawyer; b. Smartt, Tenn., Feb. 24, 1919; s. Robert White and Sarah Alma (Roggli) S.; B.S., U. Tenn., 1942, J.D., 1948; m. Harriet Chapin, June 9, 1943; children—John Madison, Jane (Mrs. Roy D. Stroud), Douglas D., Robert W., III. Admitted to Tenn. bar 1948; since practiced in McMinnville; dir. alumni affairs U. Tenn., Knoxville, 1948-69; mem. firm Fowler, Rowntree, Fowler & Robertson, Knoxville, 1969—; life mem. 6th Circuit Jud. Conf. Served to capt. AUS, 1942-46; lt. col. Res. Mem. Phi Delta Phi. Democrat. Presbyterian (mem. session 1970-73). Club: Kiwanis. Home: 4603 Holston Hills Rd Knoxville TN 37914 Office: 7th Floor First Tenn Bank Bldg Knoxville TN 37902

SMARTT, MARVIN MILLER, hosp. adminstr.; b. Hopkinsville, Ky., Nov. 11, 1941; s. Ransom Larkin and Maude (Miller) S.; B.S., L.I. U., 1974, M.Profl. Studies, 1976; m. Jacqueline Thoroughgood, Nov. 11, 1971; children—Moravia Marie, Marnese Marie, Marnique Miller. Mem. adminstrv. staff N.Y. Med. Center, N.Y.C., 1963-71; asst. dir. Bellevue Hosp. Center, N.Y.C., 1971-77; asst. hosp. adminstr. patient services Charity Hosp., New Orleans, 1977—; lectr. N.Y. Med. Sch., 1974-75, N.Y. Police Acad., 1974-77. Mem. adv. bd. N.Y.C. Bd. Edn., 1974-76; br. campaign mgr. Lindsey for Mayor. Served with AUS, 1966-70; Vietnam. Decorated Silver Star, Bronze Star. Mem. Am. Mgmt. Assn., Am. Hosp. Assn., Public Hosp. Assn., La. Young Adminstrn. Assn., Nat. Assn. Hosp. Execs. Democrat. Mem. Ch. of Christ. Club: Zulu. Office: 1532 Tulane Ave New Orleans LA 70140

SMEAD, LUCILLE CLARK, speech pathology cons.; b. Buckingham County, Va.; d. Michael Evan and Elizabeth (Morgan) Jones; Tchr.'s cert., Madison Coll., 1934; B.S., Longwood Coll., 1938; M.Ed., U. Va., 1959; m Llewellyn Smead, Feb. 1, 1980. Tchr. public schs., Virginia Beach, N.C., 1932-56; asst. prin. Portsmouth (Va.) public schs., 1960-63, prin., 1956-60, dir. speech pathology, 1964-67; speech cons. State Dept. Edn., Richmond, Va., 1967—; staff speech clinician Kirk-Cone Rehab. Center, Portsmouth, 1959-61; pvt. practice speech pathology, Richmond, 1959-67; condr. workshops for speech clinicians and classroom tchrs., Va.; dir., performer TV shows to depict diagnostic and evaluation aspects of speech pathology, 1965-66. Bd. dirs. Children's Theater of Tidewater, 1960-66, Norfolk Civic Ballet, 1960-67, Tidewater Arthritis Found., 1960-66, Portsmouth Little Theater, 1960-66, PTA, Portsmouth, 1942-67, Portsmouth Community Concert, 1946-67, Nat. Com. of Arts for Handicapped, 1975-80, Va. Com. on Aging, 1977-79. Fellow Am. Speech and Hearing Assn. (cert. clin. competence); mem. Portsmouth Edn. Assn. (pres. 1965-66), Organized Portsmouth Area Ret. Tchrs. Assn. (pres. 1960-61), AAUW, Va. Edn. Assn., NEA, Va. Speech and Hearing Assn., Council of Speech and Hearing Cons. in State Depts. Edn., Madison Coll. Alumni Assn., Longwood Coll. Alumni Assn., U. Va. Alumni Assn., Nat. Assn. state Dirs. Spl. Edn., Council Exceptional Children, Speech Assn. Eastern States, Profl. Women Orgns. of State Dept. Edn., Va. Govtl. Employees Assn., Va. Mus.

Fine Arts, Va. Hist. Soc., Portsmouth Hist. Soc., Internat. Platform Assn., English Speaking Union, Va. Soc. for Preservation of Antiquities, Portsmouth Friends of the Mus. Presbyterian. Clubs: Portsmouth Music (pres. 1960-64), Order Eastern Star (worthy matron 1953-54), Portsmouth Women's, Soroptimist, Richmond Brandon's Woman's. Contbr. articles to profl. jours. Home: 104 W Franklin St Richmond VA 23220 also 205 Butler Ave St Simons Island GA 31522 Office: PO Box 6Q Richmond VA 23216

SMEAD, WILLIAM JACKSON, ophthalmologist; b. Camden, Ark., Sept. 27, 1945; s. William and Vivian (Jackson) S.; B.A., B.S., U. Ark., 1968, M.D., 1970; m. Teddy Grace, June 8, 1968; children—Emily, Elizabeth, Ellen. Intern, Univ. Hosp., Little Rock, 1970-71; resident in ophthalmology U. Ark., Little Rock, 1974-78; practice medicine specializing in ophthalmology, Greeneville, Tenn., 1978—. Served in USAF, 1971-74. Diplomate Am. Bd. Ophthalmology. Mem. AMA, Tenn. Med. Assn., Greene County Med. Soc. (sec. 1980—), Am. Acad. Ophthalmology. Club: Lions (dir. 1979—). Home: 1204 Christy Ct Greeneville TN 37743 Office: 725 E Church St Greeneville TN 37743

SMITH, ADA MAE, educator, psychologist; b. Anson, Tex., Oct. 29, 1929; d. Loyd Isaac and Ada Grace (Turner) Blanton; student Lillie Jolly Sch. Nursing, 1948-51; B.S., U. Houston, 1954; M.Th., M.R.E., Southwestern Baptist Theol. Sem., 1957; M.Ed., U. Tex., 1965, Ph.D., 1970; m. Howard Lee Smith, May 11, 1956; children—Donna Lynn, David Lee. With purchasing dept. Sheffield Steel Co., 1947-49; field cons. Tex. Woman's Missionary Union, 1954-56; So. Bapt. missionary to Nigeria, W.Africa, 1957-59, Ghana, W.Africa, 1959-65; counselor Tex. Schs., 1965-69; counseling cons. Region 7, U.S. Office Edn., 1969-70; prof. psychology, dir. testing, counselor Dallas County Community Coll. Dist., 1970—; pvt. practice psychology, 1974—; prof. psychology Richland Coll., pres. faculty, 1979-80; also lectr., seminar leader; mem. Gov.'s Human Resources Seminar, 1974; ednl. cons. HEW, 1974-75; mem. coordinating bd. Adv. Com. for Academic Due Process, Tenure and Acad. Freedom, 1975-77; chmn. pro tem Inter-Coll. Council. Election judge, Garland, Tex., Dallas County Community Coll. Dist., 1975—; active March of Dimes; precinct chmn. Democratic party, 1976—, del. Tex. State Dem. Conv., 1976, candidate state Dem. exec. com., 1976. U.S. Office Edn. grantee, 1969-70; Acad. scholar U. Houston, 1952-53; scholar Lillie Jolly Sch. Nursing, 1948-51, Delta Kappa Gamma state and internat. scholar, 1969-70; licensed psychologist, Tex. Mem. Am., Dallas psychol. assns., Tex. Jr. Coll. Tchrs. Assn. (Meritorious Service awards 1971—, 2d v.p. 1971-72, 1st v.p. 1973-74, pres. 1974-75, exec. com. 1972-76, del. Am. Personnel and Guidance Assn. Senate 1970, task force profl. cons., ad hoc com. acad. freedom, tenure and retrenchment, chmn. resolutions com. 1970-71), Tex. State Tchrs. Assn. (life), Biofeedback Research Soc., Tex. Psychol. Assn., Am. Law Psychol. Assn., Delta Kappa Gamma, Kappa Delta Pi. Author: Study Guide for Introduction to Psychology, 1975. Contbr. articles to profl. jours. and religious publs. Home: 2417 Northridge Dr Garland TX 75043 Office: 401 W Centerville Rd Garland TX 75041 also Richland Coll 12800 Abrams St Dallas TX 75243

SMITH, ALBERT KIRK, coll. adminstr.; b. Salineville, Ohio, Dec. 21, 1922; s. Albert Thompson and Elizabeth Rachel S.; B.A., Mt. Union Coll., 1952; M.Ed., Kent State U., 1959; Ph.D., Case Western Res. U., 1974; m. Evelyn Louise Hirst, Jan. 23, 1944; children—Albert James, Alan Eugene. Accountant, Alliance Mfg. Co. (Ohio), 1946-50; owner, operator ins. agy., Salineville, 1948-59; tchr. pub. schs., Ohio, 1952-59, Dade County Schs., Miami, 1959-61; instr. accounting Miami Dade Community Coll., Miami, 1961-65, chmn. bus. dept., 1963-65, dean students, 1965-69, asst. to pres., 1969-70, exec. asst. to chief adminstr., 1970-79, dean for adminstrn., 1979—; cons. in field. Served with Signal Corps, U.S. Army, 1943-46; ETO. Found. Econ. Edn. fellow, 1964. Coll. chmn. United Fund campaign, 1970-76. Mem. Am. Assn. Jr. Colls., Am. Coll. Personnel Assn. (dir. Body Commn. XI), Am. Assn. Higher Edn., Nat. Council Student Devel., Nat. Assn. Environ. Edn. Republican. Methodist. Clubs: Order Eastern Star, Masons. Home: 10300 SW 92d St Miami FL 33176 Office: 11011 SW 104th St Miami FL 33176

SMITH, ALEXANDER GOUDY, astronomer; b. Clarksburg, W.Va., Aug. 12, 1919; s. Edgell Ohr and Helen (Reitz) S.; B.S., Mass. Inst. Tech., 1943; Ph.D., Duke U., 1949; m. Mary Elizabeth Ellsworth, Apr. 19, 1942; children—Alexander Goudy, Sally Jean. Physicist radiation lab. Mass. Inst. Tech., 1943-46; research asst. Duke U., 1946-48; mem. faculty U. Fla., Gainesville, 1948—, prof. physics and astronomy, 1956—, chmn. dept. astronomy, 1962-71, acting dean Grad. Sch., 1971-73; dir. U. Fla. Radio Obs., 1957—; cons. USN, USAF. Fellow Optical Soc. Am., Am. Phys. Soc., AAAS; mem. Soc. Photog. Scis. and Engrs., Am. Astron. Soc. (editor Photo-Bull. 1975—), Astron. Soc. Pacific, Internat. Astron. Union, Internat. Sci. Radio Union, Fla. Acad. Scis. (pres. 1963-64; medal 1965), Assn. Univs. Research in Astronomy (dir., cons.), Sigma Xi (nat. lectr. 1966, past pres. Fla. chpt.), Sigma Pi Sigma. Republican. Christian Scientist. Club: Athenaeum (past pres.). Author: Radio Exploration of the Sun, 1966; co-author: Microwave Magnetrons, 1958; Radio Exploration of the Planetary System, 1964; contbr. articles to profl. jours. Address: 1417 NW 17th St Gainesville FL 32605

SMITH, ALFORD LEE, paper mfg. co. exec.: b. Turkey, N.C., Nov. 1, 1941; s. Alton Clifton and Margaret Jane (McCullen) S.; B.S., N.C. State U., 1963; postgrad. Harvard U., 1979; m. Martha Anne Barr, June 9, 1963; children—Lee Anne, Alford Lee, Michael Jeffrey. Process engr. Tenn. River Pulp & Paper Co., Counce, 1963-66; plant chemist Austell Box Bd. Corp. (Ga.), 1966-69, v.p., gen. mgr., 1969-78, sr. v.p., 1978—, also dir.; gen. mgr. Sweetwater Paper Bd. Co., Austell, 1972—. Paper div. chmn. United Way Met. Atlanta, 1978-79; bd. dirs. N.C. State Pulp and Paper Found., 1979-81. Mem. TAPPI, Am. Paper Inst. Democrat. Baptist. Club: Rotary (pres. Austell 1974-75). Home: 1334 Arden Dr Marietta GA 30060 Office: Sweetwater Paper Bd Co PO Box 665 Austell GA 30001

SMITH, ALFRED GLAZE, JR., economist, educator; b. Urbana, Ill., Dec. 28, 1913; s. Alfred Glaze and Lucy Catharine (Prutsman) S.; A.B., Columbia U., 1934, A.M., 1939, Ph.D., 1954; m. Katharine Cushing Brown, May 9, 1936; children—Alfred Glaze III, LeRoy Fairchild. With personal div. S.H. Kress & Co., 1936-38; instr. econs. U. S.C., 1938-42, asst. prof., 1942-47, asso. prof., 1947-54, prof., 1954—, head dept. econs., 1958-70, asso. v.p. instrn., 1974-76; Fulbright prof., Bologna, Italy, 1963-64. Owner, operator farm, Lexington County, S.C. Served as officer USNR, 1943-46; comdr. Res. Mem. Am., So. econ. assns., Econ. History Assn. Author: Economic Readjustment of an Old Cotton State: South Carolina, 1820-1860, 1958. Home: 1816 Enoree Ave Columbia SC 29205

SMITH, ALFRED GOUD, educator; b. The Hague, Netherlands, Aug. 20, 1921; s. William G. and Joan (Wraslouski) S.; B.A. (scholar), U. Mich., 1943; M.A., U. Wis., 1947, Ph.D., 1956; m. Britta Helen Bonazzi, May 30, 1946. Far East analyst Dept. State, 1945-46; instr., acting instr. U. Wis., 1946-50; supr. linguistics Trust Ter. of Pacific Islands, 1950-53; asst. prof. anthropology Antioch Coll., 1953-56; asso. prof. anthropology, arts and linguistics Emory U., 1956-62; prof. anthropology, and community service and public affairs U. Oreg., 1963-73; dir., prof. Center for Communication Research, U. Tex., Austin, 1973-78, prof. communication and anthropology Sch. Communication, 1978—; cons. Served to 1st lt. OSS, U.S. Army, 1942-45. Am. Council Learned Socs. fellow, 1942. Fellow AAAS, Am. Anthrop. Assn.; mem. Internat. Communication Assn. (pres. 1973-74), Soc. for Intercultural Edn., Tng. and Research. Clubs: Rotary, Town and Gown. Author: Communication and Culture, 1956; Communication and Status, 1966; Cognitive Styles in Law Schools, 1979; contbr. articles to profl. jours. Home: 1401 Ethridge Ave Austin TX 78703 Office: Sch of Communication U Tex Austin TX 78712

SMITH, ALFRED SAMUEL, parasitologist, ednl. adminstr.: b. Miami, Fla., Jan. 7, 1940; s. Samuel and Birda (Washington) S.; B.S., Bethune Cookman Coll., 1962; M.S., Howard U., 1964, Ph.D., 1969; m. Patricia Elaine Moore, Aug. 4, 1964; 1 son, Alfred Redie. Instr. biology Gibbs Jr. Coll., St. Petersburg, Fla., 1964-65; asst. prof. biology Tuskegee Inst. (Ala.), 1969-72, asso. prof., 1974-76; asso. prof. biology, asst. v.p. for acad. affairs Ala. State U., Montgomery, 1976—; rev. panelist Sci. Faculty Profl. Devel. Program, NSF, 1978. Asso. lay leader Met. United Meth. Ch., Montgomery, tchr. young adults Sunday sch. class; pres. Washington Public PTA, Tuskegee, Ala., 1975-76. Mem. Am. Soc. Parasitologists, Helminthological Soc. Washington, Nat. Sci. Tchrs. Assn., Am. Assn. for Higher Edn., AAAS, Assn. for Supervision and Curriculum Devel., Am. Assn. U. Adminstrs., Sigma Xi, Phi Beta Sigma, Phi Delta Kappa. Club: Masons. Home: 4054 Strathmore Dr Montgomery AL 36116 Office: 915 S Jackson St Montgomery AL 36101

SMITH, ALLEN FRANKLIN, SR., educator; b. Fort Worth, Aug. 10, 1917; s. Emory Cecil and Eva Vivian (Mathis) S.; A.B., Jarvis Christian Coll., 1942; M.S., Prairie View A. and M. U., 1946; certificate alcohol studies U. Ga., 1964; m. Isabell Marshall, July 8, 1956; children—Cheryl Diane, Allen Franklin. Asst. prof. phys. edn., athletic dir., coach Jarvis Christian Coll., Hawkins, Tex., 1946-57; backfield coach, head baseball coach and golf coach Jackson (Miss.) State U., 1957-59; dean students, 1960, dean men, 1961, dir., organizer security dept., 1961, also asst. prof. health and phys. edn., golf coach; asso. VA, 1964-66. Mem. voter registration com., Hawkins, Tex., 1955. Served with M.C., USN, 1942-45. Recipient Centennial Appreciation Certificate, Jackson State U., 1977, Certificate of Appreciation, United Christian Ch., 1977. Mem. Am. Assn. Health and Phys. Edn., Miss. Assn. Health and Phys. Edn., Miss. Alumni Alcohol and Drug Studies, Omega Psi Phi. Democrat. Mem. Christian Ch. Home: 3658 Albemarle Rd Jackson MS 39213 Office: Jackson State U Jackson MS 39217

SMITH, ALLIE MAITLAND, univ. dean; b. Lumberton, N.C., June 9, 1934; s. Allie McCoy and Emma Hattie (Wright) S.; B.M.E. with honors, N.C. State U., 1956, M.S., 1961, Ph.D., 1966; m. Sarah Louise Whitlock, June 16, 1957; children—Sara Leianne, Hollis Duval, Meredith Lorren. Asso. engr. Martin Co., Balt., 1956-57; mem. tech. staff Bell Telephone Labs., Burlington, N.C., 1957-62; research project engr. Research Triangle Inst., Durham, 1962-66; research supr. Arnold Research Orgn., Inc., Arnold Air Force Sta., Tenn., 1966-79; instr. N.C. State U., 1958-60, asst. prof. (extension), Raleigh, 1961-62; adj. prof. U. Tenn., Tullahoma, 1967-79, Knoxville, 1974; dean Sch. Engring., prof. mech. engring. U. Miss., University, 1979—. Asso. fellow Am. Inst. Aeros. and Astronautics (thermophysics tech. com. 1973-77, chmn. 1976-77, session chmn. 11th aerospace scis. meeting 1973, session chmn. ann. meeting 1978, chmn. conf. with ASME 1974, 78, gen. chmn. thermophysics conf., 1975, editorial coms. publs. 1973-78, mem. energy activities task force 1976—, asso. editor jour. 1975-77, publs. com. 1976—, tech. program com. aerospace scis. meeting 1978, terrestrial energy systems tech. com. 1978-81, chmn. 1980-81; Thermophysics award 1978; gen. chmn. aerospace scis. meeting 1979); mem. Am. Soc. Engring. Edn. (long range planning com. 1975—), AAUP, ASME (K-12 tech. com. on aero. and astronautical heat transfer, session chmn. Nat. Heat Transfer Conf. 1977), N.Y. Acad. Scis., Sigma Xi, Phi Kappa Phi, Tau Beta Pi, Pi Tau Sigma. Baptist. Author: Fundamentals of Silicon Integrated Device Technology, Vol. 1: Oxidation, Diffusion and Epitaxy, 1967; contbr. articles to profl. jours.; editor: Radiative Transfer and Thermal Control, 1976; Thermophysics of Spacecraft and Outer Planet Entry Probes, 1977; reviewer for Progress in Astronautics and Aeronautics, Jour. Franklin Inst., Am. Inst. Aeros. and Astronautics Jour., ASME Jour. Heat Transfer and Internat. Jour. Heat and Mass Transfer; proposal reviewer NSF. Home: 1714 Country Club Dr Tullahoma TN 37388 Office: Sch Engring U Miss University MS 38677

SMITH, ANGIE FRANK, JR., lawyer; b. Detroit, Tex., Nov. 3, 1915; s. A. Frank and Bess Patience (Crutchfield) S.; B.A., Rice U., 1937; LL.B., U. Tex., 1940; LL.D., Southwestern U., Tex., 1976; m. Mary Hannah, June 15, 1939; children—Tweed Smith Kezziah, Karen Smith Rehm, A. Frank III, Allison Smith Campbell, Leslie Ann. Mng. partner Vinson & Elkins, and predecessor; dir. Cullen/Frost Bankers, Inc., Cullen Center Bank & Trust, Tex. Eastern Corp. Adv. bd. Internat. Oil and Gas Edn. Center, Internat. and Comparative Law Center; research fellow, trustee Southwestern Legal Found.; trustee, chmn. bd., mem. exec. com. Meth. Hosp., Houston, Southwestern U., Georgetown, Tex.; trustee Baylor Coll. Medicine, Tex. Med. Center, Cullen Found.; bd. dirs. Houston Symphony Soc., Tex. Assn. Taxpayers, Tex. Research League. Served with USNR, 1942-45. Fellow Am., Tex. bar founds.; mem. Am. Judicature Soc., Sons Republic Tex., Knight San Jacinto, Tex. Philos. Soc., Am., Tex., Houston bar assns., Houston C. of C. (dir.), Order of Coif, Phi Delta Phi. Methodist. Clubs: River Oaks Country; Broadmoor Golf, Garden of Gods (Colorado Springs). Home: 3420 Piping Rock Lane Houston TX 77027 Office: First City Nat Bank Bldg Houston TX 77002

SMITH, ANNE TAYLOR, chemist; b. Draper, Utah, Sept. 29, 1938; d. James LaDell and Mildred Louise (Aiken) Taylor; B.S. magna cum laude (Univ. scholar, 1955-59), Furman U., 1959; M.A. (So. fellow, 1959, NDEA fellow 1959-62), U. Utah, 1962; m. William Jerry Smith, Sept. 27, 1969; children—Carl Andrew, Millicent Mae, Stephanie Anne. Research chemist Gastroenterology div. VA Hosp., Salt Lake City, 1962-66; clin. chemist VA Hosp., Oteen, N.C., 1966-68; asst. clin. chemist Greenville (S.C.) Gen. Hosp., 1968-73, clin. chemist, 1973-75, adminstrv. officer lab., 1975—; faculty Sch. Med. Tech., Greenville Hosp. System, 1968—. Leader Cub Scouts, Boy Scouts Am., Greenville, 1980—. Recipient Cert. of Apprecation, CETA program, 1976. Mem. Am. Assn. Clin. Chemistry, Clin. Lab. Mgmt. Assn., Hand and Torch, Sigma Xi, Chi Beta Phi. Mormon. Clubs: Utah Oratorio Soc., Tabernacle Choir. Contbr. articles to profl. jours. Home: 7 Rangeview Circle Greenville SC 29611 Office: 701 Grove Rd Greenville SC 29605

SMITH, ANNINIAS CORNELIUS, educator; b. Pitt County, N.C., Sept. 11, 1944; s. Hulbert Hooker and Martha (Smith) Hooker; B.S., N.C. Agrl. and Tech. State U., 1966; postgrad. Md. State U.; East Carolina U. Community Outreach worker Food and Med. Services program Pitt County Dept. Social Services, 1968-71; mentally handicapped specialist Pitt County Schs., 1971—; coach Spl. Olympics. Sec. Little Creek Free Will Baptist Ch. Served with U.S. Army, 1967-69. Mem. Jaycees, N.C. Assn. Educators, Assn. Classroom Tchrs., NEA, Assn. Retarded Persons, NAACP. Democrat. Clubs: Greater Men Fellowship, Am. Legion, Masons, Shriners. Home: 1300 Ward St Greenville NC 27834 Office: PO Box 189 Winterville NC 28590

SMITH, ARTHUR REGINALD, home bldg. and land devel. co. exec.; b. Spartanburg, S.C., July 4, 1942; s. Arthur and Dorothy May (Byars) S.; student N.C. State U., 1960-62; A.S., Central Piedmont Coll., 1974; m. Judy Beal, June 6, 1964; children—Artie, Allison. Vice-pres. Arthur Smith Studios, 1964-69; account exec. Mission Broadcasting, 1969-71; v.p. Ralph Squires Constrn. Co., Charlotte, N.C., 1971-75; pres. Smith-Allen Co., Charlotte, 1975—, Devel. Marketing Enterprises, Charlotte, 1976—, Ash Devel. Co., Inc., Charlotte, 1978—; dir. Clay Music Corp., Charlotte, 1964—. Pres., N.C. Homebuilders Sales and Marketing Council, 1979; Mem. Nat. Assn. Homebuilders (dir.), Nat. Assn. Homebuilders Sales and marketing Council (life mem. Million Dollar Circle), Charlotte Homebuilders Assn. (treas. 1979, v.p. 1980), N.C. Homebuilders Assn. Democrat. Clubs: Carmel Country, Myrtle Beach Tennis. Author: Power of Love, 1959; You Are the One, 1959. Home: 5000 Rea Rd Matthews NC 28105 Office: 5507 Monroe Rd Charlotte NC 28212

SMITH, B. J., artist; b. Beaver, Okla., Aug. 22, 1931; s. Oliver Lindell and Mattie Sue (Harper) S.; B.F.A., Okla. State U., 1955; M.F.A., U. Okla., 1959. Asst. to dir. Okla. Art Center, Oklahoma City, 1961-65; asst. prof. art Okla. State U., Stillwater, 1965—, dir. Gardiner Art Gallery, 1965—; one-man shows: Town and Gown Theater, Stillwater, 1967, Summit Gallery, Oklahoma City, 1972, U. Okla. Mus. Art, Norman, 1973; two-man shows: CAF Gallery, Oklahoma City, 1968, Gardiner Art Gallery, Okla. State U., Stillwater, 1971; group shows: Philbrook Art Center, Tulsa, 1958, 64, 65, 67, 68, 73, Okla. Art Center, Oklahoma City, 1962-64, 68, 70, Springfield (Mo.) Art Mus., 1966, 70, 71, CAF Gallery, 1966, Kennedy Center Performing Arts, Washington, 1976, State Capitol Rotunda, Oklahoma City, 1979, Memphis State U., 1979, Wichita State U., 1980, others. Served with AUS, 1955-57. Recipient Purchase award 9th Midwest Biennial Joslyn Art Mus., Omaha, 1966; Okla. Biennial 1967 Okla. Art Center, 1967, painting award 38th Okla. Artists Ann., Philbrook Art Center, Tulsa, 1968. Home: 2132 W Sunset Dr Stillwater OK 74074

SMITH, BARBARA ANN, accountant; b. Dallas, May 6, 1935; d. George Jefferson and Ina Pearl (Nowlin) Gardner; Asso. Mid. Mgmt., Mountain View Jr. Coll., 1975; div.; children—Cynthia Marie Dixon, Robert Lee Dixon. Asst. cashier U.S. Rubber Co., Dallas, 1954-57; sec.-treas. Am. Graphics Co., Dallas, 1974-79; pres. Am. Way Credit Union, Dallas, 1974-76; sec.-treas. Am. Legal Printing Co., Dallas, 1964-79, Abco Inc., Dallas, 1964-79, Am. Poster & Printing Co., Dallas, 1964-79; asst. sec.-treas. Am. Equity Press Inc., Dallas, 1974-79; partner MS Services, Dallas and Chgo., 1979—; v.p., sec. Big D Bindery, Dallas, 1980—. Home: 3515 Brown 109 Dallas TX 75219 Office: Wimbledon Pl Suite 109 Dallas TX 75219 also Mdse Mart Chicago IL 60654

SMITH, BARRY SAMUEL, physician; b. Windber, Pa., Jan. 15, 1947; s. Bernard and Irene (Snyder) S.; B.S., Pa. State U., 1967, M.D., Jefferson Med. Coll., 1969; m. Jane A. Ostrosky, May 3, 1969; children—Brenda Kristine, Christopher Michael, Eric Wade. Intern, Reading (Pa.) Hosp., 1969-70; resident in phys. medicine and rehab. Inst. Phys. Medicine and Rehab., Louisville, 1970-73, jr. partner, 1975-78, asso. med. dir., 1978—; adj. asst. prof. U. Louisville. Served with M.C., USN, 1973-75. Mem. AMA, Ky. Med. Assn., Jefferson County Med. Soc., Acad. and Congress of Phys. Medicine and Rehab. Republican. Methodist. Club: Filson (Louisville). Office: 220 Abraham Flexner Way Louisville KY 40202

SMITH, BARRY WILFRED, data processing services co. exec.; b. West Point, Nebr., Nov. 24, 1942; s. Herbert Andrew and Hilda Helen (Holz) S.; B.A., U. Kans., 1964; M.B.A., Harvard U., 1967; m. Mary Alice Moore, June 12, 1965; children—Allison, Eric, Meredith. Programmer, systems analyst Sanitary Towel & Laundry Co., Lincoln, Nebr., 1967-70; pres. Unisystems Inc., Dallas, 1970—; dir. Matrix Control Systems, Inc. Mem. Textile Rental Supply Assn. Am., S.W. Linen and Indsl. Supply Assn., S.E. Textile Rental Assn. Home: 12407 Cedar Bend Dr Dallas TX 75234 Office: 2840 Walnut Hill Ln Dallas TX 75229

SMITH, BAYNARD RENNICK, electronic co. exec.; b. Chattanooga, Dec. 18, 1921; s. John Baynard and Alma Ester (Rennick) S.; student U. Chattanooga, 1940, U. Tenn., 1941-43; student U.S. Naval Acad., 1944; m. Peggy Norton Speir, Feb. 16, 1945; children—Susan, David, Alan, Margaret, Carolyn. Foreman, Am. Lava Corp., Chattanooga, 1948-52; dept. head Gen. Ceramics Corp., Keaston, N.J., 1952-54; v.p., prin. Mitronics, Inc., Murray Hill, N.J., 1954-67; v.p. Electro Oxide Corp., Palm Beach Gardens, Fla., 1973—; pres. Intermetallics Corp., North Palm Beach, Fla., 1972—, also dir.; chmn. bd. CER-TEK, Inc., El Paso, Tex., 1977—. Served with USNR, 1943-45. Decorated Silver Star medal. Mem. AAAS. Republican. Methodist. Patentee field metallurgy and tech. ceramics. Home: 701 Lakeside Dr North Palm Beach FL 33408

SMITH, BENJAMIN DENNIS, research chemist; b. Norfolk, Va., July 16, 1938; s. Prentis P. and Edwyne (Parker) S.; B.S. in Chemistry, Coll. William and Mary, 1960; Ph.D. in Chemistry, Ga. Inst. Tech., 1966. Research chemist Naval Surface Weapons Center, Dahlgren, Va., 1960—. Recipient Outstanding Young Man of Year award, 1971-72; Naval Surface Weapons Center Outstanding Performance award, 1972. Mem. Am. Chem. Soc. (chmn. radio and TV com. of Va. sect.), Va. Acad. Scis., N.Y. Acad. Scis., U.S. Coast Guard Aux. (public edn. officer and public relations officer Flotilla 14-5). Home: Potomac Gardens Apts 93A PO Box 1026 Dahlgren VA 22448 Office: Naval Surface Weapons Center Code G-54 Dahlgren VA 22448

SMITH, BENJAMIN FRANKLIN, council ofcl.; b. Holcomb, Miss., Dec. 22, 1917; s. Ben F. and Allene (DeShazo) S.; B.S., Delta State Tchrs. Coll., 1939; postgrad. George Peabody U.; m. Mary Alyce Bounds, Aug. 31, 1941; children—James Winfred, Lelia Elaine. Instr. biol. sci. Arcola (Miss.) Sch., 1939-41, Jackson City Sch., 1941-42; tng. officer VA, 1946-47; asst. mgr. Delta Council, 1947-49, sec., mgr., 1949-57, exec. v.p., 1957—; mgmt. rep. Labor Mgmt. Manpower Com. Region IV, 1957-64; mem. Nat. Cotton Adv. Com. Served as capt. AUS, 1942-46. Recipient Man of Year award Progressive Farmer, 1962; Spl. Service award U.S. Weather Bur., 1964; Outstanding Alumni award Delta State Coll., 1964; Golden Anniversary Fed. Land Bank award, 1967; Silver Beaver Boy Scouts Am. Mem. Miss., Nat., So. assns. C. of C. execs., Delta State Alumni Assn. Methodist. Club: Lions. Author articles in tech. jours.; contbr. to Delta Looks Forward, 1949; Flood Control in the Mississippi Valley, 1952; editor Delta Council News. Home: Leland MS 38756 Office: Stoneville MS 38776

SMITH, BETTYE HOPPER, hosp. food service adminstr.; b. Madison County, Tenn., Dec. 27, 1927; d. Hallie Tigrett and Linnie Elizabeth (Harris) Hopper; B.S. in Home Econs., U. Tenn., 1949, M.S. in Instn. Adminstrn., 1971; m. John Sanford Smith, Sept. 4, 1951; children—Mary Elizabeth Smith McCurry, Sue Margaret Smith Coley, Beverly Carol. Asst. home demonstration agt. Gibson County Extension Service, U. Tenn., 1950-51; tchr. high sch. home econs. Madison County (Tenn.) Bd. Edn., 1953-54; therapeutic dietitian Jackson-Madison County Gen. Hosp., 1955-61, food service dir., 1961—; cons. food service, 1966—. Recipient 20-Yr. Service award

Jackson-Madison County Gen. Hosp., 1975. Mem. Am. Soc. Hosp. Food Service Adminstrs. (Dedicated Service on Bd. Dirs. award 1974) Am. Dietetic Assn. Methodist. Home: 532 Smith Ln Jackson TN 38301 Office: 708 W Forest St Jackson TN 38301

SMITH, BILLY DEAN, educator; b. Idabel, Okla., Aug. 19, 1936; s. Billy Ray and Virginia Dean (Wright) S.; B.S., Am. Technol. U., 1976; advanced tech. diploma Tex. State Tech. Inst., 1976; m. Mary Lyda Wyatt, Oct. 4, 1975; children—Michael Dean, Jeffery Thomas, Christopher Allen, Gregory Aaron, Deborah Michelle. Enlisted U.S. Coast Guard, 1952, advanced through grades to chief petty officer, 1966; ret., 1969, instr. welding Tex. State Tech. Inst., 1975-79, sr. instr., 1979—, career counselor, 1979—. Decorated Bronze Star (3), Purple Heart (3), Cross of Gallantry. Mem. Am. Welding Soc. (dir., chmn. scholarship com., mem. edn. com.), VFW, DAV. Democrat. Roman Catholic. Club: Am. Sportsman's. Office: Tex State Tech Inst Welding Dept Bldg 1-5 Waco TX 76705

SMITH, BILLY JACK, park dir.; b. San Angelo, Tex., Feb. 23, 1931; s. George Frank and Lida Eva (Gartman) S.; student Odessa Coll., 1949-50, Howard County Coll., 1962-64; m. Carolyn D. Smith, Jan. 29, 1950; children—Gary Ray, David Jack. Sales engr. McCullough Tool Co., Andrews, Tex., 1954-60; regional park dir. Tex. Parks and Wildlife Dept., Waco, 1960—; landscape architect, 1972—. Served with USAF, 1950-54. Recipient citation Tex. Legislature, 1962. Mem. Tex. Bd. Landscape Architects, Nat. Landscape Inst., Jaycees, Southwest Park and Recreation Instn. Mason, Lion. Home: 9719 Timberview Waco TX 76710 Office: Box 4186 Waco TX 76705

SMITH, BOYCE MILES, air force officer, meteorologist; b. Detonti, Ark., Apr. 3, 1924; s. William Pinkston and Alice Vivian (Burrow) S.; B.S. in Chem. Engring., U. Ark., 1950; Meteorologist, U. Tex., 1961; M.S. in Atmospheric Sci., Colo. State U., 1965; m. Helen Marguerite Snavely, Aug. 3, 1954; children—Sherry Allyson, Stanley Miles, Sally Anne, Scott Anthony. Enlisted U.S. Army, 1943, commd. 2d lt., 1944, advanced through grades to col. USAF, navigator combat missions, World War II, Korea, chief forecaster USAF, Athens, Greece, 1961-64, dir. geophys. dept., fgn. tech. div., Wright-Patterson AFB, Ohio, 1965-69, staff meteorologist Taiwan Def. Command, USN, Taipei, 1969-71, vice comdr. 1st Weather Group, USAF, Saigon, Vietnam, 1971-72, mem. spl. staff U.S. Army Europe, Heidelberg, W.Ger., 1972-75, comdr. 5th Weather Squadron, USAF, Ft. McPherson, Ga., 1975—; environ. cons. Repub. China Air Force, Taipei, 1969-71. Active Boy Scouts Am. Decorated Legion of Merit, Meritorious Service medal with oak leaf cluster, Air medal with 4 oak leaf clusters. Mem. Am. Meteorol. Soc., Am. Geophys. Union, Alpha Chi Sigma. Methodist. Home: 4120 Morning Trail College Park GA 30349 Office: HQ 5th Weather Squadron Ft McPherson GA 30330

SMITH, BRANDON CORDER, ret. petroleum engr.; b. Electra, Tex., June 22, 1915; s. Brandon H. and Dera M. (Corder) S.; B.S. in Petroleum Engring., Tex. A. and M. U., 1966; m. Anne Gertrude Barron, May 27, 1943; children—Brandon Corder, William Theodore. Field prodn. foreman Sun Oil Co., Evansville, Ind., 1938, sec. and asst. to prodn. supt., 1938-39, jr. petroleum engr., field prodn. foreman, Gainesville, Tex., 1945-46; enlisted USAAF, 1941, advanced through grades to lt. col., 1955; flight comdr. 98th Bomb Group, 1942-43; field maintenance squadron comdr., 1947-48; policies, procedure and requirements officer Hdqrs. SAC, Omaha, 1949-52, chief maintenance 7th Bomb Wing, Carswell AFB, 1955-56; dep. comdr. maintenance Glasgow (Mont.) AFB, 1963-64, ret., 1964; petroleum engr. Lone Star Producing Co., San Antonio, 1966-70, sr. engr., Houston, 1970-72; dist. petroleum engr. Enserch Exploration, Inc., Midland, Tex., 1972-76; ret., 1976. Decorated D.F.C. with one oak leaf cluster, Air medal with two oak leaf clusters. Baptist. Clubs: Masons, K.T., Shriners, Order Eastern Star. Home: 108 Henry Ford Dr Schertz TX 78154

SMITH, CARL WAYNE, agronomist; b. Slocomb, Ala., Jan. 20, 1947; s. Carl and Laura Leola (Moss) S.; B.S., Auburn U., 1969, M.S., 1971; Ph.D., U. Tenn., 1974; m. Mary Elizabeth Gravlee, Jan. 4, 1970; children—Amy Michelle, Karen Elizabeth. Soil conservation trainee Geneva County, Ala., 1967, Coffee County, Ala., 1968; grad. research asst. Auburn U., 1970-71; grad. research asst. U. Tenn., Knoxville, 1971-74; asst. prof. U. Ark., 1974-78, asso. prof. agronomy, 1978—. Bd. dirs. St. Francis County chpt. Ark. Red Cross. Served with USMCR, 1969-75. Mem. Crop Sci. Soc. Am., Am. Genetic Assn., Sigma Xi, Phi Kappa Phi, Gamma Sigma Delta, Alpha Zeta. Baptist. Contbr. articles to sci. jours. Home: 854 Inglewood Rd Forrest City AR 72335 Office: PO Box 789 Marianna AR 72360

SMITH, CARLOS CLIFFORD, lawyer; b. Chattanooga, Nov. 6, 1939; s. Clarence Roy and Ellen Catherine (Henegar) S.; B.S., U. Chattanooga, 1961; J.D., U. Cin., 1964; m. Ann Christine Windhorn, Feb. 27, 1965; children—Mark, Catherine Ann. Admitted to Tenn. bar, 1964; mem. firm Strang, Fletcher, Carriger, Walker, Hodge & Smith, Cattanooga; spl. counsel to Atty. Gen. Tenn., 1971-79; gen. counsel Met. Govt. Charter Commn., 1969-70, Electric Power Bd. Chattanooga, 1975—; mem. Tenn. Law Revision Commn., 1971-76, chmn., 1974-76. Pres. Blood Assurance, Inc., 1971-75; v.p., treas. Team Evaluation Center, 1971-75, 77-79; bd. dirs., v.p. Chattanooga Speech and Hearing Center, 1974-79, Auditorium Bd. City of Chattanooga, 1973—; chmn. legal sect. Tenn. Valley Public Power Assn., 1978-80. Named Chattanooga Outstanding Young Man of Year, Jaycees, 1974. Fellow Am. Bar Found.; mem. Chattanooga (pres. 1975-76), Tenn. (chmn. adminstrn. of justice com. 1977-78, mem. tax sect.), Am. (public utility, real estate, probate and trust sects.) bar assns., Tenn. Def. Lawyers Assn., Chattanooga Jaycees (v.p. 1967-69, state dir. 1969-70), Chattanooga C. of C. (air pollution task force 1966-68, vice chmn. govt. affairs com.). Lutheran. Home: 1117 Applewood Circle Signal Mountain TN 37377 Office: 1200 Maclellan Bldg Chattanooga TN 37402

SMITH, CAROLE LINA, pianist, educator; b. Wilkinsburg, Pa., Oct. 25, 1934; d. Paul Arno and Edris Laura (Wilson) Guenther; B.S. in Edn. (scholar), S.W. Mo. State U., 1955; diploma piano, M.Mus., La. State U., 1957; pupil Ruth Burr, Wilfred Adler, William Van Overeem, William Armstrong, Alfred Mouledous; m. Stephen R. Wilmoth, July 22, 1979; children—Mark Tobin Everett, James Wilson Everett. Head piano dept. Labette County Community High Sch., Altamont, Kans., 1955-56; pvt. piano tchr., Houston and Dallas, then Los Altos, Calif., 1957-62, Sherman, Tex., 1962—; tchr. piano pedagogy, continuing edn. Austin Coll., Sherman, 1974-80, Richardson, 1980—; piano instr. Grayson County Coll., Sherman, 1975-80, Music Master Sch. Music, Plano, Tex., 1979-80; pres. Bomar Cramer Music Club, 1966-68; bd. dirs. Sherman Mus. Arts, 1966-69, 73-80, charter mem., pres. women's guild, 1968-69, 73-74; violist Sherman Symphony Orch., 1973-80; mem. Cliburn Council, 1980. Charter mem., v.p. Sherman Community Players Theater Guild, 1969-70, bd. dirs., 1967-70; v.p. Grayson County Humane Soc., 1978-79; mem. bd. Sherman LWV, 1974-75. Certified music tchr. Mem. Music Tchrs. Nat. Assn., Tex. Music Tchrs. Assn. (sec. student affiliate 1974—), Nat. Guild Piano Tchrs. (adjudicator 1972—), Grayson County (charter mem., pres. 1971-73), Richardson, Plano, Dallas (pres. 1980—) music tchrs. assns., Am. Symphony Orch. League, AAUW, Sigma Alpha Iota, Sigma Sigma Sigma. Home: 919 Vinecrest Richardson TX 75080 Office: PO Box 165 Plano TX 75074

SMITH, CECIL EDWARD, acct.; b. Kosse, Tex., Mar. 20, 1942; s. Billy and Juanita Faye (McCarver) S.; B.B.A., U. Tex., Arlington, 1967; m. DianaJulia Zatopek, Nov. 22, 1962. With Arthur Young & Co., Ft. Worth, 1967—, mgr., 1972-76, prin., 1976-79, partner, 1979—, office dir. personnel, recruiting and edn., 1974—. Active United Way campaigns, 1974-78. Served with USAF, 1967. C.P.A., Tex., La. Mem. Nat. Assn. Accts., Tex. Soc. C.P.A.'s (pres. Ft. Worth chpt. 1979-80). Methodist. Club: Wimbledon Racquet. Home: 5101 Hidden Oaks Ln Arlington TX 76017 Office: 2200 Ft Worth Nat Bank Fort Worth TX 76102

SMITH, CHARLENE JOHNSON, counselor; b. McComb, Miss., Dec. 31, 1942; d. Luther and Margie Ruth (Dillon) Johnson; B.S., Alcorn State U., 1963; M.S., Tenn. State U., 1972; m. Hampton Smith, Dec. 30, 1961. Tchr., J. E. Johnson High Sch., 1964-68, Willard Elem. Sch., Chgo., 1968-69; sec., receptionist Tenn. State U., Nashville, 1969-72; counselor Albany (Ga.) State Coll., 1973—. Mem. Am. Personnel and Guidance Assn., Am. Coll. Personnel Assn., Am. Sch. Counselors Assn., Prosperos. Baptist. Home: 1116 St Andrews Dr Albany GA 31707 Office: Albany State College 504 College Dr Albany GA 31705

SMITH, CHARLES FOSTER, accountant; b. nr. Scranton, S.C., Nov. 14, 1919; s. Wade H. and Kizzie (Marlowe) S.; B.S., U. S.C., 1940; m. Sarah Virginia Fore, Nov. 15, 1947; children—Sarah Dianne, Rebecca Elaine, Caroline Virginia. Practice pub. accounting, Myrtle Beach, also Conway, S.C., 1947—; dir. Peoples Nat. Bank, Conway, 1959-69; mem. action bd. C & S Bank, Myrtle Beach, 1969—; mem. S.C. Bd. Accountancy, 1969-75, chmn., 1971-74. Treas., bd. dirs. Coastal Ednl. Found., pres., 1974-77. Served with AUS, 1944-46; PTO. C.P.A., S.C. Mem. S.C. Assn. C.P.A.'s (pres. 1959-60, Service to the Profession award 1978), Am. Inst. C.P.A.'s, Civitan Club (pres. 1951-53), Horry County Hist. Soc. (pres. 1969), U. S.C. Alumni Assn. (councilor-at-large 1974-76), Phi Beta Kappa, Omicron Delta Kappa. Methodist (chmn. adminstrv. bd. 1956-57, bd. pensions S.C. conf.). Home: 3400 N Kings Hwy Myrtle Beach SC 29577 Office: 1704 Oak St Myrtle Beach SC 29577

SMITH, CHARLES HERVEY, lawyer; b. Muncie, Ind., Jan. 29, 1947; s. John Hervey and Grace June (Godwin) S.; B.B.A. in Fin., So. Methodist U., 1971, J.D., 1974; m. Linda Jo Noret, Dec. 23, 1972. Account mgr. Dun & Bradstreet, Inc., Dallas, 1966-72; admitted to Tex. bar, 1974; asso. firm Vial, Hamilton, Koch, Tubb, Knox & Stradley, Dallas, 1974-76; v.p., gen. counsel Noret Theatres, Inc., Lamesa, Tex., 1977; trial atty. firm Strasburger & Price, Dallas, 1977—; adj. instr. So. Meth. U. Law Sch., 1976. Cert. flight and ground instr., accident-prevention counselor, FAA. Mem. Am. Bar Assn., Lawyer Pilot Bar Assn., Dallas Bar Assn., Tex. Bar Assn., Order of Coif. Editor Southwestern Law Jour., 1973-74. Address: 1200 One Main Pl Dallas TX 75250

SMITH, CHARLIE HASKIN, social worker; b. Exmore, Va., May 30, 1940; s. Raymond Paul and Pearl Naomi S.; B.A., Va. State Coll., 1963; M.S.W., N.Y. U., 1966, M. Pub. Adminstrn., 1976; m. Shirley Hunter, July 30, 1972; 1 son, David Asher. Spl. caseworker family counseling unit Monroe County Dept. Social Services, Rochester, N.Y., 1966-68; sr. clin. social worker VA Hosp., East Orange, N.J., 1968-76; chief social work service VA Center, Martinsburg, W.Va., 1976—; adj. prof. social work and sociology Shepherd Coll., Shepherdstown, W.Va., 1977—. Cert. social worker, N.Y. Mem. Nat. Assn. Social Workers, Acad. Cert. Social Workers, Council on Social Work Edn., Am. Public Health Assn., Am. Hosp. Assn., W.Va. Pub. Health Assn., Soc. Hosp. Social Work Dirs., W.Va. Welfare Conf., Am. Coll. Hosp. Adminstrs. Home: 202 Shenandoah Rd Martinsburg WV 25401

SMITH, CHARLOTTE OLIVER, ednl. adminstr.; b. Lufkin, Tex., Sept. 5, 1940; d. William Boyd and Mae Isabelle (Housel) Oliver; M.Ed., U. Houston, 1967; Ed.D., 1971; m. T.C. Smith, Jr., June 12, 1971. Sr. cons. Research Inst. Advanced Tech., Killeen, Tex., 1974-75; dir. instl. research, prof. edn. Am. Tech. U., Killeen, 1976-77; dir. ednl. program devel. Research Inst. Advanced Tech., 1977-79; dean ednl. program devel. Central Tex. Coll. System, Killeen, 1979—; faculty U. Houston, 1967-71, N. Tex. State U., 1972; cons. Scottish Rites Hosp. for Crippled Children, 1972-74, RCA Ednl. Systems, 1972-74, Tex. Edn. Agy., 1972-73. Bd. dirs. Bluebonnet Girl Scout Council, 1979—. Mem. Am. Statis. Assn., Tex. Jr. Coll. Tchrs. Assn. Methodist. Club: Altrusa (pres. 1979—). Home: 601 Tower St Killeen TX 76541 Office: Central Tex Coll Hwy 190 W Killeen TX 76541

SMITH, CLAUDE KENNETH, educator; b. Gray Hawk, Ky., Feb. 10, 1932; s. Robert S. and Martha Jane (Farmer) S.; B.S., Eastern Ky. U., 1954; M.R.E., So. Bapt. Theol. Sem., 1958; M.B.A., U. Ky., 1966; m. Wanda M. Cox, June 17, 1956; children—Sherilyn Rhea, Claude Kenneth. Mem. faculty McKee (Ky.) High Sch., 1954-55; chmn. bus. dept. Bluefield (Va.) Coll., 1957-61; staff accountant Haskins and Sells, Indpls., 1961-62; sr. accountant George S. Olive & Co., CPA's, Indpls., 1962-64; partner Amick & Helm, C.P.A.'s; chmn. dept. accounting Eastern Ky. U., Richmond, 1964—, mem. faculty senate, 1969-72, chmn. faculty senate, 1969-70. Bd. dirs., sec.-treas. Home Care Centers, Inc., Richmond; city commr., Richmond, 1972-77. Recipient YMCA-YWCA award for citizenship, 1954. Mem. Ky. Soc. C.P.A.'s (chmn. career opportunities com. 1970-71), Am. Inst. C.P.A.'s (membership com. 1968-71), Am. Accounting Assn., Central Ky. Assn. C.P.A.'s. Baptist (deacon 1960—; chmn. deacons 1963-64). Home: 109 Meadowlark Dr Richmond KY 40475

SMITH, CLIFFORD JOSEPH, ocean shipping exec.; b. Mandeville, La., Oct. 22, 1919; s. Nicholas N. and Marietta Anne (Toledano) S.; student Tulane Coll., 1939-41; student Coll. of Advance Traffic and Transportation, Lamar Coll., 1947-48; m. Georgiana Clestia Oelking, Nov. 19, 1946; children—Clifford, Jr., Doris Anne, Frederick Nicholas, Kevin John, Nanette Noelle. Asst. mgr. Plant Shipping Co., New Orleans, 1948-51; v.p. Gufl Funch Edye & Co., Inc., New Orleans, 1951-65; exec. v.p. Furness Withy Agencies, New Orleans, 1965-74; chmn. Gulf Associated Freight Confs., New Orleans, 1975—; hon. consul of Denmark for La. and Miss., 1970—; dir. Furness Withy Agencies, New Orleans, New Orleans Steamship Assn. and Waterfront Employers Assn., 1965-74. Pres. New Orleans Bd. of Trade, 1977-78; annual panel chmn. Inst. of Foreign Transp. and Port Ops., New Orleans, 1970—; chmn. Transportation Industry Group United Fund, New Orleans, 1972—; industry commr. River Pilots Fee Commn., New Orleans, 1969—; economic development com. New Orleans C. of C., 1977-79. Served with USAAF, 1942-46. Decorated Order of Dannebrog (Denmark). Mem. Internat. House (dir. 1977-79), Internat. Trade Mart (dir., exec. com., 1977-79), World Trade Club of New Orleans, New Orleans Steamship Assn., New Orleans Traffic and Transp. Bureau, Fgn. Relations Assn. of New Orleans, Am. Legion. Democrat. Roman Catholic. Clubs: Empire, Timberlane Country, Plimsoll. Home: 300 Hawthorne St Gretna LA 70053 Office: 927 Whitney Bldg New Orleans LA 70130

SMITH, CRAIG CHAMPNEY, banker, mfr., cons.; b. Rochester, N.Y., Oct. 29, 1915; s. Frank George and Ina (Baker) S.; student Canadaigus Acad., 1928-33, Ind. U., 1937; m. Mary Elizabeth Leinen, Sept. 4, 1941; children—Ina Smith Welch, Eric, Marc, Lisa Smith Adams, Melanie, Paul. Pres. Parazin Corp., 1948-64, chmn., 1964—; pres. Oxford Corp., 1953-58, also dir.; pres. Magnarol Co., 1954-64, also dir.; chmn. bd. Smith-Hart Corp. 1958-60, Gen. Packaging Corp., 1958-64, Rochester Lithograph Corp., 1958-60, Wrap-Tures Gift Wrap, Inc., Gen. Packaging Corp. N.Y., Stranahan Foil Co., Ben-Mont Papers, Adams Paper Co.; dir. Provinel Co., Inc., Permalap, Inc., Central Trust, 1953-65. Served as lt. comdr. USNR, 1941-46. Decorated Silver Star. Mem. C. of C. Clubs: Oak Hill Country, Rochester, Rochester Yacht, Sarasota Yacht, Everglades Yacht, Vero Beach Yacht. Home: Provence Route 1 Box 333A Somerset VA 22972 Office: 400 18 St Vero Beach FL 32960

SMITH, CURTIS WAYNE, landscape architect; b. Wichita Falls, Tex., Sept. 18, 1929; s. Clifton O. and Maudie Faye (Johnson) S.; student Tex. A. and M. U. 1946-47, Midwestern State U., 1947-48; m. Ruth Preston, June 13, 1948; children—Katherine Ruth, Steven Wayne, Douglas Preston. With Smith Nursery, Wichita Falls, Tex., 1948-61, partner, 1954-61; owner Smith's Gardentown, Wichita Falls, 1961—; organizing dir. Am. Nat. Bank, 1975; instr. Midwestern State U., 1975. Alderman, City of Wichita Falls, 1978, mayor pro tem, 1979—. Mem. Am. (bd. govs. 1972-75), Tex. (pres. 1969) assns. nurserymen, Garden Centers Am. (dir. 1972—). Baptist (gen. sec. 1970—). Club: Wichita (Wichita Falls, Tex.). Author: Employee Training Manual, 1975. Home: 2310 Irving St Wichita Falls TX 76308 Office: 4100 Kemp St Wichita Falls TX 76308

SMITH, D. JUDY, guidance counselor; B.A., U. Tex.; M.Ed., Hardin-Simmons U. Former tchr. Big Spring (Tex.) pub. schs.; Coahoma (Tex.) pub. schs.; counselor Big Spring Ind. Sch. Dist., 1971—; instr. Webb AFB for Sul Ross U., Alpine, Tex., 1973-78. Mem. Vol. Council, Big Spring State Hosp., 1972-75; sponsor Midland Community Theater, Big Spring Community Concerts. Mem. Permiam Basin Council for Children with Learning Disabilities, Permian Basin Counselors Assn. (pres. 1978-79, legis. chmn. 1979-80), Am., Tex. personnel and guidance assns., Nat. Vocat. Guidance Assn., Tex. State Tchrs. Assn. (pub. relations chmn. 1971-72), Tex. Classroom Tchrs. Assn., Counselor Educators and Suprs., Big Spring Area C. of C. (cultural affairs com. 1978-79), Heritage Mus. Big Spring, Smithsonian Assos. Clubs: Hyperion, Potpourri, Cotillion, Lions Aux. Home: 808 Edwards Blvd Big Spring TX 79720 Office: 708 11th Pl Big Spring TX 79720

SMITH, DALE HARRIS, child care agy. adminstr.; b. Watford City, N.D., Apr. 22, 1943; s. Leslie and Marie (Bruins) S.; B.S., Tulsa U., 1968; postgrad. Wichita State U., 1973; m. Rebecca Jan Keach, Dec. 15, 1973; children—Kim, Vicki, Melissa, Eric, Jeff, Brad. Mem. acctg. dept. staff Pan Am. Petroleum Corp., Tulsa, 1962-66; counselor Tulsa Boys Home, 1967-68; supr. Continental Baking Co., Tulsa, 1969-73; exec. dir. Boys' Village, Lake Charles, La., 1974—. Bd. dirs. Ret. Sr. Vols. Program; chmn. youth care com. Gov.'s Adv. Bd. on Juvenile Justice and Delinquency Prevention. Mem. La. Child Care Assn. (v.p.), La. Assn. Child Care Agys., Nat. Assn. Homes for Children. Republican. Address: Route 10 Box 280 Lake Charles LA 70601

SMITH, DANNY COSBY, computer programmer; b. Mt. Pleasant, Tex., Jan. 16, 1935; s. Robert Glover and Mamie Maurine (Cosby) S.; B.S. in Math., E. Tex. State U., 1957, M.S. in Computer Sci., 1977; m. Margaret Ann Grau, June 20, 1957; children—Charles Robert, Stephen Dan, Lisa Ann, Michael Alan. Draftsman, Lone Star Steel Co., Lone Star, Tex., 1957; tab operator Service Bur., Dallas, 1958, Comml. Standard Ins. Co., Ft. Worth, 1958; structural analyst Gen. Dynamics, Ft. Worth, 1958-59; tchr. White Settlement (Tex.) schs., 1959-63; linesman Gen. Dynamics, Ft. Worth, 1963-66; sci. programmer E-Systems Inc., Greenville, Tex., 1966—, assembly lang. instr., 1972-77. Served with USAF, 1957-58, capt. Res. Mem. IEEE Computer Soc. Baptist. Home: 1309 Skyline Dr Greenville TX 75401 Office: PO Box 1056 Greenville TX 75401

SMITH, DAVID HERBERT, physician; b. Pauline, S.C., July 26, 1883; s. Christopher Columbus and Flora Eugenia (West) S.; M.D., Med. Coll. Charleston (S.C.), 1909; m. Elizabeth Lurania Davis, Oct. 17, 1922; 1 dau., Elizabeth Davis Smith Owens. Intern, Roper Hosp., Charleston, 1909-10, chief staff, 1910-11; gen. practice medicine, Pauline, 1911-70; resident physician Glenn Springs (S.C.) Hotel, 1920; mem. staff Spartanburg Gen. Hosp., Mary Black Hosp., Spartanburg. Served as 1st lt. M.C., U.S. Army, 1918. Mem. AMA (Fifty Yr. club), Spartanburg County Med. Soc. (named Dr. of Yr. 1955), Am. Legion. Episcopalian. Clubs: Masons, Shriners. Died Apr. 16, 1978. Address: Route 1 Box 7 Pauline SC 29374

SMITH, DIANE MARY YOUNG, mental health practitioner, educator; b. Cin., July 11, 1939; d. William L. and Christine W. (Manning) Young; B.S., Georgetown U., 1961; M.S., Tex. Woman's U., 1972, Ph.D., 1979; children—Peter, Theresa, Michele, Christopher, Geoffrey, Joseph. Staff nurse, nursing supr., dir. inservice edn. Flow Meml. Hosp., Denton, Tex., 1971-74; instr. coll. nursing Tex. Woman's U., Denton, 1974-77, part time faculty, 1978—; pvt. practice mental health Denton, 1978—; vis. grad. faculty U. Tex., El Paso, summer 1978; condr. workshops for industry, univs., continuing edn. in nursing, public groups. Bd. dirs. Denton County div. Am. Heart Assn., 1969-76 pres., 1975-76, CPR instr.; vol. community immunization and screening programs; bd. dirs. Denton Area Crisis Center; vol. nurse Denton Christian Pre-Sch.; founder health program Casa Hogar de los Pequenos, Mex. Mem. Dallas Analytical Psychology Assn., Sigma Theta Tau, Phi Delta Gamma. Author tape-slide presentation on exec. stress. Home: 1017 Oakland St Denton TX 76201 Office: 1808 N Elm St Denton TX 76201

SMITH, DOCK GARNER, JR., lawyer; b. Clayton, N.C., May 20, 1935; s. Dock Garner and Helen (Rains) S.; B.S., E. Carolina U., 1957; J.D., U. N.C., 1960; m. Peggy Faye Smith, 1957; children—Dock Garner, Douglas G., Sandra Kay, Daniel G. Admitted to N.C. bar, 1960; individual practice law, Robbins, N.C., 1961—; pres. Robbins Improvement Co., Inc. Pres. Robbins Mchts. Assn., 1963-64, Moore County Young Democrats, 1964-66; sec., dir. Northmoore Student Loan Found., Inc.; mem. Gov.'s N.C. Task Force on Adjudication, Moore County Planning Bd., 1973. Town atty., Robbins, 1964-80. Mem. N.C., Moore County, 20th Jud. Dist. bar assns., N.C. Acad. Trial Lawyers, Jr. C. of C. (pres. 1963-64). Methodist. Clubs: Elks, Lions (pres. 1978-79), Masons, Montgomery County Country; Riverside Golf and Country, Pinehurst Golf and Country. Home: 310 Frye St Robbins NC 27325 Office: 118 E Salisbury St Robbins NC 27325

SMITH, DONALD ALAN, advt. exec.; b. Newark, Ohio, Dec. 4, 1934; s. Brooks and Ella (Jaeger) S.; B.F.A., U. Ga., 1956; children—Kirk Martin, Angela. Div. designer Dairypak, Athens, Ga., 1957—; owner Don Smith Ad Creations, Athens, 1960—; design cons. Athens Daily News, Athens Banner Herald, 1965-78, Athens Observer, 1979, Ga. Outdoor Advt., 1963—, Athens Tempo mag., 1979; art dir. Athens mag., 1968-73. Served with U.S. Army, 1957-58. Recipient Design award Internat. Paper Co., 1970; 1st place awards Inst. Outdoor Advt., 1970; Awards of Excellence, Deep South Advt. Show, 1971, 72; Gold Medal award Ga./Ala. Newspaper Advt. Execs. Assn., 1971; Awards of Excellence, So. Creativity Show, 1972, 73, 79; award Ga. Press Assn., 1975; 1st place award So. Classified Advt.

Mgrs., 1978, others. Mem. Am. Advt. Fedn., Athens Ad Club, Atlanta Advt. Club (Phoenix awards 1970, 74), Athens Area C. of C. (public realtions chmn. 1965-70, Outstanding Service award 1965-66), Phi Beta Kappa, Phi Kappa Phi. Presbyterian. Home: 4 Tangelwood Ct Athens GA 30606

SMITH, DONALD EARL, educator; b. Arenzville, Ill., June 15, 1935; s. Earl D. and Helen (Spangler) S.; B.S., U. Ill., 1959, M.Ed., 1962; D.Ed. (grad. asst., hons.), Ill. State U., 1969; m. Anita Torres, June 5, 1975; children by previous marriage—Leslie, Lisa. Grad. asst. U. Ill., Champaign, 1959-60; guidance dir. Central Jr. High Sch. Rock Island, Ill., 1960-61; instr. vocat. Black Hawk Coll., Moline, Ill., 1961-64; guidance dir. Atlanta-Mc Lean, Ill., 1964-65; acad. v.p. Gulf Coast Bible Coll., Houston, 1969-73; cons. in field, research grantee, 1976-77. Mem. Am., Tex. personnel, guidance assns., Assn. Counselor Edn. Suprs., Phi Delta Kappa. Clubs: Kiwanis (bd. dirs. 1977-78), Exptl. Aircraft Assn., Nat. Rifle Assn. (life). Author numerous publs. in field; co-editor, contbg. author Dynamics of the Faith, 1972; research in field. Home: 217 S Crisp St Uvalde TX 78801 Office: Sul Ross Univ Uvalde Study Center Uvalde TX 78808

SMITH, DORETTA FRENNA, artist; b. Trieste, Italy, July 23, 1924; d. Antonio and Antonietta (Demel) Frenna; came to U.S., 1948, naturalized, 1954; grad. Comml. Inst.-Tech. Inst. Accounting, 1941; student Berlitz Sch. Lang., 1942-44, Eneukel Sch. Art and Design, Italy, 1942-46, Coastal Carolina Community Coll., 1969-74; m. William J. Smith, Oct. 16, 1948; children—Frank, George, Rose-Mary, William, Anna, Edward, John, Michael. With City of Trieste, 1942-46; instr. painting and crafts Coastal Carolina Community Coll., Jacksonville, N.C., 1974—; free-lance artist and tchr. oil painting and watercolor, Jacksonville, 1974—; one-woman shows: Onslow Art Soc., 1974, Photo and Art Supply, Greensboro, N.C., 1977, Brown Library, Washington, 1978, Art Center, Kinston, N.C., La Galerie Moufée, Paris, 1978, Gallerie Vallombreuse, Biarritz, France, 1978, Marine Resource Center, Emerald Isle, 1978, Green Valley Country Club, Fayetteville, N.C., 1979-80, others; represented in permanent collections: Onslow Meml. Hosp., Jacksonville, Waccamow Bank & Trust Co., Southport, N.C., Public Library, Southport, Hyde-Martin Regional Library, Coastal Carolina Community Coll., others. Recipient various awards for arts, crafts, needlework; purchase awards Waccamow Bank and Trust Co., 1976, Hyde-Martin Regional Library, Beaufort County, N.C., 1975; State award of Merit, Cath. Daus. Am., 1978; First Place award State Art Competition. Mem. St. John Art Gallery, Onslow County Art Soc., Onslow County Art Council, Carteret Art Council, Associated Artists of Southport, N.C. Watercolor Soc., Internat. Soc. Artists, Am. Bus. Women's Assn., Cath. Daus. Am. Roman Catholic. Home: 1334 Richlands Hwy Jacksonville NC 28540

SMITH, DOUGLAS ALDRIDGE, television exec.; b. Salt Lake City, May 17, 1925; s. Finis N. and Ada Byrd (Whitehead) S.; student U. of South, 1942-43; B.S., U. S.C., 1945; m. Ina Rose Holcombe, May 5, 1945; children—William Holcombe, April Jordan. Various advt. and pub. relations positions, 1946-56; with WFBC-TV div. Multimedia Broadcasting Co., Greenville, S.C., 1956—, sr. v.p., gen. mgr. WFBC-TV, 1966—, dir. Multimedia Broadcasting Co., 1970-77, mem. mgmt. com., 1977—; dir. Five Forks Enterprises, 1968—. Sec., vice chmn. Greenville County Mus. Commn., 1972—; chmn. S.C. Arts Commn., 1975-77. Served to lt. (j.g.) USNR, 1943-45. Recipient Printers Ink Silver Medal award Advt. Fedn. Am., 1963; named Boss of Yr., Am. Bus. Womens Assn., 1964, Nat. Secs. Assn., 1974. Mem. Nat. Assn. Broadcasters, TV Bur. Advt. (chmn. sales advisory com.), S.C. Broadcasters Assn. (pres. 1975-76), Greenville Advt. Club. Episcopalian. Clubs: Green Valley Country, Poinsett. Asso. producer, Miss Am. Pageant, 1962; producer Miss S.C. Pageants, 1957-62. Home: 7 Woodfern Circle Greenville SC 29607 Office: PO Box 788 Greenville SC 29602

SMITH, DOUGLAS OMAR, JR., lawyer; b. Birmingham, Ala., Feb. 2, 1935; s. Douglas Omar and Ople Eugenia (Beeler) S.; B.S. in Bus. Adminstrn., U. Ark., 1956; J.D., Yale U., 1959; m. Constance Jean Christopher, Dec. 7, 1968; children—Sara Frances, Douglas Omar. Admitted to Ark. bar, 1959, U.S. Supreme Ct. bar, 1971; asso. firm Warner, Warner & Ragon, Fort Smith, Ark., 1959-60; partner firm Warner & Smith, 1961—; dir. United Peoples Savs. & Loan Assn., 1970—. Mem. Fort Smith Sch. Bd., 1971-78, pres., 1973-74; mem. Ark. Comprehensive Health Planning Council, 1971-79; mem. Bost Sch. Bd., 1966-69; mem. bd. Region VI Health Planners Assn., 1972-75; mem. Juvenile Services Commn., 1973-79; mem. Ark. Dem. State Com., 1972-74, exec. com., 1973-74; bd. dirs. Western Ark. Guidance and Counseling Center, 1975—; trustee Sparks Regional Med. Center. Served with USAF, 1961-62. Fellow Ark. Bar Found. (dir. 1973-75), Am. Coll. Trial Lawyers; mem. Sebastian County (pres. 1966-67), Ark. (ho. of dels., exec. council 1972-75), Am. bar assns., Internat. Assn. Ins. Counsel, Am. Judicature Soc. Club: Town. Presbyterian. Home: 13 Berry Hill Fort Smith AR 72901 Office: 214 N 6th St Fort Smith AR 72901

SMITH, DUDLEY, trade assn. exec., sugar cons., author; b. Campbellsville, Ky., Dec. 6, 1904; s. Herbert G. and Addie (Feather) S.; B.S., U. Ky., 1931; postgrad. U.S. Dept. Agr. Grad. Sch., 1931-35; m. Verta Enid Templeton, June 9, 1935; children—Mary Lou Smith Brown, Dudley T., Elizabeth Smith Jones. Tobacco mktg. and program specialist U. Ky., 1929-31, U.S. Govt., 1931-36; ofcl. Washington and San Juan (P.R.) offices Assn. Sugar Producers P.R., 1936-72, v.p., 1941-72; tobacco and livestock farmer, Mitchellville, Md., 1941-68; internat. cons. sugar and tobacco, 1940—; exec. sec. Sugar Equipment and Services Exporters Assn., 1976—; mem., ofcl. various Md. agrl. orgns., 1947-69; chmn. Nat. Sugar Research and Mktg. Adv. Com., 1951-58; mem. Nat. Tobacco Industry Adv. Com., 1963-65, Nat. Tobacco Research Adv. Com., 1964-66. Mem. Internat., P.R., Am., Queensland sugar technologists assns., Alpha Gamma Rho, Alpha Zeta. Democrat. Methodist. Clubs: Masons, Rotary. Author: Cane Sugar World, 1977; editor Sugar y Azucar Yearbook, 1971-77. Home: 1 Benjamin Franklin Dr Sarasota FL 33577 Office: 582 S Washington Dr Sarasota FL 33577

SMITH, DUNCAN KEMP, JR., elec. engr.; b. Houston, May 22, 1934; s. Duncan Kemp and Lois (Walker) S.; B.I.S., U. Fla., 1961; postgrad. U. South Fla., 1969; m. Helen Ann Wagner, Feb. 1, 1953; children—Barry Keith, Randy Lee, Sherry Lynn. Spl. projects engr. Fla. Tile Industries, Lakeland, 1960-67; elec. engr. Am. Cyanamid Co., Brewster, Fla., 1963-66; field elec. engr. Dorr-Oliver Engring. Ltd., Bartow, Fla., 1966-67; asst. supt. planning and engring. Lakeland Dept. Electric and Water, 1967—. Vice chmn. Fire Commn. Dist. #1, Polk County, Fla., 1975—. Democrat. Episcopalian. Club: Moose. Home: 1419 Pleasant Pl Lakeland FL 33801 Office: 1000 E Parker St PO Box 368 Lakeland FL 33802

SMITH, E. F., JR., utility co. exec.; b. Brownwood, Tex., July 21, 1922; s. E.F. and Belle (Morrison) S.; B.S., Howard Payne U., 1952; m. Shirley Lois Melane, Oct. 13, 1942; children—Sandra Joann, Robert Franklin. County clk. Brown County (Tex.), 1947-50; spl. agt. Prudential Ins. Co., 1952-53; mgr. Bd. Community Devel., Coleman, Tex., 1953-54; mgr. acctg. and fin. Dallas Water Utilities, 1954—; cons. PanAm Health Orgn., Barbados, W.I., 1979. Water safety chmn. ARC. Served with U.S. Army, 1942-45. Decorated Bronze Star. Mem. Tex. Water Utilities Assn. Baptist. Club: Lions (pres., zone chmn.). Home: 1241 Toltec Dr Dallas TX 75232 Office: Dallas Water Utilities Room 5AN City Hall 1500 Marilla St Dallas TX 75201

SMITH, EARL, ednl. adminstr.; b. Jackson, Ky., Mar. 26, 1929. B.A. in Elem. Edn., English, Eastern Ky. U., 1958; M.A. in Elem. Edn., English, U. Ky., 1961. Tchr., Breathitt Bd. Edn., Jackson, Ky., 1958-60; lab. supr. tchr. Morehead (Ky.) State U., 1960-63; ednl. supr. Hazard (Ky.) Ind. Schs., 1963—. Mem. Ky. Assn. Sch. Adminstrs., Nat. Assn. Sch. Adminstrs., Ky. Edn. Suprs., (pres. 1971), Ky. Council English Tchrs. Recipient Outstanding Sch. Adminstr. Award, 1973, Outstanding Alumnus, Eastern Ky. U. Address: Hazard Ind Schs PO Box 1118 Hazard KY 41701

SMITH, EARL CONWAY, physician; b. Waldo, Ark., May 22, 1904; s. Hillyard Jackson and Zula Caldonie (Kitchens) S.; B.S., Tulane U., 1926, M.D., 1928; m. Thelma Louise Reyes, Nov. 6, 1936. Intern La. State Charity Hosp., New Orleans, 1928-29, resident, 1929-30; fellow in obstetrics and gynecology Chgo. Lying-In Hosp., U. Chgo., 1937; practice medicine specializing in obstetrics and gynecology New Orleans, 1930—; asst. dept. gynecology Tulane U. Post-Grad. Med. Sch., New Orleans, 1930-31; vis. surgeon La. State Charity Hosp., New Orleans, 1933-36, sr. vis. surgeon, 1966-71; vis. surgeon So. Bapt. Hosp., New Orleans, 1932-71, mem. cons. staff, 1971—; asso. vis. surgeon Mercy Hosp., 1930-48, Sara Mayo Hosp., 1950-71; instr. in obstetrics and gynecology La. State U. Med. Center, 1931-39, asst. prof., 1939-42, 46-52; guest lectr. U. Munich (Germany), 1968, U. London, 1968, U. San Salvador, 1969, U. Thailand (Bangkok), 1970. Served to comdr. M.C., USN, 1942-46. Decorated Purple Heart; diplomate Am. Bd. Obstetrics and Gynecology. Fellow AMA; mem. La. State Med. Soc., La. Gynecol. and Obstet. Soc. (pres. 1941-42), New Orleans Gynecol. and Obstet. Soc. (pres. 1947-48), Am. Coll. Obstetricians and Gynecologists, New Orleans Grad. Med. Assembly, Southeastern Surg. Congress. Democrat. Episcopalian. Clubs: Pickwick; Metairie Country. Contbr. numerous articles in field to profl. jours.; inventor obstetric forceps. Address: 401 Metairie Rd Apt 411 Metairie LA 70005

SMITH, EARLENE HEATON, educator; b. Capron, Okla., Sept. 19, 1931; d. Earl Campbell and Inez Belle Heaton; B.S., Northwestern Okla. State U., 1953; M.Ed., U. Okla., 1961; children—Robert, Ann, Portia, Lana. Tchr., Norman (Okla.) public schs., 1968-77, Southeast High Sch., Oklahoma City, 1953-55; asst. dean women U. Okla., Norman, 1961-64, counselor, instr. Coll. Nursing, 1977—; bd. dirs. Wesley Found., 1975—; mem. design team McFarlin Acad., 1978—. Pres., Cleveland County Democratic Women's Assn., 1965-66; mem. alumnae adv. council Okla. U., 1966-68; nat. pres. women's aux. Student Am. Med. Assn., 1957-59. Named Outstanding Mem., Norman Jr. C. of C. Aux., 1964; recipient spl. recognition Bd. Global Ministries, United Meth. Ch., 1974-78. Mem. Am. Assn. Higher Edn., Assn. Study Higher Edn., Am. Coll. Personnel Assn., Okla. Coll. Personnel Assn., Alpha Psi Omega, Kappa Delta Pi, Phi Delta Gamma. Club: Univ. Home: 1406 Westbrooke Terr Norman OK 73069 Office: 650 Parrington Oval Norman OK 73019

SMITH, EDWARD, purchasing exec.; b. Vicco, Ky., May 29, 1924; s. Albert B. and Maggie (McDaniel) S.; B.A., Morehead State U., 1948; M.A., Stetson U., 1957; m. Barbara J. Moore, Aug. 29, 1950; 1 dau., Kimberly Joy. Tchr., coach Combs High Sch., Viper High Sch., Perry County, Ky., 1948-50, Johnsville High Sch., Morrow County, Ohio, 1950-52; tchr. Perrysville High Sch., Ashland County, Ohio, 1952-53, Lakeview High Sch., Orange County, Fla., 1953-54, Boone High Sch., Orange County, 1954-58; asst. prin. Evans High Sch., Orange County, 1958-59; dir. purchasing Orange County, Fla., 1959—; adj. prof. Jones Coll., Orlando, Fla., 1968-78. Mem. Southeastern Assn. Sch. Bus. Ofcls., Fla. Bus. Edn. Assn. (sec.-treas.), Fla. Edn. Assn. (sec. area V), Fla. Assn. Sch. Bus. Adminstrs. (pres.), Fla. Assn. Govtl. Purchasing Officers, Orange County Assn. Supervision and Adminstrn., Orange County Bus. Edn. Assn. (pres.), Kappa Mu. Mem. Christian Ch. Home: 1534 Crestline St Orlando FL 32806 Office: 434 N Tampa Ave Orlando FL 32802

SMITH, EDWARD MORRIS, JR., agrl. agy. ofcl.; b. Hopewell, Va., Sept. 10, 1948; s. Edward Morris and Esther Anne (Yates) S.; B.S., Va. Commonwealth U., 1972, M.B.A., 1979. Market research analyst Smith Kline Corp., Richmond, Va. and Phila., 1972-73; mgr. mktg. div., mgr. corp. planning Blue Shield & Blue Cross of Va., Richmond, 1973-78; dir. rural health and tng. Va. Farm Bur. Fedn., Richmond, 1978—; adj. faculty Va. Community Coll. System, 1973-79. Mem. steering com. prevention of disease and disability Central Va. Health Systems Agy., Richmond, 1979-80; mem. state public edn. com. Am. Cancer Soc., 1979-80. Mem. Am. Soc. Tng. and Devel. Presbyterian. Club: Kiwanis. Home: 3510 W Broadway Hopewell VA 23860 Office: Va Farm Bur Fedn 200 W Grace St Box 27552 Richmond VA 23261

SMITH, EDWARD PATRICK, JR., surgeon; b. Balt., Mar. 26, 1922; s. Edward Patrick and Mary Loretta (Muth) S.; student Loyola at Balt., 1940-42; B.S., U. Md., 1949, M.D., 1946; m. Sarah Elizabeth Ballard, Dec. 24, 1945; children—Edward Patrick, David Middleton, Patricia Michelle. Intern, Mercy Hosp., Balt., 1946-47, resident, 1947-48; resident U. Md. Hosp., Balt., 1950-52, Lahey Clinic, Boston, 1952-53, U. Mich. Hosp., Ann Arbor, 1953-55; commd. 1st lt. USAF, 1943, advanced through grades to col., 1969; stationed in Tex., Philippines, Fla. and Calif.; ret., 1969; pvt. practice thoracic surgery, St. Petersburg, Fla., 1969—; mem. staff St. Anthony's Hosp., Bayfront Med. Center, All Children's Hosp., Apollo Med. Center; mem. med. recovery team Project Mercury, 1960-61. Spl. dep. sheriff Pinellas County (Fla.), 1971—; mem. North Redington Beach Town Commn., 1975—. Diplomate Am. Bd. Surgery, Am. Bd. Thoracic Surgery. Fellow Coll. Chest Physicians, A.C.S.; mem. Soc. Thoracic Surgeons, So. Thoracic Surg. Assn. John Alexander Soc., Southeastern Surg. Congress, U. Md. Surg. Soc., Air Force Assn. Clubs: Seminole Lake Country, Bath. Home: 454 S Bath Club Blvd North Redington Beach FL 33708 Office: 1012 27th St N Saint Petersburg FL 33705

SMITH, EDWARD WENDKOS, broadcasting co. exec.; b. Greenville, S.C., Feb. 2, 1946; s. Hoyt Thomas and Carrie Bell (Hollingsworth) S.; student Furman U.; m. Peggy A. Groves, Mar. 12, 1966; 1 son, Sterling Wendkos. Salesman, sales mgr. Sta. WGON and Sta. WYNQ-FM, Chattanooga, 1970-74; salesman Sta. WDEF AM/FM, Chattanooga, 1975; gen. mgr. Sta WTJR AM/FM, Richmond, Va., 1975—. Unit dir. March of Dimes; campaign chmn. United Way. Served with U.S. Army, 1965-67. Mem. Nat. Assn. Broadcasters, Radio Advt. Bur., Va. Assn. Broadcasters, Richmond Ad Club, Greater Richmond Broadcasters Assn. Baptist. Clubs: Richmond Bass Masters, Nat. Bass Anglers, Sportsman's Soc. Office: 3314 Cutsman Ave Richmond VA 23230

SMITH, EDWIN, telephone co. exec.; b. Providence, May 9, 1941; s. Wilbur H.E. and Ethel Lucille S.; Cert. of design, Parson's Sch. Design, 1963; m. Alicia Margaret Caesar, July 17, 1977; stepchildren—Steven, Stacey. Asst. br. mgr. 1st Jersey Nat. Bank, Newark, 1966-69; loan officer U.S. Small Bus. Adminstrn., Newark, 1969-70; bus. opportunity and devel. specialist Medic, Inc., Newark, 1970-74; dir. franchise opportunities clearinghouse Meric, Inc., N.Y.C., 1974-76; acct. exec. Southwestern Bell Telephone Co., Dallas, 1976—; staff asso. Found. Metaphys. Studies, Dallas. Bd. dirs. Park S. YMCA, Dallas. Served with NG U.S. Army, 1963-69. Mem. Am. Soc. Tng. and Devel., Dallas Black C. of C., Assn. Profl. Color Labs, Photo Mktg. Assn., Profl. Photographers Assn. Office: 5525 LBJ Regency Center I Dallas TX 75240

SMITH, ELIZABETH WIESS (MRS. LLOYD H. SMITH), civic worker; b. Beaumont, Tex., Jan. 29, 1916; d. Harry Carothers and Olga (Keith) Wiess; student Miss Porter's Sch., Miss Helen Stout's Schs.; m. Lloyd Hilton Smith, on May 25, 1940; children—Sandra K. Smith Mosbacher, Sharon L. Smith Keller, Sydney C. Smith Kerr. Trustee, Ballet Found., 1950-70, Southampton Hosp., 1958-70, Houston Mus. Fine Arts, 1951—, Houston Ballet Found., 1957—, Vis. Nurse Assn., 1947-52, Michael E. DeBakey Med. Found., 1970—, art assos. St. Thomas U., 1963—; bd. dirs. Inst. Antiquities and Christianity of Claremont Grad. Sch., 1970-74; trustee Soc. for Rehab. of Facially Disfigured, Royal Oaks Found., Research to Prevent Blindness; nat. bd. dirs. Northwood Inst., 1977—. Mem. Am. Fedn. Art, Southampton Hist. Soc. Clubs: Houston Garden, Assembly, Bayou, Ramada Allegro (Houston); River (N.Y.C.); Southampton Garden; Curzon House (London). Home: 2 Longfellow Ln Houston TX 77005

SMITH, ERNEST LEROY, chemist; b. McGaheysville, Va., Jan. 31, 1939; s. Lawrence and Rhoda Mae (Moore) S.; B.S. in Biology, Eastern Mennonite Coll., 1966. Project chemist Reynolds Metals Co., Grottoes, Va., 1966-72, analytical chemist, 1973—. Served with USAF, 1957-61. Mem. N.Am. Thermal Analysis Soc. Democrat. Baptist. Home: Route 1 Box 57 McGaheysville VA 22840 Office: PO Box 128 Caverns Blvd Grottoes VA 24441

SMITH, ETHEL LILLIE KNOTT (MRS. BUDD ELMON SMITH), librarian; b. nr. Oxford, N.C., July 21, 1915; d. Fielding and Lillie (Overton) Knott; student Queens Coll., 1933-34; A.B., Meredith Coll., 1937; B.L.S., U. N.C., 1942; M.A., Appalachian State Tchrs. Coll., 1955; postgrad. U. Chgo.; m. Budd Elmon Smith, Dec. 28, 1943; children—James Fielding, William Budd. Tchr., Guilford (N.C.) Coll. High Sch., 1937-38, Roanoke Rapids (N.C.) High Sch., 1938-42; librarian Gastonia (N.C.) High Sch., 1942-43, U.S. Army, Camp Butler, N.C., 1943-44, Cornell Library Assn. Library, 1944-45; instr. Wake Forest Coll., 1946-51; librarian Oxford City Schs., 1952-53; instr. Wingate (N.C.) Coll., 1953-55, librarian, 1955—; exec. sec. N.C. Nat. Library Week, 1963. Sec., Wingate PTA, 1957-58, Woman's Missionary Union, 1958-60, Union County Planning Bd., 1964—; mem. com. Self-Study Baptist Colls. N.C., 1964-65. Mem. AAUW (pres. N.C. 1970-72), Am., Southeastern, N.C. (past chmn. jr. coll. sect., chmn. coll. and univ. sect.) library assns., Nat. Council Tchrs. English, Modern Lang. Assn., Delta Kappa Gamma. Democrat. Baptist. Club: Woman's Garden. Asso. editor: The Junior College Library Collection; contbr. articles to profl. jours. Address: Route 2 Box 121A Benson NC 27504

SMITH, EUNICE TRASS, educator; b. Brookhaven, Miss., Mar. 2, 1937; d. Henry Bancroft and Drusie Belle (Hutchins) Trass; B.S., Alcorn State U., 1958; M.B.E. (So. Edn. Found. fellow), U. Miss., 1969; Ed.D., U. So. Miss., 1975; m. Charlie James Smith, Jan. 19, 1956; children—Olivia Delores, Lynda Kathryn, Evelyn Camille, Valerie Michelle. Tchr. bus. Bay Springs (Miss.) Vocat. Attendance Center, 1958-59, Clarke County High Sch., Enterprise, Miss., 1959-63, Brinkley Sr. High Sch., Jackson, Miss., 1963-68; sec. to dir. admissions Rust Coll., Holly Springs, Miss., 1968-69; asso. prof., head dept. bus. edn. and adminstrv. services Jackson (Miss.) State U., 1969—. Neighborhood vol. Muscular Dystrophy, 1971-73; leader Girl Scouts U.S.A., 1966-68; mem. solicitation com. Farish St. YMCA, 1979. Mem. Nat. Assn. Bus. Tchrs. Edn., Nat. Assn. Tchr. Educators for Bus. and Office Edn., Nat. Bus. Edn. Assn., So. Bus. Edn. Assn., Miss. Bus. Edn. Assn, Alpha Kappa Mu, NAACP, Delta Sigma Theta (treas. Jackson Alumnae chpt. 1965-68), Delta Pi Epsilon, Kappa Delta Pi, Phi Delta Kappa, Pi Omega Pi. Baptist. Coll. and univ. editor Miss. Bus. Edn. Assn. Jour., 1975, 77. Office: Box 17100 Jackson State U Jackson MS 39217

SMITH, FINIS W., state senator; b. Springfield, Mo., Aug. 29, 1926; s. Joseph L. and Mable (Pearcey) S.; B.S., Tulsa U., 1952, J.D., 1954; M.A., Okla. U., 1975; m. Doris Louise Harper, Oct. 18, 1974; children—Michael, David, Donald, Susan. Admitted to Okla. bar, 1954, since practiced in Tulsa; partner firm Smith, Brown, Martin & Adkisson, 1958—; chmn., chief exec. officer Community Bank & Trust Co., Tulsa, 1972—; mem. Okla. Senate from 37th Dist., 1964—, chmn. revenue and taxation com., 1969, pres. pro tem., 1972; dir. Am. Trustee Life Ins. Co., Southwest Pioneer Life Ins. Co. Past pres. Tulsa County Democrats. Served with A.C., USNR, 1942-46. Recipient Disting. Ser. award Okla. Osteo. Coll., 1974; named Okla.'s Outstanding Senator, U.P.I., 1971, 74, Most Valuable Legislator, Oklahoma City Times, 1980. Mem. Am. Bar Assn., Am. Bankers Assn., Nat. Conf. Legis. Leader, Am. Soc. Public Adminstrs., Okla. Bar Assn., Okla. Bankers Assn., Tulsa Country Jr. Bar Assn. (past pres.). Mem. Christian Ch. (Disciples of Christ). Home: 2424 W 45th Ct Tulsa OK 74107 Office: 410 Beacom Bldg Tulsa OK 74103

SMITH, FLOYD WILSON, telephone co. exec.; b. Liberty, S.C., July 1, 1928; s. Jessee Earl and Kate Alma (Hunter) S.; student Clemson U., 1945-47, Samford U., 1955-58, U. Ala., 1959-60; m. Vivian Louise Young, Sept. 6, 1952; children—Browyn Louise Cardwell, Floyd Wilson. With So. Bell, Anniston, Ala., 1952-54, Birmingham, Ala., 1954-56, Montgomery, Ala., 1956-58, Nashville, 1958-60; with Am. Tel. & Tel., N.Y.C., 1960-63; asst. sec. employees benefits com. South Central Bell, Nashville, 1963-68, Birmingham, Ala., 1968—. Instr. arts and crafts Ala. Med. Center, 1973; adv. Jefferson County Regional Health Council, 1977, Jefferson Health Found. Served with USAF, 1949-52. Mem. Birmingham C. of C. Baptist (chmn. property and grounds com. 1977—, mem. bldg. com. 1977—, chmn. deacon's caring com. 1977-79, sec. bd. deacons 1977-79, mem. mission com. 1977-79). Home: 3741 Woodvale Rd Birmingham AL 35223 Office: South Central Bell Tel Co PO Box 432 21st Floor Birmingham AL 35201

SMITH, FRANCES SCOTT, speech pathologist; b. Crystal Springs, Miss., Nov. 15, 1932; d. John William and Birdie Estelle (Parkinson) Scott; B.A., U. Miss., 1954, M.A., 1956; Ph.D., Purdue U., 1961; m. S. Allen Smith, June 5, 1955; children—Leonard, Lywin, Carl. Speech pathologist Laurel (Miss.) City Schs., 1954-55; pvt. practice speech pathology, Hammond, La., 1960-63, Jacksonville, Fla., 1970—; speech pathologist Speech and Hearing Clinic, Jacksonville, 1963-65, chief speech pathologist, 1965-69, acting dir., 1969-70; instr. Office of Continuing Edn., U. Fla., Jacksonville, 1964—; mem. Fla. State Adv. Council of Speech Pathology and Audiology, 1969-70, 72-75; cons. Kadis, 1970-74. Chmn. Fla. Health and Rehab. Services, 1976-78; chmn. task force com. on spl. edn. Community Planning Council, 1973-74. Mem. Fla. Speech and Hearing Assn. (chmn. govt. regulation com. 1971-73), Am. Speech and Hearing Assn. (cert. in speech pathology, audiology), Fla. Cleft Palate Assn. (pres. 1979-80, counselor 1973-75), Am. Acad. of Pvt. Practice in Speech Pathology and Audiology (dir. 1980—), Jacksonville Assn. for Children with Learning Disabilities (mem. adv. council 1970-75), Fla. Assn. for Mental Retardation, N.E. Fla. Lang., Speech and Hearing Assn. (pres. 1973-74). Mem. Christian Ch. Office: 230 Arlington Rd North Jacksonville FL 32211

SMITH, FRANK LOUIS, SR., ins. agt.; b. Bassett, Va., Nov. 21, 1944; s. Louis Edward and Lessie E. S.; B.S., Tex. Tech U.; M.B.A., U. Tex., 1973; 1 son, Frank Louis. Property and Casualty underwriter Allstate Ins. Co., Roanoke, Va., 1973-75; sales rep. Equitable Life Ins. Co. U.S., Roanoke, 1976—. Served with USAF, 1965-70. Mem. Va. Life Underwriters Assn., Million Dollar Round Table, Roanoke Bus. League, NAACP. Democrat. Roman Catholic. Clubs: Va. Coin, Jogging, Golf, Jefferson. Home: 5426 Twilight Rd NW Roanoke VA 24019 Office: 14th Floor FNEB Bldg PO Box 13526 Roanoke VA 24035

SMITH, FRED CARL, surgeon; b. Polk County, Ga., Sept. 20, 1923; s. Leamon Andrew and Nancy O. (Stephenson) S.; B.S., Emory U., 1944, M.D., 1950; m. Mary Katherine Hallman, Feb. 11, 1951; children—Vickie Elaine, Mary Elizabeth, Leamon Andrew, Fred Carl (dec.), Nancy Lucille. Intern in surgery Grady Meml. Hosp., Atlanta, 1950-51; resident in surgery Atlanta VA Hosp., 1951-54; fellow in surgery Emory U., Atlanta, 1954-55; individual practice medicine specializing in surgery S. Ga. Med. Center, Valdosta, 1955—, chief of staff, 1968. Served with M.C., U.S. Army, 1943-46. Ford Found. research grantee, 1955. Diplomate Am. Bd. Surgery. Fellow A.C.S., SE Surg. Congress; mem. AMA, Ga. Surg. Soc., S. Ga. med. socs., 8th Dist. Med. Soc. (pres. 1976), James C. Thoroughman, Ga. surg. socs., Sigma Xi, Alpha Kappa Kappa. Baptist. Clubs: Valdosta Country, Elks. Contbr. articles to profl. jours. Home: 906 Mill Pond Rd Valdosta GA 31601 Office: Bldg F Oak Center 11 2704 N Oak St Valdosta GA 31601

SMITH, GARY DON, TV exec.; b. Waco, Tex., Apr. 11, 1947; s. William Lloyd and Jo Nell (Pair) S.; B.S. in Indsl. Tech., Am. Tech. U., 1973; M.B.A., Pepperdine U., 1977; Ph.D., Walden U., 1979; m. Judy Carol, June 21, 1968; children—Jennifer Carol, Stephanie Jill. Chief engr. Mosley Machinery, Waco, 1970-73; pres. Hupp Systems, Inc., Waco, 1973-75; dir. systems devel., Mac Corp., Dallas, 1975-76; v.p. B.O.P. div. Ross Hill Control Corp., Houston, 1976—; pres. Gary D. Smith & Assos., Waco; now exec. v.p., gen. mgr. PTL TV Network, Charlotte; dir. Harper Oil Tool & Hupp Systems, Inc. Served with USMCR, 1966. Registered profl. engr., Calif., Can.; nat. certified mfg. engr. Mem. Soc. Mfg. Engrs. (sr.), Am. Inst. Indsl. Engrs. (sr.), Nat., Tex. socs. profl. engrs., Assn. Iron and Steel Engrs., Soc. Petroleum Engrs. Republican. Mem. Full Gospel Church. Author: The Pil Principle, 1980. Patentee winch, tractor crane, shear baler, solid waste vehicle, control system. Home: PO Box 220554 Charlotte NC 28222

SMITH, GARY LYNN, mech. engr.; b. Dallas, Nov. 10, 1951; s. William Nelson and Norma Scott (McCommas) S.; B.S., Okla. State U., 1974; m. Jean Ann Gray, Aug. 21, 1976. Segment engr. Sun Oil Co., Midland, Tex., 1974-75, Colorado City, Tex., 1975-78, dist. mech. engr., Tulsa, 1978-79; prodn. engr. Samson Resources, Tulsa, 1979—. Mem. Soc. Petroleum Engrs., ASME, Am. Inst. Aeros. and Astronautics. Home: 205 W Los Angeles Pl Broken Arrow OK 74012 Office: 2700 First Nat Tower Tulsa OK 74103

SMITH, GEORGE HUDSON, banker, devel. co. exec.; b. Cleveland, Ala., Dec. 31, 1932; s. Leo Hobson and Ruby Betty (Horton) S.; B.A., Samford U., 1960, M.A., 1969; m. Janice Foster, June 4, 1955; 1 dau., Meghan. Announcer/sales Sta. WCRL, Oneonta, Ala., 1956-57; sales Sta. WAPI, Birmingham, Ala., 1957-58; prodn. Sta. WBRC-TV, Birmingham, 1958-60; dir. pub. relations, asso. prof. journalism Samford U., Birmingham, 1960-70; v.p. First Ala. Bank, Birmingham, 1970-74; sr. v.p. Bank of SE, Birmingham, 1974-77; partner GHS Devel. Corp., Birmingham, 1977—. Bd. dirs. Birmingham Civic Ballet, 1972—; active Birmingham Festival of Arts, 1965-72, Downtown Action Com., 1971-74, Operation New Birmingham, 1968-74. Served with AC, USN, 1954-56. Mem. Birmingham C. of C. (local ambassadors com.), Profl. Journalism Soc. (dir.), Birmingham Advt. Club (dir.), Bank Mktg. Assn., Birmingham Press Club (dir.), Ala. Pub. Relation Com. (dir.). Clubs: Vestavia Country, Downtown, The Club. Author: The Life and Times of William James Samford, 1970. Home: 2637 Mountain Wood Dr Birmingham AL 35216 Office: PO Box 6697 Birmingham AL 35210

SMITH, GEORGE ROSE, justice Ark. Supreme Ct.; b. Little Rock, July 26, 1911; s. Hay Watson and Jessie Alice (Rose) S.; student Washington and Lee U., 1928-31; LL.B., U. Ark., 1933; m. Peg Newton, Dec. 3, 1938; 1 dau., Laurinda Hempstead. Admitted to Ark. bar, 1933; practiced in Little Rock, 1933-49; mem. firm Rose, Dobyns, Meek & House; asso. justice Ark. Supreme Ct., 1949—, also mem. com. jury instrns. Served to maj. AUS, 1942-46. Mem. Ark. Bar Assn., Inst. Jud. Adminstrn., Sigma Alpha Epsilon, Phi Delta Phi. Author: Arkansas Annotations to Restatement of Trusts, 1938; Arkansas Mining and Mineral Law, 1942. Home: 2 Cantrell Rd Little Rock AR 72207 Office: Justice Bldg Little Rock AR 72201

SMITH, GEORGE THOMAS, ins. co. exec.; b. Raleigh, N.C., Sept. 21, 1933; s. Gordon and Edith Lanier (Clark) S.; A.B., U. N.C., 1955; grad. mgmt. program Coll. Ins., Princeton U., 1969; m. Sarah H. Liggett, June 13, 1955; children—Susan L., George Thomas. Regional mgr. Gt. Am. Ins. Co., now div. v.p., Raleigh, N.C.; bd. govs. N.C. Rate Bur., N.C. Reins. Facility, S.C. Ins. Guaranty Fund, N.C. Ins. News Service; mem. adv. bd. Ins. Services Office N.C. Bd. dirs. Cerebral Palsy and Rehab. Center, Raleigh. Served to 1st lt. USAF, 1955-58. Mem. Carolinas Ins. Mgrs. Assn. Democrat. Episcopalian. Clubs: Carolina Country, Sphinx. Office: 401 Oberlin Rd Raleigh NC 27605

SMITH, GEORGIA ELIZABETH, univ. adminstr.; b. Ft. Riley, Kans., Nov. 28, 1954; d. John Franklin and Mary Elizabeth S.; B.A., Colo. State U., 1976; M.S., Western Ill. U., 1978. Acad. adv., student asst. Colo. State U., Ft. Collins, 1974-76; head resident adv. Western Ill. U., Macomb, 1976-78; asst. dir. residential and judicial affairs Vanderbilt U., Nashville, 1978—. Mem. Am. Personnel and Guidance Assn., Am. Coll. Personnel Assn., Nat. Assn. Student Personnel Adminstrs., Tenn. Assn. Student Personnel Adminstrs. Roman Catholic. Clubs: Young Nashvillians, Woodmont Coll. and Careers Choir. Home: Box 2934 Sta B Nashville TN 37235 Office: Vanderbilt U 4112 Branscomb Quadrangle Nashville TN 37235

SMITH, GILBERT EDWIN, geologist, inst. exec.; b. Nelsonville, Ohio, Oct. 26, 1922; s. Charles Gilbert and Inez C. (Williams) S.; B.S. in Geology, Ohio U., 1950; M.S., W.Va. U., 1951; m. Mary Anna Matheny, Nov. 22, 1951. Geologist, Ohio Div. Geol. Survey, 1951-56; sr. staff geologist Aluminum Co. Am., Ill. and Mex., 1956-61; sr. geologist, head coal sect. Ky. Geol. Survey, 1963-76; asso. dir. Inst. Mining and Minerals Research, U. Ky., Lexington, 1976—. Served with U.S. Army, 1943-46. Fellow Geol. Soc. Am. (chmn. coal geology div. 1975); mem. Mine Insps. Inst. Am., Am. Assn. Stratigraphic Palynologists, AIME, Am. Legion., Sigma Xi. Clubs: Masons, Shriners, Elks, Eagles. Home: 1710 Blue Licks Rd Lexington KY 40504 Office: KCERL PO Box 13015 Lexington KY 40583

SMITH, GLORIA QUINN, spl. edn. tchr.; b. Chattanooga, Dec. 26, 1931; d. Taylor Lee and Katherine (Bird) Quinn; B.A. (univ. grantee), U. New Orleans, 1975; children—Linda Sheryl, Cindy Renée, Donna Patrice, Zachary Quinn, Walter Daniel. Nursery attendant Paradise Lanes, Metairie, La., 1963-67; waitress Pitt Grill, Kenner, La., 1967-73, Ranch House Restaurant, Kenner, 1973-74, House of Lee, Metairie, 1974-78; spl. edn. tchr. Jefferson Parish Sch. Bd., 1975-79; spl. edn. tchr. Guntersville City (Ala.) Bd. Edn., 1979—; real estate agt. Stan Weber & Assos., Inc., LaPlace, La., 1978-79. Mem. Council for Exceptional Children, Council for Children with Behavior Disorders, Ala. Edn. Assn., Guntersville Edn. Assn., Kappa Delta Pi. Home: 405 Allicia St Albertville AL 35950

SMITH, GORDON LAIDLAW, JR., mfg. oil and gas prodn. co. exec.; b. Chattanooga, Jan. 29, 1926; s. Gordon Laidlaw and Sara (Simmons) S.; B.C.E., Duke U., 1948; m. Frances Lowrance Street, Aug. 22, 1951; children—Gordon Laidlaw III, Preston Lowrance, Sara Frances. With Wheland Co. (merged into Gordon Street, Inc. 1961), Chattanooga, 1948-61, trainee, 1948-50, supt. prodn. planning and material control, 1950-53, asst. sales mgr., 1953-56, sales mgr., 1956-58, sec., 1958-61, dir., 1959-61; sec., dir. Gordon Street, Inc. (merged into N.Am. Royalties, Inc. 1969), Chattanooga, 1961-69, sec.-treas., 1964-69; sec.-treas. N.Am. Royalties, Inc., Chattanooga, 1969-72, v.p. fin., treas., 1972-79, v.p. planning and devel., sec., treas., 1979—, also dir.; dir. First Fed. Savs. & Loan Assn. Chattanooga, Commerce Union Bank, Chattanooga. Chmn. Chattanooga-Hamilton County chpt. ARC, 1962-64, mem. exec. com., 1958-75; mem. Met. Bd. YMCA, 1966-67, mem. campaign cabinet New YMCA Fund, 1966—; mem. Duke U. Alumni Admissions Adv. Com.; bd. dirs. Boys' Club Chattanooga; trustee Mc Callie Sch. Served with USNR, 1944-46. Mem. Am. Petroleum Inst., U.S. C. of C., Greater Chattanooga Area C. of C. (pres. 1975-76), Chattanooga (pres. 1966-67), Tenn. (bd. govs. 1970—) mfrs. assns., Chattanooga Automobile Club (pres. 1973-74), Phi Delta Theta, Omicron Delta Kappa. Presbyterian (deacon 1954—, trustee 1964—). Clubs: Kiwanis (pres. Chattanooga 1963), Chattanooga Golf and Country, Mountain City (Chattanooga). Home: 1609 Edgewood Circle Chattanooga TN 37405 Office: 200 E 8th St Chattanooga TN 37402

SMITH, HARRISON HARVEY, newspaper cons.; b. Wilkes-Barre, Pa., Oct. 24, 1915; s. Ernest Gray and Marjorie (Harvey) S.; literary-sci. diploma Wyoming (Pa.) Sem., 1936; postgrad. Medill Sch. Journalism, Northwestern U., 1937-38; m. Joanne Christopher, June 7, 1940; children—Barbara Dewitt, Marjorie Harvey, Susan C.; m. 2d, Margaret Simons, July 18, 1947 (dec. May 1978); children—Rosanne Jameson, Elizabeth Simons. Asst. pub. Wilkes-Barre Times-Leader, 1938-39, v.p., asst. sec., 1939-46, pres., 1946-79; editor Wilkes-Barre Record, 1962-72; newspaper cons., Key Biscayne, Fla., 1979—; dir. 1st Eastern Bank Wilkes-Barre. Chmn., Wyoming Valley chpt. ARC, 1954-55, chmn. NE Pa. Blood Center, 1955-56; v.p. Wilkes-Barre Gen. Hosp., 1954-76. Served with U.S. Mil. Govt., Korea, 1945-46. Recipient Distinguished Service award U.S. Jr. C. of C., 1949. Mem. Am. Soc. Newspaper Editors, Nat. Conf. Editorial Writers, Pa. Newspaper Pubs. Assn. (exec. com. 1954-62), AP Pa. (pres. 1953), Wyoming Hist. Soc. (pres. 1971-74), Am. Legion, VFW, Sigma Delta Chi. Republican. Presbyterian. Clubs: Newcomen, Poor Richard (Phila.); Mirador (Geneva); Westmoreland (Wilkes-Barre); Masons (33 deg.). Home and Office: 177 Ocean Lane Dr Key Biscayne FL 33149

SMITH, HARRY MORGAN, anthropologist; b. Orlando, Fla., Dec. 31, 1926; s. Claude Earle and Pearl Adelaide (Morgan) S.; B.S., Fla. State U., 1953; postgrad. Troy State U.; m. Charlene Scrafford, Aug. 24, 1962; 1 son, Charles Michael Moras. Research asso. dept. anthropology, field research Caribbean and Central Am., Fla. State U., 1952-53; supervisory research scientist USAF, Maxwell AFB, Ala., 1954—; tchr., lectr. emergency survival, cross-cultural communications and environ. utilization planning, 1966—; dir. Fla. State U.'s Panama Archeol. and Bot. Expdn., 1952, participant Cuba Expdn., 1953; dir. Zundapp Mid-Am. Expdn., 1953-54, Peruvian Amazon River Basin Expdn., 1963. Served with USCG, 1944-46; PTO. Recipient Air Force decoration for exceptional civilian service, 1967, Air Force certificate of honor for outstanding service Am. MIA of PWs in S.E. Asia, 1970; named Civilian of Year, USAF, 1967, Hon. Air Commando, 1st Air Commando Wing, 1962. Mem. Soc. Applied Anthropology, Am. Polar Soc., Explorers Club, Ala. Acad. Sci., Assn. Tropical Biology, Nat. Audubon Soc., Isthmian Anthropology Soc. Contbr. articles to profl. jours. Home: Route 4 Box 257 Wetumpka AL 36092 Office: AUL Environ Info Div Bldg 754 Maxwell AFB AL 36112

SMITH, HELEN LAVERNE, film producer; b. Dallas, Aug. 16, 1927; d. Johnny George and Mattie Pearl (Harmon) Hamilton; student E. Tex. U., 1946, So. Meth. U., 1962-64, S.W. Christian Coll., 1964; m. Charles Ray Smith, Feb. 23, 1946; children—Nancy Sharon Smith McDonald, Charles Marcus. With Cook Paint & Varnish, Dallas, 1944-47, Butler Bros., Dallas, 1947-48; ind. auditor, various sml. bus., Dallas, 1949-53; owner-operator Charles R. Smith Import/Export, Dallas, 1960-62; with Varo Inc., Garland, Tex., 1962-74; owner, pres. Laurel Leaf, Inc., Dallas, 1977—; pres. Day Star Inc., Dallas, 1977—; pres., owner Canyon Film Distributors, Dallas, 1979—. Named Bus. Woman of the Year, Am. Bus. Women Assn., 1974-75. Mem. Am. Bus. Women Assn. (pres. 1973), Tex. Film Tape Assn. of Profls., Nat. Assn. Broadcast Employers and Technicians. Baptist. Home: 3231 Chapel Creek Dr Apt 144 Dallas TX 75220 Office: PO Box 29928 Dallas TX 75229

SMITH, HENRY LEROY, ednl. adminstr.; b. Mt. Holly, N.C., July 25, 1931; s. Henry L. and Jennie M. (Hill) S.; A.B., Lenoir Rhyne Coll., 1967; Ed.M., U. Va., 1962, Ed.D., 1967; m. La Vonne Elaine Stroupe, Nov. 12, 1955; children—Preston Browning, Robin Elaine. Tchr. elem. and secondary levels N.C. public schs., 1955-60; dir. spl. edn. Lynchburg (Va.) public schs., 1961-66, Charlotte-Mecklenburg (N.C.) public schs., 1966-69; sr. state plan officer Bur. Edn. for Handicapped, U.S. Office Edn., Washington, 1969-73; chmn. spl. edn. dept. Auburn (Ala.) U., 1973-76; dir. internat. programs Latin Am. and Africa, Goodwill Industries Am., Bethesda, Md., 1976-77; asst. state supt. edn. La. State Dept. Edn., Baton Rouge, 1976—; cons. to numerous local public sch. systems in various states, 1966-79, state edn. agys., 1967-79; lectr. various colls. and univs., 1963-79; mem. faculty U. Va., 1963-66, Lynchburg Coll., 1965. Mem. Mental Health Bd., State of Va., 1964-66, N.C., 1968-69; pres. Lynchburg Mental Health Assn., 1964-66, Lynchburg Sheltered Workshop, Inc., 1965-66, Charlotte Mental Health Assn., 1968, Charlotte Assn. Ret. Citizens, 1969, Auburn Mental Health Assn., 1975; chmn. (N.C.) Gov.'s Study Commn. Spl. Edn., 1969. Served with USN, 1947-49. Recipient Disting. Public Service award La. Assn. Ret. Citizens, 1977, Man of the Year award, City of Lynchburg, 1966, W. Kuhn Barnett award, 1967; Disting. Service award La. Assn. Gifted/Talented, 1979; Educator of Year, Phi Delta Kappa, 1979. Fellow Am. Assn. Mental Deficiency; mem. Internat. Council for Exceptional Children (gov.-at-large 1978—), NEA, La. Assn. Educators, Phi Delta Kappa, Kappa Delta Pi. Baptist. Clubs: Lions, Rotary. Home: 1526 Kenilworth Pkwy Baton Rouge LA 70808 Office: Box 44064 La State Dept Edn Baton Rouge LA 70804

SMITH, HUBERT GENE, educator; b. Ponca City, Okla., Dec. 27, 1931; s. Hubert Murel and Fern Maxine (Gabriel) S.; B.S. in Bus., Okla. State U., 1953, M.B.A. in Bus., 1971, Ed.D. in Bus. Edn., 1973; children—Sheryl Lynn, Stephen Vincent, Debra Ann. Refinery accountant Continental Oil Co., Ponca City, Okla., 1953-54, methods analyst, 1954-60, computer analyst, 1960-62, sr. computer analyst, 1962-69; asst. dir. Total Guidance Info. Support System, Bartlesville, Okla., 1969-71; research asst., research, planning and evaluation Okla. Dept. Vocat.-Tech. Edn., Stillwater, 1971-73, dir. linear programming project, 1973-74; asst. prof., mgr. systems design and computer services Sch. Occupational and Adult Edn., Coll. Edn. Okla. State U., Stillwater, 1974—. Mem. Assn. for Systems Mgmt., NEA, Am., Okla. vocational assns., Okla. Edn. Assn., Beta Gamms Sigma, Delta Pi Epsilon. Home: Rural Route 1 Kildare OK 74642 Office: Sch Occupational Adult Edn Coll Edn Okla State U Stillwater OK 74074

SMITH, HUGH ELMORE, obstetrician, gynecologist; b. Mullins, S.C., Jan. 27, 1925; s. Howard Buchanan and Ruth Celia (Bethea) S.; student The Citadel, 1942-43, U. Miss., 1946; M.D., Med. U. S.C., 1950; m. Martha Elizabeth Meares, June 21, 1947; children—Bonnie Ruth, Hugh Elmore, Jefferson H., Brian B. Intern, Roper Hosp., Charleston, S.C., 1950-51, resident in obstetrics and gynecology, 1951-54; practice medicine specializing in obstetrics and gynecology, Orangeburg, S.C., 1954—; mem. staff Orangeburg Regional Hosp. Served in USNR, 1943-46. Diplomate Am. Bd. Obstetrics and Gynecology. Fellow Am. Coll. Obstetricians and Gynecologists; mem. S. Central, S.C. obstet. and gynecol. socs., S. Atlantic Assn. Obstetricians and Gynecologists. Methodist. Clubs: Country, Rotary (past pres.) (Orangeburg). Home: 1195 Middleton St Orangeburg SC 29115 Office: 909 Summers St Orangeburg SC 29115

SMITH, IVAN HURON, architect; b. Danville, Ind., Jan. 25, 1907; s. Calvin Wesley and Irma (Huron) S.; student Ga. Tech., 1926; B.Arch., U. Fla., 1929 m. Sara Butler, Aug. 18, 1972; 1 dau., Norma Smith Benton. Prin., Ivan H. Smith, Jacksonville, Fla., 1936-41; partner Reynolds, Smith & Hills, Jacksonville, Tampa, Orlando, Merritt Island and Ft. Lauderdale, Fla., 1941—, chmn. bd., 1970-77, chmn. emeritus, 1977—; dir. So. Indsl. Bank, Jacksonville; chmn. Jacksonville Constrn. Trades Qualification Bd., 1971; mem. Duval County Govt. Study Commn., 1966-67; sec. Jacksonville Bldg. Code Adv. Bd., 1951-68. Bd. dirs. Duval County-Jacksonville Safety Council, Jacksonville U. Council. Served with USNR, 1943-45; CBI. Fellow AIA (pres. Fla. N. chpt. 1952, Jacksonville chpt. 1956); mem. Fla. Assn. Architects (chmn. profl. practice commn. 1965-67, Pullera award for Outstanding Service to Profession 1965), Jacksonville C. of C. (bd. govs. 1957-59), Beta Theta Pi, Phi Kappa Phi, Sigma Tau. Clubs: Rotary, Gargoyle (U. Fla.); River, Univ., San Jose Country (Jacksonville). Prin. works: Fla. Field Stadium U. Fla., 1953; Duval County Ct. House, 1958; Jacksonville City Hall, Student Center Jacksonville U., 1960. Tampa Airport, 1970; (with Edward Durell Stone) Fla. State Capitol Complex, 1977. Home: 10460 Sylvan Ln W Jacksonville FL 32217 Office: 4019 Boulevard Center Dr Jacksonville FL 32201

SMITH, IVAN JUAN, realtor; b. Corbin, Ky., Apr. 9, 1930; s. Alvy and Ruby (Candy) S.; A.A., U. Fla., 1954; m. Gene Frances Wynne, Sept. 28, 1951; children—Stephanie Kay (Mrs. Craig Courty), Kelly Sue (Mrs. William Gil.), Cary Lynn. Asso. mem. M.N. Weir & Sons, Inc. realty, Pompano Beach, Fla., 1954-59, v.p., 1959-64; pres., 1965-69; pres., chmn. bd. Ivan J. Smith & Co., Inc. Realtors, Pompano Beach, 1969—; pres. Barsmith Corp.; chmn. bd. 1st Nat. Bank Broward County; dir. First Bankers Corp. Fla. Mem. South Fla. council Boy Scouts Am., 1970-73. Served with USCG, 1951-54. Named Outstanding Young Man, Jr. C. of C. Pompano Beach, 1963; Pompano Beach Realtor of Year, 1967. Mem. Nat. Inst. Farm and Land Brokers, Nat. Assn. Realtors, Pomano Beach-Deerfield Beach Bd. Realtors (pres. 1967), Greater Pompano Beach C. of C. (pres. 1972). Clubs: Hundred of Broward County; Century of Univ. Fla.; Lake Toxaway (N.C.) Country; Tower (Ft. Lauderdale, Fla.). Home: B-1 212 Briny Ave Pompano Beach FL 33062 Office: 3350 E Atlantic Blvd Pompano Beach FL 33062

SMITH, JACK DARLING, machinery co. exec., publisher; b. Madison, Fla., Jan. 25, 1920; s. Amos Charles and Ida Mae (Gissendaner) S.; student S. Ga. Coll., 1948-50; A.B., Valdosta State Coll., 1952, B.S., 1952; B.D., Emory U., 1955, M.Div., 1972; LL.B., Blackstone Sch. Law, 1970, J.D., 1971; m. Jane Frances Kappel, Dec. 13, 1970; children by previous marriage—Lyndell Darling, Joan Renice Smith Cole, Walton Earle. Vice pres., gen. mgr. Nat. Pub. Relations, Inc., Thomasville, Ga., 1946-48; ordained to ministry Meth. Ch., 1952; pastor, Ludowici, Ga., 1948-52, Stockbridge, Ga., 1952-55, Wadley (Ga.) 1st Ch., 1955-60, Sylvania, Ga., 1960-64, Dublin, Ga., 1964-68; v.p. pub. relations Fulghum Industries, Inc., Wadley, 1968—, also dir.; pres. Dixie Publs. & Arts Co., Inc. County chmn. Gov. Carter's campaign, 1970; trustee Ga. Magnolia Manor, Americus, 1965—; trustee Epworth-by-the-Sea. Served with USAAF, 1940-45. Mem. Ga. gov.'s staff, 1966-68, 68-70, 71; named Adm. Ga. Navy, 1971—. Mem. C. of C. (pres. 1972—). Democrat. Clubs: Masons, Rotary. Pub., The Logger, Lumberman Mag., 1969—. Home: Box 703 Wadley GA 30477 Office: Box 487 Wadley GA 30477

SMITH, JACK GILLESPIE, engr.; b. Kansas City, Mo., Aug. 17, 1917; s. Harvey H. and Della (Gillespie) S.; student Ga. Inst. Tech., 1935-40, U. Minn., 1943-44; m. Myra Louise Johnson, Nov. 27, 1941; children—Mary Louise Smith Johnson, Jack Gillespie, Davie Clarissa Smith Milsted. Elec. engr. TVA, Knoxville, 1940-58, Army Ballistic Missile Agy., Huntsville, Ala., 1958-60; aerospace tech. mgr. NASA, MSFC, Huntsville, 1960—, now attached to Office Asso. Dir. for Mgmt., Sci. and Engring. Directorate; ordained deacon Presbyn. Ch. U.S. Served with AUS 1942-46. Registered profl. engr., Tenn. Home: 1310 Kennamer Dr Huntsville AL 35801 Office: MSFC EM 12 Bldg 4487 Huntsville AL 35812

SMITH, JACKSON STOCKS, III, advt. agy. exec.; b. Charlotte, N.C., Sept. 9, 1946; s. Jackson Stocks and Ethel Vara (Brady) S.; B.S., Auburn U., 1968; M.B.A., U. Ga., 1969; m. Dorothy Elizabeth Crutsinger, Aug. 3, 1978; children—Stacey, Katherine, Shelby. Sales rep. Scott Paper Co., Atlanta, 1969-70, sr. sales rep., Jacksonville, Fla., 1970-71; advt. mgr. Internat. Dairy Queen, Inc., Mpls., 1971-74; pres. Jackson Smith Advt., Inc., Atlanta, 1974—. Episcopalian. Clubs: Cherokee Town and Country, Horseshoe Bend Country, Atlanta Auburn. Home: 110 Dogwood Lake Ct Roswell GA 30076 Office: 1155 Hammond Dr Atlanta GA 30328

SMITH, JAMES DAVID KIMO, lawyer; b. Wiesbaden, Germany, Jan. 1, 1948; came to U.S., 1950, naturalized, 1965; s. James David and Bliss A.; B.A. in Psychology, U. Hawaii, 1969, B.S. in Geology, 1969, M.S. in Geology, 1972; J.D., U. S.D., 1976. Sci. programmer Kentron Hawaii Ltd., Honolulu, 1968-70; field engr. Fegeles Power Service Amel Co., Honolulu, 1971-72; geologist U.S. Geol. Survey, EROS Data Center, Sioux Falls, S.D., 1972-75; admitted to bar, S.D., 1977, Hawaii, 1977, Tex., 1977, Alaska, 1978, Calif., 1980; gen. counsel Kentron Internat., Inc., Dallas, 1977—. Coordinator, Drug Rehab. Center, Honolulu, 1968-70. Mem. Tex. Bar Assn., Hawaii Bar Assn., S.D. Bar Assn., Alaska Bar Assn., Calif. Bar Assn., Am. Bar Assn., Labor Law Assn., Am. Assn. Petroleum Geologists, Geol. Soc. Am., Am. Soc. Photogrammetry. Author: Tax Aspects of Coal Extraction, 1980. Home: 4137 Normandy Ave Dallas TX 75205 Office: 2345 W Mockingbird Ln Dallas TX 75235

SMITH, JAMES LESLIE, contracting co. exec.; b. Stuttgart, Ark., Oct. 26, 1936; s. Leslie Leroy and Lois Laverne (Newberry) S.; B.E.E., U. Ark., 1959. Elec. engr. Internat. Paper Co., various locations, 1961-68; elec. engr. Quality Electric Service, Panama City,

Fla., 1968-71; gen. mgr. Ener-Dyne Inc., Panama City, 1971-72; mgr. sales and engring. Wireways Inc., Panama City, 1973—; also dir. Served with U.S. Army, 1959-61. Mem. IEEE. Republican. Mem. Christian Ch. Home: 3201 Treasure Circle Panama City Beach FL 32407 Office: 2215 17th St E PO Box 1847 Panama City FL 32401

SMITH, JAMES SHELDON, oil co. exec.; b. Corpus Christi, Tex., Nov. 17, 1939; s. Francis Joseph and Geraldine Lena (Laningham) S.; A.A., del Mar Jr. Coll., 1963; student U. Corpus Christi, 1962, Tex. A & I Coll., 1966, Tex. A&I U., 1973; m. Agnes Lenora Langridge, Sept. 14, 1960; children—James Sheldon, Mark Alexander. Material analyst Tex. Hwy. Dept., Corpus Christi, 1964-66; truck operator Texaco, Inc., Corpus Christi, 1966-76; broker, owner, Landmark Realty, Corpus Christi, 1970—; pres. Marine Oil Service Co., Corpus Christi, 1976—. Mem. Corpus Christi C. of C. Republican. Clubs: Masons, Propeller. Home: 235 Ocean View Pl Corpus Christi TX 78411 Office: 2223 N Port Ave Corpus Christi TX 78401

SMITH, JANE LYNETTE, educator; b. Louisville, July 17, 1939; d. Jacob Urban and Rhoda Hildegarde (Guy) Smith; student (Monseignor Felix N. Pitt scholar), Nazareth Coll., Louisville, 1957-59; student Most Holy Sacrament Tchr. Tng. Sch., Lafayette, La., 1960-63, U. S.W.La., 1962-65; B.A. (Senator Harvey Peltier grant), Nicholls State U., 1972, M.Ed., 1974, Edn. Specialist, 1977. Bookkeeper Bourbon Stock Yard Commn., Louisville, 1957-58; tchr. N. Ala. Missions Archdiocese of Birmingham, 1958-60; joined Sisters of Most Holy Sacrament, 1960; tchr. poverty program, Sunset, La., 1963; tchr., asst. prin. St. Maurice, Star of Seas schs., New Orleans, 1964-67; tchr. Lafourche Parish Schs., Thibodaux, La., 1968, 72—, home sch. visitor, 1974—; tchr. Holy Savior Sch., Lockport, La., 1968-70; bookkeeper Valentine Sugars, Lockport, 1971. Sec. Com. for Juvenile Detention Home for Lafourche Parish, 1975-77, Lafourche Friends of the Library, Thibodaux, 1976—; organizer, pres., treas. Lockport Friends of Library, 1976—; dep. Office of Lafourche Parish Sheriff, 1976—. Mem. Am. Personnel and Guidance Assn., Am. Sch. Counselors Assn., La. Tchrs. Assn., Lafourche Tchrs. Inc. (sec. 1976—), Nicholls State U. Alumni, Phi Delta Kappa. Democrat. Roman Catholic. Home: 108 Ferdinand St Lockport LA 70374 Office: care Lafourche Parish Sch Bd Thibodaux LA 70301

SMITH, JAY CLEVELAND, ednl. adminstr.; b. Aline, Okla., Jan. 27, 1940; s. Emory Melvin and Almeda Elizabeth (Woods) S.; B.A., U. Okla., 1962; M.Ed., U. Hawaii, 1967; Ph.D., Mich. State U., 1971; m. Peggy Karen Smith, June 4, 1961; children—Gregory Jay, Cherylle Almeda. Tchr. pub. schs., Okla., 1961-63; supr. Federally Assisted Programs, Jefferson Davis Parish Sch., La., 1963-65; vis. prof. Western Mich. U. Ednl. Resources Center, summers 1969-70; asst. prof. ednl. adminstrn. Ga. State U., Atlanta, 1970-72; ednl. devel. officer, dean learning resources U. S.C., 1972-76; dir. Instructional Services Center, staff asst. to provost for television U. Okla., Norman, 1976—; cons. Acad. Humanities, Greater Columbia Forum. Mem. S.C. Council on Consumer Credit, 1973-76; chairperson Parents Adv. Council, Lexington County (S.C.) Schs., 1974-76; regional rep. Faculties of Okla. Coll. and Univ. Systems, 1978—. Named Outstanding Tchr., Midwest City Schs., 1963; Experienced Tchr. fellow U. Hawaii, 1968-69; Ednl. Professions Devel. Act fellow Mich. State U., 1969-71; Ford Found. seminar leader U. S.C., 1972-76. Mem. Am. Assn. Higher Edn., Assn. Ednl. Communications and Tech., Nat. Assn. Ednl. Broadcasters, AAUP, Div. Instructional Devel., Am. Assn. Univ. Adminstrs., Soc. Coll. and Univ. Planning, Phi Delta Kappa. Democrat. Methodist. Clubs: Masons; Kiwanis. Home: PO Box 2537 Norman OK 73070 Office: Instructional Service Center U Okla 820 van Vleet St Norman OK 73019

SMITH, JEFFERSON VERNE, state senator; b. Greer, S.C., Jan. 15, 1925; s. Jefferson Verne and Lillian (Farley) S.; student Presbyn. Coll., Clinton, S.C., 1942-43; m. Jean Myers, Nov. 27, 1947; children—Jefferson Verne, Carole Jean Smith Cofer. Pres. Tire Exchange, Inc., Greer, Mauldin, Simpsonville and Greenville, S.C.; dir. Hercules Tire & Rubber Co., Greer Fed. Savs. & Loan Assn.; mem. S.C. Senate from 2d Dist. Ruling elder 1st Presbyn. Ch., Greer, 1965—; bd. govs. Shriners Hosp., Greenville, 1971-73; commr. Greer Commn. Public Works, 1969-72; mem. bd. commrs. S.C. Sch. Deaf and Blind, 1965-69; chmn. Greenville County Democratic Party, 1970-72. Served with AUS, 1943-45. Mem. S.C. Tire Dealers Assn. (pres. 1964-65), Greer C. of C. (pres. 1961-62), S.C. Peach Festival Assn. Clubs: Shriners, Woodmen of World. Address: Box 528 Greer SC 29651

SMITH, JERRY LEE, geneticist, agrl. co. exec.; b. Springfield, Ill., Oct. 6, 1946; s. James William and Gertrude Elouise (Estill) S.; B.S., So. Ill. U., Carbondale, 1969, M.S., 1970; Ph.D., U. Ark., Fayetteville, 1975; m. Donna McQueen, Sept. 9, 1967; children—Krista, Amanda. Grad. asst. animal sci. So. Ill. U., Carbondale, 1968-69; research asst. in animal sci. U. Ark., Fayetteville, 1970-74; geneticist Shaver Poultry Breeding Farms, Cullman, Ala., 1974-76; geneticist Peterson Farms, Inc., Decatur, Ark., 1976—, dir. comml. line devel., 1976—. Pres., Decatur PTA, 1979-80. Mem. Nat. Breeders Roundtable (editor 1978—, chmn. exec. com. 1980), Ark. Poultry Fedn., Poultry Sci. Assn., World's Poultry Sci. Assn., Am. Registry of Cert. Animal Scientists, AAAS, Sigma Xi. Methodist. Home: PO Box 101 Decatur AR 72722 Office: Peterson Farms Inc PO Box 248 Decatur AR 72722

SMITH, JERRY LEE, state legislator; b. Muskogee, Okla., Dec. 6, 1943; s. Hollis C. and Eulema M. (Hall) S.; B.A., Okla. State U., 1967; J.D., U. Tulsa, 1970. Admitted to Okla. bar, 1971; mem. firm Frazier and Dyer, Tulsa, 1972-80, firm Frazier, Smith and Farris, 1980—; mem. Okla. Ho. of Reps., 1972—. Mem. Okla., Tulsa County bar assns., Okla. Trial Lawyers Assn., Phi Delta Phi. Home: 5327 E 33 St Tulsa OK 74135 Office: 1424 Terrace Dr Tulsa OK 74104

SMITH, JIM RAY, realtor; b. West Columbia, Tex., Feb. 27, 1932; s. William G. and Laura A. (Brown) S.; B.B.A., Baylor U., 1957; m. Paula M. Braden, Apr. 2, 1955; children—James Ray, Paul Braden, Ripple Alicia. Mem. Cleve. Browns Football Club, 1956-62, Dallas Cowboys Football Club, 1963-64; owner Jim Ray Smith & Co., comml. and indsl. realty, Dallas, 1965—; dir. Addison State Bank; mem. Dallas Equalization Bd., 1972-73. Vice chmn. realtors sect. com. gifts, trusts and bequests Wadley Insts. Molecular Medicine, Dallas, 1973—; bd. dirs. Baylor U. Stadium Corp., Cotton Bowl Athletic Assn. Served with AUS, 1955-56. Named to High Sch. All-Star Football Game, 1950, All S.W. Conf. Baylor U., 1953, 54, Coll. All-Star Football Team Chgo. News, 1955, Browns All-Time All-Star Team, 1962, play in Pro-Bowl Los Angeles Times, 1958, 59, 60, 61, 62, Baylor U. Hall of Fame, 1968; named Lineman of Week, UP and AP, 1953, All Am. Baylor U., 1953, All Pro Cleve. Browns, 1958, 59, 60, 61, 62. Mem. Dallas Bd. Realtors, Tex., Nat. assns. realtors, Ex-student Assn. Baylor U. Hankamer Sch. Bus. (pres. 1973), Baylor B Assn., Fellowship Christian Athletes (pres. chpt. 1969), Bill Glass Evangelistic Assn. (treas. 1971, dir.), Salesmanship Club Dallas (dir. 1976). Baptist (deacon). Club: Bent Tree Country. Home: 7049 Cliffbrook St Dallas TX 75240 Office: PO Box 182 15525 Dallas Pkwy Addison TX 75001

SMITH, JODY BRANT, educator; b. Macon, Ga., May 7, 1943; s. Jody Bass and Gladys Irene (Patterson) S.; A.B., Mercer U., 1965; M.A., U. Miami, 1969, postgrad., 1970; m. Deborah Faye Everett, Aug. 20, 1971 (div. 1978); children—Heather Deborah, Jody Brant II. Asst. prof. philosophy, humanities Pensacola Jr. Coll., 1970—; pres. Pyrrho Press, Inc., Gulf Breeze, Fla., 1974—; pres. U.S. Guadalupan Research Project, 1979—; invited reader Indian Philos. Congress, New Delhi, 1975. Bd. dirs. Pensacola Right to Life, Inc., 1973-76, Fla. State Right to Life Com., Inc., 1974-75; provider written testimony U.S. Ho. of Reps. and U.S. Senate coms. Fla. Endowment for Humanities grantee, 1974. Mem. Am. Philos. Assn., Psychical Research Found., AAAS, Beta Beta Beta; fellow Am. Soc. Psychical Research. Contbr. articles to profl. jours. Home: 1503 E Lakeview Ave Pensacola FL 32503 Office: 1000 College Blvd Pensacola FL 32504

SMITH, JOE HAROLD, air force officer; b. Frisco City, Ala., Oct. 6, 1933; s. Arthur Harold and Etta V. (Grimes) S.; student Fla. State U., 1966, Parkland Coll., 1970-73; B.S., Rollins Coll., 1976; m. Betty Fay Turner, Nov. 19, 1955; children—Joe Harold, Bettina R., Joann F. Enlisted as pvt. U.S. Air Force, 1952, advanced through grades to chief master sgt., 1978; mgmt. analysis supt. Patrick AFB, Fla., 1974—, fin. cons., 1978—. Decorated Bronze Star, Air Force Commendation medal. Mem. Am. Mgmt. Assn., Air Force Sergeants Assn., Non-Commd. Officers Assn. Democrat. Home: 360 Glenwood Ave Satellite Beach FL 32937 Office: 1035th TCHOG/ACM Patrick AFB FL 32925

SMITH, JOHN GETTYS, public relations and business exec.; b. York, S.C., Nov. 24, 1932; s. Clyde B. and Ora (Gettys) S.; A.B., U. S.C., 1956; m. Nelle Elliott McCants, June 25, 1955; children—John Gettys, Spencer McCants, Ora Elliott. Tchr., York High Sch., 1956-57; with York County Health Dept., 1957-59; York bur. chief Rock Hill (S.C.) Evening Herald, 1959-61; salesman Smith Furniture, York, 1961-63; dir. pub. relations Sea Pines Plantation Co., 1963-64, v.p. pub. relations, community devel. Sea Pines Co., Hilton Head Island, S.C., 1964-74, also dir.; v.p. Sea Pines Investment Co., 1969-74; pres. John Gettys Smith Assos., Pub. Relations Cons., 1974—; owner, v.p. CBS World Travel Service, Inc., 1976—; partner Guide Publs., 1976—; pres. Harbour Ventures, Inc., Caliboque Properties Inc.; pres. John Gettys Smith Bus. Brokerage Agy.; chmn. John Gettys Smith Real Estate Agy.; coordinator Internat. Inst. Advancement Creative Arts, 1967-70; founder York Mus. Assn. 1956, York County Meml. Mus., 1958; dir. ann. tour York homes; mem. York County Hist. Commn., 1960-63. Chmn., Western York County Crippled Children's Soc., 1959-63; advisory mem. S.C. Confederate Centennial Commn., 1961-65; exec. com. Savannah Symphony Sec., 1969-72; mem. Beaufort County Bd. Edn., 1967-69; pres. Carolina Low Country Hist. Found., 1965-74; v.p. Sea Pines Acad., Sea Pines Ednl. Found., 1965-73; chmn. Gov.'s Conf. on Travel and Tourism, 1971-72, 75; v.p. CBS Tournament Tennis Champions, 1971; chmn. CBS Tennis Classic, 1972-73, P.G.A. Sea Pines Heritage Golf Classic, 1969-74, NBC-Family Circle Tennis, 1973; pres. S.C. Travel Council, 1973-74; trustee, mem. exec. com. Hilton Head Island Inst. for Arts. Served with U.S. Army, 1954-56. Recipient 1st pl. award Discover Am. Travel Orgn., 1967, 74, also Order of CORTE, 1974. Mem. Historic Beaufort Found. (fund raising com. 1971-72), York County (charter) hist. socs., Artists' Guild York, Chester, Lancaster Counties S.C. (exec. com.), S.C. (advisory com. for tourist promotion 1959-61), Hilton Head Island C. of C. (v.p. 1964-66, pres. 1967), Hugenot Soc., S.C. Hist. Soc., South Caroliniana Soc., Hilton Head Island Homebuilders' Assn. (sec.-treas. 1965-66), Sigma Nu, Kappa Pi. Episcopalian (vestryman). Clubs: Chatham, Oglethorpe (Savannah, Ga.); Plantation (Hilton Head Island). Author: A Family of York, 1967; contbr. articles to mags., newspapers. Home: Sea Pines Plantation 48 Beach Lagoon Hilton Head Island SC 29928 Office: John Gettys Smith Assos Smith Bldg PO Box 5478 Hilton Head Island SC 29928

SMITH, JOHN JAMES, JR., environ. cons. engr.; b. Franklin, N.J., Dec. 6, 1936; s. John J. and Mary Estelle (Gurka) S.; B.S., U. Fla., 1967; m. Sondra Lanphear, Dec. 19, 1956; 1 son, James H. With Sperry Rand, Gainesville, Fla., 1956-57, Ford Motor Co., Mahwah, N.J., 1957-58, Lehigh Portland Cement Co., Miami, Fla., 1958-63; research asst. U. Fla., Gainesville, 1963-64, wastewater and water research labs., 1964-66; chemist, part owner Environ. Sci. and Engring., Gainesville, 1966-67; dir. tech. services Black Crow & Eidsness Engrs. (name changed to BCE-CH2M Hill, 1977), Gainesville, 1967-70, mgr. process design, 1970-75, v.p., dir. cons. services, 1976, v.p., coordinator water and wastewater, 1977—, v.p., regional office mgr., 1978—; v.p. CH2M Hill, Inc., CH2M Hill N.W., Inc., CH2M Calif., Inc., CH2M Hill Central, Inc., CH2M Hill S.E., Inc., CH2M Hill Internat. Corp. (Domestic). Served with USAFR, 1954-62. Mem. Am. Water Works Assn., Air Pollution Control Assn., Am. Chem. Soc., Fla. Pollution Control Assn., Water Pollution Control Fedn., Internat. Assn. Water Pollution Research, Nat. Water Supply Improvement, Am. Angus Assn., Sigma Xi. Democrat. Roman Catholic. Contbr. articles to profl. jours. Home: Jackpine Ranch Route 2 Box 148 Newberry FL 32669 Office: PO Box 1647 Gainesville FL 32602

SMITH, JOHN JOSEPH, lawyer; b. Pitts., Nov. 14, 1911; s. John Joseph and Alta Ethel (McGrady) S.; A.B., Birmingham So. Coll., 1931; A.M., U. Va., 1932, postgrad. in econs., 1932-34; J.D., U. Ala., 1937; m. Ruth Lee Snavely, July 11, 1942; children—John Joseph, Robert William. Instr., U. Ala., 1934-37; admitted to Ala. bar, 1937, bar Supreme Ct. U.S.; asso. Murphy, Hanna & Woodall, 1937; asst. prof. U. Va., 1937-39; atty. Office Solicitor Labor, U.S. Dept. Labor, 1939-42; enforcement atty. rent div. OPA, 1942-43; legal counsel aircraft div. Bechtel-McCone Corp., Birmingham, 1943-46; pvt. practice law, Birmingham, 1946—; mem. gov.'s staff, 1963-71. Active Community Chest, YMCA, Better Bus. Bur.; committeeman Boy Scouts Am.; founder, commr. Homewood Joy Open Baseball League, 1958-72, chmn. bd., 1972—; chmn. Homewood Citizens Action Com. Against Annexation. Recipient Nat. Pop Warner award for service to youth, 1961. Mem. Am., Ala., Birmingham bar assns., Farrah Order Jurisprudence (founder, nat. pres. 1969-71, historian 1973—), Am. Econ. Assn., U. Va., U. Ala. alumni assns., Birmingham, Homewood chambers commerce, Order of Coif, Pi Gamma Mu, Farrah Order of Jurisprudence, Tau Kappa Alpha, Delta Sigma Phi. Methodist (founder, dist. dir. young adult fellowship classes). Clubs: Masons, Shriners, The Club, City Salesmen's (sec.) (Birmingham). Author: Selected Principles of the Law of Contracts, Sales and Negotiable Instruments, 1938; Farrah Order of Jurisprudence, 1974. Home: 1506 Primrose Pl Birmingham AL 35209 Office: John A Hand Bldg Birmingham AL 35203

SMITH, JOHN LEE, JR., assn. exec.; b. Fairfax, Ala., Dec. 11, 1920; s. John Lee and Mae Celia (Smith) S.; B.A., Samford U., 1950; student New Orleans Bapt. Theol. Sem., 1950-51, 53; D.D., Ohio Christian Coll., 1967, Birmingham Bapt. Bible Coll., 1979; postgrad. Auburn U., 1956, Baylor U., 1972-73; LL.D., Nat. Christian U., 1974; m. Vivian Herrington, Aug. 15, 1942; children—Vicky Suzanne Smith Hawkins, Joan Marie Smith Wimbercy, Jennifer Lee Smith Ruscilli. Ordained to ministry Baptist Ch., 1947; pastor various Bapt. Chs., Ala. and Ga., 1947-59, Dalraida Bapt. Ch., Montgomery, Ala., 1959-66, 1st Bapt. Ch., Demopolis, Ala., 1966-69; asso. exec. dir. Ala. Council on Alcohol Problems, Birmingham, 1969-70, exec. dir., 1970-78; exec. dir. Am. Council on Alcohol Problems, Washington, 1972-74, sec., 1975—, also dir.; dir. missions Bessemer Bapt. Assn., 1978—; bd. advisors alcoholism unit of Jefferson County Com. for Econ. Opportunity; lectr. on alcohol and drugs to various univs.; tchr. Samford U., Mercer U. Extension; registered lobbyist Ala. State Legislature, U.S. Congress. Mem. Christian Life Commn., 1959-60; chmn. Marengo County Cancer Soc., 1967-68; mem. Gov.'s Com. on Pornography, 1970-78; bd. dirs., exec. com. Nat. Temperance and Prohibition Council, 1970—; mem. Nat. Coordinating Council on Drug Edn., 1972—; exec. dir. Temperance Edn., Washington, 1972-74; bd. trustees Internat. Reform Fedn., 1973-75. Served to capt., USAAF, 1942-45; ETO. Mem. Phi Kappa Phi. Club: Masons. Editor: ALCAP Bull., 1970-78, Bessamer Bapt. Reminder, 1978—. Contbr. articles on alcohol and drug problems to periodicals. Home: 608 Staffordshire Dr Birmingham AL 35216 Office: PO Box 298 1331 Fairfax Ave Bessemer AL 35020

SMITH, JOHN LUCIAN, JR., beverage co. exec.; b. West Point, Miss., Oct. 24, 1918; s. John Lucian and Sara Eugenia (Cottrell) S.; B.S.C., U. Miss., 1940; m. Claire Davis, Aug. 6, 1953; children—Daniel Davis, Susan Peyton. With Coca-Cola Co., Atlanta, 1940-67, field sales mgr., 1957-61; pres. foods div. Coca-Cola Co., Houston, 1967-70; pres. Coca-Cola USA, Atlanta, 1970-74; pres. Coca-Cola Co., also dir.; dir. So. Ry. System. Nat. bd. dirs., v.p. Boys Clubs Am.; trustee Spelman Coll.; mem. adv. bd. Scottish Rite Hosp., Shorter Coll., U. Miss. Engring. Sch. Mem. Am. Soc. Corporate Execs., Delta Kappa Epsilon. Clubs: Capital City, Commerce, University Yacht, Piedmont Driving (Atlanta). Home: 3444 Tuxedo Rd NW Atlanta GA 30305 Office: PO Drawer 1734 Atlanta GA 30301

SMITH, JOHN MILLARD, geologist; b. Indpls., May 20, 1922; s. Theodore Thomas and Amy (Flint) S.; B.S., Ind. U., M.A., 1954; m. Alice Lorene Spencer, Dec. 25, 1948; children—Tamara Diane, Theodore Spencer, Millard. Chief geologist, Kaolin Processing Companies, Dry Branch and Sandersville, Ga. 1957—. Mem. Ga. Bd. Registration for Profl. Geologists. Served with USNR, 1943-46. Fellow Geol. Soc. Am.; mem. Clay Minerals Soc., Am. Inst. Mining Engrs., Baptist. Mason. Contbr. profl. jours. Home: 5181 Zebulon Rd Macon GA 31210 Office: Georgia Kaolin Co Dry Branch GA 31082

SMITH, JOHN MILLEDGE, JR., sociologist; b. Aiken, S.C., Feb. 3, 1928; s. John Milledge and Lillian (Rogers) S.; B.S., U. Ga., 1949, M.Ed., 1950, Ph.D., 1972; m. Frances Clark, Dec. 9, 1973; children—Larry, Karen, Alan, Rhonda, Douglas, Laura, Caroline. Civilian cons. U.S. Army, Ft. Gordon, Ga., 1953-60; adminstrv. asst. C & S Nat. Bank, Atlanta, 1960-61; asso. prof. sociology Augusta (Ga.) Coll., 1962—; cons. Model Cities Program, Savannah, Ga., Community Devel. Program, U. Ga.; lectr. in field. Bd. dirs. Met. YMCA, Central Savannah River Area Econ. Opportunity Authority. Served with AUS, 1946-47. Mem. Ga. Sociol. Assn. (pres.), Psi Chi, Phi Delta Kappa, Alpha Kappa Delta. Presbyterian (elder). Club: Augusta Exchange (dir.). Home: 1002 Redbird Rd Augusta GA 30904

SMITH, JOHNNY EUGENE, educator; b. Berkeley, Calif., Apr. 22, 1947; s. Wiley Mathew and Jeana Marie (Griffin) S.; B.A., S.W. Tex. State U., 1970; certified Tex. A and M U., 1973; m. Martha Ann Martens, Aug. 3, 1968; children—Kristann Kelly, Brannon Mathew. Head instr. Camp Gary Job Corps Center, San Marcos, Tex., 1969—; cons. Tex. Edn. Agy. Mem. Tex. State Tchrs. Assn., Gary Profl. Assn., Cibolo-Valley Jaycees (dir. 1976, v.p. 1977, named outstanding 1st year Jaycee, Spoke leader, recipient Keyman award), Tex. Jaycees (dir. 1978, outstanding dist. dir. 1978, Roadrunner award 1976-79), U.S. Jaycees (outstanding recruiter 1977, presdl. award 1977). Methodist. Co-author elec. student resource manual for Tex. Pub. Schs. Home: 16332 #2 I H 35N Schertz TX 78154 Office: Gary Job Corps Center San Marcos TX 78666

SMITH, JOSEPH BURKHOLDER, author; b. Harrisburg, Pa., June 16, 1921; s. Robert Craighead and Margaret Elizabeth (Burkholder) S.; A.B., Harvard U., 1944; M.A., U. Pa., 1950; m. Jeanne Hoffman, Dec. 19, 1942; children—Ruthven Smith Slawsky, Julie Smith Lenk, Andrew C. Asst. prof. history and polit. sci. Dickinson Coll., Carlisle, Pa., 1946-51; ops. officer clandestine services CIA, 1951-73; public relations cons. Anderson Clayton, S.A., Mexico City, 1973-76; cons. Mexican Tourism Council, 1975; author: Portrait of a Cold Warrior, 1976; Second Thoughts of a Top CIA Agent, 1976; contbr. articles in field. Adv., N.E. Fla. Council on Aging. Served with U.S. Army, 1943-46. Mem. AAUP, Am. Hist. Soc., Smithsonian Assos., Nat. Trust Hist. Preservation. Democrat. Clubs: Harvard (Jacksonville, Fla.); Univ. (Mexico City). Home and Office: 124 Seagrape Dr Jacksonville Beach FL 32250

SMITH, JUANITA MORROW, librarian; b. Monroe County, Miss., Feb. 12, 1921; d. William and Corene (Lowe) Morrow; A.B. in English, Rust Coll., 1956; M.S. in Library Sci., Atlanta U., 1968; m. Albert Smith; children—Gwendolyn, Albert, Sheila. Tchr., West Point (Miss.) City Schs., 1944-45; tchr., librarian Calhoun County Schs., Bruce, Miss., 1945-62; tchr., librarian Amory City (Miss.) Schs., 1962—. Mem. Amory Edn. Assn., Miss. Assn. Educators, NEA, Nat. Council Negro Women, Miss. Library Assn., Nat. Assn. Colored Women's Clubs, Inc., Rust Coll. Alumni Assn. Named Woman of Year, Girls Teen In Action Federated Club, 1975; Outstanding Black Educator, 1979. Home: 1081 D Ave Amory MS 38821 Office: PO Box 330 Amory MS 38821

SMITH, JUDITH JOHNS, educator; b. Pitts., Oct. 27, 1937; d. Henry and Ruth Esther (Agar) Johns; B.A. cum laude in English, Coll. William and Mary, 1960; M.S. in Edn., Old Dominion U., 1971; postgrad. U. N.Mex., 1974-76. Tchr. jr. high sch. English and geography Norfolk (Va.) pub. schs., 1962-65; chief editor, tech. writing instr. Stanwick Corp., Norfolk, Va., and Washington, 1965-67- psychometrician, adolescent therapist, sch. dir. Psychiat. Assos. of Tidewater, also Tidewater Psychiat. Inst., Norfolk and Virginia Beach, Va., 1967-74; sr. program dir. Tchr. Edn./Spl. Edn., Alexandria, Va., and Albuquerque, 1976-79; project dir., prin. investigator Dissemin/Action, Falls Church, Va., 1979—; field reader, div. personnel preparation Bur. Edn. for Handicapped, Office of Edn., HEw, Washington, 1976—, field reader Office of Developmental Disabilities, Rehab. Services Adminstrn., 1978—; vis. lectr. Coll. Edn. U. Md., 1979—. Mem. adv. bd. Hospice Services of Lackawanna County, Scranton, Pa., 1978—; area leader Muscular Dystrophy Assn. Am., Norfolk, 1970-72; pub. info. dir. Com. for Rights of Handicapped, Albuquerque, 1976. Mem. Internat. Council for Exceptional Children, Va. Council for Children with Behavior Disorders, Am. Assn. for Edn. of Severely/Profoundly Handicapped, Washington Ind. Writers. Republican. Presbyterian. Mem. editorial bd. Am. Assn. for Edn. of Severely/Profoundly Handicapped Rev., 1977-78. Home: 3701 S George Mason Dr Apt 1613 Falls Church VA 22041 Office: Dissemin/Action 3705 S George Mason Dr Suite C-4 Falls Church VA 22041

SMITH, JULIUS CLARENCE, III, lawyer; b. Greensboro, N.C., June 16, 1922; s. Julius Clarence and Lila (Keith) S.; B.A., U. N.C., 1946, J.D., 1949; m. Marian Adams, June 21, 1951; children—Stephen, Thomas J., Marian Keith. Admitted to N.C. bar, 1949; asso. firm Smith, Wharton & Pope, Greensboro, 1950-56; partner firm Smith, Moore, Smith, Schell & Hunter, 1956—; dir. Wysong & Miles Co., Greensboro. Mem. Greensboro Parks and Recreation Commn., 1965-73, chmn., 1971-73; bd. dirs. Greensboro

Natural Sci. Center, 1974—; mem. parents council Wake Forest U. Served with AUS, 1943-46. Mem. Am., N.C., Greensboro (dir. 1956-57, 79-80) bar assns. Clubs: Rotary, Greensboro Country, Oak Island Country. Home: 310 Irving Pl Greensboro NC 27408 Office: PO Box 21927 Greensboro NC 27420

SMITH, KATHI LYNNE, fin. analyst; b. Wood River, Ill., June 11, 1950; d. Odis Lindell and Jean Elizabeth (Dorsey) C.; B.B.A. magna cum laude, Pan Am. U., 1978, postgrad. U. Tex., Austin, 1979—; m. 1980. Fin. analyst IBM, Austin, 1979—; researcher EPA, 1976-77. Mem. ACLU, AAUW, NOW. Home: 11601 February St Austin TX 78753

SMITH, KATHLEEN CARR ABLES, nurse; b. Fayetteville, Tenn., Sept. 10, 1929; d. R.A. and Virge Lee (Locker) Ables; diploma St. Thomas Sch. Nursing, Nashville, 1950; B.S. with honors in Nursing, U. Ala., 1978; 2 children. Supr., Lincoln County Hosp., Fayetteville, 1950; staff nurse Meth. Hosp., Memphis, 1951-55; nurse Patrick Clinic, Fayetteville, 1955-59; operating rm. staff nurse Med. Center Hosp., Huntsville, Ala., 1972-75, dir. central services, 1975—. Mem. Traveling Nurse Assn., Ala. Nursing Assn., U. Ala. Huntsville Alumni Assn. Democrat. Mem. Chs. of Christ. Home: 715 DeSoto Rd SE Huntsville AL 35801 Office: 911 Big Cove Rd Huntsville AL 35801

SMITH, KENNETH CLIFFORD, accountant; b. North Collins, N.Y., July 20, 1936; s. Paul Joseph and Celia Mary (Haag) S.: B.S. in Acctg., U. So. Miss., 1968; m. Sara Louise Gober, Apr. 11, 1959; children—Rebecca, Dennis, Amy. Asst. purchasing agt. Irby Steel Co., Gulfport, Miss., 1959-65; acct. Dow Chem. Co., Freeport, Tex., 1968-74, acctg. supr., 1974-77, mgr. payroll and employee benefits, 1977-79, mgr. acctg., 1979—. Fin. chmn. Boy Scouts Am., 1977-79. Served with USCG. Mem. Am. Inst. C.P.A.'s, Nat. Assn. Accts. Home: 127 Ash Ln Lake Jackson TX 77566 Office: Dow Chem Co Tex Div Freeport TX 77541

SMITH, LARRY CLAUDE, airline exec.; b. San Angelo, Tex., Dec. 31, 1939; s. Claude B. and Ella Sue S.; B.S. in Bus. Adminstrn., N.Mex. State U., 1964; m. Edith R. Rudder, Nov. 5, 1960; children—Lauri Sue, Larry Claude. Various exec. positions with ins. cos., 1964-70; controller, treas. Recognition Products, Inc., Dallas, 1970-75; pres. Air Carry, Inc., Dallas, 1972—; co-owner, pres. Kitty Hawk Airways, Inc., Dallas, 1976—; flight instr. Mem. Aircraft Owners and Pilots Assn., Nat. Assn. Underwater Instrs., Nat. Assn. Flight Instrs. Republican. Office: Kitty Hawk Airways Inc 8034 Aviation Pl Suite 200 Dallas TX 75235

SMITH, LARRY DONNEL, athletic dir.; b. Mendenhall, Miss., Feb. 2, 1953; s. Dave Lee and Lillie Mae Smith; B.S., Jackson (Miss.) State U., 1976, M.S. Ed., 1977; m. Drborah Gaines, July 21, 1979; 1 dau., Jamaal LeVardes. Grad. asst. basketball coach Jackson State U., 1976-77; athletic dir., head basketball coach Miss. Indsl. Coll., Holly Springs, 1977—, also instr. phys. edn. Mem. Nat. Athletic Dirs. Assn., AAHPER. Mem. Ch. of Christ. Club: Masons. Office: Miss Indsl Coll Holly Springs MS 38635

SMITH, LARRY FRED, sales exec.; b. Memphis, June 12, 1946; s. Fred William and Hazel Norene (Stamey) S.: B.S. in Biology, Memphis State U., 1968; postgrad. U. Calif., Santa Barbara, 1978; m. Virginia Ann Kent, Dec. 31, 1978; 1 dau., Jaclyn Leigh. Asst. plant mgr. Dean Food Co., Louisville, Memphis, Rochester, Ind., 1969-70; mgr. Lakeland Devel. Corp., Memphis, 1970-71; salesman Corning Sci. Instruments, New Orleans, Atlanta, 1971-74; area sales mgr. Ortho Instruments, Memphis, 1974—; dir. Lakeland Devel. Corp., Memphis, 1978—. City founder, Lakeland, Tenn. Served with USAF, 1968-69. Recipient Colonel V.R. Fairfax award City of Memphis, 1968; numerous sales awards. Mem. Arnold Air Soc., Omicron Delta Kappa. Baptist. Home: 9770 Pine Point Dr Arlington TN 38002 Office: 410 University Ave Westwood MA 02090

SMITH, LARRY RONALD, data processing cons.; b. Wills Point, Tex., Dec. 16, 1939; s. Woodie Archie and Cecil Clara (Burns) S.; B.S., N. Tex. State U., 1962; postgrad. U. Wis. Banking Sch., 1974; m. Jerry Lynn Jones, July 16, 1960. Programmer, Employers Casualty Co., Dallas, 1962-64; v.p., mgr. data processing Tex. Bank & Trust Co., Dallas, 1964-74; cons. Career Sales, Inc., personnel cons., Dallas, 1974-75; mgr. data center Chancellor Scis., Inc., Dallas, 1975; cons. data processing, Dallas, 1975. Mem. Data Processing Mgmt. Assn. Home: 11031 Hillcrest Rd Dallas TX 75230 Office: 7151 Envoy Ct Dallas TX 75247

SMITH, LELAND D., JR., constrn. materials co. exec.; b. Houston, June 7, 1931; s. Leland D. and Julia Elizabeth (Branard) S.; B.B.A., Tex. A&M U., 1954; married; children—Leland D. III, Bradley L., Linda D. With Raleigh A. Smith & Son, Houston, 1954-55; project purchasing agt. Brown & Root, Inc., Houston and Lufkin, Tex., 1957-60; sales rep. Corey Supply Co., Houston, 1960-62; with Gen. Portland, Inc., 1962—, successively gen. sales mgr., v.p., div. gen. mgr., Houston, v.p., div. gen. mgr., Dallas, v.p., div. gen. mgr., Los Angeles, now v.p., gen. mgr. Trinity South div. Bd. dirs. Tex. Youth Camps, 1965-72, 74—. Served to 1st lt. Anti-Aircraft Arty., U.S. Army, 1955-57. Mem. Asso. Gen. Contractors, Tex. Aggregate and Concrete Assn. (dir. 1977-79), Houston C. of C. Clubs: Lakeside Country, Warwick, Breakfast Assn. (Houston). Office: Gen Portland Inc PO Box 152 Houston TX 77001

SMITH, LENORA (WEST) COGHLAN, civic worker; b. Ft. Benning, Ga., Dec. 3, 1922; d. James Joseph and Lenora West (Bowen) C.; student Vanderbilt U., 1940-42, Randolph-Macon Woman's Coll., 1942-43; B.A. in History cum laude, Columbus Coll., 1971; m. Joseph Wilson Smith, July 17, 1943; children—Sydney Bowen, Lenora West, Joseph Wilson, Walter Clifford II. Pres. trustees and friends div. Ala. Library Assn., 1961-62, Russell County (Ala.) Hist. Commn., 1972-74; chmn. Phenix City-Russell County Library Bd., 1957-61, 62-64, Phenix City-Russell County Bicentennial Com., 1974-79, Phenix City Riverfront Devel. Com., 1979—; bd. dirs. Ala. Sunbelt Conf., 1978—; Phenix City-Russell County rep. Civilian and Mil. Council, 1979—; active Bartram Trail Conf., Russell County Community Resource Devel. Com., Russell County Extension Council, Episcopal Churchwomen. Recipient award of merit Ala. Hist. Commn., 1976. Mem. Ala. Environ. Quality Assn., Ala. Hist. Assn., Ft. Mitchell Hist. Soc., Phenix City Hist. Preservation Soc., Daus. of Colonial Wars in State of Ala., D.A.R. Chi Delta Phi, Phi Alpha Theta, Kappa Alpha Theta. Democrat. Home: 3301 14th Ave Phenix City AL 36867

SMITH, LEROY FLEMING, JR., physician; b. Savannah, Ga., Oct. 7, 1935; s. Leroy Fleming and Helen (Tuten) S.; A.B., King Coll., 1956; M.D., Med. Coll. Ga., 1960; m. Elizabeth Hilsman, July 18, 1959; children—Leslie, Powell, Edward, Abigail. Intern, Harrisburg (Pa.) Hosp., 1960-61; resident Cleve. Clinic Found., 1963-67; practice medicine specializing in hematology, med. oncology, Alexandria, Va., 1967—; asso. clin. prof. medicine Georgetown U. Med. Sch., 1970—; chief med. oncology, chmn. cancer com. Fairfax Hosp., Falls Church, Va. Served with USAF, 1961-63. Diplomate Am. Bd. Internal Medicine and Med. Oncology. Fellow A.C.P. Home: 1105 Vassar Rd Alexandria VA 22314 Office: 5226 Dawes Ave Alexandria VA 22311

SMITH, LOIS CONLEY, educator; b. Montgomery, Ala., Oct. 8; d. Prince Edward and Fannie Fostene (Thompson) Conley; B.S., Ala. State U., 1939; M.A., U. Mich., 1944; m. Lovett Smith, Oct. 14, 1943. Tchr., Montgomery Pub. Schs., 1940—; vis. prof. Ala. A. and M. U., 1966; counselor adults night sch. Carver High Sch. Active Landsmark Found. of Montgomery; trustee Day St. Bapt. Ch., Montgomery chpt. Nat. Multiple Sclerosis Soc.; mem. Montgomery Hist. Devel. Commn. Recipient grants Fulbright, NDEA, East West, Phelp Stoke, Robert A. Taft; named outstanding woman of So. Region, 1974. Mem. Overseas Educators, Nat., Ala. (pres.) councils social studies, NEA, Pi Lambda Theta (grantee to Russia 1977), Iota Phi Lambda, Phi Delta Kappa. Clubs: Les Sante Civic (pres. 1970-74), Eastern Star. Home: 3321 Cleveland Ave Montgomery AL 36105 Office: 2001 Fairview Ave Montgomery AL 36108

SMITH, LORETTA ELAINE, nurse, state ofcl.; b. Brenham, Tex., Mar. 9, 1939; d. Sherwood William and Gerdine (Sternberg) Mantzel; R.N., Meth. Hosp. Sch. Nursing, Houston, 1960; B.S. in Nursing, Incarnate Word Coll., 1973; M.S. in Health Professions, SW Tex. State U., 1978; m. Robert Vernon Smith, June 1, 1958; children—Grayson, Mark. Surg. supr. Lee Meml. Hosp., Giddings, Tex., 1960; clin. nurse Physicians and Surgeons Clinic, Dallas, 1960-61; cardiovascular nurse, Austin, Tex., 1961-64, gen. and indsl. nurse, 1965-67; nurse Tex. Dept. Mental Health and Mental Retardation, Austin, 1967-72; program specialist mental retardation services Dept. Human Resources, Austin, 1976-77, spl. asst. mental retardation services Tex. Dept. Health, Austin, 1977-79, chief mental retardation specialist, 1979—; asst. adminstr. Cresthaven Nursing Center for Mentally Retarded, Austin, 1974-76. Lic. nursing home adminstr. Mem. Am. Assn. Mental Deficiency, Tex. Assn. Mental Deficiency, Tex. Public Health Assn., Tex. Public Employee Assn., Austin Area Intergovtl. Tng. Council. Office: 1100 W 49th St Austin TX 78756

SMITH, LORETTE, sch. prin.; b. Isola, Miss., Aug. 31, 1932; d. Ruble L. and Bertha Hoke; B.A., Greenville Coll., 1956; M.A., Fla. Atlantic U., 1969; Ed.D., Nova U., 1979; m. John Smith, Oct. 27, 1960; children—Leah, Monna. Tchr., Indpls. Public Sch. System, 1956-57, 60-63; tchr. Broward County Sch. System, Ft. Lauderdale, Fla., 1963-73, prin. Westchester Elemen. Sch., Coral Springs, 1973—. Bd. govs. Nova U., 1973—. Named Outstanding Woman of Yr. Broward County Edn. Women in Communications, 1979. Mem. Nat. Assn. Elemen. Sch. Prins., NEA, Am. Assn. Sch. Adminstrs., Phi Delta Kappa, Delta Kappa Gamma, Club: Zonta. Office: 12405 Royal Palm Blvd Coral Springs FL 33065

SMITH, MARGIE FRAZIER, nursing home adminstr.; b. Mobile, Ala., Aug. 26, 1952; d. Harold Edward and Marjorie Elizabeth (Hyland) Frazier; B.M., U. South Ala., 1974; m. Craig Monroe Smith, July 27, 1974. Adminstrv. asst. Cogburn Nursing Home, Mobile, 1974-75, asst. adminstr., 1975-76; field rep., nursing home cons. Electronic Data Systems, Montgomery, Ala., 1976-78; adminstr. Hillhaven Convalescent Center, Mobile, 1978—. Vice chmn. United Fund, 1974, 76, 78; chmn. Am. Heart Assn., 1974; dir. music Roman Catholic Ch. Recipient Public Service award United Fund, 1974. Mem. Ala. Nursing Home Assn., Am. Health Care Assn., Sigma Alpha Iota (past chpt. treas.). Home: 58 Sherwood Dr Mobile AL 36606 Office: Hillhaven Convalescent Center 1758 Springhill Ave Mobile AL 36607

SMITH, MARIAN ADAMS (MRS. JULIUS CLARENCE SMITH III), civic worker; b. Winston-Salem, N.C., June 6, 1928; d. Roger Lee and Blanche Evelyn (Brann) Adams; B.F.A., U. N.C., 1951; m. Julius Clarence Smith III, June 21, 1951; children—Stephen Manly, Thomas Julius, Marian Keith. Art supr. Raleigh (N.C.) Pub. Schs., 1951; art tchr. Greensboro (N.C.) Pub. Schs., 1952-55. Pres., Southeastern Theatre Conf., 1970-71, chmn. children's theatre div., 1964-66, chmn. endowment fund, 1969-73, now adminstrv. dir.; pres. N.C. Theatre conf., 1970-71; mem. nat. com. Am. Coll. Theatre Festival, 1974-77; v.p. Theatre for Young People, Greensboro, 1962—; chmn. adv. com. of theatre U. N.C. at Greensboro, 1962—; chmn. children's theatre Jr. League of Greensboro, 1962-63, chmn. TV, 1964-65; v.p. Jr. League sustainers, 1970-71. Bd. govs. Nat. Childrens's Theatre Conf., 1967-69. Recipient Community Arts award Altrusa, 1973; Suzanne M. Davis Meml. award Southeastern Theatre Conf., 1974; Amoco gold medallion award Am. Coll. Theatre Festival, 1975; Alumni Service award U. N.C., Greensboro, 1978. Mem. Am. Theatre Assn. (dir. 1972, chmn. rules com. 1975), Children's Theatre Assn. (chmn. festival com. 1974), Greensboro Women's Investment Club (pres. 1965-66). Club: Greensboro Study (pres. 1964-65). Home: 310 Irving Pl Greensboro NC 27408 Office: 1209 W Market St U NC at Greensboro NC 27412

SMITH, MARK HARRISON, correction inst. officer; b. Atlanta, Apr. 20, 1947; s. Charles Leon and Sarah Antoinette McDonald S.; B.A., Emory and Henry Coll., 1969; M.A., Peabody Coll., Vanderbilt U., 1974. Shipping clk. Brunswick Corp., Abingdon, Va., 1969-70; salesman Combined Ins. Co., Richmond, Va., 1970; dir. student activities Emory and Henry Coll., Emory, Va., 1970-72; orientation dir. Tenn. Dept. Correction, Nashville, 1975-77; tng. officer Tenn. Corrections Inst., 1977-79, coordinator juvenile tng., 1980—; cons. on juvenile offenders. Mem. adminstrv. bd. West End United Methodist Ch., Nashville, 1973-77; chmn. transp. Nashville Symphony Guild, 1975-77. Mem. Am. Personnel and Guidance Assn., Pub. Offender Counselor assn., Am., Tenn. correctional assns., Am. Assn. Correctional Psychologists, Am. Assn. Correctional Tng. Personnel, Internat. Platform Assn., Phi Delta Kappa. Democrat. Methodist. Home: 6017 Don Allen Ave Nashville TN 37205 Office: Tenn Corrections Inst 510 Gay St Suite 208 Nashville TN 37219

SMITH, MARTHA ANN DUNCAN, speech pathologist; b. Kingsport, Tenn., July 13, 1952; d. Thomas L. and Ruby B. (Barnes) Duncan; B.S. (Chi Omega Mother's Club scholar 1973), U. Tenn., Knoxville, 1974, M.A. (U.S. Office Edn. grantee 1974-75), 1976; m. Hoke Smith, III, July 2, 1977. Summer coordinator Sullivan County (Tenn.), Neighborhood Youth Corps, 1972; speech pathologist Little Tenn. Valley Edn. Coop., Alcoa, 1975-77, Fulton County (Ga.) Sch. System, Atlanta, 1977—; judge Nat. Forensics League, 1968—, chpt. sec., 1969-70; cons. in field. Named Outstanding Sr. in Coll. of Edn., U. Tenn., 1974. Mem. Am. Speech and Hearing Assn., Nat. Soc. Autistic Children, Phi Kappa Phi, Pi Lambda Theta, Chi Omega. Republican. Presbyterian. Home: 1997D DeFoor Ave Atlanta GA 30318 Office: 710 E Temple Ave College Park GA 30337

SMITH, MARY E. LEINEN (MRS. CRAIG C. SMITH), corp. exec., cons.; b. Rochester, N.Y., July 2, 1917; d. Raymond Francis and Frances (Connor) Leinen; A.B., St. Mary of the Woods, 1938; m. Craig C. Smith, Sept. 4, 1941; children—Ina Frances Smith Welch, Eric Craig, Marc Champney, Melissa Anne Smith Adams, Melanie Lee, Paul Stacy. Exec. sec. Clarke W. O'Brien, real estate developer, Rochester, 1938-43; sec. to bus. mgr. Washington Times Herald, 1944-45; pres., dir., exec. dir. Wrap-Tures Gift Wrap, Inc., Rochester, 1959-67; dir. finance Parazin Corp., Gen. Packaging Corp., Rochester, 1959—; dir. Woman's Ednl. and Indsl. Union. Trustee Rochester Hearing and Speech Center, Rochester Cerebral Palsy Assn., 1955-58, Harley Sch., 1957-60. Republican. Clubs: Rochester Yacht, Oak Hill Country; Vero Beach (Fla.) Yacht; Sarasota Yacht (Fla.). Home: Provence Route 1 Box 333A Somerset VA 22972 Office: 400 18 St Vero Beach FL 32960

SMITH, MERYLEEN BAILEY, ret. physician; b. Rock, W.Va., Sept. 13, 1917; d. Addison Crockett and Alice Imogene (Shutt) Bailey; student Mary Baldwin Coll., 1934-35; M.D., U. Cin., 1943; postgrad. U. Pa., 1955-56; m. Robert J. Smith, Feb. 7, 1947 (div. 1955); children—Roberta Smith Matney, Alexander Moffett. Intern, Jewish Hosp., Cin., 1944; mem. staff Williamson Meml. Hosp. (W.Va.), 1944-47; gen. practice medicine, Peterstown, W.Va., Rich Creek, Va., 1947-55; resident in pediatrics Robert Packer Hosp. and Guthrie Clinic, Sayre, Pa., 1956-57; chief pediatric dept. Bluefield (W.Va.) San. Clinic, 1957-62; pediatric cons., maternal and child health div. W.Va. Dept. Health, Charleston, 1962-69, project dir. statewide family planning program, 1971-73; clinician Southern W.Va. Regional Health Council, Bluefield, 1974-75; ret. Diplomate Am. Bd. Pediatrics. Mem. AMA, Am. Acad. Pediatrics, W.Va. Med. Assn., Mercer County Med. Soc. Republican. Methodist. Club: Order Eastern Star. Home: Duncan Dr and Water St Peterstown WV 24963

SMITH, MICHAEL WILLIAM, air force officer; b. Kansas City, Kans., July 29, 1940; s. Elmer Raymond and Mary Francis S.; Asso. Engring., Clarinda (Iowa) Community Coll., 1960; postgrad. Iowa State U., 1960-61; B.S., Okla. State U., 1965; M.S., UCLA, 1977; m. Gail Ellen Bowers, Oct. 16, 1976; children—Chelli Lucille, Michael Shane. Jr. engr. Martin Marietta Co., Denver, 1961-62; served as enlisted man U.S. Air Force, 1962-65, commd. 2d. lt., 1965, advanced through grades to maj., 1976, pilot rating, 1966, combat tour SE Asia, 1970-71, engr./launch controller Titan IIIC tests, Cape Kennedy Air Force Sta., Fla., 1972-74, flight test project engr. A-10 aircraft Edwards AFB, Calif., 1974-76, asst. ops. officer 74th Tactical Fighter Squadron, 23d Tactical Fighting Wing, England AFB, La., 1978—. Decorated Silver Star, DFC with 5 clusters, Air medal with 9 clusters, Air Force Commendation medal with cluster. Mem. Soc. Flight Test Engrs., Order of Daedalians, Pi Tau Sigma. Republican. Mem. ch. of Christ. Home: 708 Post Oak Blvd Alexandria LA 71301 Office: 74TFS England AFB LA 71301

SMITH, MILDRED BIRGE, med. records cons.; b. Shreveport, La., Nov. 8, 1930; d. Harry James and Mary Leola (A'Brantes) Birge; B.S. cum laude, Med. Records Adminstrn., La. Tech. U., 1975; m. Robert Lewis Smith, Aug. 21, 1948; children—Charlotte Ann, Marilyn Jean, Ruth Ellen, Robert Lewis, Charles Wayne. Med. records clk. Schumpert Med. Center, Shreveport, La., 1969; bank teller First Nat. Bank, Shreveport, 1970; med. records clk. Willis-Knighton Hosp., Shreveport, 1971-72; substitute tchr., sec. Caddo Parish Schs., Shreveport, 1973-75; instr. med. terminology Vo-Tech Center, Shreveport, 1976-77; med. records adminstr. Bossier City (La.) Gen. Hosp., 1975-78, Northwest La. State Sch., Bossier City, 1978-80; owner, mgr. Med. Record Cons. Service, Shreveport, 1980—; med. records cons. Mid-La. Health Systems Agy., Baton Rouge, 1978; med. records cons. North La. Health Systems Agy., Shreveport, 1978, mem. adv. council bd. dirs., 1979—; med. records cons. Physicians and Surgeons Hosp., Shreveport, 1976; clin. site instr. La. Tech. U., Ruston, 1975—. Election commr., Shreveport, 1970-75; mem. La. Talent Bank of Women, 1979—. Registered med. records adminstr. Mem. Am. Med. Record Assn., La. Med. Record Assn. (mem. exec. bd. 1977-81), Northwest La. Med. Record Assn. (pres. 1977, 78), Am. Bus. Womens Assn., Am. Soc. of Law and Medicine, La. Tech. U. Alumni Assn., Phi Kappa Phi. Democrat. Clubs: Elks Ladies Aux., Club 100 (Shreveport). Home and office: 4003 Santa Monica Ct Shreveport LA 71119

SMITH, NANCY VERONICA, sch. counselor; b. Kiln, Miss., Nov. 8, 1950; d. Ray Joseph and Alicia Veronica (Necaise) Favre; A.A., Pearl River Jr. Coll., 1970; B.S., U. So. Miss., 1971, M.Ed., 1974; m. Doyle Grant Smith, Aug. 25, 1972; children—Leah, Jay, Ray. Guidance counselor Hancock North Central Sch., Pass Christian, Miss., 1975—. Mem. Miss. Assn. Gifted and Talented, Miss. Personnel and Guidance Assn., Am. Personnel and Guidance Assn. Roman Catholic. Home: Route 2 Box 176A Perkinston MS 39573 Office: Route 1 Pass Christian MS 39571

SMITH, NEALE ERICSON, mfg. co. exec.; b. Douglas, Ariz., Nov. 6, 1932; s. Roy Ellsworth and Beatrice (Neale) S.; B.S., Calif. Inst. Tech., 1954; M.E.E., Ariz. State U., 1966, M.S. in Physics, 1967; m. Ana Elva Cornejo Gardner, Nov. 21, 1969; children—Neale Ricardo, Eric David, Odin Alonso. Radar devel. engr. Goodyear Aerospace, Litchfield Park, Ariz., 1963-66; physicist, info. theory Lawrence Radiation Lab., Livermore, Calif., 1968; with Macromex, S.A., Agua Prieta, Sonora, Mex., 1968—, tech. dir., 1968—. Served with USMCR, 1954-56. Mem. IEEE, Eta Kappa Nu. Home: 1099 Calle 3ra Agua Prieta Sonora Mexico Office: Ave Panamericana Calle 2 Agua Prieta Sonora Mexico

SMITH, OLIVER ANDERSON, JR., realtor, developer; b. Knox County, Tenn., June 24, 1915; s. Oliver Anderson and Alva Belle (Seaton) S.; B.S., U. Tenn., 1939; m. Evelyn Dooley, Dec. 14, 1939; children—Oliver Anderson III, Diana Smith Rasnic, Carol Mae Smith Tombras. Supr., U.S. Dept. Agr., Clinton, Tenn., 1939-41; appraiser Fed. Land Bank, 1941-43; now realtor, developer, bldg. supply dealer, shopping center developer, real estate auctioneer, estate mgr., many other businesses. Trustee Covenant Coll., Lookout Mountain, Tenn.; organizer, trustee PCA Presbyn. Ch., Knoxville, Tenn. Mem. Nat. Realtors Assn., Nat. Auctioneers Assn., Nat. Appraisers Assn., Nat. Platform Assn. Democrat. Mason (32 deg., Jester), Optimist (organizer; past pres.). Home: Westland Dr Knoxville TN 37922 Office: F-28 West Town Center Knoxville TN 37919

SMITH, OSCAR DALLAS, JR., judge; b. Columbus, Ga., July 21, 1920; s. Oscar D. and Marie (Bertling) S.; student Ga. Southwestern Coll., 1938-40, U. Va., 1946-47; m. Jane Latane Bryan, Jan. 10, 1948; 1 son, Oscar Dallas. Admitted to Ga. bar, 1947, practiced in Columbus, 1947-62; judge City Ct. Columbus, 1962-69; 3d judge Superior Ct. of Chattahoochee Circuit (Ga.), 1970—. Served with USAF, 1941-45. Decorated D.F.C., Air medal with 2 oak leaf clusters. Mem. Am. Judicature Soc., State Bar Ga., Assn. U.S. Army. Presbyterian (elder). Clubs: Columbus Lawyers, Columbus Exec. Office: Govt Center Columbus GA 31901

SMITH, OSCAR FRANCIS, IV, dredging co. exec.; b. Norfolk, Va., Apr. 12, 1942; s. Oscar Francis III and Marjorie (Goodwin) S.; student Va. Poly. Inst., 1960-63; B.S. in Fin. and Mgmt., Old Dominion U., 1971; m. Sharon Smith, May 13, 1967; children—Oscar Francis, V, Susan Lee, Glendyn Greig. Clk., Norfolk Dredging Co., 1960, asst. supt., Cape Charles, Va., 1961, Charleston, S.C., 1962-63, supt., Miami, Fla., 1964, Merritt Island, Fla., 1965, Norfolk, 1966-68, personnel mgr., safety dir., 1968-73, dir. loss control, 1973-76, asst. sec., 1976-78, sec., 1978, also dir. Mem. Y's Mens Club YMCA, Norfolk, 1964-68; mem. Norfolk Safety Council, 1971-73; mem. exec. com. constrn. sect. Nat. Safety Council, 1972—, editor newsletter, 1973-75; asso. mem. Fed. Safety Adv. Council—Hampton Roads Area; mem. Am. Nat. Standards Com. on Safety in Constrn. and Demolition; mem. exec com., bd. dirs. Va. Safety Assn., 1974—. Cert. hazard control mgr. Mem. Am. Soc. Safety Engrs. (sec. Greater Tidewater chpt. 1972-73, v.p. 1973-74, pres. 1974-75), Vets. of Safety (v.p. Eastern region 1977—, charter pres. Old Dominion chpt.

1978—), Nat. Safety Mgmt. Soc., Va. Soc. Safety Engrs., Nat. Assn. Dredging Contractors (chmn. industry com. on Safety and noise), Soc. Am. Mil. Engrs., Omicron Delta Epsilon. Episcopalian (vestryman 1973-75, 79-81). Club: Engrs. Hampton Roads (Norfolk). Home: 1432 Gates Ave Norfolk VA 23507 Office: PO Box 539 Norfolk VA 23501

SMITH, PAUL, engr., educator; b. Winston-Salem, N.C., June 7, 1928; s. Paul and Irene (Jones) S.; B.S. in Mech. Engring., Prairie View (Tex.) A. and M. Coll., 1958; M.S. in Aeros. and Astronautics, Stanford, 1965; postgrad. U. Minn., 1971-74; m. Edith E. Boynton, May 19, 1957; children—Earl B., Roszanna M. Aero. engr. U.S. Air Force, Kelly AFB, Tex., 1958-59; asst. prof., head dept. mech. engring. Prairie View A. and M. Coll., 1959-63, asso. prof., 1965-69; asst. prof. mech. engring. So. U., Baton Rouge, 1969-74, asso. prof., 1974—, dir. Student Retention Center, 1976—; cons. in systems analysis 3M Corp., St. Paul, 1972-73; mech. engr. NASA, Houston, 1967, Cape Kennedy, Fla., 1970. Mem. Citizens Transit Council, Mpls., 1973-74; mem. 208 Citizens Adv. Com., Baton Rouge, 1978-79; del. Democratic Dist. Conv., 1972. Served with AUS, 1946-48, 50-51, USAF, 1955-57. Recipient Patterson award United Air Lines, 1953; Gen. Motors Co. faculty fellow, 1966; Shell Found. fellow, 1973-74; registered profl. engr., Tex. Mem. Am. Soc. Engring. Edn., Am. Inst. Aeros. and Astronautics, AAUP (dir. Prairie View chpt. 1958-60), United Mil. Retirees Assn. (sec. 1975-78, pres. 1978—), Alpha Phi Alpha. Baptist. Contbr. articles to profl. jours. Home: 7062 Chisholm Ave Baton Rouge LA 70811 Office: PO Box 9358 Baton Rouge LA 70813

SMITH, PAUL ABRAHAM, automobile co. exec.; b. Easley, S.C., Dec. 11, 1912; s. James Adger and Lulie Jane (Durham) S.; B.S. cum laude, U. S.C., 1938; m. Elizabeth Parrott, May 18, 1940; children—Paul Abraham, Jane Elizabeth. Tchr. accounting U. S.C., 1936-37, 38; with Oliver Motor Co., Columbia, S.C., 1938—, gen. mgr., 1958-62, v.p., 1962—, also dir.; v.p., dir. Motor Parts Co. of S.C., Inc., 1965, Oliver Leasing, Inc., 1965—. Mem. Am. Mgmt. Soc. (dir. 1957-58, 68-69, sec. 1974-75, recipient Merit award 1970), Nat. Assn. Accountants (v.p. 1966), Columbia New Car and Truck Dealers Assn. (treas. 1973, 77). Republican. Baptist. Clubs: Columbia Rotary, Palmetto. Home: 3327 Blossom St Columbia SC 29205 Office: 2101 Main St Columbia SC 29202

SMITH, PAUL EDMUND, JR., educator; b. Northampton, Mass., Feb. 6, 1927; s. Paul Edmund and Mary Jane (Murphy) S.; B.A., U. Mass., 1948; postgrad. Harvard U., 1948-49; M.A., Boston U., 1957; B.D., Columbia Theol. Sem., 1957, M.Div., 1971; postgrad. U. N.C., 1967-68. Instr. Latin and French, Chester (Vt.) High Sch., 1949-53, Loris (S.C.) High Sch., 1953-54; lectr. U. Ga., Albany, 1957-59; instr. Latin Rocky Mount (Va.) High Sch., 1959-61; minister Henderson Presbyn. Ch., Albany, 1957-59, Rocky Mount (Va.) Presbyn. Ch., 1959-64; asst. prof. religion Ferrum (Va.) Coll., 1961-68; vis. lectr. history John Tyler Community Coll., Chester, Va., 1968-69; instr. philosophy and religion Richard Bland Coll., Petersburg, Va., 1968-71, asst. prof., 1971-76, asso. prof., 1976—, chmn. dept., 1971—. Mem. Am. Hist. Assn., Fincastle Presbytery. Democrat. Presbyterian. Home: Lakewood Estates 3774 Westwood Dr Petersburg VA 23803 Office: Commerce Hall Richard Bland Coll Petersburg VA 23803

SMITH, PEGGY ANN LEVERETT (PEG), educator; b. Brownwood, Tex., Dec. 19, 1940; d. Robert Vann and Mary Louella (Spinks) Leverett; B.S. in Social Work, Tex. Woman's U., 1963; m. George Raymond Smith, Dec. 23, 1967. Social worker Tex. Dept. Public Welfare, Abilene, 1963-66; dir. generic and med. social work Christian Service Center, Abilene, 1966-72; cons. House of Christian Services, Dallas, 1974; tchr. behavior therapy modification Abilene State Sch., Tex. Dept. Mental Health and Mental Retardation, 1978—; ann. lectr. Abilene Christian Coll., 1967, 69, Okla. Christian Coll., 1970, Lubbock Christian Coll., 1974; vol. Denton State Sch.; co-group therapist Mental Health Mental Retardation Center, Abilene; bd. dirs. Am. Arthritis Found., Abilene. Mem. Nat. Council Family Relations, Nat. Rehab. Assn., Child Welfare League Am., Tex. United Community Services, Am. Assn. Mental Deficiency. Mem. Churches of Christ. Contbr. articles to Christian Woman and Christian Chronicle, 1966-72; instrumental in establishment Abilene Suicide Prevention Service, 1969. Home: 342 Ambler #1A Abilene TX 79601 Office: Staff Devel and Tng Abilene State Sch PO Box 451 Abilene TX 79604

SMITH, PHILIP LYNN, printing co. sales rep.; b. Amarillo, Tex., Dec. 25, 1949; s. James Quentin and Jimalou (Park) S.; student Amarillo Jr. Coll., 1968-70; B.S. in Zoology, Tex. Tech. U., 1973; m. Sharon Dee Bailey, Dec. 31, 1969. Sales rep. Mogul Corp., Lubbock, Tex., 1973-74, Corpus Christi, Tex., 1974-75; sales rep. Uarco Bus. Forms, San Angelo, Tex., 1975—. Mem. Data Processing Mgmt. Assn., San Angelo C. of C. Home: 217 Twin Oaks St San Angelo TX 76901 Office: Uarco Bus Forms PO Box 1202 San Angelo TX 76902

SMITH, QUINTON ELWOOD, real estate exec.; b. Sturgis, Ky., Mar. 5, 1943; s. Otto George and Evelyn (Rowell) S.; student Albany (Ga.) Jr. Coll., 1970-72, Tampa (Fla.) U., 1962-63; A.A. in Engring., DeVry Tech. Inst., Chgo., 1966; cert. Western Union and RCA Tech. Sch., 1966; LL.B., LaSalle Extension U., 1978; children—Aaron Keith, Darien Wesley. Salesman, Strout Realty, Sylvester, Ga., 1972-73, Five Points Agy., Albany, Ga., 1974-75; pres. Smith Constrn. Co., Sylvester, 1975-79; real estate broker/auctioneer, pres. Smith Realty & Auction, Inc., Albany, 1979—. Served with USAF, 1961-65. Lic. real estate broker, Ga., Fla. Mem. Nat. Bd. Realtors, Nat. Auctioneers Assn., Auctioneers Guild, Ga. Bd. Realtors, Ga. Auctioneers Assn., Albany Bd. Realtors, VFW. Democrat. Methodist. Clubs: Pineknoll Country, Shriners. Home: 2100 Rosebrier St Albany GA 31705 Office: 216 S Mock St Albany GA 31705

SMITH, RACHEL ANN THOMPSON, counselor; b. Nathalie, Va., Dec. 26, 1940; d. Avery Oscar and Esther Maude (Guthrie) Thompson; Asso. in Secretarial Sci., Bluefield Coll., 1961; B.S. in Bus. Edn., Radford Coll., 1963; M. Counselor Edn., U. Va., 1973; m. Robert Wilson Smith, Dec. 22, 1962; 1 dau., Lysaundra Camille. Sec., Ford Motor Co., Dearborn, Mich., 1963-66; tchr. Halifax County (Va.) Sr. High Sch., 1966-68, Halifax County Jr. High Sch., 1970-72, guidance counselor, 1971—, mem. spl. edn. placement com., 1974-75, mem. spl. edn. adv. com., 1976—, editor Student Handbook, 1972; peer counselor trainer Workshop of Va. State Dept. Health and Phys. Edn., 1976; mem. Substance Abuse Prevention Team for Halifax County South Boston City pub. schs., 1975-76. United Fund Drive Community vol., Aaron's Creek, Va., 1966; adult tchr. First Bapt. Ch., South Boston, Va., 1974-77; chairperson Southside Community Mental Health and Mental Retardation Services Bd., 1977—. Certified guidance counselor and tchr. Va. Mem. Am., Va. personnel and guidance assns., NEA, Va., Halifax edn. assns., Nat. Vocat. Guidance Assn., Halifax County Mental Health Assn. (1st v.p. 1978-79), Internat. Platform Assn., South Boston Jaycettes (v.p. 1970), Delta Kappa Gamma (pres. Phi chpt. 1976-78), Phi Theta Kappa. Home: 605 Arbroath Rd South Boston VA 24592 Office: Halifax County Jr High Sch Halifax VA 24558

SMITH, RALPH CHARLES, ins. co. exec.; b. Flint, Mich., July 6, 1924; s. Alfred Ernest and Emma Regina (Schuepferling) S.; A.B., U. Mich., 1948, J.D., 1950; m. Anita R. Dumont, June 21, 1947; children—Gregory, Jeffrey, Alyssa. Admitted to Mich. bar, 1950, Ohio bar, 1960; v.p. Burton Abstract & Title Co., Detroit, 1950-59; exec. v.p. Cuyahoga Title & Trust Co., Cleve., 1959-61; v.p. Lawyers Title Ins. Corp., Cleve., Akron, Ohio and Washington, 1961-69; v.p. Commonwealth Land Title, Washington, 1969-73, sr. v.p., regional mgr., 1973-79, sr. v.p., dir. Nat. Title Ser. div., Vienna, Va., 1979—, also dir. Pres. Spring Hill PTA, McLean, Va., 1968, Cooper Jr. High PTA, McLean, 1971-72; trustee Title Ins. Polit. Action Com., Washington, 1977—. Served with AC U.S. Army, 1943-46. Mem. Am. Land Title Assn., D.C. Land Title Assn. (pres. 1976-78), Mortgage Bankers Assn., D.C. Home Builders Assn., D.C. Bd. Realtors, Am. Bar Assn., Mich. Bar Assn.Assn., Nat. Assn. Corporate Real Estate Execs. Clubs: Internat. Town & Country, Nat. Press, D.C. Touchdown. Contbr. articles in field to profl. jours. Office: Suite 913 8150 Leesburg Pike Vienna VA 22180

SMITH, RANDOLPH RELIHAN, plastic surgeon; b. Augusta, Ga., Apr. 13, 1944; s. Lester Vernon and Maxine (Relihan) S.; B.S., Clemson U., 1966; M.D., Coll. Ga., 1970; m. Katherine Eugenia Cross, June 8, 1968; children—Katherine, Randolph. Intern, Bowman Gray Sch. Medicine, Winston-Salem, N.C., 1970-71; resident in surgery and otolaryngology Duke U., Durham, N.C., 1971-75; resident in plastic and reconstructive surgery Med. Coll. Ga., 1975-77; Christine Kleinert fellow in hand surgery U. Louisville, 1977; attending physician Univ. Hosp., Augusta, Ga., 1977—; asst. clin. prof. plastic surgery Med. Coll. Ga., 1978—. Served to maj. M.C., U.S. Army, 1971-77. Diplomate Am. Bd. Otolaryngology. Fellow Am. Acad. Otolaryngology. Episcopalian. Contbr. articles in field to profl. jours. Office: Suite 2F University Hospital 820 Saint Sebastian Way Augusta GA 30902

SMITH, RANKIN MCEACHERN, ins. co. exec., football exec.; b. Atlanta, Oct. 29, 1925; ed. Emory U., U. Fla., U. Ga. With Life Ins. Co. Ga., 1943—, tng. asst., 1950, dist. mgr., 1951, asst. v.p., 1954, corp. sec., 1954, v.p., 1957, exec. v.p., 1963, sr. v.p., 1968-70, pres., chief exec. officer, 1970-75, chmn. bd., 1975-79, also dir.; owner, chmn. bd. Atlanta Falcons football team; dir. Greyhound, Inc., Trust Co. Ga. Assos. Mem. exec. bd. Atlanta council Boy Scouts Am.; exec. com. Central Atlanta Progress, Inc.; Ga. chmn. Nat. Soc. Prevention Blindness, 1973-74; div. chmn. United Way campaign, 1973-74. Trustee U. Ga. Found., Reinhardt Coll., Lovett Sch.; bd. dirs. Better Bus. Bur. Atlanta; mem. exec. com. Life Insurers Conf. Mem. Atlanta C. of C. (dir.), Chi Phi. Methodist. Mason (Shriner), Rotarian. Clubs: Piedmont Driving Capital City (dir.), Commerce (dir.). Office: Atlanta Falcons 521 Capitol Ave SW Atlanta GA 30312*

SMITH, RANKIN MCEACHERN, JR., profl. football club exec.; b. Atlanta, Aug. 23, 1947; s. Rankin McEachern and Miriam (Wellman) S.; B.B.A., U. Ga., 1970, M.B.A., 1971; m. Rebecca Reid Robinson, Sept. 11, 1970. Agent, Life Ins. Co. of Ga., Atlanta, 1971-73, staff mgr., 1973-75; adminstrv. asst. Atlanta Falcons Football Club, 1975, bus. mgr., 1976, pres., 1977—, bd. dirs. Bd. dirs. Atlanta Cerebral Palsy Found., Greater Atlanta USO, Am. Humanics, Boy Scouts Am. Methodist. Clubs: Rotary, Capitol City, Piedmont Driving. Office: Suwanee Rd at I-85 Suwanee GA 30174

SMITH, RAYMOND D(ANIEL), publishing co. exec.; b. St. Johnsville, N.Y., Aug. 4, 1912; s. Emery Augustus and Ada Anna (Groff) S.; student N.Y. U., 1949; m. Blanche Virginia Wolfram, Feb. 11, 1960; 1 stepson, Charles H. Copeland. Advt. dept. Schenectady (N.Y.) Union-Star, 1929-31; pub. Schenectady Neighborhood News, 1932-33; chemist, dispatcher, gen. office Standard Oil of N.J., Schenectady, Albany, N.Y., and N.Y.C., 1934-51; freelance photographer Life, other mags., N.Y.C., 1944-50; pub. Cats mag., Pitts., Washington, Pa., 1951-79, Port Orange, Fla., 1979—, asso. pub. Cats mag. Japan, Tokyo, 1976—; editor Mag. Index, Pitts., 1958. Elder, Presbyn. Ch., N. Buffalo, Pa., 1969—. Mem. Am. Cat Fanciers Assn., Crown Cat Fanciers Fedn., Am. Cat Assn., AAAS, Henry George Found. Am. Democrat. Contbg. author: Cat Lovers Bedside Book, 1974; In Praise of Cats, 1975; Cat Catalog, 1976; contbr. articles to encys., profl. jours.; Am. editor (with Blanche V. Smith) Complete Cat Ency., 1972, Rand McNally Pictorial Ency. of Cats, 1980. Home: 1928 Vernon Pl S Daytona FL 32014 Office: Cats mag PO Box 37 Port Orange FL 32019

SMITH, RAYMOND KERMIT, ednl. adminstr.; b. Hahnville, La., July 6, 1915; married, 2 children. B.A., Xavier U., 1946, M.A. in Adminstrn. and Supervision, 1951; postgrad. in reading No. Mich. U., 1962, La. State U., 1965-66, Loyola U., New Orleans, 1966-68, Internat. Grade Sch., New Orleans, 1973. Tchr.-prin. St. Charles Parish Schs., Luling, La., 1937-42, supr. instrn., 1942-79, asst. supt. instrn., 1979—. instr. reading Loyola U., New Orleans, parttime, 1968-75. Pres., United Givers Fund St. Charles Parish, 1971-72; v.p. Bayou-River Health Planning Council, 1974-77, pres., 1977—; pres. New Orleans/Bayou River Health Systems Agy., 1978; chmn. bd. commrs. St. Charles Hosp., Luling. Mem. NEA, La. Tchrs. Assn., Internat. Reading Assn., La. Council Tchrs. English, La. Assn. Suprs. and Counsultants, La. Edn. Assn., Acad. Am. Educators. Recipient citation for directing 10 years of Head Start, Sec. HEW; contbr. articles to ednl. jours. Home: 104 Gum St PO Box 70 Hahnville LA 70057 Office: Sch Bd Office Box 46 Luling LA 70070

SMITH, REBECCA LOU, librarian; b. Murfreesboro, Tenn., Nov. 26, 1927; d. William Hoyt and Mary Pearl (Marlin) Smith; B.A., David Lipscomb Coll., 1949; M.A., George Peabody Coll. Tchrs., 1952. Tchr., Franklin (Ky.) Simpson Jr. High Sch., 1949-51; bibliographer Ohio State U., 1952-55; circulation librarian David Lipscomb Coll., 1955-59; asst. reference librarian Middle Tenn. State U., Murfreesboro, 1969—; substitute summer librarian, 1958-69. Mem. ALA, Southeastern, Tenn., Mid-State library assns., NEA, Tenn. Edn. Assn., Rutherford County Hist. Soc. (Cannonsburgh award 1977). Democrat. Mem. Ch. of Christ. Contbr. articles to profl. jours. Home: 1910 Lebanon Rd Murfreesboro TN 37130

SMITH, REGINALD BRIAN FURNESS, anesthesiologist; b. Warrington, Eng., Feb. 7, 1931; s. Reginald and Betty (Bell) S.; came to U.S., 1962, naturalized, 1967; M.B., B.S., U. London (Eng.), 1955; m. Margarete Groppe, July 18, 1963; children—Corinne, Malcolm. Intern, Poole Gen. Hosp., Dorset, Eng., 1955-56; rotating intern Wilson Meml. Hosp., Johnson City, N.Y., 1962-63; resident anesthesiology Med. Coll. Va., Richmond, 1963-64, U. Pitts., 1964-65; clin. instr. U. Pitts., 1965-66, asst. prof., 1969-71, asso. clin. prof., 1971-74, prof., 1974-78, vice chmn. dept. anesthesiology, 1974-77, acting chmn., 1977-78; prof. and chmn. anesthesiology U. Tex., San Antonio, 1978—; dir. anesthesiology Eye and Ear Hosp., Pitts., 1971-76; anesthesiologist in chief Presbyn.-Univ. Hosp., Pitts., 1976-78. Served to capt. Royal Army Med. Corps, 1957-59. Diplomate Am. Bd. Anesthesiology. Fellow Am. Coll. Anesthesiology, Am. Coll. Medicine, A.C.P., Am. Coll. Chest Physicians; mem. Internat. Anesthesia Research Soc., Am., Western Pa. (pres. 1974-75) socs. anesthesiologists. Editor: International Ophthalmology Clinics, 1973; contbr. articles to profl. jours. Home: 213 Canada Verde San Antonio TX 78232 Office: 7703 Floyd Curl Dr San Antonio TX 78284

SMITH, RELIFORD ORVIN, JR., lawyer; b. Knoxville, May 2, 1945; s. Reliford Orvin and Rova Lee (Rule) S.; B.S., U. Tenn., 1966, J.D., 1969; m. Deborah Anne Elliott, July 27, 1974. Admitted to Tenn. bar, 1969, U.S. Tax Ct., 1975; individual practice law, Erwin, Tenn., 1972—. Bd. dirs. Clinchfield Sr. Adult Center. Served with U.S. Army, 1970-71. Decorated Bronze Star. Recipient Danforth award, 1966. Mem. Erwin Jaycees (pres. 1974-75), Tenn. Jaycees (mgr. criminal justice program 1976-78). Mem. Unicoi (pres. 1976—), Tenn., Am. bar assns., Tenn., Am. trial lawyers assns. Republican. Methodist. Club: Kiwanis. Home: 108 Balsam St Erwin TN 37650 Office: 229 Main St S Erwin TN 37650

SMITH, REX CRAIG, tobacco retail chain exec.; b. Dallas, Oct. 31, 1946; s. Wilford Thomas and Sue Evelyn (Simpson) S.; student UCLA, 1967-70, U. Houston, 1970-71; m. Dona Gayle George, Oct. 7, 1973. Agt., Transco Freight Co., 1965; partner Newman's Auto, Tustin, Calif., 1968-70; exec. v.p. Pipe Pub, Inc., Houston, 1970—, also dir.; pres. S&S Distbrs. Co., Houston, 1971-74; v.p. AppleTree Contractors, Houston, 1978—, also dir.; lectr. in field. Bd. dirs. Highland Youth Ranch, 1972-73. Served with USMC, 1965-69. Mem. Retail Tobacco Dealers Am., Christian Businessmen's Com., Internat. Council Shopping Centers. Republican. Club: Optimists (pres. Highland 1972-73). Home: 10114 Trade Winds Houston TX 77086 Office: Pipe Pub Inc 5201 Mitchelldale St Suite A-9 Houston TX 77092

SMITH, RICHARD PAUL, social worker; b. Little Rock, Sept. 14, 1939; s. Harvey Elbert and Merle Elizabeth (Miller) S.; B.S., Okla. Bapt. Coll., 1962; M.S.W., U. Okla., 1968; m. Norma Dean Rye, Dec. 28, 1961; children—Rick, Denise, Jennifer. Caseworker, Okla. Dept. Public Welfare, Shawnee, 1962-65, casework supr., Wagoner, 1965-66, county dir. Ottawa County, Miami, Okla., 1969-72, programs adminstr. quality control, Oklahoma City, 1972—. Registered social worker, Okla. Mem. Nat. Assn. Social Workers, Acad. Cert. Social Workers. Baptist. Home: 3917 Kim St Del City OK 73115 Office: Box 25352 Capitol Station Oklahoma City OK 73125

SMITH, RICHARD STOWERS, investment banker, rancher; b. San Antonio, July 20, 1934; s. Luther Stevens and Hazel (Stowers) S.; B.A., Yale U., 1955; m. Josephine McRae Powell, Jan. 13, 1962; children—Elliott Stowers, Quincy McRae. Asso. investment banking Lazard Freres Co., N.Y.C., 1958-63; v.p., dir. Russ Co., San Antonio, 1964, N.Y. Securities Co. Inc., 1965-72; sr. v.p., dir. Rotan Mosle Inc., Houston, 1973—; mng. partner Stowers Ranch Co., 1967—; former dir. Mesa Petroleum Co., Chesapeake Industries, Stowers Furniture Co., David M. Lea, Chesterfield Land & Timber Corp., Thomson Industries Ltd.; dir. Rocky Mountain Exploration Co., Verna Corp. Former bd. dirs. Houston Ballet; pres., bd. dirs. Houston Child Guidance Center. Mem. Investment Assn. (N.Y.). Republican. Episcopalian. Clubs: River, Union, The Recess (N.Y.C.); Hay Harbor, Fishers Island (N.Y.) Country; Port Bay Hunting (Rockport, Tex.); Tex. Corinthian Yacht (Kema); Argyle (San Antonio); Coronado, Bayou (Houston). Home: 2233 Troon Rd Houston TX 77019 Office: 1600 S Tower Pennzoil Pl Houston TX 77002

SMITH, ROBERT ADRIAN, packaging mfg. co. exec.; b. Chgo., Oct. 13, 1941; s. Virgil A. and Mildred (McClintick) S.; student U. Ill., 1959-60; B.S., So. Ill. U., 1963; m. Nancy L. Niess, Dec. 13, 1941; children—Jeffrey, Michael. With Owens-Ill., Inc., Alton, Ill., 1963-67, personnel staff asst., Toledo, 1967-68, indsl. relations dir., Atlanta, 1968-72, indsl. relations dir., adminstrv. mgr., Streator, Ill., 1972-76, plant mgr., Toledo, 1976-78, Lakeland, Fla., 1978—. Mem. grievance panel State of Ill., 1972-76; campaign chmn. United Way, Streator, 1976—. Recipient Distinguished Service award Streator Jr. C. of C., 1975; named Outstanding Citizen Ill., Jaycees, 1975. Clubs: Streator Rotary (pres. 1976), Lakeland Rotary. Office: PO Box 850 Lakeland FL 33802

SMITH, ROBERT CHARLES, educator; b. McComb, Miss., Nov. 24, 1943; s. Thomas J. and Nona M. (Richmond) S.; B.A., Southeastern La. Coll., 1966; Ed.M., La. State U., 1971, M.A., 1971, M.S. in Library Sci., 1972, Ed.D., 1975; m. Donna Sue Smith, Aug. 12, 1967; children—Tye Wesley, Piper Lee. Parish librarian Assumption Parish Library Demonstration, Napoleonville, La., 1967-68; media specialist Basic Combat Tng. Com. Group, Fort Ord, Calif., 1969-70; media librarian Park Elem. Sch., Baton Rouge, 1971-73; asso. prof. dept. library sci. and instructional media Western Ky. U., Bowling Green, 1974—, acting head dept. library sci., summer, 1977. Mem. Task Force Personnel Edn. and Resource Person, Gov.'s Pre-White House Conf. on Libraries, 1979; tchr. Children's Ch., U Bapt. Ch., 1971-73. Served with U.S. Army, 1968-70. La. State library scholar, 1966-67. Mem. ALA, Ky. Library Assn. (exec. bd. 1977-78, editor bull. 1979—), Southeastern Library Assn. (Outstanding Author award com. 1979-80), Ky. Assn. Communications and Tech., Assn. Ednl. Communications and Tech., Ky. Sch. Media Assn. (mem. intellectual freedom com. 1976-77), Phi Kappa Phi, Kappa Delta Pi, Phi Delta Kappa. Baptist. Contbr. articles on library service to jours. in field. Home: 1721 Curling Way Bowling Green KY 42101 Office: Dept of Library Sci and Instructional Media Western Ky U Bowling Green KY 42101

SMITH, ROBERT FRANKLIN, educator; b. Atlanta, Sept. 5, 1949; s. Frank Markwalter and Edith Ruth (Holcombe) S.; B.S., U. Fla., 1971; M.A., U. Wis., 1973, Ph.D., 1976; m. Kathy Lynn Bradberry, Mar. 10, 1979. Teaching and research asst. U. Wis., Madison, 1971-76; asst. prof. psychology George Mason U., Fairfax, Va., 1976—; cons. in behavioral toxicology Lawrence Johnson & Assos., Inc., 1978—. Mem. Am. Psychol. Assn., AAAS, Midwestern Psychol. Assn., Psychonomic Soc., Sigma Xi, Phi Beta Kappa. Democrat. Contbr. articles in field to profl. jours. Home: 272 Manassas Dr Manassas VA 22110 Office: Dept Psychology George Mason University Fairfax VA 22030

SMITH, ROBERT JACKSON BATES, JR., govt. ofcl.; b. Augusta, Ga., Nov. 9, 1941; s. Robert Jackson Bates and Mary (Willis) S.; B.B.S., U. Ga., 1963, LL.B., 1965; m. Kittie Potter Graham, Aug. 11, 1962; children—Robert Jackson Bates III, Samuel T.G., Mary Willis. Admitted to Ga. bar, 1965; partner firm Yow, Lee & Smith, Augusta, 1966-67; partner Allgood & Childs, Augusta, 1968-69; U.S. atty. So. Dist. Ga., 1969—. Part time instr. law Augusta Coll., 1966-69. Legal counsel, mem. exec. com. Richmond County (Ga.), 1967-69. Bd. dirs. Augusta Easter Seal Soc., 1965-69, 1st v.p. 1967-68. Named Outstanding Young Man of Richmond County, Jr. C. of C., 1969-70. Mem. Am., Augusta, Fed. bar assns., Augusta Trial Lawyers Assn., Phi Alpha Delta. Home: 1138 Glenn Ave Augusta GA 30904 Office: PO Box 2547 Augusta GA 30903

SMITH, ROBERT LEO, ecologist; b. Brookville, Pa., Mar. 23, 1925; s. Leo F. and Josephine Elizabeth (Ferguson) S.; B.S., Pa. State U., 1949, M.S., 1954; Ph.D., Cornell U., 1956; m. Alice Elizabeth Casey, Nov. 15, 1952; children—Robert Leo, Thomas Michael, Pauline Ann, Maureen Elizabeth. Asst. prof. biology State U. N.Y., Plattsburgh, 1956-58; prof. wildlife ecology W.Va. U., Morgantown, 1958—; cons. in ecology to pubs., govt. Served with AUS, 1950-52. Mem. Ecol. Soc. Am., Am. Ornithologists Union, Wildlife Soc., Am. Soc. Mammalogists, AAAS, Am. Inst. Biol. Scis., Wilson, Cooper ornithol. socs., Sigma Xi. Republican. Roman Catholic. Club: Lakeview

Country (Morgantown). Author: Ecology and Field Biology, 3d edit., 1980; The Ecology of Man: An Ecosystem Approach, 1976; Elements of Ecology and Field Biology, 1977; adv. bd. Funk & Wagnall's Ency.; contbr. to Ency. Brit. and World Book Ency. Home: Route 7 Box 660 Morgantown WV 26505 Office: Div Forestry WVa Univ Morgantown WV 26506

SMITH, ROBERT REED, criminologist; b. Rahway, N.J., Feb. 20, 1940; s. Ralph Lacey and Catherine Marie (Reed) S.; B.A. (Harvey S. Smith award), Syracuse U., 1962, M.A., 1963; M.S., Am. U., 1969; Ed.D., Auburn U., 1978; m. Margaret Sanders Land, Nov. 5, 1966; children—Jennifer Reed, Matthew Mulherin. Research asst. Am. U., Washington, 1968-69, Fla. Div. Corrections, Tallahassee, 1969; tng. coordinator, chief ops. research Rehab. Research Found., Draper Correctional Center, Montgomery, Ala., 1969-74; assessment and evaluation specialist, psychometrist, acting dir. div. profl. services Ala. Bd. Corrections, Montgomery, 1974-75; asst. prof. criminal justice Troy State U., Maxwell AFB extension, 1975—; asst. adj. prof. Auburn U., 1971-74; asso. prof. counseling and guidance in corrections W.Va. Coll. Grad. Studies, Institute, W.Va., 1979—; cons. in field; state dir. Ala. and W.Va. Internat. Halfway House Assn., 1975—; mem. Citizens Advisory Commn. on Prosecution, 15th Circuit Ct. Ala., 1977. Served with U.S. Army, 1963-68; Res., 1968—. Mem. Ala., Am. personnel and guidance assns., Am. Correctional Assn., So. Sociol. Soc. (chmn. membership 1975-79), Res. Officers Assn., Nat. Soc. Scabbard and Blade, Phi Gamma Delta, Kappa Phi Kappa. Democrat. Roman Catholic. Contbr. articles to books, profl. jours. Home: 133 Geronimo Dr Saint Albans WV 25177 Office: WVa Coll Grad Studies Institute WV 25112 WVa Coll Grad Studies Institute WV 25112

SMITH, ROBERT RUSSELL, surgeon; b. Brewton, Ala., Dec. 22, 1932; s. James Follin and Minnie (Rentz) S.; B.S., U. Ala., 1954; M.D., Med. Coll. Ala., 1958; children—Emily Follin, Marion Leigh, Kate Finlay, Robert Russell. Intern, Denver Gen. Hosp., 1958-59; resident in surgery Med. Coll. Ala., 1961-65: practice medicine specializing in surgery, Brewton, Ala., 1965—. Served with USAF, 1959-61. Fellow A.C.S.; mem. AMA, Am. Trauma Soc. Address: 103 Elliott St Brewton AL 36426

SMITH, ROBERT SIDNEY, business exec.; b. Charlotte, N.C., Feb. 26, 1945; s. Edward Mason and Virginia Irene Smith; A.B. in Econs. and Bus. Adminstrn., Wofford Coll., Spartanburg, N.C., 1967. With mktg. dept. Humble Oil & Refining Co., 1971-72; v.p. Nat. Assn. Hosiery Mfrs., Charlotte, 1972-78; partner, v.p. Green, Smith & Crockett Inc., 1978—; cons. in field. Chmn. research com. Mecklenburg County Republican Party, 1977-78; sect. chmn. Charlotte United Way; pres. Charlotte Area Alumni Club Wofford Coll., 1977; bd. dirs. Nat. Alumni Assn. Wofford Coll.; mem. industry sector advisory com. on textile for U.S. spl. trade rep. U.S. Dept. Commerce. Served to capt. USMCR, 1967-70; Vietnam. Decorated Purple Heart; Vietnamese Cross Gallantry. Mem. Am. Statis. Assn., Textile Analysts Club N.Y.C., Am. Inst. Econ. Research, Charlotte Textile Club, DAV, Mil. Order Purple Heart. Presbyn. Home: 229 N Canterbury Rd Charlotte NC 28211 Office: 516 Charlottetown Mall Charlotte NC 28204

SMITH, ROBERT SULLINS, physician; b. Del Rio, Tenn., May 28, 1929; s. Robert Taylor and Ollie Lillie (Moore) S.; B.S., Randolph-Macon Coll., 1951; M.D., Med. Coll. Va., 1956; m. Nancy Virginia Kibler, Aug. 26, 1950; children—Carol, Michelle, Robert Sullins, Janet. Intern, Mercy Hosp., Springfield, Ohio, 1956-57; gen. practice medicine Dinwiddie, Va., 1958-69; Va. med. examiner, med. examiner FAA, Dinwiddie, 1958-69, State Va., Dinwiddie County, Dinwiddie, 1958-74; emergency physician Petersburg (Va.) Hosp., 1969-74; family practice medicine, Richmond, Va., 1974—; asso. clin. prof. dept. family medicine Med. Coll. Va., 1975—. Mem. Va. Com. Study Abortion, 1969-70, Physician Shortage, 1970-71. Vice pres. Dinwiddie Citizens Orgn. for Better Edn. and Other Improvements, 1963-64; bd. dirs. Ruritan Civic and Recreation Assn.; bd. dirs. John Tyler Community Coll., 1968-79, chmn. bd., 1974-76; dist. steward United Meth. Ch., 1976—, bd. dirs. Va. United Meth. Pensions and Related Benefito, 1976—. Served to capt. M.C., USAF, 1957-58. Named Most Outstanding Sr. Citizen Dinwiddie County, 4 Ruritan clubs Dinwiddie County, 1964. Diplomate Am. Bd. Family Practice. Charter fellow Am. Acad. Family Physicians; mem. AMA, 4th Dist. med. socs., Med. Soc. Va., Va. (rural health com.), Tri City Area (pres. 1968-74), acads. family physicians, Va. (dir. 1968-70, sec. 1970-72, v.p. 1973-74, pres. 1975-76) Am. Med. Polit. Action Com., Med. Coll. Va., South Central PSRO (chmn. long term care planning com. 1979—), Randolph Macon alumni assns., Am. Coll. Emergency Physicians, Richmond Acad. Medicine, Richmond Acad. Family Practice, Va. Council Health and Med. Care, Omicron Delta Kappa, Chi Beta Phi, Beta Beta Beta, Alpha Sigma Chi, Lamba Chi Alpha, Theta Kappa Psi. Clubs: Masons, Walter Hines Page. Address: Route 1 Box 16 Dinwiddie VA 23841

SMITH, ROBERT WAYNE, county ofcl.; b. Tullahoma, Tenn., Feb. 5, 1949; s. Floyd L. and Marjorie (Kent) S.; B.S., Middle Tenn. State U., 1971; m. Beverly Dianne Sullivan, Dec. 5, 1973; children—Kimberley Michelle, Susan Elaine. Claims examiner Life Ins. Co. Ga., Atlanta, 1971-76; exec. dir. Indsl. Bd. Coffee County (Tenn.), 1976—. Bd. dirs. Tenn. Vocat. Rehab. Center, Manchester, 1977—, Coffe County United Givers Fund, 1978—. Mem. Am. Indsl. Devel. Council, Am. Mgmt. Assn., So. Indsl. Devel. Council, Tenn. Indsl. Devel. Council, Alpha Kappa Psi. Home: 26 Central Ave Tullahoma TN 37388 Office: PO Box 247 Manchester TN 37355

SMITH, RONALD HOMER, social services adminstr.; b. Sumter, S.C., Jan. 10, 1951; s. Homer and Eunice (Duvall) S.; A.A., North Greenville Coll., 1971; B.A., U. S.C., 1973, M.S.W., 1977; m. Linda Yvonne Hodge, Aug. 16, 1975; children—Jason Adam, Whitney Anne. Child protective service worker Sumter County Dept. Social Services, 1973-75; staff devel. and tng. coordinator Dist. VI S.C. Dept. Social Services, Sumter, 1977-79; dir. Marlboro County Dept. of Social Services, Bennettsville, S.C., 1979—; part time faculty mem. Chesterfield-Marlboro Tech. Edn. Center, 1979—. Mem. Nat. Assn. Social Workers, Am. Public Welfare Assn., S.C. State Employees Assn., S.C. Youth Workers Assn., S.C. County Dirs. and Suprs. Assn. Club: Rotary. Home: 308 Pinewood St Bennettsville SC 29512 Office: Parsonage St Ext Bennettsville SC 29512

SMITH, RONALD MARTIN, computer service co. exec.; b. Columbia, Mo., Sept. 30, 1944; s. Russell Mac and Shirley Elizabeth (Fahey) S.; student S.W. Mo. State Coll., 1963-64; m. Linda Jean Collura, July 14, 1969; 1 son, Ryan Daniel. With Sunshine State Systems, Tampa, Fla., 1969—, computer systems analyst, 1971-75, asst. v.p., 1975-76, v.p., 1976-79, v.p., dept. head, 1979—. Served with USN, 1965-69. Mem. Assn. for Computing Machinery. Home: 523 Terrace Hill Dr Temple Terrace FL 33617 Office: 925 Florida Ave Tampa FL 33602

SMITH, RONALD ROY, clergyman, co. exec.; b. Los Angeles, May 17, 1931; s. Franklin Winfred and Frances Rose (Jolly) S.; student So. Calif. Coll., 1949-53; certificates Iowa U., 1963, Syracuse U., 1967, U. Okla., 1970-71; m. Dolores Jean Haws, June 17, 1951; children—Ronald F., Roseanne R. Smith Martin, Russell A. Ordained to ministry Open Bible Standard Chs., 1953; minister First Ch. of Open Bible, Des Moines, 1953-62; founder, exec. dir. Valley View Village Retirement Home, Des Moines, 1962-66; adminstrv. asst. to pres. Oral Roberts U., Tulsa, 1967-68, v.p. devel., 1968-72, exec. v.p. bus. and fin., 1972-79; developer, pres. Univ. Village Inc., Tulsa, 1968—; pres. Abundant Life Ins., Tulsa, 1972-79, TRACO Prodns. Inc., Tulsa, 1972-79; producer Oral Roberts Quar. Spls. and Weekly Half Hour Shows, 1975-79; pres., chief exec. officer Midwest Video Prodns., Tulsa, 1979—; dir. Delaware County Bank, Jay, Okla., First Nat. Bank, Miami, Okla., Bank of Grove (Okla.). Pres., Non-Profit Homes Iowa, 1965-66; commr. Tulsa Housing Authority, 1973; mem. Mayor's Charter Revision Com.; bd. dirs. Tulsa Jr. Coll. Mem. Am. Coll. Pub. Relations Assn., Tulsa C. of C. (dir.), Am. Mgmt. Assn., Am. Assn. Ret. Persons, Am. Inst. Fund Raisers, Am. Assn. Homes for Aging, Am. Gerontol. Soc., Oral Roberts Assn. (exec. v.p., trustee 1972-79). Clubs: Rotary, Petroleum of Tulsa, So. Hills Country. Home: 6803 E 73d St Tulsa OK 74145

SMITH, RUBY JERNIGAN, nurse; b. Bradyville, Tenn.; d. Willis Henderson and Pare Zettie (Bynum) Jernigan; R.N., Nashville Gen. Hosp., 1937; postgrad. George Peabody Coll., 1951-52; B.S. in Edn., U. Tenn., 1970; m. William McKinley Smith, Aug. 18, 1943. Staff nurse Vanderbilt U. Hosp., Nashville, 1937-40, Holston Valley Community Hosp., Kingsport, Tenn., 1940; staff nurse, dir. nursing Davidson County Hosp., Nashville, 1940-43; occupational health nurse Neuhoff Packing Co., Nashville, 1943-44; public health nurse Met. Life Ins. Co., Nashville, 1944-52; staff nurse, dir. nurses ARC Blood Program, Nashville, 1953-59; dir. nursing Blood Bank Found., Nashville, 1959-63; instr. Sch. Nursing, Met. Nashville Gen. Hosp., 1963-70, dir. nursing edn., 1972—, sponsor classes 1966-68, 69, coordinator nursing program for clin. practice U. Tenn., Nashville; coordinator, instr. bimonthly inservice programs Met. Gen. Hosp., 1972—; coordinator Met. Practical Nursing Program for Clin. Practice, 1972—; cons. Dist. III, Tenn. Student Nurses Assn., 1964-67. Mem. Am. Nurses Assn., Tenn. Nurses Assn. (Dist. III del. to conv. 1973-77, 78, 79; various coms.), Nat. League Nursing, Tenn. League Nursing (coms. for conv. 1978), Mid-Cumberland League Nursing, Nat. Nashville Gen. Hosp. Alumnae Assn. (pres. 1972-76, treas. 1979-80), U. Tenn. Alumni Assn., Am. Heart Assn. Democrat. Baptist. Co-author: History of Tenn. Nurses Assn., 1955-77. Home: 2318 Deerwood Dr Nashville TN 37214 Office: Met Nashville Gen Hosp Nursing Edn 72 Hermitage Ave Nashville TN 37210

SMITH, RUBY LUCILLE, librarian; b. Nobob, Ky., Sept. 19, 1917; d. James Ira and Myrtie Olive (Crabtree) Jones; A.B., Western Ky. State Tchrs. Coll., 1943, M.A., 1966; m. Kenneth Cornelius Smith, Dec. 25, 1946; children—Kenneth Cornelius, Corma Ann. Tchr. rural schs., Barren County, Ky., 1941-42; tchr. secondary sch. English, librarian Temple Hill Consol. Sch., Glasgow, Ky., 1943-47, 49-51, 53-56, sch. librarian, 1956—. Sec. Barren County Cancer Soc., 1968-70, Barren County Fair Bd., 1969-70; leader 4-H Club, 1957-72, mem. council Barren County. Trustee Mary Wood Weldon Meml. Library, 1964—; trustee Barren County Pub. Library, 1969—, sec., 1969—. Mem. NEA (life), Ky. Edn. Assn., Ky. Assn. Sch. Librarians (sec. 1970-71), 3d Dist. Library Assn. (pres. 1964, 66), Barren County Edn. Assn. (pres. 1960-62), Ky. Audio Visual Assn., Monroe Assn. Woman's Missionary Union (dir. 1968-72, 79—), Monroe Assn., Delta Kappa Gamma. Baptists (library dir. 1972—). Republican. Home: Route 1 Box 38 Summer Shade KY 42166 Office: Route 4 Box 145 Glasgow KY 42141

SMITH, RUPERT LYNDON, utility co. exec; b. Arcadia, Fla., Feb. 5, 1947; s. George Robert and Virginia Louise (Mott) S.; B.S. in Journalism, U. Fla., 1969; m. Sharon Estelle Lynn, June 14, 1969; children—Rupert Chandler, Robert Trent. Public affairs adminstr. Gen. Tel. of SE, Durham, N.C., 1972-73, external communications mgr., 1973-76, communictions mgr., 1976-79, v.p. public affairs, 1979—. Pres., N.C. Mus. Life and Sci., 1980—, Drug Rehab. Service, 1978—; v.p. Durham United Way, 1979—. Served with U.S. Army, 1970-72. Recipient Carnegie Found. Herosim award, 1966. Mem. Durham Public Relations Soc. (past pres.), Durham Jaycees (dir. 1976), Durham C. of C. (research com. chmn. 1977-78). Democrat. Methodist. Home: 3001 Marywood Dr Durham NC 27712 Office: 3632 Roxboro Rd Durham NC 27704

SMITH, RUSSELL ERNEST, ins. agt.; b. Puyallup, Wash., May 21, 1952; s. Wayne Daryl and Evelyn Lael S.; B.A., Wash. State U., 1975; m. Cynthia Baldwin Smith, July 3, 1976; 1 dau., Alison Lael. Sales rep. Southwestern Co., Nashville, 1970-75; sales mgr. Security Sales, 1975-77; pres. R.E. Smith & Assos., Inc., Knoxville, Tenn., 1977-79; owner, chmn. bd. Omni Systems, Inc., 1978—; life underwriter, fin. planner Sequoyah Assos., Inc., Knoxville, 1979—. Republican. Presbyterian. Home: 5004 Flint Hill Dr Knoxville TN 37921 Office: 1209 Euclid St Knoxville TN 37921

SMITH, SAMUEL PHIL, TV engr.; b. Ranger, Tex., July 10; s. Robert Carlton and Ollie Colene (Powell) S.; student Tarrant County (Tex.) Jr. Coll., 1967-70, Tex. Tech U., 1978; m. Joyce LaVerne Putnam, July 30, 1976. Asst. film dir. Sta. KTXS-TV, Abilene, Tex., 1964-67; prodn. analyst Gen. Dynamics Corp., Fort Worth, 1967-70; film editor Sta. WFAA-TV, Dallas, 1971-75; instructional media technician Vernon (Tex.) Regional Jr. Coll., 1975-77; TV engr. Tex. Tech U. Sch. Medicine, Lubbock, 1977—. Mem. Nat. Assn. Ednl. Broadcasters, Assn. Audio-Visual Technicians, Tex. Ednl. TV Assn., Assn. Ednl. Communications and Tech., Tex. Assn. Ednl. Tech., Internat. TV Assn., Broadcast Ednl. Assn. Democrat. Baptist. Office: 4th and Indiana Sts Lubbock TX 79430

SMITH, SAMUEL WALLACE, illustrator, photographer; b. Birmingham, Ala., Nov. 21, 1925; s. Burr Sommers and Jessie Irene (Poe) S.; B.A. in Bus. Adminstrn. and Econs., Howard Coll. (now Samford U.), 1951; m. Sara Alta Thornton, Jan. 7, 1950; children—Sandra Leigh, Samuel Scott. Tech. illustrator, supr. Hayes Aircraft Corp., Birmingham, 1952-60; art prodn. mgr., art dir. advt. dept. Loveman's Co., Birmingham, 1960-69, art dir., 1969; sr. illustrator in charge dept. photography and graphics So. Natural Gas Co., Birmingham, 1969—. Served with USN, 1943-46, 50-52. Recipient award for best internal mag. design Birmingham Bus. Communicators, 1975, for cover photo, 1975, for photo story, 1975. Mem. Lambda Chi Alpha. Republican. Baptist. Home: 803 S 78th St Birmingham AL 35206 Office: So Natural Gas Co PO Box 2563 Birmingham AL 35202

SMITH, SARAH STERDIVANT, counselor; b. Meridian, Miss., June 4, 1952; d. Clenton and Doris Katherine (Mitchell) Sterdivant; student Tougaloo Coll., 1970-71; B.S. (Pres.'s scholar), Miss. State U., 1974, M.Ed., 1976, Ed.S., 1978; m. Melvin Marvin Smith, Dec. 18, 1977. Counselor, Miss. State U., Mississippi State, 1974-77, Columbus (Ga.) Coll., 1977; dir. counselors Mary Holmes Coll., W. Point, Miss., 1978—. Vol., Clay County pub. schs., 1978-79; public relations mem. Miss. State U., 1974-76. Recipient Miss. State U. Dedication and Service award, 1977, named outstanding counselor, 1975-76; outstanding Young Woman Am., 1978, 79. Mem. Am. Personnel and Guidance Assn., So. Coll. Personnel Assn., Miss. Personnel and Guidance Assn., Am. Coll. and Sch. Assn., Student Christian Assn. (advisor 1978-79), Alpha Kappa Alpha. Democrat. Methodist. Clubs: Elks, Bible Study League, Gospel Chorus, Meth. Youth Fellowship. Home: Office: Counselor Center Mary Holmes Coll West Point MS 39773

SMITH, SHERWOOD HUBBARD, JR., utility co. exec., lawyer; b. Jacksonville, Fla., Sept. 1, 1934; s. Sherwood H. and Catharine Gertrude (Milliken) S.; A.B., U. N.C., 1956, J.D. with honors, 1960; m. Eva Hackney Hargrave, July 20, 1957; children—Marlin Hamilton, Cameron Hargrave, Eve Hackney. Admitted to N.C. bar, 1960; mem. firm Lassiter, Moore and Van Allen, Charlotte, N.C., 1960-62, Joyner and Howison, Raleigh, N.C., 1962-65; asso. gen. counsel Carolina Power & Light Co., Raleigh, 1965-70, sr. v.p., 1971-74, exec. v.p. adminstrn., 1974-76, pres., 1976—, chmn. bd., 1980—. Vice chmn. Central Selection Com. Morehead Scholars, U. N.C.; mem. Gov.'s Energy Crisis Study Commn., State of N.C.; mem. vestry, sr. Warden Christ Episopal Ch., Raleigh; chmn. Raleigh Civic Center Authority; sec. bd. dirs. Bus. Found. of N.C.; trustee Z. Smith Reynolds Found.; trustee, vice chmn. Rex Hosp., Raleigh. Served with USN, 1956-57. Mem. Raleigh C. of C. (past pres.), Am. Nuclear Energy Council (chmn., dir.), Edison Electric Inst. (vice chmn. policy com. on govtl. affaris). Democrat. Office: 411 Fayetteville St Mall Raleigh NC 27602

SMITH, SOL, cons. petroleum engr.; b. Balt., Aug. 27, 1913; s. Hyman and Betty (Katz) S.; B.S., U. Tex., 1935, M.S., 1937; m. Dorothy Rose Cohen, Dec. 30, 1945; children—Larry, Darrold, Randy. Dist. engr. R.R. Commn. of Tex., Pampa and Wichita Falls, 1937-42, asst. chief engr. Austin, 1946-48; engr. chem. warfare U.S. War Dept., Huntsville, Ala., 1942-45; dist. engr. Mobil Oil Corp., Edna, Tex., 1945-46; cons petroleum and natural gas engr., Austin, 1948—; tchr. natural gas course U. Okla., Norman, 1949. Mem. Am. Inst. Mining and Metall. Engrs., Soc. Petroleum Engrs, Am. Gas Assn., Soc. Petroleum Evaluation Engrs., Am. Petroleum Inst. Clubs: Masons, Shriners. Contbr. articles to profl. publs. in field. Home: 3221 Cherry Ln Austin TX 78703 Office: 815 Brown Bldg Austin TX 78701

SMITH, SPURGEON EUGENE, research exec.; b. San Marcos, Tex., July 17, 1925; s. Charles Spurgeon and Grace Rebekah (Berry) S.; B.S., S.W. Tex. State U., 1946; m. Linnea Bergquist, Aug. 27, 1948 (div. Feb. 1972); children—Thomas Spurgeon, Marian Elizabeth. Systems specialist Def. Research Lab. of U. Tex., 1951-56; v.p. research Textran, Inc., Austin, Tex., 1956-61; research dir., v.p. advanced research scis. and systems group Tracor, Inc., Austin, 1961—; dir. Sta. KMFA-FM. Served to lt. (j.g.) USNR, 1943-46. Mem. Am. Math. Soc., Acoustical Soc. Am., Assn. Old Crows. Episcopalian. Research on radar and countermeasures; patentee in field. Home: 1305 Bradwood Rd Austin TX 78722 Office: 6500 Tracor Ln Austin TX 78721

SMITH, STEPHEN MICHAEL, educator; b. Cin., Mar. 4, 1951; s. John Pollard and Mary Margaret (Wimsatt) S.; A.A., Winston Churchill Coll., 1971; B.A. Atlantic Christian Coll., 1973; postgrad. U. N.C., 1980—; m. Paula Pope, Aug. 10, 1974. Counselor, Boys Home of N.C., Lake Waccamaw, 1973; dir. Columbus Workshop, Whiteville, N.C., 1974-78; regional mental retardation coordinator State of N.C., Fayetteville, 1978-79; devel. officer Southeastern Community Coll., Whiteville, 1979—; established 3 programs to train handicapped adults. Trustee Mental Health Assn., 1977-78; sec. N.C. Sheltered Workshop Assn., 1976-78; chmn. local fund drive St. Jude's Children's Research Hosp. 1978; mem. Nat. Council on Resource Devel. Recipient various awards for work with handicapped. Mem. Am. Assn. on Mental Deficiency, Nat. Assn. for Retarded Citizens. Democrat. Presbyterian (past deacon). Club: Civitan. Contbr. articles to newspapers.

SMITH, STEVEN LEE, mech. engr.; b. Little Rock, Dec. 10, 1947; s. Robert Dean and Lou Ella (Rankin) S.; B.M.E., U. Ark., 1970; m. Kathleen Louise Brown, June 22, 1968; children—Richard Allen, Stephanie Lynne. Mech. engr. Reynolds Metals Co., Alumina Partners of Jamaica, St. Elizabeth, Jamaica, 1970-71, mech. maintenance engr., 1973-76, project mech. engr., 1976—. Served with AUS, 1971-73. Mem. Ark. Soc. Profl. Engrs., ASME. Democrat. Methodist. Club: Trace Creek Country. Home: 25 Bloomfield Spurtree PO Manchester Jamaica West Indies Office: care Alpart 2820 Canal St New Orleans LA 70119

SMITH, T. WOODIE, JR., cellular biologist; b. Birmingham, Ala., Sept. 30, 1945; s. T. Woodie and Lois (Russ) S.; A.A., John A. Gupton Coll., 1968; B.S., Birmingham-So. Coll., 1967; M.A., George Peabody Coll., 1971, Ph.D., U. So. Miss., 1977. Biology tchr. Bay County High Sch., Panama City, Fla., 1968-70, 71-72; asst. prof. biology Gulf Coast Community Coll., Panama City, 1972-75, 79—; fgn. med. mission bd. instr. Eku Bapt. Hosp., Nigeria, NW Africa, summer 1974; postdoctoral research fellow Delta Regional Primate Research Center, Tulane U., New Orleans, 1977-78; postdoctoral research fellow U. Melbourne, Australia, Royal Melbourne Hosp., 1978-79. Vol. fgn. med. mission bd.; bd. dirs. March of Dimes, 1971-75, chmn., 1975; vestryman St. Andrew's Episcopal Ch., 1972-75; bd. dirs. Children's Mus., 1974-75. Mem. Electron Microscopy Soc. Am., Tex. Soc. Electron Microscopy, Miss. Acad. Scis., Sigma Xi, Beta Beta Beta, Phi Kappa Phi. Clubs: Panama Country, St. Andrews Bay Yacht, Downtown Rotary (program chmn., 1975). Contbr. articles in field to profl. jours. Office: Dept Biology Gulf Coast Community College Panama City FL 32401

SMITH, TALBOT MERTON, baseball club exec.; b. Framingham, Mass., Sept. 27, 1933; s. Edward B. and Helen Irene (McClure) S.; A.B. in Bus. Adminstrn., Duke U., 1955; m. Jonnie Valeria Adams, June 10, 1956; children—Valerie Jo, Randall Edward. Asst. dir. minor league clubs and scouting Cin. Reds, 1957-60; asst. to gen. mgr. Houston Astros, 1960-61, dir. scouting and minor league ops., 1961-63, asst. to pres., 1963-65, v.p., dir. player personnel, 1965-72, dir. ops., 1972-73, exec. v.p., gen. mgr., 1975-76, pres., gen. mgr., 1976—; exec. v.p. N.Y. Yankees, 1973-75; chmn. bd. Major League Scouting Bur., also mem. adv. com. on player relations. Served to 1st lt. USAF, 1955-57. Republican. Club: Westside Tennis (Houston). Office: Houston Astros Astrodome PO Box 288 Houston TX 77001

SMITH, TERRY EMILE, ednl. adminstr.; b. Bogalusa, La., Mar. 4, 1941; s. Talmadge Hampton and Virginia Anice (Alford) S.; B.A., Southeastern La. Coll., Hammond, 1964, M.Ed., 1972; Ed.S., U. Ala., 1979; m. Nettie Lenora Sheridan, Sept. 2, 1961; children—Sandra Darlene, Susan Marlene, Teresa Christine. Tchr. 6th grade St. Tammany Parish Schs., Slidell, La., 1964-68; Slidell, La., 1964-68; tchr. 4th and 6th grades Tyndall Elem. Sch., Tyndall AFB, Fla., 1968-73; project dir. Cullman (Ala.) City Child Devel. Center, 1973-79; adminstrv. rep. to exec. com. Cullman City Edn. Assn., 1978-79; adminstrv. asst. Cullman City Schs., 1979—; instr. So. Benedictine Coll., St. Bernard, Ala., 1976-77; cons. Huntsville-Madison County Community Action Com., 1977, Ala. Headstart State Tng. Office, Tuskegee, 1974. Bd. dirs. Cullman chpt. A.R.C., 1975-76, first aid instr., 1972—; mem. adv. bd. George C. Wallace State Community Coll., 1975—; adv., mem. kindergarten com. First Bapt. Ch., Cullman, 1974-77. Mem. Ala. Edn. Assn., Kappa Delta Pi. Baptist. Club: Civitan (pres.-elect 1974-75, pres. 1975-76) (Cullman). Home: 1439 Longbrook Dr NE Cullman AL 35055

SMITH, TERRY HOWARD, security analyst; b. Greenwood, Miss., Feb. 25, 1946; s. Oswald John and Ruth (Holmes) S.; B.A., La. State U., 1969; M.B.A., Loyola U., New Orleans, 1971; m. Mary Flack, July 25, 1970; 1 son, John Henry. With Howard Weil Labouisse Friedrichs, New Orleans, 1970—, v.p., security analyst instl. dept. Mem. Fin. Analysts of New Orleans, Fin. Analysts of N.Y., Beta Gamma Sigma, Kappa Sigma. Democrat. Methodist. Clubs: Colonial Golf and Country, Rivercenter Tennis. Home: 1300 Rural St River Ridge LA 70123 Office: 211 Carondelet St New Orleans LA 70130

SMITH, TERRY JACK, poultry co. exec.: b. Cumming, Ga., Sept. 13, 1947; s. Arthur Cleveland and Elliore (Vaughan) S.; B.S.A., U. Ga., 1969; m. Debra Lenora Sanders, May 1, 1971; children—Terry Jack, Heather Nicole. With A.C. Smith Poultry Co., Cumming, Ga., 1969—, mgr. integrated broiler operation, 1973—. Trustee Gainesville (Ga.) Jr. Coll., 1979—. Served with U.S. Army, 1971. Mem. Ga. Poultry Fedn., Southeastern Poultry and Egg Assn., Nat. Broiler Council. Baptist. Club: Rotary (pres. 1976-77). Home: Route 3 Cumming GA 30130 Office: AC Smith Poultry Co Route 3 Cumming GA 30130

SMITH, THOMAS ADRIAN, ins. co. exec.; b. Houston, Aug. 15, 1939; s. Arthur Newton and Jesse (Clayton) S.; B.S., Southwest Tex. State U., 1962; M.B.A., Western New Eng. U., 1970; m. Marjorie Martin, Mar. 12, 1962; children—Cameron R., Kelly M., Erin D. Systems engr. Electronic Data Systems Corp., Dallas, 1969-71; asst. to exec. v.p. mktg. Southland Life Ins. Co., Dallas, 1971-72; dir. tech. mktg. TCC, Inc., Austin, Tex., 1972-73, mgr. systems installations, 1973-75; first v.p. methods and systems Occidental Life Ins. Co. N.C., Raleigh, 1975-77, sr. v.p. adminstrn., 1977-78; pres. Fin. Fitness, Inc., Raleigh, N.C., 1978—, also dir. Served to capt. USAF, 1963-70. Decorated Air Force Commendation medal. Mem. Ins. and Statis. Assn., Direct Mail/Mktg. Assn., Direct Mktg. Ins. Assn. Mem. editorial adv. bd. Employee Health and Fitness. Republican. Episcopalian. Home: 4100 Converse Dr Raleigh NC 27609 Office: Financial Fitness Inc 1001 Wade Ave Raleigh NC 27605

SMITH, THOMAS EARLE, JR., lawyer, state senator; b. Oxford, N.C., July 22, 1938; s. Thomas Earle and Margaret Louise (Osterhout) S.; A.B., Davidson Coll., 1960; J.D., U. S.C., 1963; m. Elizabeth Eulalia Munn, June 23, 1962; children—Mary Dresden, Amy Louise. Admitted to S.C. Bar Assn., 1963; mem. firm James P. Mozingo, 1963-65; individual practice law, Pamplico, S.C., 1965-73; partner firm Nettles, Smith, Turbeville and Reddeck, Pamplico, 1973-79; individual practice law, 1979—; dir. Pamplico Bank and Trust Co., Johnsonville (S.C.) State Bank; partner Ind. Warehouse, Pamplico, 1972—; mem. S.C. Ho. of Reps., 1966-72; mem. S.C. Senate, 1973—. Recipient Outstanding Legislator award S.C. Council Exceptional Children 1976; Senate of Year award S.C. Assn. Retarded Citizens, 1975; Legislator of year award S.C. Young Democrats, 1979. Mem. S.C. Bar Assn., Am. Bar Assn., Am. Trial Lawyers Assn. Democrat. Methodist. Clubs: Lions, Masons, Shriners. Office: 100 Walnut St Pamplico SC 29583

SMITH, THOMAS JEFFERSON, III, hardware co. exec.; b. Dublin, Ga., Oct. 12, 1930; s. Thomas Jefferson, Jr. and Lucile (Kinnebrew) S.; B.A. in Econs., U. Va., 1952; m. Gladys Anne Shearouse, Mar. 10, 1957; children—Jefferson IV, Lucile, Laura, Meda. With T.J. Smith Wholesale Hardware Co., McRae, Ga., 1954—, pres., 1964—; distbr. Chevron, USA, 1966—; pres. Telfair Auto Service, 1975—, Sellers, Inc., 1978—; chmn. De Soto Nut House, 1979—. Pres. Central Ga. council Boy Scouts Am., 1978—, recipient Eagle Scout award, 1945, Silver Beaver award, 1964; area chmn. Nat. Eagle Scout Assn., since 1976; choir dir. United Methodist Ch., 1958-75, mem. adminstrv. bd., 1956—, mem. assn. ch. adminstrs., 1977—; treas. S. Ga. Conf. United Meth. Ch., 1974—; chmn. bd. trustees Ocmulgee Acad., 1974-79. Served as lt. USNR, 1952-54. Recipient Col. Robert L. Scott award Boy Scouts Am., 1945. Mem. Nat., So. wholesale hardware assns., Nat. Fedn. Ind. Bus. (adv. council), So. Hardware Assn., Am. Numismatic Soc., Audubon Soc., Am. Legion (comdr. post 1979—), Nat. Hist. Soc., Am. Camellia Soc., Pioneer Hist. Soc. (dir.), U. Va. Alumni Assn. (life, Woodberry Forest Alumni Assn., Beta Theta Pi. Clubs: Rotary (past pres. McRae), Cadillac LaSalle, Capital City (Atlanta); Dublin (Ga.) Country; Farmington Country (Charlottesville, Va.). Home: 306 W Graham St McRae GA 31055 Office: 120 Scotland Ave McRae GA 31055

SMITH, THOMAS WYATT, hosp. adminstr.; b. Campbellsville, Ky., May 9, 1937; s. Samuel Garnett and Mary Lee (Rice) S.; A.A., Campbellsville Jr. Coll., 1955; B.S. in Commerce, U. Louisville, 1966; certificate in Health Adminstrn., Ohio State U., 1973; certificate hosp. fin. mgmt. U. S.C., 1977; m. Malinda Susan Parker, Dec. 15, 1956; children—Gregory Thomas, Bradley Wyatt, Brentley Parker. Salesman, Louisville Gas and Electric Co., 1955-63, advt. and pub. relations mgr., 1963-69; dir. pub. relations and devel. Jewish Hosp., Louisville, 1969-73, asst. dir., 1973-76, v.p., 1976—. Pres. Buechel Little League, 1973; active Boy Scouts Am., United Way, various other civic activities; mem. exec. com., treas. Hosp. Council Met. Louisville, 1975-76; bd. dirs. Louisville Emergency Med. Services. Served with AUS, 1959. Mem. Am. Mktg. Assn. (pres. Louisville chpt. 1966), Louisville Advt. Club (dir. 1970-73, v.p. 1972-73), Nat. Assn. Hosp. Devel., Louisville Area C. of C., Am. Soc. Hosp. Pub. Relations Dirs., Ky. Hosp. Assn. Baptist (deacon 1962—; dir. Sunday sch. 1972-74). Home: 2303 Tavener Dr Louisville KY 40222 Office: 217 E Chestnut St Louisville KY 40202

SMITH, TOM EUGENE, grocery chain exec.; b. Salisbury, N.C., May 2, 1941; s. Ralph Eugene and Cora Belle (Ervin) S.; A.B. in Bus. Adminstrn., Catawba Coll., 1964; m. Catherine Conway Wallace, Oct. 16, 1971; children—Leigh Ann, Nancy Thompson. With Del Monte Sales Co., 1964-70, account mgr., Hickory, N.C., 1967-68, sales supr., Charlotte, N.C., 1969-70; buyer Food Town Stores, Inc., Salisbury, 1970-74, v.p. distbn., 1974-77, exec. v.p., 1977—, also dir.; dir. N.C. Nat. Bank. Bd. dirs. United Way, Salisbury, 1977-79. Mem. Nat. Assn. Retail Grocers, Sales Execs. Club (dir. 1974-79, pres. 1980), Am. Legion. Republican. Lutheran. Clubs: Salisbury Country, Rotary (dir. 1975-76). Home: 620 Catawba Rd Salisbury NC 28144 Office: PO Box 1330 Harrison Rd Salisbury NC 28144

SMITH, VERNON DEVON, physicist; b. Waxahachie, Tex., Sept. 20, 1943; s. Vernon Lee and Margaret Narissa (Barnard) S.; B.S., N. Tex. State U., 1965, M.S., 1975; postgrad. U. Calif., San Diego, 1966-68; m. Diane Moon, Dec. 11, 1970; children—Jill Deane, Jana Susan, Jacob Devon. With Gulf Gen. Atomics, Inc., San Diego, 1966-68; with Waxahachie (Tex.) Ind. Sch. Dist., 1970-73; sr. research physicist S.W. Research Inst., San Antonio, 1976-79; sr. aerosystems engr. Gen. Dynamics, Ft. Worth, 1979—. Deacon Baptist Ch., 1972—, treas., 1971-76. Served in U.S. Army, 1968-70; Vietnam. Decorated Army Commendation medal. Mem. Am. Soc. Nondestructive Testing (chmn. sect. 1978-79), AAAS, Tex. Acad. Scis., Phi Eta Sigma, Sigma Pi Sigma. Democrat. Home: 425 Tims Rd Crowley TX 76036 Office: PO Box 748 Fort Worth TX 76101

SMITH, VINCENT L., III, musician, arranger, composer; b. Pensacola, Fla., Mar. 15, 1947; B.S. in Music Edn., Fla. A. and M. U., 1969. Interest leader Upward Bound Program in Community Action Project 347, 1967; asst. to dir. bands, arranger for coll. bands Bethune Cookman Coll., Daytona Beach, Fla., 1971—; owner, mgr. Michavin Music Co. Served with U.S. Army, 1969-71. Decorated Army Commendation medal with oak leaf cluster. Mem. Fla. Music Educators Assn., Nat. Assn. Jazz Educators, Nat. Acad. Recording Arts and Sci. Composer: Angella White; Song for A Lady; Space Funk; A Minor Bag; Monk's Blues; Ronnie's Stuff; Senorita Dee. Office: PO Box 2061 Daytona Beach FL 32015

SMITH, WALTON RAMSEY, forest products cons.; b. Charlotte, N.C., Aug. 21, 1910; s. Frank Brandon and Cora May (McNinch) S.; student Davidson Coll., 1928-29; B.S. in Forestry, N.C. State U., 1934; m. Annie Dee Leatherman, July 3, 1936; children—Deanne Smith Winiarski, Patricia Smith Adams, Dorothy Smith Sullivan, Sylvia Smith Calhoun, Walton Ramsay. With adminstrn. U.S. Forest Service, Franklin, N.C. and Jackson, Miss.; 1936-39, research, New Orleans, Madison, Wis. and Asheville, N.C., 1939-50; pres. Walton Lumber Co., Mebane, N.C., 1950-52; engaged in research U.S. Forest Service, Asheville, 1952-68, ret., 1968; forest products cons. to wood industries, 1969—; adj. prof. Sch. Forest Resources N.C. State U., Raleigh, 1965-75. Pres. N.C. Forestry Found., 1965-73. Recipient Superior Service award U.S. Dept. Agr., 1969; Distinguished Alumnus award N.C. State U. Sch. Forestry Research, 1970; Gottschalk award Forest Products Research Soc., 1967; Borden award for research Borden Co. and Forest Products Research Soc., 1969. Mem. Forest Products Research Soc. (nat. bd. 1958-62), Soc. Am. Foresters. Contbr. articles to profl. jours. Home: Route 4 Box 570 Franklin NC 28734

SMITH, WALTON WRIGHT, realtor; b. Selma, N.C., Feb. 5, 1909; s. William Exum and Addie Beatrice (Wellons) S.; student Duke U., 1927-30; m. Geraldine Mavis Bezant, Aug. 2, 1945; children—Pamela Smith Edmonds, Janet Smith Darnell, Walton Wright. Clk., J.C. Penney Co., Wilson, N.C., 1930-32; partner Smith-Anderson Service Sta., Wilson, 1933-35; investigator Retail Credit Co., Wilson, Burlington, Winston-Salem and Greenville, N.C., 1935-40; operative builder, Wilson, 1940-42; builder, realtor, developer, Wilson, 1945—; pres. Wilson Bd. Realtors, 1971; v.p. Multiple Listing Service, 1973. Served to capt. USAAF, 1942-45. Mem. Eastern N.C. Home Builders Assn. (pres. 1967). Club: Wilson Country. Home: 1208 Brookside Dr Wilson NC 27893 Office: 805 Ward Blvd N Wilson NC 27893

SMITH, WARREN HUNTINGTON, architect; b. Spokane, Wash., Jan. 23, 1925; s. Earl Robert and Esther (Hines) S.; student Wash. State U., Pullman, 1942-43; B.Arch., U. Oreg., 1949; M.Arch., Mass. Inst. Tech., 1950; m. Margaret Isabel Griffiths, June 17, 1949; children—Christopher Earl, Theodore Jesse. Architect, Bindon & Wright, architects, Seattle, 1950-55; project architect Arabian-Am. Oil Co., The Hague, Netherlands, 1955-57; chief architect Bechtel Assos., N.Y.C., 1957-60; mgr. bldg. product devel. U.S. Plywood Corp., N.Y.C., 1960-62; cons. architect Wellman-Lord Engring., Inc., Lakeland, Fla., 1962-64; prin. Warren H. Smith & Assos., Lakeland, 1964; now pres. Smith Archtl. Group, Inc., Lakeland; chmn., City of Lakeland Bd. Standards and Appeals; mem. pub. adv. panel on archtl. services GSA; mem. Polk County Citizen's Adv. Com. for Econ. Devel. Assistance; bd. dirs., pres. Lakeland YMCA. Served with USAAF, 1943-45; ETO. Decorated Purple Heart; recipient award for Excellence in Indsl. Design, Factory Mag., 1961. Mem. AIA (corporate mem., pres. Polk County sect.), Am. Soc. Interior Designers, Delta Upsilon. Unitarian. Clubs: Kiwanis, Fla. Sailing Assn. (St. Petersburg); Lakeland Yacht. Prin. works include: Fla. Technol. U., Orlando, Fed Courthouse, Orlando, Sci. and Tech. Bldg. U. South Fla., Tampa. Home: 2725 Oakland Dr Lakeland FL 33803 Office: 402 S Kentucky Ave Lakeland FL 33802

SMITH, WARREN THOMAS, clergyman, educator; b. Knoxville, Tenn., Oct. 20, 1923; s. Warren T. and Lola May (Jones) S.; student Maryville Coll., 1942-43; B.A., Ohio Wesleyan U., 1945; B.D., Emory U., 1948, postgrad., 1974-75; Ph.D., Boston U., 1953; D.D., Lincoln Meml. U., 1958; m. Barbara Ann Sullards, Dec. 27, 1949; 1 son, James Warren. Ordained deacon Methodist Ch., 1947, elder, 1949; full connection N. Ga. Ann. Conf., 1951; pastor Waldo (Ohio) Meth. Ch., 1944-45, Howard Ave. Meth. Ch., Dorchester, Mass., 1949-50; asso. pastor Peachtree Rd. Meth. Ch., Atlanta, 1950-53; pastor Sharp Meml. Meth. Ch., dir. religious life, head dept. religion Young Harris Coll., 1953-57; pastor Trinity Meth. Ch., Atlanta, 1957-60; mem. staff Bd. Edn., Meth. Ch., 1960-64; pastor Young Harris Meml. Ch., Athens, Ga., 1964-66, N. Decatur Meth. Ch., 1966-68; sr. pastor First United Meth. Ch., College Park, Ga., 1968-74; asst. prof. ch. history Interdenominational Theol. Center, Atlanta, 1974-79, asso. prof., 1979—. Recipient grant Nat. Endowment for Humanities for in-depth biography Thomas Coke, 1969. Mem. Am. Soc. Ch. History, Wesley Hist. Soc. (Eng.), Am. Hist. Assn., Omicron Delta Kappa, Delta Tau Delta. Club: Masons. Author: Thomas Coke, Foreign Minister of Methodism, 1959; Heralds of Christ, 1963; Selections from the Writings of Thomas Coke, 1966; At Christmas, 1969; Preludes: Georgia, Methodism, The American Revolution, 1976; And the Play Goes On: Characters in the Biblical Drama, 1980; Augustine: His Life and Thought, 1980; contbr. articles to religious jours. Home: 3460 Hemphill St College Park GA 30337 Office: 671 Beckwith St SW Atlanta GA 30314

SMITH, WAYNE LINEBACK, cons. engr.; b. Knoxville, Tenn., Apr. 3, 1904; s. William LaFayette and Dove (Lineback) S.; B.S., U. Tenn., 1926; m. Mildred Elizabeth Wilson, May 19, 1934. Sales promotional engr. Knoxville Iron Co., 1926-39; maintenance engr. Am. Bemberg Corp., Elizabethton, Tenn., 1939-44; co-owner, chmn. bd., prin. Wayne L. Smith & Assos., Inc., Knoxville, 1944—; exec. dir. S&S Assos., Architects and Engrs., 1964-72; sec. Farmers Mut. Fire Ins. Co., of Knox County, 1960-70; v.p. Viviane Woodard Cosmetic Co., 1972—; dir. Farmer's Mut. Fire Ins. Co. Tenn.; county surveyor Knox County, 1969—. Mem. Tenn. Constl. Conv., 1971; bd. dirs. Knox County Farm Bur., 1970—. Mem. Nat., Tenn. socs. profl. engrs., Am. Coll. Surveyors. Republican. Christian Ch. Home: 2400 Merchant Rd Knoxville TN 37912 Office: 2800 Merchant Rd Knoxville TN 37912

SMITH, WILLIAM FRED, real estate exec.; b. Cabarrus County, N.C., May 9, 1946; s. Fred Herman and Arabelle Treece S.; A.Applied Sci., Central Piedmont Community Coll., 1971; A.Arts, Key West Jr. Coll., 1969, So. Mgmt. Inst., U. Ga., 1977; m. Donna Jean Martin, Aug. 28, 1966; 1 dau., Amanda Leigh. Finished artist and designer Interstate Graphics, Inc., Charlotte, N.C., 1972; designer, art dir. E. J. Presser, Charlotte, 1972-73; art dir., designer, account exec. Francis Smith, Inc., Charlotte, 1973-74; advt. rep. Kannapolis (N.C.) Pub. Co., 1974-75; exec. v.p. Kannapolis Mchts. Assn., 1975-78, Kannapolis Credit Bur., Inc., 1978-79; real estate exec., Kannapolis, 1979—; bd. dirs. Devel. Group, Inc., Huntsville, Ala., 1978. Served with USN, 1967-71. Recipient Honor award Kimberly Clark, 1974; Nat. Exec. Achievement award Assn. Credit Burs., Inc., 1978, Nat. Gold Key Leadership award, 1978. Mem. C. of C. U.S., N.C. Assn. C. of C. Execs., Kannapolis C. of C. (exec. v.p.) N.C. Retail Execs. Assn. (bd. dirs. 1976-78), Better Bus. Bur. Greater Mecklenburg (dir. 1976-78). Republican. Lutheran. Home: 504 Dodge St Kannapolis NC 28081 Office: PO Drawer Z 1108 Centergrove Rd Kannapolis NC 28081

SMITH, WILLIAM HOWARD, physician; b. Woodward, Okla., Jan. 15, 1925; s. Charles Bernard and Catherine (Campbell) S.; B.S., Northwestern State Coll., 1944; M.D., U. Okla., 1947; m. Joy Stafford, Nov. 21, 1946 (dec. 1960); children—Su Su, Kelly, Joel; m. 2d, Joy Mock, June 13, 1971; 1 adopted dau., Karla Kay, 1 son, Tyre Smith. Intern, Kansas City Gen. Hosp., 1947-48; practice medicine, Lindsay, Okla., 1948-51, 53-62, practice medicine, surgery, Pasadena, Tex., 1962—; mem. staff Pasadena Bayshore, Pasadena Gen., Bapt. Meml. hosps., Houston; med. dir. Southmore Hosp. Mem. Lindsay Pub. Sch. Bd., 1953-54. Served as capt., M.C., AUS, 1951-53. Diplomate Am. Bd. Family Practice. Fellow Am. Acad. Family Practice; mem. AMA, Tex., Indsl., Harris County med. assns., Assn. Mil. Surgeons, Assn. Ry. Surgeons, Houston Acad. Medicine. Home: 2312 Lillian St Pasadena TX 77502 Office: 901 E Curtis St Pasadena TX 77502

SMITH, WILLIAM JAMES, mfg. co. exec.; b. Red Springs, N.C., Nov. 21, 1939; s. William James and Sarah Brown (Campbell) S.; student U. N.C., 1958-62; m. Elizabeth Ann Brown, Mar. 2, 1968; children—Patrick Scott, William Alan. Personnel mgr. Internat. Paper Co., Statesville, N.C., 1967-73, Burlington (N.C.) Industries, 1973-74, office adminstr., 1974-76; personnel adminstr. Health-tex, Inc., Danville, Va., 1978—. Cub scoutmaster Boy Scouts Am., Danville, 1979—; organizer Iredell County Com. for Info. to Youth on Industry, 1971-72; chmn. Iredell County Indsl. Opportunity Day, 1971-72; cons. adv. com. Vocat. Edn. Program, 1972-73; employer adv. com. Va. Employment Commn., 1979-80. Served with U.S. Army, 1963-67. Recipient Award for Outstanding Service, United Fund, 1971. Mem. Am. Soc. Personnel Adminstrn., Danville Area Personnel Assn. Democrat. Methodist. Club: Iredell County Personnel (pres. 1972-73). Office: 2499 N Main St Danville VA 24541

SMITH, WILLIAM MASSIE, lawyer; b. Richmond, Va., Apr. 17, 1920; s. James Gordon and Ella Williams (Buek) S.; B.A., U. Va., 1948, J.D., 1948; m. Elizabeth Catherine Haden, Dec. 27, 1941); children—Elizabeth Smith Sullivan, William Massie, Sallie Cameron Smith Foster, David Gordon. Admitted to Va. bar, 1948; practiced in Charlottesville; partner firm Smith & Danielson, 1948-51, Paxon, Marshall & Smith, 1951-73; prin. firm Paxon, Smith, Boyd, Gilliam & Gouldman, Inc., Charlottesville, 1973—; dir., chmn. exec. com. Fidelity Am. Bank, Charlottesville; dir. Citizens Commonwealth Corp., Central Fidelity Banks, Inc., So. Title Ins. Corp. Pres., United Community Funds and Councils Va., 1963-64; bd. dirs. St. Margaret's Sch., Martha Jefferson Hosp.; v.p. Va. Center for Creative Arts; chmn. U. Va. Athletic Council, 1977-78. Served with USMCR, 1942-46. Mem. Am. Judicature Soc., Marine Corps Res. Officers Assn., Am. Legion, Navy League, Am., Va. (v.p. 1958) bar assns., Va. State Bar, Alumni Assn. U. Va. (pres. 1971-72, sec.-treas. alumni fund), U. Va. Law Sch. Alumni Assn. (sec. 1948-68), Raven Soc., Beta Theta Pi, Phi Delta Phi, Omicron Delta Kappa. Episcopalian. Clubs: Farmington Country, Greencroft, Red-Land (pres. 1977-78) (Charlottesville); Commonwealth (Richmond, Va.). Home: 1834 Westview Rd Charlottesville VA 22903 Office: 500 Citizens Commonwealth Center Charlottesville VA 22902

SMITH, WILLIAM NELSON, bus. service broker; b. Bluefield, W.Va., Mar. 4, 1926; s. William Edwin and Tabitha Katherine (Bush) S.; B.S. in Bus. Adminstrn., Va. Poly. Inst. and State U., 1950; m. Miriam Mary Shewey, July 21, 1951; 1 son, Scott Nelson. With Am.-Standard Co., 1950-54; mem. sales staff A.H. Robins Co., Richmond, Va., 1955-57; trade relations mgr. S.E. Massengill Co., 1957-59, conv. mgr., 1957-61, consumer products mgr., 1959-61; v.p., gen. mgr. Truett Labs. div. Southwestern Drug Corp., Dallas, 1961-67; ind. mktg. cons., Dallas, 1967-70; mktg. dir. Partake, Inc., Dallas, 1967-70; pres. Unified Interests Interchange, bus. services, Bluefield, W.Va., 1970—. Water safety dir. ARC, Richmond, Newport News and Bristol, Va., 1956-59; div. chmn. United Fund, 1975-78; elder Presbyterian Ch. Served with AC, U.S. Army, 1944-46. Mem. Soc. Am. Magicians, Internat. Brotherhood of Magicians. Republican. Clubs: Kiwanis (v.p.), Masons, Moose, Sales Execs., Univ. Contbr. articles on mktg., corporate image, and packaging to trade publs. Home: 202 Oakhurst Ave Bluefield WV 24701 Office: PO Box 1451 321 Hancock St Bluefield WV 24701

SMITH, WILLIAM RANDOLPH, JR., systems engr.; b. Columbia, S.C., Sept. 2, 1939; s. William Randolph and Sarah Emma Mae (Abell) S.; B.S., Tex. A. and I. U., 1961; M.S., Am. U., 1977; m. Marcia Elizabeth Thompson, Dec. 28, 1974; 1 son by previous marriage—Peter William. Commd. 2d lt. U.S. Army, 1961, advanced through grades to maj., 1968; with Communications-Electronics Command and Staff, Germany, 1961-65; ADPS plans and operations officer, Vietnam, 1967; ADP logistical staff officer, Pa., 1968-69; comdr. Autodin Switch, Vietnam, 1969-70; chief EUCOM Computer Center, Germany, 1970-73; lead systems analyst, project leader, mgmt. info. systems project officer Army Computer Systems Command, 1973-76; discharged, 1976; sr. systems analyst, cons. Value Engring. Co., Alexandria, Va., 1976-78; staff engr. Northrop/Page Communications Engrs., Inc., Vienna, Va., 1978—. Decorated 2 Bronze Star medals, 2 Army Commendation medals, Meritorious Service medal, Joint Service Commendation medal; certified secondary tchr., Tex. Mem. Am. Mgmt. Assn., Soc. Mgmt. Info. Systems, IEEE (Computer Soc.), Computer Security Inst., Tech. Mktg. Soc. Am., Assn. Computing Machinery, Data Processing Mgmt. Assn., Res. Officers Assn., Armed Forces Communications-Electronics Assn., Smithsonian Assos. Methodist. Clubs: Bulldog of Am. (div. VII); Capitol Bulldog (v.p.). Home: 5616 N 34th St Arlington VA 22207 Office: 801 Follin Ln Vienna VA 22180

SMITH, WILLIAM ROBERT, III, physicist; b. San Antonio, Jan. 11, 1935; s. William Robert, Jr., and Anna (Love) S.; B.S. in Physics, U. Tex., 1957, B.A. in Math., 1958, Ph.D. in Physics, 1963; m. Jodell Power, Sept. 9, 1963. Research asso. Nuclear Physics Lab. of U. Tex., Austin, 1963, neutron physics div. Oak Ridge Nat. Lab., 1963-65; sr. research officer Nuclear Physics Lab. of Oxford U. (Eng.), 1965-66, summers 1967-68; research asso. Nuclear Physics Lab., U. So. Calif., Los Angeles, 1966-67; asso. prof. physics Trinity U., San Antonio, 1967—; research cons. Balcones Research Center, U. Tex., Cyclotron Lab., Tex. A. and M. U., 1970. Sec. Medina Bend Ranch Assn., 1971, chmn., 1972. Mem. Am. Phys. Soc., Sigma Pi Sigma, Sierra Club. Republican. Episcopalian. Editor Computer Physics Communications, 1967—; contbr. articles to profl. jours. Home: 563 E Craig St San Antonio TX 78212 Office: 715 Stadium Dr San Antonio TX 78284

SMITH, WILLIAM RUSSELL, microbiologist, educator; b. Denton, Tex., Jan. 13, 1917; s. Ira Russell and Willie (Caskey) S.; B.S., N. Tex. State U., 1937, M.S., 1938; postgrad. U. Minn., 1949; Ph.D. in Microbiology, U. Tex., 1955; m. Dorothy Youngblood, May 13, 1939; children—Barbara Ann, Christopher Ronald. Tchr. biology, high sch. and jr. coll., 1939-43; asst. prof. biology Lamar U., Beaumont, Tex., 1951-54, asso. prof., 1955-58, prof., 1958—, Univ. Regents prof., 1974—; research scientist U. Tex., 1952-53. Mem. health sect. Beaumont Community Council, 1964-68; pres., Beaumont Planned Parenthood Assn., 1968-69; trustee Schlesinger Geriatric Center, chmn., 1975-76. Served to lt. (j.g.) USNR, World War II; PTO. U.S. Army Quartermaster Corps grantee, 1951-52; registered microbiologist. Mem. AAUP, Am. Soc. Microbiology, Tex. Soc. Microbiology, N.Y. Acad. Scis., Tex. Assn. Coll. Tchrs., Sigma Xi, Kappa Delta Pi, Phi Sigma, Tri Beta. Presbyterian. Club: Lions. Home: 4785 Dellwood Ln Beaumont TX 77706 Office: Dept Biology Lamar U Box 10037 Beaumont TX 77710

SMITH, WILLIE TESREAU, JR., judge, lawyer; b. Sumter, S.C., Jan. 17, 1920; s. Willie T. and Mary (Moore) S. ; student Benedict Coll., 1937-40; A.B., Johnson C. Smith U., 1947; LL.B., S.C. State Coll., 1954, J.D., 1976; m. Anna Marie Clark, June 9, 1955; 1 son, Willie Tesreau, III. Admitted to S.C. bar, 1954; began gen. practice, Greenville, 1954; past exec. dir. Legal Services Agy. Greenville County, Inc.; state family ct. judge 13th Jud. Circuit S.C., 1977—. Mem. adv. bd. Greenville Tech. Edn. Center Adult Edn. Program and Para-Legal Program; bd. dirs. Greenville Urban League; past trustee Greenville County Sch. Dist. Served with AUS, 1942-45, USAF, 1949-52. Mem. Am., Nat., S.C., Greenville County bar assns., Southeastern Lawyers Assn., Am. Legion, Greater Greenville C. of C., NAACP, Omega Psi Phi. Presbyterian (past chmn. bd. trustees Fairfield-McClelland Presbytery). Clubs: Masons, Shriners, Rotary. Home: 601 Jacob Rd Greenville SC 29605 Office: County Office Bldg S Main St PO Box 757 Greenville SC 29602

SMITHEY, KAREN BIGGS, educator; b. Wharton, Tex., July 14, 1941; d. Robert Oscar and Mittie Deliah (Pugh) Biggs; student Wharton County Jr. Coll., 1959-60; B.S., S.W. Tex. State U., 1962; M.Ed., Sam Houston State U., 1978; m. William L. Smithey, Jr., June 6, 1964; 1 dau., Audra Karen. Tchr. vocat. homemaking edn. Wharton (Tex.) High Sch., 1962-64, Bay City (Tex.) High Sch., 1969-71; county extension agt.-home econs. Tex. Agrl. Extension Service, Tex. A&M U., Ft. Bend County, 1964-67; dir.-tchr. Westgate Nursery Sch., Westgate Ch. of Christ, Beaumont, Tex., 1972-74; tchr. vocat. homemaking edn., chmn. dept. Boling (Tex.) High Sch., 1975—; mem. area adv. com. Tex. Edn. Agy. Chmn., Boling Mental Health Orgn., 1979; bd. dirs. East Wharton County unit Am. Cancer Soc. Mem. Am. Vocat. Assn., Am. Home Econs. Assn., Tex. Vocat. Tchrs. Assn., Assn. for Childhood Edn. Internat., Vocat. Homemaking Tchrs. Assn. Tex., Phi Theta Kappa, Delta Kappa Gamma. Democrat. Mem. Ch. of Christ. Club: Lioness Internat. (pres. Boling). Home: 6711 Gwyneth St Boling TX 77420 Office: Boling High Sch 703 Atlantic St Boling TX 77420

SMITH HAYNES, LINDEN CORINE, biologist; b. Leaksville, Miss., Nov. 24, 1945; d. General Leon and Margaret (Bolton) S.; B.S., Alcorn State U., 1964; M.S., Va. State U., 1968; Ph.D., Iowa State U., 1977; m. Worth Edward Haynes, Apr. 17, 1965; 1 dau., Natasha Camille. Chmn. sci. dept., tchr. biology, zoology Harris Jr. Coll., Meridian, Miss., 1964-67; chmn. sci. dept. tchr. biology and physics Alexander High Sch., Brookhaven, Miss., 1968-69; instr. biology and comparative anatomy Utica Jr. Coll., 1968-74, instr. biology and human physiology, 1977—. Pres. usher bd., dir. vacation Bible sch. St. Paul Bapt. Ch., Brookhaven, Miss.; sec. Utica Community Devel. Assn. Named Outstanding Tchr. of Yr. Utica Jr. Coll., 1974; grantee NSF, 1979—. Mem. Miss. Assn. Educators, Miss. Acad. Sci., Sigma Xi, Iota Sigma Phi, Beta Kappa Chi, Delta Sigma Theta. Address: Utica Jr Coll Box 133 Utica MS 39175

SMITHSON, FRANCIS DANIEL, accountant; b. Alton, Ill., Feb. 6, 1945; s. Harold Oscar and Frances La Fern (Eubanks) S.; student Flight Sch., 1963-65; B.A. in Accounting, U. West Fla., 1975; m. Jane Anne Corder, May 23, 1964; children—Danese Kaye, Suzanne Marie. Served as enlisted man U.S. Marine Corps, 1963-65, commd. 2d lt., 1965, advanced through grades to maj., 1975; officer, Okinawa; logistics officer Marine Medium Helicopter Squadron-263, Vietnam; released from active duty, 1972; with Gulf Power Co., Pensacola, Fla., 1975—, supr. property records, 1976-79, supr. accounts payable, 1979—. Adviser Jr. Achievement, 1975; active Girl Scouts U.S.A. Decorated D.F.C., Purple Heart, Air medal. Mem. Nat. Mgmt. Assn. Democrat. Methodist. Participant 1st mil. landing on U.S.S. Tarawa, 1975. Home: 900 Medford Ave Pensacola FL 32505 Office: 75 N Pace Blvd Pensacola FL 32504

SMOAK, RANDOLPH DUNCAN, surgeon; b. Bamberg, S.C., May 5, 1933; s. Randolph Duncan and Mary (Farmer) S.; B.S., U. S.C., 1955; M.D., Med. U. S.C., 1959; m. Saundra Harvin, June 6, 1959; children—Saundra Elizabeth, Katherine Augusta, Anne Harvin, Eleanor Randolph. Intern, Grady Meml. Hosp., Atlanta, 1959-60; resident in gen. surgery Med. U. S.C., Charleston, 1962-66, oncology fellow surgery, 1963-64, chief resident and teaching fellow surgery, 1965-66; sr. fellow surgery M.D. Anderson Hosp. and Tumor Clinic, Houston, 1966-67; practice medicine specializing in surgery, Orangeburg, S.C., 1967—; mem. staff Orangeburg Regional Hosp., chief staff, 1979. Pres., S.C. div. Am. Cancer Soc., 1975-77; sec.-treas. S.C. Med. Care Found., 1974—; bd. dirs. ARC. Served with M.C., USAF, 1960-62. Diplomate Am. Bd. Surgery. Fellow A.C.S.; mem. AMA, Southeastern Surg. Congress, S.C. Med. Assn. (councilor 1969—, vice chmn. 1975—), So. Med. Assn., Pan Am. Med. Assn., S.C. Surg. Soc. (v.p. 1976-77), Soc. Head and Neck Surgeons, Edisto Med. Soc., MacComb Soc. (v.p.), SAR, Sons of Confederacy, French Huguenot Soc. Presbyterian (ruling elder 1975—, chmn. bd. deacons 1973-74). Club: Kiwanis (dist. lt. gov.). Home: 275 Mason Rd Orangeburg SC 29115 Office: 695 Laurel St Orangeburg SC 29115

SMOLLEN, JOSEPH WILLIAM, III, elec. engr.; b. Jackson, Miss., July 21, 1935; s. Joseph William, Jr. and Ora Mae (Jordan) S.; student U.S. Naval Acad., 1957; B.S. in Elec. Engring., Miss. State U., 1958; postgrad. So. Methodist U., 1958, U. Calif., Los Angeles, 1964; m. Shirley Elizabeth Newman, May 16, 1957; children—Carene Durno, Joseph William V. Electronic designer Chance-Vought & Dresser, Dallas, 1958-59; tech. rep. Sperry-Rand, Inc., Huntsville, Ala., 1959-60; sr. engr., asst. to sr. v.p. Brown Engring. Co., Huntsville, Houston, 1961-63; test programs mgr. reliability NASA-Michoud, New Orleans, 1963-67, systems safety following Apollo fire, 1967-70, spl. assignment to Miss. Gov.'s Emergency Council, 1970, research and tech. transfer to City of New Orleans, 1971-77, engr. Space Shuttle Project, Marshall Space Flight Center, Ala., 1977-78, engr. Strategic Petroleum Res. Project Mgmt. Office, 1978—; owner, operator cons. firm in geothermal energy; guest lectr. univs.; faculty Delgado Coll., 1965-68. Cons. to chmn., Urban Consortium, 1977—; pres. Sherwood Forest Sch. PTA, 1971-72, Marion Abramson Sr. High Sch. PTA, 1973-76, Young Men's Bus. Club, New Orleans, 1974; chmn. bd. New Orleans Floral Trail, 1974; bd. dirs. Internat. House, 1974, Boy Scouts Am. Served with U.S. Army, 1959. Recipient Spl. award NASA, 1970, awards Mayor of New Orleans, 1975, Gov. La., 1975, certificate of merit Regional Planning Commn., 1977; numerous other awards. Mem. IEEE (vice chmn. Huntsville sect., editor sect. mag.), Am. Inst. Aeros. and Astronautics, Nat. Space Inst., Nat. Geog. Soc. (life), Am. Engring. Assn. (founder), Space Studies Inst., Future Soc., Naval Acad. Alumni (pres. New Orleans 1977), Miss. State Alumni Assn. Democrat. Methodist. Clubs: Paidia, Bards of Bohemia, Deep Oil, Fifth Saturday, J.C. Newman Hunting Lodge. Home: 4934 Hauck Dr New Orleans LA 70127 Office: DOE SPR 900 Commerce Rd E New Orleans LA 70123

SMOOT, GEORGE FITZGERALD, JR., research hydrologist; b. Wetumpka, Ala., Jan. 16, 1922; s. George Fitzgerald and Ethel (Fuller) S.; student Tulane U., 1939-42; B.S., Auburn U., 1950; m. Talicia Diane Crawford, July 14, 1943; children—George Fitzgerald, Sharon Diane, Jack Edward Bowie. Engr. technician U.S. Geol. Survey, Ala. dist., 1948-50, hydraulic engr., Ala. dist., 1950-52, Alaska dist., 1952-56, Ohio dist., 1956-62, research hydrologist, Washington, 1962-68, coordinator research on instumentation, Washington, 1968-77; cons. hydrology, 1977—; expert adviser representing UN and U.S. AID Program to developing nations on problems relating to hydrology. Served with USNR, 1942-45. Mem. ASCE, Am. Geophys. Union, Internat. Assn. Hydrol. Scis. (hydrometry com. 1968—), Internat. Orgn. Standardization (chmn. subcom. group on instruments for measurement flow in open channels 1966—). Developed moving-boat method measuring flow in large rivers, 1968. Home: PO Box 126 Orange Beach AL 36561

SMOTHERS, FOUNT TILLMAN, architect; b. Nashville, Jan. 18, 1930; s. Fount Tillman and Ruth Moore (Paschal) S.; B.S., Ga. Inst. Tech., 1955; M.S., Ohio U., 1969; m. Ida Garrett Herod, Oct. 27, 1951; children—Benjamin Edward, Norman Paschal. Architect, Nick & Smothers-Architects, Naples, Fla., 1960-65; prof. Sch. Architecture, Ohio U., Athens, 1965-69; prof. Sch. Architecture and Urban Design, U. Kans., Lawrence, 1969-75; dept. head, dir. Office Bldg. Research, La. State U., Baton Rouge, 1975-79, prof. dept. architecture, 1975—; pres. La. Inst. Bldg. Research, 1979; cons. Gulf States Utilities Co., Beaumont, Tex., 1975—, AIA Research Corp., Washington, 1974—, La. State Dept. Natural Resources, Baton Rouge, 1975-79; chmn. La. State Architects Selection Bd., 1977; co-chmn. energy conservation adv. bd. Gulf States Utilities Co., 1976-79. Recipient Design award Ohio AIA and Precast Concrete Assn., 1968, Seldon Hall award Nat. Assn. Home Builders, 1978. Mem. AIA (Design Honor awards 1962, 68), Nat. Acad. Sci. (bldg. energy conservation com. 1980), Nat. Inst. Bldg. Sci., Internat. Council Bldg. Research, La. Architects Assn. Contbr. articles to profl. jours. Home: 260 La State U Ave Baton Rouge LA 70808 Office: Dept Architecture Room 136 Atkinson Hall Baton Rouge LA 70803

SMOTHERS, WILLIAM EDGAR, JR., seismograph co. exec.; b. Shawnee, Okla., July 9, 1928; s. William Edgar and Lena Rivers (Randolph) Smothers; B.S. in Acctg. and Bus. Adminstrn., Okla. State U., 1950; m. Marilyn Myrtle Cales, Sept. 6, 1952; children—William Edgar III, Susan Elaine. Auditor, Donald P. Groom, Ada, Okla., 1950; staff accountant Amoco Prodn. Co., Tulsa, 1953-56; internal auditor Seismograph Service Corp., Tulsa, 1956-60, chief internal auditor, 1961-70, mgr. tax and auditing, 1971-78, treas., 1978—. Chmn. Unied Way Drive; mem. budget com. Tulsa Area United Way. Served to capt. U.S. Army, 1950-53. Mem. Nat. Assn. Accountants Assn. for Systems Mgmt. Democrat. Presbyterian. Clubs: Petroleum, Financial, Elks, Kiwanis (Tulsa). Office: Seismograph Service Corp PO Box 1590 Tulsa OK 74102

SMYTHIES, JOHN RAYMOND, physician; b. Naini Tal, India, Nov. 30, 1922; s. Evelyn Arthur and Olive Muriel (Cripps) S.; came to U.S., 1973; M.A., U. Cambridge, 1942, M.D., 1955, M.Sc., 1958, M.B. B.Chir., 1945; M.Sc., U. B.C., 1955; D.P.M., U. London, 1952; postgrad. Worcester (Mass.) Found., 1958-59, U. Cambridge, 1955-57, U. B.C., 1953-55; m. Vanna Maria Grazia Gattorno, Dec. 2, 1950; children—Adrian Greville, Christopher John Evelyn. Sr. resident Maudsley Hosp., London, 1959-61; reader psychiatry U. Edinburgh (Scotland), 1961-73; C.B. Ireland prof. psychiat. research and biochemistry U. Ala. Med. Center, Birmingham, 1973—; cons. WHO, 1963-68. Served with Royal Navy, 1946-48. Nuffield fellow, 1955-57. Fellow Royal Coll. Physicians London, Royal Coll. Psychiatrists, Am. Psychiat. Assn., Royal Soc. Medicine; mem. Am. Coll. Neuropharmacology, Internat. Soc. Psychoneuroendocrinology (pres. 1971-74), Internat. Brain Research Orgn., Collegium Internationale Neuropsychopharmacologium, Am. Soc. Pharmacology, Soc. Biol. Psychiatry. Episcopalian. Club: Athenaeum (London). Author: Biological Psychiatry, 1968; Brain Mechanisms and Behavior, 1973; (with Arthur Koestler) Beyond Reductionism, 1969; others; editor Internat. Rev. Neurobiology, 1958—; contbr. articles to profl. jours. Patentee in field. Home: 4245 Stone River Rd Birmingham AL 35213 Office: Neurosci Program U Ala Med Center Birmingham AL 35233

SNAPP, ELIZABETH, educator, librarian; b. Lubbock, Tex., Mar. 31, 1937; d. William James and Louise (Lanham) Mitchell; B.A. magna cum laude, N. Tex. State U., Denton, 1968, M.L.S., 1969, M.A., 1977; m. Harry Franklin Snapp, June 1, 1956. Asst. to archivist Archive of New Orleans Jazz, Tulane U., 1960-63; catalog librarian Tex. Woman's U., Denton, 1969-71, head acquisitions dept., 1971-74, coordinator readers services, 1974-77, asst. to dean Grad. Sch., 1977-79, instr. library sci., 1977—, acting univ. librarian, 1979—. Co-sponsor Irish Lecture Series, Denton, 1968, 70, 73, 78; sec. Denton County Democratic Caucus, 1970. Mem. Am., Southwestern, Tex. (program com. 1978) library assns., AAUW (legis. br. chmn. 1973-74, br. pres. 1979-81), So. Conf. Brit. Studies, AAUP, Tex. Assn. Coll. Tchrs. (pres. Tex. Woman's U. chpt. 1976-77), Woman's Shakespeare Club (pres. 1967-69), Beta Phi Mu (chpt. pres. 1976-78, pres. nat. adv. assembly 1979-80), Alpha Chi, Alpha Lambda Sigma (pres. 1970-71), Pi Delta Phi. Episcopalian (directress altar guild 1966-68, 73-76). Asst. editor Tex. Academe, 1973-76; book reviewer Library Resources and Tech. Services, 1973—; Contbr. articles to profl. jours. Home: 612 Grove St Denton TX 76201 Office: PO Box 24093 TWU Sta Denton TX 76204

SNAPP, HARRY FRANKLIN, historian; b. Bryan, Tex., Oct. 15, 1930; s. H.F. and Ethel (Manning) S.; B.A., Baylor U., 1952, M.A., 1953; Ph.D., Tulane U., 1963; m. Elizabeth Mitchell, June 1, 1956. Instr., U. Coll. Tulane U., 1960-62; asst. prof. history Wofford Coll., 1963-64; asst. prof. history N. Tex. State U., Denton, 1964-69, asso. prof., 1969—. Mem. Friends Winchester Cathedral, Am. Com. for Irish Studies; mem. adv. com. on acad. freedom and tenure policy, coordinating bd. Tex. Coll. and Univ. System. Recipient N. Tex. State U. Faculty Research award, 1966, 67. Mem. AAUP (pres. North Tex. chpt. 1968-69, pres. Southwestern regional conf. 1971-72, pres. Tex. conf. 1974-76, nat. council 1976—), So. Conf. Brit. Studies (sec.-treas.), Am., So. hist. assns., Hist. Assn. (London), Northamptonshire Record Soc., Butler Soc. (Ireland), Econ. History Soc., Ch. Hist. Soc., Tulane U. Alumni Assn., Alpha Chi. Episcopalian. Editor Brit. Studies Mercury, 1970—, Tex. Academe, 1973-76; contbr. articles to profl. jours. Home: 612 Grove St Denton TX 76201 Office: PO Box 1427 Denton TX 76201

SNAPP, MATTHEW, psychologist, ednl. adminstr.; b. Bklyn., Feb. 1, 1943; s. Matthew L. and Ruth (Crane) S.; B.A., Wagner Coll., 1965; M.A., Brigham Young U., 1968; Ph.D., U. Tex., 1970; m. Sharon Budnick, June 19, 1976; children—Laurie, Scottie. Tchr. elementary sch., Old Bridge, N.J., 1965; tchr. social studies jr. high sch., Matawan, N.J., 1966; sch. psychologist Regional Child Study Service, Price, Utah, 1967-68; pres. Children's Mental Health Center, Austin, Tex., 1968-70; lectr. dept. ednl. psychology U. Tex., Austin, 1970-72, adj. asst. prof., 1972-78, adj. asso. prof., 1978—; vis. asso. prof. Coll. Edn., Pan Am. U., Edinberg, Tex., 1977; lectr. dept. psychology S.W. Tex. State U., San Marcos, 1979—; dir. dept. counseling and guidance Austin Ind. Sch. Dist., 1970-71, dir. student devel., 1971—; trainer Nat. Tng. Labs., 1974; cons. Tex. Classroom Tchrs. Assn., Austin, 1972-75, Ednl. Service Center, drug edn. program, 1971, Eanes Ind. Sch. Dist., 1971, Austin Diocese, 1971, Tex. Edn. Agy., 1973—, Tex. Youth Council, 1976—. Bd. dirs. Austin Child Guidance Center, v.p., 1971-74; trustee Austin-Travis County Mental Health—Mental Retardation Center, 1974-77, v.p., 1976-77. Mem. Am., Southwestern, Tex. psychol. assns., Tex., Central Tex. personnel and guidance assns., Nat. Assn. Sch. Psychologists, Assn. Humanistic Psychology, Assn. Women in Psychology, Am. Ednl. Research Assn., Tex. State Tchrs. Assn., Austin Assn. of Pub. Sch. Adminstrs., Austin Group Therapy Assn. Phi Delta Kappa, Phi Kappa Phi, Psi Chi. Co-author: Cooperation in the Classroom; contbr. articles to profl. jours. Home: 9005 Sam Carter Dr Austin TX 78736 Office: 6100 Guadalupe St Austin TX 78752

SNAVELY, GUY EVERETT, JR., orgn. exec.; b. Baldwin, Md., June 30, 1906; s. Guy E. and Ada (Rittenhouse) S.; A.B., Birmingham-So. Coll., 1927; L.H.D., Athens Coll., 1950; m. Helen McNeill, June 3, 1930; children—Sherry Louise, Dan McNeill. Bus. mgr. Ala. Inst. for Deaf and Blind, 1933-38; exec. sec., trustee Pickett & Hatcher Ednl. Fund, Inc., Columbus, Ga., 1938-62, exec. v.p., 1962-76, chmn. bd. trustees, 1976—. Mem. adv. com. Higher Edn. Act 1965, U.S. Office Edn., 1965-69, mem. adv. com. Nat. Vocational Student Loan Ins. Act 1965, 1965-69; mem. membership com., coll. scholarship service Coll. Entrance Exam. Bd., 1966-68. Treas., Ga.-Ala. council Boy Scouts Am., 1955-63, treas. Chattahoochie council, 1964-77, pres., 1978-79; chmn. Columbus Citadel, Salvation Army, 1974-75; dir. Family Service Bur., 1939-41, 54-58; counselor Miss Ga. Scholarship Fund, 1947-53; dir. Nat. Conf. Christians and Jews, 1950-53; dir. Columbus Appeals Rev. Bd., 1951-53; chmn. Ga. com. Am. Assn. for UN, 1952-56; pres. Columbus Community Chest, 1948-50; pres. Muscogee Mental Health Assn., 1953, v.p., 1958, 62-65. Bd. dirs. W.Ga.-E.Ala. Better Bus. Bur., 1970-72, Jr. Achievement, Columbus Sch. Speech; trustee Ga. Found. Ind. Colls., 1969—, Columbus Coll. Found., 1980—. Served as maj. F.A., AUS, 1942-46; ETO, 1944-45. Decorated Bronze Star. Mem. Columbus C. of C. (chmn. edn. com. 1948-49), Mil. Order World Wars (chpt. adj. 1961-62, comdr. 1965-66), Assn. U.S. Army (dir. chpt. 1968-71, 74—), Brimingham-So. Coll. Alumni Assn. (past pres.), So. Assn. Student Fin. Aid Adminstrs. (sec.-treas. 1963-70), Omicron Delta Kappa, Alpha Tau Omega. Presbyterian (vice chmn. com. on homes and ednl. instns. Synod Ga. 1962-66, mem. com. on campus Christian life 1965-66, elder, mem. extension com. Presbytery Southwest Ga. 1972—, chmn. candidates com. 1976-78). Kiwanian (pres. Columbus club 1941, sec. Ga. dist. 1950). Club: Big Eddy. Home: 2619 Habersham Ave Columbus GA 31906 Office: 1800 Buena Vista Rd Columbus GA 31906

SNAY, JACK ALEXANDER, accountant; b. Lansing, Mich., Oct. 27, 1939; s. Frank and Bernice (Hoffman) S.; B.S., Wayne State U., 1967; m. Sharon L. Deverna, May 11, 1961; 1 son, Scott Steven. Mgr. Price Waterhouse & Co., Detroit, 1968-70, Miami, Fla., 1970-73; controller Am. Marine Underwriters, Miami, 1973-74; chief fin. officer Walter Harvey Corp., Miami, 1974; owner, accountant Simons & Snay, P.A., C.P.A.'s, Miami, 1974—; owner, operator Condo Mgmt. & Realty, Inc., Miami, 1978—; mem. adj. faculty U. Miami, 1974-76. Served with U.S. Army, 1958-61. Mem. Am. Inst. C.P.A.'s, Mich. Assn. C.P.A.'s, Fla. Inst. C.P.A.'s, Beta Gamma. Republican. Baptist. Club: South Dade Anglers (pres. 1978-79) (Miami). Office: 10651 SW 88th St Miami FL 33176

SNEAD, ROBERT ROSE, constrn. co. exec.; b. Daytona Beach, Fla., Oct. 19, 1927; s. Walter S. and Lillie G. (Mabbette) S.; B.Arch., Rensselaer Poly. Inst., 1950; m. Peggy Liggett, June 14, 1969; children—David, Donna, Terry, Patrick, Kenneth. Sr. partner Snead & Wiggert Mapping Service, Daytona Beach, 1948-51; constrn. engr. E.I. DuPont de Nemours & Co., Jackson, S.C. and Circleville, Ohio, 1952-54; v.p., gen. mgr. Richardson Constrn. Co., Ft. Lauderdale, Fla., 1954-61; v.p. Hageman Bldg and Devel. Co., Ft. Lauderdale, 1962; pres., chmn. bd., chief exec. officer Snead Constrn. Corp., Ft. Lauderdale, 1963—. Mem. Asso. Gen. Contractors (dir. S. Fla. chpt., also mem. Mid-Fla. chpt.), Broward, Miami, Tampa, Daytona Beach, Mut. builders exchanges, Sommellier Guild, Ft. Lauderdale Symphony Assn., Opera Guild Ft. Lauderdale, Miami Ballet Soc., Community Concert Assn., Confrerie de la Chaine des Rotisseurs, Les Amis du Vin, Broward Com. of 100, Am. Orchid Soc., Ft. Lauderdale Orchid Soc. Clubs: Broward Dolphins Booster (v.p.); Coral Ridge Country, Le Club Internat., Ft. Lauderdale, Touchdown, Nat. Exchange (chpt. pres., state pres.) (Ft. Lauderdale). Home: 2711 NE 57th Ct Fort Lauderdale FL 33308 Office: PO Box 23691 Fort Lauderdale FL 33307

SNEARY, TOM FAGNER, contractor; b. Davenport, Iowa, Apr. 7, 1919; s. Loy E. and Ida Mae (Chapin) S.; B.A., Northwestern U., 1945; m. Cora Nell McAlister, Dec. 26, 1942; children—Loy Edward, Barbara Ann. With Studebaker Corp., various locations, 1946-57, asst. zone mgr., Chgo., 1955-56, Cin., 1956-57; dist. mgr. Ford Motor Co. edsel div., Dallas, 1957-58; mgr. marketing Superior Decals Inc., Dallas, 1958-61; pres., owner Jennite Co. Dallas, 1961—. Precinct chmn. Dallas Democratic Com.; election judge, Dallas, 1969—. Served to capt. AUS, 1942-45. Decorated Silver Star (2), Purple Heart (3), Bronze Star. Fellow Constrn. Specifications Inst. (nat. bd. dirs., 1972-75, recipient various awards including presidents plaque, 1975); mem. North Dallas C. of C. Mem. Christian Ch. (chmn. bd., elder). Mason. Author: Construction of Asphaltic Concrete Tennis Courts, 1973; Construction of Portland Cement Concrete Tennis Courts, 1973. Home and office: 10264 Gooding Dr Dallas TX 75229

SNEED, TOMMY LYNN, broadcasting co. exec.; b. Chattanooga, Oct. 23, 1947; s. Grady and Beulah May (Watson) S.; B.A., Tenn. Temple Coll., 1969; m. Cynthia Louise Keasler, June 15, 1968; children—David, Jason. Sta. mgr. Sta. WPJD, Daisy, Tenn., 1972-74; mgr. Sta. WMOC, Chattanooga, 1974-78; v.p., gen. mgr. Radio Paradise, Chattanooga, 1978—. Bd. dirs. Womens Gospel Mission, Chattanooga. Baptist. Office: PO Box 9452 Chattanooga TN 37412

SNELL, JOYCE JOHNSON, career planning cons.; b. Albany, N.Y., Sept. 20, 1943; d. Franklin W. and Dorothy M. Johnson; B.S. in Psychology, Washington U., St. Louis, 1965; M.S. in Personnel and Guidance, SUNY, Albany, 1971; children—Jeffrey, Jennifer. Vice pres. sales and mktg. Diversified Real Estate Services, Greenville, S.C., 1976-78; career devel. counselor Center for Continuing Edn. for Women, Greenville Tech. Coll., 1978-79; dir. career planning div. Finley O'Connor and Co., Greenville, 1979—. Mem. Greenville County Planning Commn., 1978—, sec., chmn. personnel com., 1979—; bd. dirs. Community Planning Council, 1976—, chmn. community resource com., 1979—. Mem. Am. Personnel and Guidance Assn. Episcopalian. Club: Zonta. Home: 106 Botany Rd Greenville SC 29615 Office: Piedmont E 37 Villa Rd Greenville SC 29615

SNELL, MOLLY MAUREEN, counselor; b. Marshill, Maine, June 25, 1947; d. Charles Jerold and Alice Mary (Brown) S.; B.S. in Nursing Edn., Columbia U., 1969; M.S., Alfred U., 1973; postgrad. Pepperdine U., 1977, U. Calif., San Diego, summers 1973, 74, 77, U. Miami, 1978-79, Nova U., 1979; doctoral candidate Union Grad. Sch., 1979—. Instr. med./surg. nursing SUNY, Alfred, 1969-71;

residence hall area coordinator Alfred (N.Y.) U., 1971-72, asst. dean students, 1972-73, asso. dean students, 1973-75; staff facilitator dept. edn. U. Calif., San Diego, summer 1974; asst. prof. Sch. Nursing, Barry Coll., Miami Shores, Fla., 1975-78; counselor and psychotherapist Living Skills Center for Adult Devel. Disabled, Dania, Fla., 1978—; cons. in field. Instr., ARC, Ft. Lauderdale, 1977—. Dept. Health and Rehab. Services grantee, 1978-79; registered nurse, N.Y., Fla.; lic. counselor, Fla. Mem. Nat. Assn. Student Personnel Adminstrs., Am. Personnel and Guidance Assn., Am. Coll. Personnel Assn., Am. Nurses Assn., Fla. Nurses Assn., Alpha Lambda Delta, Phi Kappa Phi. Address: 720 Conchshell Way Plantation FL 33324

SNELLINGS, GEORGE MARION, III, lawyer; b. Monroe, La., June 24, 1939; s. George Marion and Marie Louise (Wilcox) S.; student Tulane U., 1956-58; B.A., La. State U., 1960, J.D., 1962; m. Dianne King, May 6, 1964; children—George Marion IV, Satchie Breard; 1 son by previous marriage, George Wilcox. Admitted to La. bar, 1962; individual practice law Monroe, 1962-79; asso. firm Snellings, Breard, Sartor, Inabnett & Trascher and predecessors, Monroe, 1962-66, partner, 1967—; stockholder, dir. Wendy's South-Tex, Inc., Corpus Christi, 1977—; owner, pres. Ram Energy Corp., 1979—. Mem. Monroe City Dem. Exec. Com., 1966-74. Mem. 4th. Jud. Dist. Ouachita Parish (La.) Bar Assn., La. Bar Assn., Am. Bar Assn. Episcopalian. Clubs: Pine Hills Gun, Dallas Gun, Chauvin Racquet, Safari Internat., Game Coin, Lotus, Bayou DeSiard Country, Balboa of Mazatlan. Author: Hunting Southland Fields and Forests, 1976. Home: 102 Country Club Rd Monroe LA 71201 Office: PO Box 6134 1903 Tower Dr Monroe LA 71203

SNIADECKI, ALAN FRANCIS, mfg. co. exec.; b. S. Bend, Ind., July 6, 1946; s. Clement John and Evelyn Harriet (Andrezejewski) S.; B.A., Mich. State U., 1973; M.Labor and Indsl. Relations, Mich. State U., 1975; m. Sharon K. Hamilton, Aug. 20, 1977. Course instr. Lansing (Mich.) Community Coll., 1975; contracts field supr. I.B.T. Pension Fund, Chgo., 1975; compensation specialist OSD, Xerox Corp., Dallas, 1977, mgr. indsl. relations XBS/OS, 1979—. Served with USMC, 1966-69. Decorated Navy Commendation medal, Purple Heart. Mich. State U. Sch. Social Sci. grad. scholar, 1975. Mem. Am. Soc. Tng. and Devel., Am. Compensation Assn., Indsl. Relations Research Assn.

SNIBBE, ROBERT MCCAWLEY, publisher; b. Catonsville, Md., Apr. 28, 1913; s. George W. and Mildred (Robinson) S.; B.A., St. John's Coll., Annapolis, 1937; m. Ellen Hynes Heavey, Sept. 23, 1939; children—Robert McCawley, Ellen L. Dir. services Standard & Poor's Corp., N.Y.C., 1938-42; bus. mgr. Bur. Nat. Affairs, Washington, 1942-43; 46-49; dir. press relations Com. for Econ. Devel., N.Y.C., 1949-52; exec. v.p. Good Reading Rack Service, N.Y.C., 1952-55; pres. Employee Relations Inc., N.Y.C., 1955-63; chmn. bd. Snibbe Publs. Inc. promotion books, Clearwater, Fla., 1963-77; pub. TV Facts, Largo, Fla., 1979—. Pres., Belleair Civic Assn., 1970-71; commr. Town of Belleair, 1977—. Trustee, St. Paul's Sch., Clearwater, Fla., 1973—. Served to lt. (s.g.) USNR, 1943-46. Recipient Freedoms Found. honor medal, 1957, 58, 59. Mem. Pub. Relations Soc. Am., Specialty Advt. Assn., Premium Mktg. Assn. Am., Kappa Alpha. Clubs: Williams (N.Y.C.); Belleview Biltmore Country, Carlouel Yacht (Clearwater). Home: 640 Poinsettia Rd Belleair FL 33516 Office: Suite 423 2400 W Bay Dr Largo FL 33540

SNIDER, JAMES RHODES, radiologist; b. Pawnee, Okla., May 16, 1931; s. John Henry and Gladys Opal (Rhodes) S.; B.S., U. Okla., 1953, M.D., 1956; m. Lynadell Vivion, Dec. 27, 1954; children—Jon, Jan. Intern, Edward Meyer Meml. Hosp., Buffalo, 1956-57; resident radiology U. Okla. Med. Center, 1959-62; radiologist Holt-Krock Clinic and Sparks Regional Med. Center, Ft. Smith, Ark., 1962—; clin. asst. prof. radiology U. Ark. Med. Center, Little Rock, 1976—; cons. USPHS Hosp., Talihina, Okla., 1962—; dir. Fairfield Community Land Co., Little Rock. Mem. Ark. Bd. Pub. Welfare, 1969-71; bd. dirs. U. Okla. Assn., 1967-70, U. Okla. Alumni Devel. Fund, 1970-74; bd. visitors U. Okla., 1976-79. Served to lt. comdr. USNR, 1957-62. Mem. Am. Coll. Radiology, Radiol. Soc. N.Am., AMA, Am. Roentgen Ray Soc., Phi Beta Kappa, Beta Theta Pi (trustee corp.), Alpha Epsilon Delta. Republican. Baptist. Club: Hardscrabble Country. Asso. editor Computerized Tomography, 1976—. Home: 5814 Cliff Dr Fort Smith AR 72901 Office: 1500 Dodson St Fort Smith AR 72901

SNIDER, NANCY RUTH, food cons.; b. Louisville, Mar. 29, 1937; d. Hiram and Ruth (Saam) Snider; student Purdue U., 1955-57; B.S., Iowa State U., 1962, M.S., 1970; Recipe editor Gen. Foods Corp., White Plains, N.Y., 1962-63; asst. food editor McCall's mag., N.Y.C., 1963-65; home economist Pillsbury Co., Mpls., 1966-68; food and nutrition editor Instns. Vol. Feeding Mag., Chgo., 1969-75; owner Nancy Snider & Assos., food cons., Chgo., 1976—. Partner, Small Bus. Communications, Chgo., 1973-75. Mem. Nat. Press Club, Inst. Food Technologist (councilor 1971-74), Am. Home Econ. Assn., Home Economists in Bus., Women in Communications, Soc. for Nutrition Edn. Author: The Professional Chef's Soy Protein Recipe Ideas, 1971. Home: 2427 Westwood Ave Louisville KY 40220

SNIDER, NATHAN HALE, steamship co. exec.; b. Vonore, Tenn., Dec. 18, 1917; s. Fred and Frances (Gray) S.; B.A., Lincoln Meml. U., 1941, L.H.D., 1977; m. Jean Elizabeth Whitaker, Dec. 30, 1944 (dec.). Contact rep. Isbrandtsen Co. Inc., N.Y.C., N.J., Va., 1946-49, gen. mgr. southeastern div., New Orleans, 1949-53, v.p., 1953-56; v.p. Amerind Shipping Co. Inc., New Orleans, 1956-71; asst. to Gulf Mgr. Norton Lilly Co., New Orleans, 1971-74; line mgr. ops. and traffic, mgr. barges and developing lines Combi Line, Biehl and Co., New Orleans, 1974—. Bd. dirs. German Seamen's Mission, New Orleans, Mandeville (La.) Union Protestant Ch., 1950-60; steward Covington Meth. Ch., 1965-70; zoning commn. 4th Ward St. Tammany Parish, 1968-70. Served to lt. comdr. USN, 1941-46. Recipient Algernon Sidney Sullivan award N.Y. So. Soc., 1973. Mem. Nat. Cargo Bur., World Trade Clubs (Memphis and New Orleans) C. of C. (fgn. commerce com.), Internat. House, Am. Legion (post comdr. 1955-57). Republican. Methodist. Clubs: Covington Country (founding mem.); Army-Navy (N.Y.C.); France-Amerique de la Louisiane, Codifil, Propeller, Export Mgrs. Home: Upper Pontalba 540 Rue St Peter New Orleans LA 70116 also Box 5 Mandeville LA 70448 Office: Biehl and Co 416 Common New Orleans LA 70130

SNIDER, RUTH ATKINSON, ednl. counselor; b. Louisville, Jan. 7, 1930; d. Ellis Orrell and Fanola Blanche (Miller) Atkinson; student Centre Coll., 1947-48; B.S., Spalding Coll., 1965, M.Ed., 1970; postgrad. Western Ky. U., 1979; m. Arnold Wills Snider, Feb. 17, 1950; children—Yvonne Marie, Ray Wills, Mark Alan. Tchr. pub. schs., Finchville, Ky., 1950-51, Louisville City Schs., 1956-57; tchr. Jefferson County (Ky.) pub. schs., 1964-66, counselor elementary schs., 1966—. Mem. Am. (del. 1974), Ky., Jefferson County personnel and guidance assns., Ky. Sch. Counselors Assn. (v.p. for elem. 1978-79), Ky. Elem. and Middle Sch. Counselors Assn. (pres. 1975-76), Jefferson County Counselors Assn., Am. Sch. Counselors Assn., Klondike Ln PTA. Baptist. Home: 2428 Chattesworth Ln Louisville KY 40222 Office: 3807 Klondike Ln Louisville KY 40218

SNIVELY, HARVEY BOWDEN, JR., citrus prodn. and processing co. exec.; b. Winter Haven, Fla., Dec. 20, 1923; s. Harvey Bowden and Sara May (McKibben) S.; B.S. in Agr., U. Fla., 1948; m. Mary Ann Schock, Nov. 25, 1949; children—Patricia Ann Snively Herndon, Harvey Bowden III, Nancy Carol, Margaret Jane. Prodn. mgr. Lake Hamilton (Fla.) Coop., 1952-67, v.p., 1967-68, pres., 1968—; pres. Orange-Co. of Fla. Inc., Lake Hamilton, 1968—; sr. v.p., dir. Orange-Co. Columbus (Ohio); dir. First Nat. Bank Winter Haven, Holiday Bank (Fla.), Citrus Central Coop., Orlando, Fla., Lake Alfred (Fla.) Growers Fertilizer Coop. Mem. pres.'s council U. Fla., Gainesville; mem. Winter Haven Indsl. Council. Served to 2d lt. USAAF, 1943-45. Mem. Pi Kappa Alpha. Club: Lake Region Country, Rotary. Home: 694 W Lake Otis Dr Winter Haven FL 33880 Office: PO Box 99 Lake Hamilton FL 33851

SNOOK, JOHN MCCLURE, telephone co. exec.; b. Toledo, May 31, 1917; s. Ward H. and Grace (McClure) S.; student Ohio State U., 1936-43; m. Marjorie Louise Younce, Jan. 15, 1974. Instr. history, fine arts and scis. Ohio State U., Columbus; exec. v.p. Gulf Telephone Co., Foley, Ala., 1955-70, pres., 1970—. Chmn., Baldwin (Ala.) Sesquicentennial, 1969; mem. hon. staff Gov. Ala., 1967—; active civil def., community projects; asst. civil def. dir. Baldwin County, 1974; mem. Baldwin County Bi-Centennial Com., 1974-75. Hon. a.d.c. lt. col. Ala.; hon. Ala. state trooper; recipient Citizen of Year award Gulf Shores, 1956-57. Mem. Nat. Rifle Assn. (life), Am. Ordnance Assn., South Baldwin C. of C., Delaware County, Baldwin County (pres.) hist. assns., Friends of Library Assn. (pres. 1973-74), Ohio State Alumni Assn., Ala. Ind. Telephone Assn., Telephone Pioneers, Ind. Pioneers. Kiwanian, Lion. Office: Box 670 Foley AL 36535

SNOOK, JOHN MELVIN, coll. pres.; b. Topeka, Mar. 27, 1934; s. Edward Raymond and Elizabeth Ann (Madden) S.; B.A., Northwestern U., 1966, M.A., 1968; Litt. D., Houghton Coll., 1977; Ph.D., U. Calif., 1978; m. Marian Ellen Cunningham, Mar. 25, 1955; children—Carmen, Carleen, Cherie, John Melvin II. Prof. English, Northwestern U., 1965-69; supt., prin. Okla. schs.; pres. Bartlesville (Okla.) Wesleyan Coll., 1973—; mgmt. cons. Served with USAF, 1953-63; Col. Res. ret. Decorated Silver Cross with 6 oak leaf clusters. Mem. Bartlesville C. of C. (dir.). Republican. Club: Rotary. Office: 2201 Silverlake Rd Bartlesville OK 74003

SNORGRASS, JOSEPH ANTHONY, profl. planner, adminstr., educator; b. Sedalia, Mo., June 11, 1952; s. Joseph William and Edrie Joy (Brooks) S.; B.A. in Environ. Design and Planning, U. Kans., 1974; M.City and Regional Planning, Ohio State U., 1975, M.Public Adminstrn., 1976; m. Cheryl Jezelle Plummer, Aug. 14, 1976. Staff asst. AT&T, Kansas City, Mo., 1971-74; regional planner Mid Ohio Regional Planning and Devel. Commn., Columbus, 1974-77; dir. planning and mgmt. Central Ala. Regional Planning and Devel. Commn., Montgomery, 1977-78; chief planner HUD, Birmingham, Ala., 1978-80, dir. adminstrv. mgmt. div., 1980—; asst. prof. Ala. State U., Montgomery, 1977—; adj. prof. Auburn U., Montgomery, 1977-78; adj. faculty, guest lectr. Ala. A. and M. U., Huntsville, 1979—. Ford Found. scholar, 1970-72; HUD grad. study fellow, 1974-76. Mem. Am. Inst. Cert. Planners, Am. Planning Assn., Internat. City Mgmt. Assn., Kappa Alpha Psi. Author: Saving Central Ohio's Forest Tracts, 1976; Central Alabama's Regional Plan, 1978, others. Home: 2455 B 15th Ave S Birmingham AL 35205 Office: Daniel Bldg 15 S 20th St Birmingham AL 35233

SNOW, WALTER THOMAS, radiologist; b. Malvern, Ark., June 16, 1919; s. Ruffin E. and Adelaide Love (Pearce) S.; B.S., Baylor U., 1940, M.D., La. State U., 1949; m. Elaine Reneau; children—Lana, Corwin, Paul, Sarah, Jeffrey. Intern, USPHS Hosp., New Orleans; gen. practice medicine, Liberty, Miss., 1950-54; resident in radiology VA Hosp., Dallas, 1954-57; chief radiologist Man (W.Va.) Meml. Hosp., 1957-58; chief of radiology Sweetwater County Hosp., Rock Springs, Wyo., 1959-63; dir. radiology Confederate Meml. Med. Center, Shreveport, La., 1963-67; chief radiology Willis Knighton Meml. Hosp., Shreveport, 1967-78, VA Med. Center, Shreveport, 1978—; clin. asst. prof. radiology La. State U. Sch. Medicine, Shreveport. Served with USAAF, 1941-45. Diplomate Am. Bd. Radiology. Fellow Am. Coll. Radiology, Am. Coll. Nuclear Medicine; mem. Am. Lung Assn. (nat. bd. dirs. 1968, pres.), Lung Assn. La. (pres. 1966-68, dir. 1963—), AMA, Christian Med. Soc., Am. Soc. Nuclear Medicine, Radiol. Soc. N. Am., Caddo Parish Med. Soc., La. Med. Soc., Am. Thoracic Soc. (La. pres. 1971). Democrat. Baptist. Club: Masons. Home: Route 4 Box 35A Keithville LA 71047 Office: PO Box 37450 Shreveport LA 71103

SNOWEISS, HOWARD, interior designer; b. N.Y.C., Apr. 2, 1943; s. Ben and Michelle (Simon) S.; B.Design, U. Fla., 1964. Designer, Designs for Bus., N.Y.C., 1964-66, Luss/Kaplan and Assos., N.Y.C., 1966-70, Westinghouse Corp. Design Center, Pitts., 1970-73; v.p., dir. interior design Design Matrix div. Ferendino, Grafton, Spillis, Carbela, Coral Gables, Fla., 1973—; guest instr. Purdue U., U. Cin., U. Miami, Carnegia Mellon U. Mem. Inst. Bus. Designers (pres. Fla. chpt.), Miami Design Preservation League, Adv. bd. Interiors Mag.; interior design work published mags., including Interior Design, Contract Interiors, Fla. Designers Quar., Archtl. Record. Office: 800 Douglas Rd Coral Gables FL 33134

SNYDELAAR, MARGARET MARY, orgn. exec.; b. Warminster, Wiltshire, Eng., Oct. 24, 1922; d. Charles and Beatrice Lily (Robinshaw) Hardwicke; student U. Tex., Austin, 1940-42; cert. in linguistics U. Mich., 1969; lic. in English as Second Lang., Universidad Nacional Autónoma de México; m. Nicholas Adrianus Snydelaar, Nov. 3, 1943; children—Beatrice Jessie, Jeanne Margaret, Andrew Charles. Successively social worker Mexican Nat. Welfare, personal rep. of gen. mgr. Altos Hornos de México, dir. Bi-nat. Center, Monclova Coahuila; now exec. dir. Instituto Mexicano Norteamericano de Relaciones Culturales de San Luís Potosí; also consular agt. for U.S.A. in San Luís Potosí. Pres., Red Cross, Monclova Coahuila; v.p. Children's Hosp.; v.p. Pan Am. Round Table; internat. v.p. Internat. Good Neighbor Council, 1978. Mem. Associación de Institutos Mexicano-Norteamericano de Relaciones Culturales (pres.), Mexican Legion of Honor. Episcopalian. Office: 766 Venustiano Carranza San Luís Potosí México

SNYDER, ALAN HOWARD, JR., mech. engring. sales exec.; b. Marshfield, Wis., Apr. 10, 1922; s. Alan Howard and Mattie Ruth (Bartlet) S.; B.M.E., So. Meth. U., 1944; m. Dorothea Jones, Feb. 16, 1946; children—Mark Evan, Cathleen. Field rep. Benson Engring. Co., Dallas, 1946-58; v.p. engring. Roberts Industries, Inc. (merged with Fed.-Mogul Corp. 1975), Salina, Kans., 1952-75, dir., 1952-75, cons., 1975-78; v.p. Robco, Inc., Dallas, 1959—. Pres., Eye Bank Assn. Tex., 1977; v.p. Eye Bank Assn. Am. Served with USNR, 1943-46. Registered profl. engr., Tex. Mem. Tex. Soc. Profl. Engrs., Tex. Assn. Bus. (dir. TABPC), Power Transmission Reps. Assn., Antifriction Bearing Mfrs. Assn. Republican. Presbyterian (elder). Clubs: Masons, Lions (exec. v.p. Sight and Tissue Found.), Brookhaven Country. Patentee in field. Home: 4526 Harvest Hill St Dallas TX 75234 Office: 1240 Majesty St PO Box 47365 Dallas TX 75247

SNYDER, ALBERT WILLIAM, educator; b. Chgo., Aug. 16, 1930; s. Albert Waldrop and Rose Mary Snyder; B.A. in Communications, Wheaton (Ill.) Coll., 1954; M.A. in TV-Radio Broadcasting, Mich. State U., 1971; m. Ruth Evelyn Chambers, July 11, 1959; children—Steven Albert, Daniel Harold. News and public affairs dir. Radio Sta. ELWA, Monrovia, Liberia, 1955-65, mgr., 1965-72; mgr. Caribbean Radio Lighthouse, St. Johns, Antigua, W.I., 1973-76; prof., chmn. div. TV-radio-film Liberty Bapt. Coll., Lynchburg, Va., 1976—; mgr. Radio Sta. WRVL, Lynchburg, 1977—; dir. Monrovia Youth for Christ, 1957-70; instr., cons. Ministry Info., Govt. Liberia, 1968-70. Served with Signal Corps, U.S. Army, 1952-54. Decorated knight comdr. Order African Redemption (Liberia). Mem. Nat. Religious Broadcasters (sec. S.E. chpt. 1978-80), Intercoll. Broadcasting Assn., Nat. Assn. Broadcasters, Am. Film Inst., Va. TV Reps. in Higher Edn. Baptist. Contbr. articles to religious jours. Home: 109 Perrymont Ave Lynchburg VA 24502 Office: Liberty Bapt Coll Lynchburg VA 24506

SNYDER, CHARLES AUBREY, lawyer; b. Bastrop, La., June 19, 1941; s. David and Shirley Blossom (Haas) S.; B.B.A., Tulane U., 1963; J.D., La. State U., 1966; m. Sharon Rae Veta, Aug. 29, 1963; children—David Veta, Shelby Haas, Claire Frances. Admitted to La. bar, 1966; asso. firm Milling, Benson, Woodward, Hillyer, Pierson & Miller, and predecessors, New Orleans, 1966-69, partner, 1969—; dir. TANO Corp., Oil Investments Inc. Trustee Kathlyn O'Brien Register Found., 1970; bd. dirs. New Orleans Speech and Hearing Center, pres., 1978-80; Mem. New Orleans, La., Am. bar assns., La. Law Inst., Beta Gamma Sigma. Clubs: Metairie Country, Vista Shores, Petroleum, Internat. House, Plimsoll. Home: 1659 Burbank Dr New Orleans LA 70122 Office: 1100 Whitney Bldg New Orleans LA 70130

SNYDER, CLARENCE DALE, physician, health care exec.; b. Logan, N.Mex., Oct. 8, 1930; s. Clarence Edward and Lotta Mae (Meeks) S.; B.S., U. Ark., 1954, M.D., 1958; m. Dorothy Ramsett, Mar. 29, 1952; children—Kathryn Ann, Jennifer Dale. Intern, Riverside Hosp., Toledo, 1958-59; gen. practice medicine, Refugio, Tex., 1963-77; chmn. bd., chief exec. officer Emergency Medicine Physicians Asso., Dallas, 1974—, Emergency Medicine Mgmt. Systems, Dallas, 1977—, Hosp. Resources Mgmt. Inc., Dallas, 1978—, Blue Ice Inc., Dallas, 1978—. Served with U.S. Army, 1950-52, 57-63. Recipient Kanaqawa Prefectural Police award Japan, 1962. Mem. AMA, Aerospace Med. Assn., Am. Coll. Emergency Physicians, Assn. Mil. Surgeons U.S., So. Med. Assn., Tex. Med. Assn., Refugio Soaring Circle. Lutheran. Office: Emergency Med Mgmt Systems Inc Love Field Terminal Bldg LB32 Dallas TX 75235

SNYDER, DAVID FRANK, architect; b. Swiftown, Miss., Jan. 20, 1927; s. Frank L. and J. Vivian (Thompson) S.; B.S. in Archtl. Engring., U. Ill., 1951; postgrad. UCLA, 1959; m. Oct. 14, 1961. Asso. architect James Assos., Indpls., 1953-64; prin. architect Snyder Blackburn Assos., Indpls., 1964-76; architect, chief operating officer Minority Airport Architects and Planners, Atlanta, 1976—. Pres., Community Action Against Poverty Greater Indpls., 1969-71; bd. dirs. Fall Creek br. Met. YMCA, Indpls., 1961-69. Served with AUS, 1951-53. Recipient Honor award HUD, 1972. Mem. Atlanta Bus. League. Baptist. Home: 4651 Greenleaf Circle SW Atlanta GA 30331 Office: 100 Peachtree St NW Suite 1647 Atlanta GA 30303

SNYDER, GARY WAYNE, ins. co. exec.; b. Ft. Wayne, Ind., Jan. 19, 1951; s. Max J. and Rosella I. Snyder; B.A. in Sociology and Econs., U. Evansville (Ind.), 1973; postgrad. Wayne State U., Detroit; m. Suellen Cline. Mgmt. cons. epidemiology HEW, 1974-76; employee benefits specialist Union Mut. Ins. Co., Detroit, 1976-79, Tampa, Fla., 1979—. Mem. ACLU, U. Evansville Founders Club. Methodist. Club: Carrollwood Village (dir.).

SNYDER, HARRY MARTIN, state ednl. adminstr.; b. Corbin, Ky., Oct. 22, 1941; s. Harry Martin and Aileen (Edwards) S.; B.S. in Econs. and Bus. Adminstrn., Georgetown (Ky.) Coll., 1963; J.D., U. Ky., 1966; m. Carolyn Witt; children—Paige Edwards, Sara Blake. Fin. aid dir., coordinator fed. programs, legal counsel Georgetown Coll., 1966-68; asst. coordinator program budget U. Ky., 1968-70, asst. budget dir., 1970-73; asso. dir., legal counsel Ky. Council Higher Edn., Frankfort, 1973-75, exec. asst., legal counsel, 1975-76, exec. dir., 1976—; mem. So. Regional Edn. Bd. Served with U.S. Army. Episcopalian. Home: 1712 Fairway Dr Lexington KY 40502 Office: Council Higher Edn West Frankfort Office Complex US 127 S Frankfort KY 40601

SNYDER, IRVIN STANLEY, microbiologist; b. Nanticoke, Pa., May 29, 1931; s. Irvin William and Wanda Dolores (Sokolowski) S.; B.S., Wilkes Coll., 1953; M.A., U. Kans., 1958; Ph.D., 1960; m. Marlene Ann Smetana, Sept. 3, 1955; children—Mary Ellen, Carole Jeanne, Irvin John. Instr. U. Iowa, 1960-61, asso., 1961-62, asst. prof., 1962-67; research prof. microbiology Bryn Mawr (Pa.) Coll., 1966; asso. prof. U. Iowa, 1967-72, prof., 1972—; prof., chmn. dept. microbiology, W.Va. U. Med. Center, Morgantown, 1973. Served with M.C., U.S. Army, 1953-55. Diplomate Am. Bd. Microbiology. Recipient Outstanding Tchr. award W.Va. U., 1973-74, 74-75, McLachlan award, 1974. Recipient Silver medal Kaw Valley Heart Assn., 1959. Fellow Am. Acad. Microbiology; mem. South Central Assn. Clin. Microbiology, Am. Soc. for Microbiology, Assn. Med. Sch. Microbiology Chairmen, Soc. Exptl. Biology and Medicine. Roman Catholic. Co-author textbook; co-author audiovisual programs on clin. microbiology; contbr. chpts. to textbooks and articles to profl. jours. Home: 101 Forest Dr Morgantown WV 26505 Office: Dept Microbiology West Virginia U Medical Center Morgantown WV 26506

SNYDER, JAMES WILB, artist; b. Phila., Jan. 7, 1901; s. James W. and Elena Rebeca (Zelley) S.; B.F.A., U. Pa., 1924; M.A. (Penfield scholar), N.Y. U., 1929, Ph.D., 1939; postgrad. Cambridge (Eng.) U., 1928, Am. U. Beirut, 1956; children by previous marriage—Sara Ann Snyder Rusinko, James Guthrie. Instr., U. Pa., Phila., 1925-27; registrar Athens (Greece) Coll., 1927-29; faculty N.Y. U., 1929-42; analyst Exec. Agy. Fed. Govt., 1947-64; chmn. dept. intelligence analysis and research Am. U., Washington, 1964-65; one-man shows Cape Cod, N.J., Fla., Eng., France; exhibited in numerous group shows; represented in permanent collections throughout U.S., Eng., Japan, France. Served to col. USAAF, 1942-45. Decorated Bronze Star. Fellow Am. Geog. Soc.; mem. Nat. Soc. Lit. and the Arts, Internat. Platform Assn. Home: 2934 Gulf Dr Sanibel FL 33957 and 111 11th St Surf City NJ 08008

SNYDER, JOHN DENNIS, carpet mfg. co. exec.; b. N.Y.C., Aug. 3, 1945; s. John and Florence Elizabeth (Hawkins) S.; B.S., N.Y. U., 1967; m. Petra Laurene Karkula, Mar. 3, 1971; children—Erik, Andrew, Gretchen. Computer operator IBM Corp., N.Y.C., 1962-64; programmer, analyst Am. Express Co., N.Y.C., 1964-68, systems analyst Einestein Montefiore Research Complex, Bronx, N.Y., 1968-71; systems engr. Nat. Computing Industries, Atlanta, 1971-74; dir. mgmt. info. systems World Carpets Inc., Dalton, Ga., 1974-78; pres. Internat. Computer Enterprises, Inc., Atlanta, 1978—; tchr. data processing Inst. Computer Tech., Westchester County, N.Y. Mem. Smithsonian Inst. Jehovah's Witness. Club: Atlanta Chess. Home: 6851 Roswell Rd Apt 0-26 Atlanta GA 30328 Office: 6065 Roswell Rd Atlanta GA 30328

SNYDER, LEHMAN L., hosp. adminstr.; b. Hubbard, Tex., July 3, 1928; s. Cecil L. and Velma (White) S.; student U. Md., 1956-57; m. Hazel Bernice Ayers, Nov. 14, 1947; children—Russell F., Kenneth W., Cecil P. Psychiat. specialist VA Hosp., Waco, Tex., 1948-51; joined U.S. Air Force, 1951; assigned USAF Hosp., London, Eng., 1956-59, 780th Hosp., Westby, Mont., 1959-63, 794th Hosp., Newenham, Alaska, 1963-64, USAF Med. Sch., Wichita Falls, Tex., 1965-69, ret., 1969; piece goods mgr. Haggar Co., Dallas, 1969-72; chief exec. officer Coryell Meml. Hosp., Gatesville, 1973-76, Hubbard Hosp., 1977—. Bd. dirs. local chpt. ARC, blood drive coordinator, 1973-75. Served with USNR, 1945-47. Mem. Am. Legion, VFW. Roman Catholic. Author: Independent Duty, 1968. Home: PO Box 58 Gatesville TX 76528 Office: 701 N 5th E Hubbard TX 76648

SNYDER, MARION GENE, congressman; b. Louisville, Jan. 26, 1928; s. M. G. and Lois E. (Berg) S.; J.D., U. Louisville, 1950; LL.B. cum laude, Jefferson Sch. Law, Louisville, 1950; m. Patricia Creighton Robertson, Apr. 10, 1973; 1 son, Mark; 3 stepchildren. Admitted to Ky. bar, 1950, D.C. bar, 1970; real estate broker, 1948—; practiced in Louisville, 1950-78; engaged in residential constrn. bus., 1958-67, in farming, 1957-67; city atty. Jeffersontown, 1953-57; magistrate 1st dist. Jefferson County, 1957-61; mem. 88th Congress, 3d Dist. Ky.; mem. 90th-96th Congresses from 4th Dist. Ky. Vice pres. Ky. Magistrates and Commnrs., 1958. Pres., Jeffersontown Civic Center, 1953-54, legal adviser Jeffersontown Community Council, 1951-52. Pres. Lincoln Republican Club Ky., 1960-61, 1st Magisterial Dist. Rep. Club, 1955-57; mem. South End Rep. Club. Mem. Ky., D.C. bar assns., Louisville C. of C., Ky. Farm Bur., Louisville Bd. Realtors, Kenton-Boone Bd. Realtors. Optimist (pres. Jeffersontown 1957-58). Office: 140 Chenoweth Ln Louisville KY 40207 also US House Reps 2330 Rayburn House Office Bldg Washington DC 20515

SNYDER, MARK EVAN, mgmt. cons.; b. Wichita, Kans., Jan. 23, 1951; s. Alan Howard and Dorothea (Jones) S.; B.S., U. Tex. at Arlington, 1974, M.S., 1977. Planning analyst Fed. Res. Bank Dallas, 1974-77; asst. to v.p. sales Qwip Systems, Dallas, 1977; electronic funds transfer dir. Tex. Credit Union League, Dallas, 1977-79; v.p. ops. and devel. Real Save Inc., Dallas, 1979—; mgmt. cons. Lifson, Herrmann, Blackmarr & Harris, Dallas, 1979—; cons. S.W.D. Machines, Ft. Worth, Earl Carver & Assos. Mem. Am. Inst. Indsl. Engrs., Planning Execs. Inst., Soc. Ins. Research, Epsilon Nu Gamma, Alpha Pi Mu. Republican. Presbyterian. Home: 1304 Laurel St Arlington TX 76012 Office: One Turtle Creek Plaza Suite 606 Dallas TX 75219

SNYDER, RICHARD WILLIAM, mgmt. cons.; b. Twin Falls, Idaho, May 29, 1946; s. William Henry and Maurene S.; student Boise State Coll., 1964-66; B.S. in Bus. Adminstrn., U. Denver, 1968, M.B.A., 1971; m. Beverly Jo Torrey, June 22, 1968; children—Kimberly Michelle, Shelley Renee. Analyst computer systems 1st Nat. Bank Denver, 1968-71; mgmt. cons. Alexander Grant & Co., Denver, 1971-73, mgr. mgmt. cons., Dallas, 1973-77, partner mgmt. cons., 1977—. Active fund drs. Jr. Achievement. C.P.A., Colo., Tex. Mem. Am. Inst. C.P.A.'s, Colo. (Silver medal 1971), Tex. socs. C.P.A.'s, Planning Execs. Inst. Republican. Presbyterian. Clubs: Dallas Athletic Country, Chandler's Landing Yacht, Lancer's. Home: 1506 Lakeshore Dr Rockwall TX 75087 Office: 1400 One Main Pl Dallas TX 75250

SNYDER, ROBERT DOUGLAS, coll. dean; b. Lancaster, Pa., Apr. 15, 1934; s. William S. and Sarah (Hoffman) S.; B.S. in M.E., Ind. Inst. Tech., 1955; M.S., Clemson U., 1959; Ph.D., W.Va. U., 1964; m. Emma Rose Perez, May 21, 1955; children—Dallas Marie, Robert Bruce, Kenneth Eugene. Servomechanisms engr. Bell Aircraft Corp., 1955; instr. engring. Ind. Inst. tech., 1956-57; asst. prof. Clemson (S.C.) U., 1960; mem. faculty W.Va. U., Morgantown, 1962-75, prof. mech. engring., 1968-75, asso. chmn. dept., 1970-75; prof., chmn. dept., dean Coll. Engring. U. N.C., Charlotte, 1975—. Mem. Am. Soc. Mech. Engrs., Am. Soc. Engring. Edn., Nat. Soc. Profl. Engrs., Am. Nuclear Soc., Soc. Rheology, Profl. Engrs. N.C., Sigma Xi. Democrat. Lutheran. Registered profl. engr., N.C. Author: (with E.F. Byers) Engineering Mechanics of Deformable Bodies, 1964, Engineering Mechanics: Statics and Strength of Materials, 1972. Home: 5900 Lebanon Rd Charlotte NC 28212 Office: Coll Engineering Univ NC Charlotte NC 28223

SNYDER, ROBERT E., mfg. co. exec.; b. Washington, May 22, 1941; s. Harold V. and Floreine L. Snyder; B.S., Marshal U., 1965; m. Patricia Diane Marushi, Apr. 10, 1965; children—Dawn Rene, Robert Shawn. Terr. rep. Kauffman-Latimer Co., 1965-67; with Rubbermaid Comml. Products Co., 1968—, gen. products mgr., 1972-74, nat. sales mgr., 1974-77, v.p. mktg., Winchester, Va., 1977—. Active Big Bros. Served with USMC, 1960. Mem. Sales and Mktg. Assn., Nat. Assn. food Service Mfg., Nat. Office Products Assn. Presbyterian. Office: 3124 Valley Ave Winchester VA 22601

SNYDER, THOMAS DANIEL, electronics engr.; b. Phila., Aug. 30, 1925; s. Thomas Daniel and Edith May (Lees) S.; Asso. in Applied Sci. in Radio and TV Tech., Milw. Sch. Engring., 1951; m. Mary Ann Wilson, Aug. 28, 1954; children—Thomas Daniel, Ellen Mary, John W. Foreman Prime Mfg. Co., Milw., 1951; with engring. dept. No. Light Co., Milw., 1951-52; communications clk. fgn. service U.S. Dept. State, 1952-55; electronics engr. U.S. Dept. Def., Warrenton, Va., 1955—. Cons. accoustics and magnetics govt. agys., 1964—; lectr. metric conversion; participant Solid States Application Conf., Fla. Atlanta U., 1971; participant profl. seminars Mass. Inst. Tech., 1962, 64, 66, Columbia, 1963, Pa. State U., 1967, U. Wis., 1969. Pres., PTA, Fairfax, Va., 1971, county rep., 1972. Served with USNR, 1943-46; PTO. Recipient Meritorious award for outstanding design in electronics equipment, U.S. Govt., 1969. Mem. AAAS, IEEE, Optical Soc. Am., Metric Assn., Am. Nat. Metric Council, Am. Legion, Cath. War Vets. (adj. 1964-67). Roman Catholic. Contbr. articles to profl. jours. Patentee in field. Home: 4246 Worcester Dr Fairfax VA 22030 Office: Warrenton Tng Center Warrenton VA 22186

SNYDLE, FRANK EMIL, educator; b. Chgo., Jan. 11, 1945; s. Frank and Emily (Capek) S.; B.A., So. Ill. U., 1968, M.S., 1971; Ph.D., U. South Fla., 1975; postgrad. (Ford Found. fellow), Wayne State U., 1975-76; M.D., U. Fla., 1980. NSF fellow, instr. dept. obstetrics and gynecology and anatomy, U. Fla., Gainesville, 1976-77, dir. semen analysis unit, 1976-77, asst. prof. dept. obstetrics and gynecology, 1977-78, instr. and clin. asso. dept. obstetrics and gynecology and div. urology, dept. surgery, 1978—; lectr., cons. in field. Rasmussen scholar, 1979; Eva H. Wheat scholar, 1978; Mobile Chem. Grad. research grantee, 1974; Biol. Stain Commn. fellow, 1968; So. Ill. U. scholar, 1968. Mem. Pan Am. Andrology Assn., Am. Assn. Sex Educators, Counselors and Therapists (cert.), AMA, Sigma Xi, Phi Sigma. Democrat. Contbr. articles to profl. jours. Home: 1938 NW 39 Pl Gainesville FL 32605 Office: Dept Obstetrics and Gynecology PO Box J294 Univ of Fla Gainesville FL 32610

SOCARRAS-COBIAN, YOHEL, telephone co. exec.; b. Cuba, May 29, 1947; s. Yohel and Haydee (Cobian-Causa) Socarras-Blancard; B.S. Liceo De La Salle, Bogota, Colombia, 1964; B.S. in Indsl. Engring., U. P.R., 1970; m. Sonia Figueroa-Sanchez, May 30, 1971; children—Sonymarie, Yomarie, Sylmarie. Sta. performance analyst Caribbean div. Eastern Airlines, Inc., San Juan, P.R., 1970-74; manpower and adminstrn. mgr. ITT Caribbean Mfg., Inc., Rio Piedras, P.R., 1974-75; dir. human resources P.R. Telephone Co., Caparra, 1975—. Mem. Am. Inst. Indsl. Engrs. Roman Catholic. Home: 1705 Parana St Rio Piedras Heights Rio Piedras PR 00926 Office: PRTC Hdqrs 1500 Roosevelt Ave Caparra PR 00920

SOCHA, KATHLEEN FITZSIMMONS, advt. and design cons.; b. Ft. Lauderdale, Fla., Jan. 20, 1949; d. Joseph Anthony and Madeline (Zoller) Fitzsimmons; B.S. in Advt. with honors, U. Fla., 1974; m. William Matthew Socha, July 18, 1970 (div. July 1978). Graphic artist Mitralux Advt., Inc., Ft. Lauderdale, 1970-72; creative dir. Minshall Combs Advt., Inc., Gainesville, 1974-75; advt. mgr. Suntec Paint Co., Gainesville, 1975-78; advt. and design cons., Gainesville, 1978-79; exec. art dir. Miller Zell, Inc., Ga., 1979—; adj. lectr. U. Fla. Coll. Journalism and Communications. Mem. Am. Advt. Assn., Gainesville C. of C., Gainesville Advt. Fedn. (1st v.p. 1974-75, 78-79). Home: 1805 Roswell Rd Marietta GA 30062

SOEFJE, ALAN ERNST, mgmt. cons., air force officer; b. New Braunfels, Tex., Apr. 29, 1933; s. Erwin W. and Linda Marie (Heinemeyer) S.; B.B.A., Tex. A&M U., 1955; J.D., St. Marys U., 1970; M.A., U. No. Colo., 1977; m. Lois Edna Tate, Nov. 25, 1965; 1 son, Edward Alan. Tchr. in public and parochial elem. schs., San Antonio, 1960-68; commd. lt. U.S. Air Force, 1955, advanced through grades to lt. col., 1979; air force command pilot Kelly AFB, Tex., 1972-79, logistics staff officer, 1971-72, race relations facilitator, 1972-79, drug and alcohol counselor, 1972-79, tchr. seminars Hdqrs. Air Force, Washington, 1975-76; lectr. bus. and bus. law St. Phillips Coll., San Antonio, 1977-78; mgmt. cons. to industry and the mil., 1972—. Active Alamo council Boy Scouts Am., 1970-71; sec., treas. Leon Valley (Tex.) Pageant Assn., 1970-71. Recipient Texas Star award San Antonio radio sta. KBAT, 1970. Mem. Air Force Assn., Res. Officers Assn., Nat. Assn. Realtors, Tex. Assn. Realtors, Mil. Order World Wars (dir. 1979-80), Delta Theta Phi. Roman Catholic. Club: T Bar M Racquet. Home: 16404 Ledge Park San Antonio TX 78232 Office: 16404 Ledge Park San Antonio TX 78232

SOENNEKER, HENRY JOSEPH, clergyman; b. Melrose, Minn., May 27, 1907; s. Henry and Mary (Wessel) S.; B.A., Josephinum Coll. and Sem., Worthington, Ohio, 1930; J.C.L., Cath. U. Am., 1950. Ordained priest Roman Cath. Ch., 1934; asst. parish of St. Anthony, St. Cloud, Minn., 1934-40, also tchr. Cathedral High Sch., St. Cloud and chaplain VA Hosp.; chaplain Sisters of St. Francis, Little Falls, Minn., 1940-48; spiritual dir. St. John's Major Sem., Collegeville, Minn., 1950-51; bishop Diocese of Owensboro, Ky., 1961—. Office: 4003 Frederica St PO Box 364 Owensboro KY 42301*

SOFER, SAMIR SALIM, chem. engr.; b. Teheran, Iran, Oct. 10, 1945; s. Salim and Violet S.; B.S. magna cum laude, U. Utah, 1969; M.E., Tex. A. and M. U., 1971; Ph.D., U. Tex., 1973. Research asst. U. Utah Coll. Medicine, Salt Lake City, 1965-69; process design engr. Celanese Chem. Co., Bishop, Tex., 1969-72; research asso. U. Tex., 1972-73, asso. postdoctoral research, 1974; asst. prof. chem. engring. U. Okla., Norman, 1974-77, asso. prof., 1977—, chmn. dept. chem. engring. and materials sci., 1975—. Recipient effective teaching award U. Okla. Sch. Chem. Engring. and Materials Sci.; Brandon H. Griffith award Okla. Engring. Students, 1977. Mem. Am. Inst. Chem. Engrs., AAAS, Am. Soc. Engring. Edn., Am. Chem. Soc. Editorial bd. Internat. Jour. Artificial Organs. Research on stblzn. on hepatic microsomes, reaction kinetics, process design, methane from agrl. wastes. Office: 202 W Boyd St Room 23 Norman OK 73019

SOFFERIN, SAMUEL LESTER, JR., hosp. adminstr.; b. Detroit, Mar. 31, 1928; s. Samuel Lester and Margaret Katherine S.; B.A., Ariz. State U., 1953; m. Patricia Ann Wilson, Oct. 2, 1952; children—David A., Timothy L., Michael J. Co-owner, gen. mgr. Sammy Sofferin's Steak House Wonder Bar, Detroit, 1946-66; food service dir. St. John's Hosp., Detroit, 1966-67, Mary Imogene Bassett Hosp., Cooperstown, N.Y., 1967, Lakeland (Fla.) Gen. Hosp., 1967—; cons. hosp. food systems to various mfg. cos. and hosps. Served with U.S. Army, 1950-52. Mem. Am. Soc. Hosp. Food Service Adminstrs., Fla. Hosp. Food Service Adminstrs. (chpt. pres. 1977—). Clubs: Elks, K.C., Rotary. Contbr. articles to profl. jours. Home: 4535 Hallamview Ln Lakeland FL 33803 Office: Lakeland Gen Hosp PO Drawer 448 Lakeland FL 33802

SOILEAU, DAVID EMILE, state ofcl., lawyer; b. Ville Platte, La., July 15, 1942; s. Audley Joseph and Inez (Gravel) S.; J.D., La. State U., 1967; B.A., U. Notre Dame, 1964. Admitted to La. bar, 1967; law clk. La. Ct. Appeals, 3d Circuit, Lake Charles, La., 1969-70, U.S. Dist. Ct., New Orleans, 1970-71; asso. atty. Phelps, Dunbar, Marks, Claverie & Sims, New Orleans, 1971-73; law clk. U.S. Dist. Ct., New Orleans, 1973; asst. prof. law La. State U., Baton Rouge, 1973-77; research analyst div. adminstrn. Office of Budget, State of La., Baton Rouge, 1977-78; exec. dir. La. Hwy. Safety Commn., Dept. Pub. Safety, Baton Rouge, 1978—. State coordinator activities Common Cause of La., 1973. Served with U.S. Army, 1967-69. Decorated Army Commendation medal. Mem. Am. Bar Assn., La. Bar Assn. Democrat. Unitarian Universalist. Home: 12540 Warfield Ave Baton Rouge LA 70815 Office: PO Box 44061 Capitol Sta Baton Rouge LA 70804

SOILEAU, JOHN MILLARD, govt. soil scientist; b. Washington, La., July 10, 1934; s. Valmont and Melba Ann (Doucet) S.; B.S. in Agronomy, U. Southwestern La., 1956; M.S. in Soils, Iowa State U., 1958; Ph.D. in Soils, N.C. State U., 1962; m. Joanne King Piper, Feb. 8, 1964; children—John Mark, Jeffery Millard, Christopher James, Trevor Valmont. Research asso. dept. agronomy Iowa State U., Ames, 1956-58; research soil scientist TVA, Muscle Shoals, Ala., 1962—. Mem. Am. Soc. Agronomy, Soil Sci. Soc. Am., Soil Conservation Soc. Am., Blue Key, Phi Kappa Phi, Gamma Sigma Delta. Contbr. articles to profl. jours. Home: 262 McGough Blvd Florence AL 35630 Office: F137 NFDC Tennessee Valley Authority Muscle Shoals AL 35660

SOILEAU, LOUIS CLAUDMIRE, IV, petroleum engr.; b. New Orleans, Apr. 8, 1949; s. Louis Claudmire, III, and Clara Virginia (Fremaux) S.; B.S. in Petroleum Engring., La. State U., 1971; m. Denise Romero, June 12, 1971; children—Catherine, Louis Claudmire. With Arco Oil and Gas Co., Lafayette, La., 1971, ops./analytical engr., Midland, Tex., 1974-78, area engr., 1978-79; staff reservoir engr. ARCO Oil and Gas Co., Dallas, 1979—, mem. speakers bur. Dir., composer for St. Ann's Youth Choir, Midland, 1978-79. Served with USAF, 1972-74. Registered profl. engr., Tex. Mem. Soc. Petroleum Engrs. of AIME (membership chmn. Permian Basin sect. 1978-79, mem. speakers bur.). Republican. Roman Catholic. Author, composer Celebrate, 1979. Home: 2004 JJ Pearce Richardson TX 75081

SOKOLOFF, JOEL JAY, educator; b. Bklyn., July 22, 1945; s. Alexander and Evelyn (Gellman) S.; B.A., Queens Coll., 1965; M.A., U. Mass., 1967; postgrad. Rutgers U., 1967-70. Research asst. Rutgers Bur. Econ. Research, New Brunswick, N.J., 1967-69; co-adj. lectr. Livingston Coll., Rutgers U., Piscataway, N.J., 1972; instr. econs. Ky. State U., Frankfort, 1974—. NSF trainee 1969; Kellogg Found. fellow, 1978. Mem. Am. Econ. Assn., Econometric Soc., Royal Econ. Soc., Am. Agrl. Econ. Assn., So. Agrl. Econ. Assn. Club: U.S. Chess Fedn., Masons. Home: 107 Sable Ln Frankfort KY 40601 Office: Sch Bus Ky State U Frankfort KY 40601

SOLANO, FILBERTO FRANCIS, law firm mgmt. exec.; b. Somerville, Mass., June 5, 1939; s. Filberto Francis and Maria Teresa (Muscolino) S.; B.S.A., Bentley Coll. Acctg. and Fin., 1965; m. Lilia M. Yannuzzi, June 7, 1969; children—Lilia R., Lisette M. Mgr. firm Goodwin, Procter & Hoar, Attys., Boston, 1970-73, Palmar Mfg. Co., Caracas, Venezuela, 1973-76; gen. office mgr. Central Stationers, Inc., Miami, Fla., 1976-78; controller Smathers & Thompson, Attys., Miami, 1978—; cons. law firm mgmt. Served with USAF, 1957-61. Mem. Am. Mgmt. Assn. Democrat. Roman Catholic. Office: Alfred I duPont Bldg Miami FL 33131

SOLBERG, MARION PATRICE, lawyer; b. Richmond, Va., May 11, 1951; d. Marion Horace and Grace Patricia (Wynne) Walker; A.B., U. N.C., J.D. with honors, 1976; m. Robert Mitchell Solberg, Dec. 22, 1972; children—Jennifer Leigh, Michael Paul. Admitted to N.C. bar, 1976; law clk firm Lawrence A. Young, Chapel Hill, N.C., 1974, Inst. Govt., U. N.C., Chapel Hill, 1975-76, asst. prof. public law and govt., 1976—; cons. in field; coordinator, tchr. workshops. Mem. Am. Soc. Hosp. Attys. Am. Public Health Assn., N.C. Soc. Hosp. Attys., N.C. Bar Assn., N.C. State Bar. Democrat. Methodist. Author books, including: North Carolina Law and the Health Department, 1978; Public Health Nursing and the Law, 1979; contbr. articles to profl. publs. Home: 121 Hideaway Dr Chapel Hill NC 27514 Office: PO Box 990 Chapel Hill NC 27514

SOLBERG, RUELL FLOYD, JR., research and devel. engr.; b. Norse, Tex., July 27, 1939; s. Ruel Floyd and Ruby Mae (Rogstad) S.; student Tex. Lutheran Coll., Seguin, 1958-59, U. Tex. at Arlington, 1959; B.S., U. Tex. at Austin, 1962, M.S., 1967; M.B.A., Trinity U., San Antonio, 1977; m. Laquetta Jane Massey, Oct. 3, 1959; children—Chandra Dawn, Marla Gaye. Research engr. asso. II acoustics div. Applied Research Labs. (formerly Def. Research Lab.), Austin, 1962-65, research engr. asso. III, 1965-67, asst. supr. mech. engring. sect., 1966-67; research engr., dept. applied electromagnetics S.W. Research Inst., San Antonio, 1967-70, sr. research engr., 1970—. Active, Norwegian Am. Mus., Leon Valley Crime Prevention Assn., Nordland Heritage Found. (charter), Bosque Meml. Mus., Oak Hills Terr. Elem. Sch. Helping Hand Program. Served with AUS. Howell Instruments scholar. Registered profl. engr., Tex. Mem. ASME (chmn. San Antonio sect. 1972-73; Charles E. Balleisen award San Antonio sect.), Am. Soc. Metals, Nat., Tex. socs. profl. engrs., Consumer Products Tech. Interest Group, Human Factors Soc., Soc. Mfg. Engrs., Norwegian Soc. of Tex. (charter), Robot Inst. Am., Norwegian-Am. Hist. Assn., Friends of N.W. Library, Vesterheim Geneal. Center, Sigma Xi, Theta Pi Epsilon, Pi Tau Sigma, Tau Beta Pi, Sigma Iota Epsilon. Lutheran. Reviewer, Shock and Vibration Digest; contbr. articles to profl. jours. Patentee in field. Home: 5906 Forest Cove San Antonio TX 78240 Office: PO Drawer 28510 San Antonio TX 78284

SOLEMENE, WILLIAM ANGELO, advt. co. exec.; b. Tarrytown, N.Y., Dec. 12, 1935; s. Anthony W. and Beatrice (Ruck) S.; B.S. in Mktg., U. Vt., 1961; postgrad. Tech. Inst., Mexico, 1961-62. Acctg. exec. Highley Advt. Co., San Juan, P.R., 1962-63; acctg. exec. for ops. in Central Am., Young & Rubicam-P.R., Panama City, 1964-66; supr. J. Walter Thompson Co., Mexico City, Mexico, 1965-68, sr. account exec., N.Y.C., 1968, mgr. Dallas office, 1969-72; propr., mgr. William A. Solemene & Assos., Dallas, 1973—. Bd. dirs. Charity for Arts in Dallas, 1975—. Served with USAF, 1958-60, maj. Res. Mem. Dallas Ad League, Dallas C. of C., Am. Fighter Pilots Assn. Republican. Episcopalian. Clubs: Masons, Shriners. Home: 8710 Park Ln Dallas TX 75231 Office: 3131 Turtle Creek Blvd Dallas TX 75219

SOLES, WILLIAM ROGER, ins. co. exec.; b. Whiteville, N.C., Sept. 16, 1920; s. John William and Margaret (Watts) S.; B.S. in Commerce, U. N.C., 1947, postgrad., 1955; m. Majelle Marrene Morris, Sept. 22, 1956; children—William Roger, Majelle Janette. With Jefferson Standard Life Ins. Co., Greensboro, N.C., 1947—, v.p., mgr. securities dept., 1962-64, asst. to pres., 1964-66, exec. v.p., mgr. securities dept., 1966, now pres., also dir.; pres., dir. Jefferson-Pilot Corp.; pres., chmn. bd. Jefferson-Pilot Fire & Casualty Co., Jefferson-Pilot Title Ins. Co., JP Investment Mgmt. Co., Jefferson-Pilot Equity Sales, Inc.; vice-chmn. bd., dir. Jefferson-Pilot Publs., Inc.; dir. Pilot Life Ins. Co., Jefferson-Pilot Broadcasting Co. Va., Piedmont Natural Gas Co., NCNB Corp., N.C. Nat. Bank. Trustee High Point Coll., Wesley Long Community Hosp. Served with USAAF, 1941-45. Mem. Am. Life Ins. Assn. (chmn., dir.), Beta Gamma Sigma. Club: Greensboro Country. Home: 604 Kimberly Dr Greensboro NC 27408 Office: PO Box 21008 Greensboro NC 27420

SOLIMAN, KARAM FARAG ATTIA, educator; b. Cairo, Oct. 15, 1944; came to U.S., 1968, naturalized, 1979; s. Farah Attia and Elaine Giris (Kallini) S.; B.S., Cairo U., 1964; M.S., U. Ga., 1971, Ph.D., 1972; m. Samia Georgi Sichom, Aug. 30, 1973; children—John, Gina, Mark. Research asst. Nat. Research Center, Cairo, 1964-68; research asst. U. Ga., Athens, 1968-72; asst. prof. Sch. Vet. Medicine, Tuskegee Inst. (Ala.), 1972-75; asso. prof. Sch. Pharmacy, Fla. A&M U., Tallahassee, 1975-79, prof., 1979—. Named Outstanding Tchr. of Yr., Fla. A&M U., 1979. Mem. Endocrine Soc., Soc. Study of Reprodn., Am. Physiol. Soc., Internat. Soc. Chronobiology, Am. Fertility Soc., Neurosci. Soc., Gamma Sigma Delta. Christian Coptic Orthodox. Editor 2 books; contbr. articles to profl. jours. Home: 2504 Fritz Ln Tallahassee FL 32304 Office: Sch Pharmacy Fla A&M U Tallahassee FL 32307

SOLIMAN, MOSTAFA AMIN, educator; b. Cairo, Feb. 2, 1932; s. Amin Y. and Latifa A. S.; came to U.S., 1961, naturalized, 1979; B.S., Cairo U., 1952, diploma, 1955; M.S., Cornell U., 1963; Ph.D., Iowa State U., 1967; m. Nabila Mahmoud. Asst. prof. U. Minn., St. Paul, 1967-71; asso. prof. Prairie View (Tex.) A. and M. U., 1971-76, prof. dept. econs. and fin., 1976—; asso. prof. Kuwait U., 1976-78. Mem. Am. Agrl. Econ. Assn., Am. Econ. Assn., Am. Statis. Assn., Econometric Soc., So. Econ. Assn., Southwestern Soc. Econ., Educators to Africa Assn., Sigma Xi, Gamma Theta Upsilon, Omicron Delta Epsilon. Contbr. articles profl. jours. Office: PO Box 2842 Prairie View TX 77445

SOLIZ, MANUEL, health systems cons.; b. San Antonio, Sept. 30, 1946; s. Manuel A. and Manuela S. Soliz; B.A., Tex. A&I U., 1970; m. Raquel Aleman, June 24, 1972; children—Manuel III, Marco Antonio. Research analyst, program specialist Interstate Research Assos., Washington, 1971-73; dir. prepaid services El Valley Community Health Plan, Harlingen, Tex., 1973-76; exec. dir. Rio Grande Fedn. of Health Centers, Inc., San Antonio, 1976-79; health systems cons., San Antonio, 1979—; mem. Nat. Adv. Com. on Nat. Health Ins. Issues, 1977—. Mem. Am. Public Health Assn., Am. Acad. Health Adminstrn., Am. Mgmt. Assn., Forum of Nat. Hispanic Orgn., Am. Heart Assn., Regional Assn. for Non Profit Community Health Orgns. (mem. exec. com.), U.S. Mexican Border Public Health Assn., Tex. Health Maintenance Orgns. Assn., Tex. State Health Coalition, AAAS, Assn. Med. Rehab. Dirs. and Coordinators, League United Latin Am. Citizens. Democrat. Roman Catholic. Home and Office: 5871 Castle Run San Antonio TX 78218

SOLLENBERGER, ARLENE LUCILLE, musician; b. Natoma, Kans., Nov. 19, 1920; d. Jesse Clarence and Versa Elvira (Dorr) S.; B. Music Edn., Bethany Coll., 1942; M. Music Edn., U. Mich., 1947, M. Music in Voice, 1948. Music supr. Rural Consol. Schs., Garfield, Kans., 1943-44, public schs., Stafford, Kans., 1944- 46; instr. in pvt. voice lessons U. Mich., 1950-59; asso. prof. music Tex. Christian U., 1959—; auditions adjudicator; Fulbright grantee, Germany, 1956. Mem. Nat. Assn. Tchrs. Singing (regional lt. gov. 1962-63, singer at nat. conv. 1963), Ft. Worth Voice Tchrs. Forum, Music Tchrs. Nat. Assn., Tex. Music Tchrs. Assn., Ft. Worth Music Tchrs. Assn., Nat. Fedn. Music Clubs (life), Tex. Fedn. Music Clubs, AAUW (mam.-ar-large), AAUP, Profl. Women at Tex. Christian U., Sigma Alpha Iota (Sword of Honor 1966), Pi Lambda Theta, Delta Kappa Gamma, Phi Kappa Phi Pi Kappa Lambda (nat. bd. regents, 1977-79), Tau Beta Sigma (hon.). Republican. Methodist. Clubs: Woman's of Ft. Worth, Euterpean, Tex. Christian U. Fine Arts Guild, Tex. Christian U. Faculty Woman's, Altrusa (internat. com. grants-in-aid 1975-79). Office: Tex Christian U Landreth #232 Fort Worth TX 76129

SOLLENBERGER, CHARLES THOMAS, dairyman; b. Fayetteville, Pa., May 30, 1918; s. Charles William and Evelyn Hannah (Ausherman) S.; student Washington and Lee U., 1936-38; m. Elizabeth Louise Dalke, Mar. 17, 1939; children—Jean Ehlman, Conee Walser, Margaret George, Thomas, Richard. Owner, Woodstock Poultry Co. (Va.), 1939-65, Shenwood Farms, Woodstock 1960—, Shenwood Office Bldg., 1967—; pres. Pennmarva Dairymen's Fedn. Coop., 1974-75; mem. Va. Agrl. Stblzn. Bd., 1958-61; adv. bd. Old Dominion Savs. & Loan. Mem. Woodstock Town Council, 1946-54, vice mayor; chmn. Shenandoah County Republican Party, 1966-69; mem. Shenandoah County Bd. Suprs., 1968—, chmn., 1968, 74, 78. Treas., Shenandoah County Meml. Hosp., 1955-77, pres., 1977—; trustee Massanutten Acad., 1969—, pres., 1977—; hon. bd. dirs. Shenandoah Valley Music Festival, Inc. Recipient Man of Year award Woodstock C. of C., 1972, Outstanding Achievement award Lord Fairfax County Soil and Water Conservation Dist., 1973, citation ARC, 1962—. Mem. Va. Dairymen's Assn. (pres. 1973-75), Md. and Va. Milk Producers Assn. (1st v.p. 1973—). Mem. United Ch. Christ (past deacon, elder, trustee). Club: Rotary (past pres. Woodstock). Home: Shenwood Farms Box 427 Woodstock VA 22664 Office: 505 N Main St Woodstock VA 22664

SOLOMON, GASSAN NICOLA, diversified co. exec.; b. Sierra Leone, Oct. 27, 1948; s. Nicola Ibrahim and Naemeh (Jacob) S.; came to U.S., 1972, naturalized, 1975; B.B.A., Am. U., Beirut, 1971; M.B.A. (Univ. fellow), Old Dominion U., 1973. Asst. to comml. mgr. F.A. Kettaneh, Beirut, Lebanon, 1971-72; sec.-treas., comptroller Peabody's Inc., Virginia Beach, Va., 1973-78; mng. dir. Peabody's Internat., Virginia Beach, 1978—, pres., 1979—. Leader, co-founder Baino's Boy Scouts, Lebanon, 1963-71. Mem. Assn. M.B.A. Execs., Am. Mgmt. Assn. Greek Orthodox. Office: PO Box 210 Virginia Beach VA 23458

SOLOMON, HOWARD DAVID, physician; b. Burlington, Vt., July 3, 1945; s. Sam and Ethel Solomon; B.A., U. Vt., 1967, M.D., 1971; m. Lyndell Elizabeth Drum, Oct. 3, 1975; children—Norman, David. Intern, Tripler Army Med. Center, Honolulu, 1971-72; resident in urology Brooke Army Med. Center, Fort Sam Houston, Tex., 1972-76; practice medicine specializing in urology, Seguin, Tex., 1979—; commd. 2d lt., M.C., U.S. Army, advanced through grades to lt. col., 1979; mem. staff urology service Moncrief Army Hosp., Fort Jackson, S.C., 1976-77; asst. chief urology service Brooke Army Med. Center, Fort Sam Houston, Tex., 1977-79; cons. urology VA Hosp., Kerrville, Tex., 1977-79, ret., 1979; mem. staff Guadalupe Valley Hosp., Seguin, Tex., 1979—. Diplomate Am. Bd. Urology. Mem. A.C.S., Am. Urol. Assn., Soc. of Govt. Service Urologists, San Antonio Urol. Assn., Assn. of Mil. Surgeons of U.S. Contbr. numerous articles to med. jours. Home: 306 Coventry Seguin TX 78155 Office: 1255 Ashby St Seguin TX 78155

SOLOMON, MARVIN, lawyer; b. Tampa, Fla., Dec. 18, 1933; s. Rudolph and Isabel Ruth (Moed) S.; B.S., B.A., U. Fla., 1955, J.D., 1960; m. Karen Marie Melich, Oct. 23, 1965; children—Elise A., Robert B. Admitted to Fla. bar, 1961; pres. firm Marvin Solomon, Tampa, 1974—. Served with U.S. Army, 1955-57. Mem. Comml. Law League Am. Democrat. Jewish. Club: Masons. Home: 4926 W Bay Way Dr Tampa FL 33609 Office: Suite 1104 412 Madison St Tampa FL 33601

SOLOMON, RICHARD BENJAMIN, specifications cons.; b. S.I., N.Y., Sept. 3, 1942; s. Irving and Lillian Ray (Sheld) S.; B.A., U. Miami, 1968; m. Barbara Hoberman, Nov. 7, 1965; children—Martin Bradley, Daniel Louis. Specification writer T Trip Russell Assos., Miami, Fla., 1962-70; dir. ops., prin. Greenleaf/Telesca, Planners, Engrs., Architects, Inc., 1970—; instr. Miami Dade Community Coll., 1973. Pres. Kendale Homeowners Assn., 1974. Served with USNR, 1963-65. Recipient various prizes Nat. Specifications Competition, 1970-74. Fellow Constrn. Specifications Inst. (nat. dir. 1977—; pres. Greater Miami chpt. 1972-73, Ben John Small Meml. award 1975). Home: 10000 SW 102d Ave Rd Miami FL 33176 Office: 1451 Brickell Ave Miami FL 33131

SOLTERO-HARRINGTON, LUIS RUBEN, surgeon; b. San Juan, P.R., Sept. 4, 1925; s. Augusto R. Soltero and Ana (Harrington); B.S.A., U. P.R., 1945; M.B., Northwestern U., 1949, M.D., 1950; m. Alice Joyce Carpenter, Apr. 24, 1958; children—Luis, Kathleen Ann, Susan Joyce, Robert, Sharon Theresa. Intern, Michael Reese Hosp., Chgo., 1950; resident in gen. surgery Aquadilla Dist. Hosp., 1950-51; resident in surgery Baylor U. Coll. Medicine and affiliated hosps., Houston, 1954-59; instr. surgery Sch. Medicine, Baylor U., Houston, 1954-59; instr. Sch. Medicine, U. P.R., 1959-60, asst. prof. surgery, 1960-64, asst. clin. prof. surgery, 1972-73, asso. clin. prof. surgery, 1973—; practice medicine specializing in gen., thoracic, cardiovascular and pediatric surgery, Hato Rey, P.R., 1959—; chief thoracic and cardiovascular surgery Tchrs. Hosp., Hato Rey, 1959—; chief surgery Ruiz-Arnau Hosp., Bayamon, P.R., 1978—; cons. in charge, thoracic and cardiovascular service Indsl. Hosp., San Juan, 1975—. Served in USAF, 1952-54. Diplomate Nat. Bd. Med. Examiners, Am. Bd. Surgery. Mem. Am., P.R. heart assns., Am. Acad. Pediatrics, P.R. Med. Assn., Denton Cooley Cardiovascular Surg. Soc., Michael E. DeBakey Internat. Surg. Soc., Pan Am. Med. Assn., Sociedad Puertorriqueña de Cardiología, Phi Chi. Home: 9 Petunir St Urb Sta Maria Río Piedras PR 00927 Office: 400 Domenech Ave Suite 502 Hato Rey PR 00918

SOMBERG, SEYMOUR IRA, cons. forester, appraiser; b. Bklyn., May 15, 1917; s. Sidney Jack and Rose (Zuckerman) S.; B.S.F., Iowa State Coll., 1941; M.S., Duke U., 1946, D.Forestry (fellow 1960-62), 1962; m. Nedra Harriet Goldstein, May 6, 1947; children—Debra Lynn Somberg Journet, Benjamin Lawrence, Sandra Jeanne, Steven Jay. Internat. cons. forester, 1941-60; asso. prof. forestry So. Ill. U., Carbondale, 1962-64; forestry officer, adviser to Peruvian Govt., FAO/UN Devel. Program, Lima, 1964-67; asso. prof. forest econs. and biometrics Auburn (Ala.) U., 1967-70; asst. dean, dir. research Sch. Forestry, Stephen F. Austin State U., Nacogdoches, Tex., 1970-74; cons. forester and appraiser, Wilmington, N.C., 1974—; reviewer research proposals EPA, 1972—, forestry com. East Tex. C. of C., 1971—; cons. Govt. Venezuela, 1967—; mem. Wilmington Tree Commn. Bd. dirs. Southeastern Jr. Coll. Served with USAAF, World War II. Loeb Found. Research grantee, 1960-62, Forest Service Research grantee, 1965-72, FAO/UN travel grantee, 1968—. Mem. Soc. Am. Foresters (nat. chmn. licensing com. 1971-72), Am. (exec. council 1971-74), So. econs. assns., Am. Statis. Assn., Am. Soc. Appraisers, AAUP, Assn. Cons. Foresters (pres. 1960-62, chpt. chmn.), Soc. Internat. Devel., Soc. Tropical Foresters, Nat. Assn. Rev. Appraisers, Am. Soc. Photogrammetry, Internat. Union Forestry Research Workers, Sigma Xi, Xi Sigma Pi. Clubs: Elks, Lions, Civitan (past pres.). Author over 70 books; contbr. to profl. jours.; editor The Consultant, 1948-60. Home: 649 Robert E Lee Dr Wilmington NC 28401

SOMERS, DANIEL EDWARD, fast food co. exec.; b. Detroit, Dec. 9, 1947; s. Arthur Edward and Margaret Mary Somers; B.S. in Bus. Adminstrn., Stonehill Coll., 1969; postgrad. in econs. U. Hartford (Conn.), 1970-71; m. Elaine Killough, Nov. 9, 1969; 1 son, Michael Christian. Investment analyst Hartford Nat. Bank & Trust Co., 1969-71; investment analyst, portfolio mgr. Liberty Mut. Ins. Co., Boston, 1971-72; v.p., security analyst White Weld & Co., Inc., Boston and N.Y.C., 1972-77; v.p. strategic planning and investor relations Hardees Food Systems, Inc., Rocky Mount, N.C., 1977-79, v.p. fin. and strategic planning, 1979—. Mem. budget com. United Way, Rocky Mount, 1979-80. Mem. N.Y. Soc. Security Analysts, N. Am. Soc. Corp. Planning. Roman Catholic. Office: Hardees Food Systems Inc 1233 N Church St Rocky Mount NC 27809

SOMMER, KATHLEEN RUTH, toxicologist; b. Port Washington, Wis., June 2, 1947; d. Harrison W. and June K. (Hansen) S.; B.A., Ripon Coll., 1969; Ph.D. (fellow), U. Iowa, 1973; m. Glenn A. Ramsey, Oct. 4, 1975. Research asso. U. Wis., 1969; instr. Baylor Coll. Medicine, Houston, 1973-74, USPHS research fellow, 1974-76; research chemist Shell Devel. Co., Houston, 1976-77; toxicologist Shell Cos., Houston, 1977-80; dir., cons. toxicologist Toxicon Corp., Cypress, Tex., 1980—; cons. Scientists Coop. Industries, 1972-76; mem. Nat. Adv. Research Resources Council, NIH, 1974-78, cons. Div. Research Resources, 1978—; guest lectr. U. Tex. Sch. Public Health and Med. Sch., 1978—. Recipient award Nat. Research Service, 1975. Mem. Am. Coll. Toxicology, AAAS, Am. Chem. Soc., Tex. Pharmacologists Assn. (indsl. liaison 1977-78), Houston Pharmacologists, NIH Alumni Assn. Clubs: Westwood Civic (parks com. 1978-79), Houston Forum, Iota Sigma Pi. Contbr. articles to profl. jours. Office: PO Box 308 Cypress TX 77429

SOMMER, RONALD RUDOLPH, med. librarian; b. Apple Creek, Ohio, Aug. 18, 1936; s. Wilson Harold and Arlene Velma (Badertscher) S.; B.S., Fla. State U., 1959, M.S., 1965; postgrad. (Mildred Jordan scholar), Emory U., 1969; m. Betty Neill, Dec. 19, 1966. Acad. instr., librarian Fla. Sch. for Boys, Marianna, 1959-61; librarian Hernando High Sch., Brooksville, Fla., 1961-63; librarian trainee N.Y. Public Library, N.Y.C., 1964; reference librarian, instr. engrng. and physics library U. Fla., Gainesville, 1965-67, dir. GENESYS libraries, asso. librarian, asso. prof. coll. engrng., 1967-68; asso. librarian, asso. prof. med. bibliography La. State U. Med. Center Sch. Medicine, Shreveport, 1968-72; dir. sub-regional med. library program NE La. U., Monroe, 1972-73, health scis. librarian, asso. prof., 1972-74; asso. prof. med. bibliography, head readers' services U. Tenn. Center Health Scis., Memphis, 1974—; cons. hosp., med., corp. libraries. Served with U.S. Army, 1959. Mem. AAUP, Med. Library Assn. (cert.), Spl. Libraries Assn., Southeastern Library Assn., Tenn. Library Assn. Republican. Episcopalian. Contbr. articles to profl. jours. Home: 2318 Ceylon Ct Memphis TN 38138 Office: 800 Madison Ave Memphis TN 38163

SOMMERS, JOHN PAUL, state ofcl.; b. Bklyn., May 21, 1937; s. Gustave Fredrick and Frieda Marie Louise (Albrecht) S.; student U. Fla., 1955-56; cert. State Forest Ranger's Sch., Lake City, Fla., 1957; m. Phyllis Jean Carter, June 9, 1963; children—Darlene, Jean-Marie, Carrie. With U.S. Forest Service, 1957, Fla. Forest Service, 1957-59; with Fla. Park Service, Dept. Natural Resources, Tallahassee, 1959—, asst. chief field services div. recreation and parks, 1979—. Served with U.S. Army, 1960-62. Mem. Fla. Inst. Park Personnel (charter mem., chmn. dist. 1). Republican. Home: 1826 Wales Dr Tallahassee FL 32304 Office: Room 677 Larson Bldg 202 Blount St (Crown Bldg) Tallahassee FL 32301

SONES, PETER JOHN, physician; b. Haines City, Fla., Oct. 20, 1937; s. Peter John and Eleanor Dyson (Merrill) S.; student Emory U., 1955-58, M.D., 1962; m. Eleanor Spaulding, June 21, 1959; children—Eleanor Elizabeth, Evelyn Yvonne, Shari Carolyn. Intern, U. Tex. Med. Br., Galveston, 1962-63, resident in internal medicine, 1963-64; resident in diagnostic radiology Emory U., Atlanta, 1966-68, fellow in neurovascular radiology, 1968-70, instr. radiology, 1969-70, asso., 1970-72, asst. prof., 1972-76, asso. prof., 1976-80; mem. staff Emory U. Hosp.; vis. prof. radiology Lund (Sweden) U., 1978. Served to capt. USAF, 1964-66. Diplomate Am. Bd. Radiology. Mem. Atlanta Radiol. Soc. (v.p. 1977), Southeastern Angiographic Soc. (pres. 1979—), Fulton County Med. Soc., Ga., Am. med. assns., Georgia Radiol. Soc., Am. Coll. Radiology, Am. Roentgen Ray Soc., Am. Soc. Neuroradiology. Clubs: Druid Hills Golf, Peachtree World of Tennis. Contbr. articles to profl. publs. Home: 2706 Briarlake Woods Way Atlanta GA 30345 Office: 1365 Clifton Rd NE Dept Radiology Emory U Atlanta GA 30322

SONGCHAROEN, SOMPRASONG, plastic surgeon; b. Thailand, May 23, 1941; came to U.S., 1967, naturalized, 1970; s. Chockchai and Saiyood Songcharoen; B.S., Chulalongkorn U., Bangkok, 1961; M.D., U. Med. Scis. and Siriraj Hosp., Thailand, 1966; m. Suthin Nguytragool, May 18, 1967; children—Marisa, Marcy. Intern, Grace Hosp., Detroit, 1967-68, resident in surgery, 1968-69, fellow hand surgery, 1970; resident in gen. surgery U. Md., 1970-74; resident in plastic and reconstructive surgery U. Miss. Med. Center, Jackson, 1974-76, asst. prof. surgery, 1976—; chief plastic surgeon VA Hosp. Center, Jackson, 1976—. Diplomate Am. Bd. Surgery, Am. Bd. Plastic and Reconstructive Surgery. Mem. A.C.S., U. Md. Surg. Soc., Southeastern Surg. Congress, AMA, Central Med. Soc. Miss., Miss. State Med. Assn., Am. Assn. Hand Surgery, Southeastern Soc. Plastic and Reconstructive Surgery, Assn. Veteran Surgeons, AAAS. Buddhist. Contbr. articles to profl. jours. Home: Route 1 #1 Deerfield Madison MS 39110 Office: 440 E Woodrow Wilson St Suite 701 Medical Towers Jackson MS 39216

SONI, GURBACHAN PAL, surgeon; b. Amritsar, Punjab, India, Jan. 17, 1945; M.B.B.S., U. Punjab, 1968; M.Surgery, Gurunanak U., India, 1973; married. Intern, Glancy Med. Coll., Amritsar, 1968, postgrad. surg. tng., 1969-73, registrar surgery, 1971-74; postgrad. surg. tng. Cook County Hosp., Chgo., 1975-76; sr. resident in surgery Chgo. Med. Sch.-VA Med. Center, North Chicago, Ill., 1976-77, chief resident, 1977-78; cons. gen. surgeon VA Med. Center, North Chicago, 1978, Miami, Fla., 1979—; attending staff St. Mary of Nazareth Hosp. Center, Chgo., 1978, Miami, 1979—, Coral Reef Gen. Hosp., Miami, 1979—; instr. surgery U. Health Scis., Chgo. Med. Sch., 1977-78, asst. prof., 1978; clin. asst. prof. surgery U. Miami Sch. Medicine, 1979—. Recipient AMA Physician Recognition award, 1979. Diplomate Am. Bd. Surgery. Mem. AMA, Chgo. Med. Soc., Ill. Med. Soc., Dade County Med. Soc., Fla. Med. Soc. Office: Glades Profl Bldg 8353 SW 124th St Suite 205 Miami FL 33156

SONNEBORN, JAMES EGLINTON, hosp. public relations exec.; b. Wheeling, W.Va., Jan. 10, 1923; s. Alfred Kraus and Ethyl (Perkins) S.; B.A., U. Md., 1964; postgrad. U. Wis.; m. Sara Jane Quigley, Aug. 9, 1944: children—James Douglas, Suzanne. Served with U.S. Army, World War II, also 1948-65; commd. 2d lt., 1948, advanced through grades to maj.; overseas service in Japan, Korea, Germany; public affairs officer, Verdun, France, 1961-64; ret., 1965; dist. scout exec. Boy Scouts. Am., 1965-1966; dep. public affairs officer Walter Reed Army Med. Center, Washington, 1966-1968; with Office of Army Surgeon Gen., 1968-73; with U.S. Army Health Services Command, San Antonio, 1973—. Mem. exec. bd. Alamo council Boy Scouts Am., 1974—. Decorated Bronze Star, Combat Inf. badge; Medaille de Verdun. Fellow Acad. Hosp. Public Relations; mem. Am. Soc. Hosp. Public Relations, Assn. Mil. Surgeons U.S., Am. Legion. Episcopalian. Clubs: Masons, Shriners. Home: 5911 Northgap Dr San Antonio TX 78239 Office: Chief Public Affairs Hdqrs USA Health Services Command Fort Sam Houston TX 78234

SONNER, RAY VINCENT, ednl. adminstr.; b. Strasburg, Va., Mar. 15, 1925; s. Albert Maywood and Edna Agnes (Stafford) S.; A.B., Lynchburg Coll., 1949; M.Ed., U. Va., 1953, Ed.D., 1974; m. Phyllis Helen Hawthorne, June 9, 1948; children—Geoffrey, Brenda, Terry. Tchr., Hopewell (Va.) High Sch., 1949-50, Harrisonburg (Va.) High Sch., 1950-55, asst. prin., 1955-58, prin., 1958-63; coordinator Apprentice Instrn., Harrisonburg, 1953-55; adminstrv. asst. to pres. James Madison U., Harrisonburg, 1963-64, dir. field services and placement, 1967-69, exec. asst. to pres., 1969-71, dir. pub. services, 1971-74, v.p. pub. affairs, 1974-77, v.p. univ. relations, 1977—; supt. Harrisonburg Schs., 1964-66. Chmn. publicity Auction 51, 1972; sec. James Madison U. Student Aid Found., 1972—, dir., 1972—; exec. dir., sec. bd. dirs. James Madison U. Found., 1969—; mem. adv. com. on tchr. certification Va. Dept. Edn., 1974-78; mem. adv. com. pub. affairs Va. Council Higher Edn., 1975—; bd. dirs. Shenandoah Valley Ednl. TV Corp., 1965-66, Crippled Children's Rehab. Center, Harrisonburg, 1964-70; bd. dirs. United Fund Harrisonburg, 1965-67, chmn. schs. div., 1975. Served to 1st sgt. AUS, 1943-46; PTO. Recipient Ethics award Rotary, 1943. Mem. Distributive Edn. Clubs Am. (hon. life mem.), Nat. Press Club, Harrisonburg C. of C. (dir. 1974-78), Assn. Higher Edn., Am. Assn. Sch. Adminstrs., Council Advancement and Support Edn., Pub. Relations Soc. Am., Va. High Sch. League (chmn. Valley dist. 1962-63), Va. Ednl. Assn. (chmn. Dist. G. prins. 1962), Diversified Occupations Coordinators Va. (chmn. 1958), Va. Coll. Placement Assn. (sec. 1967), Phi Delta Kappa. Lutheran (mem. council 1955-60). Clubs: Elks, Rotary, Spotswood Country. Home: PO Box 1015 811 Sandtrap Ln Harrisonburg VA 22801 Office: James Madison U Harrisonburg VA 22801

SONNIER, ISADORE LEON, educator; b. Midland, La., Oct. 31, 1928; s. Numa James and Alvina (Cormier) S.; B.A. in Elementary Edn., U. Southwestern La., 1955; M.Ed. in Ednl. Adminstrn. and Psychology, La. State U., 1958; Ed.D. in Sci. Edn., U. No. Colo., 1966; m. Claudine Hazel Box, Aug. 4, 1956; children—Suzanne E. Sonnier Leggett. David L., Joan M., John S., Sharon L., Charlotte A. Tchr., Baton Rouge Schs., 1955-61, U. No. Colo. Lab. Sch., Greeley, 1961-66; mem. faculty Western State Coll. Colo., Gunnison, 1966-67; mem. faculty U. So. Miss., Hattiesburg, 1967—, prof. sci. edn., 1967—; dir. NSF programs jr. high sch. tchrs., 1968-73; cons. Colo. and Wyo. State depts. edn., 1964-66. Pres., Oak Grove Band Parents Orgn., 1969-71. Served with USMCR, 1946-49, 51-53. Recipient research grant Scripps Inst. Oceanography-Calif. Bur. Comml. Fisheries, 1967, Faculty Research grant U. So. Miss., 1971-72, Environ. Edn. grant Sears & Roebuck, 1972-73, Esso. Corp., 1972-73, Miss. Power Co., 1972-73, IBM Student grant, 1975—; Chlortrol student grantee, 1976. Mem. AAAS, Nat. Assn. Geology Tchrs. (v.p. Mountain region 1964), Assn. Edn. Tchrs. Sci., Nat. Sci. Tchrs. Assn. (book rev. com. 1970—), Miss. Swimming and Diving Assn. (v.p. 1974, pres. 1975). Democrat. Roman Catholic. Author: Cajun Boy: The Story of Acadiana, 1980; contbr. articles to profl. jours. Home: 211 Springhill Dr Hattiesburg MS 39401

SOOCH, KEWAL SINGH, chemist, food co. exec.; b. Punjab, India, Feb. 1, 1941; came to U.S., 1971, naturalized, 1978; s. Malook Singh and Ishar Kaur (Dhaliwal) S.; student Faculty Sci., Govt. Coll. Hoshiarpur, India, 1962; B.S. with honors in Chemistry, Punjab U. Chandigarh, India, 1967, M.S. with honors in Chemistry, 1968. Mem. faculty Eastern Ark. Community Coll., 1975; asst. prof. Khalsa Coll., Mahilpur, Punjab, India, 1968-71; chemist Na-Churs Plant Food Co., Marion, Ohio, 1972-74, chemist, quality control mgr., Forrest City, Ark., 1975—. Fellow Am. Chem. Soc., Am. Soc. for Quality Control. Mem. Nirankari Mission (Universal Brotherhood). Contbr. articles to profl. publs. Home: 314 Tennessee St Forrest City AR 72335 Office: 3132 Industrial Rd Forrest City AR 72335

SOODER, KARL MICHAEL, food co. exec.; b. Miami, Fla., Jan. 31, 1943; s. Evald Karl and Janet Bernice (Selig) S.; B.A. cum laude, U. Miami, 1967; M.B.A., Columbia, 1972; m. Sandra Waters, Sept. 20, 1969; children—Michael, Christopher. Legis. asst. Congressman L.A. Bafalis, Miami, 1969-70; asso. product mgr. PepsiCo, Inc., Dallas, 1972-74; product mgr. Gillette Co., Boston, 1974-76; mktg. mgr. William B. Reily & Co., New Orleans, 1976—; adj. prof. Grad. Sch. Bus., Tulane U. Mem. Republican Nat. Com., 1978—, U.S. Olympic Com., 1978—. Woodrow Wilson fellow, 1967-69. Mem. Nat. Coffee Assn., Am. Mktg. Assn. Roman Catholic. Club: Royal Palm Polo. Home: 9008 Hermitage Pl New Orleans LA 70123 Office: William B Reily & Co 640 Magazine St New Orleans LA 70130

SOPER, WILLIAM BARLOW, educator; b. Longmont, Colo., Dec. 27, 1947; s. John William and Cleta (Vae) S.; B.A., Bethel Coll., Kans., 1970; M.S., Fort Hays State U., 1974; Ph.D., U. Ga., 1977; m. Diane Kay Moberly, June 1, 1969. Asst. prof. behavioral sci. La. Tech. U., Ruston, 1977—; cons. La. Bur. Student Services, 1977—. Served with U.S. Army, 1970-72. La. Vocat. Counselor tng. grantee, 1979-80. Mem. Am. Psychol. Assn., Am. Personnel and Guidance Assn., Internat. Assn. Applied Psychology, Soc. Psychol. Study Social Issues, Southeastern Psychol. Assn., Southeastern Assn. Counselor Edn. and Supervision, Am. Mental Health Counselor Assn., AAUP, Phi Kappa Phi, Psi Chi, Phi Delta Kappa, Avanti Owners Assn., Studebaker Drivers. Contbr. articles to profl. jours. Home: Route 5 Box 13A Ruston LA 71720 Office: Edn Lab La Tech U Ruston LA 71272

SORDO-SUAREZ, JOSE ANTONIO, discount card co. exec.; b. Havana, Nov. 1, 1941; s. Jose Antonio and Gloria (Marmol) D.; came to U.S., 1973; B.A. in Advt., U. Havana, 1969, in Acctg., 1966; m. Marisel E. Castillo, Mar. 6, 1976; children—Greny, Vivian. Installment loan officer Republic Nat. Bank Miami, 1973-75; comptroller, fin. aid officer Ramirez Coll., San Juan, 1976-77; personnel mgr., comptroller Nicky Cruz Outreach of Fla., Miami, 1977-78; pres., exec. dir. Descuento Co., Miami, 1978—; pvt. practice acctg., Miami, 1966—; bus. cons., 1973—. Treas., Young Explorers U.S., 1976—; v.p., treas. Community Health Care Center, 1978—. Mem. Nat. Soc. Public Accts. Roman Catholic. Home: 1890 SW 3d St Suite 3 Miami FL 33135 Office: 1701 W Flagler St Suite A Miami FL 33135

SORENSEN, ANTON MARINUS, JR., educator; b. Granger, Tex., Feb. 5, 1925; s. Anton Marinus and Odie Bertha (Cobb) S.; B.S., Tex. A. and M. U., 1949; M.S., Cornell U., 1951, Ph.D., 1953; m. Tommie Mae Moorman, June 3, 1944; children—Susan Dee, Walter Frank. Lab. asst. Tex. A&M U., College Station, 1948-49; grad. asst. Cornell U., 1949-53; asst. prof. Miss. State U., State College, 1953-55; asst. prof. Tex. A&M U., 1955-57, asso. prof., 1957-65, prof., head physiology of reproduction sect., 1965—; cons. Wortham Research Found., 1960, Eli Lilly Co., 1966, internat. programs AID Dominican Republic, 1969, Pioneer Beef Cattle, 1971—, Curtiss Breeding Service, 1975; Piper prof. Minnie Stephens Piper Found., 1970. Mgr., coach Little League, 1963-64, umpire-in-chief, 1966; choir props A&M Consol. High Sch., 1965-70, chmn., 1965-66, 69-70; mem. bd. equalization A&M Consol. Sch. Dist., 1969-72, chmn., 1970. Served with U.S. Army, 1944-46; ETO. Recipient Faculty Disting. Achievement award Tex. A&M Former Students Assn., 1968; named Honor Prof., Coll. Agr., Tex. A&M U., 1971, Outstanding Prof., 1971. Mem. Am. Soc. Animal Sci. (Disting. Tchr. award 1969), Am. Dairy Sci. Assn., Soc. Study Fertility, Am. Assn. Lab. Animal Sci., AAAS, Soc. Study Reproduction, Nat. Assn. Colls. and Tchrs. Agr., Am. Registry Cert. Animal Scientists, Council Agrl. Sci. and Tech., N.Y. Acad. Scis., Tex. Assn. Coll. Tchrs., Tex. Acad. Sci., Sigma Xi, Alpha Zeta, Phi Kappa Phi, Gamma Sigma Delta (Disting. Service to Agr. award 1972). Author: Repro Lab., A Laboratory Manual for Animal Reproduction, 4th edit., 1979; (with W.T. Berry, Jr. and L.D. Wythe, Jr.) Basic Animal Science, 6th edit., 1978; Animal Reproduction: Principles and Practices, 1979; contbr. articles to profl. jours. Home: Route 5 Box 1130 Bryan TX 77801 Office: Animal Sci Dept Tex A&M U College Station TX 77843

SORENSON, ERIC JOHN, urologist; b. Milw., Aug. 8, 1939; s. Richard Nelson and Gertrude Marie (Monefeldt) S.; student Rice Inst., 1957-58; B.A., U. Okla., 1960, M.D., 1964; m. Linda May Baughman, Aug. 5, 1961; children—Eric John, Robert N., Amy L. Intern, U. Va., Charlottesville, 1964-65, resident in urology, 1965-70; practice medicine specializing in urology, Lynchburg, Va., 1972—. Served to maj. M.C. U.S. Army, 1970-72. Decorated Bronze Star. Fellow A.C.S.; mem. AMA, Va. Med. Soc., Lynchburg Acad. Medicine, Am. Urol. Assn., Va. Urol. Soc. Episcopalian. Home: 915 Trents Ferry Rd Lynchburg VA 24503 Office: 1915 Thomson Dr Lynchburg VA 24501

SORENSON, TERRY BRUCE, auditor; b. Garden City, Mich., Dec. 21, 1947; s. Roy E. and Margaret L. Sorenson; B.S. in Acctg. and Fin., No. Mich. U., 1972; m. Jean L. Haas, Aug. 28, 1970; children—Bente R., Kristin M. Dist. internal auditor Western Auto Supply Co., Kansas City, Mo., 1973-74; asst. fin. mgr. Maritime Terminals, Inc., Norfolk, Va., 1975-78, dir. auditing, 1979—. Mem. Inst. Internal Auditors, Tau Kappa Epsilon. Republican Presbyterian. Home: 5632 Anthony Rd Virginia Beach VA 23455 Office: Maritime Terminals Inc 7737 Hampton Blvd Norfolk VA 23505

SORIA, RAYMOND W., hosp. food service adminstr.; b. Stockton, Calif., Sept. 18, 1947; s. Raymond and Angie S.; A.A., San Joaquin Delta Coll., 1967; B.A., St. Patrick's Coll., Mountain View, Calif., 1972. Dir. food service San Domenico Sch., San Anselmo, Calif., 1975-76, Los Angeles New Hosp., Beverly Hills, Calif., 1976-77; field supr. Los Angeles Satellite System, Los Angeles, 1977-78; dir. food service West Anaheim (Calif.) Community Hosp., 1978-79, Midland (Tex.) Meml. Hosp., 1979—. Named Outstanding Trainee, ARA Food Services Co., 1972. Mem. Am. Hosp. Assn., Soc. Hosp. Food Service Adminstrn. Democrat. Roman Catholic. Home: 3212 W Wadley St Apt 157 Midland TX 79701 Office: 2200 W Illinois St Midland TX 79701

SORRELL, FURMAN YATES, educator; b. Wadesboro, N.C., July 14, 1938; s. Furman Yates and Julia Lee (Little) S.; B.S., N.C. State U., 1960; M.S., Calif. Inst. Tech., 1961, Ph.D., 1966; m. Mariam Ann Holcomb Sell, Jan. 23, 1969; 1 dau., Shannon Lea. Research engr. Pratt & Whitney Aircraft, West Palm Beach, Fla., 1961-62; research asso. joint inst. for lab. astrophysics U. Colo., Boulder, 1966-67, asst. prof. aerospace engring. sci., 1967-68; faculty N.C. State U., Raleigh, 1968—, asst. prof., 1968-70, asso. prof., dir. grad. program engring. sci. and mechanics, 1970-74, asso. prof. engring. sci. and mechanics, 1975-76, prof. mech. engring., 1976—; asso. Perry Assos. Cons. Engrs. Active energy conservation; advisor local churches. NSF research grantee, 1966-68; grantee N.C. Sci. and Tech. Com., 1975-77, NOAA, 1976—; registered profl. engr., N.C. Mem. Am. Geophys. Union, Am. Acad. Mechanica, Am. Phys. Soc., N.Y. Acad. Scis., ASHRAE. Contbr. articles to profl. jours. Home: 4808 Kaplan St Raleigh NC 27606

SORRELLS, FRANK DOUGLAS, mech. engr.; b. Toccoa, Ga., May 14, 1931; s. Ralph Price and Ila B. (Freeman) S.; B.S. in Mech. Engring., U. Tenn., 1957, M.S., 1968; m. Alma M. West, June 19, 1954; 1 dau., Desiree Grace. Project test engr. Thiokol Corp., Huntsville, Ala., 1958-59, design engr. Saco-Lowell Reserach Center, Clemson, S.C., 1959-60; chief engr. Huyck-Formex Co., Greeneville, Tenn., 1960-65; mgr. engring. Plasti-Line Co., Knoxville, Tenn., 1965-67; exec. v.p. Lee Assos. Inc., Knoxville, 1967-76; pvt. practice engring., Knoxville, 1976—; dir. engring. Optical div. Cole Nat. Corp., 1978—. Served with USAF, 1950-54. Registered profl. engr., Tenn. Mem. Nat., Tenn. socs. profl. engrs., ASME, ASTM, Soc. Plastics Engrs., Pi Tau Sigma. Lutheran. Patentee in field. Home and office: 5516 Timbercrest Trail Knoxville TN 37919

SORRIER, ISABEL LANE, librarian; b. Statesboro, Ga., Aug. 13, 1917; d. Brooks Blitch and Caroline Viola (Moore) Sorrier; B.S., Ga. So. Coll., 1938; postgrad. U. Ga., 1940; B.S., George Peabody Coll., 1942. Intern, Warder Pub. Library, Springfield, Ohio, 1942; librarian Homerville (Ga.) High Sch., 1939-41; head librarian Waycross (Ga.) Pub. Library, 1942; librarian Newnan (Ga.) High Sch., 1943; dir. Statesboro (Ga.) Regional Library, 1944—; mem. library adv. com. bldg. constrn. Ga. Dept. Edn., mem. book selection com. Sec. chpt. ARC, 1945-48; mem. library services and constrn. Act Adv. Council, 1976—. Mem. ALA, S.E., Ga. (exec. bd. 1960, chmn. sect. 1960-62) library assns., Ga. Edn. Assn., Bus. and Profl. Women's Club (treas. 1950-52). Presbyterian. Home: 112 Park Ave Statesboro GA 30485 Office: 124 S Main St Statesboro GA 30458

SOTELO-ORTIZ, FEDERICO, orthopaedic surgeon; b. Caborca, Sonora, Mex., July 4, 1913; s. Jose Maria and Concepcion (Ortiz) Sotelo-Romero; B.S., Universidad Nacional de Mex., 1934, M.D., 1940; m. Idolina Garza de Sotelo, Sept. 2, 1939; children—Lourdes Sotelo de Delgado, Abelardo Sotelo-Garza, Sigfrido Sotelo-Garza, Danilo Sotelo-Garza, Coppelia Ludmila Sotelo-Garza. Intern Gen. Hosp., Mexico City, 1938-39; resident in orthopaedic surgery Hosp. for Joint Diseases, N.Y.C., 1944-47; practice medicine specializing in orthopaedic surgery, Mexico City, 1948, Hermosillo, Sonora, Mex., 1948—; adj. orthopaedic surgeon to orthopaedic service Gen. Hosp., Mexico City, 1941-44; asso. physician Inst. Mexicano del Seguro Social, Mexico City, 1943-44; asst. prof. human anatomy U. Nacional de Mex., Mexico City, 1944-48; prof. botany and zoology secondary pub. schs. of Mexico City, 1941-44; mem. staff Hosp. General, Mexico City, 1941-44, Sanatorio Licona, Hermosillo, 1948-77, Hosp. Sonora, 1978—; guest prof. orthopaedic surgery Hadassah U. Hosp. and Sch. of Medicine, Hebrew U., Jerusalem, 1974, Rotschild U. Hosp., Technion of Haifa (Israel), 1979. Rector-pres. U. Sonora, Hermosillo, 1968-73. Named Outstanding Citizen of Tucson, 1970. Recipient Internat. Goodwill award Tucson Trade Bur., 1970. Fellow A.C.S., Internat. Coll. of Surgeons; mem. Sociedad Mexicana de Ortopedia, Am. Acad. of Surgeons, Pan Am. Med. Assn. (Latin Am. chmn. sect. on med. edn. 1969—), Pan Pacific Surg. Assn., Assn. of Bone and Joint Surgeons, Am. Fracture Assn., Acad. Nacional de Medicina, Am. Acad. Orthopedic Surgeons, Soc. Internat. de Chirurgie Orthopedique and Traumatologie, Asociacion Medica de Hermosillo, Acad. Mexicana de Cirugia, Alumni Assn. of Hosp. for Joint Diseases and Med. Center (v.p. 1969-70, 1973-74), Sociedad Latino Americana de Ortopedia y Traumatologia, AAAS, Royal Coll. Medicine (London). Contbr. articles on orthopedic surgery to med. jours. Home: Calzada de Guadalupe s/n Hermosillo Sonora Mexico Office: Matamoros and Yucatan Sts Hermosillo Sonora Mexico

SOTO-MUNOZ, MANUEL, painter; b. Caguas, P.R., Jan. 20, 1913; s. Manuel Soto and Elisa Munoz; student Art Students League N.Y., 1947-51; m. Clara Hernandez, Sept. 3, 1948. Draftsman, P.R. Water Resources Authority, San Juan, 1937-47; artist Art Award Co., Inc., Bklyn., 1950-62; art dir. La Milagrosa mag., San Juan, 1962-65; art instr. extension div. U. P.R., Rio Piedrâs, 1962-64; art instr., Rio Piedras, 1960-78. Served with U.S. Army, 1942-45. Recipient award of merit Fla. So. Coll., 1958; prize Art Students League N.Y., 1950; 1st prize Salón Arte Sacro de P.R., Aguadilla Art Center, 1979. Mem. Artists Equity Assn., Long Beach Art Assn. (N.Y.), Internat. Soc. Artists, Am. Biog. Research Assn. Roman Catholic. Club: Exchange (v.p. 1968-70) (Bayamon Sur, Bayamon P.R.). Artist practicing and teaching Art Form of Painting, 1960-80. Home and Office: 1605 Indo St El Cerezal Rio Piedras PR 00926

SOTTILE, JAMES, III, mining co. exec.; b. Miami, Fla., Aug. 3, 1940; s. James and Ethel (Hooks) S.; B.S. cum laude, U. Fla., 1962; m. Judith Horne, Dec. 5, 1959; children—James, Michael, Scott, Thomas, Jennifer. Vice pres. Goldfield Corp., Melbourne, Fla., 1970-71, pres., dir., 1971—; v.p. dir. Canaveral Indian River Groves, Inc., Micco, Fla., 1964-70, Brevard-Indian River Groves, Inc., Micco, 1964-69, Indian River Shores Groves, Inc., 1962-64; pres., dir. Indian Mound Corp., Micco, 1963-69, Original 51 Corp., Micco, 1966-69; v.p. Lake Byrd Citrus Packing Co., Melbourne, Fla., 1963-71, pres., 1971—, also dir.; v.p. Indian River Orange Groves, Inc., Micco, 1963-69, pres., 1969-74, also dir.; pres., dir. Citrus Growers of Fla., Inc., Melbourne, 1970—; v.p., dir. No. Goldfield Investments, Ltd., Inc., Melbourne, 1971-79, pres., 1979—; v.p., dir. Mamba Engring Co., Inc., Titusville, Fla., 1972—; pres., dir. Black Range Mining Corp., Albuquerque, 1972—, San Pedro Mining Corp., Albuquerque, 1972—, Goldfield Consol. Mines Co., Albuquerque, 1972—, Harlan Fuel Co. (Ky.), 1975—; v.p., dir. Valencia Center, Inc., Coral Gables, Fla., 1964—. Supr., sec. San Sebastian Drainage Dist., Melbourne, 1965-76, trustee, 1976-78. Mem. Fla. C. of C. (dir. 1972-76), Young Pres.'s Orgn. Democrat. Roman Catholic. Clubs: Eau Gallie Yacht (Melbourne); Cat Cay (Bahamas). Home: 846 Malibu Ln Indialantic FL 32903 Office: 65 E NASA Blvd Melbourne FL 32901

SOUDERS, BRUCE CHESTER, clergyman, educator; b. Richland, Pa., Dec. 27, 1920; s. Ray Levan and Sue (Hartman) S.; B.A., Lebanon Valley Coll., 1944; M.Div., United Theol. Sem., 1947; M.A., Columbia U., 1953; student Luth. Theol. Sem., Gettysburg, Pa., 1953-66, James Madison U., 1967-69; m. Patricia Marie Bartels, Aug. 18, 1945; 1 son, Gregory Allen. Ordained to ministry, United Meth. Ch., 1947; instr. Lebanon Valley Coll., 1947-49; pastor Neidig Meml. United Meth. Ch., Oberlin, Pa., 1949-57; instr. Lebanon Valley Coll. Extension Program, Harrisburg, Pa., 1957-66; dir. public relations, 1957-65, dir. publs., 1965-66; mem. staff Shenandoah Coll. and Conservatory of Music, 1966—, chmn. English dept., 1966-73, chmn. arts and scis. faculty, 1972—, prof. English, 1975—; lectr.; panelist Nat. Endowment for the Humanities. Recipient Honor medal Freedom Found., 1951; Nat. Endowment for Humanities fellow, 1971. Mem. Hist. Soc. Winchester and Frederick County, Preservation of Hist. Winchester Assn., Winchester-Frederick County Ministerial Assn., MLA, Nat. Council Tchrs. English, So. Humanities Conf., Blue Ridge chpt. Va. Mus. Fine Arts (pres. 1974-76), Poetry Soc. Va. (contest chmn. 1976, 77), Poetry Soc. Am., Smithsonian Assos. Author: To A Student Dying Young and Other Poems, 1978; editor: Lebanon Valley Coll. Alumni Rev., 1957-66; Lebanon Valley College: A Centennial History 1866-1966, 1966; contbr. poetry, articles and book revs. to jours. and religious publs. Home: 1625 Stafford Dr Winchester VA 22601 Office: Shenandoah Coll and Conservatory of Music College Dr Winchester VA 22601

SOULE, CHARLES ARTHUR, JR., wood preserving co. exec.; b. Pensacola, Fla., Apr. 14, 1941; s. Charles Arthur and Margaret Pomeroy (Washburn) S.; B.A., Yale U., 1963; M.B.A., Harvard U., 1969; m. Margherita Ligon Jones, June 5, 1965; children—Margherita Crane, Saranne Ligon. Chief fin. officer Escambia Treating Co., 1970-75, pres., 1975—, dir., 1970—; dir. Citizens & Peoples Nat. Bank Pensacola, 1971—. Bd. dirs. Pensacola Arts Council, 1970-73, Action '76 Pensacola, 1971-74, Bapt. Hosp., 1977—, Jr. Achievement, 1976-78, Asso. Industries Fla., 1976-79; bd. dirs. Pensacola Open Golf Tournament, 1971-79, chmn. 1977-78; mem. Water-Sewr Bd. Escambia County, 1973-76; trustee Pensacola Art Center, 1969-73, v.p., 1972; trustee Heritage Found., 1971-74, Bapt. Hosp. Found., 1975-78. Served with USNR, 1964-67. Mem. Am. Wood Preservers Assn., So. Pressure Treaters Assn. (dir. 1976—, sec.-treas. 1977-78, v.p. 1979-80), Pensacola Sports Assn. (dir. 1977, treas. 1978, pres. 1979), Beta Theta Pi. Democrat. Episcopalian. Clubs: Rotary, Pensacola Country, Exec. Pensacola, Pensacola Yacht. Home: 903 Fairway Dr Warrington FL 32507 Office: PO Box 17108 Pensacola FL 32522

SOULE, PHILLIP EARL, ins. co. exec.; b. Moline, Ill., Feb. 4, 1950; s. Wallace P. and Elizabeth A. (Kline) S.; B.S., U. Ill., 1972; m. Rebecca Keime, June 11, 1972; 1 dau., Ellen Marie. Group sales rep. State Mut. Life Assurance Co. Am., Greensboro, N.C., 1972-76, regional group sales mgr., Atlanta, 1976—. C.L.U. Mem. Am. Soc. Chartered Life Underwriters. Home: 730 Rio Grande Dr Alpharetta GA 30201 Office: Suite 505 2700 Cumberland Pkwy NW Atlanta GA 30339

SOULES, LUTHER HUGH, JR., food brokerage co. exec.; b. nr. San Antonio, Aug. 11, 1915; s. Luther Hugh and Frances Blanche (Harper) S.; student Draughon's Comml. Coll., 1932-34; m. Bessie Merle Myers, June 12, 1937; children—Luther Hugh, Barbara Soules Young, Joe Carlton. Bookkeeper, Bruner Bros. & Runnels, Mineola, Tex., 1933-37; office mgr. Van Winkle Motor Co., Dallas, 1937-43; SW regional mgr. Canada Dry Ginger Ale, Inc., Dallas, 1943-58; v.p. Great Western Foods Co., Fort Worth, 1958-62; pres., owner Luke Soules Inc. food broker, San Antonio, 1962—. Mem. San Antonio Sales and Mktg. Execs. (v.p. 1967-69, dir. 1967-73), Soc. Mayflower Decs., Sons Republic Tex., SAR. Club: Rotary. Presbyterian. Home: 511 Larkwood St San Antonio TX 78209 Office: 8614 Crowhill St San Antonio TX 78209

SOUTHERN, CHARLES EVERETT, physician; b. Williamson County, Tex., Apr. 21, 1907; s. Victor Anderson and Lilly Maude (Connell) S.; M.D., Baylor U., 1931; m. Carra Elizabeth Stiles, June 1, 1933; children—Thomas Charles and James Victor (twins). Intern, Scott and White Hosp., Temple, Tex., 1931-32; gen. practice medicine, Burton, Tex., 1932-50, Brenham, Tex., 1950-76; owner, operator So. Clinic, Brenham, 1959-76; med. dir. Brenham State Sch. for Mental Health-Mental Retardation, 1976-79; resident in pediatrics St. Louis Children's Hosp., 1943-44, Columbus Med. Center, N.Y.C., 1946-47, Ochsner Clinic, New Orleans, 1948-49; dir. First Nat. Bank, Brenham, 1952-79; a founder, chmn. bd. South Central Savs. Co., Brenham, 1970-79. Bd. dirs. David Crockett dist. Boy Scouts Am., 1950-60, Brenham Youth Council, 1956-60. Mem. Tex. State Med. Assn. AMA, Am. Assn. Family Physicians, Am. Assn. Physicians and Surgeons, Washington Burleston County Med. Soc. Democrat. Episcopalian. Clubs: Rotary. Brenham Country, Elks, Sons of Herman. Died Sept. 8, 1979. Home: 607 Walnut Hill Dr Brenham TX 77833

SOUTHERN, JOHN STEPHEN, researcher, counselor; b. Abilene, Tex., Dec. 30, 1953; s. John H. and Leta Faye (Fincher) S.; A.B., U. So. Calif., 1974; M.S., E. Tex. State U., 1976, Ed.D., 1979; m. Donna Lou Edwards, Feb. 14, 1975. Social worker Tex. State Dept. Human Resources, Dallas, 1975-76, social work supr., 1976-77; research asso. Occupational Curriculum Lab., E. Tex. State U., 1978-79, researcher, 1979-80, instr. dept. student personnel and guidance, 1979-80; dir. counseling Odessa (Tex.) Coll., 1980—; instr. Cedar Valley Coll., Lancaster, Tex. Mem. Assn. Advancement Behavior Therapy, Am. Personnel and Guidance Assn., Nat. Vocat. Guidance Assn., Am. Coll. Personnel Assn., Soc. Behavioral Medicine, Phi Beta Kappa, Phi Kappa Phi, Psi Chi, Phi Delta Kappa. Home: 6270 Saratoga Circle Dallas TX 75214 Office: Odessa Coll 201 W University Odessa TX 79762

SOUTHERN, PAUL MORRIS, JR., physician; b. Ft. Worth, June 26, 1932; s. Paul Morris and Margaret M. (Moore) S.; B.S., Abilene Christian Coll., 1953; M.D., U. Tex., 1959; children by previous marriage—Sheryl Ann, Mark Lee. Intern, Parkland Meml. Hosp., Dallas, 1959-60, resident, 1960-62; research fellow infectious diseases U. Tex. Southwestern Med Sch., Dallas, 1962-63, 66-68; practice medicine, specializing in internal medicine, Irving, Tex., 1963-66; asst. prof. internal medicine U. Tex. Southwestern Med. Sch., Dallas, 1968-71, asso. prof. pathology and internal medicine, 1973—; asst. prof. lab. medicine Washington U. Sch. Medicine, St. Louis, 1971-73; dir. clin. microbiology Parkland Meml. Hosp., Dallas, 1973—. Diplomate Am. Bd. Internal Medicine, Am. Bd. Infectious Diseases, Am. Bd. Pathology. Fellow A.C.P.; mem. Tex. Soc. Clin. Microbiology (pres. 1974-76), Acad. Clin. Lab. Physicians and Scientists, Am. Soc. Microbiology, Infectious Diseases Soc. Am., Am. Soc. Clin. Pathologists, So. Soc. Clin. Investigation, Am. Fedn. Clin. Research, Alpha Omega Alpha. Contbr. articles to profl. jours. Home: 9145 Drumcliffe Ln Dallas TX 75231 Office: 5323 Harry Hines Blvd Dallas TX 75235

SOUTHERN, THOMAS MARTIN, analytical chemist; b. Beaumont, Tex., June 19, 1942; s. Haskell Larry and Earline (Shaw) S.; B.S., Lamar U., 1960-64, M.S., Tex. Tech. U., 1966; Ph.D., U. Houston, 1969; M.B.A., So. Meth. U., 1977; m. Barbara Marie Lewis, June 4, 1966; children—Michelle Lea, John Wesley. Sr. chemist Tex. Eastman Co., Longview, 1969—; partner East Tex. Graphics, Longview, 1970—. Mem. Am. Chem. Soc., Nat. Assn. Thermal Analysis, Tex. Profl. Photographers Assn. Home: 2207 Paul St Longview TX 75601 Office: PO Box 7444 Longview TX 78601

SOUTHGATE, HERBERT SOMERVILLE, minister, religious orgn. exec.; b. Norfolk, Va., Apr. 21, 1901; s. Thomas Somerville and Nettie Duncan (Norsworthy) S.; B.A., Va. Mil. Inst., 1922; B.D., Emory U., 1928; D.D., Randolph-Macon Coll., 1950; m. Isobel Faye Fletcher, Oct. 9, 1932; 1 son, Herbert Fletcher. Supt., Southgate Marine Corp., Norfolk, Va., 1923-25; ordained to ministry United Methodist Ch., 1934; pastor's asst. St. Paul's Ch., Fresno, Calif., 1931-32; pastor Bassett (Va.) Meml. Ch., 1928-29, Orange Circuit, Orange County, Va., 1932-36, Trinity Ch., Smithfield, Va., 1936-40; chaplain Randlph-Macon Coll., Ashland, Va., 1940-44; pastor Dulin Falls (Va.) Ch., 1944-48, Trinity Ch., Alexandria, Va., 1948-52, Annandale (Va.) Ch., 1958-60; dist. supt. Roanoke Dist., United Meth. Ch., Roanoke, Va., 1952-58; rec. sec. bd. trustees Ams. United for Separation of Ch. and State, Washington, 1960-61, dir. ch. relations, 1961-66, treas., 1967-73, v.p., 1966—; pres. Alexandria Council Chs., 1952. Clubs: Kiwanis, Rotary, Ruritan, Exchange. Mem. Antique Car Club Am. (region pres. 1973), Kappa Alpha. Contbr. articles to religious jours. Home and Office: 1611 Larchwood Dr Venice FL 33595

SOUTHWELL, JOSEPH RAY, JR., computer cons.; b. Oklahoma City, Nov. 20, 1952; s. Joseph Ray and Grace Elizabeth S.; B.S., Okla. State U., 1979; m. Deborah Ann DeShazo, Aug. 20, 1978. Founder, pres. Freelance Computer Programming, Inc., Oklahoma City, 1977—; pres. Inc. Freelance Data Centers, Inc., Oklahoma City, 1978—; v.p. Synthetic Lubricants, Inc. Office: 2912 Classen Blvd Oklahoma City OK 73106

SOVERN, CHARLES, hotel exec., ret. army officer; b. Kansas City, Mo., May 25, 1923; s. Charles and Florence Alice (Roberts) S., Sr.; B.S., Northeastern U., 1963; grad. Command and Gen. Staff Coll., 1956, Army War Coll., 1971, Def. Lang. Inst., 1965, Indsl. Def. and Disaster Planning Inst., 1974, IBM Course for Execs., 1974; m. Betty Bell, May 9, 1969; children—Donna Marie Sovern Ellis, Charles D., Jennifer Susan. Enlisted U.S. Army, 1941, advanced through grades to col., 1974; dep. chief special security Defense Intelligence Agy., Washington, 1963-66; comdr. 470th Mil. Intelligence Group, Panama, 1966-68; dep. chief of staff intelligence Hdqrs. 3d U.S. Army, Ft. McPherson, Ga., 1968-69, Hdqrs. Mil. Assistance Command, Vietnam, 1969-70, Hdqrs. U.S. Army Forces, Pacific, Hawaii, 1970-73; asst. dep. chief of staff intelligence Hdqrs. Forces Command, Ft. McPherson, Ga., 1973-74; dir. personnel Peachtree Plaza Hotel, Western Internat. Hotels Atlanta, 1974-79, exec. com., 1977-78, corporate personnel policy com., 1977-78; dir. personnel Pinehurst Inc. (N.C.), 1979—. Cons., Vets. Outreach Program, Economic Opportunity, Atlanta, 1976-78, vice chmn., 1976-77; mem. adv. bd. Sch. of Hotel, Atlanta, 1976-77; cons. to admnstrn. Ga. State U., 1976-77, guest speaker, 1976-77; mem. adv. council Morris Brown Coll., Atlanta, 1976-77. Decorated Parachute badge, 4 Legion of Merit awards, 4 Bronze Stars, Joint Service Commendation, Army Commendation, Grand Star of Honor (China); Legion of Honor (Panama); Honor medal (2d class) (Vietnam); recipient Outstanding Service award EOA, 1976; certificate of appreciation Clark Coll., 1977. Mem. Assn. Personnel Admnstrs., Hospitality Personnel of Atlanta, Am. Soc. for Tng. and Devel., Nat. Intelligence Assn., Assn. U.S. Army, Ret. Officers Assn. Clubs: Ft. McPherson Officers; Dunwoody Country, Pinehurst Country. Home: 107 Glenwood Trail Southern Pines NC 28387 Office: Pinehurst Inc Pinehurst NC 28374

SOWA, WALTER D., educator, lawyer; b. McKeesport, Pa., Jan. 17, 1907; s. Peter and Anna (Jankowska) S.; A.B., U. Pitts., 1928, Litt.M., 1940; J.D., Duquesne U., 1933; m. Eva Ingersoll Long, Apr. 4, 1942; children—Peter William, Thomas Michael. Tchr. elementary sch., Alliquippa, Pa., 1928-30, high sch., Pa., 1930-42; probation officer Juvenile Ct., Allegheny County, Pa., 1940-41; joined U.S. Army, 1942, advanced through grades to lt. col., 1962; acad. coordinator Baylor U., 1943-44, Tex. A. and M. Coll., 1944-46; judge adv. Korea

Base Command, 1946-48; at Pa. State Coll., 1948-50; asst. judge adv. X Corps, Korea, 1950-51; sec. gen. staff X Corps, 1951-52; chief contracting div. Hdqrs. 3d Army, 1952-56; legal assistance adviser, 1956-60; trial observer-lawyer, 1960-62, ret., 1962; prof. criminal law Cumberland Law Sch. Howard Coll., Birmingham, Ala., 1963—; prof. criminal law and evidence Samford U., Birmingham, 1963-77, adj. prof. law, 1977—. Decorated Bronze Star. Mem. Am., Ga., Ala. bar assns., Pa. Edn. Assn. Methodist. Mason. Home: 2121 16th Ave S Birmingham AL 35205

SOWELL, LAVEN, musician; b. Wewoka, Okla., Jan. 9, 1933; s. Vestal Laven and Viola Jane (Jackson) S.; B.Mus., U. Okla., 1955; M.A., Columbia U., 1964; postgrad. Manhattan Sch. Music, N.Y.C., 1956-57, Aspen (Colo.) Sch. Music, 1951-53, Conservatoire de Musique de Fontainebleau (France), 1966. Dir. choral music Edison High Sch., Tulsa, 1961-70; dir. choral activities U. Tulsa, 1970—, prof. voice, 1970—; on tour with Charles L. Wagner Opera Co., 1955-56; chorus master Tulsa Opera Inc., 1962—; choirmaster 1st Presbyn. Ch., Tulsa, 1969—; instr. Evergreen Conf. Ch. Music (Colo.), summers 1972-74; clinician and adjudicator voice students. Recipient Distinguished Service award Okla. PTA, 1970, named hon. lit. gov. Okla., 1975. Mem. Nat. Assn. Tchrs. Singing, Music Educators Nat. Conf., Okla. Music Educators Assn., Music Tchrs. Nat. Assn., Am. Guild Organists and Ch. Musicians. Home: 3540 S Wheeling St Tulsa OK 74105 Office: 600 S College St Tulsa OK 74104

SOWELL, W. R. (BILL), aviation co. exec.; b. Chipley, Fla., Nov. 8, 1920; s. Claude Tee and Eunice (Richardson) S.; student Centenary Coll., 1940-42; grad. Norton Bus. Coll., Shreveport, La., 1942; m. Nadine Martin, Sept. 1942 (div. Feb. 1971); children—J. Donald, Dorris Dianne Sowell Preston, Deborah K., Sheri Denise. Owner, pres. Panama Airways, Inc., Panama City, Fla., 1946-53; pilot instr., flying supr. So. Airways, Bainbridge, Ga., 1950-53; founder, owner, pres., pilot, instr. Sowell Aviation Co., Inc., Panama City, 1954—; chmn. bd. Sowell Aircraft Service, Inc., Panama City, 1964—; founder, pres., owner Pensacola Aviation Inc., Pensacola, Fla., 1964-72; pres., co-owner Sowell Rent-A-Car, Inc., Panama City; airplane and instrument pilot examiner FAA, 1946—; mem. Panama City Airport Bd., 1959-61, chmn., 1959-61; mem. Fla. Gov.'s Aviation Com., 1972—, chmn., 1977-79. Served with AC, AUS, 1940-45. Mem. Airplane Owners and Pilots Assn., Quiet Birdmen, Nat., Fla. (pres. 1970-72, dir.) aviation trades assns., Bay County C. of C. (dir. 1956-66, chmn. aviation com. 1962-63). Baptist. Clubs: Rotary, Masons, Shriners, Elks, St. Andrew Bay Yacht. Home: 3037 W 30th Ct Panama City FL 32401 Office: Panama City Bay County Municipal Airport Panama City FL 32401

SOWELL, WENDELL LORAINE, toxicologist; b. Pemberton, W.Va., Aug. 17, 1917; s. Larkin Andrew and Sallie Lee (Brewer) S.; B.S., Auburn U., 1947, M.S., 1955; LL.B., Jones Law Sch., 1960; Ph.D. in Preventive Medicine, U. Okla., 1967; m. Alva Loree Webb, July 7, 1936; children—Bashaba Sowell Gibbons, Wendell Loraine, Darrell B. Toxicologist, Ala. Dept. Toxicology and Criminal Investigation, Auburn, 1947-60; dir., establisher Crime Lab., Ft. Worth, 1960-65; asst. supt., dir. crime lab. Ohio Bur. Criminal Identification and Investigation, London, 1968; asso. prof. biol. scis. Livingston (Ala.) U., 1968-71; asso. prof. Sch. Law Enforcement, Jacksonville (Ala.) State U., 1971-77; dir. Sch. Law Enforcement, Patrick Henry State Jr. Coll., Monroeville, Ala., 1977—; pres. Sowell Realty, Inc., Birmingham and Jacksonville, Ala., 1972—; head prof. Sowell Sch. Realty, Jacksonville; dir. N.E. Ala. Police Acad., Jacksonville, 1972. Served with U.S. Army, 1942-44. NIH trainee environ. health U. Okla., 1965-67. Mem. Nat. Acad. Criminal Justice Scis., So. Assn. Criminal Justice Educators, Forensic Sci. Soc., Internat. Assn. Forensic Toxicologists, Am. Acad. Forensic Scis., Ala. Peace Officers Assn., Gamma Sigma Delta, Sigma Delta Kappa. Baptist. Author: (with Robert A. Wilson) Institute on Homicide Investigation Techniques, 1961. Home: 1111 Buford St Monroeville AL 36460 Office: Sch Law Enforcement Patrick Henry State Jr Coll Monroeville AL 36460

SOWLE, DONALD EDGAR, mgmt. cons. firm exec.; b. Mt. Pleasant, Mich., May 27, 1915; s. Sidney Edgar and Mary Agnes (West) S.; B.S., Central Mich. U., 1940; postgrad. Harvard U., 1942, Mass. Inst. Tech., 1942; M.B.A., U. Chgo., 1950; m. Gretchen Elizabeth MacRae, July 4, 1942; children—Lisa Sowle Cahill, Mary Ann Sowle Messing. Sales rep. Armour & Co., Grand Rapids, Mich., 1940-41; commd. 2d lt. USAF, advanced through grades to col., 1958; asst. dir. Jet Propulsion Lab., Calif. Tech. Inst., Pasadena, 1965-68; group v.p. Gulf & Western Industries, Los Angeles, 1968-69; dir. studies Congressional Commn. on Govt. Procurement, Washington, 1970-73; pres., chmn. bd. dirs. Don Sowle Assos., Inc., Arlington, Va., 1973—; instr. Georgetown U., 1961-65; adj. prof. Am. U., Washington. Trustee, officer Nat. Contract Mgmt. Found., 1973—. Recipient Pub. Service award Los Angeles County, Calif., 1969. Fellow Nat. Contract Mgmt. Assn. (bd. advisers), Beta Gamma Sigma. Republican. Roman Catholic. Clubs: K.C., Capitol Hill, Nat. Aviation. Home: 6643 McLean Dr McLean VA 22101 Office: Suite 708 1911 Jefferson Davis Hwy Arlington VA 22202

SOZA, WILLIAM, accountant; b. Shafter, Tex., Apr. 14, 1936; s. Manuel G. and Rebecca (Velasco) S.; B.B.A., U. Tex. at Austin, 1960; m. Susan P. Eddy, Nov. 20, 1965; children—Stephanie, Mary Elizabeth. Sr. accountant Main Lafrentz & Co., Washington, 1964-67; mgr. audits and taxes NUS Corp., Rockville, Md., 1967-69; pvt. practice pub. accounting, Falls Church, Va., 1969-73; prin. Soza & Co., Ltd., C.P.A.'s, Falls Church, 1973—. Mem. adv. bd., vice chmn. Fairfax County Corps, Salvation Army, 1970-78. Served with AUS, 1962. Mem. Va. Soc. C.P.A.'s, Am. Inst. C.P.A.'s. Roman Catholic. Clubs: Touchdown (Washington); Annandale (Va.) Rotary (dir. 1973-74). Home: 2307 Locust Ridge Ct Falls Church VA 22046 Office: 803 W Broad St Falls Church VA 22046

SPAGNA, NENO JOHN, urban planner, inst. exec.; b. Wheeler, Ind., Sept. 12, 1924; s. Calisto and Lucia (Gabellini) S.; A.B., U. Miami, 1951; M.S., U. Tenn., 1954, M. Urban and Regional Planning, with honors, U. del Valle, Cali, Colombia, 1966; A.S. summa cum laude, Manatee Jr. Coll., 1972; M.P.A., Nova U., 1977, D.Pub. Adminstrn., 1978; m. Patricia Josephine Brewer, Oct. 9, 1954; children—John Patrick, Christina Anne. Planning technician Chattanooga Housing Authority, Chattanooga, 1951-52; planning draftsman Tenn. State Planning Commn., Knoxville, 1953-54, planning technician City of San Bernardino, Calif, 1954-56, tech. advisor San Bernardino Urban Renewal Agency, 1954-56; planning dir. City of Hollywood, Fla., 1956-64, Manatee County, Fla., 1966-73, dir. community devel., Collier County, Fla., 1973—; pres. Fla. Inst. Urban Affairs, Inc.; mem. Gov's. Council for the Handicapped, 1971-73, mem., past v.p. Manatee Comprehensive Health Planning Council, 1970-73; founder Manatee Area Planning Services Council (MAPS); mem. Manasota 88, Manatee-Sarasota bi-county environ health planning council, cons. to Cali, Colombia City Planning Dept., 1964. Served in U.S. Army Air Corps, 1943-46. Decorated WWII Victory medal. Recipient Outstanding Achievement award, Nat. Assn. of Counties; Outstanding Service award, Gov's. Advisory Com. for the Handicapped, 1973; certificate of appreciation, City of Bradenton Beach, Fla., 1973; Meritorious Service award, Manatee County Bd. of County Commrs.; Outstanding Service award, Izaak Walton League of Am. Mem. Urban Land Inst., Internat. City Mgmt. Assn., Am. Soc. Public Adminstrn., Inter-Am. Soc. Planners, Am. Inst. Cert. Planners, Am. Soc. Planning Ofcls., Am. Planning Assn. (Meritorious award 1979), Fla. Planning and Zoning Assn. (past pres. chpt.), Fla. Planning and Zoning Dirs. Assn. (past pres.), Fla. Inst. Planners (founder, interim pres.), Exptl. Aircraft Assn. Roman Catholic. Contbr. articles to profl. jours. First planner in Fla. to promote and use transfer of development rights process. Home: 3850 27th Ave SW Box 7215 Naples FL 33940 Office: 3850 27 Ave SW Naples FL 33990

SPAIN, DAVID ROWAN, govt. ofcl.; b. Providence, Feb. 6, 1929; s. Charles Green and Eva (Rowan) S.; B.A., U. Va., 1951, postgrad., 1951-53. With Navy Publs. & Printing Service, Washington, 1956-62, dep. dir. publs. Potomac River Naval Command, 1960-61, asst. head publs. standards br., 1961-62; exec. asst. for fin. mgmt. JAG, Navy Dept., 1962—. Served to sgt. AUS, 1953-56. Home: 8004 Lilac Lane Alexandria VA 22308 Office: Office of Judge Advocate General Navy Dept 200 Stovall St Alexandria VA 22332

SPAIN, NETTIE EDWARDS (MRS. FRANK E. SPAIN), civic worker; b. Alexandria, La., Oct. 9, 1918; d. John Henry and Sallie Tamson (Donald) Edwards; student Alexandria Bus. Coll., 1936-37, Birmingham-Southern Coll., 1958-59, Nat. Tng. Inst., United Community Funds and Councils Am., 1965-66; m. Frank E. Spain, Apr. 18, 1974. Reporter, Alexandria Daily Town Talk, 1942-45; staff writer Brimingham (Ala.) Post, 1945-49; pub. relations dir. Community Chest, Birmingham, 1949-53; dir. information services Pa. United Fund, Phila., 1953-55; asst. exec. dir. Ala. Assn. for Mental Health, Birmingham, 1956-57; pub. relations dir. United Appeal, Birmingham, 1958-68, asst. exec. dir., 1968-71; asst. to pres. for devel. U. Ala., Birmingham, 1971-74, acting dir., 1975. Mem. pub. relations com. Ala. Heart Assn., 1972-73; bd. dirs. Hale County chpt. ARC, Kate Duncan Smith D.A.R. Sch., Grant, Ala.; bd. dirs., charter mem. Birmingham Children's Theater; bd. dirs. Children's Aid Soc., Jefferson-Shelby Lung Assn., 1972-75, Vol. Bur. of Greater Birmingham, 1972-77; mem. community adv. com. Jr. League, 1974-75; adv. bd. dirs. Historic Hale County Preservation Soc.; mem. adv. com. Internat. Friendship program U. Ala., Birmingham, 1974-79, hon. mem. pres.'s council. Recipient 1st Place awards Nat. Photos for Fedn., 1966-67; citation Pa. United Fund, 1955, citation for service Jefferson-Shelby Lung Assn., 1975, citation Ala. Heart Assn., 1974; award of merit Ala. Hist. Commn., 1977; Distinguished Service citation Vol. Bur. Greater Birmingham, 1977. Benjamin Franklin fellow Royal Soc. Arts, London, U.S.A.; mem. Nat. Pub. Relations Council of Health and Welfare Services (dir. 1967-69), Women's Com. of 100, Progress Study Club, Hale County Council for Arts, Met. Opera Guild, Birmingham Opera Guild, English Speaking Union, Cauldron Club, Pub. Relations Council Ala. (hon. life), Am. Women in Radio and TV (historian 1968), Colonial Dames Am., D.A.R., Ala. Burgess, First Families of Va., Nat. Trust for Hist. Preservation, Guy E. Snavely Soc. Birmingham-So. Coll., Hist. Hale County Preservation Soc., Nat. Soc. Colonial Dames Am., Ala. Hist. Assn. Episcopalian. Clubs: Lakeview Country (Greensboro, Ala.); Crepe Myrtle Garden; Mountain Brook Country (Birmingham); North River Yacht (Tuscaloosa, Ala.). Home: 3100 Overhill Rd Birmingham AL 35223 also Medley PO Box 400 Greensboro AL Office: University Station Birmingham AL 35294

SPALDING, CLEM HILL, auto ins. co. exec.; b. Lebanon, Ky., Feb. 24, 1924; s. Wallace Hugh and Nell (Hill) S.; student U. Louisville, 1942-43, Trinity U. Tex., 1946; B.B.A. cum laude, St. Mary's U., 1948; m. Emma Catherine Rivas, Oct. 28, 1948; children—Emma C. Spalding Spieczny, Ann Spalding Towns, Mary C., Judith M., Theresa R., Clem H., William F., Nell E. Trainee, Sears Roebuck & Co., New Albany, Ind., 1948-49; gen. ins. adjuster, mgr. Horton Adjustment Co., Louisville, Campbellsville, and Elizabethtown, Ky., 1949-54; gen. adjuster Lloyd Caldwell Corp., San Antonio, 1954-57; underwriter, mgr., dir., v.p. United Services Automobile Assn. San Antonio, 1957—; past chmn. gov. com. Tex. Automobile Ins. Plan; mem. gov. com. Okla. Automobile Ins. Plan. Past trustee Oblate Coll. S.W.; mem. com. Boy Scouts Am. Served with AUS, 1943-46. Mem. Nat. Soc. C.P.C.U.'s (past pres. Alamo chpt.), Tex. Auto Ins. Service Office (chmn. governing com.), Nat. Assn. Ind. Insurers (chmn. auto ins. plan com.). Roman Catholic. Clubs: Austin, Turtle Creek Country. Home: 163 Skipper Dr San Antonio TX 78216 Office: USAA Bldg San Antonio TX 78288

SPALDING, HENRY A., mining engr.; b. Ky., Mar. 20, 1899; s. J.D. and Alice (Estes) S.; studied under personal tutors; m. Gertrude Petrey, Feb. 8, 1923; children—Jack P. (dec.), Richard D. Gen., widely diversified engring. practice; inventor metall. processes; pres. H.A. Spalding, Inc.; mgr., part owner Old Va. Land Co.; mem. adv. bd. Ky. Geol. Survey. Co. Recipient Outstanding Citizen award Hazard (Ky.) civic clubs, 1958. Registered profl. engr. Mem. ASCE, Am. Inst. Mining, Metall. and Petroleum Engrs. (Legion of Honor), Ky. Soc. Profl. Engrs. (pres. 1949-50, hon.), Ky. Acad. Sci., Appalachian Geol. Soc., Ky. Hist. Soc., Nat. Rifle Assn. (exec. com., dir.). Club: Filson. Co-author: Engineers Vest Pocket Book; contbr. articles to profl. jours. Home: Broadway Hazard KY 41701 Office: Baker Bldg Hazard Ky also 1028 Connecticut Av NW Washington DC 20009

SPALDING, RICHARD LEROY, hosp. adminstr.; b. LaGrange, Mo., Apr. 18, 1936; s. Edward William and Thelma (Keith) S.; student Culver-Stockton Coll., 1955-56, Hardin-Simmons U., 1964, Columbia 1965; m. Beulah Kaye Barrigar, June 3, 1956; children—Kathleen J., Richard L., John E. Announcer, account exec. Sta. WCAZ, Carthage, Ill., 1954-58; exec. v.p. Circle-S, Inc., Eastland, Tex., 1959-61; adminstr. Eastland Meml. Hosp., 1961-62; adminstrv. asst. Hendrick Meml. Hosp., Abilene, Tex., 1962-66; exec. dir. Meml. Hosp., Denison, Tex., 1966-73; sr. v.p. Hendrick Med. Center, Abilene, 1973-80, pres., 1980—, pres. Hendrick Med. Center Found., 1974—, Southwestern Health Devel. Corp., ASORA, Inc., Spalding Properties, Inc.; instr. Grayson Coll. Pres., Denison Concert Assn., 1969-70; mem. Gov.'s Conf. Health Care Costs; pres. Abilene Philharmonic Assn.; bd. dirs. Abilene Community Theatre; chmn. Abilene United Way, 1977. Named Boss of Year, Denison, 1971-72. Mem. Tex. Hosp. Assn. (chmn. council pub. edn. 1969-74, chmn. Blacklands div. 1969-70), Am. Coll. Hosp. Adminstrs. Baptist. Club: Masons. Home: 1850 Elmwood Dr Abilene TX 79605 Office: PO Box 88 Abilene TX 79604

SPANN, CHARLES HENRY, biologist; b. Brandon, Miss., Sept. 11, 1939; s. Silas Lee and Fannie Burnice (Barnette) S.; A.A., Utica Jr. Coll., 1960; B.S, Tougaloo Coll., 1962; M.S., U. Miss., 1972, Ph.D., 1974; m. Velma Richmond, Apr. 20, 1963; children—Eric L., Marcus D., Charlotte R. Tchr., coach Crystal Springs (Miss.) High Sch., 1966-70; asso. prof. biology Jackson (Miss.) State U., 1974—. Served with USAF, 1962-66. Mem. Jackson Urban League, NAACP, Miss. Acad. Scis., AAAS, Intercollegiate Studies Inst., Am. Soc. Anatomists, Beta Beta Beta, Omega Psi Phi, Baptist. Contbr. articles to profl. jours. Home: 810 Winthrop Ct Jackson MS 39206 Office: Dept Biology Jackson State U Jackson MS 39217

SPANN, GEORGE WILLIAM, mgmt. cons.; b. Cuthbert, Ga., July 21, 1946; s. Glinn Linwood and Mary Grace (Hiller) S.; B.S. in Physics with honors, Ga. Inst. Tech., 1968, M.S., 1970, M.S. in Indsl. Mgmt., 1973; m. Laura Jeanne Nason, June 10, 1967; 1 dau., Tanya Lynne. Engr., Martin Marietta Corp., Orlando, Fla., 1968-70; research scientist Engring. Expt. Sta., Ga. Inst. Tech., 1970-75; v.p., dir. Metrics, Inc., mgmt. and engring. cons., Atlanta, 1973-78, pres., dir., 1978—; mem. Ga. Energy Policy Council, Ga. Metrication Council, NASA applications survey group for landsat follow-on. Regents scholar, 1964. Mem. Am. Soc. Photogrammetry, Urban and Regional Info. Systems Assn., Atlanta Jaycees, Tau Beta Pi, Phi Kappa Phi, Sigma Pi Sigma. Author papers, reports. Home: 3475 Clubland Dr Marietta GA 30067 Office: 290 Interstate North Suite 116 Atlanta GA 30339

SPANO, JOSEPH GRIFFIN, physician; b. Lake Charles, La., Nov. 23, 1938; s. Frank and Martha Katherine (Ellis) S.; student McNeese State Coll., 1956-59; M.D., La. U., 1963; m. Valerie Jo Dosen, June 23, 1979; children—Gregory Todd, Eric Joseph, Stephen Brandon. Intern, Kings County Hosp., N.Y.C., 1963-64; resident in internal medicine VA Hosp., New Orleans, 1964-67; instr. Tulane U., 1965-67; fellow in medicine Harvard U., 1969-70; practice medicine specializing in internal medicine and gastroenterology, Naples, Fla., 1970—; chief staff Naples Community Hosp., 1973-75. Bd. dirs. Collier County Econ. Devel. Council, 1977. Served with USAF, 1967-69. Diplomate Am. Bd. Internal Medicine. Mem. AMA, Fla., So. med. assns., Collier County Med. Soc., Am. Soc. Internal Medicine. Republican. Roman Catholic. Clubs: Port Royal Beach, Naples Bath and Tennis. Home: 718 Springline Dr Naples FL 33940 Office: 385 13th Ave S Naples FL 33940

SPANO, PETER FRANCIS, banker; b. Bklyn., Mar. 24, 1943; s. Joseph P. and Catherine R. (Benedetto) S.; B.B.A., St. John's U., 1964; M.B.A., City U. N.Y., 1972. Mgr. small loans dept. N.Y. Bank for Savs., N.Y.C., 1966-68; 2d v.p. Chase Manhattan Bank, N.Y.C., 1968-77; v.p., sr. investment officer Flagship Nat. Bank of Miami (Fla.), 1977—; v.p. group head Instl. Trust Services, Miami Beach, Fla., 1979—. Mem. Inst. for Quantitative Research in Fin., Fin. Analysts Soc. of Miami (v.p. 1979-80), Econ. Soc. S. Fla. Clubs: Nat. Economists, Miami Bond (dir. 1979-80). Home: 7701 SW 88th St Miami FL 33156 Office: 777 Brickell Ave Miami FL 33131

SPARKMAN, ROBERT SATTERFIELD, surgeon; b. Brownwood, Tex., Feb. 18, 1912; s. Ellis Hugh and Ola (Stanley) S.; B.A., Baylor U., 1935, M.D., 1935, LL.D., 1974; m. Willie Ford Bassett, Feb. 21, 1942. Intern, Cin. Gen. Hosp., 1935-36, resident surgery, 1938-40; intern Good Samaritan Hosp., Lexington, Ky., 1936-37; resident pathology Baylor Hosp., Dallas, 1937-38; practice medicine specializing in surgery, Dallas, 1946—; chief dept. surgery Baylor U. Med. Center, Dallas, 1969—; mem. staff Parkland Meml. Hosp., Dallas; clin. prof. surgery U. Tex. Southwestern Med. Sch., Dallas, 1963—; chief civilian surg. cons. 5th U.S. Army Area, 1950-73, also cons. to surgeon gen. U.S. Army, 1950—. Bd. dirs. Friends of Dallas Pub. Library, 1968—, Assos. of So. Meth. U. Libraries, 1970—; trustee Dallas and Mae Smith Found., v.p., 1971—. Served to col. M.C., AUS, 1940-46; PTO. Decorated Bronze Star; recipient Distinguished Alumnus award Baylor U., 1976, Coll. Medicine, 1976. Diplomate Am. Bd. Surgery. Fellow A.C.S. (bd. govs. 1962-70); mem. Am. (2d v.p. 1977-78), So. (v.p. 1959 pres. 1978), Okla. (hon.) surg. assns., Tex. Surg. Soc. (pres. 1965), Dallas Gen. Surgeons Soc. (pres. 1961), Internat. Soc. Surgery, Dallas So. Clin. Soc., Dallas County Med. Soc., Am., Tex. med. assns., Soc. Med. Cons. to Armed Forces, James D. Rives Surg. Soc., John Shaw Billings History of Medicine Soc. (hon.), Soc. Surgery Alimentary Tract, Société Internationale de Chirurgie, Philos. Soc. Tex., Alpha Omega Alpha. Clubs: Chaparral, Petroleum, Dallas Country. Editor, also prin. author: The Texas Surgical Society, The First Fifty Years, 1965; editor: Minutes of the American Surgical Association 1880-1968, 1972; contbr. articles to profl. jours. Home: 5351 Wenonah Dr Dallas TX 75209 Office: 1004 N Washington St Dallas TX 75204

SPARKMAN, WENDELL BURL, san. engr.; b. Coleman, Tex., Mar. 21, 1913; s. William Burl and Beulah (Parker) S.; B.S. in Civil Engring., Tex. Technol. U., 1939; M.C.E., U. Okla., 1956; m. Lela Ruth Woolf, July 22, 1944; children—Mary Beth Sparkman Kennedy, John Wendell, Roy Burl. Office asst. Tex. Hwy. Dept., Sanderson, 1939; jr. hydraulic engr. U.S. Geol. Survey, Fort Smith, Ark., 1939-40, 41-42 asst. hydraulic engr., 1942-48, asso. hydraulic engr., 1948-56; civil engr. C.E., U.S. Army, 1956-58; san. engr. USAF, Tinker AFB, Okla., 1958-62, civil engr., 1962-63; civil engr. U.S. Bur. Indian Affairs, Gallup, N.Mex., 1964-67; san. engr. HUD, Houston, 1967-77; pvt. practice engring., Houston, 1977—. Mem. Long Range Water Supply Com. Oklahoma City, 1953-54. Registered profl. engr. Tex., Okla. Baptist (deacon 1959-64, 70—). Modern Woodman of Am. Home and Office: 15419 W Hampton Circle Houston TX 77071

SPARKS, CHARLES PAUL, indsl. psychologist; b. nr. Louisa, Ky., Oct. 9, 1915; s. Charles Clarence and Fannie (France) S.; B.S., Ohio State U., 1936, M.A., 1938; postgrad. Tulane U., 1949-51; m. Jean Case, Nov. 19, 1941; children—Paul E., Steven D. Psychologist pub. schs., Mansfield, Ohio, 1937-40; dir. psychol. services Indpls. Pub. Schs., 1940-42; unit head personnel research Adj. Gen. Office, U.S. Army, 1946-48; project dir. Richardson, Bellows, Henry & Co., 1948-50, regional dir., 1951-54, v.p., 1955-62, pres., 1963; personnel research coordinator Exxon Co. U.S.A., Houston, 1964—; adj. prof. U. Houston, 1970—. Served to capt., AUS, 1942-46. Fellow Am. Psychol. Assn. Author: (with D.H. Fryer, E.R. Henry) Outline of General Psychology, 1951. Home: 7715 Dashwood Dr Houston TX 77036 Office: 800 Bell St Houston TX 77001

SPARKS, JIMMIE LEE, educator; b. Belmont, Miss., Oct. 17, 1920; d. Rubin Timotheous and Mary Jane (Cranford) S.; B.S., Miss. State U., 1951, M.Bus. Edn., 1953. Tchr. bus. Burnsville (Miss.) High Sch., 1945-46, Tishomingo (Miss.) High Sch., 1947-59, Red Bay (Ala.) High Sch., 1959-67; tchr. bus. N.W. Ala. State Jr. Coll., Phil Campbell, 1967—. Mem. United Bus. Assn., Nat. Bus. Assn., NEA, Ala. Edn. Assn. Democrat. Mem. Ch. of Christ. Home: Route 1 Dennis MS 38838 Office: NW Ala State Jr Coll Route 3 Phil Campbell AL 35581

SPARKS, JOSEPHINE BEATY, real estate investor; b. El Paso, Tex.; d. Frank and Ruth (Parr) Sparks; B.F.A., B.B.A., So. Methodist U., 1945. Real estate developer Center Six Shopping Center, Village Shopping Center, Corpus Christi, Tex.; dir. Guaranty Nat. Bank & Trust. Dist. dir. U.S. Treasury Dept., 1960; v.p. Gulf Coast Humane Soc., 1960—; pres. Parent-Child Guidance Centers, 1960; mem. Nueces County Hist. Commn., 1975—; mem. Tex. Gov.'s Com. White House Conf. on Children and Youth, 1960; bd. dirs. United Seamen's Service, 1953-63, Tex. Assn. Mental Health, 1962-67, Tex. United Fund, 1962-66; bd. dirs. Goals for Corpus Christi; sec., treas. bd. dirs. Area Conv. and Tourist Bur.; trustee YWCA, 1969-74; bd. govs. Tex. Arts Alliance; adv. council Inst. Texan Cultures, U. Tex.; mem. south Tex. adv. bd. Children's Hosp., San Antonio; v.p. Corpus Christi Conv. and Tourist Bur., 1976-77; sec. bd. trustees S. Tex. Children's Med. Center. Mem. Jr. League Corpus Christi (pres. 1961), Corpus Christi Art Found., Corpus Christi C. of C. (exec. com., bd. dirs.), Corpus Christi Mus., Order of de Pineda, Las Donas de la Corte,

Cotillion Alegre, Navy League U.S., Assn. Jr. Leagues Am. (nat. bd. dirs. 1962-64). Methodist. Home: 205 Rosebud Ln Corpus Christi TX 78404

SPARKS, OTIS VERNON, elec. distbn. co. mgr.; b. Berea, Ky., June, 15, 1951; s. Gene Edward and Patsy Ann (Arnett) S.; B.S., Union Coll., 1974; m. Dinah Sue Yost, July 26, 1975; 1 son, Ryan Ashley. Asst. controller So. Dollar Stores, Inc., Richmond, Ky., 1975-76; asst. office mgr. Jackson County Rural Electric Coop. Corp., McKee, Ky., 1976, officer mgr., 1976—. Pres., Jackson County Little League, 1976-79. Mem. Ky. Electric Co-op Accts. Assn. (sec. 1978-79, v.p. 1979—). Jackson County Jaycees (external v.p. 1977). Club: Kiwanis (sec. treas. 1976-79). Home: PO Box 277 McKee KY 40447 Office: Jackson County RECC PO Box 307 McKee KY 40447

SPARKS, WILLIAM EARL, SR., developer, builder, realtor; b. Danville, Va., Dec. 13, 1945; s. Dewey C. and Irene J. (Lewis) S., Sr.; student N.C. Sch. Arts, 1965-66, Weatherford Coll., 1971-72; B.B.A. magna cum laude Cameron Brown Mortgage Bankers scholar, Alpha Kappa Psi scholar), U. Ga., 1974; m. Elizabeth Bellamy Lattimore, June 18, 1971; children—Catherine Ashley, William Earl, Jr., Robert Lattimore. Vice pres. Lattimore Land Corp., Savannah, Ga., 1974—, dir., 1974—; exec. v.p. Intercoastal Asso., Inc., Savannah, 1975—, dir., 1975—; pres. Heritage Ventures, Inc., Savannah, 1976—, dir., 1976—; pres. Sparks Constrn. Co. Inc. Sec., bd. dirs. St. Andrews on Marsh, Savannah, 1976—; bd. dirs. Islands YMCA, Wilmington Island, 1976—; active with fund raising and campaign cons. with various candidates. Served to capt. U.S. Army, 1967-72. Decorated D.F.C., Bronze Star, and various service and commendation medals; selected for participation in Leadership Savannah Program, 1976. Mem. Savannah, Ga., Nat. homebuilders assns., Savannah, Ga., Nat. assns. of realtors, Savannah C. of C., Phi Kappa Phi, Alpha Kappa Psi, Democrat. Episcopalian. Clubs: Savannah Yacht, Oglethorpe, The Debtors, Wilmington Island Lions (1st v.p. 1975-76). Home: 111 N Millward Ct Savannah GA 31410 Office: PO Box 3775 Savannah GA 31404

SPARLING, GEORGE BRYANT, helicopter co. engr.; b. St. Louis, Aug. 31, 1945; s. George Henry and Deothy Dean (Charlwood) S.; B.S. in Aerospace Engring., U. Tex., Arlington, 1968, postgrad., 1968—; m. Sherry Ann Jones, Nov. 16, 1974; children—Irene Margaret, Jessica Ann. Design engr. Ling Temco Vought Aerospace Co., Dallas, 1968-72; research engr. Bell Helicopter Co., Fort Worth, 1972-79; project engr. Aerospatiale Helicopter Corp., Grand Prairie, Tex., 1979—; pres. Sparling Enterprises, Aircraft Modification & Customizing, Arlington, Tex., 1972—. Instr., Tex. Vol. Hunter Safety Program, 1972—, Operation Orphans, Tex., 1968-72; mem. aerospace engring. curriculum adv. bd. U. Tex. at Arlington. NSF grantee, 1968; registered profl. engr.; certified res. police officer. Mem. Am. Helicopter Soc., Nat., Tex. socs. profl. engrs., Internat. Aerobatic Club, Aerobatic Club Am., Exptl. Aircraft Assn., Nat. Rifle Assn., Mensa, Tau Beta Pi. Episcopalian. Club: Arlington Sportsman's. Home: 2615 Kingston St Arlington TX 76015 Office: 2701 Forum Dr Grand Prairie TX 75051

SPATAFORE, JOHN THOMAS, sales exec.; b. Balt., Aug. 31, 1948; s. Thomas and Vivian Agatha (Fisher) S.; m. Dianna Lynn Gaberdiel, Dec. 1, 1973; children—Angela Marie, Thomas Anthony. Sales rep. metal goods div. Alcan Aluminium, 1968-73; resident sales rep. Keystone Tubular Service Co., St. Petersburg Beach, Fla., 1973-74; sales mgr. Emko Stainless Steel, Hialeah, Fla., 1974-77; sales mgr. Marmon/Keystone Corp., Doraville, Ga., 1977-79, dist. mgr., Atlanta, 1979—. Mem. ASTM, Steel Service Inst. Home: 3042 De Anna Way Lawrenceville GA 30245 Office: 4250 Blue Ridge Industrial Pkwy Lawrenceville GA 30071

SPAULDING, JAMES MICHAEL, flour mill exec.; b. Winchester, Tenn., Feb. 2, 1945; s. James Ross and Jeanette (Reynolds) S.; B.B.A., U. Miami, 1967; M.B.A., Middle Tenn. State U., 1972; m. Evelyn Rushing, Jan. 26, 1974; children—Stephanie, Michael Ross. Bus. mgr. Met. Govt. of Nashville, 1972-74; owner Huntland (Tenn.) Milling Co., 1974—. Alderman, City of Huntland, Tenn., 1976-77, mayor, 1977—. Served with U.S. Army, 1968-70. Mem. Sigma Alpha Epsilon. Democrat. Club: Lion. Home: 304 Main St Huntland TN 37345 Office: Huntland Milling Co 800 Main St Huntland TN 37345

SPAULDING, NANCY JO, educator; b. Cin., Oct. 4, 1937; d. Frank and Gertrude (Cook) Lowther; B.S., U. Tex., Austin, 1959, M.Ed., 1965, postgrad., 1966-78; m. George Winston Spaulding, Jr., Oct. 22, 1959; children—Jo Betsy, Shelley. Tchr., Austin Ind. Sch. Dist., 1959-68, 69-72; instr. U. Tex., Austin, 1968-69; tchr. Round Rock Ind. Sch. Dist. (Tex.), 1972-74, librarian, 1974-77, dir. media, 1977—; mem. adv. com. Edn. Service Center Region XIII. Mem. Tex. Library Assn., ALA, Tex. Tchrs. Assn., NEA, Assn. Ednl. Communications and Tech., Assn. Supervision and Curriculum Devel., Learning Resources Program Dirs. Tex., Phi Delta Kappa, Delta Kappa Gamma. Roman Catholic. Clubs: Ivy Trails Garden. Home: 11906 Brookwood Rd Austin TX 78750 Office: 1300 N Mays St Round Rock TX 78664

SPEAR, HAROLD CHARLES, surgeon; b. N.Y.C., Sept. 29, 1923; s. Harold and Helen (Baker) S.; B.S., Yale U., 1944; M.D., Harvard U., 1947; m. Suzanne Clare Bowmall, June 10, 1947; children—Laurinda Hope, Harold Charles, Alison L. Surg. intern and resident Yale-New Haven Med. Center, 1947-50, 53-56; fellow in surgery Mayo Found., 1950-51; practice medicine specializing in surgery, Miami, Fla., 1956—; clin. asst. prof. surgery U. Miami, 1965—; sr. attending staff North Shore, Parkway Gen., Hialeah, North Miami Gen., Palmetto Gen. hosps. Trustee, North Shore Hosp., 1977—; mem. Com. of 100, Miami Beach, 1977—. Served to capt. M.C., USAF, 1951-53. Diplomate Am. Bd. Surgery, Am. Bd. Thoracic Surgery. Fellow A.C.S.; mem. Am. Coll. Chest Physicians (past chpt. pres.), AMA, Fla. Med. Assn., Dade County Med. Assn., Am. Assn. Thoracic Surgery, Soc. Thoracic Surgeons (founder), So. Thoracic Surg. Assn. Clubs: Bath (Miami Beach); Yale, Harvard (Miami); Miami Shores Country. Contbr. articles to med. jours. Home: 9325 N Bayshore Dr Miami Shores FL 33138 Office: 909 Interama Blvd Suite 501 North Miami Beach FL 33162

SPEARS, ADRIAN ANTHONY, fed. judge; b. Darlington, S.C., July 8, 1910; s. J. Monroe and Mary Agnes (Moore) S.; LL.B., U. S.C., 1934, J.D., 1971; m. Elizabeth Wylie, June 10, 1937 (div. 1973); children—Sara Elizabeth (Mrs. Tor Hultgreen), Claude Monroe, Thomas Wylie, Carolyn Blakely, James Adrian. Admitted to S.C. bar, 1934, Tex. bar, 1937; pvt. practice, Darlington, 1934-36, San Antonio, 1937-61; spl. dist. judge, Tex., 1951; judge U.S. Dist. Ct. for Western Dist. Tex., San Antonio, 1961-62, chief judge, 1962-79. Del. 5th Circuit Jud. Conf., 1955-58; mem. com. adminstrn. criminal law Jud. Conf. U.S., 1969—; mem. faculty Seminar Newly Apptd. Judges, 1971-75; mem. bd. Fed. Jud. Center, Washington, 1971-75. Chmn. bd. adjustment, City Alamo Heights, Tex., 1947-49; charter revision com., City San Antonio, 1949. Del. Democratic Nat. Conv., 1952, 56, 60; mem. Tex. Dem. Exec. Com., 1950-52; trustee Our Lady of Lake U., 1975-77. Recipient Rosewood Gavel award St. Mary's U. Law Sch., 1971. Mem. Fed. (dir. San Antonio chpt.), Am., San Antonio (pres. 1959-60) bar assns., state bars Tex., S.C., Fifth Circuit Dist. Judges Assn. (pres. 1976-77), Pi Kappa Phi, Phi Delta Phi, Omicron Delta Kappa. Methodist. Mason (33 deg., K.T., Shriner), Rotarian. Clubs: San Antonio Country, Monday Morning Quarterback (pres. 1961) (San Antonio). Home: 9004 Wickfield San Antonio TX 78217 Office: 655 E Durango Blvd San Antonio TX 78206

SPEARS, FRANKLIN SCOTT, state supreme ct. justice; b. San Antonio, Aug. 10, 1931; s. Jacob Franklin and Lois Harkey S.; student So. Meth. U., 1948-50; B.B.A., U. Tex., 1954, J.D., 1954; m. Rebecca Errington, Dec. 3, 1977; children by previous marriage—Franklin Scott, Carleton Blaise, John Adrian. Admitted to Tex. bar, 1954; practice law, San Antonio, from 1954; judge 57th Dist. Ct., San Antonio, 1968-78; justice Tex. Supreme Ct., 1978—; mem. Tex. Ho. of Reps., 1958-60; mem. Tex. Senate, 1961-67. Office: PO Box 12248 Capitol Station Austin TX 78711

SPEARS, GEORGE HARRISON, JR., ret. textile co. exec.; b. Bruceville, Tex., June 20, 1915; s. George Harrison and Martha Eunice (Walraven) S.; A.A., Schreiner Inst., 1935; B.B.A., U. Tex.; m. Jane Thompson, Jan. 23, 1948; children—Craig, Rebecca, Mark, David. Accountant United Fruit Co., Guatemala, 1938-39; chief accountant Campbell, Taggart, Dallas, 1940-53; self-employed as C.P.A., Dallas, 1954-70; treas., dir. Facho, Inc., Dallas, 1970-77. Served to lt. USNR, 1942-46. C.P.A., Tex. Mem. Soc. C.P.A.'s. Methodist (trustee 1950-52). Home: 1239 Danville St Richardson TX 75080

SPEARS, GEORGE WOODRIDGE, educator, writer; b. East Point, Ky., Jan. 22, 1913; s. George Kelley and Julia (Clark) S.; student Transylvania U., 1931-32; A.B., Morehead State U., 1935; A.M., U. Ky., 1947, Ph.D. (Univ. grantee), 1953; m. Mary Evalena Gilbert, July 22, 1935; children—Philip and Richard (twins), Sandra. Tchr. pub. schs., Greenup County, Ky., 1935-48; instr. English, U. Ky., 1948-51; asso. prof. Georgetown (Ky.) Coll., 1953-63, prof., 1963-78, prof. emeritus, 1978—. Mem. Poetry Soc. Am., Ky. Poetry Soc., South Atlantic MLA, Ky. Hist. Soc., Phi Beta Kappa, Sigma Tau Delta. Republican. Baptist. Author: (biography) Elizabeth Madox Roberts; (verse) The Feudalist, 1946, River Island, 1963, Concord, 1975; contbr. verse and prose to mags. Home: 905 Shoshone Trail Georgetown KY 40324

SPEARS, JACK, assn. exec.; b. Fort Smith, Ark., Dec. 23, 1919; s. Clifford Grady and Josephine (Ferguson) S.; B.S. cum laude, U. Ark., 1941; m. Helen Jeanne Jackson, May 14, 1942; children—Jack, Richard Thomas. Exec. dir. Tulsa County Med. Soc., 1942; mem. bd. Tulsa County Pub. Health Nursing Service, 1959-67. Bd. dirs. Am. Cancer Soc., Tulsa County, 1945-55, Tulsa Lakes Area Health and Tb Assn., 1952-68. Recipient Distinguished Service award Salvation Army Tulsa, 1973. Mem. Am. Assn. Med. Soc. Execs. (trustee 1967-69), Beta Gamma Sigma, Alpha Kappa Psi. Author: Hollywood-The Golden Era, 1971; The Civil War on the Screen, 1977; contbr. numerous articles on history of motion pictures, films and book revs. to Films in Rev., 1955—. Home: 6208 S Utica St Tulsa OK 74136 Office: Tulsa County Med Soc 750 Utica Sq Medical Center Tulsa OK 74114

SPEARS, JAMES ERNEST, educator; b. Tyronza, Ark., Aug. 3, 1929; B.S. in English and Biology with high honors, Tenn. Poly. Inst., 1956; M.A. in English and History, George Peabody Coll. for Tchrs., 1960; postgrad. in English and Linguistics Ohio U., summers 1967-69, Rensselaer Poly. Inst., summer 1973, M.I.T., summer 1976, U. Mich., summer 1978. Asst. prof. U. Chatanooga, 1963-66, Austin Peay State U., 1966-67; asso. prof. English, U. Tenn., Martin, 1967—. Served with U.S. Army; Korea. Mem. Tenn. Folklore Soc. (pres. 1977-79), Tenn. Philol. Assn., Am. Jersey Cattle Club, Phi Kappa Phi (pres. Chpt. 127 1979-80), Kappa Delta Pi. Clubs: Masons, Shriners. Author: A History of the English Language Manual-Workbook, 1972; (with Mildred Y. Payne) Folk Miscellany of Weakley County Tennessee, 1973; Contbr. articles to folklore jours.; research in linguistics, folklore. Home: Chevy Chase Farm Herman Brooks Rd Martin TN 38237 Office: U Tenn at Martin Martin TN 38238

SPEARS, JOHN HERMAN, lawyer; b. Imboden, Ark., Oct. 10, 1901; s. Ben and Kate (Odom) S.; student U. Ark., 1927-28, Memphis State Coll., 1928-29; m. Willie Sue Robertson, Jan. 4, 1930. Admitted to Ark. bar, 1935, since practiced in West Memphis; dep. pros. atty. Crittenden County (Ark.), 1940-44; city atty. West Memphis, 1945-52; pres., dir., atty. West Memphis Fed. Savs. & Loan Assn.; atty. Bank of West Memphis; atty. Crittenden Meml. Hosp., 1968-78, trustee, 1978—. Mayor of Turrell (Ark.), 1938-39; chmn. Local Draft Bd., 1946-71; trustee So. Bapt. Coll., Walnut Ridge, Ark., Bapt. Meml. Hosp., 1963-75; trustee, Sunday Sch. tchr. First Bapt. Ch., West Memphis. Mem. Crittenden County Bar Assn. (past pres.). Club: West Memphis Country. Home: PO Box 768 West Memphis AR 72301 Office: 500 E Broadway West Memphis AR 72301

SPEARS, JOHN LEONARD, III, gasoline mktg. co. exec.; b. Paintsville, Ky., Sept. 10, 1935; s. John Leonard and Eunice (Daniel) S.; A.B., Centre Coll. of Ky., 1957; m. Donna Gayle Troutman, June 19, 1957; children—Lisa Gayle, Amy Dawn. Disbursement auditor Chevrolet div. Gen. Motors Corp., Norwood, Ohio, 1957-58; various mktg. positions Ashland Oil Inc., Louisville, 1958-72, div. mgr., 1968-72; v.p. Remote Services, Inc., Louisville, 1972-74, pres., 1974—. Dist. tng. chmn. Boy Scouts Am., 1965; bd. dirs. Parkhill Community Planning Council, 1968-72; trustee Ky. Travel Council, 1968-72, Springfield Village, 1979—. Mem. Louisville Oil Men's Club (pres. 1977), Am. Petroleum Inst., Soc. Ind. Gasoline Marketers Am., Ky. Petroleum Marketers Assn. Democrat. Baptist. Mason. Club: Owl Creek Country. Home: 1822 Knollwood Rd Louisville KY 40207 Office: 981 S 3d St Box 660 Louisville KY 40203

SPEARS, LEONARD JOSEPH, hosp. adminstr.; b. Holmwood, La., Sept. 8, 1942; s. Burnis Joseph and Nora Mae (Primeaux) S.; student McNeese U., 1960-61; B.S., Northeast State U., 1965; M.P.H., Tulane U., 1973; m. Debra Louise Keadle, Mar. 1, 1977; children—Alicia, Brian. Pharmacist Merhoff Pharmacy, Metairie, La., 1965-66; dir. pharmacy and central services Rapides Gen. Hosp., Alexandria, La., 1969-71; adminstr. Am. Legion Hosp., Crowley, La., 1973—; adj. instr. Tulane U., New Orleans, 1976-80. Served with U.S. Army, 1966-69. Decorated Army Commendation medal. Mem. Health Systems Agy., La. Hosp. Assn. (dist. pres. 1977-78), Am. Coll. Hosp. Adminstrs., Am. Hosp. Assn., Am. Pharm. Assn., Hosp. Financial Mgmt. Assn., Inst. Mgmt. Accounting, Delta Omega, Phi Delta Chi. Democrat. Roman Catholic. Home: Route 3 Box 214A Crowley LA 70526 Office: 714 N Ave K Crowley LA 70526

SPEARS, ROBERT FIELDS, lawyer; b. Tulsa, Aug. 1, 1943; s. James W. and Berneice F. Spears; B.B.A., Tex. Tech. U., 1965; J.D. with honors, U. Tex., 1968; m. Jacquelyn Castle, May 10, 1961; children—Jeffrey Castle, Sally Fields. Admitted to Tex. bar, 1968, since practiced in Dallas; partner firm Rain, Harrell, Emery, Young & Doke, 1974—. Mem. Am. Bar Assn., State Bar Tex., Chancellors, Order of Coif, Phi Delta Phi, Phi Kappa Phi. Asso. editor Tex. Law Rev., 1967-68. Home: 4001 Druid Ln Dallas TX 75205 Office: 4200 Republic Bank Tower Dallas TX 75201

SPECA, EDWARD JOHN, mgmt. cons., def. analyst; b. Rochester, N.Y., Sept. 13, 1947; s. John and Adrienne Beatrice (Galiffo) S.; B.S., Clarkson Coll. Tech., Potsdam, N.Y., 1969, M.S., 1971; m. Donna Marie Streeter, Aug. 29, 1969; children—Aaron Michael, Kirsten Roxanne. Vol. probation officer St. Lawrence County, N.Y., 1970; sr. systems analyst Def. Systems Mgmt. Coll., Dept. Def., Ft. Belvoir, Va., 1971-77; sr. program analyst Advanced Tech. Inc., Arlington, Va., 1977—; exec. v.p. John Speca Realty, East Rochester, N.Y., 1971—. Active Eastern Prince William Sports Club, youth football, and Prince William Soccer Inc., youth soccer, Woodbridge, Va., also Boy Scouts Am. Served to 1st. lt. C.E., U.S. Army, 1971-77. Cert. data processing, Inst. for Cert. of Computer Profls., 1975. Mem. ASME, Nat. Soc. Profl. Engrs. (asso.), Soc. Am. Mil. Engrs., Assn. for Computing Machinery, Data Processing Mgmt. Assn., Am. Mgmt. Assn., U.S. Golf Assn. (asso.), Triangle, Tau Delta Kappa. Club: Elks (treas. lodge 1976—) Home: 13724 Knowles St Woodbridge VA 22191 Office: Suite 300 1735 Jeff Davis Hwy Arlington VA 22202

SPECK, GEORGE WILLIAM, obstetrician-gynecologist; b. San Angelo, Tex., May 5, 1946; s. Arthur Henderson and Evelyn Eugenia (Kidd) S.; B.A., U. South, Sewanee, Tenn., 1968; M.D., U. Tex., 1972; m. Iris Teresa Watson, June 21, 1969; children—Lena Teresa, William Henderson, Charles Kenneth, Michael Christopher. Intern, U. Tex. Med. Br., 1972-73; resident Scott & White Meml. Hosp., Temple, Tex., 1973-76; practice medicine specializing in Ob-Gyn, Nacogdoches, Tex., 1978—. Served with M.C., USAF, 1976-78. Diplomate Am. Bd. Ob-Gyn. Fellow Am. Coll. Ob-Gyn; mem. AMA, Tex. Med. Assn., Tex. Assn. Ob-Gyn, Phi Beta Kappa. Episcopalian. Home: 3507 Raquet St Nacogdoches TX 75961 Office: 4800A NE Stallings Dr Nacogdoches TX 75961

SPECTOR, DANIEL EARL, educator; b. Pensacola, Fla., Dec. 19, 1942; s. Joseph and Dorothy Margaret Spector; A.B., George Washington U., 1963; postgrad. (NDEA fellow), U. Fla., 1963-64; M.A., U. Tex., 1972, Ph.D. (NDFL fellow), 1975; m. Esta Gelda Rappaport, Aug. 9, 1964; children—Warren Leigh, Susan Artemis. Teaching asst./research asso. U. Tex., Austin, 1971-75; supervisory edn. specialist Mil. Police Sch. U.S. Army, Ft. McClellan, Ala., 1975—; tchr. in field. Sunday Sch. tchr. various local churches. Served with USAFR, 1965-70. Recipient award for Arabic studies Lebanon-Am. Soc., 1973. Mem. Mil. Testing Assn., Am. Hist. Assn., Middle East Inst., Mensa, Phi Alpha Theta. Democrat. Jewish. Club: B'nai B'rith. Contbr. articles to profl. jours. Home: 1615 E Fairway Circle Jacksonville AL 36265 Office: US Army Military Police School Attn ATZN-TDE-S Fort McClellan AL 36205

SPECTOR, MICHAEL JOSEPH, recording co. exec.; b. N.Y.C., Feb. 13, 1947; s. Martin Wilson and Dorothy (Miller) S.; B.S., Washington and Lee U., 1968; m. Margaret Dickson, Sept. 14, 1977. Research chemist Am. Viscose, Phila., 1968-69; pres. MJS Entertainment Corp., Miami, Fla., 1970—, also MJS Internat., Inc.; dir. Plaza Bank of Miami, 1977; partner Old Town Key West Devel. Ltd. (Fla.), 1977—; pres. MJS Entertainment of Can. Inc., Toronto, Ont. Bd. dirs. Goodwill Industries So. Fla. Served with AUS, 1969-70. Recipient Robert E. Lee research grant Washington and Lee U., 1967-68. Mem. Nat. Assn. Record Merchandisers (dir. Nova div.), Country Music Assn., Delta Tau Delta. Clubs: Met., Jockey (Miami); Ocean Reef (Key Largo, Fla.). Patentee synthetic stretching process. Office: PO Box 52-3725 Miami FL 33152

SPEECE, LEGRANDE DETRICK, II, health program exec.; b. Wilkes-Barre, Pa., Aug. 29, 1933; s. William Legrande and Mary (Thomas) S.; student Wilkes Coll., 1955-56, Pensacola Jr. Coll., 1956-57; B.S., Fla. State U., 1959, M.S.W., 1973; m. Delores Joan Aanrud, Feb. 14, 1964. Beverage agt., 1959-67; social worker Fla. Div. Family Services, Pensacola, 1968-71; clin. social worker Pensacola Mental Health Center, 1973-74; dir. Okaloosa (Fla.) Alcohol Center, 1974-79; dir. New Life Alcohol Program, Bapt. Hosp., Pensacola, 1979—; instr. sociology, criminology Troy State U., Eglin AFB, 1975—; mem. adv. bd. Bowling Green (Fla.) Inn, 1976—. Bd. dirs. Fla. Alcohol Coalition, 1973—. Served with USNR, 1952-54. Mem. Nat. Assn. Social Workers, Acad. Cert. Social Workers. Republican. Presbyterian. Clubs: Toastmasters, Civitan. Home: 3 Utah Ct Pensacola FL 32505 Office: New Life Alcohol Program Baptist Hosp 1000 W Moreno St Pensacola FL 32505

SPEED, CLAUDE OSCAR, JR., ednl. cons.; b. Orange, Tex., July 31, 1923; s. Claude Oscar and Exa (Ray) S.; B.S., Tex. A. and M. U., 1950; M.Ed., S.W. Tex. State U., 1971, certificate in Counseling, 1971; m. Dolores Faye Seiler, June 16, 1973; children by previous marriage—Claude Oscar, Laura Annette Speed Carlson, David Robert. Various mech. positions Gulf Oil Corp., Thompson, Tex., 1945-46, Shreveport, La., 1952-60, Houston, 1960-65; mechanic H.L. Peterson Co., Dallas, 1947-48; tchr. Beaumont (Tex.) High Sch., 1950-52; drafting instr vocat. div. Gary Job Corps Center, San Marcos, Tex., 1965-71, vocat. counselor, 1971-72; cons. Tex. Edn. Agy., Austin, 1972—. Served with USAAF, 1942-45; ETO. Decorated Air medal with 2 oak leaf clusters. Mem. Nat. Rifle Assn. (life). Club: Masons. Home: PO Box 329 Flatonia TX 78941 Office: 201 E 11th St Austin TX 78701

SPEED, WORTH MONTYQUE, radio co. exec.; b. Dallas, July 25, 1921; s. Thomas Jackson and Kathleen Louise (Burton) S.; student U. Calif. extension, 1951-52; m. Mary Lou Carrell, July 7, 1945; children—Suzanne Speed Powers, Joanne Speed Miller. Commd. 2d lt., USAAF (now USAF), 1940, advanced through grades to col., 1964; pilot, 1944-45; prisoner of war, Germany, 1945; at Pentagon, 1966-70; chief logistics Hdqrs., 1970-73; ret., 1973; program mgr. Collins Radio Co. div. Rockwell Internat., Richardson, Tex., 1975—. Mem. DeSoto Library Bd., 1975-76. Decorated Legion of Merit with 3 clusters, Air medal with 6 clusters, Purple Heart; Croix de Guerre avec palme (France). Mem. DeSoto C. of C. (exec. com. 1975), Armed Forces Communications Assn., Nat. Mgmt. Assn., Combat Pilots Assn., Ret. Officers Assn., Air Force Assn., Am. Legion. Mem. Ch. of Christ. Clubs: Masons, Shriners. Home: 621 Glenview Circle Garland TX 75040 Office: Alma Rd Richardson TX 75115

SPEEKS, EMELDA LOUISE, speech pathologist, audiologist; b. Lake Providence, La., Mar. 2, 1952; d. Tumpsey Samuels Speeks and Teresa Smith Speeks Brown. B.S., So. U., 1974; M.A., Western Mich. U., 1975. Cons. Speech and hearing Hammond (La.) State Sch., 1975-76, Caddo Parish (La.) Schs., 1976-78; parttime audiologist Mollie Webb Speech and Hearing Center, Shreveport, La., 1978; cons. speech and hearing La. State U., Baton Rouge, 1978-79; early childhood (speech/lang.) therapist E. Baton Rouge Parish Schs., 1979—. Active Democratic party. Thurgood Marshall fellow, 1974-75. Mem. Am. Speech and Hearing Assn., So. U. Speech Pathology and Audiology Alumni Assn. Methodist. Home: 9818 Ave J Baton Rouge LA 70807

SPEERS, TERYL TOWNSEND, painter; b. Coronado, Calif., May 9, 1938; d. Robert Lee and Elizabeth Terrell (Archer) Townsend; student U. Tex., 1956, Froman Art Sch., Cloud Croft, N.Mex., 1970, Molno Sch. Art, N.Y.C., 1975, 76; pupil of Millard Sheets, Chen Chi, Edgar Whitney, Charles Reid, 1972-75; m. Don Philip Speers, Mar. 15, 1957; children—Don Philip, Shawn Elizabeth. One-woman shows: Robert Rice Gallery, Houston, 1976, Country Gallery, N.Y.C.,

1975, Kirby Gallery, Houston, 1977, Butler Inst. Am. Art, Youngstown, 1977, Watercolor U.S.A., Springfield, 1977, Potomac Gallery, Old Towne, Va., 1978; 2-artist show Foothills Art Center, Golden, Colo., 1976; represented in juried exhbns.: Albuquqerque Mus. Fine Art, Tucson Mus. Art, Birmingham (Ala.) Mus. Art, NAD; tchr. Canary Hill Galleries, Houston, 1974-77, Tex. Art Supply, Inc., Houston, 1976-77, Tex. Inst. Child Psychology, Houston, 1975-76, Houston Ind. Sch. Dist., 1975; mem. sch. art com. Houston Livestock Show and Rodeo, 1976-78; mem. cultural affairs com. Houston C. of C., 1977, 78. Recipient 3d award Nat. Small Painting Show, 1976; Century award merit, 1974, Art Assn. award, 1977 and Rocky Mountain Nat. Show. Mem. Watercolor Soc. Houston (pres. 1975, chmn. advisory bd. 1976; Jo Taylor award, 3d award 1975, spl. award for service 1976), Southwestern (pres. Houston 1975; Top Merit award 1976), Ala. watercolor socs., Foothills Art Center, Western Fedn. Watercolor Socs., Art League Houston. Republican. Episcopalian. Home and Studio: 3763 Westerman St Houston TX 77005 also 11 Old South Wharf Nantucket MA

SPEIGHT, DAVID LARRY, educator; b. Paris, Tenn., July 28, 1943; s. David Ernest and Frances Wilma (Duncan) S.; B.S., U. Tenn., 1965, M.S., 1967; postgrad. N.C. State U., summer 1969, U. Kans., 1967-68, Ariz. State U., summer 1971; m. Joyce Tallent, Aug. 29, 1965; children—David Henry, Jonathan Mark. Faculty, Cleveland (Tenn.) State Community Coll., 1968—, asso. prof. biology, 1968—. Deacon, Central Ch. of Christ, Cleveland, 1973—. NSF grantee, 1969-73. Mem. NEA, Tenn. Edn. Assn., E. Tenn. Edn. Assn., Cleveland State Community Coll. Edn. Assn., Tenn. Acad. Sci. Home: 4527 Lee Dr NW Cleveland TN 37311 Office: Box 1205 Cleveland State Community Coll Cleveland TN 37311

SPEIGHT, RONALD EARL, coll. adminstr.; b. Greene County, N.C., May 9, 1949; s. Claude Lee and Geneva (Forbers) S.; B.A., N.C. Central U., 1971, M.A., 1973; m. Jacqueline Sanders, June 2, 1979. Dir. Learning Center, vis. lectr. N.C. Central U., Durham, 1973-74; dir. Learning Lab., instr. edn. S.C. State Coll., Orangeburg, 1974—. Named Man of Year, Phi Beta Sigma, 1971. Mem. Assn. Ednl. Media and Tech., AAUP, Phi Delta Kappa, Phi Beta Sigma. Democrat. Methodist. Club: Masons. Home: 471 Boulevard NE Orangeburg SC 29115 Office: PO Box 1955 SC State Coll Orangeburg SC 29117

SPEIGNER, WILLIAM HENRY, deaf interpreter; b. Florala, Ala., Oct. 22, 1929; s. William Henry and Sallie Mae (King) S.; student Howard Coll., 1954-55, 57; A.B., Truette McConell Coll., 1957; grad. Bapt. Bible Inst., 1962, Associated Builders and Contractors Carpentry Schs., 1977. Interpreter, First Bapt. Ch., DeFuick Spring, Fla., 1960-61; house father Ala. Sch. for Deaf, Taladega, 1963-64; interpreter Calvary Bapt. Ch., Prattville, Ala., 1964, Westside Bapt. Ch., Jasper, Ala., 1965-69, Tabernical Bapt. Ch., Orlando, Fla., 1970-72; interpreter Grace Bible Bapt., Leesburg, Fla., 1973-75; head interpreter Tabernacle Bapt. Ch., Orlando, 1977—; now constrn. worker, interpreter for deaf. Served with AUS, 1950-52. Mem. Fla. Registery for Deaf, Register Interpreters for the Deaf, Internat. Assn. Parents of Deaf. Home: 426 N John St Orlando FL 32811

SPEIR, WILLIAM BYRD, planning cons.; b. Savannah, Ga., Nov. 21, 1921; s. Allen William and Eura Byrd (Pelham) S.; B.S. in Indsl. Engring., U. Ala., 1949; m. Lucy Kirkland, Apr. 1, 1950; children—Linda, William Byrd. Engr. div. material handling Continental Gin Co., Birmingham, Ala., 1949-50; engr. So. Services Inc., power plant engring., Birmingham, 1950-51; engr. Rust Engring. Co., engring. and constrn., Birmingham, 1952-62, mgr. indsl. planning, 1963-73, mgr. urban planning, 1971-73; pres. W. B. Speir & Assos., land use planners, Birmingham, 1973—. Mem. Gov. Ala. Cost Control Survey Team, 1972. Served with USAAF, 1942-46, USAF, 1951-52. Named Outstanding Indsl. Engr. S.E. Region Am. Inst. Indsl. Engrs., 1970. Mem. Capstone Engring. Soc. (dir.), Am. Inst. Indsl. Engrs., Am. Inst. Planners, So. Indsl. Devel. Council, Urban Land Inst., Theta Tau. Republican. Christian Scientist. Clubs: Kiwanis, The Club Inc. Contbr. articles on land use planning and site selection to profl. jours. Home: 3724 Briaroak Circle Birmingham AL 35223 Office: PO Box 7422 Birmingham AL 35223

SPELCE, FRANK, JR., mfg. tech. engr.; b. Fate, Tex., June 18, 1918; s. Frank Jones and Chellie (McLendon) S.; student Howard Payne U., 1938; m. Dona Gene Eagle, Feb. 12, 1943; 1 dau., Mary Carol. Tool and ops. planner Gen. Dynamics Corp., Ft. Worth, 1942-53, asst. supr.-tool and ops. planning, 1953-57, tool and mfg. engr., 1957-73, sr. mfg. tech. engr., 1973-79, project mfg. tech. engr., 1979—. Mem. Nat. Mgmt. Assn., Soc. for Advancement of Material and Process Engring. Specialist in the field of tooling and mfg. of advanced composites. Home: 4236 Locke Ave Fort Worth TX 76107 Office: PO Box 748 M/Z 6217 Fort Worth TX 76101

SPENCE, FLOYD DAVIDSON, congressman; b. Columbia, S.C., Apr. 9, 1928; s. James Wilson and Addie (Lucas) S.; A.B., U.S.C., 1952, J.D., 1956; m. Lula Hancock Drake, Dec. 22, 1952 (dec.); children—David, Zack, Benjamin, Caldwell. Admitted to S.C. bar, 1956; partner firm Callison and Spence, West Columbia, 1956—; mem. S.C. Ho. Reps., 1956-62; mem. S.C. Senate, 1966-70, minority leader, 1966-70, chmn. joint internal security com., 1969; mem. 92d-96th congresses from S.C.; mem. Com. on Standards Ofcl. Conduct, Armed Services Com. Past chmn. Ridge dist., also Granby dist. Boy Scouts Am., former scoutmaster, also exec. bd. S.C. council; chmn. Lexington County Mental Health Assn., 1959; mem. exec. com. bd. dirs. Mid-Carolina Mental Health Assn., 1970. Capt. USNR. Mem. Am. Legion (mem. counter-subversive activities com. 1966, 67), VFW, Res. Officers Assn., Navy League, Columbia Carillon (dir. 1966-70), West Columbia-Cayce, Lexington, S.C. chambers commerce. Lutheran. Contbr. articles on communism to profl. jours.; lectr. in field. Home: Box 869 Lexington SC 29072 Office: 1835 Assembly St Room 1449 Columbia SC 29201

SPENCE, FRANK RICHARD, cons. firm exec.; b. Lancaster County, Pa., Sept. 22, 1935; s. Frank Maynard and Mary Elizabeth (Loomis) S.; B.A. (Regents Alumni scholar), U. Mich., 1959, M.P.A., 1960; m. Marjorie Elaine Hendricks, June 20, 1958; children—Christopher Scott, Gregory Todd, Jeffrey Allan. Asst. city mgr. Park Forest (Ill.), 1960-61, Pensacola (Fla.), 1961-63; city mgr. North Palm Beach (Fla.), 1963-66; adviser to Govt. Liberia, W.Africa, 1966-68; asst. city mgr. City of Miami Beach (Fla.), 1968-72, city mgr., 1972-76; county adminstr. Alachua County (Fla.), Gainesville, 1977-80; pres. Frank Spence & Assos., Inc., govt. cons. service, Gainsville, 1980—; chmn., chief exec. ofcls. com., mem. exec. com., council mem. Manpower Planning Council of Met. Dade County, Miami, 1974-76. Bd. dirs. Meth. Ch., Alachua County United Way, 1978-79; corp. mem. United Way of Greater Miami, 1975-76; chmn. bd. trustees Bass Mus., Miami Beach, 1972-76; nat. bd. govs. Grad. Program in Pub. Adminstrn., Nova U., Ft. Lauderdale, Fla., 1974-77; charter mem. Alachua County Research and Devel. Authority, 1978—; mem. Fla. Manpower Services Council, 1977-79; mem. adv. bd. Human Resource Center, Fla. Internat. U., 1975-76. Served with Mil. Police, AUS, 1954-56; ETO. Life fellow Fla. Kiwanis Found.; mem. Am. Soc. Pub. Adminstrn. (nat. council 1974-77, exec. com., pres. S.Fla. chpt. 1971, chmn. Joint Task Force on Pub. Adminstrn. and Urban Governance 1974-76), Internat. City Mgrs. Assn. (chmn. Joint Task Force on Public Adminstrn. and Urban Governance 1974-76, Urban Task Force for Africa), Dade County (pres. 1974-75), Palm Beach County (past pres.) city mgrs. assns., Nat. Assn. County Adminstrs., Fla. Assn. County Adminstrs. (pres. 1978-79), Fla. City and County Mgrs. Assn. (dir. 1974-76), Fla. League Cities (tax and fin. com. 1974-76), U. Mich. Alumni Assn. (nat. dir. 1974-77, pres. 4th dist. 1972-74). Club: Kiwanis (pres. 1974). Home: 512 SW 80th Blvd Gainesville FL 32608 Office: 502 NW 75th St Suite 317 Gainesville FL 32601

SPENCE, JANE CAROL, rehab. services adminstr.; b. Memphis, Aug. 29, 1947; d. Herman J. and H. Christine (Brackin) Wilson; B.S.E., Ark. State U.; m. Jim Spence, Apr. 13, 1968; 1 son, Kevin Lance. Tchr., Marked Tree (Ark.) Public Schs., 1970-71; supr. client services Sheltered Workshop Crittenden County Inc., West Memphis, Ark., 1972—. Mem. Am. Vocat. Assn., Nat. Rehab. Assn., Ark. Vocat. Edn. and Spl. Needs Personnel, Vocat. Evaluation-Work Adjustment Assn. Baptist. Home: 394 LP Mann St Marion AR 72364 Office: 208 N 4th St West Memphis AR 72301

SPENCE, JOHN MORGAN, JR., utility co. exec.; b. LaFayette, Ala., Jan. 2, 1923; s. John Morgan and Edna E. (McCarley) S.; B.S., Auburn U., 1949; m. Norma Lee Chadwick, Aug. 4, 1945; 1 dau., Deborah Ellen. Extension farm agt. Ala. Extension Service, Florence, 1949; asst. mgr. Lauderdale County Coop., Florence, 1949-52; dist. and div. rural service engr. Ala. Power Co., Tuscaloosa, 1952-63; sr. agrl. engr., 1963-67, supr. sales tng., 1968-75, mgr. ednl. devel. and tng. support, 1976-78, asst. to v.p. human resources, 1978-1979, mgr. consumer affairs, Birmingham, 1979—. Served with AUS, 1943-45. Recipient hon. state farmer degree Future Farmers Am., 1959, hon. mem. Ala. 4-H Clubs, 1963; registered profl. engr., Ala. Mem. Nat. Mgmt. Assn. (Leadership award 1969), Am. Soc. Tng. and Devel., Indsl. Audio Visual Assn., Gamma Sigma Delta. Presbyterian. Home: 4521 Linwood Dr Birmingham AL 35222 Office: PO Box 2641 Birmingham AL 35291

SPENCE, JUDSON CAUTHEN, educator; b. Elizabeth City, N.C., Mar. 17, 1921; s. John Paul and Nancy Estelle (Cauthen) S.; B.A., The Citadel, 1943; Diplome, Sorbonne, 1952; M.A., Fla. State U., 1964, Ph.D., 1968; m. Mary Virginia Truett, July 1, 1943; children—Judson Cauthen, Patrick Truett, Edward Lee, Merry Lynn. Commd. 2d lt. U.S. Army, 1944, advanced through grades to lt. col., 1961; instr. EUCOM Intelligence Sch., Oberammergau, Ger., 1946-48; instr. French U.S. Mil. Acad., West Point, N.Y., 1952-55; sr. aide-de-camp, interpreter to comdg. gen., airborne advisor, Vietnam, 1955-56; ret., 1963; asst. prof. French and German, The Citadel, Charleston, S.C., 1965-66, prof. modern langs., 1970—; prof., chmn. dept. fgn. langs., dean of men Bapt. Coll., Charleston, 1966-70. Decorated Medal of Honor (Vietnam); NDEA doctoral fellow, 1963; Citadel Devel. Found. grantee, 1972, 74, 79. Mem. Am. Assn. for Higher Edn., South Atlantic Modern Lang. Assn., Am. Council Teaching of Fgn. Langs., Am. Translators Assn., S.C. Assn. Tchrs. of Fgn. Langs. Republican. Baptist. Home: 1750 I'on Ave Sullivan's Island SC 29482 Office: Capers Hall The Citadel Charleston SC 29409

SPENCE, PAUL HERBERT, librarian; b. Geraldine, Ala., Dec. 25, 1923; s. John Clardy and Leila Gertrude (Carrell) S.; student Duke U., 1942-43; A.B., Emory U., 1948, M.A., 1956; Ph.D., U. Ill., 1969; m. Ruth McCollough Schmidt, May 9, 1954; children—John Carrell, Peter Schmidt, Robert McCollough. Asst. reference librarian Emory U., Atlanta, 1950-53; chief periodical reference librarian Air Univ. Library, Maxwell AFB, Ala., 1953-56; dir. Air Force Inst. Tech., Wright-Paterson AFB, Ohio, 1957-58; social studies librarian U. Notre Dame, South Bend, Ind., 1959-60; asst. dir. social studies U. Nebr., Lincoln, 1960-63; history and polit. sci. librarian U. Ill., Urbana, 1963-66; asst. dir. public services U. Ga., Athens, 1966-70; librarian U. Ala., Birmingham, 1970—. Served with U.S. Army, 1943-46. Mem. Southeastern Library Network (past dir.), Ala. Library Assn. (treas. 1975-76), Southeastern Library Assn. (pres.-elect 1979-80), ALA, Ala. Hist. Assn., Am. Mgmt. Assn., Newcomen Soc. N. Am. Presbyterian. Home: 614 Warwick Rd Birmingham AL 35209 Office: Sterne Library U Ala in Birmingham University Sta Birmingham AL 35294

SPENCE, ROGER WILLIAM, telephone co. exec.; b. Portsmouth, Va., Jan. 28, 1949; s. Millard Walker and Grace (Nichols) S.; B.S., Va. Poly. Inst. and State U., 1970; M.B.A., Tex. Christian U., 1973. Mgr. computer ops. C. & P. (Bell) Telephone Co., Richmond, Va., 1974-78, mgr. toll and cash 1978-79, mgr. customer billing, 1979—. Active Richmond Jr. Achievement, Greater Richmond United Givers Fund. Served to 1st lt. USAF, 1971-74. Recipient Comdt.'s award USAF, 1969. Mem. Adminstrv. Mgmt. Soc., Richmond Jaycees, Va. Tech. Alumni Assn. (pres. Dallas-Ft. Worth chpt. 1973). Republican. Methodist. Home: 11810 S Briarpatch Dr Midlothian VA 23113 Office: 3011 Hungary Spring Rd Richmond VA 23228

SPENCE, TERRY GEORGE, dentist; b. Massawadox, Va., Sept. 3, 1951; s. George Dewey and Ellen Marie (Hiltebrand) S.; B.S. in Biology, Lynchburg Coll., 1973; D.D.S., Med. Coll. Va., 1977. Gen. practice dentistry, Exmore, Va., 1978—; mem. staff Nassadow Meml. Hosp. Mem. Acad. Gen. Dentistry, ADA, Va. Dental Assn., Tidewater Dental Assn., Am. Orthodontic Soc., Am. Soc. Advancement of Anesthesia in Dentistry, Am. Soc. Dentistry for Children. Republican. Methodist. Club: Ruritan. Home: Box 147 Quinby VA 23423 Office: Box 819 Exmore VA 23350

SPENCE, WILLIAM WALLACE, III, auditor; b. Balt., June 28, 1943; s. William Wallace and Mary Elizabeth (Hughes) Spence; B.S. in Accounting, Loyola Coll., Balt., 1965; m. Eileen Theresa Hall, Feb. 19, 1966; children—Stephen Robert, Matthew William, Gregory Brion. With Western Electric Co., Balt., 1968-70, sr. auditor, 1970-72, sr. auditor Atlanta, 1972-74, head dept. auditing, 1974-78, head dept. auditing, N.C., 1978-79, head dept. EDP auditing, 1979—. Pres. Community Civic Group, Norcross, Ga., 1973. Served with Ordnance Corps, U.S. Army, 1966-71. Mem. Inst. Internal Auditors (pres. Atlanta chpt. 1977-78). Republican. Roman Catholic. Home: 109 Woodleigh Ct James Town NC 27282 Office: Mt Hope Church Rd Greensboro NC 27405

SPENCER, FERN E. SMITH (MRS. LUCIAN W. SPENCER), civic worker; b. Wheeler, Tex., May 13, 1920; d. Bonner and Laura (Lamberth) Smith; student Amarillo Jr. Coll.; m. Lucian Witten Spencer, May 20, 1949; children—Patricia Ann (Mrs. W.C. McElhannon), Laura Beth (Mrs. Robert D. Hill, Jr.), Lucian W. Asso. editor The Arlington Woman mag. Bd. dirs. Moore County Concert Assn., Girl Scout council, Dallas Civic Ballet, Dallas Symphony Orch. League; vol. worker Presbyn. Hosp.; mem. San Antonio Little Theatre; bd. dirs. Arlington Community Hosp. Aux. Named Woman of Year, Beta Sigma Phi, 1962. Presbyn. (deaconess., v.p. women's assn.). Clubs: Woodlawn Garden; Arlington Woman's (bd. dirs.); Dumas Garden, 1932 Study; Tanglewood Hills Country. Home: 1119 Western Blvd Arlington TX 76013 Office: 1209 S Bowen Rd Suite 202 Arlington TX 76013

SPENCER, JOE ED, coll. adminstr.; b. San Angelo, Tex., Mar. 28, 1934; s. Joseph Edgar and Jessie Lee (Ashmore) S.; B.B.A., Sul Ross State U., 1961; M.B.A. in Mgmt., Tex. A. and M. U., 1969; m. Carolyn Ann Schwartz, July 4, 1959; children—Carla Sue, John David. Instr. bus. Sul Ross State Coll., 1962-64, dean of men, 1964-65; mgr. ElDorado Woolens, Inc., (Tex.), 1965-68; bursar Tarrant County Jr. Coll., Ft. Worth, 1968-73, dir. bus. services, 1973—. Served with U.S. Army, 1956-58. Mem. Nat. Assn. Ednl. Buyers, Tex. Tchrs. Assn., Tex. Assn. Pub. Jr. Bus. Officers, Aircraft Owners and Pilots Assn., Tex. Farm Bur., Tex. Sheep and Goat Raisers Assn. (dir.), Alpha Chi, Phi Delta Kappa. Republican. Presbyterian. Clubs: Masons; Ft. Worth Farm and Ranch. Home: 105 SE Harris St Burleson TX 76028 Office: 1400 Electric Service Bldg Fort Worth TX 76102

SPENCER, JOSE LUIZ DE CASTRO E SILVA, aerospace engr.; b. Lisbon, Portugal, Sept. 11, 1934; s. Augusto Vaz Spencer and Antónia Lúcia Sousa Dias de Castro e Silva; came to U.S., 1970; Licenciado em Matematica, U. Lisbon, 1966, Engenheiro Geografo, 1966; Ph.D. in Aerospace Engring. (Fulbright scholar), U. Tex., 1975; m. Maria Teresa Simoes da Silva Paes de Matos, Oct. 8, 1961; children—João Augusto, Maria da Graca. Sec. to gov. Dist. Inhambane, Mozambique, 1958-61; instr. dept. math. U. Lourenco Marques (Mozambique), 1966-70; teaching asst. math. and dynamics U. Tex., Austin, 1970-75; sr. engr. McDonnell Douglas Tech. Services Co., Houston, 1975-78, task mgr., 1977-78; engr. scientist Computer Scis. Corp., 1978—; lectr. astrodynamics, 1975; lectr. tech. math. U. Houston, 1976—. Registered profl. engr., Tex. Mem. Am. Inst. Aeros. and Astronautics, Smithsonian Assos., S. African Math. Soc., Nat. Mgmt. Assn., Sigma Gamma Tau. Home: 2802 Pilgrims Point Dr Webster TX 77598 Office: 1300 Bay Area Blvd Houston TX 77058

SPENCER, LORRAINE BARNEY, biologist, educator; b. Odgen, N.Y., Jan. 26, 1924; d. Elmer Cecil and Edna Justine (Zinter) Barney; B.S. (Dana scholar), Guilford Coll., 1966; M.A. (Univ. scholar), Wake Forest U., 1970, Ph.D. (Research fellow), 1973; m. Richard Earl Spencer, Sept. 12, 1942 (div. 1961); children—Linda, Susan S. Foushee, Deborah (Mrs. Curtis L. Mitchell), Nancy (Mrs. Charles L. Hertlein). Instr. biology lab. Wake Forest U., Winston Salem, N.C., 1968-72, research fellow, 1972-73; biol. researcher, Greensboro, N.C., 1973—; adj. prof. Guilford Coll., Greensboro, 1974; asst. prof. St. Augustine's Coll., Raleigh, N.C., 1974—. Mem. So. Appalachian Bot. Club, Soc. Econ. Botany, Phycol. Soc. Am., N.C. Acad. Sci., Internat. Assn. Plant Taxonomy, Bot. Soc. Am., Assn. S.E. Biologists, A.A.A.S., Am. Inst. Biol. Scis., Sigma Xi. Contbr. articles to profl. jours. Home: 315 White Oak Dr Cary NC 27511 Office: Box 554 Dept Biology St Augustine's Coll Raleigh NC 27611

SPENCER, MARY MILLER, civic worker, club woman; b. Comanche, Tex., May 25, 1924; d. Aaron Gaynor and Alma (Grissom) Miller; B.S., North Tex. State U., 1943; 1 dau., Mara Lynn. Cafeteria dir. Mercedes (Tex.) Pub. Schs., 1943-46; home economist coordinator All-Orange Dessert Contest, Fla. Citrus Commn., Lakeland, 1959-62, 64; children's services worker Fla. Div. Family Services, Lakeland, 1969-70, social worker, 1970—. Tchr. purchasing sch. lunch dept. Fla. Dept. Edn., 1960. Clothing judge Polk County (Fla.) Youth Fair, 1951-68, Polk County Federated Women's Clubs, 1964-66; pres. Dixieland Elementary Sch. PTA, 1955-57, Polk County Council PTA's, 1958-60; dist. 7. Fla. Congress Parents and Tchrs., 1961-63; chmn. pub. edn. com. Polk County unit Am. Cancer Soc., 1959-60, bd. dirs., 1962-72; charter mem., bd. dirs. Lakeland YMCA; sec. Greater Lakeland Community Nursing Council, 1965-69; trustee, vice chmn. Polk County Eye Clinic, 1962-64, pres., 1964—; bd. dirs. Polk County Scholarship and Loan Fund, Inc.; mem. exec. com. West Polk County (Fla.) Community Welfare Council, 1960-62, 65-68; mem. budget and audit com. Greater Lakeland United Fund, 1960-62; mem. adv. bd. Polk County Juvenile and Domestic Relations Ct., 1960-69,; mem. exec. com. Sun Coast Health Council, 1968-72, vol., disaster res. social worker ARC, 1970—; mem. Fla. Health and Welfare Council, 1970-73, Polk County Mental Health Assn., 1970—. Sec. bd. dirs. Fla. West Coast Ednl. Television, 1960—. Mem. Fla. Congress Parents and Tchrs. (hon. life, pub. relations chmn. 1962-66.), Fla. Assn. Health and Social Services, Fla. Pub. Health Assn., Nat. Welfare Fraud Assn., Alumni Assn. North Tex. State U. Democrat. Methodist. Mem. Order Eastern Star. Home: 535 W Beacon Rd Lakeland FL 33803 Office: PO Box 2161 Lakeland FL 33803

SPENCER, MORRIS GRADY, financial investor; b. Wynnewood, Okla., Sept. 28, 1907; s. Edward L. and Exie (Hunter) S.; B.M.E., U. Okla., 1930; postgrad. Mass. Inst. Tech., 1931-32; m. Mildred Colson, May 6, 1936; children—Nelson H., Janet W. Geophysicist, Geophys. Service, Inc., Dallas, 1930-38; supt. devel. Coronado Corp., Dallas, 1938-41; pres. Las Tecas Petroleum Co., Dallas, 1942-44; pres. Comanche Corp., Dallas, 1940-50; pvt. fin. investor, Dallas, 1950—; pres., dir. Seismogram Library Corp., Dallas, 1953—. Trustee, The Hockaday Sch., St. Mark's Sch. of Tex. Mem. Am. Assn. Petroleum Geologists, Soc. Exploration Geophysicists, Urban Land Inst., Internat. Council Shopping Centers. Clubs: Dallas Petroleum, Brook Hollow Golf. Home: 3615 Lexington Ave Dallas TX 75205 Office: 2800 Routh St Suite 200 Dallas TX 75201

SPENCER, SHERWOOD, lawyer; b. Ashland, Ky., Jan. 23, 1913; s. Holmes A. and Mary (Baker) S.; B.B.A., U. Fla., 1933, J.D., 1936; LL.D., Nova U., 1975; m. Jean Rowe, Dec. 15, 1939; children—William Sherwood, Carol Ann. Admitted to Fla. bar, 1936, U.S. Supreme Ct. bar, 1963; practice law, Hollywood, Fla., 1939—; city atty. Hollywood, 1949-53. Dir., gen. counsel Hollywood Fed. Savs. & Loan Assn.; dir. Southeast Bank of Broward. Mem. grievance com. 15th Jud. Circuit, 1950-55; mem. com. of 100. Mem. Broward County (pres. 1949), Fla. (bd. govs. 1953-63, dir. real property sect. 1971—), Am. (standing com. unauthorized practice of law) bar assns., Fla. Title Assn. (chmn. title examiners' div. 1950-51). Clubs: Rotary, Emerald Hills Country, Hollywood Yacht (vice commodore 1948), Lauderdale Yacht. Home: 1600 Rodman St Hollywood FL 33021 Office: Hollywood Fed Bldg Hollywood FL 33022

SPENCER, WARREN FRANK, educator; b. Swan Quarter, N.C., Jan. 27, 1923; s. Carroll Baxter and Lucille Gertrude (Mann) S.; student George Washington U., 1942, U. Fla., 1942-43; B.S.S. cum laude, Georgetown U., 1947; M.A., U. Pa., 1949, Ph.D., 1955; m. Elizabeth Jolanda Toth, Sept. 6, 1947; children—Lucille Mann, Carroll Baxter. Instr. history Salem Coll., Winston-Salem, N.C., 1950-53, asst. prof., 1953-56; asst. prof. Old Dominion U., Norfolk, Va., 1956-57, asso. prof., 1957-61, prof., 1961-67, chmn. div. social studies and dept. history, 1961-67; prof. history U. Ga., Athens, 1967—, Sandy Beaver teaching prof. history, 1978—. Served with AUS, 1943-45. Vis. scholar, Duke, 1952; Am. Philos. Soc. fellow, 1958, 70, 75; recipient 1st Ann. Faculty award Old Dominion U., 1961-62, Best History Book Published in 1970 award Phi Alpha Theta, 1971; named Outstanding Honors Tchr., U. Ga., Athens, 1977. Mem. Am. Hist. Assn., So. Hist. Assn. (chmn. European History sect. program com. 1970), Ga. Assn. Historians (pres. 1979-80), Soc. French Hist. Studies, Phi Alpha Theta. Democrat. Episcopalian. Co-founder, pres. Norfolk Hist. Soc., 1966-67. Author: (with Lynn M. Case) The United States and France: Civil War Diplomacy, 1970. Contbr. to profl. jours. Home: 290 Fortson Dr Athens GA 30606 Office: Dept History Univ Georgia Athens GA 30602

SPENCER, YVONNE GOOLSHY, nurse, educator; b. Pine Hill, N.C., Dec. 6, 1934; d. Massassa Joseph and Lacy (Malloy) Goolsby; R.N., M.S.Ed., N.C. A&T State U., 1969; B.S.N., U. Cin., 1973;

children—Thurman Maurice, William Gregory. Instr., N.C. A. and T. State U., Greensboro, 1971—. Mem. Nat. League Nursing, N.C. Nurses Assn., Santa Flomena Nurses Honor Soc., Delta Sigma Theta, Sigma Theta Tau. Democrat. Methodist. Office: Noble Hall Duldey St Greensboro NC 27411

SPENCLEY, GAILMARIE HANNA, temporary employment contractor; b. Winthrop, Mass., July 31, 1941; d. Galil and Maria (Sparaco) Hanna; student Burdett Coll., Boston; children—Deborah Ann Spencly Linn, Billy Ray. Terminal mgr. Air Shipper Airlines, also Asso. Air Freight, Logan Internat. Airport, East Boston, Mass.; mgr. Manpower, Inc., Great Lakes, Ill., Long Beach and Downey, Calif.; br. mgr. Adia Interim Services, Torrance and Garden Grove, Calif.; v.p. Abacus/Indsl. Labor, Inc., Virginia Beach and Richmond, Va., 1975—. Brownie and Girl Scout leader; den mother Cub Scouts; active Los Angeles C. of C. Youth Job Procurement Program, summer 1975, Irvine (Calif.) Indsl. League. Mem. Nat. Assn. Temp. Services, USN Ombudsman, Norfolk C. of C., Am. Bus. Women's Assn. (chmn.). Office: Abacus Temporary Services 5620 Virginia Beach Blvd Virginia Beach VA 23462 also 7100 W Broad Street Rd Richmond VA 23229

SPERO, MORTON BERTRAM, lawyer; b. N.Y.C., Dec. 6, 1920; s. Adolph Otto and Julia (Strasburger) S.; B.A., U. Va., 1942, LL.B., 1946; m. Louise Thacker, May 1, 1943; children—Donald Steven, Carol (Mrs. Steven A. Roen). Admitted to Va. bar, 1946, U.S. Supreme Ct. bar, 1961; mem. legal staff NLRB, 1946-48; partner Nat-Sales Co., Petersburg, Va., 1948-61; practice, Petersburg, 1961-71; partner firm Spero & Diehl, and predecessor, Petersburg, 1971—. Chmn. bd. Community Bank, 1973—. Chmn. campaign United Fund Petersburg, 1960, pres., 1964-65; chmn. Dist. IV Va. Council on Social Welfare, 1969; mem. profl. adv. staff Southside Mental Health Assn., 1963—; co-chmn. Nat. Conf. Christians and Jews, Petersburg, 1951-55; mem. council USO, Peterburg, 1965-73; organizer cub scout pack 152 Robert E. Lee council Boy Scouts Am. Chmn. Howell for Gov., Petersburg, 1973. Served with USNR, 1942-45. Recipient Service to Law Enforcement citation Petersburg Police Dept., 1965; named Outstanding mem. B'nai B'rith Petersburg, 1966. Mem. Va. State Bar (chmn. criminal law sect 1972-73, chmn. family law sect. 1979-80), Va. Trial Lawyers Assn. (v.p. 1972-74), Petersburg Bar Assn. (sec.-treas. 1964-66), Tau Epsilon Phi, Jewish religion (pres. congregation 1973-75). Elk (exalted ruler 1969), Rotarian; mem. B'nai B'rith (state v.p. 1954). Home: 210 Walnut Blvd Apt 13 Petersburg VA 23803 Office: Marshall Bldg PO Box 870 Petersburg VA 23803

SPEZZANO, VINCENT EDWARD, publisher; b. Retsof, N.Y., Apr. 3, 1926; s. Frank and Lucy Spezzano; B.A., Syracuse U., 1950; m. Majorie Elliott, Dec. 18, 1948; children—Steve, Judy, Mark, Christine. Reporter, The Livingston Republican, Geneseo, N.Y., 1950-51, The News, Lynchburg, Va., 1951-54, The Globe Democrat, St. Louis, 1954-55; polit. writer The Times Union, Rochester, N.Y., 1955-64, dir. public service and research, 1964-68; public service dir. The Gannett Co., Inc., Rochester, 1968-71, dir. promotion, 1971-75; pub., pres. Cape Publs., Inc., Cocoa, Fla., 1975—; asst. v.p. Gannett/South, Gannet Co., Inc., 1977-78, v.p., 1978-79, pres. Gannet/S.E. Newspaper Group, 1979—; dir. Barnett Bank, 1977—. Bd. dirs. Wuesthoff Meml. Hosp., 1977—, United Way of Brevard County, Cape Canaveral Hosp.; trustee Brevard Art Center and Mus., 1979—. Served with USN, 1944-46. Mem. Am. Newspaper Publishers Assn., Fla. Press Assn. (dir. 1977—), Cocoa Beach Area C. of C. (dir. 1976—), Internat. Newspaper Promotion Assn. (pres. 1970-71, award 1975). Roman Catholic.

SPICELAND, JESSE DAVID, acct., educator; b. Marshall, Mo., July 1, 1949; s. Jesse Watson and Irene (Sletoff) S.; B.S. with high honors, U. Tenn., 1971; M.B.A., So. Ill. U., 1972; Ph.D., U. Ark., 1976; m. Rebekah Carol Farrow, Mar. 28, 1971; children—Denise Rebekah, Michael David. Instr. acctg. Middle Tenn. State U., Murfreesboro, 1972, U. Ark., Fayetteville, 1974-75; asst. prof. acctg. La. State U., Baton Rouge, 1975-78, asso. prof., 1978—; cons. local firms. C.P.A., La. Mem. Am. Acctg. Assn., Nat. Assn. Accts., Am. Inst. C.P.A.'s, Assn. M.B.A. Execs., Soc. La. C.P.A.'s, Acad. Acctg. Historians, Beta Gamma Sigma, Beta Alpha Psi, Phi Kappa Phi. Republican. Christian. Contbr. articles to profl. jours. Home: 1014 Leycester Dr Baton Rouge LA 70808 Office: Dept Acctg La State U Baton Rouge LA 70803

SPICOLA, GUY WILLIAM, lawyer, state senator; b. Tampa, Fla., Feb. 27, 1938; s. Joseph G. and Alma (Norona) S.; B.A., U. Fla., 1960, LL.B., 1962; m. Georgie Ann Blevins, Sept. 1, 1973; children—Brandon Sean, Courtney Brooke. Admitted to Fla. bar, 1962; atty. finance and taxation coms. Fla. Ho. of Reps., 1963, mem., 1967-74, majority whip, 1969-74, chmn. environ. protection com.; mem. Fla. senate, 1975— atty. City of Temple Terrace (Fla.), 1963-66. Pres., bd. dirs. Young Democrats Hillsborough County, 1965-66; alt. del. Dem. Nat. Conv., 1968. Named Fla. Outstanding Conservationist, 1971, Legislator of Week, 1971, 72, Outstanding Environmentalist, 1974; recipient numerous awards. Mem. Am., Tampa-Hillsborough County bar assns., Fla. Bar, Am., Bay Area (pres.) trial lawyers assns., Acad. Fla. Trial Lawyers, Am. Arbitration Assn., Am. Judicature Soc., Tampa, Ybor City, Tampa Jr. chambers commerce, U. Fla. Alumni Assn., Sierra Club, Audubon Soc., Am. Heritage Gun Club, Fla. Wildlife Fedn. Phi Delta Phi, Alpha Tau Omega. Roman Catholic. Clubs: University (Tampa); Merrymakers. Address: 806 E Jackson St Tampa FL 33602 also Senate Office Bldg The Capitol Tallahassee FL 32304

SPIELBERGER, ADELE DERBY, hwy. safety adminstr.; b. Lynn, Mass., Apr. 1, 1932; d. Louis Irving and Pauline Marie (Zack) Derby; B.S., Tufts U., 1952; M.S., Fla. State U., 1976; div.; children—David Keith, Joan Ellen. Asst. treas., registered rep. Hays Brokerage Firm, Durham, N.C., 1955-59; instr., dir. computer application services Fla. State U., Tallahassee, 1967-71; criminal justice planner Bur. Criminal Justice, Tallahassee, 1971-74, dep. chief Bur. Comprehensive Planning, 1974-77; Fla. Gov.'s hwy. safety rep., bur. chief hwy. safety Dept. Community Affairs, Tallahassee, Fla., 1977—; mem. traffic conf. Nat. Safety Council, 1979—; mem. Nat. Hwy. Safety Adv. Com., 1979—. Mem. Leon County Democratic Exec. Com., 1977—; pres. Democratic Women's Club of Leon County, 1977—. Mem. Nat. Assn. Gov.'s Hwy. Safety Reps. (treas. 1978—). Home: 3312 North Shore Circle Tallahassee FL 32312 Office: 530 Carlton Bldg Tallahassee FL 32304

SPIELMAN, DAVID GEORGE, photographer; b. Tulsa, Jan. 23, 1950; s. Lloyd William and Martha Jean (Sloan) S.; B.A., Westminster Coll., Fulton, Mo., 1972, student art history, Vienna, Austria, 1971-72. Founder, photographer, exec. Magazine St. Studio, New Orleans, 1973-74, successor name David Spielman Photographer, 1974-79, Spielman Co., 1979—. Home and Office: PO Box 15741 New Orleans LA 70175

SPIELVOGEL, BERNARD FRANKLIN, chemist; b. Ellwood City, Apr. 23, 1937; s. Rudolph and Johanna Walberger (Frank) S.; B.S. in Chemistry and Physics, Geneva Coll., 1959; Ph.D. (Univ. Scholar fellow), U. Mich., 1963; children—Karl, Jan, Jeffrey. Inst. chemistry U. N.C. at Chapel Hill, 1963-64, asst. prof., 1964-67; program dir. Army Research Office, Research Triangle Park, N.C., 1967—. Adj. asso. prof. chemistry Duke, 1972—. Petroleum Research Fund grantee, 1964; Army Research Office grantee, 1972. Mem. Am. Chem. Soc. Contbr. research articles on chemistry to sci. publs. Office: PO Box 12211 Research Triangle Park NC 27709

SPIERS, HELEN LOUISE, ednl. adminstr.; b. Helena, Ark., Dec. 19, 1923; d. Luther M. and Florence (Larkin) Harden; B.A. in Math., Quachita Bapt. U., 1946; M.Ed. in Elem. Edn., U. Houston, 1957; m. Preston Louis Spiers; 1 son, William Preston. Tchr. San Antonio Ind. Sch. Dist., 1951-53, LaMarque (Tex.) Ind. Sch. Dist., 1953-57, coordinator, 1958-72, dir. elem. edn., 1972—; mem. Tex. State Commn. Sch. Accreditation, 1975—. Mem. Assn. Supervision Curriculum Devel., NEA, Tex. State Tchrs. Assn., Nat. Pub. Relations Assn., Nat. Council Tchrs. Mathematics, Kappa Delta Gamma. Recipient Certificate of Appreciation Commn. on Elem. Sch. So. Assn. Colls. and Schs., Delta Kappa Gamma, Epsilon Sigma. Author (with others) edn. publ. Home: 1423 Laskey Houston TX 77034 Office: PO Box 7 LaMarque TX 77568

SPIES, HERBERT AUGUST, III, computer scientist; b. Andalusia, Ala., May 15, 1945; s. Herbert August and Martha (Ward) S.; student Mobile Coll., 1963-65; B.S., U. Ala., 1967; M.S., Ga. Inst. Tech., 1972; m. Sidra Scott, Aug. 26, 1967; children—Herbert August, Lawrence Scott. With U.S. Civil Service, Eglin AFB, Fla., 1968—, timesharing team leader, 1975—. Cubmaster, pack 512 Boy Scouts Am., Shalimar, Fla., 1976-79. Recipient U.S. Civil Service Quality Salary Increase award, 1973; Sustained Superior Performance award, 1975. Mem. Assn. for Computing Machinery. Republican. Home: 31 Holly Ave Shalimar FL 32579 Office: AD/KRES Eglin AFB FL 32542

SPIKES, WILLIAM FRANKLIN, univ. dean; b. Berwyn, Ill., July 14, 1949; s. William Franklin and Joyce Elizabeth (Ernest) S.; B.S.Ed., No. Ill. U., 1971, M.S., 1973, Ed.D., 1975; postgrad. U. Tex.; m. Janice Ann Morrison, Aug. 21, 1971. Coordinator profl. devel. workshops, instr. adult edn. No. Ill. U., DeKalb, 1972-75; dir. continuing edn., asst. prof. edn. Our Lady of the Lake U., San Antonio, 1975-77; asso. dean for continuing edn. St. Mary's U., San Antonio, 1977—, asso. prof. edn., 1977—; cons. Santa Rosa Med. Center, U. Tex., Tex. A. and M. U., others. Mem. San Antonio River Corridor Com.; mem. San Antonio C. of C. Free Enterprise; mem. Urban affairs and Mil. Council; mem. advisory com. Alamo Area Council Govts.; elder Condordia Luth. Ch. Mem. Nat. Assn. Pub. Continuing Adult Edn. (com. on higher edn.), Nat. Council Urban Adminstrs. of Adult Edn., Adult Edn. Assn. U.S.A., Am. Assn. for Higher Edn., AAUP, Am. Ednl. Research Assn., Am. Mgmt. Assn., Am. Mktg. Assn. Am. Soc. for Tng. and Devel., Assn. for Continuing Higher Edn., Assn. for Continuing Profl. Edn., Assn. for Urban Edn., Phi Delta Kappa. Contbr. articles to profl. jours. Home: 5427 Princess Donna San Antonio TX 78229 Office: One Camino Santa Maria San Antonio TX 78284

SPILLERS, JAMES PARKER, geologist, petroleum exec.; b. Calhoun, La., Jan. 5, 1926; s. George Ford and Elizabeth (Honnicutt Abbott) S.; B.S., U. N.C., 1948; M.S., La. State U., 1952; m. Gwen Lois, Aug. 27, 1960; children—James Bernard, Elizabeth Ann, Patricia Faye, Annette Vester, Jennifer. Jr. geologist Gulf Oil Corp., Houston, Ft. Worth, and W. Tex., 1948-49; geologist Aminoil-Kuwait, N.Y.C., 1949-50; grad. teaching asst. geology La. State U., Baton Rouge, 1950-52; sr. geologist Humble-Calif., Houston, 1952-63; asso. prof. geology Miss. So. U., Hattiesburg, 1955-57; pres., owner Pacific-Atlantic Oil Co., Lafayette, La., 1970—. Cons. petroleum, expert witness. Served with USMCR, 1941-45. Home: 417 Shelly Dr Lafayette LA 70503 Office: 1313 Pinhook St Lafayette LA 70505

SPILMAN, DALE DEWAIN, security co. exec.; b. Oklahoma City, May 25, 1945; s. James J. and Betty Jane West; A.A., Winona (Minn.) State U., 1978; m. Tonia Kay Meshke, Oct. 5, 1978. Installation mgr. Diebold Inc., Oklahoma City, 1969-72, regional mgr., San Francisco, 1972-74; pres. N.W. Installations and Service Inc., Red Wing, Minn., 1974-77; asst. mgr. customer service Gould Inc., Lake City, Minn., 1977-78; v.p. customer service Nat. Midwest Safe, Inc., Oklahoma City, 1978-79; owner Security Design & Service, Oklahoma City, 1979—. Served with USMC, 1963-67; Vietnam. Decorated Purple Heart; Vietnamese Cross of Gallantry; recipient C. William Brownfield award Minn. Jaycees, 1975. Mem. Oklahoma City C. of C., United Assn. Mfrs. Reps. Mil. Order Purple Heart, Am. Legion, VFW. Democrat. Episcopalian. Home: 8220 Karla Ln Yukon OK 73099 Office: 501 N Meridian Bldg 408 Oklahoma City OK 73107

SPILMAN, LOUIS, editor; b. Crawfordsville, Ind., Jan. 7, 1899; s. Theodore Bruce and Susan Dale (Boughner) S.; student Wabash Coll.; m. Emily Jane Moon, Sept. 15, 1920; children—Susan (Mrs. V.F. Reynolds), Mary Emily (Mrs. E.O. Davisson), William, Louis, Robert, Martha (Mrs. Paul R. Clark). City editor Marion (Ind.) Chronicle, 1920-24; editor-mgr. Lyman Publ. Corp. div. Fed. Bus. Publ., N.Y.C., 1924-29; pres., editor, pub. News-Virginian, Waynesboro, Va., 1929-64, chmn. bd., 1964—; daily columnist, 1934—; sec., dir. Waynesboro Hotel Corp., 1937-41; corr. U.S. Atomic Bomb Tests, Bikini, 1946; chmn. bd. Glasgow (Ky.) Daily Times, 1957-76. Mem. Meth. Com. Overseas Relief, 1952-64, mem. pub. relations and Meth. info. com., 1964-68; chmn. Gov.'s Study Commn. on Vocat. Rehab., 1967-69; mem. U.S. Dept. Commerce Trade Mission to Germany, 1962. Chmn., Augusta County Flood Control Commn., 1972-73; bd. dirs. Germanna Found., 1972—. Served as sgt. U.S. inf., 1916-17, 2d lt. USAAC, 1917-18. Mem. Va. Press Assn. (pres. 1933-35), So. Newspaper Pub. Assn., Va. Farm Bur., Am. Legion, Phi Gamma Delta, Sigma Delta Chi. Democrat. Mason (Shriner), Rotarian. Author: So This Is South America, 1962. Home: 700 Locust Ave PO Box 747 Waynesboro VA 22980 Office: 531 W Main St PO Drawer 747 Waynesboro VA 22980

SPINK, WILLIAM BERTRAND, art dealer; b. Pawtucket, R.I., Jan. 25, 1914; s. Marcus and Mary Louise (Bailey) S.; B.S., Bryant Coll., 1933; B.L.I., Emerson Coll., 1938, A.M., 1940, M.A. (hon.), 1960. Dir. drama N. Providence (R.I.) High Sch., 1939-41, Hingham (Mass.) High Sch., 1941-45; head English dept. Attleboro High Sch., 1946-49; dir. extension div. Emerson Coll., 1940-50; dir. drama Newton (Mass.) High Sch., 1949-63; pres. Naples Art Gallery, Inc. (Fla.), 1963—. Pres., Mass. Drama Festival, 1950-54, N.E. Drama Festival, 1955-57, Third St. Area Mchts. Assn., Naples, 1969-71, 77-80. Served with USCGR, 1942-45. Recipient N.E. Theater Assn. award for outstanding drama directing, 1960. Home: 333 Neptune's Bight Naples FL 33940 Office: 275 Broad Ave S Naples FL 33940

SPINOSA, FRANK LEONARD, brewery exec.; b. Memphis, Feb. 7, 1941; s. Frank Anthony and Marie Louise (Pieroni) S.; B.B.A., Memphis State U., 1966; m. Norma Jean Hatten, Apr. 17, 1971; 1 son, Shane Anthony. Asst. state mgr. Miller Brewing Co., Atlanta, 1967-69, state mgr., 1969-71; with Pearl Brewing Co., San Antonio, 1971—, gen. mktg. mgr., 1978, v.p., 1978—; sr. v.p. sales, dir. Falstaff Brewing Corp., 1980—, also sr. v.p. sales Ft. Wayne plant (Ind.). Served with U.S. Army, 1963-64. Mem. Houston Livestock Show and Rodeo (life), San Antonio Livestock Show and Rodeo (life), Greater Memphis State, Memphis State Alumni Assn. Roman Catholic. Clubs: Enoch's, Univ. Home: 13710 Bluff Gate San Antonio TX 78216 Office: 312 Pearl Pkwy San Antonio TX 78213

SPIRO, CYRIL SVEN, banker; b. Toronto, Ont., Can., Dec. 26, 1942; s. Benjamin Paul and Rosemay G. (Laughrun) S.; came to U.S., 1943, naturalized, 1947; B.S. in Fgn. Service, Georgetown U., 1968; M.B.A., U. Pa., 1972; With Citibank, Geneva/London/Brussels, 1968-70; mgr. Inter Maritime Factoring, S.A., Geneva, 1971; v.p., head shipping sect., multinat. div. Bank of Am., San Francisco, 1973-75, v.p., asst. mgr. Singapore br., 1975-76, v.p., sr. lending officer, Los Angeles, 1976-78; v.p., mgr., dir. Bank of Am. Internat. of Fla., Miami, 1978—. Bd. dirs., mem. exec. com. Internat. Center, Miami, 1978—. Served with USAF, 1961-65. Mem. Am. Mgmt. Assn., Greater Miami C. of C., Coral Gables C. of C. Office: Bank of Am Internat of Fla 1000 Brickell St Miami FL 33131

SPIROLO, CAROL OLGA, surg. technologist; b. New Orleans, Dec. 23, 1944; d. Americo Martin and Olga Eugene (Capus) S.; grad. Charity Hosp. Sch. Surg. Technologists, 1962. Staff technologist Charity Hosp., New Orleans, 1962-65; staff obstetrical technologist Ochsner Found. Hosp., New Orleans, 1965-68; staff surg. technologist USPHS Hosp., New Orleans, 1968-72, VA Med. Center, New Orleans, 1972—. Mem. Nat. Assn. Surg. Technologists (cert. mem., pres. local chpt. 1969-71, treas. local chpt. 1978-79, nat. dir. 1972-74, nat. pres. 1976-77, mem. liaison council for cert. mem. 1978-79, mem. of site visitation com. for accreditation of surg. tech. schs. 1976—). Home: 2436 Joseph St New Orleans LA 70115 Office: 1601 Perdido St New Orleans LA 70146

SPITZER, CARY REDFORD, instrumentation engr.; b. New Hope, Va., July 31, 1937; s. Clyde Burke and Marion Jeanette (Redford) S.; B.S., Va. Poly. Inst., 1958; M.S. in Adminstrn., George Washington U., 1970; m. Carrie Laura Ruth Logan, June 18, 1960; 1 son, Stiegel Logan. Instrumentation engr. NASA, Hampton, Va., 1962-69, experiments mgr. Project Viking, 1969-77, dep. project mgr. NASA Avionics Planning Office, 1978—. Served with USAF, 1959-62. Mem. IEEE (sr.), sect. chmn. 1968-69), Aerospace and Electronic Systems Soc. (v.p. tech. operations, 1969-72, pres. 1973-74), Pi Delta Epsilon, Rho Tau Sigma. Methodist (lay leader 1966-67, chmn. adminstrv. bd. 1972-73). Patentee in field. Home: 1701 A Ironbound Rd Williamsburg VA 23185 Office: Langley Sta MS 472 Hampton VA 23665

SPIVEY, GERALD LYNN, computer programmer; b. Dallas, Mar. 16, 1950; s. James Amende and Minnie Legunie (Remmer) S.; B.B.A., North Tex. State U., 1974. Computer applications analyst Mobil Oil Co., Dallas. Mem. Assn. Computing Machinery, Beta Gamma Sigma. Home: 611 Devonshire St Richardson TX 75080 Office: PO Box 900 Dallas TX 75221

SPIVEY, TED RAY, educator; b. Ft. Pierce, Fla., July 1, 1927; s. Theodore Roosevelt and Etty Pearl (Sumner) S.; A.B., Emory U., 1949; M.A., U. Minn., 1951, Ph.D., 1954; m. Julia Brannon Douglass, June 30, 1962; children—Mary Leta, John Andrew. Instr. in English, Emory U., 1954-56; asst. prof. English, Ga. State U., 1956-60, asso. prof., 1960-64, prof., 1964—, dir. lower div. studies dept. English, 1961-68. Served with USN, 1945-46. Ga. State U. Urban Life Center grantee, 1977-78, 78-79. Mem. Modern Lang. Assn., South Atlantic Modern Lang. Assn., AAUP, Internat. Soc. Study Symbols. Democrat. Episcopalian. Club: Brittany. Author: (with K.M. England) A Manual of Style, 1964. The Renewed Quest, 1969; The Coming of the New Man, 1971; cons. editor Internat. Jour. Symbology, Studies in Lit. Imagination. Home: 3181 Frontenac Ct NE Atlanta GA 30319 Office: Univ Plaza Ga State U Atlanta GA 30303*

SPLITTER, LARRY ROBERT, elec. engr.; b. Lyons, Kans., June 25, 1947; s. Norman Herman and Wilda Jean (Burrell) S.; B.S. in E.E., Okla. State U., 1970; m. Janiee C. Cunningham, May 21, 1977. With E-Systems Inc., Dallas, 1972—, sr. scientific programmer, 1975-76, sr. software engr., 1976—. Cert. computer programmer Inst. Cert. Computer Profls. Baptist. Home: 1601 Plantation St Garland TX 75042 Office: PO Box 226118 Dallas TX 75266

SPOONER, CAROL LOUISE, aircraft co. exec.; b. Hornell, N.Y., Nov. 16, 1934; d. Raymond LaVern and Lilyan Rosalie (Prager) Pratt; student Hornell Bus. Sch., 1952-53, Riverside Community Coll., 1975-80; m. Karl Benjamin Spooner, Feb. 27, 1954; children—Karen, Kim, Kelley, Karrie, Kevin. Frodn. control clk. Piper Aircraft Corp., Vero Beach, Fla., 1962-72, supr. prodn. control, 1972-77, mgr. parts control, 1977-79, mgr. prodn. control, 1979—. Active Indian River County United Way. Mem. Am. Prodn. and Inventory Control Soc., Am. Mgmt. Assn., Piper Mgmt. Assn. Democrat. Episcopalian. Club: Women of the Moose. Office: Piper Aircraft Corp PO Box 1328 Vero Beach FL 32960

SPOONER, EDWARD CHARLES, architect; b. New Orleans, Dec. 11, 1942; s. Charles Alexander and Oscieola Ouida (Woods) S.; B.Arch., La. State U., 1957; m. Charlotte Lynn Sherwood, July 17, 1968; 1 son, Edward Charles. Designer, Welton, Becket & Assos., N.Y.C., 1967-69, Skidmore, Owings & Merrill, N.Y.C., 1969-75, Kennerly, Slomanson & Smith, N.Y.C., 1975-76; project mgr. Rogers, Butler & Burgun, N.Y.C., 1976-77; dir. design Folse-Henningson, Durham & Richardson, New Orleans, 1977-80; prin. Jahncke Spooner Assos., New Orleans, 1980—. Pres. bd. dirs. Hospice New Orleans, 1979. Mem. AIA. Republican. Episcopalian. Clubs: N.Y. Yacht, Essex of New Orleans, So. Yacht, Pendennis. Home: 1304 Lowerline St New Orleans LA 70118 Office: 935 Third St New Orleans LA 70130

SPOONER, RONALD LEE, research co. exec.; b. Detroit, Oct. 8, 1939; s. Clarence D. and Eleanor (White) S.; M.S. in Engring. (I.F.C. fellow 1962, Gannett fellow 1963), U. Mich., 1963, M.S. in Math., 1965, Ph.D. in Engring., 1967; m. Linda Ethel Ellis, June 15, 1962; children—Lisa, Susan, Carrie. Research engr. Cooley Electronic Lab, Ann Arbor, Mich., 1964-68; asso. dir. Bolt Beraner & Newman Co., Washington, 1968-72; v.p., founder Planning Systems Inc., Washington, 1972—. Adj. prof. dept. elec. engring. Catholic U. Am., Washington, 1968—. Treas. Annandale (Va.) Coop. Nursery Sch., 1972; mem. For Love of Children, Washington, 1968—. U. Fla. grantee, 1964. Mem. I.E.E.E., Acoustical Soc. Am., Washington Acad. Scis., U.S. Naval Inst., Sigma Xi, Eta Kappa Nu, Tau Beta Pi, Phi Kappa Phi, Alpha Tau Omega. Clubs: Fairfax Tennis (Va.), Cosmos. Asso. editor I.E.E.E. Jours. Contbr. to profl. jours. Home: 3727 Camelot Dr Annandale VA 22003 Office: 7900 W Park Dr McLean VA 22101

SPORCK, FREDERICK THOMAS, physician; b. Steubenville, Ohio, Apr. 26, 1945; s. Howard Albert and Edna Lillian (Burdge) S.; B.S., Otterbein Coll., 1967, M.D., W.Va. U., 1972; m. Victoria Louise Van Loenen, June 17, 1972; children—Aaron Thomas. Intern, W.Va. U., 1972-73, resident in otolaryngology, 1973-76; fellow in cleft lip and palate mgmt. U. Iowa, 1976; fellow in cosmetic facial surgery UCLA, 1977; instr. otolaryngology W.Va. U., Morgantown, 1976-78, asst. prof., 1978—, chief sect. facial plastic and reconstructive surgery, 1979, vice-chmn. dept. otolaryngology, 1979—; practice medicine specializing in otolaryngology, Morgantown, 1976—; cons. Clarksburg (W.Va.) VA Hosp. Mem. Am. Cleft Palate Assn., Am. Acad. Ophthalmology and Otolaryngology, W.Va. Acad. Ophthalmology and Otolaryngology, W.Va. Med. Soc., Monongalia

County Med. Soc., A.C.S. Methodist. Clubs: Masons, Shriners. Office: Div Otolaryngology Med Center WVa U Morgantown WV 26506

SPORTS, PEARLIE MAE, hosp. food service exec.; b. Dillon, S.C., Apr. 18, 1937; d. George and Leola (Dial) Lovette; student Florence Darlington Tech. Sch., 1976-77; m. Marvin Thomas Sports, May 4, 1960; children—Larry, Patricia, Charles, Laura and Leola (twins). Asst. lunch room mgr. Blenheim Schs., 1967-70; dir. food service Marlboro Hosp., Bennettsville, S.C., 1970—. Mem. Hosp. Instn. and Edn. Food Service Soc. Democrat. Methodist. Home: PO Box 22 Blenheim SC 29516 Office: PO Box 378 Bennettsville SC 29512

SPRABERRY, DAVID CARR, investment exec.; b. Lamesa, Tex., June 26, 1941; s. Carr D. and Roda M. (Parish) S.; student Hardin-Simmons U., 1959-64; B.B.A., N.Tex. U., 1966; postgrad. S.Tex. Sch. of Law, 1966-68; m. Shirley L. Greenlee, July 22, 1973; children—Donna R., Kenneth C., Paul G. Partner, O'Donnell Implement Co., 1954, Draw Farms, 1957, Howell Farms, 1961, A.J. Spraberry Estates, 1961, Redwind Farms, 1973, Wade Farm, 1977, Wheeler Farm, 1979; mng. partner D & J Implement Co., Tahoka, Tex., 1968-77; pres. Spraberry & Assos., Inc., 1979—. Mem. Tex. Numismatic Assn., Am. Numismatic Assn. Baptist. Clubs: Rotary. Home: 808 N 13th St Lamesa TX 79331 Office: 314 N Austin Lamesa TX 79331

SPRADLEY, ALVIN WAYNE, artist; b. Pell City, Ala., Nov. 11, 1937; s. James Thornton and Josephine (Whitten) S.; student Drawing Board Sch. Art, Birmingham, Ala., 1967-70; m. Patricia Ann Rich, June 8, 1959; children—Donald Dwayne, Jerry Wayne. One man shows: Coffey & Thompson, Charlotte, N.C., Ringland Gallery, Birmingham, Birmingham Trust Nat. Bank, Ala. Grand Hotel, Point Clear, Ala. Bapt. Med. Center, Birmingham; group shows include: Birmingham Festival Art, 1978, Southeastern Center Contemporary Art, Winston-Salem, 1972, 73, 74, N.C. So. Watercolor Soc., 1977, Bryant Galleries, Jackson, Miss. and New Orleans, 1978; represented in permanent collections: Birmingham Mus. Art, Columbus (Ga.) Mus. Art, Birmingham Trust Nat. Bank; lectr. in field. Served with U.S. Navy, 1956-60. Mem. So. Watercolor Soc., Birmingham Art Assn., Ala. Art League. Home: 911 Hill-Top Rd Pell City AL 35125

SPRADLEY, DON DELOY, realtor; b. Kern County, Calif., Dec. 8, 1934; s. Clyde Anderson and Veda Latan (Ellis) S.; B.S., Kans. State Coll., 1961. Ins. claims exec. Farmers Group MFA Mut. Ins. Co., Jackson, Tenn., 1963-72, Medallion Ins. Co., Kansas City, Mo., 1972-75; owner, pres. Olive Branch Realty, Arlington, Tex., 1978—. Mem. Arlington Bd. Realtors, Tex. Claims Assn., Tenn. Claims Assn. Democrat. Baptist. Club: Kiwanis Arlington Sundown (pres. 1980). Home: 1411 Waggoner Dr Arlington TX 76013 Office: 2417 Park Row W #204 Arlington TX 76013

SPRADLIN, MICHAEL COLLINS, army officer; b. Knoxville, May 19, 1947; s. William Herbert and Edith Cathrine (Collins) S.; B.S., U. Tenn., 1975, M.S. in Social Work, 1976; m. Constance Jean Borders, Sept. 7, 1968; children—Shennan Alycia, Stacy Erin. Enlisted in U.S. Army, 1970, advanced through grades to capt., 1979; social work officer Moncrief Army Hosp., Ft. Jackson, S.C., 1977-79, Dwight D. Eisenhower Army Med. Center, Ft. Gordon, Ga., 1979—. Mem. Nat. Assn. Social Workers, Acad. Cert. Social Workers. Office: Social Work Service Eisenhower Army Med Center Fort Gordon GA 30905

SPRADLING, ROBERT WESLEY, engring. exec.; b. Whitewright, Tex., Dec. 6, 1918; s. Oliver Patrick and Lula Rupert (Nash) S.; B.S. in Chem. Engring., U. Okla., 1941, M.S., 1942; postgrad. U. Ill., Chgo., 1954-55; m. Ramona Virginia Kelly, Sept. 15, 1947; 1 son, Donald F. Div. engr. Coca-Cola Export Corp., Tokyo, 1945-47; design engr. Am. Cyanamid Co., Bridgeville, Pa., 1948-52; chief engr. U.S. Rubber Co., Joliet (Ill.) Arsenal, 1952-57; chief engr. supply div. U.S. Steel Corp., Chgo., 1957-62; cons. engr., Wilmington, Del., 1962-73; mgr. projects Black, Sivalls & Bryson, Houston, 1973-76; v.p. KPS Industries, Wilmington, 1966—, Lake Louise Hills, Inc., Whitehouse Station, N.J., 1970—; v.p. Asso. Internat. Design Consultants, Nederland, Tex., 1978—. Served to lt. col. AUS, 1943-45. Registered profl. engr., Wis., Tex. Mem. Am. Inst. Chem. Engrs., Am. Chem. Soc., Aircraft Owners and Pilots Assn., Phi Gamma Delta. Clubs: Masons, Chgo. Engineers. Home: 12036 Dorrance Ln Stafford TX 77477 Office: 4242 SW Freeway Houston TX 77027

SPRAGGINS, ROBERT LEE, mass spectrometrist; b. Sedalia, Mo., Feb. 18, 1939; s. William Arthur and Esther Louise (Kurtz) S.; B.S. in Chemistry, La. Tech. U., 1963, M.S., 1966, Ph.D., U. Okla., 1970; Seagrant postdoctoral fellow Stevens Inst. Tech., 1971-72; m. Janet Elizabeth Brewton, Mar. 16, 1963; children—Robin Lee, William Robert, Leslie Brewton. Chemist, Cities Service, Lake Charles, La., 1963-65; research fellow Alza Corp., Palo Alto, Calif., 1970-71; postdoctoral fellow, research scientist Stevens Inst. Tech., Hoboken, N.J., 1971-75; mass spectrometrist Tex. A&M U., College Station, 1975-77; sr. scientist, mass spectrometrist Radian Corp., Austin, 1977, sr. scientist, group leader mass spectrometry, 1979—; mem. N.J. Marine Consortium for Research, 1974-75. Coach, Little League Baseball, 1977—. Served with U.S. Army, 1962. N.J. Heart Assn. grantee, 1974, NIH grantee, 1975-77. Mem. Am. Chem. Soc., Sigma Xi (Research award 1970), Phi Lambda Upsilon. Presbyterian. Patentee in field. Home: 10610 Hard Rock Rd Austin TX 78750 Office: 8500 Shoal Creek Blvd Austin TX 78766

SPRATLIN, WILLIAM BENNETT, II, mfg. co. exec.; b. Florence, Ala., May 24, 1937; s. William Bennett and Grace S.; B.S., Auburn U., 1959; m. Jimmie Sue Ballard, June 28, 1958; children—Terri Lynn, Patricia Diane, William Bennett III. With Agrico Chem. Co., various locations, 1959-74, asst. plant mgr., Saginaw, Mich., 1965-69, tech. service mgr. East Coast, Greensboro, N.C., 1969-74; founder, pres., gen. mgr. Johnson City Chem. Co., Inc., (Tenn.), 1974—; dir. Mountain Empire Bank. Served with Army N.G., 1953-62. Mem. Am. Mgmt. and Pres. Assn., Tenn. Plant Food Assn. (founding dir., past pres., recipient Presdl. award), Johnson City C. of C., Fertilizer Inst. Republican. Methodist. Club: Rotary (past pres.). Home: 2806 Avondale St Johnson City TN 37601 Office: PO Box 760 Johnson City TN 37601

SPRAY, PAUL, surgeon; b. Wilkinsburg, Pa., Apr. 9, 1921; s. Lester E. and Phoebe Gertrude (Hull) S.; B.S., U. Pitts., 1942; M.D., George Washington U., 1944; M.S., U. Minn., 1950; m. Mary Louise Conover, Nov. 28, 1943; children—David C., Thomas L., Mary Lynn (Mrs. Thomas Branham). Intern U.S. Marine Hosp., S.I., 1944-45; resident Mayo Found., Rochester, Minn., 1945-46, 48-50; practice medicine specializing in orthopedic surgery, Oak Ridge, 1950—; mem. staff Oak Ridge Hosp., E. Tenn. Meml., East Tenn. Baptist, Park West hosps., Knoxville, Harriman (Tenn.) Hosp., Chamberlain Meml. Hosp., Rockwood, Tenn. Cons., Daniel Arthur Rehab. Center, Oak Ridge Associated Univs.; volunteer vis. cons., CARE Medico, Jordan, 1959, Nigeria, 1962, 65, Algeria, 1963, Afghanistan, 1970, Bangldesh, 1975, 77, 79, Peru, 1980; A.M.A. voluntary physician, Vietnam, 1967, 72; vis. asso. prof. U. Nairobi, 1973; mem. teaching team of Internat. Coll. Surgeons to Khartoum, vis. prof. orthopedic surgery U. Khartoum, 1976; hon. prof. San Luis Gonzaga U., Ica, Peru; AmDoc volunteer cons., U. Biafra Teaching Hosp., 1969; sec. orthopedics overseas div. CARE Medico, 1971-76, sec. medico adv. bd., 1974-76, vice chmn., 1976, chmn., 1977-79, v.p. CARE, Inc., 1977-79, public mem. care bd., 1980—. Vice pres. Anderson County Health Council, 1975, pres., 1976-77; pres. health commn. Council So. Mountains, 1958-65, sec. bd., 1965-66. Tenn. pres. UN Assn., 1966-67. Served to capt. AUS, 1946-48. Recipient various humanitarian awards; diplomate Am. Bd. Orthopedic Surgery. Fellow A.C.S., Internat. Coll. Surgeons (Tenn. regent 1976—); mem. Societe International Chirurgie Orthopedique et de Traumatologie, Western Pacific Orthopedic Assn., Orthopedic Letters Club, Am. Fracture Assn., Am. Acad. Orthopedic Surgeons (mem. com. on injuries 1980—), AMA (Humanitarian Service award 1967, 72), Am. Assn. Vol. Physicians (pres. 1977-78), Alumni and Friends of Medico (pres. 1975-77), Indonesian Orthopedic Soc. (hon.), Peru Acad. Surgery (corr.), Peruvian Soc. Orthopedic Surgery and Traumatology (corr.). Quaker. Club: Lions (Humanitarian award 1968, Ambassador of Goodwill award 1979). Home: 507 Delaware Ave Oak Ridge TN 37830 Office: 145 E Vance Rd Oak Ridge TN 37830

SPRESSER, DIANE MAR, mathematician, computer scientist, educator; b. Welch, W.Va., Dec. 12, 1943; d. Paul Mack and Rachel Jean (DeMario) S.; B.S. with honors, Radford Coll., 1965; M.A., U. Tenn., Knoxville, 1967; postgrad. Ohio State U., summers 1970-72; Ph.D., U. Va., 1977. Instr. math. Madison Coll. (now James Madison U.), Harrisonburg, Va., 1967-68, asst. prof., 1968-77, asso. prof., 1977—, acting head dept. math., 1978-79, head dept. math. and computer sci., 1979—; cons. in field. Organist, Blessed Sacrament Ch., Harrisonburg, 1969—. Mem. Am. Math. Soc., Math. Assn. Am., Assn. for Computing Machinery, Va. Acad. Sci., AAAS, Assn. for Women in Math., Pi Mu Epsilon, Phi Kappa Phi, Delta Kappa Gamma. Roman Catholic. Office: Dept Math and Computer Sci James Madison U Harrisonburg VA 22807

SPRESSER, JAMES CLARENCE, educator; b. Taylorville, Ill., May 16, 1947; s. Clarence and Mary Francis (Collins) S.; B.S., So. Ill. U., 1970, M.S., 1973, postgrad. in communications, 1979—; m. Linda England, Apr. 12, 1969; children—Amy Lynn, Shane Clarence. Tchr. speech theatre Murphysboro (Ill.) High Sch., 1970-72; tchr. English, Holy Innocents Sch., St. Louis, 1972-73; mgmt. devel. cons. Mind, Inc., N.Y.C., 1973-75; producer, dir. Multi media program Communico Inc., St. Louis, 1975-76; head speech communication program and theatre program Columbia (Tenn.) State Community Coll., 1976—; pres. Mas Advt. Inc., Columbia, 1977—; communications cons. Pres., Maury County Creative Arts Guild, 1977-78. Recipient Young Educator of Yr. award Maury County, 1978. Mem. Tenn. Edn. Assn. (local pres. 1976-77), Gen. Semantics Inst., NEA. Roman Catholic. Contbr. poetry to jours. and mags. Home: 3006 McIntire Dr Columbia TN 38401 Office: Dept Speech Columbia State Community Coll Columbia TN 38401

SPRIGGS, CHARLES KENNETH, architect; b. Washington, D.C., July 12, 1946; s. Kahl Kenneth and Rosa Nell (Booth) S.; B.A., Princeton U., 1968; M.Arch., Harvard U., 1971; certificate in project mgmt. Air Force Inst. Tech., 1972. Transp. planner C.E. Maguire, Inc., Waltham, Mass., 1971; design mgr. Sea Pines Co., Hilton Head Island, S.C., 1973-75; architect, corp. sec. Maddox & Assos., P.C., Savannah, Ga., 1975-77; pres. Spriggs & Wilkes, P.C., Savannah, 1979—; mem. Nat. Com. Architecture for Justice, 1978—; project dir. Art in Pub. Places Program, Chatham County, Ga., 1977-78; bd. dirs. Collaborative Resources Internat., Inc., Savannah, 1979—. Bd. trustees mem., archtl. cons. Telfair Acad. of Arts and Scis., Savannah, 1977—; mem. Leadership Savannah, 1977-78. Served to capt. Civil Engring. Squadron, USAF, 1971-73. Registered architect, Ga., S.C., Md.; certificate, Nat. Council of Archtl. Registration Bds. Mem. AIA, Internat. Solar Energy Soc., Nat. Trust for Historic Preservation, Assn. for Preservation Tech., Historic Savannah, Ga. Conservancy. Clubs: Harvard Club of Washington, D.C., Harvard Club of Atlanta, Princeton Club of Washington, Savannah Golf, Columbia Country (Chevy Chase, Md.). Author documentary: Patterns of Change, The Evolution of a Courthouse, 1978; archtl. works include: Chatham County Courthouse, Savannah, 1977; Residence for Officials from Kuwait, Kiawah Island, S.C., 1975. Home: PO Box 10062 Savannah GA 31412 Office: PO Box 10062 Savannah GA 31412

SPRIGGS, GARRY LEE, coll. adminstr.; b. Portsmouth, Ohio, May 19, 1940; s. Harvey Carl and Marie Ellen (Dawson) S.; student Frankfort Pilgrim Coll., 1959-61; B.A., Hobe Sound Bible Coll., 1977; m. Eunice Junice Williams, Jan. 16, 1960; children—Kevin, Debbie, Phillip, Timmy. Ordained to ministry Pilgrim Holiness Ch. Am., 1966; pastor Pilgrim Holiness Ch., Afton, Ohio, 1961-63, Syracuse, N.Y., 1968-73; field mgr. for Ohio and Ind., Furst McNess Co., 1963-64; gen. evangelist Pilgrim Holiness Ch. of America (now Wesleyan Ch.), Marion, Ind., 1964-68; Christian service dir. Hobe Sound Bible Coll., 1973—; dir. Christian edn. Community Bible Chapel, Stuart, Fla.; dir. ch. growth seminars Interch. Holiness Conv., Inc. Republican. Home: 11468 SE Ella Ave Hobe Sound FL 33455 Office: PO Box 1065 Hobe Sound FL 33455

SPRINGER, BERL M., public service co. exec.; b. 1921; B.S., Tex. Tech Coll., 1943; married. Jr. engr. Wright Aero. Corp., 1943-44; engr. constrn. dept. Southwestern Public Service Co., Amarillo, Tex., 1946-49, rate engr., 1949-67, mgr. rates and budget dept., 1967-69, v.p. rates and budget, 1969-72, exec. v.p., 1972-76, pres., chief operating officer, 1976—, also dir.; dir. Tuco Inc., Llantex Inc. Served to 1st lt. U.S. Army, 1944-46. Office: Southwestern Public Service Co SPS Tower Bldg 6th and Tyler Sts PO Box 1261 Amarillo TX 79170*

SPRINKLE, PHILIP MARTIN, otolaryngologist; b. Greensboro, N.C., Aug. 5, 1926; s. Philip E. and Margaret S.; student Bridgewater Coll., 1943-44; M.D., U. Va., 1953; m. Mary Elizabeth Cadger, July 15, 1955; children—Philip Martin, Christian Edward. Intern, Va. Mason Hosp., Seattle, 1953-54; resident in gen. surgery Watts Hosp., Durham, N.C., 1960-61; resident in otolaryngology U. Va. Hosp., Charlottesville, 1961-64; general practice medicine, Martinsville, Va., 1954-60; practice medicine specializing in otolaryngology, Charlottesville, 1965, Morgantown, W.Va., 1965—; asst. prof. otolaryngology U. Va. Hosp., Charlottesville, 1964-65; prof. surgery W.Va. U. Med. Center, Morgantown, 1967, chmn. div. otolaryngology, 1965; physician cons. W.Va. Rehab. Center Inst., 1969—. Bd. dirs. Gallaudet Coll., Washington. Served with USAAF, 1945-46. Diplomate Am. Bd. Otolaryngology. Fellow A.C.S.; mem. Am. (award of merit 1975), W.Va. (pres. 1967-68) acads. ophthalmology and otolaryngology, Soc. Univ. Otolaryngologists, Soc. Academic Chmn. of Otolaryngology, Am. Acad. Gen. Practice, Am. Acad. Facial, Plastic and Reconstructive Surgery (dir. 1975-78), Am. Soc. Head and Neck Surgery, Royal Soc. Medicine, Am. Laryngol. Soc., AMA, Raven Soc., Am. Laryngol., Rhinological and Otological Soc., Alpha Omega Alpha. Contbr. numerous articles on otology and laryngology to profl. jours. Home: 616 Vista Place Morgantown WV 26505 Office: Div Otolaryngology WVa U Med Center Morgantown WV 26506

SPROUL, HARVEY LEONARD, judge; b. Williamsburg, Ky., Oct. 8, 1933; s. Harvey LaFayette and Ruth (Renfro) S.; B.S., U. Tenn., 1955, J.D., 1957; student Judge Adv. Gen.'s Sch., 1958; m. Sylvia Ann Moulton, May 31, 1958; children—Daniel, Susan, Jane Anne, Lyda B. Admitted to Tenn. bar, 1957, U.S. Supreme Ct. bar, 1960; claims adjustor U.S. F & G Ins. Co., Knoxville, Tenn., 1957; partner law firm Dannel, Fowler & Sproul, Lenoir City, Tenn., 1961-63, Dannel & Sproul, 1963-65, Sproul & Russell, 1968-70, Sproul & Bailey, 1972-74; judge Loudon County, Tenn., 1966-74; individual practice law, 1974—. Chmn., East Tenn. Devel. Dist., 1966-69; chmn. bd. Mid-East Community Action Agy., 1972-75; mem. State Adv. Com. for Local Planning, 1971-74; chmn. Tellico Area Planning Council, 1967-74; bd. dirs. Overlook Mental Health Center, 1972-74; mem. State Democratic Exec. Com., 1976-78. Served with J.A.G.C., AUS, 1958-60; lt. col. Res. Named Tenn.'s Outstanding Young Man, 1966; Lenoir City Distinguished Service award, 1962. Mem. Tenn. County Judges Assn. (v.p. 1972-74), Am. Bar Assn. (vice chmn. mil. law com. 1978-79), Tenn. Bar Assn., Loudon County Bar Assn. (pres. 1966-67), Tenn. Trial Lawyers Assn., Am. Soc. Hosp. Attys., Tenn. Soc. Hosp. Attys., Lenoir City C. of C. (pres. 1980), Phi Delta Phi, Kappa Sigma, Delta Sigma Phi. Methodist. Club: Rotary (pres.). Home: PO Box 444 Lenoir City TN 37771 Office: 109 W Broadway Lenoir City TN 37771

SPROULL, ROBERT CHRISTLEY, dentist, researcher, ret. officer; b. New Cumberland, W.Va., Nov. 5, 1920; s. Bert Christley and Emma (Allen) S.; D.D.S., U. Pitts., 1950; postgrad. U. So. Calif., 1956-57; m. Mary M. Moran, June 3, 1949; children—Robert M., Elizabeth A., William A., Brian E. Enlisted man U.S. Army, 1942-46; commd. officer U.S. Army, 1950, advanced through grades to col., 1967; chief fixed prosthodontic service William Beaumont Gen. Hosp., El Paso, Tex., 1966-72, chief hosp. dental clinic, 1970-72. Asst. to Dr. Berndmark Heukemes, archaeologist, Heidelberg, Germany, 1961-65. Decorated Bronze Star medal, Legion of Merit. Diplomate Am. Bd. Prosthodontics. Fellow Am. Coll. Dentists, Am. Coll. Prosthodontists (inter-soc. color council); mem. Am. Acad. History Dentistry (pres. 1975-76), Am. Dental Assn. Club: Prospectors (pres. 1972) (El Paso). Contbr. articles to profl. jours. Research on color matching in dentistry, laser and holography. Home: 10912 Gary Player Dr El Paso TX 79935 Office: 2601 McRae Blvd El Paso TX 79925

SPRUILL, STEVEN GREGORY, author; b. Battle Creek, Mich., Apr. 20, 1946; s. John Chester and Arleen Marcelle (Camp) S.; B.A. in Biology, Andrews U., 1968; M.A., Cath. U. Am., 1978, Ph.D. in Clin. Psychology, 1980; m. Nancy Lyon, Aug. 24, 1969. Life scis. researcher, writer, editor Hazelton Labs., Inc., Falls Church, Va., 1969-72; fellow NIMH, 1972-74; psychology extern Washington VA Hosp., 1977, doctoral intern Mt. Vernon Center for Community Mental Health, Fairfax, Va., 1977-78; works include: (novels) Keepers of the Gate, 1977, The Psychopath Plague, 1978, The Janus Equation, 1980. Mem. Authors Guild, NOW. Address: 123 N Park Dr Arlington VA 22203

SPULLER, GEORGE FRANCIS, printing co. exec.; b. Niagara Falls, N.Y., Apr. 28, 1915; s. Earl C. and Nettie (Dunham) S.; B.B.A., Niagara U., 1939; m. Veronica G. Bishop, May 17, 1941; children—Sharyn, Cindy. With Moore Bus. Forms, Inc., Denton, Tex., 1934—, acctg. mgr., 1939-52, sales control mgr., 1952-74, mgr. sales adminstrn., 1974—. Mem. Denton City Council, 1960-63; mayor pro tem City of Denton, 1962-63; county chmn. ARC, 1956-62; campaign chmn. United Fund, 1969. Served with Fin. Dept., U.S. Army, 1942-46. Mem. Adminstrv. Mgmt. Soc. (dir. Dallas chpt. 1967-68). Republican. Methodist. Club: Kiwanis (pres. 1966) (Denton). Home: 1205 Greenbrier St Denton TX 76201 Office: Texas Bldg Suite 350 Denton TX 76201

SPUNT, GERALD ALAN, pediatrician; b. N.Y.C., Mar. 8, 1948; s. Maurice Lester and Matilda Martha (Goldstein) S.; B.A. cum laude, Hunter Coll., 1968; M.D., SUNY, Bklyn., 1972; m. Penny Kay Effron, Jan. 6, 1973; children—Meredith Fay, Emily Anne. Intern, Nassau County (N.Y.) Med. Center, 1972, resident in pediatrics, 1972-75; practice medicine specializing in pediatrics, North Lauderdale, Fla., 1977—; mem. staff Plantation (Fla.) Gen. Hosp., Univ. Community Hosp., Tamarac, Fla. Served to maj., M.C., USAF, 1975-77. Diplomate Am. Bd. Pediatrics. Fellow Am. Acad. Pediatrics; mem. Broward County Med. Soc., Fla. Med. Assn. Jewish. Office: 8033 Kimberly Blvd North Lauderdale FL 33068

SPURLOCK, JACK MARION, research engr., educator; b. Tampa, Fla., Aug. 16, 1930; s. Joseph Marion and Gertrude (Saffold) S.; B.Chem. Engr., U. Fla., 1952; M.S., Ga. Inst. Tech., 1958, Ph.D., 1961; m. Phyllis Lowene Ridgway, June 30, 1952; children—Barbara Lynn, Scott Edward, Paul Andrew, Teresa Anne. Quality control engr. Auto-Lite Battery Co., East Point, Ga., 1954-55; research asso., asst. prof. Ga. Inst. Tech., Atlanta, 1955-62, asso. dir. Applied Scis. Lab., Engring. Expt. Sta., 1974-79, dir. Chem. and Material Scis. Lab., 1979—; mgr. aeroscis. research dept. Martin Co., Orlando, Fla., 1962-64; dir. engring. research dept. Atlantic Research Corp., Alexandria, Va., 1964-69; exec. v.p. Health and Safety Research Inst., Springfield, Va., 1969-72, pres., 1972-74; Mem., chmn. SAE Com. on Spacecraft Environmental Control and Life Support Systems, 1965—. Served to lt. USAF, 1952-54. Fellow Am. Inst. Chemists, Royal Soc. Health, Aerospace Med. Assn. (asso.), Am. Inst. Aero. and Astronautics (asso.); mem. Am. Inst. Chem. Engrs., Aerospace Med. Assn., Am. Chem. Soc., A.A.A.S. Presbyn. (elder). Author: (with Thomas W. Jackson) Research and Development Management, 1966. Home: 293 Indian Hills Trail Marietta GA 30067 Office: Interdisciplinary Programs Ga Inst Tech Atlanta GA 30332

SQUATRIGLIA, ROBERT WILLIAM, psychologist, educator; b. Waterbury, Conn., Nov. 23, 1937; s. P. William and Mary E. (Ogenskis) S.; A.B., Coll. William and Mary, 1960, M.A., 1965; Ph.D., U. S.C., 1970; m. Betty Lee Powell, Aug. 12, 1961; children—Robert William, Elizabeth Lee, Katherine Ann, Stephen Karl. Asst. dean of men Coll. William and Mary, Williamsburg, Va., 1963-67; coordinator, VA counselor U. S.C., Columbia, instr. coll. edn., 1967-70; asst. v.p. student affairs, v.p. student affairs SUNY, Brockport, 1970-72; asso. dean student affairs counseling psychologist SUNY, Albany, 1972-77; asso. chancellor and dean student devel. U. S.C. Coastal Carolina Coll., Conway, 1978—; cons. office of edn. Ft. Jackson, S.C., 1968-69; participant Am. Council on Edn. Leadership Inst., 1979. Served with U.S. Army, 1960-63. Recipient chancellor's award, grantee Research Found. SUNY, 1975, 76, 77. Mem. Am. Personnel and Guidance Assn., Am. Coll. Personnal Assn., S.C. Personnel Assn., Am. Assn. Higher Edn., AAUP, Nat. Assn. Student Personnel Adminstrs., Omicron Delta Kappa, Blue Key, Phi Delta Kappa. Clubs: Rotary, Toastmasters, Jaycees. Office: Coll Center U SC Coastal Carolina Conway SC 29526

SQUIBB, SAMUEL DEXTER, educator; b. Limestone, Tenn., June 20, 1931; s. Ben B. and Pearl (Harris) S.; B.S. in Chemistry, East Tenn. State U., 1952; Ph.D., U. Fla., 1956; m. Jo Ann Kyker, Dec. 15, 1951; children—Sandra Lavanne, Kevin Dexter. Asso. prof. chemistry Western Carolina U., Cullowhee, N.C., 1956-60; asst. prof., coordinator dept. chemistry Eckerd Coll., St. Petersburg, Fla., 1960-63, asso. prof., coordinator, 1963-64; prof., chmn. dept. chemistry U. N.C. at Asheville, 1964—. Fellow Am. Inst. Chemists (life, profl. accredited); mem. Am. Chem. Soc. (Charles H. Stone award 1979), AAUP, N.C. Assn. Educators, N.C. Inst. Chemists (pres. 1977-79), Phi Beta Kappa, Alpha Chi Sigma, Gamma Sigma

Epsilon. Presbyn. (deacon 1968-71). Author: Experimental Chemistry I, 1970; Experimental Chemistry II, 1971; Experimental Modern Organic Chemistry, 1970; Chemistry I, 1972; Chemistry II, 1974; Understanding Chemistry I, 1979. Home: 8 Honey Dr Asheville NC 28805

SQUIER, WELLS MILLER, interior designer; b. Detroit, Jan. 18, 1929; s. Ernest V. and Carma (Miller) S.; B.S. in Indsl. and Mech. Engring., U. Mich., 1951, B.S. in Indsl. Design, 1954; m. Bernadette Bentley, Mar. 10, 1969; children—Lesley, Monica, Whitney, Wells. Profl. designer Gen. Motors Tech. Center, Warren, Mich., 1954-57; designer for Victor Gruen Archtl. Office, Detroit, 1957; partner Squier & Maxwell, indsl. designers, Ft. Lauderdale, Fla., 1957-62; pres. Wells M. Squier Assos., Inc., Ft. Lauderdale, 1964—. Mem. Ft. Lauderdale Beach Adv. Bd., 1976—; pres. Archtl. Environments Inc., Ft. Lauderdale, 1978—; mem. hist. adv. bd. Ft. Lauderdale, 1976—; trustee Ft. Lauderdale Mus. Arts, 1976—. Recipient Achievement awards Instns. Mag., 1964, Ft. Lauderdale Jaycees award, 1965. Mem. Inst. Store Planners, Am. Soc. Interior Design, Indsl. Designers Am., Alpha Rho Chi. Episcopalian. Clubs: Masons, Lauderdale Yacht, Classic Jaguar Assn., Rolls-Royce Owners. Office: 1234 NE 4th Ave Ft Lauderdale FL 33304

SQUIRES, JAMES RALPH, constrn. co. exec.; b. Dillon, S.C., Jan. 2, 1940; s. William Guilford and Ruby Alice (Whittington) S.; student public schs., Charlotte, N.C.; m. Ann Newton, Apr. 17, 1965; children—Samuel Guilford, James Drew. With Squires Constrn. Co., 1959-62; pres. SBS Builders, Inc., Charlotte, 1968-70; pres. Ralph Squires Homes, Charlotte, 1970—, Squires & Assos., Realtors, 1975—, JRS Enterprises, Inc., 1976—. Mem. Charlotte Tree Commn., 1977; bd. dirs. Athletic Found. U. N.C., Charlotte, 1979. Recipient Profile award N.C. Blue Cross/Blue Shield, 1974, Albert Gallatin merit cert., 1974. Mem. Charlotte Homebuilders Assn. (pres. 1974), N.C. Home Builders Assn. (v.p. 1975), Nat. Homebuilders Assn., Charlotte Bd. Realtors. Republican. Baptist. Home: 2624 Milton Rd Charlotte NC 28212 Office: 6809 Orchard Ridge Dr Charlotte NC 28212

SQUIRES, WARREN GLENN, ret. elec. engr.; b. Sioux City, Iowa, Sept. 11, 1913; s. Glenn Samuel and Beulah Warren (Greene) S.; student U. Colo., 1932-35; B.S. in E.E., U. Tex., 1938; m. Alice Carolyn Butts, June 15, 1946. Substa. operator Dallas Power & Light Co., 1938-42; engr. Brown & Root Constrn. Co., McAlester, Okla., 1942-44; research engr. N. Am. Aviation Co., Dallas, 1944-45; mgr. S.W. Engrs., San Antonio, 1949; div. engr. Tex. Power & Light Co., Sherman, 1950-78. Named Engr. of the Year, N.E. Tex. chpt. Tex. Soc. Profl. Engrs., 1972. Registered profl. engr., Tex. Mem. I.E.E.E., Nat., Tex. socs. profl. engrs., Sigma Pi Sigma (alumnus mem.). Mem. Christian Ch. (chmn. bd. 1961-62, 65-66, elder 1961—, chmn. elders 1976, 79, 80). Home: 519 N Holly Ave Sherman TX 75090

SREBNICK, SAUL, mfg. co. exec.; b. Havana, Cuba, July 30, 1933; came to U.S., 1960, naturalized, 1970; s. Abraham David and Bertha (Perey) S.; pub. acct. U. Habana, 1960; m. Maria Horenstein, Dec. 6, 1960; children—Howard M., Scott A., Eliza A. Partner, Intramerco, S.A., Habana, 1952-60; supr. Latin Am. Dept. Bank Levmi Le-Israel B.M., N.Y.C., 1961-63; comptroller Perlin Packing Co., Inc., Norfolk, Va., 1963-66; pres. Scott Notions, Inc., Miami, Fla., 1966—; dir. Continental Nat. Bank of Miami. Bd. dirs. Temple Menorah, Miami Beach, 1978—, fin. sec., 1979—; campaign dir. Cuban Hebrew div. Greater Miami Jewish Fedn., 1978-79, pres., 1979-80. Democrat. Jewish. Club: Cuban Hebrew Congregation. Office: 545 NW 26 St Miami FL 33127

SROUJI, JACQUELINE, writer, photographer; b. Nashville, Mar. 12, 1944; d. Albert-Nicklaus Paul and Marye Louise (Haynes) Steubbel; grad. St. Bernard Acad., Nashville, 1962; m. Suheil Hanna Srouji, Jan. 1, 1967; children—John Suheil, Joseph Patrick, Yousra Claire. News reporter, photographer Nashville Banner, 1963-68; copy editor, headline writer, staff writer Tennessean, Nashville, 1970-72, 75-76; dir. dept. public info. and health edn. Middle Tenn. Health Systems Agy., Inc., Nashville, 1977—; writing cons.; facilitator Transactional Analysis. Mem. allocation panel Council Community Services, 1979—; mem. info. and referral com. United Way, 1979—, Service award. Served with U.S. Army, 1962, with USN, 1976-78. Named Woman of Year, Nat. Bus. and Profl. Women's Club, 1974; recipient award Freedoms Found., 1966; winner Spring Arts Festival, 1979. Mem. Am. Soc. Law and Medicine, AAAS, Tenn. Acad. Sci., Tenn. Conf. Social Welfare, Am. Assn. Health Planning, World Future Soc., Internat. Assn. Bus. Communicators, Public Relations Soc. Am. Greek Catholic. Author: Critical Mass, 1977. Office: Box 15702 Nashville TN 37215

STABILE, DANIEL LOUIS, educator; b. Sharon, Pa., May 14, 1942; s. Daniel Joseph and Jane Mary (Combine) S.; B.A., Kent (Ohio) State U., 1968; M.A., U. Santo Tomas, Manila, 1971, Ph.D., 1974; m. Monica Ellen Tramel, June 16, 1979. Tchr., dept. chmn. Cleve. Roman Cath. schs., 1966-69; guidance counselor, dept. chmn. Wagner Sch. USAF, Clark Field, Philippines, 1969-71; dist. supr. vocat. and career edn. USAF Dependents Schs., 1971-75; edn. specialist overseas dependents schs. Dept. Def., 1975—; prof. edn. LaVerne (Calif.) U., 1972-75, U. Santo Tomas, 1974-75; asst. dir. Inst. Devel. Ednl. Activities Fellows program, 1975-79; bd. dirs. Grad. Sch., U. Santo Tomas, 1974-75. Info. specialist, weekend vol. Smithsonian Inst., 1978—. Recipient Sustained Superior Performance award, 1973, Outstanding Performance award, 1975; named disting. fellow Inst. Devel. Ednl. Activities, 1978, summer fellow, 1973, 75, 76, 78, 79. Mem. Am. Assn. Sch. Adminstrs., Am. Personnel and Guidance Assn., Am. Vocat. Assn., Assn. Edn. Communication and Tech., Phi Delta Kappa. Author research papers. Home: 3101 S Manchester St Apt 221 Falls Church VA 22044 Office: 2461 Eisenhower Ave Alexandria VA 22331

STACEY, NORMA JEANNE, nurse; b. Houlton, Maine, Aug. 20, 1927; d. Lisle Fulton and Rena Alice (Hannigan) Hallett; R.N., Mercy Hosp. Sch. Nursing, Portland, Maine, 1947; student E. Tex. State U., 1977—; m. James Edward Stacey, Oct. 26, 1948; children—James Edward, Royal K. II, Marsha Stacey Carmichael, Catherine Stacey Shrode, John Douglas, Mark Allen, Mary Margaret, Rebecca Jane. Nurse, Maine, 1947, Tex., 1950-51, Mo., 1953-55, Colo., 1958-60, Ga., 1964-66, Okinawa, 1966-67, Hawaii, 1967-68, Ariz., 1968-70, Ky., 1970-71; nursing supr. Children's Med. Center, Oklahoma City, 1971-74, Dallas, 1975-78. Active Girl Scouts U.S.A., 1962-64, 66-67, 71-74, Nat. Council Catholic Women, 1962-64, 68-70, AAU, 1977—. Mem. Smithsonian Assos. Roman Catholic. Home: 2901 Biscayne Circle Plano TX 75075

STACK, EDWARD J., Congressman; b. Bayonne, N.J., Apr. 29, 1910; B.A., Lehigh U., 1931; J.D., U. Pa., 1934; M.A., Columbia U., 1938; m. Jean Pearce, 1954; children—Kathleen, William. Admitted to N.Y. state bar; practiced in N.Y.C.; real estate investor; bank dir.; sheriff, Broward County, Fla., 1968-78; commr., mayor City of Pompano Beach (Fla.), 1965-69; mem. 96th Congress from 12th Congressional Dist. Fla.; mem. Nat. Democratic Fin. Council, Broward County Dem. Exec. Com.; holder numerous gubernatorial and public service positions. Served with USCG, 1942-46. Recipient Man of Yr. award Council Italian-Am. Clubs Broward County, 1973, Good Govt. award Ft. Lauderdale Jaycees, 1975; County Govtl. Activities award Freedoms Found., 1975, Law Enforcement medal SAR, 1975, Man of Yr. award Civitan Club, 1977, Gt. Am. Traditions award Internat. B'nai B'rith, 1978. Mem. N.Y. Bar Assn., Fla. Sheriffs Assn., Broward County Chiefs Police Assn., Internat. Narcotic Enforcement Officers Assn., Fla. Council on Crime and Delinquency, Internat. Assn. Chiefs Police, Boys Clubs Broward County, Am. Legion, Emerald Soc., Ky. Cols., Urban League, Beta Theta Pi. Democrat. Clubs: Kiwanis, K.P. Office: Room 1440 Longworth House Office Bldg Washington DC 20515

STACKLER, LOUIS MICHAEL, planner; b. Wilmington, Del., June 28, 1948; s. Louis Joseph and Margaret Wanda (Bialkowski) S.; A.B., King's Coll., Wilkes-Barre, Pa., 1970; M.A., Okla. State U., 1974; m. Susan Camille Creider, Dec. 21, 1974; 1 dau., Elizabeth Anne. Planner intern Tulsa Model Cities Program, 1973, program evaluator, 1973-74; dir. health planning No. Okla. Devel. Assn., Enid, 1974-76; coordinator Okla. Health Systems Agy., Enid, 1976—. Chmn. fund raising com., bd. dirs. Heart Assn.; bd. dirs. Foster Grandparent Program and Ret. Sr. Vol. Program; mem. com. YMCA; bd. dirs. United Way Enid, 1979. Served with USNR, 1969-70. Recipient Man of Year award Heart Assn., 1978; registered emergency med. technician. Mem. Am. Soc. Public Adminstrn., Okla. Health and Welfare Assn., Okla. Public Health Assn., Region VI Health Planning Assn., Pi Sigma Alpha. Democrat. Roman Catholic. Clubs: K.C., Kiwanis. Home: 405 N 19th St Enid OK 73701 Office: 1909 S Van Buren St Enid OK 73701

STACY, RALPH WINSTON, physiologist; b. Middletown, Ohio, Feb. 6, 1920; s. Wayne and Elvira (Gillum) S.; B.S., Miami U., Ohio, 1942; M.S., Ohio State U., 1947, Ph.D., 1948; m. Marjorie J. Shepard, Mar. 19, 1943; children—William B., Susan M. Prof. physiology dept. Ohio State U., Columbus, 1949-61, U. N.C., Chapel Hill, 1961-69; scientist Cox Heart Inst., Kettering, Ohio, 1969-72; prof., chmn. dept. physiology So. Ill. U., Carbondale, 1972-77; research physiologist EPA, Chapel Hill, 1977—. Served with USAF, 1942-46. Mem. Biophys. Soc., Am. Physiol. Soc., Bioengring. Soc., Sigma Xi, N.C. Watercolor Soc. Roman Catholic. Author: Modern College Physiology; Computers in Biomedical Research; Physiology of Muscular Activity and Exercise; Biological and Medical Electronics; Essentials of Biological and Medical Physics; contbr. numerous articles on physiology, biophysics and biomathematics to sci. jours. Home: 609 Tinkerbell Chapel Hill NC 27514 Office: US Environmental Protection Agy Mason Farm Rd Chapel Hill NC 27514

STADELMANN, RICHARD WILLIAM, clergyman, educator; b. Lynn, Mass., Dec. 16, 1932; s. William Louis and Olga Ann (Halbich) S.; B.A., Earlham Coll., 1954; M.Div., Yale, 1958; postgrad. Tulane, 1960-65; m. Bonnie Sue Shelton, June 16, 1956 (div. Dec. 1972); children—Marcus Richard, Lowell Shelton, Mary Idell, Kristine Marie; m. 2d, Patricia Annette Perry, June 12, 1976; children—Olga Gertrude, Greta Katryn; stepchildren—Aimee Elizabeth, Lisa Annette. Ordained minister Christian Ch., 1954; minister Bethel Christian Ch., Fountain City, Ind., 1952-54, Perry (Ohio) Christian Ch., 1958-60; instr. Tulane, 1962-63, La. State U., New Orleans, 1963-67; asst. prof. philosophy Tex. A & M U., College Station, 1967—; minister Brenham (Tex.) Christian Ch., 1968-76, Smithville (Tex.) Christian Ch., 1978—. County chmn. Burleson County Republican party, 1973-74, precinct chmn. Brazos County, 1974—. Served with USNR, 1958. Lindemuth scholar, 1950-54; Elk scholar, 1950-54; Am. Legion scholar, 1950-54; Yale U. scholar, 1957-58; Tulane scholar, 1960-65; recipient Downes award, 1958. Mem. AAUP (pres. 1971-72), Am. Philos. Assn., Metaphys. Soc. Am., Soc. Process Studies, Southwestern Philos. Soc., Am. Forensic Assn., Tau Kappa Alpha. Home: 1218 S Ridgefield Circle College Station TX 77840 Office: Dept Philosophy Tex A & M Univ College Station TX 77843

STADT, BESSIE WINIFRED, Spanish linguist, educator; b. Rochester, N.Y., Aug. 7, 1914; d. Arthur Alfred and Elsie (Stanbridge) Stanford; B.A. with high distinction, U. Rochester, 1938, M.A., 1939; Ph.D., U. Ariz., 1969; m. Norman Paul Stadt, Aug. 30, 1958. Tutorial fellow Spanish, Northwestern U., 1939-40; v.p., treas. Gallia Labs., Inc., N.Y.C., 1948-57; tchr. Spanish, N.Y.C. secondary schs., 1959-60, 61-63, Dixie Hollins High Sch., St. Petersburg, Fla., 1960-61; grad. asso. Spanish, U. Ariz., Tucson, 1963-65; asst. prof. Spanish, Simpson Coll., Indianola, Iowa, 1965-66; asst. prof. Spanish, Rollins Coll., Winter Park, Fla., 1966-69, asso. prof., 1969-75, prof., 1975—, head dept. fgn. langs., 1974-77; translator, judge county and state competitions in Spanish. Research grantee Rollins Coll., summers 1970, 72. Mem. MLA, S. Atlantic MLA, Am. Assn. Tchrs. Spanish and Portuguese, Phi Beta Kappa, Phi Sigma Iota, Sigma Delta Pi. Home: 905 Garden Dr Winter Park FL 32789

STAFFORD, GEORGE TIMOTHY, JR., trailer mfg. co. exec.; b. Birmingham, Ala., Sept. 30, 1907; s. George Timothy and Margaret (Berry) S.; B.S. in Mech. Engring., Auburn U., 1929; m. Agnes Evelyn Coffin, Mar. 31, 1934; children—Evelyn (Mrs. Burns Johns), George Timothy III, Harry Coffin. Mgr. heating dept. Birmingham Gas Co., 1930-42; engr. WPB, 1943, Continental Gin, 1944; v.p. Fontaine Truck Equipment, 1945; pres. Birmingham Mfg. Co. Inc., 1946—, Birmingham Totemall Inc., 1962—. Chmn. bd. trustees Southeastern Bible Coll., Birmingham, 1979—. Patentee in field. Mem. Tau Beta Pi, Phi Delta Gamma, Alpha Phi Epsilon. Home: 3632 Montevallo Rd Birmingham AL 35213 Office: PO Box 289 Springville AL 35146

STAFFORD, JAMES POLK, JR., civil engr.; b. Oxford, Miss., Oct. 13, 1918; s. James Polk and Lottie Etoile (Smith) S.; B.S., Miss. State Coll., 1939; M.S., Iowa State Coll., 1940; m. Edna Earle Snyder, May 29, 1941; children—Jeanette Patricia, Pamela Anne, James Polk III. Engr., Soil Conservation Service, U.S. Dept. Agr., 1940, 46; civil engr. office engring. br., constrn. div. U.S. Army Engr. Dist., Vicksburg, Miss., 1947-62, resident engr. DeGray Dam, 1963-72, chief constrn. div., 1973—. Pres., Cooper High Sch. P.T.A., 1962, Arkadelphia High Sch. Booster Club, 1967, Vicksburg Community Chrous, 1975-76. Served with U.S. Army, 1941-45. Recipient George Marshall Scholastic award Command and Gen. Staff Coll., 1963; Meritorious Service medal U.S. Army Reserve, 1974. Mem. Soc. Am. Mil. Engrs. (Goethals award 1974), ASCE, U.S. Com. on Large Dams. Registered profl. engr., Miss. Methodist. Club: Lions. Home: 326 McAuley Dr Vicksburg MS 39180 Office: PO Box 60 Vicksburg MS 39180

STAFFORD, JOSEPH HOOVER, univ. adminstr.; b. Hope, Ind., June 5, 1939; s. Joseph Howard and Katherine Elizabeth (Hoover) S.; B.S., Purdue U., 1961, M.S., 1962, Ph.D., 1965; m. Margaret Ann Johnson, Aug. 10, 1963; children—Mary Ann, Don, Susan, David, Kathy. Agrl. economist U.S. Dept. Agr., 1962-64; research asso. dept. civil engring. M.I.T., 1966-67, asst. prof., 1967-70; asst. dean for acad. affairs U. Fla., Gainesville, 1971-75; vice chancellor State Univ. System of Fla., Tallahasse, 1975—; mem. Fla. State Bd. Ind. Colls. and Univs., 1975—. Served with U.S. Army, 1964-66. Author: (with R. deNeufville) Systems Analysis for Engineers and Managers, 1971. Home: 2917 Lasswade Dr Tallahassee FL 32312 Office: 107 W Gaines St Tallahassee FL 32304

STAFFORD, STEPHEN WILLIAM, educator; b. El Paso, Tex., July 21, 1948; s. Mason Lee and Christine (Warthen) S.; B.S. in Metall. Engring., U. Tex., El Paso, 1970; Ph.D. in Materials Scis., Rice U., Houston, 1975; m. Karen Day, Aug. 14, 1971. Engr. Armco Steel Corp., summer 1969, asso. process metallurgist, 1970-72; postdoctoral fellow Rice U., 1975, vis. asst. prof. mech. engring., 1975-76; faculty dept. metall. engring. U. Tex., El Paso, 1976—. Served with AUS, 1970-71. Robert A. Welch Found. fellow, 1975; Rice Fellow, 1972-75; Am. Smelting and Refining Co. scholar; registered profl. engr., Tex. Mem. Am. Inst. Metal. Engrs., Am. Soc. Metals, Tex. Soc. Profl. Engrs., Sigma Xi, Tau Beta Pi, Alpha Sigma Nu, Tau Kappa Epsilon. Office: Dept Metall Engring U Tex El Paso TX 79968

STAGG, LOUIS CHARLES, educator; b. New Orleans, Jan. 3, 1933; s. Louis Anatol and Gladys (Andrews) S.; B.A. in English, La. Coll., 1955; M.A. in English U. Ark., 1957, Ph.D. in English, 1963; m. Mary Casner, June 5, 1959; children—Robert Charles, Helen Marie. Teaching asst. English U. Ark., 1955-59; asst. prof. William Jewell Coll., 1959-60; instr. Stephen F. Austin State U., 1960-62; asst. prof. Memphis State U., 1962-69, asso. prof., 1969-77, prof., 1977—, dir. English Drama Players, 1968—. Cons. Nat. Endowment for Humanities, 1975, 76, 78. Mem. Memphis Oratorio Soc. Chorus, 1969—. Recipient summer stipend Nat. Endowment for Humanities, 1967; Memphis State U. grantee, 1965—; travel grantee to U.S. Library of Congress, summer 1971. Mem. Modern Lang. Assn., So. Humanities Conf. (sec.-treas. 1974-76, exec. com. 1976—, ad hoc com. on crisis in teaching humanities 1977—), Tenn. (exec. sec. 1970-75, pres. 1976-77, exec. com. 1977), Ark. philol. assns., Shakespeare Assn. Am., Internat. Shakespeare Assn., Renaissance Soc. Am., South Central Renaissance Conf. (chmn. nominations 1976, exec. com. 1978—), South Central (sec., chmn. English I 1971), South Atlantic modern lang. assns., South Central Coll. English Assn., Patristic Medieval and Renaissance Conf. Middle Atlantic States (sect. chmn. Medieval drama 1977), AAUP, Phi Beta Kappa, Alpha Chi. Democrat. Episcopalian (lay reader 1969—). Author: (with J. Lasley Dameron) Poe's Critical Vocabulary, 1966; author series: Index To The Figurative Language of John Webster's Tragedies, 1967, of Ben Jonson's Tragedies, 1967, of Thomas Heywood's Tragedies, 1967, of George Chapman's Tragedies, 1970, of John Marston's Tragedies, 1970, of Thomas Middleton's Tragedies, 1970, of Cyril Tourneur's Tragedies, 2d edit all 7 under title Index to the Figurative Language of the Tragedies of Shakespeare's Chief 17th Century Contemporaries), 1977; contbr. to Great Writers of the English Language, 1979. Circulation editor Interpretations, 1976—. Contbr. articles on English drama to profl. jours. Home: 5219 Mason Rd Memphis TN 38117 Office: Dept English Memphis State U Memphis TN 38152

STAGGERS, HARLEY O., congressman; b. Keyser, W.Va., Aug. 3, 1907; s. Jacob Kinsey and Frances Winona (Cumberledge) S.; A.B., Emory and Henry Coll., 1931, LL.D., 1953; postgrad. Duke U., 1935; LL.D., Davis and Elkins Coll., 1969, W.Va. U., W.Va. Wesleyan Coll., 1971; m. Mary Veronica Casey, Oct. 4, 1943; children—Margaret Ann, Mary Katherine, Frances Susan, Elizabeth Ellen, Harley Orrin, Daniel Casey. Coach, tchr sci. Norton (Va.) High Sch., 1931-33; head coach Potomac State Coll., Keyser, 1933-35; sheriff Mineral County, Keyser, 1937-41; right-of-way agt., Va. dir. Office Govt. Reports, later OWI, 1942; mem. 81st to 96th Congresses from 2d W.Va. dist. Served as lt. comdr. A.C., USNR, 1942-46; PTO. Mem. Am. Legion, V.F.W., DAV, Amvets, W.Va. Farm Bur. Democrat. Methodist. Clubs: Moose (past pres. state assn.), Elks, K.P., Lions (past dist. gov. W.Va.). Office: 2366 Rayburn House Office Bldg Washington DC 20515

STAHL, DAN L., constrn. co. exec.; b. Joplin, Mo., Nov. 15, 1948; s. Norman K. and Betty L. S.; B.A. in Bus. Adminstrn., Okla. State U., 1970; m. Linda M. McIntyre, May 29, 1970; 1 son, Jeff M. Scaleman, Evans & Assos. Constrn. Co., Inc., Ponca City, Okla., 1970-71, job. cost supr., 1971-72, accounts payable supr., 1972-73, office mgr., 1973-79, asst. treas., 1979. Chmn. allocations com., mem. exec. com., mem. bd. dirs. Ponca City United Way, 1979. Mem. Am. Bus. Club (dir. 1979), Ponca City C. of C., Indian Nations Car Assn. (pres.), Ducks Unlimited (charter mem., area chmn. 1975-77). Republican. Methodist. Home: 37 Raintree St Ponca City OK 74601 Office: Evans & Assos Constrn Co Inc 3320 N 14th St Ponca City OK 74601

STAHL, RAY EMERSON, freelance writer, public relations cons.; b. Latrobe, Pa., Mar. 24, 1917; s. Curtis E. and Josephine (King) S.; A.B., Bethany Coll., 1938; M.Div., Butler U., 1943; Ed.M., U. Pitts. 1946; postgrad. St. Vincent Coll., 1939. Pitts. Sch. Accountancy, 1939-40, U. Ky., 1955; M.A., Ohio State U., 1969; m. Faith Worrell, Aug. 25, 1941; children—Ellen Josephine (Mrs. Lawrence Carpenter), Ray Emerson. Ordained to ministry Disciples of Christ Ch., 1941; minister Brentwood Christian Ch., Pitts, 1943-46, First Christian Ch., Erwin, Tenn., 1946-50; exec. sec. in charge bus. adminstrn. and pub. relations Milligan Coll., Tenn., 1950-68; dir. pub. relations E. Tenn. State U., Johnson City, 1968-78. Bd. dirs. United Way. Mem. Tipton-Haynes Hist. Assn., Council for Advancement Small Colls. (chmn. pub. relations 1957-61), Pub. Relations Soc. Am. (accredited), East Tenn. Edn. Assn. (chmn. pub. relations 1968-76), Johnson City C. of C. (dir.), Kappa Alpha, Theta Phi, Kappa Tau Alpha. Republican. Mem. Christian Ch. (elder). Club: Kiwanis. Author: How to Finance the Local Church, 1953; Six Decades of Progress, 1976. Contbr. articles to profl. jours. Home: 108 Park Ct Johnson City TN 37601

STALCUP, JOE ALAN, lawyer, clergyman; b. Hooker, Okla., Feb. 13, 1931; s. Herbert I. and Ruby (Gantt) S.; B.B.A. cum laude, So. Methodist U., 1951, J.D. magna cum laude, 1959, M.Th. magna cum laude, 1978; m. Nancy Jo Vaughn, Sept. 3, 1950; children—Melinda Stalcup Lundy, Sondra Stalcup Goodson, Cherl Stalcup Ehley. Tchr. Dallas Ind. Sch. Dist., 1951-57; admitted to Tex. bar, 1959; asso. mem. firm Locke, Purnell, Boren, Laney & Neely, Dallas, 1959-66; asso. atty., partner firm Geary, Brice & Lewis, Dallas, 1966-67; founder, sr. partner firm Stalcup, Johnson, Meyers & Miller and predecessor firm, Dallas, 1968-75; ordained minister Christian Ch.; dean Sch. Theology for Laity, 1978-80. Pres. Dallas County Young Democrats, 1952-54. Bd. dirs., mem. exec. com. N. Tex. Christian Communications Commn., 1972-78; bd. dirs., v.p. Greater Dallas Council Chs., 1972-75. Mem. Am., Tex., Dallas bar assns., Phi Alpha Delta. Home: 7594 Benedict Dr Dallas TX 75214 Office: 505 Diamond Shamrock Tower 717 N Harwood St Dallas TX 75201

STALEY, KENNETH EUGENE, automobile mfg. co. exec.; b. Western, Nebr., Nov. 26, 1904; s. Ernest Grant and Ruby (Stevens) S.; student U. Nebr., 1922-24, Armed Forces Indsl. Coll., 1947-48; m. Nell Dowd, Oct. 23, 1928. With Gen. Motors Corp., various locations, 1929-66, gen. sales mgr., Detroit, 1959-62, v.p. distbn. and mktg., 1962-66, ret., 1966, mem. Gen. Motors Speakers Bur., 1966—; dir. First Fed. Savs. & Loan, Lake Worth, Fla. Sec. treas., mem. bd. govs. Nat. Hwy. User Conf., Washington, 1962-66. Bd. dirs. Auto Industry Hwy. Safety Com., 1962-66; trustee Fla. Atlantic U. Found., Boca Raton (Fla.) Community Hosp.; gov. U. Miami (Fla.); mem. bd. regents Gen. Motors Inst., 1962-66. Served to col. AUS, 1941-45; ETO. Decorated Bronze Star, Purple Heart, Presdl. citation; Belgian Croix de Guerre, others. Mem. Soc. Univ. Founders, Soc. Benefactors, Internat. Oceanographic Found., Automotive Orgn. Team, Lambda Chi Alpha. Republican. Roman Catholic. Clubs: Royal Palm Yacht and Country, 100, Police and Firemen Benefactors (Boca Raton); 100; D.A.C. (Detroit). Home: 1200 S Ocean Blvd Apts 15A-B Boca Raton FL 33432 Office: Gen Motors Bldg W Grand Blvd Detroit MI 48202

STALLINGS, JESSE DANIEL, logistician; b. Terrell, Tex., Apr. 20, 1915; s. William Thomas and Katherine Lee (Hall) S.; Certified Internat. Inst. Photographic Arts, 1950, Am. Mgmt. Assn., 1973, Inst. Profl. Mgrs. Trinity U., 1976, Rockwell Internat. Schedule Cost Control Systems Program, 1977; m. Toinette Marie Heffington, July 25, 1945; children—Sharon Sue, Michael Daniel, Melissa Marie, Robin Joseph. Stunt man, actor various employers, and locations, 1930-40; surveyor Ky. Nat. Gas Co., Owensboro, 1938; field supt. Municipal Service Co., Henderson, Ky., 1939-40; constrn. supt. Ky. Ice and Storage Co., Henderson, 1948; constrn. mgr. Gulf S. Utilities, Lucedale, Miss., 1949-50; mgr. Myres Photo Labs., Dallas, 1950-51; art editor and pub. relations dir. Southwestern Square Dancer Mag., Dallas, 1951-52; supv. State Farm Ins. Co., Dallas, 1952-62; mgr. provisioning dept. Collins Radio Divs., Rockwell Internat., Dallas, 1962-77; pvt. practice, Logistics cons., Garland, Tex., 1977—; mgr. provisioning dept., sr. logistics engr. Tracor Inc., 1978—. Team leader U.S. Savs. Bond Drive, Dallas, 1975; loaned exec. United Way Fund Drive, 1976; curator 112th Cavalry Mus., 1960-77; asst. to Irving (Tex.) Bicentennial Mus. Com., 1976—. Served as capt. U.S. Army, 1940-47; mem. 112th Cavalry Tex. NG, 1930-40. Decorated Bronze Star, Purple Heart. Recipient Leadership award, N.Tex. chpt. Soc. Logistics Engrs., 1974, 75; Patriotic Service award, U.S. Treasury Dept., 1975; letter of commendation Rockwell Internat., 1976; certificate of Appreciation City of Irving Bicentennial Commn., 1976; 112th Cavalry Assn., 1974. Mem. Am. Mgmt. Assn., Soc. Logistics Engrs. (chmn. N. Tex. chpt. 1974-75, organizer, chmn. Tex. chpt. 1978-79, mem. dist. bd. advs.), Electronics Industries Assn., 112th Cavalry Assn., 1st Cavalry Div. Assn., Retired Officer Assns., VFW. Mem. Christian Ch. Home: Pet Rock Ranch 15 Country Oaks Dr Buda TX 78610

STALLINGS, WILLIAM DERWART, physician, educator; b. Balt., Dec. 18, 1932; s. Bernard F. and Mary M. (Derwart) S.; B.A., U. Va., Charlottesville, 1954, M.D., 1958; m. Shelley Ann Markle, Dec. 26, 1959; children—Jeff, Valerie, Evan, Neil, Nicole. Intern, Kans. U. Med. Center, 1958-59; resident Sch. Aviation Medicine U.S. Navy, Pensacola, Fla., 1959; practice medicine specializing in family practice, Virginia Beach, Va., 1962—; mem. staff First Colonial Family Practice Center, Virginia Beach, 1970—; chief of staff Gen. Hosp. of Virginia Beach, 1965, pres. staff, 1970; asso. clin. prof. family practice Med. Coll. Va., Richmond, 1974—. Served with USN, 1959-62. Diplomate Am. Bd. Family Practice. Fellow Am. Acad. Family Practice; mem. AMA, Soc. Tchrs. Family Medicine, Med. Soc. Va. Roman Catholic. Clubs: Princess Anne Country, K.C. Home: 2508 Little Lake Ct Virginia Beach VA 23454 Office: 1120 First Colonial Rd Virginia Beach VA 23454

STALLMAN, KENNETH EDWARD, banker; b. Wausau, Wis., Mar. 4, 1941; s. Edward John and Florence Marie (Sternberg) S.; B.S. in Polit. Sci. and Econs., Wis. State U., Eau Claire, 1964; M.S. in Ibero-Am. studies, U. Wis., Madison, 1968; m. JoAnn Edythe Fenton, May 8, 1971; 1 son, Kenneth John. Mem. Peace Corps, Peru, 1964-66; asst. v.p. Bank of Am. N.T. & S.A., San Francisco, 1969-74; v.p., mgr. Bank of Am. Internat. of Tex., Houston, 1978—. Mem. Houston World Trade Assn. (dir.), Am.-Arab C. of C. (dir.), Dallas World Trade Assn., Tulsa World Trade Assn., Houston C. of C. Office: Bank of Am Internat of Tex 500 Dallas St Houston TX 77002

STALLWORTH, DANIEL TUCK, educator; b. Beatrice, Ala., Apr. 23, 1932; s. Frank Tuck and Emma Jerry S.; B.S., Ala. State U., 1956; M.S., Atlanta U., 1961; postgrad. U. Ala., Okla. State U., 1973—; m. Dorothy Mae Millender, June 21, 1958; children—Daniel Irvin, Sharran Yvette. Tchr., Booker T. Washington High Sch., Montgomery, Ala., 1956-60; mem. faculty Ala. State U., Montgomery, 1961—. Elder, minister Jehovah's Witnesses. Mem. Math. Assn. Am., Beta Kappa Chi. Author: Basic College Mathematics, 1967. Home: 2019 Grande Ave Montgomery AL 36116 Office: 232 PH Alabama State University Montgomery AL 36104

STALLWORTH, HUGH FRANCIS, physician; b. Cin., July 1, 1944; s. Alvin Jaxon and Louise Beatrice (Peoples) S.; B.S., Wayne State U., 1968, M.D., 1970; m. Patricia Ann Powe, July 1, 1966; children—Timothy, Kimberly. Intern, Detroit Gen. Hosp., 1970-71; resident in internal medicine Henry Ford Hosp., Detroit, 1973-74; practice family medicine, Detroit, 1974-78, Danville, Ky., 1978—; sch. physician Ky. Sch. for Deaf, Danville, 1979—; mem. staff Ephram McDowell Meml. Hosp., Danville; asst. prof. Coll. Medicine, U. Ky., 1980—. Served to capt. AUS, 1971-73. Diplomate Am. Bd. Family Practice. Recipient award Joseph P. Kennedy Jr. Found., 1979. Mem. Nat. Med. Assn., Am. Acad. Family Physicians, Boyle County Med. Soc. (v.p.), Danville C. of C. Home: 586 Buckingham Ln Lexington KY 40503

STAMBAUGH, HARRIETT WYNN MCCARDELL (MRS. JAMES STAMBAUGH), social worker; b. Phillipsburg, Pa., May 10, 1922; d. Horace A. and Vivian A. (Wynn) McCardell; B.A., Juniata Coll., 1942; M.S. in Social Service, Boston U., 1947; m. James Arthur Stambaugh, May 1, 1954; children—James Arthur, David Monroe, Richard Thomas. Tchr. history, Curwensville, Pa., 1942-44; social worker ARC, Lancaster, Pa., 1945-46, social work supr., Cin., 1947-54; adminstr. social work Dept. Pub. Welfare, Lexington, Va., 1958-61; area. supr. social work Ky. Dept. Child Welfare, Frankfort, 1962; intake social worker Hope Cottage, Children's Bur., Dallas, 1963; adminstr., mental health and mental retardation cons. Dallas County Health Dept., Dallas, 1963-66; dir. clin. social work dept. Childrens Med. Center, Dallas, 1966—. Instr., Southwestern Med. Sch., Dallas, 1966-67, asst. prof. pediatrics, 1967—; exec. dir. Southwestern Cons., Inc., Dallas, 1968-75; cons. Terrell State Hosp., Dallas Child Welfare Dept., 1966-67, Dallas Assn. Retarded Children, 1966-68; cons. various nursing homes, 1968-71; mem. Mental Health-Mental Retardation Profl. Adv. Bd. Dallas County, Tex., 1966-73, Mental Health Assn. Profl. Adv. Bd., Dallas, 1968-72, Dallas County Community Action Com. Bd., Dallas, 1967-68; mem. med. adv. com. Dallas chpt. Nat. Found., 1973-80, Parents Without Partners, 1967-74, mem. profl. adv. com. Creative Learning Center, 1968-74, Epilepsy Assn., 1972-80; mem. Abortion Edn. Com. Dallas, 1970-71; mem. state bd. Parents Anonymous, 1973-78; chairperson Child Abuse and Neglect Com.; mem. Region VI Task Force, HEW, 1975; mem. adv. com. Early and Periodic Screening, Testing and Diagnosis Program, 1975-78; mem. policy adv. com. Child Abuse and Neglect Regional Resource Center, 1975—; mem. human service adv. com. Eastfield Coll., Dallas County Jr. Coll. Dist., 1975-80; mem. children and youth adv. com. City of Dallas, 1976—, human devel. fund rev. com., 1976-77; mem. prof. adv. com. Vis. Nurses Assn., 1977-80; mem. dist. 23 service/rehab. com. Am. Cancer Soc., 1977-79. Bd. dirs. Dallas Mental Health Assn., 1972—, Routh St. Center, 1972—, Family Center, 1973-75; mem. profl. adv. com. Dallas Assn. Children with Learning Disabilities, 1973—. Recipient Arete award, 1969; Margaret Cone award for contbn. to children's services, 1973. Mem. Nat. Assn. Social Workers (Social Worker of Year, Dallas chpt. 1969), Acad. Certified Social Workers, Am. Assn. Marriage and Family Counselors, Tex. Soc. Hosp. Social Work Dirs. (dir. 1973-78, pres. 1977), Soc. Hosp. Social Work Dirs. of Am. Hosp. Assn. (dir. 1979—), Women's Council Dallas County. Democrat. Methodist. Home: 7138 Currin Dr Dallas TX 75230 Office: 1935 Amelia St Dallas TX 75235

STAMBAUGH, REGINALD JACK, ophthalmologist; b. West Palm Beach, Fla., Jan. 1, 1930; s. Gleason Noah and Marjorie (Hilton) S.; A.B., U. Fla., 1952; M.D., U. Miami, 1959; m. Carolyn Stroupe, Nov. 24, 1965; children—Melanie, Joette, Valerie, Reginald Giles. Intern, Grady Meml. Hosp., Atlanta, 1959-60, resident, 1960-64; individual practice medicine specializing in ophthalmology, West Palm Beach, 1963—; chief ophthalmology Good Samaritan Hosp., West Palm Beach, 1966-74; lectr. Bascom Palmer Eye Inst., U. Miami Sch. Medicine, 1964-73; mem. med. adv. bd. Fla. Soc. for Prevention of Blindness, 1972-77, Crippled Children's Soc. of Palm Beach, 1965-77. Bd. dirs. Fla. Med. Polit. Action Com., 1975-77. Served with USAF, 1952-54. Decorated Korean Presidential citation; diplomate Am. Bd. Ophthalmology, Nat. Bd. Med. Examiners. Mem. Fla., So. Am. med. assns., Am. Acad. Ophthalmology and Otolaryngology, Fla. Soc. Ophthalmology (sec.-treas. 1975-77, pres.-elect), Palm Beach County Med. Soc. (pres. 1977, trustee 1977—). Democrat. Episcopalian. Clubs: Sailfish of Fla. (bd. govs.), Bath and Tennis (Palm Beach). Contbr. numerous articles, papers in field. Home: 272 Queens Ln Palm Beach FL 33480 Office: 2707 N Flagler Dr West Palm Beach FL 33407

STAMEY, MARIYANA LOUISE, city ofcl.; b. Barberton, Ohio, Oct. 18, 1938; d. Eli and Marcella (Engel) Sekicki; student Akron U., 1957-60, Manatee Jr. Coll., 1971-77; m. Jay Stamey, Oct. 15, 1961; 1 dau., Sharon Sarita. With City of Sarasota (Fla.), 1960—, data processing supr., 1968-71, adminstrv. asst. to city auditor and clk., 1971-79, records mgr., 1979—. Mem. Assn. Records Mgrs. and Adminstrs., Nat. Microfilm Assn., Mcpl. Clks. Assn. Democrat. Home: 2453 Robinson Ave Sarasota FL 33582 Office: PO Box 1058 Sarasota FL 33578

STAMLER, ARTHUR DONALD, media prodn. exec.; b. Malden, Mass., Apr. 23, 1933; s. John Jacob and Yvette (Greenblatt) S.; B.S. cum laude, Boston U., 1954; M.S., Calif. Western U., 1977, Ph.D., 1979; m. Virginia Inez Orrison, Aug. 7, 1960; children—Bert, Frances, Blake, Ardon, Sara. News dir. Sta. WHIL, Boston, 1951-54; gen. mgr. Sta. WGUY, Bangor, Maine, 1954-56; gen. mgr. Sta. WFAX, Falls Church, Va., 1957-59; mgr. audio-visuals Nat. Assn. Broadcasters, Washington, 1959-61; owner, gen. mgr. Sta. WOHN, Herndon, Va., 1961-64; pres., chief exec. officer Ads Audio Visual Productions, Inc., Falls Church, Va., 1961-78, chmn., 1979—. Vice chmn. Fairfax Planning Commn., 1961, chmn. Fairfax Fire Commn., 1972-73; vice chmn. Fairfax Econ. Devel. Commn., 1972-73; chmn. Fairfax Bicentennial Commn., 1974-77. Served to 1st lt. AUS, 1956-58. Recipient CINE Dept. State award, gold and silver medals N.Y. Internat. Film Festival, gold award Indsl. Film Producers Assn., highest honors Nat. Soc. Films for Safety. Mem. Public Relations Soc. Am., Am. Soc. Assn. Execs., IEEE, Nat. Assn. Govt. Communicators, Fairfax C. of C. (pres. 1971-72), Audio Engring. Soc., Broadcast Pioneers Am., Acad. TV Arts and Scis., Acad. Country Music, Nat. Assn. Religious Broadcasters, Armed Forces Communications and Electronics Assn., Am. Film Inst. Home: 352C Fort Valley Saint Davids Church VA 22652 also 3612 University Dr Fairfax VA 22030

STAMLER, WILLIAM RAYMOND, materials handling machinery co. exec.; b. Beckley, W.Va., Nov. 11, 1934; s. William Raymond and Mary H. (Buford) S.; B.A., U. of South, 1956; m. Ellen Charlotte Boyd, Sept. 30, 1961; 1 dau., Rose Mary. Pres., chmn. W.R. Stamler Corp., Millersburg, Ky., 1965—, treas., 1972—; dir. Asso. Industries of Ky.; pres. Peoples Deposit Bank, Paris, Ky., 1978—. Mem. Ky. Commn. Product Liability, 1977—; chmn. bd. trustees Millersburg Mil. Inst., 1978—; bd. dirs. Bourbon County YMCA; trustee U. of South. Served with USAF, 1956-65. Decorated Air Force Commendation medal with cluster. Mem. Bourbon County C. of C. (pres. 1971, best dir. 1973), Paris High Sch. Alumni Assn. (pres. 1969), Am. Mining Congress (gov. mfrs. div. 1979—), AIME, Young Pres.'s Orgn. U.S. Power Squadron, Res. Officers Assn., Kappa Alpha. Episcopalian. Clubs: Mining, Cincinnati, Lafayette, Lexington Yacht, Stoner Creek Country. Home: 2 Mount Airy Dr Paris KY 40361 Office: W R Stamler Corp 600 Main St Millersburg KY 40348

STAMM, ROBERT CALVIN, engring. and constrn. co. exec.; b. Phila., July 2, 1925; s. William Calvin and Allis Patience (Gill) S.; student Columbia Coll., 1943, Wittenberg U., 1944; B.S.M.E., Columbia U., 1950; m. Esther Elizabeth Smith, Aug. 8, 1953. Project engr. Westvaco Corp., N.Y.C., 1950-56, mgr. design and constrn., 1956-59, engring. group mgr., 1959-69, chief engr., 1969-75, corporate mgr. energy and property conservation, 1975-76; v.p. Brown & Root, Inc., Houston, 1976—. Served with USAAF, 1944-46. Fellow TAPPI (past dir., exec. com.); mem. AAAS, Am. Concrete Inst., ASME, Can. Pulp and Paper Assn., Res. Officers Assn., Phi Kappa Psi, Tau Beta Pi. Club: Houston Engring. and Sci. Home: 1643 W Belt Dr S Houston TX 77042 Office: PO Box 3 Houston TX 77001

STAMPER, JAMES HARRIS, physicist; b. Richmond, Ind., Sept. 10, 1938; s. L.A. and Adele Stamper; B.A. magna cum laude in Physics, Miami U., Oxford, Ohio, 1960; M.S. in Physics, Yale U., 1962, Ph.D., 1965; m. Susan Diann Hayes, June 10, 1974. Asst. prof. physics Elmira (N.Y.) Coll., 1962-63, 65-66, U. Fla., Gainesville, 1967-70; asso. prof., chmn. dept. phys. scis. Fla. So. Coll., Lakeland, 1970—; cons. Battelle Meml. Inst., Columbus, Ohio, 1968-74, Agrl. Research and Edn. Center, Lake Alfred, Fla., 1977—. Mem. Am. Phys. Soc., Am. Assn. Physics Tchrs., Fla. Acad. Scis., Phi Beta Kappa, Sigma Pi Sigma, Phi Eta Sigma. Home: 98 Imperial Southgate Villas Lakeland FL 33803 Office: Fla Southern Coll Lakeland FL 33802

STAMPER, JOE ALLEN, lawyer; b. Okemah, Okla., Jan. 30, 1914; s. Horace Allen and Ann (Stephens) S.; B.A., U. Okla., 1933, LL.B., 1935; m. Johnnie Lee Bell, June 4, 1936; 1 dau., Jane Allen (Mrs. Ernest F. Godlove). Admitted to Okla. bar, 1935; practiced in Antlers, Okla., 1935-36, 46—; atty. Pushmataha County, 1936-39; mem. Okla. indsl. commn., 1939-40; spl. justice Okla. Supreme Ct., 1948. Pres., Antlers Sch. Bd., 1956-67, Pushmataha Found., 1957—; mem. Okla. Bicentennial Commn. Mgr., Okla. Democratic party, 1946; chmn. dist., 1946-50; alternate del. Dem. Nat. Conv., 1952; vice chmn. bd. Okla. U. Law Center, 1976—. Served from 2d lt. to col. AUS, 1935-46, ETO. Decorated Bronze Star. Fellow Am. Coll. Trial Lawyers, Am. Bar Found.; mem. Am. (ho. of dels.), Okla. (bd. govs. 1969-74, Pres.'s award 1977) bar assns., Okla. Bar Found. (pres. 1978), Mil. Order World Wars, S.A.R., Pi Kappa Alpha. Baptist (deacon). Mason (32 deg., Shriner), Lion. Club: Whitehall (Oklahoma City). Home: 1000 NE 2d St Antlers OK 74523 Office: PO Box 100 Antlers OK 74523

STAMPER, ORVILLE BUSH, ret. educator; b. Wheeler, Tex., July 29, 1913; s. William Clinton and Mary Audrey (Bush) S.; B.S., Okla. State U., 1936; M.Ed., U. Okla., 1949; Ed.D., Tex. Tech. U., 1958; m. Delila Murrel Cummings, July 13, 1941; children—Carol Ann Stamper Stover, Gary Lynn. Tchr., prin. Okla. Pub. Schs., 1933-44; accountant Asso. Refineries, Duncan, Okla., 1944-45; prin. N.Mex. Pub. Schs., 1945-49; prin. Tex. Pub. Schs., 1949-54, supt. Three Way Consol., Morton, Tex., 1954-55; dir. audio-visual dept. No. State Coll., Aberdeen, S.D., 1955-60; asso. prof. David Lipscomb Coll., Nashville, 1960-61; prof., dir. tchr. edn. Okla. Christian Coll., Oklahoma City, 1961-78, ret., 1978. Mem. Nat., Okla. assns. tchr. educators, Am. Assn. Colls. for Tchr. Edn., Mensa, Phi Delta Kappa. Home: 712 NW 52d St Oklahoma City OK 73118

STAMPS, DENNIS EARL, audiologist; b. Columbia, Miss., Aug. 18, 1941; s. Earl and Helen S.; B.A., U. So. Miss., 1965; M.A., U. Ill., 1967. Audiology trainee VA Hosp. and Keesler AFB Hosp., Biloxi, Miss., 1965; asst. in audiology U. Ill., Urbana, 1965-67; clin. audiologist, instr. U. Miami Sch. Medicine, 1967-69; clin. audiologist Springfield (Ill.) Clinic, 1969-70; clin. audiologist, instr. La. State U. Med. Center, New Orleans, 1970-73; clin. audiologist, supr. Baptist Hosp., Pensacola, Fla., 1973—, acting dept. head, 1977. Named Employee of Month, Bapt. Hosp., 1977, recipient Five Year Service award, 1978. Mem. Am. Speech and Hearing Assn. (cert. clin. competence), Fla. Lang., Speech and Hearing Assn. Baptist. Home: 5655 N 9th Ave Apt J-207 Pensacola FL 32504 Office: Baptist Hosp Speech and Hearing Clinic 1000 W Moreno St Pensacola FL 32501

STANALAND, WILLIAM WHIT, JR., accountant; b. Benson Junction, Fla., Mar. 15, 1930; s. William Whit and Goldie (Merritt) S.; B.S. in Bus. Adminstrn., U. Fla., 1957, postgrad., 1959; postgrad. Rollins Coll., 1964; m. Norma Lee Ober, June 24, 1961; children—Sherry D., William Whit III, Terence B., Dana Lee; m. 2d, Sandra L. Swann, Dec. 1, 1971. Jr. accountant Pepsi Cola Bottling Co., 1957-58; accountant Wells, Laney, Earlich & Baer, 1958-59, A.J. Mixner, C.P.A,, 1961-63; controller Halco Products, Inc., 1959-61; C.P.A., Orlando, Fla., 1963—. Served with USMC, 1948-52. C.P.A., Fla. Mem. Am., Fla. insts. C.P.A.'s, Asso. Builders and Contractors. Clubs: Econs. of Orlando, Kiwanis, Toastmasters. Home: 510 Crane's Way Unit 302 Altamonte Springs FL 32701 Office: 327 Whooping Loop Altamonte Springs FL 32701

STANASZEK, WALTER FRANCIS, educator, pharmacist; b. Chgo., Oct. 23, 1940; s. Walter Edward and Blanche Mary (Boots) S.; B.S., U. Ill., 1962, M.S., 1966, Ph.D., 1970, certificate Residency Hosp. Pharmacy, 1966; m. Mary Jane Weisman, May 7, 1966; children—Mary Beth, Jennifer Lynn. Pharmacist, Carson's Pharmacy, Danville, Ill., 1962-64; asst. dir. Hosp. Pharmacy Services, U. Ill. Research and Edn. Hosps., Chgo., 1966-70; instr. hosp. pharmacy U. Ill. Coll. Pharmacy, 1968-70; research fellow dept. anesthesiology Presbyn.-St. Luke's Hosp., Chgo., 1968-70; asst. prof. clin. pharmacy U. Okla. Coll. Pharmacy, Oklahoma City, 1970-76, asso. prof., 1976—; adj. prof. div. health occupations Oscar Rose Jr. Coll., Midwest City, Okla., 1973—; adj. asso. prof. nursing U. Okla., 1976—; coordinator and cons. hosp. pharmacy Presbyn. Hosp., Oklahoma City, 1972—; cons. VA Hosps., Muskogee, 1971—, Oklahoma City, 1971—; vis. prof. U. Okla. Health Sci. Center, 1975-77. Recipient Lederle Pharmacy Faculty award, 1974, 75, Outstanding Faculty Mem. award, 1978, Lyman award, 1973. Mem. Am. Pharm. Assn., Am. Soc. Hosp. Pharmacists (editor I.P.A. jour. 1970—), A.A.A.S., Am. Assn. Colls. Pharmacy, Acad. Pharm. Scis., A.A.U.P., Sigma Xi, Rho Chi, Phi Delta Chi. Author: (with M. Stanaszek) Handbook of Medical Terminology, 4th edit., 1977; (with T. Covington) Perspectives in Clinical Pharmacy Practice, 1974. Editor (with C. Blissitt and O. Webb) Clinical Pharmacy Practice, 1972; contbg. editor U.S. Pharmacist Jour., 1976—; contbr. numerous articles to profl. and sci. jours. Home: 402 N Sherry St Norman OK 73069

STANCLIFF, FREDERICK JACOB, ins. co. exec.; b. Wyoming, Ill., Mar. 3, 1902; s. David Marion and Annie Florence (Neibert) S.; B.S. in Mech. Engring., Rice U., 1926; m. Florence May Powars, Nov. 15, 1927; 1 son, Frederick Jacob. Petroleum and field Engr. Marland Oil Co. (now Conoco), 1926-31; life ins. agt., 1931-35; gen. agt. Vol. State Life Ins. Co., Houston, 1935—. Named to Hall of Fame, Rice U., 1973, recipient Distinguished R award, 1971. Mem. Gen. Agts. and Mgrs. Assn. (pres.), Am. Soc. Magicians (pres.), Tex. Shrine Clown Assn. (pres.), Harris County Grand Jury Assn. (treas.), R Assn. of Rice U. (sec.-treas.). Mason (Shriner, K.T.). Clubs: Shrine Luncheon (pres.); Salesmanship of Houston (pres.). Home: Number 4 Westlane Houston TX 77019 Office: Suite 100 3801 Kirby St Houston TX 77098

STANCZYK, MARTIN HENRY, govt. ofcl., metallurgist; b. Jersey City, Jan. 26, 1930; s. Martin John and Mary Josephine (Sajkowski) S.; B.S., U. Ariz., 1957, M.S., 1958, Metall. Engr. (hon.), 1975; m. Mary Lu Sauer, Nov. 28, 1957 (div. 1974); children—Cynthia, Rebecca, Jeanette, Brooks; m. 2d, Charlotte B. Sherrill, July 1978; stepchildren—Gayle, David, Billy. Metallurgist, U.S. Bur. of Mines, Tucson, 1957-60, research metallurgist, Tuscaloosa, Ala., 1960-68, supervisory metallurgist, College Park, Md., 1968-73, dir. research, Tuscaloosa, 1973—. Mem. Ala. Environ. Council. Coach, (Kettering) Md. Boys and Girls Club; football coach Boys Club Tuscaloosa. Mem. adv. bd. U. Ala. Mineral Resource Inst. Served with USAAF, 1949-53. U.S. Bur. of Mines fellow, 1957. Mem. Am. Inst. Mining Engrs. (sec. treas. 1968-70, award 1973), Sigma Xi, Phi Lambda Upsilon. Elk. Contbr. articles to profl. publs. Home: 8 Woodland Pines Tuscaloosa AL 35405 Office: PO Box L University AL 35486

STANDEL, RICHARD REYNOLD, JR., lawyer; b. N.Y.C., Nov. 20, 1936; s. Richard Reynold and Antoinette (Pfinder) S.; A.B., Columbia U., 1956, J.D., 1959; LL.M., N.Y. U., 1972; m. Elizabeth Curtis Hughes, Dec. 14, 1963. Admitted to N.Y. bar, 1960, Colo. bar, 1974, Tenn. bar, 1979; asso. firm Wickes, Riddell, Bloomer, Jacobi & McGuire, N.Y.C., 1959-64; successively atty., council, asso. gen. counsel Johns-Manville Corp., N.Y.C., 1964-71, dir. acquisition ops., then dir. acquisitions and divestments, Denver, 1972-76; v.p., gen. counsel, sec. No. Telecom, Inc., Nashville, No. Telecom Systems Corp., Mpls., 1976—; dir. CTSS, Inc., No. Telecom Acceptance Corp., No. Telecom Industries, Inc. Mem. Am. Soc. Corp. Secs. Club: Richland Country. Home: One Harpeth Trace Dr Nashville TN 37205 Office: International Plaza Nashville TN 37217

STANDER, ROBERT ANGUS, chem. co. exec.; b. Balt., July 7, 1928; s. Henricus Johannes and Florence Mary (Creelman) S.; student Cornell U., 1946-47; A.B. in Physics, Colby Coll., 1950; m. Maurine Masal Maust, June 4, 1951; children—Mary Stander Landry, Linda Stander Denton, Robert Angus, Timothy. Trainee physicist Texaco, Inc., 1950-51; with Chem. Service, Inc., 1955-62, br. mgr., Baton Rouge, 1956-58, gen. mgr., Lafayette, La., 1958-62; founder Chem. Applicators of Lafayette, Inc., 1963, chmn. bd., pres., gen. mgr., 1963—; dir. Burlastan. Served with USAF, 1952-55; Korea. Mem. Nat. Assn. Corrosion Engrs., Nat. Assn. Power Engrs., Natural Gas Processors Assn., Am. Petroleum Inst., Nat. Pilots Assn., Aircraft Owners and Pilots Assn., Air Force Assn., Am. Legion. Republican. Presbyterian. Club: Rotary. Inventor chem. and mechanic procedures. Home: 313 Thibodeaux Dr Lafayette LA 70503 Office: PO Box 52803 Lafayette LA 70505

STANDIFER, HUGH AVERY, city ofcl.; b. Johnson County, Tex., Dec. 19, 1932; s. Mynis William and Lucy Kate (Lomax) S.; student Sam Houston State U., 1950, 70-71, U. Tex., Arlington, 1958, Central Tex. Coll., 1971-72, St. Edwards U., 1973; B.S. in Criminal Justice,

Am. Tech. U., 1974; m. Bonnie K. Ruschmyer Juergens, Apr. 14, 1979; children by previous marriage—Hugh Marcus, William Herman, Penny Teresa, Patti Christine. Computer programmer Gen. Foods Corp., 1958-64; ops. mgr. Nat. Western Life Ins. Co., Austin, Tex., 1964-67; asst. div. chief for data processing Tex. Dept. Public Safety, Austin, 1967-73; data systems adminstr. City of Austin, 1974—; mem. rev. bd. Public Technology, Inc., 1975-76; instr. Tex. A&M U., 1969-74; mem. textbook selection com. Austin Ind. Sch. Dist., 1975-76, Gov.'s Commn. on Standards and Goals for Tex., 1975-76. Served with AUS, 1955-58. Mem. Met. Info. Exchange (pres. 1980), Govt. Mgmt. Info. Scis., Urban and Regional Info. Systems Assn., Library an Info. Tech. Assn., ALA, Tex. Assn. Govtl. Data Processing Mgrs. (exec. com., chmn. edn. com.). Lutheran. Pioneer in use of convict labor for clerical/data preparation activities. Office: PO Box 1088 Austin TX 78767

STANFIELD, LARRY ARDEN, architect; b. Mobridge, S.D., Jan. 29, 1946; s. Wesley Doyle and Samara Lathona (Scott) S.; student (Coll. Scholastic scholar) Lee Coll., 1963-65, U. Chattanooga, 1965; B.Arch. (Univ. Scholastics scholar), U. Tenn., 1970; m. Alana Fern Tharp, June 18, 1966; children—Sean Christopher, Leslee Caprice, Wesley Chandler. Draftsman, White & Thomas Architects, Knoxville, Tenn., 1966; designer, student asst. U. Tenn. Sch. Architecture, 1966-70, student tchr., 1969-70; designer Sverdrup and Parcel and Assos., Inc., Nashville, 1970-73; project coordinator Gresham and Smith Architects, Nashville, 1973-74, project architect, 1974-80, head archtl. design and sr. project architect, 1980—. Dept. Transp. research grantee, 1966, 67; Nat. Endowment for Arts grantee, 1969. Mem. AIA, Tenn. Soc. Architects, Constrn. Specifications Inst., Phi Kappa Phi. Presbyterian (deacon 1980). Designer: Palm Dr. Hosp., Sebastopol, Calif., 1974, Ukiah (Calif.) Gen. Hosp., 1974, restoration U.S. Customs House, Nashville, 1979, restoration Hermitage Hotel, Nashville, 1979, renovation and expansion King Faisal Med. Center, Saudi Arabia, 1976-80. Office: 2222 State St Nashville TN 37203

STANFORD, BILLY PATE, circuit breaker mfg. co. exec.; b. Temple, Tex., Oct. 6, 1941; s. Joe B. and Pauline Stanford; student Temple Jr. Coll., 1963, U. Tex., 1963-64; m. Diana Blight, Sept. 19, 1974; children—Lisa, Paula, Suzanne. Store dir. H.E. Butt Grocery Co., Belton, Tex., 1958-74; ops. officer Texas Bank, Temple, 1974; sales mgr. Frito-Lay, Inc., Temple, 1974-75; indsl. relations dir. Rockwool Industries, Inc., Belton, 1975-80; personnel mgr. Gould Inc., Temple, 1980—. Bd. dirs. Belton United Fund, 1972-75, Blue Bonnet council Girl Scouts U.S., 1978-80; bd. dirs. Heart of Tex. council Boy Scouts Am., 1975-77. Served with U.S. Army, 1964-69. Mem. Am. Soc. Personnel Adminstrs., Temple Personnel Assn., Tex. Safety Assn., Ind. Businessmen Am., Tex. Assn. Businessmen, U.S. Jaycees (pres. 1972-73). Methodist. Club: Rotary (pres. 1971-72). Home: 621 Estate Dr Belton TX 76513 Office: PO Box 1908 Temple TX 76501

STANFORD, HARRY WRIGHT, ednl. adminstr.; b. San Antonio, Sept. 3, 1923; s. Edward Rosemond and Elizabeth Gooch (Wright) S.; B.S., North Tex. State U., 1942; M.S., Calif. Inst. Tech., 1944; postgrad. U. Tex., Austin, 1946-47, 66, Tex. Tech., 1967-68; m. Katheryne Lucille Belser, Aug. 15, 1948; children—Rebecca (Mrs. Gene B. Christy), Janice (Mrs. Robert K. Hickman), Teresa (Mrs. John J. Davis, Jr.), Nancy Jo. Tchr., prin. Elkhart (Tex.) Pub. Schs., 1942-43; asst. state auditor, Austin, 1947-49; chief accountant, auditor N.Tex. State U., Denton, 1949-55; asst. supt., bus. mgr. Midland (Tex.) Pub. Schs., 1955-69, San Antonio Pub. Schs., 1969-77, Alamo Hts. Pub. Schs., 1977—. Chmn. supervisory com. Tchr. Credit Union, 1950-61; chmn. shelter com., disaster plans ARC, 1963-66; govt. agys. chmn. United Fund, 1964-65; sec. fin. com. Midland Citizens Adv. Com. for Pub. Schs., 1965; mem. adv. com. Tex. Bd. Edn., Edn. Mgmt. Info. System, 1968-76. Served with USAAF, 1943-46; PTO. C.P.A., Tex. Mem. Tex. Assn. Sch. Bus. Ofcls. (pres. Bexar County 1973-74), Assn. Sch. Bus. Ofcls. of U.S. and Can., Tex. Soc. C.P.A.'s, Tex. Tchrs. Assn. (life). Methodist. Mason, Lion. Author: School District Accounting Procedures Manual, 1971. Office: 141 Lavaca St San Antonio TX 78210

STANFORD, WILEY WATTS, pension cons.; b. Pine Apple, Ala., July 20, 1926; s. Wiley Watts and Lillian (McCrory) S.; student U.S. Mcht. Marine Acad., 1944-46; B.S., Auburn U., 1948; children—Susan Stanford Jemison, Charlotte Stanford Jackson. Asst. cashier Elba Exchange Bank (Ala.), 1948-50; chief accountant Life Ins. Co., Elba, 1950-54; v.p. So. Benefit Life Ins. Co., Elba, 1954-58, also dir.; ins. agt., Pine Apple, 1958-65; v.p. Carlisle and Assos., Montgomery, Ala. and Atlanta, 1965-71, pres., 1971—, also dir. Mem. council Boy Scouts Am., 1952-57. Served as ensign USNR, 1946-47. Registered securities rep., Ala., Ga. Mem. Am. Soc. Pension Actuaries (asso.), So. Pension Conf., Internat. Assn. Fin. Planners. Baptist. Clubs: Lions, Masons. Office: 3300 Northeast Expressway Suite 4M Atlanta GA 30341

STANIFER, RALPH MICHEL, ophthalmologist; b. Detroit, Dec. 14, 1946; s. Ralph Eugene and Evelyn Martha (Zellman) S.; B.S. with distinction, Wayne State U., 1968; M.D., U. Mich., 1973. Intern, St. Joseph Mercy Hosp., Ann Arbor, Mich., 1974; resident in ophthalmology U. Mich., 1974-77; cornea fellow Baylor Med. Coll., Houston, 1977-78, asst. prof., 1978—; chief ophthalmology VA Hosp., Houston. Diplomate Am. Bd. Ophthalmology. Mem. AMA, Tex. Med. Assn., Am. Acad. Ophthalmology, Contact Lens Assn. Ophthalmologists, Assn. Research in Vision and Ophthalmology. Home: 47 Chelsea Pl Houston TX 77006 Office: Dept Ophthalmology Baylor Coll Medicine Houston TX 77030

STANIFIER, JAMES WILLIAM, educator; b. Beaumont, Tex., Oct. 20, 1913; s. Samuel Francis and Zena Zora (Owens) S.; B.S., Tex. A&M U., 1944; M.Ed., U. Tex., Austin, 1945; Ed.D., U. Mich., 1957; m. Lillian Lela Hill, July 22, 1944; 1 dau., Jo Lynn. Asst. coach, intramural dir. Lamar Coll., 1940-42; instr. phys. edn., asst. intramurals Tex. A&M U., 1942-43; athletic dir. Austin Recreation Dept., 1944-46; dir. phys. edn., athletic dir. Wharton Coll., 1946-47; dir. recreation Cactus Plant, Phillips Petroleum Co., 1947-52; asst. prof. health and phys. edn. U. Dayton (Ohio), 1956-57; asso. prof. Tex. Christian U., Fort Worth, 1957-60, prof. phys. edn., 1960-79; cons. driver edn. Tex. Edn. Agy., 1971; vis. prof. Sul Ross State U., 1974; ind. cons. driver and traffic safety, Ft. Worth, 1979—. Mem. AAHPER, Nat. Coll. Phys. Edn. Assn. for Men and Women, Am. Driver and Traffic Safety Edn. Assn. (bd. dirs., award of merit), AAUP, Am. Coll. Safety Assn., Tex. Driver and Safety Edn. Assn. (bd. dirs., past pres., honor award, award named in his honor), Tex. Assn. Health and Phys. Edn., Tex. Assn. Coll. Tchrs., Ft. Worth Driver Edn. Assn., Phi Delta Kappa. Contbr. articles to profl. jours. Home: 4404 Wedgmont Circle S Fort Worth TX 76133 Office: Dept Kinesiological Studies Tex Christian U Fort Worth TX 76129

STANITSKI, CONRAD LEON, chemist; b. Shamokin, Pa., May 3, 1939; s. Leon John and Florence Filomena (Czarnecki) S.; B.S., Bloomsburg State Coll., 1960; M.A., State Coll. of Iowa, 1964; Ph.D. (NASA fellow), U. Conn., 1971; m. Barbara Sherts, July 27, 1963; children—Susan, Beth. Tchr., Lower Dauphin High Sch., Hummelstown, Pa., 1960-63; instr. Edinboro (Pa.) State Coll., 1965-67; asst. prof. chemistry Ga. State U., Atlanta, 1971-76; asso. prof., chmn. dept. chemistry Randolph-Macon Coll., Ashland, Va., 1976—; cons. NSF, W.B. Saunders Publs., Prentice-Hall Publs., McGraw-Hill Pubs. Mem. Am. Chem. Soc., AAAS, Smithsonian Assos., Sigma Xi, Phi Lambda Upsilon, Phi Sigma Pi. Presbyterian. Club: Hanover Country. Author: Chemistry for Health-Related Sciences, 1976; Lab. Manual in Chemistry for Health-Related Sciences, 1976; Aspects of Chemistry for Health-Related Sciences, 1979. Home: 117 Mullen Dr Ashland VA 23005 Office: Randolph-Macon Coll Henry St Ashland VA 23005

STANLEY, DUFFY BROCK, architect; b. Midland, Tex., Feb. 14, 1923; s. Benjamin M. and Mary (White) S.; student Tex. A. and M. U., 1941-43, B.Arch., 1948; m. Irene Marie Muller, July 31, 1948; children—Sheila, Lars, Brock, Sonya, Sharon. Draftsman-designer J.J. Black, Architect, Midland, 1948-51; job capt. Carroll & Daeuble, Architects, El Paso, Tex., 1951-57; prin. Duffy B. Stanley, Architects, El Paso, 1957—; lectr. U. Juarez (Mex.), 1978. Mem. El Paso Zoning Bd. Adjustment, 1959-69, chmn., 1970; mem. Open Space Com. El Paso, 1970-71; vice chmn. Citizens Environ. Council, 1971-72; chmn. El Paso County Hist. Commn., 1978; bd. dirs. Mission Heritage Assn. El Paso; chmn. govt. applications rev. com. W. Tex. Council Govts., 1977. Served to capt. AUS, 1943-46. Decorated Bronze Star, Silver Star, Combat Infantryman's badge with 2 battle stars. Mem. A.I.A. (chpt. pres. 1964, state dir. 1965, chmn. chpt. com. hist. bldgs.). Presbyterian. Mason. Author: Open Space in the El Paso Region, 1970. Major works include: El Paso Water Utilities Bldg., 1965; Morehead Sch., El Paso, 1964; Lincoln Intermediate Sch., El Paso, 1979. Home: 3120 Wheeling St El Paso TX 79930 Office: Bassett Tower El Paso TX 79901

STANLEY, HAZEL CARTER, hosp. nutrition services dir.; b. Clinchport, Va., Sept. 18, 1930; d. Clyde William and Mary Julie Carter; student Va. Intermont Coll., 1947-48; B.S., Madison U., 1951; postgrad. U. Iowa, Va. Poly. Inst. and State U., Radford U.; m. Robert Calhoun Stanley, Aug. 18, 1951; children—Roberta Stanley Bell, Barbara Kay, John William. Dietitian, Chesapeake & Ohio Hosp., Clifton Forge, Va., 1953-57, Catawba Hosp., Va., 1960-65, 4-H Center, Wintz, Va., 1965-66; dietitian, dir. food services Roanoke (Va.) Meml. Hosps., 1966. Mem. food service adv. com. Nat. Assn. Retarded Citizens; mem. 5th Dist. planning commn., profl. adv. com. Blue Ridge chpt. Epilepsy Assn. Am. Recipient award of merit Roanoke Meml. Hosp., 1970. Mem. Am. Dietetic Assn. (council ednl. preparation), Va. Dietetic Assn., Roanoke Dietetic Assn., Roanoke Valley Nutrition Assn., Nutrition Today Soc. Mem. Ch. of the Brethren. Club: Tinker View Swim and Tennis. Home: Route 2 Box 53 Valley Rd Troutville VA 24175 Office: PO Box 13367 Roanoke Memorial Hospitals Roanoke VA 24033

STANLEY, JACK BERRY, gas co. exec.; b. Houston, July 30, 1947; s. John Roy and Mildred K. S.; B.S. in Indsl. Tech., W. Tex. State U., 1973; m. Sonja K. Tarter, June 5, 1971; 1 son, Jerry Wayne. Draftsman, Pioneer Natural Gas Co., Amarillo, Tex., 1971-72, engrng. asst., 1972-78, sr. engrng. asst., 1978-79, field prodn. supt., 1979—. Past scoutmaster Boy Scouts Am., Amarillo. Mem. Am. Soc. Cert. Engrng. Technicians (pres. Tri-State chpt.; Outstanding Engrng. Technician Tri-State chpt. 1978), Inst. for Cert. of Engrng. Technicians, Alumni Assn. W. Tex. State U., Alpha Tau Omega. Republican. Baptist. Home: PO Box 501 Miami TX 79059 Office: Pioneer Natural Gas Co PO Box 498 Miami TX 79059

STANLEY, JOSEPH ANDREW, JR., san. engr.; b. Ft. Worth, Sept. 30, 1915; s. Joseph Andrew and Florence (Lewis) S.; student Sul Ross Coll., 1933-35; grad. Tex. Tech. U., 1939; postgrad. Vanderbilt U., 1940; m. Mildred Dutton Knox, July 28, 1940; children—Carole Ann, Joseph A. III. Jr. engr. Tex. Hwy. Dept., Pecos, Odessa, 1940; jr. engr., dist. san. engr. Tex. Dept. Health, Lubbock, 1940-46; san. engr. City of Lubbock, 1946-47; pres. Hygeia Bottled Water Inc., Lubbock, 1947—. Chmn., City County Bd. Health, Lubbock, 1951-54; chmn. Municipal Utilities Bd., 1959-65; chmn. City-County Health Bd., Lubbock, 1966-68; chmn. Citizens Adv. Com., 1966-69; flight safety officer Civil Air Patrol. Del., Tex. State Democratic Conv., 1954; sec., chmn. pro tem, then chmn. bd. mgrs. Lubbock County Hosp. Dist., 1968-80. Bd. dirs., sec.-treas. bd. Lubbock Boys Clubs, 1968-73; pres. bd. dirs. YMCA, 1957; bd. dirs. Vols. of Am., So. Plains Health Systems Agy. Served with USPHS, 1954-56. Named One of 5 Outstanding Young Men, Tex. Jr. C. of C., 1946; Engr. of Year, 1970. Lic. pilot. Mem. Nat., Tex. socs. profl. engrs., Am. (pres. 1966, sec.-treas. 1967), Tex. (pres. 1963, 65) bottled water assns., Tex. Turf Irrigation Assn. (pres. 1967), Am. Water Works Assn., Phi Kappa Psi. Baptist. Rotarian, Mason. Clubs: Lubbock, Lubbock Country, Univ. City. Patentee water purification equipment. Home: 5412 16th Pl Lubbock TX 79416 Office: 405 Ave U Lubbock TX 79401

STANLEY, MARVIN MILES, educator; b. Lexington, Miss., Mar. 1, 1922; s. Marvin and Leila Virginia (Miles) S.; student Miss. State U., 1939-42; A.B., George Washington U., 1956; M.B.A., Harvard U., 1959; Ph.D., Am. U., 1972; m. Rebecca Alice Matchett, May 21, 1943; children—Richard Matchett, Virginia Miles, Lynne Anne. Commd. 2d lt. USAF, 1943, advanced through grades to col., 1964; command pilot, chief plans and programs div., chief public info. div. Office Sec. Air Force, 1964-67; dir. info. Tactical Air Command, 1967-68; ret., 1968; asst. prof. Coll. William and Mary, Williamsburg, Va., 1968-71, asso. prof., 1971-74, prof. bus. adminstrn., 1974-77, Chessie prof. bus. adminstrn., 1977—, asso. dean Sch. Bus. Adminstrn., 1971-74; v.p. Mid-Atlantic Research, Inc., 1979—; dir. First Va. Bank of Peninsula/Tidewater; cons. Coca-Cola Co., 1974—, Chessie System, 1974—. Mem. Gov. Va. Bd. Adv. Economists, 1978—; bd. dirs. Eastern region Acad. Mgmt., 1971-74; chmn. bd. Queens Lake, Inc., 1971-73; mem. commn. to study acquisition Washington Nat. and Dulles Airports by Commonwealth Va., 1971-73. Decorated Legion of Merit (2), Air medal (2); recipient Silver Anvil award Am. Public Relations Assn., 1960.; Baker scholar Harvard Bus. Sch., 1959. Mem. Acad. Mgmt., Air Force Assn., Ret. Officers Assn., Newcomen Soc. N. Am., Beta Gamma Sigma. Republican. Episcopalian. Clubs: Army-Navy Country, Golden Horseshoe Golf Assn. Home: 103 Little John Rd Williamsburg VA 23185 Office: Sch Bus Adminstrn Coll William and Mary Williamsburg VA 23185

STANLEY, NANCY NELL, librarian-archivist; b. Blum, Tex., Nov. 26, 1924; d. James Harvey and Sadie Pearl (Luton) Stanley; student Southwestern Baptist Theol. Sem., 1952-53; B.A., Mary Hardin-Baylor Coll., 1956; postgrad. in library sci. Va. Commonwealth U., 1960-61. Dir. religious edn. First Bapt. Ch., Belton, Tex., 1956-57; dir. religious edn. for youth First Bapt. Ch., Brownwood Tex., 1957-58; mgr. library and archives Fgn. Mission Bd., So. Bapt. Conv., Richmond, Va., 1958—. Dean women, counselor Bapt. ch. camps in Tex., 1954-58. Mem. A.L.A., Soc. Am. Archivists, Va. Library Assn., So. Baptist Hist. Soc., Va. Hist. Soc., Assn. Nat. Archives, Smithsonian Instn. (asso.), Alpha Chi, Sigma Tau Delta. Contbr. articles to religious jours. Home: 4712 Patterson Ave Richmond VA 23226 Office: 3806 Monument Ave Richmond VA 23230

STANLEY, ROBERT ALTON, educator; b. Steiner, Tex., May 3, 1917; s. Lawrence B. and Margie K. (Adcock) S.; B.S., N. Tex. State U., 1946; M.A., Sul Ross State Coll., 1949; m. Anna Marie Seljos, Dec. 23, 1938; children—Lee Burnett, Randall Leighton, Warren Llewellyn. Tchr. pub. schs. Tex., 1937-42; prin. high sch. Granfills Gap, Tex., 1946-51, Brewer High Sch., Fort Worth, 1951-58; supt. Granbury Ind. Sch. (Tex.), 1958-71; tchr. Cleburn (Tex.) Ind. Sch. Dist., 1971-73; supt. Blum (Tex.) Ind. Sch. Dist., 1973-78. Served with C.E., AUS, 1942-46; PTC. Mem. Internat. Platform Assn., Nat. Wildlife Fedn. Home: 1210 Hemphill Cleburne TX 76031

STANONIS, BENEDICT ANTHONY, oil co. exec.; b. Louisville, Aug. 6, 1933; s. Frank and Lelia Elizabeth (Lehman) S.; B.S., U. Ky., 1953; student Air War Coll., 1972; m. Michaela Maria Kahlert, Apr. 15, 1974; 1 son, Anthony Joseph. Commd. 2d lt. U.S. Air Force, 1953, advanced through grades to lt. col., 1970; served in Vietnam, 1967-68; with Hdqrs. USAFE, Wiesbaden, Ger., 1968-71, Hdqrs. DCA, Arlington, Va., 1971-73 ret., 1973; founder, sr. v.p., chemist OILCO Internat. Liquids Corp., Lexington, Ky., 1975—. Decorated Bronze Star. Mem. Am. Chem. Soc., Ret. Officers Assn., Air Force Assn., Am. Legion., Alpha Chi Sigma. Democrat. Roman Catholic. Club: Circle Chess. Address: 3816 Lake Trail Dr Kenner LA 70062

STANONIS, DAVID JOSEPH, chemist; b. Louisville, Mar. 19, 1926; s. Frank and Lelia Elizabeth (Lehmann) S.; B.S., U. Ky., 1945; Ph.D., Northwestern U., 1950. Asst. prof. Clark U., Worcester, Mass., 1949-50, Loyola U., Chgo., 1950-54; research chemist So. Regional Research Center, U.S. Dept. Agr., New Orleans, 1956—. Served with AUS, 1954-56. Mem. Sci. Research Soc. N.Am. (pres. New Orleans br. 1965), Am. Inst. Chemists (chmn. La. chpt. 1971), Am. Assn. Textile Chemists and Colorists (chmn. Gulf Coast sect. 1974, 75), Fiber Soc., Am. Chem. Soc. Roman Catholic. Contbr. articles to profl. jours. Patentee in field. Home: 3406 Canal St New Orleans LA 70119 Office: 1100 Robert E Lee St New Orleans LA 70179

STANSBURY, WILLIAM BROWN, city ofcl.; b. Corydon, Ind., Mar. 18, 1923; B.A. in Econs., U. Louisville, 1947, J.D., 1950; married; 1 dau., Patricia Stansbury Beckman. Admitted to Ky. bar, 1950; with firm Mapother, Morgan and Stansbury, from 1952; sr. partner firm Wood, Goldberg, Pedley and Stansbury. Pres., mayor pro-tem Bd. of Aldermen, Louisville, 1974-75; probate commr., judge pro-tem, Jefferson County, also mem. planning and zoning com., mem. fin. and budget com.; mem. Gov.'s Com. Constitutional Revision; active numerous campaign coms., from 1963; mayor City of Louisville, 1977—. Served to capt. U.S. Army, AC, 1942; awarded Air medal with oak leaf cluster. Recipient Distinguished Citizenship award, 1972. Mem. Louisville (past pres., past mem. ethics com., past mem. bd. legal aid, past mem. exec. com., former chmn. unauthorized practice of law com.), Ky. (convention chmn. 1977, mem. lawyer-laymen advisory com., former chmn. unauthorized practice of law com.), Am. bar assns., Louisville C. of C. (cities com.), Delta Epsilon, Rotarian. Clubs: "L" (bd. dirs.), ULA, Jefferson, Big Springs Country, Holy Name Soc. Home: 766 Greenridge Lane Louisville KY 40207 Office: Office of Mayor Room 101 City Hall 601 W Jefferson St Louisville KY 40202

STANSFIELD, GEORGE JAMES, librarian, historian; b. Oak Park, Ill., Mar. 8, 1917; s. James Howard and Inez Pearl (Snyder) S.; student M.I.T., 1934-35; B.S., Harvard U., 1940; postgrad. Am. U., 1940-44, 61-64, George Washington U., 1965-66; m. Anna Bryant Hill, Oct. 20, 1945; children—Louisa Westcott, James Ross. With Nat. Park Service, 1941-42, Nat. Archives, Washington, 1942-46, World War I Declassification Bd., Dept. Army, 1946-48; with library reference sect. Nat. War Coll., Washington, 1948-61, library dir., 1961-73, historian, 1965-76; historian Nat. Def. U., Washington, 1976-78, chief spl. collection, hist. br., library div., 1978—; librarian Am. Mil. Inst., 1944-63; mem. Fed. Library Com. Task Force on acquisition of library materials and correlation of fed. library resources, 1965-72. Chmn., Hist. Records Adv. Com. City of Alexandria, 1975—. Fellow Am. Mil. Inst. (life); mem. Alexandria Library Co., Spl. Libraries Assn. (chmn. archives com. mil librarians div. 1966-76), Alexandria Assn. (pres. 1972-73), Soc. Am. Archivists, Am. Hist. Assn., Alexandria Hist. Soc. (treas. 1974-76), SAR. Episcopalian. Book rev. editor Mil. Affairs, 1944-46, 50-63; asso. editor, author chpt. Alexandria: A Towne in Transition, 1800-1900, 1977; adv. bd. No. Va. Heritage, 1978—; editorial com. Alexandria History, Vol. I, 1978; contbr. sects. to books, articles to jours., reports, ency. Address: 512 Duke St Alexandria VA 22314

STANTON, GERALD BARRY, educator, clergyman; b. Cambridge, Eng., Apr. 22, 1918; s. Percival and Florence Maidie (Richardson) S.; came to U.S., 1926, naturalized, 1936; student St. Petersburg Jr. Coll., 1936-37; B.Sc., Wheaton (Ill.) Coll., 1940; postgrad. Wheaton Sem., 1940-41; Th.M., Dallas Theol. Sem., 1945, Th.D., 1952; m. Mary Elizabeth Engstrom, Aug. 4, 1946; children—Kenneth Paul, Sharon Elizabeth, Richard Allen, Elaine Christine. Ordained to ministry Bapt. Ch., 1942; nation-wide Bible Conf. ministry, 1952—; prof. systematic theology Talbot Theol. Sem., chmn. doctrine dept. Biola Coll., Los Angeles, 1952-61; exec. dir. Christian World Found., Boca Raton, Fla., 1962-64; founder, pres. Ambassadors Internat., Inc., West Palm Beach, Fla., 1964—; asso. prof. religion Palm Beach Atlantic Coll., 1968-71. Bd. reference Internat. Missions. Republican. Author: Christian Foundations, 1954; The Person and Work of Jesus Christ, 1955; Kept From the Hour, 1956; Prophetic Highways, 1957; The Great Words of the Gospel, 1959; What Is God Like?, 1963; Why I Am a Premillennialist, 1976. Mem. revision com. The Fundamentals for Today, 1958; editorial bd King's Bus. Mag., 1955-61. Contbr. articles to Baker's Dictionary of Theology, religious publs. Home: 270 Granada Rd West Palm Beach FL 33401 Office: 1111 S Flagler Dr West Palm Beach FL 33401

STANTON, PAUL EUGENE, JR., surgeon; b. Atlanta, Dec. 28, 1944; s. Paul E. and Mary Ruth (Pollard) S.; B.A. (Latin scholar), Emory U., 1965; M.D. (Rita Bard scholar), Med. Coll. Ga., 1969; m. Nancy Lynn Brumit, July 2, 1966; children—Eric Scott, Ryan Ashley, Shelley Allison. Rotating intern surgery Tampa Gen. Hosp., U. South Fla., 1969-70; resident surgery Ga. Bapt. Med. Center, 1970-74; vascular fellow Northwestern U. Sch. Medicine, Chgo., 1974-75; practice medicine, specializing in vascular surgery, Atlanta, 1975—; mem. staff Crawford W. Long Hosp., West Paces Ferry Hosp., chief vascular surgery dept., 1977-78; dir. surg. residency edn. program Ga. Bapt. Med. Center, Atlanta, 1975—, dir. Blood Flow Lab., 1975—; clin. instr. surgery Emory U., Atlanta, 1975—; clin. asst. prof. surgery Med. Coll. Ga., 1980—; partner Atlanta Vascular Specialists, P.C., 1979—. Recipient Upjohn Intern of Yr. award Tampa Gen. Hosp., 1970; diplomate Am. Bd. Surgery. Fellow A.C.S.; mem. Internat. Cardiovascular Soc., So. Assn. for Vascular Surgery, So. Med. Assn., Atlanta Med. Assn., Ga. Med. Assn., AMA, Southeastern Surg. Congress, Theta Kappa Psi (v.p. 1967-68), Alpha Epsilon Delta. Contbr. articles to profl. jours. Home: 9490 Riverclub Pkwy Duluth GA 30136 Office: Suite 412 315 Boulevard NE Atlanta GA 30312

STANTON, RALPH EDWARD, hosp. adminstr.; b. Sevierville, Tenn., July 14, 1939; s. John Claude and Zora Rose-Ann (Whaley) S.; B.S., Cumberland Coll., 1962; M.B.A., U. Tenn., 1970; postgrad. Auburn U., 1972; M.H.A., Miss. Coll., 1978; m. Deanna Faye Ellis, July 18, 1964; 1 dau., Raecheal Elizabeth. Tchr. jr. high sch., Gatlinburg, Tenn., 1962-65 auditor Internat. Harvester Credit Corp., 1965-67; tchr. vocat. high sch., Sevierville, 1967-70; fiscal officer VA, Montgomery, Ala., Jackson, Miss., 1971—. Served with U.S. Army, 1967-68. Mem. Delta Phi Epsilon. Democrat. Baptist. Home: 5276

Brookhollow Dr Jackson MS 39212 Office: 1500 E Woodrow Wilson Dr Jackson MS 39216

STANTON, ROBERT LOWELL, physician; b. Des Moines, Feb. 18, 1924; s. Judson Horatio and Ozella (Hull) S.; B.S., U. Miami, 1948; M.D., Temple U., 1953; m. Betty Mae Tyrell Phillips, Sept. 15, 1945; children—Michael Phillips, Peter Wares, Scott Hull. Intern Temple U. Hosp., Phila., 1953-54; resident Dade County Hosp., Miami, Fla., 1954-55, resident internal medicine, VA Hosp., Miami, 1955-56; practice medicine, specializing in family practice, Miami, 1957—; mem. attending med. staff Am. Hosp., Larkin Gen. Hosp., Baptist Hosp., South Miami Hosp., Doctors Hosp., all Miami; pres. Ind. Practice Assn., Inc.; dir. South Fla. Group Health Inc. Served with USNR, 1942-45. Decorated Silver Star; diplomate Am. Bd. Family Practice. Mem. AMA, Dade County, Fla. med. assns., So. Med. Group (co-founder), Am. Acad. Family Practice, Beta Beta Beta, Alpha Epsilon Delta, Phi Chi. Unitarian (pres. congregation 1967-69). Home: 9430 SW 53d St Miami FL 33165 Office: 9090 SW 87th Ct Miami FL 33176

STANTON, THOMAS COUSAR, educator; b. Dillon County, S.C., June 13, 1929; s. Hugh Cousar and Kate Margaret (Jones) S.; B.S., U. Md., 1960; M.S., George Washington U., 1966, D.B.A., 1974; grad. Intelligence Officers advanced course, 1960; m. Sara Louise Thomas, July 20, 1950; children—Sara Kate, Thomas Cousar. commd. 2d lt., U.S. Army, 1952 advanced through grades to lt. col., 1972; Pentagon staff officer; 1964-68; advisor Imperial Iranian Armed Forces, 1968-70, Korea, 1953-55, Viet Nam, 1964; ret., 1972; lectr. George Washington U., 1970-74; prof. Fin. and Accounting James Madison U., 1974-76, v.p. for acad. affairs, 1976—; ordained to ministry Bapt. Ch., 1973; pastor Zoar Bapt. Ch., Bristersburg, Va. Decorated Meritorious Service medal Joint Service Commendation medal, Army commendation medal with 2 oak leaf clusters, Purple Heart. Mem. Assn. Govt. Accountants (Ann. authors award 1975). Office: James Madison U Harrisonburg VA 22807

STAPLETON, FANNIE EVELYN, property mgmt. co. exec.; b. Greenville, Tex., Mar. 9, 1922; d. John Plen and Nancy Vesta (Hill) Willeford; student Paris Jr. Coll., 1940-41, East Tex. State Coll., 1957-58; m. Worley Stapleton, June 15, 1961; 1 dau. by previous marriage, Carolyn C. Lambert. Various jobs, Greenville, 1946-59; owner, operator Sands Motel, Brownsville, Tex., 1960-61; with Kaplan & Kaplan Properties, San Antonio, 1962-73; property mgr. Samuel Geltman Co., Hasbrouck Heights, N.J., 1973—. Cert. apt. mgr., Tex.; Lic. real estate agt., Tex. Mem. Tex. Apt. Assn., Nat. Apt. Assn., Small Bus. Assn., San Antonio Apt. Assn. (mem. exec. bd. 1977-78, treas., 1978-79). Democrat. Clubs: Altrusa, VFW Aux. Home and Office: 8051 Broadway St San Antonio TX 78209

STAPP, WILLIAM FINKBINE, physician; b. Biloxi, Miss., Mar. 20, 1920; s. Edward H. and Gertrude May (Mosher) S.; B.S. in Pharmacy, Loyola U., New Orleans, 1943; M.D., Marquette U., 1951. Intern, Parkland Hosp., Dallas, 1951-52, resident clin. pathology, 1952-54; resident VA Hosp., McKinney, Tex., 1955-56, John Sealy Hosp., Galveston, Tex., 1962-63; Fulbright Med. Research fellow Rikshospital, U. Oslo (Norway), 1956-57; vis. research asso. in coagulation research U. Vienna (Austria) Med. Sch., 1958-61; NIH cancer trainee Baylor U. Hosp., Dallas, 1964-65; practice medicine, specializing in clin. pathology, Jackson, Miss., 1966-71, Dallas, 1971—; asst. to dir. clin. labs. U. Hosp., U. Miss. Med. Center, Jackson, 1966-71, asst. prof. dept. clin. lab. scis., 1966-71; dir. Eastlake Lab., Dallas, 1974-76; spl. med. rep. to Terry Corp., Fla., 1974-76; sec.-treas., med. cons. to Multiple Discipline Scis., Inc., 1976—, Agr. Devel. Corp., Inc. subs. Anilag AG, 1978—, Futuron, Inc., 1978—; med. dir. Biotec Labs., Inc., 1979—; co-dir. Clin. Lab., cons. clin. pathology Med. Center Hosp. of Garland (Tex.), Inc., 1975—; camp physician S.W. chpt. Nat. Hemophilia Found., 1975—. Diplomate Am. Bd. Clin. Pathology. Mem. Am. Soc. for Hematology, Am. Soc. Clin. Pathology, Internat. Soc. for Thrombosis and Haemostasis, Coll. for Am. Pathologists, Am. Diabetic Assn., Internat. Soc. for Hemophilia, Am. Hemophilia Soc., Nutrition Today Soc., Dallas County Med. Soc., So. Med. Assn., AMA, Miss. Acad. Scis., AAUP, AAAS, Alpha Kappa Kappa, Sigma Xi. Episcopalian. Contbr. articles to profl. publs. Home: 6008 Ridgecrest Apt 251 Dallas TX 75231 Office: Medical Center Hosp of Garland 2010 S Shiloh Rd Garland TX 75041

STARK, CARL DENNIS, psychotherapist; b. N.Y.C., July 10, 1946; s. Leon and Lil S.; B.A. in Social Psychology, U. Ga., 1968, masters degree in clin. social work, 1974; m. Lillian Charlene McCullough, Nov. 9, 1968; 1 son, Chad Brian. Psychiat. social worker, children's specialist N. Ga. Community Mental Health Center, Gainesville, 1973-77; dir. child and adolescent clinic Central Ga. Community Mental Health Center, Macon, 1977—; pvt. practice child psychotherapy, Macon, 1977—; cons. to group homes. Served as capt. USAF, 1968-72. Recipient cert. of merit for outstanding leadership and service State of Ga., 1978. Mem. Nat. Assn. Social Workers (chmn. Central Ga. chpt.), Acad. Cert. Social Workers, Council for Exceptional Children, Assn. Children with Learning Disabilities., Vineville Hist. Assn. Macon. Baptist. Home: 2393 Clayton St Macon GA 31204 Office: Suite 702 Ga Power Bldg Macon GA 31202

STARK, CAROL JEAN, marriage and family counselor; b. Rapid City, S.D., Apr. 8, 1936; d. Carl Wallace and Katherine Julia (Jacks) Shrum; B.S. in Nursing, North Park Coll., 1960; M.Ed., Tex. Christian U., 1972; m. Thomas Clarence Stark, Jan. 12, 1970; children—Lois Brynn Bennett, Cynthia Anne Bennett. Gen. hosp. and clin. nurse, Chgo. and Fort Worth, Tex., 1967-80; dir. health and handicap services Tarrant County Jr. Coll., Fort Worth, 1968—, instr. courses in human relations, 1972—; marriage and family counselor, Fort Worth, 1974—; lectr. in field personal growth, family living, divorce therapy. Vol. resource person Fort Worth Ind. Sch. Dist. Mem. Am., Tarrant County assns. marriage and family therapists, Am. Personnel and Guidance Assn., Internat. Transactional Analysis Assn., Am. Coll. Health Assn., Phi Delta Kappa. Home: 3729 Walton St Fort Worth TX 76133 Office: 3467 Bluebonnet Circle Fort Worth TX 76109

STARK, EDMUND FREDERICK, JR., railroad exec.; b. Richmond, Va., July 11, 1923; s. Edmund Frederick and Maude Inez (Tooms) S.; B.M.E., U. Va., 1949; M.A. in Indsl. Mgmt., Mass. Inst. Tech., 1956; m. Anna Wray Schweickert, Nov. 10, 1945; children—Frederick Diah, Wray Carroll, Pleasant Larus. Machinist apprentice, C&O Ry., Richmond, Va., 1940-44, shop engr., shop facilities office, 1950-62, asst. mechan. engr., 1962-68, sr. engr. mechan. facilities, C&O, B&O, Western Md. r.r.s., 1968-77; mgr. pier and marine maintenance C&O Ry., 1977—; dir. employees credit union C.40. Ry., 1958-62; treas. Babe Ruth Baseball League, Barboursville, W.Va., 1968-69; mem. Va. C. of C., Richmond, 1974-75. Served with USN, 1944-46. Certified prof. mgr., Va.; recipient fellowship Mass. Inst. Tech., 1956-57. Mem. Richmond Diesel Club (pres. and sec. 1952, 1953), ASME, Nat. Mgmt. Assn., U. Va. Alumni Assn., Am. Defense Preparedness Assn. Republican. Episcopalian. Clubs: Garden Farms Swim (treas. 1966-69), Elk, Mason. Co-patentee in field. Home: 49 Hardwick Rd Newport News VA 23602 Office: Terminal Bldg Newport News VA 23607

STARK, LUCIEN PAUL, pianist, educator; b. Winterset, Iowa, Mar. 4, 1929; s. Robert Walter and Naomi Marie (Simpson) S.; B.Mus., Drake U., 1950, M.Mus., 1951; D.M.A., U. Mich., 1961; m. Caroline Phillippe, Jan. 8, 1952; 1 son, Paul Andrew. Asst. prof. music Minot (N.D.) State Tchrs. Coll., 1954-55; pianist in residence Iowa State U., Ames, 1957-60; prof., chmn. piano faculty George Peabody Coll., Nashville, 1961-76; prof. piano U. Ky., Lexington, 1976—, chmn. keyboard div., 1976—. Served with U.S. Army, 1951-53. Named Distinguished Alumnus Drake U., 1974. Danforth found. grantee, 1960. Mem. Music Tchrs. Nat. Assn., Phi Mu Alpha Sinfonia (nat. pres. 1976-79), Pi Kappa Lambda, Omicron Delta Kappa. Composer Two Improvisations for Organ, 1966. Home: 124 Forest Ave Lexington KY 40508 Office: School of Music University of Kentucky Lexington KY 40506

STARK, NORMAN, actor, acting workshop exec.; b. Bronx, N.Y., Sept. 15, 1940; s. Martin and Margaret (Neuman) S.; student Newark State Coll., 1963-69; 1 dau., Michelle Allison. Owner, Acad. Music, Coral Springs, Fla., 1975-78; pres. Acad. Musical Services, musical ednl. service, Coral Springs, 1975-78; acting asst. dir. Miami Film Services (Fla.), 1979-80: dir. P.W.P. Playhouse, Ft. Lauderdale, Fla., 1978—. Pres. B.E.S.T. Group div. Jewish Community Center, Hollywood, 1979-80. Served with U.S. Army, 1963-69. Mem. Fla. Motion Picture and TV Assn. Club: B.E.S.T. Singles (Hollywood). Home: 12501 NE 13th Ave Apt 319 North Miami FL 33161 Office: 100 N Biscayne Blvd Suite 2707 Miami FL 33132

STARK, STANLEY AHART, publisher; b. Beaumont, Tex., Mar. 9, 1944; s. Douglas Ahart and Helen Maxine (Williford) S.; student S. Tex. Jr. Coll., 1966-68, U. Houston, 1968-70. Account exec. Houston Chronicle, 1963-68; cash control supr. Gulf Oil Co., 1968-71; terr. mgr. Isgo Corp., Houston, 1971-73; pub. Houston Living Mag., 1978—. Mem. Greater Houston Builders Assn. (dir. sales and mktg. council). Office: Houston Living Mag 5444 Westheimer Suite 450 Houston TX 77057

STARKE, EDGAR ARLIN, JR., metallurgist, educator; b. Richmond, Va., May 10, 1936; s. Edgar Arlin and Mary Louise (Stein) S.; B.S. in Metall. Engring., Va. Poly. Inst., 1960; M.S., U. Ill., 1961; Ph.D. in Metall. Engring., U. Fla., 1964; m. Donna Lee Frazier, June 10, 1961; children—John Arlin, Karen Lee. Metallurgist, Savannah River Lab., Aiken, S.C., 1961-62; asst. prof. Ga. Inst. Tech., 1964-68, asso. prof. metallurgy, 1968-72, prof., 1972—, dir. Fracture and Fatigue Research Lab., 1978—. Vis. scientist Oak Ridge (Tenn.) Nat. Lab., 1967, Max-Planck-Institut fur Metallforschung, Stuttgart, Germany, 1971; cons. Bell Tel. Lab., 1973-75, Lockheed Ga. Research Lab., 1965—, Southwire Co., 1967—. Served with AUS, 1954-56. Mem. Am. Soc. Metals (sec. Atlanta chpt. 1974-75), Am. Inst. Mining and Metall. Engrs. (sec.-treas. Ga. chpt. 1965-66, v.p. Ga. chpt. 1967, pres. chpt. 1968, sec. Non-Ferrous Metallurgy com. 1973-74, vice chmn. Non-Ferrous Metallurgy com. 1974-75, chmn. 1976-78, vice chmn. program metal sci.), Sigma Xi (sec. Ga. Inst. Tech. chpt. 1974-75), Tau Beta Pi, Alpha Sigma Mu, Omicron Delta Kappa, Pi Delta Epsilon. Contbr. numerous articles to profl. jours. Home: 670 Amberidge Trail NW Atlanta GA 30328

STARKEY, ROBERT GIBSON, athletic dir.; b. Cresaptown, Md., Dec. 26, 1931; s. Randall W. and Hallie G. (Anderson) S.; B.S., A.B., Shepherd Coll., Shepherdstown, W.Va., 1958; M.S., W.Va. U., 1965; m. Greta May Messick, Oct. 23, 1952; children—Randy Steve, Sandie Lynn. Coach, tchr. high schs. in W.Va., 1958-68; athletic dir., head basketball coach, asst. prof. phys. edn. Shepherd Coll., 1968—. Served with USAF, 1949-52; Korea. Mem. NEA, W.Va. Edn. Assn., Am. Health Edn. Assn., Nat. Assn. Intercollegiate Basketball Coaches, W.Va. Intercollegiate Athletic Basketball Coaches Assn. (chmn. 1978-79). Democrat. Baptist. Author articles in field. Address: RD 1 Shepherdstown WV 25443

STARKEY, RUSSELL BRUCE, JR., utility co. exec.; b. Lumberport, W.Va., July 20, 1942; s. Russell Bruce and Dorotha Mable (Field) S.; B.S., Miami U., Oxford, Ohio, 1964; grad. student U. New Haven, 1972-73, N.C. State U., 1974-75, U.S. Navy Schs., 1964-66, 68; m. Joan McClellan, May 27, 1966; children—Christine, Pamela, Joanne. Sr. engr., nuclear generation sect. Carolina Power & Light Co., Raleigh, N.C., 1973-74, sr. engr. ops. quality assurance, 1974, prin. engr., 1974-75, quality assurance supr. Brunswick Steam Electric Plant, Southport, N.C., 1975-76, supt. tech. and adminstrv., 1976, supt. ops. and maintenance, 1976-77, plant mgr. H.B. Robinson Steam Electric Plant, Hartsville, S.C., 1977—. Served with USN, 1964-73. Mem. Am. Mgmt. Assn. Club: Hartsville Rotary. Home: 62 Botany Woods Hartsville SC 29550 Office: PO Box 790 Carolina Power & Light Hartsville SC 29550

STARKS, C. ANTHONY, hosp. adminstr.; b. Mortons Gap, Ky., Feb. 10, 1945; s. James L. and Lillian M. (Noffsinger) S.; student U. Evansville (Ind.), 1969; m. Sharon A. Starks, Dec. 19, 1964. Purchasing expediter Mead Johnson & Co., Evansville, 1966-73; buyer/expediter Hahn Inc., Evansville, 1973-74; purchasing agt. Medco Centers, Evansville, 1974-76; dir. purchasing Maury County Hosp., Columbia, Tenn., 1976—. Mem. Tenn. Hosp. Assn., Middle Tenn. Purchasing Group (pres. 1978—), Tenn. Soc. Hosp. Purchasing Mgrs. Home: 102 Greely Dr Columbia TN 38401 Office: Maury County Hosp 1224 Trotwood St Columbia TN 38401

STARNES, EARL MAXWELL, urban and regional planner; b. Winter Haven, Fla., Sept. 14, 1926; s. Thomas Lowe and Kathrine Maxwell (Gates) S.; student Fla. So. Coll., 1946-48; B.Arch. cum laude, U. Fla., 1951; M.S. in Urban and Regional Planning, Fla. State U., 1973, Ph.D., 1977; m. Dorothy Jean Prather, Aug. 21, 1949; children—Thomas Oliver, William Craig, Janet Maxwell, Patricia Ann. Architect various firms, Ft. Lauderdale and Miami, Fla., 1951-57; partner Starnes and Rentscher, Architects, Miami, 1957-63, Starnes, Rontscher & Assos., 1964-70; dir. div. mass transit ops. Fla. Dept. Transp., Tallahassee, 1971-72; dir. Fla. Div. State Planning, Tallahassee, 1972-75; prof. urban and regional planning U. Fla., 1976—, chmn. dept. urban and regional planning, 1978—; adj. asst. prof. Fla. State U., Tallahassee, 1971-74. Mem. Dade County (Fla.) Bd. County Commrs., 1964-71; chmn. Joint Liaison Com. on Responsiblity for Urban Services, Dade County, 1965-71; vice mayor Dade County, 1964-68; bd. dirs. State Assn. County Commrs., Fla., 1968-71; mem. Fla. Phosphate Lands Adv. Com., 1979—. Served with USCG, 1944-46. Fellow AIA (Fla. Public Service award 1973, mem. com. on urban planning and design 1976—), Am. Planning Assn., Nat. Inst. Building Services (research adv. com. 1979—), Phi Kappa Phi. Democrat. Contbr. articles on land use to profl. jours.; research on fiscal impact of land use, devel. mgmt. systems; architect: First Unitarian Ch., Miami. Office: 431 GPB U Fla Gainesville FL 32611

STARNES, GARY BERTRAM, educator; b. Ft. Worth, Jan. 11, 1943; s. Bertram Lamar and Ita Clara (Counts) S.; B.A., Arlington State Coll., 1965; M.A., Tex. Christian U., 1967, Ph.D., 1971; m. Sonja Iris Elam, Aug. 19, 1967; 1 dau., Emily Susan. Instr. history Dallas Bapt. Coll., 1969-71, asst. prof., 1971-73, asso. prof., 1973—, dir. Bachelor of Career Arts Program, 1974—. Pres., Ridgmar Capital Fund, 1977—. Recipient Presidio la Abhia award Sons Republic of Tex., 1971. Mem. Tex. State Hist. Assn., Hispanic Am. Hist. Assn., Tex. Com. Humanities, Assn. Gen. and Liberal Studies, Council Advancement of Experiential Learning, Phi Kappa Theta, Phi Alpha Theta. Baptist. Author: The San Gabriel Missions, 1747-1756, 1967; Juan de Ugalde y los Provincias Internas de Coahuila y Texas, 1975; contbr. articles, book reviews to publs. Home: 7500 Douglas Ln Smithfield TX 76180 Office: 7007 Kiest St Dallas TX 75211

STARNES, MYRA NELL, promotional recreation and transp. exec.; b. Columbia, S.C., Feb. 1, 1952; d. William Julian and Juanita (Cox) S.; B.A. in Art, Columbia Coll., 1974. Mem. interior design staff Myrtle Beach Lumber Co. (S.C.), 1974; social dir., mktg. asst. Venture Mgmt. Inc., Atlanta, 1975-76; pres., chmn. Leisure Time Unltd. of Myrtle Beach, Inc., 1976—; pres. Horry, Georgetown, Williamsburg Transit Systems Inc., 1980—. Recipient Good Heart award Heart Assn., 1976. Mem. Transp. Assn. Carolina (pres. 1978-80), Hotel, Motel and Restaurant Assn. Episcopalian. Home: 808 65th Ave N Unit 5 Myrtle Beach SC 29577 Office: Leisure Time Unltd of Myrtle Beach Inc PO Box 332 Myrtle Beach SC 29577

STARNES, OSCAR EDWIN, JR., lawyer; b. Raleigh, N.C., May 3, 1924; s. Oscar Edwin and Marion (Fletcher) S.; B.S., Davidson Coll., 1947; LL.B., U. N.C., 1950; m. Sarah Jane Whitmire, June 1948 (dec.); children—Oscar Edwin III, Amy Elizabeth, Jane Marion; m. 2d, Lida Martin, July 1978. Admitted to N.C. bar, 1950, since practiced in Asheville; mem. firm Van Winkle, Buck, Wall, Starnes, Hyde & Davis, 1950—. Corp. counsel City of Asheville, 1959-68. Trustee, Montreat-Anderson Coll. Served with AUS, 1941-43. Decorated Purple Heart. Fellow Am. Coll. Trial Lawyers; mem. Am., N.C. (bd. govs. 1963-66), Buncombe County (pres. 1973) bar assns. Kiwanian. Home: 129 Stuyvesant Rd Asheville NC 28803 Office: 18 Church St Asheville NC 28807

STASSI, JOHN ALOYSIUS, II, lawyer; b. New Orleans, Sept. 11, 1937; s. John A. and Amy (Rivet) S.; B.A., Tulane U., 1960, LL.B., 1962; m. Kathleen Jane Judlin, Aug. 10, 1974; children—John Aloysius, III, David A., R. Matthew, Sarah. Admitted to La. bar, 1967, U.S. Supreme Ct. bar, 1965; trial atty. tax div. Dept. Justice, Washington, 1962-63; asso. firm Deutsch, Kerrigan & Stiles, New Orleans, 1963-67, partner, 1967-70; prin. firm Stassi & Rausch, New Orleans, 1971—; lectr. in field. Vice chmn. professions United Way Campaign, New Orleans, 1969-70; v.p. Oakridge Park Improvement Assn., Metairie, La., 1979—. Mem. Am. Bar Assn. (chmn. subcom. on state and local taxes 1969-70), La. State Bar Assn. Club: New Orleans Yacht. Home: 197 E Oakridge Park Metairie LA 70005 Office: 821 Gravier St New Orleans LA 70112

STATTON, SYLVIA DORETHA, guidance counselor; b. Richmond, Va., Jan. 11, 1950; d. James Arthur and Geneva (Latney) S.; B.S. in Math. Edn., Va. State Coll., 1972; M.Ed. in Guidance and Counseling, Va. Commonwealth U., 1976. Guidance counselor Benjamin A. Graves Middle Sch., Richmond, 1978—. Mem. Am. Personnel and Guidance Assn., Va. Personnel and Guidance Assn., Va. Vocat. Guidance Assn., Va. Assn. Non-White Concerns, Va. Sch. Counselor Assn., Richmond Personnel and Guidance Assn. Baptist. Home: 2303 Beck Dr Richmond VA 23223 Office: 119 W Leigh St Richmond VA 23220

STAUB, ERNEST WILSON, surgeon; b. Bronxville, N.Y., Dec. 25, 1931; s. Ernest Flury and Virginia (Wilson) S.; B.A., Colgate U., 1953; M.D., Northwestern U., 1957; M.S., U. Ill., 1960; m. Janet Ellen Lewis, Apr. 1, 1960; children—Jennifer, James, Julianne, Janet, John, Jeffrey. Intern, Evanston (Ill.) Hosp., 1957-58; resident surgery Presbyn.-St. Luke's Hosp., Chgo., 1958-62, resident thoracic and cardiovascular surgery, 1963-64, adj. attending staff cardiovascular surgery, 1965; Robertson Traveling fellow London Hosp., 1960-61, fellow surg. research, 1962; attending staff Moore Meml. Hosp., Pinehurst, N.C., 1965—, pres. med. staff, 1974-76; cons. surgery McCain Hosp. (N.C.), 1965—; asso. Pinehurst Surg. Clinic (N.C.), 1965—, pres., 1979—; asst. in surgery U. Ill. Med. Sch., 1958-62, instr., 1963-65; asst. prof. surgery Duke, 1972—. Dir., N.C. Nat. Bank, Southern Pines. Mem. Moore County home health adv. com., 1969—; mem. adv. council elementary sch., Southern Pines, 1971-76; pres. Pinehurst Forum, 1973-75; vice chmn. N.C. Bd. Human Resources, 1974-77; vice chmn. N.C. Bd. Med. Examiners, 1972-78, pres., 1977-78; bd. dirs. Moore Meml. Hosp., 1974-76; bd. dirs. N.C. Heart Assn., pres., 1977-78. Recipient Founders award N.C. Heart Assn., 1972. Diplomate Am. Bd. Thoracic Surgery, Am. Bd. Surgery. Mem. A.M.A., N.C. Med. Assn., Fifth Dist. Med. Soc. (sec.-treas. 1967-74), Moore County Med. Soc., A.C.S., N.C. Surg. Assn. (council), So. Thoracic Surg. Assn., Soc. Thoracic Surgeons. Episcopalian (vestryman 1972-74). Contbr. articles to profl. jours. Home: 375 S Valley Rd Southern Pines NC 28387 Office: Pinehurst Surg Clinic Pinehurst NC 28374

STAUBER, LESLIE EDWIN, mfg. exec.; b. Rural Hall, N.C., Mar. 28, 1903; s. William Edwin and Lillian (Felts) S.; A.B., U. N.C., 1925; m. Jessie Louise Brown, May 10, 1930; children—Leslie Edwin, Barbara June (Mrs. Fred Mexwell Fultz). Owner, Rural Telephone Co., 1927-28; partner Rural Hall Veneer Co., 1928-53, owner, 1954—, mfr. wood veneers, 1928—, plywood, 1936—. Organizing mem., sec.-treas. Rural Hall San. Dist., 1938-50; charter mem. Rural Hall Fire Dept., 1938-50; justice of peace, 1932-34. Mem. Moravian Ch. (charter, charter rep. to com. Rural Hall Meml. Park). Club: Civic (pres. 1947). Home: Corner Broad and Wall Sts Rural Hall NC 27045 Office: 1st St Rural Hall NC 27045

STAUBLIN, JUDITH ANN, computer co. exec.; b. Anderson, Ind., Jan. 17, 1936; d. Leslie Fred and Esta Virginia (Ringo) Wiley; student Ball State U., 1954-55, 69-70, Savs. and Loan Inst., 1962-67, U. Ga., 1974, Wright State U., 1975; children—Juli Jackson, Scott Jackson. Teller, Anderson Fed. Savs. and Loan Assn., Anderson, 1962-64, data processing mgr., 1965-70, loan officer, 1970-72, v.p. systems, 1972-74, fin. systems mktg., 1974-76; fin. dist. mgr. data centers div. NCR Corp., Atlanta, 1977—. Active United Way. Mem. Am. Savs. and Loan Inst., Fin. Mgrs. Soc., Ga. Exec. Women's Network, Anderson C. of C. Home: 3640 Peachtree Corners West No 1303 Norcross GA 30092 Office: 130 Technology Park Norcross GA 30092

STAVER, MICHAEL, bus. exec., fin. advisor; b. Ganado, Ariz., Feb. 6, 1946; s. Hugh and Cecilia (Birdshead) S.; A.A., N.Mex. Mil. Inst., 1966; B.S., No. Ariz. U., 1968; postgrad. La. State U., 1969; m. Joanna May Bolf, June 7, 1967 (div. Sept. 1971); 1 son, Kenneth Todd. Founder, chief exec. officer, chmn. bd. Preble Properties, Inc., Dallas, 1970—, Michael Staver & Co., Inc., Dallas, 1971—, Staver, Trent & Tisdale, Inc., Dallas, 1972—, Guyer and Staver Fin. Inc., Dallas, 1972—; owner Dallas Diamonds, Women's Profl. Basketball League. Served with U.S. Army, 1968-70. Mem. Internat. Council Shopping Centers, Nat. Home and Apt. Builders. Republican. Home: 9404 Timberleaf St Dallas TX 75231 Office: 5925 Maple Ave Dallas TX 75235

STAVROLAKIS, JAMES ALEXANDER, plumbing fixtures co. mgr.; b. Storrs, Utah, Oct. 1, 1921; s. Alexander and Crystal (Haniotis) S.; B.S., Rutgers U., 1943; Sc.D., M.I.T., 1949; postgrad. Columbia, 1963; m. Rachel Gallup, Feb. 24, 1951; children—Kristalia, Alexander, Marianthe, Stacy Ann, Andrew. Engr., Gen. Electric Co., Oak Ridge, 1949-52; supr. Armour Research Found., Chgo., 1952-55; asst. mgr. Mallinckrodt Chem. Works, St. Louis, 1955-56; devel. mgr.

Crucible Steel Co. Am., Pitts., 1956-61; v.p. Am. Standard, Inc., Louisville, 1961-67, gen. mgr., 1967-70; pres. Glasrock Products, Inc., Atlanta, 1970-73, Stanbest, Inc., Atlanta, 1973-78; gen. mgr. Gerber Plumbing Fixtures Corp., Chgo., 1978—. Served with USAAF, 1942-46. Clubs: N.Y. Engrs.; Big Spring Country (Louisville); Cherokee Town and Country (Atlanta). Home: 2879 Rivermeade Dr Atlanta GA 30327 Office: 4656 W Touhy Ave Chicago IL 60646

STAY, ELLSWORTH JAMES, pathologist; b. Detroit, Jan. 15, 1946; s. Ellsworth McQuire and Marie Theresa (Shovlin) S.; A.B., Villanova U., 1968; M.D., Mich. State U., 1973; m. Martha D. Donnelly, June 19, 1971; children—Ellsworth James, Rachel Tone, Rourke McQuire. Intern, Peter Bent Brigham Hosp., Boston, 1973-74, resident in pathology, 1974-77; asso. pathologist Winchester (Mass.) Hosp., 1977; pathologist Arlington (Va.) Hosp., 1978—; clin. instr. Harvard U. Med. Sch., Boston, 1977-78. Diplomate Am. Bd. Pathology. Fellow Am. Soc. Clin. Pathology, Coll. Am. Pathologists; mem. Va. Med. Soc., Arlington County Med. Soc., Washington Soc. Pathologists. Clubs: Washington Golf and Country; Winchester Country. Research on limb regeneration, tumor pathology. Office: Dept Surg Pathology Arlington Hospital Arlington VA 22205

STAYMAN, SAMUEL M., investment co. exec.; b. Worcester, Mass., May 28, 1909; s. Morris and Fannie R. (Mittel) S.; A.B., Dartmouth Coll., 1930, M.B.A., 1931; m. Marjorie Schmukler, May 1, 1941 (dec. Feb. 1961); 1 dau., Susan Marjorie Stayman Madorsky; m. 2d, Josephine Lewis Wacht, Sept. 21, 1962. With sales dept. Superior Products Co., Boston, 1931-37; sales mgr. Berkshire Mfg. Co., 1937-39; pres. Vt. Woolen Mills, Inc., N.Y.C., 1939-43, Stamina Mills, Inc., N.Y.C., 1952-58, S.M.S.A. Corp., N.Y.C., 1966—; chmn. Strand Consultants, Ltd., N.Y.C. Mem. Am. Contract Bridge League (trustee). Clubs: Cavendish, Dartmouth, Harmonie (N.Y.C.); Beach Point (Mamaroneck, N.Y.). Author: Expert Bidding at Contract Bridge, 1951; The Complete Stayman System of Contract Bidding, 1957; Do You Play Stayman?, 1965. Originator Stayman Conv. method of bidding at contract bridge. Home: 2500 S Ocean Blvd Palm Beach FL 33480 Office: 850 3d Ave New York NY 10022

STEAD, PRISCILLA STEERS, educator; b. N.Y.C., June 29, 1917; d. Henry Coster and Lilian Adele (Palmer) Steers; student Smith Coll., 1935-37; B.S., Columbia U., 1948; M.A., Columbia U., 1953; postgrad. N.Y. Sch. Psychotherapy, 1952; m. Rexford A. Stead, Sept. 6, 1946; children—Penelope, Mark Alden. Tchr., Country Day Sch., Gulfport, Fla., 1958-59; psychologist Adult Mental Health Clinic, Clearwater, Fla., 1959-62; curator edn. Mus. Fine Arts, St. Petersburg, Fla., 1963-66; asso. prof. psychology and anthropology St. Petersburg Jr. Coll., Clearwater, Fla., 1966—; lectr. art Mus. Fine Arts, St. Petersburg, 1975-76; lectr. anthropology Suncoast Archeol. Soc., St. Petersburg, 1977—. Bd. govs. Fla. Gulf Coast Art Center, 1979—. Served with WAC, 1943-46. Recipient Certificate of Merit-Outstanding Citizen Pinellas County, Fla., 1963, Merit award for teaching St. Petersburg Jr. Coll., 1967. Mem. AAUP, Phi Theta Kappa. Home: 13575 Oakhurst Rd Largo FL 33542 Office: Social Sci Dept St Petersburg Jr Coll Drew St Clearwater FL 33515

STEAKLEY, JOE EARL, mapping corp. exec.; b. Cleburne, Tex., Feb. 24, 1923; s. George David and Mary Launa (Poindexter) S.; B.A. in Geography, Boston U., 1957, M.A. in Geography, 1958; M.B.A., Auburn U., 1971; m. Margaret Fern Hooper, Apr. 24, 1943; children—Nancy Jean Steakley Hildebrand, Cynthia Anne Steakley Clarke. Nationalized with Tex. Nat. Guard, 1940; served with 2d inf. div., World War II; advanced through grades to capt.; transferred to USAF, aovanced through grades to maj.; served in aerial reconnaisance, ret., 1961; photogrammetric expert in intelligence work, 1961-66; chief advanced tech. div. Def. Mapping Agy., St. Louis and Washington, i966-73; founder, pres. So. Resources Mapping Corp., Greensboro, Ala., 1973—, So. Camera, Inc., Greensboro. Vestryman, St. Paul's Episcopal Ch., Greensboro. Decorated Purple Heart (2), Bronze Star (3). Fellow Am. Inst. Aeros. and Astronautics (asso.); mem. ASCE, Am. Congress Surveying and Mapping, Am. Soc. Photogrammetry (nat. pres. i974). Club: Odd Fellows. Home: 1301 Tuscaloosa St Greensboro AL 36744 Office: So Resources Mapping Corp Greensboro AL 36744

STEAKLEY, ZOLLIE C., JR., justice Tex. Supreme Ct.; b. Rotan, Tex., Aug. 29, 1908; s. Zollie Coffer and Frances Elizabeth (McGlasson) S.; B.A., Hardin-Simmons U., 1929, LL.D., 1959; LL.B., U. Tex., 1932; LL.D., U. Corpus Christi, 1958; m. Ruth Butler, June 3, 1939. Admitted to Tex. bar, 1932; practice law, 1932-39, 46-57; asst. atty. gen. Tex., 1939-42; sec. of state Tex., 1957-60; justice Supreme Ct. Tex., 1961—. Served with USNR, 1942-46. Mem. Am. Bar Assn., Am. Judicature Soc., State Bar Tex., Philos. Soc. Tex. Democrat. Home: 3302 Mt Bonnell Dr Austin TX 78731 Office: Supreme Ct Tex Austin TX 78711

STEARLEY, MILDRED SUTCLIFFE VOLANDT, former found. exec.; b. Ft. Myer, Va., Aug. 3, 1905; d. William Frederick and Mabel Emma (Sutcliffe) Volandt; student George Washington U., 1923-24, 25-28; m. Ralph F. Stearley, Sept. 19, 1931. Elementary tchr. Brent Sch., Baguio, Philippines, 1929-30; staff aide vol. services ARC, also acting chmn., Charlotte, N.C., 1943, staff asst., Washington, 1943-47, Gray Lady vol., Okinawa, 1950-53, Brazil, Ind., 1954; trustee Air Force Village Found., San Antonio, 1975-78, sec. bd., 1975-77. Mem. adv. bd. Am. Security Council; life mem. Air Force Village Found. Recipient commendation ARC, 1943. Mem. Army Daus., Am. Legion Aux., Army-Navy Club Aux., Smithsonian Instn., P.E.O. (life), Pi Beta Phi. Episcopalian. Clubs: Shakespeare Circle, Ladies Reading (Brazil, Ind.); Lackland Officers Wives, Bright Shawl (San Antonio). Home: 4917 Ravenswood Dr San Antonio TX 78227

STEARMAN, LINNIE MARIE, educator; b. Waldron, Ark.; d. Lester M. and Georgia L. (Robbins) S.; B.S. Edn. and Elementary Edn. and Spl. Edn., State Coll. Ark., Conway, 1974; M.S.E. in Learning Disabilities, U. Central Ark., 1978. Tchr. educable mentally retarded Whitten Elementary Sch., Marianna, Ark., 1974—. Mem. Nat., Ark. edn. assns. Mem. United Pentecostal Ch. Home: 184 Pearl St Marianna AR 72360 Office: 175 Walnut St Marianna AR 72360

STEARNS, E(LIZABETH) CAROLYN, hosp. exec.; b. Mooresville, Ind., Aug. 16, 1928; d. Gale Able and Ercie Louise (Smith) Rose; grad. high sch.; m. William Joseph Sawyers, Sept. 6, 1946 (div. May 1951); children—William Joseph, Sherry Lou; m. 2d, John Pershing Stearns, Oct. 4, 1954; 1 son, Dennis Gale. Sec., Lab. Equipment Corp., Mooresville, 1946-49, Hdqrs. 10th Air Force, 1949-50; with VA Hosp., Indpls., 1950-72, adminstrv. asst. to chief med. service, 1966-70, adminstrv. officer med. service, 1970-72; staff asst. med. service VA Hosp., Tampa, 1972—; adminstrv. asst. to chmn. dept. medicine U. South Fla. Coll. Medicine, Tampa, 1972—. Mem. bus. edn. adv. com. J. Everett Light Career Center, Indpls., 1969-72. Recipient Cert. of Appreciation, AMVETS, 1971. Mem. Med. Group Mgmt. Assn., Nat. Notary Assn., Nat. Assn. for Female Execs., Hillsborough County Med. Assts. Assn. Office: Dept Internal Medicine 12901 N 30th St Box 19 Tampa FL 33612

STEED, CHARLES EDGAR, state ofcl.; b. Atlanta, Ga., May 25, 1930; s. Charles Emory and Eddie Lue (Scott) S.; B.B.A., Ga. State U., 1961; children—Linda, Melanie, Charles W. Personnel dir. W. R. Bean & Son, Atlanta, 1961-67, Advance Indsl. Security, Inc., Atlanta, 1967-70; dir. adminstrn. Ga. Ports Authority, Savannah, 1971—; instr. Internal Mgmt. Council, Savannah, 1975—. Mem. bd. mgmt. YMCA, 1974-78. Served with USN, 1948-52. Recipient Ga. State U. sr. award, 1961. Certified mgr. Mem. Am. Mgmt. Assn., Am. Soc. Personnel Adminstrn. (pres. Savannah chpt. 1975), Ga. Bus. and Industry Assn., Internat. Mgmt. Council, Am. Legion, Delta Sigma Pi. Baptist. Address: PO Box 2406 Savannah GA 31402

STEED, EVELYN SUSAN CATHERINE, speech and lang. pathologist; b. San Juan, P.R., July 3, 1949; d. John Aloysius and Sue (Mendez) Finn; B.S. cum laude (Cape Henrys Womans Club scholar), Old Dominion U., 1971; M.Ed., U. Va., 1972; m. Paul Harper Steed, Jr., June 4, 1977; 1 son, John-Paul. Speech-lang. pathologist Sarasota (Fla.) public schs., 1972-73, Jacksonville (Fla.) Speech and Hearing Clinic and Hope Haven Childrens Hosp., 1973-74, Duval public schs., Jacksonville, 1974-75, Episcopal Day Care Center, Jacksonville, summer 1975; instr. speech-lang. pathology U. Tenn., Knoxville, 1975-76; clin. speech-lang. pathologist supr. Auburn (Ala.) U., 1976-79; speech-lang. pathologist Coweta public schs., Newnan, Ga., 1979—; cons. Duval public schs., Tallapoosa-Chambers County Headstart Program (Ala.), Talladega-Clay-Randolf Area Community Action Com. (Ala.). Recipient cert. of achievement Sarasota Pub. Schs. dept. speech-lang. pathology and exceptional child edn., 1973, Tchrs. cert. Fla.; pvt. license in speech-lang. pathology, Fla., Ala., Ga. Mem. Am. Speech and Hearing Assn. (cert. clin. competence). Democrat. Roman Catholic. Home: Franmar Apts #4 Newnan GA 30263 Office: 55 Savannah St Newnan GA 30263

STEED, TOM, congressman; b. nr. Rising Star, Tex., Mar. 2, 1904; m. Hazel Bennett, Feb. 26, 1923; 2 sons (Roger, officer USMCR dec. China, May 1947). Connected with Okla. daily newspapers, 20 yrs.; mng. editor Shawnee News & Star, 4 yrs. Mem. 81st to 96th congresses from 4th Okla. Dist. Served from pvt. to 2d lt. A.A.A., AUS, 1942-44, with OWI, 1944-45; CBI. Served longest tenure of any Oklahoman. Office: US House Reps 2405 Rayburn House Office Bldg Washington DC 20515

STEEDLEY, MARY LOU SNYDER, health services exec.; b. Allentown, Pa., Jan. 15, 1936; d. Diehl and Sallie (Peter) Snyder; diploma in nursing Hosp. U. Pa., 1956; B.S. in Nursing, U. Pa., 1959; M.S. in Hygiene, Tulane U., 1966. Staff nurse Hosp. U. Pa., Phila., 1956-58; staff nurse, acting head nurse USPHS Hosp., New Orleans, 1959-60; instr., public health coordinator Mather Sch. Nursing, So. Baptist Hosp., New Orleans, 1960-65; asst. prof. public health nursing Sch. Nursing, La. State U., New Orleans, 1966-68; dir. profl. services Home Health Services La., Inc., New Orleans, 1968-77, adminstr./dir. patient care services, 1979—; cons. Unihealth Services Corp., New Orleans, 1968-77, v.p. profl. services, 1975—; adj. asst. prof. sect. community health nursing Tulane U. Sch. Public Health and Tropical Medicine, 1970—; disaster nursing New Orleans chpt. ARC, 1962—; adv. bd. group profl. personnel Home Health Services La., 1968—, dir., 1977—; co-chmn. ad hoc com. Greater New Orleans Continuity of Patient Care Com., 1970-72. USPHS trainee, 1965-66. Mem. Nat. League Nursing (chmn. com. for pvt. agys. 1975—, exec. com. council home health agys. and community health services 1977—), S. La. League Nursing (dir. 1972-76, 78—), Am. Public Health Assn. (exec. bd. 1975—), Am. Public Health Assn., La. Public Health Assn., Am. Nurses Assn., La. Nurses Assn., New Orleans Dist. Nurses Assn., Nat. Assn. Home Health Agys., La. Hosp. Assn., Soc. Nursing Service Dirs., Tulane U. Alumni Assn., Tulane U. Med. Alumni Assn., U. Pa. Alumni Assn., Hosp. U. Pa. Alumni Assn., DAR, Sigma Theta Tau, Delta Omega. Author publs. in field. Office: 2001 Canal St New Orleans LA 70112

STEEDLEY, MILDRED DUNCAN, educator; b. Gainesville, Ga., Oct. 25, 1948; o. William Lester and Floestine Mildred (Nix) Duncan; student Brenau Coll., 1966-67; Asso. Sci., Gainesville Jr. Coll., 1968; B.S. in Secondary Edn., U. Ga., 1970, M.Ed. in Guidance and Counseling, 1973; m. James Wellington Steedley, June 4, 1971. Coordinator coordinated vocat. acad. edn. Jefferson High Sch., Jefferson, Ga., 1970-71; tchr. English, Jonesboro (Ga.) Sr. High Sch., 1971-72, coordinator coordinated vocat. acad. edn., 1972-74, counselor, job placement coordinator, dir. comprehensive career guidance project, 1974-77; project dir. Learning in the Community, Clayton County Bd. Edn., 1977-79; aoj. prof. Ga. State U. mem. Career Edn. Task Force, Ga. Dept. Edn.; cons. to various edni. instns. Coach Am. Jr. Bowling Congress, 1975-77, asst. dir. state bowling tournament, 1977; organist Southside Baptist Ch., 1976-78. Mem. Am., Ga. personnel and Guidance assns., NEA, Ga., Clayton County edn. assns., Ga. Sch. Counselors Assn., Ga. Vocational Guidance Assn. :sec. 1976-77, dir. 1975-76), Phi Kappa Phi, Phi Theta Kappa (sec. 1968), Kappa Delta Pi. Democrat. Editor Vocalizer, 1973-74. Home: 8552 Sheridan Dr Jonesboro GA 30236 Office: 2299 Old Rex Morrow Rd Morrow GA 30260

STEELE, BENNIE WESLEY, state ofcl.; b. Edna, Kans., Aug. 10, 1918; s. Jessie Lee and Mattie May (Poteet) S.; B.A., Oklahoma City U., 1954, postgrad., 1965; m. Ethelynn Belle Bales, Aug. 29, 1936; children—Patricia Steele Weekly, Pamela Steel Crawford. With Star Mfg. Co., 1936-37; self employed truck driver, 1937-40; welder, welding foreman Robinson Steel Co., 1940-43; mgr., co-owner Steele Brothers Machine Shop, Oklahoma City, 1946-51; jr. draftsman, sr. draftsman, design squad boss Okla. Hwy. Dept., Oklahoma City, 1951-56, mgr. data services, 1956-72, head spl. services div., 1972—; mem. indsl. art faculty Oklahoma City U., 1956-57. Ordained minister Ch. of Christ, 1959, elder, 1972. Mem. Gov. Bellman's Com. on Centralization, 1964. Served with USAAF, 1943-45; ETO. Mem. Am. Assn. State Hwy. Ofcls. Club: Toastmasters International (past pres., named Outstanding Toastmaster 1964, Best Speaker Area 2 1965) (Oklahoma City). Home: 4906 N Asbury St Bethany OK 73008 Office: State DOT Bldg Oklahoma City OK 73105

STEELE, DAVIS TILLOU, mech. engr.; b. Springfield, Mo., Jan. 10, 1923; s. Davis William and Aliene (Tillou) S.; B.S. in Mech. Engring., U. Mo., Rolla, 1950; m. Frances Eloise Van Schaick, Feb. 23, 1952; children—Michael, Cynthia, Janet, Dan. Engr. and weapons system mgr. Boeing Co., Wichita, Kans., also Seattle, 1954-63; systems support mgr. Bendix Systems Div., Ann Arbor, Mich., 1963-68, v.p. Am. Sentry N. Tex., Fort Worth, 1968-71; pres. Housing Engrs., Inc., Fort Worth, 1971—. Served with USN, 1943-46. Registered profl. engr., Tex. Mem. Am. Engring. Assn. (chpt. sec.). Clubs: Masons, Shriners. Office: 7305 Grapevine Hwy Fort Worth TX 76118

STEELE, DONALD WILLIAM, retirement center adminstr.; b. Watertown, N.Y., Apr. 30, 1949; s. Desmond Stanley and Doris Helen (Vantassel) S.; B.A. in Sociology, Oral Roberts U., 1971; A.A. in Applied Sci., Health Care Supervision, Tulsa Jr. Coll., 1977; m. LaJuana French, Aug. 23, 1970; children—Shana, Jenny. Dir. bldgs. and grounds Univ. Village, Tulsa, 1971-74, adminstr., 1976—, pres., 1978—; plant mgr. Oral Roberts U., Tulsa, 1974—. Hon. bd. dirs. Tulsa Area Safety Council. Mem. Okls. Nursing Home Assn., Tulsa Met. Nursing Home Assn. (v.p.). Republican. Mem. Assemblies of God Ch. Club: Rotary (Tulsa). Home and Office: 8555 S Lewis Ave Tulsa OK 74136

STEELE, JACK TONY, savs. and loan assn. exec.; b. Longview, Tex., Jan. 4, 1938; s. J. C. and Ludie Belle (Moreau) S.; grad. LaSalle U., 1971; m. Kathryn Elizabeth Conley, Mar. 31, 1979; children—Gregg, Stephanie, Chris, Stephen. Mgr., Household Finance Corp., Longview, 1960-73; v.p., asst. sec. Longview Savs. & Loan Assn., 1973-78; asst. v.p. First Fed. Savs., Longview, 1978—. Served with USAF, 1956-60. Recipient Spoke award Longview, Tex. Jaycees, 1963. Mem. Tex. Savs. and Loan Assn., Inst. Financial Edn. (certificate achievement 1976). Roman Catholic. Clubs: Longview Lions, Ambassadors, K.C. Home: 304 Ralph St Longview TX 75605 Office: 116 E South St Longview TX 75601

STEELE, JAMES EUGENE, ednl. adminstr.; b. South Norfolk, Va.; s. James Edward and Blanche Eugenia (Munden) S.; B.S. in Music Edn., William & Mary Coll., Norfolk, 1961; M.Ed. in Ednl. Adminstrn. and Supervision, Temple U., 1972; Ed.D. in Ednl. Adminstrn., Nova U., 1965. Piccoloist, Norfolk Symphony Orch., 1951-73; dir. choral music Hampton (Va.) City Schs., 1960-65, supr. music, 1965—. Dir. fine arts div. Hampton Assn. Arts Humanities, 1967—. Mem. NEA, Va., Hampton edn. assns., Va. Assn. Sch. Execs., Hampton Instructional Suprs. Assn., Tidewater Regional Suprs., Va. Assn. Sch. Curriculum Devel., Va. Music Suprs. Assn., Va. Music Educators Assn., Music Educators Nat. Conf., Va. Choral Dirs. Assn., Va. Band and Orchestra Dirs. Assn., Va. String Tchrs. Assn. Guest flute soloist Music Tchrs. Assn. Great Britain, 1962. Certified as tchr. supr., Va. Home: 1001 Gates Ave Apt 7B Norfolk VA 23507 Office: 1300 Thomas St Hampton VA 23669

STEELE, ROY WAYNE, copier co. exec.; b. Mineola, Tex., Jan. 10, 1943; s. Maurice E. and Lois O. (Johnston) S.; B.A., Tex. A&M U., 1966, B.B.A., 1970, M.Ed., 1973; postgrad. George Washington U., 1976—; m. Della Jane Roderick, Nov. 8, 1969; children—Amanda, Jason. Mathematician, Gen. Dynamics Corp., Ft. Worth, 1966-69; instr. math., asst. registrar Tex. A&M U., College Station, 1969-73; engr. Halliburton Corp., New Orleans, 1973-74; with Xerox Corp., Leesburg, Va., 1974—, mgmt. trainer, program developer, 1975—. Recipient sales awards Xerox Corp., 1974, 75. Mem. Nat. Micrographics Assn. Democrat. Baptist. Office: Xerox Corp PO Box 2000 Leesburg VA 22075

STEELMAN, VIOLA MARY, radiologic technologist; b. Athens, Tex., June 19, 1929; d. Herbert George and Emma Mae (Coker) Brink; student Watson's Bus. Coll., 1949; grad. Plainview Sanitarium and Clinic X-Ray Sch., 1950; student Hutchenson Flying Sch., 1948; m. Deris Steelman, Oct. 3, 1958. With Central Plains Regional Hosp., Plainview, Tex., 1946—, chief technologist, 1951, tech. dir. Sch. Radiologic Tech., 1951—; dir. dept. radiology, 1972—. Cert. radiologic technologist. Mem. Am. Soc. Radiologic Technologists, Tex. Soc. Radiologic Technologists, Hi Plains Soc. Radiologic Technologists, S. Plains Soc. Radiologic Technologists, Soc. Nuclear Medicine, Tex. Soc. Allied Health Professions, Ednl. Alliance of Tex., Beta Sigma Phi. Presbyterian. Home: 220 NE Alpine St Plainview TX 79072 Office: 2601 Dimmitt Rd Plainview TX 79072

STEENE, KARL MICHAEL, savs. and loan assn. exec.; b. Syracuse, N.Y., Mar. 25, 1948; s. Robert William and Claribel L. (Howard) S.; B.S., Fla. Atlantic U., 1970, M.B.A., 1971; m. Monica Pfreundner, Sept. 13, 1969; 1 dau., Erika Jennifer. Market analyst First Fed. of Lake Worth (Fla.), 1971-73; v.p., regional mgr. Unidex Corp., Atlanta, 1973-75; v.p., dir. research and planning Heritage Fed. Savs., Daytona Beach, Fla., 1975-79; v.p., dir. mktg. Naples Fed. Savs. and Loan Assn. (Fla.), 1979—. Mem. Savs. Instns. Mktg. Soc. Am. (vice chmn., mem. research com., 1st Place Nat. Mktg. award 1978), Am. Advt. Fedn., C. of C., Jaycees. Club: Kiwanis. Home: 3333 Binnacle Dr Naples FL 33940 Office: 900 5th Ave S Naples FL 33940

STEERE, BRUCE MIDDLETON, truck line exec.; b. Evanston, Ill., Dec. 25, 1918; s. Kenneth David and Grace (Duffield) S.; B.A., Yale, 1942; indsl. adminstrn., Harvard Bus. Sch., 1943; m. Anne MacCuen Bullivant, July 5, 1968; children—Lucy Duffield, Grace McLaurin, Mrs. Douglas E. Kliever, Richard M. H. Harper III, Patricia (Mrs. Wyman Flint, Jr.), L. Harper. Indsl. engr. Chance Vought Aircraft, Bridgeport, Conn., 1943-45; pres. Steere Tank Lines, Dallas, 1945—. Pres., dir. So. Ins. Co., Dallas, 1952—; dir. Republic Financial Services, Inc., Allied Finance Co., Indsl. Life Ins. Co., (all Dallas). Mem. Tex. Tank Truck Carriers Assn. (past pres.), Tex. Motor Transp. Assn. (past pres.), Beta Theta Pi. Democrat. Mem. Christian Ch. Clubs: Brook Hollow Golf (Dallas); Koon Kreek (Athens, Tex.) N.Y. Yacht, Cruising of Am. (N.Y.C.); Stone Horse Yacht (Harwich Port, Mass.); Athletic (Dallas). Home: 4412 N Versailles St Dallas TX 75205 Office: 2727 Turtle Creek Dallas TX 75219

STEERE, HARRY HAVELOCK, linguist, educator; b. Boston, May 7, 1933; s. Kenneth Warren and Ruth Ellen (Hanson) S.; A.B., Harvard Coll., 1956; M.A., Middlebury Coll., 1958; Ph.D., Columbia U., 1968; m. Ellen F. DeWolfe Aug. 25, 1956; 1 dau., Heather. Instr. French, Fessenden Sch., west Newton, Mass., 1956-57; chmn. French dept. Lawrence Acad., Groton, Mass., 1958-59; instr. French, Upsala Coll., East Orange, N.J., 1964-68; asst. prof. French, Bates Coll., Lewiston, Maine, 1968-74; asst. prof. French, Hendrix, Coll., Conway, Ark., 1974-79. Organist 1st Ch. Christ Scientist, Portland, Maine, 1969-74; mem. exec. bd. Community Concert Assn., Lewiston-Auburn, Maine 1973-74. Mem. Am. Guild Organists (sub-dean Lewiston chpt. 1973-74), Am. Assn. Tchrs. French (v.p. Maine chpt. 1973-74), Modern Lang. Assn., Ark. Fgn. Lang. Tchrs. Assn., Am. Council on Teaching of Fgn. Langs., Am. Soc. for 18th Century Studies, AAUF. Author: Henri-Joseph DuLaurens, a Philosophe Manque, 1968 Died Sept. 24, 1979. Home: Route 6 Box 179 Conway AR 72032

STEFADOUROS, MILTIADIS ANARGYROU, physician; b. Athens, Greece, Apr. 24, 1939 came to U.S., 1971, naturalized, 1978; s. Anargyros and Chrysoula (Boussiotou) S.; M.D., Nat. and Capodistrian U. of Athens, 1963, D.M.S., 1970; m. Frederique Nikolaidis, Sept. 23, 1968 children—Chrysoula, George Anargyros. Intern, King Paul Hosp., Athens, 1966-67; resident Alexandra Hosp., Athens, 1967-69; clin. asst. in cardiology St. George's Hosp. Med. Sch., London, 1969-71; research fellow in cardiology U. N.C. Sch. Medicine, Chapel Hill, 1971-72; asst. prof. medicine (cardiology) Med. Coll. Ga., Augusta, 1972-76, asso. prof., 1976—; mem. staff E. Talmadge Meml. Hosp., VA Hosp. Served with Greek Army M.C., 1964-66. Greek State Scholarship Found. Scholar, 1969-72; NIH grantee, 1974-77. Diplomate Am. Bd. Internal Medicine. Fellow Am. Coll. Cardiology, Am. Coll. Angiology, Am. Coll. Chest Physicians, A.C.P.; mem. Am. Heart Assn., Am. Soc. Echocardiography, Am. Fedn. for Clin. Research Med. Assn. Athens, So. Soc. for Clin. Investigation. Greek Orthodox. Manuscript cons. Circulation jour., Chest jour., Catheterization and Cardiovascular Diagnosis jour.; contbr. articles on cardiology to med. jours. Home: 409 Dorchester Dr Augusta GA 30909 Office: 1120 15th St Augusta GA 30912

STEFANU, CONSTANTINE, univ. adminstr., educator; b. Patras, Greece, June 1, 1930 (parents Am. citizens); s. James and Helen (Pappas) S.; A.B., Jacksonville State Coll., 1957; M.S., Ala. Med. Coll., 1969; Ph.D., U. Ala., 1972; m. Mary L. Pate, Jan. 4, 1975; children—Steven, Stephanie, Sonya. Computer specialist VA Hosp., Birmingham, Ala., 1964-67; epidemiologist Med. Coll. Ala.

Birmingham, 1967-72; dir. mgmt. and planning U. Tenn. Med. Sch., Memphis, 1972-75; dir. planning and resource analysis, asso. prof. dept. family practice U. Tex. Health Sci. Center at Dallas, 1975—; epidemiol. cons. St. Jude Children's Hosp., Memphis; bio-statis. cons. Children and Youth Project, Birmingham; asst. sec., accreditation/evaluation AMA Bd. mem. Greek Orthodox Ch.; sec. Ala. chpt. Nat. Multiple Sclerosis Soc. Served with U.S. Army, 1951-53. Recipient Hope Chest award Nat. Multiple Sclerosis Soc., 1970; Nat. Found. for Med. Edn. grantee, 1972-74. Mem. Assn. Am. Med. Colls. (nat. chmn. planning coordinators), Assn. Instnl. Researchers (chmn. spl. interest group), Am. Public Health Assn., Soc. Coll. and Univ. Planning, Inst. Mgmt. Sci., Ops. Research Soc. Am., Phi Delta Kappa, Alpha Mu. Gamma. Club: Masons. Contbr. articles to med. jours. Home: 7140 Baxtershire Dr Dallas TX 75230 Office: U Tex Health Sci Center at Dallas 5323 Harry Hines Blvd Dallas TX 75235

STEFFENS, ROGER CHARLES, landscape architect; city planner; b. Milw., May 18, 1934; s. Raymond Charles and Helen Anna (Jahn) S.; student St. Petersburg Jr. Coll., 1958-59; B.Landscape Architecture cum laude, U. Fla., 1962; M. City and Regional Planning, U. N.C., 1964; m. Huguette Ann Bourgery, Sept. 27, 1957; children—Marc Charles, Ashley Noelle. Prin. Planner City of Huntsville (Ala.), 1964-67; city planner asso. Ewald Assos., Memphis, 1967-68; div. mgr. Reynolds, Smith & Hills, Jacksonville, Fla., 1968-72; v.p. Reynolds, Smith Hills, 1972-77, Bos & Assos., 1978—; cons. in city planning and landscape architecture, 1977—; partner PLD LTD., Jacksonville, 1972—; trustee BNC Investors, Jacksonville. Mem. Huntsville Beautification Bd., 1965-67; spl. adviser Huntsville Bd. Adjustment, 1965-67. Bd. govs. Deerwood Homeowners Assn., Jacksonville, Fla., 1971-72. Served with USAF, 1954-58. Named Hon. Citizen of Huntsville, 1967; recipient state and nat. awards for excellence in community planning and land devel. Mem. Am. Inst. Planners, Am. Soc. Landscape Architects, Am. Soc. Landscape Architecture (mem. nat. com. on edn. and policy planning 1973-74), Am. Soc. Planning Ofcls., Urban Land Inst., Fla. Planning and Zoning Assn., World Future Soc., Porsche Club Am., Gargoyle, Phi Kappa Phi. Home and office: 7640 Windward Way W Jacksonville FL 32216

STEGER, WILLIAM M., fed. judge; b. Dallas, Aug. 22, 1920; s. Merritt and Lottie (Reese) S.; student Baylor U., 1938-41; LL.B., So. Meth. U., 1950; m. Ann Hollandsworth, Feb. 14, 1948; 1 son, Reed. U.S. atty. Eastern Dist. Tex., 1953-59; U.S. dist. judge Eastern Dist. Tex., Tyler, 1970—. Mem. Tex. Republican Exec. Com., 1966-69, chmn., 1969-70. Served to capt. USAAF, World War II. Decorated Air medal with 4 oak leaf clusters. Home: 801 Meadow Creek Tyler TX 75703 Office: PO Box 1109 Tyler TX 75710

STEGMAIER, CARL EDWARD, JR., entomologist; b. Kansas City, Kans., Jan. 18, 1921; s. Carl Edward and Clara Belle (Bancroft) S.; B.S., Kans. State U., 1949, M.S., 1950; m. Clara Louise Darling, Oct. 18, 1946; children—Bruce Dewain, Eric Lee, Gene Edward, David Brian. Regulatory entomologist U.S. Dept. Agr., Animal and Plant Health Inspection Service, Plant Protection and Quarantine Programs, N.Y.C., Miami, Fla., 1952-77; research asso. Fla. State Collection Anthropods; conducted free research Fla. Dept. Agr. Served with USMC, 1940-46. Recipient certificates of merit U.S. Dept. Agr., 1969, 73. Mem. Fla. (award for services rendered in field entomology 1973), Kans., Washington, Ga. entomol. socs., Entomol. Soc. Am., Biol. Research Inst. Am., Acarological Soc. Am., DAV, Gamma Sigma Delta. Methodist. Contbr. articles profl. jours. Home: 1948 Harriett Dr Tallahassee FL 32303 Office: US Dept Agr Animal and Plant Health Inspection Service Hyattsville MD 20782

STEHLIN, JOHN SEBASTIAN, JR., physician; b. Brownsville, Tenn., June 16, 1923; s. John Sebastian and Princess (King) S.; M.D., Marquette U., 1947; m. Mary E. Cleary, Sept. 1950 (div. Sept. 1962); 1 dau., Mary Cleary; m. 2d, Jean Waggoner, Apr. 7, 1973 (div. Oct. 1977). Intern Milw. Hosp., 1947-48, resident, 1949-52; resident Bapt. Hosp., Memphis, 1948-49; fellow surgery Lahey Clinic, Boston, 1952-53, 56; mem. staff U. Tex. M.D. Anderson Hosp. and Tumor Inst., Houston, 1955-67, sr. fellow, 1955-56, asso. prof. surgery, 1963-67, asso. surgeon, 1961-67; clin. asso. prof. surgery Baylor Coll. Medicine, Houston, 1967—, also sci. dir. Stehlin Found. for Cancer Research, 1970—. Mem. surg. staff St. Joseph Hosp., Houston; hon. prof. Faculty Medicine U. Republic Uruguay. Diplomate Am. Bd. Surgery. Fellow A.C.S.; mem. Am. Assn. Cancer Research, A.A.A.S., A.M.A., Cancer Assn. Argentina (hon.), Cancer Soc. Chile (hon.), Harris County Med. Soc., Houston Surg. Soc., Internat Platform Assn., James Ewing Soc., N.Y. Acad. Scis., Pan Am. Med. Soc., Salem Surg. Soc. (hon.), Soc. Dermatology Uruguay (hon.), Southwestern Surg. Congress, So. Med. Assn., Surg. Soc. Chile (hon.), Tex. Med. Assn., Tex. Surg. Soc., Western Surg. Assn., Royal Soc. Medicine. Home: 5981 Inwood Houston TX 77057 Office: 777 St Joseph Profl Bldg Houston TX 77002

STEIB, CHARLES JOSEPH, mathematician; b. New Orleans, Sept. 26, 1934; s. Martin Joseph and Doretta P. (Wiedemann) S.; B.S., Southeastern La. U., 1958; M.S., La. State U., 1960; m. Frances M. Musante, Aug. 22, 1959; children—Craig M., Dori F., Derryl P. Mem. faculty La. State U., 1958-60, U. New Orleans, 1962-67; mem. faculty Southeastern La. U., Hammond, 1960-62, 67—, asso. prof. math., 1974—. NSF grantee, 1965, 69. Mem. La. Assn. Tchrs. Math. (pres.), Math. Assn. Am., Nat. Council Tchrs. Math. Author: Inversion of Matrices, 1958; (with B.D. Reynolds) Introduction to Sets and Logic, 1965; (with T.K. Maddox and L.H. Davis) Polynomial Functions, 1970. Home: 1903 Cherie Dr Hammond LA 70401 Office: Box 801 University Station Hammond LA 70402

STEIDEN, WILLIAM ALAN, bus. exec.; b. Louisville, Mar. 13, 1937; s. Leonard Clarence and Elizabeth Francis (Hougland) S.; B.S.C., U. Notre Dame, 1959; M.B.A., U. Louisville 1962; m. Martha Jean Muhs, June 25, 1960; children—William Alan, Elizabeth Dawn. In sales and adminstrn. positions Procter & Gamble Co., Louisville, from 1961, Cin., to 1966; br. adminstrn. mgr. Xerox Co., Louisville, 1966-68; v.p. Dolfinger's Inc., Louisville, 1968-77, pres., 1978—; instr. bus. Bellarmine Coll., 1968—; lectr. Transylvania Coll., 1977-78. Bd. dirs. Family and Children's Agy., Louisville, from 1972, pres., vice chmn. bd., 1977—; pres. Third Order Carmelites, Roman Catholic Ch., 1974-79. Mem. Retail Merchants Assn., (pres. local chpt. 1978-80), Retail Controllers Assn. (pres. local chpt. 1972), St. Xavier Alumni Assn. (treas. 1975). Clubs: Audubon Country; Rotary, Pendennis (Louisville). Office: 325 W Walnut St Louisville KY 40202

STEIN, ALVIN, surgeon; b. Paterson, N.J., Oct. 16, 1936; s. David and Minnie (Bochner) S.; B.A., N.Y. U., 1957; M.D., Chgo. Med. Sch., 1961; m. Leona L. Greenbaum, June 22, 1958; children—Eileen Gale, Randy Sue, David. Intern, Hosp. for Joint Diseases, N.Y.C., 1961-62, resident, 1962-63; resident Met. Hosp. and Flower-Fifth Ave. Hosp., N.Y.C., 1963-64, 65-66, Hosp. for Crippled Children, Newark, 1964-65; practice medicine, specializing in orthopedic surgery, Bronx, N.Y., 1966-73, Ft. Lauderdale area, Fla., 1973—; chief Children's Orthopedic Service and Clinic, Bronx Lebanon Hosp., 1960-73; chief staff Lauderdale Lakes Gen. Hosp., 1974-75; mem. staff Bennett Community Hosp., Plantation, Fla., Plantation Gen. Hosp., Univ. Community Hosp., Tamarac, Fla., Cypress Community Hosp., Pompano Beach, Fla. Bd. dirs. Miami Hebrew Acad., 1973—, mem. exec. com. bd., 1975—; bd. dirs. Moriah Sch., Englewood, N.J., 1968—, Yeshiva Torah Vodaath and Mesifta, Bklyn., 1965—. Diplomate Am. Bd. Orthopedic Surgery. Fellow A.C.S., Am. Acad. Orthopedic Surgeons, Internat. Coll. Surgeons; mem. Fla., Eastern Orthopedic assns. Mason (Shriner). Home: 5220 N 31st Pl Hollywood FL 33021 Office: 3001 NW 49th Ave Lauderdale Lakes FL also 8251 W Broward Blvd Fort Lauderdale FL 33324

STEIN, DAVID ERIC, physicist, air force officer; b. Jacksonville, Fla., Jan. 13, 1950; s. Stanley Wolfe and Dorothy Jean (Lilley) S.; B.S. with high honors (J. Hillis Miller Meml. scholar), U. Fla., 1971, postgrad. (Ford fellow), 1971-72, M.S. in Physics, 1977. Instr. physics dept. U. Fla., Gainesville, 1971, 72-74, NSF research asst., 1974-76; commd. 1st lt. U.S. Army, 1977, transferred to Air Force, 1979, advanced through grades to capt., 1979. Mem. Am. Phys. Soc., Am. Assn. Physics Tchrs., Res. Officers Assn., Air Force Assn., Smithsonian Assos., Internat. Platform Assn., Fla. Blue Key, Scabbard and Blade, Phi Beta Kappa, Sigma Pi Sigma, Omicron Delta Kappa, Phi Kappa Phi. Home: 4331 S Bend Circle E Jacksonville FL 32207 Office: RADC-OCTM Griffiss AFB NY 13441

STEIN, WALTRAUT JOHANNA HEDWIG, psychologist; b. Berlin, Germany, Mar. 23, 1932; d. Gerhard M. and Hertha E. (Petrack) S.; came to U.S., 1939; naturalized, 1945; B.A., Youngstown U., 1957; M.A., Ohio U., 1959; Ph.D., Northwestern U., 1963. Asst. prof. philosophy State U. N.Y., Oswego, 1963-64, U. Ga., Athens, 1966-70; asso. prof. psychology W. Ga. Coll., Carrollton, 1972-79. Mem. Am. Philos. Assn., Assn. Humanistic Psychology. Author: On the Problem of Empathy, 1964. Contbr. articles to profl. jours. Home: 770 Jolly Ave S Apt K-16 Clarkston GA 30021

STEIN, WILLIAM JACOB, biochemist; b. Scranton, Pa., Oct. 4, 1925; s. William Gregory and Margaret Marie (Manweiler) S.; B.S., U. Scranton, 1950; m. Johanna Mary Petrus, June 16, 1951; children—Annie Laurie Stein Coligan, William, Gretchen Stein Kraft, Kurt, Karl. Biochemist, Eastern Utilization, Research and Devel. div. Allergens Lab., U.S. Dept. Agr., Washington, 1953-73; coordinator animal facility, sr. scientist supr. Meloy Lab., Inc., Springfield, Va., 1973—. Served in USN, 1943-46. Recipient certificate merit U.S. Dept. Agr., 1969, certificate achievement Combined Fed. Campaign of Nat. Capital Campaign, Mem. Am. Assn. Lab. Animal Sci. Roman Catholic. K.C. Home: 14027 Roanoke St Woodbridge VA 22191 Office: 6715 Electronic Dr Springfield VA 22151

STEINBACH, KARL HEINRICH, physicist; b. Bonn, Germany, Feb. 19, 1928; s. Franz and Mathilde (Braunshausen) S.; Diplom in Physics, U. Munich (Germany), 1953; Ph.D. in Elec. Engring., Tech. U. Hannover (Germany), 1971; m. Dobrila Bojanovic, Dec. 28, 1955; children—Bernhard Zdravko, Carlo Franz, Boris John. Came to U.S., 1959, naturalized, 1965. Physicist, Pintsch Electro Co., Konstanz, Germany, 1953-57; chief electronics lab. Telefunken Co., Munich, also Konstanz, 1957-59; chief microwave and electronics unit U.S. Army Mobility Equipment Research and Devel. Center, 1959-65, chief research and design br., 1965-67, chief research div., 1967-71, chief mine detection div., 1971-75, chief Advanced and Applied Concepts Office, 1975-76; asso. tech. dir. for tech. assessment U.S. Army Mobility Equipment Research and Devel. Command, 1976-78, spl. asst. for sci. and tech. Office of Comdr., 1978—. Recipient award for outstanding achievement Army Sci. Conf., West Point, 1962; research and devel. award Dept. Army, 1969, Sec. of Army research and study fellow, 1971. Mem. IEEE (pres. elect Belvoir chpt.), Sigma Xi. Patentee in field. Home: 9115 Coronado Terr Fairfax VA 22030 Office: US Army MERADCOM Fort Belvoir VA 22060

STEINBERG, ALAN WOLFE, investment mgr., corp. exec.; b. Bklyn., Oct. 26, 1927; s. Benjamin F. and Gertrude (Wolfe) S.; A.B. with honors and spl. distinction in Math., Columbia U., 1947, M.S., 1950, postgrad., 1957-59; postgrad. N.Y. U., 1955-56; m. Suzanne Nichols, Oct. 12, 1958; children—Carol, Laura, Benjamin T. Engr., U.S. Dept. Agr., 1948-50; internal computer cons. Port N.Y. Authority, 1954-56; asst. prof. indsl. engring., ops. research, N.Y. U., 1956-62; pres. Am. Computing Centers, 1962-66; v.p., dir. TBS Computer Centers Corp., N.Y.C., 1967-76; dir. R-T-W Computer Network Corp., N.Y.C.; gen. partner Alan W. Steinberg Partnership, Hartsdale, N.Y., 1968-78, South Miami, Fla., 1978—; chmn. bd. Midland Capital Corp., N.Y.C.; dir. Interpoint Corp., Chgo., Am. Patriot Health Ins. Co. Nat. adviser automation United Jewish Appeal, 1966—; bd. dirs. Herbert O. Wolfe Found., Barrett Sch. Served with AUS, 1950-53. Mem. Assn. Computing Machinery, AAUP, Inst. Mgmt. Scis., N.Y. Acad. Scis., Tropical Audubon Soc. (co-chmn. fin. com.), Phi Beta Kappa, Alpha Pi Mu. Author: The Case for a Wealth Tax, 1973; contbr. articles to profl. jours. Home: 11097 Paradela Ave Coral Gables FL 33156 Office: 7800 Red Rd Suite 203 South Miami FL 33143

STEINBERG, DONALD MICHAEL, mktg./communications co. exec.; b. Knoxville, Tenn., Feb. 3, 1954; s. Leon and Rose (Frimeth) S.; B.A. (William Randolph Hearst Found. scholar), Memphis State U., 1977. Advt. intern John Malmo Advt., Memphis, 1977; account exec. WMPS Radio, Plough Broadcasting, Memphis, 1978-79; v.p. Leavitt & Assos., mktg., mgmt. and communications, Memphis, 1979—; freelance advt. cons., 1977—. Recipient cert. of merit Am. Diabetes Assn., 1978. Mem. Memphis Advt. Fedn., Memphis State U. Alumni Assn. (dir. journalism 1978-79, editor Journalism Newsletter 1977—). Home: 1855 Poplar Woods Circle Germantown TN 38138 Office: 1755 Lynnfield Rd Memphis TN 38138

STEINBERG, LARRY JAY, accountant; b. Columbia, Mo., Dec. 3, 1942; s. Simon Carl and Margaret Carolyn (Strunck) S.; B.S. cum laude, A.B., U. Mo., 1964; m. Rita Susan Hymson, Aug. 23, 1964; children—Scott Hymson, Laura Frances. With Ernst & Ernst, Louisville, 1964-71, supr., 1969-71; mgr. Touche Ross & Co., Louisville, 1971-75, partner, 1975—. Treas., Louisville Hebrew Sch., 1966-68; treas. Chance's Nursery and Kindergarten, Inc., 1973-74, pres., 1974-75; treas. Ky. Dance Council, Inc., 1974-76, v.p., 1976-77, mem. exec. com., 1977-78; treas. Bur. Jewish Edn., 1978-80, pres., 1980—. Treas., City of Bancroft, 1973, chmn. bd. trustees, 1974-75; precinct capt. Republican party, 1973-76; treas. Louisville chpt. Am. Jewish Com., 1976-78, sec., 1978-80; mem. Louisville-Jefferson County Zool. Commn., 1979—. C.P.A., Ky. Mem. Ky. Soc. C.P.A.'s, Am. Inst. C.P.A.'s, Louisville Jr. C. of C. (treas. 1968-69). Jewish. Club: Lincoln of Ky. (treas. 1974-76). Home: 7500 Adler Way Louisville KY 40222 Office: 510 W Broadway Louisville KY 40202

STEINBERG, LEONARD LOUIS, engring. cons.; b. Phila., Nov. 29, 1923; s. Louis L. and Blanche B. (Platt) S.; B.A., Temple U., 1939; B.S. in Mech. Engring., Pa. State U., 1941, M.S. in Indsl. Engring., 1942; postgrad. N.Y. U., 1955-56; m. Janice Louise Ritchey, Feb. 11, 1948; children—Leonard Louis, Gwendolyn Steinberg Sweeney, Susan Steinberg Malecki, Cynthia Steinberg Forte. Mem. staff Curtiss-Wright Corp., Woodridge, N.J. and Quehanna, Pa., 1955-60; chief mfg. engr. Singer Co., State College, Pa., 1960-62; gen. mgr. Nuclide Corp., State College, 1962-63; project engr. Westinghouse Electric Co., Pitts., 1963-65; chief systems engring., tech. utilization The Boeing Co., Huntsville, Ala., 1965-70; sr. engring. specialist Martin Marietta Corp., Huntsville, 1973; sr. product engr. Ford Motor Co., Detroit, 1973-75; sr. project engr. United Tech. Corp., Huntsville, 1977—; engring. cons. Huntsville, 1975-77, formerly cons. to NASA, U.S. Army Ballistic Missile Command, indsl. corps., Gen. Dynamics, Singer Co., GAF Corp., Dynacolor Corp., Optimal Data Corp., Am. Tech. Services. Active Boy Scouts Am., 1948-55; Salvation Army, 1949-54; mem. Community Adv. Council, Bloomfield, N.J., 1956-58; mem. Small Bus. Devel. Council, Huntsville, 1970-73; comdr. Huntsville squadron U.S. Power Squadrons, 1969-70, mem. governing bd., 1970, dist. treas., 1970-72. Bd. dirs. Hosp. Bd., State Coll., Pa., 1960-62, Boys and Girls Ranches Ala., 1967—, Econ. Devel. Council, Huntsville, 1971-75. Served with USNR, 1942-45. Recipient certificate Noteworth Recognition NASA, 1969, certificate Contribution to Aerospace Boeing Corp., 1969, Design award Weatherhead Corp., 1958, Zero Defects Man of Month award The Boeing Co., 1968; named to Roll of Honor, Apollo/Saturn V, 1970. Mem. ASME, Am. Inst. Indsl. Engrs., Nat. Soc. Profl. Engrs., Soc. Mfg. Engrs. (cert.), Soc. Am. Value Engrs., Soc. Reliability Engrs. (pres. chpt. 1979—), Huntsville Assn. Tech. Socs. (sec. 1979), The Innovators, U.S. Power Squadrons, Smithsonian Assos., Oceanic Soc. (charter), Tau Beta Pi, Pi Gamma Mu. Democrat. Presbyterian. Clubs: Univ., Kiwanis, Elks, Whitesburg Boat and Yacht. Contbr. articles to books and profl. jour. Patentee in several fields. Home: 6014 Kimbrell Ln Huntsville AL 35810 Office: PO Box 3375 Huntsville AL 35810

STEINBERG, PAUL B., lawyer, state senator; b. Bklyn., Mar. 21, 1940; s. Morris L. and Elsie K. Steinberg; B.B.A. cum laude, U. Miami, 1961; J.D., Stetson U., 1963; m. Sandra J. Schwartz; children—Lisa Lee, Richard Lawrence, Samantha Lynn. Admitted to Fla. bar; practiced law, Miami Beach, Fla.; mem. Fla. Ho. of Reps., 1972-78; mem. Fla. State Senate, 1978—. Bd. dirs. Miami Beach Taxpayers Assn.; trustee Myasthenia Gravis, Inc., Temple Emmanu-El; chmn. City of Miami Beach Beautification Com. Named Legislator of Yr., Fla. Audubon Soc., 1978; recipient Golden Apple award Dade County Edn. Assn., 1971. Mem. Stetson Lawyers Assn. (past dir.), Fla. Bar Assn., Dade County Bar Assn., D.C. Bar Assn., Phi Alpha Delta. Home: 900 Bay Dr Miami Beach FL 33141 Office: 505 Lincoln Rd Miami Beach FL 33139

STEINE, LYON, physician; b. Montreal, Que., Can., Feb. 3, 1903; s. Maurice Bertie and Tillie (Lesser) S.; came to U.S., 1928, naturalized, 1934; B.Sc., McGill U., 1924, M.D., C.M., 1928; m. Hazel McGinnis, Apr. 18, 1946; children—Janet (Mrs. Roy Bailey), Ellen (Mrs. Donald Milner), Michael, Lynette. Surg. intern, then resident Mt. Sinai Hosp., N.Y.C., 1928-32; pvt. practice gen. medicine, Valley Stream, N.Y., 1932-73; med. dir. Hyland Plasma Donor Center, Atlanta, 1973—. Mem. med. adv. council N.Y. State Senate Com. on Health, 1970. Served to capt. M.C., AUS, 1942-45. Recipient M&R award Ross Labs., Columbus, Ohio, 1953; named Representative Family Doctor, Guidance Assn., 1971. Diplomate Nat. Bd. Med. Examiners. Fellow Royal Soc. Health; charter fellow Am. Acad. Family Practice, Nassau (N.Y.) Acad. Medicine (past trustee); mem. A.M.A., N.Y. State, Nassau med. socs., Alpha Omega Alpha. Contbr. articles to profl. jours. Home: 1585 Bainbridge Lane Roswell GA 30075 Office: 128 Harris St NW Atlanta GA 30313

STEINER, EDWARD DANIEL, educator; b. St. Louis, Sept. 16, 1948; s. William Otto and Pearl Anna Steiner; student St. Mary's Jr. Coll., 1966-67; A.S., Okla. State U., 1969, B.S., 1970, M.S., 1971; m. Sherry Lynn Laffoon, Jan. 17, 1970; children—Misty Renay, Kristi Kathlene. Technician, Okla. State U., 1969-70; firefighter City of Stillwater (Okla.), 1970-71; curriculum specialist Okla. Fire Service Tng. Dept., 1969-71; mem. faculty Okla. State U. Tech. Inst., Oklahoma City, 1970—, asso. prof. fire protection, 1979—, head dept., 1972—; cons. Mem. Nat. Fire Protection Assn., Nat. Safety Council, Internat. Assn. Fire Service Instrs., Fire Service Tng. Assn., Okla. Arson Adv. Council, Okla. Tech. Soc., Metro Area Fire Chiefs Assn., Fire Protection Alumni Assn., Oklahoma C. of C. Democrat. Methodist. Home: 8800 Northridge Terr Oklahoma City OK 73132 Office: 900 N Portland Ave Oklahoma City OK 73107

STEINER, PHILIPP LEONHARD, computer sci. co. ofcl.; b. Basel, Switzerland, Sept. 11, 1938; came to U.S., 1964, naturalized, 1972; s. Leonhard H. and Georgette Celestine Steiner; Diploma Structural Concrete Design, Basel Sch. Arts and Trade, 1959; math and physics student U. Basel, 1960-61; elec. engring. student U. Tex., 1965-67; m. Elisabeth Bruetsch, Apr. 7, 1979. Engring. technician and programmer Freese & Nichols, Ft. Worth, 1964-71, EDP mgr., 1979—; organizer, systems analyst for info. systems Ciba-Geigy, Basel, 1972-78; asst. dir. constrn. div. Soc. Computer Applications in Engring., Planning and Architecture, 1979—. Mem. U.S. Power Squadron. Republican. Club: Ft. Worth Boat. Home: 3740 Misty Meadow Dr Fort Worth TX 76133 Office: 811 Lamar St Fort Worth TX 76102

STEINERT, JEFF HUTCHINSON, hosp. adminstr.; b. Jersey City, Apr. 23, 1921; s. Clarence H. and Erma S.; student engring. Bucknell Jr. Coll., 1938-39, CUNY, 1941-42, chemistry, Columbia U., 1946; m. Mary Schepis, Dec. 26, 1943; children—Geoffrey, Susan, Barbara. Controller, asst. dir. Greenville (S.C.) Hosp. System, 1954-69; asst. v.p. Duke U. Med. Center, Durham, N.C., 1969-74; asso. dir. fin. Charlotte (N.C.) Meml. Hosp., 1974—; cons. HEW, 1966-74; lectr. health adminstrn. Duke U., 1972-74, adj. asst. prof., 1974—. Trustee, Covenant Coll., Lookout Mountain, Tenn., 1966-77. Served with U.S. Army, 1943-45. Fellow Hosp. Fin. Mgmt. Assn. (nat. pres.), mem. Am. Hosp. Assn. Presbyterian. Home: 3327 Providence Rd Charlotte NC 28211 Office: PO Box 32861

STEINFELD, JOHN ROBERT, radiologist; b. New Brighton, Pa., May 6, 1942; s. Robert Charles and Sally (Marshall) S.; B.A., Williams Coll., 1964; M.D., U. Va., 1968; m. Henrietta Hohlt, Dec. 28, 1967; children—Molly Marshall, Robert Reynolds. Intern, Wilmington (Del.) Med. Center, 1968-69; resident in radiology U. Va. Hosp., Charlottesville, 1971-74; practice medicine specializing in diagnostic radiology, Asheville, N.C., 1974—; staff radiologist, chief of ultrasound Meml.-Mission Hosp., Asheville, 1974—. Served to capt., M.C., USAF, 1969-71. Diplomate Am. Bd. Radiology. Mem. Am. Roentgen Ray Soc., Am. Inst. Ultrasound in Medicine, Am. Coll. Radiology, Radiol. Soc. N. Am., AMA, Theta Delta Chi, Phi Chi. Republican. Presbyterian. Club: Country of Asheville. Contbr. articles to profl. jours. Office: 103 Doctors Bldg Asheville NC 28801

STEINHAUER, JOHN MATHIAS, state legislator; b. Nashville, July 23, 1925; s. John M. and Martha Gertrude (Garrety) S.; student U. Tenn., 1945-46; m. Betty Jane Hagewood, June 21, 1952; children—Joni, John Mathias, Janet, Steven Harold. With Henderson Broadcasting Corp. (Tenn.), 1970—, B.A.T. Inc., 1965—; mem. Tenn. Ho. of Reps., 1967-68, 71-72, 76—, chief bill clk., 1971-72, sec. gen. welfare com., mem. judiciary com.; chmn. spl. joint com. on elderly Tenn. Legislature, mem. spl. joint com. children's services; mem. com. human resources of nat. task force Nat. Conf. State Legislatures; city commr. Hendersonville, 1974-77. Recipient George Washington Honor medal Freedoms Found., 1969. Democrat. Lutheran. Clubs: Sertoma (past pres.), Shriners (Nashville). Home: 124 Circle Dr Hendersonville TN 37075 Office: 109 War Meml Bldg Nashville TN 37219

STEINICHEN, JOHN, architect; b. Stone Mountain, Ga., Apr. 29, 1907; s. John and Ada (Wallace) S.; apprentice in sculpture under Herman Steinichen, 1922-26; student Ga. Inst. Tech., 1945; m. Laura Octavia Johnson, Aug. 5, 1929; children—John III, Joyce Kay (Mrs. Glenn E. Wiltsey). Designer, sculptor, 1926-31; freelance artist, sculptor, musician, 1931-41; with Firestone Aircraft Plant, Atlanta, 1942-45; architect with various archtl. firms, Atlanta, 1945-50; asso. architect Finch, Alexander, Barnes, Rothschild & Paschal and predecesser firms, Atlanta, 1950-73. Sculptures and paintings exhibited in group shows, Atlanta, Washington, N.Y.C., others, 1931—; represented in pvt. collections. Mem. Am. Fedn. Musicians, A.I.A., Soc. Mil. Engrs., Allied Artists Am. (asso.), Audubon Artists Assn., Rockdale C. of C. Presbyterian. Home: PO Box 59 3131 Dennard Rd Conyers GA 30207

STEINMAN, ANTON ALBERT, IV (TOM), internat. broker; b. Voorburg, Netherlands, Nov. 22, 1932; came to U.S., 1958, naturalized, 1963; s. Anton A. and Mathilda Wilhelmina (Maat) S.; ed. in aero. engring. and bus. adminstrn., Netherlands, 1950-54. With Sygma Electronics, Inc., N.Y.C., 1958, Manson Labs., Inc., Stamford, Conn., 1964-68; audio visual tech. dir. Bd. Edn., Norwalk, Conn., 1966-68, John A. Define & Co., real estate, Danbury, Conn., 1966-68; real estate, import and export broker, Danbury, 1974—; fin., real estate and commodity broker, pres., owner Internat. Resources and Intermediary Services, Inc., Johnson City, Tenn., 1974—; cons. in field. Served with Royal Dutch Naval Air Force, 1954-56. Mem. U.S. Bd. Realtors, Tenn. Bd. Realtors, Internat. Traders. Republican. Christian Ch. Translator tech. and med. pubs. from English into Dutch, for U.S. and Dutch research insts., 1961-63. Office: PO Box 3124 CRS Johnson City TN 37601

STELZER, PATRICK THEODORE, auditor, govt. ofcl.; b. Muenster, Tex., Mar. 15, 1935; s. August Charles and Lorene (Williams) S.; B.B.A., East Tex. State U., 1960; M.A., U. Okla., 1971, postgrad., 1972-76; m. Pauline Myrick, Dec. 27, 1955; children—Rene Anne, Kristy M. Supervisory auditor GAO, Dallas, 1960-73; asst. regional audit dir. HEW, Dallas, 1974—. Tchr. fin. mgmt. techniques Office Minority Bus. Enterprise, 1972—. Served with USMC, 1954-57. Mem. Inst. Internal Auditors, Assn. Govt. Accountants, Fed. Bus. Assn., Acad. Polit. Sci., Am. Acad. Polit. and Social Scis., EDP Auditors Assn., Fed. Govt. Accountants Assn. (treas. Dallas chpt. 1972-74). Roman Catholic. Home: Box 157 Muenster TX 76252 Office: 1200 Main Tower Dallas TX 75202

STEM, MARTHA SNOWDON, editor, author; b. Oil City, Pa., July 2, 1908; d. Wayne Compton and Nettie (Snowdon) Stem; grad. Va. Jr. Coll. Sch. Journalism, 1927; A.B., Pa. Coll. for Women, 1929. Columnist dir. spl. edits. schs., coll. and chs. Pitts. Press, 1932-41, St. Petersburg (Fla.) Times, 1941-42; free lance writer pub. relations, 1942-51; exec. sec. Dept. Pub. Information, Am. Optometric Assn., Pitts., 1951-53; dir. profl. relations Optometric Extension Program Found., Duncan, Okla., 1953-78, co-organizer, cons., editor Optometric Extension Program Asst.'s Course, 1958-78. Tchr. introductory psychology pvt. high sch., St. Petersburg, Fla., 1945-49. Corr. Acad. Therapy Publs., San Rafael, Cal., 1966-78. Bd. dirs. vols. for Vision, 1968-78. Mem. Chatham Coll. Alumnae Assn., Omega. Presbyn. Author: Optometric Extension Program Course series Professional and Patient Relations, 23 vols. Editor: Optometric Extension Program NEWS, 1954-78. Contbr. articles to various optometric publs. Home: 445 29th Ave N St Petersburg FL 33704

STENGLEIN, JOSEPH ARTHUR, air force officer, educator, geographer; b. N.Y.C., Apr. 28, 1916; s. Conrad and Margaret K. (Foerst) S.; B.S. in Mil. Sci., U. Md., 1953; M.S. in Geography, U. Tex., 1965; m. Mary F. Woods, Apr. 28, 1942 (div. Sept. 1969); children—Millie M. Stenglein Heine, Joseph Arthur II, Linda L. Stenglein Kaderka. Commd. 2d lt. USAAC, 1939; advanced through grades to col. USAF, 1951; ret., 1961; airline pilot Western div. Pan Am. Airways, 1940-41; test pilot Boeing Aircraft Co., Seattle, 1941-42; prof. Air Force R.O.T.C., U. Nebr., Lincoln, 1953-56; prof. geography Tex. So. U., Houston, 1965-79. Decorated Croix de Guerre with palm (France). Mem. AAUP, Internat. Platform Assn., Tex. Assn. Coll. Tchrs., Assn. Am. Geographers, Oceanic Soc., Internat. Oceanographic Found., Ret. Officers' Assn., Am. Security Council (advisory bd. 1971-75), Combat Pilots Assn., 8th Air Force Hist. Soc., Amvets, Aircraft Owners and Pilots Assn., Exptl. Aircraft Assn., Nat. Assn. Uniformed Services, Am. Mus. Nat. History, Am. Legion, Gamma Theta Upsilon. Roman Catholic. Elk, Moose, Daedalian. Club: Army and Navy (Washington). Contbr. articles to profl. jours. Home: 3215 Broadway St Apt 27 Houston TX 77017

STENHOLM, CHARLES WALTER, congressman; b. Stamford, Tex., Oct. 26, 1938; s. Lambert and Irene Strenholm; B.S. in Agr., Tex. Tech. U., 1961, M.S., 1962; m. Cynthia Ann Watson, July 1, 1961; children—Chris, Cary, Courtney. Vocat. agr. tchr., 1962-64; exec. v.p. Rolling Plains Cotton Growers, 1964-67; gen. mgr. Stamford Electric Coop., 1967-76; owner, mgr. Stenholm Farms, Stamford, 1969-76; pres. Double S. Farms, Inc., 1976-77; dir. First Nat. Bank Stamford, 1975-78, adv. dir., 1979—; charter trustee Cotton Inc.; pres. Tex. Electric Coop., 1976; v.p. Tex. Fedn. Coops., 1977; mem. Tex. Agr. Stablzn. Com.; mem. 96th Congress from 17th Dist. Tex. Pres. Stamford Little League Baseball, 1977, Stamford United Way, 1974; exec. com. 30th Senatorial Dist. Tex. Democratic Party, 1974. Named Am. Farmer, Future Farmers Am., 1959. Mem. Rolling Plains Cotton Growers (past pres.), Stamford C. of C. (past pres.). Lutheran. Club: Stamford Exchange. Address: 1610 Longworth Bldg Washington DC 20515

STENNIS, JOHN CORNELIUS, U.S. senator; b. Kemper County, Miss., Aug. 3, 1901; s. Hampton H. and Cornelia (Adams) S.; B.S., Miss. State Coll., 1923; LL.B., U. Va., 1927; Ph.D. (hon.), Millsaps Coll., U. Wyo.; LL.D., Miss. Coll., Belhaven Coll., 1972; m. Coy Hines, Dec. 24, 1929; children—John Hampton, Margaret Jane. Pvt. practice law, DeKalb, Miss.; mem. Miss. Ho. of Reps., 1928-32; dist. pros. atty., 1931-35; apptd. circuit judge, 1937, elected to same office, 1938, 42, 46; mem. U.S. Senate, 1947—, chmn. Senate Armed Services Com., mem. Appropriations Com. Mem. Am., Miss. bar assns., Phi Beta Kappa, Alpha Chi Rho, Phi Alpha Delta. Presbyn. Mason, Lion. Home: DeKalb MS 39328 Office: US Senate Washington DC 20510

STEPBACH, ROBERT FRANK, JR., clin. psychologist; b. Binghamton, N.Y., Mar. 20, 1923; s. Robert Frank and Minnietta St. Claire (Wall) S.; B.A., Syracuse U., 1950; M.A., 1952; Ed.D., George Peabody Coll. Tchrs., 1962; m. Edith Schou, June 2, 1951; children—Joseph, Sorine (Mrs. Burt Markert), Karen (Mrs. Luther E. Smith, Jr.), Marc. Speech pathologist and audiologist State of Tenn., Nashville, 1952, Bill Wilkerson Hearing and Speech Center, Nashville, 1952-57; clin. psychologist Nashville Mental Health Center, 1957-69; pvt. practice clin. and cons. psychology, Nashville, 1963—. Cons., Dede Wallace Mental Health Center, Multi-County Comprehensive Community Mental Health Center, Sumner County Guidance Center, Nashville Met. Schs.; mem. profl. adv. com. Cecil Sims Cerebral Palsy Center, 1971-76. Mem. Tenn. Bd. Examiners in Psychology, 1971-73. Bd. dirs. HELP, Inc., 1958-62, Donelson Child Devel. Center, 1967-69, Nashville Mental Health Assn., 1965-68, Robert F. Stepbach, Jr., Found., Sumner County Guidance Center; mem. exec. com. Kennedy Center, Nashville, 1966-69. Served with USNR, 1942-46. Recipient Maurice Falk Med. fund grant, 1964-65. Mem. Am., Southeastern; Tenn. (sec.-treas. 1967-69, v.p. 1969-71, pres. 1972-73) Psychol. assns., Am. Soc. Clin. Hypnosis, Am. Soc. Exptl. and Clin. Hypnosis, Sigma Nu. Editor: HELP Newsletter, 1958-62; Guideline, 1973-74; The Tenn. Psychologist, 1974-77. Home: 817 Allen Rd Nashville TN 37214 Office: 1920 Church St Nashville TN 37203

STEPHAN, CHARLES ROBERT, ret. naval officer, educator; b. Bklyn., Sept. 30, 1911; s. Charles Albert and Ella (Wallendorf) S.; B.S. in Engring., U.S. Naval Acad., 1934; D.Engring., Fla. Atlantic U., 1978; m. Eleanor Grace Storck, Feb. 14, 1937; children—Yvonne (Mrs. U.T. Brown), Joan Diane (Mrs. E. Cathcart), Charles Royal, Robert Warren. Commd. ensign USN, 1934, advanced through grades to capt., 1953; air def. officer in U.S.S. Raleigh, Pearl Harbor, 1941; comdg. officer U.S.S. Woodworth, South Pacific, 1943-44; asso. prof. naval sci. Rensselaer Poly. Inst., 1945-46; exec. officer in U.S.S. Iowa, 1951-52; comdr. Destroyer Squadron 8, 6th Fleet, 1959-60; ASW research and devel. dir. Staff Chief Naval Operations, Washington, 1960-63; prof., chmn. ocean engring. dept. Fla. Atlantic U., 1964-74, dir. coop. edn., 1974-76, prof. emeritus, 1976—. Trustee Fla. Ocean Scis. Inst. Decorated Navy Cross, Bronze Star medals (2). Fellow Marine Technol. Soc.; mem. U.S. Naval Inst., Am. Soc. Engring. Edn. (chmn. ocean engring. com. 1975-76), AAUP, Navy League, Coop. Edn. Assn. Clubs: Kiwanis (past pres. Sunrise, Boca Raton), Torch. Home: 500 S Ocean Blvd Apt 704 Boca Raton FL 33432

STEPHANS, ANDREW PAUL, lawyer; b. Harlingen, Tex., May 26, 1926; grad. Columbia Coll., 1949, Columbia Law Sch., 1952; m. Iris McDuffie, July 31, 1965; 1 dau., Melisande. Admitted to Tex. bar, 1953; atty. Harris County, Farmers Home Adminstrn. and Commodity Credit Corp., Dept. Agr., 1954; atty. Butler, Binion, Rice, Cook & Knapp, Houston, 1954-69; pvt. practice, Houston, 1969—; owner Buffalo Plaza Shopping Center, Houston, 2121 San Felipe Bldg, Houston. Tchr. hotel law U. Houston Hotel Sch., 1972-73; lectr. Am. Inst. Bankers, Inst. Internal Auditors. Served with inf. AUS, World War II; ETO. Mem. Am., Houston bar assns., State Bar Tex., Am. Judicature Soc., Phi Theta Kappa. Club: Columbia U. (pres. 1965-68) (Houston). Home: 2424 Stanmore St Houston TX 77019 Office: 2121 San Felipe Bldg Houston TX 77019 also 50 Ave Victor Hugo 75116 Paris France

STEPHENS, BERTRAM EASTMOND SAMUEL, obstetrician and gynecologist; b. St. Vincent, West Indies, Apr. 19, 1938; came to U.S., 1962; s. George S. and Beryl I. (Walker) S.; B.A., Hunter Coll., N.Y., 1966; M.D., Howard U., Washington, 1970. Intern, Howard U., 1970-71; resident in ob-gyn Freedmen's Hosp., D.C. Gen. Hosp., Greater S.E. Community Hosp. and Norfolk Community Hosp., 1971-75; practice medicine specializing in ob-gyn, Hampton, Va., 1975—; mem. staff Hampton Gen., Mary Immaculate, Whittaker Meml. hosps.; chief of surgery Whittaker Meml. Hosp., 1979-80; active Peninsula Planned Parenthood, Am. Cancer Soc. Active Beau Brummel Civic and Social Club, Youth Profls. of Tide Water, Los Aficionados Jazz Soc. (pres.), Big Bros., NAACP., Recipient service award E.R. Whittaker Meml. Hosp., 1977. Diplomate Am. Bd. Ob-Gyn. Mem. Nat. Med. Assn., AMA, Am. Soc. Psychoprophylaxis in Obstetrics, Va. Med. Soc., Am. Assn. Gynecol. Laparoscopists. Episcopalian. Home: 109 Waltham St Hampton VA 23666 Office: 2002 Kecoughton St Hampton VA 23661

STEPHENS, BETTY JO, educator; b. Little Rock, Nov. 15, 1929; d. Cottral Joseph and Jennie Mae (McDandell) Walker; B.S.E., U. Central Ark., 1952; M.S., U. Mo., 1956; m. Sidney M. Stephens, Aug. 14, 1956; children—Cynthia Louise, James Dennis. Instr. health and phys. edn. in public schs., Rolla, Mo., 1953-54; dir. elem. and sec. phys. edn., Christopher (Ill.) public schs., 1955-57; instr., coach, asst. prof. U. Ark., Little Rock, 1969-75, coordinator for women's athletics, 1976—. Mem. Ark. Womens Sports Assn., Am. Inter-Collegiate Athletics for Women, Ark. Assn. for Health, Phys. Edn. and Recreation, Sigma Sigma Psi, Alpha Kappa Gamma. Democrat. Methodist. Clubs: Order Eastern Star, Demolay Mothers, Patron of Ark. Tennis Assn. Home: PO Box 56 Bryant AR 72022 Office: Dept Women's Athletics U Ark Little Rock AR 72201

STEPHENS, CHARLES ANTHON, physician; b. Camden, Tex., Oct. 13, 1925; s. Buford Dured and Carrie (Collins) Stephens; B.A., U. Tex., 1950, M.D., 1954; m. Nancy Raisch, June 25, 1954; children—Deborah, Claudia, Charles Anthon II, Barbara, Jerry. Intern Univ. Hosp., Little Rock, 1954-55; resident U. Tex. Med. Br., Galveston, 1955-58; practice medicine specializing in obstetrics-gynecology, Odessa, Tex., 1958—; mem. staff Med. Center Hosp., chief of staff 1962; mem. staff Odessa Women's and Children's Hosp., chief ob-gyn., 1979-80. Bd. dirs. Odessa Community Chest and United Fund, 1959-60, Ector County Assn. Retarded Children, Midland-Odessa Mental Health-Mental Retardation Bd. Served with USNR, 1943-46. Diplomate Am. Bd. Obstetrics and Gynecology. Fellow Am. Coll. Obstetrics-Gynecology; mem. AMA, Tex. Med. Assn., Ector County Med. Soc., Tex. Obstetrics and Gynecology Soc., Tex. Perinatal Assn., Willard R. Cooke Obstetrics-Gynecology Soc., Pi Kappa Alpha, Phi Chi. Home: 3204 Blossom Lane Odessa TX 79762 Office: 808 Tower Dr Odessa TX 79761

STEPHENS, CHARLES RICHARD, univ. adminstr.; b. McIntosh County, Ga., Mar. 1, 1938; s. James Anthony and Lillian Belle (Frances) S.; B.A., Morehouse Coll., 1960; postgrad. Atlanta U., 1961, 64, 65, U. New Orleans, 1978; m. E. Delores Betts, Nov. 12, 1960; children—Chandra Rae, Charlita Rochelle. Membership and public relations sec. Butler Street YMCA, Atlanta, 1961-62, membership-program dir., 1964-67, asst. gen. exec., 1967-70; area dir. United Negro Coll. Fund, N.Y.C., 1970-72, regional dir., 1973-74, nat. campaign dir., 1975-76; devel. dir. Sch. Medicine, Morehouse Coll., Atlanta, 1977; v.p. for devel. Dillard U., New Orleans, 1977-79, Clark Coll., Atlanta, 1979—; cons. Robert R. Moton Devel. Consortium. Served with U.S. Army, 1962-64. Cert. dir. YMCA's of N. Am. Mem. Nat. Soc. Profl. Fund-Raising Execs., Council for Advancement and Support of Edn., Alpha Phi Alpha. Presbyterian. Home: 2853 Wright Dr SW Atlanta GA 30311 Office: Clark Coll 240 Chestnut St SW Atlanta GA 30314

STEPHENS, GEORGE GAYLE, physician, med. educator; b. Ashburn, Mo., Aug. 6, 1928; s. George Lewis and Helen Cleo (Williamson) S.; A.A., Central Coll., McPherson, Kans., 1946; student Greenville (Ill.) Coll., 1947; B.S., U. Mo., 1950; M.D., Northwestern U., 1952; m. Eula Jean Shields, July 10, 1948; children—Lynn, Joel, Scott, Jan, Julie, Ken, Jean. Intern, Wesley Hosp., Wichita, Kans., 1952-53; gen. practice medicine, Wichita, 1955-67; dir. family practice residency Wesley Med. Center, Wichita, 1967-72; prof., chmn. dept. family practice Wichita State br. U. Kans. Sch. Medicine, 1972-73; dean Sch. Primary Med. Care, U. Ala., Huntsville, 1973-77; chmn. dept. family practice U. Ala. Sch. Medicine, Birmingham, 1977—. Served with M.C., AUS, 1953-55. Home: 4300 Overlook Rd Birmingham AL 35222

STEPHENS, GRETCHEN DAVIS, ins. underwriter; b. Omaha, May 5, 1940; d. LaMonte Fulford and Virginia Gretchen (Romberg) Davis; student Northwestern U., 1958-60; B.A., Boston U., 1962; children—Gregory F., Virginia G. Asso., Nat. Life of Vt., H.V. Seger & Assos., Houston, 1971—. Mem. Pres.'s Club Nat. Life of Vt.; recipient Nat. Sales Achievement award 1977, 78; C.L.U. Mem. Houston Assn. Life Underwriters, Houston chpt. C.L.U.'s, Houston Estate and Fin. Forum, Tex., Women's leaders round tables, River Oaks Bus. Women's Exchange Club (pres. 1978). Office: 4801 Woodway St 320W Houston TX 77056

STEPHENS, JAMES, city ofcl.; b. Dublin, Ga., Nov. 27, 1946; s. Evada Faye (Perry) S.; student Talladega Coll., 1964-66; B.A., So. Ill. U., 1972; M.P.A., Nova U., 1977; m. Sandra Denette Edwards, Oct. 14, 1972; children—Ahmed, Nina. Community organizer Community Action Program, Fort Lauderdale, Fla., 1966-68, area coordinator, 1968-70; exec. dir. Dept. Human Services, Dania, Fla., 1972—; state coordinator for Haitians 1979—. Chmn. bd. dirs. Broward County Ex-Offenders Task Force, 1978, Coalition Human Services Dirs., 1979; coordinator public relations Broward County Planning Council, 1979. Recipient Broward County Human Relations award, 1977, Disting. Service award N.W. Women's Aux., 1978, Human Merit award Dade County Elks, 1979. Mem. Nat. Black Social Workers Assn., Am. Mgmt. Assn., Nat. Alliance Businessmen, Omega Psi Phi. African Methodist Episcopal Ch. Club: Masons. Office: 100 W Dania Beach Blvd Dania FL 33004

STEPHENS, JAMES MACON, clergyman; b. Corpus Christi, Tex., Jan. 4, 1935; s. Joe Key and Mary Emma (Robertson) S.; student Del Mar Coll., 1952-54; B.B.A., U. Tex., Austin, 1963; M.R.E., Southwestern Bapt. Theol. Sem., 1965; m. Vonda Lee O'Neal, May 30, 1964; 1 son, James Macon. Ordained to ministry Baptist Ch., 1965; music dir. Trinity Bapt. Ch., Corpus Christi, 1956-58, Southside Bapt. Ch., Corpus Christi, 1959-61; interim music dir. Bapt. chs., Austin, 1961-63; music and youth dir. First Bapt. Ch., Granbury, Tex., 1963-65; minister of music and edn. Coll. Bapt. Ch., Big Spring, Tex., 1965-68, Second Bapt. Ch., Odessa, Tex., 1968-74, Kiestwood Bapt. Ch., Dallas, 1974-76; asso. pastor for edn. and adminstrn. First Bapt. Ch. of Woodway, Waco, Tex., 1976-79; minister of edn. and adminstrn. Calvary Bapt. Ch., Beaumont, Tex., 1979—; v.p. Odessa Ministerial Alliance, 1971-72; associational ch. tng. dir., Waco, Tex., 1977-78; mem. adv. council Baylor U. Profl. Devel. Center. Mem. Southwestern Bapt. Religious Ednl. Assn., Nat. Assn. Ch. Bus. Adminstrs. So. Bapt. Ch. Bus. Officers Assn. Democrat. Club: Masons (master 1970-71). Home 1197 Garley Beaumont TX 77701 Office: 3650 Dowleu Rd Beaumont TX 77706

STEPHENS, JOHN CARNES, hydraulic engr.; b. Attalla, Ala., Sept. 22, 1910; s. John J. and Margaret Editha (Carnes) S.; B.S., Ala. U., 1931; postgrad. Stanford, 1931-32; m. Phelia Frances Walker, Sept. 10, 1936; children—John Carnes, Mary Louise, Margaret Editha. Agrl. engr. Soil Conservation Service, U.S. Dept. Agr., Dadeville, Ala., 1933-39, asst. project engr. Everglades Project, Ft. Lauderdale, Fla., 1939-42, project engr., 1942-46, research project supr., 1949-54, research project engr. Agrl. Research Service, 1954-61, research investigations leader, watershed engr. So. br. Soil and Water Conservation, Ft. Lauderdale, 1961-62; research investigations leader, dir. S.E. Watershed Research Center, Athens, Ga., 1962-70; chief N.W. br. Soil and Water Conservation, Agrl. Research Service, Boise, Ida., 1970-72, research area dir. Mississippi Valley area So. region Agrl. Research Service, Stoneville, Miss., 1972-75, cons. engr., geologist, collaborator Agrl. Research Service, Ft. Lauderdale, 1975—; water control engr. Dade County (Fla.), 1946-49. Collaborator Central-So. Fla. Flood Control Dist., 1949-78. Registered profl. engr., Fla.; registered profl. geologist, Ida. Mem. Am. Geophys. Union, Am. Soc. Agrl. Engrs. (John Deere Gold Medal award 1976), ASCE (exec. com. irrigation and drainage div. 1964-72, mem. mgmt. group D water resources 1972-75), Am. Water Resources Assn., Soil Conservation Soc. Am., Scabbard and Blade, Sigma Phi Epsilon. Presbyterian. Clubs: Rotary, Ft. Lauderdale Country. Contbr. articles to profl. jours. Home: 1111 NE 2d St Fort Lauderdale FL 33301

STEPHENS, KENNETH DEAN, JR., mgmt. and engring. cons.; b. Logan, Utah, Dec. 8, 1942; s. Kenneth Dean and Dorothy Clara (Hoffler) S.; student U. Utah, 1961-63, U. P.R. Grad. Sch. Physics, 1973; m. Christiana Gloria Hughes, Apr. 13, 1968; children—Trina Ridvan, Nick Jalal. Staff engr. Sta. KLOR-TV, Provo, Utah and Sta. KLRJ-TV, Las Vegas, Nev., 1958-61; chief engr. Sta. KUER-FM, Salt Lake City and Sta. KCET-TV, Ogden, Utah, 1961-63; dir. TV research U. Utah, 1964-67; pres. Electronic Research Corp., Salt Lake City, 1968-71; mgr. Tele-San Juan, Inc, owner Sta. WTSJ-TV, San Juan, P.R., Sta. WPSJ-TV, Ponce, P.R. and Sta. WMGZ-TV, Mayaguez, P.R., 1970-74 pres. Broadcast Devels. Internat., St. Just, P.R., 1974—; tech. advisor audio-visual dept. Universal House of Justice, Baha'i World Center, Haifa, Israel; cons. for UN Sci. activities Baha'i Internat. Community (New York); instr. broadcasting and communications. Mem. Internat. Inst. Communications. Baha'i. Patentee video rec., color TV projection, radar glasses for blind, color TV system, TV transmission developed color TV system used by NASA manned spacecraft. Office: PO Box 158 Saint Just PR 00750

STEPHENS, LAWRENCE WESLEY, aerospace engr.; b. Terrell, Tex., Nov. 1, 1949; s. Arnie Lawrence and Delia Bess (Welborn) S.; B.S. in Aerospace Engring., U. Tex., Arlington, 1972, M.S., 1979. Grad. teaching/research asst. U. Tex., Arlington, 1973-74; aerospace engr. Vought Corp., Dallas, 1974—; lectr. aerospace engring. U. Tex., Arlington, 1974-75, 79-80, mem. Aviation Edn. Resource Center, 1975—. Mem. Arlington Little League Baseball, 1973-77; adv. Jr. Achievement, Irving, Tex., 1979-80. Tex. Aluminum Co. scholar, 1968. Mem. Am. Inst. Aeros. and Astronautics (Outstanding Individual Achievement award U. Tex., Arlington br. 1973, young profl. com. 1978—, pub. affairs chmn. North Tex. sect. 1976-78, sect. tech. activities chmn. 1978-79, chmn. organizing com. S.W. region student conf. 1980), Tau Beta Pi, Sigma Gamma Tau. Author papers in field. Office: Unit 2-30330 Vought Corp PO Box 225907 Dallas TX 75265

STEPHENS, LEVIE BURDESHAW, ret. state ofcl.; b. Skippersville, Ala., Dec. 5, 1905; s. James Arthur and Martha (Burdeshaw) S.; B.S., U. Ala., 1926; LL.B., Jones Law Sch., 1949; m. Lottie Jackson, June 1, 1930; children—Martha (Mrs. William Stancik), Janella (Mrs. Thomas Esslinger). Admitted to Ala. bar, 1950; tchr., coach high schs. Ala., 1926-34; social case worker, A.R.C. and Jefferson County Dept. Pub. Welfare, 1934-37; probation officer Juvenile and Domestic Relations Ct., Birmingham 1937-39; probation and parole officer Ala. Bd. Pardons & Paroles, Montgomery, 1939-40, supr. probation and parole officers, 1940-43, exec. dir., 1944-75; dir. Ga. Bd. Pardons and Paroles, 1943-44; ret., 1975. Mem. profl. council Nat. Council Crime and Delinquency, mem. adv. council on parole. Mem. Ala. Probation and Parole Assn. (pres. 1952), So. States Probation and Parole Conf. (pres. 1949), Parole and Probation Compact Adminstrs. Assn. (adminstr. 1949—), Nat. Probation and Parole Assn., Assn. Paroling Authorities (exec. com.), Am. Correctional Assn. (dir. 1962—). Methodist. Kiwanian. Home: 3049 Cloverdale Rd Montgomery AL 36106

STEPHENS, LOUIS CORNELIUS, JR., ins. co. exec.; b. Dunn, N.C., Dec. 19, 1921; s. Louis Cornelius and Agnes (Warren) S.; B.S., U. N.C., 1942; M.B.A., Harvard U., 1947; m. Mary Adams, Sept. 6,

1952; children—Michael, Mary, Anne, Joan, Louis, Suzanne, Melanie, Peter. With Pilot Life Ins. Co., Greensboro, N.C., 1949—, pres., chief exec. officer, 1971—. Bd. dirs. Research Triangle Inst., N.C. Citizens Assn., Moses Cone Meml. Hosp., Salem Acad. and Coll., Belmont Abbey Coll., Jr. Achievement Greensboro; chmn. bd. trustees U. N.C., Greensboro, 1977—. Served with USN, World War II. Mem. Health Ins. Assn. Am. (chmn.), Clearinghouse on Corp. Social Responsibility (dir.). Roman Catholic. Office: Pilot Life Ins Co Box 20727 Greensboro NC 27420

STEPHENS, ROBERT EDWARD, educator; b. Montgomery, Ala., Feb. 25, 1937; s. Sidney Frazer and Dorothy Eleanor (Bach) S.; B.S., U. Ala., 1961, M.A., 1965; postgrad. Ind. U., 1967-68, Ball State U., 1968-69, Miss. State U., 1970, Ala. A. and M. U., 1971, U. Ala., 1969-75; m. Mavis Lynnette Bridges, May 31, 1964; children—Karlton Robert, Jeremy Edward. Band dir. Banks High Sch., Birmingham, Ala., 1961-65; chmn. fine arts div. John C. Calhoun Community Coll., Decatur, Ala., 1965-75, band dir. instr., woodwind instruments, 1965—; dir. Summer Musicals Orch., 1974—. Joe Wheeler Found. scholar, 1958-61. Mem. Music Educators Nat. Conf., NEA, Ala. Edn. Assn., Ala. Music Educators Assn., Ala. Band Masters Assn. Democrat. Presbyterian. Clubs: Civitan, Masons. Contbr. articles to profl. jours. Home: 1819 19th Ave SW Decatur AL 35601 Office: Bee Line Hwy Decatur AL 35601

STEPHENS, ROBERT F., state ofcl.; b. Covington, Ky., Aug. 16, 1927; student Ind. U.; LL.B., U. Ky., 1951. Admitted to Ky. bar, 1951; asst. atty. Fayette County (Ky.), 1964-69; judge Fayette County, 1969-75; atty. gen. Ky., Frankfort, 1976-79; justice Ky. Supreme Ct., 1979—. Bd. dirs. Nat. Assn. Counties, 1973-75; 1st pres. Ky. Assn. Counties; 1st chmn. Bluegrass Area Devel. Dist. Served with USN, World War II. Named Outstanding County Judge of Ky., 1972. Democrat. Office: State Capitol Frankfort KY 40601*

STEPHENS, STEVE, investment banker, TV producer; b. Newport, Ark., Apr. 22, 1930; s. Owen and Allie Mae (Rozzell) S.; student U. Little Rock, 1948; B.S. in Bus. Adminstrn., U. Ark., 1951; postgrad. U. Miss., 1954-55; L.H.D., Southwestern Coll., Oklahoma City; m. Ellen Beede, Apr. 21, 1957; children—Stanton, Steele. With CBS-TV, Little Rock, 1957-65; spl. asst. to U.S. Senator John L. McClellan, Washington, 1965-68; corporate v.p. pub. relations and advt. Nat. Investors Life Ins. Co., Little Rock, 1968-69; pres., chmn bd., owner Stephens Internat., Ltd., Little Rock, 1969—; chmn. bd., chief exec. officer Stephens Investments, Inc.; founder Stephens Internat. Travel Inc.; v.p. corporate affairs Brittenum & Assos.; dir. Bolivian Internat. Devel., Sociedad Anomina. State adviser Nat. Found., 1960-64; mem. exec. com. Radio Free Europe, 1961-62; state chmn. Arthritis Found., 1969; state adviser Youth Leadership Council, 1961-65; chmn. Little Rock City Beautiful Commn., 1961-62; mem. Pulaski County Health and Welfare Council, 1961-62; del. Inter-Am. Partners Alliance for Progress Conf., Lima, Peru, Partners of Ams. Hemispheric Conf., San Jose, Costa Rica, 1968; chmn. publicity United Fund campaign, 1968, bd. dirs., 1969-71; publicity chmn., dist. vice chmn. Pioneer dist. Boy Scouts Am., 1969-70; state chmn. March Dimes, 1973-74, mem. nat. council vols.; state chmn. Internat. Youth for Understanding; chmn. council community advisers St. Vincent Infirmary; bd. adv. trustees Direct Relief Found.; bd. dirs. Internat. Services for Blind, Inc.; internat. bd. dirs. Partners of Ams.; bd. visitors Army-Navy Acad. Named Bolivian Consul Gen. for Ark., Bolivian Pres., 1969. Served with USMC, 1951-54. Recipient Service to Humanity award Little Rock Jaycees. Mem. Internat. Assn. Polit. Consultants, Brit. Inst. Pub. Relations (overseas asso.). Clubs: Masons, Shriners, Little Rock, Racquet, Pleasant Valley Country; Bahama Sound Beach. Home: 2823 Painted Valley Dr Little Rock AR 72212 Office: Pleasant Valley Pl Hidden Valley Dr Little Rock AR 72212

STEPHENS, SYDNEY, JR., educator; b. Pine Knot, Ky., Oct. 2, 1927; s. Sidney and Maude (Stephens) S.; A.B., Cumberland Coll., 1950; B.S., Eastern Ky. State U., 1957; M.S., U. Ill., 1960; m. Edith Daisy Strunk, June 14, 1947; children—Betty Louise, Wanda Jo, Brenda Kay, Linda Sue, Robert Ralph. Tchr., McCreary County (Ky.) pub. schs., 1952-56; faculty Eastern Ky. U., Richmond, 1956—, asso. prof. math., 1980—; cons. State Dept., 1963-68. Ednl. com. chmn. State Dept. Fish and Wild Life, 1974-78; county com. chmn. Republican Party, 1974-78. Served with USN, 1944-48, 50-52. NSF grantee, 1959-60; Danforth grantee, 1960-63; NSF grantee, 1965; recipient Outstanding Alumni award in edn. Eastern Ky. U., 1974. Mem. Ky. Edn. Assn., NEA, Math. Assn. Am., Nat. Council Math. Tchrs., Nat. Rifle Assn., Pi Mu Epsilon, Kappa Mu Epsilon, Pi Kappa Alpha. Republican. Baptist. Club: Ky. League of Sportsmen. Home: Route 8 Richmond KY 40475 Office: W402 Eastern Ky Univ Richmond KY 40475

STEPHENS, TED WARREN, psychologist; b. Lawton, Okla., June 26, 1920; s. George Washington and Katie Belle (Link) S.; B.S. in Chemistry and Zoology, Okla. A. and M. Coll., Stillwater, 1948; M.S. in Psychology, Okla. State U., 1955. Part-time instr. Okla. State U., 1957-61; chief psychologist Okla. Rehab. Center, Okmulgee, 1958-61; coordinator, chief psychologist Regional Guidance Center, Lawton, 1961—. Pres. Comanche County Juvenile Bur. Adv. Com., 1975—. Vice pres. Lawton YMCA, 1972, recipient Service to Youth award, 1972; chmn. council deacons First Bapt. Ch., Lawton, 1977. Served with AUS, 1943-46. Mem. Am., Southwest, Okla. psychol. assns., Soc. Pediatric Psychology, Am., Okla. pub. health assns., Okla. Health and Welfare Assn., Okla. Assn. Children with Learning Disabilities. Club: Kiwanis (pres. downtown Lawton 1977-78). Home: 1217 SE 45th St Lawton OK 73501 Office: 1010 S Sheridan St Lawton OK 73501

STEPHENS, WILL BETH DODSON, psychologist, educator; b. Van Horn, Tex., July 14, 1918; d. John Lester and Almeda (Garner) Dodson; B.F.A., U. Tex., 1942, M.Ed., 1958, Ph.D., 1964; m. Jack Howard Stephens, Feb. 18, 1944; children—Jack Howard, Jill Johnstone. Asst. dir. U.S.O., Del Rio, Tex., 1942-45; asst. dir. YWCA, Austin, 1946-47; spl. edn. tchr., Tyler, 1956-60; research asso. U. Tex., 1962-64; research asst. prof. Inst. for Research on Exceptional Children, U. Ill., Urbana, 1965-66; asso. prof. ednl. psychology Temple U., Phila., 1966-70, prof. spl. edn., 1970-75; head spl. edn. program U. Tex., Dallas, 1975—. Mem. Pres.'s Com. on Mental Retardation, 1971-78; bd. dirs., past pres. Found. Exceptional Children; mem. ednl. adv. bd. Am. Found. for the Blind; mem. adv. com. Nat. Public Radio. Vocat. Rehab. Adminstrn. post-doctoral fellow U. Geneva (Switzerland), 1964-65. Fellow Am. Psychol. Assn., Pa. Psychol. Assn., Am. Assn. Mental Deficiency (v.p. ednl. div. 1977-79); mem. Council for Exceptional Children (past pres. div. mental retardation, chmn. nat. research coms.), Nat. Assn. Retarded Children (nat. edn. com.), Jean Piaget Soc. (internat. adv. bd.), Am. Psychol. Assn., Soc. Research Child Devel., Internat. Assn. Sci. Study Mental Deficiency, NEA, D.A.R., Geneal. Soc. Pa., Am. Ednl. Research Assn., Pi Lambda Theta. Episcopalian. Contbr. articles to profl. jours. Home: 17214 Stedman Dallas TX 75252 Office: Green 4-224 U Tex Richardson TX 75080

STEPHENSON, HARRY PRESTON, broadcasting exec.; b. Marion, Va., June 15, 1945; s. Herman Preston and Delma Kate (Anderson) S.; student Marion Jr. Coll., 1964, Southwestern Bus. Coll., 1965, U. Md., 1968, U. Tenn., 1971—; m. Linda Jean Vautier, Sept. 6, 1965; 1 dau., Heather Nichole. Surveyor, U.S. Dept. Agr., 1964; cameraman, announcer Sta. WTVK-TV, Knoxville, 1970; announcer, copy Sta. WEZK, Knoxville, 1971; sales, 1972-74, mgr. sales, 1974-75, mgr., 1975-77; gen. mgr. Sta. WZEZ, Nashville, 1977—. Bd. dirs. Tenn. Lung Assn.; hon. bd. dirs. Knoxville Zoo. Served with USAF, 1965-70; Vietnam. Recipient Excellence in Advt. award Knoxville Assn. for Blind, 1978. Mem. Sierra Club, Isshinryu Karate Assn., Nashville Advt. Fedn. Club: Masons. Office: Sta WZEZ504 Rosedale St Nashville TN 37204

STEPHENSON, JOSEPH ELMER, surgeon; b. Pikeville, Ky., Oct. 3, 1917; s. Elmer D'Ester and Emabel (Bennett) S.; A.B., U. Ky., 1939; M.D., U. Louisville, 1942; m. Juanita Jeanice (Polly) Floyd, Dec. 30, 1939; children—Joseph Floyd, John Wesley, James Gibbs Rich. Intern Charity Hosp. La., New Orleans, 1942-43; practice medicine, Elkhorn City, Ky., 1946-51; resident div. grad. medicine Tulane Med. Sch., 1951-54, fellow in gen. surgery Ochsner Found. Hosp. and Clinic, 1951-54; sr. surg. resident Lallie Kemp Charity Hosp., Independence, La., 1954-55; practice medicine specializing in gen. surgery, Ashland, Ky., 1956—. Served to capt. M.C., USAAF, 1943-46. Diplomate Am. Bd. Surgery. Fellow ACS; mem. Ky. Med. Soc., AMA, Boyd County Med. Soc., Ochsner Surg. Soc., Ky. Hist. Soc. (life), Sigma Chi (life), Alpha Kappa Kappa, Alpha Omega Alpha. Author 2 books. Home: 2726 Cumberland Ave Ashland KY 41101 Office: Suite 412 2d Nat Arcade Ashland KY 41101

STEPHENSON, LOIS CARPENTER, ednl. career devel. coordinator; b. Scott City, Kans., Dec. 2, 1929; d. Cleve Albert and Elsie Estelle (Helfrick) Carpenter; B.A., Southeastern La. U., 1967, M.Ed., 1973; m. Gerald Dwayne Stephenson, Oct. 29, 1951; children—Gerald Lane, Howard Lynn, Jeffrey Lee. Tchr. elementary schs., Kans., 1948-56, Slidell, La., 1965-73; tchr., counselor Slidell (La.) pub. schs., 1973-78, ednl. career devel. coordinator, 1978—. Mem. Am. Personnel and Guidance Assn., Am. Sch. Counselors Assn., La. Assn. Mental Health, La., St. Tammany Parish tchrs. assns. Methodist. Office: 1308 9th St Slidell LA 70458

STEPHENSON, MATILDE KEJNER, psychologist, educator; b. Tucuman, Argentina, June 25, 1927; d. Aaron and Eva (Koifman) Kejner; Ph.D. in Math., U. Cordoba, 1947, Ph.D. in Psychology, 1959; M.A. in Psychology, Northwestern U., 1954; m. Robert William Stephenson, Aug. 19, 1968. Came to U.S., 1967, naturalized, 1975. Prof. psychology, chmn. dept. U. Cordoba, 1956-66; vis. prof. Cornell U., 1960-63, U. Pitts., 1967; social scientist Standard Oil Co. N.J., 1963-64; research scientist Am. Inst. Research, 1968-70; sr. research scientist, prof. Am. U., 1970-73; mgr. research and devel. div. Urban Bus. Edn. Assn., 1973-76; prof. Grad. Sch. Bus., Fed. City Coll., 1973-76; prof. Sch. Bus. Adminstrn., St. Mary's U., 1976—. Chmn. edn. and health coms. Commn. Concerns for Spanish Speaking Peoples, 1972-76; mem. Montgomery County Pub. Sch. Hispanic Task Force, 1973, 76. Mem. Am., Interam. psychol. assns., Soc. Humanistic Mgmt., Internat. Council Psychology, Bus. and Profl. Women's Club. Contbr. articles to profl. jours. Address: 630 Sunhaven Dr San Antonio TX 78239

STEPHENSON, ROBERT JUBILEE, civil engr.; b. Vidalia, Ga., Apr. 8, 1932; s. Jubilee Smith and Annie (Hatcher) S.; B.C.E., Ga. Inst. Tech., 1954; postgrad. soil mechanics Harvard, 1963; m. Patricia Ann Kent, June 9, 1954; children—Daniel Kent, Barbara Eleanor. Coop. student-worker Ga. Hwy. Dept., 1950-52; jr. engr. C.E., Atlanta, 1954-57, staff soil mechanics br. South Atlantic div. lab., Marietta, Ga., 1957-68, br. chief, 1968-71, dir. South Atlantic Div. Lab. C.E., Marietta, 1971—; cons. in field. Mem. vestry St. James Episcopal Ch., Marietta, 1978—, jr. warden, 1979, sr. warden, 1980. Served with AUS, 1955-57. Recipient Meritorious Civilian Service award Dept. of Army, 1976; Outstanding Fed. Supr. award Atlanta Fed. Exec. Bd., 1976; registered profl. engr., Ga. Mem., Nat., Ga. (Engr. of Yr. in Govt. award 1979) socs. profl. engrs., ASCE, ASTM. Home: 399 Seminole Dr NE Marietta GA 30060 Office: PO Box 51 Marietta GA 30060

STEPHENSON, ROBERT LLOYD, educator; b. Portland, Oreg., Feb. 18, 1919; s. George A. and Myrtle L. (Smith) S.; B.A., U. Oreg., 1940, M.A., 1942; Ph.D., U. Mich., 1956; m. Georgie E. Boydstun, Jan. 5, 1946. Lab. dir. U. Tex., San Antonio, 1940-41; field dir. River Basin Surveys, Smithsonian Instn., Tex., 1946-52, Mo., 1952-63, U.S., 1963-66; coordinator Nev. Archeol. Survey, U. Nev., Reno, 1966-68; dir. Inst. Archeology and Anthropology, U. S.C., also state archaeologist, Columbia, 1968—; cons. in archeology Colville Consol. Indian Tribes, Nespelem, Wash., 1980. Bd. dirs. U. S.C. Mus., 1971-75; mem. S.C. Rev. Bd. for Nat. Hist. Preservation Act, 1969—; ex-officio mem. Camden Hist. Commn., 1971—; mem. S.C. Heritage Trust Adv. Bd., 1976—; mem. archaeol. adv. com. TVA, 1972—. Served with USMC, 1942-46. Fellow Am. Anthrop. Assn.; mem. Nat. Assn. State Archeologists (pres. 1980—), Soc. Profl. Archeologists (dir. 1977-79), Soc. Am. Archeology, AAAS, Oreg. Hist. Soc., archeol. socs. Oreg., Tex., Nev., Mo., S.C., Md., Fla., Tenn., Soc. Vertebrate Paleontology, Anthrop. Soc. Wash., Nebr. Acad. Sci., Nebr. Hist. Soc., Nat. Trust for Historic Preservation, Southeastern Archeol. Conf., Am. Assn. for State and Local History, Soc. for Hist. Archaeology, Conf. on Historic Sites Archaeology, Council of Abandoned Mil. Posts (nat. dir. 1979-80), Sigma Xi. Republican. Episcopalian. Clubs: Condon, Toastmasters (dist. lt. gov. 1967-68, 70-72). Asst. editor Am. Antiquity, 1960-63; asso. editor Plains Anthropologist, 1960-62; editor Plains Anthropologist, 1963, Nev. Archeol. Survey Reporter, 1966-68, Inst. Archeology and Anthropology's Notebook, 1969—; contbr. articles to profl. jours. Home: 5831 Satchel Ford Rd Columbia SC 29206 Office: Inst Archeology and Anthropology Univ of SC Columbia SC 29208

STEPHENSON, SAM EDWARD, JR., surgeon; b. Bristol, Tenn., May 16, 1926; s. Sam E. and Hazel Beatrice (Walters) S.; B.S., U. S.C., 1946; M.D., Vanderbilt U., 1950; m. Janet Sue Spotts, May 16, 1970; children—Sam Edward III, W. Douglas, Dorthea L., Judith Maria. Intern, Butterworth Hosp., Grand Rapids, Mich., 1950-51; resident gen. surgery Thayer VA Hosp., Nashville, Tenn., 1951-53, Vanderbilt U. Hosp., Nashville, 1953-56, Middle Tenn. Tb. Hosp., Nashville, 1956-57; instr. surgery Vanderbilt U., 1955-57, asst. prof., 1957-60, asso. prof., 1960-67; prof., chmn. dept. surgery Univ. Hosp., Jacksonville, Fla., 1967-78; prof. surgery U. Fla., Jacksonville, 1967—; individual practice medicine, specializing in surgery Jacksonville, 1979—. Served with USNR, 1944-46. Nat. Found. fellow, 1957-59; HEW research grantee, 1957-67. Mem. A.C.S., Am. Coll. Chest Physicians, Am. Surg. Assn., So. Surg. Assn., Soc. Univ. Surgeons, Soc. Vascular Surgery, Am. Assn. Thoracic Surgery, others. Republican. Episcopalian. Clubs: Ponte Vedra, Masons. Contbr. articles to profl. publs. Developer synchronized cardiac pacer, researcher atherosclerosis. Home: 10553 Scott Mill Rd Jacksonville FL 32217 Office: 223 Marshall Taylor Bldg Jacksonville FL 32207

STEPHENSON, SCOTT ALLEN, mfg. co. exec.; b. Columbus, Ohio, June 20, 1954; s. Edwin Carlton and Frances Ann (Sadler) S.; A.S. in Computer Sci., Bluefield (W.Va.) State Coll., 1975, B.S. in Bus. Adminstrn., 1979; m. Sandra Gay Bennett, July 5, 1975. Computer programmer Ammars Inc., Bluefield, 1975-76; data processing mgr. Betsy Ross Bakeries, Bluefield, 1977—, mgr. acctg., 1979—; cons. data processing. Mem. Bluefield Jaycees (internal v.p. 1979—). Republican. Baptist. Home: 530 Parkway Bluefield WV 24701 Office: PO Box 1070 Bluefield WV 24701

STEPHENSON, WILLIAM EATON, educator; b. Plymouth, Ind., Oct. 31, 1930; s. Allen Walter and Lefa Fawn (Whisman) S.; A.B., Ind. U., 1951; M.A., U. Calif. at Berkeley, 1959, Ph.D., 1963; m. Marilyn Lorraine Ramey, Dec. 16, 1967. Asst. prof. English, U. Calif. at Los Angeles, 1963-70; asso. prof. English, East Carolina U., Greenville, N.C., 1970-76, prof., 1976—; lectr. in field. Woodrow Wilson fellow, 1960-61, 61-62, Am. Council Learned Socs. fellow, 1966-67. Mem. Modern Lang. Assn., S. Atlantic Modern Lang. Assn. Am. Film Inst., Brit. Film Inst., Univ. Film Assn. Contbr. articles to profl. jours. Home: 1611 Oaklawn Ave Greenville NC 27834 Office: Dept English East Carolina U Greenville NC 27834

STEPHENSON, WILLIAM LANE, floor coverings co. exec.; b. Shreveport, May 1, 1928; s. William Lane and Corrie Edna (Pipkin) S.; student Centenary Coll., Shreveport, 1947-48; m. Freda Marie Henderson, May 12, 1950; children—Kathy (Mrs. Michael Yearwood McGovern), William Lane III, Karon. Apprentice floor layer, 1944-51; propr. Stephenson Floor Coverings, Shreveport, 1951—. Adviser to mayor of Shreveport, 1968. Mem. Shreveport-Bossier Greater Floor Covering Assn. (charter mem., pres.), Shreveport Exec. Assn. (dir.); asso. mem. Assn. Gen. Contractors. Methodist (chmn. bd. 1966, chmn. blsg. com. 1968-71). Mason (Shriner). Club: Brookwood Athletic (pres. 1956-57). Home: 3839 Betty Virginia Circle Shreveport LA 71106 Office: 3911 Southern Ave Shreveport LA 71106

STERLING, WALTER GAGE, mfg. co. exec.; b. Anahuac, Tex., May 20, 1901; s. Ross Shaw and Maude (Gage) S.; LL.B., U. Tex., 1925; m. Ruth Dermody, Jan. 30, 1941. Admitted to Tex. bar, 1925; with Royalty Properties, Houston, 1927—, v.p., 1946—; pres. Sterling Oil & Refinery 1935-50, Richmond Mfg. Co., 1951—; with Richmond Sales, 1952—; dir. Citizens Nat. Bank & Trust Co., Baytown, Living Bank, Houston; trustee Mortgage & Trust Investors. Trustee Hermann Hosp. Estate, 1950—, pres. bd. trustees, 1965—; trustee Sch. of Ozarks, Point Lookout, Mo., 1973—; regent U. Tex. System, 1975—; bd. dirs. Tex. Med. Center. Served to capt. USAAF, 1941-44. Mem. Inst. Hemotherapy, S.A.R. (pres. gen. 1968-69), Delta Kappa Epsilon. Clubs: Lakeside Country (past pres.), Petroleum (past pres.) (Houston). Home: 1600 Holcombe Blvd Penthouse A Houston TX 77030 Office: PO Box 2891 Houston TX 77001

STERN, AARON, author, ednl. cons., lectr.; b. Germany, May 20, 1918; s. David and Helen (Schurek) S.; student gymnazium, Plock, Poland, 1933-37, Warsaw U., 1937-38; B.A., Bklyn. Coll., 1956; M.A. Equiv., Columbia, 1957; student Jewish Theol. Sem. Am.; m. Bella Tcherniawska, Jan. 1940; children—Edith, David. Originator, Total Ednl. Submersion Method; conducted sch. based on method in Displaced Persons Camp, Germany, 1948-49; lectr. on method at univs., 1949—; conducted landmark study of Head Start Program for HEW, 1974. Active participant desegregation of pub. facilities, voters registration; active presdl. campaigns senators Eugene McCarthy, George McGovern. Honored by resolutions City of Miami, 1964, Fla. Legislature, 1965, U.S. Congress, 1974; Justinian Lodge scholar; Columbia grantee. Mem. Nat. Soc. Profs., Authors Guild, Authors League Am. Author: Ethnic Minorities in Poland, 1937: Nazi Atrocities in Europe; The Making of a Genius; The Joy of Learning, 1977; author sci. papers. Home: 2485 NE 214th St North Miami Beach FL 33318

STERN, ANDREW MILTON, public relations exec.; b. Cleve., Mar. 22, 1949; s. Sidney H. Stern and Sue (Friedlander) Miller; grad. U. Del., 1970; m. Sabina Bobzin, Feb. 28, 1971; children—David Patrick, Eric Thomas. Press sec. to mayor City of Wilmington (Del.), 1970-73; asst. dir., dir. public affairs Wilmington Med. Center, 1973-75; staff asst. to pres. The White House, Washington, 1975-77; mgr. pub. relations and advt. Wylain, Inc., Dallas, 1977-80; pres. Andrew M. Stern Assos., Inc., Dallas, 1980—. Mem. Public Relations Soc. Am., U. Del. Alumni Assn. (Tex. chmn.). Home: 6922 Brentfield Dr Dallas TX 75248 Office: Wylain Inc 17250 Dallas Pkwy Dallas TX 75248

STERN, GENE, mfg. co. exec.; b. N.Y.C., Jan. 6, 1933; s. Moe and Anna (Polansky) S.; B.A. (scholar), U. Rochester, 1955; M.B.A., Hofstra U., 1970; children—Dianne, Susan, Michael, Sandra. Program adminstr. Hazeltine Corp., Little Neck, N.Y., 1959-63; program planning and control mgr. Grumman Corp., Bethpage, N.Y., 1964-70; fin. analyst-internal cons. J. Walter Thompson Co., N.Y.C., 1970-72; dir. finance, v.p. Internat. Corp. Enterprises (name formerly DCI Co.), Dallas, 1972-75; controller, treas. Royal Park, Inc., Dallas, 1975-78; controller Victor Costa Inc., 1978-79; chief fin. officer Prophecy Corp., Dallas, 1979—. Served with USAF, 1956-59. Mem. Nat. Assn. Accountants. Clubs: Lancers, Brookhaven. Author: Commonality in Planning, 1970. Contbr. articles to profl. jours. Home: 4446 Mill Creek Dallas TX 75234

STERNBERG, HANS JOACHIM, dept. store exec.; b. Aurich, Germany, July 4, 1935; s. Erich and Lea (Knurr) S.; A.B. magna cum laude, Princeton, 1957; m. Donna Gail Weintraub, Feb. 19, 1967; children—Erich, Julie Ellen, Deborah Ann, Mark Samuel. Came to U.S., 1937, naturalized, 1943. With Goudchaux's, Inc., Baton Rouge, 1960—, chmn. bd., 1976—; partner Insa Sternberg & Bros., Baton Rouge, 1960—; v.p. Erich Sternberg Realty Co., Inc.; dir. Fed. Home Loan Bank Little Rock, Stas. WQXY, KQXY, WLCS; dir. Cable Systems of the South, CATV Hammond, CATV Bessemer. Pres. Baton Rouge Jewish Welfare Fedn., 1971-72; mem. young leadership cabinet United Jewish Appeal, 1970-74. Bd. dirs. La. Heart Assn., 1970-71, La. Capital Area Health Planning Council, 1970-71, Anglo-Am. Art Museum, 1973—; bd. dirs. Baton Rouge Art Gallery, 1967—, pres., 1972; chmn. U.S.S. Kidd Naval War Meml. Served to lt. (j.g.) USNR, 1957-59. Recipient Baton Rouge Booster of Yr. award, 1979. Mem. Young Presidents Orgn. Jewish (treas. temple 1971-72, sec. Men's club 1969). Clubs: City, Bocage Racquet, Irish. Patentee Quik Card. Home: 2375 Kleinert Ave Baton Rouge LA 70806 Office: PO Drawer 3478 Baton Rouge LA 70821

STERNENBERG, FRED CHARLES, aerospace co. exec.; b. Birmingham, Ala., Sept. 22, 1929; s. Fred Charles and Nettie Irene (Daniel) S.; student Auburn U., 1949; m. Delores Jean Lancaster, Mar. 8, 1957; children—Fredrick Karl, Toni Lynn. Project supr., tech. publs. Hayes Internat. Corp., Birmingham, 1953-60; supv. publications dept. aerostructures div. AVCO Corp., Nashville, 1960-63, proposals supvr. mktg. dept., 1963-67, mktg. services mgr., 1967—, mgr. pub. relations and advt., 1976-78, dir. pub. relations and advt., 1978-79, dir. communications, 1979—. Mem. Nat. Mgmt. Assn., Nashville Avco Mgmt. Club, Leica Hist. Soc. Am. (officer). Methodist. Editor: Viewfinder Jour., 1975—; contbr. articles to tech. jours. Office: PO Box 210 Nashville TN 37202

STERRETT, JANE RICHARDS, educator, soprano; b. Denver, Apr. 24, 1916; d. Vere Stiles and Virginia May (Tyler) Richards; student Columbia U. Sch. Journalism, 1933-35; Mus.B., Oberlin Conservatory (scholar), 1949; M.A., Tchrs. Coll. Columbia, 1942; m. Delbert E. Sterrett, Aug. 11, 1947; children—Jamie Christopher, Vera Kay, Tyler Orr. Soprano soloist, recitalist, N.Y.C., 1939-48, performances include: Town Hall, N.Y.C., 1940, 41, 47, 48,

Liederkranz Hall, N.Y.C., 1941; tchr. Columbia U., 1941, 44-48; pvt. instr. music, Gainesville, Fla., 1948—; appearances with N.Y. Composers Assn., 1941, 47, Tampa (Fla.) Symphony Orch., 1952, Nashville Symphony Orch., 1955, others; instr. voice George Peabody Coll., 1954-55. Scholar, La Scala Opera Sch., Milan, Italy, 1948; recipient So. div. Mason and Hamlin Tchr. of Year award, 1968, 69, 70, 72; co-recipient 1st award Am. Women Composers Concert program S. Atlantic div. Nat. Fedn. Music Clubs, 1976. Mem. Nat. Assn. Tchrs. of Singing (lt. gov. Fla. 1967-68), Music Educators Nat. Conf., Music Tchrs. Nat. Assn., Fla. Music Tchrs. Assn. (pres., state certification chmn., dir.), Gainesville Music Tchrs. Assn. (pres.), Fla., Nat. fedns. music clubs, Sigma Alpha Iota, Altrusa. Presbyterian. Contbr. articles to profl. jours. Home: 2100 NW 8th Ct Gainesville FL 32601

STETTINIUS, WALLACE, printing co. exec.; b. N.Y.C., Mar. 4, 1933; s. Edward R. and Virginia Gordon (Wallace) S.; B.A. in Psychology, U. Va., 1955, M.B.A., 1959; m. Mary Gray, June 25, 1958; children—Elizabeth G., Wallace G., Gordon. Prodn. asst. Garrett & Massie, Richmond, Va., 1959-60; office mgr. Anderson & Strudwick, Richmond, 1960-63; v.p. Virginia Capital Corp., Richmond, 1963-67; pres. William Byrd Press, Inc., Richmond, 1967—; instr. (part-time) U. Richmond Evening Coll., 1961-70; dir. Mt. Vernon Corp., Gray Lumber Co.; dir., mem. exec. com. First & Mchts. Nat. Bank. Vice pres. Richmond Area Community Council; mem. adv. bd. Salvation Army; treas. Valentine Mus., Collegiate Schs.; vestryman, sr. warden St. Mary's Episcopal Ch.; bd. dirs. Jr. Achievement, Va. Ind. Coll. Found., Friends Assn. for Children; bd. dirs., pres., Va. Home for Boys; trustee Va. Union U. Served to capt. USMC, 1955-57. Recipient Elmer G. Voight award. Mem. Graphic Computer Communications Assn. (past pres.), Greater Richmond C. of C. (dir.), Raven Soc., Phi Kappa Sigma. Author: Management Planning and Control: The Printer's Path to Profitability, 1975. Home: 206 Dryden Ln Richmond VA 23229 Office: William Byrd Press PO Box 27481 Richmond VA 23261

STETZER, LLOYD WESLEY, physician; b. McKeesport, Pa., Jan. 21, 1924; s. Lewis Austin and Irene N. (Killean) S.; B.S., Ark. State U., 1957; B.S.M., U. Ark., 1959, M.D., 1961; M.S., U. Cin., 1978; m. Grace Marie Halsema, May 1, 1947; children—Michael, Eric, Scott, Mark. Office mgr., cashier Ark. Rice Growers, Jonesboro, 1950-51; served with USAAF, 1942-46, USAF, 1951-55; commd. lt. (j.g.) M.C., U.S. Navy, 1961, advanced through grades to capt., 1977; chief regional occupational health service, Keywest, Fla., 1974-76, Naval Regional Med. Center, Charleston, S.C., 1978—. Decorated Air medal; diplomate Am. Bd. Allergy and Immunology, Am. Bd. Preventive Medicine (occupational medicine). Fellow Am. Coll. Allergists, Am. Coll. Occupational Medicine; mem. AMA, Assn. Mil. Allergists, Am. Assn. Occupational Medicine. Democrat. Roman Catholic. Home: Quarters AA Naval Base Charleston SC 29408 Office: Shipyard Branch Clinic Naval Base Charleston SC 29408

STEVENS, BEN DEE, tax cons.; b. San Angelo, Tex., Jan. 13, 1942; s. Rex and Nettie Marie (Evans) S.; B.B.A. in Personnel Mgmt., U. Houston, Clear Lake City, 1978; postgrad. S. Tex. Sch. Law; m. Patricia Bess Duncan, Jan. 1, 1975; 1 son, Andrew Duncan; 1 dau. by previous marriage, Samantha Ann. Revenue officer collection div. IRS, Houston, 1965-73, collection group mgr., dist. dir. rep., Harlingen, Tex., 1974, collection group mgr., dir's. rep., El Paso. Tex., 1975-76, collection br. chief, Austin, Tex., 1977; pvt. practice fed. tax collection cons., Pasadena, Tex., 1978—; founder, pres. C M S Profl. Sports Mag. Served with U.S. Army, 1960-62. Mem. Am. Mgmt. Assn., Am. Bar Assn. (law student div.), Phi Alpha Delta. Baptist. Home and Office: 1810 Millwood Houston TX 77008

STEVENS, DONALD KING, aero. engr., nuclear cons., ret. army officer; b. Danville, Ill., Oct. 27, 1920; s. Douglas Franklin and Ida Harriet (King) S.; B.S. with high honors in Ceramic Engring., U. Ill., 1942; M.S. in Aeros. and Guided Missiles, U. So. Calif., 1949; grad. U.S. Army Command and Gen. Staff Coll., 1957, U.S. Army War Coll., 1962; m. Adele Carman de Werff, July 11, 1942; children—Charles August, Anne Louise, Alice Jeanne Stevens Kay. Served with Ill. State Geol. Survey, 1938-40; ceramic engr. Harbison-Walker Refractories Co., Pitts., 1945-46; commd. 1st lt. U.S. Army, 1946, advanced through grades to col., 1963; with Arty. Sch., Fort Bliss, Tex., 1949-52; supr. unit tng. and Nike missile firings, N.Mex., 1953-56; mem. Weapons Systems Evaluation Group, Office Sec. of Defense, Washington, 1957-61; comdr. Niagara-Buffalo (N.Y.) Defense, 31st Arty. Brigade, Lockport, N.Y., 1963-65; chief Air Def. and Nuclear br. War Plans div. Office Dep. Chief Staff for Mil. Ops., 1965-67, chief strategic forces div., 1967-69; chief spl. weapons plans, J5, U.S. European Command, Ger., 1969-72, ret., 1972; guest lectr. U.S. Mil. Acad. 1958-59; cons. nuclear policy and plans to Office Asst. Sec. of Def., 1975—; cons. Sci. Applications, Inc., 1976-78, U.S. Army Concepts Analysis Agy., Bethesda, Md., 1973—; cons. on strategy Lulejian & Assos., Inc., 1974-75. Asst. camp dir. Piankeshaw Area council Boy Scouts Am., 1937; mem. chancel choir, elder First Christian Ch., Falls Church, Va., 1957-61, 65-69, 72—; elder, trustee Presbyn. Ch., 1963-65. Decorated D.S.M. (Army), Legion of Merit, Bronze Star. Mem. Am. Ceramic Soc., Assn. U.S. Army, U. Ill. Alumni Assn., U. So. Calif. Alumni Assn., Sigma Xi, Sigma Tau, Tau Beta Pi, Phi Kappa Phi, Alpha Phi Omega. Clubs: Rotary, Niagara Falls Country; Ill. (Washington); Terrapin. Contbr. articles to engring. jours.; pioneer in tactics and deployment plans for Army surface-to-air missiles. Address: 5916 5th St N Arlington VA 22203

STEVENS, JAMES DOUGLAS, clergyman; b. Monroe, Mich., Dec. 1, 1943; s. James L. and Helen L. Stevens; B.A., Bob Jones U.; S.T.M., Dallas Theol. Sem., 1971; M.Div., Grace Theol. Sem., 1968; m. Margaret L. Parrott, June 27, 1970; children—Mark James, Matthew Russell. Ordained to ministry Baptist Ch., 1968; minister coll. age youth Inter-City Bapt. Ch., Allen Park, Mich., 1971-72; minister Pomona Bible Ch., Copemish, Mich., 1973-75; asso. prof. religion Liberty Bapt. Coll., Lynchburg, Va., 1975—, adv. coordinator div. religion, 1977—. Mem. Soc. Bibl. Lit., Am. Personnel and Guidance Assn., Kappa Delta Pi. Contbr. to Liberty Bible Commentary, 1978. Home: Idaho Circle Sunnymead Rustburg VA 24588 Office: PO Box 1111 Candler Mountain Rd Lynchburg VA 24514

STEVENS, JOE FRANKLIN, accountant; b. Lancaster, Ky., July 7, 1944; s. Logan A. and Senia M. (Morgan) S.; student Berea Coll., 1962-65; B.S. in Accounting, Eastern Ky. U., 1967; m. Edwina Burdette, July 16, 1965; children—Randall Shane, Kelli Jo, Brook Rena. With Kelley, Galloway & Goolsby, C.P.A.'s, Ashland and Pikeville, Ky., 1967-75, partner, 1972-75; fin. v.p. Barber Paramont Coal Corp., Wise, Va., 1976—; partner Stevens & Robinson, C.P.A.'s, Pikeville, 1977-78, Robinson & Stevens Enterprises, 1977-79. Treas., Pike County Carroll for Gov. campaign, 1975. Recipient Am. Legion award, 1962; named Kiwanian of the Year, 1975; C.P.A., Ky. Mem. Am. Inst. C.P.A.'s, Ky., Eastern Ky. socs. C.P.A.'s, C. of C. (dir. 1974-75). Club: Kiwanis (v.p. 1974-75). Home: 214 Lakeview Dr Pikeville KY 41501 Office: PO Box 2889 Pikeville KY 41501

STEVENS, LOIS HARMON, vocat. counselor; b. Florence, S.C., Feb. 4, 1927; d. Ivey Pearson and Annie (Laney) Harmon; B.A., Meredith Coll., 1948; M.Ed., Miss. State U., 1973; m. John Ashley Stevens, May 29, 1949; 1 son, John Ashley. Eligibility worker State Welfare Dept., Scott County, Miss., 1970-71; tchr. Webster County Schs., Walthall, Miss., 1971-73; career edn. coordinator Winona (Miss.) Pub. Schs., 1973-76, occupational orientation instr., career edn. coordinator, 1976-77, vocat. counselor, career edn. program coordinator, 1977—; vis. instr. Miss. Coll., Clinton, 1975-76; cons. in field. Pres. Grenada Higher Edn. Council, 1974—. Mem. Am., Miss. personnel and guidance assns., Mid-Miss. Personnel and Guidance Assn. (pres. 1977-78), NEA, Miss. Assn. Educators, Miss. Assn. Career Educators (pres. 1977-78), Miss. Assn. Vocat. Educators, Am. Sch. Counselors Assn., Miss. Sch. Counselors Assn. (pres. elect 1980-81), Miss. Vocat. Guidance Assn., Meredith Coll. Alumnae Assn. (pres. Magnolia chpt. 1978—), Phi Delta Kappa, Delta Kappa Gamma. Baptist. Home: 352 Forest Hill Dr Grenada MS 38901 Office: 311 Fairground St Winona MS 38967

STEVENS, MARION BENNION, nutritionist, educator; b. Murray, Utah, Sept. 23, 1925; d. Sterling Alfred and Beryl Adella (Hamilton) Bennion; B.S., Utah State U., 1947; M.A., Columbia, 1949; Ph.D., U. Wis., 1956; m. Wayne E. Stevens. Clin. dietitian Columbia Presbyn. Med. Center, N.Y.C., 1947-49; instr. Idaho State U., Pocatello, 1949-50; mem. faculty Brigham Young U., Provo, Utah, 1953-77, prof. nutrition, 1961-77, chmn. dept. food sci. and nutrition, 1955-60, 62-69, program dir. med. dietetics, 1973-76; vis. asst. prof. U. Calif., Davis, 1960-61; del. White House Conf. Food, Nutrition and Health, 1969; mem. Gov. Utah Advisory Council Comprehensive Health Planning, 1972-76; exec. com., chmn. rev. com. advisory council Utah Office Health Planning and Research Devel., 1976-77; lectr. Coll. Family Living, 1967; Sigma Xi lect., 1968. Mem. advisory com. women in services DOD, 1965-68. Named Prof. of Month, Brigham Young U., Jan. 1972, recipient Karl G. Maeser Distinguished Teaching award, 1974. Mem. Am. Dietetic Assn. (editorial bd. jours., accrediting commn.), Am. Inst. Nutrition, Inst. Food Technologists, Nutrition Edn. Soc., Am. Home Econs. Assn., Nutrition Today Soc., Sigma Xi, Phi Kappa Phi. Mormon. Author: Introductory Foods, 1980; Clinical Nutrition, 1979; Science of Food, 1980; contbr. profl. jours. Home: 2320 Gene Littler Dr El Paso TX 79936

STEVENS, MARK LESLIE, beverage co. exec.; b. N.Y.C., Apr. 30, 1941; s. Hy and Edna S.; B.A., U. Pa., 1962, M.B.A., 1964; m. Jacqueline Lee McLaughlin, May 24, 1964; children—Victoria Joyce, Scott Paul. Mem. brand mgmt. staff Gen. Mills Co., Mpls., 1965-69, R.J. Reynolds Co., Winston-Salem, N.C., 1969-72; asst. to pres. Internat. Playtex Co., N.Y.C., 1972-73; v.p. mktg. Gen. Cinema Corp., Miami, Fla., 1973-77, group v.p., 1977, pres. Sunkist Soft Drinks Inc. subs., Atlanta, 1977—. Mem. Am. Mgmt. Assn., DeKalb C. of C. (dir.). Office: Sunkist Bldg 2600 Century Pkwy Atlanta GA 30345

STEVENS, NORMA YOUNG, educator; b. Canton, Ga., Oct. 23, 1927; d. S. Taylor and Cora Lee (Stephens) Young; B.F.A. in Landscape Architecture, U. Ga., 1949, Ed.D., 1970; M.Religious Edn., New Orleans Bapt. Theol. Sem., 1954; postgrad. Escuela de Idiomas, 1960-61; m. Howard L. Stevens, Sept. 6, 1949; children—Catherine Stevens Self, Karen Stevens Cantrell, Kristen Leslie. With Jones Ornamental Nursery, Nashville, 1950-54; tchr., counselor in sem. Fgn. Mission Bd. So. Bapt. Conv., Mex., 1960-75; prof. edn. Belmont Coll., Nashville, 1974—; cons. psychologist Colegio Americano, Torreon, Coahiela, Mex., 1970-74. Mem. Am. Psychol. Assn., Tenn. Psychol. Assn., Tenn. Assn. Tchr. Educators, Kappa Delta Pi. Baptist. Author: Go Out With Joy, 1966; co-author: The Christian Looks at Divorce, 1980; contbr. to Everyday, Five Minutes with God, 1970. Home: 3439 Stokesmont Rd Nashville TN 37218 Office: Belmont College Nashville TN 37203

STEVENS, RICHARD YATES, city ofcl., lawyer; b. Raleigh, N.C., Dec. 12, 1948; s. Floyd L. and Luna (Yates) S.; B.A. in Polit. Sci., U. N.C., 1970, J.D., 1974, M.Public Adminstrn., 1978. Asst. dean men U. N.C., Chapel Hill, 1970-71, asst. residence dir., 1971-75, asst. Office Student Affairs, 1973-75; admitted to N.C. bar, 1974; individual practice law, Chapel Hill, 1974-76; adminstrv. asst. City of Durham (N.C.), 1975-76, budget officer, 1976-78, dir. adminstrn., 1978-79, dir. fin. and program devel., 1979—; adj. prof. polit. sci. N.C. State U., 1979—; coordinator N.C. State Govt. intern program Inst. Govt., summer 1971. Mem. Internat. City Mgmt. Assn., Am. Soc. Public Adminstrn., Am. Bar Assn., N.C. Bar Assn., N.C. City-County Mgmt. Assn., U. N.C. Public Adminstrn. Alumni Assn. (pres. 1977-79), U. N.C. Gen. Alumni Assn. (dir. 1978-80). Democrat. Home: 5404 Hillsborough St Raleigh NC 27606

STEVENS, ROY ARTHUR, orgn. exec.; b. Benson, N.C., Aug. 30, 1924; s. Arthur Festus and Lalon (Strickland) S.; grad. Worth Bus. Coll., Fayetteville, N.C., 1942, Southeastern Inst. for Orgn., 1958, Bus. Mgmt. Inst., Jacksonville, N.C., 1959; m. Nora Alma Wood, June 21, 1947; children—Roy Arthur, Gloria Delilah. Clk., A.E. Rankin Co., Inc., Fayetteville, 1942-43, bookkeeper, 1946-49; chief clk., office mgr. Becker County Sand & Gravel Co., Cheraw, S.C., 1949-55; owner, operator Stevens Bookkeeping Service, 1955; asst. mgr. C. of C., Fayetteville, 1956; mgr. Jacksonville C. of C., 1957-64; dir. Resources Devel. Commn. for Brunswick County, Southport, 1965-69; mgr. Onslow County, 1969-71; dir. Carteret County Econ. Devel. Council, Morehead City, N.C., 1971—. Mem. exec. bd., past pres. Ocean Hwy. Assn.; mem. environ. affairs adv. com. Coastal Plains Regional Commn., 1973; past pres., bd. dirs. Travel Council N.C.; former dir. N.C. Indsl. Developers Assn. Served with USAAF, 1943-46. Named Tarheel of Week, 1964. Baptist. Home: West Car Meadows Morehead City NC 28557 Office: 913 Shepard St Morehead City NC 28557

STEVENS, WILLIAM EVANS, mfg. co. exec.; b. Gouverneur, N.Y., Sept. 30, 1945; s. William Weldon and Aleen Migeonette (Pease) S.; A.A.S., Central Piedmont Community Coll., 1974; m. Linda Catherine Warth, June 21, 1971; children—William Warth, Michael Evans. Design draftsman, Terrell Machine Co., Charlotte, N.C., 1968-70; tool designer Lundy Electronics & Systems, Charlotte, 1970-72; product engr. Scovill Mfg. Co., Charlotte, 1972—; tchr. Piedmont Community Coll., 1979—. Served with USAF, 1963-67. Baptist. Patentee in field. Home: Route 4 Box 393A Monroe NC 28110 Office: PO Box 25288 Charlotte NC 28212

STEVENSON, EARL, JR., cons. civil engr.; b. Royston, Ga., May 8, 1921; s. Earl and Compton Helen (Randall) S.; B.S. in Civil Engring., Ga. Inst. Tech., 1953; m. Sue Roberts, Apr. 25, 1956; children—Catherine Helen, David Earl. Engr., GSA, Atlanta, 1959-60; engr., pres. Miller, Stevenson & Steinichen, Inc., Atlanta, 1960—. Served with USAAF, 1944-45. Registered profl. engr., Ga., Ala., S.C., Miss. Mem. Ga. Soc. Profl. Engrs., Water Pollution Control Fedn. Methodist. Home: 3163 Laramie Dr Atlanta GA 30339 Office: One Perimeter Way NW Atlanta GA 30339

STEVENSON, EDWARD WARD, otolaryngologist; b. Lowrys, S.C., Jan. 9, 1926; s. Thomas M. and Annie Lou (Ward) S.; student Duke, 1943-45; M.D., U. Md., 1949; m. Dorothy Nell Giles, Sept. 2, 1947; children—Sally Anne, Laura Jean, Nancy Ruth, Molly Giles. Intern Bapt. Meml. Hosp., Memphis, 1949-50; resident otolaryngology Med. Coll. Va., Richmond, 1953-55; fellow in otolaryngology Ochsner Found. Hosp., New Orleans, 1955-56, mem. otolaryngology staff Ochsner Clinic, 1956-57; fellow otolaryngology Tulane U., New Orleans, 1955-56; practice medicine, specializing in otolaryngology, Birmingham, Ala., 1957-60, 65-79, Decatur, Ala., 1960-65; instr. dept. otolaryngology U. Ala. Med. Sch., Birmingham, 1957-66, clin. asst. prof., 1966—. Served with USNR, 1943-45, M.C., 1950-53. Mem. Morgan County (Ala.) Med. Soc. (pres. 1964), Med. Assn. Ala. (chmn. pub. relations com. 1972-73), Ala. Acad. Ophthalmology and Otolaryngology (pres. 1970). Club: Rotary. Office: 840 Montclair Rd Birmingham AL 35213

STEVENSON, EUGENE OCTAVE SYKES, surgeon; b. Washington, Oct. 24, 1932; s. Thomas and Eugenia Octavia (Sykes) S.; B.S., George Washington U., 1955, M.D., 1960; J.D., Am. U., 1973; m. Mary Lou Holliday, June 4, 1960; 1 dau., Kathryn Sykes. Intern George Washington U. Hosp., 1960-61; resident surgery Fairfax (Va.) Hosp., 1961-52, Wadsworth VA Hosp., Los Angeles, 1965-67; registrar pediatric surgery Alder Hey Children's Hosp., Liverpool, Eng., 1967-68; pvt. practice gen. surgery, No. Va., 1968—; mem. staff Fairfax, No. Va. Doctors, Commonwealth, Arlington hosps.; instr. surgery Georgetown U. Med. Sch., 1971—; admitted to Va. bar, 1973; mem. Va. Bd. Medicine. Served as lt. USNR, 1962-65. Internat. Coll. Surgeons grantee, 1967-68. Diplomate Am. Bd. Surgery. Fellow A.C.S.; mem. A.M.A., Va., Fairfax County (past pres.) med. socs., Va., Southeastern surg. socs., No. Va. Acad. Surgeons (past pres.), Brit. Assn. Pediatric Surgeons, Va., Fairfax County bar assns., Sigma Alpha Epsilon, Phi Alpha Delta. Clubs: Army-Navy Country (Arlington); Washington Golf and Country. Contbr. med. jours. Home: Aspen Grove 4300 Roberts Rd Fairfax VA 22030 Office: 6120 Brandon Ave Springfield VA 22150

STEVENSON, FERDINAN BACKER, lt. gov. S.C.; b. New Rochelle, N.Y., June 8, 1928; d. William Bryant and Ferdinanda (Legare) Backer; B.A. Smith Coll., 1949; m. Norman Williams Stevenson, Dec. 29, 1957; children—David, Ferdinan, Norman Williams, Josephine. Editorial asst. N.Y. Herald Tribune, 1952-54; former mem. S.C. Ho. of Reps.; lt. gov. State of S.C., Columbia, 1979—. Trustee, Historic Charleston Found., 1963-74; trustee, sec. Coll. of Charleston Found., 1970-74; co-chmn. Save Charleston Found., 1970-74; pres. Footlight Players in the Dock Street Theater, 1973-74. Democrat. Episcopalian. Author: (with Ruth Biemillrt) Nat Fein's Animals, 1955; (with Patricia C. Robinson) Return to Octavia, 1964, A Clearing in the Fog, 1970, Savage Summer, 1976. Office: Office of Lt Gov State Capitol Bldg Columbia SC 29211

STEVENSON, H(ARRY) B(AND), chem. engring. cons.; b. Omaha, Oct. 24, 1901; s. Robert Bigelow and Maude Eleanor (Band) S.; B.S. in Chem. Engring., U. Colo., 1925; m. Charlotte Mae Hartman, Sept. 25, 1926; children—Robert Band, Barbara Ellen. Analytical chemist Procter & Gamble Co., Cin., 1925-27, research chemist, 1927-28, head chemist, 1929-40, tech. supt. Procter & Gamble Def. Corp., Milan, Tenn., 1941-46, sect. head devel. dept., Cin., 1946-50; tech. dir. Milan Arsenal, 1951-58; mgr. ops. and planning soap products div. Procter & Gamble, Cin., 1959-66; ret., 1966; pres. Stevenson Assos., Corsicana, Tex., 1967—. Sec.-treas. Lakeway Civic Corp., 1970-73, v.p., 1974-75; chief engr. Lakeway Vol. Fire Dept., 1968-75; mem. Service Corps of Ret. Execs., 1973—, Internat. Execs. Service Corps, 1975—. Recipient spl. SCORE award Small Bus. Adminstrn., 1974; registered profl. engr., Tex. Mem. Am. Inst. Chem. Engrs., Am. Oil Chemists Soc., Am. Def. Preparedness Assn. Republican. Episcopalian. Clubs: Cin. Engrs., Lakeway Yacht and Country, Corsicana Country. Patentee instrument research and devel. Home and Office: 1203 Lexington Sq Corsicana TX 75110

STEVENSON, JAMES CURLY, JR., banker; b. Grand Prairie, Tex., Jan. 4, 1950; s. James Curly and Myrtle (Steveson) S.; B.S. in Mgmt., Dallas Bapt. Coll., 1974. Insp., Haskon, Inc., Arlington, Tex., 1968; salesman J.C. Penney Co., Inc., Grand Prairie, 1971-79; asst. v.p. Grand Prairie State Bank, 1979—. Mem. Grand Prairie Planning and Zoning Commn.; bd. dirs. Am. Heart Assn., Met. Dallas chpt. March of Dimes; precinct chmn. Democratic Party, Grand Prairie. Recipient Banker of Yr. award We Care Youth Found., 1977. Mem. Am. Inst. Banking, Grand Prairie C. of C. (past dir.). Baptist. Clubs: Lions (dir.), Rock Creek Bar B Q, Optimist (v.p.) Grand Prairie). Home: 517 SW 15th St Grand Prairie TX 75051 Office: Grand Prairie State Bank 200 W Main St Grand Prairie TX 75050

STEVENSON, JAMES PRESTON FANT, clergyman; b. Hartselle, Ala., Oct. 5, 1919; s. James Preston and Claribel (Fant) S.; grad. Fort Smith Jr. Coll., 1939; A.B. (Kneeland Theol. award), Coll. of Ozarks, 1941, D.D., 1950; B.D., Columbia Theol. Sem., 1944, M.Div., 1971; m. Kathryn McGee, Jan. 3, 1942; children—Victoria Fant (Mrs. Phillip Land II), Sarah Kay. Ordained to ministry Presbyn. Ch., 1944; pastor First Presbyn. Ch., Uniontown, Ala., 1944-46, Canal St. Presbyn. Ch., New Orleans, 1946-50, First Presbyn. Ch., Clarksdale, Miss., 1952-68, Central Presbyn. Ch., Bristol, Va., 1968-73; family relations counselor, Bristol, Va., 1972-73; pastor Tirzah Presbyn. Ch., Waxhaw, N.C., 1973—. Vice pres. New Orleans Ministerial Assn., 1949; pres. Coahoma County Ministerial Assn., Clarksdale, 1958; mem. edn. study com. Presbyn. Ch. in U.S., chmn. standing com. woman's work, 1958, chmn. permanent com. of minister and his work in gen. assembly, 1964—; chmn. com. on minister and work Presbyn. Ch. State of Miss.; chaplain Miss. Ho. of Reps., 1959; chaplain of day Ho. of Reps., Washington, 1969; Va. State chaplain. Camp chaplain Boy Scouts Am.; chaplain City of Coahoma County, City of Bristol, Va., Appalachian Crime Clinic; clergy rep. Coahoma County Parents League; youth counselor Youth Court, Coahoma County; dir. religious affairs Va. Civil Def. Col. staff Gov. Johnson of Miss., Gov. Ellington of Tenn. Bd. dirs. Columbia Theol. Sem., Decatur, Ga., A.R.C., Highlands, Union Ct. Meml. Hosp., Monroe, N.C.; bd. dirs. Presbyn. Home; bd. dirs., mem. exec. com. Va. Highlands Community Coll., Bristol Meml. Hosp.; chmn. bd. dirs. Coahoma County Nursing Sch. Served as capt., chaplain, USAF, 1950-52, Korea. Recipient Alumnus of Year award Coll. of Ozarks, 1949. Mem. Nat. Council Family Relations. Mason (chaplain New Orleans shrine 1948—). Mem. Coahoma County, Bristol chambers commerce, S.A.R., Alumni of Columbia Theol. Sem. (v.p. 1955-57). Co-author: The Manual for Ordination and Installation of Ministers, 1963. Home: RFD 4 Box 119 Waxhaw NC 28173

STEVENSON, JANE LATIMER, sch. counselor; b. Owensboro, Ky., Mar. 20, 1931; d. William Forrest and Dora Lee (Birk) S.; student Hollins Coll., 1949-51; A.B., Centre Coll., Danville, Ky., 1953; M.A., Ind. U., 1956; postgrad. Mansfield Coll., Oxford (Eng.) U., 1963. Admissions officer Ky. Wesleyan Coll., Owensboro, 1954-59; registrar U. Ky. Henderson Community Coll., 1959-61; guidance counselor Daviess County High Sch., Owensboro, 1965—. Leader, Pennyrile council Girl Scouts U.S.A., 1953-54; elder First Presbyterian Ch., Owensboro, 1972—, clk. session, 1977, chmn. Christian edn. com., 1975, 79; bd. overseers Centre Coll., 1953-54, bd. alumni dirs., 1966-74, trustee, 1974—; bd. dirs. Louisville Presbyn. Theol. Soc., 1972—. Recipient Vol. Service award Jr. League, 1975. Mem. Am. Personnel and Guidance Assn., Ky. Personnel and Guidance Assn., Green River Personnel and Guidance Assn., NEA, Ky. Edn. Assn., Sierra Club, Nat. Audubon Soc., Delta Kappa Gamma. Clubs: DAR, Filson, Jr. League, Hosp. Guild Owensboro, Owensboro Country. Home: 1610 Griffith Ave Owensboro KY 42301 Office: 4255 New Hartford Rd Owensboro KY 42301

STEVENSON, JOE LEE, acct., educator; b. Tazewell, Va., Jan. 13, 1930; s. James Melvin and Virginia (Lockhart) S.; B.S., Concord Coll., Athens, W.Va., 1962; M.E., Va. Poly. Inst. and State U., Blacksburg, 1967; m. Wanda Bailey, June 22, 1956; 1 dau., Melody. Tchr., Bluefield (W.Va.) High Sch., 1964-65; auditor IRS, Bluefield, W.Va., 1965-66; asso. prof. bus. edn. S.W. Va. Community Coll., Richlands, 1968—. Mem. steering com. Mountain-Dominion Resource Conservation and Devel. Com., 1976—. Served with U.S. Army, 1952-54. Recipient merit award Nat. Bus. Edn. Assn., 1962; C.P.A. Mem. Blue Key, Delta Pi Epsilon. Methodist. Home: Route 3 Box 135 Bluefield VA 24605 Office: Box SVCC Dept Bus Edn SW Va Community Coll Richlands VA 24641

STEVENSON, NANCY BACKER, lt. gov. S.C.; b. N.Y.C., June 8, 1928; d. William Bryant Backer and Ferdinanda Le Gare Backer Waring; B.A., Smith Coll., 1949; LL.D. (hon.), U. S.C., 1979, Columbia (S.C.) Coll., 1979; children—David, Ferdinan, Norman Williams, Josephine. Reporter, N.Y. Herald Tribune, 1949; mem. S.C. Ho. of Reps., 1975-78; lt. gov. State of S.C., Columbia, 1978—. Trustee, Historic Charleston Found., 1963-78; trustee, sec. Coll. of Charleston Found., 1970-74; co-chmn. Save Charleston Found., 1973-76; vice chmn. S.C. Com. to Re-Elect Pres. Carter, 1979-80. Named Bicentennial Career Woman of Yr., Charleston Bus. and Profl. Womens Club, 1976. Mem. S.C. Hist. Soc. (v.p. 1965-69), Trident Bus. and Profl. Women's Club. Democrat. Episcopalian. Office: State Capitol Columbia SC 29201

STEVERDING, BERNARD, physicist; b. Stadtlohn, Germany, Aug. 3, 1926; s. Herman and Francis (Nieland) S.; came to U.S., 1957, naturalized, 1962; Ph.D., U. Muenster, 1951; D.Engring., Inst. of Tech., Aachen, 1956; m. Theresa Schlösser, Dec. 29, 1958. Asst. prof. Inst. Tech., Aachen, 1953; research asst. metallurgy Deutsche Edelstahl Werke, Krefeld, 1956-57; physicist in weapons tech. U.S. Army Missile Command, Redstone Arsenal, Ala., 1960-78; part-time asst. prof. U. Ala., Huntsville, 1962—; vis. scholar U. Cal. at Berkeley, 1971-73. Past mem. materials adv. bd. NSF; mem. bd. Redstone Sci. Info. Center; mem. Tripartite Tech. Coop. Panel. Mem. Am. Inst. Aeros. and Astronautics, Deutscher Naturforscher und Ingenieure. Author, patentee in several fields. Home: 5725 Tannahill Circle Huntsville AL 35802 Office: US Army Research and Standardization Group (Europe) 223 Old Marylebone Rd London W1 England

STEVES, JOHN RICHARD, JR., aerospace co. exec.; b. Englewood, N.J., Nov. 22, 1933; s. John Richard and Elizabeth (Bigham) S.; B.A., Syracuse U., 1965; M.B.A., Auburn U., 1971; m. Helen Lucille Smith, Dec. 10, 1960; children—Debra Lynn, John Richard, Kent Walker. Commd. 2d lt. U.S. Air Force, 1957, advanced through grades to lt. col., 1972; chief adminstrn. 30th Mil. Airlift Squadron, McGuire AFB, N.J., 1951-65; exec. officer, dep. comdr. logistics, Scott AFB, Ill., 1965-67; asst. to dep. comdr. logistics, Hickam AFB, Hawaii, 1967-72; exec. officer, dep. comdr. ops., Saigon RVN, 1971-72; system mgr. internat. fighter aircraft, Kelly AFB, Tex., 1972-76; ret., 1977; mgr. integrated logistics support Gen. Dynamics, Ft. Worth, 1977—. Decorated Bronze Star medal, Meritorious Service medal. Mem. Air Force Assn., Soc. Logistics Engrs. Home: 8604 Irongate Ct Fort Worth TX 76179 Office: Gen Dynamics PO Box 748 Fort Worth TX 76101

STEWART, ALBERT, JR., physician; b. Fayetteville, N.C., Sept. 23, 1920; s. Albert and Winnie Davis (Bruton) S.; student U. S.C., 1936-37; A.B., U. N.C., 1941; M.D., Washington U., 1944; m. Mary Inglesby DuBose, Oct. 5, 1951; children—Albert III, David DuBose, Paul Finley, Charles Inglesby, James Bruton. Intern, Barnes Hosp., St. Louis, 1944-45; fellow in medicine Washington U., St. Louis, 1946-47; ships surgeon Grace Line, N.Y.C., 1947; resident physician Meml. Hosp., Charlotte, N.C., 1948; fellow in gastroenterology Lahey Clinic, Boston, 1949; practice medicine specializing in internal medicine, Fayetteville, 1950—; physician VA Hosp., Fayetteville, 1950-51, cons., 1955-70; attending physician Highsmith, Cape Fear Valley hosps.; clin. asso. prof. medicine U. N.C. Sch. Medicine, 1968-80; dir. Cross Creek Savs. & Loan Assn. Served with M.C., USNR, 1945-46, 52-54. Diplomate Am. Bd. Internal Medicine. Fellow A.C.P.; mem. AMA, N.C., Cumberland County med. socs., Am., N.C. socs. internal medicine, Fayetteville Area C. of C. (dir. 1974—), St. Andrew's Soc., Cape Fear Assembly. Democrat. Episcopalian. Kiwanian. Home: 1507 Morganton Rd Fayetteville NC 28305 Office: 114 Broadfoot Ave Fayetteville NC 28305

STEWART, BETTY SUE, psychologist, counselor; b. Pilot Point, Tex., Aug. 18, 1932; d. A.D. and Attice Lee (Silvey) Clement; B.A. cum laude, U. Houston, 1970, M.A., 1972; children—Donald Eugene, Christopher John. Psychol. asso. Almeda Clinic, Houston, 1972-77; dir. Marriage and Family Counseling Services Inc., 1977—. Mem. Am. Assn. Marriage and Family Counselors, Am., Southwestern, Tex., Houston psychol. assns., Mensa, Psi Chi, Phi Kappa Phi. Asst. author: Freedom and Growth in Marriage, 1975; author: Baby and Child Care for Physically Disabled Mothers, 1977; The Troubled Child, 1978. Editor: Human Sexuality: A Brief Edition, 1973. Home: 6 Pine Creek Ln Houston TX 77055 Office: 8552 Katy Freeway 244 Houston TX 77024

STEWART, CHARLES CARRINGTON, cons. engr.; b. Washington, Oct. 8, 1925; s. Malcolm Nebeker and Margaret Carrington (Laurens) S.; B.S., U.S. Mil. Acad., 1947; M.S., U. Mich., 1959; M.B.A., Fla. State U., 1964; m. Helen Elizabeth Weidener, June 14, 1947; children—Charles Carrington, Suzanne Stewart Myers, Arthur Malcolm. Commd. 2d lt. USAAF, 1947, advanced through grades to col. USAF, 1969; program mgr., test pilot, 1959-64; asst. air attache, Sweden, 1964-68; lectr. Indsl. Coll. Armed Forces, 1970-71; dir. plans and resources ops. USAF Systems Command, 1971-73; ret., 1973; program mgr. Braddock, Dunn & McDonald, cons., Vienna, Va., 1973—. Active local Boy Scouts Am. Decorated Legion of Merit with 1 oak leaf cluster, Joint Services Commendation medal, Air medal with 4 oak leaf clusters; Vietnamese Honor medal 1st class; named hon. col. staff gov. N.Mex.; hon. citizen Jackson, Miss.; hon. mem. Fla. Sheriffs Assn. Mem. Soc. Automotive Engrs., Am. Inst. Aeros. and Astronautics, Am. Def. Preparedness Assn., Air Force Assn., Air Force Hist. Soc., Daedalians, Ret. Officers Assn., Nat. Assn. Remotely Piloted Vehicles, Smithsonian Assos. Episcopalian. Author articles in field. Home: 65 Poquito Bayou Shalimar FL 32579

STEWART, CLARA WOODARD, advt. exec.; b. Mineola, N.Y., May 1, 1952; d. Samuel Woodard and Irene (Colm) S.; B.A. in Broadcasting and Psychology, Mich. State U., 1974; M.A. in Journalism and Communications, U. Fla., 1975. Sales rep. Sta. WSBR, Boca Raton, 1976-77; pres., media dir. Fred Wagenvoord Assos., Inc., Boca Raton, Fla., 1977—. Bd. dirs. United Way Greater Boca Raton, 1979—; bd. dirs. Boca Raton Community Theater, 1977-78, publicity chmn., 1977-78. Mem. Women in Communications, Advt. Fedn. Greater Ft. Lauderdale, Nat. Assn. Ednl. Broadcasters, Mensa (S.E. regional public relations asst. 1978—), Mommas and Poppas Broward County, Phi Kappa Phi. Home: 1401 NW 7th Ave Apt A-1 Boca Raton FL 33432 Office: Weir Plaza Exec Suite 855 S Federal Hwy Boca Raton FL 33432

STEWART, DAVID KEITH, educator; b. Olathe, Kans., May 22, 1921; s. Bernard and Louverna Adele (Brown) S.; B.A., Central Mo. State Coll., Warrensburg, 1948; M.A., Tchrs. Coll., Columbia, 1950; postgrad. U. Iowa, 1952-58, Cornell U., summer 1968; Ed.D., N.Y. U., 1970; m. Nina Farmer, Aug. 15, 1942; children—Judith (Mrs. Charles L. Brader, Jr.), Diana Kathryn (Mrs. Roger Rearden), Jeanne Elizabeth. Teaching prin. Plainville (Kans.) Elementary Sch., 1948-49; tchr. Greenwich (Conn.) pub. schs., 1949-50; prin. sch., Muncie, Kans., 1950-52; dir. elementary edn. Iowa City Pub. Schs., 1952-58; instr. State U. Iowa, summers 1955-57; dir. elementary edn. Kenosha (Wis.) pub. schs., 1958-64; prin. Murray Ave. Sch., Mamaroneck, N.Y., 1964-68; asst. supt. personnel Mamaroneck Pub. Schs., 1968-70; supt. McCracken County Pub. Schs., Paducah, Ky., 1970-73; prof. edn. adminstrn. U. So. Miss., Hattiesburg, 1973—. Vis. prof. Carthage Coll., Kenosha, summers 1963-64; editor, host Chalk Dust, ednl. radio series, weekly, Iowa City, 1955-57; cons. panelist in labor relations and policy devel. So. Region Sch. Bd. Assn. Research and Tng. Center. Served with USAAF, 1942-45; PTO. Contbr. articles to profl. jours. Home: 3422 W Adeline Hattiesburg MS 39401 Office: PO Box 8293 So Sta U So Miss Hattiesburg MS 39401

STEWART, DONALD WILBUR, U.S. Senator; b. Munford, Ala., Feb. 8, 1940; B.S., U. Ala., 1962, LL.S., 1965; m. Priscilla Runkle Black; children—Priscilla, Taylor. Admitted to Ala. bar, 1965; partner firm Wilson, Propst & Stewart, Stewart and Colvin, Stewart and Morris, Anniston, Ala.; mem. Ala. Ho. of Reps., 1970-74, Ala. Senate, 1974-78; U.S. magistrate, 1967-70; mem. U.S. Senate from Ala., 1978—. Served to 1st lt. U.S. Army, 1965. Mem. Ala. Bar Assn., Am. Bar Assn., Calhoun County Bar Assn., Anniston Jaycees, Ala. Assn. for Retarded Citizens, Calhoun County Assn. for Retarded Citizens, Phi Alpha Delta, Omicron Delta Kappa, Delta Tau Delta. Democrat. Methodist. Clubs: Civitan, Masons, Shriners. Office: 110 Russell Senate Office Bldg Washington DC 20510*

STEWART, DOROTHY ELIZABETH, ins. co. exec.; b. Thayer, Mo., Apr. 23, 1933; d. Kenneth Lawrence and Susanna Elizabeth (Low) Henning; student Draughons Bus. Coll., Memphis, 1952-54; m. Carlos Ray Stewart, Sept. 5, 1954; children—Carla Rae, Traci Deone. Sec. to chmn. bd. Time-Life Ins. Co., San Antonio, 1957-61; sec. to chmn. bd. and adminstr. v.p. Gt. Am. Res. Ins. Co., Dallas, 1961-73, underwriter life and health ins., 1973-75, asst. v.p., 1975—, mgr. records dept., 1975—; mgr. records dept. J.C. Penney Life Ins. Co., Dallas, 1976—. Fellow Life Office Mgmt. Assn.; mem. Assn. Records Mgrs. and Adminstrs., Nat. Micrographics Assn. (dir. Dallas chpt.). Methodist. Office: 2020 Live Oak Dallas TX 75221

STEWART, DUNCAN CLARK, clergyman; b. Glasgow, Scotland, Nov. 5, 1921; s. Hugh and Margaret Stewart (Clark) S.; B.A., Wheaton (Ill.) Coll., 1947; B.D., Princeton Theol. Sem., 1950; M.S. in Edn., Ind. U., 1959; Th.D., Burton Sem., 1960; m. Doris Mae Bearse, Aug. 24, 1946; children—Kathleen Margaret (Mrs. Kenneth L. Thomas), Stacy Clark, Bruce Duncan. Ordained to ministry Presbyn. Ch., 1950; pastor Alexandria 1st Presbyn. Ch., Mt. Pleasant, N.J., 1947-50, 1st Presbyn. Ch., East Boston, Mass., 1950-51; commd. 1st lt. U.S. Army, 1951, advanced through grades to col., 1971; asst. chaplain 4th Army, 1957-58; chief audiovisual research Army Chaplain Bd., 1959-62; chief profl. devel. and tng. Office Chief of Chaplains, Army Dept., 1962-64; chaplain 25th Inf. Div., Vietnam, 1968-69; dir. resident instrn. U.S. Chaplain Sch., Ft. Hamilton, Bklyn., 1969-71; exec. dir. Armed Forces Chaplain Bd., Office Sec. Def., Washington, 1971-76; staff chaplain 5th U.S. Army, San Antonio, 1976-79; ret., 1979; pastor Covenant Presbyn. Ch., San Antonio, 1979—; mem. Presbytery del Salvador. Chmn. Am. youth activities, Wurzburg, Germany, 1966-68; pres. P.T.A., Crane, Ind., 1958-59. Mem. Crane Town Council, 1958-59. Served with AUS, 1943-45. Decorated Silver Star, Legion of Merit with oak leaf cluster, Bronze Star with V and 2 oak leaf clusters, Purple Heart with cluster, Meritorious Ser. medal with 2 oak leaf clusters, Army Commendation medal with oak leaf cluster, Air medal, Combat Med. Badge, Combat Inf. Badge; Vietnamese Cross of Gallantry, Vietnamese Honor medal 1st class. Mem. Mil. Chaplains Assn., Assn. U.S. Army. Home: 205 Roleto Dr San Antonio TX 78213 Office: 211 Roleto Dr San Antonio TX 78213

STEWART, EASTON, civil engr.; b. Wybark, Okla., Sept. 11, 1922; s. Voistes Lee and Zella (Fears) S.; B.S. in Civil Engring., U. Okla., 1953; m. Maralynn E. Robertson, Dec. 29, 1949; children—Stephen, Charles, Barbara, Cheryl. Owner, Easton Stewart & Assos., Cons. Engrs., Baton Rouge, 1969—. Served with USNR, 1942-45; PTO. Registered profl. engr., Okla., Miss., La., Tenn. Mem. Cons. Engrs. Council, Am. Soc. C.E., Nat., La. socs. profl. engrs., Am. Pub. Works Assn., Inst. Transp., Inst. Municipal Engrs. Specialist in maj. hwy. design. Home: 11433 Archery Dr Baton Rouge LA 70815 Office: 6717 Goya Ave Baton Rouge LA 70806

STEWART, EVELYN JUANITA, sem. dean; b. Ft. Smith, Ark., Nov. 15, 1926; d. Orvie Rufus and Gladys Beatrice (Efurd) Stewart; B.A., Ouachita Bapt. Coll., 1948; M.R.E., Southwestern Bapt. Theol. Sem., 1953. Asso. tng. union dept. Miss. Bapt. State Conv., Jackson, 1953-60; dir. jr. and intermediate work First Bapt. Ch., Tulsa, 1960-62; children's cons. Bapt. Sunday Sch. Bd., Nashville, 1962-69; dean of women, dir. student activities Southwestern Bapt. Theol. Sem., Ft. Worth, 1969—. Mem. Southwestern Bapt. Religious Edn. Assn. (sec. 1970), So. Bapt. Religious Edn. Assn. (v.p. 1971, sec. 1976-77). Clubs: Seminary Woman's (v.p. 1971, 73), Fort Worth Woman's, Knife and Fork (Ft. Worth). Editor jr. sect. Builder mag., 1962-69. Contbr. to publs. in field. Home: 4536 Stanley St Barnard Hall Fort Worth TX 76122 Office: PO Box 22000-3F Fort Worth TX 76122

STEWART, FRANKLIN BURTON, soil scientist; b. Sparta, Tenn., Aug. 17, 1922; s. Alvin Hill and Ada Dorcas (McCulley) S.; B.S., Tenn. Technol. U., 1946; M.S., U. Tenn., 1947; Ph.D., U. Md., 1955; m. Jeanne Marie Sigourney, Dec. 17, 1944. Soil scientist Va. Truck and Ornamentals Research Sta., Virginia Beach, 1955—. Served with USMC, 1943-46, 51-52. Home: 1601 Maycraft Rd Virginia Beach VA 23455 Office: 1444 Diamond Springs Rd Virginia Beach VA 23455

STEWART, GEORGE LOUIS, parasitologist; b. Washington, Oct. 30, 1945; s. Galen C. and Geneivive Mary (Gantos) S.; B.S. in Biology, Tulane U., 1969; Ph.D. in Parasitology, Rice U., 1973; m. Julia B. Majure, Oct. 16, 1969. Research asso., lectr. Rice U., Houston, 1974-77; asst. prof. biology dept. U. Tex., Arlington, 1977—. NIH grantee, 1979-82. Mem. Am. Soc. Parasitologists, Am. Heartworm Soc., Southwestern Assn. Parasitologists, Sigma Xi. Office: Dept Biology U Tex Arlington TX 76010

STEWART, HOMER FRANCIS, lawyer; b. Little Rock, Mar. 26, 1915; s. Homer Clifford and Velma (Ruff) S.; student Ark. State Tchrs. Coll., 1935-37; B.B.A., U. Tenn., 1940, J.D., 1941; m. Nelle Yoest Dale, Dec. 22, 1940; children—Vivian Nannette Stewart Frisk, Clifford Francis, Andrew Dale, Jonathan Travis. Admitted to Tenn. bar, 1947, pvt. practice law, Nashville, 1947-56; partner Watkins, McGugin, Stewart, Finch & McNeilly, 1956-70; individual practice, 1971-72; partner Stewart & Estes, 1973-75, Stewart, Estes & Donnell, 1975—. Mem. devel. council U. Tenn., 1960-64, deans alumni adv. com. Coll. of Law, 1976-79. Served with USNR, 1943-46. Mem. Nashville, Tenn., Am., Fed. bar assns., Tenn. Def. Lawyers Assn., Internat. Assn. Ins. Counsel, Fedn. Ins. Counsel, Am. Judicature Soc., Def. Research Inst., World Assn. Lawyers of World Peace Through Law Center, Am. Soc. Hosp. Attys., Tenn. Assn. Hosp. Attys., U. Tenn. Alumni Assn. (pres. Davidson County chpt. 1957), Nashville C. of C. (chmn. edn. com. 1964-65). Presbyn. (deacon 1954—). Mason (Shriner). Club: City (Nashville). Home: 410 Wilsonia Dr Nashville TN 37205 Office: 3d National Bank Nashville TN 37219

STEWART, JAMES BENHAM, surgeon; b. Birmingham, Ala., Mar. 15, 1913; s. David and Matilda Mallette (Benham) S.; B.S., Birmingham So. Coll., 1933; M.D., Emory U., 1938; m. Katherine Eula Jordan, June 27, 1939; 1 son, J. Benham Stewart. Intern, Emory U. Hosp., Atlanta, 1938-39; resident Duval Med. Center, Jacksonville, Fla., 1941-44; practice medicine specializing in surgery, Macon, Ga., 1948—; pres. Stewart, Menendez & Rhame, P.C., Macon, 1977—; dir. Macon Tumor Clinic, 1952-72; chmn. dept. oncology Macon Hosp., 1952-74; dir. Middle Ga. Hosp., Macon, 1958—; pres., dir. Middle Ga. Doctors Bldg. Co., Macon, 1958—. Bd. dirs. Burke Found., 1973—, A.R.C., Macon, 1958—, Macon Rescue Mission, 1963—; bd. dirs. Ga. unit Am. Cancer Soc., 1965—, Bibb County unit, 1953—. Served to capt. M.C., AUS, 1944-47. Diplomate Am. Bd. Surgery, Am. Bd. Abdominal Surgeons; recipient Alumnae of the Year award Birmingham So. Coll., 1977. Fellow A.C.S.; mem. Ga. Surg. Soc., Bibb County Med. Soc., AMA, Med. Assn. Ga., So. Med. Assn., Am. Soc. Abdominal Surgeons (pres.-elect, mem. exec. com.). Methodist. Clubs: Kiwanis, Elks. Contbr. articles to med. jours. Home: 1234 Nottingham Dr Macon GA 31201 Office: 700 Spring St Macon GA 31201

STEWART, JOHN ELLIOTT, ret. investment counsellor; b. Chgo., Dec. 1, 1912; s. Robert Wright and Maude (Elliott) S.; ed. Yale, 1935; m. Mary Terry Schlamp, May 9, 1936; children—James Jeremiah, Sara Royall, John Elliott. Salesman Colonial Beacon Oil Co., N.Y.C., 1935-36; pres. Stewart, Warren & Co., N.Y.C., 1937-40; comml. aviation pilot, flight instr. A & H Flying Service, Asheville, N.C., 1940-42; asst. supt. stas. operations and flight dispatch mgr. Pan Am. Airways, Inc., Atlantic div., N.Y.C., 1947-50; asso. Neergard, Miller & Co., N.Y.C., 1950-57, Coffin & Burr, Inc., N.Y.C., 1957-61, Laird, Bissell & Meeds, 1961-62; formed own investment counseling firm, Madison, 1962; dir. North Madison Representative Orgn., 1966-68, pres., 1967-68. Sec. Federated Assns., Greenwich, 1952-54; dir. Am. Coalition, Washington, 1957-60; chmn. U.S. Day Com. Greenwich, 1954; v.p. Madison Land Conservation Trust, 1966-67, pres., 1968-70, dir., chmn. land acquistion com., 1968-71, justice of peace, 1964-71; mem. Conn. Power Facility Evaluation Com., 1971; mem. Conn. Am. Revolution Bicentennial Council, 1971—; chmn. Bicentennial Commn. of Palm Beach, 1974-76. Mem. Republican Town Com. Madison, 1964-71; dir. Palm Beach Rep. Club, 1972-74, pres., 1972-74. Bd. dirs. Palm Beach Civic Assn., 1975—. Served as lt. comdr., naval aviator USNR, 1942-46. Mem. Greenwich C. of C. (past v.p., dir. 1956-60, chmn. legislative com., edn. com.), Ky. Soc. Palm Beaches (div. 1975—), S.A.R. (bd. mgrs., sr. v.p. Conn. soc. 1962-64, pres. Conn. Soc. 1964-66, nat. trustee for Conn., 1965-67, v.p. Palm Beach chpt. 1972), C.A.R. (mem. bd. Conn. soc.; sr. pres. Lt. William Stewart Soc.). Republican. Clubs: Metropolitan (gov. 1958-62) (N.Y.C.); Racquet (Chgo.); Madison Rotary (dir. v.p. 1966-67, pres. 1968-69); Biltmore (N.C.) Forest Country; Everglades (chmn. bridge com. 1977-79) (Palm Beach, Fla.); Sailfish of Fla. Home: La Casa Pequena 730 North County Rd Palm Beach FL 33480

STEWART, JOHN HARVEY, coal co. exec.; b. Buckhannon, W.Va., Nov. 28, 1925; s. Dwight Lovall and Grace Mildred (Marteney) S.; student U. Richmond, 1943-44, W.Va. U., 1956-58, Marshall Coll., 1958-61; m. Joan Hickman, Oct. 30, 1958; children—John Russell, Kurt Harvey. Vocat. instr. Logan County Bd. Edn., 1956-61, Tri-County Vocat. Edn. Center, 1968-70, Carver Career and Tech. Edn. Center, 1970-71; tng. coordinator Fuel Supply div. Am. Electric Power Service Corp., Athens, Ohio, 1972-77; dir. tng. coal ops. Pickands Mather & Co., Charleston, W.Va., 1977—. Mem. Ohio Gov.'s Manpower Planning Council, 1974-77; active Boy Scouts Am. Served with AUS, 1943-45. Decorated Purple Heart. Mem. Am. Soc. Tng. and Devel., Am. Vocat. Assn., Mine Insps. Inst. Am. Clubs: Riverside Country, V.F.W., Moose. Home: Route 1 Woodruff Acres Ripley WV 25701 Office: 70th St Charleston WV 25304

STEWART, JONAS LEE, religious exec.; b. Brownsville, Tenn., Jan. 17, 1919; s. Lynn N. and Julia Ann (Thomas) S.; student U. Tenn., Martin, 1936-37; B.A., Union U., 1942, D.D., 1967; Th.M., Southwestern Bapt. Theol. Sem., 1946; m. Emma Lee Simpson, June 24, 1947; children—James Larry, Billy Joe. Ordained to ministry Baptist Ch., 1938; pastor rural chs., 1938-46; missionary Tenn. Bapt. Conv., 1946-48; pastor 1st Bapt. Ch., Somerville, Tenn., 1948-56, 1st Bapt. Ch., Huntingdon, Tenn., 1956-68; exec. sec.-treas. Tenn. Bapt. Found., Brentwood, 1968—; dir. So. Bapt. Fgn. Mission Bd.; trustee Sunday Sch. bd. So. Bapt. Conv.; dir. exec. bd., pres. Tenn. Bapt. Conv. Recipient Exec. Leadership award Bd. Trustees Tenn. Bapt. Found., 1978; hon. col. Staff Gov. of Tenn. Mem. Assn. So. Bapt. Found. Execs. (pres.). Clubs: Rotary (past pres.), Lions. Author: More Than Money, 1970; These Shall Never Die, 1975; contbr. to Vol. III So. Bapt. Ency., 1971. Home: 650 Harding Pl Nashville TN 37211 Office: PO Box 347 Brentwood TN 37027

STEWART, KENNETH LAMONT, sociologist, educator; b. Weiser, Idaho, Apr. 2, 1949; s. Lawrence Linden and Charlotte Juanita (Waltman) S.; student Coll. of Idaho, 1967-68; B.A., Boise State U., 1971; M.A., Colo. State U., 1973; Ph.D., Western Mich. U., 1976. Grad. asst. sociology Colo. State U., Ft. Collins, 1971-73; grad. asso. sociology Western Mich. U., Kalamazoo, 1973-75, instr., 1974; instr. sociology Angelo State U., San Angelo, 1975-76, asst. prof., 1976—. Mem. housing planning com. Concho Valley Council of Govts., 1977; mem. San Angelo Citizens Com. on Drug Abuse, 1978. Faculty research grantee, Angelo State U., 1978. Mem. Soc. for Study of Symbolic Interaction (coordinator S.W. region 1977-79), Am. Sociol Assn., Southwestern Sociol. Assn., Southwestern Social Sci. Assn. Democrat. Jewish. Home: 2209 Colorado St San Angelo TX 76901

STEWART, LYNDA JONES, broadcasting co. exec.; b. Dora, Ala., June 6, 1939; d. Charles Bernard and Kathryn Louise (Swaim) Jones; B.A. in Journalism cum laude, U. Ga., 1961; m. Charles Britton Stewart, June 5, 1966. Staff editor So. Bell Tel. & Tel., Atlanta, 1961-64; public editor Office Public Relations, U. Ga., Athens, 1964-68; editor employee mag. Cox Broadcasting, Atlanta, 1968, pub. editor, 1968-74, coordinator, 1974-75, dir. communications, 1975—, asst. sec., 1979—; cons., lectr. in field. Co-chmn. United Way Communications Council, Atlanta, 1975—; mem. Del. Assembly United Way, 1976—; bd. dirs. Atlanta unit Am. Cancer Soc., 1979—. Recipient Bolen award as outstanding pres. in dist. II, Internat. Assn. Bus. Communicators, 1974, others. Mem. Internat. Assn. Bus. Communicators (accredited, exec. v.p. 1979), C. of C. Methodist. Contbg. editor U. Ga. Alumni Mag., 1968—. Office: 1601 W Peachtree St NE Atlanta GA 30309

STEWART, MARCUS CROWDER, utilities exec.; b. Whiteville, Tenn., Dec. 14, 1907; s. Marcus Jefferson and Mattie Sue (Crowder) S.; B.S., U. Tenn., 1929, postgrad., 1953, 61; m. Mattie Reeves Patton, June 18, 1936; 1 son, Marcus Crowder. Local mgr. Tenn. Electric

Power Co., 1929-39; property recorder TVA, 1939-40; mgr. Sand Mountain Electric Coop., Ft. Payne, Ala., 1940-71, mgr. emeritus, 1971-73, mgmt. cons., 1973—. Engring. mgmt. cons. Sand Mountain Water Authority; co-organizer Farmers Telephone Coop. and Water Systems; signup coordinator N.E. Ala. Water, Sewer and Fire Protection Dist., 1975—. Bd. dirs. Choccolocco council Boy Scouts Am., United Givers Fund DeKalb County. Served to 1st lt. Officers Res. Corp., 1929-46. Recipient Max Howard award for outstanding community achievement, 1975; registered profl. engr., Ala. Mem. Am. Inst. Mgmt. (asso.), North Ala. Pub. Power Distbrs. (chmn. coms.; Outstanding Mgr. grantee 1972), North Ala. Indsl. Devel. Assn. (pres., dir.), Tenn. Valley Pub. Power Assn. (pres., treas., dir.), Ala. Rural Electric Assn. Coops. (pres., dir.), Nat. Rural Elec. Coops. Assn. (pub. relations com. chmn.), Ft. Payne (dir. 1951-54), Rainsville (dir. 1965-68) chambers commerce. Democrat. Methodist (adminstrv. bd., past chmn.). Mason; mem. Order Eastern Star (past worthy patron). Home: 206 Forrest Ave S Fort Payne AL 35967 Office: PO Box 581 Fort Payne AL 35967

STEWART, MARK HOKE, real estate developer; b. Radford, Va., Sept. 16, 1950; s. Connor Edward and Goldie (West) S.; B.A., Erskine Coll., 1972; postgrad. U. S.C. Law Sch., 1973; m. Rebecca Anthony, May 27, 1972; 1 son, Anthony Christian. Mortgage loan analyst 1st Piedmont Mortgage Co., Greenville, S.C., 1973-76; v.p. Land Lease Corp., also Land Lease Nat., Greenville, 1976-77; mem. comml. sales and devel. staff Furman Co., Greenville, S.C., 1977—. Cons. Children's Learning Centers, Spartanburg, S.C. Mem. S.C. Real Estate Brokers. Presbyterian. Clubs: Sertoma (dir. heritage, 1975-76); Poinsett. Home: 7 Bridgeton Ct Greenville SC 29615 Office: Furman Co Daniel Bldg Greenville SC 29602

STEWART, MILTON DUDLEY, JR., economist; b. Palestine, Tex., May 12, 1930; s. Milton Dudley and Alice Hazel (Eilenberger) S.; B.A., Tex. A. and M. U., 1958, M.S., 1960; Ph.D., U. Tex., Austin, 1972; m. Jaye Jean Taylor, July 25, 1979; children—Lisa Elaine, Jan Elizabeth Colwell, John Taylor Colwell. Lectr. econs. U. Md., Far East div., Tokyo, 1962-63, European div., Heidelberg, West Germany, 1963-66; asso. prof. econs. and fin. Stephen F. Austin State U., Nacogdoches, Tex., 1966—; internat. econ. cons. U.S. Dept. Commerce, Washington, 1974. Served with USAF, 1951-55. Mem. AAUP, Am. Econ. Assn., E. Tex. Estate Planning Council, Southwestern Soc. Economists, Tex. Assn. Coll. Tchrs. (mem. state exec. bd. 1973-75), World Future Soc., Omicron Delta Epsilon. Episcopalian. Editor: SFA Bus. Review, 1976-78; contbr. articles to profl. jours. Home: 133 Old Line Dr # 41 Nacogdoches TX 75961 Office: PO Box 13009 Stephen F Austin State U Dept Econs and Finance Nacogdoches TX 75962

STEWART, PATRICIA FERN HINTON, med. technologist; b. Booneville, Miss., June 13, 1932; d. Milliard Carroll and Mattie (Peeler) Hinton; B.S., Miss. State Coll. for Women, 1954; M.S., U. Miss., 1971; m. A.T. Stewart, Jr., Oct. 30, 1976. Asst. chief Univ. Hosp. Clin. Bacteriology Lab., Jackson, Miss., 1955-60; blastomycosis research lab. VA Hosp., Jackson, 1960-69; med. research in respiratory diseases VA Center, Jackson, 1969-75; instr. microbiology U. Miss. Med. Sch., Jackson, 1972-76; clin. microbiologist VA Hosp., Biloxi, Miss., 1975—. Mem. AAUW, Miss. Soc. Med. Technologists (pres. 1959-60, dir. 1963), Am. Soc. Microbiologists, Med. Mycol. Soc. Am., Am. Soc. Med. Tech., Central Dist. Soc. Med. Technologists (pres. 1958), Alpha Mu Tau. Mem. Christian Ch. Contbr. articles to profl. jours. Home: 58 54th St Gulfport MS 39501 Office: VA Hosp Clin Lab Biloxi MS 39531

STEWART, PATRICIA LUCILLE, nurse, army officer; b. Terre Haute, Ind., Dec. 31, 1946; d. Etzell L. and Virginia Pearl (Ripple) S.; diploma, St. Anthony Hosp. Sch. Nursing, 1967; B.S.N., Loretta Heights Coll., 1972; M.Hosp. Adminstrn., Baylor U., 1977. Commd. 2d. lt. Nurse Corps, U.S. Army, 1967, advanced through grades to maj., 1979; staff nurse Ft. Bragg Hosp., N.C., 1967-68, Vietnam, 1968-69, resigned, 1969, rejoined service, 1970; head nurse, supr. dept. clinics W. Ger., 1972-74, spl. projects officer dept. nursing Brooke Army Med. Center, Ft. Sam Houston, Tex., 1974-75; nursing methods analyst William Beaumont Army Med. Center, El Paso, Tex., 1977—; evening charge nurse Porter Meml. Hosp., Denver, 1969-70. Decorated Army Commendation medal with oak leaf cluster. Mem. Tex. Hosp. Assn., Am. Hosp. Assn. Democrat. Baptist. Office: William Beaumont Army Med Center Piedras St El Paso TX 79920

STEWART, PAUL DEAN, educator; b. Fouke, Ark., Jan. 23, 1938; s. Robert Floyd and Ethel Gertrude (McAdams) S.; B.S., E. Tex. State U., 1962; M.Ed., 1968; m. Ronda Ann Cole, Aug. 23, 1963; 1 son, Steven Cole. Tchr., El Paso (Tex.) Public Schs., 1962-67, Greenville (Tex.) High Sch., 1967-68; asst. football coach East Tex. State U., Commerce, 1967-68; instr. Texarkana (Tex.) Community Coll., 1968-69; asst. prof. health, phys. edn., dir. intramurals Tarrant County Jr. Coll., Ft. Worth, 1969—; ofcl. Spl. Olympics track and field meets; timer Southwestern Parks and Recreation Ann. Meet; speaker in field. Bd. dirs. ARC, Texarkana, Ark-Tex., 1968-69. Recipient award of Merit Tex. High Sch. Coaches Assn.; cert. of Appreciation, Arlington (Tex.) YMCA, 1979. Mem. Nat. Intramural Recreational Sports Assn. (cons. to region IV community colls.), Tex. Jr. Coll. Tchrs. Assn., Tex. Assn. Health, Phys. Edn., Recreation, SW Football and Basketball Ofcls. Assn., Tarrant County Jr. Coll. Faculty Assn., Tex. Assn. Intramural Dirs. Republican. Episcopalian. Co-author: Health Concepts of Physical Activity, 1974. Home: 6405 Beachview Dr Arlington TX 76016 Office: Dept Health Phys Edn Tarrant County Jr Coll 5301 Campus Dr Fort Worth TX 76119

STEWART, PRISCILLA ANN MABIE, educator; b. Iowa City, Sept. 21, 1926; d. Edward Charles and Grace Frances (Chase) Mabie; B.A., State U., Iowa, 1948; M.A., U. South Fla., 1971; m. Thomas Wilson Stewart, Aug. 28, 1949. Coordinator elem. art Manatee County (Fla.), 1953-59; tchr. art Manatee Jr. Coll., 1959—; organizer, dir. Pelican Perch Wild Bird Hosp., Bradenton, 1953—. Mem. Mensa, Intertel Soc., Nat. Art Edn. Assn., Fla. Art Edn. Assn., Fla. Ornithol. Soc., Phi Beta Kappa, Phi Kappa Phi. Republican. Episcopalian. Home: 128 N 28th St W Bradenton FL 33505 Office: Dept Art Manatee Jr Coll Bradenton FL 33507

STEWART, ROBERT H., III, banker; b. Dallas, Dec. 3, 1925; s. Robert H. Stewart; B.B.A. in Banking, So. Meth. U., 1949; children—Cynthia Caroline, Alice Partee. With Empire State Bank, Dallas, 1949-50; with First Nat. Bank, Dallas, 1951—, v.p., 1953-59, sr. v.p., pres., 1959-72; chmn. bd. First Internat. Bancshares, Inc., 1972—. Served to 1st lt. inf. U.S. Army, 1944-46, also Korea. Club: Brook Hollow Golf (Dallas). Office: First Internat Bancshares Inc PO Box 6031 Dallas TX 75283*

STEWART, ROBERT WILLIAM, III, accountant; b. Plainview, Tex., June 14, 1940; s. Robert William and Marian (McDowell) S.; student Schreiner Inst. (Kerrville, Tex.), 1958, Spartin Sch. Aeros., 1959, Yingling Sch. Aeros., 1960, Lubbock Christian Coll., 1963; B.B.A. in Accounting, Tex. Tech. U., 1966; m. Margaret Fay Chapman, Dec. 2, 1960; children—Robert William IV, Paul William. Auditor firm Ernst & Ernst, Lubbock, Tex., and Ft. Worth, 1966-68; dir. finance Mitchell Industries, Inc., Mineral Wells, Tex., 1968-70; exec. v.p. Moon & Hall, Inc., Mineral Wells, 1969-76; asso. Zack Burkett Co., Graham, Tex., 1971-76; owner Robert W. Stewart, C.P.A., Mineral Wells, 1976—; partner Stewart & Crabtree, C.P.A.'s, 1979—; pres. Steward Assos., Inc., 1978—; chmn. bd. Creative Horizons, Inc.; mem. Tex. Bd. C.P.A.'s. Sponser Cub Scouts Am., Mineral Wells, 1971-72; mem. parks bd. City of Mineral Wells, 1978-80; mem. long range water study bd. City of Mineral Wells, 1978-80; adviser Jr. Achievement, Ft. Worth, 1968-69. C.P.A., Tex. Mem. Am. Inst. C.P.A.'s, Tex. Soc. C.P.A.'s. Presbyterian. Clubs: Rotary (pres. 1980—), Holiday Hills Country, Brazos River Gun and Archery (Mineral Wells). Home: 1 Preston Pl Mineral Wells TX 76067 Office: 101 Executive Park Bldg PO Box 40 Mineral Wells TX 76067

STEWART, ROGER HAROLD, dermatologist; b. Detroit, Sept. 13, 1940; s. Meyer and Nettie (Wolk) S.; A.B., U. Mich., 1962, M.D., 1966; m. Linda Berenfield, May 23, 1964; children—Sheri Lynne, Michael Lee. Intern U. Calif., Los Angeles, 1966-67; resident U. Va., Charlottesville, 1967-68; resident Henry Ford Hosp., Detroit, 1968-70, chief resident, 1969-70; practice medicine specializing in dermatology, Fort Lauderdale, 1972—; clin. asst. prof. dermatology, U. Miami (Fla.), 1972—. Served to maj. M.C., U.S. Army, 1970-72. Diplomate Am. Bd. Dermatology. Fellow Am. Acad. Dermatology, Am. Coll. Cryosurgery; mem. Am., Fla., So., Broward County (sec.) med. assns., Miami, Broward County (sec.) dermatol. assns., Phi Beta Kappa, Alpha Omega Alpha. Contbr. articles on dermatology to med. jours. Office: 4750 N Federal Hwy Fort Lauderdale FL 33308

STEWART, SAM, chem. co. exec.; b. Bryn Mawr, Pa., July 27, 1951; d. Robert S. and Ruth D. S.; B.S., Finch Coll., 1972. Mem. sales staff Page & Biddle Co., Bryn Mawr, 1972, mgr., 1972-73; with Annandale Corp., Charlotte, N.C., 1973—, v.p., 1975, asst. to pres., 1975—. Office: 11750 Fruehauf Dr Charlotte NC 28217

STEWART, VINCENT EUGENE, artist; b. N.Y.C., May 13, 1929; s. Thomas Vincent and Margaret Mary (Mahoney) S.; student Art Students' League, N.Y.C., 1949-51, Cooper-Union, N.Y.C., 1949-51, Sch. Cartoonists and Illustrators, N.Y.C., 1950-51; m. Roberta Shannon, Sept. 20, 1970. Illustrator Blue Book Mag., N.Y.C., 1949, N.Y. Times, 1950, Colliers Mag., 1950, Seventeen Mag., 1951; instr. graphics Corcoran Sch. Art, Washington, 1968-71; alt. instr. Columbia (Md.) Inst., 1969-71; owner, operator Potomac Graphics Soc., Vienna, Va., 1971—; one-man shows: Margaret Dicky Gallery, Washington Tchrs. Coll., 1968, Lipman's Gallery, Silver Spring, Md., 1969, Patrick Henry Gallery, Vienna, Va., 1971, Antioch Coll., Columbia, Md.; represented in permanent collection: Nat. Gallery of Art. Roman Catholic. Home and office: Vienna VA 22180

STEWART, WALTER BINGHAM, educator; b. Evanston, Ill., Aug. 15, 1913; s. Walter Morgan and Elizabeth (Bingham) S.; student U. Ill., 1932-33, Northwestern U., 1939-40, U. Wis., 1961-63, Upper Iowa U., 1962-63; A.B., U. N.C., 1938; B.S., Radford Coll., 1964; postgrad. U. Fla., 1966-68; m. Janie Veda Sinclair, July 3, 1938; children—Sinclair, Donald. Account exec. Erwin, Wasey, Chgo., 1939-40; advt. mgr. Parker Pen Co., Janesville, Wis., 1940-44; sales and advt. mgr. Louis Melind Co., Chgo., 1945-47; advt. mgr. Reynolds Pen Co., Chgo., 1947-50; advt. mgr. H.W. Gossard Co., Chgo., 1950-61; mgr. Travelmats-Press Pub. Co., Prairie du Chien, Wis., 1961-63; chmn. journalism dept. Radford (Va.) Coll., 1965-67, 69-78; dean Sch. Liberal Arts, Embry-Riddle Aero. Inst., 1967-69, prof., 1978—; editor Radford Messenger, 1970-78; freelance newspaperman; advt. cons. to Western Auto Stores, Travel Bur. Fla.; radio broadcaster. Mem. Soc. Coll. Journalists (Pi Delta Epsilon-Alpha Phi Gamma) (nat. v.p. 1975-77), Kappa Delta Pi, Phi Delta Kappa, Phi Gamma Delta. Rotarian. Author: Do You Pass the Model Test, 1957; Do You Dress Like a Model, 1958; Do You Have a Model Figure, 1959; Adventures in Travel, 1962; The Complete Book of Modeling, 1974. Home: 2828 N Atlantic Ave 401 Daytona Beach FL 32018

STEWART, WILLIAM, chemist; b. New Orleans, Oct. 12, 1901; s. Thomas David and Lilly (Boone) S.; B.S., Tulane U., 1921; grad. student U. Chgo., 1936, Northwestern U., 1937; m. Claire Yvonne Philippi, Nov. 10, 1934. Chemist, Cuban Canadian Sugar Co., 1921-22; with Swift & Co., 1923-66, chief chemist Southeastern div., 1946-66; chief chemist Meeker Sugar Mill, LeCompte, La., 1968-73; part-time tchr., sugar researcher La. State U., Baton Rouge, 1972-73; research sugar cane sampling Am. Sugar Cane League, 1974; chief chemist sugar cane core sampling St. Martin Sugar Coop., St. Martinsville, La., 1975—. Recipient Smalley award Am. Oil Chemists Soc., 1954, 61, 66. Address: 218 Tennyson Cove Picayune MS 39466

STICHT, JOSEPH PAUL, indsl. exec.; b. Clairton, Pa., Oct. 3, 1917; s. Joseph Paul and Adah (Montgomery) S.; A.B., Grove City Coll., 1939, LL.D. (hon.); postgrad. U. Pitts.; m. Alta Ferne Cozad, Oct. 19, 1940; children—David S., Mark D. With U.S. Steel Co., 1939-44, TWA-ATC Internat., 1944-48; asst. to pres. Campbell Soup Co., 1948-49, v.p., 1949-57; pres. Campbell Soups Internat., 1957-60; exec. v.p., Federated Dept. Stores, Inc., 1960-65, vice-chmn., 1965-67, pres., 1967-72, also dir.; chmn. exec. com. R.J. Reynolds Industries, Inc., 1972-73, pres., chief operating officer, 1973-78, pres., chief exec. officer, 1978-79, now chmn., chief exec. officer, also dir.; dir. Celanese Corp., Wachovia Bank and Trust Co., Wachovia Corp., Foremost-McKesson, Inc., S.C. Johnson & Son, Inc. Trustee, Old Salem, Grove City Coll., Rockefeller U.; bd. visitors Med. Center and Sch. Bus., Duke U.; mem. M.I.T. Corp.; bd. govs. Corp. Fund Performing Arts at Kennedy Center; mem. N.C. Bus. Council on Arts and Humanities. Mem. Conf. Bd. (sr.), Council on Fgn. Relations, Com. Econ. Devel. (trustee), N.C. Council on Mgmt. and Devel. (chmn.). Presbyn. Clubs: Rotary, Queen City (Cin.); Lost Tree (North Palm Beach, Fla.); Links (N.Y.C.), Old Town (Winston-Salem, N.C.). Office: R J Reynolds Industries Inc PO Box 2959 Winston-Salem NC 27102

STICKNEY, ROBERT ROY, aquaculturist; b. Mpls., July 2, 1941; s. Roy Eldon and Helen Doris (Nelson) S.; B.S., U. Nebr., 1967; M.A., U. Mo., 1968; Ph.D., Fla. State U., 1971; m. LuVerne Carolan Whiteley, Dec. 29, 1961; children—Robert Roy II, Marolan Margaret. Research asso., asst. prof. Skidaway Inst. Oceanography, Savannah, Ga., 1971-75; asst. prof. wildlife and fisheries scis. Tex. A&M U., College Station, 1975-78, asso. prof., 1978—; cons. Farmland Industries, Kansas City, Mo. Served with USAF, 1959-63. Mem. Inst. Am. Fisheries Research Biologists, Am. Fisheries Soc. (editorial bd. 1978-80), Am. Soc. Limnology and Oceanography, Internat. Oceanographic Found., World Mariculture Soc., Sigma Xi. Author: Principles of Warmwater Aquaculture, 1979; contbr. articles to profl. jours. Home: 1812 Hondo St College Station TX 77840 Office: Dept Wildlife and Fisheries Scis Tex A&M U College Station TX 77843

STIDHAM, SCOTT FILMORE, chem. co. exec.; b. Pensacola, Fla., Apr. 20, 1926; s. Harold Glen and Lena Scott S.; B. Indsl. Engring., N.C. State U., 1950; m. Norma Louise Williams, June 27, 1953; children—Susan Gayle, Scott Filmore. Indsl. engr. Dan River Mills, Danville, Va., 1950-53; indsl. engr. Reynolds Metals Co., Louisville, 1953-55, Grand Rapids, Mich., 1955-56, Richmond, Va., 1956-57, Phoenix, 1957-58, ops. mgr., Richmond, Va., 1958-64, exec. asst. to ops. v.p., 1964-69, adminstrv. mgr. sheet, plate, wire, rod, and bar div., 1969-72; gen. supt. phosphate ops. Texasgulf, Inc., Beaufort County, N.C., 1972-75; adminstrv. mgr. Texasgulf Chems. Co. div. Texasgulf, Inc., Raleigh, N.C., 1975—; city dir. N.C. Nat. Bank. Chmn. bd. Meredith Coll. Assos. 1979—, Raleigh chpt. Jr. Achievement, 1979-80; bd. dirs. various civic orgns. Served with U.S. Army, 1945-47. Recipient appreciation awards from various civic orgns. Mem. Am. Inst. Indsl. Engrs., Soc. Advancement of Mgmt., Raleigh C. of C. Democrat. Methodist. Clubs: Carolina Country, Rotary (Raleigh). Home: 3420 Landor Rd Raleigh NC 27609 Office: 3100 Glenwood Ave Raleigh NC 27622

STIEG, ROBERT WILSON, JR., ednl. adminstr.; b. Clintonville, Wis., Mar. 12, 1943; s. Robert Wilson and Jane Ellen (Gibson) S.; student Faculté Catholique de Lyon, 1964-65; B.S. in Fgn. Service, Georgetown U., 1966; m. Louise Fannie Blatt, Feb. 3, 1968. Novice, Communaute de Taize, 1963-66; research asso. R.R.Bowker Assos., Washington, 1966-67; tchr. Grafton Sch., Berryville, Va., 1967-68, asst. headmaster, 1968-70, headmaster, 1970—. Mem. exec. bd. Nat. Assn. of Pvt. Schs. for Exceptional Children, dir. 1973—, rec. sec., 1973-76, treas., 1976-78, v.p., 1978, pres., 1979—; mem. exec. bd. Va. Assn. Ind. Spl. Edn. Facilities, dir. 1973—, treas. 1973, v.p. 1974, chmn. membership services com., 1975, pres., 1977-79; mem. Va. Inter-Dept. Task Force on Licensure of Children's Residential Facilities, 1977—; mem. Va. Inter-Dept. Com. on Rate Setting, 1978—; mem. Interstate Consortium on Licensure of Children's Residential Facilities, 1978—. Mem. exec. bd. Shenandoah Area council Boy Scouts Am., 1974—, advancement chmn., 1978—. Mem. Northwestern Mental Health Assn. (dir. 1973—, treas. 1976-77, pres. 1978-79, state bd. 1978—), Orton Soc., Assn. for Children with Learning Disabilities, Council for Exceptional Children. Rotarian. Home: Route 2 Box 781 Front Royal VA 22630 Office: Box 469 Berryville VA 22611

STIFF, ASHBY GORDON, JR., educator, cons.; b. Balt., Oct. 18, 1930; s. Ashby Gordon and Mary Ellen (Waring) S.; A.B., Johns Hopkins U., 1951; M.S., Fla. State U., 1957. Mgmt. trainee Sheraton Corp. Am., Balt., 1956; mgmt. trainee Hotel Corp. Am., Washington, 1957; asst. mgr. Many Glacier Hotel, Glacier Park Co., Glacier, Mont., summer 1958, gen. mgr., 1959-60; gen. mgr. Canyon Village Yellowstone Park Co., Yellowstone Park, Wyo., summers 1961, 64, gen. mgr. Lake Hotel, summer 1962; dir. food, housing NDEA French Insts., Tallahassee, 1963; instr. Sch. Bus., Hotel Adminstrn. Fla. State U., Tallahassee, 1957-61, asst. prof., 1961-68, asso. prof., 1968—, dir. European study program, 1970—; partner Ashby Stiff & Assos., 1977—. Served with USAF, 1951-55. Named Ky. col. Mem. S.A.R. (past chpt. sec.-treas.), Soc. War 1812 in Md., Order First Families Va., Council Hotel, Restaurant and Instl. Edn. (mem. research com. 1968—, head research project new concepts comml. food edn. 1968, charter mem.), Soc. Hosts, League Hospitality Execs., Soc. Scullions (past pres.), AAUP, Navy League, Alpha Kappa Psi, Alpha Psi Omega, Lambda Chi Alpha. Club: Johns Hopkins (Balt). Publs. editor League Hospitality Execs., 1964—. Contbr. articles to profl. jours. Home: 203 N Meridian St Tallahassee FL 32301 Office: Dept Hotel Restaurant Adminstrn Florida State U Tallahassee FL 32306

STIGALL, LAVERNE JOHNSTON, program analyst; b. Miami, Fla., July 10, 1925; d. John B. Johnston and Lona (Moore) Johnston; B.B.A. cum laude, Memphis State U., 1971; M.S., U. Ark., 1977; m. Eugene E. Stigall, June 21, 1947; children—Lynda, Gerald, Kevin. With staff U.S. Navy, Naval Air Station, Millington, Memphis, 1948-80; instr. Sch. Bus. Memphis State U. 1978-80. Mem. AAUW, Am. Assn. Mil. Comptrollers, Am. Soc. Tng. and Devel., Am. Mgmt. Assn., Memphis State U. Alumni Assn., U. Ark. Alumni Assn. Republican. Methodist. Home: 4634 Normandy Ave Memphis TN 38117 Office: Chief Naval Tech Tng Naval Air Station Memphis Millington TN 38054

STILES, FREDERICK ARTHUR, mathematician; b. San Antonio, May 1, 1944; s. Aden Edmund and Dorothy (Thomson) S.; B.A., U. Tex., Austin, 1965, B.S., 1966, M.A. (NDEA Title IV Fellow), 1968, Ph.D., 1971. Tchr. mathematics, St. Mary's Hall, San Antonio, 1971-74, San Antonio Acad. of Tex., 1974-75; instr. mathematics evening div. San Antonio Coll., 1972—; chmn. dept. mathematics, Tex. Mil. Inst., San Antonio, 1977—; mathematics cons. to psychologist. Mem. Math. Assn. Am., Nat. Council Tchrs. Mathematics, NEA, Nat., Tex. State rifle assns., Nat. Muzzle-Loading Rifle Assn., Am. Def. Preparedness Assn., Nat. Assn. Watch and Clock Collectors, Mensa, Phi Kappa Phi, Phi Delta Kappa. Republican. Home: 5309 Boatman San Antonio TX 78219 Office: 800 College Blvd San Antonio TX 78209

STILES, MAX CARR, sch. counselor; b. Fairview, W.Va., Aug. 3, 1929; s. Arlie and Martha Beryl (Parrish) S.; B.S., U. Cin., 1954; postgrad. Fairmont State Coll., 1954-56; M.S., W.Va. U., 1967; m. Jerilynn Lucille Stover, Dec. 30, 1969; children—Melissa Annette, Amorette Christie. Furniture designer, art tchr., Rivesville, W.Va., 1956-68; guidance counselor Jennie Dean, Stonewall Jackson middle schs., Manassas, Va., 1968—; career resource counselor. Dir. Nat. Thespians; co-coordinator WNVT workshop on ednl. TV series for Prince William County; facilitator bldg. com. Rivesville Methodist Ch., 1957-59, ch. steward, 1957, mem. bldg. com. St. Thomas United Meth. Ch. Mem. Am. Personnel and Guidance Assn., Nat. Vocat. Guidance Assn., NEA, Va., Prince William County edn. assns. Republican. Illustrator: vocat. rehab. dept. W.Va. U., 1965-66; Book, 1966. Home: 10705 Lake Jackson Dr Manassas VA 22110 Office: 10100 Lomond Dr Manassas VA 22110

STILLE, EVELYN ELIZABETH (TRUSSELL), indsl. relations exec.; b. Lagrange, Ga., July 4, 1921; d. Daniel Coley and Winnie Mae (Phillips) T.; A.A., Lagrange Coll., 1942; diploma Druitt Sch. of Speech, 1953; diploma Patricia Stevens Modeling Sch., 1954; diploma Viviane Woodard Acad., 1963; cert. Ga. State U., 1959; m. Edward Jackson Stille, Aug. 21, 1942 (div. 1948); children—Deanna Lynn Stille Strickland, Fredrick Vaughn. Tchr. Hogansville (Ga.) Public Schs., 1943-51; exec. sec. and safety coordinator Atlanta Newspapers, Inc., 1951-64; office mgr., personnel dir. Manpower, Inc., Atlanta, 1964-65, also personnel dir., 1964-65; adminstrv. div. mgr. James Pair Personnel Service, Atlanta, 1965-66; personnel and indsl relations dir. Westab div. of Mead Corp., Atlanta, 1966-73, editor co. newsletter, 1970-73; personnel and indsl. relations dir., editor 9 plant newsletter Atlantic Envelope Co., 1973—. Mem. job placement and adv. com. Atlanta public schs., 1974-76; tchr. Jr. High Sunday Sch. Grace Ch., Atlanta, 1959-70, organizer and dir. Grace Drama Group, 1960-70; mem. Mayor's Com. for Manpower Area Planning, Atlanta, 1973-74; mem. Ga. Employment and Tng. Council, 1979-80. Mem. Adminstrv. Mgmt. Soc. (mem. speakers bur. 1975—, internat. coms. 1977—, asst. area 8 dir. 1978, pres. 1978-79, Merit award 1978), Indsl. Relations Assn., Ga. Bus. Industry and Trade (mem. indsl. relations com. 1974-76, cert. of Appreciation 1974), Atlanta Womens C. of C. (asso. editor of Action publ. 1974-75), Atlanta Personnel Club (chmn. safety com. 1970-71). Democrat. Methodist. Home: 3030 Castleton Way Marietta GA 30062 Office: 1700 Northside Dr NW PO Box 1267 Atlanta GA 30301

STILLWELL, WALTER BROOKS, JR., dentist; b. Savannah, Ga., Dec. 27, 1919; s. Walter Brooks and Jane Caroline (Shuptrine) S.; student U. Md., 1938-39; D.D.S., Balt. Coll. Dental Surgery, 1943; m. Selpha Theresa Everson, Sept. 17, 1945; children—Walter Brooks, Caroline Marie, Serena Everson. Individual practice dentistry, Balt., 1946-49, Savannah, 1949—, specializing in pedodontia, 1955—; mng. partner Shuptrine Co., drug mfg. co., Savannah, 1961—; pres. Stillwell, McCaslin, McCaslin, Savannah, 1970—. Mem. Ga. Bd. Dentistry, 1972-79; pres. Ga. Bd. Dentistry, 1976-77. Mem. Savannah Symphony Soc., Little Theatre of Savannah. Served to capt. Dental Corp, AUS, 1943-46. Fellow Am. Acad. Pedodontics, Ga. Dental Assn., Am. Coll. Dentists, Internat. Coll. Dentists, Southeastern Soc. Pedodontics, Ga. Soc. Pediatric Dentistry, Savannah Dental Soc. (pres. 1955-56), ADA, Southeastern Dist. Dental Soc. (pres. 1964), Ga. Soc. Dentistry for Children (pres. 1969), S.R., Soc. Colonial Wars in Ga. Baptist (deacon 1952—). Clubs: Civitan, Savannah Yacht, Savannah Golf, Chatham, Cotillion. Home: 1 Marsh Dr Savannah GA 31404 Office: 211 E 31st St Savannah GA 31401 also 5901 Abercorn St Savannah GA 31405

STILTZ, HARRY LANGLEY, housing cons. co. exec.; b. Hereford, Md., Aug. 7, 1920; s. Emory Holton and Mamie (Langley) S.; student U. Chattanooga, 1948-49; B.S. in Elec. Engring., U. Tenn., 1951; postgrad. Columbia Theol. Sem., 1974-77; m. Mary Alleen, June 9, 1965; 1 dau., Lea Ann. Project engr. E.I. du Pont de Nemours & Co., Inc., Chattanooga, asst. prof. U. Chattanooga, 1951-53; field test engr. TVA, Chattanooga, 1953-56; project engr. Lockheed Ga. Co., Marietta, 1956-58, group engr., 1959-62; group engr. Martin Co., Orlando, Fla., 1958-59; pres., chmn. bd. dirs. Aerosci. Electronics, Inc., Atlanta, 1962-66; founded Aerospace Telementry Sch., Atlanta, 1962, dir., 1962-68; pres. Stiltz Sales & Engring. Co., Atlanta, 1966-68; research engr. Ga. Inst. Tech., 1968-69; sr. partner Manufactured Housing Cons., Atlanta, 1969—; v.p., gen. mgr. W.P. Atkinson Industries, Inc., Shawnee, Okla., 1969-71; v.p., gen. mgr. TBR Homes, Inc., Pelham, Ga., 1972-73; div. mgr. C.O. Smith Industries, Inc., Moultrie, Ga., 1973—; ordained to ministry Presbyn. Ch., 1977; pastor Fairfield Highlands Presbyn. Ch. Bd. dirs. Orchid Bowl Assn., Chattanooga, 1947-48; neighborhood commr. Boy Scouts Am., Marietta, 1960-62. Served with USAAF, 1942-45. Recipient Gen. Electric Zero Defects award Aerosci. Electronics, Inc., 1966. Registered profl. engr., Tenn., Ga., Okla. Mem. I.E.E.E., Instrument Soc. Am., V.F.W., Eta Kappa Nu, Tau Beta Pi. Presbyn. Author, editor: Aerospace Telemetry, vol. I, 1962, vol. II, 1966. Home: 903 11th Ave Birmingham AL 35228

STILWELL, WILLIAM EARLE, III, psychologist, educator; b. Cin., July 28, 1936; s. William Earle and Frances (Hunt) S.; A.B., Dartmouth, 1958; M.S., San Jose State Coll., 1966; Ph.D., Stanford, 1969; m. Doris Ann Nowak, June 7, 1969; children—Jane Belen, William Earle IV. Vocat. psychologist div. psychiat. vocat. services Dept. Mental Health, San Carlos, Calif., 1966-68; research psychologist Am. Insts. Research, Palo Alto, Calif., 1967-69; asst. prof. U. Ky. at Lexington, 1969-74, asso. prof., 1974—; cons. to sch. systems, Ky., 1972, W.Va., 1973-76, Va., 1974, Ark., 1976; v.p., dir. Ednl. Skills Devel., 1971—; cons., mem. Am. Psychol. Assn. accreditation team U. Fla., 1979, U. Iowa, 1980. Served with Intelligence Corps, USNR, 1960-63, comdr. Res., 1965—. Lic. psychologist, Ky. Mem. Am., Ky. psychol. assns., Am. Ednl. Research Assn. (chmn. nominating com. counseling and human devel. div. 1974, v.p. div. 1980—), Ky. Sch. Counselors Assn. (v.p. 1979-80), Am. Sch. Counselors Assn., Nat. Vocat. Guidance Assn., Assn. Counselor Edn. and Supervision, AAAS, Am., Ky. personnel and guidance assns., Res. Officers Assn. U.S.A. (life), Naval Res. Assn., Stanford U. Alumni Assn. (life), Hon. Order Ky. Cols., Psi Chi, Phi Delta Kappa. Co-author: Psychology for Teachers and Students, 1980; contbr. articles and revs. to profl. jours. Home: 1919 Williamsburg Rd Lexington KY 40504

STIMSON, RICHARD ALDEN, educator, fin. cons.; b. Hamden, Conn., Jan. 18, 1923; s. Frank Giles and Susie Alden (Brown) S.; B.A., Yale, 1943; postgrad. Am. U., Biarritz, France, 1945, Yale, 1947-50; M.S.M., Fla. Internat. U., 1976; postgrad. U. N.C., 1978—; m. Joan Daffodil Crabb, Apr. 19, 1947; 1 son, Richard Edgar Frank. Research asso., State of Conn., Hartford, 1946-50; exec. dir. state council for Pa. Fair Employment Practices Commn., Harrisburg, 1950-51; dir. pub. information Fedn. Protestant Welfare Agys., N.Y.C., 1951-52; asst. dir. pub. relations Am. Inst. C.P.A.'s, N.Y.C., 1952-56; asst. exec. dir. Am. Textbook Pubs. Inst., N.Y.C., 1956-59; pres. Stimson Asso., Pub. Relations, N.Y.C., 1959-64; exec. asst. communications Price Waterhouse & Co., N.Y.C., 1960-64; pub. relations dir. Wool Bur., Inc., N.Y.C., 1964-69; account mgr. Kofoed Pub. Relations Assos., Hollywood, Fla., 1969-70; pres. Stimson Assos., Inc., Ft. Lauderdale, Fla., 1970—; asst. prof. Sch. Bus. Adminstrn. and Econs., High Point (N.C.) Coll., 1977-79; treas. info. Council on Fabric Flammability, 1967-68, vice chmn., 1968-69; cons. ednl. relations Jones, Brakeley & Rockwell, Inc., N.Y.C., 1961-64; adviser U.S. Army Information Sch., Ft. Slocum N.Y., 1962. Treas., Council for Edn., Valley Stream, L.I., N.Y., 1954; v.p., trustee dist. 13 Bd. Edn., Valley Stream, 1955-58. Served with AUS, 1943-46; ETO; maj. U.S. Army Res. ret. Mem. Pub. Relations Soc. Am. (charter mem. counselors sect.), AAUP, Fla. Pub. Relations Assn. (state dir. 1971-75). Unitarian. Contbg. editor Pub. Relations Quar., 1963-72. Home: PO Box C Misenheimer NC 28109 Office: Sch Bus Adminstrn and Econs Pfeiffer College Misenheimer NC 28109

STINSON, LEE ROY, mfg. co. exec.; b. Ft. Worth, Jan. 18, 1937; s. Lee Roy and Agnes Inez S.; B.B.A., Brantley Draughon Coll., Ft. Worth, 1971; ed. Tex. Christian U., 1963; postgrad. Tarrant County Jr. Coll., Ft. Worth, 1974-75; m. Cherald Glennis Penrod, May 10, 1962; children—Kirby Lee, David Brent. Mem. dept. prodn. control Lennox Industries, Inc., Ft. Worth, 1956-67; prodn. mgr. Bell Helicopter, Ft. Worth, 1967-72; S.W. div. gen. mgr. Hancock-Gross Industries, Inc., Ft. Worth, 1972—; sponser vocat. office edn. Haltom High Sch. Bd. dirs. YMCA, Ft. Worth, 1970-76. Democrat. Baptist. Club: Masons. Home: 5428 Mallory St Haltom City TX 76117 Office: 2524 White Settlement Rd Fort Worth TX 76107

STIPE, JOHN R., fin. exec.; b. Batesville, Ark., Oct. 14, 1930; s. Ryburn Irvin and Ethel L. (Martin) S.; B.S. in Agr., U. Ark., 1953, postgrad. 1954-55; m. Mary Ann Cato, Dec. 19, 1958; children—Richard M., Roger W. Asst. county agt. St. Francis County, Ark., 1954-56, asso. county agt., 1956-58; with Forrest City (Ark.) Prodn. Credit Assn., 1959—, pres., 1967—. Mem. Ark. Adv. Council for Gifted and Talented Children, 1979—; sec. St. Francis County Fair Assn., 1954—; deacon, Sun. sch. supt. First Bapt. Ch., Forrest City, 1957—. Served to capt. Army N.G., 1947-67. Mem. Forrest City C. of C. (dir. 1977-80), Ark. Prodn. Credit Assn. (pres. 1967—), Am. Inst. Coop. and Farm Burs., Am. Soybean Assn., Rice Council, Agr. Council of Ark. Democrat. Baptist. Clubs: Rotary, Masons, Gideon.

STIREWALT, JOHN NEWMAN, coal co. exec.; b. Springfield, Ill., July 14, 1931; s. Newman Claude and Genevieve (Henton) S.; A.B., U. Miami (Fla.), 1953; grad. exec. program, Carnegie Mellon U., 1978; m. Joan McCarthy, Dec. 26, 1957; children—Genevieve, Janice, James, Christopher. Sales rep. Kaiser Aluminum Co., 1956-63; with Consol. Coal Co., 1963-79, asst. v.p., 1976-79; v.p. mktg. Y&O Coal Co. div. Panhandle Eastern Co., Martins Ferry, Ohio, 1979—. Served with AUS, 1954-56. Mem. Mich. Coal and Rail Assn., Ill. Mining Inst., Sigma Chi (life). Club: Wheeling Country. Home: Glenwood Rd Wheeling WV 26003 Office: PO Box 1000 St Clairsville OH 43950

STIRZAKER, NORBERT ARTHUR, educator; b. Lorain, Ohio, July 20, 1928; s. Herbert Aidan and Sara (Smith) S.; B. Mus. Edn., Murray State U., 1950; M.M., Ind. U., 1951; M.Ed., U. Miss., 1957, Ed.D., 1958; m. Mildred Elizabeth Parsons, July 28, 1951; children—Kim Elizabeth, Thomas Duncan, Ellen Ann, Amy Grace. Band dir., supr. music Holland (Mo.) Pub. Schs., 1951-52, band dir., county supr. music Brownsville (Tenn.) Pub. Schs., 1954-56; head dept. social scis., prof. edn. Rio Grande (Ohio) Coll., 1958-59; asst. supr. course programs U. Mich. Extension Service, Ann Arbor, 1959-61; dir. div. extended services, asst. prof. edn. Ind. State U., Terre Haute, 1961-67; chief adminstrv. officer Ind. State U. at Evansville, 1965-67; dir. U. S.C. at Spartanburg, 1967-73, asso. prof. ednl. adminstrn., 1973—. Co-founder, asst. sec. Spartanburg County Elementary Sch. Adminstrs. Study Council. Mem. Spartanburg City Long Range Planning Com., 1969-76. Bd. dirs. Spartanburg chpt. United Fund, 1969-72, Charles Lea Center, Spartanburg; chmn. bd. dirs. Speech and Hearing Clinic, Spartanburg, 1969-71. Served with AUS, 1952-54. W.K. Kellogg research fellow, 1956-58. Mem. C. of C. Greater Spartanburg (dir. 1972-75), So. Regional Council on Ednl. Adminstrn., Sigma Pi Mu, Kappa Delta Pi, Phi Mu Alpha, Phi Delta Kappa. Rotarian. Contbr. articles to profl. jours. Home: 527 Royal Oak Dr Spartanburg SC 29302 Office: Univ SC Spartanburg SC 29303

STIVERS, THEODORE EDWARD, bus. exec.; b. Cleveland, Tenn., Jan. 26, 1920; s. Theodore E. and Eulalee (Rose) S.; B.S., Kans. State U., 1941; m. Sara Jane Reid, Aug. 8, 1942; children—Samuel Reid, Karen Elaine, Joanne Elizabeth; m. 2d Mary Jackson Berry, May 24, 1973. Flour miller Theodore Stivers Milling Co., Rome, Ga., 1938-40; trainee Quaker Oats Co., Sherman, Tex., 1941, research mgr., Akron, Ohio, 1945-53; cons. engr., pres. T.E. Stivers Assos., Inc., Decatur, Ga., 1953—. Mem. Ga. Bd. Registration for Profl. Engrs. and Land Surveyors, chmn., 1972, 77, vice chmn., 1976, 79. Republican precinct committeeman, Atlanta, 1961-62. Served to lt. USNR, 1942-45. Registered profl. engr. Calif., Ga., Fla., Tenn., S.C., La., Miss., Mo., Ark., Colo., Del., Hawaii, Iowa, Kans., Ky., Maine, N.C., N.D., Pa., R.I., Utah, Vt., Va., Wyo., S. Africa. Mem. Am. Soc. Agrl. Engrs. (sr.), Cons. Engrs. Council Ga. (pres. 1970), Am. Soc. Agrl. Cons. (pres. 1972-73), Am. Soc. Testing Materials, Nat. Council Profl. Service Firms (dir. 1973-77), Nat. Soc. Profl. Engrs., Nat. Council Engring. Examiners (pres. 1976-80), Am. Assn. Cereal Chemists, Assn. Operative Millers, Ga. Poultry Assn., Ga., Fla. feed assns. Methodist. Clubs: Decatur Executive; Atlanta Stadium, Atlanta City, Druid Hills (Atlanta); Capitol Hill (Washington). Home: PO Box 608 Decatur GA 30031 Office: 1452 Church St Decatur GA 30031

STOBIE, DAVID WILLIAM, actuary; b. Pietermaritzburg, South Africa, Jan. 19, 1933; s. Gordon Kellie and Margaret Merle (Skirving) S.; came to U.S., 1958; m. Victoria Ann Tether, Feb. 2, 1963; children—Thomas Anthony, Keith William, Peter David, Jennifer Marie, Paula Margaret. Actuarial clk. Norwich Union Life Ins. Soc., Eng. and South Africa, 1951-58; actuarial asso. Equitable Life Assurance Soc., N.Y.C., 1958-61, sr. procedures analyst, 1961-64; cons. actuary, data processing cons., Okla., Kans., 1965-73; asso. actuary Ins. Systems Am., Atlanta, 1973—. Mem. Am. Acad. Actuaries, Assn. Computing Machinery. Roman Catholic. Home: 1529 Brompton Ct Dunwoody GA 30338 Office: Ins Systems of Am 6855 Jimmy Carter Blvd Norcross GA 30071

STOBS, JAMES ROBERT, constrn. co. exec., artist; b. Logan, Iowa, Nov. 30, 1913; s. Matthew and Bonnie (Twiford) S.; B.F.A., U. Fla., 1937; m. Ruby Lee Wentworth, Mar. 5, 1939; children—James Robert II, Barbara Lee (Mrs. Fredrick Merrill Macy), Gayle Anne. Chmn. bd., founder Stobs Bros. Constrn. Co., Miami, Fla., 1937—; sec.-treas. Forming Services, Inc., Miami, 1965—; developer-promoter acreage ltd. partnerships. Built Internat. Oceanographic Found. Planet Ocean, S.C.M. Bldg., Addressograph-Multigraph Dist. Offices, Eastern Air Lines Computer Reservations Center, J.F. Kennedy Meml. Library, Hialeah Sr. High Sch. (all Miami); Pier House, Key West, Fla., psychotic children's unit J. Hillis Miller Hosp., Gaineville, Fla.; exhibited in group art shows Tri-County Fair, Tampa, Fla., Soc. Four Arts, Palm Beach, Fla., others; exhibited in one-man show Witt's Gallery, 1978; mem. North Miami Art League Jury, 1976, 77-78, Ann. Dade County Poincianna Art Exhbn., Jury, 1972, 73, others. Mem. Miami Shores (Fla.) Planning Bd., 1950-53; v.p. Progress for Dade County, Inc., 1977-78. Recipient Blue Ribbon, Tri-County Fair, Tampa, 1936, cash prize Soc. Four Arts Exhbn., Palm Beach, 1937, Art award Am. Heritage Bicentennial, 1976, also others. Mem. Asso. Gen. Contractors (Safety award 1968-72, treas. nat. conv. 1952), Dade County Grand Jury Assn., Internat. Soc. Artists/U.S.A., Internat. Platform Assn., Miami Shores C. of C. (dir. 1976—), Greater Miami C. of C. (legis. action com.), Delta Sigma Phi. Republican. Presbyterian (deacon 1961-63). Clubs: Miami Shores Country (chmn. social com. 1979), Kiwanis (dir. 1977—). Home: 429 NE 101st St Miami Shores FL 33138 Office: 7010 NE 4th Ct Miami FL 33138

STOCKDELL, KENNETH GAYLE, SR., audiologist, educator; b. Sellersburg, Ind., July 3, 1929; B.S. in Bacteriology, Purdue U., 1953; postgrad. U. Ky., 1956-58; M.S. in Audiology and Speech Pathology, Vanderbilt U., 1960, postgrad., 1969-71; postgrad. U. Okla., 1965-66; m. Jo Ann Higgs, May 28, 1955; children—Kenneth Gayle, Rebecca Joan, Nancy Lynne. Clin. audiologist VA Regional Office, Louisville, Ky., 1960-61; dir. Audiology Clinic, Minot (N.D.) State Coll., 1961-65; asso. prof. audiology N.D. U., Fargo, 1965-69, head dept. audiology and speech pathology, 1966-69; mem. med. staff Neuropsychiat. Inst. and Hosp., Fargo, N.D., 1968-69; cons. audiologist Cloverbottom Hosp. and Sch., Nashville, Tenn., 1969-71; asst. prof. audiology Middle Tenn. State U., Murfreesboro, 1971—, adminstr. Speech and Hearing Clinic, 1972—; cons. to various hosps. in N.D., 1966-69; propr., dir. Ken Stockdell & Assos., Murfreesboro, 1971—; dir. Hearing Aid Specialists Workshop, Murfreesboro, 1975-77; coordinator Stuttering Workshop, 1975. Chmn. Mayor's Com. on Employment of Handicapped, Minot, N.D., 1963-65; mem. Gov.'s Com. on Employment of Handicapped, Minot, 1962-65, State Mental Health Planning Com., N.D., 1965; mem. adv. bd. Opportunity Sch., Fargo, N.D., 1966. Faculty research grantee Middle Tenn. State U., 1973-74, 78. Mem. N.D. Speech and Hearing Assn. (pres. 1964-65), Am. Speech and Hearing Assn. (del. to house state dels. 1963-64), Acad. Rehab. Audiology (mem. task force 1972-75) editor jour. 1978—), Internat. Platform Assn., Tenn. Speech and Hearing Assn., So. Audiol. Soc. Club: Sertoma (Gem award 1965). Contbr. articles on audiology to profl. jours. Office: Speech and Hearing Clinic Middle Tenn State Univ Murfreesboro TN

STOCKING, HOBART EBEY, geologist, educator; b. Clarendon, Tex., Nov. 16, 1906; s. Jerome Daniel and Sarah Maria (Ward) S.; student Clarendon Jr. Coll., 1925-27, U. Tex., 1928; M.A., Johns Hopkins, 1938; Ph.D., U. Chgo., 1949; m. Helen Berenice Smith, Aug. 25, 1934; children—Sarah (Mrs. Abdelkader Ben Bouchta), Martha, Topographic engr. Companhia de Petroleo de Angola, Portuguese W. Africa, 1929-31; asst. geologist U.S. Geol. Survey, 1933-34; geologist Shell Petroleum Co., Midland, Tex., 1936-38; asst. prof. W.Va. State U., Morgantown, 1940-43; chief geologist Dist. 1, Petroleum Adminstrn. War, 1943-45; State Dept. vis. prof. U. Costa Rica, 1945-46; prof. geology Okla. State U., Stillwater, 1946-52, 58—; chief geologist Grand Junction div., AEC, 1954-58, chief Argentine Mission, 1958; prof. Johns Hopkins, summer 1962-73; Distinguished lectr. Am. Assn. Petroleum Geologists, 1956. Dist. coordinator Common Cause, 1973-75. Named hon. prof. U. Costa Rica, 1948; scholar Johns Hopkins, 1932. Fellow AAAS, Geol. Soc. Am. Author: The Road to Santa Fe, 1971; also articles. Home: 108 Berry St Stillwater OK 74074

STOCKTON, ERNEST LOONEY, coll. pres.; b. Lebanon, Tenn., Aug. 27, 1917; s. Ernest Looney and Katherine (White) S.; B.A., Cumberland U., 1939, LL.D. (hon.), 1958; M.A., George Peabody Coll., 1947, postgrad., 1952-54; postgrad. Vanderbilt U., 1952-54; L.H.D. (hon.), Okla. Christian Coll., 1971; m. Bettye Truman Hatfield, July 10, 1942; 1 dau., Bettye Sharon. Tchr. English, asst. coach Castle Heights Mil. Acad., Lebanon, 1939-42, tchr. English, 1945-51, dir. guidance, 1950-53, dir. admissions, 1951-53, v.p., 1957-58, headmaster, 1958; pres. Cumberland Coll. of Tenn., 1958—; trustee Cordell Hull Found. Internat. Edn., 1978—. Nat. bd. dirs. U.S. Jr. C. of C., 1948-49; pres. Tenn. Jaycees, 1949-50; chmn. Tenn. March of Dimes, 1947. Served to lt. USCG, 1942-45. Rotary Internat. Paul Harris fellow, 1977. Mem. Am. Assn. Jr. Colls. (commn. on legis. 1971-74), Nat. Council Ind. Jr. Colls. (commn. on legis. 1971, dir. 1977—), So. Assn. Community and Jr. Colls. (pres. 1974-75), Tenn. Coll. Assn. (pres. 1974-75), Tenn. Council Pvt. Colls. (chmn. 1976-78), Wilson County C. of C. (dir. 1978—). Presbyterian. Club: Rotary (pres. club 1961-62, dist. gov. 1967-68). Office: Cumberland Coll Lebanon TN 37087

STOCKTON, EUGENE, counselor for deaf; b. Wagoner, Okla., Jan. 31, 1918; s. Roy Milbern and Emma Jane (Barrick) S.; B.A., U. Tulsa, 1951; M.S., Fla. State U., 1968; m. Regna Grace Aabel, Aug. 31, 1946; 1 son, Eugene Reede. With Tulsa Pub. Co., 1951-56; state mgr. Fla. Pub. Co., 1956-66; counselor for deaf Fla. Vocat. Rehab., Jacksonville, 1967—. Served with U.S. Navy, 1936-45. Named Outstanding Counselor in Community Service Programs, 1971; Dist., State and Regional Counselor of Year Nat. Rehab. Counseling Assn., 1976. Mem. Nat., Fla. assns. for deaf. Home: 6823 Waikiki Rd Jacksonville FL 32216 Office: 1325 San Marco Ave Jacksonville FL 32207

STOCKTON, ROBERT LOUIS, physician, surgeon; b. Bethany, Okla., June 12, 1932; s. Frank Howard and Lola Bess (Abbott) S.; B.S., Okla. Central State U., Edmond, 1955; M.D., U. Okla., 1959; m. Sylvia Zoe Davis, Aug. 31, 1957; children—Sheryl Kay, Scott Alan. Intern, Baylor U. Med. Center, Dallas, 1959-60, resident gen. surgery, 1960-61; resident neurol. surgery U. Tex. Southwestern Med. Sch., Dallas, 1961-66, clin. instr., jr. attending, 1970—; practice medicine, specializing in neurol. surgery, Ft. Worth and Waco, Tex., 1966—. Bd. dirs. Waco Municipal Airport, 1976-77. Served to col. M.C. Tex. Army N.G., 1949—. Diplomate Am. Bd. Neurol. Surgery. Fellow A.C.S.; mem. Am. Assn. Neurol. Surgeons, Congress Neurol. Surgeons, Univ. Assn. Emergency Med. Services, Aerospace Med. Assn., U.S. Army Flight Surgeons Assn., So. Neurosurgeon Soc., Tex. Neurosurgical Soc., Assn. U.S. Mil. Surgeons, AMA, Tex. Med. Assn. (mem. disaster med. care com. 1970—, chmn. 1979—), McLennan County Med. Soc. Baptist. Home: 4617 Scottwood St Waco TX 76708 Office: Box 3188 824 N 18th St Waco TX 76707

STOCKWELL, BENJAMIN EUGENE, lawyer; b. Oklahoma City, Aug. 28, 1931; s. Benjamin Paul and Anna (Cunningham) S.; B.A., U. Okla., 1952, LL.B., 1956; m. Marjorie Ethel Ribble, Apr. 4, 1952; children—Margaret Lynn, David Alan. Admitted to Okla. bar, 1956; practiced in Oklahoma City, 1956-60, Norman, Okla., 1961—; mem. firm Benedum and Stockwell, 1961-62; mem. firm Stockwell and Pence, 1970-77, Stockwell Law Offices, 1977—; asst. prof. law, legal adviser to pres.'s office U. Okla., 1960-61, now spl. lectr. Coll. Law; chmn. Okla. State Bd. Examiners Ofcl. Shorthand Reporters; mem. Okla. State Bd. Shorthand Reporters, 1971-76, chmn. 1974-76. Chmn. Cleveland County Bd. Health, 1963-64. Bd. dirs. Cleveland County Cancer Soc. Served to 1st lt. AUS, 1952-54. Mem. Okla. State (mem. exec. council 1965—; chmn. spl. com. on implementation of jud. reform amendments 1967; v.p. 1969), Cleveland County (past pres.) bar assns., Okla. Inst. for Justice, Order of Coif, Pi Kappa Alpha, Pi Gamma Mu. Episcopalian. Mason; mem. Order DeMolay. Home: 1201 Lee St Norman OK 73069 Office: 119 E Main St Norman OK 73069

STODDARD, NAN, oil co. exec.; b. Shreveport, La., Feb. 11, 1936; d. James Henry and Cora L. (Tucker) Boddie; student Centenary Coll., 1964-65; m. Donald Lane Stoddard, June 15, 1956; 1 dau., Peggy Sue. Acct., Lyons Petroleum, Shreveport, 1964-69; asst. controller Transcontinental Oil Corp., Shreveport, 1976—; corp. insp. Diamond Coal Co., Inc. ann. meetings, 1973-77, Transcontinental Oil Corp. ann. meetings, 1970—. Mem. Nat. Assn. Accts. Democrat. Baptist. Home: Route 2 Box 15 Shreveport LA 71109 Office: 1400 First Nat Bank Tower Shreveport LA 71101

STODGHILL, PATSY ANN, poet, educator; b. Heath, Tex., Feb. 1, 1935; d. William Curtis and Emma Lou (Lofland) Hall; B.S., N. Tex. State U., 1956; M.A., U. Tex., 1958; m. Donald Ray Stodghill, Mar. 27, 1959; children—Steven Hall, Sheri Sue. Tchr. English Dallas Ind. Sch. Dist., 1957-60, 61-65; coll. lectr., 1966-76; poet laureate of Tex., 1978-79. Lit. judge cultural arts program P.T.A., 1971-74; co-chmn. poetry, schs. program, Dallas County, 1971-72; chmn. poetry convs., Tex., 1973-74; lectr. reader poetry; participant creative writing workshops. Recipient over 50 nat. and state poetry prizes. Mem. Poetry Soc. Tex. (dir. 1970, 72-75, pres. 1976-80), Nat. Fedn. State Poetry Socs. (state presidents bd. 1976—), Tex. Assn. Creative Writing Tchrs., Internat., World poetry socs., Fine Arts Soc. Tex., Avalon Poets, Dallas Pen Women, A.A.U.W., Delta Kappa Gamma (chmn. personal growth devel. 1974-75). Author: Mirrored Images, 1975 (Nortex Press Book Publ. award 1974). Contbr. poetry to numerous anthologies and poetry mags. Address: 1424 Highland Rd Dallas TX 75218

STOECKER, PHILIP GEORGE, pharm. co. ofcl.; b. Phillips, Wis., Feb. 27, 1937; s. Gustave Eric and Katherine (Lavin) S.; B.A. in Bus. Adminstrn., U. Wis., 1962; m. Judy Lynn Ross; children—Sharon, John, Stephen, Mark. Sales rep. Western-So. Life Ins. Co., Milw., 1962-63, asso. sales mgr., 1963-67; sales rep. Reed & Carnrick Pharm. Co., Milw., 1967-70, div. mgr., Dallas, 1970-75, regional sales mgr., dir. tng. and mgmt. assessment programs, 1975—. Pres. parent-child program YMCA, Arlington, Tex.; asst. cubmaster Cub Scouts Am., Arlington. Served with U.S. Army, 1954-58. Mem. Nat. Soc. Pharm. Sales Trainers, Dallas Sales and Mktg. Execs. Methodist. Office: 2225 Randol Mill Suite 223 Arlington TX 76011

STOEHR, LEONARD ARTHUR, ops. research analyst; b. Oak Park, Ill., Aug. 11, 1929; s. Arthur Felix and Margaret Martha (Hinz) S.; B.A., Columbia, 1951; M.S., U.S. Navy Postgrad. Sch., 1967; m. Davsta Moore, May 28, 1954 (div. July 1977); children—Leonard Frederick, Katherine Lee. Commd. ensign U.S. Navy, 1951, advanced through grades to capt., 1972; comdr. minesweeper, 1954, submarine, 1964-66; ret., 1973; with Ops. Research, Inc., Silver Spring, Md.,

1973-77; sr. asso. Ketron Inc., 1977—. Decorated Meritorious Service medal. Mem. Ops. Research Soc. Am., Washington Ops. Research Council. Home: 1612 N Hartford St Arlington VA 22201 Office: 1700 N Moore St Arlington VA 22209

STOELZEL, WALLACE BLAKE, data processor; b. Denver, June 4, 1939; s. Ernest Joseph and Minnie (Wright) S.; B.A., U. No. Colo., 1961; M. Natural Sci. (NSF grantee), Ariz. State U., 1966; m. Rosemary C. Berka, June 3, 1961; children—Judith Gail, Daniel Mark. Tchr. math. and sci. Santa Maria (Calif.) schs., also Lompoc (Calif.) Fed. Correctional Inst., 1961-64; grad. asst. physics Ariz. State U., 1965-66; chmn. math.-sci. and indsl. tng. ARAMCO, Dhahran, Saudi Arabia, 1966-68, programmer-analyst, profl. devel. analyst, 1968-74; mgr. data processing Newspaper Printing Corp., El Paso, 1974-78; v.p., co-owner Dec-Plessey OEM, Kennedy Data Systems, Inc., El Paso, 1978—; owner A-AOOS, El Paso, 1979—. Served in Mil. Police, U.S. Army, 1957-58. Mem. Nat. Wildlife Assn. (life), E. African Wildlife Soc. Republican. Episcopalian. Home: 320 Sundown Pl El Paso TX 79912 Office: Kennedy Data Systems Inc El Paso TX 79901

STOESS, RAY HAMPTON, assn. exec.; b. PeeWee Valley, Ky., June 10, 1931; s. Carl Raymond and Margaret (Smith) S.; student U. Ky., 1949; U. Louisville, 1955-61; m. Donna Newcomb, June 22, 1951; children—Pamela, Janet, Sandra, Teri, Bucky. With Sealtest, Louisville, 1954-68, sales mgr. home service routemen, 1964-66, mgr. food store sales, 1966-68; asst. v.p. prodn. Hubbuch in Ky., Louisville, 1968-69; gen. mgr. Ramada Inn, Louisville, 1969-71; dir. sales Ramada Inn, Louisville, 1972; now exec. dir. Ky. Gasoline Dealers Assn., Inc.; exec. sec. Ky. Equipment Distbrs.; propr. Ray Stoess Liquors, Ray Stoess Seneca Bottle Shoppe; owner Olde Town Traders Dress Shop; also Louisville mgr. Ky. C. of C.; exec. dir. Ky. Sheriff's Boys and Girls Ranch. Chmn. Bluegrass Indsl. Park, Louisville, 1973-74. Chmn., City-County All-Star Football Game (Crippled Childrens Bowl), 1965; a founder Ky. Hall of Fame, Ky. State Fairgrounds, 1965; orginator, pres. Mini Bd. Assn. Atherton High Sch., Louisville, 1973-74; active Russell Area council Poverty Program. Served with USMC, 1950-54; Korea. Named retail salesman of year Sealtest, 1958, salesman of year, 1960-62, recipient Pres.'s Cup award, 1961; named outstanding young man in commerce and industry by bus. leaders Louisville, 1966, outstanding hotel salesman in Am., Wash. State U. chpt. Sigma Iota, also Hotel Sales Mgmt. Assn., 1975. recipient Flying Dutchman award Met. Parks & Recreation, 1969, Louisville Gen. Hosp. award for starring Pro-Celebrity Golf Tournament, 1971. Mem. Louisville (dir., 1965-66), Jefferstown (pres., 1973-74, chmn. gaslight festival 1974) chambers commerce, Am. Legion, V.F.W. Methodist. Contbg. editor Ky. Sportsworld mag. Home: 2367 Valley Vista Rd Louisville KY 40205

STOESSEL, CAROLE JEAN (MRS. ALEXANDER W. ZVONAR), physician, pianist; b. Salisbury, N.C., July 14, 1936; d. Frank William and India Beatrice (Aldredge) Stoessel; student piano with Raymond Lewenthal, 1954-55; B.A. magna cum laude, Catawba Coll., 1959; M.D. (Nancy Lybrook Lasater Reynolds scholar), Bowman Gray Sch. Medicine, Wake Forest U., 1963; m. Alexander W. Zvonar, Nov. 2, 1963. Concert pianist recitals, concerts, 1950-59, 71-75; various TV and radio appearances, 1950-55; intern pathology Columbia Presbyn. Med. Center, N.Y.C., 1963-64. resident fellow dept. microbiology, 1964-65; physician A.R.C. Bloodmobile unit, Rowan County, N.C., 1972-75. Dealer antique dolls, 1967—. Bd. dirs. Rowan County Democratic Women; trustee, mem. exec. com. Hist. Salisbury Found.; v.p. Residents of Old Salisbury. Mem. Children Am. Revolution, Historic Salisbury Found. (charter mem.; trustee, exec. com.), Residents of Old Salisbury (dir.). Democrat. Lutheran. Address: 329 S Fulton St Salisbury NC 28144

STOESSER, BRUCE CARLTON, urologist; b. Buffalo, July 5, 1942; s. Paul N. and Kathryn E. (Wolf) S.; B.A., Ohio Wesleyan U., 1964; M.D., SUNY, Buffalo, 1968; m. Linda Urmston, June 25, 1966; children—Mary Louise, William Carlton. Intern, resident in surgery Millard Fillmore Hosp., Buffalo, 1968-70; resident in urology U. Conn., Hartford, 1972-75; practice medicine specializing in urology, Tulsa, 1975—; instr. Okla. U., Tulsa Med. Sch., 1975—. Served to lt. comdr. M.C., USN, 1970-72. Fellow A.C.S.; mem. Am. Urol. Assn., AMA, Okla. State Med. Assn., Tulsa County Med. Soc. (sec.-treas. 1978-81). Republican. Presbyterian. Home: 3107 E 58th St Tulsa OK 74105 Office: 2325 S Harvard St Suite 307 Tulsa OK 74114

STOKE, CHARLES BEECHER, research analyst; b. Winchester, Va., Sept. 20, 1936; s. Irvin Franklin and Frances Ann (Hummer) S.; B.A., U. Va., 1963, M.Ed., 1965; m. Annie Sue Shelton, Aug. 17, 1968. Guidance counselor, instr. sci., coach Fork Union (Va.) Mil. Acad., 1965-66; guidance counselor Charlottesville (Va.) pub. schs., 1966-70; human factors research analyst Va. Hwy. and Transp. Research Council, Charlottesville, 1970—; baseball and soccer ofcl. and coach. Served with USNR, 1955-63. Mem. Am. Driver and Traffic Safety Edn. Assn. (sec. research div. 1973-74, vice chmn. 1974-75), Transp. Research Bd., Am. Psychol. Assn., U. Va. Student Aid Found., Kappa Delta Pi, Phi Delta Kappa. Author reports. Home: 2221 Greenbrier Dr Charlottesville VA 22901 Office: PO Box 3817 University Station Charlottesville VA 22903

STOKER, RUPERT RANDOLPH, bank dir., hardward mfg. co. exec.; b. Zephyr, Tex., Apr. 10, 1907; s. Edgar E. and Ellie Brown (Couch) S.; student So. Meth. U., 1942; m. Thelma Jo Cavitt, Sept. 1, 1935; children—Carolyn (Mrs. John T. Shinn), Lindley Randolph. Partner, Cavitt Store, Red Oak, Tex., 1935-42; co-mgr. quality control staff N.Am. Aviation, Dallas, 1942-47; pres. Trego Industries, Inc., Red Oak, 1947-79; dir. 1st Nat. Bank, Waxahachie. Active Ellis County Democratic Com. Mem. Ellis County Hist. Soc., Tex. Builders Hardware Club, Nat. Builders Hardware Assn. Mem. Christian Ch. (chmn. bd. stewardship 1966-79, worship com. 1965—). Lion. Club: Waxahachie Country. Home: 610 W Marvin St Waxahachie TX 65165 Office: Box 85 Red Oak TX 75154

STOKES, ARCH YOW, lawyer; b. Atlanta, Sept. 2, 1946; B.A., Emory U., 1967, J.D., 1970; m. Patricia Elaine Stokes; children—Jennifer Jean, Austin Christopher. Admitted to Ga. bar, 1970, U.S. Ct. Mil. Appeals, 1971; dep. asst. atty. gen. Ga., Atlanta, 1970; asso. firm Branch and Swann, Atlanta, 1973-75, partner, 1975-77; partner firm Stokes, Lazarus & Watson, Atlanta, 1977—. Served with USMCR, 1971-73. Mem. State Bar Ga., Am., Atlanta bar assns., Lawyers Club Atlanta, (editor-in-chief Atlanta Lawyer 1974-78) Omicron Delta Kappa, Phi Delta Phi, Sigma Alpha Epsilon. Methodist. Author: The Wage & Hour Handbook for Hotels, Restaurants and Institutions, 1978; The Equal Opportunity Handbook for Hotels, Restaurants and Institutions, 1979; mng. editor Emory Law Jour., 1969-70. Office: 3711 Roswell Rd Atlanta GA 30342

STOKES, BETTIE EUGENE GREEN, educator; b. New Orleans, July 18, 1907; d. Lawrence and Matilda (Taylor) Green; bus. diploma Dillard U., 1925; B.S., Tuskegee Inst., 1949, M.Ed., 1963; postgrad. Ohio State U., 1966; m. Gladstone Hodge, Jan. 9, 1944 (div. June 1948); m. Charles G. Stokes, Nov. 10, 1952. Clerical, adminstrv., sec. VA Hosp., Tuskegee, Ala., 1928-62; career devel. guidance Tuskegee Inst., 1964-71. Trustee, sec. bd. Greenwood Cemetery Assn., 1960-70. Mem. State Steering com. Ala. Women's Polit. Caucus, 1972-78, chmn., 1975-77; mem. Nat. Women's Polit. Caucus; Ala. chmn. Com. Fed. Employee Polit. Edn., 1975—; mem. human rights com. Ala. Prison System, 1976-77. Recipient Outstanding Performance award VA, 1958, Incentive award 1959. Mem. Coll. Personnel Assn., AAUW, Am. Fedn. Govt. Employees (local pres. 1950-52), NAACP (sec. Tuskegee br. 1944-46), ACLU, Civil Liberties Union Ala. (bd. dirs.), Nat., Ala. personnel and guidance assns., Southeastern Council on Family Relations, Tuskegee Civic Assn. Home: PO Box 477 Tuskegee Institute AL 36088

STOKES, CARL NICHOLAS, lawyer; b. Memphis, Jan. 26, 1907; s. John William and Edith Isabell (Burgess) S.; student Draughton's Bus. Coll., 1929-30; LL.B., U. Memphis, 1933; m. Laverne Judson, Aug. 21, 1930; 1 dau., Vicki Laverne (Mrs. Dennis Neff Koehn). Admitted to Tenn. bar, 1934; mem. firm Norvell & Monteverde, Memphis, 1934-38; with legal dept. Tenn. Unemployment Compensation Div., 1937-38; clk. City Ct. Memphis, 1938-42, Criminal Cts. Shelby County, 1946-50; judge City Ct. Memphis, 1950-52; mem. firm Shea & Pierotti, Memphis, 1952-62; v.p., gen. counsel Allen & O'Hara, Inc., Memphis, 1962-72; mem. firm McDonald, Kuhn, Smith, Gandy, Miller & Tait, Memphis, Stokes, Kimbrough, Grusin & Kizer, Memphis; dir. 1st Fed. Savs. and Loan Assn. Adv. bd. Salvation Army, chmn., 1973-75; trustee Shrine Sch. for Handicapped Children; trustee, tax atty. Shelby County. Served to capt., inf. AUS, 1942-46. Recipient award of merit Tenn. Bar Assn., 1958. Mem. Am., Tenn., Memphis and Shelby County bar assns., Memphis Estate Planning Council, Memphis Area C. of C. (chmn. welcome com. 1972-73). Mem. Christian Ch. (life elder). Mason (33 deg., K.T., Shriner), Kiwanian (pres. 1971-72, lt. gov. 1974-75). Home: 2237 Massey Rd Memphis TN 38138 Office: Law Offices Stokes Kimbrough Grusin & Kizer 6263 Poplar Towers Memphis TN 38138

STOKES, DEE HUNTINGTON, accountant; b. San Antonio, Oct. 1, 1943; s. Aldin Lowell and Wilma Susan (Redwine) S.; B.B.A. in Accounting, U. Tex., Austin, 1966; m. Janet Elaine Longway, June 6, 1970; children—Dee Huntington II, Justin Blair. From jr. accountant to staff accountant Collier, Johnson & Woods, C.P.A.'s, Corpus Christi, Tex., 1970-73; v.p., controller Weaver Potato Chip Co., Denver, 1973; partner Stokes Co., San Antonio, 1973-74; fin. analyst Mooney Aircraft Corp., Kerrville, Tex., 1974-75, mgr. acctg., 1975-78; controller Abilene (Tex.) facility Gen. Dynamics, 1978—. Active Boy Scouts Am. Served with USAF, 1966-70. C.P.A. Mem. Am. Inst. C.P.A.'s, Tex. Soc. C.P.A.'s. Baptist. Club: Kiwanis. Home: 2410 Glenwood Abilene TX 79605 Office: PO Box 1401 Abilene TX 79604

STOKES, EVERETT DONALD, physicist; b. Toledo, July 14, 1943; s. Thomas Jefferson and Mary Cassie (Pruitt) S.; B.S., Middle Tenn. State U., 1965; M.S., U. Ark., 1968, Ph.D., 1971; m. Cassandra Lynn Stokes, Cynthia Diane. Research asso. laser devel. Rice U., 1970-72; mem. tech. staff Texas Instruments Co., Dallas, 1972-74; vis. asst. prof. U. Okla., Norman, 1975-76; research asso. physics So. Meth. U., Dallas, 1976, research asst. prof., 1977—; co founder Solar Semiconductor Instruments, Dallas, 1977. NDEA fellow, 1966-70. Mem. Am. Phys. Soc., Sigma Xi, Sigma Pi Sigma. Democrat. Mem. Ch. of Christ. Contbr. articles to profl. jours. Home: 1940 Rambling Ridge Carrolton TX 75007 Office: So Meth U PO Box 472 Dallas TX 75275

STOKES, LEE DOUGLAS, psychologist; b. Rahway, N.J., Apr. 16, 1940; s. John Albert and Gladys Mildred (Eby) S.; B.A., Auburn U., 1968; M.A., La. State U., 1969, Ph.D., 1972; m. Mary Elizabeth Carter, Oct. 30, 1974; children—Edward Douglas, Thomas Andrew, Cara Lee, Melissa Anne. Asst. prof. psychology Southeastern La. U., Hammond, 1972-74; St. Joseph Sem. Coll., St. Benedict, La., 1973-75; staff psychologist SE La. Hosp., Mandeville, 1974—; dir. A Psychology Place, New Orleans, 1977—; cons. in field; dir. So. Imperial Coatings Corp. Served with U.S. Army, 1960-63. Licensed psychologist, La. Mem. Am. Psychol. Assn., Southeastern, Southwestern, La. psychol. assns., La. Acad. Scis. Roman Catholic. Contbr. articles to tech. jours. Office: 8237 1/2 Jefferson Hwy Harahan LA 70123

STOKES, MACK (MARION) BOYD, bishop; b. Wonsan, Korea, Dec. 21, 1911; s. Marion Boyd and Florence Pauline (Davis) S.; came to U.S., 1929; student Seoul Fgn. High Sch., Korea; A.B., Asbury Coll., 1932; B.D., Duke, 1935; postgrad. Boston U. Sch. Theology, 1935-37, Harvard, 1936-37; Ph.D., Boston U., 1940; LL.D., Lambuth Coll., Jackson, Tenn., 1963; D.D., Millsaps Coll., 1973; m. Ada Rose Yow, June 19, 1942; children—Marion Boyd III, Arch Yow, Elsie Pauline. Resident fellow systematic theology Boston U., 1936-38, Bowne fellow in philosophy, 1938-39; ordained to ministry Meth. Ch. as deacon, 1938, elder, 1940; vis. prof. philosophy and religion Ill. Wesleyan U., 1940-41; prof. Christian doctrine Candler Sch. Theology, Emory U., 1941-56, asso. dean, Parker prof. systematic theology, 1956-72, chmn. exec. com. div. of religion grad. sch., 1956-72, acting dean Candler Sch., 1968-69; elected bishop United Meth. Ch., 1972, now bishop, Jackson, Miss.; mem. faculty Inst. Theol. Studies, Oxford U., 1958, Del., Meth. Ecumenical conf., 1947, 52, 61, 71, Holston, Gen. confs., S.E. Jurisdictional Conf., 1956, 60, 64, 68, 72; chmn. com. ministry Gen. Conf. Meth. Ch., 1960; nat. com. Nature Unity We Seek, 1956—; mem. gen. com. ecumenical affairs theol. study com. United Meth. Ch., 1968-72, com. on Cath.-Meth. relations, 1969—. Mem. Am. Philos. Assn., Am. Acad. Religion, AAUP, Metaphys. Soc. Am., Theta Phi (nat. sec.), Pi Gamma Mu. Author: Major Methodist Beliefs, 1956; The Evangelism of Jesus, 1960; The Epic of Revelation, 1961; Our Methodist Heritage, 1963; Crencas Fundamentals Dos Methodistas, 1964; Study Guide on the Teachings of Jesus, 1970; The Bible and Modern Doubt, 1970; Major United Methodist Beliefs, 1971; Dialogues on John's Gospel, 1975; The Holy Spirit and Christian Experience, 1975; Jesus the Master Evangel, 1978; Can God See the Inside of an Apple?, 1979; The Bible in Wesleyan Heritage, 1979; Questions Asked by United Methodists, 1980. Address: PO Box 931 Jackson MS 39205

STOKES, MARION BOYD, III, lawyer, author; b. Atlanta, May 3, 1943; s. Marion Boyd and Ada Rose (Yow) S.; B.A., Emory U., 1964, J.D., 1967; postgrad. Mercer U. Law Sch., Macon, Ga., 1964-65; m. Vickie Maria, Dec. 1, 1973; 1 dau., Elizabeth Rose. Admitted to Ga. bar, 1968; asso. firm Maley & Crowe, Atlanta, 1968-69, partner, 1969-72; partner firm Stokes, Lazarus & Watson and predecessor firm, Atlanta, 1972—. Served with USMC, 1967-68; from lt. (j.g.) to lt. Judge Adv. Gen. Corps, USNR, 1968-73. Recipient U.S. Law Week award; Am. Jurisprudence award in field of unfair trade practices, 1967. Mem. Am., Ga., Atlanta bar assns., Assn. Trial Lawyers Am., Ga. Trial Lawyers Assn., Comml. Law League Am., Conf. Bankruptcy Judges, Union Internationale des Avocats, Phi Delta Phi. Republican. Methodist. Author: The Seller's Credit Guide, 1977. Office: 3711 Roswell Rd Atlanta GA 30342

STOKES, OSCAR BARKER, city mgr.; b. Durham, N.C., Aug. 28, 1928; s. Oscar Montague and Arline Bernice Feezor (Spencer) S.; ed. Ashmore Bus. Coll., U. N.C.; m. Lois Ann Marley, Oct. 26, 1956; children—Sharon Kay, Anne Carol. Mem. City of Lexington (N.C.) Police Dept., 1952-57, adminstrv. asst., tax collector, 1957-61; city mgr., dir. pub. housing Town of Valdese, N.C., 1961-67; city mgr. City of Roanoke Rapids (N.C.), 1967-72, City of Sanford (N.C.), 1972—. Water safety dir. Lexington ARC, 1950-52; dir. Roanoke Rapids Council Govtl. Law and Order, 1970-72; mem. bd. selectors Burke County Community Coll., 1965-67. Chmn. bd. Valdese Community Center. Served with USNR, 1944-46, PTO; AUS, 1949-52. Democrat. Methodist. Clubs: Moose, Elks, Rotary (dir., past pres.). Home: 2616 Chippendale Trail Sanford NC 27330 Office: PO Box 338 Sanford NC 27330

STOLL, TONI (MRS. HERBERT STOLL), artist; b. N.Y.C., Nov. 5; d. Leo and Rose (Kamerman) Rosenberg; B.F.A., Syracuse U., 1941; postgrad. Rutgers U.; m. Herbert Stoll, Dec. 31, 1941; children—Joanne Stoll Snyder, Barbara Stoll Law. Tchr. art classes USO, Denver, 1942, Lafayette Sch., Highland Park, N.J., 1953-58; painting instr. New Brunswick (N.J.) Art Center, 1953-69; decorating cons. Feverlight & Stoll Furniture Co., 1959-74; exhibited Nat. Arts Club, N.Y.C., 1961-62, Smithsonian Instn., Washington, 1961-63, Jersey City Mus., 1961-66, Douglas Coll., Rutgers U. Tercentennial, 1964, Fairleigh Dickinson U., Madison, N.J., galleries in N.Y.C., Phila., Palm Beach; one-man and group shows, Miami, Hollywood, Ft. Lauderdale, others; represented in permanent collections: New Brunswick Pub. Library, Jewish Community Center of L.I., Beach Haven, N.J., P.S.G.&E. Co., Newark, numerous pvt. collections; judge art exhibits Roebling-Boehm Art Scholar competition, New Brunswick Area, 1962, Fedn. Women's Clubs, spring, 1964, Cinema Theatre Children's Exhibit, Menlo Park, N.J., 1968-69. Artist liaison chmn. Anshe Emeth Meml. Temple Art Show, 1959-60. Recipient Grumbacher 1st prize best in oils, 1960, 62; 2d prize, honorable mention Am. Artists Profl. League, Drew U., 1962, 64; best in watercolor South River (N.J.) Art Show, 1963; award Gold Coast Watercolor Soc. 5th Ann., 1980. Mem. Am. Artists Profl. League, Am. Fedn. Arts, Art and Culture Center of Hollywood (Fla.), Broward Art Guild, Gold Coast Water Color Soc., Fla. Watercolor Soc. Home: 1703 Saint Andrews Rd Hollywood FL 33021

STOLTZ, JACQUE RAE, elec. engr.; b. Oil Hill, Kans., July 17, 1925; s. Samuel Galard and Willameta (York) S.; B.S. in Elec. Engring., Tex. Tech. U., 1949; m. Marguerite Evelyn Johnson, July 18, 1947; children—Michael Rae, Mark Alan, Teresa Ann. Chief engr. N.Mex. Electric Service, Hobbs, 1949-59; mgr. Dixie Electric Co., Hobbs, 1959-63; electronic engring. supr., computer systems Mobil Oil Corp., Houston, 1963—; adult edn. instr. Odessa (Tex.) Coll., 1971—. Served with inf. AUS, 1943-46. Decorated Silver Star, Bronze Star; Brit. Mil. medal. Registered profl. engr., Tex. Mem. Am. Inst. M.E., Am. Petroleum Inst. (adv. com. Sch. Automation Tech.), Instrument Soc. Am. (sr. mem.), Nat. Soc. Profl. Engrs., Oblates Assn., Alpha Chi, Kappa Mu Epsilon. Author, patentee in field. Home: 3719 Golden Lake Dr Kingwood TX 77339 Office: Nine Greenway Plaza Suite 2700 Houston TX 77046

STOLTZ, ROBERT EDWARD, univ. adminstr.; b. Lebanon, Ind., Oct. 9, 1930; s. Lloyd Robert and Ceres Caroline (Williams) S.; B.S., Baylor U., 1951; M.A. in Psychology (Sol Dreyfuss scholar), So. Meth. U., 1953; Ph.D. in Indsl. Psychology, Ohio State U., 1956; m. Camilla Jane Hush, May 26, 1956; children—William Edward, Douglas Paul, Karen Ann. Tng. specialist Temco Aircraft Corp., Dallas, 1953; research asst. Occupational Opportunities Service, Ohio State U., 1954-55, teaching asst. dept. psychology, 1955-56; cons. indsl. psychology to various indsl. and ednl. orgns., 1956—; asso. prof., chmn. dept. psychology So. Meth. U., Dallas, 1956-64; regional dir. So. Regional Office Coll. Entrance Exam. Bd., 1964-73, v.p. and exec. dir., 1973-74, v.p. Spl. Field Services, 1974-75; vice chancellor acad. affairs Western Carolina U., Cullowhee, N.C., 1975—; vis. lectr. and vis. prof. various colls. and univs. in so. region, 1956—. Mem. N.C. Commn. on Ann. Testing, 1977—. Served with Mil. Intelligence Corps, USAR, 1950-59. Recipient Disting. Service award So. Assn. Black Adminstrv. Personnel, 1972; named Educator of Year, Jackson County (N.C.), 1978. Mem. Am. Psychol. Assn., Am. Assn. Collegiate Registrars and Admissions Officers, Am. Ednl. Research Assn., Am. Assn. Higher Edn., Acad. Criminal Justice Scis., Tex. Psychol. Assn., Southwestern Psychol. Assn., Soc. Coll. and Univ. Planning, Nat. Council Measurement in Edn., Sigma Xi. Democrat. Episcopalian. Contbr. articles on counseling and applied psychology to profl. publs. Home: PO Box 2500 Cullowhee NC 28723 Office: Academic Affairs Office Western Carolina Univ Cullowhee NC 28723

STONE, BARBARA ANNE, mech. engr.; b. Trenton, N.J., Dec. 11, 1942; d. William Thomas and Helen Constance (Craynok) Chadwick; Asso. Sci., Trenton Jr. Coll., 1962; B.M.E., Newark Coll. Engring., 1964; M.B.A., U. W. Fla., 1976; grad. Air War Coll., 1978, Indsl. Coll. Armed Forces, 1979; m. James William Stone, June 6, 1964; children—Julie Beth, Kenneth Howard. Engr., Xerox Corp., Rochester, N.Y., 1964-67; engr. Air Force Armament Lab., Eglin AFB, Fla., 1967-74, Armament Devel. and Test Center, 1974-79; engr. space shuttle program NASA, Washington, 1979—. Active summer recreation program for handicapped, diabetic/hypertension screening clinic; chmn. Easter Seal Coffee Day, 1975. Recipient Tech. Achievement award Xerox Corp., 1966; Air Force Community Service award, 1978. Mem. ASME, Am. Def. Preparedness Assn., Pi Tau Sigma. Club: Ft. Walton Beach Jr. Woman's (pres.). Contbr. tech. articles to profl. jours. Home: 8515 Milford Ct Springfield VA 22152 Office: Hgts NASA 600 Independence Ave Washington DC 20546

STONE, BEN HARRY, lawyer, state ofcl.; b. Gulfport, Miss., Jan. 18, 1935; s. William Harry and Tressie (Lancaster) S.; B.B.A., Tulane U., 1957; LL.B., J.D., U. Miss., 1961; m. Nancy Jane Reed, Nov. 14, 1958; children—Nancy Jane, Virginia Louise, Kathleen Lancaster. With devel. dept. Tulane U., 1958-59; admitted to Miss. bar, 1961; practiced in Jackson, 1961-63; mem. firm Eaton, Cottrell, Galloway & Lang, Gulfport, 1963—; mem. Miss. Senate, 1968—. Teaching fellow U. Miss. Sch. Law. Chmn. Harrison County chpt. Am. Cancer Soc., 1965; mem. Miss. Council Devel. Marine Resources, 1969-72, Miss. Marine Conservation Commn. Bd. dirs. Salvation Army, Gulfport, 1965, Cath. Charities, Inc., 1968—. Served with USAF, 1957-58. Mem. Am., Harrison County (pres. 1967) bar assns., Miss. State Bar, Miss. Econ Council, Miss. Soc. Prevention Blindness, Miss. Research and Devel. Council (mem. exec. com. 1968—), Miss. Marine Resources Council, Gulfport Area C. of C. (dir.), Sigma Alpha Epsilon, Phi Delta Phi. Presbyn. Home: 1320 E Beach Blvd Gulfport MS 39501 Office: 2300 14th St Gulfport MS 39501

STONE, BRYCE DOUGLAS, JR., educator; b. Cookeville, Tenn., Apr. 4, 1927; s. Bryce Douglas and Mary Elizabeth (Ensor) S.; B.S. in Bus. Adminstrn., U. Tenn., Knoxville, 1949, M.S. in Mgmt., 1956, Ph.D. in Psychology, 1968; m. Barbara Jeanine Courtney, June 7, 1973. Specialist, mgr. devel. Orlando (Fla.) div. Martin-Marietta Corp., 1963-65; mgr. corporate personnel info. Tex. Instruments Inc., Dallas, 1965-68; prof., head dept. mgmt. Tex. A. and M. U., 1968—; cons. in field. Served with USNR, 1945-46. Ford Found. fellow, 1957-59; recipient Faculty Service award Nat. Univ. Extension Assn., 1975. Mem. Am. Psychol. Assn., Indsl. Relations Research Assn., Am. Soc. Personnel Adminstrn. (diplomate), Acad. Mgmt., N.Y. Acad. Scis., Sigma Xi, Phi Kappa Phi, Beta Gamma Sigma, Sigma Iota Epsilon. Home: 1305 Glade St College Station TX 77840

STONE, ERNEST, univ. pres.; b. Crossville, Ala., Dec. 24, 1912; s. Samuel W. and Belinda K. (McDaniel) S.; B.S., Jacksonville State U.; B.A., M.A., U. Ala.; postgrad. Mich. State U., Columbia U.; m. Katharine Gunn, Aug. 18, 1935; 1 son, William Ernest. Prin., Kilpatrick Jr. High Sch., Crossville (Ala.) High Sch.; supt. DeKalb County schs., Fort Payne, Ala.; prof. edn. Jacksonville State U.; dir. lab. schs., supt. Jacksonville city schs., state supt. of edn., State of Ala., 1967-70; pres. Jacksonville State U., 1971—. Pres. Gulf South Athletic Conf., 1975-76; mem.-at-large Nat. council Boy Scouts Am.; del. Nat. Dem. Conv., 1956; mem. Gov.'s Select Com. for Unified Edn. Budget, 1977. Served with USN, 1943-46. Recipient Outstanding Services to Youth citation Ala. Congress Parents and Tchrs., 1970, Outstanding Civilian Service medal Dept. Army, 1977. Mem. Ala. Acad. Honor, NEA, Am. Legion (state comdr. 1971-72), Newcomen Soc. N.Am., Phi Delta Kappa, Kappa Phi Kappa, Delta Kappa Phi, Omicron Delta Kappa. Democrat. Baptist. Clubs: Masons, Shriners. Author: Case Studies of DeKalb County Children; contbr. articles to various publs. Home: PO Box 576 730 N Pelham Rd Jacksonville AL 36265 Office: Jacksonville State Univ Jacksonville AL 36265

STONE, HARRY BENJAMIN, JR., physician; b. Ashland, W.Va., Mar. 15, 1909; s. Harry Benjamin and Mary Lu (Kearfott) S.; B.S., Hampden Syndey Coll., 1930; M.D., U. Va., 1934; m. Margaret P. Venable, Jan. 18, 1936; children—Harry Benjamin, Charles Venable, Kearfott M. Intern, U. Va. Hosp., 1934-35; resident in otolaryngology N.Y. Eye and Ear Infirmary, N.Y.C., 1935-37; practice medicine specializing in eye, ear, nose and throat, Roanoke, Va., 1937—; mem. staff Roanoke Meml., Community, Lewis-Gale hosps.; pres., dir. Roanoke Med. Bldg. Corp. Served to lt. cmdr. USNR, 1942-46. Mem. Roanoke Acad. Medicine, Med. Soc. Va., AMA, Am. Acad. Otolaryngology and Ophthalmology, Va. Soc. Ophthalmology and Otolaryngology (past pres.), Roanoke C. of C., Phi Beta Kappa. Baptist. Clubs: Rotary, Shenandoah. Home: 2215 Brambleton Ave SW Roanoke VA 24015 Office: 30 1/2 Franklin Rd SW Roanoke VA 24011

STONE, HUBERT DEAN, journalist; b. Maryville, Tenn., Sept. 23, 1924; s. Archie Hubert and Annie (Cupp) S.; student Maryville Coll., 1942-43; B.A., U. Okla., 1949; m. Agnes Shirley, Sept. 12, 1953 (dec. Mar. 1973); 1 son, Neal Anson. Sunday editor Maryville-Alcoa Daily Times, 1949; mng. editor Maryville-Alcoa Times, 1949-78, editor, 1978—; v.p. Maryville-Alcoa Newspapers, Inc., 1960—; pres. Stonecraft, 1954—. Mem. mayor's adv. com. City of Maryville. Bd. dirs. United Fund of Blount County, 1961-63, 74-76, vice chmn. campaign, 1971-72, campaign chmn., 1973, v.p., 1974, pres., 1975; bd. dirs. Maryville Utilities Bd.; trustee Smoky Mountain Passion Play Assn.; adv. bd. Harrison-Chilhowee Baptist Acad. Served from pvt. to staff sgt. AUS, 1943-45. Decorated Bronze Star; named Outstanding Sr. Man of Blount County, 1970, 77. Mem. Profl. Photographers of Am., Tenn. Profl. Photographers Assn., Internat. Postcard Distbrs. Assn., Great Smoky Mountains Conservation Assn., Ft. Loudoun Assn., Tenn. Jaycees (editor 1954-55, life mem., sec.-treas. 1955-56), Jr. Chamber Internat. (senator), Maryville-Alcoa Jaycees (life mem., pres. 1953-54), Blount County (v.p. 1971, 76, pres. 1977), Townsend (dir. 1969-71) chambers commerce, Tenn. Asso. Press News Execs. Assn. (v.p. 1973, pres. 1974), Asso. Press Mng. Editors Assn., Am. Legion, V.F.W., Chilhowee Bapt. Assn. (chmn. history com.) U. Okla. Alumni Assn. (life mem., pres. E. Tenn. chpt. 1954-55), Sigma Delta Chi (life; dir. E. Tenn. chpt.). Baptist (trustee, deacon, chmn. nominating, evangelism, fin., personnel coms.). Mason, Kiwanian (Alcoa pres. 1969-70). Club: Green Meadow Country. Author articles in field. Home: 1510 Scenic Dr Maryville TN 37801 Office: 307 E Harper Ave Maryville TN 37801

STONE, JOHN AUSTIN, nuclear chemist; b. Paintsville, Ky., Nov. 30, 1935; s. James William and Christine (Austin) S.; B.S., U. Louisville, 1955; Ph.D., U. Calif. at Berkeley, 1963; m. Helen Reynolds, June 2, 1968; children—Tracye Victoria, Philip Austin, Suzanne Reynolds. With Savannah River Lab., E.I. DuPont de Nemours & Co., Aiken, S.C., 1963—, research staff chemist, 1974—. Traveling lectr. Oak Ridge Asso. Univs., 1964-74. Served with USCG, 1955-57. Mem. Am. Phys. Soc., Am. Chem. Soc., Sigma Xi, Phi Kappa Phi, Lambda Chi Alpha. Episcopalian. Home: 2221 Morningside Dr Augusta GA 30904 Office: Savannah River Laboratory Aiken SC 29801

STONE, JOHN EVERETT, JR., thoracic surgeon; b. Knoxville, Tenn., Mar. 12, 1947; s. John Everett and Philomene Bess (Miller) S.; B.S., Wake Forest U., 1969; M.D., U. Tenn., 1972; m. Betty Frances Hyder, June 20, 1970; children—Robert Andrew, John Everett. Intern, U. Ala., 1972-73, resident in gen. surgery, 1973-77; fellow in cardiothoracic surgery U. N.C., Chapel Hill, 1977-79; attending surgeon Cardiothoracic and Vascular Surg. Assos., P.C., Mobile, Ala., 1979—; mem. staff Mobile Infirmary, Providence, Drs., U. South Ala. hosps.; instr. U. Ala., 1975-77. Diplomate Am. Bd. Surgery. Mem. AMA (Physicians Recognition award 1973), John W. Kirklin Soc., Nathan A. Womack Soc., Southeastern Surg. Congress, Mobile County Med. Soc., Sigma Chi. Methodist. Club: Pres.'s Wake Forest U. Home: 648 Falls Church Rd Mobile AL 36608 Office: 185 Louiselle St Mobile AL 36607

STONE, (MARY) KATHARINE GANN (MRS. ERNEST STONE), educator; b. Sylacauga, Ala.; d. William C. and Mary (Twilley) Gann; B.S., Jacksonville State U., 1933, LL.D., 1974; M.A., U. Ala., 1944, postgrad., 1960, 62; m. Ernest Stone, Aug. 18, 1934; 1 son, William Ernest. Prin., tchr. DeKalb County Schs., 1934-44; tchr. Jacksonville (Ala.) State U., 1944-46, dir. elementary lab. sch., 1948-75; condr. workshops for tchrs. Jefferson, Calhoun, Marshall, Butler, Cherokee counties; tchr. inst. numerous counties, cities; vice chmn. Title III Adv. Council, State of Ala., 1968-75, Title IV Adv. Council, 1975—; mem. Gov.'s Com. on Adult Edn., 1968—; mem. course of study com. State Dept. Edn., 1973—. Recipient Alumnus of Year award Jacksonville State U., 1961-62. Mem. Ala. Edn. Assn. (dist. pres. 1944-46), Edn. Profl. Standards Commn. (tchr. 1944-50), AAUW (pres. 1950-52), NEA, Dept. Elementary Sch. Prins. (pres. dist. V 1971-72), Assn. Childhood Edn., Nat. Assn. Parliamentarians, Ala. Assn. Parliamentarians (historian 1963-65, sec. 1971-73, v.p. 1973-75, treas. 1975-77, corr. sec. 1977—), Nat. Council Tchrs. Math., Am. Assn. Sch. Adminstrs. Ala. Fedn. Women's Clubs (exec. bd. 1945—; Kitty Stone grad. scholarship endowment fund established 1969), Delta Kappa Gamma (pres. chpt. 1940-44), Kappa Delta Pi, Alpha Xi Delta. Club: Prog. Study (pres. 1951-52). Home: Pres's Mansion Jacksonville State U 730 N Pelham Rd Jacksonville AL 36265

STONE, LARRY DALE, advt. agy. exec.; b. St. Louis, Dec. 15, 1947; s. Jewel and Mary Lou (Herren) S.; B.F.A., La. Poly. U., 1969; m. Donna M. Miller, Aug. 17, 1968; children—Steven Kelly, Adam Patrick. Prodn. mgr. Bill Kerr Design, Little Rock, 1969-72; v.p., art dir. Stephens Internat. Ltd., Little Rock, 1972-75; v.p., creative dir. Watkins & Assos., Little Rock, 1975—. Mem. Ark. Soc. Communication Arts (past pres.). Democrat. Office: 2030 Worthen Bank Bldg Little Rock AR 72201

STONE, MARVIN JULES, physician, educator; b. Columbus, Ohio, Aug. 3, 1937; s. Roy J. and Lillian (Bedwinek) S.; student Ohio State U., 1955-58; S.M. in Pathology, U. Chgo., 1962, M.D. with honors, 1963; m. Jill Feinstein, June 29, 1958; children—Nancy Lillian, Robert Howard. Intern ward med. service Barnes Hosp., St. Louis, 1963-64, asst. resident, 1964-65; clin. asso. arthritis and rheumatism br. Nat. Inst. Arthritis and Metabolic Diseases, NIH, Bethesda, Md., 1965-68; resident in medicine, A.C.P. scholar Parkland Meml. Hosp., Dallas, 1968-69; fellow in hematology dept. internal medicine U. Tex. Southwestern Med. Sch., Dallas, 1969-70, instr. dept. internal medicine, 1970-71, asst. prof., 1971-73, asso. prof., 1974-76, clin. prof., 1976—; adj. prof. biology So. Meth. U., Dallas, 1977—; dir. Charles A. Sammons Cancer Center, chief oncology, dir. immunology, co-dir. div. hematology-oncology Baylor U. Med. Center, Dallas, 1976—; mem. faculty and steering com. immunology grad. program Grad. Sch. Biomed. Scis., U. Tex. Health Sci. Center, Dallas, 1975-76, adj. mem., 1976—. Chmn. com. patient-aid Greater Dallas/Ft. Worth chpt. Leukemia Soc. Am., 1971-76, chmn. med. adv. com. Dallas/Ft. Worth chpt., 1978—, med. dir. Dallas Met. dist., 1979-80; med. v.p. Dallas unit Am. Cancer Soc., 1977-78, pres., 1978-80. Served with USPHS, 1965-68. Diplomate Am. Bd. Internal Medicine. Named Outstanding Faculty Mem. Dept. Internal Medicine, Baylor U., 1977-78. Fellow A.C.P.; mem. A.A.A.S., Am. Rheumatism Assn., Reticuloendothelial Soc., Am. Assn. Immunologists, Am. Fedn. Clin. Research, Am. Soc. Hematology, N.Y. Acad. Scis., Council on Thrombosis, Am. Heart Assn. (established investigator 1970-75), Am. Soc. Clin. Oncology, Am. Assn. Cancer Research, Tex. Med. Assn., Dallas County Med. Soc., Am. Soc. Preventive Oncology, Fedn. Am. Scientists, So. Soc. Clin. Investigation, Phi Beta Kappa, Sigma Xi, Alpha Omega Alpha. Contbr. articles to profl. Jours., chpts. to books. Office: Charles A Sammons Cancer Center Baylor U Med Center 3500 Gaston Ave Dallas TX 75246

STONE, MINNIE STRANGE, automotive service co. exec.; b. Palatka, Fla., Mar. 10, 1919; d. James Arrious and Pansy (Thomas) Strange; student Massey Bus. Coll., 1938-39; m. Fred Albion Stone, Nov. 30, 1939; children—Fred Albion, James Thomas, Thomas Demere. Sec., bookkeeper Sears, Roebuck & Co., Jacksonville, Fla., 1939-41; financial sec. U.S. Army, Macon, Ga., 1941, Atlanta, 1942; sec., bookkeeper Stony Heavy Vehicle Specialists (formerly) Raleigh Spring & Brake Service, Inc. (N.C.), 1953—, sec.-treas. corp., dir., 1960—. Sec., Myrtle Underwood PTA, 1958—; treas. Frances Lacy PTA, 1968—; pres. YWCA, Raleigh, 1973-76, bd. dirs., 1963-76, adv. bd., 1976-79, adminstrn. com., 1979—. Mem. Raleigh Council Smaller Garden Clubs (pres. 1960-61), N.C. Art Soc., Vol. Guild Dorothea Dix Hosp., Wake County Mental Health Assn., Monthly Investors Club. Republican. Baptist. Club: Coley Forest Garden. Home: 920 Runnymede Rd Raleigh NC 27607 Office: Hwy 70 E Raleigh NC 27610

STONE, NORMAN MICHAEL, clin. child psychologist; b. Balt., Mar. 23, 1949; s. Forrest Leon and Beverly Iola (Gendason) S.; B.A., UCLA, 1971; Ph.D., (USPHS fellow), U. Iowa, 1975; m. Kathleen Carole Flanigan, Mar. 22, 1969; children—Shannon Helen, Caroline Rebecca. Adminstrv. asst. Research and Tng. Clinic, U. Iowa, 1974-75; clin. fellow San Fernando Valley Child Guidance Clinic, Los Angeles, 1975-76; dir. youth and family services Abilene (Tex.) Mental Health-Mental Retardation Regional Center, 1976—; mem. adj. faculty Hardin Simmons U., McMurray Coll.; cons. Tex. Dept. Human Resources; chmn. youth coms. Mental Health Assn. and Community Coordinating Council, 1977-78; chmn. steering com. to form Abilene Big Brother/Big Sister, Inc., 1978; bd. dirs. Big Bros./Big Sisters of Abilene, Kenley Sch. for Learning Disabled. Lic. clin. child psychologist, Tex. Mem. AAUP, Am. Psychol. Assn., S.W. Network Youth Services, Sigma Xi. Author: Children's Level of Functioning Scale, 1979; contbr. articles to profl. jours. Home: 2410 Helena Circle Abilene TX 79606 Office: 851 Orange St Abilene TX 79601

STONE, RALPH GUYTON, mfg. co. exec.; b. Williamston, S.C., Sept. 16, 1928; s. William Mack and Mary Eliza (Hendrix) S.; student public schs., S.C.; m. Sarah Mae Waldrep, July 5, 1948; children—Zora, Mike, Don, Pam, Kenneth. With Dodd Sheet Metal Works, Anderson, S.C., 1947-71, gen. mgr., 1950-71; gen. mgr. R. G. Stone Metal Works, Anderson, 1973—; cons. Greenville Tech. Coll., 1970. Anderson dist. commr. Boy Scouts Am., 1964-69; coach Little League Baseball, Anderson, 1963-68. Served with USN, 1946-47; PTO. Mem. Am. Inst. Plant Engrs. (pres. 1969-70), VFW (post comdr. 1970-71). Office: 311 Manley Dr PO Box 3041 Anderson SC 29621

STONE, RICHARD BERNARD, senator; b. N.Y.C., Sept. 22, 1928; s. Alfred and Lily (Abbey) S.; B.A. cum laude, Harvard U., 1949; LL.B., Columbia U., 1954; m. Marlene Singer; children—Nancy, Amy, Elliot. Former sec. Royal Castle Systems, Inc.; former dir. Eagle Army Navy, Inc.; former partner firm Stone, Bittell, Langer, Blass & Corrigan; city atty., Miami, Fla., 1966-67; mem. Fla. Senate, 1967-70; sec. of state State of Fla., 1971-74; senator from Fla., 1975—. Mem. Dade County, Am., Interam. bar assns., Corp. Banking and Bus. Law Com., Fla. State Bar, Am. Judicature Soc. Jewish. Rotarian, Moose, Elk, K. P., Mason. Home: 930 Live Oak Plantation Rd Tallahassee FL 32303 Office: 1327 Dirksen Senate Office Bldg Washington DC 20510

STONE, RICHARD BERNARD (DICK), senator; b. N.Y.C., Sept. 22, 1928; s. Alfred and Lily (Abbey) S.; B.A. cum laude, Harvard U., 1949; LL.B., Columbia U., 1954; m. Marlene Singer; children—Nancy, Amy, Elliot. Former sec. Royal Castle Systems, Inc.; former dir. Eagle Army Navy, Inc.; partner Stone, Bittell, Langer, Blass & Corrigan; city atty. Miami, Fla., 1966-67; mem. Fla. Senate, 1967-70; sec. of state Fla., 1971-74; mem. U.S. Senate from Fla., 1975—. Mem. Dade County Bar Assn., Am. Bar Assn., Interam. Bar Assn., Am. Judicature Soc. Jewish. Clubs: Rotary, Moose, Elks, Masons, K.P. Office: 1327 Dirksen Senate Office Bldg Washington DC 20510 also 2639 N Monroe St Tallahassee FL also 500 Zack St Tampa FL 33602

STONE, ROBERT MICHAEL, hypnotherapist, psychotherapist; b. Union Springs, Ala., Mar. 13, 1952; s. Jack B. and Elizabeth Ann (Holmes) S.; student Pensacola Jr. Coll., 1970-71; B.A. with honors, U. Fla., 1974; M.S., Auburn U., 1976; m. Carolyn Stewart, July 14, 1978. Psychotherapist in pvt. practice, Montgomery, Ala., 1976-78, Pensacola, Fla., 1978—; cons. in field; lectr. colls., univs., TV, radio, profl. and civic groups. Mem. Am. Personnel and Guidance Assn. Author: A Key to Unlimited Consciousness, 1979; Self-Hypnosis Manual, 1979; contbr. articles to newspapers and mags. Home: 3475 Blueridge Dr Pensacola FL 32503 Office: PO Box 19050 Pensacola FL 32503

STONE, ROWENA MAUDE, ednl. adminstr.; b. Georgetown, Tex., Aug. 8, 1932; B.S. in Edn., Southwestern U., Georgetown, 1960; M.Ed. in Supervision and Adminstrn., S.W. Tex. State U., 1965; postgrad. in Edn., U. Tex., Austin; married, 2 children. Tchr., Round Rock (Tex.) Ind. Sch. Dist., 1960-66, dir. curriculum, 1972, asst. supt. curriculum and instruction, 1974—; prin. Taylor (Tex.) Ind. Sch. Dist., 1966-72. Mem. AAUW (pres.), Tex. Assn. Sch. Adminstrs., Am. Assn. Supervision and Curriculum Devel., Tex. Assn. Supervision and Curriculum Devel., Am. Assn. Sch. Adminstrs., Round Rock Women's Club, Alpha Delta Kappa. Cert. tchr., prin., supr., Tex. Home: 300 Briarwood Round Rock TX 78664 Office: 1311 Round Rock Ave Round Rock TX 78664

STONE, ROY MAXWELL, record co. and publishing co. exec.; b. Live Oak, Fla., Jan. 9, 1916; s. William E. and Lola (Miller) S.; student U. Fla., 1938-39, South Tex. Law Sch., 1954-55; m. Lulu Pryor Cloud, Dec. 8, 1940; children—Maxwell Pryor, William Robert, Mary Alice. Religious songwriter J. H. Henson Music Co., Atlanta, 1950; with Baxter Music Co., Dallas, 1950-52, Stamps Quartet Music Co., Dallas, 1952-54, Country Music Band, 1934-39; owner R & M Record Shops, Inc., 1956—, Stoneway Record Co., Houston, 1964—, Roy M. Stone Pub. Co., 1964—, Stoneway Pub. Co., 1970—; pres. Wide World Records, 1969—. Mem. Country Music Assn. Baptist. Mason. Author, Composer: Our Hymns and Gospel Songs. Composer many songs including I Know That God is Real, Out of Order. Home: 10414 Shady Ln Houston TX 77093 Office: 2817 Laura Koppe Houston TX 77093

STONE, RUBY ELIZABETH, state mental health ofcl.; b. Malvern, Ark., Dec. 30, 1915; d. William Albert and Mattie Catherine (Heard) Brown; student Ouachita Coll., Henderson State Coll. and U. Ark., 1937-40; m. Chancellor Hines Stone, Mar. 1, 1942 (dec.). Elem. tchr., Prattsville, Ark., 1936-41; personnel asst. Ark. State Hwy. Dept., Little Rock, 1941-44; personnel employee War Dept., 1945-47; successively personnel asst., sec. to personnel dir., asst. personnel dir. Ark. State Hosp., Little Rock, 1947-66, mental health personnel mgr., 1966—; chmn. credit com. Ark. State Hosp. Credit Union, 1953—. Active Community Concert Assn., Art Center, United Way, Ark. State Hosp. Aux. Cert. Public Personnel Assn.; notary public, Ark. Mem. Am. Soc. Personnel Adminstrn. (cert.), Ark. Personnel Assn. (dir. 1973-76), Ark. Assn. Hosp. Personnel Dirs., Chi Sigma. Interior decorator; dress designer; antique collector. Home: 7500 Choctaw Rd Little Rock AR 72205 Office: 4313 W Markham St Little Rock AR 72201

STONE, THOMAS JENNINGS, JR., real estate exec.; b. Sandersville, Ga., Nov. 20, 1914; s. Thomas J. and Ruby (Stanley) S.; grad. high sch.; m. Mary Linnie Harden, Sept. 28, 1944; 1 dau., Joanne H. Various clerical, auditing, acctg. positions, 1933-36; with W.L. Florence, promoter-developer, Athens, Ga., 1936-41, gen. mgr., sec.-treas. various affiliated corps., 1936-41; chief accountant Brunswick Marine Constrn. Corp., Brunswick (Ga.) Stockyard, 1941-42; accountant, auditor in pvt. practice, Augusta, Ga., 1946-49; sales and promotion work J.C. Bible, Jr., real estate Augusta, 1949-51; owner Tom Stone Real Estate, broker, developer, contractor, Augusta, 1951—; pioneered devel. Town of Martins (Ga.), 1953-55 owner, developer Lincoln Meml. Gardens, 1965—; co-developer Med. Complex, Lagos, Nigeria; co-developer nursing home, Augusta, 1969-70. Served with AUS, 1942-46. Mem. Am. Legion, Internat. Platform Assn. Baptist. Clubs: Masons (32 deg.), Shriners. Pioneered stockyard system and brine-curing of meats in So. Ga. 1930's. Home: 3462 Milledgeville Rd Augusta GA 30909 Office: RFD 1 Box 275 Hwy 56 CSRA Bldg Augusta GA 30906

STONEBURNER, DANIEL LEE, ecologist; b. Zanesville, Ohio, July 4, 1945; s. Floyd Benjamin and Harriet (Stockdale) S.; B.S., Ind. State U., 1967; Ph.D., Iowa State U., 1970; m. Ellen Louise Hansen, Mar. 13, 1971; children—Tara Elizebeth, Erin Kristen. Regional ecologist S.E. regional office Nat. Park Service, Dept. Interior, Atlanta, 1974-78; research asso. Nat. Park Service - univ. research unit coordinator Inst. Ecology, U. Ga., Athens, 1978—; cons. in field. Served with U.S. Army, 1970-74. Decorated Army Commendation medal; recipient Spl. Achievement award Dept. Interior, 1979. Mem. Audubon Soc., Brit. Ecol. Soc., Ecol. Soc. Am., Internat. Wildlife Assn., Limnology and Oceanography, Nat. Geog. Soc., Assn. Southeastern Biologists. Lutheran. Contbr. articles to profl. jours. Office: Nat Park Service Coop Research Unit Inst Ecology U Ga Athens GA 30602

STONER, EDMUND CURTIS, JR., cons. engr.; b. Riverside, Calif., Oct. 20, 1903; s. Edmund Curtis and Margaret (Copley) S.; student Lafayette Coll., 1921-22; B.S. in Elec. Engring., Yale, 1926; m. Margaret Dorman Hamilton, June 23, 1926 (dec. 1958); 1 dau., Margaret Hamilton (Mrs. John N. Schofield, Jr.); m. 2d, Mary J. Garcia, 1960. Chief engr. ITT, Peru, Cuba and Spain, 1933-41; asst. v.p. Fed. Telephone & Radio, 1945-48; cons. engr. to minister of communications Govt. of Turkey, Ankara, 1948-51; chief engr. Gen. Telephone & Electronics Corp., Muskegon, Mich., 1954-58, chief engr., Tampa, Fla., 1958-65; engr. planning dir. Gen. Telephone Co. Fla., 1965-68; cons. engr., 1969—. Served to lt. col. USAAF, World War II (col. Res. ret.), Decorated Bronze Star; Mil. Order Brit. Empire. Mem. Rochester, Muskegon, Tampa chambers commerce, Order of Daedalians, OX-5 Aviation Pioneers, SAR, Phi Kappa Psi. Presbyn. Clubs: University (Tampa, Fla.); Army-Navy (Washington); Yale (N.Y.C.). Author: Never for Me, 1968. Home: 310 S Burlingame Ave Temple Terrace FL 33617

STONESIFER, JOSEPH NOVAK, mgmt. and adminstrn. specialist; b. Oak Park, Ill., Feb. 24, 1914; s. Joseph Bernard and Bessie Sadie (Novak) S.; A.A., Morton Jr. Coll., 1933; B.S., U. Ill., 1936; M.A., George Washington U., 1946; A.B.D. in Adminstrn. and Edn., Am. U., 1973; m. Jean Ann Fisher, Mar. 5, 1955; children—Joseph Novak, John Dewitt, Jean Ann. Wholesale rep. Armour & Co., Chgo., 1932-34; personnel classification analyst CSC, Washington, 1935-38; dir. orgn. U.S. Maritime Commn., 1938-46; dir. personnel U.S. Naval Air Sta., Oahu, Hawaii, 1939-40; dir. adminstrn. Office of Chief Naval Ops. and Office of Sec. Navy, Washington, 1946-50; planning officer Office of Adminstr., CAA, Washington, 1950-54; moblzn. liaison officer Exec. Office of Pres., Washington, 1954-59; dir. mgmt. studies FAA, Washington, 1959-69; coordinator computer applications Dept. Transp., Washington, 1965-69; dir. orgn. Exec. Office of the Pres., Washington, 1966-68; faculty George Washington U., Washington, 1955-71, asso. prof. bus. and pub. adminstrn., 1969—. Asso. prof. Central Mich. U., 1974-76; propr. Janus Enterprises, cons. on mgmt., Falls Church, Va., 1965—; dir. manpower devel. Fairfax Community Action Program, 1977-79; exec. dir. No. Va. Consortium for Med. Edn., 1979—. Served to lt. comdr. USNR, 1942-46; mem. Res. (ret.). Mem. Am. Assn. Sch. Adminstrs., Am. Soc. Personnel Adminstrn. (accredited), Internat. Personnel Mgmt. Assn., Am. Soc. Public Adminstrn., Soc. for Advancement Mgmt., Am. Psychol. Assn., Am. Assn. for Higher Edn., Am. Assn. Sch. Adminstrs., Am. Ednl. Research Assn., Acad. Mgmt., Am. Polit. Sci. Assn., Beta Beta Tau, Phi Delta Kappa. Club: Toastmasters Internat. (pres. 1950-51). Author: Background and Success of Classification Analysts, 1950; The Executive Officer's Handbook, 1959; Selective Bibliography for Personnel Management, 1960; Conduct of Organization Review Programs, 1969; Regulatory Functions in the Federal Government, 1970; Solving Broad Management Problems, 1975; contbr. articles to profl. jours. Home: 3137 Valley Ln Falls Church VA 22044 Office: Janus Enterprises Falls Church VA 22044

STORAGE, T. W. (PETE), recreational bldg. exec.; b. Nitro, W.Va., Mar. 4, 1943; s. William Allen and Lucille (Clark) S.; B.S. in Tech. Sci. and Indsl. Arts, W.Va. State Coll., 1964; M.S. in Park Planning, W.Va.

U., 1967; children—Kimberlie Rae, Phillip Anthony, Kelly Jean. Instr. indsl. arts Suncrest Jr. High Sch., Morgantown, W.Va., 1964-67; state park planner W.Va. Dept. Natural Resources, Charleston, 1967-70; park planner, acting dir. Orange County Park Dept., Orlando, Fla., 1970-72; v.p. Recreation Planning div. King Helie Planning Group, Orlando, 1972-75; pres. Park Structures of Am., Ft. Lauderdale, Fla., 1975—. Mem. Nat. Park and Recreation Soc., Nat. Small Business Assn. Presbyterian. Contbr. research paper in field. Address: PO Box 8637 Fort Lauderdale FL 33310

STORES, CHARLES DINWIDDIE, lawyer; b. Portsmouth, Va., Mar. 10, 1906; s. William A. and Sarah H. (Jones) S.; B.S., Roanoke Coll., Salem, Va., 1928; LL.B., LaSalle Extension U., Chgo., 1937; m. Dorothy M. Palmer, June 6, 1931; children—Charles Dinwiddie, Virginia Ann (Mrs. John Le Page), Robert Bruce. Admitted to Va., D.C., U.S. Patent and Trademark Office, U.S. Supreme Ct. bars; with Esso Research & Engring. Co., Linden, N.J., 1929-42, Elizabeth, N.J., 1942-48, Washington, 1948-68, head Washington office, 1954-68; patent atty. Humble Oil & Refining Co., Baton Rouge, La., 1968-70; ret., 1970. Mem. Am. Patent Law Assn., Am. Sci. Affiliation, S.A.R. Fla. Baptist (deacon). Home: 15 Sunflower St Apt 36 Cocoa Beach FL 32931

STOREY, EDWARD ALBERT, II, engr.; b. Salina, Kans., Oct. 26, 1947; s. Edward Albert and Alice Louise (Parker) S.; B.C.E., The Citadel, 1969; M.C.E. (grad. teaching asst. 1969-71), U. Va., 1971; m. Carol Willis Rich, June 14, 1970; 1 son, Edward Albert. Cons. engr. Gooch & Assos., Charlottesville, Va., 1970-71; design engr. Gifford Hill & Co., Charlotte, N.C., 1972-73; project engr. Myrtle Beach (S.C.) Farms Co., 1973-75; engr., property mgr. Chicora Devel., Myrtle Beach, 1975-79; project mgr. Kiawah Island Co., Charleston, S.C., 1979—; instr. mgmt. night sch. Mem. spl. Olympics com. Horry County Assn. Retarded Children, 1977. Served with U.S. Army, 1971. Registered profl. engr., S.C.; recipient Sertoma Club Centurion award, 1977, Tribune award, 1977-78. Mem. Profl. Engring. Soc. S.C., ASCE, Am. Road Builders Assn., S.C. Bd. Realtors, Urban Land Inst., Community Assn. Inst., Tau Beta Pi. Methodist. Clubs: Grand Strand Sertoma (dir. 1976-78), Citadel Brigadier, Horry County Citadel (pres. 1978-79), Masons. Home: 679 Edmonds Dr Charleston SC 29412 Office: PO Box 12910 Charleston SC 29412

STOREY, MARY ALICE, educator; b. Perry County, Miss., July 13, 1920; d. Henry Elsworth and Elizabeth Morren; B.S., U. So. Miss., 1942; M.A., La. Tech. U., 1973; postgrad Northeast La. U., summer 1978; m. Edgar L. Storey, Jr., June 2, 1943 (dec.); children—Herman Edgar, Mary Katherine Storey Spiritosanto. Tchr. elem. sch., Picayune, Miss., 1942-45; tchr. spl. edn. Evergreen Presbyn. Vocat. Sch., Minden, La., 1969-72, dir. girls program, 1972-75; dir. tng. and habilitation G.B. Cooley Hosp., West Monroe, La., 1975—. Mem. Am. Assn. Mental Deficiency, Nat. Assn. Retarded Citizens. Prebyterian. Home: 569 Sherwood Dr West Monroe LA 71291 Office: Rt 8 Box 93 West Monroe LA 71291

STOREY, RICHARD BOYLE, trade assn. exec.; b. Washington, Apr. 12, 1945; s. Arthur and Robin (Boyle) S.; B.A. in Bus. Adminstrn., Salem (W.Va.) Coll., 1968; postgrad. U. Del.; grad U.S. Chamber's Inst. for Orgn. Mgmt.; m. Linda Lee Penrose, Sept. 1, 1965; children—Christie Lynn, Karen Lee. Dist. scout exec. Boy Scouts Am., 1968-72; dir. membership services Nat. Crushed Stone Assn., 1972-74; dir. membership Discover Am. Travel Orgns., Inc., 1974-75; exec. v.p. Pa. Restaurant Assn., Inc., 1976-77; exec. dir. Internat. Mil. Club Execs., Assn., 1977—; cons. mgmt. and tng. programs. Bd. dirs. Multi Mgmt. Assos. Cert. Assn. Exec. Mem. Am. Soc. Assn. Execs. (mem. govt. affairs com.), Washington Soc. Assn. Execs., Washington Legis. Soc., Nat. Assn. Execs. Club, U.S. C. of C., Greater Washington Mil Club Mgrs. Assn., Council on Hotel, Restaurant and Institutional Edn., Alpha Phi Omega. Republican. Episcopalian. Club: Masons (32 deg.). Asso. editor Clubs and Recreation mag. Home: 307 E Brunswick St Sterling VA 22170 Office: 1750 Old Meadow Rd Suite S-103 McLean VA 22102

STORM, MARK KENNEDY, artist; b. Valdez, Alaska, Sept. 4, 1911; s. Lynn Whippo and Bertha Katherine (Kennedy) S.; student U. Tex., 1930-34; m. Elizabeth Ferne Sweeny, Sept. 30, 1934; children—Tommie Lu, Carol Jane. Horseman, comml. artist, illustrator, painter, sculptor, horse trainer, Glencoe, N.Mex., 1928-34; comml. artist Tex. Engraving Co., Houston, 1934-37; draftsman Shell Oil Co., Houston, 1937-46; illustrator Wetmore & Co., Houston, 1946-51; illustrator, painter, sculptor, 1951—; one-man shows include Glasser Gallery, San Antonio, 1973; Brazosport (Tex.) Center Arts and Scis., 1978; group shows at Amarillo (Tex.) Art Center, 1975, 76; Snyder (Tex.) Coliseum, 1977; Abercombie and Fitch Gallery, N.Y.C., 1976; Western Heritage Sale, Houston, 1978; represented in permanent collections at Tex. Ranger Mus., Waco, Night Hawk Restaurant, Austin; executed mural Houston Mus. Natural Sci., 1970. Mem. Tex. Cowboy Artists Assn. (awards 1976, 77), Houston C. of C. (agribus. com.), Houston Livestock Show and Rodeo Assn., Nat. Fedn. Ind. Bus. Baptist. Clubs: Rotary, Briar (Houston). Author, illustrator: Gruyo of the Flying H., 1956; illustrator: Picture Tales from Mexico, 1941; Texas Brags, 1943, 50. Home: 2256 Shakespeare Houston TX 77030 Studio: 2322 University Blvd Houston TX 77005

STORM, WILLIAM JOHN, retail food co. exec.; b. Chgo., Feb. 13, 1925; s. Josef and Rose (Steirer) Somogyi; M.E., U. Ill., 1947; M.B.A., U. Chgo., 1953; married; children—Michael, David, Cynthia, Caroline, Matthew, Julie, Sara. Engr., C.E., U.S. Army, 1952-53; owner, cons. Profl. Mgmt. Service, New Orleans, 1954-68; partner Alexander Grant & Co., C.P.A.'s, New Orleans, 1968-78; sr. v.p. fin. Church's Fried Chicken Inc., San Antonio, 1979—; mem. faculty Tulane U., 1956-69, U. Ill., 1955-57, Loyola U., New Orleans, 1956-71. Mem. AAUP, Nat. Soc. Profl. Engrs., La. Engring. Soc. Republican. Presbyterian. Contbr. articles to trade jours. Office: Box BH001 San Antonio TX 78284

STORMONT, RICHARD MANSFIELD, bus. exec.; b. Chgo., Apr. 4, 1936; s. Daniel Lytle and E. Mildred (Milligan) S.; B.S., Cornell U., 1958; m. Virginia Louellen Walters, Nov. 21, 1959; children—Stacy Lee, Richard Mansfield, John Frederick. Food cost analyst, sales rep. Edgewater Beach Hotel, Chgo., 1957-58, asst. sales mgr. Marriott Motor Hotels, Inc., Washington, 1962-64; dir. sales Marriott Motor Hotel, Atlanta, 1964-68, resident mgr., 1969-71, gen. mgr., 1974-79; pres. Kenney-Stormont Assos. Inc., 1980—; gen. mgr. Marriott Motor Hotel, Dallas, 1971-73, Phila., 1973-74; pres. Hardin Mgmt. Co., 1979-80; dir. Frederick J. Walters, mgmt. cons. Pres., Atlanta Conv. and Visitors Bur., 1975-76, chmn. bd., 1976-77; bd. dirs., exec. com. Central Atlanta Progress, Inc.; bd. dirs. Better Bus. Bur.; mem. exec. council Boy Scouts Am. Served to lt. (j.g.) USNR, 1959-62. Recipient Distinguished Salesman of Year award Marriott, 1967. Mem. Sales and Mktg. (v.p. 1978), (exec. v.p. 1969-70, pres. Atlanta chpt. 1970-71, Atlanta C. of C. (v.p.), Ga. Bus. and Industry Assn. (dir.), Atlanta Hotel-Motel Assn. (pres. 1976-77), Hotel Sales Mgmt. Assn. (past chpt. pres.), Ga. Hospitality and Travel Assn. (dir. 1977-79), Cornell Soc. Hotelmen (pres. Ga. chpt. 1976), Pi Sigma Epsilon, Phi Kappa Psi. Rotarian. Home: 495 River Crest Ct Atlanta GA 30328 Office: 5600 Roswell Rd Suite 240 Prado East Atlanta GA 30342

STORMS, RAYMOND EDWIN, petroleum engr., cons.; b. Mission, Tex., Sept. 16, 1915; s. Louis Wilson and Louise Emma (Duensing) S.; B.S. in Petroleum Engring., Tex. A. and M. U., 1937, M.Engring. in Petroleum Engring., 1960; m. Doris Mae Purcelley, June 27, 1943; children—Richard Ray, Randolph Lee. Prodn. engr. Mene Grande Oil Co., Maracaibo, Venezuela, 1937-41; jr. process engr. J.S. Abercrombie Oil Co., Old Ocean, Tex., 1942-45; petroleum engr., adminstrv. asst. Mene Grande Oil Co., 1945-56; v.p. San Jacinto Venezolana, Maracaibo, 1957-58; asso. prof. petroleum engring. La. Tech. U., Ruston, 1960-77; v.p. Coutret & Assos., Inc., petroleum reservoir engring. cons., Shreveport, La., 1978—. Registered profl. engr., La., Tex. Mem. Soc. Petroleum Engrs., La. Engring. Soc., Tau Beta Pi, Pi Epsilon Tau. Baptist. Rotarian (pres. Ruston 1970-71). Author: Myths and Realities of the Energy Shortage (best publn. Coll. Engring., La. Tech. U. 1974), 1974. Home: 1006 D'Arbonne St Ruston LA 71270

STORRER, WILLIAM ALLIN, educator; b. Highland Park, Mich., Mar. 22, 1936; s. Fredrick Ray and Margaret Ann (Pitts) S.; student Albion Coll., 1954-56; A.B. in Engring. Scis., Harvard U., 1959; M.F.A. in Theatre Arts, Boston U., 1962; Ph.D. in Comparative Arts, Ohio U., 1968; m. Carol A. Tuthill, Nov. 6, 1964 (div. June 1969); 1 dau., Kirsten; m. 2d, Patricia Alice Whalley, Dec. 30, 1976. Electronics engr. Raytheon Co., Wayland, Mass., 1958-60; tech. dir. small stage Boston Arts Festival, 1961, 62; dir. dramatics Melrose (Mass.) High Sch., 1962-63; dir. playhouse and repertory theatre, instr. drama and speech Hofstra U., 1963-66, instr. opera, 1965; dir. univ. theatre, asst. prof. theatre U. Toledo, 1968-69; dir., asso. prof. theatre and film Southampton Coll. L.I. U., 1969-73; asso. prof. theater and speech World Campus Afloat, Chapman Coll., 1972; asst. prof. cinema studies and still photography Ithaca Coll., 1973-76; asso. prof. media arts U. S.C., 1976—. Mem. A Soc. Integrated Arts (founder), Am. Theatre Assn., Univ. Film Assn., Soc. Archtl. Historians, Coll. Art Assn., Assn. Ednl. Communications Tech., Speech Communications Assn., Shakespeare Oxford Soc. Author: The Architecture of Frank Lloyd Wright, 1974; contbr. articles to popular mags., profl. jours. Home: 3118 Wheat St Columbia SC 29205 Office: Media Arts U SC Columbia SC 29208

STORRS, ELEANOR EMERETT, research inst. exec.; b. Cheshire, Conn., May 3, 1926; d. Benjamin Porter and Alta Hyde (Moss) S.; B.S. with distinction in Botany, U. Conn., 1948; M.S. in Biology, N.Y. U., 1958; Ph.D. in Chemistry, U. Tex., Austin, 1967; m. Harry Phineas Burchfield, Nov. 29, 1963; children—Sarah Storrs, Benjamin Hyde. Asst. biochemist Boyce Thompson Inst. Plant Research, Yonkers, N.Y., 1948-62; research scientist Clayton Found. Biochem. Inst., U. Tex., Austin, 1962-65; biochemist Pesticides Research Lab., USPHS, Perrine, Fla., 1965-67; dir. dept. biochemistry Gulf South Research Inst., New Iberia, La., 1967-77; adj. prof. chemistry U. Southwestern La., Lafayette, 1974-77; research prof. biology, head div. comparative biochemistry Med. Research Inst., Fla. Inst. Tech., Melbourne, 1977—; cons. in rehab. and prevention deformities of leprosy. Recipient plaque La. Health Dept., 1972; Disting. Alumnus award U. Conn., 1975; Gold award Am. Coll. Pathologists and Am. Soc. Clin. Pathologists, 1974; Gerard B. Lambert award, 1975; NIH grantee, 1968—; Center for Disease Control grantee, 1969-73; WHO grantee, 1973—, leprosy program grantee, 1978—; German Leprosy Relief Assn. grantee, 1973—; Nat. Council Episcopal Ch. grantee, 1975-77. Fellow Am. Inst. Chemists, AAAS, N.Y. Acad. Scis.; mem. Internat. Leprosy Assn., Am. Chem. Soc., Internat. Soc. Tropical Dermatology, Bot. Soc. Am., Reticuloendothelial Soc., Am. Forestry Assn., Am. Soc. Mammalogy, Am. Assn. Lab. Animal Sci. (Charles A. Griffin award 1975), Wildlife Disease Soc., Sigma Xi. Episcopalian. Clubs: Appalachian (Boston); Green Mountain (Bear Mountain, N.Y.); Mystic Krewe of Iberians (mem. ct. 1972, queen 1974). Author: (with H. P. Burchfield) Biochemical Applications of Gas Chromatography, 1962; (with H. P. Burchfield, D.E. Johnson) Guide to the Analysis of Pesticide Residues, 2 vols., 1965; contbr. articles, chpt. to profl. publs.; pioneer devel. leprosy in exptl. animal (armadillo). Office: 7725 W New Haven Ave Melbourne FL 32901

STORRS, THOMAS IRWIN, banker; b. Nashville, Aug. 25, 1918; s. Robert Williamson and Addie Sue (Payne) S.; B.A., U. Va., 1940; M.A., Harvard, 1950, Ph.D., 1955; m. Kitty Stewart Bird, July 19, 1948; children—Thomas, Margaret. With Fed. Res. Bank, Richmond, Va., 1934-60, v.p. charge research, 1957-59, v.p. charge Charlotte br., 1959-60; exec. v.p. N.C. Nat. Bank, Greensboro, 1960-67, vice chmn. bd. dirs., 1967-69, pres., 1969-73, chmn. bd., 1977—; pres. NCNB Corp., 1968-73, chmn. bd., 1974—; dir. Black and Decker Mfg. Co., Cannon Mills Co. Pres., Fed. Adv. Council, 1974-75. Trustee U. N.C., Charlotte, Davidson (N.C.) Coll. Served to lt. comdr. USNR, 1941-45, 51-52; comdr. Res., ret. Mem. N.C. Citizens Assn. (pres. 1971-72), Assn. Res. City Bankers. Episcopalian. Clubs: Greensboro City; Charlotte Country, Charlotte City. Home: 2633 Richardson Dr Charlotte NC 28211 Office: NCNB Corp NCNB Plaza PO Box 120 Charlotte NC 28255

STORY, CHARLES WILLIAM, ins. co. exec.; b. Birmingham, Ala., Aug. 23, 1945; s. Tillman Stewart and Lillian Lenora (Hoglan) S.; A.B. in English and Philosophy, Birmingham So. Coll., 1967; postgrad. gen. mgmt. skills Am. Mgmt. Assn. Extension Inst., 1974-76; m. Betty Jean Smith, Feb. 25, 1977; children—Tammy, Susan. Salesman, asst. mgr., state mgr. Am. Assn. Life Ins. Co., Birmingham, 1967-68; salesman Corroon & Black Benefits, Inc. (name formerly Blair, Follin, Allen & Walker Inc.), Nashville, 1968-69, asst. v.p. for tng. and devel., 1973—, agy. coordinator, 1969—. Mem. Am. Mgmt. Assn., Am. Soc. for Tng. and Devel. Presbyterian. Home: 7917 Meadowview Dr Nashville TN 37221 Office: 301 Plus Park Blvd Nashville TN 37202

STOUDEMIRE, GEORGE WOODROW, real estate broker; b. Chapin, S.C., Sept. 24, 1912; s. Thomas O'Neal and Rilla Ellen (Amick) S.; A.B., Newberry Coll., 1934; m. Ruby Mae Marsh, Feb. 17, 1938; children—Ellen Esther, George Woodrow, Thomas Archie. With Claude E. Creason Co., Columbia, S.C., 1933-60; owner Woody Stoudemire Co., real estate and ins., Columbia, 1961—; Appraiser. Mem. Columbia (pres. 1972, named Realtor of Year, 1973, dir., 1969-74), S.C. (dir. 1969-74) bds. realtors, Multiple Listing Service (dir. 1968-73, v.p., 1968). Lutheran (chmn. fin. com.). Clubs: Newberry Coll. Indian (pres. Columbia area 1959-60), Rotary (pres. 5 Points Club 1975-76); Lions. Home: 213 Partridge Ln W Columbia SC 29169 Office: 2715 Millwood Ave Columbia SC 29205

STOUDEMIRE, STERLING A(UBREY), ret. educator; b. Concord, N.C., Sept. 4, 1902; s. Palmer and Frances (Cranford) S.; A.B., U. N.C., 1923, M.A., 1924, Ph.D., 1930; m. Irene Slate, 1925 (dec. 1940); 1 dau., Marian S. (Mrs. James A. Hawkins); m. 2d, Mary Arthur Billups, 1946; 1 son, Sterling Cranford. Instr. Spanish, U. N.C., 1924-30, asst. prof. Spanish, 1930-35; asso. prof. Spanish, 1935-41, prof. Spanish, 1941-73, prof. emeritus, 1973—, head dept. Romance langs., 1949-64. Served as lt. comdr. USNR, 1942-45. Mem. Modern Lang. Assn., S. Atlantic Modern Lang. Assn. (pres. 1962), Am. Assn. Tchrs. Spanish and Portuguese, Am. Name Soc., Phi Gamma Delta. Episcopalian. Author articles on Spanish Romanticism, Italian opera in Spain; author and editor Spanish texts and anthologies. Translator: Oviedo's Natural History of the West Indies, 1959; Christian Doctrine (Pedro de Cordoba), 1970. Home: 712 Gimghoul Rd Chapel Hill NC 27514

STOUDT, MICHELE IRENE, mfg. co. ofcl.; b. Reading, Pa., July 13, 1953; d. Donald Leroy and Kathryn Irene Stoudt; B.A. (Carnegie Mellon grantee), Lehigh U., 1975; postgrad. U. Bonn, 1975. Prodn. supr. Joseph E. Seagram & Sons, Balt., 1976-78; mfg. engr. Tex. Instruments Co., Dallas, 1978-79, supr. prodn. planning, 1979—. Mem. Am. Mgmt. Assn. Democrat. Mem. Reformed Ch. Clubs: Dallas Area Lehigh Alumni (dir.), Order Eastern Star. Office: PO Box 6015 M/S 548 Dallas TX 75222

STOUT, ALBERT WESLEY, transp. co. exec.; b. Denver, Feb. 8, 1926; s. Albert W. and Henrietta (Rabjohn) S.; student Ind. State U., 1951; m. Elsie Hernandez, Nov. 26, 1976; children—Robert W., Shirley Ann. Vice pres., treas. Eastern Express, Inc., Terre Haute, Ind., 1947-71; pres. Motor Freight Corp., Terre Haute, 1968-71; pres. Specialized Transp. div. Ryder System, Inc., Miami, Fla., 1971-79; pres. Atlantic Express, Inc., Atlanta, 1979—, Served to 1st lt. USAR, 1943-46. Mem. Nat. Assn. Shipper Motor Carrier Conf. (pres., chmn. bd.), Am. Soc. Traffic Transp. (dir.), Central States Motor Freight Bur. (dir.), Nat. Motor Freight Traffic Assn. (chmn. bd. dirs.), Ind. Motor Truck Assn. (dir.), ICC Practitioners Assn., Delta Nu Alpha (pres.). Club: Atlanta Athletic. Home: 8145 Bail Mill Rd Atlanta GA 30338 Office: 1530 Dunwoody Pkwy Suite 204 Atlanta GA 30338

STOUT, DAVID WILLIAM, counselor; b. Elwood, Ind., Aug. 8, 1942; s. George William and Mary Katherine S.; B.S. in Edn., Ball State U., 1964; M.Ed., Miss. State U., 1977, Ed.S., 1978; m. Reba L. Owens, July 2, 1968; children—Jeffrey Allen, George Edward. News dir. WCBI-TV, Columbus, Miss., 1971-72; job. devel. counselor Miss. Employment Security Commn., Columbus, 1972-74; factory rep. Cerfact Lab., Atlanta, 1974-77; counselor Placement and Career Info. Center, Miss. State U., 1977-78; dir. counseling and student personnel, mem. faculty Alcorn State U. Sch. Nursing, Natchez, Miss., 1978—; cons. area sr. citizens operations; adj. prof. U. So. Miss., Copiah-Lincoln Jr. Coll. (Natchez). Mem. adv. council Miss. Bd. Health, 1979-80. Served with USAF, 1965-71. Decorated AF Commendation medal, air medal (4). Mem. Am. Personnel and Guidance Assn., Am. Coll. Personnel Assn., So. Coll. Personnel Assn., Nat. Assn. Student Personnel Adminstrs., Nat. Vocat. Guidance Assn., Miss Personnel and Guidance Assn., Phi Delta Kappa. Baptist. Club: Masons. Home: Rt 2 Box 83B Columbus MS 39701 Office: Alcorn State U Duncan Park Natchez MS 39120

STOUT, ETHAN AUTREY, inventor, entrepreneur, corp. exec.; b. DeQueen, Ark., Dec. 30, 1932; s. Ethan Allan and Leora Mae (Stuman) S.; student McNeese State Coll., 1954-55; m. Patricia Ann Nelson, Apr. 25, 1960. Civilian health tng. instr. and various sales and mgmt. positions, 1955-62; owner, operator Comml. Bldg. Maintenance Co., Houston, 1962-76; pres. Saepas Enterprises, Inc., Houston, 1969—; pres. Houston Complete Automotive and Richmond Automotive 1969-77, Spartan Labs., Inc., 1977—. Served with USAF, 1951-55. Mem. Tex. Assn. Bldg. Service Contractors (v.p., charter). Methodist. Club: Lions (dir.). Pioneer, Mr. Goodpump. Home: 6810 Winkleman Rd Houston TX 77083 Office: 9801 A Harwin St Houston TX 77063

STOUT, JOSEPH ALLEN, JR., historian, author; b. Sioux City, Iowa, May 27, 1939; s. Joseph A. and Mary A. (Comstock) S.; B.A., Angelo State Coll., 1967; M.A. (NDEA fellow), Tex. A. and M. U., 1968; Ph.D., Okla. State U., 1971; m. Bonnie Jean Slavens, Sept. 27, 1975; children—Carolyn Ve Ann, Sherilyn LeAnn. Tchr., San Angelo (Tex.) High Sch., 1968-69; asst. prof. Mo. So. State Coll., Joplin, 1971-72; asst. prof. dept. history Okla. State U., Stillwater, 1972-74, asso. prof., 1974—, supr. grad. teaching assts., 1976-77, instr. extension courses in Am. West and history, 1969-71. Mem. Am., Okla. hist. socs., Western History Assn., Tex. State Hist. Assn., Phi Kappa Phi, Phi Alpha Theta, Alpha Mu Gamma, Sigma Delta Pi. Author 13 books including: (with Odie B. Faulk) A Short History of the American West, 1974; Frontier Adventures: American Exploration in Oklahoma, 1976; Apache Lightning: The Last Great Battle of the Oho Calientes, 1974; (with Odie B. Faulk) The Mexican War, 1973. Home: 2701 S Mar Vista Stillwater OK 74074 Office: 525 Math Sci Bldg Okla State U Stillwater OK 74074

STOUT, JOSEPH EARL, state ofcl.; b. Lake Charles, La., Apr. 27, 1927; s. Charles Earl and Mabel (Fargue) S.; student U. Tenn., 1960, La. State U., 1965, FBI Nat. Acad., 1967, Tex. A. and M. U., 1969; m. Dora Elaine Cole, Dec. 8, 1951; 1 dau., Martha Jane. Patrolman, Lake Charles (La.) Police Dept., 1948-49, sgt., 1949-53, detective sgt., 1953-56, capt., 1956-65, chief, 1965-74; mem. La. Bd. Parole, 1975—. Vice chmn. adv. com. La. State U. Law Enforcement Tng., 1965—; mem. Commn. on Law Enforcement Standards and Edn., 1969; mem. La. Commn. Law Enforcement Adminstrn. of Criminal Justice, Com. on Law Enforcement, 1969-71; chmn. Red Carpet Com., 1968. Bd. dirs. S.W. Guidance Council. Recipient recognition certificate of merit Gov. La., 1971, certificate of merit La. State U., 1971, Tourism award Lake Charles Assn. Commerce, 1967, Law Enforcement award Optimist Internat., 1968. Mem. La. Assn. Chiefs Police (pres. 1967-68), La. Peace Officers Assn. (pres. 1970-71), Internat. Assn. Chiefs Police (chmn. membership com. 1966-68), Municipal Police Officers Assn., FBI Nat. Acad. Grads. (3d v.p. La. chpt. 1971-72, pres. La. chpt. 1974), Greater Lake Charles C. of C. Methodist (dir. 1970-72). Rotarian. Club: Buccaneer (dir. 1971-72). Home: 9803 Dwyerwood Ave Baton Rouge LA 70809 Office: State Office Dept Corrections Pentagon Ct PO Box 44304 Capitol Sta Baton Rouge LA 70804

STOUT, MARY WEBB, educator; b. Richmond, Va., Dec. 24, 1947; d. Frank Edmond and Edith Harris Webb Steger; B.A., Mary Washington Coll., 1970; M.Ed., U. Va., 1972; postgrad. U. Md., 1976, Boston U., 1976; m. Ted Alvin Stout, July 8, 1972. Tchr., Harrisonburg (Va.) Public Schs., 1970-71, Buckingham County Public Schs., Buckingham, Va., 1972-73; tchr. predischarge edn. program Army Edn. Center, Vicenza, Italy, 1973-74; post dir. Army Continuing Edn. System, 1976-77, edn. counselor, 1974-76; edn. specialist U.S. Army Q.M. Sch., Ft. Lee, Va., 1978—. Water safety instr. ARC, 1971—; bd. dirs. Massanetta Springs Alumni Assn., Presbyterian Ch. U.S., 1979—. Recipient Sustained Superior Performance award CSC, 1977; Outstanding Achievement award Dept. Army, 1975, 76. Mem. Assn. U.S. Army, Am. Personnel and Guidance Assn., Nat. Vocat. Guidance Assn., Mil. Educators and Counselors Assn., Va. AAU, Antique Automobile Club Am. Democrat. Clubs: Ft. Lee Track, Ft. Lee Officers' Wives, 4-H All Stars. Home: 1008 Smithfield Ave Hopewell VA 23860 Office: US Army QM Sch Individual Tng Analysis and Design Bldg 4100 Fort Lee VA 23801

STOVALL, CLARA YUVONNE (BUNNY), mgmt. cons.; b. Brownfield, Tex., Jan. 19, 1935; d. Elmer Clay and Bernice Arlene (Donathan) Griffith; student pub. schs., Idalou, Tex.; m. Leland Zane Stovall, June 14, 1953; children—Sabrina D. Stovall Linn, Leighland Shawn. Prodn. mgr., sales mgr. Tex. Mesquite, Mesquite Daily News, 1964-74, prodn. mgr., 1965-74, account exec., 77; mgr. div. Mgmt. Recruiters Dallas, Inc., with Search Group, Lineback Assos. div., 1977—; tchr. offset printing. Tchr. Sunday sch. Northridge Baptist Ch., 1961-75, Methodist Ch., 1968-71. Named Nat. S.W. Account Exec. of Yr., 1977; other awards; accredited account exec. Mem. Bus. Women Dallas. Democrat. Club: Order Eastern Star. Home: Route 2

209 N Jobson St Sunnyvale TX 75182 Office: 8350 N Central Expressway Suite 2140 M Dallas TX 75206

STOVALL, GUY FRANKLIN, JR., investment exec.; b. El Campo, Tex., Jan. 13, 1934; s. Guy Franklin and Edith I. Stovall; B.B.A., U. Houston, 1956; m. Kay Kuhn, Feb. 7, 1956; children—Guy Franklin III, Becky, Linda, David, Eric. Trader in oil, land, cattle, rice investments; dir., chmn. bd. 1st Nat. Bank, El Campo, Tex. Trustee Gulf Coast Med. Found., former pres. and chmn. bd.; trustee Wharton County Jr. Coll. Found., also numerous trusts. Recipient Elk of year award, 1969-70. Mem. Petroleum Club. Methodist (trustee 1965-77). Home: El Campo TX 77437 Office: 202 E Jackson St El Campo TX 77437

STOVALL, HENRY CALVIN, JR., automobile and farm equipment dealer; b. Cornelia, Ga., Aug. 20, 1915; s. Henry Calvin and Elizabeth Patton (Phillips) S.; A.B., U. Ga., 1937; m. Nancy Gay Hipps, Feb. 4, 1976; 1 step-dau., Marcia Dalton Loyd. Office mgr. Comml. Credit Corp., Columbus, Ga. and Mobile, Ala., 1938-40; pres., treas. Stovall Motor Co., Inc., Cornelia, 1946—, Stovall Tractor Co., Inc., 1948—, Dual S Enterprises Inc., 1972—; dir. Cornelia Bank; treas. Wesley Homes, Inc., Atlanta. Vice chmn. Cornelia Housing Authority, 1951-75, chmn., 1975—; mem. state disciplinary bd. State Bar Ga., 1974-79. Served with U.S. Army, 1940-46; ETO; NATOUSA; col. Res. Ret. Recipient Quality Dealer award Time Mag., 1974. Mem. Nat., Ga. (pres. 1975-76) automobile dealers assns., Cornelia C. of C. (pres. 1956). Democrat. Methodist. Clubs: Masons, Shriners, Kiwanis (pres. Cornelia club 1955), Capitol City, Toccoa Country, Chattahoochee. Home: 410 Grandview Circle Cornelia GA 30531 Office: PO Box 629 Clarkesville Rd Cornelia GA 30531

STOVALL, JAMES WATTS, clergyman; b. Mobile, Ala., Apr. 27, 1912; s. Albert Bee and Rosa Lee (McDowell) S.; student pub. schs.; m. Janet Elizabeth Myers, June 19, 1935 (dec. Aug. 1967); 1 dau., Mary Elizabeth. Blacksmith's helper Mobile County, Ala., 1930-38; asst. warehouseman Mobile County, 1938-43, warehouseman, 1943; minister Belforest Christian Ch., 1953-54, Robertsdale Christian Ch., 1955-65, 67—, Azalea Christian Ch., 1966-67. Speaker, Central Baldwin County Easter Sunrise Service, 1974. Lifetime blood donor A.R.C., 1957—. Recipient Town and Country Minister of Year award Ala. Christian Chs., 1963. Mem. Baldwin County Ministers Assn. Mason. Home: 300 Stocking Mobile AL 36604

STOVALL, RANDALL HOWARD, biologist; b. Norman, Okla., Feb. 3, 1951; s. Jack William and Dorothy Lorraine S.; student U. Okla., 1969-71, Odessa Coll., 1972, Midland Coll., 1972; B.S., U. Tex., Arlington, 1973, M.A., 1975; postgrad. U. Tex., Houston, 1975-77; Ph.D., Okla. State U., 1980; m. Laraine Lois Stovall, Aug. 12, 1977. Instr. biology N. Harris County Coll., Houston, 1977-78; asst. prof. biology Northwestern Okla. State U., Alva, 1979—. U. Tex. Grad. Sch. Biomed. Sci. merit scholar, 1976. Mem. AAAS, Am. Mus. Natural History, Am. Soc. Ichthyologists and Herpetologists, Herpetologist League, Nat. Wildlife Fedn., Soc. Study Amphibians and Reptiles, Southwestern Assn. Naturalists, U. Tex. Biology Grad. Student Assn. (pres. 1974-75), Tex. Soc. Electron Microscopy, Sigma Xi, Phi Sigma. Contbr. articles to profl. jours. Office: Dept Biology Northwestern Okla State U Alva OK 73717

STOVER, WILLIAM REITZEL, educator, condominium cons.; b. Waynesboro, Pa., June 8, 1906; s. Harry Edgar and Antoinette (Reitzel) S.; B.S., Temple U., 1938, Ed.M., 1940; Litt. D., Wagner Coll., 1953; m. Anna Mary Miller, June 5, 1928. Prin. Amon Heights and Jr. High Sch., Pennsauken, N.J., 1928-47, supt., 1947-55; supt. Central Regional High Sch. Dist., Bayville, N.J, 1955-58, Mainland Regional High Sch. Dist., Linwood, 1958-64. Ofcl. local congregation Luth. Ch., 1931—, ofcl. N.J. Synod, 1953-64; mem. commn. on ministry with aging Fla. Synod; instr. Christian edn., 1950—, del. Luth. Ch. Convs., 1952-64; mem. Luth. Laymen's Movement. Troop com. chmn. Boy Scouts Am., 1936-42, mem. bd. review 1941-42; pres. Condominium Assn. and area council, 1970-72; active various civic or charity drives. Bd. dirs. Wagner Coll., Mt. Airy Sem., Phila., S.W. Fla. Retirement Center, Community Mobile Meals. Mem. N.E.A. (life), P.T.A. (life), N.J. Edn. Assn. (pres. 1951-53), Nat., N.J. assns. sch. adminstrs., Assn. Ret. Persons (local pres. 1966-68), Phi Delta Kappa. Lutheran. Mason (Shriner). Author: What You Should Know Before Buying a Condominium, 1972; cross-reference Index of Florida Condominium Laws, ann. Home: 3272 Southfield Ln Sarasota FL 33579

STOWE, CHARLES ROBINSON BEECHER, mgmt. cons.; b. Seattle, July 18, 1949; s. David Beecher and Edith Beecher (Andrade) S.; B.A., Vanderbilt U., 1971; M.B.A., U. Dallas, 1975. Account exec. Engleman Co., pub. relations and advt., Dallas, 1974-75; instr. Richland Coll., Dallas, spring 1976; accountant Arthur Andersen & Co., Dallas, 1976-78; part-time public relations cons.; dir. Productive Capital Corp.; gen. partner Productive Capital Assos.; pres. Stowe & Co., Mgmt. cons., Dallas, 1978—. Trustee, Stowe-Day Found., 1979—; mem. nat. adv. bd. Young Am.'s Found., 1979—. Served as officer USNR, 1971-74; lt. Res. Recipient Freedoms Found. award, 1969, Navy Achievement medal, 1973. Mem. Pub. Relations Soc. Am., Nat. Assn. Accountants, Dallas C. of C., Sigma Iota Epsilon. Club: Dallas Vanderbilt (pres. 1977-78). Author articles. Home: 5021 Manett Dallas TX 75206

STOWE, WILLIAM MCFERRIN, clergyman; b. Franklin, Tenn., Jan. 28, 1913; s. John Joel and Myra Anderson (McFerrin) S.; A.B., Hendrix Coll., Conway, Ark., 1932, D.D., 1956; B.D., Duke, 1935, D.D., 1967; Ph.D., Boston U., 1938; D.D., Oklahoma City U., 1955; L.H.D., Southwestern Coll.; LL.D., So. Meth. U., Baker U., 1966; m. Twila Farrell, July 28, 1943; children—William McFerrin, Twila Gayle, Martha Elizabeth. Ordained to ministry Meth. Ch., 1937; pastor Meth. Ch., Alta Loma, Tex., 1938-40, Garden Villas Meth. Ch., Houston, 1940-44; mem. staff Bd. Edn., Meth. Ch.; dir. youth work Tex. Conf. Meth. Ch., 1940-44, dir. spl. tng. enterprises, 1944-49, sec. personnel service, 1946-49; sec. vocational council Meth. Ch., 1946-48; pastor First Meth. Ch., Stillwater, Okla., 1949-51, St. Luke's Meth. Ch., Oklahoma City, 1951-64; bishop The Meth. Ch., Kansas Area, 1961-72, Dallas, 1972—. Vis. prof. The Iliff Sch. Theology, Denver, summer 1945-47, Scarritt Coll., Nashville, 1944-46; spl. lectr. Boston U. Sch. Theology, 1945, Perkins Sch. Theology, So. Meth. U., 1944-46, Westminster Theol. Sem., 1946-47, Grad. Sch. Religion, U. So. Calif., 1946, Gammon Sch. Theology, 1944-45; dean Meth. Pastors' Sch. Mem. exec. com. Okla. Council Chs., pres. Oklahoma City Council Chs., 1955-56; pres. Okla. Conf. bd. edn. The Meth. Ch.; mem. exec. com. jurisdictional bd. edn., mem. co-ordinating council, del. to world conf., 1956, 61, 66, 71, 76, jurisdictional conf., 1956, 60, 64, del. gen. conf., 1956, 60, 64; mem. exec. com. World Meth. Council; del. World Meth. Theol. Inst., Oxford, Eng., 1958, 62; exec. com. Okla. Meth. Conf. Council; pres. Okla. Conf. Meth. Commn. Christian Higher Edn., 1956-60; pres. Tex. Conf. Chs., 1976-77; chmn. Advance; trustee So. Meth. U., Southwestern U., Huston-Tillotson Coll., Perkins Sch. Theology, Kans. Wesleyan U., St. Paul Sch. Theology; chmn. bd. trustees Lydia Patterson Inst., 1976—. Recipient Distinguished Alumnus award Boston U. Sch. Theology. Mem. Sigma Chi. Mason. Club: The Mokus (Boston). Author: Characteristics of Jesus, 1962; Power of Paul, 1963; It All Began With God. Contbr. articles to religious jours. Home: 4123 Echo Glen Dallas TX 75234 Office: PO Box 8127 3300 Mockingbird Ln Dallas TX 75205

STOWELL, JEREMY AVERILL, psychiatrist; b. N.Y.C., May 31, 1941; s. Averill and Helen Louise (Smart) S.; B.A., Northwestern U., 1963; M.D., Duke, 1967; m. Susanne Renate Dassel, June 26, 1965; children—Tanya, Sasha, Raissa, Katya, Alyna. Intern USPHS Hosp., Seattle, 1967; resident U. Colo. Med. Center, Denver, 1968-70; with NIMH, 1970-72; pvt. practice child and adult psychiatry, Fairfax, Va., 1972—; mem. staff Fairfax Hosp.; dir. adolescent unit Dominion Psychiat. Treatment Center, Seven Corners, Va., 1975—, also pres. med. staff; dir. psychiat. treatment program Fairfax County Juvenile Ct., 1970—, Keystone Alcoholism Program, 1974-77; mem. Washington Psychiat. Council, 1974-76; med. dir. Acertink Acad.; cons. in field. Mem. Am. Psychiat. Assn., AMA, No. Va. Psychiat. Assn. (pres. 1974-76), Am. Soc. Adolescent Psychiatry, Fairfax County Med. Soc. (peer rev. com.), Phi Delta Theta. Episcopalian. Home: 10525 Summerwind Ln Fairfax Station VA 22039 Office: Suite 405A 10560 Main St Fairfax VA 22030

STOWERS, JACOB FURLEY, III, urban forester; b. Clearwater, Fla., Aug. 27, 1942; s. Jacob Furley and Jane (Thompson) S.; A.A., St. Petersburg Jr. Coll., 1963; B.S. in Forestry, U. Fla., 1967, M. Agr., 1971; m. Kathryn Coates, Sept. 13, 1974; children—Sheri Lynn, Christine D. Biol. technician Dept. Interior, Gainesville, Fla., 1964-67; lab. technician U. Fla. Sch. Forest Conservation and Natural Resources, 1967-70; urban forester Fla. Div. Forestry, Ft. Lauderdale, 1972; environ. planner Coral Ridge Properties, Coral Springs, Fla., 1972-74; urban forester Pinellas County (Fla.) Dept. Environ. Mgmt., 1974-76, chief environ. mgmt. div., 1976-77, asst. dir. dept., 1977-79, dir. dept., 1979—. Mem. Soc. Am. Foresters, Urban Forestry Working Group, Internat. Soc. Arboriculture (gov.), Alpha Zeta, Xi Sigma Pi. Home: PO Box 252 Crystal Beach FL 33528 Office: 315 Court St Clearwater FL 33516

STOWHAS, MARGARITA CLARA, lang. sch. and transl. service exec.; b. Santiago, Chile, Nov. 18, 1937; d. A. Raul and Graciela (Sanchez) S.; came to U.S., 1971; Ph.D., Univ. de Chile, 1961; div.; 1 son, Chris M. Cantin. Tchr., Escuela San Patricio, Santiago, 1959; prof. Spanish, Universidad Catolica, Santiago, 1960-64; head social dept. Corporacion de la Vivienda, 1964-71; laborer Childress Canvas, Dallas, 1971; order filler Paradise Corp., Dallas, 1972; mem. officer staff Franklin Stores Corp., Dallas, 1972-73; night sch. tchr. Dallas Ind. Sch. Dist., 1973-75; tchr., translator, Dallas, 1973-77; lang. instr. Eastfield Coll., Dallas, 1975-77; exec. dir. Dallas Internat. Lang. Center, 1975—. Mem. Am. Translators Assn., L'Alliance Francaise, Nat. Assn. Female Execs., North Dallas C. of C. Mem. Ch. Jesus Christ of Latter-day Saints. Office: 1450 Preston Forest Sq Dallas TX 75230

STRACENER, NEALON, savs. and loan exec.; b. Kipling, La., June 29, 1916; s. James Monroe and Mary Evelyn (Higginbotham) S.; B.A. in Journalsim, La. State U., 1942, J.D., 1948; m. Mary Helen Langlois, June 2, 1943; children—Douglas Nealon, Carol Elizabeth. Admitted to La. bar, 1947, also U.S. Supreme Ct.; practiced in Baton Rouge, 1947—; founder, pres. Guaranty Fed. Savs. & Loan Assn., 1957—. Pres., Alpha Xi Delta House Corp., 1973-75. Chmn. 6th Dist. Republican Exec. Com., East Baton Rouge Parish Exec. Com.; gen. counsel Rep. State Central Com.; editor La. Republican, 1952-62; del. Rep. Nat. Convs., 1956, 60. Mem. Am., La. State, East Baton Rouge Parish bar assns., Am. Coll. Mortgage Attys., Am. Judicature Soc., Theta Xi, Sigma Delta Chi. Baptist (deacon). Mason (Shriner). Home: 9461 Woodbine Dr Baton Rouge LA 70815 Office: 3155 Weller Ave Baton Rouge LA 70805

STRADINGER, DAVID CLARK, city adminstr.; b. Chgo., Jan. 10, 1947; s. Oscar and Mavis Marguerite (Clark) S.; B.A., Hampden-Sydney Coll., 1969; M.P.A. (Ford Found. fellow), U. Va., 1972; m. Christine DeLorme Tavel, Aug. 22, 1970; 1 son, Shane Austin. Adminstrv. intern city mgr.'s office City of Charlottesville (Va.), 1971-72; adminstrv. asst. city mgr.'s office City of Charlotte (N.C.), 1972-73, asst. city mgr., 1973-75; city mgr. City of Myrtle Beach (S.C.), 1975—. Chmn. Horry County (S.C.) United Way Campaign; trustee S.C. Hall of Fame. Mem. Am. Soc. Public Adminstrn., Internat. City Mgmt. Assn., S.C. City-County Mgmt. Assn., Myrtle Beach C. of C. (dir. 1975—), Omicron Delta Kappa. Club: Rotary. Office: PO Box 2468 Myrtle Beach SC 29577

STRAHLE, ROLF GULLMAR, educator, architect; b. Gothenburg, Sweden, May 21, 1919; s. Gunnar W. and Gerda C. (Hedlund) S.; M.Arch., Swedish State Coll. Tech., 1944; postgrad. U. Gothenburg, 1948-49, seismic design course Stanford U., 1977; m. Ivy Soriano de Strahle, Nov. 21, 1956; children—Bjorn Gullmar, Jeanne-Marie Karin. Came to U.S., 1947. Expert, adviser UN Tech. Assistance, Nigeria, Dahomey, 1961, Ethopia, Kenya, 1964-66, Peru, 1969-73; chief architect Inst. Urban Housing, San Salvador, El Salvador, C.A., 1950-57; prof. Sch. Architecture, U. El Salvador, 1950-57; cons. architect, design and planning dept. suburbs City Gothenburg, 1957-58; asso. prof. Sch. Architecture, Syracuse U., N.Y., 1958-59; prof. Sch. Architecture Tulane U., New Orleans, 1959-69; now prof. Sch. Architecture U. Southwestern La., Lafayette; adviser, cons. internat. field of housing. Served with Royal Engrs. (Sweden), 1940-44. Mem. Swedish Inst. Architects, AIA, AAUP. Home: 101 Suffolk Ave Ivanhoe Estates Lafayette LA 70508

STRAIT, MARY WELLS, speech and lang. pathologist, audiologist; b. Huntington, W.Va., Dec. 10, 1937; d. Frank Nix and Mary Frances (Robinson) Wells; A.A., U. Ky., 1968; A.B. summa cum laude, Marshall U., 1971, M.A. summa cum laude, 1972, postgrad., 1972-75; m. Aug. 6, 1955 (div. 1979); children—Wesley Shawn, Kenneth Shane. Speech and lang. pathologist, adminstr. Geiger Easter Seal Speech and Hearing Center, Ashland, 1972-79, exec. dir., 1976—; cons. com. for parents of hearing impaired children, Bur. Edn. for Exceptional Children, State Adv. Com. for Deaf, Child Find Com.; lectr. Sch. Nursing, Ashland Community Coll.; adv. Ashland Vocat.-Tech. Sch., Ironton (Ohio) Vocat. Tech. Sch. Bd. dirs. Council on Aging; cons. Jr. Achievers; commd. gov.'s task force on edn. First woman Boss of Year, Ashland Area Jaycees, 1977; named Ind. Woman, Ashland Daily Ind. Newspaper, 1976. Mem. Am. Speech, Lang. and Hearing Assn., W.Va. Speech and Hearing Assn., Ky. Speech and Hearing Assn. (Jour. editorial bd.). Clubs: Ashland Jr. Women's, Pilot. Commd. Ky. Col. Home: 1040 Amherst Dr Ashland KY 41101 Office: 2201 Lexington Ave Ashland KY 41101

STRALEY, H. W., III, geophysicist; b. Mercer County, W.Va., May 12, 1900; s. H. W., II and Rosa Lee Bearegard (Walthall) S.; B.A., Concord Coll., Athens, W.Va., 1923; Ph.D., U. N.C., 1937; Ph.D., U. Chgo., 1938; m. L. Garnet Brammer, July 24, 1927; children—H.W., IV, William F. Jr. engr. Pocatello C. & C. Co., 1927-30; asso. prof. geology Baylor U., 1939-42; with U.S. Bd. Econ. Warfare, 1942-46, mem. tech. mission to Cuba, 1942-43; cons., tchr. Cath. U. and Am. U., 1946-48; vis. prof. geology Okla. U., 1948-49; prof., cons. Ga. Inst. Tech., 1949-67; cons. geologist, 1967-69; prof. geology Morehead (Ky.) State U., 1969-71; cons. Dames & Moore, Atlanta, 1951—; cons. Mobil Oil Co., Boon-Lewis Devel. Co., Pacatello Coal & Coke Co., Pocahontas Fuel Co., Rary Coal Co., other cos.; speaker internat. Symposium Carolina Bays, Royal Astron. Soc., London, Eng., 1968. Mem. Am. Inst. Mining Engrs., Am. Assn. Petroleum Geologists, Am. Geophys. Union, Carolina (pres. 1938-39), Yorkshire (Eng.) geol. socs., Soc. Econ. Geophysicists, Geol. Soc. Am. Address: 5910 Riverwood Dr NW Atlanta GA 30328

STRANGE, BUFORD BENNETT, broadcasting co. exec.; b. Mansfield, La., July 18, 1936; s. Buford Zack and Josie (Griffith) S.; B.A., La. Coll., 1958; M.A., U. So. Miss., 1959; postgrad. U. Minn., 1960-61; m. Mayme Vera Stone, May 30, 1959; children—Jo-Ruth, Vera-Zee, Clinton Buford, Danya-Lee. Reporter Mansfield Enterprise, 1956-57, Interstate Progress, Logansport, La., 1956-57, Shreveport (La.) Times, 1955-57, 66—; news dir. WDAM-TV, Hattiesburg and Laurel, Miss., 1961-66; asst. prof. dept. communications, dir. radio-TV U. So. Miss., Hattiesburg, 1958-66; pres. Heart Dixie Broadcasting Corp., gen. mgr. KDXI radio, Mansfield, 1967—; pres. Mansfield Cablevision. Sec., Sabine River Authority. Recipient several civic awards, including La.'s Sound Citizen award La. Jr. C. of C., 1966, La. Sch. Bell award La. Tchrs. Assn., 1969. Mem. Mansfield (hon. life), La. (regional v.p. 1970-71), U.S. (dir. 1970-71) Jaycees, Pi Kappa Delta, Alpha Psi Omega, Sigma Delta Chi. Baptist (supt.). Lion. Author: (with W.E. Simonson) Techniques of Debate, 1960. Contbr. articles to profl. jours. Home: 114 Gibbs St Mansfield LA 71052 Office: Drawer 740 Mansfield LA 71052

STRASSBURG, KENNETH RUSSELL, forest products co. exec.; b. Romeo, Mich., May 9, 1924; s. Fred and Hattie (Kegler) S.; student pub. schs., Mt. Clemens, Mich.; m. Marion Geschwind, Jan. 9, 1946; children—Janet Strassburg Olson, Kenneth Russell, Kevin and Kathy (twins). With Gate City Industries, Ft. Lauderdale, Fla., 1946-67, v.p., 1967—; v.p. ops. Mack Industries, Hollywood, Fla., 1965-77; v.p. Eastern ops. Dant & Russell, Inc., Port Everglades, Fla., 1977—. Pres., Grace Lutheran Ch., Ft. Lauderdale, Fla., 1965. Served with 11th Airborne Div., U.S. Army, 1943-46; PTO. Decorated Purple Heart. Mem. Fla. Lumber and Bldg. Materials Assn. (pres. 1972-73), Luth. Layman's League, Hoo Hoo Internat. Republican. Home: 1309 Middle River Dr Fort Lauderdale FL 33304 Office: Dant & Russell Inc PO Box 13137 Port Everglades FL 33316

STRATAS, NICHOLAS EMANUEL, psychiatrist; b. Toronto, Ont., Can., Aug. 9, 1932; s. Emanuel Nicholas and Argero (Terezakis) S.; came to U.S., 1957, naturalized, 1962; B.A., U. Toronto, 1953, M.D., 1957; m. Rene Printezis, Dec. 14, 1955; children—Nicholas, Byron, Andrew. Intern Meml. Hosp., Danville, Va., 1957; resident psychiatry Eastern State Hosp., Williamsburg, Va., 1958-60, chief resident Dorthea Dix Hosp., Raleigh, N.C., 1960-61, clin. dir., also dir. residency tng., 1961-63; dir. psychotherapy clinic Rex Hosp., Raleigh, 1960-62; mem. staff N.C. Dept. Mental Health, 1963-73, dir. edn., 1963-66, dir. research, 1965-66, dep. commr., 1966-69, regional commr., 1970-73; pvt. practice, Raleigh, 1963—; mem. staff Wake Med. Center, Rex hosps.; clin. asso. prof. psychiatry U. N.C. Med. Sch., 1964—; cons. in field. Mem. Gov. N.C. Com. State Govt. Reorgn., 1970-71. Bd. dirs. Raleigh Cultural Center, 1973-74, Inst. Human Ecology, 1969-73, Wake County Mental Health Assn., 1964-65, N.C. Found. Mental Health Research, 1965-66. Recipient citation U. Toronto, 1957, AMA, 1969, 72, 75, 78, gov. N.C., 1968, 70. Diplomate Am. Bd. Neurology and Psychiatry. Fellow Am. Psychiat. Assn. (citation 1970, 79), Am. Pub. Health Assn., Am. Soc. Clin. Hypnosis, Acad. Psychomatic Medicine, Royal Soc. Health. Author: Consultation Education, 1975; also articles. Asso. editor N.C. Jour. Mental Health, 1965-73. Home: 304 Foxhall St Raleigh NC 27609 Office: 3900 Browning Pl Raleigh NC 27608

STRATE, WARREN EDWARD, metals co. exec.; b. Independence, Mo., Aug. 20, 1943; s. Warren Albert and Dorothy Lucenda (Marten) S.; B.S. in Pub. Relations and Advt., Mo. State U., 1968, M.S. in Indsl. Sociology, 1970; m. Jacqueline Kay Boyer, June 26, 1963; children—Kimberly R., Karen Dianna. Sales rep. Vernaz Drug Co., Warrensburg, Mo., 1965-68; dir. advt. and pub. relations Mo. Pub. Service Co., Kansas City, 1968-73; mgr. mktg. communications Star Mfg. Co., pre-engineered metal bldg. systems, Oklahoma City, 1973-77; pres. Strate Bros. Feed and Grain, 1977—; dir. Estates Investment, Inc., Kansas City, 1971-73. Chmn. Blue Springs (Mo.) United Appeal campaign, 1973; vice chmn. mfg. and petroleum div. Oklahoma City United Appeal campaign, 1974. Bd. dirs. Wesley Found., U. Okla. Served with USMCR, 1961-65. Named Mem. of Year, Kansas City Indsl. Advertisers, 1971. Mem. Mo. State U. Alumni Assn. (nat. pres. 1973-74), Alpha Kappa Delta. Mason (32 deg., Shriner). Home: 3906 Briarcrest Dr Norman OK 73069 Office: Strate Bros Feed and Grain Norman OK

STRATHDEE, KENNETH ALEXANDER, mgmt. cons.; b. Chgo., Nov. 27, 1928; s. Alexander and Elizabeth (Dignan) S.; B.B.A., Loyola U., Chgo., 1951; m. Mary Therese Wells, June 23, 1956; children—Kenneth Edward, Mary Carol. With Gits Molding Corp., Chgo., 1953-61; sr. asso. A.T. Kearney Co., Chgo., 1961-73; partner Coopers & Lybrand, Houston, 1973—. Served with U.S. Army, 1951-53. Mem. Inst. Mgmt. Cons., Houston World Trade Assn., Internat. Council Small Bus., St. Andrews Soc., Delta Sigma Pi. Roman Catholic. Contbg. author: The Managerial and Cost Accountant's Handbook, 1979. Office: 1010 Jefferson St Houston TX 77002

STRATON, JOHN WILLIAM, mining engr.; b. Williamson, W.Va., Sept. 29, 1922; s. Joseph Butcher and Mae Bernice (Sullivan) S.; student W.Va. U., 1940-43, B.S. in Engring. of Mines, 1947; M.B.A., U. Pa., 1949; m. Jeannette Stathers, Aug. 21, 1948; children—Joseph C., John William. Indsl. engr. Truax Traer Coal Co., Kayford, W.Va., 1949-50; indsl. engr. Princess Elkhorn Coal Co., David, Ky., 1950-51, chief engr., 1951-54, dir. indsl. engring., 1954-56, gen. supt., 1956-57; gen. mgr. Lorado (W.Va.) Coal Mining Co., 1958-60; mining engr. Gates Engring. Co., Beckley, W.Va., 1960-61, v.p. mining engring., 1961-71, exec. v.p. ops., 1971-75, exec. v.p., 1976-77, pres., 1978—; pres. Raleigh Acceptance Co., Beckley, 1973—. Bd. dirs. YMCA, Beckley, 1964-66, 68-69, treas., 1966; vestryman Beckley Episcopal Ch., 1965-66, 73-76, Key Man, 1978; mem. W.Va. Reclamation Bd. Review, 1971—, chmn., 1973-75. Served with U.S. Army, 1943-46. Recipient Pres.'s award Raleigh County C. of C., 1964. Mem. Nat. Assn. Profl. Engrs. (dir. 1970-76), W.Va. Soc. Profl. Engrs. (pres. 1970-72), Am. Inst. Mining and Metall. Engrs., Soc. Mining Engrs. (chmn. coal div. 1979, dir. 1980—), Assn. Cooperation in Engring. (chmn. coordinating com. on energy 1976), Pan. Am. Union of Engring. Socs. Democrat. Episcopalian. Clubs: Glade Springs, Black Knight, Elks. Contbr. articles to tech. jours. Home: 801 Northwestern Ave Beckley WV 25801 Office: PO Drawer AF Beckley WV 25801

STRATTON, HENRY DAVIS, lawyer; b. Pikeville, Ky., Aug 9, 1925; s. Pem Burton and Minnie M. (Davis) S.; student Asbury Coll., 1943, Pikeville Coll., 1946-47; LL.B., U. Louisville, 1950; m. Lois Jean Shipley, June 14, 1947; children—David Carey and Daniel Pemberton (twins), Teresa Louise. Admitted to Ky. bar, 1950, since practiced in Pikeville; pres., dir. Citizens Bank of Pikeville; v.p., dir. East Ky. Broadcasting Co.; dir. Campbell County Broadcasting Co., Lawrence County Broadcasting Co., Greater Ky. Broadcasting Co., Walter P. Walters Agy., London Broadcasting Co.; chmn. Fed. Jud. Selection Commn. of Ky., 1976—. Mem. Ky. Crime Commn., 1968-76. Bd. dirs., gen. counsel Meth. Hosp. Ky.; regent Eastern Ky.

U., 1970—; trustee Pikeville Coll., 1974—. Served with AUS, 1943-46. Mem. U.S. (dir.), Ky. (v.p.) jr. chambers commerce, Nat. Conf. on Uniform State Laws (commr.), Am., Ky. (mem. ho. of dels. 1964-65, gov. 1966-78, v.p. 1974, pres. 1974-75, 76-77, pres.-elect 1975-76, chmn. fed. jud. selection com. 1977—) bar assns., Ky. Hist. Soc., Phi Alpha Delta, Omicron Delta Kappa. Methodist. Mason. Clubs: Filson, Greenmeadows, Willowbrook. Home: 110 Cedar Dr Pikeville KY 41501 Office: 2d St Pikeville KY 41501

STRATTON, JOHN ROBERT, mfg. co. exec.; b. Hillsboro, Ohio, Nov. 4, 1928; s. Ronald Robert and Hazel (Duncan) S.; student Case Sch. Applied Sci., 1948-50; m. Margaret Longsdorf, Jan. 17, 1971; children—Kimberly E., Sarah L.; stepchildren—Joseph B., Cherylann. Div. exec. Cleve. Trencher Co., constrn. equipment, 1967-69; div. mgr. Long Mfg. Co., Tarboro, N.C., 1969-72; v.p. Capacity, Inc., Dallas, 1972—. Served with USMC, 1946-48. Mem. Am. Soc. Metals, AIME, Soc. Automotive Engrs., Fluid Power Soc., Am. Trucking Assn. (mem. maintenance com. 1972—, mem. ops. council 1972—). Address: 6735 Churchill Way Dallas TX 75230

STRATTON, PORTER ANDREW, historian, educator; b. Richland, N.Mex., Dec. 31, 1918; s. Earl Jefferson and Laura Elizabeth (Watson) S.; B.A., U. N.Mex., 1942; M.A., Eastern N.Mex. U., 1962; Ph.D., Tex. Tech. U., 1967; m. Mary Roseanna Carter, Feb. 7, 1947; children—Stephen Andrew, John Carter, Jo Beth. Advt. mgr. Portales (N.Mex.) Tribune, 1945-57, News-Tribune, Portales, 1957-61; prof. history Pan Am. U., Edinburg, Tex., 1964—, head dept., 1971-79. Served with USAAF, 1941-45. Decorated D.F.C., Air medal with 3 oak leaf clusters. Mem. Kappa Alpha, Phi Alpha Theta. Lion (pres. Edinburg 1970-71). Author: The Territorial Press of New Mexico, 1834-1912, 1969. Home: 1025 Ebony Dr Edinburg TX 78539

STRAUB, JOHN HENRY, photographer; b. Akron, Ohio, Feb. 13, 1932; s. Ray Elsworth and Hester Irene (Beckwith) S.; student U. Ala., 1949-50, 51-52, Auburn U., 1950-51; m. Winifred Marie Fulmer, Mar. 2, 1954; children—Barbara Sue, Patricia Ann, James Robert. Photographer, Tuscaloosa (Ala.) News, 1955; photog. supr. Gulf States Paper Corp., Tuscaloosa, 1957-77; owner, mgr. Images Plus, Tuscaloosa, 1977—; mem. faculty U. Ala., 1974—, Brewer State Jr. Coll., 1977-78. Served with U.S. Army, 1952-55. Mem. Profl. Photographers Am. (Ala. council, nat. award 1974, photog. craftsman degree; cert.), Profl. Photographers Miss.-Ala. (dir., Ala. Photographer of Yr. award 1972, profl. certified photographer 1975), Tuscaloosa Jaycees. Baptist. Club: Exchange. Home: Route 1 Box 195 Northport AL 35476 Office: 415 15th St Tuscaloosa AL 35401

STRAUSS, JEANNE H., tech. translator; b. Hamburg, Germany, Mar. 5, 1928; d. Frederic and Julie S.; came to U.S., 1948, naturalized, 1954; B.A., Roosevelt U., 1956; M.A., Loyola U., Chgo., 1960; doctoral candidate U. Wis., Madison. Legal sec. Montgomery Ward, Chgo., 1957-60; instr. Creighton U., Omaha, 1961-63; teaching asst. U. Wis., Madison, 1964-65; asst. prof. U. Wis., Stevens Point, 1965-69, Western Ill. U., Macomb, 1969-71, U. Wis., Superior, 1973-75; tech. translator Phillips Petroleum Co., Bartlesville, Okla., 1975—. Mem. Am. Assn. Tchrs. French, Am. Assn. Tchrs. Spanish and Portugese, MLA, Philbrook Art Museum. Republican. Home: PO Box 78 Bartlesville OK 74003

STRAUSS, RICHARD, counselor; b. Boston, Dec. 23, 1944; s. Alexander and Mary S.; B.A., Rollins Coll., 1966; M.Ed., Salem State Coll., 1968; postgrad. U. South Fla., 1971; m. Sandra Conrad, Apr. 9, 1977. Tchr. English, Central Jr. High Sch., Metheun, Mass., 1968, Dixie Hollins High Sch., St. Petersburg, Fla., 1968-71; ednl. cons. Patricia Stevens Coll., Tampa, Fla., 1971-72; vocat. rehab. counselor II, State of Fla., St. Petersburg, 1972-74; vocat. rehab. counselor Crawford Rehab. Services, Inc., Tampa, Fla., 1974-76, dir., Rockville, Md., 1976—. Cert. rehab. counselor Nat. Bd. Commn. on Rehab. Counselor Cert.; certified vocat. expert Social Security Adminstrn.; lic. rehab. counselor, Va.; lic. employment counselor, Md. Mem. Nat. Rehab. Assn., Nat. Rehab. Counseling Assn., Am. Personnel and Guidance Assn., Nat. Employment Counseling Assn., D.C. Rehab. Counseling Assn. Office: Crawford Rehab Services Inc 152 Rollins Ave Suite 204 Rockville MD 20852

STRAW, CLARK MASON, electronics co. exec.; b. Plymouth, N.H., Sept. 26, 1946; s. Harold I. and Edith Janet (Pasewark) S.; B.S. in Elec. Engring., Tex. Tech. U., Lubbock, 1969; M.S. in Adminstrv. Sci. and Mgmt., U. Tex., Dallas, 1975; m. Suzanne Claire Rydman, Sept. 7, 1968; children—Kelley Christine, Kevin Clark. With Hewlett-Packard Co., 1969—, field engr. calculator products div., Dallas, 1972-74, dist. mgr., 1974-77, regional mgr. for computational products, Atlanta, 1977-79, area mgr. computer products group, 1979—. Boswell scholar, 1964; recipient Internat. Radio award, France, Argentina, Ecuador, U.S., USSR and Japan. Mem. IEEE, Nat., Tex. socs. profl. engrs., Am. Amateur Radio Relay League, Dallas Amateur Radio Club, Atlanta Radio Club, Radio Amateur Satellite Soc. Republican. Presbyterian. Club: Indian Hills Country. Home: 577 Greystone Trace Marietta GA 30067 Office: PO Box 105005 Atlanta GA 30348

STRAW, JIMMIE FRANKLIN, cost reduction cons., writer, pub.; b. Pryor, Okla., Apr. 23; s. Walter L. and Katarine (Beley) S.; student public schs., Douglass, Kans.; m. DeLores Ann Satterfield, Feb. 28; children—Rebecca, Micaela, Joseph, Phillip, Andrei. Pres., TSA Import/Export Co., 1963-65, Redy Electronics Mfg. Inc., 1964-65, Trans-Global Merc., 1967-70, Internat. Trade & Devel. Corp., 1972-73, Jim Diamond Wigs, 1968-70, Discount Wig Centers, 1970-76, Peek-A-Boo Wig Shops, 1970-76, Salesway Corp., 1975-76; editor, pub. Bus. Opportunities Digest, Atlanta, 1976—; writer, editor, pub. Bus. Intelligence Network Confidential Memos, Atlanta, 1972—; founder, exec. dir. Am. Bus. Club, Atlanta, 1972—; chmn. Aalpha Royale Advt., Atlanta, 1971—. Served with U.S. Army, 1964-67. Mem. Nat. Writers Syndicate (mem. editorial bd. of rev.), Mensa, Panjandrums (founder, coordinator). Author: The Complete Book of Money Making Opportunities, 1979; Financing Sources (annually); Finders Fee Guide (annually); editor, pub. Communications, newsletter Panjandrums, 1977—. Office: PO Box 13748 Atlanta GA 30324 also Suite 114 3110 Maple Dr NE Atlanta GA 30305

STREAM, HAROLD HENRY, farmer, rancher; b. New Orleans, July 17, 1920; s. Harold Henry and Violet (Abaunza) S.; B.E. in Chem. Engring., Tulane U., 1942; m. Matilda Geddings Gray II, June 1, 1946; children—Harold Henry III, Sandra Gray, William Gray (dec.). With Union Oil Co. Calif., 1946-69; pres. MGS Co., Lake Charles, La., 1969—; dir. Pacific Moulded Products Co., Santa Barbara Mill and Lumber Co., Gulf Nat. Bank. Trustee Matilda G. Gray Found., New Orleans Museum Art, Anglo-Am. Mus.; mem. pres.'s adv. council Tulane U. Served with USNR, World War II. Home: 1315 Royal St New Orleans LA 70116 Office: Box 40 Lake Charles LA 70601

STREAM, KATHRYN SHEAFFER, audiologist; b. Pittsboro, Miss., Nov. 10, 1939; d. Jack T. Sheaffer and Mary K.S. Kirksey; B.A., Vanderbilt U., 1960; M.A., Northwestern U., 1961; postgrad. U. Tex. Med. Br., 1977—; m. Richard William Stram, Dec. 29, 1961; children—Mary, Elizabeth. Clin. audiologist Michael Reese Med. Center, Chgo., 1961-64, UCLA, 1969-71, U. Tex. Med. Br., Galveston, 1971—; pvt. practice audiology, Galveston, 1978—; lectr., workshops on parent counseling for profls. Pres., United Way of Galveston, 1977. Office of Vocat. Rehab. tng. grantee, 1960-61. Mem. Am. Speech and Hearing Assn., Tex. Speech and Hearing Assn., So. Audiol. Soc.; fellow Soc. Advancement of Ear, Nose and Throat in Children. Contbg. author: Pediatric Audiology, 1978. Office: Suite 724 200 University Blvd Galveston TX 77550

STREED, WILLIAM ERIC, reinforced plastics mfg. co. exec.; b. Mobile, Ala., May 23, 1944; s. William Raymond and Juanita (Williams) S.; B.S. in Mech. Engring., U. Miss., 1966. Project mgr. Owens Corning Fiberglas, Granville, Ohio, 1966-70; cons. to European Plastics Industry, Dublin, Ireland, 1970-73; owner Mech-Tran, Inc., Brunswick, Ga., 1973-78; ops. mgr. Koch Fiberglass Products Co. div. Koch Industries, Brunswick, 1978—. Trustee, Youth Estate. Mem. ASME, Soc. Plastics Engrs., Modern Plastics Mgmt. Adv. Com., Alpha Tau Omega (state alumni dir. 1974, state dir. 1975). Republican. Lutheran. Clubs: Jaycees, St. Simons Island Exchange (pres. 1975). Home: 316 Armstrong St Brunswick GA 31520 Office: Glynco Indsl Park Brunswick GA 31520

STRENGLEIN, DENISE DOWNEY, instl. researcher; b. Glen Ridge, N.J., June 12, 1935; d. John Benjamin and Lucy Josephine (Smith) Downey; student City Coll. N.Y., 1953; A.A. with honors, St. Petersburg Jr. Coll., 1962; A.B. with honors, U. S.Fla., 1967, M.A., 1969, postgrad., 1976—; m. Harry Frederick Strenglein, Jan. 10, 1958; 1 son, Ralph. Sec., Sperry Gyroscope Co., Great Neck, N.Y., 1955-58; grad. teaching asst., U.S. Fla., Tampa, 1967-68, research asso., 1970-76, coordinator instl. research, 1976—; instr. mathematics. Mem. Assn. Instl. Research (com. on long range goals, 1976-77, nominating com. 1979), Nat. Council Tchrs. of Mathematics, So. Conf. Instl. Research (program co-chmn., 1975, chmn., 1977, mem.-at-large 1980), Pi Mu Epsilon. Democrat. Clubs: Common Cause, Fla. Trail Assn., Royalty Players. Contbr. papers to confs. and publs. Home: 1507 Winding Way Clearwater FL 33516 Office: Univ South Florida ADM 280 Tampa FL 33620

STRENKOWSKI, JOHN SIGMUND, educator; b. Elizabeth, N.J., Feb. 6, 1950; s. Sigmund Anthony and Emily Constance (Zych) S.; B.S., U. Va., 1972; M.S. in Aero. Engring., M.I.T., 1973; Ph.D. in Applied Mechanics, U. Va., 1977; m. Deborah Gail Clevinger, June 17, 1972. Research scientist Battelle Meml. Inst., Columbus, Ohio, 1976-78; asst. prof. mech. and aerospace engring. N.C. State U., 1978—. NSF fellow, summer 1971; Dupont Meml. fellow, 1972-73; NSF grantee, 1979—. Mem. ASME, AIAA, Am. Soc. Engring. Edn., Sigma Xi, Tau Beta Pi, Sigma Gamma Tau. Club: N.C. State U. Faculty. Contbr. articles to profl. jours. Home: 1421 Harris Ct Cary NC 27511 Office: 2407 Broughton Hall NC State U Raleigh NC 27650

STRICHERZ, MATHIAS ERNEST, psychologist; b. Watertown, S.D., July 13, 1948; s. Killian Frederick and Stella Ruth (Wall) S.; B.A., Huron Coll., 1972; M.Ed., U. Guam, 1974; Ed.D., Tex. Technol. U., 1976. Head resident dormitory complex U. Guam, 1972-73; research asst. Coll. Edn., Tex. Technol. U., Lubbock, 1974-76, staff psychologist, 1977—; psychologist U. N.Mex., 1976-77, U. Houston, summer 1978. Chief adv. Reese AFB Social Actions Wing Psychologist, 1977-78. Served with USN, 1967-71. Tex. Technol. U. Grad. Sch. grantee, 1976, Ednl. Research Fund grantee U. N.Mex., 1977; Wilson Arnold lectr. Methodist Hosp., Lubbock, 1978. Mem. Am. Assn. Sex Educators, Counselors and Therapists, Am. Soc. Clin. Hypnosis, Internat. Soc. Hypnosis, Am. Personnel and Guidance Assn., Rocky Mountain Ednl. Research Assn., Rocky Mountain Psychol. Assn., Lubbock Assn. Psychologists, Nat. Vocational Guidance Assn. Roman Catholic. Author: (drama) Missing in Action, 1971. Contbr. articles to profl. jours. Home: 5315 24th St Lubbock TX 79407 Office: PO Box 4160 Tex Technol U Lubbock TX 79409

STRICKLAND, ALLEN MCGILL (MRS. GEORGE M. STRICKLAND), artist; b. Washington; d. I.J. Nota and Frances M. (Maloy) McGill; student pvt. schs.; m. George Marion Strickland, Nov. 11, 1947. Salon in Paris Artistes Français: one-man show at Daytona Beach (Fla.) Art League, Cinema Theatre Gallery, Daytona Beach, Ormond Beach (Fla.) War Meml. Gallery, 1975, Ormond Beach Library, 1979; 2-man show Daytona Beach Art League, 1972; represented in pvt. collections in U.S. and France. Mem. Nat. League Am. Pen Women (pres. Daytona Beach br.; numerous prizes Fla. Fedn. Art, Daytona Beach Art League (numerous prizes), Garden Club Am. (pres. Halifax County). Home: 487 John Anderson Hwy Ormond Beach FL 32074

STRICKLAND, EARLINE, educator; b. Forrest County, Hattiesburg, Miss., May 20; s. Bill and Daisy Lee Strickland; B.S., Alcorn State U., 1960; M.S., Iowa State U., 1969, Ph.D., 1975; postgrad. U. So. Calif., summers, 1974-77, U. So. Miss., 1978. Instr., Montgomery High Sch., Louise, Miss., 1960-68; faculty intern div. social and rehab. services HEW, Atlanta, Ga., Washington; asst. prof. dept. edn. Miss. Valley State U., Itta Bena, 1969-70, dir. Community Devel. Resource Center, prof., head dept. family and community services, 1971—; vis. prof. Alcorn State U., 1977—; vis. prof. Iowa State U., Ames, 1972, research asst., summer, 1975; vis. prof. Jackson (Miss.) State U., 1976; mem. research team for nat. research project Nat. Center on Black Aged, 1977—; condr. workshops on gerontology. Mem. Am. Home Econs. Assn., Miss. Home Econs. Assn., Miss. Consumer Edn. Assn., Am. Gerontol. Assn. in Higher Edn., Miss. Council on Social Work, Leflore Mental Health Assn., Delta Sigma Theta (treas.) Democrat. Baptist. Editor: Human Ecology Forum. Address: PO Box 306 Itta Bena MS 38941

STRICKLAND, FRANK DALLAS, mktg. exec.; b. Atlanta, Dec. 14, 1946; s. Frank Leslie and Mable Elizabeth (Jones) S.; B.B.A., Ga. State U., 1971, M.B.A., 1972; m. Dec. 16, 1968; children—Frank Dallas, Dorsey Elizabeth. Staff acct./auditor Peat, Marwick, Mitchell & Co., Atlanta, 1972-74; with Data Systems Corp., Atlanta, 1974-78, v.p., 1977-78; dir. sales/mktg. Reynolds & Reynolds Co., Atlanta, 1978—. Trustee, Met. Atlanta Crime Commn., 1980—. Served with USNR, 1966-72. Mem. Am. Mgmt. Assn., Nat. Accts. Assn., Nat. Soc. Public Accts. Club: Trout Unltd. (dir. 1978). Home: 4592 Polo Ln Atlanta GA 30339 Office: PO Box 4897 Atlanta GA 30302

STRICKLAND, GEORGE HENRY, JR., banker; b. Boston, Nov. 16, 1924; s. George Henry and Ann (Lane) S.; student Denison U., 1945-48; J.D., Ohio State U., 1951; m. Margery Wood, July 31, 1948; children—Ann, George Henry. Admitted to Ohio bar, 1952; asso. firm Estabrook Finn & McKee, Dayton, Ohio, 1952-58; partner firm Young Pryor Lynn Strickland & Falke, Dayton, 1958-71; sr. v.p., head trust dept. Bank of Beaufort, Hilton Head Island and Beaufort, S.C., 1971—. Served with AUS, 1943-45. Mem. Ohio Bar Assn., Dayton Bar Assn., Hilton Head Island C. of C. (dir.). Clubs: Dayton Country (pres.), Rotary (dir.). Home: 24 Willow Oak Ct Hilton Head Island SC 29928 Office: Bank of Beaufort PO Box 5069 Hilton Head Island SC 29928

STRICKLAND, JAMES MELL, JR., environmental engring. cons.; b. Macon, Ga., Mar. 17, 1929; s. James Mell and Doris Ester (Criswell) S.; B.S. in Civil Engring., Va. Mil. Inst., 1951; m. Velma Jean Wilburn, June 19, 1951; children—Charlotte, Susan, Teresa. Engr., Whitman Requardt & Assos., Balt., 1953-54, Newport News (Va.) Waterworks Commn., 1954-56; partner Hayes, Seay, Mattern & Mattern, architects-engrs.-planners, Roanoke, Va., 1956—. Served with C.E., AUS, 1952. Decorated Bronze Star. Registered profl. engr., Ala., Fla., Ga., Ky., Md., N.C., S.C., Tenn., W.Va., Va. Mem. Am. Acad. Environ. Engrs., Nat. Soc. Profl. Engrs., Am. Cons. Engrs. Council, Water Pollution Control Fedn., Am. Waterworks Assn. Methodist. Home: 1907 Cantle Ln Roanoke VA 24018 Office: 1315 Franklin Rd Roanoke VA 24016

STRICKLAND, LEONARD GENE, govt. support ser. co. exec.; b. Gallipolis, Ohio, July 12, 1937; s. Samual Edward and Wilma Icie (Elkins) S.; student Our Lady of the Lake U., 1977-79; m. Sarah Frances Jenkins, Dec 25, 1956; children—Leonard Gene, Bryan Wayne. Commd. airman U.S. Air Force, 1955, advanced through grades to sr. master sgt., 1978, ret., 1978; with Tech. Contract Mgmt. Inc., Austin, 1978—, v.p. in charge of tech. support div., 1978—. Decorated Bronze Star medal, Air Force Commendation medal. Named Transp. Supr. of the Year, Headquarters Air Training Command, 1973. Mem. Nat. Def. Transp. Assn. Democrat. Clubs: Masons, Order Eastern Star. Home: 1605 Sage Hollow Circle Austin TX 78758 Office: 7718 Wood Hollow Dr Suite 166 Austin TX 78731

STRICKLAND, ROBERT LOUIS, business exec.; b. Florence, S.C., Mar. 3, 1931; s. Franz M. and Hazel (Eaddy) S.; A.B., U. N.C., 1952; M.B.A. with distinction, Harvard U., 1957; m. Elizabeth Ann Miller, Feb. 2, 1952; children—Cynthia Anne, Robert Edson. Advt. mgr. Lowe's Cos., Inc., North Wilkesboro, N.C., 1957-58, ops. mgr., 1958-60, mktg. mgr., 1960-61, dir. mktg., 1961-69, v.p. mktg., 1969-70, sr. v.p., 1970-76, exec. v.p., 1976-78, office pres., 1970-78, chmn. bd., 1978—, mem. exec. com., dir., 1961—; v.p., mem. adminstrv. com. Lowe's Profit-Sharing Trust, 1961—, chmn. ops. subcom., 1972-78; mem. nat. com. Loew's Employee Stock Owners Plan, 1977—; dir. Nat. Assn. O-T-O Cos., Revelstoke Cos. Ltd., Calgary, Can. Mem. N.C. Ho. of Reps., 1962-64; mem. Republican exec. com. N.C., 1962-73. Trustee, sec. bd., mem. personnel Com. Wilkes Community Coll., 1965-73; trustee N.C. Sch. of Arts Found., 1975-78; v.p. bd. dirs. Nat. Home Improvement Council, 1972-76. Served with USN, 1952-55; lt. Res., 1955-62. Named Wilkes County (N.C.) Young Man of Yr., Wilkes Jr. C. of C., 1962; recipient Bronze Oscar of industry award Fin. World, 1969, 70, 71, 72, 73, 74, 77, 78, 79, Silver Oscar of Industry award, 1970, 72, 73, 74, 77, 78, 79, Gold Oscar, 1972; recipient certificate of Distinction, Brand Names Found., 1970, Distinguished Mcht. award, 1972. Mem. Newcomen Soc., Scabbard and Blade, Phi Beta Kappa, Pi Kappa Alpha. Clubs: Twin City, Forsyth Country (Winston-Salem, N.C.); Hound Ears (Blowing Rock, N.C.); Roaring (N.C.) Gap. Author: Lowe's Cybernetwork, 1969; Lowe's a Living Legend, 1970; Ten Years of Growth, 1971; The Growth Continues, 1972, 73; The Scoreboard, 1978; contbr. articles to profl. jours. Home: 226 N Stratford Rd Winston-Salem NC 27104 Office: Box 111 North Wilkesboro NC 28656

STRICKLAND, STANFORD ALLEN, electronic engr.; b. Seattle, Wash., Jan. 2, 1937; s. Homer Allen and Geraldine Marie Strickland; B.S. in Elec. Engring., U. Wash., 1964; M.S., U. Santa Clara, 1974; grad. IBM Middle Mgmt. Sch., Fla. Atlantic U., 1974; postgrad. Sci. Research Inst., 1975; m. Mary Sandra Sullivan, Aug. 19, 1970; children—Michael Gary, Donna Kaye. Spl. circuit designer IBM, San Jose, Calif., 1964-68, staff engr. in charge of circuit tech. dept., Boca Raton, Fla., 1968-70, mgr. power system design, 1970-74, sr. engr., 1975—, mgr. electronic tech., 1975—; instr. electronics West Palm Beach (Fla.) Jr. Coll., 1969-70. Registered profl. engr., Fla., Calif. Mem. IEEE (ednl. activities bd. 1979—, mem. engrs. council profl. devel. accreditation team). Patentee in field. Home: 1498 NW 4th Ct Boca Raton FL 33432 Office: 2000 NW 51st St Boca Raton FL 33431

STRICKLAND, THOMAS JOSEPH, artist; b. Keyport, N.J., Dec. 27, 1932; s. Charles and Clementine (Grasso) S.; student Newark Sch. Fine and Indsl. Arts, 1951-53, Am. Art Sch., 1956-59, Nat. Acad. Fine Arts, N.Y.C., 1957-59; m. Debrah J. Ponn, 1977. One man shows: Hollywood (Fla.) Art Mus., 1972, Studio Gallery, N.Y.C., 1959, 60, Le Monde, Palm Springs, Calif., 1960, 61, Binderton House, Phila., 1962, Internat. Art Exchange, N.Y.C., 1962, Art Fair Galleries, Holmdel, N.J., 1963, Libyan Gallery, N.Y.C., 1963, 64, Galerie 19, Roslyn, N.Y., 1963, Old Queens Gallery, New Brunswick, N.J., 1964, Elion Art Found., Princeton, N.J., 1965, Galerie des Deux Mondes, N.Y.C., 1967, Gabriel's Gallery, Hillsdale, N.J., 1968, Greater Miami C. of C., 1973, Elliott Mus., Stuart, Fla., 1974; group shows: 1st Ann. Met. Young Artists Show, Nat. Arts Club, 1958, Am. Artists Profl. League, Nat. Arts Club, 1958, 61, Parke-Bernet Galleries, N.Y.C., 1959, 61-64, Hashomer Hatzair, N.Y.C., 1961-64, Jewish Labor Com. Art Sale, N.Y.C., 1963-65, Butler Inst. Am. Art, Fine Arts Festival, Youngstown, Ohio, 1963, Orchestral Workshop of Westchester, White Plains, N.Y., 1964-65, Art Fair 65, Garden City, N.Y., 1965, Art 66 Sisterhood of Temple Beth El, Closter, N.J., 1966, Harmons of Guilford (Conn.), 1969, Gramercy Art Gallery, N.Y.C., 1966, Salon Rouge du Casino, Dieppe, 1967, Expn. Intercontinentale, Monaco, 1966-68, New York Galerie, Nice, 1971, 7e Grand Prix internat. de peinture de la Cote d'Azur, Cannes, 1971, Grove House, Coconut Grove, 1971-72, Art Show Temple Beth Am, Miami, 1972, Beaux Arts of Lowe Art Mus., Miami, 1972, Miami Art Center, 1973, Art Guild Boca Raton, 1973, Greater Miami C. of C., 1973, Elliott Mus., 1974, Am. Painters in Paris, 1975-76; represented in numerous collections including St. Vincent Coll., Latrobe, Pa., Hollywood (Fla.) Art Mus., St. Hugh Cath. Ch., Miami, Elliott Mus., Salem Coll., Winston-Salem, N.C.; guest appearances on TV; instr. painting and pastel Grove House, 1979. Recipient Julius Hallgarten prize Nat. Acad. Sch. Fine Arts, 1956, Dr. Ralph Weiler prize, 1957; Bertrum R. Hulmes Meml. Medal award Am. Vets. Soc. Artists, N.Y.C., 1965; Digby Chandler prize Knickerbocker Artists Exhbn., 1965; 1st prize Hollywood Arts and Crafts Guild Ann. Mems. Art Exhbn., 1972, Seven Lively Arts Festival Circle Art Show, Hollywood, 1972, Hollywood Art Mus., 1973, Blue Ribbon award Cape Coral Nat. Art Show, 1973, Met. Miami Flower Show, 1974; Charles Hawthorne Meml. award Nat. Arts Club Exhbn., 1977, others. Mem. Pastel Soc. Am., Grove House, Internat. Platform Assn., Blue Dome Art Fellowship. Club: Miami Palette. Contbr. articles to mags. Address: 2598 Taluga Dr Miami FL 33133

STRICKLETT, MARK EDWARD, educator; b. Omaha, Mar. 18, 1952; s. Dale William and Kittie Irene (McNeely) S.; B.A., Bellevue Coll., 1975; M.A., Calif. Western U., 1979; cert. Iowa Sch. Deaf, 1975; m. Sharon Kathleen Washka, July 4, 1976; 1 dau., Tandi Lee. Psychiat. technician Nebr. Psychiat. Inst., 1971-73; supr. residential services Douglas County Mental Health, 1973-74; dir. vocat. indsl. tng. Eastern Nebr. Community Office of Retardation, 1975-77; regional coordinator The Calif. Project, Ventura, 1977-78; state dir. Ga. Project, Athens, 1978—. Mem. vocat. adv. bd. Ga. Assn. Retarded Citizens, 1977-80; mem. youth adv. bd. YMCA, Omaha, 1975-77; cons. Mayor's Commn. on Employment of Handicapped, Santa Barbara, Calif., 1977-78. Mem. Am. Assn. Edn. of Severely/Profoundly Handicapped, Ga. Assn. Retarded Citizens, Nat. Assn. Retarded Citizens, Am. Assn. Mental Deficiency (chmn. region VII vocat. div. 1979—), Calif. Assn. Rehab. Facilities, Vocat. Evaluation and Work Adjustment Assn. Episcopalian. Home: 281

Rhodes Dr Athens GA 30606 Office: 850 College Station Rd Athens GA 30605

STRICKS, MAX, fin. exec.; b. N.Y.C., Nov. 20, 1924; s. Joseph and Rachael (Streitzer) S.; B.B.A., Pace U., 1956; postgrad. Bernard M. Barach Sch. Bus. and Pub. Adminstrn., 1956-59; m. Bernice Geller, Feb. 15, 1947; children—Mark David, Rochelle Sandra. Chief cost accountant, asst. treas. Gahagan Constrn. Corp., N.Y.C., 1956-65; mgr. finance constrn. div. Koppers Co., Pitts., 1965-68; controller Alsan Constrn. Corp., New Brunswick, N.J., 1968-71; v.p. finance Urban Home Ownership Corp., N.Y.C., 1971-73; treas., chief financial officer, mem. exec. com. First Fla. Bldg. Corp., Miami, 1973-76; controller Gany Corp., Miami, 1976-77; fin. exec. Fininvest, Ltd., 1978-79. Officer, Ocean Home Owners Civic Assn., 1964-65. Trustee, First Fla. Savs. and Profit Sharing Trust. Served with AUS, 1943-46. Decorated Combat Inf. badge, Leadership Green Stripe award. Mem. Nat. Assn. Accountants, Am. Accounting Assn., Am. Arbitration Assn. (nat. panel arbitrators 1967), Jewish War Vets. Democrat. K.P.

STRICKS, RICHARD BERT, lawyer; b. Cin., June 12, 1951; s. William and Eva (Lesser) S.; student Inter-Am. U. P.R., 1969-70; B.A. in Sociology, U. Cin., 1973; J.D., Tulane Sch. Law, 1976. Admitted to La. bar, 1976; clk., Bagert & Bagert, attys., 1974-76; practiced in New Orleans, 1976—; mem. firm Stein, Stricks & Assos., New Orleans, 1978—; pres. Bienville Mortgage Co., New Orleans, 1975-76. Mem. Nat. Assn. Criminal Def. Lawyers, Am. Trial Lawyers Assn., Am. Bar Assn., La. Trial Lawyers Assn., La. Bar Assn., Phi Alpha Delta. Democrat. Jewish. Club: B'nai B'rith (New Orleans). Home: 4213 St Charles Ave New Orleans LA 70115 Office: 2735 Tulane Ave New Orleans LA 70119

STRIEGLER, BERT CROWLEY, oil co. exec.; b. Brady, Tex., May 21, 1931; s. Cecil and Neva (Moseley) S.; B.S. in Bus., Trinity U., San Antonio, 1956; m. Beverly Irene Engdahl, June 12, 1950; 1 dau., Michele Lynn. With Conoco Inc., 1956—, sales mgr. aviation sales, 1970-77, mgr. tech. services N. Am. mktg., Houston, 1977—; contest dir. Acad. Model Aeros. Mem. Mayor Houston Commn. Parks, 1974-78; sponsor Cambodian refugees. Served with USAF, 1950-55. Mem. Soc. Automotive Engrs. Republican. Methodist. Clubs: Houston Radio Control, Manned Spacecraft Center Radio Control. Author papers in field. Home: 5831 McKnight St Houston TX 77035 Office: 5 Greenway Plaza E Houston TX 77046

STRILER, RAYMOND JOSEPH, army officer; b. Crystal City, Mo., Dec. 21, 1938; s. Hugo James and Mary Jane (Coleman) S.; B.S. in Edn., Southwest Mo. U., 1961; postgrad Command and Gen. Staff Coll., 1973-74; M.S. in Counseling, George Peabody Coll., 1978; postgrad. Okla. U., 1979-80; m. Heidi Marie Buettner, Apr. 26, 1965; children—Alexander, Michael. Commd. 2d lt. U.S. Army, 1962; advanced through grades to lt. col., 1978; inf. officer, Germany, 1962-65, 74-76, Vietnam, 1966-67, 69-70, Eng., 1977-78; adv. Okla. N.G., 1978—. Decorated Bronze Star, Air medal with 9 clusters, Vietnamese Cross Gallantry. Mem. Am. Personnel and Guidance Assn., Assn. U.S. Army, N.G. Assn., Sigma Pi (past pres.). Democrat. Roman Catholic. Club: Toastmasters. Author: Military Training Manual, 1972. Home: 1304 Winding Creek Rd Moore OK 73160 Office: 3501 Military Circle NE Oklahoma City OK 73111

STRIMBU, JERRY LEE, indsl. psychologist; b. Gary, Ind., Sept. 10, 1945; s. Thomas and Rosemary S.; B.A. in Psychology, Fla. Atlantic U., 1968; M.S., U. Ga., 1971, Ph.D. (Zimmer scholar), 1973; m. Pamela Blake, Aug. 12, 1967; childern—Christopher, Elizabeth. Asst. v.p., dir. personnel research and planning dept. Nat. Bank of Detroit, 1973-76; mgr. corp. staffing and employee relations H.E. Butt Grocery Co., Corpus Christi, Tex., 1976-78; sr. v.p., dir. human resources div. Tex. Fed. Savs. & Loan Assn., Dallas, 1978—. Mem. Am. Psychol. Assn., Tex. Psychol. Assn., Sigma Xi., Psi Chi. Club: Royal Oak Country. Contbr. articles to profl. jours. Home: 9602 Windy Terr Dallas TX 75231 Office: 8300 Preston Rd Dallas TX 75225

STRING, SAMUEL TIMOTHY, surgeon; b. Phila., May 13, 1939; s. Samuel Weber and Prudence (Dedrick) S.; B.A., U. Pa., 1961; M.D., 1966; m. Elizabeth Ann Thomas, June 18, 1965; 1 son, Samuel Timothy. Intern, U. Hosps. of Cleve., 1966-67, resident surgery, 1967-72; research U. Calif., San Francisco, 1969-70, fellow in vascular surgery, 1974-75; practice medicine specializing in vascular surgery, Mobile, Ala., 1975—; instr. surgery U. Calif. Med. Center, San Francisco, 1974-75; asst. prof. surgery U. South Ala., Mobile, 1975-77, asso. prof., 1977—; chief vascular surg. service U. South Ala. Med. Center, Mobile, 1975—; mem. staffs U. South Ala. Med. Center, Providence Hosp., Mobile Infirmary. Served in M.C., U.S. Army, 1972-74. Decorated Army Commendation medal. Diplomate Am. Bd. Surgery. Mem. Am. Heart Assn. (fellow stroke council), So. Soc. Vascular Surgery, A.C.S., AMA, Internat. Cardiovascular Soc., Assn. for Acad. Surgery. Republican. Contbr. articles in field to profl. jours. Home: 21 Kings Way Mobile AL 36608 Office: Dept Surgery U South Ala Med Center Fillingim St Mobile AL 36617

STRINGER, DONALD HALL, ins. co. exec.; b. Brookhaven, Miss., Aug. 13, 1938; s. Flavil Hall and Ella V. (Bowman) S.; B.A., Harding Coll., Searcy, Ark., 1967; m. Betty Lee Cox, Nov. 30, 1973; children—Caroline, Kip, Colleen, Clint. Vice pres. Shannon Supply Co., Clinton, Ark., 1961-65; sci. tchr. Bradford (Ark.) public schs., 1967-68; group rep. Conn. Gen. Life Ins. Co., Houston, 1969-74; regional group mgr. Home Life Ins. Co., New Orleans, 1974-79, Dallas, 1979—. Mem. pres.'s devel. council Harding Coll., 1974—; mem. Congressman Livingston's ins. and pension adv. com., 1978. Served with U.S. Army, 1959-65. Named Mgr. of Year, Home Life Ins. Co., 1977. Mem. Gen. Agts. and Mgrs. Assn., Life Underwriters Assn., Employee Benefit Planning Assn. La., Mensa. Republican. Mem. Ch. of Christ. Home: Rt 1 Country Club Estates Argyle TX 76226 Office: One Turtle Creek Village Suite 500 Dallas TX 75219

STRINGER, HERMAN EMERY, personnel exec.; b. Eva, Ala., Aug. 22, 1937; s. Herman Illie and Ester Irene (Kelley) S.; student Coastal Carolina Community Coll., 1967, U. Wis., 1957, 58, 76-78, Wallace State Jr. Coll., 1976-78; m. Betty Sue Dawson, Sept. 6, 1958; children—Herman Paul, Susie, Scott David. Enlisted pvt. E-1 USMC, 1954, advanced through grades to Master Sgt., 1976; security officer Birmingham First Nat. Bank (Ala.), 1976; employment officer, affirmative action officer, corporate awards officer, Employee Retirement Income Security Act, then officer, govt. contracts officer, Cullman, Ala., 1979—. Bd. mem. Boy Scouts Am., N. Ala. dist., 1979—; mem. Wallace State Profl. Council, 1977-79; sect. capt. Brewer for Gov., 1978, campaign mgr. Entrekin for Mayor, 1977; Cullman dist. Chmn. Job Ser. Improvement Program, 1979. Mem. Am. Soc. Personnel Mgmt., Ala. Community Relations Assn., Ala. Indsl. Relations Assn., North Ala. Community Assn. Baptist. Club: Moose. Home: 1548 Rose St NW Cullman AL 35055 Office: 2000 Hwy 157 W Cullman AL 35055

STRINGER, JAMES FRANK, JR., oil exploration co. exec.; b. Houston, Oct. 2, 1948; s. James Frank and Nina Reece (Crawford) S.; B.B.A., So. Meth. U., 1970; m. Ann Elizabeth Roberts, July 12, 1969; children—Allison Ann, James Frank. Landman, The Stringer Corp, San Angelo, Tex., 1970-75, pres., 1975—; dir. S.W. Bank of San Angelo. Bd. dirs. San Angelo Symphony, San Angelo YMCA. Mem. San Angelo Ramrods Civic Orgn., chmn., 1977. Mem. Am., Permain Basin assns. petroleum landmen, W. Central Tex. Oil and Gas Assn. (dir.). Republican. Baptist. Home: 911 Montecito San Angelo TX 76901 Office: 2402 College Hills San Angelo TX 76901

STRINGER, MARY LEE, educator; b. Heflin, La., May 5, 1941; d. Cleve and Lancy Ree (Caldwell) Calloway; B.S., Grambling State U., 1962; M.A., Atlanta U., 1969; cert. French Inst., Tex. So. U., 1964; cert. French Workshop, N.E. State U., 1966; postgrad. Sorbonne U., Paris, 1972; m. Johnny Ray Stringer, Nov. 23, 1974. Tchr., Lincoln High Sch., Ruston, La., 1962-69; faculty Alcorn State U., Lorman, Miss., 1969-73, chmn. dept. fgn. lang., 1972-73; asst. prof. French, Grambling (La.) State U., 1973—. Mem. AAUW, Am. Assn. Tchrs. French., MLA, Coll. Lang. Assn., Am. Council Teaching Fgn. Langs., Assn. Tchr. Educators, S. Central Assn. Modern Langs., La. Fgn. Lang. Tchrs., Assn., Elizabeth Robinson Alumni Assn., Atlanta U. Alumni Assn., Epsilon Psi Omega, Alpha Kappa Alpha. Democrat. Baptist. Office: Dept Fgn Lang Grambling State U Grambling LA 71245

STRINGER, ROBERT LYNN, banker; b. Killeen, Tex., Dec. 11, 1923; s. James Benjamin and Myrtle Lucille (Arnold) S.; B.B.A., Baylor U., 1949; grad. Rutgers U. Grad. Sch. Banking, 1955; m. Ora Belle Sharp, June 6, 1947; 1 son, Robert Lynn. Asst. cashier to v.p. Nat. City Bank, Waco, Tex., 1946-57; v.p. Tex. Nat. Bank, Houston, 1957-58; pres. Waxahacie Bank & Trust Co. (Tex.), 1958-60, Fed. Nat. Bank, Shawnee Okla., 1960-65, Ark. Valley Bank, 1965-70, 1st Nat. Bank of Mena (Ark.), 1971-77; chmn. bd. Security Nat. Bank, Cowette, Okla., 1977—, Bank of Commerce, Jenks, Okla., 1978—; v.p. FABCO. Bd. dirs. West Ark. council Boy Scouts Am., 1965-70. Served with AUS, 1943-46. Mem. Bankers Assn., Am. Mgmt. Assn., Mena C. of C. (dir. 1973). Baptist. Clubs: Rotary (past pres.); Masons (Shriner), Lion. Home: 5912 S Jamestown Ave Tulsa OK 74135

STRINGFELLOW, MARVIN ELLIOT, athletic dir.; b. Birmingham, Ala., Oct. 25, 1945; s. Carl Raymond and Julie (Elliott) S.; B.S. in Math. Edn., Fla. State U., 1967, M.S. in Ednl. Adminstrn., 1968; Ed.D. in Phys. Edn., U. Ala., 1972; m. Carol Kellam, Sept. 14, 1968; children—Laura Lynn, Christine Louise. Substitute tchr., 1968; freshman baseball coach Fla. State U., 1968; asst. mgr. S. Central Bell Telephone Co., Birmingham, 1968-70; teaching fellow, asst. baseball coach, recreation dir. speech and hearing clinic U. Ala., 1970-72; asso. prof. Jackson State U., 1972-77, baseball coach Sports Ambassadors Internat., summers 1972-75; dir. athletics, chmn. dept. health, phys. edn. and recreation Georgetown (Ky.) Coll., 1977—. Tchr. Sunday sch. Georgetown Baptist Ch. Mem. Nat. Assn. Intercollegiate Athletics (dist. rep. 1979-80; Dist. Coach of Year award 1979), AAHPER, Nat. Recreation and Parks Assn., U.S. Baseball Fedn., Am. Baseball Coaches Assn., Nat. Assn. Intercollegiate Baseball Coaches, Nat. Assn. Intercollegiate Athletic Dirs., Ky. Alliance Health, Edn. and Phys. Recreation, Ky. Intercollegiate Athletic Conf. (Coach of Year 1979). Author papers in field. Home: 400 Pocohontas Trail Georgetown KY 43023 Office: Dept Phys Edn and Athletics Georgetown Coll Georgetown KY 40324

STRIPLING, LEE BURNETT, engring. cons., tech. co. exec.; b. Beaumont, Tex., Feb. 27, 1929; s. Bonnie Duke and Willie Valda (Cariker) S.; B.S., U. Colo., 1950; M.S., UCLA, 1960; m. Mary Ann Favorito, June 25, 1955; children—Susan Ann, Cindy Lee, Cathleen Marie. Sr. tech. specialist Rocketdyne Co., Canoga Park, Calif., 1953-63; sr. tech. specialist Aerojet-Gen. Co., Sacramento, 1963-66; free-lance engring. cons., Neptune Beach, Fla., 1966—; pres. Intratec, Inc., Neptune Beach, 1975—; specialist on hydrodynamics and cavitation applied to turbomachinery design, 5 axis numerical control machining. Mem. ASME (Moody award Fluids div. 1962), Numerical Control Soc., Fla. Solar Energy Soc., Pi Mu Epsilon, Pi Tau Sigma, Sigma Tau. Democrat. Baptist. Home and office: 573 Pine St Neptune Beach FL 32233

STRITE, JACOB JAY MILLER, clergyman; b. Greencastle, Pa., Dec. 19, 1904; s. John Calvin and Daisy Belle (Miller) S.; A.B., Lynchburg Coll., 1930; student Christian Theol. Sem., Indpls., 1933-37; B.D., Lexington Theol. Sem., 1958, Th.M., 1959; m. Anna Irene Eckert Foltz, Aug. 9, 1929 (dec. 1953); children—Georgia Annabelle (Mrs. Carl Ray Flock), Martha Eckert (Mrs. Tony Lee Trexler); m. 2d, Clara Belle Fleishman, Oct. 23, 1954. Ordained to ministry Disciples of Christ Ch., 1933; minister North Eastwood Christian Ch., Indpls., 1933-35, Daleville (Ind.) Christian Ch., 1935-44, Corydon (Ind.) Christian Ch., 1945-50, Melrose Christian Ch., Roanoke, Va., 1950-57, Mt. Carmel Christian Ch., Winchester, Ky., 1957-60, Christian Coll. Ga., Athens, Ga., 1960-61 (also counselor, tchr.), Friendship Christian Ch., Athens, 1962-64, minister at large, 1964-69; asso. Bethany Christian Ch., Roanoke, Va., 1969—; mem. council on Christian Unity, Christian Ch. Mem. Disciples of Christ Hist. Soc., Nat. Audubon Soc., Smithsonian Assos., Postal Commemorative Soc., Am. Assn. Ret. Persons, Va. Christian Ministers Conf., Am. Conservative Union, Nat. Taxpayers Union, Nat. Wildlife Fedn., Automobile Club Va. Republican. Club: Pioneer (Lynchburg Coll.) (dir.). Home: 1678 Springbrook Rd NW Roanoke VA 24017

STRITE, LEWIS EDGAR, steel fabricating co. exec.; b. Hagertown, Md., Nov. 7, 1920; s. Edgar Irvin and Mary Magdeline (Martin) S.; m. Ethel Showalter, Dec. 22, 1945; children—L. Gerald, Elaine Hess, Carmen Miller. With Shenandoah Mfg. Co., Harrisonburg, Va., 1942—, sales mgr., 1945-53, gen. mgr., 1958-68, exec. v.p., gen. mgr., 1968—; pres. Mennonite Broadcast Inc., 1952-72; dir. Rockingham Nat. Bank, Wetsel Seed Co. Pres., Mennonite Christian Leadership Found.; bd. dirs. Mennonite Bd. Missions, James Madison U. Found. Mem. Harrisonburg-Rockingham County C. of C. (pres. 1969, Businessman of Year award 1976), Nat. Platform Assn. Club: Rotary Internat. (Paul Harris fellow award 1977). Home: 1325 Hillcrest Dr Harrisonburg VA 22801 Office: PO Box 711 Harrisonburg VA 22801

STROBUSH, EARL MORRIS, air force non-commd. officer; b. Nashville, July 30, 1944; s. James Russell and Ruby Christeen (Pittard) S.; student Lake Superior State Coll., 1972-73; cert. City Coll. of Chgo., 1974; B.S., William Carey Coll., 1978; m. Pauline Patricia Wallace, Oct. 23, 1969. Enlisted U.S. Air Force, 1963, advanced through grades to tech. Sgt., 1976; assigned to 39th Bombardment Wing, Eglin AFB, Fla., 1964-65, 70th Bombardment Wing, Clinton-Sherman AFB, Okla., 1965-66, 9th Reconnaissance Tech. Squadron, 9th Reconnaissance Wing, Beale AFB, Calif., 1966-67, 15th Reconnaissance Tech. Squadron, March AFB, Calif., 1967-68; non-commd. officer in charge chem. mix unit 12th Reconnaissance Intelligence Tech. Squadron, Vietnam, 1968-70; non-commd. officer in charge photog. printing 15th Reconnaissance Tech. Squadron, March AFB, Calif., 1970-72; combined system team mem. 449th Airborne Missile Maintenance Squadron, Kincheloe AFB, Mich., 1972-73, also instr. Base Leadership Sch., 1972-73; precision photog. processing technician 30th Tactical Reconnaissance Squadron, Alconbury Royal AFB, U.K., U.S. Air Force Europe, 1973-76; non-commd. officer in charge print sect. 16th Tactical Reconnaissance Squadron, 363rd Tactical Reconnaissance Wing, Shaw AFB, S.C., 1976-79; non-commd. officer in charge print unit 18th Tactical Reconnaissance Squadron, 363rd Tactical Reconnaissance Wing, Shaw AFB, 1979; unit OJT mgr. 38th Tactical Reconnaissance Squadron, 26th Tactical Reconnaissance Wing, Zweibruchen AFB, Germany, 1979—. Mem. Air Force Assn., Non-commd. Officers Acad. Graduates Assn. (publicity chmn. Shaw AFB chpt. 1978-79, v.p. Rheinland-Pfalz chpt. 1979-80), Nat. Rifle Assn. Am. Clubs: Order Eastern Star, Masons. Home: 46 Brabhan Dr Dalzell SC 29040 Office: 38th TRS/CCT APO New York NY 09860

STRODE, STEVEN WAYNE, physician; b. Dallas, Jan. 4, 1949; s. Royall Maurice and Maida (Sommerville) S.; B.S., So. Meth. U., 1969; M.D., U. Tex. Southwestern Med. Sch., 1974; m. Peggy Lee O'Neill, Sept. 21, 1974; children—Sean Wayne, Colleen Leigh. Intern, U. Ark. for Med. Scis., Little Rock, 1974-75; resident in family practice U. Ark. for Med. Scis., Little Rock, 1974-77, chief resident in family medicine, 1976-77, asst. prof. dept. family and community medicine, 1978—; teaching fellow in family medicine U. Western Ont., London, Can., 1977; practice family medicine, Jacksonville, Ark., 1977; cons. McAlmont Community Health Clinic, 1979. Diplomate Am. Bd. Family Practice. Mem. Am. Acad. Family Physicians, Ark. Acad. Family Physicians, Soc. Tchrs. Family Medicine, Am. Med. Holistic Assn., Conf. Family Practice Residents (Ark. del. 1975-76), Phi Beta Kappa, Beta Beta Beta. Methodist. Home: 1003 N McKinley St Little Rock AR 72207 Office: 1700 W 13th St Little Rock AR 72202

STROM, E(DWIN) THOMAS, chemist; b. Des Moines, June 11, 1936; s. Edwin Lewis and Maria Kristina (Johannson) S.; B.S., U. Iowa, 1958; M.S., U. Calif. at Berkeley, 1961; Ph.D., Iowa State U., 1964; m. Charlotte Faye Williams, June 14, 1958; children—Laura Christine, Eric William. With Mobil Co., Dallas, 1964, 66—, sr. research chemist, 1967—. Vis. lectr. Dallas Bapt. Coll., 1969-70, El Centro Community Coll., 1970-72, U. Tex. at Dallas, 1974; adj. prof. chemistry U. Tex., Arlington, 1978—. Bd. dirs. Greater Dallas Council Chs., 1978-79; mem. Dallas Council Chs., 1978-79; mem. Dallas Tri-Ethnic Com., 1976—, vice-chmn., 1978; founding chmn. Project Hope Met. Dallas, 1969, S.W. Oak Cliff Assn. for Human Relations, 1971. Served to 1st lt. AUS, 1964-66. Mem. Am. Chem. Soc. (councilor, 1972-74, chmn., 1975), Theta Xi, Phi Eta Sigma, Phi Lambda Upsilon, C. of C. Lutheran. Republican, Lion. Contbr. articles to profl. jours. Home: 1134 Medalist Dr Dallas TX 75232 Office: PO Box 900 Mobil Field Research Lab Dallas TX 75221

STROM, JAMES LEE, univ. adminstr.; b. McCormick, S.C., Dec. 13, 1933; s. Charles Lee and Ruby Cornelia (Jernigan) S.; B.S.E.E., Clemson U., 1956; B.B.A., Augusta Coll., 1970; Ph.D. in Engring., Clemson U., 1975; m. Margaret Faye Adams, Sept. 10, 1960; children—Mark Adams, Stephen Lee, Nancy Faye, Sharon Elizabeth. Aircraft engr. Lockheed Aircraft Co., Marietta, Ga., 1956-57, 59-61; supr. Polaris Fire Control, Missile Guidance and Computer Systems, Dept. Navy, Charleston, S.C., 1961-64; sr. research engr. Continental Groups, Inc., Augusta, Ga., 1964-67, mgr. process control, 1967-71; dir. planning and corporate relations Office Devel., Clemson (S.C.) U., 1971—; mem. vol. support com. Nat. Assn. State Univs. and Land-Grant Colls., 1980—; owner, operator Strom Enterprises; prof. mgmt. Tri-County Tech. Coll., 1978—. Mem. steering com. Republican Party, Richmond County, Augusta, 1966-69; mem. S.C. Ednl. TV Com., 1963-64; mem. bd. Clemson YMCA, 1975—, chmn., 1976—; mem. troop com. Boy Scouts Am., 1973—, chmn., 1977-79, mem. finance com. Blue Ridge dist., 1976-79; mem. bd. dirs., budget com. Pickens County United Way, 1977—; mem. adv. com. Outdoor Edn.-Recreation Lab., 1978—; mem. S.C. Appalachian Council Govts. Manpower Study Commn., 1973-75. Served with Signal Corps, U.S. Army, 1957-59. Mem. Soc. Coll. and Univ. Planning, Council Advancement and Support Edn., Coll. and Univ. Systems Exchange, Coll. and Univ. Machine Records. Baptist. Patentee in field. Home: 102 Winchester Ct Clemson SC 29631 Office: 302 Sikes Hall Clemson U Clemson SC 29631

STROM, L(EWIS) D(OBSON), govt. ofcl.; b. Edgefield, S.C., Dec. 23, 1910; s. William Augustus and Susie (Dobson) S.; B.S., Clemson U. (S.C.), 1933; m. Eloise Fisher, Nov. 27, 1969; 1 dau., Diane Strom Groseclose; stepchildren—R. James and Coy A. Short. With Fed. Land Bank, Columbia, S.C., 1933-39; regional dir. to zone adminstr. War Assets Adminstrn., Atlanta, 1946-49; with GSA, 1949—, dep. commr. transp., Washington, 1969, adminstr. region 4, Atlanta, 1969—; chmn. Atlanta Fed. Exec. Bd., 1973—. Bd. dirs. Met. Atlanta chpt. ARC, 1972-75. Served from lt. to col. U.S. Army, 1939-46; ETO. Mem. Atlanta Assn. Fed. Execs. (pres. 1964). Recipient Commendation award War Assets Adminstrn., 1947; Meritorious award GSA, 1955, 65, Commendable Service award 1961, Adminstr.'s Exceptional Service award, 1973. Home: 19 Olde Ivy Sq NE Atlanta GA 30342 Office: 1776 Peachtree St NE Atlanta GA 30309

STROMAN, SAMUEL DAVID, ret. army officer, educator; b. Orangeburg, S.C., Dec. 18, 1924; s. Moses Clay and Clara Beatrice S.; A.B., S.C. State Coll., 1950; M.A., Howard U., 1964; M.S., U. Wis., 1972; Ph.D., Am. U., 1976; m. Cleo Jane Ables, Aug. 10, 1950; children—Sandra Dianne, Sherolyn Debra, Synthia Diane, Samuel David. Enlisted U.S. Army, 1941, advanced through grades to first sgt., 1942, discharged, 1945, commd. 2d lt. U.S. Army, 1950, advanced through grades to col., 1970; co. comdr. 373d Armored Inf. Bn., Germany, 1953-54, 82d Airborne Div., Ft. Bragg, N.C., 1956-57; bn. comdr., Ft. Jackson, S.C., 1966-67; chmn. dept. mil. sci. U. Wis., Milw., 1970-72, Howard U., Washington, 1973-76; ret., 1976; asst. prof. dept. behavioral sci. S.C. State Coll., Orangeburg, 1976—; dir. Vasquez Assos. Decorated Legion of Merit with oak leaf cluster, Bronze Star. Mem. Am. Personnel and Guidance Assn., Assn. for Counselor Edn. and Supervision, D.C. Sch. Counselors Assn., S.C. Personnel and Guidance Assn., S.C. Assn. of Counselor Edn. and Supervision, S.C. Sch. Counselors Assn., S.C. Assn. Non-White Concerns in Personnel and Guidance, VFW, Phi Kappa Phi, Kappa Delta Pi, Phi Delta Kappa, Kappa Alpha Psi. Club: Masons. Editorial bd. Edn. Mag., 1971—, Jour. Instructional Psychology, 1971—. Home: PO Box 1601 South Carolina State College Orangeburg SC 29117 Office: Dept Behavioral Sciences SC State Coll Orangeburg SC 29117

STRONACH, CAREY ELLIOTT, physicist, educator; b. Boston, Aug. 8, 1940; s. Ralph Howard and Frances Burns (Maynard) S.; B.S., U. Richmond (Va.), 1961; M.S. (duPont fellow 1961-63), U. Va., 1963; Ph.D., Coll. William and Mary, Williamsburg, Va., 1975; m. Joan Alice Louise Venner, Aug. 20, 1966; children—John Maynard, Howard Stanley. Instr. physics Va. State U., Petersburg, 1965-66, asst. prof., 1966-71, 72-76, asso. prof., 1976—; vis. asso. prof. U. Alta., 1978-79. Pres., Petersburg area chpt. Va. Council Human Relations, 1965-67; mem. Petersburg Commn. Community Relations Affairs, 1974-77; corr. sec. Petersburg Democratic Com., 1974-77; mem. Va. Nat. Dems. NSF sci. faculty fellow, 1971-72; NASA summer faculty fellow, 1976. Mem. Am. Phys. Soc., Am. Assn. Physics Tchrs., AAUP (chpt. pres. 1968-70), AAAS, Va. Acad. Sci., Nat. Inst. Sci., Fedn. Am. Scientists, Phi Beta Kappa, Sigma Xi (chpt. sec. 1977-78), Sigma Pi Sigma, Pi Mu Epsilon. Episcopalian. Club: Richmond Physics. Author papers in field. Home: 2241 Buckner St Petersburg VA 23803 Office: Box 358 Va State U Petersburg VA 23803

STRONG, ANN BROWN, chemist; b. Utica, Miss., Apr. 7, 1938; d. Charlie Julian and Olie Rebecca (Pickett) Brown; B.S., Miss. Coll., 1961; postgrad. U. Fla., 1961-62; m. Lenton W. Strong, Aug. 31, 1962; children—Barbara, Steve, David. Chemist, USPHS, Montgomery, Ala., 1962-66, research chemist, supr. milk sect., 1966-69, supervisory chemist, chief environ. analysis unit, 1969-71; supervisory chemist, chief analytical services br. U.S. EPA, Montgomery, 1971-76, chief monitoring and analytical sects., 1976-79; phys. scientist U.S. Army C.E., Vicksburg, Miss., 1979—. Mem. Health Physics Soc. (sec. Ala. chpt. 1972-73), Internat. Radiation Protection Assn., Phi Theta Kappa. Contbr. in field. Home: PO Box 59 Utica MS 39175 Office: USAE/WES/EL PO Box 1631 Vicksburg MS 39180

STRONG, FRANK RANSOM, educator; b. Lawrence, Kans., Apr. 4, 1908; s. Frank and Mary Evelyn (Ransom) S.; B.A., Yale U., 1929, J.D., 1934; LL.D., N.C. Central U., 1978, Ohio State U., 1978; m. Gertrude Elizabeth Way, Aug. 31, 1929; children—John William, Mary Elizabeth (Mrs. Lawrence J. Brennan). Instr. econs. U. Del., 1929-31; instr., asst. prof. law U. Iowa, 1934-37; asst. prof., asso. prof., prof. law Ohio State U., 1937-65, dean, 1952-65, dean, prof. emeritus, 1965—; prof. law U. N.C., Chapel Hill, 1965—, Cary C. Boshamer Univ. Disting. prof., 1970-78, emeritus, 1978—; vis. asso. prof. law Duke, 1940-41; J. DuPratt White prof. law Cornell U., 1963; faculty, orientation program in Am. law Princeton, 1966-67, seminar chmn., 1967; dir. law teaching clinics Assn. Am. Law Schs., 1968-75; mem. faculty Salzburg Seminar Am. Studies, 1959; summer vis. prof. law Brigham Young U., Duke, U. Mich., U. N.C., Northwestern U., U. Tex., Tex. Tech U., Willamette U.; vis. prof. Sixty-Five Club, Hastings Coll. Law, spring 1974; Rice vis. prof. U. Kans., fall 1977. Chmn. bd. trustees Ohio Legal Center Inst., 1961-65; chmn. bd. visitors N.C. Central U. Sch. Law, 1979—. Recipient Distinguished Service award Ohio State U., 1956, fellows award Ohio Bar Assn. Found., 1964. Mem. Assn. Am. Law Schs. (pres. 1960), Order of Coif (nat. sec.-treas. 1970-80), Phi Beta Kappa. Independent. Home: 211 Markham Dr Chapel Hill NC 27514

STRONG, HAROLD S., educator; b. Memphis, Mar. 14, 1914; s. Autry P. and Bessie L. (Brown) S.; B.Music Edn., Cosmopolitan Sch. Music, 1950; M.Music Edn., Chgo. Musical Coll., 1951; children—Harold L., Carl L. (both dec.). Substitute tchr. Chgo., 1951-52; band dir. Douglass High Sch., Columbia, Mo., 1952; faculty U. Ark., Pine Bluff, 1952—, prof., dir. bands, 1980—; clinician, cons. Ark. bands. Served with U.S. Army Band, 1942-46. Recipient community service award Townsend Park Sch., 1969; cert. Army ROTC, 1970, 71, 72; named Band Dir. of Yr., Southwestern Activity Assn., 1968-69; cert. of appreciation Little Rock Unlimited Progress, Inc., 1972; five 1st place band certificates Memphis Cotton Makers Jubilee. Mem. AAUP, Coll. Band Dirs. Nat. Assn., Ark. Band Dirs. Assn., Music Edn. Nat. Assn., Kappa Kappa Psi, Omega Psi Phi (man of yr. 1968-69, cert. of outstanding community service in music, 1973). Presbyterian. Club: Am. Legion. Researcher hist. instruments. Home: 2633 Filmore St Memphis TN 38114 Office: Box 21 University of Arkansas Pine Bluff AR 71601

STRONG, LEAH AUDREY, educator; b. Buffalo, Mar. 14, 1922; d. Robert Leroy and Dorothy Sinclair (Kennedy) Strong; B.A., Allegheny Coll., 1943; M.A., Cornell U., 1944; Ph.D., Syracuse (N.Y.) U., 1953. Instr. English, Syracuse U., 1947-52; asst. prof. English, Cedar Crest Coll., Allentown, Pa., 1953-61; prof. Am. studies Wesleyan Coll., Macon, Ga., 1961—. Mem. Am., Southeastern (v.p. 1979—) Am. studies assns., So. Humanities Conf. (exec. sec. 1980—), South Atlantic MLA, AAUP, Am. Motorcycle Assn. Mem. Order Eastern Star. Club: Altrusa (Macon). Author: Joseph Hopkins Twichell: Mark Twain's Friend and Pastor, 1966. Contbr. articles to profl. jours. Home: 1173 Forest Hill Rd Macon GA 31210 Office: Am Studies Wesleyan Coll Macon GA 31201

STROSNIDER, JOHN STEVEN, mental health adminstr., psychologist; b. Winchester, Va., Oct. 17, 1949; s. James Arthur and Marcelene (Craun) S.; A.S., Lees McRae Coll., 1970; B.S., Va. Commonwealth U., 1972; M.A., Appalachian State U., 1974; postgrad. Coll. of William and Mary, 1975-79; m. Robin Gayle Read, July 29, 1972; children—Rebecca Lynn, Mollie Anne. Grad. asst. Appalachian State U., Boone, N.C., 1972-73; staff psychologist, coordinator psychol. testing Community Mental Health Center Psychiat. Inst., Norfolk, Va., 1974-77, clin. adminstr. adult inpatient service, 1977-78; dir. outpatient services Mental Health Services, Roanoke, Va., 1978—; asst. instr. dept. psychiatry Eastern Va. Med. Sch., 1975-77; pvt. practice counseling, Roanoke, 1978—; instr. Tidewater Community Coll., Virginia Beach, Va., 1974-77; pres. Weastro Enterprises Inc., Woodstock, Va.; chmn. Southwestern Va. Conf. on Group and Family Psychotherapy, 1979, 80. Mem. Va. Mental Health Counselors Assn., Am. Mental Health Counselors Assn., Va. Psychol. Assn., Va. Personnel and Guidance Assn. Lutheran. Contbg. editor Going to College Handbook, 1970; contbr. articles to profl. publs. in field. Home: 3102 Corbieshaw Rd SW Roanoke VA 24015 Office: Box 4622 Roanoke VA 24015

STROUD, DAVID, JR., chem. co. exec.; b. Kennett, Mo., July 2, 1913; s. David and Mary Maude (Striefler) S.; student S.E. Mo. State Coll., 1931-34; m. Mildred Ward Harrison, Jan. 14, 1939; 1 dau., Susan Elizabeth. Asst. purchasing agt. Mo. Utilities Co., Cape Girardeau, Mo., 1934-37; purchasing agt. Ark. Utilities Co., Helena, 1937-42; gen. mgr. A. S. Kelly Co., West Helena, Ark., 1946-47; comptroller, Lewis Supply Co., Inc., Helena, Ark., 1947-52; sec.-treas. Helena Wholesale, Inc. (Ark.), 1952-73, financial v.p., 1968-73, also dir.; chief accountant Eagle River Chem. Corp., West Helena, 1973—. Chmn. West Helena Mayor's Adv. Council, 1966-68; West Helena Planning Commr., 1962—; ex-officio mem. Phillips County Planning Commn., 1964—, Area Planning Commn., 1966—; vice-chmn. West Helena Water Commn., 1964-71, chmn., 1971—; vice-chmn. West Helena Sewer Commn., 1964-71, chmn., 1971—; v.p. West Helena Promotional Assn., 1971, vice chmn. Phillips County Port Authority 1971—. Bd. dirs., v.p. Mid-South Sight Service Inst., Memphis, 1962-70. Served to lt. (j.g.) USNR, 1942-46. Decorated Bronze Star medal; recipient Key to City West Helena, 1971, award Mid-South Sight Service Inst., 1971. Republican. Methodist. Lion. Club: Ark. Razorback Booster. Home: 216 Richmond Hill West Helena AR 72390 Office: Jerry Williams Indsl Park West Helena AR 72390

STROUD, ROBERT EDWARD, lawyer; b. Chester, S.C., July 24, 1934; s. Coy Franklin and Leila (Caldwell) S.; A.B., Washington and Lee U., 1956, LL.B., 1959; m. Katherine E. Clark, Apr. 8, 1961; children—Robert Gordon, Margaret Lathan. Admitted to Va. bar, 1959; asso. McGuire, Woods & Battle, Charlottesville, 1959-64, partner 1964—; lectr. Washington and Lee U., 1957-59; lectr. bus. taxation Grad. Sch. Bus. Adminstrn., U. Va., 1969—, also legal edn. insts., others. Pres. Charlottesville Housing Found., 1968-73; mem. Montreat (N.C.) Mgmt. Council, 1974-77; mem. council Synod of Virginias, Presbyn. Ch. U.S., 1973-77, moderator, 1977-78. Trustee Presbyn. Found., 1972-73; mem. gen. exec. bd. Presbyn. Ch. U.S., 1972-73. Served to 2d lt. with AUS, 1957. Mem. Am., Va. bar assns., Tax Inst. Am., Am. Judicature Soc., Washington and Lee Law Sch. Assn. (pres. 1979-80), Phi Eta Sigma, Omicron Delta Kappa, Phi Delta Phi. Presbyn. Co-author: Buying, Selling and Merging Businesses, 1975. Editor: Advising Small Business Clients, Vol. I, 1978. Editor-in-chief Washington and Lee Law Rev., 1959. Home: 104 Woodstock Dr Charlottesville VA 22901 Office: PO Box 1191 Charlottesville VA 22902

STRUBY, CHESTER ALBERT, JR., newspaper pub.; b. Macon, Ga., Jan. 19, 1917; s. Chester Albert and Julia (Riley) S.; A.B. magna cum laude, Mercer U., 1938; m. Jane Whitfield Spearman, May 24, 1947; children—Cynthia Jane, Neil Albert. Reporter, Macon Telegraph, 1938-40, state editor, 1940-41; state editor, asst. city editor Macon News, 1946-47; exec. editor Macon Telegraph and Macon News, 1947-57, editor The Telegraph, 1954-57, gen. mgr. Macon newspapers, 1957-78, exec. v.p. Macon Telegraph Pub. Co., 1958-76, pres., pub. Macon Telegraph and Macon News, 1976—. Chmn. bd. trustees Mercer U., 1978—, So. Ednl. Reporting Service, 1962-64; pres. Forward Macon, 1977, Macon United Way, 1979; chmn. Macon Housing Authority, 1975-77; v.p. Ga. Boy Scouts Am., 1978-80, pres., 1980—; trustee Sen. Richard Russell Found., 1970—; pres. Ga. State Fair Assn., 1975. Served to lt. comdr. USNR, 1941-46. Recipient cert. of merit Freedoms Found., 1950; Silver Beaver award Boy Scouts Am., 1967; others. Mem. So. Newspaper Pubs. Assn. (pres. 1966-67, chmn. bd. trustees Found. 1967-69), Ga. AP (chmn. 1963-64), Am. Newspaper Pubs. Assn., Ga. Press Assn., Air Force Assn., N.C. Soc. of Cincinnati, Greater Macon C. of C. (pres. 1974), Sigma Delta Chi, Phi Delta Theta. Democrat. Baptist. Clubs: Rotary, Idle Hour Golf, River North Country, Elks. Office: PO Box 4167 Macon GA 31213

STRUELENS, MICHEL MAURICE JOSEPH GEORGES, fgn. affairs cons., lectr., writer; b. Brussels, Belgium, Mar. 10, 1928 (came to U.S. 1960, naturalized 1966); B.A., Coll. St. Pierre, Brussels, 1944; M.A., Antwerp (Belgium) U., 1949; Ph.D., Am. U., Washington, 1968; m. Godelieve De Wilde, Aug. 2, 1949; children—Alain, Patricia, Brigitte, Bernard, Jean Paul (dec.). Insp. econ. affairs Congo Govt., Leopoldville, 1950-54, chief insp. econ. affairs, 1954-55, dep. commr. transp., 1955-57; dir. Information and Pub. Relations Office for Congo, Brussels, 1957-58, Congo Tourism Pavillion, Internat. World's Fair, Brussels, 1958-59; dir. gen. Belgian Congo and Ruanda Urundi Tourist Office, Congo, 1959; chmn. African Commn. Internat. Union Ofcl. Travel Orgns., Geneva, Switzerland, 1959-60; ofcl. Katanga rep. in U.S., N.Y.C., 1960-63; dir. gen. Internat. Inst. for African Affairs in Can., 1963-64; spl. asst. to prime minister Democratic Republic Congo, fgn. affairs minister, adviser to Congo UN delegation, adviser Congo embassy, Washington, N.Y.C., 1964-65; dir. Eurafrica, Consultants on Fgn. Affairs, Washington, 1966—. Prof. polit. sci., French, internat. bus. Am. U., 1968—, dir. Center Research and Documentation on European Community, 1971—, dir. E.C. Inst. in Europe, 1978—, dir. U. Antwerp exchange program, 1979, chmn. internat. bus. dept. Coll. Bus. Adminstrn., 1980—; adminstr. Congo Touring Clubs, Brussels, Leopoldville, 1959-78; adminstr. French parish, exec. v.p. Eglise Saint Louis Corp., French-Speaking Union Inc., Washington, 1974-75; investment adviser, 1977—. Recipient Internat. Union Ofcl. Travel Orgns. Poster award, Brussels, 1958; Etoile de Service en Argent, King of Belgium, 1956, chevalier de l'Ordre Royal du Lion, 1957; Faculty award Am. U. Coll. Bus. Adminstrn., 1979. Mem. Phi Sigma Alpha. Rotarian. Club: Bukavu Royal Sports (founder Congo 1950; pres. 1951-54; hon. pres. 1957). Author: (with Inforcongo) Congo Belge et Ruanda-Urundi, 1958; (monograph) Le Canada à l'Heure de l'Afrique, 1964; The United Nations in the Congo—or ONUC—and International Politics, 1976. Home and office: 1374 Woodside Dr McLean VA 22102

STRUL, GENE M., cons., former TV news dir.; b. Bklyn., Mar. 25, 1927; s. Joseph and Sally (Chartoff) S.; student journalism U. Miami (Fla.), 1945-47; m. Shirley Silber, Aug. 7, 1949; children—Ricky, Gary, Eileen. News dir. sta. WIOD AM-FM, Miami, 1946-56; assignment editor, producer sta. WCKT-TV, Miami, 1956-57, news dir., 1957-79; dir. broadcast news Miami News, 1957; free-lance writer newspapers and mags.; cons. dept. communications U. Miami, 1979—, acting dir. public relations, 1979—. Served with AUS, 1945. Recipient Preceptor award Broadcast Industry Conf., San Francisco State U.; Abe Lincoln award So. Baptist Radio-TV Conf.; Nat. Headliners award; Sta. WCKT has received numerous awards for news, including 3 Peabody awards, Emmy award, Nat. Sigma Delta Chi award. Mem. Nat. Acad. Television Arts and Scis. (past gov. Miami chpt.), Radio-TV News Dirs. Assn., Fla. AP Broadcasters (past pres.), Greater Miami C. of C., Nat. Broadcast Editorial Assn., Sigma Delta Chi. Home: 145 SW 49th Ave Miami FL 33134

STRUPP, HANS HERMANN, psychologist, educator; b. Frankfurt am Main, Germany, Aug. 25, 1921; s. Josef and Anna (Metzger) S.; came to U.S., 1939, naturalized, 1945; A.B. with distinction, George Washington U., 1945, A.M., 1947, Ph.D., 1954; m. Lottie Metzger, Aug. 19, 1951; children—Karen, Barbara, John. Research psychologist Human Factors Ops. Research Labs., Dept. Air Force, Washington, 1949-54; supervisory research psychologist, personnel research br. Adj. Gen.'s Office, Dept. of Army, Washington, 1954-55; dir. psychotherapy research project Sch. Medicine, George Washington U., Washington, 1955-57; dir. psychol. services dept. psychiatry U. N.C. Sch. Medicine, Chapel Hill, 1957-64, asso. prof. psychology, 1957-62, prof., 1962-66; prof. dept. psychology Vanderbilt U., Nashville, 1966-76, dir. clin. tng., dept. psychology, 1967-76, Distinguished prof., 1976—. Recipient Helen Sargent meml. award Menninger Found., 1963; Alumni Achievement award George Washington U., 1972; Distinguished Profl. Achievement award Am. Bd. Profl. Psychology, 1976; diplomate in clin. psychology Am. Bd. Profl. Psychology; licensed clin. psychologist, Tenn. Fellow Am. (chmn. ad. hoc com. for 2d conf. on research in psychotherapy 1958-62, mem. exec. council 1964, exec. bd. 1969-72, council of reps. 1970-73, chmn. com. on fellows div. psychotherapy 1970-74, pres. div. clin. psychology 1974-75, chmn. policy and planning com. div. clin. psychology 1976-77; Disting. Profl. Psychologist award 1973, Disting. Scientist award div. clin. psychology 1979), Tenn. psychol. assns., AAAS; mem. Eastern, Southeastern psychol. assns., Am. Psychopathol. Assn., Soc. for Psychotherapy Research (pres. 1972-73), Psychologists Interested in Advancement of Psychoanalysis, Phi Beta Kappa, Sigma Xi. Mem. editorial advisory bd. Psychotherapy: Theory, Research and Practice, 1963—, Jour. Cons. and Clin. Psychology, 1964—, Jour. Nervous and Mental Disease, 1965—, Jour. Am. Acad. Psychoanalysis, 1972—; contbr. chpts. to books, articles and revs. to profl. jours. Home: 5058 Villa Crest Dr Nashville TN 37220 Office: Dept Psychology Vanderbilt U Nashville TN 37240

STRUVE, CLEMENS ARAM, ophthalmologist; b. Campbellton, Tex., Sept. 29, 1929; s. Guido Louis and Alice Eloise (Sisk) S.; B.A. with honors, U. Tex., Austin, 1950, M.D., U. Tex. Med. Br., Galveston, 1954; m. Cynthia Anne Salinas, Nov. 11, 1975; children—Stephen Douglas, Joseph Aram Ernest, Frank Andrew, Cynthia Ann, Paul Aram, John Louis. Intern, U.S. Naval Hosp., Great Lakes, Ill., 1954-55; resident in ophthalmology U. Tex. Med. Br. Hosps., Galveston, 1958-61, instr. Med. Br., 1960; clin. instr. in ophthalmology U. Tex. Med. Sch., Houston, 1972—; practice medicine specializing in ophthalmology, Corpus Christi, Tex., 1961—; mem. staffs Doctors, Spohn, Meml., Driscoll Found. Children's hosps. (all Corpus Christi). Served with USN, 1954-57. Mem. Am. Acad. Ophthalmology and Otolaryngology, Am. Assn. Ophthalmology, Tex. Ophthalmol. Assn. (pres. 1977), Nueces County (Tex.) Med. Soc., Tex., Am. med. assns., Corpus Christi Surg. Soc. Episcopalian. Club: Rotary. Author: (movie) Lint Free Eye Surgery, 1966. Home: 5033 Cascade St Corpus Christi TX 78413 Office: PO Box 6374 3166 Reid Dr Corpus Christi TX 78411

STUART, EDWARD, JR., forest engr.; b. Boston, June 15, 1917; s. Edward and Helen (Fox) S.; B.S. in Forestry, U. Maine, 1937; F.E. (hon.), Biltmore Forest Sch., Weisbaden, Germany, 1946; children—Edward, Diane, Bruce. Forester, Maine and Can., 1937; forester U.S. Forest Service in Mass., Colo., S.D., Wyo., 1938-42; cons. and practicing forester, Va., N.C., S.C., Md., W.Va., 1946-56; pres., chmn. bd. dirs. Eastern Forestry, Inc., Hampton, Va., 1956—. Guest lectr. U. Maine, U. Nev., U. Wash., Stephen F. Austin U., La. State U.; forestry cons.; real estate appraiser. Served from lt. to capt. AUS, 1942-46; mil. govt. Forestry Office, Great Hesse, Germany, 1945-46. Decorated Commendation medal Croix Militaire (Belgium); recipient Va.'s Forest Conservationist of Yr. award, 1976. Mem. Nat. Assn. Cons. Foresters (pres. 1948-50; exec. council 1950-60, exec. sec. 1960—, editor The Consultant), Nat. Council Forestry Assn. Execs., Am. Soc. Appraisers, Am. Forestry Assn. (forest progress adv. council 1950-51), Soc. Am. Foresters (chmn. Rappahannock sect. 1960), Mil. Govt. Assn., Va. Forestry Council (sec.), Practicing Foresters Inst. (dir.), Gloucester, Mathews, Middlesex Realty Bd. (dir.), Nat. Assn. Real Estate Bds., Va. Real Estate Assn., SAR, Nat. Forest Products Assn. (mem. forestry adv. com.), Nat. Def. Exec. Res., Am. Legion, Explorers Club. Author numerous tech. articles on forestry and appraising. Home: PO Box 369 Yorktown VA 23690

STUART, HELEN GWINN, assn. exec.; b. Poplar Bluff, Mo., Nov. 13, 1920; d. Frank Abner and Ida Leona (Hickman) Gwinn; A.B., U. Miami (Fla.), 1943; student LaSalle Extension U., 1958-60; grad. N.Y. Inst. Photography, 1957; m. Hardin V. Stuart, Sept. 1, 1945 (dec.); 1 son, Jonathan Vereen. Nat. field rep. Girl Scouts U.S.A., N.Y.C., 1955-60, United Cerebral Palsy, Columbia, S.C., 1960-65; exec. dir. S.C. Retarded Children, 1965-73; program coordinator S.C. Heart Assn., Columbia, 1973-74, dir. hypertension control project, 1974-77; mem. staff Horry-Georgetown Tech. Coll., 1977—; mem. S.C. Adv. Council on Vocat. and Tech. Edn.; mem. adv. councils The Blind and Deaf Child, the Handicapped Child, Dept. Edn. Stuart Manor for retarded women, half way house, named in her honor, 1971. Mem. Nat. Rifle Assn., Nat. Wildlife Fedn., Nat. Council Resource Devel., Delta Zeta. Democrat. Episcopalian. Home: PO Box 277 Murrells Inlet SC 29576

STUART, JAMES WALLACE, quality control exec.; b. Newport, Ark., Apr. 5, 1950; s. Herschel Albert and Helen Madeline (Bishop) S.; B.Physics, U. Ark., 1975. Inhalation therapist Wash. Regional Hosp., Fayetteville, Ark., 1972-73; cardiac nurse Newport Hosp. & Clinic, Newport, Ark., 1975; tchr. sci. Plaquemines Parish Sch. Bd., Port Sulphur, La., 1975-76; organic chemist Empire (La.) Menhaden Co., 1976, quality control mgr., 1976—; quality control cons. La. Menhaden Co., Cameron, 1978—. Served with M.C., U.S. Army, 1969-71. Mem. Costeau Soc., Oceanic Soc., Assn. Energy Engrs., Am. Oil Chemists Soc., AAAS, Nat. Fish Meal and Oil Assn. (chmn. tech. com.), Am. Chem. Soc., Plaquemines Parish Art Guild. Home: PO Box 98 Hwy 23S Empire LA 70050 Office: Empire Menhaden Co Inc Empire LA 70050

STUART, MARY LOUISE WHEAT, counselor, diagnostician; b. Quanah, Tex., Nov. 22, 1928; d. Henry Ray and Mattie (Isaacks) Wheat; student Lubbock Christian Coll., 1965-66, Draughons Business Coll. of Dallas, 1945; B.S. in Edn., Tex. Tech U., 1968, M.S. in Edn., 1971, grad. student, 1971-76; m. Carroll Winferd Crelia (dec.); m. 2d, Frankie Adell Stuart, Feb. 2, 1962; children—Rita Crelia Ritter, Donna Carroll Crelia Arledge, Bruce Ray Crelia, Mary Nell Crelia Benham; step-children—Franklin Stuart, Mary Susan Stuart Osborne. Sec. Watkins, Inc., Quanah, 1945-46, Joskie's of Tex., San Antonio, 1946-47, Dept. Pub. Welfare, Quanah, 1953-54, Radio Sta. KOLJ, Quanah, 1953-54; office mgr. devel. office Lubbock Christian Coll., Lubbock, 1956; civil service sec. Reese AFB, Lubbock, 1956-58, 59-62; tchr. 2d grade Lubbock Pub. Schs., 1968-71, 2d and 3d grades, 1971-72, elementary counselor, 1972-75, counselor, diagnostician, 1975—. Certificates elementary edn., mentally retarded, physically handicapped, counselor, lang. and/or learning disabilities, ednl. diagnostician, special edn. counselor, spl. edn. supr., supr., mid-mgmt. admnstr., Tex. Mem. Tex. State Tchrs. Assn., Am., Tex., W.Tex. personnel and guidance assns., Lubbock Educators Assn., Lubbock Classroom Tchrs. Assn., Delta Kappa Gamma. Democrat. Baptist. Home: 2704 57th St Lubbock TX 79413

STUART, WILLIAM HOOD, JR., rancher, distbn., agrl. lime co. exec.; b. Bartow, Fla., July 7, 1936; s. William Hood and Margrette Kennedy (Moore) S., Sr.; B.S., Wash. State U., 1959; M.B.A., U. Pa., 1965; m. Nancy Emily Sell, Aug. 4, 1961; children—Margrette Kennedy, Lenore Crosland. Exec. dir. pvt. semi-scientific expdn. to S. Pacific and S.E. Asia, 1958-63; mgr. retail hardware co., Bartow, Fla., 1963-66; pres. Sea Research & Devel. Inc., Bartow, 1966-76; v.p., sec., dir. W.H. Stuart Ranch, Inc., Bartow, 1973—, River Constrn. Co., Inc., Bartow, 1974—, Am. Constrn. & Engring., Inc., Bartow, 1976—, Am. Resources, Inc., Bartow, 1976—, Moffatt Bearings Co., Phila., 1976—, Doline, Inc., Bartow, 1980—, Indsl. Drives, Inc., Knoxville, Tenn., 1980—. dir. Nat. Trust Bank of Fla., 1976—, Bearings & Transmissions Spltys., Inc., Mineco, Inc., Falcon Transport, Inc., Dolime Minerals Co., Holland Groves, Inc., Pembroke Lab., ARI Properties, Inc. Trustee, Erskine Coll. and Theol. Seminary, Due West, S.C., 1974—, treas., 1979—; mem. Fla. Gov.'s Com. on Handicapped, 1975-79; chmn. Fla. Sheriffs' Girls' Villa Classic Exec. Com., Bartow, 1975-76; bd. dirs. Tri-County Mental Health Center, Winter Haven, Fla., 1976-77; pres. Polk County (Fla.) C. of C., 1976; mem. Polk County Bicentennial Commn., 1975-76; pres. Youth Opportunities Unlimited, Polk County, 1970-71; bd. dirs. Polk County Juvenile Home, 1972-74; treas., bd. dirs. Mental Health Center Polk County, 1973-79; pres. Bartow C. of C., 1973; chmn. adv. bd. Downtown Redevel. Assn. Bartow, 1972—; pres. Bartow Rotary Club, 1971-72, pres. Camp Rotary Operating Assn., 1977-79, gov. Rotary Dist. 695, Central Fla., 1974-75, mem. internat. research com., 1979-80; elder Asso. Reformed Presbyterian Ch., Bartow, 1970—, moderator Fla. Presbytery, 1979. Recipient distinguished service award Youth Opportunities Unlimited, 1972; outstanding citizen award Bartow Lion's Club, 1973; meritorious service award Rotary Found., 1976; named Paul Harris fellow Rotary, 1975. Mem. Am., Eastern brahman breeders assns., S.E. Council of Foundations, Polk County Council on Econ. Edn., Fla. C. of C. (dir. 1975—). Club: Acacia Nat. Author: Fifty Years of Service, 1978; contbr. to multi-media presentations and handbook on underwater photography and diving. Home: 205 E Hooker St Bartow FL 33830 Office: PO Box 1378 Bartow FL 33830

STUBBLEFIELD, GERRY GERALDINE, dietitian, hosp. ofcl.; b. Horry County, S.C., Mar. 23, 1938; d. Ashley Gleston and Ida Louise (Hought) Hardee; student E. Tex. State Coll., 1972-73, Eastfield Coll., Dallas, 1973-74, Tyler Jr. Coll., 1977; m. Roy Stubblefield, Sept. 17, 1954; children—Jack, Tony, Lesa, Terry. Owner, operator florist shop, Sulphur Springs, Tex., 1973-78; dir. foods Meml. Hosp. Hopkins County, Sulphur Springs, 1977—; lectr. in field. Mem. Am. Hosp. Assn., E. Tex. Dietetic Assn., E. Tex. Hosp. Assn., Nat. Fedn. Bus. and Profl. Women's Clubs. Republican. Baptist. Address: 1429 Doris Dr Sulphur Springs TX 75482

STUBBS, FRANK SPENCER, physician, surgeon; b. Galveston, Tex., Oct. 16, 1926; s. Frank Spencer and Cecelia Gertrude (Gottlob) S.; student N.W. Inst. Med. Tech., 1949-50, Sam Houston State U., 1951-52, U. Tex., 1952-53; M.D., U. Tenn., 1957; B.S., Thomas A. Edison Coll., 1970, Ph.D., 1971, D.Sc. (hon.), 1972; children—Louise Cecilia, Frank Spencer III. Intern, Robert B. Green Hosp., San Antonio, 1957-58; resident anesthesiology Baylor U. Hosp., Houston; practice medicine and surgery, San Antonio, 1958-61, Karnes City, Tex., 1961—; sec. staff Otto Kaiser Meml. Hosp.; chmn. bd., pres. Karnes County Savs. & Loan Assn., 1970—. Health officer City of Karnes City, 1965—. Served with U.S. Maritime Service, 1944-49; maj. Air N.G., 1958-72. Diplomate Am. Bd. Family Practice, Am. Bd. Abdominal Surgeons. Fellow Am. Soc. Abdominal Surgeons, Internat. Coll. Surgeons, Am. Acad. Family Practice, Am. Geriatric Soc., Royal Soc. Health (London), Am. Soc. Colposcopy and Colpomicroscopy, Am. Acad. Behavioral Scis.; mem. St. Anthony Club, Sons of Herman, Karnes Hosp. Assn. (dir. 1968-73), Karnes-Wilson County Med. Soc. (pres. 1966, 78, 79), AMA (physician recognition award 1969, 72), Phi Rho Sigma. Designer, builder Stubbs Clinic, Karnes City, 1975. Office: 515 S Panna Maria St Karnes City TX 78118

STUBBS, GORDON EUGENE, mgmt. analyst; b. Austin, Tex., July 21, 1926; s. Homer Albert and Emily Violet (Armstrong) S.; student U. Ala., 1943-44, San Antonio Coll., 1949-51, U. Puget Sound, 1962-64; B.G.S., Chaminade Coll., 1969; postgrad. U. So. Calif., 1969-70; M.S., U. Hawaii, 1971, Ph.D., 1972; M.A., Central Mich. U., 1974; m. Ruby Mae Durham, Feb. 28, 1946; 2 sons, Lester Eugene, Gordon William. Prodn. mgr. Dept. Def., San Antonio, 1950-51; recalled to active duty with U.S. Air Force, 1951, served as aircraft maintenance mgr., San Antonio, 1952-58, chief flight engr., Europe, 1958-61, records mgr., Tacoma, Wash., 1961-64, mgmt. analyst advisor, Riverside, Calif., 1964-66, chief performance engr., Honolulu, 1966-68, adminstrn. mgr., Honolulu, 1968-69, ret. 1969; br. mgr. Profl. Tax Service, Waipahu, Hawaii, 1970-71; lead indsl. engr. technician Dept. Def., Honolulu, 1972-74; lead computer programmer FDA, USPHS, HEW, Washington, 1974-76; mgmt. analyst, Office Asst. Sec. Health, USPHS, HEW, Rockville, Md., 1976—; propr. Stubbs Profl. Enterprises, Honolulu and Washington, 1971—. Served with USAF, 1943-46. Recipient flying safety award, 1965, outstanding achievement award, Pacific Air Force, 1973. Democrat. Baptist. Clubs: Masons, Shriners. Author: The Development of Human Resources, 1969; Developing Responsive Personalities for Interactive Computer Systems, 1972; An Automated Central Supervisory System, 1974; developer computer systems areas of fin. bus. mgmt., operational controls, taxes, edn., medicine, health care, 1969-78. Home: 5414 Juliet St Springfield VA 22151 Office: 5600 Fishers Ln Room 17-75 Rockville MD 20857

STUBBS, MARSHALL, def. cons.; b. Superior, Nebr., June 13, 1906; s. Frank Hale and Avis Idona (Long) S.; B.S., U.S. Mil. Acad., 1929; M.S., Mass. Inst. Tech., 1939; student Nat. War Coll., 1951-52; m. Harriett Clotilde Rodes, June 22, 1929; children—Harriett Stubbs Johnson, Helen Stubbs Smyly. Commd. 2d lt., U.S. Army, 1929, advanced through grades to maj. gen., 1958, ret., 1963; inf. officer Marchfield (Calif.), Ft. Crook, Nebr., Ft. Benning, Ga., Schofield Barracks, Hawaii, 1929-34; chem. corps. officer Edgewood Arsenal, Md., Washington, Rocky Mt. Arsenal, Colo., 1934-43, Eng., France, Belgium, Germany, 1943-47; commanding gen. Chem. Corps Materiel Command, Balt., 1954-55, Army Chem. Center, Md., 1955-57; commanding gen. 1st logistical command, Ft. Bragg, N.C., 1957-58; chief chem. officer Washington, 1958-62; cons. on chem. and biol. weapons and def., 1963—. Decorated D.S.M., Legion of Merit, Bronze Star Medal, Order of Leopold with Palm and the Croix de Guerre with Palm (Belgian). Mem. Assn. U.S. Army, Am. Chem. Soc., Am. Def. Preparedness Assn. Republican. Episcopalian. Club: Masons. Address: 6631 Wakefield Dr Alexandria VA 22307

STUCK, ROGER DEAN, physicist; b. Ventura, Calif., Nov. 6, 1924; s. William Henry and Grace Marion (Ready) S.; B.S. in Elec. Engring., Calif. Inst. Tech., 1947; M.S. in Elec. Engring., N.C. State U., 1957; postgrad. U. Calif., Berkeley, 1966, San Diego State U., 1971; m. Opal Christine Phillips, July 25, 1948; children—Roger Dean II, Phyllis Jean Stuck Munns, Sandra Lynne Stuck Swiers. Elec. engr., Warren Wilson Vocat. Jr. Coll., Swannanoa, N.C., 1947-69; dean student affairs Warren Wilson Coll., Swannanoa, 1969-72, mem. faculty dept. physics, 1972—. Served to lt. (j.g.) USNR, 1943-46; PTO. Mem. Am. Phys. Soc., Am. Assn. Physics Tchrs., N.C. Acad. Sci., Sigma Xi. Republican. Presbyterian. Author: The Periodic Table of Physical Concepts, 1977. Address: Box 5085 Warren Wilson Coll Swannanoa NC 28778

STUCKEY, JAMES RONALD, ins. exec.; b. Enterprise, Ala., Oct. 5, 1947; s. James D. and Eunice S.; A.A., Enterprise State Jr. Coll., 1968; B.S., Auburn U., 1971; M.B.A., Troy State U., 1977; student Jones Law Sch.; m. Elizabeth Menges, Aug. 3, 1974; 1 dau., Heather Elizabeth. Salesman, Mut. Savs. Life Ins. Co., Elba, Ala., 1971-73, mgr., 1973-75; salesman Liberty Nat. Life Ins. Co., Enterprise, Ala., 1975—. Chmn. Muscular Dystrophy City of Enterprise, 1978. Mem. Boll Weevile Jaycees (dir. 1978), Nat. Assn. Life Underwriters, Enterprise Assn. Life Underwriters (pres., v.p., program chmn.), Auburn U. Alumni Assn., Ala. Life Underwriters Assn. Baptist. Home: 107 Auburn St Enterprise AL 36330 Office: PO Box 1080 Enterprise AL 36330

STUDENMUND, WALTER RUSSELL, educator; b. Phila., June 12, 1916; s. Morris F. and Edna (Russell) S.; B.S., U. Pa., 1947; M.B.A., N.Y. U., 1963; Ph.D., Walden U., 1977; m. Elisabeth P. Harwood, Nov. 21, 1942; children—Arnold H., Sarah Elisabeth, Barbara Ann, David Russell. Clk., Atlantic Richfield Corp., Phila., 1934-47; office mgr. Presbyn. Ch., N.Y.C., 1947-53; office mgr. Simon & Schuster, N.Y.C., 1953-54; personnel and office mgr. Harcourt Brace Jovanovich, N.Y.C., 1954-69; asso. prof. bus. adminstrn. Davis and Elkins Coll., 1969—; cons. Island Creek Coal Co.; Bata Shoe Co.; W.Va. Correction System; Ernst & Ernst. Vice-pres. bd. dirs. Appalachian Mental Health Center, 1972-75. Served to lt. comdr. USNR, 1941-45. Mem. Adminstrv. Mgmt. Assn. (v.p. 1961), Nat. Office Mgmt. Assn., Am. Mktg. Assn., Am. Acctg. Assn. Republican. Presbyterian. (elder). Club: Mountain State Stamp (treas. 1974). Home: 118 Grandview Ave Elkins WV 26241 Office: Davis & Elkins Coll Elkins WV 26241

STUDER, DALE FREDERICK, coal co. exec.; b. nr. New Philadelphia, Ohio, Oct. 2, 1921; s. John W. and Louise (Finzer) S.; grad. high sch.; grad. Dale Carnagie course, 1973; m. Kathryn L. Andreas, Aug. 25, 1946; children—Paula Gay, Deborah Elaine. Prin. owner Walden's Ridge Coal Co., 1953—, Tri-State Coal Sales, Chattanooga, 1957—, Pioneer Coal Co., Chattanooga, 1974—, Sequatchie Valley Coal Corp., 1975—, Mid-South Treatment Systems, 1975—, Pine Tree Farms, Dale F. Studer & Assos. Republican Central committeeman, Sugarcreek, Ohio, 1946-49; adv. Tenn. State Legis., 1966-67; adv. SE Tenn. Devel. Dist., 1977; mem. nat. finance council Nat. Dem. Com., 1979—; Reclamation Review Bd. Tenn., 1978—; prin. stockholder, bd. dirs. Chattanooga Choo-Choo, 1975—. Served with USAAF, 1942-46; ATO; ETO. Mem. hon. staff Gov. Tenn. Mem. Ind. Coal Operators Assn. Tenn. (v.p. 1971-72), Tenn. State Coal Operators Assn. (pres. 1975-76, dir. 1974-80), Inst. Explosive Engrs., Inst. Mining Engrs., Am. Legion (comdr. post 1946-49), Nat. Coal Assn., Mining and Reclamation Council Am. (dir. 1978—), Am. Security Council, Internat. Platform Assn. Methodist (dir. 1955-58). Home: 952 Runyan Dr Chattanooga TN 37405

STURCKEN, EDWARD FRANCIS, materials scientist; b. Charleston, S.C., Nov. 13, 1927; s. Edward Frederick and Eulalie Marie (Seyle) S.; B.S. (scholarship), Coll. Charleston, 1948; M.S. (teaching fellow), St. Louis U., 1950, Ph.D., 1953; spl. studies Mass. Inst. Tech., 1958, Poly. Inst. Bklyn., 1959; m. Shirley Ann Stirrat, June 6, 1953; children—Edward Francis, Lynda Marie. Scientist Savannah River Lab., ERDA, E.I. duPont de Nemours & Co., Inc., Aiken, S.C., 1953—, sr. scientist, 1962—, research asso., 1970—; vis. scientist U. Calif. at Berkeley, 1966-68. Pres. Sturcken Ltd., real estate, 1960—; owner, mgr. Doral Apts., Atlanta, 1974—, Fairwood Apts., North Augusta, S.C., 1979—; dir. Augusta Racquetball Center, Inc. Mem. Am. Crystallographic Soc., Am. Soc. Metals (award electron microscopy), Am. Phys. Soc., Internat. Metallographic Soc., Pi Kappa Phi. K.C. Contbr. articles to profl. jours. Home: 823 Woodlawn Ave N Augusta SC 29841 Office: Savannah River Lab Aiken SC 29801

STURDIVANT, VERNON RAY, elec. engr.; b. Hermliegh, Tex., Sept. 20, 1933; s. Ira Ray and Ona Gertrude (Vernon) S.; B.S., U. Tex., 1956; M.S., So. Meth. U., 1966; m. Judy Lynn Weber, Mar. 12, 1976; children—Daniel Lee, Michael Ray, Amy Lyn, Tammy Lynn. Aerosystems engr. Gen. Dynamics Co., Ft. Worth, 1956-62; aerospace technologist NASA, Houston, 1962-63; sr. aerosystems engr. Gen. Dynamics Co., 1963-68; staff engr. SW Research Inst., San Antonio, 1968—; instr. San Antonio Coll., 1975—. Mem. Sigma Xi. Home: 11014 Bar X Trail Helotes TX 78023 Office: PO Drawer 28510 San Antonio TX 78284

STURGESS, ROBERT WILLIS, mgmt. cons.; b. London, May 12, 1938; s. Walter Deane and Vanda Lena S.; came to U.S., 1975; B.S. in Engring., U. London, 1962, D.Eng., 1968. Project engr. various cos. Middle East including Fluor, Bechtel, Iranian Oil Operating Cos., Internat. Mgmt. and Engring Group, 1964-70; mgmt. cons. to oil co., Saudi Arabia, 1970—. Mem. ASME, Iranian Petroleum Inst. Clubs: Royal Dutch Shooting (patron HRH Prince Bernhardt of The Netherlands), Masons (32 deg.). Pvt. pilot. Office: 1705 First City Nat Bank Houston TX 77002

STURGIS, JAMES DORSEY, engr.; b. Baton Rouge, Mar. 26, 1937; s. Madison B. and Adah Elizabeth (Proctor) S.; B.S., La. State U., 1959, M.S., 1964; Ph.D., U. Ala., 1969; m. Priscilla Jo Head, Dec. 17, 1960; 1 dau., Dana Jo. Test engr. Gen. Dynamics, Ft. Worth, 1959-62; instr. U. Ala., Tuscaloosa, 1968-69; sr. scientist Harris Corp., Melbourne, Fla., 1969—. NASA trainee, 1964-67. Mem. Sigma Xi, Tau Beta Pi, Pi Tau Sigma, Pi Mu Epsilon, Phi Kappa Phi. Presbyterian. Home: 284 Cimarron Circle Palm Bay FL 32905 Office: PO Box 37 Melbourne FL 32901

STURM, JOHN EDWARD, educator; b. Pitts., Oct. 6, 1927; s. John E. and Elizabeth Louise (Sexauer) S.; A.B. in Econs., Bowdoin (Maine) Coll., 1951; M.Ed., U. N.H., 1962; Ed.D., U. Mass., 1973; m. Jean Moses, Dec. 29, 1951. With Ketchum, McCleod & Grove, advt., Pitts., 1952-54; prin. N.H. pub. schs., 1956-65; asst. prof. edn. State Univ. Coll., Buffalo, 1966-73; bus. mgr., dir. devel. Stuart Hall Sch., Staunton, Va., 1973-75; asso. prof. edn. Mt. Senario Coll., Ladysmith, Wis., 1975-76, James Madison U., Harrisonburg, Va., 1976—. Served with AUS, 1945-47. Recipient poetry awards N.C. State U., 1978, Gertrude Saucier Hist. Soc., Nat. State Fedn. of Poetry Socs., 1979; grantee Am. Fedn. Tchrs., 1966, 68. Fellow Royal Soc. Health; mem. N.Y. Poetry Forum, Pa. Poetry Soc., Ariz. Poetry Soc., Poetry Soc. Am., Am. Assn. Supervision and Curriculum Devel., Phi Delta Kappa. Author: (poetry) Keystone Drummer Boy, 1978; co-editor: Substantive Readings in Education, 1968; Democratic Legacy in Transition, 1971; Critical Essays on Education, 1979. Address: Dept Secondary Edn and Sch Adminstrn James Madison U Harrisonburg VA 22801

STURROCK, THOMAS TRACY, horticulturist, educator; b. Havana, Cuba, Dec. 9, 1921 (parents Am. citizens); s. David and Ruth (Earle) S.; diploma Palm Beach Jr. Coll., 1941; B.S.A. with honors, U. Fla., 1943, M.S.A., 1943, Ph.D., 1961; m. Betty Jeanne Norquist, June 30, 1948; children—Nancy Elizabeth, John David, Barbara Jeanne, Catherine Ann, Robert Charles. Grove maintenance Sturrock Tropical Fruit Nursery, West Palm Beach, Fla., 1946-56; insp. Fla. Plant Bd., West Palm Beach, 1956-57; tchr. biology Palm Beach High Sch., West Palm Beach, 1957-58; research asst. U. Fla., Gainesville, 1958-60; tchr. biology Palm Beach Jr. Coll., Lake Worth, Fla., 1960-64; asst. prof. biol. scis. Fla. Atlantic U., Boca Raton, 1964-68, asso. prof., 1968-74, prof., 1974—, asst. dean Coll. Sci., 1971—. Cubmaster, Boy Scouts Am., West Palm Beach, 1960-62, scoutmaster, 1946-54, dist. chmn., 1961-63, mem. exec. bd. Gulf Stream council, 1961—, v.p., 1969-70, 80—. Served to capt. USAAF, 1943-46; PTO; lt. col. Res. Recipient Silver Beaver award Boy Scouts Am., 1951. Mem. Fla. State Hort. Soc., Fla. Acad. Scis., Sigma Xi. Presbyterian. Home: 1010 Camellia Rd West Palm Beach FL 33405 Office: Fla Atlantic U Boca Raton FL 33431

STUTTS, WILLIAM FLOYD, orthodontist; b. Tuscaloosa, Ala., Dec. 14, 1926; s. Floyd D. and Rubye (Park) S.; B.S., U. Ala., 1948; D.D.S., Northwestern U., 1952; m. Marilyn Martin, June 9, 1951; children—Billy, Janet, Debbie, Pamela, Michael. Pvt. practice orthodontics, 1960—; orthodontic staff Children's Med. Center; instr. Baylor U. Sch. Dentistry. Diplomate Am. Bd. Orthodontics. Fellow Am. Coll. Dentists; mem. Am. Dental Assn., Dallas Country Dental Soc., Southwestern Soc. Orthodontics (pres. 1977-78), European, Tex. (pres. 1977-78) orthodontic socs., Am. Assn. Orthodontist, Am. Soc. Dentistry for Children, AAAS, Biol. Photographic Assn., Fedn. Dentaire Internat., Alpha Tau Omega, Delta Sigma Delta. Office: 7912 Spring Valley Rd Dallas TX 75240

STYLES, JIMMIE CARTER, coll. adminstr.; b. Bellville, Ga., Oct. 17, 1931; s. Roy Thelmer and Hellon Berton S.; B.S., Ga. So. Coll., 1956; M.S., George Peabody Coll., 1958, Ed.D., 1962; m. Jimmie Mae Strickland, Jan. 4, 1951; children—Dennis Carter, Denise Hellon, Duaine Lester. Jr. high and high sch. tchr., Savannah, Ga., 1955-57; grad. asst. George Peabody Coll. for Tchrs., 1957-58; instr. Gulf Coast Jr. Coll., Panama City, Fla., 1958-60, Troy (Ala.) State U., 1960-61; instr., dir. data systems Broward Jr. Coll., Fort Lauderdale, Fla., 1961-65; asst. to pres. Tarrant County Jr. Coll. Dist., Fort Worth, 1965, v.p., 1966-69, vice chancellor research and devel., 1969—; computer and data processing cons. Amarillo Coll., Austin Community Coll., Vernon Regional Coll., El Paso Community Coll., DeKalb Community Coll., Clarkston, Ga., Gulf Coast Community Coll. Dist., Gulfport, Miss., 1968-79; cons. HEW, 1967-72. Mem. planning council Greater Fort Worth Manpower Consortium, 1976-77; mem. manpower adv. com. Tex. Employment Commn., 1968; area leader United Fund, 1971. Served with USN, 1950-54. Recipient Cert. of Appreciation, Tarrant County United Fund Crusade of Hope, 1972, Appreciation award Fort Worth Founders Lions Club, 1972-73, Second Step Service award Bapt. Radio and TV Commn., 1973, Lion of Year award Fort Worth Founders Lions Club, 1977-78. Mem. Am. Tech. Edn. Assn. (trustee 1972-73), Am. Vocat. Assn. (policy com. tech. edn. div. 1973-74), Tex. Assn. Ednl. Data Systems (dir. 1969-70), N. Tex. Higher Edn. Council (chmn. 1979), Nat. Assn. Ednl. Data Systems, Tex. Jr. Coll. Tchrs. Assn., Fort Worth C. of C. (Marshal's award 1971), Delta Pi Epsilon. Baptist. Club: Fort Worth Founders Lions. Author: (with Denny Pace) Guidelines for Work Experience Programs in the Criminal Justice System, 1969; Law Enforcement Training and the Community College: Alternatives for Affiliation, 1970; Handbook of Narcotics Control, 1972; Organized Crime: Concepts and Control, 1975. Home: 1800 Calais Rd Fort Worth TX 76116 Office: 1400 The Electric Service Bldg Fort Worth TX 76102

STYLES, WILLIAM ANDREW, coal co. ofcl.; b. Charleston, W.Va., Oct. 27, 1954; s. William H. and Katherine C. S.; B.B.A. magna cum laude, Marshall U., 1976. Adminstrv. mgr. Land Use Corp., Summersville, W.Va., 1976-77, asst. supt., mgr. preparation and distbn., 1978—. Mem. Marshall U. Alumni Assn. Republican. Home: 436 Ashley Ln Summersville WV 26651 Office: Box 460 Summersville WV 26651

STYS, MICHAEL STANLEY, elec. engr.; b. Mt. Vernon, N.Y.; s. Z. Stanley and Danuta U. (Buzdygan) S.; B.S. with distinction, Cornell U., 1974; M.S., U. Calif. at Berkeley, 1975. Sr. asso. engr. IBM Corp., Austin, Tex., 1976—. Mem. IEEE, Eta Kappa Nu, Tau Beta Pi. Home: 203 Faubion Dr Georgetown TX 78626 Office: IBM 11400 Burnet Rd Austin TX 78758

SUAREZ, JOSE JOAQUIN, JR., cement co. exec.; b. Penuelas, P.R., Sept. 6, 1935; s. Jose Joaquin and Elisa (Matos) S.; student Columbia U., 1953-55; B.S. in Elec. Engring., U. Pa., 1959; m. Iris Garrastazu, Feb. 8, 1958; children—Jose J., Rosario. Plant elec. engr. Puerto Rican Cement Co., Inc., Ponce, 1959-64, chief elec. engr., 1964-69, plant mgr., 1969—. Registered profl. engr., P.R. Mem. Nat. Soc. Profl. Engrs., IEEE. Roman Catholic. Office: Puerto Rican Cement Co Inc PO Box 1349 Ponce PR 00731

SUAREZ, MANUEL LAURENTINO, educator; b. Havana, Cuba, Nov. 8, 1945; s. Laurentino and Aida Menendez (Llado) S.; came to U.S., 1963, naturalized, 1968; B.A., Bloomfield Coll., 1967; M.A. (Univ. fellow), U. Iowa, 1969; Ph.D., U. Ga., 1973; m. Cynthia Ann Rummel, June 7, 1970; children—Laurentino Suarez, Cynthia Cristina. Actuarian firm Woodward, Ryan, Sharp & Davis, Montclair, N.J., also N.Y.C., 1963-67; teaching asst. U. Iowa, 1967-69; mgr. internat. div. Am. Hosp. Supply Corp., Evanston, Ill., 1969-70; teaching asst. U. Ga., 1970-72; chmn. dept. fgn. langs. Tift Coll., 1972-73; Wesleyan Coll., Macon, Ga., 1973-74; asso. prof. romance langs. East Tenn. State U., 1974—; pres. Mountain Interstate Fgn. Lang. Conf., 1977. Recipient Scholarship Key Bloomfield Coll., 1966; East Tenn. State U. grantee, 1975-76. Mem. A.A.U.P., Modern Lang. Assn. Am., South Atlantic Modern Lang. Assn., Tenn., Mountain Interstate (v.p. conf.) fgn. lang. assns., Pi Delta Phi, Sigma Delta Pi, Phi Sigma Iota. Presbyn. Lion. Author: La Espana de Erasmo, 1973; El teatro en verso del siglo XX, 1975; Intermediate Spanish, 1977; editor jour. Crítica Hispánica. Home: 1907 Clearwood Dr Johnson City TN 37601

SUAREZ, ROBERTO ERNESTO, newspaper adminstr.; b. Havana, Cuba, Nov. 20, 1951; came to U.S., 1960, naturalized, 1973; s. Roberto J. and Miriam (Campuzano) S.; B.A. in Econs., Rutgers Coll., 1973; M.B.A., Wake Forest U., 1975. With Miami Herald, 1975—, West Coast circulation mgr., Ft. Myers and Naples, Fla., 1977-79, circulation mgr. Palm Beach County, 1979—. Mem. So. Circulation Mgrs. Assn., Delta Upsilon. Roman Catholic. Club: Kiwanis (Miami, Fla.). Home: 1690D Forest Lakes Circle West Palm Beach FL 33406 Office: 1218 S Olive Ave West Palm Beach FL 33401

SUAREZ, ROBERTO JOSE, publishing co. exec.; b. Havana, Cuba, May 5, 1938; came to U.S., 1961, naturalized, 1969; s. Miguel A. and Esperanza (DeCardenas) S.; B.S. in Econs., Villanova Coll., 1949; m. Miriam Campuzano, Nov. 5, 1950; children—Roberto, Miriam, Elena, Antonio, Miguel, Carlos, Armando, Raul, Teresa, Gonzlao, Esperanza, Ana. Partner, Suarez & Smith, Real Estate, Havana, 1950-58; pres., chmn. Financiera Nacional De Cuba, Havana, 1959-61; with Miami Herald Publishing Co., 1961-69, controller subs. ops., 1964-69; owner Institutional Equipment Co., Honduras, Central Am., 1969-72; controller Knight Publishing Co., Charlotte, N.C., 1972-77, v.p., gen. mgr., 1978—. Treas. Charlotte Symphony Orch., 1976-79; bd. advisors Belmont Abbey Coll., 1977-79; bd. dirs. Spirit Square, Charlotte, 1978-79; bd. dirs. Family & Children's Services, Charlotte, 1978-79; bd. dirs. Greater Charlotte Urban League, 1979. Mem. Charlotte C. of C. (v.p. 1976-78). Clubs: Charlotte City, Carmel Country. Office: 600 S Tryon St Charlotte NC 28202

SUBASIC, FRANK JOSEPH, trailer facility gen. mgr.; b. Pitts., Nov. 26, 1940; s. Michael Edwin and Helen (Ojnowski) S.; student Pitts. Tech. Inst., 1960-61, Ednl. Inst. Pa., 1961-62; grad. Indsl. Mgmt. Tech., 1962; student Corning Community Coll., 1964, U. Pa. Night Sch., 1965-68; m. Patricia A. Carns, June 9, 1962; children—Frank, Jr., Scott, Shawn, Stephen, Kelly Jo. Project engr. Ingersoll Rand Co., Painted Post, N.Y., 1963-65; mfg. engr. Elliott div. Carrier Corp., Jeannette, Pa., 1965-68; asst. chief indsl. engring. Howes Leather Co., Boston, 1968-70; gen. mgr. Gichner Mobile Systems div. Union Corp., Berkeley Springs, W.Va., 1970-72; mgr. tng. Prowler Industry of Md., Hancock, 1972; gen. mgr. Fleetwood Co., Wilderness Industry of Ind., Frankfort, 1972-74; gen. mgr. Fleetwood Enterprises, Prowler Industry of Md., Hancock, 1974—; adv. bd. Morgan County State Bank. Bd. dirs. Potomac Bend Med. Center; pres. Berkeley Springs Little League Assn. Republican. Roman Catholic. Mem. Soc. Barbershop Quartets. Home: Route 4 Grove Hts Berkeley Springs WV 25411

SUBER, JOHN THOMAS, JR., architect; b. Columbia, S.C., Mar. 24, 1949; s. John Thomas and Mattie Reid (Green) S.; B.A., Clemson U., 1971, B.Arch., 1972. Staff architect, specification writer Lyles, Bissett, Carlisle & Wolff, Columbia, 1972-75; dir. archtl. div., specification writer Wilbur Smith & Asso., Columbia, 1975-77; dir. archtl./interior design div. Bonitz of S.C., Columbia, 1977—. Mem. AIA, Columbia Council Architects, Nat. Council Archtl. Registration Bds., Constrn. Specifications Inst. Lutheran. Home: 509 Ott Rd Columbia SC 29205

SUCHINA, LUCILE FENZL, oil co. exec.; b. Houston, Dec. 18; d. Gustav John and Sarah (Ludtke) Fenzl; student Southwestern Bus. U., 1941-42; m. Andrew Harry Suchina, Aug. 29, 1942; children—Carole Ann Robertson, Pamela Jean Suchina Gillan, John Andrew. Stenographer C.E., U.S. Army, Galveston, Tex., 1942; sec. Aviation Enterprises, train-air ferry, Houston, 1943-44; sec. to supt. maintenance Pioneer Air Lines (now Continental Air Lines), Houston, 1944-47; account payable clk. Tellepsen Constrn. Co., Houston, 1950-51; stenographer City of Houston, 1953-54; sec. Exxon Co. U.S.A., Houston, 1954—. Nat. chmn. So. Conf. Youth Activities and Voice of Democracy Scholarship, 1973-74; mem. Tex. Medal of Honor Grove Com., 1976. Hon. citizen Lubbock, Tex., 1974; hon. mayor San Antonio, 1976. Mem. Am. Mem. Am. Inst. Parliamentarians, Nat. Secs. Assn., Houston Parliamentary Soc., Internat. Platform Assn., Am. Mgmt. Assn. Republican. Roman

Catholic. Clubs: Toastmistress (chpt. pres. 1969-70), VFW Aux. (pres. Tex. 1976-77)., nat. chmn. jr. girls So. Conf. 1977-78). Home: 7314 Cayton St Houston TX 77061 Office: PO Box 2180 Houston TX 77001

SUD, ISH, mech. engr.; b. Calcutta, India, Oct. 6, 1949; s. Inder Sain and Santosh Vati (Law) S.; B.Tech., Indian Inst. Tech., Kanpur, 1970; M.S., Duke U., 1971, Ph.D., 1975; came to U.S., naturalized, 1978. Design engr. T.C. Cooke, P.E., Inc., Cons. Engrs., Durham, 1974-77, dir. sect. energy mgmt. and spl. projects, 1978; sr. project engr., systems analyst Duke U., Durham, 1976—; pres. SUD Assos., Cons. Engrs., Durham, 1979—. Mem. India Assn. (pres. 1973-74), ASHRAE, ASME. Hindu. Contbr. articles to profl. jours. Home: 1812 Birmingham Ave Durham NC 27704 Office: 433 W Main St Box 3593 Durham NC 27702

SUDDATH, MARY LOUISE, educator; b. Roane County, Tenn., July 1, 1920; d. Frank Kenner and Ruth Amelia (Dahl) S.; student McMurry Coll., 1935-38; B.A., Tex. Wesleyan Coll., 1939; M.S., Case Western Reserve U., 1961. Elem. tchr., Tex., 1939-45; staff phys. therapist Walter Reed Army Hosp., Washington, 1946-47; staff therapist, asst. chief VA Hosp., Temple, Tex., 1947-60; chief phys. therapist VA Hosp., Fayetteville, N.C., 1960-75; dir. phys. therapist asst. program Fayetteville Tech. Inst., 1975—. Served with WAC Service Corps., 1945-47. Office of Vocational Edn. grantee, 1960-61. Mem. Am. Phys. Therapy Assn., N.C. Phys. Therapy Assn. Methodist. Club: Pilot (pres. 1978-79). Book reviewer: Physical Therapy, 1969—. Home: 421 McRae Dr Fayetteville NC 28305 Office: Fayetteville Tech Inst PO Box 32356 Fayetteville NC 28303

SUDIA-SKEHAN, SHAWN DAVIS, assn. exec.; b. Atlanta, Sept. 5, 1951; d. William Daniel and Marguerite Elizabeth (Delony) Sudia; B.A., Ga. State U., 1973, postgrad., 1973-75; m. Paul Stephen Skehan, Mar. 27, 1976. Mem. bicentennial staff Ga. C. of C., Atlanta, 1976; dir. public info. Ga. Hosp. Assn., Atlanta, 1977—; mem. com. on health edn. Med. Assn. Ga. Recipient Pres.'s award Ga. Soc. Hosp. Public Relations, 1977. Mem. Am. Soc. Hosp. Public Relations, Am. Soc. Assn. Execs., Atlanta Press Club. Presbyterian. Editor Ga. Hosp. Affairs, Ga. Hosp. Assn., 1977—, Yearbook, 1977—; author: A History-Georgia Hospital Association, 1979. Home: 2801 Hollywood Dr Decatur GA 30033 Office: Ga Hosp Assn 92 Piedmont Ave NE Atlanta GA 30303

SUEHS, OLIVER WILLIAM, physician; b. Carmine, Tex., Nov. 17, 1911; s. Paul E. and Laura (Marburger) S.; B.A., U. Tex., 1932, M.D., 1936; m. Helen Margaret Budd, June 28, 1941; children—Peggy Ann, Oliver William. Intern, U. Pa. Grad. Hosp., 1936-38; resident in otolaryngology and broncho-esophagology Jefferson Med. Coll. Hosp., Phila., 1938-41; pvt. practice medicine, specializing in otolaryngology, Austin, Tex., 1941—; mem. staff St. David's Hosp., Seton Med. Center (both Austin). Served to maj. U.S. Army, 1943-45. Mem. Travis County Med. Soc. (pres. 1947), Tex. Med. Assn. (chmn. Eye, Ear, Nose and Throat sect. 1953), Tex. Soc. Ophthalmology and Otolaryngology (pres. 1968), Am. Broncho-Esophagol. Assn. (v.p. 1968), Am. Laryngol. Assn. (v.p. 1970), Am. Council Otolaryngology (Tex. State chmn. 1973-75), A.M.A., Am. Acad. Ophthalmology and Otolaryngology, Tex. Otolaryngol. Assn., Am. Triol. Soc., Pan-Am. Assn. Otolaryngology and Broncho-Esophagology, Internat. Broncho-Esophagol. Soc. Republican. Episcopalian. Clubs: Austin Country, Coronet, Headliner's, Doctors Journal Club (pres. 1958). Contbr. numerous articles to med. jours. Office: 14 Med Arts Sq Austin TX 78705

SUELL, ROBERT MAY, wholesale dry goods co. exec.; b. Nicholasville, Ky., July 7, 1917; s. Albert and Sarah Frances (English) S.; student War Manpower Commn. Bur. Tng., 1945, Am. Sch. Chgo., 1947, Dun & Bradstreet Bus. Coll., 1950; m. Nona Christine Brumfield, June 15, 1957. Mgr., Park Theatre, 1941-43, 46-47; asst. credit mgr. Ades-Lexington Dry Goods, Co., Inc., Lexington, Ky., 1947-57, credit mgr., 1957—. Chmn., Jessamine County (Ky.) Republican Com., 1972-76, campaign chmn., 1972-73, 74-76. Served with AUS, 1943-46. Mem. Nat., Ky., Jessamine County (pres. 1971-73, dir. 1969-75) hist. socs., Lexington C. of C., Ky. Farm Bus., Spirit of '76 Soc. (charter). Mem. Christian Ch. Mason (32 degree, Shriner), Odd Fellow (grand chaplain Ky. 1975-76, lodge dep. grand master 1976-77). Author: Union Lodge No. 10, I.O.O.F., 1970; The History of Freemasonry in Jessamine County, Kentucky, 1974. Home: 121 Bell Ct Nicholasville KY 40356 Office: 249 E Main St Lexington KY 40507

SUGGS, JOHN THOMAS, lawyer; b. Denison, Tex., Dec. 22, 1904; s. John Thomas and Ruby Edna (Bunch) S.; B.B.A., U. Tex., 1925; LL.B., 1927; m. Mary Hope Robinson, Jan. 31, 1929; children—Ann Lee Suggs Smith, Mary Shelly Suggs Miller. Admitted to Tex. bar, 1927, U.S. Supreme Ct. bar, 1931; practice law, Denison, Tex. and Dallas, 1927-38; dist. judge Grayson and Collin Counties, Tex., 1938-44; gen. counsel Tex. & Pacific Ry. Co., Dallas, 1944-51, v.p., 1951-59, pres., chmn. bd., 1959-69, also dir.; individual practice law and cattle raiser, 1969—; dir. State Nat. Bank, Denison, First Nat. Bank of Van Alstyne (Tex.); lectr., instr. So. Methodist U. Mem. Am., Tex., Dallas bar assns., Tex. Bar Found., Dallas Citizens Council, Mexican Acad. Internat. Law. Democrat. Episcopalian. Clubs: Dallas Country, Dallas City, Hurricane Creek Country, Masons. Contbr. articles in field to profl. jours. Home: 4206 Fairfax St Dallas TX 75205 Office: 3033 First International Bldg Dallas TX 75270

SUGGS, MARION JACK, univ. ofcl., clergyman; b. Electra, Tex., June 5, 1924; s. Claude F. and Lottye M. (Gibson) S.; B.A., U. Tex., 1946; B.D., Tex. Christian U., 1949; Ph.D. (Guerney Harris Kearns fellow), Duke U., 1954; m. Ruth Barge, Nov. 13, 1943; children—Adena Ruth Suggs Beck, James Robert, David Nathan. Ordained to ministry Disciples of Christ Ch., 1948; minister First Christian Ch., Gladewater, Tex., 1948-50, Wendell (N.C.) Christian Ch., 1950-52; asst. prof. N.T., Brite Divinity Sch., Tex. Christian U., Fort Worth, 1952-54, asso. prof., 1954-56, prof., 1956—, dean Brite Divinity Sch., 1977—. Recipient Disting. Alumnus award Tex. Christian U., 1973, Book award Christian Research Found., 1969. Mem. Soc. Bibl. Lit. (chmn. research and publ. com. 1975-78, mem. fin. com. 1978—), Studiorum Novi Testamentum Societas, Phi Beta Kappa, Kappa Alpha Delta, Pi Gamma Mu. Democrat. Club: Ridglea (Ft. Worth). Author: The Layman Reads His Bible, 1957; The Gospel Story, 1960; Wisdom, Christology and Law in Matthew's Gospel, 1967; contbr. articles and essays to religious and scholarly jours.; N.T. annotations editor Oxford Study Edit. of New English Bible, 1976. Home: 5605 Winifred Dr Ft Worth TX 76133 Office: Brite Divinity School Tex Christian Univ Ft Worth TX 76129

SUHLER, MICHAEL JOHN, mfg. co. exec.; b. Houston, Dec. 9, 1951; s. William Henry and Eileen (Heaner) S.; B.B.A., U. Houston, 1974. Budget adminstr. U. Tex. Med. Sch., Houston, 1973-75; product mgr. Brinkmann Corp., Dallas, 1975—; Founder, Tex. Mobile Health Care Program, 1978. Recipient Outstanding Public Ser. award in health care Tex. Health Care Assn., 1978. Mem. Am. Mgmt. Assn., Nat. Sporting Goods Assn., Dallas Jaycees. Democrat. Home: 14010 Marsh Ln Apt 110 Dallas TX 75234 Office: 4215 McEwen Rd Dallas TX 75234

SUHR, GEORGE RASMUS, Bahamian govt. ofcl.; b. Sulhamstead, Eng., July 15, 1920; s. Frederik John and Beatrice Mary (Leake) S.; M.B.A., Royal Comml. Coll., Copenhagen, 1941; diploma Social Sci., London U. Poly., 1949; m. Ruth Andersen, Dec. 26, 1942; children—Hannah Suhr Stewart, George-Henrik, John; came to U.S., 1957. With Autourist Rent-a-Car, Copenhagen, 1950-61, exec. v.p., 1957-61; exec. v.p. Kemwel Group, N.Y.C., 1961-68; v.p. Arthur Frommer Orgn., N.Y.C., 1968-69; pres. Hotel Rep., Inc., N.Y.C., 1969-76, chmn. bd., 1971-76; chmn. bd., chief exec. officer Hotelworld Mgmt. Group Inc., 1976-78; cons., 1978—; dir. mktg. Bahamas Ministry of Tourism, Nassau, 1980—; dir. Auto-Europe Inc., N.Y.C., Selected European Travel, Inc., N.Y.C.; lectr. Cornell Sch. Hotel Adminstrn., 1971—. Scoutmaster Morris-Sussex council Boy Scouts Am., Chatham, N.J., 1964-69, adminstr. World Jamboree, 1967. Served with Intelligence Corps, Brit. Army, 1943-49. Fellow Inst. Cert. Travel Agts., Tourism Soc.; mem. Am. Soc. Assn. Execs. (adv. com. 1972-76), Assn. Group Travel Execs. (v.p. 1970-76), Am. Soc. Travel Agts. (adv. com. 1964-66), Hotel Sales Mgmt. Assn., French C. of C. (councillor 1973—), Chavaliers du Tastevin (comdr.), Newcomen Soc., Spanish Am. C. of C. Lutheran (mem. ch. council 1958-69). Clubs: Rotary, Skal (N.Y.C.); Royal So. Yacht (Hamble, Eng.); Royal Danish Yacht (Copenhagen). Author: Great Hotels and Resorts of the World. Contbr. articles to profl. jours. Home: 2342 NE 29th St Lighthouse Point FL 33064 Office: Nassau Ct Nassau Bahamas

SUITER, JOHN WILLIAM, indsl. engring. cons.; b. Pasadena, Calif., Feb. 16, 1926; s. John Walter and Ethel May (Acton) S.; B.S. in Aero. Sci., Embry Riddle U., 1964; m. Joyce England, Dec. 3, 1952; children—Steven A., Carol A. Cons. indsl. engr., Boynton Beach, Fla., 1955—. Instr. U. S.C. Tech. Edn. Center, Charleston, 1967-69. Served as pilot USAF, 1944-46. Registered profl. engr., Fla. Mem. Am. Inst. Indsl. Engrs., Soc. Mfg. Engrs. (sr.), Computer and Automated Systems Assn., Methods-Time Measurement Assn. (asso.). Home: 190 SE 27th Ave Boynton Beach FL 33435 Office: PO Box 1797 Delray Beach FL 33444

SUKI, WADI NAGIB, physician; b. Khartoum, Sudan, Oct. 26, 1934; s. Nagib Khalil and Fahima Hamdi (Hariz) S.; B.S., Am. U. Beirut, 1955, M.D. with distinction, 1959; m. Lailah Janet Stephan, May 6, 1967; children—Leila, Ramzy, Lenora, Wade. Came to U.S., 1959, naturalized, 1964. Fellow in exptl. medicine U. Tex. Southwestern Med. Sch., Dallas, 1959-61; resident in internal medicine Parkland Meml. Hosp., Dallas, 1961-63; fellow in nephrology U. Tex. Southwestern Med. Sch., 1963-65, instr., 1965-66, asst. prof. internal medicine, 1966-68; asso. prof. medicine Baylor Coll. Medicine, Houston, 1968-71, prof., 1971—, chief renal sect. 1968—; practice medicine, specializing in internal medicine and kidney diseases, Dallas, 1965-68, Houston, 1968—; chief renal sect. Meth. Hosp., Houston; attending physician Ben Taub Gen. Hosp., Houston; cons. medicine VA Hosp., Houston. Chmn. med. adv. bd. Kidney Found. Houston and Greater Gulf Coast, 1969-71; chmn. nat. med. adv. council Nat. Kidney Found., 1971-73, mem. sci. adv. bd., 1972-80, sec., 1977-78, chmn., 1979-80; mem. exec. com. council on kidney in cardiovascular disease Am. Heart Assn., 1971-75; cons. in nephrology Wilford Hall USAF Med. Center, Lackland AFB, Tex.; mem. gen. med. B study sect. NIH, USPHS, 1975-79; mem. VA Med. Research Rev. Bd. in Nephrology, 1974-77, chmn., 1976-77. Research and tng. grantee, NIH, USPHS, 1968—. Fellow A.C.P.; mem. Internat., Am. socs. nephrology, A.A.A.S., Am. Fedn. Clin. Research, Am. Physiol. Soc., Am., So. (sec.-treas., pres.) socs. clin. investigation, European Dialysis and Transplantation Assn. (asso.), Alpha Omega Alpha. Editor: Kidney in Systemic Disease, 1976, 80; editorial bd. The Kidney, 1970-73, Jour. Clin. Investigation, 1975-80, Kidney Internat., 1976—, Mineral and Electrolyte Metabolism, 1977—, Renal Physiolog, 1978—, Nephron, 1979—. Contbr. articles to profl. jours. Home: 2330 N Braeswood Houston TX 77030 Office: 6565 Fannin St Houston TX 77030

SULLENBERGER, HAL JOSEPH, architect; b. Stephenville, Tex., Mar. 26, 1933; s. Hal McCallom and Madeline (Funkhouser) S.; student Arlington State Coll., 1952-53, Amarillo Coll., 1953-54; B.Arch., Tex. Tech. U., 1962; m. Ara Broocks Cox, Nov. 2, 1952; children—Hal Joseph Jr., Ara Broocks. Archtl. draftsman firm Wilson, Patterson, Sowden, Dunlap, & Epperly, Fort Worth, 1962-63; draftsman firm Preston M. Geren, Fort Worth, 1963-67, job capt., 1968-71; field supr. firm Albert S. Komatsu, Fort Worth, 1967; job capt. firm Lawrence D. White, Fort Worth, 1967-68, 71-72; asso. architect firm Robert L. Wright, Fort Worth, 1972-73; project architect firm Thomas E. Stanley, Dallas, 1973, chief prodn. architect, 1973-75; project architect J.L. Williams & Co., 1975-76; architect Mid-United Contractors, Ft. Worth, 1976; field insp. (architect) Vantage Planning Systems, Dallas, 1976—, v.p., 1978—. Served with USNR, 1950-64. Mem. A.I.A. (corporate mem.; chmn. edn. com.), Constrn. Specifications Inst. (dir. 1973-75, pres.-elect 1975-76, pres. 1976-77, dir. 1977-78). Episcopalian. Home: 600 Eastwood Dr Fort Worth TX 76107 Office: 2525 Stemmons St Dallas TX 75207

SULLINS, WILLIAM DAVID, JR., optometrist; b. Athens, Tenn., Aug. 3, 1942; s. William David and Mildred (Falk) S.; B.S., Tenn. Wesleyan Coll.; O.D., So. Coll. Optometry; m. Judith Kay Jones, June 11, 1964; children—William David III, Stuart Andrew. Optometrist, Athens; sec.-treas. Sullins and Sullins, Optometrist, P.C. Past mayor, Athens; vice chmn. Athens Regional Planning Commn. Served with USN, 1967-70. Named Tenn. Optometrist of Year, 1978-79, Optometrist of the South, 1980. Mem. Am. Optometric Assn., Tenn. Optometric Assn., Eastern Tenn. Optometric Assn., Nat. Eye Research Found., C. of C. Methodist. Clubs: Kiwanis, Elks. Home: 1831 Crestwood Athens TN 37303 Office: Box 661 517 Jackson St Athens TN 37303

SULLIVAN, ALLEN R., sch. dist. adminstr.; b. Cambridge, Mass., July 15, 1941; s. Fernando and Dorothy (Alleyne) S.; B.S. in Social Studies Edn., Northeastern U., Boston, 1965; M.S. in Spl. Edn., Syracuse (N.Y.) U., 1966, Ph.D. in Spl. Edn., 1970; married; children—Raylene, Reginald. Tchr., Syracuse pub. schs., 1966-68; asso. prof. dept. spl. edn., dir. tng. of tchr. trainees program U. Minn., Mpls., 1970-75; dir. spl. edn. Dallas Ind. Sch. Dist., from 1975, now dep. asso. supt. Mem. Gov. of Minn. Adv. Bd. for Gifted, Handicapped and Exceptional Children, 1972-74; mem. Minn. State Commr. Edn.'s Spl. Edn. Adv. Bd., 1974-75; mem. sci. mgmt. panel Collaborative Perinatal Study, NIH; mem. Ft. Worth State Sch. Adv. Bd.; chmn. region X Spl. Edn. Dirs. Adv. Com. Mem. Nat. Alliance of Black Sch. Educators, Assn. Black Psychologists, Soc. Research Child Devel., Council Exceptional Children, Assn. Supervision and Curriculum Devel., Tex. Council Adminstrs. Spl. Edn., Am. Acad. Polit. and Social Sci., Nat. Soc. Study Edn., Psi Chi. Recipient Meyer O. Grunberg award for profl. promise Northeastern U. Office: 3700 Ross Ave Dallas TX 75204

SULLIVAN, EDWARD JAMES, JR., neurosurgeon; b. Trenton, N.J., Feb. 22, 1920; s. Edward James and Sara Elizabeth (Gaskill) S.; B.S., U. Notre Dame, 1942; M.D., Georgetown U., 1945; m. Mignonne Mary Martin, Aug. 17, 1944; children—Edward James III, William Patrick, Kathleen Elizabeth (Mrs. Robert P. Mellor). Intern U.S. Naval Hosp., Pensacola, Fla., 1945-46; instr. neuro-anatomy Georgetown U. Sch. Medicine and Dentistry, 1948; resident neurosurgery St. Vincent's Hosp., Jacksonville, Fla., 1948-49; resident gen. surgery St. Luke's Hosp., Jacksonville, 1949-50; resident neurosurgery Christ Hosp., Cin., 1951-52; chief neurosurgery VA Center, Dayton, Ohio, 1952-54; pvt. practice, Jacksonville, 1954—; chief neurosurgery St. Vincent's Hosp., 1958-64; chief neurosurgery St. Luke's Hosp., 1964-77, chief staff, 1977-79; chmn. med. staff Cathedral Health and Rehab. Center, 1973-74; asst. clin. prof. neurosurgery U. Fla. Jacksonville Hosps. Edn. Div., 1975-77. Served to lt. M.C., USNR, 1943-47, 50-51. Diplomate Am. Bd. Neurol. Surgeons. Fellow A.C.S.; mem. Congress Neurol. Surgeons, Am. Acad. Neurology, Am. Assn. Neurol. Surgeons, Jacksonville C. of C. (com. of 100). Home: 1636 Woodmere Dr Jacksonville FL 32210 Office: 2545 Riverside Ave Jacksonville FL 32204

SULLIVAN, HOLLAND ARTHUR, gen. agt.; b. Boston, July 28, 1945; s. Leo F. and Marguerite (Holland) S.; B.S., Spring Hill Coll., Mobile, Ala., 1968; postgrad. Am. Coll., Bryn Mawr, Pa., 1975—; m. Cynthia Sullivan, Dec. 6, 1974; 1 son, Holland A. Ins. agt. Aetna Life Ins. Co., Memphis, 1972-74, sales mgr., 1974-77, sales mgr., Houston, 1977-78; gen. agt. Aetna Life and Casualty, San Antonio, 1978—. Mem. Nat. Assn. Life Underwriters, Am. Soc. C.L.U.'s, San Antonio Assn. Life Underwriters, Gen. Agts. and Mgrs. Assn. Club: Rotary. Office: Suite 1050 6243 Interstate Hwy 10 San Antonio TX 78201

SULLIVAN, JAMES LENOX, clergyman; b. Silver Creek, Miss., Mar. 12, 1910; s. James Washington and Mary Ellen (Dampeer) S.; B.A., Miss. Coll., 1932, D.D., 1948; Th.M., So. Bapt. Theol. Sem., 1935; m. Velma Scott, Oct. 22, 1935; children—Mary Beth (Mrs. Bob R. Taylor), Martha Lynn (Mrs. James M. Porch, Jr.), James David. Ordained to ministry of Baptist Ch., 1930; pastor Bapt. Ch., Boston, Ky., 1932-33, Beaver Dam, Ky., 1933-38, Ripley, Tenn., 1938-40, Clinton, Miss., 1940-42, First Bapt. Ch., Brookhaven, Miss., 1942-46, Belmont Heights, Nashville, 1946-50, Abilene, Tex., 1950-53; exec. sec., treas. Bapt. Sunday Sch. Bd., Nashville, 1953-73, pres., 1973-75; exec. sec. Broadman Press, 1953-75, Conv. Press, 1955-75; vis. prof. So. Bapt. Theol. Sem., 1973-79. Pres., So. Bapt. Conv., 1977; trustee Union U., Cumberland U., So. Bapt. Theol. Sem., Hardin-Simmons U., Midstate (Tenn.) Bapt. Hosp., Hendrick Meml. Hosp. (Tex.). Recipient E.Y. Mullins Denominational Service award, 1973. Mem. Baptist World Alliance (exec. com., v.p. 1975—). Clubs: Rotary (Ripley, Tenn.); Lions (Brookhaven, Miss.); Kiwanis (Abilene, Tex.). Author: Your Life and Your Church, 1950; John's Witness of Jesus; Memos for Christian Living; Reach Out; Rope of Sand with Strength of Steel; God Is My Record. Contbr. articles religious publs. Address: PO Box 167 Hermitage TN 37076

SULLIVAN, JOSEPH EDWARD, concert promotion/artist mgmt. co. exec.; b. Tullahoma, Tenn., Jan. 27, 1942; s. Rufus James and Mildred (Crowder) S.; student pub. schs., Manchester, Tenn.; m. Barbara Jean Lawson, Apr. 1, 1961; children—Kimberly Jo, Tracy Leigh. Disc jockey, WMSR, Manchester, Tenn., 1958, WJIG, Tullahoma, Tenn., 1961-62, WAAY, Huntsville, Ala., 1962-63; program dir., disc jockey WKGN, Knoxville, 1964-67; program dir. WMAK, Nashville, 1967-72; group program dir. Mooney Broadcasting Corp., Nashville, 1968-72; pres. The Sound Seventy Corp., Nashville, 1973—, Sound Seventy Mgmt., Inc., Nashville, 1973—; chmn. bd. Sound Seventy Prodns., Inc., Nashville, 1973—. Named Nat. Program Dir. of the Year, by Bill Gavin Radio Programming Conf. 1971. Mem. Country Music Assn. (dir. 1980-81), Nashville Songwriters Assn. (dir. 1978-79). Methodist. Office: 210 25 Ave N Nashville TN 37203

SULLIVAN, JOSEPH VINCENT, bishop, Roman Cath. Ch.; b. Kansas City, Mo., Aug. 15, 1919; s. John Lawrence and Anastasia Agnes (Prosser) S.; grad. Cath. U., 1946, S.T.L., S.T.D., 1949; postgrad. Creighton U., 1951. Ordained priest Roman Catholic Ch., 1946; asst. supt. schs. Diocese of Kansas City (Mo.), 1948-50, supt. schs., 1951-57, chancellor, 1957-67; consecrated aux. bishop, 1967; vicar gen. diocese, from 1967; diocesan consultor, from 1957; pastor Our Lady of Good Counsel parish, Kansas City, Mo., from 1967; now bishop Diocese of Baton Rouge; Cath. chaplain Kansas City (Mo.) Police Dept.; mem. Diocesan Sch. Bd., from 1957. Bd. dirs. N.Am. Coll., Louvain, Belgium. Author: Catholic Teaching on the Morality of Euthanasia, 1948; Mercy Killing, 1950. Address: PO Box 2028 Baton Rouge LA 70821

SULLIVAN, W. D., charitable orgn. adminstr.; b. Mayfield, Ky., Dec. 11, 1923; s. Iseman and Birdie (Melton) S.; student Murray Coll., 1939-40; m. Sue Nell Gardner, Apr. 30, 1944; children—Stephen, Elizabeth, David, Rodney. Buyer mgr. Sears Roebuck & Co., Paducah, Ky., 1940-60; dir. Community Chest Paducah (Ky.), 1964-76; exec. dir. United Way Paducah, 1976—. Chmn. Youth Advisory Com. Paducah; treas. Sr. Citizens Inc.; pres. Market House Mus., Paducah Heart Assn., 1965, Paducah Cancer Assn., 1966. Recipient Ky. Gov's. award Youth Advancement, 1973; Paducah Mayor's award Community Advancement, 1974; Duke of Paducah award, 1964. Presbyterian. Home: 1203 Lone Oak Rd Paducah KY 42001 Office: 124 1/2 S 7th St Paducah KY 42001

SULLIVAN, WALTER FRANCIS, clergyman; b. Washington, June 10, 1928; s. Walter Francis and Catherine Jeanette (Vanderloo) S.; B.A., St. Mary's Sem. U. Balt., 1947, S.T.L., 1953; J.C.L., Catholic U., Washington, 1960. Ordained priest Roman Cath. Ch., 1953; asst. pastor St. Andrews Ch., Roanoke, St. Mary's, Star of Sea, Ft. Monroe, 1956-58; sec. Diocesan Tribunal, 1960-65; chancellor Diocese of Richmond, VA., 1965; rector Sacred Heart Cathedral, Richmond, 1967; ordained aux. bishop of Richmond, 1970; succeeded to the See, 1974. Office: 807 Cathedral Pl Richmond VA 23220*

SULLIVAN, WILLIAM LITSEY, lawyer, state senator; b. Harrodsburg, Ky., Nov. 1, 1921; s. Charles Blount and Anne (Litsey) S.; B.A., Centre Coll. of Ky., 1949; LL.B., U. Ky., 1948; m. Elizabeth Dorsey, Apr. 21, 1951; children—William Litsey, John Charles. Admitted to Ky. bar, 1948; with firm Dorsey and Sullivan, Henderson, Ky., 1956-77; commr. aeros. State of Ky. 1958-60; mem. Ky. Senate, 1954-57, 66—, majority leader, 1956, pres. pro tem, 1968-76. Served with USAAC, 1942-45; ETO. Named Outstanding Young Man of Ky., U.S. Jr. C. of C., 1956. Rotarian (pres. 1962). Internat. Formula I air race champion, 1976. Home: 517 N Main St Henderson KY 42420 Office: 140 N Main St Henderson KY 42420

SULLIVAN, WILLIAM STANLEY, lawyer; b. Birmingham, Ala., Sept. 17, 1931; s. Andrew J. and Era Kathryn (Stanley) S.; student Va. Poly. Inst., 1947; B.A., U. Richmond, 1951, LL.B., 1954; m. Jacquelyn Scott Bryant, Aug. 17, 1954; children—William Stanley, Elizabeth Scott. Admitted to Va. bar, 1954, practiced in Richmond, 1958—; partner William, Sullivan & Cabell, 1958-61, Sadler, Parker & Sullivan, 1962-63, Parker & Sullivan, 1963-71, Sullivan & Kane, 1971—; pres. Rox Industries, 1968-69. Mem. staff ARC Nat. Aquatics Sch., 1968—; bd. dirs. Saints and Sinners, 1961-64, pres., 1965. Served with USNR, 1954-58. Mem. Assn. Trial Lawyers Am., Am., Va., Richmond bar assns., Press Club Va., MacNeil Law Soc., Fraternal Order Police (counsel to chair, Va.), Fraternal Order Police Assos. (chmn. bd. trustees Richmond), Phi Gamma Delta, Delta Thgta Phi. Methodist. Home: 4012 Hermitage Rd Richmond VA 23227 Office: 4002 Hermitage Rd Richmond VA 23227

SULZBY, JAMES FREDERICK, JR., Realtor; b. Birmingham, Ala., Dec. 24, 1905; s. James Frederick and Annie (Dobbins) S.; student Howard Coll., Birmingham, 1925-26, A.B., Birmingham-So. Coll., 1928; grad. Am. Inst. Banking, 1934; Litt.D., Athens Coll., 1953; m. Martha Belle Hilton. Nov. 9, 1935; children—James Frederick III, Martha Hilton (Mrs. Robert J.B. Clark). Mem. staff trust dept. First Nat. Bank of Birmingham, 1929-43; pres. Sulzby Realty Co., 1943—; dir. Home Fed. Savs. & Loan Assn.; pres. Norwood Gardens, Inc. Mem. humanities adv. council Auburn U.; mem. Jefferson County Personnel Bd.; chmn. Planning Com., 1948-61; dir. Ala. Bapt. publ., 1945—; historian 75th anniversary celebration for Birmingham, 1946, also treas. deacon, mem. exec. com. Southside Baptist Ch.; pres. Ala. Baptist Young Peoples Union, 1932-33; chmn. Jefferson County Nat. Found. Infantile Paralysis, 1951-52. Bd. govs. Civic Theatre of Birmingham, 1946-48; trustee Birmingham Civic Symphony Assn., Rushton Lectures, Ala. Hall of Fame; bd. dirs. Birmingham Sunday Sch. Assn. Recipient Distinguished Service award Ala. Hist. Commn., 1972. Mem. Newcomen Soc. N.Am. (Ala. com.), Ala. Hist. Assn. (pres. 1947-49, sec. 1950—), Ala. Baptist (pres. 1947-49), Birmingham (sec. 1945-50, trustee) hist. socs., Avondale Civic Assn. (pres. 1946), Am. Planning and Civic Assn., Nat. Assn. Real Estate Bds. (dir. 1952-56), Birmingham Bd. Realtors (pres. 1953), Ala. Assn. Realtors (pres. 1952), Ala. Writers Conclave (pres. 1950), Birmingham Area Ednl. Television Assn. (treas., dir.), Ala. Acad. Sci. (pres. 1965-66), Birmingham C. of C. (chmn. edn. com. 1949-51), Birmingham So. Coll. Alumni Assn. (pres. 1960). Phi Beta Kappa, Delta Sigma Phi, Omicron Delta Kappa. Clubs: Mountain Brook Country; University (Tuscaloosa); The Club, Downtown. Author: Birmingham As It Was in Jackson County, 1944; Birmingham Sketches, 1945; Annals of the Southside Baptist Church. 1947; Historic Alabama Hotels and Resorts, 1960; Authur W. Smith: A Birmingham Pioneer, 1855-1944, 1961. Democrat. Baptist. Home: 3121 Carlisle Rd Birmingham AL 35213 Office: Massey Bldg Birmingham AL 35203

SUMERELL, CRAVEN HOWARD, ednl. and mgmt. cons.; b. Fort Barnwell, N.C., Nov. 7, 1930; s. Mark H. and Neva (Jolly) S.; B.S., Atlantic Christian Coll., 1953; M.A., East Carolina U., 1962; postgrad. Duke U., 1972; m. Amy Dee Davis, June 18, 1970; children—Dee Allison, Patrick Craven, Amy Shannon. Tchr., coach Hall's High Sch., Clinton, N.C., 1953-54; machine acct. Carolina Tel. & Tel. Co., Tarboro, N.C., 1956-62; sr. systems analyst, computer mgr. United Mchts. and Mfrs., Inc., N.Y.C., 1962-67; dean instrn. Catawba Valley Tech. Inst., Hickory, N.C., 1967-70; pros. Piedmont Tech. Inst., 1970-73; pres. Ednl. Indsl. Systems, Inc., Spartanburg, N.C., 1973—; guest lectr. various univs. Served with U.S. Army, 1954-56. Mem. Am. Assn. Community and Jr. Colls., Am. Vocat. Inst., Am. Inst. Mgmt., Textile Data Processing Assn., N.C. Public Community Coll. Pres.'s Assn., So. Mgmt. Assn., Nat. Speakers Assn. Democrat. Baptist. Club: Rotary. Contbr. articles to profl. jours. Home: Petty St Gaffney SC 29340

SUMMER, VIRGIL C., utility co. exec.; b. Spartanburg, S.C., 1920; grad. Internat. Corr. Schs.; M.S., U. S.C.; married. With S.C. Electric & Gas Co., Columbia, 1937—, v.p. electric ops. and engring., 1966-67, sr. v.p., 1967-77, pres., chief operating officer, 1977—, also dir. Fellow ASME; mem. Nat. Soc. Profl. Engrs. Office: SC Electric & Gas Co 328 Main St Box 764 Columbia SC 29202*

SUMMERLIN, GLENN WOOD, JR., advt. agy. exec.; b. Dallas, Ga., Apr. 1, 1934; s. Glenn Wood and Flora (Barrett) S.; student Ga. Inst. Tech., 1951-52; B.B.A., Ga. State U., 1956, M.B.A., 1967; m. Rebecca Anne Valley, Oct. 16, 1971; 1 son, Wade Hampton; children by previous marriage—Glenn Wood III, Edward Lee. Prodn. mgr. Fred Worrill Advt., Atlanta, 1956-65; v.p. sales Grizzard Advt., Inc., Atlanta, 1965-74, pres., 1974—. Vice chmn. Polaris dist. Boy Scouts Am., 1967; chmn. distributive edn. adv. com. DeKalb Coll., 1974-75. Trustee Ga. State U. Found., 1967-75, vice chmn., 1974; bd. founders George M. Sparks Scholarship Fund; mem. Council on Abandoned Mil. Outposts. Named Outstanding Young Man in DeKalb County N. DeKalb Jr. C. of C., 1967, Alumnus of Year, Ga. State U., 1973; recipient C.S. Bolen award So. Council Indsl. Editors, 1967, Humane award Atlanta Humane Soc., 1971. Mem. Asso. Mail Advt. Agys. (pres. 1976-77), Ga. Assn. Bus. Communicators (pres. 1966-67), Mail Advt. Service Assn. (pres. N. Ga. chpt. 1959-60), Am. Mktg. Assn. (dir. Atlanta chpt. 1969-75, pres. 1973-74), Ga. Bus. and Industry Assn. (gov. 1972-75), Atlanta Humane Soc. (dir. 1970—, treas. 1973-74, 80), Ga. State U. Alumni Assn. (pres. 1971-72), Co. Mil. Historians, Mensa, Ga. Arms Collectors Assn. (President's award 1973), Assn. Am. Sword Collectors, Tex. Gun Collectors Assn., Tenn. Gun Collectors Assn., Omicron Delta Kappa, Sigma Phi Epsilon. Home: 1133 Ragley Hall Rd NE Atlanta GA 30319 Office: 1144 Mailing Ave SE Atlanta GA 30315

SUMMERS, ALAN GRABLE, graphic designer; b. Nanking, China, Aug. 25, 1948; s. George Edwin, Jr., and Janie Louise (Campbell) S.; B.Design, U. Fla., 1974; m. Dorothy Elaine Deaux, Mar. 3, 1972; 1 dau., Katheryn Elaine. Founder, pres. Graphic Design Assos., Gainesville, Fla., 1975—; cons. Harvard Polit. Review. Vice pres., treas., bd. dirs. Gainesville Jaycees, 1974-80. Served with Signal Corps, U.S. Army, 1968-71; Vietnam. Decorated Air Medal, Purple Heart, Army Commendation medal (2). Recipient awards of excellence, Nat. Graphics Competition, 1975, 76, eight Addy Awards. Mem. Graphic Artists Guild, Am. Advt. Fedn., U.S. Parachute Assn. Democrat. Methodist. Clubs: U.S. Water Ski Assn., Am. Skydivers Assn. Profl. Graphic Artists. Home: 1937 NE 6th Terr Gainesville FL 32601 Office: 1705 NW 6th St Gainesville FL 32601

SUMMERS, JAMES WILLIAM, chief justice; b. Rusk, Tex., July 8, 1914; s. James Lee and Constance (Rook) S.; B.B.A., J.D., U. Tex., 1937; grad. Inst. for Juvenile Ct. Mgmt., Nat. Coll. for State Judiciary; m. Inez Thompson Steed, Nov. 22, 1969; children—Julia Ann (Mrs. Charles E. Tucker), Raymond C. Steed. Admitted to U.S. Supreme Ct. bar, Tex. bar, 1937, practiced in Rusk, 1937-56; city atty., 1937-41; county atty. Cherokee County, 1941-42, 47-48, county judge, 1949-56; judge 2d Jud. Dist. Tex., Rusk, 1957-78; chief justice Ct. Civil Appeals, 12th Supreme Jud. Dist. Tex., Tyler, 1978—. Dir. Southwestern Title & Guaranty Co. First State Bank, 1937-78; partner Summers Bros., land, cattle, timber. Faculty, Tex. Coll. for judiciary, 1975-76. Dir. Civil Def., Cherokee County, 1949-56; mem. Cherokee County Heritage Assn., Cherokee Civic Theatre; mem. adv. council Criminal Justice Program, Stephen F. Austin U., vice chmn. Rusk Housing Corp.; chmn. Nacogdoches-Cherokee Counties Probation Bd. Bd. dirs. East Tex. area council Boy Scouts Am., Rusk Indsl. Found., Rusk United Way, Rusk Bicentennial Commn.; bd. dirs., exec. com. Rusk Civic Service, Inc. Served as lt. USNR, 1942-46. Fellow Tex. Bar Found. (life); mem. Am. Judicature Soc., Am., East Tex., Cherokee, Smith County bar assns., State Bar Tex. (mem. nominating com. judicial sect., vice chmn. juvenile judges continuing legal edn. com.), Nat. Conf. State Trial Judges, Am., Tex., East Tex. Aberdeen-Angus assns., U. Tex. Ex-Students Assn. (exec. council Austin, past pres. Cherokee County alumni club), Rusk C. of C. (chmn. govt. affairs com.), Tex. Farm Bur. Fedn., Tex. State Hist. Found., Cherokee County Hist. Commn. (dir.), Am. Legion, Beta Gamma Sigma, Phi Delta Phi, Phi Eta Sigma, Phi Delta Theta (v.p. East Tex. alumni). Democrat. Methodist (chmn. ofcl. bd. 1955-56, 73-74, trustee, charge lay leader, dist. steward 1975-77). Clubs: Masons (Shriners), Kiwanis (past pres.), Willow Brook Country, Plaza (Tyler). Contbr. to profl. publs. Home: 200 W 5th St Rusk TX 75785 also 567 Towne Oaks Dr Tyler TX 75701 Office: 306 Smith County Courthouse Tyler TX 75702

SUMMERS, JOSEPH FRANK, automation cons.; b. Newnan, Ga., June 26, 1914; s. John Dawson and Anne (Blalock) S.; B.A. in Math., U. Houston, 1942; profl. certificate meteorology, U. Calif. at Los Angeles, 1943, U. Chgo., 1943; postgrad., U. P.R., 1943-44; M.A. in Math., U. Tex. at Austin, 1947; postgrad. (fellow math.) Rice U., 1947-49; m. Evie Margaret Mott, July 8, 1939; children—John Randolph, Thomas Franklin, James Mott. With Texaco Inc., Houston, 1933-42, 49—, mgr. data processing, 1957-67, asst. gen. mgr. computer services dept., 1967-79, automation cons., 1979—; instr. math. AAC, Ellington Field, Tex., 1941-42, U. Tex. at Austin, 1946-47. Pres. Houston Esperanto Assn., 1934-39. Served to capt. AAC, 1942-46. Mem. Assn. Computing Machinery (pres. 1956-58), Nat. Assn. Accountants (past dir.), Am. Petroleum Inst. (mem. data processing and computing com. 1955-59), A.A.A.S., Nat. Trust for Historic Preservation, Smithsonian Instn., World Future Soc. Author: Mathematics for Bombadiers and Navigators, 1942. Contbg. author: American Petroleum Institute Drilling and Production Practices. Home: 5517 Tilbury Dr Houston TX 77056 Office: PO Box 53462 Houston TX 77052

SUMMERS, PATTI PRATT, health educator; b. Uniontown, Pa., Jan. 14, 1938; d. M. Wayne and Helen J. (Burke) Pratt; R.N., Presbyn. Hosp.-U. Pitts. Sch. Nursing, 1958; B.A., Marietta (Ohio) Coll., 1976; postgrad. W.Va. U., 1976—; m. James C. Summers, June 14, 1977; children—William W., Marian L., Douglas L. Med.-surg. clin. instr. Presbyn.-U. Pitts. Sch. Nursing, 1960-64; instr. staff devel., human resources dept. Camden-Clark Hosp., Parkersburg, W.Va., 1976-78; dir. public relations Greensboro (N.C.) Hosp., 1980—; past bd. dirs. Mid-Ohio Valley chpt. ARC. Mem. Pitts. Symphony Women's Aux., 1970-72, Parkersburg Art Center, 1974—; mem. alumni council Marietta Coll., 1978-81, v.p., 1979-80. Recipient commendation Freedoms Found. Mem. AAUW (bd. dirs. Parkersburg 1977—), Greensboro Civic Ballet Guild. Republican. Presbyterian. Clubs: Parkersburg Country, Greenmont Racquet. Home: 3617 Gramercy Rd Greensboro NC 27410 Office: 1501 Pembroke Rd Greensboro NC 27408

SUMMERS, ROBERT LEROY, transp. co. exec.; b. Granite City, Ill., Dec. 9, 1942; s. Joseph Patrick and Genevia (Dykes) S.; B.S., U. So. Ill., 1962; m. Judith Ann Hudson, Dec. 28, 1979; 1 dau. by previous marriage—Maria Christina. Asst. gen. mgr. St. Louis Tchr.'s Credit Union, 1967-71; gen. mgr. RAC Credit Union, St. Louis, 1971-73, Greater Indpls. Firefighters Fed. Credit Union, 1973-74; benefit adminstr., asst. to exec. v.p. Pacemaker Driver Service, Inc., Indpls., 1974-79; dir. labor relations Progressive Driver Services, Inc., Jacksonville, Fla., 1979—. Served with USMC, 1961-66. Mem. Credit Union Exec. Soc., Cuna Sch. Alumni Assn. (bd. dirs. 1971-75), Am. Mgmt. Soc., Am. Mgmt. Assn., Am. Legion (post comdr. 1968-69, nat. comdrs. advisor 1967-71). Republican. Roman Catholic. Club: Royal Order Christian Ams. Young Men's. Home: 4560 Grassy Cay Ln Jacksonville FL 32224

SUMMERS, THOMAS EUGENE, entomologist; b. Seneia, Ga., June 7, 1919; s. Elijah Gary and Tinie (Cheek) S.; B.S.A., U. Ga., 1941; M.S., Iowa State Coll., 1947, Ph.D., 1950; m. Nancy Morgan, Dec. 1943; m. 2d, Edith Hernandez, June 30, 1961; children—Thomas Morgan, Gary Robert, Ruth Anne, Elizabeth Christine. Plant pathologist Dept. Agr., State College, Miss. and Belle Glade, Fla., 1950-65, entomologist sugarcane insects investigations Agrl. Research Sta., Canal Point, Fla., 1965-79; entomologist/pathologist U.S. Sugar Corp., Clewiston, Fla., 1979—; mem. grad. faculty U. Fla., 1966. Served with USAAF, 1941-46. Decorated Purple Heart, Air medal, D.F.C. Mem. Entomol. Soc. Am., AAAS, Internat. Orgn. for Biol. Control, Fla. Entomol. Soc., VFW. Clubs: Elks, Rotary. Research on small grains diseases, diseases of stem and leaf fiber crops; developer program for control of insect pests which attack sugarcane and cattle through biol., cultural and chem. control methods, diseases of sugar cane. Home: 111 Ridgewood Ave Clewiston FL 33440 Office: PO Box 1207 Clewiston FL 33440

SUMMERSELL, CHARLES GRAYSON, educator; b. Mobile, Ala., Feb. 25, 1908; s. Charles Fishweek and Sallie Rebecca (Grayson) S.; A.B., U. Ala., 1929, A.M., 1930; Ph.D., Vanderbilt U., 1940; m. Frances Sharpley, Nov. 10, 1934. Instr. history U. Ala., University, 1935-40, asst. prof., 1940-46, asso. prof., 1946-47, prof., 1947—, head dept. history, 1954-71; radio commentator, Tuscaloosa and Selma, Ala., 1941-43. Mem. Ala. Hist. Commn., Tannehill Furnace and Foundry Commn., Tuscaloosa County Preservation Authority. Commd. lt. (j.g.), USNR, 1942; active duty, 1943; served with USN, in PTO; lt. comdr., comdr. Res., 1954; officer charge Naval Tng. School, Norfolk, Va., 1951-53; mem. steering com. organizing Tuscaloosa unit Organized Res. of Navy, 1947. Recipient Letter of Commendation USNR, 1945. Mem. So., Mississippi Valley, Ala. (pres. 1955-56) hist. assns., Orgn. Am. Historians, U.S. Naval Inst., Naval Hist. Found., SAR (pres. Ala. 1957-58), Am. Assn. State and Local History (council 1965-71), Am. Hist. Assn., Hakluyt Soc., Phi Beta Kappa (pres. Ala. chpt. 1953-54), Phi Alpha Theta. Democrat. Clubs: University; Tuscaloosa Country; Army-Navy (Washington). Author: Historical Foundations of Mobile, 1949; Mobile History of a Seaport Town, 1949; Alabama History for Schools, 1957, rev., 1965, 70; (with Howard W. Odum and G.H. Yeuell) Alabama Past and Future, 1941, rev. edit. (with G.H. Yeuell and W.R. Higgs), 1950; (with Frances C. Roberts) Exploring Alabama, 1957, rev., 1961; (with Frances S. Summersell) Alabama History Filmstrips, 1961; (with F.S. Summersell and Rembert W. Patrick) Florida History Filmstrips, 1963; (with others) Texas History Filmstrips, 1965; The Cruise of the C.S.S. Sumter, 1965; Ohio History Filmstrips, 1967; (with others) California History Filmstrips, 1968, Illinois History Filmstrips, 1970; (with others) Atlas of Alabama, 1973. Editor: The Journal of George Townley Fullam: Boarding Officer of the Confederate Sea Raider Alabama, 1973; Colonial Mobile (Peter J. Hamilton), 1976. Mem. editorial adv. bd. Am. Neptune, 1946—; mem. editorial bd. Ala. Rev., 1964—. Contbr. articles and revs. to encys. and profl. jours. Home: 1411 Caplewood Dr Tuscaloosa AL 35401 Office: PO Drawer CZ University AL 35486

SUMMERSELL, FRANCES SHARPLEY (MRS. CHARLES GRAYSON SUMMERSELL), club woman; b. Birmingham, Ala.; d. Arthur Croft and Thomas O. (Stone) Sharpley; student U. Montevallo, Peabody Coll., Nashville; m. Charles Grayson Summersell, Nov. 10, 1934. Partner, artist, writer Asso. Educators, 1959—. Mem. Ft. Morgan Hist. Commn., 1959-63. Mem. D.A.R., Magna Charta Dames, U. Women's Club (pres. 1957-58), U.D.C. (state historian 1956-58, pres. Robert Emmet Rodes chpt. Tuscaloosa 1953-55), Daus. Am. Colonists (organizing regent Tuscaloosa 1956-63), English Speaking Union, Marquis Biog. Library Soc. (adv. mem.), Tuscaloosa County Preservation Soc. (trustee 1965-75, service award 1975), West Ala. Art Assn., Nat. Trust. Clubs: Univ., Country (Tuscaloosa). Co-author: Alabama History Filmstrips, 1961; Viewing Alabama History Filmstrips, 1961; Florida History Filmstrips, 1963; Texas History Filmstrips, 1965-66; Ohio History Filmstrips (Merit award Am. Assn. State and Local History 1968), 1967; California History Filmstrips, 1968; Illinois History Filmstrips, 1970. Home: 1411 Caplewood Tuscaloosa AL 35401

SUMMERSON, GEORGE WILLIAM, hotel exec.; b. Richmond, Va., Nov. 18, 1903; s. George Ralph and Eula Mead (Ford) S.; B.S., Washington and Lee U., 1927; m. Champe Grant, Dec. 24, 1932; children—Champe (Mrs. Don Hyatt), Sue (Mrs. Irvin Wells III), George William. Gen. auditor Robert E. Lee Hotel, Winston-Salem, N.C., 1929-35; mgr. Washington Duke Hotel, Durham, N.C., 1935-39; gen. mgr. Hotel Gen. Shelby, Hotel Bristol (Va.), 1939-56; pres., gen. mgr. Martha Washington Inn, Abingdon, Va., 1956—. Pres. Bristol Community Chest, 1950-51, Washington County United Fund, 1964-65; mem. state adv. com. Salvation Army, 1972—, vice chmn. divisional adv. bd., 1973-75. Mayor, mem. City Council, Bristol, 1951-57; vice mayor, mem. Town Council, Abingdon, Va., 1968-70, 71—, mayor, 1972-78. Bd. visitors Sullins Coll., Bristol, Va., 1972-76; bd. dirs., exec. com. Mt. Rogers Planning Commn., 1969—, chmn., 1973-74; mem. Va. Statewide Health Coordinating Council, 1977-79. Recipient Bristol's Outstanding Citizen award V.F.W., 1953; City of Bristol Pub. Service Recognition award, 1954-56; Bristol Centennial Celebration award, 1956; Distinguished Service award Hotel-Motel Greeters, 1969, Va. Hotel-Motel Assn., 1971. Mem. Am. Hotel and Motel Assn. (trustee ednl. inst. 1958-78, pres. inst. 1967-69), Am. (dir. 1949), Va. (pres. 1948), So. (pres. 1952) hotel assns., Hotel Greeters (chpt. pres. 1932), Bristol C. of C. (pres. 1952), Va. Travel Council (pres. 1950-51, outstanding service citation 1952), Abingdon C. of C. (pres. 1959-60), Va. State C. of C. (certificate appreciation 1961, v.p. 1969-71, dir. 1960, 62, 67, 69, 70). Methodist (chmn. adminstrv. bd. 1966-69, lay leader 1970-72). Mason (Shriner), Kiwanian. Club: Glenrochie Country (pres. 1961) (Abingdon). Home: 150 W Main St Abingdon VA 24210 Office: Martha Washington Inn 150 W Main St Abingdon VA 24210

SUMNER, FLORENCE GREIS, educator; b. Hammonton, N.J., Aug. 20, 1914; d. George Rehmann and Florence (Cottrell) Greis; A.B., U. N.C. at Greensboro, 1936; M.A., Western Carolina U., 1961; Edn. Specialist, U. Ga., 1971; m. Joseph Kenneth Sumner, July 29, 1939 (dec.); children—Vida Sumner Fiser, Joann C., Georgene Sumner Gay. Tchr., guidance counselor, speech therapist pub. schs., Gastonia, N.C., 1936-39, Wilmington, N.C., 1942-45, Charlotte, N.C., 1956-67; instr. speech pathology U. Ga., 1967-69; speech pathologist Charlotte Rehab. Hosp., 1969-70; asst. to asso. prof. speech pathology Western Carolina U., 1970—; speech cons. Jackson County Day Care Centers. NIH fellow 1967-68. Mem. Am. Speech and Hearing Assn. (certificate of clin. competence in speech pathology), N.C. Speech, Hearing and Lang. Assn., Council Exceptional Children, NEA, N.C. Assn. Educators, Internat. Reading Assn. Methodist. Clubs: Univ. Book, Yoke-fellows. Home: Box 526 Cullowhee NC 28723 Office: Western Carolina University Cullowhee NC 28723

SUMNERS, LESTER FURR, lawyer; b. Blytheville, Ark., June 2, 1926; s. Chester Lamar and Bessie (Furr) S.; B.A., U. Miss., LL.B., 1950; m. Mary Joyce Bonner, Feb. 12, 1956; children—Thomas Bonner, Melinda Watson, Leslie Elizabeth. Admitted to Miss. bar, 1950; mem. staff Office of Solicitor, USDA, Washington, 1951-52; practiced in New Albany, Miss., 1952—; mem. firm Darden & Sumners, New Albany, 1954-76, Darden, Sumners, Carter & Trout, P.A., 1976—. Trustee, N.E. Miss. Jr. Coll., 1961-66. Recipient Silver Beaver award Boy Scouts Am. Fellow Internat. Acad. Trial Lawyers; mem. Miss. State (commr. 1950-63, 65-67, complaint commr. 1963, 65, v.p. 1970-71, pres. 1971-72), Am. bar assns., Miss. Bar Found. (pres. 1979-80), Am. Assn. Forensic Scientists, U. Miss. Law Alumni Assn. (chpt. pres. 1976-77), Delta Kappa Epsilon. Presbyn. Asso. editor Miss. Law Jour., 1949-50. Home: 418 Pine Ridge Dr New Albany MS 38652 Office: PO Box 123 New Albany MS 38652

SUMRELL, GENE, research chemist; b. Apache, Ariz., Oct. 7, 1919; s. Joe B. and Dixie (Hughes) S.; B.A., Eastern N.Mex. U.; Ph.D., U. Calif. at Berkeley, 1951. Asst. prof. chemistry Eastern N.Mex. U., 1951-53; sr. research chemist J.T. Baker Chem. Co., Phillipsburg, N.J., 1953-58; sr. organic chemist S.W. Research Inst., San Antonio, 1958-59; project leader Food Machinery & Chem. Corp., Balt., 1959-61; research sect. leader El Paso Natural Gas Products Co. (Tex.), 1961-64; project leader So. utilization research and devel. div. U.S. Dept. Agr., New Orleans, 1964-67, investigations head, 1967-73, research leader Oilseed and Food Lab., So. Regional Research Center, 1973—. Served from pvt. to staff sgt. AUS, 1942-46. Mem. Am. Chem. Soc., A.A.A.S., N.Y. Acad. Scis., Am. Inst. Chemists, Am. Oil Chemists Soc., Am. Assn. Textile Chemists and Colorists, Research Soc. Am., AAUP, Sigma Xi, Phi Kappa Phi. Home: PO Box 24037 New Orleans LA 70184 Office: 1100 Robert E Lee Blvd New Orleans LA 70179

SUMWALT, ROBERT LLEWELLYN, JR., constrn. co. exec.; b. Columbia, S.C., Dec. 29, 1927; s. Robert Llewellyn and Caroline M. (Causey) S.; B.S. in Civil Engring., U. S.C., 1949; M.S. in Civil Engring., Mass. Inst. Tech., 1950; m. Mary Joyce Mills, Mar. 8, 1952; children—Elizabeth Ladson, Robert Llewellyn III. Area engr. E. I. duPont de Nemours & Co., Camden, S.C., 1950-52; constrn. engr. Columbia City Sch. System, 1952-58; sr. v.p., dir. McCrory-Sumwalt Constrn. Co., Inc., Columbia, 1958-77; chmn. bd., treas., dir. Sumwalt-Mashburn Engring. & Constrn. Co., Inc., Columbia, 1977-79; pres., treas., dir. Sumwalt Constrn. Co., Inc., Columbia, 1979—. Pres., Richland County unit Am. Cancer Soc., 1956, Carolina Carillon Ball, 1963; sect. chmn. United Community Services, 1957; div. chmn. constrn. div. United Way, 1973. Bd. dirs. Am. Cancer Soc., S.C. chpt., 1957, Richland County unit ARC, 1955-56. Served to comdr., C.E.C., USNR. Named Young Man of Year, Columbia Jr. C. of C., 1958. Registered profl. engr., S.C. Mem. Asso. Gen. Contractors Am., (chmn. bldg. div., dir. Carolinas br. 1977), Am. Inst. Constructers, Columbia Contractors Assn. (pres. 1969), S.C. Soc. Engrs., S.C. Soc. Profl. Engrs., U. S.C. Alumni Assn. (circuit v.p. 1956), Sigma Alpha Epsilon, Phi Beta Kappa, Omicron Delta Kappa, Tau Beta Pi. Presbyn. (chmn. bd. deacons 1968, elder). Kiwanian (pres. 1962). Clubs: Forest Lake Country, Palmetto, Cotillion, Wildwood Country, Columbia Ball, Centurion (Columbia); Litchfield Country (Litchfield Beach, S.C.). Home: 1420 Belmont Dr Columbia SC 29205 Office: 4600 Forest Dr Suite 10 Columbia SC 29206

SUNDBERG, ALAN CARL, state supreme ct. justice; b. Jacksonville, Fla., June 23, 1933; s. Robert C. and Gertrude (Rudd) S.; B.A., Fla. State U., 1955; LL.B., Harvard U., 1958; m. Barbara Lester; children—Allison, Angela, Laura, Alan, William. Admitted to Fla. bar, 1958; practice law, St. Petersburg, Fla., 1958-75; justice Fla. Supreme Ct., Tallahassee, 1975—; bd. govs. Fla. Bar, 1970-75, mem. exec. com., 1973-74. Mem. Adv. Bd. Salvation Army, St. Petersburg; chmn. bd. trustees Canterbury Sch. of Fla., dir. Fla. Gulf Coast Symphony, dir. St. Petersburg Symphony; trustee Pinellas County Law Library; mem. Pres.' Roundtable Eckerd Coll., St. Petersburg. Mem. St. Petersburg Fla. Bar Assn., Pinellas Trial Lawyers Assn., Fla. Bar Found. (past v.p.), St. Petersburg C. of C. (past bd. govs., v.p.), Phi Beta Kappa, Phi Kappa Phi, Omicron Delta Kappa, Phi Delta Phi. Office: Supreme Ct of Fla Supreme Ct Bldg Tallahassee FL 32304

SURBER, DAVID FRANCIS, pub. relations, advt. cons., TV producer, journalist; b. Covington, Ky., May 16, 1940; s. Elbert and Dorothy Kathryn (Mills) S.; B.A. in Physics, Thomas More Coll., 1960; LL.D. (h.c.), London Inst. Applied Research, 1973. Owner, The P.R. Co., pub. relations and advt. counseling, Covington, 1960—. Spl. corr. Am. newspapers to Vatican II, Rome, Italy, 1965. Mem. Bd. Adjustment (Zoning Appeals), Covington, 1964—, chmn., 1971—; chmn. Covington Environ. Commn., 1971-72, Commn. Strip Mining, 1967-68; mem. pub. interest adv. com. Ohio River Valley Water Sanitation Commn., 1976—; mem. water quality adv. com. Ohio-Ky.-Ind. Regional Council Govts., 1975—. Mem. rehab. com. Community Chest Greater Cin., 1972—, mem. agy. admissions com., 1972—, mem. priorities com., 1972—. Pres. bd. dirs. Cathedral Found., 1968—; trustee Montessori Learning Center, 1973—; mem. Ky. Nature Preserves Commn., 1976-79. Recipient Community Service award Thomas More Coll., 1975. Mem. AFTRA, Tri-State Air Com. (chmn. 1973-74), Izaak Walton League (pres. Ky. 1973, dir. Ky.; nat. dir.), ACLU. Producer: Make Peace with Nature, WKRC-TV, Cin., 1974, Strip Mining Must Be Stopped, 1972; Energy: Where Will It Come From; How Much Will It Cost, 1975; Atomic Power for Ohio, 1976; A Conversation With The Vice President, 1976; The Bad Water, 1977; The Trans-Alaska Pipeline: A Closeup Report, 1977. Home and office: 9 E Southern Ave Covington KY 41015

SURBER, JOE ROBERT, ednl. adminstr.; b. Pawhuska, Okla., Apr. 11, 1942; s. Hugh Richard and Odema (Harris) S.; B.A., Northeastern State U., 1964; M.S., Okla. State U., 1969, Ed.D., 1974; m. Jo Del Novak, Jan. 27, 1967; children—Robert Brian, Karrie Jo. Tchr. lang. arts Jefferson (Colo.) Schs., 1964-65; tchr. English, counselor jr. high sch. Ponca (Okla.) City Schs., 1965-70, prin. Unity High Sch., 1970-71; counselor/psychometrist Bi-State Mental Health Found., Ponca City, 1971-74; dir. spl. services Ponca City Schs., 1974—. Chmn. Community Relations Com. Ponca City, 1973-75; bd. dirs. Help Line, Inc., 1974-76; bd. dirs. Ponca City chpt. ARC, 1974—. Named 1 of 3 outstanding young Oklahomans, 1976. Mem. Am., Okla. personnel and guidance assns., Nat. Assn. Sch. Psychologists, Okla. Sch. (v.p. 1976), Okla. psychol. assns., Am. Sch. Counselors Assn., Okla. Edn. Assn. (v.p. psychol. sect. 1975). Democrat. Presbyterian. Clubs: Lions, Elks. Home: 1308 De Sota St Ponca City OK 74601 Office: 613 E Grand Ave Ponca City OK 74601

SURRATT, JERRY LEE, educator; b. Winston-Salem, N.C., Oct. 18, 1936; s. Robert Lee and Cleo Shirley (Phelps) S.; A.A., Wingate Coll., 1957; B.A., Wake Forest Coll., 1959; B.D., Southeastern Baptist Theol. Sem., 1962; Ph.D., Emory U., 1968; m. Alice Andrea Allen, June 16, 1963; children—Andrea Leigh, Emily Elizabeth, Maria Katherine. Instr. and acting chaplain, Salem Coll., Winston-Salem, 1965-67; prof. Wingate Coll. (N.C.), 1967—, acad. dean, 1968-77, Homer V. Lang prof. religion and history, 1977—. Chmn. joint com. on coll. transfer N.C. Bd. Higher Edn., 1970; v.p. N.C. Assn. Jr. Colls., 1971, pres., 1973; mem. exec. com. N.C. Assn. Colls. and Univs., 1973; sec. Charlotte Area Ednl. Consortium, 1973, chmn., 1975-77. Bd. dirs. Charlotte Speech and Hearing Clinic, 1976—. Mem. Am. Acad. Religion, Am. Soc. Ch. History, Moravian Hist. Soc., N.C. Hist. and Lit. Soc., Wachovia Hist. Soc., Assn. Acad. Deans N.C., Conf. Acad. Deans So. States. Mason. Home: PO Box 487 Wingate NC 28174

SUSKO, MICHAEL, aerospace engr.; b. Monessen, Pa., July 10, 1921; s. Alexander and Mary (Boiwka) S.; student Calif. (Pa.) State Coll., 1940-42, U. Va., 1943, Yale, 1944; B.A., Duquesne U., 1948; postgrad. in math. and engring. U. Pitts., 1948-50, Fla. State U., 1954-59, U. Fla., 1956-59, U. Ala., 1962-75, Pa. State U., 1963; M.S. in Engring. Sci., U. Tenn., Knoxville, 1977, postgrad. m. Margaret Elaine Priecko, Feb. 2, 1950; children—Justine Susko Manis, Michael Alexander, John Edward, Andrew Franklin, Mark Stephen. Project mathematician Air Proving Ground Command, U.S. Air Force, Eglin AFB, Fla., 1951-54, aero. engr., 1954-57, supervisory aero. engr., aircraft performance engr., 1957-61; aerospace engr. NASA, George C. Marshall Space Flight Center, Huntsville, Ala., 1961—; cons. atmospheric diffusion problems. Baseball mgr. Little League, 1963, 74-75, Babe Ruth League, 1953-67. Served with USAAF, 1943-46; PTO. Recipient certificate of participation for Saturn, 1967, Apollo achievement award, 1969, letter of commendation Marshall Space Flight Center, 1973, Skylab achievement award, 1974. Mem. AIAA (charter; asso. dir. tech. panel 1978-79), Am. Meteorol. Soc. (chmn. No. Ala. chpt. 1975), Am. Def. Preparedness Assn., Am. Geophys. Union, Am. Legion. Club: Elks. Contbr. articles to profl. jours. Mem. team manning meterol. tower at Kennedy Space Center for Saturn V mission to moon, 1969; prin. investigator experimental research in use of electrets in performing air quality expts. Launch Complex 41, Kennedy Space Center for Titan III Viking A mission to Mars, 1975; exptl. investigator on air quality analyses for space shuttle vehicle to be flown in the 1980's; mgr., player semi-profl. baseball, 1937-41. Home: 7108 Jones Valley Dr SE Huntsville AL 35802 Office: NASA George C Marshall Flight Center Space Sciences Lab Huntsville AL 35812

SUSMAN, MORTON LEE, lawyer; b. Detroit, Aug. 6, 1934; s. Harry and Alma (Koslow) S.; B.B.A., So. Meth. U., 1956, LL.B., 1958; m. Nina Meyers, May 1, 1958; 1 son, Mark Lee. Admitted to Tex. bar, 1958, Fed. bar, 1961; law clk. Wynne & Wynne, Dallas, 1958; asst. U.S. atty., Houston, 1961-65, 1st asst. U.S. atty., 1965-66, U.S. atty., 1966-69. Mem. Tex. Bill of Rights Found., 1967-69. Past mem. bd. dirs. Am. Jewish Com. Houston, S.W. Regional council Am. Jewish Com. Houston Council Human Relations, Planned Parenthood Houston, S.W. Region Planned Parenthood; bd. dirs. Ct. Vol. Services, Houston, 1969—; bd. visitors Law Sch., So. Meth. U., 1974-77. Served to lt. with USNR, 1958-61. Recipient Younger Fed. Lawyer award Fed. Bar Assn., Washington, 1968. Mem. Am., Fed., Houston bar assns., State Bar Tex., Barristers, Sigma Alpha Mu (pres. 1954), Phi Eta Sigma, Phi Alpha Delta, Delta Sigma Pi. Jewish (trustee congregation 1968-72). Rotarian. Club: Houston. Case note editor Southwestern Law Jour., 1957-58. Home: 338 Hunters Trail Houston TX 77024 Office: 2290 Two Shell Plaza Houston TX 77002

SUSMAN, STEPHEN DAILY, lawyer; b. Houston, Jan. 20, 1941; s. Harry and Helene Gladys (Daily) S.; B.A. magna cum laude, Yale U., 1962; LL.B. summa cum laude, U. Tex., Austin, 1965; m. Karen Lee Hyman, Dec. 26, 1965; children—Stacy Margraeta, Harry Paul. Admitted to Tex. bar, 1965, U.S. Supreme Ct. bar, 1970; law clk. Chief Judge 5th Circuit, 1965-66, to Asso. Justice Hugo Black, U.S. Supreme Ct., 1966-67; partner firm Fulbright & Jaworski, 1966-75; spl. cons. atty. gen. of Tex., 1975; partner firm Mandell & Wright, 1975—; vis. prof. law U. Tex., Austin, 1975. Bd. dirs. Jewish Family Service, 1967-75, Am. Jewish Com., 1967—. Recipient Leon Green Outstanding Ex Editor award U. Tex. Law Sch., 1970. Research fellow Southwestern Legal Found., 1975—. Mem. Am. Law Inst., Am. Bar Assn., Tex. Law Rev. Pubs. (dir.). Clubs: Yale (pres.), Houston, Athletic, Houstonian (Houston); Yale (N.Y.C.). Home: 9211 Kenilworth St Houston TX 77024 Office: 806 Main St Houston TX 77002

SUSSMAN, MARION BEATRICE BAUM, counseling psychologist, ednl. cons.; b. Paterson, N.J.; d. Samuel and Adele (Gerstein) Baum; student U. Ala., 1940-42; B.Ed. cum laude, U. Miami, 1953, M.Ed., 1956, Ph.D., 1973; postgrad. U. N.C., 1969; m. Irving Sussman, Nov. 21, 1943 (div. Apr. 1979); children—Nicki Sussman Horowitz, Roberta Joy. Sci. tchr. Kinloch Park Jr. High Sch., Miami, Fla., 1953-56, counselor, guidance chmn., test chmn., 1956-63, asst. prin. for guidance, 1969-73; counselor, test chmn. S.W. Miami High Sch., 1963-68; grad. asst. U. Miami, Coral Gables, Fla., 1968-69; mem. staff Piedmont summer program Wake Forest U., Winston-Salem, N.C., 1972-75; dir. Piedmont winter program Biscayne Coll., Miami, 1974; pvt. practice as counselor, 1973—; sch. services cons. N.C. Advancement Sch., Winston-Salem, 1974-75; partner Human Effectiveness Assos., Winston-Salem, 1975-80. Cons. on peer-group counseling; clin. cons. Council on Drug Abuse, Winston-Salem, 1975—; psychotherapist cons. Mandala Psychiat. Hosp., 1976-79; psychotherapist Salem Psychiat. Assos., Winston-Salem, 1979—. Active various community drives. Mem. NEA, Am., Dade County (pres. 1967-68) personnel and guidance assns., Fla. Edn. Assn., Am. Psychol. Assn., Assn. for Humanistic Psychology, Common Cause, N.C. Group Behavior Soc., Internat. Transactional Analysis Assn., NOW. Home: 747 Yorkshire Rd Winston-Salem NC 27106 Office: 3637 Old Vineyard Rd Winston-Salem NC 27104

SUSTENDAL, DIANE MARIE, fashion editor; b. New Orleans, Aug. 30, 1944; d. George and Mary (Anderson) S.; student La. State U., 1963-64; certificate John McCrady Sch. Fine Arts, 1966; m. John Marshall Miller. Asst. art critic Times-Picayune, New Orleans, 1966-68; asst. mng. spl. studies div. Frederick A. Praeger, N.Y.C., 1969; fashion and beauty editor Times-Picayune Pub. Corp., New Orleans, 1970—, women's news editor, 1974-75. Bd. dirs. Ballet Hysell, New Orleans, 1971-73. Recipient award La. Press Anns., 1972. Mem. Fashion Group (dir. New Orleans chpt. 1973-74), New Orleans Symphony (women's com.), New Orleans Mus. Art, La. Council Music and Performing Arts, Art Assn. New Orleans. Republican.

SUTER, PAUL LABARRER, banker; b. N.Y.C., July 22, 1914; s. Roland LaBarrer and Bertha Jane (Wheeler) Suter; B.A., Upsala Coll., 1937, certificate in teaching, 1937; postgrad. N.J. State Coll., 1938-40; certificate in banking Bank Adminstrv. Inst., U. Wis., 1955-57; m. Susan Robertson Wilsey, Mar. 6, 1948; children—Bruce Wilsey, George Wheeler, Paula Sue. Dept. and br. examiner 1st Nat. City Bank N.Y., 1945-52; comptroller Marine Bank & Trust Co., Tampa, Fla., 1953-62; asst. v.p., auditor Bank Clearwater (Fla.), 1962-79; v.p., auditor N.E. Bank of Clearwater, 1980—. Served with U.S. Army, 1940-45. Certified internal auditor. Mem. Nat. Assn. Accountants, Inst. Internal Auditors (pres. local chpt. 1972-73), Bank Adminstrv. Inst. (dir. local chpt. 1973-74). Home: 5552 Pentail Circle Tampa FL 33624 Office: 600 Cleveland St Clearwater FL 33517

SUTHERLAND, GEORGE WARREN, govt. ofcl.; b. Plains, Ga., Mar. 27, 1943; s. Amos Hiott and Grace (Rees) S.; A.S., Abraham Baldwin Coll., 1974; B.S., U. Ga., 1974, M.S., 1976; m. Phyllis Margie Williams, July 1, 1967; children—Warren Foster, Stephen George, Mark Philip. Tchr., Oconee County (Ga.) Public Schs., 1967-68; economist Ga. Mountains Area Planning and Devel. Commn., Gainesville, 1968-70; exec. dir. N. Ga. Area Planning and Devel. Commn., Dalton, 1970—; pres. Assn. Appalachian Local Devel. Dists. Pres. Cheerhaven Mental Retardation Center, 1979-80; deacon 1st Bapt. Ch., Dalton. Mem. Ga. Planning Assn., Nat. Assn. Regional Councils, Nat. Assn. Devel. Orgns. Club: Rotary. Home: 1608 Southmont Dr Dalton GA 30720 Office: 503 W Waugh St Dalton GA 30720

SUTHERLAND, RAYMOND CARTER, educator; b. Horse Cave, Ky., Nov. 5, 1917; s. Raymond Carter and Ruth (Veluzat) S.; student Transylvania Coll., 1935-36; A.B., U. Ky., 1939, M.A., 1950, Ph.D., 1953; grad. Gen. Theol. Sem., 1942, now postgrad. Ordained to ministry Episcopal Ch., 1942; curate St. Luke's Ch., Anchorage, Ky., 1942-44; prof. U. Tenn., 1953-57; prof. Ga. State U., Atlanta, 1957—, now dir. grad. studies in English; research grant U. Oxford, 1959. Served as chaplain, capt. AUS, 1944-47, PTO, ETO. Recipient research grant from Georgia State Coll. for work on medieval manuscripts. Mem. Am. Archaeol. Assn., New Chaucer Soc., Heraldry Soc. Eng., Medieval Acad. Am., Modern Lang. Assn., Oriental Ceramic Soc. (London), Heraldry Soc. (London), Phi Kappa Phi, Omicron Delta Kappa. Am. Author: Medieval English Conceptions of Hell as Derived from Biblical, Patristic, and Native Germanic Sources, 1953; The Religious Background of Swift's A Tale of A Tub, 1958; Mechanics of Versification, 1963, 2d edit., 1964; The Celibate Beowulf, the Gospels and the Liturgy (Ga. State Coll. Monograph series), 1964. Contbr. articles profl. jours. Home: 50 Polo Dr NE Atlanta GA 30309

SUTHERLAND, THOMAS (TUCKER) LEE, JR., newspaper publisher, editor; b. Mathis, Tex., July 8, 1938; s. Thomas Lee and Betty (Collins) S.; B.A., Tex. A. and M. U., 1960; m. Carole Sparks, June 8, 1960; children—Tom, Scott, Craig, Beth. Advt. mgr., sportswriter Robstown (Tex.) Record, 1960-61; gen. mgr., editor Mathis News, 1961-63; Pasadena (Tex.) Citizen, 1963-65; self-employed in pub. relations and advt., 1965; dir. info. and service Tex. Daily Newspaper Assn., Houston, 1968-69; asst. to pub. Horvitz Newspapers of Ohio, 1966-69; bus. mgr. Abilene (Tex.) Reporter-News, 1969-70; pub., editor Corsicana (Tex.) Daily Sun, 1970-71, Hamilton (Ohio) Journal-News, 1971-74, San Angelo (Tex.) Standard-Times, 1974—; asst. instr. journalism Angelo State U., 1977—. Bd. dirs. Tom Green County United Way, Ft. Concho Mus., Tex. Arts Alliance, Chihuahuan Desert Research Inst., Fiesta Del Concho, West Tex. Conf. on State Affairs, Angelo State U. Found.; mem. adv. bd. St. John's Hosp. Mem. Am. (com. on journalism edn.), So. newspaper pubs. assns., Tex. Daily Newspaper Assn. (dir.), Am. Soc. Newspaper Editors, Internat. Newspaper Advt. Execs., West Tex., San Angelo chambers commerce. Roman Catholic. Clubs: San Angelo Press, San Angelo River (pres. bd. dirs.). Editor: Ohio Almanac 1968, Ohio Almanac 1969. Contbr. articles to mags. Home: 2710 Vista del Arroyo San Angelo TX 76901 Office: 34 W Harris St San Angelo TX 76903

SUTTER, EVERETT LEE, psychologist; b. Seward, Pa., Nov. 14, 1920; s. Edward Wayne and Jennie Elizabeth (Reynolds) S.; B.A., W. Va. Wesleyan Coll., 1948; M.S., Pa. State U., 1948; Ph.D., U. Tex. at Austin, 1952; m. Mary Ann Law, Sept. 4, 1948; children—Cynthia Ann, David Lee, Lynn Marie. Pvt. practice clin. psychology, San Angelo, Tex., 1954-66; asso. prof. clin. psychology Stephen F. Austin State Coll., Nacogdoches, Tex., 1966-68; dir. Univ. Counseling Center, Memphis (Tenn.) State U., after 1968, Univ. Health Center, to 1978; dir. Lauderdale County Counseling Center, Ripley, Tenn., 1978—; cons. schs., hosps., govt. agys., Tenn. Vocat. Rehab. Center. Served with USNR, PTO, 1943-46. Mem. Am., Southeastern, Southwestern, Tenn. psychol. assns. Home: 128 Wardlaw Pl Ripley TN 38063 Office: Lauderdale County Counseling Center Ripley TN 38063

SUTTER, NORMA JEAN, sch. counselor, marriage counselor; b. Indpls., Dec. 27, 1926; d. H. Nathan and Clara L. (Kenner) Swaim; B.A., DePauw U., Greencastle, Ind., 1948; M.A. in Counseling Psychology, Ball State U., Muncie, Ind., 1974; m. Jack Geyer Sutter, Aug. 8, 1948; children—John Robert, Joseph Swaim, Julia Jean, Janice Ann. Service dir. Grant County (Ind.) Crippled Children and Adults Soc., 1962-65; asst. dir. Eastern Pageant, Marion, Ind., 1965-66; exec. dir. Grant County Mental Health Assn., 1966-67; dir. selfdevised therapeutic program for emotionally disturbed children, juvenile delinquents, Marion, 1969-71; bd. dirs. Hot-Line, Inc., Marion, 1969-73; dean girls Jones Jr. High Sch. and psychol. cons. Westminster Presbyn. Day Care Center (both Marion), 1971-73; elem. sch. counselor, West Palm Beach, Fla., pvt. practice marriage counseling, 1974—; guest lectr. Marion Coll., Taylor U., Ball State U., Palm Beach Atlantic U.; vol. therapist South County Mental Health Clinic, 1978-79; lectr.; cons. Parent Edn. Workshop, Boca Raton, Fla., 1979. Chmn. small bus. div. Marion Gen. Hosp. fund raising, 1964. Mem. Am. Personnel and Guidance Assn., Nat. Assn. Women Deans, Adminstrs. and Counselors, Fla. Personnel and Guidance Assn., Kappa Kappa Gamma, Phi Delta Kappa. Home: 218 SE 26th Ave Boynton Beach FL 33435

SUTTERFIELD, LYNDLE JEWELL, metals co. exec.; b. Reynolds County, Mo., Mar. 1, 1930; s. Oather E. and Olive G. (Shults) S.; student Jr. Coll., Flat River, Mo., 1948; m. Diana Ruth Rapp, Oct. 14, 1950; children—Phyllis, Thomas, Linda, Jeffrey. Acct., Mo.-Kans.-Tex. R.R., St. Louis, 1949-54; divisional mgr. adminstrn. Reynolds Metals Co., St. Louis, 1954-64, Kansas City, Mo., 1964-70, mgr. adminstrn. chem. div., Richmond, Va., 1970-79, Little Rock, 1979—. City councilman, chief budget officer Crystal Lake Park, Mo., 1965. Mem. Am. Ceramic Soc. Baptist. Home: 15 Portia Dr Little Rock AR 72212 Office: 10720 Harris Rd Suite 103 Little Rock AR 72211

SUTTLES, WILLIAM MAURRELLE, clergyman, educator; b. Ben Hill, Ga., July 25, 1920; s. Wiley Maurrelle and Eddie Lou (Campbell) S.; B.C.S., Ga. State U., 1942; M.Div., Yale U., 1946; Th.M., Emory U., 1947, M.R.E., 1953; Ed.D., Auburn U., 1958; D.D. (hon.), Mercer U., 1972; Hum.D. (hon.), Tift Coll., 1978; m. Lanette Lovern, Jan. 28, 1950. Ordained to ministry Bapt. Ch., 1938; pastor Haralson (Ga.) Bapt. Ch., 1950—, Luthersville (Ga.) Bapt. Ch., 1951-62; asst. registrar Ga. State U., Atlanta, 1942-44, asst. prof. English and speech, 1946-55, asso. prof. speech, 1955-57, prof., 1957—, prof. ednl. adminstrn. and higher edn., 1970—, also chmn. dept. speech, 1955-62, dean students, 1956-62, v.p. academic affairs, 1964-69, exec. v.p., provost, 1970—; personnel dir. Rich's, Inc., Atlanta, 1962-64; dir., mem. exec. com. Ga. Fed. Savs. and Loan Assn., 1968—; dir., mem. audit com. 1st Ga. Bank. Mem. Southeastern regional manpower advisory com. U.S. Dept. Labor, 1972-74; trustee George M. Sparks Scholarship Fund, 1962—, Ga. State U. Found., 1963—, Tift Coll., 1967-77, John and Mary Franklin Found., 1967—, Hillside Cottages, 1968-79. Served with USN, 1944-46. Named Ga. Rural Minister of Year, Progressive Farmer Mag. and Emory U., 1959; Ga. Clergyman of Year, Ga. region NCCJ, 1971; One of 300 Who Have Shaped Atlanta, Atlanta Mag., 1976; recipient Medal of St. Paul, Archbishop of Greek Orthodox Archdiocese N. and S.Am., 1976. Mem. Internat. Communication Assn., Speech Communication Assn., So. Speech Communication Assn., So. Anthrop. Soc., Ga. State U. Alumni Assn. (pres. 1967), Kappa Delta Pi, Phi Delta Kappa, Omicron Delta Kappa, Sigma Nu, Sigma Pi Alpha, Sigma Tau Delta, Phi Kappa Phi, Beta Gamma Sigma, Phi Eta Sigma, Alpha Kappa Psi, Kappa Phi Kappa, Alpha Lambda Delta, Blue Key. Clubs: Commerce, Kiwanis (pres. 1966), Masons (Shriner). Office: University Plaza Atlanta GA 30303

SUTTON, DORIS GREENE, educator; b. London, Ky., Nov. 6, 1935; d. Kenneth C. and Jamie E. (Stacey) Greene; A.B. in English, Georgetown Coll., 1955; M.A., U. Ky., 1966, Ph.D. in English and Curriculum, 1973, postgrad., 1977; 1 son, Charles William. Tchr., Ky. public schs., 1956-69; asst. prof. English, Eastern Ky. U., Richmond, 1969-76, asso. prof., 1976—; bus. writing cons. IBM, 1978, VA Hosp. campaign, 1978; instr. extension and continuing edn. div. various Ky. communities, 1970—; chairperson Nat. Task Force on Testing in English. Judge, Ky. High Sch. Speech Festival, Civitan Internat. Oratorical contest; community vol. U.S. Bur. Prisons, 1971-76. Mem. Nat. Council Tchrs. English, Conf. Coll. Composition and Communication (nat. exec. com.), Ky. Philos. Assn., Ky. Philological Assn. Democrat. Club: Arlington Country. Contbr. articles to profl. publs. Home: 5 Governor's Manor Richmond KY 40475 Office: 217 Wallace Bldg Eastern Ky Univ Richmond KY 40475

SUTTON, FREDERICK ISLER, JR., Realtor; b. Greensboro, N.C., Sept. 13, 1916; s. Fred I. and Annie (Fry) S.; grad. Culver (Ind.) Mil. Acad., 1934; A.B., U. N.C., 1939, postgrad. Law Sch., 1939-41; grad. Realtor's Inst., 1956, postgrad. Grad. Sch., 1957; m. Helen Sykes Morrison, Mar. 18, 1941; children—Fred Isler III, Frank Morrison. Propr., Fred I. Sutton, Jr., realtor, Kinston, N.C., 1946—; dir. Hotel Kinston; dean Realtors Inst., U. N.C., 1966, 67. Chmn. Kinston Parking Authority; v.p., dir. Ednl. Found., 1966; sec. Indsl. Devel. Com.; chmn. Kinston Water Resources Commn.; pres. United Fund, 1969-71. Trustee Florence Crittenton Services, 1971, bd. dirs., 1972-74. Served from ensign to lt. comdr. USNR, 1941-46. Mem. N.C. (v.p. 1957), Kinston (pres., Realtor of Year 1963) bds. realtors, N.C. Assn. Real Estate Bds. (dir.), Nat. (rep. N.C. Realtors State Assns. com. 1969, 70), N.C. (v.p. 1959, 61-63, chmn. edn. com. 1964, regional v.p. 1966) assns. realtors, Realtor's Inst. (trustee 1961-63, v.p. 1966), S.R., Kinston C. of C. (v.p. 1967, 69). Presbyterian (deacon). Clubs: Masons (32 deg.), Shriners, Kiwanis (pres. 1964). Home: 1101 N Queen St Kinston NC 28501 Office: Sutton Bldg Kinston NC 28501

SUTTON, GLORIA JEAN, counselor; b. Salisbury, Md., Oct. 2, 1948; d. Paul Weldon and Doris Mabel (Tribeck) S.; B.S., Towson State U., 1971; M.Ed., Western Md. Coll., 1977. Tchr., counselor Carroll County Bd. Edn., Westminster, Md., 1971-77; vocat. evaluatdr Goodwill Industries, Austin, Tex., 1977-78; vocat. rehab. counselor Tex. Rehab. Commn., Austin, 1978—. Mem. Nat. Vocat. Guidance Assn., Am. Personnel and Guidance Assn., Am. Rehab. Counseling Assn. Home: 7909 Creekmere Ln Austin TX 78745 Office: Career Development Center 55 N IH 35 Austin TX 78702

SUTTON, JOHN F., JR., coll. dean, lawyer, rancher; b. Alpine, Tex., Jan. 26, 1918; s. John F. and Pauline (Elam) S.; J.D. with honors, U. Tex., 1941; m. Nancy Ewing, June 1, 1940; children—Joan (Mrs. Tom Parr), John E. Admitted to Tex. bar, 1941; mem. firm Matthews, Nowlin, Macfarlane & Barrett, San Antonio, 1945-48, Sutton, Steib & Barr, San Angelo, Tex., 1949-57; prof. law U. Tex., Austin, 1957-69, William Benjamin Wynne prof. law, 1969-79, dean, 1979—; spl. agt. FBI, 1942-45. Mem. Am., Travis County bar assns., State Bar Tex., Tex. Bar Found. (life), Soc. Former Spl. Agts. FBI, Tex.-S.W. Cattle Raisers Assn., Order Coif, Phi Delta Phi. Author: (with Charles McCormick and Frank Elliott) Cases and Materials on Evidence, 1971. Home: Route 1 Box 36C Buda TX 78610 Office: 2500 Red River St Austin TX 78705

SUTTON, OLEN RAY, mgmt. educator; b. Garvin County, Okla., May 23, 1936; s. Ardie Preston and Percy Mae (Bond) S.; B.B.A., Central State U., Edmond, Okla., 1971; postgrad. Northeastern U., Boston, 1974; M.S., Okla. State U., Stillwater, 1975, postgrad., 1976; postgrad. Okla. U., 1977; m. Roberta Lee Steele, May 20, 1966; children—Steven Ray, Jeffry Alan, Olen Craig, Douglas Scott. Chief of police, also fire and safety officer Med. Center, Okla. U., Oklahoma City, 1965-71; mfg. supr. Wilson Cert. Food Inc., Oklahoma City,

1971-73; instr. mgmt. Connors State Coll., Warner, Okla., 1973—, dir. co-op edn., 1973—; cons. in field. Active Boy Scouts Am., 1974, Little League, 1977, 1st. Baptist Ch. Warner, 1978. Served with USAF, 1956-64. Decorated Republic of Vietnam Gallantry Cross with device, Air Force Commendation medal. Mem. Am. Edn. Tech. Soc., Okla. Tech. Soc., Okla. State U. Alumnus Assn., Higher Edn. Alumnus Council of Okla. Office: Dept of Mgmt Connors State Coll Warner OK 74469

SUTTON, PHILIP GARLAND, JR., marketing cons.; b. New Albany, Ind., May 8, 1936; s. Philip Garland and Ona (Tucker) S.; student Western Mich. U., 1954-56; B.S., Purdue U., 1958; postgrad. Northeastern U., 1962-63, Union Coll., 1964-65; m. Marsha Anne McCauley, June 10, 1961; children—Philip Garland III, David Maurice, Elizabeth Tucker. Tech. rep. Am. Cyanamid Co., Boston, 1958-63; market devel. specialist Gen. Electric Co., Waterford, N.Y., 1963-66, mgr. southwestern dist., Dallas, 1966-69, mgr. plastic additive project, Waterford, 1969-71, mgr. fluids sect., 1971-72; pres. Sutton Assos., marketing cons., Houston, 1972—, also Cypress Assos., Inc., Houston. Served with USCGR, 1959-60. mem. Soc. Plastics Industries, Soc. Aerospace Materials and Process Engrs. Delta Chi. Unitarian. Lion. Clubs: Cy-Fair Swim (chmn. bd.), Wimbledon Racquet. Home: 10711 Creektree Dr Houston TX 77070 Office: 13029 Champions Dr Houston TX 77069

SUZUKI, HOWARD KAZURO, univ. dean; b. Ketchikan, Alaska, Apr. 3, 1927; s. George K. and Tsuya S.; B.S., Marquette U., 1949, M.S., 1951; Ph.D., Tulane U., 1955; m. Tetsuko Fujita, Sept. 12, 1952; children—Georganne, Joan, James, Stanley. Instr. anatomy Yale U. Sch. Medicine, 1955-58; asst. prof. U. Ark. Med. Center, Little Rock, 1958-62, asso. prof., 1962-67, prof. anatomy, 1967-70; prof., asso. dean U. Fla. Coll. Health Related Professions, Gainesville, 1970-71, prof., acting dean, 1971-72, dean, prof., 1972—; mem. gen. research support program NIH, 1972-77, Health Manpower Program, VA, 1974-77. Bd. dirs. Civitan Regional Blood Bank; div. chmn. United Way; pres. Gallery Guild, State Adv. Council Vocat. Edn.; regional v.p. Fla. Assn. Retarded Citizens, 1974-76. Fellow AAAS; mem. Soc. Exptl. Biology and Medicine, Am. Soc. Anatomists, Am. Soc. Allied Health Professions, So. Assn. Allied Health Deans at Acad. Health Centers (chmn. 1979—), Sigma Xi. Episcopalian. Home: 4331 NW 20th Pl Gainesville FL 32605 Office: Box J-185 J Hillis Miller Health Center U Fla Gainesville FL 32610

SVACINA, TERRY LOUIS, retail data processing exec.; b. Manitowoc, Wis., Nov. 19, 1946: s. Louis S. and Dorothy T. (Gerl) S.; student U. Wis., 1974-75; m. Gail Ann Pech, June 21, 1969; 1 son, Todd Terry. Mgr. systems and programming H.C. Prange Co., Sheboygan, Wis., 1968-76; mgr. electronic data processing Popular Dry Goods Co., El Paso, Tex., 1976—; lectr. in field. Mem. NCR Retail Computer Users Group (v.p. 1976-79, pres. 1979—), Fedn. NCR Users Group (retail vocat. adv. com.), Data Processing Mgmt. Assn. Home: 10717 Camaro Ct El Paso TX 79935 Office: PO Box 1890 El Paso TX 79999

SVENSON, ERNEST OLANDER, psychiatrist and psychoanalyst; b. Duluth, Minn., Oct. 16, 1923; s. Ernest G. and Mabel A. (Benson) S.; B.A., Augustana Coll., 1948; B.S., Wayne State U., 1948, M.D., 1952; children—Ernest E., Stuart K. Intern, Gorgas Hosp., Panama Canal Zone, 1952-54; resident La. State U.-Charity Hosp., New Orleans, 1954-57; psychoanalytic trainee New Orleans Psychoanalytic Inst., 1958-62; practice medicine, specializing in psychoanalysis and psychiatry, New Orleans, 1958—; asso. prof. La. State Med. Sch., New Orleans, 1968—; chief dept. psychiatry Touro Infirmary, New Orleans, 1972-75; tng. and superivising analyst New Orleans Psychoanalytic Inst., 1972—; sr. vis. physician Charity Hosp., 1967—; courtesy staff DePaul Hosp. Vice chmn. project rev. com. New Orleans Health Planning Commn., 1978—; bd. dirs. New Orleans Assn. for Mental Health, 1975-78; bd. dirs., exec. com. New Orleans Area Health Systems Agy., 1978—, chmn. project rev. com., 1979—. Served to lt. (j.g.) USNR, 1941-46; PTO. Diplomate Am. Bd. Psychiatry and Neurology. Fellow Am. Psychiat. Assn., Am. Coll. Psychiatrists, AAAS, N.Y. Acad. Scis.; mem. La. (pres. 1969-71), New Orleans (pres. 1969-70) psychiat. assns., New Orleans Psychoanalytic Soc. (pres. 1971-73), New Orleans Psychoanalytic Inst. (sec.-treas. 1975—), Internat., Am. psychoanalytic assns., Alpha Omega Alpha. Club: New Orleans Lawn Tennis. Home: 2925 Palmer Ave New Orleans LA 70118 Office: 1301 Antonine St New Orleans LA 70115

SWAEBE, RICHARD, diamond and precious gem dealer; b. N.Y.C., Dec. 4, 1938; s. Leslie and Rosa (Landau) S.; m. Lily Kalkstein, Sept. 25, 1963; children—Theodore Aaron, Daniela. Pres., chmn. bd. Diamond Sales Co., Miami, Fla., 1963—; chmn. bd. Jewelers Comml. Fin. Co.; cons. Diamond and Precious Gem Index, Smithsonian Instn. dept. mineral sci. Treas., mem. exec. bd. Fla. region Anti-Defamation League. Served with U.S. Army, 1956-59. Mem. Diamond Dealers Assn., Diamond Trade Assn., Jewelers Security Alliance, Jewelers Bd. Trade, Ocean Power Boat Racing Assn. Republican. Jewish. Clubs: Bankers, Palm Bay, Cricket, Jockey (Miami). Office: Ainsley Bldg Suite 1500 14 NE 1st Ave Miami FL 33132

SWAFFORD, WILLIAM BRYSON, lawyer, educator; b. Monterey, Tenn., Aug. 23, 1912; s. William Carlin and Pearl (Kidwell) S.; B.S., U. Tenn., 1948; M.S., U. Miss., 1955; M.A., Memphis State U., 1958; LL.B., So. U., 1962; m. Violet Jeannette Lain, Nov. 28, 1943; children—Barbara Lain Swafford Stanton, William Bryson, Patricia Ann Swafford O'Brien. Instr., U. Tenn. Coll. Pharmacy, Memphis, 1945-55, asst. prof., 1955-61, asso. prof., head dept. pharm. adminstrn., 1961-63, prof., chmn. dept. pharmaceutics, 1963-71, asst. dean, 1971-77, emeritus prof., 1977—; exec. dir. Tenn. Bd. Pharmacy, 1977-79; individual practice law, 1979—; cons. VA hosps., Memhis, Nashville; mem. research team Marion Labs. Indsl. Pharm. Research; sec.-treas. dist. 3 Nat. Assn. Bds. Pharmacy-Am. Assn. Colls. Pharmacy, 1967-78. Served to maj. AUS, 1941-46; ETO; col. Res., ret. Decorated Silver Star medal, Bronze Star medal, Purple Heart; French Fouragerre; named hon. citizen Knoxville, 1973. Dilomate Am. Bd. Pharm. Dilomates. Fellow Am. Coll. Apothecaries; mem. Am., Tenn. (Pharmacist of Year 1973), Memphis, Shelby County pharm. assns., Mil. Order World Wars, Res. Officers Assn., Am. Assn. Colls. Pharmacy (chmn. conf. tchrs. 1970-71), Delta Chi Delta, Phi Delta Kappa, Kappa Psi, Rho Chi. Author: Pharmacy and the Law, A Manual For Practicing Pharmacists, 1969; A Correspondence Course in Pharmaceutical Law, 1969; A Correspondence Course Non-Prescription Drugs, 1971; co-author other corr. courses. Home: 1840 Poplar Estates Pkwy Germantown TN 38138 Office: 874 Union Ave Memphis TN 38163

SWAIM, GARY DALE, educator; b. Houston, Nov. 17, 1934; s. Glyn Dale and Juanita Jeannine (Oxford) S.; A.B., U. Calif., Riverside, 1966; Ph.D., U. Redlands and Claremont Grad. Sch., 1971; m. Mary Lou Cumming, July 23, 1954; children—Gary Don, Steven Randall. Mktg. rep. IBM, Dallas, 1959-63; instr. English, U. Redlands, Calif., 1966-69, dean undergrad. studies and asso. prof. English, 1973-78; asst. prof. Ark. State U., Jonesboro, 1969-72; faculty North Lake Coll., Irving, Tex., 1979—, also div. chmn. communications and humanities. Mem. MLA, Conf. Christianity and Lit., Council Advancement Experiential Learning, Western Assn. Summer Sch. Adminstrs., Democrat. Mem. Ch. of Christ. Contbr. poems to numerous jours. Home: 524 Campana Court Irving TX 75061 Office: North Lake College 2000 Walnut Hill Ln Irving TX 75062

SWAIN, ALICE MARIE MCNEELY, reading specialist; b. Oklahoma City, Feb. 3, 1924; d. William Henry and Lucy Bruce (McCuiston) McNeely; B.S., Langston U., 1946; M.E., U. Okla, 1952; m. Robert Alphonso Swain, Aug. 24, 1946; children—Robert Alphonso II, Lecia Danee. Tchr. schs., Oklahoma City, 1950—; pres. Together Enterprises, Oklahoma City, 1971—; asst. prof. edn., coordinator reading Langston (Okla.) U. Recipient S.W. Regional Sigma of Year award, 1962, Outstanding Citizen award local chpt. Omega Psi Phi, 1976; U. Okla. math. grantee, 1963, Livingtext book grantee, 1964; named one of 10 outstanding nat. Sigma women, 1965. Mem. Urban League Guild, NAACP, YWCA, Okla. Edn. Assn., NEA, Nat. Pan-Hellenic Council (sec. 1970-72, v.p. 1972—, nat. pres. 1974-75, Excellence in Service award 1974-76), Sigma Gamma Rho (past chmn. bd. dirs., Hall of Fame; nat. grand episloleus 1974, 1st grand anti-basileus 1976—, Leadership award Zeta Sigma chpt., 1st v.p. 1978-80). Mem. Christian Ch. Club: Tes Trams Social (Oklahoma City). Editor: Alice's Short Stories, 1972. Contbr. column The Black Dispatch, 1974; social columnist Black Chronicle, 1978. Home: 3016 Norcrest Dr Oklahoma City OK 73111 Office: 3016 Norcrest Dr Oklahoma City OK 73111

SWAIN, JAMES O(BED), educator; b. Greenfield, Ind., Dec. 31, 1896; s. Ashbell Willard and Laetitia (Lambert) S.; A.B., Ind. U., 1921, A.M., 1923; Ph.D., U. Ill., 1932; student U. Madrid, summer 1933, U. Chile, 1951-52; m. Nancy Jane Cox, June 19, 1923; children—James Maurice, Juan Robert. Mem. faculty Mich. State Coll., 1931-37, asst. prof. modern langs., 1935-37; prof. chmn. dept. Romance langs. U. Tenn. 1937-58; guest dir. summer langs. sch. Western Colo. Coll., 1937; guest lectr. Am. lit. U. Chile, summer session, 1952; guest lectr. U. Madrid, summer 1958, Maracaibo, Venezuela, 1959; exec. sec. Mountain Interstate Fgn. Lang. Conf., 1963-64; vis. prof. U. Ky., 1964—, Maryville Coll., 1966, Roanoke Coll., 1967, Lee Coll., 1969-70. Served with C.E., U.S. Army, 1918-19. Mem. Modern Lang. Assn. Am. (sectional officer various times), Central, So. States, South Atlantic (pres. 1948-49) modern lang. assns., Am. Assn. Tchrs. Spanish (exec. com. 1949-52), Am. Assn. Tchrs. French, Am. Assn. Tchrs. Italian, Institute de Literature Iberoamericana, Sigma Delta Pi (nat. exec. sec. 1947-63). Methodist (deacon). Author: Rumbo a Mexico, 1942; Ruedo Antillano, 1946; Vicente Blasco Ibanez, Realistic Techniques, 1959; Juan Marin-Chilean, the Man and his Writings, 1971. Co-editor: Les Chemins de la Mer. Asso. editor Hispania, 1936-42; asst. bus. mgr. Modern Lang. Jour., 1938-51. Travel Europe, Latin Am., South Am. Contbr. to Compton's Pictured Ency., Latin Am. and Spanish Lit. Home: 414 Forest Park Blvd Carlton Towers Knoxville TN 37919

SWAIN, NANCY JANE COX, former educator; b. Elwood, Ind., Dec. 19, 1901; d. Alfred Thomas and Emma (Allen) Cox; A.B. with high distinction, Ind. U., 1923, postgrad., 1928; M.A., U. Tenn., 1951, postgrad., 1953; m. James Obed Swain, June 24, 1923; children—J. Maurice, J. Robert. Teaching missionary M.E. Ch., Costa Rica, 1923-28; instr. U. Tenn., Knoxville, 1943, 45, non-resident instr. corr. Extension Div., 1959-71; tchr. Oak Ridge High Sch., 1943-67, Hollins Coll., 1967. Mem. Am. Assn. Tchrs. Spanish and Portuguese, E. Tenn. Edn. Assn., S. Atlantic Modern Lang. Assn., P.E.O., Phi Beta Kappa, Phi Kappa Phi, Sigma Delta Pi, Pi Delta Phi, Pi Lambda Theta. Republican. Methodist. Home: 414 Forest Park Blvd Knoxville TN 37919

SWAISGOOD, HAROLD EVERETT, educator; b. Ashland County, Ohio, Jan. 19, 1936; s. Ray Weaver and Jennie Mable (Morr) S.; B.S., Ohio State U., 1958; Ph.D., Mich. State U., 1963; m. Janet E. Cromwell, Sept. 15, 1956; children—Mark Harold, Ronald Ray. Research asst. Mich. State U., East Lansing, 1958-63; postdoctoral research asso. NIH, 1963-64; asst. prof. N.C. State U., Raleigh, 1964-67, asso. prof., 1967-72, prof. food sci. and biochemistry, 1972—; vis. prof. U. Lund (Sweden), 1974. NIH fellow, 1962-63; USPHS fellow, 1963-64. Mem. Am. Chem. Soc., Am. Soc. Biol. Chemists, AAAS, Am. Dairy Sci. Assn. (milk protein nomenclature and methodology com. 1966-77, chmn. milk synthesis com. 1978-79), Inst. Food Technologists, Sigma Xi, Phi Kappa Phi, Phi Eta Sigma. Democrat. Methodist. Editorial bd. Jour. Food Sci., 1977, Jour. Dairy Sci., 1975; patentee in field; contbr. articles to profl. jours. Home: 3711 Corbin St Raleigh NC 27612 Office: Dept Food Sci NC State Univ Raleigh NC 27650

SWANK, CHRISTINE HYLTON, furniture co. exec., interior designer, accountant; b. Appomattox, Va., Nov. 26, 1925; d. William Preston and Sammie Ella (Ferguson) Hylton; student Nat. Bus. Coll., 1945-46, Kenny Sch. Accounting, 1947-48; m. Eugene C. Swank, July 16, 1960; 1 son, Patrick Shreve. Sec., George H. Glover, Inc., Birmingham, Mich., 1949-52; sec.-treas. Wilson GMC, Inc., Pontiac, Mich., 1952-54; office mgr. Vic Francis, Inc., Pompano Beach, Fla., 1958-60; pres. Swank's Furniture-Interiors, Inc., Delray Beach, Fla., 1960—. Vice-chmn. Palm Beach County, Senator Edward J. Gurney Campaign, 1968; pres. Delray Beach Woman's Republican Club, 1969-71. Mem. Nat. Home Furnishings Assn. Episcopalian. Clubs: Bus. and Profl. Women's, Am.-German. Home: 6230 N Ocean Blvd Ocean Ridge FL 33435 Office: 1440 N Federal Hwy Delray Beach FL 33444

SWANSON, CARL DAVID, educator; b. Kansas City, Mo., Jan. 8, 1932; s. Carl O. and Alice Rae (Johnson) S.; B.S., Washington and Lee U., 1954, J.D., 1957; M.A., Western Mich. U., 1969, Ed.D., 1971; m. Janice C. Vanderstoep, Aug. 31, 1961; children—David Andrew, Adrain Rae. Actively practiced law, church work, Kansas City, Mo., 1957-69; instr. counseling, asst. dir. scholarship Western Mich. U., Kalamazoo, 1969-71; v.p., dean, chmn. div. social sci. Elkins (W.Va.) Coll., 1971-73, head dept. psychology, 1971-73, pres. faculty, 1971-73; coordinator, prof. counselor edn. programs James Madison U., Harrisonburg, Va., 1973—; cons. in field; adj. prof. law Washington and Lee U., Lexington, Va., 1976—; chmn. Va. Licensure Bd. Profl. Counselors, 1975-76, Counselor Cert. Com. Va., 1974-75; vis. scientist NSF, Am. Psychol. Assn., 1974—, Va. Acad. Sci., 1969—; bd. dirs. Va. Bd. Behavioral Sci., Shenandoah Lodge Treatment Center, Pear St. Treatment Center. Served with U.S. Army, 1957. Recipient Outstanding Faculty Contbn. award James Madison U., 1976-77, Counselor of Yr. award Va. Personnel and Guidance Assn., 1976, Outstanding Educators of Am. award Wall St. Jour., N.Y. U., 1954; Menckeller grantee, 1954-57; honored by Profl. Assns. Conv., 1975. Mem. Va. Assn. Specialists in Group Work (pres.), Valley Personnel and Guidance Assn. (pres.), So. Assn. Counselor Educators. Episcopalian. Clubs: Torch, Rotary. Contbr. articles to profl. jours. Home: Cottage Plains Farm Grottoes VA 24441 Office: James Madison U Harrisonburg VA 22801

SWANSON, DONALD CHARLES, geologist; b. Canon City, Colo., Sept. 22, 1926; s. Charles William and Josephine Anne (Kramer) S.; B.S. in Gen. Arts and Sci., Colo. State U., 1950; B.S. in Geology, Tulsa U., 1956; postgrad. U. Okla., 1965-67; m. Helen Kathyrn Smith, June 10, 1950; children—Charles Richard, Jeffrey Stuart. Tax engr. and geologist Carter Oil Co., Tulsa, 1951-61; explorationist Humble Oil Co., Tex. and Okla., 1961-67; research geologist Exxon Prodn. Research Co., Houston, 1967-79; cons. geologist Swanson Petroleum Enterprises, Houston, 1979—; partner Swanson & Crow, 1979—. Fellow Geol. Soc. Am.; mem. Am. Assn. Petroleum Geologists (recipient A.I. Levorsen awards 1969, Sigma 79), Chi. Lutheran. Contbr. articles to profl. jours. Home: 13611 Kingsride St Houston TX 77079 Office: 11999 Kady Freeway Suite 310 Houston TX 77079 also Box 2189 Houston TX 77001

SWANSON, GENE EARL, orthopedic surgeon; b. Sioux City, Iowa, May 26, 1941; s. Ernest Clarence and Bertha (Hansen) S.; B.S., U. Iowa, 1963, M.D., 1966; m. Edythe E. McDougall, Dec. 28, 1963; children—Molly, Kyle, Heidi, Andrew. Intern, Tripler Army Med. Center, 1967; resident in orthopedic surgery Mayo Grad. Sch. Medicine Clinic, Rochester, Minn., 1970-73, chief resident asso. to staff, 1973-74; practice medicine specializing in orthopedic surgery Winchester (Va.) Surg. Clinic, 1974—; staff Winchester Meml. Hosp., 1974—; mem. Va. State Bd. Medicine, 1977—; chmn. Multiple Hosp. Com., 1976—; adv. bd. Bank of Fredrick County, Stephens City, Va., 1976—. Chmn., State Leadership Com., Winchester, 1978. Served to maj. M.C., AUS, 1966-70. Diplomate Am. Bd. Orthopedic Surgery. Mem. AMA, Va. Med. Soc., No. Va. Med. Soc., Am. Acad. Orthopedic Surgeons. Presbyterian. Home: Route 1 Box L41 Stephens City VA 22655 Office: Winchester Surg Clinic 20 S Stewart St Winchester VA 22607

SWANSON, HENRY DAVID, theatre dir., designer; b. Springfield, Ill., May 26, 1930; s. Henry David and Gertrude Carolyn (Dreska) S.; B.A., La. State U., Baton Rouge, 1952; M.A., U. Denver, 1957; m. Alice Ellen Holbrook, Dec. 28, 1957 (div. June 1972); children—Ellen Terry, David Lance, Amy Christine; m. 2d, Jo Anne Murphy Jerit, Dec. 23, 1972. Designer Dunes Summer Theatre, Michigan City, Ind., 1956-58; instr. drama Christian Coll., Columbia, Mo., 1957-62; asst. to designer Elitch Gardens Theatre, Denver, 1959-60; founder, exec. dir. Arrow Rock (Mo.) Lyceum Repertory Theatre, 1961—; tchr. acting, designer U. Fla., Gainesville, 1962-66; designer St. Louis U., 1966-68; dir. theatre Memphis State U., 1968-75. Guest designer Front St. Theatre, Memphis, 1968; guest designer Memphis Opera Theatre, 1969-70, Asolo Theatre, Sarasota, Fla., 1970-72; cons. in theatre. Mem. theatre adv. com. Mo. State Council Arts, 1964-72. Bd. dirs. Red Balloon Players, Memphis, 1968-71. Served to lt., J.G., USNR, 1952-55; Korea. Mem. United Scenic Artist Am., A.A.U.P., Southeastern Theatre Conf., Am. Theatre Assn. Home: 3899 Poplar Av Memphis TN 38111 Office: Arrow Rock Lyceum Arrow Rock MO 65320

SWANSON, LAWRENCE LEMONTE, mfg. co. exec.; b. Ottumwa, Iowa, Feb. 27, 1926; s. Roy Benjaman and Mary Jane (Springer) S.; student Iowa Success Bus. Coll., 1944-46; m. Dorothy Eleanor Dingle, Aug. 29, 1947; children—Theresa Lorraine, Cynthia Kay. Vice-pres. Griffin Lamp Co., Shelby, Miss., 1953—, bd. dirs. Dir. Fed. Housing Authority, Shelby, 1970-77. Mem. Miss. Assn. Purchasing Mgrs. Republican. Episcopalian. Clubs: Shelby Country, Big Eddy Fishing, Rotary, Lions. Home: 402 Louisiana St Shelby MS 38774 Office: Hwy 61 S Shelby MS 38774

SWANSON, MARY HELEN, civic worker; b. Oklahoma City, Dec. 2, 1926; d. Guy Carylton and Elsie Virginia (Vaughn) Jones; student Okla. State U., 1945-47; m. Charles Henry Swanson, Feb. 14, 1948; children—Linda Jean Swanson Ristow, David Charles, Kristina Anne, Joy Virginia Swanson Blaschke. Pres., Oklahoma City Republican Women's Club, 1972-74; mem. exec. com. Okla. County Rep. Party, 1969-77; corr. sec. Okla. Fedn. Rep. Women, 1971-73, pres., 1979—; del. Okla. Rep. Conv., 1969-76; mem. Okla. Rep. State Com., 1969-77; del. Rep. Nat. Conv., 1976; active numerous polit. campaigns; publicity chmn. Okla. Hospitality, 1971; mem. women's com. Okla. Symphony, Women's Music Club, Okla. Heritage Assn.; active local Big Sisters, Girl Scouts, hosp. aux. Recipient various service awards. Baptist. Address: 2716 NW 60th St Oklahoma City OK 73112

SWARINGIN, DAVID GLEN, constrn. co. exec.; b. Roystown, Tex., Oct. 8, 1935; s. Hollis Green and May Floriene (Smith) S.; student Tarleton State Coll., 1958; B.B.A., Tex. Tech. U., 1963; m. Kay Sharon Maynard, June 7, 1975; children—Dallas Deniese, Elizabeth Elaine. Working leadman Nat. Gypsum Co., Rotan, Tex., 1954-58; utility supr. Ford Motor Co., Dallas, Kansas City, Mo., 1963-65; installation engr. Alexander Proudfood Co., Chgo., 1965-66; dir. indsl. relations RSR Corp., Dallas, 1966-79; dir. human resources Sam P. Wallace Co., Dallas, 1979—; cons. Giesen & Assos.; chmn. bd. So. Lead Employees Credit Union. Served with U.S. Army, 1958-60. Mem. Am. Soc. Tng. and Devel., Dallas Personnel Assn., Indsl. Relations Research Assn. Republican. Baptist. Home: 5707 Overridge Dr Arlington TX 76017 Office: Sam P Wallace Co 2102 Empire Central Dallas TX 75235

SWARTHOUT, GERARD, JR., constrn. co. exec., civil engr.; b. Ft. Clayton, C.Z., May 14, 1922; s. Gerard and Marguerite Simmons (Downman) S.; B.C.E., Ga. Inst. Tech., 1947; m. Evelyn L. Presler, Nov. 10, 1945; children—Edith S. Cheek, Gerard III. Engr., Ga. Hwy. Dept., 1947-54; engr. B.P. Lamb Co., Statesboro, Ga., 1954-65; engr., adminstr. Scott Bridge Co., Opelika, Ala., 1965—, exec. v.p., 1969—. Served to sgt. AUS, 1942-46. Registered profl. engr., Ga., Ala. Mem. Ala. Road Builders Assn. (dir. 1967-71, treas. 1971, sec. 1972, v.p. 1973, pres. 1974), Am. Road and Transp. Builders Assn. (nat. dir. 1979—). Episcopalian (vestryman, layreader, warden 1950—). Elk. Home: 407 N 4th St Opelika AL 36801 Office: PO Box 2038 Opelika AL 36801

SWARTZ, HARRY, physician; b. Detroit, June 21, 1911; s. Isaac and Anne (Srere) S.; A.B., U. Mich., 1930, M.D., 1933; postgrad. N.Y. U., 1936-38; m. Eve Sutton, Oct. 3, 1942. Intern, Michael Reese Hosp., Chgo., 1933-35; resident allergy N.Y. U. Med. Colls. and Clinics, 1936-38; asst. attending physician Inst. of Allergy, Roosevelt Hosp., N.Y.C., 1946-74; chief allergy clinic, attending physician, prof. medicine N.Y. Polyclinic Med. Sch. and Hosp., N.Y.C., 1957-73; med. dir. Soluble Products Corp., Edison, N.J., 1965-74; pres. Health Field Validation Corp., N.Y.C., 1965-79; med. editor Med. Opinion and Rev., 1965-69; editor-in-chief Investigación Médica Internacional, 1974—. Served from 1st lt. to maj., M.C., AUS, 1942-46. Diplomate Am. Bd. Clin. Immunology and Allergy. Emeritus fellow Am. Acad. Allergy, Am. Coll. Allergists, Am. Assn. Clin. Immunology and Allergy, Internat. Acad. Applied Nutrition; mem. Internat. Allergologic Soc., AAAS, N.Y. County Med. Soc., Phi Beta Kappa, Alpha Omega Alpha, Phi Kappa Phi. Author: Allergy: What It Is and What To Do About It, 1949, rev. 1966, also several fgn. edits.; Your Hay Fever, 1951, rev., 1962; The Allergic Child, 1954; Laymans Medical Dictionary, 1956; The Allergy Guide Book, 1962, rev., 1966; Your Body (juvenile), 1962. Editor: Simplified Med. Dictionary. Patentee safety and med. devices. Home: APDO 752 Cuernavaca MOR Mexico Office: 155 E 55th St New York NY 10022 also Matias Romero 116 Mexico 10 DF Mexico

SWARTZ, JON DAVID, psychologist, educator; b. Houston, Dec. 28, 1934; s. Orville Elmo and Nina June (Baker) S.; student S.W. Tex. State U., 1953; B.A., U. Tex., 1956, M.A., 1961, Ph.D. (U.S. Office Edn. fellow), 1969, postgrad (sr. fellow community psychology and community mental health), 1973-74; m. Carol Joseph Hampton, Oct.

20, 1966; children—Eric Jason McFarland, Sally Katherine Baker, Edward Joseph Bryson. Mem. faculty U. Tex., Austin, 1956—, research and teaching asst. dept. psychology, 1956-62, field dir. Austin Longitudinal Research Project, 1962-65, asst. dir., 1965-69, co-dir., 1969-74, asso. research dir. SEIMC, 1970-71, asst. prof. dept. ednl. psychology, 1969-72, research scientist Hogg Found. for Mental Health, 1972-74, asso. prof., chmn. psychology, Permian, 1974-78, chmn. psychology, anthropology, sociology, 1975-78; Brown prof. edn. and psychology Southwestern U., Georgetown, Tex., 1978—, also dir. testing and guidance; vis. lectr. Nat. U. Mexico, 1962, cons., 1962-74; cons. Rehab. Research and Tng. Center in Mental Retardation, U. Tex., 1966-70; vice chmn. psychology sect. AAAS-SWARM div., 1976-77. Mem. Mayor's Drug Abuse Panel, Odessa, Tex., 1975-78; chmn. adv. bd. Human Potentials Center, Permian Basin Community Centers for Mental Health and Mental Retardation, Midland and Odessa, Tex., 1975-78. Recipient Franklin Gilliam prize bibliography, 1965, Spencer Research award Nat. Acad. Edn., 1972; U. Tex. Research Inst. Faculty Research grantee, 1971; Hogg Found. grantee, 1979—. Fellow, Am. Anthrop. Assn., Am. Psychol. Assn., AAAS, Soc. Applied Anthropology, Am. Assn. Mental Deficiency, Soc. Personality Assessment; mem. Western Research Conf. Mental Retardation (exec. com.), Interam. Soc. Psychology, Soc. Applied Anthropology, Southwestern Sociol. Assn., Tex. Assn. Mental Deficiency, Am. Sociol. Assn., Tex. Soc. Coll. Tchrs. of Edn., AAUP, Am. Acad. Mental Retardation, Council Anthropology and Edn. (founding), Internat. Council Edn. for Teaching, Internat. Assn. Applied Psychology, Tex., Southwestern psychol. assns., Internat. Soc. Study Behavioral Devel., Tex. Acad. Sci., Sigma Xi, Psi Chi, Mu Alpha Nu, Delta Tau Kappa, Phi Kappa Phi (editorial adv. bd. jour. 1976—). Democrat. Unitarian. Author: (with W.H. Holtzman) Inkblot Perception and Personality, 1961; (with C.C. Cleland) Mental Retardation, 1969; Administrative Issues in Institutions for the Mentally Retarded, 1972; Holtzman Inkblot Technique Annotated Bibliography, 1973, rev. edit., 1978; Multihandicapped Mentally Retarded, 1973; (with W.H. Holtzman, R.Diaz-Guerrero) Personality Development in Two Cultures, 1975; (with C.C. Cleland and L.W. Talkington) The Profoundly Mentally Retarded, 1976; Profound Mental Retardation, 1978; editorial cons. Interam. Jour. Psychology, 1970-75, Mental Retardation, 1972-77; editorial asso. Current Anthropology, 1971-77; asso. editor Am. Corrective Therapy Jour., 1971—; editorial bd. Tex. Psychologist, 1979—; editor GRANT-S, 1979—; book review editor Jour. Biol. Psychology, 1972—; spl. manuscript cons. Jour. Ednl. Psychology, 1971-72; manuscript reviewer Am. Jour. Mental Deficiency, 1979—, Jour. Cons. & Clin. Psychology, 1977—, Developmental Psychology, 1978—; manuscript cons. Jour. Psychol. Anthropology, 1977—; manuscript rev. bd. Human Orgn., 1976—; spl. reader Social Sci. Quar., 1979—; manuscript cons. Nelson-Hall Pubs., Inc., 1975—, Allyn & Bacon, 1976—, Prentice-Hall Pubs., 1976—, Melton Book Co., 1977—; contbr. over 250 articles and revs. to profl. jours. Home: 1401 E 18 St Georgetown TX 78626 Office: Southwestern U Georgetown TX 78626

SWARTZ, PHILLIP RALEIGH, coll. adminstr.; b. Hominy, Okla., July 23, 1930; s. Merle David and Martha Mae (Buchannan) S.; A.A.S., Amarillo Coll., 1948-51; B.B.A., W.Tex. State U., 1953; M.B.A., 1963; postgrad. U. Ky., 1958-63; m. Barbara Belle Brooks, Aug. 26, 1951; children—Kassandra Kay, Cherlyn Jo, Kristi Lynn. Bus. mgr. Amarillo (Tex.) Coll., 1964-65; dir. fiscal affairs Coordinating Bd., Tex. Coll. and Univ. System, Austin, 1965-67; treas. Am. Technol. U., Killeen, Tex., 1973-76; dep. chancellor Central Tex. Coll., Killeen, 1967—; dir. Fort Hood Nat. Bank (Tex.). Mem. So. Assn. Colls. and Schs. (vis. coms.), So. Assn. Coll. and Univ. Bus. Assn. Computing Machinery, Am. Soc. Mil. Comptrollers. Methodist. Club: Masons. Home: 2005 Prather St Killeen TX 76541 Office: Hwy 190 W Killeen TX 76541

SWARZMAN, HERBERT GEORGE, investment banking exec.; b. N.Y.C., May 29, 1937; s. Herman and Mollie (Mosberg) S.; B.A., Dartmouth Coll., 1958; LL.B., Bklyn. Law Sch., 1960; m. Abby Levingson, Jan. 29, 1961 (div. May 1971); 1 son, David; m. 2d, Joyce Burick, Feb. 12, 1976. Sales and mgmt. Dempsey-Tegeler Co., N.Y.C., 1961-62; with A.G. Becker & Co., N.Y.C., 1963-68; founder, mng. partner Dryfoos & Co., N.Y.C., 1969-73; cons. security firms, 1974-75; founder, pres. Gulfcoast Cons. and Investors Corp., Tampa, Fla., 1976—; pres. Herand Inc., Real Estate Investments, Tampa, 1978—; chmn. N.Am. Steel Corp., Lakeland, Fla., 1979—. Mem. finance com. Horace Mann Elementary Sch., N.Y.C., 1971-72; chmn. N.Y.C. interviewing com. for applications for admission Dartmouth, 1965-75, dist. dir. enrollment for N.Y.C., 1974-75, chmn. reunion fund, 1974, pres. Class of 1958, 1974-79; co-chmn. basic gifts Tampa Jewish Fedn., 1977-78; treas., Democratic Com., N.Y.C., 1971-73. Bd. dirs. Univ. Settlement, 1966-68; bd. dirs., treas. Tampa Jewish Fedn., 1978—. Mem. Dartmouth Alumni Assn. N.Y.C. (founder, pres. 1975-76). Clubs: Dartmouth (dir., bd. govs. 1974-75), Lawyers (N.Y.C.); Carrollwood Village Golf and Tennis. Home: 4214 Fairway Run Tampa FL 33624

SWEARINGEN, EUGENE LAURREL, banker; b. Grant, Nebr., Aug. 21, 1920; s. Laurrel Brooks and Edna Ruth (Frank) S.; B.S., Okla. State U., 1941, M.S., 1948; Ph.D., Stanford, 1955; J.D. (hon.), Okla. Christian Coll., 1972; m. Aasalee Chace, Sept. 19, 1941; children—Linda Sue Swearingen Miller, Sandra Kay Swearingen Grant, Sherry Jean Swearingen Peet. Field scout exec. Boy Scouts Am., Texarkana, Ark., 1941-43, Perry Okla., 1946-47; instr. Okla. State U., Stillwater, 1948-49, prof. economics, 1951-56, dean Coll. Bus., 1957-65, v.p. for devel., 1964-66, v.p. for acad. affairs, 1964-65, v.p. for bus. and fin., 1966-67; pres. U. Tulsa, 1967-68; pres. Nat. Bank of Tulsa (now Bank Okla.), 1968-69, pres., chief exec. officer, 1969-72; chmn. bd., chief exec. officer Bank of Okla., Tulsa, 1973-78, chmn. exec. com., 1978—; dean of bankers Southwestern Grad. Sch. Banking, So. Meth. U., Dallas, 1975-79. Pres., Downtown Tulsa Unltd., 1972-73; mem. Okla. Bd. Regents for Higher Edn., 1976—; pres. Indian Nations council Boy Scouts Am., 1976-77; chmn. Tulsa Area United Way, 1979. Served with USN, 1943-46. Recipient Mktg. Man of the Year award Tulsa chpt. Am. Mktg. Assn., 1971; Downtown Tulsa Unltd. Man of the Year award, 1969; NCCJ Brotherhood award, 1977; award of Spl. Recognition, Arts Commn. of City of Tulsa, 1975; named to Okla. Hall of Fame, 1973. Mem. Tulsa C. of C. (pres. 1975), Okla. Bankers Assn. (dir. 1972-75), Assn. Reserve City Bankers, Phi Kappa Phi, Beta Gamma Sigma, Omicron Delta Kappa, Beta Alpha Psi, Delta Sigma Pi. Democrat. Methodist. Clubs: So. Hills Country, Tulsa, Tulsa. Editor: (with Merwin M. Hargrove and Ike H. Harrison) Business Policy Cases with Behavioral Science Implications, 1963. Home: 2650 E 66th St Tulsa OK 74136 Office: PO Box 2300 Tulsa OK 74192

SWEEN, TRUDY LOCKE, artist; b. Pitts., Jan. 24, 1933; d. John Paul and Catherine Claire (Wild) Locke; B.F.A., U. Houston, 1967; postgrad. Instituto de San Miguel, Mexico, 1967-68; m. Curtiss A. Sween, Oct. 10, 1953 (div. 1972); 1 dau., Lisa Brooke. One-woman shows: Galeria Trilce, Barcelona, Spain, 1970, L'Angle Aigu Galerie, Brussels, Belgium, 1970, Tyler (Tex.) Mus. Art, 1973, Ars Longa Gallery, Houston, 1974, Loft-on-Strand, Galveston, 1975, Nacional Museo de Arte, La Paz, Bolivia, 1978, Centro Boliviano-Américano, Cochabamba, Bolivia, 1978, Art Mus. S. Tex., Corpus Christi, 1980; group shows include: Contemporary Arts Mus., Houston, 1965, 75, Seattle Print Internat., 1971, Dallas Mus. Fine Arts, 1972; represented in permanent collections: Shell Oil Co., Mitchell Energy Corp., Exchange Bank, Esso Eastern Corp., Exxon Corp., Art Mus. South Tex., Corpus Christi, Museo Nacional de Arte, La Paz, Bolivia; art cons. Houston Grand Opera, 1973-79; designed vestments for Houston's woman Episcopal priest; nat. panelist Women in Art, U. Tex. Mischner Art Mus. Mem. adv. bd. Houston Grand Opera, 1977-79; nat. panelist Nat. Women's Conf., Houston, 1977; bd. dirs. Equinox Theater, Houston, 1980—. Mem. Houston Cultural Arts Council (exec. bd. 1978-79, dir. 1977-78), Artists Equity, Nat. Women's Caucus for Art. Author: Innerscapes, 1979; Doors: Houston Artists, 1979. Home and Office: 8423 Hunters Creek Dr Houston TX 77024

SWEENEY, DONALD EUGENE, JR., chem. engr.; b. Little Rock, Dec. 4, 1936; s. Donald Eugene and Martha Eugenia (Chrisp) S.; B.Ch.E., Cornell U., 1959, M.Ch.E., 1960. Asso. chem. engr. Texaco, Inc., Port Arthur, Tex., 1959-61, chem. engr., 1961-65, sr. chem. engr., 1965-67, project engr., 1967-74, sr. project engr., 1975-77, ops. research analyst, Houston, 1977—. Mem. Am. Inst. Chem. Engrs., AAAS, Tau Beta Pi. Patentee various control and optimization techniques for petroleum alkylation and gas absorption processes. Office: PO Box 52332 Houston TX 77052

SWEENEY, GEORGE BERNARD, JR., cons., holding co. exec.; b. Cleve., May 9, 1933; s. George Bernard and Ethel E. (Wise) S.; B.S. in Bus. Adminstrn., John Carroll U., 1955; M.B.A., Wharton U. Pa., 1957; m. Molly Jane O'Neill, July 13, 1963; children—Brian, Kelly, Mark, Kevin, Kim. With Exxon Corp., 1956-78, v.p., chmn., pres. Esso Pakistan Fertilizer Co., Karachi, 1969-74, v.p. Exxon Corp. and Exxon Chem. U.S.A., Houston, 1974-78; dir., prin. Chagrin Valley Co. Ltd., Cleve., 1977—; dir. Nevamar Corp., Odenton, Md., Evergreen Capital Corp., Houston, Exec. Confs. Ltd., Houston; chmn. bd. A/L Sports, Inc., Chgo., 1979—; pres. Questers, Inc., Houston, 1979—. Bd. dirs., exec. com. Houston Symphony, 1976—; trustee John Carroll U., Cleve., 1977, Strake Jesuit Coll. Prep., Houston, 1979—; trustee, chmn. bd. Trinity Coll., Washington, 1974—; exec. bd. Wharton Grad. Sch., U. Pa., 1980—. Served with Transp. Corps, U.S. Army, 1958. Recipient in Pakistan U.S. State Dept. citation of appreciation, 1974. Mem. Fin. Execs. Inst., Houston World Trade Assn., Houston C. of C. (future studies com. 1977). Home: 589 Magnolia Circle Houston TX 77024 Office: 7700 San Felipe Suite 180 Houston TX 77063

SWEENEY, JAMES LYNWOOD, psychologist; b. Floyd, Va., June 28, 1944; s. Fred Douglas and Allene Gertrude S.; B.A., Lynchburg Coll., 1966; M.A. in Psychology, U. W. Fla., 1973; m. Doris L. Urmson, Aug. 30, 1975. Spl. edn. tchr. Marianna, Fla., 1971-72; psychologist, unit dir. A.P. Brewer Developmental Center, Mobile Ala., 1973—, residential living dir., 19—; ednl. cons. Mobile County Public Schs., 1975; bd. dirs. L'Arche Internat., Mobile, 1976-78, com., 1976—. Served with USAF, 1966-70, with USAFR, 1970—. Mem. Am. Assn. on Mental Deficiency, Friends of Brewer (program chmn.), Mobile Assn. for Retarded Citizens, Nat. Assn. Developmental Disabilities Mgrs. Republican. Nazarene. Joint author Curriculum Guide in Occupational Preparation for the Disadvantaged and Handicapped, State of Fla., 1973. Home: Route 5 Box 81 BC Mobile AL 36608 Office: PO Box 8467 Mobile AL 36608

SWEENEY, ROBERT JOSEPH, JR., oil co. exec.; b. Montpelier, Vt., Oct. 23, 1927; s. Robert Joseph and Glenna Ethyln (Little) S.; B.S. in Engring. Physics, Auburn (Ala.) U., 1948; M.S. in Petroleum Engring., La. Tech. U., 1961; m. Hazel Miller, Mar. 7, 1947; children—Robert Joseph, III, Theodore C., James Bradford. With Murphy Oil Corp., 1952—, v.p. prodn. and exploration, 1966-69, pres., chief operating officer El Dorado, Ark., 1972—; pres. Murphy Eastern Oil Co., 1969-72; dir. First Fed. Savs. & Loan Assn. El Dorado, Ocean Drilling and Exploration Co. Bd. dirs., past pres. Boys Club El Dorado, S.Ark. Arts Center. Served with USNR, 1945-46. Mem. AIME. Roman Catholic. Club: K.C. Home: 1502 N Euclid St El Dorado AR 71730 Office: 200 Jefferson Ave El Dorado AR 71730

SWEET, JAY LINCOLN, land surveyor; b. Hepburnville, Pa., Feb. 12, 1929; s. Garner Meredith and Anita May (Schultz) S.; student elec. drafting Chgo. Tech. Coll., 1951; student Utah State U., 1966-67; B.S. in History, SUNY, 1978; m. Allura Maude Wickham, Jan. 2, 1951; children—Karen (Mrs. James L. Knox), Janice (Mrs. Verlan P. Miller), Jay Lincoln, Gifford Lyle. Party surveyor Western Geophys. Co., Los Angeles, 1953-54; chief of party Met. Engrs., Salt Lake City, 1954-56; transit man Utah Road Commn., 1956-57; instrument man, draftsman Utah Power & Light Co., 1957; chief of surveyor Coon & King Engrs., Salt Lake City, 1957-59; pres., gen. mgr., dir. Geotech Land Surveyors, Salt Lake City, 1959-65; surveyor, design draftsman Kaiser Engrs., Magna, Utah, 1965-66; instr. civil tech. Utah Tech. Coll., 1966-68; sr. design draftsman, chimney div. M.W. Kellogg Co., Williamsport, Pa., 1968-72; land surveyor firm Robert E. Owen & Assos., Inc., West Palm Beach, Fla., 1972-74; owner Jay Sweet & Sons, Cons. Land Survey, West Palm Beach, 1974; asst. dir. survey div. Engring. and Pub. Works Dept. Palm Beach County (Fla.), West Palm Beach, 1974—. Legis. chmn. Granger P.T.A., Salt Lake City, 1964-65. Candidate for county surveyor Salt Lake County, 1962, 66; chmn. Republican Voting Dist., county conv. del., 1966. Registered profl. land surveyor, Ky., Fla., Ariz., Ida., Utah. Mem. Am. Congress on Surveying and Mapping (past sec.-treas. Utah chpt.), Fla. Soc. Profl. Land Surveyors (past pres.). Mem. Ch. Jesus Christ of Latter-day Saints (pres. br. 1968-71, 2d counselor in bishopric 1973-74). Home: 400 Rome Dr Palm Springs FL 33461 Office: PO Box 2429 West Palm Beach FL 33402

SWEETEN, JOHN MARBROOKS, JR., extension agrl. engr.; b. Rocksprings, Tex., Jan. 11, 1944; s. John Marbrooks and Johnnie Rachel (Johnson) S.; student Austin Coll., 1961-62, U. Tex. at Austin, 1963; B.S., Tex. Tech. U., 1965; M.S., Okla. State U., 1967, Ph.D., 1969; m. Mary Claire Kinney, Mar. 25, 1967; children—Jessica Lynn, Patrick Kinney. Grad. research asst. Okla. State U., 1965-68, NSF grad. fellow, 1968-69; san. engr. USPHS, Cin., 1969, U.S. EPA, Cin., 1970-71; extension agrl. engr. Tex. A. and M. U., 1971—; research engring. and edn. cons. livestock waste mgmt. and feedlot pollution control; engring. cons. EPA, also industry; cattle feeder and rancher; tech. adviser to state and nat. livestock assns., to state air and water pollution control agencies. Served to lt. comdr. USPHS, 1969-71. Plains Cotton Ginners scholar, 1964. Registered profl. engr. Mem. Am. Soc. Agrl. Engrs. (paper award 1970), Nat., Tex. (Outstanding Young Engr. award), socs. profl. engrs., Sigma Xi, Phi Kappa Phi, Gamma Sigma Delta, Alpha Zeta. Presbyterian. Contbr. articles to profl. jours. and nat. livestock publs. Home: 1804 Leona St College Station TX 77840

SWEIGERT, MILTON EDWARD, architect; b. Atlanta, Mar. 2, 1934; s. Ray Leslie and Edna (Powers) S.; B.S., Ga. Inst. Tech., 1956, B.Arch., 1959; m. Helen LaRue Horne, June 16, 1956; children—Vicki LaRue, Valerie Lea. Designer, L. Miles Sheffer, Architect, Atlanta, 1960; job capt. Cunningham & Forehand, Architects, Inc., Atlanta, 1961-65; project architect Lockwood Greene Engrs., Inc., Spartanburg, S.C., 1965-67, archtl. dept. head, Atlanta, 1967-68; v.p., chief architect Zachary W. Henderson & Assos., Atlanta, 1968-70; chief architect Sheetz & Bradfield, Architects, Inc., 1970-73; corp. architect Financial Bldg. Consultants, Inc., Atlanta, 1973-74 individual practice architecture, 1974—. Asst. prof. So. Tech. Inst., Marietta, Ga., 1975-80, asso. prof., 1980—. Supporting mem. Arthritis Found., 1969—, Haggai Inst., 1974—, Growth Ministries, Inc., 1976—. Served with USNR, 1956-58. Registered architect, Ga. Ala., Fla., S.C. Mem. Ga. Archtl. and Engring. Soc. (dir. 1974-76, pres. 1976), Ga. Assn. Architects, Constrn. Specifications Inst., Ga. Conservancy, Ga. Tech. Nat. Alumni Assn., Dunwoody North Civic Assn. (dir. 1978-79), Tau Sigma Delta, Delta Tau Delta. Republican. Mem. Riverside Ch. Atlanta (bd. deacons 1980—). Clubs: Dunwoody N Driving (dir., v.p. 1974-75), Bent Tree Property Owners Assn. Home: 4518 Kingsgate Dr NE Atlanta GA 30338 Office: Archtl Civil Bldg Room 556a So Tech Inst Marietta GA 30060

SWENSON, ANN MARIE, mag. editor; b. Buenos Aires, Argentina, Dec. 29, 1932; d. Erhardt Sven and Anna (Granberg) Swenson; A.B., Wheaton Coll., 1955; M.A., U. Wis., 1957; M.R.E., Southwestern Baptist Theol. Sem., 1962; M.Ed., U. Tex., El Paso, 1970; D.Min., Luther Rice Sem., 1978. Missionary Fgn. Mission Bd., So. Baptist Conv., El Paso, Tex., 1962-79, Mex., 1979—; editor Ensayo sobre la Obra Estudiantil Bautista, Baptist Spanish Publishing, also editor Marchemos. House editor La Preparacion de Los Jovenes de la Iglesia Mag., pres. bd. trustees, 1973-75; former editor Ancla, Adelante!. Pres. Union Nacional Femenil Bautista Misionera Sara Alicia Hale, Mexico, 1971—. Home: 4204 Edgar Park El Paso TX 79904

SWENSON, GEORGE EDWIN, mfg. co. exec.; b. N.Y.C., Sept. 17, 1931; s. Edwin Lofquist and Alma (Murch) S.; B.S., U.S. Naval Acad., 1954; m. Elsie Milli Gronbach, June 13, 1954; children—Kenneth Scott, Denis Wayne, Eric Jon, Derek George. Prodn. services mgr. Alumina Partners of Jamaica (W.I.), 1968-72; plant engr. Kaiser Aluminum & Chem. Corp., Halethorp, Md., 1972-74; maint. mgr. Howmet Aluminum Co., Rockwell, Tex., 1974-77; plant mgr. Sid Richardson Gasoline Co., Kermit, Tex., 1978—. Served with USN, 1950-59. Mem. Gas Processors Assn., Am. Mgmt. Assn. Lutheran. Club: Monahans Swim (dir. 1979-80). Home: 1106 S Gary St Monahans TX 79756 Office: PO Drawer R Kermit TX 79745

SWETMAN, GLENN ROBERT, educator, poet; b. Biloxi, Miss., May 20, 1936; s. Glenn Lyle and June (Read) S.; B.S., U. So. Miss., 1957, M.A., 1959; Ph.D., Tulane U., 1966; m. Margarita Ortiz, Feb. 8, 1964 (div. 1979); children—Margarita June, Glenn Lyle Maximilian, Glenda Louise. Teaching fellow U. So. Miss., 1957-58, asst. prof., 1964-66; instr. Ark. State U., 1958-59, McNeese U., 1959-61; instr., teaching fellow Univ. Coll. Tulane U., 1961-64, spl. asst. dept. elec. engring., 1961; asso. prof. La. Inst. Tech., 1966-67; prof., head dept. langs. Nicholls State Coll., Thibodaux, La., 1967-69, head dept. English, 1969-71, prof., 1971—. Partner, Breeland Pl., Biloxi, Miss., 1960—; stringer corr. Shreveport (La.) Times, 1966—; partner Ormuba, Inc., 1975—; cons. tech. writing Union Carbide Corp., Am. Fedn. Tchrs. State v.p. Nat. Com. to Resist Attacks on Tenure, 1974—. Subdiv. coordinator Republican party, Hattiesburg, Miss., 1964. Served with AUS, 1957. Recipient Poetry awards KQUE Haiku contest, 1964, Coll. Arts contest, Los Angeles, 1966, Black Ship Festival, Yoqosuka, Japan, 1967; Green World Brief Forms award Green World Poetry Editors, 1965. Mem. Modern Lang. Assn., S. Central Modern Lang. Assn., Coll. Writers Soc. La. (pres. 1971-72), IEEE, Am. Assn. Engring. Edn., La. Poetry Soc. (pres. 1971-74), Internat. Boswellian Inst., Nat. Fedn. State Poetry Socs. (2d v.p., nat. membership chmn. 1972-74, pres. 1976-77), Am. Fedn. Tchrs. (chpt. pres. 1973-78), Nat. Fedn. State Poetry Socs. (1st v.p. 1975-76), Phi Eta Sigma, Omicron Delta Kappa. Book reviewer Jackson (Miss.) State Times, 1961. Poems pub. in various publs. including Poet, Prairie Schooner, Trace, Ball State U. Forum, Film Quar.; (books of poems) Tunel de Amor, 1973; Deka #1, 1973; Deka #2, 1979; Shards, 1979; Concerning Carpenters, 1980; cons. editor (poetry) Paon Press, 1974—, Scott-Foresman, 1975; editorial bd. Scholar and Educator, 1980—. Home: 2127 Audobon Dr #28 Thibodaux LA 70301

SWETONIC, MARJORIE ANN, naval officer; b. Pitts., Sept. 26, 1935; d. Thomas Paul and Anna (Reha) S.; B.S. in Nursing, U. San Francisco, 1958; M.S. in Nursing Adminstrn., U. Wash., 1965. Commd. lt. (jg.) Nurse Corps, U.S. Navy, 1960, advanced through grades to capt., 1979; service in Guam and Vietnam; ednl. coordinator Naval Regional Med. Center, Portsmouth, Va., 1977—; adj. instr. Old Dominion U. Sch. Nursing, 1977—; mem. clin. faculty U. Va. Sch. Nursing, 1978—, Hampton (Va.) Inst., 1978—; adv. com. nursing options Roakoke-Chowan Tech. Sch., 1979—; adv. nd. bacjerlor's degree nursing program Norfolk State U., 1980; cons. in field. Bd. dirs. Catholic Family Services, Portsmouth, 1978—, pres., 1979-80. Decorated Navy Achievement medal; recipient Mother Baptiste Russel award U. San Francisco, 1959, Beatrice Bowman award Naval Regional Med. Center, Camp Pendleton, Calif., 1973; cert. appreciation Am. Heart Assn., 1973, Meritorious Service award, 1974. Mem. Am. Nurses Assn., Va. Nurses Assn., Nat. League Nursing, Va. League Nursing, Am. Hosp. Assn., Am. Soc. Health Educators and Trainers Va. Soc. Health Educators and Trainers, Assn. Mil. Surgeons, Assn. Bus. Bus. and Profl. Women, Gamma Pi Epsilon. Roman Catholic. Office: NRMC Portsmouth VA 23708

SWICK, LEO EMMETT, JR., geologist; b. Lima, Ohio, July 2, 1917; s. Leo E. and Mildred May (Kennedy) S.; B.A., Ohio State U., 1939; M.S., 1941; m. Margaret Kathryn Nunemaker, Sept. 28, 1938; children—Sue (Mrs. Robert Henry), Nancy (Mrs. W. James Carmichael), Kathryn (Mrs. Wayne Locke), David Edward. Geol. engr. Mickel Plate R.R., Cleve., 1941-43; indsl. engr. B. & O. R.R., Balt., 1943-44; geologist Magnolia Petroleum Co., Mt. Vernon, Ill., 1944-46, Gainesville, Tex., 1946-48; prin. L.E. Swick, geologist, oil operator, Gainesville, 1948—; v.p., dir. Geodata Internat. Inc., Dallas, 1973—. Cons. in petroleum geology, 1948—. Mem. Gainesville City Council, 1951-52; chmn. bd. edn., Gainesville, 1954-59. Mem. Am. Assn. Petroleum Geologists (life), Am. Inst. Profl. Geologists, Gainesville C. of C. (pres. 1954). Home: 820 S Dixon St Gainesville TX 76240 Office: Box 734 411 E California St Gainesville TX 76240

SWIETER, ROBERT KIETH, telecommunications co. exec.; b. Lake View, Ia., Oct. 12, 1928; s. William Dewey and Gladys Margaret (Webster) S.; m. Virginia Rae Varian, Dec. 19, 1953; children—Varian, Robert Kieth, Steven, Mark. Field engr. Western Electric Co., Winston-Salem, 1956; mgr. test operations Burroughs Corp., Phila., 1957-61; v.p. ITT Fed. Electric, Paramus, N.J., 1961-72; v.p. AEL Service Corp., Colmar, Pa., 1972-74; program mgr. Ford Aerospace & Communications Corp., Willow Grove, Pa., 1974-77; exec. v.p. Superior Cable Corp., Hickory, N.C., 1977—. Served with USN, 1947-56. Mem. Ind. Telephone Pioneer Assn. Club: Lake Hickory Country. Home: Route 2 Box 491 Hickory NC 28601 Office: 1928 Main Ave SE Hickory NC 28601

SWIFT, EDWARD VIRGINIUS, JR., physician; b. Palestine, Tex., Sept. 1, 1910; s. Edward Virginius and Rena (Egan) S.; M.D., U. Tex., 1933; M.S., U. Minn., 1939; m. Ann Peck, June 30, 1938; children—Virginia A., Charles E. Intern, resident in internal medicine Parkland Hosp., Dallas, 1933-35; fellow in medicine Mayo Found., Rochester, Minn., 1935-38, 1st. asst. Mayo Clinic, 1938-39; cons. medicine Malone-Hogan Found., Big Springs, Tex., 1947-66, Allen Clinic, Burnet, Tex., 1966—; pres. Malone-Hogan Found., 1965-66;

individual practice medicine, specializing in internal medicine Burnet, 1966—; mem. staff Shepperd Meml. Hosp., Burnet. Served with M.C., U.S. Army, 1941-46. Diplomate Am. Bd. Internal Medicine. Mem. Am. Soc. Internal Medicine, Tex. Acad. Internat. Medicine, Tex. Rheumatism Assn., Am., Tex., Tri-County med. assns., Alpha Omega Alpha. Rotarian (pres. Burnet 1977-78). Home: Route 1 Box 135 Marble Falls TX 78654 Office: 410 S Water St Burnet TX 78611

SWIFT, ROY ALLEN, occupational therapist, army officer; b. Emporia, Kans., June 22, 1943; s. Harold H. and Thelma Margaret (Prichett) S.; B.S., U. Kans., 1966; M.S. in Edn., U. So. Calif., 1971; m. Susan Jane Lanning, Aug. 6, 1966; children—Gregory, Holly, Cheryl, Anne. Commd. 2d lt. U.S. Army, 1965, advanced through grades to maj., 1975; occupational therapist William Beaumont Med. Center, El Paso, Tex., 1966-68, 97th Gen. Hosp., Frankfurt, Germany, 1968-71; occupational therapist, instr., dir. Occupational Therapy Tech. Sch., Valley Forge Gen. Hosp., Phoenixville, Pa., 1971-72; instr., project officer, dir. Occupational Therapy Tech. Sch., Acad. Health Scis., Ft. Sam Houston, Tex., 1973-77; chief occupational therapy sect. Womack Army Hosp., Ft. Bragg, N.C., 1977—. Mem. Assn. U.S. Army, Am. (mem. accreditation com. 1973-77), N.C. occupational therapy assns., Adult Edn. Assn. U.S. Presbyterian. Contbr. articles to profl. jours. Home: 2437 Torcross Dr Fayetteville NC 28304 Office: Box 353 Occupational Therapy Sect Womack Army Hosp Ft Bragg NC 28307

SWIGERT, JAMES LYNWOOD, zoo ofcl.; b. Carlisle, Pa., May 18, 1941; s. Clarence Mentzer and Evelyn Elizabeth (Shearer) S.; B.S. in Animal Sci., W.Va. U., 1966; m. Esther Earlene Adams, Sept. 14, 1963; 1 son, Earl Trent. Zoologist, Mesker Park Zoo, Evansville, Ind., 1968-69; zool. dir. Jungle Larry's Safari, Naples, Fla., 1969-72; dir. Randolph Park Zoo, Tucson, 1972-75, Jackson (Miss.) Zool. Park, 1975—, exec. dir. Friends of Jackson Zoo. Fellow Am. Assn. Zool. Parks Aquariums (profl.); mem. Am. Game Bird Breeders Fedn., World Pheasant Assn., Am. Fedn. Aviculturists, Internat. Wild Waterfowl Assn., Pheasant Trust, Audubon Soc. Home and Office: 2918 W Capitol St Jackson MS 39209

SWIGGETT, HAL, writer, photographer; b. Moline, Kans., July 22, 1921; s. Otho Benjamin and Mildred (Spray) S.; ed. high sch.; m. Wilma Caroline Turner, Mar. 1, 1942; children—Gerald, Vernon. Staff photographer San Antonio Express-News, 1946-67, head dept., 1955-67; free-lance writer/photographer San Antonio, 1947—, full-time, 1967—. Served with USAAC, World War II. Mem. Wildlife Unltd. (pres. chpt. 1955-58), Outdoor writers Assn. Am. (dir. 1969-72), Tex. Outdoor Writers Assn. (pres. 1967-68), Ducks Unltd., Nat. (life), Tex. (life) rifle assns., Internat. Handgun Metallic Silhouette Assn. (life), Game Conservation Internat. Republican. Baptist. Contbg. author books game hunting, gun-oriented paperbacks; author: Hal Swiggett on North American Deer, 1980; asso. editor Gun World; handgun editor Guns, Game and Shooting; contbg. editor Gun Digest. Home: 539 Roslyn St San Antonio TX 78204

SWIHART, JOHN DONALD, JR., elec. engr.; b. Hobart, Okla., Aug. 3, 1936; s. John D. and Mary (Madden) S.; B.S. in Elec. Engring., U. Okla., 1959; postgrad. U. Fla., 1967, Tarrant County Jr. Coll., 1969, ranch mgmt. program Tex. Christian U., 1976-79; M.B.A., N. Tex. State U., 1974; m. Mary Ann Nixon, Jan. 30, 1958; children—Susan LaRue, Timothy George, David Gerard, Mary Kathryn. Electronic engr. FAA, Oklahoma City, 1959-66, elec. engr. aircraft systems, Fort Worth, 1967—; electronic engr. Naval Tng. Device Center, Orlando, Fla., 1967. Asst. cubmaster, Webelos den leader, scoutmaster Boy Scouts Am., 1967—; class rep. U. Okla. Alumni Devel. Fund. campaign, 1968. Served to lt. U.S. Army, 1959. Registered profl. engr., Okla., Tex. Mem. Okla. Cattlemens Assn., Okla. Wheat Growers Assn., Tau Beta Pi, Eta Kappa Nu, Sigma Tau, Sigma Iota Epsilon. Democrat. Roman Catholic. K.C. Home: 7313 Janetta Dr Fort Worth TX 76118 Office: FAA PO Box 1689 Fort Worth TX 76101

SWINNEN, JAMES EDWARD, cons. engring. co. exec.; b. Alexandria, La., Dec. 1, 1948; s. Roy Victor and Mary Aline (Barron) S.; B.A. in Communications, Loyola U., New Orleans, 1970; M.A. in English, U. New Orleans, 1972; Ph.D. in English, Tulane U., 1978; postgrad. Loyola U., New Orleans, 1979—; m. Daria Joan Smythe, May 24, 1970. Field engr. asso. Ralph M. Parsons Co., Garyville, La., 1976; project adminstr. spl. projects office Walk, Haydel & Assos., Inc., New Orleans, 1977—. Mem. Renaissance Soc. Am. Democrat. Roman Catholic. Book reviewer New Orleans Rev., 1971—. Home: 8109 Freret St New Orleans LA 70118 Office: 600 Carondelet St New Orleans LA 70130

SWISHER, RHAE MARTIN, JR., univ. adminstr.; b. Hammond, Ind., Dec. 18, 1921; s. Rhae Martin and Ruth (Dixon) S.; B.S. in Acctg., Ind. U., 1943, J.D., 1950; m. Barbara Burns, Apr. 4, 1946; children—Deborah Ann, Rhae Martin III, Karen Lee. Admitted to Ind. bar, 1950; dir. mgmt. services, asso. prof. bus. adminstrn. Sch. Bus., Kans. State U., 1965-69; v.p. fin. Simpson Coll., 1969-72; asso. dean Sch. Bus. and Commerce, Troy State U., 1972-75, dean, 1975—; dir. Troy Fed. Savs. & Loan Assn.; public panelist Am. Arbitration Assn.; chmn. Ala. Assn. Higher Edn. in Bus., 1979-80. Mem. adv. com. Ala. Manpower Adv. Council, 1975—; commr. Troy Housing Authority, 1978—. Served with USN, 1943-47. Mem. Acad. Mgmt., Delta Sigma Pi, Phi Delta Phi, Phi Eta Sigma. Methodist. Office: Sch Bus and Commerce Troy State U Troy AL 36081

SWISHER, ROBERT LEE, JR., investment broker; b. Marion, N.C., Dec. 4, 1943; s. Robert Lee and Lucille Daniels S.; B.A., U. of the South, 1966; M.B.A., U. Pa., 1968; m. Linda Verne Siemoneit, Nov. 9, 1974. Brand mgr. Procter & Gamble Co., Cin., 1968-70; v.p. Goldman Sachs & Co., St. Louis, 1970-76; v.p. Bear Stearns & Co., Dallas, 1976—; v.p. U.S. Resources, Inc., Dallas, 1977—; pres. Sooner Investment Corp., Dallas, 1979—. Served with USMCR, 1968. Mem. Dallas Securities Dealers. Presbyn. Home: 7716 Willow Winds Ct Dallas TX 75230 Office: One Main Pl Suite 100 Dallas TX 75250

SWITZER, BARRY, football coach; b. Crossett, Ark., Oct. 5, 1937; ed. U. Ark.; m. Kay, 1963; children—Greg, Kathy, Dove. Asst. football coach U. Ark., 1960-65; asst. football coach U. Okla., 1966-72, head coach, 1973—. Served with U.S. Army. Named Coach of Yr., 1973. Office: U Okla Room 201 180 W Brooks St Norman OK 73019

SWITZER, JAMES REGINALD, educator; b. Gulfport, Miss., July 4, 1917; s. Henry Shelby and Lottie (Garner) S.; B.S., U. So. Miss., 1941; M.S., La. State U., 1947; Ed.D. (Gen. Edn. Bd. fellow), U. Tex., 1952; m. Sara Ann Jackson, Aug. 5, 1941; children—Carolyn, Jan, Sally, Reggie, Hank. Faculty U. So. Miss., Hattiesburg, 1946—, instr., 1946-49, dean student affairs, 1952-68, prof. health edn., 1968—; cons., lectr. on stress mgmt. and other health edn. topics. Served with USAF World War II. Named distinguished prof. of year U. So. Miss., 1975; recipient U. So. Miss. alumni certificate of award, 1963. Mem. AAHPER, Am. Assn. for Advancement of Tension Control, Phi Delta Kappa, Omicron Delta Kappa, Phi Kappa Phi. Baptist. Club: Beaver Lake Recreational Center. Condr. seminars on stress and stress mgmt.; contbr. articles to health jours. Home: PO Box 434 Purvis MS 39475 Office: Box 5105 Hattiesburg MS 39401

SWITZER, RICHARD ALAN, mfrs. rep.; b. Oklahoma City, May 31, 1943; s. Charles and Jo (Tarpley) Lamb; B.S., U. Tex., Arlington, 1966; m. Dawn Laurel Breitwieser a.k.a. Dawn Michaels, Feb. 19, 1972; 1 son, Charles Edward (Ched). Asst. designer Executive Aircraft, Dallas, 1966-68; staff engr. interiors Braniff Airways, Dallas, 1968-74; dir. engring. Trans Aero Industries, Los Angeles, 1974-76; mgr. engring. Hydraflow, Inc., Los Angeles, 1976-78; v.p. engring. and mktg. Geo. Harris Co., Tulsa, 1978—. Served as capt., navigator, Tex. Air N.G., 1966-74. Cert. engring. technician. Mem. Interior Designers Guild, Tex. Guard Assn. Republican. Christian. Home: 3415 E 85 Pl Tulsa OK 74136 Office: Box 21 Cleveland OK 74020

SWOFFORD, DICKEY LYNDELL, JR., accountant; b. Griffin, Ga., Aug. 22, 1946; s. Dickey Lyndell and Julia Mell (Wilson) S.; B.B.A. in Mktg., U. Ga., 1968, B.B.A. in Accounting and Fin., 1971; m. Beverly Jean Foster, Apr. 18, 1969; children—Aubrey Lyndell, Benjamin Foster, Joseph Beaty II. Fin. analyst Massey Ferguson Credit Corp., Chamblee, Ga., 1969-70; accountant Peat, Marwick, Mitchell & Co., Greenville, S.C., 1971-74; audit mgr. Blount Inc., Montgomery, Ala., 1974-76; dir. internal auditing Gen. Telephone Co. of the S.E., Durham, N.C., 1976-78; individual practice acctg., Atlanta, 1978-79; partner Swofford & Abernathy, Atlanta, 1979—. C.P.A., S.C., Ala., N.C., Ga. Mem. Am. Inst. C.P.A.'s, S.C., N.C. assns. C.P.A.'s, Ala. Soc. C.P.A.'s, Ga. Soc. C.P.A.'s, Nat. Assn. Accountants (dir. 1976—), Am. Mgmt. Assn., Inst. Internal Auditors, Lambda Chi Alpha. Republican. Clubs: Rotary, Terminus Internat. Home: 540 Park Ln Marietta GA 30067 Office: Suite 775 Tower Place 3340 Peachtree Rd Atlanta GA 30326

SWONK, JOSEPH LEO, educator; b. Kalamazoo, Mich., Aug. 9, 1935; s. Casper Leo and Ethel Mae (Graham) S.; B.A., Western Mich. U., Kalamazoo, 1957, M.A., 1961; postgrad. Fla. State U., Tallahassee, 1970-72; m. Patricia Ann Hardy, Oct. 27, 1956; children—Stephen, Katherine. Instr. of English, Litchfield (Mich.) High Sch., 1957-58; instr. of English, Berrien Springs (Mich.) High Sch., 1958-62, also debate coach, 1959-62, drama dir., 1957-62, golf coach, 1961; instr. of English, Niles (Mich.) High Sch., 1962-64; asst. prof. of English, Ferris State Coll., Big Rapids, Mich., 1964-68, Indian River Community Coll., Fort Pierce, Fla., 1968-70; grad. asst. Fla. State U., Tallahassee, 1971-72; asso. prof. of English, Rappahannock Community Coll., Warsaw, Va., 1972—, also forensic judge, designer, dir., tchr. systems workshop for elementary, secondary tchrs., 1974-75; ednl. cons. in systems tng., 1974-75. Dir., Essex County (Va.) Bicentennial Pageant, 1975, 76. Mem. Distinguished Service to Community award, 1977. Mem. AAUP, Modern Lang. Assn., Nat. Council Tchrs. English, Southeastern Conf. on English in Two-Year Coll., Va. Assn. Tchrs. English, Full Gospel Businessmen's Fellowship (pres. chpt. 1976-77), Phi Kappa Phi. Democrat. Roman Catholic (lay minister). Club: Tappahannock Lions Internat. (pres. 1974-75, 75-76). Home: Star Route 1 Box 220 Dunnsville VA 22454 Office: Box 318 Warsaw VA 22572

SWOPE, JEFFREY GORDON, mfg. co. exec.; b. LaGrange, Tex., Mar. 1, 1950; s. James Sidney and Bobbye Sue (McGill) S.; student Tex. Tech. U., 1968-71. With CIC Cosmetics Internat., Dallas, 1970—, area dir., 1973-74, v.p. sales and mktg., 1974—; dir. Justin of Dallas, Inc. Mem. Republican Nat. Com., 1976— Home: Route 3 Box 175X1 Roanoke TX 76262 Office: 1414 Round Table Dallas TX 75247

SWORDS, HENRY LOGAN, physician; b. Terrell, Tex., May 12, 1918; s. John Henry and Mattie Ethel (Logan) S.; B.S., East Tex. State U., 1939; M.S., 1947; M.D., Southwestern Med. Sch., 1947; m. Ruth C. Riley, June 20, 1940; children—Henry Logan II, Sylvia Lorraine. Tchr., Ft. Worth Pub. Schs., 1939-41, prin., 1941-44; intern John Peter Smith Hosp., Ft. Worth, 1947-48; gen. practice medicine, Ft. Worth, 1948—; mem. staff St. Joseph's, Harris Meml., All Saints hosps., Ft. Worth; chief div. gen. practice St. Joseph Hosp., 1970-71. Served as cadet USAAF, 1942. Mem. Am., Tex. med. assns., Am., Tex. acads. gen. practice, Am. Geriatric Soc., Tarrant County Med. Soc. (v.p. 1967), Phi Beta Pi. Methodist (chmn. bd. 1957-58, pres. bd. trustees 1959-60). Rotarian (pres. N. Ft. Worth 1969-70). Home: 5808 Blue Ridge Dr Fort Worth TX 76112 Office: 301 W Central St Fort Worth TX 76106

SWORDS, RUTH CLIFFORD RILEY (MRS. HENRY LOGAN SWORDS), dentist, univ. ofcl.; b. Itasca, Tex., Nov. 1, 1916; d. Philip Eugene and Ruth (Love) Riley; B.A., East Tex. State U., 1938; B.S., Tex. Wesleyan Coll., 1961; D.D.S., Baylor U., 1961; m. Henry Logan Swords, June 20, 1940; children—Henry Logan II, Sylvia Lorraine. Tchr., Ft. Worth Pub. Schs., 1938-42; engring. draftsman Gen. Dynamics Co., Ft. Worth, 1942-48; dir. Caruth Sch. Dental Hygiene, Baylor Coll. Dentistry, Dallas, 1962—. Named Alumna of Year, Tex. Wesleyan Coll., 1964, Distinguished Alumna, East Tex. State U., 1974. Fellow Internat., Am. colls. dentists; mem. Am., Tex. dental assns., Ft. Worth Dist. Dental Soc., Am. Assn. Dental Schs., Baylor Odontological Honor Soc. (charter), Tex. Dental Hygienists Assn. (hon.), Dallas Dist. Dental Hygienists Soc. (hon.), Sigma Tau Delta, Alpha Chi, Sigma Phi Alpha, Omicron Kappa Upsilon (chpt. pres. 1969), Alpha Delta Pi, Upsilon Alpha. Methodist. Rotarian (pres. Ft. Worth woman's chpt. 1954-56). Club: Rejebian Afternoon (treas. 1956-57). Home: 5808 Blueridge Dr Fort Worth TX 76112 Office: Baylor College Dentistry 3302 Gaston Ave Dallas TX 75246

SYBRANT, TERRY DEAN, clin. social worker; b. Hobart, Okla., Nov. 11, 1945; s. Dean Donald and Eileen S.; B.A., Warren Wilson Coll., 1972; M.S. in Social Work, U. Tenn., 1974; m. Brenda Dale Brady, Dec. 27, 1974. Dir. social services USAF Regional Hosp., March AFB, Calif., 1974-76; chief mental health clinic, dir. social services USAF Hosp., Little Rock AFB, Ark., 1976—, child advocacy officer, drug and alcohol rehab. officer. Bd. dirs. Blue Ridge Community Mental Health Center, Asheville, N.C., 1972. Served with USN, 1965-70. Registered master social worker, Ark. Mem. Acad. Social Workers, Nat. Assn. Social Workers, Ark. Assn. Social Workers (licensing com. 1978-79), Soc. Hosp. Social Work Dirs., Soc. Air Force Social Workers, Air Force Assn. Democrat. Presbyterian. Contbr. paper to profl. symposium. Home: 9002 Peach Tree St North Little Rock AR 72116 Office: Mental Health Clinic (SGHMA) USAF Hospital Little Rock AFB AR 72076

SYLVESTER, JOHN CAIUS, microbiologist; b. Mauston, Wis., Feb. 14, 1915; s. C.P. and Edith M. (Organ) S.; B.S. with high honors, U. Wis., 1939, M.S., 1940, Ph.D., 1943; m. Helen E. McKnight, May 21, 1940; children—Michael Jon, Steven Carl. Instr. bacteriology Ind. U., Bloomington, 1942; research bacteriologist Abbott Labs., North Chicago, Ill., 1943-45, mgr. prodn. fermentation, 1946-49, asst. mgr. microbiol. research, 1950-51, mgr. fermentation research, 1952-55, mgr. microbiol. labs., 1956-62, dir. microbiologic research div., 1963-65, research specialist div. of exptl. therapy, 1966-68, dir. exptl. biology div., 1969-71, cons. clin. microbiology, 1972—. Chmn. Intersci. Conf. on Antimicrobial Agts. and Chemotherapy, 1962. Trustee Am. Type Culture Collection, chmn., 1974. Mem. Am. Chem. Soc. (sec. fermentation div. 1952-58, chmn. fermentation div. 1960, chmn. div. food and agrl. chemistry 1961), Am. Acad. of Microbiology (bd. govs. 1963-65), Assn. of Clin. Scientists, Am. Pub. Health Assn., Am. Soc. for Microbiology (mem. publs. bd. 1962-64, 67-71), Am. Inst. Biol. Scis., AAAS, Sigma Xi, Phi Eta Sigma, Phi Kappa Phi, Alpha Zeta, Gamma Alpha. Editor Applied Microbiology, 1967-68, editor-in-chief, 1969-71. Contbr. numerous articles on microbiology to sci. jours. Address: 157 SW 51st St Cape Coral FL 33904

SYLVESTER, JOSEPH EDWARD, wine co. exec.; b. N.Y.C., Jan. 12, 1921; s. Joseph Edward and Harriet (Fox) S.; B.A., Johns Hopkins U., 1942; postgrad. U. Berlin, 1957; m. Suzanne Esther May, Jan. 4, 1975; children—Norman, Timothy. Propr., Chappaqua Wine and Liquor (N.Y.), 1946-73; Met. N.Y. account exec. Browne Vintners wine div. Joseph E. Seagram & Sons, 1974-77; wine mgr. Sigels Wines & Liquors, Dallas, 1977—; lectr. Les Amis du Vin; wine columnist Patent Trader, Westchester, N.Y. Bd. dirs. Chappaqua Symphony, 1950-52; vol. fireman Chappaqua Fire Dept., 1945-50. Served to maj., inf., AUS, 1942-45. Decorated Bronze Star, Silver Star; recipient Ed Gibbs Newsletter award for brand name mdsg., 1958. Mem. Moore County Hounds (life). Clubs: N. Dallas Racquet, Willow Bend Polo and Hunt, Hickory Creek Hunt (Dallas). Home: 15517 Preston Rd Dallas TX 75248 Office: 15003 Inwood Rd Dallas TX 75240

SYLVESTER, JOSEPH ROBERT, marine biologist; b. Fayetteville, N.C., Nov. 2, 1942; s. Joseph Augustus and Sally Parker S.; B.S., U. Hawaii, 1965, M.S., 1969; Ph.D., U. Wash., 1971; m. Joan Gwendolyn Blaylock, Dec. 20, 1978. Fishery biologist Nat. Marine and Fishery Service, Honolulu and Seattle, 1969-74, fishery mgmt. specialist, St. Petersburg, Fla., 1978—; fishery biologist Oceanic Inst., Waimanalo, Hawaii, 1974-76; dir. Bur. Fish and Wildlife, Govt. of V.I., 1976-78; pres. Aquatic Syntox Inc. Mem. Am. Fisheries Soc. (cert. fishery scientist), Am. Inst. Fishery Research Biologists, Sigma Xi. Office: Nat Marine and Fishery Service 9450 Koger Blvd Saint Petersburg FL 33702

SYNAR, MICHAEL L., congressman; b. Vinita, Okla., Oct. 17, 1950; B.B.A., U. Okla., 1972, J.D., 1977; postgrad. in econs. (Rotary scholar) U. Edinburgh, 1973; M.A., Northwestern U., 1973. Admitted to Okla. bar, 1977; rancher; real estate broker; mem. 96th Congress from 2d Congressional Dist. Okla. Democrat. Office: Room 1338 Longworth House Office Bldg Washington DC 20515

SYRDAHL, SUSAN BOWMAN, nurse; b. Lenoir, N.C., Nov. 1, 1947; d. Lindsey Odell and Delia Christine (Triplett) Bowman; R.N., Gaston Meml. Hosp., Gastonia, N.C., 1968; B.S., Greensboro (N.C.) Coll., 1975; m. Tor Jan Syrdahl, Oct. 19, 1975; 1 son, Slade Alf. Nurse epidemiologist infectious disease lab., dept. pediatrics U. N.C. Med. Sch., Chapel Hill, 1968-72; clin. nursing instr. Guilford (N.C.) Tech. Inst., 1975-76, 79—; supr. central sterile supply High Point (N.C.) Meml. Hosp., 1976-79. Recipient Service award March of Dimes, 1973. Mem. N.C. Assn. Hosp. Central Service Personnel, Beta Sigma Phi. Office: Guilford Tech Inst Jamestown NC 27282

SYRON, EDWARD PHILIP, air force officer; b. Schenectady, July 13, 1949; s. Joseph Thomas and Dorothy Jean (Knapp) S.; B.S., Ithaca Coll., 1971; M.H.A., Washington U., St. Louis, 1977; m. Suzan Clare Klokis, Oct. 13, 1973; 1 dau., Kelly Kristen. Adminstrv. asst. Mary Imogene Bassett Hosp., Cooperstown, N.Y., 1971-72; commd. 2d lt. U.S. Air Force, 1972, advanced through grades to capt., 1976; asst. adminstr. resources USAF Hosp., Plattsburg AFB, N.Y., 1972-75; mental health adminstr. USAF Regional Hosp., Sheppard AFB, Tex., 1976-77, asst. adminstr. hosp. services, 1977-78, asso. adminstr. registrar services, 1978-79, comdr. med. squadron sect., 1979, congressional liaison officer Office of Surgeon Gen., USAF, Washington, 1979—. Decorated Air Force Commendation medal, Meritorious Service medal. Mem. Am. Coll. Hosp. Adminstrs., Air Force Assn., Am. Hosp. Assn., Assn. Mental Health Adminstrs., Assn. Mil. Surgeons U.S., Tex. Hosp. Assn., Officer's Mixed Bowling League (pres. 1978-79), Pi Lambda Chi. Roman Catholic. Home: 2409 Alden Ct Woodbridge VA 22192 Office: Office Surgeon Gen USAF Bolling AFB Washington DC 20332

SZABUNIEWICZ, CHARLES HENRY, constrn. co. exec.; b. Jadotville, Belgian Congo, Feb. 29, 1952; came to U.S., 1961; s. Michael and Izabella S.; B.A., Tex. A&M U., 1974, B.B.A., 1974. Asst. aquatics mgr. Tex. A&M U., College Station, 1970-74; prin. Real Estate Investment Assos., Bryan, Tex., 1975-77; fiscal agt. Center for Energy and Mineral Resources, Tex. A&M U., 1977-78; v.p. Brazos Gen. Services Corp., Bryan, 1978-79; aquatics dir. City of College Station, 1979—; pres. C. Henry's Homes, Bryan, 1979—. Bd. dirs. Univ. Found. for Medicine, 1977—, chmn. bd., 1978; bd. mem. Brazos Gen. Services Corp., 1977-78. Mem. Tex. Recreation and Parks Soc., Nat. Soc. Lic. Realtors. Republican. Roman Catholic. Home: 307 North Ave Bryan TX 77801

SZEBEHELY, VICTOR GYÖZÖ, aero. engr.; b. Budapest, Hungary, Aug. 10, 1921; s. Victor and Vilma (Stöckl) S.; came to U.S., 1947, naturalized, 1952; M.E., U. Budapest, 1943, Dr. Engring., 1945; m. Jo Betsy Lewallen, May 20, 1970; 1 dau., Julia. Asst. prof. U. Budapest, 1945-47; research asso. State U. Pa., 1947-48; asso. prof. Va. Poly. Inst., 1948-53; research asso. Model Basin, US. Navy, 1953-57; research mgr. Gen. Electric Co., Phila., 1957-62; asso. prof. Yale U., 1962-68; prof. dept. aerospace engring. U. Tex., Austin, 1968—, chmn. dept., 1977—, L.B. Meaders prof., 1979—; cons. NASA-Johnson Space Center. Knighted by Queen Juliana of the Netherlands for sci. activities, 1956; recipient Brouwer award in dynamical astronomy, 1978. Fellow AIAA, AAAS: mem. Commn. Celestial Mechanics (pres.), Internat. Astron. Union, Am. Astron. Soc., Author 12 books in field celestial mechanics, 1968—; contbr. numerous sci. articles to profl. jours. Home: 2501 Jarratt Ave Austin TX 78703 Office: Dept Aerospace Engring U Tex Austin TX 78712

SZENAS, JAMES JOSEPH, social service agency adminstr.; b. Leechburg, Pa., Apr. 28, 1930; s. Julius and Mary (Bobak) S.; B.A., U. Conn., 1952; M.S., Trinity U., 1954; postgrad. Bryn Mawr Coll., 1956-57; m. Virginia Nave, Aug. 19, 1955; children—Gregory J., Mark A. Dir. personnel, operations dir. Goodwill Industries, Phila., 1957-60; exec. dir. Goodwill Industries, Tacoma, 1960-66; field services dir. Goodwill Industries of Am., Washington, 1966-68; pres. Goodwill Industries Suncoast, St. Petersburg, Fla., 1968—. Bd. dirs. Pasadena Community Ch., 1971-75; com. chmn. Boy Scouts Am., Pinellas Council, 1972-74. Served with USAF, 1952-56. Named Goodwill Exec. of Year, 1975. Mem. Assn. Rehab. Facilities (past bd. dirs., past pres. Fla. assn.), Nat. Rehab. Assn., Am. Psychol. Assn. Methodist. Elk, Rotarian. Home: 13355 Park Blvd Seminole FL 33542 Office: 10596 Gandy Blvd PO Box 14456 St Petersburg FL 33733

SZYLLER, LEON A., constrn. co. exec.; b. Paris, Oct. 14, 1927; s. Salomon and Anna (Zonenlicht) S.; came to U.S., 1943, naturalized, 1945; B.A., Tulane U., 1962; m., 1950; children—Anna, Marcel, Rene. Tchr., Phila. Pub. Schs., 1950-52; constrn. estimator, New Orleans, 1952-57; pres. L.A.S. Enterprises, New Orleans, 1957—; dir. E. Jefferson Hosp. Served with U.S. Army, 1944-46; ETO. Mem. Home Builders Assn. (dir.), Home Builders Assn. Greater New Orleans (pres.), Nat. Home Improvement Council, Nat. Remodelers

Assn., Better Bus. Bur., C. of C. Office: PO Box 10567 New Orleans LA 70181

TABER, JIM MARTIN, broadcasting co. exec.; b. Austin, Tex., June 29, 1940; s. F. Wally and Mable (Martin) T.; student Denver U., 1958-59, Colo. State U., 1959-60. Announcer, Sta. KOSI, Denver, 1958-59; program dir., announcer Sta. KXXI, Golden, Colo., 1959-60; program and music dir. Sta. WABB, Mobile, Ala., 1960-63, Sta. WSGN, Birmingham, 1963-68; music dir. Sta. KLIF, Dallas, 1968-73; ops., program and music dir. Sta. KROQ, Los Angeles, 1973; pres., gen. mgr. Taber Broadcasting Co., Inc., El Paso, Tex., 1974—. Mem. El Paso Ad Club (dir. 1976-77, recipient Addie award 1975), El Paso C. of C., Tex. Assn. Broadcasters, El Paso Broadcasting Assn., Democrat. Roman Catholic. Clubs: Kiwanis (dir. 1977-78, Outstanding Citizen 1977). Office: Radio Center 5710 Trowbridge St El Paso TX 79925

TACKETT, CHARLES WILLIAM, univ. ofcl.; b. Lexington, Ky., June 11, 1928; s. William and Marie (Farmer) T.; B.S. cum laude (State of Tex. scholar), Sam Houston U., 1972, postgrad. (Alpha Chi scholar), 1972—; m. Betty Lou Greene, June 27, 1954; children—Cheryl K., Charleen K. With Corpus Christi (Tex.) Police Dept., 1950-73, lt. detectives (homicide, robbery), 1963-68, comdr. police, 1968-73; mem. teaching staff Del Mar Coll., 1972-73, Bee County Coll., 1972-73; dir. pub. safety (adminstrn.) Sam Houston State U., Huntsville, Tex., 1973—; mem. spl. study coms. for tng. and edn. in law enforcement. Served with USMCR, 1947-50. Mem. Internat. Assn. Chiefs of Police, Tex., N.Mex. assns. dirs. univ. police, Alpha Kappa Delta. Baptist. Clubs: Masons (32 deg.), Kiwanis, Rotary. Home: 112 Magnolia Way Huntsville TX 77340 Office: Pub Safety Services Sam Houston State U Huntsville TX 77341

TAFFEE, WILLIAM FRANCIS, JR., chem. engr.; b. Calhoun County, Mich., May 22, 1922; s. William Francis and Pearl Louise (Wildt) T.; B.S., Mich. State U., 1948, M.S. in Chem. Engring., 1949; m. Lois Elizabeth Luedders, Feb. 19,1942; children—Kathleen, Patrick, Mary, Beth. With Monsanto Co., Anniston, Ala., 1949—, start up supt., 1964-68, engring. supr., 1968-78, engring. specialist, 1978—; adj. asst. prof. chem. engring. Auburn U. Stage hand, tech. dir., bd. dirs. Anniston Little Theater, 1971—; permanent deacon Roman Catholic Diocese of Birmingham (Ala.), 1975—. Served with USAAC, 1941-45; PTO, CBI. Registered profl. engr., Mo., Ala. Club: K.C. (Ala. treas. 1975-78, sec. 1978-80, state dep. 1980—). Home: 1405 McCall Dr Anniston AL 36201 Office: PO Box 249 Anniston AL 36202

TAHAMI, ALI S., univ. adminstr.; b. Tehran, Iran; October 23, 1949; came to U.S., 1974; s. Hosien and Eran (Mottaghi) T.; M.S. in Operation Research, George Washington U., Washington, 1977; M.S. in Engring. Mgmt., So. Meth. U., 1980. Internal mgr. housing office So. Meth. U., Dallas, 1978—, research asst. dynamic measurement lab., 1978—; lectr. in field. Served with Iranian Army, 1972-74. Mem. Inst. Mgmt. Scis., Am. Inst. Indsl. Engring. Office: PO Box 3272 So Meth U Dallas TX 75275

TAIT, COLUMBUS DOWNING, JR., psychoanalyst, educator; b. Valdosta, Ga., Sept. 3, 1923; s. Columbus Downing and Mary L. (Jacobs) T.; B.A., U. Va., 1943, M.D., 1947; m. Nancy Kirk Reep, Aug. 25, 1956; children—Carl Downing, Jennifer Bradshaw. Intern, Bellevue Hosp., N.Y.C., 1947-48; resident in psychiatry Compton (Cal.) Sanitarium, 1948-49, Rockland (N.Y.) State Hosp., 1950; AEC postdoctoral research fellow in med. scis. Duke, 1949, Yale, 1950; psychoanalytic student Columbia, N.Y.C., 1950, 53-57; practice medicine specializing in psychiatry and psychoanalysis, N.Y.C., 1953-64; instr. Psychoanalytic Clinic, Columbia, 1957-64; asso. prof. psychiatry Emory U. Sch. Medicine, Atlanta, 1964-67; prof. 1967-77, part-time prof., 1977—; dir. research Ga. Mental Health Inst., 1965-71; part-time practice psychoanalysis; geog. tng. psychoanalyst. Research and cons. psychiatrist Washington Youth Council, 1954-61, Mblzn. for Youth, N.Y.C., 1962-64. Served to lt., M.C., USNR, 1951-53. Diplomate Am. Bd. Psychiatry and Neurology. Fellow Am. Psychiat. Assn. (com. on history of psychiatry 1969-76); mem. Am., Internat. psychoanalytic assns., AMA, AAAS, Ga., Atlanta med. socs., Phi Beta Kappa, Alpha Omega Alpha. Author: (with Hodges) Delinquents, Their Families, and the Community, 1962. Contbr. articles to profl. jours. Home: 820 Douglas Rd NE Atlanta GA 30342 Office: Lenox Towers 3400 Peachtree Rd NE Atlanta GA 30326

TAJ, KOKAB, home economist, educator; b. Pakistan, Jan. 2, 1945; d. Din and Sardar Saytth T.; came to U.S., 1957, naturalized, 1960; B.S. in Home Econs., Punjab U., Pakistan, Ed.B., 1962, M.S., 1963; Ph.D. in Home Econs. Edn., So. Ill. U., 1969. Lectr., Coll. Home Econs., Lahore, Pakistan, 1963-67; grad. fellow and asst. So. Ill. U., Carbondale, 1967-69; asst. prof. Southwest Mo. State Coll., Springfield, 1969-70; asso. prof. So. U., Baton Rouge, 1970—, dir. Internat. Population Studies Center, 1973—; guest speaker various secondary schs. and women's clubs in Ill. and Mo., 1969—; lectr. radio programs, 1950-67. Future Homemakers Am. fellow, 1969; Fulbright Hays Travel grantee, 1967. Mem. Am. Home Econs. Assn., Am. Population Assn., Am. Fertility Soc., Internat. Fedn. Home Econs., WHO, World Med. Assn., Internat. Univ. Women Fedn., Smithsonian Inst., Internat. Alliance Women U.K. Author: (text in Urdu) Home Economics for Intermediate Classes, 1967, Home Economics for BA Classes, 1967; Family Life Federal Research, 1976; contbr. articles on home econs. to publs. in Pakistan and U.S. Office: Dept Home Economics Southern Univ Baton Rouge LA 70813

TALBERT, ROY, JR., coll. adminstr.; b. Cheraw, S.C., Aug. 1, 1943; s. Roy and Betty Jean (Harper) T.; B.A. (Furman Scholar), Furman U., 1965; M.A. (NDEA fellow), Vanderbilt U., 1967, Ph.D., 1971; m. Linda Diane Thompson, Aug. 1, 1975; children—Matthew, Rebecca Anne. Sr. teaching fellow Vanderbilt U., Nashville, 1967-70; asst. prof. history Ferrum (Va.) Coll., 1974-76, dir. curriculum and programs, 1976-79; vice chancellor, dean acad. affairs Coastal Carolina Coll. of U. S.C., Conway, 1979—; producer, host The Public Eye, TV show, 1978-79; project dir. numerous film, TV and pub. programming projects for community and civic groups, 1975-79. Served to capt. U.S. Army, 1970-72. Mem. So. Hist. Assn., Horry County Hist. Soc. Baptist. Author: (with Rex Stephenson) Too Free for Me, 1979; editor: Studies in the Local History of Slavery, 1978. Home: Route 6 Box 120 Conway SC 29526 Office: Coastal Carolina Coll Conway SC 29526

TALBOT, GWENDOLYN EDITH, speech and lang. pathologist; b. Lowell, Mass., Oct. 6, 1946; d. Charles Robert II and Eleanor Marion (Morse) T.; B.A., U. Ariz., 1969, M.A. (Office Edn. grantee), 1971; postgrad. Pima Coll., 1971. Speech-lang. clinician Flowing Wells Public Sch. Dist., Tucson, 1969; speech-lang. pathologist with diagnostic team for HEW, Childrens Evaluation Center, Tucson, 1971-73; chief speech-lang. pathologist Blue Ridge Speech and Hearing Center, Inc., Manassas and Leesburg, Va., 1973-75; pres., speech-lang. pathologist Speech Pathology Cons. Services, P.C., Manassas, 1976—; founder, pres. Chronic Pain Outreach, 1976—; cons. speech-lang. pathologist Prince William Hosp., Manassas, 1973—, Potomac Hosp., Woodbridge, Va., 1974—, Prince William County Health Dept., 1976—; chief exec. officer, incorporator Rehab. Day Centers, Inc., 1980—; participant White House Conf. for Handicapped Individuals, 1977. Instr. CPR, ARC, 1977—; emergency med. technician, 1971—; mem. Prince William County child abuse steering com., 1976-78; bd. dirs. Manassas Area Assn. Retarded Citizens, 1976-79, Manassas Park spl. edn. adv. com., 1977—; chpt. head Nat. Jr. Tennis League, 1976-77; pres. Wheelchair Sports Devel. Programs for No. Va., 1979; speech pathologist for New Voice Club of Am. Cancer Soc., 1973-77, bd. dirs., 1975—. Recipient Disting. Service commendation Tucson-Pima County CD Commn. for search and rescue ops., 1973; lic. speech pathologist, Va. Mem. Am. Speech, Lang. and Hearing Assn. (cert. clin. competence), Speech and Hearing Assn. Va., Internat. Assn. Logopedics and Phoniatrics (conf. participant 1980), DAR, Sigma Alpha Eta. Methodist. Clubs: Soroptimist Internat., Jr. Woman's (Manassas). Contbr. to The Politics of Pain, 1978. Home and Office: 8222 Wycliffe Ct Manassas VA 22110

TALBOTT, FRANK, III, lawyer; b. Danville, Va., Mar. 26, 1929; s. Frank and Margaret (Jordan) T.; B.A., U. Va., 1951, LL.B., 1953; m. Mary Beverley Chewning, July 11, 1952; children—Beverley, Frank IV. Admitted to Va. bar, 1952; gen. practice law, Danville, 1956-66; with Dan River Inc., 1966-76, v.p., gen. counsel, 1968-76; partner firm Clement, Wheatley, Winston, Talbott & Majors, Danville, 1976-78; individual practice law, Danville, 1979—; dir. Danville region First & Mchts. Nat. Bank. Vice chmn. Danville Sch. Bd., 1964-70; sec. Danville Democratic Com., 1962-63; trustee U. Va. Student Aid Found., 1963-68; bd. dirs. United Fund Danville, 1959-63; bd. mgrs. U. Va. Alumni Assn., 1971-73. Served with AUS, 1953-56. Decorated Commendation medal. Mem. Am., Va. (v.p. 1965-66, exec. com. 1967-70), Danville (pres. 1965-66) bar assns., Am. Judicature Soc., Newcomen Soc., Delta Psi, Phi Alpha Delta. Methodist. Clubs: Golf, German (Danville). Home: 420 Maple Lane Danville VA 24541 Office: 621 Masonic Bldg Danville VA 24541

TALBOTT, IRVIN DURWARD, JR., coll. adminstr.; b. Elkins, W.Va., Aug. 27, 1942; s. Irvin D. and Jean Elizabeth (Kittle) T.; B.A., W.Va. U., 1964, M.A., 1971, M.S., 1977, Ph.D., 1976; m. Linda Carol Gibson, May 29, 1971; children—Amanda Carol, Jason Matthew. Vol., Peace Corps, Somali Republic, 1964-66; instr. history W.Va. U., 1973-77; dir. community devel. and research center Glenville (W.Va.) State Coll., 1977-78, dir. office resource devel., 1978—. Mem. project dirs. council W.Va. Elderhostel; bd. dirs. Gilmer County Med. Center, 1977—; pres. adv. council Region VII Area Agy. on Aging, 1978-80; v.p. Gilmer County Recreation Council, 1978—. Served with AUS, 1967-69. Decorated Bronze Star; W.Va. U. Found. overseas research grantee, 1974; Overseas Conf. Found. grantee, 1975. Mem. Am. Hist. Assn., W.Va. Hist. Soc., Agrl. History Soc., W.Va. Continuing Edn. and Community Service Assn. Democrat. Baptist. Home: 915 Mineral Rd Glenville WV 26351 Office: Glenville State Coll Glenville

TALIAFERRO, WILLIAM, educator; b. Arlington, Ga., Aug. 16, 1933; s. Ben Seaborn and Willie Mae (Sasser) T.; A.A., Chipola Jr. Coll., 1951; B.A., U. Fla., 1953; M.S., Fla. State U., 1968; Ed.D., U. Houston, 1979; m. Pamela Sue Bryen, Nov. 23, 1973; children—Beth, Dan, Rosemarie, Ben. Commd. 2d lt., U.S. Air Force, 1953, advanced through grades to col., 1969, ret., 1975; prof. polit. sci. and history Alvin (Tex.) Community Coll., 1976—. Decorated D.F.C., Air medal, Air Force Commendation medal. Recipient Arnold Air Soc. Gold medal, 19—. Mem. Am. Edn. Research Assn., Tex. Jr. Coll. Tchrs. Assn., Alvin Community Coll. Tchrs. Assn. Baptist. Clubs: Kiwanis, Masons. Contbr. articles in field to profl. jours. Home: 227 W Castle Harbour Friendswood TX 77546 Office: 3110 Mustang Rd Alvin TX 77511

TALKINGTON, THOMAS WALTON, JR., orthopedic surgeon; b. Bogalusa, La., June 28, 1922; s. Thomas Walton and Dora Geneva (Clement) T.; B.S., Miss. Coll., 1943; postgrad. U. Miss., 1945; M.D., Tulane U., 1947; m. Gloria McGee, July 4, 1949; children—Thomas William, James McGee. Gen. practice medicine, Waterproof, La., 1948-50, Natchez, Miss., 1952-63; resident in orthopedic surgery Jackson, Miss., 1963-66; practice medicine, specializing in orthopedic surgery, Jackson, Miss., 1966—; pres. Talkington & Wilder, Orthopedics, Jackson, 1969—; staff, Hinds Gen. Hosp., Jackson. Served to lt., M.C., USNR, 1950-52. Diplomate Am. Bd. Orthopedic Surgery. Fellow Am. Acad. Orthopedic Surgeons; mem. Am., Miss. med. assns., Central Med. Soc., So. Med. Assn., Miss. Orthopedic Soc. Home: 370 Elms Ct Circle Jackson MS 39204 Office: 1814 Hospital Dr Jackson MS 39204

TALLENT, ROBERT LEE, pharmacist; b. Monroe County, Tenn., July 31, 1938; s. Robert F. and Sue Lee (Leslie) T.; B.S. in Pharmacy, Samford U., 1962; m. Kay Sexton, Aug. 28, 1960; children—Michael Keith, Rodney Lee, Robert Stanton. Dir. pharmacy Epperson Hosp., 1962-66, dir. pharmacy Tallent Drug Co., Jefferson City, Tenn., 1966-72, Athens (Tenn.) Community Hosp., 1972—. Mem. Monroe County Bd. Health. Mem. Tenn. Soc. Hosp. Pharmacists, Am. Soc. Hosp. Pharmacists. Republican. Baptist. Clubs: Jaycees, Masons, Shriners. Office: Athens Community Hosp Box 250 Athens TN 37303

TALLEY, CLARENCE, artist; b. Pineville, La., June 12, 1951; s. Albert and Susie (Edmond) T.; B.A., So. U., 1973; M.F.A., La. State U., 1975; m. Carolyn Ann Westley, Nov. 18, 1972. Mem. part-time faculty So. U., 1974; asst. prof. art Prairie View (Tex.) A&M U., 1975; one-man exhbns. include Sutton Gallery, Houston, 1978, Prairie View A&M U., 1979, O'Kane Gallery, U. Houston, 1980; group shows include: Huntsville (Ala.) Mus. Art, 1979, Wash. State U., 1978, Art League of Houston, 1977, 78, 79, HUD Office, Houston, 1979, U.S. Dept. Health, Nassau Bay, Tex., 1980; lectr. regional aspects of art; participant Caribbean-Am. Exchange Program, 1979. Mem. Nat. Conf. Artists, Coll. Art Assn., Tex. Fine Art Assn., Houston Watercolor Soc. Democrat. Baptist. Address: PO Box 2134 Prairie View TX 77445

TALLEY, WILLIAM GILES, JR., container mfg. co. exec.; b. Adel, Ga., Sept. 25, 1939; s. William Giles and Mary (McGlamry) T.; B.S. in Bus. Adminstrn., U. S.C., 1961; m. Jacqueline Vickery, Apr. 14, 1962; children—William Giles III, John Lindsey, Bronwyn Ashley. Mgmt. trainee Talley Veneer & Crate Co., Inc., Adel, 1961-62, plant mgr., salesman, Waynesboro, Ga., 1965-67; with Talley's Box Co., Leesburg, Fla., 1962-65, plant mgr., 1967-69; partner, gen. mgr. Growers Container Cooperative, Inc., Leesburg, 1969—; dir. First Nat. Bank Leesburg. Bd. dirs. Leesburg Hosp. Assn. Served with USAAF, 1961. Mem. Fla. Forestry Assn. (dist. v.p. 1980, dir. 1978—), Leesburg C. of C. (dir.), Sigma Alpha Epsilon. Democrat. Methodist. Clubs: Elks, Kiwanis. Home: Lake Griffin Leesburg FL 32748 Office: PO Box 817 Leesburg FL 32748

TALLEY, WILLIAM WOODROW, II, energy mgmt. cons., resource analyst; b. Hobart, Okla., Aug. 17, 1942; s. William Woodrow and Jacquita Elizabeth (Surber) T.; B.S. in Chem. Engring., U. Okla., 1964, M.S., 1971, M.S. in Nuclear Engring., 1971, Ph.D. in Nuclear and Chem. Engring., 1973; m. Sandra Jean Smith, Sept. 12, 1964; children—Kimberly Veda Michelle, Britani Suzanne. Chem. engr. Continental Oil Co., Ponca City, Okla., 1963-64; with Coll. of Engring., U. Okla., 1970-73; exec. dir. Okla. Energy Advisory Council, Oklahoma City, 1973-74; asst. to dir. Fossil Fuel and Advanced Systems, Electric Power Research Inst., Palo Alto, Calif., 1974; asso. Resource Analysis and Mgmt. Group, 1974-75; chmn. Okla. Gov.'s Adv. Council on Energy, Oklahoma City, 1975-79; pres., chief exec. officer William W. Talley II, Inc., Oklahoma City, 1976—; mng. partner Resource Analysis and Mgmt. Group, 1976—; pvt. practice cons. energy mgmt. and fuels tech., 1969-74. Vice-chmn. Okla City C. of C. Energy Council, 1975-79; bd. dirs. Allied Arts Found., 1977—; bd. dirs. Frontiers of Sci. Found., 1977—, Okla. Symphony Orch., 1978—; commr. parks and recreation Norman (Okla.). Served as nuclear submarine officer USN, 1964-69. Mem. Am. Nuclear Soc. (founding mem. process heat application com.). Author: Energy in Oklahoma, 1974; Industrial Development in Oklahoma, 1974; Enhanced Recovery Alternatives, 1975; Oklahoma Energy Facts, 1977; numerous others; author energy mgmt. model MANERGY, 1973. Office: 2500 1st National Center 120 N Robinson St Oklahoma City OK 73102

TALLMAN, CLIFFORD WAYNE, supt. schs.; b. Columbus, Ohio, June 13, 1932; s. Frank Albert and Ella Louise (Ott) T.; B.S., Capital U., 1954; M.A., Ohio State U., 1960; postgrad. U. Alaska, 1956, Ohio State U., 1957-60, Bowling Green State U., 1961-65, U. Toledo, 1962, Kent State U., 1968-75, Akron U., 1971-72, Cleve. State U., 1973; m. Ruth Anne Fletcher, Apr. 6, 1958; children—Martin Wayne, David Edwin, Kathryn Anne. Tchr., Grove City (Ohio) High Sch., 1954-56; adminstr.-tchr. Southwestern City Schs., Grove City, 1956-60; supt. Scipio-Republic (Ohio) Schs., 1960-63; supt. Columbus Grove (Ohio) Schs., 1963-65; supt. Jackson Local Schs., Massillon, Ohio, 1965-73; supt. Brecksville (Ohio) city schs., 1973-78, Kenton County (Ky.) Schs., 1978—. Cons. AMA Conv. on Schs., Physicians, 1963; athletic dir. Seneca County; chmn. Seneca County Health Com., 1960-63; bd. dirs. YMCA, Cuyahoga Spl. Edn. Bd., No. Ky. Transp. Authority, Eastern Ky. Devel. Center; chmn. Ohio Right to Read program, 1970-73. Served with U.S. Army, 1954-56, USNR, 1950-54. I.D.E.A. fellow, 1969; F.E.E. fellow, 1971. Mem. Am., Ky., Kenton County, Buckeye assns. sch. adminstrs., NEA, Ohio Edn. Assn., Ohio Historic Assn., Central, Ohio (pres.) tchrs. assns., Cuyahoga County Supts. Assn., Phi Delta Kappa, Ben Hur. Lutheran. Lion. Home: 570 Erlangen Erlangen KY 41018 Office: 5535 Madison Pike Ind KY 41051

TALMADGE, HERMAN E(UGENE), U.S. senator; b. McRae, Ga., Aug. 9, 1913; s. Eugene and Mattie Thurmond (Peterson) T.; grad. Druid Hills Sch., Atlanta, 1931; LL.B., U. Ga., 1936; student Midshipman's Sch., Northwestern U., 1942; m. Leila Elizabeth Shingler, Dec. 24, 1941 (div.); children—Herman Eugene, Robert Shingler (dec.). Admitted to Ga. bar, 1936; practiced with father, Atlanta, 1936-41, 45-48; gov. Ga., 1948-55; gen. practice law, Atlanta, 1955-57; U.S. senator, 1957—. Served with USN, 1941-45; commd. ensign and advanced through grades to lt. comdr.; participated in invasion of Guadalcanal aboard U.S.S. Tryon; served as flag sec. to comdt. of Naval Forces at New Zealand, June 1943-Apr. 1944; exec. officer U.S.S. Dauphin, participated in engagements with Japanese Fleet and in Battle of Okinawa; entered Tokyo Bay, V-J Day. Mem. Navy League, Am. Legion, V.F.W., S.C.V., S.A.R., Am., Ga., Atlanta bar assns., Farm Bur., Sigma Nu, Sigma Delta Kappa, Sphinx. Democrat. Baptist. Mason (Shriner), Elk. Club: Touchdown (Athens, Ga.). Author: You and Segregation. Office: 109 Russell Senate Office Bldg Washington DC 20510*

TAM, THOMAS YIU-TAI, chem. engr.; b. Hong Kong, Dec. 20, 1946; came to U.S., 1969, naturalized, 1977; s. Chi and Wei (Yung) T.; M.S., Ohio U., 1971, Ph.D., 1975; m. Nancy Gouw, Sept. 8, 1973; 1 son, Michael W. H. Teaching and research asst. Ohio U., Athens, 1970-75; engr. III in advance tech. Fiber Div., Allied Chem. Corp., Petersburg, Va., 1975-76, engr. operation-tech., 1976—. Treas., Richmond (Va.) Cinens Congregation, 1978-79. Clipinger fellow, 1973. Mem. Soc. Plastic Engrs. Christian Ch. Contbr. articles to profl. jours.; patentee in field. Home: 3918 Harvette Dr Richmond VA 23234 Office: PO Box 31 Petersburg VA 23803

TAMBONE, PETER JOHN, mktg. firm exec.; b. N.Y.C., June 24, 1938; s. Vito A. and Clara (Riccardi) T.; student Cooper Union, 1958; m. Barbara Gail Yadeska, Feb. 1, 1968; children—Adam, Brian. Account exec. Wunderman, Ricotta & Kline, N.Y.C., 1964-66; account supr. firm Rapp & Collins, N.Y.C., 1966-69; v.p. Jamian Advt. Inc., N.Y.C., 1969-70; pres. firm Campbell Advt. Inc., N.Y.C., 1974-75; v.p. Downe Communications Inc., 1973—; pres. Greenland Studios, Inc., 1974—, Tambone Direct Mktg., Inc., 1975—, G.L.S. Communications, Inc., 1976—; exec. v.p. Natural Interiors, Inc. Mem. Direct Mail Advt. Assn., Direct Mail Writers Club, Assn. Third Class Mailers, Parcel Post Assn. Home: 6579 Racquet Club Dr Fort Lauderdale FL 33319 Office: 1200 Sterling Rd Dania FL 33004 also 1345 Ave of Americas New York NY 10019

TAN, BILLY TOO SENG, accountant; b. Johor Bahru, Johor, Malaysia, July 22, 1954; s. Hong Saw and Siew Heuw (Khoo) T.; B.S. in Acctg. (211D fellow), So. U., 1974; M.B.A., La. State U., 1979. Salesman, Orchard Motor Ltd., Johor Bahru, Johor, Malaysia, 1972-74; maintenance clk. East State Rental Co., Baton Rouge, 1974-78, mgr., 1979—; acct. Harriss and Harrisson Ltd., C.P.A.'s, Baton Rouge, 1975—; fin. cons.; instr. So. U., Baton Rouge. Recipient Gold award Southwestern Co. of Tenn., 1974, Tough Minded Bus. award, 1974. Home: 3238 Carlotta St Baton Rouge LA 70802

TAN, KIM-HOCK, biochemistry; b. Java, Indonesia, Dec. 4, 1939; came to U.S., 1970, naturalized, 1979; s. Ah-Choo and Soh-Goh Tan; B.S., Nanyang U., 1964; M.S., U. Minn., 1970; Ph.D., Loyola U., Chgo., 1974; m. Chio-Hoon, Dec. 28, 1968; children—Timothy C.S., Joshua C.W., John. Instr., Nanyang U., 1964-65; postdoctoral fellow U. Chgo., 1973-74; NIH postdoctoral trainee M.I.T., 1974-77; asst. prof. biochemistry Winston-Salem (N.C.) State U., 1977-80, asso. prof., 1980—. NIH grantee, 1977—. Mem. Am. Chem. Soc., N.Y. Acad. Scis., Sigma Xi. Baptist. Contbr. articles to profl. jours. Home: 1587 Northwest Blvd Winston-Salem NC 27104 Office: Biology Dept Winston-Salem State Univ Winston-Salem NC 27102

TANDY, MICHAEL JON, banker; b. Colchester, Ill., Oct. 18, 1941; s. Chester Eugene and Valda Nellie (Taylor) T.; B.S., E. Tex. Baptist Coll., 1964; B.B.A., Tex. Wesleyan U., 1966; m. Nelda Jane Martin, July 30, 1965; children—Jon Andrew, Jennifer Lynn, Jason Michael. Tchr., Los Fresnos (Tex.) schs., 1964-65; asst. v.p. mktg. Central Security Life Ins. Co., Ft. Worth, 1965-67; agt. Conn. Gen. Life Ins. Co., Ft. Worth, 1967-70; sales rep. Minn. Mining & Mfg. Co., Dallas, 1970-72; mgr. Hertz Truck Rental, Dallas, 1972-73; trust officer Continental Nat. Bank, Ft. Worth, 1973-76; v.p., mgr. trust dept. Tex. Bank & Trust Co., Sweetwater, 1976—. Bd. dirs. Ft. Worth Opera Soc., 1974-76; adv. dir. Ft. Worth Salvation Army, 1975-76; pres. Sweetwater Humane Soc., 1976-80; co-chmn. Nolan County United Way, 1977-78, chmn., 1978-79. Mem. Am. Inst. Banking, Bank Adminstrn. Inst., Tex. Bankers Assn. Republican. So. Bapit. Club: Rotary. Home: 1403 Stanley St Sweetwater TX 79556 Office: PO Box 630 Sweetwater TX 79556

TANNEBAUM, SAMUEL HUGO, certified pub. accountant; b. Oklahoma City, Aug. 15, 1933; s. Simon L. and Eva (Kapp) T.; B.B.A. with spl. distinction, U. Okla., 1955; m. Nita Mae Levy, June 12, 1955; children—Lori L., Marilyn J. Staff accountant Alford, Meroney & Co., Dallas, 1955-61 pvt. practice accounting, Dallas, 1961-63; partner Tannebaum & Bindler, C.P.A.'s, Dallas, 1963-67; mng.

partner Tannebaum, Bindler & Lewis, C.P.A.'s, Dallas, 1967-80, Tannebaum, Bindler & Co., C.P.A.'s, Dallas, 1980—. Bd. dirs. Dallas Home and Hosp. for Jewish Aged, 1973-76; trustee Temple Emanu-El, Dallas, 1976—. Named C.P.A. of Year, Dallas chpt. Tex. Soc. C.P.A.'s, 1976; C.P.A., Tex. Mem. Am. Inst. C.P.A.'s (council), Tex. Soc. C.P.A.'s (dir., past v.p., past chpt. pres.), Nat. Assn. Estate Planning Councils (dir. 1978—), Dallas Estate Planning Council (past pres.). Club: Lancers. Home: 5820 Meletio Ln Dallas TX 75230 Office: 300 Metropolitan Savings Bldg Dallas TX 75202

TANNEHILL, JOHN FRANKLIN, physician; b. Hattiesburg, Miss., Aug. 11, 1938; s. Antone Walter and Marjorie (Wyman) T.; B.A., Vanderbilt U., 1960; M.D., Tulane U., 1964; m. Suzanne Haley, July 3, 1965; children—John Franklin, Brett, Wyman. Intern, Charity Hosp., New Orleans, 1964-65; resident in internal medicine Tulane U., New Orleans, 1968-69, resident in gen. surgery, 1969-70, resident in otorhinolaryngology, 1970-73; fellow in head and neck surgery U. Cin., 1973-74; mem. staff Ochsner Clinic, New Orleans, 1974-76; practice medicine specializing in otorhinolaryngology and maxillo facial surgery, Waynesville, N.C., 1976—; mem. staff Hagwood County Hosp.; asst. clin. prof. Tulane U. Sch. Medicine, 1974-76. Served in USAF, 1965-68. NIH grantee, 1963. Mem. AMA, Acad. of Otorhinolaryngology, So. Med. Assn., N.C., Haywood County med. socs. Methodist. Club: Rotary. Home: 107 Glendale Dr Waynesville NC 28786 Office: 120 Hospital Dr Clyde NC 28721

TANNER, BILLY CHARLES, real estate and holding co. exec.; b. Hartselle, Ala., July 27, 1935; s. Orville Wright and Mabel Nettie (Landers) T.; B.S., U. Ala., 1958; m. Frances Leah Puckett, Jan. 26, 1961; children—Terry Charles, Billy Renea. Developer, builder homes and shopping centers Circle T Devel. Inc., Hartselle, 1959—; builder Han-O-Way Markets, chain convenience stores, 1964—; pres. Tanner Cos., holding co., Hartselle, 1975—, The Gen. Stores, 1979—. Coordinator North Ala. for Gov. George Wallace, 1964-68. Served with AUS, 1957-58. Mem. Commerce Execs. Soc. of U. Ala. Baptist. Clubs: Masons, Rotary (pres. 1979). Home: 303 Crescent Dr Hartselle AL 35640 Office: Tanner Heights Plaza Hartselle AL 35640

TANNER, GLORIA ANN, nurse, educator; b. Macon, Ga., Dec. 18, 1931; d. Hillman Bennett and Gladys Corinne (McKinney) T.; Ed.D., Teachers Coll. Columbia (N.Y.) U., 1974. Instr. sch. nursing Savannah, Ga., and Atlanta, 1956-71; asst., prof., asso. prof. coll. of nursing Clemson (S.C.) U., 1974-77, asst. to dean for research devel., 1977-79, dir. nursing research, 1979—, univ. faculty research grantee, 1978-79; So. Regional Edn. Bd. Com., Demonstration Project in Grad. Edn. Active Hypertension Screening in Clemson. Mem. Am. Nurses Assn. and Council of Nurse Researchers, Nat. League for Nursing, AAUP, Am. Heart Assn., S.C. Heart Assn. (nursing edn. com.), S.C. Nurses Assn. Continuing Edn. and Recognition program com.). Club: Clemson U. Faculty. Contbr. article in field to profl. publ. Office: Clemson University College of Nursing Room 536 College of Nursing Bldg Clemson SC 29631

TANNER, JOHN PAUL, electronics co. exec.; b. Cleve., Sept. 22, 1927; s. William and Lucille (McKenney) T.; B.B.A., U. Miami, 1951, B.S. in Indsl. Engring., 1954; M.B.A., Rollins Coll., 1966; m. Mary Magdalen Johnson, Nov. 6, 1948; children—Timothy, Thomas, Christina, John, Roy, William, Joseph, Julia, Daniel, David, Mary Ellen. Engr., Chemstrand Corp., Pensacola, Fla., then sr. engr. Bendix Corp., South Bend, Ind., 1951-58; supr. prodn. engring. Radiation Inc., Melbourne, Fla., 1958-64; chief plans and programs LTV Aerospace Corp., Kennedy Space Center, Fla., 1964-67; dir. indsl. and prodn. engring. Electronic Communications Inc., St. Petersburg, Fla., 1967-74; mgr. mfg. engring. Scott Electronics Corp., Orlando, Fla., 1974-76, McDonnell Douglas Astronautics Co., Titusville, Fla., 1976-78; dir. mfg. Applied Devices Corp., Kissimmee, Fla., 1978—; pres. John P. Tanner & Assos., cons. engrs., Orlando, Fla., 1969—; lectr. engring. tech. St. Petersburg Jr. Coll., 1968-70, Valencia Community Coll., 1973-75; adj. prof. U. Central Fla., 1975—. Served to lt. USNR, 1951-53; Korea. Registered profl. engr., Fla., Ga. Mem. Am. Inst. Indsl. Engrs. (sr.). Democrat. Roman Catholic. Home: 1410 Pinar Dr Orlando FL 32807 Office: 2931 N Poinciana Blvd Kissimmee FL 32741

TANNER, PAUL FRANCIS, clergyman; b. Peoria, Ill., Jan. 15, 1905; s. Frank John and Laura (McGowan) T.; A.B., St. Francis (Wis.) Sem., 1930, A.M., 1931, S.T.B., 1931; student Marquette U., 1923-25, 33-36, Kenrick Sem., St. Louis, 1925-27. Ordained priest Roman Catholic Ch., 1931; sec. Cath. Action, also dir. Confrat. Christian Doctrine, and dir. Cath. Youth activities Archdiocese Milw.; asst. dir. youth dept. 1940-42, dir., 1942-45, asst. gen. sec. N.C.W.C., 1945-58, gen. sec., 1958-68; bishop, St. Augustine, Fla., 1968-79; ret., 1979; apptd. Papal Chamberlain, 1948; domestic prelate, 1954; consecrated Titular Bishop Lamasba, 1965. Author: (with Dr. Edward Fitzpatrick) Methods of Teaching Religion in Elementary Schools, 1939. Editor: Catholic Action, 1943-53. Home: 881 Ocean Dr Apt 27C Key Biscayne FL 33149

TANNER, TERRELL BENSON, physician; b. nr. Clermont, Ga., July 25, 1932; s. Fred Homer and Alice (Haynes) T.; grad. Emory Jr. Coll., 1951; B.A., U.S. Naval Sch. Aerospace Medicine, 1953, M.D., 1959; m. Jane Davidson, 1954 (dec. 1967); children—William Davidson, Sarah Rogers; m. 2d, Martha Cash, Apr. 11, 1969; children—Robert Benson, John Cash. Intern. U.S. Naval Hosp., Pensacola, Fla., 1959-60; resident U.S. Naval Sch. Aerospace Medicine, 1960-61; practice medicine specializing in family practice, Hartwell, Ga., 1964-69, Gatlinburg, Tenn., 1969-75, Oxford, Ga., 1975—; mem. staff Anderson (S.C.) Meml. Hosp., 1964-69; chief staff Hart County Hosp., 1967-69; mem. med. staff Sevier County (Tenn.) Hosp.; vice chief staff Newton County (Ga.) Hosp., 1979; coll. physician Oxford Coll. of Emory U., 1975—. Sec. Hart County (Ga.) Republican Party, 1967-68; speaker E. Tenn. Heart Assn., 1973-74; bd. dirs. Gatlinburg Community Chest. Served with USN, 1958-64. Fellow Am. Acad. Family Physicians (charter); mem. Royal Soc. Health (London), Ga. Acad. Gen. Practice (dir. 1964-67), Omicron Delta Kappa, Phi Chi. Home: Historic Alexander Means Home 1008 Emory St Oxford GA 30267 Office: 110 Clarke St PO Box 68 Oxford GA 30267

TANNER, WALTER RHETT, lawyer; b. Athens, Ga., May 16, 1938; s. John Bryson and Walterette (Arwood) T.; A.B. cum laude, U. Ga., 1960, J.D. cum laude, 1962; m. Carolyn Laverne Watson, Nov. 11, 1967; 1 son, Walter Rhett. Admitted to Ga. bar, 1961; asso. firm Hansell, Post, Brandon & Dorsey, Atlanta, 1962-66, partner, 1966—. Mem. bd. sponsors Atlanta Symphony Orch., 1975—, mem. exec. com., 1977—, v.p., 1978—, chmn. maj. gifts campaign, 1980—; mem. Leadership Atlanta, 1979-80. Served to lt. USNR Res., 1964-72. Mem. Atlanta, Am. bar assns., State Bar Ga. (vice-chmn. bar and media com. 1979-80), U. Ga. Alumni (pres. chpt. 1973-74, chmn. Atlanta/Met. council 1975, mem. state bd. mgrs., v.p. 1976—), Atlanta Lawyers Club, Gridiron, Phi Beta Kappa, Omicron Delta Kappa, Phi Kappa Phi, Phi Delta Phi, Delta Tau Delta. Club: Capital City. Office: 3300 First Nat Bank Tower Atlanta GA 30303

TANNOUS, AFIF, social scientist, former govt. ofcl., cons. rural devel.; b. Lebanon, Sept. 25, 1905; came to U.S., 1937, naturalized, 1943; s. Ishak I. and Theodora (Yazbik) T.; B.A., Am. U. of Beirut (Lebanon), 1929; M.A., St. Lawrence U., 1938; Ph.D., Cornell U., 1940; m. Josephine S. Milkey, Sept. 16, 1941; children—David, Paul. Tchr., American High Sch., Tripoli, Lebanon, 1923-25; adminstrv. ofcl. Sudan Govt., 1929-31; leader rural devel. work in Palestine, Lebanon, Syria, 1931-37; tchr. Am. U. of Beirut, 1933-37; teaching fellow St. Lawrence U., Canton, N.Y., 1937-38, Cornell U., Ithaca, N.Y., 1938-40; mem. faculty sociology dept. U. Minn., 1940-43; Middle East regional specialist Office Fgn. Agrl. Relations, U.S. Dept. Agr., 1943-51; lectr. agrl. economy and social orgn. of Middle East, Sch. of Advanced Internat. Studies, Washington, 1948-51; dep. dir. U.S. Ops. Mission to Lebanon, 1951-54; liaison for U.S. Dept. Agr. with ICA and chief Africa and Middle East Analysis br. Fgn. Agrl. Service, Washington, 1954-61, area officer Africa and Middle East, 1961-71, ret., 1971; lectr. on Middle East affairs to profl. orgns. and civic groups, 1940-71; cons., bd. dirs. Internat. Center for Dynamics of Devel., Arlington, Va., 1971—; dep. dir. U.S. Agr. Exhibit, Cairo, 1960; cons. on food prodn. project in Morocco, Tunisia and Sudan, AID, 1974; mem. U.S. Dept. Agr. team for Egypt, 1975; adv. editor Middle East Jour., 1947—; mem. FAO Mission to Greece, 1946, U.S. Agrl. Mission to Middle East, 1946, UN Econ. Survey Mission to Middle East, 1949, U.S. Tech. Task Force to Egypt to organize Egyptian-Am. Rural Devel. Service, 1953, U.S. govt. team to survey wheat relief needs in Tunisia, 1956. Mem. Am. Sociol. Assn., Rural Sociol. Soc., Am. Acad. Polit. and Social Sci., Soc. Applied Anthropology, Middle East Inst., AAAS, Sigma Xi. Contbr. numerous articles on Middle East affairs to profl. publs., including Science, Am. Scientist, The Humanist, also chpts. to books.

TANONA, CHARLES CARROLL, chem. engr.; b. Worcester, Mass., Nov. 20, 1922; s. Michael and Josephine Mary (Klewiec) T.; B.S., Worcester Poly. Inst., 1944, M.S., 1948. With Union Carbide Corp., South Charleston, W.Va., 1948—, project mgr., 1977—. Served with USAAF, 1943-46. Registered profl. engr., Tex., W.Va., Calif. Mem. Am. Chem. Soc., Am. Inst. Chem. Engrs., ASME (power test code com. 25, 1971-78), Nat. Fire Protection Assn. (com. on storage flammable liquids 1972-75). Patentee in field. Home: 1330 Kanawha Blvd E Charleston WV 25301 Office: PO Box 8361 South Charleston WV 25303

TANOUS, HELENE MARY, physician; b. Zanesville, Ohio, Oct. 22, 1939; d. Joseph Carrington and Rose Marie (Mokarzel) Tanous; B.A., Marymount Coll., 1961; M.D., U. Tex., 1967; m. James A. Bell. Intern County Hosp., Los Angeles, 1967-68; resident in radiology U. So. Calif. Hosp., Los Angeles, 1969-71; instr. radiology U. So. Calif. Med. Sch., Los Angeles, 1971-72; practice medicine specializing in radiology, Los Angeles, 1972-73; asst. prof. diagnostic radiology Baylor Med. Sch., Houston, 1973—; dir. med. student elective in diagnostic radiology Ben Taub Hosp., Houston, 1973-75, chief radiologist Diagnostic Clinic, 1975-79; practice radiology, Tampa, Fla., 1979—. Founder, pres. Children's Advocates, Inc. Diplomate Am. Bd. Radiology. Mem. Am. Med. Women's Assn. (del. to Internat. Med. Women's Assn., Paris), Pinellas County Med. Soc., W. Coast Radiology Soc., Am. Trauma Soc. Office: 3000 Medical Park Dr Suite 101 Tampa FL 33612

TANT, EMMA JEAN, marriage and family therapist; b. Miami, Fla., Dec. 21, 1928; d. Roy Hamilton and Clara Agnes (Thomason) Green; B.S., Auburn U., 1950; M.A.T., U. N.Mex., 1970; postgrad. U. N.Mex., 1970-71, Tex. Christian U., 1972-78; m. James P. Tant, Feb. 9, 1968; 1 son, Billy Gene. Tchr. pub. schs., Ala., 1950-54, N.Mex., 1956-65; dist. mgr. Field Enterprises, Albuquerque, 1955-57; planner, coordinator family living program Albuquerque Job Corps for Women, OEO, 1964-65; owner, mgr. Temporary Help Service, 1965; pvt. practice marriage and family counseling, Fort Worth, 1973—; dir. Get Slim Internat., Inc.; instr. Tex. Christian U., 1976—. Chmn. Democratic Precinct Com., 1960-62; mem. Gov.'s Commn. on Status of Women N.Mex., 1969-71; mem. Mayor's Com. on Status of Women Fort Worth, 1973-77; mem. Mech. Bd. Fort Worth, 1973—; mem. personnel com. YWCA; mem. adv. bd. Womens Haven Home for Battered Wives; bd. dirs. Fort Worth Ballet; mem. steering com. Texans for ERA. Mem. AAUW, Am., Tex. home econs. assns., Am. Humanistic Psychology Assn., Am. Assn. Marriage and Family Counselors (asso.), Internat. Transactional Analysis Assn. Clubs: Fort Worth Newcomers, El Paso, Elks. Home: 2325 Edwin St Fort Worth TX 76110 Office: 1415 Hurley St Fort Worth TX 76104

TANT, LARRY RAY, aerospace engr.; b. Central, S.C., Oct. 29, 1932; s. Felton Ray and Lucy Lavenia (Rogers) T.; B.S. in Civil Engring., Clemson U., 1962; M.S. in Engring. Mgmt., George Washington U., 1970; m. Jo Anne Alexander, June 4, 1952; children—Martin Ray, Ginger Carol. Aerospace technologist Langley Research Center, NASA, Hampton, Va., 1962—, project engr. on constrn. research facilities, 1962-69, head mission integration for scout launch vehicle Scout Project Office, 1969—, now mgr. ops. Scout Program. Merit badge counselor Boy Scouts Am., Hampton, 1965-69, scoutmaster, 1967-69. Served with USN, 1952-56. Lic. comml. pilot; cert. fallout shelter analyst. Recipient achievement awards NASA, 1977, 80, Apollo achievement award, 1978. Mem. ASCE (asso.). Republican. Clubs: Langley Aero, Peninsula Engrs. Home: 4007 Threechopt Rd Hampton VA 23666 Office: NASA Langley Research Center MS158A Hampton VA 23665

TANZOSCH, JOHN A., assn. exec.; b. Bronx, May 19, 1942; s. Alois and Teresa (Relich) T.; B.B.A., City Coll. N.Y., 1969, M.B.A., 1972; m. Felicia M. Schillaci, Jan. 22, 1968; children—Lori Anne, Christopher Lewis. Acct., Am. Inst. Indsl. Engrs., N.Y.C., 1963-67, officer mgr., 1967-70, dir. ops. and fin., N.Y.C. and Norcross, Ga., 1970-74, mng. dir. adminstrn., Norcross, 1974—. Mem. Ga. Soc. Assn. Execs., Council Engring. and Sci. Soc. Execs. Roman Catholic. Club: Lions (treas. 1977—). Home: 669 S Wind Dr Lilburn GA 30247 Office: 25 Technology Park/Atlanta Norcross GA 30092

TAPP, JOHN CECIL, physician; b. Horse Cave, Ky., Dec. 1, 1940; s. Ernest and Lottie Belle (Gill) T.; student David Lipscomb Coll., 1958-59, Western Ky. U., 1959-61; postgrad. Sch. Pharmacy, U. Ky., 1962; M.D., U. Louisville, 1966; m. Carolyn Sue Frank, July 29, 1972; children—John Randolph, Gregory Patrick. Intern, U. Louisville, 1966-67, resident in internal medicine, 1969-70; practice medicine, Bowling Green, Ky., 1971—; mem. staff Greenview Hosp., Bowling Green Warren County Med. Center, dir. Farmboy Meats, Inc.; owner, operator Tappland Ranches. Served as maj. USPHS, 1967-69. Fellow Am. Acad. Family Physicians; mem. Am. Acad. Bariatric Physicians, Tri-County Med. Soc., Alpha Omega Alpha, Alpha Kappa Kappa, Kappa Psi, Bowling Green-Warren County C. of C. Office: 414 Old Morgantown Rd Bowling Green KY 40201

TAPP, TOMMY VON, bank ofcl.; b. Faulkner, Miss., Aug. 18, 1943; s. Thomas Claude and Mattie Lee (Jones) T.; B.S., Union U., 1965; m. Sherry Ann Reaves, June 11, 1965; children—Teresa Elise, Kristina Vonette. Programmer, Miss. Hwy. Dept., Jackson, 1965-72; project mgr. Hatco, Corinth, Miss., 1972-77; data processing mgr. Security Bank, Amory, Miss., 1977—. Baptist (deacon). Clubs: Sertoma (pres. 1972), Exchange (sec. 1974), Masons. Home: 1319 Rogers Dr Amory MS 38821 Office: PO Box 270 Amory MS 38821

TAPPAN, CHARLES STRANAHAN, lawyer; b. Des Moines, July 25, 1940; s. Clarence Stranahan and Katharine (Short) T.; B.B.A., U. Mich., 1962, LL.B., 1965; m. Joyce Hannah Dillon, Dec. 25, 1970; children—Preston Charles, Viva Katharine. Admitted to Mich. bar, 1966, Ky. bar, 1975; coordinator wage and benefits dept. Chrysler Corp., Highland Park, Mich., 1965-67; asst. sec. Great Lakes Gas Transmission Co., Detroit, 1967-72; div. counsel Litton Industries, Florence, Ky., 1972-77; treas., gen. counsel Carlisle Constrn. Co., Wilder, Ky., 1977—. Pres., founder Lake Waynoka Property Owners Assn., 1975-76; mem. M.B.A. adv. bd. No. Ky. U., 1980—. Mem. Am. Bar Assn., Am. Mgmt. Assn., Ky. Bar Assn., No. Ky. C. of C. (chmn. air quality monitors com. 1978—, Walter L. Pieschel award for outstanding service 1980). Club: Bankers. Home: 6 Dartmouth St Fort Mitchell KY 41017 Office: 840 Licking Pike Wilder KY 41071

TAPPAN, WILLIAM BURGESS, entomologist; b. DeFuniak Springs, Fla., May 9, 1928; s. Walter Lebaron and Bessie (White) T.; B.S., U. Fla., 1953, M.S., 1954; m. Barbara Ann Love, June 5, 1960. Plant insp. Fla. State Plant Bd., Gainesville, 1954-55; agrl. nematologist U.S. Dept. Agr., Lake Alfred, Fla., 1955; entomologist U. Fla., Quincy, 1955—. Served with USAAF, 1946-49; PTO. Registered profl. entomologist. Mem. Am. Phytopathol. Soc., Tobacco Workers Conf. (vice-chmn. 1975-76, chmn. 1977-79), Tobacco Sci. Council (chmn. 1978-79), Lepidoptera Found., Am., ASTM, Fla., Ga. entomol. socs., Am. Inst. Biol. Sci., Nat. Eagle Scout Assn., Alpha Zeta, Gamma Sigma Delta, Phi Sigma. Democrat. Baptist. Club: Quarterback (Quincy). Contbr. articles to profl. jours. Home: 106 Cheeseborough Ave Quincy FL 32351 Office: Agrl Research and Edn Center Quincy FL 32351

TARBOX, GURDON LUCIUS, JR., museum dir.; b. Plainfield, N.J., Dec. 25, 1927; s. Gurdon Lucius and Lillie (Hodgson) T.; B.S., Mich. State U., 1952; M.S., Purdue U., 1954; m. Milver Ann Johnson, Sept. 25, 1952; children—Janet Ellen Tarbox Lamb, Joyce Elaine Tarbox Gant, Paul Edward, Lucia Ann. Asst. dir. Brookgreen Gardens, Murrells Inlet, S.C., 1954-59, trustee, 1959—, dir., 1963—. Chmn. Georgetown County Mental Health Commn., 1964-66; mem. exec. council Confedn. S.C. Local Hist. Socs., 1976—; trustee S.C. Hall Fame, 1976—. Served with AUS, 1946-48. Mem. Soc. Am. Foresters, Am. Assn. Bot. Gardens and Arboreta (dir. 1971-74), Georgetown County Hist. Soc. (pres. 1970-74), Am., Royal hort. socs., Am. Assn. Museums, Southeastern Museums Conf. (dir. 1977-80), S.C. Fedn. Museums (pres. 1974-76), Am. Assn. State and Local History, S.C. Confedn. Local Hist. Socs. Episcopalian. Club: Rotary (pres. 1979-80). Home: Brookgreen Gardens Murrells Inlet SC 29576 Office: Brookgreen Gardens Murrells Inlet SC 29576

TARKENTON, ALLAN RAY, ship repair co. purchasing exec.; b. Portsmouth, Va., Dec. 30, 1946; s. Samuel Rufus and Mary Lou (Shingleton) T.; B.S., Frederick Coll., 1968; M.B.A., U. Md., 1973. Mgmt. trainee Firestone Tire & Rubber Co., Virginia Beach, Va., 1970-71; dir. East Coast Tennis, Ltd., Virginia Beach, 1973-75; dir. purchasing Moon Engring. Co., Norfolk, Va., 1975—. Served with AUS, 1968-70. Mem. Am. Inst. Indsl. Engrs., Nat. Assn. Purchasing Mgmt. (achievement awards), Nat. Contract Mgmt. Assn. (chmn. exec. bd.). Presbyterian. Club: Propeller (Norfolk). Home: 3646 Ship Chandler Wharf Virginia Beach VA 23456 Office: 545 Front St Norfolk VA 23510

TARKINGTON, RAIFE GIDEON, mgmt., research and photog. cons.; b. Columbia, N.C., Feb. 10, 1915; s. Luid Ceylon and Mary Alene (Pritchard) T.; B.S., Va. Poly. Inst., 1936; m. Mary Eleanor Peters, Oct. 20, 1944; children—Pamela Ann, John Luid. Research engr. Research Labs., Eastman Kodak Co., Rochester, N.Y., 1936-41, asst. to dir., 1946-56, head mil. photography dept., 1956-58, asst. dir. photog. research div., 1958-60, asso. dir., 1960-65, dir., 1965-71, research, mgmt. and photog. cons., 1971—. Past chmn. elections East Irondequoit (N.Y.) Sch. Bd.; past mem. Irondequoit Bay Commn.; mem. Tyrrell County (N.C.) Bicentennial Commn.; past dist. chmn. Monroe County (N.Y.) Republican Com. Served to lt. col. USAAF, 1941-46. Decorated Legion of Merit. Fellow AAAS, Am. Inst. Chemists; mem. Soc. Photog. Scientists and Engrs., Am. Soc. Photogrametry (dir. 1961-63), Am. Inst. Chem. Engrs., Am. Mgmt. Assn., Soc. Photo-Optical Instrumentation Engrs., Reserve Officers Assn. (past v.p. N.Y. dept., past pres. Rochester chpt.), N.Y. Acad. Sci., Phi Kappa Phi, Phi Lambda Upsilon. Club: Rotary (treas. 1977-78, v.p. 1978-79, pres. 1979—). Author articles, chpts. in books. Inventor photog. materials and processes. Address: Box 462 Columbia NC 27925 also 791 Hampshire Ln Virginia Beach VA 23462

TARRILLION, THOMAS LEE, data processing cons.; b. San Antonio, Apr. 9, 1946; s. Paul William and Annie Ruth (Jansky) T.; B.A., St. Mary's U., 1968, M.B.A., 1971; m. Sylvia Olivia Evans, Aug. 26, 1967; children—Stephen, Mark, Michelle Lynn, Cynthia Marie. Asst. dir. Computer Center, St. Mary's U., San Antonio, 1964-68, asst. registrar, 1968-69, registrar, 1969-73; data processing cons., San Antonio, 1973—. Cubmaster, Boy Scouts Am., 1977-79, asst. scoutmaster, 1979—; mem. parish council Roman Catholic Ch., 1977, chmn. fin. com., 1976-77. Cert. data processor. Mem. Data Processing Mgmt. Assn. Home: 4402 Lark Ave San Antonio TX 78228 Office: Suite 112 1747 Citadel Plaza San Antonio TX 78209

TARTELL, JOSEPH SPADARO, psychologist; b. N.Y.C., June 17, 1943; s. Joseph John and Elvira Marie (Spadaro) T.; B.S., Manhattan Coll., 1965; M.A., U. Okla., 1972; m. Judith Loise Geis, Apr. 16, 1966; children—Joseph Lawrence, Deborah Allison. Research psychologist U.S. Air Force, 1965-77; dir. med. job analysis U.S. Army Acad. Health Sci., Ft. Sam Houston, Tex., 1977-78; sr. analyst Occupational Measurement Center, Randolph AFB, Tex., 1978—; cons. in field. Mem. Mil. Testing Assn. Contbr. articles to profl. jours. Home: 3227 Canaveral Dr San Antonio TX 78217 Office: USAF Occupational Measurement Center Randolph AFB TX 78236

TARWATER, WILLIAM RAYMOND, ins. agt., state legislator; b. Duncan, Okla., Nov. 24, 1921; s. Olin Proctor and Ola (Carmichael) T.; student Okla. U., 1938-40; m. Jean Johnson, Apr. 4, 1943; children—William O., Judy A. Owner, Tarwater Ins. Agy., Duncan, 1948—; mem. Okla. Ho. of Reps., 1966—; trustee Okla. Housing Fin. Agency, 1975—. Bd. dirs. Duncan Community Chest, 1950-53. Chmn. Stephens County (Okla.) Democratic central com., 1960-65. Trustee Okla. Housing Finance Agy. Mem. Am. Legion, Okla. State Golf Assn. (dir. 1959—; pres. 1962). Elk, Rotarian. Home: 1001 N 9th St Duncan OK 73533 Office: 1301 W Main St Duncan OK 73533

TATAM, WILLIAM MACK, psychotherapist; b. Hampton, Ark., Oct. 8, 1932; s. Ernest and Myrtle Lee (McKinnie) T.; B.S., Miami U., Oxford, Ohio, 1954; M.S.W., U. Pitts., 1956; postgrad. U. Denver, 1963-66; m. Miriam Shaw, Dec. 22, 1956; children—Karen, Mark, Kris. Commd. 2d lt. U.S. Army, 1956, advanced through grades to lt. col., 1976, ret., 1976; pvt. practice marital, family and individual psychotherapy, Lawton, Okla., 1976—. Founder, Parents Anonymous, Lawton. Recipient Okla. Gov.'s award for work in child abuse, 1976; registered therapist Assn. for Research and Enlightenment, Edgar Caycee Found. Mem. Nat. Assn. Social Workers, Am. Assn. Marital and Family Therapy, Assn. Sex Educators, Counselors and Therapists, Comanche County Mental Health Assn., Group for Psychosocial Research (chmn.). Unitarian.

Contbr. articles to profl. jours.; editor-in-chief Lawton Home and Lifestyle; weekly newspaper humor columnist. Home: 332 Warwick Way Lawton OK 73501 Office: Suite 203 Security Bldg 501 C Ave Lawton OK 73501

TATE, ALBERT, JR., judge; b. Opelousas, La., Sept. 23, 1920; s. Albert and Adelaide (Therry) T.; student La. State U., 1938-39, certificate, 1948; B.A., George Washington U., 1941; LL.B., Yale, 1947; m. Claire Jeanmard, Apr. 23, 1949; children—Albert III, Emma Adelaide, George J., Michael F., Charles E. Admitted to La. bar, 1948; practiced in Ville Platte, 1948-54; judge Ct. Appeal 1st Circuit La., Baton Rouge, 1954-60; presiding judge Ct. Appeal 3d Circuit, Lake Charles, 1960-70; asso. justice La. Supreme Ct., 1958, 70-79; judge 5th circuit U.S. Ct. of Appeals, 1979—; prof. law La. State U., 1967-68; mem. La. Jud. Council, 1960-70; mem. com. and council La. State Law Inst., 1954-59; faculty Inst. Jud. Adminstrn., N.Y. U., 1965—, Appellate Judges Seminar, U. Ala., 1966, 70, U. Nev., 1967; chmn. La. Judiciary Commn., 1969-70; mem. adv. council Nat. Center for State Cts., 1970-71; del. La. Constl. Conv., 1973. Chmn. La. Commn. on Aging, 1956-59; pres. La. Cotton Festival, 1955-57; mem. Evangeline Area council Boy Scouts Am., 1948—, dist. chmn., 1949-50. Served with AUS, 1942-45. Recipient Am. Trial Lawyers judiciary award, 1971. Mem. Am. (chmn. exec. com. appellate judges conf. 1966-76), La. bar assns., Am. Judicature Soc. (dir. 1969-73), La. Conf. Ct. of Appeal Judges (pres. 1967-70), Am. Legion, V.F.W., Order of Coif (hon.), Blue Key (hon.), Delta Kappa Epsilon. Clubs: K.C., Woodmen of World, Rotarian. Author: Louisiana Civil Procedures, 1968, 3d edit., 1977; Treatises for Judges, 1971, 3d edit., 1977. Contbr. articles to profl. jours. Home: Box 309 Ville Platte LA 70586 also 2414 Octavia St New Orleans LA 70115 Office: Room 324 600 Carp St New Orleans LA 70130

TATE, ELLIENNE NELL TODD, nurse, educator; b. Lake Charles, La., Sept. 30, 1940; d. Donald W. and Marie (Young) Todd; B.S., Northwestern La. U., 1962; M.S., U. Md., 1964; Ed.D., La. State U., 1978; m. W.O. Tate, Jr., Nov. 19, 1966; 1 son, Walton Todd. Staff nurse Lake Charles (La.) Meml. Hosp., 1962-63; instr. Northwestern La. U., 1964-67; instr. Southeastern La. U., Hammond, 1967-69, prof., dean Sch. Nursing, 1969—. Mem. Am. Nurses Assn., La. State Nurses Assn., Sigma Theta Tau, Alpha Kappa Gamma. Republican. Presbyterian. Home: Route 4 Box 158 Hammond LA 70401 Office: Box 781 University Station Hammond LA 70402

TATE, HORACE EDWARD, assn. exec.; b. Elberton, Ga., Oct. 6, 1922; s. Henry Lawrence and Mattie Beatrice (Harper) T.; B.S., Ft. Valley (Ga.) State Coll., 1943; M.A., Atlanta U., 1951; Ed.D., U. Ky., 1961; m. Virginia Barnett, 1949; children—Calvin, Veliosa, Horacena. Tchr., secondary sch. prin. in Ga., 1942-59; asso. prof. edn. Fort Valley State Coll., 1959-61; exec. sec. Ga. Tchrs. and Edn. Assn., 1961-70; asso. exec. sec. Ga. Assn. Educators, 1970-77, exec. sec., 1977—; mem. Nat. Commn. Libraries and Info. Services, 1978. Mem. Ga. Senate from 38th Dist., 1975-76, 77-78, 79-80. Mem. NEA (life), Ft. Valley State Coll. Alumni Assn., Phi Delta Kappa. Democrat. Methodist. Author articles in field. Home: 621 Lilla Dr SW Atlanta GA 30310 Office: 3951 Snapfinger Pkwy Decatur GA 30035

TATE, JOYCE ELAINE, counselor; b. Dallas, Oct. 15, 1946; d. Chester Thomas and Clara Bruce (Gay) T.; B.A., Bishop Coll., 1969; M.Ed., Tex. So. U., 1973. Receptionist for Postmaster Gen., Mr. McMillian, Dallas, 1966; speech asst. Dr. Joyce Bell, Bishop Coll., Dallas, 1967-68; first black coll. bd. model of Sanger Harris, Dallas, 1968-69; tchr. pub. schs., Lamar and Houston, Tex., 1969-77; Magnet Sch. counselor, Houston, 1977—. Organizer young adults group Antioch Missionary Baptist Ch., 1976-77, recipient Disting. Service in Edn. award, 1974, 75, 76, 78; active YWCA, NAACP; sponsor entertainment for sick ARC, 1970—; founder, sponsor Charm Club, 1969—. Named Tchr. of Year, Lamar Sch., 1971. Mem. NEA, Tex. Tchrs. Assn., Houston Tchrs. Assn., Am. Personnel and Guidance Assn., Am. Sch. Counselors Assn., Tex. Personnel and Guidance Assn., Houston Counselors Assn. Home: 6610 Kassarine Pass Houston TX 77033 Office: 4801 La Branch Houston TX 77004

TATE, NATHAN WASHINGTON, entertainment agt.; b. Decatur, Ala., May 26, 1938; s. Willie Benford and Bessie Lucille (Washington) T.; grad. high sch.; m. Frances Inez Davis, June 1963; 1 son, Nathan Washington. Pub. safety officer Wheeler Dam (Ala.) Plant, TVA, 1969—; owner, pres. Nat Tate Enterprises, Decatur, 1969—; franchise owner, operator New Orleans Famous Fried Chicken, Huntsville, Ala.; gen. sales mgr. Radio Sta. WEUP, Huntsville. Served with USAF. Recipient Bronze medal Carnegie Found., 1950. Mem. Internat. Mil. Club Execs., AGVA, VFW, Am. Legion. Democrat. Club: Masons. Home: 506 Monroe Dr NW Decatur AL 35601 Office: Nat Tate Enterprises PO Box 1125 Decatur AL 35601

TATE, PAUL CALVIN, lawyer; b. Mamou, La., July 11, 1922; s. Hosea and Lovina (Guillory) T.; LL.B., La. State U., 1950; m. Anna Soileau, Jan. 7, 1941; children—Sandy, Paul C.; m. 2d, Janice Farris Adam; children—Adam, Frank. Admitted to U.S. Supreme Ct. bar, La. bar, 1950, since practiced in Mamou, asst. dist. atty. 13th Jud. Dist., 1954-61; city atty., Mamou, 1950-61. Dir. Guaranty Bank of Mamou. Dir., Pub. Housing Adminstrn., 1952-54; pres. Young Democrats of La., 1958-62; pres. La. Folk Found., La. Ednl. and Cultural Found., La. Mass Media Found.; mem. La. Ednl. and TV Authority, 1979. Served with Signal Corps, AUS, 1942-46. Recipient Silver Beaver award Boy Scouts Am., 1967, Ordre de la Pleiade, Paris, 1967, Ordre des Francophone d'Amerique, Que., 1979. Fellow Am. Acad. Law and Sci.; mem. Am. Judicature Soc., Am., La. bar assns., La. Law Inst. Council, Nat., La. assns. claimants' compensation attys., Nat. Folk Festival Assn. (nat. adv. com.), Am. Legion (comdr. 1951; dist. comdr. 1961-62), Council for Devel. of French in La., Internat. Assn. French Speaking Parliamentarians (sec. La. chpt.), New Orleans Young Men's Bus. Club. Woodman of World (head consul of La. 1957-58), Rotarian (pres. 1950). Home: Route 2 Box 27 Mamou LA 70554 Office: 6th St at Chestnut St Mamou LA 70554

TATOM, THOMAS JACKSON, indsl. distbg. co. exec.; b. Edmond, Okla., Oct. 4, 1948; s. Thomas Mearl and Anna Juanita (Morris) T.; student Tex. Luth. Coll., 1966-68, Fla. Jr. Coll., Jacksonville, 1969, Mountain View Jr. Coll., 1972, Tarrant County Jr. Coll., 1974-76; m. Mary Lou Little, Jan. 16, 1976; children—Karen Sue, Heather Alanna. Asst. to treas. Morrison Supply Co., Ft. Worth, 1973-76; controller Well Machinery & Supply Co., Ft. Worth, 1976-78; treas. Triangle Supply Co., Dallas, 1978-79; v.p. ops. Well Machinery & Supply Co., Ft. Worth, 1979—. Treas., Morsco Fed. Credit Union, Ft. Worth, 1975-76. Served with USN, 1968-72. Cert. LP gas insp. R.R. Commn. Tex. Mem. Nat. Assn. Credit Mgrs. Home: 5468 Wedgmont Circle N Fort Worth TX 76133 Office: Well Machinery & Supply Co PO Box 1659 Fort Worth TX 76101

TATUM, ALLYN CARR, lawyer, state ofcl.; b. Portia, Ark., Jan. 27, 1942; s. Algin Carr and Nina Ruth (Turney) T.; B.S. in Bus. Adminstrn., U. Ark., 1967, J.D., 1970; m. Lois Ann Galloway, Apr. 30, 1977; children—Leslie Rochelle, Juliet Kee. Admitted to Ark. bar, 1970; asso. Highsmith, Harkey & Walmsley, Batesville, 1970-72; partner Highsmith, Tatum, Highsmith, Gregg & Hart, 1972-77; regional atty. Ark. Dept. Social Services, 1973-77; chmn. Ark. Workers Compensation Commn., 1977—; vis. prof. Ark. Coll., 1971-74; trust dept. adviser Citizens Bank, 1971-75; legal cons. White River Planning and Devel. Dist., 1972-77. Area Wide Comprehensive Health Planning Council, 1974-75; dir. Independence Savs. & Loan Assn. Pres., E. Side PTA, 1974-75; mem. pres. adv. council Ark. Coll., 1974-75; mem. adv. bd. Gateway Vo-Tech Sch., 1977-78; mem. Batesville (Ark.) Planning Commn., 1971-73, Community Sch. Bd., 1972-77; bd. dirs. Ark. Health Systems Found., 1974-75; bd. dirs. Delta-Hills Health Systems Agy., 1976—, exec. com., 1977; bd. dirs., exec. com. Ark. Health Coordinating Council, 1976-77; bd. dirs. N. Central Ark. Mental Health Center, 1972—, pres., 1974-80; chmn. exec. com. Region VI SW Assn. Mental Health Centers, 1977-80; bd. dirs. Batesville Community Theater, 1972; bd. dirs. Nat. Community Mental Health Inst., 1976—, exec. com., 1977-78; bd. dirs. Nat. Council Community Mental Health Centers, 1975—, pres.-elect, 1980—. Recipient So. Senator award So. Bapt. Coll., 1974. Mem. So. Assn. Workers Compensation Adminstrs. (exec. com. 1971—, v.p. 1977, pres. 1978-79), Am., Ark., Independence County (pres. 1971-72) bar assns., Ark. Trial Lawyers Assn., Nat. Health Lawyers Assn., Internat. Assn. Indsl. Bds. and Commns. (nominating com. 1978-79), Scot Booster Club, Ark. Mental Health Assn., Batesville C. of C., Pi Kappa Alpha, Delta Theta Phi. Baptist. Clubs: Kiwanis, Batesville Country (pres. 1974-75, dir. 1975-76). Home: 2708 Northeastern Ave Jacksonville AR 72076 Office: Office of Chmn Ark Workmen's Compensation Commn Justice Bldg State Capital Grounds Little Rock AR 72201

TATUM, H. MICHAEL, accountant; b. ElDorado, Ark., Dec. 23, 1928; s. H.M. and Clara (Greenwood) T.; B.B.A., So. Meth. U., 1967; m. Edna Beatrice Brashier, May 22, 1946; children—Louis M., David C., Jeanne M. Acct., Am. Liberty Oil Co., Dallas, 1954-69; v.p., sec. Callon Petroleum Co., Natchez, Miss., 1969—; acctg. instr. Co-Lin Jr. Coll., Natchez, 1974-78. Trustee Jefferson St. United Meth. Ch., 1977—, vice chmn., 1979-80. Served with USN, 1946-48. Mem. Am. Soc. Corporate Secs. Methodist. Home: 507 Orleans St Natchez MS 39120 Office: 300 Franklin St Natchez MS 39120

TATUM, SPENCER MCCOY, ins. agt.; b. Repton, Ala., Jan. 13, 1947; s. Cornelia Tatum Ryland; grad. U. N.D., 1970; 1 dau., Amanda Jill. Ins. agt. Andrew Jackson Life Ins. Co., 1978—, Lamar Life Ins. Co., 1978—, New Eng. Life Insurance Co., 1979—. Dir. youth tng. First Baptist Ch. Named Most Valuable Asso., New Eng. Ins. Co., 1979. Mem. Nat. Assn. Life Underwriters, La. Assn. Life Underwriters, Acadiana Assn. Life Underwriters (pres.-elect 1980), Million Dollar Round Table. Republican. Baptist. Home: Route 1 Box 107K Carencro LA 70520 Office: PO Box 3742 Lafayette LA 70502

TAUCHER, GREGORY MICHAEL, advt. exec.; b. Salt Lake City, Jan. 25, 1954; s. Joseph R. and Carolyn D.; B.S., U. Utah, 1976; M.S. in Journalism, Northwestern U., 1977; m. Julie Ann Cook, June 2, 1976. Account exec. Richards Group, Dallas, 1977-78; v.p., account supr. Rosenberg & Co., Dallas, 1978—. Home: 6061 Village Bend Dr #614 Dallas TX 75206 Office: Two Turtle Creek Village Suite 1300 Dallas TX 75219

TAYLOR, ANDREWENA ALEXANDER HOLLOWAY, educator for the deaf; b. Murfreesboro, Tenn., July 17, 1951; d. Watt Weakley, Jr., and Louanna Harris (Robertson) Holloway; B.A., Birmingham-Southern Coll., 1973; M.S., Vanderbilt U., 1975; m. Murrey Thomas Taylor, Jr., May 18, 1974. Asst. in developmental studies Shelby State Community Coll., Memphis, 1975-76; speech-lang. specialist Memphis State U. Deaf Edn. Program, 1976-78; specialist deaf edn. for S.Central Dist. Tenn., Columbia, 1978—; instr. sign lang. for parents and tchrs. of hearing impaired. Active Williamson County-Heritage Found., Assn. for the Preservation of Tenn. Antiquities, Youth in Govt. Com. of Sen. Howard Baker, 1968. Cert. educator of the deaf; cert. in speech and hearing, deaf edn., Tenn. Mem. Am. Speech and Hearing Assn., Tenn. Speech and Hearing Assn. Methodist. Clubs: Pi Beta Phi Alumni Assn., Birmingham-Southern Alumni Assn., Vanderbilt Alumni Assn. Home: 230 Jennings St Franklin TN 37064 Office: 805 1/2 Nashville Highway Columbia TN 38401

TAYLOR, BELINDA LAVEEDA, educator; b. Vicksburg, Miss., Mar. 7, 1952; d. James Oscar and Annie Pearl (Smith) Taylor; B.S., Tuskegee Inst., 1972, M.Ed., 1973. Grad. asst. Tuskegee Inst. (Ala.), 1972-73; counselor spl. services Mary Holmes Coll., West Point, Miss., 1973-76, coordinator Upward Bound program, 1976—. Sec., edn. com. Clay County Community Fed. Credit Union, 1975—. Mem. Mary Holmes Coll. Edn. Assn. (asst. sec. 1974), Am., Miss., 5th Dist. Miss. personnel and guidance assns., Southeastern Assn. Ednl. Opportunity Program Personnel, Am. Coll. Personnel Assn., Kappa Delta Pi. Democrat. Baptist. Club: Ladies of Essence Social (pres. 1975). Home: PO Box 2066 Mary Holmes College West Point MS 39773 Office: Upward Bound Project West Point MS 39773

TAYLOR, BERNARD, univ. adminstr.; b. Birmingham, Ala., Oct. 30, 1943; s. Willie and Edna (Lee) T.; B.A., Wiley Coll., Marshall, Tex., 1966; postgrad. U. Okla. Coordinator fin. aid, instr. humanities Daniel Payne Coll., Birmingham, 1968-70; asst. to pres. for devel. Mary Holmes Coll., West Point, Miss., 1970-73; dir. public relations Miss. Valley State U., Itta Bena, 1973-75; dir. fund raising Tex. So. U., Houston, 1975-76; v.p. devel. Ky. State U., Frankfort, 1976—; cons. in field. Bd. dirs. Big Bros./Big Sisters Franfort, Frankfort Community Council; bd. dirs., pres. elect Frankfort Arts Found.; vice chmn. bd. dirs. Franklin County chpt. ARC; adv. council Bluegrass Regional Criminal Justice Com. Served with USAR, 1966-68; Vietnam. Decorated Army Commendation medal. Mem. Council Advancement and Support Edn. in Ky. (pres. 1979-80), Phi Delta Kappa, Phi Beta Sigma. Democrat. Presbyterian. Author, editor in field. Home: 1750 Galbraith Rd Frankfort KY 40601 Office: Office Devel Ky State Univ Frankfort KY 40601

TAYLOR, BOYD EUGENE, writer, newspaper exec.; b. Atlanta, July 31, 1901; s. Eugene Helm and Minnie (Jarrell) T.; B.S., Emory U., 1923; M.S., Sorbonne, 1926; Certificate, Louvre Mus. (France), 1926, Prado Mus., Spain; M.A., U. Madrid, 1925; Ph.D., Cranmer, 1975; m. Cora Mina Moses, Feb. 22, 1922 (dec. 1927). Sci. writer Hearst Newspapers, 1919-40; tchr. Fulton High Sch., Atlanta, 1922-27; asst. night chief Atlanta bur. A.P., 1920; city editor Atlanta Constn., 1941-44; gen. mgr. Ind. Press, Atlanta, 1944—; pres. Southland, Inc., Stone Mountain Food Products, Inc., Community Newspapers, Inc. Pres. Separate Schs., Inc., Pvt. Sch. Found., Nat. Laymens Com. to Crush Communism in Chs.; co-founder Hartsfield Internat. Airport, 1925. Bd. dirs. Ga. Taxpayers Relief Assn., Genetics Research Library; founder Friends of Rhodesia; chmn. Historic House Mus. Corp. Served to 2d lt., Signal Corps, U.S. Army, World War I; to maj. USAAF, World War II. Recipient plaque Fulton County Tchrs. Assn., 1963; holder 3 world passenger car records. Life fellow Royal Soc. (London); asso. Nat. Archives; mem. Am. Soc. Human Genetics, Genetics Soc. Am. (life), Am. Genetic Assn., Population Assn. Am., Ga. Acad. Sci., Am. Inst. Biol. Scis., AAAS (life), Brit. Assn. for Advancement Sci. (life), Anglican Soc., Soc. For Study Evolution, Internat. Assn. for Advancement Eugenics and Ethnology, Am. Soc. Health Assn., Council For Basic Edn., Planned Parenthood Fedn. Am., Am. Acad. Polit. and Social Sci., Soc. for Preservation English Lang. and Lit. (founder), Nat. Wildlife Fedn., Nat. Rifle Assn. (life), Nat. Hist. Assn., Nat. Trust for Historic Preservation. Anglican Orthodox (co-founder, trustee). Club: Atlanta Billiard (founder, pres.). Inventor Taylorscope aerial stereo viewer '40. Home: 327 Saint Paul Ave SE Atlanta GA 30312 Office: PO Box 1 Atlanta GA 30301

TAYLOR, CARL BECK, former educator; b. Cogan House, Pa., July 20, 1913; s. Albert Delos and Myrtle Estella (Beck) T.; A.B., Hobart Coll., 1935; A.M., Kalamazoo Coll., 1936; postgrad. Columbia, 1936-37; Ph.D., Pa. State U., 1962; m. Florence Theola Ayres, Aug. 23, 1938; children—Jeffrey Ayres, Kevin Larue. Instr. sociology Hobart and William Smith Colls., Geneva, N.Y., 1937-47; tchr. Lycoming (Pa.) Sch. Dist., 1948-50; agent Nationwide Ins. Co., Lycoming, 1950-57; research asst. Pa. State U., 1957-61; vis. prof. Shippensburg (Pa.) State Coll., 1961; prof. family relations W.Va. U., Morgantown, 1961-78, prof. emeritus, 1978—. Mem. exec. bd. W.Va. Council on Children and Youth, 1961-74, v.p., 1964-65, pres., 1965-69; pres. W.Va. U. Employees Credit Union, 1965—. Mem. Am., Sociol. Assn., Rural Sociol. Soc., Nat. Council Family Relations, S.E. Council Family Relations, Am., W.Va. (mem. exec. bd.) home econs. assns., Phi Beta Kappa, Alpha Kappa Delta, Pi Gamma Mu, Phi Kappa Phi, Omicron Nu, Phi Upsilon Omicron, Phi Delta Kappa. Home: 773 Augusta Ave Morgantown WV 26505

TAYLOR, CHARLES PAT, univ. dean; b. Salem, Ky., Dec. 10, 1945; s. Charles A. and Georgia Patmor T.; B.S., U. Tenn., Martin, 1968; M.A., Western Ky. U. 1971; Ed.D., Memphis State U., 1975; m. Judith Couch, June 8, 1968; children—Marijo, Charla. Tchr.-coach Crittenden County High Sch., Marion, Ky., 1968-70, Geeter High Sch., Memphis, 1970-72; admissions counselor Union U., Jackson, Tenn., 1972-73; asst. prof. edn. Belmont Coll., Nashville, 1975-79; asso. acad. dean Union U., Jackson, Tenn., 1979—; social studies cons. Memphis City Schs., 1974-75; tchr. edn. cons. Metro-Nashville Public Schs., 1975-79; chmn. Metro Council for Tchr. Edn., 1977-78, vice-chmn., 1978-79. Mem. Com. Tenn. Educators to elect Jimmy Carter, 1976. Recipient Outstanding Prof. of Year award Belmont Coll., 1978. Mem. Assn. Tchr. Educators (Tenn. rep. to nat. conv. 1978-80), Tenn. Council Social Studies, AAUP, Kappa Delta Pi, Phi Delta Kappa. Democrat. Baptist. Home: 27 Windale St Jackson TN 38301 Office: Acad Center Union U Jackson TN 38301

TAYLOR, DALLAS JEFFREY, architect; b. Abington, Pa., Dec. 24, 1944; s. William C. and Helen S. (Schmidt) T.; B.S., John Brown U., 1966; B.A., U. Ark., 1969, B.Arch., 1969; m. Veta Ruth Taylor, Dec. 21, 1965; children—Dallas Christopher, Jeffrey Michael, Scott Ryan. Architect, Woodward Cape, Dallas, 1969-72; project mgr. Southwestern Dynamics, Dallas, 1972-74; dir. housing Jordan Co., Dallas, 1974-75; architect Bank Bldg. Corp., Dallas, 1975-77; pres. Counsel Corp., 1977-79; exec. v.p. Woodward/Taylor, 1979—; dir. Prestonwood Assn. Mem. AIA, Tex. Soc. Architects. Home: 15642 Kingscrest Dallas TX 75248 Office: Counsel Corp 3627 Howell St Dallas TX 75204

TAYLOR, DORIS ELVIRA, hosp. adminstr.; b. Jamaica, L.I., N.Y., Oct. 13, 1929; d. James Polk and Elizabeth Mae (Lytle) Stone; student U. Miami, 1952; A.S.N., Miami Dade Jr. Coll., 1965; B.S.H.E., Appalachian State U., Boone, N.C., 1979; m. Edwin Drunmond Taylor, Mar. 24, 1948; children—Edwin Drummond, Charles G., James L., Suzanne E. Head nurse Mercy Hosp., Miami, 1966-69; charge nurse Watauga County Hosp., Boone, N.C., 1970; inservice instr. Caldwell Community Coll., Lenoir, N.C., 1971; dir. nursing Cannon Meml. Hosp., Banner Elk, N.C., 1971-74; asst. adminstr. patient care Caldwell Meml. Hosp., Lenoir, N.C., 1974—; mem. state adv. council Vocat. Edn.-Health Occupations Com., Caldwell County, N.C., 1979—; mem. adv. bd. Home Health Agy., 1977—; chmn. adv. bd. asso. degree nursing program Caldwell Community Coll., 1975-76. Registered nurse, N.C., Fla. Mem. Foothills Soc. Nursing Service Adminstrs., Gamma Beta Phi, Alpha Chi. Republican. Home: Route 5 Box 573 Boone NC 28607 Office: 321 Mulberry St Lenoir NC 28645

TAYLOR, DOUGLAS JENNINGS, process safety and fire protection specialist; b. Worcester, Mass., Mar. 12, 1917; s. Henry and Lavena Alice (Jennings) T.; B S. in Chem. Engring., Mass. Inst. Tech., 1939; m. Edith Louise Harding, June 10, 1967. Devel. engr. Linde Air Products Co., Tonawanda, N.Y., 1939-55; safety engr. Union Carbide Corp., Sistersville, W.Va., 1955-67, process safety and fire protection specialist Ohio Valley Plant Engring., Sistersville and Marietta, 1967—; chief engr., sec.-treas. IVS, Inc., Waverly, W.Va., 1972—; gen. chmn. Central Ohio Valley Indsl. Emergency Orgn., 1963. Dir. Pleasants County (W.Va.) Emergency Services, 1961—; chmn. Pleasants County Housing Com., 1975; sec. bd. dirs. Pleasants County Community Action, 1975-79; bd. dirs. Pleasants County Housing Rehab. Program, 1980—; mem. Pleasants County Democratic Exec. Com. Named Ky. col. Mem. Am. Soc. Safety Engrs. (profl.), Nat. Fire Protection Assn. (asso.), Am. Def. Preparedness Assn. (life). Episcopalian. Clubs: Kiwanis (gov. W.Va. dist. 1971-72) (St. Marys, W.Va.); Masons, Elks. Home: 501 Sycamore St Saint Marys WV 26170 Office: PO Box 245 Waverly WV 26184

TAYLOR, EDWIN DESHA, engr.; b. Cynthiana, Ky., Oct. 15, 1923; s. Howard Graves and Garnetta (Stewart) T.; B.S., U. Calif., Berkeley, 1964; m. Jacqueline Ann Avery, Dec. 16, 1977; children—Charles, Lee, Alex, Garnetta, Linda, Lyna, Rosemary, Edwin, William. Served with U.S. Navy, 1940-61; ret., 1961; mgr. facility ops. Beverly Enterprises, Castro Valley, Calif., 1970-72; dir. health services facilities Govt. of Micronesia, Trust Territory of Pacific Islands, 1972-75; dir. phys. plant Sacred Heart Med. Center, Eugene, Oreg., 1975-76; dir. engring., chief engr. Highlands Bapt. Hosps., Louisville, 1976-79; asst. works engr. Louisville works Marley Cooling Tower Co., 1979—. Vice chmn. Louisville Fire Prevention Council, 1977-78; bd. dirs. Seven Counties Service. Decorated Purple Heart (2). Mem. Am. Inst. Plant Engrs. (regional dir.), Ky. Soc. Hosp. Engrs. (pres.), Nat. Fire Protection Assn., Hon. Order Ky. Cols. Democrat. Clubs: Masons, Shriners. Home: PO Box 4336 Louisville KY 40204 Office: 6333 Strawberry Ln Louisville KY 40214

TAYLOR, ERNEST AUSTIN, JR., devel. engr.; b. Balt., Jan. 18, 1918; s. Ernest A. and Alma (Robinson) T.; B.S. in Elec. Engring., Ga. Inst. Tech., 1948; m. Rachel Charleen Morgan, Feb. 14, 1944; children—Rachel Alma Taylor Clay, Charles Ernest. Elec. engr. Phillips Petroleum Co., Bartlesville, Okla., 1948-51, Elec. Equipment Co., Augusta, Ga., 1951-52; elec. design engr. Patchen & Zimmerman, Augusta, 1952-56; elec. engr. Monsanto Co., Decatur, Ala., 1956-61, sr. engr., 1961-66, devel. asso., 1966-70, sr. specialist, 1970—. Bd. dirs. Internat. Bible Coll., Florence, Ala., 1972—, sec., 1976—. Served with USN, 1943-45. Norbett P. No-No fellow award, 1972. Mem. Nat. Soc. Profl. Engrs., Ala. Soc. Profl. Engrs., Fluid Power Soc. Mem. Ch. of Christ. Patentee elec. engring. equipment and design. Home: 2202 Cleveland Ave SW Decatur AL 35601 Office: Monsanto Co PO Box 2204 Decatur AL 35602

TAYLOR, GLORIA SMITH, social worker; b. Cleve., Oct. 21, 1945; d. Albert and Mamie (Ross) Smith; M.S.W., SUNY, Stony Brook, 1974; m. Eric B. Taylor, July 10, 1965; children—Larry, Veronica, Cassandra, Patrice. Counselor for underachieving girls Port Jefferson (N.Y.) Jr. High Sch., 1972; med. social worker St. Charles Hosp., Port Jefferson Station, N.Y., 1973; med. social worker St. Joseph Hosp. East, Inc., Memphis, 1975—, also dir. med. social service; bd. dirs.

Upjohn Health Care Services. Mem. Soc. for Hosp. Social Work Dirs., Am. Hosp. Assn., Tenn. Soc. Health Care Social Workers, Tenn. Hosp. Assn., Health and Social Services Communications Council (treas.). Baptist. Home: 2157 Maplecrest Rd Memphis TN 38116 Office: St Joseph Hosp East Inc 5959 Park Ave Memphis TN 38117

TAYLOR, JAMES BOYD, cons.; b. Owensboro, Ky., May 30, 1919; s. James Hays and Marie Bruce (Boyd) T.; student pub. schs. N.Y.C., Louisville and Owensboro; m. Frances M. Taylor. With IRS, 1943-47; with Glenmore Distilleries Co., Owensboro, 1933-43, 47—, asst. v.p., 1955-64, v.p., gen. mgr., 1964-78; cons. mgmt. and operational skills systems installations, 1978—; dir. Citizens State Bank, Owensboro. Mem. Adv. Council on Naval Affairs; mem. Louisville dist. adv. com. SBA. Trustee Brescia Coll., 1974-76; chmn. bd. Owensboro Daviess County Hosp., 1968-75, Tri State Health Council, 1972-75; mem. Green River Area Health Council, 1972-75. Chosen by U.S. Pres. to receive Loyalty award VFW, 1972. Mem. Owensboro Daviess County (dir. 1967-69), Ky. chambers commerce, Distilled Spirits Inst. Presbyterian. Clubs: Pendennis (Louisville); Petroleum (Evansville); Campbell (Owensboro). Pioneer bulk gauging distilled spirits. Home: 1515 Dean Ave Owensboro KY 42301 Office: APC Skills Co 252 Royal Palm Way Palm Beach FL 33480

TAYLOR, JAMES DANIEL, beverage refrigeration co. exec.; b. Rahway, N.J., Nov. 21, 1928; s. James Daniel and Ella Sophie (Sneedse) T.; student Bates Coll., 1948, Sch. Fgn. Service, Georgetown U., 1949-61, U. Mex., summer 1949; M.B.A., Ateneo of Manila, 1964; postgrad. Bus. Sch., Harvard U., 1978; m. Teresa Frances Lavers, Dec. 18, 1965; children—Anita Teresa, Andrea Ella, Alex James. With Standard Vacuum Oil Co., Philippines, 1951-65; mktg. exec. Esso Standard Oil Co., C.Am., 1965-68; dir. mgmt. consultants Price Waterhouse Co., N.Y.C., Tampa, Fla., 1968-74; pres. Jim Taylor Corp., Orlando, Fla., 1974—, Cubes Inc., Orlando, 1976—; dir. So. Data Co., So. Cons. Co. Mem. Mountainside (N.J.) Sch. Bd., 1971-72; patron Rollins Coll., U. Central Fla.; mem. panel United Cerebral Palsy Found.; bd. dirs. Union County Sch. Bd., 1972; cons. Fla. Senate, 1974; Jaycee senator, 1969—. Served with U.S. Army, 1946-48. Recipient Inner Circle award Jos. Schlitz Brewing Co., 1979, C.Am. award Govt. of Honduras, 1950. Mem. Am. Mgmt. Assn., Sales Execs. Club, Central Fla. Wholesalers Assn. (pres.), Georgetown U. Alumni Assn. Republican. Episcopalian. Clubs: Winter Park Racquet, University, Tar Boosters; Manila Polo. Contbr. articles to profl. publs. Office: 187 Atlantic Dr Maitland FL 32751

TAYLOR, JERRY ALLAN, architect, civil and structural engr.; b. Frankfort, Ky., Mar. 21, 1946; s. Charles and Mary Helen (Long) T.; B.S. in Civil Engring., U. Ky., 1969, B.Arch., 1973; m. Nancy Louise Pullen, Apr. 1, 1967; children—Jeffrey Allan, Trisha Lynn. Spl. projects engr. Ky. Dept. Transp., Frankfort, 1964-70; prin. Chrisman, Miller, Wallace, Inc., Lexington, 1970—; vis. prof. U. Ky. Sch. Arch. Unit commr. Boy Scouts Am., recipient 20 yr. service award. Registered profl. engr. and architect, Ky. Ky. Hwy. scholar, 1964-66. Mem. AIA, Ky. Soc. Architects, Ky. Devel. Council, Am. Soc. Energy Engrs., Ky. Assn. Counties, Internat. Soc. Solar Engrs. Baptist. Chmn. energy adv. com. Ky. Dept. Edn., 1978—; mem. adv. com. So. Solar Energy Center, 1979—; mem. planning com. for energy conservation and solar energy U. Ky., 1978—. Author: Energy Audit Manual for Educational Facilities, 1978; (with others) Kentucky Solar Energy Handbook, 1979; Energy Audit Manual for Schools, Hospitals and Public Buildings, 1979. Home: 132 Bellemeade St Frankfort KY 40601 Office: 326 S Broadway Lexington KY 40508

TAYLOR, JESSE FREDERICK, govt. ofcl., found. exec.; b. Phoenix, Apr. 8; s. Frederick J. and Grace S. Taylor; B.A., Ariz. State U., 1952, M.A., 1957; Ph.D. (hon.), Rochdale Coll., Toronto, Ont., Can.; m. Willene Pulliam, Aug. 25, 1967; 1 son, Darryl Kenyatta. Instr. English, Prairie View (Tex.) Coll., 1957-59; teaching fellow English dept. Ariz. State U., Tempe, 1959-60; asso. prof. English, humanities So. U., New Orleans, 1960-65; lectr., cons., counselor Inst. Afro-Am. and Comparative Cultures, New Orleans, 1965-73; counselor Div. Vocational Rehab., New Orleans, 1973-75; instl. counselor La. Family Planning Program, New Orleans, 1974-75; med. and social services specialist Mental Health Services, New Orleans, 1975-76; personal and rehab. counselor, New Orleans, 1976-77; acad. adviser legal tng. program, cons. communication, part-time tutor English, Am. Found. Negro Affairs, New Orleans, 1977—; social services worker New Orleans City Council, 1977—. Served with USAF, 1952-56. Certified rehab., family, marriage and counselor. Mem. Nat., La. rehab. assns., Nat. Rehab. Counselors Assn., Am. Soc. Adlerian Psychology, Am. Personnel and Guidance Assn., Nat. Council Tchrs. English, Assn. Black Psychologists, Nat. Psychol. Assn., Am. Psychotherapy Assn., Am. Acad. Polit. and Social Scis., Assn. Black Anthropologists, Am. Humanist Assn. Home: 3140 New Orleans St New Orleans LA 70122

TAYLOR, JIM E., auto parts aftermarket exec.; b. Hot Springs, Ark., June 29, 1925; s. James Edward and Winifred Mart (Farmer) T.; student St. Louis U., San Jacinto Coll., Memphis State U.; children—James Edward, Thomas W., Mary Carol, Pamela Joann, Angelia Paris. With Automotive Aftermarket div. TRW, 1952-61; owner Univ. Auto Supply, Houston, 1962-71; dir. personnel and human resources Bass & Meineke Mgmt. Co., Inc., Pasadena, Tex., 1972—; lectr. in field.; guest lectr. San Jacinto Coll.; cons. in field. Mem. adv. bd. vocat. edn. dept. Houston and Pasadena Ind. Sch. Dists.; Tex. chmn. regional public events Am. Heart Assn., 1978-79, bd. dirs. Pasadena area. Lutheran. Club: Lions. Home: 621 W 16th St Houston TX 77008 Office: 1001 E Shaw Pasadena TX 77506

TAYLOR, JOHN LIPPINCOTT, marine biologist; b. Phila., Oct. 29, 1932; s. Thomas Thompson and Anna Lippincott (Engle) T.; B.S., Antioch Coll., 1955; M.S., U. Fla., 1961, Ph.D., 1971; m. Patricia May, Oct. 12, 1967; children—Elizabeth Richie, John Richie. With Nat. Marine Fisheries Service, St. Petersburg, Fla., 1961-72, chief, environ. assessment div., region 2, 1971-72; owner, dir., marine biologist Taylor Biol. Co., Lynn Haven, Fla., 1972—; instr. marine ecology U. West Fla., 1977, Gulf Coast Community Coll., Panama City, Fla., 1977-79. Served with USMC, 1956-58. Mem. Internat. Oceanographic Found., AAAS, Am. Soc. Limnology and Oceanography, Biol. Assn. of U.K., Fla. Acad. Sci., Sigma Xi, Phi Sigma. Republican. Quaker. Home and office: 801 Delaware Ave Lynn Haven FL 32444

TAYLOR, JOHN RENFORD, JR., banker; b. Lubbock, Tex., June 15, 1933; s. John Renford and Lucille (Grier) T.; grad. Sch. Banking, So. Methodist U., 1972; LL.B., LaSalle Ext. U., 1962; m. Rosalie Fore, Oct. 1, 1977; children—Perry, Michael. Pres., Continental Nat. Bank, San Antonio, 1974-77; adv. dir., v.p. League City (Tex.) Bank, 1978—; v.p. Citizens State Bank, Dickinson, Tex., 1978—, Bay Area Bank, Webster, Tex., 1978—, Alvin (Tex.) State Bank, 1978—; mem. faculty U. Houston, Clear Lake, 1978—, Coll. of Mainland, Texas City, 1978—, Am. Inst. Banking, Houston, 1970—. Mem. adv. bd. Sch. Profl. Studies, U. Houston, 1978—. Served with USAF, 1952-56. Mem. Robert Morris Assos., Am. Inst. Banking, Internat. Platform Assn., Fedn. Ind. Bus., Nat. Assn. Bus. Economists, Authors Guild, Mensa. Methodist. Author: How to Start and Succeed in a Business of Your Own, 1977; columnist Across the Counter. Office: 2401 Termini Dickinson TX 77539

TAYLOR, JON GUERRY, engring. cons.; b. Columbia, S.C., Nov. 8, 1939; s. Edward Lee and Sadie Margaret (Sessions) T.; B.S. in Civil Engring., U. S.C., 1965, postgrad., 1967; m. Faye Elizabeth Taylor, June 3, 1961; children—Jon Guerry, Sally Suzanne, Joy Valerie. Systems mgr. LBC & W, Architects and Engrs., Columbia, 1968-69, v.p., asst. exec. dir. ops., 1969-70; v.p. tech. services Lowell Dunn Co., Miami, 1970-71; v.p. spl. projects Capeletti Bros. Inc., Miami, 1971-77; dir. Concrete Promotion Council Fla., Inc., Winter Park, 1977-78; prin. engr. Wilbur Smith & Assos., Charleston, S.C., 1978—; lectr. in field. State chmn. Fla. Citizens for Right-to-Work, 1976—. Served with AUS, 1959. Registered profl. engr., S.C., Fla.; registered land surveyor, Fla. Mem. Asso. Builders and Contractors (chpt. pres. 1976-77, Man of Year award 1977), ASCE. Methodist (adminstrv. bd.), Engring. Contractors Assn. (dir. 1976-77). Contbr. articles to tech. and community publs. Home: 2062 Dogwood Rd Charleston SC 29407 Office: 194 E Bay St Charleston SC 29401

TAYLOR, JOSEPH TALIAFERRO, III, physician; b. Charleston, S.C., July 24, 1937; s. Joseph Taliaferro and Eloise (Lanier) T.; B.S., Coll. Charleston, 1959; M.D., Med. U. S.C., 1961; m. Susan Dwight Walker, July 11, 1959; children—Ellen Walker, Susan Sloan, Joseph Taliaferro. Intern, Med. U. S.C. Teaching Hosps., 1961-62; gen. practice medicine, Ridgeville, S.C., 1962-63, Summerville, S.C., 1963—; chief staff Dorchester County Hosp., 1969-72, North Trident Regional Hosp., 1975-77, chief dept. medicine, 1979. Trustee, Summerville Acad., pres., 1968—; trustee N. Trident Regional Hosp., 1980—. Served as capt. M.C., AUS, 1966-68. Decorated Bronze Star medal. Diplomate Am. Bd. Family Practice. Fellow Am. Acad. Family Physicians; mem. Am., S.C. med. assns., Coastal Med. Soc. (sec.-treas. 1974-77, pres. 1977-79), Am. Acad. Family Practice, Dorchester County Med. Soc. (pres. 1969-71), Alpha Omega Alpha. Episcopalian (vestryman 1971-74). Lion. Home: 108 Old Country Club Rd Summerville SC 29483 Office: 435 N Cedar St Summerville SC 29483

TAYLOR, JUDY CARVER, nursing home exec.; b. Stephenville, N.F., Mar. 29, 1951; d. Wiley Carroll and Charlotte Lorraine Kenney (Beaver) Carver; student Middle Tenn. State U., 1969-70, E. Tenn. State U., 1970-73; m. Joseph Larry Taylor, Apr. 4, 1976; 1 dau., Tiffany Charlotte. Patient care coordinator, social dir., co-owner, pres. Ivy Hall Nursing Home, Inc., Elizabethton, Tenn., 1971—. Mem. Tenn. Health Care Assn., Tenn. Nursing Home Assn., Soc. Care of Aging, Carter County C. of C. Club: Elizabethton Jr. Women's. Home: 305 Watauga Ave Elizabethton TN 37643 Office: 301 Watauga Ave Elizabethton TN 37643

TAYLOR, KENNETH MICHAEL, social worker; b. Galax, Va., June 16, 1949; s. Squire O. and Hope B. T.; A.A., Hiwassee Coll., 1969; B.A., Scarritt Coll., 1973, M.C.W., 1973; M.S. in Social Work, U. Tenn., 1975; 1 dau., Mary Joan. Social group worker Magness Center, Nashville, 1971-73; psychiat. social worker Mental Health Clinic, Inc., Wise, Va., 1975—; lectr. in social welfare Clin. Valley Coll., U. Va., 1976—. Bd. dirs. planning dist. I, Community Mental Health and Mental Retardation Services Bd., 1979—. Mem. Nat. Assn. Social Workers, Am. Assn. Marriage and Family Therapists, Acad. Cert. Social Workers. Home: 139 11th St NW Norton VA 24273 Office: Mental Health Clinic Inc PO Box 920 Wise VA 24293

TAYLOR, LAWRENCE HUFF, JR., cable TV exec.; b. Roanoke Rapids, N.C., Dec. 27, 1921; s. Lawrence Huff and Lillian Carter T.; student N.C. State U., 1939-40, Duke U., 1945, 46; m. Doris J. Taylor, July 6, 1949; children—Larry Wesson, Stephen Robert. Mem. N.C. Hwy. Patrol, 1947-53; chief dept. Northampton County Sheriff's Dept., Jackson, N.C., 1954-63; investigator Allsbrook, Benton, Knott, Cranford, Allsbrook, Whitaker & White, attys., Roanoke Rapids, 1963-64; mgr. Roanoke Rapids TeleCable (N.C.), 1964—. Mem. Bd. Edn. Northampton County. Served with USAAF, 1940-45; PTO. Decorated Bronze Star. Mem. So. Assn. Cable TV (dir.), N.C. Cable TV Assn. (pres.), C. of C. (dir.), Am. Legion (exec. bd.), VFW. Democrat. Methodist. Clubs: Masons, Shriners, Lions (past pres., dist. gov.), Tower (charter mem.). Home: 332 Starke Dr Roanoke Rapids NC 27870 Office: Roanoke Rapids TeleCable 20 E 11th St Roanoke Rapids NC 27876

TAYLOR, MARSHALL BENNETT, transp. services co. exec.; b. Portland, Maine, May 16, 1946; s. Clifford Brenton and Anne (Marshall) T.; B.S. in Mech. Engring., Worcester Poly. Inst., 1968; M.B.A., Babson Coll., 1972; m. Nancy Hamilton Smith, June 7, 1969; children—Prescott Bennett, Cameron Clark. Supr. inventory and prodn. control Allis Chalmers Corp., Boston, 1968-71; supr. systems and fin. analysis Mobil Oil Corp., Scarsdale, M.Y., 1972-74; mgr. capital planning Ryder System, Inc., Miami, Fla., 1974, dir. corp. planning, 1974-75, asst. treas., 1975-78, treas., 1978-79, v.p., treas., 1979—. Home: 12790 SW 64th Ct Miami FL 33156 Office: 3600 NW 82nd Ave Miami FL 33152

TAYLOR, MARVIN ELLIOTT, hosp. adminstr.; b. Greenville, S.C., Oct. 13, 1920; s. Robert Lafayette and Theodosia (McCall) T.; grad. George Washington U., 1950; m. Roberta Lou Owen, Nov. 26, 1954; children—Davis Hamilton, Jonathan Elliott, Gregory Franklin. Reporter, Greenville News, 1939-43; writer Dept. State, Washington, information officer U.S. embassy, Pusan, Korea, 1952-54; cultural officer U.S. embassy, Bonn, Germany, 1954-59; spl. asst. in edn. and cultural affairs USIA, Dept. State, Washington, 1959-62; consul U.S. embassy, Nairobi, Kenya, 1962-63; dir. pub. relations Greenville Hosp. System, 1963—. Chmn. pub. information Greenville County (S.C.) Found., 1968-78; mem. exec. com. S.C. Health and Sci. Fair, 1965-73. Served with AUS, 1943-46; PTO. Mem. S.C. (pub. relations cons.), Am. (adv. com. pub. relations) hosp. assns., C. of C., Am. Soc. for Hosp. Pub. Relations, Carolinas Hosp. Pub. Relations Soc. (dir., officer), Advt. Club Greenville. Republican. Presbyterian. Kiwanian. Home: 53 Woodvale Ave Greenville SC 29605 Office: 100 Mallard St Greenville SC 29601

TAYLOR, NANCY JANE, hosp. adminstr.; b. Gowanda, N.Y., Feb. 17, 1941; d. Bedford D. and Helen L. (Shultz) Pickup; R.N., Buffalo Gen. Hosp., 1962; B.S. in Nursing Edn. U. Buffalo, 1969; M.S. in Health Care Adminstrn., Fla. Internat. U., 1974; m. Olmon P. Taylor, Jr., May 20, 1978; stepchildren—Gale, Michael, Wayne. Supr. Lake Sumter Community Mental Health Center, Eustis, Fla., 1970-72; exec. dir. Lake County Boys Ranch, Altoona, Fla., 1972-74; dir. public relations Lake Community Hosp., Leesburg, Fla., 1974-75, asso. adminstr., 1976-77, adminstr., 1977—; tech. advisor Lake County Vo-Tech Center; ednl. bd. Lake Sumter Community Coll. Bd. dirs. Am. Cancer Soc., Lake County Boys Ranch; active Central Fla. chpt. Am. Heart Assn., Nat. Fedn. Bus. and Profl. Women. Mem. Am. Hosp. Assn., Fla. Hosp. Assn., Am. Acad. Med. Adminstrs. (program com.), Fla. League of Hosps., Hosp. Fin. Mgmt. Assn., Profl. Standards Review Orgn. Central Fla. (bd. dirs.), Emergency Med. Council for Health and Rehabilitative Services State of Fla., E.Central Fla. Hosp. Council, Leesburg Area C. of C. (v.p.), Lake County Fla. C. of C. (bd. dirs., 1979). Methodist. Club: Elks Aux. (bd. dirs., budget com. chmn., chmn. program com.). Home: PO Box 688 Leesburg FL 32748 also Inglewood Dr Lake Miona Heights Wildwood FL 32785 Office: 700 N Palmetto Leesburg FL 32748

TAYLOR, ORVILLE WALTERS, historian; b. El Dorado, Ark., Sept. 20, 1919; s. William Oscar and Minnie Belle (White) T.; A.B., Ouachita Baptist U., 1947; M.A., U. Ky., 1948; Ph.D., Duke U., 1956; m. Evelyn Adelle Bonham, Dec. 5, 1942; children—Michael, Priscilla Taylor Norvell, Melissa, Penelope. Instr. history Little Rock Jr. Coll., 1950-55; prof. history Baptist Coll., Iwo, Nigeria, 1955-62, U. N.C., Asheville, 1963-65; prof., chmn. dept. Wesleyan Coll., Macon, Ga., 1965-69, Ga. Coll., Milledgeville, 1969—; exec. sec., state historian Ark. History Commn., 1959; cons. Ministry of Edn., Nigeria, 1956-62; cons. Nat. Endowment for Humanities, 1972—. Justice of peace, Pulaski County, Ark., 1952-55; bd. dirs. Ark. Ednl. TV Assn., 1953-55; mem. nat. advisory com. Civil War Centennial Commn., 1959. Served to Capt. U.S. Army, 1941-46; Lt. Col. USAF (ret.), 1977—. Am. Philos. Soc. grantee, 1968-69. Mem. AAUP, Royal African Soc. (life), Am., So., Ark. (sec.-treas. 1954-55) hist. assns., Ga. Assn. Historians (pres. 1973-74), Ga. Polit. Sci. Assn. (pres. 1970-71), Assn. for Study Afro-Am. Life and History, Phi Beta Kappa, Phi Kappa Phi. Democrat. Baptist. Author: Negro Slavery in Arkansas, 1958; contbr. articles and revs. to profl. jours. and encys. Home: 590 W Lakeview Dr Milledgeville GA 31061 Office: Box 528 Georgia Coll Milledgeville GA 31061

TAYLOR, PATRICIA ROBERTSON, ins. saleswoman; b. Jackson, Miss., Oct. 23, 1932; d. James Zetus and Addie (Grady) Robertson; m. Hiran Burgoyne Taylor, Sr., Dec. 22, 1951; children—Hiram Burgoyne, Jane Taylor Shropshire. Various secretarial positions, 1950-67; field underwriter Mut. Life Ins. Co. N.Y., Mobile, 1967—. Mem. Million Dollar Round Table; recipient various other ins. sales awards. Mem. Nat. Assn. Life Underwriters, Women's Leaders Roundtable, Ala. Assn. Life Underwriters, Mobile Assn. Life Underwriters (pres. 1979-80). Republican. Methodist. Home: 573 Markham Dr Mobile AL 36609 Office: 2700 Grant St Mobile AL 36606

TAYLOR, PAUL FRANKLIN, coll. adminstr.; b. Portsmouth, Ohio, Oct. 28, 1946; s. Frank Claude and Ruth (Jones) T.; B.A., U. Ky., 1970; M.A., Georgetown Coll., 1972; children—Matthew, Kate. Counselor, dir. financial aid Shawnee State Gen. and Tech. Coll., Portsmouth, 1970-72; guidance counselor Central Ky. State Vocat.-Tech. Sch., Lexington, 1972-74; dir. tng. Bluegrass Employment and Tng. Program, Lexington, 1974-76; asst. prof., career counselor Lexington Tech. Inst., 1976-77, asst. prof., asst. dir., chief adminstr. for student services, 1977—. Vice-chmn., Bluegrass Employment and Tng. Program's Citizens Adv. Council to Mayor, 1979-80; mem. Lexington Edn. Work Council, Equal Employment Opportunity Rev. Com. Recipient Outstanding Service awards Bluegrass Employment and Tng. Program, 1977, 78, Lexington Edn. Work Council, 1977. Mem. Am. Personnel and Guidance Assn., Am. Coll. Personnel Assn., Ky. Personnel and Guidance Assn., Coll. Personnel Assn. Ky., Coop. Edn. Assn. Ky., So. Assn. Collegiate Registrars and Admission Officers, Ky. Assn. Collegiate Registrars and Admissions Officers, U. Ky. Alumni Assn. Democrat. Home: 1100 Mt Rushmore Way Lexington KY 40502 Office: 206A Oswald Bldg U Ky Lexington KY 40506

TAYLOR, PRISCILLA DEAN, nurse, psychologist; b. Greenville, S.C., July 5, 1936; d. Joseph Wilson and Ruth Mozelle (Brown) Hunt; Asso. in Nursing, Bapt. Coll. Charleston, 1973, B.S., 1973; M.S. in Nursing, Med. Coll. Ga., 1976; M.S.Ed., Southern Ill. U., Edwardsville, 1976; m. William Haynie Taylor, Jr., Oct. 7, 1955; children—Billy, Cindy, Mandy. Instr. clin. nursing Bapt. Coll., Charleston, 1973-74, instr. nursing, 1974-76; instr. nursing Med. U. S.C., Charleston, 1976—; instr. psychology Trident Tech. Coll., 1977; vol. counseling Dorchester Mental Health Clinic, Crisis Intervention Workshop for Emergency Med. Technicians. Pub. mem. Palmetto Low Country Health Systems Agy., 1976—. NIH trainee, 1974-76. Mem. Am., S.C. nurses assns., Flowertown Bus. and Profl. Womens Club. Baptist. Home: 104 Race Club Rd Summerville SC 29483 Office: 171 Ashley ave Charleston SC 29403

TAYLOR, RALPH WAYNE, constrn. co. exec.; b. Felda, Fla., Aug. 5, 1927; s. Homer Raymond Taylor and Mildred Vance (Manley) Taylor Feller; B.S., Asbury Coll., 1950; E.E., U. Miami, 1952; m. Norma Jean Booth, Jan. 5, 1950; children—Jean Jonelle, Alan Wayne, Cheryl Lynn, Angela Roseanne, Scott Ward. Tchr. sch., 1950-51; design engr. Gen. Electric Co., Cin., 1953-57; elec. engr. Martin Marietta Corp., Cape Canaveral, Fla., 1957-60, supr., 1960-65, activation mgr., 1965-73; pres. Eden-Roc Homes, Inc., Ft. Myers, Fla., 1979—, Fla. Frontier Steakhouse System, Inc., Ft. Myers, 1979—; v.p. Taylor Industries, Inc., Ft. Myers, 1979—. Served with USN, 1945-47. Mem. AIAA. Republican. Home: 3334 McGregor Blvd Fort Myers FL 33901 Office: 9150 Cleveland Ave S Fort Myers FL 33907

TAYLOR, RANDALL OWEN, constrn. co. exec.; b. Ft. Worth, Aug. 19, 1949; s. Wayne Cullen and Mary Gerdaline T.; student U. Tex., Arlington, 1968-70; cert. in programming Acad. Computer Tech., 1972; m. Elizabeth Ann Switzer, Oct. 7, 1978. Plant mgr. Western Dynamics Action Co., Princeton, Tex., 1971-72; cost acct. Tex. Hwy. Dept., McKinney, 1972-73; head engring. dept. Brown & Root Inc., Glen Rose, Tex., 1973—.

TAYLOR, RANDY RAY, psychologist; b. Miles City, Mont., Mar. 6, 1950; s. Duane Rowland and Elizabeth Frances (Erdelt) T.; B.S., U. Wyo., 1972, M.S., 1973, Ph.D., 1976; m. Susan Lillian Schmidt, Dec. 18, 1975; 1 son, Nikolas Kristen. Clin. psychology intern, Northside Community Mental Health Center, Tampa, 1976-77; dir. psychol. services Gaston Lincoln Psychiat. Hosp., Gastonia, N.C., 1977-79; pvt. practice family and individual therapy, 1978-79; adj. faculty U. N.C., Charlotte, 1978-79. Bd. dirs. Gaston County Rape Companion Program. Mem. N.C. Psychol. Assn., Sigma Xi (asso.). Lutheran. Club: YMCA. Home: 2512-I Cherbough Way Gastonia NC 28052 Office: 401 N Highland St Gastonia NC 28052

TAYLOR, RAYMOND MASON, lawyer, librarian; b. Washington, N.C., Jan. 1, 1933; s. Thaddeus Raymond and Mary Ada (Mason) T.; A.B. in Polit. Sci., U. N.C., 1955, J.D., 1960; grad. U.S. Army Intelligence Sch., 1956; m. Rachel High, Apr. 3, 1965; 1 dau., Elizabeth Lee. Staff reporter Washington Daily News, summers, 1952, 54; adminstrv. asst. CD Orgn., Winston-Salem and Forsyth County, N.C., 1955; adminstrv. intern City of Winston-Salem, summer, 1958; admitted to N.C. bar, 1960, U.S. Supreme Ct. bar, 1970; research asst. to justice Supreme Ct. N.C., 1960-61; asso. firm Gardner, Connor and Lee, Wilson, N.C., 1961-64; adj. instr. bus. law Atlantic Christian Coll., Wilson, 1962-63, adj. prof., 1963-64; marshal, librarian Supreme Ct. N.C., 1964-77; project dir. Fed. Jud. Center Study of Fed. Ct. Libraries, 1976-77; spl. lectr. econs. and bus. N.C. State U., Raleigh, 1967—; individual practice law, Raleigh, 1977—; dir. N.C. Law Research Facilities Study, 1970; chmn. State and Ct. Law Libraries U.S.-Can., 1973-74; sec. Wake County Library Commn., 1979—. Sec., Southeastern area council Am. Jr. Red Cross, 1949-50, study visitor to Europe, 1950; Democratic chmn. Pineville Precinct, Beaufort County, N.C., 1954-57; parliamentarian Wilson County Dem. Exec. Com., 1962-64; mem. N.C. 2d Solicitorial Dist., Dem. Exec. Com., 1962-64. Served with Intelligence Corps, U.S. Army, 1955-57. Recipient award of excellence Soc. Tech. Communication, 1976; named Tar Heel of Week, 1971. Mem. Am. Bar Assn. (mem. spl. com.

on law book pub. practices 1970-76, chmn. law sch. bds. visitors com. 1976-77), N.C. Bar Assn., N.C. Acad. Trial Lawyers, Am. Bus. Law Assn., Am. Assn. Law Libraries, Internat. Assn. Law Libraries (chmn. ct. libraries com. 1977—), Order Golden Fleece (pres. 1958-59), Am. Bar Found. (mem. library services com. 1969-73), Asso. Clubs (Topeka) (nat. speaker 1974—), Pi Sigma Alpha, Phi Delta Phi. Presbyterian. Clubs: Capital City, Raleigh, Execs. Contbr. articles to legal jours.; asst. editor Tar Heel Barrister, 1958-59; student editorial bd. N.C. Law Rev., 1960. Home: 3073 Granville Dr Raleigh NC 27609 Office: Suite 200 Insurance Bldg 336 Fayetteville St Mall PO Box 1590 Raleigh NC 27602

TAYLOR, REX ALAN, city adminstr.; b. Crawfordsville, Ind., May 23, 1948; s. Denvil Marion and Helen Alberta T.; B.S., Ind. State U., 1970, M.S., 1971; m. Lana Kay Palm, Apr. 25, 1970; children—Lyana, Aaron. Teaching fellow Ind. State U., 1970-71; adminstrv. aide to city mgr. City of Decatur (Ill.), 1971-73; asst. city mgr. City of Ames (Iowa), 1973-77, acting city mgr., 1975-76; city mgr. City of Paris (Ky.), 1977—; dir. Indsl. Promotion Corp. Mem. Bourbon County (Ky.) Allocation Com., United Way.; mem. adminstrv. bd. So. Hills United Methodist Ch. Mem. Internat. City Mgmt. Assn., Ky. City Mgmt. Assn. (1st v.p.), Am. Soc. Public Adminstrn. Democrat. Clubs: Masons; Rotary (Paris). Office: 800 Pleasant St Paris KY 40361

TAYLOR, RICHARD DOUGLAS, county ofcl.; b. Mt. Clemens, Mich., Sept. 8, 1948; s. William H. and Myrtle (Gullion) T.; student Bluefield State Coll., 1966-67, 77-79; m. Norma Jean Webb, Oct. 15, 1969; children—Robert Matthew, Adam Christopher. Field service mgr. Carter Machinery Co., Bluefield, W.Va., 1968-70; supr. ops. So. W.Va. Regional Health Council, Inc., Bluefield, 1970-75; asst. country adminstr. Tazewell (Va.) County, 1976—. Cons. advisor Tazewell County Vocat. Tech. Sch. Served with USAF, 1967-68. Mem. Va. Solid Waste Mgmt. Assn. (bd. dirs.), Valley Info. Systems Assn. (bd. dirs.), S.W. Va. Solid Waste Mgmt. Assn. (v.p.). Office: PO Box 68 Tazewell VA 24651

TAYLOR, ROBERT ANDREW, cons. engr.; b. Port Royal, Pa., Mar. 10, 1935; s. Cahuncey Steely and Pearl Esther (McCormick) T.; B.S., Pa. State U., 1961, M.S., 1963; m. Mary Frances Barker, June 1, 1957; children—Stephen Kent, Daniel Barker, Bart Andrew. Mech. engr. researcher Pa. State U., Univ. Park, 1961-65; engr. Caterpillar Tractor research, Peoria, Ill., 1963-64; aerospace engring. exec. Chrysler Corp., New Orleans, 1964-75; mech. engr. U.S. Dept. Agr. so. regional research center, New Orleans, 1974-75, Agrl. Exp. Sta., Clemson, S.C., 1975—; cons. to univs., corps in field. Church deacon, elder Mt. Zion Presbyterian Ch.; active little theater. Served with U.S. Army, 1954-57. Registered profl. engr., La. Mem. ASME. (textile adv. bd. S.C.), Fiber Soc. Am. Republican. Clubs: Golf, Yacht. Contbr. articles to profl. jours. Home: RD # 3 Box 275 Anderson SC 29621 Office: Box 792 Clemson SC 29631

TAYLOR, ROBERT EARL, city ofcl.; b. Syracuse, N.Y., Aug. 4, 1946; s. Earl Herman and Mary (Welch) T.; children—Mary Christina, Eric Michael. With Eastern Airlines, Ft. Lauderdale, Fla., 1967—; councilman City of N. Miami Beach (Fla.), 1973—. Served with USAF, 1965. Mem. Dade County League Cities (1st v.p. 1979—), Fla. League Cities (chmn. intergovtl. relations 1976—), Gold Coast League Cities, Nat. League Cities, Am. Legion. Democrat. Methodist. Clubs: K.P., City of Hope. Home: 1951 NE 157th Terr North Miami Beach FL 33162 Office: 17011 NE 19th Ave North Miami Beach FL 33162

TAYLOR, ROBERT LADDIE, patent agent; b. Carter County, Tenn., Dec. 26, 1946; s. Robert Love and Pansy Maude (Morrell) T.; B.S. in Chemistry and English, E. Tenn. State U., 1969; m. Christine Ann Crumley, Nov. 22, 1969; 1 son, Robert Shaun. Sr. research tech. Great Lakes Research Corp., Elizabethton, Tenn., 1968-72, patent searcher analyst, 1972-75, patent agent, 1975—; admitted to U.S. Patent bar, 1974. Active Stoney Creek Vol. Fire Dept., safety/first aid instr., 1976—. Baptist. Clubs: Elks, Moose. Home: Route 7 Box 323-B Elizabethton TN 37643 Office: PO Box 1031 Elizabethton TN 37643

TAYLOR, ROBERT WAYNE, assn. exec.; b. McKinney, Tex., Aug. 16, 1938; s. Alvin Wilson and Alice Loraine (Wyatt) T.; student U. Wis., 1967; m. Judith Ann Smith, Nov. 13, 1959; children—Randall, Leigh, Lesli. Various positions Okla. Credit Union League, Tulsa, 1966—, pres., 1970—; pres. Okla. Corp. Credit Union; dir. Okla. Central Credit Union. Served with USAF, 1958. Mem. Tulsa C. of C., Internat. Assn. Mng. Dirs. Baptist. Home: 10319 S Sandusky St Tulsa OK 74136 Office: 214 E Skelly Dr Tulsa OK 74105

TAYLOR, ROD ALLEN, artist, educator; b. Feb. 29, 1932; s. Fred and Susie (Hill) T.; B.S., Va. State U., 1959; M.A., Am. U., 1961; Ed.M., Ala. State U., 1972; Ph.D., Pa. State U., 1974; m. Ora Williams, Aug. 25, 1967; 1 son, Rodney Alan. Tchr. art Hine Jr. High Sch., Washington, 1961-63; instr. art Shaw U., Raleigh, N.C., 1963-64; cons. Nat. Security Agy., Washington, 1964-66; instr. art St. Augustine Coll., Raleigh, 1966-68, Ala. A&M U., 1968-70; edn. cons. in humanities U. So. Ala., 1970-72; instr. Pa. State U., 1972-74; chmn. fine arts dept. Norfolk (Va.) State U., 1974—; exhbns. include: Smithsonian Instn., 1963, Atlanta U., 1965, Corcoran Art Gallery, 1965, Bonbonniere Gallery, Nicaragua, 1962, Pa. State U., 1972, Cath. U. Am., 1967. Bd. dirs., chmn. Norfolk Com. Improvement of Edn. Served with U.S. Army, 1953-55. Mem. NEA, Assn. Supervision and Curriculum Devel., Nat. Sculptors Soc., So. Sculptors Guild, Alpha Phi Delta. Author: An Empirical Investigation of the Art/Personality Relationship. Home: 432 Longdale Crescent Chesapeake VA 23325 Office: Norfolk VA

TAYLOR, RONALD JAMES, ins. exec.; b. Sennett, N.Y., Feb. 9, 1941; s. Lloyd A. and Mary Elizabeth (Manzer) T.; B.A., Colgate U., 1963; multiple line degree Coll. Ins., N.Y.C., 1964; m. Betsy Ann Hull, Aug. 31, 1963; children—Mary Elizabeth, Ronald James, Robin Lynn, Wendy Allison. Account asst. Delaney Offices, Inc., N.Y.C., 1963-66; account exec. G.L. Hodson & Son, Inc., N.Y.C., 1966-69; v.p., dir. E.W. Blanch Co., Mpls., 1969-75; pres., dir. Reins. Services of Am., Inc., Atlanta, 1975—; vice chmn., pres., dir. RSA Mgmt., Inc., Atlanta, 1979—. Clubs: Cherokee Town and Country, Colgate Alumni of Atlanta. Home: 6460 River Chase Circle NW Atlanta GA 30328 Office: 1700-B Commerce Dr NW Atlanta GA 30318

TAYLOR, RUTHFORD T., mech. engr.; b. Leesburg, Fla., Jan. 14, 1933; s. Berle W. and Martha A. Taylor; A.A., Northeastern Okla. A. and M. Coll., 1952; B.S., Okla. State U., 1961; m. Frances L. Erion, May 20, 1953; children—Beverly, Brenda, Barbara, Beth, Paul. With Employers Casualty Ins. Co., Amarillo, Tex., 1961-63; with Mason & Hanger-Silas Mason Co., Amarillo, 1963—, various engring. positions, 1963-71, sr. project engr., supervisory head work analysis and control sect., 1971-74, sr. project engr., supervisory head estimating sect. plant design dept., 1974-75, sr. project engr., supr. head maintenance and modification sect. plant design dept., sect. engr., 1975—. Served with U.S. Army, 1951-57. Registered profl. engr., Tex. Mem. Full Gospel Bus. Men's Fellowship Internat. (v.p. Amarillo chpt. 1978). Presbyterian. Home: 3413 Lipscomb St Amarillo TX 79109 Office: PO Box 30020 Amarillo TX 79177

TAYLOR, SHAHANE RICHARDSON, JR., ophthalmologist; b. Greensboro, N.C., Sept. 5, 1928; s. Shahane Richardson and Mary Hoke (Hooker) T.; A.B., U. N.C., 1955, M.D., 1959; m. Betty Jane Teague, Aug. 2, 1952; children—Shahane R. III, Anne Teague, Mary Hooker. Intern, N.C. Meml. Hosp., Chapel Hill, 1959-60; resident in ophthalmology U. N.C.-McPherson Meml. Hosp., 1960-63; practice medicine specializing in ophthal. surgery, Greensboro, N.C., 1963—; chief ophthalmology Wesley Long Hosp.; staff Moses Cone, Greensboro hosps. (all Greensboro); vis. instr. surgery U. N.C., Chapel Hill, 1964-73; pres. Mgmt. Systems N.C., 1969-72; dir. Profl. Automated Mgmt., 1972—; dir. Warner London, Inc., 1973—, sec., 1976—. Served to capt., M.I., U.S. Army, 1951-54. Diplomate Am. Bd. Ophthalmology. Mem. AMA, So. Med. Assn., N.C. Med. Soc. (exec. council 1979—), Guilford County Med. Soc. (pres. 1977), Am. Acad. Ophthalmology and Otolaryngology, Pan Am. Ophthal. Soc., Soc. Eye Surgeons, Mensa, Quarter Century Wireless Assn., Intertel. Episcopalian. Clubs: Greensboro Whist, Greensboro Country, Greensboro City (dir.), Core Banks, Mchts. and Mfrs. Assn. Home: 2207 Carlisle Rd Greensboro NC 27408 Office: 348 N Elm St Greensboro NC 27401

TAYLOR, WILLIAM BARRETT, III, internat. marketing exec., lawyer; b. Winston-Salem, N.C., July 7, 1919; s. William Barrett, II, and Frances Dinsdale (Swann) T.; A.B., U. Tenn., 1941; J.D., U. Fla., 1950; postgrad. Oxford U., 1943, George Washington U., 1948, U. Denver, 1957, U. Md., 1958; m. Gwendoline Madge Abbott, May 1, 1945; children—Sally Hill (Mrs. Christopher Brunton), William Barrett IV, Richard A., Michael A. Admitted to Fla. bar, 1950, U.S. Supreme Ct. bar, 1953; commd. 2d lt. U.S. Air Force, 1941, advanced through grades to col., 1954; with 8th AF, 1942-45; with Office of Legislative Liaison, Office Sec. of Air Force, 1950-54; asst. chief of staff USAF Acad., 1955-58; with Joint U.S. Mil. Group, Spain, 1958-62; with Office of Asst. Sec. of Def., 1962-64; ret., 1964; internat. liaison McDonnell Douglas Corp., Washington, 1964-75; dir. internat. devel. Lykes Youngstown Corp., 1975-77; pres. Wm. B. Taylor Assos., 1978—; commr. South Pacific Commn., Noumea, New Caledonia, 1969, sr. commr., 1970-74, with rank of dep. asst. sec. of state; v.p. Taylor Bros., Inc., Winston-Salem, 1947-50. Mem. Trans Atlantic council Boy Scouts Am., 1960-62; bd. dirs. Nat. Alliance Sr. Citizens. Mem. Am., Inter-Am., Fla. bar assns., Air Force Assn., Navy League, Am. Def. Preparedness Assn., Middle East Inst., Iran Am. Soc. Author: Pictorial History 14th Combat Bomb Wing, 1946. Home: 3209 N Columbus St Arlington VA 22207 Office: Suite 404 2201 Wilson Blvd Arlington VA 22201

TAYLOR, WILLIAM BROCKENBROUGH, SR., engring. co. exec.; b. Norfolk, Va., Mar. 11, 1925; s. Lewis Jerome and Roberta Page (Newton) T.; B.S., U.S. Mil. Acad., 1945; M.S.E., Johns Hopkins U., 1951; m. Nancy Dare Aitcheson, June 12, 1945; children—William Brockenbrough, Anne Taylor Cregger, Paul K., Katharine C., David A. With U.S. Army C.E., Washington and Ft. Belvoir, Va., 1955-62, NASA Manned Space Flight Program, Washington, 1962-67; sci. adv. U.S. Army Research and Devel., Pentagon, 1967-69; tech. dir. U.S. Army Research and Devel. Center, Ft. Belvoir, Va., 1969-73; chief research and devel. U.S. Army Corps Engrs., 1974-77; cons. engr., Alexandria, Va., 1973-79; dir. corp. energy growth Planning Research Corp., McLean, Va., 1979; pres., bd. dirs. VMI Research Labs., Lexington, Va., 1972—; cons. in field. Mem. Fairfax County Schs. PTA, 1953-79; chmn. Episcopal Diocesan Com. on Alternatives for Children in Trouble, 1977-79; pres. Region VI Episc. Diocese Va., 1979—. Served with U.S. Army, 1945-54. Recipient Superior Achievement award NASA, 1967; Meritorious Civilian Service award U.S. Army, 1962, 77; registered profl. engr., Va., D.C. Fellow Soc. Am. Mil. Engrs.; mem. AIAA, Sigma Xi. Republican. Contbr. articles to profl. jours. Home: 4001 Belle Rive Terr Alexandria VA 22309 Office: PRC Energy Analysis Co 7600 Old Springhouse Rd McLean VA 22102

TAYLOR, WILLIAM LADALE, ednl. adminstr.; b. West Point, Ga., Nov. 23, 1946; s. Horace William and Geraldine (Hall) T.; B.A., U. Ala., 1970, M.B.A., 1976; m. Nancy Yates, Aug. 19, 1969; 1 dau., Lindsey McCall. Dormitory dir. U. Ala., University, 1974-77, Greek adv., 1976-77, asst. dir. student union, 1976-77, asso. dir., 1977, dir. Ferguson Center, 1977—. Served with Signal Corps, U.S. Army, 1970-74. Recipient citation of honor, alumni award Theta Chi, 1978; decorated Meritorious Service medal. Mem. Nat. Assn. Student Personnel Adminstrs., So. Coll. Personnel Assn., Assn. Coll. Unions-Internat. (research com), Tuscaloosa County Alumni Assn. (sec.-treas. 1978-79, pres.-elect 1979—), Phi Delta Kappa, Kappa Delta Pi. Mem. United Ch. of Christ. Office: PO Box CQ University AL 35486

TEAGUE, BILL TRUMAN, med. tech. adminstr.; b. Freer, Tex., Oct. 24, 1937; s. Carl L. and Gladys E. (Wade) T.; B.S., Hardin Simmons U., 1961; cert. Hendrick Meml. Hosp. Sch. Med. Tech., 1961; Med. Tech., U. Tex. Med. Br. Sch. Blood Bank Tech., 1964; m. Mary Ann Herrington, Dec. 26, 1958; children—Timothy Ray, James Wade. Instr., U. Tex. Sch. Blood Banking, Galveston, 1963-66; blood bank technologist U. Tex. Med. Br., Galveston, 1964-66; instr. edn. services Philip Levine Lab. Immunohematology, Raritan, N.J., 1966-67; instr. Bayfront Med. Center, Inc., St. Petersburg, Fla., 1967-72; dir. Community Blood Bank, St. Petersburg, 1967-72; dir. Travis County Med. Soc. Blood Bank, Austin, Tex., 1972-75; exec. dir. The Blood Center, Houston, 1975—; clin. instr. dept. med. tech. U. Tex., Houston, 1978—; mem. com. blood and blood component utilization Am. Blood Commn., 1977-78. Trustee, Nat. Hemophilia Found., Tri-City chpt., 1968-72, chmn., 1971-72. Served to lt. U.S. Army, 1961-62. Named Med. Technologist of Year, Fla. Soc. Med. Tech., 1971-72. Mem. Am. Assn. Blood Banks v.p. 1978-79, dir. 1975-78, pres. elect 1979-80, pres. 1980-81), Am. Soc. Med. Tech. (dir. region VII 1973-75, pres. Fla. div. 1971-72), South Central Assn. Blood Banks (pres. 1979—). Presbyterian. Contbr. articles on med. tech. adminstrn. and donor service to profl. publs. Home: 5318 Havenwoods Dr Houston TX 77066 Office: 5303 Caroline PO Box 8371 Houston TX 77004

TEAGUE, CLAUDE EDWARD, JR., mfg. co. exec.; b. Sanford, N.C., Sept. 9, 1924; s. Claude Edward and Mary (Spaugh) T.; A.B., U. N.C., Chapel Hill, 1947, Ph.D., 1950; div.; children—Penny Renee, Brian Howard, Claude Edward, 3d. Research chemist Am. Viscose Corp., Marcus Hook, Pa., 1950-51; with R.J. Reynolds Tobacco Co., Winston-Salem, N.C., 1952-75, asst. dir. research, 1970-75; planning mgr. R.J. Reynolds Industries, Winston-Salem, 1975-76, dir. corp. research, 1976—; teaching asst. U. N.C., 1947. Served with U.S. Army, 1943-45. Decorated Bronze Star, Purple Heart; research fellow Office Naval Research, 1948-50. Mem. Am. Chem. Soc., N.Y. Acad. Sci., Winston-Salem C. of C., Sigma Xi. Club: Westwood. Home: 716 Archer Rd Winston-Salem NC 27106 Office: RJ Reynolds Industries PO Box 2959 Winston-Salem NC 27102

TEAGUE, PEYTON CLARK, chemist, educator; b. Montgomery, Ala., June 26, 1915; s. Robert S. and Sara McGehee (Clark) T.; ed. Huntingdon Coll., 1932-34; B.S., Auburn U., 1936; M.S., Pa. State U., 1937; Ph.D., U. Tex., 1942; m. Patricia Cussons Lamb, June 12, 1937; 1 dau., Norah Teague Grimball. Research chemist Am. Agrl. Chem. Co., Newark, 1937-39; instr. dept. chemistry Auburn (Ala.) U., 1941-42, asst. prof., 1943-45; research chemist U.S. Naval Research Lab., Washington, 1942-45; asst. prof. U. Ga., Athens, 1945-48, U. Ky., Lexington, 1948-50; asso. prof. dept. chemistry U. S.C., Columbia, 1950-56, prof., 1956—, deptl. dir. grad. studies, 1971—; vis. prof. U. Coll., Dublin, Ireland, 1963-64, 77; dir. Teague Hardware Co., Montgomery, Ala., 1955-74. Vestryman, Trinity Episcopal Cathedral, 1968-71, lay reader, 1963—. Recipient Outstanding Tchr. award U. S.C., 1976. Mem. Am. Chem. Soc. (chmn. S.C. sect. 1958-59), Phytochem. Soc. N. Am. (pres. 1969-70), S.C. Acad. Sci., Sigma Xi (pres. U. S.C. chpt. 1962-63), Phi Kappa Phi, Phi Lambda Upsilon, Blue Key, Phi Delta Theta. Clubs: Kiwanis, Forest Lake Country. Contbr. articles to sci. jours. Home: 1550 Adger Rd Columbia SC 29205 Office: Dept Chemistry U SC Columbia SC 29208

TEAGUE, WILLIAM JOSEPH, historian; b. Seagraves, Tex., Sept. 2, 1941; s. Henry Joseph and Ruth (Cody) T.; B.A., U. Tex., Austin, 1963; M.A., So. Meth. U., 1971; Ph.D., N.Tex. State U., 1977. Instr. history El Centro Coll., Dallas, 1972-79, N. Tex. State U., Denton, 1974-77; asso. prof. history, chmn. social scis. dept. Tex. Coll., Tyler, 1978—; free lance author; grants cons. Nat. Endowment for Humanities. Served with USNR, 1963-65; Vietnam. Postdoctoral grantee Lyndon B. Johnson Found., So. Fellowships Fund, Nat. Endowment for Humanities; postdoctoral fellow Am. Studies Assn., Am. Hist. Records and Publs. Commn. Mem. Am. Hist. Assn., Am. Polit. Sci. Assn., So. Hist. Assn., AAUP, So. Labor Studies Assn., Soc. Historians of Early Am. Rep. Episcopalian. Home: 2808 Throckmorton St Apt 108 Dallas TX 75219 Office: Texas College Tyler TX 75701

TEASLEY, EDGAR WILLIAM, assn. exec., realtor; b. Toccoa, Ga., Oct. 7, 1912; s. Edgar Carl and Pearle (Brown) T.; A.B. in Econs., George Washington U., 1936; m. Margaret Pitney, Sept. 15, 1939; children—Stewart P., Russell W. Jr. exec. W.R. Grace & Co., N.Y.C., 1936-41; gen. mgr., owner radio sta. WTNT, Augusta, Ga., 1947-49; self-employed land developer, home builder, realtor, Greenville, S.C., 1950-63; exec. v.p. Home Builders Assn., Greenville, 1963—. Trustee Home Builders Ins. Trust, Home Builders Self Insurers Fund, Home Builders Pension Fund. bd. dirs. Greenville Housing Found. Served with USNR, 1941-46. Recipient 8 awards as exec. v.p. Home Builders Assn. Greenville. Mem. Am. Soc. Assn. Execs. (certified assn. exec.), Nat. Assn. Home Builders (life dir., econ. adviser), Home Builders S.C. (dir.). Presbyterian (ruling elder). Editor, pub. Home Building Newsletter, 1962—. Home: 8 Sunset Dr Greenville SC 29605 Office: 702 E McBee Ave Greenville SC 29601

TEASLEY, SIDNEY WESLEY, hosp. food service adminstr.; b. Carrobor, N.C., Aug. 26, 1926; s. Thomas Lee and Ethel Mary (Ragen) T.; student U. Calif., 1951-53, in Instl. Mgmt., Air. U., Gunter AFB, Ala., 1955; B.S.B.A., Evans Coll., 1958; m. Elsie Annie Davis, Apr. 28, 1944. With VA Hosp., Salisbury, N.C., 1955-57; with Cabarrus Meml. Hosp., Concord, N.C., 1957—, food service adminstr., 1958—. Served with USAF, 1951-55; PTO. Mem. Hosp. Food Service Adminstrs., Food Service Exec. Assn. Republican. Mem. Assemblies of God. Home: 1105 Highland Ave Landis NC 28088 Office: 920 Church St N Concord NC 28025

TECKLENBURG, JANE MARIE, sr. citizens center adminstr.; b. Wichita, Dec. 28, 1935; d. William Castner and Marie Catherine (Arthur) Boyle; B.A., Tex. Christian U., 1957, M.A., 1968; m. Harvey Howard Tecklenburg, Mar. 14, 1959; children—Kerry Howard, Luci Rae, Brian Kay. Girls worker Bethlehem Center, Fort Worth, 1957-60; spl. project dir. Camp Fire Girls, Fort Worth, 1967-68; program dir. Sr. Citizens Center, Inc., Fort Worth, 1968-71, exec. dir., 1971—. Mem. Gerontol. Soc., Western Gerontol. Soc., Nat. Council Aging, Nat. Inst. Sr. Centers (v.p. 1977-79), Nat. Assn. Nutrition and Aging Services, Tex. United Community Services, Tex. Assn. Sr. Centers (sec. 1976-77, v.p. 1978-79), Tex. Assn. Title VII Projects (sec. 1976-77, pres. 1978-80), Nat. Inst. Sr. Centers (chmn.-elect 1980—). Methodist. Clubs: Leadership, Forum, Press. Home: 1424 Porto Bello Ct Arlington TX 76012 Office: 1000 Macon St Fort Worth TX 76102

TEDDER, CHLOE JEAN, vol. service adminstr.; b. Ft. Smith, Ark., Aug. 7, 1929; d. Eric Norquest and Roberta Luella (McLaughlin) Jordan; student Ft. Smith Jr. Coll., 1947-50, Newspaper Inst. Am., 1954-56; m. Robert F. Tedder, Jr., Apr. 3, 1947; children—Michael Eric, Stephen Mark, Robert David, Daniel Lee. With advt. sales SW Times Record, Ft. Smith, Ark., 1962-70; office div. mgr. Manpower, Ft. Smith, 1970-72; dir. vol. service Sparks Regional Med. Center, Ft. Smith, 1972—. Christmas seal chmn. Ark. Lung Assn.; active Ft. Smith Community Concert, Ft. Smith Art Center, Ft. Smith Hist. Soc., Sparks Aux., Sparks Guild. Mem. Am. Soc. Dirs. of Vol. Service, Ark. Soc. Dirs. of Vol. Service (pres., 1975-76). Republican. Baptist. Contbr. to Volunteer Leader. Office: 1311 South I St Fort Smith AR 72901

TEDFORD, WILLIAM HOWARD, JR., psychologist; b. Charlotte, N.C., May 26, 1936; s. William Howard and Sara Elizabeth (Cromer) T.; B.S. in Physics, Davidson Coll., 1958; M.S. in Physics, U. Nev., 1963; M.A. (fellow), Emory U., 1966, Ph.D. in Psychology, 1967; m. Jean Thomas Mabry, Feb 20, 1960; children—William Howard, Sara Louise. Instr in physics So. Meth. U., 1963-64, asso. prof. psychology, 1969-76, prof., 1976—; asst. prof. Oberlin (Ohio) Coll., 1967-69; adj. prof. U. Tex. Health Sci. Center, Dallas, 1978—. Served with Ordnance Corps, U.S. Army, 1958-61. NIMH fellow, 1965-67; NSF grantee, 1968, 70. Mem. Am. Psychol. Assn., Midwestern Psychol. Assn., Southwestern Psychol. Assn., Tex. Psychol. Assn., Psychonomic Soc., AAUP, Mensa, Sigma Xi, Sigma Pi Sigma, Psi Chi. Republican. Methodist. Contbr. articles, revs. to profl. publs; research on psychol. perception of time. Home: 1622 Centenary Dr Richardson TX 75081 Office: Psychology Dept So Meth U Dallas TX 75275

TEGTMEYER, CHARLES JOHN, physician; b. Hamilton, N.Y., July 25, 1939; s. Charles Edwin and Eusebia (Petgrave) T.; B.A. (N.Y. Regents scholar) with honors, Colgate U., 1961; M.D. USPHS Research scholar), George Washington U., 1965; m. Virginia Peters, June 1, 1963. Extern in surgery French Hosp., N.Y.C., 1964; surg. intern George Washington U. Hosp., Washington, 1965-66, surg. resident, 1966-68, resident in radiology, 1968-71; fellow in cardiovascular radiology Peter Bent Brigham Hosp., Boston, 1971-72; practice medicine specializing in radiology, Charlottesville, Va., 1972—; asst. prof. of radiology U. Va. Med. Center, Charlottesville, 1972-75, asst. prof. anatomy, 1973-77, dir. radiology edn. for med. students, 1972—, asso. prof. radiology, 1975-78, prof., 1978—, asso. prof. of anatomy, 1977—, dir. of angiography dept. radiology, 1974—; mem. staff U. Va. Hosp. Served to maj. AUS, 1966-72. Diplomate Am. Bd. Radiology (examiner June 1979), Nat. Bd. Med. Examiners. Fellow Am. Coll. Angiology; mem. Radiol. Soc. N.Am., Am. Coll. Radiology, Med. Soc. Va., Am. Roentgen Ray Soc., Eastern Radiol. Soc., AMA, Albemarle County Med. Soc., Soc. Cardiovascular Radiology, Trout Unltd., Salt Water Fly Rodders Am. Nu Sigma Nu, Sigma Chi. Contbr. numerous articles on angiology to med. jours.; inventor of lymph duct cannulator. Home: Bass Hollow Route 1 Box 207A Earlysville VA 22936 Office: Dept Radiology U Va Med Center Charlottesville VA 22901

TELFORD, DONALD MCCREA, educator, mathematician; b. Mt. Ida, Kans., June 22, 1903; s. George Baldridge and Carrie (Holiday) T.; B.S., Kans. State U., 1930; M.A., E. Tenn. State Coll., 1971; m. Nelle Rose Young, Dec. 24, 1946; children—Janet Telford Petzelt, Dianne Telford Biscoglia. Tchr. pub. schs. Tex., 1930-42; served with U.S. Army, 1918; commd. 2d lt. U.S. Army, 1942, advanced through ranks to lt. col., 1948; ret. 1961; mem. faculty Gordon Mil. Coll., Barnesviile, Ga., 1962-69; tchr. St. Joseph High Sch., Atlanta, 1969-72; mem. faculty Coll. Brenau, Gainesville, Ga., 1972-73; mem. faculty math. Ga. Mil. Coll., Milledgeville, 1973—, chmn. dept. math., 1975—; chmn. dept. math. Thomas County (Ga.) Community Coll., 1978, recipient citation, 1978. Umpire profl. baseball, 1933-41. Named Spot Light Tchr. Gordon Mil. Coll., 1966. Mem. Res. Officers Assn., VFW, Am. Legion, Ret. Officers Assn., DAV, AAUP, Nat. Math. Assn., NEA. K.C. Author: A Teaching Guide for Chemical Biological and Radiological Warfare, 1958; A Comparison of Grades Made at Junior Colleges vs Senior Colleges, 1971; Why Some People Are Problem Drinkers. Home: 1708 Delowe Dr Atlanta GA 30311 Office: Thomas County Community Coll Thomasville GA 31792

TELLEEN, JUDY GERTRUDE JOHNSON, educator; b. Chgo., Dec. 13, 1942; d. Kurt Theodore and Gertrude Lillian (Lockwood) J.; B.A., Lawrence Coll., Appleton, Wis., 1964; M.A., U. Mich., 1967; Ph.D., U. Mich., 1970; m. David Roger Telleen, June 15, 1964; children—Karin, Kirstin, Erik. High sch. English tchr., Mich., 1964-67; spl. asst. to v.p. student affairs U. Mich., 1967-68; pvt. practice guidance and counseling, West Berlin, 1971-72, Arlington, Va., 1973—; lectr., participant Counseling and Guidance Tng. Seminar for Coll. Tchrs., Madras, India, 1980. Welfare chmn. German-Am. Women's Club, West Berlin, 1971-72; mem. religious edn. council Unitarian Ch., Arlington, 1973-76, chmn. ednl. adv. div., 1977; chmn. edn. com. Harrington House Sch., Madras, 1979-80; mem. welfare com. Overseas Women's Club, Madras, 1979-80. Doctoral research grantee U. Mich., 1969. Mem. Am. Personnel and Guidance Assn., Am. Coll. Personnel Assn., Assn. Counselor Edn. and Supervision, Nat. Vocat. Guidance Assn., Am. Sch. Counselor Assn., Pi Lambda Theta, Pi Beta Phi, Phi Kappa Phi. Author: A Predictive Model of the Cumulative Academic Achievement of Graduate Students From India, 1970; Guidance Factors Influencing Indian Students to Attend the University of Michigan, 1971. Address: 1941 N Vermont St Arlington VA 22207

TELLER, DAVID NORTON, neurochemist; b. Bklyn., Oct. 1, 1936; s. Frank and Ruth (Goldberg) T.; B.S., Bklyn. Coll., 1957; M.S., N.Y. U., 1960, Ph.D., 1964; m. Sonia Ruth Safir, Jan. 18, 1959. Biologist, Fine Organics, Inc., N.Y.C., 1956-57; research asst. pediatric hematology and nutrition Flower-5th Ave. Hosp., N.Y.C., 1957-59; sr. research scientist N.Y. State Dept. Mental Hygiene, Wards Island, N.Y.C., 1959-65; asso. research scientist, 1965-76; asso. prof. psychiatry U. Louisville Med. Sch., 1976-79, prof., 1979—; lectr. grad. sch. Fairleigh Dickinson U., 1970-73. Mem. AAAS, Am. Chem. Soc. (sect. chmn. 1977), ASTM (subcom. chmn. 1968—), Am. Soc. Neurochemistry, Coll. Internat. Neuropsychopharmacology, Brit. Biochem. Soc., Am. Soc. Pharm. Exptl. Therapeutics, N.Y. Acad. Scis., Sigma Xi. Contbr. numerous articles in field to profl. jours. Home: 8013 Devonia Ave Louisville KY 40222 Office: U Louisville Med Sch Psychiatry and Behavioral Sciences PO Box 35260 MDR 517 Louisville KY 40232

TELSON, RICHARD, computer cons.; b. Passaic, N.J., May 28, 1929; s. John Charles and Francis (Kurowski) T.; student Black Hills State U., Spearfish, S.D., 1967-69, Rollins Coll., 1978—; m. Renee Patricia Long, Feb. 7, 1949; children—Linda Lee Telson Lohr, Richard. Enlisted U.S. Air Force, 1948; advanced through grades to chief master sgt., 1968; various assignments Seymour Johnson AFB, N.C., Ellsworth AFB, S.D.; ret., 1970; tchr. mathematics Seminole Sch. Bd., Sanford, Fla., 1970-71; sr. systems analyst, mgr. data processing, programmer Lake County Sch. Bd., Tavares, Fla., 1971-77; sr. systems analyst, mgr. data processing, programmer, computer auditing specialist Advanced Distributors, Consol. Book Pubs. and Assos., 1977-79; computer cons., Winter Park, Fla., 1979—; tchr. data processing Lake Sumter Community Coll. Mem. Seminole County Democratic Exec. com., bd. dirs. De Paugh Nusing Home, Winter Park, Fla. Certified adult edn. tchr., Fla. Mem. Assn. Systems Mgmt., Data Processing Mgmt. Assn., Air Force Sergeants Assn. Lutheran. Club: Kiwanis. Home: 120 Arla Ct Winter Park FL 32792

TEMPLE, GRAY, clergyman; b. Lewiston, Maine, Mar. 13, 1914; s. Charles Hosea and Eleanor (Gray) T.; A.B., Brown U., 1935; B.D., Va. Theol. Sem., 1938, D.D., 1961; m. Maria Drane, Jan. 29, 1940; children—Gray, Robert Brent, Charles Adams. Ordained priest P.E. Ch., 1939; rector, Rocky Mt., N.C., 1942-53, Charlotte, N.C., 1953-56, Columbia, S.C., 1956-61; bishop of S.C., 1961—. Successively mem. standing com., exec. council and bd. exam. chaplains P.E. Diocese N.C., 1942-56; successively mem. standing com., exec. com. and bd. exam. chaplains P.E. Diocese Upper S.C., 1956-61; del. Gen. Conv. P.E. Ch., 1949-52, 55, 58; mem. nat. exec. council P.E. Ch. U.S.A., 1970-76. Vice pres. East Carolina council Boy Scouts Am., 1950-53. Trustee Porter-Gaud Sch., Voorhees Coll., Ch. Home for Children, Ch. Home Ladies, Kanuga Conf. Center. Home: 1 King St Apt 605 Charleston SC 29401 Office: PO Drawer 2127 Charleston SC 29403

TENCH, KAREN ELIZABETH, ednl. career counselor; b. Pitts., Oct. 12, 1952; d. Clinton, Jr., and Ruth Mae (Bowman) T.; B.S. in Edn., Clarion State Coll., 1974; M.A. in Guidance and Counseling, Atlanta U., 1978. Customer personnel clk. Western Pa. Water Co., Pitts., 1975-76; elementary guidance worker Atlanta Bd. Edn., 1977-78, ednl./career counselor, 1978—; coordinator career devel. program; cons. in field. Counselor YMCA; mem. NAACP. Mem. Am. Personnel and Guidance Assn., Ga. Div. Spl. Services Programs. Methodist. Researcher: Reading Among the Disadvantaged, 1977; Counseling Ethics Among Counselors, 1977. Home: 425 10 St NE Atlanta GA 30309 Office: 965 Martin Luther King Dr Atlanta GA 30314

TEN EYCK, HOWARD JUDSON, financial planner; b. N.Y.C., May 26, 1935; s. Howard Judson and Colleen Maude (Roache) Ten E.; student Farmingdale A. and T. U., 1954-56, N.Y. State Police Acad., 1958; grad. Coll. Fin. Planning, 1977; B.A. in Bus., Internat. U., 1980; m. Elaine Alma Grahn, Feb. 12, 1964; children—Lynn Elizabeth, Virginia Beth, Alicia Francis, Robert Grahn. Trooper, N.Y. State Police, 1957-62; investigator Bur. Criminal Investigation, State of N.Y., 1962-69; owner, operator White Store Restaurant, Cooperstown, N.Y., 1969-73; chmn. bd., pres. Howard Ten Eyck & Co., Inc. & Exec. Planning Services, Inc., St. Petersburg, Fla., 1973—. Fellow Am. Inst. Fin. and Mgmt.; mem. fin. com., adminstrv. bd. St. James United Meth. Ch., 1978-79. Mem. Nat. Assn. Life Underwriters, Internat. Assn. Financial Planners, Inst. Cert. Fin. Planners. Republican. Clubs: Feather Sound Country, Sertoma, Masons. Home: 1290 87th Ave N Saint Petersburg FL 33702 Office: 9720 Executive Center Dr N Suite 110 Saint Petersburg FL 33702

TENG, LINCOLN, computer scientist; b. Leiyang, Hunan, China, May 5; s. Wenhen K. and Yun Sue T.; came to U.S., 1948; naturalized, 1955; B.A., Nat. Central U., Nanking, China, 1948; M.A., U. Mich., 1949, M.S., 1953, M.S.L., 1961; Ph.D., U. Minn., 1970; m. Ruth Hu, Aug. 27, 1960; children—Sanford P., Wayne G., Yung Sue. Research asst. Statistics Lab., U. Mich., 1951-53, research asso. Inst. Tech., 1958-61; research asso. Mass. Inst. Tech., 1953-58; sr. systems engr. aerospace systems div. Bendix Corp., 1961-63; prin. systems design engr. UNIVAC div. Sperry Corp., 1963-69; pres., tech. dir. Optimal Data Corp., Huntsville, Ala., 1969-77; asso. prof. computer and info. sci. Ala. A. and M. U., Normal, 1977—. Served with Chinese Army, World War II. Chinese Nationalist Govt. scholar, 1948-50. Mem. Am. Math. Assn., Am. Econ. Assn., IEEE, Sigma Xi. Baptist. Clubs: Elks, Ala. A. and M. U. Pres.'s. Patentee in field. Home: 5605 Alta Dena St Huntsville AL 35802 Office: Computer and Info Scis Dept Ala A and M U Normal AL 35762

TENNANT, RALPH BOYD, dentist; b. Gaffney, S.C., Sept. 8, 1929; s. Boyd Bryan and Ellen Christine (Fincher) T.; student U. Fla., 1951-52, U. Miami, 1955-56; A.A., Charlotte Coll., 1957; D.D.S., Emory U., 1961; children—Cynthia Ruth, Christine Elizabeth, Ralph Boyd II, Georgia Noel. Individual practice dentistry, Temple Terrace, Fla., 1961—; dir. Interbay Citizens Bank, Tampa, Fla. Golf coach King High Sch., 1966-71; pres. Community Health Services Assn., 1971-72; mem. Hillsborough County Adv. Com. for Gov. Reuben Askew, 1971-76; team doctor U. Tampa, 1968-75, Tampa Bay Rowdies Profl. Soccer, 1974-79; team dentist Tampa Bay Buccaneers, NFL, 1976-79, pres. team dentist assn. Bd. dirs. Tampa Sports Found. Served with USMCR, 1952-54. Recipient Coach of the Year award Fla. Athletic Coaches Assn., 1969, 70; Distinguished Service award Fla. Coaches Assn., 1970. Mem. Am. Soc. Dentistry for Children, Am. Dental Assn., West Coast Dist., Hillsborough County (dir. 1967-75, pres. 1972) dental socs., Temple Terrace C. of C. (dir. 1963-65), Delta Sigma Delta. Clubs: Suncoast Alpine Ski (v.p. 1975, pres. 1976, dir. 1974—) Optimist (pres. 1964-65) (Temple Terrace, Fla.). Home: 11008 Ridgedale Rd Temple Terrace FL 33617 Office: 5202 Busch Blvd Temple Terrace FL 33617

TENNENT, LOIS-NEAL HAMILTON, historian; b. Davidson, N.C., Dec. 20, 1914; d. Charles Harvey and Martha Cornelia (Deaton) Hamilton; B.A., Converse Coll., 1935; M.A. (scholar), Columbia U., 1939; m. Edward Smith Tennent, June 18, 1942; children—Edward Smith, Martha H., Charles H., Anne H. Tchr., Taylorsville (N.C.) High Sch., 1935-38, Glynn Acad., Ga., 1939-40; asst. dean students, instr. history Mary Baldwin Coll., Va., 1940-42; mem. faculty dept. history Spartanburg (S.C.) Methodist Coll., 1958-79, emeritus, 1979—, organizer, dir. travel study programs Europe. Bd. dirs. United Way; mem. bd. Council Spartanburg County; sec. bd. Spartanburg Legal Aid and Defenders; pres. Evans Jr. High PTA. Mem. AAUP, Hist. Assn. Spartanburg County, S.C. Hist. Assn., S.C. Hist. Soc., Alpha Mu Gamma, Delta Kappa Gamma. Democrat. Presbyterian. Clubs: Jr. League, Assembly, Thursday Study, Modern Lit., Book Reporters, Garden Study. Home: 1024 Glendalyn Circle Spartanburg SC 29302

TENNEY, WILLIAM FRANK, pediatric nephrologist; b. Shreveport, La., June 5, 1946; s. William Bonds and Pat (Patton) T.; B.A., Vanderbilt U., 1968; M.D., La. State U., New Orleans, 1972; m. Elizabeth Carter Steadman, Oct. 4, 1973; 1 dau., Amy Karen. Intern, Grady Meml. Hosp., Atlanta, 1972-73; resident pediatrics Emory U. Affiliated Hosps., Atlanta, 1973-74, pediatric nephrology fellow, 1974-76; pediatrician Columbia Dist. Hosp. Health Center, St. Helene, Oreg., 1976-79; practice medicine specializing in pediatric nephrology, Shreveport, La., 1979—; clin. asst. prof. dept. pediatrics La. State U. Sch. Medicine, Shreveport, 1979—; regional med. adv. Nat. Found. March of Dimes, St. Helens, Oreg., 1976-79. Diplomate Am. Bd. Pediatrics. Mem. AMA, Am. Acad. Pediatrics, N. Pacific Pediatric Soc., La. State Med. Soc., Shreveport Med. Soc., Empirical Soc. of Emory U. Office: 940 Margaret Pl Suite 306 Shreveport LA 71101

TENNEY, WILLIAM PAUL, civil engr.; b. San Francisco, Sept. 30, 1924; s. Leon Paul and Vera Belle (Stough) T.; student Okla. A. and M. U., 1943-44, Colo. Sch. Mines, 1948-50; B.S. in Civil Engring., U. So. Calif., 1953; m. Maxine D. Paulson, Oct. 4, 1945; 1 dau., Jill Anne. Surveyor, Alaska Road Commn., summers 1950-51; civil engr. freeway design Calif. Div. Hwys., 1951-52; with Dames & Moore-Geotech. and Environ. Scis., 1952—, mng. partner, Houston, 1976—. Served to lt. as navigator USAAF, 1943-45; ETO. Registered profl. engr., Calif., Ariz., N.Mex., Tex., La. Fellow ASCE; mem. Structural Engrs. Assn. So. Calif. (asso.), Cons. Engrs. Assn. Calif., Soils and Found. Assn. (past dir.), U.S. Com. on Large Dams, Am. Cons. Engrs. Council, Houston Engring. and Sci. Soc., Los Angeles, Houston chambers commerce. Republican. Home: 9468 Briar Forest Dr Houston TX 77063 Office: 2020 N Loop West 200 Houston TX 77018

TENNY, RALPH FERRELL, electronics designer; b. Kansas City, Mo., Sept. 5, 1931; s. Ralph and Gertrude (Ferrell) T.; Asso. Sci., Arlington State Coll. (now U. Tex. at Arlington), 1956; m. Jo Nell Reed Brock, Nov. 8, 1962; stepchildren—Kevin, Kristi, Kerry. Research analyst Gen. Dynamics, Fort Worth, 1957-58; electronics technician Collins Radio Co., Richardson, Tex., 1958-60; sr. research asst. Tex. Instruments Inc., Dallas, 1960-76; sr. designer Pavco Electronics Inc., Dallas, 1976-78; hardware cons. George Goode & Assos., Inc., 1978—. Youth choir sponsor 1st Methodist Ch., Richardson, Tex., 1974—; team mgr. U.S. Model Airplane Team, Indoor World Championships, Debrecen, Hungary, 1966, Cardington, Eng., 1972. Served with USAF, 1950-54. Mem. Computer Hobby Group N.Tex., Acad. Model Aeronautics (asso. v.p. dist. VIII), Nat. Indoor Model Airplane Soc. (co-founder). Republican. Editor Indoor News and Views, 1961—; contbg. editor Am. Aircraft Modeler, 1970-73; Model Aviation, 1975—. Contbr. articles to profl. and hobby jours. Home: 432 Lynn St Richardson TX 75080

TENZEL, RICHARD RUVIN, ophthalmologist; b. Phila., Jan. 19, 1929; s. Jack and Pauline (Korenblat) T.; B.A., Vanderbilt U., 1950; M.D., U. Tenn., 1954; m. Shirley Ruth Baum, May 19, 1956; children—Jack, David, Vicki Gail. Intern, Jackson Meml. Hosp., Miami, Fla., 1955; resident Manhattan Eye, Ear, Nose and Throat Hosp., N.Y.C., 1956-60; practice medicine specializing in ophthalmology, Miami Beach, Fla., 1960—; clin. prof. ophthalmology U. Miami, 1975—; chief ophthalmic plastic surgery service Bascom Palmer Eye Inst., Miami. Served with USNR, 1956-58. Fellow A.C.S.; mem. Am. Acad. Ophthalmology and Otolaryngology, Am. Soc. Ocularists (med. adviser 1971-75), Am. Soc. Ophthalmic Plastic and Reconstructive Surgery (pres. 1974-75), AMA. Mason (32 deg.). Contbr. articles to profl. jours. Home: 19231 NE 20th Ct North Miami Beach FL 33179 Office: 1100 NE 163d St North Miami Beach FL 33162

TENZER, FLORENCE GILDA, nurse; b. Bklyn., Sept. 5, 1929; d. Max and Rose (Tatz) Yurowitz; R.N., Jewish Hosp., Bklyn., 1950; B.S. cum laude, U. Miami, 1967; postgrad. in health sci. Fla. Atlantic U., 1970-72; m. Seymour Tenzer, May 5, 1951; 1 dau., Barbara. Public health nurse, N.Y.C., 1953-54; staff nurse U. Miami (Fla.) Infirmary, 1955-56; charge nurse recovery room Meml. Hosp., Hollywood, Fla., 1956-59; pvt. duty nurse, 1959-61; med., surg. supr. So. Fla. State Hosp., Hollywood, 1961-67; dir. edn., asso. dir. nursing Parkway Gen. Hosp., N. Miami Beach, Fla., 1967—; adv. to Trainex Corp., Miami-Dade Community Coll., Fla. Internat. U. Recipient Chmn. award United Fund, 1969. Mem. Nat. League Nursing, Am. Nursing Assn., Fla. Nursing Assn., Fla. Nurses Assn. (pres. 1959-61), So. Fla. Inservice Educators (pres. 1974-75), S. Fla. Public Relations Group (sec. 1969-70), Am. Soc. Health, Manpower, Edn. and Tng., Am. Soc. Tng. and Devel. (dir. Miami chpt. 1978—), Heart Assn. Greater Miami, U. Miami Alumni Assn., Jewish Hosp. Alumni Assn., Tau Theta Sigma. Club: Toastmasters. Home: 1753 NW 74th Ave Plantation FL 33313 Office: 160 NW 170th St North Miami Beach FL 33169

TEPLY, MARK LAWRENCE, educator; b. Lincoln, Nebr., Jan. 11, 1942; s. Lawrence Joseph and Gertrude Margaret (Kupfer) T.; B.A., U. Nebr., 1963, M.A., 1965, Ph.D., 1968; m. Kathleen K. McGrayel, Aug. 3, 1968; 1 son, David Lawrence. Asst. prof. math. U. Fla., Gainesville, 1968-73, asso. prof., 1973—; vis. asso. prof. Fla. State U., 1976; speaker in field. Recipient various NSF research grants. Mem. Am. Math. Soc., Math. Assn. Am., Phi Beta Kappa, Sigma Xi. Lutheran. Contbr. research articles to math. jours. Home: 2011 NW 7th Ln Gainesville FL 32603 Office: Dept Mathematics University of Florida Gainesville FL 32611

TEPPER, ARTHUR, health care co. exec.; b. N.Y.C., June 26, 1936; s. Louis A. and Florence Tepper; B.A., Allegheny Coll., 1958; M.B.A., N.Y. U., 1964; m. Elizabeth Ernst, Oct. 26, 1960; children—Lee, Gregory. Mng. partner, then partner Stanley Heller & Co., N.Y.C., 1964-74; pres. Medicare Equipment Rental Corp., Tampa, Fla., 1975—, DME Systems Inc., Tampa, 1978—. Served with Army N.G., 1959-64. Mem. Nat. Assn. Durable Med. Equipment Suppliers, N.Y. Soc. Security Analysts, Fla. Assn. Home Health Agencies. Office: 11620 Florida Ave Tampa FL 33612

TEPPER, DAVID JONATHAN, pediatrician; b. Cin., Oct. 22, 1942; s. Jack and Rene Bernice (Kaplan) T.; B.A., U. Chattanooga, 1964; M.D., U. Tenn., 1968; m. Cheryl Lee Klemisch, Mar. 29, 1979; children—Jacqueline Renee, Michael David, William Nelson. Intern, City of Memphis Hosp., 1968-69, resident, 1969-71; practice medicine, specializing in pediatrics, Chattanooga, 1973—; adj. prof. dept. spl. edn. U. Tenn., Chattanooga, 1974—; sec.-treas. Tepper Hosp., Chattanooga, 1974—; chmn. bd. dirs., pres. Chattanooga Testing & Counseling Services, Ltd., 1976—; regional cons. Head Start program, 1974—. Rep. diabetes central council Am. Diabetes Assn., 1977—; pres. Chattanooga Opera Assn., 1978—, bd. dirs., 1976; pres. Chattanooga Hamilton County Assn. for Retarded Children and Adults, 1977—; chmn. Multi-Disciplinary Child Abuse Team, 1977—; bd. dirs. Jewish Day Sch., 1975, Diabetes Assn., 1975, Scenic Land Sch. for Exceptional Children, 1975—, Blood Assurance, 1974-77, Cerebral Palsy, 1976—, Jewish Welfare Fedn., 1976—, Orange Grove Center for Retarded Children, 1977—. Served with USAF, 1971-73. Decorated Air Force Commendation medal; recipient Annual Recognition award Assn. Children with Learining Disabilities, 1973; citation Am. Diabetes Assn., 1976; Physicians Recognition award AMA, 1972. Diplomate Am. Bd. Pediatrics. Mem. Chattanooga-Hamilton County Med. Soc., Chattanooga Pediatric Soc., Am., Tenn. med. assns., Assn. Mil. Surgeons U.S., Am. Acad. Pediatrics, Am. Diabetes Assn., Nat. Assn. Retarded Children and Adults, Jr. C. of C. (dir. 1974-76), Kappa Sigma Epsilon. Republican. Jewish. Home: 107 Circle Dr Signal Mountain TN 37377 Office: 511 McCallie Ave Chattanooga TN 37402

TEREKHOV, MIGUEL R., educator, choreographer; b. Montevideo, Uruguay, Aug. 22, 1928; came to U.S., 1954, naturalized, 1963; s. Miguel George and Antonia (Rodriguez) T.; grad. Montevideo public schs.; m. Yvonne Chouteau, Aug. 31, 1956; children—Christina, Elizabeth. Soloist, Teatro Sodre, Montevideo, 1941-43; soloist, lead dancer Original Ballet Russe, 1943-49, prin. dancer Teatro Sodre, Montevideo, 1949-51; prin. dancer Boris Kniaseff Ballet Co., Buenos Aires, 1951-52; choreographer weekly TV program Night at the Ballet, Havana, Cuba, 1954; lead dancer Ballet Russe de Monte Carlo, 1954-58, regisseur gen., 1957; prin. dancer Teatro Sodre, Montevideo, 1952-54; staged own choreography ballet Don Quixote, Tex. Christian U. Ballet, Ft. Worth, 1976; staged own choreography Arensky Variations for Allegro Ballet Co., Houston, 1976; artist-in-residence Okla. U., 1961-63, asst. prof. ballet, 1963-67, asso. prof., 1967-70, prof., 1970—, chmn. dept. dance, 1973—; choreographer full length ballets of The Nutcracker, Coppelia, Undine, Romeo and Juliet, Giselle, Okla. City Civic Ballet, also U. Okla. Ballet; choreographer one act ballets; choreographer operas La Traviata and Carmen, Oklahoma City Lyric Opera; Die Fledermaus and The Unicorn, The Gorgon, The Manticore, Okla. U. Sch. Music; guest lectr. Ballet Club, N.Y.C.; instr. master classes Southwest Regional Ballet Festival; dir. Oklahoma City Civic Ballet, 1963-71; co-dir. Okla. Indian Ballerina Festival, 1967. Bd. dirs. Oklahoma Summer Arts Inst. Mem. Nat. Assn. for Regional Ballet, Okla. Arts and Humanities Adv. Bd., Okla. Summer Arts Inst. Roman Catholic. Office: Dept Dance 563 Elm Ave Room 209 U Okla Norman OK 73019

TERNEUS, WILLIAM FRANCIS, mfg. co. exec.; b. Clarksburg, W.Va., Sept. 12, 1951; s. Robert Louis and Dorothea G. (Wyatt) T.; asso. degree in electronics United Electronics Inst., 1971; m. Christina A. Stout, June 26, 1971; 1 dau., Suzanne. Service technician Sodaro Electronics, Charleston, W.Va., 1969-71, 73-74, N.C.R., Charleston, 1971-73; service mgr. Charleston Cash Register Co., 1974-79; sr. technician test dept. controls div. Harris Corp., Melbourne, Fla., 1979—. Mem. Christians Family Movement, St. Albans (W.Va.) Jr. C. of C. Democrat. Roman Catholic. Club: Moose. Home: 5421 Vevey Turn Orlando FL 32810

TERRELL, CECIL ROLAND, ednl. adminstr.; b. Bartow, Fla., Sept. 14, 1937; s. R.C. and Florrie Emma (Weaver) T.; B.S. in Edn. and English, Troy State U., 1962; M.A. in Secondary Edn., U. Ala., 1966, Ed.D., 1970; postgrad. Jacksonville U., 1970-72, U. Fla., 1972, U. N. Fla., 1977; m. Mary Sue Morrow, June 30, 1963; children—Thomas Roland, James Morrow. Asst. prof. curriculum Jacksonville (Fla.) U., 1970, chmn. dept. secondary edn., 1971, chmn. curriculum and instrn., 1972; asst. prof. Exptl. Sch., U. Ala., Birmingham, 1972; adj. prof. curriculum U. N. Fla., Jacksonville, 1973-77; dir. ednl. program devel. Fla. Jr. Coll., Jacksonville, 1973-74, dir. staff and program devel., 1974—, dir. internat. edn., 1975—; adj. asso. prof. adminstrn. and higher edn. Grad. Faculty, U. Ala., Tuscaloosa, 1977-78. Dir. trustees Mandarin (Fla.) Meth. Ch., 1979—. Recipient Merit Tchr. award Brevard County, 1967; NDEA fellow, 1967-70. Mem. Nat. Council Tchrs. English, Nat. Assn. for Supervision and Curriculum Devel., Am. Edn. Research Assn., Nat. Council for Staff, Program and Organizational Devel. (founding pres. 1977-79), Fla. Assn. for Staff and Program Devel. (founding pres. 1975-77, Outstanding Service award 1977), Fla. Assn. Tchr. Educators, Fla. Assn. Community Colls., Fla. Collegiate Consortium for Internat. Intercultural Edn., Beta Theta Pi. Democrat. Methodist. Club: Moose. Contbr. articles on ednl. programs and higher edn. to profl. jours. Home: 3463 Cypresswood Dr South Jacksonville FL 32217 Office: 21 W Church St Jacksonville FL 32202

TERRELL, MARYANN WATKINS, nurse; b. Olean, N.Y., Mar. 18, 1947; d. Lawrence William Watkins and Alice D. (Stannis) Watkins Petsch; B.S. in Nursing, U. Ariz., 1970; m. Jennings Bryan Terrell, III,

Nov. 25, 1970. Unit dir. psychiat. programs St. Mary's Hosp. and Health Center, Tucson, 1970-75; psychiat. nurse, caseworker Harris County Mental Health-Mental Retardation, Houston, 1975-76, Bernalillo County Mental Health Center, Albuquerque, 1976-77; dir. nursing Hamlin (Tex.) Meml. Hosp., 1977—. Registered nurse, Ariz., N.Mex., Tex. Mem. Am. Assn. Critical Care Nurses, Tex. Nurses Assn. Presbyterian. Office: Hamlin Meml Hosp 632 NW 2d St Hamlin TX 79520

TERRY, ALICE EDITH, artist; b. N.Y.C., June 23, 1925; d. Leon and Rose (Smithline) T.; B.A., Brown U., 1945; M.F.A., U. Miami (Fla.), 1975; m. Ben Johnson, 1950 (dec. 1967); children—Leon Axel, Susan Bedsaul, Benjamin Franklin Johnson. Artist-in-residence Lowe Art Mus., Miami, 1977-78; graphic artist and designer Fusion Dance Co., Miami, 1978-80; one-artist shows include: Fleishman Gallery, N.Y.C., 1960, Hacker Gallery, N.Y.C., 1961, Jervis Public Library, Rome, N.Y., 1962, Wesleyan Coll., Macon, Ga., 1966, Lowe Mus. Gallery, Coral Gables, Fla., 1966, Rose Fried Gallery, N.Y.C., 1963, Interch. Center, N.Y.C., 1973, Eckerd Coll., St. Petersburg, Fla., 1968, 70, 72, Edison Jr. Coll., Ft. Myers, Fla., 1970, Krannert Mus., Urbana, Ill., 1961, Robinson Gallery, Naples, Fla., 1979, 80, Gallery 24, Miami, 1980; group shows: Martha Jackson Gallery, N.Y.C., 1962, St. Petersburg Mus. Fine Arts, 1969, David Anderson Gallery, N.Y.C., 1962, Knox-Albright Mus., Buffalo, 1963, Mus. Modern Art, N.Y.C., 1963, Whitney Mus., N.Y.C., 1953, Corcoran Gallery, Washington, Gallery 24, Miami, 1979; represented in permanent collections: Guggenheim Mus., N.Y.C., N.Y. U., N.Y.C., Wesleyan Coll., Macon, Ga. Mem. Women's Caucus for Art (founder S. Fla. br. 1973). Address: 3201 Aviation Ave Miami FL 33133

TERRY, ALVIN EUGENE, advt. exec.; b. Houston, Nov. 28, 1950; s. Edward Thomas and Ruby (Terry) Thomas; student U. Houston, 1972-77, Houston Community Coll., 1977-78; m. Brenda Gail McGruder, June 24, 1972; children—Erika Natasha, Vanessa Renee. Vice-pres. B.B.B.B. Prodns., Inc. & Assos., Houston, 1976—, Tex. Souvenirs Unlimited, Houston, 1979—; pres. Advt. Agy. Unlimited, Houston, 1976—. Speaker, Houston Ind. Sch. Dist., 1978-79. Served with USAF, 1969-72. Mem. Houston C. of C., Bus. and Profl. Advt. Assn., Better Bus. Bur., Direct Mail Club Houston, Houston Citizens C. of C., Houston Retail Mchts. Assn., Tex. Retail Mchts. Assn. Home: 4426 Penhurst St Houston TX 77093 Office: 7227 Fannin St Suite 203 Houston TX 77030

TERRY, ESMOND ARNOLD, radio sta. exec.; b. Patrick County, Va., June 22, 1933; s. Otey Kemper and Verona Kathleen (Spangler) T.; student public schs., Va.; m. Sara Watts, Oct. 24, 1953; children—Wanda, Jennifer, Laurie, Scott. Profl. country musician, guitar and bass; with Jim Eanes and Shenandoah Valley Boys, Benny Jarrell and The Flinthill Playboys, Bill Monroe and The Bluegrass Boys; radio announcer 1959-61; ordained to ministry Baptist Ch., 1971; owner Radio Sta. WODY, Bassett, Va., 1970—; pastor Hillcrest Bapt. Ch., Ridgeway, Va., 1976—. Served with U.S. Army, 1953-55. Home: 206 Woodlawn Rd Collinsville VA 24078 Office: Drawer 231 Bassett VA 24055

TERRY, FRANK WOMACK, state ofcl.; b. Chatham, Va., Apr. 21, 1924; s. Charlie Lynch and Maggie Mae (Lester) T.; student LaSalle U., 1961-63; m. Kathleen Coleman Gammon, May 31, 1979. Aircraft technician Glen L. Martin Aircraft Co., Balt., 1942-43; asst. mgr. Darling Shops Corp., New Orleans, 1947-48; asst. mgr. McCarthy Harris Hotel Corp., Danville and Warrenton, Va., 1949-55; state tax dist. supr. Commonwealth of Va. Dept. of Taxation, Harrisonburg, 1956—. Served with USAAF, 1943-46. Recipient longevity service awards State of Va. Mem. Va. Govt. Employees Assn. Baptist. Home: 42 Monument Ave Harrisonburg VA 22801 Office: Commonwealth of Va Dept of Taxation 350 N Main St Harrisonburg VA 22801

TERRY, HAROLD KNIGHT, orthodontist; b. Durham County, N.C., June 30, 1916; s. Isaac Holt and Lillian Margaret (Lunsford) T.; B.S., Duke U., 1936; D.M.D., Harvard U., 1940; cert. Washington U., St. Louis, 1946, U. Havana, 1948; m. Doris Hattersley, Nov. 28, 1942; children—Janet Louise, James Lee, Thomas Holt, Paul Knight. Research asst. in biochemistry Duke U., 1936; practice dentistry specializing in orthodontics, Miami, Fla., 1940—; pres. Camplands U.S.A., Inc.; v.p. Aviation Engring. Research and Devel. Corp.; grad. instr. orthodontics Washington U., 1949-66; guest lectr. U. Pa., U. N.C., U. Chile, Boston U., European and C. Am. univs. and clinics. Chmn., Citizens Com. for 14th St. Causeway, Broward County, Fla. Served to lt. comdr. USNR, 1942-46; PTO. Diplomate Am. Bd. Orthodontics. Fellow Am. Coll. Dentistry, Internat. Coll. Dentistry, Fla. Dental Soc. (hon.); mem. Am. Assn. Orthodontics (pres. 1970-71), So. Soc. Orthodontics (pres. 1963), Greater Miami Acad. Orthodontics (pres. 1954-58), ADA (chmn. orthodontic sect. 1954), Aircraft Owners and Pilots Assn., Methodist. Clubs: Lauderdale Yacht, Duke Alumni of S. Fla. (past pres.), Harvard of Miami (past v.p.). Contbr. to Orthodontics in Daily Practice (J.A. Salzmann), 1976; articles to Am. Jour. Orthodontics. Home: 600 NE 55th Terr Miami FL 33137 Office: 259 NE 28th St Miami FL 33137

TERRY, JAMES CROCKETT, parapsychologist, acct.; b. Nevada City, Calif., Apr. 4, 1948; s. Seth Sprague and Crystal (Crockett) T.; B.A., Allegheny Coll., 1971; M.A., Calif. State Coll., Sonoma, 1972; Ph.D. (Garner Murphy fellow), Humanistic Psychology Inst., 1975. Research asst. Inst. for Parapsychology, Durham, N.C., 1972-73; asst. researcher Maimonides Med. Center div. parapsychology and psychophysics, 1973-75; dir. Community Mental Health Center program Maimonides Med. Center, Bklyn., 1973-75; asso. researcher Inst. for Parapsychology, Durham, N.C., 1975, Mind Sci. Found., San Antonio, 1975-77; adminstr. resocialization program Dr. Paul Obert, Inez, Tex., 1977-80; divisional controller Coca-Cola Co. of San Antonio, 1979—; v.p. Crockett Investments, 1979—. Parapsychology Found. grantee, 1974, 75. Mem. Parapsychol. Assn., Assn. for Humanistic Psychology. Episcopalian. Contbr. articles to profl. jours. Home: 143 W Lovera St San Antonio TX 78212 Office: 162 Exposition Dr San Antonio TX 78291

TERRY, JOHN VERLIN, educator; b. Hagerstown, Ill., Oct. 8, 1920; s. William Bergen and Clester (Hopkins) T.; B.A., John Brown U., 1949; M.B.A., U. Ark., 1966; L.H.D., Linda Vista Baptist Coll. and Sem., San Diego, 1967; m. Fern Nadine Stradley, Feb. 14, 1942; children—John Mark, Joan Elizabeth, Luanne, Clay Thomas. Ordained to ministry Bapt. Ch., 1946; pastor chs. Tex., Ark., 1948-58; asst. to pres. Peterson Industries, Decatur, Ark., 1958-62; head bus. dept. John Brown U., Siloam Springs, Ark., 1966-70, head div. devel., 1971—; guest lectr. U. Ark., 1966—; prin. firm John V. Terry & Assos., Siloam Springs, 1969—; corp. cons. indsl. and public affairs Allen Canning Co., Inc. Mem. exec. com., bd. dirs. Ark. Council Econ. Edn., 1968—; commr. Edn. Commn. U.S., 1969—; chmn. adv. council Small Bus. Adminstrn., Ark., 1970—. Served with AUS, 1942-44; PTO. Mem. Am., So. econ. assns., Southwestern Social Sci. Assn., Ark Coll. Tchrs. Econs. and Bus. (pres. 1969), Modern Woodmen Am., Beta Gamma Sigma. Contbr. articles to profl. jours. Home: PO Box 28 Siloam Springs AR 72761

TERRY, PERCY, JR., tool and die co. exec.; b. Shreveport, La., Apr. 19, 1919; s. Percy and Marianne (Woodall) T.; student Centenary Coll., 1941-42, U. Mich., 1945-46, Walsh Coll. Accountancy, 1946-48; m. Margaret Ellen Spencer, Dec. 1, 1945; 1 son, Kim Woodall. Office mgr. Glendale Machine & Tool Co., 1948-49; office mgr. Springfield Detail & Machine Parts Co., 1949-56; treas., gen. mgr., dir. Springfield Tool & Die, Inc., Greenville, S.C., 1956—. Mem. devel. com. Henry Ford Community Coll., 1956, mem. library planning com., chmn. sch. naming com., 1964-72; mem. bus. industry edn. adv. com. Wayne County Sch. Dist.; mem. machine tool tech. com. Spartanburg (S.C.) Coll. Served with USAAF, 1936-45. Recipient Recognition award U. Mich. Alumni Club, Dearborn, 1974. Mem. Detroit Tooling Assn., Am. Ordnance Assn., U. Mich. Alumni Assn. (pres. 9th dist. 1973-74, dist. dir.). Lutheran. Clubs: Western Golf and Country (Detroit); University of Mich. of Dearborn (past pres., gov.), Rotary; Palmetto Dunes Resort Golf (Hilton Head Island, S.C.); Holly Tree Golf (Simpsonville, S.C.). Home: 112 Honey Horn Dr Simpsonville SC 29681 Office: PO Box 6787 Sta B Greenville SC 29606

TERRY, RONALD ANDERSON, banker; b. Memphis, Dec. 5, 1930; B.S., Memphis State U., 1952; grad. Southwestern Grad. Sch. Banking, 1961, Advanced Mgmt. Program, Harvard U., 1971; m. Beth Howard, Feb. 1, 1953; children—Natalie, Cynthia. With First Nat. Bank Memphis N.A., 1957—, chmn., chief exec. officer, 1973—; pres. parent co. First Tenn. Nat. Corp., 1971-73, chmn. bd., chief exec. officer, 1973—. Bd. dirs. Future Memphis; bd. dirs., past pres. Boys Clubs Memphis, Arts Appreciation Found. Memphis; trustee Memphis State U. Found. Served to lt. USNR, 1953-57. Mem. Am. Bankers Assn. (past legis. chmn.), Assn. Res. City Bankers (legis. chmn.), Assn. Bank Holding Companies, Econ. Club Memphis (past pres.). Presbyterian. Office: PO Box 84 Memphis TN 38101

TERRY, T(AYLOR) RANKIN, JR., lawyer; b. Louisville, Sept. 17, 1946; s. T. Rankin and C. Ruth (Ochs) T.; B.S. in Mech. Engring., U. Ky., 1968; J.D., Washington U., 1971; LL.M., U. Fla., 1976; m. Kristine Ann Luther, May 24, 1969. Admitted to Ky. bar, 1971, Fla. bar, 1971; asso. firm Boehl, Stopher, Graves & Deindoerfer, Louisville and Paducah, Ky., 1971-72; asso. firm Roberts, Watson, Bright, Adams & Terry, 1972-76, partner, 1976-77; partner Terry, Adams & Corbin, Ft. Myers, Fla., 1977—; vis. lectr. engring. U. Ky., 1972, U. Fla., 1976. Asst. atty. City of Ft. Myers, 1971-75. Mem. ASME, Fla. Bar, Ky. Bar Assn., Fla. Engring. Soc. Democrat. Presbyterian. Club: Royal Palm Yacht (Ft. Myers). Home: 1245 Hanton Ave Fort Myers FL 33901 Office: 2132 McGregor Blvd Fort Myers FL 33901

TERRY, WARREN BERGEN, bottling co. exec.; b. Patoka, Ill., Aug. 11, 1918; s. William Bergen and Clester (Hopkins) T.; student U. Tex., 1939-44; m. Frances LaVerne Schnasse, Feb. 14, 1938; children—Warren Bergen, Sumner Patrick, William Michael, Timothy Edward. With Am. Bottling Co., Corpus Christi, Tex., 1936-49; co-owner, mgr., v.p. Coca-Cola Bottling Co., San Jose, Cal., 1949-53, also dir.; co-owner, v.p., gen. mgr. Quaker State Bottling Co., Pitts., 1953-59; advt. bus., Boston, 1959-61; co-owner, pres., gen. mgr. Ft. Wayne Coca-Cola Bottling Co. (Ind.), 1961-68; chmn. bd. Blue Grass Coca-Cola Bottling Co., Inc., Lexington, Ky., 1963—, Mount Sterling, Danville, Campton, Richmond and Somerset, Ky., 1965—, Coca-Cola Bottling Co. So. Ill., Inc. 1973—; pres., co-owner Sprite-Flite Jets, Inc., Lexington, 1973-78; pres. Renwar Corp., 1975—, Terry Properties, 1972—. Bd. dirs. Lexington unit Nat. Multiple Sclerosis Soc., 1967—; mem. adv. com. Lexington Jr. League Horse Show, 1972—; bd. curators Transylvania U., 1969—; mem. devel. com. U. Ky., 1970—, bd. dirs., 1978—; bd. advisors Patterson Sch. Diplomacy, 1975—. Fellow U. Ky., 1968—. Mem. Lexington C. of C. (dir. 1969—), Ky. C. of C. Clubs: Country (Lexington); Thunderbird Country, Desert Island (Rancho Mirage, Calif.); Port Royal, Naples (Fla.) Yacht; Carmel (Calif.) Valley Golf and Country; Jockey (Miami, Fla.). Home: Russell Cave Pike PO Box 11761 Lexington KY 40577 Office: Leestown Rd and Greendale Pike PO Box 12330 Lexington KY 40582

TERRY, WILLIAM RAY, apparel mfg. co. exec.; b. Roanoke, Ala., June 29, 1949; s. Jesse Arnold and Velma G.; B.A., Morehouse Coll., 1971; grad. Weaver Sch. Real Estate, 1974; div.; 1 dau., Tamara M. Vice-pres. Hillcrest Corp., Roanoke, Ala., 1973—; sec. Terry Properties, Roanoke, Ala., 1972—; v.p. Terry Constrn., Roanoke, 1973—, Terry Mfg. Co. Inc., Roanoke, 1971—. Lic. real estate broker, Ala.; notary public, Ala. Baptist (deacon 1979, asst. adult Sunday sch. tchr.). Home: 927 South St Roanoke AL 36274 Office: 924 South St Roanoke AL 36274

TEVIS, MARTHA MAY, educator; b. Wichita Falls, Tex.; d. John Felix and Valerie (McLamore) T.; B.A., Our Lady of the Lake U., 1964, M.A., 1965; Ph.D., U. Tex., 1967. Asso. prof. Pan Am. U., Edinburg, Tex., 1967—; editor The Curriculor, publ. Tex. Council Community Mental Health/Mental Retardation Centers, Inc., 1977—. Vice chmn. bd. Trop. Tex. MHMR Center, 1969—; mem. exec. bd. Tex. Council Community MHMR Centers, Inc., 1976—; vice-chmn. bd. Trinity Episcopal Sch., 1973-79; bd. dirs. Pan Am. Univ. Alumni, 1978—. Alexander Caswell Ellis fellow, 1965-67. Fellow Philosophy of Edn. Soc.; mem. Am. Ednl. Studies Assn., AAUP, NEA, Tex. Tchrs. Assn., Tex. Assn. Coll. Tchrs., Southwestern Philosophy of Edn. Soc. (pres. 1977), Am. Classical League, Pi Beta Phi, Kappa Delta Pi (counselor), Pi Lambda Theta, Alpha Chi. Episcopalian. Club: Daus. Republic of Tex. Contbr. articles to profl. jours. Office: Edn Bldg Pan Am Univ Edinburg TX 78539

TEW, E. JAMES, JR., electronics co. exec.; b. Dallas, July 7, 1933; s. Elmer James and Bessie Fay (Bennett) T.; student Arlington State Jr. Coll., 1955-57; B.B.A. in Indsl. Mgmt., So. Meth. U., 1969; M.S. in Quality Systems, U. Dallas, 1972, M.B.A. in Mgmt., 1975; m. Barbara Dean Evans, Dec. 12, 1952; children—Teresa Annette, Linda Diane, Brian James. Mgr. quality assurance ops. and corp. reference standards lab. Tex. Instruments Inc., Dallas, 1957—, chmn. corp. metric implementation com., mem. credit com. Texis Credit Union; adj. faculty Richland Coll., Mountain View Coll. Precinct chmn., election judge, 1961-64, del. several county and state convs. Served with U.S. Army, 1953-55. Decorated Army Commendation medal with oak leaf cluster; registered profl. engr., Calif. Fellow Am. Soc. for Quality Control (cert. as quality and reliability engr., chmn. Dallas-Ft. Worth sect. 1974-75); mem. Optical Soc. Tex. (charter), Am. Nat. Metric Council, Tex. Metric Council (charter; dir. Dallas region), U.S. Metric Assn., Res. Officers Assn., Dallas C. of C. (chmn. world mfg. com. 1974-77, chmn. spl. task force career edn. adv. bd. 1973-74), Nat. Rifle Assn., Mensa. Baptist. Clubs: Texins Rod and Gun (pres. 1969-70), Texins Flying, Masons (32 deg.). Contbr. articles to profl. jours. Home: 10235 Mapleridge Dallas TX 75238 Office: PO Box 226015 MS 415 Dallas TX 75266

TEW, SUZETTE PETTIS, banker; b. Meridian, Miss., Sept. 17, 1953; d. Tollie Calvin and Joyce Jerome (McDevitt) Pettis; B.S. in Acctg., U. So. Miss., 1974; postgrad. Miss. State U., 1979—; m. Philip Rush Tew, Mar. 25, 1979; 1 son, Kenneth Lightsey. Ins. clk. Forrest Gen. Hosp., Hattiesburg, Miss., 1975; asst. auditor Peoples Bank Miss., Meridian, 1975, acctg. officer, 1976-79, controller, 1979—. Active United Way Lauderdale County. Mem. Nat. Assn. Bank Women, Meridian Bus. and Profl. Women (named Young Career Woman 1978), Meridian Area C. of C., U. So. Miss. Alumni Assn., Phi Chi Theta. Baptist. Clubs: Navy League, Downtown (Meridian). Home: 4516 15th St Meridian MS 39301 Office: 905 22d Ave Meridian MS 39301

TEXTER, E(LMER) CLINTON, JR., physician; b. Detroit, June 12, 1923; s. Elmer Clinton and Helen (Rotchford) T.; B.A., Mich. State U., 1943; M.D., Wayne State U., 1946; postgrad. U. Detroit, 1946-47, N.Y. U. Postgrad. Med. Sch., 1948-49, Northwestern U., 1959-60, Williams Coll., 1975; m. Jane Starke Curtis, Feb. 19, 1949; children—Phyllis Cardew, Patricia Ann, Catherine Jane. Intern, Providence Hosp., Detroit, 1946-47; Heart Assn. research fellow in medicine Cornell U. Med. Coll., N.Y.C., 1948-50; asst. physician to outpatients N.Y. Hosp., N.Y.C., 1949-50; asst. resident medicine 3d div. N.Y. U., Goldwater Meml. Hosp., N.Y.C., 1950-51; instr. medicine Duke U. Sch. Medicine, Durham, N.C., 1951-53; asst. physician Duke Hosp., Durham, 1951-53; asso. medicine Northwestern U. Med. Sch., Chgo., 1953-56, asst. prof. medicine, 1956-61, asso. prof., 1961-68, dir. tng. program in gastroenterology, 1954-65; attending physician Northwestern Meml. Hosp., VA Lakeside Hosp., Chgo., 1953-68; asso. med. dir. Profl. Life & Casualty Co., Chgo., 1965-68; cons. gastroenterology U.S. Naval Hosp., Great Lakes, 1963-68; mem. adv. bd. Skokie Valley Community Hosp., 1959-68; chmn. dept. clin. physiology, cons. gastroenterology and publs. sects. Scott & White Clinic, Temple, Tex., 1968-72; cons. William Beaumont Army Med. Center, El Paso, Tex., 1968—; surgeon gen. U.S. Army, 1970—; prof. physiology adj. U. Tex. S.W. Med. Sch., Dallas, 1969-72; coordinator allied health programs Temple (Tex.) Jr. Coll., 1969-72, prof. medicine, physiology, biophysics, head div. gastroenterology Coll. Medicine, 1972—, asst. dean Coll. Health Related Professions, 1972-73, asso. dean Coll. Health Related Professions, U. Ark., Little Rock, 1973-75; mem. active staff Univ. Hosp., Little Rock, 1972—, asso. chief staff for edn., 1972-75; chief gastroenterology VA Hosp., Little Rock, 1972-79; cons. St. Vincent Infirmary, Little Rock, 1973—, Doctors Hosp., Little Rock, 1975—, Jefferson Hosp., Pine Bluff, Ark., 1975—; dir. Ark. Digestive Disease Center, 1975—; cons. Ark. regional med. program Ark. Health Systems Found., 1972—, Council on Drugs, 1958—. Active Ark. Art Center, Ark. Symphony Soc.; bd. dirs. Wayne State Fund, Detroit, 1975—. Served with USNR, 1947-49. Recipient Distinguished Service awards Wayne State U., 1969, 74; Clarence F. G. Brown fellow Inst. Medicine, Chgo., 1953-56. Diplomate Am. Bd. Internal Medicine. Fellow A.C.P.; mem. AMA (com. on med. rating phys. impairment 1960-64), Am. Gastroent. Assn., Am. Fedn. Clin. Research (chmn. gastroenterology 1956, 63), Am. Med. Writers Assn. (pres. 1973-74), Am. Assn. Study Liver Disease, Am. Soc. Gastrointestinal Edoscopy, Am. Physiol. Soc., Am. Soc. Clin. Pharmacology and Therapeutics (dir. 1971—), So. Soc. Clin. Investigation, Central Soc. Clin. Research, Sigma Xi, Theta Alpha Phi, Delta Chi, Nu Sigma Nu. Episcopalian (lay reader 1967-79, chalicer 1979—). Clubs: Lit. (Chgo.); John Evans of Northwestern U.; Country of Va. Author: Peptic Ulcer-Diagnosis and Treatment, 1955; Physiology of the Gastrointestinal Tract, 1968; contbr. articles to profl. jours. Home: 11519 Tahoe Ln Little Rock AR 72212 Office: U Ark 4301 W Markham St Little Rock AR 72205

THACKER, ALVIN MONROE, JR., mgmt. cons.; b. Charleston, W.Va., Oct. 3, 1942; s. Alvin Monroe and Mary Elizabeth (Isaac) T.; B.A., Morris Harvey Coll., 1965; certificate in counseling Marshall U., 1966; m. Pamela Lea Schepman, Apr. 13, 1968; children—Andrew Monroe, Elizabeth Anne. Probation officer Kanawha County (W.Va.) Juvenile Ct., 1964-65; with W.Va. Dept. Welfare, Charleston, 1966-78, adminstrv. asst., 1958-70, supr., 1970, dir. office adminstrv. rev., 1970-78; v.p. Maximus Inc., tech. cons. to mgmt., McLean, Va., 1978—. Mem. alumni council Morris Harvey Coll.; bd. dirs. Eastern Regional Council on Welfare Fraud. Served with Air N.G., 1965-71, USAF, 1966. Recipient Cause II Program award Dept. Labor. Mem. Am. Pub. Welfare Assn., Am. Mgmt. Assn., Nat. Welfare Fraud Assn., W.Va. Welfare Conf., Nat. Reciprocal and Family Support Enforcement Assn., Nat. Eligibility Workers Assn., Theta Xi. Republican. Lutheran. Home: 5006 Lone Oak Pl Fairfax VA 22032 Office: McLean Office Bldg Suite 101 6723 Whittier Ave McLean VA 22101

THACKER, DONALD PHILIP, social worker; b. Danville, Ky., Sept. 3, 1931; s. Philip Oliver and Mae (McBee) T.; B.A., Centre Coll. of Ky., 1953; M.S.S.W., U. Louisville, 1957; m. Ruth Gerkins, Aug. 6, 1955; children—Philip Scott, Sara Ruth, Molly McBee. Clin. social worker, asst. prof. dept. psychiatry Ohio State U., 1959-64; program supr. VA Med. Center, Battle Creek, Mich., 1965-67; chief social work services Dorn Vets. Hosp., Columbia, S.C., 1968—; social work cons. Kershaw County Hosp.; mem. adv. bd. on hospice S.C. Bapt. Hosp.; mem. Broad River subcouncil Three Rivers Health Systems Agy. Registered social worker, S.C. Mem. Nat. Assn. Social Workers. Club: Lower Richland Lions. Home: 1013 Coatesdale St Columbia SC 29209 Office: Dorn VA Hospital Columbia SC 29201

THACKER, JOSEPH LEROY, JR., geologist; b. Kansas City, Mo., Oct. 20, 1942; s. Joseph Leroy and Edna Louise T.; B.S., U. Mo., Kansas City, 1965, M.S., Rolla, 1974; m. Janet Ann Pursley, Sept. 1, 1962; children—Jeffrey Michael, Jon Mathew. Grad. teaching asst. U. Hawaii, Honolulu, 1965-67; geologist Mo. Geol. Survey, Rolla, 1968-77; exploration geologist Texasgulf Inc., Norman, Okla., 1977—. Mem. Soc. Econ. Paleontologists and Mineralogists, Soc. Mining Engrs. of AIME, Assn. Mo. Geologists, Sigma Xi. Republican. Mem. Christian Ch. (Disciples of Christ). Speaker profl. sci. conf. and symposium; author: Traverse in Late Cambrian Strata from the St. Francois Mountains, Missouri to Delaware County, Oklahoma, 1975; Guidebook to the Geology Along Interstate 55 in Missouri, 1977; contbr. sect. to book; series of maps. Home: 1113 Merrymen Green Norman OK 73069 Office: 2241 W Lindsey St Suite 502 Norman OK 73069

THACKRAY, RICHARD IRVING, psychologist; b. Wausau, Wis., Jan. 27, 1927; s. Irving Brownsell and Virginia (Weaver) T.; B.A., Lawrence Coll., 1950; M.A., U. Mo., 1952; Ph.D., Purdue U., 1956; m. Marilyn Ann Patterson, June 20, 1953; children—Richard, Susette. Asst. prof. psychology Allegheny Coll., Meadville, Pa., 1956-59; research psychologist Wright-Patterson AFB, Dayton, Ohio, 1959-65; psychophysiologist Inst. Pa. Hosp., 1965-67; chief stress behavior research FAA, Oklahoma City, 1967—; prof. psychology U. Okla., 1972—. Asso. fellow Aerospace Med. Assn.; fellow Am. Psychol. Assn.; mem. Soc. Psychophysiol. Research, Internat. Assn. Applied Psychology, Sigma Xi, Psi Chi. Contbr. articles in field to profl. jours. Home: 1615 Chestnut Ln Norman OK 73069 Office: CAMI FAA PO Box 25082 Oklahoma City OK 73125

THAMES, REDDEN JEFFERSON, state ofcl.; b. Elba, Ala., Oct. 31, 1932; s. Aaron Preston and Ruth (Bass) T.; A.B., Stetson U., 1958; B.D., So. Baptist Theol. Sem., 1962, M.Div., 1970; m. Joanne Ellen Reeves, Sept. 1, 1952; children—Ruth, Nancy, Joe, Jim. Ordained to ministry So. Bapt. Ch., 1952; pastor chs., Lake View, S.C., 1962-67, Loris, S.C., 1967-70; dir. Horry County Dept. Social Services, Conway, S.C., 1970-73; dist. dir. S.C. Dept. Social Services, Columbia, 1973—; dir. Catawba Regional Planning Council, 1973—. Bd. dirs. Dillon County Rural Recreation Commn., 1964—, Central Midlands Regional Planning Council, 1973—, Coastal Plains Mental Health Commn., 1971-73, Coastal Plains Regional Home Health Council, 1971-73. Named Rural Minister of Yr., Progressive Farmer mag., 1965, Outstanding Alumnus, Stetson U., 1971. Mem. Am. Mgmt. Assn., Adminstrv. Mgmt. Soc., Child Welfare League Am., Am. Public Welfare Assn. (human resources adv. com. 1975-79). Club: Masons. Author: Dynamic Supervision, 1977. Home: 741 Shadow Mist Ln Columbia SC 29210 Office: SC Dept Social Services PO Box 1520 Columbia SC 29202

THARP, MARVIN OSCAR, mgmt. cons.; b. Vineland, N.J., Nov. 9, 1946; s. Marvin Oscar and Alberta Steudle (Quairoli) T.; B.S. in Engring., N.C. State U., 1970; M.S. in Mgmt., Fla. Internat. U., 1975; m. Terril Stone, Dec. 14, 1969. Field engr. Leeds & Northrup Co., Cleve., 1970-71; asst. to pres. Bernardo, Inc., Miami, Fla., 1971-73; airport engr., supt. support services, mgmt. systems engr. Met. Dade County (Fla.) Aviation Dept., Miami, 1973-76; mgr. mgmt. adv. services dept. Price Waterhouse & Co., Miami, 1976—; mem. adj. faculty Embry Riddle U., Barry Coll.; lectr. other local colls.; adv. com. fin. mgmt. and adminstrn. M.P.A. program U. Miami, 1979—; corp. sec., treas. Productivity Center. Vice chmn. S. Fla. council Jewish com. scouting Boy Scouts Am., 1976-78, chmn., 1978-80. Recipient Shofer award Nat. Jewish Com. Scouting. Mem. Am. Inst. Indsl. Engrs. (sr. mem., sec. Miami chpt. 1977-78, pres. 1978-79, dir. 1979-80, asst. dir. govt. div. 1979—), Soc. Am. Valve Engrs., Greater Miami C. of C. (transp. action com. 1979—). Club: B'nai B'rith (lodge trustee 1977-79). Contbr. articles to tech. jours. Home: 16665 SW 91st Ave Miami FL 33157 Office: 3500 One Biscayne Tower Miami FL 33131

THAXTON, CARLTON JAMES, librarian; b. Tucson, May 23, 1935; s. Carl Newton and Daisy (Conard) T.; A.B., U. Ga., 1957; M.S., Fla. State U., 1958; m. Donna Jean Bradley, Aug. 25, 1957; children—James Bradley, Carl Stanton. Dir. Coastal Plain Regional Library, Tifton, Ga., 1958-60, 61-68, Kingsport (Tenn.) Pub. Library, 1960-61; dir. div. pub. library services Ga. State Dept. Edn., Atlanta, 1968—; instr. library sci. U. Ga. Sch. Edn. at off campus centers in Albany and Tifton, 1960—. Mem. Am., Ga., Southeastern library assns. Democrat. Methodist. Home: 3207 Oxbridge Way Lithonia GA 30058 Office: 156 Trinity Ave SW Atlanta GA 30303

THAXTON, JOHNNY PAUL, edn. adminstr.; b. Dardanelle, Ark., Mar. 15, 1939; s. Frank L. Thaxton and Ellen L. (Kupfer) Stoddard; B.A. in Math., Ark. Tech. U., 1961; M.A., U. Ark., 1969, Specialist, 1974; m. Leora Faye Miller, Jan. 2, 1959; children—John, Teresa, Andrea, Ernest, Darin. Tchr. mat. Dardanelle (Ark.) High Sch., 1961-65, Gardner Jr. High Sch., Russellville, Ark., 1965-69, asst. prin., 1969-72; prin. Russellville Middle Sch., 1972—; pres. Classroom Tchrs. Assn., 1967. Mem. Ark. Assn. Secondary Sch. Prins., Ark. Middle Sch. Assn. (pres., 1977), Nat. Middle Sch. Assn., Ark. Assn. Ednl. Adminstrs., Phi Delta Kappa. Mem. Church of Christ. Home: Route 1 Box 192 Dardanelle AR 72834 Office: 1100 S Arkansas St Russellville AR 72801

THAYER, PAUL, diversified co. exec.; b. Henryetta, Okla., Nov. 23, 1919; s. Paul Ernest and Opal Marie (Ashenhurst) T.; student U. Wichita, 1937-38, U. Kans., 1939-41; m. Margery Schwartz, Feb. 14, 1947; 1 dau., Brynn. Pilot, Trans World Airlines, 1945-47; chief exptl. test pilot Chance Vought Corp., 1948-50, sales mgr., 1951, sales and service mgr., 1952-54, v.p. sales and service, 1954-58, v.p. Washington operations, 1958-59, v.p., gen. mgr. Vought Aeros. div., 1959-63, pres., 1963; chief flight test Northrop Aircraft Co., 1950-51; sr. v.p. Ling-Temco-Vought, Inc., Dallas, 1963, exec. v.p., 1964, chmn. bd., chief exec. officer, 1970—; chmn. bd., chief exec. officer LTV Aerospace Corp., Dallas, 1965-70, LTV Corp., 1970—. Served from ensign to lt. comdr. USNR, 1941-45. Decorated D.F.C., Air medal with nine oak leaf clusters. Recipient Distinguished Service award sec. navy, 1962. Mem. Soc. Exptl. Test Pilots, NAM (dir.), Nat. C. of C. (dir.), Bus. Round Table, Conf. Bd., Phi Gamma Delta. Home: 10200 Hollow Way Dallas TX 75229 Office: PO Box 225003 Dallas TX 75265

THAYER, PAUL ARTHUR, marine geologist, educator; b. N.Y.C., Apr. 30, 1940; s. Francis Marion and Ruth Helen (Laudage) T.; B.A., Rutgers U., 1961; postgrad. Ohio State U., 1961-62; Ph.D., U. N.C., 1967; m. Carolyn S. King, Feb. 5, 1966; 1 son, Christopher B. Geologist Chevron Oil Co., Lafayette, La., 1967-68; asst. prof. geology Tex. Agrl. Indsl. U., Kingsville, 1968-70; vis. asst. prof. marine geology Inst. Marine Scis. U. N.C., Chapel Hill, 1969-71, adj. prof., 1973—; prof. marine geology U. N.C., Wilmington, 1970—; cons. Va. Div. Mineral Resources, 1970-75, Brit. Petroleum Alaska, 1973-76, E.I. DuPont, 1978—, U.S. Army, 1978, U.S. Geol. Survey, 1978-80. Recipient 2 prizes for Paper, Gulf Coast Assn. Geol. Socs., 1973, 74; grantee NSF, 1972-74, AEC, 1974-75, Dept. Energy, 1979—. Fellow Geol. Soc. Am.; mem. Am. Assn. Petroleum Geologists, Internat. Assn. Sedimentologists, AAAS, Soc. Econ. Paleontologists Mineralogists, Sigma Xi, Sigma Gamma Epsilon. Contbr. articles in geology to profl. jours. Office: Dept Earth Sciences Univ North Carolina Wilmington NC 28401

THAYER, WILLIAM ALFRED, civil engr.; b. Queens, L.I., N.Y., Nov. 17, 1945; s. Richard Francis and Irene Teresa (Cody) T.; A.A. in Civil Engring., Miami-Dade Community Coll., 1975; B.S. in Civil Engring., Fla. Internat. U., 1979; m. Sharon Wood Kunkel, Sept. 16, 1978; children—Hank, Matthew. Draftsman, City of Coral Gables, Fla., 1964-67; technician Fla. Dept. Transp., Miami, 1968-78, engr., coordinator, 1978—. Mem. exec. council, dist. VI liaison com. Fla. Dept. Transp. Served with AUS, 1968-71. Decorated Army Commendation Medal, Vietnam Commendation Medal. Mem. Am. Concrete Inst., ASCE (affiliate), Dade County Constrn. Coordination Council, Monroe County Coordination Council, World Future Soc., Dade County Citizens' Safety Council, Smithsonian Assos., Fla. Utility Liaison Council. Home: 11600 SW 181st Terr Perrine FL 33157 Office: 401 NW 2d Ave Suite 520 Miami FL 33128

THEISEN, JEROME GEORGE, aerospace scientist; b. St. Cloud, Minn., July 1, 1928; s. George Vincent and Edna Ella (Rupp) T.; B.S., U. Minn., 1951; M.S., Va. Poly. Inst., 1956; postgrad. Ga. State U., 1969-71; m. Dannie Ann Buckhalt, Nov. 8, 1952; children—Larry Jerome, Linda Ann, Gregory Wayne. Research scientist Nat. Adv. Com. for Aeros., Hampton, Va., 1952-56; structural specialist Lockheed-Ga. Co., Marietta, 1956-65, staff scientist research lab., 1965—; pres. H.H. Johnson Assos., Inc., Architects, Ft. Myers, Fla., 1971—; dir. engring. and founding bd. Deep-Space Found., Ltd., Atlanta, 1979—; co-chmn. ad hoc com. on loads and dynamics Aerospace Industries Assn., 1960-61. Pres. Chenney Woods Civic Club, Smyrna, Ga., 1958-60. Served with U.S. Army, 1951-52. Certified civil engr., Minn.; registered profl. engr., Ga. Mem. Nat. Mgmt. Assn., Simulation Councils, Inc., Natural Philos. Soc. Am., Jimmy Carter Talent Com. Democrat. Methodist. Home: 2951 Octavia Circle Marietta GA 30062 Office: 86 S Cobb Dr Marietta GA 30063

THELANDER, MARION FUNK (MRS. PETER VICTOR THELANDER), ednl. psychologist; b. Phila., June 17, 1905; d. Martin Engle and S. Agnes (Kreider) Funk; B.S., U. Pa., 1931; M.S., Franklin and Marshall Coll., 1956; postgrad. Temple U., 1957-62; m. John Herr Smith, June 19, 1931; 1 dau., Glenna Mary (Mrs. Edgar David McClure); m. 2d, Peter Victor Thelander, Nov. 28, 1963. Tchr. spl. edn. Bd. Edn., Lancaster, Pa., 1931-34, 46-56; tchr. spl. edn., jr. high sch. English, Bd. Edn., Haverford, Pa., 1935-38; psychol. intern Millersville (Pa.) State Coll., 1957; dir. spl. services, psychologist Bd. Edn., Roselle, N.J., 1958-65; psychologist Bd. Edn. of Charlotte County (Fla.), Punta Gorda, 1965-68; mem. Council Tng. and Research in Mental Health, Dept. State, Fla., 1970-74; writer column Herald News, Punta Gorda, Fla. Cons. psychologist on mental retardation various states, 1954—; cons. Charlotte County Mental Health Assn., 1967, v.p., 1969; pres. Charlotte County Health Plus Community Action, Inc., 1969-71, v.p., exec. dir., 1972—; chmn. rehab. facilities adv. com.-area of retarded Lee, Collier, Charlotte counties div. vocat. rehab. Fla. Dept. Edn., Tallahassee, 1967-70; tchr. lip reading Port Charlotte U., 1970—; Fla. del. White House Conf. on Aging, 1971; bd. dirs. West Central Comprehensive Health Planning Council, Inc., 1971-73; sec. South Central Comprehensive Health Planning Council, 1972; pres., 1973; v.p. SW Comprehensive Health Planning Council, 1973; pres. Charlotte County (Fla.) Comprehensive Health Planning Council, 1974. Named One of Women of Achievement, N.J. Zeta Tau Alpha, 1963; named to Charlotte County Sr. Hall of Fame, 1974. Mem. Am. Assn. Sch. Adminstrs., NEA, Provisional LWV (Charlotte County pres. 1966), Am. Speech and Hearing Assn., Speech Assn. Eastern States, Internat. Council Exceptional Children (pres. Lancaster chpt. 1934), N.J., Fla. psychol. assns., Psi Chi. Republican. Author: Children at the Window, 1953; Teaching the Slow Learning Child, 1954: ednl. series, documentary film for TV; contbr. articles to publs. Home: 809 NE Conway Blvd Port Charlotte FL 33950

THELEN, EARL, communications co. exec.; b. Carrol, Iowa, June 27, 1936; s. Paul H. and Alma P. (Schulte) T.; Asso. Cert., Brown Inst., 1959; student UCLA, 1959-61, Brevard Jr. Coll., 1965-66; m. Carol Maag, July 25, 1959; children—Steve, Keith, Gary, Nick, Scott. Electronic technician Fed. Electric Co., Santa Maria, Calif., 1959-60; sect. mgr. RCA, Alaska, 1960-65, mgr. ops., Fla., 1965-68, dist. mgr., New Orleans/Atlanta, 1968-71; area mgr. Telex Computer Co., Dallas, 1971-74; chief operating officer, Carterfone Communications Corp., Dallas, 1974—. Exec. council Cable & Wireless N. Am., 1979—. Served with Airborne, U.S. Army, 1954-57. Mem. Assn. Field Service Mgrs. Republican. Roman Catholic. Home: Rural Route 2 Box 142 McKinney TX 75069 Office: Carterfone Communications Corp 1111 W Mockingbird Ln Suite 1400 Dallas TX 75247

THERIOT, ANTOINE, JR., boating corp. exec.; b. Breaux Bridge, La., Oct. 17, 1932; s. Antoine and Marie Louise (Angelle) T.; B.S., U. Southwestern La., 1954; M.A., Central Mich. U., 1974; postgrad. U.S. Air Force Air Command and Staff Coll., 1966-67, U. Utah, 1972, U.S. Air Force Air War Coll., 1973; m. Beverly Mary Broussard, Sept. 5, 1954; children—Brad, Guy, Denise, Karen. Commd. officer U.S. Air Force, 1954, advanced through grades to lt. col., 1971, ret., 1977; pres. Theriot Investments Corp., Breaux Bridge, La., 1962—; gen. mgr. Lafayette Crewboats, Inc. (La.), 1977—. Active Boy Scouts Am.; treas. Mil. Council of Cath. Men, European Region, 1971-73; Cath. Lay Eucharistic minister, 1972-75. Decorated Bronze Star, Meritorious Service medal with oak leaf cluster, Air Force Commendation medal. Mem. Air Force Pilots, Air Force Assn. Democrat. Office: 606 Canal St Delcambre LA 70528

THERRIEN, FRANCOIS XAVIER, JR., bus. and tax cons.; b. Amesbury, Mass. June 6, 1928; s. Francis Xavier and Doris Alma (Cote) T.; B.S., U.S. Mil. Acad., 1950; M.S., U. Ariz., 1962; m. Yoshiko Kashima, July 22, 1969; children—Francois Xavier, Norman, Sakura, Izumi. Commd. 2d lt., U.S. Army, 1950, advanced through grades to lt. col., 1965, ret., 1970; dist. dir. R. J. Carroll Asso., Inc., Atlanta, 1970-71; with Treasure Lake, Atlanta, 1971; pres. Identiseal of Fla., Orlando, 1972-74; owner Yoshiko Enterprises, Winter Park, Fla., 1974—; instr. Seminole Community Coll., 1974-79; sec. Buck Enterprises, Orlando, 1978—, Cosmic Corp., Orlando, 1978—; dir. E. J. Air Services, Inc., Art Works, Inc., Arabian Express, Inc. Decorated Army Commendation medal, Air medal, Bronze Star medal, Silver Star; Croix DeGuerre with palm. Mem. Nat. Assn. Enrolled Agts. Roman Catholic. Home: 1492 Canterbury Circle Casselberry FL 32707 Office: 1850 Lee Rd Suite 309 Winter Park FL 32789

THIBODEAUX, JOHN SULIE, physician; b. Abbeville, La., July 9, 1950; s. Sulie Joseph and Therese (Rodrigue) T.; B.S. with honors, U. Southwestern La., 1971; M.D., La. State U., 1974; m. Pamela Alicia Richard, May 30, 1970; children—Richmond Sully, Jan Alicia, Micah Antoine. Intern, Lake Charles (La.) Charity Hosp., 1974-75, chief resident in family practice 1975-78; mem. Med. Arts Group, Lake Charles, 1978; practice medicine specializing in family practice, Erath, La., 1979—; propr. Erath Family Doctor Clinic; chief staff, bd. dirs. Erath Meml. Hosp. Fellow Am. Acad. Family Physicians; mem. AMA, Nat. Assn. Residents and Interns, La. Med. Soc., Vermilion Parish Med. Soc., Am. Paint Horse Assn., La. Wildlife Fedn., Vermilion Parish Farm Bur., Erath Jaycees, Phi Kappa Phi. Democrat. Roman Catholic. Home: Route 2 Box 867 Erath LA 70533 Office: 506 E Edwards Ave Erath LA 70533

THIBODEAUX, MARY SHEPHERD, educator; b. Minden, La., Aug. 11, 1945; d. Ross and Arquilla (Amos) Shepherd; B.S. (Merit scholar), Grambling State U., 1965; M.Bus. Edn., Eastern N.Mex. U., 1966; Ph.D., N. Tex. State U., 1976; m. Alton Thibodeaux, Jr., Aug. 20, 1966; 1 son, Edward Shepherd. Research asst. Grambling State U., 1965; counselor Upward Bound program HEW, 1966; instr., asst. prof. bus. Grambling State U., 1966-72; asst. prof. bus. N. Tex. State U., Denton, 1976—; cons., trainer for devel. in bus., industry, edn., public instns. Kellow Found. grantee, 1977-79; recipient Disting. Tchr. award N. Tex. State U., 1979. Mem. Nat. Acad. Mgmt., So. Mgmt. Assn., S.W. Fedn. Acad. Disciplines, Small Bus. Dirs. Inst. Assn., Alpha Kappa Mu, Pi Omega Pi, Kappa Delta Pi, Phi Chi Theta. Democrat. Roman Catholic. Club: Order Eastern Star. Home: 2011 W Oak St Denton TX 76201 Office: Coll Bus N Tex State U Denton TX 76203

THIEL, JOHN ELLSWORTH, social worker; b. Lockport, N.Y., July 20, 1943; s. Ellsworth John and Marjory (Porter) T.; B.A., Roberts Wesleyan Coll., 1966; M.S.W., U. Buffalo, 1970; m. Vivian Elizabeth Little, June 11, 1966; children—Julie, Laurie. Sr. psychiatric social worker DePaul Clinic, Rochester, N.Y., 1971-77; clinic dir. Newberry (S.C.) Mental Health Clinic, 1977—; pvt. practice psychotherapy, Newberry, S.C., 1977—. Exec. bd. dirs. Diet, Discipline and Discipleship, Rochester, N.Y., 1977—; bd. dirs. Vocat. Therapy Coop., 1978—; chmn. adv. bd. for protective services Dept. Social Services, 1979—; co-chmn. Newberry Human Resources Com., 1979—. Mem. Nat. Assn. Social Workers, Acad. Certified Social Workers. Democrat. Presbyterian (deacon). Club: Rotary. Writer newspaper column Thinking Mental Health, 1977—. Home: 1168 Crosshill Ln Newberry SC 29108 Office: Newberry Mental Health Clinic 1306 Hunt St Newberry SC 29108

THIEL, PAUL JOSEPH, distbn. exec.; b. Racine, Wis., Dec. 16, 1926; s. Joseph John and Julia Ann (Bahl) T.; B.S. in Mech. Engring., Marquette U., 1949; m. Rita Mary Madden, June 23, 1951; children—Paula, Christine, Julie, Bruce, Janet, Kevin, Kurt, Susan. Pres., gen. mgr. Gateway Equipment Co., Syracuse, N.Y., 1965-67; v.p. western div. WABCO Distbn. Co., San Leandro, Calif., 1967-68; mgr. field ops. contrn. equipment div. W. Air Brake Co., Peoria, Ill., 1968-70; pres. State Machinery Co., W. Columbia, S.C., 1971-79; v.p., gen. mgr. Ann Realty Group Inc., Lexington, S.C., 1979—; former dir. Furnival Machinery Co., MBR Corp., Vivian Equipment Co. Served with USN, 1944-46. Mem. S.C. Distbrs. Assn., Asso. Equipment Distbrs. Assn., W. Columbia C. of C. Roman Catholic. Club: Coldstream Country (Irmo, S.C.). Home: Route 2 Box 338 K-2 Columbia SC 29210 Office: PO Box 43 West Columbia SC 29169

THIELE, JOHANNES PETER, thoracic and cardiovascular surgeon; b. Chemnitz, Germany, Aug. 5, 1934; s. Walter Emil and Gertha Helen (Romer) T.; came to U.S., 1968; candidate medicine U. Cologne, 1956; M.D., U. Marburg (Germany), 1959; m. Martha Cecilia Tellez, July 10, 1965; children—Christina, Stefan. Intern, Darmstadt, Germany, 1959-61; resident in gen., thoracic and cardiovascular surgery, Cologne and Dallas, 1963-73; asst. clin. prof. U. Tex. Southwestern Med. Sch., Dallas, 1973—; asso. attending staff Baylor, St. Paul hosps., Children's Med. Center; asso. to Drs. Mitchel, Adam & Assos., Dallas, 1974—. Diplomate Am. Bd. Surgery, Am. Bd. Thoracic Surgery. Fellow Am. Coll. Chest Physicians, Am. Coll. Cardiology, A.C.S., Soc. Thoracic Surgeons; mem. AMA, Tex., Dallas County med. socs. Lutheran. Home: 4108 High Summit St Dallas TX 75234 Office: 3434 Swiss Ave Dallas TX 75204

THIERSTEIN, ELDRED A., musicologist, opera dir.; b. Newton, Kans., June 5, 1935; s. Christian B. and Ella A. (Regier) T.; student Wuppertal Tchrs. Acad., Germany, 1956-57; A.B., Bethel Coll., 1958; M.Music Edn., Ind. U., 1963; Ph.D., U. Cin., 1974; m. E. Joan Voth, Mar. 17, 1959; children—Joel Peter, Gretchen Susanne. Tchr. pub. elementary sch. Woodstock, Nfld., Can., 1960-61, Harding Jr. High Sch., Hamilton, Ohio, 1963-66; profl. singer Cin. Summer Opera Co., Cin., 1964-72; musicologist and dir. opera Ky. State U., Frankfort, 1972—; summer lectr. in music dept. gerontology U. D.C., Washington, 1977. Mem. Nat. Assn. Tchrs. Singing, Am. Guild Musical Artists, Am. Musicol. Soc., Coll. Music Soc., Pi Kappa Lambda. Mennonite. Author papers, articles. Home: 8415 Conover Pl Alexandria VA 22308

THIGPEN, CHARLES ALLEN, lawyer; b. Greensboro, Ala., Dec. 7, 1941; s. Francis Marion and Rosalie (Johnson) T.; B.S., U. Ala., 1965, J.D., 1972; m. Peggy Whittington, Jan. 25, 1965; children—Christopher Allen, Margaret Marion. Admitted to Ala. bar, 1972, Fed. bar, 1972; mem. firm Dishuck & Dishuck, Tuscaloosa, 1972-73; partner firm Tucker, Gray & Thigpen, Tuscaloosa, 1973-77, firm Burke & Thigpen, Greensboro, 1977—; municipal judge, Greensboro, 1977—; dir. Univ. Community Coop. Del. Young Dem. State Conv., 1974; bd. dirs. Citizens Conf. Criminal and Juvenile Justice in Ala., 1974—, Citizens Conf. on Ala. State Cts., Inc., 1974—; bd. dirs. Tuscaloosa County Mental Health Assn., 1973—, pres., 1976—; mem. research and human rights rev. com. Ridgecrest Children's Center. Served to capt. USAF, 1965-69: Vietnam. Decorated Bronze Star. Mem. Am., Ala. (governing body Lawyer Referral Service), Hale County bar assns., Young Lawyers Assn., Ala. Trial Lawyers Assn., Phi Alpha Delta, Delta Sigma Pi, Farrah Law Soc. Methodist. Clubs: Univ., Lakeview Country, Rotary. Home: 1803 Main St Greensboro AL 36744 Office: 1113 Main St Greensboro AL 36744

THIGPEN, ROGER STEPHEN, hosp. ofcl.; b. Atlanta, Oct. 8, 1946; s. Joe Randolph and Mary Willie (Knott) T.; B.S. in Acctg., Auburn U., 1970; m. Joan Helmey, Aug. 29, 1970; 1 son, Tyler Stephen. Staff acct. George G. Scott & Co., Rock Hill, S.C., 1974-75, Larry D. French, C.P.A., Rock Hill., 1975-76; with Hosp. Affiliates Internat., Inc., 1976—, asst. controller, then controller Coral Reef Med. Center, Miami, Fla., 1976-77, controller Lykes Meml. Hosp., Brooksville, Fla., 1977-79, Alleghany Regional Hosp., Clifton Forge, Va., 1979—. Sec. Jaycee Boys Homes Inc., 1974-75, chmn., 1976. Named Jaycee of Year, Rock Hill, S.C., 1975; C.P.A., S.C. Mem. Am. Inst. C.P.A.'s, Hosp. Fin. Mgmt. Assn., S.C. Assn. C.P.A.'s. Lutheran. Office: Alleghany Regional Hosp PO Box 627 Clifton Forge VA 24422

THOENNES, LINDA LU, dietitian; b. Iowa City, Iowa, Oct. 12, 1951; d. Robert James and Helen Grace (Key) T.; B.S., Iowa State U., 1973. Dietetic intern, U. Iowa, 1973-74; therapeutic dietitian U. Iowa Hosp., 1974; gen. dietitian Children's Hosp., Iowa City, 1974-75; clin. dietitian Presbyn. Hosp., Dallas, 1976-79; dietary dir. Mesquite (Tex.) Meml. Hosp., 1979—. Mem. Am. Dietetic Assn., Tex. Dietetic Assn., Dallas Dietetic Assn. (yearbook chmn. 1977-78, program chmn. 1978-79, nominating com. 1979-80), Am. Soc. Hosp. and Sch. Food Service Adminstrs., Kappa Delta. Office: 1011 Gus Thomasson St Mesquite TX 75149

THOMAS, ALAN TOY, chem. engr.; b. Louisville, May 15, 1921; s. M(oses) A(lan) and Ruth (Lacefield) T.; B. Chem. Engring., U. Louisville, 1943, M. Chem. Engring., 1947, Ph.D., 1964; m. Joycelyn Jane Markert, Mar. 18, 1945; children—Thomas Douglas, Tucker Craig. With Brown-Forman Distillers Corp., 1943—, apprentice supr., tech. supr., research engr. and statistician, research asso., project and devel. engr., asst. to v.p. and dir. prodn., 1943-64, asst. dir. prodn., 1964-73, asst. v.p., dir. prodn., 1973-79, v.p., tech. dir., 1979—, v.p., dir. prodn. Canadian Mist Ltd. subs., 1974-79, v.p., tech. dir., 1979—; lectr. math. U. Louisville, 1957-59, lectr. bus. mgmt., 1964—, adj. asst. prof. liberal studies, 1976—. Registered profl. engr., Ind. Fellow AAAS; mem. Am. Chem. Soc., Am. Mgmt. Assn., Am. Math. Soc., Ops. Research Soc. Am., Distillers Feed Research Council (dir.), Distilled Spirits Council U.S. (tech. com. 1980—), Inst. Mgmt. Sci., Am. Soc. Quality Control, Inst. Math. Statistics, N.Y. Acad. Sci., Phi Lambda Upsilon, Sigma Xi. Presbyterian. Contbr. articles to profl. jours. Home: 708 Arbor Dr N Anchorage KY 40223 Office: PO Box 1080 Louisville KY 40201

THOMAS, ALVIN IGNACE, univ. adminstr.; b. New Orleans, Sept. 7, 1925; s. Clarence P. and Lillian P. Thomas; A.S., Xavier U., 1943; B.S., Kans. State Coll., 1948, M.S., 1949; Ph.D., Ohio State U., 1957; postgrad. Pa. State Coll., 1951, U. Mich., 1963; m. Iris A. Butler, June 2, 1951; children—Kenneth C., Michael D., Janet M., Julie E. Dean, Sch. of Indsl. Tech., Prairie View (Tex.) A&M Coll., 1963-66; pres. Prairie View A&M U., 1966—; cons. Dow Chem., Litton Industries, Westinghouse Corp.; chmn. bd. dirs. Houston br. Fed. Res. Bank of Dallas. Served with U.S. Army, 1941-43. Mem. Nat. Assn. Land-Grant Colls. (exec. com. 1971-74), Tex. Council of Coll. Presidents, Tex. Rural Devel. Commn., Am. Council Indsl. Arts, Am. Mgmt. Assn., Tex. Indsl. Edn. Assn., Office for Advancement of Negro Colls. Roman Catholic. Author: Technical Education In Liberia, 1963; Accelerating Curriculum Change in Black Colleges, 1973. Home: 224 Elm Prairie View TX 77445 Office: PO Drawer W Prairie View TX 77445

THOMAS, ANDREW CHRISTIE, educator; b. Lynn, Mass., Apr. 26, 1936; s. Christie Andrew and Alice (Mortis) T.; B.S., Boston U., 1959; M.A., Salem State Coll., 1965; M.A., State U. Coll. at Buffalo, 1970; Ed.D., U. Ga.; m. Peggy Ann Carney, Mar. 1, 1974. Tchr., Revere (Mass.) Public Schs., 1961-68, Buffalo Public Schs., 1968-69; asso. prof. Tenn. Technol. U., 1973—. Cons., Jackson County Assessment Program. Served with USMCR, 1959-60. Recipient learning and behavioral disorders fellowship, 1969-70. Mem. Am. Edn. Research Assn., Am. Personnel and Guidance Assn., Tenn. Edn.

Assn., Reserve Officers Assn., Phi Delta Kappa. Greek Orthodox. Office: Tenn Tech U PO Box 5141 Cookeville TN 38501

THOMAS, BERL MICHAEL, nursery co. exec.; b. Jonesboro, Ark., Nov. 24, 1940; s. Berl E. and Prudy Mae (Meurer) T.; B.S.A. in Vocat. Agr., Ark. State U., 1962; M.S. in Agronomy and Plant Breeding, La. State U., 1964; Ph.D. in Genetics and Agronomy, Botany and Weed Control, Miss. State U., 1972; m. Wilma Wood, June 3, 1960; 1 son, Michael Thomas. Chief agronomist La. Land & Exploration Co., Houma, 1967-70; dir. research Fla. Celery Exchange, Belle Glade, 1970-73; dir. prodn. and research Speedling, Inc., Sun City, Fla., 1973-76, v.p., 1976-79, pres., 1979—; lectr. in field. Mem. Crop Sci. Soc. Am., Soil Sci. Soc. Am., Am. Soc. Agronomy, Bedding Plants Inc. (dir.), Profl. Farmers Am., Ohio Florists Assn., Fla. State Hort. Soc., Council for Agrl. Sci. and Tech., So. Nurserymen's Assn., Fla. Nurserymen and Growers Assn., Fla. Foliage Assn. Home: 808 60th St Bradenton FL 33505 Office: PO Box 98 Sun City FL 33586

THOMAS, CHARLES EDWARD, writer, historian, educator; b. Ridgeway, S.C., Nov. 17, 1903; s. Robert Charlton and Rosa Woodruff (Taft) T.; B.A., U. of South, 1927. Instr. English, U. of South, Sewanee, Tenn., 1927-28, v.p. for endowment, 1947-48, dir. admissions, 1948-51; instr. English, Syracuse (N.Y.) U., 1928-29; editor The Delta, asst. sec. Sigma Nu fraternity, Indpls., 1929-39; exec. dir. Ch. Soc. for Coll. Work, Episcopal Ch., Washington, 1940-42; v.p. Resort Airlines, N.Y.C., 1946-47; commr. bldgs. and lands, Sewanee, 1953-54; free lance writer-historian, Greenville, S.C., 1955—. Historiographer, registrar Diocese of Upper S.C., 1957-60; vestryman Otey Parish, Sewanee, 1953-54; historiographer Christ Ch., Greenville, 1968-75; mem. Greenville Hist. Preservation Commn., 1971-75; sec. bd. regents, trustee U. of South; trustee St. Marys Coll., Raleigh, N.C. Served with USN, 1942-46, 51-53, to comdr. Res., 1942-60. Recipient citation Sec. Navy, 1943, Alumni Exonarti award U. of South, 1977. Mem. Huguenot Soc. S.C., English Speaking Union, Fairfield County, Greenville County, S.C., Dalcho hist. socs., Found. for Hist. Restoration Pendleton Area, Caroliniana Soc. (exec. council), Blue Key, Sigma Nu (Hall of Honor award 1976), Omicron Delta Kappa. Author: Sewanee, the Oxford of America, 1933; European Universities, 1936; St. Stephen's Church, Ridgeway, S.C., 1934; Know Your Church-Christ Church, Greenville, S.C., 1972; editor: Posthumous Poems of Louis Archibald Douglass, 1931; contbr. to Purple Sewanee, 1932, A Fairfield Sketchbook, 1963, St. Philip's, Greenville, S.C., 1973, Biographical Tribute to the Rt. Rev. Albert Sidney Thomas, LL.D., D.D., S.T.D., Bishop of South Carolina, 1977. Home: 200 Fairview Ave Alta Vista Greenville SC 29601

THOMAS, CLARENCE LEE, JR., elec. engr.; b. Groesbeck, Tex., Aug. 25, 1925; s. Clarence L. and Nettie (Oates) T.; B.S.E.E., U. Houston, 1949; m. Helen Petrey, Dec. 16, 1951; children—Helen Pamela, Stephen Lee, Raymond Andrew. Instr., Sch. Tech., U. Houston, 1948-49; sr. elec. engr. Palmer & Baker Engrs., Inc., Mobile, Ala., 1950-76; chief estimator, supt. Meador Contracting Co., Mobile, 1975-76; v.p., sec., chief elec. engr., asso. Owen S. Posey & Assos., Inc., Mobile, 1976—. Served with AUS, 1943-46. Mem. Illuminating Engring. Soc. (chmn. Gulf Coast chpt.), IEEE (chmn. Mobile sect.), Am. Cons. Engrs. Council, Mystic Mardi Gras Orgn. Mem. Ch. of Christ. Club: Masons. Contbr. articles on tunnel and roadway lighting standards to mags. Home: 122 N Julia St Mobile AL 36604 Office: 622 Azalea Rd Mobile AL 36609

THOMAS, DAVID, export co. exec.; b. N.Y.C., Dec. 8, 1930; s. Max Henry and Edith Caroline (Bott) T.; student Bethany Coll., 1947-48; A.B. summa cum laude, N.Y. U., 1958; M.B.A. with distinction, 1963; m. Joyce Buchanan, Dec. 6, 1958; 1 son, David Buchanan. Adminstrv. officer N.Y. U. extension, 1958-59; with Standard Oil Co. (N.J.), 1959-69, tng. dir. Esso Research, Linden, N.J., 1959-61; mgr. Employment and tng. Enjay Chem. Co. div., N.Y.C., 1961-63; mgr. mktg. services, 1964-66, regional sales mgr., 1966-67, mktg. mgr. Esso Chem. S.A., Brussels, Belgium, 1967-68, mgr. capital investment dept. Enjay Chem. Co. div., N.Y.C., 1968-69; mktg. mgr. Internat. Paper Co., N.Y.C., 1969-71; v.p. mktg. Columbia Precision Corp., Hudson, N.Y. and N.Y.C., 1971-72; v.p. mktg. Huyck Corp., Wake Forest, N.C., 1972-73, v.p. fluid control products, 1973-75, v.p. mktg. and new bus. devel., 1975-78; chmn. subs. Chronister Valve Co., Houston, 1973-75; chmn. Export Fundamentals, Inc., 1979—; dir. N.C. Internat. Trade Center, 1978—; lectr. N.Y. U., 1958-59, N.C. State U.; participant profl. seminars and confs. Mem. dist. export council U.S. sec. Commerce. Served with AUS, 1948-54. Recipient Alumni Achievement award N.Y. U., 1963. Mem. Am. Mgmt. Assn. (mktg. council 1972—), Am. Soc. Tng. and Devel., N.C. World Trade Assn. (dir.), Am. Mktg. Assn. Episcopalian. Author: (with P.W. Maloney) Interviewing the Professional Employee, 1961. Home: 5018 Shamrock Dr Raleigh NC 27612 Office: 100 E Six Forks Rd Raleigh NC 27619

THOMAS, DAVID ORMONDE, radio sta. exec.; b. Pensacola, Fla., Mar. 24, 1929; s. John Douglas and Sybil (Addenbrooke) T.; B.A. in Econs., Southwestern U., Memphis, 1951; m. Mary Elizabeth Hickman, June 3, 1955; children—Rebecca, David. Account exec. King & Stanley Outdoor, Memphis, 1963-65; account exec., Sta. WHBQ, Memphis, 1965-69, sales mgr. 1969-73; v.p., gen. mgr. Sta. WEZI, Memphis, 1973-79; v.p. Southern Broadcasting Co., Memphis, 1979—. Div. chmn. United Way, Memphis, 1977; bd. dirs. Cystic Fibrosis Soc., Memphis, 1977. Mem. Sales and Mktg. Execs. Memphis (sec.-treas. 1979), Memphis Area Broadcasters Assn. (pres. 1978), Tenn. Assn. Broadcasters (West Tenn. v.p. 1977-80), Memphis Advt. Fedn. Republican. Presbyterian. Clubs: Stonebridge Country. Office: 5900 Poplar St Memphis TN 38138

THOMAS, DAVID RAYMOND, physician; b. Jackson, Miss., Apr. 26, 1946; s. Raymond Pierce and Dot (Ballard) T.; B.S., U. Miss., 1968, M.D., 1971; m. Janice Lynn Nichols, June 30, 1967; children—Sandra, Heather, Michael. Resident in internal medicine U. Miss. Med. Center, 1971-75; practice medicine, specializing in internal medicine, Starkville, Miss., 1975—; clin. instr. medicine U. Miss., 1975—; adj. prof. microbiology Miss. State U., 1975—; mem. staff Univ. Med. Center, Jackson, Oktibbeha County Hosp. Diplomate Am. Bd. Internal Medicine. Mem. Prairie Med. Soc., Am. Soc. Internal Medicine, A.C.P., Miss. State Med. Soc. Mem. Ch. of Christ. Club: Optimist. Office: 517 University Dr Starkville MS 39759

THOMAS, DAVID WALTER, JR., mfg. co. exec.; b. Asheville, N.C., May 19, 1938; s. David Walter and Francis (Warren) T., Sr.; B.S. in Mech. Engring., N.C. State U., 1962; M.S. in Indsl. Mgmt., U. Tenn., 1974; m. Mary Ruth Gordon, June 10, 1961; children—David, Anne. Field service engr. Huyck Corp., Tenn. and N.C., 1962-63, sales engr., 1963-64, product mgr., 1964-66, mgr. product mgmt., 1966-68, project mgr., 1969-70, mgr. mfg. services, 1968-69, constrn. mgr., 1970-71, start-up engr., 1971, plant mgr., 1971-72, mfg. mgr., 1972-74, v.p., gen. mgr. div., 1974-79, corp. dir. planning, Wake Forest, N.C., 1979—. Dist. chmn. Boy Scouts Am., 1977-78, exec. com. East Tenn. council, 1976-78; mem. budget com. United Way, 1977-78; chmn. personnel com. 1st Bapt. Ch., Greeneville, 1975-77, adult discussion leader, 1970-79. Served with U.S. Army, 1960-61. Elected pres. of class U. Tenn. Exec. Devel. Program, 1974, Issues Speaker, 1977; recipient various hon. coll. leadership awards. Mem. Paper Industry Mgmt. Assn., Golden Chain, Blue Key, Beta Gamma Sigma. Baptist. Clubs: Lions, Exchange. Contbr. research paper, articles to profl. jours. Home: 14204 Crosscreek Rd Raleigh NC 27614 Office: Huyck Corp Wake Forest NC 27612

THOMAS, EZEKIEL FRED, JR., veterinarian; b. Ocala, Fla., June 10, 1936; s. Ezekiel Fred and Buna Estell (Gladin) T.; D.V.M. magna cum laude, U. Ga., 1960; m. Mary Emily Blanchard, Aug. 19, 1961; children—Jewel Kathryn, Ezekiel Fred III. Veterinarian, River Forest Animal Hosp. (formerly Thomas Animal Hosp.), Sarasota, Fla., 1960-63, owner, 1964—; pres. Ezekiel F. Thomas, Jr., D.V.M., Profl. Assn., 1974—. Longhouse chief Myaca Nation, YMCA Indian Guides, 1975—. Mem. Am., Fla. vet. med. assns., Am. Animal Hosp. Assn. (hosp. dir. 1964-79), S.W. Fla. Vet. Med. Assn. (pres. 1972-73), Sigma Chi (pres. Sarasota alumni soc. 1968), Phi Kappa Phi, Phi Zeta, Blue Key. Democrat. Clubs: Rotary, Field, Yacht (Sarasota). Home: 4536 Riverwood Ave Sarasota FL 33581 Office: 4937 S Tamiami Trail Sarasota FL 33581

THOMAS, FORREST BENJAMIN, III, toxicologist; b. Yokohama, Japan, Oct. 14, 1947 (parents Am. citizens); s. Forrest Benjamin, Jr., and Betty Kikuye (Ohashi) T.; B.S., Tulane U., 1969; M.S., U. Tex. Health Sci. Center, Houston, 1971, Ph.D., 1973; m. Diane Marie Jewasko, Mar. 9, 1974. Cancer research trainee sect. exptl. pathology, dept. pathology, U. Tex. System Cancer Center, M.D. Anderson Hosp. and Tumor Inst., Houston, summers 1968, 69, predoctoral fellow, 1969-73, postdoctoral fellow sect. nucleotide metabolism, dept. biochemistry, 1973-74, Rosalie B. Hite postdoctoral fellow, 1974-75, 76-77, research asso., 1975-76, toxicologist, health, safety and environ. Shell Oil Co., Houston, 1977—. Recipient Am. Legion award, 1962. Mem. Am. Coll. Toxicology, AAAS, Sigma Xi. Methodist. Club: Forum of Houston (charter). Contbr. papers in field to profl. publs. and confs. Home: 13815 Almeda School Rd Houston TX 77047 Office: PO Box 4320 Houston TX 77210

THOMAS, FRANCIS THORNTON, surgeon, educator; b. Hibbing, Minn., June 24, 1939; s. Gerald M. and Patricia E. (Thornton) T.; B.S., U. Minn., 1962, M.S., 1963, M.D., 1964; m. Judith M. Jannino, June 26, 1969; children—Francis Scott, David Randolph, Jason Hunter. Intern Bellevue Hosp., N.Y.C., 1965-66, resident in surgery, 1966-68, chief resident in surgery, 1968-69; fellow in thoracic surgery Case-Western U., 1969-71; instr. surgery Med. Coll. Va., Richmond, 1971-72, asst. prof., 1972-74, asso. prof., 1974—; practice medicine specializing in surgery Pitt Meml. Hosp., 1979—; prof. surgery Eastern Carolina Sch. Medicine, Greenville, N.C., 1979—; cons. in field; sci. cons. Nat. Inst. Heart, Lung and Blood Diseases, Nat. Inst. Allergy and Infectuos Diseases, Nat. Inst. Gen. Med. Research. Diplomate Am. Bd. Surgery, Am. Bd. Thoracic Surgery. Fellow A.C.S.; mem. AAUP, Am. Assn. Immunologists, Transplantation Soc., Soc. Univ. Surgeons, Med. History Club, Am. Soc. Transplant Surgeons (founding mem.), Southampton Recreation Assn., Sigma Xi. Democrat. Episcopalian. Club: Greenville Country. Contbg. author to med. books. Cons. editor Transplantation Jour., 1976—, Jour. of Surg. Research, 1975—. Office: East Carolina Sch Medicine Greenville NC 27834

THOMAS, GARNETT JETT, accountant; b. Farmington, Ky., July 27, 1920; s. Pinkney Madison and Ethel (Drinkard) T.; B.S., Lambuth Coll., 1947; student U. Notre Dame, 1943-44; M.S., Miss. State U., 1949; m. Katherine Gardner, Mar. 26, 1948. Clk./acct. Ill. Central R.R., Paducah, Ky., 1941-42; mgr. Coll. Bookstore, Lambuth Coll., Jackson, Tenn., 1946-47; acct. Miss. Agrl. and Forestry Expt. Sta., Mississippi State, 1948-60, chief acct., 1960-75, adminstrv. officer and chief acct., 1975—; adv. bd. Nat. Bank of Commerce of Miss., 1974—; pres. PBR Corp., Starkville, Miss., 1977—. Served with USN, 1942-46. Decorated Bronze Star medal. Mem. Nat. Assn. Accts., Assn. Govt. Accts., Am. Assn. Accts., So. Assn. Agrl. Scientists. Republican. Methodist. Club: Rotary (pres. 1959-60, dist. gov. dist. 682, 1977-78, adv. com. to pres. 1979—). Home: 72 Ridge Dr Route 1 Starkville MS 39759 Office: PO Drawer AT Mississippi State MS 39762

THOMAS, GEORGE BELL, SR., coll. pres.; b. Ninety-six, S.C., July 1, 1929; s. James Wesley and Cattie (Davis) T.; B.S., S.C. State Coll., 1952; M.A., Am. U., 1960; Ed.D., George Washington U., 1968; m. Mary Ethel Myles, Nov. 10, 1950; children—George Bell, Marvin Eliho, Clinton Cornell, David Robert, Joseph William. Bus. edn. tchr. Montgomery County (Md.) Public Schs., 1957-65, curriculum specialist, 1965-68, prin., adult edn. tchr., 1962-68, asst. prin., 1968-69, prin., 1969-71, area dir. instruction, 1971-76, asso. supt., 1971-76; vis. instr. Howard U., 1972-73; pres. Voorhees Coll., Denmark, S.C., 1978—, also trustee. Served with USAF, 1952-56. Mem. Am. Assn. Sch. Adminstrs., S.C. Coll. Council, So. Assn. Colls. and Schs., United Negro Coll. Fund, Am. Council Edn., Assn. Episcopal Colls., Nat. Assn. Equal Opportunity in Higher Edn., Nat. Congress Ch.-Related Colls. and Univs., Coalition for Concerns of Blacks in Post-Secondary Edn. in S.C., Episcopal Commn. for Black Ministries, Bamberg County C. of C., NAACP, Columbia Urban League, Omega Psi Phi (chpt. Man of Yr. 1970), Delta Sigma Theta (award), Md. Congress Parents and Tchrs. (hon. life). Club: Sandy Spring Comml. (v.p.). Democrat. Baptist. Contbr. articles to bus. edn. jours. Home and Office: Voorhees College Denmark SC 29042

THOMAS, JAMES WELDON, geophysicist; b. Gainesville, Tex., Apr. 2, 1909; s. Charles M. and Gladys Pearl (Moon) T.; B.A., N. Tex. State U., 1929, B.S., 1930; postgrad. U. Tex., Austin, 1930; D.C.L. (hon.), Atlanta Law Sch., 1975; m. Isabel Cunningham Edwards, Aug. 23, 1930 (dec. 1968); children—Ann Tamsin Thomas McElyea, William Lee, Diana Craig Thomas Childress; m. 2d, Bess Fleming. With Geophys. Service Inc. (now subs. Tex. Instruments, Inc.), Dallas, 1930—, pres., to 1960, mem. pres.'s council, 1960—, past dir. U.S. and fgn. subs.; cons. geophysics, Dallas, 1960—; pres. Diversified Properties Inc., Dallas. Trustee Tex. Presbyterian Found.; bd. dirs. Presbyn. Pan Am. Sch., Kingsville, Tex., Internat. Linguistics Center, Dallas; past mem., chmn. Good Neighbor Commn. Tex.; past chmn. bd. dirs. Salvation Army Advisory Bd., Mexico City; hon. counsul Rep. of Korea, Dallas-Fort Worth. Mem. Am. Assn. Petroleum Geologists (emeritus), Soc. Exploration Geophysicists (emeritus), Dallas Geophys. Soc., Dallas Geol. Soc. Clubs: Lions (past chpt. pres.), Dallas Petroleum, Brook Hollow Golf, Cadence, Thalia, Dallas Dinner Dance, Masons.

THOMAS, JANICE MARY, career counselor; b. Jackson, Miss., Jan. 22, 1948; d. Leon and Ruby Betrous T.; B.S., Loyola U., 1970, M.Ed., 1972. Head resident, program coordinator Loyola U., New Orleans, 1970-73; tchr., guidance counselor Lourdes Community Sch., New Orleans, 1972-76; asst. prin., guidance counselor St. Angela Merici Sch., New Orleans, 1976-78; dir. career services Our Lady of Holy Cross Coll., New Orleans, 1978—. Mem. La. Assn. Religious and Values Issues in Counseling (pres.), Assn. Religious and Value Issues in Counseling (nat. sec. 1978-79), Am. Personnel and Guidance Assn., Am. Sch. Counselors Assn., Am. Coll. Personnel Assn., La. Personnel and Guidance Assn., Coll. Placement Council, Loyola U. Alumni Assn. (dir.). Roman Catholic. Office: 4123 Woodland New Orleans LA 70114

THOMAS, JOHN HARLEY, union exec.; b. Christina, Fla., June 17, 1915; s. John William and Lena Pearle (Hall) T.; student pub. schs., Mulberry, Fla.; m. Ester Lee Rhodes, Sept. 29, 1934 (dec. 1970); children—Rose Mary, John Harley; m. 2d, Zeni Inez May, June 17, 1972; stepchildren—Ed Hanberry, Linda Blackledge. Joined Internat. Chem. Workers Union, 1934; officer local 22056 Fed. Labor Union, 1934-44; v.p., Fla., Am. Fedn. Labor, 1955; mem. staff Internat. Chem. Workers Union, 1954-58, internat. v.p., 1958—, dir. S.E. region, from 1958, subsequently v.p. and regional dir. southeastern states. Served with USNR, 1944-45. Democrat. Baptist. Home: 17315 Simmons Rd Lutz FL 33549 Office: 402 Reo St Suite 215 Exec Sq Tampa FL 33609

THOMAS, JOSEPH MURRAY, JR., traffic engr.; b. Atlanta, Jan. 29, 1939; s. Joseph M. and Ruby L. (Davis) T.; certificate in traffic engring., Northwestern U., 1961; grad. Ga. Inst. Tech., 1967; m. Barbara N. Nicholson, Jan 3, 1957; children—Joseph Murray, J. Lynn, Matthew L. Civil engr. City of Atlanta Planning Dept., 1958, dist. traffic engr., 1959-64, traffic ops. engr., 1964-72, dep. dir. traffic engring., 1972-78, chief Div. of Traffic Engring., 1979—; instr. Ga. Inst. Tech., Atlanta, 1964—. Recipient Hensley award, So. sect. Inst. Transp. Engrs., 1976; registered profl. engr., Ga. Mem. Nat. Soc. Profl. Engrs., Ga. Soc. Profl. Engrs., Inst. Transp. Engrs., Inst. Transp. Engrs. (pres. So. sect. 1973, chmn. dist. bd. 1980). Baptist. Contbr. articles, chpts. in books to profl. publs. Home: 5071 Kurt Ln Conyers GA 30207 Office: City of Atlanta 1003 City Hall Atlanta GA 30303

THOMAS, JULIA MAE, ednl. pub.; b. New Orleans; d. Posey and Mary Wilson (Gardette) Stewart; B.A. in Elementary Edn., So. U., Baton Rouge, 1955; M.A. in Curriculum Devel., DePaul U., Chgo., 1977; div.; 1 son, Clyde L. Thomas. Elementary tchr. New Orleans pub. schs., 1955-61; technician Ohio State U., 1960-61; elementary tchr. Chgo. Bd. Edn., 1961-64, New Orleans Bd. Edn., 1964-68; elementary tchr., Chgo., 1968-74, reading resource tchr., 1974-78; reading specialist So. U., Baton Rouge, from 1978; now pres. Julia M. Thomas Inc. Vol. Profl. Womans Aux. of Provident Hosp., 1962-64, 74—. Mem. Chgo. Area Reading Assn., Internat. Reading Assn. (resolutions com. 1979-80, speaker), Assn. Supervision and Curriculum Devel., Am. Assn. Sch. Adminstrs., Assn. Ednl. Communications and Tech., Am. Assn. Ednl. Research, Council for Basic Edn., Nat. Assn. Elementary Sch. Prins., Black Alliance, Phi Delta Kappa, Eta Phi Beta, Kappa Delta Pi. Author: The Achievement of Continuous Progress Level C Children as Measured by Norm-Referenced and Criterion Referenced Tests on Reading Comprehension, 1976. Office: PO Box 52484 New Orleans LA 70152

THOMAS, LANGLEY CARSWELL, baking co. exec.; b. Tampa, Fla., Oct. 2, 1928; s. Preston and Evie (Lee) T.; student U. Ga., Waycross, 1953-55; m. Wynelle Walker, Feb. 6, 1949; children—Lang, Anna, Linda. Postal clk. U.S. Post Office, Waycross, 1945-56; salesman Nabisco, Jacksonville, Fla., 1956-65, sales supr., Atlanta, 1965-67, sales driver, br. mgr., 1967-73, regional mgr., 1973—. Deacon, Central Baptist Ch., Waycross, 1955, Parkview Bapt. Ch., Gainesville, Fla., 1963-65; tchr. men's bible class First Bapt. Ch., Morrow, Ga., 1977—. Served with U.S. Army, 1946-47, 50-51. Recipient sales awards. Mem Ga. Automatic Mdsg. Council, N.C., S.C. and Va. Vending Assn. Democrat. Home: 1846 Argonne Dr Morrow GA 30260 Office: Mt Zion Rd Morrow GA 30260

THOMAS, LEE BALDWIN, mfg. exec.; b. Alma, Neb., Sept. 17, 1900; s. Rees and Fannie (Baldwin) T.; B.B.A., U. Wash., 1923; m. Margaret Thomas, 1924 (dec.); children—Lee Baldwin, Margaret Ellen (Mrs. Wallace Dunbar), Susan Jane (Mrs. A. Scott Hamilton); m. 2d, Elizabeth Cawthorn Bromley. Advt. mgr. Ernst Hardware Co., Seattle, 1923-24, sales mgr., 1926-29; buyer R. H. Macy Co., N.Y.C., 1924-25; dir. home goods merchandising Butler Bros., Chgo., 1929-41; pres. Ekco Products Co., Chgo., 1941-47, Am. Elevator & Machine Co., Louisville, 1947-48; chmn. bd. Vermont Am. Corp. and subsidiaries, Am. Saw & Tool Co., Louisville, Vt. Tap & Die Co., Lydonville, Vt., Multi Metals, Inc., Louisville, DeLuxe Saw & Tool Co., Louisville and High Point, N.C.; chmn. bd. Thomas Industries, Inc. and subsidiaries; owner Honey Locust Valley Farms, Cloverport, Ky., Bd. dirs. Honey Locust Found., Louisville. Mem. N.A.M. Clubs: Delray Dunes Golf and Country (Delray Beach, Fla.); Owl Creek Country (Anchorage, Ky.); Harmony Landing Country, Hunting Creek Country (Prospect, Ky.); Pendennis (Louisville); Union League, Mid-day (Chgo.), Lake Region Country (Winter Heaven, Fla.); Mountain Lake (Lake Wales, Fla.). Home: Evergreen Rd Anchorage KY 40223 Office: Vermont American Bldg 100 E Liberty Suite 401 Louisville KY 40202

THOMAS, LORENZO ROBERTO, author; b. Panama, Republica de Panama, Aug. 31, 1944; s. Herbert Hamilton and Luzmilda Henrietta (Gilling) T.; naturalized U.S. citizen, 1956; B.A. in English Lit., Queens Coll., City U. N.Y., 1967; postgrad. Pratt Inst., 1967. Writer-in-residence Tex. So. U., 1973, Black Arts Center, Houston, 1974-76, Tex. Commn. Arts and Humanities, 1974-78, Ark. Arts Council, Little Rock, 1976—, State Arts Council Okla., Oklahoma City, 1978—. Mem. adv. bd. KPFT-FM, 1975-76; bd. dirs. Coordinating Council Lit. Mags., 1975-79; mem. lit. panel Nat. Endowment Arts, 1980. Served with USN, 1968-71. Recipient Dwight Durling prize in poetry Queens Coll., 1963, John Golden award 1963; Lucille Medwick award, 1974; Com. on Poetry grantee, 1973. Author: Fit Music, 1972; Dracula, 1973; Jambalaya: Four Poets, 1975; Chances Are Few, 1979; editor Lost World, 1961-62, Ear, 1963; Roots, 1974; ANKH, 1974. Adv. or guest editor: NIMROD, 1977, HOODOO, 1978. Home: PO Box 14645 Houston TX 77021

THOMAS, MAMIE JACKSON, educator; b. Decatur, Ga., Feb. 12, 1919; d. Andrew and Mamie (Bowdre) Jackson; A.B., Clark Coll., 1941; M.A., Atlanta U., 1960, Ph.D., 1973; m. Joseph E. Thomas, Dec. 27, 1948 (dec.). Asst. to actuary Atlanta Life Ins. Co., 1942-54; tchr. French and English, Clayton County Bd. Edn., Jonesboro, Ga., 1959-60, secondary sch. counselor, 1960-75; asso. prof. edn. Clark Coll., Atlanta, 1975—; supr. practicum NDEA Guidance and Counseling Inst., Atlanta U., 1961-63. Certified sch. counselor, Ga.; certified in prins. of life ins. Life Office Mgmt. Assn. Mem. Am. Personnel and Guidance Assn., NEA, Am. Assn. Colls. Tchr. Edn., Am. Psychol. Assn. Episcopalian. Home: 2566 Hightower Ct Atlanta GA 30318

THOMAS, MICHAEL ALFRED, architect; b. Jackson, Tenn., Oct. 13, 1943; s. Edward Michael and Myra Alma (Risky) T.; B.Arch., U. Fla., 1967; m. Kay Wilson, Jan. 25, 1972; children—Errin, Marc, Shawn. Group leader-project mgr. Lockwood-Greene, Spartanburg, S.C., 1968-72; mgr. comml. multi-family projects Ervin Co., Charlotte, N.C., 1972-73; asst. v.p. architecture Teledyne Architects, Huntsville, Ala., 1973-74; chief architect Daniel Internat. Corp., Greenville, S.C., 1974—. Recipient Young Profl. award Bldg. Design and Constrn., 1978. Mem. AIA. Home: 107 Whittlin' Way Taylors SC 29687 Office: Daniel Internat Corp 5th floor Daniel Bldg Greenville SC 29602

THOMAS, MICHAEL EARL, air force officer; b. Columbus, Ohio, Nov. 30, 1944; s. Roderick M. and Virginia A. (Middleton) T.; B.A. in Communications, Ohio State U., 1967; M.A. in Polit. Sci. cum laude, Okla. State U., 1979; m. Susan K. Thomas, June 21, 1968; 1

dau., Dana. Commd. 2d lt. U.S. Air Force, 1967, advanced through grades to maj., 1979; logistics plans officer 67th Tactical Reconnaissance Wing, Bergstrom AFB, Tex., 1971-73; tech. assistance field team liaison officer, Iran, 1973-74; chmn. working group for air force logistics support of European wideband microwave system Hdqrs. U.S. Air Force Europe, Ramstein AFB, W. Ger., 1974-75; exec. officer, dep. chief of staff for logistics, 1975-76; capt. Air Force Logistics Command Career Broadening Program, 1976-78; B-52 program mgr. for airframe systems Tinker AFB, Okla., 1978-79; mem. tech. assistance field team Secretariat Air Force Weapon System Acquisition Study Group, Hdqrs. U.S. Air Force, Washington, 1979—. Mem. Soc. Logistics Engrs., U.S. Tennis Assn., Air Force Assn., Phi Kappa Phi. Methodist. Home: 5346 Rawlings St Oklahoma City OK 73145 Office: OC-ALC/MM Tinker Air Force Base OK 73145

THOMAS, (MARY) MICHELE BURHARD, educator; b. Columbus, Ohio, Oct. 28, 1941; d. Carl Leo and Mary Monica (McGonagle) Burhard; B.A. summa cum laude in Chemistry, Ohio Dominican Coll., 1963; M.Ed. in Guidance and Counseling, U. Miss., 1970, Ph.D. Student Personnel Services in Higher Edn., 1972; m. Jack Anthony Thomas, July 27, 1963; children—Maria Theresia, Jacqueline Ann, Renate Margareta. Biology tchr. Am. Internat. Sch., Vienna, Austria, 1964-65; English tchr. Rieseikan Gakuin, Nishinomiya, Japan, 1966-68; math. tchr. Granville (Ohio) Jr. High Sch., 1968-69; instr. U. Miss., University, 1970-72; asst. prof. ednl. psychology and guidance U. Tenn. at Nashville, 1973-75; asso. prof. psychology Tenn. State U., Nashville, 1975—, vice-chmn. steering com. Univ. Self-Study for So. Assn. Colls. and Schs., 1977—. Recipient Merit award Student Govt. Assn. Tenn. State U., 1977; lic. psychol. examiner in counseling, sch. psychology Tenn. Bd. Examiners in Psychology. Mem. Am., Tenn. (exec. sec. 1975-76) personnel and guidance assns., Tenn. Psychol. Assn., Am., So., Tenn. assns. counselor edn. and supervision, Tenn., Am. assns. non-white concerns in personnel and guidance, Nat., Tenn. vocat. guidance assns., Nat. Cath. Guidance Conf., Psi Chi, Phi Kappa Phi, Kappa Delta Pi. Democrat. Roman Catholic. Clubs: Nashville Dem. Women's, W. Meade Swim and Tennis. Author various manuals on vocat. and career devel. and guidance Tenn. State Dept. Edn., 1974-76; contbr. articles to profl. jours. Home: 818 Cammack Ct Nashville TN 37205 Office: PO Box 644 Tenn State U Nashville TN 37203

THOMAS, PATSY RUTH, speech-lang. pathologist; b. Ozark, Ala., Apr. 7, 1943; d. James Wyatt and Nellie Lee (Andrews) Trotter; M. Speech Pathology, M. Gen. Speech, Auburn U., 1972; 1 son, Derrick; 1 ward, Michael Hartzog. Sales clk., Kress, Ala., 1964, 66, Dothan, Ala., 1966-73; bookkeeper, 1973-76; speech-lang. pathologist, Dothan, 1976—. Adv. bd. health Project Headstart, Dothan, 1974-76, chmn., 1975; chmn. S.E. Ala. Quality Assurance Com., 1977—; bd. dirs. Alamed and S. Ala. Home Health Service; active CAP. Auburn U. fellow, 1970-71; Montgomery (Ala.) Crippled Children Service scholar, 1969-71. Mem. Am. Speech and Hearing Assn. (cert. clin. competence), Wiregrass Speech and Hearing Assn. (founder 1975), Speech and Hearing Assn. Ala., Strokers' Club for CVA's (founder 1973). Lutheran. Researcher auditory perceptual problems, speech reading; asso. editor SHAA Jour., 1979—. Home: 513 Haisten Dr Dothan AL 36301

THOMAS, PENDLETON EMMETT, III, gynecologist; b. Suffolk, Va., Feb. 19, 1929; s. Otey Perkins and Ursula Magdelene (Towell) T.; B.A., U. Va., 1950; B.S., Med. Coll. Va., 1954, M.D., 1954; postgrad. Drexel Inst. Tech., 1963-64; m. Jacalyn Morecock, Sept. 2, 1978; children—Robert E., Randall J., Ronald S., John P., Anne E., Hilary Q., Mary C. Intern, Mt. Carmel Hosp., Detroit, 1954-55, resident, 1955-58; practice medicine specializing in gynecol. surgery, Richmond, Va., 1958-62, 63—. Served with U.S. Army, 1946-48, U.S. Navy, 1962-63. Diplomate Am. Bd. Obstetrics and Gynecology. Fellow A.C.S., Am. Coll. Obstetricians and Gynecologists; mem. Med. Soc. Va., AMA, Richmond Acad. Medicine, Va., Richmond obstet. and gynecol. socs., Am. Soc. Sex Educators and Counsellors, Flying Physicians Assn., First Flight Soc., Nat. Assn. Flight Instrs., Silver Wings Soc., Aircraft Owners and Pilots Assn. Roman Catholic. Home: 9907 Kingsbridge Rd Richmond VA 23233 Office: 5700 Old Richmond Rd Richmond VA 23226

THOMAS, PHILIP ROBINSON, operational mgmt. cons. co. exec.; b. Torquay, Devon, Eng., Dec. 9, 1934; s. Leslie Robinson and Margaret (Lilford) T.; came to U.S., 1963, naturalized, 1969; B.Sc., U. London, 1959, M.Sc., 1961, postgrad., 1961-64; m. Wayne Laverne Heirtzler, Apr. 6, 1973; children by previous marriage—Martin N. R., Stephen D. R. With Tex. Instruments Corp., 1961-72, ops. mgr., Dallas, 1963-72, Bedford, Eng., 1961-63; v.p., gen. mgr. MOS/LSI div. Gen. Instruments Co., N.Y.C., 1972-73; gen. mgr. MOS Products div. Fairchild Camera and Instrument Corp., Mountainview, Calif., 1973-75; v.p. Integrated Circuits div. RCA, Somerville, N.J., 1975-78; pres., chief exec. officer Thomas Group Inc., Ethel, La., 1978—. Mem. IEEE, Brit. Inst. Radio and Electronics Engrs. Contbr. articles to profl. jours.; patentee semicondrs. Home: Route 1 Box 181-D Ethel LA 70730 Office: Thomas Group Inc Route 956 Ethel LA 70730

THOMAS, RANDALL ELWOOD, constrn. co. exec.; b. Tulsa, Sept. 22, 1949; s. Jack Elwood and Betty Jean T.; B.S. in Indsl. Mgmt., Purdue U., 1971; m. Melissa Kay; 1 son, Justin Earl. Mgr. metal bldg. div. Jack Thomas Constrn. Co. Inc., Tulsa, 1971-74, sec., 1974-77, exec. v.p., 1977—. Mem. Nat. Metal Bldg. Dealers Assn. (Bldg. of Yr. award 1975), Asso. Builders and Contractors Okla. (dir. 1978), Metal Bldg. Mfg. Assn., Laminated Fiberglass Insulation Producers Assn., Thermal Insulation Mfg. Assn., Tulsa Metal Bldg. Dealers Assn. (dir. 1978—, pres. 1977), Theta Chi. Republican. Presbyterian. Home: 8730 E 27th St Tulsa OK 74129 Office: Jack Thomas Constrn Co Inc 301 N Walnut St Broken Arrow OK 74012

THOMAS, RICK LEE, civil engr.; b. Neon, Ky., Aug. 24, 1953; s. Hairm and Shirley (Collins) T.; A.A. in Mining Tech., Pikeville Coll., 1974; A.A. in Sci., Hazard Community Coll., 1976; B.S. with distinction in Civil Engring., U. Ky., 1978, postgrad. in law, 1980—; m. E. Darlene Wright, June 8, 1973; 1 dau., Charity Darlene. Underground miner Beth Elkhorn, Jenkins, Ky., 1972-74; instrument specialist Mine Enforcement and Safety Adminstrn., Whitesburg, Ky., 1974-76; head mining engring. Cawood Engring., Harlan, Ky., 1978-79; constrn. engr. Monterey Coal Co., Huntington, W.Va., 1979—; tchr. elec. classes Pikeville Coll., 1973-74; cons. to local mining industry. Ky. Mining Engrs. Scholar, 1974-78. Mem. AIME, ASCE, Jr. C. of C. Home: Gen Delivery Neon KY 41840

THOMAS, ROBERT EARL, drilling co. exec.; b. Weatherford, Tex., July 14, 1926; s. Earl M. and Louise M. Harrington (Kimmell) T.; student Cisco Jr. Coll., 1946-47; B.B.A., Lamar State Coll., 1964; m. Brenda Mae Harris, Dec. 2, 1971; children—Wesley Earl, Katherine Gail Thomas Litt; stepchildren—Debbi Dell Head, Kris Baker. Profl. baseball player Pitts. Pirate Orgn., 1946-47; with patrol div. Tex. Dept. Pub. Safety, Abilene, 1947-50; claim adjuster, claims mgr. Highlands Ins. Co., Dallas, 1950-72; personnel and ins. dir. Penrod Drilling Co., Dallas, 1972—. Served with USAF, 1944-46. Mem. Am. Soc. Personnel Adminstrn., Dallas Personnel Assn., Am. Mgmt. Assn., Ind. Assn. Drilling Contractors (adv. com.), Risk and Ins. Mgmt. Soc. Home: 2143 Kessler Ct Dallas TX 75208 Office: 3300 1st National Bank Bldg Dallas TX 75202

THOMAS, RUBLE ANDERSON, utility co. exec.; b. Birmingham, Ala., July 14, 1921; s. James A. and Grace (Smith) T.; B.S. in Mech. Engring., Ga. Inst. Tech., 1947, B.S. in Elec. Engring., 1948, M.S. in Elec. Engring., 1949; student Oak Ridge Sch. Reactor Tech., 1953-54; m. Mary Jo Bass, Feb. 16, 1941; children—James, Janice Thomas Jones. Electric design engr. Commonwealth & So. Corp., Birmingham, 1948; with So. Co. Services Inc., Birmingham, Ala., 1949—, mgr. nuclear power, 1959-65, asst. to pres., 1965-66, v.p., 1966—. Mem. So. Interstate Nuclear Bd., 1966-77; dir. Power Reactor Devel. Co., Detroit, 1968-73; trustee High Temperature Reactor Devel. Assos., 1967-73. Served to 1st lt. AUS, 1943-44, USAAF, 1944-46. Registered profl. engr., Ala., Fla., Ga., Mich., Miss. Mem. Am. Nuclear Soc. (dir.), ASME, Atomic Indsl. Forum, Edison Electric Inst., Electric Power Research Inst., IEEE. Clubs: Kiwanis, Downtown, Inverness Country. Home: 5033 Kerry Downs Rd Birmingham AL 35243 Office: PO Box 2625 Birmingham AL 35202

THOMAS, WADE HAMILTON, accountant; b. Jackson, Miss., May 12, 1922; s. Harrison Spurgeon and Lealer (Bandy) T.; B.S. with distinction, Tenn. A. and I. U., 1949, postgrad., 1950; m. Mary Katherine Scruggs, Oct. 8, 1958; 1 dau., Michelle L., Korda, Renee, Wade, Karl, Harrison, Kenneth, George, Rex, Axel. Faculty, So. Tng. Inst., Nashville, 1947-51; spl. ordinary rep. Universal Life Ins. Co., Memphis, 1951-52; gen. clk. U.S. Post Office, Nashville, 1953-63; partner Drake & Thomas, Nashville, 1954-60; owner W. H. Thomas, Pub. Accountant, Nashville, 1960-63; mgmt. intern, field mgr. Pub. Bldg. Service, GSA, Atlanta, 1963-72; owner W. H. Thomas, Pub. Accountant, Nashville, 1973—. Adv. council Asheville (N.C.) Civic Center, 1977. Served in Armed Forces, World War II. Recipient A. and I. State U. Golden Anniversary Citation, 1962; U.S. Post Office Superior Accomplishment award, 1960; GSA Spl. Accomplishments award, 1971; Omega Psi Phi Distinguished and Outstanding Service award, 1974. Mem. Asheville Fed. Exec. Assn., Nat. Assn. Ret. Fed. Employees, Nat. Soc. Pub. Accountants, Tenn. Assn. Pub. Accountants, N.C. Soc. Accts. (v.p.), Asheville Bd. Realtors, N.C. Bd. Realtors, Tenn. A. and I. State U. Alumni Assn., Omega Psi Phi. Roman Catholic. Clubs: Asheville Optimist, W. Asheville Civic Community, Carlton. Home: 2 Mardell Circle Asheville NC 28806 Office: PO Box 2202 Asheville NC 28802

THOMAS, WILLIE LEE, educator, artist; b. Morston, Tex., Sept. 25, 1915; d. Sidney and John Etta (Watts) Cannon; student Tex. State U., 1930-32, U. Boulder, 1934-37, Art Inst. Chgo., 1944-46; B.S., Tillotson U., 1934; M.A., U. Calif. at Berkeley, 1946; M.S., Tex. So. U., 1952; m. Joel Lafayette Thomas, June 22, 1940; 1 dau., Arillian Ruth. Tchr. Houston Pub. Schs., 1935-36, Crawford Elementary Sch., Houston, 1944-77; tchr. art, chmn. dept. Jack Yates Sr. High Sch., Houston, 1944-77; instr. art Tex. So. U., Houston, 1952-55; exhibited in one-woman shows Mus. Fine Arts, Houston, 1948, 49, 50, Art League Houston, 1976, Coll. of Mainland, Texas City, 1976, Bay City, 1977; group show Tex. So. U. Youth art chmn. Area II, Ethel Ransom Club, Houston, 1970-74, art chmn., 1972-76; dist. art chmn. Women's Federated Clubs of Tex., Houston, 1970-74. Recipient 1st prize Art League of Houston, 1952, hon. mention Museum of Fine Arts of Houston, 1949. Mem. Nat., Houston, Tex. assns. art educators, Nat. Am. Crafts Council of Arts, Contemporary Handweavers Tex., Museum of Fine Arts, Art League of Houston, Tex. Designer Craftsmen, Orgn. of Artists, Tex., Houston tchrs. assns., NEA, Alpha Kappa Alpha, Democrat. Baptist. Co-author bull. Houston Sch. Dists., 1976; Houston's 1st Black art educator. Address: 2519 Wichita St Houston TX 77004

THOMASON, GARY DAN, electronic instrument mfg. co. exec.; b. Polk County, Ga., Aug. 29, 1935; s. Daniel Webster and Stella Irene (Denson) T.; B.A., Ga. State U., 1973; postgrad. Harvard Bus. Sch., 1974; m. Jo Ann Lenning, Nov. 24, 1955; children—Gary Wayne, Geoffrey Daniel. Prodn. mgr. Pepperell Mfg. Co., Lindale, Ga., 1952-55; weaver Lockheed Ga. Co., Marietta, 1955; installer Inland Container Corp., Rome, Ga., 1955-58; instrumentation prodn. mgr. Sci. Atlanta, Inc., 1961—. Corp. exec. dir. Jr. Achievement, 1976-77. Served with U.S. Army, 1958-61. Mem. Am. Mgmt. Assn. Democrat. Baptist. Home: 1371 Spring Valley Ln Stone Mountain GA 30087 Office: 3845 Pleasantdale Rd Atlanta GA 30340

THOMASSON, RAYMOND FRANKLIN, adminstrv. chemist; b. Ansted, W.Va., Nov. 17, 1914; s. Charles L. and Mary Margaret (Holley) T.; A.B., W.Va. U., 1940, B.S., 1940. Jr. chemist Wright Aero. Corp., Lockland, Ohio, 1940-41; chemist U.S. Rubber Co., Indpls., 1945-47; sr. health surveyor Monsanto Chem. Co., Miamisburg, Ohio, 1947-53; chemist C.& N.W. Ry., Chgo., 1953-57; sr. chemist Santa Fe R.R., 1957—; pvt. practice as cons. chemist, Cin., 1947-50, Dayton, Ohio, 1950-53; sr. health surveyor Chgo. Bd. Edn., 1971—. Served with AUS, 1942-45. Mem. AAAS, Am. Inst. Chemists, Am. Chem. Soc., W.Va., Ind., Chgo. acads. sci., Franklin Inst., Armed Forces Chem. Assn., Am. Ordnance Assn., Am. Soc. Testing Materials, Am. Accounting Assn., Art Inst. Chgo., NEA, Entomol. Soc., Washington, ALA, DAV, Am. Legion, others. Methodist. Clubs: Masons; Moose; Odd Fellows. Research in field. Home: 211 Wyoming St Charleston WV 25302

THOMISON, JOHN BROWN, pathologist; b. Chattanooga, Apr. 17, 1921; s. John Greer and Mary (Brown) T.; B.A., Vanderbilt U., 1942, M.D., 1944; m. Elva Smith Hollins, Sept. 11, 1944; children—Mary Ann Thomison Zink, John, Elva Hollins Thomison Palmer, Robert Hollins. Intern, Ohio State U. Hosp., Columbus, 1944-45; resident surgery Erlanger Hosp., Chattanooga, 1947-49, pathology Vanderbilt Hosp., 1949-52; vis. pathologist Vanderbilt Hosp., Nashville, 1952—, chief gynecol. pathology sect., 1955-66, chief cytopathology service, 1955-66; pathologist Park View Hosp., Nashville, 1966—, chief lab. services, 1970-75; pres. Associated Pathologists, P.C., Nashville, 1969-78; sec. Internat. Clin. Labs., Inc., Nashville, 1972-78; instr. to asso. prof. Vanderbilt Med. Sch., 1951-66, asso. clin. prof., 1966—. Bd. dirs. Tenn. div. Am. Cancer Soc., 1963—, chmn. profl. edn. commn., 1965-70, pres., 1977-78. Served with U.S. Army, 1945-47. Nat. Institution of Allergy and Infectious Disease grantee, 1960-66; recipient Am. Cancer Soc. Nat. Divisional award for Distinguished Service in Cancer Control, 1975. Diplomate Am. Bd. Pathology. Fellow Am. Soc. Clin. Pathology, Coll. Am. Pathologists; mem. AMA (council continuing physician edn. 1976—, vice chmn. 1979—), Internat. Acad. Pathology, Tenn. Med. Assn., Nashville Acad. Medicine, Tenn. Soc. Pathologists (pres. 1961-62), Am. Soc. Cytology, Am. Soc. Microbiology, Sigma Xi. Clubs: Exchange Nashville, Belle Meade Country, Nashville City. Editor Jour. Tenn. Med. Assn., 1972—; So. Med. Jour., 1977—. Home: 714 Darden Pl Nashville TN 37205 Office: 230 25th Ave N Nashville TN 37203

THOMPSON, A. LEON, JR., realtor, investor; b. Waxahachie, Tex., Mar. 16, 1948; s. Aubrey Leon and Mary Ann (West) T.; B.B.A., Tex. A. and M. U., 1970; J.D., U. Tex., 1973. Admitted to Tex. bar, 1973; head, farm and ranch dept. Jim Stewart Realtors, Waco, Tex., 1971-75; owner Thompson Properties, Waco, 1975—; partner Thompson and Farrar Investments, Waco, 1975—; v.p., dir. Webster Distbg. Co., Waco, 1976—; dir. Kindler Jewelers; instr. investment real estate McLennan Community Coll. Area coordinator for Bob Krueger Senate campaign, Waco, 1978. Mem. State Bar Tex., Waco-McLennan County Bar Assn., Nat. Assn. Realtors, Realtors Nat. Mktg. Inst., Tex. Assn. Realtors. Democrat. Presbyterian. Home: 3624 Castle St Waco TX 76710 Office: 704 Citizen's Tower Waco TX 76701

THOMPSON, ALVONZO, retail exec.; b. Memphis, Mar. 3, 1951; s. Buford Rogers and Pearlean (Frison) T.; B.S. in Bus. Mgmt., Tenn. State U., 1973; postgrad. U. Tenn., Nashville, 1978—; m. Eloise M. Link, Apr. 28, 1979; children—Tosha, Artemis. Store mgr. Sears, Roebuck & Co., Memphis, 1973-76; gen. mgr. univ. bookstores Tenn. State U., Nashville, 1976—, mgr. univ. retail entities; dist. mgr. Nat. Safety Assos., Nashville. Active Young Nashvillians, NAACP, Bros. of Harambee, co-founder, treas., 1970-73, organizer fund drive for Meharry Med. Coll. Sickle Cell Anemia Fund. Mem. Nat. Assn. Coll. Stores, Am. Booksellers Assn. (certified), SE Assn. Coll. Stores, Tenn. Assn. Coll. Stores, Tenn. State U. Alumni Assn. (v.p. 1977-78), Phi Beta Lambda. Democrat. Baptist. Clubs: Sean Social, Royal Gents Civic. Home: 270 Tampa Dr Nashville TN 37211 Office: 3500 Centennial Blvd Nashville TN 37203

THOMPSON, ANDREW BOYD, JR., pub. co. exec.; b. West Point, Ga., Mar. 30, 1930; s. Andrew Boyd and Frieda Jaqueline (Smith) T.; student Auburn U., 1948-49; m. Laura June Guy, Mar. 13, 1959; children—Guy Bradly, Eric Kiepp. Materials engr. asst. Ala. Hwy. Dept., Montgomery, 1949-51, 54-55; lab. technician So. Testing Labs., Montgomery, 1955; salesman, mgr. Mel's Photo Shop, Montgomery, 1955-57, 58-66; agt. Prudential Ins. Co. Am., Montgomery, 1957-58; furniture salesman Sears, Roebuck & Co., Montgomery, 1966; v.p. Nat. Photo Pricing Service, Inc., Montgomery, 1966—, dir., 1972—. Bd. dirs. Friends of Epilepsy, 1977—, pres., 1977-78, sec., 1978—. Served with U.S. Army, 1951-54; lt. col. Res. Recipient Medal Am. Legion, 1948. Mem. Photo Mktg. Assn. Internat., Photog. Mfrs. and Distbrs. Assn., Res. Officers Assn., Internat. Platform Assn., Montgomery C. of C., Am. Biog. Inst. Research Assn. (asso.). Methodist. Home: 4353 Amherst Rd Montgomery AL 36116 Office: PO Box 3008 Eastbrook Sta Montgomery AL 36109

THOMPSON, ANNIE LAURA, educator; b. Henderson, Tenn., July 8, 1937; d. Wesley Sylvester and Letha Irene (Jones) T.; B.A., U. Ala., 1959; M.A., Duke U., 1961; Ph.D., Tulane U., 1973. Instr., U. Miss., Oxford, 1960-64, Auburn (Ala.) U., 1964-66; teaching asst. Tulane U., New Orleans, 1966-70; asso. prof. Spanish, Delgado Coll., New Orleans, 1970—; instr. Spanish for physicians and med. persons Tulane U., La. State U. Med. Sch., Ochsner Clinic and Hosp. Active New Orleans Mental Health Assn. Recipient Outstanding Tchr. award Delgado Coll. Student Govt. Assn., 1974; Woodrow Wilson fellow, 1956-60; NDEA fellow, 1968-69. Mem. MLA, AAUP, Spring Fiesta Assn., Phi Beta Kappa, Phi Alpha Theta, Sigma Delta Pi. Mem. Ch. of Christ. Asst. editor The Crusader, 1961-64. Office: 615 City Park Ave New Orleans LA 70119

THOMPSON, CATHERLENE SHAW, educator; b. Guilford County, N.C., July 3, 1921; d. Stone Walter and Lena Leorenza (Blackwell) Shaw; A.B., Shaw U., 1943; M.A., Columbia U., 1959; postgrad. U. N.C., Chapel Hill, 1961, U. Besancon (France), 1963, Middlebury Coll., 1974; m. James Lafayette Thompson, Sr., Aug. 11, 1950; 1 son, James Lafayette. French tchr. DuBois High Sch., Wake Forest, N.C., 1943-45; directress Somerville Mission Sch., St. Marc, Haiti, 1945-50; ofcl. rep. Lott-Carey Bapt. Fgn. Mission Conv., Govt. Haiti, 1947-50; French tchr. Jordan Sellars High Sch., Burlington, N.C., 1950-64; asso. prof. dept. fgn. lang. Fayetteville (N.C.) State U., 1964—, dir. lang. lab., supr. student interns; dir. instl. self study So. Assn. Colls. and Schs., 1968-69. Mem. Am. Assn. Tchrs. French, NEA, Coll. Lang. Assn., AAUP, Nat. Assn. Lang. Lab. Dirs., Fgn. Lang. Assn. N.C. (adv. bd.), N.C. Tchrs. Assn. (chmn. sec. fgn. lang. sect.), N.C. Assn. Educators, N.C. State Employees Assn., Zeta Phi Beta. Club: Fayetteville State U Faculty Women's. Home: 1820 Cascade St Fayetteville NC 28301 Office: PO Box 963 Fayetteville State U Fayetteville NC 28301

THOMPSON, CHARLES ROBERT, environ. engr.; b. Seattle, Sept. 2, 1949; s. Robert Cecil and Gloria Elizabeth (Smith) T.; B.S. in Chem. Engring., Va. Poly. Inst., 1971, M.S. in Environ. Sci. and Engring., 1972; m. Rosemary Ayres, May 22, 1971; 1 son, Ryan Charles. With Environ. and San. Engring. Atlantic Div., Naval Facilities Engring. Command, Norfolk, Va., 1972—, program mgr. air quality control, 1972—. Mem. Am. Inst. Chem. Engrs., Air Pollution Control Assn. Methodist. Home: 3961 Shady Oaks Dr Virginia Beach VA 23455 Office: Code 114 Atlantic Div Naval Facilities Engring Command Norfolk VA 23511

THOMPSON, CLARK WALLACE, JR., investment exec.; b. Galveston, Tex., Aug. 28, 1919; s. Clark Wallace and Libbie (Moody) T.; B.B.A., U. Tex., 1947; m. Charlene Quitter; 1 dau., Anne Thompson McNeilis. With Arthur Anderson & Co., Houston, 1947-56, partner, 1956-61; personal investment mgmt., Houston, 1961—; now also dir. Southwestern Savs. Assn., Houston. Mem. accounting adv. com. U. Tex., Austin, 1958—; mem. adv. com. Salvation Army; trustee Northwood Inst., Midland, Mich.; steering com. Tex. Futures, Austin. Served to capt. AUS, 1943-46. Mem. Am. Inst. C.P.A.'s, Fat Stock Show Assn., Beta Theta Pi, Beta Alpha Psi. Democrat. Episcopalian. Clubs: Houston Country, Houston; Port Bay (Rockport, Tex.); Broadmoor Golf, Garden of the Gods, Kissing Camels Golf (Colorado Springs). Home: 4911 Tilbury Dr Houston TX 77056

THOMPSON, DEAN ALLAN, cattleman; b. Peru, Ind., Jan. 29, 1934; s. Paul Franklin and Pauline St. Clair (Thrush) T.; student Purdue U., 1952-54. Mgr. Thompson Farms, breeders registered Hereford cattle, Peru, 1956-69; owner Thompson Farms, Wartrace, Tenn. and Peru, 1970—, Dean Thompson Prodns., Wartrace, Wartrace Records; chmn. bd. Instant Copy and Printing, Inc., Monterrey, Calif., Trenton Energy Inc., Bloomfield, Ind.; profl. beef cattle judge. Bd. dirs. H.A. Thrush Found., Peru; precinct committeeman, chmn. Miami County (Ind.) Young Republican Com., 1962-67; treas. 5th Dist. Young Reps., 1965-66. Served with U.S. Army, 1955-56. Mem. Nat. Western (dir.), Ind. (dir. 1958-68, pres. 1960) polled Hereford assns., Ind. Cattleman's Assn. (founding dir.), Ind. Livestock Breeders Assn., Tenn. Hereford Assn. (dir. 1977—, v.p. 1979, pres. 1980). Methodist. Clubs: Toastmasters Internat. (pres., area gov.); Columbia (Indpls.). Home and office: Box 230 Route 1 Wartrace TN 37183

THOMPSON, ETHBERT CLAY, III, ceramic engr.; b. Greenville, Miss., Aug. 8, 1944; s. Ethbert Clay and Nellie Rivers (Tribble) T.; B.S. in Ceramic Engring., Miss. State U., 1966; M.B.A., Augusta Coll., 1977; m. Donna Frances Sudduth, Nov. 23, 1963; children—Donna Teresa, Stephanie Kay. Devel. engr. refractories div. Babcock & Wilcox Co., Augusta, Ga., 1969-79, project engr., 1969-74, sr. project engr., 1974—; corp. coll. recruiter, 1977—. Pres. sanctuary choir, mem. music com. Curtis Baptist Ch., Augusta, 1979—. Served with Ordnance Corps, U.S. Army, 1966-69. Decorated Army Commendation medal with oak leaf cluster. Mem. Instrument Soc. Am. (sr. mem. mgmt. div. and glass and ceramics div.), Assn.

M.B.A.'s. Patentee high strength hot press die. Home: 3122 Fieldstone Circle Augusta GA 30907

THOMPSON, F(RANCIS) NEAL, fin. planning corp. exec.; b. N.Y.C., Oct. 21, 1940; s. M. Weldon and Mary Temple (Meacham) T.; B.A., Lynchburg Coll., 1962; M.B.A., U. Richmond, 1966; postgrad. Purdue U., 1971; m. Patricia Turner, June 16, 1962; children—Melissa Temple, Turner Jennings. Vice pres. Fidelity Bankers Life, Richmond, Va., 1965-72; dir., founder, chmn. exec. com. Wheat Ins. Survices, Richmond, 1972-74; pres. Corporate Consultants, Inc., Richmond, 1974—; adj. prof. fin. and ins. Va. Commonwealth U., Richmond, 1976—; dir. F.C. Mgmt. Co., Nashville Artists and Repetoire Co. Vol. worker Boy Scouts Am., 1963—, instl. rep., 1976—. C.L.U., cert. fin. planner, Va. Mem. Assn. Advanced Life Underwriters, Million Dollar Round Table, Richmond Assn. Life Underwriters, Internat. Assn. Fin. Planners. Republican. Mem. Christian Ch. Clubs: Bull and Bear, Westwood Racquet. Author: Assessing Individual Managerial Performance, 1966. Home: 12305 Lullington Dr Richmond VA 23233 Office: 1145 Gaskins Rd Richmond VA 23229

THOMPSON, HORACE EDWARDS, physician, educator; b. Pampa, Tex., Jan. 12, 1921; s. Marion and Clara T.; student U. Denver, 1941-44; M.D., U. Colo., 1948; m. Edith Marguerite Hamilton, David Edwards, Susan Nanette, Carol Jean. Intern, Gen. Hosp. Fresno County, Fresno, Calif., 1948-49; resident Johns Hopkins Hosp., 1951-52, Presbyterian Hosp., Chgo., 1952-54; gen. practice medicine, Fairplay, Colo., 1949-50; practice medicine specializing in ob-gyn, Denver, 1954-55, 57-66; asst. clin. prof. dept. ob-gyn U. Colo., 1966-67, asso. clin. prof., 1967-71, asso. prof., 1971-73, prof., 1974-78, dir. ob-gyn service Denver Gen Hosp., 1974-78; prof., chmn. La. State U., 1978—. Served to maj. U.S. Army, 1955-57, maj., 1961-62; lt. col. USAR (ret.). Mem. Shreveport Med. Soc., La. Med. Soc., Denver Med. Soc., Colo. Med. Soc., Colo. Gynecol. and Obstet. Soc., Am. Coll. Obstetricians and Gynecologists, Central Assn. Obstetricians and Gynecologists, Am. Inst. Ultrasound in Medicine (recipient William Fry Meml. award, 1978), Assn. Advancement Med. Instrumentation. Presbyterian. Author: Diagnostic Ultrasound in Clinical Obstetrics and Gynecology, 1978. Asso. editor: Jour. Clin. Ultrasound, 1978. Home: 5619 Mirador Circle Shreveport LA 71119 Office: 1501 Kings Hwy Shreveport LA 71130

THOMPSON, HORACE KENT, JR., banker; b. Wilmington, N.C., Dec. 12, 1933; s. Horace Kent and Hortense Josephine (Hopkins) T.; B.A., U. N.C., 1956; m. Flavia Josephine Seeger, Nov. 10, 1956; children—Benjamin Garrett, Ashley Ellen, Daniel Kent, Cyrus Scott, Laura Hadley, David McKinney. Sales-mgmt. trainee Polymer Chems. div. W.R. Grace & Co., Clifton, N.J., 1956-57; with Wachovia Bank & Trust Co., N.A., 1959—, v.p., city exec., Fayetteville, N.C., 1973—. Mem., chmn. Fayetteville Revitalization Commn.; mem. budget rev. com. ESEA Title I; v.p., bd. dirs. Methodist Coll. Found.; officer migrant ministry Albermarle Council Migratory Labor, 1965-70; bd. dirs. Elizabeth City Boys Club, 1971; mem. ciitzens adv. council Emergency Sch. Assistance Program. Served with U.S. Army, 1957-59. Mem. Am. Inst. Banking (instr.), Nat. Assn. Accountants, N.C. Bankers Assn., Fayetteville C. of C. (chmn. revitilization com. 1977). Espicopalian. Clubs: Exchange, Lions, Optimist, Highland Country, Dark Branch Racquet. Home: 506 Thorncliff Rd Fayetteville NC 28303 Office: PO Box 1888 Fayetteville NC 28302

THOMPSON, HOWARD ARTHUR, coll. dean; b. Russellville, Ala., May 16, 1931; s. William McGary and Mary Cuthbert (Hatch) T.; B.B.A., U. Calif., Berkeley, 1953; M.B.A., Tulane U., 1958; Ph.D., U. Ala., 1968; m. Eunice Eickemeyer, Nov. 2, 1958; children—Julie, Peter, Betsy. Sales rep. Continental Can Co., Milw., Chgo. and Louisville, 1958-63; instr. U. No. Ala., Florence, 1963-65, U. Ala., Tuscaloosa, 1966-68; lectr. U. New South Wales (Australia), 1968-70; asso. prof., dir. Mgmt. Devel. Center, U. Tulsa, 1970-74; prof., dean Coll. Bus., Eastern Ky. U., Richmond, 1974—. Served with USN, 1954-57. Mem. Am., So., Southwestern (treas., pres. 1974-76) mktg. assns., Mem. Ch. of Christ. Club: Rotary. Author: Australian Cases in Marketing, 1975; The Great Writings in Marketing, 1976; Cases in Marketing, 1979; contbr. articles to profl. jours. Home: 330 University Dr Richmond KY 40475 Office: Coll Business Eastern Ky U Richmond KY 40475

THOMPSON, JACK WARREN, state govt. ofcl.; b. Frankfort, Ky., July 11, 1932; s. William McKinley and Ella (Mitchell) T.; student Ky. State U., 1968-69; m. Mary Frances Evans, Jan. 21, 1954; 1 son, Mark Warren. Data processing mgr. Ky. Dept. Finance, 1951-61, Hoover Ball & Bearing Co., 1961-65; pres. Lexington Computer Service (Ky.), 1965-68; operations mgr. Ky. Dept. Edn., Frankfort, 1968-76, dir., div. program design and maintenance, 1976—; chmn. Ky. Info. Processing Adv. Com. Scoutmaster, Boy Scouts Am., 1967-70. Served with U.S. Army, 1953-55. Ky. col. Mem. Data Processing Mgmt. Assn., Ky. Farm. Bur. Mem. Disciples of Christ. Home: Rural Route 9 Hanly Ln Frankfort KY 40601 Office: 628 Teton Trail Frankfort KY 40601

THOMPSON, JAMES WILLIAM, educator; b. Overton, Tex., Sept. 24, 1937; s. King Daniel and Lucile (Reaney) T.; B.A. in Religion and Philosophy, Southwestern U., 1960; M.A. in Sociology, U. Houston, 1971; m. Verdine Mae Ford, Jan. 25, 1963; 1 dau., Susan Marie. Dir. Christian edn. First United Meth. Ch., Lufkin, Tex., 1961-64, First United Meth. Ch., Conroe, Tex., 1964-68; asst. prof. sociology Tenn. Wesleyan Coll., Athens, 1971—; dir. tng. contact McMinn-Meigs Co., 1973-76. Diaconal minister United Meth. Ch. Mem. Am. Sociol. Assn., So. Sociol. Soc., Nat. Council on Family Relations, Christian Educators Fellowship of United Meth. Ch., Blue Key, Pi Delta Epsilon, Kappa Alpha. Club: Optimist (past pres.). Home: 1110 Sioux St Athens TN 37303 Office: Tenn Wesleyan College Athens TN 37303

THOMPSON, JERE WILLIAM, retail food and dairy co. exec.; b. Dallas, Jan. 18, 1932; s. Joe C. and Margaret (Philp) T.; grad. high sch., 1950; B.B.A., U. Tex., 1954; m. Peggy Dunlap, June 5, 1954; children—Michael, Jere W., Patrick, Deborah, Kimberly, Christopher, David. With Southland Corp., Dallas, 1954—, v.p. stores, 1962-73, exec. v.p., 1973-74, pres., 1974—, dir., 1962—. Bd. dirs. St. Paul Hosp. Endowment Fund; mem. Coll. Bus. Adminstrn. Found. Advisory Council U. Tex. at Austin. Served to lt. (j.g.) USNR, 1954-56. Home: 4217 Armstrong Pkwy Dallas TX 75205 Office: 2828 N Haskell Ave Dallas TX 75221*

THOMPSON, JOHN P., retail food co. exec.; b. Dallas, Nov. 2, 1925; s. Joe F. and Margaret (Philp) T.; B.B.A., U. Tex., 1948; m. Mary Carol Thomson, June 5, 1948; children—Mary Margaret, Henry Douglas, John P. With Southland Corp., 1948—, pres., 1961-69, chmn. bd., chief exec. officer, 1969—. Office: 2828 N Haskell Ave Dallas TX 75221*

THOMPSON, JOYCE CAROLYN, elec. contracting co. exec.; b. Houston, Aug. 7, 1923; d. Robert Harris and Ruth Morse (Fisk) Davis; B.B.A., Baylor U., 1944; comml. law certificate Nat. Inst. Credit, 1971, certificate in parliamentary procedure, 1975; m. Billy Morris Thompson, Dec. 27, 1945. Accounting clk. comptroller dept. Texaco Corp., Houston, 1944-45; office mgr., dir., corporate sec.-treas. Fisk Electric Co. Inc., Houston, 1945—; corporate sec.-treas., dir. Fisk Telephone Systems Inc., Houston, 1971—, Fisk Line Co., Houston, 1974—. Active, Reach to Recovery program Am. Cancer Soc. Mem. Nat. Assn. Women in Constrn., Houston Assn. Credit Mgmt. Exec. Women Internat. Republican. Methodist. Club: Woodlands Country. Office: 111 TC Jester Blvd Houston TX 77007

THOMPSON, K(ENNETH) REED, elec. engr.; b. Alma, Ga., Feb. 20, 1931; s. Howard and Larue (Head) T.; B.E.E., Ga. Inst. Tech., 1953, M.S. in Elec. Engring., 1954; m. Margaret Louise Drody, Mar. 22, 1952; children—Larry Stephen, Fred Lamar. With Ga. Power Co., Atlanta, 1950-52; with Gen. Electric Co., 1954—, systems engr., 1958-61, sr. systems engr., 1961-66, engring. unit mgr., 1966-71, GE Drive Systems Dept. engring. subsect. mgr., 1971-78, mgr. metal industry engring., Salem, Va., 1978—; adj. faculty Ga. Inst. Tech., 1953-54, U. Va. Extension, Roanoke, 1955-58. Recipient Gen. Electric Cordiner award, 1963; registered profl. engr., Va. Mem. Va. Soc. Profl. Engrs. (sec.-treas. 1978—), IEEE (sr. mem., region 3 vice chmn. 1980—), Nat. Soc. Profl. Engrs., Assn. Iron and Steel Engrs., Tau Beta Pi, Eta Kappa Nu, Phi Kappa Tau. Club: Briaereans. Patentee in field. Office: 1501 Roanoke Blvd Rm 246 Salem VA 24153

THOMPSON, LAFE ALFRED, textile mill exec.; b. Greeneville, Tenn., July 26, 1938; s. James Hazel and Gladys Mae (Burkhart) T.; student Limestone Coll., 1964-65, U. Tenn., Knoxville, 1958-59, 66-68; m. Sally Lorraine Hunter, Sept. 6, 1963; children—Lafe Hunter, Lee Meredith, Matthew Ryan. Service mgr. Dictaphone corp., Knoxville, Tenn., 1962-65; asst. ops. mgr. Copeland & Co., Knoxville, 1967-68; mgmt. trainee Hartsville (S.C.) Mill., Deering Milliken Co., 1968-71, dept. mgr., 1971-73; supt. mid-fiber Nat. Spinning Co., Washington, N.C., 1973; supt. spun yarn open-end Texfi Corp., Liberty, N.C., 1973-75; mgr. spin plants Aileen, Inc., Abilene, Tex., 1975-76; tech. supt. Walton Mill, Inc., Monroe, Ga., 1976-79, corp. tng. dir., 1979-80; mgr. corp. quality control tng. J.P. Stevens Co., Greenville, S.C., 1980—. Pres., Monroe Elem. PTA, 1979, 80; com. chmn. Cub Scouts, Monroe; PTA rep. to Bd. Edn., 1978-79; chmn. bd. deacons Ray Meml. Ch., Monroe, 1977. Mem. Inst. Textile Tech. Republican. Clubs: Monroe Golf and Country, Kiwanis. Home: 117 Pierce St Monroe GA 30655 Office: JP Stevens & Co Inc PO Box 2267 Greenville SC 29602

THOMPSON, LEE BENNETT, lawyer; b. Miami, Indian Ter., Mar. 2, 1902; s. P.C. and Margerie Constance (Jackson) T.; B.A., U. Okla., 1925, LL.B., 1927; m. Elaine Bizzell, Nov. 27, 1928; children—Lee Bennett, Jr., Ralph Gordon, Carolyn Elaine. Admitted to Okla. bar, 1927, since practiced in Oklahoma City; spl. justice Okla. Supreme Ct., 1967-68; sec., gen. counsel, dir. Mustang Fuel Corp. and other corps. Past sec. Masonic Charity Found. Okla.; chmn. Okla. County chpt. ARC, 2 terms; chmn. resolutions com. Nat. ARC Conv., 1953. Served from capt. to col. AUS, 1940-46; PTO. Decorated Legion of Merit; recipient Distinguished Service citation U. Okla., 1971. Fellow Am. Bar Found., Am. Coll. Trial Lawyers; mem. Oklahoma City C. of C. (past dir.), Oklahoma City Jr. C. of C. (past pres.), U.S. Jr. C. of C. (past dir. and v.p.), Oklahoma City Symphony Orch. (past dir.), Oklahoma City Community Fund (past dir.), Okla. County (past pres.), Am. (ho. of dels.), Okla. (pres. 1972) bar assns., Okla. Bar Found. (trustee 1970—), U. Okla. Alumni Assn. (past mem. exec. com.), U. Okla. Meml. Student Union (pres.), Oklahoma City Zool. Soc. (past dir.), Am. Judicature Soc., Mil. Order World Wars, Mil. Order Carabao, Am. Legion, Beta Theta Pi (past v.p., trustee), Phi Beta Kappa. Democrat. Mem. Christian Ch. (past deacon and elder). Clubs: Masons (33 deg.), Shriners, Jesters, Rotary (past pres.), Seventy Five, Men's Dinner (past mem. exec. com.), Beacon, Oklahoma City Golf and Country. Home: 539 NW 38th St Oklahoma City OK 73118 Office: 2120 First Nat Bldg Oklahoma City OK 73102

THOMPSON, LEROY, JR., army res. officer, radio engr.; b. Tulsa, July 7, 1913; s. LeRoy and Mary (McMurrain) T.; B.S. in Elec. Engring., Ala. Poly Inst., 1936; m. Ola Dell Tedder, Dec. 31, 1941; 1 son, Bartow McMurrain. Commd. 2d lt. U.S. Amy Res., 1935, advanced through grades to col., 1963; signal officer CCC, 1936-40; radio engr. Officer Hdqrs. 4th C A., 1941, signal officer OSS, Burma, 1945, signal officer Hdqrs. OSS, China, 1945, radio engr., tech. liaison officer, Central Intelligence Group, CIA, 1945-50; chief radio br. Hdgrs. FEC, Tokyo, 1950-53, chief radio engring br. Signal C Plant Engring. Agy., 1953-55; radio cons. to asst. dir. def. research and engring. communications, 1960-62; ret., 1973; pvt. research and devel. on communication and related problems, 1963—; owner Thompson Research & Exptl. Devel. Lab. Licensed profl. radio engr., Ga. Mem. IEEE (sr.), Vet. Wireless Operators Assn., Am. Radio Relay League, Nat. Rifle Assn., Mil. Order World Wars, Res. Officers Assn., Am. Motorcycle Assn., Nat. Wildlife Fedn. Baptist. Home: 6450 Overlook Dr Alexandria VA 22312

THOMPSON, LULA BELLE (MRS. GORDON THOMPSON), author, educator; b. Birmingham, Ala., Oct. 19, 1889; d. R. Whitfield and Mary Frances (Wood) Beck; student East Lake Athenaeum Coll.; m. Gordon Thompson, Dec. 31, 1914; 1 son, Robert Gordon. Tchr. pub. schs., Jefferson, Montgomery Counties, Birmingham, 1908-13; free lance writer, 1925—; lectr. Birmingham City Schs., Masonic Home, Montgomery; tchr. writing VA Hosp., Birmingham, 1969—. Mem. staff Internat. Fair, Birmingham, 1970—; mem. speaker's bur. Birmingham Centennial celebration, 1971. Mem. Women in Communications, Nat. League Am. Pen Women (pres. Birmingham br. 1960-62), Berean Club (Woman of Year 1962, 64, plaque award 1973). Baptist (tchr. 1906—). Contbr. numerous articles, stories to various publs. Home: Essex House Apt 408 605 N 21st St Birmingham AL 35203

THOMPSON, MACK AUTREY, former state legislator; b. Paragould, Ark., Dec. 16, 1922; s. J. Ed and Mattie L. (Miller) T.; student Ark. State U., 1945-46; m. Allean Lively, Jan. 13, 1951; children—Mack Edward, Richard Allen. High sch. coach, Oak Grove, Ark., 1946-47; trooper Ark. State Police, Little Rock, 1947-67; maj., 1961-67. Mem. Paragold (Ark.) Pub. Sch. Bd., 1971-74; mem. Ark. Ho. of Reps., 1973-75, 77-79. Served with AUS, World War II. Democrat. Baptist. Mason, Kiwanian. Home: 1025 W Emerson St Paragould AR 72450 Office: 220 W Highland St Paragould AR 72450

THOMPSON, MARGARET INEZ, health club exec.; b. Padadena, Tex., Feb. 1, 1950; d. O. B. and Marie Emily (Cripwell) Lynam; student San Jacinto Jr. Coll., 1979; m. Mike R. Thompson, Oct. 16, 1979; 1 dau. by previous marriage, Jennifer Marie Kitts. Exercise and nutrition physiologist Lockheed Electronic Co., Houston, 1970-76; supr., data analyst Data Transformation Corp., Houston, 1976-79; owner, operator Elegance, Health, Fitness & Beauty Center, Friendswood, Tex., 1979—; cons., tchr. in field. Mem. Internat. Phys. Fitness Assn. Address: PO Box 5866 San Leon TX 77539

THOMPSON, MARGUERITE MYRTLE GRAMLING (MRS. RALPH B. THOMPSON), librarian; b. Orangeburg, S.C., Apr. 23, 1912; d. Thomas Laurie and Rosa Lee (Stroman) Gramling; B.A. in English cum laude, U. S.C., 1932, postgrad., 1937; B.L.S., Emory U., 1943; m. Ralph B. Thompson, Sept. 17, 1949 (dec. Oct. 1960). Tchr. English pub. high schs., S.C., 1932-43; librarian Rockingham (N.C.) High Sch., 1943-45, Randolph County (N.C.) Library, Asheboro, 1945-48, Colleton County (S.C.) Library, Walterboro, 1948-61; dir. Florence (S.C.) County Library, 1961-78. Sec. com. community facilities, services and instns. Florence County Resources Devel. Com., 1964-67; vice chmn. Florence County council on Aging, 1968-70, 78-79, sec., 1976-77, exec. bd., 1968—, treas., 1974-75; mem. Florence County Bicentennial Planning Com., 1975-76; mem. agy. relations and allocations com. United Way, 1979-80. Named Boss of Year Florence County chpt. Nat. Secs. Assn., 1971; named Career Woman of Year, Florence Bus. and Profl. Women's Club, 1974. Mem. ALA (council 1964-72), Southeastern, S.C. (pres. 1960, chmn. assn. handbook revision com. 1967-69, sect. co-chmn. com. standards for S.C. pub. libraries 1966-75, mem. planning com. 1976-78, fed. relations coordinator 1972-73) library assns., Delta Kappa Gamma (state scholarship chmn. 1967-73, internat. scholarship com. 1970-74, dir. SE region 1978-80, coordinator Golden Anniversary Conf. SE region 1979, state 2d v.p. 1971-73, 1st v.p. 1973-75, pres. 1975-77, chmn. state handbook com. 1977—, exec. bd. 1971—), Greater Florence C. of C. (div. vice chmn. 1968; women's div. chmn. 1969-70, dir. 1975-77), Southeastern Regional Conf. Women in Chambers Commerce (dir. 1970-71), Florence Lit. Club (pres. 1970-72, v.p. 1972-74 sec. 1979—). Methodist (chmn. ch. library com. 1965-71, chmn. com. ch. history, 1968-69, sec. adminstrv. bd. 1979-80, chmn. ch. circle 1980—). Home: 1012 Woodstone Dr Florence SC 29501

THOMPSON, MARILYN ANDERSON, med. editor; b. Sacramento, July 27, 1932; d. Andrew Gustave and Cleo Lou (Osoinach) Anderson; A.B. U. Calif., Berkeley, 1953; m. James C. Thompson, Apr. 14, 1967; 1 dau., Laura Victoria Fargas. Tech. writer Hughes Aircraft Corp., 1958-61; editor surgery dept. U. Calif. Med. Sch., Los Angeles, 196 -71; med. editor Office Dean Medicine, U. Tex. Med. Br., 1972-74; manuscript editor Continuing Edn. for Family Physician jour., 1974-77; dir. publs. office continuing med. edn. U. Tex. Med. Br. at Galveston, 1977—. Pres. Venice (Calif.) Democratic Club, 1960. Mem. Am. Med. Writers Assn. (co-founder Los Angeles chpt. 1963, v.p. 1964), Galveston Hist. Found., Galveston County Cultural Arts Council, NOW. Home: 1421 Bayou Shore Dr Galveston TX 77550 Office: Office Dean Medicine Univ Tex Med Branch Galveston TX 77550

THOMPSON, NORMAN RAY, computer analyst; b. Hesperia, Mich., Nov. 11, 1912; s. Harvey Roy and Jessie May (Bunting) T.; B.S., Mich. State Coll., 1940; M.S. (fellow), U. Tenn., 1942; Ph.D., Mich. State U., 1955; m. Irene McCall, Feb. 2, 1943; children—Irene, David Ray, James Roy, Ellenore Ann. Tchr. vocat. agr., Rudyard, Mich., 1946-48; asst. prof. dairy husbandry Va. Poly. Inst., Blacksburg, 1948-53, asso. prof., 1953-70; biostatistician USN, Gt. Lakes, Ill., 1970-72; statistician USCG, Washington, 1974-79; computer analyst Computer Scis.-Technicolor Assos., Greenbelt, Md., 1979—; statis. cons. Served in USN, 1942-45. Mem. Am. Dairy Sci. Assn., Am. Soc. Animal Sci., AAAS, Biometric Soc., Am. Statis. Assn., Am. Genetic Assn., Assn. Computing Machinery, Sigma Xi, Alpha Zeta. Presbyterian. Clubs: Toastmasters; Buick Am. Home: 504 Russell Rd Alexandria VA 22301 Office: 10210 Greenbelt Rd Seabrook MD 20801

THOMPSON, PRESTON GLENN, hosp. exec.; b. Birmingham, Ala., Aug. 25, 1940; s. Robert Gordon and Mattie Sue (Jordan) T.; B.S., U. Ala., Birmingham; m. Judy Ellen Baver, Nov. 25, 1977; children—Preston Scott, Barri Susanne, Bryan Oliver. Asst. to v.p. student affairs U. Ala., Birmingham; dir. recruitment U. Ala. Hosps., asst. mgr. hosps. personnel, dir. recruitment, to 1979; dir. profl. services St. Margaret's Hosp. Montgomery, Ala., 1979—; cons. Am. Hosp. Assn., Ala. Hosp. Assn., Nat. Student Nurses Assn., Inter-Med Communications, Inc., Health Careers Council Ala. Camp dir. Cystic Fibrosis Found.; campaign chmn. United Way; chmn. ARC Blood Drive. Served with USN. Mem. Nat. Assn. Nurse Recruiters (past pres.), Am. Soc. Personnel Adminstrn., Ala. Soc. Hosp. Personnel Adminstrs., Birmingham Council Hosp. Personnel Adminstrs. Republican. Baptist. Home: 1458 Pampas Dr Montgomery AL 36117 Office: PO Drawer 311 Montgomery AL 36101

THOMPSON, RICHARD JOHN, chemist; b. Chapman Ranch, Tex., Aug. 2, 1927; s. Burch and Leone (Brown) T.; B.S. in Chemistry, U. Tex., Austin, 1952, M.A. in Organic Chemistry, 1956, Ph.D. in Inorganic Chemistry, 1959; m. Virginia Lee Malmstrom, June 2, 1952; children—Richard John, Margaret Lee. Asst. prof. chemistry Lamar State U., 1957-58; asst. prof. N. Tex. State U., 1959-62; asso. prof. Tex. Tech. U., 1962-68; chief analytical chemistry br. EPA, Cin., 1968-71, Research Triangle Park, N.C., 1971-79, acting dir. Environ. Monitoring div., 1979—; adj. prof. N.C. State U., 1974. Tex. Eastman fellow, 1958-59; Research Corp. grantee, 1960-68, R.A. Welch Found. grantee, 1961-68; NSF grantee, 1965-68. Mem. Am. Chem. Soc. (chmn. S. Plains sect. 1965, N.C. sect. 1974), Air Pollution Control Assn., Sigma Xi, Phi Lambda Upsilon. Contbr. articles to profl. jours. Home: PO Box 337-C Route 1 Hillsborough NC 27278 Office: Environmental Protection Agency Research MD-78 Triangle Park NC 27711

THOMPSON, RICHARD WAITE, educator; b. N.Y.C., May 7, 1941; s. Maurice Bainton and Mary Frances (Waite) T.; B.A., Rutgers U., 1963; M.A., U. Iowa, 1968, Ph.D. in Hosp. and Health Adminstrn., 1968; m. Amelia Marie Wolf, Dec. 27, 1974; children—Bridget, Timothy, Todd, Kristi, Brandi. Clin. asso. prof. nursing Sch. Nursing, U. Ala. Birmingham, 1975, asso. prof. family practice Sch. Medicine from 1975, prof. dept. health services adminstrn. Sch. Community and Allied Health, 1979—, co-dir. grad. program in health services adminstrn., 1978—. Mem. Am. Coll. Hosp. Adminstrs. Episcopalian. Editorial adv. Contemporary Adminstrator, 1977—. Office: Sch Community and Allied Health U Ala University Sta Birmingham AL 35294

THOMPSON, ROBERT FRANKLIN, otolaryngologist; b. Newnan, Ga., May 6, 1931; s. Joseph Frank and Dora Rebecca (Ingram) T.; B.S., U. Ga., 1952; M.D., Emory U., 1956; m. Debra Leigh Alford, May 21, 1977; children by previous marriage—Pamela Rene and Cynthia Ann (twins), Robert Mills. Intern, Piedmont Hosp., Atlanta, 1956-57, resident in internal medicine, 1957-58; resident in otolaryngology Bowman-Gray Sch. Medicine, Winston-Salem, N.C., 1960-64; practice surgery specializing in otolaryngology, Atlanta, 1964-74, Newnan, 1974—; mem. staffs Crawford W. Long, St. Joseph, Northside, Piedmont hosps., Atlanta, Coweta Gen., Newnan hosps., Newnan, Tanner Meml. Hosp., Carrollton, Ga.; chief ear; nose and throat Piedmont Hosp., 1970-74; asst. clin. prof. Bowman-Gray Sch. Medicine, 1964; asso. prof. Ga. Tech. Inst., 1971-77; founder Cochlear Microphonic Research Lab. Served to capt., flight surgeon SAC, USAF, 1958-60. Diplomate Am. Bd. Otolaryngology. Fellow Southeastern Surg. Congress, Am. Acad. Ophthalmology and Otolaryngology, Floyd McRae Surg. Soc., Ga. Surg. Soc.; mem. AMA, Ga., Coweta County med. socs., Ga. Otolaryngology Soc., Soc. Mil. Otolaryngologists. Baptist. Home: Route 1 Box 323 Emmett Young Rd Grantville GA 30220 Office: PO Box 1155 Newnan GA 30264

THOMPSON, SYBIL COOK, hosp. adminstr.; b. El Dorado, Ark., May 30, 1925; d. Benjamin Alexander and Stella Mae (Dean) Cook; R.N., Warner Brown Sch. Nursing, 1943-46; m. David Allen Thompson, Nov. 26, 1953; 1 son, David Henry. Night supr. Magnolia

City Hosp., 1946-47; office nurse for Joe F. Rushton, physician, Magnolia, Ark., 1947-53; pvt. duty nurse, El Dorado, 1953-54; asst. sch. nurse, Crane, Tex., 1965-67; floor supr. Jennings (La.) Am. Legion Hosp., 1967-69; supr. nursing Allen Parish Hosp., Kinder, La., 1969-72, hosp. adminstr., 1972—. Mem. La. Nurses Assn., Ark. Nurses Assn., Wash. State Nursing Home Adminstrs. Assn. Republican. Methodist. Home: PO Box 81 Kinder LA 70648 Office: Allen Parish Hosp PO Box 370 Kinder LA 70648

THOMPSON, THOMAS GLOVER, JR., social worker; b. St. Jo, Tex., Mar. 23, 1930; s. Thomas Glover and Gladys Maureen (Rone) T.; B.A., Midwestern U., 1962; M.S.W., Our Lady of the Lake, 1968; m. May 25, 1957. Caseworker, Tex. Dept. Pub. Welfare, 1962-66; field cons. various state insts., 1968-69; chief instl. services Tex. Dept. Public Welfare, 1969-77; utilization review officer Tex. Dept. Health, Austin, 1977—. Pres., Midwestern U. Young Dems., 1961-62. Served with USN, 1951-53. Mem. Nat. Assn. Social Workers (chpt. treas. 1973-76), Tex. Public Employees Assn. (chpt. v.p. 1964-65, treas. 1971-72), Tex. Public Health Assn. Democrat. Baptist. Home: 2303 A Mahone St Austin TX 78758 Office: 1100 W 49th St Austin TX 78756

THOMPSON, THOMAS TERRY, physician; b. Elkhorn, W.Va., Feb. 18, 1933; s. Charles Frederic and Rosalee (Mills) T.; B.A., Lenoir Rhyne Coll., Hickory, N.C., 1960; M.D., Med. Coll. Va., Richmond, 1964; m. Nancy Long White, Dec. 31, 1976; children by previous marriage—Mark Christopher, Carol Marie. Intern, DePaul Hosp., Norfolk, Va., 1964-65; resident in radiology Duke U. Med. Center, Durham, N.C., 1967-69; practice medicine specializing in radiology, Durham, 1970—; chief radiology service VA Hosp., Durham, N.C., 1970-75; asso. dean sch. medicine Duke U., 1975—, asso. prof. radiology, 1975—, asso. prof. community health scis., 1975—. Served with USMCR, 1952-55. Diplomate Am. Bd. Radiology. Mem. N.C. Med. Soc., AMA, Radiol. Soc. N.Am., Am. Coll. Radiology. Lutheran. Author: Primer of Clinical Radiology, 1973; A Guide for Automatic Processing and Film Quality Control, 1975; A Practical Approach to Modern X-Ray Equipment, 1978; Cahoon's Formulating X-Ray Techniques, 9th edit., 1979. Home: 3303 Stoneybrook Dr Durham NC 27705 Office: PO Box 3312 Duke U Med Center Durham NC 27710

THOMPSON, VIVIAN OPAL, nurse; b. Lebanon, Va., Nov. 30, 1925; d. Luther Smith and Cora Belle (Baugh) Thompson; R.N., Knoxville (Tenn.) Gen. Hosp., 1947. Supr. obstetrical dept. Knoxville Gen. Hosp., 1947-48; gen. duty nurse Clinch Valley Clinic Hosp., Richlands, Va., 1948-52, supr., 1957-61, 68-78; indsl. nurse, Morocco, Africa, 1952-56; charge nurse Bluefield Sanitarium, W.Va., 1961-65, Rochingham Meml. Hosp., Harrisonburg, Va., 1965-68, Clinch Valley Community Hosp. Mem. Nat. League Nursing. Democrat. Presbyterian. Home: 205 Pennsylvania Ave Richlands VA 24641

THOMPSON, WAYNE DOUGLAS, real estate broker; b. Roanoke, Va., July 8, 1944; s. Curtis and Ellen (Fogle) T.; student public schs., Roanoke; m. Marzetta Hunt, Sept. 23, 1963; 1 son, Wayne Douglas. Police officer, Salem, Va., 1963-64; asst. supt. Walker Machine & Foundry, Roanoke, 1964-68; agt. Perry Realty Co., Roanoke, 1968-70; v.p. Hite-Thompson Realtors, Roanoke, 1970-72; sales mgr., sec., treas. Davis, Cox & Thompson, Vinton, Va., 1972-74; pres., real estate broker W.D. Thompson Realty Co., Inc., Roanoke, 1974—. Mem. Nat., Va. home builders assns., Roanoke Valley Bd. Realtors, Nat., Va. realtors assns. Republican. Morman. Home: 5048 Cherokee Hills Dr Salem VA 24153 Office: 4137 Brandon Ave SW Roanoke VA 24018

THOMPSON, WAYNE WRAY, historian; b. Wichita, Jan. 30, 1945; s. Clarence William and Elaine Maxine (Wray) T.; B.A., Union Coll., Schenectady, 1967; ed. U. St. Andrews, Scotland, 1965-66; Ph.D., U. Calif., San Diego, 1975; m. Lillian Evelyn Hurlburt, June 28, 1969. Historian, USAF, 1975—. Served with AUS, 1971-72. Decorated Army Commendation medal. Mem. Am. Hist. Assn., Orgn. Am. Historians, AF Hist. Found., Am. Mil. Inst., AF Assn., Armed Forces Communications and Electronics Assn., Phi Beta Kappa. Contbr. to Congress Investigates (Arthur M. Schlesinger, Jr., and Roger Bruns, eds.), 1975. Home: 11110 Lone Shadow St San Antonio TX 78233 Office: ATC H History and Research Div Randolph Air Force Base TX 78148

THOMPSON, WILLIAM MITCHELL, JR., banker; b. Bridgeton, N.J., July 21, 1940; s. William Mitchell and Ethel Jean (Smith) T.; B.A., Stetson U., 1963; m. Shirley Jane Pomeroy, Jan. 20, 1968; children—Huntleigh Carol. Mem. personnel staff Boeing Co., Cocoa Beach, Fla., 1966-68, Schlumberger Co., Sarasota, Fla. and Houston, 1968-72; dir. personnel Palmer Bank Corp., Sarasota, 1972-76; regional v.p. personnel Flagship Banks Inc., Tampa, from 1976, now sr. v.p. personnel; instr. U. South Fla., Fla. Bankers Assn., Supervision Acad. Campaign mgr., county commr., 1970; asst. campaign mgr. Pres. Ford, Sarasota County. Served to 1st lt. U.S. Army, 1964-65. Mem. Stetson U. Alumni Assn. (dir. 1976), Sarasota Personnel Assn. (pres.), Am. Soc. Personnel Adminstrn., Fla. Bankers Assn., Delta Sigma Phi. Republican. Presbyterian. Clubs: St. Petersburg Racquet. Commerce Tampa. Author: Supervision, 1977. Home: 3330 Maple St NE St Petersburg FL 33704 Office: Box 3303 Madison and Franklin Sts Tampa FL 33601

THOMPSON, WILLIAM RONALD, educator, cons.; b. Pottsville, Pa., Dec. 10, 1946; s. Ronald William and Mary Barbara (Betz) T.; B.S. in Edn., Millersville State Coll., 1968, M.Ed., 1970; postgrad. W.Va. U., 1972-75, Marshall U., 1972-75; m. Carole Ann Houser, May 26, 1967; 1 dau., Susan. Tchr. indsl. arts Manheim (Pa.) Central Sch. Dist., 1968-71; asso. prof. technology Fairmont State Coll., 1971—, coordinator tech. edn. programs, 1976—; adj. prof. Marshall U., 1976; project dir. Edn. Personnel Devel. Act Insts., 1975-77, cons. inservice workshops, 1972-77; owner TAU Assos., Inc. Mem. Am., W.Va. indsl. arts assns., Am., W.Va. vocat. assns., World Future Soc., Am. Council Indsl. Arts Tchr. Edn. (asso.), Epsilon Pi Tau. Home: 1250 Woodland Crescent Fairmont WV 26554 Office: Div Tech Fairmont State Coll Fairmont WV 26554

THOMPSON, WILLIS HERBERT, JR., petroleum industry exec.; b. Mpls., 1934; B.A. in Geology, U. Minn., 1956, M.S. in Geology, 1959; married. Exploration geologist, geophysicist Standard Oil Co. Tex., 1959-64; former pres., chief exec. officer Signal Oil & Gas Co.; former pres. Burmah Oil & Gas Co., AMINOIL USA Inc.; pres., chief operating officer MAPCO, Inc., Tulsa, 1976-80, pres., chief exec. officer, 1980—, also dir. Served to 1st lt. C.E., U.S. Army. Mem. Am. Assn. Petroleum Geologists, Tex.-Midcontinent Oil and Gas Assn. (dir.), Ind. Petroleum Assn. Am. (dir.), Am. Petroleum Inst. Office: Mapco Inc 1800 S Baltimore Ave Tulsa OK 74119

THONHOFF, ROBERT HENRY, educator; b. Salida, Colo., Dec. 12, 1929; s. Harold and Lula Mae (Graham) T.; B.A., St. Mary's U., 1953; M.A., S.W. Tex. State Tchrs. Coll., 1963; m. Victoria Marie Balser, June 1, 1951; children—Margaret, Robert Henry, Susan. Tchr., coach Jourdanton (Tex.) High Sch., 1953-56; prin., tchr. Fashing (Tex.) Elementary Sch., 1956—; research asso. Tex. Hist. Assn., summer 1965, Inst. Texan Cultures, summer 1967. Community leader, Fashing, 1956—. Served with USAF, 1947-50. Recipient Presidio La Bahia award, 1970. U. Idaho fellow, 1966. Mem. Tex. Folklore Soc., Tex. (Leadership award 1977), W.Tex. hist. assns., Tex. Cath., Karnes County hist. socs., Tex. Old Missions and Forts Restoration Assn. Methodist. Club: Masons. Author: The First Ranch in Texas, 1964; San Antonio's Stage Lines, 1847-1881, 1971; Drama and Conflict: The Texas Saga of 1776, 1976; contbr. to Southwestern Hist. Quar., 1966. Home: Star Route 1 Box 36 Fashing TX 78020 Office: Fashing Elementary Sch Fashing TX 78020

THOR, DANIEL EINAR, immunologist; b. Davenport, Iowa, Sept. 4, 1938; s. Harry Raymond and Florence Elvira (Berglund) T.; student Monmouth Coll., 1956-59; M.D., U. Ill., 1963, Ph.D., 1968; m. Lois Anita Vistain, Jan. 9, 1971; children—Emaly Alida, Carlton George James Vistain. Intern, Presbyn. St. Luke's Hosp., Chgo., 1963-64, resident, 1964-66; instr. surgery, medicine and microbiology U. Ill. Hosps., Chgo., 1966-68; research investigator NIH, Bethesda, Md., 1968-71; asso. prof. microbiology and pathology U. Tex. Health Sci. Center, San Antonio, 1971-76, prof., 1976—, chmn. med. faculty assembly, 1979-80; mem. com. immunodiagnosis Nat. Cancer Inst., NIH, 1973—. Bd. dirs. Cancer Therapy and Research Found. S. Tex., Asthma and Immunology Found., San Antonio. Served to sr. surgeon USPHS, 1968-71. Recipient Landsteiner Centennial award, 1969. Fellow Am. Soc. Exptl. Biology; mem. Am. Assn. Immunologists, Am. Soc. Clin. Oncology, Am. Assn. Cancer Research, AAAS, Reticuloendothelial Soc., AAUP, Gideons Internat. (pres. San Antonio North Camp 1974—), Sigma Xi. Author articles in field. Home: 2743 Whisper Path San Antonio TX 78230 Office: U Tex Health Sci Center 7703 Floyd Curl Dr San Antonio TX 78284

THOR, STEVEN JAY, educator; b. N.Y.C., June 5, 1946; s. Sidney and Helen (Pick) T.; B.A. in Psychology, Syracuse U., 1968; M.A., U. Mo., 1971; postgrad. Fairleigh Dickinson U., 1972-74. Tchr. public relations N.Y.C. Bd. Edn., 1968-76; creative dir. Harold Bader Assos., Miami, Fla., 1976; instr. public relations, journalism Broward Sch. Bd., Dillard High Sch., Ft. Lauderdale, Fla., 1977—. Recipient Newsletter award United Fedn. Tchrs., 1972, 74, Eli Trachtenberg award, 1973; named Outstanding Elem. Sch. Tchr., 1975. Mem. Fla. Scholastic Press Assn., Journalism Edn. Assn., Sigma Delta Chi. Home: 3401 NW 47th Ave Lauderdale Lakes FL 33319 Office: 2501 NW 11th St Fort Lauderdale FL 33311

THORBURN, JAMES ALEXANDER, educator; b. Martins Ferry, Ohio, Aug. 24, 1923; s. Charles David and Mary Edna (Ruble) T.; B.A., Ohio State U., 1949, M.A., 1951; postgrad. U. Mo., 1954-55; Ph.D., La. State U., 1977; m. Lois McElroy, July 3, 1954; children—Alexander Maurice, Melissa Rachel. Head English dept. high sch., Sheridan, Mich., 1951-52; instr. English, U. Mo. at Columbia, 1952-55, Monmouth (Ill.) Coll., 1955-56, U. Tex. at El Paso, 1956-60, U. Mo. at St. Louis, 1960-61, La. State U. at Baton Rouge, 1961-70; asso. prof. Southeastern La. U., Hammond, 1970—. Served with F.A., AUS, 1943-46. Mem. MLA, Linguistic Assn. S.W., Avalon World Arts Acad., Internat. Poetry Soc., Internat. Acad. Poets, Sigma Delta Pi, Phi Kappa Phi. Republican. Presbyterian. Contbg. author: Exercises in English, 1955; also poetry. Book rev. editor Experiment, 1958—; asso. editor Innisfree, 1980—. Home: 721 St Landry St Baton Rouge LA 70806 Office: Southeastern La Univ Dept English Hammond LA 70402

THORLAND, RODNEY HAROLD, JR., educator; b. Lake Mills, Iowa, Feb. 16, 1941; s. Rodney Harold and Geneva Marie (Reines) T., Sr.; B.A., Luther Coll., 1964; M.S., Emory U., 1969, Ph.D., 1971; m. Lynda Taylor, June 16, 1979. Mem. Peace Corps, Nigeria, 1964-67; asst. prof. physics Kennesaw Jr. Coll., Marietta, Ga., 1971-72; NSF traineeship Emory U., Atlanta, 1969-71, research asso., 1972-73; asst. prof. Vol. State Community Coll., Gallatin, Tenn. 1973-76, asso. prof., 1976—; panel mem. rev. cause proposals NSF, 1978. Mem. Am. Phys. Soc., Am. Assn. Physics Tchrs., AAAS, Sigma Xi, Sigma Pi Sigma. Lutheran. Contbr. articles in field to profl. jours. Home: 168 Hickory Heights Hendersonville TN 37075 Office: Nashville Pike Vol State Community Coll Gallatin TN 37066

THORMAN, GARETH LYNN, field engr.; b. Santa Monica, Calif., Jan. 17, 1944; s. Kenneth Russell and Marian Ruth T.; student Auburn U., 1963, Athens Coll., 1965, Brevard Engring. Coll., 1966, U. South Ala., 1970; m. Connie Lee O'Brien, Feb. 17, 1964; 1 dau., Heather Lynn. Draftsman, Chemstrand, Decatur, Ala., 1965; designer Chrysler Space Div., Cape Kennedy, Fla., 1965-67; weight engr. Lockheed Aircraft, Marietta, Ga., 1967-69, Ling-Temco-Vought, Arlington, Tex., 1969-70, Litton Ship Systems, Pascagoula, Miss., 1970-73, Bell Aerospace, New Orleans, 1973-74; field engr. Marion Corp., Theodore, Ala., 1974—. Mem. Soc. Allied Weight Engrs., Soc. Mech. Engrs. Democrat. Methodist. Contbr. studies and reports to profl. publ. Home: 302 Sienna Vista Mobile AL 36607 Office: PO Box 526 Theodore AL 36582

THORN, WILLIAM E(RNEST), coll. pres.; b. McAlester, Okla., Feb. 27, 1923; s. Floyd B. and Irma (Roller) T.; B.A., Hardin-Simmons U., 1948, D.D., 1972; B.D., Southwestern Baptist Theol. Sem., 1954; D.S.T., S.W. Bapt. Coll., 1974; m. Jessie D. Holder, 1947; children—Jenny Lynn, Martha Jane, Rebecca Rae, Karen Irene. Ordained to ministry So. Baptist Ch., 1942; pastor Calvary Bapt. Ch., Lubbock, Tex., 1954-64, Met. Bapt. Ch., Wichita, Kans., 1964-75; pres. Dallas Bapt. Coll., 1975—; mem. fgn. mission bd. So. Bapt. Conv.; pres. Kans. Conv. So. Bapts., 1970; chaplain Lions Internat., 1970; v.p. Bapt. Gen. Conv. Tex., 1971; mem. bd. devel. Hardin-Simmons U., 1956; mem. bd. curators Redford Sch. Theology, S.W. Bapt. Coll., 1974; speaker in field. Served with USN, 1942-45. Recipient Service award Pres. Lions Internat., 1970. Mem. Tex. Bapt. Sch. Adminstrs. Assn. (pres. 1977). Author: A Bit of Honey, 1957; Wake Up, Make Up and Go., 1974; Famous for the Gospel, 1975; Little Foxes that Destroy the Vines, 1980. Home: Route 1 109 Meadowbrook Red Oak TX 75154

THORNBERG, ALAN FRANCIS, dental cons. co. exec.; b. Rochester, N.Y., May 22, 1944; s. Arnold Frederick and Muriel Marie (Stutsman) T.; student public sch.; m. Shar Ron Scott Leach, Sept. 17, 1977; children—Lynn Marie, Jeff Alan. Dist. mgr. Seimens Corp., Islin, N.J., 1970-72; pres. Aftco Enterprises, Summerville, N.J., 1972-75; founder, pres. Aftco Assos., Atlanta, 1975—; lectr. dental schs.; cons. to physicians and dentists establishing a practice. Club: 200. Home: 1505 Northridge Rd Atlanta GA 30338

THORNE, DARLENE CHERYL, pathologist; b. Wilson, N.C., Oct. 27, 1948; d. Leonard Western and Lucille Ferrell (Thorne) T.; B.S., U. N.C., Chapel Hill, 1970, M.D., 1974. Resident in pathology U. N.C., Chapel Hill, 1974-78, fellow in immunohematology, 1978-79; pathologist St. Joseph's Hosp., Savannah, Ga., 1979—. Mem. Am. Soc. Clin. Pathology, Coll. Am. Pathologists, Phi Beta Kappa. Office: 11705 Mercy Blvd St Josephs Hosp Savannah GA 31406

THORNE, H(AROLD) WALTER, engring. psychologist; b. Peekskill, N.Y., July 31, 1916; s. Terry Helmer and Lydia Josephine (Jansson) T.; B.A., U. Tex., El Paso, 1964; M.Ed., Boston U., 1970; Ph.D., Ga. State U., 1979; m. Leba Sue Kellar, Feb. 1, 1974; children—Raymond Walter, Vanessa Joan. Research asso. psychologist George Washington U. Ft. Bliss Field Unit, El Paso, 1958-65; asso. research scientist Am. Insts. Research, Bedford, Mass., 1965-66; sr. human factors engr. Raytheon Service Co., Burlington, Mass., 1967-68; mem. profl. staff TRW Systems, Bedford, 1968-70; dir. edn. YMCA Learning Center, Lowell, Mass., 1971-72; engring. psychologist Dept. of Army, Ft. Benning, Ga., 1972—; cons. Episcopal Diocese of Mass., 1970-71. Certified quality engr., Calif. Mem. Human Factors Soc., Southeastern Psychol. Assn., Am. Def. Preparedness Assn., Assn. U.S. Army. Episcopalian. Author: VD Is for Squares, 1967. Home: 3866 Hawaii Way Columbus GA 31906 Office: Bldg 76 USAIB HF Branch Fort Benning GA 31905

THORNE, JOHN THOMAS, indsl. instrument control system engr. and designer; b. Port Arthur, Tex., Apr. 17, 1926; s. Ernest Eugene and Mary (Wooldridge) T.; student Tex. Coll. Mines, 1944-45, LeTourneau Tech., 1949-50, Lamar Coll., 1952-53, Lee Coll., 1964-65; U. Houston, 1967-68, 78-79; m. Patricia McBride, Feb. 12, 1949; children—John Thomas, Ernest E., Alida Diane, Jerry Allen. Instrument technician Texas City Refining Inc. (Tex.), 1953-63; instrument and electronics instr. Lee Coll., 1963-66; instrument supr. Tech. Maintenance, Inc., Pasadena, Tex., 1963-67; ind. cons., Houston area, 1967-68; ind. cons. Diamond-Shamrock, Tenneco, U.S. Indsl. Chems., Olin Corp., 1967-68; instrument tech. dept. head San Jacinto Coll., 1966-68; regional systems mgr. Robertshaw Controls Co., Houston and Anaheim, Calif., 1968-70; ind. cons. Olin Corp., Pasadena Ind. Sch. Dist., 1970-72; mgr. tng. sales Tex-A-Mation Engring., La Porte, Tex., 1971-72; ind. cons. Forney Engring., Dallas also J.E. Sirrine Co., Houston, 1972; instrument designer Stubbs, Overbeck & Assos., Houston, assigned to Celanese Chm. Co., Bishop, Tex., 1972; instrument design supr. S.I.P., Inc., Houston, assigned to Shell Chem. Co., Houston, 1972-74; sr. instrument engr., design supr. Tellepsen Petro-Chem. Constrn. Co., Houston, 1974-79; prin. Thorne Cons. Service, Houston, 1979—. Mem. Tex. Senate Com. for Tech. and Vocational Edn., 1971-75; Tex. rep. for instrumentation HEW Conf., Los Alamos, 1967. Served with AUS, 1946, 50-53; with USAAF, 1946-49. Registered profl. engr. Mem. Instrument Soc. Am. (edn. dir. Houston sect. 1972-74), Am. Soc. Engring. Technicians, Internat. Platform Assn. Mason. Home: 16922 Blackhawk Friendswood TX 77546 Office: PO Box 37 Friendswood TX 77546

THORNE, MELVIN QUENTIN, JR., mental health center dir.; b. Houston, Feb. 23, 1939; s. Melvin Quentin and Ruby Marie (Bauerkemper) T.; B.A., Sam Houston State U., 1961; M.S.W., U. Tex., 1964; m. Denise Dale Brockman, Dec. 2, 1961; children—Dana Marie, Lorrie Denise. Asst. prof. U. Houston, 1970-74; cons. Trims, Houston, 1974-75; dir. mental health services Mental Health-Mental Retardation Center for Greater West Tex., San Angelo, 1975-76; exec. dir. Multi-County Community Mental Health Center, Tullahoma, Tenn., 1976—. Mem. Nat. Registry Health Care Providers in Clin. Social Work (dir. 1975—), Nat. Assn. Mental Health Adminstrs., Nat. Assn. Hosp. Social Work Dirs. Lutheran. Home: 501 Hohldale Houston TX 76901

THORNHILL, BONNIE ELIZABETH BREWER THOMAS, nurse, educator; b. Milw., Nov. 29, 1941; d. Benjamin J. and Hazel Pearl (Denman) Brewer; B.S. in Nursing (NDEA scholar), U. Ala., 1964; M.S. in Nursing (fellow), Med. Coll. Ga., 1977; m. Cebourn Edgar Thornhill, Dec. 11, 1976; children by previous marriage—Tanya Cherie Thomas, Melissa Eve Thomas. Asst. head nurse Sacred Heart Hosp., Pensacola, Fla., 1967-68; instr. Sch. Nursing, Anniston (Ala.) Meml. Hosp., 1968-70; instr. Gadsden (Ala.) State Jr. Coll., 1970-76; asst. prof. maternal-child health nursing Lurleen B. Wallace Sch. Nursing Jacksonville (Ala.) State U., 1976—. Mem. Am., Ala. (dir. 1976) nurses assns., Nat. League for Nursing, Am. Edn. Assn. Lutheran. Home: Route 1 Box 397 Anniston AL 36201 Office: Jacksonville State U Jacksonville AL 36201

THORNHILL, PAUL BERYL, indsl. engr.; b. Ellwood City, Pa., June 23, 1925; s. Paul Gordon and Mildred Marie (Bishop) T.; B.S., Westminster Coll., New Wilmington, Pa., 1949; postgrad. U. Youngstown, 1950-53, U. Louisville, 1953-54; m. Elizabeth Albin Pierce, Aug. 2, 1946; children—Laurell Sue, Wayne Paul. Plant engr. Am. Cyanamid, New Castle, Pa., 1946-52; sales engr. Logan Co., Louisville, 1952-61; sales engr., production mgr. Rexnord, Inc., Ellwood City, Pa., 1961—, mgr. field services, Danville, Ky. and Chico, Calif. Leader, Boy Scouts Am., 1949-74; mem. Boyle County Juvenile Disposition Panel, Danville, Ky., 1978-80. Served with USMC, 1943-46. Mem. Am. Meterial Handling Soc., Am. Inst. Indsl. Engrs., Am. Legion. Republican. Presbyterian. Clubs: Wilderness Shrine, Masons, Shriners. Home: 412 Meadowbrook Dr Danville KY 40422 Office: Rexnord Inc Danville KY 40422

THORNSBERRY, WILLIS LEE, JR., chemist; b. Sturgis, Ky., Aug. 10, 1940; s. Willis Lee and Jane (Hall) T.; B.S., Murray State U., 1963; M.S., U. Ark., 1967; Ph.D., Tulane U., 1974; m. Mary Elizabeth Gaswint, June 19, 1965; children—Brian, Michele. Chemist, Freeport Minerals Co., Belle Chasse, La., 1967-78; sr. research chemist 1978—. Webelos den leader, asst. scoutmaster Boy Scouts Am., 1973—; coach, bd. dirs. Oakdale Athletic Dist. Served with AUS, 1963-65. Mem. Am. Chem. Soc. (treas. La. sect. 1977—, Congressional sci. counselor 1979—), Sigma Xi, Alpha Tau Omega. Democrat. Patentee chem. process devel. Contbr. articles to sci. jours. Home: 549 Lynnmeade Rd Gretna LA 70053 Office: PO Box 26 Belle Chasse LA 70037

THORNTON, DANNETTA KENNON, linguist, educator; b. Birmingham, Ala., Dec. 15, 1938; d. Daniel and Verna Ynez (Herron) Kennon; B.A., Fisk U., 1959; M.A., Ind. U., 1960; postgrad. Carleton U., Ottawa, Can., 1967; A.A. certificate U. Ala., Birmingham, 1972, Ph.D., 1977; m. William Cullen Thornton, Feb. 11, 1961; children—Verna Alberta, William Kennon. Chmn. fgn. langs. dept. Ullman High Sch., Birmingham, 1962-66; chmn. fgn. langs. dept. Lawson State Community Coll., Birmingham, 1966—; cons. Spl. Tutorial Services, Miles Coll., Birmingham, 1977-79, Birmingham Ednl. Film Festival, 1973-74. Bd. dirs. Jefferson County Child Devel. Council; bd. mem. Bradford's Indsl. Ins. Co. and Bradford's Funeral System, Planned Parenthood, Birmingham Area, Campfire West; den leader Cub Scout Troop; bd. deaconess Sixth Ave. Bapt. Ch. Recipient Excellence in Teaching award Lawson State Community Coll., 1968, Citizen's award of merit Beta Psi, 1972, Educator of Year award Omega Psi Phi, 1979; NDEA scholarship grantee, 1963. Mem. Am. Assn. Tchrs. French, NEA, Nat. Assn. Black Women Academicians, Ala. Edn. Assn., Ala. Assn. Women's Clubs, Inc., Kappa Delta Pi, Phi Delta Kappa, Alpha Kappa Alpha. Clubs: Jack and Jill of America, Inc. (v.p. 1979-80), Semper Fidelis (pres. 1978-79), Club Entre Nous (sec. 1975-77), Links, Inc. (reporter 1978-79). Home: 420 W 10th Ct Birmingham AL 35204 Office: Lawson State Community Coll 3060 Wilson Rd Birmingham AL 35221

THORNTON, HOWARD LEE, profl. recruiting co. exec.; b. Springfield, Mo., July 14, 1934; s. Homer O. and Edith Christine (Pierce) T.; student public schs., Hartville, Mo.; m. Sandra L. Kluball, Mar. 2, 1962; children—Tali Jay, Danielle Lee. Served as 1st sgt. U.S. Army, 1954-74; assignments in Korea, Vietnam, Okinawa, Germany; ret., 1974; mgr. Western Man Temporary Service, Columbus, Ga., 1973-74; mgr., tech. recruiter Dunhill of Columbus, Inc., 1974-76; pres. Plas-Tech Personnel, Inc., Columbus, 1976—. Decorated Meritorious Service medal, Bronze Star, Army Commendation medal; recipient numerous certs. of appreciation. Mem. Nat. Employment

Network, Nat. Assn. Personnel Consultants, Nat. Fedn. Ind. Businesses, Better Bus. Bur., Columbus C. of C. Office: 3228 Cody Rd Suite 107 Columbus GA 31907

THORNTON, PETER BENEDICT, educator; b. New Orleans, May 31, 1919; s. Peter and Katie (Johnson) T.; A.B. (Seymour Straight award 1941), Dillard U., New Orleans, 1941; M.A., Northwestern U., 1949; Ed.D. (Danforth fellow), U. No. Colo., Greeley, 1963; m. Evelyn Louise Burroughs, Jan. 11, 1945; 1 son, Peter Byron. Asst. prin., coach, tchr. Vernon (La.) High Sch., 1941-43; phys. dir. New Orleans YWCA, 1943; asst. instr., mgr. coop. Dillard U., 1946-48; instr. Texas Coll., Tyler, 1949-50; prof. guidance and counseling Tex. So. U., Houston, 1950—; vocat. cons. HEW; bd. dirs. Harris County Mental Health Assn. Bd. dirs. Julia C. Hester House, Houston, 1958, asst. sec., 1958; asst. sec. Harris County Grand Jury, 1967, 70; mem. bd. Episcopal Pastoral Center, Houston, 1963. Served with AUS, 1943-46. Mem. Nat. Vocat. Guidance Assn., Am. Personnel and Guidance Assn., Southwestern Psychol. Assn., Tex. Assn. Coll. Tchrs., Tex. Personnel and Guidance Assn., Tex. Assn. Counselor Educators and Suprs., Dillard U. Alumni Assn. (pres. Houston chpt. 1957-58), Kappa Alpha Psi, Phi Delta Kappa. Democrat. Episcopalian. Contbr. articles profl. jours. Home: 4406 Fernwood St Houston TX 77021 Office: Tex So Univ Houston TX 77004

THORNTON, RAY, ednl. adminstr.; b. July 16, 1928; B.A., Yale, 1950; J.D., U. Ark., 1956; m. Betty Jo Mann, Jan. 27, 1956; children—Nancy, Mary, Stephenie. Admitted to Ark. bar; dep. pros. atty. 6th Jud. Circuit, 1956-57; atty. gen. State of Ark., 1970-73; mem. 93d-95th congresses from 4th dist. Ark.; exec. dir. Joint Ednl. Consortium, Henderson State U. and Ouachita Bapt. U., Arkadelphia, Ark.; adv. bd. N.Y. U. Center Sci. and Tech. Policy; chmn. risk assessment subcom. adv. com. recombinant DNA research NIH. Past chmn. Ark. Bd. Law Examiners; del. to 7th Constl. Conv. Ark., 1969-70. Served with USNR, Korean War. Democrat. Home: 301 N Rose St Sheridan AR 72150 Office: PO Box 499 Arkadelphia AR

THORNTON, ROBERT STRONG, otorhinolaryngologist; b. Camden, Ark., May 10, 1945; s. Robert Bleakly and Christine (Jackson) T.; B.A., U. Ark., 1968, M.D., 1970; m. ChloeAnn Tierney, May 5, 1973; children—Robert Henry, Kimberly Christine. Intern, Tulane U., 1970-71, resident in otolaryngology, 1974-77; resident in surgery Emory U. Med. Sch., Atlanta, 1973-74; practice medicine specializing in otorhinolaryngology, Drs. Pou, Quinn, Watkins & Thornton, P.C., Shreveport, La., 1977—; mem. staff Shumpert Med. Center, Physicians and Surgeons Hosp.; clin. asst. prof. La. State U., Med. Sch., Shreveport, 1977—; clin. instr. surgery Tulane U. Med. Sch., New Orleans, 1977—. Served to lt. USN, 1971-73. Diplomate Am. Bd. Otolaryngology. Mem. Am. Acad. Otolaryngology, F.A.C.S., Am. Acad. Facial Plastic and Reconstructive Surgery, AMA, Shreveport Med. Soc., U.S. Power Squadron, U. Ark. Alumni Assn. Office: 2121 Line Ave Shreveport LA 71104

THORNTON, SUE BONNER, librarian; b. nr. Fairfield, Tex.; d. John Carder and Mary (Bonner) Thornton; A.B., U. Okla., 1920. A.B. in L.S., 1938, Mus.B. in Piano, 1921; M.A., Columbia, 1932; postgrad. U. Hawaii, summer 1936. Music supr. Okla. pub. schs., 1921-25; head music dept. Northeastern State Coll., Tahlequah, Okla., 1925-32, librarian, 1932—. Freestone county chmn. hist. markers and landmarks Tex. Hist. Survey Com.; chmn. bd. trustees Freestone County (Tex.) Mus. Mem. N.E.A., A.L.A., Daus. Am. Colonists, Colonial Dames 17th Century (rec. sec. Okla. state chpt.), Nat. Soc. Magna Charta Dames, Tahlequah C. of C., United Ch. Women Tahlequah (chmn. 1960), D.A.R. (chmn. good citizens com. for state 1958-60), Huguenots of S.C., U.S. Daus. War 1812, Daus. Colonial Wars, Ams. Royal Descent, Colonial Order of Crown, Platagenet Soc., Tex. Federated Women's Clubs (chmn. edn. dept.) Order of Washington, Soc. Descs. Order of Garter, P.E.O., Okla., Tex. geneal. socs., Tex. Hist. Found., Tex., Southwestern Cattle raisers assns., Alpha Gamma Delta. Democrat. Presbyn. (pres. local women's dept. 1965—). Clubs: Dallas Garden, History (Fairfield), Pan American Round Table, Freestone County Country; Harvey Woman's (Palestine, Tex.). Author: The Bonner Family History. Home: Fairfield TX 75840

THORNTON, WILLIAM BASS, utility exec.; b. Huckaboy, Tex., Jan. 2, 1910; s. Daniel and Marguerite Virginia (Bass) T.; student U. Tulsa, 1928-30, U. So. Calif., 1931, S. Tex. Law Sch., Houston, 1940-41; m. Josephine Luther, Mar. 16, 1952; children—Nancy Thornton Schumacher, Mary Virginia. Constrn. supt. Brown & Root, Inc., Houston, 1932-38; mgr. land and right of way dept. Houston Lighting & Power Co., 1938-75, cons. on lands, right of way, land mgmt. and land acquisition, 1975—; pres. INT Enterprises Inc.; v.p. Ametco. Chmn. Harris County ARC, 1943; pres. Bd. Equalization Sugarland and Ft. Bend Ind. Sch. Dists., 1955-66. Mem. Am. Right of Way Assn. (sr. mem.; pres. 1968, nat. dir. 1969-70, Man of Year award 1969), Am. Soc. Appraisers (sr.), Houston C. of C. Democrat. Roman Catholic. Clubs: Masons, K.C., Plaza (Houston), Sugar Creek Country. Contbr. articles to mags. Home: 839 Chevy Chase Dr Sugarland TX 77478 Office: 15119 Memorial Dr Houston TX 77024

THORNTON, WILLIAM LEWIS, surgeon; b. San Antonio, Oct. 21, 1923; s. Daniel Raymond and Rhoda (Lewis) T.; B.S., U. Miss., 1945; M.D., U. Pa., 1947; m. Mae Carroll Harrison, June 14, 1945; children—Carroll Hodges, Rhoda Gayle, William Lewis, Lee Kinsey. Intern, Parkland Hosp., Dallas, 1947-48, surg. resident, 1948-52; pvt. practice medicine, specializing in gen. surgery, Meridian, Miss., 1952—; pres. Med. Arts Surg. Group, Meridian, 1972—; chief of staff Anderson Hosp., Meridian, 1976-77. Pres., Lauderdale County Cancer Soc., 1954—; pres. Meridian Mus. Art, 1975—; steward Central United Methodist Ch., Meridian, 1956—; 1st v.p. Meridian C. of C. Jr. Aux. Mardi Gras, 1972. Served with U.S. Army, 1943-46. Diplomate Am. Bd. Surgery. Mem. A.C.S. (pres. Miss. chpt. 1960), Meridian C. of C. (dir. 1970-73), Southeastern Surg. Soc., Am., So., Miss. med. assns., E. Miss. Med. Soc., Meridian C. of C. (pres. 1980). Methodist. Clubs: Exchange (pres. Meridian 1960), Northwood Country (pres. 1971-72). Home: 4000 Country Club Dr Meridian MS 39301 Office: 2111 14th St Meridian MS 39301

THORPE, LARRY WAYNE, immunologist, exptl. pathologist; b. Portland, Oreg., Apr. 29, 1947; s. Robert Eugene and Lillian (Anderson) T.; B.S., U. Oreg., 1970; postgrad. Med. Center, U. Ill., 1970-73; Ph.D., Med. Br., U. Tex., 1978. Research asso. Med. Br., U. Tex., Galveston, 1974-76, transplantation immunologist, 1976-78, McLaughlin fellow, 1978-80, research fellow in pathology, 1978-80, adj. instr. Sch. Allied Health, 1979, research scientist dept. medicine, 1980—; lectr. pathology, immunology. NSF fellow, summer 1968. Mem. Electron Microscopy Soc. Am., Internat. Acad. Pathology, N.Y. Acad. Scis., Sigma Xi. Author book in field. Home: 1324 Postoffice St Galveston TX 77550 Office: 202 Keiller Bldg Med Br U Tex Galveston TX 77550

THORPE, MARION DENNIS, univ. chancellor; b. Durham County, N.C., Sept. 25, 1932; s. Ulysses and Minne Thorpe; B.A., M.A., N.C. Coll.; Ph.D., Mich. State U., 1961; m. Lula Glenn; children—Pamela Monique, Marion Dennis. Asst. instr. ednl. psychology Mich. State U., East Lansing, 1959-61; from asst. prof. to asso. psychology N.C. Coll., 1961-65; nat. leader Job Devel. Task Force, U.S. Dept. Labor, 1966; asst. dir. N.C. Bd. Higher Edn., 1966-67; v.p. Central State U., Wilberforce, Ohio, 1967-68; prof. psychology and edn. Elizabeth City (N.C.) State U., 1968—, pres., 1968-72, chancellor, 1972—; mem. intern program So. Regional Edn. Bd.; dir. Wachovia Bank; pres. Herrington Village Apts., Inc.; cons. U.S. Office Edn. Mem. exec. bd. Tidewater council Boy Scouts Am.; mem. President Nixon's N.C. Com. on Public Edn.; mem. Durham Com. on Negro Affairs, Martin Luther King Scholarship com. Woodrow Wilson Found.; mem. Human Relations Council, Elizabeth City, Mayor's Com. Jobs for Vets, Elizabeth City, 1971; bd. dirs. Elizabeth City Boys Club, Manpower Devel. and Tng. Project, Wilberforce, Ohio, Operation Breakthrough, Mus. of the Albemarle, The Daily Advance publ., Elizabeth City State U. Found., United Negro Coll. Fund; trustee White Rock Bapt. Ch., Durham, N.C., N.C. Symphony Soc. Served with USAF, 1952-56. Named Hon. Citizen, Hazard, Ky., 1966. Mem. Am. Assn. for Higher Edn., Am. Acad. Polit. Sci., Am. Personnel and Guidance Assn., N.C. Psychol. Assn., Am. Psychol. Assn., N.C. Assn. Colls. and Univs. (exec. com.), Assn. Eastern N.C. Colls. (exec. com.), Eastern N.C. Psychol. Assn., Internat. Platform Assn., So. Assn. Colls. and Schs. (commr.), Am. Assn. Sch. Adminstrs., Omega Psi Phi, Alpha Phi Omega, Sigma Pi Phi, Psi Chi, Alpha Kappa Mu, Phi Delta Kappa. Democrat. Baptist. Contbr. articles to profl. publs. Home: 1304 Parkview Dr Elizabeth City NC 27909 Office: PO Box 10 Parkview Dr Elizabeth City State Univ Elizabeth City NC 27909

THOTA, VYKUNTAPATHI, educator; b. Purushothamapatnam, Andhra State, India, Nov. 3, 1940; came to U.S., 1961; s. Seshadri and Lakshmamma (Byra) T.; B.Sc., Osmania U., 1961; M.S., Kans. State U., 1962; Ph.D., Mich. State U., 1966; m. Kunapareddy Ratnagirijakumari, Dec. 20, 1968; 1 dau., Sri Lakshmi. Grad. asst. Audiovisual Center, Mich. State U., 1963-64, research asso. Instructional Media Center, 1966-67; asst. prof. dept. instructional tech. So. Ill. U., Edwardsville, 1967-72; asst. prof. dept. library sci. and ednl. media Va. State U., Petersburg, 1972-76, asso. prof., 1976-79, prof. ednl. tech., 1979—; continuing edn. prof. U. Va.; cons. Mem. Assn. for Ednl. Communications and Tech., Assn. for Supervision and Curriculum Devel., Va. Ednl. Media Assn., Jack and Jill of Am., Kappa Delta Pi, Phi Delta Kappa, Beta Kappa Chi. Named gold medalist, prof. of yr. Contbr. articles to profl. publs. Office: Va State U Box 5002-N Petersburg VA 23803

THRALL, ROBERT MCDOWELL, educator; b. Toledo, Ill., Sept. 23, 1914; s. Charles Haven and Gertrude (Gerking) T.; B.A., Ill. Coll., 1935, Sc.D., 1966; Ph.D., U. Ill., 1937; m. Natalie Hunter, Sept. 3, 1936; children—Charles Alexander, James Hunter, Mary Emily. Teaching fellow U. Ill., 1935-37; instr. math. U. Mich., 1937-42, asst. prof., 1942-48, asso. prof., 1948-55, prof., 1955-69, prof. ops. analysis Research Inst., 1956-69, head ops. research dept., 1957-60; prof., chmn. dept. math. scis. Rice U., Houston, 1969-78, Noah Harding prof. math. scis., 1978—; pres. Robert M. Thrall and Assos., Inc., Houston, 1971—. Recipient Henry Russell award, U. Mich., 1947, Disting. Faculty award, 1965. Mem. AAAS, AAUP, Am. Statis. Assn., Assn. Computing Machinery, Econometric Soc., Inst. Math. Statistics, Math. Assn. Am., Inst. Mgmt. Sci., Ops. Research Soc. Am., Psychometric Soc., Gen. Systems Research, Soc. Indsl. and Applied Math., Phi Beta Kappa, Sigma Xi, Phi Kappa Phi. Author: (with E.B. Miller) College Algebra, 1960; (with L. Tornheim) Vector Spaces and Matrices, 1957; (with A. Spivey) Linear Optimization, 1970. Mem. editorial bd. Operational Research Quar., 1960-69, Behavioral Science, 1964—. Home: 12003 Pebble Hill Houston TX 77024 Office: Department of Math Sciences Rice University Houston TX 77001

THRASH, ARTHUR FRANKLIN, lab supr.; b. Myrtlewood, Ala., Jan. 9, 1944; s. Olin Leslie and Mary Elizabeth (Barlow) T.; student Internat. Corr. Sch., 1969-70; B.S. in Tech. Mgmt., Athens State Coll., 1980; m. Mae Boozer, Dec. 23, 1962; children—Kenneth Steven, Mona Lisa, Traci Marie. Quality control staff Gulf State Paper Corp., Demopolis, Ala., 1966-68; head paper tester MacMillian & Bloedel, Pine Hill, Ala., 1968-70; evniron. specialist Water and Waste Treatment, Champion Papers, Courtland, Ala., 1970-78, pres. supervisory commn. employees' credit union, 1976-78; chemist Champion Paper Co., Courtland, Ala., 1978-80, dir. credit union, 1979-80. Mem. Water Pollution Control Fedn., Ala. Water and Pollution Control Assn., Ala. Wildlife Fedn. Club: Bowhunters of Ala. Home: 2409 Murphree Rd SE Decatur AL 35601 Office: Box 189 Courtland AL 35618

THRASH, SARA ARLINE, educator; b. Jefferson City, Tenn., Mar. 14, 1928; d. Arlie Eugene and Leola (McDonald) Cate; B.A., Carson Newman Coll., 1949; M.A., U. South Fla., 1969, Ed.S., 1974; Ph.D., Brunnel U. (Eng.), 1977; m. Willard D. Thrash, Jan. 1, 1952; children—Douglas, Diane, Mark, David. Tchr. pub. schs. Tenn., Miss., 1949-52; tchr. gifted children Mid City Sch., New Orleans, 1961-63; tchr. Fla. pub. schs., 1966-71; tchr. spl. edn., ednl. dir. Escambia Assn. Retarded Children, Pensacola, Fla., 1971-73; adj. tchr. U. West Fla., Pensacola, 1971-73; coordinator learning disabilities Western Carolina U., Cullowhee, N.C., 1975-78; cons. Polk County Child Devel. Center U. N.C., Ashville, 1975-78, Cherokee Reservation, 1975-78; organizer parent therapy groups in learning disabilities, 1975—; staff writer Bapt. Sunday Sch. Bd., 1973-78; vis. prof. spl. edn. St. Leo's (Fla.) Coll., 1979; ednl. coordinator Eckerd Wilderness Therapeutic Camping Program, 1980—; condr. workshop First World Congress on Future Spl. Edn., 1978. Steering com. Jackson County Family Life, 1977-78; tchr. couples class St. Petersburg (Fla.) First Bapt. Ch., 1973-75, Cullowhee First Bapt. Ch., 1977-78; guest lectr. in chs. Recipient Presdl. Citation Award, Carson Newman Coll., 1977; First Bapt. Ch. Family Life recognition, 1977; U.S. Fla. fellow, 1968-69, 73. Mem. AAUW, Council of Exceptional Children, Assn. Children with Learning Disabilities, Assn. Retarded Children, Fla. Writers Guild, Assn. Gifted and Talented Appalachian Writers, Phi Kappa Phi. Baptist. Clubs: Spl. Olympics Booster, Appalachian Writers, Swim, Jogging, Parents are People. Author: Little Things that Keep Families Together, 1976; contbr. articles in field to profl. jours. Home: 4200 14th Way NE Saint Petersburg FL 33703

THRASHER, EMMA REID (MRS. HAROLD MORGAN THRASHER), city extension agt.; b. East Orange, N.J., Nov. 8, 1921; d. William Albert and Hope (Forman) Reid; B.S. in Child Devel. and Home Econs., Pa. State U., 1940-44; student Coll. William and Mary, 1955, 58, U. Va., 1957; M.S., Va. Poly. Inst., 1979; m. Harold Morgan Thrasher, June 22, 1944; children—Henry Taylor, William Seay, Lee-Hope. Tchr., Friend's Community Sch., West Chester, Pa., 1944-45, Chesapeake (Va.) Pub. Sch., 1951-53, 55-61; extension agt. Extension div. Va. Poly. Inst. and State U. Coop. Extension Service, 1961—, supr. 4-H youth program, 1970—; saleswoman, unit mgr. Tupperware Home Parties, Inc., 1953-56; treas. Seay Hope Taylor Corp., Chesapeake, Va., 1970—; adv. bd. J.C. Penney, Inc. Pres. Gt. Bridge Band Parents Assn., 1968; patron Norfolk Civic Ballet, 1968-75; mem. Chrysler Museum, Norfolk, Va. Museum, Richmond, Smithsonian Instn.; mem. Chesapeake Human Services Com.; bd. dirs. S.E. dist. 4-H Edn. Center, Chesapeake, 1974—; mem. area com. Ret. Sr. Vol. Program (RSVP); bd. dirs. Chesapeake Meals on Wheels. Mem. Nat. (Disting. Service award 1973), Va. (policy com. 1971, 4-H com. 1971) assns. extension home economists, Am., Va. (dir. 1964-69, dist. chmn. 1962-65) home econs. assns., Nat. (Distinguished Service award 1976; long range com. 1976-79, nominating com. 1977), Va. (v.p. 1973, pres. 1975) assns. extension 4-H agts., Va. Extension Service Assn., Pa. State U. Alumni Assn. (life mem., area chmn. 1969-70), Am. Bible Soc., Nat. Hist. Soc., Chesapeake C. of C. (dir. women's div. 1977-79), Epsilon Sigma Phi (unit citation 1979). Home: 710 Sign Pine Rd Chesapeake VA 23322 Office: Agr Dept 300 Cedar Rd Chesapeake VA 23320

THREET, STEPHEN WAYNE, ednl. adminstr.; b. Crossville, Tenn., Dec. 5, 1951; s. Denton Mitchel and Goldie Irene (Farley) T.; B.S., Tenn. Tech. U., 1973, M.A., 1975; postgrad., George Peabody Coll., 1976—; m. Lorraine Gayle Walker, Dec. 21, 1974; 1 son, Jack Denton. Prevocat. instr. for mentally retarded blind persons project Orange Grove Center, Chattanooga, 1973-74; bus driver, instr. Pacesetter Inc., adult activity center for mentally retarded, Cookeville, Tenn., 1974-75, program coordinator Pacesetters Inc. and 2 satellite centers, 1975-77; exec. dir. King's Daus. Sch., pvt. sch. for mentally retarded, Columbia, Tenn., 1977—; adj. faculty spl. edn. Tenn. Tech. U. Active United Giver Fund. Mem. Council Exceptional Children, Am. Assn. Mental Deficiency, Nat. Assn. Retarded Citizens, Nat. Rehab. Assn. Tenn. Dirs. Assn. Baptist. Club: Rotary. Home: 1502 Jewell Dr Columbia TN 38401 Office: King's Daus Sch 412 W 9th St Columbia TN 38401

THURER, RICHARD JEROME, thoracic and cardiovascular surgeon; b. Amityville, N.Y., June 1, 1936; s. Carl and Rose (Friedman) T.; A.B., Princeton U., 1957; M.D., Columbia U., 1961; m. Priscilla Sue Arlen, Apr. 17, 1966; children—Margaret Anne, Katherine Arlen. Intern, Columbia Presbyn. Med. Center, N.Y.C., 1961-62, resident, 1964-70; instr. surgery Columbia U., N.Y.C., 1970; asso. in surgery U. Pa. Sch. Medicine, Phila., 1970-71; asst. prof. surgery U. Miami (Fla.), 1972-77, asso. prof., 1977—; chief thoracic and cardiovascular surgery VA Hosp., Miami, 1972. Served as lt. USNR, 1962-64. Mem A.C.S., Am. Coll. Cardiology, Am. Coll. Chest Physicians, Am. Assn. Thoracic Surgery, Soc. Thoracic Surgeons, Internat. Cardiovascular Soc., Am. Thoracic Soc., So. Thoracic Surg. Assn., AMA. Club: Princeton of S. Fla. Contbr. article in field to profl. jour. Home: 7400 SW 133 St Miami FL 33156 Office: PO Box 016960 Miami FL 33101

THURMAN, CLARENCE, psychologist; b. Louisville, Dec. 20, 1922; s. Clarence Younger and Jessie America (O'Brien) T.; B.B.A., Baylor U., 1952, Ph.D. 1973; B.D., So. Bapt. Theol. Sem., 1959; M.A., U. Louisville, 1965; postdoctoral resident in clin. psychology U. Miss. Med. Center, 1978-79; m. Eddie Lee Tilden, July 29, 1947; children—Cheryl Lynn, Charles Douglas, Marsha Lee. Sales mgr. Froelich Co., Louisville, 1946-49, 56-59; ordained to ministry Bapt. Ch., 1954; minister Victory Bapt. Ch., Tex., 1954-56; minister of edn. Hazelwood Bapt. Ch., Louisville, 1956-59; So. Bapt. fgn. missionary to Malaysia, 1959-71; instr. Hill Jr. Coll., Hillsboro, Tex., 1970-73; asso. prof. psychology William Carey Coll., Hattiesburg, Miss., 1973-74, prof., 1974—, chmn. dept. edn. and psychology, 1974-78, chmn. psychology dept., 1978—, asst. dean grad. studies, 1974—; dir. Bapt. Bldg. Loan Fund Malaysia, Ltd.; mgr. Golden Sands Bapt. Assembly (Port Dickson, Malaysia). Served with USAAF, 1943-45; ETO. Decorated Air Medal. Mem. Am., Southeastern, Miss. psychol. assns., Assn. Heads of Depts. of Psychology, Miss. Assn. Higher Edn., Miss. Acad. Scis., Assn. Christian Counselors and Psychotherapists, Phi Delta Kappa, Phi Kappa Phi, Kappa Delta Pi, Delta Sigma Pi, Alpha Chi. Clubs: Hattiesburg Rotary, Psychology, Masons, DeMolay. Author: The Effect of Hypnosis on Learning Meaningful Material, 1973; A Historical Study of Educational Developments in Malaysia, 1950-64, 65; Self-Scoring Multiple Choice Test with Immediate Knowledge of Results, 1975; Zip Code Quick Quiz Cards, 1973; also articles. Home: 2005 Mamie St Hattiesburg MS 39401 Office: Box 177 William Carey College Hattiesburg MS 39401

THURMOND, ROGER CHANEY, real estate co. exec.; b. Little Rock, Aug. 2, 1945; s. Frank Russell and Frances (Chaney) T.; student Hendrix Coll., Conway, Ark., U. Ark., Little Rock, 1967; m. Edith Karen Snell, Aug. 2, 1969; 1 dau., Ashley Elizabeth. Mgr., Riviera Apts., Little Rock, 1965-69; salesman Rector-Phillips-Morse, Inc., Little Rock, 1969-71; salesman Fausett & Co., Little Rock, 1971-72; v.p., gen. mgr. May Devel. Corp., Little Rock, 1972-73; pres. Universal Properties, Inc., Little Rock, 1973—. Mem. Greater Little Rock C. of C., Nat. Assn. Realtors, Realtors Nat. Mktg. Assn., Inst. Real Estate Mgmt., Ark. Real Estate Assn., Nat. Real Estate Exchange, Inc. Mem. Fellowship Bible Ch. Club: Country of Little Rock. Contbr. articles to profl. jours. Home: 2121 Old Forge Dr Little Rock AR 72207 Office: Suite 926 Savers Fed Bldg Little Rock AR 72201

THURMOND, STROM, U.S. senator; b. Edgefield, S.C., Dec. 5, 1902; s. John William and Eleanor Gertrude (Strom) T.; B.S., Clemson Coll., 1923; 13 hon. degrees; m. Jean Crouch, Nov. 7, 1947 (dec. Jan. 1960); m. 2d, Nancy Moore, Dec. 22, 1968; children—Nancy Moore, Juliana Gertrude, J. Strom, Paul Reynolds. Tchr. in S.C. schs., 1923-29, supt. edn., 1929-33; admitted to S.C. bar, 1930; city atty., county atty., state senator, 1933-38; circuit judge, 1938-46; gov. S.C., 1947-51; mem. Thurmond, Lybrand & Simons, 1951-55; U.S. senator, 1954—; del. Democratic Nat. Conv., 1932, 36, 48, chmn. S.C. del. and nat. committeeman, 52, 56, 60; chmn. S.C. del. Republican Nat. Conv., 1968, del., 1972, 76; States' Rights Dem. candidate for Pres., 1948. Served with U.S. Army, 1st Army, ETO and PTO; attached to 82d Airborne Div. for invasion of Europe, 1942-45; ret. maj. gen. U.S. Army Res. Decorated 18 medals and awards, including Legion of Merit with oak leaf cluster, Bronze Star medal with V., Purple Heart, Presdl. Distinguished Unit citation, 5 battle stars (U.S.), Croix de Guerre (France), Order of Crown (Belgium). Recipient Patriots award Congl. Medal of Honor Soc., 1974. Past trustee Winthrop Coll. Mem. Am. Bar Assn., Res. Officers Assn. (past nat. pres.; Minuteman of Year award 1971), Am. Legion (nat. def. com., Distinguished Pub. Service award 1975), Mil. Govt. Assn. (past nat. pres.), numerous other vets., civic and fraternal orgns. Baptist. Republican. Author: The Faith We Have Not Kept, 1968. Home: Aiken SC 29801 Office: Senate Office Bldg Washington DC 20510

TIANO, JUDITH JORDAN, nurse; b. Hartford, Conn., Dec. 21, 1942; d. Clifford Castree and Cora Ruth (Simpson) Williams; B.S. in Nursing, U. Cin., 1964; M.Ed., Xavier U., 1974; m. Samuel Louis Tiano, Nov. 24, 1976; children by previous marriage—Melanie Lynn Jordan, Tracey Anne Jordan. Staff nurse burn unit Cin. Gen. Hosp., 1964-65; instr. Bethesda Hosp. Sch. Nursing, Cin., 1965-71; dir. staff devel. and tng. Bethesda Instns., Cin., 1971-72; instr. Christ Hosp. Sch. Nursing, Cin., 1972-73; dir. nursing United Hosp. Center, Inc., Clarksburg, W.Va., 1973—; nurse and edn. cons.; asst. prof. Salem (W.Va.) Coll. Active Girl Scouts U.S.A., 1973-78, W.Va. Lupus Found. Mem. Nat. League for Nursing, Am. Soc. Hosp. Nursing Service Adminstrs. (W.Va. pres. 1976-77), Am. Hosp. Assn., W.Va. Planning Com. for Perinatal Health, W.Va. League for Nursing (pres. 1979-81), Health Systems Agy. W.Va., Sigma Theta Tau. Republican. Home: 723 Brightridge Dr Bridgeport WV 26330 Office: United Hosp Center Inc PO Box 1680 Clarksburg WV 26301

TICE, GEORGE ARTHUR, engring. cons.; b. Munhall, Pa., Feb. 19, 1934; s. George and Christine (Pelger) T.; B.S.C.E., U. Pitts., 1958; m. Eileen Elizabeth Reisinger, Feb. 27, 1960; children—Daniel Edward, John Michael, Julie Ann. Designer-detailer Howard, Needles, Tammen & Bergendoff, Cleve., 1958-60; design, mcpl. engr. Vegeler-Ramsey Co., Mt. Lebanon, Pa., 1960-64; with Holley Kenney, Schott, Inc. (became div. Babcock Contractors Inc. 1979), 1964—, mgr. Beckley office ops. (W.Va.), 1971-79, v.p., 1979—; mem. engring. adv. com. W.Va. Water Devel. Authority. Mem. Beckley Hwy. Devel. Com. Registered profl. engr., Pa. W.Va., Va., Md. Mem. Water Pollution Control Fedn., Am. Waterworks Assn., Am. Public Works Assn., Am. Congress Surveying and Mapping, Nat. Soc. Profl. Engrs., W.Va. Soc. Profl. Engrs. (chmn. public relation-publs. com. 1975-76, 77-78; pres. 1980—), Soc. Am. Mil. Engrs., AIME. Democrat. Lutheran. Clubs: Variety, Masons, Elks, Moose; Black Knight Country (Beckley). Home: 101 Perdue St Beckley WV 25801

TIDMORE, JIM TODD, petroleum landman; b. Midland, Tex., Aug. 4, 1952; s. B. Jim and Myra Nell (McReynolds) T.; student San Antonio Coll., 1972-73; B.B.A. in Acctg., Baylor U., 1975; m. Ann Elizabeth Howell, Aug. 5, 1972; children—Donn, Stephen. Staff acct. tax dept. Peat, Marwick, Mitchell & Co., San Antonio, 1975-77; sr. acct. Michael Kelley & Co., San Antonio, 1977-78; v.p. fin. Sulo Oil Co., San Antonio, 1978-80; ind. petroleum landman, San Antonio, 1980—. Mem. San Antonio Exec. Alliance, Alpha Beta Psi. Office: 1231 Milam Bldg San Antonio TX 78205

TIDWELL, MURRAY FRANKLIN, JR., bank exec.; b. Grimes, Okla., Mar. 27, 1940; s. Murray Franklin and Florence Frankie (Ely) T.; B.S. in Agronomy, Panhandle State U., 1963; postgrad. Okla. State U. Okla. Bankers Intermediate Sch. Banking, 1974, Agrl. Lending Sch., 1969; m. Jody, Jan. 21, 1967; children—Donna Denise, Kenneth Anson, Jennifer Jo. Salesman, Hitch Grain Co., Hitchland, Tex., 1963-65; mgr. Tex-co Grain Co., Mouser, Okla., 1965-69; agrl. rep. Security State Bank, Cheyenne, Okla., 1969-74, v.p., 1974—. Chmn., Roger Mill's County (Okla.) Devel. Council, 1975; chmn. Upper Washita Conservation Dist., Cheyenne, 1979—. Served with USAR, 1962-68. Mem. Okla. Bankers Assn. (dir. 1973), Nat. Range Soc., Panhandle State Alumni. Democrat. Clubs: Kiwanis (pres. club 1973-74), Masons, K.T. Home: Route 1 Box 28 Crawford OK 73638 Office: PO Box 497 Cheyenne OK 73628

TIEDEMANN, ALBERT WILLIAM, JR., chemist; b. Balt., Nov. 7, 1924; s. Albert William and Catherine (Madigan) T.; B.S., Loyola Coll., Balt., 1947; M.S., N.Y. U., 1949; Ph.D., Georgetown U., 1958; m. Mary Therese Sellmayer, Apr. 6, 1953; children—Marie Therese, Donna Elise, Albert William III, David Lawrence. Teaching fellow N.Y. U., 1947-50; instr. chemistry Mt. St. Agnes Coll., 1950-55; chief chemist Emerson Drug div. Warner Lambert Pharm. Co., Balt., 1955-60; analytical supr. Hercules Powder Co., Allegany Ballistics Lab., Cumberland, Md., 1960-68; tech. service supt. Hercules Inc., Radford, Va., 1968-72; dir. Va. Div. Consol. Labs., Richmond, 1972-78; vice-chmn. Va. Toxic Substances Adv. Council, 1978—; dep. dir. for labs. Va. Dept. Gen. Services, 1978—. Served to lt. (j.g.) USNR, 1943-46; capt. Res., 1946—. Fellow Am. Inst. Chemists; mem. Am. Mgmt. Assn., Soc. Advancement Mgmt., Am. Soc. Quality Control (chmn. Richmond sect. 1975-76, councilor biomed. div. 1978-80), U.S. Naval Inst., Naval Res. Assn. (dist. pres. 1954-57; nat. v.p. 1962-63, 65-69; nat. chmn. Navy Sabbath Program 1969-75; Nat. Meritorious Service award 1971), Central Atlantic States Assn. Food and Drug Ofcls. (exec. bd. 1977—). Home: 10511 Cherokee Rd Richmond VA 23235 Office: Div Consolidated Labs 1 N 14th St Richmond VA 23219

TIEMEIER, DAVID ALAN, oil well services co. exec.; b. Burlington, Iowa, May 28, 1947; s. Walter Bernard and Idabel (Goepel) T.; B.S., Iowa State U., 1969; postgrad. Tex. Christian U., 1972, Tex. Woman's U., 1975, Central State U., 1977; m. Julia Marie Cross, June 26, 1971; 1 son, Joel. Trainee, Western Co. N. Am., Lindsay, Okla., 1975-76, adminstrv. asst. to region mgr., Oklahoma City, 1976-78, regional salesman, 1978, dist. mgr., Garden City, Kans., 1979—. Served with USAF, 1970-75. Decorated Air medal. Mem. Soc. Petroleum Engrs., Am. Petroleum Inst., Am. Legion. Republican. Roman Catholic. Club: Elks. Home: 2519 N 3d St Garden City KS 67846 Office: RFD 1 Garden City KS 67846

TIEMEYER, CHRISTIAN, orch. condr.; b. Balt., Sept. 21, 1940; s. Henry Christian, Jr. and Bertha Hegler (Kappler) T.; B.Mus., Peabody Conservatory, 1962, M.Mus., 1963; D.M.A., Catholic U. Am., 1977; m. Patti Jeanine Farriss, June 22, 1968; children—Jeanine Elizabeth, Henry Christian, IV. Cellist, Balt. Symphony, 1959-60; mem. faculty Peabody Inst., 1961-63; asst. and acting prin. cellist Am. Symphony Orch., N.Y.C., 1962-64; prin. cellist Utah Symphony, 1968-75; chmn. conducting and string faculties U. Utah, 1968-77; mem. adj. faculty Brigham Young U., Provo, Utah, 1968-75; asso. condr. Dallas Symphony, 1978—; condr. Greater Dallas Youth Orch., 1978-79; founding condr. Dallas Chamber Orch., U. Tex. and Brookhaven Coll., 1978; music dir. Salt Lake City chpt. Young Audiences, Inc., 1974-76. Served with USAR, 1964-67. Office: Dallas Symphony Music Hall PO Box 26207 Dallas TX 75226

TIERNEY, CECILIA VERONICA, accountant; b. Newark, Del., July 13, 1922; d. William Aloysius and Helen Irene (O'Rourke) Tierney; B.A., U. Del., 1943; M.B.A., U. Pa., 1952; Ph.D., U. Tex., Austin, 1970. Mem. audit staff Price Waterhouse & Co., Phila., 1944-47; mem. faculty U. Del., 1947-50, Syracuse U., 1950-51, Bridgeport U., 1953-55, U. Tex., 1955-60, U. Wash., 1966-68, U. Calif., Berkeley, 1974-75, Wash. State U., 1968-77; mem. internal audit staff RCA Service Co., Gloucester City, N.J., 1952-53; with accounting research div. Am. Inst. C.P.A.'s, 1960-66; with tech. activities div. Financial Accounting Standards Bd., Stamford, Conn., 1975-76; research accountant, mgmt. info. and control Phillips Petroleum Co., Bartlesville, Okla., 1977—. Adv. bd. Coll. Bus. Research, U. Tulsa. C.P.A., N.Y. Mem. Am. Inst. C.P.A.'s, Am. Accounting Assn., Okla. Soc. C.P.A.'s, Desk and Derrick Club, Beta Alpha Psi. Democrat. Roman Catholic. Home: 2074 SE Osage St Bartlesville OK 74003 Office: 617 ICB Bartlesville OK 74004

TIETKE, WILHELM, gastroenterologist; b. Niengraben, Germany, Oct. 15, 1938; came to U.S., 1969, naturalized, 1979; s. Wilhelm and Frieda (Schmeding) T.; M.D., U. Goettingen (W.Ger.), 1968; m. Imme Schmidt, Oct. 15, 1965; children—Cornelia, Claudia, Isabel. Intern, Edward W. Sparrow Hosp., Lansing, Mich., 1970; resident in internal medicine Henry Ford Hosp., Detroit, 1971-73; fellow in gastroenterology, 1973-75; practice medicine specializing in gastroenterology, Huntsville, Ala., 1975—; mem. vol. faculty, cons. U. Ala., Huntsville, 1976; clin. asst. prof. internal medicine, 1979—; pres. Gastroenterology Assos. P.A., Huntsville, 1979—. Diplomate Am. Bd. Internal Medicine. Mem. AMA, Ala. Med. Soc., Am. Soc. Gastrointestinal Endoscopy. Lutheran. Home: 2707 Westminster Way Huntsville AL 35801 Office: 204 Lowe Ave Suite 11 Huntsville AL 35801

TIGNER, WILLIE JAMES, govt. ofcl.; b. Cusetta, Ala., Apr. 24, 1939; s. James and Flora Mae (Huggerly) T.; B.S. in Edn., Daniel Payne Coll., 1970; postgrad. U. Ala., Birmingham, 1974-76; m. Johnnie Mae Tinch, Oct. 27, 1969; children—Arthur Warren, Jacques Leon, Jonathan Kenyatte. Compliance officer Employment Standards Adminstrn. Office, Fed. Contract Compliance Program, Dept. Labor, Birmingham, Ala., 1973—; v.p. ops., dir. Four J and Assos., Birmingham, 1979—; alternate bd. mem. Jefferson County Com. for Econ. Opportunity, 1969-74, bd. dirs., 1970-73. Served with USCG, 1958-62. Mem. Am. Assn. Compliance Officers, Am. Fedn. Govt. Employees (v.p. local 2206, 1973, steward local 2519, 1979), Birmingham Urban League, United Negro Coll. Fund of Ala., Am. Bowling Congress, VA Metro Bowling League, Pi Lambda Sigma. Democrat. Baptist. Home: 616 Tree Haven Dr Birmingham AL 35214 Office: Dept Labor Room 300 908 S 20th St Birmingham AL 35205

TILLER, DAVID CLYDE, mfg. co. exec.; b. Robstown, Tex., Dec. 19, 1938; s. William Clyde and Sally (Jones) T.; B.F.A., U. Tex., 1961; m. Martha Russell, Nov. 26, 1966; 1 son, John Russell. Sr. research asso. Inst. Tex. Cultures, San Antonio, 1967-68; real estate cons. Lane Realtors, Austin, Tex., 1968-69; owner, operator Mrs. Robinson's 1912 Sandwich Bars, Austin, San Marcos, Tex., 1969-75; polit. fund-raiser, advance man Presdl. candidate U.S. Senator Lloyd M. Bentsen, 1975-76; adminstrv. asst. Wylain, Inc., Dallas, 1976-77, dir. corp. pub. affairs, 1977-78, v.p. corporate communications, 1978-80; v.p. Sunshine Mining Co., Dallas, 1980—. Co-chmn. hospitality for vis. dignitaries LBJ Library Dedication, 1971; bd. dirs. March of Dimes, Austin, Fine Arts Council, Austin, Laguna Gloria Art Museum, Austin, U.S.A. Film Festival, Dallas; public affairs council Machinery and Allied Products Inst.; vestryman, mem. day sch. bd., lay reader All Saints Episcopal Ch., Austin; lay reader St. Michaels and All Angels Ch., Dallas. Served with U.S. Army, 1961-66. Mem. Pub. Relations Soc. Am., Dallas Mus. Fine Arts. Clubs: Bent Tree Country, Chaparral. Home: 4316 Shenandoah Dallas TX 75205 Office: 500 Plaza of the Americas S Dallas TX 75201

TILLER, WENDELL HOWARD, orthopedic surgeon; b. Spartanburg, S.C., Oct. 17, 1920; s. Wendell and Ruth Howard (Lanham) T.; B.S., Wake Forest U., 1942, M.D., 1945; m. Martha Ivey, May 28, 1949; children—Linda Tiller McHam, W. Howard, Barbara Tiller Barragan, Frank, Martha I. Intern, N.C. Bapt. Hosp., Winston-Salem, 1945, asst. resident orthopedic surgery, 1948-50; resident orthopedic Children's Hosp., Boston, 1950-51; chief orthopedics U.S. Naval Hosp., Quantico, Va., 1952-54; practice medicine specializing in orthopedics, Spartanburg, 1951—; mem. staff Spartanburg Gen. Hosp., 1947, 51-52, 54—, Mary Black Hosp., Spartanburg, 1956—; asso. clin. prof. orthopedic surgery Med. U. S.C., Charleston, 1971—; dir. Blue Cross and Blue Shield S.C., 1965-74. Mem. Airport Commn. Spartanburg, 1961-63. Bd. dirs. YMCA Family Center, Spartanburg, 1955—; elder 1st Presbyn. Ch., Spartanburg, 1966—. Served to lt. comdr. M.C., USN, 1946, 52-54. Diplomate Am. Bd. Orthopedic Surgery. Fellow A.C.S.; mem. Am., Pan. Am., So., S.C. med. assns., Spartanburg County Med. Soc. (pres. 1969), S.C. Orthopedic Assn. (pres. 1970-71), Am. Acad. Orthopedic Surgeons, Southeastern Surg. Congress, Pan Pacific Surg. Assn., N.Y. Acad. Scis. Rotarian. Home: 210 Edgecombe Rd Spartanburg SC 29301 Office: 711 N Church St Spartanburg SC 29303

TILLEY, WILLIAM JESSE, JR., structural steel mfr.; b. Bristol, Va., June 24, 1932; s. W.J. and Annette (Ferguson) T.; B.B.A., U. Mich., 1954; M. Indsl. Mgmt., Ga. Inst. Tech., 1958; M. Indsl. Admininstrn., Yale U., 1959; m. Cynthia Muller, Nov. 19, 1971; children—Laura, Carl, Linda, Gary Robinette II, Sara Robinette, Christina. With Bristol Steel & Iron Works, Inc., 1952—, asst. exec. v.p., 1959-66, pres., chief exec. officer, 1966—; pres., chief exec. officer Miss. Valley Structural Steel Co., St. Louis, 1978—, Chattanooga Boiler & Tank Co. (Tenn.), 1978—, Debron Internat., Galway, Ireland, 1978—; officer, dir. numerous mfg. cos., 1966—; dir. Dominion Nat. Bank, Bristol; Adv. bd. Liberty Mut. Va., 1974—. Chmn. fin. com. State St. United Meth. Ch., 1976—, fund raising chmn., 1976; bd. dirs. Boys Club of Bristol, 1974—, Downtown Mchts. Assn., 1975—, Nat. Jr. Tennis League, 1975—. Served to 1st lt. U.S. Army, 1954-56. Mem. Am. Inst. Steel Constrn. (1st. vice chmn. 1978—), Nat. Assn. Mfrs. (dir. 1972-74), Va. Mfrs. Assn. (chmn. 1979), Va. State C. of C. (dir. 1972-76), Young Presidents' Orgn., Newcomen Soc. N. Am., Aircraft Owners and Pilots Assn. Clubs: Country of Bristol; Yale of N.Y.C.; Yale of Va.; Barkley, Internat., Whitehall (Chgo.). Home: Greentree Circle Bristol VA 24201 Office: 300 Piedmont Ave Bristol VA 24201

TILLMAN, CELESTINE, educator; b. Trout, La., Dec. 12, 1933; d. Elbert Lee and Lillie (Mays) T.; B.S., So. U., 1955; M.S., Howard U., 1957; postgrad. Pa. State U., 1958-61, La. State U., 1968-72. Instr. chemistry So. U., Baton Rouge, 1957-63, asst. prof., 1963—; NORCUS fellow, research chemist Atlantic Richfield Hanford Co. (Wash.), summers 1973, 77, cons., 1976-77; research fellow Pa. State U., 1958-60 NSF chem. faculty fellow La. State U., summers 1968, 69, 71. Active ARC, NAACP, La. Council on Human Relations, Audubon council Girl Scouts U.S.A., YWCA, Leadership Conf. on Civil Rights, LWV, Nat. Assn. Land Grant Colls., Center for Urban Environ. Sci., Women in Community Service, Nat. Pan Hellenic, others. Atlantic Richfield Hanford Co. research grantee, 1976-77; recipient Chemistry Tchr. of Year award So. U., 1978-79. Mem. AAAS, Am. Chem. Soc., La. Acad. Sci., Baton Rouge Analytic Instrument Discussion Group, Assn. for Women in Sci., Nat. Orgn. for Profl. Advancement of Black Chemists and Chem. Engrs., Phi Delta Kappa, Iota Sigma Pi, Sigma Delta Sigma Theta. Manuscript reviewer for publs. Home: 10761 S Gibbens Dr Baton Rouge LA 70807 Office: Chemistry Department Southern University Baton Rouge 70813

TILLMAN, JAMES ALBERT, JR., urban affairs and mgmt. cons.; b. Atlanta, Aug. 10, 1926; s. James Albert and Grace (O'Neill) T.; A.B. (Honors fellow), Morris Brown Coll., 1948; A.M. (Univ. fellow), Atlanta U., 1948; Ph.D. (Carnegie fellow 1949-50, Ford fellow 1951-52), Syracuse (N.Y.) U., 1952; m. Mary Spalding Norman, Apr. 11, 1951; children—James Albert III, Gina Grace. Personnel dean, prof. Ft. Valley State U., 1948-52, Fisk U., 1952-56; fgn. service officer Dept. State, Far Eastern and Latin Am. Areas, 1956-59; exec. dir. Greater Mpls. Interfaith Fair Housing Program, Inc., 1959-65; asso. dir., program adminstr. Community Action Tng. Center, Syracuse U., 1965-66; exec. dir. Crusade for Opportunity, Community Action Agy., Syracuse and Onodaga County, N.Y., 1966-68; pres. Tillman Assos., Syracuse, N.Y.C., Atlanta, 1968—; adj. prof. Gordon-Conwell Theol. Sem., 1977—. Mem. Assn. Social Sci. Tchrs., Am. Sociol. Soc., Am. Acad. Polit. and Social Sci., Religious Edn. Assn. U.S. and Can., Am. Fgn. Assn., Assn. Fgn. Student Advisers, Minn. Council for Civil and Human Rights, A.C.L.U., Nat. Assn. Intergroup Relations Ofcls., Nat. Planning Assn., Nat. Conf. on Religion and Race, Internat. Platform Assn., Dirs. Assn. and Am. Acad. Cons. (dir. N.Y. Community Action Program), Alpha Kappa Delta, Sigma Rho Sigma. Author: To Secure These Rights, 1963; Not By Prayer Alone, 1964; Annotated Action Guide, 1965; (with Mary Norman Tillman) Why America Needs Racism and Poverty, 1969, What Is Your Racism Quotient?, 1969, The White Racism Seminar/Practicum: A New Race Relations Change Methodology, 1973, The Minneapolis Public Schools: An Analytic Profile, 1974; The Community Action Agency as a Weapon in the War Against Poverty, 1966; Segregation and the Minneapolis Public Schools: An Overview with Recommendations for its Arrest and Reversal, 1974. Contbr. articles to profl. jours. Address: 1765 Glenview Dr SW Atlanta GA 30331

TILLMAN, MASSIE MONROE, lawyer; b. Corpus Christi, Tex., Aug. 15, 1937; s. Clarence and Artie Lee (Stewart) T.; B.B.A., Baylor U., 1959, LL.B., 1961; m. Jerra Sue Comer, July 27, 1957; children—Jeffrey Monroe, Holly. Admitted to Tex. bar, 1961, since practiced in Ft. Worth; partner firm Herrick & Tillman, 1961-66, Brown, Herman, Scott, Dean & Miles, 1970-78; individual practice law, 1978—. Fellow Tex. Bar Found.; mem. Fort Worth-Tarrant County Bar Assn. (dir. 1970-72, chmn. med.-legal liaison com. 1968-75, sec.-treas. 1976-77), Tex. Assn. Def. Counsel (dir. 1976-77), Tex. Bar Assn., State Bar Tex. (chmn. pilot project Right of Trial by Jury 1969—), Assn. Trial Attys. Am., Tex. Trial Lawyers Assn. Democrat. Presbyn. Author: Tillman's Trial Guide, 1970. Home: 4612 Briarhaven Rd Fort Worth TX 76109 Office: 2703 Fort Worth Nat Bank Bldg Fort Worth TX 76102

TILLOTSON, REX FOUNT, coll. ofcl.; b. Mt. Airy, N.C., Dec. 20, 1920; s. Squire Fount and Mattie Florence (Reynolds) T.; B.S., Wake Forest Coll., 1943; postgrad. Med. Coll. Va., 1943, 46; Ed.M., Coll. of William and Mary, 1969; m. Mary Alice Smith, Feb. 11, 1950; children—Mary Susan Tillotson Morse, Nancy Elizabeth, Nita Jo, Patricia Fount. Instr., coach Lynchburg (Va.) Coll., 1946, dir. admissions, 1954-64, exec. sec. Alumni Assn., 1954-60; tchr., coach Shoals High Sch., Surry County, N.C., 1947-48, Copeland High Sch., Surry County, 1948-52; med. research asst. in heart physiology Baylor U. Coll. Medicine, Houston, 1950; stockbroker Mason & Co., Williamsburg, Va., 1964-65; tobacco farmer, King, N.C.; asso. dean admissions Coll. of William and Mary, Williamsburg, Va., 1965—. Served with U.S. Army, 1942-45; PTO. Decorated Silver Star medal Bronze Star medal with oak leaf cluster; lic. pvt. pilot. Mem. Va. Personnel and Guidance Assn. (pres. 1972-73), Va. Assn. Collegiate Registrars and Admissions Officers (pres. 1957-58), Peninsula Personnel and Guidance Assn. (past pres.) Am. Personnel and Guidance Assn., Am. Legion, VFW, Am. Legion Boys State of Va. (dir. 1975—), U.S. Lawn Tennis Assn., Nat. Assn. Parliamentarians, Lynchburg Coll. Alumni Assn., Kappa Delta Pi, Kappa Sigma. Club: Toastmasters (gov. dist. 66 1974). Home: Drawer KJ Williamsburg VA 23185 Office: Office Admissions Coll William and Mary Williamsburg VA 23185

TILLY, LOIS AMELIA, educator; b. Chgo., Jan. 27; d. Andrew Thomas and Leona Gloria (Arsheal) T.; B.S. in Vocal Music Edn., So. U., 1969; M.A., Xavier U., 1978; postgrad. Loyola U., New Orleans. Vocal music tchr. P.A. Capdau Jr. High Sch., New Orleans, 1979—; minister of music Central Missionary Bapt. Ch., New Orleans, 1964—, Second Bethlehem Bapt. Ch., New Orleans, 1974—; organ accompanist vocal recs.; organist weekly radio program Quiet Music, Sta. WVOG, New Orleans. Mem. Music Educators Nat. Conf., Am. Choral Dirs. Assn., Fellowship of Christian Musicians, Middle Schs. Assn. Home: PO Box 3442 New Orleans LA 70177

TIMCHAK, LOUIS JOHN, JR., lawyer; b. Johnstown, Pa., June 7, 1940; s. Louis John and Edna Ann (Bonistall) T.; A.B., Georgetown U., 1962; LL.B., U. Pitts., 1965; m. Susan Truesdale Mueller, June 3, 1972; children—Louis John, Alexander Mueller, Christopher Truesdale. Admitted to Pa. bar, 1965, D.C. bar, 1966, Fla. bar, 1970, N.Y. State bar, 1973; individual practice law, Johnstown, 1968-69; real estate atty. Marriott Corp., Washington, 1969-73; asso. firm Finley, Kumble, Wagner, Heine & Underberg, N.Y.C., 1973-74; asst. v.p., asst. corp. counsel Phipps Land Co., Atlanta, 1974-75, v.p., corp. counsel, 1976; regional v.p. IDS Mortgage Devel. Corp., Atlanta, 1976-78; regional v.p. IDR Mgmt., Inc., Atlanta, 1978—. Served to lt. JAGC, USNR, 1965-68. Lic. real estate broker, Ga. Mem. Am., Fla. bar assns., Bar Assn. D.C., Atlanta Hist. Soc., High Mus. Art, Nat. Audubon Soc. Clubs: City Tavern (Washington); Univ. (Pitts.); Ponte Vedra (Fla.); Ocean Reef. Office: Suite 505 550 Pharr Rd NE Atlanta GA 30305

TIMM, EVERETT L., musician, univ. adminstr.; b. Highmore, S.D., Jan. 8, 1914; s. Henry R. and Bertha (Hoffman) T.; B.M., Morningside Coll., 1936, D.Mus. (hon.), 1967; M.Mus., Eastman Sch. Music, 1943, Ph.D., 1948; m. Marguerite Jeanne Anderson, 1940; children—Gary, Laurance. Instr., dir. bands Morningside Coll., 1936-42; instr. flute Eastman Sch. Music, 1946-48; mem. faculty dept. music La. State U., Baton Rouge, 1942-43, 48-55, dean Sch. Music, prof. woodwinds, 1955-79; staff conductor Sta. KSCJ, 1939-42; asst. conductor Sioux City Symphony Orch., 1943-46; 1st flutist Sioux City Symphony, 1931-42; 1st flutist Baton Rouge Symphony, 1948-49; soloist Rochester Symphony, La. State U. Symphony, Eastman Symphony. Bd. dirs. Baton Rouge Civic Symphony Assn.; v.p., bd. dirs. Community Concerts, Baton Rouge. Mem. Nat. Assn. Schs. of Music (pres. 1971-76), Music Educators Nat. Conf. (past pres. So. div.), Music Tchrs. Nat. Assn. (past chmn. coll. music So. div.), La. Music Educators Assn. (past sec.-treas., past chmn. coll. and univ. com.), Soc. Research in Music Edn., Omicron Delta Kappa, Phi Mu Alpha, Kappa Kappa Psi. Contbr. articles to profl. jours. Office: Sch Music La State Univ Baton Rouge LA 70803

TIMMINS, LOIS FAHS, hosp. ofcl.; b. N.Y.C., July 3, 1914; d. Charles Harvey and Sophia (Lyon) Fahs; B.S., Northwestern U., 1935; M.A., Columbia U., 1936, Ed.D., 1941; m. Aug. 12, 1942 (div.); children—Nancy Fahs, Kathy Fahs. Instr. phys. edn. Mt. Allison U., N.B., Can., 1936-39; asst. prof. phys. edn. Willimantic (Conn.) State Tchrs. Coll., 1941-43; staff UNESCO, Paris and Austria, 1950; asst. prof. recreation Tex. Woman's U., Denton, 1953-57; dir. recreation therapy Timberlawn Psychiat. Hosp., Dallas, 1957-72, dir. halfway house, cons. day hosp., 1972-77, asst. to adminstr., dir. publicity, 1977—. Author: Swing Your Partner: Old Time Dances of New Brunswick and Nova Scotia, 1939; Understanding Through Communication, 1972; Life-Time Charts, 1978; contbr. articles to profl. publs. Home: 6145 Anita St Dallas TX 75214

TIMMONS, BANNER PHILDELLIA, oil co. exec.; b. Connersville, Okla., June 5, 1935; s. Lloyd James and Minnie Ruth (Cobble) T.; B.B.A., U. Tex., 1969; m. Janice Mozell Van Deventer, June 5, 1959; children—Steven Phil, Bret Duane, Jeffrey Lloyd. Sr. accountant, gas control unit Atlantic Richfield, Dallas, 1974-75, supr. info. support, 1975-76, dir. gas devel. and compliance, 1976-78, dir. oil acctg., 1978—. Served with U.S. Army, 1957-59. C.P.A., Tex. Mem. Petroleum Accts. Soc. Baptist. Club: Mason. Home: Rural Route 1 Box 178D Mansfield TX 76063 Office: Atlantic Richfield PO Box 2819 Dallas TX 75221

TIMMONS, ROBERT DEAN, state legislator Ala.; b. Birmingham, Ala., July 3, 1932; s. Joe and Stella Golden (Livingston) T.; seminars U. Chattanooga, U. Ala.; m. Emily Loyd, Apr. 3, 1965; children—Chirsty, Todd, Leslie. Owner life ins. agy., Birmingham, 1965—; mem. Ala. Ho. of Reps., 1970—. Bd. dirs. Jefferson County Sheriffs Acad.; trustee Ala. Sheriffs Boys Ranch. Democrat. Methodist. Club: Sertoma (past sec.-treas.). Author first ins. code for Ala. Home: 3431 Kildare Dr Birmingham AL 35226 Office: PO Box 8302 Birmingham AL 35218

TINDALL, GEORGE TAYLOR, neurosurgeon, educator; b. Magee, Miss., Mar. 13, 1928; s. George Earl and Lyda (Smith) T.; B.A., U. Miss., 1948; M.D., Johns Hopkins U., 1952; m. Suzie Cunningham, Sept. 4, 1971; children—Catherine, George Taylor, Suzanne, Annelle. Intern, Johns Hopkins Hosp., Balt., 1952-53; resident Duke U.,

Durham, N.C., 1955-56, 65-60, chief resident, 1960-61, asst. prof. neurosurgery, 1961-67, asso. prof., 1967-68; chief neurosurgery Durham (N.C.) VA Hosp., 1961-68; prof. and chief div. neurosurgery U. Tex. Med. Br., Galveston, 1968-73; prof. surgery, chief neurosurgery Emory U., Atlanta, 1973—. Served to capt. USAF, 1953-55. Diplomate Am. Bd. Neurol. Surgery. Mem. Am. Acad. Neurol. Surgery (editor jour. 1971—), Am. Assn. Neurol. Surgeons, Congress Neurol. Surgeons (pres. 1973-74), Soc. Neurol. Surgeons, Neurosurg. Soc. Am., Soc. Univ. Neurosurgeons (pres. 1966), A.C.S., AMA, Ga. Med. Assn., Johns Hopkins Med. and Surg. Assn., Alpha Omega Alpha.

TINDALL, GEORGE WILLIAM, chemist; b. Niagara Falls, N.Y., Aug. 12, 1943; s. George L. and Gladys (Czupryua) T.; B.S. in Chemistry, Clarkson Coll., Potsdam, N.Y., 1965; Ph.D. in Chemistry, U. Minn., Mpls., 1969; m. Judith A. Ames, July 2, 1965; children—Cynthia, Debra. Sr. chemist Tenn. Eastman Co., Kingsport, 1979—. Home: Route 10 Kingsport TN 37664

TINDELL, BILLY EUGENE, architect; b. Springfield, Mo., Jan. 21, 1925; s. Benjamin H. and Effie M. (McClure) T.; B.Arch., U. Okla., 1959; m. Zola Ernestine Biggs, Jan. 8, 1950; children—Lee Ann, Billy Stephen. Sr. research architect Southwest Research Inst., San Antonio, 1965-67; chief architect Hudgins Thompson Ball, Tulsa, 1967-69; chief architect, dir. archtl. control com. Cooper Communities, Inc., Bentonville, Ark., 1969-71; architect B.E. Tindell, Rogers, Ark., 1971-73; archtl. supr. Bechtel Power Corp., Houston, 1974—. Served with AUS, 1943-46. Decorated Purple Heart. Mem. A.I.A., U. Okla. Alumni Assn. (life). Address: 2111 Teague St Houston TX 77080

TING-BEALL, HIE PING, med. researcher, educator; b. Sibu, Sarawak, Malaysia, Dec. 15, 1940; came to U.S., 1959, naturalized, 1975; d. Lik Hung and Ngu Cheong Ting; B.S., Greensboro Coll., 1963; M.S., Tulane U., 1965, Ph.D., 1967; m. Harry Clark Beall, Aug. 15, 1970; 1 son, Allen. Postdoctoral fellow Mich. State U., East Lansing, 1967-69; postdoctoral trainee Johnson Research Found., U. Pa., Phila., 1969-70; research asso. Mich. State U., 1970-72; research asso. Duke U. Med. Center, 1972-75, asst. med. research prof. depts. anatomy and physiology, 1975—. Mem. Biophys. Soc., So. Soc. Anatomists, N.C. Acad. Sci., Sigma Xi. Contbr. articles to profl. jours. Home: 1008 Horton Rd Durham NC 27704 Office: Box 3011 Duke U Med Center Durham NC 27710

TINGLER, LOYD, retail trade co. exec.; b. Daviess County, Mo., Aug. 27, 1920; s. Lawrence Henry and Leah Mae (Robinson) T.; grad. Chillicothe (Mo.) Bus. Coll., 1941; postgrad. Harvard U., 1947; m. Arlene Marie Preston, Aug. 8, 1948; children—Elizabeth, Charles, James. Mgr., Webb's Furniture Store, St. Petersburg, Fla., 1949-62; propr., dir. Loyd Tingler Furniture Inc., Pinellas Park, Fla., 1962—; dir. S.E. Bank of Pinellas Park, 1976—. Chmn. Pinellas Park Water Mgmt. Dist., 1976—; trustee 5th Ave Bapt. Ch., St. Petersburg, 1960—; bd. dirs. Boys' Club of Pinellas Park, 1965-73, Pinellas Park Girls' Club, 1971-72, Child Guidance Clinic of Pinellas Park, 1973-75, Bay Vista Civic Assn., 1957-72. Served with USN, 1942-47. Mem. Fla. Furniture Dealers Assn. (dir. 1972—), Nat. Home Furnishing Assn., Contractors and Builders of Pinellas County, Pinellas Park C. of C. (dir. 1972-75, transp. chmn. 1972-75 named Citizen of Year 1979). Republican. Baptist. Clubs: Optimist (dir. 1967-70, Friend of the Boy award 1971), Kiwanis (Layman's award 1975); Feather Sound Country, Moose. Home: 8800 60th St Pinellas Park FL 33565 Office: 8010 US Hwy 19 Pinellas Park FL 33565

TINGLEY, GLENN VINCENT, clergyman; b. Fields Corner, Ohio; July 31, 1901; s. Nelson Eugene and Edith G. (Gage) T.; student Los Angeles Sem., 1915-20, Los Angeles Pacific Coll., 1919-20; A.B., Mt. Vernon U., 1942, Th.B., 1942; D.D., Christ Sem., 1944; m. Elva Eunice Allen, Sept. 10, 1921; children—Ruth Eunice Tingley Teer, Pauline Elsie Tingley Sawyer (dec.), Alice Mae Tingley Schafer, Marjorie Tingley Blount, Peggy Glenn Iris Tingley Barker, Glenn Vincent. Ordained to ministry, Christian and Missionary Alliance, 1926; pastor Birmingham Gospel Tabernacle, 1929-56; pres. Birmingham Bible Inst., 1930-50; pastor Alliance Ch., Rochester, N.Y., 1956-60; pres. Radio Revival, Inc., 1929—; pastor Fort Payne; Ala., 1969-80; pres. Courier Broadcasting Service, Inc., 1944-51, Fair Haven Conf. Grounds, Birmingham, Ala., 1952-60. Evangelist interdenominational crusades various countries, 1959—; conf. speaker for The Evang. Alliance Mission, Aruba and Curacao, 1961; speaker Slovak Bapt. Union of Europe, 19 countries, 1954, Oriental Missionary Soc. in Greece, 1954; evangelist Christian and Missionary Alliance, Lebanon, Syria, Jordan and Ivory Coast. French West Africa, 1954, nat. evangelist, 1963-69; crusades in Peru, Colombia, Japan, Hong Kong, Philippines, Singapore, Malaysia, Israel. Pres. DeKalb County Mental Health Assn., 1967-80. Trustee Toccoa Falls Bible Coll., CED Mental Health Hosp. Mem. Christian and Missionary Alliance, Nat. Religious Broadcaster (dir. 1941-61), Rochester Ministers Fellowship (pres. 1957-58), Rochester Fedn. Chs. (dir. 1957-58), Fort Payne Ministerial Assn., Pastors' Assn. Ft. Payne (pres. 1972). Home: PO Box 656 309 NW 21st St Fort Payne AL 35967 Office: PO Box 10684 Birmingham AL 35202

TINKLER, ARLENE TAD, architect; b. Gypsum, Kans., Jan. 3, 1927; d. Merrill Wayne and Winnifred Arlene (Schultz) T.; B.S. in Architecture, Kans. State U., 1949, M.S. in Architecture, 1952. Job capt. Charles W. and John A. Shaver, Architects, Salina, Kans., 1949-51; pvt. practice architecture, Manhattan, Kans., 1951-52; architect Wyatt C. Hedrick, Architects and Engrs., Houston, 1952-57, Ft. Worth, 1957-65; architect Kirk, Voich & Smith, Architects and Engrs., Ft. Worth, 1965-66, Parker, Croston & Assos., Architects and Engrs., Ft. Worth, 1966-75; architect, contracting officer constrn. mgmt. div. Public Bldgs. Service, GSA, Ft. Worth, 1975—. Registered architect, Kans., Tex. Mem. AIA, Nat. Assn. Women in Constrn. Methodist. Home: 7304 Marilyn Ln Fort Worth TX 76118 Office: 819 Taylor St Fort Worth TX 76102

TINNON, JOSEPH EUGENE, educator; b. Ellisville, Miss., Feb. 9, 1939; s. Joseph Earl and Wilbur Doris (Herrington) T.; A.A., Jones County Jr. Coll., 1958; B.S., U. So. Miss., 1960; M.S. (NSF grantee), U. Miss., 1964, Ed.D., 1977; m. Bobbie Nell Jenkins, Dec. 18, 1960; children—Jeffrey Eugene, Tracey Lea. Tchr. math. Jones County Schs., 1961, Laurel City Schs., 1961-65; indsl. engr. Masonite Corp., 1965-67; instr. math. U. So. Miss., Hattiesburg, 1967-69, dir. corr. study and confs., 1969-71, dir. confs. and workshops, 1971-77, asst. dean div. continuing edn., 1977-79, asso. dean, 1980—, adj. instr. dept. curriculum and instrn., 1978-79, asst. prof., 1980. Bd. dirs. N.E. Lamar Fire Dept., 1978-79; mem. Hattiesburg Area Sports Adv. Council, 1977—. Mem. Nat. U. Extension Assn., Assn. Continuing Higher Edn., Miss. Assn. Higher Edn., U. So. Miss. Alumni Assn., U. Miss. Alumni Assn., Phi Delta Kappa, Kappa Mu Epsilon. Methodist. Clubs: University Civitan, U. So. Miss. Hardwood. Home: 606 Lamar Ave Hattiesburg MS 39401 Office: U So Miss Southern Sta Box 5055 Hattiesburg MS 39401

TINSLEY, JAMES ROBINSON, librarian, historian, educator; b. Shreveport, La., Feb. 15, 1944; s. James Madison and Norma Elise (Robinson) T.; A.B., Centernary Coll., 1966; M.A., E. Tex. State U., 1967; M.L.S., U. Ala., 1975. Grad. asst. E. Tex. State U., 1967; instr. history William Carey Coll., 1967-68; instr. history Morehead (Ky.) State U., 1968-72, asst. prof., 1972-74; grad. fellow U. Ala., University, 1974-75, reader in history, 1975-77; asst. librarian, archivist Lafourche Parish Library, Thibodaux, La., 1977-78; tchr. spl. edn., St. Mary Parish, La., 1978—; book reviewer, 1968—. Jr. warden St. Alban Episcopal Ch., 1970-74, lay reader Diocese of Lexington, 1969-74, Diocese of Ala., 1974-76, jr. warden Christ Episc. Ch., Napoleonville, La., 1977-79, observer Gen. Conv. Lexington Diocese, 1970-74; del. Episcopal Conv. of La., 1978. Recipient Order Merit of Lexington, Order St. John of Jerusalem; named Ky. Col., Adm. Mem. Am., So., Ch. hist. assns., ALA, Pi Gamma Mu, Phi Alpha Theta, Gamma Theta Upsilon, Alpha Beta Alpha, Tau Kappa Epsilon, Blue Key. Republican. Home: 1039 Sheridan St Shreveport LA 71104 Office: 12 Venus St Morgan City LA 70380

TIPPS, CHARLES WALKER, mech. engr., clergyman; b. El Dorado, Ark., Feb. 22, 1927; s. Jesse Charles and Loree (Walker) T.; A.A., Kilgore Jr. Coll., 1947; B.S., Tex. A. and M. U., 1950; m. Dorothy Glenda Elam, June 4, 1948; 1 son, Charlie Bill. Corrosion engr. City Pub. Service Co., San Antonio, 1950-55; service mgr. Bob Tipps Lincoln-Mercury Co., Tyler, Tex., 1956; well logging engr. Halliburton Co., Houma, La., 1956-57, Wellex Co., Harvey, La., 1957-59; corrosion engr. City Pub. Service Co., San Antonio, 1959-69, sr. engr., 1969-76, engr. in charge gas engring. design, 1970—; cons. in field; ordained minister Ch. of Christ, 1974; asso. minister Highland Hills (Tex.) Ch. of Christ, 1967-73; minister Bellaire (Tex.) Ch. of Christ, 1974-76, now elder. Served with USNR, 1945-46. Named boss of year San Antonio Jaycees, 1966. Registered profl. engr., Tex. Mem. Tex. Soc. Profl. Engrs. (outstanding service award 1967), Nat. Assn. Corrosion Engrs. (regional membership chmn. 1974-75; nat. publicity chmn. 1964-66; corrosion specialist; Outstanding Service award S. Central Region 1974), I.E.E.E., Tex. Gas Assn. Club: Toastmasters. Contbr. articles to profl. publs. Home: 1043 Vanderbilt St San Antonio TX 78210 Office: PO Box 1771 San Antonio TX 78296

TIPTON, JANIS CLARK, state ofcl.; b. Jeffersonville, Ind., Mar. 4, 1953; d. Horace Edward and Olive E. (Gayhart) Clark; B.S., Western Ky. U., 1975; M.P.A. (HEW Title IX fellow), U. Ky., 1978; m. Carl David Tipton, Dec. 20, 1975. Adminstrv. specialist Office Planning and Research, Ky. Dept. for Natural Resources and Environ. Protection, Frankfort, 1975-77; grad. asst. Office Policy and Analysis, U. Ky., Lexington, 1977; grad. intern Bluegrass Area Devel. Dist., Lexington, 1978; dep. dir. Office Planning and Evaluation, Ky. Dept. Energy, Lexington, 1978—. Cert. in environ. law and program evaluation CSC. Mem. Am. Soc. for Public Adminstrn., Am. Mgmt. Assn. (cert. project mgmt.), Presdl. Classroom for Young Ams. Alumnae, Alpha Xi Delta. Democrat. Presbyterian. Club: Sin The Karate. Contbr. articles to profl. publs. Home: 2733 Stetson Ln Lexington KY 40502 Office: PO Box 11888 Iron Works Rd Lexington KY 40578

TIPTON, JUDY SCHMITT, guidance counselor; b. Dallas, Dec. 17, 1952; d. James Wesley and Helen (Pierce) Schmitt; B.S. in Elem. Edn., U. Houston, 1973, M.Ed. in Guidance and Counseling, 1978; m. Gary Lee Tipton, Mar. 24, 1978. With Houston Ind. Sch. Dist., 1973—, guidance counselor Clifton Middle Sch., 1979—. Mem. Am. Personnel and Guidance Assn., Houston Personnel and Guidance Assn., Houston Sch. Counselors Assn., Congress Houston Tchrs. Assn. Baptist. Address: 6011 Ogden Forest St Houston TX 77088

TIPTON, WILLIAM VERNON, corp. exec.; b. Ft. Worth, Apr. 19, 1944; s. Zeke and Cecile Evelyn (Taylor) T.; student S. Tex. Jr. Coll., 1965-67; Jerry Diane Rhodes, Aug. 19, 1969; 1 son, Tyson Matthew. Warehouseman, Tipton Co., Houston, 1965, sales rep., 1966, chmn. bd., 1967—; chmn. bd. Component Mfg. Corp., Houston, 1966—, Producers Splty. & Mfg. Corp., Ft. Worth, 1976—, Plumb Easy, Inc., Houston, 1979—, Easy Data, Inc., Houston, 1979—; mem. Plumbing, Heating and Cooling Info. Bur., 19—. Commd. dep. constable Parent Tchrs. League. Served with AUS, 1962-65. Recipient appreciation award Houston Plumbing Industry Golf Assn., 1978, standards and edn. award Tex. Commn. Law Enforcement Officers, 1970; lic. pvt. pilot; cert. in real estate, Tex. Mem. Mfrs. Agts. Nat. Assn., Assn. Industry Mfrs. Reps. (dir., pres. S. Tex. chpt.). Methodist. Clubs: Spring-a-Lings Square Dance, Suburban Ranches Riding. Home: 14102 Sandy Ln Tomball TX 77375 Office: 3301 Commerce St Houston TX 77003

TIRRE, WERNER EDWARD, pharm. mfg. co. exec.; b. Bremen, Germany, Apr. 21, 1925; s. Hugo Walther and Johanna (Windhorst) T.; came to U.S., 1953, naturalized, 1959; D.Econs., U. Hamburg (Germany), 1948; m. Evelyn Kaiser Deichman, Dec. 5, 1951; children—Barbara JoAnn, Andrea Michelle, Amy Noelle, Emelie Christine. Exec. v.p. Midwest Farm & Cattle Co., Atkinson, Ill., 1966-73; controller Camstaff Constrn. Co., Ocean Reef Club, Key Largo, Fla., 1973-74; asst. to vice chmn. First Mortgage Investors Co., Miami, 1974-75; v.p., treas., chief fin. officer N. Am. Biologicals, Inc., Miami, 1975—. Served to 1st lt. German Army, 1942-45. Home: Ocean Reef Club Key Largo FL 33037 Office: 16500 NW 15th Ave Miami FL 33169

TISCH, JOSEPH LESAGE, clergyman, social work exec.; b. Mt. Vernon, N.Y., Sept. 3, 1933; s. Joseph Francis and Deborah Theresa (LeSage) T.; B.A. in History, Notre Dame U., New Orleans, 1956, M.A. in History, 1958; D.D. (hon.), Addison State U., Can., 1979. Ordained priest Catholic Ch., 1960; asst. pastor, Newman Club chaplain, dir. rural mission, Woodworth, La., 1960-63; prin. St. Joseph High Sch., Plaucheville, La., 1963-67; social worker Fla. State Welfare Bd., 1968-70; asst. exec. dir. Brevard County Community Action Agy., Inc., 1970-73; dir. City of Melbourne (Fla.) Human Services Dept., 1973—; bd. dirs. Provincial Clerical Synod, Liberal Cath. Ch. Chmn., City of Cape Canaveral Recreation Bd., 1968-74. Named Humanist of Yr., Space Coast chpt. Am. Humanist Assn., 1974. Mem. Nat. Assn. Social Workers (chmn. Central East Coast unit Fla. chpt.), Nat. Assn. City Human Service Ofcls. (nat. organizing com., dir.), Theosophical Soc. Democrat. Club: Kiwanis. Author: French in Louisiana, 1959; The Big Step, 1963; editor: The Evolving Universe, 1979—, Catholic Critiques, 1973—. Home: PO Box 1117 Melbourne FL 32901 Office: 635 E New Haven Ave Melbourne FL 32901

TISCHLER, SAMUEL GORDON, health care adminstr.; b. Miami Beach, Fla., Oct. 12, 1948; s. Stanley Phillip (stepfather) and Anita Muriel (Frankel) Kessel; B.S. in Journalism, U. Fla., 1970; M.A. in Health Care Adminstrn., George Washington U., 1973; m. Suzanne Marie Bowman, Jan. 18, 1975. Sr. adminstrv. asst. Borgess Hosp., Kalamazoo, 1973-75; adminstrv. asst. S. Suburban Hosp., Hazel Crest, Ill., 1975-76; v.p. Ambucare Internat., Miami, Fla., 1976-78; asst. dir. Cedars of Lebanon Health Care Center, Miami, 1978—. Div. head United Way Dade County (Fla.). Mem. S. Fla. Hosp. Assn., Fla. Hosp. Assn., Am. Hosp. Assn., Am. Coll. Hosp. Adminstrs., Sigma Delta Chi. Club: Lions (Coral Gables). Home: 150 SE 715 NE 205th Terr North Miami Beach FL 33179 Office: 1400 NW 12th Ave Miami FL 33136

TISDALE, JOE REESE, broadcasting co. exec.; b. Andalusia, Ala., Aug. 18, 1943; s. Newton Daniel and Alice Hazel (Leonard) T.; B.M.E., Troy (Ala.) State U., 1966; M.S. in Edn., 1979; m. Faye Allen, Nov. 27, 1974; children—Robert Warren, Brandon Ray, Patrick Allen. Announcer, WJSB and WAAZ-FM, Crestview, Fla., 1956-66; newsman WAMI AM-FM, Opp, Ala., 1967-77; dir. choral music Opp City Schs., 1966—; v.p., gen. mgr. Tisdale Video, Inc./TV-6, Opp, 1970—; show-choir dir. Auburn U. summer music camp, 1978, 79. Mem. adminstrv. bd. Opp 1st United Meth. Ch., 1966—, choir dir., 1966—; adv. bd. theatre Ala. Council on Arts and Humanities, 1976-78. Recipient Educator of Yr. award Opp Jaycees, 1975; named condr. of yr. Troy State U. Honors Choral Festival, 1980. Mem. Ala. Vocal Assn. (dir.), Music Educators Nat. Conf., Am. Choral Dirs. Assn., NEA, Ala. Edn. Assn., Opp Edn. Assn. Composer vocal pieces. Home: 511 Jeffcoat Ave Opp AL 36467 Office: PO Drawer TV Opp AL 36467

TISDALE, LLOYD BRENT, indsl. environ. systems mfg. co. exec.; b. Olney, Ill., Dec. 26, 1946; s. Paul Theodore and Thelma Eileen (Scheetz) T.; student Lee Coll., 1974-75; A.A., San Jacinto Coll., 1976; B.S., U. Houston, 1980; m. Jana Beth Arnold, Oct. 24, 1979; 1 dau., Brooke Michelle. Field labor, Tisdale Co., Baytown, Tex., 1968-69, service dept., 1969-71, service mgr. and parts distbn., 1971-74, supt. mfg. prodn., 1974-75, corp. sec., 1975-77, head sales and engring., corp. v.p., 1977—; cons. in field. Active Republican Congl. Election campaigns, Howard Jarvis' Proposition 13. Served with USAF, 1967. Cert., licensed master air conditioning technician, contractor, sr. parachute rigger. Mem. Internat. Solar Energy Soc., ASHRAE, Baytown Home Builders Assn., Republican. Developer mktg., worldwide, of heating, air conditioning, and refrigeration equipment in highly volatile and highly corrosive atmospheres. Home: 400 Red Bud St Baytown TX 77520 Office: Tisdale Co 115 N Main St Baytown TX 77520

TISE, LARRY EDWARD, govt. archivist; b. Winston-Salem, N.C., Dec. 6, 1942; s. Russell Edward and Lena Irene (Norman) T.; A.B., Duke U., 1965, M.Div., 1968; Ph.D. (Ford Found. fellow, Research Triangle fellow), U. N.C., Chapel Hill, 1974; m. Alice Brandon Smith, Aug. 21, 1965; children—Larry Edward, Nicholas Allen. Part time editor John Fries Blair, pub., Winston-Salem, 1969-72; instr. dept. history U. N.C., Chapel Hill, 1972-73; dir. hist. publs. N.C. Bicentennial Com., Raleigh, 1973-74; asst. dir. N.C. Div. Archives and History, Raleigh, 1974-75, dir., 1975—, N.C. State Hist. Preservation Officer, 1975—; sec. N.C. Hist. Commn., 1975—; bd. dirs. Hist. Preservation Fund of N.C., Inc. Chmn., USS Monitor Tech. Adv. Com., 1977—. Recipient William R. Davie History award, 1979. Mem. Am. Hist. Assn., Orgn. Am. Historians, So. Hist. Assn., Soc. Am. Archivists, Am. Assn. State and Local History, Nat. Trust Hist. Preservation, Nat. Conf. State Hist. Preservation Officers (dir. 1975-79, pres. 1979—). Methodist. Author: The Yadkin Melting Pot, 1968; gen. editor: Winston-Salem in History, 13 vols., 1976; editor in chief N.C. Hist. Rev., 1975—; co-editor: Southern Experience in the American Revolution, 1978; Writing North Carolina History, 1979. Home: 328 Wildwood Dr Durham NC 27712 Office: NC Div Archives and History 109 E Jones St Raleigh NC 27611

TISON, ROBERT WARREN, ins. agt.; b. Jacksonville, Fla., Oct. 11, 1942; s. Arthur M. and Mildred H. Tison; student public schs.; m. Alice Hinton, Feb. 26, 1970; children—Kathi, Ronald, Pauline, Paulette. Engaged in ins. sales, 1965—; agy. mgr. Franklin Life Ins. Co., Jacksonville, 1973—. Elder, past deacon Mardarin Christian Ch. Served with USAF, 1960. Mem. Million Dollar Round Table, 1974; recipient various ins. salesmanship awards. Mem. Life Underwriters Assn. Jacksonville (past dir.). Home: 5448 Contina Ave Jacksonville FL 32211 Office: 101 Century 21st Dr Suite 113 Jacksonville FL 32216

TITONE, RUSSELL EMIL, planning exec.; b. New Brunswick, N.J., Mar. 11, 1948; s. Nicholas and Clara (Cassano) T.; A.S. in Bus. Adminstrn. cum laude, Tidewater Community Coll., 1979; m. Maureen Linda Murphy, June 15, 1968; children—Nicole Colette, Elise Marie, Brenna Beth, Summer Renee, Fawn Noelle. Engr. technician with licensing and quality control Va. Electric Power Co., Surry, 1976-77, sr. engr. technician in prodn., ops. and maintenance Surry Nuclear Power Sta., 1977-79, engring. supr. in prodn. ops. and maintenance, 1979—. Served with USN, 1968-76. Mem. Am. Soc. Quality Control, Am. Mgmt. Assn., Phi Theta Kappa. Republican. Roman Catholic. Home: 4509 High St W Portsmouth VA 23703 Office: Surry Power Station PO Box 315 Surry VA 23883

TITSWORTH, TOBIE RICHARD, III, coll. adminstr.; b. Henryetta, Okla., May 13, 1945; s. Tobie Richard and Thelma Edith (Stephens) T.; B.S., Okla. State U., 1967, M.S., 1973, Ed.D., 1976; m. Laura Jeanne Barnes, Dec. 24, 1966; children—Scottie Richard, Stephanie Ann. Tchr. vocat. agr. Miami (Okla.) Public Sch., 1971-74; asst. prof. agrl. engring. Tex. A&M U., College Station, Tex., 1975-79; dean community and tech. edn. Claremore (Okla.) Coll., 1979—. Active Sunday Sch., Baptist Ch., 1976-78. Served to capt. USAF, 1966-71; maj. Res. Named outstanding tchr. Collegiate FFA, Tex. A&M U. Mem. Am. Soc. Agrl. Engrs. (chmn. com. 218 agrl. mechanization 1979-80), Am. Soc. Engring. Edn., Am. Assn. Tchrs. Educators in Agr., Res. Officers Assn., Phi Kappa Phi, Phi Delta Kappa, Alpha Zeta. Designer, constructor 1848-sq.-foot energy-efficient home, 1979. Home: 1461 Paradise Park Claremore OK 74017

TITUS, GEORGE FRANCIS, accountant; b. Clarendon, Pa., Jan. 2, 1898; s. Smith Luther and Mary Frances (McBride) T.; B.S., U. Okla., 1927; M.S., Columbia, 1928; postgrad. Harvard Grad. Sch. Arts and Sci., 1932; M.A. Yale, 1932; m. Edna Mae Brown. Accountant various accounting firms, N.Y.C., 1928-32; chief field auditor, Dept. Agr., 1934-35; financial analyst, Dept. Internal Revenue, 1935-40; chief auditor Dept. Navy, Phila., 1941-45, mem. Navy Contract Renegotiation Bd., 1945-46, chief accountant Pearl Harbor Naval Shipyard Hawaii, 1947-49, dep. controller Mil. Sea Transport Service N.Y., 1949-50; financial analyst ECA, 1950-53; deptl. internal auditor, Treasury Dept., Washington, 1953-63; former prof. econ. history Southeastern U., now ret. Mem. Am. Inst. C.P.A.'s, Yale Engring. and Sci. Assn., Acacia, Chi Beta, Sigma Alpha Epsilon. Home: 4501 Arlington Blvd Arlington VA 22203

TOBAL, MARCOS ANDRÉS, recording studio exec.; b. Buenos Aires, Argentina, Sept. 19, 1952; s. José Salomón and Salha Joyce T.; came to U.S., 1969, resident, 1978; B.S. in E.E., U. Miami, 1975. Bus. asso. Panam Colombia de Plásticos, S.A., Bogotá, Colombia, 1965—; elec. engr. Nat. Electronics, Mexico City, 1975; adminstr., chief elec. engr. Studio Center Sound Recs., Inc., North Miami, Fla., 1975—; pres. Overtone, Inc., Electronics Research, North Miami; sec.-treas. Train Tracks Pub., North Miami, 1975—; pres. Avatar Prodns., Inc., North Miami, 1979—; pres. Harbour Terr., Inc., land devel. corp., Bay Harbor Islands, Fla., 1980—. Recipient Gold Record awards for Do You Wanna Get Funky With Me, 1977, Fantasy Love Affair, 1978, Foxy, 1978, Dance With Me, 1978, Get Off, 1978. Mem. Audio Engring. Soc., IEEE. Office: care Harbour Terr Inc 1160 Kane Concourse Bay Harbor Islands FL 33154

TOBIN, NEIL WILLIAM, priest, ednl. adminstr.; b. Worthington, Iowa, July 14, 1932; s. Frd and Eleanor Margaret (Welter) T.; B.A., Loras Coll., 1954; S.T.B., Gregorian U., 1956, S.T.L., 1958; M.A., Fordham U., 1965, Ph.D., 1967; H.C.D. (hon.) Palmer Coll., 1974. Ordained priest Roman Catholic Ch., 1957; tchr. St. Patrick's High Sch., Cedar Rapids, Iowa, 1959-60; faculty Loras Coll., Debuque, Iowa, 1960-77, acad. dean, 1972-74, v.p. for acad. affairs, 1975-77; pres. Belmont (N.C.) Abbey Coll., 1978—; mem. Iowa State Advisory Com. on Tchr. Edn. and Certification, 1970-77, chmn., 1974-76. Bd. dirs. Dubuque Symphony Orch., 1974-76, 2d v.p., 1975-76; bd. dirs. Worldwide Marriage Encounter, 1979—. Mem. Am. Assn. Higher Edn., Delta Epsilon Sigma (nat. sec-treas. 1972—). Home: 8308 Meadow Lakes Dr Charlotte NC 28210 Office: Presidents Office Belmont Abbey College Belmont NC 28012

TOBOLOWSKY, JACK LEHMAN, textile co. exec.; b. Dallas, Jan. 16, 1917; s. Reuben and Etta Gertrude (Tobolowsky) T.; B.B.A., U. Tex., 1937; m. Josephine Pergament, Feb. 7, 1943; children—Dona Tobolowsky Stiffel, Ira, George, Myra Tobolowsky Prescott. Sr. engr. Western Electric Co., N.Y., 1944-49; gen. mgr. Tex Style Mfg. Co., Midlothian, 1949-59; pres. Midlo Textile Co., Midlothian and Dallas, 1959-63; pres. Wolf Textile Co., Dallas, 1963—; also engaged in ranching. Served with AUS, 1942-44. Mem. Phi Sigma Delta. Home: 5909 Waggoner Dr Dallas TX 75230 Office: 2214 Pacific Ave Dallas TX 75201

TOBON, HECTOR, physician; b. Argelia, Colombia, Dec. 5, 1931; came to U.S., 1969, naturalized, 1980; s. Emilio Tobon and Mercedes Escobar de Tobon; B.S., U. Antioquia, 1952; M.D., Nat. U. Colombia, 1959; m. Miryam Castrellon, Jan. 30, 1961; children—Beatriz L., Paula C. Intern, St. John of God Hosp., Bogotá, Colombia, 1960-61; plant physician, coordinator med. edn. Ecopetrol Refining Plant, Barrancabermeja, Colombia, 1961-69; resident Franklin Sq. Hosp., Balt., 1969-72, Md. Rehab. Center, Balt., 1973; practice medicine specializing in family medicine, Austin Tex., 1976—; cons. physician Oak Crest Manor Nursing Homes, 1978—, IRS, 1979—. Active, Travis County Anti-Alcoholic Program. Diplomate Am. Bd. Family Practice. Fellow Am. Acad. Family Physicians; mem. Am. Occupational Med. Assn., Am. Soc. Tropical Medicine and Hygiene. Editor-in-chief: U-235, Generation. Office: 2404 S Interstate Hwy 35 Austin TX 78704

TOCHAROEN, AHRAYA, physician; b. Samuthprakarn, Thailand, July 22, 1938; s. Tavin and Yaun T.; student Chulalongkorn U., Bangkok, Thailand, 1958-59; M.D., U. Med. Scis., Dhonburi, Thailand, 1963; diplomate tropical medicine and hygiene U. Mahidol, Thailand, 1969; m. Gridsana Tocharoen, Aug. 15, 1969; children—Aunchana, Aunyika. Staff officer Thailand Ministry Public Health mobile unit N.E. Thailand, 1964-69; rotating intern Middlesex Meml. Hosp., Middletown, Conn., 1970-71; resident in pediatrics Richland Meml. Hosp., Columbia, S.C., 1971-73; staff Beaufort-Jasper Comprehensive Health Service Inc., Ridgeland, S.C., 1973—. Diplomate Am. Bd. Family Practice. Fellow Am. Coll. Angiology, Am. Acad. Family Physicians, Am. Acad. Pediatrics (asso.), Am. Coll. Chest Physicians (asso.); mem. Am. Coll. Emergency Physicians, Am. Geriatrics Soc., Am. Coll. Cryosurgery, Am. Public Health Assn. Buddhist. Home: 1614 Battery Creek Rd Beaufort SC 29902 Office: PO Box 357 Ridgeland SC 29936

TODD, EDWARD PAUL JOSEPH, surgeon, educator; b. Chgo., Aug. 12, 1941; s. Edward William and Georgine Marilyn T.; B.A., Baylor U., 1963, M.D., 1968, Ph.D., 1969; m. Marilyn Debner, Dec. 26, 1965; children—Erin, Edward, Rachael, Daphne. Intern, U. Minn. Hosp. and Clinics, 1969-70; resident in surgery, 1970-74; asst. prof. surgery U. Ky. Med. Center Hosp., Lexington, 1974-77, asso. prof. surgery, chmn. cardio-thoracic surgery, 1977—; cons. staff VA Hosp., Lexington, 1977—. Fellow Am. Coll. Chest Physicians, Am. Coll. Cardiology A.C.S.; mem. So. Thoracic Surg. Assn., Thoracic Surgery Dirs. Assn., Soc. Thoracic Surgeons, Am. Heart Assn., Ky. Surg. Soc., Ky. Thoracic Soc., Assn. Acad. Surgery, Southeastern Pediatric Cardiology Soc., Ky. Med. Assn., Fayette County Med. Assn., Lexington Surg. Soc. Contbr. articles to med. jours. Home: 604 Galaxie Dr Lexington KY 40502 Office: Cardio Thoracic Surgery Ky Med Center Lexington KY 40536

TODD, GRANT EDWARD, carpet co. exec.; b. Eugene, Oreg., Mar. 9, 1939; s. Roy Texas and Gladys Katherine (Stofiel) T.; B.S. in Sociology, U. Oreg., 1961; m. Kathleen Ann Chasse, Dec. 13, 1969; children—Jennifer Leigh, Adam Kelleher. Asst. sales promotion mgr. U.S. Plywood, N.Y.C., 1966-69; nat. promotional mgr. Sylvania Electronic Components, N.Y.C., 1969-70; dir. communications Trend Mills, Rome, Ga., 1970-74; v.p. market devel. Interface Flooring Systems, LaGrange, Ga., 1974—. Mem. Sales Promotion Execs. Assn. Club: Optimist. Home: Cameron Mill Rd LaGrange GA 30240 Office: Orchard Hill Rd LaGrange GA 30240

TODD, LEE BARNHARDT, physician; b. Newport News, Va., Mar. 13, 1905; s. Lee Resser and Mary (Barger) T.; B.S., Coll. William and Mary, 1927; M.D., Med. Coll. Va., 1932; m. Daisy Burns, May 13, 1935; children—Jane Elizabeth Todd Young, John Richard, Ann Lee Todd Jones. Intern hosp. div. Med. Coll. Va., Richmond, 1932-34; gen. pvt. practice Quinwood, W.Va., 1934-43, 1951—; dir. Health Dept., Newport News, Va., 1946-51; mem. staff Greenbrier Valley Hosp.; examiner Draft Bd., 1946-51. Bd. dirs. Salvation Army; mem. Pres.'s Council Coll. William and Mary. Served to maj. U.S. Army, 1943-46. Fellow Royal Coll. of Health; mem. Am. Geriatrics Soc., AMA, Greenbrier, W.Va. med. socs., Trudeau Soc., W.Va. Pediatric Soc., Am. Heart Assn., Nat. Geog. Soc., Internat. Platform Assn., Order White Jackets (pres.), Pi Kappa Alpha, Alpha Omega Alpha, Omicron Delta Kappa, Chi Beta Phi, Theta Chi Delta, Phi Chi. Mason (Shriner). Club: Willow Wood Country (Hinton, W.Va.); Rainelle Golf. Address: Quinwood WV 25981

TODD, M(ALYN) ALFRED, radiologist; b. Memphis, Apr. 24, 1943; s. Alfred Cleo and Myra (Lowry) T.; B.A., Southwestern U. at Memphis, 1965; M.D., U. Tenn., 1968; m. Elizabeth Odom, Feb. 28, 1964; children—Beth, Meri, Rebecca. Intern, Roanoke (Va.) Meml. Hosp., 1968-69; resident U. Tenn., Memphis, 1975-78, chief resident, 1978; family practice medicine, Lafayette, Tenn., 1971-75; practice medicine specializing in diagnostic radiology, Gallatin, Tenn., 1978—; staff radiologist Sumner County Meml. Hosp., Gallatin, 1978—. Served to capt. M.C., U.S. Army, 1969-71. Diplomate Am. Bd. Radiology. Mem. Tenn. Med. Assn., Sumner County Med. Soc., Tenn. and Middle Tenn. Radiol. Socs. Baptist. Clubs: Rotary, Bluegrass Country. Home: Route 3 Grassland Shores Gallatin TN 37066 Office: Medical Mall Gallatin TN 37066

TODD, PATRICIA HOVATTER, ecologist; b. Salisbury, Md., July 23, 1952; d. Elston Gerald and Myra Ella (Howard) Hovatter; B.S. in Biology, Salisbury State Coll., 1974; M.S. in Biology, Tenn. Tech. U., 1976; m. Robert Millard Todd, Jr., Oct. 5, 1974; Grad. teaching asst. Tenn. Tech. U., Cookeville, 1975-76; hatchery mgr. I Tenn. Wildlife Resources Agency, Nashville, 1976, wildlife mgr. I, 1976-77; environ. planner II Tenn. Dept. Transp., Nashville, 1977, environ. planner III, 1977—. Mem. Nat. Wildlife Fedn., N.Am. Benthol. Soc., Phi Kappa Phi, Sigma Xi, Beta Beta Beta. Democrat. Methodist. Contbr. articles to profl. publs. Home: 340 Cane Ridge Rd Antioch TN 37013 Office: 706 Church St 516 Doctors Bldg Nashville TN 37219

TODES, JAY LITTMAN, educator; b. Galveston, Tex., Sept. 26, 1925; s. Lew and Dorothy T.; B.A., U. Tex., Austin, 1946, M.A., 1949; Ed.D., U. Houston, 1967; m. Nancy P. Goldberg, June 29, 1967; children—Jennifer Leslie, Douglas Matthew. Asst. prof. econs. Trinity U., San Antonio, 1949-52; personnel dir. Battelstein's, Houston, 1953-54; prin. Galveston Ind. Sch. Dist., 1954-62, Dallas Ind. Sch. Dist., 1962-66; chmn. bus. div. Richland Coll., Dallas County Community Coll. Dist., 1967-74, dir. mid-mgmt. North Lake Coll., 1977—; organizer Island Tchr. Credit Union, pres., 1954-62. Mem. Am. Vocat. Assn., Tex. Vocat. Assn., Adminstrv. Mgmt. Soc., Tex. Jr. Coll. Mgmt. Educators Assn. (pres. 1970-72), Phi Delta Phi. Club: Masons. Author: Management and Motivation: An Introduction to Supervision, 1977. Home: 4623 Melissa Ln Dallas TX 75229 Office: North Lake College 2000 Walnut Hill Ln Irving TX 75062

TOFFANELLO, ANGELO GIUSEPPE, hotel exec.; b. Venice, Italy, Mar. 12, 1940; s. Pietro and Angela (Bisson) T.; came to U.S., 1969, naturalized, 1975; student LaSalle Extension U., 1975-79. With various restaurants, hotels throughout Switzerland, Eng., British Isles, 1958-65; chef saucier and gardemanger Inverurie Hotel, Paget, Bermuda, 1965-66; chef de cuisine Cafe Valencia, Freeport, Grand Bahama Island, 1966-68, chef saucier Princess Hotels Internat., Grand Bahama Island, 1968-69; banquet chef Eden Roc Hotel, Miami Beach, Fla., 1969; exec. chef Playboy Towers Hotel, Chgo., 1970-71; partner, chef Del Vecchio's Restaurant, San Francisco, 1971-72; exec. chef, ops. mgr. for gourmet in-flight catering, Eastern Airlines, Voisin of Miami Beach, 1972-75; food and beverage dir. Caribbean Harbour Club, St. Thomas, U.S. V.I., 1975, MRC Motel Corp., Orlando, Fla., 1975-77, Hospitality Mgmt. Corp., Wichita (Kans.) Royale, 1977—; tchr. continental cooking Alliance Francaise of Wichita, 1978-79. Recipient First Prize award Mid-Am. Culinary Show, Wichita, 1977. Mem. Food Services Exec. Assn., Am. Culinary Fedn., Fla. Restaurant Assn., Kans. Restaurant Assn., Am. Mgmt. Assn. Home: 11102 Heathrow St Orlando FL 32809 Office: 125 N Market St Wichita KS 67202

TOFTOY, CHARLES NELSON, systems engring. co. exec., former army officer; b. West Point, N.Y., Mar. 18, 1935; s. Holger Nelson and Hazel E. (Schweikert) T.; B.S. in Engring., U.S. Mil. Acad., 1958; M.B.A., Tulane U., 1969, postgrad., 1977—; m. Patricia Louise Nollenberger, Feb. 8, 1964; children—Eric Nils, York Robert Holger. Commd. 2d lt. U.S. Army, 1958, advanced through grades to lt. col., 1978; comdr. 82d Airborne Div., Ft. Bragg, N.C., 1963-64; advisor 7th VN Airborne Bn., 1965-66; dep. G3 and Bn. S3, 1st Inf. Div., 1969-70; chief ops. research analyst Orgn. of Joint Chiefs of Staff, Pentagon, Washington, 1971-73; exec. officer U.S. Army Inf. Brigade, C.Z., 1973-75; chief ops. research analyst Office of Dep. Chief of Staff for Research Devel. and Acquisition, Dept. of Army, Pentagon, Washington, 1975-78, ret., 1978; adj. prof. mgmt. Golden Gate U., Southeastern U., Washington, 1975—; dir. planning Analytical Systems Engring. Corp., Arlington, Va., 1978-80; mgr. Raytheon Service Co., Washington, 1980; mgmt. cons., 1976—; Active Nat. Capital Area council Boy Scouts Am., 1976-79; chmn. Youth Activities Center, C.Z., 1973-75. Decorated D.F.C., Legion of Merit, Bronze Star (6), Air medal (7), Purple Heart (2); Gallantry Cross (Vietnam). Mem. Ops. Research Soc. Am., Active Corps of Execs., AAUP, Small Bus. Inst. Assn., Tulane Bus. Soc., AAU. Episcopalian. Clubs: Road Runners Am. Masons. Home: 3800 24th St N Arlington VA 22207 Office: 2341 Jefferson Davis Hwy Suite 826 Arlington VA 22202

TOKOLY, MARY ANDREE, clin. microbiologist; b. Manila, Dec. 4, 1940; d. Robert Francis and Ruby Waunita (Shriner) T.; B.S., Tex. Woman's U., 1962, M.S., 1964, Ph.D., 1974. Instr. microbiology Victoria (Tex.) Coll., 1964-66; asst. prof. microbiology Kans. State Coll., Pittsburg, 1966-68; grad. teaching asst. microbiology Tex. Woman's U., Denton, 1968-74; asst. prof. microbiology Kans. Newman Coll., Wichita, Kans., 1974-75; clin. microbiologist Nix Clin. Lab., San Antonio, 1975-77, Met. Gen. Hosp., San Antonio, 1977—. Mem. San Antonio Intercity Infection Control Com., 1978—. Robert A. Welch research fellow, 1972-73. Mem. Am. Soc. Clin. Pathologists (cert. microbiologist), Am. Soc. Med. Technologists (cert. med. technician), AAUW (dir. San Antonio br.), N.Y. Acad. Scis., Am. Soc. Microbiology, Soc. Indsl. Microbiology, AAUW, Sigma Xi. Club: Altrusa of San Antonio (dir.).

TOLEDO, TONY MILTON, internist; b. Miami, Fla., Sept. 21, 1939; s. Anthony Arnau and Polly (Reid) T.; B.S., Rollins Coll., 1961; M.D., Tulane U., 1965; m. Sandra Rainey, Aug. 19, 1962; children—Clark Anthony, Katherine Rainey, Blair Dewitt. Intern, Brooke Gen. Hosp., Ft. Sam Houston, San Antonio, 1965-66, resident in internal medicine, 1966-69; practice medicine specializing in internal medicine Internal Medicine Assos., San Antonio, 1972—; med. staff Nix., Baptist, Santa Rosa, Met., Methodist, Community hosps., Normandy Terr., Carriage Sq., St. Benedict, Morningside Manor nursing homes; clin. asst. prof. Med. Sch., U. Tex., San Antonio, 1969—; adivser to com. for med. assts. San Antonio Coll., 1975—. Active YMCA, Tex. Polit. Action Com. Served to maj. M.C., U.S. Army, 1965-72. Decorated Bronze Star medal. Mem. AMA (physicians recognition award 1972), Tex. Med. Assn., Bexar County Med. Soc., Am., Tex. thoracic socs., Tex. Soc. Internal Medicine, A.C.P., Am. Coll. Chest Physicians, Am. Soc. Internal Medicine, Tex. Diabetic Assn., Am. Lung Assn. (pres. Alamo Area 1977), Am. Assn. Med. Assts. (state adviser Tex. chpt. 1975), San Antonio Power Squadron, Lambda Chi Alpha, Nu Sigma Nu. Republican. Baptist. Contbr. articles to med. jours. Home: 11414 Destiny St San Antonio TX 78216 Office: 1420 Nix Profl Bldg San Antonio TX 78205

TOLF, ROBERT WALTER, writer; b. Chgo., Aug. 3, 1929; s. Carl Oscar and Margarethe (Zeltner) T.; B.A., Harvard U., 1951; Ph.D., U. Rochester, 1957; m. Nancy E. List, Aug. 9, 1952; 1 dau., Carolyn Anne. With Fgn. Service U.S. Dept. State, 1957-70, assigned to Scandinavia, 1957-65, Switzerland, 1965-70; editor, writer, columnist, Fla., 1971—; restaurant editor Fla. Trend mag., 1972—; columnist Ft. Lauderdale News/Sun-Sentinel, 1975—; lectr. to acad., ch. and community groups. Served with U.S. Army, 1954-57. Mem. Nat. Speakers Assn. Clubs: Fox; Harvard (Palm Beach)(Broward County); Varsity. Author: How to Survive Your First Six Months in Florida, 1972; Best Restaurants Florida, 1977; Country Inns of the Old South, 1978: Best Restaurants on Florida's Gold Coast, 1979; The Russian Rockefellers: The Saga of the Nobel Family and the Russian Oil Industry, 1976; contbr. articles to N.Y. Times, Mainliner, others. Home and Office: 1980 Sharon St Boca Raton FL 33432

TOLLIVER, OLLIE BELL, guidance counselor; b. Lamont, Miss., Sept. 21, 1944; d. Booker T. and Mary Lee (Hawkins) Wright; B.S. in English, Jackson State Coll., 1966; M.S.Ed. in Guidance and Counseling, Jackson State U., 1976; m. Johnny Edward Tolliver, June 18, 1966; children—Felicia, Johnny, Patricia Denise. Tchr., Madison County Public Schs., Madison, Miss., 1966, Indianaola (Miss.) Public Schs. 1966-67; sec. Harvard U. Housing, 1968-70, Jackson State U., 1973-77; counselor Jackson State U. Grad. Sch., 1977—. Cons. to commissary rep. for Dean's Office, U.S. Mil. Acad., West Point, N.Y., 1972-73. Mem. Am. Personnel and Guidance Assn., Jackson State U. Alumni Assn., Jack and Jill Am., Inc., Alpha Kappa Alpha. Baptist. Home: 327 Overlook Circle Jackson MS 39217 Office: Jackson State U Counseling Center Jackson MS 39217

TOLO, KENNETH WILLIAM, univ. adminstr.; b. Bemidji, Minn., Nov. 21, 1940; s. Modolf W. and Evelyn Irene (Larsen) T.; B.A. in Math., summa cum laude, Concordia Coll., 1962; M.A. in Math., U. Nebr., 1964, Ph.D., 1968; M.A. in Public Affairs, U. Minn., 1972; m. Roselyn JoAnn Solberg, June 27, 1964; children—Kristi-Anne, Julie Elizabeth. Asst. prof. math. U. Tenn., Knoxville, 1968-70; asst. prof. Lyndon B. Johnson Sch. Public Affairs, U. Tex., Austin, 1972-74, asso. prof., 1974-80, prof. public affairs, 1980—, asso. dean, 1975, acting dean, 1975-76, asso. v.p. acad. affairs univ., 1979—; dir. Office Policy Devel. and Coordination, Office Sec., U.S. Dept. Commerce, Washington, 1977; cons. to Pension Benefit Guaranty Corp., U.S. Dept. Commerce, HEW, Inst. for Ednl. Leadership, 1971—; co-dir. vocat., higher and adult edn. group, Ednl. Study Mission to USSR, 1974; dir. Tex. Ednl. Seminar (for state legislators), 1973-76; project dir. U.S. Dept. Labor, 1978-79; mem. U.S. del. Internat. Assn. Schs. and Insts. Adminstrn. Roundtable, Yugoslavia, 1976. Recipient 1st Sec.'s Medal award U.S. Dept. Commerce, 1977; NDEA, NSF fellow, 1962-66. Mem. Policy Studies Orgn., Soc., AAAS, Sigma Xi. Lutheran. Author: Higher Education in Texas: Student Aid and Governance, 1978; Preparation for Apprenticeship through CEIA, 1979; Coordination of State and Federal Apprenticeship Administration, 1980; editor: Beyond Today's Energy Crisis, 1975; The American City: Realities and Possibilities, 1974; Educating A Nation: The Changing American Commitment, 1973; others. Home: 9000 Currywood Dr Austin TX 78759 Office: MAI 201 Univ of Tex Austin TX 78712

TOM, BALDWIN HENG, immunobiologist; b. San Francisco, Sept. 19, 1940; s. Fred and Lily Tom; B.A., U. Calif., Berkeley, 1963; M.S., U. Ariz., 1967, Ph.D., 1970; m. Madeline Reiko Nobori, June 13, 1964; children—Darren Christopher, Alyson Lindsy. Research fellow Stanford U., 1970-73; asst. prof. Northwestern U., 1973-77; asst. prof. immunology U. Tex. Med. Sch., Houston, 1977—; organizer, program chmn. Nat. Symposium on Liposomes and Immunobiology, 1980. Recipient Research Career Devel. award Nat. Cancer Inst., 1979. Mem. AAAS, Am. Assn. Cancer Research, Am. Assn. Cancer Research, Am. Assn. Immunologists, Fedn. Am. Scientists, Soc. Exptl. Biology and Medicine, Tissue Culture Assn., N.Y. Acad. Scis. Presbyterian. Patent on process of producing carcinoembryonic antigen. Office: U Tex Med Sch Houston TX 77030

TOMAN, JOSEPH ALBERT, tooling co. exec.; b. Chgo., July 30, 1938; s. Joseph Thomas and Elsie Ann (Doubek) T.; B.S., Purdue U., 1961; m. Joyce Lynn McKee, Sept. 2, 1961; children—John Murray, Jane Ellen. Indsl. engr. Timken Bearing Co., Canton, Ohio, 1961-62; v.p., gen. mgr., dir. McKee Engring. Co., Marianna, Fla., 1963—. Jackson County chpt. chmn. ARC, 1973-76, div. council rep., 1978—. Mem. Marianna Rotary (sec. 1968-70, pres. 1979-80, dir. 1971-73), Jackson County C. of C. (dir.), Soc. Mfg. Engrs., Nat. Fedn. Ind. Business, Lambda Chi Alpha. Methodist (ofcl. bd. fin. chmn., ch. lay leader). Clubs: Marianna Country (pres. 1971), Olympia Spa Country. Home: 301 Berkshire Rd Marianna FL 32446 Office: 1100 Indsl Pk Marianna FL 32446

TOMCZAK, CHRISTINA MARY, banker; b. Yonkers, Sept. 24, 1946; d. Henry Peter and Jane Mary (Brzozowski) T.; B.S., Fla. State U., 1968. Sr. examiner, Fed. Res. Bank Atlanta, 1968-77; v.p. Am. Bancshares, Inc., Miami, now sr. v.p.; dir. 2d Nat. Bank Clearwater (Fla.), Exec. Bank, Ft. Lauderdale, Fla., Univ. City Bank, Gainesville, Fla., 2d Nat. Bank North Miami Beach (Fla.), Gt. Am. Bank of Pinellas, Clearwater, Gt. Am. Bank of Broward County, Ft. Lauderdale, Gt. Am. Bank of Gainesville, Gt. Am. Bank of North Miami Beach, Gt. Am. Bank of Davie. Mem. Bank Adminstrn. Inst., Planning Execs. Inst., Am. Bankers Assn., Am. Mgmt. Assn., Gamma Sigma Sigma (nat. pres., nat. dir., 1969—). Home: 10812 Kendall Dr N Q-26 Miami FL 33176 Office: 11755 Biscayne Blvd North Miami FL 33161

TOMLINSON, CLIFTON HARVEY, ins. co. exec.; b. Lott, Tex., Sept. 5, 1923; s. Clifton Robert and Cora Jo (Sills) T.; B.B.A., U. Tex., Austin, 1950; m. Norma Lee Stephens, Oct. 6, 1962; 1 stepson, Leslie Earl Sorrels, Jr. Purchasing agt. Wilson X-Ray and Surg. Co., Austin, Tex., 1950-51; with Farmers Ins. Group, Austin, 1952—, regional personnel mgr., 1973—; asst. sec. Tex. Farmers Ins. Co., 1976—; dir. Farmers Tex. County Mut. Ins. Co. Served with USAAF, 1942-45, 47-52. Mem. Austin Personnel Assn., Am. Soc. Personnel Adminstrs., CAP. Baptist. Club: Balcones Country. Home: 5303 Ridge Oak Dr Austin TX 78731 Office: 2100 S Interregional Hwy Austin TX 78704

TOMLINSON, LAWRENCE ARCHDALE, III, mfg. co. exec.; b. Charlotte, N.C., Dec. 30, 1952; s. Lawrence Archdale and Sarah Venerable (Sutton) T.; B.S., Wofford Coll., 1975. Mgr. mktg. services Homelite Co., Charlotte, N.C., 1976-77, mgr. advt. and sales promotion, 1977-79, mgr. nat. accounts Homelite div. Textron, 1979—. Adv., Jr. Achievement. Republican. Episcopalian. Office: 14401 Carowinds Blvd Charlotte NC 28217

TOMLINSON, WILLIAM HOLMES, educator; b. Thornton, Ark., Apr. 12, 1922; s. Hugh Oscar and Lucy Gray (Holmes) T.; B.S., U.S. Mil. Acad., 1943; student Air Command Staff Coll., 1958; M.B.A., U. Ala., 1960; M.S. in Internat. Affairs, George Washington U., 1966; grad. U.S. Army War Coll., 1966; Ph.D. in Bus. Adminstrn., Am. U., 1974; postgrad. Advanced Mgmt. Program, Harvard U., 1968, 69; m. Dorothy Payne, June 10, 1947 (dec.); children—Jane Axtell, Lucy Gray, William Payne; m. 2d, Florence Mood Smith, May 1, 1969 (div.); m. 3d, Suzanne Scollard Gill, Mar. 16, 1977. Commd. 2d lt., arty., U.S. Army, 1943, advanced through grades to col., 1966; aide de camp comdg. gen. 8th Army, 1945-48; mem. Office of Under Sec. Army, Pentagon, Washington, 1961-64; comdr. 2d Bn., 8th Arty. and 7th Div. Arty., S. Korea, 1964-65; faculty Indsl. Coll. Armed Forces, Ft. McNair, Washington, 1966-72, ret., 1973; faculty U. North Fla., Jacksonville, 1973—, asso. prof. mgmt., 1976—; mem. Nat. Def. Exec. Res., Fed. Emergency Mgmt. Agy., 1976-80. Decorated Bronze Star, Legion of Merit, Philippine Liberation medal, Japanese Occupation medal; recipient Freedom Found. award, 1973; accredited personnel diplomate. Mem. Acad. Mgmt., So. Mgmt. Assn., Am. Soc. Personnel Adminstrn., Indsl. Relations Research Assn., Acad. Internat. Bus., Co. Mil. Historians, Nat. Eagle Scout Assn., West Point Soc. N. Fla. (pres. 1976), Mil. Order Stars and Bars. Presbyterian (elder). Clubs: Army Navy, Army Navy Country, Kappa Alpha Order, Masons (32 deg.). Contbr. articles and case studies to profl. jours. and books. Home: 1890 Shadowlawn Jacksonville FL 32205 Office: U North Fla PO Box 17074 Jacksonville FL 32216

TOMPKINS, CURTIS JOHNSTON, indsl. engr.; b. Roanoke, Va., July 14, 1942; s. Joseph Buford and Rebecca (Johnston) T.; B.S., Va. Poly. Inst., 1965, M.S., 1967; Ph.D., Ga. Inst. Tech., 1971; m. Mary Katherine Hasle, Sept. 5, 1964; children—Robert, Joseph, Rebecca. Indsl. engr. E.I. DuPont de Nemours, Richmond, Va., 1965-67; instr. Sch. Indsl. and Systems Engring., Ga. Inst. Tech., Atlanta, 1968-71; asst. prof. Grad. Bus. Sch., U. Va., Charlottesville, 1971-72, asso. prof., 1972-77; prof., chmn. indsl. engring. W.Va. U., Morgantown,

1977-80, dean Coll. Engring., 1980—; cons. maj. corps. and govt. agys. Chmn. Wesley Found. Council on Ministries, U. Va., 1972-75, 1st United Meth. Ch. Council on Ministries, Charlottesville, 1973-74; bd. dirs. YMCA, Charlottesville, 1973-75; mem. Epilepsy Program Adv. Bd., 1975-77. Mem. Ops. Research Soc. Am., Am. Inst. Indsl. Engrs. (sr.), Inst. Mgmt. Scis., Am. Statis. Assn., Am. Soc. Engring. Edn., Sigma Xi, Alpha Pi Mu, Phi Kappa Phi. Methodist. Editor: (with L.E. Grayson) Management of Public Sector and Nonprofit Organizations, 1980; author chpt. Encyclopedia for Professional Management, 1978. Home: 1453 Anderson Ave Morgantown WV 26505 Office: WVa U Coll Engring Morgantown WV 26506

TOMPKINS, ROBERT GEORGE, physician; b. Portland, Oreg., May 29, 1923; s. George Henry and Minnie (Davies) T.; B.S., U. Wash., 1943; M.B., Northwestern U., 1947, M.D., 1949; M.S., U. Minn., 1954; m. Rosemarie Nowicki, June 6, 1948 (dec. 1960); children—Timothy Michael, Mary Eileen, George Henry, Robert George. Intern, King County Hosp., Seattle, 1948-49, resident, 1949-50; fellow, 1st asst. Mayo Found., Rochester, Minn., 1950-54; practice medicine specializing in cardiology and internal medicine, Tulsa, 1954—; mem. staff St. Francis Hosp., chief of staff, 1964, med. dir., 1968—; asso. clin. prof. medicine Tulsa Med. Coll.-U. Okla.; v.p. William K. Warren Med. Research Center. Med. chmn. Guatemala Mission Hosp., Diocese Oklahoma City and Tulsa; coordinator Tulsa planning program Okla. Regional Med. Program; mem. Tulsa Health and Hosp. Planning Council; trustee St. Francis Hosp. Diplomate Am. Bd. Internal Medicine; decorated Knight of Equestrian Order Holy Sepulchre of Jerusalem (Vatican). Fellow Am. Coll. Physicians, Royal Coll. Medicine, Am. Coll. Cardiology; mem. AAAS, AMA, Am. Diabetic Assn., Am., Tulsa County (pres. 1959) heart assns., Am. Rheumatism Assn., Mayo Alumni Assn., Alpha Kappa Kappa. Club: K.C. Contbr. articles in field to prof. jours.; editor Jour. Okla. State Med. Assn., 1974—. Home: 2221 E 22d Pl Tulsa OK 74114 Office: 6161 S Yale St Tulsa OK 74136

TONK, EDWARD S., educator; b. Raleigh, N.C., Jan. 16, 1945; s. James William and Emily (Rogers) T.; B.A. in English Lit., U. N.C., 1967, M.A. in Comparative Lit., 1969; Ph.D. (fellow), Northwestern U., 1973; m. Elizabeth Susan Creamer, June 20, 1975; children—Allen Stewart, Susan Rogers. Asst. prof. English, N.C. State U., Raleigh, 1973-75, asso. prof., 1975—, chmn. dept., 1979—; project leader studies in Renaissance lit. Northwestern U., Evanston, Ill., 1980— (on leave). Mem. MLA, Renaissance Studies Soc., Southeastern Modern Lang. Assn., Phi Beta Kappa, Phi Delta Theta. Contbr. articles to profl. jours. Home: 7396 Bright Oaks Ln Raleigh NC 27396 Office: 413 Desmond Dr Schaumburg IL 60193

TOOHIG, MICHAEL FRANCIS, elec. products co. exec.; b. Lawrence, Mass., Dec. 9, 1924; s. Timothy Michael and Catherine (Walsh) T.; B.S. cum laude, Boston Coll., 1949, M.S., 1950; postgrad. Ind. U., 1964; m. Barbara Jean Bissonnette, June 30, 1956; children—Delsina M., Timothy J., Terrence M., Michele T., Aimee L. Supr. def. research div. Firestone Tire & Rubber Co., Akron, O., 1950-53; v.p., gen. mgr. ITT Tube and Sensor Labs., Fort Wayne, Ind., 1953-72; v.p., dir. engring. Electron Tube div. ITT, Roanoke, Va., 1972-79; pres., gen. mgr. Aerospace Optical Products div. ITT, Roanoke, 1979—. Chmn. radiation def. Ft. Wayne Civil Def., 1957-60. Chmn. bd. Second Act. Inc., Roanoke, 1975-77. Served with AUS, 1943-46. Decorated Bronze Star. Mem. I.E.E.E., Assn. U.S. Army. Roman Catholic. Patentee in field. Home: 5207 N Spring Dr Roanoke VA 24019 Office: 7635 Plantation Rd Roanoke VA 24019

TOOL, H. RAYMOND, mfg. co. exec.; b. Kansas City, Mo., Feb. 3, 1938; s. Herman R. and Lillian M. (Pruitt) T.; B.S., U. Kansas City, 1960; M.S., U. Mo., 1963; Ph.D., Heed U., 1979; m. Brenda L. Toot, Mar. 25, 1961; children—Harold R., Carol D. Sales mgr. Hach Chem. Co., 1965-74; v.p., sec. Branchemco, Inc. Jacksonville, Fla., 1974—; pres. Indsl. Materials Corp., Jacksonville, 1977—, Designs Unltd., 1977—; partner Western Way Warehouse, 1976—. Mem. Am. Chem. Soc., Am. Soc. Heating, Refrigerating and Air Conditioning Engrs., Tech. Assn. Pulp and Paper Internat. Republican. Presbyterian. Clubs: Masons, Shriners. Home: 1301 1st St S Jacksonville Beach FL 32250 Office: 8286 Western Way Circle Jacksonville FL 32216

TOOMBS, BARRY DONALD, radiologist; b. Dallas, June 9, 1949; s. Donald Royce and Wanda Marcille (Heavener) T.; B.A., U. Tex., Austin, 1971; M.D., U. Tex., Galveston, 1974; m. Linda Dianne Pittard, Aug. 5, 1972; children—Gretchen Linsay, Jonathan Barry Edward. Intern, Baylor Med. Coll., 1974-75; resident, clin. fellow in diagnostic radiology Mass. Gen. Hosp./Harvard Med. Sch., Boston, 1975-78; asst. prof. radiology U. Tex. Med. Sch., Houston, 1978—, chief gastrointestinal radiology Hermann Hosp., 1978—. Diplomate Am. Bd. Radiology. Mem. AMA, Harris County Med. Assn., Tex. Med. Assn., Am. Coll. Radiology. Baptist. Home: 2344 Watts St Houston TX 77030 Office: 6431 Fannin St Houston TX 77030

TOPOREK, EDWARD JOSEPH, security exec.; b. Lackawanna, N.Y., Oct. 14, 1927; s. Frank and Stella (Sopecki) T.; student pub. schs., Lackawanna; m. Mary Eileen Hennessy, Dec. 2, 1953; children—Edward Joseph, Victoria, James. Joined U.S. Air Force, 1945, ret., 1965; with Martin Marietta, Orlando (Fla.) Aero Space Div., 1966-70; with Sentinel Star Co., Orlando, 1970—, now mgr. security and safety. Adv. com. Valencia Community Coll., 1978—, Seminole Community Coll., 1978—; vol. ARC, 1956—. Mem. Am. Soc. Indsl. Security, Nat. Fire Protection Assn., Assn. Chiefs of Police, Orange County Criminal Justice Council. Republican. Roman Catholic. Home: 201 Jennie Jewel Dr Orlando FL 32806

TOPPE, JONATHAN RICHARD, architect; b. Ann Arbor, Mich., Jan. 4, 1946; s. Morris and Mary Loretta (Boyle) T.; B.Arch. with honors, U. Fla., 1969, M.A. in Architecture, 1971. Architect firms in Tampa and St. Petersburg, Fla., 1971-78; asso. Harvard, Jolly, Marcet & Assos. architects, P.A., St. Peterburg, 1979—; vis. critic, lectr. U. Fla., 1971—; project architect for Freedom Fed. Gandy & Brandon offices, 1972, Humanities and Fine Arts Complex, U. Central Fla., 1972, Sandy Lane and Walsingham elem. schs., Pinellas County, Fla., 1974, Kennedy Sq., Tampa, 1975, Knights Elem. Sch., Hillsborough County, Fla., 1976, Gibbs High Sch. additions and renovation, St. Petersburg, 1977, proposed Jacques Cousteau Marine Scis. Conv. Center, St. Petersburg Beach, 1978, Van Dyck Office Center, St. Petersburg, 1979, 500 room resort hotel, St. Petersburg Beach, 1979. Mem. AIA (chmn. Fla. commn. edn. and research 1977), Nat. Council Archtl. Registration Bds., Suncoast Bus. Roundtable (charter, sec., treas.), Leadership St. Petersburg, Gargoyle Soc., Tau Sigma Delta, Omicron Delta Kappa. Democrat. Club: Suncoast Tiger Bay. Mem. editorial bd. Fla. Architect, 1980. Contbr. articles to profl. jours. Home: 210 14th Ave N Saint Petersburg FL 33701 Office: 2714 9th St N Saint Petersburg FL 33704 also 512 N Florida Ave Tampa FL 33602

TORBERT, CLEMENT CLAY, JR., state justice; b. Opelika, Ala., Aug. 31, 1929; s. Clement Clay and Lynda (Meadows) T.; student U.S. Naval Acad., 1948-49; B.S., Auburn U., 1951; postgrad. U. Md., 1952; LL.B., U. Ala., 1954; m. Gene Hurt, May 2, 1952; children—Mary Dixon, Gene Shealy, Clement Clay III. Admitted to Ala. bar, 1954; practiced in Opelika; city judge, Opelika, 1954-58; partner firm Samford, Torbert, Denson & Horsley, 1959-74; chief justice Ala. Supreme Ct., 1977—; dir. First Nat. Bank Opelika, Opelika-Auburn Broadcasting Co. Mem. Ala. Ho. of Reps., 1958-62, Ala. Senate, 1966-70, 74-76. Served to capt. USAF, 1952-53. Mem. Ala. Acad. Honor, Phi Delta Phi, Phi Kappa Phi, Alpha Tau Omega. Methodist (trustee). Club: Kiwanis. Home: 611 Terracewood Dr Opelika AL 36801 Office: 445 Dexter Ave Montgomery AL 36130

TORBICK, WILLIAM, elec. mfg. exec.; b. Chgo., Dec. 13, 1923; s. Nicholas and Mary (Shuga) T.; student Milw. Sch. Engring., 1946-48; m. Elizabeth Evans, Mar. 5, 1949; children—Susan, Marita J., William D., Nicholas J., Ellen S. With Gen. Elec. Co., 1948—, beginning as service engr. x-ray dept., successively sales rep., dist. sales mgr. mobile radio dept., regional mgr., nat. sales mgr., 1948-75, mgr. mktg. mobile communications bus. div., Lynchburg, Va., 1975—. Served with USAAF, 1942-46. Mem. Assn. Police Communications, Petroleum Engring. Assn., Radio Club Am. Office: General Electric Co Mountain View Rd Lynchburg VA 24502

TORCHIA, AUGUSTUS GERALD, advt. art dir.; b. Utica, N.Y., Sept. 13, 1939; s. Joseph Louis and Anne Marie (Potaro) T.; B. Design, U. Fla., 1961; m. Mary Lynn McNutt, Apr. 15, 1962; children—Michelle, Elizabeth, Andrea. Package designer Package Products, Charlotte, N.C., 1964-67; jr. art dir. Kincaid Advt., Charlotte, 1967-69; with Cargill, Wilson & Acree Advt., Charlotte and Richmond, Va., 1969-76, corp. creative dir., 1974-76; art dir., v.p. Thompson, Torchia & Dymond, Inc., Charlotte, 1976—. Served with AUS, 1961-64. Recipient awards local and internat. advt. competitions; named One of Top 100 Creative People in U.S., Ad Day, 1975. Office: 1323 Durwood Dr Charlotte NC 28204

TORIAN, MERVILLE RUSSELL, SR., constrn. co. exec.; b. Birmingham, Ala., Nov. 28, 1933; s. Ezra Sullivan and Leona (Friend) T.; student U. Ala., 1956; m. Doris Willene Davis, Aug. 28, 1952; children—Merville Russell, William Michael, James Gregory. Supr., Rust Engring. Co., Birmingham, New Orleans, Cleveland, Tenn. and Escanaba, Mich., 1956-70; resident constrn. mgr. Pullman-Swindell Co., Salt Lake City and Ahwaz, Iran, 1970-76; exec. v.p., dir. John Price Assos., Inc., Salt Lake City, 1976-79; mgr. constrn. mktg. Rust Engring. Co., Birmingham, 1979—. Dir., state dir. Cleveland Jaycees, 1962-65. Recipient several public service awards Jaycees. Mem. Soc. Mining Engrs. Presbyterian. Club: Rotary. Home: 1724 Valpar Dr Birmingham AL 35226

TORKELSON, LEIF OSCAR, physician; b. Shelby, Mich., Apr. 5, 1926; s. Ingolf and Anne Martine (Bergsmark von Rockmann) T.; student George Washington U., 1943, U. N.Mex., 1946-47; B.A., Ohio State U., 1949; postgrad. U. Va., 1952-53, M.D., 1957; m. Betty Kirsch, Aug. 29, 1954; children—Kirstann Lee, Leif Erik, Kari Ingabert, Kirk Torleif, Kai Oscar, Inger Kristus. Intern, Mary Fletcher Hosp., Med. Coll. Vt., Burlington, 1957-58; resident in medicine DePaul Hosp., Norfolk, Va., 1958-59; resident in psychiatry N.C. Meml. Hosp., U. N.C., 1959-60; resident medicine Duke U. Affiliated Hosps., Durham, N.C., 1960-61; instr. medicine Sch. Medicine, Western Res. U., Cleve., 1961-62; instr. medicine, asst. prof. medicine U. Ky. Coll. Medicine, 1963-67; vis. physician U. Va. Sch. Medicine, 1967—; pvt. practice internal medicine, Madison, Wis., 1962-63; pvt. practice internal medicine and cardiovascular disease, Harrisonburg, Va., 1968—; clin. investigator for L-Dopa, 1970-71; lectr. in field; conduct of cardiac stress testing studies James Madison Coll., Harrisonburg, 1975-77, also adj. prof. health, 1975-77. Regional cons. Nat. Center Chronic Disease Control of USPHS, Charlottesville, Va., 1967-68. Served with USNR, 1944-45, to lt., 1949-52. Recipient research grants for studies cardiac rehab. and cardiac stress testing Sch. Medicine, Western Res. U. and Crile VA Hosp., 1961-62, Coll. Medicine, U. Ky., 1965-67. Mem. A.M.A. (Physician Recognition award 1969, 72, 76-79), Am. Heart Assn., Acad. Medicine Cleve., State Med. Soc. Va., Albemarle, Rockingham County med. socs., Am. Soc. Internal Medicine, Assn. Am. Indian Affairs, Conservation and Wildlife Socs., Pi Kappa Alpha. Republican. Lutheran. Contbr. articles profl. jours. Home: Route 1 Box 240D Mount Crawford VA 22841 Office: 635 S Main St Harrisonburg VA 22801

TORNBERG, DAVID NORMAN, orthopedic surgeon; b. Camden, N.J., June 5, 1941; s. John Norman and Cleonice Mary (De Marco) T.; B.S., U.S. Naval Acad., 1964; M.D. (Rudin scholar), Columbia U., 1973; m. Diane Hill, June 27, 1964; children—Elizabeth Anne, David Robert. Research asso. Orthopedic Research Lab., Columbia U., N.Y.C., 1972-77; intern Columbia U. Hosp., 1973-74, resident, 1974-77; practice medicine specializing in orthopedic surgery, Newport News, Va., 1977—; attending surgeon, instr. family practice tng. program Riverside Hosp., Newport News. Served to lt. nuclear submarine force USN, 1964-69. Diplomate Am. Bd. Orthopedic Surgery. Mem. Orthopedic Research Soc., Va. Med. Soc., Va. Orthopedic Soc., U.S. Naval Acad. Alumni Assn. Episcopalian. Clubs: James River Country (Newport News); Corinthian Yacht (Cape May, N.J.). Contbr. articles to med. jours. Office: 324 Main St Newport News VA 23601

TORRANCE, JOHN W., chem. engr.; b. Birmingham, Ala., Nov. 13, 1941; s. Walter Sylvester and Clara (Lott) T.; B.S. in Chem. Engring., Auburn U., 1965; M.B.A., U. S.C., 1973; m. Catherine Ella Hoyt, July 31, 1965; children—Evelyn Elizabeth, Catherine Denise. With Allied Chem. Corp., 1965—, supr. polymer prodn., Columbia, S.C., 1965-73, environ. engr., Petersburg, Va., 1973—, supr. environ. services, 1978—. Mem. Am. Inst. Chem. Engrs., Air Pollution Control Assn., Chester Jaycees (pres. 1977—), Chester YMCA (bd. mgrs.), Beta Gamma Sigma. Republican. Baptist. Home: 5825 Buxton Dr Chester VA 23831 Office: PO Box 31 Petersburg VA 23803

TORRE, GORDON THOMAS, hosp. adminstr.; b. Canton, Ohio, Mar. 9, 1951; s. Gerald Phillip and Mae Alice Ruth Hodge; student Pearl River Jr. Coll., Poplarville, Miss., 1971-73; student U. So. Miss., 1973—; m. Nancy Robinson, Aug. 16, 1974; 1 son, Jeffery Thomas. With Forrest Gen. Hosp., Hattiesburg, Miss., 1974—, mgr. dept. central service, 1976-79, dir. dept. material mgmt., 1979—. Little League soccer coach. Mem. Am. Soc. Hosp. Central Services Personnel. Republican. Roman Catholic. Home: 206 Weathersby Rd Hattiesburg MS 39401 Office: 400 S 28th Ave Hattiesburg MS 39401

TORRENCE, DANIEL DEAN, clergyman; b. Wehutty, N.C., Jan. 25, 1931; s. Emory James and Edith Ruby Torrence; B.S., E. Tex. Baptist Coll., 1960; M.R.E., New Orleans Bapt. Theol. Sem., 1962; m. Dee Ann Hartley, Aug. 19, 1955; children—Denita Kaye, Karen Denise. Ordained to ministry Bapt. Ch., 1959; minister music and edn. chs. in La., 1954—; minister music and edn. Highland Bapt. Ch., W. Monroe, 1978-79, Grawood Bapt. Ch., Keithville, La., 1979—; pres. bd. dirs. Okaloosa Bapt. Encampment, 1975-78; chaplain CAP, 1968—. Pres., Haynesville (La.) Cancer Soc., 1966-67. Served with USAF, 1950-54; Korea. Mem. La. Religious Edn. Assn. (v.p. 1976-77), N.E. La. Bapt. Assn. Staff Fellowship (v.p. 1979), La. Bapt. Religious Edn. Assn., Music Ministers La. Home: 6091 Dorchester Circle Keithville LA 71047 Office: Route 1 Box 267 Keithville LA 71047

TORRES, JOSE ERASMO, instr., counselor; b. Holquin, Cuba, Dec. 2, 1934; s. Jose Matias and Lilia Elda (Peralta) T.; came to U.S., 1958, naturalized, 1970; A.B., Asbury Coll., 1962. Dir. Christian edn. United Methodist Ch., Fitts., Balt., 1962-65; instr. Spanish, Park Sch. of Balt., 1966-67; chmn. fgn. langs., dir. counseling Pennington (N.J.) Sch., 1967-72; dean acad. student affairs St. Edward's Sch., Vero Beach, Fla., 1973-75, dir. counseling, 1975—; instr. adult edn. Indian River County Pub. Schs., Vero Beach, 1973—. Vol. with Salvation Army, N.Y.C., dir. fresh air camp, 1962; chaplain Boy Scouts Am., 1965-72; mem. exec. bd. Indian River County chpt. ARC, 1979. Cert. tchr., Fla. Mem. Am. Personnel and Guidance Assn., Am. Assn. Tchrs. of Spanish and Portuguese, Am. Assn. Christian Counselors. Office: St Edward Upper Sch Rt 2 Box 26 South A-1-A Vero Beach FL 32960

TORRES, JUAN BAUTISTA, business exec.; b. Maunabo, P.R., Apr. 25, 1939; s. Augustin and Leoncia (Morales) T.; B.B.A., U. P.R., 1964; m. Delia J. Robles; children—Alice Jeanette, Juan B., Katherine, Caroline, Nancy, Donna, Michael, Glorisol. Investigator, U.S. Dept. Labor, San Juan, P.R., 1958-59; chief accountant U.S. Industries Worldwide, Inc., San Juan, 1959-64; controller Empacadora de Carnes, Inc., Caguas, P.R., 1964-67; supv. cost accounting, asst. controller Fibers Internat., Inc., Guayama, P.R., 1967-69; controller, treas. Capitol Transp., Inc., San Juan, 1969—; Transport Adjustment Bur., Inc., San Juan, 1969—; Darmanin Devel. Corp., San Juan, 1969-80. Mem. P.R. (dir. banquet honoring 10 Young Outstanding Men in P.R., 1974, 76, 77, 78, named best v.p. of ops., 1975; recipient Presidential award, 1974; senator, 1973—, sec. senate 1977, Outstanding Young Man award 1979), Rio Piedras (pres. 1973, 78) Jaycees, Nat. Assn. Accts. Republican. Seventh-day Adventist. Home: Camino Andres Rosas Rd PR-842 KMG 1 RFD 6 Box 643F Bo Caimito Rio Piedras PR 00928 Office: GPO Box 3008 San Juan PR 00936

TORRES, PAUL DELMAS, accountant; b. Mobile, Ala., June 23, 1936; s. Frank Bernard and Claire Lilian (Delmas) T.; B.Sc. cum laude (Univ. scholar), Spring Hill Coll., 1958; M.B.A., U. Ala., 1959, Ph.D., 1971; m. Mary Paula McKenzie, June 17, 1961; children—Paul Delmas, Malcolm, Mary Claire, Matthew. Asst. prof. acct. Okla. State U., 1960-64, 65-69; tax sr. Arthur Andersen & Co., Atlanta, 1964-65, tax researcher, New Orleans, 1970; asso. prof. U. So. Miss., 1970-73, prof., 1973—; tchr. C.P.A. courses. Recipient Toolen medal Spring Hill Coll., 1958, Haskins & Sells Found. award, 1965, Gold medal Okla. C.P.A.'s, 1962; South Central Bell Outstanding Prof. award U. So. Miss. 1974, Excellence in Teaching award, 1976; U. Ala. fellow, 1958-59; C.P.A., Ga., Okla., Miss. Mem. Am. Inst. C.P.A.'s. Democrat. Roman Catholic. Author: Responsibilities in Tax Practice, 1979; contbr. articles to profl. publs. Home: 323 Emerson Dr Hattiesburg MS 39401 Office: PO Box 8434 Sou Sta Hattiesburg MS 39401

TORRES-AYBAR, FRANCISCO GUALBERTO, pediatrician, pediatric cardiologist; b. Santurce, P.R., July 12, 1934; s. Francisco Javier Torres and Maria Aybar; B.S., U. P.R., 1956; M.D., Barcelona Sch. Medicine, 1963; m. Elga Arroyo, Oct. 30, 1965; children—Elga, Jo Ann Marie. Intern Ponce (P.R.) Dist. Gen. Hosp., 1963-64, resident, 1964-66; fellow in pediatric cardiology Baylor Coll. Medicine, Houston, 1967-69 attending pediatrician Ponce Dist. Gen. Hosp., 1966-67, chief pediatric cardiology, 1969—, asst. chief pediatrics, 1970-71, chief pediatrics, 1971—, chmn. med. edn., 1970-72, v.p. med. staff 1970-72, 76-77, pres. med. staff, 1972-73; asst. clin. prof. pediatrics U. P.R. Sch. Medicine, Rio Piedras, 1975-79, asso. prof., 1979—; prof., chmn. dept. pediatrics Cath. U. P.R. Sch. Medicine, 1979—. Fellow Am. Acad. Pediatrics, A.C.P., Am. Coll. Cardiology, Royal Soc. of Health; mem. Am. Acad. Med. Adminstrn., P.R., Am. med. assns., Phi Sigma Alpha. Roman Catholic. Club: Ponce Rotary. Contbr. 39 articles to profl. jours. Home: A 26 Jacaranda Ponce PR 00731 Office: 13 Mayor St Ponce PR 00731

TORRES-DELGADO, RENE, educator; b. N.Y.C., June 10, 1947; s. Angel-Rene and Eva-Angelina (Delgado-Pasapera) T.; B.A. magna cum laude, U. P.R., 1969; M.A., Middlebury Coll., 1970; Ph.D., Pacific So. U., 1977; postgrad. Princeton U., N.Y. U. Asst. in instruction Romance Langs. dept. Princeton (N.J.) U., 1971; instr. classics Ponce Coll., U. P.R., San Juan, 1971-72, instr. fine arts, 1973-77, asst. prof. fine arts, 1977—. Mem. Am. Assn. Tchrs. French, Am. Assn. Tchrs. Spanish and Portuguese, AAUP. Republican. Roman Catholic. Office: Fine Arts Dept University of Puerto Rico at Rio Piedras San Juan PR 00931

TORRES-OLIVER, JUAN FREMIOT, clergyman; b. San German, P.R., Oct. 28, 1925; s. Luis N. and Amalia (Oliver) Torres; student St. John's Sem., 1944-50; M.A. in Musicology, Cath. U. Am., 1952; LL.B., U. P.R., 1959; LL.M., St. John's U., 1964. Instr., Cath. U. P.R., Ponce, 1952-56; vice chancellor Diocesan Curia, 1961-64; prof., asso. dean Sch. Law, Cath. U. P.R., 1961-64, grand chancellor, 1964—; apptd. bishop Ponce, 1964; installed and consecrated bishop Ponce, 1964—; v.p. P.R. Episc. Conf., 1976. Decorated Cross of Order Juan Pablo Duarte, Dominican Republic. Mem. Academia de Artes y Ciencias, Phi Alpha Delta. Club: Ponce Yacht. Home: Bishop's House PO Box 205 Sta 6 Ponce PR 00731 Office: PO Box 205 Sta 6 Ponce PR 00731

TORREY, PAUL DWIGHT, petroleum geologist, engr.; b. West Feliciana, La., June 28, 1903; s. Henry Marion and Louise Harriet (Winter) T.; B.S. with high honors in Petroleum Geology, U. Pitts., 1935, Petroleum Engr., 1927; D.Sc. in Petroleum Engring. (hon.), Marietta Coll., 1952; m. Jennie Pierson Mays, June 18, 1958. Geologic aide U.S. Geol. Survey, 1925-27; chief geologist Northwestern Pa. Oil Producers Assn., 1928-32; cons. geologist, Pa. and N.Y., 1932-35; chief engr. Sloan and Zook Co., Tex. and La., 1935-43; exploration geologist, prodn. specialist radioactive minerals War Dept., Can. and Africa, 1943-46; cons. engr. Standard Oil Co. of Calif., Tex. and Calif., 1947-52; mem. faculty U. Tex., 1952-67, disting. lectr. petroleum engring., 1958-67; ind. oil producer and petroleum cons., 1967—; pres. Lynes, Inc., 1940-43, Orchem Corp., 1952-58; chmn. standing com. on secondary recovery, chmn. central com. on drilling and prodn. practice Am. Petroleum Inst.; chmn. secondary recovery and pressure maintenance com. Interstate Oil Compact Commn. Decorated Purple Heart, Legion of Merit; recipient Bicentennial award Nat. Parks and Conservation Assn., 1976; registered profl. engr., Tex. Mem. Am. Assn. Petroleum Geologists (cert. petroleum geologist), Soc. Petroleum Engrs. (John Franklin Caroll award 1978), AIME (hon.). Republican. Presbyterian. Clubs: Petroleum (Ft. Worth); Masons, Shriners. Editor: Secondary Recovery of Oil in the United States, 1942, rev. edit., 1950. Home: 404 A Buena Vista Circle Austin TX 78746 Office: 5000 E Bee Cave Rd Austin TX 78746

TORSON, VICTOR JUNIOR, engring. co. exec.; b. Garden City, Kans., Jan. 6, 1930; s. Victor and Marion Francis (Holland) T.; B.A., U. Wichita, 1951; m. Patricia Ann Martin, May 1, 1977; children—Victor Jay, Georja E., John S., Bruce E., Theron K. Gen. mgr. Shamrock Constructors, Inc., Dodge City, Kans., 1962-70; v.p. D&R Constrn. Co., Springfield, Mo., 1971-75; area mgr. Saleh & Abdulaziz, Abahsain, Inc., Dammam, Saudi Arabia, 1976-77; asst. to pres. KM Engring Co., Enid, Okla., 1977—. Mem. Pipeline Contractors Assn., Mensa. Democrat. Mormon. Home: 2701 N

Adams St Enid OK 73701 Office: KM Engring Co 1118 N Polk St Enid OK 73701

TOTTRESS, RICHARD E., clergyman; b. Newby, Okla., Nov. 25, 1917; B.A., Pacific Union Coll., 1943; B.A., Oakwood Coll., 1969; student Langston U. Ministerial intern, 1943-47; ordained to ministry Seventh Day Adventist Ch., 1947; dist. pastor, Okla., 1947-52, S.C., 1952-58, Ga., 1958-61, N.C., 1961-63; dean Oakwood Coll., 1963-66, pastor, chaplain, 1965—, also tchr. Bible and social studies; producer dir. radio broadcasts Chaplain's Cheer, 1952—, Your Bible Speaks, Meditation, others; now dir. broadcasting, asso. pastor Berean Seventh Day Adventist Ch., Atlanta. Active March of Dimes, ARC, others. Recipient awards from Oakwood Coll., Tex. A&M. U., Seventh Day Adventist Ch., others. Fellow Am. Bible Inst., Internat. Bible Assn.; mem. Internat. PlatformPlatform Assn., Ministerial Assn., Assn. Seventh Day Adventist Historians, Huntsville Interdenominational Ministerial Assn. Author: Truth Speaks, 1975. Office: PO Box 41772 Atlanta GA 30331*

TOUPS, PATRICIA ANN TOUCHSTONE, librarian; b. Meridian, Miss.; d. Huie Hyman and Sibyl Christine (Sessions) Touchstone; B.A., Ga. State U., 1972; M.Ln., Emory U., 1973. Asst. librarian Fed. Res. Bank Atlanta, 1973-77; librarian Life Office Mgmt. Assn., Atlanta, 1978—. Active Egleston Hosp. Aux. Mem. Spl. Libraries Assn., ALA. Author: Life Office Management Association Index to Information, 1978. Home: 1789 Noble Dr Atlanta GA 30306 Office: 100 Colony Sq Atlanta GA 30361

TOUS DE TORRES, LUZ M., bank exec.; b. San Juan, P.R., Apr. 23, 1944; d. Rafael Tous Cortes and Iris Fernos; B.B.A., U. P.R., 1965; M.B.A., Interam. U., 1976, also P.R. Sch. Banking, 1976; m. Manuel A. de Torres, Jr., Feb. 17, 1967; children—Rosa Iris, Lara Sofia. With Banco Popular, San Juan, 1965—, 2d v.p., employee relations dir., 1969—. Co-founder P.R. Indsl. Editors Assn., pres., 1970-72; dir. bank's blood program for ANRC, 1972—. Recipient Outstanding Acad. Achievement award Interam. U., 1976. Mem. Am. Soc. Personnel Adminstrs. (accredited personnel mgr.), Am. Mgmt. Assn., Internat. Assn. Bus. Communicators, Internat. Platform Assn. Office: GPO Box 2708 San Juan PR 00936

TOW, JAMES L., army officer; b. Fort Eustis, Va., Feb. 10, 1930; s. William Melton and Marion Juliana (Lyons) T.; B.S., U.S. Mil. Acad., 1952; B.A.E., M.S., Ga. Inst. Tech., 1962; grad. Army War Coll., 1970; m. Barbara Lucille Freeman, May 31, 1958; children—Alicia Leigh Tow, Patricia Lynn. Commd. 2d lt. U.S. Army, 1952, advanced through grades to col., 1973; bn. comdr. and exec. officer, Vietnam, 1967-68; ops. research analyst Office Asst. Vice Chief of Staff, U.S. Army, Washington, 1968-69; staff officer, br. chief, acting chief airmobility div. Office Chief Research and Devel., Washington, 1970-73; project mgr. 2.75 Inch Rocket System, Redstone Arsenal, 1975-78; aviation systems dir., dep. dir. and acting dir. battlefield systems integration Army Devel. and Readiness Command, Alexandria, Va., 1978—. Decorated Legion of Merit, D.F.C., Purple Heart, Air medal with 29 oak leaf clusters, others. Mem. Army Aviation Assn. Am., Am. Helicopter Soc., Am. Def. Preparedness Assn., Assn. U.S. Army, AMVETS. Methodist. Home: 7611 Gaylord Dr Annandale VA 22003 Office: Comdr DARCOM/DRCBSI Alexandria VA 22333

TOWER, JOHN GOODWIN, U.S. senator; b. Houston, Sept. 29, 1925; s. Joe Z and Beryl (Goodwin) T.; A.B. in Polit. Sci., Southwestern U. Tex., 1948, also LL.D.; M.A. in Polit. Sci., So. Meth. U., 1953; student London Sch. Econs. and Polit. Sci. U. London, 1952-53; LL.D., Howard Payne Coll., Alfred U.; m. Lilla Burt Cummings, May 29, 1977; children—Penelope, Marian, Jeanne. Announcer radio sta. KFDM, Beaumont, Tex., 1948, KTAE, Taylor, Tex., 1948-49; ins. agt., Dallas, 1950-51; asst. prof. polit. sci. Midwestern U., Wichita Falls, Tex., 1951-60; U.S. senator from Tex., 1961—, mem. banking, housing and urban affairs, ranking minority armed services, ethics coms., chmn. senate Republican Policy Com., 1973—. Del., Republican nat. convs., 1956, 60, 64, 68, 72, mem. platform com., 1960, 64, 68, 72, chmn. tax delegation, 1972, chmn. senatorial campaign com., 1969-70. Trustee So. Meth. U., Southwestern U. Enlisted man USNR, World War II, PTO. Mem. Am. Polit. Sci. Assn., S.W. Social Sci. Assn., Tex. Hist. Soc., Am. Legion, U.S. Naval Inst., Am. Assn. U. Profs., Kappa Sigma. Methodist. Kiwanian, Mason (32 deg., Shriner). Home: Wichita Falls TX 76302 Office: 142 Russell Senate Office Bldg Washington DC 20510

TOWLER, WILLIAM ALBERT, III, title and trust co. exec.; b. Charlottesville, Va., Nov. 19, 1935; s. William Albert, Jr. and Jane Nolan (Cotten) T.; B.S. in Econs., cum laude, Washington and Lee U., 1958; M.B.A., U. N.C., Charlotte, 1970; m. Martha Lois Jackson, Dec. 18, 1971; children—Bill, Mark, Lynn. Fin. trainee internat. div. Gen. Electric Co., N.Y.C., 1960-61; v.p. adminstrn. Wachovia Bank & Trust Co., Charlotte, 1961-70, Communications Inst. Am., Inc., Dallas, 1970-71; v.p., mgr. adminstrn. div. Rattikin Title Co., Ft. Worth, 1971-74, exec. v.p., 1974-77; pres., chief exec. officer, dir. Am. First Title & Trust, Oklahoma City, 1977-79; pres., chief exec. officer, dir. Am. First Corp., 1980—; chmn. bd., chief exec. officer Am. First Land Title Ins. Corp., 1980—; dir. First Life Assurance Co. Served as 2d lt. U.S. Army, 1958-60. Mem. Am., Okla. mortgage bankers assns., Okla., Central Okla. home builders assns., Oklahoma City Met. Bd. Realtors, Ft. Worth Execs. Assn. (pres. 1973, dir. 1974), Am. (chmn. young people's title com. 1975—, chmn. edn. com. 1975—), Tex. (dir. 1976-77, named Titleman of Year 1977), Okla. land title assns., Oklahoma City C. of C., Delta Tau Delta. Episcopalian. Clubs: Green Country, Beacon (Oklahoma City). Home: 6325 N Villa 127 Oklahoma City OK 73112 Office: 133 W Main St Box 25225 Oklahoma City OK 73125

TOWLER, WILLIAM RUSSELL, elec. systems designer; b. Chatham, Va., Aug. 17, 1921; s. Joab Washington and Nannie (Pickrel) T.; B.E.E., U. Va., 1951, M.E.E., 1967; postgrad. U. Calif. at Los Angeles, 1952-54; m. Virginia Anne Wood, Feb. 16, 1949 (div. Apr. 1961); children—Antonia Russell, Sam Channing, Barbara Hayes. Elec. engr. Convair div. Gen. Dynamics Corp., San Diego and Pomona, Calif., 1951-57; project. engr. Sperry Piedmont Co., Charlottesville, Va., 1957-63; research scientist Research Labs. for Engring. Scis., U. Va., Charlottesville, 1963—. Mem. elec. adv. group Danville (Va.) Community Coll. 1968—. Served with USAAF, 1942-46. Mem. IEEE, AAAS. Patentee in field. Office: RLES Thornton Hall U Va Charlottesville VA 22903

TOWNLEY, FINOS JOHN, brokerage co. exec.; b. Birmingham, Ala., Aug. 26, 1902; s. Stephen Mountville and Mellar Elizabeth (Johnson) T.; student Birmingham Med. Coll., 1922; student marketing Miss. So. U., 1943; m. Nellie Estelle Jones, Sept. 25, 1924; children—Finos Jack, Thomas Richard. Salesman Swift & Co., Nashville, 1924, br. mgr., 1927-29, dist. mgr., 1930-36, asst. gen. sales mgr., 1937-46, v.p. sales, 1946-47, dir., 1960—; asst. to pres. Murray Biscuit Co., Augusta, Ga., 1967-70; pres. Nova Sales, Inc., Lakeland, Fla., 1967—, also dir.; chmn. bd. Inland Distbg. Inc. Dir. Nat. Sales Execs., Chgo. Mayor Lone Palm, Fla., 1968—. Bd. dirs. Am. Meat Inst., Chgo. Mem. Nat. Assn. Food Research (dir. 1955—; pres. 1953-53). Republican. Baptist. Mason. Clubs: Lone Palm Golf (Lakeland, Fla.); Hidden Hills Golf (Jacksonville, Fla.); Lincolnshire Country (Crete, Ill.) (v.p. 1958-59, 60-61). Home: 540 Lone Palm Dr Lakeland FL 33801 Office: 3710 New Tampa Hwy Lakeland FL 33802

TOWNS, HOWARD DONAL, bus. exec.; b. Bienville Parish, La., Jan. 29, 1926; s. Howard Donal and Zelma Lee (Dodson) T.; student La. Tech. U. 1947-50; B.S. in Bus. Admnstrn., U. Miami, Fla. 1950; m. Francis Marian Cadle, Dec. 31, 1946; children—Virginia Anne, Howard D., III. Wholesale distributor Cities Service Oil Co., Miami and Lake Wales, Fla., 1950-61, Texaco Inc., Lake Wales 1961-71, Union Oil of Calif., Lake Wales, 1971-77; owner, operator Towns Oil Co. Petroleum Products, Lake Wales, 1950-79, Towns Enterprises real estate and investments co., Lake Wales, 1978-79; mng. dir. Peach Bowl, Atlanta, 1979—. Active with various civic orgns., Lake Wales and Polk County (Fla.); deacon First Baptist Ch., Lake Wales, 1978—. Served with USAAF, 1943-45; ETO. Decorated Air medal, Purple Heart. Mem. Am. Mgmt. Assn., La. Tech. U. Alumni Assn. Clubs: Lions (dir. 1974-76), Elks, Am. Campers and Hikers, Fla. Lions Tarnished Brass. Home: 1526 Rainier Falls Dr NE Atlanta GA 30329

TOWNSEND, CHARLES RAY, author, educator; b. Nocona, Tex., Nov. 5, 1929; s. Claude Webster and Dot Jane (Keck) T.; B.A., Midwestern State U., 1960; M.A., Baylor U., 1961; Ph.D., U. Wis.-Madison, 1968; m. Mary Louise Smith, Apr. 9, 1950; children—William Donald, Mary Jane, Charles. Frederick Jackson Turner research asst. U. Wis., Madison, 1965; asso. prof. history Hardin-Simmons U., Abilene, Tex., 1965-67; asso. prof. W. Tex. State U., Canyon, 1967-74, prof., 1975—. Recipient Grammy award Nat. Acad. Rec. Arts and Scis., 1975, Western Heritage award Nat. Cowboy Hall of Fame, 1975. Mem. AAUP, Am. Hist. Assn., Orgn. Am. Historians. Democrat. Baptist. Club: Masons. Author: Homecoming: Reflections on Bob Wills and His Texas Playboys 1915-73, 1974; San Antonio Rose: The Life and Music of Bob Wills, 1976; contbr. articles in field to profl. jours. and books. Home: 507 25th St Canyon TX 79015 Office: West Tex State U Canyon TX 79016

TOWNSEND, JAMES BAKER, state legislator; b. Haileyville, Okla., Nov. 23, 1927; s. John Dunn and Rose Isabel (Baker) T.; grad. high sch.; m. June Marie Childers, Aug. 8, 1949; children—James Lawrence, Jeffrey Paul, Jay Arthur. Mem. Okla. Ho. of Reps., 1965—, Democratic caucus chmn., 1967-70, 1st asst. to majority floor leader, 1973—. Served with AUS, 1946-47. Mem. Okla. Farmers Union, Pottawatomie Cattlemens Assn., United Transp. Union. Lion. Home: Route 6 Box 216 Shawnee OK 74801 Office: Room 504 State Capitol Bldg Oklahoma City OK 73105

TOWNSEND, KILIAEN VAN RENSSELAER, state legislator; b. Garden City, N.Y., Oct. 6, 1918; s. Edward Nichol and Beatrice (Nicholas) T.; A.B., Williams Coll., 1939; LL.B., U. Va., 1942; m. Elizabeth Webb, June 27, 1970; children—Kiliaen Van Rensselaer, Carter Webb. Admitted to Ga. bar, 1946; mem. firm Dorsey & Dorsey, Atlanta, 1947-49; pres. Dixie Ray Glassheat Co., Atlanta, 1949-58; pres. Atlanta Motor Lodges, Inc., 1958-69; pres., operator Townsend Properties Inc., Atlanta, 1969—; mem. Ga. Ho. of Reps., 1965—; dir. Merc. Nat. Bank, Atlanta. Pres. Atlanta Humane Soc., 1964-65. Del. Rep. Nat. Conv., 1952. Bd. dirs. Atlanta YMCA, Boy Scouts, Planned Parenthood, Legal Aid Soc., Mental Health Assn. Served with AUS, 1942-45. Mem. Order of Coif, Chi Psi, Phi Delta Phi. Contbr. articles to various publs. Home: 208 Townsend Pl NW Atlanta GA 30327 Office: 214 Townsend Pl NW Atlanta GA 30327

TOWNSEND, ROBERT LEE, cons., ret. adminstrn. and aerospace co. exec.; b. Clarksville, Ark., Aug. 2, 1911; s. John Darius and Eula (Johnson) T.; B.S., U.S. Naval Acad., 1934; M.S., Mass. Inst. Tech., 1943; student Nat. War Coll., 1956; m. Elizabeth Terrell Archer, July 24, 1937; 1 dau., Terrell Archer Townsend Speers. Commd. ensign USN, 1934, advanced through grades to vice adm., 1969; assigned to USS Trenton, Lexington, Tripoli, capt. Kearsarge, comdr. carrier divs. 17 and 6, comdr. Naval Air Systems Command, 1966-69, comdr. Naval Air Force U.S. Atlantic Fleet, 1969-72; ret., 1972; pres., chmn. Grumman Internat. Co., Bethpage, N.Y., 1972-76; cons., 1976—. Mem. Am. Ordnance Assn. U.S. Naval, M.I.T., Nat. War Coll. alumni assns., Tex. State Soc. Baptist. Home and Office: 3433 Malbrook Dr Falls Church VA 22044

TOWNSEND, TERRY ERWIN, energy systems mfg. co. exec.; b. Cleveland, Tenn., Nov. 11, 1949; s. Erwin and Pauline (Campbell) T.; B.S. in Mech. Engring., Tenn. Tech. Inst., 1971, M.S. in Mech. Engring., 1972; m. Betty Louise Rominger, June 21, 1970; 1 dau., Tiffany Elaine. Research asst. Tenn. Tech. U., Cookeville, 1971-72; supr. research and devel. Combustion Engring. Co., Chattanooga, Tenn., 1972-76; broker, developer Townsent R/E/ Constrn., Cleveland, Tenn., 1976-77; pres. Tech. Energy Corp., Cleveland, 1977—; cons. in field. Coach Tyner Civitan Basketball and Baseball leagues, 1972-73. Alcoa scholar, 1970; Fleetguard fellow, 1971-72. Mem. Am. Soc. Mech. Engrs., Am. Inst. Chem. Engrs., Am. Soc. Heating, Refrigeration and Air Conditioning Engrs., Solar Energy Constrn. Assn., Realtors Nat. Marketing Inst., Phi Kappa Phi, Pi Tau Sigma, Tau Beta Pi, Kappa Mu Epsilon. Republican. Baptist. Home: 505 W Inman St Cleveland TN 37311 Office: 505 W Inman St Cleveland TN 37311

TOYNE, MARGUERITE CASTLES, adminstr., educator; b. Batesburg, S.C., Jan. 7, 1942; d. Hal Ross and Myrtle (McKeown) Castles; A.B., U. South Fla., 1970; M.B.E., Ga. State U., 1971, Ph.D., 1974; m. Brian Toyne; children—Susanne Marguerite, Ross Brian. Bookkeeper, Erlangen (Germany) Rod and Gun Club, 1964, Inmark, Inc., Kensington, Md., 1968; evening instr. DeKalb Tech. Sch., Clarkston, Ga., 1971; grad. instr. Ga. State U., Atlanta, 1972; instr. DeKalb Community Coll., Clarkston, 1974; mgmt. cons. Mescon, Inc., Atlanta, 1974-75; chairperson dept. bus. and econs. Columbia (S.C.) Coll., 1975-79, founder adv. bd. dor dept.; dir. mgmt., edn. and tng. programs Office Textiles and Apparel, Dept. Commerce, Washington, 1979—; planner, organizer, leader seminars, workshops for women in mgmt., careers, 1975, 76; teaching scholar S.C. ETV Network, Columbia, 1976—; mem. S.C. Commn. Higher Edn., 1976, Ednl. Resources Found., Columbia. Leader presentations at Ga. State U., Ga. State Data Processing Schs. Com., Ga. Vocat. Assn. Bus. and Office Edn., Ga. Library Assn., Nat. Am. Bus. Communications Assn., S.C. Women's Banking Assn. Vice pres., liaison Am. Field Service, NDEA fellow, 1971-74; faculty forum fellow Exxon Corp., Houston, 1976. Mem. Am. Bus. Communication Assn. (nat. bus. practice and problems com. 1975), Am. Soc. Tng. and Devel., Data Processing Mgmt. Assn., Am. Mktg. Assn., Assn. Computing Machinery, Columbia Sales and Mktg. Execs. (dir. 1977-78, chmn. constn. and by-laws com. 1977-78), Kappa Delta Pi, Delta Pi Epsilon. Clubs: Coldstream Country (bd. govs.), Bus. and Profl. Women's Assn. Contbr. articles on edn., data processing to publs. Home: Rt 2 Box 489 Chester SC 29706 Office: Dept Commerce Room 2815 Washington DC 20230

TOZER, WILLIAM THOMAS, ins. co. exec.; b. Petersburg, Ill., Jan. 19, 1934; s. Clarence W. and Winona (Armstrong) T.; B.S., U. Ill., 1956; m. Joan Marie Heberlein, July 31, 1955; children—Barbara, Theodore, Marilyn. Acturial asst. State Farm Life Ins. Co., Bloomington, Ill., 1956-60; sr. v.p., actuary Am. Republic Ins. Co., Des Moines, 1960-70; v.p., actuary Am. Republic Assurance Co., Des Moines, 1967-70; dir., 1967-70; v.p., actuary United Ins. Co. of Am., Chgo., 1970-72; v.p., chief actuary Ky. Central Life Ins. Co., 1972—; v.p. Ky. Central Ins. Cos., 1975—. Frequent speaker on computers at profl. meetings, seminars; pres. Actuarial Club of Des Moines, 1965. Mem. actuarial adv. bd. Drake U., 1967-70; chmn. computer adv. com. Iowa Ins. Dept. 1967-68. Mem. Polk County Tax Payers Computer Com., 1965; agy. affairs com. United Way, 1973—. C.L.U. Fellow Soc. Actuaries, Life Office Mgmt. Inst.; mem. Southeast Actuaries Club, Am. Acad. Actuaries, Internat. Actuarial Assn., Am. Council Life Ins. (com. 1973—), Lexington C. of C., Hon. Order Ky. Cols., Phi Kappa Phi, Phi Eta Sigma, Beta Gamma Sigma. Presbyn. (elder, deacon, trustee). Contbr. articles to profl. jours. Home: 647 Tateswood Dr Lexington KY 40502 Office: Kincaid Towers Lexington KY 40508

TRABANT, PETER KURT, oceanographer, geophysicist; b. N.Y.C., Sept. 25, 1942; s. Warren Edwin and Jean (Cowen) T.; B.S., U. Miami, 1968; M.S., Ph.D., Tex. A&M U. With radar meteorology dept. Inst. of Marine Scis., U. Miami, 1965-68; geophysicist Pan Am. Petroleum Corp., Fort Worth, 1968-69; research asso. Tex. A&M U., Coll. Sta., 1969-74; cons. Offshore Engring. Hazards & Platforms; cons., Houston, 1974—. Served with U.S. Navy, 1961-65. Mem. Marine Tech. Soc., Am. Assn. of Petroleum Geologists, Sigma Chi. Democrat. Unitarian. Clubs: YMCA, Houston Yacht. Contbr. articles on geology, oceanography and geophysics to profl. jours., and chpts. to books on marine geology. Sci. mem. aboard Glomar Challenger. Home and Office: 615 Kipling St Houston TX 77006

TRAHAN, JO ELLEN BROUSSARD, speech pathologist; b. Lake Arthur, La., July 26, 1933; d. Cyrus James and Thelma Audell (Hughart) Broussard; B.A., U. Southwestern La., 1964, M.Ed., 1971; m. Curtis Kirby Trahan, Nov. 2, 1953; children—David Scott, Paul William. Speech pathologist Vermilion Parish Sch. Bd., Abbeville, La., 1956—, chmn. speech and hearing, 1974—, supervising pathologist student tchrs., 1971—. Mem. Am. Speech and Hearing Assn., La. Speech and Hearing Assn., Acadiana Speech and Hearing Assn., Delta Kappa Gamma. Author: (with Jeanette Laguaite) Guidelines for Services for Communication Disorders, 1974. Home: 107 St Mary St Abbeville LA 70510 Office: PO Drawer 520 Abbeville LA 70510

TRAMEL, JAMES TURNER, mfg. co. exec.; b. Camp Polk, La., Nov. 26, 1944; s. Nathan Turner and Maudie Ineta (Boatman) T.; B.B.A. in Fin., Tex. A. and M. U., 1966; m. Canda Beth Flanagan, June 4, 1966; children—Stacy Diane, Stephany Dawn. Dir. property mgmt. Russo Properties, Inc., Houston, 1978-80; contract adminstr. Tex. Instruments, Inc., Houston, 1980—. Served with USAF, 1966-73. Decorated D.F.C. with oak leaf cluster, Purple Heart, Air medal with 8 oak leaf clusters (U.S.); Gallantry medal with device (Vietnam). Mem. Air Force Assn. (sec. treas. chpt.), Tex. A. and M. Former Students, Disabled Am. Vets, Mil. Order Purple Heart, Houston C. of C., Res. Officers Assn. (jr. v.p. chpt. 1976, sec. chpt. 1978, state historian 1978). Methodist. Club: S.W. Houston Aggie. Home: 12838 Westella Dr Houston TX 77077 Office: Texas Instruments Inc Houston TX

TRAMONTANA, JOSEPH, clin. psychologist; b. New Orleans, Aug. 18, 1942; s. Rosario and Theresa (Greiner) T.; B.A., La. State U., New Orleans, 1965; M.A., U. Miss., 1967, Ph.D., 1971; children—James Michael, Jody Lynn. Clin. psychologist Group Aid for Retarded Children, Mobile, Ala., 1970-71; instr. child devel., psychologist U. Tenn. Child Devel. Center, Memphis, 1971-72; dir. Regional Mental Health and Retardation Center, Oxford, Miss., 1972-75; dir. spl. services Gulf Coast Mental Health Center, Gulfport, Miss., 1975-78, clin. psychologist, 1978—; pvt. practice clin. psychology, Gulfport, 1978—; part-time clin. psychologist Delta Region Mental Health and Retardation Program, Bolivar County Center, Cleveland, Miss., 1971-72; part-time instr. dept. psychology, U. South Ala., 1971; cons. pediatric and adult referrals, 1971, 73-75; diagnostician Keesler AFB Children's Program, 1977—; cons., instr. child mgmt. Delta Hills Head Start Program, 1974-75; clin. psychologist Pine Belt Mental Health Center, Hattiesburg, Miss., 1975-76; task force So. Regional Edn. Bd., 1973-74; small grants reviewer HEW, 1974; cons. Miss. Interagy. Commn. Developmental Disabilities Tng. Program, 1974. Active Miss. Mental Health Assn., Harrison County Mental Health Assn., Harrison County Assn. for Retarded Citizens. Dir., author, co-author grants, projects in field; lic. psychologist, Ala., Miss., Tenn. Mem. Nat. Register Health Service Providers in Psychology, Am. Psychol. Assn. (clin. and cons. psychology), Southeastern Psychol. Assn., Miss. Psychol. Assn., Am. Assn. Mental Deficiency, Southeastern Assn. Behavior Therapy, Acad. Psychologists Marital and Family Therapy, Am. Soc. Clin. Hypnosis. Reviewer Jour. Applied Behavior Analysis; workshop leader, panel discussant profl. confs.; contbr. chpt. to book, articles, papers to profl. publs. Home: 1620 Oak Ave Gulfport MS 39501 Office: 640 16th St Gulfport MS 39501

TRANBARGER, RUSSELL EUGENE, nurse; b. Woodson, Ill., July 11, 1936; s. Andrew Russell and Dorothy Edith (Orris) T.; A.A., Blackburn Coll., 1958; B.S.N., DePaul U., Chgo., 1966; M.S.N., U. N.C., Chapel Hill, 1970; m. Theresa Isek, June 10, 1961. Staff nurse Children's Meml. Hosp., Chgo., 1959, VA Hosp., Durham, N.C., 1967-68; staff nurse, asso. dir. nursing, dir. nursing service N.C. Meml. Hosp., Chapel Hill, 1968-72; dir. nursing services Moore Meml. Hosp., Pinehurst, N.C., 1972-77; adminstr. nursing Moses H. Cone Hosp., Greensboro, N.C., 1977—; asso. clin. prof. nursing U. N.C. (Greensboro); mem. N.C. Bd. Nursing, 1979—. Chmn. Eureka precinct Democratic Party, 1977. Served with Nurse Corps, AUS, 1960-63, 64-67. Mem. N.C. Nurses Assn. (pres. 1977-79), N.C. Fedn. Nursing Orgns. (dir. 1977-80), Am. Nurses Assn., Am. Soc. Nursing Service Adminstrs., Sigma Theta Tau. Democrat. Roman Catholic. Club: K.C. Home: 4805 W Friendly Ave Greensboro NC 27410 Office: 1200 N Elm St Greensboro NC 27420

TRANQUILLO, MARY DORA, educator; b. Pitts., Apr. 14, 1943; d. Guy and Maria Dora (Grossi) Caranfa; B.F.A., Pratt Inst., 1965; M.A., N.Y. U., 1971; postgrad. U. South Fla., 1973-74, Fashion Inst. Tech., 1978; m. Joseph A. Tranquillo, June 26, 1965; 1 dau., Maria Nannette. Asst. buyer Frederick Atkins, 1965-66; art tchr. Christ The King High Sch., 1966-67, St. Joseph High Sch., 1967-68; home econs. tchr. Derby (Conn.) High Sch., 1968-71, Mann Jr. High Sch., Brandon, Fla., 1971-72, Plant City (Fla.) High Sch., 1972-74; program coordinator fashion merchandising St. Petersburg (Fla.) Jr. Coll., 1974—. Recipient Deca Outstanding Service award, 1979. Mem. Am. Home Econs. Assn., Am. Vocat. Assn., Assn. Coll. Profs. Textiles and Clothing, Fla. Assn. Community Colls., Fla. Vocat. Assn. Democrat. Roman Catholic. Club: Kiwanis Aux. Home: 3005 St Croix Dr Clearwater FL 33519 Office: 2465 Drew St Clearwater FL 33515

TRAPP, CLAYTON LESLIE, JR., civil engr.; b. Wellington, Kans., Mar. 13, 1929; s. Clayton Leslie and Lee Fern (Goff) T.; B.S. in Civil Engring., Kans. State U., 1951; m. Dixie Jeanne Bradshaw, Apr. 15, 1972. Airworthiness dir. Boeing Co., Wichita, Kans., 1970-71; sec., treas. Tyson Bldg. Corp., Ft. Worth, 1971—; pres., chief exec. officer Multisound Corp., Ft. Worth, 1975—; chmn. bd., chief exec. officer Comml. Floorcovering Co., Houston, 1977—; v.p. Ronco Properties

Co., Ft. Worth, 1977—. Recipient various certs. appreciation; Registered profl. engr., Tex. Mem. Metal Bldg. Dealers Assn., Tex. Soc. Profl. Engrs. Address: PO Box 1952 Fort Worth TX 76101

TRAXLER, W. A., x-ray technologist; b. Morton, Miss., Apr. 9, 1921; s. Willie Peke and Phenie Jane (Finch) T.; student LaSalle Extension U., 1939-42, Lamar U., 1952-54, N. Tex. State U., Lee Coll., Baytown, Tex., 1962-64; grad. Burroughs Sch. Bus. Machines, Houston, 1947; m. Ila B. Skipper, July 28, 1949; children—Kathryn Lynn, Patrick Allen. Surveyor's apprentice C.L. Cain, C.E., Dayton, Tex., 1939-40; gen. supt., bookkeeper C.L. Carr Constrn., Dayton, 1941-42; bookkeeping positions Gulf Oil Co., Houston, 1946, Minimax Stores, Houston, 1947; lab. and x-ray technologist Drs. Delaney & Schulz, Liberty, Tex., 1947-48, Ft. Bend Hosp., Rosenberg, Tex., 1949, Nightingale Hosp., El Campo, Tex., 1950; lab. and x-ray technologist, asst. adminstr. Mansfield Hosp. (La.), 1951-52, Chambers Meml. Hosp., Anahuac, Tex., 1959-76; lab. and x-ray technologist Drs. Delaney, Schulz & Castle, Liberty, 1952-59; head x-ray dept., asst. adminstr. in charge purchasing Otto Kaiser Meml. Hosp., Kenedy, Tex., 1976—. Treas., 1st Baptist Ch., Karnes City, Tex., Gambrell Bapt. Assn., Karnes City. Served with USN, 1941-46. Recipient Order of Golden Microscope award Am. Med. Technologists, 1960. Mem. Am. Med. Technologists, Am. Cardiology Technologist Assn., Am. Registry Radiologic Technologists, Am. Soc. Radiologic Technologists, Tex. Soc. Radiologic Technologists, Inc., Am. Soc. Hosp. Purchasing Agts. Democrat. Baptist. Home: 901 E Main St Karnes City TX 78118 Office: Otto Kaiser Meml Hosp Hwy 181 N Kenedy TX 78119

TRAYER, DAVID MCGUIRE, indsl. hygiene engr.; b. Bluefield, W.Va., Aug. 23, 1932; s. Raymond Andrew and Myrtle Jane (Hoops) T.; B.S. cum laude, Emory and Henry Coll., 1954; M.S. (AEC fellow), Harvard U., 1962; m. Myralin Anne Gillenwater, Aug. 22, 1953; children—Carol Allison, Catherine Jane, Cheryl Dianne. Research chemist Union Carbide Nuclear Co., Oak Ridge, 1954-61; chemist Tenn. Eastman Co., Kingsport, 1962-64; research engr. ARO, Inc., Tullahoma, Tenn., 1964-69; supr. indsl. hygiene engring. TVA, Muscle Shoals, Ala., 1969—, asst. br. chief, 1977—. Mem. Am. Conf. Govtl. Indsl. Hygienists (gen. chmn. 1978-79), Am. Indsl. Hygiene Assn. (pres. Tenn. Valley sect. 1976), Am. Acad. Indsl. Hygiene, Nat. Safety Council. Democrat. Mormon. Contbr. articles to profl. jours. Home: 562 Hazelwood Dr Florence AL 35630 Office: TVA Florence Indsl Park Bldg Muscle Shoals AL 35660

TRAYLOR, BARBARA CARLTON, hosp. public relations adminstr.; b. Washington, June 3, 1942; d. Clayton C. and Ann S. Carlton; B.A., U. Ala., 1963, M.A., 1967; m. J.W. Traylor, July 29, 1972. Dir. public info. Ala. Ednl. TV Commn., Birmingham, 1968-69; public relations dir. Greater Birmingham Conv. and Visitors Bur., 1969-70, Ala. Hosp. Assn., Montgomery, 1970-74; dir. public affairs St. Thomas Hosp., Nashville, 1974-79; dir. public affairs and devel. St. Vincent's Hosp., Birmingham, Ala., 1979—. Recipient awards in field. Mem. Public Relations Soc. Am. (officer Nashville chpt.), Am. Soc. Hosp. Public Relations (past dir.), Ala. Soc. Hosp. Public Relations, Phi Beta Kappa, Pi Beta Phi Alumnae. Methodist. Club: Birmingham Press. Home: 3641 Brookwood Rd Mountain Brook AL 35223 Office: St Vincent's Hosp PO Box 915 Birmingham AL 35201

TRAYLOR, JERRY LYNN, mfg. co. ofcl.; b. Jacksonville, Tex., Mar. 14, 1945; s. Simon B. and Ella K. T.; B.S. in Civil Engring., Tex. Tech. U., 1970, M.S. in Civil Engring., 1971; m. Susan Smyrl, Aug. 17, 1968; children—Stacy Lynn, Robert Thomas. Design engr. Star Mfg., Oklahoma City, 1971-73, chief design engr., 1973-75, mgr. material and prodn. control, 1975—. Served with USAF, 1963-67. Fellow level cert. practitioner in inventory mgmt.; registered profl. engr., Tex. Mem. ASCE, Nat. Soc. Profl. Engrs., Am. Prodn. and Inventory Control Soc. (v.p. Oklahoma City chpt. 1977, pres. 1978-79, instr. short courses in prodn. control 1977-79). Republican. Home: 908 NE 5th St Moore OK 73160 Office: PO Box 94910 Oklahoma City OK 73109

TRAYLOR, JOSEPHINE ZANANIRI, educator; b. Alexandria, Egypt, June 22, 1925; d. Joseph and Martha Eychenne (Koury) Zananiri; came to U.S., 1946, naturalized, 1949; B.A., U. Mo., 1950; M.A., Middlebury (Vt.) Coll., 1952; postgrad. N.Y. U., 1971-79; m. Orba F. Traylor, Nov. 17, 1945; children—Joseph Marion, Robert Forest, John Christopher. Mem. faculty Christian Coll., Columbia, Mo., 1950-51, Capital Day Sch., Frankfort, Ky., 1956-58, U. Md., Far East div., 1960-65; mem. faculty U. Ala., Huntsville, 1965—, asst. prof. modern langs., 1969—, chmn. modern fgn. lang. dept., 1976—; lang. adviser Marshall Space Flight Center, 1973, 77, U.S. Army Missile Command, 1975; sr. lang. cons. Passias Found., 1979. Recipient Mention tres hon. Inst. de Phonetique, U. Paris, 1952. Research grantee U. Ala., 1973. Mem. Alliance Francaise (pres. Huntsville 1969), Modern Lang. Assn., Am. Assn. French Tchrs., Huntsville Art League and Mus. Assn., Phi Sigma Iota. Democrat. Roman Catholic. Club: Huntsville Rotaryann (pres. 1971). Author: Les Reves et les Songes Chez Marcel Proust, 1972; also articles. Home: 216 Westmoreland Huntsville AL 35801 Office: Univ Ala Huntsville AL 35807

TRAYLOR, ORBA FOREST, economist; b. Providence, Ky., June 16, 1910; s. Eddie Ewing and Dillie (Stuart) T.; B.A., Western Ky. U., 1930; M.A., U. Ky., 1932, Ph.D., 1948; J.D., Northwestern U., 1936; m. Josephine Zananiri, Nov. 17, 1945; children—Joseph Marion, Robert Forest, John Christopher. Admitted to Ky. bar, 1941; legal asst. 1st Nat. Bank of Chgo., 1936-37; dir. research and statistics Ky. Dept. Welfare, 1941; asso. econ. analyst U.S. Treasury Dept., 1942; asst. prof. econs. and bus. U. Denver, 1946-47, U. Mo., 1947-50; tax specialist ECA, Greece, 1950-53; commr. fin. State of Ky., 1958-59; dir. econ. affairs and fin. Office High Commr., Ryukyus Islands, 1960-65; prof. econs. and public adminstrn. U. Ala., Huntsville, 1965-75; vis. prof. public adminstrn. San Diego State U., 1975-76, Western Ky. U., 1977; fin. economist Dept. State, 1977-78; adj. prof. econs. Ala. A&M U., 1979—; fiscal cons. Johns Hopkins U., 1957-61; sr. adv. Bank of Ryukyus, 1960-65; chmn. bd. Ryukyuan Devel. Loan Corp. and Joint Fgn. Investment Bd., 1960-65; intern counselor Oak Ridge Univs., 1965-66, Teledyne Brown Engring., 1970-72, TVA, 1972-74, AID, 1974-75; research adv. Southeastern Inst. Tech., 1978—. Served to lt. col., AUS, 1942-46. Mem. Am. Econ. Assn., So. Econ. Assn., Am. Soc. Public Adminstrn. (nat. council 1973-75), Am. Bar Assn., Ky. Bar Assn., Nat. Tax Assn.-Tax Inst. Am. (dir. 1971-74), Res. Officers Assn., Beta Gamma Sigma, Delta Sigma Pi. Democrat. Baptist. Club: Rotary. Mem. editorial bd. Pub. Adminstrn. Rev., 1973-79. Home: 216 Westmoreland St Huntsville AL 35801

TRAYWICK, HILDEGARDE ANNE, speech pathologist; b. Dutton, Ala., Jan. 1, 1938; d. Hulton Arthur and Audrey (Griffith) Spears; B.A., Middle Tenn. State U., Murfreesboro, 1971; M.A. (grad. asst.), Memphis State U., 1972; divorced; children—Victoria, Laura Leigh. Speech clinician Memphis Speech and Hearing Center, 1971-72; speech pathologist Huntsville (Ala.) Rehab. Center, 1972-74; coordinator speech and hearing services Madison County (Ala.) schs., Madison, 1974—. Active local Girl Scouts Am.; pres. Birmingham (Ala.) Jaycetes, 1962. Mem. Am. Speech and Hearing Assn., NEA, Speech, Hearing and Deaf Educators, Ala. Edn. Assn., Speech and Hearing Assn. Ala. Republican. Methodist. Home: 2231 Tollgate Rd Huntsville AL 35801 Office: Madison County Bd Edn County Courthouse Huntsville AL 35801

TREACY, JAMES BERNARD, mfg. co. exec.; b. Indpls., Nov. 1, 1921; s. Aloysius Bernard and Alice (Klaus) T.; B.S. in Elec. Engring., U. Notre Dame, 1944; postgrad. Inst. for Internat. Mgmt., Burgenstock, Switzerland, 1968; m. Francesca Maenza, May 10, 1947; children—Mark J., Paul B., Stuart C., Brian C. From sales engr. to v.p., group exec. Bendix Corp., 1950-76; with Teldix G.m.b.H., Heidelberg, W. Ger.; now chmn., chief exec. officer Facet Enterprises, Inc., Tulsa; dir. Bank of Okla., Tulsa. Trustee, Bishop Kelley High Sch., Tulsa, Philbrook Art Center, Tulsa. Mem. Soc. Automotive Engrs., World Wildlife Fund. Roman Catholic. Club: Southern Hills Country (Tulsa). Office: 7030 S Yale Ave Tulsa OK 74136

TREAT, CAROL LOU, sch. counselor; b. Annapolis, Md., Aug. 29, 1931; d. Burnett Forrest and Carol Moyne (Deane) Treat; B.S., U. Tex., 1952; M.Ed., 1960, postgrad., 1967; postgrad. U. Ariz., 1965; Tchr. phys. edn. and scis. Dallas Pub. Schs., 1952-59; counselor Pearce Jr. High Sch., Austin, Tex., 1960-61, Burnet Jr. High Sch., Austin, 1961-74, Dobie Jr. High Sch., Austin, 1974—; cons. in field; mem. profl. advisory bd. Austin Mental Health-Mental Retardation Assn., 1977—; partner Draper's Cove Craftspeople. Mem. Am., Tex., Central Tex. personnel and guidance assns., Am., Tex. sch. counselors assns., Assn. for Humanistic Edn. and Devel., Austin, U.S. women's polit. caucuses, Lago Vista Women's Golf Assn., Phi Delta Kappa (corr. sec. 1977—). Democrat. Presbyterian. Author: (with Jeffrey Bormaster) Talking, Listening, Communicating, 1975, Talking, Listening, Communicating II, 1978, Counseling, Consulting, Coordinating, 1979. Home: 8807 Merion Circle Austin TX 78754 Office: 1200 E Rundberg Ln Austin TX 78753

TREECE, CORDELLA LOUISE WEISENBORN (MRS. ROBERT EARL TREECE), artist, musician, educator; b. Van Wert, O., Mar. 11, 1917; d. Thomas H. and Clarissa (Riley) Weisenborn; student Defiance Coll., 1937-38, Toledo Mus. Art, 1958-60; m. Robert Earl Treece, Aug. 6, 1939; children—Thomas Zane, Susan Clarissa (Mrs. Walter Grabner). Comml. artist Adams Studio, Toledo, 1946-69; instr. art Toledo Artists Club, 1963-77, adminstrv. pres., 1966-77; music instr. Toledo U., 1958-59; resident-in-a-day art instr. Toledo Pub. Schs.; juror local and nat. art shows; one man shows Toledo Pub. Libraries, World of Sound, Park Lane Hotel, Toledo Artists' Club, Defiance Soc. Artists, Toledo Artists Club, others; exhibited juried shows at county fairs, 1st Nat. Bank, Toledo Artists Club, Toledo Mus. Art, Cinema I and II, others; gallery shows include internat. Platform Assn., 1970—, Put-In-Bay Gallery, 1972, 73, Studio Gallery Point Place, McGinnis Gallery, Toledo, Bertrand Russel House, Nottingham, Eng.; represented in many pvt. collections, permanent collection Waite High Sch., Toledo. Affiliate mem. City Toledo Arts Commn., 1973-77. Recipient awards Toledo Artists' Club, 1958, 68, 69, 70, 71-76, also Artist of Year, 1971; Honor award Toledo Fedn. Art, 1968; awards Internat. Platform Assn. Art Show, Washington, 1970, 73, 77, Promenade Park Show, Toledo, 1972, 74, 7th Ann. Rose Garden Arts Festival, Toledo, Secor Park Ann. Show, Toledo, 8th Festival of Arts, Toledo, 1973, Parkway Plaza Show, 1973, 1st place modern painting Pine Hill Art Festival, 1978, Lake Eola Festival of Arts and Crafts, 1978, Apopka (Fla.) Arts and Crafts, 1978; various awards Lucas County and Wood County fairs; numerous other art awards. Mem. Toledo Fedn. Musicians (life), Toledo Fedn. Artists (rec. sec. 1964-75), Toledo Fedn. Art Soc. (sec. 1963-75, trustee), Ohio China Painters (pres. 1966), Toledo Womens Orch. League, Northwestern Ohio Watercolor Soc. (founding mem.), Internat. Platform Assn. (gov. 1975, mem. arts com., editor letter for artists 1976—), Central Fla. Artists Assn. (v.p. 1979-80), Maitland Art Assn. (rec. sec. bd. dirs. 1979—), Fla. Watercolor Soc., Nat. League Am. Pen Women (Winter Park br.), Soroptimists (v.p. 1971, corr. sec. 1972-74). Methodist. Clubs: Toledo Women's Art League (pres. 1963-64, treas. 1965, corr. sec.), Samagama, Toledo Artists (pres., trustee 1966-77, editor Sketch Pad 1970-76). Home: Box 1211 606 Arvern Altamonte Springs FL 32701

TREEN, DAVID CONNER, gov. La.; b. Baton Rouge, July 16, 1928; s. Joseph Paul and Elizabeth (Speir) T.; B.A., Tulane U., 1948, LL.B., 1950; m. Dolores Yvonne Brisbi, May 26, 1951; children—Jennifer Anne Neville, David C. and Cynthia Lunceford (twins). Admitted to La. bar, 1950; with firm Deutsch, Kerrigan & Stiles, New Orleans, 1950-51; v.p. Simplex Mfg. Corp., New Orleans, 1952-57; mem. firm Beard, Blue, Schmitt & Treen, New Orleans, 1957-73; mem. 93d-96th congresses from 3d La. Dist., chmn. House Republican Study Com., 1978; gov. La., 1980—; Rep. candidate for Congress from 2d Congl. dist. La., 1962, 64, 68, candidate gov., 1972, 79; del. Nat. Rep. Conv., 1964, 68, 76, chmn. La. del., 1968, 72; mem. Rep. State Central Com., 1962—; chmn. Jefferson Parish exec. com., 1962-67; Rep. nat. committeeman, 1972-74. Served as 1st lt. USAF, 1951-52. Mem. La. Bar Assn., Order of Coif, Phi Delta Phi, Kappa Sigma. Methodist. Club: Metairie (La.) Country. Home: Gov's Mansion Baton Rouge LA 70804 Office: State Capitol Baton Rouge LA 70804

TREGLE, JOSEPH GEORGE, historian; b. New Orleans, Dec. 22, 1919; Ph.B., Loyola U., New Orleans, 1939; M.A., La. State U., 1941; Ph.D. (Harrison fellow), U. Pa., 1954. Instr. to prof. history Loyola U., New Orleans, 1945-58; prof. history U. New Orleans, 1958—, dean acad. affairs, 1959-64; lectr. in field. Mem. La. Coll. Conf. (pres. 1962), Gulf Coast History and Humanities Conf., La. Hist. Soc., Am., So. (chmn. nominating com. 1962, exec. council 1980—), La. (pres. 1962) hist. assns. Editor: An Historical Narrative and Topographical Description of Louisiana and West Florida (Thomas Hutchins), 1968; History of Louisiana (Antoine Le Page Du Pratz), 1976; mng. editor La. Hist. Quar., 1954-57; editor La. Bicentennial Reprint Series, 1976—; contbr. articles on So. and La. history to profl. jours., encys. Home: 540 Turquoise St New Orleans LA 70124 Office: Edn Bldg 154 U New Orleans New Orleans LA 70122

TREIMAN, EDWARD S., elec. engr.; b. Toledo, Iowa, July 29, 1910; s. Samuel E. and Dorothy (Walker) T.; B.S. in Elec. Engring., Iowa State Coll., 1933, E.E., 1943; m. Selma White, June 24, 1942; children—Sue, Terri, Larry. With Western Electric Co., Chicago and New York, engring., research and transcontinental line experimentations, 1933-37; asst. purchasing agent Allied Machinery Corp., 1937; with Internat. Western Electric Co., 1938-39; mng. dir. Nat. Electric Light Assn., 1946-52; cons. engr., Chgo., 1952—; sec. St. Lawrence Commn. of U.S., 1944-46, Second Nat. Radio Conf., 1945. Commd. 1st lt., Signal Corps, U.S. Army, 1937, later capt. Mem. IEEE, Edison Electric Inst., NAM, Tau Beta Pi, Delta Upsilon. Republican. Clubs: Union League, University, Recess (N.Y.C.); Univ. (Chgo.). Address: 2918 W Fargo St Chicago IL 60645

TRELAWNY, GILBERT STERLING, microbiologist; b. Cin., Nov. 12, 1929; s. Charles Harold and Marguerite (Sterling) T.; B.S., Del. Valley Coll., 1957; M.S., Lehigh U., 1960, Ph.D., 1966; m. Florence Ann Mulholland, Nov. 19, 1950; children—Edward, Janice, James. Lab. technician for doctor, Jamaica, L.I., 1947-51; research asso. Del. Valley Coll., Doylestown, Pa., 1953-57; instr., 1957-60, asst. prof., 1960-66; prof. biology James Madison U., Harrisonburg, Va., 1966—, head dept. biology, 1972—. Served with U.S. Army, 1951-53. Mem. Va. Acad. Scis., Mycological Soc. Am., Assn. Southeastern Biologists. Clubs: Elks. contbr. articles to profl. jours. Home: 85 Emery St Harrisonburg VA 22801 Office: Dept Biology James Madison U Harrisonburg VA 22801

TRELLES PEREZ-YANEZ, TONY, advt. agy. exec.; b. Havana, Cuba, Mar. 22, 1931; s. Tomas and Carmen P.-Y.; came to U.S., 1960, naturalized, 1968; C.P.A., Havana U., 1954; diploma TV prodn. Havana Advt. Sch., 1956; m. Juany Sauto, June 19, 1965; children—Tony, Tanya. Various positions Esso Standard Oil Co., Havana, 1949-60; writer, producer, dir. programs C.M.Q. Radio and TV Network, Cuba, 1955-60; writer TV programs Sta. WAPA, San Juan, P.R., 1960-61; writer Sociedad Española Radiodifusión, Radio Network, Madrid, 1961-62; staff Nestle's AFICO Publicidad Internacional, Vevey, Switzerland, 1962-63; mgr. advt. and public relations Nestlé Products Inc., San Juan, 1963-66; copy dir., radio and TV dir., creative dir. Young & Rubicam of P.R. Inc., San Juan, 1966-69; creative dir. West Indies Advt. Co., San Juan, 1969-75; founder, owner, operator Tony Trelles Advt., Inc., Santurce, P.R., 1976—. Recipient 1st prize Am. Brewers Assn. ann. conv., 1973, numerous other awards. Roman Catholic. Home: 233 FD Roosevelt Ave Hato Rey PR 00917 Office: PO Box 6035 Loiza Sta Santurce PR 00914

TRENT, GEORGE ELDER, hosp. adminstr.; b. Kingsport, Tenn., June 5, 1932; s. James Luther and Beulal I. (Bull) T.; A.B., Carson-Newman Coll., 1960; postgrad. E. Tenn. State U., 1962; m. Dianne Vaughn, Feb. 24, 1978; children—James David, Michelle, Melissa. Adminstr., Jefferson Meml. Hosp., Jefferson City, 1963-67; asst. dir. Vanderbilt U. Med. Sch., Nashville, 1967-68; adminstr. Donelson Hosp., Nashville, 1968-77, Muhlenberg Community Hosp., Greenville, Ky., 1977—; cons. Am. Hosp. Assn., 1963-79, Hosp. Corp. Am., 1968-77, NIH, 1967-68, Mehamy Med. Coll., 1967-68, Med. Coll. S.C., 1967-58; vice chmn. Western Ky. Hosp. Services. Served with USN, 1952-55. Fellow Am. Coll. Hosp. Adminstrs., Royal Soc. Health; mem. Am. Hosp. Assn., Ky. Hosp. Assn., Tenn. Hosp. Assn. (chmn. bd. 1976-77), Am. Coll. Nursing Home Adminstrs. (asso.). Baptist. Club: Kiwanis. Author: Health Planning for Emerging Multi Hospital Systems, 1978. Home: 113 Paradise St Greenville KY 42345 Office: 440 Hopkinsville St Greenville KY 42345

TRENT, NORA CATRON, speech pathologist; b. Morristown, Tenn.; d. Samuel Neill and Jessie Myrtle (Harrison) Catron; B.S., U. Tenn., 1958, M.S., 1962; m. Gaston Hugh Trent; children—Samuel, Hugh, Marilyn, Stephan. Speech pathologist Knox County (Tenn.) Bd. Edn., 1955-63. Tenn. Dept. Public Health, Nashville, 1963—, dir. speech and hearing service, 1976—. Adv. council hearing and speech center U. Tenn., 1968-75; adv. council Project Headstart, Nashville, 1973-76; bd. dirs. League for Hearing Impaired, 1976—. Mem. Am. Speech and Hearing Assn. (cert. clin. competence), Tenn. Speech and Hearing Assn., Tenn. Public Health Assn., Council Exceptional Children, Am. Assn. Ret. Persons, Delta Kappa Gamma. Baptist.

TRENTHAM, HAROLD LEE, chem. engr.; b. Jefferson City, Tenn., Nov. 3, 1923; s. Shannon Otis and Ina Davis (Rankin) T.; A.A., Mars Hill Coll., 1942; B.Chem. Engring., N.C. State U., 1943; m. Marjorie Valentine, June 24, 1944; children—Marsha Trentham Hunter, Harold Lee, Gary. Research engr., Tenn. Eastman Corp., Kingsport, 1943-45; process engr. Celanese Corp., Bishop, Tex., 1945-47, Fish Engring. Corp., Houston, 1947-54; v.p. Delta Engring. Corp., Houston, 1955-60; pres. Trentham Corp., Houston, 1960—; dir. Austin Rankin Corp., Environ. Tectonics Corp., Republic of Tex. Savs. Assn., Trentham Corp., Graff Engring. Corp., and others. Scoutmaster, Cub Scouts; Republican precinct chmn. Mem. Houston C. of C., Nat. Fedn. Ind. Businessmen, Natural Gas Processors Assn., SAR, Internat. Platform Assn., Tex. Law Enforcement Officers Assn., Galveston Hist. Found., Am. Inst. Chem. Engrs., AAAS, Tex. Soc. Profl. Engrs. Republican. Baptist. Club: University. Patentee in field. Contbr. profl. jours. Home: 1502 Broadway Galveston TX 77550 Office: 811 Westheimer Houston TX 77006

TREVEY, JOHN EDWIN, state senator, physician; b. Big Island, Va., May 2, 1933; s. John T. and Mary Elizabeth (Horton) T.; B.A., Va. Mil. Inst., 1955; M.D., Med. Coll. Va., 1959; m. Mary Jo Dove, July 9, 1960; children—John Harrison, Mary Elizabeth. Intern, Roanoke (Va.) Meml. Hosp., 1959-60; gen. practice medicine, Galax, Va., 1962-66; physician IBM Corp., Lexington, Ky., 1966—; mem. courtesy staff Central Bapt., Good Samaritan, St. Joseph hosps.; chief of staff Galax Gen. Hosp., 1964-65; asso. clin. prof. community medicine U. Ky. Sch. Medicine, Lexington, 1967—; med. examiner Galax and Grayson County, Commonwealth of Va., 1962-66. Vice pres. Eastern Little League, 1973-74; state rep. Ky. Gen. Assembly, 1977; mem. state senate Ky. Gen. Assembly, 1979—; mem. Fayette County (Ky.) Republican Exec. Com., 1971-79; bd. dirs. United Way of the Bluegrass, 1972-80, campaign chmn., 1974; bd. dirs. Family Counseling Service, 1969-76; trustee Lexington-Fayette County Drug Edn. Com., Ky. State Bd. Health, 1971-73. Served as capt., M.C., USAF, 1960-62; now lt. col. Res. Diplomate Am. Bd. Fellow Am. Occupational Med. Assn. (ho. of dels. 1975-79); mem. Am. Acad. Occupational Medicine, Am. Coll. Preventive Medicine, Va., Ky., Fayette County (v.p. 1972-73) med. socs., Ky. Indsl. Med. Assn. (pres. 1969-70), AMA, Alpha Sigma Chi. Baptist. Clubs: Lexington Kiwanis, Lexington Country. Home: 5241 Tates Creek Pike Lexington KY 40503 Office: 740 New Circle Rd Lexington KY 40511

TREVINO, FERNANDO MANUEL, health services researcher; b. Brownsville, Tex., Aug. 20, 1949; s. Manuel Emilio and Consuelo Ivern T.; A.A., Laredo Jr. Coll., 1970; B.S., U. Houston, 1971; M.P.H., U. Tex., 1975, Ph.D., 1979. Caseworker, Tex. State Dept. Pub. Welfare, Laredo, 1972 instr. allied health scis. U. Tex. Med. Br., Galveston, 1973-74, coordinator Office of Spl. Programs, 1974—. Sec., Gulf Region, Tex. Assn. Chicanos in Higher Edn., 1978—. Bd. dirs. Galveston Youth Shelter, Inc.; bd. dirs. Chicano Health Policy Devel., Inc. Served with M.C., U.S. Army, 1971-72. Mem. Am. Public Health Assn., Am. Acad. Health Adminstrn., Tex. Assn. Chicanos in Higher Edn., Sigma X. Roman Catholic. Contbr. articles to profl. jours. Office: 165 Gail Borden U Tex Med Br Galveston TX 77550

TREVINO, LEE BUCK, profl. golfer; b. Dallas, Dec. 1, 1939; s. Joe and Juanita (Barrett) T.; ed. pub. schs.; m. Claudia Ann Fenley, Aug. 24, 1964; children—Richard Lee, Lesley Ann, Tony Lee, Troy Liana. Head profl. Hardy's Driving Range, Dallas, 1961-65; asst. profl. Horizon Hills Country Club, El Paso, Tex., 1966-67; chmn. bd. Lee Trevino Enterprises, Inc.; touring profl. Santa Teresa Country Club, Sunland Park, N.Mex., 1967—; tournament winner Tex. Open 1965, 66, N.Mex. Open, 1966, U.S. Open, 1968, 71, Hawaiian Open, 1968, Tucson Open, 1969, 70 Nat. Airlines Open, 1970, World Cup, 1969, 71, Brit. Open, 1971, 72, Canadian Open, 1971, 77, 79, Danny Thomas Memphis Classic, 1971, 72, Sahara Internat., 1971, Tallahassee Open, 1971, Greater St. Louis Classic, 1972, Greater Hartford Open, 1972, Jackie Gleason Classic, 1973, Doral Eastern Open, 1973, Mexican Open, 1973, 75, Chrysler Classic, Australia, 1973, Greater New Orleans Open, 1974, PGA Championship, 1974, World Series of Golf, 1974, Fla. Citrus Open, 1975, Colonial Nat., 1976, 78; 6th ofcl. money winner, 1968, 1st money winner, 1970, 2d place money winner, 1971, 72; 4th place money winner, 1974; 1st golfer to have scored four sub-par rounds in U.S. Open Competition, 1968; co-holder of all time low scoring record U.S. Open Competition.

Hon. chmn. Christmas Seal campaign, 1969, 70, 71, Nat. Sports Ambassador, 1971; hon. chmn. Trans Pecos Tb and Respiratory Diseases Assn.; grand marshal Sun Carnival Parade, 1969-70, 71-72; mem. Pres.'s Conf. on Phys. Fitness and Sports; mem. sports com. Nat. Multiple Sclerosis Soc. Served with USMC, 1956-60. Named Tex. Profl. Athlete of Year, 1970, Profl. Golf Assn. Player of Year, 1971, Golf mag. Player of Year, 1971, Sportsman of Year Sports Illus. mag., 1971, Internat. Sports Personality of Year Brit. Broadcasting Assn., 1971, A.P. Male Athlete of Year, 1971; recipient Ann. Hickok Belt award, 1971, Gold Tee award, 1971, Vardon Trophy, 1970, 71, 72, 74; named to Tex. Hall of Fame, 1974, El Paso Hall of Fame, 1974. Star TV golf program. Home: 11737 St Michaels Dr Dallas TX 75230 Office: 1341 W Mockingbird Ln Suite 718E Dallas TX 75247

TRIAS-MONGE, JOSE, chief justice P.R. Supreme Ct.; b. San Juan, P.R., May 5, 1920; s. Jose Trias-Duffrent and Belen Monge; B.A., U. P.R., 1940; M.A., Harvard, 1943, LL.B., 1944; J.S.D., Yale U., 1947; m. Jane G. Trias, June 3, 1943; children—Jose E., Peter J., Arturo. Admitted to P.R. bar, 1945; 1st asst. atty. gen., then atty. gen. P.R., 1949, 53-57; mem. P.R. Constl. Conv., 1951-52; U.S. rep. Caribbean Commn., 1954-60, Inter-Am. Jud. Com. of OAS, 1966-67; mem. Gov. P.R. Commn. for Reform Jud. System P.R., 1973-74; pvt. practice, 1957-74; chief justice P.R. Supreme Ct., 1974—; mem. faculty U. P.R. Law Sch., intermittently, 1947-49, trustee, 1962-72; pres. various coms. Jud. Conf. P.R. Vice pres. Festival Casals, 1957-69, 73-74. Mem. Am., P.R. bar assns. Roman Catholic. Author: El Sistema Judicial de Puerto Rico, 1978. Contbr. profl. jours. Home: PO Box 4006 San Juan PR 00905 Office: PO Box 2392 San Juan PR 00903

TRIBLE, PAUL SEWARD, JR., Congressman; b. Balt., Dec. 29, 1946; s. Paul Seward and Katherine (Schilpp) T.; B.A., Hampden-Sydney Coll., 1968; J.D., Washington and Lee U., Lexington, Va., 1971; m. Rosemary Dunaway; 1 dau., Mary Katherine. Admitted to Va. bar, 1971; law clk. to U.S. dist. judge Albert V. Bryan, 1971-72; asst. U.S. atty. Eastern Dist. Va., 1972-74; commonwealth's atty. Essex County, Va., 1974-76; mem. 95th-96th Congresses from 1st Va. dist. Bd. govs. St. Margaret's Sch., Tappahannock, Va.; trustee Hampden-Sydney Coll. Named Outstanding Young Man of Va., Jaycees, 1978. Republican. Episcopalian. Mem. Law Rev., Washington and Lee U. Office: 326 Cannon House Office Bldg Washington DC 20515

TRICE, JOHNNIE CLARENCE, psychiatrist, med. service adminstr.; b. Clarendon, Ark., Nov. 22, 1931; s. Richard H. and Lena C. (Ferguson) T.; B.A., Hendrix Coll., Ark., 1952; M.D., U. Ark., 1957; m. Iva Maye Jeffery, Sept. 27, 1958; children—John Richard, Charlotte Anne. Intern St. Vincent Infirmary, Little Rock, 1957-58; resident psychiatry U. Okla. Med. Center, Oklahoma City, 1958-61; chief resident VA Hosp., Oklahoma City, 1959-60; practice medicine specializing in psychiatry, Athens, Ga., 1965—; psychiat. cons. El Reno (Okla.) Fed. Reformatory, 1961, U. Okla. Med. Center, Oklahoma City, 1961, Community Psychology Clinic, Ardmore, Okla., 1961, La. State Penitentiary, Angola, 1964-65, Ga. Pardons and Parole Bd., Atlanta, 1965-66, Gilbert Meml. Infirmary, U. Ga., Athens, 1965-67, Western Judicial Circuit Ct., Athens, 1965—, Clarke County (Ga.) Alcoholism and Drug Rehab. Center, Athens, 1966-72, Vocat. Rehab. Center, Athens, 1965—, Probation and Parole Office, Athens, 1965-71, Ga. Indsl. Inst., Alto, 1965—; psychiatrist VA Hosp., Dept. of Medicine and Surgery, Atlanta, 1965—; asst. prof. psychiatry U. Ga., Athens, 1965-71; dir., chief forensic psychiat. div. East La. State Hosp., Jackson, 1961-62, 64-65; staff psychiatrist female admissions ward Central La. State Hosp., Pineville, 1962-64; med. dir. and psychiat. cons. Electroencephalographic Lab., Athens, 1965-67; psychiat. dir. Child Psychiat. Clinic, Clarke County Pub. Health Center, Athens, 1965-68; psychiat. dir. Athens Gen. Hosp. Mental Health Clinic, 1965-69; dir. Avalon Psychiat. Clinic, 1966—. Served with USNR, 1949-53. Recipient Outstanding Service award State Dept. of Hosps., La., 1962. Mem. A.M.A., Am. Psychiat. Assn., Ga. Med. Assn., So. Med. Assn., Internat. Acad. Forensic Psychology, Alpha Chi. Contbr. articles on forensic psychiatry to profl. jours. Home: Deerfield Rd Bogart GA 30622 Office: 150 Talmadge Dr Athens GA 30601

TRICE, MARY SUE WILLIAMS, counselor; b. Marietta, Ga., Aug. 9, 1950; d. Pembroke Whitfield and Cora Virginia (Swanson) Williams; B.A. Art Edn., W. Ga. Coll., 1971, M.Ed. in Guidance and Counseling, 1972; m. Richard Alan Trice, Dec. 15, 1972. Resource room tchr. jr. high mentally retarded Anderson Sch. Dist. (S.C.), 1973; substitute tchr., tutor, Boone, N.C., 1973-75; dir. guidance, tchr. art Monroe Acad., Inc., Forsyth, Ga., 1975-78; art instr. Gwin Oaks Elementary Sch., Lawrenceville, Ga., 1978—. Mem. Am. Personnel and Guidance Assn., Am., Ga. sch. counselors assns., Assn. Measurement and Evaluation in Guidance, Gwinnett County Art Educators Assn., Alpha Gamma Delta. Home: 1706 Corinth Circle Stone Mountain GA 30087 Office: 400 Gwin Oaks Dr Lawrenceville GA 30245

TRICK, OTHO LEE, psychiatrist; b. Anderson, Ind., Aug. 4, 1931; s. Homer Forest and Juanita Mertie (Turner) T.; student Anderson Coll., 1950-52; pre-med. student, Ind. U., 1952-54, M.D., 1958; m. Reita Ann Meyerowitz Troum, June 2, 1974; children—David Lee, Kevin Lee, Bryan Lee, Cynthia Lee. Rotating intern Blodgett Meml. Hosp., Grand Rapids, Mich., 1958-59; gen. practice medicine, Durand, Mich., 1959-64; resident in psychiatry, Duke U. Med. Center, 1964-67; chief inpatient service VA Hosp., Albuquerque and instr. in psychiatry U. N.Mex., 1967-68; dir. inpatient program dept. behavioral medicine and psychiatry W.Va. U., 1968-73, asst. chmn. dept. behavioral medicine and psychiatry, 1972-74, dir. Charleston div., 1973-74, asst. prof. psychiatry, 1968-70, asso. prof., 1970-74, prof., 1974; co-dir. Family Inst. of the S.W., Inc., Houston, 1974—; mem. staffs Bapt. Meml. Hosp., Houston, Sharpstown Gen. Hosp., Houston; psychiat. cons. Harris County (Tex.) Dept. Edn. Div. Psychol. Services, 1974-77; speaker to civic groups. Active Boy Scouts Am. Named 1 of 10 Most Outstanding Tchrs., W.Va. U. Sch. Medicine Sr. Class, 1970; recipient Outstanding Tchr. award W.Va. U., 1972; diplomate Am. Bd. Psychiatry and Neurology. Mem. AMA, Harris County Med. Soc., Tex. Med. Assn., Am. Psychiat. Assn. (sec. W.Va. dist. br. 1970-71), Am. Group Psychotherapy Assn. Clubs: Masons, K.T. Contbr. articles to profl. jours. Home: 10002 Green Tree Houston TX 77042 Office: 6601 Tarnef St Suite 206 Houston TX 77074

TRICKETT, A. STANLEY, historian, educator; b. Swinton, Yorks, Eng., Aug. 3, 1911; came to U.S., 1914, naturalized, 1921; s. Albert and Maud Mary (Stanley) T.; A.B., Asbury (Ky.) Coll., 1932; M.A., U. Ky., 1933; diploma Sch. of Internat. Studies, Geneva, Switzerland, 1934; Ph.D. in History, Victoria U. Manchester (Eng.), 1935; m. Mary Patton, Dec. 27, 1938. Instr. in history Northwestern U., Evanston, Ill., 1936; instr. dept. history Drew U., Madison, N.J., 1936-39, asst. prof., 1939-44, asso. prof., 1944-46; prof. history, dean univ. Kans. Wesleyan U., 1949-54, pres., 1950-54; prof. history U. Nebr., Omaha, 1957-74, prof. emeritus history, 1974—; guest lectr. various radio and TV programs, 1936-74. Served from 2d. lt. to col., U.S. Army, World War II; ETO, NATOUSA. Decorated Legion of Merit, Meritorious Service medal; Research Travel grantee, 1934, 35, 69. Fellow Royal Hist. Soc. of Great Britain; mem. Am. Hist. Assn., Phi Alpha Theta (internat. council 1971-73, internat. v.p. 1973-75, internat. pres. 1975-77, chmn. internat. adv. bd. 1977-79). Republican. Methodist. Clubs: Masons (32 deg.), Sojourners, Jesters, Shriners, Lehigh Acres Country; Mirror Lake Golf. Contbr. numerous articles and revs. to hist. jours.; editorial bd. The Historian, 1966-73. Address: 236 S Lake Dr Lehigh Acres FL 33936

TRIGGS, MARY ELLEN BANFIELD, mktg. exec.; b. South Amboy, N.J., Dec. 25, 1939; d. Henry Joseph and Mary Catherine (Vail) Banfield; student Syracuse (N.Y.) U., 1972; B.G.S., Rollins Coll., Winter Park, Fla., 1975; m. William M. Triggs, Sept. 10, 1960; children—William Joseph, Matthew Henry, Anne. Art dir. Durable Techniques, Inc., advt., Syracuse, 1969-71; campaign dir. for Fla. Senator Lori Wilson, 1972; founder, 1st chmn. S. Beaches Exec. Council, homeowners lobby, 1971-73; mem. Fla. com. for ERA, League Women Voters, 1974-75; area sales rep. Xerox Corp., Orlando, Fla., 1976, sales rep., 1976-78, br. mktg. support mgr., 1978, br. mktg. mgr., 1978-79, sales mgr. Fla. E. Coast, 1979, br. sales mgr. Central Fla., 1980—; polit. cons., 1975—. Bd. dirs. Brevard Council, 1975—; mem. Fla. Commn. Human Relations. Brevard Legis. Tax Study Commn. Advisory council WEWDI and WOW programs Brevard Community Coll. Home: 190 Sand Pine Rd Indialantic FL 32903 Office: 1980 N Atlantic Ave Cocoa Beach FL 32931

TRIGGS, WILLIAM MICHAEL, elec. engr.; b. South Amboy, N.J., Aug. 15, 1937; s. William and Stella (Szatkowski) T.; B.S. in Metall. Engring., Lafayette Coll., Easton, Pa., 1960; M.S. in Metallurgy, Stevens Inst. Tech., Hoboken, N.J., 1965; m. Mary Ellen Banfield, Sept. 10, 1960; children—William J., Matthew H., Anne. Research investigator Asarco Co., S. Plainfield, N.J., 1960-61; engr. RCA, Somerville, N.J., 1961-66; engring. unit mgr. Gen. Electric Co., Syracuse, N.Y., 1966-71; wafer fabrication mgr. Semiconductor div. Harris Corp., Melbourne, Fla., 1971—; tchr. indsl. courses in phys. metallurgy. Bd. dirs. Liverpool (N.Y.) Nursery Sch., 1967; founder, 1st pres. of Sand Pine Home Owners Assn., 1972-73; co-founder, charter mem. S. Beaches exec. council Homeowners Lobby, 1972. Recipient Bausch & Lomb award, 1955; N.J. State scholar, 1955-57. Mem. Electrochem. Soc., Am. Mgmt. Assn., Tau Beta Pi, Alpha Sigma Mu. Club: Pines Tennis. Patentee in field. Home: 190 Sand Pine Rd Indialantic FL 32903 Office: PO Box 883 Melbourne FL 32901

TRILLO, ALBERTO ALFONSO, physician; b. Mexico City, Mexico, Aug. 7, 1936; s. Alfonso A. and Consuelo J. (Nieto) T.; came to U.S., 1975; M.D., Nat. U. Mexico, 1961; Ph.D. in Pathology, U. Western Ont., Can., 1972; m. Hermina Borgerink, Nov. 3, 1965; children—Alexander, Patrick. Resident in pathology Nat. Med. Center, Mexico City, 1961-62; research fellow dept. pathology Queen's U., Kingston, Ont., Can., 1963-65; resident in pathology Victoria Hosp. and U. Hosp., London, Ont., 1972-74; postdoctoral fellow dept. pathology U. Western Ont., 1974-75; practice medicine specializing in pathology, Winston-Salem, N.C., 1975—; sr. investigator and dir. Lab. Electron Microscopy, Nat. Inst. Cardiology, Mexico City, 1965-69; demonstrator in pathology dept. pathology U. Western Ont., 1969-74; asst. prof. pathology Bowman Gray Sch. Medicine, Winston-Salem, 1975—; dir. Cytopathology Lab., N.C. Bapt. Hosp., Winston-Salem, 1975-78. Diplomate Am. Bd. Pathology. Fellow Coll. Am. Pathologists; mem. Am. Soc. Cytology, Internat. Acad. Pathology, Electron Microscopy Soc. Am., N.C. Soc. Cytology, Can. Assn. Pathologists, Internat. Soc. Gynecol. Pathologists. Roman Catholic. Contbr. articles to sci. jours. Home: 939 Peace Haven Rd N Winston Salem NC 27104 Office: 300 Hawthorne Rd Winston Salem NC 27103

TRIMBLE, LINDA FRANCES, mfg. co. exec.; b. Dallas, Feb. 11, 1948; d. Joseph Leon and Frances Elise (Manship) T.; student Stephen F. Austin U., 1966-67; B.B.A., N. Tex. State U., 1970; postgrad. bus. adminstrn. U. South Fla., 1976—. Sr. control analyst Southwestern States Bankcard Assos., Dallas, 1970-72; mgmt. acct. Redman Devel. Corp., Dallas, 1972-74; exec. officer, asst. mgr. accounts payable Lincoln Property Co., Dallas, 1974-75; mgr. acctg. and internal auditor, Tampa, Fla., 1975-76; mgr. acctg. and data services S.E. div. Duo Fast Corp., Tampa, 1976—. Mem. Am. Mktg. Assn., Nat. Assn. Accts., LWV, Phi Chi Theta (nat. officer 1973-78). Democrat. Methodist. Club: Pilot. Home: 2812 Ebony Pl Seffner FL 33584 Office: 1212 N 39th St Tampa FL 33605

TRIMBLE, LORA NELLE GARRETSON (MRS. JAMES CURTIS TRIMBLE), writer; b. Wichita Falls, Tex., Aug. 12, 1935; d. Jesse Columbus and Alma Geneva (Higgenbottom) Garretson; student Sul Ross State Tchrs. Coll., 1954, Midwestern U., 1956; B.A., So. Meth. U., 1961; m. James Curtis Trimble, Sept. 4, 1954; children—James Curtis, Mary Christiana. Dir., Royal Lane Lang. Center, Dallas, 1969-75; English lang. tchr. to fgn. adults, 1969-75. Theta Sigma Phi. Address: 9445 Hunters Creek Dallas TX 75243

TRINDAL, WESLEY STEELE, mech. engr.; b. Superior, Wis., July 21, 1925; s. Glen William and Mabel Elda (Steele) T.; B.S. in Mech. Engring., La. State U., 1956; m. Mary Elizabeth Steger, Aug. 12, 1949; 1 son, Joseph William. Test and devel. engr. Ford Motor Co. and Chrysler Corp., Detroit, 1956-58; prin. engr. vehicles U.S. Army Mobility Equipment Research and Devel. Command, Ft. Belvoir, Va., 1958—. Served to sgt., AUS, 1943-52. Decorated Purple Heart with oak leaf cluster. Mem. Soc. Automotive Engrs., Regular Common Carrier Conf., Am. Def. Preparedness Assn. Contbr. articles profl. jours. Home: 8526 Old Mount Vernon Rd Alexandria VA 22309 Office: DRDME HK US Army MERADCOM Fort Belvoir VA 22060

TRINER, EDWIN GEORGE, govt. ofcl.; b. Yonkers, N.Y., Feb. 22, 1924; s. Moe and Grace S. Triner; B.S., U.S. Mil. Acad., 1949; M.A., U. Calif., Berkeley, 1953, Ph.D., 1954; M.S., U. Ariz., 1963; m. Ernestine R. Rudiak, Feb. 11, 1950; children—Kandi J., Bruce. Commd. 2d lt. U.S. Air Force, 1949, advanced through grades to col., 1967; ret., 1967; asso. dean Coll. Bus. Adminstrn., U. Houston, 1969-72; dir. planning, analysis, regulation AEC, Washington, 1972-74; dir. resources planning, evaluation, controller U.S. Nuclear Regulator Commn., Alexandria, Va., 1974—; adj. prof. George Washington U., 1969—, Central Mich. U., 1974—. Mem. Am. Psychol. Assn., Human Factors Soc., Newcomen Soc. Home: 4001 Sulgrave Dr Alexandria VA 22309 Office: US Nuclear Regulatory Commn 7022 Fairmont St Bethesda MD 20555

TRINGALE, ANTHONY ROSARIO, life ins. co. exec.; b. Syracuse, N.Y., Apr. 20, 1942; s. Anthony and Susan Marie (Cerio) T.; B.S.F.S., Georgetown U., 1967; CLU, Am. Coll. Life Underwriters, 1973; m. Myranda Lou Atwell, Aug. 1, 1964; children—Anthony William, Michael Paul, Mark David, Amber Marie. Office mgr. trainee N.Y. Life Ins. Co. No. Va., 1965-66, office mgr., Fairfax office, 1966, field underwriter, 1966-68, asst. mgr., 1968-73, mgmt. asst., home office, N.Y.C., 1973, gen. mgr. Pitts. gen. office, 1973-76; gen. mgr. Acacia Mut. Life Ins. Co., Annandale, Va., 1976—; lectr. in field. Founding vice chmn. Fairfax Orgn. Christians/Jews United in Service (FOCUS); vol. ARC, Children to Children Found.; panelist Washington Multiple Sclerosis Soc. C.L.U. Mem. No. Va. Assn. Life Underwriters (treas. 1972), Sales Marketing Execs. Met. Washington (pres. 1979-80), Nat. Assn. Life Underwriters (nat. mgmt. award Gen. Agts. and Mgrs. Conf., 1976-79), No. Va. Estate Planning Council, No. Va. Gen. Agts. and Mgrs. Assn. (v.p. 1979-80). Roman Catholic (lector, instr.). Home: 8805 Sandy Ridge Ct Fairfax VA 22031 Office: 7700 Little River Turnpike Suite 600 Annandale VA 22003

TRISSEL, RONALD LEROY, hosp. food service adminstr.; b. Rockingham County, Va., Sept. 19, 1945; s. D. Lloyd and Alice Virginia (Blosser) T.; B.S., Eastern Mennonite Coll., Harrisonburg, Va., 1967; postgrad. Va. Commonwealth U., 1968; m. Doris Jean Reynolds, Oct. 13, 1979; children—Vanessa Aline, Marci Jeannine. Dir. hosp. food services Servomation Mathias, Inc., Clarkston, Ga., 1967-73; dir. food services S. Fulton Hosp., East Point, Ga., 1973-75; dir. hosp. food services, hosp. food mgmt. staff analyst ARA Food Services, Inc., Atlanta, 1975—. Treas., South Fulton Mental Health Assn., 1975. Mem. Am. Soc. Hosp. Food Service Adminstrs. (past pres. Ga. chpt.), Jaycees (regional treas. 1974-75, Outstanding Regional Officer, 1974-75, regional v.p. 1975-76), Am. Hosp. Assn. (cert. health care food adminstr.), Internat. Food Service Exec. Assn. Republican. Baptist. Home: 301 Woodbrook Ln Marietta GA 30067 Office: 57 Executive Park S NE Suite 460 Atlanta GA 30329

TRITICO, FRANK EDWARD, historian, ednl. adminstr.; b. Houston, Aug. 1, 1930; s. Leonard Frank and Aletha Agnes (McBride) T.; B.A., U. St. Thomas, 1955; M.Ed., U. Houston, 1963; postgrad. U. Va., 1967, Columbia U., 1968; m. Marilyn Ann Stewart, Sept. 8, 1956; children—Robert Blakey, Mark Douglas, Mary Lindsey, Frank Edward. Chmn. dept. Houston Ind. Sch. Dist., 1960-67; cons. Harris County (Tex.) Dept. Edn., Houston, 1967-71, dir. adult edn., 1968-70; dir. curriculum and instruction Katy (Tex.) Ind. Sch. Dist., 1971-79; guest lectr. Am. Petroleum Inst., U. Houston, 1962—, Rice U., 1978; chmn. Spanish Tex. Microfilm Center, 1975—, LaBahia Research Awards, 1975—. Mem. Tex. Civil War Centennial Commn., 1959-63; chmn. Harris County Hist. Commn., 1968—; commr. Battleship Tex., 1971-77; mem. Tex. Medal of Honor Grove Com., 1976; chmn. San Jacinto Battleground Hist. Adv. Bd., 1979. Recipient Tex. Heritage Distinguished Service medal, 1963; knight comdr. Knights of San Jacinto, 1963; Freedom Fellowship award, 1970; SAR Gold Good Citizenship medal, 1970; Alcalde de La Villita Honorary Mayor of San Antonio, 1971; Jefferson Davis award, 1973; DAR medal of Honor, 1973; William Paca award, 1975; Marianer Knight of Teutonic Order, 1977; knight Equestrian Order of Holy Sepulchre of Jerusalem, 1977, George Washington Honor medal Freedoms Found., 1978; cert. of commendation Tex. Hist. Commn., 1979. Mem. Tex. State Tchrs. Assn., Nat., Tex. assns. supervision and curriculum devel., Am., Tex. assns. sch. adminstrs., Katy Edn. Assn., Tex. State Hist. Assn., Tex. Hist. Found., Am. Assn. State and Local History, Harris County Heritage Soc., Philos. Soc. Tex., Tex. Hist. Found. (dir. 1979—). Roman Catholic. Author: (with E.M. Carrington) Women in Early Texas, 1975; editorial bd. Heraldry, 1976—; contbr. articles in field to profl. jours. Home: 11931 Kimberley Ln Houston TX 77024

TROGDON, DEWEY LEONARD, textile co. exec.; b. Summerfield, N.C., Feb. 17, 1932; s. Dewey Leonard and Ethel (Miller) T.; A.B. in Econs., Guilford (N.C.) Coll., 1959; postgrad. U. N.C., Greensboro, 1967-68, U. Va., 1970, Harvard U., 1978; m. Barbara Jean Ayers, Sept. 10, 1955; children—Mark, Leonard. With Cone Mills Corp., 1958—, v.p., then exec. v.p., 1977-79, pres., Greensboro, 1979—, also dir. Bd. dirs. Greensboro Jr. Achievement. Served with USNR, 1949-53. Mem. Am. Textile Mfrs. Inst. Methodist. Office: 1201 Maple St Greensboro NC 27405

TROMBINO, ROGER A., fin. exec.; b. Kenosha, Wis., Sept. 23, 1939; s. Paul and Lena (Lenconi) T.; B.S., U. Wis., 1962; m. Joann M. Buchholtz, Nov., 1961; children—Tracey, Suzanne, Steven. Sr. v.p., treas. Norin Corp., N. Miami, Fla.; dir. Homosassa Springs, Inc. Bd. dirs. Villa Maria Hosp. Mem. Am. Inst. C.P.A.'s, Fin. Execs. Inst. Home: 14501 SW 79 Ave Miami FL 33158 Office: 12100 NE 16 Ave North Miami FL 33161

TROMBLEY, CHARLES CYPRIAN, clergyman, author; b. Littleton, N.H., Aug. 24, 1928; s. Carroll Cyprian and Beulah Ashell (Bradshaw) T.; theology grad. Am. Div. Sch., 1970; postgrad. Immanual Bapt. Coll., 1972, Moody Bible Inst., 1972; m. Gladys Allen, Jan. 27, 1951; children—David, Darlene, Deborah, Deanna. Ordained to ministry Baptist Ch., 1959; founder, pastor Full Gospel Tabernacle, Bellows Falls, Vt., 1956-59; pastor Christian Fellowship Ch., Sarasota, Fla., 1960-62; exec. sec., crusade evangelist The Gospel Crusades, Inc., Sarasota, 1960-63; conf. Bible tchr., evangelist, Sarasota, 1962-69; founder, editor The Expositor Publs., Sarasota, from 1966, Broken Arrow, Okla., 1979—; dir. The Gospel Light Telecast, Ottumwa, Iowa, 1970-72; pastor Sheridan Assembly Christian Center, Tulsa, 1972-73; founder, dir. The Charismatic Teaching Ministries, Tulsa, 1973; dir. CTM Publs., Broken Arrow, 1972—; supr. Mfulu Za Yehova Mission, Luchenza, Malawi, 1976—. Served with USCG, 1946-49. Mem. World Ministry Fellowship, Full Gospel Businessmen's Fellowship. Republican. Author: Visitation-The Key to Church Growth, 1970; Christian Answers for the Jehovah's Witnesses, 1975; Kicked Out of the Kingdom, 1974; Praise-Faith at Work, 1976; Released to Reign, 1979. Mem. adv. editoral staff Logos Mag., Plainfield, N.J., 1979—. Contbr. articles in field to profl. jours. Home: 293 W Ithica St Broken Arrow OK 74012 Office: Charles Trombley Ministries 500 N Elm Place Broken Arrow OK 74012

TROPF, WALTER DAVID, educator; b. Cleve., Nov. 5, 1927; s. Ralph and Gladys Celestia (Rickel) T.; student Case Western Reserve U., 1947-48; B.A., Taylor U., 1951; M.S.W., U. Mich., 1959; postgrad. U. Fla., 1976—; m. Annabelle Emilie Strange, Dec. 26, 1954; children—Judith Ann, Ralph Kelvin, Elizabeth Sue. Program sec. YMCA, Toledo, 1951-53; caseworker Lucas County Public Welfare Dept., Toledo, 1953-57, Lucas County Chico Welfare Bd., Toledo, 1957-61; dir. group life Summit County Child Welfare Bd., Akron, Ohio, 1961-63; dir. social services and dir. campus life Fla. United Meth. Children's Home, Enterprise, 1963-72; asst. prof. social work U. Central Fla., Orlando, 1972—; U. Fla. grad. asst., 1976-77; cons. Group Child Care Project, U. N.C., 1965-68, Fla. Group Child Care Assn., 1972-75. Served with U.S. Army, 1946-47. Mem. Nat. Assn. Social Workers, Nat. Council on Family Relations, Fla. Council on Family Relations (state sec. 1979-80), Am. Sociol. Assn. Presbyterian. Editor: Group Child Care Training Manual, 1977. Office: Dept of Sociology PO Box 25000 Univ of Central Fla Orlando FL 32816

TROSPER, MILTON FRENCH, JR., dist. engr.; b. Monte Vista, Colo., June 2, 1948; s. Milton French and Wilam Oleta (Wallis) T.; B.A. in Physics, Adams State Coll., 1971. Quality control technician Johns Manville Co., Florence, Colo., 1971-73, engr. research center, Denver, 1973-74, research engr., 1974-78, dist. engr., Ft. Worth, 1978—; instr., coordinator curtain wall constrn. seminars, indsl. asbestos cement seminars, roofing constrn. seminars, mini-computer applications in constrn., mini-computer applications bldg. design. Advisor Explorer Post 293 N. Glen, Thornton, 1974; 2d lt. N. Glen Ambulance Corps, 1974-75; instr. BLS-CPR Colo. Heart Assn., 1977-78, EMT Wilderness Extrication, 1978. Recipient A Award for Outstanding Performance Johns Manville, 1976. Mem. Asbestos Info. Assn. N. Am. (tech. advisor), ASTM, Am. Inst. Chem. Engring., AAAS, Latent Acoustical Soc., Emergency Med. Technicians Assn. of Colo. (chmn. tng. com. 1976-78), Nat. Registry Emergency Med. Technicians, Nat. Assn. Emergency Med. Technicians, Assn.

Paramed. Edn., Republican. Methodist. Patentee high velocity low volume dust collection for portable tools, fire resistant plywood, fire resistant celleluar foam insulation. Home: 101 700 Leisure Dr Fort Worth TX 76112 Office: PO Box 9096 Fort Worth TX 76107

TROTH, WILLIAM ANDREW, psychologist; b. Monesson, Pa., Aug. 3, 1935; s. Andrew William and Esther (Johnston) T.; B.A., Wittenberg U., 1959, M.Ed., 1961; Ph.D., Ohio State U., 1966; m. Anita Louise Sailor, May 8, 1977; children—Andrew, William, Lisa. Tchr., counselor pub. schs., Fairborn, Ohio, 1959-62; asst. instr. edn. Ohio State U., Columbus, 1962-64; instr. Otterbein Coll., Westerville, Ohio, 1964-66; asso. prof., coordinator psychol. services E. Tex. State U., Commerce, 1966—. Mem. Am. Psychol. Assn., Am., Tex. personnel and guidance assns., Nat. Vocat. Guidance Assn., Tex. Career Guidance Assn. (founding pres.), Biofeedback Soc. Tex. (founding dir.). Lutheran. Home: 5828 Marina Dr Garland TX 75043 Office: Center for Student Devel East Tex State Univ Commerce TX 75428

TROTTER, IRVIN WHITFIELD, land surveyor; b. Largo, Fla., Mar. 26, 1925; s. James Whitfield and Rosa Carolyn (Kilgore) T.; student Mass. State Coll., Amherst, 1943-44; m. Norma Jean Deinhardt, June 2, 1951; children—Jo Ann (Mrs. Douglas Wayne Johnson), Lavon (Mrs. Michael Carl James). Rodman, Leo Butler, Land Surveyor, Clearwater, Fla., 1946-48; engr. aide Wash. State Hwy. Dept., Spokane, 1948-56; field supr. Wolf Bros. Surveying, Winter Park, Fla., 1956-62; v.p. Tinklepaugh Surveying Services, Orlando, Fla., 1962-71; v.p. Henrich, Inc., Winter Park, 1971-79; pres. Henrich, Trotter, Carter & Ayres, Inc., 1979—. Served with AUS, 1943-46; ETO. Decorated Bronze Star medal. Mem. Fla. Soc. Profl. Land Surveyors (sec.-treas. 1967-74). Home: 1824 Pineview Circle Winter Park FL 32792 Office: 636 Wymore Rd Winter Park FL 32789

TROTTER, LARRY ALLEN, furniture co. exec.; b. Asheboro, N.C., Oct. 7, 1945; s. Lester Merritt and Leocia Daisy (Allen) T.; student public schs., Asheboro; m. Nancy Jane Kearns, Oct. 30, 1965; children—Brent Dudley, Marty Allen. With B.B. Walker Co., Asheboro, 1964-69, computer programmer, 1967-69; systems analyst, programming mgr. Internat. Computer Services Inc., High Point, N.C., 1970-71; systems analyst B.B. Walker Co., Asheboro, 1971-75; data processing mgr. Stuart Furniture Industries Inc., Asheboro, 1975—. Pres., PTA, 1976-77; mem. local sch. adv. council, 1977—, chmn., 1979; trustee Tabernacle Vol. Fire Dept.; ch. treas., del. to Western N.C. Ann Conf., mem. dist. council on ministries United Methodist Ch.; chmn. bd. mgrs. Mt. Shepherd Retreat Center. Mem. Carolina-Va. N.C.R. Computer Users Group (pres. 1979—). Republican. Home: Route 3 Box 331 Asheboro NC 27203 Office: Stuart Furniture Industries Inc PO Box 220 Asheboro NC 27203

TROTTER, NORMAN LEROY, indsl. engr.; b. Pickens County, S.C., Nov. 26, 1942; s. Norman Leroy and Jessie (Trotter) Justice; B.S. in Indsl. Mgmt., Ga. Inst. Tech., 1971; m. Patricia Lightsey, Mar. 6, 1965; children—Kathleen, Jennifer. Sales engr. Trane Co., Atlanta, 1971-72; plant indsl. engr. Vanity Fair, Robertsdale, Ala., 1972-75; staff indsl. engr. Garan, Inc., Starkville, Miss., 1975-76; canned meats indsl. engr. Bryan Foods Inc., West Point, Miss., 1976-77, asst. prodn. supt. canned meats, 1977-79; corporate indsl. engr. Uncle Ben's Foods, Houston, 1979—. Fund-raising chmn. PTA, 1978; chmn. Ga. Tech. Young Alumni, 1971-72. Served with USN, 1965-68. Mem. Am. Inst. Indsl. Engrs., Delta Sigma Pi. Republican. Presbyterian. Home: 6327 Alden St Houston TX 77084 Office: 13001 Westheimer Rd Houston TX 77077 also PO Box 1752 Houston TX 77001

TROTTER, RICHARD PATRICK, savs. and loan assn. exec.; b. Atlanta, Oct. 4, 1933; s. Richard Adelbert and Nell Lucile (Hamilton) T.; B.B.A., U. Ga., Athens, 1955, LL.B., 1964; postgrad. U. Pa., Phila., 1959-61, M.A. (Pub. Finance Center fellow, Univ. teaching fellow), 1967; m. Frances Elizabeth Goodwin, June 12, 1964; 1 dau., Carmen Nell. Mem. profl. staff Joint Com. on Internal Revenue Taxation, U.S. Congress, Washington, 1967-70; asst. to bd. mem. Fed. Home Loan Bank Bd., Washington, 1970-73; legis. counsel Nat. Assn. Realtors, Washington, 1973-75; sr. v.p. finance and adminstrn., treas., dir. Ga. Fed. Savs. and Loan Assn., 1975—. Served with USMCR, 1956-59. Mem. Res. Officers Assn., Marine Corps Res. Officers Assn., Fin. Execs. Inst., Fin. Mgrs. Soc., Blue Key, Chi Phi, Phi Delta Phi, Omicron Delta Kappa. Home: 1085 Edgewater Dr Atlanta GA 30328 Office: 20 Marietta St Atlanta GA 30303

TROUGHT, JOHN HERBERT, corp. ofcl.; b. Niagara Falls, Ont., Can., Aug. 1, 1933 (parents Am. citizens); s. Herbert Hall and Madalyn Benedicta (Campbell) T.; student Palm Beach Jr. Coll., 1967-69; m. Charlene Elaine Gore, June 17, 1976; 1 dau. by previous marriage, Brenda Jeanne. With RCA Corp., Palm Beach Gardens, Fla., 1966-69; process engr. Burroughs Corp., 1970-71; sr. mfg. engr. Phils Wholesale Auto Parts, West Palm Beach, Fla., 1971-72; warehouse mgr. Pratt & Whitney Aircraft, West Palm Beach, 1972-74; materials analyst Cordis Corp., Miami, Fla., 1974-76; supr. documentation and records Intermedics, Inc., Freeport, Tex., 1976, corp. mgr. internat. regulatory affairs, 1976—. Served with USN, 1950-54. Mem. Soc. Mfg. Engrs., Am. Soc. Quality Control, Nat. Geog. Soc., Acad. Model Aeros., Brazoria County Modelers Assn. Democrat. Inventor Steri-vu packaging system for intraocular lenses. Home: 30 Robin Hood Ln Richwood TX 77531 Office: 240 Tarpon Inn Village Freeport TX 77541

TROUP, ALEXANDER GORDON, III, steel co. exec.; b. Chgo., July 13, 1938; s. Alexander Gordon and Hazel Purdy (Hall) T.; student N. Tex. State U., 1956-59; m. Sally Elizabeth Carpenter, July 29, 1973; children—Andrew C., Alexander Gordon IV. Inside salesman Russell Steel, Grand Prairie, Tex., 1960-62; inside salesman, metal goods div. Alcan Aluminum Corp., Chgo. and Dallas, 1962-67, outside salesman, 1967-72, sales mgr., 1972-76; dist. mgr. Steel Service Center Warehouse, Russell Steel div. Van Pelt Corp., Grand Prairie, 1976—. Served with USMC, 1956-64. Named Salesman of Year, E. Tex. Purchasing Mgmt. Assn., 1970. Mem. ASTM, ASME. Republican. Mem. Ch. of Christ. Home: 2801 Augusta Ln Arlington TX 76012 Office: 2602 Pinewood Dr Grand Prairie TX 75051

TROUT, MARGIE MARIE MUELLER, civic worker; b. Wellston, Mo., Apr. 27, 1923; d. Albert Sylvester and Pearl Elizabeth (Jose) Mueller; student Webster Coll., 1944-45; m. Maurice Elmore Trout, Aug. 24, 1943; children—Richard Willis, Babette Yvonne. Sec. offices Robertson Aircraft Corp., St. Louis, 1942; speed lathe and drill press operator Busch-Selzer Diesel Engine Co., St. Louis, 1942-43; Cub Scout den mother, Vienna, Austria, 1953-55, Mt. Pleasant, Mich., 1955, London, Eng., 1956-57; leader Nat. Capitol council Girl Scouts U.S.A., Bethesda, Md., 1963-65; co-chmn. Am. Booth YWCA and Red Cross Annual Bazaars, Bangkok, Thailand, 1970-72; worker ARC, Vientiane, Laos, 1959-60, Bangkok, 1970-72; activities co-chmn., exec. bd. mem. Women's Club Armed Forces Staff Coll., Norfolk, Va., 1975-77; mem. Am. Women's Clubs, Embassy Clubs, Internat. Women's Clubs Vienna, 1952-55, London, 1956-59, Vientiane, 1959-61, Bangkok, 1969-72, Munich, Germany, 1965-69, Norfolk, 1975-77. Crochet articles exhibited Exhibition of Works of Art by the Corps Diplomatique, London, Eng., 1958. Home: 6203 Hardy Dr McLean VA 22101

TROUTMAN, EDWIN GLENN, physician; b. Olathe, Kans., July 31, 1927; s. Edwin Glenn and Maude Roxanne (Seaton) T.; student U. Ariz., 1944-45, 46-47; M.D., U. So. Calif., 1952; m. Mary Olena Flesher, Sept. 4, 1949; children—Clinton Edwin, David Glenn. Intern, resident Barlow Sanatorium, Los Angeles, 1951-54; resident 1st Med. Div. Bellevue Hosp., N.Y.C., 1955, 56; teaching resident fellow Nat. Tb. Assn., Am. Trudeau Soc., 1955, 56; practice medicine, specializing in internal medicine, Ft. Worth, 1961—; mem. staff numerous Ft. Worth hosps.; instr. medicine U. So. Calif., 1954; instr. medicine U. Tex. Med. Br., 1957-59, asst. prof. medicine, 1959-61, asst. to dean of medicine 1957-59, med. dir. outpatient dept., asst. dir. for planning, 1959-60; clin. asst. prof. medicine U. Tex. Southwestern Med. Sch., 1961—; dir. med. edn. and research Harris Hosp., Ft. Worth Found., Ft. Worth, 1961-65; pres. Tex. Allergy Labs., Inc., Med. Computers, Inc., Doctors Operational Computer Service, Inc. Bd. dirs. Tarrant County Hist. Soc. Served with USNR, 1945-46. Mem. Am., Tex. diabetes assns., Am., Tex. State, Tarrant County med. assns., Am. Thor. Soc. Republican. Author various articles pub. in profl. jours. Home: 2026 Ward Parkway Fort Worth TX 76110 Office: 712 7th Ave Fort Worth TX 76104

TROUTMAN, JANET KAY, radio broadcasting exec.; b. Austin, Tex., July 12, 1954; d. Arthur Young and Clarice (Lee) T.; student San Antonio Coll., 1972-75. With Sta. KONO, San Antonio, 1973-74, Sta. KBUC, San Antonio, 1974-75, Sta. WOAI, San Antonio, 1975-76, Sta. KLIF, Dallas, 1976-77; mem. sales staff Sta. KTXQ, Dallas, 1977-79, account exec., Ft. Worth, 1979—. Mem. Ft. Worth Ad Club. Republican. Mem. Christian Ch. Clubs: Playboy (Dallas); Horseshoe Bend Country. Home: 1505 Carol Oaks Trail Apt 1309 Fort Worth TX 76112 also 26-67A Horseshoe Bend Trail W Weatherford TX 76086 Office: Sta KTXQ 1215 Country Club Dr Fort Worth TX 76112

TROWBRIDGE, EDMUND HARRISON, bus. adminstr.; b. Cambridge, Mass., Aug. 9, 1936; s. Edmund Harrison and Viola (Vail) T.; B.B.A. with honors, U. Miami, 1962; postgrad. Sch. Law, U. S.C., 1963; m. Carol Ann Arand, July 17, 1965; children—Kimberlee Anne, Kyle Harrison. Claims adjustor Gt. Am. Ins. Co. and So. Fire Adjustors, Ft. Lauderdale and Coral Gables, Fla., 1963-67; claims supr. Kemper Ins. Co. Fla., 1967-70; regional claims mgr. Stuyvesant Ins. Group, Miami, 1970-74; legal adminstr. Stephens, Magill, Thornton and Sevier, Miami, 1974-77; claims mgr. Frank B. Hall & Co., Inc., Coral Gables, 1977—; bus. cons., Coral Gables, 1970—. Vol. worker Nat. Republican Com., United Fund, Goodwill Industries, 1970—; mem. Fla. Adv. Com. on Arson Prevention. Served with U.S. Army, 1963. Recipient Nat. Subrogation Recovery award, named Nat. Claimsman of month, 1966. Mem. Assn. Legal Adminstrs., S. Fla. Para-Legal Assn., Southeastern Ins. Claims Execs. Council, Miami Claim Mgrs. Council, Atlanta Claims Assn., Miami Inter-Co. Arbitration Com., S. Fla. Claims Assn., U. Miami Alumni Assn., U. Miami Athletic Fedn., Sigma Phi Epsilon, Alpha Delta Sigma, Delta Sigma Phi. Clubs: Miami Touchdown, Country of Coral Gables. Creator of negligence def. litigation Bring Up system, 1975; innovator of telephone claims handling procedures, 1966-68; founder first and third party desk adjustment procedures, 1971-72. Home: 732 Santander Ave Coral Gables FL 33134 Office: PO Box 343800 Coral Gables FL 33134

TROWELL, CHRISTY TUTTLE, educator; b. Oliver, Ga., May 9, 1934; s. Christian Samuel and Ivey Mae (Tuttle) T.; B.S. in Edn., Ga. So. Coll., 1954, M.Ed., 1961, Ed.S., 1965; m. Frances Nannette Register, July 26, 1958; children—Mary Nannette, Christina Kay, Christian Samuel, Robert. Tchr., Coffee High Sch., Douglas, Ga., 1957-65; social sci. instr., asso. prof. S. Ga. Coll., Douglas, 1965—; instr. 8th Congressional Dist. Honors Program, 1966, 67. Mem. adv. com. Agrirama, 1979-80; mem. Douglas Community Devel. Com., 1976-79; mem. natural areas com. Ga. Dept. Natural Resources, 1976-79. Served in U.S. Army, 1954-57. NSF grantee, 1976. Mem. Assn. Am. Geographers, Nat. Council Geog. Edn., Southeastern Archaeol. Conf., Eastern States Archaeol. Fedn., Soc. Ga. Archaeology, Ga. Acad. Sci., Fla. Anthrop. Soc., Ga. Hist. Soc., Ala. Archaeol. Soc., Tall Timbers Research Assn., Soc. Ga. Archaeology (v.p. 1976, pres. 1977, co-editor Early Ga. 1977). Methodist. Contbr. articles to profl. jours. Home: RFD 3 Douglas GA 31533 Office: S Ga Coll Douglas GA 31533

TRUAX, ROBERT CHARLES, edn. cons.; b. Rochester, Minn., Oct. 15, 1936; s. Clair Joseph and Muriel A. (Whitcomb) T.; B.A., U. R.I., 1972; M.Ed., Providence Coll., 1975; m. Patricia Ann Clark, Aug. 27, 1960; children—Heidi, Alan Scott. Enlisted U.S. Navy, 1956, served aviation electronics technician, 1956-57; commd. ensign, 1959, advanced through grades to comdr., 1974, served Mediterranean/Atlantic areas, 1959-63, staff of chief of naval personnel, 1963-66, served U.S.S. Kearsarge, Vietnam, 1966-68, exec. officer Keflavik, Iceland, 1975-77, faculty U.S. Navy War Coll., 1972-75, ret., 1979; edn. cons., Springfield, Va., 1977-79; lectr. in social sci. No. Va. Community Coll. Active Boy Scouts Am., 1966-77. Recipient commendation for course design, War Coll., 1974. Mem. U.S. Naval Inst., Am. Personnel and Guidance Assn. Roman Catholic. Lodge: Eagles (Minn.). Editor Anti Submarine Operations, Nuclear Operations, Strike Operations, 1976; contbr. articles in field of mgmt., edn., data analysis to publs. Home and Office: 7709 Mulberry Bottom Ln Springfield VA 22153

TRUAX, ROBERT LISLE, physicist; b. Mobridge, S.D., July 1, 1929; s. Ross Haines and Olga Marie (Wilson) T.; B.S., Iowa State U., 1963; m. Patricia Stratton Jones, Dec. 31, 1959. Mgr. govt. avionic products Collins Radio Co., Cedar Rapids, Iowa, 1957-64; mgr. ionospheric sounder and avionic products Granger Assos., Palo Alto, Calif., 1964-68; research engr. Dayton Aircraft Products, Ft. Lauderdale, Fla., 1968-71; pres. Truax Co., Fort Myers, Fla., 1971—, also chmn. bd.; pres., chmn. TCO Mfg. Corp., DanePole Inc. Served with AUS, 1951-57. Mem. Aircraft Owners Pilots Assn., Nat. Pilots Assn., Nat. Rifle Assn., Smithsonian Assos., Kappa Sigma. Republican. Club: Masons. Patentee low noise static discharger device. Home: 1615 Avalon Pl Fort Myers FL 33901 Office: 604 Danley Dr Fort Myers FL 33907

TRUDNAK, STEPHEN JOSEPH, landscape architect; b. Nanticoke, Pa., Feb. 25, 1947; s. Stephen Adam and Marcella (Levullis) T.; B.S. in Landscape Arch., Pa. State U., 1970. Jr. landscape architect Kling Partnership, Phila., 1970-72; landscape architect firm Keith French Assos., Washington, 1972-73; head dept. landscape architecture Linganore Center Design, Frederick, Md., 1973-74; head dept. landscape architecture Toups and Loiederman, Rockville, Md., 1974-76; project landscape architect Dade County Transit Improvement Program, Kaiser Transit Group, Harry Weese & Assos., Ltd., Miami, Fla., 1976—. Mem. Am. Soc. Landscape Architects, Nat. Speleol. Soc. SCARAB. Home: 1425 Obispo Ave Coral Gables FL 33134 Office: Flagler Center Bldg 44 W Flagler St Suite 731 Miami FL 33130

TRUE, DEWITT SIDNEY, gynecologist; b. Boston, July 19, 1916; s. Sidney John and Esther Hutchins (Ramsay) T.; A.B., Harvard U., 1939, M.D., 1943; m. Anna Mae McMennamin, Mar. 25, 1943; children—Dewitt Ramsay, Sandra True Conrad, Candace True Harding, Kristen Converse. Commd. lt. (j.g.) USN, 1943, advanced through grades to capt., 1957; intern, U.S. Naval Med. Center, Bethesda, Md., 1943-44; resident in ob-gyn U.S. Naval Hosp., Chelsea, Mass., 1946-48, 51-52; chief dept. U.S. Naval Hosp., Beaufort, S.C., 1948-51, exec. officer, 1960-62; asst. chief dept. U.S. Naval Hosp., Portsmouth, Va., 1954-60; ret., 1964; practice medicine specializing in ob-gyn, Portsmouth, Va., 1964—; mem. staff Maryview Hosp., Portsmouth Gen. Hosp.; instr. Eastern Va. Med. Sch., Norfolk. Bd. dirs. Va. Cancer Soc. Am., 1962-64, 67-69, 72-76, Portsmouth unit, 1959—. Diplomate Am. Bd. Ob-Gyn. Fellow Am. Coll. Obstetricians and Gynecologists; mem. Med. Soc. Va., Va. Ob-Gyn. Soc., Tidewater Ob-Gyn Soc., Portsmouth Acad. Medicine, Nat. Philatelic Soc., Nat. Audubon Soc. Deacon, tchr., choir mem. Churchland Bapt. Ch. 1955—. Club: Kiwanis. Home: 4426 Point West Dr Portsmouth VA 23703 Office: 500 Rodman Ave Portsmouth VA 23707

TRUETT, CASEY, physician; b. Gatesville, Tex., Sept. 26, 1944; s. Herbert Winters and Gladys (Reed) T.; student U. Ala., 1962-63; B.S. with honors, U. Okla., 1965, M.D., 1969; m. Lisa A. Truett, Jan. 20, 1979; 1 dau., Melinda Katherine. Intern St. Francis Hosp., Tulsa, 1969-70; practice medicine, Norman, Okla., 1972—; cons. MEDCOM, N.Y.C., 1974—; asso. clin. prof. dept. family practice and community medicine and dentistry U. Okla. Coll. Medicine, 1975—; med. examiner Cleveland County (Okla.), 1973; asst. prof. Oral Roberts U. Sch. Medicine, 1979—. Chmn. Okla. Med. Polit. Action Com., 1976-77; bd. dirs. Norman C. of C., 1975-77, Norman Christian Fellowship, 1978, Norman Alcohol Info. Center, 1978-79; mem. health occupations adv. com. Moore/Norman Vocat.-Tech. Sch.; mem. Norman Mayor's Task Force, 1974; mem. Republican State Com., 1973-75; bd. dirs. Campfire Girls, Norman, 1974-75. Served with USPHS, 1970-72. Recipient Kiwanis Spl. award, Tahlequah, Okla., 1972; elected as Eagle Scout, 1958, to Student AMA Com. on Med. Edn., 1968; USPHS grantee, 1966-67; diplomate Am. Bd. Family Practice. Fellow Am. Acad. Family Practice; mem. Okla. Med. Assn. (trustee 1974-77), So. Med. Assn., Okla. Acad. Family Practice, Cleveland McClain County Med. Soc. (pres. 1979), Royal Soc. Medicine (London) (affiliate), U. Okla. Alumni Assn. Republican. Club: Kiwanis. Home: 8001 S Quebec St Tulsa OK 73071 Office: Oral Roberts Family Practice Center 7306 S Lewis St Tulsa OK

TRUITT, DARRELL WARREN, coll. dean; b. Arnett, Okla., May 19, 1935; s. P.W. and Bonnie (Lee) T.; B.A., W. Tex. State U., 1957, M.Ed., 1967; postgrad. Tex. Tech. U., Am. U.; grad. U.S. Command Gen. Staff Coll., 1976; m. Jo Anne Montgomery, Aug. 27, 1954; children—Terri Lynne, Tanya Layne. Tchr., football coach River Rd. Ind. Sch. Dist., Amarillo, Tex., 1963-70; dir. student activities Amarillo Coll., 1970-73, dean of students, 1974—. Deacon 1st Presbyterian Ch., 1979—. Served to lt. col., AUS, 1957-63. Decorated Army Commendation Medal; cert. public sch. supt., prin., adminstr., tchr., Tex. Mem. Jr. Col. Student Personnel Assn. Tex. (dir. 1975-79), Western Jr. Coll. Assn. (v.p. 1975-76), Tex. Assn. Coll. and Univ. Student Personnel Adminstrs., Tex. Tchrs. Assn., Am. Personnel and Guidance Assn. Democrat. Home: 7116 Gainsborough St Amarillo TX 79106 Office: PO Box 447 Amarillo TX 79178

TRUITT, WILLIAM JAMES, economist; b. Dallas, Mar. 4, 1940; s. William Alton and Nova Merle (Hamilton) T.; B.A., So. Meth. U., 1960; M.S. (Ford Found. fellow), Purdue U., 1962; Ph.D., U. Ill., 1968; m. Catherine Cecile Butts, Aug. 25, 1962; children—Susan Narceille, Catherine Nova. Asst. prof. econs., La. State U., 1965-68; asso. prof. Baylor U., 1968-71, prof., 1971—, dir. grad. studies, 1970-71, chmn. dept. econs., 1971—; sec. TRUMAS, Inc., Red River Timberline, Inc. Chmn. com. on edn., mem. bldg. com., mem. council on ministries, mem. adminstrv. bd., mem. personnel com. First United Meth. Ch., Waco, Tex., 1977—; bd. dirs. Wesley Found., Baylor U. Mem. Am., So. econs. assns. Club: Fish Pond Country. Office: Hankamer Sch Bus Baylor U Waco TX 76706

TRUMBLE, GLENN EDWARD, chem. engr.; b. Moline, Ill., July 4, 1937; s. Thomas Joseph and Marian (Thorngren) T.; student St. Mary's Coll., 1955, Ill. Inst. Tech., 1956-61, St. Ambrose Coll., 1958; B.S. in Chem. Engring., Johns Hopkins U., 1966; postgrad. U. Tenn., Chattanooga, 1971, Chattanooga State Tech., 1973; 1 dau., Julie Ellen. Analytical chemist, metallurgist Internat. Harvester Co., Chgo., 1956-59; research metallurgist Steel City, Chgo., 1960; owner, operator Seaway Research Co., cons., East Chicago, Ind., 1960-62; head analytical chemist Huntingdon Research Co., Balt., 1966-69; sr. project engr. Chattem Drug Co., Chattanooga, 1970-75; asst. to plant mgr. Ill. Nitrogen Co., Marseilles, 1976-77; environ. coordinator Velsicol Chem. Co., Memphis, 1977-79; project mgr. Matrix Engring. Co., Beaumont, Tex., 1980—; cons. environ. engr., new products. Served with U.S. Army, 1962-65. Mem. Water Pollution Control Fedn., Air Pollution Control Fedn., Am. Inst. Chem. Engrs., ASTM, Am. Chem. Soc. Roman Catholic. Club: Cherokee Sportsman's. Patentee in field. Home: 975 Iris St Beaumont TX 77706 Office: Matrix Engring Co PO Box 3731 Beaumont TX 77704

TRUSLER, MARTHA DAY, nurse; b. DeValls Bluff, Ark., Feb. 28, 1926; d. Clarence Charles and Hortia (Moss) Day; R.N., U. Tenn., 1946; m. Jack Edward Trusler, Oct. 30, 1948; 1 dau., Karen Sue (dec.). Med./surg. nurse City of Memphis Hosp., 1946-57; nurse central service and recovery room LeBonheur Children's Hosp., Memphis, 1957-73; nurse central service and infection control Meth. S. Hosp., 1973-78; infection control coordinator Meth. Hosps. of Memphis, 1978—. Mem. Am. Nurses Assn., Assn. Practitioners in Infection Control (bd. dirs. regional chpt.), Am. Soc. Hosp. Central Service Personnel. Republican. Methodist. Home: 184 Palisade St Memphis TN 38111 Office: 1265 Union St Memphis TN 38104

TRUSSELL, GALE RAGAN, state ofcl., recreation and tourism specialist; b. Minden, La., Nov. 5, 1940; s. George Reuben and Lurline (Shaw) T.; B.S., La. State U., 1962; M.F., La. State U., 1967; m. Glenda Rae Stott, June 15, 1963; 1 son, Joel Ragan. Farm forester Mo. Dept. Conservation, West Plains, 1965-66; chief planner Mo. State Park Bd., Jefferson City, 1966-70; recreation planner Gov.'s Office of Planning, Jefferson City, 1970-78; recreation and tourism specialist Ala. Coop. Extension Service, Mobile, 1978—; chmn. Gov.'s Open Space Com., 1971—; mem. Mo. U. Sch. Forestry Adv. Council; chmn. land and transp. com. Tenn.-Tom Waterway, 1975-77. Mem. Ala. Park and Recreation Assn., Coastal Environ. Edn. Council, State Outdoor Recreation Plan Adv. Com., Farm Bur. Democrat. Baptist. Contbr. articles to profl. jours. Home: 7662 Adobe Ridge N Mobile AL 36609 Office: 3940 Government Blvd Mobile AL 36609

TRYBUL, THEODORE, engr., govt. ofcl.; b. Chgo., Apr. 12, 1935; s. Theodore and Sophie (Mihalik) T.; B.S., U. Ill., 1957; M.S., U. N.Mex., 1963; Sc.D., George Washington U., 1976; m. Barbara Jane Reynolds, Aug. 22, 1959; children—Adrienne, Barbie, Catherine, Diane, Elizabeth, Theodore. Engr., Internat. Harvester Co., Chgo., 1954-56; staff scientist Sandia Corp., Albuquerque, 1957-64; engring. dept. mgr. Gen. Dynamics Corp., Pomona, Calif., 1964-65; tech. dir. Aerospace Corp., San Bernardino, Calif., 1965-67; project mgr. Raytheon Co., Bedford, Mass., 1967-68; div. chief AMC, Washington, 1968-74; chief estimates and studies DARCOM, Alexandria, Va., 1974—; prof. mgmt. U. No. Colo., 1971-76; prof. engring. George Washington U., 1976—; prof. bus. adminstrn. Am.

U., 1977—. Pres. Gunston Sch. PTA, Lorton, Va., 1971, 77; mem. Woodridge (Va.) Parish Council, 1975; bd. dirs., chmn. Our Lady of Angels Ch., 1976-77; mem. Fairfax County Bd. Edn., 1971-77. Served with C.E., U.S. Army, 1959-61. Recipient award for pub. service PTA, 1971. Mem. ASME, Am. Ordnance Assn., Armed Forces Mgmt. Assn., Am. Soc. Mil. Comptrollers, Ops. Research Soc. Am., Washington Ops. Research Council, Internat. Soc. for Technology Assessment, World Future Soc., Washington Acad. Sci., Mil. Ops. Research Soc., Smithsonian Instn. Roman Catholic. Clubs: Aquia Harbor, Sea Pines, Plantation, Millionaires, George Washington U. Faculty, K.C. Contbr. numerous articles to profl. jours. Home: 203 Yoakum St Alexandria VA 22304 Office: 5001 Eisenhower Ave Alexandria VA 22333

TSAI, KUO-CHUN, water pollution engr.; b. Taiwan, Aug. 16, 1937; s. See Fang and Mu Chiao (Tseng) T.; came to U.S., 1968, naturalized, 1977; B.S. in Civil Engring. (fellow Nat. Sci. Council Rep. of China), Cheng Kung U., 1960; M.S. in Environ. Engring., U. Fla., 1969; Ph.D. in San. Engring. (Chancellor fellow), U. Mo., Rolla, 1977; m. Helena F. Tseng, Dec. 22, 1967; children—Flora, Jeanne. Instr. civil engring. Cheng Kung U., Taiwan, 1964-70, asso. prof. san. engring., 1970-73; project engr. AWARE, Inc., Nashville, Tenn., 1979—; del. to Internat. Assn. Water Pollution Research, Johannesburg, S. Africa. Mem. Nat. Soc. Profl. Engrs., Water Pollution Control Fedn. Baptist. Home: 232 Hickory Trace Dr Nashville TN 37211 Office: 40284 Nashville TN 37204

TSAI, STANLEY T. H., microbiologist; b. Taiwan, Apr. 20, 1924; s. H. C. and I. C. (Chun) T.; B.S., Nat. Taiwan U., 1952; M.S., U. Tenn., 1962; m. Jesusa Guzman, Apr. 25, 1964. Chemist, Taiwan Serum and Vaccine Lab., 1955-57; research asst. Chgo. Med. Sch., 1962-67; research asso. La. State U. Med. Center, 1967-70; instr. anatomy U. Ark. Med. Center, Little Rock, 1970—. Mem. Internat. Soc. Chronobiology, Sigma Xi. Contbr. articles to profl. jours. Home: 1400 N Hughes Little Rock AR 72207 Office: 4301 Markham Little Rock AR 72201

TSAO, MING JYI, anesthesiologist; b. Taiwan, Jan. 16, 1944; S. Ho Song and Wu Hou Tsao; M.D., Kaohsiung Med. Coll., Taiwan, 1970; m. Yieh-Ying Yang, Jan. 6, 1972; children—Alice S., Benjamin E. Intern, St. Anne's Hosp., Chgo., 1972-73; resident in surgery Lakeland (Fla.) Gen. Hosp., 1973-74, in anesthesia, Milwaukee County Gen. Hosp., Milw., 1974-77; practice anesthesia, Ocala, Fla., 1977—; dir. anesthesia dept. Munroe Meml. Hosp. (name now Munroe Regional Med. Center), Ocala, Fla., 1977—. Served as ensign Chinese Navy, 1970-71. Diplomate Am. Bd. Anesthesiology. Fellow Am. Coll. Anesthesiologists; mem. AMA (Physicians Recognition award 1978), Am. Soc. Anesthesiologists, Internat. Anesthesia Research Soc., Fla. Med. Assn., Marion County Med. Soc. Buddhist. Home: 2115 SE 38th St Ocala FL 32671 Office: 131 SW 15th St Ocala FL 32670

TSCHANTZ, BRUCE ALLEN, civil engr., educator; b. Akron, Ohio, Sept. 15, 1938; s. Miles Emerson and Gladys Marcella (Krichbaum) T.; B.S. in Civil Engring., Ohio No. U., 1960; M.S., N.Mex. State U., 1962, Sc.D., 1965; m. Penelope Ann Ford, Dec. 20, 1962; children—Peter Allen, Michael Ford. San. engr. Bur. Indian Affairs, Albuquerque, 1962-63; civil engr. White Sands (N.Mex.) Missile Range, 1965; asst. prof. civil engring. U. Tenn., Knoxville, 1965-69, asso. prof., 1969-74, prof., 1974—; chief fed. dam safety Fed. Emergency Mgmt. Agy., Washington, 1979-81; cons. hydrologist U.S. Geol. Survey, Knoxville, 1973-76; cons. Exec. Office of Pres., Office Sci. Tech. Policy, Washington, 1977—, Tenn. Dept. Transp., 1976—; mem. Gov.'s Adv. Com. on Dams, Tenn., 1972, Tenn. Legislative Land Use Planning Task Force, 1973; cons. Tenn. Dept. Conservation, 1978. Recipient Engring. Coll. Faculty Achievement award, 1977, M.E. Brooks Disting. Prof. award, 1978. Registered profl. engr., Ohio, Tenn., Va. Mem. ASCE (Faculty of Year award Student chpt. 1968, dam safety task com. of nat. water policy com.), Am. Soc. Engring. Edn. (civil engr. chmn. S.E. sect. 1972, Southeastern Young Faculty award, Dow Chem. award 1970, Western Electric Outstanding Educator award 1980), Nat., Tenn. (v.p., pres. Knoxville br. 1973-75, Knoxville Young Engr. award 1970) socs. profl. engrs., Knoxville Tech. Soc., Sigma Xi, Chi Epsilon, Tau Beta Pi. Contbr. articles on dam safety, flood control and hydrologic impacts of strip mining to profl. jours. Home: 1508 Meeting House Rd Knoxville TN 37921 Office: 63 Perkins Hall U Tenn Knoxville TN 37916

TSCHOEPE, THOMAS, bishop; b. Pilot Point, Tex., Dec. 17, 1915; s. Louis and Catherine (Sloan) T.; student St. Thomas Sch. Pilot Point, 1930, Pontifical Coll. Josephinum, Worthington, Ohio, 1943. Ordained priest Roman Catholic Ch., 1943; asst. pastor in Ft. Worth, 1943-46, Sherman, Tex., 1946-48, Dallas, 1948-53; adminstr. St. Patrick Ch., Dallas, 1953-56; pastor St. Augustine Ch., Dallas, 1956-62, Sacred Heart Cathedral, Dallas, 1962-65; bishop of San Angelo, Tex., 1966-69, Dallas, 1969—. Home: 3915 Lemmon Ave Box 19507 Dallas TX 75219

TU, KEVIN KUEN-CHING, microbiologist; b. Canton, China, Oct. 16, 1936; came to U.S., 1965, naturalized, 1976; Ph.D. in Bacteriology, Utah State U., 1972; m. Connie Kung-Lin Tso, June 20, 1970; children—Charlene, Shawn. Research and teaching asst. Utah State U., Logan, 1967-72; postdoctoral fellow Erie County Med. Center and SUNY, Buffalo, 1972-74; asst. prof. pathology Wayne State U., 1974-76; chief microbiologist Charleston (W.Va.) Area Med. Center, 1976—; mem. clin. faculty U. Charleston, W.Va. U. Med. Sch. Mem. Am. Soc. Microbiology, Am. Soc. Clin. Pathology (cert. specialist in med. microbiology and public health), Sigma Xi. Baptist. Contbr. articles to profl. jours. Office: 3200 MacCorkle Ave SE Charleston WV 25304

TUBB, GLORIA LUKE, educator; b. Shuqualak, Miss., May 3, 1926; d. Green Van and Mary Elizabeth (Stokes) Luke; B.A., Miss. U. Women, 1948; M.S., U. So. Miss., 1971; m. Jackson McWhirter Tubb, Jr., Sept. 4, 1947; children—Van Jackson, James Benson, William Luke. Instr. public schs., Toccopola and Skene, Miss., 1949, 51; instr. Delta State Coll., 1951; instr. public schs., Louin, Miss., 1956-57, Bay Springs, Miss., 1958-60, Ellisville, Miss., 1960-61, West Jones, Miss., 1962-63; instr. English, Jones County Jr. Coll., Ellisville, 1970-78, coordinator devel. skills program, 1979—; judge sci. fairs. Mem. Zoning Commn. Bay Springs, 1974-76. Mem. Faculty Assn. Jones County Jr. Coll. (pres. 1978), Miss. Faculty Assn. (sec. 1979), Miss. Assn. Educators, NEA, Miss. Polit. Action Council Tchrs., Southeastern Conf. Two Year Colls. English, Delta Kappa Gamma (v.p. 1978, 79), Phi Upsilon Omicron. Methodist. Home: 42 Broadmoor Dr Laurel MS 39440 Office: Jones County Jr Coll Ellisville MS 39437

TUBBS, LAWRENCE ALLEN, elec. engr.; b. Dunkirk, N.Y., May 11, 1940; s. Wesley Blake and Esther Grace (Lowell) T.; B.E.E., Clarkson Coll. Tech., 1962; M.S. in E.E., Purdue U., 1969; m. Ann Whitworth Stokes, Nov. 26, 1976; stepchildren—Whitworth Stokes Jones, Gina Payne Jones. Electronic engr. Advanced Ballistic Missile Def. Agency, Huntsville, Ala., 1972-75; electronic engr. Ballistic Missile Def. Advanced Tech. Center, Huntsville, 1975—. Bd. dirs. Huntsville Amateur Hockey Assn., 1972—. Served to maj. U.S. Army, 1962-72. Mem. IEEE, Assn. U.S. Army, Eta Kappa Nu. Home: 1012 Appalachee Rd Huntsville AL 35801 Office: PO Box 1500 Huntsville AL 35807

TUCCIARONE, JOHN ROBERT, electronics engr.; b. Bronx, N.Y., July 26, 1949; s. John and Madeline (Strychacki) T.; B.E.E., Poly. Inst. Bklyn., 1972; M.E.E., Poly. Inst. N.Y., 1977; m. Linda Ann Mader, Aug. 8, 1976. Electronics engr., telemetry div., tech. support directorate Picatinny Arsenal, Dover, N.J., 1972-77; electronics engr., hydro power test sect. C.E., U.S. Army, Clark Hill, S.C., 1977—. Mem. Nat. Assn. Skin Diving Schs. (instr.). Home: 3912 Creekwood Ln Martinez GA 30907 Office: Corps Engrs US Army Clark Hill SC 29821

TUCKER, ELLIS EUGENE, educator; b. Booneville, Miss., Sept. 15, 1931; s. Ocie Eugene and Ethel Irene (McCutchen) T.; B.A.E., U. Miss., 1952; M.Div., Emory U., 1958; M.S., La. State U., 1967; advanced M.L.S., Fla. State U., 1973, Ph.D., 1974. Ordained to ministry United Meth. Ch., 1952; minister chs., Miss., 1952-55, 58-63; librarian Lepanto (Ark.) High Sch., 1963-64; cataloger, acting librarian Frederick Coll., Portsmouth, Va., 1964-67; asst. librarian, audio visual dir. Allegany Community Coll., Cumberland, Md., 1967; dir. Ala. Library Learning Center, Jacksonville, 1968-69; asst. prof., chmn. dept. library sci. U. Miss., 1967-76, asso. prof., dir. Grad. Sch. Library and Info. Sci., 1976—. Bd. dirs. U. Miss. Wesley Found. Mem. ALA, Southeastern, Miss. library assns., Continuing Library Edn. Network, Beta Phi Mu, Phi Kappa Phi, Phi Delta Kappa. Democrat. Editor Southeastern Librarian; mem. editorial bd. Jour. Library Automation. Home: 601 Manor Dr Oxford MS 38655 Office: Grad Sch of Library and Info Sci U of Miss University MS 38677

TUCKER, EVERETT, JR., real estate devel. co. exec.; b. Tucker, Ark., July 7, 1912; s. Dewitt Everett and Will Lynn (Alexander) T.; B.S., Washington and Lee U., 1934; postgrad. U. N.Mex. Sch. Law, 1948; m. Francis Marion Williams, Oct. 9, 1943; children—Robert Williams, Everett III, Marion Clarke. With Standard Oil Co., Little Rock, 1934-36; asst. mgr. S.E. Tucker Co. (Ark.), 1936-41; indsl. mgr. Little Rock C. of C., 1949-59; pres. Indsl. Devel. Co. of Little Rock, 1960—; dir. Ark. Nat. Stockyards, Comml. Nat. Bank, Commonwealth Fed. Savs. and Loan, Little Rock, Capitol Cable Corp., Austin, Tex. Mem. Little Rock Sch. Bd., 1958-65, pres., 1959-63; trustee Little Rock U., 1958-59; mem. Little Rock City Planning Commn., 1959. Served to maj. USAAF, 1942-47. Named Disting. Alumnus, Washington and Lee U., 1979. Mem. Am. (past pres.), So. (past pres.) indsl. devel. councils. Democrat. Episcopalian. Clubs: Little Rock, Little Rock Country. Home: 4601 Kavanaugh Blvd Little Rock AR 72207 Office: 1780 Tower Bldg Little Rock AR 72201

TUCKER, JACK NORRIS, lawyer, former state senator; b. Charleston, Miss., May 15, 1921; s. Harry Randolph and Lucy (Rolfe) T.; grad. Holmes Jr. Coll., 1942; B.A., U. Miss., 1948, LL.B., 1950, J.D., 1968; m. Pattye Sue Williams, Sept. 12, 1948. Admitted to Miss. bar, 1950; pvt. practice law Tunica, 1950—; mem. Miss. Senate, 1960-80. Commr. election Tunica County, Miss., 1952-56, chmn. bd., 1952-56; dir. Miss. Heart Assn., 1952-56, 60-64; chmn. Tunica Heart Fund, 1952—; lay-del. Miss. to Am. Heart Assn., 1960-61; chmn. Tunica County Heart Council, 1961—; Boy Scout commr. Tunica County. Served from ensign to lt. (j.g.), USNR, 1942-46; USNR (ret.). Mem. Am., Tunica, Coahoma County bar assns., Miss. State Bar Am. Legion, V.F.W., Delta Kappa Epsilon, Phi Delta Phi. Democrat. Methodist. Rotarian. Home: PO Box 1256 Tunica MS 38676

TUCKER, JOHN ANDREW, III, newspaper exec.; b. Atlanta, July 11, 1929; s. John Andrew and Dorothy Matthew T.; B.S. in Communications, U. Fla., 1955; m. Eugenia Rosignol, Jan. 29, 1955; children—Angel, John, Nancy, Chris, Clay, Lee, Jill. Mgr. telephone ops. So. Bell, Orlando, 1955-65, dist. mgr., Jacksonville, 1965; dir. bus. devel. Fla. Publ. Co., Jacksonville, 1965-66, v.p., 1966-77, pres., gen. mgr., 1977—; dir. Flagship Banks. Bd. dirs. Mental Health Assn., Jacksonville, Meml. Hosp., Jacksonville; pres. Jr. Achievement, Jacksonville. Served with USAF, 1950-53. Recipient Jacksonville Jr. C. of C. Disting. Service award, 1964. Mem. Sales and Mktg. Execs., Gator Bowl Assn. (pres.), Fla. Press Assn. (past pres., dir. 1978-79). Roman Catholic. Club: Jacksonville Quarterback. Office: 1 Riverside Ave Jacksonville FL 32202

TUCKER, MARGARET JONES, trust co. exec.; b. Livingston, Tex., June 14, 1919; d. Roland Ward and Edna Juanita (Munsell) Jones; student U. Houston, 1940-41; m. James Edward Tucker, July 1, 1961; children—James Montgomery Smith, Sally Margaret Smith. Agy. and corp. sec. Columbia Gen. Life Ins. Co., Houston, 1955-62; account exec. Hand & Assos. Employee Benefit Cons. and Actuaries, Houston, 1962-63; exec. v.p. Am. Industries Trust Co., Houston, 1965-77, pres., 1977—, also dir. Mem. governing bd. dirs. Elva Lobit Acad. Performing Arts, 1979-80. Enrolled to practice before IRS; lic. Nat. Assn. Security Dealers, Tx. Bd. Securities. Mem. Am. Bus. Women's Assn., Tex. Assn. Bus., Internat. Found. Employee Benefit Plans, Assn. Pvt. Pension and Welfare Plans, Am. Soc. Pension Actuaries (asso.), Houston C. of C., DAR, P.E.O. Republican. Presbyterian. Home: 8403 Carvel St Houston TX 77036 Office: 600 Jefferson St Houston TX 77002

TUCKER, RICHARD DAVID, educator; b. Richmond, Va., Feb. 7, 1927; s. Joseph and Alease (Hill) T.; B.A., Va. Union U., 1949; M.S., Va. State Coll., 1951; Ed.D., UCLA, 1964. Grad. asst. Va. State Coll., Petersvurg, Va., 1950-51; tchr. Randolph (Richmond, Va.) Sch., 1951-54, Luther Jackson High Sch., Merrifield, Va., 1954-59; faculty Summer Session, Hampton (Va.) Inst., 1962; asst. prof. Tuskegee (Ala.) Inst., 1964-65; prof. history Miss. Valley State Coll., Itta Bena, 1965-70; instr. psychology, econ., sociology Mary Holmes Coll., W. Point, Miss., 1970—, faculty senate pres., 1974-75; cons. Nat. Endowment for the Humanities, 1974-77; dir. acad. honors program Mary Holmes Coll., 1978—, advisor student newspaper, 1978—, dir. edn. and social sci. div., 1979—. Minority Student fellowship scholar, 1972-73. Mem. Mary Holmes Coll. Edn. Assn. (pres. 1975-76), Miss. Edn. Assn., NEA, Am. Hist. Soc., AAUP, Assn. for Supervision and Curriculum Devel., Phi Theta Kappa, Phi Delta Kappa, Alpha Phi Alpha, NAACP. Roman Catholic. Contbr. articles to profl. jours.; author: The Psychology of Personality, 1977 (booklet). Home: Mary Holmes Coll West Point MS 39773 Office: PO Box 2217 Mary Holmes Coll West Point MS 39773

TUCKER, SAMUEL JOSEPH, psychologist; b. Birmingham, Ala., Nov. 5, 1930; s. Daniel L. and Lucille M. (McGhee) T.; B.A., Morehouse Coll., 1952; M.A., Columbia U., 1956; Ph.D., Atlanta U., 1969; m. Arlene Kelly, July 12, 1958; children—Samuel, Sabrina, Sharon, Sterling. Sr. clin. psychologist N.Y. State Dept. Mental Hygiene, 1957-63; dean students Morehouse Coll., 1964-71; asst. prof. counselor edn. U. Fla., 1971-73; pres. Edward Waters Coll., Jacksonville, Fla., 1973-76; dean Univ. Coll., Ala. State U., Montgomery, 1976-78; pres. Langston (Okla.) U., 1978-79; pres. Atlanta Human Devel. Center, 1979—; cons. in field. Mem. Jacksonville Area Planning Bd.; mem. exec. com. Boy Scouts Am. Served with U.S. Army, 1952-54. Danforth Found. grantee, 1967-68. Mem. Am. Psychol. Assn., Am. Personnel and Guidance Assn., Ga. Psychol. Assn., Assn. Black Psychologists, Jacksonville Area C. of C. (past bd. govs.), Alpha Phi Alpha. Author: Phoenix From the Ashes, 1976; syndicated weekly columnist, 1979—. Home: 735 Peyton Rd SW Atlanta GA 30311 Office: 1123 Gordon St SW Atlanta GA 30310

TUCKER, SCOTT, banker; b. West Point, N.Y., May 18, 1948; s. Reuben Henry, III, and Helen Justine (McAlister) T.; B.S. in Bus. (scholar), The Citadel, 1970; M.B.A., U. Utah, 1972; grad. Sch. Banking of South, La. State U., 1979; m. Mary Linda Bercume, May 31, 1970; children—David Bruce, Kelly Ann. Successively adminstrv. asst., asst. cashier, asst. v.p. 1st Nat. Bank fo S.C., Charleston, 1972-78, v.p., comml. loan officer charge credit and discount depts., 1978—. Chm. bd. dirs. East Cooper Sch. Bd., 1977—. Served to 1st lt., USAF, 1970-72. Mem. Nat. Assn. Accts. (dir. Charleston chpt. 1975), Robert Morris Assos. (paper award 1973), Bishop England Alumni Assn. (pres. 1975), AF Assn. (sec.-treas. 1975-76, sec. 1976-77). Roman Catholic. Clubs: Propeller of U.S., East Cooper Booster (treas. 1976-77). Home: 998 Scotland Dr Mount Pleasant SC 29464 Office: 18 Broad St Charleston SC 29401

TUCKER, STEPHEN GUYNN, systems engr.; b. Atlanta, Aug. 14, 1946; s. Benton Aubry and Marion Lee (Haymore) T.; B.S. with honors in Bus. Edn., U. Ga., 1977; children—Adam, Carrie. Programmer, analyst Service Bur. Corp., Dallas, 1968-70; devel. programmer, analyst IBM, White Plains, N.Y., 1970-74, systems engr., Atlanta, 1974-77, systems engr., Jacksonville, Fla., 1977—. Served with USAF, 1969-70. Cer. in data processing Inst. Cert. Computer Profls., also cert. in computer programming (systems). Mem. Data Processing Mgmt. Assn., Assn. Systems Mgmt. Home: PO Box 10309 Jacksonville FL 32207 Office: IBM PO Box 2900 Jacksonville FL 32203

TUCKER, THOMAS JOSEPH, hosp. adminstr.; b. Bement, Ill., Jan. 3, 1932; s. Benjamin John and Gertude Cecilia (Cannon) T.; B.S., U. Ill., 1972; M.B.A., Corpus Christi State U., 1980; m. Jacquelyn Stewart, July 18, 1962; 1 son, Michael Joseph. With Nat. Distillers, Tuscola, Ill., 1955-70; public accountant, Corpus Christi, Tex., 1972-75; asst. adminstr. fin. Spohn Hosp., Corpus Christi, 1975—. Served with USN, 1951-54. Fellow Hosp. Fin. Mgmt. Assn. (pres. South Tex. chpt. 1979-80); mem. Am. Inst. C.P.A.'s, Tex. Soc. C.P.A.'s, Tex. Hosp. Assn., Tex. Assn. Hosp. Accts., U. Ill. Alumni Assn. Republican. Roman Catholic. Home: 350 Peerman Corpus Christi TX 78411 Office: 1436 3d St Corpus Christi TX 78411

TUCKER, TROY LEE, city ofcl.; b. Cisco, Tex., Sept. 16, 1931; s. M.C. and Flora Faye (Sutton) T.; B.S., Mich. State U., 1965; M.B.A., Angelo State U., 1975; m. Layla Carline Pinkston, Feb. 1, 1954; children—Rhonda Ann, Renie Carol. Commd. officer U.S. Air Force, 1951, advanced through grades to maj., 1968, ret., 1970; dir. San Angelo (Tex.) Council on Alcoholism, 1976-79; mem. Regional Health Services Bd., 1977-79; city commr. City of San Angelo, 1976—; indsl. security and bus. cons.; mayor-pro-tem, City of San Angelo, 1978-79. Bd. dirs. Tex. Assn. Children with Learning Disabilities, 1976-78, San Angelo Cath. Charities; mem. Gov.'s Council Mcpl. Affairs. Decorated Air Force Commendation medal, Bronze Star medal. Mem. Tex. Mcpl. League, DAV, VFW. Democrat. Christian Ch. Clubs: Masons, Shriners, Elks, Knights of Round Table. Home: 1802 N Van Buren St San Angelo TX 76901 Office: PO Box 1751 San Angelo TX 76901

TUCKWILLER, PAT ALEXANDER, physician; b. Morgantown, W.Va., Apr. 13, 1905; s. David and Lucie (Watts) T.; B.S., W.Va. U., 1926; M.D., U. Chgo., 1929; m. Carline C. Hazlebeck, July 1, 1936; children—David W., Alan Ross. Intern, Presbyn. Hosp., Chgo., 1928-29, City Hosp., Cleve., 1929-30; resident Univ. (Lakeside) Hosp., Cleve, 1930-32; practice medicine, specializing in internal medicine, Charleston, W.Va., 1932—; chief of staff Meml. Hosp., Charleston, 1951-54, chief of medicine, 1951-57; med. cons. Charleston Area Med. Center, 1974—, chmn. com. on continuing edn. and hosps., 1965-77; prof. medicine emeritus W.Va. U. Extension Sch., Charleston, 1978—. Served to col. U.S. Army, 1942-47. Diplomate Am. Bd. Internal Medicine. Fellow A.C.P.; mem. Kanawha Med. Soc., AMA, So. Med. Soc. Club: Kiwanis. Home: 4308 Kanawha Ave SE Charleston WV 25304 Office: 3416 MacCorkle Ave SE Charleston WV 25304

TUDER, SANDRA CHARLEEN, banker; b. Chattanooga, Oct. 29, 1951; d. Fred Marshall and Mary Catherine (Lofty) Pitts; student profl. courses Northwestern U., 1977, U. Tenn., Chattanooga, 1977; m. Roger D. Tuder, Aug. 25, 1972; 1 son, Roger Dale. With Blue Cross-Blue Shield, Chattanooga, 1967-71; staff Diagnostic Hosp., Chattanooga, 1971-72; with Am. Nat. Bank, Chattanooga, 1972—, asst. operation mgr., 1977—. Mem. Am. Bus. Women's Assn. Baptist. Club: Order Eastern Star. Address: Box 140 Lookout Mountain TN 37350

TUDOR, BYNUM ELLSWORTH, JR., diversified co. exec.; b. Winston-Salem, N.C., Apr. 27, 1933; s. Bynum Ellsworth and Ruth Catherine (Heath) T.; A.B., U. N.C., 1955; m. Mary Esther Seay, Feb. 7, 1959; children—Bynum Ellsworth III, Elizabeth Hanes. Adminstr. employee benefit plans R.J. Reynolds Tobacco Co., Winston-Salem, 1965-70, mgr. employee benefits, 1970-73; corporate dir. employee benefits R.J. Reynolds Industries, Inc., 1973—; v.p., treas., dir. Winston-Salem Health Care Plan, Inc., 1976—, Winston-Salem Dental Care Plan, Inc., 1978—. Bd. dirs. Piedmont Med. Found., Amos Cottage-Bowman Gray Sch. Medicine. Served with U.S. Army, 1955-57. Mem. Nat. Assn. Employers on Health Maintenance Orgns. (dir. 1976—, pres. 1977-78), Washington Bus. Group on Health, NAM. Republican. Presbyterian. Clubs: Bald Head Island Golf and Tennis, Tortuga, Grand Cayman Islands (B.W.I.). Home: 625 Arbor Rd Winston-Salem NC 27104 Office: R J Reynolds Industries Inc Winston-Salem NC 27102

TUGGLE, PAUL DAVID, mobile home co. exec.; b. Kansas City, Kans., Jan. 16, 1951; s. Frank David and Ruby (Blackburn) T.; student Miami Dade Jr. Coll., 1971, U. South Fla., 1974; m. Elsa Agnes Sweatt, Aug. 9, 1974. With Market Research, Inc., St. Petersburg, Fla., 1972-73; mgr. men's dept. Montgomery, Ward & Co., Tampa, Fla., 1973-75; sales mgr. J.G. Home Sales Co., Clearwater, Fla., 1975-77; mgr. Japanese Garden Mobile Estates, Clearwater, 1975-77; area mgr. Mobile Home Communities, Inc., Riviera Beach, Fla., 1977—; sales mgr. Ramada Homes, Inc. div. Skyline Corp., 1977—. Recipient Dade County Outstanding Citizen award, 1968; named hon. citizen of Cancun, Quintana Roo, Mex., 1977. Mem. Nat. Assn. Underwater Instrs., Fla. Ocean Racing Assn., Fla. Mobile Home and Recreational Vehicle Assn., Contractors and Builders Assn. Pinellas County, Greater Miami Underwater Council, Fla. Land Owners Assn. Republican. Methodist. Clubs: Windjammers (past pres.), Fla. Skin Divers, Marine Biology, Ocala Sailing, Gulf and Atlantic Yacht. Home: 1 Spring Drive Pl Ocala FL 32672 Office: 1714 SW 17th St Ocala FL 32670

TULLIS, RICHARD BARCLAY, communications and info. handling equipment mfg. co. exec.; b. Western Springs, Ill., July 12, 1913; s. Lauren Barclay and Izelah (Gilmore) T.; A.B., Principia Coll., Elsah, Ill., 1934; m. Chaille Handy, Aug. 17, 1935; children—Sarah Tullis de Barcza, Barclay J., Garner H. With Miller Printing Machinery Co., Pitts., 1936-56, pres., 1952-56; with Harris Corp.,

Cleve., 1956—, exec. v.p., 1957-61, pres., 1961-72, chief exec. officer, 1968-78, chmn., 1972-78, chmn. exec. com., Melbourne, Fla., 1978—, also dir.; dir. Cleve. Electric Illuminating Co., Gen. Tire & Rubber Co., Akron; trustee First Union Real Estate Investments, Cleve. Trustee Principia Coll., Elsah, Ill., Musical Arts Assn., Cleve. Home: 221 Indian Harbor Rd Vero Beach FL 32960 Office: Melbourne FL 32919

TULLOS, S. J., guidance counselor; b. Wyatt, La., July 6, 1928; s. Sherwood John and Lena Melinda (Walker) T.; B.S. in Agr. La. Tech. U., 1950, B.A. in Elementary Edn., 1956; M.A. in Supervision and Adminstrn., U. N.C., 1959, Ed.D. in Psychology and Guidance, 1967. Tchr. pub. schs., Shreveport, La., 1956-64; asst. prof. edn. La. Tech. U., Ruston, 1964-71, asso. prof., 1971—; cons. in field. Supt. Sunday sch. Highland Baptist Ch., Shreveport, 1960-64. Served with USAF, 1950-54. Mem. La. Tchrs. Assn., Am. Personnel and Guidance Assn., Assn. for Counselor Edn. and Supervision, La. Personnel and Guidance Assn. Democrat. Contbr. articles to tech. jours. Home: 1109 Barnett Springs Rd Apt 8 Ruston LA 71270 Office: PO Box 6307 Tech Sta Ruston LA 71270

TULLY, CHRISTOPHER CARL, physician; b. Charleston, W.Va., June 22, 1913; s. Christopher Columbus and Eva Lena (Lanham) T.; B.S. magna cum laude, Morris Harvey Coll., 1937; B.S., W.Va. U., 1945; M.D., Med. Coll. Va., 1947; m. Virginia Belle Tully, Apr. 9, 1937 (dec. 1963); children—Christopher Carl II, Richard R.; m. 2d, Margaret A. Plumley, Oct. 29, 1966. With Charleston Fire Dept., 1935-39, U.S. P.O., Charleston, 1939-43; intern U.S. Marine Hosp., 1947-48; gen. practice medicine, South Charleston, W.Va., 1948—; mem. staff H. J. Thomas Meml. Hosp., South Charleston, 1948—, pres., 1966; prof. family practice Kanawha Valley Family Practice Center, 1973—. Dir., mem. exec. com. First Nat. Bank of South Charleston. Mem. South Charleston Recreation Com.; chmn. South Charleston Park Bd.; mem. Kanawha County Bd. Edn., 1959-70, pres., 1963-64; mem. Charter Bd. South Charleston, W.Va. Served with U.S. Army, 1944-46, 47-48, 51-53, 71. Diplomate Am. Bd. Family Practice. Fellow Am. Acad. Family Physicians; mem. Am. Acad. Family Practice (pres. Kanawha chpt. 1962-63; pres. W.Va. chpt. 1969-70, chmn. bd.), W.Va. Acad. Family Practice (dir. 1960-64), AMA, W.Va., Kanawha med. socs., So. Med. Assn., Am. Soc. Contemporary Medicine and Surgery, Phi Beta Pi. Mason (Shriner), Lion (pres. Spring Hill 1957-58, citizen of year South Charleston 1956-57). Home: 4530 Spring Hill Ave South Charleston WV 25309 Office: 4605 McCorkle Ave South Charleston WV 25309

TULLY, CHRISTOPHER CARL, JR., dentist; b. Charleston, W.Va., May 30, 1939; s. Christopher Carl and Virginia Bell (Tully) T.; B.S. in Chemistry, Morris Harvey Coll., 1962; M.S. in Biochemistry, W.Va. U., 1965, D.D.S., 1969; m. Susan Watson Sturgis, Apr. 1, 1978; children by previous marriage—Christopher Carl III, Karen Lynn, Deborah Ann. Practice dentistry, Morgantown, W.Va., 1969; North Augusta, S.C., 1969—. Chmn., North Augusta area Nat. Childrens' Dental Health Week, 1972; dental coordinator United Fund, 1970-71; mem. North Augusta Area Hosp. Planning Com., 1971, Alcohol and Drug Referral Com., 1971-73; chmn. North Augusta Am. Cancer Soc., 1970—, Aiken County Dental Disaster Assn.; chmn. judges com. Miss North Augusta-Miss S.C., 1970; coach Optimist Basketball League, 1969—, Football League, 1970—, Baseball League, 1969-72. Mem. ADA, Acad. Gen. Dentistry, S.C. Dental Assn., Am. Soc. Dentistry for Children, Am. Endodontic Soc., Am. Soc. Preventive Dentistry, Augusta Dental Soc., W.Va. Dental Alumni Assn., Jr. C. of C., Sigma Nu, Delta Sigma Delta. Republican. Methodist. Lion. Clubs: Seratoma, North Augusta Booster. Home: 1934 Bolin Rd North Augusta SC 29841 Office: 501 A East Martintown Rd North Augusta SC 29841

TUMAY, MEHMET TANER, geotech. cons., educator; b. Ankara, Turkey, Feb. 2, 1937; came to U.S., 1959; s. Bedrettin and Muhterem (Uybadin) T.; B.S. in C.E., Robert Coll. Sch. Engring. (Turkey), 1959; M.C.E., U. Va., 1961; postgrad. UCLA, 1963-64; Ph.D., Tech. U. Istanbul (Turkey), 1971; postdoctoral fellow U. Fla., 1976; m. Karen Nuttycombe, June 15, 1962; children—Peri, Suna. Instr. civil engring. U. Va., Charlottesville, 1961-62; asst. prof. civil engring. U. Louisville, 1962-63; teaching fellow UCLA, 1963-64; asst. prof. civil engring. Robert Coll. Sch. Engring., Istanbul, 1966-71; asso. prof. dept. civil engring. Bogazici U., Istanbul, 1971-75; asso. prof. civil engring. La. State U., Baton Rouge, 1976—; Fugro-Cesco research fellow U. Fla., Gainesville, 1975-76; research asst. Va. Council Hwy. Investigation and Research, 1961-62; geotech. cons. BOTEK, Ltd., Istanbul, 1975—, D.E.A., Cons. Engrs., Istanbul, 1974-75, SOFRETU-RATP, Paris, 1972-73, Sauti, Spa, Cons. Engrs., Italy, 1969-72; cons. in field. AID scholar, 1975-76; NSF internat. travel grantee, 1979; lic. nuclear reactor operator, AEC; qualified fallout shelter analyst and instr. Dept. Def.; lic. civil engr., La., Turkish Chamber of Civil Engring. Mem. ASCE, Am. Soc. Engring. Edn., ASTM, La. Engring. Soc., Turkish Soil Mechanics Group (charter), Turkish Chamber Civil Engrs., Soil Mechanics Research Council of Istanbul Tech. U., Internat. Soc. Soil Mechanics and Found. Engring., Sigma Xi, Chi Epsilon, Tau Beta Pi. Contbr. articles to profl. jours. Home: 1915 W Magna Carta Pl Baton Rouge LA 70815 Office: Dept Civil Engring La State Univ Baton Rouge LA 70808

TUNE, JOHN CHILDRESS, lawyer; b. Nashville, July 16, 1931; s. John Clark and Harriet Bailey (Childress) T.; B.A., Vanderbilt U., 1954; J.D., YMCA Law Sch., Nashville, 1962; grad. Air War Coll., 1975; m. Carolyn Mai Norman, May 21, 1955; children—John Edward, Julian W., David C., Admitted to Tenn. bar, 1962, U.S. Supreme Ct., 1968, since practiced in Nashville, partner firm Tune, Entrekin & White, 1962—; chmn. bd. Music Country Motors Co., Nashville, 1960—; dir. Nashville br. Fed. Res. Bank Atlanta, 1970-75, chmn., 1971, 75. Chmn., Met. Nashville Airport Authority, 1970-73, commr., 1970—; pres. Nashville unit Am. Cancer Soc., 1976, chmn. exec. com., 1977; bd. dirs. Middle Tenn. council Boy Scouts Am., 1970—, Cumberland Mus. and Sci. Center, 1973—, Nashville Symphony Assn., 1974—, Leadership Nashville; adv. bd. U. Tenn. at Nashville, 1974—. Served with USAF, 1951-53, col. Res., dep. chief staff Tenn. Air N.G. Mem. Am., Nashville (dir. 1975-77), Tenn. (gov. 1974—) bar assns., Am., Tenn., Nashville trial lawyers assns., Tenn. Criminal Def. Lawyers Assn., Am. Judicature Soc., Nashville Area C. of C. (dir. 1968-75, pres. 1974), Barristers Club Nashville (pres.), Nashville Automobile Trade Orgn. (pres. 1962), Kappa Sigma (chpt. pres. 1953-54). Home: 217 Brookhollow Rd Nashville TN 37205 Office: First American Center 26th Floor Nashville TN 37238

TUNE, RAYMOND LOYD, mfg. plant exec.; b. Woodward, Okla., Jan. 9, 1945; s. James P. and Imo C. (Gaston) T.; B.A., St. Edward's U., 1969; M.B.A., East Tex. State U., 1978; m. Celinda Leigh Drake, Feb. 25, 1956; children—Steven Loyd, Kristina Rayann. Field auditor Tex. Edn. and Rehab. Commn., Austin, 1971-73; mng. partner Mountain Meats Inc., Aspen, Colo., 1973-75; personnel rep. Otis Engring., Carrollton, Tex., 1975-79; instr. bus. (part-time) Brookhaven Coll., Dallas, 1979—; prodn. mgr. Tidel Systems, Dallas, 1979—. Democratic precinct chmn., Austin, Tex., 1971-72; chmn. adv. com. Tex. State Tech. Inst.; adv. com. Okla. State Tech. Served with USN, 1962-66. Mem. Am. Prodn. and Inventory Control Soc. Home: 3120 Valley Meadow Dallas TX 75220 Office: 2615 E Beltline Dallas TX 75006

TUNNER, WILLIAM SAMS, urol. surgeon; b. San Antonio, Nov. 14, 1933; s. William Henry and Sarah Margaret (Sams) T.; student Washington and Lee U., 1952-55; M.D., U. Va., 1960; m. Sallie Berry Woodul, Dec. 4, 1965; children—William Woodul, Jonathan Sams. Intern in surgery, then asst. surg. resident Duke Hosp., 1960-62; fellow cancer surgery Cancer Inst. NIH, Bethesda, Md., 1962-64; resident in urol. surgery Cornell-N.Y. Hosp., 1964-68, fellow transplantation, dialysis and biochemistry, instr. surgery, 1968-70; asst. prof. urol. surgery U. Tex. Med. Sch., San Antonio, 1970-72; practice medicine specializing in pediatric and adult urology, Richmond, Va., 1972—; mem. staff St. Mary's, Henrico County, Retreat hosps.; asst. clin. prof. urology Med. Coll. Va., 1972—. Valentine research fellow, 1970-72; grantee Hearst Research Found., 1970-72. Diplomate Am. Bd. Urology. Fellow A.C.S., Am. Acad. Pediatrics (affiliate); mem. AMA, Transplantation Soc., Am. Urol. Assn., Am. Nephrology Assn., Alpha Epsilon Delta, Beta Theta Pi. Episcopalian. Clubs: Westwood Racquet, Lester Manor, Ware River Yacht. Contbr. to med. jours., films. Home: 4705 Rolfe Rd Richmond VA 23226 Office: St Mary's Hosp Profl Bldg 5855 Bremo Rd Richmond VA 23226

TUNSTILL, GARLAND ALBERT, cons. in finance and govt. relations; b. Eastland County, Tex., Nov. 16, 1901; s. William Austin and Eula (Compton) T.; LL.B., Cumberland U., Lebanon, Tenn., 1923; m. Clover Dell Hill, Feb. 23, 1937 (dec. July 1972). Admitted to Tex. bar, 1924; practice law, Ft. Worth, 1924-26; ind. oil operator, Houston, 1926-40; bus. economist and entrepreneur, 1941-47; financial and govt. relations cons., 1948—. Precinct chmn. Republican party, 1954—. Mem. com. on sociol. conditions in South, Tulane U. Bd. dirs., cons. Movimiento Pro Federacion Americana. Mem. Tex. Bar Assn. Christian Scientist. Author: (essay) Can the Monroe Doctrine Bring Peace and Prosperity to the Americans? (in library of James Monroe Meml. Found., Fredericksburg, Va.). Home and office: 7420 Haywood Dr Houston TX 77061

TURCOTTE, JOHN WINFIELD, state agy. exec.; b. Jackson, Miss., June 14, 1948; s. William Henry and Annie Cook (Tribble) T.; student Millsaps Coll., 1966-68; B.A. with highest honors, U. So. Miss., 1970, M.A., 1974; m. Terry Hightower, June 4, 1970; 1 dau., Leigh Anne. Tchr., Greene County Schs., Leakesville, Miss., 1970-71; polit. sci. instr. Hinds Jr. Coll., 1971-73; staff Miss. Joint Legis. Com. on Performance Evaluation and Expenditure Rev., 1973-74, div. coordinator, 1974-78, exec. dir., 1978—; chmn., mem. exec. com. legis. program evaluation sect. Nat. Conf. State Legislatures, 1978. Mem. Am. Soc. Pub. Adminstrn., Govtl. Research Assn., Phi Kappa Phi, Pi Gamma Mu. Office: PO Box 1204 Jackson MS 39212

TURK, JAMES CLINTON, judge; b. Roanoke, Va., May 3, 1923; s. James Alexander and Geneva (Richardson) T.; A.B., Roanoke Coll., 1949; LL.B., Washington and Lee U., 1952, J.D., 1972; m. Barbara Duncan, Aug. 21, 1954; children—Ramona Leah, James Clinton, Robert Malcolm Duncan, Mary Elizabeth, David Michael. Admitted to Va. bar, 1952; mem. firm Poff & Turk, Radford, Va., 1952-72; mem. Va. Senate, 1959-72, minority leader; chief U.S. dist. judge Western Dist. Va., Roanoke, 1972—. Trustee Radford Community Hosp., 1959-74. Served with AUS, 1943-46. Mem. Order of Coif, Phi Beta Kappa, Omicron Delta Kappa. Baptist (deacon). Home: 1002 Walker Dr Radford VA 24141 Office: Fed Bldg Roanoke VA

TURK, JOHN COBB, architect; b. Buffalo, Oct. 16, 1930; s. Roswell Lester and Alice Knoche (Cobb) T.; B.A., Colgate U., 1952; postgrad. Taliesin, Frank Lloyd Wright Found., 1955-57; m. Sandra Miriam Baruch, Mar. 18, 1967; stepchildren—Gary Chesman, Gail Chesman, Kristine Paulat, Craig Chesman. Asst. supt. George W. Walker & Sons, contractors, Buffalo, 1958-59; instr. fine arts Colgate U., Hamilton, N.Y., 1959; archtl. designer various firms, Buffalo, 1959-70; asst. to pres. Bennett Lumber Co., North Tonawanda, N.Y., 1970; owner John C. Turk, Designer, Buffalo, 1970-72; instr., head dept. archtl. engring. tech. Midlands Tech. Coll., Columbia, S.C., 1972-79, head dept. constrn. tech., 1979—; teaching asso. U. S.C., Columbia, 1973-78. Served with C.E., U.S. Army, 1953-55. Mem. AIA, Constrn. Specifications Inst. Republican. Unitarian-Universalist. Home: 260 Shoreline Dr Columbia SC 29210 Office: Drawer Q Columbia SC 29250

TURK, MICHAEL ANTHONY, marketing exec.; b. Memphis, Tenn., July 3, 1951; s. Edward Joseph and Marie Francis T.; B.B.A. cum laude, Memphis State U., 1973; m. April M. Grant, July 14, 1979. Asst. advt. and promotion mgr. McDonald Bros. Co., Memphis, 1973-74; asst. mktg. dir. Keystone Labs., Inc., Memphis, 1975-77, mktg. dir., 1977—. Home: 416 Allison Cove Memphis TN 38122

TURKHEIMER, ARNOLD IVAN, communication co. exec.; b. Mt. Vernon, N.Y., June 20, 1939; s. Milton S. and Lillian G. (Goldberg) T.; B.A., U. Iowa, 1961, M.A., 1962; m. Andrea J. Widelitz, June 13, 1965; children—Mitchell, Roberta. Dist. mgr. United World Films, div. Universal Pictures, N.Y.C., 1962-67; pub. relations mgr. spl. projects British Airways, N.Y.C., 1967-76; v.p., div. mgr. Booke & Co., Vicom Communications div., Winston-Salem, N.C., 1976-78; mgr. Southeastern U.S. employee benefit communications William M. Mercer Inc., Atlanta, 1979—. Recipient gold medals, N.Y. Film Festival, 1969, 72, 73. Mem. Internat. Communications Council, Soc. Motion Picture TV Engrs., Nat. Audio-Visual Assn. (cert. media specialist). Club: Masons. Home: 4752 Big Oak Bend Marietta GA 30062 Office: 3340 Peachtree Rd Atlanta GA 30326

TURLEY, STEWART, retail drug chain exec.; b. Mt. Sterling, Ky., July 20, 1934; s. R. Joe and Mavis (Sternberg) T.; student Rollins Coll., 1952-53, U. Ky., 1953-54; m. Judith Anne Hall, July 10, 1953; children—Carol Anne, Karen Elaine. With Crown Cork & Seal Co., Phila., and Orlando, Fla., 1955-66, plant mgr., Phila., 1964-66; with Jack Eckerd Corp., Clearwater, Fla., 1966—, sr. v.p., 1971-74, pres., 1974-75, pres., chmn. bd., 1975—; dir. Barnett Banks of Fla., Jacksonville. Chmn. fund raising Jr. Achievement Pinellas County, 1976; bd. dirs. Gulf Coast Art Center. Mem. Am. Retail Fedn. (dir.), Nat. Assn. Chain Drug Stores (dir.), Young Pres.'s Orgn. Republican. Clubs: Carlouel Yacht, Rotary, Belleview Biltmore Country, Feather Sound Country. Office: PO Box 4689 Clearwater FL 33518

TURNER, ALICE KATHRYN, tchr., pianist, organist; b. Greenville, Miss., Jan. 27, 1921; d. Robert Abner and Clara Lee (Johnson) Ireland; B.Mus. cum laude, Miss. State Coll. Women, 1943; postgrad. Juilliard Sch. Music, 1943, Northwestern U., 1943-45; m. David Wilson Turner, June 11, 1947; children—David Wilson, Ada Lee Turner Wichman. Organist, 1st Baptist Ch., Greenville, 1936—; mem. Greenville Piano Quartet, 1943—; judge Nat. Piano Guild auditions, 1970—. Certified Nat. Guild Piano Tchrs. Mem. Sigma Alpha Iota. Address: 1018 Cedar St Greenville MS 38701

TURNER, BRUCE EDWARD, lawyer; b. Wichita, Falls, Tex., Oct. 31, 1947; s. Charles William and Marie Jeanne (Masson) T.; B.A., Tex. Tech. U., 1970, J.D., 1973; LL.M., N.Y. U., 1974. Admitted to Tex. bar, 1974; mem. firm Dillingham, Schlieder & Marquelette, Houston, 1974-76, firm Johnston & Feather, Dallas, 1976—; seminar tchr. Northlake Coll. Community Service, 1979—. Active Big Bros., Dallas, 1978—. Mem. ICC Practitioners, Tex. Bar Assn. Republican. Roman Catholic. Clubs: Downtown Men's, K.C. Contbr. articles to profl. jours. Home: 4504 Normandy St Dallas TX 75225 Office: 3303 Lee Pkwy Dallas TX 75219

TURNER, CHARLES ARTHUR, artist, educator; b. Houston, Tex., Nov. 17, 1940; s. Lloyd T. and Modest A. (Wainwright) T.; B.A., N. Tex. State U., 1962; M.F.A., Cranbrook Acad. Art, 1966. Instr., Birmingham (Mich.) Art Assn., 1965-66; asst. prof. Madison Coll., Harrisonburg, Va., 1966-68; guest instr. U. Houston, Tex., 1973, Glassell Sch. Art, Mus. Fine Arts, Houston, 1968—; one-man shows include: Columbia Mus. Art, Columbia, S.C., 1968, Circle Gallery, New Orleans, 1969, Beyond Baroque Gallery, Venice, Calif., 1969, Art Gallery, Sam Houston State U., Huntsville, Tex., 1971, Beaumont (Tex.) Art Mus., 1972, Art Mus. of S. Tex., Corpus Christi, 1973, Art Gallery, Madison Coll., Harrisonburg, Va., 1967, 74, Sol Del Rio Gallery, San Antonio, Tex., 1975, 78, Moody Gallery, Houston, Tex., 1976, 77, 78; numerous group shows, latest being: Blaffer Gallery, U. Houston, 1974, Longview Mus., Longview, Tex., 1974, 75, U. Minn., Mpls., 1975, Moody Gallery, Houston, 1975, The Art Center, Waco, Tex., 1977, Mus. Fine Arts, Houston, 1978; represented in permanent collections: Mus. of Fine Arts, Houston, First City Nat. Bank, Bellaire, Tex., Alcoa Corp., Detroit, Cranbrook Acad. Art, Bloomfield Hills, Mich., Del Mar Coll., Corpus Christi, Tex., AT&T, N.Y.C., East Tenn. State U., Johnson City, Dresser Industries Inc., Houston. Mem. Coll. Art Assn. Am., Tex. Fine Arts Soc., Tex. Watercolor Soc. Home: 2419 Julian St Houston TX 77009 Office: 5101 Montrose St Houston TX 77005

TURNER, DEBORAH MADELINE, financial exec.; b. Louisville, Feb. 28, 1948; d. Samuel Elwood and Katherine (Kennedy) Green; student Wheelock Coll., 1973, Ind. U., 1979, U. Louisville, 1979; m. Charles Turner, Sept. 16, 1967; children—Michelle Lynnette, Camille Yvette. Teller time credit dept. Citizens Fidelity Bank, Louisville, 1968-72; asst. dir., fin. mgr. Community Coordinated Child Care, Louisville, 1972—, dir., 1977; cons. So. Regional Edn. Bd., 1977, Ky. Dept. Edn., 1978; workshop leader Louisville Assn. Children Under Six, Ky. Citizens for Child Devel., 1979. Bd. mem. Human Services Coordination Alliance. Nat. Achievement scholar. Mem. Am. Mgmt. Assn. Democrat. Home: 7409 Crawfordshire Ln Louisville KY 48220 Office: 1355 S 3d St Louisville KY 40208

TURNER, DILLARD DEAN, II, fin. cons.; b. Hazard, Ky., Sept. 17, 1940; s. Dillard Dean and Thelma D. (Clark) T.; student Cumberland Coll., 1963, Eastern U., 1965; B.S., Western State Coll. Law, 1975; m. Doris Lee, Jan. 6, 1979; children by previous marriage—Mark, Pamla. With Barker Adjustment Co., Corbin, Ky., 1965, Gay and Taylor, Inc., Corbin, 1966-67, Adjustment, Inc., Lexington, Ky., 1967-69; pres. D. Turner & Assos., Inc., London, Ky., 1979—. Pres. fin. commn. Cumberland Valley Regional Mental Health, 1979—; mem. City Council London, 1978-79; adv. Gov. Julian Carroll's Econ. Dept. task force on fin., 1978-79; county chmn. John Y. Brown for Gov., 1979; mem. London County Devel. Assn., 1969—. Mem. London Jaycees (nat. dir. 1970-72). Home: 114 Hill St London KY 40741 Office: Rm 210 First Nat Bank Bldg London KY 40741

TURNER, EDWARD MASON, bishop, Episcopal Ch.; b. Chgo., Nov. 13, 1918; s. Allen Bowden and Frances Marjory (Miller) T.; B.A., Marquette U., 1941; B.D., Nashotah House Sem., U. Nashville, 1944; m. May 29, 1944; 2 children; m. 2d, Shirley Louise Dittmer, May 1958. Ordained priest Episcopal Ch.; priest in charge St. Peter's Ch., Seward, Alaska, 1944-49; asst. to dir. dept. Episcopal Ch., 1949-53; canon St. John's Cathedral, Santurce, P.R., 1953-59; rector St. Paul's, Frederikstec, V.I., 1959—; now bishop V.I. Del. Gen. Conv. Episcopal Ch., 1964-70. Address: PO Box 7488 St Thomas VI 00801

TURNER, ELBERT DAYMOND, JR., educator; b. Gainesville, Fla., Nov. 15, 1915; s. Elbert D. and Lena (Baird) T.; B.A. with honors, Davidson Coll., 1937; M.A., U. N.C., 1939, Ph.D., 1949; m. Irma Aboy, Aug. 2, 1945; children—Carmen Irma (Mrs. Joseph Lipe), Ana Maria (Mrs. Timothy Lomperis), Victoria (Mrs. Todd Powers), Elbert D. III, Rosa. Teaching fellow U. N.C., 1937-38, part-time instr. 1938-39; instr. Ga. Tchrs. Coll., 1939-41; instr. Spanish, U. N.C., 1946-49; asst. prof. U. Del., 1949-58, dir. lang. lab., 1955-66, asso. prof. modern langs., 1958-61, prof. modern languages, 1961-66; prof., chmn. dept. fgn. langs. U. N.C., Charlotte, 1966-71, dir. grad. studies, 1970—; vis. prof. NDEA Inst., Utah State U., 1963-64, Utah State U., Oaxaca, Mexico, summer 1966; cons. pub. schs. Del., 1951-52, 56, Delaware Dept. Pub. Instrn., 1959-66, Memphis State U., 1967-70, Profl. Child Care Centers, Inc., 1969-73. Chmn. test devel. Nat. Spanish Exams., 1965-74. Served from 1st lt. to lt. col. AUS, 1941-46; col. Res. ret. Research grantee Nat. Endowment Humanities, 1979-82. Fellow Southeastern Inst. Medieval and Renaissance Studies, 1968. Mem. Am. Assn. Tchrs. Spanish and Portuguese, AAUP, Council Grad. Schs. U.S., Conf. So. Grad. Schs., Assn. for Latin-Am. Studies, Am. Council on Teaching Fgn. Langs., Charlotte Area Ednl. Consortium (sec. 1971-72), S. Atlantic Modern Lang. Assn., Instituto de Literatura Iberoamericana, Renaissance Soc. Am., Phi Beta Kappa, Delta Sigma Pi, Eta Sigma Phi, Sigma Phi Epsilon. Republican. Presbyn. (elder). Clubs: Charlotte Swimming, U. N.C. Faculty. Author: Gonzalo Fernandez de Ovideo y Valdes: An Annotated Bibliography, 1967; The Conquest and Settlement of Puerto Rico, 1975. Contbr. to numerous profl. publs. Mem. adv. bd. N.C. Fgn. Lang. Tchr., 1970—. Home: 233 Fenton Pl Charlotte NC 28207

TURNER, ELIZABETH ADAMS NOBLE (MRS. JACK RICE TURNER), ednl. adminstr.; b. Yonkers, N.Y., May 18, 1931; d. James Kendrick and Orrel (Baldwin) Noble; B.A., Vassar Coll., 1953; M.A., Tex. A. and I. U., 1964; m. Jack Rice Turner, July 11, 1953; children—Jay Kendrick, Randall Ray. Ednl. cons. Noble & Noble Pub. Co., N.Y.C., 1956-67; psychometrist Corpus Christi (Tex.) Guidance Center, 1967-70; psychologist Corpus Christi State Sch., 1970-72, dir. programs, 1972, dir. vol. service, 1972-76; program coordinator Rio-Grande Mental Health and Mental Retardation Center, 1976—, dir. staff devel., 1978-80; dir. alumni affairs Corpus Christi State U., 1977—. Real estate salesman Tompkins-Young, Corpus Christi, 1967-70; coordinator vols. Summer Head Start Program, Corpus Christi, 1967. Mem. allocations com. United Fund, Corpus Christi, 1970; bd. dirs. YWCA, Corpus Christi Hearing and Speech Assn., Coastal Bend Mental Health Assn., Suicide Prevention Inc., Tb Assn., Council Govts., Corpus Christi Mus., Art Mus. of South Tex., Corpus Christi, Vol. Action Center, Conv. and Tourist Bur., Big Bros./Big Sisters of Nueces County; mem. scholarship com. Lulac Ednl. Service Center; adv. com. U. Tex. Sch. Social Work; mem. Corpus Christi City Council, 1979-81. Recipient Love award YWCA, 1970. Mem. Tex. Psychol. Assn. (pres., mem. exec. bd.), Psychol. Assos. (pres.), Am. Psychotherapy Assn., Am. Assn. Mental Deficiency, Leadership Corpus Christi, Goals 100 Com., Jr. League Corpus Christi, Tex. Bookman's Assn., Tex. Assn. Realtors, Corpus Christi C. of C. (dir.), Kappa Kappa Gamma. Clubs: Corpus Christi Country, Corpus Christi Yacht, Junior Cotillion, Press. Home: 4466 Ocean Dr Corpus Christi TX 78404 Office: PO Box 3070 Corpus Christi TX 78404

TURNER, ELVIE, JR., zool. park dir.; b. Walnut Springs, Tex., Feb. 16, 1929; s. Elvie Lee and Rosa Mae (Hudson) T.; B.S. in Animal Husbandry, Tex. Tech. U., 1956; M.L.A., Tex. Christian U., 1978; m. Elaine Henserling, Dec. 27, 1958; children—Karen Sue, Timothy

Craig, Tracy Lea. Gen. zool. curator Dallas Zool. Park, 1956-63; dir. Macom World Wildlife Preserve, Mecom Ranch, Laredo, Tex., 1963-67, Ft. Worth Zool. Park and Aquarium, 1967—. Served with USAF, 1949-52. Fellow Am. Assn. Zool. Parks and Aquariums (dir.); mem. Ft. Worth Zool. Assn. Home: 2419 Kensington St Fort Worth TX 76110 Office: 2727 Zoological Park Dr Fort Worth TX 76110

TURNER, FREDERICK CORNELIUS, physician; b. New London, Conn., Mar. 14, 1942; s. Frederick Cornelius and Gladys (Beattie) T.; A.B., Providence Coll., 1964; M.D., U. Tex., 1968; m. Gladys Marie Haynes, June 24, 1977; children—Kristin Marie, Jennifer Marie. Intern, U. Mo. Med. Center, Columbia, 1968-69, resident in internal medicine, 1969-70; resident in gastroenterology Boston VA Hosp., 1972-74; chief resident internal medicine U. Mo. Med. Center, Columbia, 1974-75, asst. prof. internal medicine and gastroenterology, 1975-77, asst. prof. pharmacology, 1976-77; practice medicine specializing in internal medicine and gastroenterology, Mountain Home, Ark., 1977—; cons. physician various hosps. No. Ark., So. Mo., 1977—. Served with USNR, 1970-72. Mem. A.C.P., Am. Soc. Gastrointestinal Endoscopy. Contbr. articles to profl. jours. Address: PO Box 333 Hwy 201 N Mountain Home AR 72653

TURNER, GALE NORMAN, sales exec.; b. Meridian, Miss., Aug. 27, 1937; s. John and Elizabeth Manning (Moore) Norman; B.S., U.S. Naval Acad., 1959; M.B.A., Ga. State U., 1973; m. Sylvia Ann Salter, Oct. 9, 1959; children—Tracey Michele, Lane Manning. Commd. ensign U.S. Navy, 1959, advanced through grades to lt., 1967, naval aviator; project engr. Holder Constrn. Co., 1967-69; ops. officer, asst. v.p. cash mgmt. 1st Nat. Bank of Atlanta, 1969-76; product mgr., dist. sales mgr. Nat. Data Corp., Atlanta, 1976—; guest lectr. numerous cash mgmt. and data processing seminars, 1975-79. Vice pres. Decatur (Ga.) Coralwood PTA, 1975; pres. Graydon Sunday Sch., Bible instr. Oak Grove Methodist Ch., 1978. Mem. Am. Inst. Banking (v.p. Atlanta chpt. 1967), Am. Nat. Standards Inst., U.S. Naval Acad. Alumni Assn. Clubs: Wings of Gold Toastmasters (pres. 1966), 5 Points Optimist (v.p. 1970). Editor: Cash Management Forum, 1975-76. Home: 3139 Boxwood Dr Atlanta GA 30345 Office: One NDC Plaza Atlanta GA 30327

TURNER, JAMES HENRY, lawyer; b. Atlanta, Dec. 16, 1918; s. Thomas Morgan and Mary (Jenkins) T.; B.A., U. Fla., 1940; J.D., Stetson U., 1969; m. Virginia Lanning, Aug. 15, 1951. Admitted to Fla. bar, 1969, U.S. Dist. Ct. bar, 1970, U.S. Ct. Appeals bar, 1970, U.S. Supreme Ct. bar, 1972, U.S. Tax Ct. bar, 1976, U.S. Ct. Claims bar, 1976, U.S. Ct. Customs and Patent Appeals bar, 1976; individual practice law St. Petersburg, Fla., 1969—; spl. counsel Dreyfus Corp., Shareholders Corp., Phoenix Mut. Life Ins. Co. Served with USN, 1942-46, comdr. Res. ret. Mem. Am., Fed., Fla., D.C. bar assns., Sigma Nu, Delta Theta Phi, Nu Beta Epsilon. Presbyterian. Club: St Petersburg Yacht. Contbr. articles to profl. jours. Home: 1201 Seville Ln NE St Petersburg FL 33704 Office: Suite 511 300 Bldg W 3151 3d Ave N St Petersburg FL 33713

TURNER, JAMES WILLIAM, educator; b. Gainesville, Tex., Dec. 24, 1933; s. Whaley and Amy Lois (Thomas) T.; B.S., N. Tex. State U., 1956, M.Ed., 1958; Ed.D., U. Mo., 1961; m. Janelle Saxon, Mar. 30, 1957; children—James William, Robin. Tchr. math. and English, Dallas Schs., 1956-59; adminstrv. asst. Columbia (Mo.) Public Schs., 1959-61; prof. Coll. Edn., N. Tex. State U., Denton, 1961—; cons. public schs. Mem. Assn. Supervision and Curriculum Devel., Assn. Tchr. Edn., Phi Delta Kappa. Republican. Presbyterian. Home: 1902 Archer Trail Denton TX 76201 Office: PO Box 5431 NT Sta Denton TX 76203

TURNER, JOE MICHAEL, indsl. sociologist, constrn. co. exec.; b. Scottsville, Ky., Jan. 9, 1941; s. Jack Redford and Helen (White) T.; B.A., Western Ky. U., 1963, M.A., 1971; Ph.D., Fla. State U., 1974; m. Judy Anderson, Aug. 19, 1960; children—Ginger, Jon, Jason. Asst. supt. Blue Ridge Mfg. Co., Christiansburg, Va., 1963-64; personnel mgr. Houchens Industries, Bowling Green, Ky., 1964-69; asst. prof. sociology Clemson U., 1971-77; dir. personnel ops. Daniel Internat., Greenville, S.C., 1977—. Bd. dirs. Housing Inst. Clemson U. Mem. Am. Soc. Personnel Adminstrn., So. Sociol. Soc., Am. Soc. Tng. and Devel., Human Resources Planning Soc., World Future Soc., Alpha Kappa Delta. Republican. Ch. Christ. Home: 205 Couch Ln Easley SC 29640 Office: Daniel Internat 12th Floor Daniel Bldg Greenville SC 29602

TURNER, JOE STEWART, elec. engr.; b. Sherman, Tex., 1909; s. Ethelbert and Annie Lee (Stewart) T.; grad. Chgo. Radio and T.V. Inst., 1932; B.A. with honors, U. Tex., 1934; m. Vivian Dybwad, Jan. 7, 1932; children—Jo Ann (Mrs. Lawrence Albert Westhaver), Robert Roger. Elec. engr. Cooney Mining Co., Glenwood, N.M., 1934-35, Internat. Milling Co., Greenville, Tex., engr., sect. supr. CAA, Ft. Worth, Tex. and Washington, 1937-47, supt. Pacific area communications, Honolulu, 1948-52; chief radar div. FAA, Washington, 1953-59; project dir. systems div. dir. Collins Radio Co., Dallas, 1960-65; supr. cost control and new tech. reporting Bendix Launch Support, Kennedy Space Center, Fla., 1966-73; research and devel. on alternate energy sources, Titusville, Fla., 1974—. Coach, Annandale (Va.) Swim Team, 1956. Bd. dirs. Annandale Recreation Center, 1956. Served with AUS, 1943-44. Named Bendix/NASA launch honoree, Nov. 1973, Man of Month, Dec. 1973; honored by astronauts for work on Apollo Program. Sr. mem. I.E.E.E. (chmn. Pacific sect. 1951); mem. Bendix Mgmt. Club. Author: DOD/Commerce Joint Use of Radar Agreement, 1958; Airport Surface Detection Equipment, 1959; Performance Standards for Communications Systems, 1960. Home: 2825-614 Washington St Titusville FL 32780

TURNER, JOE VERNON, JR., discount store exec.; b. Lubbock, Tex., Oct. 22, 1944; s. Joe Vernon and Estelle (Arp) T.; student Tex. Technol. U., 1963-66; m. Elizabeth Ann Haynes, Aug. 23, 1966; 1 dau., Mary Elizabeth. Asst. store mgr. Howard Bros. Discount Stores, Ft. Walton Beach, Fla., Ft. Lauderdale, Fla., Smyrna, Ga., 1966-69; regional softlines supr. Arlans Dept. Stores, Atlanta, 1969-70; buyer, v.p. softlines Howard Bros. Discount Stores, Monroe, La., 1970—. Republican. Covenant Presbyn. Home: 2213 Redwood Dr Monroe LA 71201 Office: 3030 Aurora St Monroe LA 71201

TURNER, JOHN HENRY, ins. co. exec.; b. Rome, Ga., Jan. 30, 1933; s. Jesse S. T.; student Auburn U., 1957-59; grad. Ga. Inst. Tech., 1961. With Continental Ins. Co., Atlanta, 1959-67, expense clk., 1961-62, gen. accountant, 1963-67; with Moore Group, Inc., Atlanta, 1967-73, accountant, 1967-70, asst. controller, 1970-72, asst. treas., 1972-73; v.p., treas. Atlanta Casualty Co., Atlanta, 1973—. Served with USN, 1951-54. Baptist. Home: 647 Bellemeade Dr Marietta GA 30060 Office: PO Box 81168 Atlanta GA 30366

TURNER, JOHN SIDNEY, JR., otolaryngologist; b. Bainbridge, Ga., July 25, 1930; s. John Sidney and Rose Lee (Rogers) T.; B.S., Emory U., 1952, M.D., 1955; m. Betty Jane Tigner, June 5, 1955; children—Elizabeth, Rebecca, Jan Marie. Intern, U. Va. Hosp., 1955-56; resident in otolaryngology Duke Med. Center, 1958-61; prof., chmn. dept. otolaryngology Emory U., 1961—, also ear specialist, chief otolaryngology Emory U. Clinic, 1961—; area cons. otolaryngology U.S. 3d Army, 1962-69; asso. dir. heart disease control program Fla. Bd. Health, 1956-58; Ga. state chmn. Deafness Research Found., 1968—. Served with USPHS, 1956-58. Recipient award of appreciation Children of Fulton County/Fulton County Health Dept., 1975; named outstanding clin. tchr. Emory U. students, 1972. Diplomate Am. Bd. Otolaryngology. Mem. So. Med. Assn. (certificate of appreciation 1974, chmn. otolaryngology sect. 1974), Ga. Soc. Otolaryngology (pres, 1973), AMA, Med. Assn. Ga., Med. Assn. Atlanta, Am. Acad. Otolaryngology, Triological Soc., Am. Council Otolaryngology, Alpha Omega Alpha. Democrat. Methodist. Club: Atlanta Optimist (pres. 1975-76). Contbr. articles on ear disease to profl. jours., chpts. in books. Home: 1388 Council Bluff Dr NE Atlanta GA 30345 Office: 1365 Clifton Rd NE Atlanta GA 30322

TURNER, JOSEPHINE, family economist; b. Morgan County, Ala., July 2, 1939; d. Lannie Odell and Ethel May (Davis) T.; B.S., U. Ala., 1966, M.S., 1968; Ph.D., Purdue U., 1975. Instr. Tex. Tech. U., Lubbock, 1968-72; asst. prof. home mgmt. and child devel. U. Southwestern La., Lafayette, 1972-73; asst. prof. family resource mgmt. Oreg. State U., Corvallis, 1975-78; family resource mgmt. specialist Ala. Co-op Extension Service, Auburn (Ala.) U., 1978—. Treas., Auburn-Opelika area Youth for Christ, 1978-80; field and camp dir. Tombigbee council Girl Scouts U.S., 1966-67. Recipient Dissertation Research award Am. Council of Consumer Interest, 1977. Mem. Ala. Home Econs. Assn., Am. Home Econs. Assn., Ala. League of Women Voters, Tex. Consumers League (regional dir. 1970-72), Southeastern Family Econs. and Home Mgmt. Edn., AAUW, Phi Upsilon Omicron, Delta Kappa Gamma. Democrat. Mem. Ch. of God. Contbr. numerous articles on home econs. to profl. jours. Home: 881 Cherokee Rd Auburn AL 36830 Office: Duncan Hall Auburn Univ Auburn AL 36830

TURNER, LORETTA FRANCES, nurse; b. Morgantown, W.Va., Feb. 24, 1940; d. Guy Charles and Frances Virginia (Dyer) Findley; B.S. in Nursing, Alderson-Broaddus Coll., Philippi, W.Va., 1962; M.S. in Edn., Madison U., Harrisonburg, Va., 1975; children—Mary Frances, Kay Lee, Samuel Charles. Head nurse Calhoun County (W.Va.) Hosp., Grantsville, 1962-63; staff nurse Newborn Nursery, Charleston, W.Va., 1963-64; charge nurse Nat. Orthopaedic and Rehab. Hosp., Arlington, Va., 1964-65; staff nurse, supr. Winchester Meml. Hosp., Winchester, Va., 1965-77, coordinator nursing edn., 1977—; asst. prof. nursing Shenandoah Coll., Winchester, 1973-77; vis. prof. psychiat. nursing Shepherd Coll., Shepherdstown, W.Va. Bd. dirs. no. region Va. Lung Assn., 1979—; bd. deacons Sunnyside Presbyterian Ch., Winchester, 1978—, vice chmn., 1979; sec. Dowell J. Howard Vocat. Sch., 1979, mem. gen. adv. com., 1978—, nursing craft com., 1978—. Mem. Am. Nurses Assn., Va. Nurses Assn. Republican. Home: Route 5 Box 614 Winchester VA 22601 Office: South Stewart St Winchester VA 22601

TURNER, LOYD LEONARD, business exec.; b. Claude, Tex., Nov. 5, 1917; s. James Richard and Maude (Brown) T.; B.A., Baylor U., 1939, M.A., 1940; postgrad. U. Pa., 1940-42; m. Lee Madeleine Barr, Apr. 13, 1944; children—Terry Lee, Loyd Lee. Instr., U. Pa., 1940-42; pub. relations coordinator Consol. Vultee Aircraft Corp., San Diego, 1946-48, dir. pub. relations, Ft. Worth, 1948-53; asst. to pres. Ft. Worth div. Gen. Dynamics Corp., 1953-71, dir. pub. affairs Convair Aerospace div., Ft. Worth, 1971-72; exec. asst. to chmn. bd. and pres. Tandy Corp., Ft. Worth, 1972-76, v.p., 1976—. Pres., Ft. Worth Pub. Library Bd., 1958-63, Casa Manana Musicals, Inc., 1978—; v.p. Ft. Worth Bd. Edn., 1962-65, pres., 1965-71; mem. exec. com. Tex. Assn. Sch. Bds., 1966-71, v.p., 1970-71; mem. steering com., council big city bds. Nat. Sch. Bds. Assn., 1967-69, mem. Gov's Com. on Pub. Sch. Edn., 1966-69; pres. Tex. Council Maj. Sch. Dists., 1968-69. Bd. dirs. Tarrant County chpt. A.R.C., 1956-59, Tex. Com. Pub. Edn., 1961-69; bd. dirs. Pub. Communication Found. North Tex., 1970-76, One Broadway Plaza, 1978—, Tex. Research League, 1979—, Longhorn council Boy Scouts Am., 1976—, Child Study Center, 1974—, Parenting Guidance Center, 1976-78, Planning and Research Council of United Way Met. Tarrant County, 1976-80, Ft. Worth Safety Council, 1980—, Christian Edn. Coordinating Bd. Bapt. Gen. Conv. Tex., 1976—. Served with USAAF, 1942-46. Named Library Trustee of Year, Tex. Library Assn., 1961, Pres. of Best Bd. of Large Sch. Systems in U.S., N.E.A., 1968; recipient citation Air Force Assn., 1962; Leadership award West Tex. C. of C., 1966, 69. Mem. Pub. Relations Soc. Am. (pres. North Tex. chpt. 1977), Tex. Assn. Bus. (bd. dirs. 1977—, exec. com. 1979—), Assn. for Grad. Edn. and Research (bd. dirs. 1978—), Air Force Assn., Nat. Mgmt. Assn., Advt. Club Ft. Worth (pres. 1977-78), Friends Ft. Worth Library (v.p. 1971), Ft. Worth C. of C. (dir. 1974-76, 78—), Arts Council Ft. Worth and Tarrant County (dir. 1980—), Baylor U. Devel. Council (pres. 1975-77), Baylor U. Alumni Assn. (dir. 1958-61), Sigma Delta Chi (pres. Ft. Worth 1961-62). Baptist. Rotarian (pres. Fort Worth 1974-75, dir. 1972-76). Clubs: Knife and Fork (dir. 1963-66, pres. 1965-66), Colonial Country, Century II, Press of Fort Worth. Author: The ABC of Clear Writing, 1954. Home: 3717 Echo Trail Fort Worth TX 76109 Office: 1800 One Tandy Center Fort Worth TX 76102

TURNER, MARIANN LOUISE, speech pathologist; b. Jacksonville, Fla., Oct. 27, 1949; d. Stephen William and Dorothy Louise (Taylor) Yanetovich; A.A., St. Petersburg Jr. Coll., 1971; M.S., U. S. Fla., 1973; m. Robert Henry Turner, Aug. 9, 1974; 1 dau., Moriah Louise. Speech pathologist Pinellas County Sch. System, Clearwater, Fla., 1974—. Mem. Am. Speech and Hearing Assn., Bay Area Speech and Hearing Assn. Democrat. Methodist. Home: 808 Woodcrest Dr Clearwater FL 33516

TURNER, MAXINE THOMPSON, educator, writing cons.; b. Butler, Ga., Mar. 27, 1935; d. Mack Thompson and Jessie (Jones) Turner; B.A., Huntingdon Coll., Montgomery, Ala., 1957; M.A., Auburn (Ala.) U., 1961, Ph.D., 1970; postgrad. U. Md., summer 1961, U. Edinburgh (Scotland) summer 1967. Mem. faculty Columbus Center, U. Ga., 1958, Montgomery Coll., Tacoma Park, Md., 1961-62, Upper Iowa Coll., Fayette, 1962-63, Auburn U., 1957-58, 63-68, Am. U., Ft. Benning (Ga.) br., 1970; asso. prof. English, Ga. Inst. Tech., 1970—. Mem. Modern Lang. Assn., S. Atlantic Modern Lang. Assn., Am. Soc. for Engring. Edn., (exec. bd. liberal studies div., Soc. for Tech. Communication (exec. bd. Atlanta chpt., nat. membership data processing com.), Am. Med. Writers Assn., Magna Carta Dames, Descs. of Knights of Order of Garter, Assn. Tchrs. Tech. Writing, AAUW, DAR. Democrat. Episcopalian. Contbr. articles to profl. jours. Office: English Dept Ga Inst Tech Atlanta GA 30332

TURNER, MYRA BROOKS (MRS. RONALD JOSEPH TURNER), composer; b. Knoxville, Tenn., Jan. 13, 1936; d. Paul David and Lillie Mary (Ray) Brooks; student Juilliard Sch. Music, 1947-51; Mus.B., So. Meth. U., 1955, Mus. M., 1956; m. Ronald Joseph Turner, June 11, 1960; children—Stacy Lynn, Cheryl Leigh, Teresa Jeanne. Mus. specialist Dallas schs., 1956-60; mus. dir. choral music, Knoxville, 1960-64; composer-in-residence Birmingham (Ala.) Children's Theatre, 1967-69; composer, lectr., performing artist, Atlanta, 1969—; instr. electronic keyboard lab. Mercer U., Atlanta, 1975-77, press sec. music prep. sch., 1976-77; dir. St. Martin in the Fields Church St. Cecilia Choir, 1973—; instr. improvisation and composition Maryville (Tenn.) Coll., 1977-79; founder Camelot Fine Arts Club, Atlanta, 1975. Bd. dirs. Atlanta Fine Arts Symposium, Allegro Children's Theatre, Atlanta; pres. Youth Orch. Guild, Knoxville. Recipient award Seattle Nat. Playwriting Contest, 1968; Nat. Merit award Phi Mu Epsilon, 1972; named Composer of Yr., Knoxville Music Tchrs. Assn., 1979. Mem. Nat., Ga. (dist. festival chmn. 1970—; state festival chmn. 1972) federated mus. clubs, Nat., Ga., Atlanta (v.p. 1972) music tchrs. assns., Internat. Soc. Known Poets and Writers, Tenn. Fedn. Music Clubs (state dir. youth div.), Mu Phi Epsilon (pres. Atlanta alumnae 1972-74), Pi Kappa Lambda, Alpha Delta Pi. Composer: (three act plays) Cinderella, 1966, Pinocchio, 1965, The Green Dragon, 1965, Mid-Summer Nights Dream, 1965, Flibbertygibbet, 1972, Javoho Junction, 1959; (piano solos) Praise The Lord, Christ Jesus, 1966, Man Speaks Through Music, 1965, The Jazz Man Suite, 1968, Fantasy in A Minor, 1968. Contbr. poem to Images and Reflections. Club: Atlanta Woman's. Address: 8629 Highlark Ln Knoxville TN 37919

TURNER, RALPH (CHIP) WILSON, JR., clergyman, religious orgn. adminstr.; b. Shreveport, La., Jan. 18, 1948; s. Ralph W. and Gladys Pearl (Ma Gouirk) T.; B.A. cum laude in Speech Edn., La. Coll., 1970; M.R.E., New Orleans Bapt. Theol. Sem., 1973; m. Sandra Elaine Aymond, May 23, 1970; children—Christopher Layne, Cory Wilson. Ordained to ministry Baptist Ch., 1972; asso. pastor and minister edn. 1st Bapt. Ch., Farmerville, La., 1968-71, 1st Bapt. Ch., Summit, Miss., 1971-73, 1st Bapt. Ch., Slidell, La., 1973-75, 1st Bapt. Ch., Port Arthur, Tex., 1975-76; minister edn. and bus. adminstr. 1st Bapt. Ch., Beaumont, Tex., 1976-79; asso. dir. missions, teaching and tng. Greater New Orleans Bapt. Assn., 1979—; Sunday sch. dir. St. Tammany Bapt. Assn., Slidell, 1973-75; ch. tng. dir. Concord Bapt. Assn., Farmerville, 1970-71; mem. nat. bd. Ch. Commn. on Civic and Youth Serving Agys. Merit badge counselor, exec. bds. New Orleans Area and Three Rivers councils Boy Scouts Am., 1973—; dist. rep. Nat. Eagle Scout Assn., 1975-79; faculty mem. Bapt. Week at Philmont Scout Ranch, 1978, 80. Recipient Alexandria (La.) Civitan Citizenship award, 1969, 70. Mem. Nat. Assn. of Ch. Bus. Adminstrs., La. Bapt. Religious Edn. Assn., Bapt. Public Relations Assn., Met. Assn. of Religious Edn. Dirs., So. Bapt. Religious Edn. Assn., Golden Triangle Religious Edn. Assn., Tex. Bapt. Public Relations Assn., Southwestern Bapt. Religious Edn. Assn., Assn. Bapt. for Scouting (nat. bd. 1978—), Internat. Platform Assn., Young Men's Bus. League of Beaumont. Democrat. Clubs: Lions, Rotary (newsletter editor 1976, chorister 1976), Masons. Contbr. articles to religious publs. Office: 2222 Lakeshore Dr New Orleans LA 70122

TURNER, ROBERT ALEXANDER, JR., rheumatologist; b. Englewood, N.J., Oct. 12, 1937; s. Robert Alexander and Marie Antoinette (Fensterer) T.; A.B., U. N.C., 1959; M.D., Med. Coll. Ala., 1966; m. Florence Elizabeth McGowan, June 25, 1960; children—John Alexander, Katheryn Elizabeth, Robert Andrew. Intern, N.C. Bapt. Hosp., Winston-Salem, 1966-67, resident in internal medicine, 1967-69; fellow in rheumatology Hosp. U. Pa., 1969-71; asst. prof. medicine (rheumatology) Bowman Gray Sch. Medicine, Winston-Salem, 1971-75, asso. prof. medicine, 1975—, chief sect. rheumatology, 1979—. Bd. dirs., mem. med. adv. com. N.C. chpt. Arthritis Found., 1975—, chmn., 1978-79. Served to 1st lt. USMCR, 1959-62. Diplomate Am. Bd. Internal Medicine. Fellow A.C.P.; mem. Am. Soc. Clin. Pharmacology and Therapeutics, Am. Rheumatism Assn., N.Y. Acad. Scis., Am. Fedn. Clin. Research, So. Soc. Clin. Investigation, Am. Assn. Immunologists, Soc. Exptl. Biology and Medicine, Chi Psi. Republican. Episcopalian. Contbr. articles to various med. jours. Home: 2801 Robinhood Rd Winston-Salem NC 27106 Office: Rheumatology Sect Dept Medicine Bowman Gray Sch Medicine Winston-Salem NC 27103

TURNER, ROBERT EDWARD (TED), III, communications co. exec., sports exec.; b.Cin., 1939; ed. Brown U.; m. 2d Jane; children—Rhett, Beauregard, Jean; children by previous marriage—Laura Lee, Robert E., IV. Pres. Turner Communications Corp., Atlanta, Atlanta Braves, Sta. WTCG-TV, Atlanta, 1976—; chmn. Atlanta Hawks. Named U.S. Yachtsman of Yr.; recipient Congl. Cup, Champion award So. Ocean Racing Circuit, America's Cup, 1977. Mem. Office: Turner Communications Corp 1018 W Peachtree St NW Atlanta GA 30309*

TURNER, ROBERT FOSTER, author; b. Atlanta, Feb. 14, 1944; s. Edwin Witcher and Martha Frances (Williams) T.; B.A., Ind. U., 1968; J.D., U. Va., 1981; m. Debra Lou Herwig, Apr. 13, 1979. Research asso., public affairs fellow Hoover Instn. on War, Revolution and Peace, Stanford (Calif.) U., 1971-74; spl. asst., legis. asst. Sen. Robert P. Griffin, Washington, 1974-79; author: Vietnamese Communism: Its Origins and Development, 1975; Myths of the Vietnam War: The Pentagon Papers Reconsidered, 1972; cons. nat. security affairs, 1979—. Served with AUS, 1968-71; Vietnam. Recipient book grants Hoover Press, 1972, Earhart Found., 1979-81; Eisenhower Found. scholar, 1979-80; Youth Found. scholar, 1979-80. Mem. Am. Soc. Internat. Law, Thomas Jefferson Lit. and Debating Soc., U.S. Chess Fedn. Republican. Sr. editor: Va. Jour. Internat. Law, 1980—; contbr. articles to N.Y. Times, profl. jours. Home: 116 Roberts Ln Apt 401 Alexandria VA 22314

TURNER, ROBERT RANDOLPH, educator, clergyman; b. Bondtown, Va., Dec. 11, 1927; married, 1 child. B.A. in English, Carson-Newman Coll., 1951; M.A. in English, U. Tenn., 1955; Ph.D. in English, George Peabody Coll. and Vanderbilt U., 1970; married; 1 child. Tchr., Coeburn (Va.) High Sch., 1945-48, Jefferson County (Tenn.) Sch. System, 1951-55; prof. English Carson-Newman Coll., 1955—. Vis. storyteller Jefferson County Schs., 1970—; storyteller Bales Meml. Library, Jefferson City, Tenn., 1973—. Mem. Nat. Council Tchrs. English, South Atlantic Modern Lang. Assn., East Tenn. Edn. Assn., Am., Tenn. folklore socs., Assn. Preservation of Tenn. Antiquities (pres. chpt. 1976-80, state trustee 1978—). Teaching fellow, 1963-64; Danforth fellow, 1966; Student Found. Research grantee, 1975; developed teaching aids for early childhood through middle sch. children's lit. Certified in teaching, Tenn., Va.; specialist in children's lit., folklore, Am. lit., children's lang. devel. and edn. Home: 208 Deborah St Jefferson City TN 37760 Office: Carson-Newman Coll PO Box 1927 Jefferson City TN 37760

TURNER, SCOTT (GRAHAM MORRISON TURNBULL), record producer, musician, composer, publisher; b. Sydney, N.S., Can., Aug. 23, 1931; s. Allison D. and Evelyn (Peters) Turnbull; came to U.S., 1952; B.A., B.S., U. Dubuque, 1956; postgrad. Tex. Tech. U., 1956-57; children by previous marriage—Trevor Graham Turnbull, Adrienne Tracy Turnbull. Mem. Brit. Empire Games track team, 1954, All-Canadian track team, 1950-56; lead guitarist Tommy Sands and the Raiders, 1957-60, Guy Mitchell, 1960-61, Eddie Fisher, 1961-62; writer/producer A&M Records, then mgr. Central Songs, Inc., 1963-64; exec. producer country div. Liberty/Imperial Records, Hollywood, Calif., 1964-69; exec. producer country div. United Artists Records, Nashville, 1970-71; producer Starcrest Records, 1975-76; ind. producer for Slim Whitman, Del Reeves and Jimmy Clanton, 1976—, also Gold Albums, U.K.; composer over 350 songs, including 48 with Audie Murphy, including: Shutters and Boards, When the Wind Blows in Chicago; Comin' in the Back Door; (with Nilsson) A Travellin' Man; The Great American Classic Cowboy; Hicktown; Does He Love You Like I Do; (with Herb Alpert) Mexican Drummer Man; songs recorded by Roy Clark, Dean Martin, Charley Pride, Eddy Arnold, Tammy Wynette, Herb Alpert, Nilsson; TV appearances include Perry Como Show, Milton Berle Show, Mike Wallace Show, Mike Douglas Show, A.M. Chgo.; live performer in Las Vegas, Miami, Chgo. Mem. ASCAP, Country Music Assn., Nat. Assn. Rec. Arts and Scis. Mem. United Ch. Can. Home and Office: 524 Doral Country Dr Nashville TN 37221

TURNER, SHIRLEY SUE, med. technologist; b. Danbury, Iowa, Nov. 17, 1935; d. Wilmer and Aleva Alice (Diment) Earnest; student Nebr. State Tchrs. Coll., 1953-55; Med. Technologist, St. Joseph Mercy Hosp. Sch. Med. Tech., 1956; m. Edmund B. Turner, Sept. 30, 1965; 1 dau., Lisa Kay. Med. technologist Magic Valley Meml. Hosp., Twin Falls, Idaho, 1956-57, Buena Vista County Hosp., Storm Lake, Iowa, 1957-59, Rockwood Clinic, Spokane, Wash., 1959-60, Greene County Hosp., Jefferson, Iowa, 1961-65, Great S.W. Gen. Hosp., Grand Prairie, Tex., 1965-71, Internat. Clin. Labs., Ft. Worth, 1971-72, Pathology Asso. of Tex., Ft. Worth, 1973-75, Grand Prairie Community Hosp., 1975—. Mem. adv. council El Centro Community Council, Dallas, 1977—. Mem. Am. Soc. Clin. Pathologists, Am. Soc. Med. Technologists. Home: 3544 Granada St Fort Worth TX 76118 Office: 2709 Hospital Blvd Grand Prairie TX 75051

TURNER, THOMAS RICHARD, physician; b. Arp, Tex., May 19, 1917; s. Leonard W. and Rosamond (Dean) T.; B.A., Baylor U., 1938, M.D., 1941; M.S., U. Minn., 1945; m. Donnie Martha Goodner, Aug. 29, 1941; children—Nancy Ethel Turner Lang, Ann Rosemond Turner Jordan, Richard Leonard. Intern, Baylor U. Hosp., Dallas, 1941-42; fellow Mayo Clinic, Rochester, Minn., 1942-45, asso. Springer Clinic, Tulsa, 1945-47, partner, 1947-60; pvt. practice medicine specializing in neurology and psychiatry, Tulsa, 1960—; mem. staff St. John's, Hillcrest, St. Francis hosps. (all Tulsa). Diplomate Am. Bd. Psychiatry and Neurology, Am. Bd. Electroencephalography. Fellow Am. Psychiat. Assn., Am. Acad. Neurology; mem. AMA, Am. Med. EEG Assn., Central Neurol. Psychiat. Assn., So. Med. Assn. (life), Pan Am. Med. Assn. (diplomate sect. on neurology), Beta Beta Beta, Alpha Chi, Alpha Epsilon Delta. Home: 1831 E 31st Pl Tulsa OK 74105 Office: 3102 S Harvard Ave Tulsa OK 74135

TURNER, ULYSSES GRANT, III, physician; b. Charlottesville, Va., May 3, 1937; s. Ulysses Grant and Margaret Saunders (Boyer) T.; B.A., U. Va., 1959, M.D., 1966; m. Barbara Burgess Turner, Oct. 16, 1960; children—Page Errin-Saunders, Margaret Olivia-Newbold, Joan Fisher. Intern, U. Va. Hosp., 1966-67, resident in obstetrics and gynecology, 1967-72; asst. prof. obstetrics and gynecology U. Va., Charlottesville, 1971-74, clin. asst. prof., 1974—; practice medicine specializing in obstetrics-genecology and sex therapy, Charlottesville, 1974—; mem. staff Martha Jefferson Hosp., U. Va. Hosp. Mem. adv. bd. Central Va. Planned Parenthood; v.p. Am. Cancer Soc., Charlottesville; mem. nat. adv. bd. Southeastern Family Forum. Served with USN, 1959-61. Diplomate Am. Bd. Obstetrics and Gynecology. Mem. Am. Assn. Sex Educators and Therapists (certified sex educator and therapist), Albermarle County Med. Soc., Med. Soc. Va., Am. Coll. Obstetrics and Gynecology, Am. Fertility Soc., Va. Obstetrics and Gynecology Soc. Clubs: Farmington Hunt, Greencroft, Farmington Polo, Fraternal Order Police. Home: Beaulieu Route 2 Charlottesville VA 22901 Office: 920 High St E Charlottesville VA 22901

TURNER, VANGIE LUELLA, elec. wholesale and lighting co. exec.; b. Lawndale, N.C., June 26, 1920; d. Lawrence Thomas and Lillie Mae (Norman) T.; student Blantons Bus. Coll., Asheville, N.C., 1940-41, U. S.C., 1960, LaSalle U., 1967-70, S.C. Sch. Real Estate, 1977. Supr. proof dept. Citizen & So. Nat. Bank, Spartanburg, S.C., 1941-43; supr. bookkeeping dept., cashier First Nat. Bank, Morgantown, N.C., 1943-47; asst. to clerical supr., jr. accountant Durham (N.C.) City and County Health Dept., 1950-52; sr. accountant Greensboro (N.C.) County Welfare dept., 1952-53; office mgr., accountant Dodge-Plymouth Dealer, Shelby, N.C., 1953-58; corporate accountant Capital Electric Supply Co., Columbia, S.C., 1959—, exec. sec.-treas., 1965—, also dir., trustee retirement plans. Trustee Coll. Place Methodist Ch., Columbia, 1976-78. Mem. Nat., Eau Claire (treas. 1978-79) bus. and profl. women's clubs. Democrat. Club: Off-Beat Organ, Bridge. Home: 600 Glenthorne Rd Columbia SC 29203 Office: 2015 Marion St Columbia SC 29201

TURNER, WILLIAM WOOD, JR., physician; b. Miami, Aug. 30, 1947; s. William Wood and Melba Ailene (Wilson) T.; student Williams Coll., 1965-67, Tulane U., 1967-68; M.D., Tulane U., 1972; m. Rosemary Wurster Chandler, Aug. 31, 1968. Intern, Southwestern Med. Sch., Dallas, 1972-73; resident in surgery Southwestern Med. Sch., Dallas, 1973-77; asst. prof. surgery Southwestern Med. Sch., Dallas, 1977—; practice medicine specializing in surgery, Dallas, 1972-77, 79—, Oklahoma City, 1977-79; mem. staff Parkland Meml. Hosp., Dallas; asst. chief surgery Dallas VA Med. Center. Served with USAF, 1977-79. Mem. Dallas County Med. Soc., Tex. Med. Assn., AMA, Assn. Acad. Surgery, Alpha Omega Alpha. Republican. Episcopalian. Contbr. articles to profl. jours.; research in gastrointestinal surgery, trauma surgery, surgical nutrition. Home: 615 Durango Circle S Irving TX 75062 Office: 5323 Harry Hines Blvd Dallas TX 75235

TURNEY, WILLIAM OTTIS, JR., corp. exec.; b. Decatur, Ala., Oct. 3, 1945; s. William O. and Libbie (Legg) T.; B.S., Austin Peay State U., 1966; M.B.A., Memphis State U., 1968; m. Patricia Maroney, Feb. 28, 1970; children—Robert Travis, Karen Marie. Asst. to v.p. fin. LTV Aerospace Corp., Dallas, 1968-71; dir. planning and bus. devel. Addressograph Multigraph Corp., Cleve., 1971-73; dir. fin. services Internat. Systems and Controls Corp., Houston, 1973-74; exec. v.p., sec., chief fin. officer Stratford of Tex., Inc., Houston, 1974-79; sr. v.p. fin. and adminstrn. Ridgeway's Inc., 1980—; dir. Jr. Glazier Food Co., Brazos Capital Corp. Served to 2d lt. USAR, 1967. Republican. Episcopalian. Clubs: Westside Tennis, Met. Tennis, Met. Racquet, Houston City. Home: 11623 Highgrove Dr Houston TX 77077 Office: 5711 Hillcroft Houston TX 77036

TUROFF, ROBERT ENNIS, producer, dir.; b. Kansas City, Mo., Nov. 8, 1932; s. Cecil Sidney and Fannie Rose Turoff; B.A., U. Denver, 1953; postgrad. N.Y. U., 1957; m. Roberta MacDonald, Sept. 7, 1961; children—Benjamin MacDonald, Kyle Ennis. Asst. stage dir. Kansas City (Mo.) Starlight Theatre, 1958-59; dir. Town and Country Musicals, Rochester, N.Y., 1960-61, Lambertville (N.J.) Music Circus, 1962; dir., writer, producer Allied Concert Series, 1960, 62, 64; dir. Theatre Under the Stars, Atlanta, 1964-65, Nat. Opera, Raleigh, N.C., 1963, 65, 67, 69, Ford Found. Opera, N.Y.C. Center, 1963, Pocono (Pa.) Playhouse, 1966, Casa Manana Musicals, Ft. Worth, 1967-70; founder, 1971, since exec. producer, dir. Golden Apple Dinner Theatre, Sarasota, Fla., 1971—; pres. Coastal Theatre Prodns., Inc., Sarasota, 1971--; pres., founder Plato, Inc., Sarasota, 1977—; guest dir., prof. U. S. Fla., Tampa; dir., producer 4 world premiere prodns.; author: (musical) Hello Sucker!, 1969; script writer adaptations of New Moon, Naughty Marietta, Merry Widow, Vagabond King; bd. dirs. arts grants program Sarasota Women's Exchange. Bd. dirs. Old Folks Aid Home, Sarasota. Served with M.C., AUS, 1954-56. Recipient various certs. merit. Mem. Actors Equity Assn., Soc. Stage Dirs. and Choreographers (charter), Fla. Theatre Conf., S.E. Theatre Conf., Nat. Restaurant Assn., Fla. Restaurant Assn., Am. Dinner Theatre Inst. (charter), Sarasota C. of C., Venice, Longboat Key and Manatee chambers commerce. Democrat. Jewish. Club: University. Office: 25 N Pineapple Ave Sarasota FL 33577

TURPEN, BEN LYNN, control engr.; b. Salt Lake City, Aug. 12, 1935; s. Don Ralph and Evelyn (Hawkins) T.; B.S. in Chem. Engring., Tex. Tech. U., 1960; A.A., Amarillo Coll., 1956; m. Martha Jane Hoover, Oct. 12, 1961; children—Carolyn, Evelyn, David, Laura, Eric. Plant engr. Phillips Petroleum Co., Borger, Tex., 1960-62, spl. problems spectro analyst, Phillips, Tex., 1962-65; plant engr. El Paso Products Co., Odessa, Tex., 1965-68, instrument engr., 1968-74, sr. control engr., 1974—; instr. Odessa Coll., 1975—; cons. in field. Dist. scouting chmn., scoutmaster Boy Scouts, 1974—. Served with USNR, 1953-67. Registered profl. engr., Tex. Mem. Am. Inst. Chem. Engrs., Instrument Soc. Am. (sr. mem.), Inst. Measurement and Control, Tex. Soc. Profl. Engrs., Soc. Mining Engrs. Mem. Ch. of Jesus Christ of Latter-day Saints. Club: Toastmasters. Home: 6315 Montana St Odessa TX 79763 Office: El Paso Products Co PO Box 3986 Odessa TX 79760

TURTUR, MARIO, JR., ins. cons.; b. Elizabeth, N.J., Feb. 1, 1930; s. Mario and Mary T.; A.B., Colgate U., 1952; postgrad. Rutgers U., 1954; m. M. Bonnie Newbatt, Feb. 22, 1952; children—Christopher, Stephen, Andrea. Sales rep. Perlfoam, Inc., Houston, 1957-59; zone mgr. sales Lightolier, Inc., Houston, 1959-61; estate planning agt. Conn. Gen. Life Ins. Co., Houston, 1961—; dir. Holly Resources, Inc., Portfoloio Mgmt., Inc. Mem. fin. com. Young Republicans. Served to 1st lt., USAF, 1952-54. Named Man of Year, Conn. Gen. Life Ins. Co., Houston, 1961-79 inclusive. Roman Catholic. Contbr. articles to ins. jours. Home: 2311 River Oaks Blvd Houston TX 77019 Office: 2000 W Loop S Suite 1400 Houston TX 77027

TUSH, MASON LEE, SR., distilling and importing co. exec.; b. Louisville, Dec. 26, 1918; s. John Otha and Elsa Louise (Stein) T.; A.B., U. Louisville, 1941; M.A. (Univ. scholar), Northwestern U., 1946; m. Anna Lucille Coldiron, June 24, 1946; children—Lesleigh, Mason Lee, John William, Patti Lynn. Dir. mktg. research Reynolds Metals Co., Louisville, 1946-48; asst. prof. econs. U. Louisville, 1948-50; dir. promotion Ky. C. of C., Louisville, 1950; with Brown-Forman Distillers Corp., Louisville, 1951—, v.p., area dir., 1966-69, v.p., 1966—; with Jos. Garneau Co., Louisville, 1951—, exec. v.p., 1969-71, dir. mktg., 1971—, pres., 1971—. Mem. psychiat. council Norton Meml. Infirmary Psychiat. Clinic, Louisville. Served to maj., fin. dept. AUS, 1941-46. Decorated Bronze Star. Mem. Confrerie de la Chaine des Rotisseurs, Confrerie des Chevaliers du Tastevin, Mensa. Club: Masons. Office: PO Box 1080 Louisivlle KY 40201

TUTTLE, ROGER LEWIS, lawyer; b. Wyandotte County, Kans., Nov. 9, 1930; s. Emmett Joseph and Freda Alberta (Lewis) T.; B.A., U. Kans., 1958; J.D., U. Miss., 1958; m. Beverly Jean Campbell, Aug. 3, 1957; children—Pamela Anne, Deborah Jean. Admitted to Miss. bar, 1958, N.C., bar, 1964, Va. bar, 1965; mem. firm Neill, Clark & Townsend, Indianola, Miss., 1958-61, Heidelberg, Woodliff & Franks, Jackson, Miss., 1961-62; area atty. Exxon, New Orleans, Charlotte, N.C., 1962-65; asso. counsel Lawyers Title Ins. Corp., Richmond, Va., 1965-71; gen. atty. A.H. Robins Co., Richmond, 1971-76; asst. gen. counsel Dan River, Inc., Danville, Va., 1976—. Served with M.I., U.S. Army, 1952-55. Decorated Commendation medal with oak leaf cluster; Mil. Cross of Kingdom of Belgium. Mem. State Bar Va., Am. Bar Assn., Am. Coll. Legal Medicine, Am. Trial Lawyers Assn., Lawyers Assn. Textile Industry, Phi Alpha Delta, Nat. CIC Assn., Assn. Former Intelligence Officers, Pi Kappa Alpha. Republican. Presbyterian. Clubs: Danville Golf, Masons, Shriner. Home: 129 Acorn Lane Danville VA 24541 Office: Dan River Inc 2291 Memorial Dr Danville VA 24541

TWEED, PAUL BASSET, crisis intervention exec.; b. Zvinigorodka, Russia, Sept. 22, 1913; s. Jacob and Ida (Basset) T.; came to U.S., 1914, naturalized, 1921; B.S., Rensselaer Poly. Inst., 1934, M.S., 1935; M.A., N.Y. State Coll. Tchrs., 1937; m. Mildred Emma Haycock, June 15, 1942; children—Bradford, Joel. Chemist, Am. Hard Rubber Co., Butler, N.J., 1936-40; chem. engr. Picatinny Arsenal, Dover, N.J., 1940-62; cons. engr. Avco Corp., Wilmington, Mass., 1962-66; engr. Martin Marietta Aerospace Co., Orlando, Fla., 1966-76; bus. mgr. We Care Inc., Orlando, 1976—. Mem. Lake Holden Water Adv. Bd., Fla. Mem. Sigma Xi. Patentee in field explosive tech. Home: 4624 Tinsley Dr Orlando FL 32809 Office: 112 Pasadena Pl Orlando FL 32803

TWIDDY, RAYMOND L., artist, educator; b. Elizabeth City, N.C., Aug. 25, 1940; s. Raymond Lee and Elizabeth (Mansfield) T.; B.S., U. N.C., 1962; M.F.A., George Washington U., 1967. Art tchr. Public Sch. System D.C., 1967; instr. painting Corcoran Sch. Art, 1967; instr., asst. prof., asso. prof. studio art, chmn. studio art dept., curator Sweet Briar Coll. (Va.), 1968—; one-man shows Ward-Nasse Gallery, N.Y.C., Queens Coll., 2d St. Gallery, Charlottesville, Va., Washington and Lee U., Sweet Briar Coll.; group shows include: Met Mus. and Art Center, Miami, Fla., Corcoran Gallery Art, Washington, Franz Bader Gallery, Chrysler Mus., N.C. Mus. Art, Greenville (S.C.) Mus. Art, Va. Commonwealth U., George Washington U., Ga. So. Coll.; represented in permanent collections: Queens Coll., City U. N.Y., Flushing, Washington and Lee U., Lexington, Va., Sweet Briar Coll., George Washington U., Washington; also pvt. collections. Served with U.S. Army, 1962-63. Recipient Purchase awards 2d St. Gallery, Charlottesville, Va., 1975, S.E. Center Contemporary Art, Winston-Salem, N.C., 1971, Norfolk (Va.) Mus. Arts and Scis., 1968; Andrew W. Mellon Found. faculty grantee Sweet Briar Coll., 1974, Sweet Briar Coll. Ford research grantee, 1970. Mem. Coll. Art Assn. Am., Southeastern Coll. Art Conf., So. Graphics Council. Home: PO Box AR Sweet Briar VA 24595 Office: 034 Babcock Fine Arts Center Sweet Briar Coll Sweet Briar VA 24595

TWIGG, DAVID KEITH, county adminstr.; b. Columbus, Ohio, Apr. 16, 1950; s. Duane C. and Roberta J. (Huggens) T.; B.A., Fla. So. Coll., 1972; M.S.M., Fla. Internat. U., 1973. Adminstrv. asst. Met. Dade County (Fla.) Comprehensive Drug Program, 1974-75, adminstrv. officer, 1975-78, dir. evaluation Comprehensive Alcohol Program, 1978-79, asst. adminstr., 1979—; clin. instr. Barry Coll., 1975-77; adj. instr. dept. public adminstrn. Fla. Internat. U., 1978—. Asst. scoutmaster S. Fla. council Boy Scouts Am., Miami, leader tng. chmn. Tequesta dist., 1979. Mem. Am. Soc. Public Adminstrn. (mem. exec. bd. S. Fla. chpt. 1978—), Fla. Alcohol Coalition, Dade County Council on Alcoholism, Fla. Trail Assn. Democrat. Methodist. Editorial bd. So. Rev. Public Adminstrn.

TWIGGS, DENNIS GLENN, psychologist; b. Marion, N.C., Feb. 5, 1946; s. James Glenn and Velva (Ledford) T.; B.S., Appalachian State U., 1969, M.A., 1972; Ph.D., Tulane U., 1977; m. Tamara Hatley, July 13, 1969; 1 son, Jason Scott. Psychologist, Mexia (Tex.) State Sch., 1977-78; psychologist San Antonio State Hosp. Sch., 1978—, dir. rehab. therapy, 1978—; lectr. in field. Served with spl. forces, U.S. Army, 1969-71. Tulane U. teaching fellow, 1974-77. Mem. AAAS, Am. Assn. on Mental Deficiency, Sigma Xi. Democrat. Baptist. Home: 227 Emporia St San Antonio TX 78218 Office: San Antonio State Hosp Sch Box 23310 Highland Hills San Antonio TX 78223

TWIGGS, LEO FRANKLIN, artist, educator; b. St. Stephen, S.C., Feb. 13, 1934; s. Frank and Bertha Lee (Myers) T.; B.A., Claflin Coll., 1956; student Art Inst. Chgo., 1960; M.A., N.Y. U., 1964; postgrad. U. Ga., Ed.D., 1970; m. Rosa Johnson, June 15, 1962; children—Kenneth, Darryl, Keith. Instr. art Lincoln High Sch., Sumter, S.C., 1958-64; asst. prof. art S.C. State Coll., Orangeburg, 1964-69, asso. prof., 1970-72, prof., 1972—, also dir. art program and Whittaker Gallery; mem. S.C. Arts Commn., 1970-73; mem. S.C. Museum Commn., 1973-76, S.C. Art Collection Com., 1970-72, S.C. Adv. Com. on Film, 1972. Served with Signal Corps U.S. Army, 1956-58. Recipient Citizenship award Am. Legion, 1956. Mem. Alpha Kappa Mu, Phi Kappa Phi. Mason, Shriner. Contbr. profl. jours.; developed batik painting process. Office: PO Box 1691 Dept Art SC State College Orangeburg SC 29115

TWISDALE, KENNETH LAUGHTON, JR., controller; b. Tarboro, N.C., Oct. 28, 1944; s. Kenneth Laughton and Gwendolyn (Marks) T.; student Wingate Jr. Coll., 1964-65, Chowan Jr. Coll., 1969-70; B.S. in Acctg., Atlantic Christian Coll., 1972; m. Carolyn Gay Overton, Apr. 17, 1970. Acct. SCA Services, Inc., Raleigh, N.C., 1972-73, Harrison & Judge, C.P.A.'s, 1973-75; controller, sect. Tulloss Tractor Co., Rocky Mount, N.C., 1975—. Served with AUS, 1966-69. Decorated AF Commendation Medal, 2 Bronze Star Medals, Bronze Star for Valor. Republican. Baptist. Home: 816 Jeffries Rd Rocky Mount NC 27801 Office: PO Box 1480 S Church St Rocky Mount NC 27801

TWITCHELL, DOROTHY, psychiatrist; b. Owatonna, Minn., Dec. 22, 1926; d. Caryl Emory and Dorothy (Buxton) Twitchell; student Cornell Coll., Mt. Vernon, Iowa, 1944-46; B.A., U. Calif. at Berkeley, 1948; M.D., Harvard, 1952; m. Clarence Benson Clark, Apr. 2, 1952 (div. Feb. 1969); children—Elizabeth Dorothy, Susan Elizabeth. Intern Orange Meml. Hosp., Orlando, Fla., 1952-53; gen. practice medicine, Winter Park, Fla., 1953-60; resident psychiatry VA Hosp., Augusta, Ga., 1961-63, Med. Coll. Ga., Augusta, 1963-64; practice medicine specializing in psychiatry, Cocoa Beach, Fla. 1967—; mem. staff Cape Canaveral Hosp., Cocoa Beach, Wuesthoff Hosp., Rockledge, Fla. Mem. exec. com. Dist. VII B, Brevard County Mental Health Dist. Bd. Mem. Brevard County Med. Soc., Fla. Med. Assn., A.M.A., Am., Fla., Central Fla. psychiat. assns., Cape Kennedy C. of C., Boylston Soc. Harvard Med. Sch., AAUW, Am. Women's Med. Assn. Republican. Episcopalian. Club: Woman's. Office: 30 N Woodland Ave Cocoa Beach FL 32931

TWITTY, ROBERT STEVEN, systems analyst; b. Clearwater, Fla., Jan. 29, 1950; s. Robert Gwynn and Edith Marie (Eckroth) T.; A.A., St. Petersburg Jr. Coll., 1970; B.S. with honors, U. Fla., 1972; C.C.P., Inst. Certification of Computer Profls., 1977; m. Gayle Linda Waldron, Nov. 17, 1973. With Fla. Power Corp., St. Petersburg, 1972—, sr. programmer, 1975-77, engring. application supr., 1977—. Mem. Phi Beta Kappa. Republican. Lutheran. Home: 4398 50th Ave S Saint Petersburg FL 33711 Office: 3201 34th St S Saint Petersburg FL 33711

TWITTY, WILLIAM BRADLEY, fin. and tax cons.; b. Allsboro, Ala., Jan. 5, 1920; s. Clarence Hudson and Lyda (Blackburn) T.; student U. North Ala., 1939-41, U. Ala., 1941-43; A.B., U. N.C., 1944; m. Gaila Northing, 1941; children—Tralelia, Camille, Gaila, Eugenia; m. 2d, Edith Bolling, July, 1951; children—Hannah, William. Vice-pres. Twitty & Twitty, Inc., Cherokee, Ala., Muscle Shoals, Ala., Birmingham, Ala., Pompano Beach, Fla., Houston, 1948-54, pres., 1954—. Chmn., Ala. State Planning Bd., 1947-51. Served with U.S. Army, 1944-45. Julius Rosenwald fellow U. Ala., 1943, U. N.C., 1944. Mem. Am. Mgmt. Assn., Nat. Hist. Assn. Democrat. Methodist. Clubs: Exchange, Masons, Elks. Author: Beyond The Leaves, 1964, Y'All Come, 1962, The Flying Green Whale and Other Poems, 1963, Sacred Chitimacho Indian Beliefs, 1971. Home: Route 2 Box 126 Cherokee AL 35616

TWOMEY, MORRIS OGDEN, photographer; b. Electra, Tex., Apr. 30, 1929; s. Benjamin James and Verna Ena (Porter) T.; student pub. schs. Vernon, Tex.; m. Marinel Bacon, Sept. 2, 1950; children—Sherinel, Marianna, Suzanna, Annelle. Comml. photographer KTBS TV, Shreveport, La., 1956-66; ind. dog show photographer, Shreveport, 1966—. Democrat. Baptist. Club: Shreveport Kennel (pres.). Contbg. photographer Great Show Dogs Am., 1969, Internat. Ency. Dogs, 1970. Home and office: 3423 Broadmoor Blvd Shreveport LA 71105

TWYMAN, JOSEPH PASCHAL, univ. pres.; b. Prainie Hill, Mo., Nov. 21, 1933; s. William L. and Hazel (Dry) T.; B.A., U. Mo. at Kansas City, 1955, M.A., 1959, Ph.D., 1962; m. Patricia Joanne Harper, July 26, 1953; children—Mark Kevin, Patricia Lynn. Asst. prof., then asso. prof. Okla. State U., 1960-66, asso. dir. Research Found., 1965-66; dir. research U. Mo. at St. Louis, 1966-67; v.p. U. Tulsa, 1967-68, pres., 1968—; cons. in field, 1960—; dir. Sooner Fed. Savs. & Loan Assn., Atlas Life Ins. Co.; mem. Commn. on Instns. Higher Edn., North Central Assn. Colls. and Schs., 1975—. Mem. adv. panel Southwestern Coop. Ednl. Lab., 1967-68; adv. bd. Tulsa Opera, 1968—, St. John's Hosp., Tulsa, 1969-76. Bd. dirs. Okla Council Econ. Edn., 1968—, Tulsa Area United Way, 1968—, Tulsa Civic Ballet, 1968—, Arts Council Tulsa, 1970-77, Thomas Gilcrease Museum Assn., 1970—, Goodwill Industries of Tulsa, Inc., 1975—; bd. dirs., acting chmn. Tulsa Area Health Edn. Center, 1977—; trustee Undercroft Montessori Sch., Tulsa, 1967-72, Children's Med. Center, Tulsa, 1968-73, Tech. Edn. Research Center Inc., Cambridge, Mass., 1977—; Hillcrest Med. Center, Tulsa, 1969—; mem. exec. com. Frontiers of Sci. Found. Okla., 1968—; bd. dirs. Tulsa Mental Health Assn., 1967-74, 75—, Mid-Continent Research and Devel. Council, 1967-68. Ford Found. grantee, 1963-66, U.S. Office Edn. grantee, 1958-60, 61-62, 62-63, 64-65, 64-66. Mem. A.A.A.S., Am. Acad. Polit. and Social Sci., Okla. Cattlemen's Assn., Belted Galloway Soc., Phi Delta Kappa, Omicron Delta Kappa. Presbyn. Clubs: Southern Hills, University and Summit (Tulsa). Author: (with others) The Concept of Role Conflict, 1964; also articles. Home: 1775 E 31st St Tulsa OK 74105

TYLER, JOHN KEITH, lawyer; b. Spring Valley, Ill., Mar. 9, 1941; s. Allen Charles and Mildred L. (Anderson) T.; student U. Tex., 1959-61; B.B.A. in Finance, So. Meth. U., 1963; J.D., U. Houston, 1973; m. Meta R. Bernard, June 17, 1972; 1 dau., Kathryn Anderson; children by previous marriage—John Bradford, Stephen Craig. Systems engr., mktg. rep. IBM, 1963-70; admitted to Tex. bar, 1973, U.S. Supreme Ct. bar, 1976, U.S. Tax Ct. bar, 1976; asso. firm Wheat, Thornton & Shaw, Houston, 1973-75; sec., treas., dir. firm Shaw & Tyler, P.C., Houston, 1975—; guest lectr. Law Sch., U. Houston. Mem. Am., Houston bar assns., State Bar Tex., Sigma Phi Epsilon, Phi Alpha Delta. Democrat. Episcopalian (vestryman). Clubs: Briar (Houston); Masons. Home: 2137 W Main St Houston TX 77098 Office: 1717 Saint James Pl Suite 136 Houston TX 77056

TYLER, JOHNNIE MAE WEEKS, ret. educator, civic worker; b. Ozark, Ala., July 28, 1913; d. John Calvin and Lena Lee (Boyett) Weeks; B.S. in Edn., Troy State Coll., 1946; postgrad. Auburn U., 1955-57; diploma in Christian tng. Baptist Sunday Sch. Bd., Nashville, 1961; m. Saxon DeWitt Dykes, Sr., Sept. 23, 1933 (div. Oct. 1963); children—Saxon DeWitt, Catherine Malissa Dykes Nolin; m. 2d,

William Deval Barefoot, Nov. 25, 1964 (dec. Oct. 1968); m. 3d, E. J. Tyler, June 12, 1969. Tchr. elementary schs. Barbour and Dale counties, Ozark, Ala., 1940-69, 6th group Emma P. Flowers Elementary Sch., Ozark Ala., 1955-69, ret., 1969. Grey lady Dale county chpt. ARC, Ozark, 1942-44, 1st aid instr., 1942-69; instr. CD, Ozark, 1963-69, 74—; CD coordinator for Ariton, Ala.; notary pub., justice peace Barbour County, 1963-64; trustee Ariton Library, 1971-77. Founding fellow So. Soc. Geneologists; mem. Am. Legion Aux. (charter unit 148), Fedn. Womens' Clubs (chmn. Dale County 1949-51), Beta Sigma Phi. Baptist (librarian ch. 1963). Clubs: Clio Study (pres. 1956-57), Progressive Study (Clio) (pres. 1959-60); Maud Martin Study (charter) (Ozark). Contbr. papers to tech. lit., book revs. Ch. Paper Monthly Publ., Clio, 1963. Home: Route 2 Box 281 Ariton AL 36311

TYLER, LOWELL PEARDON, real estate broker, ins. agt.; b. Dover-Foxcroft, Maine, Nov. 3, 1928; s. Carroll Linwood and Alice (Brawn) T.; Bus. Mgmt. degree, LaSalle U., 1963; LL.B., Blackstone Sch. Law, Chgo., 1973; m. Elisabeth Eleanor Allen, Oct. 22, 1951; children—Joyce E., Valarie Yvone. Ins. agt. Prudential Ins. Co., Bangor, Maine, 1952-73; ins. agt. New Eng. Mut. Life, Palm Beach, Fla., 1973-74; gen. agt. and broker, Lake Worth, Fla. and Palm Beach, 1973—; real estate broker, Lake Worth, 1978—. Served with USAF, 1948-52. Mem. Nat. Assn. Underwriters (past v.p. local chpt.), Nat. Assn. Realtors, Am. Legion (past post comdr., dist. comdr., past county adjutant Maine). Clubs: Elks, Kiwanis. Home: 1432 S Lakeside Dr Lake Worth FL 33460 Office: 3923 Lake Worth Rd Suites 214-215 Lake Worth FL 33461

TYNDALL, MARSHALL CLAY, JR., banker; b. Wilmington, Del., Feb. 20, 1943; s. Marshall Clay and Dorothy Mabel (Batten) T.; B.S., U. Del., 1965, M.B.A., 1975; m. Bonnie Gay Blankenburg, June 19, 1965; children—Steven Marshall, Michael Edward, Julie Anne. Mem. mgmt. tng. program First Pa. Bank, 1965-68, cash mgmt. mgr., 1968-70, comml. mktg. mgr., 1970-71, sr. mktg. officer, 1971-73; v.p., dir. mktg. Tex. Commerce Bank, Houston, 1973-76, sr. v.p., 1976—; sr. v.p., dir. mktg. Tex. Commerce Bancshares, Inc., Houston, 1976—; dir. Tex. Commerce Bank-Campbell Center, Dallas. Mem. exec. bd. Sam Houston Area council Boy Scouts Am., Houston; bd. dirs. Bluebonnet Bowl Assn., Greater Houston Conv. and Visitors Council, Houston Mayor's Civic Center Improvement Com. Mem. Bank Mktg. Assn. (nat. dir. 1977-80), Houston C. of C. (aviation steering com.). Methodist. Home: 14714 Kellywood St Houston TX 77079 Office: 712 Main St Houston TX 77002

TYNER, MAX RAYMOND, clergyman, business exec.; b. Kokomo, Ind., Nov. 21, 1925; s. Paul Raymond and Dora May (Schroeder) T.; student Ind. U. extension, 1946; B. Liberal Studies, U. Okla.; postgrad. Calif. State U.; m. Marjorie Jane Tobias, Dec. 30, 1949; children—Renita (Mrs. Thomas Odom), Shawnee Marthel (Mrs. James Overstreet). Gen. mgr. Becraft Motor Express, Inc., Kokomo, 1946-58; owner Tyner Realty & Ins., McAllen, Tex., 1959-72; buyer Summer Inst. Linguistics, Mexico City, 1972-73; ordained to ministry Methodist Ch., 1968; pastor 1st United Meth. Ch., George West, Tex., 1973-77. Bd. dirs., sec. Rio Grand Children's Home, Mission, Tex., 1968-72; bd. dirs. Alliance Village Nursing Home, McAllen, 1970-72, Salvation Army, 1965-69. Served with USNR, 1944-45. Named hon. citizen, Guadalajara, Mexico, 1964, Xalapa, 1963; named outstanding mem. Kokomo Jr. C. of C., 1956. Mem. Am. Assn. Christian Counselors, Tex. Assn. Realtors, Mc Allen Real Estate Bd., Internat. Platform Assn., Am. Legion, United Comml. Travelers, Wycliffe Assn., Christian Writers Guild. Republican. Clubs: Masons, Shriners. Home: 6213 N 17th St McAllen TX 78501 Office: PO Box 2453 McAllen TX 78501

TYREE, JAMES EDWARD, gas co. exec.; b. Sperry, Okla., 1922; B.S., U. Okla., 1948; married. With Okla. Natural Gas Co., 1949—, asst. dist. operating supr., 1954-55, dist. operating mgr., 1955-64, dist. v.p., Shawnee, Okla., 1964-68, Oklahoma City, 1968-72, exec. v.p., Tulsa, 1972-76, pres., 1976—, also dir. Office: Okla Natural Gas Co 624 S Boston Ave Box 871 Tulsa OK 74102

TYROCH, RUTH CECILIA, nurse, hosp. ofcl.; b. Temple, Tex., Apr. 26, 1924; d. Joe R. and Cecelia A. (Doskocil) Pitrucha; diploma King's Daus. Sch. Nursing, 1945; student Temple Jr. Coll., 1963-65; m. Jerry Daniel Tyroch, June 29, 1947; children—Grady Lynn, Jerry Daniel Jr., Elizabeth Ann. Supr. operating room Nursing Service, King's Daus. Hosp., Temple, 1945-46; staff and head nurse operating room nursing service VA Hosp., Temple, 1946-55; instr. nursing Vocat. Nursing Sch., Navarro County Hosp., Corsicana, Tex., 1956; asst. supr. operating room nursing service VA Hosp., Temple, 1957-76; supr. operating room nursing service Olin E. Teague VA Med. Center, Temple, 1976—. Pres., Freeman Heights (Tex.) PTA, 1958; pres. Christian Sisters Assn., Seaton, Tex., 1959-60; active Seaton Brethren Ch., 1960-78. Mem. Assn. Operating Room Nurses (pres. Central Tex. 1962-63), Am. Nurses Assn. Democrat. Home: 4305 Hickory St Temple TX 76501 Office: Olin E Teague VA Med Center 1901 S 1st St Temple TX 76501

TYSON, BRUCE CARROLL, JR., pharm. co. exec.; b. Greenville, N.C., Aug. 17, 1936; s. Bruce Carroll and Lila Erle (Taylor) T.; B.S. magna cum laude, Duke U., 1958; M.A. (Gulf Research fellow), Princeton U., 1960; Ph.D., U. Del., 1969. Analytical chemist U.S. Army Edgewood (Md.) Arsenal, 1963-67; research asso. A.H. Robins Co., Richmond, Va., 1968-75, dir. analytical research, 1975—. Served to 1st lt. AUS, 1961-63. Mem. Am. Chem. Soc., Phi Beta Kappa, Sigma Xi, Pi Mu Epsilon. Phi Lambda Upsilon. Contbr. articles to sci. jours. Home: 2003 Hanover Ave Richmond VA 23220 Office: 1211 Sherwood Ave Richmond VA 23220

TYSON, KENNETH ROBERT THOMAS, surgeon, educator; b. Houston, July 30, 1936; s. Howard Ellis and Myrle Henrietta (Daunoy) T.; B.A., U. Tex., 1956; M.D., U. Tex. Med. Br., 1960; m. Sue Ann Delahoussaye, Nov. 20, 1971; children—Deborah, Kenneth, Michael, Jill. Intern Ind. U. Med. Center, Indpls., 1960-61, resident gen. and thoracic surgery, 1961-66; resident pediatric surgery Children's Hosp. Med. Center, Boston, 1966-67; chief pediatric gen., thoracic surgery U. Tex. Med. Br. at Galveston, 1967—, asst. prof. surgery, 1967-71, asso. prof., 1971-75, prof., 1975—, surgeon-in-chief Child Health Center, 1974—. Diplomate Am. Bd. Surgery, Am. Bd. Thoracic Surgery. Fellow ACS, Am. Acad. Pediatrics, Am. Coll. Cardiology; mem. Am. Assn. Thoracic Surgery, Soc. Surgery Alimentary Tract, Soc. U. Surgeons, So. Thoracic Surg. Assn., Am. Pediatric Surg. Assn., Tex. Surg. Soc., So. Surg. Assn., Alpha Omega Alpha, Delta Kappa Epsilon, Alpha Kappa Kappa. Episcopalian. Home: 2824 Dominique St Galveston TX 77550 Office: Dept of Surgery U of Tex Galveston TX 77550

TYSON, PHOEBE WHATLEY, painter; b. Wichita Falls, Tex., May 5, 1926; d. Mertic Boyd and Susie Phoebe (Creath) Whatley; student Abilene Christian U., 1943-45; B.A., N. Tex. State U., 1946, M.A., 1951; m. Josiah William Tyson, Jr., Dec. 20, 1946; children—Josiah William III, Phoebe Creath. Elementary art tchr. Ft. Worth Ind. Sch. Dist., 1946-47; pvt. tchr. art, Haskell, Tex., 1948-50; painter watercolors, acrylics, Seabrook, Tex., 1971-79, Austin, Tex., 1979—; exhibitor Biennial Exhbn., Nat. League Am. Pen Women, Kennedy Center, Washington, 1976, Rocky Mountain Nat. Watermedia Exhbn., Golden, Colo., 1977; pres. McLean (Va.) Art Club, 1971. Mem. Tex. Fine Arts Assn., Nat. League Am. Pen. Women (nat. art bd. 1972-74, Tex. v.p. 1972-74, Meml. br. pres. 1976-78, award of distinction 1976), Art League Houston, AAUW (v.p. Austin 1955-56), Clear Creek Art League, Watercolor Art Soc. Houston, San Antonio Water Color Group. Mem. Church of Christ. Home and Office: 8600 Appalachian St Austin TX 78759

UDELL, HELEN BROOKS, psychologist, educator; b. College Park, Md., Oct. 4, 1936; d. William J. and June (Ammons) Brooks; B.S., U. Western Carolina, 1959; M.S., Nova U., 1963; Ph.D., Heed U., 1975; m. Monroe Udell, Dec. 3, 1973; 1 dau. by previous marriage, Helen (Heidi) Brooks Sher. Tchr. English, Spanish, Music Haywood County schs., Waynesville, N.C., 1959-63; tchr. English, Spanish Jefferson County schs., Louisville, Ky., 1963-65; tchr. English Plant City (Fla.) schs., 1965-67; tchr. English Broward County (Fla.) schs., 1967—, also counselor, psychologist. Organizor Parent Awareness of Drug Abuse Program, Dania, Fla., 1976; v.p. Olsen Jr. PTA, Dania, 1976-77. Certified profl. hypnosis, 1977. Mem. NEA, Fla. English Tchrs., Am. Personnel and Guidance Assn., Am. Assn. Ethical Hypnosis, AAUW, Fla. Assn. Practicing Hypnotherapists, Broward Tchrs. Union, S. Broward High Band Parents Assn. Clubs: Order of the Eastern Star, Dania Opti-Mrs. (v.p.). Contbr. poems to mags. Home: Dania FL 33004

UDOUJ, RICHARD JOHN, furniture mfg. co. exec.; b. Fort Smith, Ark., May 6, 1936; s. John J. and Olivia Katherine (Vorster) U.; student U. Ark., 1956-57; B.A., Creighton U., 1959; m. Mary Youmans, Sept. 5, 1959; children—Natalie Marie, Richard John, Cristelyn Catherine, Frank Youmans. With Riverside Furniture Corp., Fort Smith, 1959—, exec. v.p., 1959-74, pres., 1974—, also dir.; dir. Ark. Best Corp. Mem. adv. bd. St. Edward Mercy Hosp., 1971-74, chmn., 1973-74; bd. dirs. Salvation Army, 1970-73; trustee St. Edward Mercy Hosp., 1975—; active Boy Scouts Am., 1943—, recipient Silver Beaver award, Order of Arrow, 1977. Served to capt. U.S. Army, 1959-63. Mem. Southwestern (pres. 1975), So. furniture mfrs. assns., Dallas Trade Mart (furniture bd. govs. 1974—, chmn. 1976), Mfrs. Exec. Assn. (pres. 1978), Furniture Industry Adv. Panel (consumer affairs com.), Fort Smith C. of C. (dir. 1970-74, Outstanding Young Man 1967, 69). Roman Catholic. Clubs: Hardscrabble Country, Fianna Hills Country, Town, K.C. Home: 3535 Royal Scots Way Fort Smith AR 72903 Office: 1400 S 6th St Fort Smith AR 72901

UEHLINGER, AUGUST FRANCIS, refinery supr.; b. Corpus Christi, Tex., Dec. 26, 1929; s. Cecil Francis and Marion Theresa U.; grad. Corpus Christi Coll., 1948; m. Janet Ruth Bitler, Oct. 29, 1963; children—Larry, Marjory, Randall, Greg, August Francis, Christopher, Joyce. With Champlin Petroleum Co., Corpus Christi, 1948—, pumper, pumper foreman, blender, dispatcher, 1948-77, terminal supr., 1977—. Mgr. youth baseball, 1956-74, umpire, 1961-62, league pres., 1965-67; active PTA, sch. activities. Club: Propeller of U.S. Democrat. Home: 9302 Moonbear Terr Corpus Christi TX 78409 Office: PO Box 9176 Corpus Christi TX 78408

UHDE, GEORGE IRVIN, physician; b. Richmond, Ind., Mar. 20, 1912; s. Walter Richard and Anna Margaret (Hoopes) U.; M.D., Duke, 1936; m. Maurine Elizabeth Whitley, July 27, 1935; children—Saundra Uhde Seelig, Thomas Whitley, Michael, Janice. Intern, Reading (Pa.) Hosp., 1936-37, resident in medicine, 1937-38; resident in otolaryngology Balt. Eye, Ear Nose and Throat Hosp., 1938-40, U. Oreg. Med. Sch., Portland, 1945-47; practice medicine specializing in otolaryngology, Louisville, 1948—; asst. prof. otolaryngology U. Louisville Med. Sch., 1945-62, prof. surgery (otolaryngology), head dept., 1963—, dir. otolaryngology services, 1963—; mem. staff Meth., Norton's-Children's, Jewish, St. Joseph's, St. Anthony's, St. Mary and Elizabeth's hosps.; cons. Ky. Surg. Tb Hosp., Hazelwood, VA Hosp., Louisville; cons. U. Louisville Speech and Hearing Center. Bd. dirs. Easter Seal Speech and Hearing Center. Served to lt. col. M.C., AUS, 1940-45; ETO; chief gas casulty and biol. warfare ETOUSA; Research Officer under Sir Lovatt Evans. Recipient Distinguished Service award U. Louisville, 1972. Fellow A.C.S., Am. Acad. Ophthalmology and Otolaryngology, So. Med. Soc.; mem. N.Y. Acad. Scis., Am. Coll. Allergists, Am. Acad. Facial Plastic and Reconstructive Surgery, A.A.A.S., Assn. U. Otolaryngologists, A.A.U.P., Assn. Mil. Surgeons U.S., Am. Laryngol., Rhinol. and Otol. Soc., Am. Audiology Soc., Soc. Clin. Ecology, Am. Soc. Otolaryngology Allergy, Centurian Otol. Research Soc. (Ky. rep.), Am. Council Otolaryngology (Ky. rep. 1968—), Hoopes Quaker Found., Alpha Kappa Kappa. Democrat. Methodist. Clubs: Filson, Big Spring Country, Jefferson. Author 4 books; contbr. articles to profl. jours. Home: 708 Circle Hill Rd Louisville KY 40207 Office: Med Towers South Louisville KY 40202

UHLAND, HOMER EDWARD, mining co. exec.; b. Breckenridge, Mo., Jan. 2, 1921; s. Russel Edward and Sarah Elizabeth Ann (Linger) U.; B.S., U. Md., 1943; m. Mary Blandford Burgess, Nov. 5, 1943; children—Edward Christopher, John Russell. With Internat. Minerals and Chem. Corp., 1948-65; v.p. mining cos. Reynolds Metals Co., 1965-69; v.p. Lithium Corp. Am., Gastonia, N.C., 1969—. Pres., Cerebral Palsy of Fla., 1965. Mem. N.C. Mining Assn. (pres. 1976-79), AIME, Am. Ceramic Soc. Clubs: Catawba Country, Kiwanis (past pres.). Patentee in field. Home: 121 Saddletree Rd Lincolnton NC 28092 Office: 449 Cox Rd Gastonia NC 28052

UHLIG, RICHARD HERBERT, educator; b. Cleve., May 12, 1923; s. Herbert and Emily Christine (Klug) U.; Ph.B., U. Wis., 1947; M.S.W., U. Calif., Berkeley, 1950; Ph.D., Brandeis U., 1970; m. L. Susanna Chabinak, Nov. 28, 1978; children by previous marriage—Barbara Joan, David Bruce, Jane Elizabeth; 1 stepdau., Suzette Snyder. Research sec. Health and Welfare Council of Louisville, 1950-52; research dir. Social Planning Council, St. Louis, 1953-56, Health and Welfare Council, Phila., 1956-66; research cons. Socio-Tech. Systems Asso., Boston, 1970-73; asso. dean, asso. prof. Sch. of Social Work, U. N.C., Chapel Hill, 1973—; cons. in field. Served to 2d lt. USAAF, 1942-45. NIMH spl. research fellow, 1966-69. Mem. Nat. Assn. Social Workers, Am. Sociol. Assn., Council on Social Work Edn., Gerontol. Assn. Democrat. Unitarian. Contbr. articles to profl. jours. Home: 7 Bluff Trail Chapel Hill NC 27514 Office: 223 E Franklin St Chapel Hill NC 27514

UHLL, JOSEPHINE THERES, hosp. adminstr.; b. Morrisonville, Ill., Oct. 22, 1918; d. James Benjamin and Laura Josephine (Young) U.; ed. DePaul U., St. Louis U. Joined Sisters of St. Dominic, Roman Cath. Ch., 1935; med. records adminstr. St. Anthony's Hosp., 1948; with St. Joseph's Hosp., Wellington, Tex., 1948-55, hosp. adminstr., 1952-55; adminstrv. asst. St. Dominic-Jackson (Miss.) Meml. Hosp., 1959-64, hosp. adminstr., chmn. bd., 1964—; dir. Blue-Cross/Blue Shield of Miss., 1969-72. Mem. Civil Service Commn., City of Jackson; bd. dirs. Epilepsy Found. Am.; pres. Miss. Blood Services, Inc., 1979-80. Fellow Am. Coll. Hosp. Adminstrs.; mem. Cath. Hosp. Assn., Miss. Hosp. Assn., Jackson C. of C. Home and office: 969 Lakeland Dr Jackson MS 39216

UHRHANE, PHILIP FREDERICK, mfg. co. exec.; b. Marietta, Ohio, May 26, 1924; s. Frederick J. and Marie L. (Trapp) U.; B.A., Marietta Coll., 1949; m. Mary E. Grudier, June 7, 1947; 1 dau., Ann Louise Uhrhane Campbell. Draftsman, Reminton Rand, Inc., Marietta, 1949-53; with Parkersburg Rig & Reel Co. (W.Va.), 1953-59, Parkersburg Aetna Corp., 1959-64, Walker Parkersburg Textron Corp., 1964—, engring. mgr. bldg. systems, 1972—; dir. Parkline Inc., 1972—, Parkline Systems, 1977—. Mem. bd. deacons 1st United Presbyn. Ch., 1970-72, trustee, 1973-75, v.p., 1973-74, pres., 1974-75. Served with M.C., U.S. Army, 1943-45. Mem. Nat. Mgmt. Assn., Am. Chem. Soc., Am. Contract Bridge League, Metal Bldg. Mfrs. Assn. (construction com. 1970—). Republican. Club: Elks. Patentee roof jack, eave strut bracket. Home: 28 Willowbrook Acres Parkersburg WV 26101 Office: Walker Parkersburg Textron 620 Depot Parkersburg WV 26101

ULLERY, JAMES RODNEY, environ. engr.; b. Columbia, S.C., July 15, 1953; s. William Gerald and Jane Elizabeth (Shealy) U.; B.Ch.E., Ga. Inst. Tech., 1975; M.P.A., U. S.C., 1979; m. Sandra Kaye Elliott, Aug. 23, 1975; Engr. I, S.C. Dept. Health and Environ. Control, Columbia, 1975-76, engr. II, 1976-78, engr. III, 1978—. Mem. Traveler's Protective Assn., Columbia. Mem. Am. Inst. Chem. Engrs., S.C. Pub. Health Assn., Phi Eta Sigma, Chi Epsilon Sigma, Sigma Phi Epsilon. Republican. Lutheran. Clubs: Lexington (S.C.) Optimist (dir. 1976-77, pres. 1977—). Home: 729 Ball Park Dr Lexington SC 29072 Office: 2600 Bull St Columbia SC 29201

ULLOCK, DONALD SARGEANT SINCLAIR CAMERON, engring. cons.; b. Chgo., July 14, 1901; s. William George and Anna Mete Gesina Christina (Wenke) U.; B.S., Ill. Inst. Tech., 1926; Ph.D., U. Mich., 1935; m. Charlotte Caroline Waldschmidt, June 25, 1927; children—Malcolm Henry William, Juanita Carol-Ann Luoni. Instr. chem. engring., curator chem. engring. labs. Ill. Inst. Tech., Chgo., 1926-31; with Union Carbide Corp., South Charleston, W.Va., 1934-66, design engr., 1939-44, sr. design engr., 1944-50, staff engr., 1950-61, engring. cons., 1961-66; pvt. practice mech. and chem. engring. cons., Lehigh Acres, Fla., 1966—. Active Boy Scouts Am., 1922-68. Chmn. South Charleston Planning Commn., 1944-50. Registered profl. engr. W.Va. Mem. Am. Chem. Soc., Nat. Soc. Profl. Engrs., Am. Inst. Chem. Engrs., Am. Soc. M.E., Am. Orchid Soc., Am. Amateur Radio Relay League, Ft. Myers Amateur Radio Club, Sigma Xi, Phi Lambda Upsilon. Presbyn. Lion. Contbr. articles to profl. jours. Home and office: 339 Dellwood Ave Lehigh Acres FL 33936

ULLRICH, JAMES ANTHONY, communications exec.; b. Indpls., June 13, 1941; s. Arlie John and Kathleen Cecilia (Bender) U.; B.A. in Philosophy, St. Francis Sem., 1963, M.Th., 1967; m. Anne Olvera, Sept. 25, 1970; children—Jennifer Anne, James Anthony. Ordained priest Roman Catholic Ch., 1967; parish priest, youth dir., Laredo, Tex., 1967-69; dir. communications Diocese Corpus Christi, Tex., 1969-70; coordinator sch. services KLRN-TV, Austin, San Antonio, Tex., 1970-73, dir. sch. services, 1973-78, 79—, mgr. sta. ops., 1978-79; state lobbyist for instructional TV, 1977—; also producer local TV programs. Mem. Greater San Antonio C. of C. (issues forum task force, urban affairs council), Tex. Ednl. TV Assn. (past pres.), Tex. Assn. Ednl. Tech. (dir.). Home: 5903 Royal Point San Antonio TX 78239 Office: PO Box 9 San Antonio TX 78291

ULRICH, PAUL THEODORE, social agy. ofcl.; b. Phila., Mar. 19, 1916; s. Paul Edmund and Catherine Henrietta (Eichley) U.; B.A., Lebanon Valley Coll., 1938; postgrad. N.Y. U., 1941-42, U. Pa., 1946; M.S.W., U. Houston, 1970; m. Elizabeth Teall Bender, Feb. 12, 1942; children—Paul Stanley, John Kenneth, George Henry, Walter Alan, Nancy Elizabeth. Tchr., Allentown (Pa.) Prep. Sch., 1938-39; draftsman, chemist Bethlehem Steel Co., Lebanon, Pa., 1939-40; tchr., Everett High Sch., 1940-41; tchr. coach Whitpain Twp. High Sch., Blue Bell, Pa., 1945-46; math. instr. Muhlenberg Coll., Allentown, 1946-47; tchr. Shaker Heights (Ohio) High Sch., 1947-48; production foreman RCA Corp., Lancaster, Pa., 1948-49; edn. adminstrn. instr., meteorol. cons. Inst. Storm Research, Houston, 1970-71; health planner Houston-Galveston Area Council, 1971-74, mgr. Area Agy. on Aging, 1974—; mem. adv. com. Tex. Research Inst. Mental Scis., Long Term Care Gerontology Center, 1979-80; sec.-treas. Tex. Assn. Area Agys. on Aging, 1979-80. Vice-chmn. Civic Assn., Clear Lake City, Tex., 1965. Served with USAF, 1941-45, 50-68; ETO. Mem. Acad. Cert. Social Workers, Am. Meteorol. Soc., Nat. Assn. Social Workers, Nat. Assn. Area Agys. on Aging. Presbyterian. Home: 1702 Silverpines St Houston TX 77062

UMANA, CESAR ROBERT, physician; b. Guatemala City, Guatemala, Aug. 16, 1934; came to U.S., 1959, naturalized, 1971; s. Jorge O. and Marta Aragon (Arroyo) U.; M.D., U. San Carlos (Guatemala), 1959; Ph.D. in Biochemistry, U. Rochester, 1963; m. Elizabeth Perdomo, Nov. 23, 1957; children—Isabel, George Robert, Maria Elena. Intern, Gen. Hosp., Guatemala City, 1958, Roosevelt Hosp., Guatemala City, 1958; resident family practice U. Minn., 1971-72; practice medicine specializing in family practice, Mpls., 1972-73, Arlington, Tex., 1973—; asso. prof. Sch. of Dentistry and Medicine, U. Minn., Mpls., 1967-71; mem. staff Abbot Hosp., Mpls., Meth. Hosp., St. Louis Park, Minn., Oak Cliff Med. and Surg. Hosp., Dallas, Arlington (Tex.) Meml. Hosp., Community Hosp., Dallas. Diplomate Am. Bd. Family Practice. Mem. Am. Acad. Family Physicians, Soc. for Exptl. Biology and Medicine, Am. Soc. of Human Genetics, Am. Chem. Soc., AMA, Tex. State Med. Soc., Dallas County Med. Soc., Sigma Xi. Contbr. articles to profl. jours.

UMHOLTZ, CLYDE ALLAN, fin. analyst; b. Du Quoin, Ill., Dec. 20, 1947; s. Frederick Louis and Opal Kathleen (Beard) U.; B.S., U. Ill., 1969; postgrad. U. Ark., 1969-70; M.S., U. Miss., 1972. Supr. quality control Champion Internat. Corp., Oxford, Miss., 1971-72; mgr. div. quality control Cook Industries, Memphis, 1973; engring. planner Northwest Industries and subsidiaries, Memphis, 1974-75; long range planning and analysis, W.R. Grace & Co. and subsidiaries, Memphis, 1975-78, on loan Center Nuclear Studies, Memphis State U., 1979—; cons. in field. Active presdl. election campaigns, 1968, 72, 80, mayoral campaign Memphis, 1975, Mid-South Billy Graham Crusade, 1978. Recipient Oratorical award Optimist Club, 1963, Leadership and Human Relations award Dale Carnegie Inst., 1977; NSF fellow, 1970-72. Mem. Memphis Jaycees, AAAS, U. Ill. Alumni Assn., U. Miss. Alumni Assn., Am. Mgmt. Assn., Am. Rose Soc., Am. Inst. Chem. Engrs., Am. Chem. Soc., Planning Execs. Inst. Baptist. Clubs: Admirals, Order of De Molay. Inventor angle trisector, 1966; researcher energy considerations of Haber cycle, 1969, comprehensive bus. and fin. studies of sulfur, sulfuric acid, and phosphates, 1975-78, cost and materials sci. studies for nuclear industry, 1979, 80. Home: 3580 Hanna Dr Memphis TN 38128

UNDERDOWN, DAVID R., tech. co. exec.; b. Dallas, Nov. 29, 1944; s. Revel Arvil and Edith Rose (Walker) U.; Ph.D., U. Houston, 1972; m. Glenda Faye Morgan, Jan. 22, 1967; children—Damon Ryan, Aimee Nicole. Supr. spl. services Imco Services Co., Houston, 1972-74; group leader prodn. ops. chemistry Getty Oil Co., Houston, 1974-78; dir. chem. research Baker Sand Control Co., Houston, 1978—. Mem. Town of Alvin (Tex.) Planning Commn., 1973-78. Mem. Soc. Petroleum Engrs., Am. Chem. Soc. Presbyterian. Office: Baker Sand Control Co PO Box 61486 Houston TX 77208

UNDERWOOD, BENJAMIN HAYES, SR., mental health adminstr.; b. Savannah, Ga., Mar. 10, 1942; s. Frank Callaway and Marion (Hayes) U.; B.B.A., U. Ga., 1964; m. Olga K. Underwood; children—Ashley Hayes, Benjamin Hayes. Asst. adminstr. Northside Manor Hosp., Atlanta, 1965-67; adminstr. Met. Psychiat. Center, Atlanta, 1967-76, also bd. dirs.; adminstr. Ridgeview Inst., Smyrna, Ga., 1977—. Bd. dirs., exec. com. Family Learning Centers, Atlanta. Served with USAF, 1966-67. Recipient Boss of Year award Am. Bus. Women's Assn., Atlanta, 1973. Mem. Am. Acad. Med. Adminstrs., Am., Ga. (mental health com. 1974—, proprietary hosp. com. 1974—, council on investor owned hosps. 1978) hosp. assns., Assn. Mental Health Adminstrs. (mem. U.S. pub. affairs com., pres. elect nominating com.), Hosp. Financial Mgmt. Assn., Am. Soc. Hosp. Purchasing Agts., Am. Soc. Hosp. Pub. Relations Dirs., Ga. Assn. Pvt. Psychiat. Hosp. (chmn.), Nat. Assn. Pvt. Psychiat. Hosps. (chmn. edn. com., Ga. legis. rep.), Cobb County C. of C. (dir.). Club: Smyrna Rotary (dir.). Home: 2156 Cedar Forks Dr Marietta GA 30062 Office: 3995 S Cobb Dr Smyrna GA 30080

UNDERWOOD, DAVID MILTON, security co. exec.; b. Houston, Mar. 5, 1937; s. Milton Ramon and Catherine (Fondren) U.; grad. Phillips Acad., Andover, Mass., 1954; B.A., Yale, 1958; postgrad. Inst. Investment Banking, Wharton Sch. Finance, U. Pa., 1969; m. Lynda Knapp, Nov. 21, 1964; children—David Milton, Catherine F., Duncan Knapp. With Morgan Stanley & Co., N.Y.C., 1962; with Underwood, Neuhaus & Co., investment bankers, Houston, 1962—, v.p., 1966-74, sr. v.p., 1974—, dir., 1968—; pres. Feliciana Corp., Houston, 1966—, Pano Tech Exploration Co., Houston, 1972—; dir. Fannin Bank. Trustee, Fondren Found., Kinkaid Sch.; bd. dirs. Meth. Hosp., Tex. Med. Center, Inc. Served to capt. AUS, 1958-60, 61-62. Decorated Army Commendation medal. Mem. Zeta Psi. Republican. Episcopalian Clubs: Houston Country, River Oaks Country, Bayou, Ramada, Houston, Allegro, Sarabande (Houston); Yale (N.Y.C.). Home: 3645 Willowick Rd Houston TX 77019 Office: 724 Travis St Houston TX 77002

UNDERWOOD, OLGA MARIA CEHELSKY (MRS. BENJAMIN HAYES UNDERWOOD), music therapist; b. Czamz, Austria, Apr. 6, 1946; d. George Michael and Veronica Bronislava (Drozdovska) Cehelsky; came to U.S., 1949, naturalized, 1960; B. Music Edn. magna cum laude, Temple U., 1968; Mus. M. in Music Therapy, U. Miami (Fla.), 1978. Tchr. music Phila. Pub. Sch. System, 1967-71; flight instr. Tamiami Airport, Homestead Airport, Homestead, Fla., 1973-74, Fulton County Airport, Atlanta, 1974-75; intern in activity therapy Ga. Mental Health Inst., Atlanta, 1974; dir. activity therapy Met. Psychiat. Center, Atlanta, 1974-75; coordinator adult psychiat. day treatment North DeKalb Community Mental Health Center, 1975—; cons. DeKalb County Day Program, 1975—. Certified music educator N.J.; certified flight instr. FAA; certified music therapist Nat. Assn. Music Therapy. Mem. Mental Health Assn., Nat., Ga., Atlanta mental health assns., Therapeutic Activities Assn. Ga. (treas. 1977-79), Day Treatment Assn. Ga., Nat. Assn. Music Therapy, Ukrainian Women's League Am., Nat. Assn. Flight Instrs., Ukrainian-Am. Assn. Ga. (musical dir. 1976—), Sigma Alpha Iota Alumni. Club: Ukrainian Am. (Miami). Contbr. article to music jour. Home: 2156 Cedar Forks Dr Marietta GA 30062 Office: 3007 Hermance Dr Atlanta GA 30319

UNDERWOOD, WILLIAM LESLIE, JR., therapist; b. Pansacola, Fla., Dec. 11, 1945; s. William Leslie and Ruby Gonzales U.; B.A. in Humanities, Bob Jones U., 1967; postgrad. Luth. Theol. Sem., 1967-69; M.S. in Counseling, Troy State U., 1975; m. Ana Maria Pendleton. Counselor, program coordinator, day treatment dept. Escambia County Community Mental Health Center, Pensacola, 1971-78; dir. partial hospitalization S. Central Ala. Mental Health Center, Andalusia, Ala., 1978—; day treatment supr. univ. and jr. coll. practicum intern grad. students; day treatment con. Halfway House. Fellow Menninger Found.; mem. Mental Health Counselors Assn., Ala. Mental Health Counselors Assn. Lutheran. Home: College Heights Apt 3 Andalusia AL 36420 Office: S Central Ala Mental Health Center Box 1013 Andalusia AL 36420

UNROE, LARRY JAMES, hosp. adminstr.; b. Charleston, W.Va., Aug. 22, 1947; s. Lawrence Adam and Frances Elizabeth (Clifton) U.; B.B.A. in Acctg., Marshall U., Huntington, 1969; M.H.A., Med. Coll. Va., 1974; m. Susan Chris Fraser, Dec. 27, 1969; 1 son, Mark Alexander. Internal auditor Ashland Oil, Inc. (Ky.), 1969-74; adminstrv. resident Charleston Area Med. Center, 1973-74; v.p. adminstrn. St. Joseph's Hosp., Parkersburg, W.Va., 1974—. Bd. deacons First United Presbyn. Ch., Parkersburg; bd. dirs. W.Va. Kidney Found.; chmn. region V adv. council Emergency Med. Services; mem. com. profl. edn. W.Va. Cancer Soc. Mem. USAR, 1969-76. Mem. Am. Coll. Hosp. Adminstrs., Am. Hosp. Assn., W.Va. Hosp. Assn., W.Va. Young Adminstrs. Assn. (past pres.). Republican. Club: Optimist. Home: 103 Woodshire Dr Parkersburg WV 26101 Office: St Joseph's Hosp 19th St and Murdoch Ave Parkersburg WV 26101

UNRUH, HENRY CORNELIUS, life ins. co. exec.; b. Barmstedt, Holstein, Germany, Mar. 25, 1914; s. Cornelius and Martha (Woltmann) U.; came to U.S., 1946, naturalized, 1952; B.Sc., Acadia U., 1933; A.M., Brown U., 1935; m. Mary Olive Facey, Oct. 4, 1941; children—Sandra Jane, David John. Actuarial clk. No. Life Assurance Co. Can., London, Ont., 1937-46; asst. actuary Provident Life & Accident Ins. Co., Chattanooga, 1946-48, actuary, 1948-55, chief actuary, from 1955, v.p., 1957-70, pres., 1970-72, chmn. bd., 1972—, also chief exec. officer, from 1972, also dir. Fellow Soc. Actuaries. Presbyterian. Office: Provident Life & Accident Ins Co Fountain Sq Chattanooga TN 37402*

UNTERKOEFLER, ERNEST LEO, bishop; b. Phila., Aug. 17, 1917; s. Ernest L. and Anna Rose (Chambers) U.; A.B., Cath. U. Am., 1940, S.T.L., 1944, J.C.D., 1950. Ordained priest Roman Cath. Ch., 1944; asst. pastor Richmond, Va., 1944-47, 50-60, Arlington, Va., 1947-50, sec. Richmond Diocesan Tribunal, 1954-60; moderator Council Cath. Women, 1956-61; chancellor Richmond Diocese, 1960-62, vicar gen., 1962-64, papal chamberlain, 1961; aux. bishop Richmond, titular bishop Latopolis, 1962-64; bishop of Charleston (S.C.), 1965—. Sec., U.S. Cath. Bishops Meeting, 1963; asst. sec. adminstrv. bd. Nat. Cath. Welfare Conf. (now U.S. Cath. Conf.), 1963-66, sec., mem. com. on budget and finance, adminstrv. bd., 1966-69; sec. Nat. Conf. Cath. Bishops, 1966-69, mem. com. for Dept. Internat. Affairs (now Social Devel. and World Peace), 1971—, ad hoc com. on women in church and society, 1971—, chmn. region IV, 1972-74, mem. adminstrv. com., 1975-77; chmn. Bishop's Com. Permanent Diaconate, 1975-77. Mem. Nat. Conf. Cath. Bishops' Commn. for Ecumenical and Interreligious Affairs, 1965-69, cons., 1969—, chmn. sub-commn. for dialogue with Presbyn. and Reform Roman Catholic-Anglican Joint Sub-Commn. on Theology of Marriage, 1967—, mem. advisory com., 1975—; mem. Com. on Social Devel. and World Peace, 1971—; chmn. Bishops' Com. on Permanent Diaconate, 1968-71, 75-77; dir. Center for Applied Research in the Apostolate, 1969—, pres., 1972—; co-chmn. Charleston Religious Com. for Bicentennial, 1976. Mem. alumni bd. govs. Cath. U. Am.; adv. com. Ams. for Energy Independence. Decorated Grand Cross Panama; recipient Pax Christi award St. John's U., 1970; Pro-Life Citizen of Yr. award S.C. Citizens for Life, 1978; Nat. Dirs. of Permanent Diaconate award, 1978. Home: 114 Broad St Charleston SC 29401 Office: 119 Broad St Charleston SC 29401

UPP, FRANKLIN HERBERT, govt. ofcl.; b. Kilbourne, Ill., Mar. 8, 1936; s. Marshall Herbert and Geneva Arlene (Sisson) U.; A.A., Cisco Jr. Coll., 1960; B.S., Abilene Christian U., 1968; M.B.A., Tex. Technol. U., 1974; m. Tellie McWilliams, Aug. 20, 1960; children—Shellie A., Jeffrey F., Angela K. Asst. mgr. Spartan Dept. Stores, San Antonio, 1960-63; with Social Security Adminstrn., 1963—, ops. supr., Abilene, Tex., 1966-69, staff asst., Dallas, 1969-71, asst. dist. mgr., Lubbock, Tex., 1971-74, dist. mgr., San Angelo, Tex., 1974—, chmn. regional goals work group, 1976-79, mgmt. hearing rep., 1974—, chmn. govt. applications rev. com., 1974-75. Chmn., Area Agy. on Aging, 1977-78; mem. adv. bd. W. Tex. Christian Found., 1975—. Served with USAF, 1954-58. Recipient Supervisory Excellence award Social Security Adminstrn., 1972; day named in his honor Mayor San Angelo, 1978. Mem. Am. Mgmt. Assn., Mensa. Mem. Ch. of Christ. Club: S.W. Kiwanis. Home: 3617 Willowbrook St San Angelo TX 76901 Office: Social Security Adminstrn 2214 Sherwood Way San Angelo TX 76901

UPTON, BILLY EUGENE, R.R. adminstr.; b. Laurel, Miss., Jan. 13, 1934; s. Walter Luther and Irma Elizabeth U.; student El Camino Coll., 1955, 56, UCLA, 1957-58; m. Bonnie Jean Meyer, May 28, 1977; children—Mark Allyn, Carla Elane. Enlisted USAF, 1950, advanced through grades to m./sgt., 1971, service in Korea, Japan, Eng. and Viet Nam, ret., 1974; dir. communications Tex. R.R. Commn., Austin, 1975—; cons. in field. Pres., Am. Youth Council of London, 1959-61. Decorated Bronze Star, Cross of Gallantry, Air Force Commendation Medal. Mem. Air Force Sgts. Assn. (pres. chpt. 213 1972-73), Asso. Public Safety Communications Officers, Tex. Agy. Radio Adv. Com. Republican. Roman Catholic. Author: Diversified Frequency Control of the Magnetron, 1972; Improving Life and Power Output of the Klystron, 1973.

UPTON, RAYMOND HOOVER, educator; b. Soddy, Tenn., Oct. 13, 1929; s. Roy Elmer and Willie Elizabeth (Legg) U.; B.S., U. Tenn., 1956; M.Ed., U. Miami (Fla.), 1971; m. Phyllis N. Gooden, May 8, 1959; children—Rebecca, Carmen. With United Fruit Co., Guatemala, 1958-60; with Fla. Dept. Edn. Sch. Systems, Dade County Pub. Schs., Goulds, Fla., 1961—, work experience coordinator, 1974-79. Mem. transp. com. Rep. Nat. Conv., 1972. Served with USN, 1946-51. Mem. NEA, Am. Vocat. Assn., Fla. Vocat. Assn., VFW, Phi Delta Kappa, Lambda Chi Alpha, Phi Gamma Mu. Republican. Methodist. Club: Masons. Contbr. articles to profl. jours. Home: 10471 SW 202d Terr Miami FL 33189 Office: 11700 SW 216th St Goulds FL 33170

URBAN, JOHN CARL, JR., development co. exec.; b. Woodbury, N.J., Aug. 28, 1942; s. John Carl and Anne Elizabeth (Marville) U., Sr.; student Am. U., 1960-61, U. of Va., 1961-64. Accounting clk. IBM, Washington D.C., 1961-63; real estate salesman Herring Realty, Falls Ch., Va., 1964-66, Regent Realty, 1969-70; real estate broker Rosslyn Asso., Arlington, Va., 1970—; builder, developer, Sarasota, Fla., 1971—; owner, pres. Wexford Inc., Sarasota, 1975—. Pres. Shadybrook Village, Fla., 1972—. Mem. Builders Nat. Adv. Council, 1978, Nat. Assn. Review Appraisers (cert.). Served to 1st. lt. with U.S. Army, 1966-69. Mem. Nat. Assn. of Home Builders. Home: 707 S Gulfstream Ave Sarasota FL 33577 Office: 1500 Whitfield Ave Sarasota FL 33580

URBAN, THOMAS F., educator; b. Pottsville, Pa., Oct. 22, 1939; s. Simon A. and Marguerite U.; B.S., U. Detroit, 1961; M.B.A., Ind. U., 1967, D.B.A., 1971; m. Nada M. Klucka, July 14, 1962; children—Thomas F. II, Becky, Carrie. Spl. agt., IRS, Detroit, 1961-65; mem. faculty Miami U., Oxford, Ohio, 1969-75, U. Iowa, 1975-76, Tex. A&M U., College Station, 1976—. Nat. Merit scholar, 1957-61; NDEA fellow, 1965-68. Mem. Am. Inst. Decision Scis., Acad. Mgmt., Case Research Assn., Indsl. Relations Research Assn., Soc. Profls. in Dispute Resolution, Assn. Bus. Simulation and Exptl. Learning. Author: Kubsim: Simulation in Collective Bargaining, 1975; contbr. articles to profl. jours. Home: 1817 Shadowwood St College Station TX 77840 Office: Dept Mgmt Tex A&M U College Station TX 77843

URBANSKI, JAMES FRANCIS, newspaper exec.; b. Bloomington, Ill., Oct. 4, 1927; s. Vincent S. and Cecelia U.; B.S. in Journalism, U. Ill., 1950; s. Ann Anderson, May 29, 1954; children—Cissy, Betsy, William, Mark. Advt. salesman Jackson (Miss.) Daily News, 1951-55; asst. advt. dir. Gary (Ind.) Post Tribune, 1955-60; retail mgr. Tampa (Fla.) Trib-Times, 1960-65, advt. dir., 1965-74, bus. mgr., 1974-77, gen. mgr., v.p., 1977—. Pres. Gulfridge council Boy Scouts Am. Served with U.S. Army, 1946-48. Recipient Silver Beaver, Boy Scouts Am., 1979. Mem. Am. Newspaper Publishers Assn., Internat. Newspaper Advt. Execs. (past pres.), Newspaper Advt. Bur., Tampa Sports Authority (vice chmn.). Roman Catholic. Clubs: Tampa Yacht & Country, Univ., Mystic Krewe of Gasparilla. Office: PO Box 191 Tampa FL 33601

URRUTIA, ROSA CELESTE, physician; b. Vega Baja, P.R., Sept. 21, 1942; d. Raul Octavio and Celeste Violeta (Lugo) Urrutia; B.S. magna cum laude, U. P.R., 1963, M.D., 1967; m. Rene A. Morell, June 3, 1967; children—Javier, Eduardo. Intern, Mercy Hosp., Buffalo, 1967-68; family practice of medicine, Smyrna, Ga.; mem. staffs Smyrna, Ga., Cobb Gen. Hosp. Diplomate Am. Bd. Family Practice. Fellow Am. Acad. Family Physicians; mem. Ga. Med. Assn., Ga. Acad. Family Practice, Cobb County Med. Soc. Roman Catholic. Office: 3903 S Cobb Dr Suite 209 Smyrna GA 30080

URSCHLER, FRIEDRICH KARL, physician; b. Fuerstenfeld, Austria, Aug. 26, 1927; s. Karl and Helene (Mann) U.; came to U.S., 1953, naturalized, 1961; M.D., Karl Franzens U., Graz, Austria, 1952; m. Judith Ann Sheets, July 10, 1972; 1 son, Mark Brian. Intern, Swedish Hosp., Seattle, 1954-56; resident Grant Hosp., Columbus, Ohio, LK Hosp., Fuerstenfeld, 1955, Miami Hosp., Dayton, Ohio, 1964, Ohio State U., 1965-66; practice medicine specializing in family practice Columbus, Ohio, 1957-69; mem. staff Grant Hosp., Ohio State U. Hosp., Mercy Hosp., Childrens Hosp., St. Anns Hosp., Community Hosp. of New Port Richey, Tampa Gen. Hosp., U. Community Hosp. Tampa, Tarpon Springs Gen. Hosp., West Pasco Hosp. Diplomate Am. Bd. of Family Practice, apptd. consulate physician by consulate Gen. of Fed. Republic of Germany in Atlanta, 1977, Austria, 1979; Medical Licenser, in Ohio, Fla., Wash., Wyo. Mem. Am. Acad. of Family Physicians, Am. Health Care Med. Dirs. Assn. (Fla. pres.), AMA, Ohio Acad. of Family Practice FMA, Pasco County med. assns., FAFP Am. Med. Soc. of Vienna, Am. Geriatrics Soc. Clubs: Elks, German Cultural Soc. Home: 143 Colonial Dr New Port Richey FL 33552 Office: 515 Forest Ave New Port Richey FL 33552

USANIS, RICHARD ANTHONY, univ. adminstr.; b. Hartford, Conn., July 28, 1941; s. Anthony William and Bernice Agnus (Gardas) U.; B.S., SUNY, Syracuse, 1963, Syracuse U., 1963; M.F., N.C. State U., 1966, Ph.D., 1972. Programmer genetics dept. N.C. State U., Raleigh, 1967-70, statis. analyst and programmer Computing Center, 1970-72, asst. dir. center, 1974-76, dir., 1976—; pres. Usanis and Assos., Raleigh, 1972—; cons. in computing field. Weyerhaeuser Corp. fellow, 1967. Mem. Assn. Computing Machinery, AAAS. Democrat. Episcopalian. Home: PO Box 10794 Raleigh NC 27605 Office: PO Box 5445 Raleigh NC 27650

USHER, EARL STATHAM, assn. exec.; b. Richland, Ga., Oct. 5, 1927; s. George W. and Lucile Ella (Statham) U.; B.S., U. Ala., 1952; postgrad. Howard Coll. Samford U., 1955, Springfield Coll. Extension, Blue Ridge, N.C., 1956-57; m. Edith Elizabeth McLennan, July 19, 1952; children—Linda Marie, James M., Anne E., Robert S. Phys. dir., dir. youth program Five Points South Br. YMCA, Birmingham, Ala., 1954-56, exec. dir., 1959-64; program dir. Met. Bd. YMCA, Birmingham, 1956-57; youth dir., camp dir. Louisville YMCA, 1957-59; exec. dir. W. J. William Br. YMCA, Cin., 1965-70; asso. gen. dir. Met. Bd. YMCA, Richmond, Va., 1970-73; gen. dir. Bessemer (Ala.) YMCA, 1974—. Served with USNR, 1952-54. Mem. Assn. Profl. Dirs., Bessemer Area C. of C. Baptist. Kiwanian, Optimist, Lion, Mason. Club: Metropolitan Dinner. Contbr. articles to profl. jours. Producer audio-visual prodns. of YMCA history in Birmingham, Cin., Richmond, Bessemer. Home: 109 Hillside Rd Bessemer AL 35020 Office: 1501 4th Ave SW AL 35020

USRY, LUTHER WALLACE, realtor; b. Gadsden, Ala., Sept. 2, 1913; s. Henry H. and Eliza (Bryant) U.; A.B., Samford U., 1937; m. Lillian Ruth Royal, Oct. 5, 1932; 1 dau., Charlotte Jane Usry Bobo. Ordained to ministry Bapt. Ch., 1936; pastor Bellevue Bapt. Ch., Gadsden, 1936-46, James Meml. Bapt. Ch., Gadsden, 1946-54; broker Harris-Usry Co., Gadsden, 1964—; now owner Usry Realty Co., Gadsden. Mem. Ala. Real Estate Bd. (dir. 1965—, fin. com. 1967—), Gadsden Real Estate Bd. (pres. 1966—, dir. 1967—), Etowah Bapt. Assn. (exec. com. 1935-54, clk., treas., 1949-54), Ala. Real Estate Assn. (dir. 1969), C. of C. Club: Masons. Home: 147 Washington Circle Gadsden AL 35901 Office: 1137 Forrest Ave Gadsden AL 35901

USSERY, JAMES C. (JAKE), lawyer; b. Cotton Plant, Ark., May 23, 1923; s. Mabel (Rodgers) U.; B.S. in Pharmacy, Loyola U., New Orleans, 1950, J.D., 1977; children—Sandra, Jim, Jill. Chief hosp. pharmacist St. Francis Hosp., Monroe, La., 1958-67; owner pharmacy chain, Monroe, 1967-73; corp. comml. pilot Gibson's Rx Pharmacy, Monroe, 1967-77; admitted to La. bar, 1978; individual practice law, Baton Rouge, 1978—; pres. Gibsons Prescription Pharmacy, 1967—. Served with AC, USN, 1941-45, 50-52. Decorated D.F.C., Air medal with 5 stars. Mem. La. Bar Assn., Baton Rouge Bar Assn., Jaycees (life mem. Monroe, named outstanding young man 1957, internat. senator). Democrat. Roman Catholic. Club: Rotary (pres.-elect 1973-74) (Monroe). Home: 4029 Pine Park Dr Baton Rouge LA 70809 Office: 4726 Government St Suite B Baton Rouge LA 70806

UTHE, ELAINE F., educator; b. Boone, Iowa, Feb. 14, 1930; d. A. R. and Ottilia M. (Leininger) U.; B.A., Marycrest Coll., 1951; M.A., Cath. U. Am., 1955; Ph.D., U. Minn., 1966. Bus. tchr. public schs., Iowa, Ill., 1951-63, U.S. Army Dependent's Schs., Poitiers, France, 1958-59; faculty Mich. State U., E. Lansing, 1966-72, U. Ga., Athens, 1972-77; asso. prof., head bus. edn. program U. Ky., Lexington, 1977—; mem. adminstrv. com. Slaughter Research Award, 1977—. Recipient Delta Pi Epsilon Research award, 1967. Mem. Am. Vocat. Assn. (mem. policy com. 1977-80), AAUP, Ky. Bus. Edn. Assn., Nat. Bus. Edn. Assn., So. Bus. Edn. Assn., Am. Ednl. Research Assn., Phi Delta Kappa. Contbr. articles to profl. jours.; author: (with others) Executive Secretarial Procedures, 5th edit., 1980; contbr. Nat. Bus. Assn. Yearbooks, 1980 81. Office: 145 Taylor Edn Bldg Univ of Ky Lexington KY 40506

UTTLEY, FRANK J., acct.; b. McRae, Ark., July 9, 1923; s. Otto George and Bessie Lucille (Horton) U.; B.B.A., Harding Coll., 1948; m. Fayra Lavonne Williams, July 3, 1948; children—Deborah, Frank, Rise. Sr. acct. Midsouth Gas Co., Little Rock, 1951-55, Fish Engring. Corp., Houston, 1955-59; chief acct. Valley Gas Prodn., Houston, 1959-63; acctg. mgr. Houston Natural Gas Corp., 1963—; v.p., sec.-treas., dir. Uttley Realty, Inc., Houston, 1972—; asst. controller Houston Pipe Line Co., 1979—. Mem. Timbergrove Manor Civic Club, 1965—; del. Republican Party precinct and dist. convs. Served with USAAF, 1943-45, USAF, 1950-51; ETO. Decorated Air medal. Mem. Houston Bd. Realtors, Nat. Assn. Realtors. Baptist. Home: 6534 Wynnwood St Houston TX 77008 Office: 1200 Travis St Houston TX 77002

UWAYDAH, IBRAHIM MUSA, medicinal chemist, pharmacologist; b. Qalqiliya, Jordan, Sept. 18, 1943; s. Musa Mahmud and Sa'adiya Yusif (Ismail Hassan) U.; came to U.S., 1969, naturalized, 1976; B.S. in Pharmacy with distinction, Am. U. Beirut, 1967; Ph.D., U. Kans., 1974; m. Afifeh Muhamed Kasem, Sept. 18, 1968; children—Nema, Basem, Hani. Profl. sales rep. Bristol-Myers Middle East Inc., Beirut, 1967-69; teaching asst. U. Kans., 1969-70, research asst., 1970-72, NIH research trainee, 1972-74; postdoctoral research asso. Med. Coll. Va., Richmond, 1974-77; sr. research chemist A.H. Robins Co., Richmond, 1977—; adj. asst. prof. pharmacology Med. Coll. Va., 1978—. Pres., Islamic Center Va., 1975-76. Mem. Am. Chem. Soc., Chem. Soc. (London), Internat. Soc. Heterocycl. Chemistry, Sigma Xi. Contbr. articles to profl. jours. Home: 7100 Able Rd Chesterfield VA 23832 Office: AH Robins Research Labs 1211 Sherwood Ave Richmond VA 23220

UZZELL, MINTER, emeritus educator; b. Baird, Tex., Aug. 6, 1909; s. Minter Womack and Ada Estelle (Cooke) U.; A.A., Wayland Baptist Coll.; A.B., Hardin Simmons U., 1930; Th.M., S.W. Bapt. Theol. Sem., 1933; Th.M., Berkeley Bapt. Div., 1937; M.A., U. Tulsa, 1951, P.D.E., 1952, Ed.D., 1954; m. Pauline Dykes, Nov. 14, 1937; children—Carol Sue (Mrs. Rex Wayne Kay), Carey Lee. Ordained to ministry Bapt. Ch., 1928; pastor, Tex., Idaho, Washington, Calif., Okla., 1928—; tchr. pub. schs., Muskogee, Okla., 1945-47; asso. sec. YMCA, Ga. Inst. Tech., 1947-48; instr. Bacone Coll., 1949-59; prof. English, Northeastern Okla. State U., Tahlequah, 1959-75, prof. emeritus, 1975—, dean of students, 1961-68. Active ARC. Served with AUS, 1941-45, 53; ETO. Mem. AAUP, Nat., Okla. edn. assns., Assn. Higher Edn., Am. Legion, Res. Officers Assn., Cherokee Hist. Soc., Indian Ter. Geneal. Soc. (pres.), SAR, Phi Lambda Chi, Phi Delta Kappa, Kappa Delta Pi. Democrat. Baptist. Club: Kiwanis. Author: Uzzell Ancestry. Home: 269 Redbud Ln PO Box 119 Tahlequah OK 74464

VACC, NICHOLAS A., counselor, sch. psychologist, educator; b. Cleve., Sept. 22, 1939; B.S., Western Res. U., 1961; M.S., Syracuse U., 1963; Ed.D. (fellow) State U. N.Y., 1967; m. Nancy Nesbitt, July 4, 1964. Tchr., South Euclid-Lyndhurst pub. schs., Lyndhurst, Ohio, 1961; personnel intern Office of the Dean of Men, Syracuse (N.Y.) U., 1962-63, research asst. Ford Found. project, 1962; sch. psychologist Bd. of Co-op Ednl. Services, Chautauqua County, N.Y., 1963-65; VA counselor State U. N.Y., Albany, 1966-67; dir. counseling Coll. Counseling Center, State U. Coll., Fredonia, N.Y., 1967-73, prof., chmn. div. tchr. edn., 1973-79; prof. Sch. Edn., U. N.C., Greensboro, 1979—; cons. to N.Y. State Edn. Dept., 1968; cons. reader for Psychol. Reports, 1978. Chmn. subcom. for mental retardation Chautauqua County Mental Health Bd., 1976-79; bd. visitors J.N. Developmental Center, 1978-79; Mem. Am. Psychol. Assn., Am. Ednl. Research Assn., Am., N.C. personnel and guidance assns., Council for Exceptional Children, Assn. of N.Y. State Educators for the Emotionally Disturbed, Am. Orthopsychiat. Assn. Club: Torch of Am. Contbr. articles to profl. jours. Home: 3705 Henderson Rd Greensboro NC 27410 Office: Sch Edn 109 Curry U NC Greensboro NC 27412

VACHE, CLAUDE CHARLES, bishop; b. New Bern, N.C., Aug. 4, 1926; s. Jean Andre and Edith Virginia (Fitzwilson) V.; student U. N.C., 1949; M.Div., Seabury Western Theol. Sem., 1952, D.D., 1976; D.D., St. Pauls Coll., 1976, Va. Theol. Sem., 1977. Ordained priest Episcopal Ch., 1953, bishop, 1976; rector St. Michaels Ch., Bon Air, Va., 1952-57, Trinity Episcopal Ch., Portsmouth, Va., 1957-76; bishop coadjutor Diocese of So. Va., Norfolk, 1976-77, bishop, 1978—; tchr. St. Christophers Sch., Richmond, Va., 1953-55. Chpt. chmn. ARC, 1955-56, mem. Eastern Area adv. council, 1960-63; chmn. Mayor's Sr. Citizens Commn., Portsmouth, Va., 1974—; pres. Tidewater Regional Health Planning Council, 1975-76. Served with USN, 1944-46. Club: Portsmouth Kiwanis. Author: History of Trinity Church, Portsmouth Parish, 1762-1962, 1962. Address: 600 Talbot Hall Rd Norfolk VA 23505

VAIL, CHARLES CONRADY, JR., indsl. relations exec.; b. N.Y.C., Oct. 19, 1933; s. Charles Conrady and Virginia (Snow) V.; B.A., Roanoke Coll., 1955; M.S., 1968; m. Mary Paula Pilkenton, Dec. 22, 1960; children—Charles Conrady III, Elizabeth Risen. Indsl. relations trainee Old Dominion Candies Co., Roanoke, 1957-60; guidance counselor Roanoke City Public Schs., 1960-64; with Roanoke Valley Industries, 1964—, pres., 1977—; v.p. Indsl. Learning Corp., Roanoke, 1970—. Co chmn., Cancer Crusade, 1967, chmn., 1968; mem. Gov.'s Com. on Employment Handicapped; bd. dirs. Am. Cancer Soc., Roanoke Valley, Roanoke Symphony Soc.; trustee Va. Council Econ. Edn. Served as officer USN, 1955-57. Mem. Va. Coll. Placement Assn. (dir.), Nat. Indsl. Council, NAM, Am. Soc. Personnel Adminstrs., Personnel Assn. Roanoke, Am. Soc. Assn. Execs. Club: Rotary. Home: 2614 Richelieu St Roanoke VA 24014 Office: 204 S Jefferson St Roanoke VA 24011

VAIL, CHARLES ROWE, elec. engr., ednl. adminstr.; b. Glens Falls, N.Y., Oct. 16, 1915; s. Charles Herbert and Grace Evangeline (Rowe) V.; B.S. in Elec. Engring., Duke U., 1937; M.S., U. Mich., 1946, Ph.D., 1956; m. Helen Hall Wilson, Sept. 4, 1939; children—Helen Winifred Vail Sites, Charles Wilson, Theodore Wakefield. Elec. engr. Gen. Electric Co., 1937-39, summers, 1940, 41, 49; instr. Duke U., 1939-45, asst. prof. elec. engring., 1945-52, asso. prof., 1952-57, prof., 1957-67, chmn. dept. elec. engring., 1953-64, asso. dean Coll. Engring., 1964-67; prof. elec. engring. and electronic scis. So. Meth. U., 1967-73, asso. dean Inst. Tech., 1967-70, v.p. univ., 1970-73; prof. elec. engring. Ga. Inst. Tech., 1973—, asso. dean Coll. Engring., 1973-79, dir. dept. continuing edn., 1979—; pres. Ga. Engring. Found., 1977. Recipient Distinguished Alumnus award Duke U. Sch. Engring., 1967, Exceptional Service in Engring. Professionalism award Atlanta chpt. Am. Inst. Plant Engrs., 1975; Rackham Spl. fellow, 1945-46; Gen. Edn. Bd. fellow, 1950-51; registered profl. engr. Fellow IEEE (chmn. N.C. sect. 1963-64); mem. Am. Soc. Engring. Edn., Nat. Soc. Profl. Engrs., Ga. Soc. Profl. Engrs. (pres. Atlanta chpt. 1977-78, state pres. elect 1980-81, Engr. of Yr. in Edn. award 1976, Engr. of Yr. in Ga. award 1979), AAAS, Soc. History Tech., Assn. Media-Based Continuing Edn. for Engrs. (initial registered agt., corp. sec.), Phi Beta Kappa, Sigma Xi. Tau Beta Pi, Eta Kappa Nu, Phi Eta Sigma, Pi Mu Epsilon. Republican. Methodist. Author: Circuits in Electric Engineering, 1950; research, publs. on high voltage phenomena, dielectric breakdown, superconducting circuitry; contbr. articles on engring. edn., especially on TV as ednl. medium, to profl. jours. Home: 2669 Peppermint Dr Tucker GA 30084 Office: Dept Continuing Edn Ga Inst Tech Atlanta GA 30332

VAIL, DAVID GEORGE, food broker; b. Salisbury, Md., July 31, 1944; s. George Raymond and Lorraine Alice (Furch) V.; B.S., U. Iowa, 1967. Sales rep. Gen. Foods, L.I., 1967-69, account mgr., 1969-70; regional mgr. Nabisco, N.Y.C., 1971-73; nat. sales mgr. Freezer Queen Foods, Buffalo, 1970-75; pres., owner Vail-Inman Asso., Miami Lakes, Fla., 1975—, chief exec. officer, 1979—. Sect. chmn., United Way, Miami, Fla., 1978-79. Recipient Nabisco Million Dollar sales award, 1973; Key Broker award Freezer Queen, 1977. Mem. Am. Food Inst., Nat. Food Brokers Assn., Nat. Frozen Food Council, Miami Food Brokers Assn., Am. Mgmt. Assn. Lutheran. Club: Palm Bay (Pro-Am champion 1977). Home: 15538 Braemar Ct Miami Lakes FL 33014 Office: 6150 NW 153 St Miami Lakes FL 33014

VAIL, PETER ROBBINS, geologist; b. N.Y.C., Jan. 13, 1930; s. Donald Bain and Eleanor (Robbins) V.; grad. Deerfield Acad.; A.B., Dartmouth Coll., 1952; M.S., Northwestern U., Evanston, Ill., 1955, Ph.D. (Shell fellow 1954-56), 1959; m. Carolyn Flesher, Sept. 15, 1956; children—Andrea, Susan, Timothy Edward. Teaching asst. Northwestern U., 1952-54; asst. geologist U.S. Geol. Survey, Spokane, Wash., also Evanston, 1952-56; research geologist Carter Oil Co., Tulsa, 1956-58; research geologist Jersey Prodn. Research Co., Tulsa, 1958-62, sr. research geologist, 1962-65; sr. research specialist Exxon Prodn. Research Co., Houston, 1965-66, research asso., 1966, research supr., 1966-70, sr. research asso., 1970-72, sr. research adv., 1972-76, research scientist, 1976—. com. mem. Consortium for Continental Reflection Profiling, 1974-80; pres., mem. internat. subcomn. on stratigraphic classification Internat. Union Geol. Scis. Comn. on Stratigraphy, 1976—. Fellow Geol. Soc. Am. (research grants com. 1977-78, councilor 1980-82); mem. Am. Assn. Petroleum Geologists (distinguished lectr. 1975-76, research com. 1978-80, co-recipient Pres.' award 1979), Soc. Exploration Geophysicists (Virgil Kaufman Gold medal 1976), Joint Oceanographic Insts. for Deep Earth Sampling (passive margin panel 1978-81), Geol. and Geophys. Soc. Houston, Am. Petroleum Inst., AAAS, Mayflower Soc., U.S. Nat. Acad. Sci. (ocean sci. bd. 1979-81), Sigma Xi. Sci. contbns. in seismic stratigraphy, global changes of sea level, tectonics. Home: 3745 Del Monte Dr Houston TX 77019 Office: Exxon Prodn Research Co Box 2189 Houston TX 77001

VAJDA, STEVEN ALAN, data processing ofcl.; b. Milw., Nov. 18, 1943; s. George F. and Lois B. (Feldman) V.; B.S. in Elec. Engring. (Alumni Scholar), Purdue U., 1965; M.B.A., Northwestern U., 1971; m. Anita Marian Zimbler, Nov. 14, 1965; 1 son, Jeffrey Matthew. Systems mgr. RCA Info. Systems, Chgo., 1965-71; mgr. MIS planning and control Ryder System, Inc., Miami, Fla., 1972—; lectr. NCC, 1979. Vocat. data processing com. Dade County Sch. Bd. and Miami-Dade Community Coll., 1975—; counselor in data processing Boy Scouts Am.; active Kendale Homeowners Assn., 1972—. Mem. Data Processing Mgmt. Assn. (pres. Miami chpt. 1975, internat. dir. 1976—, govt. and industry relations com. 1977—; nat. award 1975), Northwestern U., Purdue U. alumni assns. Founder student chpt. Data Processing Mgmt. Assn., Miami Dade North, 1974. Home: 9681 Kendale Blvd Miami FL 33176 Office: PO Box 520816 Miami FL 33152

VALCHAR, JERRY EDWARD, ins. co. exec.; b. Oakland, Tex., Dec. 13, 1917; s. Jerry Joe and Annie (Malinovsky) V.; student Blinn Jr. Coll., 1953, Temple (Tex.) Jr. Coll., 1954; student in farm mut. prins. U. Tex., 1966-67; m. Vlasta Ermis, Jan. 21, 1946; children—Gladys Ann, Bernice Jane (Mrs. Nicolas K. Henry). Sec.-adjuster lodge Farmers Mut. Protective Assn., Weimar, Tex., 1947-52, treas., Temple, 1953-58, pres., 1959—, also dir.; pres. Tex. R.V.O.S. Ins. Co., 1978—. Notary pub., Bell County (Tex.), 1953—; translator birth certificates from Czech lang. Dist. Social Security Office, Temple, 1966—. Mem. Temple Citizens Adv. Com., 1962-67; mem. housing study group, Temple, 1966-67; mem. nat. council U.S.O., 1971—, v.p. Temple council, 1971-72, pres., 1973. Sec., Planning Commn., Temple, 1968-71, mem. City Zoning Bd., 1970-71. Bd. dirs. Temple United Fund. Served with AUS, 1941-45; PTO. Decorated Bronze Star. Adm., Tex. Navy, 1969—. Mem. Tex. Assn. Mut. Fire and Storm Ins. Cos. (pres. 1965-67), Western Fraternal Life Assn., Slavonic Benevolent Order Tex., V.F.W. Mem. Ch. of Brethren (ch. bd. 1954-55, pres. Men's Brotherhood 1965-66). Modern Woodman. Club: Farm and Ranch. Contbr. articles to co. publs. Home: 12 E Young St Temple TX 76501 Office: PO Box 426 Temple TX 76501

VALDES, JOSEPH RAYMOND, diversified mfg. co. exec.; b. Savannah, Ga., Aug. 3, 1939; s. Joseph Richard and Ruth Ann (Rogers) V.; B.B.A., U. Ga., 1960; M.B.A., Northwestern U., 1969; m. Denisa Helene Valdes, Apr. 5, 1974; children—J. Ron, Vicki L., Bart R. Corp. staff supr. U.S. Steel Corp., Chgo., 1960-67; div. mgr. lift trucks Allis-Chalmers Co., Harvey, Ill., 1967-69; v.p. ops. Condecor Inc., Mundelein, Ill., 1968-74; adminstrv. mgr. Lennar Corp., Miami, Fla., 1974-77; div. v.p. Ralston Purina Co., Apopka, Fla., 1978—; officer and dir. Victory Enterprises Inc., Arlington Heights, Ill., 1973—, Hartwood Manor Inc., Fredericksburg, Va., 1972—, South Market Inc., Tampa, Fla., 1967—; ltd. partner Spruce Hill Assos., Mt. Prospect, Ill., 1973—. Chmn. Young Republicans Cook County, Ill., 1963-64; campaign mgr. 2d. Congl. Dist., Ill., 1966. Mem. Am. Mgmt. Assn., Profl. Photographers Am., Aircraft Owners and Pilots Assn. Presbyterian. Club: Hollywood Scuba. Home: 104 Hill Crest Dr Longwood FL 32750 Office: 1350 S Sheeler Rd Apopka FL 32703

VALDÉS-CHAO, JOSÉ ANTONIO, advt. agy. exec.; b. Havana, Cuba, Feb. 19, 1930; s. Pedro Sergio and María Josefa (Chao) V.; Advt. Agt., Profl. Sch. Commerce, Havana, Cuba, 1954; Profl. in Advt., U. Havana, 1956; m. Nee Hilda R. Villavol, Dec. 15, 1957; 1 dau., Viviana. Co-owner, gen. dir. Aguila Publicitaria, Havana, Cuba, 1954-61; office mgr. Internat. Rescue Com., Miami, 1961-63; copywriter, ad divisional supr. Milw. Boston Store, 1963-64; copywriter, creative coordinator, account rep., account supr. J. Walter Thompson Co., San Juan, P.R., 1965-68; v.p., gen. mgr. Ross Roy N.Y., Inc., San Juan, 1968-70; pres. J. A. Valdes-Chao, Inc., San Juan, 1971—; prof. sales and advt. Profl. Sch. Commerce, Havana, Cuba, 1954-61. Recipient Silver Medal, Internat. Film and TV Festival, 1971, Bronze Medal, 1975. Mem. Am. Mgmt. Assn., Advt. Agy. Assn. P.R. (v.p. 1973-74), C. C. P.R. Democrat. Roman Catholic. Club: Caribe Hilton Swimming and Tennis (San Juan, P.R.). Contbr. articles in field to profl. jours. Home: 902 Ponce de León Ave Apt 1001 Miramar Santurce PR 00907 Office: 804 Ponce de León Ave Suite 202 Santurce PR 00907

VALDEZ, ESTHER MIRANDA, educator; b. Binan, Laguna, Philippines, July 1, 1921; Certificate in Elementary Edn., Harvardian Coll., Philippines, 1955; B.A. in Elementary Edn., Salem (W.Va.) Coll., 1967; M.A. in Spl. Edn., W.Va. U., Morgantown, 1972; married; 3 children. Prin. Binan Elementary Sch., Laguna, 1955-58; prin. Cebu (Philippines) City Elementary Sch., 1958-65, Davao (Philippines) Elementary Sch., 1965-66; tchr. spl. edn. Weston (W.Va.) Central Sch., 1968—. Mem. NEA, W.Va. Edn. Assn., Nat., W.Va. councils exceptional children, Assn. Classroom Tchrs. Assn. Mental Retardation, Mental Health Assn., Kappa Delta Pi. Specialist in behavior modification of spl. edn. children. Home: 183 Archwood Dr Bridgeport WV 26330 Office: Weston Central Sch Weston WV 26452

VALENTI, ELAINE ARLT, ednl. counselor; b. New Orleans, May 3, 1923; d. William and Angeline Catherine (Mendel) Arlt; B.A. in Edn., St. Mary's Dominican Coll., 1969; M.Ed., Tulane U., 1970, postgrad., 1975; m. Saverio Edward Valenti, Nov. 20, 1941; children—Keith, Craig, Donna, Kurt, Robin. Tchr. Archdiocese of New Orleans, St. Agnes Sch., Jefferson, La., 1960-64, Wonderland Pvt. Sch., Metairie, La., 1964-68; tchr. Live Oak Jr. High Sch., New Orleans Public Schs., 1968-71, counselor, 1971-75; adj. prof. guidance program Center for Tchr. Edn. Tulane U., New Orleans, 1972-76; counselor St. Charles Parish Public Schs. Hahnville (La.) Jr. High Sch., 1974-79; cons. public and pvt. schs.; parish test coordinator state competency assessment, 1977-79; parish rep., chmn. state adoption com. textbooks in career edn., secondary level. Certified guidance and counseling, adminstrn., supervision, parish supr., family therapy. Mem. La. Group Psychotherapy Soc. (affiliate), Nat. Council on Family Relations, La. Council on Family Relations, Am. Personnel and Guidance Assn., La. Personnel and Guidance Assn., Am. Sch. Counselors' Assn., La. Sch. Counselors' Assn., Kappa Delta Pi, Delta Epsilon Sigma. Democrat. Roman Catholic. Researcher, co-author: The Effects of Student Transiency on Education, 1978. Home: 9401 Francine Dr River Ridge LA 70123 Office: St Charles Parish Public Schools PO Box 46 Luling LA 70070

VALENTINE, MELINDA STAUFFER, speech and lang. pathologist; b. Wichita Falls, Tex., Aug. 20, 1954; d. Charles Dee and Loretta Jean (Webster) Stauffer; B.S., Okla. State U., 1976; M.S., So. Meth. U., 1977; m. James Thurston Valentine, July 31, 1976. Speech and lang. pathologist Dallas Ind. Sch. Dist., 1977—. Bur. Educationally Handicapped grantee, 1976-77. Mem. Tex. Speech Lang. Hearing Assn. (ethical practices com. 1979-82), Am. Speech Lang. Hearing Assn., Dallas Assn. Speech—Lang. Pathologists and Audiologists, N.W. Tex. Pediatric Group Assn. Home: 12832 Noel Rd #1029 Dallas TX 75230 Office: 1515 S Ravinia St Dallas TX 75211

VALLANCE, WINFRED DAN, mfg. co. exec.; b. Memphis, Tex., Apr. 4, 1937; s. Marvin Carter and Ruby Dell (Thomas) V.; B.S., U. Tex., Austin, 1963; M.S. in Nuclear Physics, Naval Postgrad. Sch., Calif., 1971; postgrad. U. Tex., Arlington, 1975-77; m. Beverly Ann Clements, Dec. 6, 1957; children—Robbie Dee, Dan Keith, Norma Ann. Served to lt. comdr. U.S. Navy, 1958-75; submarine officer, engring. duty officer; engring. mgr. Champion Parts Rebuilders, Inc., Fort Worth, 1975-76, gen. mgr. Hope div. (Ark.), 1976—. Bd. dirs. United Way, 1978-80. Mem. Ret. Officers Assn., DAV (life), VFW. Home: Route 5 Box 262 Hope AR 71801 Office: PO Box G Hope AR 71801

VALLBONA, CARLOS, physician; b. Granollers, Barcelona, Spain, July 29, 1927; s. Jose and Dolores (Calbo) V.; B.A., B.S., U. Barcelona, 1944, M.D., magna cum laude, 1950; came to U.S., 1953, naturalized, 1967; m. Rima Gretel Rothe, Dec. 26, 1956; children—Rima Nuria, Carlos Fernando, Maria Teresa, Marisa. Child health physician sch. child health Barcelona, 1952; staff Stagier Etranger Hôpital Enfants Malades, Paris, 1952-53; intern, resident in pediatrics U. Louisville, 1953-55; resident in pediatrics Baylor Coll. Medicine, Houston, 1955-56, asso. prof. physiology and pediatrics, 1962-69, prof. rehab. medicine, 1967—, prof., chmn. dept. community medicine, 1969—. French govt. Ministry of Edn. fellow, 1952; Children's Internat. Center fellow, 1953; Fulbright vis. prof. Autonomous U., Guadalajara, Mex., 1967; co-recipient gold medal 6th. Internat. Congress Phys. Medicine, 1972; named Pub. Citizen of Yr., San Jacinto chpt. Nat. Assn. Social Workers, 1974. Fellow Am. Coll. Preventive Medicine, Am. Coll. Chest Physicians; mem. Soc. Pediatric Research (emeritus), AMA, Am. Pub. Health Assn., Am. congress Rehab. Medicine, AAAS, Sigma Xi. Roman Catholic. Contbr. articles to profl. publs. Home: 3002 Ann Arbor St Houston TX 77063 Office: 1200 Moursund St Houston TX 77030

VALLEY, CHRISTOPHER RICHARD, JR., social worker; b. New Orleans, Oct. 14, 1947; s. Christopher Richard and Clare Veronica (Gardner) V.; A.B. magna cum laude, Boston Coll., 1971; A.M., U. Chgo., 1973; m. Elanna Lee Roach, Sept. 8, 1979. Youth worker W.Va. Mountain Project, 1971; asst. dir. div. social concerns Catholic Charities Diocese of Gary (Ind.), 1973-75; dir. program devel. and research Child Service and Family Counseling Center of Atlanta, 1975—. Mem. DeKalb County Democratic Com., Ga. Dem. Com., Young Dems. of Ga., named Young Dem. of Yr., 1978. NSF fellow, 1970. Mem. Nat. Assn. Social Workers, Ga. Conf. Social Welfare, Ga. Planning Assn., Village Writers Group, Ind. Media Artists of Ga., Phi Beta Kappa. Roman Catholic. Contbr. articles to profl. jours.

VALLOTTON, WILLIAM WISE, surgeon, educator; b. Valdosta, Ga., Nov. 26, 1927; s. Joseph Edward and Mattie (Rouse) V.; A.B., Duke, 1947; M.D., Med. Coll. Ga., 1952; postgrad. Harvard, 1956; m. Hulda Roberta Jones, Sept. 3, 1950; children—Stephen Ralph, Amie, Mark Hugh, William Wise. Intern, U. Wis., 1952-53; resident ophthalmology Duke U., 1953-55, instr., 1953-55, asso., 1955-56; asso. prof. ophthalmology Med. U. S.C., Charleston, 1958-65, prof., 1965—, dir. residency program ophthalmology, 1960-70, chmn. dept. ophthalmology, 1967—, dir. Storm Eye Inst., 1976—; v.p. Vallorbe Inc., Valdosta, 1955—. Cons., USN Hosp., Charleston, 1962—, State Hosp. S.C., Columbia, 1963—, U.S. Vets. Hosp., Charleston, 1966—; faculty home study Am. Acad. Ophthalmology and Otolaryngology. Bd. dirs. S.C. Commn. for Blind, 1975-76. Served to lt. M.C., USNR, 1956-58. Diplomate Am. Bd. Ophthalmology. Fellow A.C.S.; mem. S.C. Ophthal. and Otolaryn. Soc. (pres. 1965), Charleston Duke Alumni Assn. (past pres.), Assn. Research in Ophthalmology (chmn. S.E. sect. 1966-67), Am. Acad. Ophthalmology and Otolaryngology (Honors award 1968), Pan Am. Ophthal. Assn., So. Med. Assn. (asso. councilor 1972-75, councilor 1975—), N.Y. Acad. Scis., Pi Kappa Phi, Alpha Kappa Kappa, Alpha Omega Alpha. Republican. Methodist. Clubs: Charleston Country, Elks. Research and publs. in ophthalmology. Home: 15 Broughton Rd Charleston SC 29407 Office: Eye Inst Med U of SC Charleston SC 29403

VALLS, RALPH, customhouse broker; b. Laredo, Tex., Mar. 24, 1909; s. Antonio and Rafaela (Mendiola) V.; grad. high sch.; m. Clotilde Withoff, May 24, 1934; 1 son, Richard R. Farmer, San Rafael Farm, 1928-41; insp. Customs Service, 1941-48; farmer, Laredo, 1948-50; customhouse broker, Laredo, 1950—, Galveston, Tex., 1960—, Houston, 1967—, Corpus Christi, Tex., 1960—; pres. Ralph Valls & Son, Inc., Corpus Christi, 1968—, now dir.; ocean freight forwarder, 1962—; a founding dir. Gulf Internat. Trader (now Houston Bus. Jours.), Houston, 1964—; dir. Ralph Valls & Son (Houston) Inc., Desi & Dick's, Inc. Lectr. internat. trade Del Mar Coll., Corpus Christi. Mem. Tex. Internat. Trade Assn. (dir. 1965, 66, 68, 71, 72). Republican. Roman Catholic. Rotarian. Club: Propellers. Home: 4601 Jarvis Dr Corpus Christi TX 78412 Office: Suite 109 Oil Industries Bldg Corpus Christi TX 78403

VAN ALSTYNE, W. SCOTT, JR., lawyer, educator; b. East Syracuse, N.Y., Sept. 21, 1922; s. Walter Scott and Cecil Edna (Folmsbee) Van A.; B.A., U. Buffalo, 1948; M.A., U. Wis., 1950, LL.B., 1953, S.J.D., 1954; m. Margaret Reed Hudson, June 23, 1949; children—Gretchen A., Hunter S. Admitted to Wis. bar, 1953; individual practice law, Milw., 1954-56; asst. prof. law U. Nebr., Lincoln, 1956-58; individual practice law, Madison, Wis., 1958-72; prof. law U. Fla., Gainesville, 1973—; vis. prof. law Cornell U., 1977; spl. counsel for Gov. Wis., 1966-70, Cambridge-Warsaw Internat. Trade Program, Cambridge (Eng.) U., 1976. Mem. Gov.'s Commn. on Edn., Wis., 1969-71. Served with AUS, 1942-45, 61-62; served to col. USAR. Decorated Legion of Merit. Mem. State Bar Wis., Phi Delta Phi, Phi Beta Kappa, Order of Coif, Omicron Delta Kappa. Republican. Presbyterian. Clubs: Madison, Ft. Rensselaer, Holland Soc. (N.Y.), SR (N.Y.). Contbr. articles to profl. jours. Home: 2726 SW 5th Pl Gainesville FL 32607 Office: Holland Law Center Univ Florida Gainesville FL 32611

VAN ARNAM, WILLIAM LEGRAND, III, cigarette co. exec.; b. Troy, N.Y., Mar. 26, 1937; s. William LeGrand and Virginia Gertrude (Doring) Van A.; B.A., U. Md., 1962; M.Ed., Coll. William and Mary, 1972; m. Joan Wiley Foster, Feb. 3, 1962; children—Cheryl Lynne, Susan Elizabeth. History tchr., Prince Georges County, Md., 1962-64; exec. Goodwill Industries of Am., Washington, 1964-69; supt. mgmt. devel. Allied Chem. Corp., Hopewell, Va., 1969-73; mgr. mgmt. devel. Philip Morris, Inc., Richmond, Va., 1973-80, dir. tng. and devel., 1980—. Pres., Richmond (Va.) Ronald McDonald House, 1978—; bd. dirs. Assn. for Study of Childhood Cancer, 1977—. Served with U.S. Army, 1957-60. Mem. Am. Soc. Tng. and Devel. (chpt. pres. 1975-76). Republican. Episcopalian. Home: 4261 Daniel St Chester VA 23831 Office: Philip Morris USA PO Box 26603 Richmond VA 23261

VAN AUKEN, ROBERT DANFORTH, univ. adminstr.; b. Chgo., Oct. 31, 1915; s. Howard Robert and Mable (Hanlon) Van A.; student Guilford Coll., 1933-35, Gen. Motors Inst. Tech., 1936-37, U. Pitts., 1953-54; B.S., U. Dayton, 1958; M.A., U. Okla., 1967; m. Ruth Bowen Cutler, Nov. 24, 1939; children—Robert Hanlon, Joseph Marshall, David Danforth, Howard Evans, Jonathan Lewis. Flying cadet USAF, 1938, advanced through grades to lt. col., 1961; fighter pilot, ops. officer, squadron comdr., 1939-45; asst. air attache, Paris, 1946-49; staff officer Pentagon, 1950-53, Wright-Patterson AFB, 1954-58, Tinker AFB, 1958-60, Holloman AFB, 1960-61; personnel officer U. Okla., Norman, 1962-65, dir. student programs and career devel., asst. prof. Coll. Bus. Adminstrn., 1965—; mgmt. cons., 1963—. Decorated Silver Star, Purple Heart. Mem. Am. Soc. Personnel Adminstrn., Acad. Mgmt., Nat. Assn. Student Personnel Adminstrs., Retired Officers Assn., Mil. Order World Wars, Beta Gamma Sigma, Delta Sigma Pi. Republican. Clubs: Lions, Masons. Home: 420 Highland Rd Midwest City OK 73110 Office: 307 W Brooks St Norman OK 73069

VAN BLARCUM, BARBARA HAPPE, exec.; b. Toronto, Ont., Can., Mar. 27, 1945; d. William Henry and Jane Hammond (Barnes) Happe; B.A., Purdue U., 1968, M.S., 1969; m. James Corbett Van Blarcum, June 19, 1965. Secondary sch. French tchr., Ind. and Ga., 1969-71; with Marriott Corp., Washington, 1972-79; dir. corp. relations Deltona Corp., Miami, Fla., 1980—. Vol. tchr. English to foreigners, 1973-76. NDEA fellow, 1968; Rotary scholar, 1963. Mem. Pub. Relations Soc. Am. (accredited; nat. exec. com. investor relations sect. 1977—), Nat. Investor Relations Inst. Republican. Episcopalian. Home: 6331 SW 49th St Miami FL 33155 Office: 3250 SW 3d Ave Miami FL 33129

VANCE, BARBARA ANN, computer co. exec.; b. Dallas, Dec. 30, 1951; d. Arthur and Adele (Petcavage) V.; B.A., U. Tex., 1973, M.B.A., 1976. With Burroughs Corp., San Antonio, 1976—, account mgr. computer sales, 1979—. Mem. Am. Mktg. Assn., U. Tex. Ex-Students Assn. Roman Catholic. Home: 135 Sheila St San Antonio TX 78209 Office: 827 E Elmira St San Antonio TX 78209

VANCE, BETTY L. WILLIAMS, ednl. adminstr.; b. Aiken County, S.C., Feb. 23, 1937; d. Tolbert Alfonza and Mamie Lucille (Robinson) Williams; B.S. in Bus. Adminstrn., S.C. State Coll., 1959, M.A. in Guidance, 1977; postgrad. Savanah State Coll., 1963-64, Augusta Coll., 1971-72, U. S.C., 1973-74; m. Bernard Berlin, Feb. 2, 1962. With Colliers mag., N.Y.C., 1953; sec. A.L. Corbitt Schs., Wagnor, S.C., 1959-62; tchr. lang. arts Winnsboro (S.C.) Elem. and Jr. High Sch., 1960-62; tchr. bus. edn. Blackney High Sch., Waynesboro, Ga., 1963-65; instr. bus. Augusta (Ga.) Tech., 1965-78, dir. admissions, 1978—; cons. in field. Mem. NEA, Ga. Edn. Assn., Ga. Bus. Edn. Assn., Sch. Counselors Am. Assn., Ga. Counselors Affiliate, Am. Vocation Assn., Ga. Vocation Assn., Am. Bell Assn., S.C. State Alumni Assn., Nat. Council of Negro Women, Ga.-Carolina Paralyzed Vets. Assn. (hon.), Iota Phi Lambda, Tau Gamma Delta. Democrat. Roman Catholic. Home: 417 Colorado St Augusta GA 30901 Office: 2025 Lumpkin Rd Augusta GA 30906

VANCE, COY MCMILLON, state ofcl.; b. Kernersville, N.C., Apr. 28, 1922; s. Marvin Dewitt and Hattie Vestal (Mabe) V.; student N.C. State Coll., 1946-52; m. Rosella Brown, May 28, 1954; children—Patricia, Coy McMillon, Gale, Deborah, Gary. With Vance Machine Co., 1940-42, Hercules Powder Co., 1942-44, Western Electric Co., Winston-Salem, N.C., 1946-76; mem. N.C. Indsl. Commn., Raleigh, 1973—, N.C. Med. Care Commn., 1972-76. Mem. Kernersville Sch. Com., 1952-56, Forsyth Meml. Hosp. Authority, 1969-73; pres. bd. mgrs. Kernersville YMCA. Served with AUS, 1944-46. Club: Kernersville Civitan (pres.). Home: 741 Mills St Raleigh NC 27608 Office: 430 N Salisbury St Raleigh NC 27611

VANCE, NINA ELOISE WHITTINGTON, theatrical exec.; b. Yoakum, Tex.; d. Perry and Minerva (Dewitt) Whittington; B.A., Tex. Christian U.; postgrad. U. So. Cal., Columbia, Am. Acad. Dramatic Art. Dir. Players Guild, Houston, 1944-46; founder, permanent dir., artistic dir. Alley Theatre, Houston, 1947—; guest dir. Arena Stage, Washington, Playhouse-in-the-Park, Phila. Participant Am. Assembly meeting Asian-Am. Assembly, Kuala Lumpur, Fedn. Malaya; adv. com. Nat. Cultural Center; adv. com. on arts U.S. Adv. Commn. Ednl. and Cultural Affairs. Recipient grant English Speaking Union, 1958; Matrix award for contbn. to field of fine arts Theta Sigma Phi; Personal Dir.'s grant for travel and study Ford Found. Home: 1400 Hermann Dr Houston TX 77004 Office: Alley Theatre 615 Texas Ave Houston TX 77002

VANCE, ROBERT MERCER, banker; b. Clinton, S.C., July 9, 1916; s. Robert Berly and Mary Ellen (Bailey) V.; B.S., Davidson Coll., 1937; m. Virginia Sexton Gray, Dec. 27, 1949; children—Mary Bailey, Robert Mercer, Russell Gray. Paymaster, Lydia Cotton Mills, Clinton, 1937-41; with M.S. Bailey & Son, Bankers, Clinton, 1946—, pres., 1948-75, chmn., 1975—; dir., asst. treas. Clinton Cotton Mills, 1948-58, v.p. 1956-58, pres., treas., 1958-64; dir., asst. treas. Lydia Cotton Mills, Clinton, 1948-58, v.p., 1953-58, pres., treas., 1958-64; pres. Clinton Mills, Inc., 1964-79, chmn. bd., 1979—, treas., 1964-70; dir. Clinton Cottons, Inc., N.Y.C., 1948—, v.p., asst. treas., 1953-58, treas., 1958—; dir. Textile Hall Corp., Greenville, S.C. Pres. Community Chest Greater Clinton, 1958; mem. nominating com. United Community Services S.C., 1959; trustee exec. com. Ednl. Resources Found., 1965; mem. State Adv. Commn. on Higher Edn., 1965-67; mem. State Commn. on Higher Edn., 1967-71, chmn., 1967-71. Bd. visitors Davidson (N.C.) Coll., 1959-62; trustee, chmn. bd. Presbyn. Coll., Clinton, 1953-67; trustee, sec. bd. Thornwell Orphanage, Clinton, 1959-67; trustee Inst. Textile Tech., Charlottesville, Va., S.C. Found. Ind. Colls. Served with Signal Corps, AUS, 1941; served to lt. comdr. USNR, 1941-46. Named Man of Year, Clinton Lions Club, 1955. Mem. Am. Textile Mfrs. Inst. (dir. 1965-68), Am. (v.p. 1953-55), S.C. (pres. 1963-64) bankers assns., S.C. Textile Mfrs. Assn. (dir. 1965—, Textile Man of Yr. 1978), S.C. Textile Assn. (pres. 1967-68), Am. Legion, S.C. State (dir. 1959-60), Clinton (dir. 1951-54) chambers commerce, Kappa Alpha. Presbyn. (elder 1958—). Mason (Shriner), Moose, Kiwanian. Clubs: Lakeside Country (Clinton); Poinsett (Greenville, S.C.); Piedmont (Spartanburg, S.C.). Home: 311 S Broad St Clinton SC 29325 Office: 211 N Broad St Clinton SC 29325

VAN CLEAVE, ROBERT FRANKLIN, geophys. exploration cons.; b. Indpls., Apr. 28, 1911; s. Benjamin F. and Almeda Margaret (Cline) Van C.; student DePauw U., 1928-30; A.B., Wabash Coll., 1933; M.S., Okla. U., 1935; m. Doris Thibodeaux, Apr. 10, 1938; children—Nancy Elizabeth, Margaret Anne, Robert Hamilton. Seismic computer operator Western Geophys. Co., 1935-37; seismic crew chief Nat. Geophys. Co., 1937-42, seismic supr., 1942-46; dist. and area geophysicist Atlantic Refining Co., 1946-51; partner Interstate Exploration Co., 1951-60; chief geophysicist Austral Oil Co., Houston, 1960-62, v.p., 1962-76; pres. Robert F. Van Cleave, Inc., Houston, 1976—; dir. Am. Tchrs. Life Ins. Co., Alexandria Ice and Cold Storage Co. (La.), Ampersand, Inc.; geophys. cons. R. Brewer & Co. Registered geophysicist, Calif. Mem. Assn. Profl. Geol. Scientists, Soc. Exploration Geophysicists, Am. Assn. Petroleum Geologists, European Assn. Exploration Geophysicists, Sigma Xi. Mem. Disciples of Christ. Clubs: Houston, Masons. Home: 12426 Woodthorpe Ln Houston TX 77024 Office: 1210 Americana Bldg Houston TX 77002

VAN CLEAVE, ROY LYNN, modular bldg. co. exec.; b. Wichita Falls, Tex., June 19, 1950; s. Elmer Ray and Frances Faye (Latch) Van C.; student Cisco Coll., 1968-69, San Antonio Coll., 1969-71; m. Janice Armine Yelvington, Oct. 2, 1971; children—David Blakely, Mark Ryan. Gen. mgr. devel. modular bldg. systems Capital Structure Co., San Antonio, 1971-76; partner, cons. modular bldg. applications Van Cleave Assos., San Antonio, 1976—; guest lectr. Trinity U., 1974-75. Served with U.S. Army Res., 1970-76. Mem. Nat. Assn. Bus. Economists, Project Mgmt. Inst., Am. Soc. Bus. and Mgmt. Cons.'s. Republican. Baptist. Club: Olmos Kiwanis. Home: 15743 Eagle Cliff San Antonio TX 78232 Office: PO Box 17002 San Antonio TX 78217

VAN CLEVE, ROY RAY, mgmt. cons.; b. Hazard, Ky., July 27, 1926; s. John Henry and Faye (Ray) Van C.; Student U. Ala., Birmingham, 1957-59; B.S., U. Omaha, 1961; M.S., Naval Postgrad. Sch., 1967; Ph.D., U. Tex., Austin, 1976; m. Winifred Mae Hart, Dec. 29, 1945; children—Roy Ray, Kathleen C. Enlisted U.S. Marine Corps, 1943, sgt., 1947; commd. 2d lt., 1948, advanced through grades to col., 1969; ret., 1971; dir. Office of Manpower Utilization, Washington, 1969-71; research asso. Center Study of Human Resources, U. Tex., Austin, 1973-74, asso. dir., 1974-75; asst. comptroller manpower services State of Tex., 1975-76; pres. Applied Job Analysis, Inc., Austin, 1976—; lectr. U. Tex., Austin, 1976-79. Decorated Legion of Merit with V, Meritorious Service Medal, Purple Heart. Mem. Acad. Mgmt., Am. Mgmt. Assn., Indsl. Relations Research Assn., Internat. Personnel Mgmt. Assn., Phi Kappa Phi. Republican. Contbr. articles to profl. jours. Home and Office: 3935 Lago Vista Dr Austin TX 78734

VANDAGRIFF, JON ROY, journalist; b. Weatherford, Tex., Feb. 22, 1935; s. John Roy and Jewel Nora (Jones) V.; A.A., Weatherford Coll., 1955; B.A., Howard Payne U., 1957; postgrad Tex. Christian U., 1965; M.A., N. Tex. State U., 1977; children—Pamela Ann Vandagriff Gruben, Philip Jon. Printer, sports writer Weatherford (Tex.) Democrat, 1952-55; asst. sports editor Brownwood (Tex.) Bull., 1955-57; sports editor Weatherford Democrat, 1957-62; prin. Wampler Elemen. Sch., Weatherford, 1962-64; editor Weatherford Democrat, 1964-70; tchr. Weatherford Ind. Sch. Dist., 1970-71; instr. journalism and communications specialist Tarrant County Jr. Coll. Dist., Fort Worth, 1971—. Hon. mem. 4-H Club; recipient awards USMC, VFW, Goodwill Industries. Mem. Tex. Jr. Coll. Tchrs. Assn., Nat. Geog. Soc., Parker County Geneal. Soc., Parker County Hist. Commn. (co chmn.), Tex. Hist. Found., Tex. Hist. Assn. Baptist. Club: Optimist. Author: The Democrat Years: A Growing Process, 1977; author, editor: The History of Parker County. Home: 1202 S Rusk St Weatherford TX 76086 Office: 1400 Electric Service Bldg Fort Worth TX 76102

VAN DAM, DIRK ENNO, airport exec.; b. Mt. Hope, N.Y., Sept. 16, 1934; s. Enno and Marjorie (Zwart) Van D.; diploma Moody Bible Inst., 1955; student Chgo. Tchrs. Coll., 1961-62; m. Camilla Rae Schut, June 17, 1960; children—Scott, Sandra, Linda, Sharon. Chief flight instr. Moody Aviation, Elizabethton, Tenn., 1960-65, asst. dir., 1966-69, dir., 1970—; mgr. Elizabethton Mcpl. Airport, 1970—; dir. Mission Aviation Fellowship, Fullerton, Calif. Deacon, tchr. Sunday sch. Immanuel Baptist Ch. Aviation Safety counselor FAA. Mem. Assn. Airport Mgrs., Aircraft Owners and Pilots Assn., Amateur Radio Relay League, Flight Safety Found. Home: Route 5 Box 148 Johnson City TN 37601 Office: Box 429 Municipal Airport Elizabethton TN 37643

VANDERLUGT, MARILYN JOAN, counselor; b. Harvey, Ill., Sept. 26, 1937; d. William and Nettie Matilda (Staat) Monsma; B.A., Calvin Coll., Grand Rapids, Mich., 1959; M.Ed. in Guidance, Stetson U., Deland, Fla., 1976; m. Anthony VanderLugt, June 27, 1959; children—Elizabeth Ann, Robert Andrew. Tchr., Saline (Mich.) Area Schs., 1959-60, tchr. high sch. English, 1960-63; facilitator for continuing edn. for women Brevard Community Coll., Cocoa, Fla., 1975-76, counselor, 1976—. Mem. Dist. 7B Mental Health Bd. of Brevard County, 1979; mem. panel United Way Brevard, Merritt Island, Fla., 1979; bd. dirs. Family Aid Soc., Brevard County, 1978-79. Mem. Am. Personnel and Guidance Assn., Internat. Transactional Analysis Assn. Home: 232 Cocoa Ave Indialantic FL 32903 Office: 1519 Clear Lake Rd Cocoa FL 32922

VANDERMEER, SHIRLEY, hosp. ofcl.; b. Ft. Worth, Aug. 28, 1927; d. Willis Collins McMahan and Mary Cleveland McMahan Robinson; student N. Tex. State U., 1943-45, Richmond Profl. Inst., 1945; m. Dan Denney, Aug. 22, 1947 (div. Mar. 1957); 1 dau., Donna Lee Denney Lamb; m. 2d., Ben Vandermeer, Mar. 16, 1963. Advt. sales Dallas Times Herald, 1951; staff Hepworth Advt. Agy., Southland Corp., Dallas, 1959-60, Dallas, 1960-61; advt. mgr. Fedway Dept. Stores, Corpus Christi, Tex., 1964-65; advt. dept. Montgomery Ward & Co., Houston, 1965-66; staff Foley's Dept. Store, Houston, 1966-67; dir. public info. St. Joseph Hosp., Houston, 1967—. Mem. Houston Area Hosp. Public Relations Soc. (pres. 1973-74), Am. Soc. Hosp. Public Relations (area rep. 1975—), Tex. Soc. Hosp. Public Relations (pres. elect. 1979), Am. Women in Radio and TV, Internat. Assn. Bus. Communicators, Tex. Public Relations Assn. Democrat. Presbyterian. Home: Route 25 Box 351-J Conroe TX 77302 Office: St Joseph Hosp 1919 LaBranch St Houston TX 77002

VANDERPOOL, BRICE DAVID, JR., physician, surgeon; b. Dallas, Nov. 2, 1932; d. Brice David and Sarah Inez (Elmore) Vanderpool; m. Marjorie Louise Martin, Dec. 17, 1955; 1 son, David Martin. Intern, Confederate Meml. Med. Center, Shreveport, La., 1956-57; resident in surgery Parkland Meml. Hosp., Dallas, 1957-61, now mem. staff; practice medicine specializing in surgery, Dallas, 1963—; partner with Drs. Vanderpool, Lane & Winter, 1974—; mem. staffs Baylor U. Med. Center, Presbyn. Hosp. Dallas. Mem. Urban Rehab. Standards Bd. Dallas, 1968-73; adv. bd. Abilene Christian U., 1970—. Served with USAF, 1961-63. Recipient certificate of service City of Dallas, 1974. Mem. AMA (physician's recognition award), Southwestern Surg. Congress, Dallas Soc. Gen. Surgeons, Tex. Med. Assn., Dallas County Med. Soc., A.C.S., Tex. Surg. Soc., Tex. Med. Found. (corp. body). Mem. Ch. of Christ. Clubs: Chaparrel of Dallas, Royal Oaks Country. Contbr. articles to profl. jours. Home: 6936 Lupton Dr Dallas TX 75230 Office: 1008 N Washington Ave Dallas TX 75204

VANDERPOOL, JAMES ALBERT, clin. psychologist, clergyman; b. Perryville, Ky., Nov. 4, 1916; s. William Sherman and Nettie Mae (Ware) V.; student Okla. U., fall 1935; B.A. magna cum laude, Oklahoma City U., 1937; M.S. in Chemistry, Northwestern U., 1939; grad. Gen. Theol. Sem., N.Y.C., 1942, St. Meinrad (Ind.) Sem., 1947; postgrad. St. Mary's Sem., Balt., 1943-44, Loras Coll., summer 1946; M.A. in Psychology, Loyola U., Chgo., 1965, Ph.D. in Psychology, 1967. Instr. chemistry Oklahoma City U., 1937; chemistry tutor Northwestern U., 1937-39; ordained to ministry Anglican Ch., 1942; rector Calvary Episcopal Ch., Batavia, Ill., 1942-43; ordained priest Roman Catholic Ch., 1947; adminstr. St. Patrick's Ch., McHenry, Ill., 1947; asst. pastor St. James Pro-Cathedral, Rockford, Ill., 1948-49; pastor Christ the King Ch., Wonder Lake, Ill., 1949-66; chief psychol. services D.C. Govt. Center for Alcoholics, Occoquan, Va., 1967-68, clin. dir. center, 1969—; adj. prof. Washington Theol. Coalition and Washington Theol. Consortium, Silver Spring, Md., 1969—. Licensed psychologist, D.C.; registered psychologist, certified sch. psychologist, Ill. Diplomate Am. Bd. Profl. Psychology; mem. Am., D.C., Va. psychol. assns., North Am. Assn. Alcoholic Programs, Am., D.C. pub. health assns., AAAS. Republican. Author: Person to Person, 1977; People in Pain, 1979. Home: 8119 Oaklake Ct Alexandria VA 22309 Office: Rehab for Alcoholics Box R Occoquan VA 22125

VAN DER VEER, BRUCE BERT, mgmt. cons.; b. Sault Ste Marie, Mich., Nov. 21, 1947; s. Arburtes and Margaret (Thompson) Van Der Veer; B.S. in Indsl. Engring., Northeastern U., 1970; M.B.A., 1971. Indsl. engr. Johnson & Johnson, North Brunswick, N.J., 1966-69, mfg. supr., 1969-70; mgmt. cons. Lifson, Wilson, Ferguson & Winick, Inc., Houston, 1972—. Served with AUS, 1971-72. Mem. Am. Inst. Indsl. Engrs., Assn. M.B.A. Execs., Tex. Soc. Profl. Engrs., Tau Beta Pi, Alpha Pi Mu. Episcopalian. Home: 5410 Pine St Bellaire TX 77401 Office: 3223 Smith St Suite 212 Houston TX 77006

VAN DE STEEG, GARET EDWARD, analytical chemist; b. Mpls., Feb. 8, 1940; s. Clarence Henry and Dolorous Estelle (Greeley) Van De S.; B.S., Marquette U., 1962; Ph.D., U. N.M., 1968; m. Dorothy Joan Henry, Sept. 5, 1965; children—Garet Erik, Leigh Bryan. Sr. research chemist Am. Potash & Chem. Corp., Trona, Calif., 1968; sr. research chemist, Whittier, Calif., 1968-69; sr. research chemist Kerr-McGee Corp., Oklahoma City, 1969-75, project research chemist, 1975-78, sr. staff analyt. chemist, 1978—; owner, mgr. Van De Steeg, Inc.; mgr. Van De Steeg Farms. Recipient AEC grant, 1963-68. Mem. Am. Chem. Soc., Sigma Xi. Republican. Lutheran. Elk. Home: 2312 NW 113th Pl Oklahoma City OK 73120 Office: 3301 NW 150th St PO Box 25861 Oklahoma City OK 73125

VANDEVER, WILLIAM GARY, banker, investor; b. Tulsa, June 17, 1925; s. Gary York and Allene (Vawter) V.; M.S., St. John's Mil. Acad., 1943; student Tulsa U., 1945-47, N.Y. U., 1948; m. Margaret Glenn, Dec. 1967; children—John York, William Eric; children by previous marriage—Gary York, William Gary. Chmn. bd., pres. The Vandever Co. Inc., Tulsa, 1959-68, dir., 1956-70; pres., dir. 1st Fidelity Co., Inc., Tulsa, 1964—; dir. MidAm. Fed. Savs. & Loan Assn., 1959—; v.p., chmn. exec. com., dir. 1st Nat. Bank Stigler (Okla.), 1966—; pres., dir. WGVI Fin. Advisors Inc., Tulsa, 1971—, W.G. Vandever & Co., Inc., Tulsa, 1974—, Okla. Conveyance Corp., 1979—, Tulsa Petroleum Corp., 1978—, Okla. Drilling Corp., 1978—, Mohawk Oil & Gas Corp., 1979—. Trustee, Am. Youth Performs Found., Inc., N.Y.C., 1966—; bd. dirs. Tulsa Philharmonic Soc., 1952—, v.p., 1960-70; mem. Pres.'s Nat. Office of Emergency Planning, 1963—; bd. dirs. Ark. Basin Devel. Assn., Tulsa, 1956-70; adv. bd. NCCJ, 1956-70, Indian Nations council Boy Scouts Am., Tulsa, 1960-65, Tulsa Civic Ballet Assn., 1965—, Tulsa Opera Inc., 1960-75; mem. Pres. Kennedy's Bi-racial Com., 1963-64, council Met. Opera N.Y., 1960-63; bd. dirs. Tulsa Psychiat. Found., 1964-68, Tulsa Broadway Theatre League, 1958-65, Tulsa Community Chest, 1962-69, YMCA of Tulsa, 1960-68; adv. bd. Downtown Tulsa Unltd., 1962-69. Served with USAF, 1943-45. Mem. Tulsa C. of C. (dir. 1956-69), Alpha Tau Omega Alumni Assn. Clubs: Tulsa, S. Hills Country, Summit. Home: 1306 E 25th St Tulsa OK 74114 Office: 1919 Fourth Nat Bank Bldg Tulsa OK 74119

VAN DUSEN, DENNIS ALAN, cons.; b. Albany, N.Y., Mar. 24, 1949; s. John A. and Ellen (Parser) VanD.; A.A., Orange Coast Coll., 1973; B.S., Pa. State U., 1974, M.S., 1975; S.M. in Applied Math., Harvard U., 1977, M.E. in Info. Scis., 1977. Cons., U.S. Senate, 1976, First Data Corp., Washington, 1976; bus. devel. mgr. Tex. Instruments, Lubbock, 1977-78; cons. Peat Marwick, Mitchell & Co., Washington, 1978—; owner Video Dynamics Co., 1978—; pres. Consumer Automation, 1979—; dir. HBS, Inc. Instr. Georgetown U., 1979—. Adv., Jr. Achievement. Served with USMC, 1966-73. Mem. Am. Mgmt. Assn., Assn. Computing Machinery, IEEE, Soc. Cert. Data Processors, ACLU, Common Cause, Upsilon Pi Epsilon, Alpha Chi Sigma. Office: 1990 K St NW Washington DC 20006

VAN EATON, EARL NEAL, ednl. adminstr.; b. Chillicothe, Mo., July 9, 1940; s. O. Neal and Grace M. (Perry) Van E.; B.S., U. Mo., 1962, M.Ed., 1966, Ph.D., 1970; m. Glenda Jean See, June 6, 1965; 1 son, John Preston. Instr. vocat. agr., Carrollton (Mo.) High Sch., 1962-65; asst. to dean of agr., U. Mo., Columbia, 1965-70; asso. dean student affairs, Okla. State U., Stillwater, 1970-72, asso. prof., 1972-77, prof., 1977—, asst. dean for resident instruction in agr., 1972—; cons. on civilian employee ednl. programs, Kelly AFB, San Antonio; faculty advisor Omicron Delta Kappa, Alpha Zeta, Student Govt. Assn., Agr. Student Assn., Student Supreme Ct., Campus Action Council. Div. chmn. United Fund, 1973-74; elder, tchr., mem. Christian edn. and Christian outreach coms. Presbyterian Ch. Recipient Dean Frank McFarland award, Okla. State U., 1974. Mem. Nat. Orientation Dirs. Assn. (chmn., 1971-72), Nat. Research and Evaluation Center (coordinator, 1973-75), Nat. Steering Com. (cons., 1974—), Nat. Assn. Student Personnel Adminstrs. (steering com. Region IV West., research com.), Phi Kappa Phi, Alpha Zeta, Kappa Delta Phi, Gamma Sigma Delta, Phi Kappa Delta. Democrat. Editor of The National Orientation Bulletin, 1971-75; contbr. articles to profl. jours. Home: 4817 Country Club Dr Stillwater OK 74074 Office: 136 Agriculture Hall Oklahoma State Univ Stillwater OK 74074

VAN FOSSEN, HELEN KEY, physician; b. Lake Providence, La., May 19, 1926; d. Harry Thomas and Maude Olivia (McPhate) Van F.; B.S., La. State U. A&M Coll., 1948, M.D., 1955. Intern and resident in internal medicine Charity Hosp. La., New Orleans, 1955-59; NIH tng. fellow in gastroenterology La. State U., New Orleans, 1959-62; practice medicine specializing in gastroenterology and internal medicine Memphis, 1962—. Bd. dirs. Memphis Ballet Soc.; v.p. Ballet South, 1970—; guarantor Met. Opera, 1970—; angel Memphis Opera Theater, 1979—; mem. Brooks Art Gallery, Dixon Gallery. Diplomate Am. Bd. Internal Medicine. Fellow Am. Coll. Gastroenterology; mem. Am. Soc. Internal Medicine, Memphis Acad. Internal Medicine, Tenn. Soc. Internal Medicine, AMA, Am. Med. Women's Assn., Tenn. Med. Soc., Memphis and Shelby County Med. Soc., So. Med. Assn., Am. Soc. Gastrointestinal Endoscopy, Tenn. Soc. Gastrointestinal Endoscopy. Democrat. Episcopalian. Contbr. article to profl. jour. Home: 4317 Burgundy Rd Memphis TN 38111 Office: 920 Madison Ave Suite 501 Memphis TN 38103

VAN FOSSEN, JOHN MELVIN, govt. ofcl.; b. Belmont Ridge, Ohio, Mar. 20, 1924; s. Robert Melvin and Ella Mae (Wright) Van F.; grad. Honolulu Conservatory Music, 1950; B.S., Oxford Syms Coll., 1964, M.B.A., 1965; Ph.D. in Bus. Adminstrn., Plato Coll., 1976; H.H.D. (hon.), Southeastern Fla. U., 1976; m. Holland Marie Yarborough, June 5, 1945; children—Raymond Melvin, Jill Lynn. Vice pres. Tidewater Mortgage Co., Hampton, Va., 1948-61; real estate appraiser HUD, Richmond, Va., 1965—; pres., adj. prof. bus. adminstrn. Essex Coll., Haverhill, Mass., 1976-77. Chmn. young profl. men's div. United Givers Fund, Hampton and Newport News, Va., 1954; instl. rep. Boy Scouts Am., Hampton, 1955-70. Served with USNR, 1942-46; PTO. Decorated Silver Star, Navy Cross. Mem. Soc. Real Estate Appraisers, Assn. Fed. Appraisers (nat. treas. 1972-74, nat. sec. 1975-76, 2d v.p. 1976-77, pres. 1978), DAV, VFW. Episcopalian. Club: Shriners, Masons (32 deg.). Home: 8504 Aldeburgh Dr Richmond VA 23229 Office: 701 E Franklin St Richmond VA 23219

VAN FRANK, RICHARD NEWELL, architect; b. Bastrop, La., Aug. 29, 1928; s. James and Louise Violet (Curle) Van F.; B.Arch., U. Ark., 1956; m. Phyllis Ann Krauss, Oct. 26, 1957; children—Laura Liane, Bradley Matthew, Jana Carol. Practice architecture, Memphis, 1952-65; with Walk Jones & Francis Mah, Inc., Memphis, 1965—, dir. corp., prin., 1970—; lectr. Caracas (Venezuela) Coll. Engring., 1977. Served with U.S. Army, 1954-56. Mem. AIA, Tenn. Soc. Architects (dir. 1978—), Am. Hosp. Assn., Constrn. Specifications Inst. Presbyterian. Club: Rotary. Office: 825 Ridgelake Blvd Memphis TN 38138

VANGELOFF, GEORGE, hosp. adminstr.; b. Lorain, Ohio, Dec. 30, 1930; s. Joseph and Julia (Spiroff) V.; student U. S.C., 1973, Tulane U., 1975; m. Betty Ann Wood, Nov. 11, 1950; children—Krystal Julia, Kurtis Jay. Seaman recruit U.S. Navy, 1948, advanced through grades to chief hosp. corpsman, 1961, ret. 1967; unit mgr. Ben Taub Gen. Hosp., Houston, 1968-69; patient accounts mgr. St. Luke's Episcopal and Tex. Children's Hosps., Houston, 1969-72; sr. health standards survey officer Ga. Dept. Human Resources, Atlanta, 1974-76; adminstr. Effingham County Hosp. and Extended Care Facility, Springfield, Ga., 1976—. Served with USN, 1972-74. Mem. Nat. Fire Protection Assn., Am. Hosp. Assn., Am. Health Care Assn., Ga. Hosp. Assn. (dist. pres. 1979—), Ga. Health Care Assn. (dist. pres. 1979—), Ga. Assn. County Health Facilities Adminstrs. (dir. 1979—), Am. Legion, V.F.W. Episcopalian. Clubs: Lions (2d v.p. 1979—), Moose. Home: PO Box 339 Springfield GA 31329 Office: PO Box 386 Springfield GA 31329

VAN HOOZER, WILLIAM ROBERT, chem. co. exec.; b. Girard, Kans., Nov. 22, 1933; s. Henry Howard and Maude M. (Mulkins) Van H.; B.S., Kans. State Coll., Pittsburg, 1955, M.S., 1961; m. Walheide Barbara Mondorf, July 26, 1958; children—Janet Kathleen, James Robert, Walter Henry. Research chemist Continental Oil Co., Ponca City, Okla., 1955-67; sr. process control chemist Continental Oil Co., Lake Charles, La., 1967-70, tech. service chemist, Trainer, Pa.,

1971-72; sr. lab. supr. analytical instrumentation PPG Industries, Lake Charles, La., 1973—. Served with Signal Corps, U.S. Army, 1956-58. Decorated Meritorious Service medal. Mem. Instrument Soc. Am., Am. Chem. Soc. (chmn. SW La. sect. 1978), Gulf Coast Instrumental Analysis Group (program chmn. 1975-76, sec.-treas. 1976-77, pres. 1977-78). Research, publs. and patents in organic chem. processes and analytical instrumentation. Home: 1031 Timberlawn Dr Lake Charles LA 70605 Office: PO Box 1000 Lake Charles LA 70602

VAN HORN, CURTIS WRIGHT, ednl. adminstr.; b. Ft. Smith, Ark., Sept. 9, 1935; s. Lynn Allen and Mary Rebecca (Wright) Van H.; B.A., Central State U., 1965, M.Ed., 1969; Ed.D., U. Okla., 1978; 1 son, Erik. Tchr. social studies Crooked Oak High Sch., Oklahoma City, 1965-69, counselor, 1969-71, asst. prin., 1971-72, prin., 1972-73; asst. supt. Crooked Oak Pub. Schs., Dist. I53, Oklahoma City, 1973—; adj. prof. Oklahoma City U., summer 1979. Active United Cerebral Palsy of Greater Oklahoma City, 1974-75; ex-officio mem. Oklahoma City Plan Adv. Com., 1978-79. Served with U.S. Army, 1954-57. Mem. Am. Assn. Sch. Adminstrs., Assn. for Supervision and Curriculum Devel., Internat. Reading Assn., Oklahoma County Tchrs. Assn. (past treas. 1969-70). Address: 1901 SE 15th St Oklahoma City OK 73129

VAN HUSS, SUSIE HESS, educator; b. Bunkie, La., Dec. 5, 1939; d. Andrew James and Laura Martin Hess; B.S. in Bus. Edn. and English, U. Southwestern La., 1970; M.B.A., Ind. U., 1960, Ph.D., 1969; m. Patrick Ray VanHuss, Dec. 10, 1977. Asst. prof. Loyola U., New Orleans, 1961-66, N.E. La. U., Monroe, 1967-69; prof. U. Southwestern La., 1969-74; prof., program dir. office adminstrn. U. S.C., Columbia, 1974—; trustee Ednl. Resources Found. Mem. Nat. Bus. Edn. Assn., Nat. Collegiate Assn. for Secs. (nat. pres. 1970-72), Am. Vocat. Assn., So. Bus. Edn. Assn. (pres. 1978), S.C. Bus. and Office Edn. Assn., Delta Pi Epsilon, Beta Gamma Sigma, Phi Kappa Phi, Pi Lambda Theta, Kappa Delta Pi. Roman Catholic. Author: (with Alfred Patrick) Century 21 College Shorthand Textbook, 1975; (with others) Shorthand: Learning and Instruction Textbook, 1980. Home: 4822 Carter Hill Dr Columbia SC 29206 Office: Coll of Bus Adminstrn U SC Columbia SC 29208

VAN LENNEP, FREDERICK LEAS, horse breeder, mfg. co. exec.; b. Phila., July 6, 1911; s. Gustave A. and Florence (Leas) Van L.; student Haverford Sch., 1920-28; grad. Philips Exeter Acad., 1929; A.B., Princeton, 1933; m. Celeste F. McNeal, Apr., 1933 (div. 1948); 1 son, Hector; m. 2d, Frances Dodge Johnson, Jan. 22, 1950; children—Fredericka D., John F.; m. 3d, Mary Hazen Sprow, June 12, 1971. Head, Castleton Farm, Lexington, Ky., horse board and breeding farm, 1946—, Castleton Farm of Trenton (Fla), 1963-78; chmn. bd., pres. Castleton Industries, Inc., Pompano Beach, Fla., 1968—; pres. Castleton, Inc., horse breeding farm; dir. Boca Raton Nat. Bank (Fla.), 1972-76. Chmn. adv. com. on horse industry Dept. Agr., 1972-76. Trustee Gulf Stream Sch. Served to lt. USNR, 1942-46. Mem. Am. Horse Show Assn. (dir. 1962—), Am. Saddle Horse Assn. (dir.), Am. Horse Council (trustee 1971—), Hambletonian Soc. (dir. 1951—), Fla. Council of 100. Presbyterian. Clubs: Royal Palm Yacht and Country (Boca Raton); Merion Cricket (Haverford, Pa.); Bloomfield Hills (Mich.) Country; Everglades (Palm Beach, Fla.); Metropolitan (N.Y.C.); Iroquois Hunt, Idle Hour (Lexington); Gulf Stream Golf. Home: Castleton Farm 2469 Iron Works Rd Lexington KY 40505 Office: 1800 SW 3d St Pompano Beach FL 33060

VAN METER, JAMES COMBS, oil co. exec.; b. Lexington, Ky., Apr. 15, 1938; s. Robert H. and Nancy (Combs) Van M.; M.S. in Math., U. Ky., 1963; m. Mary Bailey, Nov. 28, 1957; children—Solomon L., Ben Hardin, John Middelton. Instr., Centre Coll., 1963-66; with Ashland Oil, Inc., 1968—, treas.-internat., Ashland, Ky., 1972-78, v.p., 1978-80, adminstrv. v.p., 1980—; Danforth fellow Washington U., St. Louis, 1966-68; instr. Ashland Community Coll. Mem. bd. advs. Ramey Children's Home, Ashland. Office: PO Box 391 Ashland KY 41101

VAN METER, KENNETH DON, sales exec.; b. Clarksburg, W.Va., Mar. 4, 1947; s. Beatrice Virginia (Parsons) Van M.; B.S. with honors, W.Va. U., 1969; M.B.A., with highest honors, U. Ga., 1979; m. Kay Joann Mason, June 10, 1971; children—Ryan Jeffrey, Adam Jeremy. Sales rep. chem. div. Pfizer, Inc., Doraville, Ga., 1977—; dir. Diversified Chem. Industries, Duluth, Ga. Bd. dirs. N. Fla. Spl. Olympics for Retarded, 1975; coordinator United Way, Gt. Falls, Mont., 1971-75. Served with USAF, 1969-77. Mem. Am. Chem. Soc., Nat. Fertilizer Solutions Assn., Inst. Food Tech., Air Force Assn., W.Va. U. Alumni Assn., Phi Kappa Phi. Republican. Home: 528 Brookview Trail Lawrenceville GA 30245 Office: 4360 NE Expressway Doraville GA 30340

VANN, JOSEPH WILLARD, JR., health care center adminstr.; b. Coffeyville, Kans., Sept. 7, 1929; s. Joseph Willard and Ora Lee (Young) V.; B.S., Central State U., Wilberforce, Ohio, 1950; postgrad. U. Tulsa, 1966-68; m. Josie Ruth Hammond, June 24, 1958; 1 dau., Kay Frances Vann Wright. Commd. 2d lt. U.S. Army, 1950; advanced through grades to capt., 1954; asst. prof. mil. sci. and tactics So. U., Baton Rouge, 1957-58; chief instr. 4th Army Non-Commd. Officers Acad., Ft. Hood, Tex., 1958-61; chief ops. 4th Logistical Command, Europe and U.S., 1961-66; ret., 1966; community relations analyst U.S. Dept. Justice, 1967; dir. comprehensive planning Tulsa Model Cities Program, 1968-69, dir. ops., 1969-71, exec. dir., 1971-74; ops. supr., dir. program planning and devel. City of Tulsa, 1974-78; exec. dir. Moton Health Systems, Inc., 1978—; dir. Downtown Tulsa Unltd.; bd. dirs. Tulsa Area Council on Aging, 1973-77, Tulsa Area Manpower Authority, 1972—. Decorated Bronze Star, Purple Heart, Army Commendation medals; recipient Tulsa Urban League award, 1976; YWCA Distinguished Service award, 1973, 75. Mem. Nat. Assn. Community Health Centers, Nat. Assn. Housing and Rehab. Ofcls., Am. Mgmt. Assn., Am. Soc. Pub. Adminstrn., Nat. Community Devel. Dirs. Assn. (dir. 1971-78), Alpha Phi Alpha, Sigma Pi Phi, Phi Alpha Delta. Clubs: Masons, Shriners. Home: 506 E 40th St N Tulsa OK 74106 Office: 603 E Pine St Tulsa OK 74106

VANNEST, MICHAEL ANTHONY, mfg. engr.; b. Jackson, Mich., Sept. 3, 1942; s. Peter Maurice and Genevive (Hinkle) V.; student Jackson Community Coll., 1960-62, Wayne State U., 1966-67, Macomb Coll., 1969-71; Florence Darlington Tech. Center, 1973-74; m. Irene Mejc, Feb. 8, 1964; children—Michelle Marie, Stacey Lynn. Sr. process and tool engr. Clark Equipment Corp., Jackson, Mich., 1965-69; design and research engr. Mich. Tool div. Excello Corp., Detroit, 1969-72; gear mfg. engr. Perfection American div. Rexnord Corp., Darlington, S.C., 1972-74; machine tool analyst Tremec, Queretaro, Mexico, 1974-75; mfg. engr. Stanley Tools, Cheraw, S.C., 1975—. Scoutmaster, 1966-67. Served with USAF, 1961-65. Mem. Soc. Mfg. Engrs. (chmn. 1978-79), Am. Legion. Roman Catholic. Club: Moose. Home: 1217 Manorway St Florence SC 29501 Office: PO Box 190 Cheraw SC 29520

VAN PATTEN, JAMES JEFFERS, educator; b. North Rose, N.Y., Sept. 8, 1925; s. Earl F. and Dorothy (Jeffers) Van P.; B.A., Syracuse U., 1949; M.E., Tex. Western Coll., 1959; Ph.D., U. Tex., Austin, 1962; m. Sept. 10, 1961. Asst. prof. philosophy and edn. Central Mo. State U., Warensburg, 1962-64, asso. prof., 1964-69; asso. prof. vis. overseas U. Okla., Norman, 1969-71; asso. prof. edn. U. Ark., Fayetteville, 1971—. Served with inf., U.S. Army, 1944-45. Decorated Purple Heart. Mem. Am. Ednl. Studies Assn., Mid S. Future Soc., World Future Soc., Am. Philosophy Assn., Southwestern Philosophy of Edn. Soc. (pres. 1970), Ark. Edn. Assn. (pres. chpt. U. Ark.), Phi Delta Kappa (pres. chpt. U. Ark. 1976-77). Club: Kiwanis. Editor: Conflict, Permanency and Change in Education, 1976; contbr. articles to books, profl. jours.; editor Jour. of Thought. Home: 434 Hawthorn St Fayetteville AR 72701

VAN SCOIK, WILBER GLEN, acct.; b. Glen Cove, N.Y., Jan. 12, 1930; s. Glen and Inez Catherine (McFann) Van S.; B.S. in B.A., U. Notre Dame, 1951; postgrad. Tampa U., 1957-60; children—Charles Glen, Gregory Lee. Carol Jean. With M. A. Montenegro & Co., C.P.A.'s, Tampa, 1959-66, partner, 1965-66; partner Harper, Van Scoik & Co., C.P.A.'s, Clearwater, Fla., 1966—. Pres., Pinellas County Estate Planning Council, 1971-72, dir., 1979; chmn. Com. on Estate Planning Conv., 1979—; mem. Pinellas County Budget Review com., 1977-78; treas. Pinellas Area council, Boy Scouts Am., 1972-78; mem. Com. of 100, Pinellas County, Fla., 1976-79. Served with USN, 1951-54. Recipient Joseph S. Clark award for outstanding service, Kiwanis, 1978-79. Mem. Am. Inst. C.P.A.'s (fin. and estate planning subcom. fed. tax div. 1977—), Fla. Inst. C.P.A.'s (chmn. estate planning com. 1973-74, chmn. legis. policy com. 1976-77, treas. W. Coast chpt. 1980—), Fla. Quarter Horse Assn. Republican. Methodist. Clubs: Harborview, Kiwanis (v.p. 1970-71, dir. 1965-69). Home: 1831 East Dr Clearwater FL 33515 Office: 2111 Drew St PO Box 4989 Clearwater FL 33518

VAN SLOOTEN, DALE ALLEN, surgeon; b. Washington, Nov. 5, 1945; s. David John and Blanche Van S.; B.A. with honors, Rutgers U., 1967; M.D., SUNY, Buffalo, 1971; m. Kay Ann Young, Nov. 3, 1969; children—Christina, Chad Allen. Intern and resident in gen. surgery, Monmouth Med. Center, Long Branch, N.J., 1971-75; practice medicine specializing in gen. surgery, Lewisburg, Tenn., 1975—; chief of surgery Lewisburg Community Hosp. Diplomate Am. Bd. Surgery. Fellow A.C.S., Am. Soc. Abdominal Surgeons; mem. AMA (physician recognition award, 1977), Tenn. Med. Assn. Methodist. Clubs: Elks, Rotary. Home: 951 Galloway St Lewisburg TN 37091 Office: 701 Cornersville Rd Lewisburg TN 37091

VAN VALEY, GEORGE WILLIAM, oil refining co. exec.; b. St. Marys, W.Va., Jan. 22, 1922; s. C. Lyle and Gaynelle Elizabeth (Hemsworth) Van V.; B.S. in Bus. and Petroleum, Marietta Coll., 1949; m. Lucile Keith, Sept. 21, 1946; children—Debra Todd, Jeffrey Lyle. Accountant, Quaker State Oil Refining Corp., Parkersburg, W.Va., 1949-50, asst. office mgr., 1950-51, office mgr., 1951—. Com. chmn. Shrine Circus for Benefit of Crippled Children Hosps., 1969-79; bd. dirs. SSS, 1968-76. Served with inf. U.S. Army, 1942-45; PTO. Recipient certs. of appreciation for serving on Selective Service Bd. Mem. 40 and 8. Republican. Lutheran. Clubs: Masons, Shriners, Elks. Home: 1304 16th St Parkersburg WV 26101 Office: PO Box 1327 Parkersburg WV 26101

VAN VLACK, MELVA BULLINGTON (MRS. WILLIAM CLARK VAN VLACK), ret. home economist; b. Vesta Community, Charleston, Ark., Apr. 3, 1909; d. Baxter Lee and Ella Emma (McConnell) Bullington; B.S., U. Ark., 1932, M.S., 1965; postgrad. U. Calif. at Berkeley, 1939, U. Ala., 1948, Jacksonville State U., 1949; m. William Clark Van Vlack, Aug. 9, 1946. Home econs. instr., Prairie Grove, Ark., 1932-33; elementary tchr., Liberty-Tulsa County, Okla., 1933-34; home demonstration agt., Magnolia, Ark., 1934-36, Hope, Ark., 1936-39, Pine Bluff, Ark., 1939-47; jr. high sch. home econs. instr., Atalla, Ala., 1949-57; extension home economist, Ft. Smith, Ark., 1957-75. Ofcl. home econs. div. Ark.-Okla. Livestock Show and Fair, Ft. Smith U., 1958-72. Recipient Distinguished Service award Nat. Assn. Extension Home Economists, 1970. Mem. Am. Home Econs. Assn., Ark. Assn. Extension Home Economists (dist. counselor), Bus. and Profl. Women Pine Bluff and Ft. Smith, Sebastian County 4-H Club Found. (life), Epsilon Sigma Phi, Delta Gamma Sigma. Methodist. Clubs: Sorosis (Magnolia); Soroptimist, Altrusa. Home: 11 Salome St Fort Smith AR 72901

VAN WAGNER, KAREN ANN, health care adminstr.; b. Zeeland, Mich., July 2, 1949; d. Orman Gerald and Catherine Jeannette (Dykstra) Van Haitsma; B.S., Western Mich. U., 1970, M.A., 1971, Ph.D., 1973; m. Bill Van Wagner, June 19, 1970. Instr., grad. asst. Western Mich. U., Kalamazoo, 1972-73; asst. prof. sociology Trinity Coll., Chgo., 1973-75; human relations specialist City of Kansas City (Mo.), 1975; asst. prof. grad. program public adminstrn. U. Kans., Lawrence, 1975-76; dir. planning and data mgmt. Okla. Health Systems Agy., Oklahoma City, 1976—; cons. in field; mem. Okla. Health Statistics Task Force, 1976—; health info. task force Region VI, Dept. HEW, Dallas, 1976; mem. Okla. Health Manpower Task Force, 1976—; mem. Mid-Am. Regional Council Steering Com., 1976; mem. learning community task force U. Kans., 1975-76. Exec. bd. Community Resource for Youth, Palos Heights, Ill., 1975; faculty devel. bd. Trinity Coll., 1975, career devel. and planning bd., 1975. Western Mich. scholar, 1968-69; Waldo-Sangren scholar, 1969-70; Western Mich. U. fellow, 1970-71, NSF trainee, 1971-72. Mem. AAUP, Am. Sociol. Assn., Am. Soc. Public Adminstrs., Am. Health Planning Assn., Am. Public Health Assn., Alpha Kappa Delta. Democrat. Methodist. Contbr. articles to profl. jours. Home: 4233 Cherry Hill Ln Oklahoma City OK 73120 Office: 11212 N May St Oklahoma City OK 73120

VAN WINKLE, PETER KEMBLE, bank exec.; b. Providence, Dec. 30, 1941; s. E. Kingsland and Kate Louise (Vondermuhll) Van W.; B.A., Denison U., 1964; M.B.A., Columbia U., 1968; C.F.A., U. Va., 1979; m. Prudence Anderson Bridges, Aug. 16, 1969; children—Trintje Anderson, Prudence Elizabeth. Trust investment officer State St. Bank, Boston, 1969-73; v.p. Lemire & Van Winkle Investment Counselors, Boston, 1973-74; chief investment officer Choate Hall & Stewart, Boston, 1974-75; v.p. First Nat. Bank in Palm Beach (Fla.), 1975—; pres. Palm Beach Water Sports Inc.; prof. Palm Beach Atlantic Coll. Treas., Parents and Teachers of Montessori Children. Served with Army N.G., 1964-70. Chartered fin. analyst. Mem. Fin. Analysts Fedn., Boston Soc. Security Analysts, Fin. Analysts Soc. Miami, Internat. Water Hockey Assn. (v.p.). Republican. Episcopalian. Club: Holland Soc. (N.Y.). Home: 110 Seaspray Ave Palm Beach FL 33480 Office: 255 S County Rd Palm Beach FL 33480

VAN ZANDT, ISAAC LYCURGUS, orthopedic surgeon; b. Ft. Worth, Nov. 12, 1911; s. Isaac Lycurgus and May Blossom (Beaumont) Van Z.; B.A., U. Tex., 1934, M.D., 1937; M.S. in Orthopedic Surgery, U. Tenn., 1951; m. Helen B. Gillespie, June 5, 1971; children by previous marriage—Neil, Eugenia. Intern, U. Pitts. Med. Center, 1937-38; resident Campbell Clinic-Hosp., Memphis, 1948-51; practice medicine specializing in orthopedic surgery, Ft. Worth, 1951—; mem staff All Saints, Harris, St. Joseph hosps. (all Ft. Worth); instr. pathology dept. U. Tex., Galveston, 1939-40. Fellow A.C.S.; mem. Tex. Med. Assn., AMA, Tex. Surg. Soc., Willis Campbell Orthopedic Club, Am. Acad. Orthopedic Surgeons, Western Orthopedic Assn. Republican. Mem. Christian Ch. Clubs: Ft. Worth Petroleum, Steeplechase. Home: 5141 Crown Rd Fort Worth TX 76114 Office: 1650 W Magnolia Suite 111 Fort Worth TX 76104

VARELMAN, DIAN WACHSMANN, speech pathologist; b. Wichita Falls, Tex., June 29, 1947; d. Anton John and Frances Adell (Frerich) Wachsmann; B.A. magna cum laude, Memphis State U., 1969, M.A., 1970; m. Jerry Lee Varelman, June 3, 1967; children—Lee Anthony, Eric Val. Speech pathologist Memphis City Schs., 1969-74; speech pathologist, coordinator Wichita Falls (Tex.) Ind. Sch. Dist., 1974—. Bd. dirs. N. Tex. chpt. Am. Diabetes Assn., 1978—. Mem. Red River Registry Interpreters for Deaf. Mem. Am. Speech, Lang. and Hearing Assn., Tex. Speech and Hearing Assn., N. Central Tex. Speech and Hearing Assn. Roman Catholic. Home: Route 3 Box 636 Wichita Falls TX 76308 Office: Wichita Falls Independent School District PO Box 2570 Wichita Falls TX 76307

VARGAS, CLARK, environ. engr.; b. Barranquilla Colombia, Jan. 16, 1945; came to U.S., 1962, naturalized, 1972; s. Carlos Guillermo and Edna O. (Sheets) V.; B.S. in Civil Engring., U. Fla., 1971, M.E., 1972; m. Donna Lee Ankeny, Apr. 25, 1976; children—Susan Kathleen, Sean Patrick. Draftsman, Waverly J. Ray & Assos., Jacksonville, Fla., 1963-65, chief engr., 1969-73; project mgr. Flood & Assos., Jacksonville, 1973-79; pres., chief engr. C. Vargas & Assos. Ltd., Inc., Jacksonville, 1979—, also chmn. bd. Served as 1st lt. U.S. Army, 1966-69. Decorated Army Commendation medal. Registered profl. engr., Ga., Fla. Mem. Nat. Soc. Profl. Engrs., Fla. Engring. Soc., Am. Soc. Mil. Engrs., Am. Water Works Assn., ASCE, Fla. Pollution Control Assn., Internat. Game Fishing Assn. (charter mem.), Sigma Tau, Tau Beta Pi. Democrat. Contbr. articles to profl. jours. Home: 716 Oaks Field Rd Jacksonville FL 32211 Office: 8808 Arlington Expressway Jacksonville FL 32211

VARGAS, YOLANDA, dietician; b. Santurce, P.R., Jan. 1, 1950; d. Ramon Vargas and Judith A. Rodriguez; B.S., U. P.R., 1969; postgrad. law Interam. U., 1979—; children by previous marriage—Reynaldo, Javier Alfonso. Food prodn. dietician main kitchen P.R. Med. Center, 1971-73, cafeteria adminstrv. dietician main cafeteria, 1974, clin. and adminstrv. dietician, 1975-77; chief dietician Profl. Hosp., Santurce, P.R., 1977—; cons. dietician for Elderly Home Care Center, Carolina, P.R., 1977—. Mem. Am. Dietetic Assn., Nutritionist and Dietitians Coll. P.R. Mem. Unity Ch. Home: G-1 2nd St Cupey Gardens Rio Piedras PR 00926 Office: PO Box 41268 Santurce PR 00940

VARHOLY, JOSEPH ROBERT, broadcasting co. exec.; b. Lebanon, Pa., Nov. 30, 1932; s. Joseph Charles and Dorothy Marion V.; B.S., Pa. State U., 1954; m. Mary C. Trolier, June 15, 1957; 1 son, John Robert. Ops. dir. Sta. WGAL-TV, Lancaster, Pa., 1957-61; asst. public affairs dir. NBC-TV, Phila., 1961-62, spl. events producer, dir., 1962-65, prodn. mgr., 1965-67, program mgr., Cleve., 1967-73, sta. mgr., 1973-76; gen. mgr. Sta. WSPA-TV, Spartanburg, S.C., 1976—. Chmn., Cleve. Orch. TV Adv. Com., 1966-76. Served with U.S. Army, 1955-57. Mem. Nat. Acad. TV Arts and Scis. (trustee, past pres. Cleve. chpt.), Nat. Assn. TV Program Execs., Nat. Assn. Broadcasters, S.C. Broadcasters Assn. Democrat. Roman Catholic. Home: 110 Lorraine Ct Spartanburg SC 29302 Office: Box 1717 Spartanburg SC 29304

VARNADORE, DONALD GENE, assn. exec.; b. San Angelo, Tex., Mar. 7, 1947; s. Henry Clell and Mary Theo (Lord) V.; B.S.E., State Coll. Ark., 1971; m. Renee White, Mar. 16, 1968; children—Lauri, Christy. Educator, Little Rock, 1971-73; program mgr. individual devel. U.S. Jr. C. of C., Tulsa, 1973-75, exec. dir. mem. devel., 1975-78, exec. v.p., 1978—. Nat. v.p. Muscular Dystrophy Assn.; mem. bd. advs. Citizens Choice. Mem. Am. Soc. Assn. Execs. (mem. profl. assn. adv. com.), Am. Mgmt. Assn., Alpha Chi. Editor Personal Dynamics, Leadership Dynamics, 1973-75. Home: 10129 E 29th St Tulsa OK 74129 Office: PO Box 7 Tulsa OK 74121

VARNER, JOHN BOFINGER, gynecologist and obstetrician; b. Athens, Ga., Jan. 19, 1915; s. Fulton Espy and Helene (Shewell) V.; M.D., Emory U., 1937; m. Theodore Lamar Davis, June 24, 1938; children—Page Nelson Frankel, John Bofinger Jr., Fulton Avery, Helene Elizabeth Varner Strahan. Intern, St. Louis City Hosp., St. Louis Maternity Hosp., 1937-40; resident in psychiatry St. Louis City Sanitarium, 1938-39; resident in obstetrics John Gaston Hosp., Memphis, 1940-41; practice medicine specializing in gynecology, Atlanta, 1946—; clin. asst. prof. obstetrics and gynecology Emory U. Med. Sch., 1960—; cons., past pres. staff Crawford W. Long Hosp. of Emory U. Served with M.C., AUS, 1941-46. Diplomate Am. Bd. Obstetrics and Gynecology. Mem. ACS, S. Atlantic, Ga. State, Atlanta assns. obstetrics and gynecology, Am. Coll. Obstetrics and Gynecology. Episcopalian. Club: Cherokee Town and Country. Home: 181 Peachtree Battle Ave NW Atlanta GA 30305 Office: 490 Peachtree St NE Atlanta GA 30308

VARNER, JULIA BROOKS, designer; b. Leaksville, N.C., Jan. 25, 1936; d. Bernard L. and Sadie (Young) Brooks; student Chgo. Sch. Interior Decoration, 1959-61; m. James Marshall Varner, June 15, 1956; children—John Stuart, Amanda, Amy, Scott. Sec., Fieldcrest Mills Co., Eden, N.C., 1954-56, Mize Motors, Eden, 1960-62, First Nat. Bank, Eden, 1962-63; propr. Julia's Interiors, Eden, 1964—; designer cons. wall furniture, 1977—; tchr. design Rockingham Community Coll., Wentworth, N.C., 1968-72. Sec. N.C. Heart Assn., 1970-71. Recipient Founders award N.C. Heart Assn., 1971. Mem. Internat. Platform Assn., Am. Soc. Interior Designers (provisional profl. mem.). Democrat. Baptist. Home: 205 Kelso Ct Cary NC 27511

VASA, ROHITKUMAR BHUPATRAI, pediatrician, neonatologist; b. Rajula, India, July 26, 1947; came to U.S., 1973; s. Bhupatrai J. and Vijalaxmi B. V.; M.BBS., Maharaja Sayajirao, U., Baroda, India, 1968, D.C.H., 1971, M.D., 1973; m. Usha R. Vasa, Feb. 26, 1970; children—Falguni, Monisha. Intern, Sayaji Gen. Hosp., Baroda, 1968-69; resident in pediatrics Beth Israel Med. Center, N.Y.C., 1973-75; fellow in neonatology N.Y. U. Med. Center, 1975-77, teaching asst., 1975-77; attending pediatrician Gouverneur Hosp., N.Y.C., 1977-79; pediatrician, neonatologist U.S. Army Hosp., Ft. Campbell, Ky., 1979—. Served with U.S. Army, 1979—. Diplomate Am. Bd. Pediatrics. Fellow Am. Acad. Pediatrics; mem. Nat. Assn. Residents and Interns. Home: 406 Ambrose Dr Clarksville TN 37040 Office: US Army Hospital Dept Pediatrics Fort Campbell KY 42223

VASILAKIS, SUSAN TILLMAN, hosp. adminstr.; b. El Paso, Tex., Nov. 27, 1947; d. Barney Nathan and Anetta Jean (McElhannon) T.; m. Anthony Joseph Vasilakis, June 8, 1968; 1 dau., Casey Annette. Staff technologist Hotel Dieu Hosp., El Paso, Tex., 1972-73, edn. coordinator, 1973-75, supr. dept. hematology, 1974-77, lab. tech. dir., 1977-79; lab. dir. Eastwood Hosp., El Paso, 1979—. Cert. med. technologist Am. Soc. Clin. Pathology. Mem. Am. Bus. Women's Assn. (sec. 1975-77, treas. 1977-78, pres. 1978-79). Democrat. Home: 10921 Tom Weiskopf St El Paso TX 79935 Office: 10301 Gateway W St El Paso TX 79925

VASILIADES, JOHN, educator; b. Kastoria, Greece, Jan. 20, 1945; came to U.S., 1955, naturalized, 1963; s. Evangelos and Alexandra (Sotiropoulos) V.; B.S., Hunter Coll., 1967; Ph.D., U. Nebr., 1971; m. Ann Stephens, Apr. 16, 1977; 1 dau., Elizabeth. Instr. chemistry U. Nebr., 1969-71; research asso. dept. chemistry Purdue U., 1971-72;

instr. clin. pathology U. Ala., 1973-75, asst. prof., 1975—, dir. spl. chemistry-toxicology, 1975—. Mem. Am. Chem. Soc., Am. Assn. Clin. Chemists. Greek Orthodox. Contbr. articles to profl. jours. Home: 933 S 39th St Birmingham AL 35222 Office: Dept Pathology U Ala 620 S 19th St Birmingham AL 35233

VASILOFF, ANGELOS, JR., civil engr.; b. Ft. Myers, Fla., July 20, 1934; B.S. in Civil Engring., U. Fla., 1956; M.S.P.A., Troy State U., 1976; D.P.A., Nova U., 1978; m. Diane A. Warner, Dec. 23, 1956; children—Andrew S., Dwayne A. Structural project engr. U.S. Air Force, Wright Patterson AFB, Ohio, 1956-60, tech. area mgr. research program Air Force Aero Propulsion Lab., 1960-68, dir. munitions containers and support directorate, Eglin AFB, Fla., 1968-74, dir. munitions container and handling equipment systems program office, 1974-76, dir. acquisition mgmt. directorate, 1976-78, chief range devel. div., 1978—. Active Baptist Ch. Served USAF, 1956-59. Mem. ASCE, Air Force Assn., Def. Preparedness Assn. Patentee in field. Home: 7 Rue de le Roi Fort Walton Beach FL 32548 Office: Armament Div TEER Eglin AFB FL 32542

VASKO, PETER FREDERICK, motor club exec.; b. N.Y.C., Nov. 28, 1943; s. Theodore and Catherine (Buday) V.; B.A., Catholic U., 1966, B.D., 1969. Adminstrv. asst. to pres. Woodlawn Meml. Gardens, Inc., Norfolk, Va., 1971-76; dir. pub. relations Carolina Motor Club, AAA, Charlotte, N.C., 1976-77, N.C. State Motor Club, Charlotte, 1977-79; dir. Health Care Inst., New Orleans, 1979—. Bd. dirs. N.Central chpt. Easter Seal Soc., 1974-75, N.C. Central U. Art Mus., 1974-76. Recipient award VFW, 1974. Mem. Better Transp. for N.C., Contact, Raleigh (Pres.'s Silver Cup 1975), Am., Charlotte, Durham (co-founder, pres.) pub. relations socs. Clubs: Rotary, Jaycees (named Jaycee of year Durham chpt. 1972). Roman Catholic.

VASQUEZ, ROBERTO JOSE, savs. and loan exec.; b. Del Rio, Tex., Mar. 18, 1949; s. Roberto and Eloisa (Sanchez) V.; B.A., San Antonio Coll., 1970; B.B.A. in Acctg., St. Mary's U., 1973; m. Noram Cardenas, Sept. 23, 1967; children—Roberto Antonio, Sarah Lynette. Cashier, HEB Food Stores, San Antonio, 1968-69, Sunshine Cleaners, San Antonio, 1969-71; intelligence trainee IRS, San Antonio, 1971; loan officer, acct. United Businessman of San Antonio, 1971-73; acctg. dept. mgr. First Fed. Savs. and Loan, San Antonio, 1973—; instr. Inst. Fin. Edn. Mem. Fin. Mgrs. Soc. Democrat. Roman Catholic. Club: K.C. (treas. 1975-77). Home: 6547 David St San Antonio TX 78239 Office: First Fed Savs and Loan 1100 NE Loop 410 San Antonio TX 78286

VASSER, RICHARD EDWARD, state ofcl.; b. Spokane, Wash., Sept. 29, 1942; s. Roy and Mary Elizabeth (Johnson) V.; student Emory U., Atlanta, 1960-61, Schreiner Inst., Kerrville, Tex., 1961-62; B.S., S.W. Tex. State U., 1965, M.P.A., 1977; m. Sue Dodgen, June 16, 1973; children—Elizabeth, Sharon. Dir. evaluation San Antonio Dept. Parks and Recreation, 1971, grant adminstr. youth services project, 1971-72; project mgr. planning div. Tex. Dept. Human Resources, Austin, 1972-74, acting dir. analysis sect. planning div., 1974-75, project mgr. planning bur., 1975-79, adminstr. research and demonstration div., med. programs, 1979, project and grant mgr. policy planning div., 1979-80, dir. research and demonstration, policy and planning div., med. programs, 1980—. Served with USAF, 1965-71. Decorated D.F.C., Air medals. Mem. Am. Mgmt. Assn., Lambda Chi Alpha (pres. 1976—). Republican. Episcopalian. Club: Austin Skiers (v.p. programs 1977-78, asst. v.p. trips 1978-79, v.p. trips 1979-80). Home: 5107 Saddle Circle Austin TX 78759 Office: PO Box 2960 Dept Human Resources Austin TX 78769

VATH, JOSEPH G., bishop. Ordained priest Roman Catholic Ch., 1941; vicar gen., aux. bishop Mobile-Birmingham (Ala.) and titular bishop of Novaliciana, 1966-69, bishop of Birmingham, 1969—. Office: PO Box 2086 Birmingham AL 35201*

VATUNA, MICHAEL ROBERT, chem. co. exec.; b. Rockaway, N.J., July 24, 1946; s. Frank and Veronica V.; B.S., Midwestern Coll., Denison, Iowa, 1969; M.S. in Indsl. Mgmt., U. Ark., 1975; m. Marcia Cornelius, June 28, 1969; 1 dau., Stephanie. Mgr. phys. distbn. Mobil Chem. Co., Frankfort, Ill., 1974-75, prodn. control, customer service supt., Frankfort, 1975-76, prodn. and material control supr. Southeast region, Covington, Ga., 1976—. Served with USAF, 1969-74. Mem. Assn. MBA Execs., Nat. Council Phys. Distbn. Mgrs. (asso.). Roman Catholic. Home: 469 Sweetwater Conyers GA 30208 Office: PO Box 71 Covington GA 30209

VAUGHAN, CLYDE WAYNE, med. products co. exec.; b. Decatur, Ala., Nov. 2, 1936; s. William Clyde and Irene Agnes (Holland) V.; A.B. in Chemistry and Biology, Florence State U., 1958; m. Karen Lee Jensen, Aug. 4, 1979; children by previous marriage—Gregory Wayne, Timothy Eric. Bacteriologist, So. Research Inst., Birmingham, Ala., 1958-60; biochemist U. Ala. Med. Coll., Birmingham, 1960-62, tech. dir. cardiac catheterization labs., 1962-70; regional mgr. Cook Inc., Bloomington, Ind., 1970—; cons. to physicians. Minister of music, various Ala. chs., 1960-70. Mem. Am. Heart Assn., U.S. Tennis Assn. Club: Cherokee Town and Country (Atlanta).

VAUGHAN, DANIEL GLEN, contracting co. exec.; b. McComb, Miss., Jan. 24, 1933; s. John Alexander and Elma Virginia (Humphreys) V.; B.S. in E.E., U. Miami, 1955; M.S. in I.E., Stanford U., 1961; m. Gloria Brister, Sept. 12, 1953; children—Daniel Glen, Gloria Dawn. Elec. engr. Gen. Electric, Syracuse, N.Y., 1955; commd. 2d lt. U.S. Air Force, 1955, advanced through grades to capt., 1966; engring. mgr. Gen. Electric, Bay St. Louis, Miss., 1966-71; pres. Vaughan Engring. Co., Gulfport, Miss., 1971; resident mgr. Global Asso., Bay St. Louis, 1971-78, project mgr., New Orleans, 1979—. Mem. Gulfport-Biloxi Regional Airport Adv. Com., 1977-79; mem. Harrison County Republican Exec. com., 1976-79. Decorated Air Force Commendation medal; registered profl. engr., Fla., Miss., Tex. Republican. Methodist. Clubs: Masons (Shriner). Home: 143 Molokai Bay Saint Louis MS 39520 Office: PO Box 29400 New Orleans LA 70189

VAUGHAN, DENNIS JOSEPH, chemist, fiberglass mfg. co. exec.; b. Gt. Britain, Mar. 25, 1932; s. Howard Joseph and Ivy May V.; came to U.S., 1970; B.Sc., U. London, 1953; B.Sc., U. Birmingham (Eng.), 1956, Ph.D., 1960; m. Gladys Slater, June 21, 1957; children—Gavin Mark, Gareth David, Giles Steven. Lectr., biochemist U. Birmingham; chemist Tufnol Ltd., Birmingham; now dir. research and devel. Clark-Schwebel Fiberglass Co., Anderson, S.C.; lectr. polymer tech. U. Aston (Eng.). Fellow Royal Inst. Statistics, Co-Polymer Soc.; mem. Plastics Inst. (asso.), Royal Inst. Chemistry (asso.). Methodist. Contbr. numerous articles to profl. jours.; patentee in field. Home: Route 10 Longview Dr Anderson SC 29621 Office: PO Box 2627 Anderson SC 29621

VAUGHAN, EUGENE H., JR., investment co. exec.; b. Brownsville, Tenn., Oct. 5, 1933; s. Eugene H. and Margaret (Musgrave) V.; B.A., Vanderbilt U., 1955; M.B.A., Harvard, 1961; m. Susan Bolinger Westbrook, May 11, 1963; children—Margaret Corbin, Richard Bolinger. Investment analyst Putnam Mgmt. Co., Boston, 1961-64; v.p. research, dir. Underwood, Neuhaus & Co., Inc., Houston, 1964-70; pres. Vaughan, Nelson & Boston, Inc., investment counsel, Houston, 1970—; dir. Founders Growth Mut. Fund, Founders Spl. Mut. Fund, S.H. Bolinger, Ltd., Moncrief-Lenoir Mfg. Bd. dirs. Houston Grand Opera Assn., 1970—; trustee Vanderbilt U., 1972—, Financial Analysts Research Found., 1973-74. Served to lt. (j.g.), USN. Mem. Financial Analysts Fedn. (chmn. bd., chief exec. officer 1973-74, dir. 1969—, exec. com. 1971—), Inst. Chartered Financial Analysts (trustee 1973-74), Houston Soc. Financial Analysts (pres. 1967-68, dir. 1966-70), Vanderbilt U. Alumni Assn. (dir. 1966-70), Sigma Alpha Epsilon. Presbyterian (elder). Clubs: Harvard Bus. Sch. (pres. 1970-72, dir. 1966-73), Houston Country, Houston Athletic. Home: 3465 Inwood Dr Houston TX 77019 Office: 2150 Two Shell Plaza Houston TX 77002

VAUGHAN, JACK CHAPLINE, ret. physicist, author; b. Sarasota, Fla., Dec. 17, 1912; s. Alfred Jefferson and Blossom Creighton (Chapline) V.; B.A. in Physics and Math., Tex. Christian U., 1967; postgrad. U. Tex. at Arlington, 1967-68, Ark. Law Sch., 1934-35; m. Anne Gwin, Sept. 4, 1942 (div. Mar. 1955); children—Jack Chapline, Gwin Vaughan Barnum (dec.), Thomas A.J., Anne; m. 2d, Lanette Worthington, Mar. 12, 1965. Propr. cattle ranch, Chicot County (Ark.), 1950, Adams County (Miss.), 1945-52; specifications writer Navy carrier-based aircraft programs Douglas Aircraft Corp. Los Angeles, 1952-55; head specifications group TITAN intercontinental ballistic missile nosecone Research and Adv. Devel. div. AVCO, Boston, 1956; analyst, writer research and devel. proposals LTV Aerospace Corp., Dallas, 1956-59, sr. analyst progress reporting and contractually required data submissions LTV-NASA-SCOUT launch vehicle program, 1959-74. Served to maj. inf. AUS, 1940-45. Mem. Am. Phys. Soc., A.A.A.S., Honourable Soc. of Cymmrodorion (Wales). Author: (all Vaughan's American Histories) Frontier Ambassador, 1957; Vaughan's Brigade Army of Tennessee, vols. 1-10, 1960-75; The British History of Geoffrey of Monmouth, 1975; The Chronicles of Wales, 1976; Martha Jane, 1977; William Vaughan. . .Renaissance Scholar; American Colonist, 1978; Gyges, Ancient Lydians, 1978; Conquest of the South (1861-1865), Part I, 1979; Welsh Colony of Virginia, 1980; translator: (from Russian) Pre-Greek Etymology, 1973. Address: PO Box 7632 Little Rock AR 72217

VAUGHAN, JERRY LYNN, coll. adminstr.; b. Galveston, Tex., May 11, 1939; s. Bert R. and Olivia (Stanley) V.; B. Applied Sci., U. Houston, 1962; M.S., Nova U., 1973; m. Maridell Roark, Aug. 11, 1962; children—Jerry Lynn, Kristen Lea, Karen Colleen. Oil well logging engr. Pan Geo Atlas Corp., Tex. and Calif., 1962-64; test engr. Gen. Dynamics Co., Ft. Worth, 1964-65; instrumentation engr. Monsanto Co., Alvin, Tex., 1965-66; gen. sales mgr. Scott Engring./Technovate Co., Pompano Beach, Fla., 1966-71; asst. to v.p. Nova U., 1971-72; v.p. adminstrn. Profl. Ins. Corp., Jacksonville, Fla., 1973-74; instr., chmn. div. indsl. edn. Coll. Mainland, Texas City, Tex., 1974-79, pub. speaker Bicentennial Speaker's Bur., 1976. Certified adminstr. fed. monies, instr. electronics and mathematics, Tex.; certified part-time post-secondary tchr., Fla. Mem. Am. Soc. Engring. Edn., Am. Radio Relay League, Am. Vocat. Assn., Tex. Jr. Coll. Tchr's. Assn., Tex. Tech. Soc., Am. Tech. Edn. Assn., Phi Delta Kappa. Club: K.C. Home: Route 1 Box 14N Alta Loma TX 77510 Office: 8001 Palmer Hwy Texas City TX 77590

VAUGHAN, JOHN NOLEN, clergyman; b. Memphis, Nov. 23, 1941; s. Nolen Lewis and Ethel Montez (Cannon) V.; B.A., Memphis State U., 1964; M.Div., Southwestern Bapt. Theol. Sem., 1967; m. Sara Joanne Wooten, Jan. 26, 1962; children—Johnna, John Nathan. Ordained to ministry Baptist Ch., 1962; youth dir. Berclair Bapt. Ch., Memphis, summer 1960; pastor Cockrum (Miss.) Baptist Mission, 1961-62; chaplain intern Methodist Hosp., Tex. Med. Center, Houston, summer 1967; asso. pastor Westridge Bapt. Ch., Euless, Tex., 1964-67; pastoral intern Travis Ave. Bapt. Ch., Ft. Worth, 1965-66; asst. pastor Hunter St. Bapt. Ch., Birmingham, Ala., 1967-69; pastor Univ. Bapt. Ch., Iowa City, 1969-73; asst. pastor Trinity Bapt. Ch., Memphis, 1973-77; asst. pastor E. Park Bapt. Ch., Memphis, 1977—; ch. growth cons. adults Tenn. Bapt. Conv., 1979—; mem. pub. relations com. Shelby Bapt. Assn., 1976-77; mem. exec. bd. Assn. Religious Leaders Iowa City, 1971-72. Mem. Creation Research Soc., So. Bapt. Pastors Conf., Tenn. Alumni Assn. Southwestern Bapt. Sem. (sec.-treas. 1978-79), Sigma Alpha Epsilon. Author, editor: (with others) Church Growth for the 80's, 1980; contbr. articles to religious jours. Home: 2116 McKellar Hills Memphis TN 38116 Office: 842 Sweetbriar Rd Memphis TN 38138

VAUGHAN, JOHN THOMAS, veterinarian, univ. adminstr.; b. Tuskegee, Ala., Feb. 6, 1932; s. Henry Asa and Mary (Howard) V.; D.V.M., Auburn U., 1955, M.S., 1963; m. Ethel Evelyn Sell, July 7, 1956; children—J.T., Faythe, Michael Sell. Mem. faculty Sch. Vet. Medicine, Auburn (Ala.) U., 1955-70, 74—, prof., head dept. large animal surgery and medicine, 1974-77, dean Sch. Vet. Medicine, 1977—; prof., dir. large animal hosp., dept. large animal medicine, obstetrics and surgery N.Y. State Vet. Coll., Cornell U., Ithaca, N.Y., 1970-74. Mem. Am. Vet. Med. Assn., Ala. Vet. Med. Assn., Am. Assn. Equine Practitioners (pres.-elect 1980), Am. Coll. Vet. Surgeons (pres. 1980-81), Sigma Xi, Phi Eta Sigma, Phi Kappa Phi, Alpha Zeta, Gamma Sigma Delta, Phi Zeta. Methodist. Club: Rotary. Author: (with D.F. Walker) Bovine and Equine Urogenital Surgery, 1980; contbr. articles to profl. jours., chpts. to books. Office: Dean Sch Vet Medicine Auburn U Auburn AL 36830

VAUGHAN, ODIE FRANK, JR., drilling co. exec.; b. Camden, Ark., Feb. 3, 1936; s. Odie Frank and Bernece (May) V.; student So. State Coll., 1954-55; B.S., La. Tech. U., 1959; m. Sandra Kay Beard, Sept. 8, 1962; children—Laura Elizabeth, Christopher Michael. With Peat, Marwick, Mitchell & Co., Dallas, 1959-61; mgr. taxes Murphy Oil Corp., El Dorado, Ark., 1962-72; treas., chief financial officer Ocean Drilling & Exploration Co., New Orleans, 1973-77, v.p., treas., chief fin. officer, 1977—. Mem. Am. Petroleum Inst. (gen. tax com. 1968—, chmn. tax com. 1977-78), Am. Inst. C.P.A.'s, Tax Exec. Inst., Fin. Exec. Inst. Baptist. Club: Lions. Home: 546 Topaz St New Orleans LA 70124 Office: 1600 Canal St New Orleans LA 70112

VAUGHAN, RICHARD DUGGER, san. engr.; b. Evanston Ill., Dec. 18, 1926; s. Merlon Gilchrist and Beatrice Vivian (Dugger) V.; B.S.C.E., Ga. Inst. Tech., 1951; M.S. in Engring., U. Mich., 1962, M.P.H., 1962; m. Laura May Henderson, Sept. 15, 1951; children—Cynthia Lynn, Robert Bruce, Kathryn Ann. Commd. ensign USPHS, 1951, advanced through grades to asst. surgeon gen., 1970; dir. Robert S. Kerr Water Research Center, Ada, Okla., 1964-66; dir. Fed. Bur. Solid Waste Mgmt. Program, 1968-71; ret., 1971; dir. environ. affairs and quality assurance ITT Community Devel., Inc., Palm Coast, Fla., 1973—. Pres. Daytona Play House, Daytona Beach, Fla., 1977-79; pres. Civil Music, Daytona Beach, 1980—. Served with U.S. Army, 1945-46. Recipient William Gibson award U. Mich., 1962; Commendation medal USPHS, 1962; Meritorious Service medal, 1970. Fellow Am. Public Health Assn.; mem. Am. Waterworks Assn., Am. Public Works Assn., ASTM, Water Pollution Control Fedn., Air Pollution Control Assn., Am. Acad. Environ. Engring. (diplomate), U. Mich. Sch. Public Health Alumni Soc. (past pres.), Delta Omega, Chi Epsilon, Phi Kappa Phi, Alpha Tau Omega. Contbr. articles to profl. jours. Office: ITT Community Devel Corp Environ Affairs Palm Coast FL 32051

VAUGHAN, VERMEILLIA ANN, sch. counselor; b. Perry, Okla., Oct. 21, 1936; d. Adam G. and Sophia B. (Brady) Stermer; B.S. in Bus. Edn., Okla. State U., 1958; M.Ed., N. Tex. State U., 1966; m. Ronald W. Vaughan, Oct. 25, 1961. Tchr. Hunter (Okla.) High Sch., 1958-59; tchr. Sandia High Sch., Albuquerque, 1959-63; counselor W. Jr. High Sch., Richardson, Tex., 1966-70, Richardson (Tex.) High Sch., 1970-72, Westwood Jr. High Sch., Richardson, 1972—. Mem. Am., Tex., N. Central Tex. personnel and guidance assns., Assn. Tex. Educators (v.p.). Presbyterian. Home: Route 2 Apt 101A Perry OK 73077 Office: 7630 Arapaho Rd Dallas TX 75048

VAUGHN, DON SEALY, trade show ser. co. exec.; b. Santa Anna, Tex., Sept. 15, 1935; s. Russell M. and Irene S. V.; B.B.A., U. Corpus Christi, 1958; m. Barbara Fay Duncan, June 24, 1955; 1 dau., Connie. Conv. mgr. Kiwanis Internat., Chgo., 1963-67; Houston conv. mgr. Nat. Assn. Home Builders, Washington, 1967, nat. dir. convs. and meetings, 1969-71; v.p. Astrodomain Corp., Houston, 1971-74; exec. v.p. Freeman Decorating Co., Dallas, 1974—; pres. Expn. Service Contractors Assn., Dallas, 1976-77; pres. AVW Audio Visual, Inc., Dallas, 1976—. Served with USAF, 1962. Named Distinguished Alumnus U. Corpus Christi, 1970. Mem. Tex. Assn. Bus. (chmn. Dallas chpt.), Trade Show Bur. (pres.), Sales and Mktg. Execs. Republican. Office: Freeman Decorating Co 1300 Wycliff Dallas TX 75207

VAUGHN, DORIS MARIE, educator; b. New Orleans, May 25, 1944; d. Albert B. and Inez Marie (Trouillier) Cousin; B.S., So. U., 1963; M.Ed., Ohio U., 1965; Ph.D., Tex. Tech. U., 1975; m. Percy Joseph Vaughn, Aug. 24, 1968; 1 dau., Tracy Lydricka. Instr., counselor So. U., Baton Rouge, La., 1965-72; asst. to v.p. and dean and instr. Tex. Tech. U., Sch. Medicine, Lubbock, 1972-75; asso. prof. psychology and counseling Ala. State U., Montgomery, 1975-77, chmn. dept. personnel sers., 1977—; cons. Emergency Sch. Aid Act project, Mobile, Ala., 1977—. Mem. sch. bd. for Queen of Mercy Sch., Montgomery, 1977-78; mem. Montgomery's Community Action bd., 1976-77; active Continental Socs., 1978—. Ohio U. grad. assistantship, 1963-65. Mem. NOW, Am. Personnel and Guidance Assn., Ala. Personnel and Guidance Assn., NEA, Am. Coll. Personnel Assn., Phi Delta Kappa, Kappa Delta Pi, Alpha Kappa Mu, Pi Gamma Mu, Phi Kappa Phi. Democrat. Roman Catholic. Home: 5794 Carriage Barn Ln Montgomery AL 36116 Office: 915 S Jackson St Montgomery AL 36105

VAUGHN, EDGAR ALBERT, JR., state ofcl. S.C.; b. Fairburn, Ga., Nov. 2, 1935; s. Edgar A. and Mary Eleanor (Kinnett) V.; B.B.A., Ga. State U., 1961; S.M. (Alfred P. Sloan fellow), Mass. Inst. Tech., 1970; m. Carol Ann Stone, June 8, 1957; children—Cynthia M., Greggory T., Catherine S. Accountant, Nat. NuGrape Co., Atlanta, 1957-61; sr. accountant James B. Carson & Co., C.P.A.'s, Atlanta, 1961-65; dep. dir. finance City of Atlanta, 1965-72; dir. auditing State of S.C., Columbia, 1972-77; asst. state auditor State of S.C., 1977-78, State auditor, 1978—; Instr. accounting Clayton Jr. Coll., Morrow, Ga., 1970-72. C.P.A., Ga., S.C. Mem. Am. Inst. C.P.A.'s, Ga. S.C. socs. C.P.A.'s Nat. Council Govtl. Acctg., Mcpl. Fin. Officers Assn., Nat. Assn. State Auditors, Comptrollers and Treasurers, Soc. of Sloan Fellows, Pi Kappa Phi. Home: 816 Kingsbridge Rd Columbia SC 29210 Office: PO Box 11333 Columbia SC 29211

VAUGHN, GEORGE PARKER, architect; b. Austin, Tex., May 12, 1949; s. Carroll Lee and Opal Florine (Parker) V.; B.Arch. with honors, Tex. Tech. U., 1972; m. Carol Jean Holland, Jan. 9, 1970; children—Greg Parker, Shelly Renee. With W. G. McMillan Constrn. Co., Lubbock, Tex., 1970-72; apprentice architect Ken Rehler & Assos., Inc., San Antonio, 1972-76; v.p., prin. architect Rehler, Vaughn, Beaty & Koone, Inc., San Antonio, 1976—; tchr. Acad. Real Estate, San Antonio, 1978—. Deacon, Sunset Ridge Ch. of Christ, San Antonio, 1976—. Wad Edn. Fund. scholar, AIA, 1971. Mem. Constrn. Specifications Inst. (pres. 1979—), AIA, Nat. Council of Archtl. Registration Bds., Tex. Soc. Architects, Tau Sigma Delta. Club: Alamo Heights Rotary (v.p. 1980—). Home: 132 Chevy Chase St San Antonio TX 78209 Office: 1901 NW Military Hwy Suite 210 San Antonio TX 78213

VAUGHN, HOWARD BEECHER, educator; b. Cullman, Ala., Aug. 1, 1922; s. Ponder Cleveland and Mary Myrtle (Allison) V.; B.Ed., U. Miami, 1955; M.A., U. Western Ky., 1967; postgrad. (U.S. Govt. grantee), Clemson U., 1967; m. Mary Ann Bank, Nov. 24, 1960; children—Pamela, Douglas, Thomas. Union carpenter, Miami, Fla., 1946-50; tchr. Dade County (Fla.) Bd. Pub. Instruction, Redland Jr. High Sch., 1955-56, S. Miami Jr. High Sch., 1956—; extension course tchr. Miami Dade Jr. Coll. N., 1963; chmn. text book com. indsl. arts, Dade County, 1965-66; dist. pres. indsl. arts State of Fla., 1968-69. Active coms. to campaign for local elections; active Boy Scouts Am., 1960-65; co-pres. Homeowners of Tamiami, 1975-77. Served with USAAF, 1942-45. Recipient Outstanding Indsl. Arts Tchr. award State of Fla., 1969; Dade County Outstanding Citizen of Week award, 1969. Mem. Am. (life), Fla. (life), Dade County (treas. 1965-66) indsl. arts assns., United Tchrs. Dade Union, Epsilon Pi Tau. Democrat. Baptist. Club: Masons. Home: 5815 SW 19th St Miami FL 33155 Office: 6750 SW 60th St Miami FL 33143

VAUGHN, HUBERT ARNOLD, ret. banker; b. Corbin, Ky., July 30, 1912; s. Jack Lewis and Ollie Mae (Black) V.; student Eastern Ky. U., 1932-35, Ohio State U., 1959; m. Clara Gibson, Feb. 7, 1936; children—Hubert Byron, Judith Ann (Mrs. David Bennett Hill), Jerry (Mrs. George Litton Kline). With Jellico Grocery Co., Inc., various locations, 1935-68, mgr., Somerset, Ky., 1941-60, mgr. Oneida, Tenn., 1960-68; dir. 1st Trust & Savs. Bank Oneida, Tenn., 1965-80, adminstr. customer service, 1969-72, v.p., trust officer, 1973-76, exec. v.p., trust officer, 1977-78, sr. v.p., 1979-80. Mem. Oneida Water Works Bd., 1969-76, chmn., 1973-76; pres. Somerset (Ky.) Rotary, 1948-49. Mem. Scott County C. of C. (dir. 1961-64, treas. 1962-64). Home: 627 Lakeshore Dr Kingston TN 37763

VAUGHN, LARRY JODY, hosp. ofcl.; b. Nashville, Sept. 15, 1945; s. Winslow Hunter and Lillian Christine (Coggin) V.; student U. Tenn., Knoxville, 1970-72; B.S., Middle Tenn. State U., 1967; m. Sherry Kaye Wallace, Aug. 12, 1972; children—Wallace Hunter, Jason Reece. Chief personnel officer Lakeshore Mental Health Inst., Knoxville, 1970-73; dir. personnel Bristol (Tenn.-Va.) Meml. Hosp., 1973-76; instr. bus. Bristol (Tenn.) Community Coll., 1974-75; personnel dir. Oak Ridge Hosp. of United Meth. Ch., 1976—. Pres., Orchard Knob Homeowners Assn., 1978—; bus. and office edn. adv. com. Oak Ridge High Sch.; bd. dirs. United Way of Bristol and Oak Ridge, Bristol Regional Speech and Hearing Center. Served with U.S. Army, 1967-69. Decorated Purple Heart with cluster, Air medal. Mem. Knoxville Hosp. Personnel Soc. (pres. 1972-73), Am. Soc. Personnel Adminstrn. (accredited exec. in personnel, v.p. Upper East Tenn. chpt. 1975-76), Tennessee Valley Personnel Assn., Am. Soc. Hosp. Personnel Adminstrn., Tenn. Hosp. Assn., DAV, Alpha Kappa Psi. Club: Elks. Home: 306 Crest Dr Clinton TN 37716 Office: Oak Ridge Hosp of United Meth Ch 125 W Tennessee Ave Oak Ridge TN 37830

VAUGHN, LUD WILSON, banker; b. Gaffney, S.C., Aug. 2, 1950; s. Joseph Wilson and Cleo Carver (Moss) V.; B.S. in Adminstrv. Mgmt., Clemson U., 1973; postgrad. Sch. Banking, La. State U.,

1979—; m. Pollianne Seegars, Nov. 10, 1973; 1 dau., Carmen Moss. Asst. auditor Citizens & So. Corp., Greenville, S.C., 1973-74, regional auditor, Rock Hill, S.C., 1974; loan officer Citizens & So. Nat. Bank, Gaffney, 1974-77, asst. v.p. in charge comml. loan dept. and br. coordination, 1977—; Am. Inst. Banking instr. Limestone Coll., 1978. Bd. dirs. Cherokee County Boys Club, pres., 1976-78; bd. dirs. Cherokee County Family YMCA, 1979—; officer Cherokee County Internat. Mgmt. Council, 1979—; chpt. Cherokee County United Way, 1976-79. Mem. Am. Inst. Banking. Baptist. Clubs: Sertoma (pres. elect 1979-80, Leadership award 1977), Ducks Unltd., Gaffney Country, Cherokee Nat. Golf. Home: PO Box 913 207 Trenton St Gaffney SC 29340 Office: PO Box 580 N Limestone Gaffney SC 29340

VAUGHN, MICHAEL JEFFERY, educator, lawyer; b. Palestine, Tex., May 26, 1943; s. J.E. and Catherine W. (Wright) V.; B.A., Baylor U., 1964, J.D., 1966; LL.M., Yale, 1967; m. Martha Ballenger, July 5, 1967; children—Russ Wright, Mary Elizabeth, Sarah Eleanor, Clay Ballenger. Admitted to Tex. bar, 1966, since practiced in Waco; mem. firm Vaughn and Sullivan, 1971-74; asso. prof. law Baylor U., Waco, 1967-71; vis. prof. law South Tex. Coll. Law, Houston, 1971; chmn. bd. Lott (Tex.) State Bank, 1974-77, First State Bank, Chilton, Tex., 1974-77; chmn. bd. Consol. Bankers Life Ins. Co., Waco, pres., 1972-74; pres., chief exec. officer First Security State Bank of Cranfills Gap (Tex.), 1973-75, chmn. bd., 1976-77; chmn. exec. com., chief exec. officer Am. Bank of Waco, 1974-76; v.p. Coracorp Mortgage Services, Inc., 1977-78; prof. law South Tex. Coll. Law, Houston, 1979—. Justice of peace Anderson County (Tex.), 1964-67; mem. Henderson County Hist. Survey Com., 1968-71. Mem. Internat. Acad. Forensic Psychology (bd. govs. 1968-71), Assn. Am. Law Schs., State Bar Tex., SCV. Club: Masons. Author: History of Cayuga and Crossroads, Texas, 1967; (with William Q. de Funiak) Principles of Community Property, 2d rev. edit., 1971; contbr. articles to profl. jours. Home: 7802 Hornwood Houston TX 77036 Office: 1303 San Jacinto Houston TX 77002

VAUGHN, RUFUS MAHLON, psychiatrist; b. Ensley, Ala., Oct. 31, 1924; s. Rufus Samuel and Anna Martina (Fink) V.; A.B., Birmingham So. Coll., 1949; M.D., U. Ala., 1953; children—Stephan Andrew, Alexander. Intern, USPHS Service, San Francisco, 1953-54; resident in psychiatry Ind. U. Med. Center, 1954-56, UCLA Med. Center, 1956-57; research asso. Boston State Hosp., 1959-61; asso. prof. U. Fla., Gainesville, 1961-70; dir. Community Mental Health Center, West Palm Beach, Fla., 1970-71; dir. research and edn. South Fla. State Hosp., Hollywood, 1973-74; bur. chief Div. Mental Health Tallahassee, 1974-75; pvt. practice psychiatry, West Palm Beach, 1975—; dir. Pride, Inc., West Palm Beach, 1976—. Served with USNR, 1943-46, USPHSR, 1953—. Diplomate Am. Bd. Psychiatry and Neurology. Mem. Am. Psychiat. Assn., Am. Coll. Psychiatrists, Am. Acad. Psychiatry and Law. Home: 3218 Spruce Ave West Palm Beach FL 33407 Office: 1897 Palm Beach Lakes Blvd West Palm Beach FL 33409

VAUGHN, SILAS MAX, coll. pres.; b. Collinsville, Tex., Mar. 20, 1926; s. Robert H. and Odessa (Graham) V.; B.S. in Bus. Adminstrn., Austin Coll., 1949, M.S. in Ednl. Adminstrn., 1950; postgrad. N. Tex. State U., 1950, U. Ky., 1955; LL.D. (hon.), King Coll., 1974; m. Catherine Watts Stewart, July 30, 1953; children—Robert Stewart, Andrew Graham. Asst. prof. bus. Gordon Mil. Coll., Barnesville, Ga., 1951-52; bursar Am. U., Cairo, 1952-54; bus. mgr. Davis & Elkins Coll., 1954-56; asst. bus. mgr. Southwestern U., 1956-59; chief bus. officer St. Andrew's Presbyn. Coll., 1959-69; vice chancellor bus. affairs U. N.C., Charlotte, 1969-72; pres. Montreat-Anderson Coll., Montreat, N.C., 1972—; cons. to colls., univs.; mem. N.C. Adv. Com. on Higher Edn. Facilities. Vice pres. Cape Fear council Boy Scouts Am.; bd. dirs. Swannanoa Valley Med. Center, Montreat; div. chmn. United Fund, Community Library Bldg Fund, Montreat. Served with USMC, 1944-46. Mem. N.C. Assn. Ind. Colls. and Univs., So. Assn. Colls. and Schs., Austin Coll. Alumni Assn. (regional v.p.), Pi Gamma Mu. Clubs: Biltmore Forest Country, Rotary (dir.), Toastmasters (pres.). Office: Montreat-Anderson Coll Montreat NC 28757

VAUGHN, WILLIAM EARL, banker; b. Pleasants County, W.Va., Nov. 18, 1950; s. William Howard and Betty Jane (Shingleton) V.; student West Liberty State Coll., 1968-69, Parkersburg (W.Va.) Community Coll., 1969-72, W.Va. Grad. Sch. Banking, 1974-77, U. Wis. Sch. Banking, 1978—; m. Patsy Lee McCutcheon, Aug. 16, 1969; children—Tracy Lee, Erica Michelle. Trainee, Comml. Banking & Trust Co., Parkersburg, 1969-70; v.p. 1st Nat. Bank, St. Marys, W.Va., 1970-76; exec. v.p. ops. and investments Bank of Paden City (W.Va.), 1976—. Mem. Jaycees state dir. St. Marys area 1975, pres. 1976, chmn. bd. 1978, outstanding local pres. 1976-77, external v.p. W.Va. 1978, outstanding external programmer 1978). Mem. W.Va. Bankers Assn., Am. Bankers Assn. Club: Paden City Lions. Home: 914 Meadow Heights Paden City WV 26159 Office: Bank of Paden City 4th and Main Sts Paden City WV 26159

VAUGHN, WILLIAM PRESTON, historian; b. East Chicago, Ind., May 28, 1933; s. James Carl and Georgiana (Preston) V.; A.B., U. Mo., Columbia, 1955; M.A., Ohio State U., 1956, Ph.D., 1961; m. Virginia Lee Meyer, June 10, 1961; 1 dau., Rhonda Louise. Instr. in history U. So. Calif., 1961-62; asst. prof. history North Tex. State U., 1962-65, asso. prof., 1965-69, prof., 1969—. Served with arty. U.S. Army, 1956-57. Mem. So. Hist. Assn. (life), Orgn. Am. Historians, Tex. Assn. Coll. Tchrs., Phi Beta Kappa, Phi Alpha Theta (Manuscript Competition winner 1972), Phi Delta Kappa. Republican. Episcopalian. Clubs: Hi Noon Lion's, Masons, Shriners. Author: Schools for All: The Blacks and Public Education in the South, 1865-77, 1974; contbr. numerous articles on black edn. and polit. antimasonry to profl. jours. Home: 908 Hilton Pl Denton TX 76201 Office: History Dept North Tex State U Denton TX 76203

VÁZQUEZ, ANTONIO, lithographic blanket co. exec.; b. San Juan, P.R., Sept. 2, 1943; s. Emilio and Agripina (Febres) V.; B.S. in Chem. Engring., U. P.R., 1964; M.S., Stevens Inst. Tech., 1966; children—Rafael, Iorna Iris, Marili. Chief chemist David M Co., San Juan, P.R., 1966-70; pres. P.R. Polymer Labs., San Juan, 1970-72; prof. Interam. U., San Juan, 1970-72; pres. Litho Enterprises, Inc., Chgo., 1972—, also dir.; v.p. Coatings, Inc., San Juan, 1972—; gen. mgr. Coatings, Inc. & Co., Bayamón, P.R., 1972—, also dir. Trustee, Caribbean Center for Advanced Studies, 1973—. Mem. P.R. Mfrs. Assn., Am. Mgmt. Assn., Colegio de Ingenieros y Agrimensores de P.R. Patentee in field. Home: H23 Febles Guaynabo PR 00657 Office: 85 E Minillas Indsl Park Bayamón PR 00619

VAZQUEZ, CESAR DAVID, guidance counselor; b. Mayaguez, P.R., Aug. 10, 1949; s. Cesar Noel and Virginia (Pietri) V.; A.B. in Psychology, U. P.R., 1971, M.Ed. in Guidance, 1973. Bilingual tchr., N.Y.C., 1971-72, 73-74, 75-76, 77—; sub dir. Consortium for Bilingual Counselor Edn., Cath. U., Ponce, P.R., 1974-75, dir. Consortium for Continued Edn. for Guidance Counselors and Sch. Adminstrs., 1976. Consortium for Bilingual Counselor Edn. grantee, 1972-73. Mem. Am., P.R. personnel and guidance assns., Am. Coll. Personnel Assn., Nat. Vocat. Guidance Assn., Nat. Cath. Guidance Conf., Am. Assn. Higher Edn., Phi Delta Kappa (treas., 1976-77). Home: 1PO Box 201 Sabana Grande PR 00747

VAZQUEZ, SALVADOR, labor relations exec.; b. Mayaguez, P.R., Jan. 28, 1915; s. Jose A. and Marta (Vargas) V.; B.S.A., Coll. of Agri. and Mech. Arts, 1941; m. Blanca Balaguer, Mar. 28, 1942; children—Awilda, Salvador. Tech. advisor Ministry of Edn., Colombia, 1949-50; supt. vocat. edn. Dept. Edn., San Juan, P.R., 1951-53; adminstr. norms and standards Dept. of Labor, Ponce, P.R., 1953-60; gen. adminstr. Seafarers Internat. Union, AFL-CIO, San Juan, 1960-61; mediator labor disputes Dept. of Labor, Whole Island, P.R., 1961-66; personnel dir. Indsl. Siderurgica, Bayamon, P.R., 1966—, Auxilio Mutuo Hosp., Hato Rey, P.R.; tchr. vocat. agri. Certified master tchr. of vocat. edn., 1951; labor relations practitioner. Mem. Am. Soc. Personnel Adminstrn. in P.R. (founder), P.R. Coll. of Agronomists Alumni Assn. of Coll. of Agr. and Mech. Arts, Hotel Industries in Antigua (mem. inquiry com., 1964). Republican. Roman Catholic. Clubs: Pan Am Shooting, Masons. Contbr. article in field. Home: 1701 Diamel St Urban San Francisco Rio Piedras PR 00927

VAZQUEZ-RODRIGUEZ, CARLOS DANIEL, clin. psychologist; b. Cayey, P.R., June 11, 1925; s. Abraham Vazquez Arguinzoni and Rosa Rodríguez Díaz; B.A., U. P.R., 1951; licentiate clin. psychology U. Barcelona (Spain), 1954; diploma indsl. psychology Instituto Indsl. Psicotécnico, Diputación Provincial, Barcelona, Spain, 1955; M.A., Columbia U., 1957; postgrad. Fordham U., 1958; Ph.D., Caribbean Center Advance Studies, Santurce, P.R., 1974; m. Adelaida Carrero Quiñones, Apr. 18, 1957; children—Carlos Daniel, Mirza Morilda, Zaira Namir. Staff psychologist Office Services to Handicapped, Div. Public Welfare, Dept. Health P.R., San Juan, 1955-59; clin. psychologist III, coordinator mental health services So. region, Ponce, P.R., 1959-64; selection officer Peace Corps, Cath. U. P.R., Ponce, 1960-64; prof. psychology dept. psychology Coll. Social Scis., U. P.R., Rio Piedras, 1965—, prof. clin. psychology and group dynamics dept. psychiatry Sch. Medicine, 1965—; cons., staff clin. psychologist Instn. Mentally Retardate, Instituto Psicopedagogico de P.R., Bayamon, 1965-72; staff clin. psychologist Community Mental Health, Children Clinic, Rio Piedras State Psychiat. Hosp., Dept. Health, 1965-71; cons. Commonwealth P.R., Office Personnel, 1970-75; dir. tng. program dept. psychiatry Sch. Medicine U. P.R., 1970-73; cons. Nat. Tng. Labs., Washington, 1966-75; dir. psychol. services Secretariat Mental Health, Dept. Health P.R., 1972-74, dir. human resources and prevention unit, 1974-79; prof. community psychiatry dept. psychiatry Sch. Medicine, U. P.R., 1974—; cons. Dept. Police, Office Supt., Govt. P.R., 1974-75; prof. psychopathology Caribbean Center Advance Studies, Santurce, 1974—, prof. psychotherapy, 1974—; planner, coordinator, cons. Div. Extensión, U. P.R., 1975—; mem. com. ethics Research Projects with Human Subjects, Dept. Health P.R., 1974-76, Cath. U., Ponce, P.R., 1974—; mem. steering com. continuing edn. program mental health professionals U. P.R., Rio Piedras, 1976—; cons. mental health com. San Juan Municipal, Dept. Health, Office Dir. Health Services, San Juan, P.R., 1976—; cons., trainer psychology of orgn. Bur. Budget, Gov's. Office, San Juan, 1979, Sec. Transp. and Public Works, San Juan, 1979; cons., adv. Dept. Health and Adminstrn Health Services and Facilities, Govt. P.R., 1979; pvt. practice psychotherapy, San Juan, Ponce, P.R., 1974—. Served with U.S. Army, 1943-46. Mem. Am. Psychol. Assn., Am. Acad. Psychotherapy, Assn. Mental Retardation, AAAS, P.R. Assn. Psychologists in Public Service (pres.), P.R. Psychol. Assn. (past v.p.), P.R. Public Health Assn., Caribbean Center Advance Studies Assn. Ex-Alumnae (pres.). Roman Catholic. Club: Exchange. Home: 2024 Bécquer St El Señorial Rio Piedras PR 00926 Office: Suite 404-A Las Américas Profl Bldg 400 Domenech Ave Hato Rey PR 00919

VAZQUEZ-RUIZ, FRANCISCO, psychologist, educator; b. Caguas, P.R., Nov. 6, 1942; s. Manuel and Dolores (Ruiz-Rivera) Vazquez-Daumont; B.A. in Psychology cum laude, U. P.R., 1964, M.A. in Psychology magna cum laude, 1967; Ph.D., Union Grad. Sch., 1976; m. Nereida Gonzalez, Dec. 22, 1967; children—Francisco, Juan Carlos, Fernando Luis. Psychologist State Psychiatric Hosp., San Juan, P.R., 1965-67; instr., psychology U. P.R., 1967-72, asst. prof., 1972-77, asso. prof., 1977—, research asso., 1969-71, dean studies, 1969-71; cons. P.R. Police Dept., 1971-77; asso. G. Cirino Gerena and Assos., Rio Piedras, P.R., 1975—; dir. Test Devel. Corp. Mem. Am., P.R. psychol. assns. Jehovah Witness. Author: The Effects of Promising and Reinforcing on an Operant Response under Specific and non Specific Instructions, 1962; Verbal Aptitude Test for Policemen, 1972; a Job Analysis of the P.R. Police, 1973; A Psychology Based on the Bible, 1976. Home: 2100 Antioquia St Rio Piedras PR 00927 Office: Dept Psychology Univ PR Rio Piedras PR 00931

VEAUDRY, WALLACE FRANCIS, hosp. adminstr.; b. Attleboro, Mass., Dec. 9, 1924; s. Edward Leon and Viola (Nickerson) V.; B.S., U.S. Mil. Acad., 1947; M.S. in Psychology, Tulane U., 1961; M.Ed., Ga. State U., 1974-76; student U.S. Army War Coll., 1966-67, Dept. State Fgn. Service Inst., 1970; m. Pauline Riley, Apr. 2, 1948; children—Paula Dean, Patricia May Veaudry Wells. Commd. 2d. lt. U.S. Army, 1947, advanced through grades to col., 1968; comdr. of brigade, 1968-69; mem. faculty U.S. Army War Coll., 1969-71; sr. province adviser Vietnam, 1972-73; dir. U.S. Army Assessment Center, 1973-74; asst. comdr. The Inf. Center, Ft. Benning, Ga., 1974-77, ret., 1977; dir. outpatient dept. The Med. Center, Columbus, Ga., 1977-78, dir. gen. services and clinics, 1978—. Bd. dirs., chmn. combined fed. campaign United Way, 1974-77. Decorated Legion of Merit with 2 oak leaf clusters, Bronze Star with V for Valor, Mertorious Service medal with oak leaf cluster, Army Commendation Ribbon with oak leaf cluster, Air medal; recipient plaque and honor certificate Freedoms Found., 1967, 70. Mem. Am. Hosp. Assn., Mil. Order World Wars, Assn. U.S. Army (v.p. local chpt. 1977—), Ret. Officers Assn., Four Chaplains Legion of Honor, Tulane Alumni Assn., U.S. Mil. Acad. Alumni Assn. Club: Rotary. Home: 3141 Shire Hill Ln Columbus GA 31904

VEAZEY, JOHN HOBSON, physician; b. Van Alstyne, Tex., June 27, 1901; s. James and Malta Augusta (Blassingame) V.; student Austin Coll., 1918-22; M.D., U. Tex., 1926; m. Elizabeth May Chandler, Mar. 14, 1935; children—Samuel James. Intern Sherman (Tex.) Hosp., 1926-28; pvt. practice medicine, Madill, Okla., 1929-35, Ardmore, Okla., 1935—; co-founder Med. Arts Clinic, Ardmore, Okla., 1952—; pvt. practice internal medicine, Ardmore, 1957—; chief staff Meml. Hosp., So. Okla., 1958—, chmn. dept. Internal Medicine, 1973; mem. staff Ardmore (Okla.) Hosp.; pres. Med. Arts Bldg. Co. Ardmore, Med. Arts Clinic of Ardmore. Co-chmn. profl. div. United Fund, 1969. Mem. Am. (Physician's Recognition award 1976, 79), Okla. State (council 1944-56) med. assns., Carter-Love-Marshall Med. Soc. (pres. 1955), Ardmore C. of C. (dir., v.p.), Am. Soc. Internal Medicine. Presbyn. (trustee). Mason. Home: 2 Overland Route Ardmore OK 73401 Office: 921 14th St NW Ardmore OK 73401

VEDELLI, JOEL, educator; b. Engelwood, N.J., Apr. 26, 1947; s. Joseph Anthony and Helen (Loshe) V.; B.S., Eastern Ky. U., 1969, M.A., 1973, Ed.S., 1974; Ed.D., U. Va., 1980; m. Marcie Sissman, Dec. 23, 1969; children—Jonathan, Jodi. Tchr. elem. phys. edn., Paterson, N.J., 1969-72; grad. teaching asst. Eastern Ky. U., Richmond, 1972-74; asso. prof., coordinator undergrad. phys. edn. James Madison U., Harrisonburg, Va., 1974—. Served with U.S. Army, 1969-71. Recipient Scholarship Key award, 1976; Va. faculty fellow, 1978. Mem. AAHPER, AAUP, Va. Assn. Health, Phys. Edn. and Recreation, Phi Epsilon Kappa. Contbr. articles to profl. jours. Home: 581 N Blueridge Dr Harrisonburg VA 22801 Office: 304 Godwin Hall James Madison U Harrisonburg VA 22801

VEGLIANTE, FRANCIS EDWARD, JR., computer co. exec.; b. New Haven, Sept. 8, 1944; s. Francis Edward and Marguerite Eleanor (Bruno) V.; M.B.A., U. Tampa, 1971; m. Stella Eve Wacelitz, June 3, 1968; children—Francis Edward III, Eve. Br. mgr. Olivetti Corp., N.Y.C., 1971-75; br. mgr. Burroughs Corp., Tampa, 1975-77; Southeast regional mgr. Microdata Corp., Tampa, 1977-79; pres. Message Center Internat., 1979—; with Mini-Computer Systems, Inc., 1979—. Mem. Am. Mgmt. Assn., Computer Assn., Tampa Jaycees., Delta Sigma Pi. Home: 13801 Supreme Pl Tampa FL 33612 Office: PO Box 22643 Tampa FL 33622

VEITCH, DOUGLAS STUART, army officer; b. Fargo, N.D., Apr. 15, 1943; s. Hope Douglas Stuart and Myrtle Jenne (Peterson) V.; B.A. in Math., N.D. State U., 1968; grad. command and Gen. Staff Coll., 1978; M. Urban Planning, Tex. A. and M. U., 1979; m. Barbara Louise Hongess, July 1, 1963; 1 son, Douglas Stuart. Commd. 2d lt. U.S. Army, 1968, advanced through grades to maj., 1979; with 2d Bn. Airborne, 508th Inf., Ft. Bragg, N.C., 1968-69; comdr. 82d Pathfinder Detachment, Ft. Bragg, 1969; aero rifle platoon comdr. Troop D 4th Cavalry, Rep. of Vietnam, 1969; with 1st Bn. Airborne, 509th Inf., West Germany, 1970; comdr. D Co. Airborne, 708th Maintenance Bn., West Germany, 1970-72, 8th S-T Bn., West Germany, 1972-74; div. ammunition officer 8th Inf. Div., West Germany, 1974-75; asst. prof. mil. sci. Tex. A. and M. U., College Station, 1976—. Served with USMC, 1961-64. Decorated Bronze Star with V Device, Army Commendation medal, Air medal, Purple Heart. Mem. Assn. U.S. Army, Am. Def. Preparedness Assn., Nat. Rifle Assn., Am. Inst. Planners, Assn. Student Planners, VFW. Republican. Unitarian. Home: 3602 Windridge Bryan TX 77801 Office: Dept of Military Science Texas A and M University College Station TX 77893

VELASCO, RALPH ESTEBAN, JR., food co. exec.; b. San Antonio, June 12, 1926; s. Ralph Esteban and Maria (Gonzalez) V.; grad. U.S. Mcht. Marine Acad., 1946; student U. Tex., 1947-50; m. Barbara J. Zizelman, Dec. 4, 1953; children—Steven, David. With Amigos Food Co., Inc., San Antonio, 1950—, sales rep., 1950-66, v.p., 1966-67, pres., 1967—. Bd. dirs. N.W. YMCA, San Antonio, 1964-66; co-founder, v.p. Tex. Pepper Improvement Found., 1971; adv. council U. Tex. Coll. Bus. Adminstrn. Found., 1978—. Recipient award SBA, 1976; Disting. Alumnus award Coll. Bus. Adminstrn., U. Tex. Mem. Nat. Canners Assn., Tex. Food Processors (v.p. 1976-79, pres. 1979—), Inst. Food Technologists (chmn. Alamo chpt. 1976—), Delta Sigma Pi, Pi Kappa Alpha. Home: Route 4 Box 4116 Boerne TX 78006 Office: 4535 W Commerce St San Antonio TX 78237

VELKER, GLEN GEORGE, radio sta. exec.; b. Ann Arbor, Mich., Sept. 12, 1938; s. Henry George and Anne Irma (Saltz) V.; B.A., U. Mich., 1962; m. Shirley Ann Black, June 8, 1962; children—Stacey, Randy, Daniel, Benjamin. Operations mgr. Sta. WOIA-FM, WOIB, Ann Arbor, 1967-69; dir. Elkins Inst., Miami Beach, Fla., 1969-72; mgr. Sta. WMCU-FM, Miami, 1972—. Served with U.S. Army, 1962-63. Mem. Nat. Religious Broadcasters (pres. Southeast chpt. 1978-80). Evangelical. Office: 2300 NW 135th St Miami FL 33167

VELLER, MARGARET PAXTON, physician; b. Beaver Dam, Ky., Dec. 14, 1925; d. Darrell K. and Gladys (Myers) Veller; B.A., Vanderbilt U., 1947, M.D., 1950. Intern, resident Vanderbilt U. Hosp., Nashville, 1950-54; pvt. practice, 1954—. Mem. Am., Miss. (com. maternal and child welfare 1956-73) med. assns., Homochitto Valley Med. Soc., Natchez Assn. of Commerce, Miss. Obstet. and Gynecol. Soc., Phi Beta Kappa, Alpha Omega Alpha. Baptist. Club: Pilgrimage Garden. Home: 28 S Circle Dr Natchez MS 39120 Office: Natchez Med Clinic 49 Sgt S Prentiss Dr Natchez MS 39120

VELTRI, ROBERT WILLIAM, microbiologist; b. McKeesport, Pa., Dec. 1, 1941; s. Anthony and Desdemona V.; A.B. in Biology, Youngstown U., 1963; M.S., Ph.D., W.Va. State U., 1968; m. Suzanne Jones, Apr. 15, 1961; children—Anthony Joseph, Katherine Marie (dec.). Asst. prof., dir. otolaryngic research U. W.Va., Morgantown, 1968-72, asso. prof., 1972-76, prof. surgery and microbiology, 1976—. Named Outstanding Teacher, W.Va. U., 1976. Mem. Am. Assn. Immunologists, Soc. Exptl. Biologists, Am. Assn. Cancer Research, Am. Soc. for Microbiology, Am. Acad. Ophthalmology and Otolaryngology (award of merit 1978), Am., English socs. for infectious diseases. Contbr. articles to profl. jours. Address: Route 4 Box 500-1 Morgantown WV 26506

VENABLE, EUGENE GEORGE, historian; b. Washington, Mar. 15, 1945; s. James Carey and Marie Louise (DeVouges) V.; B.A., U. N.Mex., 1967, M.A., 1972; postgrad. Tex. A&M U., 1977—. Grad. teaching asst., dept. history U. N.Mex., Albuquerque, 1968-69; chief historian Hdqrs. U.S. Army Health Services Command, Ft. Sam Houston, Tex., 1975—; hist. cons. U.S. Army Med. Mus. Served to capt. USAF, 1969-75. Mem. Am. Hist. Assn., Orgn. Am. Historians, Am. Mil. Inst., Res. Officers Assn., Adult Edn. Assn. U.S., Pi Alpha Theta. Club: Ft. Sam Houston Officer's. Home: 9614 Nona Kay Dr San Antonio TX 78217 Office: Hdqrs US Army Health Services Command Hist Office Fort Sam Houston TX 78234

VENABLE, JAMES HEISKELL, physician; b. Wichita Falls, Tex., Mar. 6, 1930; s. Douglas Randolph and Esther (Lewis) V.; A.B., Mercer U., 1951; M.D., Tulane U., 1955; m. Martha Elizabeth Bush, Oct. 2, 1955; children—Elizabeth Anne, Douglas Randolph, Katherine Louise. Intern, Charity Hosp., New Orleans, 1955-56; resident in gen. practice H.P. Long Hosp., Pineville, La., 1956-57; gen. practice medicine, Columbus, Ga., 1957-59; resident in obstetrics and gynecology Tulane/Charity Hosp., New Orleans, 1959-62; practice medicine specializing in obstetrics and gynecology, Columbus, Ga., 1962—; mem. staff St. Francis Hosp., Columbus, chief staff, 1975-78; asso. prof. Emory U. Med. Sch., 1970—. Diplomate Am. Bd. Obstetrics and Gynecology. Mem. South Atlantic Assn. Obstetricians and Gynecologists, Continental Gynecol. Soc., Am. Coll. Obstetricians and Gynecologists, AMA, Ga. Obstetrics and Gynecology Soc., Ga. Surg. Soc., Med. Assn. Ga. Republican. Presbyterian (deacon). Home: 2912 Wingfield Dr Columbus GA 31906 Office: 104 Physicians Bldg Columbus GA 31901

VENABLE, JOSEPHINE DOTT (JO DOT), nurse; b. Pulaski County, Va., May 31, 1934; d. Effort Wayne and Opal Ola (Phillips) Akers; diploma Pulaski Hosp. Sch. Nursing, 1955; m. Wilburn Eugene Venable, Aug. 18, 1952; 1 son, Joseph Eugene. Staff nurse Pulaski (Va.) Hosp., 1955-59; occupational health nurse Pulaski (Va.) Furniture Corp., 1960-69; nursing supr. Pulaski (Va.) Gen. Hosp., 1969-73; asst. dir. nursing services Pulaski (Va.) Community Hosp., 1973—; adj. faculty New River Community Coll., Dublin, Va., 1979—. Recipient Dr. Thomas F. Frist Humanitarian award, 1977. Home: 1222 Newbern Rd Pulaski VA 24301 Office: 2400 Lee Hwy Pulaski VA 24301

VENDITTO, JAMES JOSEPH, engr.; b. Dobbs Ferry, N.Y., Nov. 13, 1951; s. Vincenzio Rocco and Maria Nichola (Cassetti) V.; B.S.Ch.E., U. Okla., 1973; m. Annabelle Ruth Carson, Dec. 26, 1972; children—Vincent James, Joseph Ryan. Engr.-in-tng., Victoria, Tex.,

1973-74; field engr. Halliburton Services, Alice, Tex., 1974-75, dist. engr., Mission, Tex., 1975-77, regional service sales engr., New Orleans, 1977-80, asst. div. engr., Corpus Christi, Tex., 1980—; cons. in field. Active United Way. Registered profl. engr., Tex. Mem. Am. Inst. Chem. Engrs., Soc. Petroleum Engrs., AIME, Am. Petroleum Inst., Internat. Platform Assn., Nat. Soc. Profl. Engrs., Tex. Soc. Profl. Engrs. Republican. Roman Catholic. Contbr. article to jour. Researcher chem. stimulation S. Tex. sandstones, devel. cementing procedures to prevent gas leakage in hot, geopressured formations; developed procedures for density controlled fracturing technique. Home: 123 Seco St Portland TX 78374 Office: 1220 Bank and Trust Tower Corpus Christi TX 78477

VENKATESH, ESWARAHALLI SUNDARARAJAN, metallurgist, petroleum engr.; b. Bangalore, India, Jan. 30, 1949; came to U.S., 1971; s. Eswarahalli R. Sundararajan and K.R. Lokamata; B.Sc., Bangalore U., 1969; B.E., Indian Inst. of Sci., India, 1971; M.S., Brown U., 1973, U. Okla., 1980; Ph.D., N.Mex. Inst. Mining and Tech., 1977; m. Vijaya H. Kasturirangaiyengar, Apr. 22, 1977. Teaching fellow Cornell U., Ithaca, N.Y., 1972-73; research asst. div. engring. Brown U., Providence, R.I., 1971-74, N.Mex. Tech., Socorro, 1974-77; research fellow U. Rochester, 1977-78; teaching asso. dept. petroleum engring. U. Okla., Norman, 1978—; petroleum engr. Tex. Pacific Oil Co., Inc., Abilene, Tex., summer, 1979; hon. cons. Metals and Materials Assos., Bangalore, India, 1977. Nat. Merit scholar, 1965-69. Mem. Am. Soc. Metals (Best Speaker award 1977), Soc. Petroleum Engrs., Metall. Soc. of I.I.Sc., India, Electron Microscopy Soc. Am., Alpha Sigma Mu, Sigma Xi. Hindu. Contbr. articles on metallurgy to tech. jours. Home: 604 Lindsey St Norman OK 73069 Office: Dept Petroleum Engring Felgar Hall Univ Oklahoma Norman OK 73019

VENSEL, VIRGINIA MARJORIE, chem. corp. exec.; b. Wakefield, Va., Oct. 28, 1925; d. Abram Joseph and Frances Cora (Walker) Burkett; student George Washington U., 1943-45, Marietta Coll., 1964-65; m. Robert Newton Vensel, Apr. 27, 1945; children—Robert Newton, Kenneth Bruce, Sheila Kay, Raymond Joseph, Jenifer Sue. Mgr. loan dept. Parkersburg Nat. Bank (W.Va.), 1953-58; with Borg-Warner Corp., Parkersburg, 1958—, credit mgr., 1965-68, gen. credit mgr., 1968—; coordinating com. mem. Corporate Internat. Funds Mgmt., 1977—. Sec.-treas. PTA, 1956-60; treas. Woodmar Employees Activities Club, 1961-62; active YWCA. Mem. Nat. Assn. Credit Mgmt., Nat. Chem. Credit Assn. Republican. Methodist. Club: Ladies Oriental Shrine. Mem. advisory panel Chem. Week Mgmt., 1976-78. Home: 1604 7th St Parkersburg WV 26101 Office: Borg-Warner Chems Internat Center Parkersburg WV 26101

VENTURINO, ANNE KING, educator; b. Blacksburg, Va., Apr. 13, 1941; d. Edward Oakley and Margaret (Brice) King; B.A. in English, Madison Coll., Harrisonburg, Va., 1962; M.Ed. in Supervision, U. Richmond, Va., 1975; m. Adam Ernest Venturino; children—Lee Anne, Amy Susan. English tchr. Henrico (Va.) County Schs., 1962-73, chmn. English dept. J.R. Tucker High Sch., 1973-75, coordinator Henrico County high Sch. English, 1975—; instr. effective teaching. Vol. Heart Fund; co-dir. Camp Gwynn. Mem. Va. Assn. Tchrs. English (treas. dist. chpt.) Va. Conf. English Educators (sec.), Assn. Supervision and Curriculum Devel., West End Cultural Soc., Nat. Council Tchrs. English, Delta Kappa Gamma. Home: 9305 Lyndonway Dr Richmond VA 23229 Office: PO Box 40 Highland Springs VA 23075

VERBECK, RONALD JOSEPH, petroleum co. exec.; b. Butte Mont., Mar. 19, 1948; s. Andrew Frank and Blanche May (Williams) V.; B.S., Mont. Tech. Coll., 1970; m. Billie Kay Landes, Sept. 29, 1973. Petroleum engr. Amoco Prodn. Co., Powell, Wyo., 1970-73; drilling engr. Amoco Internat. Oil Co., Lafayette, La., 1973-74; ops. mgr. Buttes Gas & Oil Co., United Arab Emirates, 1974-76; div. engr. Buttes Resources Co., Houston, 1976-78; ops. mgr. Dernick Resources, Inc., Houston, 1978—. Mem. Soc. Petroleum Engrs. Republican. Home: 12722 Scouts Lane Cypress TX 77429 Office: Dernick Resources Inc 12600 Northborough Dr Suite 200 Houston TX 77067

VERCHOW, CARY MARK, food mfg. co. exec.; b. Bklyn., Aug. 18, 1941; s. Philip and Edna V.; B.Chem. Engring., City U. N.Y., 1964, postgrad., 1968-72; children—Scott, Jennifer. Exptl. engr. Pratt & Whitney Aircraft Co., West Palm Beach, Fla., 1964-66; project engr. Thiokol Chem. Corp., Denville, N.J., 1966-67; project engr. Gulf Degremont Co., Liberty Corner, N.J., 1967-69, proj. mgr., 1969-73; mgr. engring. Belco Pollution Control Corp., Fairfield, N.J., 1973-74; mgr. project mgmt. Nichols Engring. Co., Belle Mead, N.J., 1974-77; tech. mgr. environ. systems Frito-Lay Inc., Dallas, 1977-79, mgr. engring. support, Irving, Tex., 1979—. Mem. Am. Mgmt. Assn., Assn. Purchasing Mgmt., Phi Lambda Delta (pres. chpt. 1963-64). Office: Frito-Lay Inc PO Box 2231 Irving TX 75061

VERDIER, FAITH IRENE, educator; b. St. Louis, June 24, 1924; d. Albert and Oneta (Russell) Cagle; B.S. in Spl. Edn., U. Ark., Fayetteville, 1964, M.S. in Elementary Edn., 1971; m. James C. Verdier; children—Sally Cox, Oneta Winkler, John, Mary. Tchr. Benton (Ark.) Pub. Schs., 1961-66; tchr. hearing impaired Little Rock Pub. Schs., 1971—; cons. Ark. Coalition for Handicapped; reader Ark. Dept. Publs. for Hearing Impaired. Internat. Parents Orgn. Certified in elementary edn. Secondary edn., tchr. deaf, Ark. Home: 10712 Chicaf Rd Mabelvale AR

VEREEN, WILLIAM JEROME, uniform mfg. co. exec.; b. Moultrie, Ga., Sept. 7, 1940; s. William Coachman and Mary Elizabeth (Bunn) V.; student Episcopal High Sch.-Va., 1954-57; grad. Culver Mil. Acad., 1959; B.S. in Indsl. Mgmt., Ga. Inst. Tech., 1963; m. Lula Evelyn King, June 9, 1963; children—Elizabeth King, William Coachman. Engr. Riverside Mfg. Co., Moultrie, Ga., 1967-70, v.p., 1970-73, exec. v.p., 1973-77, pres., 1977—, also dir.; v.p., dir. Moultrie Cotton Mills, 1969—; v.p., dir. Riverside Industries, Inc., Moultrie, 1973-77, pres., 1977—; pres., dir. Riverside Uniform Rentals, Inc., Moultrie, 1971—; pres. Riverside Mfg. Co. (Ireland) Ltd., 1977—, Riverside Mfg. Co. (Germany) GmbH, 1979—. Bd. dirs. Moultrie-Colquitt County (Ga.) Devel. Authority, 1973—, Moultrie-Colquitt County United Givers, Moultrie YMCA, Colquitt County Cancer Soc.; trustee Community Welfare Assn., Moultrie, Pineland Sch., Moultrie, Leadership Ga. Served to capt. USMC, 1963-67. Decorated Bronze Star, Purple Heart. Mem. Am. Apparel Mfrs. Assn., Young Pres.'s Orgn. (Rebel chpt.), Nat. Assn. Uniform Mfrs., Sigma Alpha Epsilon. Presbyn. (chmn. bd. deacons). Elk, Kiwanian. Home: 21 Dogwood Circle Moultrie GA 31768 Office: PO Box 460 Moultrie GA 31768

VERGNE-MARINI, PEDRO JUAN, nephrologist; b. Mayaquez, P.R., July 29, 1942; s. Pedro J. and Olga M. (de Vergne) Vergne-Roig; B.S. in Chemistry, U. P.R., 1964; M.D., U. Md., 1968; m. Olga Morell, Sept. 1, 1968; children—Pedro Juan, Francisco Javier. Intern, U. P.R. Sch. Medicine, San Juan, 1968-69, resident in internal medicine, 1969-71, clin. instr., 1971-73, NIH fellow in cardiology, 1971-73; NIH fellow in nephrology U. Tex. Southwestern Med. Sch., 1973-75, chief clin. research in nephrology, 1975—, asst. prof. internal medicine, 1977—, clin. prof. medicine, 1977—; practice medicine specializing in nephrology, Dallas; mem. staff Parkland Meml., Meth., St. Paul, Presbyn. hosps., Baylor U. Med. Center; med. dir. Southwestern Dialysis Center and B.M.A. of P.R., 1979. Fellow Am. Coll. Physicians, Am. Coll. Angiology, Am. Coll. Cardiology; mem. Am. Soc. Nephrology. Roman Catholic. Contbr. articles in field to med. jours. Home: 4315 Mill Creek Rd Dallas TX 75234 Office: 1525 W Mockingbird St Suite 317 Dallas TX 75235

VERKAUF, BARRY STEPHEN, physician; b. Tampa, Fla., Dec. 28, 1930; s. Oscar and Rose V.; student Emory U., 1961; M.D., Tulane U., 1965; m. Arline Laviage, Aug. 22, 1964; children—Stefanie, Leslie. Resident in ob-gyn Johns Hopkins Hosp., Balt., 1966-72; asst. chief of service Balt. City Hosp., 1972; asst. prof. ob-gyn, dir. div. reproductive endocrinology U. South Fla. Coll. Medicine, Tampa, 1974-76, asso. prof. ob-gyn, dir. reproductive endocrinology, 1976—; practice medicine, specializing in ob-gyn, reproductive endocrinology and infertility, Tampa, 1974—. Served to maj., M.C., U.S. Army, 1972-74. Diplomate Am. Bd. Ob-Gyn. Mem. AMA, Fla. Med. Assn., Johns Hopkins Med. and Surg. Soc., Fla. Ob-Gyn Soc., Pacific Coast Fertility Soc., Am. Fertility Soc., Am. Coll. Obstetricians and Gynecologists. Guest editor Collected Letters of Ob-Gyn, 1975—. Home: 4922 W Bay Way Dr Tampa FL 33609 Office: 2708 Azeele St Tampa FL 33619

VERKLER, BILLY DUAN, educator; b. Black Rock, Ark., Sept. 6, 1929; s. Jewel Thomas and Sylvia Loraine (Thomas) V.; B.S., Ark. State Coll., 1951; M.S., Mich. State U., 1955; Ph.D., Miss. State U., 1970; m. Billie Ruth Krummel, Mar. 27, 1958; children—Melinda, Wenoka. Work supr. State Prison So. Mich., Jackson, 1954; asst. prof. sociology Harding Coll., Searcy, Ark., 1957-68; prof. sociology Harding U., Searcy, 1970—; social work cons. Served with U.S. Army, 1951-53; Korea. Title I grantee, 1976-77. Mem. Am. Sociol. Assn., So. Sociol. Soc., Southwestern Sociol. Assn., Ark. Sociol. Assn. Mem. Ch. of Christ. Club: Civitan. Home: Box 522 Rt 2 Searcy AR 72143 Office: Box 656 Harding U Searcy AR 72143

VERNON, FRANCES EUNICE, health care exec.; b. Syracuse, N.Y., June 16, 1944; d. Edgar Willis and Josephine Mary Darlington; B.A., SUNY, Buffalo, 1962; M.B.A., Baylor U., 1978; m. Ivan Reed Vernon, Dec. 23, 1967; children—Nancy Kay, Cynthia Grace, Joan. Speech pathologist Onondaga County Bd. Coop. Ednl. Sers., Syracuse, 1966-67, Taylor (Mich.) Sch. Dist., 1968-69, Streetsboro (Ohio) Sch. Dist., 1970-71; adminstr. Childrens Guidance Center, Meth. Home, Waco, Tex., 1979—. Mem. Southwestern Mktg. Assn., Beta Gamma Sigma, Sigma Iota Epsilon. Home: 8920 Raven Dr Waco TX 76710 Office: 1111 Herring Ave Waco TX 76708

VERNON, HARRY ROWE, food co. exec.; b. Milw., Nov. 7, 1915; s. Harry Arthur and Ella Celeste (Rowe) V.; B.S. in Organic Chemistry, Elmhurst (Ill.) Coll., 1939; m. Alev Watts, July 26, 1938; children—Lorel Jean, Barbara Ann, Patricia Lyn. Dir. tech. services, Swift and Co., 1939-56; with Anderson Clayton Foods, 1956—, dir. indsl. product devel., 1972-80, dir. tech. service indsl. products, Dallas, 1980—; cons. in field. Mem. ofcl. bd. Spring Valley United Methodist Ch., Dallas, 1970; pres. Prestonwood Homeowners Assn., 1969-72. Mem. Am. Soc. Bakery Engrs., Inst. Food Technologists, Am. Assn. Cereal Chemists, Am. Assn. Candy Technologists, Nat. Potato Chip Inst. (Service award 1965), Elmhurst Coll. Alumni Assn. (pres. 1942-45, Service award 1970). Republican. Club: Brookhaven Country. Author papers in field. Home: 15615 Kingscrest Circle Dallas TX 75248 Office: 3879 Churchill Way Dallas TX 75251

VERNON, SAMUEL DAVID, physician; b. Smyth County, Va., May 2, 1947; s. C.H. and Glenna (Pugh) V.; B.A. in Biology, Emory and Henry Coll., 1969; M.D., Med. Coll. Va., 1973; m. Gertrude Jelf, July 12, 1970; children—David, Neal, Anna Laura. Intern and resident in internal medicine Med. Coll. Va., Richmond, 1973-76; practice medicine specializing in internal medicine, Marion, Va., 1976—; pres. med. staff Smyth County Community Hosp. Adv. bd. Smyth County Mental Health Assn. Mem. A.C.P., Southwestern Va. Med. Soc., Smyth County Med. Soc. (sec.). Republican. Methodist. Club: Lions. Home: 115 W Cherry St Marion VA 24354 Office: Radio Hill Rd Marion VA 24354

VERNOR, JAMES LEO, oil co. exec.; b. Corpus Christi, Tex., Sept. 16, 1936; s. V. L. and Ruth I. (Pierce) V.; B.S. in Gen. Engring., Tex. A&I U., 1960; postgrad. U. Southwestern La., 1965; m. Judith Louise Watts, Dec. 16, 1961; children—James Leo, Jeffrey, Jennifer. Field engr. Pan Geo Atlas Corp., Houston, 1961-64; drilling engr. Tenneco Oil Co., Lafayette, La., 1964-69; drilling supt. Conoco North Sea, London, 1969-74; mgr. internat. production Tex. Pacific Oil Co., Inc., Dallas, 1974—, v.p. fgn. subsidiaries, 1975—. Mem. AIME, Soc. Petroleum Engrs. Republican. Methodist. Office: 1700 1 Main Pl Dallas TX 75250

VERRET, MERLIN JAMES, geologist; b. Loreauville, La., June 27, 1927; s. Louis Alphonse and Marie Louise (Bellot) V.; B.S. in Geology, U. Southwestern La., 1951; m. Betty Elaine Guillory; children—Cynthia Louise, Merlin Madison, Wavelyn Cheri, Suzanne Marie, Matthew William. Geol. draftsman Phillips Petroleum Co., 1947-48, geologist, Lafayette, La., 1951-53; geologist Tex. Gulf Producing Co., Lafayette, 1953-55, Charles H. Lawrence, Jr., Lake Charles, La., 1955-58; cons. geologist, ind. oil operator, Houston and Lake Charles, 1958-68; exec. v.p. Damson Oil Corp., 1969-73; pres. Delta Energy Resources, Inc., Lake Charles, 1973—, also dir.; cons. Chmn. benefit program St. Patrick's Hosp., 1979. Served with USMC, 1943-45. Mem. Houston Geol. Soc., Am. Assn. Petroleum Geologists, Am. Geol. Inst. Democrat. Methodist. Home: 4717 Pine Bluff Dr Lake Charles LA 70605 Office: 3002 Country Club Rd Lake Charles LA 70605

VERRY, WILLIAM ROBERT, social systems engr.; b. Portland, Oreg., July 11, 1933; s. William Richard and Maurine Houser (Braden) V.; B.S., Portland State U., 1958; B.A., Reed Coll., 1955; M.A., Fresno State U., 1960; Ph.D., Ohio State U., 1972; m. Bette Lee Ronspiess, Nov. 20, 1951 (separated Nov. 1979); children—William David, Sandra Kay, Steven Bruce, Kenneth Scott. Faculty, Redley Coll., Reedley, Calif., 1957-70; ops. research analyst U.S. Navy, China Lake, Calif., 1960-63; sr. design engr. Honeywell, Litton Industries, UNIVAC, Mpls., 1963-67; project leader Tech. Operations, Inc., Alexandria, Va., 1968-70; research asso. Ohio State U., Columbus, 1970-72; prin. staff engr. Computer Scis. Corp., Falls Church, Va., 1972-77; mem. tech. staff The MITRE Corp., McLean, Va., 1977—; cons. in field. Pres., Indian Wells United Fund, 1963; active Boy Scouts Am., 1958—, recipient Scouter's Key, 1959, Council award, 1962. Mem. Am. Inst. Indsl. Engrs., Operations Research Soc. Am., Washington Operations Research Council, Am. Def. Preparedness Assn. Christian Ch. Contbr. articles to profl. jours. Home: 2251 Pimmit Dr #1423 Falls Church VA 22043 Office: MITRE Westgate Research Park McLean VA 22101

VERSEN, GREGORY RYAN, social worker; b. Vicksburg, Miss., Dec. 22, 1942; s. Joseph Louis and Vera (Cobb) V.; B.A., Miss. Coll., Clinton, 1965; M.S.S.W., U. Tenn., Nashville, 1967; m. Susie Eugenia Patridge, Mar. 19, 1966; children—Christopher Ryan, Jill Patridge, Stephen Gregory. Child welfare worker Leflore County (Miss.) Dept. Public Welfare, 1967; asst. prof. social work Miss. U. for Women, 1972-77; asso. prof. social work James Madison U., Harrisonburg, Va., 1977—, social work program coordinator, 1977-79; nursing home cons. Deacon, 1st Baptist Ch. of Columbus, Miss., 1976; bd. dirs. Lowndes County Council Aging, 1974-76, Lowndes County Nutrition Program, 1975-77, Golden Triangle Contact Teleminsistry, 1975-77, Valley Program for Aging Services, Va., 1979. Served with M.S.C., AUS, 1968-72. Decorated Army Commendation medal; NIMH grantee, 1965-67; NSF grantee, 1979; cert. Acad. Cert. Social Workers. Mem. Nat. Assn. Social Workers, Va. Council Social Welfare, Council Social Work Edn., Social Work Educators Conf. Va. Baptist. Club: Harrisonburg Exchange (dir. 1979). Home: 1320 Star Crest Dr Harrisonburg VA 22801 Office: Dept of Sociology Anthropology and Social Work James Madison University Harrisonburg VA 22807

VES'SELLS, JAMES J., counselor, educator, former air force officer; b. Shawnee, Okla., Oct. 23, 1918; s. Edward F. and Grace G. S. Ves'sells; B.S., Sophia U., 1957; M.A. in Counseling and Guidance, Ohio State U., 1964; postgrad. Fla. State U., 1968, Auburn U., 1969, U. Ga., 1971; grad. Fla. Sch. Alcoholic Studies, 1975; doctoral candidate Nova U., 1979—; m. Pearl E. Clark, July 15, 1979. Enlisted in USAF, 1941, commd., 1943, advanced through grades to maj., 1960; bombardier, 1943, 44; nav. instr., Harlingen AFB, Tex., 1950-53; press censor, corr.'s liaison officer UN and Far East Command, 1953-58 nat. hdqrs. CAP-USAF, Washington and Houston, 1958-61; asst. dir. candidate adv. service USAF Acad., 1961-63; ret., 1963; counselor Brandon (Fla.) High Sch., 1964-65; counselor Div. Vocat. Rehab. State of Fla., 1965-75; exec. dir. The First Step of Sarasota, Inc. (Fla.), 1975-76; mgr. Siesta House, Siesta Key Beach, Fla., 1976—; cons. drug and alcohol abuse, 1970—; instr. U. Tampa (Fla.), 1972—; notary public, 1970—; public relations officer Fla. Community Services Assn., 1973; bd. dirs., mem. exec. bd. Fla. Rehab. Assn., 1973-75. Bd. dirs. Acacia Fraternity, Ohio State U., 1963-64; pres. Prof. Leaders Associated with Youth, 1970-71. Decorated Air medal with six oak leaf clusters; Croix de Guerre with palm (France); recipient Boss of Year award Southeast Region Assn. Rehab. Secs., 1975. Mem. Fla. Rehab. Assn. (Achievement award 1975, dir. 1974-78, awards chmn. 1974), Nat. Rehab. Counseling Assn., Fla. Rehab. Counseling Assn. (sec. 1970-71), Internat. Transactional Analysis Assn. Clubs: Masons, Shriners. Author: (with Samuel Angus) Careers in Space Science and Technology, 1964. Home: 2907 E Crawford St Tampa FL 33610 Office: Fla Health and Rehab Services Office Vocat Rehab 9350 Bay Plaza Blvd Tampa FL 33619

VEST, DEED LAWRENCE, univ. ofcl.; b. San Antonio, Mar. 21, 1944; s. Deed Lafayette and Martha (Lee) V.; B.A. cum laude, U. Tex., 1968, M.B.A., 1970; m. Carol Ann Hanna, Aug. 28, 1964; children—Kelly Rene, John David. Asso. auditor Trans World Airlines, Kansas City, Mo., 1970-71, auditor, 1971-72, sr. fin. analyst, 1972, div. controller, sales and services Tex. Internat. Airlines, Houston, 1972-73, dir. inflight services, 1973-74; asso. mgr. M.D. Anderson Hosp., U. Tex., Cancer Center, Houston, 1974-75, sr. asso., adminstrv. officer physicians referral service med. practice, 1976-77, managerial advisor to the exec. council, exec. retirement bd., univ. cancer found., 1976-77; mng. dir. central food service facility U. Tex., Houston, 1977—, bus. dir. Cancer Bull. Med. publ., sec., treas. to bd. dirs., and med. arts publ. found. Mem. Sigma Iota Epsilon. Home: 11126 Sageburrow St Houston TX 77089 Office: University of Texas 7777 Knight Rd Houston TX 77054

VEST, DONALD B., state ofcl.; b. Montezuma, Iowa, Jan. 18, 1915; s. Cyrus Wilson and Helen Olivia (Bone) B.; B.S., Colo. State U., 1938; diploma Pasadena Community Theatre, 1940; children by previous marriage—Patricia Jane, Margret Kris. Announcer, newscaster stas. Chgo., Denver, Colorado Springs and Cheyenne, Wyo., 1942-49; prodn. supr. Sta. WRVA-Radio, Richmond, Va., 1949-56, pub. service dir. Channel 12, 1956-68; dir. info. Va. Commn. for Visually Handicapped, Richmond, 1968—; lectr. Va. Commonwealth U., Richmond U. Bd. dirs., v.p. Va. Thanksgiving Festival, 1958-68. Mem. Am. Assn. Workers for Blind, Nat. Rehab. Assn., Richmond Public Relations Assn., Va. Soc. for Prevention Blindness. Methodist. Club: Va. Press. Home: 3107 Monument Ave Apt 3 Richmond VA 23221 Office: 3003 Parkwood Ave Richmond VA 23221

VESTER, MICHAEL ELIJAH FRANCIS, hosp. personnel adminstr.; b. Rocky Mount, N.C., Sept. 28, 1937; s. Elijah Francis and Berdie Frank (Lane) V.; B.A., U. N.C., 1959. Adminstr. asst. Lenox Hill Hosp., N.Y.C., 1967-72, supr. admissions, 1972-77; dir. admissions Rutherford Hosp., Inc., Murfreesboro, Tenn., 1977-78, personnel dir., 1978—. Mem. Am. Hosp. Assn. Hosp. Personnel Adminstrn., Tenn. Hosp. Assn., Middle Tenn. Health Care Personnel Adminstrn. Assn., Tenn. Hosp. Assn. for Health Care Personnel Adminstrn. Home: Route 1 Box 308B Pleasant View TN 37146 Office: 423 N University St Murfreesboro TN 37130

VETTER, CYRIL EDWARD, communication co. exec.; b. Donaldsonville, La., July 31, 1942; s. Bernard A. and Joel (LeBlanc) V.; B.A., La. State U., 1965, J.D., 1972; m. Donna Truman Staples, Mar. 21, 1967; children—Heather S., Gabrielle D. Admitted to La. bar, 1973; pres. Sta. WRBT-TV, Baton Rouge, 1976—; pres. Vetter Communications Co., Baton Rouge, 1976—; dir. Manhattan Dist., Inc. Served with U.S. Army, 1966-70. Decorated Bronze Star. Mem. Nat. UHF Broadcasters Assn. (founding dir., treas.), Nat. Assn. Broadcasters. Office: 5220 Essen Ln Baton Rouge LA 70808

VETTER, JOSEPH GERARD, clergyman, editor; b. Greensboro, N.C., Feb. 1, 1947; s. Raymond Edward and Regina Dolores (Murray) V.; B.A. in Philosophy, Pontifical Coll. Josephinum, 1969, M.Div., 1973. Ordained priest Roman Catholic Ch., 1973; asso. pastor St. Michael's Roman Catholic Ch., Cary, N.C., 1973-74, Immaculate Conception Cath. Ch., Durham, N.C., 1974-76; chaplain Duke U. Med. Center, Durham, N.C., 1974-76; editor N.C. Catholic, Raleigh, 1976—; communications dir. Roman Cath. Diocese of Raleigh, 1977—. Mem. N.C. Press Assn., Cath. Press Assn. of U.S. and Can. Office: North Carolina Catholic 300 Cardinal Gibbons Dr Raleigh NC 27606

VIAR, CHARLES RICHARDS, guidance counselor; b. Memphis, June 24, 1944; s. W.C., Jr. and Geneva (Curnutte) V.; student U. Chattanooga, 1962-67; B.S., U. Tenn. at Martin, 1972, M.S., 1973; postgrad. Memphis State U., 1975—; m. Julia Page Wood, June 12, 1965; children—Lee Page (dec.), Charles Richards. Tchr. English, Halls (Tenn.) High Sch., 1972-74, guidance counselor, 1974—; adj. instr. psychology Dyersburg (Tenn.) State Community Coll., 1976—; sponsor Halls Tiger newspaper; sports writer Dyersburg State Gazette, 1973-75. Vice pres. Halls Booster Club, 1974-76; sponsor for Alpha Phi Omega. Push for St. Jude Hosp., Memphis. Served with U.S. Army Intelligence, 1967-70. Certified in psychology and counseling Tenn. Dept. Edn. Mem. Am., Tenn. personnel and guidance assns., Am. Mental Health Counselors Assn., Smithsonian Soc., Tenn. Edn. Assn., Met. Soc. (sponsor), Nat. Geog. Soc., U.S., Tenn. Jaycees, Alpha Phi Omega, Sigma Chi. Methodist. Clubs: U. Tenn. Century, Halls Gates Rotary (dir.). Home: Viar Rd Halls TN 38040 Office: 800 W Tigrett St Halls TN 38040

VICAIN, LESTER EMANUEL, JR., data processing co. exec.; b. Cheyenne, Wyo., June 1, 1945; s. Lester Emanuel and Alma V.; B.S. in Chemistry, Baylor U., 1967; M.S. in Mgmt. Sci., U. Tex., Dallas, 1974; m. Sylvia Ann Toone, Dec. 13, 1969; children—Victoria Lesa, Valeria Ann. Process engr. Tex. Instruments, Dallas, 1971-74; systems analyst Hughes Tool Co., Houston, 1974-77; sr. systems analyst FMC, Houston, 1977; industry rep. Brown & Root, Houston, 1977-78, project leader, 1978—. Active mem. Nat. Tax Referendum Com.; deacon 1st Baptist Ch., Houston. Served to capt. USMCR, 1969-71; Vietnam. Mem. Assn. for Systems Mgmt. Home: 6218 Brown Bark St Houston TX 77092 Office: Brown & Root PO Box 3 Houston TX 77001

VICK, GILES WESLEY, JR., coll. adminstr.; b. Kannapolis, N.C., Jan. 7, 1918; s. Giles Wesley and Annie Elizabeth (Pitts) V.; B.A., Duke U., 1938; M.A., E. Carolina U., 1974; m. Frances Austine Cuthbertson, Jan. 30, 1949; children—Giles Wesley III, John Cuthbertson. Tchr. high sch., Harmony, N.C., 1938-39; prof. mathematics Wood Coll., Mathiston, Miss., 1939-42; commd. 2d. lt. U.S. Air Force, 1943, advanced through grades to maj., 1958; hurricane forecaster, 1949-51; forecaster SAC, 1956-61, Lakenheath, Eng., 1961-63; ret., 1963; prof. sci. Wingate (N.C.) Coll., 1963-74, dir. financial aid, 1974—. Mem. Meteorol. Soc. (certified profl.), Am. Geophys. Union, So. Assn. Student Financial Aid Adminstrs. Methodist. Lion (v.p. Wingate 1968-70). Contbr. articles to profl. publs. Home: Route 1 Box 56 Monroe NC 28110 Office: Wingate Coll Wingate NC 28174

VICK, JOHN EDWARD, pine plywood mfr.; b. Enterprise, Ala., Mar. 10, 1939; s. Frank and Carrie Lee (Palmer) V.; B.S. in Mech. Engring., Auburn U., 1962; m. Faye Aman, Jan. 20, 1970; children—Patricia, Claire, Amanda. Vice pres. plywood operations Dixon Lumber Co. Inc., Andalusia, Ala., 1969-78, also dir.-gen. mgr. Dixon Plywood div., 1970-78; partner, dir. D&G Devels. Pty. Ltd., Perth, Australian, Andalusia Broadcasting Co., 1970-77; owner, mgr. John Vick & Co., farm operation; dir. Citibanc of Andalusia. Bd. dirs. Ala. Sheriffs Boys Ranch, 1967-72, Ala. Eye-Sight Found.; mem. forestry adv. com. Auburn U., chmn. subcom. on forest products; mem. So. Forest Resource Council. Served to lt. USNR, 1962-66. Mem. Am., Ala. (past dir.), forestry assns., Forest Farmers Assn., Am., Ala., Covington County (past pres.) cattlemen's assns., Ala.-Guatemala Partner of Alliance for Progress, U.S. Naval Inst., U.S., Andalusia (past dir.) chambers commerce, Am. Philatelic Soc., Confederate Stamp Alliance, Nat. Hist. Soc., Nat., Ala. (dir., pres.) wildlife fedns., Am. Soybean Assn. Methodist (past pres. men's Club). Lion (past pres. Andalusia). Home: 511 Chapman St Andalusia AL 36420 Office: Box 369 Andalusia AL 36420

VICKERS, GEORGE MAX, food co. exec.; b. Mt. Pleasant, Tex., Mar. 26, 1940; s. George Henry and Ruth Delmar (Skipper) V.; B.S., La. Poly. U., 1962; m. Margaret Ann Barlow, June 5, 1965; children—Jeffery Owen, Elizabeth Ann, Jason Henry. Claims adjuster Liberty Mut. Ins., Little Rock, 1964-66; personnel supr. Timex Corp., Little Rock, 1966-71;personnel dir. Baptist Med. Center, Little Rock, 1971-73; div. mgr. rice processing Riceland Foods, Stottgard, Ark., 1973—. Ark., 1973—. Dep. sheriff res. Arkansas County, 1975—; chmn. Ark. County CD, 1975; dist. chmn. Grand Pacific dist. Quapan council Boy Scouts Am. Served with USCGR, 1962-70. Mem. Rice Milers Assn., Stuttgart C. of C. Baptist. Home: 2008 N Henderson Stuttgart AR 72160 Office: PO Box 927 Stuttgart AR 72160

VICKERS, JOEL ELLISON, educator; b. Durham, N.C., Feb. 5, 1939; s. Andrew Jackson and Elizabeth (Wilson) V.; A.B., U. N.C., 1960, M.P.H. (fellow), 1973, Dr.P.H., 1980; m. Jeannette Marilyn VanBoskerck, Sept. 7, 1957; children—Joseph Scott, Kenneth Wayne, Robert Daniel, Kevin Brett. Bus. mgr. W.B. Jones Alcoholic Rehab. Center, Greenville, N.C., 1969-70; asso. prof. dept. community health East Carolina U., Greenville, 1973—, asst. to vice chancellor for health affairs, 1974-75; dep. dir. Eastern Area Health Edn. Center, Greenville, 1975—; cons. N.C. Div. Mental Health, 1970-73. Mem. Farmville Arts Council, 1977—. Served with USAF, 1960-68. Decorated Commendation medal; HEW mgmt. devel. tng. grantee, 1979-80. Mem. Am. Public Health Assn., N.C. Public Health Assn., N.C. Hosp. Assn., Acad. Mgmt., Am. Soc. for Tng. and Devel., Am. Soc. Law and Medicine, Alliance for Continuing Med. Edn., Am. Edn. Assn., Greenville Area C. of C. Democrat. Baptist. Contbr. articles to profl. jours. Home: 201 Grimmersburg St Farmville NC 27828 Office: PO Box 7224 Greenville NC 27834

VICKERY, ARTHUR PERRY, book mfg. co. exec.; b. Beaumont, Tex., Mar. 20, 1941; s. Frank Leslie and Nettie Newton (Collier) V.; B.S., Lamar U., 1963; M.B.A., Ga. State U., 1975; m. Mary Anne Copenhaver, Aug. 31, 1968; children—Anne Reynolds, Arthur Perry. Systems engr. IBM Corp., Atlanta, 1967-69, mktg. rep., 1969-73; supr. mgmt. adv. services Laventhol & Horwath C.P.A.s, Atlanta, 1973-75; mgr. adminstrv. services Arcata Corp. Kingsport, Tenn., 1975—. Mem. gen. adv. bd. Tri Cities State Tech. Inst. Served with AUS, 1964-67. Decorated Bronze Star, Air medal, Purple Heart; Vietnamese Cross of Gallantry, Vietnamese Civil Action Honor medal. Mem. Greater Kingsport Area C. of C., Kingsport Symphony Orch. Assn. Republican. Methodist. Home: 553 Dogwood Dr Kingsport TN 37663 Office: PO Box 711 Kingsport TN 37660

VICKERY, CHARLES EUGENE, lawyer, state senator; b. Greenville, S.C.; s. Victor Van and Edna Freeman V.; B.S., The Citadel, 1965; J.D., U. N.C., 1969; m. Jean Marshall, June 6, 1970; children—Andrew Marshall, Mary Claire. Admitted to N.C. bar; asst. dist. N.C. 19th Jud. Dist., 1970, asst. dist. atty. N.C. 15th Jud. Dist., 1971; partner firm Winston, Coleman and Bernholz, Chapel, Hill, N.C., 1972-74; partner Vickery, Culpepper and Wolfington, Chapel Hill, 1974—; mem. N.C. State Senate, 1974—. Trustee, U. N.C. Public TV; mem. N.C. Symphony Council. Mem. Am. Bar Assn., N.C. Acad. Trial Lawyers, N.C. State Bar. Democrat. Baptist. Office: 135 E Rosemary St Chapel Hill NC 27514

VICKREY, JAMES FRANK, JR., coll. pres.; b. Montgomery, Ala., Feb. 6, 1942; s. James F. and Mildred K. (Murray) V.; A.B., Auburn U., 1964, M.A., 1965; Ph.D. in Speech Communication, Fla. State U., 1972; postgrad. Harvard Bus. Sch., 1974; 1 son, John Robert. Instr. speech and forensics Auburn (Ala.) U., 1965-68; asst. debate coach U. Ala., 1968-69; instr. bus. communication Fla. State U., Tallahassee, 1969-70, adminstrv. asst. to exec. v.p., 1970-71; asst. to pres. and dir. univ. relations U.S. Fla., Tampa, 1971-75; exec. asst. to chancellor and dir. public affairs Univ. System of Fla., Tallahassee, 1975-77; pres. U. Montevallo (Ala.), 1977—. Mem. edn. com. Fine Arts Council, Tampa, 1973-75; bd. dirs. United Way, Birmingham, Ala., 1979—; mem. Ala. Film Commn. S. Allen Edgar fellow, 1965. Mem. Am. Assn. State Colls. and Univs., Am. Council Edn., Am. Assn. Univ. Adminstrs., Ala. Assn. Coll. Adminstrs., Phi Eta Sigma, Phi Kappa Phi, Omicron Delta Kappa. Democrat. Methodist. Clubs: Rotary, Kiwanis. Contbr. articles on speech communication to scholarly jours. and movie-related materials to popular mags. Office: Calkins Hall Sta 1 U Montevallo Montevallo AL 35115

VICKREY, ROBERT EDWARD, JR., cons. civil engr.; b. Wayne County, Ky., Nov. 20, 1912; s. Robert Edward and Idell (Wade) V.; B.S., Okla. State U., 1934; postgrad. U. Dallas, 1970-71; m. Dixie Richards Green, June 5, 1971; children—Jeanie Vickrey Dalton Sutherland, Paul Edward. Prodn. engr. Sun Oil Co., Tulsa, 1934-41, gas engr., Dallas, 1942-46, prodn. supt., Carthage, Tex., 1947-49, head gas measurement dept., 1950-71; adviser to head ops. Nat. Iranian Gas Co., Tehran, 1972-74; pres. Vickrey Engring. Inc., Dallas, cons. natural gas ops. and measurement, 1974—; lectr. in field. Registered profl. engr., Tex. Mem. Am. Petroleum Inst. (Citation for Service award 1975), Instrument Soc. Am. (pres. N. Tex. sect. 1955), Soc. Petroleum Engrs., Am. Inst. M.E. (chmn. Dallas sect. 1961), Dallas Geol. Soc., Gas Processors Assn., Tex., Nat. socs. profl. engrs., N.E. Tex. Gas Measurement Assn. Mem. Ch. of Christ. Clubs: Exchange Oak Cliff (pres. 1958), Elmwood Dads Dallas (sec.-treas. 1952), Petroleum Engrs. Dallas (pres. 1960), Nomads. Contbr. articles to profl. jours. Home: 3832 Periwinkle Dr Dallas TX 75233

VIDAL-CAYRO, SERGIO, Realtor, developer, builder; b. Havana, Cuba, Dec. 15, 1928; came to U.S., 1960, naturalized, 1968; s. Joaquin and Georgina (Cayro) V.; student Havana Bus. U., 1948; C.P.A., U. Havana, 1950, spl. public relations and sales degrees, 1955, mktg. and radio surveying specialist, 1958; m. Teresa, Dec. 26, 1952; children—Sergio Carlos, Ana Cecilia. Treas., comptroller Havana (Cuba) Internat. Airport, 1952-59; dir. Cubana Airlines, owner-pres. Internat. Airport Radio, Havana, 1954-59; mktg. dir., sales mgr. Spanish news dir. sta. WFAB, Radio Miami, Fla., 1962-70; realtor, pres. Gran Realty Inc., Miami, 1970-79, pres. Gran Realty Inc. of Fla., 1970—; pres. Gran Travel Agy. Inc., Miami, 1979—; developer Portofino's Shopping Centers; pres. Metro Contractors Co. Inc., Superior Mortgage. Active Christian Commitment Found., major Miami adv. bd. for civil and polit. activities, major City of Hialeah advisor for Latin bus., Tigertail Polit. Club. Awarded key Dade County, 1972, key City of Miami, 1965, award City of Hialeah, 1969, Lincoln-Marti award, U.S. Govt., 1966. Mem. Fla. Assn. Mortgage Brokers, Miami Bd. Realtors, Coral Gables Bd. Realtors, Hialeah Bd. Realtors, Nat. Bd. Realtors, Am. Club, Fla. Builders Assn., Fedn. Am. Clubs, Latin Am. C. of C. Democrat. Roman Catholic. Clubs: Ocean Reef (Key Largo, Fla.); Standard of Greater Miami. Home: 19220 Royal Birkdale Dr Country Club of Miami Estates FL 33015 Office: 2351 W Flagler St Miami FL 33135

VIDAURRETA, LUIS EDUARDO, educator; b. Havana, Cuba, Dec. 15, 1920; came to U.S., 1966, naturalized, 1971; s. Jose Luis and Maria Caridad (Bellow du Hamel) V.; Ph.D., U. Havanna, 1944; m. Alicia S. Suarez, Dec. 27, 1943; children—Jose Luis, Alicia dela Caridad. Faculty, U. Havana, Cuba, 1944-66, prof. chemistry, until 1966; faculty La. State U., Baton Rouge, 1966—, asso. prof., 1972—. Mem. Am. Chem. Soc., Am. Ofcl. Analytical Chemists, Am. Assn. Sugar Cane Technologists, La. Acad. Scis., Sigma Xi. Roman Catholic. Club: K.C. Home: 1246 Seyburn Dr Baton Rouge LA 70808 Office: Dept Chemistry La State U 211 Choppin Hall Baton Rouge LA 70803

VIDRICK, ROBERT LOUIS, transp. ofcl.; b. Cleve., Oct. 7, 1931; s. Louis John and Julia Anne (Cernic) V.; B.A., U. Md., 1964; M.S., Shippensburg State Coll., 1973; m. Amelia E. Parrish, June 4, 1955; children—Robert Louis, Julie Ann. Commd. 2d lt. U.S. Army, 1953, advanced through grades to col., 1974; served with Transp. Corps; ret., 1977; mgr. internat. transp. Robertshaw Controls Co., Richmond, Va., 1977—. Decorated Legion of Merit (3), Bronze Star (4), Meritorious Service medal (2), Air medal (3), Army Commendation medal. Mem. Nat. Council Phys. Distbn., Traffic Club Richmond, Import/Export Club Richmond, Gideons Internat. Baptist. Contbr. articles to mags. including Distbn. Worldwide, Jour. Commerce, Traffic Mgmt., Harper Circle. Office: 1910 Byrd Ave Richmond VA 23230

VIDRINE, ARTHUR, JR., surgeon; b. New Orleans, Sept. 10, 1934; s. Arthur and Kathleen V.; B.S., La. State U., 1956, M.D., 1959; m. Beverly Joan Dodson, Aug., 1956; children—Babette Anne, Arthur, Stephen Mark, Marguerite D. Intern, Charity Hosp. of La., New Orleans, 1959-60, resident in gen. surgery, 1960-64; practice medicine specializing in surgery, Lafayette, La., 1964—; asst. clin. dir. surgery Charity Hosp. La., New Orleans, 1963-64; mem. staff Our Lady of Lourdes, Rayne Meml., Erath Meml., Lafayette Gen., Lafayette Charity hosps., clin. dir., sr. surgeon, 1964-70; sr. surgeon Lafayette Tb Sanitarium, 1964-70; clin. asso. prof. surgery La. State U. Sch. Medicine, New Orleans, 1969—; vis. lectr. Coll. Nursing, U. Southwestern La., Lafayette, 1968—; med. adviser Acadian Ambulance Service, 1970—, Acadiana Ostomy Assn., 1974—. Bd. dirs. Acad. Sacred Heart, Grand Coteau, La., 1970—, chmn., 1972-74. Recipient Pfizer award of Merit, U.S. CD Council, 1976; research fellow dept. pharmacology, summer 1957, 58. Diplomate Am. Bd. Surgery (guest examiner 1971). Fellow A.C.S. (pres. La. chpt. 1977, state chmn. com. on trauma 1970-76); mem. Surg. Assn. La. (dir. 1969-72, pres. 1975), Am. Coll. Chest Physicians, La. State (disaster med. care com. 1974—), Lafayette Parish (pres. 1974) med. socs., Southeastern Surg. Congress, La. Thoracic Soc., Am. Trauma Soc., James D. Rives Surg. Soc., Am. Cancer Soc. (dir. La. div. 1975—, med. adviser Lafayette parish unit 1970—), Delta Kappa Epsilon, Eta Sigma Phi, Alpha Epsilon Delta, Phi Eta Sigma, Nu Sigma Nu. Roman Catholic. Contbr. articles in field to med. jours. Home: 160 Twin Oaks Blvd Lafayette LA 70503 Office: 116 Hospital Dr Lafayette LA 70503

VIERA, CRISTOBAL EUGENIO, surgeon; b. Camaguey, Cuba, Sept. 6, 1941; s. Cristobal J. and Luz Marina (Garcia) V.; came to U.S., 1959, naturalized, 1966; student Candler Coll., Havana, Cuba, 1960; B.S., U. Miami, Fla., 1966, M.D., 1970; m. Estela Mendez, Jan. 23, 1965; children—Estelle Marie, Christopher. Straight surg. intern Sch. Medicine, U. Miami, 1970-71, asst. resident in surgery, 1971-72, resident, 1972-73, sr. resident, 1973-74, chief resident, 1974-75, clin. instr., 1976—; individual practice medicine specializing in gen. and vascular surgery, Miami, 1975—; staff Am., Mercy, Hialeah hosps. Co-chmn. Philharm. chpt. Interam. Found. for Endowment of Fine Arts, 1978—; bd. dirs. League Against Cancer. Diplomate Am. Bd. Surgery. Fellow A.C.S.; mem. Dade County Med. Soc., Fla. Med. Assn., So. Med. Assn., Am. Cancer Soc., Phi Chi. Republican. Roman Catholic. Clubs: Racquet of Royal Biscayne, Big Five. Home: 1421 Blue Rd Coral Gables FL 33146 Office: Mercy Profl Bldg Suite 910 3661 S Miami Ave Miami FL 33133

VIERS, JIMMY DON, acct., coal co. exec.; b. Grundy, Va., June 13, 1943; s. Charles L. and Roberta V.; student U. Richmond, 1963-65, Clinch Valley Coll., 1960-62; B.B.A., East Tenn. State U., 1980; m. Lois M. Owens, Feb. 17, 1962; children—Jimmy Don, Shane L. Acct., Va. Electric and Power Co., Richmond, 1962-63; store acct. Internat. Harvester Co., Richmond, 1963-67; acct. Flanary and Hoover, C.P.A.'s, Williamsburg, Va., 1967-69; sr. acct. Dent K. Burk Assos, C.P.A.'s, Bristol, Va., 1969-75; v.p., controller Gen. Energy Corp., Abingdon, Va., 1975-76; dir. corp. taxes United Coal Corp., Bristol, 1976—. C.P.A., Tenn. Mem. Bristol Jaycees (treas. 1972), Bristol C. of C., Am. Inst. C.P.A.'s, Tenn. Soc. C.P.A.'s. Baptist. Home: 201 Ambers Dr Bristol TN 37620 Office: PO Box 1280 Bristol VA 24201

VIGEE, KENNARD O'NEIL, chem. co. exec.; b. Crowley, La., June 7, 1940; s. Edward B. and Eva (Simon) V.; math. degree U. Southwestern La., 1965; m. JoAnn Witherspoon, Feb. 3, 1968; 1 dau., Heather Eve. Sales engr. NL Baroid Co., Lafayette, La., 1969-72, dist. ops. mgr., 1972-74, dist. mgr., 1974-77, asst. regional sales mgr., 1977—. Served with U.S. Army, 1962-63. Mem. Soc. Petroleum Engring., Am. Petroleum Inst., Nat. Skeet Shooters Assn. Democrat. Roman Catholic. Clubs: S. La. Gun, Safari. Home: 110 Shipley Dr Lafayette LA 70503 Office: PO Box 51287 Lafayette LA 70505

VIGLE, JOHN BARRY, JR., librarian; b. Chattanooga, Sept. 11, 1925; s. John Barry and Louie-Pearl (Conn) V.; B.A., U. Ky., 1949, M.S. in L.S., 1956; m. Marjorie Maye Britton, June 9, 1954; children—Gregory Owen, Sean Carl. With Ky. Insp. Bur., 1953-55; with Bklyn. Pub. Library, 1956-59; with U. Dayton, 1959-72, instr. philosophy, part-time, 1962-65, asst. dir. univ. libraries, 1965-72; dir. univ. library Xavier U., Cin., 1972-79; dir. library services Eckerd Coll., St. Petersburg, Fla., 1979—. Pres. Greater Cin. Library Consortium, 1974-75, Tampa Bay Library Consortium, 1980. Served with USNR, 1943-45. Mem. AAUP, ALA, Sports Car Club Am., Phi Kappa Tau. Asso. editor: Union List of Serials in the Libraries in the Miami Valley (1st edit.) 1968. Home: 4354 50th Terr S Saint Petersburg FL 33711 Office: Library Eckerd Coll Saint Petersburg FL 33733

VIGNESS, DAVID MARTELL, historian; b. LaFeria, Tex., Oct. 12, 1922; s. Lewis Martell and Nina (Hegge) V.; B.A., U. Tex., Austin, 1943, M.A., 1948, Ph.D., 1951; m. Winifred Woods, Jan. 29, 1949; children—Margaret, Richard. Instr., U. Tex., Austin, 1951; prof. history, head dept. social scis. Schreiner Inst., Kerrville, Tex., 1951-55; mem. faculty Tex. Tech. U., Lubbock, 1955-79, chmn. dept., 1961-78; vis. prof. Pan Am. U., summer 1973, U. N.Mex., 1979; cons. Peace Corps, 1966, 67; mem. Tex. Commn. Humanities, Nat. Endowment Humanities, 1971-78. Trustee, Austin Presbyterian Theol. Sem., 1973—. Served with USNR, 1943-46. Fulbright lectr. U. Chile, Cath. U. Santiago, 1957-58; recipient H. Bailey Carroll award S.W. Hist. Quar., 1972. Fellow Tex. State Hist. Assn.; mem. So. Hist. Assn., Am. Hist. Assn., Southwestern Council Latin Am. Studies (pres. 1972-73), Latin Am. Studies Assn., Western History Assn., Conf. Latin Am. History, Southwestern Social Sci. Assn. (exec. council), Phi Kappa Phi, Phi Alpha Theta, Pi Sigma Alpha, Sigma Delta Pi. Presbyterian. Club: Rotary. Author: The Revolutionary Decades, 1965; (with others) Estudios de Historia del Noreste de Mexico, 1972; contbg. author: The Texas Heritage, 1980; asst. editor: Documents of Texas History, 1964; contbr. articles to profl. jours. Home: 3523 58th St Lubbock TX 79413 Office: Dept History Tex Tech U Lubbock TX 79409 Died July 16, 1979

VILES, ARDLE LEE, cable mfg. co. exec.; b. Tenn., Aug. 4, 1936; s. John Mose and Manora (Cook) V.; B.S. in Acctg., U. Tenn.; postgrad. in law YMCA Night Law Sch., Nashville; m. Patricia W. Wreyford, Dec. 21, 1957; children—Eric Andrew, Janelle Anne. With Price Waterhouse & Co., 1959-62, AVCO Corp., 1962-63, Beaunit Corp., 1963-68, Hanes Corp., 1968-70; pres., dir. Superior Cable Corp., Hickory, N.C., 1970—. Bd. dirs. YMCA of Catawba County (N.C.); mem. Catawba County Indsl. Revenue Bond Authority. C.P.A., Tenn. Mem. Am. Inst. C.P.A.'s, Fin. Execs. Inst. Republican. Club: U. Tenn. Pres.'s. Office: 1928 Main Ave SE Hickory NC 28601

VILES, HENRY, pathologist; b. Cali, Colombia, Dec. 24, 1938; s. Pedro and Tulia V.; M.D., U. del Valle (Colombia), 1968; m. Lyda Benítez, Feb. 26, 1960; children—Maurice, Andrés. Rotating intern Hosp. U. del Valle, Cali, 1967-68; resident in pathology Stamford (Conn.) Hosp., 1971-75, chief pathology resident, 1975-76; dir. labs. Mayfield (Ky.) Community Hosp., 1976—; dep. coroner Graves County (Ky.), 1978—. Diplomate Am. Bd. Pathology. Mem. Coll. Am. Pathologists, AMA, Am. Soc. Clin. Pathologists, Am. Soc. Microbiology, AAAS. Home: Lakeview Dr Mayfield KY 42066 Office: 206 W South St Mayfield KY 42066

VILLAFRANCA, EMIL L., hosp. adminstr.; b. Guinoyoran, Bukidnon, Philippines, Feb. 8, 1936; s. Zosimo D. and Fortunata L. V.; came to U.S., 1963, naturalized, 1971; B.S.C., Philippine Union Coll., Manila, 1962; M.S., Internat. U., Kansas City, Mo., 1977, Ph.D., 1978; m. Katherine Lucille Todd, Oct. 31, 1965; children—FeAimee, Emilee Joy, Micheline Sue. Acct., Mid-Am. Nursing Homes, Inc., Marshfield, Wis., 1968-69; adminstr. Ranger Park Hosp. and Ranger Park Inn Nursing Home, Santa Anna, Tex., 1969-73, McCamey (Tex.) Hosp. Dist., 1973-75, Callahan Gen. Hosp., Baird, Tex., 1975—; sec.-treas. FIL AM, Inc. Mem. Tex. Hosp. Assn., Baird C. of C. Republican. Adventist. Club: Lions. Home: 211 Manor Dr Comfort TX 78013 Office: 700 Faltin Comfort TX 78013

VILLARREAL, JOSEPH L., sales exec.; b. Monterrey, Mex., Nov. 1, 1939; s. Nicholas and Socorro V.; came to U.S., 1955, naturalized, 1978; student DePaul U., Chgo., 1966-68. Advt. mgr. LaRaza Publs., Chgo., 1975-76; with Am. Airlines, Chgo. O'Hare Field, 1965-66; inflight dir. sales United Airlines, Chgo., 1966-75; sales mgr. U.S. Spanish TV Network, Chgo. and Dallas, 1977-79. Served with AUS, 1963-65; ETO. Recipient award of merit Chgo. Assn. Commerce and Industry, 1975, Inflight Sales award United Airlines, 1973. Mem. Dallas C. of C., Mex.-Am. C. of C. Roman Catholic. Club: North Park Raquet Ball (Dallas).

VINCENT, BRUCE HAVIRD, ind. oil and gas co. ofcl.; b. Laramie, Wyo., Nov. 7, 1947; s. Dale Leon and Mildred Sara (Havird) V.; A.B. in Bus. Adminstrn., Duke U., 1969; M.B.A. in Fin., U. Houston, 1976; m. Pamela Jean Benson, Dec. 20, 1968; children—Jenifer Jean, Bryce Havird. With First City Nat. Bank of Houston, 1973-80, asst. v.p., 1975-77, v.p. and group mgr. dept. petroleum and minerals, 1977-80; exec. v.p., chief operating officer Peninsula Resources Corp., Corpus Christi, Tex., 1980—; cons. fin. Served to lt., j.g., USN, 1969-73. Mem. Ind. Petroleum Assn. Am., Tex. Mid-Continent Oil and Gas Assn., Internat. Assn. Drilling Contractors, Am. Inst. Banking, Houston C. of C. Home: 15806 Brookvilla Dr Houston TX 77059 Office: 823 N Tancahua TX Corpus Christi TX 78403

VINCENT, DANIEL ASHLEY, educator; b. Jacksonville, Fla., Dec. 20, 1927; s. Daniel Boscawen and Virginia (Ashley) V.; B.S., Ga. Inst. Tech., 1950; M.A., U. S. Fla., 1969; Ph.D., U. Va., 1974; m. Evelyn Grace Polk, Oct. 20, 1961; children—Daniel Ashley, Julia Grace. Engr., v.p. Dan B. Vincent, Inc., Tampa, Fla., 1950-69; research asso. low temp. physics U. Va., Charlottesville, 1974; sr. physicist Superconducting Tech., Inc., Mountain View, Calif., 1974-76; v.p. Vincent Processes, Inc., Tampa, 1976—; asso. prof. Coll. Engring., U. S. Fla., Tampa, 1977—; cons. Rockwell Internat. Corp., 1978—, U. Va., 1976—. Served with USN, 1955-59. Mem. Am. Phys. Soc., Sigma Xi. Episcopalian. Contbr. articles to profl. jours.; patentee in field. Home: 166 Baltic Circle Tampa FL 33606 Office: Univ of S Fla Coll of Engring Tampa FL 33620

VINCENT, PATRICIA JANE, speech and hearing adminstr.; b. Chattanooga, Mar. 13, 1936; d. Clarence E. and Jennie Arlene (Babb) V.; B.S., E. Tenn. State Coll., 1958, M.A., 1968; postgrad. Northwestern U., summer 1962. Speech clinician Georgetown County Schs., Georgetown, S.C., 1958-61; speech pathologist Hearing & Speech Center, Columbia, S.C., 1961-67; exec. dir. Pee Dee Speech & Hearing Center, Florence, S.C., 1968—; faculty U. S.C., Lander Coll. Mem. planning and devel. bd. Pee Dee Regional Health Systems Agy., 1978—; cons. Pee Dee area Girl Scouts, 1977-79, mem. public relations com., 1973, 80—; bd. dirs. Florence County (S.C.) Assn. for

Retarded Children, 1970. Recipient 20 year award Girl Scouts. Mem. S.C. Speech and Hearing Assn. (v.p. 1961, honors 1979), Am. Speech and Hearing Assn., Nat. Rehab. Assn. Club: Civitan (v.p. Palmetto 1979, dir. 1980). Kenfield Meml. scholar, 1967. Home: 600 Sandra Terr Florence SC 29501 Office: Pee Dee Speech & Hearing Center 153 N Barody St Florence SC 29503

VINCENT, RICHARD CLEO, plastics mfg. co. exec.; b. Kirksville, Mo., Jan. 29, 1924; s. Cleo Nathan and Ethel Ada (Crowder) V.; student La. Poly. Inst., 1944, Oberlin Coll., 1944-45; B.S., Purdue U., 1947; student Pa. State U., 1947-50, U. Calif., Los Angeles, 1952, 56, San Luis Rey Coll., 1953-56. Research asso. Ordnance Research Lab., Pa. State U., 1947-50; asst. to dir. transducer engring. Bendix Corp., North Hollywood, Calif., 1951-53; cleric Franciscan Fathers, Oakland, Calif., 1953-56; sr. engring. project adminstr. Nortronics, Northrop Corp., Hawthorne, Calif., 1956-59; sr. mem. engring. staff RCA, Van Nuys, Calif., 1959-64; sr. project staff engr. Rocketdyne div. N. Am. Rockwell, Canoga Park, Calif., 1964-66; teleprocessing services supr. Vought Aeros. div. LTV, Grand Prairie, Tex., 1968-70; ordained to ministry, 1970; minister various locations, 1970-77; tech. tng. mgr. Plastics Mfg. Co., Dallas, 1977—; v.p., dir. Master Mortuary Service, Inc. Del., Tex. Republican Conv., 1972; vol. chaplain Dallas County Jail, 1971-73. Served with USMCR, 1943-46. Mem. IEEE, Assn. for Research and Enlightenment, Pi Kappa Alpha. Club: Ind. Order of Foresters. Home: 926 Turner Ave Dallas TX 75208 Office: Plastics Mfg Co 2700 S Westmoreland PO Box 24645 Dallas TX 75224

VINEKAR, SHREEKUMAR SANJIV, physician, psychiatrist; b. Trivandrum, Kerala, India, Sept. 14, 1942; s. Sanjiv Lakshman and Krishnabai Sanjiv (Mudbhatkal) V.; M.B.,B.S. (M.D.), Seth G.S. Med. Coll., U. Bombay (India), 1966; m. Shyamala H. Sashittal, Mar. 1, 1966; children—Sanjivani, Jay. Intern, Church Home and Hosp., Balt., 1966-67; resident U. Okla. Health Scis. Center, Oklahoma City, 1969-74; practice medicine specializing in child and adolescent psychiatry, Oklahoma City, 1974-76; cons. psychiatrist So. Okla. Alcohol Program and Guidance Clinic, Ardmore, 1974-76; staff psychiatrist Central State Hosp. and chief inpatient service Norman (Okla.) Community Mental Health Center, 1976-78; dir. inpatient service Phil Smalley Children's Center, Hayden H. Donahue Mental Health Inst., Norman, 1978-80; group pvt. practice Oklahoma City Neuropsychiat. Clinic, 1976—; clin. asst. prof. dept. psychiatry and behavioral scis. U. Okla. Health Scis. Center, Oklahoma City, 1974—. Bd. dirs. Oklahoma County Council for Mentally Retarded, 1975-77. Diplomate Am. Bd. Psychiatry and Neurology. Mem. Oklahoma City C. of C., AMA, Am. Psychiat. Assn., Am. Acad. Psychiatry and the Law. Office: 1111 N Lee St Suite 437 Oklahoma City OK 73103

VINES, LARRY PAUL, SR., elec. engr., naval officer; b. Clanton, Ala., Jan. 25, 1943; s. L. P. and Marie Josephine (Jones) V.; B.S.E.E., Purdue U., 1970; M.S.E.E., Naval Postgrad. Sch., 1976; m. Patricia Lynn Stock, June 27, 1960; children—Larry, Lynn, Laura, Lane. Served as enlisted man U.S. Navy, 1960-70, advanced through grades to lt. comdr., 1980; fire control technician, 1960-66; exec. officer bn., 1969-70; missile officer USS Belknap, 1970-73; ops. officer USS Talbot, 1976-79; chief engr. USS Barnstable, 1979—. Decorated Sec. of Navy Achievement. Mem. Naval Inst., Nat. Geog. Soc., Sigma Xi. Home: 1059 Tradewinds Rd Virginia Beach VA 23464

VINES, WILLIAM DUANE, dental lab adminstr.; b. Monett, Mo., Dec. 25, 1936; s. William Loren and Ava V.; student bus. U. Ark., 1955-59; m. Carolyn Sue Dickson, Aug. 2, 1958; children—Laura Sue, Elizabeth Anne. Mem. pub. relations staff H. Dickson Inc., Ft. Smith, Ark., 1960-66, v.p., gen. mgr., 1970-78, pres., 1979—; dir. personnel and pub. relations Hickory Springs Mfg. Co., Ft. Smith, 1966-70. Bd. dirs. City of Ft. Smith, 1967-70; adv. bd. Sparks Hosp., 1977—. Served to major Air N.G. Named Man of Yr., Ft. Smith Jr. C. of C., 1969. Mem. N.G. Assn. Ark., Western Ark. Counseling and Guidance Center (dir.), Res. Officers Assn. (pres. 1968-69), Ark. Athletic Union (co-chmn. 1962-75), Ark. Dental Lab. Assn. (pres. 1974, 75), Kappa Sigma. Methodist. Club: Exchange Internat. Home: 5419 Country Club Ln Fort Smith AR 72901 Office: PO Box 287 Fort Smith AR 72901

VINEYARD, RONNIE MAC, electric co. exec.; b. Comanche, Tex., Aug. 29, 1942; s. Howell Morton and Jesse Ernestine (Mewborn) V.; B.B.A. in Mktg., Tex. Christian U., 1965; m. Garry Etola Martin, June 14, 1963; children—Dana, Amy, Hal. Spl. rep. Southwestern Bell Telephone Co., Ft. Worth, 1963-70; state mktg. mgr. Continental Telephone Co., Russellville, Ark., 1970-77; Southwest sales and service rep. Cook Electric Co., Chgo., 1977—. Named Salesman of Yr., Ft. Worth Sales and Mktg. Execs. Internat., 1967; Man of Yr., Russellville C. of C., 1974. Mem. Ind. Telephone Pioneers Assn., La. Telephone Assn., Kans. Telephone Assn., Tex./Okla. Telephone Assn., Ark. Telephone Assn. (rep. to bd., dir.), Russellville C. of C. (past dir.). Democrat. Methodist. Clubs: Masons, Kiwanis (past dir. Russellville), Russellville Country (dir., v.p.). Home: 705 W 17th Terr Russellville AR 72801 Office: Cook Electric Co 6201 W Oakton St Morton Grove IL 60053

VINEYARD, RUTH ANNE, historian; b. Seymour, Ind., Jan. 11, 1944; d. Avis Aaron and Olive Jane (Johnson) Ruddick; B.S. in Edn., Ball State U., 1966, M.A., 1972; m. James Roscoe Vineyard, Sept. 4, 1965; children—Jane Marie, James David. Tchr. public schs. in Ind. and Ala., 1966-70, 73-74; mem. faculty Nat. Chung Hsing U., Taichung, Taiwan, 1973, U. Md., Ching Chuan Kang Air Base, Taiwan, 1973, San Antonio Coll., 1975-77; tchr. Am. and world history Highland Park High Sch., Dallas, 1977—. Recipient Service award USAF Family Services, 1970, 72. Mem. Am. Hist. Assn., Nat. Hist. Soc., Highland Park Educators Assn., Consumers Union, Delta Zeta. Episcopalian. Club: USAF Officers Wives. Home: 3142 Bluestem Dr Garland TX 75042 Office: Highland Park High Sch 4220 Emerson St Dallas TX 75205

VINING, WILLIAM DAVID, advt. exec.; b. Atlanta, Oct. 31, 1954; s. William Maurice and Florence Fling V.; A.A., Armstrong State Coll., 1975; B.S., U. Tenn., 1977. Announcer WTOC AM/FM-TV, Savannah, Ga., 1972-75; producer/dir. WTVK-TV, Knoxville, Tenn., 1975-77; exec. v.p. Communication Concepts, Inc., Knoxville, 1977-78; advt. mgr. Clayton Cos., Knoxville, 1978—. Team capt. membership drive Boy Scouts Am., 1978. Mem. Greater Knoxville Advt. Club. Office: PO Box 12144 Knoxville TN 37912

VINSON, CLARENCE DAVID, JR., educator; b. Ohatchee, Ala., June 23, 1933; s. Clarence David and Vera Pearl V.; B.S., Jacksonville State U., 1954, M.S., 1959; Ph.D., U. Ala., 1977. Tchr. sci., math., coach Saks High Sch., Anniston, Ala., 1957-65; tchr., coach Munford (Ala.) High Sch., 1965-69; asso. prof. sci. Jacksonville (Ala.) State U., 1969—. Served with U.S. Army, 1955-57. Mem. NEA, Ala. Edn. Assn., Am. Numismatic Assn. Democrat. Baptist. Club: Anniston Bowling Assn. (bd. dirs.). Home: 435 Arnold Dr Anniston AL 36201 Office: Gen Sci Dept Jacksonville AL 36265

VINTURELLA, JOHN BARRY, bldg. supplies co. exec.; b. New Orleans, Nov. 11, 1942; s. John Joseph and Josephine (Anselmo) V.; M.S. in Communication Research, Boston U., 1974; Ph.D. (NDEA fellow), Tulane U., 1968; m. Janet Bourque, Aug. 17, 1974; children—Victoria Jane V., David Joseph V. Systems engr. IBM, New Orleans, 1966-68; mgmt. scientist Kaiser Aluminum & Chem. Corp., Oakland, Calif.. 1968-69; project dir. Internat. Data Systems, New Orleans, 1969-70; dir. Computer Research Center U. New Orleans, 1970-72; dir. academic computing Bentley Coll., Waltham, Mass., 1973-74; mgr. New Orleans Computer Center, La. Info. Processing Authority, 1975; v.p. Southland Plumbing Supply Inc., Metairie, 1975-78, Covington, La., 1978—; pres. Tammany Group, Covington; cons. Digi-Sci. Ltd., Calgary, Alta., Can., Chinese Petroleum Corp., Taipei, Taiwan, Office of La. Gov.; mem. La. Joint Legis. EDP Com., 1970-72; judge Internat. Sci. Engring., Fair, 1972; councilman dist. 3 St. Tamonany Parish, 1980—. Recipient commendation La. House of Reps., 1971. Author: Introduction to Fortran, 1975; author papers in field. Home: 323 Robin Hood Rd Covington LA 70433 Office: Rt 3 Box 352 Covington LA 70433

VIOHL, FREDERICK ALBERT, educator; b. N.Y.C., May 25, 1941; s. Fred W. and Margarete R. V.; B.S., N.Y. U., 1966, M.B.A., 1968; Ed.D., U. Ga., 1979; children—Lisa, Andrew. Mktg. researcher Cunningham & Walsh, Inc., 1965-67; mktg. mgr. Trane Co., 1976-77; zone mgr. Kelly Health Care, Kelly Services, Inc., 1977-79; asst. prof. mktg. Troy (Ala.) State U., 1979—; cons. mktg. Served to capt. USAF, 1967-76. Decorated AF Commendation Medal. Mem. Sales and Mktg. Execs. Montgomery, Am. Mgmt. Assn., AFFAssn., AAUP, Alpha Delta Sigma. Club: Maxwell Officers. Home: 3413 Woodhill Rd Montgomery AL 36109 Office: Troy State University Troy AL 36081

VIOLA, R(EBECCA) ANNE, nurse; b. Durham, N.C., Aug. 1, 1942; d. Willie Derring and Rebecca Mae (Elliotte) Norris; R.N. diploma Watts Hosp. Sch. Nursing, Durham, 1963; m. Michael David Viola, Sept. 26, 1964; 1 son, Michael David. Asst. head nurse Watts Hosp., 1963-65; supr. dept. fed. employees Hosp. Savs. Assn., Chapel Hill, N.C., 1965-68; operating room supr. McPherson Hosp., Durham, 1968—. Mem. Assn. Operating Room Nurses (dir. local chpt.). Methodist. Home: 5318 Revere Rd Durham NC 27713 Office: 1110 W Main St Durham NC 27701

VIRGIN, HERBERT WHITING, JR., orthopedic surgeon; b. Nevada, Mo., Oct. 12, 1906; s. Herbert Whiting and Isabelle (Goff) V.; student Washington and Lee U., 1923-24; A.B., Northwestern U., 1927, M.B., 1931, M.D., 1932; m. Frances Patterson True, June 2, 1934; children—Herbert Whiting III, Charles Edward, Frances Elizabeth. Rotating intern Evanston (Ill.) Gen. Hosp., 1931-32; chief resident in orthopedic surgery Shriners' Hosp. for Children, 1932-33, Meth. Hosp., Madison, Wis., 1933-34, Jackson Clinic, 1934-35; practice medicine specializing in orthopedic surgery, Pensacola, Fla., 1940-42, Miami, Fla., 1942—; mem. staff Jackson Meml. Hosp.; sr. orthopedic surgeon Mercy Hosp.; orthopedic surgeon Doctors Hosp.; team physician Miami Dolphins Profl. Football Team, Miami Orioles Profl. Baseball Team, Ft. Lauderdale Strikers Profl. Soccer Team, Miami Jai Alai. Trustee Boys Club of Miami. Served as lt. USNR, 1935-41. Diplomate Am. Bd. Orthopedic Surgery. Fellow A.C.S., Southeastern Surg. Congress, Am. Acad. Orthopedic Surgeons; mem. Internat. Coll. Surgeons, AMA, Fla., Dade County med. assns., Fla. Orthopedic Soc., Am. Fractures Assn., Com. of One Hundred, Beta Theta Pi, Nu Sigma Nu. Clubs: Biscayne Bay Yacht, Coral Reef Yacht, Masons. Home: 3635 St Gaudens Rd Coconut Grove FL 33133 Office: 1333 S Miami Ave Miami FL 33130

VISE, JOYE LAWSON, educator; b. Pauline, S.C., Dec. 20, 1924; d. Robert Clyde and Bonnie Lee (Nichols) Lawson; B.S., Wofford Coll., 1964; M.Ed., U. S.C., 1975; m. Carol Fredrick Vise, June 8, 1945; children—Aletia, Sharon, Kennon, Marshia, Timothy. Tchr. home econs. Pacolet (S.C.) High Sch., 1945-46, Pauline and Glenn Springs elementary schs., 1956-64, Roebuck (S.C.) Jr. High Sch., 1963-71, Jesse Bobo Elementary Sch., 1972—. Tchr. Sunday sch. Friendship Bapt. Ch. Mem. PTA, NEA. Home: Box 527 Pauline SC 29374

VISENTIN, THOMAS ANTHONY, ship's agt.; b. Pawtucket, R.I., Feb. 12, 1948; s. Louis Roy and Claudia Nora (Bernardi) V.; B.S., Maine Maritime Acad., 1969; m. Arlyn Kay Eckerman, July 30, 1972; children—Eric Micheal, Kevin Mark. Served aboard various chem. tankers and gen. cargo ships U.S. Mcht. Marine, 1969-74; port capt., ops. asst. Steuber Co. Inc., N.Y.C., 1974-77; port mgr. Texana Marine Agy., Texas City, Tex., 1977—; port capt., loading cons. Overseas Enterprises, Inc. Multimedia instr. ARC; sec. Seabrook (Tex.) Vol. Fire Dept. Mem. Propeller Club U.S., Maine Maritime Acad. Alumni Assn. Office: Texana Marine Agy PO Box 712 Texas City TX 77590

VISK, ANTHONY GUY, advt./promotion cons., syndicator; b. Troy, N.Y., Oct. 5, 1925; s. Guy and Mary (LaPosta) V.; student Brown U., 1960; grad. Palmer Inst. Authorship, Hollywood, Calif., 1948; m. Marie Patricia Cioffi, Sept. 14, 1952; children—Anthony Guy (dec.); Nadine Lillo, Robert. Comedy writer, radio and TV network shows, 1952-63; continuity dir., promotion writer WROW-AM, WTEN-TV, Albany, N.Y., 1955-57; promotion mgr., writer WPTR Radio, Albany, 1957-59; promotion dir., sales promotion mgr. WPRO Radio, Providence, 1959-70; promotion mgr. WXIA-TV, Atlanta, 1970-72; pres. Tony Visk Creative Broadcasting, Atlanta, 1972—; instr. radio/TV advt. writing Emory U., Atlanta, 1977—. Served with AUS, 1944-46. Decorated Bronze Star medal. Mem. Nat. Acad. TV Arts and Scis., Broadcasters Promotion Assn. Club: Atlanta Advertising. Author spl. comedy material Humorous Introductions for Emcees, 1953. Office: Tony Visk Creative Broadcasting 3802 Greenrock Ct Atlanta GA 30340

VITALE, JOSEPH JAMES, printing co. exec.; b. Chgo., Feb. 2, 1931; s. Joseph C. and Mary Elizabeth (Lile) V.; student pub. schs., Beaver, Ark., Louisville; m. Carol Lee Frankensteen, Nov. 15, 1974; children—Mary Beth, Joseph James, Michael, Anthony; stepchildren—Richard, Grace, John. Asst. buyer Stewarts Dry Goods Co., Louisville, 1947-54; rate clk. L.&N. R.R., Louisville, 1954-55; propr., mgr. Thompson Bros. Florist & Tropical Fish, Louisville, 1955-57; asst. production mgr. A.D. Weiss Litho Co., Hollywood, Fla., 1960—; cons. to various aquarium publs., 1970—. Proctor Broward County Mensa. Served with U.S. Army, 1955. Mem. Everglades Aquarium Soc. (parliamentarian 1977-78), Am. Catfish and Loach Assn. (pres. 1976—). Democrat. Contbr. articles on tropical fish to tech. jours. Home: 3840 NW 3 Terrace Pompano Beach FL 33064 Office: 2025 McKinley Hollywood FL 33020

VITO, RAYMOND PETER, engr., educator; b. Buffalo, July 26, 1942; s. Gasper and Elizabeth (DeVincentis) V.; B.S. in Engring. Sci., SUNY, Buffalo, 1964, M.S., 1965; Ph.D., Cornell U., 1971; m. Virginia Anne Williams, Mar. 18, 1972. Research engr. Worthington Corp., Buffalo, 1965; structural research engr. Bell Aerospace Corp., Niagara Falls, N.Y., 1966-67; mem. tech. staff Aerospace Corp., El Segundo, Calif., summer, 1969; instr. dept. theoretical and applied mechanics Cornell U., Ithaca, N.Y., 1971; Nat. Research Council of Can. fellow McMaster U., Hamilton, Ont., 1971-73; asst. prof. dept. engring. sci. and mechanics Ga. Inst. Tech., Atlanta, 1974-80, asso. prof., 1980—. NASA fellow, 1976, 78; NSF grantee, 1977-79. Mem. ASME, Am. Acad. Mechanics, Sigma Xi. Contbr. articles on engring. sci. to profl. jours. Home: 2224 Riada Dr NW Atlanta GA 30305 Office: 210 North Ave Atlanta GA 30332

VITTETOW, FRANCIS HOYT, state ofcl. Ky.; b. Evansville, Ind., Apr. 3, 1921; s. Green Thomas and Ida Mae (Ligon) V.; B.A., Murray (Ky.) State U., 1949; M.A., George Peabody Coll. for Tchrs., 1950; m. Elizabeth Ruth Prather, Oct. 15, 1949; children—Diane, Frank, James, Thomas. With Sebree (Ky.) Banner, 1936-39; ins. salesman, 1939-40; asst. mgr. chain grocery store, 1940-42; tchr., Louisville, 1950-51; tchr. Cloverport (Ky.) High Sch., 1951-52; supt. schs. Cloverport Ind. Sch. Dist., 1952-53; cons. in-ser. tchr. edn. Ky. Dept. Edn., Frankfort, 1953-58; elementary and secondary edn. adviser AID, Philippines, 1958-62; edn. adviser, Vientiane, Laos, 1963-66; asst. supt. pub. instrn. for state and fed. relations Ky. Dept. Edn., Frankfort, 1966-77, state dir. adult basic edn., 1977-80, ret., 1980. asso. prof. edn. Morehead (Ky.) State U. summers 1956-58. Pres., Vittetow Realty Corp., Inc., Lexington, Ky. Merit badge counselor Boy Scouts Am. Chmn. sc. bd. Am. Dependent Sch., Vientiane, 1965-66; bd. govs. Kilometer 6 Housing Assn., Vientiane. Served with AUS, 1942-45. Recipient Meritorious Ser. award AID, 1965. Mem. Nat., Ky. edn. assns., Order Ky. Cols. (hon.), Phi Kappa Phi. Methodist (dist. lay leader, mem. bd. standards). Democrat. Mason (Shriner). Home: 208 Steele St Frankfort KY 40601 Office: Plaza Tower Frankfort KY 40601

VIVIAN, JOHN, electronic engr.; b. Edgware, Middlesex, U.K., Sept. 15, 1946; s. Henry and Queenie (Winfield) V.; B.Sc. in Elec. Engring., Portsmouth (Eng.) Poly., 1969. Jr. engr. Plessey Radar, U.K., 1967-70; field engr. Satellite Positioning Corp., Houston, 1972-73, systems engr., 1973-76, supr. hardware, 1976-77; mgr. navigation support services Seiscom-Delta, Houston, 1977-78; project mgr. Litton Resources Systems, 1978-79, product line mgr., 1979—. Mem. IEEE, Inst. Nav., Inst. Elec. Engrs. (U.K.). Contbr. articles on ice nav., satellite and geodetic positioning to profl. lit. Home: 3804 Villanova West University Place TX 77005 Office: 3930 Westholme Dr Houston TX 77063

VIVIANO, SAMUEL THOMAS, food co. exec.; b. Detroit, Dec. 11, 1913; s. Salvatore and Gustine (Palazolla) V.; student. pvt. schs.; m. JoAnn Maxwell, June 21, 1971; children by previous marriage—Samuel Thomas III, Sara Jean Dobb. With Viviano Marcaroni Co., Carnegie, Pa., 1930—, pres., chmn. bd., 1967—. Served with U.S. Army, 1942-46. Home: PO Box 339 Land O Lakes FL 33539 Office: Box 546 Carnegie PA 15106

VIVONA, ALDO FRANCIS, broadcasting co. exec.; b. Kingston, N.Y., Apr. 6, 1947; s. Vito and Joan Frances (Bozzo) V.; student Orange County Vocat. Sch., 1966-67, Orange County Adult Edn., 1973-76, Valencia Community Coll., 1976-79; m. Terri Rae Parker, June 22, 1968. Radio talent WLOF Radio, Orlando, Fla., 1964-73; broadcast engr. WFTV TV, Orlando, 1966-67; transmitter supr. WMFE-TV, Orlando, 1967-73, asst. chief engr., 1973-75, adminstrv. services coordinator, 1975-78, v.p. for adminstrn. and fin., 1978—. Mem. job. service improvement com. Fla. State Employment Service, 1978—. Mem. Am. Mgmt. Assn., Assn. Small Computer Users. Club: Toastmasters. Office: 11510 E Colonial St Orlando FL 32807

VLIET, GARY CLARK, mech. engr.; b. Bassano, Alta., Can., June 3, 1933; s. Lowell Clark and Maria (Riste) V.; B.S. in Chem. Engring., U. Alta., Edmonton, 1955; M.S. (Fluor fellow), Stanford U., 1957, Ph.D. in Mech. Engring., 1962; m. Donna Mae Love, Dec. 15, 1962; children—Kirsten, Joanne, David. Research scientist Lockheed Research Labs., Palo Alto, Calif., 1961-71; asso. prof. mech. engring. U. Tex., Austin, 1971-79, prof. mech. engring., 1979—; dir. Energy Engring. Assos., Austin; cons. solar energy. Recipient Canadian Chem. Engring. Inst. prize U. Alta., 1953, award of honor for allied professions Austin chpt. AIA, 1977. Mem. ASME (Best Heat Transfer Paper award 1970), Internat., Tex. (pres., dir.) solar energy socs. Republican. Presbyterian. Club: Austin Yacht. Contbr. articles on heat transfer to profl. jours. Office: Dept Mech Engring U Tex Austin TX 78712

VOGEL, DOUGLAS JAMES, univ. adminstr.; b. Bradford, Pa., Aug. 15, 1940; s. James John and Margaret Mary (Douglas) V.; B.A., U. Kans., 1965, M.B.A., 1974; m. Janice Lee Jones, June 11, 1966; children—Andrew Wade, Matthew Douglas, Adam John, Katherine Marie. Research asst. Menninger Found., Topeka, 1964-67; researcher, asst. dir. U. Kans., Lawrence, 1967-74, instr., 1969-71, asso. dir. bus. affairs, 1978-79; v.p. fiscal affairs Trinity U., San Antonio, 1979—. dep. legis. post auditor State of Kans., Topeka, 1974-78; cons. auditor tng. com. Council State Govts., 1976-78, Eagleton Inst., Rutgers U., 1976-78, Booz, Allen Systems, 1970-71. Chmn. bd. dirs. Achievement Place, Inc., 1970-73. Served with USAF, 1960-61. Mem. Am. Soc. Pub. Adminstrn., Nat. Assn. Coll. and Univ. Bus. Officers, Am. Mgmt. Assn., Lawrence Jr. C. of C. (dir., 1967, Outstanding Jaycee award, 1966). Republican. Office: Office of Vice Pres Fiscal Affairs Trinity U San Antonio TX 78284

VOGEL, MICHAEL LOUIS, social worker; b. San Francisco, Sept. 12, 1947; s. Philip and Lorraine Maxine (Slavin) V.; A.A., City Coll. San Francisco, 1968; B.A., Ohio State U., 1970; M.S.W., Va. Commonwealth U., 1973; m. Ellen Ann Hunt, June 6, 1971; 1 son, Philip Edwin. Regional dir. B'nai B'rith Youth Orgn., San Francisco, 1973-75; chief social work Westbrook Psychiat. Hosp., Richmond, Va., 1976-79; dir. residential services Florence Crittenton Services, Lynchburg, Va., 1979-80; pvt. practice, 1980—. Mem. Hanover County Mental Health Services Bd., 1977-78. Cert. reality therapist. Mem. Acad. Cert. Social Workers, Assn. Clin. Social Workers, Nat. Assn. Social Workers. Jewish. B'nai B'rith. Home: 304 Lake Forest Pl Lynchburg VA 24502 Office: 2316 Atherholt Rd Suite 204 Lynchburg VA 24501

VOGTLE, ALVIN WARD, JR., electric utility exec.; b. Birmingham, Ala., Oct. 21, 1918; s. Alvin Ward and Ollie (Stringer) V.; B.S., Auburn U., 1939; LL.B., U. Ala., 1941; m. Kathryn Drennen, Apr. 20, 1945 (dec.); children—Kathryn D., Anne Moore Vogtle Baldwin, Alvin Ward; m. 2d, Rachael Giles, 1966; children—Bryant Wade, William Patrick, Rachael Giles, Robert Jackson. Admitted to Ala. bar, 1941; asso. Martin Vogtle, Balch & Bingham, and predecessors, Birmingham, 1945-50, mem. firm, 1950-62; exec. v.p., dir. Ala. Power Co., 1962-65; pres. So. Electric Generating Co., 1960-62, dir., 1962—; exec. v.p. The So. Co., 1966-69, pres., dir., 1969—; chmn. bd., dir. So. Services Inc.; dir. Seaboard Coast Line Industries, Inc., Union Camp Corp., Protective Life Ins. Co., Ala., Ga., Gulf, Miss. power cos. Past chmn. Edison Electric Inst.; trustee Com. for Econ. Devel., Tax Found. Served from 2d lt. to capt. USAAF, 1941-45. Mem. Newcomen Soc. N.Am., Soc. Colonial Wars, The Conf. Bd., SAR, Ala. Hist. Assn., Sigma Nu. Episcopalian. Home: Batesville Rd King's Lea Farms Woodstock GA 30188 Office: 64 Perimeter Center E Atlanta GA 30346

VOIGHT, JESSELYN WINSTON, nurse, educator, health cons.; b. Milw., Mar. 26, 1923; d. Edwin Peter and Ruby (Winston) Eggert; nursing diploma Walther Meml. Sch., 1944; B.S. in Nursing Edn., Loyola U., Chgo., 1949; M.A., U. Mich., 1970, Ph.D., 1972, visiting scholar, 1975; m. Byron Edward Voight, Aug. 21, 1948; children—Stephanie, Bradley, Alison, Keith, Geoffrey, Andrea. Instr. nursing Oakland Community Coll., Union Lake, Mich., 1969-73, asst. prof., 1973-75, asso. prof. nursing Oakland U., Rochester, Mich., 1975-76; nursing educator, cons. WHO, Ministry of Health, Sri

Lanka, 1976-77; prof., dir. special programs for Allied Health and Nursing, E. Ky. U., Richmond, 1977; cons. gerontol. nursing, aging and gerontol. nursing research. Trustee Pleasant Ridge Found., Pleasant Ridge, Mich., 1967-69; vol. Detroit Art Inst., 1968-76, Am. Archives Art, Detroit, 1974-76, Republican Party, Royal Oak, Mich., 1952-76, Ky. Gov.'s Council on Aging, 1978; mem. Founders Soc., Detroit Art Inst. Served with U.S. Army Nursing Corps, 1945-46. Recipient service award Detroit Art Inst., 1974. Mem. Am. Nurses Assn., Ky. League for Nursing, Ky. Nurses Assn. (nursing edn. commn.), Am. Nurses Assn. Council Continuing Edn., AAUW, Pi Lambda Theta, Sigma Epsilon Sigma. Republican. Episcopalian. Club: Zonta. Researcher clin. nursing fields. Home: 208 C Barnes Mill Rd Richmond KY 40475 Office: Coll Allied Health Nursing E Ky U Richmond KY 40475

VOITH, GEORGE GERARD, sales exec.; b. Balt., Aug. 27, 1922; s. Gerard A. and Bertha K. (Krumm) V.; B.A., Washington Coll., 1949; m. Gloria Mae Buschman, Apr. 27, 1951; children—Karren, Jerry, Chris, Susan. Salesman, J.J. Haines & Co., Balt., 1948-50; salesman R.A. Siegel Co., Atlanta, 1950-52, sales mgr., 1952-65, v.p. sales, 1965—; adv. com. rep. Armstrong Cork Co., 1965, 70, 79; producer, owner ednl. tape programs, 1964—. Served to lt. (j.g.) USN, World War II. Club: Atlanta Country (dir.). Home: 4612 Club Circle Atlanta GA 30319 Office: 1175 Chattahoochee Ave Atlanta GA 30325

VOLDNESS, ARLEN RALPH, home for aged adminstr.; b. Chgo., Sept. 1, 1932; s. Albin Olie and Edna L. (Olsen) V.; student No. Ill. U., 1955-56; m. Helen Ferguson, Oct. 27, 1956; children—James R., Barbara A., Paul E., H. Katrina, Mark A., Francis D. Research engr. HRB-Singer, State College, Pa., 1961-65, tng. dir., 1965-66; sr. research engr. Technology, Inc., Dayton, Ohio, 1967; owner Arby's Franchise, Winter Park, Fla., 1968-69; nat. electronic adminstr. Bell & Howell Corp., Chgo., 1970-71, prin. elec. engr. Magnacraft div., 1972-76; owner Hopkins Electric and Maintenance Co., Cin., 1977-78; adminstr. St. Francis Village, Crowley, Tex., 1978—; cons. electronic controls; instr. religion. Founder, St. Francis Hospice, 1979; regional minister prefect 3d Order of St. Francis. Served with USAF, 1951-55. Mem. Internat. Assn. Elec. Insps., Tex. Assn. Homes for Aging. Democrat. Roman Catholic. Club: K.C. Co-inventor Unicolor photo process, 1966-67; co-author: Aborne Infrared Surveillance, 1963. Home: 6316 Whitman St Fort Worth TX 76133 Office: 1 Chapel Plaza Crowley TX 76036

VOLKER, JOSEPH FRANCIS, coll. ofcl.; b. Elizabeth, N.J., Mar. 9, 1913; s. Francis Joseph and Rose G. (Hennessey) V.; D.D.S., Ind. U., 1936; A.B., U. Rochester, 1938, M.S., 1939, Ph.D., 1941; D.Sc. (hon.), U. Med. Sci., Thailand, 1967; Dr. honoris causa, Lund U., Sweden, 1968, U. Louis Pasteur de Strasbourg, 1972; D.Sc. (hon.), Ind. 1970, U. Ala., 1970, Coll. Medicine and Dentistry, N.J., 1973, U. Rochester, 1975, Georgetown U., 1978, Fairleigh Dickinson U., 1978; Professor (honoris causa), Universidade Federal do Rio de Janeiro, 1977; m. Juanita Berry, Feb. 6, 1937; children—Joseph Francis, Juanita Anne, John Berry. Dental intern Mountainside Hosp., Montclair, N.J., 1936-37; Carnegie fellow in dentistry U. Rochester, 1937-41, asst. prof. biochemistry, 1941-42; prof. clin. dentistry Dental Sch., Tufts Coll., 1942-47, dean, 1947-49, Sch. Dentistry, U. Ala., 1948-62, dir. research and grad. studies U. Ala. Med. Center, 1955-65; v.p. health affairs, 1962-66; v.p. Birmingham Affairs, 1966-68, dir. Med. Center, Birmingham, 1966-68, exec. v.p. U. Ala. Birmingham, 1968-69, pres., 1969-76, chancellor U. Ala. System, 1976—; dir. Ariz. Med. Sch. Study, 1960-61, U.S. Dept. State teaching specialist, Thailand, 1951; mem. Unitarian Service committee's med. teaching mission to Czechoslovakia, 1946, Germany, 1948. Bd. regents Nat. Library Medicine, 1973-77. Decorated Order White Lion (Czechoslovakia), Most Noble Order Crown (Thailand); comdr. Order Falcon, Republic Iceland, 1969; fellow in dental surgery Royal Coll. Surgeons Eng., 1962; fellow faculty dentistry Royal Coll. Surgeons Ireland, 1973. Diplomate Am. Bd. Oral Medicine. Mem. Inst. Medicine of Nat. Acad. Scis., Soc. Exptl. Biology and Medicine, ADA, Am. Chem. Soc., Internat. Assn. Dental Research, Sigma Xi, Omicron Kappa Upsilon, Alpha Omega Alpha. Club: Cosmos. Home: 8 Central Highlands Tuscaloosa AL 35404 Office: University of Ala System PO Box BT University AL 35486

VOLLBEER, FRED H., fin. exec.; b. Davenport, Iowa, Jan. 3, 1944; s. Walter H. and Fern J. (Holst) V.; B.B.A., U. Iowa, 1966; m. Bonnie J. Deur, Dec. 28, 1968; 1 son, Robert Scott. With Berlage Bernstein Builders, Alexandria, Va., 1971-72; v.p. finance L.A. Clarke & Son, Inc., Washington, 1972-76, also dir.; controller Micro Systems, Inc., Vienna, Va., 1976-77; chief fin. officer Williams Lumber Co. Inc., Rocky Mount, N.C., 1977-78; personal bus. mgr. to Roy J. Carver, founder, chmn. bd. Bandag, 1978—; gen. mgr. Carver Enterprises, Miami, Fla., 1978—; dir. Lancaster Masonry, Inc. (Fairfax, Va.); owner Fred H. Vollbeer Fin. Services. Founding bd. dirs. Carver Med. Research Inst. Served with USAF, 1968-71. Mem. Alpha Kappa Psi. Club: Benvenue Country (Rocky Mount). Home: 6885 Cassia Pl Miami Lakes FL 33014 Office: 880 NE 69th St Suite 1E Miami FL 33138

VOLMAR, PETER JON, architect; b. Northport, L.I., N.Y., Feb. 6, 1938; s. Paul George and Lucille Grace (Bailey) V.; B.Arch., U. Fla., 1962; m. Judith Elliott, Aug. 25, 1958 (div.); children—Jon Robie, Julie Ellen; m. 2d, Cynthia Ann Stokes, Feb. 23, 1974 (div.). Designer, Harvard & Jolly, 1961-63; asso. architect C. Randolph Wedding & Assos., 1963-71; pvt. practice architecture, St. Petersburg, Fla., 1971—; archtl. cons. St. Petersburg Waterfront Re-devel., 1964; archtl. critic Tulane U.; lectr. in field; works include 1st Fed. Savs. & Loan Assn. Annex, Sheen residence, John Knox Apts., Fla. Power Corp. Hdqrs., Treasure Island Municipal Center, Treasure Sands Condominium Apts., Chateau Towers. Past chmn. Treasure Island (Fla.) Planning and Zoning Bd., Pinellas County Bd. Adjustments and Appeals; mem. plans rev. com. Pinellas County Sch. Bd. Recipient award AIA, 1961, 64, county archtl. awards, 1969, 71; Energy award Pinellas County Contractors and Builders Assn. Mem. AIA (past treas. Fla. Central chpt., past pres.), St. Petersburg Assn. Architects (past pres.), Archtl. Prescast Assn., St. Petersburg C. of C., Gargoyle. Presbyn. Clubs: St. Petersburg Yacht; Treasure Island Tennis and Yacht. Home: 12274 1st St W Treasure Island FL 33706 Office: 265 108th Ave Treasure Island FL 33706

VON BERGEN, JOHN DAVID, elec. engr.; b. Scranton, Pa., Jan. 24, 1939; s. John David and Beulah Evelyn (Greene) VonB.; B.E.E., Cath. U. Am., 1962; m. Kwon Sim Kim, Feb. 24, 1973; children—James H., John D., Kim S. Research asst., dept. elec. engring. Cath. U., Washington, 1961; lab. technician Nat. Sci. Labs., Washington, 1961-62; project engr., program mgr. Northrop Page Communications Engrs., Inc., Vienna, Va., 1962-77; dir. engring. Northrop Page Tech. Services Inc., Vienna, 1977—. Mem. IEEE (sr.), Am. Soc. Mil. Engrs., Armed Forces Communications Electronics Assn., Washington Telecommunications Soc., Communications Soc. Republican. Roman Catholic. Club: K.C. Home: 2267 Marginella Dr Reston VA 22091 Office: 307A Maple Ave W Vienna VA 22180

VON BOMHARD, MORITZ, opera dir.; b. Berlin, June 19, 1908; came to U.S., 1936, naturalized, 1942; s. Ernst and Hanna (Schmid) B.; Referendar, U. Leipzig (Germany); diploma Conservatory Leipzig, 1932; diploma Juilliard Sch. Music, 1941; M.A., Columbia U. Tchrs. Coll., 1947; Ph.D. (hon.), Ursuline Coll., 1958, Center Coll.; m. Charme Elizabeth Risley, Aug. 31, 1962. Dir. Princeton U. Orch.-Glee Club, to 1942; founder, dir. New Lyric Stage opera co., eastern U.S.; founder, dir. Ky. Opera Assn., Louisville, 1952—; condr. Hamburg (Germany) Opera; stage dir. various European houses; guest condr. European symphony orchs.; publicity mgr., guest condr. Louisville Orch. Served with USAAF, 1942-45. Juilliard fellow; recipient Giorami Martini award Bellarmin Coll. Mem. Musicians Union. Roman Catholic. Composer 2 symphonies, chamber music, songs.

VON BUEDINGEN, RICHARD PAUL, urologist; b. Rochester, N.Y., Sept. 14, 1938; s. Wilmer Edward and Clara Elma Buedingen; B.S., U. Wis., 1960, M.A. in Philosophy, 1961, M.D., 1965; m. Bari Luwe Solesky, Nov. 26, 1966; children—Kirsten Karla, Christian Karl. Commd. ensign U.S. Navy, 1964, advanced through grades to capt., 1975, intern, U.S. Naval Hosp., St. Albans, N.Y., 1965-66, resident in internal medicine, in plastic and thoracic surgery, in urology affiliate programs Naval Regional Med. Center, Oakland, Calif., and U.S. Hosp., Oakland, U. Calif. San Francisco, Stanford U., 1969-73, resident in pediatric urology, 1973, scientist astronaut trainee Naval Aerospace Med. Inst., Pensacola, Fla., 1966-67, group flight surgeon Marine Corp Air Sta., Beaufort, S.C., 1967-69, chief urology Naval Regional Med. Center, Long Beach, Calif., 1973-75, asst. clin. prof. urology, U. Calif., Irvine, 1973-75, resigned, 1975; pvt. practice urology, Aiken, S.C., 1975—; bd. trustees Aiken Community Hosp., 1977-78. Fellow A.C.S.; mem. AMA, Am. Urol. Assn., S.C. Med. Assn., S.C. Urol. Assn., So. Med. Assn., Soc. Govt. Urologists, Aiken County Med. Soc. Club: Whiskey Rd. Fox Hounds (Master of Fox Hounds). Contbr. articles to profl. publs. Home: 217 Easy St Aiken SC 29801 Office: 154 Waterloo St Aiken SC 29801

VON DER HAAR, FRANK ANTHONY, fin. exec.; b. New Orleans, Aug. 26, 1927; s. Frank A. and Lucy (Ventura) Von Der H.; B.B.A., Tulane U., 1949; M.S., Columbia U., 1950. With Peat, Marwick, Mitchell & Co., New Orleans, 1950-52, 54-68; self-employed, 1952-54; with Williams, Inc. and related cos., New Orleans, 1968—, v.p. fin., sec.-treas., 1973—; treas. City Center Realty Co., Inc., New Orleans, 1972—, sec.-treas., 1973—; treas. Sea Energy Corp., New Orleans, 1977—. Sec.-treas., trustee Wildlife Preserve Found., 1975—; bd. dirs. New Orleans Symphony, 1978-80. Served with U.S. Army, 1945-46. C.P.A., La. Mem. C. of C. (mem. steering com. Central Area Council 1979), Tax Execs. (pres. 1974-75), La. Soc. C.P.A.'s, Am. Inst. C.P.A.'s, Internat. Trade Mart, Internat. House. Democrat. Roman Catholic. Home: 622 Dumaine St New Orleans LA 70116 Office: 1323 Whitney Bldg New Orleans LA 70130

VONDERHAAR, WILLIAM PURCELL, family practice physician; b. Davenport, Iowa, Oct. 21, 1930; s. Bernard Herman and Dorothy Elizabeth (Purcell) V.; A.B., U. Louisville, 1952, M.D., 1956; m. Elayne Elizabeth Roose, Sept. 8, 1954; children—Lisa Maret, Denys Laurent, Mark Roose, Niel Gerard, Gregory Jude, Julie Elayne, Kurt Barnard, Franz Purcell. Intern, U.S. Army Hosp., El Paso, Tex., 1956-57; gen. practice medicine, Vine Grove, Ky., 1957-58, Louisville, 1972—; first chairperson dept. family medicine U. Louisville, 1972—, asst. v.p. health affairs, 1974—, prof., 1973—; chmn. bd. subarea council Western Ky. Health Systems Agy. Bd., 1979—. Bd. dirs. Roman Catholic Sch., 1970—; chmn. County Sch. Bd., 1974—; bd. dirs. Community Action Commn., Neighborhood Health Assn.; active United Appeal. Served with USAF, 1950-52, Army N.G., 1952-56, U.S. Army, 1956-57. Named Man of Year, WHAS, WHAS-TV, 1963. Mem. AMA, Soc. Tchrs. Family Medicine, Am. Acad. Family Physicians, Am. Sch. Bds. Assn., Jefferson County Med. Soc. (pres. 1975). Democrat. Club: Kiwanis. Home: 1908 Tyler Ln Louisville KY 40205 Office: 500 S Preston St Louisville KY 40201

VON DER LANCKEN, CARL, lawyer, educator, lectr.; b. Rochester, N.Y., Apr. 22, 1910; s. Frank Louis and Giulia (Ulbrich) von der L.; student Western Res. U., 1929-30, George Washington U., 1930-31; LL.B., Cumberland U., 1932; B.A., U. Tulsa, 1933; M.A., Tulane U., 1936; postgrad. Harvard U., 1937-38; J.D., Samford U., 1969; m. Mary-Ellen Collins, Nov. 29, 1945; children—Carla, Paula. Admitted to Tenn. bar, 1932; mem. polit. sci. faculty U. Tulsa, 1936-37; account exec. Harry Caylor Assos., pub. relations, Chgo., 1942-43; legal counsel Nat. Labor Bur., Chgo., 1943-44; ednl. dir., editor United Shoe Workers Am., Chgo., 1944-46; exec. dir. Chgo. Council Am. Soviet Friendship, 1946-47; dir. Progressive Party of Okla., 1948-50, mem. nat. com., 1949-50; lectr. on Am. culture Brazil-U.S.A. Cultural Union, Sao Paulo, 1950-51; chmn. nat. pub. affairs Am. Ethical Union, 1954-56; exec. dir. L.I. Com. for Sane Nuclear Policy, 1955-57; chmn. L.I. Friends of Kefauver, also speech writer 1956 vice Predsl. campaign, 1956; chmn. N.Y.C. area Wayne Morse for Pres. campaign, 1960; prof. polit. sci. Westchester Community Coll., Valhalla, N.Y., 1959-75, prof. emeritus, 1975—; moderator pub. affairs program Radio Sta. WFAS, White Plains, N.Y., 1971-72. Co-ordinator Common Cause, 1st Congl. Dist., Fla., 1977-79; writer and lectr. on pub. affairs, 1977—. Mem. Greenburgh (N.Y.) Bd. Edn., 1963-66; Democratic nominee Westchester County Legislature, 1972; mem. Nat. Com. Dem. Alternative, 1979-80. Recipient Spl. Service award Am. Fedn. Tchrs. AFL/CIO, 1975; elected to Nat. Horseshoe Pitching Hall of Fame, 1977. Mem. Am. Judicature Soc., ACLU, Am. Acad. Polit. Sci., N.Y. State United Tchrs., United Fedn. Coll. Tchrs. (sec. N.Y.C. 1971-73). Common Cause, Nat. Horseshoe Pitchers Assn. Democrat. Club: Harvard. Cinema critic Westchester County News, 1970-71. Home: 2100 W Beach Dr Apt Y-102 Panama City FL 32401

VON KUTZLEBEN, BERND EBERHARD, nuclear engr.; b. N.Y.C., May 23, 1950; s. Siegfried Edwin and Ursula Herta (Klotz) von K.; B.Sc. equivalent in Physics, U. Hamburg (Germany), 1974; B.Sc. equivalent, Fachhochschule Wedel (Germany), 1976, M.Sc. equivalent in Phys. Engring., 1977. Lab. asst., head gas chromatography dept. Fachhochschule Wedel, Wedel, Germany, 1977-79; asst. shift test dir. Combustion Engring., Inc., Russellville, Ark., 1979—. Home: 1910 S El Paso Ave Apt 6 Russelville AR 72801 Office: Combustion Engring Inc 1000 Prospect Hill Rd Windsor CT 06095

VON ROSENBERG, DALE URSINI, chem. engr.; b. Austin, Tex., Sept. 5, 1928; s. Hermann Ursini and Lucy Marie (Goldthwaite) vonR.; B.S., U. Tex., 1949; Sc.D., Mass. Inst. Tech., 1953; m. Marjorie Ann Taylor, June 12, 1953; children—Carol Sue, Eugene Dale, Byron Alonzo, Clyde Hermann. Sr. research asso. Humble Oil & Refining Co., Houston, 1953-57; asso. prof. La. State U., Baton Rouge, 1957-63; prof. chem. engring. Tulane U., New Orleans, 1963-76, U. Tulsa, 1976-79; research asso. Mobil Research and Devel. Corp., Dallas, 1979—. Mem. Soc. Petroleum Engrs. Republican. Presbyterian. Author: Methods for the Numerical Solution of Partial Differential Equations, 1969. Office: Mobil Research and Devel Corp PO Box 900 Dallas TX 75221

VONSIATSKY, ANDRÉ ANASTASE, acct.; b. St. Petersburg, Fla., July 2, 1950; s. Anastase A. and Edith Priscilla (Royster) V.; A.A., St. Petersburg Jr. Coll., 1973; B.A. in Fin., U. South Fla., 1976; M.B.A., Wake Forest U., 1978; m. Jeanne Hunt Myers, Aug. 21, 1976; children—Dominique Marion, Anastase André. Gen. auditor First Nat. Bank, St. Petersburg, Fla., 1973-75; acct. Coopers & Lybrand, Tampa, Fla., 1978—; adj. instr. bus. St. Petersburg Jr. Coll., 1979—. Mem. Com. of 100, Pinellas County, new enterprise com., 1978—; campaign treas. Dorothy Sample for Fla. House, 1976, 78. C.P.A., Fla. Mem. Nat. Assn. Accts., Assn. of MBA Execs., Am. Inst. C.P.A.'s, Fla. Inst. C.P.A.'s, Phi Kappa Phi, Beta Gamma Sigma, Beta Alpha Psi, C. of C. Republican. Russian Orthodox. Home: 1601 Park St N Saint Petersburg FL 33710 Office: 1220 Exchange Bank Bldg Tampa FL 33602

VON TUNGELN, GEORGE ROBERT, educator; b. Golconda, Ill., July 18, 1931; s. Cecil Ernest and Rachel Elizabeth (Wright) von T.; B.S., So. Ill. U., 1951, M.S., 1956; Ph.D., U. Ga., 1974; m. Marilyn Ruth Burris, Nov. 6, 1955; children—Stuart, Cheryl, Brenda, Sonya, Eric. Asst. prof. to asso. prof. agrl. econs. Clemson U., 1958-68, coordinator spl. instrnl. programs, prof. agrl. scis., 1968-77, asst. to dean internat. programs, coordinator spl. instrnl. programs, prof., 1977—; cons. Pres., P.T.O., 1972. Served with AUS, 1952-54. Mem. Assn. State Univ. Dirs. Internat. Agrl. Programs, Assn. So. Agrl. Scientists. Baptist. Contbr. articles to research jours. Home: 101 Brookwood Dr Clemson SC 29631 Office: 102 Barre Hall Clemson Univ Clemson SC 29631

VOOS, WILLIAM JOHN, coll. exec.; b. St. Louis, July 2, 1930; s. William Fred and Dolly May (Hall) V.; B.F.A., Washington U., St. Louis, 1952; M.F.A., U. Kans., 1953; m. Louise M. Huddle, July 27, 1954; children—Nancy E., Susan L., Patricia A. Designer, Advertiser's Displays & Exhibits, Inc., St. Louis, 1953; chmn. art dept. McCluer High Sch., Florissant, Mo., 1956-64; chmn. div. humanities Florissant Valley Community Coll., 1964-68; asso. dean, asso. prof. art Washington U. Sch. Fine Arts, 1968-73; dean Atlanta Coll. Art, 1973-75, pres., 1975—. Mem. Marta Council on Arts; mem. adv. bd. art Atlanta Public Library; mem. adv. panel on art Atlanta GSA. Served with U.S. Army, 1953-55. NEA fellow in fine arts adminstrn. N.Y. U., 1967. Mem. Coll. Art Assn., Ga. Alliance for Arts, Union Ind. Colls. Art (vice chmn.). Exhibited art in one-man shows. Office: 1280 Peachtree St Atlanta GA 30309

VORISEK, ELMER ALBERT, ret. ophthalmologist; b. Chgo., Nov. 7, 1900; s. Albert O. and Louise O. (Kucera) V.; B.S., U. Chgo., 1921; M.D., Rush Med. Coll., 1923; m. Matilde Pekny, Nov. 6, 1928. Resident in ophthalmology Presbyterian Hosp., Chgo., 1928-29, med. instn., Vienna, Austria, 1929; prof. Elschnig Clinic, Prague, Czechoslovakia, 1930; asst., dept. ophthalmology Rush Med. Coll., Chgo., 1929-31; practice medicine specializing in ophthalmology, Chgo., 1923-51, Des Moines, 1952-72; asso. attending ophthalmologist St. Lukes Hosp., Children's Meml. Hosp., Chgo., 1931-51; chief eye service Lawson U.S. Army Gen. Hosp., Atlanta, 1941-46. cons. Municipal Contagious Diseases Hosp., Chgo., 1931-51; mem. ophthalmology staff Iowa Meth. Hosp., Mercy Hosp., Iowa Luth. Hosp., Des Moines, 1951-71; cons. in ophthalmology Knoxville (Iowa) VA Hosp., 1952-72; med. adviser Iowa State Dir. SSS, 1952-72; ret., 1972. Diplomate Am. Bd. Ophthalmology. Col. M.C. USAR ret. Mem. AMA., Am-Ophthal. Soc. Club: K.C. (past grand knight, 4 deg.). Contbr. articles to med. jours.; radio speaker. Home: Rt 1 Eureka Springs AR 72632

VORSANGER, FRED S., univ. adminstr.; b. Calumet City, Ill., Apr. 20, 1928; s. Fred and Hannah (Steifel) V.; B.S. in Bus. Adminstrn., Ind. U., 1951; M.B.A., George Washington U., 1970; postgrad. U. Ark., 1971; m. Doreen D. Carter, Apr. 24, 1965; children—Diana, Bruce, Bob; 1 stepson, Mark Carter. Accountant, Ernst & Ernst, Chgo., 1951-53; internal auditor Purdue U., Lafayette, Ind., 1953-59; treas., bus. mgr. Am. Council on Edn., Washington, 1959-68; v.p. U. Ark., Fayetteville, 1968—; trustee Common Fund, N.Y.C.; dir. Tyson Foods, Inc.; pres. Sacubo; faculty Coll. Bus. Mgmt. Curriculum, U. Ky. and U. Calif. at Santa Barbara, 1975—. Spl. cons. Meridian House Found., Washington, 1960-68; treas. Inst. for Service to Edn., Washington, 1967-68; examiner N. Central Commn. on Accrediting, 1971—. Pres., Washington County unit Am. Cancer Soc., 1971-72. Bd. dirs. Nationwide Edn. Conf. Centers, N.W. Ark. Regional Planning Commn., Ark. Regional Med. Program, U. Ark. Found., Fayetteville Community Concert Assn., Nat. Assn. Land Grant Colls. and State Univs. Served with AUS, 1945-47. Mem. Nat. Assn. Ednl. Buyers (treas., dir.), Nat. (profl. devel. com., dir.), So. (pres.) assns. coll. and univ. bus. officers, Am. Council Edn. (com. taxation), Fayetteville C. of C. (dir., treas.), Blue Key, Delta Sigma Pi, Sigma Phi Epsilon. Clubs: Rotary; Fayetteville Country; Capitol (Little Rock). Author: (with Julian H. Levi) Patterns of Giving to Higher Education, 1968. Contbr. articles to profl. jours. Editorial adv. bd. Commerce Clearing House, Inc., 1963-68; editorial adv. com. Coll. and Univ. Bus. Mag. Home: 1315 E Ridgeway Dr Fayetteville AR 72701

VOSS, KENNETH WILLIAM, II, county ofcl.; b. Los Angeles, Nov. 22, 1943; s. Kenneth William and Madeline Liana (Bajiot) V.; B.A., E. Carolina U., Greenville, N.C., 1970; m. Judi Ann Kline, Aug. 24, 1969; children—Heidi Elizabeth, Kenneth William, III. Comml./resident appraiser Snohomish County, Everett, Wash., 1970-74; valuation specialist N.C. Dept. Revenue, Raleigh, 1974-75; dir. revaluation Cumberland County, Fayetteville, N.C., 1975—; instr. Fayetteville Tech. Inst., Harold Walters Sch. Real Estate. Pres. Sunday sch. for adults 1st Baptist Ch., Fayetteville, 1978-80, chmn. youth council, 1979; pres. Better Homes for Families, 1978; bd. dirs. Royal Ambassadors Youth Group, 1977-80. Served with USMCR, 1963-66. Norman Register scholar, 1975. Mem. Am. Inst. Real Estate Appraisers, Soc. Real Estate Appraisers, Internat. Assn. Assessing Officers, Am. Right-of-Way Assn., Nat. Assn. Rev. Appraisers, Am. Soc. Appraisers, Green Valley Watch Assn. Clubs: N.C. Track, E. Carolina Priate, Elks. Author, speaker in field. Home: 1602 Snead Ave Fayetteville NC 28303 Office: 121 Franklin St Fayetteville NC 28302

VOSS, STEPHEN CULWELL, petroleum co. exec.; b. McAllen, Tex., Oct. 27, 1948; s. John William and Lila Beth (Culwell) V.; B.S. in Petroleum Engring., Tex. A&M U., 1971; M.B.A., Harvard U., 1976; m. Elizabeth Anne Baltis, Jan. 2, 1970; children—Matthew Bradley, Austin Grant, Michelle Leigh. Petroleum engr. Chevron Oil Co., Lafayette, La., 1971-72; drilling engr. Aminoil, Lafayette, 1973-76; drilling engr.; coordinator Goldrus Drilling Co., Lafayette, 1976-77, mgr. drilling ops., 1978, v.p. drilling ops., 1979—. Registered profl. engr., Tex. Mem. Internat. Assn. Drilling Contractors (dir., chmn. So. La. chpt.), So. Petroleum Engrs., Tex. Soc. Profl. Engrs., Lafayette C. of C., Tau Beta Pi, Pi Epsilon Tau. Republican. Mem. Ch. of Christ. Home: 106 Eton Circle Lafayette LA 70508 Office: Goldrus Drilling Co 300 Whitney Sq Lafayette LA 70501

VOTRAL, RONALD ANDREW, pharm. co. exec.; b. Fountain Hill, Pa., May 19, 1953; s. Michael and Mary Bridget (Ulincy) V.; B.S. in Pharmacy, Temple U., Phila., 1976; m. Catherine Louise Blaisse, Feb. 26, 1977. Pharmacist, Allentown (Pa.) and Sacred Heart Hosp. Center, 1976-77; nuclear pharmacist Pharmatopes, Inc., Toledo, 1977; dir. pharmacy Driscoll Found. Children's Hosp., Corpus Christi, Tex., 1977-78; sales rep. Eli Lilly Co., Corpus Christi, 1978—. Mem. Am. Soc. Hosp. Pharmacists, Tex. Pharm. Assn., Kappa Psi. Democrat. Roman Catholic. Club: Racquetball (Corpus Christi). Address: 6029 Norvel St Corpus Christi TX 78412

VRANEK, ERIC ANTHONY, air force officer; b. Chgo., Nov. 6, 1947; s. Anthony Otto and Marjorie Constance (Boquist) V.; B.A., Grinnell Coll., 1969; M.B.A., U. Utah, 1975; m. Lynda Renee Lamberth, Dec. 30, 1970; children—Jennifer Lynn, Jon David. Commd. 2d lt. U.S. Air Force, 1970, advanced through grades to capt., 1974; assigned to Mountain Home AFB, Idaho, 1972-73, 74-76, Anderson AFB, Guam, 1973-74, Webb AFB, Tex., 1976-77; ops. staff officer, T-37 instr. pilot 14 Flying Tng. Wing, Columbus AFB, Miss., 1977—. Mem. adminstrv. bd. Broadacres United Methodist Ch., Columbus, 1979—. Decorated Air Force Commendation medal. Mem. Air Force Assn., Beta Gamma Sigma. Republican. Home: 3303 Wisteria Rd Columbus MS 39701 Office: 14 Flying Tng Wing/Door Columbus AFB MS 39701

VROOM, JAMES RANDALL, hosp. adminstr., acct.; b. Balt., Sept. 12, 1954; s. Henry Joseph and Janet Louise V.; B.A. cum laude, Duke U., 1976, M.Hosp.Adminstrn., 1978. Adminstrv. intern N.C. Justice Dept. for James H. Pou Bailey, sr. resident judge, 10th. Jud. Dist., Raleigh, 1975; asst. chief Outpatient Adminstrn. Ser., Naval Regional Med. Center, U.S. Navy, Charleston, S.C., 1978, asst. chief Manpower Mgmt. Service, 1979, projects and plans officer, 1979-80, asst. chief Fin. and Material Mgmt. Service, 1980—; commd. ensign U.S. Navy, 1976, advanced through ranks to lt., 1979; staff acct., Dennis P. Baars, Acctg., Charleston, 1979—. C.P.A. Duke Health Adminstrn. Merit scholar, 1976-78. Mem. Am. Coll. Hosp. Adminstrs., N.C. Assn. C.P.A.'s, Am. Hosp. Assn. Democrat. Roman Catholic. Club: Charleston Officers. Home: Apt I-8 Boone Hall Dr Charleston SC 29407 Office: Naval Regional Med Center McMillian and Rivers Ave Charleston SC 29408

VROOMAN, WILLIAM PAUL, mgmt. engr., hosp. adminstr.; b. Schenectady, N.Y., Feb. 2, 1944; s. Foster Paul and Mary Lucille (Rowe) V.; B.S., Rensselaer Poly. Inst., Troy, N.Y., 1966; M.S., Union Coll., Schenectady, N.Y., 1971; children—Deborah Ann, Tammy Lynn, Kelly Ann. Quality engr. Norton Co., Troy, N.Y., 1966-67; co. planning analyst Gen. Electric Co., Schenectady, 1967-71; mgmt. engr., Hosp. Assn. N.Y. State, Albany, 1971-73; sr. research analyst N.Y. State Dept. Health, Albany, 1973-74; pres. James Rowe Pubs. and James Rowe Assos., Schenectady, 1974-78; sr. cons. Medicus Systems Corp., Chgo., 1975-78; sr. mgmt. engr., Vanderbilt U. Hosp., Nashville, 1978—. Mem. Hosp. Mgmt. Systems Soc. Conservative. Home: 155 Bay Shore Dr Hendersonville TN 37075 Office: Mgmt Engring Vanderbilt U Hosp 3200 W End Ave Nashville TN 37203

WAAS, GEORGE LEE, lawyer; b. N.Y.C., July 12, 1943; s. George and Anne W.; B.S. in Journalism, U. Fla., 1965; J.D., Fla. State U., 1970; m. Harriet Issner, July 18, 1971; children—Elaine Beth, Amy Michelle. Newspaper reporter Palm Beach Post, Fort Lauderdale News, 1966-67; admitted to Fla. bar, 1970, U.S. Supreme Ct. bar, 1973; legal research asst., asst. atty. gen., Tallahassee, 1968, 69-71; staff atty. Fla. League Cities, 1971; asst. to dir. of labor Sec. of Commerce, Tallahassee, 1971-73; asst. dir. Fla. Bar, 1973-74; asst. dean Fla. State U. Coll. Law, 1974-75; staff atty. Fla. Dept. Transp., 1975-77; asst. gen. counsel Fla. Dept. Health and Rehab. Services, Tallahassee, 1977—; cons. Fla. Legal Services. Mem. Leon County Democratic Com., 1970-71. Mem. Fla. Govt. Bar Assn. Tallhassee Bar Assn. Jewish. Club: Capital Tiger Bay. Home: 400 Collinsford Rd Tallahassee FL 32301 Office: Suite 406 1323 Winewood Blvd Tallahassee FL 32301

WACHTEL, THOMAS DELL, state ofcl.; b. Dumas, Ark., Apr. 6, 1940; s. Carl D. and Juddie L. (Fornea) W.; B.S., U. Central Ark., 1962; M.B.A., Loyola U., 1971; children—Thomas Scott, Ruston Dee, John Randall. With Martin Co., Little Rock and Denver, 1962-64, space div. Chrysler Corp., New Orleans and Detroit, 1964-68, Boeing Co., Seattle and New Orleans, 1968-70, Litton Industries, Pascagoula, Miss. and Los Angeles, 1970-71, LTV, Dallas and Detroit, 1971-76; quality assurance adminstr. Ark. Dept. Computer Scis., Little Rock, 1976—; cons. in field. Mem. Am. Logistics Soc., Nat. Eagle Scout Assn. Democrat. Methodist. Club: Elks. Home: 6900 Cantrell Rd Apt D3 Little Rock AR 72207 Office: PO Box 3155 Little Rock AR 72203

WADDELL, HAROLD EDWARD, JR., computer programmer; b. Rome, Ga., June 19, 1951; s. Harold Edward and Mary Sue (Gresham) W.; student Coosa Valley Vocat. Tech. Sch., 1969-71, Reinhardt Coll., 1978—; m. Victoria Kaye Cleveland, Feb. 26, 1971; children—Ryan, Adam. Contract programmer NCR, Atlanta, 1971-72; computer programmer Canton (Ga.) Textile Mills, Inc., 1972-73, programmer analyst, 1973-74, mgr. programmers, 1974—. Reinhardt Coll. scholar, 1979, Polit. Sci. Honors award, 1979; cert. data processor. Mem. Data Processing Mgmt. Assn. Baptist. Club: Trout Unltd. Home: Route 6 Canton GA 30114 Office: PO Box 827 Canton GA 30114

WADDELL, JAMES MADISON, JR., state senator; b. Boydell, Ark., Nov. 1, 1922; s. James Madison and Mable Waddell; B.S. in Civil Engring., The Citadel, 1947, LL.D., 1972; m. Natalie Lavis, Jan. 2, 1946; children—James M.V., Michael, John. Pres. Citizens Ins. Agy., Beaufort, S.C., also gen. agt. Pilot Life Ins. Co.; mem. S.C. Ho. of Reps., 1954-58; mem. S.C. Senate, 1960—, chmn. fish, game and forestry com., 1st vice chmn. fin. com. Served to capt. AUS, 1943-46; ETO. Decorated Bronze Star, Purple Heart, Combat Inf. badge; named Outstanding Senator of Year, Greenville News, 1977, 78; Outstanding Legislator S.C. Council Exceptional Children, 1977; Soil Conservationist of Year, S.C. Wildlife Fedn., 1973, Legis. Conservationist of Year, 1977. Mem. Assn. Citadel Men, DAV, Navy League, Ret. Officers Assn., VFW. Democrat. Presbyterian. Club: Shriners. Home: 1500 Riverside Dr Beaufort SC 29902 Office: PO Box 1026 Beaufort SC 29902

WADDELL, JOHN ROY, constrn. components co. ofcl.; b. Greeneville, Tenn., Dec. 17, 1947; s. Walter Woodrow and Ida Mae (Shenault) W.; student U. Tenn., 1965-68, E. Tenn. State U., 1968-69; m. Frances Ann Gosnell, June 10, 1969; children—Benjamin John, Robin Anne. Draftsman, Garland Constrn. Co., Johnson City, Tenn., 1969-73; owner Waddell Constrn. Co., Greeneville, Tenn., 1973-76; asst. plant mgr. Truss Inc., Knoxville, Tenn., 1976, gen. mgr., 1976—. Mem. Component Mfg. Council. Democrat. Methodist. Home: 7812 E Sesame Ln Knoxville TN 37918 Office: Route 13 Norris Freeway Knoxville TN 37918

WADDELL, KAREN VINYARD, hosp. exec.; b. Oklahoma City, Sept. 16, 1949; d. Marvin Randal and Thelma Ida May (Thomas) Vinyard; B.A. in Journalism, U. Okla., 1971; m. Bruce Lee Waddell, Aug. 22, 1970; children—Joshua Douglas, Jill Dru. Writer, Daily Oklahoman, Oklahoma City, 1970-71; dir. pub. relations Okla. Heart Assn., Oklahoma City, 1971-73; account exec., writer Ackerman Inc., Oklahoma City, 1973-75; dir. community relations Presbyterian Hosp., Oklahoma City, 1976—, asst. to pres., 1977—. Mem. pub. relations com. Okla. Heart Assn., 1974—; adj. instr. U. Okla. Sch. Journalism. Mem. Pub. Relations Soc. Am. (accredited), Internat. Assn. Bus. Communicators, Okla. Hosp. Assn. Pub. Relations Soc. (pres.), Am. Hosp. Assn. Soc. Public Relations Dirs., Sigma Delta Chi. Baptist. Editor Perspectives, Prebyn. Hosp. quar., 1976—. Home: 7310 NW 106 Oklahoma City OK 73132 Office: Presbyterian Hosp NE 13th at Lincoln Blvd Oklahoma City OK 73104

WADDELL, RAYMOND LEE, sch. adminstr.; b. Marks, Miss., June 24, 1931; s. Robert Lee and Ollie Mae (Gilmore) W.; B.A., Mid-South Bible Coll., 1967; B.A., Memphis State U., 1970, M.A., 1973, postgrad., 1973—; m. Mary Kathryn Grace, Aug. 5, 1950; children—Stanley Ray, Sandra Kaye. Customer rep. Memphis Light, Gas and Water div., Tenn., 1952-71; tchr. C. H. Spurgeon Acad., Memphis, 1971-73; tchr. First Assembly Christian Sch., Memphis, 1974-75, elem.-secondary adminstr., 1975-79; prin. Lake County High Sch., Tiptonville, Tenn., 1979—; ednl. cons., Munford, Tenn., 1978. Served with AUS, 1950-51. Mem. Nat. Assn. Elem. Sch. Prins., Am. Hist. Assn., Memphis Assn. Ind. Schs., Tenn. Assn. Ind. Schs., Tenn. Assn. Middle Schs. First Assembly of God. Home: 4471 Dunn St Memphis TN 38117

WADDINGTON, HENRY RICHARD, restaurateur; b. Phila., Jan. 20, 1939; s. Robert McCoy and Dorothy Jane (Young) W.; B.S. in Bus. Adminstrn., Buckenell U., 1961; m. Caroline Scheidt, July 8, 1967; children—Shelley Jane, Douglas Karl; 1 son by previous marriage, Henry R. Asst. mgr. restaurant div. Stauffer Foods Corp., 1961-64; gen. mgr. New Orleans Playboy Club, Playboy Internat., 1968-69; gen. mgr. Segefield Country Club, Greensboro, N.C., 1970-72, Officers Club, Naval Sta., Charleston, S.C., 1972-76; sec.-treas., operation mgr. The Colony House and Wine Cellar restaurants Trigon, Inc., Charleston, S.C., 1976—; dir. Sprouts & Krouts, Inc.; mem. adv. bd. Coll. Gen. Studies, Hotel, Restaurant and Tourism Sch., U. S.C. Vice-pres., Charleston Travel Council, 1978—; mem. food com. Spoleto Arts Festival, 1977—; chmn. food com. Miss U.S.A. Beauty Pageant, 1977-78; bd. dirs. E. Copper Sch., 1978-79; fin. chmn. Charleston Invitation Tennis Tournament, 1979, chmn., 1980. Served from ensign to lt. USNR, 1964-68; Vietnam. Mem. S.C. Restaurant Assn. (1st v.p. 1978-79, Restaurateur of Yr. 1979, dir. 1977—, pres. 1979—), Charleston-Trident C. of C. (dir.), Internat. Mil. Club Execs. Assn. (v.p. 1975-76, dir. 1974-76). Republican. Presbyterian. Clubs: Charleston Tennis (dir.), Seabrook Country; Rotary (dir. 1979—) (Charleston). Contbr. articles to profl. mag. Home: 721 Creekside Dr Mount Pleasant SC 29464 Office: Trigon Inc 35 Prioleau St Charleston SC 29401

WADDLE, TED W., state legislator; b. Somerset, Ky., July 9, 1928; James K. and Jessie L. (Kelly) W.; student Internat. Corr. Schs.; m. Barbara Westbrook, June 4, 1949; children—Ted W., Donna Lynn, Debra K., Timothy B. Pres., Waddle & Co., Warner Robins, Ga., 1955—; mem. Ga. Ho. of Reps. from 113th Dist., 1973—. Mem. Ga. Soc. Profl. Engrs., Surveying and Mapping Soc. Ga. Republican. Baptist. Club: Morning Optimist. Address: 113 Tanglewood Dr Warner Robins GA 31093

WADE, CHARLES RONALD, ins. exec.; b. Monroe, La., Dec. 26, 1950; s. Alex Melvin and Loree Davenport (Hunter) W.; B.B.A., Tex. So. U., 1979; m. Callie Marie Cheeks, Aug. 4, 1973; 1 son, Charles Ronald. Owner, operator Wade's Upholstery, Houston, 1972-75; sr. accountant S.R. Wade & Assos., Houston, 1975-78; v.p. Saratoga Enterprises, Inc., Houston, 1977—; agt., prin. Charles Wade Ins. Agy., Houston, 1976—. Served with USN, 1969-71. Mem. CORE, Tex. Black Polit. Caucus, NAACP, Amvets, Houston Assn. Life Underwriters. Democrat. Baptist. Home: 1807 Thorbrook Missouri City TX 77459 Office: PO Box 943 Missouri City TX 77459

WADE, GERALDINE ELIZABETH, ednl. counselor; b. Oklahoma City, Jan. 13, 1929; d. John Reed and Mildred Virginia (Mobley) Raymer; B.S. in Edn., U. Okla., 1950, M.Ed., 1963; children—Christopher L. Kerns, Stephen M. Kerns. Tchr. English and French, Midwest City (Okla.) Sch. System, 1959-64; counselor Mid-Del Sch. System, Midwest City, 1964—, Carl Albert Jr. High Sch., 1971—; admissions counselor, evening asst. to registrar, psychology tchr. Oscar Rose Jr. Coll., Midwest City, part-time, 1975—. State of Okla. and Central State U. grantee to Career Inst. for Counselors, 1977. Mem. U. Okla. Alumni Assn., Am., Okla. personnel and guidance assns., NEA, Okla. Edn. Assn., Assn. Classroom Tchrs., Midwest City C. of C. Democrat. Methodist. Author: Occupational Information: Focus on Guidance, 1974. Home: 3700 S Anderson Rd Choctaw OK 73020 Office: 2515 S Post Rd Midwest City OK 73130 also 6420 SE 15th St Midwest City OK 73110

WADE, JAMES ALBERT, oil co. exec.; b. Paris, Tex., Sept. 4, 1953; s. Lawrence Albert and Betty Jo (Norvell) W.; B.B.A., E. Tex. State U., 1974; postgrad. So. Methodist U.; m. Karon Jean Vickers, May 25, 1974; 1 son, Kristopher James. Fin. acct. Mobil Oil Corp., Dallas, 1975-77, tax acct., 1977—; self-employed fin. cons., 1977—. Mem. ch. council, pre-sch. coordinator Urbandale 1st Baptist Ch. Mem. Tex. Assn. Public Accountants, Phi Theta Kappa, Alpha Chi. Home: 10517 Checota St Dallas TX 75217 Office: PO Box 900 Dallas TX 75221

WADE, KENNETH DALLAS, mfg. co. exec.; b. Switchback, W. Va., Oct. 29, 1936; s. John Emmett and Gertrude Lee (Crigger) W.; B.S. in Edn., Concord Coll., 1961; M.S. in Personnel Adminstrn., George Washington U., 1967; Ph.D. in Bus. Adminstrn., Calif. Western U., 1977; m. Pamela Alta Meadows, Aug. 4, 1960; children—Tammy Ann, Kenneth Dallas, Shannon Kanett. Instr. McLain Coll., Bluefield, W. Va., 1961-62; personnel asst. N. & W Rys., Bluefield, 1962-63; coordinator distributive edn. Virginia Beach (Va.) pub. schs., 1963-66; personnel mgr. Universal Elec. Co., Altavista, Va., 1966-72; personnel dir. Lane Co., Altavista, 1972-73; pres. Central Va. Industries, Inc., Lynchburg, 1973—; dir. Greater Lynchburg Transit Co., Lynchburg Devel. Corp.; vice-chmn. Gov.'s Pvt. Industry Council; pub. mem. Blue Cross Va. Bd. dirs. Jr. Achievement Lynchburg, 1973—; Central Va. Planning Dist. Commn., 1973—; Central Va. Manpower Planning Council, 1973-76; Central Va. Health Planning Council, 1973-76; Central Va. Speech & Hearing Center, 1973-76. Served with USAF, 1954-58. Mem. Lynchburg Rotary (v.p. 1975), Va. Parents and Tchrs. Assn., Am. Soc. for Personnel Adminstrn., Central Va. Personnel Assn., Nat. Indsl. Council. Democrat. Baptist. Clubs: Hill City Swim and Tennis, Piedmont. Editor Central Va. Industires Bulletin; editor: Survey of Compensation and Benefits for Central Va., 1973—. Home: 108 Village Rd Lynchburg VA 24502 Office: 604 F & M Bldg Lynchburg VA 24504

WADE, KENNETH RAND, motor carrier co. exec.; b. Knoxville, Tenn., Aug. 12, 1944; s. Dwight Robert and Kate (Reagan) W.; B.S., U. Tenn., 1966; postgrad. East Tenn. State U., 1978; m. Georgene Mitchell Stevens, July 7, 1979; 1 dau., Kathryn Alexis; 1 stepson, Jay Ragan Stevens. Mgmt. trainee Mason and Dixon Lines, Inc., Atlanta, 1971-72, platform supr., Chattanooga, 1972-73, sales rep., Ft. Wayne, Ind., 1973-75, supr. personnel recruiting and tng., Kingsport, Tenn., 1975-76, mgr. personnel, 1976—. Chmn. vocat. office edn. adv. bd. Dobyns-Bennett High Sch., Kingsport, 1977—; mem. adv. bd. Tri-Cities State Tech. Inst., Blountville, Tenn., 1978—; mem. adv. bd. Alcohol and Drug Council, Kingsport, 1978—. Served to capt. USMC, 1967-71; Vietnam. Decorated Air medal (22). Mem. Am. Soc. Personnel Adminstrs., Tenn. Coll. Placement Assn., Ft. Wayne Traffic Club. Democrat. Methodist. Clubs: Elks, Eagles. Home: 108 Leslie Ct Kingsport TN 37663 Office: PO Box 969 Kingsport TN 37662

WADE, LENNIS PRESTON, engring. co. exec.; b. Lynchburg, Va., June 30, 1933; s. Lennis Bob and Dolah (Carey) W.; B.C.E., Va. Poly. Inst. and State U., 1955, postgrad., 1955-56; m. Jett Gale Preble, July 1, 1955; children—Gale Preble, Larke Lizette, Stephanie Preston. Instr. applied mechanics Va. Poly. Inst. and State U., Blacksburg, 1955-56; engr. Wiley & Wilson Engrs., Architects, Planners, Lynchburg, 1958— asso., 1964-69, partner, 1969-72, v.p., 1973, pres., 1973-79, chmn. bd., 1980—; dir. First & Mchts. Nat. Bank. Mem. adv. bd. Lynchburg Salvation Army, 1978—; bd. dirs. Lynchburg Fine Arts Center, 1979—. Served to 1st lt. USAF, 1956-58. Recipient The Societas Cincinnatorum Inst. award, 1955. Mem. Arnold Air Soc., Va. Poly. Inst. and State U. Alumni Assn. (dir. 1975—, pres. Lynchburg chpt. 1966-67), Greater Lynchburg C. of C. (dir. 1974-78, pres 1976-77), Va. Soc. Profl. Engrs. (state pres. 1970-71, Distinguished Service award 1971, Engr. of Year 1977), Nat. Soc. Profl. Engrs. (nat. dir. 1975-79), Va. Assn. Professions, ASCE, Newcomen Soc., Tau Beta Pi, Chi Epsilon, Omicron Delta Kappa, Scabbard & Blade. Presbyn. (deacon 1967-69, elder 1970-73, 76-79). Clubs: Boonsboro Country, Piedmont. Home: 1515 Langhorne Rd Lynchburg VA 24505 Office: PO Box 877 2310 Langhorne Rd Lynchburg VA 24501

WADE, THOMAS EDWARD, educator; b. Jacksonville, Fla., Sept. 14, 1943; s. Wilton Fred and Alice Lucyle (Hedge) W.; B.S. in E.E., U. Fla., 1966, M.S., 1969, Ph.D., 1974; m. Ann Elizabeth Chitty, Aug. 6, 1966; children—Amy Renee, Nathan Thomas. Illumination and power distribution engr. Reynolds, Smith & Hill Archtl. and Engring., Jacksonville, summer, 1964; TV studio engr. U. Fla. Genesis system, Gainesville, 1966-63, elec. engring. instr., 1968-74, interim asst. prof., 1975, adminstr. Electron Device Research Center, 1976; asst. prof. elec. engring. Miss. State U., Mississippi State, 1976—, pres. faculty council, 1980; session chmn. Internat. Electron Devices Meeting, 1978, Univ./Industry/Govt. Microelectronics Symposium, 1979, gen. chmn., 1980; pubs. chmn. Southeastern Symposium on System Theory, 1977. Bd. deacons First Bapt. Ch., Starkville, Miss., 1979—, mem. fin. com., 1979—, chancelor choir, 1976—. Recipient Outstanding Undergrad. Engring. Teaching award, U. Fla., 1976; Leadership Certificate, Fla. Engring. Soc., 1973; Leadership Key, Benton Engring. Soc., 1969, 70, 72. Mem. IEEE, Am. Assn. Engring. Edn., Am. Sci. Affiliation, AAAS, Miss. Engring. Soc., Soc. Photo. Optical Instrumentation, Internat. Soc. Hybrid Microelectronics, Electronics Internat. Adv. Com., Miss. Acad. Sci., Sigma Xi, Tau Beta Pi, Eta Kappa Nu, Sigma Tau, Omicron Delta Kappa, Blue Key, Epsilon Lambda Chi, Alpha Phi Omega. Democrat. Baptist. Club: Rotary Internat. Contbr. articles to profl. jours. Home: 707 Old West Point Rd Starkville MS 39759 Office: PO Drawer EE Mississippi State MS 39762

WADE, WILLIAM HALL, physician; b. El Paso, Tex., Jan. 26, 1928; s. Edward Charles and Avis Mary (Hall) W.; student U. Tex., El Paso, 1944-46; M.D., Northwestern U., 1950; m. Karen B. Rodenbush, Sept. 26, 1971; children—Michele, William II, Edward, James, David Matthew. Intern, N.Y. U., 1950-51, resident in surgery, 1953-57; asst. prof. surgery U. Mo., 1958; asso. prof. Bellevue Med. Center, N.Y. U., N.Y.C., 1959; practice medicine specializing in general and vascular surgery, El Paso, 1960—; attending surgeon Providence Meml. Hosp., 1960—, chief of surgery, 1966; attending surgeon Hotel Dieu Hosp., 1960—, chief staff, 1978-80, chief of surgery, 1968-76; attending surgeon Sun Towers Hosp., 1966—, chief of surgery, 1970, chief staff, 1971; attending surgeon Southwestern Gen. Hosp., Sierra Med. Center. Served with AUS, 1951-53. Diplomate Am. Bd. Surgery. Fellow A.C.S. (pres. N.Mex.-El Paso chpt. 1975); mem. El Paso County Med. Soc. (pres. 1978), AMA, Tex. Med. Assn. (com. profl. ins. 1974—), Tex. Surg. Soc. Episcopalian (vestry 1978—). Club: Rotary. Pres., El Paso Sheriff's Posse, 1978. Contbr. articles to profl. jours. Home: 4245 Park Hill El Paso TX 79902 Office: 1501 Arizona St 15-E El Paso TX 79902

WADHWANI, PRAKASH KISHINCHAND, engring. and planning co. exec.; b. Karachi, Pakistan, Oct. 21, 1944; s. Kishinchand Roopchand and Gopi Kishinchand (Samtani) W.; naturalized, 1977; B.S. in Civil Engring., M.S. U. Baroda (India), 1968; m. Rita Parasram Gidwani, Nov. 1, 1975. Regional rep. in W. India, Harper & Row Publishers, 1969-70; mgr. airport div. Raike Assos., Inc., Ashland, Ohio, 1971-73; sr airport planner Ralph M. Parsons Co., Pasadena, Calif., 1973-75; sr. airport engr. Modam Cons. Engrs., Tehran, 1975-76; exec. dir Raike Assos., Inc., Atlanta, 1976— pres. Wadwani Assos., Inc., Atlanta, 1979—. Mem. Airport Operators Council Internat., Am. Assn. Airport Execs., S.E. Airport Mgrs. Assn., Airport Cons. Council, Am.-Indian Cultural Soc. Club: Pinetree Country (Kennesaw). Home: 1411 Shiloh Trail E Kennesaw GA 30144 Office: PO Box 525 Kennesaw GA 30144

WAGAR, JOE A., constrn. co. exec.; b. Belcourt, N.D., Oct. 13, 1932; s. James E. and Clara A. (Thiefault) W.; studnet pub. schs., N.D.; m. Maxine Ruark, Nov. 24, 1962; 4 stepchildren. Constrn. supt. Goodman & Rossman, Orlando, Fla., 1967, United Fla., Orlando, 1968; project mgr., v.p. C & H Constrn. Co., Jacksonville, Fla., 1970-77; project mgr Ramar Group, Sarasota, Fla., 1977—. Served with U.S. Army, 1952-54. Roman Catholic. Address: PO Box 1832 Venice FL 33595

WAGENER, JAMES W., univ. pres.; b. Edgewood, Tex., Mar. 18, 1930; s. James W. and Ima (Crump) W.; B.A., So. Meth. U., 1951; M.A., U. Tex., Austin, 1967, Ph.D., 1968; m. Ruth Elaine Hoffman, May 31, 1956; children—LuAnn Wagener Powers, Laurie Kay. Instr. U. Tex., Austin, 1967-68, asst. prof., 1970-74; asst. prof. U. Tenn., 1968-70; asst. to chancellor for academic affairs The U. Tex. System, 1974; asso. prof U. Tex., San Antonio, 1974-79, prof. div. edn., 1978—, acting pres., 1978, pres., 1978—, asst. to pres. Health Sci. Center, 1974-75, exec. asst. to pres., 1975-77, acting dean, 1976-77. Bd. govs. Southwest Found. for Research and Edn., San Antonio, 1978—; bd. dirs., trustee Southwest Research Inst., San Antonio, 1978—. Ellis fellow, 1967-68. Mem Greater San Antonio C. of C., Am. Ednl. Studies Assn., Assn. Institutional Research, Soc. Profs. Edn., Soc. Coll. and Univ. Planning, Phi Delta Kappa, Phi Theta Kappa. Clubs: Rotary, Torch. Contbr. articles and book revs. in field. Home: 209 Sir Arthur Ct San Antonio TX 78213 Office: The Univ of Texas San Antonio TX 78285

WAGENER, KATHRYN LOUISE, nurse; b. Pitts., Feb. 2, 1935; d. Raymond Daniel and Stella (Keller) W.; B.S. in Nursing, U. Pitts., 1958. Staff nurse Western Psychiat. Inst. and Clinic, Pitts., 1958-59, Lee Meml. Hosp., Ft. Myers, Fla., 1959-61, head nurse recovery room, 1961-73, supr. operating room and recovery room, 1973-79; supr. operating and recovery rooms Lehigh Acres Gen. Hosp., 1979—; admissions com. surg. technologists program Lee Vocat. Tech. Sch.; nurse panel Davis & Geck Co. Mem. Assn. Operating Room Nurses. Republican. Presbyterian. Club: Greater Ft. Myers Dog. Home: 966 Hyacinth St North Fort Myers FL 33903

WAGENER, LEE EDSON, airport exec.; b. Chgo., June 21, 1920; s. William F. and Charlotte (Williams) W.; B.B.A., Northwestern U., 1941; m. Anne E.; children—Carol J., David L. With Western Electric Co., 1941-48; cir. airports Broward County, Ft. Lauderdale, Fla., 1948—; dir. Barrett, Inc., Joliet, Ill., Barrett Hardware Co., Joliet; dir. Airport Ops. Council Internat. Served to lt. comdr. USNR, 1942-46; PTO. Recipient Top Mgmt. award Sales and Mktg. Execs. Club, Ft. Lauderdale, 1962. Mem. Southeastern Airport Mgrs. Assn. (pres. 1957), Am. Assn. Airport Execs. (pres., 1968-69), Ft. Lauderdale C.

of C., Am. Legion, Quiet Birdmen, Assn. Naval Aviation. Mason. Club: Congressional Flying (Washington). Home: 1668 S Ocean Ln Fort Lauderdale FL 33316 Office: Broward County Dept Airports 290 SW 41st Ct Fort Lauderdale FL 33315

WAGES, ORLAND JACK, clergyman, librarian; b. Canton, Tex., Aug. 2, 1915; s. Homer DeWitt and Della (Crabtree) W.; student Tex. Tech. Coll., 1936-39; B.S. in L.S., Stephen F. Austin State Coll., 1954; M.S. in L.S., E. Tex. State Coll., 1958, postgrad., 1960-63; m. Alice Ella Humphreys, Aug. 31, 1956. Librarian, instr. speech Jacksonville (Tex.) Coll., 1951-59; asst. librarian, instr. library sci. E. Tex. State Coll., Commerce, 1959-63; librarian, extension instr. library sci. Bridgewater (Va.) Coll., 1963—; extension instr. U. Va., 1967—. Ordained to ministry Baptist Ch., 1951; pastor chs. in Maydelle, Tex., 1953-57, Edom, Tex., 1957-59, Jackson, Tex., 1959-63, Fulks Run, Va., 1963-64, West Side Bapt. Ch., Harrisonburg, Va., 1967-69. Served to capt. with USAAF, 1940-48. Mem. A.L.A., Southeastern, Va. (editor Va. Librarian 1965-69) library assns., Am. Ednl. Research Assn., Christian Librarians Fellowship (pres. 1967-69), Va. Microfilm Assn. (v.p. 1975), Ministerial Assn., Shenandoah Valley Folklore Soc., Rockingham Hist. Soc., Nat. Geneal. Soc., Phi Delta Kappa. Democrat. Clubs: Civitan (v.p. Jacksonville 1958-59), Rotary (pres. Bridgewater 1966-67). Author: Church Librarian's Handbook, 1961. Home: 210 W Bank St Bridgewater VA 22812 Office: Bridgewater College Bridgewater VA 22812

WAGGONER, JAMES MILAN, clergyman; b. Jacksonville, Fla., Aug. 24, 1933; s. George Jamison and Stella Lorene (Vest) W.; student Temple Coll., 1951-53; A.B., Elon Coll., 1955; student So. Theol. Sem., 1955-56; M.Div., Southeastern Theol. Sem., 1961; m. Margaret Delores Johnson, Sept. 30, 1967; children—Robert, Barbra. Ordained to ministry Meth. Ch., 1958; minister Whitney Cross Meth. Charge, 1957-61, Trinity Ch., 1961-65, Whitley Meml. Ch., 1965-68; chaplain Meth. Home for Children, Raleigh, N.C., 1968-75, Southeastern Distbrs. Assn., 1975-77; supr. chaplaincy services div. youth services N.C. Dept. Human Resources, 1977—. Chaplain Boy Scouts Am., 1965-75. Exec. sec. John A. Wilkinson Meml. Found., 1964-65. Recipient Harvard Book prize, 1948, Citizenship award Am. Legion, 1950, Distinguished Citizen award Belhaven (N.C.) C. of C., 1964, Trailblazer award, Boy Scouts Am., 1967. Mem. Internat. Platform Assn., Group Child Care Assn., Southeastern, N.C. child care assns., Am. Protestant Hosp. Assn., Coll. of Chaplains, Butner Ministerial Assn. (v.p.), Am. Correctional Assn., Assn. Evang. Instl. Chaplains, N.C. Chaplains Assn., Assn. Clin. Pastoral Edn., Health and Welfare Assn. Composer: Boy Scout Pilgrimage Theme Song, 1968; John A. Wilkinson High School Alma Mater, 1964. Home: 3212 Barker Pl Raleigh NC 27604

WAGGONNER, JOSEPH DAVID, JR., banker; b. Plain Dealing, La., Sept. 7, 1918; s. Joseph David and Elizzibeth (Johnston) W.; B.A., La. Poly. Inst., 1941; m. Mary Ruth Carter, Dec. 14, 1942; children—Carol Jean, David. Mem. 87th-95th Congresses, 4th Dist. La. Mem. Bossier Parish Sch. Bd., 1954-61, pres., 1956-57; mem. La. Bd. Edn., 1960-61. Pres. United Sch. Com. La., 1961, La. Sch. Bds. Assn., 1961. Served to lt. comdr. USNR, World War II, Korea. Mem. Am. Legion, 40 and 8, Kappa Sigma (Man of Year 1973, worthy grand master). Democrat. Methodist. Mason (33 deg.), Shriners (Grand Cross Ct. of Honor), Elks, Lions. Home: Benton LA 71006

WAGLEY, MARJORIE IRENE CORLEY (MRS. ALTON CADE WAGLEY), educator; b. Florien, La., Nov. 4, 1914; d. Luther Franklin and Nancy (Miller) Corley; B.A., Northwestern U., 1936; M.Ed., U. Houston, 1950; postgrad. S.W. Tex. State Coll., 1946, Brigham Young U., 1958; m. Alton Cade Wagley, Jan. 16, 1937; children—Margie Katherine (Mrs. Gene Barry), Alton Carlin. Tchr. pub. schs., Sabine Parish, La., 1936-42, Beaumont, Tex., 1945-53; dir. spl. edn. S. Parks Sch., Beaumont, 1953—. Dir. Services Unlimited, Beaumont. Mem. NEA, Tex. Tchrs. Assn., Council Adminstrs. Spl. Edn. (sec. 1967-69), Tex. Council Adminstrs. Spl. Edn. (past pres., past sec.), Council for Exceptional Children, Tex. Council for Exceptional Children (pres. 1966; membership chmn. 1967-70), Delta Kappa Gamma. Baptist. Club: Soroptimist (charter; corr. sec. pres. chpt. 1972-74, treas. 1975) (Beaumont, Tex.). Author: Organizing and Administering Special Education. Home: PO Box 206 Nome TX 77629 Office: 1025 Woodrow St Beaumont TX 77705

WAGNER, ALAN BURTON, mfg. co. exec.; b. Balt., June 8, 1938; s. Robert Ellsworth and Anna Margaret (Schnitzlein) W.; B.Engring. Sci. (scholastic leadership award) John Hopkins, 1960; M.M.E., Case-Western Res. U., 1962, Ph.D. in Bus. Mgmt., 1965; m. Lynn Felton Wynant, June 26, 1964; children—Brian Alan, David Scott, Elizabeth Lynn. Mgr. orgn. planning and devel. Internat. Minerals & Chem. Corp., Libertyville, Ill., 1964-67, dir. indsl. relations, 1967-70, v.p. div. orgn. and indsl. relations, 1970-73, corporate v.p. adminstrn., 1973-79; pres. Taylor Tot Products, Inc., 1979—; dir. Sobin Chems., Inc., Great Lakes Container Corp., 1972-76; lectr. in field. Fellow Alfred P. Sloan Nat. Found.; mem. Chgo. Assn. Commerce and Industry, Chem. Industries Council of Midwest, ASME, Am. Mgmt. Assn., ASHRAE (Homer Addams award), AAAS, Ky. Coal Assn. (dir. 1977—), Sigma Xi, Omicron Delta Kappa. Clubs: Knollwood (Lake Forest, Ill); Greenbriar Golf and Country, Lafayette (Lexington, Ky.). Home: 1523 Lakewood Ct Lexington KY 40502 Office: Box 636 Taylor Tot Rd Frankfort KY 40602

WAGNER, ANDREW JAMES, meteorologist; b. Greenwich, Conn., Apr. 12, 1934; s. Andrew and Ruth Howard (Machette) W.; B.A., Wesleyan U., Middletown, Conn., 1956; M.S., Mass. Inst. Tech., 1958, postgrad., 1958-65; m. Betty Christina Ritenour, Aug. 9, 1969. Meteorologist, Long Range Prediction Group and Climate Analysis Center, Nat. Weather Service, Suitland, Md., 1965—. Pres. Lake Beverly Forest Civic Assn., 1977-79, v.p., 1979—. NSF summer fellow, 1959. Fellow Washington Acad. Sci.; mem. Am. Meteorol. Soc., Am. Geophys. Union, Am. Sci. Affiliation, Royal Meteorol. Soc., Creation Research Soc., SAR (1st v.p. and chaplain chpt. 1979—), Sigma Xi. Conglist. (elder, trustee, treas.). Contbr. articles to profl. jours. Home: 7007 Beverly Ln Springfield VA 22150 Office: World Weather Bldg 5200 Auth Rd Suitland MD 20023

WAGNER, ARTHUR WARD, JR., lawyer; b. Birmingham, Ala., Aug. 13, 1930; s. Arthur Ward and Lucille (Lockheart) W.; B.S.B.A., U. Fla., 1954, LL.B., 1957; m. Ruth Alice Shingler, May 11, 1957; children—Celia, Julia, Helen. Admitted to Fla. bar, 1957, since practiced in West Palm Beach; mem. firm Cone, Wagner, Nugent, Johnson & McKeown, 1957—. Dir. Flagler Nat. Bank of Palm Beach. Fellow Internat. Acad. Trial Lawyers, Am. Coll. Trial Lawyers; mem. Am., Palm Beach County bar assns., Assn. Trial Lawyers Am. (pres. 1975-76), Phi Delta Theta. Episcopalian (vestry 1972-74). Clubs: Tuscawilla, Mayacoo Lakes Country. Contbr. articles to profl. jours. Home: 2631 S Flagler Dr West Palm Beach FL 33405 Office: PO Box 3466 West Palm Beach FL 33402

WAGNER, B. DAVID, athletic adminstr.; b. Canton, Ohio, Sept. 16, 1939; s. Oscar T. and Evelyn C. (Bowman) W.; B.S. in Edn., Ohio U., Athens, 1961; M.Ed., 1965; Ph.D., Fla. State U., 1972; m. Ann Snee, Aug. 4, 1962; children—Michelle, Michael, Robert. Head freshman football coach, asst. prof. Phys. edn. Ohio U., 1961-63, asst. coach, 1967-69; part-time instr. Fla. State U., 1969, acad. adv. athletes, 1970-71, asst. dir. community coll. affairs, 1971-73; dir. matriculation affairs, 1973-75, acting dean student services, 1977-78; asst. athletic dir. Vanderbilt U., Nashville, 1978—. Mem. Am. Assn. Community and Jr. Colls., Fla. Assn. Community Colls., AAHPER, Am. Football Coaches Assn., Nat. Assn. Coll. Dirs. Athletes, Coll. Assn. Bus. Mfrs. Athletics, Fellowship Christian Athletes, Phi Delta Theta, Phi Epsilon Kappa. Baptist. Club: Toastmasters. Author papers in field. Office: PO Box 120158 Nashville TN 37212

WAGNER, BERNARD RICHARD, assn. exec.; b. Broken Arrow, Okla., Aug. 16, 1940; s. Bernie Paul and Edith Rebecca Wagner; student U. Okla., 1961, Insts. for Orgn. Mgmt., 1972-76, Tex. Christian U., So. Meth. U.; m. Pamela Jean White, Mar. 30, 1968; children—Craig Richard, Susan Diane. Mem. staff lease dept. ARCO Corp., Tulsa, 1958-60; mgr. lease dept. Lubell Oil Co., Tulsa, 1961-70; exec. dir. Broken Arrow C. of C., 1971—. Recipient awards Tulsa YMCA, 1969, United Way, 1973. Mem. Tulsa YMCA (mem. membership bd.), Broken Arrow Hist. Soc. (dir.), Indian Nations Council of Govts. (dir.), Okla. C. of C. Execs. Baptist. Clubs: Rotary, Broken Arrow Lions, Tail Twister. Home: 1000 W Boston Pl Broken Arrow OK 74012 Office: 114 N Main St Broken Arrow OK 74012

WAGNER, BILL, lawyer; b. Daytona Beach, Fla., Apr. 13, 1933; s. Adam A. and Nella (Schroeder) W.; B.A., U. Fla., 1955, LL.B. with honors, 1960; m. Joan Handley, Jan. 24, 1955; children—Alan Frederick, Darryl William, Thomas Adam. Admitted to Fla. bar, 1960, U.S. Supreme Ct. bar, 1967; practiced in Miami, 1960-63, Orlando, Fla., 1963-65, Tampa, Fla., 1965—; asso. firm Mershon, Sawyer, Johnston, Simmons and Dunwody, 1960-61; asso. firm Nichols, Gaither, Beckham, Colson and Spence, Miami, 1961-63, Orlando, 1963, partner, 1963-65; partner firm Nichols, Gaither, Beckham, Colson, Spence and Hicks, Tampa, Fla., 1965-67; partner firm Wagner, Cunningham and Vaughan, Tampa, 1967-70, firm Wagner, Cunningham, Vaughan, Genders and McLaughlin, Tampa, 1970—. Mem. Gov.'s Judicial Nominations Commn. for Hillsborough County, Fla., 1971-72, Judicial Nominations Commn. for Hillsborough County, 1972-75, Fla. Bd. Bar Examiners, 1974-79. Served to capt., USAF, 1955-57. Roscoe Pound fellow Am. Trial Lawyers Found., 1973—. Fellow Am. Coll. Trial Lawyers; mem. Assn. of Trial Lawyers of Am. (mem. bd. govs. 1973-79, exec. com. 1975-76, chmn. nat. membership com. 1975-76, vice chmn. election procedures com. 1975-76, dir. internal affairs 1976-77, mem. commn. on profl. ethics 1979—), Acad. of Fla. Trial Lawyers (pres. 1972-73, pres.'s spl. award for legis. work 1971, pres.'s award for outstanding service 1979), Fla. Bar (bd. govs. 1979—, mem. attorney fees com. 1971—, chmn. 1972; civil rules procedures com. 1965—, vice chmn. 1968, 74-77, chmn. 1977—; med. malpractice com. 1975—), Am., Lawyer-Pilot, Hillsborough County bar assns., Bay Area Trial Lawyers Assn. (v.p. 1966-68), N.Y. State, Calif. trial lawyers assns., U. Fla. Law Center Assn., Order of the Coif, U. Fla. Alumni Assn., Fla. Blue Key, Commerce Club of Tampa, Beta Theta Pi, Phi Kappa Phi. Democrat. Contbr. chpts. on law to profl. publs. Home: 6090 River Trace Tampa FL 33617 Office: 708 Jackson St Tampa FL 33602

WAGNER, EILEEN NAUSE, educator; b. Jefferson City, Mo., July 4, 1948; d. Frank Xavier and Mary Ellen (Kielty) Nause; B.S., Va. Commonwealth U., 1969; M.Ed., U. Va., 1970, Ed.D., 1975; m. Lester A. Wagner, Jan. 23, 1971; 1 dau., Lauren Ashley. Tchr. secondary schs., Henrico County, 1970-72; asst. prof. developmental English John Tyler Community Coll., 1972-75; asst. prof. English Va. Union U., Richmond, 1976—; mem. adj. faculty dept. English Va. Commonwealth U., 1970—. Recipient Golden Nugget award Pub. Broadcasting Ser. Wall Street Week, 1977. Mem. Nat. Council Tchrs. English, Va. Assn. Tchrs. English. Democrat. Roman Catholic. Author: For the Sake of Argument: Writing Editorials and Position Papers, 1979. Contbr. articles to profl. jours. including English Jour., English Edn., Va. English Bull., others. Home: 3811 Sulgrave Rd Richmond VA 23221 Office: 1500 N Lombardy St Richmond VA 23221

WAGNER, HARRY MAHLON, educator; b. Iola, Kans., June 1, 1924; s. Harry L. and Ruby E. (Davis) W.; B.S., U.S. Naval Postgrad. Sch., 1954; M.S., Kans. State Tchrs. Coll., 1964; Ed.D., U. Ark., 1969; m. Mary Lou Jones, Dec. 12, 1944; children—Chris M., Derrick A., Jon D., Marc A., Margaret E. Commd. aviation cadet U.S. Navy, 1942, advanced through grades to lt. comdr., 1956, ret., 1963; faculty John Brown U., Siloam Springs, Ark., 1964-67; faculty Cameron U., Lawton, Okla., 1969—, asso. prof. math., 1972—. Chmn., Lawton USO Council, 1975-76; v.p. Inst. of Great Plains, 1973-79; bd. dirs. Am. Inst. Discussion, Oklahoma City, 1979—, Cameron Campus Ministry, 1970—. Mem. Math. Assn. Am. Democrat. Methodist. Home: 307 NW Tanglewood Ln Lawton OK 73505 Office: Cameron Univ Lawton OK 73502

WAGNER, JACQUELINE ANN, city planner; b. N.Y.C.; B.S. magna cum laude in Bus. Adminstrn., N.Y. Inst. Tech., 1974; M.B.A., Nova U., 1976, D.B.A., 1980. Asst. to v.p. sales Gianinni Sci. Corp., N.Y.C., 1964-67; planning analyst City of Hollywood (Fla.), 1968-72, zoning adminstr., 1973-77, city planner, 1977—, prin. planner, 1980—; staff advisor Planning and Zoning Bd., City Commn. Youth advisor, counselor St. John's Episcopal Ch., Hollywood, 1973-75. Mem. Acad. Mgmt., Am. Inst. Planners, Fla. Planning and Zoning Assn., Am. Soc. Public Adminstrs. Club: Zonta. Home: 2822 Monroe St Hollywood FL 33020 Office: 2600 Hollywood Blvd Hollywood FL 33020

WAGNER, JOHN BARTON, JR., elec. engr.; b. Ashland, Ky., June 5, 1952; s. John Barton and Virginia Gaynelle (Shoemaker) W.; A.A., St. Petersburg Jr. Coll., 1974; B.S., U. South Fla., 1976; m. Judith Ann Barnes, Sept. 1, 1973. Distbn. engr. Ky. Power Co., Ashland, 1976-77; elec. engr. Withlacoochee River Electric Coop., Inc., Dade City, Fla., 1976—, also Head distbn. systems engring. Cert. computer programmer. Mem. IEEE, Tau Beta Pi, Phi Kappa, Phi. Home: 1401 E Young Dr Zephyrhills FL 33599 Office: N 21st St Dade City FL 33525

WAGNER, KENNETH WALTER, computer center mgr.; b. St. Louis, Aug. 9, 1929; s. George Edward and Myrtle Minnie (Schneider) W.; B.S. in Chem. Engring., Washington U., St. Louis, 1957; postgrad. La. State U., 1966-67, So. Meth. U., 1973-74; m. Carol Sue Waterhouse, Nov. 4, 1961; children—Richard Michael, Robert Charles, Gregory Christopher. Process design engr. Monsanto Chem. Co., St. Louis, 1957-59, prodn. supr., 1960-66; systems engr. Kaiser Aluminum Co., Gramercy, La., 1966-72; systems cons. Walk Haydel Consultants, New Orleans, 1972-73; mgr. computer center Ford, Bacon & Davis, Dallas, 1973—; cons. computer systems. Served with C.I.C., U.S. Army, 1951-53. Registered profl. engr., Tex. Mem. Tex. UNIVAC Users Assn., Nat., Tex. socs. profl. engrs. Republican. Presbyterian. Author: (with Dr. William Osborne) Computer Design of Bayer Alumina Plants, 1969. Home: 610 Briarcrest Dr Richardson TX 75081 Office: PO Box 38209 Dallas TX 75238

WAGNER, LESTER ANDREW, mortgage banker; b. Hamburg, Germany, Dec. 3, 1946; s. Joseph and Marianna W.; came to U.S., 1950; B.A., U. Va., 1968; M. Commerce, U. Richmond (Va.), 1973; m. Eileen Marie Nause, Jan. 23, 1971. Urban intern HUD, Richmond, 1972-73, multifamily housing rep. insured housing, 1973-74, insured and coll. housing, 1974-76, pub. housing and elderly housing, 1976-79; asst. v.p. Va. Nat. Bank Mortgage Corp., Richmond, 1979—. Mem. schs. com. U. Va. Mem. Richmond Jaycees. Club: Westwood Racquet. Home: 3811 Sulgrave Rd Richmond VA 23221 Office: 201 E Gary St Richmond VA 23219

WAGNER, MICHAEL GRAFTON, fin. adviser; b. Greenville, Ohio, May 31, 1935; s. Chester and Mary Elizabeth (Palmer) W.; B.A., Vanderbilt U., 1957, asso. (hon.) Grad. Sch. Bus., 1969; m. Jo Anne McIlwain, June 16, 1956 (div. Jan. 1980); children—Kurt McIlwain, Charles Hammock, Krista Kathleen, Kerstin Kayne, Mary Gretchen, Michael Grafton. With Henny Penny Corp., Eaton, Ohio, 1957-79, dir. advt., 1960-63, dir. mktg., 1963-68, pres., chief exec. officer, after 1968, also of Henny Penny, Ltd., Toronto, Ont., Can.; pres. Schaefer Corp., Madison, Ala., 1979—. Area chmn. Vanderbilt U. Endowment Fund, Nashville, 1961-66, 70-74; chmn. Tobacco Bowl, Hartsville, Tenn., 1969; finance chmn. Tenn. Republican Party, 1977-78. Bd. dirs. Green Hills Golf and Country Club. Mem. Am. Rifle Assn., Am. Ordnance Assn., Am. Forestry Assn., Am. Mgmt. Assn., Nat. Restaurant Assn., Nat. Assn. Food Equipment Mfgrs., Internat. Food Service Mfgrs. Assn., Commadore Boosters, Ohio Forestry Assn., Pres.' Assn., Alpha Tau Omega. Episcopalian (sec., treas., warden 1969-71), Mason. Home: PO Box 2124 Huntsville AL 35804 Office: 1200 Wall Triana Rd Madison AL 35758

WAGNER, MURRAY ROBERT, controller; b. Phila., July 4, 1948; s. Abraham and Edith (Silver) W.; student public schs., Coral Gables, Fla.; m. Cheryl Lynn Whitlock, Mar. 4, 1972; 1 dau., Karla Amalie. Bookkeeper, Hoffman Septic Tank Mfg., LaBelle, Fla., 1970-72, Sanders Mobile Home Sales, Ft. Myers, Fla., 1972-74; acct. Henry Southworth, C.P.A., Asheville, N.C., 1974-75; controller Sronce Automotive Supply, Inc., Asheville, 1976—; part-time acctg. practice, Asheville, 1975—. Jehovah's Witness. Home: 189 Fairfax Ave Asheville NC 28806 Office: 100 S Lexington Ave Asheville NC 28801

WAGNER, PATRICIA D'ANGELO, educator; b. New Orleans, Dec. 14, 1929; d. Peter M. and Freida W. (Harrell) D'Angelo; B.B.A. cum laude, N. Tex. State U., 1969, M.B.Ed., 1970; postgrad. U. Houston; m. George William Wagner, Oct. 16, 1962; children—Carl Edmond Whorton, Priscilla Anne Whorton Morris. Sec., office mgr. legal firms, Houston, 1958-62; sec. Hart Willis, Jr., civil atty., 1964-65; adminstrv. sec. N. Tex. State U. Grad. Sch., Toulouse, 1970-71; substitute tchr. Spring Branch Ind. Sch. Dist., Cypress-Fairbanks Ind. Sch. Dist., Houston Skill Center, 1971-74; instr. Houston Community Coll. Systems, 1974—. Mem. Tex. Jr. Coll. Tchrs. Assn., Am. Vocat. Assn., Nat. Bus. Edn. Assn., Tex. Bus. Edn. Assn., N. Tex. State U. Alumni Assn., N. Tex. State U. Alumni Assn. (sec. 1973-74), Houston Community Coll. Systems Faculty Senate, Mensa, Beta Gamma Sigma, Delta Pi Epsilon, Kappa Delta Pi, Pi Omega Pi. Methodist. Club: Eastern Star. Home: 9905 Westview Dr Houston TX 77055 Office: 2800 Main St Houston TX 77002

WAGNER, WILLIAM VERNON, JR., assn. exec.; b. New Castle, Pa., Nov. 27, 1921; s. William Vernon and Mary Lavina (Jacobs) W.; B.S., Pa. State U., 1942; m. Sara Margaret Bailey, Mar. 24, 1945; children—Mary Louise, William Vernon. With Eastern States Farmers Exchange, 1946-50; engring. positions Portland Cement Assn., 1950-72; tech. dir. Wire Reinforcement Inst., McLean, Va., 1972-76, pres., mng. dir., 1976—. Served with AC, U.S. Army, 1942-46. Registered profl. engr. Fellow Am. Concrete Inst.; mem. Nat. Soc. Profl. Engrs., ASCE, Am. Soc. Agrl. Engrs., Am. Soc. Assn. Execs., ASTM, Reinforced Concrete Research Council, Transp. Research Bd. Republican. Lutheran. Author tech. manuals. Home: 9639 Cinnamon Creek Dr Vienna VA 22180

WAGONER, BETTIE RODERMUND, govt. adminstr.; b. Detroit, May 29, 1923; d. Carl William and Vina (Powell) Rodermund; student Anderson Coll., 1940-41; certificate U. S.C., 1956; m. Donald W. Wagoner, Apr. 26, 1947. Sec. Sumter (S.C.) City Schs., 1941-42; traffic mgr. Pan Am. Airways, Miami, Fla., 1942-44; cost accountant Coble Dairies, Lexington, N.C., 1944-46; adminstrv. officer Dept. Army, Ft. Jackson, S.C., 1955—. Mem. Riverbanks Zool. Soc., Smithsonian Assos., Am. Rose Soc. Presbyterian. Home: 142 Miot St Columbia SC 29204 Office: Fort Jackson Columbia SC 29207

WAHLQUIST, JACK RAINARD, ins. co. exec.; b. Omaha, Oct. 10, 1933; s. Kenneth Dudley and Dot (Sesler) W.; B.A. magna cum laude, Yale U., 1955; J.D. with honors, U. Tex., 1958; m. Elizabeth Jean Bailey, July 8, 1960; children—Laura Alice, Elizabeth Jennifer. Admitted to Tex. bar, 1958; atty. Great Nat. Life Ins. Co., Dallas, 1958-65, v.p., sec., 1965-67, exec. v.p., dir., 1967-69; chmn. bd., pres. Transport Life Ins. Co., Fort Worth, 1969-70; v.p. Southland Life Ins. Co., Dallas, 1970-73, sr. v.p. mktg., 1973-74, sr. v.p., dir. gen. agys., 1974-77, sr. v.p. agy. planning, 1977-78; sr. v.p., chief mktg. officer Lone Star Life Ins. Co., Dallas, 1978—; sec., treas., dir. Sch. Life Ins. Mktg., Lafayette, La., 1975-79. Bd. dirs., v.p., sec. Goodwill Industries, 1977—; bd. dirs. Dallas Theatre Center, 1964-76, Mcpl. Radio Adv. Bd., 1976-79; bd. dirs., sec. Dallas Arts Found., 1973-76. Registered health underwriter. Fellow Life Mgmt. Inst.; mem. Am. Soc. C.L.U.'s, Nat. Assn. Life Underwriters, Tex. Health Ins. Council, Am. Bar Assn., Tex. Bar Assn., Yale Alumni Assn. Home: 7019 Gateridge Dallas TX 75240 Office: 200 Treadway Plaza Dallas TX 75235

WAIDELICH, CHARLES J., oil co. exec.; b. Columbus, Ohio, May 2, 1929; s. Bernard Howard and Alberta (Poth) W.; B.S., Purdue U., 1951, D.Eng. (hon.), 1978; m. Margaret Ellen Finley, Jan. 26, 1952; children—Michael Brian, Sharon Ann. Engr., Cities Service Oil Co., Bartlesville, Okla., 1951-54; asst. to pres. Cities Service Pipeline Co., Bartlesville, 1956-59; pipeline coordinator Cities Service Co., N.Y.C., 1959-65, transp. coordinator, 1965-66, staff v.p. ops. coordination, 1966-68, exec. v.p. ops., dir., 1970-71, pres. 1971—; v.p. ops. Tenn. Corp., N.Y.C., 1968-70; chmn. bd. Colonial Pipeline Co., Atlanta, 1967-70. Bd. dirs. Transp. Assn. Am. Served with C.E., AUS, 1954-56. Mem. Am. Petroleum Inst., AIME, Theta Xi. Clubs: Sky, Econ. (N.Y.C.); Internat. (Washington); So. Hills Country, Summit, Utica 21 (Tulsa); Masons. Home: 2161 Forest Blvd Tulsa OK 74114 Office: Cities Service Co Cities Service Bldg Tulsa OK 74102

WAIDHOFER, SALLY DICKENS, food service adminstr.; b. Beaumont, Tex., Jan. 11, 1948; d. Wayne and Althea (Kemp) Dickens; B.A. in Teaching, San Houston State U., 1970; m. Ben Waidhofer II, Oct. 9, 1975. Library asst. San Houston Library, Huntsville, Tex., 1967-70; various clerical positions San Houston Bus. Office, 1970-72; sr. acctg. clk. Tex. Instruments, Houston, 1972-75, food service adminstr., 1975—. Mem. Assn. for Food Service Mgmt., Soc. for Food Service Mgmt. Republican. Baptist.

WAITS, EMMETT MOORE, clergyman, hosp. adminstr.; b. Indpls., Apr. 6, 1923; s. Emmett Moore and Marie Church (Williams) W.; B.A., Transylvania U., 1945; M.Div., U. of the South, 1949; S.T.M., So. Meth. U., 1961, postgrad., 1960-61, D.Min., 1980; grad. St. Augustine's Coll., Canterbury, Eng., 1954-55; postgrad. Oxford (Eng.) U., 1956. Instr., U. of the South, 1946-49; ordained priest Episcopal Ch., 1949; rector Emmanuel Ch., Winchester, Ky., 1949-54; chaplain North Tex. State U. and Tex. Woman's U., 1956-63; dir. univ. div. Episc. Ch. in S.W., Tex. and N.Mex., 1960-63;

rector St. Barnabas's Ch., Denton, Tex., 1967-73; dir. pastoral and social services Gaston Episc. Hosp., Dallas, 1973—; prof. systematic theology Episc. Sem. Ky., 1950-54. Chmn. service and rehab. Area V, mem. state bd. dirs. Tex. div. Am. Cancer Soc.; mem. med. adv. bd. Dallas Ostomy Assn. Served with U.S. Army, World War II. Named Outstanding Priest, Episc. Diocese Dallas, 1961. Fellow Am. Protestant Hosp. Assn. Coll. Chaplains; mem. Soc. Social Work Dirs., Am. Hosp. Assn., Tex. Hosp. Assn., Augustan Soc., Ky. Hist. Soc., SAR, Soc. Colonial Wars, Nat. Huguenot Soc., Ams. Royal Descent, Magna Carta Barons, Sons Republic of Tex. Democrat. Club: Mil. and Hospitaller Order of St. Lazarus of Jerusalem (sr. chaplain, knight of grace). Home: 5005-A Cedar Springs Rd Dallas TX 75235 Office: 3505 Gaston Ave Dallas TX 75246

WALBORSKY, HARRY M., chemist; b. Lodz, Poland, Dec. 25, 1923; s. Israel and Sara (Miedowicz) W.; B.S., Coll. City N.Y., 1945; PH.D., Ohio State U., 1949; m. Paula Levitt, Nov. 28, 1970; children—Edwin, Eric, Lisa, Irene. Research asso. Calif. Inst. Tech., 1948-49, U. Calif. at Los Angeles Atomic Energy Project, 1949-50; prof. chemistry Fla. State U., 1950-54, asso. prof., 1954-58, prof., 1962—. NIH Fellow, 1952; NSF fellow, 1962. Mem. Am. Chem. Soc. (Fla. award 1978), Chem. Soc. (London), Sigma Xi. Democrat. Jewish. Contbr. numerous articles to profl. jours. Home: 2223 Ruadh Ride Tallahassee FL 32303 Office: Chem Dept Fla State U Tallahassee FL 32306

WALBY, THOMAS FRANCIS, airline pilot, author, educator; b. N.Y.C., May 3, 1940; s. Thomas Frederick and Edith Helena (Carlson) W.; B.S., Manhattan Coll., 1962; M.S., Embry-Riddle U., Fla., 1977; doctoral candidate Calif. Western U.; m. Lilian Andersen, Apr. 1, 1970; 1 dau., Karen. Pilot, Eastern Air Lines, 1967—; chmn. council 18, legis. action com. Airline Pilots Assn., 1977—; mem. council 18 aviation safety com., aircraft accident investigator, 1974—; lectr. career opportunities; asst. prof. aero. Sci. Embry-Riddle U.; U.S. adv. Transp. Industry Tng. Bd. Gt. Britain, 1979—; author numerous articles in profl. jours. Served to capt. USMCR, 1962-66. Decorated Air medal; recipient Alenwick Mannix award N.Y. High Schs., 1956, Eastment award, 1957, Presdl. award of merit, 1978. Mem. Aviation Writers Assn., Am. Soc. Aerospace Edn., Am. Legion, Alpha Eta Rho (founder, pres. grad. chpt.), Phi Kappa Theta. Republican. Roman Catholic. Clubs: K.C., Danish-Am., Sword and Marlin Miami. Address: 7655 SW 173d St Miami FL 33157

WALCH, JOHN LEO, clergyman, artist; b. Oklahoma City, Jan. 14, 1918; s. John L. and Montie Cecilia (Muller) W.; A.B., Loyola U., Chgo., 1939; grad. (scholar), Sch. Chgo. Art Inst., 1941, Kenrick Sem., St. Louis, 1945. Ordained priest Roman Catholic Church, 1945; asst. pastor Christ the King Ch., tchr. Marquette High Sch., Tulsa, 1945-49, tchr. sch.; pastor Our Lady of Sorrows Ch., Chandler, Okla., 1949-53, St. Francis of Assisi Ch., Newkirk, Okla., 1953-58; apptd. mem. Diocesan Bldg. Commn., charter mem., 1953—; mem. diocesan Liturgical Commn., 1964—, priests senate, 1976-79; founder St. John Damascene Studio of Liturgical Art, Oklahoma City, 1958—; pastor Holy Angels Ch., Oklahoma City, 1971—; instr. Briar Cliff Coll., Sioux City, Iowa, 1965-66; exhibitor more than 40 one-man shows including Okla. Art Center, 1950, 63, 68, Philbrook Art Center, Tulsa, 1957; exhibitor Internat. Exposition Modern Sacred Art, Rome, Italy, 1950, pictured in catalog; artist paintings, sculpture, liturgical design for over 65 Cath. instns. including Center for Christian Renewal, Resurrection Cemetery Chapel, Church of Christ the King, Oklahoma City, Ch. of St. James, Ch. of St. Eugene, Archbishop's Chapel, St. Anthony Hosp., Oklahoma City, St. Francis Hosp., Tulsa, Ch. of St. Anne, Albuquerque, Sem. of Immaculate Conception, Huntington, N.Y.; illustrator The Roman Missal, 1964; mem. restoration team Mabee-Gerrer Mus., Shawnee, Okla., 1974—; instr. workshops in field. Bds. dirs. Okla. Art Guild, Okla. Mus. Art (Oklahoma City), Mabee-Gerrer Mus.; mem. deSaisset Art Gallery (U. Santa Clara, Calif.), Philbrook Art Center (Tulsa). Winner prize Nat. Sacred Heart art contest, 1954, over 90 prizes juried art shows. Mem. Cath. Art Assn., Southwestern Watercolor Soc. (charter Oklahoma City chpt.), Cloisonne Collectors Club. Democrat. Contbr. articles to Cath. Art Quar. Home: 317 N Blackwelder St Oklahoma City OK 73106

WALCHKO, JACK COLLIN, audiologist; b. Lorain, Ohio, Feb. 2, 1942; s. Mike and Gloria Walchko; B.S., Kent State U., 1965, M.A., 1967; postgrad. U. Iowa, 1968-69; Ed.D., U. Sarasota, 1975; m. Barbara Sakowski, Aug. 28, 1965; 1 son, Kevin. Coordinator hearing services 4-County Area, Toledo, Iowa, 1967, dir. speech and hearing services, 1968-69; state dir. audiology services State of Minn., 1969-71; dir. speech pathology and audiology services Happiness House Rehab. Center, Sarasota, Fla., 1971-75; exec. dir., audiologist Manatee Hearing and Speech Center, Bradenton, Fla., 1975—; cons. to Fla. State Health Dept., 1977-80. Recipient Golden Ear award Fla. State Hearing Aid Dealers Assn., 1973, Gov.'s award State of Fla., 1974; Research grantee Kent State U., 1965. Mem. Am. Speech and Hearing Assn., Fla. Speech and Hearing Assn., So. Assn. of Audiologists, Council for Exceptional Children, Nat. Assn. of Speech Agys. Club: Sertoma (Tribune award 1975, Centurion award 1976). Author: (with Robert Mullin) Practical Procedures in Public School Hearing Conservation, 1968; contbr. articles on audiology to profl. jours. Home: 3700 Gulf Dr Sun Bow Bay Holmes Beach FL 33510 Office: 2010 59th St W Bradenton FL 33505

WALDEN, PHILIP MICHAEL, rec. and publishing co. exec.; b. Greenville, S.C., Jan. 11, 1940; s. Clemuel Barto and Carolyn (McLendon) W.; A.B. in Econs., Mercer U., 1962; m. Peggy Hackett, Sept. 13, 1969; children—Philip Michael, Amantha Starr. Pres., Phil Walden Artists & Promotions, 1961, Walden Artists & Promotions, 1963-69, Phil Walden & Assos., 1965—, Capricorn Records, Inc., 1969—, Rear Exit Pub. Co., 1969—, No Exit Music Pub. Co., 1969— (all Macon, Ga.). Campaign chmn. Muscular Dystrophy Assn., 1975; past mem. Macon-Bibb County Planning and Zoning Commn.; mem. Com. for Preservation of White House; chmn. Macon Heritage Found., Inc.; mem. In-Town Macon Neighborhood Assn.; mem. nat. fin. com. Jimmy Carter Presdl. Campaign. Served to 1st lt. AUS. Recipient 14 Gold Record awards, 3 Platinum Record awards, 11 pub. awards; Rolling Stone Red Suspenders award, 1977; named a Top Exec. of Tomorrow, Billboard Mag., 1976; Martin Luther King Jr. Humanitarian award, 1977; Big Bear award Mercer U., 1975; Shriners plaque, 1976, 77; Human Relations award Am. Jewish Com., 1978. Mem. Rec. Industry Assn. Am. (dir.), Nat. Assn. Rec. Merchandisers, Nat. Assn. Rec. Arts and Scis. (past v.p., trustee), Nat. Trust Historic Preservation, Middle Ga. Hist. Soc., Brandywine Conservancy, Common Cause Ga. (dir.), Phi Delta Theta Alumni Assn., Phi Mu Alpha Sinfonia (hon.). Clubs: Elks; River North Golf and Country; Gov.'s of Ga.; Pres.'s (Mercer U.); Sea Pines. Founder Otis Redding Scholarship fund and Phil Walden Scholarship, Mercer U. Home: 1121 Jackson Springs Rd Macon GA 31201 Office: 535 Cotton Ave Macon GA 31201

WALDO, ALBERT LEON, cardiologist; b. N.Y.C., Nov. 25, 1936; s. Maxim and Susan Gertrude (Cohen) W.; B.A. (N.Y. State scholar, Schoelkopf scholar, LeFevre scholar), Cornell U., 1958; M.D., State U. N.Y., 1962; m. Rosa Ines Torres Rodriguez, Dec. 28, 1973; children—Miguel A., Richard E., Eric. W. Intern, Kings County Hosp., Bklyn., 1962-63, chief resident in medicine, 1965-66; asst. med. resident Balt. City Hosps., 1963-65; fellow in medicine Johns Hopkins U. Sch. Medicine, 1963-65; postdoctoral fellow in cardiac electrophysiology Coll. Physicians and Surgeons, Columbia U., N.Y.C., 1966-68, vis. fellow in medicine, 1968-69; practice medicine specializing in cardiology, N.Y.C., 1969-72, Birmingham, Ala., 1972—; asst. physician Vanderbilt Clinic, Presbyn. Hosp., N.Y.C., 1966-69, asso. in Cardiovascular Lab., 1969-70, asst. surgeon, 1969-72; asso. dept. pharmacology Coll. Physicians and Surgeons, Columbia U., 1969-70, asst. prof., 1970-72; asso. prof. dept. medicine U. Ala., Birmingham, 1972-76, prof., 1976—, scientist Cardiovascular Research and Tng. Center, 1972-76, sr. scientist, 1976—; staff physician Univ. Hosp. Mem. exec. bd. Birmingham Music Club, 1973-78. Diplomate Am. Bd. Cardiology, Am. Bd. Internal Medicine. Fellow A.C.P., Am. Coll. Cardiology, Council on Clin. Cardiology of Am. Heart Assn.; mem. Birmingham Cardiovascular Soc., Cardiac Electrophysiol. Soc., Am. Physiol. Soc., Am., So. socs. for clin. investigation, Assn. Univ. Cardiologists, Jefferson County Med. Soc., Am., Ala. heart assns., AAAS, N.Y. Acad. Sci., Alpha Epsilon Delta. Editorial bd. Circulation, 1974-78, 80—, PACE, Heart and Lung, 1978—. Office: Univ of Alabama Medical Center Birmingham AL 35294

WALDO, TOMMY RUTH BLACKMON (MRS. SELDEN FENNELL WALDO), educator; b. Dallas, Jan. 14, 1916; d. Gulie Hargrove and Mary Lee (Craig) Blackmon; B.A., Agnes Scott Coll., 1938; M.A., U. Fla., 1955, Ph.D., 1961; m. Selden Fennell Waldo, Oct. 28, 1941 (dec. Nov. 1950); children—George Selden (dec.), Andrew Blackmon. Cons., Washington, 1975—; instr., 1955-61, asst. prof. English, 1961-68, asso. prof., 1968-76, prof., 1976—; pvt. tchr. piano and organ, 1938-55; organist Holy Trinity Episcopal Ch., Gainesville, 1941-42; asso. organist First Bapt. Ch., 1943-58, organist, 1958—. Dir., v.p. League Women Voters, 1947-50. Mem. Modern Lang. Assn., S. Atlantic Modern Lang. Assn., Fla., Gainesville music tchrs. assns., Southeastern Renaissance Conf., Phi Beta Kappa (chpt. pres. 1974-75), Delta Kappa Gamma (v.p. 1972-74), Sigma Alpha Iota. Democrat. Baptist. Author: Musical Terms as Rhetoric. Contbr. articles to profl. jours. Home: 719 NE 1st St Gainesville FL 32601

WALDRON, ROBERT FRANCIS MCDONNELL, trade exec.; b. Yonkers, N.Y., Nov. 27, 1929; s. Charles A. and Frances B. (McDonnell) W.; B.A., St. Bonaventure U., 1951; children—Robert Patrick, Mary Pat, Elizabeth Ann, Stacey Kathryn. Area mgr. C. Am., Colgate Palmolive Co., Guatemala City, 1955-57; v.p., gen. mgr. Larin Food & Candy div. Richardson-Merrell Mexico, Mexico City, 1957-72; mng. dir. Tabacalera Mexicana, Mexico City, 1972-73; partner Alyarez Waldron Mktg. Mgmt. Cons., Mexico City, 1973-75; pres. Mextrade, Inc., San Antonio, 1975—. Served with USAF, 1951-56. Home: 8715 Starcrest Dr Apt 15 San Antonio TX 78217 Office: 42 N Star Mall San Antonio TX 78216

WALDROP, BENNY EARL, heating and air conditioning exec.; b. Spartanburg County, S.C., Apr. 2, 1943; s. Oriss Lowel and Carrie Mae (Reid) W.; student Spartanburg public schs.; m. Vicky Collins, Nov. 6, 1965; 1 dau., Lori Ann. Owner, mgr. Benny E. Waldrop Heating and Air Conditioning, Inman, S.C., 1970—; pres. adv. bd. Spartanburg Tech. Coll. Mem. S.C. Mech. Contractors Assn., Refrigeration Ser. Engrs. Soc. Baptist. Clubs: Masons, Shriners. Home: 11 Humphrey St Inman SC 29349 Office: 38 1st St Inman SC 29349

WALDROP, GERRY LUTHER, army officer, data processing analyst; b. Kilgore, Tex., May 13, 1943; s. Curtis Luther and Gladys Miriam (Cox) W.; B.A., Austin Coll., 1965; M.B.A., Tex. Tech. U., 1974; m. Joyce Janelle Buchanan, Nov. 6, 1965; children—Elbridge Gerry, Sara Kathleen, Amy Allison. Dept. mgr. J. C. Penney Co., Dallas, 1965-66; enlisted in U.S. Army, 1966, advanced through grades to maj., 1977; platoon leader, Vietnam, 1967-68; co. comdr., Ft. Bragg, N.C., 1968-70, div. chief project corps automation requirements, 1975-77; co. comdr., Ft. Huachuca, Ariz., 1970-72; div. chief project combat service support test hdqrs., Ft. Hood, Tex., 1974-75; requirements analyst Supreme Hdqrs. Allied Powers Europe, Mons, Belgium, 1977—; grad. asst. Tex. Tech. U., 1972-74, instr. in ADP, 1972-74. Cubmaster Occoneechee council Boy Scouts Am., 1975-77. Decorated Bronze Star, Meritorious Service medal; Vivian Thyng scholar, 1961-65; Bruce McMillan Jr. scholar, 1961-65; Austin Coll. scholar, 1961-65. Mem. Assn. U.S. Army, Sigma Iota Epsilon. Presbyterian. Author: Corps Information Requirements Analysis Methodology, 1975 Command and Control Requirements Analysis Methodology. Home: PO Box 28 Kilgore TX 75662 Office: Infor Systems Div Supreme Hdqrs Allied Powers Europe Hdqrs APO NY 09055

WALDROP, WILLIAM ALLEN, JR., govt. ofcl.; b. Atlanta, May 31, 1951; s. William Allen and Susan Hixie (Brewer) W.; B.B.A., W. Ga. Coll., 1974; children—Patrick Alan, Jason Craig. With IRS, 1974, U.S. Postal Service, 1974; with EPA, 1974—, chief of classification, southeast regional office, Atlanta, 1979—. Recipient Sustained Superior Performance award EPA, 1976; cert. of appreciation Atlanta Clean City Commn., 1977. Mem. Internat. Personnel Mgmt. Assn., Classification and Compensation Soc., Fed. Classification Assn. Atlanta, Atlanta Assn. Fed. Execs. Democrat. Baptist. Club: Toastmasters (club pres. 1976, dist. gov. 1979—, Able Toastmaster award 1978, Outstanding Toastmaster, Peachtree Center club 1976, Disting. Toastmaster 1980). Home: 127 Jonathan Rd Riverdale GA 30274 Office: EPA 345 Courtland St Atlanta GA 30308

WALEWSKI, KARL STEVEN, bank exec.; b. Jackson, Mich., Nov. 25, 1942; s. Walter Joseph and Helen Mary (Bogdynski) W.; B.A., Mich. State U., 1969; student Nat. Sch. Bank Investments, 1977, Nat. Comml. Lending Sch., 1977; m. Marjorie Ann McCombs, Oct. 30, 1965; children—Joseph Walter, Edward Francis. Sales engr. Mech. Reps., Dearborn, Mich., 1967-68; sect. chief Western Electric Corp., Columbus, Ohio, 1969-71; asst. v.p. Huntington Nat. Bank, Columbus, 1971-74; v.p., cashier First Carolina Nat. Bank, Hartsville, S.C., 1974—; cons. banking. Bd. dirs. mchts. div. Hartsville C. of C., 1976-77; chmn. bus. div. Hartsville United Way., 1976; v.p. Parent-Tchr. Orgn., St. Mary's Roman Catholic Sch., Hartsville, 1976-77. Served with USAF, 1960-64. Mem. Am. Inst. Banking, Bank Adminstrn. Inst. (dir. chpt.). Clubs: Rotary (chmn. internat. service com.), Hartsville Country. Office: PO Drawer 40 South Fifth Hartsville SC 29550

WALGAMA, UPALI SANATH, physician; b. Ceylon, Dec. 22, 1941; s. Sumanadasa and Alencina Walgama; grad. Ananda Coll., Ceylon, 1959; M.D., U. Ceylon, 1967; m. Preeni Fernando, Apr. 18, 1968; children—Ruwani, Rehan. Intern, Perth Amboy (N.J.) Gen. Hosp., 1972-73; resident Episcopal Hosp., Phila., 1974-77; practice medicine, specializing in internal medicine, Henderson, Tex., 1977—; cons. internal medicine Henderson Meml. Hosp. Bd. dirs. Rusk County Heart Assn., 1979—. Diplomate Am. Bd. Internal Medicine. Mem. Tex. Med. Assn., Rusk County Med. Soc. Home: 1601 Timothy St Henderson TX 75652 Office: 601 Laylon St Henderson TX 75652

WALIGURA, CHARLES LEO, engring. co. exec.; b. Houston, May 15, 1944; s. Charles Mike and Alma Olga (Peter) W.; B.S. in Chem. Engring., U. Houston, 1969, M.S., 1976; m. Sally Lu Cashman, Aug. 2, 1969; 1 son, Eric Charles. With Brown & Root, Inc., Houston, 1967—, staff mgr. process design dept., 1977—. Bd. dirs. Village Fire Dept., 1979—; mem planning and zoning commn. City of Bunker Hill Village, 1979—. Registered profl. engr., Tex. Mem. Nat. Soc. Profl. Engrs., Am. Inst. Chem. Engrs., Project Mgmt. Inst., Phi Kappa Theta. Republican. Roman Catholic. Home: 1 Valley Forge St Houston TX 77024 Office: Brown & Root Inc PO Box 3 Houston TX 77001

WALK, DARLENE MARIE, city ofcl., data cons.; b. Johnstown, Pa., June 3, 1950; d. Donald Edward and Lois Theresa (Lauland) W.; B.A., U. Southwestern La., 1972, M.A., 1974; postgrad. Tulane U., 1973—. Urban policy specialist I, Mayor's Office of Policy Planning, City of New Orleans, 1974-76, urban policy specialist II, 1976—, project coordinator data analysis unit, 1976-77, coordinator planning unit, 1977-78, neighborhood planning unit, 1978, analysis unit, 1979—; data cons., 1979—. Mem. Am. Planning Assn., Am. Polit. Sci. Assn., So. Polit. Sci. Assn., Am. Hist. Assn., Am. Mgmt. Assn., Am. Acad. Polit. and Social Scis., AAUW, Phi Kappa Phi, Sigma Tau Delta, Kappa Delta Pi, Pi Gamma Mu, Phi Sigma Alpha, Pi Mu Epsilon. Democrat. Roman Catholic. Editor: Neighborhood Profiles, 70 vols., 1979; Blight Index, 3 edits., 1978; Neighborhood Summary, 2 vols., 1977; Citizen Attitude Survey, 3 edits., 1980. Home: Box 53067 New Orleans LA 70153 Office: 1300 Perdido St New Orleans LA 70112

WALKER, ALMENA NORRIS, librarian, counselor; b. Wake County, N.C., Sept. 13, 1935; d. Fred and Nellie Ann (Jones) Norris; B.A., N.C. Central U., Durham, 1976, M.A., 1978; postgrad. doctoral program U. N.C., Chapel Hill; m. Alvis Walker, July 22, 1956; children—Aljoesor, Alvernon, Alvin. Asst. dir. recreation D.C. Recreation Dept., Washington, 1958-61; asst. dir. N.C. Deaf and Blind Sch., Raleigh, 1963-64; dir. adult program YWCA, Durham, N.C., 1965-66; specialist recreation Murdock Center, Butner, N.C., 1966-68; asst. dir. for after-sch. care Durham County Schs., Durham, to 1979; supr., residence counselor N.C. Central U., Durham, 1968—; librarian Durham County, Durham, 1978—. Pres., Carr Jr. High Sch. PTA, 1974-76; mem. exec. com. Durham Democratic Party; mem. Durham Com. Women in Action. Recipient cert. Pan Hellenic Council, 1978-79, Salvation Army award, 1979. Cert. tchr. N.C. Mem. Am. Personnel and Guidance Assn., N.C. Personnel and Guidance Assn., Sigma Gamma Rho (adviser chpt.), Beta Lambda chpt. Address: 1308 N Mangum St Durham NC 27701

WALKER, BURLIAN O'NEAL, coll. adminstr., journalist; b. Magee, Miss., Oct. 31, 1941; s. Cordas Burlian and Arlee (Williamson) W.; student Copiah-Lincoln Jr. Coll., 1960-62; B.S., U. So. Miss., 1964, postgrad., 1965-66, 70-71; postgrad. (Newspaper Fund fellow) U. Miss., 1970. English tchr. Simpson County Schs., 1964-65, 66-67; clk. U.S. Ho. of Reps., 1966; dir. pub. relations and alumni affairs, instr. journalism Copiah-Lincoln Jr. Coll., Wesson, Miss., 1967—. Chmn. bd. dirs., dir., actor, publicity chmn. Brookhaven Little Theatre, 1968—; asst. publicity chmn. Miss. Theatre Assn. Conv., 1972; publicity chmn. Am. Cancer Soc., Copiah County chpt., 1972; exec. dir. Miss Co-Lin Pageant, Inc., 1970—. Alt. del. Miss. Republican party state conv., 1968; county del., Rep. precinct chmn., 1976. Mem. Miss. Assn. Journalism Edn. (pres. 1973-74), Miss., Copiah-Lincoln edn. assns., Miss. Coll. Pub. Relations Assn. (pres., v.p., officer, mem. bd. 1974-78, 79-80), Miss. Journalism Assn., Copiah-Lincoln Jr. Coll. (pres. 1970-71), U. So. Miss. alumni assns., Nat. Soc. Pub. Poets, Wesson Jr. C. of C., Delta Psi Omega. Club: Lions (v.p. Wesson). Contbr. articles to profl. jours. Home: Route 2 Box 25 Wesson MS 39191 Office: Copiah Lincoln Jr Coll Wesson MS 39191

WALKER, CLYDE LEWIS, athletic dir.; b. Poplar Branch, N.C., Nov. 17, 1929; s. Clyde Vernon and Annie Lee (Howard) W.; A.B., Catawba Coll., Salisbury, N.C., 1951; M.Ed., U. N.C., Chapel Hill, 1961; m. Ruby Wilkerson, Sept. 3, 1950; children—Ginger, Clyde Lewis, Kim. Tchr., coach high schs. in N.C., 1951-67; asst. athletic dir., head football recruiter U. N.C., 1967-73; dir. athletics U. Kans., Lawrence, 1973-78, U. N.C., Charlotte, 1978—. Mem. Nat. Assn. Collegiate Dirs. Athletics. Democrat. Baptist. Clubs: Carmel Country, Charlotte N.E. Kiwanis (pres. 1979). Home: 5827 Beckett Ct Charlotte NC 28211 Office: UNCC Station Charlotte NC 28223

WALKER, DANIEL JOSHUA, JR., lawyer; b. Gibson, N.C., Nov. 27, 1915; s. Daniel Joshua and Annie (Hurdle) W.; A.B., U. N.C., 1936, J.D., 1948 m. Sarah Elizabeth Nicholson, June 14, 1941. Claim dept. Barnwell Bros. Trucking Co., Burlington, N.C., 1936-42; admitted to N.C. bar, 1948; clk. Superior Ct., Alamance County, Graham, N.C., 1948-53; partner Long, Ridge, Harris & Walker, Graham, 1953-67; county atty. Alamance County, Graham, 1964-77, county mgr., 1971-76; sr. mem. firm Walker Harris & Pierce, Graham, 1967-71; partner firm Allen, Allen, Walker & Washburn, Burlington, N.C., 1977—. Mem. Human Relations Council, Alamance County, 1963-71, chmn., 1970; mem. N.C. Environ. Mgmt. Commn., 1972-77. Pres., Alamance County Young Democratic Club, 1950; chmn. Alamance County Dem. Exec. Com., 1956-58; mem. N.C. Dem. Exec. Com., 1958-66. Trustee Tech. Inst. of Alamance, 1964-71; bd. dirs. Alamance County United Fund, Cherokee council Boy Scouts Am., Community YMCA, Burlington; trustee Presbyn. Found., Presbyn. Ch. U.S., 1969-73, mem. exec. com., 1971-73, moderator Orange Presbytery, 1980. mem. council Orange Presbytery, 1972-74. Served with AUS, 1942-46. Decorated Bronze Star. Mem. Am. Judicature Soc. Alamance County C. of C. (pres.-elect 1980), Am., N.C., Alamance County (pres. 1977) bar assns., N.C. Assn. County Attys. (v.p. 1971, pres. 1972, named county atty. of yr. 1971), Phi Alpha Delta. Democrat. Presbyn. (elder; trustee ch.). Home: 215 Long Ave Graham NC 27253 Office: 500 S Main St Burlington NC 27215

WALKER, DAVID AARON, counselor; b. Ada, Okla., Nov. 20, 1947; s. Aaron Eugene and Betty Jean (Kidwell) W.; B.A., East Central U., Ada, 1975; 1 dau., Angela. Adminstrv. asst. Ada Area Youth Services, 1975, dir., coordinator and counselor Ada Alternative Edn. Program, 1975-76; counselor Okmulgee (Okla.) County Council Youth Services, 1976-79; exec. dir./counselor Turning Point, Inc., Tillman County (Okla.) Youth Services, Frederick, 1979—; mem. criminal justice adv. council Assn. S. Central Okla. Govts., 1979—. Pres., People Helpers, 1977—. Served with USAF, 1967-69. Mem. Am. Personnel and Guidance Assn., Okla. Assn. Youth Services. Bahai (treas. Frederick). Home: 300 S 17 St Frederick OK 73542 Office: 100 1/2 N Main St PO Box 429 Frederick OK 73542

WALKER, DEE BROWN, judge; b. Royse City, Tex., Dec. 3, 1912; s. Dee Alexander and Lela Blanche (Jones) W.; LL.B., So. Meth. U., 1935; m. Ruthe Elizabeth Edwards, Mar. 28, 1942; children—Susan Hays, Stephen Craig; m. 2d, Anna Lee Gandy, Sept. 13, 1952. Admitted to Tex. bar, 1935; atty. Tex. Fire & Casualty Underwriters, 1935-36, Standard Accident Ins. Co., 1936-41, Glens Falls Indemnity Co., 1941-42; gen. practice law, Dallas, 1946-59; atty. Southland Life Ins. Co., 1959-63; judge 162d Jud. Dist. Ct. Dallas County, 1963—. Mem. Dallas County Democratic Com., 1952-63. Trustee Dallas Pub. Library; v.p., dir., trustee Royse City Cemetery Found., Chisholm Cemetery Found., Cottonwood Cemetery Found. Served from pvt. to 1st lt. AUS, 1942-46. Mem. Am., Dallas bar assns., State Bar Tex., Dallas County Criminal Bar Assn., Am. Judicature Soc., Southwestern Legal Found., So. Meth. U. Alumni and Law Sch. Alumni Assn., Res. Officers Assn., Dallas Geneal. Soc. Dallas (pres.

dir. 1963-65), S.A.R. (past pres. Dallas), Am. Legion, Mil. Order World Wars, D.A.V., V.F.W., Soc. Colonial Wars, Sons Confederate Vets., Phi Alpha Delta. Mem. Christian Ch. Mason (K.T., 33 deg., Shriner), Lion. Home: 5918 Vanderbilt Dallas TX 75206 Office: 162d Dist Ct House Dallas TX 75202

WALKER, DONALD IRVINE, petroleum product cons.; b. Winnipeg, Man., Can., July 21, 1911; s. John Irvine and Alberta Louise (Wahn) W.; student Park Coll., 1928-31; A.B., Grinnell Coll., 1933; postgrad. State U. Iowa, 1934, Iowa State Coll., 1935, Princeton U., 1944; m. Marie Hubbard, July 9, 1931; 1 dau., Donna Marie Walker Wheeler. Tchr. chemistry, high sch., Newton, Iowa, 1933-37; chief chemist Maytag Co., Newton, 1937-39; with AMOCO Oil Co. (formerly Standard Oil Co., Ind.), Chgo., 1939-74, product mgr., 1961-74; petroleum product cons., Ormond Beach, Fla., 1974—. Mem. fund raising com. Child Care Center, Evanston, Ill., 1966-67; trustee Park Coll., Parkville, Mo., 1975—. Served to lt. USNR, 1943-45. Mem. ASTM (sec. 1959-68, Outstanding Service award 1976), TAPPI (sec. 1959-68, Outstanding Service award 1967), Am. Chem. Soc., Am. Petroleum Inst. Congregationalist (Ill. State Bd. 1955-57, local ch. trustee 1975-77). Patentee in field; contbr. articles to profl. jours. Home: 910 Old Mill Run Ormond Beach FL 32074

WALKER, DONALD ROY, counselor, historian; b. Beaumont, Tex., Oct. 2, 1941; s. Gaus Wilburn, Jr., and Juanita (Sellars) W.; B.A. in Zoology, U. Tex., Austin, 1969; M.A. in History, Lamar U., Beaumont, 1974; postgrad. Tex. Tech. U., Lubbock, 1975-79; m. Jonette McElroy, Mar. 21, 1977; children—Jennifer Debs, Jolie Marguerite. Counselor, Tex. Sch. for Deaf, Austin, 1964-65; Peace Corps vol., Mekambo, Gabon, 1965-58; with Dept. of State, AID, Hue, South Vietnam, 1969-72; teaching asst. Lamar U., 1972-74; instr. Tex. Tech. U., 1975—, internat. student counselor Internat. Programs Office, 1978—; instr. history Western Tex. Coll., Snyder, 1978—. Bd. govs. Lubbock County ACLU, 1978-79; pres. Llano Estacado Audubon Soc., 1978—. Recipient Grad. Student Teaching award Tex. Tech. U., 1976-77. Mem. Am. Hist. Assn., Orgn. Am. Historians, So. Hist. Assn., Nat. Assn. Fgn. Student Affairs, Delta Phi Epsilon, Phi Alpha Theta, Phi Kappa Phi, Omicron Delta Kappa. Editor: (with others) Studies in History, 1978-79; contbg. editor Stirpes, 1979. Home: 3205 31st St Lubbock TX 79410 Office: PO Box 4248 Texas Tech University Lubbock TX 79409

WALKER, DORA FOGARTY (MRS. HAROLD FRANCIS WALKER), librarian; b. New Haven, June 4, 1905; d. James Augustine and Grace (Hyland) Fogarty; B.S., Columbia U., 1930; M.A., Yale, U.-So. Conn. State Coll., 1956; 6th year diploma U. Conn., 1962; m. Harold Francis Walker, June 28, 1937 (dec. Nov. 1953); children—John James, Margaret Grace Walker Gaffney, Elizabeth Rose Walker Catelli, Francis Edward. Elementary sch. tchr., West Haven, Conn., 1923-29; training tchr. Danbury State Coll., 1930-42; reading tchr. Haley Sch., West Haven, 1952-57; library tchr. Bailey Jr. High Sch., West Haven, 1957-63; library head West Haven High Sch., 1963-71; sch. library cons., West Haven, 1957-71; bldg. rep. Lake Clarke Gardens, Lake Worth, Fla., 1972-74, recreation supr., 1971—; media dir. St. Luke Sch., Lake Worth, 1971—. Adminstrv. asst. Coll. Park Sch., West Haven, 1951-52; spl. Conn. state media cons. part-time, 1964-70; asst. prof. So. Conn. State Coll., New Haven, 1960-70. Water safety chmn. ARC, West Haven, 1967-71. Mem. Conn. Sch. Library Assn. (pres. 1961-62), Nat. Council Parents and Tchrs. (West Haven v.p. 1956-57), Conn. Ret. Tchrs. Assn., Fla. Ret. Tchrs. Assn., ALA, Fla. Library Assn., Palm Beach County Library Assn., New Eng. Ednl. Media Assn., Fla. Assn. for Media in Edn. Contbr. articles to publs. Home: Lake Clarke Gardens 2606 S Garden Dr Apt 110 Lake Worth FL 33461

WALKER, DORIS ANN, nurse; b. Tenn., Dec. 30, 1925; d. Charlie and Patience L.G. (Hickman) Coleman; diploma licensed practical nurse Milw. Inst. Tech., 1950; diploma nursing City Memphis Hosp. Sch. Nursing, 1959; B. Profl. Studies, Memphis State U., 1977, postgrad., 1977—; m. Ossie B. Walker, Nov. 27, 1958; 1 son, Duncan Eric. Staff nurse Highland Park (Mich.) Hosp., 1952-54, John Gaston Hosp., Memphis, 1954-55; staff nurse with E. H. Crump Hosp., Memphis, 1959-60, head nurse operating room, 1960-61, operating room supr., 1961-68; with City of Memphis Hosp., 1968-77, asso. dir. nursing, 1973-75, acting asso. adminstr.-nursing, 1975-77; dir. nursing Shelby County Hosp., Memphis, 1977—; asst. clin. prof. U. Tenn., 1977—; mem. rev. com. Regional Med. Program. Bd. govs. Memphis Health Center, 1969-71; exec. com. MMCC HSA Agy., 1976-77. Mem. Am. Nurses Assn., Tenn. Soc. Nursing Service Dirs., City Memphis Hosp. Sch. Nursing Alumni Assn., Chi Eta Phi. Baptist. Club: Elks. Home: 2174 Albany St Memphis TN 38108 Office: 1075 Mullins Station Rd Memphis TN 38134

WALKER, ESPER LAFAYETTE, JR., civil engr.; b. Decatur, Tex., Sept. 22, 1930; s. Esper Lafayette and Ruth (Mauldin) W.; B.S., Tex. A. and M. U., 1953; B.H.T., Yale, 1958; m. Sara Lynn Dunlap, Oct. 2, 1955; children—William David, Annette Ruth. Design engr. Tex. Hwy. Dept., Austin, 1956-57; dir. Dept. Traffic Engring., High Point, N.C., 1958-63; v.p. Wilbur Smith & Assoc., Houston, 1963—. Pres. Meadowbrook PTA, 1976-77; chmn. pack com. Sam Houston council Boy Scouts Am., 1973, treas. troop com., 1976—; baseball team mgr. Spring Br. Sports Assn., 1975-77. Served to 1st lt. C.E., AUS, 1953-56. Recipient Key Man award High Point Jaycees, 1962. Registered profl. engr., Tex., S.C., Colo., Ark., Wis., La. Mem. Nat., Tex. socs. profl. engrs., High Point Jaycees (dir.), Houston C. of C. (chmn. transit com.) Inst. Transp. Engrs. (pres. So. sect. 1963). Methodist (adminstrv. bd. 1971—, bldg. com. 1974-77). Clubs: Warwick, Summit, Beaumont. Home: 14216 Kellywood Ln Houston TX 77079 Office: 1535 West Loop S Suite 200 Houston TX 77027

WALKER, EVELYN, ret. public radio-tv broadcasting exec.; b. Birmingham, Ala.; d. Preston Lucas and Mattie (Williams) Walker; A.B., Huntingdon Coll., 1927, L.H.D., 1974; postgrad. Cornell U., 1927-29; M.A., U. Ala., 1963, postgrad., 1965-75; spl. TV course U. Ill., summer 1953. Tchr. speech Phillips High Sch., Birmingham, Ala., 1930-34; head speech dept. Ramsay High Sch., Birmingham, 1934-52; chmn. schs. radio, TV, 1944-75, producer, coordinator TV-radio Birmingham Pub. Schs., 1952-69; head instrnl. TV programming services, 1969-75; broadcaster daily childrens program, Birmingham, 1946-57; staff producer Birmingham Ednl. TV Studio for Ala. Pub. TV Network, 1954-75; cons. Gov.'s Ednl. TV Legis. Study Com., 1953. Mem. Def. Adv. Com. on Women in the Services, 1958-60; chmn. TV and radio competition Festival of Arts, 1962-65; bd. dirs. Women's Com. of 100 for Birmingham, 1968—; TV radio co-chmn. Gov's Adv. Bd. to State Safety Com., 1965-68; nat. del. Asian-Am. Women Broadcaster's Conf. 1966; media chmn. Gov.'s Commn. Ala. Yr. of Child; mem. Salvation Army Aux.; audio visual chmn. Birmingham Council P.T.A., 1966-75. Bd. dirs. Women's Army Corps Found. Recipient Educator's Medal award Freedoms Found., 1963; Spl. award for the Arts Birmingham Festival of Arts. 1962; Red Cross TV award, 1964; Nat. Headliner award Women in Communications, 1965; Key to City of Birmingham, 1966; Ala. service award Nat. Exchange Club, 1969; named Ala. Woman of Achievement, 1964, Birmingham Woman of Yr., 1965; Ala. Woman of Yr., Progressive Farmer mag., 1966; named hon. col. Ala. militia, hon. lt. a.d.c.; 20-Year Service award Ala. Ednl. TV Commn.; Obelisk award Children's Theatre, 1976; certificate of appreciation USMC, 1959, Air Force Recruiting Service, 1961, 3d Army Corps, 1961, N.Am. Air Def. Command, 1962. Mem. Nat. League Am. Pen Women, Nat. Assn. Ednl. Broadcasters, Am. Women in Radio and TV (local pres. 1959-60; dir.), Marquis Biog. Library Soc., Ala. Hist. Assn., Colonial Dames XVII Century, Daus. Am. Colonists (state TV chmn. 1966-76), Noble Order of Crown, Colonial Order of Crown, Am. United Daus. 1812 (TV chmn.), Huntingdon Coll. Alumnae Bd. (achievement award, 1958, 1st nat. v.p. 1959-60, internat. pres. 1961-63, 2d v.p. 1973-76), Ams. Royal Descent, Royal Order Garter, Magna Charta Dames (sec.-treas. 1963-64), DAR (state program chmn. 1979—), UDC, Plantagenet Soc., English Speaking Union, Humane Soc., Internat. Platform Assn., Birmingham-Jefferson Hist. Assn., Women's Golf Assn., Freedom Ednl. Found. (bd. dirs.), Ala. Congress PTA (audio visual chmn. 1966-75), Arlington Hist. Assn. (dir. 1969—), Women in Communications, Ala. Dist. Exchange Clubs (hon. life, bronze plaque award 1969), Art Assn., Art Mus., Bot. Soc., Symphony Women, Women for Patriotic Events Ala., Delta Delta Delta Alumna (past local pres). Methodist. Clubs: Press, The Club, Downtown, Birmingham Country. Home: 744 Euclid Ave Birmingham AL 35213

WALKER, EVELYN BADGER, educator; b. Pensacola, Fla., Aug. 8, 1930; d. Earl Badger and Rita Mae (Davis) Badger Outing; B.S. with honors, Bethune-Cookman Coll., 1955; M.Ed., Fla. A&M U., 1971; m. William E. Walker, Aug. 4, 1949 (div.). Tchr. phys. edn. Washington Jr. High Sch., 1955-69, Scenic Heights Elem. Sch., Pensacola, 1969—; community counselor, 1971—; participant People Organized for Community Devel., Tchrs. for Polit. Action. Recipient cert. for outstanding service Scenic Heights Sch. PTA, 1973; Disting. ser. award Bethune-Cookman Coll. Alumni Assn., 1979, Mary McLeod Bethune Medallion, 1979. Mem. Escambia Edn. Assn., NEA, Am. Personnel and Guidance Assn., Nat. Council Negro Women, Bethune Cookman Coll. Alumni Assn., Kappa Delta Pi, Alpha Kappa Alpha. Democrat. Roman Catholic.

WALKER, EVERITT DONALD, ednl. adminstr.; b. Haynesville, La., Apr. 27, 1922; s. Samuel Bethel and Marjorie Lavada W.; B.S., Sam Houston State U., 1948; M.B.A., U. Tex., 1949; LL.D., Southwestern U., 1976; m. Kathryn Marie Keneaster, Sept. 17, 1943; 1 son, Everitt Donald. Asst. prof. acctg. and fin. Sam Houston State U., Huntsville, Tex., 1949-50, asso. prof., 1950-51, auditor, 1950-51; auditor Tex. Tech U., Lubbock, 1951-55; bus. mgr. U. Tex. Med. Br., Galveston, 1955-59, bus. mgr., comptroller of hosps., 1959-64, asso. dir., 1964-65, prof. preventive medicine and community health, 1972—; dir. facilities planning and constrn. U. Tex. System, Austin, 1965-66, vice chancellor for bus. affairs, 1966-68, exec. vice chancellor for bus. affairs, 1968-70, dep. chancellor for adminstrn., 1970-75, dep. chancellor, 1975-77, pres., chief operating officer, 1977-78, chancellor, 1978—; chmn. region II fed. legis. network Nat. Assn. State Univs. and Land-Grant Colls., 1978—. Vice chmn. fin. com. United Fund, Galveston, 1964. Served to maj. USAAF, 1942-47. Named Disting. Alumnus, Sam Houston State U., 1978; C.P.A., Tex. Mem. Assn. Am. Univs. Nat. Assn. State Univs. and Land-Grant Colls. (chmn. 1977-79), Council of Presidents of Tex. State Sr. Colls. and Univs., Am. Council on Edn., Tex. Soc. C.P.A.'s, Tex. Philos. Soc., Beta Alpha Psi. Office: 601 Colorado St Austin TX 78701

WALKER, GEORGE KONTZ, educator; b. Tuscaloosa, Ala., July 8, 1938; s. Joseph Henry and Catherine Louise (Indorf) W.; B.A., U. Ala., 1959; LL.B., Vanderbilt U., 1966; M.A., Duke, 1968; LL.M., U. Va., 1972; postgrad. (Sterling fellow), Yale, 1975-76; m. Phyllis Ann Sherman, July 30, 1966; children—Charles Edward, Mary Neel. Admitted to Va. bar, 1967, N.C. bar, 1976; law clk. Judge John D. Butzner, Jr., U.S. Dist. Ct., Richmond, Va., 1966-67; asso. atty. Hunton, Williams, Gay, Powell & Gibson, Richmond, 1967-70; practiced in Charlottesville, Va., 1970-71; asst. prof. Wake Forest U. Law Sch., Winston-Salem, N.C., 1972-73, asso. prof. law, 1974-77, prof., 1978—; vis. prof. law Marshall-Wythe Sch. Law, Coll. William and Mary, Williamsburg, Va., 1979-80; staff researcher project commentaries Va. Constn., Va. Gen. Assembly, 1971-72; dir. research Va. County Suprs. manual 3rd edit. Va. Assn. Counties, 1972-74; cons. Naval War Coll., 1976—. Served from ensign to lt. (j.g.), USNR, 1959-62; comdr. Res. Woodrow Wilson fellow Duke, 1962-63. Mem. Am., Va. bar assns., Va. State Bar, N.C. State Bar, Am. Soc. Internat. Law, Order of Barristers, Phi Beta Kappa, Sigma Alpha Epsilon, Phi Delta Phi. Democrat. Episcopalian (lay reader). Author: International Law for the Naval Commander. Contbr. articles to profl. jours. Home: 2845 Wesleyan Ln Winston Salem NC 27106

WALKER, GEORGE PINCKNEY, III, geologist; b. El Paso, Tex., June 28, 1934; s. George Pinckney and Helen (Griffith) W.; Profl. in Petroleum Engring., Colo. Sch. Mines, 1956; M.A. in Geology, U. Tex., Austin, 1967; m. Estella Jeanne Livingston, Sept. 4, 1955; children—George Pinckney, Charlisa Ann, Betsy Kim. Petroleum engr., dist. engr. Tenneco Oil Co., Wichita Falls, Tex., Great Bend, Kan., Lafayette, La., 1956-64; geologist sr. grade Amoco Prodn. Co., Midland, Tex., Ft. Worth, 1966-71, Houston, 1971—, sr. geologist, 1971-73, staff geologist, 1973-74, staff geologist sr. grade, 1974-75, area geologist, 1975-76, project geologist, 1976-77, div. geol. supr., 1977-78, div. geologist-exploitation, 1978-80; owner Walker Exploration Co., 1980—; part-owner, mgr. Bluff Creek Ranch, Center Point, Tex., 1966—. First vice chmn., chmn. program Lafayette Republican Club, 1963; mem. Rep. Parish Exec. Com., Lafayette, 1963-64; candidate Police Juror Ward 9, Lafayette Parish, 1964; Registered profl. engr., La.; certified profl. geol. scientist Assn. Profl. Geol. Scientists. Mem. Am. Petroleum Inst. (3d vice chmn. adv. bd. 1962-64), Am. Inst. Mining, Metall. and Petroleum Engrs., Am. Assn. Petroleum Geologists, West Tex., N.Mex., Ft. Worth (chmn. field trip registration com. 1969), Houston geol. socs., Soc. Econ. Paleontologists and Mineralogists, Geol. Soc. Am., Sigma Gamma Epsilon. Research in subsurface geology of Kerr Basin and adjacent areas, South Central Tex. Home: 9814 Fox Run Ct Houston TX 77080 Office: Amoco Prodn Co 500 Jefferson St PO Box 3092 Houston TX 77001

WALKER, GLYNDA MARIE, assn. exec.; b. Alton, Ill., May 31, 1940; d. Robert Glenn and Ethel Marie (Conyer) Walker; B.S., So. Ill. U., 1962; M.A., Ohio State U., 1968. Speech and hearing therapist Wheeling (W.Va.) Soc. Crippled Children, Inc., 1962-66, dir. speech and lang. dept., 1968—; counselor, student personnel dept. Ohio State U., Columbus, 1966-67, speech, hearing clinician, 1967-68. Bd. dirs. W.A.T.C.H., Headstart Assn. for Retarded Citizens. Mem. Am. Speech and Hearing Assn., W.Va. Speech and Hearing Assn., Council for Exceptional Children, W.Va. Jaycee-ettes (awards), Wheeling Jaycee-ettes, Sigma Alpha Eta, Delta Zeta, Zeta Phi Eta. Club: Order Eastern Star. Home: 200 B Betty St Wheeling WV 26003 Office: Wheeling Society for Crippled Children Inc 1305 National Rd Wheeling WV 26003

WALKER, HARVEY GLENN, media mfg. corp. exec.; b. Altamahaw, N.C., Nov. 25, 1949; s. Harvey Amos and Beatrice (Ashley) W.; grad. Tech. Inst. of Alamance, 1972; m. Jean Elaine Darnell, Sept. 26, 1973; children—Amanda Dawn. Insp., Heritage Casket Co., Burlington, N.C., 1971-72; shipping clk. Carolina Biol. Supply Corp., Burlington, 1972-73; transp. mgr. Granite Diagnostics Inc., Burlington, 1973—. Baptist. Home: 2225 Wilkins St Burlington NC 27215 Office: Granite Diagnostics Inc 1308 Rainey St Burlington NC 27215

WALKER, HELEN ROSALIE, county ofcl.; b. Victoria, Tex., Feb. 14, 1937; d. Frank Henry and Beatrice (Vanek) Dusek; A.A., Victoria Coll., 1956; m. Walter C. Walker, Mar. 20, 1956; children—Randy, Vicki. Proofreader, Victoria Advocate, 1956—; dep. treas. Victoria (Tex.) County, 1956-73, treas., 1973—. Adult leader O'Connor 4-H Club, 1971-75; bd. dirs., treas. Victoria County Democratic Women's Club; bd. dirs. Victoria County United Way; past treas., sponsor Victoria Girls' Fastpitch Assn. Mem. County Treasurers Assn. Tex. (2d v.p.), Nat. Assn. County Treasurers and Fin. Officers, Tex. Assn. Elected Women. Clubs: Pilot (past pres., dir.), Toastmistress (past pres.). Recipient New Counties U.S.A. Achievement award Nat. Assn. Counties, 1975. Home: 3601 Bobolink Ln Victoria TX 77901 Office: 115 N Bridge St Room 116 Victoria TX 77901

WALKER, HIAWATHA BROWN, educator; b. Lauderdale County, Ala., July 11, 1918; s. Andrew John and Jennie Eldora W.; B.S., Florence State Tchrs. Coll., 1939; M.A., George Peabody Coll. Tchrs., 1946; M.P.H., U. N.C., 1947, Ph.D., 1959. Tchr., Lauderdale County, 1939-41; sanitarian Talladega (Ala.) County Health Dept., 1941-42; tchr. Cullman County, Ala., 1948; health educator TVA, 1948-49; health educator Spartanburg (S.C.) Health Dept., 1949-50, 53-55; research asso. U. N.C., 1957-59, asso. prof. health edn., 1959-71; prof. health edn. E. Tenn. State U., Johnston City, 1971—. Served with U.S. Army, 1942-46. Mem. N.C. Assn. Health Educators (pres. 1971), Am. Public Health Assn. (chmn. health edn. sect. 1977), Soc. Public Health Edn. (pres. 1977, historian Tenn. chpt. 1979), Am. Sch. Health Assn., Tenn. Public Health Assn., Tenn. Acad. Health Edn., Kappa Mu Epsilon, Delta Omega, Phi Delta Kappa, Kappa Delta Pi. Mem. Ch. of Christ. Home: 1818 Brook Hollow Rd Johnson City TN 37601 Office: PO Box 24414 University Station Johnson City TN 37601

WALKER, JACK D., banker; b. Cullman, Ala., Aug. 26, 1938; s. Doyle B. and Stella (York) E.; student West Point High Sch., Cullman, Ala.; m. Sept. 4, 1964; children—Belinda, Steven, Clete. Clk., State Nat. Bank, Cullman, 1956-62, mgr. proof, bookkeeping, transit, Huntsville, Ala., 1962-64; with Central Bank Ala., 1964-69, 70—, v.p., regional gen. auditor, 1973—; auditor Bankers Trust S.C., Columbia, 1969-70. Bd. dirs. Wesley Meml. United Meth. Ch., 1971-79, also trustee, tchr. Sunday Sch., choir mem. Chartered bank auditor; cert. data processing auditor. Mem. Bank Adminstrn. Inst. (past pres., dir. Tenn. Valley chpt.), Inst. Internal Auditors, Electronic Data Processing Auditors Assn. Republican. Home: 1206 Noble Ave SW Decatur AL 35601 Office: 251 Johnson St SE Decatur AL 35601

WALKER, JAMES CLINTON, JR., radiologist; b. Birmingham, Ala., Dec. 1, 1946; s. James Clinton and Margaret Emily (McShan) W.; B.S., U. Ala., 1968, M.D., 1972; m. Darlene Shikle, Dec. 18, 1965; 1 dau., Kelley Darlene. Intern, St. Vincent's Hosp., Birmingham, 1972-73; resident in diagnostic radiology Baptist Med. Centers, Birmingham, 1973-76; radiologist Birmingham Radiol. Group, P.A., 1976—; mem. staff Bapt. Med. Center Hosp., E. End Hosp., Birmingham, 1976—. Diplomate Am. Bd. Radiology. Mem. Am. Coll. Radiology, Radiol. Soc. N. Am., AMA. Baptist. Home: 819 Conroy Rd Birmingham AL 35222 Office: 940 Montclair Rd Suite 200 Birmingham AL 35213

WALKER, JAMES GORDON, educator; b. Jones County, Miss., Aug. 27, 1947; s. James Alton and Janie Mae (Tullos) W.; A.A., East Central Jr. Coll., 1968; B.S. in Edn. (Sperry scholar 1968), Miss. Coll., 1970, M.Ed., 1971; Ed.D. (univ. fellow 1974), U. So. Miss., 1975; m. Senita Ann Arthur, Nov. 5, 1967; children—James Gordon, Arthur Merkel Kelly. Tchr., then prin. elementary schs. in Miss., 1970-72; prin. Harrison Central Elementary Sch., Harrison County (Miss.) Schs., Gulfport, 1972-76, county dir. instrn., 1976-80; supt. schs. Grenada (Miss.) Separate Sch. Dist., 1980—; mem. adj. faculty William Carey Coll., Hattiesburg, Miss., U. So. Miss.; cons. in field. Treas. Harrison County PTA, 1972-75; bd. dirs. Miss. PTA, 1978-80. Mem. Am. Assn. Sch. Adminstrs., Miss. Assn. Sch. Adminstrs., Miss. Assn. Asst. Supts., Miss. Assn. Educators, Assn. Supervision and Curriculum Devel., Miss. Edn. Assn. (del. 1973-76), Kappa Delta Pi, Phi Delta Kappa (v.p. 1980—). Baptist. Clubs: Orange Grove Civitan (sec. 1978-80), Masons. Home: 1985 Tuscola Grenada MS 38901

WALKER, JEWETT LYNIUS, clergyman, ch. ofcl.; b. Beaumont, Tex., Apr. 7, 1930; s. Elijah Harvey and Ella Jane (Wilson) W.; B.A., Calif. Western U., 1957; M.A., Kingdom Bible Inst., 1960; B.R.E., St. Stephens Coll., 1966, D.D., 1968; LL.D., Union Bapt. Sem., 1971; m. Dorothy Mae Croom, Apr. 11, 1965; children—Cassandra Lynn, Jewett L., Kevin, Michael, Ella, Betty Renne, Kent, Elijah H. Ordained to ministry A.M.E. Zion Ch., 1957; pastor Shiloh A.M.E. Zion Ch., Monrovia, Calif., 1961-64, Martin Temple A.M.E. Zion Ch., Los Angeles, 1964-65; 1st A.M.E. Zion Ch., Compton, Calif., 1965-66; Met. A.M.E. Zion Ch., Los Angeles, 1966-73; Logan Temple A.M.E. Zion Ch., San Diego, Calif., 1973-74, Rock Hill A.M.E. Zion Ch., Indian Trail, N.C., 1974-79, Bennettsville A.M.E. Zion Ch., Norwood, N.C., 1979—; sec. dept. home missions, brotherhood pensions, and relief A.M.E. Zion Ch., Charlotte, N.C., 1974. Trustee Clinton Coll., Rock Hill, Lomax-Hannon Coll., Greenville, Ala., Union Bapt. Theol. Sem., Birmingham, Ala.; pres. Am. Ch. Fin. Service Corp., Carolina Home Health Service Inc., Methodist Life Ins. Soc. Inc. Mem. NAACP (life). Clubs: Shriners, Masons (33 deg.). Author articles. Home: 910 Bridle Path Ln Charlotte NC 27211 Office: PO Box 30846 401 2d St Charlotte NC 28202

WALKER, JO NEWLIN, educator; b. Canyon, Tex., Aug. 13, 1921; d. Burt and Ora Etta (Thompson) Newlin; B.S., W. Tex. State U., 19—, M.Ed., 19—, M.A., 19—; m. Jack Harrison Walker, Mar. 27, 1941; 1 son, Billy Kenneth. Various secretarial positions, 1941-45; tchr. pub. schs., Amarillo, Tex., 1955; instr. dept. English, Amarillo, 1957-68, asst. prof., 1968-72, asso. prof., 1972-77, prof., 1977—. Mem. Tex. Jr. Coll. Tchrs. Assn., Council Coll. Tchrs. English. Presbyterian. Home: WT Box 656 Canyon TX 79016 Office: Amarillo Coll PO Box 447 Amarillo TX 79178

WALKER, JOANNE BRINTON, real estate mktg. exec.; b. Rochester, N.Y., July 11, 1949; d. Albert Donald and Phyllis Margaret (Noll) Brinton; B.S. in Bus. Adminstrn., East Carolina U., 1971; m. William H. Walker, Jan. 21, 1973. Asst. to pres. Lester Bros. Furniture Co., St. Petersburg, Fla., 1971-75; mktg., ops. dir. Tourtelot, Inc., Realtors, St. Petersburg, 1976-79, asst. v.p., 1979—, pres. Tourtelot Sales, Inc. subs., real estate brokers, 1980—. Active Girl Scouts Am. Mem. St. Petersburg Advt. Fedn. (dir. 1980—). Republican. Roman Catholic. Club: St. Petersburg Jr. Woman's. Home: 5631 Denver St NE Saint Petersburg FL 33703 Office: 127 Central Ave Saint Petersburg FL 33701

WALKER, KENNETH HOUSTON, SR., bus. cons.; b. Enterprise, Ala., Oct. 1, 1927; s. Homer Lee and Julia (Spears) W.; B.S. in Edn., U. Ga., 1953; m. S. Kathryn Bowden, Sept. 11, 1942; children—Ken H., Jr., Keith B., Kris C. Edn. cons. Sears Roebuck Found., Chgo., 1951-59; aircraft technician Northrup World Wide Air Services, Fort Rucker, Ala., 1965-73; exec. v.p., instr. C.W. Parker & Asso., Troy, Ala., 1974—; cons. speed learning, time mgmt., supr. motivation; div.

mgr. Life Investors Ins. Co. Am. Active state and local politics. Served with USN, 1943-46, to lt. col. Ala. State Militia, 1974—. Recipient award for outstanding ability in aircraft tech. USAF, 1967, USN, 1969, Royal Australian Air Force, 1970, Norwegian Air Force, 1970. Mem. Democrats of Ala., Am. Vets Assn., SCV (local dir.), Assn. USN, Assn. U.S. Army, Am. Legion, VFW, ACLU. Club: Masons. Address: Box 368 Brundidge AL 36010

WALKER, L(ESLIE) BRENT, social worker; b. Memphis, Tex., July 24, 1948; s. William Jackson and Betty Dale(West) W.; B.S., Midwestern U., 1970; M.S. in Social Work, U. Tex., Arlington, 1973; m. Vicki Gene Meyer, Nov. 6, 1970; children—Natalie, Kristen, Luke. With Wichita Falls (Tex.) State Hosp., 1969-73, ward social worker, 1973; asst. coordinator outreach services Terrell (Tex.) State Hosp., 1973—; mem. undergrad. social work adv. bd. E. Tex. State U., 1974—, chmn., 1975, 80. Mem. vestry Episcopal Ch., Dallas, 1975-78. Mem. Acad. Cert. Social Workers, Assn. Rural Mental Health (exec. bd.), Nat. Assn. Social Workers. Home: 6018 Highcrest St Garland TX 75034 Office: Box 70 Terrell TX 75160

WALKER, LEE RICHMOND, psychologist; b. Providence, Jan. 16, 1950; s. LeRoy Richmond and Elsie Kelley W.; B.A., R.I. Coll., 1973; Ph.D., U. Tex., Austin, 1978; m. Luci Mary Savino; 1 dau., Cynthia Lee Walker. Mental health worker Butler Hosp., Providence, 1972-73; dir. children's program Cumberland County Mental Health/Mental Retardation Center, Fayetteville, N.C., 1978—; instr. Fayetteville Tech. Inst., 1978—; vis. asst. prof. N.C. State U., 1979—. Lic. sch. psychologist, N.C. Mem. Am. Psychol. Assn., N.C. Psychol. Assn., Cumberland County Mental Health Assn., Phi Kappa Phi. Democrat. Office: Cumberland County Mental Health Center 801 Arsenal Ave Fayetteville NC 28305

WALKER, LYNN WESLEY, librarian; b. Okeechobee, Fla., Aug. 30, 1928; s. Benjamin Franklin and Neva Gertrude (Williams) W.; B.A., U. Fla., 1950; M.A., Fla. State U., 1953; m. Joyce Roberta Orr, June 9, 1950; children—John Michael, Richard Allen, Jacqueline Lynne. Cataloger, U. Tenn. Library, 1950-52; sci. cataloger U. Fla. Library, 1952-53; sci. reference librarian U. Fla., 1953-54, librarian Engring. and Physics Library, 1954-66; dir. libraries U. Central Fla. (formerly Fla. Technol. U.), Orlando, 1966—; cons. microfilm retrieval systems, 1972—; instr. library sci. and engring. graphics U. Fla., 1953-57. Bd. dirs. Southeastern Library Network, 1978—. Mem. ALA (councilor 1971-74), Fla. Library Assn. (pres. 1970-71), Southeastern Library Assn., Nat. Micrographics Assn., Naval Res. Assn., Fla. Assn. of AAU (v.p. 1971-74), Beta Phi Mu. Democrat. Episcopalian. Contbr. articles to library jours. Home: 640 Berwick Dr Winter Park FL 32792 Office: U Central Fla PO Box 25000 Orlando FL 32816

WALKER, MARK ANTHONY, judge; b. Covington, Tenn., Sept. 3, 1908; s. Mark Anthony and Ella (Simonton) W.; B.S., U. Tenn., 1931; student U. Tenn. Coll. Law, 1930-31, U. Wis. Sch. Law, 1934; m. Lulie Reynolds Eddins; children—Mark Anthony, Nathalie Eileen, Lawrence Eddins. Admitted to Tenn. bar, 1935; practiced in Covington, 1935-46; circuit judge 16th Jud. Circuit of Tenn., 1946-67; judge Ct. Criminal Appeals, State Tenn., 1967—, presiding judge, 1967-77, 79-80. Mem. Tenn. Ho. of Reps., 1939-42. Mem. Tenn. Democratic Exec. Com., 1940-43; v.p. Tenn. Young Dem. Club, 1946. Served with USNR, 1942-46; comdr. Res. Mem. Am. Bar Assn., Bar Assn. Tenn., Am. Judicature Soc., Kappa Sigma. Presbyn. Mason (Shriner). Address: 315 S Main St Covington TN 38019

WALKER, MELFORD WHITFIELD, state ofcl.; b. Manning, S.C., Sept. 21, 1924; s. James Allen and Daisy Elizabeth (Jones) W.; A.B., Va. Union U., 1949. B.D., 1952; Th.M., Union Theol. Sem., 1953; M.S., Va. Commonwealth U., 1973; m. Ruth Blackwell, May 27, 1954; children—Melford Whitfield, Margaret, Reginald, Darryl. With Va. Dept. Vocat. Rehab., Richmond, 1966—, trust fund coordinator, 1977-78, rehab. tng. coordinator, 1975-77, asst. dir., 1978—; faculty Storer Coll., 1953-55, Va. Union U., Richmond, 1960-66. Served with Signal Corps, U.S. Army, 1942-46. Cert. rehab. counselor. Mem. NAACP (pres. Va. conf. 1970-74, chmn. region 7, 1972-73, chmn. nat. nominating com. 1973-74, pres. Hanover County br. 1964-79), Va. Rehab. Assn., Nat. Rehab. Assn., Regional Council of Non-White Mems. Democrat. Baptist. Home: 2526 Northumberland Ave Richmond VA 23220

WALKER, P. DUANE, hosp. mgmt. co. exec.; b. McKeesport, Pa., June 5, 1931; s. Percy Theodore and Bertha I. (Westerberg) W.; B.S., Pa. State U., 1953; M.B.A., N.Y. U., 1969; m. Doris Jane McClymont, Dec. 12, 1969; children—Jeannine Cherie, Andrea Lee, Edward Duane. Systems engr. IBM Corp., Pitts, 1955-58; cons. controller's staff Westinghouse Electric Co., Pitts., 1958-59; mgr. mgmt. adv. services Price Waterhouse & Co., Pitts., 1959-62; mgr. bus. systems planning IBM Corp., 1962-74; sr. v.p. mgmt. systems Humana Inc., Louisville, 1974—. Mem. Fund for the Arts, Louisville, 1976-77; bd. dirs. Jr. Achievement, 1978-79; mem. athletic com. Ky. Country Day Sch.; mem. Louisville Schs. and Bus. Coordinating Council, 1979; dir. father's asso. Hanover Coll. Mem. Soc. Mgmt. Info. Systems, Am. Inst. Indsl. Engrs., Pa. State U. Alumni Assn. Presbyterian. Clubs: Nittany Lions, Harmony Landing Country. Home: 1309 N Buckeye Ln Goshen KY 40026 Office: Box 1438 Louisville KY 40201

WALKER, ROBERT EDWARD, sales exec.; b. Waxahachie, Tex., Apr. 17, 1951; s. William Campbell and Sara Frances (Utley) W.; student Southwestern Jr. Coll., 1969, 70; B.B.A., Tex. Christian U., 1972, postgrad., 1973-74; m. Caryn Jane Henderson, Apr. 10, 1976. Youth dir. First United Methodist Ch., Mansfield, Tex., part-time, 1971-73; account exec. KXOL/Sigmor Broadcasting, Ft. Worth, 1973-74, WFAA/Belo Broadcasting, Dallas, 1974-76; nat. prodn. sales mgr. AVW Prodns., Dallas, 1976—; public relations cons. Here's Life, Dallas, 1976. Deacon, McKinney Bible Ch., Ft. Worth, 1978—. Anderson Clayton Labs. scholar, 1969-73. Mem. Mktg./Communications Execs., Dallas Advt. League, Mktg. Planners Internat., Lambda Chi Alpha (alumni adv. 1978—). Home: 7308 Laurie Dr Fort Worth TX 76112 Office: 2241 Irving Blvd Dallas TX 75207

WALKER, ROBERT LUTHER, oil co. exec.; b. Colorado City, Tex., Dec. 25, 1921; s. James Thomas and Jennie Mae (Jones) W.; student N. Tex. Agr. Coll., 1939-49, U. Tex., 1941-42; m. Ruth Odette Bevill, Sept. 19, 1942; children—Robert Craig, Karen Kay, James Louis. Oil scout Amerada Petroleum Co., Midland, Tex., 1946-48; asst. dist. landman Continental Oil Co., Midland, 1948-49; dist. landman Champlin Petroleum Co., 1949-64, supt. of land, 1964-71, div. landman, 1971-74, regional land mgr. 1974-78, dist. exploration mgr., Midland, 1978—, asst. sec., 1964—. Served with USAAF, 1942-46. Decorated Air medal. Mem. Am. Assn. Petroleum Landmen, Permian Basin Landmen Assn. Republican. Baptist. Club: Ranchland Hills Country. Home: 1203 Neely St Midland TX 79701 Office: 300 Wilco Bldg Midland TX 79701

WALKER, ROBERT MICHAEL, project engr.; b. Los Angeles, May 27, 1940; s. George Frank and Roberta Ruth (Potts) W.; B.S. in Mech. Engring., N.Mex. State U., 1963, M.S. in Mech. Engring., 1964, D.Sc. (fellow), 1967; m. Dickie Tighe, May 20, 1967; children—Katherine Marie, Robert Tighe, Ann Michelle. Grad. asst. mech. engring. dept. N.Mex. State U., 1963-64, instr., 1964-67, instr. extension sch., White Sands Missile Range, 1968-70; prin. scientist BDM Corp., McLean, Va., 1971-79, sr. scientist, El Paso, Tex., 1967-71, project mgr., Tucson, 1971-75, prin. investigator nuclear survivability communication systems, McLean, 1975-77, nat. expert NATO integrated communication system design, The Hague, Netherlands, 1977-78, prin. scientist, McLean, 1978-79; sr. project engr. TRW Def. and Space Systems Group, McLean, 1979—. Cub scout webelos den master Boy Scouts Am., Tucson, 1972-73, asst. scoutmaster, Annandale, Va., 1975-77; mem. archtl. com. Canterbury Woods Civic Assn., 1979—. Served to capt. Ordnance Corps, U.S. Army, 1968-70. Decorated Commendation medal; registered profl. engr., N.Mex., Pa. Mem. Armed Forces Communications and Electronics Assn., Air Force Assn., Engring. Guidance Council El Paso, SAR (sec.-treas. Tucson chpt. 1971-74), Soc. Pershing Rifles, Sigma Xi, Tau Beta Pi, Pi Tau Sigma. Club: Classic Thunderbird Internat. Home: 4928 Althea Dr Annandale VA 22003 Office: 7600 Colshire Dr McLean VA 22003

WALKER, RONALD HUGH, bus. cons.; b. Bryan, Tex., July 25, 1937; s. Walter Hugh and Maxine (Tarver) W.; B.A., U. Ariz., 1960; m. Anne Lucille Collins, Aug. 8, 1959; children—Lisa Anne, Marjorie Maxine, Lynne Jeanice. Exec. Allstate Ins. Co., Pasadena, Calif., 1964-67; gen. mgr. Hydson Co., Los Angeles, 1967-69; spl. asst. to Sec. Interior, Dept. Interior, 1969-70; dir. advance office, spl. asst. to Pres., Washington, 1970-73; dir. Nat. Park Service, 1973-75; asso. dir. World Championship Tennis, 1975-77; pres. Ron Walker and Assos., Inc., bus. and polit. cons., Dallas, 1977-79; v.p., partner Korn/Ferry Internat., Dallas, 1979—. Recipient Disting. Citizen award U. Ariz., 1973; Outstanding Service award Dept. Interior, 1975. Republican. Methodist. Club: Bent Tree Country. Home: 7231 Hillwood Dallas TX 75248 Office: One Dallas Centre 350 North St Paul Suite 1675 Dallas TX 75201

WALKER, SUSAN LEE, nurse, hosp. ofcl.; b. Spartanburg, S.C., Feb. 4, 1952; d. Jack Swann and Harriett B. (Pentrack) Beeler; A.D., U. Tenn., Martin, 1974, B.S., 1975; m. Danny Ray Walker, June 8, 1973; 1 son, Matthew. Staff, head nurse ICU, Vol. Gen. Hosp., Martin, Tenn., 1974-75; tchr. sci. Beulah High Sch., Riverview, Ala., 1975-77; head nurse postpartum-urology, med.-surg. units Lee County Hosp., Opelika, Ala., summer 1976, ednl. cons., inservice instr., 1977—; CPR instr. Am. Heart Assn., ednl. chmn. Lee County, 1977—. Mem. Am. Vet. Assn. (parliamentarian student aux. 1978-79), Am. Soc. Health Educators and Trainers, Am. Nurses Assn., Alpha Psi Wives Aux. (treas. 1977-78, service chmn. 1978—). Mem. Ch. of Christ. Office: Regional Edn Dept Lee County Hosp 2000 Pepperell Pkwy Opelika AL 36801

WALKER, THOMAS CHARLES, fin. cons.; b. Trenton, N.J., Jan. 19, 1933; s. Thomas Charles and Anne Marie (Reagan) W.; B.S. in Indsl. Engring., Lafayette Coll., 1954; m. Carolyn Francis Wolff, Apr. 13, 1957; children—Thomas Charles, Joseph Fredrick. Various mgmt. positions Tex. Instruments, Dallas, 1959-66; pres. Superior Circuits Corp., Dallas, 1966-68; chmn., chief exec. officer Intermed Corp., Dallas, 1968-71; pres. Waste Resources Corp., Phila., 1971-72; v.p. Browning-Ferris Industries, Houston, 1972-76; v.p. Criterion Capital Corp., Houston, 1976-77; prin. Thomas C. Walker Assos., Dallas, 1977—. Served with USNR, 1955-59. Mem. Nat. Solid Waste Mgmt. Assn., NAM. Republican. Roman Catholic. Clubs: Dallas Country, Dallas City, T-bar-M Tennis. Home: 4353 Edmondson Ave Dallas TX 75205

WALKER, WALTER JACKSON, food co. exec.; b. Knoxville, Tenn., Sept. 30, 1919; s. John Wesley and Mattie Alma (Gilbert) W.; student U. Tenn., 1938-40; m. Learah Loraine Ford, Aug. 15, 1940; 1 dau., Gayle Walker Threet. Ins. agt. Shenandoah Life Ins. Co., Roanoke, Va., 1938-41; salesman H.T. Hackney Co., Knoxville, 1941-42; owner, operator Jack Walker's Market, 1946-65; pres. Family Pantry Markets Inc., Knoxville, 1965—; dir. 1st. Tenn. Bank. Bd. dirs. Jr. Achievement Knoxville, 1976—; trustee Arthritis Found. Knoxville, 1976—; bd. dirs. Presbyn. Homes Tenn., 1975—, E. Tenn. Children's Hosp., 1977—. Interest Rate Info. Bd. Knoxville, 1977—, Expo 82, 1977—; pres. elect Knoxville chpt. ARC, 1975—; chmn. United Way Knoxville, 1974-75. Served with USCGR, 1942-45. Recipient Red Triangle award YMCA, 1975; named retailer of yr. Tenn. Retail Mchts. Assn., 1977. Mem. Knoxville C. of C. (pres. 1976—), Nat. Assn. Retail Grocers, Nat. Assn. Convenience Stores. Republican. Baptist. Clubs: Rotary, Executive, City, Masons (32 deg.), Shriners. Home: 9627 Tunbridge Ln Knoxville TN 37922 Office: PO Box 12330 Knoxville TN 37912

WALKER, WARD WINSTON, editor, publisher; b. Huron, S.D., Oct. 12, 1916; s. Don Glen and Florence Edith (Ward) W.; student Central State Tchrs. Coll., Stevens Point, Wis., 1934-36; m. Mary Ellen Beil, Apr. 1, 1946; children—Ward Winston, Pamela, Gretchen, Richard. Staff, City News Bur. Chgo., 1937-38; reporter, feature writer, fgn. corr. Chgo. Tribune, 1938-48; pvt. practice pub. relations counseling, Chgo., 1948-63; editor, pub. Brownsville (Tex.) Times, 1967—. Served with USMCR, 1942-45. Mem. Tex. Press Assn. Republican. Episcopalian. Clubs: Rancho Viejo Country, Elks. Home: 5212 Rancho Viejo Country Club PO Box 3918 Brownsville TX 78520 Office: PO Box 472 Brownsville TX 78520

WALL, BENNETT HARRISON, educator; b. Raleigh, N.C., Dec. 7, 1914; s. Bennett Louis and Evie David (Harrison) W.; A.B., Wake Forest Coll., 1933; M.A., U. N.C., 1941, Ph.D., 1946; m. Neva Olive White, Sept. 7, 1968; children by previous marriage—Maie (Mrs. John E. Clark), Diana (Mrs. John Freckman), Ann Bennett. Instr., N.C. State U., 1942-43; instr. U. N.C., 1943-44; instr. U. Ky., 1944-46, asst. prof., 1946-52, asso. prof., 1952-64; prof. history dept. Tulane U., New Orleans, 1968-80, head dept., 1968-73, dir. Tulane Center Bus. History Studies, 1974-80; lectr. Am. history U. Ga., Athens, 1980—. Mem. Orgn. Am. Historians, Agrl. History Soc., Bus. History Soc., Econ. History Assn., Newcomen Soc., Western History Assn., La. (pres. 1974-75), So. (sec.-treas. 1953—) hist. assns., Omicron Delta Kappa, Phi Alpha Theta. Co-author: Teagle of Jersey Standard, 1974. Contbr. numerous articles to profl. jours. Home: 150 Ashton Dr Athens GA 30606

WALL, CHARLES BUFORD, ednl. EDP ofcl.; b. Clarksville, Tenn., Oct. 23, 1947; s. Robert Buford and Mary Lillian (Kennedy) W.; student Case Inst. Tech., 1965-66; B.A., Austin Peay State U., 1969; m. Linda Jean Tyree, Mar. 15, 1969; children—Shannon Lynn, Wendy Melinda. Computer programmer, Cumberland Elec. Membership Corp., Clarksville, Tenn., 1968; student programmer, Austin Peay State U., Clarksville, 1967-69, dir. computer center, 1972—; date processing mgr., U. Tenn., Nashville, 1969-72; cons. C & W Enterprises; bd. dirs. Queen City Telecommunications; instr. computer programming, U. Tenn., 1969-72. Active Montgomery County Civil Defense, 1966; advisory bd. high sch. data processing courses, 1973. Baptist. Club: Kiwanis (dir., 1972-74, pres., 1976-77; Clarksville Hilldale, Kiwanian of Year, 1974-75). Home: Route 3 Wingate Clarksville TN 37040 Office: Austin Peay State Univ Clarksville TN 37040

WALL, CHARLES INGLEFIELD, corp. exec.; b. Sedan, Kans., 1904; B.S. in Bus. Adminstrn., U. Kans., 1927; married. With Pioneer Corp. (name formerly Pioneer Natural Gas Co.), Amarillo, Tex., 1927—, v.p. distbn., then exec. v.p., 1954-55, pres., 1955-68, chmn. bd., pres., chief exec officer, 1968-69, chmn. bd., chmn. exec. com., 1969-70, chmn. bd. 1970—, also dir.; pres. West Tex. Gas Co., 1951-54; dir. Quanah Acme Co., Pacific R.R., 1st Nat. Bank Amarillo. Office: Pioneer Corp 301 Taylor St PO Box 511 Amarillo TX 79105*

WALL, EDWIN CRAIG, banker, wood products co. exec.; b. Lilesville, N.C., Feb. 14, 1911; s. Ben R. and Annie Lee (Shuford) W.; student U. N.C., 1933; LL.D., Clemson U., 1967; m. May Howard, Mar. 14, 1936; children—Edwin Craig, May Ervin, Harriet Wall Martin, Nell Wall Otto. Dep. chmn. bd. Fed. Res. Bank of Richmond (Va.), 1972—; chmn. bd Canal Industries, Inc., Canal Devel. Corp., Canal Wood Corp.; pres., dir. Seacoast Industries, Inc.; dir. Myrtle Beach Lumber Co., Inc., Waccamaw Lumber & Supply Co., Inc., Red Hill Chip Corp. Chmn. S.C. Commn. on Higher Edn., 1967-71; trustee Queens Coll., Charlotte, N.C., 1967-76, Belle Baruch Found., 1969-76. Recipient Silver Beaver award Boy Scouts Am., 1960; Outstanding Community Service award Am. Legion, 1971. Mem. Am. Pulpwood Assn. (dir. 1968), Forest Farmers Assn. (dir. 1965). Presbyn. (elder 1955-76). Home: 303 Lakeland St Conway SC 29526 Office: Canal Industries Inc PO Box 830 Conway SC 29526

WALL, FURMAN GRESHAM, JR., investment co. exec.; b. Richmond, Va., Sept. 23, 1944; s. Furman Gresham and Jane Winfield (Pearce) W.; B.B.A., U. Ga., 1966; M.B.A., U. Va., 1968; certificate N.Y. Inst. Finance, 1969, C.F.A., 1972; m. Mary Curtis McGregor, June 9. 1965; children—Furman Gresham III, Anne Winfield, Robert Scott, Kathleen McGregor. First v.p., dir. Investment Corp. Va., Norfolk, 1971—; pres., treas., dir. Back Bay Ltd., 1976-77; v.p., dir. Gresham Wall Realty, Inc., 1977—; dir. Wedgewood Carpet Co., Richmond, 1971-72, The Delta Group, Inc., 1980—. Bd. dirs. Alanton Civic League, 1972-74; sponsor Colgate Darden Grad. Sch. Bus. Adminstrn., U. Va., 1968—; trustee, pres. parents group Cape Henry Collegiate Sch., 1973-74. Chartered fin. analyst. Mem. Fin. Analysts Fedn., Richmond Soc. Fin. Analysts, Securities Assn. Va., Inc., N.Y. Soc. Security Analysts, U. Va. Alumni Assn. (dir., pres. 1979-80, sec. 1978-79), Chi Phi. Republican. Episcopalian. Home: 1633 Cutty Sark Rd Virginia Beach VA 23454 Office: 5 Main Plaza East Norfolk VA 23510

WALL, GLENN RAY, cons. engr.; b. Ludlow, Ky., Jan. 25, 1932; s. Raymond and Bertha Alice (Denham) W.; B.S., Auburn U., 1959; M. Pub. Adminstrn., U. Ala., 1968; M.C.E., U. Tenn., 1969; m. Lloydene Sanderson, Dec. 28, 1957; children—Glenna Rene, Raymond Lloyd, Cindy Rachelle. Engr.-in-tng. So. Ry., 1952-53; civil engr. TVA, Knoxville, 1960-64, asst. to chief local flood relations, 1964-73, staff coordinator local flood relations, 1973-75, supr. flood plain mgmt. services, 1975-79; prin. Flood Loss Reduction Assos., 1979—; chief airfield mgmt. McGhee Tyson, Air NG Base, Knoxville, 1965-75, mobilization asst., dir. engring. Armament Devel. and Test Center, Eglin AFB, Fla.; interagy. loan to Fed. Ins. Adminstrn., HUD, Washington, 1973. Co-chmn. TVA div. United Fund-ARC Appeal, 1966; mem. Tenn. Wing staff CAP, 1975—, N.Ga. Water Resources Adv. Com., 1976-77, N.Ga. Natural Resources and Environ. Quality Com., 1977—. Served to 1st lt. USAF, 1953-57; ETO; col. Res., 1979—. Decorated Air Guard Commendation medal, Air Force Commendation medal; recipient certificate of merit as bd. dirs. TVA Employees Credit Union, 1967; fellow So. Regional Tng. Program in Pub. Adminstrn., 1968; Ky. Col.; registered profl. engr., Tenn.; cert. profl. mgr. Mem ASCE, Nat. Assn. Govt. Engrs. (past v.p.), Knoxville Tech. Soc. (chmn. youth devel. com. 1971-72, pres. 1973), Am. Soc. Pub. Adminstrn. (past pres. E.Tenn. chpt., Meritorious Service award 1973), Nat. Mgmt. Assn. (organizational steering com. 1974, chmn. pub. relations com. 1976), Nat. Soc. Profl. Engrs., Tenn. Soc. Profl. Engrs., Res. Officers Assn. Mem. Ch. of Christ (deacon). Author: Administrative Law and Use of Flood Plains, 1968; Establishing an Engineering Basis for Flood Plain Regulations, 1969; Interdisciplinary Approach to Solving Flood Problems, 1972; Decision-Making Process for Flood Plain Managers, 1973; Two Decades of Flood Plain Management-The TVA Regional Experience, 1974; Interdisciplinary Approach to Improve Public Works Projects, 1974; TVA-Theatre of Innovation, 1975; Interdisciplinary Cooperation Can Work, 1975; How to Develop Flood Plain Lands but Avoid Flood Problems, 1977. Home: 329 Sevenoaks Trail Concord TN 37720 Office: 7481 Weeping Willow Rd Germantown TN 38138

WALL, JERRY EUGENE, mech. engr.; b. Harding, Pa., July 31, 1939; s. John and Kathryn (Nolleran) W.; student U. Md., 1959-60; m. Mildred Weitzel, July 31, 1971; children—Jennifer, Stephanie. With Garwood Industries, Exeter, Pa., 1960-76, chief engr. dump body, trailer and hydraulic hoist products, until 76; chief engr. Old Dominion Mfg. Co., Culpeper, Va., 1980—. Past mem. various civic coms. Moscow Boro, Pa.; mem. Moscow Boro Council, 1972-76. Served with U.S. Army, 1957-60. Republican. Methodist. Club: Lions. Patentee hydraulic valves and systems. Home: Route 3 Box 48 Culpeper VA 22701 Office: Old Dominion Mfg Co PO Box 711 Culpeper VA 22701

WALL, JOHN MCKNIGHT, elec. engr.; b. Charlottesville, Va., Oct. 24, 1945; s. James Graham and Mary Virginia (Leazer) W.; B.Engring., Auburn U., 1968; m. Mary Elizabeth Durham, July 7, 1972; children—John Michael, James Warren. Elec. engr. Fla. Power and Light Co., Naples, 1972—. Served with U.S. Army, 1968-72. Mem. IEEE. Democrat. Baptist. Home: 4465 19th Ave SW Naples FL 33999 Office: PO Box 1187 Naples FL 33939

WALL, NANCY NEAL, med. social worker; b. Cornelia, Ga., Oct. 3, 1949; d. Woodrow Brock and Florine Kansas (Farmer) Neal; B.A., U. Ga., 1971; m. James Barnard Wall, Dec. 19, 1969; 1 dau., Kathryn Neal. Social worker Center Creative Living and Spiritual Growth, Athens, Ga., 1971-73; dir. supportive living program Athens-Clarke County Mental Health Center, 1973-74; social work asso. Lenwood VA Hosp., Augusta, Ga., 1974-75; social worker rheumatology service Med. Coll. Ga., 1974-76; dir. social work service St. Joseph Hosp., Augusta, 1976-79; social worker Univ. Hosp., Augusta, 1979—; bd. dirs Lyndale Pvt. Sch. Mentally Retarded, Lyndale Pvt. Sch. Mentally Retarded Group Home. Mem. Ga. Soc. Hosp. Social Workers (pres. elect 1979-80), Ga. E. Central Dist. Soc. Hosp. Social Workers, Augusta Jr. League. Methodist. Home: 628 Carlton Dr Augusta GA 30909 Office: Univ Hosp Walton Way Augusta GA 30901

WALL, OSCAR EDWARD, JR., chem. co. exec.; b. Newton, Miss., Dec. 4, 1934; s. Oscar Edward and Mildred Buena Vista (O'Donnell) W.; B.S. cum laude in Chem. Engring., U. Miss., 1957; m. Nellie Opal Burns, June 3, 1956; children—Summer Kathleen, Melanie Lynn, Robert Edward. Production dept. head Union Carbide Corp., Charleston, W.Va., 1957-65, market mgr., N.Y.C., 1965-72; v.p. First Chem. Corp., Jackson, Miss., 1972—. Exec. com. PTA, Stamford, Conn., 1962; health com. Miss. Econ. Council, 1975; bd. dirs. St. Albans (W.Va.) Library, Goodwill Industries Miss., 1978-79; dir. Miss. Opera Assn., 1977, pres., 1979; precinct leader Republican Party, Jackson 1975; deacon Northminster Baptist Ch., Jackson, 1975-77, chmn. bd. deacons, 1979-80. Mem. Mfg. Chemists Assn., Synthetic Organic Chems. Mfrs. Assn., Miss. Internat. Trade Club (pres. 1978), Drug, Chems. and Allied Trades Assn. Club: Country of Jackson. Home: 1739 Saint Ann St Jackson MS 39202 Office: 700 North St PO Box 1249 Jackson MS 39205

WALL, RALPH ALAN, artist; b. Hobart, Ind., Aug. 1, 1932; s. Ralph Albert and Helen Alwilda (Ferren) W.; B.S., Oklahoma City U., 1957; m. Marcia Ann McKinney, Aug. 30, 1957; children—Frank, Stefanie, Eric. Partner, Wall & Herndon, art and design studio, Houston, 1960-69; exhibited in one-man shows: Okla. Mus. Art, Oklahoma City, 1973, Lodge on Desert, Tucson, 1971, Goddard Center Performing and Visual Arts, Ardmore, Okla., 1972, Ponca City (Okla.) Art Center, 1972, Andersons Gallery, Oklahoma City, 1974-75, Glasser's Gallery, San Antonio, 1980; group shows: Glasser's Gallery, 1978-79, Western Heritage Sale, Houston, 1979, Stamford (Tex.) Art Found., 1979, Mountain Oyster Club, Tucson, 1972-79; represented in permanent collections; v.p. football history yearbook SW Conf. Football, 1968-70. Served with USNR, 1953-55. Recipient Gold Medal, Franklin Mint Portfolio Am. Art, 1974; Am. Inst. Graphic Art award, 1967; Gold award Tex. Ranger Hall of Fame, 1979. Clubs: Mountain Oyster, Tucson (hon. life artist), Art Dirs. Houston (pres. 1966-67). Home: Rt 1 Box 63-H New Braunfels TX 78130

WALL, VINSON, state legislator Ga.; b. Athens, Ga., Oct. 17, 1947; s. Clarence Jacob and Fannie Lucile W.; student pub. schs., Ga.; m. Linda Gail Mason, Dec. 6, 1969; 1 son, Jeffrey Vinson. Mem. Ga. Ho. of Reps., 1973—. Democrat. Baptist. Address: 1694 Little Fawn Dr Lawrenceville GA 30245

WALLACE, BEATRICE GAY, ednl. adminstr.; b. Farmville, Va., June 19, 1939; d. Phillip Franklin and Lucy Jane (Barr) Gay; B.S., Longwood Coll., 1961, M.S., 1969, postgrad., summers 1974-76; postgrad. U. Va., 1969-70, Layne's Bus. Sch., summer 1961; m. Richard Floyd Wallace, June 25, 1961; children—Denise Anjanette, Michele Evon. Sec. Prince Edward Sch. Found., Farmville, Va., 1961-63; tchr. Randolph Henry High Sch., Charlotte Court House, Va., 1963-64, Prince Edward Acad. Upper Sch., Farmville, 1965-68, Crewe (Va.) High Sch., 1969-70, Nottoway Sr. High Sch., Nottoway Court House, Va., 1970-71; learning lab. dir., instr. devel. studies John H. Daniel Campus, Southside Va. Community Coll., Keysville, 1971-74, coll. coordinator learning labs., asst. prof. edn. and health Christanna Campus and John H. Daniel Campus, Alberta, Va. and Keysville, 1974-79, speakers bur., 1972-75; cons., resource person individualized and mediated instrn. ten counties, 1971-79. coordinator lay instr. insts. for emergency med. technicians Southside Va., 1975, 76, 77; cert. instr. CPR, first aid and emergency care ARC; active Ladies Aux. to Farmville Vol. Fire Dept., 1961—, pres., 1978; Sunday Sch. tchr. Farmville Baptist Ch., 1961-63, 74-76, Heritage Bapt. Ch., Farmville, 1976—, dir. jr. dept., 1977—; first aid asst./instr. camping trips Girl Scouts U.S.A. Mem. Va. TV Reps. in Higher Edn., Community Coll. Assn. for Instructional Tech., Assn. Ednl. Communications Tech., Va. Ednl. Media Assn., Internat. Soc. for Semantics, Longwood Coll. Alumnae Assn., Phi Delta Kappa. Democrat. Club: Modern Woodmen Am. (adv. Tenn Club, 1976-79, merit awards, 1977, 78). Home: Route 2 Box 126 Farmville VA 23901 Office: Southside Virginia Community Coll John H Daniel Campus State Route 40 Keysville VA 23947

WALLACE, BETTYE M., educator; b. Malvern, Ark., Oct. 22, 1929; d. David E. and Jannie E. (Greer) W.; B.S.E., Henderson State U., 1950; M.A., U. No. Colo., 1953; postgrad. U. Ark., 1964, 67, 70, 75, 78. Tchr., coach Murfreesboro (Ark.) High Sch., 1950-51, Rison (Ark.) High Sch., 1951-54, Malvern (Ark.) High Sch., 1954-63; instr. Henderson State U., Arkadelphia, Ark., 1963-66, asst. prof., coach, 1966-78, athletic dir. for women, 1978—. Mem. Ark. Assn. Health, Phys. Edn. and Recreation, Ark. Women's Intercollegiate Sports Assn. (chairperson), AAHPER, Ark. High Sch. Coaches Assn., Ark. Bd. Women Ofcls., Lambda Sigma Tau. Methodist. Home: 1447 Welch St Arkadelphia AR 71923 Office: Box H 1060 Henderson State Univ Arkadelphia AR 71923

WALLACE, GLADYS BALDWIN, librarian; b. Macon, Ga., June 5, 1923; d. Carter Shepherd and Dorothy (Richard) Baldwin; B.S. in Edn., Oglethorpe U., 1961; M.Librarianship, Emory U., 1966; postgrad. U. Ga., 1970-71, Ga. State U., 1979, 80; m. Hugh Loring Wallace, Jr., Oct. 14, 1941; (div. Sept. 1968); children—Dorothy, Hugh Loring III. Librarian pub. elementary schs., Atlanta, 1956-66; head librarian Northside High Sch., Atlanta, 1966—. Ga. Dept. Edn. grantee, 1950; NDEA grantee, 1963, 65. Mem. ALA, NEA, Ga., Atlanta assns. educators, Atlanta Symphony Orch. League (individual gifts campaign com.), Emory U. Alumni Assn., Madison-Morgan Cultural Center, Ga. (intellectual freedom com. 1976-80), Southeastern library assns., Oglethorpe U. Nat. Alumni Assn. Home: 136 Peachtree Memorial Dr NW North Carolina 6 Atlanta GA 30309 Office: 2875 Northside Dr NW Atlanta GA 30305

WALLACE, JACK CARPENTER, farmer; b. Starksville, Miss., Feb. 3, 1925; s. Jamew Wade and Martha Virginia (Carpenter) W.; E.E., U. Tex., Austin, 1947; m. Martha L. Rene Soens, Aug. 22, 1952; children—Martha Lorene, Margaret Ann, Cynthia Jane, Jack Carpenter, Susan Lee. Farmer, Edinburg, Tex., 1947—; mem. Hidalgo County Agrl. Stabilization Conservation Com. Former mem. Edinburg Consol. Sch. Dist. Bd. Edn. Served to lt. (j.g.), USNR, 1943-46. Home and Office: 328 Enfield Rd Edinburg TX 78539

WALLACE, JACK EUGENE, pharmacologist; b. Harrisburg, Ill., Jan. 5, 1934; s. Harry H. and Ruby V. (Burroughs) W.; B.S., So. Ill. U., 1955, M.A., 1957; Ph.D., Purdue U., 1961; m. Verla Ann Standerfer, Aug. 14, 1955; children—Michael Eugene, Kimberly Ann. Supervisory pharmacologist USAF, chief forensic toxicology USAF Sch. Aerospace Medicine, Brooks AFB, Tex., 1962-72; pharmacologist, clin. chemist Bexar County Hosp. Dist. and dept. pathology U. Tex. Med. Sch., San Antonio, 1972-77, dir. biochem. pathology; dir. research and devel. S.W. Bio-clin. Labs., San Antonio, 1969-72; clin. asso. prof. U. Tex. Med. Sch., San Antonio, 1967-72; asst. prof. dept. pathology U. Tex. Health Sci. Center, San Antonio, 1972-74, asso. prof., 1974-79, prof., 1979—; asso. prof. Inst. Clin. Toxicology, Houston, 1973—; cons. in clin. chemistry Santa Rosa Med. Center, San Antonio, 1968—, Audie Murphy VA Hosp., San Antonio, 1973—, U.S. Army Med. Lab., Ft. Sam Houston, Tex., 1973—; cons. in toxicology Pathology Assos. of Tex., Ft. Worth, 1976-78; cons. Epilepsy Found. Am., 1976—, Ft. Worth Lab., 1978—. Served with USAF, 1962-64; lt. col. Res. Recipient Sci. Achievement award USAF, 1966. Diplomate Am. Bd. Forensic Toxicology (dir. 1975-80, chmn. examinations com. 1975—), Am. Acad. Forensic Scis., Forensic Scis. Found. Fellow Am. Inst. Chemists, Nat. Acad. Clin. Biochemistry; mem. Internat. Assn. Forensic Toxicologists, Am. Chem. Soc., Am. Assn. Clin. Chemists, Sigma Xi, Phi Lambda Upsilon. Contbr. numerous articles to profl. jours. Home: 9215 George Kyle Dr San Antonio TX 78240 Office: Dept Pathology U Texas Health Sci Center San Antonio TX 78284

WALLACE, JOAN EDAIRE SCOTT, social scientist; b. Chgo., Nov. 8, 1930; d. William Edouard and Esther (Fulks) Scott; A.B. with honors, Bradley U., 1952; M.S.W., Columbia, 1954; postgrad. U. Chgo. Sch. Social Service Adminstrn., 1963-64; Ph.D. in Psychology, Northwestern U., 1973; H.H.D., U. Md., 1979; m. John H. Wallace, June 12, 1954 (div. 1977); children—Mark Scott, Eric Matthew, Victor Paul; m. 2d, Maurice Dawkins, Oct. 1979. Social worker St. Mary's Home for Children, 1954-58, casework dir., 1965-67, also field instr.; social worker United Charities Family Service Bur., 1959-61; social work analyst Midway research project U. Chgo. Sch. Social Service Adminstrn., 1962-65; asso. prof. social work Jane Addams Grad. Sch. Social Work U. Ill., Chgo. Circle campus, 1967-73; lectr. psychology Barat Coll., U. Ill.; asso. dean, prof. Howard U. Sch. Social Work, Washington, 1973-75; dep. exec. dir. Nat. Urban League, 1975-76; v.p. adminstrn. Morgan State U., 1976-77; currently asst. sec. adminstrn. U.S. Dept. Agr. Bd. dirs. Child Care Assn. Ill., 1968-69, chmn. adoption sect., 1967-69, chmn. adoption workshop, 1968-69; chmn. planning com. Inst. Child Care Workers, 1968; bd. execs. Wilmette (Ill.) Human Relations Com., 1968-69; mem. advisory com. Fish (vols. in social service), 1969; mem. advisory com. Project for Emergency Care of Children, 1968-69; mem. Ill. Welfare Assn., 1967-69; mem. Council on Social Work Edn., 1968—; mem. psychologists for Social Action, 1969-73; mem. Pres.'s Com. on Handicapped, N.Y.C. Mayor's Com. on Aging. Chmn. sect. Child Welfare League Conf., 1968; coordinator Inst. Child Care Workers, 1968. Vol. Wilmette Urban Gateways. Trustee St. Mary's Services for Children. Recipient Robert S. Abbott award, 1948; Episcopal Service for Youth fellowship in social work, 1952-54; Northwestern U. fellowship for grad. study, 1969-70; Outstanding Educators award, 1971; Distinguished Alumni award Bradley U., 1978. Mem. Pi Gamma Mu. Office: USDA Independence & 14th Streets Washington DC 20050

WALLACE, JOHN RAY, ins. agy. exec.; b. Cameron, Tex., Apr. 10, 1927; s. Leslie Ray and Hattie Gertrude (Sparks) W.; B.B.A., U. Tex., Austin, 1949; m. Sallie Daniel, Aug. 18, 1946; children—Nancy Eileen, John Ray, Leslie Howard, David Alan. Salesman, Brydson Lumber Co., Austin, 1948-49, Wm. Cameron Co., San Antonio, 1950, Certain-Teed Products, San Antonio, 1951-52, Dallas, 1954-55, New Process Steel Co., Dallas, 1955, Riverwood Lumber Co., Dallas, 1955; pres., gen. mgr. Imperial Supply Co., Dallas, 1955-69; exec. sales dir. Tex. Am. Life Ins. Co., Amarillo, 1969-74; agt. Bankers Life Ins. Co., Dallas, 1969-74; owner John Wallace Agy., Dallas, 1974—; tchr. profl. courses. Troop chmn. Boy Scouts Am., 1955-65; precinct chmn. Republican Party, 1965; election judge, 1964. Served with USN, 1944-45, 52-54. Mem. Nat., Tex., Dallas assns. life underwriters, Dallas Estate Council. Baptist. Clubs: East Dallas Lions, South Park YMCA, Masons, Order DeMolay. Bd. govs. Shrine Burns Hosp. Home: 6232 Hollis St Dallas TX 75227 Office: 3330 Hwy 80 Mesquite TX 75150

WALLACE, MINOR GORDON, JR., architect, landscape architect; b. Texarkana, Tex., Oct. 30, 1936; s. Minor Gordon and Dessie (Bledsoe) W.; B.A., U. Ark., 1961, B. Arch., 1961; m. Judy Marie Mullen, Jan. 25, 1975; children—Rayma, Minor Gordon III. Project architect Bruce R. Anderson, Architect, Little Rock, 1964-67; univ. architect U. Ark., Fayetteville, 1968—; prin. Wallace & Estes, Architects, Fayetteville, 1978-80; dir. facilities planning and constrn. U. Ark. System, Fayetteville, 1968—; cons. ednl. planning, architecture. Chmn. bd. dirs. NW Ark. Arts and Crafts Guild, 1977-79; bd. dirs. NW Ark. Cultural Center, 1978—. Mem. AIA, Am. Soc. Landscape Architects, Council Ednl. Planners, Soc. for Coll. and Univ. Planning, Nat. Trust for Historic Preservation, Assn. Univ. Architects. Democrat. Unitarian. Campus landscaping Pine Bluff and Fayetteville campuses U. Ark., 1977-78, indoor tennis center, Fayetteville campus, 1979-80. Home: PO Box 423 Fayetteville AR 72701 Office: PO Box 1384 Fayetteville AR 72701

WALLACE, RAYMOND HOWARD, JR., geologist, hydrologist; b. Columbus, Ga., July 29, 1936; s. Raymond Howard and Fannie Serelle (Rutland) W.; student Asbury Coll., Wilmore, Ky., 1954-56; B.S. in Geology, Fla. State U., 1960; M.S. in Geology, La. State U., Baton Rouge, 1966; m. Katharine Frances Ritter, Apr. 4, 1958; children—Raymond Howard III, Haviland. Geologist-trainee Gulf Oil Corp., New Orleans, 1964; grad. teaching asst. geology La. State U., 1964-65, research asst. La. Water Resources Research Inst., 1965-66; geologist water resources div. U.S. Geol. Survey, Baton Rouge, 1966-69, hydrologist, St. Louis, 1969-71, Bay St. Louis, Miss., 1971—, chief Gulf Coast hydrogeology projects, 1975—. Mem. tech. adv. task force on non conv. sources of natural gas FPC, also sub-task force on gas dissolved in water. Served to capt. USMCR, 1960-63. Mem. Am. Assn. Petroleum Geologists, Soc. Econ. Paleontologists, Mineralogists, Sigma Xi. Author various sci. publs. Home: 506 N Beach Blvd Bay St Louis MS 39520 Office: US Geol Survey Water Resources Div NASA/NSTL Bay St Louis MS 39529

WALLACE, RONALD LESTER, mgmt. cons.; b. Cleburne, Tex., Dec. 22, 1942; s. Ruel Lester and Minnie Lucille Walker W.; B.S. in Indsl. Engring., Gen. Motors Inst., 1967; M.B.A., U. Tex., Arlington, 1975; m. Carol Ann Glenn, Aug. 8, 1964; children—Gregory Todd, Chandra LeAnn. With Gen. Motors Assembly div. Gen. Motors Corp., Arlington, Tex., 1962-77, labor relations rep., 1968-71, gen. supr. plant engring. and maintenance, 1971-72, dir. orgn. devel., 1972-77; dir. orgn. devel. Western Co. N. Am., Ft. Worth, 1977-78; pres. Ronald L. Wallace & Assos., Arlington, 1978—, Planning Inst., Inc., Arlington, Tex., 1979—; adj. prof. Grad. Sch. Mgmt., U. Dallas, 1976-79, M.J. Neeley Sch. Bus., Tex. Christian U., 1979—. Coach various youth sports programs. Mem. Am. Soc. Tng. and Devel., Am. Soc. Personnel Adminstrn., Assn. M.B.A. Execs., Nat. Orgn. Devel. Network. Republican. Methodist. Club: Optimist. Home: 1606 Forest Glen Ct Arlington TX 76013 Office: PO Box 13585 Arlington TX 76013

WALLACE, WESLEY HERNDON, broadcaster, educator; b. Denver, Apr. 18, 1912; s. William Harvey and Lillian Frances (Parker) W.; B.S., N.C. State U., 1932; M.A., U. N.C., Chapel Hill, 1954; Ph.D., Duke U., 1962; m. Mary Carolyn Andrews, Feb. 23, 1956; 1 dau., Sue Daniels. Broadcaster, writer, producer, announcer Sta. WPTF, Raleigh, N.C., 1934-42; gen. mgr. Manila Broadcasting Co., Philippines, 1948-50; lectr. in radio and TV, U. N.C., Chapel Hill, 1952-54, asst. prof., 1954-57, asso. prof., 1957-66, prof., 1966—, chmn. dept. radio, TV, motion pictures, 1962-74, acting chmn., 1976-77; cons. So. Regional Edn. Bd., 1964-67; mem. Gov.'s Ednl. TV Commn., 1962-64, also mem. central steering com. of commn.; cons. U.S. GAO, 1977-78; spl. cons. N.C. Task Force Public Telecommunications, 1978-79; adminstrv. bd. Sta. WUNC-FM, also adv. council sta.; v.p. Triangle Advt. Fedn., 1977-78. Bd. dirs. Orange County chpt. N.C. Symphony Soc. Served with U.S. Army, 1942-47. Decorated Bronze Star; recipient Silver Medal award Triangle Advt. Fedn., 1978. Mem. N.C. Assn. Broadcasters (Earle Gluck Disting. Service award 1975, Broadcasting Hall of Fame 1976), Broadcasting Edn. Assn., Nat. Assn. Ednl. Broadcasters, Radio-TV News Dirs. Assn., Radio-TV News Dirs. of Carolinas (hon. life), Nat. Assn. TV Program Execs., Internat. Radio and TV Soc., N.C. Hist. Soc., So. Hist. Assn., Kappa Phi Kappa, Phi Kappa Phi. Democrat. Baptist. Writer, producer, dir. program Compact Day, 1953; contbr. articles to profl. and hist. publs. Home: 102 Carol Woods Chapel Hill NC 27514 Office: 209A Swain Hall 044A Univ North Carolina Chapel Hill NC 27514

WALLACH, NEAL LLOYD, retail exec.; b. Bronx, N.Y., Nov. 1, 1947; s. Lawrence and Lena W.; student Harvard U., summers 1965-68; B.A. cum laude, Boston U., 1969; M.B.A. in Fin. and Acctg., U. Houston, 1977; 1 dau. by previous marriage, Jacqueline Beth. With Foley's div. Federated Dept. Stores, Houston, 1970—, corp. expense cons., 1974, selling supt. Downtown Store, 1975, dir. corp. compensation, 1975-76, mgr. human resources info., 1976-78, mgr. internal audit, 1979—; acctg. instr. Houston Community Coll.; chmn. bd. Foley's Asso. Credit Union. Mem. budget allocation com. United Way, employee chmn. Foley's, 1976-78. Served with USAR, 1969-75. Mem. Nat. Assn. Accts., Inst. Internal Auditors, Data Processing Mgmt. Assn., EDP Auditors Assn., Am. Compensation Assn. (cert. compensation profl.), Am. Soc. Personnel Adminstrn., Houston C. of C. Home: 12800 Briar Forest Dr No 156 Houston TX 77077 Office: 1110 Main St Houston TX 77002

WALLECK, SYLVESTER BERNARD, ednl. adminstr.; b. Vanderbilt, Tex., Feb. 21, 1943; s. Carl R. and Alma (Scheel) W.; A.A. in Math., Wharton (Tex.) County Jr. Coll., 1963; B.Ed. in Math., SW Tex. State Coll., San Marcos, 1965; M. Ed. in Math., Southeastern State Coll., Durant, Okla., 1971; m. Diann R. Thompson; 1 dau., Heather Rae. Tchr. math. Calhoun County Ind. Sch. Dist., Port Lavaca, Tex., 1965-74, secondary coordinator, 1974-79; prin. Jefferson Elementary Sch., Port Lavaca, Tex., 1979—. Dir. on alumni council SW Tex. State U., 1969—, pres. alumni, 1978-79; pres. Calhoun County United Way, 1978-79, Calhoun Tchrs. Fed. Credit Union, 1979—, South Tex. Sq. and Round Dance Assn., 1978-79. Certified tchr., supr.; profl. adminstr. cert. NSF grantee. Named An Outstanding Young Man of Am., U.S. Jaycees, 1979. Home: 728 Brookhollow Dr Port Lavaca TX 77979 Office: Box 406 Port Lavaca TX 77979

WALLENBORN, PETER AMBROSE, JR., otolaryngologist; b. Salisbury, N.C., Nov. 25, 1920; s. Peter A. and Elizabeth (Keeling) W.; student U. N.C., 1938-41; M.D., U. Va., 1944; postgrad. Tulane U., 1948; m. Dolly Virginia Franklin, Mar. 2, 1946; children—Elizabeth Wallenborn Green, Dolly Ann, Peter Ambrose, David L., Ellen M., Robert C. Intern, U. Va. Hosp., 1944-46; resident New Orleans EENT Hosp., 1948-50; practice medicine, specializing in otolaryngology, Roanoke, Va., 1950-65, Roanoke E.N.T. Clinic, 1965—; clin. prof. otolaryngology U. Va., Roanoke, 1974-77. Vestryman, St. John's Episcopal Ch., 1966. Served with M.C., U.S. Army, 1946-48. Diplomate Am. Bd. Otolaryngology. Recipient Key Man award State of Va. Jr. C. of C., 1953. Mem. Med. Soc. Va., Roanoke Acad. Medicine (pres. 1968), S.W. Va. Med. Soc., AMA, Am. Laryngol., Rhinol. and Otol. Soc., Va. Soc. Ophthalmology and Otolaryngology (pres. 1967). Contbr. articles in field to med. jours. Home: 3596 Peakwood Dr SW Roanoke VA 24014 Office: 201 McClanahan St SW Roanoke VA 24014 and PO Box 8306 Roanoke VA 24014

WALLER, CHARLES PAYTON, oil and gas exploration co. exec.; b. Dallas, Mar. 5, 1939; s. Lorenzo Payton and Pearl Cleo W.; B.S., N. Tex. State U., 1970, postgrad. in clin. psychology, 1971-72; m. Linda Kay Scott, Nov. 22, 1968; children—Michael Payton, Kristin Elizabeth. Cost acctg. specialist Fleming & Sons, Dallas, 1962-66; exec. asst. to pres. Fabricators, Dallas, 1964-68; mgmt. cons. FMB Assos., Dallas, 1972; cons. mgmt., Arlington, Tex., 1972-76; corp. tng. dir. Atlantic Pacific Marine Corp., Houston, 1977—; cons to industry on mfg. systems, human resource devel. Recipient Spoke award Nat. Jr. C. of C., 1961. Mem. Internat. Assn. Drilling Contractors, Am. Soc. Tng. and Devel., Am. Soc. Personnel Adminstrn., Young Republicans. Baptist. Subject of industry mag. interviews; participant in design of maintenance tech. courses for drilling industry at U. Tex.; established 1st skills tng. center in drilling industry. Home: 1003 Apache Falls Dr Katy TX 77450 Office: 2425 Fountainview Suite 300 Houston TX 77057

WALLER, HARRY EDWARD, telecommunications engr.; b. Verona, Ky., May 26, 1922; s. Charles Marvin and Mary (Alexander) W.; B.S. in Elec. Engring., U. Ky., 1949; m. Bernice Mae Connely, Aug. 21, 1948; children—Shellye Waller White, Connie Waller Allen. Installer Gen. Telephone Co. Ky., Lexington, 1949-50; field engr. REA, Washington, 1953-56; pres. Bruce Telephone Co. (Miss.), 1956—. Served with Signal Corps, U.S. Army, World War II. Mem. U.S. Ind. Telephone Assn., Nat. Soc. Cable TV Engrs., Ind. Telephone Pioneer Am. (nat. pres. 1978-79), Nat. Cable TV Assn., Ala.-Miss. Telephone Assn., Miss. Econs. Council, C. of C. (past pres.). Baptist. Club: Lions (past pres.). Home and Office: PO Box 489 Bruce MS 38915

WALLER, JIM DALE, mktg. exec.; b. Denton, Tex., May 26, 1940; s. James Lauelle and Allie Blankenship W.; B.B.A., Baylor U., 1962; m. Carron V. Sanderson, June 3, 1960; 1 dau., Luanna Dale. Dept. mgr. J. C. Penney Co., Waco, Tex., 1960-62; territory mgr. Lever Bros., Waco, Tex., 1963-64, account exec., Dallas, 1964-65, field coordinator, Charlotte, N.C., 1965-66, sales mgr., Atlanta, 1966-67; southeastern sales mgr. Vulcan Industries, Birmingham, Ala., 1967-68; v.p. mktg. Collins & Aikman Hosiery div., Clinton, S.C., 1968—. Dr. W. P. Ball scholastic scholar Baylor U., 1958-62. Mem. Am. Marketing Assn., C. of C. (dir.). Republican. Baptist. Office: Box 525 Clinton SC 29325

WALLER, LOUIS CLINTON, physician; b. Candler, N.C., Aug. 16, 1918; s. Eugene Clinton and Anna Louise (Anderson) W.; student So. Missionary Coll., Collegedale, Tenn., 1936-39; M.D., Loma Linda (Cal.) U., 1943; m. Minnie Sue Bruce, Aug. 7, 1941; children—John, Robert, Adele (Mrs. Daryll Ward), Karen (Mrs. Richard Henderson), Benton, Celia, Michael. Intern Nashville Gen. Hosp., 1943-44; practice medicine specializing in family practice, Asheville, N.C., 1946—; mem. staffs St. Joseph's Hosp., Meml. Mission Hosp., chief dept. family practice, 1958-59, 62-63, 66-67, 70-71, vice-chief dept. medicine, 1960 (all Asheville). Med. dir. Pisgah Sanitarium, Candler, N.C., 1946-57; v.p. MPA Corp., Asheville, 1968—. Bd. dirs. Buncombe County (N.C.) Human Relations, 1969-70, So. Missionary Coll. Com. of 100, 1965—; trustee So. Missionary Coll. Served to capt., M.C., 1944-46; ETO, PTO. Diplomate Am. Bd. Family Practice. Fellow Am. Acad. Family Practice; mem. Buncombe County, N.C., So., Am. med. assns., Asheville C. of C. (dir. 1968-70), West Asheville Bus. Assn. (chmn. com. urban renewal 1968-69). Seventh Day Adventist (elder). Inventor in field. Home: Box 369 Route 4 Candler NC 28715 Office: 1425 Patton Ave Asheville NC 28806

WALLER, SAMUEL CARPENTER, lawyer; b. Augusta, Ga., May 3, 1918; s. Harcourt E. and Josephine (Carpenter) W.; A.B., Princeton, 1940; LL.B., Harvard, 1948; m. Anna Bacon Maxwell, Apr. 18, 1952; children—Anna M., Laura G., Amelia C. Admitted to Ga. bar, 1947, since practiced in Augusta; mem. firm Cumming, Nixon & Eve, 1948-51; partner firm Nixon, Yow, Waller & Capers, and predecessor firm, 1951—; city atty. City of Augusta, 1964-69; dir. Ga. R.R. Bank & Trust Co.; mem. Nat. Conf. Commrs. Uniform State Laws, 1965-72, Ga. Criminal Justice Council, 1975-79. Pres., Augusta Library, 1956-58; mem. Augusta Coll. Found., 1963—, chmn., 1979—; pres. Augusta Symphony League, 1974-75; mem. Augusta City Council, 1950-56; mem. Richmond County (Ga.) Democratic Exec. Com., 1962-76, chmn., 1962-66. Served to capt. AUS, 1941-45, now maj. Res. Decorated Bronze Star medal. Mem. State Bar Ga. (bd. govs. 1967-77, exec. com. 1975), Am., Augusta (pres. 1971-72) bar assns., Harvard Law Sch. Assn. Ga. (pres. 1960-61). Episcopalian (sr. warden; registrar Diocese of Ga.). Kiwanian (pres. Augusta 1976-77). Clubs: Augusta Country, Pinnacle. Home: 600 Gary St Augusta GA 30904 Office: Ga R R Bank Bldg Augusta GA 30902

WALLEY, WILLIAM CARL, physician; b. Guntersville, Ala., Feb. 7, 1939; s. Billy Carl and Ora Frances (Williams) W.; B.S. in Chem. Engring., Auburn U., 1962; M.D., U. Ala., 1969; m. Jane Elizabeth Copeland, Sept. 11, 1960; children—Marc Ashley, Elizabeth Dawn, Anthony Dee, Patton Shawn. Compounding engr. Goodyear Tire & Rubber Co., Gadsden, Ala., 1962-63; project chem. engr. Internat. Pulp & Paper Co., Georgetown, S.C., 1963-65; intern Mobile (Ala.) Gen. Hosp., 1969-70; occupational physician Tenn. Eastman Co., Kingsport, Tenn., 1973-75; asso. prof. East Tenn. State U., Kingsport, 1975-77; practice medicine specializing in occupational, indsl. and emergency medicine Kingsport, Tenn., 1978—; mem. staff Holston Valley Community Hosp., Indian Path Hosp., Kingsport; also aviation med. examiner. Bd. dirs. Sullivan County chpt. Am. Cancer Soc., 1972-73, Kingsport Speech and Hearing Center, 1977-79. Served with AUS, 1970-73. Diplomate Am. Bd. Family Practice. Fellow Am. Acad. Family Practice; mem. So. Med. Assn., Am. Acad. Family Practice, Am. Acad. Occupational Medicine, Am. Occupational Med. Assn., Sullivan Johnson County Med. Soc., Tenn. Med. Soc., Aerospace Med. Assn. Republican. Baptist. Home: Rt 6 Box 172 Kingsport TN 37660 Office: PO Box 908 Kingsport TN 37662

WALLING, ALBERT CLINTON, II, clergyman; b. Ft. Lauderdale, Fla., Sept. 24, 1925; s. Jacob Biffie and Nora Maurine (Stone) W.; B.A., Trinity U., 1948; M.Div., Episcopal Div. Sch., 1953; postgrad. Harvard, 1961-63, So. Meth. U., 1972, Vanderbilt U., 1975; D.Min., U. of South, Sewanee, Tenn., 1977; m. Carroll Langlois Wicher, Dec. 26, 1964; children—Maurine Carroll, Elizabeth Hancock. Ordained priest Episcopal Ch., 1954; vicar All Saints Ch., Pleasanton, Tex., 1953-54; asst. rector St. Davids Ch., Austin, Tex., 1954-60; vicar Holy Family Ch., prin. St. Saviours Sch., McKinney, Tex., 1960-61; vicar St. Nicholas Ch., Ft. Worth, 1961-64; asso. rector St. Johns Ch., Ft. Worth, 1964-66; rector Ch. of Good Shepherd, Terrell, Tex., 1966-71, Ch. of Ascension, Dallas, 1971-74; asso. rector St. Mark Ch., Houston, 1974-77; rector St. Alban's Ch., Houston, 1977—. Mem. ecumenical relations com. Diocese of Dallas, 1969-73; Episcopal chaplain Terrell State Hosp., 1966-71. Marker chmn. Dallas County Hist. Survey Com., 1971-73; pres. Austin Ministerial Alliance, 1957-58, Mental Health Assn. Austin-Travis County, 1958-59, Greater Ft. Worth Gen. Ministers Assn., 1963; bd. dirs. Austin Pre-Sch. Hearing Center, 1957-58; mem. Tex. Hist. Found., 1968—; trustee U. of South, 1971-74; mem. council on aging City of West University Place (Tex.), 1976, vice chmn., 1977; founder, pres. emeritus trustee San Jacinto Descendants; diocesan trustee Grace Hall, U. Tex., Austin, 1958-60, Clergy House, Episcopal Diocese Dallas, 1971-74; adv. bd. Aging Programs of Houston Met. Ministries, 1977—; bd. overseers Houston Met. Ministries, 1976—; chmn. Community Standards Coalition of Houston, 1976—; mem. Christians and Jews Concerned for Israel Com. of Houston, 1977—. Hon. Ky. Col. (life). Mem. Greater Houston Clergy Assn. (1st v.p. 1975, pres. 1976-78), Sons Republic Tex. (past historian gen., chaplain Dallas chpt., dist. rep. 1971-73), Nat. Trust Historic Preservation, Tex. State Geneal. Soc. (state chaplain 1976-77, 1st v.p. 1977—, contbr. to Stirpes), Jamestowne Soc. (life), Huguenot Soc. Founders of Manakin, Va. (pres. Tex. br. 1975-77, Tex. chaplain 1972-74), Ch. Hist. Soc., Nat. Soc. Ams. of Royal Descent (life). Democrat. Club: Harvard (Houston). Contbr. to Internat. Clan Chisholm Soc. Jour., Inverness, Scotland, Citizens of the Republic of Texas, 1977. Home: 1115 Beaver Bend Rd Houston TX 77088 Office: 420 Woodard St Houston TX 77009

WALLING, BERT HEYWARD, JR., physician; b. Union, S.C., July 28, 1921; s. Bert Heyward and Sarah Ethel (Weber) W.; B.S., Coll. of Charleston, 1943; M.D., S.C. Med. Coll., 1945; m. Florence Audrey Hill, Jan. 1, 1945 (dec. 1961); children—Bert Heyward III, Randolph Richard; m. 2d, Sarah Ellen Jones, Nov. 28, 1963. Intern, Columbia (S.C.) Hosp., 1945-46; resident obstetrics and gynecology Columbia Hosp., 1948-50, Charlotte (N.C.) Meml. Hosp., 1950-51; pvt. practice ltd. to obstetrics and gynecology, Walla Walla, Wash., 1951-52, Johnson City, Tenn., 1952, Kingsville (Tex.) Clinic, 1952—; staff Kleberg County Hosp., Kingsville; courtesy staff Meml. Hosp., Corpus Christi, Tex., Brooks County Hosp., Falfurrias, Tex. Served to lt. (j.g.) M.C., USNR, 1946-48. Diplomate Am. Bd. Obstetrics and Gynecology. Fellow Am. Coll. Obstetrics and Gynecology; mem. AMA, So., Tex. med. assns., Tex. Assn. Obstetrics and Gynecology, Internat. Fertility Assn., Am. Fertility Soc., Nat. Rifle Assn., Phi Rho Sigma. Episcopalian. Mason. Home: 528 E Shelton Ave Kingsville TX 78363 Office: 227 W Kleberg Ave Kingsville TX 78363

WALLIS, THOMAS LEE, educator; b. Baldwyn, Miss., Feb. 7, 1942; s. William I. and Mary Irene (Snell) W.; A.S., Northeast Miss. Jr. Coll., 1963; B.A., William Carey Coll., 1965; M.Ed., U. Miss., 1978. Elem. tchr., Ga. and Miss., 1965-75; adult edn. tchr. NE Miss. Jr. Coll., Booneville, 1975-77; dir. adult edn. Northeast Miss. Jr. Coll., 1977—. Mem. Miss. Assn. Educators, Miss. Assn. Pub. Continuing and Adult Edn., Nat. Assn. Pub. Continuing and Adult Edn. So. Baptist. Home: Route 1 Box 151 Baldwyn MS 38824 Office: Box 1591 NE Miss Jr Coll Booneville MS 38829

WALLS, CARL EDWARD, JR., communications co. ofcl.; b. Magnolia, Ark., Sept. 9, 1948; s. Carl E. and Melba Rene (Garrard) W.; student San Antonio Coll., 1966-68; m. Doris Duhart, Aug. 1, 1970; children—Carl Edward, Forrest Allen. With Sears Roebuck & Co., San Antonio, 1967—, div. mgr., 1969-73, area sales mgr., 1973-78; service cons. Southwestern Bell, 1978-79, account exec., 1979—. Mem. citizens advisory com. Tex. Senate, 1975—; commr. Alamo Area council Boy Scouts Am., 1970-79, Capitol Area council, 1980—, nat. jamboree staff, 1973, 77, 81. Recipient Patriotic Service award U.S. Treasury Dept., 1975, 76; Scouters Key and Commrs. award also Dist. Merit award, 1978, Boy Scouts Am. Mem. Scouting Collectors Assn. (pres. S. Central region 1979-80). Baptist. Home: 11712 D-K Ranch Rd Austin TX 78759 Office: 712 E Huntland Austin TX 78752

WALLS, JOSEPH KYLE, orgn. exec.; b. Booneville, Ark.; B.F.A., U. Okla., 1969, M.F.A., 1971; cert. in arts adminstrn., Harvard U., 1970; postgrad. (fellow) Fla. State U., 1971-74. Dir. publicity office, univ. theatres Coll. Fine Arts, U. Okla., Norman, 1970, adminstr. studio theatre program Sch. of Drama, 1970-71, adminstrv. intern, office of budget and research Nat. Endowment for Arts, Washington, 1972; exec. asst. to exec. dir. State Theatre of Fla., 1971-73, research fellow sch. of Theatre, Fla. State U., Tallahassee, 1974; adminstr. Clarence Brown Theatre Co., dept. speech and theatre U. Tenn., Knoxville, 1974-75; dep. dir. for adminstrn. and dir. of performing arts programs Colorado Springs (Colo.) Fine Arts Center, 1976-77; devel. officer, adminstr. Changing Scene Theatre, Denver, 1978; exec. dir. Arts and Humanities Council Greater Baton Rouge, Inc., 1978—; sec. Rocky Mountain Arts Consortium, 1976-77; cons. Colo. Council on Arts and Humanities, 1977-78; bd. dirs. Colorado Springs Dance Theatre, 1977-79; mem. theatre panel La. State Arts Council, 1979-80; chmn. Baton Rouge Met. Cultural Corsortium, 1978-80; mem. planning task force Baton Rouge Fine Arts Mus., 1979-80. Recipient Faculty Service award La. State U., 1979; Western States Arts Found. grantee, 1977. Mem. Am. Council of Arts, Assn. Coll. Univ. and Community Arts Adminstrs., Am. Soc. for Theatre Research, Am. Theatre Assn. (dir. 1971-73), Brit. Soc. for Theatre Research, Assn. La. Arts and Artists (treas. 1979-80), Nat. Assembly of Community Arts Agys. Clubs: Kiwanis, Camelot. Office: Arts and Humanities Council Greater Baton Rouge Inc PO Box 3893 Baton Rouge LA 70821

WALLS, MARGARET SUSAN, occupational specialist; b. Tampa, Fla., Mar. 13, 1951; student Fla. Coll., 1969-70, U. South Fla., 1979—. Free lance public relations cons., Tampa, 1974—; occupational specialist Hillsboro County (Fla.) Schs., Tampa, 1977—; mktg. Dance Scene Mag.; coordinator Artswatch, Greater Tampa C. of C., 1979; guest lectr. in field. Vocalist Tampa's 91st Birthday Celebration. Mem. Fla. Vocat. Assn., Fla. Public Relations Assn., Fla. Personnel and Guidance Assn., Dance Masters Am. (faculty). Republican. Club: Tampa Jr. Woman's. Author slide presentation: You and the World of Work, 1975. Office: 4401 W Cypress St Tampa FL 33607

WALLS, MARTHA ANN WILLIAMS (MRS. B. CARMAGE WALLS), newspaper exec.; b. Gadsden, Ala., Apr. 21, 1927; d. Aubrey Joseph and Inez (Cooper) Williams; student pub. schs., Gadsden; m. B. Carmage Walls, Jan. 2, 1954; children—Byrd Cooper, Lissa Williams. Sec.-treas., So Newspapers, Inc., Montgomery, Ala., 1954-67, also dir.; pres., dir. Walls Newspapers, Inc., Montgomery, 1967-70, So. Newspapers, Inc., Baytown, Tex., 1970—; sec.-treas., dir. Portales (N.Mex.) News-Tribune Pub. Co., Summer Camps, Inc., Guntersville, Ala., 1954-69, Quay County Sun Newspaper, Inc., Tucumcari, N.Mex.; v.p., dir. Dixie Newspapers, Inc., Gadsden, Ala., Fort Payne (Ala.) Newspapers, Inc., Scottsboro (Ala.) Newspapers, Inc., Reidsville (N.C.) Newspapers, Inc., Review Publishers, Inc., Freeport, Tex.; dir. Franklin County Newspapers, Inc., Russellville, Ala., Rockport (Tex.) Pilot, Angleton (Tex.) Times, Inc., Brenham (Tex.) Banner-Press, Inc., Cedartown (Ga.) Standard, Madisonville (Tex.) Metero, Port Lavaca (Tex.) Wave. Bd. dirs. Montgomery (Ala.) Acad., 1970-74. Episcopalian. Home: 623 Shartle Circle Houston TX 77024 Office: 7700 San Felipe Suite 111 Houston TX 77063

WALLS, MARTHA SHARPE, nurse; b. Statesville, N.C., June 21, 1946; d. Luther and Sadie (Milam) Sharpe; R.N. (Physician's Med. Aux. scholar 1965-67), Lowrance Sch. Nursing, Mooresville, N.C., 1968; B.S. in Health Edn., Appalachian State U., Boone, N.C., 1979; m. Ronnie Walker Walls, Dec. 20, 1965; 1 dau., Heather Michelle. Mem. nursing staff Lowrance Hosp., 1968-69, 70-76, head nurse pediatrics, 1977-78, dir. inservice edn., 1978—; intensive care nurse Charlotte (N.C.) Meml. Hosp., 1969-70; adv. com. practical nurse edn., health service adv. council Mitchell Coll. Cert. nurse, N.C. Mem. Am. Nurses Assn. (dir. dist. 4, 1978, chmn. dist.4 public relations com. 1978), Am. Acad. Health Adminstrn., Carolina's Soc. Health Care Edn. Democrat. Methodist. Home: Route 7 Box 99 Mooresville NC 28115 Office: PO Box 360 Mooresville NC 28115

WALSH, JAMES ANTHONY, law enforcement officer; b. New Castle, Pa., June 9, 1940; s. James Garett and Blanche (Nene) W.; A.S., Broward Community Coll., 1970; B.S., Fla. Internat. U., 1974; J.D., Nova U., 1977; m. Leanne Denise Gagnon, May 15, 1969; children—Pam, Danny, Jodi. With Hollywood (Fla.) Police Dept., 1963—, lt., 1973—; admitted to Fla. bar, 1977; individual practice law, Hollywood, Fla., 1978—; mem. faculty Broward Community Coll., 1973—; dir. Mcpl. Mgmt. Cons. Inc. Mem. Internat. Assn. Chiefs of Police, Am. Bar Assn., Am. Judicature Soc., Fla. Bar Assn., Fla. Assn. Police Attys., Soc. Advancement Ethical Hypnosis, Asso. Public Safety Communications Officers, Phi Alpha Delta. Club: Masons. Home: 4978 SW 102d Ave Cooper City FL 33328 Office: Hollywood Police Dept 3250 Hollywood Blvd Hollywood FL 33021

WALSH, JOSEPH JAMES, gen. contractor; b. Hamilton, Ont., Can., Mar. 22, 1931; s. Francis Lenton and Mary Ann (McInally) W.; B.B.A., U. Miami, 1961; children—Kathleen, Thomas, Joanne. Project mgr. Frank J. Rooney, Inc., Ft. Lauderdale, Fla., 1962-65; projects mgr. Collins Constrn. Corp., Ft. Lauderdale, 1965-71; pres. J.J. Walsh Constrn., Inc., Ft. Lauderdale, 1971—. Mem. adv. com. Broward County Bd. Rules and Appeals. Served with U.S. Army, 1953-54. Mem. Broward Builders Exchange (2d v.p. 1975—). Democrat. Roman Catholic. Office: 1187 SW 26th Ave Fort Lauderdale FL 33312

WALSH, MARY D., civic worker; b. Whitewright, Tex., Oct. 29, 1913; d. William Fleming and Anna Maud (Lewis) Fleming; B.A., So. Meth. U., 1934; LL.D. (hon.), Tex. Christian U., 1979; m. F. Howard Walsh, Mar. 13, 1937; children—Richard, Howard, D'Ann (Mrs. Wm. F. Bonnell), Maudi Walsh Willson, William Lloyd. Pres. Fleming Found.; v.p. Walsh Found.; partner Walsh Co.; bd. dirs. Lloyd Shaw Found., Colorado Springs, Colo. Guarantor Fort Worth Arts Council, Fort Worth Opera, Fort Worth Symphony Orch.; hon. v.p. Opera Bd., 1967--. Co-founder Am. Field Service in Ft. Worth; mem. Tex. Commn. for Arts and Humanities, 1968-72, mem. adv. council, 1972—. Bd. dirs. Van Cliburn Internat. Piano Competition, Colorado Springs Day Nursery, Colorado Springs Symphony, Ft. Worth Symphony, Wm. Edrington Scott Theatre; hon. chmn. Opera Ball, 1975, Opera Guild Internat. Conf., 1976. Recipient numerous awards, including Altrusa Civic award at 1st Lady of Ft. Worth, 1968; (with husband) Distinguished Service award So. Bapt. Radio and Television Commn., 1972; Opera award Girl Scouts, 1977; award Streams and Valleys, 1976-79; (with husband) Brotherhood citation Tarrant County chpt. NCCJ, 1978, Royal Purple award Tex. Christian U., 1979; spl. recognition award Ft. Worth Ballet Assn., 1978; named (with husband) Patron of Arts in Ft. Worth, 1970, Edna Gladney Internat. Grandparents of 1972. Mem. Ft. Worth Boys Club, Ft. Worth Children's Hosp., Jewel Charity Ball, Ft. Worth Pan Hellenic (pres. 1940), Opera Guild, Fine Arts Found. Guild, Girl's Service League, AAUW, Goodwill Industries Aux., Child Study Center, Tarrant County Aux. of Edna Gladney Home, YWCA (life), Ft. Worth Art Assn., Ft. Worth Ballet Assn., Tex. Boys Choir Aux., Round Table, Colorado Springs Fine Art Center, Am. Automobile Assn., Nat. Assn. Cowbelles, Ft. Worth Arts Council (dir.), Rae Reimers Bible Study Class (pres. 1968), Tex. League Composers (hon. life), Chi Omega (pres. 1935-36), others. Baptist. Clubs: Rejebian Book Review, Kappa Sigma Wives and Mothers, The Woman's (Club Fidelite), Dinner Dance (1st v.p. 1968). Home: 2425 Stadium Dr Fort Worth TX 76109 also 1801 Culebra Ave Colorado Springs CO 80907

WALSH, SARA ELIZABETH ECHART, educator; b. Commerce, Tex., Dec. 11, 1938; d. Thomas Vester and Lindel Faye (Carrington) Echart; B.S., E. Tex. State U., 1960, M.S., 1962; postgrad. U. Houston, 1974—. Tchr., Public Schs., Galena Park (Tex.), 1962-65; mem. faculty S. Tex. Jr. Coll., Houston, 1965-74, U. Houston, 1974—; sec., clk. Western Gillette, Inc., Houston, 1966—. Mem. AAUW, Nat., Tex. (dist. sec.-treas. 1980) bus. edn. assns., Internat. Word Processing Assn. (exec. dir. 1980), Am. Bus. Communication Assn., Nat. Secs. Assn., Delta Pi Epsilon, Pi Omega Pi, Phi Beta Lambda, Gamma Phi Beta, Alpha Lambda Delta, Phi Eta Sigma. Republican. Home: 9023 Gaylord #102 Houston TX 77024 Office: 1 Main St Houston TX 77002

WALSTAD, PAUL MARION, surgeon; b. Mpls., Mar. 29, 1915; s. Julius Oscar and Hilma (Latt) W.; B.A., U. Minn., 1939, B.S., 1941, M.B., 1943, M.D., 1944; m. Marjorie Jane Vandenberg, Jan. 24, 1945; children—Diana, Marilyn, David, Linda, Paula. Intern Hosp. of Good Samaritan, Los Angeles, 1944; resident in gen. Surgery Mary's Help Hosp., San Francisco, 1947-49, U. Pa. Grad. Sch. Medicine, 1949-50; resident in thoracic and cardiovascular surgery Highland-Alameda County Hosp., Oakland, Calif., 1958-59, Children's Hosp., Oakland, 1958-59, U. Oreg. Med. Sch., 1959-61; surgeon Travis AFB, Calif., 1950-51; pvt. practice medicine specializing in surgery, Turlock, Calif., 1953-58, 62-64; chief of surgery Stanislaus County Hosp., Modesto, Calif., 1955-56, 63-64; surgeon Daniel Boone Clinic, Harlan, Ky., 1964—; chief of surgery Harlan Appalachian Regional Hosp., 1965—, chief surg residency tng. program, 1965-77, chief staff, 1971-72; cons. in thoracic surgery, Middleboro, Whitesburg Appalachian Regional Hosps., 1965—; chief surgery VA Hosp., Phoenix, 1975-76; vol. physician, Vietnam, 1969; surgeon Kijabe Med. Center, Kenya, East Africa, 1971. Bd. dirs. County chpt. Am. Cancer Soc., 1962-64, Ky. Lung Assn., 1976—. Served with M.C., AUS, 1944-47, 51-53. Diplomate Am. Bd. Surgery, Am. Bd. Thoracic Surgery. Fellow A.C.S. (Ky. cancer liaison fellow), Am. Coll. Chest Physicians (pres. Ky. chpt. 1972), U. Pa. Grad. Sch. Medicine Surg. Soc.; mem. AMA, Ky., Harlan County (pres. 1973) med. socs. Am., Ky. (pres. 1974) thoracic socs., Southeastern Surg. Congress, So. Thoracic Surg. Assn., Ky. Med. Assn., Christian Med. Soc., Soc. Thoracic Surgeons. Contbr. articles to profl. jours. Home: Woodland Hills Harlan KY 40831 Office: Daniel Boone Clinic Harlan KY 40831

WALSTON, VIRGIL ALFRED, civil engr. cons., real estate broker; b. Palestine, Tex., Dec. 20, 1903; s. William Watts and Nora (Featherstone) W.; student Tex. A. and M. U., 1923-26; B.C.E., U. Houston, 1953; m. Dorothy May Darden, July 15, 1928; children—Dorothy Jean (Mrs. Charles W. Alcorn, Jr.), Virgil Alfred, Jr., Sally Darden (Mrs. Sweeney J. Doehring, Jr.). Chainman civil engring. dept. Mo. Pacific R.R., Palestine, Tex., 1926-27, rodman, 1927-29; with Humble Oil & Refining Co., Houston, 1929-68, office sr. supervising engr. Hqrs. Civil Engring. Dept., Houston, 1948-56, regional engr. Southwest Region, 1964-65, sr. tech. adv., Chief Prodn. Engr.'s staff, 1965-68, ret., 1968; engring. cons. Alyeska Pipeline Service Co., Houston, 1969-74; cons. Michael Baker, Jr., Inc., 1974-75. Mem. Tex. State Bd. Registration for Public Surveyors, 1963-68, chmn. bd. 1967-68. Mem. Am. Petroleum Inst., ASCE, Nat., Tex. socs. profl. engrs, Tex. Surveyors Assn. Baptist. Mason. Home: 3609 Overbrook Ln Houston TX 77027

WALSTON, WOODROW WILLIAM, hosp. adminstr.; b. Pinetops, N.C., July 12, 1918; s. Joe and Minnie L. (Little) W.; B.S. in Commerce, N.C. Central U., 1946; m. Hazel R. Howell, Aug. 31, 1958; 1 son, Reginald H. Office mgr. Kate Bitting Reynolds Meml. Hosp., Winston-Salem, N.C., 1946-52; adminstr. Community Hosp., Martinville, Va., 1952-58, Richmond (Va.) Community Hosp., 1958-69; asst. adminstr. Provident Hosp., Balt., 1969-70, asst. dir., 1970-71, asso. dir. adminstrn., 1971-72, dir. adminstrn., 1972-73; bd. dirs. Central Va. Hosp. Council. Bd. dirs. Leigh St. Br. YMCA, 1960-69, Richmond Br. NAACP; dist. commr., chmn. orgn. and extension com. Robert E. Lee Council Boy Scouts Am., 1960-69, dist. commr. Blue Ridge Council, Martinsville, 1953-58; bd. dirs. Big Bros. of Richmond; deacon, ch. treas. All Souls Presbyn. Ch.; hosp. rep. Blue Cross/Blue Shield of Va.; bd. dirs. Met. Jr. Baseball League, Richmond, chmn., 1973—; bd. dirs. Rubicon Alcoholism Program, Richmond. Recipient Order of Merit, Boy Scouts Am., 1963. Mem. Am. Hosp. Assn. (advisory panel small and rural hosps., 1976—), Hosp. Fin. Mgmt. Assn. (treas. Md. chpt., 1970-73, bd. dirs., 1970-73), Central Va. Hosp. Council, Va. Hosp. Assn. and Roanoke Area Hosp. Council, Va., Md.-Del.-D.C., Hosp. Assn., Am. Coll. Hosp. Adminstrs., Nat. Assn. Health Services Execs. (pres. Va.-Carolinas chpt., 1973—), N.C. Coll. Central U. Alumni Assn. (pres. Richmond chpt., 1973-79). Clubs: Kappa Alpha Psi (keeper of records and exchequer Greensboro alumni chpt., 1947-49, Roanoke alumni chpt., 1953-56, charter mem. Martinsville alumni chpt., keeper of records and exchequer, 1956-58, bd. dirs. Eastern Province Council, Richmond alumni chpt.), Pan Hellenic Council of Richmond (treas.), Spartans Social and Civic Club (treas.), Club 533 (treas.), Spring Lake Golf, Masons, Shrine. Home: 1720 Shewalt Dr Richmond VA 23228 Office: Richmond Community Hospital 1219 Overbrook Rd Richmond VA 23220

WALTER, JOHN PAUL, economist; b. Gainesville, Tex., Oct. 7, 1939; s. Joseph Bernard and Anna Marie (Walterschied) W.; B.S.Econs., Benedictine Coll., 1961; M.B.A. in Mgmt., North Tex. State U., 1962, M.A. in Econs., 1965; Ph.D. in Econs. (Univ. fellow), U. Notre Dame, 1970; m. Carol Diane Atkins, Aug. 17, 1974. Vis. Fulbright-Hayes prof. econs. Universidad Nacional de Trujill (Peru), 1970; indsl. research economist Fed. Res. Bank, Dallas, 1971-72; dir. econ. research Turner, Collie & Braden, Houston, 1972-73; corp. economist Shell Oil Co., Houston, 1973—; adj. prof. U. Houston, U. St. Thomas. Mem. Mayorial Com. to Study Airspace Rights in Houston, 1972-73; adviser on econ. impacts of changing weather patterns in Houston Mayor of Houston, 1972-76; mem. advisory com. NSF Chambers County (Tex.) Environ. Controls System Study, 1973-75. Served with USN, 1963-65. UNICEF grantee, 1969. Mem. Western Econs. Assn., Assn. Social Econs., Nat. Assn. Bus. Economists (pres Houston chpt. 1976, dir. chpt. 1977-78), Notre Dame Alumni Assn. of Houston (v.p. 1976—), Nat. Notre Dame Alumni Assn., Omicron Delta Epsilon. Author: Deprived Urban Youth, 1975; contbr. numerous articles to econ., sociol. jours., 1969—; pioneer in econs. of nutrition. Home: 10805 Villa Lea Houston TX 77071 Office: PO Box 2463

WALTER, VICTOR ARNOLD, engring. co. exec.; b. N.Y.C., Aug. 6, 1925; s. Victor Arnold and Theresa Minerva (Koster) W.; B.S., U.S. Merchant Marine Acad., 1946; B.S.M.E., La. State U., 1948; m. Beverly J. Beauchamp, May 13, 1950; children—Victor John, Timothy Arthur, Beverly Anne. Field engr. Chevron Co., Natchez, Miss., 1948-51; project engr., project mgr. Pure Oil Co., Chgo., 1953-62; chief utilities engr. Union Oil Co. of Calif., Chgo., 1962-67, supt. utilities div., Beaumont, Tex., 1967-72; v.p. Incon Inc., Houston, 1972-78; v.p. Turner Collie & Braden, Inc., Houston, 1978-79; chief energy systems engr. Bechtel, Inc., Houston, 1979-80; mgr. indsl. projects Stone & Webster Engring. Corp., Houston, 1980—. Served to lt. USNR, 1946-47, 51-53; ETO, Korea. Registered profl. engr., Tex. Mem. ASME (chmn. com. hydrocarbon processing petroleum div. 1973-75), Nat., Tex. socs. profl. engrs., Assn. Energy Engrs., Houston Engring. and Sci. Soc., Tau Beta Pi, Kappa Mu Epsilon, Phi Eta Sigma. Lutheran. Club: Quail Valley Golf. Home: 2723 W Pebble Beach Dr Missouri City TX 77459 Office: 1160 Dairy Ashford Houston TX 77079

WALTERS, DONN LEE, social worker; b. New London, Wis., July 19, 1946; s. Ralph H. and Alice E. (McNutt) W.; B.A., U. Evansville, 1968; M.Div., McCormick Sem., 1972; M.S.W., U. Ill., 1972; m. Alice D. Hardie, Dec. 27, 1969; children—Bradford LeBron, Sarah Alice, Donald Benjamin. Exec. dir. Greater Little Rock Presbyn. Urban Council, 1972—; dir. Adolescent Protective Services, Little Rock, 1975—; acting dir. Presbyn. Family and Child Services, Little Rock, 1979—; chmn. bd. Suspected Child Abuse and Neglect; bd. dirs. Ecumenical Retirement Center; cons. for detection and treatment of child abuse. Mem. Ark. Radio Bd.; mem. mission com. Ark. Presbytery, Presbyterian Ch. Mem. Nat. Assn. Social Workers, Acad. Certified Social Workers, Nat. Assn. Police Chaplains. Home: 5915 Stonewall Rd Little Rock AR 72207 Office: 2200 Gaines St Little Rock AR 72216

WALTERS, FREDERICK J(AMES), mgmt. cons.; b. N.Y.C., Feb. 18, 1906; s. Frederick J. and Laura Patricia (O'Connor) W.; A.B., Princeton, 1927; m. Virginia Cross, Jan. 18, 1934; children—Rosa Lee (Sister Marie Virginia O.P.), Virginia (Mrs. R. M. Stormont), Frederick James (dec.), James Anthony. With Gen. Motors Corp.,1927-45; mem. exec. staff Gen. Electric Co., 1945-46; v.p. Hotpoint, Inc., 1946-52, Packard Motor Car Co., 1952-53; pres. Fred Walters Oldsmobile, Atlanta, 1953-62; v.p. Boyden Assos., Inc., 1962-73; pres. Walters & Co., mgmt. cons., 1973—; dir. Flex-Comm Internat. Guest lectr. Ga. Inst. Tech., U. Ga., Ga. State U. Roman Catholic. Clubs: Capital City, Princeton, Rotary. Author: Handbook for District Representatives, 1939; A Summary of Veterans' Reemployment Rights, 1944. Home: 4418 Davidson Ave NE Atlanta GA 30319 Office: 4418 Davidson Ave NE Atlanta GA 30319

WALTERS, JACKSON HENRY, bus. exec.; b. Tampa, Fla., Mar. 27, 1953; s. Jackson Carey and Florence Lillian (Noxtine) W.; B.S.E., U. Pa., 1975; m. Patricia Lynn Litsinger, May 6, 1978; 1 dau., Kathleen Michelle. With Poe and Assos., Inc., Tampa, 1975—, mgr. loss control nat. programs, 1978—; lectr. legal and dental malpracticg prevention. Democrat. Methodist. Office: 102 W Whiting Tampa FL 33602

WALTERS, KENNETH VAN, media cons.; b. St. Louis, Dec. 16, 1948; s. Leland Edgar and Beverly Rae W.; B.F.A., So. Meth. U., 1971. Announcer, Sta. KNUS-FM, Dallas, 1968, Sta. KVIL, Dallas, 1969; mem. prodn. staff Sta. WFAA-TV, Dallas, 1970-71; accouncer Sta. KERA-TV, Dallas, 1970, Sta. WRR, Dallas, 1972-73; gen. mgr. Sta. KRSM-FM, Dallas, 1973—; dir. media services St. Mark's Sch. of Tex., 1973—; mem. adv. council media instruction Tex. State Tech. Inst.; mem. steering com. Tex. Student Film Festival. Methodist. Home: 7518 Colgate Dallas TX 75225 Office: 10600 Preston Dallas TX 75230

WALTERS, MICHAEL Y., theatre dir.; b. Oneida, Ky., Dec. 17, 1943; s. Francis Russell and Amnie (Young) W.; B.S., Cumberland Coll., 1965; M.A., U. Ky., 1969; m. Betty S. Smith, Mar. 22, 1963; 1 dau., Andrea Michele. Asst. prof., dir. speech and theatre Cumberland Coll., Gatlinburg Summer Opera, 1964, Lexington Children's Theatre, 1967—; mng. dir. The Legend of Daniel Boone, Williamsburg, Ky., 1976-80; regional mgr. Ky. High Sch. Speech League, 1974-77. Mem. Ky. Gov.'s Inst. Aging, 1977—, Ky. Gov.'s Econ. Devel. Commn. Tourism and Travel Bd., 1976-79; bd. dirs. Cin. Center Civic Opera, 1980—. Mem. Am. Theatre Assn. (project chmn. 1976-77), Am. Film Inst., Ky. Theatre Assn. (pres. 1975), Southeastern Theatre Conf. (dir. 1976). Democrat. Baptist. Office: Dir Speech and Theatre Cumberland Coll Williamsburg KY 40769

WALTERS, STANLEY CRAIG, shipyard exec.; b. Laurel, Miss., Sept. 26, 1921; s. Luther Marvin and Elizabeth (Craig) W.; B.S., U. Ala., 1942; m. Sarah Elizabeth Gann, Dec. 22, 1945; m. Sarah Elizabeth Gann, Dec. 22, 1945; children—Mary Elizabeth, Peggy Craig. Served as enlisted man U.S. Marine Corps, 1942-46; transferred to U.S. Navy, 1946, advanced through grades to chief petty officer, 1958, ret., 1958; corp. dir. indsl. relations U.S. Plywood—Mengel Wood Industries, Laurel, Miss., 1958-67; div. mgr. personnel and labor relations Nicholson File Co., Greenville, Miss. and Portland, Oreg., 1967-73; exec. v.p. Mainstream Shipyards, Greenville, 1973—. Decorated Navy Commendation medal; accredited personnel exec. Mem. Miss. Mfrs. Assn., Am. Soc. Personnel Adminstrs., Am. Waterways Operators, Nat. Waterways Assn., Greenville C. of C. (dir. 1978-70), Propeller Clubs U.S. (nat. v.p. 1976-77, sec. Greenville club 1974—). Republican. Methodist. Clubs: Rotary, Greenville Golf and Country, Masons. Home: 1737 W Azalea Greenville MS 38701 Office: Lake Ferguson Greenville MS 38701

WALTERS, TED WILSON, oil co. exec.; b. Jasper, Tex., Aug. 9, 1947; s. Ted Welborn and Mary Frances W.; B.B.A., U. Tex., Austin, 1967; 1 son by previous marriage—Logan Marquis. Sales corr. Tyler Pipe Co. (Tex.), 1970-74; constrn. supr. Baker Crow Constrn. Co., Dallas, 1974-76; ind. landman, Tyler, 1976; v.p. Herd Producing Co., Tyler, 1977—; Served with Tex. N.G., 1970-76. Mem. E. Tex. Landmans Assn. (dir. 1978, treas. 1979), Am. Assn. Petroleum Landmen. Episcopalian. Clubs: Centurions, Willowbrook Country, Tyler Tennis and Swim, Plaza. Home: 1413 Belmont St Tyler TX 75701 Office: 915 Peoples Nat Bank Bldg Tyler TX 75702

WALTERS, WILFRED NELSON, JR. (BUD), engring. co. adminstr., state ofcl.; b. Tarentum, Pa., Mar. 31, 1942; s. Wilfred Nelson and Rebecca I. (Hamilton) W.; student Air War Coll., 1967; B.S. in Engring. Mgmt., Clayton U., 1979, M.B.A. candidate; children—Quentin Scott, Amy Beth, Kristian Jil. Constrn. mgr. Walters & Haas, Inc., 1963-65, Walters & Walters, Ltd., Mgmt. and Design Cons., 1965-67; staff cons. U.S. Ho. of Reps. Select Com. on Small Bus., Washington, 1969-70; project mgr., v.p. Del E. Webb of Colo., 1971-72; sr. project engr., asst. to v.p. project mgmt. Alyeska Pipeline Service Co., Anchorage, 1973-77; asst. to pres., mgr. corp. devel. and govt. relations Resource Sci. Corp./Williams Bros. Engring. Co., Tulsa, 1978-79; mem. Gov.'s Cabinet, State of Pa., exec. dep. sec. Dept. Community Affairs, Harrisburg, 1980—; past pres. Pitts. Contractors Assn. Co-chmn. fund dr. Heart Assn., 1966. Co-recipient Westinghouse Design award of excellence, 1970; Presdl. Sports award, 1973. Mem. Am. Soc. Mil. Engrs. (v.p. local chpt.), Pitts. Athletic Assn. Democrat. Club: Masons (Shriner). Home: 5949 E 55 St Tulsa OK 74135

WALTNER, BEVERLY RULAND, artist; b. Kansas City, Mo.; d. Harry George and Ruth Anna (Laitner) Waltner, Jr.; student Columbia U., 1950-51, Yale U., 1951-53; B.A., U. Miami, Fla., 1955; M.F.A., No. Ill. U., 1968; postgrad. Kent State U., summer 1968. Tchr. art pub. schs. of N.Y., 1960-61, Fla., 1961-62, Mo., 1962-63, Ill., 1963-65; instr. art Barry Coll., Miami Shores, Fla., 1969-70; artist-designer, Coral Gables, Fla., 1972—; one person shows: Art Gallery, No. Ill. U., DeKalb, 1968, Lyons Meml. Library, Point Lookout, Mo., 1968, Jewish Community Center Gallery, Kansas City, Mo., 1969; juried exhbns. include: New Horizons in Painting, N.Shore Art League, 1966, 68, Chautauqua Exhbn. Am. Art, 1968-73, 10th Mid-Western Bienniel, Joslyn Mus., 1968, Mid-Am. I, Nelson Gallery and St. Louis Mus., 1968, Nat. Soc. Painters in Casein and Acrylic, 1969, 70, 72, 73, Ark. Nat., Ark. State U., 1970, 35th Ann. Mid-Yr. Show, Butler Inst. Am. Art, 1970, Ann. Exhbn. Am. Painting, Soc. Four Arts, 1971, 74, IV and V Ann. Pan. Am. Exhbns., 1972, 73; represented in permanent collections: No. Ill. U., Arlen Realty Mgmt., Inc., Alexander Muss and Sons, Equitable Life Assurance Soc. of the U.S., Gen. Devel. Corp., Zuckerman-Vernon Corp., also numerous private collections. Recipient First Place award Ann. Chautauqua Exhibition of Am. Art, 1968, Louis E. Selden award, 1972; Top award New Horizons in Painting Show, 1966, honorable mention, 1968. Mem. Artists Equity Assn., Cultural Execs. Council Profl. Artists Guild (treas. 1977-78, v.p. 1978-79, editorial staff newsletter 1977—), Chautauqua Art Assn. Address: 7500 Almansa St Coral Gables FL 33143

WALTON, CONRAD GORDON, SR., architect; b. Houston, June 18, 1928; s. John Edward and Evelyn Lucille (Gordon) W.; B.S. (Walsh scholar), Rice U., 1951; postgrad. U. Houston, 1955; m. Rilda Ellen Akin, Dec. 10, 1954; children—Conrad Gordon, Evelyn Coleman, Roberta Agnes. Asso. mem. Hamilton Brown & Assos., Houston, 1960-61; chief supt. Welton Becket & Assos., Houston, 1961-63; partner Alexander, Walton & Hatteberg, Houston, 1963-68; owner Conrad G. Walton, Houston, 1968—, D.C.W. Asso., A & E, 1974—. Co-owner subdiv. Holiday Oaks, Lake Somerville, Tex., 1964—; registered fallout shelter analyst Def. Dept., 1966—. Pres. Woodrow Wilson Elementary PTO, Houston, 1969-70, Houston Great Books Council, 1976-77; chmn. Troop 345, Roberts Sch., Boy Scouts Am., 1960-71; Republican precinct chmn., 1964-71; trustee Fair Haven United Meth. Ch., 1976-77. Served with AUS, 1952-54; Korea. Mem. AIA (treas. 1968), Tex. Soc. Architects, Houston C. of C. (civic affairs com.). Methodist. Optimist. Architect U. Houston Arch. Bldg. addition, 1969. Home: 9014 Springview Houston TX 77080 Office: 3203 Mercer St Houston TX 77027

WALTON, MRS. LADY BOGGS, ret. librarian; b. nr. Scottsville, Va., Dec. 5, 1909; d. Walter Francis and Melissa (Frame) Boggs; B.S., Longwood Coll., Farmville, Va., 1935; postgrad. William and Mary, 1939, U. Va., 1953; m. Leslie H. Walton, Aug. 17, 1940. Tchr., Mt. Tabor Sch., Buckingham County, Va., 1927-28, 29-32, Oak Grove Sch., Gilmer County, W.Va., 1928-29, Warren Sch., Albemarle County, Va., 1932-33, Greenwood High Sch., Albemarle County, 1933-35, 51-53, Scottsville High Sch., 1935-47; librarian at Albemarle High Sch., Charlottesville, Va., 1953-63, Greenbrier Sch., Charlottesville, 1963-74. County program chmn. Extension Homemakers Clubs. Recipient Rotary Fgn. Travel fellowship for tchrs., 1968. Mem. Am. (mem. recruitment com.), Va. (past chmn. recruitment com., sch. corr. Va. Librarian, 2d v.p., 1st v.p., pres.-elect 1965, pres. 1966) library assns., Nat., Va. edn. assns., Nat. Council English, Math. and Social Studies, Pi Gamma Mu, Kappa Delta Pi, Delta Kappa Gamma (chpt. pres.). Baptist (deacon). Home: RFD 1 Crozet VA 22932

WALTON, ROBERT ALDRIDGE, internist; b. Jacksonville, Fla., Nov. 18, 1934; s. Levi Larkin and Vernell Lee (Huband) W.; A.B., Duke U., 1957; M.D., U. Miami, 1962; m. Nancy Cook, Oct. 19, 1963; children—Scott, Todd, Cathy. Intern, Duval Med. Center, Jacksonville, 1962-63; resident in medicine Lloyd Noland Hosp., Fairfield, Ala., 1966-68; fellow in pulmonary disease U. Ala., Birmingham, 1965, med. dir. emphysema research, 1964-65; med. dir. Indsl. Health Council, Birmingham, 1968-72; practice medicine specializing in internal medicine and pulmonary disease, Birmingham, 1968—; asst. prof. publ health U. Ala., 1968; cons. Black Lung Program Social Security Adminstrn. Served with USPHS, 1963-65. Bd. dirs. Birmingham Civic Opera, So. Regional Opera Assn. Mem. Ala., Jefferson County med. socs., Soc. of Internists, Am. Thoracic Soc. (rep. councilor Am. Lung Assn. 1976-79), Am. Coll. Chest Physicians, Alpha Kappa Kappa, Beta Theta Pi. Democrat. Mem. Christian Ch. (Disciples of Christ). Home: 3705 Briar Oak Circle Birmingham AL 35223 Office: 800 Montclair Rd Birmingham AL 35213

WALTON, WILLIAM HENRY, coll. adminstr.; b. Percilla, Tex., Dec. 29, 1927; s. Douglas Edmond and Luna May (Bridges) W.; B.A., Stephen F. Austin State U., 1956; M.Ed., Sam Houston State U., 1961; Ph.D., U. Tex., Austin, 1968; postgrad. So. Meth. U., 1956-57, U. Houston, 1961-65; m. Martha Messer, July 22, 1956; children—Nancy Elizabeth, William Harold, Wyche Henry, Kathleen Rebecca. Tchr. public schs., Tex., 1957-65, also counselor, adminstr.; dir. student services Wharton County Jr. Coll., 1965-66; dean coll., pres. coll. Tex. Southmost Coll., Brownsville, 1968-71; v.p., acad. affairs Navarro Coll., Corsicana, Tex., 1971-74; dean arts and sci. Panola Jr. Coll., Carthage, Tex., 1974—. Pres., Panola County council Camp Fire Girls. Served with USN, 1948-50. Kellogg Found. fellow, 1966-68; Kettering Found. fellow, 1967-68; recipient award United Fund, Camp Fire Girls. Mem. Panola County C. of C., Consortium Border Colls. (pres. 1970-71), Tex. Assn. Community Jr. Coll. Instructional Adminstrs. (charter), Tex. Jr. Community Coll. Assn., Phi Delta Kappa. Methodist. Clubs: Lions, Masons. Office: Panola Jr Coll Carthage TX 75633

WALWICK, PAUL ALBERT, communication specialist, educator; b. Terre Haute, Ind., Apr. 17, 1926; s. Anton and Bertha (Krampe) W.; B.S., Ind. State U., 1949, M.S., 1953; L.T.D., Concordia Coll., 1964; D.Ed., Pa. State U., 1967; m. Joyce Ann Stuart, Aug. 9, 1952; children—Claudia Jane, David Stuart, Paula Marie. Tchr. Luth. High Sch., St. Louis, 1949-57; asso. prof. speech Concordia Coll., Seward, Nebr., 1957-68; prof., chmn. dept. speech, East Tenn. State U., Johnson City, 1968—; minister Luth. Ch., Mo. Synod, 1963; minister Bethlehem Luth. Ch., Johnson City, 1972—. Bd. dirs. Luth. Family Services, Omaha. Served with USNR, 1944-46. Luth. Aid Assn. fellow, 1966-67. Mem. Speech Communication Assn., So. Speech Communication Assn., Tenn. Speech Communication Assn., NEA, Internat. Communication Assn., Phi Delta Kappa, Psi Chi, Delta Sigma Rho-Tau Kappa Alpha, Alpha Lambda Phi. Home: 7 Beechwood Circle Johnson City TN 37601 Office: PO Box 21760A East Tenn State U Johnson City TN 37601

WALZ, ROBERT BRADSHAW, historian; b. Ashdown, Ark., Sept. 27, 1918; s. Joe and Lolla (Bradshaw) W.; A.A., Magnolia A. and M. Coll., 1939; B.A., Henderson State Tchrs. Coll., 1941; M.A., U. Tex., Austin, 1952, Ph.D., 1958; m. Curtistine Parsons, Apr. 28, 1951. Instr., Texarkana Coll., 1946-51; teaching fellow U. Tex., Austin, 1952-55; instr., asst. prof. history E. Tex. State U., Commerce, 1955-58; mem. faculty dept. history So. Ark. U., Magnolia, 1958—, prof., 1968—. Served with USAAF, 1943-45. Mem. Orgn. Am. Historians, So. Hist. Assn., Western Hist. Assn., Tex. State Hist. Assn., Ark. Hist. Assn. (mem. bd. 1963—, pres. 1968-69, 69-70), Ark. Archaeol. Soc. Democrat. Methodist. Home: 1502 N Jackson St Magnolia AR 71753 Office: PO Box 1292 So Ark Univ Magnolia AR 71753

WAMPLER, WILLIAM CREED, congressman; b. Pennington Gap, Va., Apr. 21, 1926; s. John Sevier and Lillian (Wolfe) W.; B.B.A., Va. Poly. Inst., 1948; postgrad. law U. Va., 1948-50; m. Mary Elizabeth Baker, Aug. 29, 1953; children—Barbara Irene, William Creed. Reporter, Bristol Va.-Tennessean, 1950-51; reporter, editorial writer Big Stone Gap (Va.) Post, 1951; reporter, copy editor Bristol Herald Courier, 1951-52; asst. campaign mgr. congl. candidate, 1948; keynote speaker, conv. chmn. 9th Dist. Va., Republican Conv., 1950, nat. vice chmn. congl. campaign com.; mem. 83d, 90th-96th Congresses from 9th Dist. Va. Mem. at large Sequoyah council Boy Scouts Am. Pres. Young Rep. Fedn. Va., 1950; chmn. 9th Va. Rep. Dist., 1965-66. Bd. visitors Emory and Henry Coll., Emory, Va.; bd. dirs. Youth Devel. Found. Served as air cadet USNR, 1943-45. Recipient Freedoms Found. award, 1954; Watchdog of Treasury award Nat. Asso. Businessmen; Appreciation plaque Va. State Letter Carriers Assn., 1968; Outstanding Citizen of Year award Bristol V.F.W. Sesquicentennial award U. Va., 1969; Distinguished Service award Ams. for Constl. Action, 1969. Mem. Am. Legion, Travelers Protective Assn., 40 and 8, Sigma Nu Phi. Clubs: Moose, Lions. Office: 2422 Rayburn Office Washington DC 20515*

WANDERMAN, RICHARD GORDON, pediatrician; b. N.Y.C., Apr. 17, 1943; s. Herman L. and Helen L. (Cohen) W.; B.A., Western Res. U., 1965; M.D., State U. N.Y., Bklyn., 1969; children—Richard Gordon Jr., Gregory Lloyd. Intern, Kings County Hosp. Center, 1969-70, resident in pediatrics, asst. clin. instr. pediatrics, 1970-71; resident in pediatrics L.I. Jewish Med. Center, 1971-72; practice medicine specializing in pediatrics, Merrick, N.Y., 1972-74, Charleston, W.Va., 1974-78, Memphis, 1978—; mem. staff, dir. adolescent clinic Charleston Area Med Center, 1974-78; clin. asst. prof. pediatrics W.Va. U. Med. Sch., 1974-78; clin. asso. prof. U. Tenn. Med. Sch., 1978—. Chmn. W.Va. Sch. Health Task Force, 1974-76; chmn. parenting com. Dist. III W.Va. PTA; chmn. health services advisory com. Headstart, Kanawha, Boone, Clay and Putnam counties, 1978; swim coach Memphis Jewish Community Center, 1979—; religious sch. tchr. Temple Israel, Memphis, 1978—. Diplomate Am. Bd. Pediatrics. Fellow Am. Acad. Pediatrics; mem. Tenn., Memphis and Shelby County med. socs., Memphis and Shelby County Pediatric Soc., S.E. Pediatric Cardiology Soc., Soc. for Adolescent Medicine, Am. Physicians Fellowship for Israel Med. Assn., Mensa, Zeta Beta Tau. Liberal Democrat. Club: South Hills Swim (dir. 1976-77). Home: 6748 Meadow Oak Pl Memphis TN 38138 Office: 6263 Poplar Ave Memphis TN 38138

WANDERS, HANS WALTER, banker; b. Aachen, Germany, Apr. 3, 1925; s. Herbert and Anna Maria (Kusters) W.; came to U.S., 1929, naturalized, 1943; B.S., Yale U., 1947; postgrad. Rutgers U. Grad. Sch. Banking, 1961-64; m. Elizabeth Knox Kimball, Apr. 2, 1949; children—Crayton Kimball, David Gillette. With Gen. Electric Co., 1947-48, Libbey-Owens-Ford Glass Co., 1948-53, Allied Chem. Co., 1953-55, McKinsey & Co., Inc., 1955-57; asst. cashier, then 2d v.p., v.p. No. Trust Co., Chgo., 1957-65; v.p. Nat. Blvd. Bank, Chgo., 1965-66, pres., 1966-70, also dir.; exec. v.p. Wachovia Bank & Trust Co., N.A., Winston-Salem, N.C., 1970-74, chmn., dir., 1977—; pres., dir. Wachovia Corp., 1974-76, chmn., dir., 1977—; v.p., dir. Winton Mineral Co., dir. Hanes Dye & Finishing Co.; trustee Wachovia Realty Investments. Mem. com. on bank relationships Council on Founds., Inc., 1973-74; mem. com. Winston-Salem Found.; bd. dirs. N.C. Engring. Found., Inc., N.C. Textile Found., Inc. Served to lt. USNR, 1943-46, 51-53. Mem. Am. Bankers Assn. (chmn. mktg. div.; dir. 1971-73), Assn. Res. City Bankers, Internat. C. of C. (trustee U.S. council), Conf. Bd. (So. regional adv. council), Newcomen Soc. N.Am. Clubs: Commonwealth, Chgo. (Chgo.); Old Town (Winston-Salem); Roaring Gap (N.C.). Home: 2760 Old Town Club Rd Winston-Salem NC 27106 Office: 301 N Main St Winston-Salem NC 27101

WANG, KENNETH YIN, mech. engr.; b. Peking, China, Mar. 18, 1937; s. Meng Hsiung and May Ling (Yu) W.; arrived U.S., 1958, naturalized, 1971; B.M.E., Mass. Inst. Tech., 1962, M.M.E., 1964; m. Louisa Kit-Chi Tsang, Sept. 19, 1964; children—Rebekah, Evangeline, Joshua. Mech. engr. Burlington Industries, Inc., Greensboro, N.C., 1964-71, sr. research and devel. engr., 1976-78, mgr., 1979—; v.p. W.W. Faith Corp., Framingham, Mass., 1971-73; dir. RCN Trading Co., Hong Kong, 1973-75. Recipient Wunsch award for machine design Mass. Inst. Tech., 1961. Mem. Sigma Xi, Tau Beta Pi, Pi Tau Sigma. Presbyterian. Patentee in field. Home: 2121 Churchill Dr Greensboro NC 27410 Office: PO Box 21327 Greensboro NC 27420

WANG, MING HSIEN, aero. engr., educator; b. China, Jan. 1, 1921; s. P. F. and L. S. (Leu) W.; M.S. in Aerospace Engring., W.Va. U., 1964; m. Helen Lai, Jan. 2, 1948; children—Lucy H., James H., Rosalie H., Hsiao-Jung Lai. From instr. to prof. aero. engring. Embry-Riddle Aero. U., Daytona Beach, Fla., 1965—. Mem. AIAA. Home: 1420 Mardrake Rd Daytona Beach FL 32019 Office: Regional Airport Daytona Beach FL 32014

WANG, RUEY-HWA, chem. engr.; b. Taipei, Taiwan, Mar. 2, 1948; came to U.S., 1971, naturalized, 1975; s. Si-Dong and Tzu (Chiang) W.; B.S., Nat. Taiwan U., 1970; M.S., Kans. State U., 1974, M.S. in statistics, 1975, Ph.D. in chem. engring., 1977; m. Betty Pochen Hsu, May 27, 1972; children—Leslie T., Grant J. Research asst. dept. chem. engring. Kans. State U., Manhattan, 1971-77; engr. Exxon Chem. Co., Baton Rouge, 1977-80; research engr. ARCO Polymers, 1980—; mem. U.S.-Japan Solids Mixing Coop. Research Team, 1976-77; mem. Chem. Engring. Product Research Panel, 1979. Mem. Am. Inst. Chem. Engrs., Sigma Xi, Phi Lambda Upsilon. Clubs: Formosan Assn. (pres. 1975), KSU Go (pres. 1975-76); Baton Rouge Formosan (v.p. 1979-80). Contbr. articles to profl. jours. Home: 547 Winston Way Berwyn PA 19312 Office: 440 College Park Dr Monroeville PA 15146

WANG, TSENG CHEN, chem. engr.; b. Tainan, Taiwan, Apr. 26, 1943; s. Ken Sun and Lain (Chun) W.; came to U.S., 1967, naturalized, 1975; B.S., Chun Yuan Coll. Sci. and Tech., 1966; M.S., U. Iowa, 1969, Ph.D., 1972; m. Huei Li Lee, Aug. 29, 1970; children—Clifford Lee, Sol Sean. Research asst. dept. chem. engring. U. Iowa, Iowa City, 1967-69, 1969-72; chemist Dunn Edwards Co., Los Angeles, 1969; Smithsonian Presidential fellow Smithsonian Instn. Ft. Pierce Bur., Fla., 1972; chem. engr. Harbor Branch Found., Inc., Ft. Pierce, 1973-75, chief chem. engr., 1976—; mem. grad. faculty Fla. Inst. Tech. Active YMCA. Registered profl. engr., Fla; certified water and wastewater treatment facilities operator, Fla.; Am. Soc. Heating, Refrigerating, Air-Conditioning Engr.'s Inc. grantee, 1969-72. Mem. Am. Chem. Soc., Am. Inst. Chem. Engrs., Fla. Acad. Scis., Sigma Xi, Alpha Xi Sigma. Contbr. articles to profl. jours. Research in environmental sci. and technology. Home: 2215 50th Ave Vero Beach FL 32960 Office: Rural Route 1 Box 196 Fort Pierce FL 33450

WANG, WILLIAM HSOUTAI, educator; b. An-Whei, China, Sept. 24, 1936; s. Chea Minning and Fu Fong W.; B.A., Nat. Taiwan, U., 1958; M.B.A., Atlanta U., 1971; postgrad. U. Ark., 1976, 77; m. Mary Lee, Mar. 3, 1963; children—Joseph, Peter. Accountant, Hdqrs. Chinese Air Force, 1958-60, Central Trust China, 1960-63, Bank Communications, 1963-68; dir. research and devel. Jefferson County Progress Inc., Pine Bluff, 1971-72; instr. U. Ark., Pine Bluff, 1972—; pres. Far East Imports, Pine Bluff, 1977—. Fed. Title III fellow, 1976, 77. Mem. Am. Accounting Assn., Southwestern Marketing Assn., Ark. Bus. and Econs. Tchrs. Assn., Ark. Chinese Assn. (counselor). Home: 14 Mocking Bird Ln Pine Bluff AR 71603 Office: U Ark at Pine Bluff Pine Bluff AR 71601

WANG, YUAN REAU, computer scientist; b. China, June 3, 1934; came to U.S., 1958, naturalized, 1969; m. Kai Hua and Hui Ying (Liu) W.; B.S.E.E., Nat. Taiwan U., 1955; M.S.E.E., U. Iowa, 1960; Ph.D., Northwestern U., 1967; m. Betty S. T. Yang, Apr. 2, 1961; children—Gary C., Lisa C., Alan C., Jean C. Devel. engr. Western Electric Co., 1960-63; asst. prof. U. Pitts., 1967-70; asso. prof. U. Nebr., Lincoln, 1970-76; sr. programming lang. researcher U.S. Army Computer Systems Command, Fort Belvoir, Va., 1976-77; asso. prof. Tex. A&I U., 1977—; session chmn. 1975 Internat. Computer Symposium; 1977 COMPSAC; Ford Found. tuition fellow Faculty Advancement Short Course, 1968. Troop com. mem. Gulf Coast council Boy Scouts Am., 1977-79. Am. Soc. Engring. Edn.-NASA summer faculty research fellow, 1970. Mem. Am. Soc. Engring. Edn., Assn. Computing Machinery, IEEE, Sigma Xi, Alpha Pi Mu, Upsilon Pi Epsilon. Contbr. articles to profl. jours. Home: 216 Pasadena Dr Kingsville TX 78363 Office: Dept Elec Engring Tex A&I U Kingsville TX 78363

WANG, YUH-YUN DAVID, food scientist; b. Foochow, China, June 18, 1940; came to U.S., 1970; s. Way and Gui-jan (Shen) W.; B.S., Nat. Taiwan U., 1961; M.S., U. Hawaii, 1972; Ph.D., U. Mo., 1977; m. Sui-Hua Sylvia Wang, July 24, 1976. Tchr., Shi-Yu Jr. High Sch., Taipei Hsein, Taiwan, 1962-63; teaching asst./instr. Nat. Taiwan U., Taipei, 1964-69; grad. research asst. U. Hawaii, Honolulu, 1970-72, U. Mo., Columbia, 1973-77; postdoctoral research asso. U. Ga. Agrl. Expt. Sta., 1977—. Served to 2d lt. Nat. Chinese Army, 1961-62. Eugene V. Nay scholar, 1975. Mem. Inst. Food Technologists, Am. Soc. Microbiology, Ga. Nutrition Council, Chinese Students Assn. (pres. 1975-76), Food Sci. Assn. (treas. 1974-75), Gamma Sigma Delta, Sigma Xi. Baptist. Contbr. articles to profl. jours. Home: 4086 Hwy 16 W Griffin GA 30223 Office: Dept Food Sci Ga Experiment Sta Experiment GA 30212

WANKO, GEORGE JOSEPH, coll. dean; b. Drums, Pa., Feb. 27, 1937; s. John Paul and Mary (Merker) W.; B.A. (Resident Advisor scholar), Pa. State U., 1964; M.S. (Resident Advisor' scholar), Syracuse U., 1966; Ph.D., Cath. U. Am., 1975. Dir. men's residences Cath. U. Am., 1966-67, asst. dean of men, 1967-69, asso. dean resident life, 1969-73, dean student life, 1973-78; dean student affairs Barry Coll., Miami, Fla., 1978—; organizer workshops in student personnel services; guest lectr. George Washington U., Md. Sch. Nursing; dir. Cath. U. Fed. Credit Union, 1977-78. Served with AUS, 1957-60. Recipient Stephen Dean Service award Cath. U. Athletic Dept., 1977; named adminstr. of year Cath. U. Student Govt., 1978. Mem. Am. Assn. Higher Edn., Am. Personnel and Guidance Assn., Nat. Assn. Student Personnel Adminstrs., Nat. Cath. Ednl. Assn. Home and office: 11300 NE 2d Ave Miami FL 33161

WANN, LAYMOND DOYLE, petroleum research scientist; b. Magazine, Ark., Apr. 25, 1924; s. Vernon Cecil and Emma (McCrary) W.; B.S. in Physics (Phi Eta Sigma scholar), Okla. State U., 1949, M.S., 1950; m. Betty Lou Brown, Nov. 6, 1948; children—Jacqueline, Lyndall Doyle. With Continental Oil Co., Ponca City, Okla., 1951—, sr. research scientist, 1957-60, research group leader, 1960—. Served with AUS, 1942-46; ETO. Decorated Bronze Star. Mem. Am. Petroleum Inst., IEEE, Aircraft Owners and Pilots Assn., Civil Air Patrol, VFW, Phi Kappa Phi, Pi Mu Epsilon, Sigma Phi Sigma. Episcopalian (vestryman). Contbr. articles in fields of elec. and radioactive well-logging, elec. design to profl. jours. Patentee in field. Home: 1501 Monument Rd Ponca City OK 74601 Office: 1000 S Pine St Ponca City OK 74601

WANNAMAKER, WILLIAM WHETSTONE, III, chem. engr.; b. Orangeburg, S.C., Nov. 1, 1926; s. William Whetstone and Evelyn (Townsend) W.; B.S., The Citadel, 1949; B.Chem. Engring., Cornell U., 1952; postgrad. U. S.C., 1954-55; m. Betty Ray Davis, Sept. 13, 1947; children—Ray (Mrs. Robert Sabalis), Harriet Wannamaker Gettys, III, William Whetstone IV, Preston Davis, Amelia Townsend, Sarah Boyd, Mary DuPre. Tech. engr. E.I. duPont de Nemours & Co., Inc., Camden, S.C., 1952-59; pres. chief chemist Wateree Chem. Co., Lugoff, S.C., 1956—; v.p., asst. gen. mgr. Hynes Chem. Research Corp., Lugoff, 1968-73; sec.-treas Manoa Metals, Inc., Ashepoo, S.C., 1972-76. Headmaster, sci. tchr. Thomas Sumter Acad., Dalzell, S.C., 1965-68; lectr. Wade Hampton Acad., Orangeburg, 1969, Joseph Kershaw Acad., 1971-72. Pres., County Republican conv., 1960, 62, 64, 66; chmn. Rep. party Kershaw County, 1961-64, 66; chmn. 5th Congl. Dist., 1961-66; 2d vice chmn. state conv., 1966; alternate del. nat. conv., 1960, 68, 72, 76, del., 1964; state exec. dir. Nixon for Pres., 1968. Bd. dirs. Joseph Kershaw Acad., Camden, chmn., 1971-72. Served with USNR, 1944-46. Registered profl. engr., S.C., Del. Fellow Am. Inst. Chemists; mem. Am. Chem. Soc., V.F.W., Alpha Chi Sigma. Episcopalian. Rotarian. Home: 902 Sunnyhill Dr Camden SC 29020 Office: PO Box 7 Lugoff SC 29078

WANTLING, BRIAN DOUGLAS, data processing dir.; b. Columbus, Ohio, Apr. 16, 1942; s. George Kenneth Dale and Leola Mary (Ross) W.; B.S. in Bus. Econs., U. Tenn., 1964; m. Bonnie Darlene Wiener, Aug. 9, 1963; children—Wendy Denise, Brian Keith, Melissa Lynn. Systems analyst Sperry UNIVAC, Richmond, Va., 1965-68; mgr. systems and programming Med. Data Services, Richmond, 1968-69; systems analyst mgr. Sperry UNIVAC, Richmond, 1969-76; data processing dir. County of Henrico Va., Richmond, 1977—. Bd. dirs. Henrico Credit Union, 1979. Named to UNIVAC Hall of Fame, 1967, 68; recipient Excellence award UNIVAC, 1976. Mem. UNIVAC Users Assn., Commonwealth of Va. Information Scis., Govt. Mgmt. Information Scis. Assn. Home: 112 Chasnell Rd Richmond VA 23235 Office: PO Box 27032 Richmond VA 23273

WARBURTON, LAWRENCE HENRY, JR., lawyer; b. San Diego, Sept. 6, 1926; s. L. H. and Estellane (Smith) W.; student Coll. Pacific-Stockton, 1945, U. Calif., Berkeley, 1945-46; B.B.A., U. Tex., Austin, 1949, LL.B., 1950; m. Jeanelle Golden, Sept. 3, 1955, children—Patrick Allison, William Perry, Lane Golden. Admitted to Tex. bar, 1950; individual practice law, Freer, Tex., 1950-54; asst. atty. gen., Tex., 1954-55; asst. dist. atty. 79th Jud. Dist. Tex., 1955-60; partner firm Perkins, Davis, Oden & Warburton, Alice, Tex., 1960—. Mem. exec. bd. Gulf Coast council Boy Scouts Am., 1960—; pres., campaign chmn. United Fund, 1960-62. Served with USNR, 1944-46. Named 1 of 5 Outstanding Young Texans, Tex. Jr. C. of C., 1960; recipient Silver Beaver award Boy Scouts Am., 1968. Mem. State Bar Tex. (mem. grievance com. for dist. 14-A 1968-69, mem. com. on profl. efficiency and econ. research 1968-69, dir. 1969-72, chmn. bar jour. com. 1972-79), Coastal Bend Bar Assn. (pres. 1960), Am. Bar Assn., Am. Judicature Soc., Tex. Trial Lawyers Assn., Alice C. of C. (dir., v.p. 1965-66), Alpha Phi Omega (pres. Tex. Alpha chpt. 1949), Sigma Phi Epsilon. Club: Rotay (pres. 1966). Methodist. Contbr. articles law jours. Home: 1821 Helen St Alice TX 78332 Office: Alice Nat Bank Alice TX 78332

WARBURTON, RALPH JOSEPH, architect, engr., urban planner; b. Kansas City, Mo., Sept. 5, 1935; s. Ralph Gray and Emma Frieda (Niemann) W.; B.Arch., Mass. Inst. Tech., 1958; M.Arch., Yale, 1959, M.C.P., 1960; m. Carol Ruth Hychka, June 14, 1958; children—John Geoffrey, Joy Frances. With various archtl., planning and engring. firms, Kansas City, Mo., Boston, N.Y.C., Chgo., 1952-64; asso., chief of planning Skidmore, Owings & Merrill, Chgo., 1964-66; spl. asst. for urban design HUD, Washington, 1966-72, cons., 1972-77; adviser to govts. Iran, 1970, France, 1973, Ecuador, 1974; prof. architecture, archtl. engring. and planning U. Miami, Coral Gables, Fla., 1972—, chmn. dept., 1972-75, asso. dean engring. and environ. design, 1973-74; cons. practice, 1972—; lectr., critic, design juror, 1965—. Chmn. community future com. Lake Barcroft Community Assn., 1971-72; mem. Met. Housing and Planning Council of Chgo., 1965-67; mem. exec. com. Yale Arts Assn., 1965-70; mem. ednl. adv. com. Fla. State Bd. Architecture, 1975. Skidmore, Owings & Merrill Traveling fellow Mass. Inst. Tech., 1958; vis. fellow Inst. for Architecture and Urban Studies, N.Y.C., 1972-74; recipient W. E. Parsons medal Yale, 1960; Spl. Achievement award HUD, 1972; commendation Fla. State Bd. Architecture, 1974; group achievement award NASA, 1976. Registered architect, Colo., Fla., N.J., Md., Ill., N.Y., Va., D.C.; registered profl. engr., Fla., N.J.; registered community planner, Mich., N.J. Mem. AIA (nat. housing com. 1968-72, 80—, nat. regional devel. and natural resources com. 1974-75, nat. systems devel. com. 1972-73, nat. urban design com. 1968-73; dir. Fla. S. chpt. 1974-75), Am. Inst. Cert. Planners (mem. exec. com. dept. environ. planning 1973-74), ASCE, Am. Soc. Engring. Edn. (chmn. archtl. engring. div. 1975-76), Nat. Soc. Profl. Engrs., Nat. Trust for Hist. Preservation (mem. principles and guidelines com. 1967), Am. Soc. Landscape Architects (hon. mem., chmn. design awards jury 1970-72), Am. Planning Assn., Internat. Fedn. Housing and Planning, Am. Soc. Interior Designers (hon. mem.), Greater Miami C. of C. (chmn. new neighborhoods action com. 1973-74), Tau Beta Pi. Christian Scientist. Mason. Clubs: Bath (Miami Beach, Fla.); Cosmos (Washington). Asso. author: Man-Made America: Chaos or Control, 1963. Editor: New Concepts in Urban Transportation, 1968; Housing Systems Proposals for Operation Breakthrough, 1970; Focus on Furniture, 1971; National Community Art Competition, 1971; Defining Critical Environmental Areas, 1974. Contbg. editor Progressive Architecture. Contbr. articles to profl. jours.; mem. adv. panel Industrialization Forum Quar., 1969-79. Home: 6910 Veronese St Coral Gables FL 33146 Office: Dept Architecture and Planning McArthur Bldg U Miami Coral Gables FL 33124

WARD, BENJAMIN PORTER, ret. naval officer, educator; b. LaFayette, Ind., July 2, 1897; s. Harry Van Devanter and Nellie Clara (Armbruster) W.; B.S., U.S. Naval Acad., 1919; M.S., Columbia U., 1927; m. Mary Ellen Estes, May 6, 1928; 1 son, Benjamin Porter. Commd. ensign USN, 1919, advanced through grades to capt., 1942, ret., 1950; asso. prof. mech. engring. Auburn U., Auburn, Ala., 1950-68, emeritus, 1968—. Decorated Victory medal, World War I, World War II, Korean War. Registered profl. engr., N.Y., Washington. Mem. Am. Soc. Naval Engrs., Soc. Naval Architects and Marine Engrs., U.S. Naval Acad. Alumni Assn., Pi Tau Sigma. Mason. Clubs: N.Y. Yacht (N.Y.C.); Ponte Vedra (Fla.); Saugahatchee Country (Auburn). Home: 815 S College St Auburn AL 36830

WARD, CHARLES HARPER, physician; b. Pocahontas, Va., June 26, 1918; s. Ballard Ernest and Lucy Butler (Anderson) W.; B.S., Coll. William and Mary, 1939; M.D., Med. Coll. Va., 1943; m. Elspeth Mitchell Hall, June 13, 1942; children—Lucy Lindsey, Charlotte Hall, James Harper. Intern U.S. Marine Hosp., San Francisco, 1943-44; practice medicine, Montross, Va., 1946-66; emergency physician St. Mary's Hosp., 1966-77, St. Luke's Hosp., Richmond, 1977—; med. advisor Richmond Area Vol. Rescue Squads. Served with M.C., USNR, 1944-46. Diplomate Am. Bd. Family Practice. Fellow Am. Acad. Family Physicians; mem. Richmond Acad. Medicine, Am. Coll. Emergency Medicine, Med. Soc. Va. Roman Catholic. Home: 5 Raven Rock Ct Richmond VA 23229

WARD, CHARLES LOWELL, JR., advt. agy. exec.; b. Houston, Dec. 27, 1940; s. Charles and Judy A. (Schley) W.; B.J., U. Tex., 1974. Founder, pres., chief exec. officer Media Communications, Austin, Houston, Dallas, 1967—. Served with Tex. N.G., 1966-72. Recipient Silver Spur, Tex. Pub. Relations Assn., 1972, 73; N.Y. Internat. Film and TV Festival Comml. Bronze award, 1972; Nat. Addy Merit award, 1976, others. Mem. Am. Assn. Advt. Agys. Tex. Public Relations Assn., Houston C. of C. Episcopalian. Clubs: Univ., The Houstonian (Houston); Westward Country (Austin, Tex.). Home: 5001 Woodway St Houston TX 77056 Office: 7575 San Felipe St Suite 125 Houston TX 77063

WARD, CRAIG BLOSS, lawyer; b. Neenah, Wis., Jan. 20, 1938; s. Taylor Dudley and Helen Williams (Bloss) W.; A.B., Rollins Coll., 1964; LL.B., Duke U., 1965; m. Paula Ann Cloys, Aug. 2, 1969; 1 dau., Lindsay Cloys. Admitted to Fla. bar, 1965, N.Y. bar, 1966, U.S. Supreme Ct. bar, 1974; asso. firm Donovan, Leisure, Newton & Irvine, N.Y.C., 1965-68; asst. gen. counsel Buena Vista Distbn. Co., Inc., N.Y.C., 1968-69; co-counsel Walt Disney World Co., Lake Buena Vista, Fla., 1969-73; partner Helliwell, Melrose & DeWolf, and predecessors, Orlando, Fla., 1973-76, Ward & Formet, P.A., Orlando, 1976-79, van den Berg, Gay & Burke, 1979—. Pres. John Young Mus. and Planetarium; bd. dirs. Orlando Opera Co., PESO. Served with AUS, 1960-61. Mem. Am., Orange County bar assns., Assn. Bar City N.Y., Fla. Bar, Phi Delta Phi, Orlando Area C. of C. Clubs: Country Orlando, Univ. Orlando. Home: 711 Alba Dr Orlando FL 32804 Office: 16 S Magnolia Ave Orlando FL 32801

WARD, DOROTHY BALL, clin. psychologist; b. Cuyahoga Falls, Ohio, Aug. 24, 1928; d. William Arthur and Effa Gay (Lee) Ball; B.A. in English Lit., U. Akron (Ohio), 1949; M.A. in Psychology, U. Fla., 1966, Ph.D., 1968. Editorial asst. The Kiwanis Mag., Chgo., 1950-54; asst. to promotion mgr. Dayton (Ohio) Newspapers, 1957-59; sec. The Mead Corp., Dayton, 1960-62, Rollins Coll., Winter Park, Fla., 1962-63; part-time psychologist Sunland Tng. Center, Gainesville, Fla., 1967; psychology intern Daytona Beach Guidance Center (Fla.), 1967-68; staff psychologist Henderson Clinic, Ft. Lauderdale, Fla., 1968-75, chief psychologist, 1975-77, chief adult service unit, 1977—; pvt. practice clin. psychology, Ft. Lauderdale, 1970—. Mental Health Tng. fellow State of Fla., 1962-65. Mem. Am. Acad. Psychotherapists, Am., Fla., Broward County psychol. assns., Kappa Kappa Gamma, Mensa. Home: 2509 Middle River Dr Fort Lauderdale FL 33305 Office: 330 SW 27th Ave Fort Lauderdale FL 33312

WARD, GEORGE TRUMAN, architect; b. Washington, July 24, 1927; s. Truman and Gladys Anna (Nutt) W.; B.S., Va. Poly. Inst., 1951, M.S., 1952; postgrad. George Washington U., 1966; m. Margaret Ann Hall, Sept. 10, 1949; children—Carol Ann (Mrs. Ronald G. Allushuski), Donna Lynne (Mrs. John H. Hale), George Truman, Robert Stephen. Archtl. draftsman Charles A. Pearson, Radford, Va., 1950; head archtl. sect. Hayes, Seay, Mattern & Mattern, Radford and Roanoke, 1951-52; with Joseph Saunders & Assos., Alexandria, Va., 1952-57, asso. architect, 1955-57; partner Vosbeck-Ward & Assos., Alexandria, 1957-64, Ward & Hall & Assos., Springfield, Va., 1964—; dir. United Va. Bank/Nat. Pres. PTA Burke (Va.) Sch., 1970-71. Bd. mgrs. Fairfax (Va.) County YMCA, 1964-76; pres. Springfield Rotary Found., 1978-79; mem. Gen. Bd. Va. Bapts. Served with AUS, 1946-47. Registered profl. architect, Va., Md., D.C., W.Va., Ohio, N.J., Del., Pa., Tenn., Ga., N.C., N.Y., Tex. Mem. AIA (corp.), Guild for Religious Architecture, Va. Assn. Professions, Va. C. of C., Tau Sigma Delta, Omicron Delta Kappa, Phi Kappa Phi, Pi Delta Epsilon. Baptist (deacon, moderator). Mason (Shriner, K.T.), Rotarian (charter mem., pres. Springfield 1973-74). Home: 9600 Burke View Ave Burke VA 22015 Office: 6320 Augusta Dr Springfield VA 22150

WARD, HARRY M., educator, author; b. Lafayette, Ind., July 30, 1929; B.A., William Jewell Coll., 1951; M.A., Columbia U., 1954, Ph.D., 1960. Mem. faculty Georgetown (Ky.) Coll., 1959-61, Morehead (Ky.) State U., 1961-65, So. Ill. U., Carbondale, 1967-68; faculty history U. Richmond (Va.), 1965—, prof., 1978—; cons. U.S. Bicentennial Media Corp., 1974-76; mem. com. Am. history coll. level exams. Ednl. Testing Service, Princeton, N.J., 1969. Mem. Am., So., Va. hist. assns., Richmond Independence Bicentennial Commn. Fellow Pilgrim Soc. Author: The United Colonies of New England, 1643-90, 1961; Department of War, 1781-95, 1962; Unite or Die: Intercolony Relations, 1690-1763, 1971; Statism in Plymouth Colony, 1973; Duty, Honor or Country: General George Weedon and the American Revolution, 1979; co-author: Richmond During the Revolution, 1775-83, 1977; contbr. chpts. and abstracts to Am. history publs. Address: Univ Richmond Dept History PO Box 155 Richmond VA 23173

WARD, HERBERT NORMAN, shoe co. exec.; b. Lunenburg County, Va., Dec. 1, 1926; s. William Norman and Marion Louise (Moore) W.; cert. bus. adminstrn. U. Richmond, 1951; m. Joyce Pankhurst, Mar. 29, 1947; children—Norman Donnan, Debra Joyce. Salesman, Edison Bros. Stores, Richmond, Va., 1942-44; teller Va. Trust Co., 1946-47; creditman Cities Service Oil Co., 1947-49, Reliable Stores Corp., Norfolk, Va., 1949-53; credit mgr. Stephen Putney Shoe Co., Richmond, 1953—, pres., treas., 1977—. Served with USN, 1944-46. Mem. Am. Legion (comdr. 1966), Nat. Assn. Credit Mgmt. Republican. Methodist. Clubs: Ruritan (pres. 1977), Masons. Home: RFD 14 Box 197-C Richmond VA 23231 Office: 3904 Jefferson Davis Hwy Richmond VA 23234

WARD, JACQUELINE ANN, nursing adminstr.; b. Somerset, Pa., Oct. 23, 1945; d. Donald C. and Thelma (Wable) Beas; B.S. in Nursing, U. Pitts., 1966; M.A., W.Va. Coll. Grad. Studies, 1976; div.; children—Charles L., Shawn Michael. Staff nurse W.Va. Univ. Hosp., Morgantown, W.Va., 1956-67; staff nurse, head nurse Charleston (W.Va.) Meml. Hosp., 1967-69; staff nurse Santa Rosa Hosp., San Antonio, Tex., 1969; staff nurse, supr. Bexar County Hosp., San Antonio, 1970; staff nurse, asst. charge nurse Rocky Mountain Osteo. Hosp., Denver, 1971; staff nurse, 3-11 charge nurse Charleston Area Med. Center, Meml. Div., 1972; staff nurse, relief charge nurse Charleston Area Med. Center, 1972-74, asst. dir. nursing Gen. div., 1974—. Mem. W.Va. Health Systems Agy., Alpha Tau Delta. Home: 702 Churchill Dr Charleston WV 25314 Office: Charleston Area Med Center Gen Div PO Box 1393 Charleston WV 25325

WARD, JAMES EVERETT, librarian; b. Dardanelle, Ark., Apr. 10, 1934; s. Norman E. and Nellie Ina (Ross) W.; B.A., Hendrix Coll., 1954; M.Ed., U. Ark., 1956, Ed.D., 1962; M.L.S., George Peabody Coll., 1968; m. Betty Jo Wells, Dec. 20, 1964; children—Bradlee Milton, David Everett. Tchr., Carlisle (Ark.) High Sch., 1955-57, Rogers (Ark.) High Sch., 1960-61; chmn. dept. phys. edn., dir. athletics Central Meth. Coll., Fayette, Mo., 1961-63; dir. library, prof. health, phys. edn. and recreation David Lipscomb Coll., Nashville, 1963—; lectr. health edn George Peabody Coll., Nashville, 1965-68, vis. prof. Sch. Library Sci., 1970; vis. prof. Tenn. State U., 1979. Served with U.S. Army, 1957-59. Mem. ALA, Southeastern Library Assn., Tenn. Library Assn., AAHPER and Dance Tenn. Assn. Health, Phys. Edn. and Recreation, NEA, Tenn. Edn. Assn., Phi Delta Kappa, Kappa Delta Pi, Beta Phi Mu. Mem. Ch. of Christ. Home: 3710 Rosemont Ave Nashville TN 37215 Office: David Lipscomb Coll Nashville TN 37203

WARD, LAWRENCE RAY, utility exec.; b. Dallas, Apr. 1, 1929; s. James Ray and Emma Elizabeth (Elam) W.; B.S. in Journalism, So. Methodist U., 1950; m. Betty Jane Blankinship, Oct. 16, 1953; children—Catharine L., J. Steve. News reporter Galveston (Tex.) Daily News, 1950-51, San Antonio Light, 1952-55; with advt. and public relations dept. Southwestern Bell Telephone Co., 1955-61; communications mgr. Dallas Power & Light Co., 1962—; chmn. advt. subcom. mass. communications adv. bd. Tex. Tech. U., 1978—. Trustee Tex. Tech. U. Dad's Assn., 1976-80. Served with AUS, 1950-52. Mem. Am. Advt. Fedn. (past dist. dir.), Public Utilities Communicators Assn. (regional chmn. 1976, nat. dir. 1978—), Tex. Electric Utilities TV Prodn. Group (chmn. 1970—), Assn. Broadcasting Execs. Tex. (past dir., sec.-treas.), Tex. Public Relations Assn., Dallas Adv. League (pres. 1976-77), Sigma Delta Chi. Methodist. Clubs: Preston North Lions (v.p. 1979-80), Press (treas. 1978-79, dir. 1977-79, mem. Gridiron exec. com. 1969—), Lancers (Dallas). Office: DP&L 1506 Commerce St Dallas TX 75301

WARD, LEW O., oil producer; b. Oklahoma City, July 24, 1930; s. Llewellyn Orcutt and Addie (Reisdorph) W. II; student Okla. Mil. Acad. Jr. Coll., 1948-50 B.S., Okla. U., 1953; m. Myra Beth Gungoll, Oct. 29, 1955; children—Casidy Ann, William Carlton. Dist. engr. Delhi-Taylor Oil Corp., Tulsa, 1955-56; partner Ward-Gungoll Oil Investments, Enid, Okla., 1956—; owner L.O. Ward Oil Operations, Enid, 1963—; v.p. 1420 Lahoma Rd. Inc., Enid, 1967—, also dir.; dir. Community Bank & Trust Co., Mag. of Okla. Bus. Vice chmn. Indsl. Devel. Commn., Enid, 1968—; mem. Okla. Gov.'s Adv. Council on Energy. Active YMCA. Chmn., Garfield County Republican Com., 1967-69; bd. dirs. Okla. Polit. Action Com., now chmn. mem. bus. adv. council Phillips U.; bd. dirs. Bass Meml. Hosp. Served as 1st lt. C.E., AUS, 1953-55. Registered profl. engr., Okla. Mem. Am. Inst. Mining and Metall. Engrs., Okla. Ind. Petroleum Assn. (dir., pres.), Ind. Petroleum Assn. Am. (dir., v.p.), C. of C. (dir., chmn. indsl. devel. com. 1970-72), Am. Bus. Club (pres. 1964), Order Ky. Cols., Alpha Tau Omega. Methodist. Mason (Shriner), Rotarian. Clubs: Metropolitan Dinner (dir. Enid), Falcon, Toastmasters (pres. Enid 1966). Home: 900 Brookside Dr Enid OK 73701 Office: 1420 Lahoma Rd Enid OK 73701

WARD, PHILLIP LAUGHTON, life ins. co. exec.; b. Carlisle, Pa., Jan. 10, 1948; s. Myris Laughton and Mavis (Everee) W.; B.A. in Edn., U. Ky., 1970; m. Betsy Ogden, June 21, 1975; children—Angela E., Aimee R. Agt., Equitable Life Ins. Co., Radcliff, Ky., 1971-72, dist. asst. mgr., 1972-73 agt. Bankers Life, Radcliff, 1973, unit supr., 1974, unit mgr., 1974—. Recipient several ins. and civic awards. Mem. Nat. Assn. Life Underwriters, Central Ky. Assn. Life Underwriters (1st v.p.), Radcliff C. of C. (dir. 1977), Radcliff Jaycees (pres. 1974, regional dir. 1975 Jaycee of Yr. 1975). Democrat. Baptist. Club: Sunrise Optimist (dir.). Home: 366 Terrace Dr Radcliff KY 40160 Office: 709 N Dixie Rd Radcliff KY 40160

WARD, ROBERT MITCHELL, social worker; b. Alexandria, La., Apr. 4, 1950; s. David Leonard and Susan Maurine (Malone) W.; B.A., Northwestern State U., 1972; M.S.W., La. State U., 1975; m. Janis Ann McDonald, Aug. 16, 1974. Tchr. spl. edn. State of La., Franklin, 1972-73; med. social cons. State of Tex. Dept. Human Resources, Waco, 1975-76, undergrad. field placement supr., 1976-80; counselor Family Counseling and Children's Services, Waco, 1980—; mem. adj. faculty Baylor U. Mem. adminstrv. bd., fin. com., chancel choir, also Sunday Sch. tchr. First Meth. Ch., Waco.; mem. Waco Civic Chorus. VA grantee, 1973-75. Mem. Nat. Assn. Social Workers, Acad. Cert. Social Workers, Weight Watchers Internat. (life), Phi Kappa Phi. Democrat. Home: 701 N 60th St Waco TX 76710 Office: Box 464 201 W Waco Dr Waco TX 76703

WARD, SAMUEL JOSEPH, JR., banker; b. Savannah, Ga., Jan. 7, 1928; s. Samuel Joseph and Frankie Inez (Ward) W.; Asso. Sci., Armstrong Coll., 1949; B.S. in Indsl. Mgmt., Ga. Inst. Tech., 1951; postgrad. Indsl. Coll. Armed Forces, 1974-75; m. Barbara Sue McDuffee, June 27, 1951; children—Samuel Joseph III, Raymond Curtis, Dana Reginald, James Grady, Robert Edwin, Glenn William. Asst. mgr. Savannah Area C. of C., 1954-59; asst. to pres. Savannah Gas Co., 1959-66; v.p. sales promotion First Nat. Bank of Atlanta, 1966-70; v.p. mktg. First Ga. Bank, Atlanta, 1970-72; v.p., dir. pub. relations Bank of Va. Co., Richmond, 1972—. Mem. So. Indsl. Devel. Council, 1972—. Mem. Ga. Tech. Athletic Recruitment, 1966—; treas. Va. Boy Scouts Am., 1973—. Mem. Chatham County (Ga.) Bd. Edn., 1959-66; trustee Ga. Found. Ind. Colls., 1962-72. Served with AUS, 1946-47, USAF, 1951-53 (col. Res.). Recipient Outstanding

Man of Year award Savannah and Ga. State Jr. C. of C., 1960; award Savannah Hist. Found., 1962; Community Relations award Am. Gas Assn., N.Y.C., 1962, 63. Mem. Bank Mktg. Assn., Va. Bankers Assn., Am. Pub. Relations Soc., Richmond Pub. Relations Soc., Am. Soc. Tng. and Devel. (pres. Ga. chpt. 1970-71). Presbyn. (chmn.). Home: 2635 Radstock Rd Midlothian VA 23113 Office: Bank of Va Co 11011 W Broad St Richmond VA 23260

WARD, WAYLON O'NEIL, marriage, family, personal therapist; b. Pittsburg, Tex., Feb. 4, 1942; s. Winston O'Neil and Melba (Stanley) W.; B.A., Tex. A&M U., 1965; M.A. in Bibl. Studies cum laude, Dallas Theol. Sem., 1975; postgrad. Asbury Sem., 1965-66, N.Tex. State U., 1972-73, E. Tex. State U., 1978—; m. Rebecca Ann Reese, Jan. 30, 1965; children—Timothy Winston, Jean Ashley, Guy David, Anna Rebecca. With Campus Crusade for Christ, Internat., Lubbock, Tex., 1966-71; v.p. Mt. Pleasant (Tex.) Broadcasting Co. and Idabel (Okla.) Broadcasting Co., 1968—; co-founder, co-dir. Christian Family Life, Dallas, 1972-73; adminstrv. coordinator Probe Ministries Internat., Dallas, 1973-74; founder, dir. Dallas Christian Counseling Services, Inc., Richardson, Tex., 1975—; instr. Dallas Bible Coll., 1974-78. Author: The Bible in Counseling, 1977. Home: 2210 Custer Pkwy Richardson TX 75080 Office: 324 N Central Expy Suite 100 Richardson TX 75080

WARD, WILLIAM TERRY, community agy. exec.; b. Lebanon, Ky., Sept. 3, 1944; s. William Richard and Elizabeth Gertrude (Downs) W.; A.B., U. Notre Dame, 1968; M.A., Eastern Ky. U., 1969; postgrad. St. Mary's Sem. and Univ., Balt., 1970-73. Tchr., Lebanon (Ky.) High Sch., 1966-68; instr. St. Mary's Coll., St. Mary, Ky., 1969-70; exec. dir. Central Ky. Community Action Agy., Lebanon, 1973—. Bd. dirs. North Central Comprehensive Care, Nat. Center for Appropriate Tech. Mem. Lebanon City Council, 1978—, chmn. budget com., 1978—. Mem. Nat. Assn. Community Action Agy. Exec. Dirs., Ky. Assn. Community Action Agys. (pres. 1977-78), S.E. Assn. Community Action Agys. (dir. 1977—, sec. 1979), Jr. C. of C. Democrat. Roman Catholic. Club: Kiwanis. Home: 226 E Mulberry St Lebanon KY 40033 Office: 406 W Main St Lebanon KY 40033

WARD-MCLEMORE, ETHEL, research geophysicist, mathematician; b. Sylvarena, Miss., Jan. 22, 1908; d. William Robert and Frances Virginia (Douglas) Ward; B.A., Miss. Woman's Coll., 1928; M.A., U. N.C., 1929; postgrad. U. Chgo., 1931, Colo. Sch. Mines, 1941-42, So. Meth. U., 1962-64; m. Robert Henry McLemore, June 30, 1935; 1 dau., Mary Frances. Head math. dept. Miss. Jr. Coll., 1929-30; instr. chemistry, math. Miss. State Coll. for Women, 1930-32; research mathematician Humble Oil & Refining Co., Houston, 1933-36; ind. geophys. research, Tex. and Colo., 1936-42, Ft. Worth, 1946—; geophysicist United Geophys. Co., Pasadena, Calif., 1942-46; tchr. chemistry, physics, Hockaday Sch., Dallas, 1958-59, tchr. math., 1959-60; tchr. chemistry Ursuline Acad., Dallas, 1964-67, Hockaday Sch., 1968-69. Mem. Am. Math. Soc., Math. Assn. Am., Am. Geophys. Union, Seismol. Soc. Am., Soc. Exploration Geophysicists, AAAS, Soc. Indsl. and Applied Math., Tex Acad. Sci., Sigma Xi. Contbr. various articles to profl. jours. Home: 11625 Wander Ln Dallas TX 75230

WARE, FREDERICK ANDERSON, JR., mgmt. scientist, educator; b. Melbourne, Australia, Apr. 27, 1935; came to U.S., 1937, naturalized, 1937; s. Frederick Anderson and Runa (Erwin) W.; B.M.E., Ga. Inst.Tech., 1957; M.B.A., Emory U., 1962; Ph.D., Ga. State U., 1973; m.Rose Marie Voorhees, Mar. 14, 1964; children—Frederick Anderson III, Laura Frances, Runa Henderson. Value design engr. Lockheed-Ga. Co., Marietta, Ga., 1962-64, mgmt. systems analyst, 1965-70; asst. prof. mgmt. Valdosta (Ga.) State Coll., 1971-73, asso. prof., 1973-76, prof., 1977—, chmn. dept. mgmt., 1975—; cons. in field. Served with Ordnance Missile Command, U.S. Army, 1958-61. Mem. Soc. Am. Value Engrs. (pres. Atlanta chpt. 1968-69), Valdosta and Lowndes County (Ga.) C. of C., Acad. Mgmt., So. Mgmt. Assn., Ga. Soc. for Textile Engring. and Devel. Presbyterian. Clubs: Valdosta Country, Rotary (pres. North Valdosta, Ga., 1977-78). Office: Dept Mgmt Valdosta State Coll Valdosta GA 31601

WARE, GRAYDON LEROY, educator; b. Springfield, Mass., Oct. 2, 1925; s. George Aaron and Dora Lenora (White) W.; B.S., Adelbert Coll., Case-Western Res. U., 1946, M.S., 1947; postgrad. U. Ill., 1949-50. Instr. Rio Grande (Ohio) Coll., 1947-49, acting chmn. dept. biology, asst. dean men, 1947-48; instr. Coll. Liberal Arts, Mercer U., Macon, Ga., 1950-52, asst. prof. biology, 1952-59, asso. prof. biology, 1959-74, prof., 1974—. Mem. AAAS, Ga. Acad. Sci., Am. Inst. Biol. Scis., Am. Soc. Mammalogy, Am. Mus. Natural History, Internat. Oceanographic Found., Blue Key, Beta Beta Beta, Sigma Alpha Epsilon (hon. province pres. 1972-74), Order of Omega. Baptist. Author: Laboratory Manual for Comparative Vertebrate Anatomy, 1973; Laboratory Manual of Parasitology, 1973; Laboratory Manual of Microbiology, 1963; Laboratory Manual for Experimental Biology, 1951. Home: 3147-C Brookwood Dr S Macon GA 31204 Office: Willet Sci Center Mercer U Macon GA 31207

WARE, PAUL DEAN, psychiatrist; b. Haynesville, La., Jan. 5, 1934; s. Leroy and Audie (Pride) W.; B.S., Centenary Coll., 1956; M.D., Tulane U., 1960; m. Margaret Adele Ferguson, Oct. 23, 1960; children—Paul Dean, Paula Denise, Dana Elizabeth, Danelle Yvonne, Paul Derek. Intern Confederate Meml. Med. Center, Shreveport, La., 1960-61; asst. resident in psychiatry U. Md., 1961-62; resident in psych- iatry, neurology Tulane U. Sch. Medicine, New Orleans, 1962-66, asst. prof., 1968—; practice medicine specializing in psychiatry, neurology, Shreveport, 1966—; mem. staff Brentwood Hosp., Shreveport, Schumpert Hosp., Shreveport. Organized community orgn. Drug Abuse Control, Shreveport, 1971-73, then pres. Named Intern of the Year, Confederate Meml. Med. Center, Shreveport, 1961. Fellow Am. Group Psychotherapy Assn., Am. Acad. Psychoanalysis, Am. Psychiat. Assn.; mem. Am., La. (pres. 1977-78) group psychotherapy assns., Internat. Transactional Analytic Assn. Contbr. articles to profl. jours. Home: 2049 Pepper Ridge Dr Shreveport LA 71106 Office: 713 Southfield Rd Shreveport LA 71106

WARES, MARGARET BONDS, educator; b. Quinton, Ala., Oct. 30, 1940; d. Hobart Aston and Martha (Brewer) Bonds; A.B., Ala. Coll., 1965; postgrad. U. Nev., 1973; 1 dau., Sabrina Evelyn. Basic skills tchr. U.S. Army Project 100,000, Ft. Benning, Ga., 1968-69; asst. prof. Nashville State Tech. Inst., 1970-74; instr., U. Nev., Reno, 1972-73; family counselor Family Counseling No. Nev., Reno, 1973; prof. reading Chattahoochee Valley Community Coll., Phenix City, Ala., 1974-76; dir. Learning Resources Lab., Sch. Community and Allied Health, U. Ala., Birmingham, 1976—; asso. dir. Exemplary Remediation Project, State Tenn., 1970-73. Treas., Ala. Coalition Citizens with Disabilities; mem. Pres.'s Com. Employment Handicapped, 1979; adv. bd. Human Resources Devel. Inst.; bd. dirs. Ala. Devel. Disabilities Advocacy Program. Hon. sergeant at arms Tenn. Ho. of Reps., 1974. Home: 108 23d Ave S Birmingham AL 35205 Office: 1700 9th Ave S Birmingham AL 35294

WARFORD, LEWIS MARSHALL, sound reinforcement co. exec.; b. McCracken County, Ky., May 15, 1943; s. Wilson Leon and Mary Emma (Young) W.; B.S. in Broadcasting Mgmt., Ind. U., 1965; m. Betty Ann Brown, June 25, 1977. Gen. mgr. WDXR radio and TV, Paducah, Ky., 1971-72; pres. Mobilsound Corp., La Center, Ky., 1972—; dep. commr. Ky. Dept. Pub. Info., 1976. Served with U.S. Army Res., 1967. Mem. Phi Gamma Delta. Democrat. Baptist. Home: Box 372 Biscayne Dr LaCenter KY 42056 Office: Mobilsound Corp 206 Broadway LaCenter KY 42056

WARK, DAVID LYNES, bank exec.; b. Detroit, Feb. 9, 1936; s. James Gordon and Marion Elaine (Wassink) W.; B.A., Dartmouth Coll., 1958; M.B.A., Syracuse U., 1963, (Ford Found. fellow), U. Chgo., 1967; postgrad. Am. U., 1965-66; m. Catharine Creed, Mar. 20, 1971; 1 son, Christopher David. Asst. to dir. dept. stats. Reader's Digest, Pleasantville, N.Y., 1969-70; dir. corp. planning Am. Express Co., N.Y.C., 1970-73; asst. v.p. planning and budgeting Am. Express Internat. Bank, N.Y.C., 1973; sr. v.p., chief fin. officer Nat. Bank of Commerce, Memphis, 1973—; sec.-treas., v.p. Nat. Commerce Bancorp., Memphis, 1977—; chmn. bd. Commerce Gen. Corp. subs. Nat. Bank of Commerce, Memphis, 1979—; speaker in field. Treas. Memphis Urban League; mem. budget com. United Way of Greater Memphis; mem. nat. fin. com. Assemblies of God Ch.; trustee Germantown (Tenn.) Assembly of God Ch.; bd. dirs. Teen Challenge of Memphis. Served with USAF, 1958-61. Mem. Fin. Execs. Inst. Office: One Commerce Sq Memphis TN 38150

WARMANN, ROBERT THEODORE, univ. ofcl.; b. St. Louis County, Mo., Sept. 8, 1932; s. John William and Amanda Anna (Hischke) W.; B.A., Valparaiso U., 1954; postgrad. U. Mo., Columbia, 1957, 58; M.A., U. Mich., 1965; postgrad. Ariz. State U., 1970-71, U. Tenn., 1972; m. Suzanne R. Magel, Aug. 12, 1961; children—Jeffrey K., RaeAnn K., Bradley J. Tchr. biology Hillsboro (Ill.) High Sch., 1956-62, Hazelwood (Mo.) High Sch., 1962-66; asst. to dean U. Mich. Sch. Music, Ann Arbor, 1966-68; instr. biology U. Wis., Whitewater, 1968-71, Jr. Coll. of Albany, N.Y., 1971-75; registrar Russell Sage Coll., Albany, 1973-77; dir. admissions, registrar U. Tex., Permian Basin, Odessa, 1977—. Bd. dirs. Permian Merit Scholarship Found., 1978-81, chmn. scholarship nominations com., 1978-80. Served with AUS, 1954-56. NSF scholar, 1965, grantee, 1970-72. Mem. Am. Assn. Collegiate Registrars and Admissions Officers, Tex. Assn. Collegiate Registrars and Officers of Admission, Nat. Assn. Fgn. Student Advisors. Lutheran. Home: 6464 Richwood Rd Odessa TX 79763 Office: Registrar's Office U Tex of Permian Basin University and Parkway Aves Odessa TX 79762

WARMBROD, BRUCE CLAY, elec. engr.; b. Arlington, Va., Dec. 24, 1948; s. Grover and Sylvia (Mullican) W.; B.S. in Elec. Engring., Va. Poly. Inst., 1972; m. Thresa Kay Jones, July 5, 1969; children—Nathan Bruce, Amy Lynnete. Design engr. Tex. Instruments Co., Dallas, 1972-78; sr. engr. Recognition Equipment Co., Dallas, 1978-79; owner, mgr. Lone Oak Nursery, Dallas, 1979—. Served with Army N.G., 1970-76. Mem. IEEE, Tex. Christmas Tree Growers Assn. Mem. Ch. of Christ. Home: 1504 Windy Meadow St Plano TX 75023 Office: 2701 E Grauwyler St Irving TX 75222

WARMING, KARL EMIL, coll. ofcl.; b. Derby, Eng., Apr. 16, 1918; s. Emil Andreas and Gladys Barry (Claxton) W.; came to U.S., 1921, naturalized, 1936; student U. Tenn., 1935-36, 42-43; student Berea Coll., 1938-41, B.A., 1947; postgrad. Harvard Inst. for Ednl. Mgmt., summer 1972, Eastern Ky. U., 1974-76, 77-78; m. Virginia Eloise Oliver, Aug. 13, 1947; children—Karla, Robert. Hosp. adminstr. Berea (Ky.) Coll. Hosp., 1949-53, Murray (Ky.) Hosp., 1953-57, Hardin County (Ky.) Meml. Hosp., 1957-62, Riverside Hosp., Jacksonville, Fla., 1962-64; bus. v.p. Berea Coll., 1964—. Bd. dirs. Hardin County chpt. ARC, 1960-63, chmn. blood program, 1958-60, del.-at-large exec. com. regional blood program, 1960-62, chmn. fin. regional blood program, 1960-61; chmn. program com. Blue Grass Hosp. Council, 1960-61; chmn. ednl. com. Hardin County chpt. Am. Cancer Soc., 1960-61; chmn. Ky. Joint Commn. for Improvement of Care of Patient, 1958-60; mem. Health Facilities Planning Council of Jacksonville, 1962-63; chmn. Berea Sewer Commn., 1964-65; mem. planning com. New Community Sch., Berea, 1964-65; bd. dirs. Berea Hosp., 1964-74; mem. Berea Planning and Zoning Commn., 1971-74, Gov.'s Task Force on State Prks Devel., 1979. Served with AUS, 1943-46. Ky. col. Fellow Am. Coll. Hosp. Adminstrs.; mem. Nat. Assn. Coll. and Univ. Bus. Officers (com. for small colls. 1978-80, chmn. com. for risk mgmt. and ins. workshops 1979-80), Council Ind. Ky. Colls. and Univ. Bus. Officers (charter, pres. 1971), Berea C. of C., Phi Kappa Phi. Democrat. Presbyterian. Clubs: Berea Indsl. Mgmt. (charter, v.p. 1972—), Arlington Country (pres. 1977), Rotary (hon.), Kiwanis, Meninak. Home: Route 4 Box 39 Berea KY 40403 Office: Berea Coll CPO 2292 Berea KY 40404

WARNER, ADDISON WHEELOCK, oil producer; b. Geneva, Ill., June 5, 1899; s. Henry Dimock and Harriette King (Young) W.; student Dartmouth, 1917; B.S., Stanford, 1922; m. Helen Christopher, Dec. 25, 1924; children—Ann Wheelock (Mrs. Kimball), Addison Wheelock. Mgr. investor's aid dept. Chgo. Jour. Commerce, 1922-26; mgr. statis. dept. Stevenson, Perry & Stacy, 1926-27; sales mgr. Robert Stevenson & Co., 1927-28; gen. mgr. Kissell, Kinnicutt & Co., Chgo., 1929-30; sr. partner Addison Warner & Co., 1930-38, pres., 1938-43; now oil producer, also chmn. bd., pres. Imco Inc.; treas., dir. Aviation Industries. Bd. dirs. Chgo. Area Project, 1934-53; trustee Union League Boys' Club, 1933-53, pres., 1938-40; chmn. finance com., trustee South Side Boys' Club, 1938-53. Served as flying cadet, U.S. Army, 1918-19; apptd. 2d lt., A.S.S. Res. Corps, 1919. Mem. Order Founders and Patriots Am., Chgo. Stanford Alumni Assn. (pres. 1938-47), SAR, Mayflower Soc., Chi Psi. Clubs: Adventurers, Econ. (life), Union League (Chgo.); Petroleum (Ft. Worth). Address: 6119 Thorpe Springs Rd Weatherford TX 76086

WARNER, ALLEN RUSSELL, educator; b. Chgo., Aug. 26, 1943; s. Henry Carl and Ann Marie (Kiefer) W.; student Elmhurst Coll., 1965-66; B.S. in Edn., No. Ill. U., 1968, M.S., 1969, Ed.D., 1973; m. Hildegard Ann Herbst, Aug. 26, 1967; children—David Eric, Robin Leigh. Tchr. high sch., Downers Grove, Ill., 1969-72; instr. No. Ill. U., DeKalb, 1972-73; asst. prof. U. Houston Victoria campus, 1973-74, asst. prof. curriculum and instruction, dir. field experiences, Coll. of Edn., 1974-79, asso. prof. curriculum and instrn., dir. field experiences, 1979—; cons. in field. Vice pres. Belle Park Community Assn., 1977-78; chmn. Ednl. Ministry com., St. Martin's Luth. Ch., Houston, 1976-78; lay ministry St. Martin's Luth. Ch., 1975—. Served with U.S. Army, 1961-64. Mem. Assn. Tchr. Educators (bd. dirs. 1978—), NEA, Nat. Council for Social Studies, AAUP, Assn. for Supervision and Curriculum Devel., Tex. Tchrs. Assn., Phi Delta Kappa. Democrat. Contbr. articles to profl. jours. Home: 4232 Belle Park Dr Houston TX 77072 Office: Field Service Office Coll of Edn Univ of Houston Houston TX 77004

WARNER, ISIAH MANUEL, chemist, educator; b. DeQuincy, La., July 20, 1946; s. Humphrey and Irma Priscilla (St. Romain) W.; B.S. (scholar), So. U., 1968; Ph.D., U. Wash., 1977; m. Della Faye Blount, June 1, 1968; children—Isiah Manuel, Chideha Charles. Co-op. student TVA, Muscle Shoals, Ala., 1967; research chemist Battelle-N.W., Richland, Wash., 1968-73; research, teaching asst. U. Wash., Seattle, 1973-77; asst. prof. chemistry Tex. A. and M. U., 1977—. Del. Wash. State Dem. Conv., 1970, Benton County Dem. Conv., 1972. Recipient Grad. Research award, Nat. Orgn. Black Chemists and Chem. Engrs., 1976; Am. Chem. Soc. summer fellow, 1975. Mem. Am. Chem. Soc. Democrat. Roman Catholic. Contbr. articles in field to profl. jours. Home: 1222 Neal Pickett College Station TX 77840 Office: Dept of Chemistry Tex A and M U College Station TX 77843

WARNER, JOHN WILLIAM, senator; b. Washington, Feb. 18, 1927; s. John William and Martha Stuart (Budd) W.; B.S., Washington and Lee U., 1949; LL.B., U. Va., 1953; m. Elizabeth Taylor, Dec. 4, 1976; children by previous marriage—Mary Conover, Virginia Stuart, John William IV. Law clk. to U.S. judge, 1953-54; spl. asst. to U.S. atty., 1956-57; asst. U.S. atty. Dept. Justice, 1957-60; partner firm Hogan & Hartson, 1960-68; undersec. of Navy, 1969-72, sec. of Navy, 1972-74; adminstr. Am. Revolution Bicentennial Adminstrn., 1974-76; mem. U.S. Senate from Va., 1979—. Trustee Washington and Lee U. Served with USNR, 1944-46; to capt. USMCR, 1949-52. Mem. Bar Assn. D.C., Washington Inst. Fgn. Affairs, Beta Theta Pi, Phi Alpha Delta. Republican. Episcopalian. Clubs: Metropolitan, Burning Tree, Chevy Chase, Alfafa, Alibi. Office: 6239 Dirksen Senate Office Bldg Washington DC 20510

WARNER, JOHN WILLIAM, U.S. senator, former sec. of navy; b. Washington, Feb. 18, 1927; s. John William and Martha Stuart (Budd) W.; B.S., Washington and Lee U., 1949; LL.B., U. Va., 1953; m. Elizabeth Taylor, Dec. 4, 1976; children by previous marriage—Mary Conover, Virginia Stuart, John William IV. Law clk. to U.S. judge, 1953-54; spl. asst. to U.S. atty., 1956-57; asst. U.S. atty. Dept. Justice, 1957-60; partner firm Hogan & Hartson, 1960-68; undersec. of navy, 1969-72, sec. of navy, 1972-74; adminstr. Am. Revolution Bicentennial Adminstrn., 1974-76; U.S. Senator from Va., 1979—. Trustee Washington and Lee U. Served with USN, 1944-46; to capt., USMCR, 1949-52. Mem. Bar Assn. D.C., Washington Inst. Fgn. Affairs, Beta Theta Pi, Phi Alpha Delta. Republican. Episcopalian. Clubs: Met.; Burning Tree; Chevy Chase; Alfalfa; Alibi. Office: 2311 Dirksen Senate Office Bldg Washington DC 20510

WARNER, KENNETH OREN, mgmt. cons., polit. scientist; b. Stewardson, Ill., Jan. 23, 1904; s. Andrew and Rose Leah (Hancock) W.; student Coll. of Puget Sound, 1922-23; A.B., U. Wash., 1926, M.A., 1927, Ph.D., 1931; m. Elizabeth Thompson, July 23, 1938; children—Martha Louise Warner McIntyre, Sarah Kathryn Warner Carter, Kenneth Thompson. Asst. dept. polit. sci. U. Wash., Seattle, 1927-29; research fellow Brookings Instn., Washington, 1929-31; asst. prof. polit. sci. U. Ark., Fayetteville, 1931-32, asso. prof., 1933-34; organizer, exec. dir. Ark. Municipal League, 1934-35; cons. Am. Municipal Assn., Chgo., 1935-37; dir. personnel State of Ark., 1937-38; exec. dir. N.W. Regional Council, Portland, Oreg., 1938-41; prof., head dept. polit. sci. U. Tenn., Knoxville, 1941-42; 1941-42; dir. personnel OPA, Washington, 1942-43; asst. adminstr. Fgn. Econ. Adminstrn., Washington, 1943-45; exec. asst. to U.S. Commr. of Edn., 1945-48; dir. institutional resources survey div. Nat. Security Resources Bd., Washington, 1948-49; exec. dir. Pub. Personnel Assn., Chgo., 1949-71; cons. to pub. agys. on mgmt. problems, 1971—. Lectr. pub. personnel adminstr. U. Chgo., 1953-65, Loyola U., Chgo., 1965, Roosevelt U., 1966, No. Ill. U., 1968, others. Mem. industry adv. com. on job evaluation U.S. Civil Service Commn., 1970-71; bd. dirs. Spring River Entertainment Assn. Mem. Am. Polit. Sci. Assn., Internat. Personnel Mgmt. Assn., Internat. City Mgmt. Assn., Pi Sigma Alpha. Democrat. Methodist. Club: Thayer-Mammoth Spring Rotary (pres. 1977-78). Author: Problems of Arkansas Government, 1932; Australian Federalism, 1933; Arkansas State and Local Government, 1934; (with Arnold Miles) Toward Competant Government, 1934; (with M.L. Hennessy) Public Management at the Bargaining Table, 1967. Editor Pub. Personnel Rev., 1949-71, Pub. Employee Relations Library, 1968-71; editor Practical Guidelines to Public Pay Adminstrn., vol. 1, 1963, vol. II, 1965. Contbr. articles on personnel mgmt. to profl. jours. Address: Route 2 Mammoth Spring AR 72554

WARNER, MARY HELEN, musician; b. Birmingham, Ala., Nov. 22; d. John Franklin and Lena (King) Sparks; Mus.B., U. Ala., 1949; Mus.M., Fla. State U., 1951; m. Henry L. Warner, June 8, 1950 (div. 1977); children—Judith Virginia Warner Johnson, Cynthia Ann. Voice instr. Fla. State U., 1950-52; choral dir. Everett Jr. High Sch., Panama City, Fla., 1957-58; choir dir. St. Andrews Episcopal Ch., Panama City, 1952-60; instr. music Gulf Coast Community Coll., Panama City, 1962-75, asso. prof. music, 1975—; dir. coll. musicals and plays; dir. plays Mine Def. Lab., Panama City Players; participant prodns. of Kaleidoscope Theatre; soprano soloist chs., oratorios, cantatas. Nominee for best actress Kaleidoscope Theatre, 1979. Mem. Nat. Assn. Tchrs. of Singing, Fla. Assn. Community Colls., Sigma Alpha Iota, Phi Kappa Lambda. Episcopalian. Home: 209 Woodlawn Dr Panama City FL 32407 Office: 5230 W Hwy 98 Panama City FL 32401

WARNER, RICHARD WRIGHT, JR., educator; b. New Castle, Pa., Nov. 10, 1938; s. Richard Wright and Emily Ruth (Curtiss) W.; B.A., Westminster Coll., 1962; M.Ed. (NDEA fellow), State U. N.Y. at Buffalo, 1966, Ed.D. (NDEA fellow), 1969; m. Lois Ann Woltner, May 28, 1966; 1 dau., Terri Lynn; children of previous marriage—Richard Wright III, Halden A. Tchr. schs., Pennsbury, Pa., 1961-62, Ashtabula, Ohio, 1962-65; counselor high sch., Cheektowaga, N.Y., 1966-68; instr. counselor edn. SUNY, Buffalo, 1968-69; mem. faculty Pa. State U., 1969-72; asso. prof. counselor edn. Auburn (Ala.) U., 1972-77, asso. dean, prof. edn., 1977—; practice psychology, Auburn, 1972—. Cons. East Ala. Mental Health Assn., Opelika, 1973—, Baldwin County Mental Health Center, 1975—, Ala. Gov.'s Com. Drug Abuse, 1974-75, Ind. U., 1976, E. Tex. State U., 1976, Pyramid, 1976-80, The Door, Orlando, Fla., 1977. Pres. Ashtabula County Young Republican Club, 1963-64 vestryman Holy Trinity Episcopal Ch., 1978—, sr. warden, 1979, 80; bd. dirs. Auburn Crises Center, 1976-78, chmn., 1978, chmn. bd. trustees 1979, 80. NSF fellow, 1964. Cert. clin. mental health counselor. Mem. Am., Ala. psychol. assns., Am. (chmn. licensure commn. 1977-80, chmn. profl. preparation and standards com. 1980—; Disting. Legis. Service award 1980), Ala. (Pres.'s award 1974, 75, 76, Disting. Service award 1978, Disting. Legis. Service award 1979) personnel and guidance assns., Nat. Juvenile Detention Assn., Assn. Univ. Adminstrs., Assn. Supervision and Curriculum Devel., Soc. Research Adminstrs., Phi Delta Kappa. Rotarian (chmn. Halloween carnival, Auburn 1974, dir. 1976-77). Author: (with J. Hansen and R. Stevic) Counseling: Theory and Process, 1972, 3d edit., 1980; (with J. Hansen and E. Smith) Group Counseling: Theory and Process, 1976, 2d edit., 1980; editor Ala. Personnel and Guidance Jour., 1975-79, column Research, Personnel and Guidance Jour., 1975-76. Contbr. articles to tech. lit. Home: 101 N Ryan St Auburn AL 36830

WARR, HOLLIS JEFFERSON, JR., educator; b. Amarillo, Tex., Oct. 16, 1949; s. Hollis Jefferson and Kathleen (Stevens) W.; B.A., Abilene Christian U., 1972, M.A., 1974; postgrad. (Bickle scholar), U. Tenn., 1976-78. Co-owner advt. agy. Drake & Warr Communication, Abilene, Tex., 1971-74; instr. communication Abilene Christian U., 1974-76, asst. prof., 1978—; teaching asst. communications U. Tenn., Knoxville, 1976-78; coordinator broadcasting, mgr. KACU Radio, 1978—; communications cons., 1974—; tchr. Dyass AFB, Abilene, part-time 1978-79. Mem. Assn. for Edn. in Journalism, Phi Kappa Phi, Kappa Tau Alpha. Republican. Mem. Ch. of Christ. Home: 733

Kenwood Way Abilene TX 79601 Office: Dept Communication Abilene Christian U Abilene TX 79699

WARR, (CLIFFORD) MICHAEL, educator, clergyman; b. Ellijay, Ga., Oct. 23, 1918; s. Clifford William and Dorothy O'Della (Kincaid) W.; A.B., Mercer U., 1944; M.Div., Southwestern Bapt. Theol. Sem., 1947, M.Ed., 1957; D.Min., Luther Rice Sem., Jacksonville, Fla., 1976; m. Sara Nelle Vaughn, Sept. 3, 1946; 1 son, Daniel Lee. Accountant, Home Owners Loan Corp., Atlanta, 1936-40; ordained to ministry Bapt. Ch., 1941; asso. pastor Met. Bapt. Ch., Washington, 1947-48; pastor Luther Rice Meml. Bapt. Ch., Washington, 1948-53, Coll. Av. Bapt. Ch., Fort Worth, 1953-57, First Bapt. Ch., Rock Hill, S.C., 1957-68; So. Bapt. evangelist, Atlanta, 1968-71; pastor Jackson Hill Bapt. Ch., Atlanta, 1971-77; mem. faculty Luther Rice Sem., 1977—. Guest tchr., numerous churchwide and area wide Bible confs. Trustee Southwestern Bapt. Theol. Sem., 1949-54, Midwestern Bapt. Theol. Sem., 1961-69; pres. Pastors Conf., Rock Hill, 1961-62, Fort Worth, 1955-56; bd. mgmt. Atlanta Downtown YMCA, mem. health club com., 1972-77, dir. mem. residence counseling, 1975-77. Mem. York County Bapt. Assn. (moderator 1963-64), Blue Key. Address: 7927 Rondeau Dr Jacksonville FL 32217

WARREN, BARRY ALAN, county ofcl.; b. Lenoir, N.C., Aug. 16, 1947; s. Rufus Gwyn and Hazel Lee (Dunn) W.; B.S., Appalachian State U., 1974, M.A., 1979; m. Judy Louise Greene, Apr. 12, 1975; children—Matthew Grant, Joseph Alan. Planning cons., Traffic & Planning Asso., Hickory, N.C., 1974-76; county planning dir. County of Caldwell, Lenoir, N.C., 1976—. Served with U.S. Army, 1966-69. Mem. Am. Inst. Planners, Nat. Assn. County Planning Dirs., Pi Gamma Mu. Democrat. Baptist. Home: Route 1 Box 579C Lenoir NC 28645 Office: PO Box 1078 Lenoir NC 28645

WARREN, CHARLENE, assn. ofcl.; b. Olney, Ill., Dec. 27, 1930; d. Charles Jerome and Dorothy Mae (Daubs) Warren; A.A., Stephens Coll., 1949; B.J., U. Tex., 1951; children—Lisa Booth, Martha Alison Booth. Advt. copywriter Radio Sta. KTAE, Taylor, Tex., 1952; with Hogg Found., U. Tex., Austin, 1965—, editor Hogg Found. News, 1971—, planning coordinator The Human Condition pub. radio series, 1971—. Active in civic and charity drives. Mem. Women in Communications (dir. 1973—), Alpha Chi Omega. Methodist (mem. adminstrv. bd. 1966-67). Home: 2102 Kipling Dr Austin TX 78752 Office: Box 7998 University Station Austin TX 78712

WARREN, CHARLES CALVIN, JR., farm machinery mfg. co. exec.; b. Harnett County, N.C., June 9, 1947; s. Charles Calvin and Ora Grave (Beasly) W.; A.A., Southwood Coll., Salemburg, N.C., 1968; postgrad Campbell Coll., Buies Creek, N.C., 1968-69; m. Lena Faye Faulkner, Aug. 29, 1976. Gen. mgr. Warren Tractor & Implement Co., Four Oaks, N.C., 1969-71; service mgr. Warren Bros. Tractor Co., Inc., Clinton, N.C., 1971-74, sales dept., 1974, gen. mgr., 1974—. Mem. North Grove Rescue Squad, 1973—. Mem. Carolina Farm Power and Equipment Assn. (dir. 1977-78). Office: 408 Smithfield Rd Clinton NC 28328

WARREN, DAVID GRANT, lawyer; b. Chgo., July 2, 1936; s. Kenneth L. and Sarah (Crain) W.; A.B., Miami U., Oxford, Ohio, 1958; J.D., Duke U., 1964; m. Marsha White, June 20, 1959; children—Douglas, Amy, Jeffrey. Admitted to N.C. bar, 1964; from instr. to prof. Inst. Govt., U. N.C., Chapel Hill, 1964-75; vis. prof. U. London, 1972-73; acting dir. N.C. Office Emergency Med. Services, 1973; dir. Health Policy Center, Georgetown U., 1975; prof. health adminstrn. Duke U. Med. Center, 1975—, acting dir. dept., 1979-80; dir. Triangle Hospice, Inc., 1978-81; mem. primary care com. Inst. Medicine, Nat. Acad. Scis., 1975-78. Pres., N.C. Health Council, 1975. Served as officer USNR, 1958-61. Mem. Am. Bar Assn., Am. Public Health Assn., Nat. Health Lawyers Assn., Am. Soc. Hosp. Attys., Royal Soc. Health, N.C. Bar Assn., N.C. Public Health Assn. (Disting. Service award 1967), N.C. Soc. Hosp. Attys. (pres. 1978). Republican. Episcopalian. Author: Problems in Hospital Law, 3d edit., 1978, A Legal Guide for Rural Health Programs, 1979; news and notes editor Jour. Health Politics, Policy and Law, 1977—. Home: 408 Lyons Rd Chapel Hill NC 27514 Office: Box 3018 Duke Univ Med Center Durham NC 27710

WARREN, FOREST GLEN, economist, agrl. cons.; b. Kouts, Ind., Dec. 15, 1913; s. Joseph Allen and Mary (Philpott) W.; B.S., Purdue U., 1937; Ph.D., U. Ill., 1945; m. Olive Louise Lauterbach, Oct. 17, 1942; children—Mary Anne, Richard Henry. Asst. to mgr. Grassmer Land Co., Kouts, Ind., 1932-33; asst. in agrl. econs. U. Ill., Urbana, 1937-41; economist Lend Lease Adminstrn. and Fgn. Econs. Adminstrn., 1942-45, U.S. Dept. Commerce, 1945-60; sr. economist Export-Import Bank U.S., Washington, 1960-66; economist U.S. Dept. Agr., Chgo., 1941-42, agrl. economist in charge farm mortgage credit research, Washington, 1966-73; agrl. cons., 1973—. Pres., Warren Lands, Inc., Kouts, 1948—. Mem. Am., Am. Farm econ. assns., Am. Soybean Assn., Nat. Econ. Club, Ceres, Sigma Xi, Gamma Sigma Delta, Alpha Chi Rho. Methodist. Club: Blue Ridge Mountain Country (Harpers Ferry, Va.). Contbr. articles to profl. publs. Home: 216 Lawton St Falls Church VA 22046

WARREN, FRANK RAYMOND, gen. contractor; b. Ft. Towsen, Okla., Mar. 7, 1915; s. Frank Homer and Ethel Estell (Mann) W.; student Lamar Jr. Coll., Beaumont, 1935, U. Tex., Austin, 1937; m. Sept. 17, 1938; m. Edith Van Riper; children—Carol Temple, Frank R., Elaine Sutherland. Research dir. Foley's of Houston, 1946-47; asst. v.p. Tenn. Gas Transmission Co., Houston, 1960-66; pres., chmn. bd. Mid-S. Corp. Tex., Pinehurst, 1967—, Central Testing Co. Inc., Lake Charles, La., 1969—; dir. Tex. Commerce Nat. Bank, Conroe; pres., chmn. bd. Mid-South Devel. Corp. Active Big Bros. Houston, Nat. Right to Work Com.; trustee Montreat-Anderson Coll., Montreat, N.C.; bd. dirs. Covenant Fellowship of Presbyterians, St. Louis. Named Outstanding Citizen of Houston Big Bros. Am., 1972. Presbyterian. Clubs: Panorama Country (pres. bd. dirs.), Rotary (Conroe). Home: 4 Winged Foot Dr Conroe TX 77301 Office: PO Box 428 Pinehurst TX 77362

WARREN, FREDERICK MARSHALL, ret. army officer, former judge; b. Newport, Ky., Aug. 23, 1903; s. William Ulysses and Katherine (Lampe) W.; A.B., LL.B., LL.M., LL.D., U. Cin.; m. Peggy Beaton, Feb. 20, 1926; 1 son, Frederick Marshall. Various positions with lumber and millwork cos., 1926-32; police judge, Southgate, Ky., 1932-35; admitted to Ky. bar, 1935; city atty., Southgate, 1935-40, 46-49; city solicitor, Newport, 1950-52; county judge, Campbell County, 1954-58; cons. to under sec. army, 1958; spl. asst. to asst. sec. army for manpower personnel and res. forces, 1959; recalled to active duty as maj. gen. U.S. Army, 1959; chief U.S. Army Res. and ROTC Affairs, 1959-63; circuit judge 17th Jud. Dist. Ky., Newport, 1964-76. Field rep. Alcoholic Beverage Control Bd. Ky., 1949; mem. U.S. Army Gen. Staff com. N.G. and army res. policy, 1953-56; mem. res. forces policy bd. Dept. Def., 1958-59. Served to col. AUS, 1941-46. Decorated D.S.M., Silver Star, Bronze Star, Army Commendation medal (U.S.); Croix de Guerre (France, Belgium). Mem. Am., Ky., Campbell County (past pres.) bar assns., Am. Legion, VFW, DAV, Assn. U.S. Army, Res. Officers Assn. (past nat. v.p.), Mil. Order World Wars. Mason, Elk. Home: 20 Crow Hill Fort Thomas KY 41075

WARREN, HENRY LEE, utility exec.; b. Humprey, Ark., Aug. 27, 1940; s. Henry and Rissie (Combs) W.; B.S., U. Ark., Pine Bluff, 1968, M.S., 1979; m. Edna Jean Henderson, Aug. 21, 1960; children—Jacqueline, Gregory, Sandra. Design asst. engring. Ark. Power & Light, Pine Bluff, 1968-70, methods analyst, 1970-74, office mgr., 1974-77, mgr. equal employment, Little Rock, 1978, mgr. employment and recruiting, 1978, dist. mgr., 1978-80, dir. internal auditing, 1980—. Pres., St. Peters Parents Tchrs. Conf., 1972-73; mem. Engring. Explorer Post Com., 1978—; bd. dirs. Sr. Citizens Activities Today. Recipient Recognition of Appreciation, Pulaski County Comprehensive Edn. Tng. Act, 1978. Mem. Edison Elec. Inst., Ark. Personnel Assn., S.W. Placement Assn. Republican. Baptist. Home: 24 McKee St North Little Rock AR 72116 Office: Ark Power & Light 5th and Broadway Little Rock AR 72203

WARREN, HERBERT ALBERT, lawyer; b. Birmingham, Ala., Dec. 18, 1922; s. Herbert Allen and Ethel Virginia (Price) W.; student Auburn U., 1940-43; B.S., U. Chgo., 1947; LL.B. magna cum laude, U. Miami, 1951; m. Marjorie Mathis, June 6, 1953; children—Richard Alan, Pamela Jayne. Admitted to Fla. bar, 1951, U.S. Supreme Ct. bar, 1960; law clk., U.S. Dist. Judge J. Holland, 1950-51; mem. firm Carr & Warren, 1951-74; individual practice, 1974—. Lectr., U. Miami Law Sch., 1951-54. Served with USAF, 1943-46. Mem. Fla., Am. bar assns., Fla. Acad. Trial Lawyers, Am. Trial Lawyers Assn., Phi Delta Phi. Presbyn. (deacon). Lion, Kiwanian. Club: Miami Shores Country. Home: 398 NE 100th St Miami Shores FL 33131 Office: 1401 Brickell Ave Suite 604 Miami FL 33131

WARREN, JOHN LEAMING, ret. air force officer; b. Holdenville, Okla., Nov. 6, 1906; s. Frank L. and Annie G. (Leaming) W.; student U. Mo., Okla. U., 1923-26; LL.B., Cumberland U., 1928; m. Shelagh D. MacKey, Apr. 30, 1949; 1 dau., Valery Anne. Admitted to Okla. bar, 1928; mem. law firm Warren & Warren, Holdenville, 1928-40. Served with USAF, 1940-63, ret. Decorated Legion of Merit, Republic Korea Mil. Merit Choongmoo medal. Mem. SAR, Okla. Bar Assn., Kappa Alpha, Episcopalian. Club: St. Petersburg Yacht. Home: 858 Placido Way Saint Petersburg FL 33704

WARREN, LAWRENCE DALE, ins. co. owner; b. Scottsburg, Ind., Jan. 4, 1944; s. Lionel G. and Edna Marie (Hollin) W.; student Purdue U., 1961-65; m. Esther S. Warren; children—Alana Kay, Douglas Dale, Kirsten. Owner, pres. Products Unltd., Inc., Houston, 1967-69; territory mgr. W. R. Grace & Co., Houston, 1970-76; owner L. Warren & Co., Houston, 1965—; pres. Warren Internat., Inc., 1976—; dir. Delta Gulf Industries, Houston. Mem. Producers Council, Inc. (pres. 1975-76), Constrn. Specifications Inst. (membership chmn. 1973-74). Republican. Methodist. Home: 506 Magic Oaks Dr Spring TX 77373 Office: 3400 Montrose Suite 718 Houston TX 77006 also PO Box 3611 Houston TX 77001

WARREN, LILLIE BELLE WATSON, real estate exec.; b. Ico, Ark., Feb. 24, 1909; d. Finis Bascum and Maude Eleanor (Ashe) Watson; B.S., U. Central Ark., 1933; m. Truman John Warren, Sept. 3, 1939 (dec. 1964); children—Mary Louise Warren Wilson, Truman John, Eleanor Ruth. Tchr. home econs. Mabelvale (Ark.) High Sch., 1929-33; asst. buyer, mgr. dept. Gus Blass Stores, Ark., 1933-39; pres. Warren Enterprises, Inc., Morrilton, Ark., 1964—. Leader, Cub Scouts Am., 1952-60; leader Girl Scouts U.S.A., 1951-62, mem. 10 county council, 1952-62; chmn. bldg. com. for preservation nat. historic places in Conway County, Ark. Arts Center, 1973—; pres. Morrilton Garden Club, 1940-42, Pathfinder Club, 1939-43; active conservationist of historic places and wild life. Mem. Morrilton Retail Mchts. Assn., Ark. Retail Mchts. Assn., Morrilton C. of C., U.S. C. of C., Nat. Bus. Assn., Small Bus. Assn. Ark. Democrat. Presbyterian. Home: 201 W Church St Morrilton AR 72110 Office: PO Box 517 Morrilton AR 72110

WARREN, MARYLOU DENNY, nurse; b. Buffalo Valley, Tenn., June 13, 1919; d. William Timothy and Effie Dora (Rippetoe) Denny; R.N., U. Md., 1946, B.S. in Nursing, 1950, M.S. in Nursing (pub. health grantee), 1963; postgrad. U. Md., 1963-65, Cath. U., 1965-66; m. Chesley Warren, Dec. 25, 1950; children—Linda Barksdale, Micki Warren Knott. Staff nurse, head nurse Dozier Hosp., Balt., 1946-48, supr. maternity, 1948-50; dir. nursing service, Carrollton, Ga., 1950-53; instr. Sch. of Nursing, City Hosp., Balt., 1953-56; faculty coordinator Sch. of Nursing, Church Hosp., Balt., 1956-63; dir. nursing service, Church Hosp., Hanover, Pa., 1970-77; dir. nursing service Cookeville (Tenn.) Gen. Hosp., 1978—, also mem. adv. bd. lic. practical nurse program; mem. faculty Tenn. Tech. U. Recipient Nurse of Yr. award Md. chpt. ARC, 1963; registered nurse, Md., Pa., Tenn. Mem. Am. Hosp. Assn., Tenn. Hosp. Assn., Nursing Service Adminstrns. Soc., Sigma Theta Tau. Democrat. Mem. Ch. of Christ. Club: Rose Growers. Home: Route 1 Box 44 Baxter TN 38544 Office: Cookeville Gen Hosp 142 W 5th St Cookeville TN 38501

WARREN, PHILIP COLLINS, architect; b. Asheville, N.C., Jan. 12, 1936; s. Ralph Brookshire and Virginia Rives (Collins) W.; B.Arch., U. Fla., 1960; m. Mary Alice McDowell, Apr. 14, 1960; 1 son, Collins McDowell. Partner, Warren & Hopson, architects, Titusville, Fla., 1963-64, Warren & Paras, architects, Tampa, Fla., 1967; owner, architect Philip Warren, Tampa, Ft. Myers, Fla., 1968, 75—; partner Warren & Fisher, architects, Ft. Myers, 1969-75; founder One Hundred and Eighty Degrees, solar energy research co. Bd. dirs. Montessori Sch. Ft. Myers, 1973-75. Served with AUS, 1961-62. Named Kiwanian of Year, Kiwanis Club, Ft. Myers, 1972. Democrat. Roman Catholic. Builder, occupant solar energy research house. Home and office: Route 15 Box 900A Nalle Grade Rd North Fort Myers FL 33903

WARREN, RICHARD ERNEST, advt. agy. exec., producer; b. Managua, Nicaragua, Jan. 27, 1942; s. Ernest Reynolds and Marina (Echevirra) W.; B.C.S., Loyola U. South, 1970; m. Cindee A. Welch, Sept. 13, 1975; children—Deborah Marie, James Kendrick. Sales office mgr. Avoncraft div. Avondale Shipyards, Inc., 1964-68; bus. mgr. Info. Council Ams., New Orleans, 1968-69, exec. dir., 1969-71, internat. dir. gen., 1971-74, pub. affairs cons., 1974-75; advt. account exec. Ladas Agy., 1974-77; regional mgr. Mace Advt. Agy, Inc., New Orleans, 1977-79; regional account exec. J. Walter Thompson, Atlanta, 1979—; editor Singles Critique, 1974—; pres. Warren Enterprises; exec. dir. La. Epilepsy Assn., 1976-77; cons. Patrolman's Assn. New Orleans, 1969-76; producer Spirit 76 internat. TV series, 1973, TV series Sportsman's Paradise, 1976-77; cons. Metro Public Relations, 1973-74, Michael The Archangel Police and Fire Legion, 1976. Organizer, Jefferson Parish Am. Revolution Townhall Bicentennial Program, 1973-74; coordinator Freedoms Found-Young Men's Bus. Club Awards Presentation, 1972-73; celebrity chmn. Miss New Orleans Pageant, 1973-74; judge Baton Rouge Pageant, 1973; bd. dirs. Muscular Dystrophy Assn., Goals to Grow Found., Crippled Children's Hosp. Served with USAF, 1960-64. Recipient Citation of Merit, Profl. Bus. Women Am., 1970; Outstanding Bur. Chmn. award Young Men's Bus. Club, 1969; certificate of Appreciation, New Orleans Pub. Sch. System, 1971; Merit citation Am. Fedn. Police, 1972, Loyalty Day award VFW, 1970; Merit citation Execs. Club New Orleans, 1970, certificate of Appreciation, Kiwanis Club, 1969; Merit award Info. Council Am., 1968; Plaque of Appreciation, Alton Ochsner Med. Found., 1970; plaque of Merit, Muscular Distrophy Assn. Am. Jerry Lewis Telethon, 1972, 73; Key to City, certificate of Merit, New Orleans, 1973, Westwego, 1977, Hammond, 1975, Houma, 1975, Morgan City, 1977, Lafayette, 1977, Alexandria, 1977, Shreveport, 1977, (all La.); named hon. sheriff various La. Parishes, also hon. La. atty. gen., hon. State Senator. Mem. Am. Legion, Am. Fedn. Police, Italian Cultural Soc., Radio Free Asia, Info. Council Ams., SAR, Adminstrv. Mgmt. Soc., So. Karate Assn., Young Men's Bus. Club Greater New Orleans, New Orleans C. of C. (Americanism com. 1969-72), Loyola U. Alumni Assn., Cross Keys. Club: Masons. Contbr. articles to profl. jours. Office: PO Box 53186 New Orleans LA 70153

WARREN, RICHARD LYNN, media producer, dir.; b. St. Johns, Mich., Aug. 12, 1951; s. Donald Clifton and Loreta Irene (Binger) W.; student Mich. State U., 1969-70; m. Nina Louise Carper, Jan. 11, 1974; children—Gretchen Christina Carr, Gary Keith Carr, Diana Lynn Warren. Asst. to press sec. for cinematography, Office of Gov., State of Mich., Lansing, 1970; enlisted in U.S. Navy, 1970; dir. multi-media prodns. center Navy Recruiting Exhibit Center, Washington, 1971-75; leading petty officer multi-media projects div. U.S. Navy Atlantic Fleet Audio-Visual Command, Norfolk, Va., 1976—; asst. to press secy. Republican Party of Mich. Central Com., 1968. Recipient commendations from comdg. officer Naval Air Tech. Tng. Center, Jacksonville, Fla., 1971, dir.-leader U.S. Navy band, Washington, 1975, comdg. officer Tactical Support Wing One, 1977, comdg. officer Attack Squadron 35, Norfolk, 1977. Recipient Gold and Silver medals N.Y. Internat. Film and TV Festival, 1977. Mem. Audio Engring. Soc., Nat. Press Photographers Assn. Republican. Pentecostal Christian. Contbr. multi-media presentation J.F. Kennedy Center for Performing Arts, Washington, 1975. Address: 408 Kingswood Pl Virginia Beach VA 23452

WARREN, RUSSELL GLEN, univ. adminstr.; b. Balt., Apr. 29, 1942; s. Clarence and Kathryn B. (Butler) W.; B.S. in Bus. Adminstrn., U. Richmond, 1964 Ph.D. in Econs., Tulane U., 1968. Asst. prof. econs. U. Richmond (Va.), 1972-74, dean Richmond Coll., 1974-75, asst. to pres. and provost, asso. prof., 1976-78; v.p. acad. affairs U. Montevallo (Ala.), 1978—. Served to capt. Fin. Corps., U.S. Army, 1969-71. Decorated Army Commendation medal. Named Outstanding Young Man of Va., Va. Jaycees, 1976; Am. Council on Edn. fellow, 1975-76. Mem. Omicron Delta Kappa, Beta Gamma Sigma, Omicron Delta Epsilon, Phi Eta Sigma, Tau Kappa Alpha, Alpha Tau Omega, Alpha Kappa Psi. Author: Antitrust in Theory and Practice, 1976; contbr. numerous articles to profl. jours. Office: Office Acad Vice Pres U Montevallo Montevallo AL 35115

WARREN, SAMUEL KELLY, elec. products co. exec.; b. Chesapeake, Va., Apr. 5, 1946; s. Joseph Kelly and Jessie Neal W.; B.A. in Bus. Mgmt., Coll. William and Mary, 1971; m. Lois Gurkin, Nov. 24, 1968. Mktg. ops. analyst Gen. Electric Co., Portsmouth, Va., 1971-72; product cost analyst Gen. Electric Co., Portsmouth, 1972-73, mgr. engring. analysis, 1973-75, mgr. product cost estimating and engring. analysis, 1975—. Chmn. Concerned Citizens for Constl. Govt., 1977—; mem. Chesapeake Republican Com. Served with USAF, 1964-68. Decorated Air Force Commendation medal. Republican. Baptist. Home: 3009 Golden Hind Rd Chesapeake VA 23321 Office: Gen Electric Co College Blvd Portsmouth VA 23705

WARREN, THOMAS LARRY, ins. agt.; b. Tampa, Fla., Sept. 16, 1942; s. Thomas J. and Doris M. Warren; B.S. in Bus. Adminstrn., Central Fla. U., 1975; m. Janice L. Childress, Aug. 29, 1962; children—Thomas L., Cheryl Kay. Mgr., Household Fin. Corp., St. Petersburg, Fla., 1964-65; sales rep., mgr. Met. Life Ins., Clearwater and Daytona Beach, Fla., 1966-77; v.p. George W. Link & Assos. Inc., Clearwater, 1977-79; gen. agt. Gulf Life Ins., Clearwater, 1979—. Served with USMC, 1960-64. Mem. Deland C. of C., Deland Jaycees, Nat. Life Underwriters Assn., Fla. Life Underwriters Assn. Democrat. Baptist. Home: 1957 E Druid Rd Clearwater FL 33516 Office: PO Box 1728 Clearwater FL 33517

WARREN, WILLIAM DAVID, data processor; b. Austin, Tex., Sept. 3, 1931; s. William Frederick and Eleanor Faver (Hill) W.; B.A., U. Tex., 1957; certificate data processing Inst. for Certification Computer Profls., 1963. Tabulating equipment operator data processing div. U. Tex., Austin, 1958-61, computer programmer, systems analyst, 1961—. Served with AUS, 1952-53. Mem. Data Processing Mgmt. Assn (sec. Austin chpt. 1969-70), Am. Philatelic Soc. (life), U. Tex. Ex-Students Assn. (life), Order DeMolay (sr.). Episcopalian. Club: Stamp (pres. 1951-52) (Austin). Home: 1502 Hardouin Ave Austin TX 78703

WARREN, WILLIAM HERBERT, educator; b. Newport News, Va., July 21, 1924; s. William Herbert and Helen Virginia (Cofer) W.; B.S., U. Richmond, 1948; M.S., Purdue U., 1950, Ph.D., 1969; m. Mary Virginia Shaw, Sept. 11, 1948; children—Katherine Warren Butt, Constance, Suzanne, David, John. Dir. indsl. relations Albemarle Paper Co. div. Ethyl Corp., Richmond, Va., 1961-64, personnel mgr., 1954-61, plant mgr., 1964-66; prof. Purdue U., West Lafayette, Ind., 1966-70; dir. labor relations Newport News Shipbldg. Co. div. Tenneco (Va.), 1970-72; prof. bus. adminstrn. Coll. William and Mary, Williamsburg, Va., 1972—; newspaper columnist, Lafayette, Ind., 1967-70. Served with USNR, 1943-46. Named Young Man of Yr., Roanoke Rapids (N.C.) Jr. C. of C., 1957. Mem. Am. Psychol. Assn., Acad. Mgmt., Sigma Xi, Kappa Sigma. Republican. Baptist. Club: Kiwanis. Home: 110 Bowstring Dr Williamsburg VA 23185 Office: Coll William Mary Williamsburg VA 23185

WARRICK, TOM POWELL, ednl. program analyst, govt. ofcl.; b. Kingsport, Tenn., Dec. 9, 1934; s. John Paul and Ruth Thorne (Eanes) W.; B.S., E. Tenn. State Coll., 1961; postgrad. Emory U., 1962; tchr. cert. Ga. State Coll., 1963; YMCA dir. cert. Springfield Coll. Extension, 1966; M.P.H. (John R. Mott YMCA scholar), U. Hawaii, 1973; m. Shirley Janet Sanders, Aug. 28, 1962; children—Tom Powell, Wesley Sanders, Melissa Grace. Tchr. pub. schs., Dekalb County, Ga., 1962-64; tchr., counselor Brandon Hall Sch., Dunwoody, Ga., 1964-65; field sec. Va. Dist. YMCA So. Area Council, 1965-67; program dir. Armed Services YMCA, Honolulu, 1967-71; residence program dir. Atherton U. YMCA, Honolulu, 1971-73; drug/alcohol edn. cons. Human Resource Mgmt. Center, Pearl Harbor, Hawaii, 1973-75; personnel research psychologist, chief naval tech. tng. Naval Air Sta., Millington, Tenn., 1975—. Mem. regional tng. com., drug/alcohol abuse cons. ARC Community Programs; mem. gov.'s Com. on Substance Abuse; mem. sch. bd. Immanuel Lutheran Ch.; v.p., pres. Parent Tchr. Group, Immanuel and Eastdale Luth. Schs., 1976, 78; cubmaster Boy Scouts Am., 1975-77. Mem. Am. Soc. Tng. and Devel., Am. Pub. Health Assn., Tenn. Pub. Health Assn., Alumni Assn. Sch. Pub. Health U. Hawaii, Western Govtl. Research Assn., Common Cause. Democrat. Editor: Y's Owl Newsletter of Va. Dist. YMCA, 1965-67; author publs. in field. Home: 7115 Hilshire Dr Memphis TN 38134 Office: Chief Naval Tech Tng Code 0164 Memphis (75) Millington TN 38054

WARRIOR, ROY WILLIAMS, educator; b. Checotah, Okla., Mar. 18, 1941; s. Zenophon and Roberta (Edwards) W.; A.B., Northeastern State Coll., 1967, M.Ed., 1974; m. Nora Jean Conard, Aug. 20, 1968; children—Karen D., Ronora A., Roy Williams. Tchr. elementary schs., Summit, Okla., 1967-68; tchr. social studies, Wichita, Kans., 1968-70; edn. services asst., Army Edn. Center, Ft. Leavenworth,

Kans., 1970-71, edn. specialist, Ft. Leavenworth, 1971-72, edn. specialist, Ednl. Devel. Br., Ft. Sam Houston, Tex., 1972-75, edn. services officer, W. Germany, 1975-78. Served with U.S. Army, 1960-63. Recipient certificate of achievement, Dept. Army, 1973. Mem. Am. Personnel and Guidance Assn. and European Br. Democrat. Baptist. Clubs: Toastmasters, Alpha Phi Alpha. Office: Ed Dev Br PSD DPCA Ft Sam Houston TX 78234

WARTA, CLARENCE EMMETT, psychologist; b. Lindenhurst, N.Y., Aug. 20, 1928; s. Anthony J. and Katherine Marie W.; A.B., Duke U., 1949; M.A., Appalachian State U., 1972; Ph.D., U. Ga., 1975; m. Dorothy L. Waldeck, Dec. 7, 1952; children—Stephanie Anne, Melanie Erna, Keith Joseph. With Warta Motors, Inc., Merrick, N.Y., 1954-69, Sales mgr., officer, dir., 1954-69; partner Kay-Tone Realty, Merrick, 1958—; counselor-supr. N.C. Div. Vocat. Rehab., Statesville, N.C., 1970-74; pvt. practice psychology, Hickory, N.C., 1975—. Bd. dirs. Foothills Mental Health Center, Morganton, N.C. Mem. Am. Psychol. Assn., Am. Personnel and Guidance Assn., Nat. Rehab. Assn., Internat. Assn. Applied Psychology, Am. Assn. Marriage and Family Therapy, N.C. Psychol. Assn., Am. Soc. Adlerian Psychologists. Office: 1015 2d St NE Hickory NC 28601

WARTON, JERRY LEE, drilling co. exec.; b. Olney, Tex., Aug. 21, 1930; s. Jesse Lee and Lola Mae (Seals) W.; m. Nina Hord, June 17, 1976; children—Michael Lee, James Lee, Jana Marque; stepchildren—Gregg Hand, Rodney Hand. With Warton Drilling Co., Odessa, Tex., 1946—, pres., 1977—. Republican. Home: 6315 Nevada St Ponderosa Estates Odessa TX 79763 Office: PO Box 3747 Odessa TX 79760

WARYAS, CAROL LYNN BROWN, educator; b. Flint, Mich., June 14, 1946; d. William Robert and Mary Louise (Lastrapes) Brown; B.A., U. Mich., 1968; M.A., Ohio U., 1969; Ph.D., U. Kans., 1974; m. Apr. 26, 1968; 1 dau., Melissa. Research asst. Bur. of Child Research, U. Kans., Parsons, 1971-74, research asso. and asst. prof. Dept. Speech and Drama, 1974-77; asst. prof. Dept. Communicative Disorders, U. Miss., University, 1977-80, asso. prof., 1980—. Cert. in clin. competence and speech pathology Am. Speech and Hearing Assn., 1973. Mem. Am. Speech and Hearing Assn. (chmn. com. on mental deficiency 1979-80), Am. Assn. Mental Deficiency (pres. Miss. chpt. 1980), Assn. for Retarded Citizens, Council on Exceptional Children, Phi Beta Kappa. Roman Catholic. Contbr. articles to profl. books and jours. Home: 204 Beacon Point Oxford MS 38655 Office: Dept Communicative Disorders Univ of Miss University MS 38677

WASDIN, JOHN TREADWELL, lawyer; b. Atlanta, Jan. 13, 1937; s. Gelon Etheridge and Marion Treadwell (Brown) W.; B.B.A., U. Ga., 1958, LL.B., 1960; postgrad. Oglethorpe U., 1963, Ga. State U., 1960-62; m. Brenda Elaine Lewis, Dec. 28, 1972; children—Marion Gelene, William Scott. Accountant, atty. firm G.E. Wasdin, Sr., Bremen, Ga., 1960-70; admitted to Ga. bar, 1960; individual practice law, Bremen, 1970—; pres., dir. Bremen Service Co., 1960—; dir. Comml. Bank, Tallapoosa, Ga., 1967—. Mem. Am. Bar Assn. (taxation sect.), State Bar Ga., Atlanta Bar Assn., Practicing Law Inst., Tallapoosa Jud. Circuit, Am. Judicature Soc., Phi Delta Theta, Phi Delta Phi, Bremen Jr. C. of C. (founder 1960). Baptist. Clubs: Athletic, City (Atlanta); Shriners (pres. W.Ga. 1965); Lions (dir. Bremen, 1962,76); Sunset Hills Country, Masons. Home: 347 Parrish Ave Bremen GA 30110 Office: PO Drawer 645 629 S Buchanan St Bremen GA 30110

WASHER, FRANCIS GENE, newspaper exec.; b. Logan County, Ky., July 9, 1940; s. Thomas Francis Washer and Martha (Miller) Hurt; B.S., Austin Peay State U., 1979; div.; children—Thomas Francis II, Jonathan Robert Winters. Cub reporter Clarksville (Tenn.) Leaf-Chronicle, 1963-64, sports editor, 1964-77, mng. editor, 1977—. Recipient several awards as sports editor and mng. editor. Mem. AP Mng. Editors, Tenn. AP Mng. Editors, Tenn. Press Assn. Episcopalian. Club: Montgomery County Sportsman's (founder, pres. 1976-79). Contbr. articles to mags. and newspapers. Home: 2272 Wildwood Clarksville TN 37040 Office: 200 Commerce Clarksville TN 37040

WASHINGTON, FRED GEORGE, health care adminstr.; b. Edwardsville, Ill., Oct. 6, 1933; s. Willie and Ada W.; B.S., Ill. Wesleyan U., 1961; M. Hosp. Adminstrn., U. Minn., 1973; m. Florence A. Johnson, Feb. 19, 1967. Personnel mgmt. specialist VA Med. Center, Hines, Ill., 1966-67, Mpls., 1967-70; spl. asst. to dir. VA Center, Fargo, N.D., 1973-74; hosp. adminstrn. specialist VA Central Office, Washington, 1974—; adv. for health care affairs White House Staff, 1974. Mayor, Town of Fort Snelling (Minn.), 1969-70. Served with USMC, 1951-54. Decorated Purple Heart. Mem. U. Minn. Program in Hosp. and Health Care Adminstrn. Alumni Assn., Am. Hosp. Assn., Assn. Mil. Surgeons U.S., Am. Mgmt. Assn., N.Y. Acad. Scis. Baptist. Home: 2335 N Quantico St Arlington VA 22205 Office: 810 Vermont Ave NW Washington DC 20420

WASHINGTON, WILLIE BARNARD, athletic dir.; b. Joiner, Ark., Oct. 27, 1951; s. George Milton and Dessie Lee Washington; B.S., Tougaloo (Miss.) Coll., 1974; M.Edn.S. in Phys. Edn., Jackson (Miss.) State U., 1976; m. Genoise Marcia Gaylor, Dec. 21, 1975; 1 son, Willie Torrain. Profl. basketball player, Brussels, 1974-75; asst. basketball coach Barber-Scotia Coll., Concord, N.C., 1975-76; athletic dir. Allen U., Columbia, S.C., 1976—, head varsity basketball coach, 1976—, asst. prof. health, phys. edn. and recreation, 1976—. Recipient Outstanding Coll. Athlete Am. award, 1973, 74, Herff Jones award, 1974, Community Service award St. Luke's Community Center, Columbia, 1979. Mem. S.C. Athletic Dirs. Assn. (exec. bd.), S.C. Alliance Health, Phys. Edn. and Recreation, Phi Beta Sigma. Author papers in field. Home: 3215 Truman St Columbia SC 29204 Office: 1530 Harden St Columbia SC

WASNESS, DONALD STANFORD, elec. engr.; b. Northwood, N.D., Aug. 17, 1932; s. Ingvald and Bertha (Bjerke) W.; diploma in Electronics, N.D. State Sch. Sci., 1952, pre-engring. diploma, 1958; B.S., N.D. State Coll., 1960; m. Dolores Marlene Olson, Sept. 7, 1957; children—James Donald, Marlene Rose. Instrumentation engr. Hercules Powder Co., Allegany Ballistics Lab., Cumberland, Md., 1960-62, engring. supr., 1962-68; sr. project engr. Hoechst Fibers Industries, Spartanburg, S.C., 1968-78, asst. plant elec. and instrumentation engr., 1978—. Liaison officer Allegany County CD Agy.-Instrument Soc. Am., 1962; adviser Jr. Achievement, 1973-75; consumer panel mem. U. S.C., 1975—; trustee St. Paul United Methodist Ch., 1973-75, 77-79, chmn., 1975, mem. adminstrv. bd., 1968—, pres. Mens Club, 1969. Served with AUS, 1952-54. Registered profl. engr., S.C. Mem. Instrument Soc. Am. (program chmn. 1963-64, 75—, v.p. 1964-65, 74-75, pres. 1965-66), Am. Bus. Club (sec. chpt. 1979-80), Soaring Soc. Am. Republican. Home: 462 Webber Rd Spartanburg SC 29302 Office: PO Box 5887 Spartanburg SC 29301

WASSALL, DONALD EVERETT, mfg. co. exec.; b. St. Louis, July 19, 1926; s. Clifford Green and Edith Idel (Tuttle) W.; B.S. in E.E., Washington U., 1949; m. Marilyn Dufficy, Sept. 28, 1968; 1 son, Michael. Research engr. Petrolite Corp., St. Louis, 1949-54; engring. mgr. Bendix Co., Calif., 1954-60; research mgr. Lockheed Electric, 1960-63; dir. sales and mktg. United Control, Seattle, 1963-64; mgr. product mgmt. Ampex, Culver City, Calif. and Reading, Eng., 1964-69; v.p. internat. Tally Corp., Kent, Wash., also Reading, 1969-70; European gen. mgr. Electronics Assos. Inc., N.J. and Eng., 1971-74; v.p., gen. mgr. Electronics Corp. Am., Cambridge, Mass., also Brussels, Belgium, 1974-77; pres., chief operating officer Fluid Measurement Systems, Inc., Tulsa, Okla., 1977—; lectr. No. Poly., London, 1968. Served with U.S. Navy, 1944-46. Mem. IEEE, Am. Mgmt. Assn., Electronic Industry Assn., Am. Inst. Mgmt., Petroleum Electric Suppliers Assn., Pi Mu Epsilon. Roman Catholic. Home: 2317 North Union Pl Tulsa OK 74127 Office: PO Box 2903 Tulsa OK 74101

WASSALL, HARRY WILLIAM, III, petroleum geologist; b. N.Y.C., May 28, 1921; s. Harry and Hattie (Leon) W.; B.S. in Petroleum Geology, U. Tulsa, 1942; m. Gladys Bello del Rio, Feb. 28, 1947; children—Richard, Rosana. Subsurface geologist Shell Oil Co., Wichita Falls, Tex., 1946-49; field geologist Gulf Oil Co., Havana, Cuba, 1950-55; prin., founder Petrocons. S.A., Geneva, Switzerland, 1955—; internat. energy cons. Served as lt. USNR, 1942-45. Mem. Am. Assn. Petroleum Geologists. Republican. Home: 5345 SW 92d St Miami FL 33156 Office: 1307 Capital National Bank Bldg Houston TX 77002

WASSOM, JOHN STANLEY, biologist; b. Rockwood, Tenn., May 1, 1941; s. Jess Raymond and Hazel Millicent (Garrison) W.; student Western Ky. State U., 1959-61, Tenn. Technol. U., 1962-63; m. Judith Ann Owings, Dec. 21, 1963; 1 dau., Zoe Millicent. Research asso. biology div. Oak Ridge Nat. Lab., 1965-69, dir. Environ. Mutagen Info. Center, 1969—. Served as lt. Chem. Corps, U.S. Army, 1963-65. Mem. Am. Coll. Toxicology, Environ. Mutagen Soc., N.Y. Acad. Sci., Sigma Xi. Methodist. Mem. editorial bd. Mutation Research (Genetic Toxicology Testing), 1976—, Environ. Mutagenesis, 1978—; asso. editor Mutation Research (Reviews in Genetic Toxicology), 1975—. Office: Environmental Mutegan Information Center Bldg 9224 PO Box Y Oak Ridge Nat Lab PO Box Y Oak Ridge TN 37830

WASSUM, CHARLES STEVENS, III, physician; b. Richmond, Va., July 28, 1939; s. Charles Stevens and Elizabeth Venable (Warriner) W.; B.A., Washington and Lee U., 1961; M.D., U. Va., 1965; postgrad. U. Wash., 1966-67, U. Calif., Berkeley, 1968; m. Ruth Anna-Stine Eriksson, July 18, 1964; children—Michelle, Charles, Christopher, Mary, Christina. Intern, U. Va., Charlottesville, 1965-66; resident U. Wash., Seattle, 1960-67, Kern County Hosp., Bakersfield, Calif., 1968-69; practice medicine specializing in pediatrics, Johnson City, Tenn., 1972-79, Marion, Va., 1979—; mem. staff Smyth County Community Hosp. Served with U.S. Army, 1970-72. Diplomate Am. Bd. Pediatrics. Mem. Assn. Am. Physicians and Surgeons, Tenn. Med. Assn. Mormon. Home: Water Mill Rd Marion VA 24354 Office: Smuth County Community Hosp Marion VA 24354

WATERS, BETTY HALE (MRS. JULIAN LAFAY WATERS), educator; b. Atlanta, Dec. 21, 1927; d. Robert Lorin and Blondyne (Cooper) Hale; Mus.B., Converse Coll., 1949; M.Elementary Edn. (Optimist scholar 1966), Ga. State U., 1968, Edn. Specialist (Delta Kappa Gamma state fellow 1970, internat. fellow 1972), 1971; Ed.D., U. Ga., 1973; m. Julian Lafay Waters, June 3, 1950; 1 son, John Robert (dec.). Classroom tchr. Dekalb County (Ga.) Schs., 1956-70, in-service lectr., 1965-68, learning disabilities clinician, 1968-70; mem. faculty, coll. supr. Oglethorpe U., Atlanta, 1970-71; coll. supr. U. Ga., Athens, 1971-73; dir.-tchr. learning disabilities program Newton County (Ga.) Pub. Schs., 1973-75; faculty Coll. Edn., N. Ga. Coll., Dahlonega, 1975-79; tchr. Lanier Sch., Gainesville, Ga., 1979—. Co-chmn. Julian L. Waters Dr. For Retarded Children, Decatur, 1962; pres. Lumpkin County ARC, 1977—. Recipient Tchrs. medal Freedoms Found., 1965, Tchr. of Yr. award Dogwood chpt. Council Exceptional Children, 1970. Mem. Assn. Childhood Edn. Internat. (local pres. 1964-66, state pres., mem. publs. com. 1977—), AAUW, Assn. for Supervision and Curriculum Devel., Assn. Tchr. Educators, Assn. Children with Learning Disabilities, Delta Kappa Gamma, Kappa Delta Epsilon. Mem. publs. com. Childhood Edn. Jour. Home: PO Box 456 Dahlonega GA 30533 Office: Hall County Schs Gainesville GA 30501

WATERS, ELEANOR LOIS YOUMANS, librarian; b. Waycross, Ga., Aug. 25, 1928; d. Jacob Edward and Hazel Lois (Hendrix) Youmans; student Perry Bus. Sch., 1944-45, U. Wis., 1966, Loyola U., 1968; m. Thomas Edward Waters, Mar. 28, 1948; children—Belinda Waters Wheeler, Thomas Bruce, Sharon Lois Waters Faircloth, Steven Edward. Sec. to supt. shipbuilding Brunswick Marine Constrn. Corp., Brunswick, Ga., 1945; library technician Nat. Marine Fisheries Service, Brunswick Lab., 1959-73, Ga. Dept. Nat. Resources Coastal Fisheries, 1974—. Recipient Superior Performance award U.S. Dept. Interior, 1965, 68. Mem. Ga. Library Assn., Soc. for Bibliography Natural History. Presbyterian. Home: 2606 Starling St Brunswick GA 31520 Office: Ga Dept Natural Resources Coastal Fisheries Div 1200 Glynn Ave Brunswick GA 31520

WATERS, HARRY GARDNER, indsl. engr.; b. Norwich, Conn., Sept. 20, 1908; s. Frank G. and Leanora (Hampson) W.; LL.B., U. Conn., 1932; Asso. Sci., New Haven Jr. Coll., 1946; m. Gwendolyn F. Thomas, Feb. 11, 1933 (dec. 1964); children—Noranne Gardner Waters Moore, John Thomas, Harry Gardner; m. 2d, Anne Howard, 1966. Clk., treasury dept. State of Conn., 1932-38; time study engr. Dravo Corp., Wilmington, Del., 1942-43; time study and method engr. Cuno Engring. Co., Meriden, Conn., 1943-44; chief methods engr. Corbin Screw div. Am. Hardware Corp., New Britain, Conn., 1944-46; indsl. engr. Miller Co., Meriden, Conn., 1946-48; mgmt. cons. Albert B. Cord Co., Cin., 1948-58; propr. H.G. Waters & Assos., 1959-80; dir. health and safety Scholze Tannery, Chattanooga, Tenn., 1971—; cons. profl. indsl. engr., 1958-71. Registered profl. engr., Ga. Mem. Am. Soc. Safety Engrs. (profl. mem., charter mem. cons. div.), Am. Indsl. Hwy. Soc. (asso. Tennessee Valley chpt.), Engrs. Club of Chattanooga. Presbyterian. Club: Masons. Home: 600-A Cauthen Way Signal Mountain TN 37377 Office: 3100 St Elmo Ave Chattanooga TN 37408

WATERS, JOHN BENNET, ins. co. exec.; b. Alexandria, La., June 23, 1943; s. John W. and Rosemary (Bennet) W.; B.B.A., 1965, postgrad., 1971; postgrad. La. State U., 1971-72; m. Madelyn Ringgold, Aug. 15, 1970; children—John Bennet, Michael Armstrnog. Pres., Air Charter, Inc., Alexandria, 1968-71; treas. Fireside Comml. Life Ins. Co., Alexandria, 1972-74, exec. v.p., 1974-77, pres., 1977—; treas. Fireside Mut. Life Ins. Co., 1972-74, exec. v.p., 1974-77, pres., 1977—; pres. Beauregard Funeral Home, Alexandria, 1974—; sec.-treas. J-2 Ranch, Inc., 1972—; exec. v.p. McArthur Corp., 1975-77, pres., 1977—; owner Waters' Flight Services, 1977—; pres. Hammer Funeral Homes, Inc., S.W. Holding Co., 1979; v.p. Creole Gold Enterprises, Inc., 1979; dir. Arian Investment Corp., 1978—, Cornerstone Devel., 1977—, Bank of S.W. La., 1978—, Moreauville State Bank, 1974—. Active Rapides United Givers, 1978—. Served to lt. USNR, 1965-67. C.P.A. Mem. Life Ins. Agy. Mgmt. Assn., Pres.'s Assn. Democrat. Episcopalian. Clubs: Kiwanis, Masons. Home: 4201 Bayou Rapides Rd Alexandria LA 71301 Office: PO Box 7478 Alexandria LA 71306

WATERS, JOHN ROBERT, clergyman; b. Inman, S.C., Aug. 9, 1923; s. John George and Carrie Esther (Lawrence) W.; student Furman U., 1940-42, Fundamental Bible Inst., Los Angeles, 1943-46, San Diego State Coll., 1950-52; B.A., Immanuel Coll., Atlanta, 1955, D.D., 1968; m. Helen Eugenia Brownlee, Aug. 28, 1943; children—Linda Gail, John Enoch, Robert David, Daniel George, Paul Stephen, Philemon Lynn, Joy Rene. Ordained to ministry Baptist Ch., 1945; pastor chs. in Calif., 1945-52; mem. faculty Fundamental Bible Inst., 1949-52, Tabernacle Bapt. Coll., Greenville, S.C., 1975—; pastor Faith Bapt. Ch., Laurens, S.C., 1952—; editor Bapt. Bible Trumpet, 1952—; sec.-treas. Southwide Bapt. Fellowship, 1958-72, treas., 1972-78; dir. Holy Land Tours, 1966—; mem. planning com. N. Am. Fundamental Bapt. Congress, 1976—. Commr., Laurens City Planning and Zoning Bd., 1977—. Mem. S.C. Bapt. Fellowship (editor Bapt. Bible Trumpet), Southwide Bapt. Fellowship. Democrat. Author: The Christian Home, 1965; The Greatest Invitation in the Bible, 1975; God's Five Books in Heaven, 1977; The High Cost of Backsliding, 1972; also articles, tracts. Home: 308 Crescent Dr Laurens SC 29360 Office: 1607 Greenwood Rd Laurens SC 29360

WATERS, MARILYN COLLAR, constrn. co. exec.; b. Senoia, Ga., Aug. 22, 1928; d. Lynn Henry and Frances Smith (Williams) Collar; student Brenau Coll., 1947, Fla. State U., 1947; children—Sunny Collar, Bany Waters Cranmer, Dwight Collar, Lester Lynn. Partner, Casa de Artes, Miami, Fla., 1965-69; exec. v.p. Sherdak Developers Corp., Miami, 1970—, v.p. Palmsea Corp., Miami, 1970—; sec.-treas. Argus Realty Services, Inc., 1970—, Internat. Realty Mktg. Corp., 1976—, Mirasol Constrn., Miami Beach, Fla., 1973—. Mem. Lowe Art Mus., Mus. of Sci. and Planetarium, Met. Mus. and Art Centers, Alpha Chi Omega. Presbyterian. Home: 8218 SW 81 Ct Miami FL 33143 Office: 2655 Collins Ave Miami Beach FL 33140

WATERS, ROLLIE ODELL, cons. firm exec.; b. Charleston, S.C., Oct. 14, 1942; s. Rollie Robert and Mary Olivia (Brown) W.; A.A., Spartanburg Coll., 1968; B.S., U. S.C., 1969; M.B.A., Pepperdine U., 1980; m. Nancy Yvonne Chapman, May 3, 1975; 1 dau., Wendie Kay. Supr. communications and spl. activities Owens-Corning Fiberglas, Aiken, S.C., 1970-71, asst. personnel dir., Fairburn, Ga., 1971-72; personnel dir. Meisel Photochrome Corp., Atlanta, 1972-73, dir. corporate personnel, Dallas, 1973-76, asst. v.p., dir. human resources, after 1976; owner/partner cons. firm Waters-Trego, 1979—; publicity dir., program dir. 35th and 36th N. Tex. Personnel Confs. Served with USAF, 1962-66. Mem. Am. Soc. Personnel Adminstrs., Dallas Personnel Assn. (v.p. membership 1977-78), Am. Mgmt. Assn., Am. Soc. Tng. and Devel., Mensa, Psi Chi, Phi Theta Kappa, Omicron Delta Kappa, Beta Phi Gamma. Democrat. Home: 5826 Morningside Dallas TX 75206

WATERS, WALLACE BRYANT, security co. exec.; b. Johnstown, Pa., Jan. 10, 1925; s. Walter Gordon and Myrtle Lois (Cartwright) W.; B.S., Butler U., 1951; m. Ina V. Day, July 24, 1953; 1 dau., Tamela Sue. Pres., gen. mgr. Sta. KLTR, Blackwell-Ponca City, Okla., 1963-67; gen. mgr. Sta. WKTR-TV, Dayton, Ohio, 1967-68; dist. sales mgr. Westinghouse Security Systems, Fort Lauderdale, Fla., 1971-78, gen. mgr. Benham Industries, Westinghouse Security Systems, 1978—. Served with U.S. Army, 1946-48. Mem. Am. Soc. Indsl. Security, Alpha Epsilon Rho. Club: Mason, Shriner. Author: The Presidents, 1976. Home: 292 Allenwood Dr Fort Lauderdale FL 33308 Office: Westinghouse Security Systems Suite 118 1001 NW 62nd St Fort Lauderdale FL 33309

WATERS, ZENOBIA MARGUERITE PETTUS, ednl. adminstr.; b. Little Rock, Mar. 4; d. Henry Augustus and Lillie Liddell (Edwards) Pettus; B.A., Philander Smith Coll., 1964; M.Ed. (Ford Found. grantee, 1967), U. Wash., 1968; children—Pamela Waters Reed, Zenobia Waters Carter. Faculty Philander Smith Coll., Little Rock, 1966—, lectr., 1966-67, instr., 1968-69, co-chmn. bus. edn. dept., 1968-70, asst. prof. bus. edn., 1969—, acting bus. mgr. summer 1969, adminstrv. asst. to v.p. for acad. affairs, 1975—, summer session coordinator, 1979—; part time instr. bus. adminstrn. Ark. Bapt. Coll., 1970—; asst. to adminstrv. mgr. Fed. Highway Adminstrn., 1970. Active Urban League; hon. and spl. mem. United Meth. Women, 1972, 76, cert. lay speaker Little Rock Conf. United Meth. Ch., 1979, del. gen. and jurisdictional confs., 1976, 80, pres. United Meth. Women, White Meml. United Meth. Ch., 1976-79; exec. com. Little Rock Conf. Council on Ministries, 1975-79, Episcopacy com. Little Rock Conf., 1978-79; asso. registrar Ark. Area Sch. Christian Mission, 1979. Union Nat. Bank grantee, 1946. Mem. Nat. Assn. Coll. and Univ. Bus. Officers, Nat. Bus. Edn. Assn., AAUW (treas. 1979—), AAUP (exec. com., dir. Aldersgate 1978-79), Phi Delta Phi. Author supervisors handbook Fed. Hwy. Adminstrn., 1970. Home: 1700 Westpark Dr Apt 212 Little Rock AR 72204 Office: 812 W 13th St Little Rock AR 72203

WATERSTREET, JOHN RICHARD, savs. and loan exec.; b. Rockford, Ill., Apr. 10, 1928; s. William Morris and Malinda Elizabeth (Weber) W.; student U. Ill., 1947-51; B.B.A., Jackson Coll., Honolulu, Hawaii, 1961; postgrad. U. Nebr. at Omaha, 1966-68; m. LaVerne Virginia Zavertnik, May 29, 1954; children—Sharon Lynn, Ronald Wayne. Mgmt. trainee Am. Airlines, N.Y.C., 1951-52; commd. 2d lt. USMC, 1952, advanced through grades to lt. col. 1968; comdg. officer Marine Attack Squadron 211, Vietnam, 1968-69; comdr. in chief Pacific Rep. Joint Strategic Target Planning Staff, 1969-72; ret., 1972; mgr. bldg. adminstrn. Ryder System, Inc., Miami, Fla., 1972-75; v.p. Dade Fed. Savs. & Loan Assn., Miami, 1975—. Swimming ofcl. AAU, 1964—; cons. Jr. Achievement, 1972-73. Decorated Legion of Merit, D.F.C., Bronze Star; recipient citation Jr. Achievement, 1973; cert. of achievement Internat. Security Conf., 1977. Cert. protection profl. Mem. Am. Soc. Indsl. Security (chpt. chmn. 1978-79, banking and fin. com. 1979—), Am. Records Mgmt. Assn. (lectr.), Bldg. Owners and Mgrs. Assn. (dir. 1977-79), Marine Corps League, Res. Officers Assn., Fin. Instn. Security Officers, Valley Forge Mil. Acad. Alumni Assn. (dir. 1979—), Delta Kappa Epsilon, Phi Alpha Theta. Republican. Episcopalian (vestryman). Club: Yale (N.Y.C.). Home: 11950 SW 63d Ave Miami FL 33156 Office: 101 E Flagler St Miami FL 33131

WATKINS, CLIFFORD EDWARD, I, educator; b. Chgo., June 7, 1940; s. Edward Fred and Fannie Wheeler W.; B.A. in Music, Clark Coll., 1961; M.Music Edn., So. Ill. U., 1966, Ph.D., 1975; m. Sally Martin, Sept. 25, 1962; children—Rebehka, Clifford Edward. Band dir. Washington High Sch., Greenville, S.C., 1961-62; band dir. C. E. Murray High Sch., Greeleyville, S.C., 1966-67; asst. prof. music, band dir. S.C. State Coll., Orangeburg, 1967-72; asso. prof. Tenn. State U., Nashville, 1972—; adjudicator and cons. in field. Served with USAF, 1962-66. Tenn. State U. faculty devel. grantee, 1979. Mem. Coll. Band Dirs. Nat. Assn., Jack and Jills Am., Kappa Delta Pi, Phi Delta Kappa, Kappa Kappa Psi, Kappa Alpha Psi. Baptist. Condr. musical performances for pres. James E. Carter, Malawi pres. Hastings Banda. Home: 713 McMurray Dr Nashville TN 37211 Office: Music Dept Tenn State U Nashville TN 37203

WATKINS, DAWSON EDWARD, III, motor carrier exec.; b. Waynesboro, Va., Mar. 12, 1941; s. Dawson Edward Jr., and Evelyn Mary (Stephenson) W.; B.A. in Polit. Sci., Lynchburg (Va.) Coll., 1966, postgrad. bus., 1968; m. Nancy Elizabeth McDaniel, Aug. 29, 1964; children—Patricia Ann, Benjamin Edward; m. 2d, Jeannie Leigh Farris, July 14, 1979; 1 dau., Leigh Galan. Employment interviewer Va. Employment Commn., 1966; personnel asst. Imperial Reading div. N.W. Industries, 1966-70; dir. personnel Smith's Transfer Corp., Staunton, Va., 1970—; tchr. personnel adminstrn. Blue Ridge Community Coll. Mem. industrywide negotiating com. for equal employment opportunity in trucking industry. Mem. grievance com. City of Staunton; mem. Commonwealth of Va. Consortium for Higher Edn. Deacon, Covenant Presbyterian Ch.. 1974; chmn. equal employment opportunity commn. City of Staunton, 1978—; gen. chmn. United Way, Staunton, 1979. Mem. Am. Soc. Personnel Adminstrn. (accredited exec. in personnel), Am. Soc. Tng. and Devel., Am. Trucking Assn. (nat. chmn. personnel council 1978-79, chmn. equal employment opportunity task force, 1978—), Shenandoah Valley Personnel Assn. (pres. 1978-79), BNA Personnel Forum, Staunton, Va. chambers commerce. Presbyn. Club: Capital Dist. Kiwanis (past dist. gov. internat.). Home: 314 Woodmont Dr Staunton VA 24401 Office: PO Box 1000 Staunton VA 24401

WATKINS, DERREL RAY, social worker; b. DeWitt, Ark., Aug. 31, 1935; s. Steve and Annie (Wheeler) W.; B.A., Ouachita U., 1965; M.R.E., Southwestern Bapt. Theol. Sem., 1968, Ed.D., 1972; M.S.W., U. Ga., 1974; m. Janis Nutt, Jan. 19, 1962; children—Derrelynn Ruth, Stephen Ray. Ordained to ministry Baptist Ch., 1955; pastor, Francis St. Bapt. Ch., Jackson, Mich., 1960-63; dir. Bapt. Good Will Center, Fort Worth, 1969-72; researcher Nat. Interfaith Coalition on Aging, Athens, Ga., 1973; asso. prof. social work Southwestern Sem., Fort Worth, 1974—. Mem. Nat. Assn. Social Workers, Council Social Work Edn., Am. Assn. Marriage and Family Therapists, Gerontol. Soc., Southwestern Social Sci. Assn., Nat. Council Family Relations, Nat. Assn. Christians in Social Work. Author: And Thy Neighbor: An Introduction to Christian Social Ministry, 1978. Home: 6513 Sabrosa Ct E Fort Worth TX 76133 Office: PO Box 22306 Fort Worth TX 76122

WATKINS, JAMES MELVIN, real estate appraiser, lending exec.; b. Atlanta, Oct. 14, 1929; s. Leroy Melvin and Mildred Lorraine (Burden) W.; student N. Ga. Coll., 1947-48; B.B.A., Ga. State U., 1959; m. Nancy Virginia Powell, Jan. 20, 1950; children—James Melvin Jr., Thomas R., Wesley D. Mortgage loan supr. Life Ins. Co. of Ga., Atlanta, 1953-71; v.p., mgr. income property loans Wortman & Mann, Inc., Jackson, Miss., 1971-75; v.p., mgr. mortgage loan div. Unifirst Fed., Jackson, 1975-78; v.p., dir. income property investments Unifirst Fed. Savs. & Loan and Wortman & Mann, Inc., Jackson, 1978—. Pres., Coralwood PTA, Atlanta, 1969-70; coach Little League, Atlanta, 1969-71; bd. dirs. Manhattan Boosters Club, 1974-75. Licensed sr. residential appraiser, Ga., 1970; certified review appraiser, Miss., 1977. Mem. Soc. Real Estate Appraisers (pres. Jackson chpt. 1976-77, dir. 1977-78), Jackson Mortgage Lenders (dir. 1977—), Jackson Realtors. Home: 6049 Lake Trace Circle Jackson MS 39211 Office: 525 E Capitol St Jackson MS 39211

WATKINS, JOHN WOODLEY, educator; b. Smithfield, N.C., June 25, 1932; s. Ulysses S. and Pauline L. W.; B.S., Hampton Inst., 1955, M.S., 1974; M.S., Va. Commonwealth U., 1979; m. Oreta Barnes, June 9, 1956; children—Cynthia Kaye, Patricia Raye (twins). Commd. 2d lt. U.S. Army, 1955, advanced through grades to lt. col., 1969; instr. Field Arty. Sch., Ft. Sill, Okla., 1964-67; chief radar instrn., Ft. Sill, 1967-70; insp. nuclear weapons, Nurnburg, W. Ger., 1970-71, adviser to intelligence officer, Vietnam, 1963-64; adviser to Korean gen. officer, 1970-71; prof. mil. sci. Hampton (Va.) Inst., 1971-75, ret., 1975; dir. upward bound Hampton Inst., 1975—. Decorated Meritorious Service medal with oak leaf cluster, Army Commendation medal with oak leaf cluster. Mem. Am. Personnel and Guidance Assn., Kappa Delta Pi, Omega Psi Phi. Home: 26 Meadowbrook Dr Hampton VA 23666 Office: Hampton Inst Tyler St Hampton VA 23668

WATKINS, LOWRY, Realtor; b. Paducah, Ky., Jan. 23, 1897; s. Rush C. and Porter (Lowry) W.; ed. public and pvt. schs.; m. Barbara Bullitt, June 20, 1942; children—Barbara Porter, Lowry, Marshall Bullitt. Prin., Lowry Watkins, Realtors, Insurors, Prospect, Ky., 1980—. Owner, Iroquois Steeplechase Meml. Cup; mem. bd. aldermen City of Louisville, 1926-28. Served as 2d lt. U.S. Army, 1917-18. Master of fox hounds, 1936-76. Mem. Louisville Real Estate Bd. (dir.), Nat. Assn. Real Estate Bds., Nat. Assn. Realtors (Realtor emeritus 1976), Ky. Hist. Soc., Nat. Aeros. Assn., Soc. Cincinnati, SAR. Clubs: Filson, River Valley, Hunting Creek (Louisville); Bath and Tennis, Seagate (Delray Beach, Fla.). Office: 6520 Montero Dr Prospect KY 40059

WATKINS, LOWRY, JR., real estate exec.; b. Louisville, Jan. 28, 1946; s. Lowry and Barbara (Bullitt) W.; B.S.C., U. Louisville, 1968. With Louisville Trust Co., 1969-73; pilot Ky. Flying Service, Louisville, 1973-76, 76—, Trans World Airlines, Saudi Arabia, 1976; sec.-treas., dir. Watkins Co., Inc., Louisville, 1970—; dir. Oxmoor Farming Corp., Louisville. Mem. Nat. Aeros. Assn., English Speaking Union, Ky. Hist. Soc. (life), U.S.P.A. (asso.), Louisville Free Pub. Library (life). Club: Filson (life) (Louisville). Address: 7500 Shelbyville Rd Louisville KY 40222

WATKINS, NELSON PAYNE, assn. exec.; b. Hornell, N.Y., June 7, 1915; s. Frank Billings and Dorothy Elizabeth (Payne) W.; B.S., U.S. Naval Acad., 1937; postgrad. Renssalaer Poly. Inst.; m. June Marie Fickel, Jan. 15, 1947; children—Clayton H., Frank L., Suzanne M., Clark C. Dir. econ. devel. Portsmouth (Va.) C. of C., 1966-71; pres. Elizabeth City (N.C.) C. of C., 1971—. Commd. ensign USN, 1937, advanced through grades to capt., 1955, comdr. submarines, destroyer and amphibious squadron, Pacific fleet, 1942-66; comdg. officer amphibious base, Norfolk, Va., 1962-66, Naval War Coll., Newport, R.I., 1952-55; asso. prof. naval sci. U. Rochester (N.Y.), 1948-51, asst. football coach, 1948-50; prof. naval sci. Rensselaer Poly. Inst., Troy, N.Y., 1958-61, varsity lacrosse coach, 1959-60, ret., 1966. Pres. Lakewood Players (Calif.), 1956; council commr., exec. bd. Boy Scouts Am., 1962-70, recipient Silver Beaver award, 1964, vice-chmn. dist., 1973-75; pres. Portsmouth Little Theatre, 1970; v.p. United Fund Elizabeth City, 1974-79; chmn. Elizabeth City ARC, 1975. Decorated Bronze Star, Meritorious Service Medal. Mem. So. Indsl. Devel. Council, N.C. Indsl. Devel. Assn., Am. C. of C. Execs., So., Va. (pres. 1970, dir.), N.C. (dir. 1976-79) assns. C. of C. execs. Episcopalian. Clubs: Rotary, Pine Lakes Country. Author: Elements of Strategy, 1955. Home: 503 W Main St Elizabeth City NC 27909 Office: 615 E Main St Elizabeth City NC 27909

WATKINS, REFORD GEORGE, sailboat designer; b. Jamaica, N.Y., Aug. 29, 1946; s. Reford Oneil and Lillian Olga Watkins; student Suffolk Community Coll., Seldon, N.Y., 1970; m. Diana Marie Meaton, Dec. 22, 1970; children—Anne Marie, Kathleen Elizabeth, Reford Joseph. Fiberglas finisher Irwin Yacht & Marine Co., St. Petersburg, Fla., 1970-71; mold repairer Starfire Boats, Salt Lake City, 1971-72; tooling engr. Heritage Yachts, Clearwater, Fla., 1973-74; owner Watkins Yacht & Marine, Inc., Clearwater, 1974—. Served with USMC, 1965-68; Vietnam. Decorated Purple Heart. Recipient 2d place Fla. Addy award, 1978, local cert. of merit Addy award, 1978, Golden Wings Advt. award St. Petersburg Times, 1978. Mem. Marine Industries Assn. (dir.), St. Petersburg Advt. Fedn. Roman Catholic. Home: 9995 54th St N Pinellas Park FL 33565 Office: 12645 49th St N Clearwater FL 33520

WATKINS, TED ROSS, social worker; b. Kaufman County, Tex., Dec. 2, 1938; s. Daniel Webster and Iva Lucy (Lowrie) W.; B.A., N. Tex. State U., Denton, 1961; M.S.W. (NIMH fellow), La. State U., 1963; D.S.W. (NIMH fellow), U. Pa., 1976; m. Betty Diane Dobbs, May 30, 1959; children—Evan Scott, Brett Dobbs, James David. Psychiat. social worker Family Guidance Center, Sharon, Pa., 1963-65; chief social worker Talbot Hall, Johnestown, Pa., 1965-70; chief social worker Harrisburg (Pa.) Mental Health Center, 1970-71; asst. prof. social work U. Tex., Arlington, 1971-76, asso. prof., 1979—; bd. dirs. counseling services Family and Individual Services Assn., Ft. Worth, 1976-79; cons. instnl. child care, mental health, family counseling, alcoholism treatment; dir. Tarrant Council Alcoholism, 1974-76, Salvation Army Alcoholism Treatment Program, 1974-76; mem. Tex. State Bd. Cert. of Alcoholism Counselors, 1974-77. Vice pres., program chmn. Metroplex Assn. Gifted and Talented; former dir. Arlington Vol. Center. Named Outstanding Profl. in Human Services, 1974; cert. Acad. Cert. Social Workers; lic. social psychotherapist, Tex. Mem. Nat. Assn. Social Workers (state bd. dirs, chair Ft. Worth Unit), Tex. Assn. Alcoholism Counselors (charter). Methodist. Contbr. articles on sibling relationships, community mental health, residential treatment of children and alcoholism treatment to profl. jours. Home: 2806 Crowley Ct Arlington TX 76012 Office: 421 University Hall University of Texas Arlington TX 76019

WATKINS, THOMAS MORRIS, audiologist; b. Ft. Clayton, C.Z., Feb. 28, 1948; s. Royal Eppes and Mary (Watkins) Stuart; B.A. magna cum laude, Met. State Coll., Denver, 1974; M.A. in Audiology, U. No. Colo., Greeley, 1975. Physician's audiological evaluator, Tulsa, 1971; audiologist U. Colo. Med. Center, Denver, 1971-73, Rocky Mountain Otolaryngology Group, Denver, 1972-73; pvt. practice audiology, Ft. Collins, Colo., 1975, Rocky Mount, N.C., 1980—; dir. mobile speech and hearing program, dept. speech pathology and audiology U. Wyo., Cheyenne, 1975-76; audiologist Kresge Hearing Lab. South, New Orleans, 1976; commd. 1st lt. U.S. Army, 1977, advanced through grades to capt., 1978; clin. coordinator audiological services Dwight David Eisenhower Army Med. Center, Ft. Gordon, Ga., 1977-80; clin. instr. Acad. Health Scis., Ft. Sam Houston, Tex., 1977-80. Mem. Am. Speech and Hearing Assn., Am. Auditory Soc., So. Audiol. Soc., Mil. Audiol. Soc., Deafness Research Found. Presbyterian. Author papers in field. Address: 3068 Sunset Ave Rocky Mount NC 27801

WATKINS, WESLEY WADE, congressman; b. DeQueen, Ark., Dec. 15, 1938; B.S. in Agr. Edn., Okla. State U., 1960; M.S. in Ednl. Adminstrn., 1961; m. Elizabeth Lou Rogers, June 9, 1963; children—Sally, Martha, Wade. Mem. staff Dept. Agr., Washington, 1963; asst. dir. admissions Okla. State U., 1963-66; exec. dir. Kiamichi Econ. Devel. Dist., Okla., 1966-68; owner, operator constrn. bus., from 1968; mem. Okla. Senate, 1975-76; mem. 95th-96th Congresses from 3d Okla. Dist. Pres. Higher Edn. Alumni Council Okla.; Okla. chmn. Nat. Future Farmers Am. Found.; mem. Okla. Health Planning Council; pres. Ada (Okla.) Growth and Devel. Assn. Served with Air N.G., 1961-67. Recipient award Nat. Fedn. Ind. Bus., 1977, Okla. State U. Alumni, 1977. Democrat. Presbyterian. Clubs: Masons, Lions. Office: 424 Cannon House Office Bldg Washington DC 20515*

WATKINS, WILLIAM CAREY, san. service co. exec.; b. Abilene, Kans., July 11, 1934; s. Carey Andrew and Ada (Gulley) W.; student public schs., Jacksonville, Fla.; m. Dorothy Cornelia Hodges, Aug. 15, 1954; children—Cynthia Elaine, William Carey, Scott Andrew. Sales and office mgr. Gulf States Plywood, Jacksonville, 1953-59; office mgr. King Concrete Products, Jacksonville, 1959-61; asst. sec., treas., billing and credit mgr. Port-O-Let Co., Inc., Jacksonville, 1961—, also dir. Democrat. Baptist. Club: Southside Bus. Men's (bd. govs. 1970-71). Home: 1761 Lilly Rd Jacksonville FL 32207 Office: 2300 Larsen Rd Jacksonville FL 32207

WATKINS, WILLIAM LAW, lawyer; b. Anderson, S.C., Dec. 26, 1910; s. Thomas Franklin and Agnes (Law) W.; A.B., Wofford Coll., 1932; LL.B., U. Va., 1933; m. Frances Sitton, Oct. 23, 1937; children—Sarah (Mrs. Allen S. Marshall), Anna (Mrs. Alexander C. Hattaway III), Elizabeth (Mrs. Anderson Mills Kinghorn, Jr.), Jane (Mrs. Roger W. Mudd). Admitted to S.C. bar, 1933; since practiced in Anderson; mem. firm Watkins & Prince, 1936-46, Watkins & Watkins, 1946-54, Watkins, Vandiver & Freeman, 1954-64, Watkins, Vandiver, Kirven & Long, 1964-67, Watkins, Vandiver, Kirven, Long & Gable, 1968-77, Watkins, Vandiver, Kirven, Gable & Gray, 1977—. Dir. Duke Power Co., Perpetual Bldg. & Loan Assn.; adv. bd. S.C. Nat. Bank. Mem. S.C. Ho. of Reps., 1935-36; mem. S.C. Probation, Parole and Pardon Bd., 1954-69. Trustee Presbyn. Coll., Clinton, S.C., 1966-75, Anderson County Hosp. Assn., 1964-74. Served with AUS, 1942-46. Decorated Bronze Star with oak leaf cluster. Fellow Am. Coll. Trial Lawyers, Am. Bar Found.; mem. Am., S.C., Anderson bar assns., Phi Beta Kappa, Sigma Alpha Epsilon. Presbyn. Rotarian. Home: 317 North St Anderson SC 29621 Office: 500 S McDuffie St Anderson SC 29621

WATSON, ABBIE I., ret. pub. health nurse; b. Greenville, Mich., July 27, 1905; d. Alfred T. and Effie (Henry) Watson; R.N., Harper Hosp. Sch. Nursing, Detroit, 1929; B.S. in Pub. Health Nursing, Wayne U., 1947; M.S. in Nursing Edn., Western Res. U., 1948. Clinic nurse outpatient dept. Harper Hosp., 1930-33; staff nurse, supr. Vis. Nurse Assn., Detroit, 1933-35, 38-42; supr. Tulare County Health Dept., Visalia, Calif., 1935-38; adminstrv. chief nurse, capt. Army Nurse Corps, AUS, 1942-46; exec. dir. Instructive Vis. Nurse Assn., Richmond, Va., 1948-57; dir. bur. pub. health nursing Instructive Vis. Nurse Assn. and City of Richmond, 1952-57; dir. bur. pub. health nursing pub. health div. Health and Hosp. Corp. of Marion County, Indpls., 1957-61; chief bur. pub. health nursing Pub. Health Dept. D.C., 1961-65; dir. pub. health nursing Met. Health Dept., Nashville, 1965-72. Mem. nursing services com. D.C. chpt. ARC, 1960-61; spl. services dept. D.C. Tb Assn., 1961—; co-chmn., club rep. Festival U.S.A. Winter Haven Bicentennial Com. Fellow Am. Pub. Health Assn. (past vice chmn., past research chmn. pub. health nursing sect. So. br.), Am. Sch. Health Assn., Royal Soc. Health (London); mem. Am. Nurses Assn., Nat. League Nursing (past chmn. program planning com. pub. health nursing biennial conv.), D.C. Pub. Health Assn. (1st v.p., chmn. constn. and by-laws com.). Club: Woman's of Winter Haven (rec. sec., pres. 1978—). Contbr. articles to profl. publs. Address: 530 Ave K NE Winter Haven FL 33880

WATSON, BENJAMIN EXCELL, real estate broker; b. Dale County, Ala., Mar. 7, 1918; s. Benjamin Arthur and Emmaline Elizabeth (Fralish) W.; student pub. schs., Dale County, Ala.; m. Allie Elizabeth Dykes, Aug. 8, 1937; children—Judy Elizabeth, Benjamin Michael. Salesman, McGough Bakeries, Montgomery, Ala., 1939-41, Collins Baking Co., Dothan, Ala., 1942-43; sales supr. Colonial Baking Co., Dothan, 1945-52; owner, broker Excell Watson Realty Co., Dothan, 1952—. Chmn., United Fund, Dothan, 1961-62; pres. Boys Club of Dothan, 1970; chmn. ofcl. bd. First United Meth. Ch., Dothan, 1970; chmn. Ala.-West Fla. Conf. Minister Retirement Fund Drive, United Meth. Ch., 1977; gen. chmn. Ford Philpot Crusade, Dothan, 1971. Served with AUS, 1944-45. Licenced real estate broker, Ala., 1952. Mem. Nat. Bd. Realtors, Ala. Bd. Realtors, Dothan Bd. Realtors. Club: Kiwanis (pres. 1963). Home: 107 Camelia Dr Dothan AL 36301 Office: 1835 Montgomery Hwy Dothan AL 36301

WATSON, GERALD JAMES, JR., indsl. engr.; b. Fort Benning, Ga., Jan. 1, 1945; s. Gerald James and Martha Nell (Clark) W.; B.S. in Indsl. Mgmt., Ga. Inst. Tech. 1967, M.S. in Indsl. Mgmt., 1969; postgrad Ga. State U, 1971-72; m. Carole Lynn Kirkland, June 17, 1967. Plant indsl. engr. Del-Mar div. U.S. Plywood Co., Atlanta, 1967-69, 72-73; plant mgr. Bobby Dodd Workshop, Atlanta, 1973-74; indsl. engring. mgr. Star Paper Tube Co., Austell, Ga., 1974—; mem. faculty Ga. Inst. Tech. 1968-69, Ga. State U., 1971-72, Mercer U. Atlanta, 1971-72. Served to 1st lt. AUS, 1969-71. Decorated Bronze Star, Air medal. Mem. Am. Inst. Indsl. Engrs. Republican. Office: PO Box 8 Austell GA 30001

WATSON, GREGORY HARRISS, defense systems analyst; b. Englewood, N.J., July 16, 1948; s. Robert John and Anne Faye (Bellotte) W.; B.A. cum laude, Taylor U., 1970; M.S., U. So. Calif., 1975; m. Cynthia Sue Sandberg, June 6, 1971; 1 son, Andrew Daniel. Grad. fellow in philosophy Am. U., Washington, 1970-71; commd. ensign U.S. Navy, 1971, advanced through grades to lt., 1976, resigned, 1977; regional mgr., sr. analyst San Jose (Calif.) Office for Atlantic Analysis Corp., 1977-78; profl. staff Center for Naval Analyses (affiliate U. Rochester), Alexandria, Va., 1978—; instr. continuing edn. Naval Postgrad. Sch., 1977. Mem. Mil. Ops. Research Soc., Ops. Research Soc. Am., Naval Inst., Officers Christian Fellowship. Republican. Researcher employment of naval forces, antisubmarine warfare tactics devel. and evaluation. Home: 4754 Tapestry Dr Fairfax VA 22032 Office: 2000 N Beauregard St Alexandria VA 22311

WATSON, JACK CROZIER, justice La. Supreme Ct.; b. Jonesville, La., Sept. 17, 1928; s. Jesse Crozier and Gladys (Talbot) W.; B.A., U. Southwestern La., 1949; LL.B., La. State U., 1956; m. Sue Carter, Dec. 26, 1958; children—Carter, Wells. Admitted to La. bar, 1956; practiced in Lake Charles, La., 1956-64; mem. firm Watson & Watson, 1960-64; prosecutor City of Lake Charles, 1960; asst. dist. atty. 14th Jud. Dist. La., 1961-64; dist. judge 14th Jud. Dist. La., Lake Charles, 1964-72; judge ad hoc 1st Circuit Ct. Appeal, 1972-73, 3d Circuit Ct. Appeal, 1974-79; justice La. Supreme Ct., 1979—. Faculty, adviser Nat. Coll. State Judiciary, 1970, 73; mem. La. Jud. Council, 1972-74. Served to 1st lt. USAF, 1950-54. Mem. Am., La., S.W. La. bar assns., Nat. Council Juvenile Ct. Judges (pres. La. council, 1969-70), Am. Legion, S.W. La. Camellia Soc. (pres. 1973—), Blue Key, Sigma Alpha Epsilon, Phi Delta Phi, Pi Kappa Delta. Club: Lake Charles Yacht (commodore 1970). Home: 311 Shell Beach Dr Lake Charles LA 70601 Office: 301 Loyola Ave New Orleans LA 70112

WATSON, JAMES CHESTNUT, physician; b. Trenton, N.J., June 16, 1936; s. Reed and Grace (Chestnut) W.; A.B., Lincoln U., 1958; M.D., Howard U., 1964; M.P.H., U. Tex., 1970; m. Pauline Kathryn Thomas, Apr. 1, 1951; children—Jamie Lyn, Juliette Grace, Paula Elise, Debra Patrice. Intern, Meml. Hosp., South Bend, Ind., 1964-65; practice pub. health and preventive medicine, Houston, 1967-69, 1969—; asst. clin. prof. community medicine Baylor Coll. of Medicine, 1970—; city health dir. City of Houston, 1978—; mem. active staff Riverside Gen. Hosp., Park Plaza Hosp. adj. prof. health adminstrn. U. Tex. Sch. Public Health, Houston; prof. public affairs Tex. So. U. Pres., chmn. bd. Freedmen's Pub. Co., Inc., pub. The Informer, Tex. Freemen, 1972—; trustee U.S. Conf. City Health Officers, 1979—. Bd. mgrs. Harris County Hosp. Dist., 1973-78. Served with USAF, 1965-67. Diplomate Am. Bd. Family Practice. Mem. Am., Tex. pub. health assns., Nat. Med. Assn., Houston Med. Forum, Omega Psi Phi. Episcopalian (mem. standing com. Diocese Tex. 1971-74). Home: 5339 Trail Lake Dr Houston TX 77045 Office: 1115 N MacGregor Houston TX 77030

WATSON, JAMES DANA, ophthalmologist; b. N.Y.C., July 1, 1941; s. James Edward and Mary Elizabeth (Muller) W.; B.A., Linfield Coll., 1963; M.D., U. Oreg., 1967; m. Joyce Carlene Fricke, July 7, 1962; children—James Dana, Amy Elizabeth. Commd. 2d lt. U.S. Army, 1967, advanced through grades to maj., 1975; intern Tripler Army Med. Center, Honolulu, 1967-68; resident Walter Reed Army Med. Center, Washington, 1969-72; staff ophthalmologist Madigan Army Med. Center, Tacoma, Wash., 1972-75, discharged, 1975; practice medicine specializing in ophthalmology, Harlingen, Tex., 1975—; ophthalmologist Valley Eye Center, P.A., Harlingen, 1975—; mem. staffs Valley Bapt. Med. Center, Dolly Vinsant Meml. Hosp. Decorated Army Commendation medal; diplomate Am. Bd. Ophthalmology. Fellow Am. Acad. Ophthalmology; mem. Am. Assn. Ophthalmology, Pan Am. Assn. Ophthalmology. Home: 1615 Sam Houston Dr Harlingen TX 78550 Office: 2001 Ed Carey Dr Harlingen TX 78550

WATSON, JERRY FRANKLIN, gen. surgeon; b. Martin, Tenn., Aug. 30, 1936; s. Paul Leon and Alta Mae (Stringer) W.; student David Lipscomb Coll., Nashville, 1954-55; A.A., U. Tenn. at Martin, 1957; M.D., U. Tenn., Memphis, 1960; m. Doris Maurine Harris, June 15, 1957; children—Edith Maurine, Susan Kay, Anne Marie. Intern John Gaston Hosp., Memphis, 1960-61; commd. capt. AUS, 1961, advanced through grades to lt. col., 1972; resident surgery Brooke Gen. Hosp., San Antonio, 1964-68; comdg. officer 44th Surg. Hosp., Korea, 1969-70; chief dept. surgery DeWitt Army Hosp., Ft. Belvoir, Va., 1970-72; pvt. practice gen. surgery, North Wilkesboro, N.C., 1972—; mem. staff Wilkes Gen. Hosp., North Wilkesboro, 1972—. Diplomate Am. Bd. Surgery. Fellow A.C.S., Southeastern Surg. Congress; mem. AMA, Assn. Mil. Surgeons, Alpha Omega Alpha. Baptist (deacon 1974—). Club: Kiwanis. Home: 605 Magnolia Rd North Wilkesboro NC 28659 Office: Corner C and 8th Sts North Wilkesboro NC 28659

WATSON, K. BERT, energy co. exec.; b. Ranger, Tex., June 22, 1925; s. Max K. and Martha Elizabeth (Slaughter) W.; B.S.Ch.E., U. Colo., 1945, LL.B., 1948; grad. Advanced Mgmt. Program, Columbia U., 1970; m. Joy Marie Willhoite, Dec. 29, 1947; children—Sandra, Randall, Kenneth, Delk, David. Admitted to Tex. bar; asst. atty. gen. State of Tex., 1949-52; gen. counsel Amarillo Oil Co., 1952-53, now chmn. bd.; sec., atty. Pioneer Natural Gas Co., 1955-56, v.p., 1965-70, also dir.; exec. v.p. Pioneer Corp., Amarillo, Tex., 1970-73, pres., chief exec. officer, 1973—, also dir.; chmn. bd. Pioneer Transmission Corp., Pioneer Gas Products, Pinaga, Inc.; dir. Pioneer Nuclear, Inc., Sharp Drilling Co. Inc., Internat. Tool & Supply Co., Inc.; pres., mem. exec. com., dir. Water, Inc.; chmn. water adv. group to Tex. Water Devel. Bd.; mem. adv. com. Tex. Water Resources Research Inst.; bd. dirs. Tex. Research League; mem. Tex. Energy Adv. Council, 1977, 78, 79. Active Boy Scouts Am.; campaign dir. March of Dimes; mem. Potter-Randall Counties (Tex.) Citizens Com.; bd. dirs. Amarillo United Fund; mem. Amarillo Solicitations Rev. Bd.; past pres. Amarillo Legal Aid. Served with USN, 1943-46. Mem. So. Gas Assn., Am. Gas Assn. (dir.), Ind. Natural Gas Assn., Fed. Power Bar Assn., Tex. Bar Assn. (commr. legal aid. com.), Amarillo Bar Assn. (pres.), Tex. Utility Lawyers Assn. Office: PO Box 511 Amarillo TX 79163

WATSON, LARRY EDWARD, bus. services co. exec.; b. Mobile, Ala., Aug. 12, 1949; s. Ben and Bessie (Turner) W.; B.A., Morehouse Coll., 1971; m. Shirley Walker, Dec. 31, 1971. Mgmt. devel. trainee So. Pacific Transp. Co., San Francisco, 1971, employment asst., 1972-73, asst. mgr. employment, Houston, 1973-76; indsl. relations adv. II, Aramco Services Co., Houston, 1976-77, indsl. relations adv. I, 1977-79, adminstr. N. Am. employment, 1979—. Active NAACP;

mem. Houston Council on Human Relations. Mem. Houston Citizens C. of C. (dir.), Am. Soc. for Personnel Adminstrn., Houston Personnel Assn. Baptist. Home: 9244 Beechnut St Houston TX 77036 Office: Aramco Services Co 1100 Milam St Houston TX 77002

WATSON, LESTER ALONZO, JR., instrument mfg. co. exec.; b. Birmingham, Ala., May 27, 1926; s. Lester Alonzo and Eunice Kyle (Wright) W.; student Ga. Inst. Tech., 1946-47, Howard Coll., 1947-48; m. Mary Viola Brown, Apr. 7, 1951; children—Betty Lynn, Judith Ann, Robert Lee. Salesman, Alemite Co. Ala., Inc., Birmingham, 1948-56, sales mgr., 1956-64, pres., 1964-67; v.p., gen. mgr. Stewart-Warner Alemite Sales Co., Inc., Birmingham, 1967—. Sec., treas. Pell City Athletic Boosters, 1977-78; mem. Nat. Adv. bd. Am. Security Council, 1970-78. Served with A.C., USN, 1944-46; PTO. Mem. Paint and Decorating Contractors Am., Alemite Sales Execs. Club (pres. 1954-55), Alemite 1610 Club (pres. 1975), Alemite A-336 Club. Clubs: Pine Harbor Country, The Club, Racquet Place, Highland Racquet. Home: PO Box 86 Cropwell AL 35054 Office: 2911 3d Ave N Birmingham AL 35203

WATSON, MARY THOMPSON, ednl. cons.; b. Bon Weir, Tex., Sept. 13, 1927; d. Clarence Leslie II and Fannie Ann (Spikes) Thompson; B.A., Tex. So. U., 1953, M.Ed., 1962; postgrad. U. Houston; m. Paul Q. Watson; 1 son, Ralph Doyle. Tchr., instrnl. coordinator, to 1979; cons. tchr. facilitator Houston Ind. Sch. Dist, 1979—; workshop leader. Zone leader Home Improvement Assn., Houston. Recipient cert. Muscular Dystrophy Assn, 1976. Mem. NEA, NAACP, Tex. Tchrs. Assn., Houston Council Edn., Nat. Council Negro Women, Classroom Tchrs., Houston Tchr. Assn., Prin. Assn., Council English, YMCA (life), Am. Bus. Women's Assn., Tex. So. U. Execs., Amicia, Zeta Phi Beta (life; pres. 1978-80), Bus. and Profl. Women. Democrat. Mem. Churches of Christ. Home: 3851 Arbor Houston TX 77004 Office: 7115 Lockwood Houston TX 77093

WATSON, ROY HERMAN, JR., state legislator; b. Wellston, Ga., Apr. 20, 1937; s. Roy Herman and Maude M. (Howard) W.; grad. Ga. Mil. Coll., 1954; student Mercer U., 1955; m. Jeanne Phillips, Feb. 26, 1956; 1 dau., Cynthia R. Adminstr., Houston County (Ga.), 1957-75; mem. Houston County Bd. Tax Assessors, 1965-69; ins. agt., Warner Robins, Ga., 1975—; mem. Ga. Ho. of Reps., 1975—. Democrat. Baptist. Clubs: Civitan, Optimists, Masons, Shriners, Moose. Home: PO Box 1905 Warner Robins GA 31093 Office: 1538 Watson Blvd Watson Robins GA 31093

WATSON, SARA CURRIE, hosp. food service adminstr.; b. Hoke County, N.C., July 3, 1924; d. Hector Fleet and Annie Peterson (McPhaul) C.; B.S. in Home Econs., Flora MacDonald Coll., 1946; m. Hector McNeill Watson, Sr., Mar. 12, 1949; children—Rebecca Ann, Hector McNeill, Carolyn Louise. Dir. food service Columbus County Hosp., Whiteville, N.C., 1946-48, Scotland Meml. Hosp., Laurinburg, N.C., 1948, Southeastern Gen. Hosp., Lumberton, N.C., 1948—, tchr. nutrition Sch. Nursing, 1948-60. Mem. Bicentennial Com., 1975-76; deacon Presbyterian Ch. Mem. Am. Soc. Hosp. Food Service, Adminstrs. of Am. Hosp. Assn., D.A.R. (regent Upper Cape Fear chpt., dist. sec.-treas.), Women of Church (hon. life; pres.). Democrat. Club: Red Springs Dilettante Book (pres.). Home: 803 W 2d Ave Red Springs NC 28377 Office: Box 1408 Southeastern General Hospital Lumberton NC 28358

WATSON, TOMMY GENE, librarian; b. Ardmore, Okla., Apr. 10, 1938; s. James Eugene and Juanita (Todd) W.; A.B. with honors, Okla. Baptist U., 1960; M.A., U. Ark., 1962, postgrad., 1965-66; M.S. in L.S., Simmons Coll., 1971; m. Ellen Gail Hill, June 4, 1963; children—James Todd, Thomas Gregory. Asst. prof., dir. freshman English, U. So. Miss., Hattiesburg, 1962-67; English master Tabor Acad., Marion, Mass., 1967-68; asst. prof. Bridgewater (Mass.) State Coll., 1968-71, asst. dir. library, 1971-73; dir. library and media services Newberry (S.C.) Coll., 1973-76; univ. librarian U. of South, Sewanee, Tenn., 1976—; chmn. So. Coll. and Univ. Union Library Group; mem. Inst. on Librarian as Learning Cons., U. Pitts., 1975. Trustee Cecil Clarke Davis Gallery and Art Center, Marion, Mass., 1970-72, Freedom to Read Found.; chmn. Little Theatre Bd., Marion, 1971-72; sr. warden St. Luke's Episcopal Ch., Newberry; bd. dirs. Newberry Arts Council, 1974-76. So. Univs. research grantee, Harvard U., 1964. Mem. ALA (com. on accreditation for grad. library schs.), Southeastern, Tenn. (vice-chmn. elect coll. and univ. sect.; chmn. intellectual freedom com., continuing edn. com.) library assns., Tenn. Assn. Coll. and Research Libraries, S.C. Found. Ind. Coll. Librarians (chmn. 1974-76). Home: Box 110 South Carolina Ave Sewanee TN 37375 Office: Jessie Ball duPont Library Univ of South Sewanee TN 37375

WATTS, ANN REANEY, systems analyst; b. Highland Park, Ill., Aug. 23, 1948; d. Burnell Vauk and Carolyn June (Turner) Reaney; student Duke U., 1966-68; B.A., Wellesley Coll., 1970; M.P.H. in Health Systems and Hosp. Adminstrn., Tulane U., 1975; m. Ralph Joseph Watts, Sept. 5, 1975. Systems analyst Travelers Ins. Cos., Hartford, Conn., 1971-73; research asst. U. Conn. Sch. Medicine, 1973; dir. systems and procedures Blue Cross of La., New Orleans, 1975-78, provider systems cons., 1978—; adj. instr. and preceptor for adminstrv. resident Tulane U. dept. health systems mgmt.; cons. hosp. systems and procedures. Mem. plan devel. com., chair service area policy task force New Orleans/Bayou-River Area Health Systems Agy.; mem. fiscal ops. sub-com. La. Title XIX Adv. Com.; vestry mem. Ch. of Annunciation, Episcopalian ch., New Orleans. Mem. New Health Care Mgrs. Assn. New Orleans, Assn. Systems Mgmt. Home: 4416 Walmsley Ave New Orleans LA 70125 Office: 2026 Saint Charles Ave New Orleans LA 70130

WATTS, GENECILE, speech pathologist; b. Columbus, Miss., Jan. 18, 1954; d. Dwight Moody and Mary Eugenia (Woolbright) W.; B.A.E. in Speech Pathology, U. Miss., 1975, M.A. in Communicative Disorders, 1976. Intern speech pathology U. Miss. Med. Center, 1975-76; speech and lang. pathologist Easter Seal Speech and Lang. Clinic, Vicksburg, Miss., 1977-78; speech and lang. pathologist, coordinator area speech and lang. therapists Miss. Learning Resources System, Miss. Dept. Edn., Cleveland, 1978-79; speech pathologist Columbus (Miss.) Separate Sch. Dist., 1979—; condr. lang. stimulation classes Miss. Action for Progress-Headstart, Vicksburg, 1978. Mem. tour com. Vicksburg Pilgrimage Orgn., 1978. Mem. Am. Speech and Hearing Assn., Miss. Speech and Hearing Assn., Miss. Edn. Assn., Zeta Tau Alpha. Methodist. Club: Cleveland Canoe. Home: 608 9th St N Columbus MS 39701 Office: Columbus Separate Sch Dist 7th St N Columbus MS 39701

WATTS, JOHN DANIEL, map co. exec.; b. Knoxville, Tenn., Sept. 29, 1942; s. Daniel Monroe and Bernice C. (Creel) W.; student U. Alaska, 1963; m. Penny D'Anne Rhea, Oct. 19, 1974. Supr. J & R Map Co., Van Buren, Ark., 1964-74, Midland, Tex., 1974-75; pres. Impact Map Co., Lubbock, Tex., 1975—. Served with USAF, 1960-64; Vietnam. Recipient Ednl. Achievement award USAF, 1963; Photog. Excellence award Photo Five Photog. Soc., 6 times, 1968-74, award of Merit, USAF, 1964; Mgr. of Yr. award Impact Map Co., 1974. Mem. Profl. Photographers Tex., Nat. Free Lance Photographers Assn., Asso. Photographers Internat., Printing Industries Am. Republican. Methodist. Home: 8210 Kenosha Ave Lubbock TX 79423 Office: 3805 Ave A Lubbock TX 79408

WATTS, VIRGINIA SHERRILL, ednl. adminstr.; b. Meridian, Miss., July 15, 1937; d. Lonnie and Dora Virginia (Lewis) Glenn; B.A. (AAUW scholar 1956), Miss. So. Coll., Hattiesburg, 1959, M.S. in Phys. Chemistry, 1961; Ph.D. (univ. fellow 1961-63), Emory U., 1965; m. Robert Claude Watts, Sept. 2, 1961; children—Adrian Rachelle, Zaran Claude. Postdoctoral research asso. Emory U., 1965-67, research asso., summer 1968; asst. prof. chemistry Agnes Scott Coll., 1967-68; asso. prof. math., then asso. prof. chemistry Atlanta Baptist Coll., 1968-71; exam. adminstr. Nat. Assessment Ednl. Progress, part-time, 1972-73; asso. prof. chemistry Morehouse Coll., Atlanta, part-time 1973-74; asst. to dean Coll. Scis. and Liberal Studies, Ga. Inst. Tech., Atlanta, 1973-76, asst. dean, 1976—. Ga. Inst. Tech. grantee, 1977. Mem. Am. Assn. Higher Edn., Assn. Gen. and Liberal Studies (exec. council), Soc. Field Experience Edn., Am. Chem. Soc., Druid Hills Civic Assn., Sigma Xi. Methodist. Author papers in field. Home: 826 Springdale Rd NE Atlanta GA 30306 Office: Ga Inst Tech Atlanta GA 30332

WAUGH, ELIZABETH ANN, social worker; b. Houston, Feb. 6, 1940; d. B. Eugene and Ruth Duffield (Parker) Waugh; B.A. in Biol. Scis., Tex. Woman's U., 1961; M.Ed. in Guidance and Counseling, U. Houston, 1970. Biochemistry technician Southwestern Med. Sch., Dallas, 1961-62; bacteriologist Alcon Labs., Ft. Worth, 1962-63; clin. bacteriologist Terrell Lab., Ft. Worth, 1964; vocat. counselor Tex. Employment Commn., 1964-74; project adminstr., therapist heroin and alcohol detoxification Harris County Psychiat. Hosp., Houston, 1974-75; supr. emergency social services Ben Taub Gen. Hosp., Houston, 1973-79; field instr. Grad. Sch. Social Work, U. Houston; cons. in field, condr. workshops; specialist in crises intervention with victims of rape and battered women. Mem. Nat. Assn. Social Workers, Am. Mental Health Counselors Assn., Am. Personnel and Guidance Assn., Nat. Vocat. Guidance Assn., Assn. Measurement and Evaluation, Assn. Specialists in Group Work, Mensa. Office: 2708 Weslayan Houston TX 77027

WAVRO, RICHARD HAROLD, ins. and oil co. exec.; b. Orlando, Fla., Aug. 15, 1939; s. Paul Kenneth and Aileen (Leiden) W.; B.A. with honors, Fla. State U., 1963; m. Susan Varner, Jan. 22, 1963 (div. June 1972); children—William Kendall, Stacey Elizabeth. Pension cons. Hand & Assos., Houston, 1969-71; treas., chief financial officer Property Investments, Inc., Houston, 1972-74; v.p., treas. Gen. Devel. Corp., Houston, 1970—; chief fin. officer Dial Dunkin & Assos., Harlingen, Tex., 1974—; v.p., treas., dir. Miller-Dunkin Oil Corp., Harlingen, 1974—; sec.-treas., dir. Cameron Life Ins. Co., Harlingen, 1974—; owner Mobile Home Ins. Specialists of Tex., Harlingen. Fin. cons. various small businesses. Mem. Am. Inst. C.P.A.'s, Tex. Soc. C.P.A.'s, Am. Soc. Pension Actuaries. Mason. Home: 1623 Clarke St Harlingen TX 78550

WAX, GEORGE LOUIS, lawyer; b. New Orleans, Dec. 6, 1928; s. John Edward and Theresa (Schaff) W.; LL.B., Loyola U. of South, 1952, B.C.S., 1960; m. Patricia Ann Delaney, Feb. 20, 1965; children—Louis Jude, Joann Olga, Therese Marie. Admitted to La. bar, 1952; practice in New Orleans, 1954—. Served with USNR, 1952-54. Mem. Am., La., New Orleans bar assns., Am. Legion. Roman Catholic. Kiwanian. Clubs: New Orleans Athletic, Suburban Gun and Rod, Pendennis. Home: 5635 Pratt Dr New Orleans LA 70122 Office: First Nat Bank Commerce Bldg New Orleans LA 70112

WAYLAND, RUSSELL GIBSON, JR., geologist, mining engr.; b. Treadwell, Alaska, Jan. 23, 1913; s. Russell Gibson and Fanchon Dudley (Borie) W.; B.S., U. Wash., 1934; M.S., U. Minn., 1935, postgrad., 1934-36, 37-39, Ph.D., 1939; A.M., Harvard U., 1937; m. Mary Mildred Brown, May 19, 1943 (div. 1964); children—Nancy, Paul R.; m. 2d Virginia Bradford Phillis, Dec. 24, 1965. Instr. geology U. Minn., 1937-39; geologist U.S. Geol. Survey, Washington, 1939-42; staff engr., office of dir., 1952-58, regional geologist, Los Angeles, 1958-66, chief conservation div., Washington, 1966-78, research scientist office of dir., Reston, Va., 1978-80, energy minerals cons., 1980—; mem. Office of Mil. Govt. (U.S.) and Allied High Commn., Berlin and Essen, Germany, 1945-52, alt. mem. U.S. Nat. com. World Energy Conf., 1974-79. Served to lt. col. U.S. Army, 1942-46. Decorated Army Commendation medal; recipient Disting. Service award Dept. Interior, 1968. Mem. AIME, Soc. Econ. Geologists, Am. Inst. Profl. Geologists, Assn. Engring. Geologists, Geol. Soc. Am., Mineral. Soc. Am., Geochem. Soc., Sigma Xi, Tau Beta Pi, Phi Gamma Delta, Sigma Gamma Epsilon, Gamma Alpha, Phi Mu Alpha. Episcopalian. Club: Cosmos (Washington). Author geol. and engring. bulls., maps; contbr. articles to profl. jours.

WAYMAN, LINDA LEE, speech pathologist; b. San Angelo, Tex., May 8, 1947; d. William Leroy and Norene Ethelda (Anderson) Blanchard; A.A., Tyler Jr. Coll., 1967; B.A., Stephen F. Austin State U., 1969, M.A., 1970; m. Michael Allen Wayman, Aug. 30, 1975; 1 dau., Kimberly Ann. Speech pathologist Jacksonville (Tex.) Ind. Sch. Dist., 1970-71, Mesquite (Tex.) Ind. Sch. Dist., 1971—, chmn. range admit rev., dismiss com., 1977-79. Named Outstanding Elem. Tchr. of Am., 1975; Stephen F. Austin State U. grad. assistantship, 1969-70. Mem. Am. Speech and Hearing Assn., Tex. Speech and Hearing Assn., Mesquite Tchrs. Assn., Sigma Alpha Eta, Kappa Pi. Methodist. Home: Route 3 4408 Sachse Rd Wylie TX 75098 Office: 2600 Bamboo St Mesquite TX 75149

WAYMAN, PATRICIA DIANE, sch. counselor; b. Enid, Okla., Nov. 11, 1946; d. Dean C. and Violet M. (Becker) W.; student Northwestern State Coll., 1964-65; B.S., Okla. State U., 1968, M.S., 1979. Tchr., Balt. County Sch. Dist., Towson, Md., 1968-69, Conway Springs (Kans.) Pub. Sch. System, 1969-76, Enid (Okla.) Sch. System, 1976-77; sch. counselor Morrison (Okla.) pub. schs., 1978—. Mem. Am. Personnel and Guidance Assn., Okla. Personnel and Guidance Assn., NEA, Okla. Edn. Assn., Noble County Tchrs. Assn., Kappa Delta Pi, Phi Kappa Phi. Democrat. Presbyterian. Address: PO Box 246 Goltry OK 73739

WAYNE, ALAN, educator; b. N.Y.C., June 18, 1909; s. Adolph Otto Johann and Martha (Horvath) Wiesenburg; B.S., Coll. City N.Y., 1931, M.S. in Edn., 1937; postgrad. Columbia, 1945-49, (A.A.A.S. Secondary Sch. fellow) N.Y. U., 1961-68; m. Muriel Rothstein, Aug. 25, 1934; children—Linda Wayne Weiss, Susan Wayne McKee. Tchr. math. and sci. Rhodes Sch., N.Y.C., 1930-45; tchr. math. James Fenimore Cooper Jr. High Sch., N.Y.C., 1940-45, Williamsburgh Vocational High Sch., N.Y.C., 1945-51; asst. prin., supr. math. and sci. Eli Whitney Vocational High Sch., N.Y.C., 1951-72; adj. instr. math. Cooper Union, N.Y.C., 1949-67, adj. prof., 1967-72; instr. math. edn. N.Y. U., 1950-51, Yeshiva U. Grad. Sch., 1959-61; adj. asst. prof. math. Queensborough Community Coll., N.Y.C., 1965-72; instr. math. and physics Pasco-Hernando Community Coll., Fla., 1975-80; editorial cons. vocat.-indsl. edn. SUNY, 1949-57; mem. curriculum devel. coms. N.Y.C. Bd. Edn., 1950-70. Vice chmn. finance com. Beacon Sq. Pool Assn.; sec. Richey Symphony Soc., 1973-77. Committeeman, N.Y. County Democratic Com., 1940. Mem. Sch. Sci. and Math. Assn., Council Supervisory Assns., AAUP, Am. Math. Soc., Soc. for Indsl. and Applied Math., Math. Assn. Am., Nat. Council Tchrs. Math., Assn. Tchrs. Math. N.Y.C. (pres. 1948-50; exec. bd., historian 1951-71), Assn. Tchrs. Math. N.Y. State (charter, county chmn. 1951-72), Math. Chmns. Assn. N.Y.C. (v.p. 1971-72), Epsilon Pi Tau. Club: N.Y. Riddlers (pres. 1952). Author: Basic Mathematics I, 1951; Basic Mathematics II, 1954; (with Olivo) Basic Applied Science, 1957; (with Bold) Number Systems, 1971; (with Peters, Schor, Meng) Exploring Mathematics, 1974. Editor: Metals Technology, 1955. Home: 6614 Springfield Dr Holiday FL 33590

WAYTE, ROSEMARY FLINT, speech pathologist; b. Carlsbad, N.Mex., Apr. 3, 1940; d. Theodore T. Flint and Emily Grant (Woods) Flint Ray; B.S., Northwestern U., 1962; M.S., U. Okla., 1964, Ph.D., 1971. Speech-lang. pathologist Speech and Hearing Center, U. Okla., Oklahoma City, 1963-69, dir. diagnostic services Keys Speech and Hearing Center, 1970-72, asst. prof. dept. otorhinolaryngology, 1972-75, asst. prof. dept. communication disorders, 1971-76, asso. prof. dept. communication disorders, 1976—, chief speech-lang pathology services U. Hosps. and Clinics, 1972-75, adj. asso. prof. dept. otorhinolaryngology, 1975—; cons. Community Speech and Hearing Center, Enid, Okla., 1978—; due process hearing officer Bur. of Indian Affairs, 1978—, Okla. State Dept. Edn., 1978—; speech-lang pathologist of the day, Ho. of Reps., State of Okla., 1979; guest lectr. various univs. and profl. assns., 1971—. Mem. council Okla. Health Systems Agy., 1978—, chmn. nominations com., 1978—; mem. adv. bd. Community Action Program of Oklahoma City and County, Inc., 1976—. Recipient Service citation Okla. Ho. of Reps., 1979. Mem. Am. Speech-Lang.-Hearing Assn. (Cert. of Appreciation 1976, asso. editor lang.-speech-hearing services in schs. 1978—), Okla. Speech and Hearing Assn. (pres. 1978, mem. numerous publs. com. 1972—), Assn. for Children with Learning Disabilities, Orton Soc., Am. Cleft Palate Assn., Council of State Assn. Presidents (fiscal officer 1979), Am. Cancer Soc. (mem. profl. edn. com. 1978—), Higher Edn. Alumni Council. Contbr. numerous articles on lang. disorders to profl. publs. Home: 1422 Glenbrook Terrace Oklahoma City OK 73116 Office: 825 NE 14th St Oklahoma City OK 73190

WEANT, JOHN THOMAS, textile mfg. co. exec.; b. Randolph County, N.C., Oct. 7, 1922; s. George Henry and Fannie (Victoria) W.; student in radar tech. N.C. State U., 1942-43, in textile finishing Ga. Inst. Tech. Extension Sch., 1961-62; m. Mary Catherine Simmons, Dec. 26, 1943; children—John Thomas, James Henry. Asst. in time study Highland Cotton Mills, High Point, N.C., 1943-47; time study engr. Walker County Hosiery Mills, LaFayette, Ga., 1947-50; indsl. engr. Standard Coosa Thatcher Co., Rossville, Ga., 1952-63; indsl. engr. Threads Usa, Inc., Gastonia, N.C., 1963-78, v.p. mfg., 1978—. Served with Signal Corps, U.S. Army, 1942. Mem. N.C. Textile Mfrs. Assn. Democrat. Clubs: Civitan (pres. club 1976, Outstanding Sec. award 1972, Spl. award 1976). Masons. Office: PO Box 759 Gastonia NC 28052

WEAST, PHILIP GRAHAM, coll. adminstr.; b. Concord, N.C., Dec. 23, 1948; s. Albert Graham and Dorothy Ruth (Kluttz) W.; B.S., Appalachian State U., 1971, M.A., 1972. Tchr. biology Millbrook High Sch., Raleigh, N.C., 1971; 1971-72; asst. mgr. restaurant Appalachian Ski Mt., Blowing Rock, N.C., 1971-72; dir. coll. union Mars Hill Coll., N.C., 1972-78; with U. Ga. Inst. Higher Edn., Athens, 1979—. Mem. Greater Mars Hill Bicentennial Commn., 1975-76; big brother to handicapped resident W. Carolina Center, Morganton, N.C., 1975—. Recipient award of appreciation, graduating class, Mars Hill Coll., 1976. Mem. Assn. Coll. Unions-Internat., Am. Personnel and Guidance Assn., Am. Coll. Personnel Assn., Nat. Entertainment and Campus Activities Assn. Lutheran. Developer leadership workshop, Mars Hill Coll. Home: 1907 S Milledge Apt D-1 Athens GA 30605 Office: U Ga Inst Higher Edn Candler Hall Athens GA 30602

WEATHERFORD, LYNDA SUE, off-shore drilling co. exec.; b. Beaumont, Tex., Aug. 12, 1947; d. Ira Dewayne and Doris Annabel (Hingle) W.; B.S. in Edn., U. Tex., Austin, 1969; M.Ed. in Counseling, Sam Houston State U., 1971. Tchr., Cypress Fairbanks Ind. Sch. Dist., Houston, 1969-70, 71-73; dir. overseas family services Storm Drilling Co., Houston, 1973-74; sr. compensation and relocation rep. Zapata Off-Shore Co., Houston, 1975—. Mem. Am. Bus. Women's Assn. Houston Personnel Assn. Researcher overseas living. Office: PO Box 4240 Houston TX 77001

WEATHERFORD, WENDELL LEON, mfg. co. exec.; b. Middlebrook, Ark., July 28, 1940; s. Frank Carter and Opal Wynona (Luter) W.; B.S. (honor scholar), Ark. Poly. Coll., 1961; M.A., U. Ark., 1964, postgrad, 1964-65; m. Lee Ann Dedrick, Sept. 7, 1962; 1 dau., Barbara Ann. With Tex. Instruments Inc., Dallas, 1968—, sr. systems analyst, Amstelveen, The Netherlands, 1972-75, supr. systems analysts, 1975-76, supr. computer systems analysts, Austin, 1976—. Served with AUS, 1965-68. NSF fellow, 1961-64. Mem. Assn. Computing Machinery. Conservative. Office: PO Box 2909 M/S 2016 Austin TX 78769

WEATHERSBY, DOROTHY GERTRUDE THOMPSON, humanist, educator; b. Franklin, Tenn., Jan. 15, 1944; d. George Clay and Laura Gertrude (Law) T.; B.A., George Peabody Coll. for Tchrs., 1966, M.A., 1967; Ed.D., U. Tenn., 1975; m. Robert Warren Weathersby II, July 26, 1969; 1 dau., Laura Priscilla. Instr. English, John C. Calhoun Jr. Coll., Decatur, Ala., 1967-70; tchr. Bearden High Sch., Knoxville, Tenn., 1970-74; adj. faculty theatre and speech English Dept. and Sch. Edn., U. Tenn., Chattanooga, 1975—; lectr. teaching techniques, censorship in secondary schs. Mem. Tunnel Hill-Varnell (Ga.) Joint Planning Commn., 1978—. U. Tenn. Non-Service fellow, 1974-75. Mem. Chattanooga-Hamilton County Tchrs. English (liaison officer 1977—), Nat. Council of Tchrs. of English, S. Atlantic MLA, Conf. English Edn., Tenn. Assn. Tchr. Educators. Methodist. Club: Tunnel Hill Jr. Woman's (sec. 1975-77). Contbr. articles to profl. jours. Home: PO Box 73 Tunnel Hill GA 30755 Office: Theatre and Speech Dept U Tenn Chattanooga TN 37402

WEATHERSBY, TROY ELBERT, data processing exec.; b. New Orleans, Aug. 27, 1950; s. Fred E. and Betty W. (Britton) W.; B.S., Miss. State U., 1973; m. Kathryn Weir, July 22, 1972; 1 dau., Kathryn Odel. Pres., Miss. Data Mgmt. Services (name changed to CEDACO, 1979), Jackson, 1973—, also dir. Mem. vestry St. Andrew's Cathedral, 1979-81. Mem. Data Processing Mgmt. Assn., Sales and Mktg. Execs. Republican. Episcopalian. Home: 4122 Woodvale St Jackson MS 39211 Office: PO Box 4273 Jackson MS 39216 also 3820 I-55 N Jackson MS 39211

WEATHERSPOON, TOMMYE LEE, elec. engr.; b. Madison, Fla., Feb. 6, 1951; s. Donnie and Kathryn W.; B.S. in Electronics, Fla. A. and M. U., 1974; M.B.A. in Mgmt., Barry Coll., 1978; postgrad. in Engring., Ga. Inst. Tech., 1980—. Coop. student Ames (Iowa) Research Lab., 1972-73; relay engr. Fla. Power and Light Co., Miami, 1974—. Active Big Bro. program Dade County. Recipient outstanding engring. award Soc. Black Engrs., 1976. Mem. IEEE, Fla. Engring. Soc., Nat. Soc. Profl. Engrs. Democrat. Baptist. Home: 2101 NW 178th St Opa-Locka FL 33056 Office: 9250 W Flagler St Miami FL 33174

WEATHINGTON, DONALD WAYNE, mental health center adminstr.; b. Gadsden, Ala., Sept. 14, 1945; s. Clarence Wesley and Wilma (Johnson) W.; B.A., Auburn U., 1971; M.A., U. S. Fla., 1974; postgrad. Auburn U., 1978—; m. Faith Joan Myer, Nov. 18, 1968; children—Buffy Ann, Nathaniel Myer. Coordinator, New Mind,

Tampa, Fla., 1973-74; dir. Chemotreatment Center, Tampa, 1974-75; exec. adminstr. Fla. Lions Camp for Visually Handicapped, Lake Wales, 1975; research asst. Auburn Inst., Auburn (Ala.) U., 1976-78; dir. Talladega (Ala.) Community Mental Health Center, 1979—; cons. human relations Gadsden (Ala.) Sch. System, 1977-78; program coordinator Assn. Grad. Students in Counseling Services, Auburn U., 1978-79. Served with M.C., U.S. Army, 1968-70. Decorated Bronze Star medal. Rotary scholar, 1964-65. Mem. Am. Personnel and Guidance Assn. (nat. com. on grad. students), Ala. Personnel and Guidance Assn., Talladega Jaycees, Phi Delta Kappa. Democrat. Episcopalian. Home: 102 Porter Dr Talladega AL 35160 Office: 1 Medical Park Talladega AL 35160

WEAVER, BARRY ROLAND, resource analyst; b. Tulsa, Nov. 11, 1933; s. Carmen S. and Ruby (Trent) W.; B.A., U. Ark., 1955; postgrad. U. N.C., 1956-57. Corr. instr. history U. Ark., Fayetteville, 1955-56; research asst. Inst. for Research in Social Sci., Chapel Hill, N.C., 1956-57; exec. dir. Human Engring Lab., Tulsa, 1958-64; sr. test adminstr. Johnson O'Connor Research Found., N.Y.C., 1965; resource analyst Office of Emergency Preparedness, Exec. Office of Pres., Washington, 1965-70; environ. writer, 1971-72; family services coordinator Econ. Opportunity Agy., Fayetteville, Ark., 1973-74; program coordinator N.W. Ark. Econ. Devel. Dist., 1974-78; research faculty U. Ark., Fayetteville, 1978—. Trustee Human Engring. Lab., asst. treas., 1959-63; trustee Johnson O'Connor Research Found. Inc., asst. treas., 1959-63; trustee Human Engring. Lab., Ont., asst. treas., 1959-64; trustee Fundacion de Investigaciones Johnson O'Connor, Mexico, 1962-65. Served with AUS, 1957. Named Honorary Citizen of Little Rock, 1963. Mem. Sierra Club (nat. council 1969-70), Newton County Wildlife Assn., Am. Collegiate Polit. League (pres. 1952-53), Phi Alpha Theta. Author tech. reports: Princeton University Aptitude Differences, 1963, Roman Catholic Colleges and Universities, 1963, Research Thesis of the American History Survey, 1964. Editor: Item-by-Item Study of English Vocabulary, 1961. Contbr. to various publs. Home: Route 2 Springdale AR 72764

WEAVER, BILL R., wholesale co. exec.; b. Vernon, Tex., Aug. 28, 1925; s. Charles Robert and Beaulah Lillian (Miller) W.; B.S. in Petroleum Engring., U. Okla., 1948; m. Linda C. Culp, Feb. 12, 1973; children—Janet K., Mark D., Bill R. II; 1 stepdaughter Tammy Lynn Taylor. Mgr. opns. Blackwood & Nichols Co., 1951-60; owner, mgr. Weaver Engring. and Weaver Operating Cos., Oklahoma City, 1960-72; v.p. Devon Corp., Oklahoma City, 1972-77; exec. v.p. Locke Supply Co., Oklahoma City, 1977—; also dir.; cons. petroleum engring. Served with A.C., USN, 1943-45. Mem. Soc. Petroleum Engrs., Full Gospel Bus. Men's Fellowship Internat. (internat. dir. 1976—). Author: Give LIFE to Your Business, 1979. Home: 2604 NW 58th Pl Oklahoma City OK 73112

WEAVER, BILL THOMAS, furniture co. exec.; b. Nashville, Dec. 6, 1925; s. Frank L. and Mamie Sue (Black) W.; B.S., Manchester Coll., 1952; M.A., Ball State U., 1964; LL.B., Blackstone Sch. Law, 1971, J.D., 1975; m. Kathryn Eloise Smith, Dec. 7, 1946; children—Kim William, Kevin Todd (dec.), Jan Kathryn, Noel Thomas, Valerie Jill. With Gen. Tire & Rubber Co., Wabash, Ind. and Akron, Ohio, 1944-60, govt. sales-tech. rep., 1959-60; with Firestone Indsl. Products Co., various locations, 1960-67, West coast sales mgr., San Leandro, Calif., 1966-67; with Graham Mfg. Inc., Auburn, Ky., 1967-78, pres., 1977-78, agt., 1967—; owner, mgr. Weaver Enterprises, Bowling Green, Ky., 1952—; asst. prof., head dept. furniture prodn. mgmt. Vincennes U., 1978—; v.p. Tri-State Bedding Co., Inc., Bowling Green, 1979—. Mem. Warren County (Ky.) Election Commn., 1972-76; scoutmaster, explorer adv. Boy Scouts Am.; chmn. Republican City Com. Wabash (Ind.), 1958-59; mem. exec. com., Warren County Rep. Com., 1977—; bd. dirs. S. Union Shaker Assn., Inc. (Ky.), v.p., 1975; bd. dirs. Shakertown Revisited, Inc. Japanese Soc. N.Y. fellow, 1959. Mem. Soc. Auto Engrs., Nat. Assn. Furniture Mfrs., Travelers Protective Assn. Episcopalian (warden, vestryman). Club: Auburn Rotary (pres. 1973-74). Home: 619 Ironwood Dr Bowling Green KY 42101

WEAVER, CHARLES HORACE, educator; b. Statesville, N.C., Nov. 11, 1927; s. L. Stacy and Elizabeth (Halliburton) W.; A.B. in English, Wofford Coll., Spartanburg, S.C., 1951; M.A. in Edn. Columbia, 1956; Ph.D. in Edn., U. N.C., Chapel Hill, 1961; 1 son, Charles Horace Asst. supt. Asheboro (N.C.) City Schs., 1962-65; supt. Elizabeth City (N.C.) Pasquotank Schs., 1965-69. Burke County Schs., Morganton, N.C., 1969-79; cons. Div. Sch. Planning, State Dept. Public Instrn., Raleigh, N.C., 1979—; dir. Western Carolina Bank & Trust Co. Bd. dirs. Western Piedmont Symphony, United Fund, Burke County Council on Alcoholism, Flynn Christian Home. Mem. NEA, N.C. Assn. Educators, Am. Assn. Sch. Adminstrs., Horace Mann League (pres. 1976-77), Phi Delta Kappa. Club: Rotary. Home: 4701 New Hope Rd Raleigh NC 27604 Office: Div Sch Planning State Dept Public Instrn Raleigh NC 27609

WEAVER, FRANK JOSEPH, ednl. adminstr., pub. relations exec.; b. Harrisburg, Pa., Aug. 9, 1945; s. Francis J. and Rita Marie (Wilson) W.; B.A., U. Houston, 1969; postgrad. U. Tex., 1969-70, Mgmt. Health Program, Harvard U., 1979; m. Patsy R. Keen, Dec. 23, 1967. Asst. to dir. devel. U. Houston, 1967-69; asst. to dir. dept. devel. and pub. relations Baylor Coll. Medicine, Houston, 1970-71, asst. dir. devel., 1971, asst. dir. dept. devel. and pub. relations, 1971-74, dir. and prin. investigator pub. edn. sect. Nat. Heart and Blood Vessel Research and Demonstration Center, 1974—, dir. pub. relations, dept. devel. and pub. relations, 1974, dir. pub. affairs, 1975—, dep. dir. Jerry Lewis Neuromuscular Disease Research Center, 1975—; cons. U. Ark. Med. Sch. Alumni Assn., Robert Wood Johnson Found., VA, Am. Heart Assn., Nat. Heart, Lung and Blood Inst., Tex. So. U., 1974; cons. med. scis. to TV and radio. Mem. exec. com. Muscular Dystrophy Assn., 1975—. Recipient Baylor Med. Alumni Assn. award, 1970-72; Disting. Achievement award Ann. Conf. S.W. Dist., Council Advancement and Support of Edn., 1978. Mem. Assn. Am. Med. Colls. (chmn. group on pub. relations 1977-78, chmn. So. region 1975-76; chmn. membership com. 1974-75, nat. chmn. 1977—; Achievement award 1978), Pub. Relations Soc. Am. (chmn. edn. com. Houston chpt. 1974, chmn. 1979-80), Am. Public Health Assn., Am. Heart Assn. (chmn. pub. relations com. 1975-76; vice-chmn. Houston chpt. 1979-80, dir. Houston chpt. 1974—, exec. com. 1978-79, dir. Tex. affiliate 1977—; Leadership award 1975), San Jacinto Lung Assn. (mem. pub. relations com. 1974-76), Council Advancement and Support of Edn. (by-laws com. 1975, dist. sec.-treas. 1974-75, editor newsletter 1973-74), Am. Coll. Pub. Relations Assn. (awards 1973, 74, sec. treas. southwest dist. 1974-75, editor southwest dist. newsletter 1973-74), Tex. Soc. Hosp. Pub. Relations Dirs., Hosp. Pub. Relations Soc. (pres. Houston area 1972-73), Harris County Med. Soc. (mem. media relations adv. com. 1972—), Tex. Med. Assn. (mem. com. on gen. arrangements 1974 ann. session), Muscular Dystrophy Assn. (mem. exec com. Houston Gulf Coast chpt. 1975—), Houston C. of C. (mem. Houston mag. adv. com. 1974-76, mem. communications com. 1977—), Alpha Epsilon Rho, Sigma Delta Chi. Home: 1611 Cherry Ridge Dr Houston TX 77077 Office: Baylor College of Medicine Texas Medical Center Houston TX 77030

WEAVER, HENRY, aircraft parts mfg. co. exec.; b. Dayton, Ohio, Oct. 5, 1916; s. Johnathon Sylvester and Marie Etta (Davis) W.; B.B.A., U. Miami (Fla.), 1945; m. Ruth Esther Heisey, July 26, 1941; children—Pamela, J. Davis. Asst. supt. Pan Am. Airways, Miami, 1941-50; tech. engr. rep. Air Assos., Miami, 1950-53; gen. mgr. So. Engring. Corp., Miami, 1953-56; pres. Wencor Inc., Miami, 1956—, Wencor Mfrs., Griffin, Ga., 1970-75, Wencor Ltd., London, 1970-75; pres. Rocnew Corp., 1976—, Lentern Internat. Inc., 1978-79; owner Tall Tree Farms, Jackson, Ga.; dir. Internat. Power & Pipe Line, Inc. Mem. adv. staff U. Miami, U. Fla., 1966—. Flight Safety Found. grantee, 1966. Mem. Value Engring. Soc., ASTM, Am. Paint Horse Assn., Am. Quarter Horse Assn. Contbr. articles on reliability, inspection and testing of aircraft, hydraulic seals to tech. jours. Home: 1240 Campamento St Coral Gables FL 33156 Office: 1820 NW 42d Ave Miami FL 33126

WEAVER, JAMES HERBERT, JR., mfg. exec.; b. Denison, Tex., Sept. 7, 1942; s. James H. and Velma Faye W.; B.B.A. with honors, U. Tex., Austin, 1967, M.B.A., 1979; m. Mary Ann Cunningham, Oct. 22, 1973; children—Chad, Chris. Mfg. and mktg. positions Johnson & Johnson, 1968-74; dir. mktg. Precept, 1974-77; v.p. ops. Tecnol, Ft. Worth, 1977—, also asst. sec. Mem. Am. Mgmt. Assn., Ft. Worth C. of C., Republican. Baptist. Office: Tecnol Inc 7450 Whitehall Fort Worth TX 76118

WEAVER, JERRY, mfg. co. exec.; b. Sextons Creek, Ky., May 21, 1931; s. Joe Bob and Jackie (Baker) W.; LL.D. (hon.), Union Coll., 1976; m. Susan Irene Ball, Mar. 8, 1952; children—Harold Ray, Daryle Robert. With Internat. Tool Co., Dayton, Ohio, 1951-57; plant supt. Ala. Tool Co., Gadsden, 1957-62; owner Dixie Tool & Die, Inc., Gadsden, 1962-64, Etowah Mfg. Co., Inc., Gadsden, from 1964; pres., chmn. bd. Mid-South Industries, Inc., Gadsden, Dixie Tool & Die, Gadsden, Mid-South Controls, Inc., Carthage, Miss., EMCO, Inc., Gadsden, Mid-South Electrics, Inc., Gadsden and Manchester, Ky., Mid-South Stamping Co., Inc., Gadsden, Sutton Bridge, Inc., Gadsden, Mid-South Leasing Co., Inc., Gadsden; chmn. bd. dirs. Coosa Valley Bank, Gadsden. Mem. Rainbow City Planning Commn., 1974; adv. com. Ala. Tech. Coll., Gadsden, 1975; bd. trustees Annville Inst., 1974—, Union Coll., 1979—; mem. Nat. Def. Exec. Res., U.S. Dept. Commerce, 1977—. Named Outstanding Alumnus, Annville Inst., 1973. Mem. Gadsden C. of C. (pres. 1972), Nat. Tool, Die and Precision Machining Assn. (pres. 1980—). Baptist. Clubs: Masons, Moose. Home: Route 4 Rainbow Dr Gadsden AL 35901 Office: PO Box 322 Gadsden AL 35902

WEAVER, JOSEPH DUDLEY, physician; b. nr. Winton, N.C., Sept. 11, 1912; s. Jesse Robert and Claudia C. (Hall) W.; B.S., Howard U., 1934, M.D., 1938; m. Rossie Mae Phenis Clay, Apr. 22, 1958; children—Jesse Robert, Patricia (adopted), Claudia. Intern Freedmen's Hosp., Washington, 1938-39; pvt. practice medicine Hartford, N.C., 1939-46, Ahoskie, 1946—; owner, operator Weaver Clinic, Ahoskie; active staff Roanoke Chowan Hosp., chief staff, 1973-75; asst. nat. med. dir. Elks, dir. Med. Clinics; treas. Hobson R. Reynolds Elk's Nat. Shrine, Inc., 1969—; med. examiner Hertford County (N.C.); mem. N.C. Air Quality Council, 1978—; bd. dirs., exec. com. Eastern N.C. PSRO. Served from 2d lt. (Res.) to 1st lt. M.C., AUS, 1942-44. Named Dr. of Year, Old North State Med. Soc., 1963. Mem. Ahoskie C. of C., Eastern N.C. Med., Dental and Pharm. Soc., Old North State, Hertford County, 1st Dist. (pres. 1975) med. socs., Nat. Med. Assn., Med. Soc. State N.C., Acad. Family Physicians, AMA, Am. Geriatric Soc., Nat. Rehab. Assn., Kappa Alpha Psi, Beta Kappa Chi. Democrat. Baptist. Clubs: Masons (32 deg.), Elks, Ambassador (pres. 1948—). Home: RFD 2 256-D Ahoskie NC 27910 Office: 111 N Maple St Ahoskie NC 27910

WEAVER, MABLE MCCONATHA, accountant; b. Alpine, Ala., Oct. 13, 1916; d. Charles Edward and Eula Mabel (Holman) McConatha; student Internat. Accountants Soc., 1962-64, U. South Ala., 1969-74; m. Randolph Stinton Weaver, Feb. 25, 1938; children—Randolph Stinton, Sherry Anne. Bookkeeper, Star Fruit & Produce Co. Inc., Mobile, 1936; office mgr. Golden Eagle Gasoline Stas. Inc., Mobile, 1959-62; accountant James Mayton, C.P.A., Mobile, 1962-71, Wilk, Reimer & Sweet, C.P.A.'s, Mobile, 1971-74; pvt. practice accounting, Mobile, 1974—. C.P.A., Ala. Mem. Am. Inst. C.P.A.'s, Am. Women's, Ala. socs. C.P.A.'s. Baptist. Home: 1918 Old Government St Mobile AL 36606 Office: PO Box 6101 1916B Government St Mobile AL 36606

WEAVER, MACON MOORE, educator; b. Littleton, N.C., Nov. 7, 1935; s. William Blackwell and Beulah Rebecca (Moore) W.; A.B., U. N.C., 1957, M.S., 1962; Ph.D., U. Miss., 1972; m. Evelyn Knisley, Sept. 24, 1958; 1 son, Macon Moore. Med. technician, dept. mycology Duke U., Hosp., Durham, N.C., 1959-61; prof. biol. sci. Chowan Coll., Murfreesboro, N.C., 1962-65; instr. biol. sci. Miss. Coll., Clinton, 1965-68; NIH trainee U. Miss. Med. Center, Jackson, 1968-71, asst. prof. anatomy, 1974—; asst. prof. Hahnemann Med. Center, Phila., 1972-74. Served with U.S. Army, 1957-59. Miss. Heart Assn. fellow, 1974, grantee, 1975. Mem. So. Soc. Anatomists, Am. Heart Assn., Am. Assn. Anatomy, Miss. Acad. Scis., Sigmi Xi. Democrat. Methodist. Contbr. articles to profl. jours. Home: 153 Riviera Dr Jackson MS 39211 Office: Dept Anatomy University of Mississippi 2500 N State St Jackson MS 39216

WEAVER, MARILYN GAIL, nurse; b. Louisville, Dec. 6, 1946; d. James Blair and Dorothy Emma (McDermott) Swartzwelder; B.S. in Nursing, U. Ky., 1968; postgrad. in Counseling Psychology, Spalding Coll., 1974-79. Staff nurse pediatrics Univ. Hosp., Lexington, Ky., 1968-69, medicine and surgery Meth. Evang. Hosp., Louisville, 1969-71; instr. nursing Ky. Bapt. Hosp., Louisville, 1973-79; psychiat. staff nurse Our Lady of Peace Hosp., Louisville, 1979—. Active Citizens Advocacy Program for Retarded, 1977, Hospice, 1978—. Recipient Outstanding Achievement award Optimist Club, 1961. Mem. Am. Nursing Assn., Ky. Nurses Assn., Am. Personnel and Guidance Assn. Home: 4305 Norene Ln Louisville KY 40219 Office: 2020 Newburg Rd Louisville KY 40205

WEAVER, MARILYN LEWIS, ednl. aminstr.; b. Pitts., May 29, 1938; s. Joseph Edwards and Mary Elizabeth (Dolan) Lewis; B.S., U. Houston, 1959, M.A., 1962; m. James E. Weaver, Jr., Jan. 28, 1970; children—Joseph Lewis, Jefferson Lee, Robert Christopher. Therapist Houston Speech and Hearing Center, 1960-62; dir. Spl. Care Sch., Dallas, 1964-68; dir. edn. and day care service Dallas County Mental Health and Mental Retardation Center, 1968-70; program dir. Children, Inc., Dallas, 1970-72, Angels, Inc., Dallas, 1971-76; pres. Package Deal, Inc., 1977—; exec. dir. Creative Children's Center, 1977—. Instr. community service div. El Centro Jr. Coll., Dallas, 1968-78; faculty Richland Community Coll., 1975-78. Mem. Adv. Bd. Helping Hand Sch., Irving, Tex., 1969-78; human services adv. com. Eastfield Coll., 1975-77. Mem. Am. Assn. Mental Deficiency, Council for Exceptional Children, Gamma Phi Beta. Home: 7018 Spring Valley Rd Dallas TX 75240 Office: 1015 Newberry Richardson TX 75080

WEAVER, MARY CARLA, oil co. ofcl.; b. Houston, Dec. 2, 1946; d. Carnes Wesley and Mary Loraine (West) W.; B.A. in Math., Randolph-Macon Woman's Coll., 1968; postgrad. N.Y. U., 1970-71; M.B.A., U. Houston, 1973. Operations research analyst Sinclair Oil, Tulsa, 1968-69; operations research analyst Sperry & Hutchinson Co., N.Y.C., 1969-70; instr. math. St. John's Sch., Houston, 1971-73; planning annalyst, staff analyst, mgr. planning systems and support Pennzoil Co., Houston, 1973-78, mgr. contbns. and community relations, 1978—. Obs., White House Conf. Balanced Growth and Econ. Devel., 1978; dir., chmn. fin. com. Houston Com. for Humanities and Public Policy; vol. polit. campaigns; fund raising adviser After Dinner Players; dir. Mountain Top Ministries. Mem. Planning Execs. Inst., Houston C. of C. (future studies com.). Methodist. Contbg. author: Corporate Financial Planning Models, 1977. Home: 5807 Beverly Hill St Apt 3 Houston TX 77057 Office: Pennzoil Co PO Box 2967 Houston TX 77001

WEAVER, OUIDA JONES, health agy. exec.; b. Ellabelle, Ga., Jan. 9, 1929; d. Hardee Bartow and Violet Vermelle (Morgan) Jones; nursing diploma Jefferson Davis Hosp. Sch. of Nursing, 1951; B.S., U. Houston, 1956; M.S., Tex. Woman's U., 1973; m. Walter William Weaver, Aug. 5, 1948; children—James David, Debra Suzanne Weaver McKelvey, Pamela Camille. Staff nurse Jefferson David Hosp., 1951, communicable disease nurse, polio center, 1952; clin. instr. Southwest Polimyelitis Rehab. Center, 1952-53; staff nurse Houston-Harris County chpt. Am. Nat. Red Cross, 1953-54, asst. dir. nursing service, 1954-56, dir. nursing service, 1956-68, Tex. regional dir. nursing service, 1967-68; exec. dir. Vis. Nurse Assn. Houston, Inc., 1968—. Mem. Montgomery County Child Welfare Bd., 1977; mem. nursing adv. bd. Houston-Harris County chpt. ARC; mem. alternative care com. Tex. Dept. Humon Resources, 1979-80. Recipient certificate of Appreciation, Houston Jr. C. of C., 1968. Mem. Am. Bus. Women's Assn., Am., Tex. (dir. 1971-77, treas. 1975-77, pres. 1979—) nurses assns., Nat., Tex., Houston Area leagues for nursing, Am., Tex. pub. health assns., Nat., Tex. (dir. 1971-77, pres. 1978-80) assns. home health agys., Internat. Inst. for Edn. Republican. Methodist. Home: 1993 O'Grady Dr McDade Estates Conroe TX 77301 Office: 3100 Timmons Ln Houston TX 77027

WEAVER, PRESTON DOUGLAS, govt. program adminstr.; b. Montclair, N.J., Apr. 8, 1940; s. Richard Edward and Alma Barbara (Bass) W.; B.A., N.C. Central U., 1962, postgrad., 1963; postgrad. Va. State U., 1964; 1 son, Derrick R. Guidance counselor Charles E. Perry High Sch., Roseboro N.C., 1963-64; adminstrv. asst., programmer Operation Breakthrough, Inc., Durham, N.C., 1965-67; exec. project dir. GROW, Inc., Raleigh, N.C., 1967-68; project writer N.C. Manpower Devel. Corp, Durham, 1968; vocat. counselor Joint Orange/Chatham Community Action Program, Chapel Hill, N.C., 1969-70; model cities liaison specialist, govtl. relations div. N.C. Dept. Natural and Econ. Resources, Raleigh, 1970-71; exec. dir. region IV Citizens Council, Inc., Atlanta, 1971—. Vice pres. D.M. Therrell High Sch. Parent-Tchrs.-Student Assn., 1977—; mem. Parents for Action, Ga. PTA. Mem. Am. Soc. for Public Adminstrn., Am. Personnel and Guidance Assn. Democrat. Baptist. Club: Young Dems. Fulton County. Home: 4570 St Andrews Dr SW Atlanta GA 30331 Office: 859 1/2 Martin L King Jr Dr NW Atlanta GA 30314

WEAVER, ROBERT SAMUEL, IV, marine instn. adminstr.; b. Richmond, Va., Mar. 30, 1950; s. Robert Samuel and Vera Nolen W.; B.A. magna cum laude, U. South Fla., 1978; m. Gloria Ann Brunelle, Apr. 14, 1974. Instr. phys. edn. Horizon Sch. for Gifted, Miami, Fla., 1971-74; instr. scuba diving Dade Marine Inst., Miami, 1974-75; tng. dir. Pinellas Marine Inst., St. Petersburg, Fla., 1975-78; v.p. Asso. Marine Inst., Tampa, 1978—. Instr. sailing ARC, also water safety; instr. scuba YMCA. Cert., 1st aide, CPR., lic. C.G. capt. Mem. Nat. Assn. Underwater Instrs., Nat. Assn. Cave Diving. Home: 2930 166 Ave N Clearwater FL 33520 Office: 1311 N Westshore Blvd Suite 202 Tampa FL 33607

WEAVER, RONALD RAY, geophysicist; b. Amarillo, Tex., Apr. 17, 1940; s. Z. G. and Effie G. (McNeese) W.; B.S., W. Tex. State U., 1962; m. Linda Lee Sims, Sept. 16, 1977; children by previous marriage—Patricia Leanne, Douglas Ray; stepchildren—Lori Beth and Leslie Dawn Sims. Geophys. engr. Geophys. Service, Inc., Houston, 1965-67, party chief, 1968-69, area geophysicist, 1970-73, processing mgr., 1974-75, U.S. marine exploration mgr., 1976-78, mgr. Latin Am./Caribbean marine exploration, 1978-79, mgr. Western U.S. land exploration, Midland, Tex., 1979—. Served to 1st lt. AUS, 1963-65. Mem. Soc. Exploration Geophysicists, Am., Pacific Coast, Houston, Permian Basin geophys. socs., Kappa Alpha. Patentee in field. Home: 4307 Valley Dr Midland TX 79703 Office: PO Drawer 1802 Midland TX 79702

WEAVER, SARAH COLBY, rehab. counselor; b. Hinton, W.Va., Feb. 7, 1954; d. Colby Sawyers and Frances Carroll (Hedrick) Weaver; student (public service student intern 1975-76) Concord Coll., 1973-76; B.A. in Psychology, W.Va. U., 1977, M.S. in Rehab. Counseling, 1978. Rehab. coordinator, counselor W.Va. Workmen's Compensation Fund, Charleston, 1979; systems coordinator emergency med. services for six so. counties W.Va., Beckley, 1979—. Pres. Young Republican Club, 1972-73; chmn. March of Dimes Drive for Summers County Schs., 1972-73; adv. council Am. Lung Assn., 1980—. Recipient Danforth award for outstanding leadership, 1973; Citizenship award Am. Legion, 1973. Mem. Am. Personnel and Guidance Assn., Nat. Rehab. Assn., Nat. Paraplegic Assn. Republican. Office: Box 1514 North Eisenhower Dr Beckley WV 25801

WEAVER, WILLIAM KISER, JR., coll. pres., clergyman; b. Oxford, Ala., Dec. 23, 1918; s. William K. and Roberta (Cooper) W.; A.B., Samford U., 1940, D.D., 1957; Th.M., So. Bapt. Theol. Sem., 1943; m. Annie Boyd Parker, Nov. 4, 1948; 1 dau., Anne Parker Weaver Reed. Ordained to ministry Bapt. Ch., 1943; dir. religious activities Samford U., Birmingham, 1946-48; dir. dept. Bapt. student work Ala., 1948-50 pastor First Bapt. Ch. Sylacauga (Ala.), 1950-61; founding pres. Mobile (Ala.) Coll., 1961—. Mem. edn. commn. So. Bapt. Conv., 1968-73; chmn. Citizens' Com. for Juvenile Delinquency Study, 1966-69; bd. dirs. Mobile area council Boy Scouts Am., 1964—, ARC, Mobile chpt., 1966—, Community Chest and Council, 1967-75, pres., 1974-75; bd. dirs. Gordon Smith Center, 1969—; bd. dirs. Mobile Museum Bd., 1964-77, chmn., 1976-77; mem. adv. com. Rotary Rehab. Center, 1973—; bd. dirs. United Fund Mobile, 1976—, Vol. Mobile, 1975-79, America's Jr. Miss Scholarship Found., 1969-72, Bapt. Sunday Sch. Bd., 1964-67; chmn. Jr. Miss. Adv. Com., 1961-64; trustee So. Bapt. Theol. Sem., 1974—, Gulf Coast Inst. Research and Tech., 1966-68. Served with USN, 1944-46. Mem. Mobile Area C. of C. (dir. 1975-79), Council Advancement of Small Colls. (dir. 1965-68, 70-76), Ala. Assn. Ind. Colls. (v.p. 1975), Assn. So. Bapt. Colls. and Schs. (pres. 1977-78), Ala. Hist. Soc., Newcomen Soc., Phi Kappa Phi, Omicron Delta Kappa. Club: Rotary (pres. 1974-75, dir. 1970-76, dist. gov. 1978-79). Home: Route 4 Box 460 Mobile AL 36609 Office: PO Box 13220 Mobile AL 36613

WEBB, CHARLES ROYCE, psychologist, coll. adminstr.; b. Prattville, Ala., Jan. 12, 1939; s. Judson Leonard and Helen Elette (Hunt) W.; B.S., U. Tenn., 1961; M. Ed., Memphis State U., 1970; Ed.D., Auburn U., 1975; m. Ruth Copeland, July 27, 1963; children—Charles Royce, Timothy Newton, Maria Gayle. Tchr. Bemis Jr. High Sch., Madison County, Tenn., 1965-68; counselor Halls (Tenn.) High Sch., 1968-70, Ga. Christian Sch., Valdosta, 1970-72; counselor sch. engring. Auburn (Ala.) U., 1973-75; tchr. psychology Freed-Hardeman Coll., Henderson, Tenn., 1975-76, dir. academic and career planning, and testing, 1976—; ordained minister

Ch. of Christ, 1964, pastor, Lexington and Halls, Tenn., Valdosta, Ga., Madison, Fla., 1964—. Pres., Mental Health Assn. Chester County, Tenn., 1977; active Boy Scouts Am. Served with USN, 1961-64. Certified tchr., counselor, Tenn., Ga. Mem. Am., Tenn. personnel and guidance assns., Am., So., Tenn. coll. personnel assns., Nat. Vocat. Guidance Assn. Club: Civitan (pres. Henderson 1978-79). Home: Jacks Creek TN 38347 Office: Freed-Hardeman Coll Henderson TN 38340

WEBB, EARL SHERMAN, educator; b. Moody, Mo., Sept. 23, 1915; s. Millard Henderson and Nora Francis (Strickland) W.; B.S., U. Mo., 1949, M.Ed., 1955, Ed.D., 1959; m. Ruth Naomi Rhodes, Apr. 13, 1940; 1 dau., Debra Ann. Tchr., Howell County Public Schs., West Plains, Mo., 1938-47, Iberia and Washington (Mo.) Public Schs., 1949-56; mem. faculty U. Mo., Columbia, 1956-61; mem. faculty Tex. A.&M. U., College Station, 1961—, asst. prof. agrl. edn., 1959-67, prof., 1967—. Served with USAAF, 1943-46. Recipient Faculty Disting. Achievement award Tex. A.&M. U., 1970; hon. state FFA degree, 1965. Mem. Am. Vocat. Assn., NEA, Tex. Tchrs. Assn., Phi Kappa Phi, Phi Delta Kappa, Gamma Sigma Delta. Mem. Ch. of Christ. Clubs: Rotary, Lions. Contbr. articles to Agrl. Edn. Mag. Home: 1011 Winding Rd College Station TX 77840 Office: Dept Agrl Edn Tex A&M U College Station TX 77843

WEBB, ELLSWORTH RUSSELL, urologist; b. Detroit, Mar. 22, 1945; s. Ellsworth Russell and Virginia Eloise (Bess) W.; M.D., U. Mich., 1971; m. Camille Elizabeth Gollon, June 21, 1969; children—Nathan, Deirdre, Luke. Intern, William Beaumont Hosp., Royal Oak, Mich., 1971-72, resident in urology, 1972-76; practice medicine specializing in urology, Mountain Home, Ark., 1978—; mem. staff Baxter County Gen. Hosp., Fulton County Hosp., Marion County Hosp., Calico Rock Med. Center. Served with AUS, 1976-78. Fellow Am. Bd. Urology. Mem. Baxter County Med. Soc., Ark. Med. Soc. Club: Elks. Home: 119 Parkview Circle Mountain Home AR 72653 Office: 10 Medical Plaza Mountain. Home AR 72653

WEBB, ERNEST PACKARD, publisher; b. Junta, W.Va., Aug. 30, 1907; s. Robert Moses and Josephine (Harvey) W.; student Fed. Schs. Comml. Designing, Mpls., 1926-29; student advt. Internat. Corr. Schs., 1946-48, Alexander Hamilton Bus. Sch., 1948-52. Artist, Mountain State Engraving Co., 1929, Huntington Engraving Co. (W.Va.), 1930, Charleston Engraving Co. (W.Va.), 1931; owner, mgr. Profl. Art Studio, Roanoke, Va., 1931-40; v.p., treas. Roanoke Engraving Co., 1940-48; pres. Va. Engraving Co., Richmond, 1947—; v.p. Dixie Engraving Co., Roanoke, 1961—; pres. W. & H. Corp., Richmond, 1968—. Served with USAAF, 1942-45. Mem. Va., Richmond chambers commerce, Internat. Craftsman's Club. Republican. Baptist. Clubs: Richmond Industrial, Willow Oaks Country, Westwood (Richmond). Home: 2000 Riverside Dr Richmond VA 23225 Office: 2003 Roane St Richmond VA 23222

WEBB, FRANK RONALDSON, retail furniture co. exec.; b. Homestead, Fla., Apr. 23, 1942; s. Andrew Franklin and Gladys Beatrice (Freeman) W.; B.S. in Indsl. Mgmt., Ga. Inst. Tech., 1964; m. Brenda Carol Yount, Dec. 29, 1967; children—Frank R., Ashleigh, Hiliary, William. Sales staff Homestead Furniture Co., 1964-68, treas., 1968—; treas. Webb-Leiby Enterprises, Homestead, Fla., 1966—; bd. dirs. 1st Nat. Bank Homestead. Bd. dirs. Nat. Bicycle Found., 1977; mem. Homestead City Primary Health Task Force, 1977, Homestead Downtown Redevel. Com., 1977. Mem. Greater Homestead C. of C. (pres. 1975-76). Democrat. Methodist. Clubs: Rotary (pres. 1970-71), Com. of 100 Miami Beach. Home: 16200 SW 200 St Miami FL 33187 Office: 35 N Krome Ave Homestead FL 33030

WEBB, JACK WILLIAMS, JR., ins. agt.; b. Bluefield, W.Va., Feb. 26, 1948; s. Jack Williams and Faye (Nimmo) W.; B.S., Va. Poly. Inst. and State U., 1970, M.B.A., 1971; m. Carolyn Parker, Aug. 22, 1970; 1 son, Jack Williams, III. With Nansemond Ins. Agy., Inc., Suffolk, Va., 1971—, comml. lines agt., 1973—, comml. lines supr., 1975-79, treas., 1977—. Pres., Tri-County Assn. for Retarded Children, Suffolk, 1976, treas., 1977-79. Named to Outstanding Young Men of Am., U.S. Jaycees, 1975. Mem. Nat. Assn. Ins. Agts., Suffolk Assn. Ins. Agts. (pres. 1976), Suffolk Jaycees (pres. 1976, chmn. bd. 1977), Suffolk C. of C. (dir. 1979), Va. Bluewater Gamefish Assn. Baptist. Home: 101 Brewer Ave Suffolk VA 23434 Office: PO Box 1626 Suffolk VA 23434

WEBB, JOHN ROBERT, personnel service co. exec.; b. Leland, Miss., July 22, 1940; s. Robert Melvin and Hazel Louise (McDaniel) W.; m. Cheryl Ann Hardin, Dec. 14, 1979. Process engr. Uniroyal, Inc., Baton Rouge, 1963-64; pilot plant engr. Copolymer Rubber & Chem. Co., Baton Rouge, 1964-67; asst. prodn. supt. Baxter Labs., Kingstree, S.C., 1967-68; research engr. Celanese Chem., Corpus Christi, Tex., 1968-70; pres., chmn. bd. W-J Enterprises, Inc., San Antonio, 1970—; dir. Dunhill Personnel Service, San Antonio, 1973—. Registered profl. engr., Tex. Mem. Nat. Employment Assn., Am. Inst. Chem. Engrs., Tex. Pvt. Employment Assn., San Antonio Pvt. Employment Assn. Republican. Baptist. Office: W-J Enterprises Inc 464 GPM South San Antonio TX 78216

WEBB, LARRY WAYNE, counselor; b. Leeds, Ala., Apr. 3, 1948; s. Chester Lee and Essie Mae (Martin) W.; B.S. in Social Welfare, U. Ala., 1974, M.A. in Guidance and Counseling (CEEB upper div. scholar 1972-74), 1979. Social worker I, Ala. Dept. Pensions and Security, Birmingham, 1974-75; youth services counselor trainee Ala. Youth Services, Roebuck Campus, Birmingham, 1979—; vol. worker Bryce (Ala.) State Hosp., 1971-73. Served with USAF, 1966-70, USAR, 1975-78. Recipient Youth Devel. Ednl. Achievement award Jefferson County (Ala.) Commn. Equal Opportunity, 1972. Mem. Am. Personnel and Guidance Assn., Nat. Rehab. Assn., Shorin-ryu Matsumura Orthodox Karate-Do Assn. Mem. Mensa, Kappa Delta Pi. Home: 316 Wendy Ave SW Leeds AL 35094 Office: 8950 Roebuck Blvd Birmingham AL 35255

WEBB, LEOTA FAYE, gas utility exec.; b. Nitro, W.Va., Nov. 2, 1932; d. Fred Franklin and Allegra Faye (Johnson) Behen; ed. extension course Harvard U., Berlitz Sch. Langs., 1951; children—Keith Alan, John Scott, Kelly Rae. Exec. sec. John Hancock Mut. Life Ins. Co., Boston, 1950-56; exec. sec. Columbia Gas Transmission Corp. (W.Va.), 1956-76, gen. services office mgr., 1976-79, mgr. office and spl. services, 1979—. Mem. Am. Mgmt. Assn. Club: Zonta Internat. Office: PO Box 1273 Charleston WV 25314

WEBB, LINDA JEAN, educator; b. Chgo., Sept. 25, 1946; d. Bert Williamson and Mary Ethel Webb; B.S., U. Fla., 1968; M.P.H., U. Tex., 1972, D.P.H., 1975. With Tex. Research Inst. Mental Scis., 1968-78, 78-79, research specialist program evaluation, 1975-78, chief evaluation research, 1978-79; mem. adj. faculty U. Tex. Sch. Public Health, 1977—; dir. continuing edn. Tex. Dept. Mental Health and Mental Retardation, 1979—; bd. dirs. Tex. Center of A.K. Rice Inst., Southwest Rehab. Inst. Fellow Tex Dept. Mental Health and Retardation, 1973-74; Allied Health Professions scholar, 1968. Mem. Am. Public Health Assn., A.K. Rice Inst., Nat. Assn. Mental Health, Soc. Psychotherapy Research, Assn. Women in Psychology, Mortar Board, Eto Rho Pi. Democrat. Methodist. Author articles in field; editorial bd. Jour. Personality and Social Systems, 1978—. Home: 1511 Kipling St Houston TX 77006 Office: 1300 Moursund St Houston TX 77030

WEBB, PAUL SANDY, city govt. ofcl.; b. Louisville, May 25, 1945; s. Robert Shields and Juanita (Coker) W.; student Carson-Newman Coll., 1963-64, U. Tenn., 1968-69; m. Louise Ogle, Sept. 10, 1965; children—Charla Rene, Shonna Lynn. With Sta. WJFC, 1964-65, Sta. WLIK, 1965-66; news dir. WATE-TV, Knoxville, Tenn., 1969-78; fire and bldg. insp. Sevierville (Tenn.), 1979—; owner motel, 1971—. Sevier County detective Sheriff's Dept., 1978-79; bd. dirs. Community Center, Tourist Ministry; mem. Bicentennial Commn., Swim Team Bd. Served with AUS, 1966-68; Africa. Mem. Internat. Assn. Fire Marshals, Nat., Tenn. sheriffs assns., Nat. Fire Protection Assn., Am. Hotel-Motel Assn., Fraternal Order Police (asso.), Radio and TV News Dirs. Assn., Sevier County Jaycees (service awards). Baptist. Home: Route 6 Birchwood Sevierville TN 37862 Office: City Hall Sevierville TN 37862

WEBB, RICHARD HENRY, IV, banker; b. Miami, Fla., July 16, 1951; s. Richard Henry and Eleanor (Myers) W.; B.B.A., U. Miami, 1974; m. Ana Luisa Naranjo, Aug. 24, 1974. Trust officer Miami Beach 1st Nat. Bank, 1969-74; programmer Flagship Services Corp., Miami Beach, 1974-76; trust systems officer Flagship Nat. Bank Miami, 1976—; adj. instr. Miami Dade Community Coll., 1979—. Mem. conservative caucus Republican Nat. Com., 1978—. Mem. Internat. Word Processing Assn., Miami Lakes Jaycees (chmn. bd., 1979-80, best dist. chpt. pres. 1978-79). Home: 13957 Lake Lure Ct Miami Lakes FL 33014

WEBB, ROBERT MACHARDY, geographer; b. Hamilton, Ohio, Dec. 2, 1915; s. Walter and Margert (MacHardy) W.; B.S., Memphis State Coll., 1949; M.A., Ohio State U., 1950; Ph.D., U. Kans., 1962; m. Bernice Larson, July 14, 1961. Instr. geography Ohio Wesleyan U., 1951-53; mem. faculty U. Man., Winnipeg, Can., summer 1964, 65, Chapman Coll., World Campus Afloat, 1972; mem. faculty U. Southwestern La., Lafayette, 1956—, prof. geography, 1964—, coordinator geography, 1973—; mem. Tamil-Nadu Seminar on Community Devel. in India, 1976. Served with USAAF, 1942-45. Mem. Assn. Am. Geographers, La. Acad. Scis. (pres. 1979). Unitarian. Author articles in field. Home: 159 Whittington Dr Lafayette LA 70503 Office: Box 40861 Univ Southwestern La Lafayette LA 70504

WEBB, ROBERT WATKINS, physician, educator; b. Chickasha, Okla., Jan. 25, 1906; s. Napoleon B. and Mary Elizabeth (White) W.; B.A., So. Meth. U., 1926; M.D., Tulane U., 1933; grad. Washington Sch. Psychiatry, 1952, Washington D.C. Psychoanalytic Inst., 1952; m. Elisabeth N. Nutting, Sept. 13, 1952. Intern Hotel Dieu Hosp., New Orleans, 1933-34; resident Pa. Hosp. Mental and Nervous Diseases, Phila., 1934-36, Inst. Pa. Hosp., 1936; asso. physician Silver Hill Found., New Canaan, Conn., 1936-37, resident Payne-Whitney Psychiat. Clinic, N.Y. Hosp., 1937-38; clin. asso. prof. psychiatry Southwestern Med. Sch., Dallas, 1953—; pvt. practice, Dallas, 1939-41, 52—; sr. attending staff physician Parkland Hosp., Dallas, 1953—. Trustee Dallas Art Assn.; bd. dirs. Dallas Theater Center. Served with M.C., AUS, 1941-46. Mem. AMA, Internat., Am. psychoanalytic assns., Am. Coll. Psychiatrists, Am. Coll. Psychoanalysts, Tex. Neuropsychiat. Assn., Am., So. psychiat. assns. Home and office: 5530 Farquhar Ln Dallas TX 75209

WEBB, TERENCE HAROLD EUGENE, chemist; b. Jacksonville, Fla., Aug. 18, 1938; s. Lewis Eugene and Emma Irene (Grossarth) W.; B.S. (scholar), Stetson U., 1960; M.S., La. State U., 1966. Petrochemist, Lab. Service, Inc., Good Hope, La., 1962-65; reliability engr. Westinghouse Molecular Electronics, Elkridge, Md., 1966; chemist Catalyst Research Corp., Balt., 1967-70; lab. scientist Md. Air Quality Lab., Balt., 1970-71; chemist Jacksonville Electric Authority, Jacksonville, Fla., 1973—. Leader, North Fla. and New Orleans area Boy Scouts Am., 1954-61. Nat. Cottonseed Products Assn. fellow, 1960-61. Recipient award Math. Assn. Am., Howarth Found., Fla. Acad. Scis. Fellow Am. Inst. Chemists; mem. Electrochem. Soc., Am. Chem. Soc., ASTM, Nat. Assn. Corrosion Engrs., Mensa, Ft. George Island Preservation Assn., Gamma Sigma Epsilon, Kappa Kappa Psi, Sigma Alpha Omega. Codeveloper 12 year lithium battery for implanted cardiac pacemaker, 1968-70. Contbr. articles to profl. jours. Home: 10023 Heckscher Dr Fort George Island FL 32226 Office: 4377 Heckscher Dr Jacksonville FL 32218

WEBB, WILLIAMS WILSON, ret. educator; b. Wagener, S.C., Apr. 20, 1914; s. Mac Williams and Marie Pearle (Wilson) W.; B.S., Clemson U., 1935, M.Ed., 1975; postgrad. Furman U., 1971, N.C. State U., 1972; m. Millie Louise Turner, July 26, 1942; children—Clark Wilson, John Mac (dec.); m. 2d, Annie Ducworth Elrod, Dec. 16, 1977. Textile chemist United Mchts. & Mfrs. Mgmt. Corp., Clearwater, S.C., 1935-37; chief textile chemist Kerr Bleaching and Finishing Works, Inc., Concord, N.C., 1937-38; textile chemist Burlington Mills Corp., Greensboro, N.C., 1938-39; farm crop surveyor Anderson County Agrl. Dept., Anderson, S.C., 1939-41; textile chemist Am. Thread Co., Willimantic, Conn., 1946, Deering-Milliken Research Trust, Clemson, S.C., 1946-47, LaFrance Industries (S.C.), 1947-48; overseer Abbeville (S.C.) Mills div. Deering-Milliken, Inc., 1948-56, Mooresville (N.C.) Mills div. Burlington Industries, Inc., 1956-62; textile chemist, colorist, lab. mgr. Am. and Efird Mills, Inc., Mount Holly, N.C., 1962-65; textile chemist Belle Chem. Co. (name now Harshaw Chem. Co.), Lowell, N.C., 1965-66; instr. textile mgmt. dept. Greenville (S.C.) Tech. Coll., 1966-71, dept. head, instr. textile mgmt. dept., 1971-72, instr. textile mgmt. dept., 1972-78. Merit badge counselor Boy Scouts Am., 1970-71. Served to capt. AUS, 1941-46. Decorated Bronze Star with oak leaf cluster. Fellow Am. Inst. Chemists, S.C. Inst. Chemists (mem. accreditation com. 1973-76); mem. Am. Chem. Soc., Am. Assn. Textile Chemists and Colorists, S.C. State Employees Assn., 101st Airborne Div. Assn., Phi Psi. Baptist. Clubs: Clemson U. Alumni, Clemson U. Iptay, Lions. Home: PO Box 395 Anderson SC 29622 also Route 1 Box 116-B Williamston SC 29697

WEBBER, JANE TURPIN, dietitian; b. Greenwood, Miss., Aug. 6, 1942; d. Charles Franklin and Emilye (Sayle) Turpin; B.S. in Food and Nutrition, Tex. Woman's U., Denton, 1964; m. Robert William Webber, July 11, 1964. Mem. dietetic staff Baylor U. Med. Center, Dallas, 1965—, adminstrv. dietitian central food service, 1968-70, dir. dietary services Hoblitzelle Meml. Hosp., 1970—; mem. food service cluster adv. com. Dallas Ind. Sch. Dist., 1970—, chmn., 1978-79. Mem. Am. Soc. Hosp. Food Service Adminstrs. (regional dir. 1977-78, chmn. scholarship com. 1978, pres. N. Tex. chpt. 1972), Am. Dietetic Assn., Tex. Dietetic Assn., Dallas Dietetic Assn. (chmn. adminstrv. dietetics sect. 1975-76), Tex. Restaurant Assn. Presbyterian. Office: 3500 Gaston Ave Dallas TX 75246

WEBER, CARL HAROLD, JR., physician, ret. air force officer; b. Lakewood, Ohio, July 28, 1933; s. Carl Harold and Betty Ruth (Stowe) W.; M.D., Duke U., 1960; m. Rosemary Ormand, Dec. 28, 1951; children—Carl Harold III, Benjamin O., Robert B. Commd. 2d lt. USAF, 1959, advanced through grades to col., 1977; ret., 1979; intern Duke Hosp., Durham, N.C., 1960-61, resident in surgery and urology, 1964-68; chief urology USAF Hosp., Lakenheath, Eng., 1968-72; acting chief urology Wilford Hall USAF Med. Center, San Antonio, 1972-73, asst. chief urology, 1973-79, tng. officer in urology, 1973-79; med. staff San Antonio Community, S.W. Tex. Meth., St. Luke's Luth. hosps., Santa Rosa Med. Center (all San Antonio), 1979—. Diplomate Am. Bd. Urology. Fellow ACS; mem. Assn. Mil. Surgeons U.S., Govt. Services Urologists Soc. (dir. 1976-78), Soc. Air Force Clin. Surgeons, Am. Urol. Assn., San Antonio Urol. Assn., San Antonio Surg. Soc. Presbyn. Contbr. articles to profl. jours. Home: 13902 Flying W Trail Helotes TX 78023 Office: 8042 Wurzbach Rd Suite 260 San Antonio TX 78229

WEBER, EARL C., cons. engring.; b. Newport, Ky., July 14, 1912; s. Christian M. and Viola (Mauer) W.; Chem.Engr., U. Cin., 1935; m. Estella Rees Deschler, Nov. 4, 1937; children—Earl C., Sandra Kay Weber Scheckelhoff. Prodn. mgr. by-products Schenley Distillers; asst. to chmn. bd. Vucan Corp., Cin.; v.p. indsl. div. H.J. Ross Assos., Inc., Miami, Fla.; engring. cons., Sarasota, Fla., 1980—. Various positions Boy Scouts Am., 1935-55. Registerd profl. engr., Ohio, Ind., Ill., N.J., Tex., La., Miss. Mem. Am. Inst. Chem. Engrs., Air Pollution Control Assn., Alpha Chi Sigma. Presbyterian. Clubs: Mason, Shriners. Home: 2320 Tanglewood Dr Sarasota FL 33579

WEBER, GEORGE H., ret. editor and pub.; b. Springville, N.Y., Nov. 1, 1910; s. Arthur Newton and Harriet Turpening (Coddington) W.; B.S. in Petroleum Engring., U. Okla., 1934; m. Christine E. Rader, June 8, 1940; children—Arthur George, William Eric. With Oil & Gas Jour., 1934-41, 46-76, refining editor, N.Y.C., 1948-58, editor-in-chief, 1958-72, editor, pub., Tulsa, 1972-76, ret., 1976. Served to maj. F.A., U.S. Army, 1941-45. Recipient Crain award Am. Bus. Press, 1977. Mem. Am. Chem. Soc., Am. Petroleum Inst., Natural Gas Processors Assn. (Hanlon award 1972), Soc. Petroleum Engrs., Am. Inst. Mining, Metall., Petroleum Engrs. Republican. Presbyterian. Club: Petroleum of Tulsa. Home: 3741 S Xanthus Ave Tulsa OK 74105

WEBER, JEROME CHARLES, univ. adminstr.; b. Bklyn., Sept. 1, 1938; s. Meyer and Ethel (Shier) W.; B.S., Bklyn. Coll., 1960; M.A., Mich. State U., 1961, Ph.D., 1966; m. Elizabeth Lynn Wiley, July 18, 1975; children—Amy Elizabeth, Jeffrey Glenn. Grad. asst. Mich. State U., 1960-64; asst. prof. U. Okla., 1964-68, asso. prof., 1968-72, prof. edn. and phys. edn., adj. prof. human relations, clin. prof. social work, 1973—, dean Univ. Coll., vice provost for instructional services, 1979—; cons. VISTA. Mem. S.W. Center for Human Relations Bd.; mem. Norman Bd. Park Commrs., 1972—. Mem. Am. Assn. Higher Edn., Am. Council Sports Medicine, Am. Council Edn., Council Sports Psychology. Democrat. Jewish. Author: Statistics and Research in Physical Education, 1970. Home: 1133 Robinhood Ln Norman OK 73069 Office: 650 Parrington Oval Norman OK 73070

WEBER, LAWRENCE KIRKWOOD, JR., real estate broker; b. San Francisco, May 20, 1930; s. Lawrence Kirkwood and Grace Laile W.; A.A., City Coll. San Francisco, 1949; B.A., U. Calif., Berkeley, 1951; m. Owene Phillips Hall, Nov. 26, 1954; children—Owene, Cathleen, Lawrence Kirkwood III, Nicholas, Louise. With Wells Fargo Bank 1951; commd. ensign U.S. Navy, 1953, advanced through grades to comdr., 1967, ret., 1972; comml. investment real estate salesman Stockton, Whatley, Davin & Co., Jacksonville, Fla., 1973-75; v.p. Walter Dickinson Inc., Jacksonville, 1976-78; pres., dir. United Property Investors, Inc. Jacksonville, 1978—; pres., dir. Security Research Consultants; partner Hook-Weber Properties. Warden St. Margarets Episcopal Ch., 1970-78; mem. Republican Exec. Com. Clay County, 1973-75. Decorated Navy Commendation medal. Mem. Nat. Assn. Corporate Real Estate Execs., Jacksonville C. of C., Alpha Tau Omega. Home: 783 Hibernia Route Green Cove Springs FL 32043 Office: 200 W Forsyth St Suite 932 Jacksonville FL 32202

WEBER, LAWRENCE M., fund raising cons.; b. Harleysville, Pa., May 8, 1939; s. Russell H. and Naomi L. (Moyer) W.; student Hagerstown (Md.) Jr. Coll., 1958, Indiana U. of Pa., 1965; m. Sally Ruth Launtz, Aug. 15, 1959; children—Lori Jo, Jeffrey Todd, Bradley Harwood. With Sta. WJEJ, Hagerstown, Md., 1957-59; gen. mgr. Sta. WEEC-FM, Springfield, Ohio, 1959-62; dir. music Sta. WRYT, Pitts., 1962-65; announcer Sta. WTAE-TV, Pitts., 1965-67; newsman Sta. WJAS, Pitts., 1967-69; with Ketchum, Inc., 1969—, v.p., Charlotte, N.C., 1979—. Pres., Charlotte Christian Sch.; public relations cons. Youth Guidance, Inc., Pitts., 1964-69. Mem. Nat. Assn. Hosp. Devel., Council Advancement and Support Edn. Clubs: City, Charlotte Athletic. Home: 2143 Sharon Rd Charlotte NC 28207 Office: 808 American Bldg Charlotte NC 28286

WEBER, LEVI BURKHOLDER, realtor; b. Petersburg, Va., Mar. 23, 1911; s. Henry S. and Mary Ann (Burkholder) W.; student Eastern Mennonite Coll., Harrisonburg, Va., 1929, Coll. William and Mary, Williamsburg, Va., 1949; m. June E. Birkholder, Feb. 26, 1939; children—Richard, Kenneth, Helen. Co-owner, sales mgr. Burkholder Dairy, Newport News, Va., 1934-48; owner, broker Key Real Estate, Inc., Newport News, 1948—; owner, pres. Edgemoor Homes, Inc., Newport News, 1948—. Trustee Eastern Mennonite Coll., 1966-70; chmn. African affairs Mennonite Econ. Devel. Assn., 1962—. Recipient award of merit Am. Assn. State and Local History, 1969. Home: 603 Windemere Rd Newport News VA 23602 Office: PO Box 2428 Newport News VA 23602

WEBSTER, BRIAN WILLIAM, promotion advt. exec.; b. London, Nov. 30, 1931; came to U.S., 1970; s. William and Mary Catherine (Conroy) W.; B.A. in Lit., Oxford U., 1949; m. Wilma J. Hynes, June 5, 1969. With Irish Times, London, 1948; newspaper reporter London Airport, 1955; owner, pub. Brit. Am. Press, Los Angeles, 1956-59; co-pub., editor Missile Industry Bull., Los Angeles, 1960-65; advt. dir. Guide to Britain, Cunard Shipping, 1966-69; pres. So. Bus. Devel. Co., Atlanta, 1969—. Served with RAF, 1949-54. Mem. N. Am. Darting Assn. (v.p.). Democrat. Anglican. Editor Dart News, Dem. Party News of DeKalb County, 1976. Office: Suite 202 2793A Clairmont Rd Atlanta GA 30329

WEBSTER, BURNICE HOYLE, physician; b. Leeville, Tenn., Mar. 3, 1910; s. Thomas Jefferson and Martha Anne (Melton) W.; B.A. magna cum laude, Vanderbilt U., 1936, M.D., 1940; D.Sc., Holy Trinity Coll., 1971; Ph.D., Fla. Research Inst., 1973; m. Georgia Kathryn Foglemann, May 6, 1939; children—Brenda Kathryn, Phillip Hoyle, Adrienne Elise. Intern St. Thomas Hosp., Nashville, 1940-42, resident, 1942-43; practice medicine, specializing in chest disease, Nashville, 1943—; mem. staff St. Thomas, Bapt., Nashville Gen., Westside hosps.; clin. prof. allied health Trevecca Coll.; cons. VA Hosp.; asso. in medicine Vanderbilt Med. Sch., 1943—; prof. anatomy Gupton-Jones Sch. Mortuary Sci., 1941-43. Pres., Middle-E. Tenn. chpt. Arthritis Found. Served with USPHS. Recipient Disting. Service award Arthritis Found. Fellow Am. Coll. Chest Physicians, Am., Internat. colls. angiology, Royal Soc. Health, Internat. Biog. Assn. (life); mem. Am. Cancer Soc. (dir., past pres. Nashville), AMA, Am. Thoracic Soc., So. Med. Soc., Tenn. Med. Assn., Nashville Acad. Medicine, SCV (surgeon-in-chief), Order St. John of Jerusalem. Research in mycotic and parasitic diseases. Home: 2315 Valley Brook Rd Nashville TN 37215 Office: Mid-State Med Center Nashville TN 37203

WEBSTER, CHERRIE JONES, mathematician; b. Colfax, La., Apr. 22, 1932; d. William Luther and Nora Margaret (Roberts) Jones; B.S., Northwestern La. State U., 1963, M.S., 1967; postgrad. U. Wis., 1968, U. Southwest Tex., 1970; m. Ray D. Webster, Aug. 12, 1949; children—Robert Dale, Charles Glynn, Cynthia. Tchr. math. Bossier High Sch., Bossier City, La., 1963; tchr. sci. Montgomery (La.) High Sch., 1963-65; instr. math. Northwestern State U., Natchitoches, La., 1967-73, asst. prof., 1973-79, asso. prof., 1979—, dir. remedial and basic math. program, 1976—. Mem. Math. Assn. Am., Nat. Council Tchrs. Math., Assn. Supervision and Curriculum Devel., Kappa Delta Pi. Roman Catholic. Home: Rt 1 Box 72B Montgomery LA 71454 Office: Dept Math Northwestern State U Natchitoches LA 71457

WEBSTER, HARVEY CURTIS, journalist; b. Chgo., Nov. 6, 1906; s. Ira Gilbert and Beatrice Dunham (Curtis) W.; A.B., Oberlin Coll., 1927, A.M., 1929; Ph.D., U. Mich., 1935; m. Lucille Audine Jones, Apr. 12, 1932. Teaching fellow U. Mich., 1929-35; instr. Colo. State Coll., 1935-36; asst. prof. to prof. English, U. Louisville, 1936-76, chmn. dept. English, 1967-68, prof. emeritus, 1976—; lit. journalist New Leader, New Republic, Poetry, Austin, Tex., 1976—. Chmn., West End Community Council, 1966-67; chmn. Ky. Democrats for Adlai Stevenson, 1960. Recipient awards Yaddo Writers Colony, Saratoga Springs, N.Y., 1947, 54, 64, 65; Fulbright prof. U. Durham, Eng., 1950-51, U. Leeds, Eng., 1962-63. Mem. AAUP (pres. Louisville chpt. 1949-50), Am. Fedn. Tchrs. (pres. Louisville chpt. 1944-45, 49-50), NAACP, Modern Lang. Assn., Modern Humanities Research Assn., Urban League. Democrat. Quaker. Author: On A Darkling Plain, 1947; After The Trauma, 1970; Selected Poems of Hortence Flexner, 1975; foreword Graham Greene: A Descriptive Catalog, 1979. Home and Office: 1201 S Congress St Austin TX 78704

WEBSTER, JEAN BROOKS, middle sch. prin.; b. Rock Hill, S.C., Jan. 21, 1926; d. Roger Malcolm, Sr., and Myrtle Thornton (Naylor) Brooks; A.B., Winthrop Coll., 1950; M.A., George Peabody Coll., 1957. Tchr., Mocksville (N.C.) High Sch., 1947-48, Lexington (N.C.) High Sch., 1948-54, Bartow (Fla.) Jr. High Sch., 1954-56, Rogers Jr. High Sch., Ft. Lauderdale, Fla., 1956-58; dean Rogers Jr. High Sch., 1958-68, asst. prin., 1968-73; prin. McNicol Middle Sch., Hollywood, Fla., 1973-76, Crystal Lake Middle Sch., Pompano Beach, Fla., 1976—; dir. Ft. Lauderdale Oral Sch., 1964-70. Chmn. Am. Heart Assn. fund drive, Lexington, 1952-53. Mem. Broward County Asst. Adminstrs. Assn. (chmn. 1965-66, dir. 1970-73), NEA (life), Nat., Fla. assns. secondary sch. prins., Assn. Supervision and Curriculum Devel., Fla. League Middle Schs., AAUW, Broward Prins. and Assts. Assn., Kappa Delta Pi, Sigma Epsilon Alpha. Democrat. Baptist. Home: 192 SW 62d Ave Plantation FL 33317 Office: 3551 NE 3d Ave Pompano Beach FL 33064

WEBSTER, REX, advt. agy. exec.; b. Gatesville, Tex., May 29, 1918; s. Roscoe and Fannie (Hooser) W.; B.A., Tex. Tech. U., 1938, M.A., 1939; m. Madge Malone, June 1, 1941; children—Len Rex, Robin. Program dir., commercial mgr. Radio Sta. KFYO, Lubbock, Tex., 1935-47; partner, Buckner, Craig & Webster Advt. Agy., 1947-52; partner, Craig & Webster Advt. Agy., Lubbock, 1952-59; partner, Webster, Harris, Weiborn Advt. Agy., Lubbock, 1959-72; partner, Webster & Harris Advt. Agy., Lubbock, Tex., 1972—; v.p., pub. relations dir. Great Plains Life Ins. Co., Lubbock, Tex., 1955-57. Advt. and pub. relations cons., instr. Tex. Tech. U., 1953-71. Pres. Lubbock council Camp Fire Girls, 1960; v.p. South Plains Council Boy Scouts Am., 1958-59; pres., Lubbock (Tex.) Better Bus. Bur., 1965. Chmn. bd. dirs. Lubbock Symphony Orch., 1949-50, charter mem., 1947, vocal soloist, dir. Pops Nite Chorus, 1963-71; chmn. bd. dirs. Lubbock (Tex.) Cerebral Palsy Treatment Center, 1962-63, 72-74; bd. dirs. Goodwill Industries, Lubbock. Served as lt. USNR, 1943-45. Recipient Distinguished Service award Lubbock Jr. C. of C., 1955, Silver Medal award for distinguished service to advt. Lubbock Tex. Advt. Club, 1967. Mem. Am. (chmn. S.W. council 1957-58), Southwestern (pres. 1955) assns. advt. agys., Am. Automobile Assn., Panhandle Plains Auto Club (v.p. 1971—), Lubbock Advt. Club (pres. 1954-55), Tex. Pub. Relations Assn. (dir. 1958-60), Rotary Internat. (pres. Lubbock 1947-48, dist. gov. 1956-57, dir. 1967-69, v.p. 1968-69, chmn. planning com. 1977-78). Baptist (mem. exec. com. gen. conv. Tex. 1968-74, chmn. bd. deacons 1972-73). Mason (32 deg.). Home: 3305 44th St Lubbock TX 79413 Office: 1313 Broadway Lubbock TX 79401

WEBSTER, ROBERT ESMONDE, III, glass co. exec.; b. Chester, Pa., Mar. 13, 1946; s. Robert E. and Edith Clara (Rue) W.; B.A., Pa. Mil. Coll., 1968; m. Nancy Marie Hamilton, Sept. 28, 1968; children—Stephen R., David A., Jeffrey M. Asst. br. mgr. Girard Bank, Phila., 1968-69, 71; foreman Corning Glass Works, 1971-74, supr. customer service, 1974-76, mfrs. sales rep., Longwood, Fla., 1976-79, Houston, 1979—. Served with U.S. Army, 1969-71. Mem. Am. Sci. Glassblowers Soc., Am. Chem. Soc. Republican. Methodist. Club: Masons. Address: 19811 Sundance Dr Humble TX 77338

WECHSBERG, HENRY, dentist; b. Germany, June 29, 1919 (came to U.S. 1935, naturalized 1941); s. Edward and Sara (Kaufmann) W.; D.D.S., Washington U., 1951; m. Florence Orin, Aug. 18, 1945; children—Orin, Wendy. Pvt. practice dentistry, Miami, Fla., 1951—. Served with CIC, AUS, 1942-45. Recipient award Am. Acad. Dental Medicine. Fellow Royal Soc. Health; mem. Am., Fla., East Coast Dist. dental assns., South Dade Dental Soc., Southeastern Acad. Prostodontics, Alpha Omega, Omicron Kappa Upsilon. Jewish (temple dir.). Mem. B'nai B'rith. Office: 3542 Coral Way Miami FL 33145

WECHSLER, DONALD BYRON, telecommunications systems engr.; b. Bklyn., Sept. 7, 1941; s. Milton and Dorothy (Biren) W.; B.S., N.C. State U., 1963; M.E.A., Washington U., St. Louis, 1967; m. Barbara Warren, July 1, 1971. Indsl. engr. McDonnell-Douglas Corp., Ampex Corp., 1963-69; prodn. engr. Tex. Instruments, Dallas, 1969-75; staff indsl. engr. U.S. Postal Service, Dallas, 1975-76; systems engr. in data communications Rockwell Internat., Dallas, 1976—. Active Big Bros. Dallas. Registered profl. engr., Tex. Mem. Nat. Mgmt. Assn., Soc. Mfg. Engrs., Computer and Automated Systems Assn., Am. Inst. Indsl. Engrs. Home: 15731 Regal Hill Circle Dallas TX 75248 Office: PO Box 10462 MS 401-102 Dallas TX 75207

WEDDLE, L. STEVE, banker; b. Jasper, Ala., July 12, 1948; s. I. Hershel and Margaret D. (Daniel) W.; B.A., U. Ala., 1970; diploma Vanderbilt U. Banking Sch., 1972; J.D., Nashville Law Sch., 1978; m. Patricia Rich, Aug. 18, 1979. Mgmt. trainee Am. Nat. Bank, Chattanooga, 1970, banking officer, 1971-73; asst. v.p. Commerce Union Bank, Chattanooga, 1974, v.p., 1975, sr. v.p., 1976, exec. v.p., dir., 1977—; dir. Chattanooga World Trade Council, Chattanooga Speech and Hearing Center, C. U. Leasing Corp. Treas. Cherokee Regional Chpt. Tenn. Easter Seal Soc.; chmn. Chattanooga Jr. Achievement; co. chmn., mem. allocations com. United Fund Chattanooga; co-chmn. Heart Fund of Chattanooga. Mem. U. Ala. Alumni Assn., Phi Sigma Kappa Alumni Assn., Mcpl. Treas.'s Assn. U.S. and Can., Am. Inst. Banking, Nashville Law Sch. Alumni Assn. Methodist. Clubs: Jaycees, Chattanooga Rotary. Contbr. articles in field (2d pl. award Robert Morris Assos. Fin. Inst. 1972). Home: 720 Bacon Trail Estate 30 Chattanooga TN 37412 Office: Commerce Union Tower 633 Chestnut St Chattanooga TN 37450

WEDDLE, LEO FRANKLIN, psychologist; b. Somerset, Ky., June 4, 1929; s. Leo Fletcher and Bessie Phine (Carney) W.; B.A., U. Ky., 1958, M.A., 1959; postgrad. Morehead State U., 1970-79; m. Laura Mildred Thomas, June 15, 1955; children—Laura Lynn, Leo Jeffrey. Grad. teaching fellow U. Ky., 1959; asst. prof. psychology Campbellsville Coll., 1961-65, dean of men, 1962-65, dean of students, 1962-65; prof. Prestonsburg Community Coll., 1966—. Mem. exec. bd. Big Sandy Community Action Program, Paintsville, Ky., 1967-76; mem. Prestonsburg Planning Commn., 1968-79; bd. dirs. Jenny Wiley Drama Assn., 1979—. Served with USMC, 1950-53. Decorated Purple Heart; named Most Popular Prof., Campbellsville Coll., 1963, Outstanding Lion, Somerset Lions Club, 1964. Mem. Ky. Assn. Community and Jr. Colls., Folk Coll. Conf. Am. (nat. sec.), Ky. Assn. Communications Tech., Kappa Delta Pi, Phi Delta Kappa. Democrat. Baptist. Home: 1125 Riverview Prestonsburg KY 41653 Office: Prestonburg Community Coll Prestonsburg KY 41653

WEDGWOOD, COLIN DAVID, acct.; b. Altrincham, Cheshire, Eng., Dec. 13, 1934; s. Stanley and Beatrice (Ordish) W.; came to U.S., 1969. Accountant in Eng., 1952-58; European internal auditor Pfizer Inc., Brussels, 1960-64; internat. internal auditor Syminston Wayne, Corp., Bracknell, Eng., 1965-68; sr. internal auditor Dresser Industries, Dallas, 1968-75, tech. staff acct., 1975—. Treas., First Unitarian Ch. of Dallas, 1978—. C.P.A., Tex. Fellow Inst. Chartered Accts. in Eng. and Wales; mem. Nat. Assn. Accts. Home: 3618 Gillespie St Apt 105 Dallas TX 75219 Office: 1505 Elm St Dallas TX 75201

WEEKLEY, FRANCES ETHEL, librarian; b. Birmingham, Ala., Feb. 27, 1919; d. Harold Hudson and Nota Leigh (Windham) W.; B.A. in Edn., U. Ala., 1941; B.A. in Library Sci., Emory U., 1945; m. Henry Odessa Hurst, Sept. 8, 1947 (dec. 1962); children—Rosalind Frances Hurst Minderhout, Walter Henry. Tchr. public schs. Ala., 1941-44, 50-52, 58-62; librarian TVA, Wilson Dam, 1945-46; librarian U. Ala., Tuscaloosa, 1946-50, 62-69; caseworker Talladega (Ala.) County Dept. Pension and Securities, 1953-54; librarian Jefferson State Jr. Coll., Birmingham, 1969—. Mem. NEA, Ala. Jr. and Community Coll. Assn., Ala. Jr. Coll. Library Assn., Ala. Library Assn. (scholarship 1944-45), Ala. Edn. Assn., Kappa Delta Pi, Pi Tau Chi, Triangle. Democrat. Methodist. Home: 1641 5th St NW Birmingham AL 35215 Office: 2601 Carson Rd Birmingham AL 35215

WEEKLEY, HAROLD J., civic orgn. exec.; b. Pennsboro, W.Va., Oct. 24, 1913; A.B. and B.S. cum laude, Salem Coll., 1936; M.S., Sch. Phys. Edn. and Athletics, W.Va. U., 1939; m. Edna Ilene Kellison, Mar. 10, 1945; children—Robert, Deanna, Richard, Sharon, Sandra, Susan. Tchr., coach Coalwood (W.Va.) Jr. High Sch., 1936-37; tchr., coach Washington Jr. High Sch., Parkersburg, W.Va., 1939-40; coach Radford (Va.) High Sch., 1940-41; mem. faculty Radford State Coll., 1940-41; instr. Sch. Phys. Edn. and Athletics, W.Va. U., 1941-42; field rep. Office of Community War Services, Charleston, W.Va., 1942-45; exec. dir Community Chest and Council, Burlington, N.C., 1945-49, Community Chest and Council and United Fund, Greenville, S.C., 1949-57, United Fund, Chattanooga, 1957—. Mem. United Community Funds and Councils of Am. (dir. 1967-70, pres. Southeastern conf. 1955-57), Am. Recreation Soc. (dir. 1946-48), Tenn. Conf. Social Welfare (treas. 1957-63), Nat. Conf. Social Welfare, Chattanooga Indsl. Personnel Club. Presbyterian (bd. deacons chmn. 1976-78, treas. 1980—). Clubs: Torch (treas. 1966-70), Tennis (treas. 1976-78), Rotary (dir. 1968-69, treas. 1979-80) (Chattanooga). Contbr. articles to profl. mags. Home: 25 Fairhills Dr Chattanooga TN 37405 Office: United Fund 420 Frazier Ave Chattanooga TN 37405

WEEKS, CHARLES, JR., pub. co. exec.; b. Palo Alto, Calif., Apr. 25, 1919; s. Charles and Mary Alice (Johnson) W.; student U. Fla., 1936-38; m. Patricia Anne Blair, Apr. 7, 1949; children—Patricia Alice, Charles Blair, Clayton Brian, Phyllis Anne. Prin., Fla. Airmotive, Inc., Lantana, Fla., 1946-50; v.p., dir. Perry Publs., Inc., West Palm Beach, Fla., 1950-69; asst. sec., dir. Perry Oceanographics, Inc., Riveria Beach, Fla., 1969—, Perry Ocean Engring., Inc., Riviera Beach, Palm Beach Cable TV Co., Palm Beach Gardens, Fla., Martin County Cable Co., Inc., Stuart, Fla.; v.p., sec., dir. Perry Bldg. Systems, Inc., Riviera Beach; v.p., dir. Bahama Publishers Ltd., Freeport, Bahamas; asst. treas., dir. Perry Ocean Engring., Inc.; dir. First Marine Bank & Trust Co. of the Palm Beaches, Inc. Mem. Planning and Zoning Bd., Lantana, 1962-65. Served to 1st lt., pilot, USAF, 1943-46: ETO. Decorated Air medal. Recipient Pilot Safety award Nat. Bus. Aircraft Assn., 1970, 74, 78. Mem. Quiet Birdman. Episcopalian. Democrat. Clubs: LaCoquille (Manalapan, Fla.); Handersonville (N.C.) Country. Home: PO Box 3411 Lantana FL 33462 Office: 100 E 17th St Riviera Beach FL 33404

WEEKS, ELIE, ret. govt. ofcl., rancher; b. Columbia, Mo., Apr. 12, 1903; s. Raymond and Mary Sophronia (Arnoldia) W.; B.S., U. Va., 1926; postgrad. L'Ecole des Sciences Politique, Paris, France, 1926-27; m. Helen George, Sept. 13, 1930. So. sales mgr. Charles Englehard, Inc., Newark, 1928-30; v.p. Weeks Engring., Richmond, Va., 1931-33; with Fed. Res. Bank, Richmond, 1933-37; sec. Beverley Heating, Richmond, 1937-42; statistician VA, Richmond, 1946-48; asst. sci. dir., tech. adviser U.S. Army Gen. Equipment Test Activity, Ft. Lee, Va., 1948-66; ret., 1966; owner-mgr. plantation and cattle ranch, Manakin-Sabot, Va., 1966—. Mem. Open Spaces Planning Bd. Goochland County, 1972-73; vice chmn. Goochland County Independence Bicentennial Commn., chmn. com. to prepare mil. map Va.; Va. chmn. and coordinator Washington-Rochambeau Nat. Hist. Route Com.; ed. dirs. Family Service Soc., 1969-72. Served with USAAF, 1942-46. Decorated Bronze Star. Mem. Va. Acad. Sci., AAAS, Am. Statis. Soc., Va. Geneal. Soc., Va. Hist. Soc., Alliance Francaise, Va. Mus. Fine Arts, Va. History Fedn., Nat. Trust for Historic Preservation, Am. Boxwood Soc., Goochland County Hist. Soc. (pres. 1968-73, editor-pub. mag. 1968-79), SAR (bd. mgrs. Va. soc. 1974-77), McGuire's U. Sch. Alumni Assn. (trustee). Clubs: Soixante Plus, Medmenham, Ruritan (charter mem., past pres. Goochland), Va. Writers. Address: Rochambeau Manakin-Sabot VA 23103

WEEKS, GEORGE ARTHUR, bus. exec.; b. Toledo, June 8, 1943; s. George Edward and Eleanore M. W.; B.S., Fla. State U., 1965; m. Julie Mercurio, Feb. 11, 1967; children—Kimberly Lynne, Scott Weeks. State mktg. coordinator Addressograph Multigraph Co., 1970-72; with ITT Community Devel. Corp., Palm Coast, Fla., 1973—, dir. community relations, 1979—, v.p. Admiral Investment Corp., Sun Sport Recreation Corp. Mem. State of Fla. Unemployment Compensation Adv. Bd., 1977-78; mem. State of Fla. Motion Picture and Television Adv. Bd., 1978-79; bd. dirs. East Flagler Mcpl. Service Dist. Served with U.S. Army, 1967-70. Mem. Am. Mgmt. Assn., Nat. Golf Found. Lutheran. Office: Club House Dr Palm Coast Exec Offices Palm Coast FL 32051

WEEKS, KENT MCCUSKEY, lawyer; b. Cleve., Nov. 21, 1937; s. John H. and Helen (McCuskey) W.; B.A., Coll. Wooster, 1959; M.A., U. N.Z., 1961; LL.B., Duke U., 1964; Ph.D., Case Western Res. U., 1969; m. Karen Hanke, July 27, 1962; children—Kevin, Barton, Kristen. Admitted to Ohio bar, 1964, Iowa bar, 1972, Tenn. bar, 1976; mem. firm and pvt. practice, Cleve., 1964-67; asst. prof. polit. sci. Coll. Wooster (Ohio), 1967-72; dean coll., prof. polit. sci. U. Dubuque, 1972-75; asso. dir. Nat. Commn. on United Meth. Higher Edn., Nashville, 1975-77; mem. firm Weeks & Anderson, Nashville, 1977—. Mem. Iowa Humanities Adv. Council, 1973-75, nursing adv. bd. Finley Hosp., 1973-75; chmn. troop com. Boy Scouts Am., 1978—. Fulbright scholar, 1960; NDEA fellow, 1966-67; Office Edn fellow, 1970-71. Mem. Am. Polit. Sci. Assn., Iowa Bar Assn., Tenn. Bar Assn. Author: Adam Clayton Powell and the Supreme Court, 1971; contbr. articles to profl. jours. Home: 6025 Sherwood Dr Nashville TN 37215 Office: 2211 Crestmoor Rd Nashville TN 37215

WEEMS, JOHN EDWARD, writer; b. Grand Prairie, Tex., Nov. 2, 1924; s. J. Eddie and Anna Lee (Scott) W.; B.J., U. Tex., 1948, M.Journalism, 1949; M.A. in L.S., Fla. State U., 1954; m. Jane Ellen Homeyer, Sept. 11, 1946; children—Donald, Carol, Mary, Barbara, Janet. Telegraph editor Temple (Tex.) Daily Telegram, 1950; instr. Calif. State Poly. Coll., San Dimas, 1950-51; night news editor San Angelo (Tex.) Standard-Times, 1951; copy editor Dallas Morning News, 1952-53; asst. prof., head cataloger main library Baylor U., 1954-57; asst. prof. U. Ala., also asst. mgr. Ala. Press Assn., 1957-58; asst. to dir. U. Tex. Press, 1958-68; prof. English, Baylor U., 1968-71, lectr. creative writing, fall 1979; reference librarian McLennan Community Coll., Waco, Tex., 1969-70; free-lance writer, 1971—. Served with USNR, 1943-46, 51-52. Am. Philos. Soc. grantee, 1964. Mem. Nat. Book Critics Circle, Authors Guild, Tex. Inst. Letters, AAUP, Sigma Delta Chi, Beta Phi Mu. Author: A Weekend in September, 1957; The Fate of the Maine, 1958; Race for the Pole, 1960; Peary: The Explorer and the Man, 1967; Men Without Countries, 1969; Dream of Empire (Amon G. Carter award), 1971; To Conquer a Peace: The War Between the United States and Mexico (Richard Fleming award), 1974; Death Song, 1976; The Tornado, 1977; (with John Biggers and Carroll Simms) Black Art in Houston, 1978. Address: 2012 Collins Dr Waco TX 76710 also care Raines & Raines Lit Agy 475 Fifth Ave New York NY 10017

WEEREN, MILO PERSHING, savs. and loan assn. exec.; b. Burton, Tex., Sept. 16, 1918; s. William Henry and Jennie Ellis (Laas) W.; student Blinn Coll., Brenham, Tex., 1936-37; m. Agnes Winifred Beaumier, Apr. 19, 1952; children—Gayle Nichols, Lana Kendall Weeren Plunkett. Material coordinator Brown Shipbuilding Co., Greens Bayou, Tex., 1941-44; work schedule coordinator Hughes Tool Co., Houston, 1944-47; mgr.-coordinator sales and pub. relations, materials insp. So. Inspection Service, Houston, 1947-56, 57-59; multi-state expediter, coordinator Austin Co., Houston, 1956-57; account exec. Top Value Enterprises, Houston, 1959-64; exec. v.p. Heights Savs. Assn., Houston, 1964—, also dir., officer; dir., officer Heights Developers, Inc., 1971—, Old Bridge Lake Community Service Corp., 1972—. Mem. speaker's adv. com. Tex. Ho. of Reps., 1970, Champions Community Improvement Action, 1968-76. Mem. Tex. Savs. and Loan League, Inst. Fin. Edn., Greater Houston Home Builders Assn. Democrat. Baptist. Clubs: 100 Club of Houston, Champions Golf, Masons. Home: 4 Colony St E Houston TX 77069 Office: 204 W 19th St Houston TX 77008

WEESE, JOHN AUGUSTUS, univ. ofcl., mech. engr., educator; b. Topeka, Kans., July 24, 1933; s. Ray A. and Margaret M. (Richmond) W.; B.S. in Mech. Engring., Kans. State U., 1955; M.S. in Engring. Mechanics, Cornell U., 1958, Ph.D. (Standard Oil Found. fellow), 1959; m. Betty Kay Dietrich, June 5, 1955; children—Carol, Katherine. Instr. engring. mechanics Cornell U., Ithaca, N.Y., 1955-57; structural dynamics engr. Boeing Co., Wichita, Kans., 1959-60, acting supr. structural dynamics research, 1962-63; faculty asso. engr. Martin-Marietta Corp., Denver, summer, 1963; mem. faculty Coll. Engring., research engr. Denver Research Inst., U. Denver, 1963-74, prof. mech. engring., 1967-74, chmn. grad. program mech. Scis. and environ. engring., 1968-70, dean Coll. Engring., 1970-74; dean Sch. Engring. Old Dominion U., Norfolk, Va., 1974—, prof. mech. engring. and mechanics, 1974—. Served to lt. USAF, 1960-62. Recipient Disting. Faculty award U. Denver, 1969, Boss of the Year award Am. Bus. Women's Assn., 1978. Mem. ASME, Va. Soc. Profl. Engrs. (Outstanding Service award 1978), AIAA, Nat. Soc. Profl. Engrs., Am. Soc. Engring. Edn., Engrs. Club of Hampton Roads, Soc. Exptl. Stress Analysis, Va. Acad. Scis., AAAS. Author: (with A. Higdon, W.B. Stiles, et al) Engineering Mechanics, all edits., 1962-79; (with A. Higdon, E.H. Ohlsen, E.H. Stiles, et al) Mechanics of Materials, 1967; also research papers on engring. mechanics. Home: 5289 Fairfield Blvd Virginia Beach VA 23462 Office: School of Engineering Old Dominion Univ Norfolk VA 23508

WEESE, WINSTON HOLBROOK, obstetrician, gynecologist; b. Jonesboro, Ark., Feb. 21, 1924; s. Newton Bicknell W.; B.S., Cornell U., 1944; M.D., U. Ark., 1946; grad. Leadership Forum Tulane U., 1969; m. Martha McIlwaine Chaffe, Jan. 30, 1954; children—Margaret, Winston, Jr., Stuart, John. Intern, St. Vincent's Infirmary, Little Rock, 1946-47; resident in pathology Charity Hosp. La., New Orleans, 1949-50, resident in obstetrics gynecology, 1950-52, chief resident in obstetrics gynecology, 1952-53; postgrad. trainee Am. Hosp., Paris, 1953-54; practice medicine specializing in obstetrics-gynecology, New Orleans, 1954—; clin. instr. La. State U. Med. Sch., 1954, asso. clin. prof. obstetrics-gynecology, 1960—; sr. attending surgeon Charity Hosp. La., New Orleans; pres. Lab. Leasing, G & O Lab., Inc.; dir. Med. Electronics div. So. Communication Corp.; bd. dirs. Custon Audio. Active Boy Scouts Am.; founding mem. Opened Door (drug treatment center; del., nat. bd. dirs. Am. Cancer Soc., 1972—, pres. New Orleans 1966-68. Served as lt j.g. USNR, 1946-49, rear adm. M.C., Res., 1974—, liaison officer chief Naval Res. to Assn. Mil. Surgeons U.S. Diplomate Am. Bd. Obstetrics-Gynecology. Fellow A.C.S., Am. Coll. Obstetrics and Gynecology; mem. AMA, La. State, Orleans Parish, So. med. socs., Am. Soc. for Colposcopy and Colpomicroscopy (pres.), S. Central Obstetrics-Gynecology Soc. (pres. 1973), Am. Fertility Soc. (bd. dirs., various offices 1962—), Naval. Res. Assn. (nat. surgeon 1970-72), Soc. Cons. to Surgeon Gen. Armed Forces, New Orleans Soc. Obstetricians-Gynecologists, New Orleans Post Grad. Med. Assembly, Royal Soc. St. George in New Orleans (charter, pres.), Clubs: La., Stratford, New Orleans Tennis, So. Yacht, Plimsoll, Lakeshore, Tally-Ho Hunting and Fishing. Contbr. articles in field to med. jours. Home: 1136 Second St New Orleans LA 70139 Office: Weese Kemmerly & Steele Suite 404 4440 Magnolia St New Orleans LA 70115

WEGNER, MARY SUE, nuclear field engr.; b. Centralia, Ill., Feb. 27, 1941; d. Clarence Frank and Mabel Arwood (Collie) Wehlage; A.A. in Physics, McLennan Community Coll., 1972; B.S. in Nuclear Engr., Tex. A and M, 1974; postgrad. Ga. Inst. Tech., 1980—; m. Lloyd Arthur Wegner, May 7, 1961; children—Diana Teresa, Kathleen Marie, Karl David. Draftsman USAF, Keesler AFB, Miss., 1959-60; clk. Mid-State Electric Co., Alexandria, La., 1963-66; draftsman Dresser Indsl. Valve and Instrument Div., Alexandria, 1966-67; aircraft inspector Gen. Dynamics, Waco, Tex., 1968-70; draftsman Lone Star Gas, Waco, 1971-72; nuclear field engr. Gen. Elec. Co., Atlanta, 1974—. Served with USAF, 1959-60. Certificate of governance, Am. Nuclear Soc. Mem. Am. Nuclear Soc. (Huntsville, Ala. chpt., v. chmn. programs, 1976, chmn., 1977). Home: 1309 Halter Ln Lithonia GA 30058 Office: PO Box 4659 Atlanta GA 30302

WEHRENBERG, THOMAS MILTON, ceramic products mfg. co. exec.; b. Nashville, June 20, 1931; s. John M. and Eva E. (Murell) W.; B.S. in Chem. Engring., Tenn. Technol. U., 1952; postgrad. Purdue U., 1954; m. Trudy Lenora Lewis, Sept. 10, 1950; children—Thomas, Bruce, Mary Ann, Mark. Chem. engr. E.I. du Pont de Nemours Co., Charlestown, Ind., 1952-58; mgr. ceramic tech. Corning Glass Works, Louisville, Ky., 1958—. Scoutmaster, George Rogers Clark council Boy Scouts Am., 1972-76. Mem. Nat. Inst. Ceramic Engrs., Am. Ceramic Soc. Lutheran. Contbr. numerous articles on refractories to tech. publs. Patentee refractory processes. Home: 1303 Tranquil Dr Jeffersonville IN Office: 1600 W Lee St Louisville KY 40210

WEHRMEISTER, ALLEN EDWARD, energy industry exec.; b. Chgo., Mar. 28, 1942; s. Edward O. and Lydia (Schweitzer) W.; B.S. in E.E., Northwestern U., 1964; m. Karen E. Kostelny, Sept. 23, 1963; children—Dawn, Leanne, Julie. Asso. engr. Douglas Aircraft Co., Santa Monica, Calif., 1964-65; application engr. Magnaflux Corp., Chgo., 1965-71; sr. research engr. Babcock & Wilcox, Lynchburg, Va., 1971-73, group supr., 1973-76, sect. mgr., research and devel., 1976-79, lab. mgr. research and devel., 1979—. Registered profl. quality engr., Calif. Mem. Am. Soc. Nondestructive Testing, ASTM, Am. Soc. Metals, Acoustic Emission Working Group. Lutheran (mem. ch. council, fin. sec.). Patentee apparatus for the in-situ detection and location of flaws in welds. Office: PO Box 1260 Lynchburg VA 24505

WEI, CHIU-NAN, chem. engr.; b. Taiwan, China, Sept. 20, 1943; came to U.S., 1970; s. Teh-Wang and Nu-Ing (Wang) W.; B.S., Nat. Taiwan U., 1968; M.S., Cath. U. Am., 1973, Ph.D., 1975; m. Suh-Shiang Shen, June 9, 1970; children—Helen, Grant. Teaching asst. Nat. Taiwan U., Taipei, 1969-70; teaching and research asst. Cath. U. Am., Washington, 1970-74; staff systems engr. Singer Co., Link Div., Silver Spring, Md., 1974-77; sr. process analysis engr. Celanese Chem. Co., Inc., Corpus Christi, Tex., 1977—; cons. in field. Mem. Am. Chem. Soc., Am. Inst. Chem. Engrs., Sigma Xi. Contbr. articles to profl. jours. Home: 5014 Wingfoot Ln Corpus Christi TX 78413 Office: PO Box 9077 Corpus Christi TX 78408

WEI, I-YUAN, chemist; b. Taipei, Republic of China, Nov. 1, 1940; s. Kuan-te and Kuan (Lu) W.; came to U.S., 1967; B.S., Taiwan Normal U., 1964; M.S., Nat. Taiwan U., 1966; Ph.D., Tufts U., 1971; m. Shirley Shiow-chih Chen, Dec. 28, 1968; children—Jerray, Jiaying. Research asso. Worcester (Mass.) Poly. Inst., 1971-72, U. N.C., Chapel Hill, 1972-75; scientist Sprague Electric Co., North Adams, Mass., 1976-77; mgr. research and devel. electrochem. div. Republic Foil, Nat. Aluminum, Salisbury, N.C., 1977—. Mem. Am. Chem. Soc., Sigma Xi. Contbr. research papers to profl. publs. Office: Klumar and Old Concord Rd Salisbury NC 28144

WEIDINGER, HERBERT HENRY, engring. co. exec.; b. Chgo., June 9, 1936; s. Andrew and Emma W.; B.A. in Econs., Loras Coll., 1958; M.L.A., So. Meth. U., 1975; M.A., U. Tex., Dallas, 1978; m. Beverly Ann Conlon, Feb. 9, 1957; children—Anita, Kathleen, David. Bank trainee Nat. Blvd. Bank, Chgo., 1958-59; credit rep. Sinclair Refining Co., Chgo., 1959-64, U.S. Steel, Chgo., 1964-66; dist. credit mgr. Kaiser Aluminum, Chgo., Dallas, 1966-71; credit mgr. Mesco Metal Bldgs., Dallas, 1972-74; credit mgr. Otis Engring. Corp., Carrollton, Tex., 1975—; tchr. evening bus. program North Lake Community Coll., Irving, Tex., 1978-79. Mem. Farmers Br. Library Bd., 1977-79, chmn., 1978-79; mem. Farmers Br. City Council, 1979—. Named Library Trustee of Year, Tex. Library Assn., 1979. Mem. Nat. Assn. Credit Mgmt., Internat. Credit Execs., Fgn. Credit Interchange Bur (pres. Dallas chpt.), Dallas Assn. Credit Mgmt. Home: 14232 Rawhide Farmers Branch TX 75234 Office: PO Box 34380 Dallas TX 75234

WEIDLER, SHIRLEY ANN, brokerage co. exec.; b. Bellville, Tex., Aug. 6, 1937; d. Hugho and Mattie Walker (Matthews) Frank; student Taylor Bus. Sch., 1955-56; m. John W. Weidler, Sept. 2, 1967; 1 son, Curtis Lee. IBM proof operator Fed. Res. Bank, Houston, 1956-57; supr. collections in transit 1st City Nat. Bank, Houston, 1960-65, stock transfer clk., 1966; payroll clk. Rotan Mosle Inc., Houston, 1966-70, supr. payroll and personnel, 1970-76, salary and benefits adminstr., 1976—. Mem. Houston Personnel Assn., Nat. Assn. Female Execs. Democrat. Methodist. Home: 5005 Georgi Ln Unit 206 Houston TX 77092 Office: 1500 S Tower Pennzoil Pl Houston TX 77002

WEIGEL, JAMES ARNOLD, computer systems analyst; b. Hamilton, Ohio, Oct. 29, 1947; s. Elmer John and Della Jane (Hill) W.; student Miami U., 1967; m. Marilyn Jean Orr, Sept. 23, 1977; 1 dau., Lori Jean. Computer operator, programmer NCR, 1969-74; sr. programmer 1st Fed. Savs. and Loan of Broward County, Ft. Lauderdale, Fla., 1974-76; sr. system analyst, project mgr. Anacomp, Inc., Sarasota, Fla., 1976-80; dir. centralized-systems software div. Data Systems Cons.'s, Dayton, Ohio, 1980—. Republican. Roman Catholic. Home: 3242 Kingswood Dr Sarasota FL 33582 Office: 5450 Far Hills Ave Suite 205 Dayton OH 45429

WEIGEL, PAUL HENRY, biochemist; b. N.Y.C., Aug. 11, 1946; s. Helmut and Jeanne Blanche (Wakeman) W.; B.A. in Chemistry, Cornell U., 1968; M.A., Johns Hopkins U. Sch. Medicine, 1969, Ph.D. in Biochemistry, 1975; m. Nancy Lynn Shulman, June 15, 1968; 1 dau., Dana Jeanne. Nat. Cancer Inst. postdoctoral fellow dept. biology Johns Hopkins, U., 1975-78; asst. prof. biochemistry, dept. human biol. chemistry and genetics U. Tex. Med. Br., Galveston, 1978—. Served with U.S. Army, 1969-71. Mem. Am. Chem. Soc., AAAS, Sigma Xi. Unitarian. Research, publs. in field. Home: 5100 Ash Ct Dickinson TX 77539 Office: Div Biochemistry U Tex Med Br Galveston TX 77550

WEILER, JOHN HENRY, indsl. engineer; b. New Orleans, Feb. 17, 1944; s. Donald Alfred and Marjorie Jane (Pons) W.; B.S. in Indsl. Engring. Tech., La. State U., 1966, postgrad., 1967-68; postgrad. Oak Ridge Inst. Nuclear Studies, 1966, 68; m. Nancy Rita Bernard, May 3, 1969; children—Kristina Leigh, Katherine Renee. Sr. Physicist La. Bd. Nuclear Energy, Baton Rouge, La., 1966-69; mgr. radiol. services Ingalls Nuclear Shipbuilding Co., Pascagoula, Miss., 1969-71; dir. safety and training Essex Corp., Houston, 1971-73; mgr. nondestructive examination Offshore Power Systems Co., Jacksonville, Fla., 1973-78, mgr. quality control and nondestructive examination, 1978—; cons. in field. Scoutmaster, Boy Scouts Am., Baton Rouge, 1964-66, explorer scout advisor, New Orleans, Pascagoula, 1966-69. Registered profl. engr., Calif. Mem. ASME, Am. Soc. for Nondestructive Testing (personnel tng. and cert. com.), Am. Welding Soc., Health Physics Soc., Am. Nuclear Soc., ASTM, Am. Soc. for Quality Control, Internat. Radiation Protection Assn., Tau Kappa Epsilon. Republican. Roman Catholic. Club: Weekenders. Contbr. articles to profl. jours. Home: 2303 Shipwreck Dr Jacksonville FL 32224 Office: 8000 Arlington Expressway Jacksonville FL 32211

WEIMER, CHARLES ERNEST, univ. adminstr.; b. Boutte, La., July 13, 1917; s. Frank J. and Lucy (Guedry) W.; B.A., La. State U., Baton Rouge, 1938, M.Ed., 1947, Ph.D., 1974; m. Mary Louise Claudet, Apr. 20, 1944; children—Charles Ernest, Chester, Catherine, James. High sch. tchr., 1938-41; prin. St. James (La.) High Sch., 1947-63; mem. faculty Nicholls State U., Thibobaux, La., 1963—, prof. edn., 1968—, asst. dean edn., 1976—, dir. student teaching, 1968—; cons. in field. Served to maj. AUS, 1941-46. Mem. Assn. Tchr. Educators, La. LTA (past exec. com.), Phi Delta Kappa, Kappa Delta Phi. Democrat. Roman Catholic. Club: K.C. (past grand knight). Home: 417 Country Club Blvd Thibodaux LA 70301 Office: Nicholls State Univ Thibodaux LA 70301

WEIMER, CLARENCE DAVID, JR., mgmt. cons.; b. Pitts., Dec. 11, 1934; s. Clarence David and Agnes (Morris) W.; B.S., U. Pitts., 1956; M.S. (grad. fellow in physics), George Washington U., 1972, D.B.A. (grad. fellow in mgmt. sci.), 1975; m. Maureen Mae Dunaway, Aug. 16, 1958 (div. 1979); children—Darin Lynn, C. David, Diana Gale; m. 2d, Ellen Roberts, 1979. Propulsion engr. Rockwell Internat. Co., Los Angeles, 1957-59; sr. devel. engr. Lockheed Missiles & Space Co., Sunnyvale, Cal., 1959-61; program mgr. United Techs. Corp., Sunnyvale, 1961-69; sr. staff mem. Inst. for Def. Analyses, Arlington, Va., 1969-78. Mem. Def. Sci. Bd. Task Force on Avionics and Electronics Mgmt., 1971; instr. physics U. Buffalo, 1957; mem. Army Materiel Acquisition Com., 1974. Mem. Am. Inst. Aeros. and Astronautics, IEEE, Acad. Mgmt., Am. Mgmt. Assn., AAAS, Inst. for Mgmt. Sci., Am. Fin. Assn. Republican. Presbyterian. Home: 2121 Westmoreland St Falls Church VA 22043 Office: 5001 Seminary Rd Suite 1022 Alexandria VA 22311

WEINBAUM, ELEANOR PERLSTEIN, estate mgr., writer; b. Beaumont, Tex., Sept. 3; d. Hyman Asher and Mamie (Gordon) Perlstein; student Ward-Belmont Coll., 1920, Benjamins' Coll., N.Y.C., 1922, Boulder U., 1931; L.H.D., U. Libre, 1972; m. Charles Weinbaum, Aug. 25, 1923 (div.); 1 son, Charles H. Partner estates mgmt. 23d. St. Shopping Center, Beaumont, 1956—; founder Eleanor Poetry Room at Lamar U., 1960, Pulse, lit. mag., 1962. Donor Poetry Room So. Methodist U., Dallas, 1965, sponsor ann. lecture by internat. poet, 1960—. Named D. Modern Humanities, Internat. Acad., 1969, one of internat. women of year with laureate honors Poet Laureate Internat., 1975; recipient Distinguished Service citation World Poetry Soc., 1970. Mem. Beaumont C. of C., Heritage Soc., Tex., Nat. Press Women, Internat. Acad. Poets, Acad. Am. Poets, Tex. Council Promotion Poetry, World and Nat. Poetry Day Com. (hon. life), Dr. Stella Woodall Poetry Soc. (pres.), Sigma Tau Delta. Jewish. Club: Beaumont. Author: From Croup to Nuts, 1941; The World Laughs With You, 1950; Jest for You, 1954; Shalom, America, 1970; Conrad's Scrabble Babble, 1977; God's Eternal Word, 1978; contbr. to Adventures in Poetry mag. Home: Hotel Beaumont Apt 415 Beaumont TX 77701 Office: 1215 Beaumont Savs Bldg Beaumont TX 77701

WEINBERG, ALEXANDER, civil engr.; b. Warsaw, Poland, Sept. 5, 1921; s. Hanan and Natalia (Friedman) W.; came to U.S., 1964, naturalized, 1971; B.S., Politechnic of Silesia, 1948; m. Anita Bergerman, June 11, 1957; children—Annette, Ohr, Shirley. Resident engr., project mgr. J. Lustig Constrn. Co., Tel Aviv, Israel, 1948-54; dist. engr. Israeli Ministry Def. Constrn. Dept., 1954-59; chief engr. Nigersol Constrn. Co., Ibandan, Nigeria, 1959-63; chief engr. Nat. Constrn. Co., Kathmandu, Nepal, 1963-64; project mgr. R. Chuckrow Constrn. Co., N.Y.C., 1964-65; chief engr. Diesel Constrn. Co., N.Y.C., 1965-68; pres. Amis Constrn. and Cons. Services, Inc., N.Y.C., 1968—. Mem. Am. Mil. Engrs. Assn., Am. Value Engrs. Club: Capitol Hill. Home: 482 E Royal Flamingo Dr Sarasota FL 33577 Office: 21 W 38th St New York NY 10018

WEINBRENNER, GEORGE RYAN, aero. engr.; b. Detroit, June 10, 1917; s. George Penbrook and Helen Mercedes (Ryan) W.; B.S., Mass. Inst. Tech., 1940, M.S., 1941; A.M.P., Harvard U., 1966; m. Billie Marjorie Elwood, May 2, 1955. Commd. 2d lt. USAAF, 1939, advanced through grades to col., 1949; def. attaché Am. embassy, Prague, Czechoslavakia, 1958-61; dep. chief staff intelligence Air Force Systems Command, Washington, 1962-68; comdr. fgn. tech. div. U.S. Air Force, Wright-Patterson AFB, Ohio, 1968-74; comdr. Brooks AFB, Tex., 1974-75; ret., 1975; exec. v.p. B.C. Wills & Co., Inc., Reno, Nev., 1975—; lectr. Sch. Aerospace Medicine Brooks AFB, Tex., 1976; dir. Hispaño-Technica S.A. Inc., San Antonio, 1977—; cons. Def. Dept., 1976, Dept. Air Force, 1975-80. Bd. dirs. San Antonio Inst. of Americas. Decorated D.S.M., Legion Merit, Bronze Star, Air medal, Purple Heart; Ordre National du Merite, Medaille de la Resistance, Croix de Guerre (France). Fellow AIAA (asso.); mem. San Antonio C. of C., Air Force Assn. (exec. sec. Tex. 1976-80), Assn. Former Intelligence Officers (nat. dir.), Am. Def. Preparedness Assn., U.S. Strategic Inst., Am. Astronautical Soc., Mil. Order World Wars, Am. Legion, Kappa Sigma. Roman Catholic. Clubs: Army-Navy, Univ. (Washington); Army-Navy Country (Arlington, Va.); St. Anthonys, Optimist (San Antonio); Spl. Forces (London). Home: 1236 Wiltshire Ave San Antonio TX 78209 Office: PO Box 35342 San Antonio TX 78235

WEINER, BERNARD KARL, physician; b. Gary, Ind., Jan. 2, 1929; s. Isidore and Anna (Alterman) W.; B.S., Ind. U., 1950, M.D., 1953; m. Marcia Myra Spitzer, Sept. 15, 1952; children—Audrey, Jodi, Karen. Intern, Methodist Hosp., Gary, 1953-54; gen. practice medicine, San Antonio, 1958—; active staff Meth. Hosp., chief dept. family practice, 1969—, sec. staff, 1974, vice chief staff, 1975, chief staff, 1977—; courtesy staff Bapt. Meml. Hosp., St. Luke's Luth. Hosp., Community Gen. Hosp., Santa Rosa Hosp. Trustee Jewish Community Center, 1970-73. Served to capt. USAF, 1954-58. Recipient Nat. Membership award Zionist Orgn. Am., 1969, Citation of Honor, 1972; Physician's Recognition award AMA, 1972, 75, 78, 79; Nat. Retention award B'nai B'rith, 1974; Maimonides award State of Israel, 1977. Diplomate Am. Bd. Family Practice. Fellow Am. Acad. Family Physicians, Royal Soc. Health, Am. Geriatrics Soc.; mem. Am., Tex., So., Pan American med. assns., Tex., Alamo acads. family physicians, Internat. Med. Assembly (trustee 1963-65), Bexar County Med. Soc. (counselor 1976-79, mem. peer rev. com. 1973-76), Zionist Orgn. Am. (dist. pres. 1968-72), Assn. Am. Physicians and Surgeons, Am. Physicians Fellowship, Phi Chi. Jewish (pres. synagogue 1975-78). Mem. B'nai B'rith (pres. lodge 1973-74). Home: 6603 Moss Oak St San Antonio TX 78229 Office: 929 Manor Dr San Antonio TX 78229

WEINER, MARCIA MYRA, lawyer; b. Chgo., Apr. 12, 1934; d. Adolph Carl and Esther (Kahan) Spitzer; student U. Ariz., 1952, 54, Ind. U. extension Indpls., 1953; B.A., St. Mary's U., San Antonio, 1965, J.D., 1970; m. Bernard K. Weiner, Sept. 15, 1952; children—Audrey Cheryl, Jodi Weiner Groff, Karen Elizabeth. Tchr. history Congregation Agudas Achim, San Antonio, 1965-69; admitted to Tex. bar, 1971; atty-adviser HUD, San Antonio area office, 1971—, spl. achievement awards HUD, 1972, 75, 77. Mem. Am., Tex., Fed. bar assns., Pi Gamma Mu, Delta Epsilon Sigma, Phi Alpha Theta, Kappa Beta Pi. Jewish. Clubs: Hadassah, Rodfei Sholom Sisterhood. Home: 6603 Moss Oak Dr San Antonio TX 78229 Office: PO Box 9163 800 Dolorosa St San Antonio TX 78285

WEINER, MORTON DAVID, bus. exec.; b. Balt., Aug. 19, 1922; s. Max and Rose (Wolfe) W.; B.S., Towson State Coll., 1942; grad. exec. program, U. Calif. at Los Angeles, 1959; m. Joan M. Maggin; children—Bruce, Susan, Lori, Julie. Pres., dir. AVNET, Inc., N.Y.C., 1963-69; pres., owner Morton D. Weiner & Co., investment bankers, N.Y.C., 1969-70; pres., chief exec. officer Norin Corp., North Miami, Fla., 1971-78; exec. v.p., dir. Norris Grain Co., 1971-78; chmn. bd. Maple Leaf Mills, Ltd., Toronto, 1974-78; pres., chief exec. officer, dir. South Atlantic Fin. Corp., 1978—; pres., dir. Atico Fin. Corp., 1979—; dir. Pan Am. Bank, Miami. Served to capt. Signal Corps, AUS, 1942-46; CBI. Office: PO Box O 13131 150 SE 3d Ave Miami FL 33101

WEINGARTNER, HANS MARTIN, educator; b. Heidelberg, Germany, Apr. 4, 1929; came to U.S., 1939, naturalized, 1944; s. Jacob and Grete (Kahn) W.; A.B., U. Chgo., 1950, S.B., 1950, A.M., 1951; M.S., Carnegie Mellon U., 1956, Ph.D., 1962; m. Joyce Trellis, June 12, 1955; children—Steven M., Susan C., Eric H., Kenneth L. Economist, U.S. Dept. Commerce, 1951-53; instr. Grad. Sch. Indsl. Adminstrn. Mellon U., 1956-57; instr. Grad. Sch. Bus., U. Chgo., 1957-61, asst. prof., 1961-63; asso. prof. fin. Alfred P. Sloan Sch. Mgmt., M.I.T., 1963-66; prof. Grad. Sch. Mgmt., U. Rochester, 1966-77; Brownlee O. Currey prof. fin. Owen Grad. Sch. Mgmt., Vanderbilt U., Nashville, 1977—; cons. Gen. Fin. Corp., 1958-64, 1st Nat. Bank Chgo., 1966-71, Marine Midlands Banks, 1971-76; dir. Computer Consoles, Inc., 1974—. Served with U.S. Army, 1951-53. Mellon fellow, 1954-55, Ford Found. fellow, 1955-56. Mem. Inst. Mgmt. Scis. (v.p. fin. 1978—), Am. Econ. Assn., Am. Fin. Assn. Author: Mathematical Programming and the Analysis of Capital Budgeting Problems, 1963; also numerous articles on banking and fin. Departmental editor Mgmt. Sci., 1967-73. Home: 1616 Ash Valley Dr Nashville TN 37215 Office: 2505 West End Ave Nashville TN 37203

WEINHAUER, WILLIAM GILLETTE, bishop, Episc. Ch.; b. N.Y.C., Dec. 3, 1924; s. Nicholas Alfred and Florence Anastasia (Davis) W.; B.S., Trinity Coll., 1948; S.T.B., Gen. Theol. Sem., N.Y.C., 1951, S.T.M., 1956, Th.D., 1970; m. Jean Roberta Shanks, Mar. 20, 1948; 3 children. Ordained priest, 1951; curate Ch. of the Resurrection, Queens, N.Y., 1951-52; vicar St. George's Ch., Bronx, N.Y., chaplain N.Y. U., 1952-53; chaplain Hunter Coll., Coll. City N.Y., Bronx, 1952-56; dir. religious edn. St. James Ch., Scarsdale N.Y., 1953-56; prof. St. Andrew's Theol. Sem., Philippines, 1956-60; vicar St. Paul Ch., Pleasant Valley, N.Y., 1960-61; instr. Gen. Theol. Sem., 1961-64, prof., 1964-71; rector Christ Ch., Poughkeepsie, N.Y., 1971; bishop Diocese of Western N.C., 1971—. Office: Box 368 Black Mountain NC 28711*

WEINMAN, PHYLLIS EVELYN, hosp. ofcl.; b. San Antonio, Jan. 22, 1932; d. John Philip and Ruby Evelyn (Stewart) Hopkins; grad. Incarnate Word, 1948; student U. Fla., 1950; m. Irvin Kenneth Weinman, Aug. 9, 1953 (div.); children—Phillip D., Russell M., Raymond S., Bruce H., James W. Editorial asst. Dept. Public Relations/Devel., SW Tex. Meth. Hosp., San Antonio, 1966-70, dir. public relations, 1970-76, coordinator community relations, 1976-77, dir. vol. services, 1977—; cons. in field. Bd. dirs. Blue Bird aux. SW Tex. Meth. Hosp., 1963—, 3d v.p., 1965. Mem. Am. Hosp. Assn., Am. Soc. Dirs. Vol. Services, Tex. Hosp. Assn., Tex. Soc. Hosp. Public Relations (chmn. state awards com. 1971-72, state dir. 1972-73, chmn. state nominating com. 1973-74, pres. San Antonio chpt. 1971), Tex.Assn.Dirs. Vol. Services, San Antonio Council Vol. Service Dirs. (sec. 1978). Office: SW Tex Meth Hosp 7700 Floyd Curl Dr San Antonio TX 78229

WEINSTEIN, MARK BERTON, physician; b. Wichita Falls, Tex., May 8, 1945; s. Samuel N. and Esther Rose (Persky) W.; B.S., Tulane U., 1967; M.D., U. Tex. Med. Sch., 1973; m. Ellen Weinstein, Jan. 31, 1970; children—Abbe, Drew, Brent. Intern, Bexar County Hosp., San Antonio, 1973-74; resident U. Pitts. Med. Center, 1974-75, Columbia Presbyn. Med. Center, 1975-77; practice medicine specializing in dermatology, San Antonio, 1977—; mem. staff Bexar County, Meth., St. Luke's, Community hosps. (all in San Antonio); clin. asst. prof. U. Tex. Health Sci. Center, San Antonio, 1977—. Diplomate Am. Bd. Dermatology. Fellow Am. Acad. Dermatology; mem. Bexar County Med. Soc. Home: 11233 Whisper Willow St San Antonio TX 78230 Office: 7950 Floyd Curl Dr #906 San Antonio TX 78229

WEIR, EUGENE ARNOLD, architect, indsl. real estate ofcl.; b. Baton Rouge, Sept. 15, 1926; s. Claude Arnold and Myrtis (Downing) W.; student La. State U., 1944-46, 47; B.S. in Archtl. Engring., Kan. State U., 1950, B.S. in Architecture, 1951; m. Nancy Jean Fitzgerald, Apr. 3, 1954; children—Eugene Marcus, Jefferson Arnold, Nancy Kathryn. Constrn. aide Fed. Housing Adminstrn., Birmingham, Ala., 1950; with Ethyl Corp., Baton Rouge, 1951—, dir. corporate real estate, 1974—. Mem. Downtown Baton Rouge Beautification Com., 1970-72; bd. dirs. Baton Rouge Art Gallery. Served with USNR, 1944-46. Mem. AIA, La. Architects Assn., Internat. Real Estate Fedn., Indsl. Devel. Research Council, Nat. Assn. Corporate Real Estate Execs. (chmn. archtl. com. 1974, dir. dist. VI, Sigma Tau, Tau Sigma Delta, Kappa Alpha. Episcopalian. Clubs: City of Baton Rouge, Camelot. Home: 6410 LaSalle Ave Baton Rouge LA 70806 Office: Ethyl Tower 451 Florida St Baton Rouge LA 70801

WEIR, GLORIA JANE, physician; b. Baton Rouge, Jan. 18, 1921; d. Claude Arnold and Peggy (Downing) Weir; student Sullins Coll., 1936-37; B.S., La. State U., 1940, M.D., 1943; m. N. Lyle Evans, July 26, 1952; children—Peggy Jane, David Lyle. Intern Charity Hosp. La., New Orleans, 1944, resident, then chief resident in pediatrics, 1949-51; practice medicine specializing in pediatrics, Baton Rouge, 1952—; staff mem. Baton Rouge Gen. Hosp., vice-chief staff, 1965, vice-chief pediatrics, 1969, chief pediatrics, 1970-71; mem. staff Our Lady of Lake Hosp., Baton Rouge, vice chief pediatrics, 1959-60; mem. staff Women's Hosp., chief pediatrics, 1969-70, mem. staff Drs. Meml. Hosp.; mem. cons. staff Mary Bird Perkins Treatment Center of Cancer, Radiation and Research Found.; vis. staff Earl K. Long Meml. Hosp.; clin. instr. pediatrics La. State U. Med. Sch.; pediatric cons., chief med. cons. Baton Rouge Gen. Hosp. Child Day Care Center, Disability Determination Services State of La.; bd. dirs. Baton Rouge Assn. Retarded Citizens, 1974-77; adv. bd. East Baton Rouge Parish Med. Aux. Diplomate Am. Bd. Pediatrics. Fellow Am. Acad. Pediatrics (alt. state chmn. 1975-78); mem. AMA, La. 6th Dist., East Baton Rouge Parish med. socs., La. Heart Assn., La., Baton Rouge pediatric socs. (v.p. 1968-69, pres. 1969-70), Children's Hosp. Found., Cancer Soc. Baton Rouge (dir. 1963-67, 76—), Sullins Alumnae Assn., Baton Rouge Civic Symphony Aux., Delta Zeta (mem. house corp.), La. State U. Alumni Fedn., La. Concert Ballet Aux. Episcopalian. Clubs: Harlequins (v.p. 1979-80). Home: 5885 Eastwood Dr Baton Rouge LA 70806 Office: 2730 Wooddale Blvd PO Box 66498 Baton Rouge LA 70896

WEIR, JAMES ROBERT, JR., metall. engr.; b. Middletown, Ohio, Dec. 29, 1932; s. James Robert and Kathleen (Lawson) W.; B.S., U. Cinn., 1955; M.S., U. Tenn., 1961; children—James R., David Jeffrey, Joseph Todd, Patrick Allen, Scott Anthony. With Oak Ridge Nat. Lab., 1955—, group leader, 1961-68, sect. head, 1968-73, div. dir. metals and ceramics, 1973—. Served with U.S. Army, 1957-59. Fellow Am. Soc. Metals (bd. dirs.), AAAS; mem. Am. Welding Soc. Club: Concord Yacht. Contbr. articles to profl. jours. Home: 105 Davidson Ln Oak Ridge TN 37830 Office: PO Box X Oak Ridge TN 37830

WEIR, JOHN HOWARD, real estate and banking exec.; b. Binghamton, N.Y., Jan. 18, 1925; s. Milton N. and Mildred L. (Young) W.; student pub., pvt. schs.; m. Jamesena G. Hardee, Aug. 31, 1950; children—Deborah Suzanne, John Howard. Gen. mgr. Weir

& Sons of Fla., Inc., Boca Raton, Fla., 1952-58, 61—; v.p., gen. mgr. Arvida Corp., 1958-61; exec. v.p., dir. Boca Raton Nat. Bank, 1961—. v.p., treas., dir. Castleton Industries, Inc., 1968-69; pres., dir. Citizens Nat. Bank, Boca Raton; chmn., pres., dir. Fidelity Nat. Bank, Pompano Beach, Fla. Trustee, vice chmn. Boca Raton Community Hosp. Served with USNR, 1943-46. Mem. Am. Legion. Republican. Presbyterian. Clubs: Wings (N.Y.C.); Boca Raton Bath and Tennis, Royal Palm Yacht and Country (Boca Raton), Masons. Home: 2840 Banyan Blvd Circle NW Boca Raton FL 33431 Office: 77 E Camino Real Boca Raton FL 33432

WEIR, RONALD LEE, educator; b. Monroe, La., Apr. 13, 1943; s. John Alexander and Geneva (Brantley) W.; B.S., N.E. La. U., 1965, M.B.A., 1967; D.B.A., Miss. State U., 1971; m. Mary Hannah Ware, Dec. 18, 1965; children—John Edward, Ronald Jason, James Austin. Instr., Northwestern La. U., Natchitoches, La., 1967-68, Miss. State U., Starkville, 1970-71; asst. prof. E. Tenn. State U., Johnson City, 1971-78, asso. prof. mktg., 1979—; mem. Bus. Econ. Planning Team—Directions 2,000, 1979; lectr., cons. Coll. of Bus. team leader Washington County United Way, 1978, 79. Named Outstanding Faculty mem. E. Tenn. State U., 1976; recipient Project Horizon award, 1976. Mem. Am. Acad. Advt., So. Mktg. Assn., Johnson City Area C. of C., Omicron Delta Kappa, Beta Gamma Sigma, Pi Sigma Epsilon, Delta Sigma Pi. Mem. Churches of Christ. Author articles. Home: 1304 Beechwood Dr Johnson City TN 37601 Office: Sam Wilson Hall E Tenn State U Johnson City TN 37601

WEIR, WILLIAM MANNING, real estate firm exec.; b. Binghamton, N.Y., May 17, 1929; s. Milton Nelson and Mildred Lydia (Young) W.; grad. high sch.; m. Dorothy Dee Willis, June 18, 1953; children—William Manning, Patricia C. Gen. mgr. Weir Contractors div. M.N. Weir & Sons, Inc., 1954-73; pres. M.N. Weir & Sons, Inc., Boca Raton, Fla., 1973-76, Weir & Sons of Fla., Inc., Boca Raton, 1976—; v.p. Boca Raton Plaza, Inc., 1962-76; dir. Security Exchange Bank, 1965-69; vice chmn., dir. Fidelity Nat. Bank, 1972—; dir. Boca Raton Nat. Bank, Fidelity Bank West Delray Beach, 1972-73. Served with USCG, 1951-54. Mem. Am. Legion, Nat. Assn. Realtors, Boca Raton C. of C., Boca Raton Bd. Realtors, Fla. Assn. Realtors. Republican. Presbyterian. Club: Royal Palm Yacht and Country (Boca Raton). Home: 444 Maya Palm Dr Boca Raton FL 33432 Office: 855 S Federal Hwy Boca Raton FL 33432

WEIRICH, THOMAS EUGENE, petroleum geologist; b. White City, Kans., Nov. 10, 1897; s. Thomas and Josephine Henrietta (Farbridge) W.; student Coll. of Emporia (Kans.), 1914-16; B.S. in Geology, U. Okla., 1922; m. Lela Marie Smith, June 10, 1925; 1 dau., Nancy Jo. Asst. geologist Empire Gas and Fuel Co., Augusta and Eldorado, Kans., 1916-18; resident geologist Marland Refining Co., Ponca City and Tonkawa, Okla., 1922-25; sub-surface geologist Skelly Oil Co., Tulsa, 1925-26; chief geologist Tidal Oil Co., Tulsa, 1926-29; geologist Phillips Petroleum Co., Bartlesville, Okla., 1929-61; cons. petroleum geologist, Bartlesville, 1961—. Served with USNRF, 1918-19. Mem. Am. Assn. Petroleum Geologists (emeritus), Tulsa Geol. Soc. (hon.), Sigma Xi (Okla. U. Alumni mem.), Bartlesville C. of C. (pecan culture). Democrat. Episcopalian. Clubs: Elks, Masons, Order Eastern Star (patron Unity chpt., 1951-52). Contbr. articles to profl. publs. Home and Office: 1308 Rockdale Rd Bartlesville OK 74003

WEIS, KATHLEEN ANN, nurse practitioner; b. Newark, Sept. 26, 1948; d. Lester Wilbur and Helen Marie (Wroblewski) W.; B.S.N., U. Iowa, 1970; certified emergency nurse practitioner U. Va., 1976. Staff nurse Dartmouth-Hitchcock Mental Health Center, Hanover, N.H., 1970-71; commd. ensign Nurse Corps, U.S. Navy, 1971, advanced through grades to lt.; staff Naval Regional Med. Center, Newport, R.I., 1971-75, dir. alcohol rehab. unit, 1973-75; ret.; commd. capt. Nurse Corps, U.S. Army, 1976; acting comdg. officer 130th Sta. hosp., attached to 30th field hosp., Heidelberg, W. Ger., 1976-77; commd. sr. nurse officer. Nat. Health Service Corps, USPHS, 1978; adviser rural health clinics, 1978—; practitioner intern, Nashville, 1976; lectr. emergency medicine. Recipient Order of Paul Revere Patriots from Mass. Gov. Francis F. Sargent, 1974; lic. emergency nurse practitioner, N.C. Mem. Am. Emergency Dept. Nurses Assn., Am. Nurses Assn., R.I. Nurses Assn., Assn. Mil. Surgeons of U.S., U. Iowa Alumnae Assn., Coll. Nursing Constituent Soc. U. Iowa, Alpha Xi Delta. Roman Catholic. Home: Flint Ridge Apts 56 Hillsborough NC 27278

WEISBARD, MARSHALL PAUL, ins. co. exec.; b. Miami, Fla., May 13, 1953; s. Ralph M. and Ruth O. W.; A.A., Fla. State U., 1973, B.S. cum laude, 1975; m. Denise R. Weinstock, Aug. 31, 1975. Sales rep. Met. Life Ins. Co., Gainesville, Fla., 1976-78, sales mgr. Ocala (Fla.) dist., 1978-79, Miami, Fla., 1979—. Mem. Nat. Assn. Life Underwriters, Phi Beta Kappa. Democrat. Jewish. Club: B'nai Brith (dir.). Home: 1130 NW 93d Terr Pembroke Pines FL 33023 Office: Met Life Ins Co 8355 NW 53d St Miami FL 33166

WEISBERG, AARON, gastroenterologist, internist; b. Bklyn., July 21, 1915; s. Joseph and Yetta W.; A.B., N.Y. U., 1935; M.D., Cin. Eclectic Med. Coll., 1939; m. Ruth Hannah Mintz, Feb. 5, 1949; children—Harlene Edith, Sharon Esta Weisberg Shapiro. Intern, Coney Island Hosp., Bklyn., 1939-40, resident in medicine, 1941-42; pvt. practice medicine specializing in internal medicine, Bklyn., 1946-74, St. Petersburg, Fla., 1974—; chief medicine Meth. Hosp., Bklyn., to 1974, cons. medicine and gastroenterology, 1977—; dir. medicine Carson C. Peck Meml. Hosp., Bklyn., 1962-71; attending emeritus Coney Island Hosp., Bklyn.; mem. staffs St. Petersburg Gen. Hosp., Palms Pasadena Hosp., St. Petersburg; attending staff medicine and gastroenterology VA Hosp., Tampa, Fla.; clin. asst. prof. medicine and gastroenterology Med. Coll., U. South Fla., 1975—; med. dir. Sperry Microwave Electronics, Clearwater, Fla. Served to capt. M.C., U.S. Army, 1942-46. Recipient Gold Medal award Coney Island Hosp., 1971; diplomate Am. Bd. Internal Medicine. Fellow A.C.P., Am. Coll. Gastroenterology, Royal Soc. Medicine, Am. Soc. Gastroenterology, Royal Soc. Internal Medicine, N.Y. Acad. Gastroenterology; mem. Internat., Am., Fla. socs. internal medicine, Pan Am. Med. Assn. (diplomate in internal medicine and gastroenterology), AMA, Fla. Med. Assn., Pinellas County, Kings County med. socs., Am. Soc. Gastrointestinal Endoscopy, Am. Fedn. Clin. Research (sr.), Fla. Soc. Gastroenterology, Am. Soc. Occupational Medicine, Am. Chem. Soc., Brotherhood of Israel, Phi Lambda Kappa. Club: N.Y. U. Contbr. articles on gastroenterology, cardiology and cancer to med. jours. Research thymus gland, anti-peptic ulcer agents. Home: 6595 Augusta Blvd Seminole FL 33543 Office: 6499 38th Ave N Saint Petersburg FL 33710

WEISBORD, NORMAN EDWARD, geologist; b. Jersey City, Oct. 1, 1901; s. Edward and Clara (Mirsky) W.; A.B., Cornell U., 1923, M.S., 1926; m. Nettie Schein, Dec. 19, 1939. Paleontologist, geologist Atlantic Refining Co., Venezuela, Colombia, Mexico, Guatemala, Cuba, 1923-33; instr. Cornell U., 1926; sr. field geologist Standard Oil Co. of N.J., Argentina, Bolivia, 1933-35; geologist, asst. chief geologist Standard Vacuum Oil Co., Java, Sumatra, Borneo, New Guinea, Papua, 1935-42; chief geologist Mobil Oil Corp., Venezuela, 1942-57; research asso. geology Fla. State U., Tallahassee, 1957-64, prof., 1964—. Fellow AAAS, Geol. Soc. Am., Geol. Soc. London, Geol. Soc. France, Geol. Soc. Switzerland, Am. Geog. Soc., Paleontol. Research Inst., Sigma Xi; mem. Am. Assn. Petroleum Geologists, Fla. Acad. Sci., Soc. Econ. Paleontologists and Mineralogists, Southeastern Geol. Soc., Am. Malacological Soc. Contbr. articles on geology and paleontology to profl. jours. Home: 1910 Gibbs Dr Tallahassee FL 32303 Office: Dept Geology Fla State Univ Tallahassee FL 32306

WEISMANTEL, GUY EDWARD, chem. engr.; b. Geneva, Ill., Dec. 9, 1936; s. Leo Joseph and Ellen Elizabeth (Zudis) W.; B.S. in Chem. Engring., U. Notre Dame, 1958; m. Cathy June Black, June 17, 1972; children—Michael, Christianne, Robert, Gregory, Matthew. Plant mgr. GMG div. O'Brien Paint Co., San Francisco and Los Angeles, 1959-66; Western editor Chem. Engring. mag., 1966-78, Gulf Coast editor, Houston, 1978-79. Recipient cert. Soc. Profl. Engrs., 1972, Service to Mankind award Sertoma Club, 1977. Mem. Am. Inst. Chem. Engrs., Water Pollution Control Assn., Am. Assn. Petroleum Writers. Republican. Roman Catholic. Club: Houston Press. Address: 1826 Spruce St Kingwood TX 77339

WEISS, ARMAND BERL, economist; b. Richmond, Va., Apr. 2, 1931; s. Maurice Herbert and Henrietta (Shapiro) W.; B.S. in Econs., Wharton Sch. Fin., U. Pa., 1953, M.B.A., 1954; D.B.A., George Washington U., 1971; m. Judith Bernstein, May 18, 1957; children—Jo Ann Michele, Rhett Louis. Officer, U.S. Navy, 1954-65; spl. asst. to auditor gen. Navy, 1964-65; sr. economist Center for Naval Analyses, Arlington, Va., 1965-68; project dir. Logistics Mgmt. Inst., Washington, 1968-74; dir. systems integration Fed. Energy Adminstrn., Washington, 1974-76; sr. economist Nat. Commn. Supplies and Shortages, 1976-77; tech. asst. to v.p. System Planning Corp., 1977-78; pres. Assns. Internat., Inc., 1978—; v.p., treas. Technology Frontiers, Inc., 1978—; sr. v.p. Weiss Pub. Co., Inc., Richmond, Va., 1960—; adj. prof. Am. U., 1979—; vis. lectr. George Washington U., 1971; chmn. U.S. del., session chmn. NATO Symposium on Cost-Benefit Analysis, The Hague, Netherlands, 1969, NATO Conf. on Operational Research in Indsl. Systems, St. Louis, France, 1970; pres. Nat. Council Assns. Policy Scis., 1971-77; chmn. adv. group Def. Econ. Adv. Council, 1970-74; resident asso. Smithsonian Instn., 1973—; expert cons. Dept. State, GAO. Del. Pres.'s Mid-Century White House Conf. on Children and Youth, 1950; scoutmaster Japan, U.S., leader World Jamborees, France, Can., U.S., 1945-61; U.S. del. Internat. Conf. on Ops. Research, Dublin, Ireland, 1972; organizing com. Internat. Cost-Effectiveness Symposium, Washington, 1970; speaker Internat. Conf. Inst. Mgmt. Scis., Tel Aviv, 1973, del., Mexico City, 1967. Mem. bus. com. Washington Nat. Symphony Orch., 1968-70, Washington Performing Arts Soc., 1974—; exec. com. Mid Atlantic council Union Am. Hebrew Congregations, 1970-79, treas., 1974-79, mem. nat. MUM com., 1974-79; mem. dist. com. Boy Scouts Am., 1972-75. Bd. dirs. Nat. Council Career Women, 1975-79. Fellow AAAS, Washington Acad. Scis.; mem. Ops. Research Soc. Am. (chmn. meetings com. 1969-71; chmn. cost-effectiveness sect. 1969-70), Washington Ops. Research Council (editor newsletter 1969—; sec. 1971-72, pres. 1973-74, trustee 1975-77, bus. mgr. 1976—), Internat. Inst. Strategic Studies (London), Inst. for Mgmt. Sci., Am. Econ. Assn., Wharton Grad. Sch. Alumni Assn. (exec. com. 1970-73), Am. Acad. Polit. and Social Sci., Alumni Assn. George Washington U. (governing bd. 1974—, chmn. univ. publs. com. 1976-78, Alumni Service award 1980 pres. 1978-79), Alumni Assn. George Washington U. Sch. Govt. and Bus. Adminstrn. (sr. v.p. doctoral assn. 1968-69, exec. v.p. 1977-78). Jewish (pres. temple 1970-72). Club: Wharton Grad. Sch. Washington (sec. 1967-69, pres. 1969-70). Co-editor: Systems Analysis for Social Problems, 1970; The Relevance of Economic Analysis to Decision Making in the Department of Defense, 1972; Toward More Effective Public Programs: The Role of Analysis and Evaluation, 1975. Editor: Cost-Effectiveness Newsletter, 1966-70, Operations Research/Systems Analysis Today, 1971-73, Operation Research/Mgmt. Sci. Today, 1974—; Feedback, 1979—; asso. editor Ops. Research, 1971-75. Home: 6516 Truman Ln Falls Church VA 22043

WEISS, GREGORY LEE, educator; b. Canton, Ohio, Aug. 19, 1949; s. Lester Dean and Betty Jane Rowley; B.A., Wittenberg U., 1971; M.S. (USPHS fellow), Purdue U., 1972, Ph.D., 1975; m. Linda Sue Fulmer, June 17, 1972. Instr. Sch. Continuing Edn., Purdue U., West Lafayette, Ind., 1974-75; asst. prof. sociology Roanoke Coll., Salem, Va., 1975—, chmn. dept. sociology, 1977-79. Vice-pres., pres. bd. dirs. Planned Parenthood Roanoke Valley, 1979-80; bd. dirs. Free Clinic Roanoke Valley; mem. profl. adv. com. Roanoke Vol. Action Center; vol. United Way, Alumni scholar Wittenberg U., 1967-71. Mem. Am. Sociol. Assn., Am. Public Health Assn., So. Sociol. Assn., Va. Sociol. Assn., Va. Social Sci. Assn., Va. Council Social Welfare. Contbr. articles to profl. jours. Home: 2839 W Club Dr Salem VA 24153 Office: Dept Sociology Roanoke Coll Salem VA 24153

WEISS, JEFFREY J., business exec.; b. Bklyn., July 13, 1943; s. Louis M. and Miriam (Solow) W.; student Miami Dade Jr. Coll., 1961-63, U. Miami, 1974—; m. Glenda Joyce Penner, June 26, 1965; children—Lara J., Gina J. Pres., chmn. bd., founder Atlantic Industries, Inc., Miami, Fla., 1965-74, spl. cons., 1974-76; chmn. bd., v.p. Exposition Corp. of Am., Miami, 1968—; v.p., dir. Scarlet O'Hara, 1970-79, Glenda Products Inc., 1972—, Gazebo Food Corp., 1973-74; founder, prin., dir. First Bank of North Kendall Assos., 1974-76; prin., dir. Allstate Realty & Investment Co., 1974—; pres., founder Advance Devel. Corp., 1975—, Custom Land, Inc., 1975—, Advance Investmen Properties, Inc., 1977—; gen. partner Flagler St. Ltd., 1979—; founder, dir. Miami Dinnerkey Boat Show, 1970—, So. Marine, 1965-68; v.p., founder Kitchencraft Inc., 1976-77; founder, chmn. bd. Advance Fin. Corp., 1977—; dir. Underwriters Fin. of Fla., Inc. Exec. com. Ednl. Community TV, 1973—. Recipient ann. corp. award March of Dimes Walkathon. Mem. Direct Selling Assn. (dir.), Smithsonian Instn. Office: 1320 S Dixie Hwy Penthouse Suite Coral Gables FL 33146

WEISS, MARVIN ARNOLD, mfg. co. exec.; b. Chgo., Oct. 10, 1924; s. Nathan and Sarah (Kushner) W.; B.S., Sch. Bus., Northwestern U., 1948; m. Martha Hirsh, Feb. 1, 1948; children—Michael Joel, Robert Steven. Sales rep. Nikoh Tube Co. div. Internat. Rolling Mills, Chgo., 1948-53; pres. Marvin Weiss & Assos., mfrs. rep., Chgo., 1953-63; v.p. mktg. Unarco Industries, Oklahoma City, 1964—. Pres. Oklahoma City Jewish Community Council, 1979-80. Served as sgt. U.S. Army, 1942-46. Mem. Mgmt. Group. Clubs: Petroleum, Oak Tree Golf, B'nai B'rith. Office: 1316 W Main St Oklahoma City OK 73106

WEISS, TANIS ELLYN COOPER, educator; b. Chgo., Apr. 29, 1941; d. Ben and Dorothy (Mogilner) Cooper; B.A., U. Tex., 1962; M.Liberal Arts, So. Methodist U., 1970; doctoral candidate N.Tex. State U., 1975—; m. Jack Weiss, Aug. 10, 1963; children—Kira Lauren, Krenna Anne. Tchr. French and Spanish, Dallas Ind. Sch. Dist., 1963-73; adv. guidance counselor Dallas Ind. Sch. Dist., 1973—. Mem. Met. Day Care Com., 1974-75; voter registration dep. City of Dallas, 1976; bd. dirs. Jr. Players Guild, 1977; tchr. Sunday sch. Unitarian Ch. Mem. NEA, Am., N. Central Tex. personnel and guidance assns., Am. Vocat. Assn., Nat. Vocat. Guidance Assn., Tex. Tchrs. Assn., Classroom Tchrs. Dallas, Dallas Assn. Counselors, NOW. Democrat. Home: 6239 Lafayette Way Dallas TX 75230

WEISSBERG, STEVEN MARVIN, obstetrician, gynecologist; b. Bklyn., May 17, 1941; s. Sidney J. and Lilyan (Katz) W.; B.A., N.Y. U., 1962; M.D., N.Y. Med. Coll., 1966; m. Linda R. Silverman, June 21, 1964; children—Michael W., Craig E. Intern, Kings County Hosp., Bklyn., 1966-67; resident Jackson Meml. Hosp., Miami, Fla., 1969-71; practice medicine specializing in obstetrics and gynecology, South Miami, Fla., 1972—; mem. staffs South Miami Hosp., Coral Reef Gen. Hosp., Larkin Gen. Hosp., Am. Hosp.; asst. clin. prof. Sch. Medicine, U. Miami. Pres. Cherry Grove Homeowners Assn., 1974-76, 79-80. Served with USPHS, 1967-69. Diplomate Am. Bd. Obstetrics and Gynecology. Fellow Am. Coll. Obstetricians and Gynecologists, Am. Fertility Soc.; Mem. Am. Assn. Gynecologic Laparoscopists, So. Med. Assn., Fla. Med. Assn., Royal Soc. Medicine, Fla. Ob-Gyn Soc., Dade County Med. Assn. (exec. com. 1978-79). Jewish. Contbr. articles to med. jours. Office: 6201 SW 70th St South Miami FL 33143

WEISSER, HERMAN MARTIN, investment banker, mortgage broker, hotel corp. exec.; b. N.Y.C., Apr. 26, 1926; s. Israel and Rose (Adler) W.; student City U. N.Y.; B.S. in Aero. Engring. U. Md. Vice pres. Powers Enterprises, Inc., N.Y.C., 1946-55; real estate builder and investor Rose Realty Co. and Daytona Motel Corp., N.Y.C. and Daytona Beach, Fla., 1952-70; pvt. practice fin. cons., appraiser, investment real estate motels, N.Y.C. and Daytona Beach, 1954—; co-owner Desert Inn, Daytona Beach, 1957-67, chmn. bd. Daytona Motel Corp., 1960—; dir. Day Realty Corp., Fla. Security Service, Inc., 800 Orange, Inc., Gwaltney Motels, Inc.; lectr. on accommodations, real estate, financing. Mem. Motel Industry Fla., 1965, bd. dirs., 1966-67; v.p. Halifax Area Council Assns., 1962, pres., 1963, 64, bd. dirs., 1962-65, chmn. coms., 1963-64; mem. Daytona Beach Mayor's Study Com., 1963, City Mgr.'s Adv. Com., 1965; mem. Daytona Beach Com. of 100. Named Motel Hall of Fame, Hospitality mag., 1967; recipient Key to City of Daytona Beach, 1966. Mem. A-1-A Motel Assn. (v.p. 1962, pres. 1963-65, dir. 1964-65, Daytona Man of Year 1963), Motel Assn. Am. (dir. 1967-69), Nat. Assn. Rev. Appraisers (sr.), Fla. Real Estate Exchangors, Nat. Assn. Mortgage Brokers, Fla. Assn. Mortgage Brokers (dist. v.p. 1980), Ormond Beach C. of C., Am. Mgmt. Assn., UN Assn. (com. mem. 1976-77), Nat. Realty Club. Clubs: Kiwanis, Halifax. Author: Manual for Operations and Control of the Complete Resort, 1968; Hotel Sales Promotion, 1969. Home: 1108 Waverly Dr Daytona Beach FL 32018 Office: Box 5631 Daytona Beach FL 32018

WEISSKOPF, BERNARD, pediatrician, child behavior, genetic and devel. specialist, educator; b. Berlin, Dec. 11, 1929; s. Benjamin and Bertha (Loew) W.; came to U.S., 1939, naturalized, 1944; B.A., Syracuse U., 1951; M.D., U. Leiden (Netherlands), 1958; m. Penelope Allderdice, Dec. 26, 1965; children—Matthew David, Stephen Daniel. Intern, Meadowbrook Hosp., East Meadow, N.Y., 1958-59; resident Meadowbrook Hosp., 1959-60, Johns Hopkins Hosp., Balt., 1962-64; fellow child psychiatry Johns Hopkins U. Sch. Medicine, Balt., 1962-64; asst. prof. pediatrics U. Ill. Coll. Medicine, Chgo., 1964-66; faculty U. Louisville, 1966—, prof. pediatrics, 1970—, dir. Child Evaluation Center, 1966—, project dir. Nat. Found.-March of Dimes Birth Defect Center, 1966-79; trustee Jewish Hosp., Louisville, 1974-77. Served to capt. USAF, 1960-62. Fellow Am. Acad. Pediatrics, Am. Assn. on Mental Deficiency; mem. Am. Soc. Human Genetics, So. Soc. for Pediatric Research. Contbr. articles to profl. jours. Home: 6409 Deep Creek Dr Prospect KY 40059 Office: Child Evaluation Center 334 E Broadway Louisville KY 40202

WEISZ, HARRY, educator, author; b. N.Y.C., May 8, 1906; s. Joseph and Mari (Berkowitz) W.; student Chgo. Law Sch., 1925-26; m. Claire A. Heller, Dec. 1, 1934; children—Nancy Sandra, Richard Allen and Michael Barry (twins). Sales dir., merchandising cons. Harry Weisz Co., Chgo., 1935-55; pres., owner Valley View Bridge Studio, Dallas, 1955-78; contract bridge instr. City of Richardson, Tex., Richland Coll., YMCA, Sanger Harris Dept. Stores, s.s. cruises. Mem. Am. Contract Bridge League (Outstanding Service award, 1974-75), Dallas Bridge Assn. (past v.p., Appreciation award, 1977), Internat. Bridge Press Assn. Club: Corinthian Sailing. Author: Practical Bridge, 1962; How To Run Duplicate Bridge At Home, 1972; columnist Richardson Daily News, White Rock News. Home: 15255 Preston Rd Dallas TX 75248

WEITZ, RONALD WAYNE, hosp. ofcl.; b. Providence, Apr. 22, 1948; s. Emil Francis and Barbara Edith W.; B.A., Pa. State U., 1969; R.T., Sch. Nuclear Medicine Tech., Mt. Sinai Med. Center, 1973; M.B.A., U. Miami (Fla.), 1978; m. Regina Ursula Weitz, May 27, 1972; children—Jennifer Michele, Allison Jean. Chief technologist, Mercy Hosp., Miami, 1973-78, dir. fin. planning and budgets, 1978—; adj. prof. health care Fla. Internat. U., 1979—. Adv. bd. Am. Assn. Nephrology Nurses and Technologists. Mem. Soc. Nuclear Medicine, Soc. Clin. Pathologists, Mgmt. Systems Soc., Am. Coll. of Hosp. Adminstrs., Hosp. Fin. Mgmt. Assn., Beta Gamma Sigma. Home: 12251 SW 94th St Miami FL 33186 Office: Mercy Hosp 3663 S Bayshore Dr Miami FL 33133

WEITZEL, WILLIAM DAVID, psychiatrist; b. Detroit, Sept. 16, 1942; s. William Howard and Mary Ann (Buscanics) W.; B.S. cum laude, Xavier U., 1964; M.D., St. Louis U., 1968; m. Joan Carol Heiser, June 8, 1968 children—Erica Marie, Jennifer Joan, Sarah Elizabeth. Intern, William Beaumont Gen. Hosp., El Paso, Tex., 1968-69; psychiat. resident Walter Reed Gen. Hosp., 1969-72; postgrad. tng. family therapy The Washington Sch. Psychiatry, 1971-72; chief dept. psychiatry and neurology Moncrief Army Hosp., Columbia, S.C., 1972-74; asst. prof. psychiatry and dir. Hosp. Inpatient Psychiatry Service, Coll. Medicine, U. Ky., Lexington, 1974-78, asso. prof. psychiatry, 1979—, lectr. Coll. Law, 1977—; supervising and cons. psychiatrist William S. Hall Psychiat. Inst., Columbia, S.C., 1973-74; psychiat. cons. Commn. on Ministry Episcopal Diocese of Lexington, 1975—; psychiat. cons. Clin. Research Center Project, Ky. Bur. Health Services, Homestead Nursing Center, Lexington, Ky., 1978—; mem. adv. com. U. Ky. Grant on Rural Aging and Mental Health, 1978—; mem. profl. adv. bd. Mental Health Assn. Central Ky., 1979—. Mem. Ky. Gov.'s Task Force on Welfare Reform, 1978—; mem. Ky. Mental Health Task Force, 1977-79. Served to maj. MC AUS, 1968-74. Diplomate Am. Bd. Psychiatry and Neurology. Mem. Group for Advancement of Psychiatry, AAAS, Am. Psychiat. Assn., (pres. Ky. dist. br. 1979-80), Am. Acad. Psychiatry and the Law. Contbr. numerous articles to profl. jours. Home: 330 Chinoe Rd Lexington KY 40502 Office: U Ky Coll Medicine Room MN 362 Lexington KY 40536

WELCH, CHARLES ROOSEVELT, JR., ins. agt.; b. Norfolk, Va., July 28, 1944; s. Charles Roosevelt and Mary Dora (Twine) W.; student Old Dominion U., 1973-74; m. Mary Ida Braithwaite, Feb. 8, 1964; 1 dau., Dorretta Jane. Cloth cutter Atlantai Furniture Mfg., 1962-67; with U.S. Postal Services, 1966-67; dist. mgr. N.C. Mut. Life Ins. Co., Norfolk, Va., 1967—. Sec.-treas. Nat. Epileptic Found., 1977-78. Mem. Detroit Exec. Council of Life Ins. Mgrs. Office: 1050 E Brambleton Ave Norfolk VA 23518

WELCH, EMILY JANE, chemist; b. Augusta, Ga., July 15, 1938; d. Foster Hudson and Clara Belle (Nickles) Templeton; B.S. magna cum laude, N. Ga. Coll., 1960; M.S., Emory U., 1960; 2 sons, Jonathan David, James Montgomery. Research asst., Vanderbilt Hosp.,

Nashville, 1960-61; dir. clin. lab., Gracewood (Ga.) State Hosp., 1962; chemist, pesticide lab., Dept. Agr., Tallahassee, 1963-68, Columbia Nitrogen Corp., Augusta, Ga., 1968; research chemist, erythropoietin research, VA Hosp., Augusta, 1969-77; chemist, spl. chem. sect., Dwight David Eisenhower Army Med. Center, Ft. Gordon, Ga., 1977—. Sec., Blythe Elementary PTA, 1969-70, 72-73, pres., 1974-75; den mother, Cub Scouts, 1972-73; sec., HAJAL, 1970-75; tchr. intermediate and sr. ch. sch., Blythe Methodist Church, 1969—. Ty Cobb Scholar, 1956-59; NSF Fellow, 1959-60. Registered research chemist. Mem. Am. Chem. Soc., Ga. Acad. Scis., Sigma Nu, Phi Beta Kappa, Nu Gamma. Republican. Author, co-author articles on erythropoietin research. Home: PO Box 88 Blythe GA 30805 Office: Dept Pathology DDEAMC Fort Gordon GA 30905

WELCH, LOUIE, assn. exec.; b. Lockney, Tex., Dec. 9, 1918; s. Gilford E. and Nora (Shackelford) W.; B.A. magna cum laude, Abilene Christian U., 1940; m. Iola Faye Cure, Dec. 17, 1940; children—Guy Lynn, Gary Dale, Louie Gilford, Shannon Austin, Tina Joy, Mitchell. Pres. Louie Welch & Co., Inc., real estate and investment brokers; pres., chief exec. officer Houston C. of C., 1974—; mem. dist. export council U.S. Dept. Commerce. Pres. Tex. Municipal League, 1959-60, pres. U.S. Conf. Mayors, 1972-73. Councilman-at-large City of Houston, 1950-52, 56-62, mayor, 1964-74. Trustee Abilene Christian U., South Tex. Jr. Coll.; bd. dirs. Goodwill Industries, Am. Cancer Research Center and Hosp., Houston Symphony, Houston Grand Opera, Energy Research and Edn. Found., Named Key Houstonian, 1973, Distinguished Eagle Scout, 1974; recipient Kennedy Peace medal, 1971, Internat. B'nai B'rith Humanitarian award, 1973, Am. Med. Center Humanitarian award, 1975. Mem. C. of C. U.S. (govt. ops. and mgmt. com.). Home: 5013 Happy Hollow Houston TX 77018 Office: Houston C of C Houston TX 77002

WELCH, MARIE ELLA, ins. agy. exec.; b. Hanna, Ind., July 17, 1913; d. Reese Kester and Myrtle Ella Sutton; B.A., Baker U., 1935; children—Paul R. McDaniel, Ronald T. McDaniel. Lang. tchr., Abilene and Enterprise, Kans., 1945-46; pres. Okla. Gen. Agy., Oklahoma City, 1953—; dir. Ins. Agts. Sch., Mng. Gen. Agts. Assn. Orgn., Profl. Ins. Agts., 1977—. Mem. adv. bd. Nat. Fedn. Ind. Bus., 1979—; dir. fund raising Opportunities Industrialization, 1979—. C.P.C.U. Mem. Mng. Gen. Agts. Assn., PIA (Disting. Service award 1977), Nat. C. of C. Republican. Methodist. Home: 4900 Woodland Dr Oklahoma City OK 73105 Office: 809 NW 36th St Oklahoma City OK 73118

WELCH, MARY ALICE, bottling co. exec.; b. Marshall, Ark., Feb. 24, 1922; d. Christopher Frederick and Laurie Annie (Guthrie) Hattenhauer; student Okla. Sch. Bus., 1951-52, Sam Houston U., 1978; m. W.J. Bryson, July 17, 1941 (div. 1952); children—Ann Irene, Jacqueline; m. 2d, James W. Welch, Sept. 29, 1957; 1 dau., Karen Sue. Sec., Douglas Aircraft Co., 1943-45, Tide Water Oil Co., 1946-48, W.E. Brown, M.D., 1949-50; steno C.E., 1951-52, USAF, 1952-53; sec. Gulf Oil Co., 1954-56; sec. Petroleum Engring. Co., Tulsa, 1957-59; with Beverage Products Corp., Tulsa, 1959—, asst. corp. sec., 1960—, editor, 1967—. Mem. adv. com. Tulsa Jr. Coll., Daniel Webster High Sch. Served with AUS, 1945-46. Mem. Nat. Secs. Assn., Inst. Cert. Secs. Democrat. Home: 508 E 117th St S Jenks America OK 74037 Office: PO Box 7427 Tulsa OK 74105

WELCH, NANCY MAE, physician; b. Daytona Beach, Fla., June 21, 1946; B.S., Lynchburg Coll., 1968; M.D., Duke U., 1972; M.S., U. Colo., 1979. Intern, U. Colo., 1972-73, resident, 1973-75, mem. clin. faculty Med. Center, 1975; instr. pediatrics Montifiore Med. Center, N.Y.C., 1975-76; asst. clin. prof. pediatrics U. Va., Charlottesville, 1978; health dir. Alleghany Health Dist., Salem, Va., 1976—; med. dir. Coordinated Health and Med. Program, Daleville, Va., 1978—. Mem. Am. Acad. Pediatrics, Am. Assn. Comprehensive Health Planners, Am. Inst. Planners, Am. Assn. Public Health, Va. Med. Soc., Va. Acad. Pediatrics, Va. Public Health Assn., S.W. Va. Pediatric Soc., Roanoke Acad. Medicine (mem. sch. health adv. com.), Roanoke Acad. Medicine Found. Home: 1046 Finney Dr Vinton VA 24179 Office: PO Box 1074 Salem VA 24153

WELCH, NATHANIEL, trade assn. exec.; b. Selma, Ala., Mar. 23, 1920; s. William Pressley and Lucille (Burt) W.; A.B. cum laude, Furman U., 1952; postgrad. U. N.C., 1942, U. Ala., 1946; m. Gloria Constance Ljunglof, Sept. 11, 1948; children—Gustaf Lindstrom, Shannon Constance, Melanie Rebecca. Advt. rep. So. Farm & Home Mag., Montgomery, Ala., 1947-52; account exec. WABT, Birmingham, Ala., 1952-53; v.p. sales Orradio Industries, Opelika, Ala., 1953-58; mgr. mktg. Orr div. Ampex Corp., Opelika, 1958-60; exec. v.p. Electronics for Edn., Kensington, Md., 1961-63; fed. rep. So. Interstate Nuclear Bd., Atlanta, 1963-68; exec. dir. Community Relations Commn., Atlanta, 1968-74; exec. v.p. Ga. Freight Bur., Atlanta, 1974—. Mem. gov. com. Investigation Voter Registration for Vets., State of Ala., 1950; mem. Nat. Citizens Com. for Community Relations, 1964-68; bd. dirs. Ala. Council Human Relations, 1959-66, pres., 1965-66; mem. charter commn. Democratic Party Ga., 1974-75; chmn. Urban Action Inc., N. Ga. conf. United Methodist Ch., 1975-79; mem. alumni bd. dirs. Furman U., 1967-72; vice-chmn. Ga. State Humanics Bd., 1979—; exec. com. Nat. Small Shipments Traffic Conf., 1975-78. Mem. U.S. Ry. Assn. (dir.), So. Traffic League, Nat. Indsl. Traffic League, Transp. Club Atlanta (Man of Year 1979, exec. com. 1980). Clubs: Rotary, Commerce. Home: 2122 Castleway Dr Atlanta GA 30345 Office: 57 Forsyth St Atlanta GA 30303

WELCH, PAUL CLAUDE, business exec.; b. Horton, Kans., Sept. 24, 1900; s. Frank and Grace (Walker) W.; m. Lucile Irene Sherman, May 1, 1920 (dec.); children—Robert Paul, Byron Eugene, William Frank. Asst. to pres. Bankers Mortgage Co., Kansas City, Mo., 1926-28; C.P.A., Mo Pac Lines, Kansas City, Mo., 1928-44; sales mgr. William B. Ward Co., Kansas City, 1944-45; dist. traffic mgr. Mid-Continent Airlines Co., Houston, 1946-48; gen. traffic mgr. Trans-Tex. Airways, Houston, 1949-51; dist. salesman Ada Oil Co., Houston, 1951-54; partner Tex. Gulf Coast Distributors, Houston, 1949-69; pres. Tex. Sales Reps. Co., Houston, 1954-69; exec. v.p., treas. Welch Assos., Inc., Houston, 1965—. Mem. Am. Soc. Safety Engrs., Nat. Soc. Fund Raising Execs., Houston Soc. Fund Raising Execs. Republican. Home: 4215 Tennyson St Houston TX 77005 Office: 3701 Kirby Center Suite 1010 Houston TX 77098

WELCH, RIZPAH L., educator; b. Wilmington, N.C., Sept. 13, 1920; d. H.M. and A. Louise (Sampson) Jones; married W. Bruce Welch; B.S. in Elementary Edn., Elizabeth City (N.C.) State Coll., 1944; M.S. in Elementary Edn. and Remedial Reading, Ind. U., Bloomington, 1952, Ed.D. in Elementary Edn. and Spl. Edn., 1966. Tchr. elementary grades Richmond (Va.) Pub. Schs., 1956-60, spl. edn. tchr., 1960-66, spl. edn. cons., 1966-67; asso. prof. edn. Va. Commonwealth U., Richmond, 1967-75, prof. edn., 1975—, chmn. dept. spl. edn., 1970-79, dir. Ednl. Devel. Centers Complex, 1979—; cons. early childhood edn. programs, P.R., 1968. Chmn., Commonwealth of Va. Developmental Disabilities Planning and Adv. Council, 75-77; mem. (Va.) Gov.'s Com. on Edn. of Handicapped, 1976-77; adv. bd. New Community Sch., Richmond, 1975—; mem. vestry St. Philip's Episc. Ch., Richmond, 1978—; 1st v.p., sec. Friend's Assn. for Children, 1969-75. Mem. AAUP, Council for Exceptional Children, Am. Assn. on Mental Deficiency, Va. Edn. Assn., Orton Soc., AAUW, Internat. Reading Assn., Nat. Council Tchrs. of English, Richmond Assn. for Retarded Citizens. Developed a model for tng. spl. edn. resource tchrs. Certified in reading, mental retardation, elementary edn., Va.; specialist in lang. devel., reading and lang. disabilities. Contbr. articles in field to profl. jours. Home: 1728 Forest Glen Rd Richmond VA 23228 Office: 2095 Oliver Hall Va Commonwealth U Richmond VA 23284

WELCH, ROBERT LAWRENCE, fire flow engr.; b. Newport, R.I., Sept. 23, 1940; s. Robert Allison and Mary Belle (Swanger) W.; B.S. in Chem. Engring., U. Pitts., 1963; m. Reina Kanarek, Sept. 20, 1974. With Goodyear Tire & Rubber Co., Akron, Ohio, 1963-66; head pliofoam tech. service Goodyear Tire & Rubber Co., Ltd., Owen Sound, Ont., Can., 1966-69; pollution control engr. Met. Dade County (Fla.), 1973-76, fire flow engr., fire engring. and water supply services, 1976—. Mem. Am. Inst. Chem. Engrs., Nat. Soc. Profl. Engrs., Am. Soc. Heating, Refrigeration and Air Conditioning Engrs., Am. Astronautical Soc., Fla. Engring. Soc. Home: 5810 SW 89th Ave Miami FL 33173 Office: 909 SE 1st Ave Miami FL 33131

WELCH, TIMOTHY WHITNEY, mental health agy. adminstr.; b. Cowley, Wyo., July 10, 1942; s. Arthur Marchant and Mary (Whitney) W.; B.S., Utah State U., 1966; M.S.W. (VA trainee), Ariz. State U., 1968; cert. in Health Care Adminstrn., UCLA, 1975; m. Phyllis Bingham, Aug. 14, 1964; children—Natalie, Michelle, Kristi. Social worker Camelback Mental Health Center, Scottsdale, Ariz., 1968-69; chief psychiat. social worker Scottsdale Psychiat. Center, 1969-72; dir. social services, dir. young adult program Camelback Hosp., Phoenix, 1972-77; clin. adminstr. Dillon Family and Youth Services, Tulsa, 1977—; guest faculty Ariz. State U., Phoenix Coll., Mesa Community Coll., Scottsdale Coll., Oral Roberts U. Elder Ch. of Jesus Christ of Latter-day Saints; bd. dirs., exec. com. Big Sisters of Ariz., 1970-71; bd. dirs. Community Orgn. Drug Abuse Control, Phoenix, 1971-72; pres. Durfee Found., Scottsdale, 1970-72. NIMH grantee, 1967-68. Fellow Am. Orthopsychiat. Assn.; mem. Nat. Assn. Social Workers, Acad. Cert. Social Workers, Am. Group Psychotherapy Assn., Am. Assn. Marriage and Family Therapists (pres. Okla. div.), Am. Coll. Hosp. Adminstrs., Am. Assn. Sex Educators, Counselors and Therapists (cert. sex therapist). Republican. Home: 6728 E 26th Pl Tulsa OK 74129 Office: 2525 E 21st St Tulsa OK 74114

WELCH, WILLIAM EDWARD, elec. switch gear co. exec.; b. Clarksburg, W.Va., June 29, 1939; s. Edward Melvin and Opal A. (Dodd) W.; A.B. in Chemistry, U. N.C., 1961; m. Norma Jean Welch; children—Cynthia Leigh, Cheryl Lynn, David William. Plant mgr. Union Carbide Corp., Clarksburg, W.Va., 1976-79, Gould-Brown Boveri, Florence, S.C., 1979—; pres. Robwel Assos., Inc., Florence; dir. Harrison County (W.Va.) Indsl. Devel. Authority. Bd. dirs. United Way, Salvation Army, ARC. Mem. Assn. Indsl. Devel. (dir.). Club: Rotary Internat. Home: 2507 W Keswick Rd Florence SC 29501 Office: PO Box F-7 Florence SC 29501

WELCH, WILLIAM MAUK, dermatologist; b. Somerset, Pa., June 21, 1933; s. Joel Jacobs and Helen (Mauk) W.; B.S., U. Pitts., 1955, M.D., 1959; m. Susan Elaine Reefman, July 17, 1960; children—Joan Elaine, Mark Jacob, Edward Bryan, Rachel Jane. Intern, Santa Barbara (Calif.) Cottage Hosp., 1959-60, gen. practice resident, 1960-61; resident in dermatology U. Wis., Madison, 1961-64; practice medicine specializing in dermatology, Corpus Christi, Tex., 1964—. Pres., Am. Cancer Soc., Nueces County, 1970-71. Served with U.S. Army, 1966-68. Mem. Nueces County Med. Soc., Tex. Med. Soc., AMA, Tex. Dermatol. Soc., Am. Acad. Dermatology, Internat. Soc. Dermatology. Methodist. Home: 226 Cape Aron Corpus Christi TX 78412 Office: 1415 Third St Suite 206 Corpus Christi TX 78404

WELCH, WILLIAM TERRY, III, telephone co. exec.; b. Los Angeles, Sept. 23, 1944; s. William Terry and Mary Olive (Hughes) W.; student in elec. engring. Ohio State U., 1962-66; m. Doris Helen Jones, May 31, 1975; children—Andrew Terry, Joanna Elizabeth. Design draftsman Exact Weight Scale Co., Columbus, Ohio, 1966-70; elec. engr. N. Electric Co., Galion, Ohio, 1970-72; service bur. supr. United Intermountain Telephone Co., Bristol, Tenn., 1972—. Served with U.S. Army, 1966-68. Mem. Am. Radio Relay League (life), Nat. Speleol. Soc., Holston Valley Grotto Cavers. Lutheran. Club: Piney Flats Kiwanis. Inventor custom electronic telephone test equipment. Home: 320 Dogwood Trail Piney Flats TN 37686 Office: 2 Spruce St Bristol TN 37620

WELCOME, VERGIE MAE ISAAC, business exec.; b. Alexandria, La., Jan. 25, 1948; d. L.D. and Viola (Tezeno) Davis; student Houston Community Coll., 1976-78, U. Houston, 1979; children—Tammy Marie Welcome, Samuel Lewis Welcome, Shatara Lynn Welcome. Lab. technician Hermann Hosp., Houston, 1968-70; glassware insp. Anchor Hocking Glass Corp., Houston, 1970-72; office asst. James G. Brown & Assos., cons. engring., Houston, 1972-75; computer operator, supr., office mgr. Jefferson Assos., Inc., Houston, 1975-76, personnel dir., 1976—. Vol. various polit. campaigns, 1978—. Mem. Clear Lake Personnel Assn., Kashmere Gardens Community Civic Club. Baptist. Club: Order of Eastern Star. Home: 4520 Majestic St Houston TX 77026 Office: 1840 NASA Rd One Suite 200 Houston TX 77058

WELDON, JOHN JOSEPH, coll. adminstr.; b. Owensboro, Ky., Aug. 15, 1921; s. Reuben Landis and Mary Ruth (Wright) W.; student St. Meinrad Coll., 1940-42; B.A. in Econs., U. Dayton, 1947; M.A. in Edn., Western Ky. U., 1968; Ph.D. (NDEA fellow), So. Ill. U., Carbondale, 1970; m. Catherine Louise Dudley, Nov. 22, 1948; children—John Joseph, Mary Loretta, Richard Dudley, Clifford Landis, James Stephen, Michael Timothy, Robert Matthew, Paul Anthony, Daniel Geoffrey, William Lawrence. Office equipment salesman with various cos., Ky. Ind. area, 1947-64; elem. tchr. Catholic Diocese of Owensboro (Ky.), 1964-66; tchr. Latin and social studies Hopkinsville (Ky.) Public High Sch., 1966-68; asst. prof. secondary edn. So. Ill. U., 1970-71; asst. prof. edn., chmn. dept. edn. Mt. Mercy Coll., 1971-73; asso. prof. edn. and social sci. Biscayne Coll., 1973-77, prof., 1977—, acad. dean, 1973—; cons. to state depts. edn. Adult leader Audubon council Boy Scouts Am. Served with USN, 1943-46. Mem. Am. Assn. Acad. Deans, Assn. Supervision and Curriculum Devel., Classical League, Phi Delta Kappa, Kappa Delta Pi. Democrat. Roman Catholic. Office: 16400 NW 32d Ave Miami FL 33054

WELDON, WILSON OSBOURNE, editor, clergyman; b. Camden, S.C., Mar. 15, 1911; s. John Wesley and Leila (Wilson) W.; B.A., U. S.C., 1931; B.D., Duke, 1934; D.D., High Point Coll., 1952; m. Margaret Hammond Lyles, July 19, 1939; children—Nanci Leila (dec.), Wilson Osbourne, Alice Adelaide. Ordained to ministry Meth. Ch., 1938; pastor Meth. chs., China Grove, N.C., 1938-42, High Point, N.C., 1942-48, Meml. Meth. Ch., Thomasville, N.C., 1948-52, 1st Meth. Ch. Gastonia, N.C., 1952-58, Myers Park Meth. Ch., Charlotte, N.C., 1958-63, West Market St. Meth. Ch., Greensboro, N.C., 1963-67; editor Upper Room, Nashville, 1967-75, dist. supt., Charlotte, 1975—. Del., Meth. Ecumenical Conf., Oxford, Eng., 1951, World Meth. Conf., London, Eng., 1966, Denver, 1971, Gen. Conf. Meth. Ch., 1956, 60, 64, 68, 70, 72, Meth. S.E. Jurisdictional Conf., 1952, 56, 60, 64, 68, 72; mem. Gen. Bd. Evangelism, 1960-67; mem. Am. exec. com. World Meth. Council, 1967—. Trustee Greensboro Coll., Duke U. Mem. Lake Junaluska Assos. (pres. 1968-72). Mason (32 deg., K.T., Shriner), Rotarian. Author: Thrill of Christian Living, 1966; Discoveries in the Lord's Prayer, 1968; A Plain Man Faces Trouble, 1971; Mark the Road, 1973. Editor: When Fires Burn. Compiler: Breakthru; Words To Live By, 1978. Home: 2318 Richardson Dr Charlotte NC 28218 Office: Box 18005 Charlotte NC 28218

WELLER, CYNTHIA PATTY, dietary cons.; b. Beaumont, Tex., Aug. 11, 1920; d. William Byrn and Sadie Alma (Malone) Patty; B.S. in Foods and Nutrition, Tex. Womans U., 1941; m. John Walker Weller, Mar. 14, 1945; children—Patty Weller Cwalinski, John W., Margaret M. Intern, Vanderbilt U. Hosp., 1941-42; asst. dietitian Miss. State Sanatorium, 1942-43; dietitian, dir. food service Orange (Tex.) City Hosp., 1943-45; clin. dietitian St. Mary's Hosp., Fort Arthur, Tex., 1963-65; Hotel Dieu Hosp., Beaumont, Tex., 1966-71; pvt. practice dietary consulting, Beaumont, Tex., 1966—; cons. dietitian health care facilities. Mem. Am. Dietetic Assn., Am. Hosp. Assn., Am. Soc. Hosp. Food Service Adminstrs., South Tex. Dietetic Assn., Tex. Dietetic Assn., Tex. Public Health Assn., Nutrition Today Soc. Methodist. Home and Office: 1107 Threadneedle St Beaumont TX 77705

WELLER, LLOYD DAVID, watch mfg. co. exec.; b. Phila., Apr., 25, 1920; s. John Jacob and Mary Gertrude (Snyner) W.; student Pa. State U., 1947-49, Northwestern U., 1946-47, Hamilton Watch Sch. Horology, 1937-39; m. Florence Wolpert Spicer, May 14, 1941; 1 son, Lloyd David, Jr. Exec., devel. engr., sales engr. Hamilton Watch Co., Lancaster, Pa., 1951-57; exec. div. 45 public relations and service, Montgomery Ward Co., Chgo., 1946-48; v.p., gen. mgr. mfg. and internat. Gen. Time Corp., Stanford, Conn.; now regional mgr. public relations and service Bulova Watch Co. Adminstr., ARC, Virgin Islands, Boy Scouts Am., Virgin Islands. Served with USNR, 1941-46. Mem. Am. Mgmt. Assn., Tex. Watchmakers and Jewelers, Am. Legion, VFW. Episcopalian. Club: Masons. Home: 5787 Caruth Haven Dallas TX 75206 Office: Suite 133 11181 Harry Hines Dallas TX 75229

WELLINGTON, JAMES ELLIS, educator; b. Arlington, Mass., July 9, 1921; s. William Edward and Jessie (Dennett) W.; A.B., Dartmouth Coll., 1948; M.A., Boston U., 1950; Ph.D., Fla. State U., 1956; m. Mary Canfield Grier, July 22, 1952; children—Georgia Grier (Mrs. Randall N. Smith), Anne Ross. Instr. dept. English, U. Nebr., 1950-53; teaching asst., instr. English, Fla. State U., 1953-56; instr., asst. prof. English, U. Miami, Coral Gables, Fla., 1956-63, asso. prof., 1963-70, prof., 1970—. Lang. cons., 1958—. Served with USNR, 1941-46. Mem. Modern Lang. Assn., AAUP, South Atlantic Modern Lang. Assn., Southeastern Renaissance Conf., Augustan Reprint Soc., Delta Upsilon. Democrat. Anglo-Catholic. Author: Alexander Pope's Epistles to Several Persons, 1963; Pope's Eloisa to Abelard, with the Hughes Letters, 1965. Home: 1200 Mariposa Ave Apt D-104 Coral Gables FL 33146 Office: Dept English U Miami Coral Gables FL 33124

WELLS, ALLAN JOEL, mfg. co. exec.; b. Kennett, Mo., Aug. 15, 1939; s. Orville David and Kitty Wayne (Muse) W.; student O'Fallon Jr. Coll., 1969; m. Carolyn Sue Williams, Jan. 9, 1958; children—Teresa Lynn, David Allan. With McDonnell Douglas, St. Louis, 1957-58, 60-69, Sperry Vickers, Tulsa, 1970-74; materials mgr. Braden Winch Co., Broken Arrow, Okla., 1974—. Multimedia first aid instr. ARC, Tulsa, 1978—. Served with USAF, 1958-60. Mem. Soc. Mfg. Engrs. Mem. Assemblies of God. Office: 800 E Dallas St Broken Arrow OK 74012

WELLS, CARL EDWARD, sales exec.; b. LaFollette, Tenn., May 14, 1953; s. James Winford and Stacy H. (Green) W.; student public schs., LaFollette. Co-owner Wells Prodns., LaFollette, 1973-75; co-owner Wimpy's Lunch, LaFollette, 1971-79; sales rep. Gattuso Foods Co., Clinton, Tenn., 1979-80; with Rose's Store, LaFollette, 1980—. Mem. LaFollette Jr. C. of C. Democrat. Baptist. Home: 701 E Beech St LaFollette TN 37766

WELLS, CARL PIERSON, JR., clergyman; b. Johnson Station, Miss., June 17, 1934; s. Carl Pierson and Mattie (Kennedy) W.; B.S., Miss. Coll., 1956; M.R.E., So. Baptist Theol. Sem., 1960; m. Eleanor Walden, June 10, 1956; children—Carla Lyn, Steve. Ordained to ministry Bapt. Ch., 1970; minister edn. Campbellsville (Ky.) Bapt. Ch., 1960-63, First Bapt. Ch., Tuscaloosa, Ala., 1963—; cons. Sunday sch. dept. Ala. Bapt. Conv. Pres. bd. dirs. W. Ala. Rehab. Center, 1979—. Served with AUS, 1956-57. Mem. So. Bapy. Religious Edn. Assn., Ala. Religious Edn. Assn. Baptist. Clubs: Kiwanis, Masons.

WELLS, CECIL MONROE, chemist; b. Madison, Wis., Feb. 22, 1934; s. Cecil Gale and Ethel Florence (Cook) W.; B.S., U. New Orleans, 1966, M.S., 1970; m. Karen Marie Cucullu, Jan. 21, 1961; children—Michael Scott, John Patrick. Chef, Hoffman House, Madison, Wis., 1950-54; chemist U. New Orleans, 1962—, sci. materials mgr., 1974—; cons. USDA Research Lab., New Orleans, 1974. Bd. dirs. Brother Martin Parents Club, 1976-78. Recipient St. Louis medallion, 1977. Mem. U. New Orleans Alumni Assn. (rep. at large 1975-76), Nat. Assn. Sci. Materials Mgrs. (organizer, 1975, pres. 1977, treas. 1979). Democrat. Roman Catholic. Home: 2526 Barracks St New Orleans LA 70119 Office: Dept Chemistry U New Orleans LA 70122

WELLS, CLIFTON TURNER, publisher, editor; b. Little Rock, Dec. 16, 1928; s. John Fenton and Arra Graves (Turner) W.; A.A., Tex. Mil. Coll., 1949; B.A., U. Ark., 1954; m. Betty Baughman, June 15, 1951; children—Leslie Jane, John Baughman, Meribeth Glenn. News writer-broadcaster Sta. KXLR, N. Little Rock, Ark., 1944-46; reporter Ft. Smith (Ark.) Times Record, 1951; reporter AP, Little Rock, 1954-59, Chattanooga, 1959-61, Nashville, 1961-62; pub. Daily Record, Little Rock, 1962-63; mem. staff Ark. Legis. Digest, Little Rock, 1962—; pres. Headlight Newspapers Inc., Morrilton, Ark., 1967—, pub., editor Conway County Petit Jean Country Headlight, Perry County Petit Jean Country Headlight, 1964—; editor Morrillton Dem. and Perry County News, 1964; v.p. Gen. Pub. Co. Inc., Little Rock; mem. printing advisory com. Petit Jean Vocat.-Tech. Sch., 1970—. Served with U.S. Army, 1951-54. Decorated Bronze Star. Mem. Ark. Press Assn. (Sweepstakes award 1967, Agr. Promotion award 1971, Editorial Writing award 1971, Indsl. Promotion award 1973, 75), Morrilton C. of C., Nat. Newspaper Assn., W. Highland White Terrier Club Am., Trinity Valley W. Highland White Terrier Club, Sigma Delta Chi, Phi Theta Kappa, Kappa Alpha. Democrat. Presbyterian. Clubs: Morrilton Country; Pleasant Valley Country (Little Rock); Midnighters Dance. Home: 15 Pilot Point Little Rock AR 72205 Office: 908 W Broadway CPO Box 5407 Morrilton AR 72110

WELLS, DAMON, JR., investment co. exec.; b. Houston, May 20, 1937; s. Damon and Margaret Corinne (Howze) W.; B.A. magna cum laude, Yale U., 1958; B.A., Oxford U., 1964, M.A., 1968; Ph.D., Rice U., 1968. Owner, chief exec. officer Damon Wells Interests, Houston, 1958—. Mem. sr. common room Pembroke Coll., Oxford U., 1972—. Bd. dirs. Child Guidance Center of Houston, 1970-73; trustee Christ Ch. Cathedral Endowment Fund, 1970-73, Kinkaid Prep. Sch.,

Houston, 1972—, Jefferson Davis Assn., 1973—, Episcopal Diocese of Tex. Retreat at Camp Allen (Tex.), 1976-79. Recipient prize for biography Tex. Writers Roundup, 1971. Mem. English-Speaking Union (nat. dir. 1970-72, v.p. Houston br. 1966-72), Brit. Inst. U.S. (founding dir. 1978—), Phi Beta Kappa, Pi Sigma Alpha. Episcopalian. Clubs: Coronado, Houston Country, Houston; Yale (N.Y.C.). Author: Stephen Douglas: The Last Years, 1857-1861, 1971. Home: 1861 Post Oak Park Dr Houston TX 77027 Office: River Oaks Bank Bldg 2001 Kirby Dr Houston TX 77019

WELLS, DONALD THOMAS, electronics mfg. co. exec.; b. Henderson, Ky., Dec. 26, 1931; s. Melvin Jackson and Laura Bell Wells; B.S. in Fin. and Mktg., U. Ky., 1957; postgrad. Ind. U., 1957-59; m. Josephine Gibbs, June 12, 1954; children—Renetta G., Kathy L. Asst. sec. treas. Von Hoffmann Press, Inc., St. Louis, 1963-68; gen. mgr., treas. Amelco Leasing Corp., St. Louis, 1968-71; group controller Interlake Steel Co., Dallas, 1971-73; corp. controller, asst. sec. treas. Multi-Amp Corp., Dallas, 1973—; chmn. bd., treas. Prairie Creek Bottery Inc.; lectr., fin. cons. Deacon, office of adv. council, chmn. budget com., chmn. fin. com. Baptist Ch. Served with U.S. Army, 1951-53. Mem. Nat. Assn. Accountants, Am. Mgmt. Assn., C. of C. Clubs: Kiwanis, Masons. Office: Multi-Amp Corp 4271 Bronze Way Dallas TX 75237

WELLS, ELIZABETH MCCALLISTER, programmer-analyst; b. Chilhowie, Va., June 10, 1923; d. Thomas Albert and Texie Josephine (Love) McC.; student Johnson City Bus. Coll., 1941-42; m. Jack Hilton Wells, Sept. 23, 1943. With ET & WNC Transp. Co., Johnson City, 1942-78, supr. programming, 1971-72, supr. systems and programming, 1972-78; programmer-analyst ITT North Electric Co., 1978—. Mem. Data Processing Mgmt. Assn. (pres. 1977). Methodist. Club: Monday. Home: 810 Forest Ave Johnson City TN 37601 Office: PO Box NCRS Johnson City TN 37601

WELLS, KENNETH DALE, economist; b. Akron, Ohio, June 23, 1908; s. Alfred Richard and Lonia Idella (Dales) W.; student U. Akron, 1928-30; B.S., Northwestern U., 1936; postgrad. U. So. Calif., Calif. Inst. Tech.; hon. degrees: L.H.D., Temple U., 1953; LL.B., LL.D., Fla. So. Coll., 1953; LL.D., Trinity Coll., 1955, Tex. Christian U., 1959; L.H.D., Salem Coll., 1962; D.B.A., Lincoln Meml. Coll., 1968; Dr. Public Service, Brigham Young U., 1969; m. Ruth Elizabeth Van Allen, Apr. 19, 1930; children—Kenneth D., Richard J. With Wells and Bliss Inc., Akron, Ohio, 1930-38; asst. to pres. Union Oil Co. Calif., Los Angeles, 1939-47; instr. economics dept. mgmt. U. So. Calif., 1947-48; dir. ops. Joint Economic Com. of Advt. Industry on Economic Edn., 1948-49; chmn. bd. trustees Family Found. of Am., Williamsburg, Va., 1977—; pres. Freedom Fraternity, Williamsburg, 1976—; co-founder, pres. emeritus, sr. vice-chmn. Freedoms Found. at Valley Forge, Pa., 1970—, pres., 1949-70. Served to 2d lt. USAR, 1930-46. Recipient numerous citations, awards and recognitions including: Nat. Assn. of Foremen award, 1949; Honor citation Mil. Order of Purple Heart, 1951; Gold medal of merit VFW, 1953; Good Citizenship medal Nat. Soc. SAR, 1956; Silver Antelope award Boy Scouts Am., 1962; Nat. Sojourners Presdl. award, 1966; Congressional Medal of Honor Soc. award, 1966; Humanitarian award Lions Internat., 1970; award of excellence Center of Am. Living, 1970; Establishment of Dr. Kenneth Dale Wells Freedom Archives, Brigham Young U., 1978. Mem. All Am. Indian Days (adv. bd. nat. chmn.), Invest-In-Am. (nat. adv. bd.), Inst. Polit. Studies (Liechtenstein), Newcomen Soc. N.Am., Nat. Assn. Bus. Economists. Clubs: The Penn, Masons (33 deg.), N.Y. Advt., Union League Phila., Capitol Hill (Washington). Mormon. Author: Economic Theory, 1959; Awake Thruout the Land, 1968; Principles of Economics (series), 1974; Mom-Family Fundamentals-Manners and Morals and Family Morale, 1975. Home: 1525 S Riverside Dr Edgewater FL 32032 Office: 402 Duke Gloucester St Williamsburg VA 23185

WELLS, LOUIS LANE, educator; b. Atlanta, Apr. 18, 1936; s. Emmett Lee and Hazel (Lane) W.; A.B., Georgetown Coll., 1959; M.A., Ind. U., 1960; m. Martha Ann Campbell, Aug. 9, 1960; children—Bryan Campbell, Leesa Lane. Asst. prof., mgr. radio sta. Georgetown (Ky.) Coll., 1962-66; instr., TV producer-dir. dept. radio-TV St. Petersburg (Fla.) Jr. Coll., 1966-69; dir. ops. Protestant Radio-TV Center, Atlanta, 1969-73; instr. dept. drama-speech DeKalb Community Coll., Clarkston, Ga., 1973—, Cons. asso. degree program in radio-TV prodn., 1978—; cons. mktg. and audio-visual aids. Den leader Webelo Cub Scouts, Boy Scouts Am., Atlanta, 1970-72. Recipient award for outstanding work in radio prodn. Ind. U., 1960. Mem. Nat. Assn. Ednl. Broadcasters, Pi Kappa Delta, Iota Beta Sigma. Democrat. Baptist. Author handbook for Ednl. FM Broadcast Sta., Georgetown Coll., 1962; contbr. research article to profl. jour. Home: 3151 Randolph Rd NE Atlanta GA 30345 Office: Dept Drama-Speech DeKalb Coll N Indian Creek Dr Clarkston GA 30021

WELLS, MARIUS HUGHEY, surgeon; b. Winnsboro, S.C., May 16, 1925; s. Lionelle Dudley and Mary Hunter (Hughey) W.; B.S., U. S.C., 1948; M.D., Med. U. S.C., 1952; m. Ruth Brice McCracken, Nov. 14, 1953; children—Katherine Ruth, Jane McCracken, Susan Brice, Marian Hughey, Marius Hughey. Intern surgery Strong Meml. Hosp., Rochester, N.Y., 1952; resident surgery Med. Center Hosp., Charleston, S.C., 1955-59; practice medicine, specializing in gen. surgery, Asheville, N.C., 1959-60, Brevard, N.C., 1960—; dir. Newland Clinic PA; coroner, med. examiner Transylvania County, N.C. Chmn., Western N.C. Emergency Med. Services Council, 1974-76, chmn. task force HSAI Emergency Med. Services, 1975; mem. Transylvania County Bd. Edn., 1976—; bd. dirs. N.C. div. Am. Cancer Soc., 1975-79; bd. dirs. N.C. affiliate Am. Diabetic Assn., 1975—, pres., 1978-79, past pres., 1979-80; past Democratic precinct chmn.; Transylvania County rep. Region B-EMS, 1974—. Served with AUS, 1944-46. USPHS grantee, 1954-55; Am. Cancer Soc. fellow (S.C.), 1956-57. Mem. A.C.S., Am. Soc. Abdominal Surgeons, Am. Trauma Soc., Am. Geriatric Soc., N.C., Western N.C. assns. rescue squads, Brevard Rescue Squad, AMA, N.C. Med. Soc. Clubs: Masons, K.T., Shriners, Rotary. Office: Newland Clinic PA Brevard NC 28712

WELLS, MICHAEL EUGENE, psychologist; b. Greensboro, N.C., Dec. 29, 1953; s. Aubrey Eugene and Betty Lou (Connell) W.; A.B. with honors, U. N.C., Chapel Hill, 1976; M.A. with honors, Western Mich. U., 1978. Program facilitator nonambulatory unit Murdoch Center, Butner, N.C., 1975; aide Orange County Devel. Center, Chapel Hill, 1975-76; cottage counselor C. A. Dillon Sch., Butner, N.C., 1976; resident coordinator Family and Children's Services, Kalamazoo, Mich., 1977; coordinator, grader Seminar in Mental Retardation, Western Mich. U., Kalamazoo, 1977-78; psychologist Murdoch Center, Butner, N.C., 1978—; vol. Oxford Orphanage, John Umstaed Psychiat. Hosp., Assn. Retarded Citizens.; trustee Orange County Mental Health Assn., 1974-76; scoutmaster Boy Scouts Am., Kalamazoo, Mich., 1977-79, cubmaster, Butner, 1980. Mem. Assn. Behavior Analysis, Am. Assn. Mental Deficiency, Assn. Advancement Behavior Therapy, N.C. Assn. Mental Deficiency (chmn. govtl. affairs com.). Home: 401 Sunset Ave Oxford NC 27565 Office: Psychology Services Murdoch Center Butner NC 27509

WELLS, MICHAEL TAYLOR, ednl. adminstr.; b. Mobile, Ala., Nov. 21, 1945; s. William Franklin and Ena Lurline (McIlwaine) W.; B.S., U. So. Miss., 1967; M.Ed., Southeastern La. U., 1973; postgrad. Loyola U., New Orleans, 1975-77; m. Linda Gay Williams, May 2, 1965; children—Sharla Gay, Michael Taylor. Tchr. English, Clara (Miss.) High Sch., 1967, Hahnville (La.) High Sch., 1967-75; adminstrv. intern Mimosa Park Elem. Sch., St. Charles Parish Pub. Schs., Luling, La., 1975; dir. div. human resources St. Charles Parish Pub. Schs., Luling, 1975—. Tchrs. lic., La. Mem. Am. Assn. Sch. Personnel Adminstrs., La. Sch. Personnel Adminstrs. Assn., La. Assn. Sch. Execs. (charter). Democrat. Methodist. Home: PO Box 144 Luling LA 70070 Office: PO Box 46 Luling LA 70070

WELLS, PAUL DENWENY, direct mktg. co. exec.; b. Chgo., Nov. 8, 1926; s. Harry L. and Ella H. Wells; student Northwestern U., 1946-47, Loyola U., Chgo., 1947-48; m. Jeanne Carey, Mar. 31, 1951; children—Cynthia, Paul, James P. Direct mail head copywriter Allstate Ins. Co., Skokie, Ill., 1953-56; sales promotion mgr. Popular Mechanics mag., Chgo., 1956-59; v.p. Key Products Inc., Lake Alfred, Fla., 1960-69; pres. Commerce Kings, Lakeland, Fla., 1969—; dir. corps. Mem. Republican Exec. Com. Polk County. Mem. Direct Mail Advt. Assn., Direct Mail Writers Assn., Polk Advt. Assn. (past pres.). Roman Catholic. Club: K.C. (past grand knight, fast faithful navigator). Editor children's activities mag., 1951-53. Home: Route 1 Box 660 Auburndale FL 33823 Office: Commerce Kings PO Box 1300 Lakeland FL 33802

WELLS, ROBERT HARTLEY, mfg. co. exec.; b. Springfield, Mass., Mar. 23, 1926; s. Cecil and Anna (Coates) W.; student Va. Poly. Inst., 1944-45; B.S., U. Maine, 1948, M.S., 1950; m. Alice G. Asplund, June 2, 1970; children—Michael, Brian Donald. Cellulose research chemist Celanese Co., 1952-54, S.D. Warren Co., 1954-58; research chemist epoxy resin research and engring. CIBA Co., Toms River, N.J., 1959-66; sect. head Borden Chem. Co., Bainbridge, N.Y., 1966-70; sr. research engr. polypropylene resins Amoco Chem. Co., Naperville, Ill., 1970-73; product mgr. Wilmington Chem. Co. (Del.), 1973-76; product mgr. for product devel. tech. services and sales AZ Products Co., Lakeland, Fla., 1976—; cons. epoxy formulations and applications, 1974—. Mem. Toms River Sch. Bd., 1962-66; bd. dirs. Garden State Symphony, Toms River, 1963-66; pres. Toms River Jaycees, 1962. Served in U.S. Army, 1944-46. Mem. Am. Chem. Soc., Photog. Soc. Am., Polk County Museum, Sigma Xi, Kappa Phi Kappa. Republican. Methodist. Clubs: Del. Camera, Stills and Reels Camera. Research on epoxy resin systems; patentee in field; exhibited photos in 3 one-man shows, 1978-79. Home: 3424 Royal Ct Lakeland FL 33803 Office: 2525 S Combee Rd Lakeland FL 33801

WELLS, THOMAS ARTHUR, musician, clergyman; b. Gowanda, N.Y., Jan. 6, 1947; s. Herbert William and Elsie Lorraine (Wallin) W.; B.S., Baylor U., 1970; M. Ch. Music, New Orleans Baptist Theol. Sem., 1978; m. Jennifer Lynn Jones, Mar. 4, 1972. Sales rep. Crown Zellerbach Corp., Tampa, Fla., 1974-75; mktg. rep. Burroughs Corp., Tampa, 1975-76; co-dir. Innovative Evangelism, New Orleans, 1976-79; ordained to ministry So. Baptist Conv., 1976; minister of music/youth 1st Bapt. Ch., Ocala, Fla., 1979—. Active Bold Missions Thrust, Balt. Served with USAF, 1970-74. Decorated D.F.C.; named outstanding grad. New Orleans Theol. Sem., 1979. Mem. Fla. Bapt. Ch. Music Conf., Phi Mu Alpha Sinfonia. Republican. Home: PO Box 1748 Ocala FL 32670 Office: 1st Baptist Ch 611 SE 3d St Ocala FL 32670

WELLS, WILLIAM LOCHRIDGE, chem. engr.; b. Mayfield, Ky., Oct. 12, 1939; s. Kenneth Morgan and Sarah Elizabeth (Lochridge) W.; student Vanderbilt U., 1957-59; B.S. in Chem. Engring., U. Ky., 1962; M.S., U. Ill. 1964, Ph.D., 1967; M.S. in Chem. Engring., U. S.C., 1974. Asst. prof. chemistry Murray State U., 1967-69; postdoctoral research asso. Wayne State U., 1969-71; asst. prof. S.W. Bapt. Coll., 1971-72; prof. Midlands Tech. Coll., 1972-74; program mgr. in air pollution research TVA, Chattanooga, 1975—; lectr. in field. NSF grantee, 1968-69; registered profl. engr., S.C. Mem. Am. Chem. Soc., Chem. Soc. (London), Am. Inst. Chem. Engrs. (past chmn. Chattanooga sect.), Nat. Soc. Profl. Engrs., Alpha Chi Sigma, Tau Beta Pi, Phi Lambda Upsilon, Sigma Chi. Club: Chattanooga Engrs. Contbr. articles to profl. publs. Home: 3522A Taft Hwy Signal Mountain TN 37377 Office: TVA 1120 Chestnut St Tower 2 Chattanooga TN 37401

WELSH, ANNE HOLBROOK, educator; b. Bourbon County, Ky., Mar. 27, 1926; d. Campbell Scotland and Mary Anne (Flanery) Holbrook; A.B. in Edn. with Distinction, U. Ky., 1964, M.A. in Edn., 1966, postgrad., 1966-74; m. John Anthony Welsh, Jr., June 28, 1943; children—Julia Ann Welsh Long, James William, Teresa Campbell Welsh Swiggett. Elementary tchr. for educable mentally retarded Fayette County Schs., Lexington, Ky., 1964-69, coordinator spl. edn., 1969—, dir. coop. summer program with U. Ky., 1969; supervising tchr. summer program U. Ky., 1966-68. Mem. state certification com. for revision of certification for tchrs. of exceptional children, 1974—. Recipient Sta. WHAS Crusade for Children award, 1967. Certified in teaching elementary grades, orthopedically handicapped, mentally retarded, supervision spl. edn. programs. Mem. Ky. Assn. Sch. Adminstrs., Nat. Assn. Profl. Educators, Profl. Educators Fayette County, Council for Exceptional Children, Council Adminstrs. Spl. Edn. Republican. Presbyterian. Home: 333 Irvine Rd Lexington KY 40502 Office: 701 E Main St Lexington KY 40502

WELSH, JAMES NEAL, process equipment mfg. co. exec.; b. Ft. Worth, July 17, 1942; s. Wiley Alfred and Jennie Ruth W.; B.A., Rice U., 1964, B.S., 1965; M.B.A., Harvard U., 1969; m. Jayne Alice Wann, Aug. 7, 1965; children—Alisha, Ryan. Indsl. sales Procter & Gamble Co., Houston, 1965-67; corp. fin. asso. Eppler, Guerin & Turner, Dallas, 1969-72; pres. Highland Capital Corp., Dallas, 1972-73; pres. Welsh Assos., Dallas, 1973-76; v.p., chief fin. officer First Corporate Fin. Corp., Dallas, 1974-76; pres., Shirco Inc., Dallas, 1976—; partner Bright & Co., Dallas, 1978—; dir. various cos.; lectr. seminars U. Dallas. Mem. Harvard Bus. Sch. Dallas; class sec. Harvard Bus. Sch. Alumni, 1976—. Conoco scholar Rice U., 1964-65. Mem. Am. Inst. Chem. Engrs., Water Pollution Control Fedn., WWEMA. Republican. Methodist. Office: Shirco Inc 2451 Stemmons Freeway Dallas TX 75207

WELSH, THOMAS J., bishop; b. Weatherly, Pa., Dec. 20, 1921; ed. St. Charles Borromeo Sem., Phila., Catholic U. Am. Ordained priest Roman Catholic Ch., 1946, bishop, 1970; titular bishop of Scattery Island and aux. bishop of Phila., 1970-74; first bishop of Arlington (Va.), 1974—. Office: care Chancery Office Suite 704 200 N Glebe Rd Arlington VA 22203*

WELTY, CHRISTAL GALE, fin. exec.; b. Freeport, Tex., Feb. 3, 1952; d. William E. and Zelma (Bourg) W.; B.B.A., U. Houston, 1973. Project analyst Zapata Tech. Service Corp., Houston, 1974-77; risk analyst Zapata Corp., Houston, 1977-78; audit scheduling mgr. Touche Ross & Co., Houston, 1978—. Mem. steering com. Bloodonor Programs, Inc., Houston, 1978-79. Mem. Am. Mktg. Assn., Profl. Bus. Women's Assn. Home: Houston TX 77057 Office: 2 Allen Center 25th Floor Houston TX 77002

WENDLAND, ROBERT ERNEST, farm products mfg. co. exec.; b. Killeen, Tex., June 25, 1900; s. Herman and Mattie Iceley (Wells) W.; student U. Tex., 1918-21; m. NoraLee Mayhew, Aug. 6, 1924; children—Bobbye Lee (Mrs. Charles P. Godbey), Erroll. Grain mcht. Wendland's Farm Products Inc., Killeen, 1922-28, Temple, Tex., 1928-36, owner, 1957—; owner Wendland Grain Co., Temple, 1936-57; owner Wendland's Farm Products, Inc., Temple, 1957—. Pres., Wendland Trust, Temple, 1949—. Served with U.S. Army, 1918. Mem. Tex. Grain Dealers Assn. (pres. 1934-35), Tex. Feed Mfrs. Assn. (pres. 1944-46), Grain and Feed Dealers Nat. Assn. (dir. 1960-64), Am. Feed Mfg. Assn. (dir. 1953-56, 60-63). Methodist (pres. bd. trustees 1954—, mem. adminstrv. bd.; chmn. bd. trustees Found., 1971—, pres. 1936-37). Rotarian (pres. club 1936-37, Dist. 587 Roll of Honor 1966, Paul Harris fellow 1979). Home: 1406 N 11th St Temple TX 76501 Office: 405 S 2d St Temple TX 76501

WENDT, CHARLES WILLIAM, soil physicist, agronomist; b. Plainview, Tex., July 12, 1931; s. Charles G. and Winnie Mae (Bean) W.; B.S. in Agronomy, Tex. A&M U., 1951, Ph.D. in Soil Physics, 1966; M.S. in Agronomy, Tex. Technol. Coll., 1957; m. Clara Anne Diller, Oct. 15, 1955; children—Charles Diller, John William, Elaine Anne, Cynthia Lynne. Research asst. Tex. Technol. Coll., Lubbock, Tex., 1953-55, instr., 1957-61, asst. prof. agronomy, 1961-63; tchr. math. and chemistry Hale Center, Tex., 1956-57; research asst. and asso. Tex. A&M U., College Station, 1963-66; asst. prof. Tex. Agrl. Expt. Sta., Lubbock, 1966-69, asso. prof., 1969-74, prof., 1974—; cons. on cotton prodn. Ministry of Agriculture, Republic of Sudan, Africa, summer, 1960; sec., treas. Hale County (Tex.) Farm Bur., 1954. Del. to Lubbock County Republican Conv., 1978; clk. session Westminister Presbyn. Ch., Lubbock, 1979—. Served with U.S. Army, 1951-53. EPA grantee, 1970-76, Dept. of Interior grantee, 1967-79. Mem. Soil Sci. Soc. Am., Agronomy Soc., Am. Soc. Plant Physiologists, Agronomy Soc., Sigma Xi, Phi Kappa Phi, AAAS. Republican. Clubs: Lions (sec. treas. 1962), Optimist (dir. 1978-79). Contbr. numerous articles on agronomy and water quality research to sci. jours.; contbr. numerous revs. on soil sci. to profl. jours. Home: 4518 22nd St Lubbock TX 79407 Office: Texas Agril Experiment Station Route 3 Lubbock TX 79401

WENDT, RICHARD PAUL, educator; b. St. Louis, Oct. 6, 1932; s. Walter Meredith and Minnie Katherine (Walters) W.; A.B., Washington U., St. Louis, 1954; Ph.D., U. Wis., Madison, 1960; m. Mary Jeannette Chopin, Feb. 7, 1970; children—Meredith Katherine, Richard Paul. Asst. prof chemistry La. State U., Baton Rouge, 1962-66; asso. prof. Loyola U., New Orleans, 1966-74, prof., 1974—; cons. VA Hosp., New Orleans, Gulf S. Research Inst., New Orleans. Served with U.S. Army, 1954-56. Mem. AAAS. Contbr. articles to profl. jours.

WENGERT, EUGENE MARK, educator; b. Knoxville, Tenn., Aug. 31, 1942; s. Norman Irving and Janet (Mueller) W.; B.S., U. Wis., Madison, 1964; M.S., Colo. State U., 1968; Ph.D., U. Wis., Madison, 1975; m. Barbara Irene Buehler, Aug. 22, 1964; children—Paul, Thad, Laura. Research forest products technologist U.S. Dept. Agr., Forest Service, Forest Products Lab., Madison, 1964-76; asso. prof., ext. specialist Dept. Forest Products, Va. Poly. Inst. and State U., Blacksburg, 1976—; cons. Sao Paulo (Brazil) Govt., 1977-78. Mem. Forest Products Research Soc. (chmn. Carolina-Chesapeake sect. 1980-81), Sigma Xi. Lutheran. Home: 206 Primrose Dr Blacksburg VA 20460 Office: 210 Cheatham Hall Va Polytech Inst and State Univ Blacksburg VA 24061

WENNER, LINDA SUE, educator; b. Phila., May 8, 1936; d. Dan Bradley and Sylvia W. (Segal) Cooper; student Huntingdon Coll., 1954-57; B.A., Chapman Coll., 1968, M.A., 1970; m. Warren Wenner, Dec. 15, 1956; children—Warren M., Charlotte Louise. Tchr., Lompoc, Calif., 1968-71, Sedalia, Mo., 1971-72; substitute tchr. Knob Noster, Mo., 1972-77; tchr. Ga. Mil. Coll., Whiteman AFB, Mo., 1974, Central Mo. State U., 1975-76; needlepoint instr. Officers' Wives Club, Whiteman AFB, 1974-78; tchr. 5th grade La Monte (Mo.) Elem. Sch., 1978—. Active Boy Scouts Am., Red Cross; craft chmn. Officer's Wives Club, 1974-78; chmn. volunteers Whiteman AFB, 1976-78. Recipient many needlepoint awards: named Woman of the Yr., Vandenburg AFB, 1968, Woman of the Yr., Bus. and Profl. Women's Club, Knob Noster, Mo., 1976. Republican. Lutheran. Clubs: Officers' Wives, Bus. and Profl. Women's Club. Author: Knob Noster: A Little History of a Little Town, 1976. Home: 832 Haulover Dr River Run S Altamonte Springs FL 32701

WENSEL, RONALD HERMAN, publishing co. exec.; b. Galveston, Tex., Feb. 2, 1937; s. Robert H. and Nora (Timmerman) W.; B.A., Baylor U., 1958; m. Julia Henington, Aug. 29, 1959; children—Marc, Tom, Kirk, Sandra. Sales engr. U.S. Gypsum Co., Shreveport, La., 1959-60; self-employed photographer, Little Rock, 1960-74; pres., gen. mgr. Henington Pub. Co., Wolfe City, Tex., 1974—; pres. Henington Industries; dir. Colonial Bank of Greenville (Tex.), Responsive Terminal Systems, Dallas. Mayor, City of Wolfe City, 1976—; bd. dirs. United Way of Hunt County (Tex.), 1978. Mem. Profl. Photographers Assn. Methodist. Club: Kiwanis. Home: 104 Crockett St Wolfe City TX 75496 Office: PO Box 29 Wolfe City TX 75496

WENTE, LEILA IBRAHIM, art historian, archaeologist; b. Cairo; came to U.S., 1957, naturalized, 1971; d. Tewfik Khalil and Nazira (Guindi) Ibrahim; student Am. U., Cairo, Western Res. U., Cleve.; B.A., U. N.C., Chapel Hill, 1958; postgrad. U. London, 1958, 61; M.F.A., U. Chgo., 1961, Ph.D., 1968; m. Edward F. Wente, Apr. 2, 1970. Docent, research asso. Oriental Inst., U. Chgo., 1961-67; research asso. art dept U. Chgo., 1967-68; mem. faculty art history dept. Pa. State U., University Park, 1969-70; prof. art history and archeology Pierce Coll., Athens, 1973; asso. prof. dept. fine arts La. State U., Baton Rouge, 1974—; cons. Ryerson fellow, summers 1963-68; Ryerson research fellow, 1965-66, 67; La. State U. summer research fellow, 1974. Mem. Archaeol. Inst. Am., Coll. Art Assn., AAUP, Soc. for Promotion of Roman Studies, Midwestern Art History Soc. Mem. Orthodox Ch. Home: 325 Embassy Apts 3942 Gourrier Ave Baton Rouge LA 70808 Office: Dept Fine Arts La State U Baton Rouge LA 70803

WENTHE, LEILA SKIDMORE, educator; b. Charleston, S.C., Nov. 26, 1941; d. Stephen Earl and Leila Belle (Smith) Skidmore; A.B., U. S.C., 1962, M.A., 1965; m. James Francis Wenthe, May 17, 1969; children—Michael Earl, Mark Raymund. Copywriter, Leslie Advt. Agy., Greenville, S.C., 1962-64; instr. advt., public relations U. S.C., Columbia, 1965-73; dir. mktg. and public relations Charleston (S.C.) Naval Shipyard Fed. Credit Union, 1974-77; asst. prof. advt. Henry W. Grady Sch. Journalism, U. Ga., Athens, 1977—. Chmn. public info. ARC, Richland County, 1967; mem. communications com. Trident 2000, Charleston, 1976-77. Recipient Charleston 1st place Addy award, 1975; Advt. Week fellowship Crain Communications/Am. Acad. Advt., 1979. Mem. Charleston Advt. Fedn. (sec. bd. 1975-77), Assn. Educators in Journalism, Am. Acad. Advt. (dir.), Athens Advt. Club, DAR, Kappa Tau Alpha, Pi Beta Phi. Roman Catholic. Home: Rt 1 Box 385-A Edisto Island SC 29438 Office: Sch Journalism U Ga Athens GA 30602

WENTLAND, THOMAS JOSEPH, speech-lang. pathologist; b. Rockford, Ill., May 30, 1934; s. Stanley Walter and Josephine Bertha (Westphal) W.; B.S., No. Ill. U., 1956; M.S., U. Wis., 1965, Ph.D., 1970; m. Phyllis Woods Wentland, Aug. 16, 1975; children—Ruth Ann, Julie Lynn, Alison Dana, Lauren Michelle. Asso. prof. speech pathology, also clin. dir. U. Wis., Stevens Point, 1966-72; prof., chmn. dept. speech pathology U. Miss., University, 1972-79; prof., head dept. speech pathology Columbus (Ga.) Coll., 1979—; cons. in field. U.S. Office of Edn. fellow, 1965-66, 68-69. Mem. Am. Speech-Lang.-Hearing Assn., Assn. Spl. Educators, Internat. Assn. Logopedics and Phoniatrics. Democrat. Unitarian. Editor: Exceptional People, 1978. Home: 5818 Old Dominion Rd Columbus GA 31904 Office: 42 Clearview Columbus Coll Columbus GA 31907

WENTWORTH, THEODORE THOMAS, JR., real estate broker, museum ofcl.; b. Mobile, Ala., July 26, 1898; s. Theodore Thomas and Elizabeth (Goodloe) W.; student pub. schs.; LL.D. (hon.), U. West Fla., 1977; m. Rosabel Howington, Sept. 5, 1920; children—Thomas Warren, Aubrey Dean, Jane. Employed in real estate field, 1916—; real estate broker T.T. Wentworth, Jr., Realtor, 1945—; dir., curator T.T. Wentworth, Jr. Mus., Pensacola, 1957—. Mem. Fla. Library and Hist. Commn., 1963-65; charter mem. Pensacola Interstate Fair, 1935—, pres., 1965—. County commr. Escambia County, 1920-24, tax collector, 1928-41. Recipient award of Merit, DAR, 1954, Realtor of Year award Pensacola Bd. Realtors, 1960, Liberty Bell award Freedoms Found., 1972, Kiwanian of Year award; Liberty Bell award W. Fla. Bar Assn., 1974; Gov.'s award Fla. Arts Council, 1974; Am. Patriot award, 1976, Action 76 Recognition award, 1976, others. Mem. Nat. Inst. Real Estate Brokers, Nat., Fla. assns. realtors, Pensacola Bd. Realtors (pres. 1960, hon. life mem.), Am. Assn. State and Local History, Greater Pensacola C. of C., Fla. (v.p.), Pensacola (charter and life mem., pres. 1936-47, pres. emeritus), Jacksonville, Ala., Walton County hist. socs., Hist. Assn. W. Fla., Hist. Assn. S. Fla., Fla. Civil War Centennial Commn., Fla. Sheriffs Assn. (hon.). Methodist (chmn. trustees 1934-58). Clubs: Masons (32 deg.), Shriners, Odd Fellows, Rebekahs, Woodmen of World, Lions. Home: 8380 Palafox Hwy Pensacola FL 32504

WENTZ, EVANS NELSON, govt. adminstr., mgmt. exec. and cons.; b. Pittsburg, Kans., Aug. 11, 1933; s. Arter Barney and Leo (Atchison) W.; B.S., Abilene Christian U., 1954; M.B.A., Columbia U., 1958. Fin. mgmt. positions Devel. and Resources Corp., N.Y.C., 1960-65, Compagnie des Bauxites de Guinee, Pitts. and Conakry, Guinea, 1970-77; exec. Wentz Investment Co., Hillsboro, Tex., 1977—, also dir.; exec. dir. Tex. Commn. for the Blind, Austin, 1979—; cons. on bauxite projects to six Arabic speaking nations. Served with U.S. Army, 1954-56. Recipient award Am. Mgmt. Assn., 1965. Republican. Home: 601 W 11th St Austin TX 78701

WENZLAU, JOHN NORBERT HANS, real estate and investment exec.; b. Meissen, Germany, Aug. 20, 1946; s. Otto Olgerd and Ursula Jutta W.; came to U.S., 1965; student Golden Gate Bapt. Sem., 1968-69, Southwestern Sem., 1979—; B.A., U. Oreg., 1968, M.A., 1970; m. Katherine Kickliter, Dec. 28, 1968; 1 son, Matthew Brian. Sales and staff mktg. Xerox Corp., Calgary, Can., 1971-74; regional sales mgr. Rentway Can. Ltd., Calgary, 1974-76; v.p., gen. mgr., sec. Maple Leaf Enterprises, Inc., Phoenix, 1977—; pres., sec. MLE, Inc., Arlington, Tex., 1978—. Mem. Republican Nat. Com., 1979—. Baptist. Home: 4409 Woodland Park Blvd Arlington TX 76013

WERBY, DON LAWRENCE, container service corp. exec.; b. Kansas City, Mo., Jan. 15, 1934; s. Manuel and Marjorie Werby; B.S. in Bus. Adminstrn., U. Mo., 1956; m. Cheryl E. Wise, Apr. 21, 1968; children—Olivia L., Jason Bryce. Dir. flexi-van sales N.Y. Central System, N.Y.C., 1964-68; dir. trailvan sales Penn Central Co., N.Y.C., 1968-69; asst. v.p. corp. mktg. Seatrain Lines, 1969-71, Interway Container Service, Inc., Houston, 1973-77, regional mgr. and area mktg. mgr. N. and S. Am., since 1977—. Served with AUS, 1956-58. Clubs: World Trade of Houston, Transp. of Houston, Walden Yacht and Country. Office: Interway Container Service Inc Suite 1509 609 Fannin St Houston TX 77002

WERDER, PAMELA ROSE, psychologist; b. Louisville, Oct. 28, 1947; d. John Joseph and Edna Mae (Gilpin) W.; B.S., Murray State U., 1969, M.S., 1971; Ph.D., Tex. Tech. U., Lubbock, 1975. Research asst. psychology Murray (Ky.) State U., 1969-71, Tex. Tech. U., 1972-74; staff psychologist U. Ky., Lexington, 1975-76; dir. developmental disabilities Cave Run Comprehensive Care Center, Morehead, Ky., 1976-77; program dir. Learning and Habilitation Service, Eastern State Hosp., Lexington, Ky., 1977—. Mem. Am. Assn. on Mental Deficiency (treas. Ky. chpt. 1977-78, pres. 1980), Am. Psychol. Assn., Nat. Assn. for Retarded Citizens. Contbr. articles to profl. publs. Home: 361 Larkwood Dr Lexington KY 40509 Office: Eastern State Hosp 627 W 4th St Lexington KY 40508

WERNAU, RICHARD JOSEPH, textile mfg. co. ofcl.; b. Passaic, N.J., Mar. 16, 1945; s. Wilson Anderson and Claire (Horsfall) W.; B.B.A., Kent State U., 1967; M.B.A., Miami U., Oxford, Ohio, 1968. Sales rep. Chesebrough-Ponds Co., Houston, 1968-72; sales rep. Riegel Textile Corp., Houston, 1972-77, product mgr., Johnston, S.C., 1977-78, product mgr. new products, 1978-79, regional sales mgr., Atlanta, 1979—. Active Young Republicans, Houston, Columbia, S.C., 1972-76; mem. Spl. Olympics Com., Houston, 1972-76. Served with U.S. Army, 1969. Mem. Am. Mktg. Assn., Am. Mgmt. Assn. Methodist. Club: Atlanta Sporting. Contbr. articles to profl. publs. Home: 701 Serramonte Marietta GA 30367 Office: 1 Corporate Sq Suite 201 Atlanta GA 30329

WERNER, DOROTHY JOHNSON, pub. relations exec.; b. Lexington, Tenn., Jan. 22, 1923; d. Arthur and Anna Laura (Pearson) Johnson; student Lambuth Coll., 1940-43, N.Y. U., 1949, U. Vienna (Austria), 1958-59; m. Merle McDougald Werner, Jan. 27, 1951; children—Michael, Douglas. Writer, photographer Memphis Pub. Co., 1944-47; catalog advt. mgr. Butler Bros., Inc., N.Y.C., 1947; publicity dir. Skillmill, Inc., N.Y.C., 1947-53; editor Women's News, mag., Korea, 1966-67; pub. info. officer No. Va. Regional Park Authority, Fairfax, 1972—. Washington rep. Nat. Council Women of U.S., 1977—; del. to State Dept., Non-Govtl. Orgn., 1977—; del.-at-large Fairfax County United Way, 1978—. Mem. Assn. Am. Fgn. Service Women, Public Relations Soc. Am., Nat. Soc. D.A.R. Presbyterian. Club: No. Va. Press (dir. 1972—). Home: 3405 Mansfield Rd Falls Church VA 22041 Office: 11001 Popes Head Rd Fairfax VA 22030

WERNER, JAMES TAYLOR, mech. engr.; b. Newark, Jan. 19, 1924; s. James Taylor and Lilly Mae (Weigel) W.; B.S. in M.E., Ford Engring. Sch., 1949; m. Doris Marion Fishel, July 15, 1944; 1 son, Keith Douglas. Sr. design engr. Ford Motor Co., Dearborn, Mich., 1943-51; sr. engring. specialist Gen. Dynamics Corp., Fort Worth, Tex., 1951—. Fellow Soc. Allied Weight Engrs. (sr., sr. internat. v.p. 1973-74, 78-79, exec. internat. v.p. 1979-80, dir., 1971-73). Home: 8317 Lupine St Fort Worth TX 76135 Office: PO Box 748 Fort Worth TX 76101

WERRING, LANA DUKE, advt. agy. exec.; b. St. Catharines, Ont., Can., Nov. 16, 1944; came to U.S., 1963, naturalized, 1968; d. Allen Edwin Duke and Bonnie Grant; student in Bus. Adminstrn., Loyola U., New Orleans, 1972-74; 1 son, R. David. Engaged in sales promotion and public relations Jr. C. of C., various cities, 1963-66; dir. advt. Clarion Herald Pub. Co., New Orleans, 1975—. Bd. dirs. Keep Christ in Your Christmas Com. Recipient New Orleans ADDY awards; Gold cert. New Orleans Art Dirs. and Designers Assn., 1976, Merit cert., 1977. Mem. Cath. Press Assn. (dir.), So. Cath. Newspaper Group (sec.-treas.), C. of C., Am. Women in Radio and TV (pres.-elect), Advt. Club New Orleans. Presbyterian. Office: Duke Advt Agy Inc 535 Gravier St Suite 702 New Orleans LA 70130

WERSHOW, HAROLD J., sociologist; b. N.Y.C., Jan. 8, 1920; s. Shamai and Sonia (Yankelich) Werchovsky; B.S. with honors in Social Sci., CCNY, 1941; M.S.W., U. Pa., 1948, D.S.W., 1960; m. Jeanette E. Garfinkel, Nov. 11, 1944; 1 son, Daniel. Social worker with various agys., 1948-60; cons. on aging to nursing homes, also to Model Cities Program, Huntsville, Ala., 1969-70; asso. dir. Community Action Program and Regional Med. Program, Birmingham, Ala., 1972; prof. sociology U. Ala., Birmingham, 1963—. Served to lt. U.S. Army, 1942-46. HEW grantee, 1973-74; cert. social worker, Ala. Fellow Am. Sociol. Assn., Gerontol. Soc.; mem. AAUP (U. Ala.-Birmingham v.p.), Acad. Cert. Social Workers. Contbr. articles to profl. publs. Home: 12 Vine St Birmingham AL 35213 Office: Ullman Bldg U Ala Birmingham AL 35294

WERTZ, DAVID FREDERICK, clergyman; b. Lewistown, Pa., Oct. 5, 1916; s. Jesse Price and Ada (Barratt) W.; A.B., Dickinson Coll., 1937; M.A., Boston U., 1939, S.T.B., 1940; m. Betty Jean Rowe, Aug. 25, 1938; children—Robert Gary, Joan Rowe Wertz Monoski, Donna Jean Ream, Elizabeth Barratt Maisonpierre. Ordained to ministry United Methodist Ch.; pastor in Boiling Springs-Hickorytown, Pa., 1934-37, Doylesburg, Pa., 1940-43, Stewartstown, Pa., 1943-46, Camp Curtin Ch., Harrisburg, Pa., 1946-49; dist. supt. Williamsport (Pa.) Dist., United Meth. Ch., 1953-55; pres. Lycoming Coll., Williamsport, 1955-68; resident bishop W.Va. Area, United Meth. Ch., Charleston, 1968—. Pres., West Branch council Boy Scouts Am., 1968, Buckskin council, 1975-76; pres. bd. local ministries United Meth. Ch., 1976-80, chmn. commn. on religion and race, 1972-76, chmn. commn. on religion in Appalachia, 1975-76; bd. dirs. Little League Baseball, Inc., 1956-66. Republican. Home: 1401 Mt Vernon Rd Charleston WV 25314 Office: 900 Washington St E Charleston WV 25301

WERTZ, DONALD LLOYD, accountant; b. Sharon Springs, Kans., Oct. 14, 1941; s. Claude DeClifton and Freda Marie (Walker) W.; B.S. in Bus. Adminstrn., Kans. State U., 1964; m. Connie Sue Moore, Jan. 27, 1963; children—Shaun Bryant, Kimberly Dawn. Audit mgr. Arthur Young & Co., Kansas City, 1964-72, Tulsa, 1972-74; fin. v.p. Dale-Carter Lumber Co., Tulsa, 1974-76; individual practice as C.P.A., Tulsa, 1977-80; partner Ostrander, Sugg & York, Tulsa, 1980—. Active YMCA, Indian Guide Program, 1974-77. C.P.A., Kans., Mo., Okla. Mem. Am. Inst. C.P.A.'s, Okla. Soc. C.P.A.'s. Mem. Christian Ch. Clubs: Shadow Mountain Swim (pres., treas. 1974-76), Men's Breakfast. Home: 6323 S 69th E Pl Tulsa OK 74133 Office: 5043 S Fulton St Tulsa OK 74135

WERTZ, HOWARD EDWARD, ins. exec.; b. Moulton, Iowa, May 14, 1924; s. Paul Lazzell and Hazel Fern (Ballew) W.; student Howard Coll., 1946-50; B.S., U. Ala., Birmingham, 1952; m. Mary Lou Vann, Aug. 23, 1947; children—Howard Edward, John Paul. Test analyst U.S. Steel Co., Birmingham, Ala., 1950-51; purchasing agt., dept. mgr. Blue Cross and Blue Shield, Ala., Birmingham, 1953-66; purchasing mgr., personnel mgr. Kennesaw Life Ins. Co., Atlanta, 1967-68; field rep. Am. Cancer Soc., Birmingham, 1968-69; dir. adminstrv. services Blue Cross and Blue Shield Ala., Birmingham, 1969—. Served with USMC, 1943-46. USAF, 1951-52. Recipient Silver Beaver award Boy Scouts Am. Mem. Purchasing Mgmt. Assn. Ala. Baptist. Office: 450 Riverchase Pky E Birmingham AL 35298

WERTZ, MARCUS EMMONS, JR., mfg. co. exec.; b. Belleville, N.J., Dec. 29, 1917; s. Marcus Emmons and Roberta Chapman (Struble) W.; B.S., Lehigh U., 1939; m. Georgieanna Cecile Campbell, Apr. 24, 1943 (dec. Nov. 1972); children—Nancy Jeanne (Mrs. James G. Kerridge), Roberta Carol (Mrs. C.M. Sutter), Marcus Emmons III; m. 2d, Constance Josephine Weil, June 23, 1973. With Lehigh Structural Steel Co., Allentown, Pa., 1949-54, 57-60, asst. supt., 1953-54, dir. indsl. relations, 1958-59, asst. to exec. v.p., 1959-60; v.p., dir. Crandall Corp., Warren, N.H., 1954-57; prodn. mgr. Gulf States Tube Co., Rosenberg, Tex., 1961-66, gen. mgr., 1966-67; cons., Houston, 1967-69; plant mgr. Rheem Superior div. Rheem Mfg. Co., Pearland, Tex., 1969-70; contract mgr. Bethelehem Fabricators Inc. (Pa.), 1970, adminstrv. v.p., 1970-72, sr. v.p., 1972-74, exec. v.p., 1974-76, chief operating officer, 1974-76, also dir.; v.p. Whitehead & Kales Co., Detroit, 1975-76; pres., dir. Gulfport Steel Co. (Miss.), 1976—. Bd. dirs. Lehigh Valley chpt. Nat. Safety Council, Bethlehem, 1971. Served to lt. comdr, USNR, 1941-45. Me. Assn. Iron and Steel Engrs., Am. Welding Soc., Newcomen Soc., Pa. Soc., Beta Theta Pi. Republican. Mason (32 deg.). Home: 113 Lakeview Dr Biloxi MS 39531 Office: Lorraine Rd PO Box 2097 Gulfport MS 39503

WERTZ, RICHARD DAVID, ednl. adminstr.; b. Indiana, Pa., Sept. 20, 1942; s. David Lee and Fern Margaret (McIntyre) W.; B.S., Pa. State U., 1964; M.Ed., 1965; Ed.D., Columbia U., 1972; m. Sandra Lanasa Wertz, Aug. 21, 1965; 1 dau., Nicole Leigh. Residence dir. Wagner Coll., Staten Island, N.Y., 1965-66, dean of men, 1966-71; asst. dean of residential life U. Pa., Phila., 1971-74; dean for residence life U. S.C., Columbia, 1974-75, asst. v.p. student affairs, 1975-78, asso. v.p. student affairs, 1978—. Mem. Am. Assn. Higher Edn., Nat. Assn. Student Personnel Adminstrs, Am. Coll. Personnel Assn., Phi Delta Kappa. Lutheran. Home: 290 Hunters Blind Dr Columbia SC 29210 Office: Residential Life Services University South Carolina Columbia SC 29208

WESLAR, JOHN BRIAN, mktg. exec.; b. Binghamton, N.Y., Dec. 30, 1942; s. George Bernard and Elaine Margaret W.; B.S. in Econs., LeMoyne Coll., 1965; M.B.A., Dartmouth Coll., 1967; m. Karen Irene Flanigan, Aug. 20, 1966; children—Brian John, Mark Andrew. Asso. product mgr. Maxwell House Coffee, Gen. Foods Corp., White Plains, N.Y., 1967-69; v.p. mktg. Hardee Products, Denver, 1969-70; product mgr. Dove Liquid Detergent, Lever Bros., N.Y.C., 1970-72, brand mgr. refrigerated products Coca Cola Foods div., Houston, 1972-77, mktg. mgr. Latin Am., 1977-79, group brand mgr. Hi-C products, 1979—; mng. dir. Sucobrisil (Brazil). Home: 1903 Corral Dr Houston TX 77090 Office: PO Box 2079 Houston TX 77001

WESLEY, EDWARD CARROLL, lawyer; b. Jacksonville, Tex., Sept. 26, 1946; s. Jessie Edward and Asalee (Holsomback) W.; A.A., Coll. of Mainland, 1969; B.A., U. Houston, 1971; J.D., Thurgood Marshall Sch. Law, Houston, 1975; LL.M., U. Tex., 1977; m. Barbara Stallworth, Sept. 21, 1968; 1 dau., Lee Ann. Admitted to Tex. bar, U.S. Dist. Ct. bar, So. Dist. Tex.; pipefitter, welder Pipefitter's Local 211, Houston, 1965-76; agt. Prudential Ins. Co., Houston, 1971-72; asst. counsel Nat. Treasury Employees Union, Austin, Tex., 1975-76; individual practice law, Dickinson, Tex., 1976—; part-time instr. Coll. of Mainland. Served with USAR, 1965-71. Mem. Am. Bar Assn., State Bar Tex., Galveston County Bar Assn., Mainland Bar Assn., Assn. Trial Lawyers Am., Dickinson C. of C. (dir. 1978—). Democrat. Presbyterian. Clubs: Dickinson Rotary (dir. 1979—), Am. Karate of Dickinson. Sculptor numerous metal sculptures. Office: 2716 Main St Dickinson TX 77539

WESLEY, THERESSA GUNNELS, writer; b. Morrilton, Ark., Sept. 2, 1945; d. Fred Jonathan and Florence (Pledger) Gunnels; B.A. in English, Philander Smith Coll., 1967; M.A., Kent State U., 1971; postgrad. U. Minn., 1973-74, Mankato State U., 1974-75; m. John W. Wesley, June 18, 1976; children—Rashida, Kameelah, Jameel. 1 son by previous marriage, Dwayne. High sch. English tchr. Springfield (Mo.) Public Schs., 1967-69, Pulaski County Sch. System, Little Rock, 1969-70; instr. U. Wis., Eau Claire, 1972-74; reading specialist Mpls. Public Schs., 1974-75; asst. prof., placement dir. Philander Smith Coll., Little Rock, 1975-78; author: Black American Writers: Past and Present, 1975. Baptist. Home and Office: 14508 Sara Dr Little Rock AR 72206

WESOLOWSKI, MICHAEL DAVID, psychologist; b. South Bend, Ind., Aug. 29, 1947; s. Joseph Anthony and Adeline June (Garber) W.; B.A., Ind. U., 1971; M.S., So. Ill. U., 1973, Ph.D., 1977. Psychologist, No. Ind. Children's Hosp., South Bend, Ind., 1971-72; psychologist dept. treatment devel. Anna (Ill.) Mental Health and Developmental Center, 1976-78, research fellow, 1973-76; research asso. Research and Tng. Center, prof. ednl. psychology W.Va. U., Morgantown, 1978—. Bd. dirs. W.Va. Advocacy for Developmentally Disabled, 1978—. Mem. Assn. Advancement Psychology, Nat. Rehab. Assn., AAAS, Am. Psychol. Assn., Am. Assn. Mental Deficiency, Assn. Advancement Behavior Therapy, Midwestern Assn. Behavior Analysis. Editorial bd. Edn. and Treatment of Children, 1978—. Home: 442 Medical Center Dr Morgantown WV 26506 Office: 509 Allen Hall West Virginia U Morgantown WV 26506

WESP, ARTHUR PHILIP, chem. co. exec.; b. Bklyn., Jan. 30, 1947; s. Arthur Philip and Virginia Helen (Marshall) W.; B.S. in Chemistry, Ohio U., 1969; m. Karen Sue Werner, Aug. 23, 1969; children—Scott, Laurie, Carrie. Sales analyst Shell Chem. Co., Cleve., 1969-70; sales asso., Houston, 1971-72, tech. sales rep., Cin., 1972-74, tech. sales rep., Cleve., 1974-77, product sales mgr. oxygenated solvents, Houston, 1977—. Pres. bd. of equalizations YMCA Indian Guides/Princesses, 1978; v.p., dir. Louette Road Utility Dist., 1978—; chmn. utility and maintenance com. Terra Nova Subdiv., 1978, trustee maintenance fund, 1979. Served with Air Def. Arty., U.S. Army, 1970-71. Mem. Am. Mgmt. Assn., Assn. Water Bd. Dirs., Blue Key, Sigma Phi Epsilon. Presbyterian. Home: 5215 Springton Ln Spring TX 77373 Office: Shell Chem Co PO Box 2463 Houston TX 77001

WESSELS, CHARLES HENRY, lawyer; b. Savannah, Apr. 26, 1940; s. Frederick and Rosalie (Childress) W.; A.B., Wittenberg U., 1962; J.D., U. Ga., 1965; m. Marcia Hancock, July 19, 1969; children—Charles Henry, Anne Meriwether. Admitted to Ga. bar, 1964; partner firm Bouhan, Williams and Levy, Savannah, 1964-72, firm Brannen, Wessels & Searcy, Savannah, 1972—; pres. So. Bank Holding Co.; dir. Atlantic Ins. and Investment Corp.; vice chmn. bd. Atlantic Mut. Fire Ins. Co.; mem. Ga. Senate, 1977—, vice chmn. jud. com. Served as lt. comdr. USNR, 1965-68. Mem. Am. Bar Assn. (past vice chmn. econs. com., mem. internat. exchange com.), Ga. Bar Assn. (chmn. govt. relations com.), State Bar Ga. (chmn. ann. meeting 1968-76). Democrat. Lutheran. Office: 22 E 34 St Savannah GA 31412

WESSELS, ROBERT DELANO, court adminstr.; b. Houston, Tex., Mar. 21, 1949; s. Delano Eugene and Grace (Moriarity) W.; B.B.A., Sam Houston State U., 1974; M.A., U. Houston, 1978; m. Mary Louise Wessels, Sept. 11, 1976; 1 son, Robert Delano. Sub-systems info. coordinator Harris County Ct. Mgrs. Office, 1974-75, adminstrv. asst., 1975-76, ct. mgr. County Criminal Cts. Law, 1976—; adj. prof. ct. mgmt. and adminstrn. U. Houston, Clear Lake City, 1977—; evaluation tech. assistance cons. Tex. Jud. Planning Com., Gov.'s Office criminal justice div., 1978; cons. Gov.'s Speedy Trial Task Force, 1977. LEAA grantee County Criminal Cts. Law, 1975-77. Mem. Am. Judicature Soc., Inst. Jud. Adminstrn., Am. Bar Assn., Am. Soc. Public Adminstrn., Tex. Assn. Ct. Adminstrn. Methodist. Home: 9638 Cedardale St Houston TX 77055 Office: 301 San Jacinto Room 401 Houston TX 77002

WESSELS, ROBERT ROGERS, cons. engr.; b. Atlanta, Oct. 27, 1922; s. Theodore Francis and Mildred Mayrant (Thatcher) W.; B.S., U.S. Mil. Acad., 1944; postgrad. Cornell U., 1948-49; m. Mary Jane Luethke, Aug. 21, 1946; children—William Robert, Kirtley. Commd. 1st lt. C.E., U.S. Army, 1946, advanced through grades to col., 1965; ret., 1973; dir. shuttle constrn. office, dir. facilities NASA Marshall Space Flight Center, Huntsville, Ala., 1972-76; cons. engr. in pvt. practice, Huntsville, 1976—; pres. Wescope Corp., 1978—. Active Boy Scouts Am.; bd. dirs. Aid to Retarded Citizens Assn., 1975—. Registered profl. engr., Ala., Pa. Mem. Nat. Soc. Profl. Engrs., Soc. Am. Mil. Engrs., Assn. U.S. Army, SAR. Republican. Episcopalian. Home: 2005 Shadecrest Rd Huntsville AL 35801 Office: PO Box 204 Huntsville AL 35804

WEST, BURTON CAREY, physician, educator; b. Pitts., Feb. 21, 1941; s. Pemberton Burton and Maree (Van Scoyoc) W.; A.B., Amherst Coll., 1963; M.D., Cornell U., 1967; m. Katherine Ann Young, Dec. 27, 1963; children—Amy, Holly, John, Abigail, Emily. Intern, Univ. Hosps., Seattle, 1967-68, asst. resident, 1968-69; clin. asso., sr. staff fellow NIH, Bethesda, Md., 1969-72; sr. resident and Hugh Morgan chief resident in medicine Vanderbilt Hosp., Nashville, 1972-74; asso. prof. medicine La. State U., Shreveport, 1977—; chief sect. of infectious diseases La. State U. Med. Center, 1974—; cons. Shreveport VA Med. Center, 1974—. Served with USPHS, 1969-71. Fellow ACP; mem. Am. Soc. Microbiology, Infectious Diseases Soc. Am., Am. Fedn. Clin. Research, Am. Soc. Trop. Medicine and Hygiene, La. Med. Soc., Shreveport Med. Soc. Office: La State Univ Med Center PO Box 33932 Shreveport LA 71130

WEST, DAN CARLOS, coll. pres.; b. Galveston, Tex., May 29, 1939; s. Embry Carlos and Mildred Louise (Junker) W.; student U. Tex., 1957-58, U.S. Naval Acad., 1958-61, Tex. Christian U., 1961; B.A., Austin Coll., 1962; B.D., Union Theol. Sem., Va., 1965; D.Div., Vanderbilt U., 1969; m. Sidney Claire Childs, June 29, 1963; children—Elizabeth Claire, Andrew Childs. Ordained to ministry United Presbyterian Ch.-Presbyterian Ch., U.S., 1965; pastor Smyrna (Tenn.) Presbyn. Ch., 1965-68; dir. ch. relations, asst. prof. interdisciplinary studies, campus minister, coordinator research and devel. Austin Coll., 1968-72; pres. Ark Coll., 1972—, prof. humanities, 1965—; Ark. mem. Edn. Commn. of States; mem. Ark. Student Loan Authority; dir. Coca-Cola Bottling Co. South Ark. Served with USN, 1958-61. Mem. Assn. Am. Colls., Nat. Assn. Ind. Colls. and Univs., Assn. Presbyn. Colls., Ark. Council Ind. Colls. and Univs. Office: Ark Coll PO Box 2317 Batesville AR 72501

WEST, DANNY FRANKLIN, funeral dir.; b. Randolph County, Asheboro, N.C., Dec. 9, 1945; s. Samuel Henry and Berta Lorraine W.; student Randolph Tech. Inst., 1969, 74; m. Barbara Lane Parks, June 11, 1967; 1 son, Ryan Stuart. Supr., Ridge Ambulance Service, Asheboro, 1967-77; with Ridge Funeral Home, Asheboro, 1967—, emergency med. technician, 1974—, bookkeeper, office mgr., 1970-78, supr. funeral home, 1970-77, funeral dir., 1970—; pres.

Asheboro Mut. Burial Assn., 1978—. Treas., Eastside Vol. Fire Dept., 1978—. Served with USAF, 1965-67. Mem. Nat. Funeral Dirs. Assn., N.C. Funeral Dirs. Assn., Woodmen of World, Asheboro Jr. C. of C. Republican. Mem. Soc. of Friends. Office: 261 N Fayetteville St Asheboro NC 27203

WEST, DOROTHY ANNE, speech and hearing therapist; b. Grand Forks, N.D., Mar. 21, 1936; d. Philip William and Tenney Constanse (Johnson) West; B.S., La. State U., 1958, M.Edn., 1973; 1 child—Jeffrey West Freeman. Speech and hearing therapist St. Helena Parish Schs., Greensburg, La., 1959-61; asst. to Dean of Women, La. State U., Baton Rouge, 1961-66; speech and hearing therapist E. Baton Rouge Parish Schs., 1966—; mem. special speech therapy study com. La. State Dept. of Edn., Baton Rouge, 1969-70; supv. student tchg. La. State U., Baton Rouge, 1967-68, 1970—. Active with Republican Party, Baton Rouge, 1968—; pres. Mortar Bd. Alumnae Chpt., Baton Rouge, 1960-62. Recipient grad. assistantship La. State U., 1958, OEO grant for grad. study, La. State U., 1969. Mem. E. Baton Rouge Parish Speech Therapists (chmn. 1969-70), La. Tchrs. Assn., Am., La. speech and hearing assns., Assn. of Classroom Tchrs., Assn. of Tchr. Educators, Lakeside Villa Condominium Assn. (sec.-treas. 1978-80, pres. 1980—), Delta Gamma (membership study com. 1962-64, scholarship chmn., 1965-69, nominating com., 1968-70, province ix collegiate chmn. 1970-75, awards chmn. 1975-79, Cable award 1980). Republican, Presbyterian. Home: 976 Baird Dr Baton Rouge LA 70808 Office: 444 Halfway Tree Baton Rouge LA 70810

WEST, HOUGHTON HENRY, JR., computer co. exec.; b. New Orleans, July 23, 1938; s. Houghton Henry and Fannie (Taylor) W.; B.S., Stephen F. Austin U., 1960; postgrad. U. Houston, 1966-67; m. Neville Jones, July 24, 1959; children—Sylvia Annette, Nancy Jane. Systems analyst Service Bur., IBM Corp., Houston, 1960-65; asst. treas. Camco, Inc., Houston, 1965-69; mgr. fin. planning No. Electric Co., Laurel, Miss., 1969-70; pres., chmn. bd. Systems Communications Corp., Houston, 1970—. Certified data processor. Mem. Data Processing Mgmt. Assn., Delta Sigma Phi. Republican. Episcopalian. Home: 5607 Havenwoods Houston TX 77066 Office: 1721 Pech Suite 300 Houston TX 77055

WEST, JAMES EARNEST, coll. dean.; b. Townley, Ala., Jan. 4, 1930; s. Young Uluar and Laura Belle (Ferguson) W.; B.S., U. Ala., 1950, M.A. in Polit. Sci., postgrad., 1969-71. Mgmt. intern Dept. Navy, 1957; pub. adminstrn. adviser ICA, 1957-62; adminstrv. attache San Diego County (Calif.), 1962-63; sr. asso. Pub. Adminstrn. Service Chgo., 1963-66, sr. asso. cons., 1966—; instr. polit. sci. Walker Coll., Jasper, Ala., 1966-78, dean acad. affairs and admissions, 1978—. Chmn. Walker County Council on Aging, 1972-73; pres. Ala. N.W. Mental Health Center, 1976-78; bd. dirs. Walker County Concerned Citizens for Youth, 1974-78, Walker Coll. Civic Concert Assn., 1976-78; chmn. Walker County Health Adv. Com., 1975-77. Served with USN, 1951-55. Decorated Disting. Service medal; recipient Disting. Service award Council on Aging, 1974, United Appeal, 1975, Ala. Dist. Circle K, 1975, Kiwanis Club, 1976. Mem. Am. Acad. Polit. and Social Scis., Am. Assn. Collegiate Registrars and Admissions Officers, So. Polit. Sci. Assn., So. Assn. Collegiate Registrars and Admissions Officers, Ala. Polit. Sci. Assn., Ala. Assn. Collegiate Registrars and Admissions Officers, Theta Chi. Democrat. Baptist. Clubs: Masons, Kiwanis (dir., v.p. Jasper 1970—). Home: 1304 Willowbrook Dr Jasper AL 35501 Office: 1400 Gamble Ave Jasper AL 35501

WEST, JATON HOLDER, social worker; b. Alexandria, La., Jan. 22, 1945; d. William Jennings Holder and Bobby (Terrell) Cowart; B.A. (Jr. League scholar), Lamar U., 1967; M.S.S.W. (NIMH scholar), U. Tex., Austin, 1973; m. Harvey Gordon West, Jr., Dec. 21, 1967; 1 son, Stephen MacPherian. Supr. S.E. Neighborhood House, Washington, 1973-74; clin. social worker Family and Child Services of Washington, 1974-78, Divorce and Marital Stress Clinic, Arlington, Va., 1978—; pvt. practice clin. social work specializing in therapy with individuals, couples, 1978—; cons. Divorce and Marital Stress Edn. Resources, Arlington, 1978—. Council mem. Am. Cancer Soc., 1974—, sec. S.E. div., Washington, 1976-77, recipient Service award, 1977. Lic. clin. social worker, Va. Mem. Nat. Assn. Social Workers, Acad. Cert. Social Workers. Home: 9965 Wood Wren Ct Fairfax VA 22032

WEST, JIMMY EDWARD, ins. co. exec.; b. Palestine, Tex., Sept. 12, 1945; s. John Dale and Hazel (Cook) W.; student U. Tex., Arlington, 1964-65; B.B.A., Sam Houston State U., 1968; m. Mary Darlene Roberts, Jan. 28, 1972; children by previous marriage—Kevin, Rhonda. Budget analyst, internal auditor Gulfatlantic Warehouse, Houston, 1969-70; prodn. mgr. First Bus. Computing Co., Houston, 1970-72; with Am. Gen. Life Ins. Co., Houston, 1972—, sr. buyer, purchasing. Steward, Methodist Ch. Served with U.S. Army, 1968-69. Mem. Nat. Purchasing Assn. Clubs: Toastmasters (treas. 1978), Masons. Home: 22118 Kenchester St Houston TX 77073 Office: Am Gen Life Ins Co 2727 Allen Pkwy Houston TX 77019

WEST, JOHN CLIFFORD, assn. exec.; b. Grand Rapids, Mich., Oct. 2, 1938; s. James C. and Elizabeth F. (Furtrell) W.; B.S., E. Tex. State U., 1961; M.Ed., Memphis State U., 1963; m. Charlotte Ann Dickerson, Sept. 12, 1959; children—Teri Deann, Elizabeth Ann, John Clifford. Head track coach Furman U., Greenville, S.C., 1964-68, dir. athletics, 1972-79; head track coach U. S.C., 1968-72; pres. SHARE, Inc., 1979—. Mem. Nat. Assn. Dirs. Athletics, Nat. Assn. Basketball Coaches, Fellowship Christian Athletes (trustee), Greenville Track Club. Baptist. Address: SHARE Inc Rt 5 Box 620 Travelers Rest SC 29690

WEST, JOSEBELL LUCILLE, educator; b. Hialeah, Fla., Dec. 2, 1925; d. Willie and Willie Alfred (Thompson) Akers; student Oakwood Coll., Acad., 1946; early childhood certificate Broward Community Coll., 1963; m. Eddie West, Mar. 28, 1946; children—Frank A., Bernard E., Marva L., Dwayne E. Tchr., Mt. Olivet Seventh-Day Adventist Ch. Sch., Dania, Fla., 1951-52, West's Kindergarten, Dania, 1952-69; social educator Broward County (Fla.) Sch. Bd., Ft. Lauderdale, 1969—. Committeewoman, Dania Democratic Com., 1958-69; pres. Collins Elementary Sch. PTA, Dania, 1960-69, Bethune Elementary Sch. PTA, Hollywood, Fla., 1969-70. Mem. NEA, Am. Legion Aux. Adventist. Clubs: Cheerful Workers, Westside Civic (sec. 1959-65, pres.) (Dania), Dania Dem., Adventist Edn. (Ft. Lauderdale, Fla.). Home: 621 NW 3d Terr Dania FL 33004 Office: 1004 NW 4th St Fort Lauderdale FL 33311

WEST, KATHRYN ALICE, educator; b. Sevierville, Tenn., Mar. 18, 1947; d. William Paul and Sara Kathryn (McMahan) Rogers; B.A., Middle Tenn. State U., 1967, M.S., 1969; 1 son, James Ronnie. Asst. prof. biology Cleveland (Tenn.) State Community Coll., 1970—. Mem. NEA, Tenn. Edn. Assn., Eastern Tenn. Edn. Assn., Cleveland State Community Coll. Edn. Assn., AAUW, DAR. Democrat. Baptist. Home: 2755 Greenbrier Dr NW Cleveland TN 37311 Office: Shiloh Church Rd Cleveland TN 37311

WEST, NORTH E., psychologist; b. Lapeer County, Mich., July 7, 1910; s. Almond Glenn and Julia Anne (Brown) W.; B.A. cum laude, Battle Creek Coll., 1938; M.R.E., No. Bapt. Theol. Sem., 1942, B.D. (Kallenbach Acad. scholar), 1946; M.Ed., U. Ark., 1960, Ed.D., 1962; m. Frances Camille Borders, Nov. 24, 1932; children—David Almond, Mary Margaret, Paul Edgar, Carol Julia. Ordained to ministry Baptist Ch., 1939; pastor, Mich., N.D., 1935-42, Wis., 1946-50; counselor, ednl. supr. Ark. ch.-related acads., 1950-59; grad. asst. U. Ark., 1960-62; faculty, head psychology dept. Wayland Bapt. Coll., 1962-68, 70-72, Hogg Mental Health Found. grantee, 1965; staff psychologist VA Hosps., Tuskegee, Ala., 1968-70, Ft. Meade, S.D., 1972-75, Murfreesboro, Tenn., 1975—, coordinator Nat. Acad. Sci. Research Project with VA, 1975-76; adj. prof. psychology Middle Tenn. State U., 1976—; bd. dirs. S.W. Christian Counseling Center, Tex., 1973—; mem. exec. bd. Concord Bapt. Assn., Tenn., 1975—. Bd. dirs. High Plains Children's Tng. Center, Tex., 1965-68, Meade-Pennington (S.D.) Counties Mental Health Assn., 1973-75, S.D. Mental Health Assn., 1973-75. Served as chaplain AUS, 1942-45. Recipient certificate commendation for service to retarded children High Plains Children's Tng. Center, 1968. Mem. Am. Soc. Clin. Hypnosis, Am., Southeastern, Tenn. psychol. assns., Psi Chi, Phi Delta Kappa, Pi Kappa Delta. Democrat. Contbr. papers in field to profl. lit. Home: 510 Eventide Dr Murfreesboro TN 37130 Office: VA Hosp Murfreesboro TN 37130

WEST, OTUS THERON, obstetrician-gynecologist; b. McConnols, Ala., Feb. 27, 1914; s. Otus Napoleon and Mada (Windham) W.; A.B., U. Ala., 1935; M.B., Northwestern U., 1939, M.D., 1940; m. Clara Amanda Hutchins, Sept. 7, 1938; children—Carolyn Fay, Clara Ann, Connie Elizabeth. Intern, Employees Hosp., Fairfield, Ala., 1939-40, resident in obstetrics and gynecology, 1940-43; chief dept. obstetrics and gynecology Lloyd Noland Hosp., Fairfield, 1943-64; practice medicine specializing in obstetrics-gynecology, Birmingham, Ala., 1964—; mem. active staff Birmingham Bapt. Med. Center, Princeton, Bapt. Med. Center, Montclair, St. Vincent, Brookwood hosps., Birmingham; clin. asso. prof. obstetrics and gynecology Sch. Medicine, U. Ala. Diplomate Am. Bd. Obstetrics and Gynecology. Fellow A.C.S.; mem. AMA, So., Ala. med. assns., Jefferson County Med. Soc., Am. Coll. Obstetrics and Gynecology, Central, Ala. assns. obstetricians and gynecologists, Birmingham Obstet. and Gynecol. Soc. (pres. 1962). Presbyterian. Clubs: Vestavia Country, The Club. Home: 3332 Faring Rd Birmingham AL 35223 Office: Suite 4E St Vincent Profl Bldg 2660 10th Ave S Birmingham AL 35205

WEST, RHEA HORACE, JR., educator; b. Loudon, Tenn., Oct. 5, 1920; s. Rhea Horace and Verna (Quillen) W.; B.S. in Accounting, U. Tenn., 1947; postgrad. (Sloan fellow, Mass. Inst. Tech. fellow), Mass. Inst. Tech., 1959-60, 63, Case Inst. Tech., summer 1960; Ph.D., U. Ala., 1964. Asso. prof. mgmt. Wake Forest Coll., 1950-51; budget and reports analyst AEC, Oak Ridge, 1951-55; teaching fellow U. Ala., Tuscaloosa, 1956-57; asst. prof. mgmt. U. Ark., Fayetteville, 1957-59; Sloan teaching intern Mass. Inst. Tech., Cambridge, 1959-60; asso. prof. econs. Carson-Newman Coll., Jefferson City, Tenn., 1960-65; prof. mgmt. Ga. State Coll., 1965-70; prof. mgmt., dir. grad. studies Auburn (Ala.) U., 1970-75; acad. dean Cooper Inst., Knoxville, Tenn., 1976—; mgmt. cons.; cons. Cape Kennedy and Huntsville (NASA), Lockheed Aircraft Co., U.S. Civil Service Commn., others; exec. v.p. Enviro South. Active Center for Study Democratic Instns., Atlanta High Mus. Art; mem. men's com. Internat. Debutantes Ball, N.Y.C., 1976—; supr. registration U. Tenn., 1946-50. Served with AUS, 1943-46. Mem. Am. Accounting Assn., Am. Mgmt. Assn., Am. Soc. Personnel Adminstrn. (nat. dir. industry edn. com. 1958-60), Inst. Mgmt. Scis., Soc. Advancement Mgmt., Acad. Mgmt., Soc. Sloan Fellows, Opelika Arts Assn., Acad. Polit. Sci., Am. Acad. Polit. and Social Scis., AAUP, Am. Legion, Opelika C. of C., Am. Ordnance Assn., Smithsonian Assos., Am. Acad. Arts and Scis., AAAS, Am. Inst. Aeros. and Astronautics, Am. Inst. Decision Scis., Am. Judicature Soc., N.Y. Acad. Scis., Internat. Platform Assn., UN Assn. U.S., Newcomen Soc. N.Am., East Tenn. Personnel and Guidance Assn., Sigma Iota Epsilon, Alpha Kappa Psi (dist. dir. 1965—), Alpha Phi Omega, Kappa Phi Kappa (pres. 1969-70), Alpha Iota Delta. Baptist. Clubs: Mass. Inst. Tech., Harvard Faculty, Kiwanis (pres. 1965). Book rev. editor Personnel Adminstr., 1960—. Contbr. numerous articles and book revs. to profl. publs. Home: 4819 Skyline Dr Knoxville TN 37914 Office: 720 N 5th Ave Knoxville TN 37917

WEST, ROBERT MIDDLETON, JR., banker; b. Austin, Tex., Aug. 3, 1945; s. Robert Middleton and Elizabeth (Kilburn) W.; student Sam Houston State Tchrs. Coll., 1963-65, Sch. Banking, Tex. Tech. U., 1978; m. Linda Ann Faron, May 10, 1969; children—Kerri Lynn, Kelly Lee. Asst. v.p. City Nat. Bank, Austin, 1966-76; v.p., cashier Bank of Austin, 1976—. Served with Army N.G., 1965-71. Mem. Tex. Capital Area Law Enforcement Assn., Bank Adminstrn. Inst. (chpt. pres. 1974-75), Forgery Investigators Assn. Tex., Capital Area Security Council, Am. Soc. Personnel Adminstrn. Methodist. Home: 4404 Balcones Woods Austin TX 78759 Office: 2501 S Congress St Austin TX 78704

WEST, ROBERT VAN OSDELL, JR., petroleum co. exec.; b. Kansas City, Mo., Apr. 29, 1921; s. Robert Van Osdell and Alma Josephine (Quistgard) W.; B.S., U. Tex., 1942, M.S., 1943, Ph.D., 1949; div.; children—Robert Van Osdell, III, Kathryn Anne, Suzanne Small, Patricia Lynn. Pres., Slick Secondary Recovery Corp., San Antonio, 1956-59; pres. Texstar Petroleum Co., San Antonio, 1959-64; pres. Tesoro Petroleum Corp., San Antonio, 1964-71, chmn. bd., 1971—; dir. Frost Nat. Bank of San Antonio, Commonwealth Oil Refining Co., San Antonio, Continental Telephone Corp., Atlanta. Past. sr. warden St. Lukes Episcopal Ch., San Antonio; chmn. bd. Tiwanaku Archeol. Found., La Paz, Bolivia; past trustee City Pub. Service Bd., San Antonio; mem. Engring. Found. Adv. Council, U. Tex., Austin; mem. adv. council Sch. Bus. Adminstrn., St. Mary's U., San Antonio; trustee SW Research Inst., San Antonio; bd. dirs. Cascia Hall Prep. Sch., Tulsa. Mem. Am. Petroleum Inst. (nat. dir.), Ind. Petroleum Assn. Am. (dir.), Tex. Mid-Continent Oil and Gas Assn. (dir.), Greater San Antonio C. of C. (dir.), All-Am. Wildcatters, 25 Year Club of Petroleum Industry. Home and office: 8700 Tesoro Dr San Antonio TX 78286

WEST, SYNTHA JANE, counselor; b. Gladewater, Tex., Oct. 22, 1938; d. Jesse Jimmy and Virginia Lavon (Wood) Traughber; B.A., Baylor U., 1961; M.Ed., E. Tex. State U., 1965, Ph.D. (fellow), 1971; m. Royce Glen West, Dec. 22, 1961; children—Rock David, Royal Jim. Tchr. elemen. sch., Denver, 1961-62, Terrell, Tex., 1962-65, Sulphur Springs, Tex., 1965; counselor Rains High Sch., Emory, Tex., 1966, Kerens (Tex.) Ind. Sch. Dist., 1966-69; dir. guidance Brewer High Sch., White Settlement, Tex., 1971-75; head counselor Longview (Tex.) High Sch., 1975-77, Marshall (Tex.) High Sch., 1977—. Mem. Am. Personnel and Guidance Assn., Tex. Personnel and Guidance Assn., Am. Sch. Counselors Assn., Piney Woods Area Counselors Assn., Tex. Congress Parents and Tchrs. (hon. life), Tex. Tchrs. Assn. (life), NEA, DAR, Phi Delta Kappa, Baylor Alumni Assn. Baptist. Home: 305 Brassell Dr Marshall TX 75670 Office: 201 S College St Marshall TX 75670

WEST, THOMAS CLYDE, welding engr.; b. Statesville, N.C., July 22, 1939; s. Troy C. and Edna E. (Shoemaker) W.; B.S. in Mech. Engring., Va. Poly. Inst., 1962; m. Alice E. Cosner, June 3, 1961; children—Paul, Troy. Design engr., welding engr. Norfolk Naval Shipyard, Portsmouth, Va., 1958-66; welding engr. Naval Ship Engring. Center, Hyattsville, Md., 1966-76; dir. welding Oceaneering Internat., Morgan City, La., 1976-80, Houston, 1980—. Pres., Collingswood Civic Assn., 1964. Recipient Spl. Achievement award Dept. Def., 1971, 75. Mem. Am. Soc. Metals, Am. Welding Soc., Jaycees (external civic improvement second place award 1966). Baptist. Office: PO Box 19464 Houston TX 77024

WESTBURY, JOHN BURNET, educator; b. Dorchester County, S.C., May 7, 1933; s. John Andrew and Malvina Ruth (Avinger) W.; student Wofford Coll., 1951-53; B.S., U. S.C., 1955; M.Ed., U. Ga., 1966; postgrad. U.S.C., 1956, 60, 62, 63, Birmingham So. Coll., summer 1961, Cornell U., 1967, St. Cloud State Coll., 1968, U. San Francisco, 1970, 75, The Citadel, 1970-71, 73, Mich. State U., 1971, Clemson U., 1972. Tchr. math. Andrews (S.C.) Pub. Schs., 1955-57, North Charleston (S.C.) High Sch., 1959-60; tchr. math., head dept. Walterboro (S.C.) Jr. High Sch., 1960-64, 65-69; tchr. math., supr. St. George (S.C.) High Sch., 1969—. Program participant Charleston (S.C.) Nat. Council Tchrs. Math. meeting, 1973, Orlando (Fla.) meeting, 1976. Mem. regional adv. com. S.C. Instructional TV, 1973-76, mem. com. to develop TV geometry series, 1972-74; mem. com. to develop. math. learning activities packages Dorchester Vocat. Sch., 1977. Served with AUS, 1957-59. Shell Merit fellow, summer 1967; NSF grantee, summers 1961-63, 66, 68, 70, 71, 75, also 1964-65; S.C. Commn. on Higher Edn. grantee, summers 1972-73. Mem. Nat. Council Tchrs Math., Math. Assn. Am., Assn. Tchrs. Math (U.K.), Sch. Sci. and Math. Assn., Metric Assn., NEA, S.C. Edn. Assn., Dorchester County Edn. Assn. (sec. 1975-76), Assn. S.C. Math Tchrs. (v.p. 1973-74, treas. 1974-75, 77-78), S.C. Math Council (v.p. 1973-74), S.C. Council Tchrs. Math. (sec. 1978-79). Methodist. Home: 423 N Parler Ave St George SC 29477 Office: 600 Minus St St George SC 29477

WESTENBERGER, JOHN MARSHALL, assn. exec.; b. Livingston, Tenn., May 13, 1940; s. Wilford Curtis and Mildred Louise (Estes) W.; B.A., Birmingham-So. Coll., 1962; m. Margaret Cornelia Stuckenschneider, Sept. 10, 1966; 1 dau., Michelle. Dir. devel. and pub. relations Reinhardt Coll., Waleska, Ga., 1967-69, Tenn. Wesleyan Coll., Athens, 1969-71; exec. asst. Tenn. Med. Assn., Nashville, 1971-73; exec. dir. Nashville Acad. Medicine, 1973-78; dir. Med. Soc. Services, Inc. Exec. v.p. Tennesseans for Better Transp., 1979—. Served with USN, 1962-65. Named one of Outstanding Young of Am., U.S. Jaycees, 1969, 74, 75, Leadership Nashville, 1977. Mem. Pub. Relations Soc. Am. (accredited), Nashville Acad. Medicine (hon.), Am. Soc. Assn. Execs., Nashville Area C. of C., Birmingham-So. Coll. Alumni Assn. (pres. chpt. 1972-74), Sigma Alpha Epsilon. Republican. Methodist. Clubs: Wildwood Swim and Tennis (Brentwood, Tenn.); Capitol Exchange (Nashville); Temple Hills Country (Franklin, Tenn.). Home: 1904 Harpeth River Dr Brentwood TN 37027 Office: 626JC Bradford Bldg Nashville TN 37219

WESTER, MICHAEL O'RAN, editor; b. Lubbock, Tex., Sept. 9, 1941; s. Jack Daniel and Rosanelle (Gray) W.; B.S., Sam Houston State U., 1961; postgrad. Tex. Tech. U., 1976; m. Frances Jane Lorenz, May 27, 1961; children—Tammy Lynn, William Michael, Jerry Daniel. Sports info. dir. Sam Houston State U., Huntsville, Tex., 1959-61; sports writer Houston Post, 1961, San Antonio Express-News, 1961-63, Abilene (Tex.) Reporter-News, 1963-64, Orange (Tex.) Leader, 1964-66; with UPI, 1966—, mgr. W. Tex. Bur., Lubbock, 1967-77, Tex. broadcast editor, Dallas, 1977-78, S.W. Div. overnight broadcast editor, 1978—, Tex. high sch. football editor, 1979—; Shaklee distbr., 1979—. Pres., Little League, Lubbock, 1972-75, dist. adminstr. 1975-77, nat. media advisor to public relations chmn., 1977—; public relations chmn. First Bapt. Ch., Plano, Tex., 1977—. Named Lone Star Conf. Sports Writer of Year, 1963-64. Mem. Tex. Sports Writers, Nat. Football Writers Assn., Tex. Bapt. Public Relations Assn., Tex. Assn. Broadcasters, UPI Tex. Broadcasters Assn., Sigma Delta Chi. Democrat. Club: Lions (sec.-treas. 1975-77, dir. 1974-77, editor dist. gov. newsletter 1975-76). Home: 2701 Lemmontree Ln Plano TX 75074 Office: 13900 Midway Rd Dallas TX 75234

WESTERLUND, ALBERT FOCH, JR., hotel chain exec.; b. Charleston, S.C., Jan. 1, 1947; s. Albert Foch and Grace Myers (Beck) W.; B.S. in Bus. Adminstrn., U. N.C., 1969; m. Sally Jo Singer, Oct. 25, 1970; children—Singer Scott, Jefferson David, Lacy Myers. Mktg. rep. Chrysler Motors Corp., Orlando, Fla., 1974; dist. sales mgr. Trust Houses Forte Hotels Inc. (London), Atlanta, 1975-76; regional sales mgr. Holiday Inns, Inc., Atlanta, 1977-78, dir. sales N. Am. Memphis, 1978-79, dir. internat. sales and mktg., 1979—; mem. European Travel Commn. Served to lt. USN, 1969-73; Vietnam. Decorated Air medal; recipient Outstanding Sales Achievement award Caribbean div. Holiday Inns, Inc., 1978, named Outstanding Regional Sales Mgr., 1977; European Mktg. award European Travel News, 1979. Mem. Am. Mgmt. Assn., Pacific Area Travel Assn., Meeting Planners Internat., Nat. Passenger Traffic Assn., Am. Soc. Travel Agts., Hotel Sales Mgrs. Assn., Skal Internat. Club: Benedicts (Atlanta). Office: Holiday Inns Inc 3796 Lamar Ave Memphis TN 38118

WESTERMAN, CAROLE JOAN, psychologist; b. Phila., Oct. 20, 1937; d. Albert John and Melva Grace (Kuhn) Westerman; B.A., Bucknell U., 1959; M.S. in Edn., U. Pa., 1963, Ed.D., 1973. Tchr., counselor Haverford Twp. (Pa.) Sch. Dist., 1959-65; asst. prof. home econs., counselor Cornell U., Ithaca, N.Y., 1965-68; counseling psychologist U. Pa., Phila., 1968-74; counseling psychologist in pvt. practice, Drexel Hill, Pa., 1974-77; counseling psychologist VA Center, Phila., 1977-78, VA Med. Center, Hampton, Va., 1978—. NDEA fellow, 1962; licensed psychologist, Pa., Mem. Am., Eastern psychol. assns., Am., Pa. personnel and guidance assns. Home: 2013 N Armistead Ave A-5 Hampton VA 23666 Office: VA Med Center Bldg 61 Hampton VA 23667

WESTERMAN, ROBERT DEAN, dentist; b. Malvern, Ark., July 29, 1936; s. Jewell Archie Lafayette and Evelyn Jean (Hunnicutt) W.; ed. La. State U.; D.D.S., Loyola U., New Orleans, 1963; m. Peggy Frances Day, Mar. 2, 1978; children—Rhett Jeffrey, Lecia Kay, Todd Douglas, Sheri Deanne, Jenny Elizabeth. Practice dentistry, Baton Rouge, 1965—; guest lectr. La. State U. Sch. Dentistry, Sch. Medicine, Sch. Vet. Medicine. Bd. dirs. 1st Meth. Ch., 1966-68; chmn. bd. trustees Fellowship Ch., 1971; mem. Gov.'s Commn. on Internat. Year of Child, 1979. Served with USAF, 1963. Mem. ADA, La. Dental Assn., Ark. Dental Assn., Am. Soc. Dentistry for Children (chmn. peer rev. com. 1974-79). Patentee in field of dental instruments. Office: 7931 Jefferson Hwy Baton Rouge LA 70809

WESTFALL, HAZEL ANN (HIGGINBOTHAM), hosp. dietitian; b. Oconee County, Ga., Nov. 30, 1934; d. Joseph Paul and Eula Mae (Murray) Higginbotham; student Young Harris Jr. Coll., 1953; B.S.H.E., U. Ga., Athens, 1955, tchrs. cert. elem. edn., 1969; children by previous marriage—Vickie Lynn Scott, Donna Gail Scott; m. Robert F. Westfall, Nov. 24, 1971; children—Lisa Ann, Robin Michele. Staff dietitian Piedmont Hosp., Atlanta, 1955-59, chief therapeutic dietitian, 1963-67; clinic dietitian Grady Meml. Hosp., Atlanta, 1959-61; dir. dietetics St. Mary's Hosp., Athens, 1967-68; tchr. Gwinnett Bd. Edn., Lawrenceville, Ga., 1969-72; cons. dietitian to nursing homes, Athens, 1972-75; chief therapeutic dietitian Athens Gen. Hosp., 1975—. Mem. Am. Dietetic Assn. (registered), Am.

Diabetes Assn., Am. Heart Assn. Baptist. Home: Route 2 Box 112 Bogart GA 30622 Office: 797 Cobb St Athens GA 30606

WESTFALL, RICHARD OKEY, fin. co. exec.; b. Phila., Dec. 25, 1947; s. Elmer Thompson and Beatrice Lois (Muschenheim) W.; B.S., U. Pa., 1969; M.B.A., U. S.C., 1975; m. Ellen Legare Moss, Mar. 1, 1975; children—Richard Okey, Ellen Legare. Loan officer C & S Nat. Bank of S.C., Orangeburg, 1974-77, asst. v.p. credit adminstrn., 1977-78, v.p., 1978-79; v.p. C & S Corp. of S.C., Columbia, 1979—. Mem. Inst. Internat Auditors. Club: Sertoma (dir. Orangeburg 1975). Home: 4850 Portobello Ct Columbia SC 29206 Office: C & S Corp of SC PO Box 1798 Columbia SC 29202

WESTMORELAND, THOMAS DELBERT, JR., chemist; b. near Vivian, La., June 2, 1940; s. Thomas Delbert and Marguerite Beatrice (Moore) W.; B.S., N. Tex. State U., 1963, M.S., 1965; Ph.D., La. State U., 1971, postdoctoral fellow, 1971-72; m. Martha Verne Beard, Jan. 1, 1966; children—Anne Laura, Kyle Thomas. Chemistry tchr., research dir. Lewisville (Tex.) High Sch., 1964; summer devel. program student Tex. Instruments, Inc., Dallas, 1966; sr. exptl./analytical engr. Power Systems div. United Technologies, South Windsor, Conn., 1972-76; sr. research chemist Pennzoil Co., Shreveport, La., 1976—; chem. cons. Active Parent Tchrs. Orgn. Recipient E.I. du Pont tching. award La. State U., 1968-69. Mem. Am. Chem. Soc. (treas. 1978-79, chmn. 1979-80), Sigma Xi (sec.), Phi Eta Sigma (pres. 1959-60), Alpha Chi Sigma, Kappa Mu Epsilon. Clubs: Jaycees (state dir. Conn. 1976, gov.'s civic leadership award Conn. 1975-76, C. William Brownfield Meml. award 1976), Masons. Contbr. sci. articles to profl. jours. Home: 9319 Midvale Dr Shreveport LA 71118 Office: PO Box 6199 Shreveport LA 71106

WESTON, EDWARD HENRY DRUMMOND, ins. agt.; b. Ft. Worth, Mar. 19, 1937; s. Robert Dixon and Adilee Drummond (Wall) W.; B.A. in English, U. Tex., Austin, 1958; student, scholar Oxford U., Eng., 1958-59. Unit mgr. Transport Ins. Co., 1962-65; personal lines supr. Nat. Union Ins. Co., 1965-68; state agt. No. and Western Tex., Continental Ins. Co., 1968-77; partner Premier Ins. Agy., Dallas, 1977—; instr. Ind. Ins. Agts. Pres., Camp Caddo Homeowners, 1978; sr. warden St. Christopher's Episcopal Ch.; nat. dir. U.S. Jaycees, 1969. Recipient Disting. Service award Tex. Jaycees. Mem. Ind. Ins. Agts. Dallas and Tex. Club: Toastmasters. Home: Rt 1 Box 21A Quinlan TX 75474 Office: 8533 Ferndale St PO Box 38181 Dallas TX 75238

WESTON, WILLIAM DAVID, univ. adminstr.; b. Melrose, Mass., Mar. 16, 1932; s. Wilbur Franklin and Eleanor Bailey (Slocomb) W.; B.S., Castleton State Coll., 1953; M.Ed., Boston U., 1954; postgrad. Syracuse U., 1960, U. Miami, 1963, Duke U., 1969, N.C. State U., 1969, U. N.C. Chapel Hill, 1974—; m. Francenia Strayhorn, Jan. 1, 1980; 1 dau., Holly Louise. Tchr. pub. schs., Vt., 1954-57; guidance dir. pub. schs. Walpole, N.H., 1959-60; counselor Palm Beach (Fla.) Jr. Coll., 1960-61; counselor N.C. State U. Raleigh, 1962-65; guidance dir. Colegio Americano de Quito (Ecuador), 1965-66; asso. dir. counseling, dean men, dean student devel. N.C. State U., Raleigh, 1966-76, dir. coop. edn., 1977—. Served with U.S. Army, 1957-59. Gen. Electric fellow, 1960; Univ. fellow Fla. State U., 1964. Mem. Am., N.C. personnel and guidance assns., Am., N.C. coll. personnel assns., AAUP, Acad. Affairs Adminstrs., Coop. Edn. Assn., N.C. Coop. Edn. Assn. Democrat. Mem. United Ch. of Christ. Home: Rt 4 Box 675 Raleigh NC 27606 Office: PO Box 5036 NC State Univ Raleigh NC 27650

WESTPHELING, ROBERT PAUL, JR., newspaper publisher; b. St. Joseph, Mo., Jan. 2, 1914; s. Robert Paul and Martha Theresa (Amelunxen) W.; B.J., U. Mo., 1936; m. Johanna Serio, Feb. 4, 1940; children—Robert Paul III, Mary Johanna. With St. Joseph News-Press, 1936-37, Effingham (Ill.) Daily Record, 1937, Gallatin (Tenn.) Examiner, 1937-38, Racine (Wis.) Day, 1938-39, Clarksdale (Miss.) Daily Register, 1939-41, Clarksdale (Miss.) Daily Press, 1941-42; mgr. advt. Washington Post, 1946-47; pub. Fulton (Ky.) News, 1947-72; pub. Hickman (Ky.) Courier, 1972—; pres. Ken-Tenn Broadcasting Corp., Fulton, 1962-67. Mem. Ky. Econ. Devel. Commn., 1963-70; activity chmn. Internat. Banana Festival, Fulton, 1964-68; chmn. Hickman-Fulton County River Port Authority, 1976—. Served to maj. AUS, 1942-46; ETO, PTO. Decorated AF Commendation Medal; hon. Rotarian; Ky. col.; recipient 57 excellence awards in newspaper publishing Ky. Press Assn., 1948-76. Mem. Ky. Press Assn. (pres. 1960), Am. Fedn. Musicians, Fulton C. of C., Delta Tau Delta. Democrat. Roman Catholic. Clubs: Rotary (pres. Fulton 1960), K.C. Home: The Highlands PO Box 598 Fulton KY 42041 Office: PO Box 70 Hickman KY 42050

WETCHER, KENNETH, psychiatrist; b. Siberia, Apr. 16, 1941; came to U.S., 1947, naturalized, 1953; s. Morris and Judith W.; B.S., CCNY, 1963; M.D., SUNY, Bklyn., 1967; m. Goldie B. Cohen, Apr. 11, 1976; children—Elyssa, Serena. Intern, Sinai Hosp. Balt., 1967-68; resident in psychiatry Psychiat. Inst., U. Md., 1968-69, Baylor U., 1971-73; practice medicine specializing in psychiatry Wetcher Clinic, Houston, 1973—; co-owner ComputerLand. Pres., Congregation Shaar Hashalom, 1974. Served to capt. USAF, 1969-71. Mem. Am. Psychiat. Assn., Tex. Med. Assn., Harris County Med. Soc., Houston Group Psychotherapy Soc., Am. Group Psychotherapy Assn., Houston Psychiat. Soc. Home: 2010 Port Royal Dr Houston TX 77058 Office: 16902 El Camino Real 2C Houston TX 77058

WETHINGTON, THOMAS DEWEY, petrochem. co. exec.; b. Delta, Colo., Dec. 5, 1926; s. Herbert Omer and Jenny Marie (Smith) W.; B.S.M.E., U. Colo., 1950; M. Engring., Tex. Tech. U., 1971; m. Jennevieve Laverne Rieke, Mar. 6, 1951; children—Lynette Diane, Susan Marie, David Thomas, Karen Rae. Insp., Cadillac motor div. Gen. Motors Co., Detroit, 1950; warehouse receiving clk. Crane-O'Fallon Co., Pueblo, Colo., 1950-51; time study and methods engr. Gates Rubber Co., Denver, 1951-57; with Phillips Petroleum Co., 1957—, supr. mech. engring. design, 1957-72, supr. planning and materiel control, Phillips, Tex., 1972-75, maintenance and services supt., 1975-78, chief constrn. planning engr., 1978—; instr. Frank Phillips Jr. Coll. Del., Hutchinson County (Tex.) Democratic Conv., 1958-72, Tex. Republican Party Conv., 1976. Served with USAAF, 1945. Registered profl. engr., Tex. Mem. Borger C. of C., Tex. Tech. U. Dad's Assn. (co-chmn. publs. com. and recognitions com. 1972—). Mem. Christian Ch. (Disciples of Christ). Home: 1305 Melmart Dr Bartlesville OK 74003 Office: Phillips Petroleum Co Bartlesville OK 74004

WETZEL, ALBERT JOHN, univ. adminstr., systems analyst, cons.; b. New Orleans, Dec. 29, 1917; s. Albert John and Emelie (Willoz) W.; B.Engring., Tulane U., 1939; M.S., Johns Hopkins U., 1950; postgrad. U. Calif., Los Angeles, 1956; m. Helen Elizabeth Zurad, Sept. 7, 1946; children—Albert John, Elizabeth Ann, Joan Clark, Edward Russel. Commd. 2d lt. C.E., U.S. Army, 1941, advanced through grades to col. USAF, 1956; service in Europe, Asia, Middle East; wing comdr. SAC, 1955-57; dir. Titan ICBM and Gemini Space Program, 1957-62; exec. dir. U.S. Air Force Council, 1962-63; dir. strategic programs, def., research and engring., Office Sec. Def., 1963-65; ret., 1965; dir. research and sponsored programs, then dir. univ. devel. Tulane U., 1965-76, v.p. alumni and univ. affairs, 1976—, adj. prof. mgmt. and engring. mgmt., 1965—; mem. rocket and space panel President's Sci. Adv. Com., 1965—; bd. dirs. Gulf South Research Inst., Inst. Def. Analysis, Washington; del. Nat. Conf. Advancement Research. Bd. dirs. Walter Clark Teagle Found., N.Y.C., Oak Ridge Asso. Univs., Navy League U.S., Crippled Children's Hosp., New Orleans, La. Council Music and Performing Arts, Council Devel. French in La., Delgado Jr. Coll., Girl Scouts; exec. com. local Boy Scouts Am.; commr. La. Ednl. TV Authority; v.p. New Orleans Cath. Found. Decorated Legion of Merit, Armed Forces and Air Force Commendation medal. Registered profl. engr., Ohio. Mem. Greater New Orleans Area C. of C. (v.p.), Sigma Xi, Kappa Sigma, Tau Beta Pi, Omicron Delta Kappa. Clubs: Internat. House, Plimsoll (New Orleans); University (N.Y.C.); Army-Navy (Washington); Rotary. Home: 7 Richmond Pl New Orleans LA 70115 Office: 206 Gibson Hall Tulane Univ New Orleans LA 70118

WETZEL, (HUGH) DONALD, supermarket exec.; b. Owensboro, Ky., Oct. 24, 1945; s. Hugh Thomas and Lovie (McGehee) Wetzel Mitchell; B.A., Ky. Wesleyan Coll., 1968; m. Sara Ann Ireland, June 17, 1967; children—Shannon, Melanie, Ross. Sch. tchr. Daviess County Pub. Sch. System, 1968-70; part owner, v.p. Wetzel's Super Markets, Inc., Ownesboro; dir. Lincoln Fed. Savs. & Loan Assn. Named Ky. Col., Outstanding Young Man Am., 1972. Mem. Super Market Inst. Mem. Christian Ch. Office: PO Box 1665 Owensboro KY 42301

WETZEL, JOSEPH PAUL, JR., med. equipment co. exec.; b. N.Y.C., May 6, 1935; s. Joseph Paul and Grace Bertha (Kremer) W.; B.S. in Bus., U. Conn., 1957. Regional mgr. Hyland Labs. div. Baxter-Travenol Co., Los Angeles, 1959-68, v.p. diagnostic research dir., 1968-70; dir. Gen. Sci. Corp., Bridgeport, Conn., 1969-71; sr. v.p., dir. Hycel Inc., Houston, 1972—; dir. Ames Packaging Co., BWH Corp. Served with USAF, 1957, 61-62. Mem. Sci. Apparatus Mfrs. Assn., Health Industry Mfrs. Assn. Clubs: Univ. (Houston); Tex. Nat. Golf (Willis). Home: 10203 Chevy Chase St Houston TX 77042 Office: Hycel Inc 7800 Westpark St Houston TX 77042

WEYHRAUCH, ERNEST EMIL, librarian, univ. dean; b. N.Y.C., July 20, 1926; s. Frederick and Martha (Ingber) W.; B.A., N.Y. U., 1951; M.S., Columbia U., 1959; M.A., Eastern Ky. U., 1980; postgrad. CCNY, 1955-57, Ind. U., 1965-66; m. Mary Ekris, July 8, 1955; children—Ernest Christopher, Anne Martha. Tech. asst. N.Y. Pub. Library, 1952-55; tchr. pub. schs., N.Y.C., 1955-57; cataloger, asst. edn. librarian, chief circulation Bklyn. Coll. Library, 1957-64; edn. librarian Ind. U., 1964-66; dir. libraries Eastern Ky. U., Richmond, 1966-75, dean libraries and learning resources, 1975—; mem. Ky. Gov.'s Pre-White House Conf. on Libraries. Mem. Ky. Library Assn. (v.p., pres. elect 1972-73), Ky., Madison County hist. socs., Nat. Rifle Assn., Phi Alpha Theta. Contbr. articles to profl. mags. Home: 211 Ridgeway Richmond KY 40475

WEYL, W. LEONARD, surgeon; b. Frankfurt, Maine, May 28, 1921; s. Herrmann and Ruth (Frank) W.; A.B., Earlham Coll., 1942; B.S., U. Ill., 1944, M.D., 1945; M.S. in Surgery, Georgetown U., 1953; m. Nancy Schmidt, Sept. 18, 1944; children—John Michael, Nancy Katherine. Intern, Henrotin Hosp., Chgo., 1945-46; resident Georgetown U. Hosps., 1949-53; practice medicine, specializing in surgery, Arlington, Va., 1953—; v.p., dir. NVDH Corp., Arlington, 1961—; dir. U.S. Savs. & Loan, Arlington, 1976-78; chief surgery N. Va. Doctors Hosp., 1961-78, emeritus, 1978—; asst. clin. prof. surgery Georgetown U., Washington, 1953—; cons. to U.S. EPA, 1972-78, Med. Service of D.C., 1977—. Trustee, Med. Service of D.C., 1957-58, 64-70; mem. Commonwealth of Va. Bd. Health, 1978—, Washington Drama Soc., 1979—. Served to capt. AUS, 1943-48. Diplomate Am. Bd. Surgery; recipient Vicennial medal Georgetown U., 1974. Fellow ACS; mem. Arlington County Med. Soc. (pres. 1972; Welburn award 1977), Med. Soc. Va. (pres. 1976-77), No. Va. Acad. Surgery (pres. 1958), AMA, Southeastern Surg. Congress. Republican. Presbyn. Clubs: Army Navy Country, Washington Golf and Country, Farmington Country, Rotary. Contbr. articles in field to profl. jours.; editor emeritus The Med. Bull. of No. Va., 1976—. Home: 1330 Mercer Ln McLean VA 22101 Office: 4625 Old Dominion Dr Arlington VA 22207

WEYSHAM, ALCIDE JOHN, lawyer; b. New Orleans, Oct. 17, 1914; s. Arnold J. and Clare (Knight) W.; A.B., Tulane U., 1939, LL.B., 1939; m. Frances Lillian Badalamenti; 1 dau. by previous marriage, Sheryl Clare (Mrs. Robert Fleming, Jr.); stepchildren—Ilene (Mrs. Edmond Catoire III), Alvin Joseph Carriere, Rosalyn Carriere. Admitted to La. bar, 1939, since pvt. practice, New Orleans; pvt. practice ltd. to notarial proc., 1975—; counsel criminal div. Legal Aid Bur. New Orleans, 1942-44; asst. counsel New Orleans Levee Bd., 1948-50; atty. fire marshall La., 1950-52; instr. real estate Our Lady of Holy Cross Coll., New Orleans. Pres. Central Gentill Civic and Improvement Assn., 1956—; chmn. Citizens' Com. Lake Pontchartrain; song dir., soloist Our Lady of Guadalupe Ch., New Orleans, 1976—. Mem. Am., La., New Orleans bar assns., Am. Judicature Soc., Internat. Platform Assn. Home: 5615 Bancroft Dr New Orleans LA 70122 Office: 4948 Chef Menteur Hwy New Orleans LA 70126

WHALEY, PERRY, educator; b. Beulaville, N.C., Oct. 25, 1928; s. William Franklin and Nellie Jane W.; A.A., Lenoir Community Coll., 1971; B.S. in Vocat. Indsl. Edn. with honors, N.C. State U., 1976, M.S. in Vocat. Indsl. Edn., 1980; m. Ruby Inez Hall, Mar. 21, 1953; children—Marisa Inez, Anita Perrie, Aleta Charlotte. Owner radio and TV service, Beulaville, 1953-58; field engr. Bendix Field Engring. Corp., Owings Mills, Md., 1958-66; instr. electronic servicing James Sprunt Tech. Coll., Kenansville, N.C., 1966—; mem. accreditation program Commn. Occupational Edn. Instns.; team mem. So. Assn. Colls. and Schs. Organizer, Little League for Girls softball, Duplin County, 1974. Served with USAF, 1948-52. Cert. Internat. Soc. Cert. Electronic Technicians. Mem. Faculty Assn. N.C. Community Coll. System (treas. 1976-81), N.C. Vocat. Assn., Am. Vocat. Assn., VFW (past post comdr.), Iota Lambda Sigma. Democrat. Clubs: Rose Hill Optimist (pres. 1978-79), Masons (past master), Shriners, Eastern Star (dist. dep. grand patron 1976-77). Home: 102 E Center St Rose Hill NC 28458 Office: James Sprunt Tech Coll PO Box 398 Kenansville NC 28349

WHALEY, RICHARD W., bus. exec.; b. Dallas, Feb. 6, 1948; s. Jack W. and Ola B. W.; B.J., U. Tex., 1971; m. Kathey Whaley. With Elfab Corp., Dallas, 1971—, quality assurance mgr., 1973-77, sales mgr., 1977-78, dir. mktg. and sales, 1978—. Mem. Am. Soc. Quality Control, Am. Mgmt. Assn. Office: 4200 Wiley Post Addison TX 75001

WHALING, ANNE, educator; b. Houston, Mar. 30, 1914; d. Horace Morland and Annie Byrd (Ward) Whaling; B.A., So. Meth. U., 1933, M.A., 1934; Ph.D., Yale U., 1946. Cataloger, specialist in music, fgn. langs. So. Meth. U., 1947-55; tchr. English dept. Arlington State Coll., 1955, instr., 1955-57, asst. prof., 1957-60, asso. prof., 1960-68; asso. prof. English, U. Tex. at Arlington, 1968-71, prof., 1971—. Program annotator for chamber music series Dallas Mus. Fine Arts, 1956—; bd. dirs. Dallas Chamber Music Soc., 1954—; chmn. Pro Musica, Dallas, 1960-62. Recipient Decima Lantern award, So. Meth. U., 1933; named Woman of Achievement, So. Meth. U. Assn., 1968. Mem. Am. Studies Assn. Tex. (councilor 1961-62), South Central Modern Lang. Assn., AAUW (chmn. fellowship com. Dallas br. 1959-64), Modern Lang. Assn., Am. Studies Assn. (co-founder Tex. chpt. 1956), Phi Beta Kappa, Delta Kappa Gamma. Methodist. Home: 3320 Daniels Ave Dallas TX 75205 Office: Dept English U Tex Arlington TX 76010

WHARRIE, JOHN ROBERT, environ. scientist; b. Red Bud, Ill., Mar. 6, 1950; s. John Dale and Ellen Marie (Wooden) W.; B.S., U. Ariz., 1972; m. A. Jana Vasey, May 27, 1971; children—John R., Robert T., Elizabeth M. Environ. test chemist Phelps Dodge Corp., Tucson, 1973-77; environ. engr. Ariz. Electric Power, Chochise, Ariz., 1977-78; mgr. pollution control Marquette Co., Nashville, 1978—. Mem. Air Pollution Control Assn. Home: 365 Binkley Dr Nashville TN 37211 Office: 1st American Center Nashville TN 37238

WHATLEY, JACQUELINE BELTRAM (MRS. JOHN W. WHATLEY), lawyer; b. West Orange, N.J., Sept. 26, 1944; d. Quirino R. and Eliane (Gruet) Beltram; B.A., U. Tampa, 1966; J.D., Stetson U., 1969; m. John W. Whatley, June 25, 1966. Admitted to Fla. bar, 1969, Alaska bar, 1971; practiced in Anchorage, 1971-73; mem. firms Gibbons, Tucker, McEwen, Smith, Miller & Whatley, Tampa, Fla., 1969-71, 1973—; dir. Fla. Investment and Devel. Corp., Carrollwood State Bank. Arbitrator Am. Can Co., Continental Can Co., United Steelworkers Am., Tampa, 1974—. Bd. dirs. Traveler's Aid Soc. Tampa. Mem. Am., Alaska, Fla., Tampa-Hillsborough County, Anchorage bar assns., Fla. Walking Horse Assn. (pres., dir.), Athena Soc., Nu Beta Epsilon, Delta Phi Epsilon, Phi Alpha Theta. Home: PO Box 17595 Tampa FL 33612 Office: 606 Madison St Tampa FL 33601

WHATLEY, ROD WARNER, architect; b. Gadsden, Ala., May 11, 1947; s. Charles Warner and Betty (Dobbins) W.; B.Arch., Auburn U., 1970; M.Arch., M. Landscape Architecture, Harvard U., 1976; 1 dau., Elizabeth Ann. Architect, J. Robert Hillier, Princeton, N.J., 1970-71, Teledyne Architects, Huntsville, Ala., 1970-74; prin. Rabun Whatley & Hatch, Architects and Planners, Atlanta, 1976—; designer Huntsville Madison County Mental Health Center, 1975, U. Ala. Sch. Nursing, Huntsville, 1977. Hon. staff mem. Huntsville Madison County Mental Health Bd.; bd. dirs. Montessori Schs. of Huntsville, 1972-73, chmn. bd. dirs., 1973-74. Registered architect, Ala.; cert. Nat. Council Archtl. Registration Bds. Mem. AIA, High Mus. Art. Methodist. Club: Harvard (Atlanta). Office: Suite 710 Two Piedmont Center 3565 Piedmont Rd NE Atlanta GA 30305

WHEATLEY, DAVID COE, architect; b. St. Louis, Feb. 21, 1929; s. Thomas and Nora (Allen) W.; student Washington U., St. Louis, 1950-53, Frank Lloyd Wright Sch. Architecture, 1953-59; m. Susan Jacobs, Mar. 30, 1957. Staff architect Frank Lloyd Wright Found., Spring Green, Wis. and Phoenix, 1959-69; participated in constrn. Guggenheim Mus., N.Y.C., 1958-60, Marin County Govt. Center, San Raphael, Calif., 1960-63; architect Wheatley-Merritt Assos., Dallas, 1969-73; v.p. planning and design Centex Homes Corp., Dallas, 1973—. Mem. City of Dallas Task Force, Historic Preservation Commn., Nat. Adv. Panel, 1979. Served with USMC, 1946-49. Registered architect, Ariz., Calif., Colo., Fla., Ga., Ind., Ill., Iowa, Kans., Md., Minn., N.J., N.Y. State, Nev., S.C., Tex., Va., Wis., D.C. Mem. AIA, Soc. Archtl. Historians, Tex. Soc. Architects, Historic Preservation League, Nat. Council Archtl. Registration Bds., Nat. Trust for Historic Preservation, Internat. Conf. Bldg. Ofcls., Bldg. Ofcls. Code Adminstrs., Nat. Acad. Code Adminstrs., Constrn. Specifications Inst., Urban Land Inst. Prin. works include Aitken residence, Woodside, Calif., 1961, Warren residence, St. Joseph, Mich., 1962, Kittleson residence, Scottsdale, Ariz., 1972, Royse residence, LaGrange, Tex., 1973, Holmdel Garden Center, N.J., 1973, Menard residence, Hillsboro, Tex., 1973, Harborside, Foster City, Calif., 1974, La Laderas, Hercules, Calif., 1975, Pitcairn, Foster City, 1976, Langley Oaks, McLean, Va., 1976, Woodbury Village, Miami, 1978, Burke Village, Va., 1979. Home: 5109 Swiss Ave Dallas TX 75214 Office: 4600 Republic Bank Tower Dallas TX 75201

WHEATLEY, EUGENE AUSTIN, JR., physicist; b. Cin., Aug. 12, 1928; s. Eugene Austin and Grace (Appleton) W.; M.E., U. Cin., 1951, M.S. in Physics, 1954; m. Dolores Gerhardt, June 9, 1956 (div. Dec. 1965); m. 2d, Carol Betty Houck, Nov. 8, 1969. Controls systems engr. Gen. Electric Co., Evendale, Ohio, 1955-58; staff mem. nuclear rocket div. Los Alamos Sci. Lab., 1958-61; asst. sr. engr. NERVA nuclear rocket div. Aerojet Gen., Azusa, Calif., 1961-63; staff mem. AC spark plug div. Gen. Motors, El Segundo, Calif., 1963-64; prin. engr. Saturn V flight evaluation working group Boeing Co., Huntsville, Ala., 1964-69; cons. Code Research Corp., Huntsville, 1970; sr. engr. Skylab, Space Shuttle Martin Marietta Corp., Huntsville, New Orleans, 1971—. Mem. Am. Phys. Soc., Am. Nuclear Soc., ASME, Am. Inst. Aeros. and Astronautics, Internat. Platform Assn., Pi Tau Sigma. Club: Point Aquarius (Ala.) Country. Contbr. articles in field to profl. jours. Home: 1619 Drake Ave SE Huntsville AL 35802 Office: Martin Marietta Corp PO Box 29304 New Orleans LA 70189

WHEATLEY, RICHARD LINDSAY, JR., banker, lawyer; b. Vinita, Okla., July 17, 1933; s. Richard L. and Mary E. (Hooks) W.; B.A., U. Okla., LL.B., 1957; m. patience Fullerton, June 17, 1956; children—Richard, Gibson, Mary Faith, Ben. Admitted to Okla. bar, 1957; practice law, Vinita, Okla., 1957-69; adminstr. consumer affairs, State of Okla., 1969-71; chmn. Univ. Bank, Stillwater, Okla., 1971—, pres., 1975—; pres. Orion Capital Corp., 1979—; dir. 1st State Bank, Ketchum, Okla., 1964-69; mem. Okla. Ho. of Reps., 1957-59. Bd. dirs. Stillwater Ind. Authority, 1978—. Served to capt. U.S. Army. Mem. Okla. Bar Assn., Am. Bankers Assn., Okla. Bankers Assn. Democrat. Episcopalian. Club: Rotary. Office: University Bank Box 1067 Stillwater OK 74074

WHEATON, ELIZABETH LEE, educator; b. Sherman, Tex.; d. Percival King and Minerva Fay (Ratzel) Fulton; student Rice Inst., 1920-21, San Angelo Coll., 1949-51; certificate S.W. Tex. State Coll., 1922, Kansas City-Horner Conservatory, 1929; B.S., McMurray Coll., 1952; postgrad. A. and I. Coll., 1953-54; m. Grant Wiltsie Wheaton, Dec. 23, 1923. Tchr. pub. schs., Texas City, Tex., 1922-24; tchr. speech, 1922-29, voice and speech, 1929-47; reporter, soc. editor Texas City Sun, 1930-36; corr. Galveston (Tex.) News, 1934; dir. The Texas City Hour, radio sta. KGBC, 1947; elementary tchr. La Feria (Tex.) Pub. Schs., 1952—; tchr. voice, speech, 1956-57; originator, writer, dir., master Story Book Time TV series sta. KRGV-TV, 1957; mem. staff S.W. Writers Conv., Corpus Christi, Tex., 1954—. Chmn. pub. relations La Feria Garden Club, Bicentennial Commn. of La Feria, display chmn. Friends of Library. Recipient Thomas Jefferson Southern award E.P. Dutton Co. and Va. Quar. Rev., 1941; U.S. Bicentennial award D.A.R. Mem. Composers, Authors and Artists Am. (chpt. pres.; mem. nat. pub. com. 1960), Tex. Woman's Press Assn., Tex. Tchrs. Assn., Poetry Soc. Tex. (charter Lower Rio Grande chpt., dir.), Tex. Inst. Letters, Am. Legion Aux. (pres. Texas City, San Angelo and LaFeria units, Tex. music chmn. 1960), Lower Rio Grande Valley Hist. Soc., Community Concert Assn. (dir.), Poetry Soc. Am. (charter mem. Lower Rio Grande Valley chpt.), D.A.R. (pub. relations com. Lt. Thomas Barlow chpt., Excellence in Journalism award Tex. Soc. 1973, 74), Delta Kappa Gamma (scholarship com. Zeta Rho chpt.). Mem. Order Eastern Star (past matron Texas City). Author: Mr. George's Joint, 1941; Texas City Remembers, 1948; also poems, articles, revs. in various mags. and newspapers. Home and office: Valley Vista Box 1026 La Feria TX 78559

WHEATON, GRANT WILTSIE, journalist; b. Kewanee, Ill., Apr. 27, 1895; s. Jeremiah Grant and Myrtle Mable (Hubbard) W.; student Draughan's Bus. Coll., Galveston, Tex., 1920, McMurray Coll., Abilene, Tex., 1951-52; m. Elizabeth Lee Fulton, Dec. 23, 1923. Various positions from sec. to v.p., gen. mgr. to corp. sec., asst. gen. mgr. Texas City (Tex.) Terminal Ry. Co., 1922-48; sec. Terminal Indsl. Land Co., 1943-48; asso. E. Gordon Perry Real Estate, Ins. Agy., San Angelo, Tex., 1948-51; owner Valley Vista Farm, La Feria, Tex., 1953-79; originator, mgr., editor Suez Scribblings San Angelo, 1950-51; field editor H. L. Peace Publs., New Orleans, 1953-57; free lance writer, 1957-79; staff lectr. Southwestern Writers Conf., Corpus Christi, Tex., 1956-60. Treas. March Dimes, Texas City, 1936-38; dir. La Feria March of Dimes, 1959-66, dir. Cameron County chpt., 1961-67. Served wtih F.A., U.S. Army, 1917-18. Decorated Silver Star medal, Purple Heart. Mem. Lower Rio Grande Valley Hist. Soc., La Feria C. of C., La Feria Live Stock Club, Am. Legion, Vets. World War I. Am. Security Council. Presbyterian (elder). Clubs: Mason (Shriner), Rotary, La Feria (past pres.). Contbr. to newspapers, non-fiction mags. Died July 7, 1979. Address: Valley Vista Box 1026 La Feria TX 78559

WHEELBARGER, JOHNNY J., educator, minister; b. Dayton, Va., Feb. 15, 1937; s. Charles W. and Rosie B. (Minnick) W.; A.B., Bethany Nazarene Coll., 1963; M.Ed., U. Va., 1967, Ed.D., 1971; M.L.S., George Peabody Coll. for Tchrs., 1975, Ph.D., 1977; m. Bonnie M. Propst, Nov. 28, 1957. Ordained to ministry, 1964; pastor, Va. Dist. Ch. of the Nazarene, Manassas, Va., 1963-67; tchr. Va. Pub. Schs., 1964-68; asst. prof. Eastern Nazarene Coll., Quincy, Mass., 1970-71; dir. learning resources Trevecca Nazarene Coll., Nashville, Tenn., 1972—, prof. edn., 1975—; pastor Santa Fe Circuit of Chs. of the Nazarene, 1973—. Served with USAF, 1954-58. Mem. Assn. for Ednl. Communications and Tech., Am. Tenn. library assns. Tenn. Audiovisual Assn., Assn. of Tchr. Educators, Phi Delta Kappa, Kappa Delta Pi, Beta Phi Mu, Phi Delta Lambda. Contbr. articles to profl. jours. Home: 210 Perlen Dr Nashville TN 37206 Office: Trevecca Nazarene College Nashville TN 37210

WHEELER, ARLINE ZILPHA FRANK (MRS. DOCK WHEELER), ret. educator; b. Sapupa, Okla., July 16, 1908; d. Wiley C. and Rosa E. (Fuqua) Frank; B.S. in Edn., S.W. State Coll., Mo., 1948; M.S., U. Kans., 1954; diploma Advanced Study in Vocat. Counselor Edn., U. Ark., 1964; m. Dock Wheeler, Feb. 26, 1927. Tchr. pub. schs., Ozark County, Mo., 1936-42; tchr. social studies high sch., Gainesville, Mo., 1942-48; tchr. social studies high sch. Bur. Indian Affairs, Haskell Inst., Lawrence, Kans., 1948-53, tchr., counselor Haskell Indian Jr. Coll. (formerly Haskell Inst.), 1963-71; tchr., adviser Stewart (Nev.) Indian Sch., 1953-54, Steamboat Boarding Sch., Ganado, Ariz., 1954-55, Cheyenne River Boarding Sch., Cheyenne Agy. S.D., 1957-60; prin. Klagetoh Community Boarding Sch., Ganado, 1955-57; prin., tchr. Dilcon Trailer Sch. (Ariz.) and Coal Mine Mesa, 1960-62; head dept. guidance Tuba City Boarding Sch. (Ariz.), 1962-63; engaged in cattle bus., 1971—. Chmn., Klagetob chpt. ARC, 1955-57; chmn. Ft. Defiance Sub-Agy. Safety Com., 1955-57. Recipient Superior Service award Bur. Indian Affairs, 1972. Mem. Benton County Anti-Cruelty Soc., Internat. Platform Assn., Am. Personnel and Guidance Assn., Nat., Ark., Northwest Ark. ret. tchrs. assns., AAUW. Democrat. Mem. Christian Ch. (ways and means chmn., past pres. Christian Women's Fellowship, tchr. adult Sunday Sch. class). Mem. Order Eastern Star, White Shrine. Home: Rural Route 2 Rogers AR 72756

WHEELER, CARLTON EDWARD, plastics co. exec.; b. Elmira Heights, N.Y., June 14, 1923; s. Irvine Dewitt and Margaret Pearl (Shaffer) W.; student Ill. Inst. Tech., 1942—, W.Va. U., 1943-44; B.S. in Chemistry, Antioch Coll., 1950; m. Anne Mitchell Wilson, June 25, 1949; children—Scott Marshall, David Charles, Elizabeth Boone. Tech. dir. Dicks Armstrong Pontius Co., Dayton, Ohio, 1950-57; v.p. Interex Corp., Guanica, P.R., 1957-58, pres., 1958—; mgr. Brockton Plastics Co. (Mass.), 1966-68; mgr. plastics div. Compro Corp., Pawtucket, R.I., 1968-70; pres. Interex Internat., Inc., 1972—. Served with U.S. Army, 1943-46. Home: Playa San Jacinto Guanica PR 00653 Office: Box 805 Guanica PR 00653

WHEELER, CHARLES BOWEN, oil co. exec.; b. Toronto, Canada, Mar. 12, 1931; s. Orby Clinton and Katherine (Riggs) W.; B.S., Stanford U., 1952, M.S., 1953; m. Jan Nette Moses, Apr. 12, 1954; children—Katherine F., Margaret B., Jan Kristan. Research geologist Exxon Corp., Tulsa, 1953-55, various geol. positions, Venezuela, Colombia, Peru, 1955-65, asst. mktg. mgr., Lima, Peru, 1965-66, mgr., Cartagena, Colombia, 1966-67, Latin Am. area advisor, N.Y.C., 1967-68, U.S. wholesale fuel bus. mgr., Houston, 1968-70, dir., pres., Buenos Aires, Argentina, 1970-73, dir., v.p., Coral Gables, Fla., 1973-79, exec. v.p., dir., 1979—. Mem. Am. Assn. Petroleum Geologists, Geol. Soc. Am., Phi Beta Kappa. Club: Riviera Country. Office: 396 Alhambra Circle Coral Gables FL 33134

WHEELER, EDWIN DERRICK, assn. exec.; b. Austin, Tex., Jan. 20, 1947; s. Dixie Lee and Atrelle (Powell) W.; A.S., Henderson County Jr. Coll., 1967; B.A., U. Tex., 1969; postgrad. S.W. Tex. State U., 1972; m. Nancy Lee Kownslar, May 31, 1969; children—Karen Lee, Ryan Derrick. Tchr., coach Waco (Tex.) Ind. Sch. Dist., 1969-70, Austin (Tex.) Ind. Sch. Dist., 1970-73; programmer/analyst data processing dept. U. Tex., Austin, 1973-76; asso. dir., mgr. Western Data Processing Center, Am. Cancer Soc., Austin, 1976—. Baptist. Home: 11600 Natrona St Austin TX 78759 Office: 3834 Spicewood Springs Rd Austin TX 78766

WHEELER, ISABEL CRICHLOW, educator; b. Jonesboro, Ark., June 9, 1929; d. Joseph Wilson and Daisie (Dawson) Crichlow; A.B., U. Mo., 1950; M.A., Ohio State U., 1951; Ph.D., St. Louis U., 1979; m. Raymond T. Wheeler, June 23, 1956; children—Sophia, Daisie, Lucy, Laurie. Copy editor C. V. Mosby Co., St. Louis, 1952-54; fellow dept. English, Washington U., St. Louis, 1954-56; faculty Bethel Coll., McKenzie, Tenn., 1969—, asso. prof. dept. English, 1976—, chmn. student life com., 1979—. Mem. Paris-Henry County Library Bd., 1968-74; bd. dirs. Paris-Henry County Friends of Library, 1968-71; neighborhood chmn. Girl Scouts U.S.A., 1968-69; pres. Atkins-Porter PTA, 1969-70; adminstrv. bd., chmn. pastor-parish relations com. First United Meth. Ch., Paris, Tenn., 1976-80. Lottye McCall scholar, 1974. Mem. Women's Soc. of Christian Service, MLA, AAUP (pres. chpt. 1976-77), Tenn. Philol. Assn., Nat. Soc. Collegiate Journalists, Nat. Council Coll. Publs. Advisers, Tenn. Fedn. Women's Clubs, Delta Kappa Gamma. Democrat. Methodist. Contbr. articles to profl. jours. Home: Route 3 PO Box 195 Paris TN 38242 Office: PO Box 63B Bethel Coll McKenzie TN 38201

WHEELER, JAMES LEON, gen. contractor, real estate developer, Army capt.; b. Sedalia, Mo., Dec. 4, 1946; s. Thomas Greer and Lelia (Hogan) W.; A.S. in E.E., Grantham Tech. Sch., 1967; certificate in engring., Chgo. Tech. Sch., 1968; A.S., State U. N.Y., Albany, 1975; student Memphis State U., 1979; m. Larna Joy Coston, Jan. 1, 1980; children—Monica Lee, James Leon Jr., Kenneth Coston. Asso. engr. Gen. Telephone Co. of the S.E., Cookeville, Tenn., 1971-73, engr., 1973, div. system engr., 1973-75, div. sr. systems engr. for Tenn., 1975-79; founder, exec. v.p. Putnam Realty Co. Inc., 1973—; res. asso. prof. mil. sci. Tenn. Tech. U., 1974-77; admissions coordinator in Tenn., U.S. Mil. Acad., 1976-78. Vice pres. Boys Club of Am., 1975-77; dir. Willow Park Apts. Corp., 1975-76; mem. financial bd. Algood Ch. of Christ. Served to capt. F.A., AUS, 1964-71; capt. USAR. Certified elec. contractor, licensed real estate broker, Tenn. Mem. Cookeville Jaycees (v.p. 1976-77), NAACP, Am. Legion, VFW. Democrat. Home: 4121 Buford Ellington Dr N Memphis TN 38111 Office: PO Box 3946 Front St Memphis TN 38103

WHEELER, JOHN INGRAHAM, JR., clin. psychologist; b. St. Louis, Nov. 27, 1925; s. John Ingraham and Nan (Donlan) W.; B.S., St. Louis U., 1949, M.S., 1951; Ph.D., U. Tex., 1955; m. Marian Huffman, Jan. 21, 1956; children—John I., Kevin D., Marian Martha, Genevieve Tighe. Pvt. practice psychol. counseling, Houston, 1957—; psychologist U. Tex.-M.D. Anderson Hosp. and Tumor Inst., 1976—; clin. prof. dept. medicine U. Tex. System Cancer Center, 1976—; clin. aseo. prof. dept. pediatrics and dept. psychiatry Baylor Coll. Medicine, 1969—; chmn. Tex. State Bd. Examiners of Psychologists, 1973-74, vice chmn., 1969-73, 74-77, mem., 1977-79; dir. Human Resources, Inc., 1980—; owner Wheel-R Charolais Farm, Anderson, Tex. Pres. Historic Anderson Inc., 1972-76. Served with AUS, 1943-46. Mem. Am., Southwestern, Tex. (disting. psychologist award 1979), Houston psychol. assns., Am. Soc. Clin. Hypnosis, Soc. Clin. and Exptl. Hypnosis, Am. Soc. Pediatric Psychology, Am. Assn. Psychologists in Pvt. Practice, Am. Acad. Psychotherapists, Am. Internat. Charolais Assn., Tex. (dir.), Gulf Coast (dir.) Charolais breeders assns. Home: 11201 Wilding Ln Houston TX 77024 Office: Suite 222 Honeywell Bldg 1535 W Loop S Houston TX 77027 also PO Box 243 Anderson TX 77830

WHEELER, LAWRENCE ALLAN, oil co. exec.; b. Leavenworth, Kans., July 30, 1939; s. Thomas Joseph (stepfather) and Jean Catherine (Howard) Reitz; B. Chem. Engring, Cornell U., 1962; M.B.A., U. Houston, 1972; m. Margaret Anne Hildebrandt, Feb. 2, 1963; 1 son, Steven Thomas. Technologist Shell Oil Co., Deer Park, Tex., 1962-66, engr. mfg. ops., N.Y.C., 1967-69; asst. mgr., ops., Deer Park, 1970-72, staff engr., Houston, 1973-76, mgr. econ. analysis Saudi Arabia petrochem. venture, 1976—. Sec. zoning bd. adjustment, City of El Lago, Tex., 1976-78; lector, mem. Parish Council, St. Mary's Cath. Ch., Humble, Tex., 1979—. Served with U.S. Army, 1963-65. Mem. Am. Inst. Chem. Engrs., Cornell Soc. Engrs., Beta Gamma Sigma. Roman Catholic. Home: 20411 Dawnmist Ct Humble TX 77338 Office: PO Box 2463 Houston TX 77001

WHEELER, ORVILLE EUGENE, engr., educator; b. Memphis, Dec. 31, 1932; s. Eugene Lloyd and Sarah Josephine (Craig) W.; B.E. cum laude, Vanderbilt U., 1954; M.S.C.E., U. Mo., 1956; postgrad. U. Ala., 1962-64; Ph.D., Tex. A. and M. U., 1966; m. Mary Bea Rychlik, June 6, 1956; 1 dau., Lynnette Layne. With Chance Vought, Dallas, 1959-60, Hayes Aircraft, Birmingham, Ala., 1960-61, Brown Engring., Huntsville, Ala., 1961-62, NASA, Huntsville, 1962-66; design specialist Gen. Dynamics, Ft. Worth, 1966-72; chief structures engr. Bucyrus Erie, Milw., 1972-78; prof. civil and mech. engring. and dean Herff Coll. Engring., Memphis State U., 1978—. Served with USN, 1956-59. Registered profl. engr., Ala., Tenn., Wis. Mem. Nat. Soc. Profl. Engrs., ASCE, ASTM, Am. Inst. Steel Constrn., Am. Soc. Engring. Educators. Methodist. Club: Memphis Engrs. Office: Memphis State U Memphis TN 38152

WHEELER, OTIS BULLARD, univ. adminstr.; b. Mansfield, Ark., Feb. 1, 1921; s. Clarence Charles and Georgia Elizabeth (Bullard) W.; B.A., U. Okla., 1942; M.A., U. Tex., 1947; Ph.D., U. Minn., 1951; m. Doris Louise Alexander, Jan. 17, 1943; children—Ann Carolyn, Ross Charles. Instr. English, La. State U., 1952-54, asst. prof., 1954-60, asso. prof., 1960-65, prof., 1965—, asso. dean grad. sch., 1962-67, chmn. dept. English, 1974, vice chancellor for acad. affairs, 1974—. Served with U.S. Army, 1942-46, 51-52. Decorated Bronze Star. Mem. MLA, South Atlantic Modern Lang. Assn., South Central Modern Lang. Assn., AAUP. Contbr. articles to profl. jours. Home: 162 Clara Dr Baton Rouge LA 70808 Office: Office of Acad Affairs La State Univ Baton Rouge LA 70803

WHEELER, RALPH ALLEN, surgeon, air force officer; b. Grand Forks, N.D., Nov. 17, 1942; s. George Carlos and Jeanette Elizabeth (Norris) W.; student Rice U., 1960-62; B.A., U. N.D., 1964, B.S., 1965; M.D., McGill U., 1967; m. Cynthia Ann Allen, Dec. 24, 1978; children—Lezlie Charlene, Scott Allen. Intern, Detroit Gen. Hosp., 1967-68; resident Wayne State U., Detroit, 1968-70, Walter Reed Army Med. Center, 1973-75; commd. 2d lt., U.S. Air Force, 1968, advanced through grades to lt. col., 1976—; staff surgeon Chief of Emergency Services, Chief Intensive Care Unit, U.S. Air Force Hosp., Homestead AFB, Fla., 1975-78; staff surgeon dept. gen. surgery, chmn. dept. emergency services Wilford Hall Med. Center, Lackland AFB, San Antonio, 1978—; clin. asst. prof. surgery U. Tex. Health Sci. Center, San Antonio, 1979—. Decorated Bronze Star, Meritorious Service medal, Air Force Commendation medal; recipient Cecile Lehman Meyer Research award, 1970. Diplomate Nat. Bd. Med. Examiners, Am. Bd. Surgery. Fellow A.C.S.; mem. Assn. Mil. Surgeons U.S. Office: Dept Emergency Services Wilford Hall Med Center San Antonio TX 78236

WHEELER, RONALD WENDELL, JR., psychologist, educator; b. Ft. Worth, June 1, 1914; s. Ronald Whitehead and Kathryn (McMillion) W.; B.A., Tex. Christian U., 1936, M.A., 1940; postgrad. Kilgore Coll., 1937-38, So. Meth. U., 1938-39, U. Tex., 1940-42, Harvard, 1942-43; Ed.D., U. Okla., 1959; m. Mary Florence Cogswell, Aug. 5, 1938; children—Wendelyn Florence (Mrs. Edwin D. White) (dec.), Marilyn Anne (Mrs. Jon D. Kindred), Gregg Alan, Carol Kay (Mrs. Thomas R. Johnson), Ronald Scott. Dir. ofcl. guide band Tex. Central Centennial Expn., Dallas, 1936; music supr., dir. bands Salem Consol. Schs., nr. Troup, Tex., 1936-39; dir. mus. therapy USPHS Hosp., Ft. Worth, 1939-42; partner, gen. mgr. Radio Sta. KTAT, Frederick, Okla., 1948-62, owner, pres., 1956-62; instr. dept. psychology East Tex. State U. at Commerce, 1961-62, asst, prof., 1962-64, asso. prof., 1964-69, prof., 1969-77, dir. reading lab., 1963-77, ret., 1977. Area III adviser S.W. Ednl. Developmental Lab.; tech. asst. Right to Read, Southwestern region U.S. Office Edn. Pres. Tillman County Mental Health Assn., 1958-61. Bd. dirs. Wesley Found., E. Tex. State U.; co-facilitator Nat. Right to Read Conf., Washington, 1976. Served to capt. USNR, 1942-48, 50-51, 59, 61, ret., 1974. Decorated China War Meml. medal Republic of China. Named commodore Okla. Navy, 1953, adm. of fleet, Okla., 1958. Certified psychologist, Tex. Mem. Am., Southwestern, Tex. psychol. assns., Nat. Reading Conf., Internat. Reading Assn., Coll. Reading Assn., Res. Officers Assn. (liaison officer Greater Dallas chpt.-E. Tex. State U.), NEA, Tex. Tchrs. Assn., Tex. Soc. Coll. Profs. Edn., Tex. Assn. Coll. Tchrs. (chpt. pres. 1965-67); mem. state nominating com. state chmn. research com. faculty and classroom, mem. state exec. com. 1968-69), Assn. Higher Edn., Tex. Christian U. Ex-Students Assn., Tex. Christian U. Letterman's Assn., Tex. Christian U. Ex-Bandsmens Assn. (pres.), N.E. Tex. Schs. Men's Club, Lambda Chi Alpha (faculty adviser), Tex. Student Edn. Assn. (faculty adviser), Student Nat. Edn. Assn. (faculty adviser), Am. Legion (post comdr.), VFW, Okla. Broadcasters Assn. (dir. 1959-61), C. of C. (pres.), Phi Delta Kappa (emeritus), Psi Chi (nat. service award 1977). Mem. Christian Ch. (Sunday sch. supt., mem. ch. bd., elder). Clubs: Webb Hill Country, Sand Hills Golf and Country. Author: Read with Speed, 3d edit., 1975; co-author: Reading Laboratory Handbook. Contbr. articles and revs. to profl. jours. Home: 2810 Tanglewood Dr Commerce TX 75428

WHEELER, WILLIAM BRYAN, III, sr. planner; b. Kissimmee, Fla., June 21, 1940; s. William Bryan and Olive Mae (Criner) W.; student U. Fla., 1958-59, U. Md., 1967-68; B.L.A., U. Ga., 1975; m. Mary Sue Wheeler, Dec. 29, 1961; children—Alicia Nanette, Bryan. Meteorol. supr. Pan Am. World Airways, 1962-63; asst. engr. Fla. Road Dept., Orlando, 1963-64; tech. supr. Xerox Corp., 1964-65; sr. field engr. Fed. Electric Corp., Rome, Italy, 1965-66; systems engr. Bendix Corp., 1966-70; devel. dir. East Coast Stainless Steel, Lanham, Md., 1970-71; regional planner Middle Flint Planning and Devel. Commn., Ellaville, Ga., 1975-78; planning dir. NE Ga. Area Planning and Devel. Commn., Athens, Ga., 1978—. Vice pres. Sumter County Bicentennial Beautification Com., 1976-77. Served with USMC, 1958-61. Mem. Am. Soc. Landscape Architects, Am. Planning Assos. Democrat. Author: The Quest—The Discovery of the Cauldron of Immortality. Home: 160 Kings Circle Athens GA 30606 Office: 305 Research Dr Athens GA 30605

WHICHARD, WILLIS PADGETT, state senator; b. Durham, N.C., May 24, 1940; s. Willis Guilford and Beulah (Padgett) W.; A.B., U. N.C., Chapel Hill, 1962, J.D., 1965; m. Leona Paschal, June 4, 1961; children—Jennifer Diane, Ida Gilbert. Admitted to N.C. bar, 1965; law clk. to justice N.C. Supreme Ct., 1965-66; partner firm Powe, Porter, Alphin & Whichard, P.A., Durhan, 1966—; mem. N.C. Ho. of Reps., 1970-74, N.C. Senate, 1974—. Mem. N.C. Army NG, 1966-72. Recipient Disting. Service award Durham Jaycees, 1971, Outstanding Legislator award N.C. Acad. Trial Lawyers, 1975, Outstanding Youth Service award N.C. Juvenile Correctional Assn., 1975. Mem. Am. Bar Assn., N.C. Bar Assn. Clubs: Durham Tobaccoland Kiwanis, Durham-Chapel Torch. Home: 5608 Woodberry Rd Durham NC 27707 Office: PO Box 3843 Durham NC 27702

WHIDDON, GENE AUSTIN, lumber co. exec.; b. Lenox, Ga., July 30, 1928; s. Oscar Ray and Mary Alma (Rutherford) W.; student U. Fla., 1946-47; student Broward Bus. Coll., 1947-48, hon. Asso. Bus. Adminstrn., 1962; m. Angelyn Sylvia Gatlin, May 19, 1950; children—Tari Lynn, Gene Austin, Michael Scott. Salesman, Causeway Lumber Co., Inc., Ft. Lauderdale, Boca Raton, Fla., 1950-53, asst. to mgr., 1953-55, sec., treas., gen. mgr., 1955-70, pres., gen. mgr., 1970—; pres. Causeway Lumber Co. Inc., 1970—; dir. Fla. Power & Light, Landmark 1st Nat. Bank, Ft. Lauderdale. Chmn. Broward Met. area Nat. Alliance Businessmen, 1972—; mem. Fla. Local Govt. Study Commn., 1972-74; bd. dirs. Fla. Council of 100, South Fla. Coordinating Council; mem. Fla. Jud. Qualifications Commn.; campaign dir. United Fund of Broward County, Ft. Lauderdale, 1963, pres., 1964; bd. dirs. Opera Guild of Ft. Lauderdale; chmn. bd. dirs. Broward Community Coll. Found.; trustee Stetson U., 1969-78; chmn. Broward County Adv. Com. to Gov., 1973-76. Served with USAF, 1948-50. Named One of 5 Outstanding Young Men, Ft. Lauderdale Jr. C. of C., 1960-61; Boss of Year, PBX Club Broward County, 1964, Boss of Year Ft. Lauderdale chpt. Nat. Secs. Assn., 1965-66; Layman of Year award Kiwanis, 1967; Outstanding Citizen of Year, Fraternal Order Police, 1976; Liberty Bell award Law-Day, Broward County Bar Assn., 1965; Top Mgmt. award Ft. Lauderdale Sales and Mktg. Execs. Club, 1965; George Washington medal honor Freedoms Found. at Valley Forge, 1976. Mem. Fla. Lumber and Bldg. Material Dealers Assn. (bd. dirs.; pres. 1968-69), Fla. (exec. com. 1970-72), Greater Ft. Lauderdale (pres. 1969-72) chambers commerce, Aircraft Owners and Pilots Assn., Christian Businessmen's Com., Execs. Assn. Ft. Lauderdale, Broward Builders Exchange (pres. 1956-57). Baptist (deacon 1955—, chmn. 1959-60). Clubs: Tower (bd. govs.), Lauderdale Yacht, Propeller (Fort Lauderdale), One Hundred (Broward County, Fla.); Kiwanis (pres. 1969-70), Masons, Shriners. Home: 1131 SW 9th Ave Fort Lauderdale FL 33315 Office: 2627 S Andrew Ave Fort Lauderdale FL 33316

WHIGHAM, BARNEY RAY, employment counselor; b. Winters, Tex., Dec. 10, 1923; s. Clyde L. and Iva (Lawrence) W.; student San Angelo Coll., 1946-49; B.A., Sul Ross State Coll., 1952; M.A. equivalent in Counseling Psychology, Tex. Tech U., 1965, M.Ed. in Spl. Edn., 1967; m. Thelma Georgia Shepard, Sept. 17, 1955. Materials checker Gasoline Plant Constrn. Co., Wingate, Tex., 1952-53; ammunitions worker Lone Star Arsenal, Texarkana, Tex., 1953; placement counselor Tex. Commn. for Blind, Austin, 1954-55, Dallas, 1955-61; employment counselor Tex. Employment Commn., Lubbock, 1965—. Mem. Lubbock County Employ the Handicapped Com., 1967—; rep. Gov.'s Com. on Employment of Handicapped, 1967, 71; bd. dirs. South Plains Guidance Center, 1969-71, S.W. Lighthouse for Blind, 1976—; mem. adv. bd., rehab. counselor tng. program Tex. Tech U., 1971, 72, 74—; bd. dirs. Nat. Youth Programming Using Mini-Bikes, 1972. Elementary and high sch. certification, Tex. Mem. Internat. Assn. Pub. Employment Services, Tex. Pub. Employee Assn., Am. Personnel and Guidance Assn., Nat. Employment Counselors Assn., Am. Psychol. Assn., Nat. Rehab. Assn. Club: Lions (dir. 1976-77) (Lubbock). Home: 7002 Vicksburg Ave Lubbock TX 79424 Office: 1602 16th St Lubbock TX 79408

WHINERY, ROBERT, engring. co. exec.; b. N.Y.C., Oct. 24, 1922; s. Samuel Brent and Mabel (Riker) W.; student Newark Coll. Engring., 1940-43; B.M.E., Cornell U., 1944; m. Larissa de Falevitch, Mar. 17, 1978; children—Pamela (Mrs. Kenneth H. Knowles), Patricia (Mrs. Steven Gilpin), Sharon (Mrs. Nick Daniloff), Elizabeth, Andrew. Engr., Standard Oil Devel. Co., Bayway, N.J., 1946-53; sales engr. Mason-Neilan Regulator Co., N.Y.C., 1953-56; br. mgr. Jay Instrument & Sp.ty. Co., Louisville, 1956-59; owner, pres. Whinery Engring. Co., Louisville, 1959—. Served with USNR, 1943-46. Registered profl. engr., Ky. Republican. Episcopalian. Clubs: Sara Bay Country, Longboat Key Golf and Tennis. Home and Office: 1335 Whitfield Ave Sarasota FL 33580 Office: PO Box 107 Anchorage KY 40223

WHIPKEY, JAMES WILBUR, journalist; b. Cameron, W.Va., July 20, 1933; s. H. Wilbur and L. Lucille (Slonaker) W.; student Marshall U., 1951-52, Ohio U., 1952-53; children by previous marriage—David, Stephanie, Crystal. News dir. Sta. KWBE, Beatrice, Nebr., 1954-55, Sta KFOR, Lincoln, Nebr., 1955-57, Sta. WTTH, Port Huron, Mich., 1957-58, Sta. WAVY-AM-TV, Portsmouth, Va., 1958-64, Sta. WSB-TV, Atlanta, 1965-71, Sta. WRNG, Atlanta, 1975-76; asso. news dir. Sta. KWK, St. Louis, 1964-65, Sta. KSOO-AM-TV, Sioux Falls, S.D., 1965; free-lance corr. various radio-tv networks, Atlanta, 1975-77, state reporter, 1965-71; senate info. officer Ga. State Senate, Atlanta, 1971-72; info. officer Ga. Bankers Assn., Atlanta, 1973-75; free lance commentator and journanlist for Ga. networks, Atlanta, 1976. Recipient award for outstanding program Corp. Pub. Broadcasting, 1971. Mem. Pub. Relations Soc. Am., Sigma Delta Chi. Presbyterian. Club: Masons. Inaugurator daily telecasts of Ga. legislature, 1971, weekly live talk show series, Ga. Pub. TV 1973. Home: 1800 Ridgeway Ave NW Atlanta GA 30318

WHIPPLE, WILLIAM UPSHAW, ednl. adminstr.; b. Lakeland, Fla., Nov. 2, 1920; s. Charles Spurgeon and Lillian Hester (Upshaw) W.; student U. Fla., 1940-41, 45-47; m. Mary Evelyn Stedham, Aug. 19, 1955; children—Carolyn Lee, Pamela Kay. Realtor, H.W. Stockard and Co., Lakeland, Fla., 1948-55; campaign dir. Wells Orgn., Chgo., 1956-57; pres. William Whipple and Assos., Lakeland, 1957-74; v.p. devel. U. of South, Sewanee, Tenn., 1974—; cons. stewardship Episcopal Dioceses of Ga., S.C. Vice pres. Lakeland YMCA, 1971-73. Served with USAF, 1942-45. Mem. Internat. Fund-Raising Assn., Nat. Soc. Fund Raisers, Council for Advancement and Support Edn., Soc. Real Estate Appraisers, U. Fla. Alumni Assn. Democrat. Baptist. Clubs: Univ., Lakeland Yacht and Country, Toastmasters (pres. Lakeland chpt. 1954). Home and Office: U of South Sewanee TN 37375

WHISENHUNT, GARY WAYNE, systems co. mgr.; b. San Antonio, Mar. 3, 1954; s. C. C. and Charlotte W.; B.B.A., S.W. Tex. State U., 1976. Asst. mgr. McDonald's Restaurant, San Antonio, 1971-76; sales rep. Charlott's Clocks, San Antonio, 1970-76; field sales engr. Tex. Instruments, Houston, 1976-77; customer support rep. Qwip Systems, Houston, 1977-78, advanced customer support rep., 1978-79, regional CSR mgr., Dallas, 1979—. Mem. Alpha Kappa Psi. Club: Houston Jaycees (dir.). Home: 8272 Spring Valley Rd Dallas TX 75240 Office: 700 Promenade Nat Bank Bldg Dallas TX 75080

WHISENTON, JOFFRE TRUMBULL, ednl. adminstr.; b. Hattiesburg, Miss.; student Tougaloo Coll., Springfield Coll.; Ph.D., U. Ala., 1968; m. Zadie E. Bedford; 1 son, Joffre Conrad. Faculty, Stillman Coll., Tuscaloosa, Ala., instr. phys. edn., prof. ednl. psychology, basketball, baseball and track coach, dean of men, chmn. phys. edn. dept., dir. athletics; with So. Assn. Colls. and Schs., Atlanta, 1969—, asso. exec. sec. commn. on colls.; program asso. Office for Student Devel., U. Ala.; spl. asst. for ednl. policy to sec. HEW. Mem. Urban League, NAACP, Am. Psychol. Assn., AAHPER, AAUP, Phi Delta Kappa, Omega Psi Phi. Address: 795 Peachtree St NE Atlanta GA 30308

WHITACRE, WALTER EMMETT, aero. engr.; b. Detroit, Sept. 28, 1931; s. Arthur James and Reba Adeline (England) W.; B.S. in Aero. Engring., Purdue U., 1959, M.S. in Indsl. Mgmt., 1968; m. Donna Lee Longstreet, Nov. 26, 1950; children—Donn Arthur, Kirk Alexander, Chris Martin. Project engr. Lockheed Missiles & Space Co., 1959-63; advanced systems engr. Marshall Space Flight Center, NASA, Huntsville, Ala., 1963—. Active Tenn. Valley council Boy Scouts Am. Recipient Valley Scouter award Boy Scouts Am., 1971, Silver Beaver award, 1974, Spurgeon award, 1977; Liberty Bell award Madison County Bar Assn., 1979. Methodist. Home: 301 Belvidere Dr Huntsville AL 35803 Office: Marshall Space Flight Center Huntsville AL 35812

WHITAKER, GLADELLE, ofcl. Stephens County (Ga.); b. Jackson, Ga., June 19, 1925; d. Ben Hill and Dillah Idain (Smith) Moss; A.B., Bessie Tift Coll., 1946; m. Howard Baine Whitaker, May 16, 1948; children—Stephen Moss, Dana Lisa. Lab. technician Ga. Dept. Health, Atlanta, 1946-52; caseworker child welfare Stephen County Dept. Family and Children Services, Toccoa, 1968—; mem. adv. bd. Stephens County Child Devel. Center; mem. adv. council Tng. Center for Developmentally Disabled. Bd. dirs. Notation on Aging, Project Developmental Continuity. Mem. Ga. County Welfare Assn. (staff devel. com.), Ga. Conf. on Social Welfare, Am. Pub. Welfare Assn. Methodist. Club: Pilot. Home: 223 Lucille Ln Toccoa GA 30577 Office: Courthouse Annex 222 North Blvd Toccoa GA 30577

WHITAKER, HALFORD SNYDER, physician; b. Oliver Springs, Tenn., July 27, 1934; s. Lorenzo Robert and Virginia Belle (Snyder) W.; B.S., U. S.C., 1954; M.D., U. Tenn., 1956. Intern, U. Tenn., City of Memphis Hosp., 1956-57; asst. resident pediatrics Crawford Long Hosp. of Emory U., 1960; resident pediatrics Bapt. Meml. Hosp., Memphis, 1961; chief resident pediatrics U. Ky., Lexington, 1962; asst. resident neurology N.C. Bapt. Hosp., Bowman Gray Sch. Medicine, 1962-64; asst. resident child neurology Children's Hosp., Boston, 1964-65; practice medicine, Morristown, Tenn., 1971-77, Columbia, S.C., 1978—; teaching fellow neurology Harvard Med. Sch., 1964-65; vis. lectr. psychology Grad. Sch. U. Ga., 1965; asso. prof. psychiatry and neurology Med. Coll. Ga., 1966-68; dir. evaluation and rehab. Gracewood (Ga.) State Sch. and Hosp., 1967-68; prof. psychology (part-time) U. Tenn., Knoxville, 1968-69, asso. prof. biomed. engring. (part-time), 1973-74; dir. Developmental Evaluation Center, Greene Valley (Tenn.) Hosp. and Sch., 1968-69, Caswell (N.C.) Developmental Center, 1969-71; staff Emergency Physicians Group, Columbia, 1976-78, Midlands Devel. Center, Columbia, 1979—. Served with USPHS, 1958-60. Diplomate Am. Bd. Family Practice, Am. Bd. Pediatrics. Fellow Am. Acad. Pediatrics; mem. So. EEG Soc., Internat. Neuropsychology Soc. (founding), So. Soc. Pediatric Research, Am. Coll. Emergency Physicians (charter), Am. Med. EEG Soc. Club: Rotary.

WHITAKER, MARK BOONE, JR., pub. utility co. exec.; b. Knoxville, Tenn., May 5, 1938; s. Mark Boone and Hewlett (Williamson) McReynolds W.; B.S.E.E., The Citadel, 1960; M.B.A., U. S.C., 1964; J.D., 1969; grad. U.S. Army Command and Gen. Staff Coll., 1974; m. Kathleen Carol Stuart, Aug. 30, 1969; children—Elizabeth McReynolds, Mark Boone III. With S.C. Electric & Gas Co., Columbia, 1964—, exec. asst. to sr. v.p. ops., 1969-71, asso. mgr. production operations, 1971-72, mgr. production operations, 1972-73, atty., 1973-75, accountant, 1975-76, asso. mgr. distribution operations, 1976, mgr. nuclear licensing, 1976—; admitted to S.C. bar, 1969. Vice chmn. Central S.C. chpt. ARC. Served with U.S. Army, 1960-62; now dep. staff judge adv. USAR. Mem. Am. Bar Assn., S.C. Bar Assn., Richland County Bar Assn., Am. Nuclear Soc. (dir. Columbia chpt.), Assn. U.S. Army, Res. Officers Assn., Mil. Order of World Wars. Episcopalian. Clubs: Summit, Forest Lake Country. Home: 3707 Northshore Rd Columbia SC 29206 Office: 328 Main St Columbia SC 29202

WHITBY, CHARLES LLOYD, JR., hosp. mgmt. engr.; b. Sherman, Tex., Mar. 29, 1954; s. Charles Lloyd and Jean Davis W.; B.S., Ga. Inst. Tech., 1976; postgrad. Augusta Coll., 1979—; m. Dianna Sue Durham, Aug. 28, 1976 (div.); 1 son, Robert Charles. Systems engr. Systems and Computer Services div. Med. Coll. Ga., 1976-78; mgmt. engr. Univ. Hosp., Augusta, 1978-80; systems engr. Med. Coll. Ga., 1980—. Mem. Hosp. Mgmt. Systems Soc., Am. Hosp. Assn. Democrat. Methodist. Home: 2148 Alfred Ln Augusta GA 30906 Office: Med Coll Ga Augusta GA 30902

WHITCOMB, JOHN MERVIN, mfg. co. exec.; b. Danbury, Conn., Aug. 25, 1949; s. Mervin Wesley and Ella Elisabeth (Hallington) W.; B.S. in Mgmt. Sci., Rensselaer Poly. Inst., 1972; M.B.A., U. Wis., 1975; m. Barbara Ann Liyana, June 20, 1970; 1 dau., Joy Ellen. Counselor, T. E. Bell Employment Agy., Latham, N.Y., 1972; mgmt. trainee Albany Internat. Corp., (N.Y.), 1972, personnel asst., personnel mgr., Appleton, Wis., 1973-74, mgr. personnel and purchasing, 1975; labor relations rep. Plough, Inc., Memphis, 1975-77, asst. dir. indsl. relations, 1977-78, dir. labor relations, 1979—. Mem. City of Germantown (Tenn.) Personnel Advisory Com., 1978, 79. Mem. Am. Soc. Personnel Adminstrn. (v.p. Memphis chpt. 1978, pres. 1979; charter mem. internat. chpt., nat. public affairs com. 1978—), Memphis C. of C. (govtl. affairs com.). Home: 1530 Stonegate Pass Germantown TN 38138 Office: PO Box 377 Memphis TN 38151

WHITE, AUSTIN EUGENE, data processing exec.; b. Saulsbury, Tenn., Apr. 2, 1941; s. James Andrew and Mamie (Poole) W.; student Memphis State U., 1965-69; m. Avis Marie Woods, Dec. 22, 1962; children—Glenda Susan, Kenneth Lee. Computer programmer elevator div. Dover Corp., 1969-71, Medicenters of Am., 1971-74; pres. Data-Tec, Inc., Memphis, 1974—. Served with USNG, 1958-62. Home: 1687 Mary Dr Memphis TN 38111 Office: PO Box 231 Southaven MS 38671

WHITE, BERNARD HENRY, scientist; b. Chgo., Oct. 15, 1947; s. Leonard Raymond and Hadassah Ruth (Frankel) W.; B.S., U. Cin., 1969; M.S., U. Wash., 1971; Ph.D. (Robert A. Welch fellow), U. Houston, 1976; m. Joan Ilene Fierst, Dec. 29, 1968; children—Simma Gorchov, Miriam Cohen, Chaim Pincus. Staff scientist Exxon Research & Engring. Co., Baytown, Tex., 1976—. Mem. Am. Chem. Soc., Am. Phys. Soc. Jewish. Club: Masons. Author: Flame Inhibition by Aliphatic Halides, 1976. Home: 3304 Grennoch Ln Houston TX 77025 Office: Exxon Research & Engring Co PO Box 4255 Baytown TX 77520

WHITE, CHARLES EDWARD, surgeon; b. Memphis, Aug. 20, 1935; s. Marvin Walker and Cleo Haltom (Jester) W.; student Memphis State U., 1957-60; M.D., U. Tenn., 1964; M.S., U. Miss., 1970; m. Mary Jane Grantham, May 31, 1959; children—Heather Lea, David Walker, Knox Grantham. Intern, Methodist Hosp., Memphis, 1965, resident, 1965-69; resident in plastic surgery U. Miss., 1970-72; asst. prof. anatomy U. Miss., 1970-72; practice medicine specializing in plastic surgery, Memphis, 1972—; asso. prof. plastic surgery, chmn. plastic surgery sect. City of Memphis Hosps. and U. Tenn. Center for Health Scis., 1978—. Bd. dirs. Memphis Orchestral Soc., 1976—. Served with USMC, 1954-57. Diplomate Am. Bd. Surgery, Am. Bd. Plastic Surgery. Fellow Am. Coll. Surgeons; mem. Am. Soc. Plastic and Reconstructive Surgery (recipient 1st prize Ednl. Found. Essay, 1972), Southeastern Soc. Plastic and Reconstructive Surgeons, Plastic Surgery Research Council, Am. Burn Assn., AMA, Tenn. Med. Assn., Memphis, Shelby counties med. socs., Tenn. Soc. Plastic Surgeons, Memphis Wine and Food Soc. (pres. 1977-79). Republican. Research in transplantation immunology. Home: 195 S Goodlett St Memphis TN 38117 Office: 220 S Claybrook St Memphis TN 38104

WHITE, CHARLES MARTIN, JR., physician; b. Greenville, S.C., Sept. 17, 1928; s. Charles Martin and Pansy Pamela (Jenkins) W.; B.S., Furman U., 1948; M.D., Med. Coll. S.C., 1953; m. Violet Gillespie, Sept. 18, 1948. Intern, Greenville Gen. Hosp., 1953-54; resident in psychiatry Med. Coll. Va., 1965-68; gen. practice medicine, Greenville, 1957-65; practice medicine, specializing in psychiatry, Greenville, 1968—; mem. teaching staff Greenville Gen. Hosp., 1968—; mem. teaching staff Marshal I. Pickens Hosp., 1968—, chmn. dept. psychiatry, 1978—; chmn. dept. psychiatry Greenville Hosp. System, 1978—; clin. asso. psychiatry and behavioral scis. Med. U. S.C., 1973—; cons. VA, St. Francis Hosp., N. Greenville Coll., Furman U., Family and Children's Ct., Greenville Gen. Hosp., S.C. Dept. Youth Services, Cherokee County Schs. Pres., Southeastern Mortgage Corp., Travelers Rest, S.C., 1960—; dir. Bank of Travelers Rest. Served to capt. M.C., USAF, 1954-56. NIMH grantee, 1966-68. Diplomate Am. Bd. Psychiatry and Neurology. Fellow Am. Acad. Gen. Practice; mem. AMA (Physician's Recognition award 1969, 79), So., S.C. med. assns., Am. Psychiat. Assn. (Physician's Recognition award 1979), Greenville County Med. Soc., Am. Soc. Adolescent Psychiatry, Neuropsychiat. Soc. Va., Phi Rho Sigma. Clubs: Masons (32 deg.), Shriners. Home: Route 2 Hwy 253 Mountain Creek Rd Taylors SC 29687 Office: 220 Arlington Ave Box 8577 A Greenville SC 29604

WHITE, CHARLES MAURICE, coll. adminstr.; b. Logan, W.Va., Mar. 2, 1950; s. Maurice Ambrose and Joyce Ann (Phillips) W.; student So. W.Va. Community Coll., 1971-72; B.A. in Polit. Sci., Marshall U., 1976, M.S. in Adult and Continuing Edn., 1978; postgrad. Va. Poly. Inst. and State U., 1979—; m. Connie Bailey, Dec. 21, 1974; 1 son, Brandon Derek. Eligibility supr. W.Va. Dept. Welfare, 1974-76; dir. fin. aid So. W.Va. Community Coll., 1976-77, coordinator fed. programs, 1977-78, dir. career and continuing edn., 1978—. Co-founder Deaf Awareness Council, 1977. Served with W.Va. N.G., 1970-76. Mem. Adult Edn. Assn. U.S., Am. Vocat. Assn., W.Va. Adult Edn. Assn., W.Va. Continuing Edn. and Community Service Assn., Logan Jaycees (past sec.). Republican. Club: Lions (pres.) (Logan). Home: PO Box 262 Stollings WV 25646 Office: University Ave Logan WV 25601

WHITE, DANIEL LYMAN, educator; b. Sault Ste. Marie, Mich., Mar. 7, 1941; s. Lewis Charles and Lillian May (Tackaberry) W.; B.S. in Bus. Adminstrn., Georgetown U., 1965; Ph.D., Northwestern U., 1970; m. Anita Marie Stevenson, Sept. 15, 1967; children—David Lewis, Daniel Steven. Auditor, Peat, Marwick, Mitchell, C.P.A.'s, Washington; instr. Northwestern U., 1965-70; asst. prof. fin. Ga. State U., Atlanta, 1970-75, asso. prof. fin., 1975—; fin. analyst Fed. Energy Adminstrn., 1974—. Am. Assembly Collegiate Schs. Bus.-Sears Roebuck & Co. Fed. Govt. fellow, 1974-75. Contbr. articles to profl. jours. Home: 2694 Twigg Circle Marietta GA 30067 Office: Dept Finance Ga State U Univ Plaza Atlanta GA 30303

WHITE, DEE WAYNE, musician, educator; b. Cardin, Okla., Aug. 24, 1919; s. Ed E. and Maude M. (Martin) W.; B.Mus., Okla. Baptist U., 1949; M.Mus., George Peabody Coll., 1953; M.Ed., George Mason U., 1979; m. Thelma L. King, June 9, 1965; children—Barbara June, Dee Bergen. Chmn. div. fine arts Belmont Coll., Nashville, 1952-63, Campbellsville (Ky.) Coll., 1963-72; chmn. communications and human studies No. Va. Community Coll., Sterling, 1972—; ch. musician, 1946—. Served with USAAF, 1943-45. Decorated D.S.M. Mem. Nat. Assn. Tchrs. Singing, Choral Condrs. Guild Am., Music Educators Nat. Conf. Democrat. Baptist. Contbg. editor Ch. Musician, 1965—. Home: 8428 Little River Turnpike Annandale VA 22003 Office: Leesburg Hwy Rural Route 2 Box 165 Sterling VA 22170

WHITE, ETHYLE HERMAN (MRS. S. ROY WHITE), artist; b. San Antonio, Apr. 10, 1904; d. Ferdinand and Minnie (Simmang) Herman; ed. pvt. schs., instrs.; m. S. Roy White, Mar. 3, 1924; children—De Lois Eileen (Mrs. William Marion Mohrle), Patsyruth (Mrs. Henry Wheeler). Exhibited numerous one-man, group shows, Tex.; represented pub. collections in U.S., pvt. collections in Switzerland, Germany, Sweden. Del. Internat. Com. Centro Studi E. Scambi Internationali. Mem. Anahuac Fine Arts Group, San Antonio, Beaumont, Galveston, Houston art leagues, Daus. Republic Tex., UDC, Watercolor Soc., Nat. League Am. Pen Women. Episcopalian. Mem. Order Eastern Star. Clubs: Fine Arts (Anahuac); Artist and Craftsmen (Dallas); Conservative Arts (Houston). Author, illustrator: Arabella. Author: Poet's Hour. Home: PO Box 176 Anahuac TX 77514

WHITE, FRANCIS ALONZO, counselor, educator; b. Port Gibson, Miss., Mar. 1, 1943; s. Francis A. and Lucille C. W.; B.S., Alcorn State U., 1963; M.S., Ind. U., 1971; Ed.D., Va. Inst. Tech., 1978; m. Jeanette Pope, Mar. 27, 1964; children—Regenia, Angelia. Tchr. social studies Addison High Sch., Port Gibson, 1963-71; counselor Port Gibson High Sch., 1972-76; coordinator career edn. Port Gibson, 1978-79; asst. prof. counselor edn. Jackson (Miss.) State U., 1979—; cons. career edn. Mem. Am. Personnel and Guidance Assn., Miss. Personnel and Guidance Assn., NEA, Alpha Phi Alpha, Phi Delta Kappa. Mem. Christian Ch. Home: 605 Coffee St Port Gibson MS 39150 Office: Jackson State U Jackson MS 39217

WHITE, FRANK DURWARD, fin. co. exec.; b. Texarkana, Tex., June 4, 1933; s. Loftin E. and Ida (Clark) W.; B.S., U.S. Naval Acad., 1956; m. Gay Daniels, Mar. 22, 1975; children—Elizabeth, Rebecca, Kyle. Account exec. Merrill Lynch, Pierce, Fenner & Smith, Inc., 1961-73; v.p. Comml. Nat. Bank, 1973-74; dir. Ark. Indsl. Devel. Commn., 1975-76; pres. Capital Savs. & Loan Assn., Little Rock, 1977—; dir. Ark. Missouri Power Co. Trustee Ark. Childrens Hosp., also chmn. long range planning com. Served to capt. USAF. Mem. Nat. Assn. State Devel. Agys. (dir. 1976), Pulaski County Savs. and Loan League (pres.), Ark. State Council on Econ. Edn., Little Rock Port Authority, Little Rock C. of C. (v.p.). Democrat. Mem. Christian Ch. Clubs: Capital of Little Rock (pres.), Country of Little Rock. Home: 912 McAdoo Little Rock AR 72207 Office: PO Box 2621 Little Rock AR 72203

WHITE, FRANK FREDERICK, JR., ins. exec.; b. Whiteville, Tenn., Jan. 3, 1938; s. Frank Frederick and Gracie Maxine W.; student Middle Tenn. State U., 1956-57; m. Mary Beth, Feb. 21, 1976; children—Frank Frederick, Thomas Alan. Salesman, Interstate Life & Accident, Chattanooga, 1957-60; group ins. salesman Blue Cross of Tenn., Nashville, 1960-65; with Blair Follin Allen & Walker, Inc., Nashville, 1965-79; exec. v.p., chief operating officer, sr. v.p. Corroon and Black Benefits, Inc., Nashville, 1979—, also dir. credit union; bd. govs. Synercon Corp., 1973-76. Served with USNR, 1953-62. Mem. Nat. Assn. Life Underwriters (active seminars). Republican. Baptist. Club: Capitol of Nashville. Home: Route 4 Lakeview Dr Mount Juliet TN 37122 Office: 301 Plus Park Blvd Nashville TN 37217

WHITE, GARNETT LEE, historian, philosopher, educator; b. Newport News, Va., July 30, 1944; s. David F. and Louise (Atwood) W.; B.A. (Seay fellow), U. Richmond (Va.), 1965, M.A., 1967; M.A. (teaching fellow), Vanderbilt U., 1970, Ph.D., 1975. Adj. asso. prof. philosophy Old Dominion U., Norfolk, Va., 1976, 78-79, philosophy and humanities, 1979—; parttime instr. philosophy Va. Wesleyan Coll., Norfolk, 1978-79; asso. prof. Paul D.Camp Community Coll., Franklin, Va., 1971—. Chmn., Franklin-Southampton Bicentennial Commn., 1974-76. Mem. AAUP (pres. Va. Conf. 1979-80), Am. Hist. Assn., Am. Soc. Reformation Research, Am. Soc. Ch. History, Soc. for Philosophy of Religion. Baptist. Home: Route 2 Box 304 Franklin VA 23851

WHITE, GEORGIA JOANNE JABER, banker; b. Springfield, Mass., Nov. 13, 1941; d. George Samuel and Margaret (Arnold) Jaber; student U. Fla., 1973, Jacksonville U., 1977; m. Bevis Valine White, Aug. 14, 1959; children—Daniel Edward, Stephen Samuel, Debra Anne. Clk., Atlantic Nat. Bank, Jacksonville, 1959-65; adminstrv. asst. Fairfield County Trust Co., Danbury, Conn., 1965-69; asst. tax officer Atlantic Nat. Bank, Jacksonville, 1969-76, asst. ops. officer, 1976; asst. tax officer Barnett Banks Trust Co., Jacksonville, 1977, tax officer, estate tax specialist, 1978—; lectr. in field. Bd. fin. Gateway council Girl Scouts U.S., 1974—; bd. fin. St. Paul United Meth. Ch., Jacksonville, 1977—, trustee found., 1978—. Mem. Fla. Bankers Assn. Democrat. Clubs: Captains, Jacksonville Offshore Sport Fishing. Home: 2310 Shipwreck Circle W Jacksonville FL 32224 Office: Barnett Banks Trust Co PO Box 40200 Jacksonville FL 32231

WHITE, JAMES PATRICK, author; b. Wichita Falls, Tex., Sept. 28, 1940; s. Joseph Brodie and Minnie Orlene (Mann) W.; B.A. with honors, U. Tex., 1961; M.A. in History, Vanderbilt U., 1963; M.A. in Creative Writing (Marston fellow), Brown U., 1973; m. Janice Lou Turner, Sept. 11, 1961; children—Christopher Jules. Asso. prof. history Blue Mountain (Miss.) Coll., 1964-66; free lance writer, 1967-70; asst. prof. creative writing U. Tex., Permian Basin, 1973-74, asso. prof., chmn. dept. creative writing, 1974-76; dir. Tex. Center for Writers, Dallas, 1976-77; vis. prof. U. Tex., Dallas, 1977-78; founding editor, pub. Tex. Books in Review, 1975—. Chmn. adv. bd. Down Center Stage, Dallas Theater Center, 1978-79; chmn. Tex. Joint English Com., Dist. XVIII, 1973-75. Mem. Am. Lit. Translators Assn. (internat. editorial bd. 1978—), Asso. Writing Program (nat. editorial bd. 1973-75), Tex. Assn. Creative Writing Tchrs. (pres. 1973-74), Conf. Coll. Tchrs. English, S. Central MLA. Christian Ch. Author: Birdsong, 1977, 2d edit., 1979; The Ninth Car, 1978, paperback edit., 1979; editor: The Bicentennial Collection of Texas Short Stories, 1974; New and Experimental Literature, 1975; King's S.W., 1975; author: Poems, 1978; editor: (with W. McDonald) Texas Stories and Poems, 1978; (with Janice White) Poetry Dallas, 1978. Home: 2525 Turtle Creek Blvd Dallas TX 75219 Office: PO Box 19876 Dallas TX 75219

WHITE, JAMES WILLIAM, hosp. adminstr.; b. Cin., May 7, 1941; s. James Harvey and Ruth Irwin (Golden) W.; B.S. in Pharmacy, U. Tex., Austin, 1964; M.S. in Hosp. Adminstrn., Trinity U., San Antonio, 1971; m. Katherine Winifred Golly, Apr. 9, 1966; children—Jeffrey Michael, Steven Patrick, Andrea Marie. Hosp. and profl. rep. S.E. Tex., Eli Lilly and Co., 1965-68; pharmacist, San Antonio, 1968-70; adminstrv. resident St. Luke's Hosp., Denver, 1970-71; asst. adminstr. St. Mark's Hosp., Salt Lake City, 1971-77; adminstr. Brownwood (Tex.) Community Hosp., 1977—; mem. sub-area council Tri-Region Health Service Agy. Bd. dirs. Brownwood State Sch., United Way Brownwood; lay reader, chalice bearer Episcopal Ch. of Good Shepherd, Brownwood. Served as officer USAR, 1964-66, USAFR, 1966-70. Mem. Am. Coll. Hosp. Adminstrs., Tex. Hosp. Assn. (chmn. council plant ops. and constrn. 1979-80, chmn. Forts and Pecos Trails div.), N.W. Tex. Hosp. Assn. Club: Brownwood Rotary. Home: 207 Quail Run Brownwood TX 76801 Office: PO Box 760 Brownwood TX 76801

WHITE, JOHN CHAPPELL, govt. ofcl.; b. Blackshear, Ga., Oct. 9, 1929; s. John Bealle and Mildred Ada (Roberts) W.; B.S. in Civil Engring., U. Ala., 1957; J.D., Emory U., 1968; m. Patricia Ann Jones, May 27, 1978; children by previous marriage—John Chappell, Kelly Ann, Christopher Williams. Hwy. engr. Palmer & Baker Engring. Co., Mobile, Ala., 1957-59; propr. J.C. White & Assos., Mobile, 1959-61; sr. design engr. Brown Engring. Co., Huntsville, Ala., 1961-63; civil engr. HUD, Atlanta, 1963-66; staff engr. S.E. region Fed. Water Pollution Control Adminstrn., HEW, Atlanta, 1966-68, dir. state planning and program grants office, 1968-69; dir. regulatory programs office S.E. region Fed. Water Quality Adminstrn., Atlanta, 1969-70; dir. enforcement div. EPA, region IV, Atlanta, 1970-73, dep. regional adminstr., 1973-75, regional adminstr., region VI, Dallas, 1975-77, regional adminstr., Atlanta, 1977—; admitted to Ga., Fla. bars, 1969. Served with USN, 1946-48, 51-52. Registered profl. engr., Ala. Mem. Ga. State Bar, Fla. State Bar. Democrat. Methodist. Home: 145 15th St NE Atlanta GA 30361 Office: 345 Courtland St NE Atlanta GA 30308

WHITE, JOHN CHARLES, historian; b. Washington, Apr. 14, 1939; s. Bennett Sexton, Jr. and Mary Elizabeth (Wildman) W.; B.A. magna cum laude, Washington and Lee U., Lexington, Va., 1960; M.A., Duke U., 1962, Ph.D., 1964; m. Carolyn Ruth West, July 6, 1963. Mem. faculty U. Ala., Huntsville, 1967—, prof. history, 1976—, chmn. dept., 1970-79; dir., sec.-treas. Consortium on Revolutionary Europe, 1979. Served to capt. USAR, 1964-67. Recipient award merit Ala. Historic Commn., 1978; Robert E. Lee scholar, 1956-60; So. fellow, 1960-63. Mem. Nat. Trust Historic Preservation, Ala. Hist. Soc., Ala. Assn. Historians (pres. 1978—), Huntsville Lit. Assn., L'Alliance Française Huntsville (pres. 1970), Phi Kappa Phi, Phi Alpha Theta. Club: Huntsville Rotary. Author articles, revs. in field; editor Proc. on Revolutionary Europe, 1977. Home: 220 Longwood Dr Huntsville AL 35801 Office: Box 1247 UAH Huntsville AL 35807

WHITE, JOHN STERLING, spectroscopist; b. Elizabeth City, N.C., Jan. 5, 1935; s. Calvin Miller and Mallie (Boyles) W.; B.A. in Chemistry, Gallaudet Coll., 1959; m. Lucie Moffatt, Aug. 8, 1959. Infrared spectroscopist R.J. Reynolds Tobacco Co., Winston-Salem, N.C. Pres. N.C. Assn. Deaf, 1972-76. Recipient Handicapped Employee of the Year award, 1975. Mem. Am. Chem. Soc., Coblentz Soc., Inc. Baptist. Club: Piedmont Deaf Lions. Office: R J Reynolds Company Research Department Winston Salem NC 27102

WHITE, JOHN WESLEY, mfg. co. exec.; b. St. Joseph, Mo., Oct. 1, 1938; s. John Olen and Lucille Madge W.; B.S., Central Mo. State U., 1960; M.S., Kans. U., 1962; m. Marilyn Marshall, Jan. 1, 1965; children—Shannon, Kevin Marshall, Andrew Olen. Mem. tech. staff Tex. Instruments, Inc., Dallas, 1961-69, asst. v.p. info. systems, 1973—; software devel. mgr. Electronic Data Systems, Dallas, 1969-72; systems software mgr. Tres Computer Systems, Dallas, 1972-73; dir. Geophys. Services, Inc., S. Am., 1979. Mem. Pi Mu Epsilon, Kappa Mu Epsilon, Phi Sigma Pi, Sigma Zeta, Tau Kappa Epsilon. Methodist. Office: Texas Instruments Inc 13500 N Central Expy Dallas TX 75265

WHITE, JOHN WILLIAM, civil engr.; b. Oxford, Miss., Apr. 19, 1918; s. Ralph Reynolds and Imogene Penn (Owens) W.; B.S. in Civil Engring., U. Miss., 1942; m. Annie Grace Kimmons, Aug. 1, 1954; children—John Paul, Connie Diane, Martha Marie. Constrn. insp. TVA, 1942; field engr., bldgs and grounds U. Miss., University, 1946-49, supt. bldgs. and grounds, 1949-53, dir. phys. plant dept., 1953—. Life mem. bd. dirs. Yocona Area council Boy Scouts Am.; treas. United Way; v.p., bd. dirs. CD Council. Served with Constrn. Bn., USNR, 1943-46. Recipient Silver Beaver award Boy Scouts Am., 1970; registered profl. engr., Miss., Mem. Nat. Soc. Profl. Engrs. (Devel. award 1977), Miss. Soc. Profl. Engrs. (devel. award 1976), Nat. Assn. Phys. Plant Adminstrs. (past dir.), Southeastern Assn. Phys. Plant Adminstrs. (past pres.), Chi Epsilon, Omicron Delta Kappa, Sigma Pi Epsilon. Presbyterian. Club: Masons. Home: 304 Phillip Rd Oxford MS 38655 Office: Phys Plant Dept U Miss University MS 38677

WHITE, JOSEPH ELLISON, business exec.; b. San Jose, Calif., Dec. 16, 1947; s. Joseph Thomas and Lorraine (Harris) W.; B.A., Old Dominion U., 1977; m. Minnie Elizabeth Mills, Sept. 10, 1972; children—Michael, Mary. Editor, Virginia Beach Guide, Lisky Lithograph, Inc., Norfolk, Va., 1969-74; tchr., vocat. coordinator Rehab. Sch. Authority, Chesapeake, Va., 1974-78; mgr. Stihl, Inc., Virginia Beach, 1978—. Mem. Am. Mgmt. Assn., In-Plant Printing Mgmt. Assn., Va. Athletic Assn. Author: Lithography I and II Curriculum Text. Home: 5501 Shadowwood Dr Virginia Beach VA 23455 Office: 536 Viking Dr Virginia Beach VA 23452

WHITE, JOSEPH OLIN, lawyer; b. Nashville, June 21, 1907; s. Hugh Couch and Olive Mae (Soper) W.; LL.B., YMCA Law Sch., 1934; postgrad. Vanderbilt U., 1955-57, U. Miss., 1956-57; m. Anna Margaret Johnson, Apr. 6, 1954. Admitted to Tenn. bar, 1934; partner firm Manier, White, Herod, Hollabaugh & Smith, Nashville, 1936—. Chmn. civil service com., Nashville, 1939-42; mem. Tenn. Senate, 1947-48; mem. Davidson County (Tenn.) Sch. Bd., 1955-63; mem. county ct., Davidson County, 1946-55. Bd. dirs. Family and Children's Services, Nashville, 1957-62. Served to maj. AUS, 1942-45. Decorated Bronze Star medal. Fellow Am. Coll. Trial Lawyers, Internat. Acad. Trial Lawyers, Internat. Soc. Barristers, Am. Bar Found.; mem. Assn. Ins. Attys. (pres. 1971-73), Nashville Bar Assn. (dir., pres. 1954-55), Tenn. Bar Assn. (dir., pres. 1964-65), English Speaking Union (nat. dir. 1956-71). Mason. Clubs: Cumberland; Masons, Elks. Home: 6417 Panorama Dr Brentwood TN 37027 Office: 230 4th Ave Nashville TN 37219

WHITE, JOSHUA WARREN, JR., state legislator; b. Norfolk, Va., Aug. 27, 1916; s. Joshua Warren and Emily Fuller (Johnston) W.; student Washington and Lee U., 1939; m. Dorothy Lee Winstead, Aug. 30, 1941; children—Joshua Warren, Dorothy Lee White Van Tassell, William C., Emily J. White Preston. Pres., treas. Old Dominion Paper Co., Norfolk, 1960—; dir. Dillard Paper Co., Greensboro, N.C., Va. Nat. Bank; mem. Va. Ho. of Dels. from 39th Dist., 1962—, asst. majority floor leader, 1974, vice chmn. com. priviledges and elections, 1974, chmn. Chesapeake and its tributaries com., 1972; mem. So. Regional Edn. Bd., 1962-66. Bd. dirs. United Communities Fund, Tidewater Cancer Soc., Norfolk Gen. Hosp., Va. Coll. Fund; trustee Mary Baldwin Coll., Jamestown Found.; pres. Young Democratic Clubs Va., 1946; treas. 2d Dist. Dem. Com., 1958. Served to lt. comdr. USNR, 1940-45. Mem. Norfolk C. of C. (past dir.), Navy League U.S. (past chpt. dir.). Presbyterian. Clubs: Princess Anne Country; Norfolk Yacht and Country, Norfolk German; Commonwealth (Richmond, Va.). Address: 3666 Progress Rd Norfolk VA 23502

WHITE, KENNETH JOEL, educator; b. Chgo., Mar. 14, 1947; s. Harvey and Reva White; B.A., Northwestern U., 1968, M.A., U. Wis., 1970, Ph.D., 1973. Economist, U.S. Treasury, 1969; prof. econs. Rice U., 1972—; vis. prof. U. B.C., 1975-76, U. Hawaii, 1978; cons. in field. Ford Found. grantee, 1970-71, NSF grantee, 1972-73. Mem. Am. Econ. Assn., Econometric Soc., Am. Statis. Assn., So. Econ. Assn., Western Econ. Assn. Contbr. articles to profl. jours. Office: Dept Econs Rice U Houston TX 77001

WHITE, LARRY RUSSELL, elec. engr.; b. Woodville, Ala., Mar. 23, 1949; s. William Quindolyn and Grace Theola (Batey) W.; B.S. in Elec. Engring., Auburn U., 1972, M.S. in Elec. Engring., 1973; postgrad. Ga. Inst. Tech., 1973-74; m. Lynda Kaye Culpepper, July 2, 1971; 1 dau., Pepper WarEagle. Co-op student IBM Corp., Huntsville, Ala., 1968-71; research asst. Auburn (Ala.) U., 1972-73; engr. So. Co. Services, Inc., Birmingham, Ala., 1974-78, mgr. load forecasting, 1978—; instr. elec. engring. U. Ala., Birmingham, 1974—. Tchr. Sunday sch. Homewood Ch. of Christ, Birmingham, 1976—. Schlumberger fellow, 1973. Mem. IEEE, Nat. Mgmt. Assn., Tau Beta Pi, Eta Kappa Nu. Contbr. articles to profl. jours. Home: 5173 Wellstone Circle Birmingham AL 35244 Office: PO Box 2625 Birmingham AL 35202

WHITE, LINDA NELL, chem. mfg. co. exec.; b. Charleston, W.Va., Nov. 24, 1941; d. Frederick Paul and Frances Eloise (Hale) Farley; student Eastern Mont. Coll., 1959-60; student W.Va. State Coll., 1973-74; m. Bernard Jerome White, May 27, 1964. Gymnastics instr. Lawrence Frankel Inst., Charleston, W.Va., 1961; sec. Union Carbide Corp., Institute, W.Va., 1961-73, office services supr., 1973-76, sr. office supr., publ. editor, 1976—. Publicity and communications United Way Kanawha Valley, 1975-79. Mem. Nat. Assn. Female Execs. Democrat. Presbyterian. Editor The Carbider, 1976—. Home: 141 Shawnee Estates Winfield WV 25213 Office: Union Carbide Corp PO Box 2831 Charleston WV 25330

WHITE, LOUIS EDWARD, JR., personnel tng. and devel. co. exec.; b. New Orleans, Jan. 27, 1945; s. Louis E. and Grace W.; B.A., So. U., New Orleans, 1971; postgrad. bus. adminstrn. Loyola U., New Orleans, 1976—; m. Mary Hughes, Feb. 17, 1968; 1 son, Rashaan A. Job placement specialist Jefferson Parish Manpower Dept., 1971-72; office mgr. N.Y. Life Ins. Co., New Orleans, 1972-76; cons. So. Devel. Found., Lafayette, La., 1977; agy. mgr. 70001 Ltd., New Orleans, 1977—. Pres., NAACP, Metairie, 1974-75, Jefferson Parish Manpower Council, 1976-77; pres. bd. dirs. Jefferson Community Action, 1977-79.Served with AUS, 1963-66. Mem. Adminstrv. Mgmt. Soc., Am. Coll. Life Underwriters. Republican. Lutheran. Club: Masons. Home: 1412 Compromise St Kenner LA 70062 Office: 344 Camp St Suite 1200 New Orleans LA 70130

WHITE, LOUISE HUMPHRIES, counselor; b. Grayson, La., Mar. 30, 1926; d. Ernest Christopher and Mary Vina (Elder) Humphries; B.A., Centenary Coll. of La., 1962; M.S. in Counseling, Ga. State U., 1971; m. Verlin Ralph White, Mar. 11, 1944; children—Carol Louise White Kelly, Verlin Ralph, Jr. Employment counselor, La. State Employment Service, Shreveport, 1966-68; master counselor Ga. Dept. of Labor, Profl. Office, Job Service Center, Atlanta, 1968—. Mem. Cathedral of St. Philip, Atlanta, 1968—, Sunday sch. tchr., 1975-78, Daughter of the King, 1973—, Episcopal ch. women, 1973—, Internat. Christian Community Network, 1973—; Foyer group leader for reconciliation, 1974—. Recipient Jongleurs award for service to Marjorie Lyons Playhouse, Centenary Coll., 1963. Mem. Am. Personnel and Guidance Assn., Nat. Employment Counselors Assn., Internat. Assn. of Personnel in Employment Service, AAUW, LWV, Atlanta Hist. Soc. Episcopalian. Club: Northside Womans (dir., chmn. arts dept. 1979—). Home: 3200 Lenox Rd NE Atlanta GA 30324 Office: One Peachtree St Atlanta GA 30303

WHITE, MARJORIE GLENN, social service adminstr.; b. Valdosta, Ga., Nov. 25, 1934; d. Joseph Max and Willie Amelia (Wall) Glenn; A.B., Valdosta State Coll., 1954, M.S., 1980; children—Sharon, David, Patrick. Tchr. English, Trion (Ga.) High Sch., 1954-55; ednl. counselor Moody AFB, Valdosta, 1956-61; casework supr. Lowndes County Dept. Family and Children Services, Valdosta, 1962-74, dep. dir., 1974—; resource speaker Valdosta State Coll. Pres., Valdosta Civic Roundtable, 1979; mem. Moody AFB Child Advocacy Com., 1977-79; mem. Lowndes County Spl. Edn. Adv. Com., 1977-79; bd. dirs. Big Bros./Big Sisters Com. of South Ga., 1978-79; mem. screening com. Mental Health Adolescent Day Care Treatment Program, 1978-79; bd. dirs. Mental Health Assn., 1978-79; mem. spl. edn. adv. com. Valdosta City Sch. System, 1978-79. Mem. Ga. County Welfare Assn., Valdosta C. of C., Alpha Kappa Delta. Democrat. Methodist. Club: Quota. Home: PO Box 386 Valdosta GA 31601 Office: PO Box 1246 Valdosta GA 31601

WHITE, MORRIS EDWARD, lawyer; b. Yazoo City, Miss., Aug. 13, 1892; s. Andrew and Fannie (Middleton) W.; B.S., U. Miss., 1913, M.A., 1915, LL.B., 1915; m. Louise Ruffin, Oct. 8, 1920; children—Louise (Mrs. W. C. Cooke), Frances Ruffin (Mrs. James B. Klay), Martha Morris (Mrs. Daniel S. Blalock, Jr.). Admitted to Miss. bar, 1915; practiced in Columbus, 1915-17; mem. firm Bell & White, Greenville, 1919-25; admitted to Fla. bar, 1925, since practiced in Tampa; mem. firm Shackleford, Brown, White & Tillman, 1925-28, Mabry, Reaves, Carlton & White, 1930-44, Fowler, White, Gillen, Yancey & Humkey, 1944-59, Fowler, White, Gillen, Humkey & Trenam, 1959, now mem. firms Fowler, White, Gillen, Boggs, Villareal, and Banker, Tampa, also Fowler, White, Burnett, Hurley, Banick & Strickroot, Miami, Fla. Mem. Hillsborough County Def. Council, 1941-42; bd. dirs. U.S.O., 1941-45; chmn. Hillsborough County Port Authority, 1945-48; pres. Tampa Community Chest, 1938. Served to capt. U.S. Army, 1918. Mem. Am., Fla., Hillsborough County bar assns., Internat. Assn. Ins. Counsel, Maritime Law Assn. U.S., Am. Judicature Soc., Am. Legion (past post comdr.). Episcopalian. Clubs: Masons (33 deg.), Shriners, Rotary (past pres.; dist. gov. internat. 1948-49), Univ., Palma Ceia Golf and Country, Tampa Yacht and Country. Home: 916 Golfview Ave Tampa FL 33609 Office: Freedom Federal Bldg 220 Madison St Tampa FL 33602

WHITE, NANCY BROWN, counselor; b. Milano, Tex.; d. Willie and Elnora Lavan Brown; B.S., Tex. So. U., 1970, M.Ed., 1976; m. June 30, 1979. File clk. Gulf Oil Co., Houston, 1970-71; elem. tchr. Houston Ind. Sch. Dist., 1971-78, counselor, 1978, elem. counselor, 1979—. Cert. in guidance. Mem. NEA, Am. Personnel and Guidance Assn., Tex. Tchrs. Assn., Houston Tchrs. Assn. Methodist. Home: 4417 Coke St Houston TX 77020 Office: Houston Ind Sch Dist 3830 Richmond St Houston TX 77020

WHITE, PERRY MERRILL, physician; b. Texarkana, Ark., Oct. 11, 1925; s. Perry Merrill and Mary Gladys (Shelton) W.; B.S., Baylor U., 1948, M.D., 1953; postgrad. Vanderbilt U., 1948-49; m. Lucy Katherine Freeman, Dec. 27, 1947; children—Perry Merrill III, Georgia Lynette, Katherine Landis, John David. Intern, VA Hosp., Houston, 1953-54; practice gen. medicine and surgery, Spearman, Tex., 1955-57; resident orthopedic surgery Talmadge Meml. Hosp., Augusta, Ga., 1957-61; practice medicine, specializing in orthopedic surgery, Atlanta, 1961—; chief Ga. Adult Amputee Clinic, 1970-78; panelist Ga. Dept. Vocat. Rehab.; instr. Ga. Baptist Hosp. Orthopedic Surgery Residency Program. Cons. Ga. Crippled Childrens Service. Mem. Circle-R Republican Support Com., North by Northwest Civic Assn.; bd. dirs. Haggai Inst. for Advanced Leadership Tng., Singapore and Atlanta. Served with USNR, 1944-46. Diplomate Am. Bd. Orthopedic Surgery. Fellow Am. Acad. Orthopedic Surgeons, A.C.S.; mem. AMA, So., Ga., Atlanta med. assns., Eastern Orthopedic Assn., Ga., Atlanta orthopedic socs., Am. Coll. Sports Medicine, Alpha Kappa Kappa. Baptist (deacon). Club: Cherokee Town and Country. Home: 1547 Cave Rd NW Atlanta GA 30327 Office: 315 Boulevard NE Atlanta GA 30312

WHITE, POLLY ANN, educator; b. Natchez, Miss., Apr. 9, 1919; d. William Pink and Callie (Thompson) Ratliff; B.S., So. U., Baton Rouge, 1949; M.S., Duquesne U., 1950; postgrad. N.Y. U., 1954-55; m. Calvin Sherman White, Dec. 4, 1951. Asso. prof., chmn. bus. dept. Alcorn Coll., Lorman, Miss., 1950-63; asso. prof. Ala. Agrl. and Mech. Coll., 1963-65, Grambling (La.) Coll., 1965-70; prof. accounting and bus. adminstrn. Alcorn Coll., 1970—. Ford Found. fellow, 1962. Mem. Am. Accounting Assn., Nat. Assn. Accountants, AAUP, Miss. Bus. Edn. Assn., Alpha Kappa Mu. Roman Catholic. Home: 907 N Union St Natchez MS 39120 Office: Box 133 Alcorn Coll Lorman MS 39096

WHITE, RALPH DALLAS, health ins. exec.; b. Oklahoma City, Feb. 11, 1919; s. Ralph Allen and Ora Della (Lamberson) W.; grad. Okla. Sch. Bus., 1938; B.Comml.Sci., Okla. Sch. Accountancy, Law and Finance, 1941; postgrad. U. Tulsa, 1947-48, U. Mich., 1965-66; m. Ramona Corrine Cafee, Aug. 29, 1943; children—Richard Dallas, Linda Diane. With Gen. Motors Acceptance Corp., Tulsa, 1939-42, Douglas Aircraft Corp., Tulsa, 1942-45; accounting supr. Blue Cross & Blue Shield of Okla., Tulsa, 1945-50, mgr. personnel and systems, 1950-51, office mgr., 1951-57, dir. adminstrn., 1957-62, sec.-treas., 1962-67, v.p., sec.-treas., 1967-70, v.p., treas., 1970-74, exec. v.p., treas., 1974—. Mem. Internat. Com. of Tulsa, 1967-68; mem. Ark. Basin Devel. Assn., 1968—. Recipient Merit award key, Nat. Office Mgrs. Assn./Adminstrv. Mgmt. Soc., 1958, Diamond Merit Award key, 1968; Boss of the Year award, Am. Bus. Women's Assn., 1961. Mem. Nat. Office Mgmt. Assn./Adminstrv. Mgmt. Soc. (pres. 1957-58), C. of C. Methodist. Clubs: Tulsa Farm, Kiwanis. Contbr. articles to profl. jours. Home: 4709 E 22 Pl Tulsa OK 74114 Office: 1215 S Boulder St Tulsa OK 74119

WHITE, RAYMOND DUTTON, civil engr.; b. Hattiesburg, Miss., Nov. 1, 1939; s. Walter Howard and Dorothy (Dutton) W.; B.S., M.I.T., 1961; postgrad Sch. Internat. Affairs, Columbia U., 1963-64; m. Lorene Dandridge Sharp, Dec. 31, 1972. Project engr. to v.p., dir. J. R. Wauford & Co., Cons. Engrs., Inc., Nashville, 1964-76; pres., chmn. bd. White Taylor Walker Cons. Engrs., Inc., Nashville, 1977—; mem. civil engring. vis. com. Nashville Tech. Inst., 1975—. Bd. dirs. Hope, Inc., 1974—; pres. Home, Inc., 1970—; deacon Donelson Presbyterian Ch. Served to lt. (j.g.) USN, 1961-63, to lt. comdr. USNR, 1963—. Internat. fellow Columbia U., 1963-64; registered profl. engr., Tenn., Ala., Ky., Ga., Miss., Ark., N.C., Fla.; diplomate Am. Acad. Environ. Engrs. Mem. Am. Water Works Assn., ASTM, ASME, Nat. Soc. Profl. Engrs., Cons. Engrs. Tenn., U.S. Naval Inst., Sigma Xi, Pi Tau Sigma. Home: 3901 Harding Rd Apt 504 Nashville TN 37205 Office: PO Box 40421 Nashville TN 37204

WHITE, RICHARD CRAWFORD, congressman; b. El Paso, Tex., Apr. 29, 1923; s. James Crawford and Lela (Mueller) W.; B.A., U. Tex., 1946, LL.B., 1949; m. Katherine Huffman, Dec. 18, 1949 (dec. Mar. 1972); children—Rodrick James, Richard Whitman, Raymond Edward; m. 2d, Kathleen Fitzgerald, Sept. 29, 1973; children—Bonnie Kathleen, Sean Carroll, Kenneth Corin. Admitted to Tex. bar, 1949; trial atty., El Paso, 1949-64; mem. 89th-96th congresses from 16th Dist. Tex. Active civic and vets. orgns. Mem. Tex. Ho. of Reps., 1955-58; chmn. El Paso County Democratic Com., 1962-64. Served with USMCR, World War II; PTO. Mem. El Paso County Bar Assn., State Bar Tex., Phi Alpha Delta, Sigma Alpha Epsilon. Episcopalian. Club: 89th Democratic Congress (dir.). Home: 146 US Courthouse El Paso TX 79901 Office: Rayburn House Office Bldg Washington DC 20515

WHITE, RICHARD LYNN, controller; b. Jonesboro, Ark., Mar. 7, 1944; s. Lavell and Lola Marie (Mays) W.; B.S. in Acctg., Ark. State U., 1969, M.S. in Bus. Adminstrn., 1976; m. Judy Lyndal Brown, June 2, 1963; children—Richard Andrew, David Wayne, Jamie Lynn. Jr. cost acct. Colson Corp., Jonesboro, 1967; controller Frolic Footwear div. Wolverine World Wide, Inc., Jonesboro, 1967—. Deacon, treas., tchr., fin. com. Needham Baptist Ch. Served with USAF, 1963-67. Mem. Acctg. Club. Democrat. Office: Frolic Footwear 1020 Aggie Rd Jonesboro AR 72401

WHITE, ROBERT ANDERSON, lawyer; b. Norfolk, Va., Dec. 12, 1928; s. Warren T. and Clara (Anderson) W.; B.A., Va. Mil. Inst., 1950; LL.B., U. Va., 1955; m. Alice Peyton Stansbury, May 19, 1951; children—Warren Thomas, Anne Peyton, Charles Stansbury, Margaret Preston. Admitted to Va. bar, 1955, Fla. bar, 1956; partner Mershon, Sawyer, Johnston, Dunwody & Cole, Miami, 1956—; mem. jud. nominating commn 3d Dist. Ct. Appeals, 1975-79 Mem. Orange Bowl Com., 1969—, pres., 1978-79; trustee Met. Mus. Art, Miami, chmn. bd. trustees, 1979—; bd. dirs. SE div. Children's Home Soc. of Fla., 1964-75, pres., 1970-71. Served with AUS, 1951-53. Mem. Am., Fla., Va., Dade County (pres. 1972-73) bar assns., Am. Coll. Probate Counsel, Phi Delta Phi, Kappa Alpha. Clubs: Miami, University, Riviera Country. Home: 9205 SW 59th Av Miami FL 33156 Office: 1600 1st Nat Bank Bldg Miami FL 33131

WHITE, ROBERT MILES FORD, life ins. co. exec.; b. Lufkin, Tex., June 9, 1928; s. Sullivan Miles and Faye Clark (Scurlock) F.; B.A., Stephen F. Austin State U., 1948; B.B.A., St. Mary's U., San Antonio, 1955; m. Mary Ruth Wathen, Nov. 10, 1946; children—Martha, Robert, Benedict, Mary, Jesse, Margaret, Maureen, Thomas. Tchr., Douglas (Tex.) Pub. Schs., 1946-47, Houston Pub. Schs., 1948-51; office mgr. Heat Control Insulation Co., San Antonio, 1951-53; accountant S.W. Acceptance Co., San Antonio, 1953-55; sec.-treas. Howell Corp., San Antonio, 1955-64; agent New Eng. Mutual Life Ins. Co., San Antonio, 1964-71; br. mgr. Occidental Life Ins. Co. of Calif., San Antonio, 1971—. Mem. Equal Employment Opportunity Council, 1974—; active Wolverine Boys Council, 1969—. Mem. San Antonio C. of C., San Antonio Estate Planners Council, S.W. Pension Conf., Nat., Tex., San Antonio assns. life underwriters, Am. Soc. Chartered Life Underwriters, San Antonio, S.E. Tex. geneal. and hist. socs., Sons of Republic of Tex., SAR, Children Am. Revolution (sr. pres. Denny Anderson soc.), Kappa Pi Sigma. Republican. Roman Catholic. Home: 701 Sunshine Dr E San Antonio TX 78228 Office: 6243 IH 10 North Suite 330 San Antonio TX 78201

WHITE, RONALD LYNN, ins. co. exec.; b. Fayetteville, Tenn., Oct. 11, 1951; s. Lylburn and Martha Katherine W.; B.S., U. Tenn., 1973; m. Eloise Ann Boling, Feb. 18, 1978; 1 stepson, Jeffrey Allen; children from previous marriage—Amy, Jill, Meg. Agt., Equitable Life Assurance Soc., Chattanooga, 1975, asst. dist. mgr., 1976, asst. dist. mgr., Nashville, 1977-78, dist. mgr., Murfreesboro, Tenn., 1978—; moderator Life Underwriter Tng. Council, 1979-80. Mem. Nat. Assn. Securities Dealers (registered rep.), Murfreesboro C. of C. (econ. devel. council), Nat. Assn. Life Underwriters, Gen. Agts. and Mgrs. Conf., Am. Mgmt. Assn. Republican. Methodist. Clubs: Lions, Elks. Home: 1315 E Castle St #p-3 Murfreesboro TN 37130 Office: PO Box 157 Murfreesboro TN 37130

WHITE, ROSALYN ELIZABETH, speech pathologist; b. Cumberland, Md., May 27, 1954; d. Howard Albert and Rosalyn Elizabeth Buchanan; M.S., Fla. State U., 1976; m. Wesley Gayden White, Apr. 2, 1977. Speech therapist Taylor County Sch. System, Perry, Fla., 1977—. Mem. Am. Speech and Hearing Assn. (cert. clin. competence, cert. public adminstrn.), Sigma Kappa (chmn. adv. com., chmn. edn. com.). Republican. Methodist. Club: Tallahassee Spa. Author: Articulation Stuttering and Hearing Loss-A Teacher's Guide, 1979. Home: 2855 Apalachee Pkwy #A-24 Tallahassee FL 32303 Office: Aquanaldo St Perry FL 32347

WHITE, SARA JANE WARREN, local govt. adminstr.; b. Waco, Tex., Jan. 1, 1936; d. Charles Alexander and Mary Frances (Stevens) Westbrook; B.A. in Sociology, Incarnate Word Coll., San Antonio, 1970; M.S. in Urban Studies, Trinity U., 1972; m. Robert E. White; children—Sally Anne, Stevens Westbrook, John William. Planner, Community Welfare Council, San Antonio, 1971-72, Dept. Planning, City of San Antonio, 1972-73; asst. coordinator Econ. Devel. Planning Services, San Antonio, 1973-76; coordinator Office of Inner City Devel. San Antonio, 1976-78; dir. planning City of Bellaire (Tex.), 1978—. Chmn. program devel. Profl. Conf. Jr. Leagues, 1975-76, sustainer advisor, 1976-77; v.p. Project Free, Econ. Opportunity Devel. Corp., Del. Agy., 1976-78; 2d. v.p. Ecumenical

Downtown Christian Asst. Ministry, 1977-78. Mem. Am. Inst. Cert. Planners, Am. Planning Assn. (sec. Houston sect.). Mem. Disciples of Christ. Research in field. Home: 718 Montclair Sugarland TX 77478

WHITE, SUSAN ANN BODER, educator, guidance counselor; b. Sharon, Pa., Jan. 18, 1943; d. William Dunbar and Claretta Ann (Kelso) Boder; student Westminster Coll., 1960-61; B.S., Ohio State U., 1964; M.A., Rollins Coll., 1978; m. James Marion White, Dec. 26, 1964; children—Jill Susann, James Marion, Jeremy William. Tchr., Robert Louis Stevenson Sch., Grandview Heights Sch. System, Columbus, Ohio, 1964-67, West End Sch., Moore County, West End, N.C., 1967-68, Robert Louis Stevenson Sch., Grandview Heights, Columbus, 1969-70; pvt. practice counseling, Sanford, Fla., 1978—. Sunday sch. tchr.; treas., sec., 2d v.p. Idyllwilde PTA, Sanford, 1974-76; pres. Mariners, 1976-77. Mem. Am. Personnel And Guidance Assn., Fla. Personnel and Guidance Assn., P.E.O., Kappa Delta Pi. Republican. Presbyterian. Address: 201 Vinewood Dr Sanford FL 32771

WHITE, SUSAN ELLIOTT, counselor; b. San Antonio, Dec. 13, 1941; d. Aubrey and Helen (Shapard) Elliott; B.A., So. Meth. U., 1963; M.Ed., U. Tex., El Paso, 1976; postgrad. N.Mex. State U., 1977—; m. William A. White, Apr. 18, 1964; children—David, Elliott, Reagan. Tchr. English, Ardsley (N.Y.) High Sch., 1964-66; counselor El Paso Center for Mental Health and Mental Retardation, 1976; marriage and family counselor, El Paso, 1977—; sex therapist William Beaumont Army Med. Center, El Paso, 1978—; mem. adv. bd. Women's Resource Center, 1977—; counselor Rape Crisis, 1979—. Chmn. membership LWV, El Paso, 1972-74; bd. dirs. El Paso Children's Day Care Assn., 1974-76, Planned Parenthood El Paso, 1973-78. Cert. Am. Assn. Sex Educators, Counselors, and Therapists. Mem. Am. Personnel and Guidance Assn., Nat. Council Family Relations, El Paso Women's Polit. Caucus, Sierra Club, Phi Kappa Phi. Presbyterian. Home: 4911 Meadowlark Dr El Paso TX 79922

WHITE, THOMAS HARRY, photographer; b. Spartanburg, S.C., Sept. 5, 1930; s. Jimmie A. and Clara (Cothran) W.; student N.Y. Inst. Photography, 1947; student journalism U. N.C., 1950; m. Lillian Ruth Hughes, Mar. 15, 1949; children—Diane Elizabeth, Karen Patryce, Thomas Harry. With editorial staff Spartanburg Herald Jour., 1947-50; organized B. & B. Studios, Inc., Spartanburg, 1950, pres., gen. mgr., 1962—; pres. Kaminers Art and Frame Co., Spartanburg, 1965—; exec. v.p. Graphico, Inc., 1971—, King Photo. Recipient awards including Nat. Art League award, 1948, S.C. Press Assn. award, 1949. Mem. Photog. Soc. Am., Nat. Press Photographers Assn., Royal Order of Scotland. Mem. United Methodist Ch. (lay leader). Clubs: Masons (33 deg.), Shriners, Sertoma. Photog. works in traveling photog. exhbns. Home: 230 Cart Dr Spartanburg SC 29302 Office: 268 E Main St Spartanburg SC 29302

WHITE, THURMAN JAMES, former univ. ofcl.; b. Ponca City, Okla., Nov. 7, 1916; s. Charles L. and Winona Faye (Enfield) W.; A.B., Phillips U., 1936; M.S., U. Okla., 1941; Ph.D., U. Chgo., 1950; m. Corrine Laura Hartson, June 13, 1939; children—Sue Ann, Charles Frank. Instr. prison edn. U. Okla., 1937-39, supr. Statewide Mus. Service, 1940-42, dir. audio-visual edn., 1942-46, asst. dir. extension div., 1946-47, acting dir., 1947-48, dir., 1949-50, dean extension div. 1950—, dean Coll. Continuing Edn., 1961—, v.p. univ., 1961-79, v.p. emeritus for continuing edn., 1980—, also regents' prof. higher edn.; exec. sec. Film Council of Am., 1946-47, bd. trustees, 1950. Mem. Def. Adv. Com. Edn. Armed Forces, 1957-60; exec. vice chmn. 1961 White House Conf. on Aging; mem. UNESCO Com. for Advancement of Adult Edn., mem. nat. adv. council Adult Basic Tchr. Tng. Program, 1966; mem. Pres.'s Nat. Adv. Council on Extension and Continuing Edn.; mem. White House Conf. on Internat. Cooperation, 1965, White House Conf. on Edn., 1965, mem. commn. acad. affairs Am. Council Edn. Bd. dirs. Gt. Books Found., Center Study Liberal Edn. Adults. Mem. NEA, Ednl. Screen (mem. editorial bd. 1947-50), Adult Edn. Assn. U.S.A. (pres. 1965-66), C. of C., Okla. Congress Parents and Tchrs. (state bd. mgrs. 1942—), Okla. Edn. Assn., Am. Legion, Okla. Mental Health Assn. (1st v.p.), Nat. U. Extension Assn. (chmn. liberal edn. com., chmn. on Extension Services in Armed Forces, rep. Am. Council on Edn., 1958-60, pres. 1960-61), S.W. Adult Edn. Assn. (exec. com.), Okla. Adult Edn. Assn., Phi Beta Kappa, Phi Delta Kappa, Psi Chi, Pi Kappa Alpha. Clubs: Internat. (Washington); Rotary. Editor: Adult Education. Contbr. articles to ednl. jours. Home: 1105 Woodland Dr Norman OK 73069

WHITE, TIMOTHY JOSEPH, physicist, indsl. co. exec.; b. Nashville, Apr. 3, 1942; s. Francis Peter and Frances Rita (Marcisovsky) W.; B.A., Vanderbilt U., 1964; M.S., U. Ala. in Huntsville, 1974, M.A.S., 1976; M.P.A., Nova U., 1978, D.P.A., 1978; m. Christine Helen Spond, Sept. 5, 1964; children—Marcia Ann, Angela Marie, Charlene Kay. Jr. engr. Air Reduction Co., Jersey City, 1964-66; physicist Sperry Rand Corp., Huntsville, 1966-67, sr. physicist, 1967-74, sr. staff physicist, group leader, 1974-77; sr. staff analyst, asst. security supr. Consol. Industries, Inc., Huntsville, 1977-78; sr. staff engr. SCI Systems, Inc., 1978-79; sr. staff scientist Sci. Applications, Inc., 1979—; pres. Dynamic Enterprises, Inc., 1979—; cons. NASA, 1966-67, 1976—, TAI Corp., 1978-79, Lyndra Corp., 1978-79, SCICOM, Inc., 1978-79. Pres. Holy Spirit Sch. PTA, 1974-76; mem. Radio Amateur Civil Emergency Service, 1974—; mem. crafts com. J.F. Drake State Tech. Coll., 1976—; instr. Christian Formation Program, 1973-75; vol. donor ARC, 1973—. Recipient Apollo Achievement award NASA, 1959, Skylab Achievement award NASA, 1974; Outstanding Service award J.F. Drake Coll., 1979. Mem. Am. Mgmt. Assns., Am. Phys. Soc., Ala. Acad. Sci., Am. Def. Preparedness Assn., Am. Soc. for Pub. Adminstrn., Policy Studies Orgn., Tech. Mktg. Soc. Am., Vanderbilt U. Alumni Assn., U. Ala. in Huntsville Alumni Assn., Sigma Pi Sigma, Mu Alpha Theta. Roman Catholic. Clubs: Am. Radio Relay League. Contbr. articles to profl. jours. Home: 11230 Hillwood Dr Huntsville AL 35803 Office: Sci Applications Inc 2109 W Clinton Ave Huntsville AL 35805

WHITE, TOM WILLINGHAM, accountant; b. McAllen, Tex., Feb. 16, 1943; s. Louis Thomas and Leota Faye (Grimm) W.; B.B.A., U. Tex., 1965; m. Lauryn G. Longwell, Mar. 8, 1968; children—Brad Edward, Parker Thomas, Landan Allen. Accountant, Haskins & Sells, C.P.A.'s, Houston, 1965-67, Paul Veale, C.P.A., McAllen, Tex., 1967-68; self-employed as C.P.A., Corpus Christi, Tex., 1969-75; pres. White, Bemis & Sluyter, Inc., C.P.A.'s, Corpus Christi, 1975—; officer Andrews Distbg. Co., Inc., Corpus Christi, 1976—. Bd. dirs., pres. Corpus Christi Bus. and Estate Council. C.P.A., Mem. Am. Inst. C.P.A.'s, Tex. Soc. C.P.A.'s (chmn. com. Corpus Christi 1971-73), U. Tex. Ex-Students Assn. (officer Corpus Christi chpt. 1970-71, bd. dirs. 1971-72). Clubs: Corpus Christi Country, Corpus Christi Town, Beachcombers, Conquistadores (officer, mem. bd.) (Corpus Christi). Home: 6121 Lost Creek Corpus Christi TX 78413 Office: 4421 Agnes St Corpus Christi TX 78405

WHITE, VEDA LANELL, nurse; b. Big Spring, Tex., Dec. 9, 1934; d. Glem Marvin and Cora Lee (McCann) Gilkerson; student Howard County Jr. Coll., 1964; L.V.N., Med. Arts Sch. Nursing, 1954; m. William J. White, Sept. 19, 1953; children—Sharon K., Ronald Craig. Supr. operating rm., supr. labor and delivery Med. Arts Clinic Hosp., Big Spring, Tex., 1960-63; instr. vocat. sch. nursing, 1963-73; operating rm. technician Galveston County Meml. Hosp., Texas City, Tex., 1973-75; asst. dir. sterile processing U. Tex. Med. Br., Galveston, 1975—. Mem. Cert. Operating Room Technicians (v.p. Galveston County 1974-75), Am. Soc. Hosp. Central Service Personnel Am. Hosp. Assn., Assn. Surg. Technicians. Home: 5113 Cottonwood Circle Dickinson TX 77539 Office: John Sealy Hosp Sterile Processing U Tex Med Br Galveston TX 77550

WHITE, WANDA MARIE, math. edn. cons.; b. Hall County, Ga., June 27, 1937; d. James Heron and Inez Ruby (Johnson) W.; B.A. in Edn., Ga. State Coll. for Women, 1959; M.Ed., Emory U., 1969; Ph.D., Ga. State U., 1979. Tchr., Fulton County Schs., Atlanta, 1959-62, 71, Lovett Sch., Atlanta, 1962-67, Decatur City, Ga., 1967-68, Atlanta, 1969-70, Emory U., Atlanta, 1968-69, 70-71, Mercer U., Atlanta, 1975-76; math. edn. cons. Ga. Dept. Edn., Atlanta, 1972-74, 76—. Mem. Nat. Council Tchrs. Math., Assn. State Suprs. Maths., Ga. Assn. Suprs. Math., Ga. Council Tchrs. Math. Home: 1188 Gordon Combs Rd Marietta GA 30064 Office: Ga Dept Edn State Office Bldg Atlanta GA 30334

WHITE, WILBER SIDNEY, JR., dentist; b. Beaumont, Tex., Mar. 15, 1922; s. Wilber Sample and Florence Viola (Lloyd) W.; A.A., Lamar Jr. Coll., 1941; B.S., Sam Houston State Tchrs. Coll., 1943; Certified in Meteorology, U. Cal. at Los Angeles, 1944; D.D.S., Baylor U., 1950; m. Margaret Culver, June 5, 1949; children—Susan, Mary Katherine, Marilyn, Patricia, David, John, Paul, Sarah. Practice of dentistry, Beaumont, Tex., 1950—; dir. dental clinic City Health Clinic, 1967—; chmn. adv. com. Lamar Sch. Dental Hygiene, 1969—. Bd. dirs. Tex Found. Dental Health and Edn., Tex. Dental Plans, Inc., Citizens Nat. Dental Plan; exec. bd. Southeast Tex. Health Council, 1973—. Served to capt. USAAC, 1943-47; CBI. Fellow Am. Coll. Dentistry; mem. Am. (council dental health 1971—, alt. mem. ho. dels. 1972—, del. nat. health council), Tex. (chmn. council dental health 1969-70, v.p. 1971-73, council on edn. 1974—) dental assns., Sabine Dist. Dental Soc. (pres. 1963, gen. chmn. spring clinic meetings 1963—), Am. Acad. Gen. Practice, Internat. Assn. Orthodontists, Tex. Pub. Health Assn., Pierre Fauchard Acad. Dentistry, Chgo. Dental Soc. (asso.), Baylor Dental Alumni Assn. (dir.), Lamar U. Alumni Assn. (dir.). Methodist. Mason (K.T., Shriner). Clubs: Sertoma (pres. 1963) Optimist (pres. 1954, lt. gov. 1958), Baylor Century (dir.), Knife and Fork, Bus. and Profl. (pres. 1962) (Beaumont). Home: 3495 Kenwood Dr Beaumont TX 77706 Office: PO Box 5453 Beaumont TX 77702

WHITE, WILLIAM VANNOY, assn. exec.; b. Lenoir, N.C., Mar. 24, 1924; s. Frank Boyd and Cornelia (Miller) W.; B.A., U. N.C., 1950; postgrad. U. Miss., 1950-51; m. Joan Robinson, Sept. 11, 1948; children—William Vannoy II, Cynthia Elma, Melinda Carol. Pub. health adviser USPHS, N.C., 1949, Miss., 1950-51, U. Ala. Med. Sch., 1952, chief family safety br., Washington, 1961-65, dir. communicable disease program, Pa., 1954-57; chief cons. region III, HEW, P.R., V.I., 1957-61; legis. liaison Bur. Disease Prevention and Environ. Control, 1966; exec. dir. Nat. Commn. on Product Safety, 1967-70; dir. Injury Data and Control Safety Center, Bur. Product Safety, FDA, Washington, 1970-73, dir. Bur. Info. Edn., U.S. Consumer Product Safety Commn., Bethesda, Md., 1973-77; v.p. Shannondale Club Ltd., 1978, dir., 1978-79; pres., dir. Citizens of Shannondale, Inc., 1979—; real estate developer, Charlestown, W.Va.; vis. prof. U. N.C., U. Mich., Columbia U., U. Minn., Purdue U.; dir. Nat. Safety Council, 1967-75; chmn. Nat. Info. Council, 1967-70. Chmn. community devel. com. City of Charles Town; bd. dirs. The Old Opera House, Charles Town, 1977-80; sr. warden and trustee St. Andrew's Episcopal Ch., Mt. Mission, W.Va., 1978-79. Served with USNR, 1942-46. Recipient Superior Service award HEW, 1959, Meritorious Service award Nat. Commn. on Products Safety, 1970, Merit award FDA, 1972. Mem. Sigma Nu, Phi Mu Alpha. Clubs: Thomas Jefferson (program chmn. 1960), Washington civitan clubs. Contbr. articles on consumer product safety to profl. publs. Home: Route 2 PO Box 615 Harpers Ferry WV 24525 Office: PO Box 289 Charles Town WV 25414

WHITEBIRD, JOANIE, poet, author, editor, educator; b. Houston, July 1, 1951; d. John Henry and Betty Sue (Bledsoe) Green; 1 adopted son, Stephen McMillan. Asst. editor Varsity Tattler Mag., Houston, 1966-67; freelance journalist Post and Chronicle newspapers, Houston, 1967-68; poet in residence Houston Lab. Theatre, 1973; mem. staff, layout artist Southern Voice bi-weekly, Houston, 1973-74, spl. features editor, 1974; curator poetry and performing arts Contemporary Arts Mus., Houston, 1974-75; instr. poetry workshop U. Houston, 1975; poet in residence Houston Ind. Sch. Dists., 1975-76; asso. editor Wings Press, Houston, 1977—; v.p. Western Ind. Pubs., Houston, 1978-79; numerous readings and performances; poetry editor Breakthrough newspapers, 1977-78; artist-in-residence U. St. Thomas, Houston. Dir., coordinator womens poetry reading Internat. Womens Yr. Conf., 1977; coordinator programs Houston Pub. Library; mem. performing arts com. Main St. Festival, 1976. Recipient grants Poetry in Schs., 1975-76, Tex. Commn. on Arts and Humanities, 1976-77. Editor: Small Change (Vassar Miller), 1976; Nolo Contendere (Judson Crews), 1978; author: (short stories) And Then There Was. . ., 1980; 24, 1978; Birthmark, 1977; Spare Poems, 1976; Naked, 1976; Bootstrap Chronicles, 1975; The Family Hand Anthology and Collected Letters, 1971. Zen Buddhist. Home: 305 Fargo St Houston TX 77006 Office: PO Box 66285 Houston TX 77006

WHITED, JOHN WALLACE, III, real estate co. exec.; b. Beckley, W.Va. Mar. 18, 1941; s. John Wallace and Jessie A. (Wauhop) W.; student Gulf Coast Community Coll., Panama City, Fla., 1959-60, Tenn. Tech. U., 1963; m. Dorothy Anne Pringle, June 22, 1961; children—John Wallace, James Robert, Elizabeth Victoria, Kristi Marie. Div. mgr. Sears Roebuck & Co., 1960-70; v.p. Belleisle Corp., Inc., Panama City, 1970—; pres. Whited Wilhite & Assos., Inc. and Four Star Investment Corp., Panama City, 1974—. Bd. dirs. Salvation Army, Panama City, 1977-78. Mem. Nat. Bd. Realtors, Associated Photographers Internat., Panama City Bd. Realtors, Associated Photographers Internat., Panama City Bd. Realtors. Republican. Methodist. Clubs: Masons, Shriners. Office: 1815 W 15th St Panama City FL 32401

WHITEFIELD, CAROLYN LEE, lawyer; b. Texarkana, Ark., Mar. 1, 1946; d. William Parker, Sr. and Julia Arabella (Rayburn) Whitefield; B.S., So. State Coll., 1970; J.D., U. Ark., 1973; m. Jerry Allen McDowell, Sept. 21, 1974. Admitted to Ark. bar, 1973, Tex. bar, 1974; individual practice law, Texarkana, 1973—. Mem. Am., Ark., Tex. bar assns. Democrat. Baptist. Home: Route 7 Box 536 Texarkana AR 75502 Office: Box 8007 State Line Plaza Room 611 Texarkana AR 75502

WHITEHEAD, DAVID CALLOWAY, JR., family physician; b. Danville, Va., May 12, 1947; s. David Calloway and Audrey (Worshon) W.; B.A. in chemistry, U. Richmond, 1969; M.D., Med. Coll. Va., 1973; m. Janice Scott, Aug. 5, 1972; children—David Calloway, Scott Hamilton. Intern, Med. Coll. Va., Richmond, 1973-74; resident in family practice Blackstone (Va.) Family Practice, 1973-76; dir. med. dept. Staunton (Va.) Correctional Inst., 1976—; dir. med. edn. Rockingham Meml. Hosp., Harrisonburg, Va., 1977—, pres., founder family practice dept., 1977; dir. First Va. Bank, Planters. Diplomate Am. Bd. Family Practice. Mem. Am. Acad. Family Physicians, Alumni Assn. Med. Coll. Va. (chpt. pres.-elect), Med. Soc. Va. (sec. chpt. 1980), Va. Acad. Family Physicians (del. 1979—), Am. Heart Assn. (dir. Rockingham County 1979—), Am. Cancer Soc. (dir. Rockingham County 1979—). Roman Catholic. Club: Rotary. Home: 881 Blueridge Dr Harrisonburg VA 22801 Office: 1015 Harrison St Harrisonburg VA 22801

WHITEHEAD, JACK OAKLEY, JR., telephone co. mgr.; b. Williamsburg, Ky., Oct. 23, 1943; s. Jack Oakley and Tennessee (Mays) W.; B.S., U. Tenn., 1968; m. Joyce Fussell, Aug. 26, 1966; children—Shelley, Brian. Bus. mgr. Daily Beacon, U. Tenn., 1966-68; mem. advt. staff Knoxville News Sentinel, 1967; bus. office mgr. South Central Bell Tel. Co., Knoxville, 1968-69, Memphis, 1970-71, Paris, Tenn., 1972-73, dist. supr., Shreveport, La., 1973-79, dist. mgr. Residence Service Center/Phone Center, New Orleans, 1979—. Chmn., Henry County chpt. Jr. Achievement, 1971-72; dist. chmn. Bedford Forrest council Boy Scouts Am., 1972-73; chmn. Henry County Democratic Com., 1972-73. Served with USNR, 1961-64. Mem. Am. Mgmt. Assn. Democrat. Presbyterian. Clubs: Rotary, Jaycees. Office: 1101 Franklin St New Orleans LA 70053

WHITEHEAD, MARVIN DELBERT, educator; b. Paoli, Okla., Dec. 18, 1917; s. Chester Arthur and Lola Elizabeth (Donnell) W.; B.S., Okla. State U., 1939. M.S., 1946; Ph.D., U. Wis., 1949; m. Verna Mae Johnson, Dec. 24, 1942; 1 son, James Mark. Asst. agrl. aide, soil conservation service U.S. Dept. Agr., Okla., 1936-38; asst. in agronomy Okla. State U., 1939-40; sr. seed analyst Fed. State Seed Lab., Ala., 1940-42; asst. plant pathology U. Wis., 1946-48, research fellow, 1948-49; asst. prof. Tex. A. & M. U., 1949-55; asso. prof. U. Mo., 1955-60; prof. botany Edinboro State Coll., 1960-63; prof. plant pathology Ga. So. Coll., 1963-68; prof. botany Ga. State U., Atlanta, 1968—; owner, operator Marvern Plant Health, Inc., Atlanta. Served with USAAF, 1941-46; PTO. Mem. A.A.A.S., Am. Phytopath. Soc., Mycol. Soc. Am., Bot. Soc. Am., Am. Inst. Biol. Sci. Crop Sci. Soc. Am., Am. Soc. Agronomy. Ofcl. Seed Analysis N. Am., Ga. Acad. Sci., Wis. Acad. Sci. Club: David Hills Golf (Atlanta). Author: College Biology, 1963. Editor: Ga. Jour. Sci. (formerly Bull. Ga. Acad. Sci.), 1974—. Contbr. articles to jours. Home: 817 Clifton Rd NE Atlanta GA 30307 Office: Ga State U Univ Plaza Atlanta GA 30303

WHITEHEAD, OREN WENDELL, educator; b. Wichita Falls, Tex., Jan. 21, 1927; s. John B and Ruth Elizabeth (Lovorn) W.; student So. Meth. U., 1946-49; A.B., William Jewell Coll., 1951; M.S., N. Tex. State U., 1953; postgrad. U. Mich., 1959-61; m. Martha Carol Carver, June 15, 1957; children—Laura Ann, James Barron, William Wendell. Asst. prof. biology William Jewell Coll., Liberty, Mo., 1953-56; cons. sci. Tex. Edn. Agy.-Tex. Dept. Edn., 1956-57; asst. prof. biology N. Tex. State U., 1957-59; teaching/research fellow U. Mich., 1959-61; tech. rep. Spinco div. Beckman Instrument Co., 1961-67; asst. prof. biology Northwestern State U., Natchitoches, La., 1967-72; chmn. dept. sci. Scotland High Sch., Laurinburg, N.C., 1978—; dir. Sci. Fair. Served with USNR, 1945-46. NSF Scholar, 1952. Mem. AAAS, Nat. Sci. Tchrs. Assn., NEA, N.C. Assn. Educators, N.C. Sci. Tchrs. Assn., Sigma Xi, Phi Delta Kappa, Sigma Nu. Democrat. Episcopalian. Club: Kiwanis. Home: Route 6 Box 224 Laurinburg NC 28352 Office: Scotland High Sch US 74 W Laurinburg NC 28352

WHITEHEAD, SAMUEL EARLE, accountant; b. Greenville, S.C., Mar. 8, 1947; s. Clarence J. and Barbara M. (Matthews) W.; student Truett McConnell Coll., 1965-67; m. Kathy Melissa Ivie, June 5, 1970; 1 dau., Melissa Joy. With Southeastern Pubs., Inc., Athens, Ga., 1970-71, Carbaugh, Jaynes & Carbaugh, Accountants, Greenville, 1971-75, Masters Machinery Inc., Mauldin, S.C., 1975-76, controller, 1975-76; accountant Plus, Inc., Greenville, 1977-78; owner Complete Bus. Services, Greenville, 1978-79; accountant Gen. Wholesale Distbrs., 1979-80; accountant Mgmt./Bookkeeping Services, 1980—. Mem. Carolina Fedn. Stamp Clubs (v.p. 1977-79, pres. 1979-80), Am. Philatelic Soc., Am. First Day Cover Soc., Am. Topical Assn. Methodist. Club: Greenville Stamp (pres. 1976, 79, sec. 1977, treas. 1978). Home: 9 Bridgeview Condos Greenville SC 29611 Office: PO Box 1871 Greenville SC 29602

WHITEHOUSE, GARY EDWARD, indsl. engr., educator; b. Trenton, N.J., Aug. 13, 1938; s. Edward E. and Lorraine L. (Baker) W.; B.S., Lehigh U., 1960, M.S., 1962; Ph.D., Ariz. State U., 1966; m. Marian Greenhalgh, Aug. 24, 1963; children—Gail Lynn, Glenn Alan. Instr., Lehigh U., 1962-63, Ariz. State U., 1963-65; mem. faculty dept. indsl. engring. Lehigh U., 1965-78, prof., 1978—; prof. indsl. engring. and mgmt. systems, chmn. dept. U. Central Fla., Orlando, 1978—; cons. in field. Registered profl. engr., Pa., Fla. Mem. Ops. Research Soc. Am., Mgmt. Scis. Inst., Am. Inst. Indsl. Engrs., Am. Soc. Engring. Edn., Fla. Engring. Soc., Alpha Pi Mu (regional v.p., exec. bd. 1966-78). Author: Systems Analysis and Design Using Network Techniques, 1973; Applied Operations Research, 1976; contbr. articles to profl. jours. Home: 355 Spring Lake Hills Dr Maitland FL 32751 Office: Univ of Central Florida Orlando FL 32816

WHITEHURST, BROOKS MORRIS, chem. engr.; b. Reading, Pa., Apr. 9, 1930; s. David Brooks and Bessie Ann (Lowry) W.; B.S., Va. Poly. Inst. and State U., 1951; m. Carolyn Sue Boyer, July 4, 1951; children—Garnett, Anita, Robert. Sr. process asst. Am. Enka Corp., Lowland, Tenn., 1951-56; sr. process devel. engr. Va.-Carolina Chem. Corp., Richmond, Va., 1956-63; project engr. Texaco Inc., Richmond, 1963-66; mgr. engring. services Texasgulf, Inc., Aurora, N.C., 1967—; solar cons. Carteret Tech. Inst., Northampton County Schs.; instr. solar energy application Beaufort Tech. Inst., 1976—; lectr. on energy subjects at tech. insts. and univs. Co-chmn. N.C. state supt. task force on secondary edn., 1974—; mem. N.C. state adv. com. on trade and indsl. edn., 1971-77; chmn. State Adv. Council Career Edn., 1977—; gov.'s liaison for edn. and bus., 1978-79. Registered profl. engr., N.C. Mem. Am. Inst. Chem. Engrs., Am. Inst. Chemists, N.C. Inst. Chemists (pres. 1975-77), Nat. Assn. Industry-Edn. Coop. (dir.), Solar Energy Inst. Am., Internat. Solar Energy Soc. Patentee in field. Home: 1983 Hoods Creek Dr New Bern NC 28560 Office: PO Box 48 Aurora NC 28560

WHITEHURST, GEORGE WILLIAM, congressman; b. Norfolk, Va., Mar. 12, 1925; s. Calvert Stanhope and Laura (Tomlinson) W.; B.A., Washington and Lee U., 1950; M.A., U. Va., 1951; student W.Va. U., 1956-57, Ph.D., 1962; m. Jennette Seymour Franks, Aug. 24, 1946; children—Frances Seymour, Calvert Stanhope. Mem. faculty Old Dominion U., 1950-68, dean students, prof. history, 1963-68; news analyst Sta. WTAR-TV, 1962-68; mem. 91st-96th congresses from 2d Dist. Va. Mem. Norfolk Council Alcoholism; past chmn. Norfolk crusade Am. Cancer Soc.; mem. nat. adv. bd. Multiple Sclerosis Assn. Bd. dirs. Tidewater Zool. and Aquarium Soc. Served with USNR, 1943-46. Decorated Air medal with oak leaf cluster. Mem. Am. Hellenic Ednl. and Progressive Assn., V.F.W., Am. Legion, Delta Upsilon. Methodist (past chmn. bd.). Lion, Rotarian. Office: Cannon House Office Bldg Washington DC 20515*

WHITEHURST, LAWRENCE ROWE, physician; b. Norfolk, Va., Feb. 29, 1948; s. Ivey Johnson and Louise (Caton) W.; B.S., U. Va., 1970; M.D. Med. Coll. Va., 1974; m. Patricia Jean Wilson, Aug. 16, 1975; children—Carrie Ann, Joseph Lawrence. Commd. 2d lt. U.S.

Army, 1970, advanced through grades to maj., 1978; intern Womack Army Hosp., Ft. Bragg, N.C., 1974-75, resident in family medicine, 1974-77; family physician, dir. med. edn. Fox Army Hosp., Redstone Arsenal, Ala., 1977-78; flight surgeon U.S. Army Aeromed. Research Lab., Fort Rucker, Ala., 1978-80; resigned, 1980; pvt. practice family medicine Buchanan Gen. Hosp., Grundy, Va., 1980—. Diplomate Am. Bd. Family Practice. Fellow Am. Acad. Family Medicine; mem. Aerospace Med. Assn., Med. Assn. Ala., Assn. U.S. Army Flight Surgeons. Methodist. Decorated Air medal. Home: Route 1 Box 187 Grundy VA 24614 Office: Profl Bldg Buchanan Gen Hosp PO Box 786 Grundy VA 24614

WHITELEY, MARY LOUISE, speech tchr.; d. W.R. and April Whiteley; b. Allen, Okla. B.S. in Speech and Psychology, Lindenwood Coll., 1935; M.S. in Speech and Edn. magna cum laude, Okla. State U., 1943; also postgrad. several colls. Speech tchr. Riverview Elementary Sch., Tulsa, 1943-66, Patrick Henry Sch., Tulsa, 1972—; library tchr. Paul Revere Sch., Tulsa, 1966-72. Active, Ch. of Christ, March of Dimes, Community Chest, Jr. Achievement; chmn. edn. com. Goals for Tulsa; mem. casting coms. Children's Theatre, Little Theatre; bd. dirs. Broadway Theatre League. Mem. Tulsa Classroom Tchrs. Assn. (treas., parliamentarian, dir., public relations com.), Okla., Nat. edn. assns., PTA (award for service to children), Okla. (sec.), Dist. library assns., Am. Council Edn. C. of C. (citizenship chmn.), DAR (Thatcher award for outstanding service 1970), Delta Kappa Gamma, Phi Kappa Phi, Phi Gamma Mu (Math.-Sci. Achievement award). Recipient citation for year around teaching Americanism Am. Legion, 1st pl. Quiz Kids Best Tchrs. Contest, Brown Dunkin Tchr. salute, Okla. Edn. award, Valley Forge medals Freedoms Found., Charles Mason George Washington Patriotism award; Freedom Shrine award Exchange Club of Tulsa, 1970. Cert. in teaching, Okla.; specialist in elem. speech, drama, elem. library. Home: PO Box 528 Holderville OK 74848 Office: 3820 E 41st St Tulsa OK 74135

WHITEMAN, BERNICE GOODE, cons. engr.; b. Gainesville, Fla., Oct. 21, 1926; d. Loring Lucian and Cordelia (Crown) Goode; B.S., Wesleyan Coll., 1946; m. James O. Whiteman, Jan. 16, 1949. Understudy to adminstrv. mgr. U. Fla., Gainesville, 1946-49; sec., asst. treas. Black, Crow & Eidsness (purchased by CH2M Hill 1977) Gainesville, 1952-77, personnel mgr., 1976—. Mem. Am. Soc. Personnel Adminstrs., Santa Fe Regional Personnel Assn. (pres. 1979—). Club: Altrusa. Office: PO Box 1647 Gainesville FL 32602

WHITEMAN, HAROLD BARTLETT, JR., coll. pres.; b. Nashville, Apr. 22, 1920; s. Harold Bartlett and Emma Morrow (Anderson) W.; A.B., Yale U., 1941, Ph.D., 1958; M.A., Vanderbilt U., 1950; m. Edith Uhler Davis, July 13, 1946; children—Bartlett, Machin, Priscilla. Adminstrv. asst. Pan Am. Airways Africa, Ltd., 1941-42; instr. Taft Sch., 1946-47, trustee, 1950-55; teaching fellow Vanderbilt U., 1947-48; asst. dean freshmen, dean undergrad. affairs, 1948-54; dean of freshmen Yale U., 1954-64, lectr. in history, 1956-64; asst. to pres. N.Y. U., 1964-67, asst. chancellor, 1967-69, vice chancellor, 1969-71, prof. govt. and internat. relations, 1966-71; pres., prof. history Sweet Briar Coll., 1971—. Bd. dirs. Episcopal Ch. Found.; trustee Chatham Hall, Va. Mus.; chmn. bd. trustees Berkeley Div. Sch. Served as maj. USAAF, 1942-46. Mem. Phi Beta Kappa, Delta Kappa Epsilon, Scroll and Key. Author: Neutrality 1941, 1941. Editor: Charles Seymour, Letters from the Paris Peace Conf., 1965. Home: Sweet Briar Coll Sweet Briar VA 24595

WHITENER, STERLING HEGNAUER, educator; b. Kuling, China, June 27, 1921; s. Sterling Wilfong and Marie (Hegnauer) W.; A.B., Catawba Coll., 1942, D.D. (hon.), 1965; M.Div., Yale U., 1945, M.A., 1946, S.T.M., 1952; M.S.W., U. N.C., 1965; m. Barbara B. Brown, July 1, 1944; children—Karen, Chris, Kim, Bonnie Dana, Katrina. Ordained to ministry United Ch. of Christ, 1945; missionary educator, adminstr. for United Ch. Bd. of World Ministries, China and Hong Kong, 1945-67; faculty Livingstone Coll., Salisbury, N.C., 1967—, prof., chmn. social welfare/sociology dept. 1972—. Pres., Rowan County Council on Aging, 1979—. Mem. Internat. Council Social Welfare, Internat. Community Devel. Assn., Nat. Assn. Social Workers, Acad. Certified Social Workers, Council on Social Work Edn. Democrat. Contbr. articles to profl. jours. Home: 357 Grove St Salisbury NC 28144 Office: Livingstone College Dept Social Welfare and Sociology Salisbury NC 28144

WHITESCARVER, KENNETH TYREE, lawyer, mil. acad. pres.; b. Salem, Va., Apr. 3, 1920; s. Kenneth Tyree and Eulalia Elizabeth (Surface) W.; student Roanoke Coll., 1938-40; B.A., Hardin-Simmons U., 1942; J.D., George Washington U., 1954; postgrad. Memphis State U., summers 1969-70, U. Mass., 1979; m. Alice Clare King, Mar. 9, 1946; children—Kenneth Tyree, Robert Hunt, William King. Commd. 2d lt. USMC, 1942, advanced through grades to lt. col., 1963; with 3d Marine Div., 1957-58; post legal officer Quantico, Va., 1958-61; with Office Legis. Asst. to Comdt. USMC, 1961-63; ret., 1963; admitted to Va. bar, 1954; partner Whitescarver & Scaife, Fredericksburg, 1963-68; pres. Fork Union (Va.) Mil. Acad., 1968—. Substitute county judge, Spotsylvania County, Va., 1963-68; commr. in Chancery, 1963-68; mem. adv. bd. Fork Union br. Nat. Bank & Trust Co. of Charlottesville, 1970—. Chmn., Rappahannock River Basin Area Adv. Com., 1966-68, Rappahannock Area Devel. Commn., 1965-68. Bd. dirs. Frank C. Pratt Mental Health chpt., Vocat. Council Pvt. Edn., 1979—; chmn. bd. Piedmont (Va.) Community Coll., 1977; bd. dirs., pres. Va. Assn. Mil. Schs.; v.p. So. Assn. Bapt. Colls. and Schs., 1977-78; pres. Va. Assn. Ind. Schs., 1980—. Recipient Judge Adv. Gen. Navy award lit. merit, 1959, Citizenship award City of Fredericksburg, 1968. Mem. Am., Va., 39th Jud. Circuit bar assns., Am., Va. trial lawyers assns., Assn. Mil. Colls. and Schs. U.S. (exec. com., pres. 1977—), Fredericksburg Area C. of C. (dir., Citizenship award 1966), Am. Legion, Phi Delta Phi, Sigma Chi. Baptist. Clubs: Masons (32 deg.), Shriners, K.P., Army Navy Country; Quantico Officers; Fredericksburg Country. Address: Fork Union VA 23055

WHITFIELD, HENRY CLAYTON, III, telephone co. ofcl.; b. Dublin, Ga., Sept. 8, 1951; s. Henry Clayton and Mary Lois Whitfield, Jr.; student Ga. So. Coll., 1969-73; B.S. in Gen. Bus., Ga. Southwestern Coll., 1974; m. Deborah Karen Sellers, Nov. 3, 1979. Communications cons. So. Bell Telephone Co., Albany, Ga., 1974-75, employee relations supr., Atlanta, 1975-76, seminar leader Communication Center, Macon, Ga., 1976-78, account exec., Savannah, Ga., 1978-79, Atlanta, 1979—. Mem. Kappa Sigma. Methodist. Home: 2120 North Sound Trail Marietta GA 30066

WHITFIELD, HERSCHEL LARRY, data processer; b. San Angelo, Tex., Mar. 10, 1940; s. William Herschel and Lou Ellen (Cole) W.; A.A., Hillsborough Community Coll., 1976; certificate in data processing, U. South Fla., 1977; m. Marquetta Ann Owens, Dec. 17, 1964; children—Carol Lee, Rector David, Eliza Ellen, Christopher Floyd. Programmer, Gen. Telephone Co. of Southwest, San Angelo, 1959-65; systems rep. Honeywell Co., Houston, 1965-67, sr. systems analyst Gen. Telephone Co., San Angelo, 1967-68; pres. Computer Command Corp., Victoria, Tex., 1968-70; ops. mgr. Lykes Youngstown Computer Services, Houston, 1970-71; mgr. data center TRW Controls Co., Houston, 1971-72; ops. staff adminstr. GTE Data Services, Tampa, 1972-78; sales rep. Comdisco, Inc., Ft. Worth, 1978—. Mem. Data Processing Mgmt. Assn. Office: 2806 SE Loop 820 Fort Worth TX 76119

WHITFIELD, JOSEPH CHARLES, lawyer; b. Beaumont, Tex., Dec. 16, 1921; s. Joseph Charles and Grace (See) W.; B.B.A., U. Tex., 1943; J.D., S. Tex. Coll. Law, 1957; m. Mary Florence Ingalls, Oct. 17, 1944; children—James Charles, Charlotte Marie Muckelroy. Admitted to Tex. bar, 1957; practicing atty., 1958—. Mem. Tex. Ho. Reps., 1959-67; candidate for U.S. Congress, 1976. Served with USNR, 1943-46, 50-53; lt. comdr. Res. ret. Mem. Nat. Assn. Def. Lawyers in Criminal Cases, Tex. Assn. Criminal Def. Lawyers. Clubs: Univ.; Inns of Court. Home: 5808 Charlotte St Houston TX 77005 Office: 2617 Richmond at Kirby Houston TX 77098

WHITFIELD, MILTON LOUIS, instrument maker; b. Durham, N.C., Sept. 5, 1923; s. James Hastings and Ethel Cuthrell (Brinn) W.; student Duke U., N.C. State U., U. N.C.; m. Rosebud Poole Whitfield, Sept. 7, 1951; children—Milton Louis, Elizabeth Anne. Foreman, instrument shop Duke U., Durham, N.C., 1947-64, mgr., 1964—. Mem. Instrument Soc. Am., AAAS. Democrat. Baptist. Home: 425 Valley Dr Durham NC 27704 Office: Dept Physics Instrument Shop Duke Univ Durham NC 27706

WHITFIELD, SYLVIA GAYLE, biologist; b. Picayune, Miss., Nov. 14, 1933; d. Fred Worth and Ruby (Williams) W.; A.A., Pearl River Coll., 1953; B.S., Miss. So. Coll., 1955; M.S., U. So. Miss., 1959. Research asst. La. State U. Med. Sch., New Orleans, 1958-60; research asso. Tulane U., New Orleans, 1960-63; prodn. mgr. Our Way, Inc., Atlanta, 1963-65; staff fellow Nat. Communicable Disease Center, Atlanta, 1965-67; research biologist Center for Disease Control, Atlanta, 1967—; cons., 1970-74. Mem. fin. com. Peachcrest Baptist Ch., 1972-73; dir. group leaders Our Sheperd's Ch., 1976-77, mem. adv. bd. Our Sheperd's Inst., 1976-77; bd. dirs. Christ for Am. Bible Inst., 1977—. Mem. Electron Microscopy Soc. Am., La. Soc. Electron Microscopy, Southeast Electron Microscopy Soc. (exec. council 1974-75), AAAS, Research Soc. Am., Sigma Xi, Beta Beta Beta. Democrat. Contbr. articles to profl. jours. Office: 1600 Clifton Rd Atlanta GA 30333

WHITFIELD, WILL WHITE, TV sta. ofcl.; b. Columbus, Miss., Sept. 9, 1913; s. Henry Lewis and Mary Dampeer (White) W.; student U. Miss.; m. Mabel Dixon Ewing, May 20, 1944; 1 dau., Mary Clare Whitfield Johnson. Audit supr. FHA, Washington, 1935-40; partner laundry bus., Vicksburg, Miss., 1947-51; sales rep. Biedenharn Co., Vicksburg, 1948-56; comml. mgr. WCBI-TV, 1956-64, gen. mgr., 1964-86; group mgr. Imes TV Stas., sec.-treas. WBOY-TV, Clarksburg, W.Va., 1976-80, exec. v.p. TV stas. WCBI, Columbus, Miss., WBOY, Clarksburg, KDUB, Dubuque, Iowa, 1980—. Served with AUS, 1940-45. Mem. Nat. Assn. Broadcasters, CBS Affiliates Assn., ABC Affiliates Assn. Baptist. Clubs: Magnolia Tennis (Columbus), Elks. Home: 1102 Southdown Pkwy Columbus MS 39701 Office: 514 Main St Columbus MS 39701

WHITFILL, DONALD RAYMOND, econ. cons.; b. Wewoka, Okla., May 22, 1939; s. Raymond Edwin and Velma Ruth (Vaughan) W.; B.S. in Chem. Engring., Okla. State U., 1961; m. Donna Faye Moseley, July 22, 1940; children—Melisa Lynn, Laura Lee. Plant engr. Exxon, Baton Rouge, 1961-65; process engr. Phillips Petroleum Co., Bartlesville, Okla., 1965-69; project mgr. Reynolds, Smith & Hills, Inc., Jacksonville, Fla., 1969-74; v.p., dir. Process Assos., Inc., Jacksonville, 1970-71; pres., dir. Faith Enterprises, Inc., Durant, Okla., 1971-72; sr. v.p., dir. PLANTEC Corp., Jacksonville, 1974—. Registered profl. engr., Fla., Okla. Mem. Fla. Engring. Soc., Nat. Soc. Profl. Engrs., Am. Inst. Chem. Engrs., Urban Land Inst., Nat. Assn. Realtors, Fla. Assn. Realtors, Navy League, Air Force Assn., Am. Def. Preparedness Assn., Tau Beta Pi, Phi Lambda Upsilon, Tau Kappa Epsilon. Republican. Baptist. Home: 707 Montego Rd E Jacksonville FL 32216 Office: 3986 Boulevard Center Dr Suite 1 Jacksonville FL 32201 also 1629 K St NW Suite 800 Washington DC 20006

WHITING, GEORGE WASHINGTON BURKE, internat, shipping co. exec.; b. Phila., Mar. 23, 1921; s. George Burke and Daisy (Gilbert) W.; student Newport Bus. Coll., 1948; B.S., Bryant Coll., 1950; m. Dale Joan Canulla, May 30, 1942; children—Merrily (Mrs. Harvey Karter), Carolyn (Mrs. Charles G. Smith, Jr.), George Washington Burke III, Richard Giles. Pres., Frontier Freight Forwarders, Inc., Miami, Fla., 1955—, Frontier Freight Brokers, Inc., Miami, 1964—, Frontier Travel Agy., Inc., Hialeah, Fla., 1961—; dir. S.E. 1st Nat. Bank of Miami Springs (Fla.); farmer, Asheville, N.C. Mem. regional export expansion council U.S. Dept. Commerce, 1971-73. Served with USN, 1939-45. Named Man of Year, Customs Brokers and Forwarders Assn. Miami, 1969-70. Mem. Customs Brokers and Forwarders Assn. Am. (mem. nat. adv. bd. 1962-73), Am. Soc. Travel Agts., Am. Soc. Internat. Execs., DAV, Customs Brokers and Forwarders Assn. Miami (pres. 1962-63), Hialeah-Miami Springs C. of C. Republican. Roman Catholic. Lion. Clubs: Century (Hialeah); Tiger Bay Political (Miami). Home: 10195 SW 84th Ct Miami FL 33156 Office: 2150 NW 70th Ave Miami FL 33122

WHITING, LYNN ERNEST, educator; b. Medina, N.Y.; s. Victor E. and Muriel Joyce (Tompkins) W.; B.S., Troy State U., 1965; M.S. in Edn., Miss. State Coll., 1969, Reish Auction Coll., 1972; postgrad. U. Tenn., 1976; m. Daisy J. Whiting, July 1, 1961; children—Victor, Nicholas. Food technician Gen. Foods Corp., Albion, N.Y., 1959-61; chmn. English dept. Monroe County High Sch., Monroeville, Ala., 1965-70; founder S. Ala. Theater Guilde, Patrick Henry Jr. Coll., Monroeville, 1967; mem. faculty Tenn. Wesleyan Coll., 1970—, chmn. speech-theater dept., 1972—, dir. theater, 1980—. Chmn., Campus Bicentennial Com.; dir. Athens (Tenn.) Halloween Festival; bd. dirs. Athens Arts Council; mem. Tenn. Arts Commn., 1976; radiol. monitoring officer Ala. CD, 1967-70. Named Tchr. of Yr. in Monroe County, 1967, in Athens, 1976, Tenn. Wesleyan Coll., 1977; Ford Found. fellow, 1968. Mem. Speech Communications Assn., Alpha Psi Omega, Alpha Psi Gamma. Methodist. Home: 1402 Willett Dr Athens TN 37303 Office: Tenn Wesleyan Coll PO Box 112 Athens TN 37303

WHITIS, REBECCA ANNE, adminstr. hosp. vols.; b. Balt., Nov. 22, 1945; d. John Ross and Sara Carolyn (Davis) Nicholason; B.S., So. Meth. U., 1964; M.S.W., Fla. State U., 1969; m. Mar. 5, 1965 (div. May 1976); children—Daniel, Dana. Supr. children's services State of Fla., Lake County, 1966-70; psychiat. social worker The Help Center, Wichita Falls, Tex., 1970; dir. homemaker-home health aide services City County Health, Wichita, Kans., 1971; dir. vols. Hissom Meml. Center, San Springs, Okla., 1974-76, State of Okla., Oklahoma City, 1976-78, Hillcrest Med. Center, Tulsa, 1978—; cons. and mem. various adv. councils on volunteerism; co-owner B & L Promotions, Sand Springs, Okla., 1980—. Trustee, A New Leaf, 1977. Recipient certs. and awards for local civic activities. Mem. Am. Assn. for Dirs. Vols., Okla. Soc. for Dirs. Vols., Nat. Assn. Social Workers, Bus. and Profl. Women, Tulsa Assn. Vol. Adminstrs. (pres. 1976), Tulsa Hosp. Council (pres. pub. relations sect. 1976). Democrat. Home: Route 1 Box 137 Sand Springs OK 74063 Office: Hillcrest Med Center Tulsa OK 74063

WHITLEDGE, ESTHER MAE, constrn. co. exec.; b. Hartshorn, Okla., May 5, 1918; d. Charles N. and Laura Mae (Miller) Whitledge; student LaSalle Extension U. (Chgo.), 1954, U. Tenn., 1958-60. Owner, operator Mae's Service Sta. & Cafe, Portageville, Mo., 1942-44; co-owner Whitledge & Beis Constrn. Co., 1944-46, Twin Oaks Hotel, 1947-51; office mgr., accountant McAlister Constrn. Co., Memphis, 1951—, also corporate officer; pres. Happy Acres, Inc., 1975-76; corp. sec., treas. Martha-Mac Corp., 1964—; 1st v.p. Central States Dredging Co., Memphis; 1st v.p. McAlister Grain Co., Friars Point, Miss., 1979—. First v.p. Women's Exec. Council, Memphis, 1965-66 pres., 1970-71 chmn. Downtown Action Unltd., 1975. Bd. dirs. Happy Acres Home for Mentally and Physically Retarded Children, pres., 1973-76; mem. St. Jude Assn. Found. Named Outstanding Woman in civic participation Downtown Assn. Memphis, 1969, Woman of Year Memphis, 1973. Mem. Nat. Assn. Women in Constrn. (pres. 1960-61, nat. conv. chmn. 1964, nat. activities regional chmn. 1965-66, regional dir. 1969), Brooks Art Meml. Gallery, Altrusa Internat. Club: Quota. Home: 3685 Hazelhedge Dr Memphis TN 38116 Office: PO Box 16806 Memphis TN 38116

WHITLEY, CHARLES ORVILLE, SR., Congressman; b. Siler City, N.C., Jan. 3, 1927; s. J.B. and Mamie G. (Goodwin) W.; B.A., Wake Forest U., 1948, LL.B., 1950; M.A. George Washington U., 1974; m. Audrey Kornegay, June 11 1949; children—Charles Orville, Martha, Sara. Admitted to N.C. bar, 1950; individual practice law, Mt. Olive, 1950-60; town atty Mt. Olive, 1951-56; adminstrv. asst. Congressman David Henderson, 1961-76; mem. 95th Congress from 3d N.C. Dist., mem. agr. and armed services coms. Served with U.S. Army, 1944-46. Democrat. Baptist. Clubs: Masons, Woodmen of World. Office: 502 Cannon House Office Bldg Washington DC 20515

WHITLEY, LENA KNIGHT, chem. co. exec.; b. LaGrange, Ga., Oct. 5, 1932; d. Waymon Terrell and Sarah (Davis) Knight; A.B., LaGrange Coll., 1954; postgrad. Auburn U., summer 1958; m. John Hamilton Whitley, June 26, 1955; children—Lena Frances, Juana Lynn. Tchr., Hill St. Jr. High Sch., LaGrange, 1954-57, LaGrange High Sch., 1957-62; sec.-treas. Franlynn, Inc., LaGrange, 1970—. Mem. LaGrange Coll. Alumni Assn. (chpt. pres., 1961-62), AAUW (br. pres. 1967-69), Kappa Phi Delta. Club: LaGrange Woman's (chaplain 1980). Baptist. Home: 811 Wisteria Way PO Box 454 LaGrange GA 30241 Office: PO Box 1345 LaGrange GA 30241

WHITLEY, TONY HAMPTON, security systems co. exec.; b. Stanly County, N.C., Dec. 27, 1941; s. Clyde Hampton and Opal (Almond) W.; student Wingate Coll., 1959-60; m. Brenda Rochelle Morton, Oct. 28, 1958; children—Tony Hampton, Karmann Chandre, Kari Shannon. Design engr. Fed. Pacific Electric Co., Albemarle, N.C., 1967-72, mktg. mgr., Newark, 1972-75; exec. v.p., chief operating officer Gen. Switch Co., Middletown, N.Y., 1975-77; v.p. sales Unican Security Systems Corp., Rocky Mount, N.C., 1977—. Served with USN, 1960-67. Republican. Baptist. Clubs: Northgreen Country, Stanly County Country. Author: Electrical Improvements You Can Make, 1976. contbr. articles to profl. jours. Home: 828 Short Spoon Circle Rocky Mount NC 27801 Office: 400 Fawn Dr Rocky Mount NC 27801

WHITLOCK, ALMA GAYNELLE, counselor; b. Mineral, Va., Apr. 10, 1939; d. Edward Jackson and Lottie Alma (Talley) Whitlock; B.A., Coll. William and Mary, Williamsburg, Va., 1961; M.Ed., U. Miami, Coral Gables, Fla., 1969; Ed.D., U. Va., Charlottesville, 1976. Elementary tchr., Virginia Beach and Henrico County, Va., 1961-68; elementary sch. counselor Henrico County Schs., 1969-74, supr. guidance, 1975-76; asst. prof. counselor edn. U. Ga., Athens, 1976-79; asso. prof. counselor edn. Va. State U., 1979—; cons. Child and Family Guidance Center of U. Ga. Co-chmn. Va. Commn. on Elementary Guidance, 1979—. Social service teaching grantee HEW, 1977-79; U. Va. grad. fellow, 1974-75; NDEA Inst. Guidance and Counseling fellow, 1968-69; named counselor of year Va. Personnel and Guidance Assn., 1973-74. Mem. Am. Personnel and Guidance Assn., Va. Personnel and Guidance Assn., Assn. Counselor Edn. and Supervision, Assn. Specialists in Group Work, Am., Va. sch. counselors assns., Nat., Va. vocat. guidance assns., Phi Mu. Baptist. Editorial bd. Personnel and Guidance Jour., 1976-78; guest editor Va. Personnel and Guidance Jour., 1975. Contbr. articles to profl. jours. Home: 97 Ivy Ln Petersburg VA 23803 Office: Harris 120 Va State U Petersburg VA 23803

WHITLOCK, CHARLES HENRY, III, civil engr.; b. Richmond, Va., Mar. 24, 1939; s. Charles Henry and Laura Ella (Knighten) W.; B.Aero. Engring., U. Va., 1961, M.Aero. Engring., 1965; M. B.A., Coll. William and Mary, 1970; Ph.D. in Civil Engring., Old Dominion U., 1977; m. Audry Jean Gregory, June 23, 1962; children—Todd Anthony, Craig Stephen. With NASA Langley Research Center, Hampton, Va., 1961—, head sect. data analysis, 1974-76, group leader spectral signature and optical modeling teams, 1976—; instr. math. Hampton Inst., 1965-67. Active alumni fund raising Coll. William and Mary, 1977. Recipient award for scholarship U. Va., 1960, 9 tech., managerial accomplishment awards NASA, 1965-76; registered profl. engr., Va. Mem. ASCE, Am. Soc. Photogrammetry. Methodist. Contbr. numerous articles to profl. jours. Home: 4-B Brook Blvd Quinton VA 23141 Office: NASA Langlay Research Center Hampton VA 23665

WHITLOCK, JAMES THOMAS, radio station exec.; b. Gravel Switch, Ky., Sept. 10, 1924; s. Oscar James and Betty (Lanham) W.; grad. high sch.; m. Francis Colleen Dye, Sept. 10, 1944; children—Betty Louise, James Thomas. Farmer nr. Grave Switch, Ky., 1947-49; elec. contractor, Lebanon, Ky., 1945-48; with Radio St. WLBN, Lebanon, Ky., 1954—, pres., gen. mgr., 1954—; owner Marion Falcon Newspaper, Lebabon, 1948-56; dir., co-owner Radio Sta. WPHN, 1968-70; dir. Farmers Nat. Bank. Chmn. Marion County Red Cross, 1948-75, Ky. Emergency Broadcast System, 1960-79; commr. Lebanon Fire and Police Depts., 1962-70; chmn. SSS, 1954-74; mem. Lebabon (Ky.) City Council, 1962-70; chmn. Gov.'s Fin. Disclosure Rev. Commn.; bd. dirs. St. Mary's Coll., 1974-75, Central Ky. Community Action Agy., 1968—; v.p., bd. dirs. Ky. Boy Scouts Am., 1965-75; bd. dirs., mem. exec. com. Lincoln Trail Area Devel. Dist., 1968— bd. dirs. Ky. Girl Scouts U.S.A., 1971-74. Served with AUS, 1944-45. Decorated Purple Heart; recipient Outstanding Businessman award, 1970, Ky. Mike award, 1973, Outstanding Citizen award, 1974. Mem. Nat. Assn. Broadcasters (bd. dirs., legis. chmn for Ky. 1968-77), Ky. Broadcasters Assn. (pres. 1968, exec. dir. 1971—, editor News), Internat. Assn. Aux. Police, Am. Legion, VFW, DAV. Democrat. Kiwanian (pres. 1968-69). Editor Forty-Niner Legion, 1960-75. Home: 224 N Spalding Ave Lebanon KY 40033 Office: PO Box 680 Lebanon KY 40033

WHITLOW, LARRY CARL, retail carpet center exec.; b. Forest City, N.C., May 19, 1943; s. Carl William and Lillian Anna Maria (Jasper) W.; B.S., E. Carolina Coll., 1967; m. Nancy Bruton Syme, Nov. 5, 1964; children—Lisa Suzanne, Randolph Lawrence, Jason Scott. Supr., Deering Milliken, Gainesville, Ga., 1966; adult edn. instr. Fayetteville (N.C.) Tech. Inst., 1967-68; pres. The Linen Closet, Greenville, N.C., 1972-80; pres. Larry's Carpetland, Inc., Greenville, 1968—; v.p. Riverhills, Inc., Greenville, 1973-75; mem. Allied Chem. Retail Info. Panel. Community adv. Pitt County Meml. Hosp.,

1979—. Served with U.S. Army, 1966-67. Mem. Retail Floor Covering Inst. (bd. dirs. 1975—), Nat. Assn. Dealers in Carpet (v.p.), Greenville Homebuilders Assn., Smithsonian Assos., Greenville Area C. of C., Greenville Jaycees. Democrat. Methodist. Clubs: Greenville Golf and Country, E. Carolina U. Pirate, Optimists (dir. 1972), Kiwanis (dir. 1975), Elks. Home: 1008 W Wright Rd Greenville NC 27834 Office: 3010 E 10th St Greenville NC 27834

WHITLOW, MICHAEL DALE, accounting co. exec.; b. Roanoke, Va., Dec. 11, 1951; s. Leo Dale and Ethel June (Gore) W.; B.S. in Mass Communications, Va. Commonwealth U., 1974; m. Isabel Jane Dowrick, Aug. 29, 1975. Info. dir. Va. Task Force on Criminal Justice Goals and Objectives, Richmond, 1975-76; pub. relations cons. Morrison and Kline Pub. Relations, Richmond, 1974-75; dir. communications Va. group Coopers & Lybrand, C.P.A.'s, Richmond, 1977-79; mgr. Public Relations Inst., Inc., Richmond, 1979—; free lance pub. relations counselor. Mem. Pub. Relations Soc. Am. (Outstanding Student award Old Dominion chpt. 1974), Va. Council Econ. Edn. (trustee), Va. Museum, Sigma Delta Chi (Outstanding Journalism Grad award 1974). Club: Downtown (Richmond). Research asst. for books, 1973, 76. Office: Suite 1000 7th and Franklin Bldg Richmond VA 23219

WHITLOW, TED WILSON, constrn. co. exec.; b. Belton, Tex., Dec. 15, 1930; s. Ted and Merle Lusk W.; B.B.A., Tex. A. and M. U., 1956; m. Sherry Melane, Aug. 13, 1965. Constrn. supt. So. Bldg. and Investment Constrn., Dallas, 1956-65; property mgr. Huie Properties, Dallas, 1965-68; pres. Whitlow Constrn., Dallas, 1968-77; constrn. supt. Mahaffey Constrn., Lewisville, Tex., 1977—; cons. Tex. Christian U., 1965-66, Tex. Tech. Inst., 1975-77. Served with USMC, 1951-52. Democrat. Methodist. Mem. Hunting Hall of Fam Found. Nat. Rifle Assn. (life), Tex. State Rifle Assn. (life). Clubs: Safari, Ducks Unlimited, Dallas Woods and Waters, Boone and Crockett. Home: 124 Lakeland St Route 4 Lewisville TX 75067 Office: PO Box 28759 Dallas TX 75228

WHITLOW, WILLIAM NEWTON, coll. adminstr.; b. Newport, Ark., Dec. 12, 1940; s. Calvin W. and Ruthel (Burge) W.; B.S.E. in Chem., Ark. State U., 1963; M.Ed., Stephen F. Austin State U., 1970; m. Beth Kaye Henegar, Dec. 6, 1942; children—Todd, Terri, Trent. Vocat. counselor Alvin (Tex.) Jr. Coll., 1970, dir. counselors, 1972, asso. dean students, 1973, dir. student services, 1975—; faculty Stephen F. Austin State U., Nacogdoches, Tex., 1968-70, Prairie View A. and M., 1972-74. Served with U.S. Army, 1963-70. Decorated Bronze Star, Air medal; cert. vocat. counselor. Mem. Am. Personnel and Guidance Assn., Nat. Vocat. Guidance Assn., Am. Coll. Personnel Assn., Tex. Personnel and Guidance Assn., Jr. Coll. Student Personnel Assn. Tex., Tex. Jr. Coll. Tchrs. Assn., Alvin C. of C. Baptist. Club: Rotary. Home: 501 Point Clear Dr Friendswood TX 77546 Office: 3110 Mustang Rd Alvin TX 77511

WHITMAN, HOMER WILLIAM, JR., investment counseling co. exec.; b. Sarasota, Fla., Jan. 8, 1932; s. Homer William and Phoebe Burke (Corr) W.; B.A. in Econs., U. of South, 1953; grad. Advanced Mgmt. Program, Emory U., 1969; m. Anne Virginia Sarran, May 8, 1954; children—Burke William, Michael Wayne. Various positions 1st. Nat. Bank Atlanta, 1956-73, group v.p., 1971-73; pres. Palmer 1st. Nat. Bank & Trust Co., Sarasota, 1973-74, Hamilton Bank & Trust Co., Atlanta, 1974-76; v.p., Lionel D. Edie & Co. Inc., Atlanta, 1977—. Trustee St. Stephen's Sch., Bradenton, Fla., 1973-74, Ringling Sch. Art, Sarasota, 1973-74, Asolo State Theatre, 1973-74, Selby Found., 1973-74; crusade chmn. Sarasota County unit Am. Cancer Soc., 1974, bd. dirs. Fulton County unit, 1974—; trustee West Paces Ferry Hosp., 1975-77; active United Way Atlanta; bd. visitors Emory U., 1975—; mem. So. Pension Conf. Served as officer USNR, 1953-56. Named hon. consul France, 1971-72. Mem. Newcomen Soc. Am., Atlanta C. of C. (life), Blue Key, Confrerie des Chevaliers du Tastevin, Atlanta Soc. Fin. Analysts, Alpha Tau Omega, Omicron Delta Kappa. Episcopalian. Clubs: Sewanee (pres. Atlanta 1962-63), Ga. Motor (dir. 1974—, pres. 1978—), Piedmont Driving, Capital City, Peachtree Golf, Commerce, Breakfast. Named outstanding young man of yr. Atlanta, 1963. Home: 3241 Rockingham Dr NW Atlanta GA 30327 Office: Suite 2205 229 Peachtree St NE Atlanta GA 30303

WHITMAN, REGINALD NORMAN, railroad ofcl.; b. Jasmin, Sask., Can., Oct. 15, 1909; s. Norman L. and Irene (Haverlock) W.; student St. Joseph Coll., Yorkton, Sask.; grad. Advanced Mgmt. Program, Harvard, 1958; m. Opal Vales, Jan. 31, 1932; children—James, Richard, Donna Whitman Throener. With Great No. Ry., 1929-69; gen. mgr. Alaska R.R., Dept. Interior, 1955-56; fed. railroad adminstr. Dept. Transp., 1969-70; chmn. bd., chief exec. officer M.-K.-T. R.R., Dallas, 1970—. Mem. Alaska North Commn., 1967-69. Served with AUS, 1943-44. Mem. Nat. Def. Transp. Assn., Am. Legion. Republican. Roman Catholic. Office: 701 Commerce St Dallas TX 75202

WHITMER, LESLIE GAY, state ofcl. Ky.; b. Lexington, Ky., July 31, 1941; s. Leslie Allen and Gaynelle Kimbrell (McPherson) W.; B.S., U. Ky., 1963, J.D., 1965; m. Patricia Ann Welch, July 5, 1969; 1 dau., Mary Gay. Admitted to Ky. bar, 1966, U.S. Supreme Ct. bar, 1972, U.S. Dist. Ct. bar, 1972, U.S. Ct. Appeals for 6th Circuit bar, 1976; atty. adviser gen. Office Gen. Counsel, USDA, Chgo., 1966-69; asst. dir. Ky. Bar Assn., asst. editor Ky. Bar Jour., 1969-72, editor, 1973—, bar counsel, 1972-73; dir., treas., bar counsel, asst. sec.-treas. Ky. Bar Found., 1973—; registrar Supreme Ct. Ky., 1974; exec. dir. bd. trustees Ky. Bar Center, 1978—; sec.-treas. Ky. Bar Title Ins. Agy., Inc., 1975—; sec.-treas., dir. Ky. Legal Services Plan, Inc., 1978—. Mem. Fed., Fayette County bar assns., Nat. Assn. Bar Execs., Nat. Orgn. Bar Counsels, Psi Chi. Club: Filson. Contbr. to Ky. Bar Jour., 1973-76. Editor: Ky. Bench and Bar, 1976—. Home: 273 Fontaine Circle Lexington KY 40502 Office: 403 Wapping St Frankfort KY 40601

WHITMORE, DONNELL RAY, linguist; b. Houston, Apr. 18, 1933; s. Fletcher Ames and Linnie Irene (Sharp) W.; B.A., North Tex. State U., 1955, M.A. in Teaching Spanish, 1963; Ph.D. (NDEA fellow), U. N.Mex., 1972; m. Mary Evelyn Layman, June 11, 1934; children—Marcus Evan, Keith Ames, Bruce Alan, Eric Lane. Tchr. pub. schs., Katy, Tex., 1955-60, Rockdale, Tex., 1960-65; instr. Temple (Tex.) Jr. Coll., 1965-69; fellow U. N.Mex., Albuquerque, 1969-72; prof., head dept. fgn. langs. Hardin Simmons U., Abilene, 1972-75; prof. bilingual edn. Tex. Woman's U., Denton, 1975—. Mem. Abilene Library Bd., 1973-75. Recipient grants Jesse Jones Houston Endowment Corp., 1959, 68, NDEA, 1962-63. Mem. Tex. Tchrs. Assn., NEA, AAUP, Tex. Assn. Coll. Tchrs., Modern Lang. Assn., Am. Assn. Tchrs. Spanish and Portuguese, Tex. Fgn. Lang. Assn., Tex., Nat. assns. bilingual edn., Phi Delta Kappa, Alpha Mu Gamma, Sigma Delta Pi. Baptist. Author: Music and Modernist Poetry: A Re-evaluation, 1972. Home: 2228 Picadilly St Denton TX 76201 Office: Box 23029 Tex Woman's U Denton TX 76204

WHITMORE, JOHN EDWIN, banker; b. Tucumcari, N.Mex., Dec. 17, 1907; s. John Elias and Margaret (Neafus) W.; student U. N.Mex., 1926-29; LL.B., Jefferson Law Sch., 1937; student U. Tex., 1925-26; m. Clara Bauman, Mar. 28, 1942; children—John Edwin III, Maria, James, Margaret. With Tex. Commerce Bank, Houston, 1945-72, pres., 1965-69, chmn. bd., 1969-72, chief exec. officer, 1966-72; sr. chmn. Tex. Commerce Bancshares, Inc., Houston, 1972—; adv. dir. Tex. Commerce Bank, Tex. Commerce Bankshares, Inc., Gordon Jewelry Corp. Bd. dirs. Houston Symphony Soc., 1965—; trustee Baylor Coll. Medicine, 1969—. Served to lt. comdr. USNR, 1942-45. Mem. Pi Kappa Alpha. Mason. Clubs: River Oaks, Ramada, Houston, Sugar Creek. Home: 5555 Del Monte St Houston TX 77056 Office: 712 Main St PO Box 2558 Houston TX 77001

WHITMORE, KENNETH LANE, civil engr.; b. Columbus, Ga., July 16, 1951; s. Ralph Ernest and Virginia Gray (Roberson) W.; B.S. in Civil Engring., Auburn U., 1973; M.B.A., U. Ala., Birmingham, 1976; m. Deborah Jo Harkins, Mar. 17, 1973; 1 son, Kenneth Lane. Structural engr. So. Co. Services, Inc., Birmingham, 1973—. Registered profl. engr., Ala. Mem. Nat. Mgmt. Assn., M.B.A. Assn. Birmingham, Auburn Alumni Assn., Am. Contract Bridge League, Chi Epsilon, Omicron Delta Epsilon, Beta Gamma Sigma. Home: 1540 Portsouth Dr Alabaster AL 35007 Office: PO Box 2625 Birmingham AL 35202

WHITNEY, A(DELBERT) GRANT, merc., ins. co. exec.; b. Lowell, Mass., July 25, 1917; s. Adelbert Howard and Julia (Sheehan) W.; B.S. in Bus. Adminstrn., Boston U., 1940; m. Lillian Ritch DeArmon, Nov. 17, 1950; children—Julia Woodley, Adelbert Grant, Frank DeArmon. Asst. to v.p. Belk Stores, Charlotte, N.C., 1946-52, asst. to pres., 1952-55, v.p., sec.-treas. Belk Stores Ins. Reciprocal, Belk Underwriters, Inc., Charlotte, 1950-58, exec. v.p., sec.-treas., 1958—; sec.-treas. Archdale Mut. Ins. Co., 1962-65, exec. v.p., sec.-treas., 1965—; gen. mgr. ins. dept. Belk Stores Services, Inc., 1951—, sec., mem. exec. com., 1959-68, v.p., 1964-68, mem. employee ins. operating com., 1971, 72; v.p., sec.-treas. Providence Realty Corp., Charlotte, 1950-63, pres., 1959-60, pres., treas., 1964-75; v.p. Queen City Investors, Inc., Charlotte, 1959-62; sec. Thrifty Investors, Inc., Charlotte, 1961-62, investment chmn., 1964-65, v.p., 1967-68. Mem. exec. com. Arthritis and Rheumatism Found., Charlotte, 1959-60, dir., 1959-60; mem. Eagle Scout exec. bd. Mecklenburg council Boy Scouts Am., 1949—, v.p., 1962-66; chmn. N.C. U.S.O., 1959-73; spl. gifts chmn. N.C. div. Am. Cancer Soc., 1967, crusade chmn., 1969, 70, bd. dirs., 1968—, pres., 1972-73; active numerous other councils and civic activities; program chmn. Charlotte Bi-Centennial Celebration Com., 1968; chmn. Charlotte-Mecklenburg Bicentennial Com.; gen. chmn. Shrine Bowl of the Carolinas, 1967, 68, Freedom Celebration Day, 1954, Mecklenburg Declaration of Independence-Freedom Celebration Day, 1975; industry chmn. laymen's nat. com. Nat. Bible Week, 1967-70; chmn. advance gifts and profl. div. United Appeal, 1955-56; chmn. spl. gifts div. bldg. fund campaign YWCA, 1952, 56. Bd. dirs. Mecklenburg Citizens Better Libraries, 1967-71, Charlotte Symphony Soc., 1949-55; bd. dirs. Charlotte Council on Alcoholism, Contact of Charlotte Goodwill Industries Charlotte, Inc., N.C. Multiple Sclerosis Soc.; founder, bd. dirs. Festival in the Park; bd. visitors Brevard Music Center; mem. nat. alumni council Boston U., 1962; chmn. promotional activities planning com. Downtown Charlotte Assn., 1965-68; parents' council Davidson Coll., 1972-73; trustee United Community Services, United Arts Council. Served as officer AUS, World War II. Recipient Distinguished Service award Jr. C. of C., 1952; named Charlotte Young Man of Year, 1952; recipient Silver Beaver award Boy Scouts Am., 1956, 8th Ann. Franklin Medallion award, Soldiers Medal for Heroism U.S. Army; selected as Man of Year, Charlotte News, 1975; elected to Exec. and Profl. Hall Fame, 1966, mem. selection com., 1967—; recipient Distinguished Service award Charlotte Exchange Club, 1967, Distinguished Service award Charlotte Rotary Club, 1966, certificate of commendation U.S. Conf. Mayors, 1976, Service to Mankind award Sertoma Club, 1977. Mem. Am. Soc. Ins. Mgmt. (pres. Carolinas chpt. 1963-64, nat. v.p. conf. activities 1965-66, 1st v.p. 1966-67, pres. 1967-68, Man of Yr. award, Pres.'s award 1971), Am. Mgmt. Assn. (participant confs., seminars), Nat. Assn. Ind. Insurers (v.p. 1953-67), Ins. Hall of Fame (internat. bd. electors 1968-70, chamber electors 1972), Captive Ins. Cos. Assn. (v.p. 1973—), U.S. (mem. ins. com. 1967-69), Charlotte chambers commerce, Am. Legion, Carolina Carrousel (dir. 1952-57, 70-71), Jr. Achievement, Inc., Newcomen Soc. N.Am., Royal Soc. Knights Carrousel (pres. 1955-64, chmn. governing council 1964-68, hon. guard marshall parade 1976), Soc. 1st Div. Inf., Res. Officers Assn., Assn. U.S. Army, Am. Found. Religion and Psychiatry (gov. 1959—), French Fgn. Legion (hon.), Inst. Religion and Health (bd. govs.), Mil. Order World Wars. Presbyn. (elder). Mason (33 deg., Shriner), Lion. Clubs: Boston University Alumni of the Carolinas (pres. 1949-51), Executives (pres. 1963-64), Myers Park Country, Charlotte City, Goodfellows (Charlotte). Home: 684 Colville Rd Charlotte NC 28207 Office: 308 E 5th St Charlotte NC 28202

WHITNEY, A(DELBERT) GRANT, merc., ins. co. exec.; b. Lowell, Mass., July 25, 1917; s. Adelbert Howard and Julia (Sheehan) W.; B.S. in Bus. Adminstrn., Boston U., 1940; m. Lillian Ritch DeArmon, Nov. 17, 1950; children—Julia Woodley, Adelbert Grant, Frank DeArmon. Asst. to v.p. Belk Stores, Charlotte, N.C., 1946-52, asst. to pres., 1952-55, v.p., sec.-treas. Belk Stores Ins. Reciprocal, Belk Underwriters, Inc., Charlotte, 1950-58, exec. v.p., sec.-treas., 1958—; sec.-treas. Archdale Mut. Ins. Co., 1962-65, exec. v.p., sec.-treas., 1965—; gen. mgr. ins. dept. Belk Stores Services, Inc., 1951—, sec., mem. exec. com., 1959-68, v.p., 1964-68, mem. employee ins. operating com., 1971, 72; v.p., sec.-treas. Providence Realty Corp., Charlotte, 1950-63, pres., 1959-60, pres., treas., 1964-75; v.p. Queen City Investors, Inc., Charlotte, 1959-62; sec. Thrifty Investors, Inc., Charlotte, 1961-62, investment chmn., 1964-65, v.p., 1967-68. Mem. exec. com. Arthritis and Rheumatism Found., Charlotte, 1959-60, dir., 1959-60; gen. chmn. Billy Graham Appreciation Day, 1968; mem. Eagle Scout exec. bd. Mecklenburg council Boy Scouts Am., 1949—, v.p., 1962-66; chmn. N.C. U.S.O., 1959-73; spl. gifts chmn. N.C. div. Am. Cancer Soc., 1967, crusade chmn., 1969, 70, bd. dirs., 1968—, pres., 1972-73; active numerous other councils and civic activities; program chmn. Charlotte Bi-Centennial Celebration Com., 1968; chmn. Charlotte-Mecklenburg Bicentennial Com.; gen. chmn. Shrine Bowl of the Carolinas, 1967, 68, Freedom Celebration Day, 1954, Mecklenburg Declaration of Independence-Freedom Celebration Day, 1975; industry chmn. laymen's nat. com. Nat. Bible Week, 1967-70; chmn. advance gifts and profl. div. United Appeal, 1955-56; chmn. spl. gifts div. bldg. fund campaign YWCA, 1952, 56. Bd. dirs. Mecklenburg Citizens Better Libraries, 1967-71, Charlotte Symphony Soc., 1949-55; bd. dirs. Charlotte Council on Alcoholism, Contact of Charlotte Goodwill Industries Charlotte, Inc., N.C. Multiple Sclerosis Soc.; founder, bd. dirs. Festival in the Park; bd. visitors Brevard Music Center; mem. nat. alumni council Boston U., 1962; chmn. promotional activities planning com. Downtown Charlotte Assn., 1965-68; parents' council Davidson Coll., 1972-73; trustee United Community Services, United Arts Council, Elmira (N.Y.) Coll., 1978. Served as officer AUS, World War II. Recipient Distinguished Service award Jr. C. of C., 1952; named Charlotte Young Man of Year, 1952; recipient Silver Beaver award Boy Scouts Am., 1956, 8th Ann. Franklin Medallion award, Soldiers Medal for Heroism U.S. Army; selected as Man of Year, Charlotte News, 1975; elected to Exec. and Profl. Hall Fame, 1966, mem. selection com., 1967—; recipient Distinguished Service award Charlotte Exchange Club, 1967, Distinguished Service award Charlotte Rotary Club, 1966, certificate of commendation U.S. Conf. Mayors, 1976, Service to Mankind award Sertoma Club, 1977, numerous other awards. Mem. Am. Soc. Ins. Mgmt. (pres. Carolinas chpt. 1963-64, nat. v.p. conf. activities 1965-66, 1st v.p. 1966-67, pres. 1967-68, Man of Yr. award, Pres.'s award 1971), Am. Mgmt. Assn. (participant confs., seminars), Nat. Assn. Ind. Insurers (v.p. 1953-67, dir. 1968—, nat. chmn. 1978-79), Ins. Hall of Fame (internat. bd. electors 1968-70, chamber electors 1972), Captive Ins. Cos. Assn. (v.p. 1973-74, sec. 1974—), U.S. (mem. ins. com. 1967-69), Charlotte chambers commerce, Am. Legion, Carolina Carrousel (dir. 1952-57, 70-71), Jr. Achievement, Inc., Newcomen Soc. N. Am., Royal Soc. Knights Carrousel (pres. 1955-64, chmn. governing council 1964-68, hon. guard marshall parade 1976), Soc. 1st Div. Inf., Res. Officers Assn., Assn. U.S. Army, Am. Found. Religion and Psychiatry (gov. 1959—), French Fgn. Legion (hon.), Inst. Religion and Health (bd. govs.), Mil. Order World Wars. Presbyn. (elder). Mason (33 deg., Shriner), Lion. Clubs: Boston University Alumni of the Carolinas (pres. 1949-51), Executives (pres. 1963-64), Myers Park Country, Charlotte City, Goodfellows (Charlotte). Home: 684 Colville Rd Charlotte NC 28207 Office: 308 E 5th St Charlotte NC 28202

WHITNEY, HAROLD TICHENOR, JR., engring. co. exec.; b. Evansville, Ind., Oct. 1, 1938; s. Harold Tichenor and Ruth (Schomburg) W.; B.S., U. Cin., 1961; M.S., Northwestern U., 1962, Ph.D., 1969; m. Doris Guinevere Phillips, Apr. 16, 1961; children—Gregory Alan, Jennifer Lynn. Soil testing technician U.S. Army C.E., Cin., 1956-61, found. engr., Louisville, Ky., 1961-63; found. engr. E. D'Appolonia Assos., Pitts., 1965-69; dept. mgr. Law Engring. Testing Co., Birmingham, Ala., 1969-72, found. cons., Atlanta, 1972-73; project mgr., found. cons. Met. Atlanta Rapid Transit Project, 1973—; project dir. Dade County Transp. Improvement Program, Miami, Fla., 1977—; asst. v.p. Law Engr. Testing Co., 1977—. Bd. dirs. Murphey Candler Youth Sports, 1975—. Mem. ASCE (com. on earth retaining structures 1971—), ASTM, Internat. Soc. Soil Mechanics and Found. Engrs., Sigma Xi, Chi Epsilon, Tau Beta Pi, Delta Tau Delta. Contbr. articles to profl. jours. Office: Suite 1205 57 Forsyth St NW Atlanta GA 30303

WHITSETT, CHARLES EDWARD, JR., aerospace engr., ret. air force officer; b. Mobile, Ala., Oct. 18, 1936; s. Charles Edward and Idora Lucile (Green) W.; B.S. in Aero. Engring., Auburn (Ala.) U., 1957; M.S., Air Force Inst. Tech., 1962; m. Evelyn Wheeler, June 1, 1958; children—Edith L., Steven A., Benjamin C. Project engr. McDonnell Aircraft Corp., St. Louis, 1957; commd. 2d lt. USAF, 1957, advanced through grades to maj.; ret., 1977; aero. engring. assignments in U.S., 1957-65; prin. investigator Skylab expt. M509, Johnson Space Center, Houston and Space and Missile Systems Office, Los Angeles, 1966-74; manned maneuvering unit project mgr. Johnson Space Center, 1975—. Trustee Clear Lake United Methodist Ch., Houston, 1976-77; council treas. local troop Boy Scouts Am., 1977-79. Decorated Meritorious Service medal; recipient Sci. Achievement award Air Force Systems Command, 1970; Victor A. Prather award Am. Astron. Soc., 1975. Registered profl. engr., Ohio. Asso. fellow Am. Inst. Aeros. and Astronautics; mem. Tau Beta Pi. Author papers in field. Home: 1110 Buoy Rd Houston TX 77062 Office: EC5 Johnson Space Center NASA Houston TX 77058

WHITTAKER, BURTON EDWARD, crime lab. exec.; b. Columbia, S.C., Nov. 5, 1921; s. Burton Edward and Ruth (O'Brien) W.; student U. Md., 1938-41; B.S., U. Miami, 1951, postgrad., 1951-54; children—Jill (Mrs. Robert Hoog), Marsha, Holly. Faculty, research biochemist U. Miami, Coral Gables, Fla., 1954; criminalist Dade County Crime Lab., Miami, 1955-57, lab. dir., 1957—; project dir. S.Fla. Satellite Crime Lab. System; project adv. com. Forensic Scis. Found. Project; mem. joint adv. com. Nat. Inst. Law Enforcement and Criminal Justice Project; vice chmn. Fla. Gov.'s Council on Crime Labs. Served with USAF, 1942-45. Fellow Am. Acad. Forensic Scis. (sec. criminalists sect. 1970-71, chmn. 1971-72, exec. com. rep. 1973-76, program chmn. Ann. Meeting, Chgo. 1975, chmn. fellow of distinction com. 1975, pres. 1977); mem. Am. Soc. Crime Lab. Dirs. (bd. govs., chmn. membership com.), So. (membership chmn.), Midwestern assns. forensic scientists, Assn. Firearms and Tool Mark Examiners, Am. Chem. Soc. Contbr. chpt. to Crime Lab. Mgmt. Forum, 1976. Home: 1324 SW 16th St Miami FL 33145 Office: 1320 NW 14th St Miami FL 33125

WHITTAKER, JOHN ROGER, urologist; b. Woodbourne, N.Y., Apr. 27, 1943; s. John George and Dorothy Lydia (Beers) W.; A.B., U. Rochester (N.Y.), 1965; M.D., U. Cin., 1969; m. Carol Sue Cottrell, June 21, 1969. Successively med.-surg. intern, resident in gen. surgery, resident in urology, fellow in transplanatation Montefiore Hosp. Med. Center-Albert Einstein Coll. Medicine, Bronx, N.Y., 1969-75; practice medicine specializing in urology, St. Augustine, Fla., 1975-76; urol. surgeon, bd. dirs. McIver Urol. Clinic, Jacksonville, Fla., also clin. asst. prof. U. Fla. Med. Sch., 1976—; cons. Univ. Hosp., Jacksonville; trustee Flagler Hosp., St. Augustine, 1976-77. Mem. A.C.S., Assn. Acad. Surgeons, Transplanation Soc., Am. Urol. Assn., AMA, Am. Assn. Clin. Urologists, Fla. Urol. Assn., Fla. Med. Assn., Duval County Med. Soc., Duval Urol. Soc. Democrat. Mem. Reformed Ch. Am. Contbr. numerous articles med. jours. Office: 710 Lomax St Jacksonville FL 32204

WHITTEMORE, DOROTHY JANE, librarian; b. San Jose, Calif., Nov. 9, 1920; d. Glen James and Jane Dorothy (Katz) Gordon; A.B., San Jose State Coll., 1941, certificate of librarianship, 1942, postgrad., 1952-53; m. Robert Clifton Whittemore, June 15, 1959; children by previous marriage—Stanley Allen Lawton, Shirley Anne (Mrs. Anthony Kopcych). Sch. library supr. Piedmont (Calif.) Sch. Dist., 1942-43; asst. post librarian Presidio of San Francisco, 1943-49; jr. librarian San Jose (Calif.) State Coll., 1951-53; reference librarian Tulane U. Library, New Orleans, 1953-76, acting dir., 1976-78, asst. librarian for public services, 1978—. Bd. dirs. New Orleans chpt. League Women Voters, 1964-66, dir. La. chpt., 1967-69, 73-78; mem. citizens adv. com. City Planning Commn. of New Orleans, 1965-67; sec. New Orleans chpt. La. Consumers League, 1972-74; adv. council La. State Bd. Nursing, 1977—; active Pub. Affairs Research Council. Council on Library Resources research grantee, 1972. Mem. Spl. Libraries Assn. (pres. La. chpt. 1975-76), La. Library Assn. (chmn. coll. and reference sect. 1968-69, exec. bd. 1973-74), New Orleans Library Club (past pres.), Am. Soc. Info. Sci., Nat. Microfilm Assn. Author: (with others) Citizen's Guide to Louisiana Government, 1969. Home: 7521 Dominican St New Orleans LA 70118 Office: Tulane U Library New Orleans LA 70118

WHITTEMORE, FRANK JACKSON, investment banker; b. Morgan County, Tenn., Jan. 11, 1918; s. Frank and Annie (Penn) W.; B.A., LL.B., U. N.C., 1942; m. Valor M. Snyder (div.); 1 son, Stephen Rand; m. Ann M. Seaman; children—Derek, Jon, Paula (Mrs. Fred Russ III). Various positions family interest in tobacco, comml. and mortgage banking, savs. and loan assn., farming, ranching, energy, 1939—; exec. v.p., dir. Kassler & Co. (now Security Pacific), mortgage bankers, Denver, 1945; pres. dir. Franklin Investment Co., dir. chmn. bd. Met. Co., other land devel., bldg. cos., 1956—; v.p., asst. to exec. v.p. Douglas L. Elliman & Co., N.Y.C., 1960; asso. Ben G. McGuire & Co., Houston; dir., chmn. Intebon Corp., Wilmington, Del.; pres. Met. Mortgage Co., Franklin Investors; dir. Continental Corp., Franklin Financial, other corps. Cons. State of Fla., 1963-64. Served to lt. comdr. USNR, World War II Mem. Am. Savs. and Loan Inst. (past pres. 4th dist.) Mortgage Bankers Assn. (past pres. Colo.), other profl. orgns., Mil. Order World Wars. Episcopalian (vestryman). Contbr. articles to profl. jours. Office: PO Box 24201 Tampa FL 33623

WHITTEN, DAVID ROCK, lawyer; b. High Point, N.C., Aug. 19, 1947; s. Guyon Eugene and Margaret (Rock) W.; A.B., Western Carolina U., 1970; J.D., U. N.C., 1973; m. Monica Russ Felton, Nov. 24, 1976; 1 son, Barrett Rock. Admitted to N.C. bar, 1973, U.S. Dist. Ct. for Eastern Dist. N.C. bar, U.S. Circuit Ct. Appeals 4th Circuit bar, U.S. Supreme Ct. bar; asso. partner firm Frink, Foy & Gainey, Southport, N.C., 1973-75; individual practice law, Wilmington, N.C., 1975-76, 77—; partner firm Whitt & Whitten, Wilmington, 1976-77; instr., lectr. Cape Fear Tech. Inst., Wilmington, 1976-78; pres., dir. instrn. Real Estate Careers, Inc., Wilmington, 1977—. Mem. adv. com. N.C. Supt. Public Instrn., 1978-78; mem. citizens adv. com. Wilmington City Council, 1976-79, Parks and Recreation Commn., 1976-79. Mem. Am. Bar Assn., N.C. Bar Assn., N.C. Acad. Trial Lawyers, Am. Acad. Trial Lawyers. Democrat. Episcopalian. Home: 161 Cliffside Dr Wilmington NC 28403 Office: 106 N 5th Ave Wilmington NC 28401

WHITTEN, JAMIE LLOYD, congressman; b. Cascilla, Miss., Apr. 18, 1910; s. Alymer Guy and Nettie (Early) W.; student lit. and law depts. U. Miss., 1926-31; m. Rebecca Thompson, June 20, 1940; children—James Lloyd, Beverly Rebecca. Prin. Cowart Pub. Sch., 1931; elected Miss. State Legislature, 1931; dist. atty. 17th Dist. of Miss., 1933, reelected, 1935 and 1939; mem. 77th-96th congresses from 2d Miss. Dist., chmn. house appropriations com. Mem. Beta Theta Pi, Phi Alpha Delta, Omicron Delta Kappa. Democrat. Mason. Home: Charleston MS 38921 also 5804 Nebraska Ave Washington DC 20015 Office: House of Representatives Washington DC 20515

WHITTIER, CHARLES TAYLOR, JR., investment co. exec.; b. Cedar Falls, Iowa, Nov. 29, 1941; s. Charles Taylor and Sara Jane (Leckrone) W.; student Montgomery Jr. Coll., 1959-62; B.S., Morehead U., 1964; M.B.A., Temple U., 1968; postgrad. U. Okla., 1971—; m. Wendi Lynn Davis, June 18, 1978. Cost analyst Philco-Ford Corp., Ft. Washington, Pa., 1967, programs adminstr., 1967-69, sr. salary adminstr., 1969-70, mgr. indsl. relations for U.S. and Third Country nats., Saigon, Vietnam, 1970, Southeast Asia liason, Phila., 1971; pres. Internat. Enterprises, Norman, Okla., 1971-76, Transnational Corp., Norman, Okla. and San Antonio, Tex., 1977—, v.p., treas. mining co., 1977—; pres. CTEC Inc., 1979—; past cons. to Okla. Aeronautical Commn.; past cons. and acting pres. Aviation FBO Co. Mem. Internat. Assn. of Students in Econs. and Commerce (bd. advisers; mem. nat. com.), AAUP, Aircraft Owners and Pilots Assn., Oklahoma City Internat. Trade Club, Licensing Execs. Soc., World Mariculture Soc., Catfish Farmers Am., Am. Fisheries Soc., Nat. Gasohol Commn. Mem. Christian Ch. (Disciples of Christ). Co-editor: The Conduct of Bus. Overseas: An Okla. Perspective, 1974. Home: 2226 Lindenwood Ln Norman OK 73071 Office: PO Box 68 Norman OK 73070

WHITTLE, JOSEPH FRANCIS, JR., geotech. engr.; b. N.Y.C., Mar. 5, 1943; B.S. in Geology, Rensselaer Poly. Inst., 1967; M.S. in Civil Engring., M.I.T., 1974. Asst. geologist Dames & Moore, Inc., N.Y.C., 1967-68; geologist and asst. soil engr. Haley & Aldrich, Inc., Cambridge, Mass., 1970-74; geotech. engr. Law Engring., Tampa, Fla., 1974-80, sr. geotech. engr., 1980—; cons. coil. rock and found. engring., 1967—. Served with C.E., U.S. Army, 1968-70. Decorated Bronze Star; registered profl. engr., Fla. Mem. ASTM, Deep Founds. Inst., Internat. Soc. Soil Mechanics, ASCE, Sigma Xi, Phi Kappa Theta. Home: 4525 S Hesperides St Tampa FL 33611 Office: Law Engring 4919 W Laurel St Tampa FL 33607

WHITTLE, MICHAEL ROY, pathologist; b. Donalsonville, Ga., Nov. 6, 1946; s. Seaborn Roy and Mildred Elouise (Sheffield) W.; B.S., Valdosta State Coll., 1966; M.D., U. Tenn., 1970. Resident in pathology U. Tenn., 1970-74; pathologist Coffee Gen. Hosp., Douglas, Ga., 1974-76, Jeff Davis Hosp., Hazelhurst, Ga., 1975-76, sec. med. staff, 1975-76; pathologist Phoebe Putney Meml. Hosp., Albany, Ga., 1977—; med. advisor med. lab. tech. Albany Jr. Coll. Exec. bd. Alapatha council Boy Scouts Am., 1976; med. v.p. Coffee County Am. Cancer Soc., 1974-75, citation, Ga. chpt., 1975. Diplomate Am. Bd. Pathology. Mem. AMA (Physicians recognition award 1975), Coll. Am. Pathologists (pathologists recognition award 1976), So. Med. Assn., Am. Soc. Clin. Pathologists, Med. Assn. Ga. Methodist. Home: 2800 N Doublegate Rd Albany GA 31707 Office: 417 3d St Albany GA 31702

WHITTON, C. T., mgmt. cons.; b. Rock Hill, S.C., July 17, 1921; s. Willard Brooks and Mamie (Gardner) W.; B.S. in Psychology, Bowling Green State U., 1950; M.A., George Peabody Coll., 1951; m. Evelyn Nancy Shook, June 14, 1950; 1 dau., Beth. With Am. Enka Corp. (N.C.), 1951-55; mgmt. engr., indsl. relations mgr. nuclear div. Martin Co., Balt., 1955-58; indsl. relations mgr. Vulcan Materials Corp., Birmingham, Ala., 1958-75, v.p. indsl. relations, 1975-78; pres. Whitton Assos., Asheville, N.C., 1978—. Served with USNR, World War II. Mem. Am. Mgmt. Assn., Soc. for Advancement Mgmt., Am. Psychol. Assn., Am. Soc. Personnel Adminstrn., Am. Compensation Assn., NAM. Home: 3 Ronsanne Pkwy PO Box 8638 Asheville NC 28804

WHITWORTH, BILLIE JOE, tools mfg. co. exec.; b. Lubbock, Tex., July 10, 1921; s. Vivian Halbert and Cora Belle W.; B.S. in Indsl. Engring., Tex. Technol. U., 1949; M.S. in Mech. Engring., William P. Rice U., 1956; m. Mary Elizabeth Cornelius, Aug. 11, 1940; children—Billie Joe, Donna Jean. With Hughes Tool Co., Houston, 1949—, product engr., 1949-76, chief engr., 1976-77, v.p. product reliability, 1977—. Indsl. advisory bds. Windham Sch. Dist., Tex., 1975—, Tex. Tech. Indsl. Engring. Dept., 1974-77. Served with USN, 1941-43. Named engr. of year Tex. Technol. U., 1976. Mem. Am. Soc. Engring. Edn., Am. Petroleum Inst., ASME, Profl. Engrs. Tex. Republican. Baptist. Patentee improvement comml. destruction tool. Home: 2114 Lillian St Pasadena TX 77502 Office: 5425 Polk St Houston TX 77023

WHORTON, ELBERT BENJAMIN, JR., univ. dean; b. Rule, Tex., Nov. 10, 1938; s. Elbert Benjamin and Bessie Allene (Allen) W.; B.S., Baylor U., 1962; M.S., Tulane U., 1964; Ph.D., Okla. U., 1968; m. Evangeline Ann Loessin, Jan. 27, 1962; children—Lalise Loessin, Anna Linae. Statistician, survey dir. La. Health Dept., New Orleans, 1964-65; asso. prof. biostatistics U. Vt., Burlington, 1968-72; asso. dean grad. sch., dir. Div. Biometry, U. Tex. Med. Br., Galveston, 1972—; statis. cons. Pres., chmn. bd. Galveston Hist. Found., 1975-77; exec. com. United Way of Galveston, 1974-78; mem. Galveston Tax Policy Commn., 1974-79. Baylor U. scholar, 1957-62; NIH fellow, 1962-68; named Citizen of the Year, Am. Legion, 1957. Mem. Council of Grad. Deans, Am. Statis. Assn., Biometric Soc., So. Regional Edn. Bd., Galveston C. of C., Sigma Xi. Presbyterian. Clubs: Rotary, Masons, Shriners. Contbr. articles to profl. jours.; mem. editorial bd. Tex. Reports in Biology and Medicine, 1972-79. Home: 20 Colony Park Circle Galveston TX 77551 Office: U of Tex Med Br Galveston TX 77550

WICK, ROBERT SENTERS, mech. engr.; b. Port Washington, N.Y., Dec. 4, 1925; s. Harold Martin and Irene Marie (Senters) W.; B.S., Rensselaer Poly. Inst., 1946; M.S., Stevens Inst. Tech., 1948; Ph.D., U. Ill., 1952; m. Nancy Bartlett Gallison, June 13, 1947; children—Stephen, Bruce, Carol, James John. Sr. research engr., research group supr. Jet Propulsion Lab., Pasadena, Calif., 1952-55; mgr. physics dept. pressurized water reactor Shippingport (Pa.) project Bettis Atomic Power Lab., 1962-64, mgr. reactor engring. and analysis dept., 1964-66; asst. mgr. naval plants Westinghouse Co., Pitts., 1966; prof. aerospace engring., nuclear engring. Tex. A. and M. U., College Station, 1966—. Mem. Whitehall (Pa.) Youth Com., 1964-66. Served with USN, 1943-46. Recipient Faculty Distinguished Achievement award in teaching Tex. A. and M. U., 1969; registered profl. engr., Tex. Mem. Am. Inst. Aeros. and Astronautics, Am. Nuclear Soc., ASME, Am. Soc. Engring. Edn., Sigma Xi, Phi Kappa Phi, Pi Tau Sigma. Episcopalian. Contbr. articles in field to tech. jours.; reviewer Applied Mechanic Revs., 1956—; chpt. editor Naval Reactor Physics Handbook, Vol. 1, 1964. Home: 1204 Neal Pickett St College Station TX 77840 Office: Dept Nuclear Engring Tex A and M Univ College Station TX 77843

WICKER, THOMAS CAREY, JR., judge; b. New Orleans, Aug. 1, 1923; s. Thomas Carey and Mary (Taylor) W.; B.B.A., Tulane U., 1944, LL.B., 1949; m. Lilliemae Hansen, Dec. 20, 1946 (div. June 1965); children—Thomas Carey III, Catherine Anne; m. 2d, Veronica Jean Di-Carlo, Dec. 10, 1965. Admitted to La. bar, 1949; law clk. La. Supreme Ct., New Orleans, 1949-50; asst. U.S. Atty., 1950-53; practiced in New Orleans, 1953-72; mem. firm Simon, Wicker & Wiedemann, 1953-67; partner firm Wicker, Wieldemann & Fransen, 1967-72; dist. judge Jefferson Parish (La.), 1972—, mem. faculty Nat. Jud. Coll., Tulane U. Sch. Law. Past bd. visitors Tulane U; bd. dirs. La. Jud. Coll.; mem. exec. com. Sugar Bowl. Served from ensign to lt. (j.g.), USNR, 1944-46. Mem. Am., La. (chmn. jr. bar sect. 1958-59, gov. 1958, mem. ho. of dels. 1960-72), Jefferson Parish, bar assns., Tulane U. Alumni Assn. (past pres.), Am. Judicature Soc., Order of Coif, Beta Gamma Sigma (chmn. nat. alumni adv. council), Pi Kappa Alpha. Democrat. Episcopalian. Clubs: Rotary (pres. 1971-72), Metairie (La.) Country. Home: 3700 Cleveland Pl Metairie LA 70003 Office: New Courthouse Bldg Gretna LA 70053

WICKS, ROBERT HAROLD, b. Houston, Feb. 15, 1926; s. Albert H. and Maude (Thompson) W.; married Marie Young; children—Sue Ellen Wicks West, Kathleen Wicks Hinojosa; B.A. in History, Bible, English, Baylor U., Waco, Tex., 1950; M.A. in Edn., Tex. A and I U., Kingsville, 1957. With Mission (Tex.) Ind. Sch. Dist., 1950—, prin., 1955-66, bus. mgr., from 1966, now asst. supt. bus. Chmn., Mission Citizen's Traffic Commn., 1957—; deacon Conway Ave. Bapt. Ch., Mission. Mem. Assn. Tex. Educators, Valley Assn. Sch. Adminstrs., Tex. Assn. Sch. Bus. Ofcls. Named Man of the Year, Mission, 1973. Served on advisory com. for budgeting, accounting and auditing of Tex. Edn. Agency. Club: Mission Rotary (pres. 1976-77). Home: 1016 Country Club Mission TX 78572 Office: 1116 Conway Ave Mission TX 78572

WICKWAR, WILLIAM HARDY, polit. scientist; b. London, Eng., May 22, 1903; s. John William and Rose (Hardy) W.; B.A., U. London, 1924, M.A., 1926; student U. Paris, 1927-28; Heidelberg U., 1931; m. Margaret Beauchamp, May 19, 1934; 1 son, Vincent Beauchamp. Lectr. London Sch. Econs., 1937; asst. prof. Rockford Coll., 1938-43; asso. prof. Conn. Coll. for Women, 1943-44; prof. govt. Hamilton Coll., 1946-49; social affairs officer UN, N.Y.C., 1948-65; prof. polit. sci. U. S.C., Columbia, 1965-71; dir. planning Richland County Hosp., Columbia, 1972-75; pres. Pub. Service Assos., Inc., 1975—; vis. prof. Am. U. Beirut, 1961-62; lectr. Grad. Sch. Pub. Adminstrn., N.Y. U., 1962-63. Cons. UN, 1966—, State Econ. Opportunity Office, 1966, State Bd. Health, 1967, State Dept. Mental Health, 1968, State Water Resources Commn., 1970, State Dept. Corrections, 1973, USCG, 1976. Adviser, Govt. Burma, 1953, Govt. Lebanon, 1954-55, Govt. Ivory Coast, 1969, Govt. of Togo, 1974; dir. regional seminar for govts. in S.E. Asia, Bangkok, 1959; leader community devel. study tour Africa, 1960; interim dir. S.C. Econ. Opportunity Bd., 1967. Mem. Plainsboro (N.J.) Planning Commn., 1953; pres. UN Fed. Credit Union, 1952; chief world food program sect. UN, N.Y.C., 1963-65; vice chmn. Columbia Area Community Mental Health Bd., 1971; mem. S.C. Comprehensive Health Planning Council, 1974-76. Served as social welfare officer UNRRA, 1944-46. Recipient Rockefeller Found. fellowship, 1927-31. Mem. Internat. Inst. Adminstrv. Scis., Am. Soc. Pub. Adminstrn. (pres. S.C. chpt. 1973), Alliance Francaise (pres. S.C. chpt. 1972), Am. Polit. Sci. Assn. Clubs: Palmetto (Columbia); British Schools and Universities (N.Y.); Explorers (N.Y.C.). Author: The Struggle for the Freedom of the Press, 1928; Baron d'Holbach, 1935; Social Services, 1936, 2d edit., 1948; Public Services, 1938; Modernization of Administration in the Near East, 1963; Anti-poverty in South Carolina, 1967; Health in South Carolina, 1968; Criminal Policy in South Carolina, 1968; Community Mental Health in South Carolina, 1969; Political Theory of Local Government, 1970; 300 Years of Development Administration in South Carolina, 1970; Administration of Public Social Programs, 1971; Place of Criminal Justice in Developmental Planning, 1977. Home: PO Box 12151 Columbia SC 29211

WIDENER, ANNA LOUISE, audiologist; b. Paducah, Ky., Dec. 9, 1949; d. Emmett David and Mary Frances (Kneer) Hannan; student St. Mary's of the Woods Coll., 1967-69; B.A., George Washington U., 1971; M.S. (David Ross research fellow), Purdue U., 1973, PhD., 1975; m. George Hoy Widener, III, June 19, 1971; children—Justin Wood, Colin English. Dir. dept. speech and audiology St. Vincent Hosp., Indpls., 1975-78; pvt. practice audiology, Winchester, Ky., 1978—, also audiologist VA Hosp., Lexington and Lexington Hearing and Speech Center; cons. seminars in parenting St. Vincent Hosp., Indpls. Mem.-at-large Library Com. Concerned with Deafness, 1978-79; projects chmn. Spouses Am. Med. Students, 1978-79; pres., co-founder Central Ky. Hearing Aid Bank, 1979—. Licensed audiologist, Ky.; cert. hearing aid dealer, Ky. Mem. Am. Speech and Hearing Assn. (cert.), Ky. Speech and Hearing Assn., Am. Council Learning Disabilities. Republican. Roman Catholic. Home: 107 Lackawanna Rd Lexington KY 40503 Office: 1109 W Lexington Ave Winchester KY 40391

WIEBE, MICHAEL JOHN, psychologist; b. Wichita, Kans., Sept. 20, 1945; s. Carl Edward and Ella Marie (Warkentin) W.; B.S., Bethel Coll, 1967; M.S., Kans. State Tchrs. Coll., 1970, Edn. Specialist, 1970; Ph.D., George Peabody Coll. for Tchrs., 1973; m. Norma Jean Buller, Aug. 12, 1967; children—Michael John II, Matthew Carl, Mark Edward. Adjunctive therapist, edn. unit Menninger Found., Topeka, Kans., 1967-69, sch. psychologist, edn. unit, 1970-71; asso. prof. spl. edn. Tex. Woman's U., Denton, 1973—, coordinator Inst. of Mental and Phys. Devel., 1973—; cons. psychology to various local sch. systems. Certified and lic. psychologist, Tex. Mem. Am. Psychol. Assn., Council for Exceptional Children, Sigma Xi, Phi Delta Kappa. Home: 905 Hilton Pl Denton TX 76201 Office: Box 23029 Tex Woman's U Station Denton TX 76204

WIECHMANN, GERALD HELMUT, health edn. co. exec.; b. Ellensburg, Wash., Sept. 19, 1933; s. Helmut Henry and Ruth Louise (Krahn) W.; B.S., Valparaiso U., 1956; M.S., Ind. U., 1962; Ph.D., So. Ill. U., 1965; m. Lois Ann Ollinger, Aug. 23, 1958; children—Kelley Kay, Bret Nickolaus. Instr., Valparaiso (Ind.) U., 1958-62, So. Ill. U., Carbondale, 1962-65; asst. prof. community health and preventive medicine U. Kans. Health Center, Kansas City, 1965-69; asst. prof. clin. health edn. Med. Coll. Wis., Milw., 1969-72, asst. dean for student affairs, 1969-72; asso. prof. community health and family medicine, asso. dean U. Fla. Health Center, Gainesville, 1972-73; exec. dir. Health Edn. Research Corp., Gainesville, Fla., 1975—; vis. prof. Med. Coll. Ga.; scholar-diplomat trainee Dept. State, Washington, 1974. Served with U.S. Army, 1956-58. Fellow Am. Sch. Health Assn.; mem. Am. Public Health Assn., Am. Coll. Health Assn., Am. Assn. Tchrs. of Preventive Medicine, Am. Assn. Sex Educators and Counselors, Phi Delta Kappa. Author: Personal and Community Health. Office: Health Edn Research Corp 4510 NW 19th Ave Gainesville FL 32605

WIELER, ERIC HANS, mgmt. scientist; b. Catskill, N.Y., Apr. 21, 1934; s. Hans Joachim and Helene Gertrud (Wundt) W.; B.S., U.S. Naval Acad., 1955; M.S. in Mgmt., U.S. Naval Postgrad. Sch., 1970; m. Patricia Ann Powell, Mar. 31, 1956; children—Eric Powell and Phoebe Alis (twins), Victoria Elizabeth. Commd. 2d lt. U.S. Marine Corp, 1955, advanced through grades to lt. col., 1971; assignments include Vietnam combat, 1968-69, hdqrs. duty, Washington, 1971-73, joint staff duty U.S. Readiness Command, Fla., 1973-75, ret., 1975; purchasing mgr. First Nat. Bank of Fla., Tampa, 1975-78, asst. v.p., 1977-78; dir. purchasing and personnel Uiterwyk Corp., Tampa, 1978-79; Eastern region personnel mgr. Hertz Equipment Rental Corp., Tampa, 1979-80. Pres., PTA, 1972-73, 74-75, 77-78; mem. Hillsborough County Republican Exec. Com., 1975—. Decorated Army Commendation medal, Bronze Star with V, Meritorious Service medal; recipient George Washington Honor medal Freedoms Found., 1967; cert. purchasing mgr.; lic. real estate salesman, Fla. Mem. Nat. Assn. Purchasing Mgmt. (dir. local chpt. 1976-79), Am. Soc. Personnel Adminstrs., U.S. Naval Inst., U.S. Marine Corps Inst., Ret. Officers Assn., U.S. Naval Acad. Alumni Assn. Lutheran. Home: 4206 W Cleveland St Tampa FL 33609 Office: 8910 N Dale Mabry Hwy Suite 30 Tampa FL 33614

WIELER, THEODORE PAUL, air force officer; b. Mineola, N.Y., Aug. 30, 1951; s. Robert and Norma W.; B.A., Davis and Elkins Coll., 1973; M.B.A., La. Tech. U., 1979; m. Georgia Mary Jones, July 28, 1973; children—Kimberly, Pamela. Reporter, Elkins (W.Va.) Intermountain, 1973-74; commd. 2d lt. U.S. Air Force, 1974, advanced through grades to capt., 1976; squadron navigator, 1975-76, instr. navigator, 1976-78, standardization-evaluation navigator, 1978-79, squadron radar navigator, Barksdale AFB, La., 1979—, also summary ct. officer, acad. instr. wing level. Mem. Arnold Air Soc., Phi Beta Lambda, Sigma Phi Epsilon. Republican. Baptist.

WIEMER, KLAUS CHRISTIAN, physicist, engring. mgr.; b. Duisburg, Germany, Aug. 8, 1937; s. Wilhelm and Ingeborg Elisabeth (Johannsen) W.; came to U.S., 1960, naturalized, 1964; B.S., U. Tex., El Paso, 1963, M.S. in Physics, 1965; Ph.D. in Physics, Va. Poly. Inst., 1969; m. Stella Marie Velasquez, Aug. 1, 1959; children—Klaus Enrique, Monica Yvette. Research physicist Schellenger Research Labs., U. Tex., El Paso, 1963-66, instr. math. and physics, 1965-66; mem. tech. staff Tex. Instruments, Inc., Dallas, 1969-73, engring. mgr., 1973—, sr. mem. tech. staff, 1978—; cons. physicist, 1964-66. Served to lt., West German Air Force, 1957-60. Fund for Excellence scholar U. Tex., El Paso, 1963-65; NASA fellow Va. Poly. Inst., 1966-69. Mem. AAAS. Lutheran. Contbr. articles to profl. jours. Patentee in field. Home: 24 Grant Circle Richardson TX 75081 Office: PO Box 1443 MS623 Houston TX 77001

WIESEL, BERT HIRSH, physician; b. Tuscaloosa, Ala., Apr. 26, 1912; s. Samuel S and Alice (Hirsh) W.; B.A., U. Ala., 1933; M.D., U. Pa., 1937; m. Anneliese Wolff, Jan. 9, 1941; children—Sam, Bert Hirsh. Intern, resident in pathology Phila. Gen. Hosp., 1937-41; practice medicine specializing in internal medicine, Tuscaloosa, Ala., 1941-44, Birmingham, Ala., 1944—; chief staff St Vincents Hosp., Birmingham, 1966-72; clin. asso. prof. medicine U. Ala., Birmingham, 1950—. Diplomate Am. Bd. Internal Medicine. Fellow ACP; mem. Jefferson County Med. Soc., Med. Soc. Ala., AMA, Am. Heart Assn., Am. Diabetes Assn., So. Med. Assn., Phi Beta Kappa, Alpha Epsilon Delta. Clubs: Shoal Creek Country, The Club, Willow Point Golf and Country. Home: 3905 Hillock Dr Birmingham AL 35213 Office: 2608 10th Ave S Birmingham AL 35205

WIGGINS, BENJAMIN STINSON, Realtor; b. Columbia, S.C., May 20, 1932; s. Stinson Oliver and Sophia Harriett (Alford) W.; B.S., Clemson U., 1956; m. Barbara Jean Conder, Mar. 17, 1956; children—Michael Benjamin, Lauri Denise. Owner, operator Wiggins Equipment Co., Columbia, 1959-62; owner, pres. Imperial Realty Co., Inc., Columbia, 1962—; dir. Townhouse Constrn., Inc.; lectr. in field; pres. Columbia Bd. Realtors, 1980. Bd. dirs. Cancer Soc., 1970-71; pres. Columbia Multiple Listing Service, 1974. Served with USAF, 1956-59. Named Realtor of Year, Columbia, 1977. Mem. S.C. Assn. Realtors (dir. 1976—), Nat. Assn. Realtors, Columbia Homebuilders Assn., Nat. Assn. Realtors, Realtors Nat. Mktg. Inst. Methodist. Clubs: Sertoma (pres.; award of merit 1970; (life), S.C. Master. Author: Real Estate Training Manual, 1979. Developer comprehensive tng. program in real estate. Home: 2046 Shady Ln Columbia SC 29206 Office: Imperial Realty Co Inc 3508 Devine St Columbia SC 29205

WIGGINS, RALPH CANNON, JR., psychologist, educator; b. Florence County, S.C., July 24, 1933; s. Ralph Cannon and Hannah (Merchant) W.; A.B., U. N.C., 1955; postgrad Miami U., 1958-59, U. Colo., 1960-61, U. Denver, 1962-63; M.A., Temple U., 1970, Ph.D., 1976; m. Bernice Joyce Maslowitz, June 28, 1960; children—Frederick Wayne, Stephen Edward, Brian David. Asst. prof. Naval sci. Miami U., 1958-60; personnel technician City and County of Denver, Colo., 1962-65; personnel specialist Gen. Electric Co., Bay St. Louis, Miss. and Phila., 1965-69; mgmt. cons. Arthur Young & Co. Phila., 1969-71; psychology intern Friends Hosp., Phila., 1973-74, State Maximum Security Forensic Diagnostic Hosp., Phila., 1974; sr. psychologist Harry J. Woehr & Asso., Phila., 1974-75; asst. prof. psychology Va. Commonwealth U., 1975—; exec. v.p. Hackman & Assc., Inc., Elkins Park, Pa., 1975—, also dir.; pvt. practice counseling and psychol. services, 1979—. Served with U.S. Navy, 1955-60. NIMH fellow, 1960-61, NDEA fellow, 1971-73; licensed psychologist, profl. counselor. Mem. Am., Va., Richmond Area psychol. assns., Va. Personnel and Guidance Assn., Richmond Personnel and Guidance Assn., Am. Personnel and Guidance Assn., Nat. Vocat. Guidance Assn., Assn. Transpersonal Psychology, Va. Acad. Sci. Baha'i Faith. Home: 2845 Clarendon Dr Richmond VA 23235 Office: Department of Psychology 810 W Franklin St Richmond VA 23284 also 2819 Parham Rd Suite H Richmond VA 23229

WIGLESWORTH, MICHAEL BLAND, advt. agy. exec.; b. Balt., Apr. 13, 1949; s. Reginald A. and Janice P. (Peppler) W.; B.S., Va. Commonwealth U., 1976; m. Barbara Atkinson, Aug. 5, 1972. Account exec. Richmond (Va.) Newspapers, 1973-75; v.p. mktg. Bunch & Laughon Advt., Richmond, 1975-76; pres. Collier & Wiglesworth Advt., Inc., Richmond, 1976—, M&W Ventures, real estate investment; pres., gen. partner Recreation Unlimited, Inc., 1979—. Mem. Am. Assn. Pres.'s, Am. Advt. Fedn., Am. Mktg. Assn., Phi Kappa Sigma. Republican. Clubs: Advt. (Richmond); Lacrosse. Home: 28 N Lombardy St Richmond VA 23220 Office: 7 S 1st St Richmond VA 23219

WIGLEY, PERRY BRASWELL, geologist; b. DeKalb County, Ala., Jan. 24, 1941; s. Perry Braswell and Ida Leola (Sterling) W.; B.S., Birmingham So. Coll., 1963; M.S., Va. Poly. Inst., 1965, Ph.D., 1968; m. Juanita Faye Landrum, June 2, 1963; children—Laura Anne, Beverley Michelle, Mary Susan. Asst. prof. Eastern Ky. U., 1967-70, asso. prof., 1970-76, prof., 1976—; vis. asso. prof., U. Waterloo (Ont.), 1973-74; geologist, U.S. Geol. Survey, 1968-77; lectr. on energy and environment U.S. Dept. Energy; environ. geology cons. to industry, 1979. NASA fellow, 1974. Mem. Ky. Geol. Soc., Paleontol. Soc., Sigma Xi. Democrat. Methodist. Contbr. articles to profl. and govtl. jours. Home: 130 Buckwood Dr Richmond KY 40475 Office: Dept of Geology Eastern Ky Univ Richmond KY 40475

WIGODSKY, HERMAN SAUL, ednl. researcher, educator; b. Sioux City, Iowa, June 12, 1915; s. Harry David and Riva (Rozran) W.; B.A., Yankton Coll., 1936; B.S., U. S.D., 1937; B.Med., Northwestern U., 1940, M.S., 1938, M.D., 1941, Ph.D., 1940; m. JoAnn Pincus, Mar. 6, 1946; children—John David, Daniel Ellis, Ann. Instr. Northwestern U., Chgo., 1937-47; prof. asso. Com. on Atomic Casualties Nat. Acad. Scis., D.C., 1947-50; lectr., dir. San Antonio div. U. Tex. Postgrad. Sch. Medicine, San Antonio, 1950-61; sec., treas. The Pincus Co., San Antonio, 1950—; mng. partner Rozran & Wigodsky Tree Farms, DeFuniak Springs, Fla., 1951—; lectr. dept. pathology U. Tex. Health Sci. Center at San Antonio, 1967-78, clin. prof., 1978—; vice chmn. Tex. Ednl. Found., San Marcos, 1969—; asso. scientist SW Found. for Research and Edn., San Antonio, 1972—; asso. prof. U. Tex. Sch. Nursing, San Antonio, 1973—; sec., treas. Olmos Co., San Antonio, 1960—, C-Z Realty Co., San Antonio, 1960—, Biomed. Engring. Assos., N. Scituate, R.I., 1963—; dir. Continental Fidelity Life Ins. Co., Phoenix, 1969-79. Dir. Jewish Social Service Fedn., San Antonio, 1951—, pres. 1955-56; trustee Childrens' Hosp. Found., San Antonio, 1956—; founder, dir. 1st pres. Downtown Assn., San Antonio, 1959—; trustee St. Mary's U., San Antonio, 1960-66; cons. Gov.s Commn. Edn. Beyond High Sch., Austin, Tex., 1964-65; dir. Research and Planning Council, San Antonio, 1968-79; trustee Yankton Coll., Yankton, S.D., 1966—. Served with USAF, 1941-47. Fellow AAAS; mem. Am. Physiol. Soc., Am. Inst. Biol. Scis., Federated Biol. Socs., AMA, Soc. for Exptl. Biology and Medicine, Am. Acad. Polit. and Social Sci., Menswear Retailers Am., Fla., Tex. forestry assns., Forest Farmers Assn., Am. Men's Fashion Assn. (dir. N.Y. 1968-75), Sigma Xi. Clubs: St. Anthony, (San Antonio); English Speaking Union (London). Contbr. numerous articles to sci. jours.; contbr. editor Prescription Writing, 1938, De Re Medica, 1947. Home: 300 Primera Dr San Antonio TX 78212 Office: 420 E Houston St San Antonio TX 78205

WILBANKS, JOHN FLANDERS, city ofcl.; b. Eastman, Ga., June 21, 1938; s. Hollis W. and Florence E. (Flanders) W.; B.S., Coll. of Charleston, 1960, postgrad. Coll. of Charleston/U. S.C., 1979—; m. Patricia Anne Jamison, June 11, 1961; children—Shannon, Shelly, John. Supr., Retail Credit Co., Charleston, S.C., 1960-68; fin. rep. Integon Corp., Charleston, 1968-72; city mgr. Folly Beach, S.C., 1972-76; county adminstr. Dorchester County (S.C.), 1976-79; town clk.-treas. Summerville (S.C.), 1979—; cons. govtl. affairs. Mem. Town Council Folly Beach, 1968, mayor, 1969-72. Served with U.S. Army, 1961-64. Mem. Internat. City Mgmt. Assn., S.C. City County Mgmt. Assn. Lutheran. Home: 116 Spring St Summerville SC 29483 Office: City Hall Main St Summerville SC 29483

WILDE, JANE HANNA, ednl. adminstr.; b. Milw., Dec. 9, 1923; d. F.E.J. and Erna A. W.; B.S., Milw. State Tchrs. Coll., 1946; M.A., U. Wis., 1951, Ph.D., 1955. Asso. prof. history Eureka (Ill.) Coll., 1957-69; asso. prof. history and polit. sci. Bethany Coll., Lindsborg, Kans., 1969-74; asso. prof. Voorhees Coll., Denmark, S.C., 1974—, chmn. social sci. div., 1977-78, dir. curriculum devel., prof. history. Del., Kans. White House Conf. on Aging, 1972. NSF grantee, 1976. Mem. Am. Assn. Higher Edn., Am. Hist. Assn., Am. Soc. Ch. History, Luth. Hist. Conf. (dir. 1974—, newsletter editor 1972-78), Soc. History of Edn., Assn. Ednl. Data Systems, AAUP (pres. Eureka Coll. chpt. 1962-67), Sierra Club. Lutheran. Contbr. articles to profl. publs. Office: Voorhees College Denmark SC 29042

WILDER, ANNETTE BEDFORD (MRS. EUGENE WILDER), librarian; b. Natchez, Miss.; d. George Madison and Ella (Ford) Bedford; B.A., Miss. Woman's Coll., 1929; postgrad. Tulane U., 1932, U. So. Miss., 1940; M.L.S., Vanderbilt U., 1948; m. Eugene Wilder, July 10, 1919; 1 son, Eugene. Instr. French and Spanish, U. So. Miss., 1928-33, librarian Demonstration Sch., 1940-55, acquisitions librarian, asst. prof. library sci., 1955-60, reference librarian, 1960-64, reference librarian, asso. prof., 1964-70. Pres., Hattiesburg Music Club, 1927-28; chmn. bd. dirs. Hattiesburg Civic Music Assn., 1927-29; v.p. Original Home and Garden Club, 1938-39; pres. Hattiesburg High Sch. P.T.A., 1938-39; bd. dirs. Garden Clubs of Miss., 1938-42; sec. bd. dirs. Hattiesburg Community Chest, 1942-43; chmn. bd. dirs. Hattiesburg council Girl Scouts Am., 1942; with Canteen Corps, ARC, 1942-45; pres. Womans Club, 1954-55; trustee Hattiesburg Pub. Library, 1955-75, chmn., 1958-61; bd. dirs. Miss. dist. YWCA, 1956-60; bd. dirs. Hattiesburg br. AAUW Scholarship Fund, 1953. Mem. Am., Southeastern, Miss. library assns., D.A.R. (regent John Rolfe chpt. 1955-57, registrar Norvell Robertson chpt. 1961-80), Daus. Am. Colonists (state regent 1964-67, So. regional chmn. 1967-70), Daus. Founders and Patriots Am. (state sec. 1952-60, state registrar 1970-74), Magna Charta Dames, Order Americans of Armorial Ancestry, Colonial Dames Am., Order First Families of Miss. 1699-1817, Miss. Geneal. Soc., Delta Kappa Gamma, Sigma Delta Pi, Pi Delta Phi, Kappa Delta Pi. Baptist. Address: PO Box 785 902 W Pine Hattiesburg MS 39401

WILDER, CHARLES RAY, chemist; b. Dimmitt, Tex., July 15, 1929; s. Jesse J. and Nellie M. (Millard) W.; B.A., W. Tex. State U., 1951; M.S., U. Tex., 1952; m. Charlene Davis, Dec. 18, 1949; children—Tanya, Steven. Polymerization chemist Phillips Petroleum Co., Borger, Tex., 1952, research chemist, rubber compounding, Bartlesville, Okla., 1957-65, supervising research chemist, 1965—. Served with Chem. Corps, U.S. Army, 1953-55. Mem. Am. Chem. Soc., So. Rubber Group. Methodist. Patentee in field; contbr. articles to profl. jours. Home: 144 Ramblewood St Bartlesville OK 74003 Office: Bldg 91G Research Center Phillips Petroleum Co Bartlesville OK 74003

WILDER, ELBA JENNINGS, govt. ofcl.; b. Saltillo, Tex., June 18, 1917; d. Pender Leroy and Maggie (King) Jennings; student So. Meth. U., 1962-63; m. C.W. Wilder, Dec. 28, 1939 (dec.); children—Carl Wayne, Weyland. Chief gen. services div. Insp. of Navy Material, Dallas, 1951-65; purchasing agt. Def. Contract Adminstrn., Dallas, 1965-72; records adminstr. S.W. div. U.S. Army Corps Engrs., Dallas, 1973—. Baptist. Club: Order Eastern Star. Home: 541 Sharp Dr DeSoto TX 75115 Office: 1200 Main St Dallas TX 75202

WILDER, JOHN SHELTON, state ofcl.; b. Fayette County, Tenn., June 3, 1921; ed. U. Tenn. Coll. Agr; U. Memphis; m. Marcelle; 2 children. Admitted to Tenn. bar, 1957; practiced law, Somerville, Tenn., 1957—; pres. Lonstown Supply Co., Inc; dir. Somerville Bank & Trust Co., Oakland Deposit Bank. Mem. Tenn. Senate, 1959-60, 66—; lt. gov. State of Tenn., 1971—. Served with U.S. Army, World War II. Named Watershed Man of Yr., Nat. Assn. Watershed Dists., 1961. Mem. Tenn., Am. bar assns., Nat. Assn. Soil and Water Conservation Dists. (prres. 1970-71), Tenn. Cotton Ginners Assn. (pres. 1948-50). Democrat. Methodist. Office: Lt Gov's Office Legis Plaza Suite 1 Nashville TN 37219*

WILDER, LAWRENCE BERNARD, research engr.; b. Castro County, Tex., Aug. 4, 1922; s. Jesse Jay and Nellie Gertrude (Millard) W.; student W. Tex. State U., 1939; B.S.M.E., Tex. Tech. U., 1943; postgrad. U. Tulsa, 1950-54; m. Alice Marie Mackey, Feb. 24, 1945; children—Larry, Jane, Gordon, Kathleen, David. Stress engr. Douglas Aircraft Co., Tulsa, 1943-44; Gen. Dynamics Co., Ft. Worth, 1946, Boeing Airplane Co., Wichita, 1946; research engr. Amoco Prodn. Co., Tulsa, 1947-54, project engr., 1954-69, research asso., 1969-76, drilling research supr., 1976—; cons. Dept. Energy, marine bd. Nat. Assembly Engring. Republican precinct committeeman; cubmaster Indian Nations council Boy Scouts Am.; coach Tulsa Little League Baseball. Served with AC, U.S. Army, 1944-46. Registered profl. engr., Okla. Mem. ASME, Soc. Petroleum Engrs. of AIME, Am. Petroleum Inst. Republican. Methodist. Club: Elks. Drilling editor ASME Jour. Energy Resources Tech., 1979-80. Patentee in field; author numerous profl. papers. Office: Amoco Prodn Co Research Center PO Box 591 Tulsa OK 74102

WILDING, RICHARD RICHMOND, mining engr.; b. Logan, W.Va., Dec. 6, 1929; s. Thomas J. and Dixie (Harwood) W.; B.S., W.Va. U., 1952; m. Sydney Mabry, Apr. 22, 1961; 1 dau., Stacy Paige. Tech. rep. Austin Powder Co., Chapmanville, W.Va., 1952-54, sales rep., 1954-60, product mgr. seismic explosives, Huntington, W.Va., 1960-68, div. mgr. seismic and pipeline explosives, Cleve., 1968-74; sales mgr. Celtite Inc., Huntington, 1974—. Bd. dirs. W.Va Coal Mining Inst., 1978. Mem. Soc. Mining Engrs. of AIME, Soc. Exploration Geophysicists, Soc. Explosive Engrs. (treas. 1975). Republican. Presbyterian. Clubs: Guyan Golf and Country, Masons. Home: 73 Hamill Rd Huntington WV 25701 Office: 624 6th Ave Huntington WV 25701

WILDMAN, GARY CECIL, chemist; b. Middlefield, Ohio, Nov. 25, 1942; s. Gerald Robert and Frances Jane W.; A.B. in Chemistry, Thiel Coll., 1964; Ph.D. in Chemistry Duke U., 1970; m. Nancy Jackson, June 5, 1965; children—Debbie, Eric. Research asst. B.F. Goodrich Research, Brecksville, Ohio, summer 1964; instr. Duke U., 1966-67; research chemist Hercules Research Center, Wilmington, Del., 1968-71; asso. prof. polymer sci. U. So. Miss., 1971-76, prof., 1976—, chmn. dept. polymer sci., 1971-76, dean Coll. Sci. and Tech., 1976—; cons. to numerous cos.; speaker in field. Mem. Am. Chem. Soc., So. Soc. Coatings Tech., Soc. Plastics Engrs., Am. Crystalographic Assn., Phi Beta Kappa, Sigma Xi, Phi Lambda Upsilon, Sigma Pi Sigma, Omicron Delta Kappa. Methodist. Club: Rotary. Contbr. articles to profl. publs.; editor symposium proc. Home: 322 S 36th Ave Hattiesburg MS 39401 Office: So Sta PO Box 5165 Hattiesburg MS 39401

WILDMAN, JOHN HAZARD, educator; b. Mobile, Ala., Jan. 22, 1911; s. Alexander James and Rachel Greene (Whitaker) W.; Ph.B., Brown U., 1933, M.A., 1934, Ph.D., 1937. Instr. English, Brown U., Providence, 1937-40; instr. English, La. State U., Baton Rouge, 1940-46, asst. prof., 1946-51, asso. prof., 1951-58, prof., 1958—. Served to USAAF, 1942-45; ETO. Mem. AAUP, MLA, South Central Modern Lang. Assn., AAAS, Catholics United for the Faith, Phi Beta Kappa. Democrat. Roman Catholic. Contbr. short stories to various publs. Office: Dept English La State U Baton Rouge LA 70803

WILEMS, PAUL JON, petroleum engr.; b. Victoria, Tex., July 9, 1945; s. Hubert William and Helen (Reifschlager) W.; B.S., Tex. A. and I. U., 1968; m. Bonnie Janelle Tate, June 4, 1966; children—Kelli Janelle, Dawn Sheree. With Natural Gas Pipeline Co. of Am., Houston, 1968-75, sr. supply planning engr. exec. br., 1974-75; dir. supply planning Mich. Wis. Pipe Line Co., Houston, 1976-77, dir. gas contracts, 1978-79, v.p. gas supply, exploration staff, 1979—. Registered profl. engr., Tex. Mem. Am. Inst. Mining, Metall. and Petroleum Engrs., natural gas men of Houston, New Orleans, Rocky Mountains, Okla., North Tex., Sigma Tau. Clubs: Quail Valley Country, Univ. Home: 3306 Meadowcreek Missouri City TX 77459 Office: Suite 1100 Galleria Towers W 5075 Westheimer Houston TX 77056

WILES, DAVID ERNEST, coll. adminstr.; b. Washington, Jan. 19, 1954; s. Ernest G. and Dorothy G. (Buglass) W.; B.S., Miami (Fla.) Christian Coll., 1976; M.S. in Edn., U. Miami, 1979; m. Esther Ann Parkes, June 12, 1976; 1 dau., Heather Joy. Admissions counselor Miami Christian Coll., 1976—, fin. aid dir., 1979—. Named Outstanding Grad., Miami Christian Coll., 1976. Mem. Am. Personnel and Guidance Assn., Am. Coll. Personnel Assn., Fla. Assn. Student Fin. Aid Adminstrs., Delta Epsilon Chi. Office: 2300 NW 135th St Miami FL 33167

WILFORD, DAN SEWELL, hosp. adminstr.; b. Memphis, June 11, 1940; B.A., U. Miss., 1962; M.Hosp. Adminstrn., Washington U., St. Louis, 1966. Adminstrv. resident Hillcrest Med. Center, Tulsa, 1965-66, asst. adminstr., 1966-69, sr. asso. adminstrn., 1969-74; exec. dir. North Miss. Med. Center, Tupelo, Miss, 1974—; pres. Tulsa Hosp. Council, 1971. Chmn. bd. Salvation Army Home and Hosp. Served as lat lt. Med. Service Corps, U.S. Army, 1962-64. Fellow Am. Coll. Hosp. Adminstrs. (regent Miss. 1975—); mem. Am., Okla. (chmn. com. on vols. 1969-70) hosps. assns., Nat. League Nursing, Am. Mgmt. Assn. Contbr. articles to profl. jours. Office: 830 S Gloster St Tupelo MS 38801

WILHELM, WILLIAM JEAN, civil engr., educator; b. St. Louis, Oct. 5, 1935; s. Maurice Ferdinand and Eileen Winifred (McClintock) W.; B.M.E., Auburn U., 1958, M.S., 1963; Ph.D., N.C. State U., 1968; m. Patricia Jane Zietz, Aug. 17, 1957; children—William, Robert, Andrew, Mary, David. Structural engr. Palmer & Baker Engrs., Mobile, Ala., 1958-60; instr. engring graphics Auburn U., 1960-64; asst. prof. civil engring. W.Va. U., Morgantown, 1967-72, asso. prof., 1972-76, prof., 1976-79, chmn., 1974-79; dean engring. Wichita (Kans.) State U., 1979—. Served with C.E., U.S. Army, 1959, 62. Fellow ASCE, Am. Concrete Inst.; mem. Am. Soc. for Engring. Edn., Nat. Soc. Profl. Engrs., Prestressed Concrete Inst., Phi Kappa Phi, Tau Beta Pi, Sigma Xi, Pi Tau Sigma, Chi Epsilon. Republican. Roman Catholic. Contbr. articles to profl. jours. Home: 2500 Banbury Circle Wichita KS 67226 Office: Coll Engring Wichita State U Wichita KS 67208

WILHOITE, DAVID LAWRENCE, phys. therapist; b. Chattanooga, Nov. 8, 1946; s. Finley Vines and Joan Naomi (Poe) W.; B.S., U. Tenn., 1969; B.S., U. Ala., Birmingham, 1973; m. Margaret Ann Pope, Aug. 8, 1970; 1 son, Brian David. Asst. dir. safety programs, ARC, Birmingham, 1970, vol. instr., 1962—, vol. disaster cons., 1969—; dir. phys. therapy services Lakeshore Hosp., Birmingham, 1973-74; dir., instr. phys. therapy U. Ala. Health Service Coll. Community Health Scis., Tuscaloosa, 1974-78; dir. phys. therapy services NE Ala. Regional Med. Center, Anniston, 1978-79; pres. Phys. Therapy Assos., P.C., 1979—; cons. in field; adj. clin. supr. U. Ala., Birmingham, 1973—, acad. adviser, Tuscaloosa, 1977. Recipient Five Yr. Service award ARC, 1973, Ten Yr. Service award, 1974; lic. phys. therapist, Ala. Mem. Am. Phys. Therapy Assn. (treas. and mem. exec. com. Ala. chpt. 1974—, book reviewer and jour. abstractor Phys. Therapy 1975—, orthopedic sports medicine sect.), Nat. Athletic Trainers Assn., East Ala. Athletic Ofcls. Assn., Phi Kappa Psi. Methodist. Club: Kiwanis Internat. Home: 707 Sugar Loaf Ln Anniston AL 36201 Office: Phys Therapy Assos PO Box 1407 Anniston AL 36202

WILKERSON, ANTHONY CARLYLE, educator; b. Dewar, Okla., Mar. 27, 1949; s. Willie Lee and Neoma Lee (Dodson) W.; B.S. in Printing Mgmt., E. Tex. State U., 1972; student Navarro Jr. Coll., 1967-69; m. Linda Kay Hand, July 5, 1969; children—Scott Franklin, Chad Carlyle. Printer, newspaper cameraman Hansford Plainsman, Spearman, Tex., 1961-67; printer, cameraman Navarro Jr. Coll. Print Shop, Corsicana, Tex., 1967-69; photographer Corsicana Daily Sun, 1969-70; printer E. Tex. State U. Print Shop, Commerce, 1970-72, also cameraman, pressman Echo News, Sulphur Springs, Tex., 1971-72; program chmn., instr. printing Tex. State Tech. Inst., Amarillo, 1972—. Ednl. Opportunity grantee, 1967-71. Mem. Printers Industry Am., Graphics Arts Tech. Found., Internat. Graphic Arts Ednl. Assn. Baptist. Home: Route 2 Box 257 Amarillo TX 79101 Office: Box 11016 Amarillo TX 79111

WILKERSON, LUTHER RICHARD, real estate co. exec.; b. Midland, Tex., Sept. 23, 1945; s. Viron Luther and Ella Margaret (Tyner) W.; ed. N. Tex. State U., 1964-69; m. Karen Thornhill Moore, Feb. 28, 1974; children—Mathew Troy, Stacy Elizabeth. Asso. sales dept. Claude R. McClennehan Real Estate, Dallas, 1971-73; pres. 1st Comml. Realty, Dallas, 1973-74; pres., chief exec. officer Boman Property Investors, Dallas, 1976—; dir. deLavreal, Monroe & Co., Scurlock & Asso., King William Enterprises. Served with USNR, 1965-71. Mem. Houston Apt. Assn. Republican. Clubs: Great Southwest Golf, Sparkman. Home: 3376 Camelot Dallas TX 75229 Office: Boman Property Investors 1720 Regal Row Dallas TX 75235

WILKERSON, MARY SHANNON, educator; b. Hickory Grove, S.C., Nov. 2, 1917; d. Samuel Claude and Lucile (Rabb) W.; B.A., Erskine Coll., 1937; postgrad. N.Y. U., 1946, Colo. U., 1954; M.A., Appalachian U., 1960; postgrad. Oreg. U., 1978. Tchr. history and phys. edn., coach Floyds High Sch., Nichols, S.C., 1937-40, Marion (S.C.) High Sch., 1940-67; prof. history Spartanburg (S.C.) Meth. Coll., 1967—; head counselor Camp Ton-A-Wandah, Hendersonville, N.C. Elected to Naismith Nat. Basketball Hall of Fame, S.C. Athletic Hall of Fame, Sports Illustrated Century Club. Mem. S.C. Hist. Assn., Spartanburg County Hist. Assn., Delta Kappa Gamma, Pi Gamma Mu. Presbyterian. Author: Straight Talk to Teens, 1966, rev. edit., 1969. Home: 804A Rutledge Ave Spartanburg SC 29302 Office: Spartanburg Meth Coll Spartanburg SC 29302

WILKERSON, VERNON FRANCIS, JR., textile co. exec.; b. Danville, Va., June 3, 1928; s. Vernon F. and Katheryne Maie (Scruggs) W.; B.S. in Mech. Engring., Va. Poly. Inst. and State U., 1950; m. Carolyn Ann Cook, Jan. 19, 1950; children—Vernon Frederick, Katheryne Wilkerson Helms, John Franklin, Dennis Charles, Carolyn Ann. Tech. service cons. Allied Chem. Corp., Syracuse, N.Y., 1950-56; asst. to pres. Rock Hill (S.C.) Printing & Finishing Co., 1956-57; corp. engr. N.C. Finishing Co., Salisbury, 1957-66, dir. engring. and services, 1966—; tchr. Salisbury High Sch., 1961-63, Rowan Tech. Coll., Salisbury, 1966-68, mem. adv. bd., 1970-71. Chmn. property com. Salisbury-Rowan YMCA, 1967—; active Rowan County United Fund Drive, 1973-78. Mem. ASME, Am. Assn. Textile Chemists, Am. Textile Mfrs. Inst. (mem. energy subcom. 1976—), Episcopalian. Clubs: Elks, Moose (Spencer, N.C.); Masons (Salisbury); Salisbury Country (v.p. 1970). Inventor mercerizer tenter frame washing system; designer textile dyeing and finishing equipment and elec. control systems. Home: 717 W Henderson St Salisbury NC 28144 Office: North Carolina Finishing Co PO Box 1100 Salisbury NC 28144

WILKES, GLENN NEWTON, athletic dir.; b. Mansfield, Ga., Nov. 28, 1928; s. Homer Thomas and Dorothy Frances (Blasingame) W.; A.B., Mercer U., Macon, Ga., 1950; M.A., Peabody Coll., Nashville, 1956, Ed.D., 1965; widower; children—Glenn Newton, Scott, Tommy, Robert. Athletic dir., basketball coach Brewton Parker Jr. Coll., Mt. Vernon, Ga., 1951-57, Stetson U., DeLand, Fla., 1957—; pres. Athletic Motivation Corp. Served with AUS, 1951-53. Decorated Commendation medal. Mem. Nat. Assn. Basketball Coaches. Baptist. Clubs: DeLand Rotary, DeLand Quarterback. Author: Winning Basketball Strategy, 1959, Basketball Coach's Complete Handbook, 1962, Men's Basketball, 1969; also articles, taped motivational athletic program. Home: 1044 W Rich Ave DeLand FL 32720 Office: Stetson Univ DeLand FL 32720

WILKINS, FRANCES MARIE, educator; b. Paden, Okla., Aug. 21, 1930; d. Charlie George and Julia Emaline (Osborn) Davis; B.S., E. Central State U., 1951; postgrad. U. Okla., 1956, Okla. State U., 1971-76, Central State U., 1975-79; m. William C. Wilkins, Dec. 28, 1951; children—Janice Marie Wilkins Hamner, William C. (dec.), Mary Sue. Tchr. bus. McLoud (Okla.) High Sch., 1951-59; tchr. bus., coop. vocat. edn. Yukon (Okla) High Sch., 1959—, coordinator, 1971—. Active Yukon Pep Club, Distributive Edn. Clubs Am.; mother adv. Yukon Order of Rainbow; mem. adv. bd. bus. dept. El Reno Jr. Coll. Mem. Okla. Edn. Assn., NEA, Okla. Distributive Edn. Assn., Nat. Assn. Distributive Edn. Tchrs., Am. Vocat. Assn., Okla. Vocat. Assn., Yukon Profl. Edn. Assn. Democrat. Baptist. Club: Order of Eastern Star. Home: 510 Kingston Dr Yukon OK 73099 Office: Yukon High Sch 1000 Yukon Ave Yukon OK 73099

WILKINS, GERALD LEE, mktg. and fin. mgmt. cons.; b. Cicero, Ind., June 24, 1934; s. James Page and Hester Elizabeth (Illges) W.; B.S., Purdue U., 1956; postgrad Washington U., St. Louis, 1957; m. Martha Ann Rogers, Sept. 29, 1962; children—Margaret Elizabeth, Maria Paige, Gregory Todd, Melanie Rebecca, Garlan Hay. Asso. editor Doane Agr. Service, St. Louis, 1956-63; v.p. Franchise Publ. Co., Chgo., 1963-67; v.p. Miller Brothers Indsl. Metals Co., Chgo., 1967-71; v.p., editorial dir. Agr. Bus. Publs., Glenview, Ill., 1971-73; v.p. Century Communications, Skokie, Ill., 1973-74, dir. seminars, 1974-76; pres. AMR Group, Eustis, Fla., 1976—. Mem. Ravenswood Conservation Commn., Chgo., 1971-74; v.p. Cul-View-Son Civic Assn., 1968-69; mem. exec. com. North Side Coop. Ministry, 1966; mem. Chgo. council Boy Scouts Am., 1974-76, chmn. Cub Scouts Lake dist. Central Fla. council, 1977-79; mem. citizens adv. com. Lake County (Fla.) Sch. System, 1979. Mem. Nat. Agri Mktg. Assn., Am. Agrl. Editors Assn., Agrl. Relations Council, Agrl. Council Am., Sigma Delta Chi. Presbyterian. Clubs: Bay St. Players (Eustis); Svithiod Singing (Chgo.). Editor: Farm Estate and Business Planning, 1973. Home: 509 Lemon Ave Eustis FL 32726

WILKINS, HENRY, III, state legislator Ark.; b. Pine Bluff, Ark., Jan. 4, 1930; s. Henry, Jr. and Minnie Bell (Jones) W.; B.A. in Polit. Sci., Ark. M. and N. Coll., 1957; M.A., Atlanta U., 1961; postgrad U. Pitts., 1966-67; m. Josetta Edwards, 1954; children—Henry, IV, Cassandra Felecia, Mark R., Angela J. Teletype technician Pine Bluff Comml., 1954-59; instr. history and govt. Ark. M. and N. Coll., 1959-60; asst. prof. urban affairs U. Pitts., 1966-67; project dir. coop. coll. devel. program Phelsp-Stocks Fund, N.Y.C., 1967-68; asso. prof. polit. sci. U. Ark., Pine Bluff, 1968—; mem. Ark. Ho. of Reps. from 54th Dist., 1972—. Sec. Ark. NAACP, 1964; mem. Jefferson County Democratic Com., 1964; mem. Ark. Dem. Com., 1972—, Ark. Dem.

Exec. Com., 1976—; del. Ark. Constl. Conv., 1968. Served with U.S. Army, 1952-54. Merrill, Lynch fellow, 1960; Ford Found. intern, 1966; recipient Distinguished Service in Politics and Govt. award 12th Episcopal dist. A.M.E. Ch., 1973; Babe Ruth Little League award, 1975; award Morris Booker Meml. Coll., 1975. Mem. Am. Assn. Coll. and Univ. Profs., Am. Polit. Sci. Assn., Ark. Polit. Sci. Assn., Ark. Wildlife Assn., Jefferson County Forum, Omegs Psi Phi. Methodist. Club: Elks. Author: Some Aspects of the Cold War, 1945-1950, 1963. Home: 303 N Maple St Pine Bluff AR 71601 Office: U Ark Pine Bluff AR 71601

WILKINS, JAMES ELMUS, JR., ednl. adminstr.; b. Millry, Ala., Sept. 25, 1933; s. James Elmus and Nannie Lou (Reynolds) W.; B.S., Livingston U., 1955; M.A., U. Ala., 1961; m. Amanda King, July 24, 1960; 1 son, James King. History tchr. Leroy (Ala.) High Sch., 1957-60, counselor, 1963-69; tchr. McAdory High Sch., McCalla, Ala., 1960-61; counselor Hewitt-Trusville High Sch., Trussville, Ala., 1961-63; prin. So. Choctaw High Sch., Silas, Ala., 1969-75; night sch. dir. Patrick Henry State Jr. Coll., Jackson, Ala., 1975—. Served with AUS, 1955-57. Mem. Nat. Assn. Secondary Sch. Prins., Ala. Assn. Secondary Sch. Prins., Ala. Jr. Coll. Assn., Ala. Hist. Assn. Baptist. Club: Woodmen of World (state escort 1969-70). Home: 316 Fairview Circle Jackson AL 36545 Office: Patrick Henry State Jr Coll 107 Broad St Jackson AL 36545

WILKINS, LEWIS LANGLEY, JR., ch. assn. exec.; b. Kerrville, Tex., Dec. 25, 1936; s. Lewis Langley and Antoinette (DeMauri) W.; A.A., Schreiner Inst., 1956; A.B., Southwestern Coll., Memphis, 1958; M.Div., Austin Presbyn. Theol. Sem., 1961; postgrad. U. Mainz (Germany), 1961-65; D.Min., McCormick Theol. Sem., 1978; m. Harriet Adamson, Feb. 5, 1960; children—Alisa Antoinette, Timothy Pack. Info. sec. World Alliance Reformed Chs., Geneva, 1965-68; communications officer Presbyn. Bd. Christian Edn., Richmond, Va., 1968-70; dir. La. Interch. Conf., Baton Rouge, 1971-74; resourcing exec. Presbyn. Synod of Mid South, Nashville, 1974-80; instr. Vanderbilt U. Div. Sch., 1977—; mem. adj. faculty McCormick Theol. Sem. Mem. Henrico County (Va.) Democratic Com., 1970. Mem. Presbyn. Judicatory Staff Assn., Amnesty Internat. Editor: Reformed and Presbyterian World, 1965-68, Dimensions in Christian Education, 1968-69; contbr. articles to profl. jours. Home: 3000 Hillsboro Rd #87 Nashville TN 37215 Office: 1701 21st Ave S #416 Nashville TN 37212

WILKINS, LORRAINE HUNT, counselor, educator; b. Forest, Miss., May 11, 1919; d. David Quincy and Mary Quin (Love) Hunt; A.B., Miss. U. for Women, 1941; M.Ed., Miss. State U., 1968; postgrad. U. Southwestern La., 1976-78; m. Don Wilkins, Dec. 8, 1945; 1 dau., Donna Virginia Wilkins Bordelon. Tchr. English, Scott County Schs., Forest, 1941-42; acctg. clk. U.S. Army, Washington and Chgo., 1942-44, Immigration and Naturalization Service, El Paso, Tex., 1944-45; librarian Scott County Library, Forest, 1947-50; tchr. Paris (Tenn.) City Schs., 1954-55; bookkeeper McConnell-Dupree Clinic, Bunkie, La., 1955-61; tchr. Avoyelles Parish Schs., Marksville, La., 1961—; counselor Bunkie High Sch. Mem. Avoyelles Assn. Educators, La. Assn. Educators, NEA, La. Personnel and Guidance Assn., Am. Personnel and Guidance Assn., Nat. Council Tchrs. English, Am. Bus. Women's Assn., La Commn. des Avoyelles, Alpha Delta Kappa, Pi Gamma Mu. Presbyterian. Home: PO Box 553 Bunkie LA 71322 Office: Bunkie High Sch Avoyelles Parish Schs 308 Cypress St Bunkie LA 71322

WILKINS, ROBERT PEARCE, lawyer; b. Jesup, Ga., Sept. 10, 1933; s. Ransome Little and Sarah (Pearce) W.; B.S., U. S.C., 1953, LL.B., 1954; LL.M., Georgetown U., 1957; m. Rose Truesdale, Jan. 7, 1956; children—Robert Pearce, Chisolm Wallace, Sarah Ruth, Rose Anne. Admitted to S.C. bar, 1954; atty. Office Gen. Counsel Sec. Army, Washington, 1956; trust officer First Nat. Bank S.C., Columbia, 1957-60; practiced law, 1960-64; partner firm McLain, Sherrill & Wilkins, Columbia, 1964-68, McKay, Sherrill, Walker, Townsend & Wilkins, Columbia, 1969-75; practiced in Columbia and Lexington, S.C., 1975—; pres. Sandlapper Press, Inc., 1967-72, pub. Sandlapper Mag. of S.C., 1968-72, editor, 1968-69; editor, pub. S.C. History Illustrated, 1970. Lectr. law U. S.C. Law Sch., 1971-78. Del., Spl. Liaison Tax Com. Southeastern Region, 1967-70; exec. com. Richland County Republican Com., 1960-64; sec.-treas. Richland County Rep. Club, 1960; bd. dirs. Central Tb-RD Assn.; trustee Sch. Dist. 1, Lexington County, S.C., 1971-78, sec., 1972-75, chmn., 1975-78; mem. S.C. Commn. on Higher Edn., 1978-80, S.C. Commn. on Lawyer Competence, 1980—. Served with AUS, 1954-55. C.L.U., S.C. Fellow Am. Coll. Probate Counsel; mem. Am. (chmn. valuation subcom., estate and gift tax com., taxation sect. 1967-73, vice chmn. service and assistance to law student div. com. gen. practice sect. 1971-72, vice chmn. corporate counsel com. gen. practice sect. 1972-74, editor econs. of law practice sect. Legal Econs. 1974-78, sec. 1977-78, vice chmn. 1978-79, chmn. elect 1979-80), S.C. (tax coordinating com. 1968-70, chmn. legal econs. com. 1973-75, ho. of dels. 1978-80), Richland County (chmn. probate sect. 1973-74, unauthorized practice of law com. 1976) bar assns., Columbia Jr. C. of C. (sec.-treas. 1958-59), Columbia Estate Planning Council (pres. 1964-65), Am. Y-Flyer Yacht Racing Assn. (area v.p. 1971, internat. dir. 1972-73), Omicron Delta Kappa, Sigma Chi. Clubs: Columbia Sailing (dir. 1968-71), Columbia Tip-Off (dir. 1968-73, pres. 1971-72). Author: Drafting Wills and Trust Agreements in South Carolina; Wills and Trust System (Arkansas); Drafting Wills and Trusts Agreement in Michigan; Drafting Wills and Trust Agreements: A Systems Approach; (with others) Word Processing for a Law Office. Contbr. articles to profl. publs. Home: PO Box 729 Lexington SC 29072 Office: One Cool Springs Ln Lexington SC 29072

WILKINS, WILLIAM THOMAS, JR., investment banker, polit. party ofcl.; b. Cotton Plant, Ark., Jan. 17, 1940; s. William Thomas and Sue Ellen (Brown) W.; student Millsaps Coll., 1958-60; B.Pub. Adminstrn., U. Miss., 1962, M.A., 1966; m. Martha Ann Huddleston, Aug. 18, 1961; children—Martha Ellen, William Thomas IV, Nathaneil Jeffries. Part-time research asst. U. Miss. Bur. Research in Bus. and Govt., 1961-62; field rep., dir. research Miss. Republican Com., Jackson, 1962-64, exec. dir., adminstrv. asst. to state chmn., 1964-73; owner, developer timber, agr. and income properties throughout U.S.; active in internat. trade and finance; dir. Bank of Miss. Exec. dir. So. Assn. Rep. State Chmn., 1969-74, So. Rep. Conf., 1969, 71, Miss. state chmn. gubernatorial campaign Rep. candidate, 1979. Mem. Kappa Sigma, Delta Sigma Phi, Pi Sigma Alpha. Presbyterian. Home: 4820 Northampton Dr Jackson MS 39211 Office: 1217 Prairie Houston TX 77002

WILKINSON, BRUCE HERBERT, educator; b. Kearny, N.J., Sept. 4, 1947; s. James S. and Joan M. (Heddy) W.; B.A., Northeastern Bible Coll., N.J., 1969, Th.B., 1970; Th.M., Dallas Theol. Sem., 1974; m. Darlene Marie Gahres, Aug. 23, 1969; children—David Bruce, Jennifer Sue. Lic. to ministry Baptist Ch., 1969; editorial asst. Dallas Theol. Sem., mem. faculty, public relations dir. Dallas Theol. Sem. Lay Inst., 1972-74; prof. Bible, Multnomah Sch. Bible, Portland, Oreg., 1974-77; pres., founder Walk Thru the Bible Ministries, Atlanta, 1972—, pres. Center for Bibl. Studies, 1979—; seminar leader, 1972—. Bd. dirs. Nat. Inst. Bibl. Studies, 1979; pres., club mgr. Christian Growth Club, 1980—. Named Alumnus of Year, Northeastern Bible Coll., 1976. Mem. Am. Mgmt. Assn. Author: Walk Thru the Old Testament, 1974; Walk Thru the New Testament, 1975; Walk Thru Personal Bible Study Methods, 1978; exec. editor monthly mag. Daily Walk, 1978—. Office: 230 Peachtree NW Suite 2100 Atlanta GA 30303

WILKINSON, EDWIN REX, ch. ofcl.; b. Buffalo, Okla., Apr. 10, 1932; s. Virgil Elwin and Lillie (Prophet) W.; B.S., Okla. Bapt. U., 1954; M.R.E., Southwestern Bapt. Sem., 1966; m. Carrie Joye Craighead, July 31, 1953; children—David, Michael, Karen, Kent, Kevin. Ordained to ministry First Baptist Ch., Buffalo, Okla., 1954; pastor South Persimmon Bapt. Ch., Sharon, Okla., 1956-58, N.W. Bapt. Mission, Woodward, Okla., 1958-65; minister of edn. First Bapt. Ch., Ardmore, Okla., 1965-73, First Bapt. Ch., Muskogee, Okla., 1973—; bd. dirs. Bapt. Gen. Conv. Okla. Mem. Southwestern Bapt. Religious Edn. Assn., Okla. Bapt. Religious Edn. Assn. (pres.). Club: Civitan. Home: Route 2 Box 383 B Muskogee OK 74401 Office: First Bapt Ch 111 S 7th St Muskogee OK 74401

WILKINSON, HAZEL WILEY, microbiologist; b. Birmingham, Ala., Aug. 4, 1941; d. Joseph Edgar and Alida Van Rensselaer (Livingston) Wilkinson, Jr.; student Salem Coll., 1959-60, U. Ala., 1960-62; B.S., U. Ga., 1963, M.S., 1965, Ph.D., 1972; m. James Nathanial Parkman. Research microbiologist Center for Disease Control, Atlanta, 1965—, now chief spl. immunology lab.; sr. faculty mem. com. continuing edn. Am. Soc. Clin. Pathologists, 1975—; adj. asst. prof. lab. practice Sch. Pub. Health, U. N.C., Chapel Hill, 1972—. Vice pres. bd. dirs. Fontaine Owners Assn., 1975-76. Mem. Am. Soc. for Microbiology (Pres's. award for Research, Southeastern br. 1971), Sci. Research Soc. Am. (sec. chpt. 1977-78), Nat. Registry Microbiologists, AAAS, Am. Assn. Immunologists, Lancefield Soc. Episcopalian. Mem. editorial bd. Jour. Clin. Microbiology, 1978—; contbr. articles to profl. jours. Home: 400 Sassafras Rd Roswell GA 30076 Office: Center for Disease Control Atlanta GA 30333

WILKINSON, ONA MARLENE, civic worker; b. Okmulgee, Okla., Sept. 26, 1932; d. Carl Jack and Ona May (Burton) Rathbun; B.A., Okla. A. and M. Coll., 1953; postgrad. Memphis State U., 1978—; m. Edward L. Wilkinson, Apr. 1, 1956; children—Edward L., Martha, Mary. Hon. chmn. Navy Memphis ARC, 1979, Nursery Bd., Child Care Center, Memphis, 1974-77; bd. dirs. Frayser-Millington Mental Health Center, Millington, Tenn., 1978—, Tenn-Ark-Miss Girl Scout Council, 1979—. Recipient Navy Relief Soc. Meritorious Service award, 1978. Mem. Am. Personnel and Guidance Assn., Navy Relief Soc. (sr. interviewer 1971—, chmn. vols. 1974-77, layette chmn. 1975-78. Episcopalian. Clubs: Delta Zeta, King's Daus., Bookmarkers Book, Memphis Symphony League, Mensa, Navy Memphis Officers Wives (hon. chmn. 1977-79), Navy Wives of Am. (advisor 1971-77), NAS Memphis Officers Wives (hon. pres. 1974-77). Address: 4644 Cedar Ridge Dr Millington TN 38053

WILKINSON, WILLIAM SCOTT, lawyer; b. Coushatta, La., Feb. 5, 1895; s. John D. and Alice M. (Scott) W.; B.A., La. State U., 1915, LL.B., 1917, J.D., 1960; m. Margaret West, Apr. 9, 1919; children—Susybelle Wilkinson Lyons, Margaret (Mrs. R.A. Wilson). Admitted to La. bar, 1917, U.S. Supreme Ct. bar, 1923; practiced in Shreveport, La., 1919—; mem. firm Wilkinson, Carmody, Peatross & Caverlee, Shreveport, 1919—; spl. asst. atty. gen. of La., 1955-65. Vice pres., dir. Hunter Co., Shreveport 1946—; dir. La. div. Mid-Continent Oil & Gas Assn.; chmn. emeritus Lee Nat. Life Ins. Co. Lectr. Inst. of Mineral Law, La. State U., Baton Rouge, Tulane U., New Orleans. Chmn. adv. council YWCA, Shreveport, 1950—; chmn. Housing Authority of City of Shreveport, 1940-41. Bd. dirs. Am. Cancer Soc., N.W. La. div. Arthritis Found., La. State U. Found., Frost Found. Mem. La. Ho. of Reps., 1920-24. Served to capt., arty. U.S. Army Res., World War I; served to col., AUS, World War II. Fellow Am. Coll. Trial Lawyers; mem. Internat., Am., La., Fed. Power, Shreveport bar assns., Am. Judicature Soc., La. Law Inst., Blair Soc. of Edinburgh, Selden Soc. of London, Shreveport C. of C. (pres. 1947-48), Res. Officers Assn., S.R., Am. Legion, VFW, Soc. War of 1812, Sigma Nu, Omega Delta Kappa. Clubs: Shreveport Country, Demoiselle, Masons, Rotary, Univ. Home: 7525 Creswell Rd Shreveport LA 71106 Office: PO Box 1707 Shreveport LA 71166

WILL, FRITZ, III, chemist; b. Richmond, Va., Oct. 24, 1926; s. Fritz and Julia Maria (Lindner) W.; B.S., U. Va., 1949, M.S., 1951, Ph.D., 1953; m. Betty Jane Ramey, Apr. 3, 1954; children—Fritz IV, Kathrine E. Chemist, Alcoa Research Labs. Aluminum Co. Am., New Kensington, Pa., 1953-65; research scientist Philip Morris Research center, Richmond, 1965-69, mgr. analytical div., 1969-79; mgr. S.D. Applications Lab., Philip Morris Inc., Richmond, 1980—. Served with AUS, 1945-46. Research fellow U. Va., 1951-53. Mem. Am. Chem. Soc., Soc. Applied Spectroscopy (pres. Va. 1970-71), U. Va. Alumni Assn. (life), Sigma Xi, Alpha Chi Sigma. Contbr. articles to profl. jours. Home: 2301 Astoria Dr Richmond VA 23235 Office: PO Box 26583 Richmond VA 23261

WILL, OSCAR, JR., hosp. adminstr.; b. Hazelton, N.D., Nov. 15, 1947; s. Oscar and Irene (Heberle) W.; B.S., U. N.D., 1973. Internal auditor Genesco, Inc., Nashville, 1973-75; asst. controller Baron's Mens Stores, Miami Beach, Fla., 1974-75; auditor Hosp. Corp. Am., Nashville, 1975-76; controller Brigham City (Utah) Community Hosp., 1976-78; dir. fin. Rockingham Community Hosp., Harrisonburg, Va., 1978-79; controller Health Scis. Center Hosp., Lubbock, Tex., 1979—. Served with U.S. Army, 1968-71. Decorated Army Commendation medal. Mem. Nat. Assn. Accountants, Hosp. Fin. Mgmt. Assn., DAV. Home: 3218 90th St Lubbock TX 79423 Office: Health Services Center Hosp 602 Indiana St Lubbock TX 79408

WILLARD, GENEVA MAE, med. asst.; b. Hugo, Okla., Aug. 24, 1933; d. Harry C. and Thelma M. (Walker) Kizer; student pub. schs., Hugo; m. Bob G. Willard, Sept. 6, 1963; children—Shelley D. Campbell, Bruce G. Campbell. Partner, Campbell's Ins. Agency Oklahoma City, 1959-61; med. asst. to Dr. Thomas E. Burleson, Oklahoma City, 1962-64; ch. sec. SW Church of Christ, Oklahoma City, 1964-66; med. asst., receptionist to Drs. Robison & Carter (name changed to Clin. Surgeons, Inc., 1971), Oklahoma City, 1967-69, personnel dir., 1969—; bus. mgr., 1971—; guest speaker Woman's Aux. to Student AMA, 1973, 76, 78. Mem. Am. Assn. Med. Assts. (certified in basic and adminstrv. procedures 1977, Okla. chmn. edn. 1977-78, instr. ins. adminstrv. course 1978, Sec. county chpt. 1979-80). Republican. Mem. Churches of Christ. Club: Brookside, Altrusa. Home: Route 5 Box 6 Blue Stem Norman OK 73069 Office: 5700 NW Grand Blvd Suite 711 Oklahoma City OK 73112

WILLARD, RALPH LAWRENCE, osteo. physician, coll. adminstr.; b. Manchester, Iowa, Apr. 6, 1922; s. H.B. and Ruth A. (Hazelrigg) W.; student Cornell Coll., 1940-42, Coe Coll., 1945; D.O., Kirksville Coll. Osteo. Medicine, 1949; m. Margaret Dyer, Sept. 26, 1969; children—Laurie, Jane, Deanette, Ann, Tom. Intern, Kirksville (Mo.) Osteo. Hosp., 1949-50, resident in gen. surgery, 1954-57; practice osteo. medicine specializing in gen. surgery, Davenport, Iowa, 1957-68; dean Kirksville (Mo.) Coll. Osteo. Medicine, 1969-73; asso. dean and acting dean Coll. of Osteo. Medicine, Mich. State U., East Lansing, 1974-75; dean Tex. Coll. Osteo. Medicine, Ft. Worth, 1975—; v.p. health affairs N. Tex. State U., Denton, 1976—. Mem. exec. com. Tex. Area 5 Health Systems Agy., 1977—. Served with USAAF, 1942-45, USAF, 1952-53, M.C., USAFR, 1975—. Decorated D.F.C., Air medal with four oak leaf clusters. Fellow Am. Coll. Osteo. Surgeons; mem. Am. Assn. Colls. of Osteo. Medicine (chmn. council of deans 1970-73, pres. 1979—), Am. Osteo. Assn., Tex. Osteo. Med. Assn., Assn. for Hosp. Med. Edn., Aerospace Med. Assn., Assn. of Mil. Surgeons of U.S., Soc. of Air Force Flight Surgeons, Am. Coll. Osteo. Surgeons. Democrat. Episcopalian. Clubs: Ft. Worth, Century II, Masons, Shriners. Office: PO Box 9074 Fort Worth TX 76107

WILLCOX, LAWRENCE AUSTIN, agrl. cons.; b. Wyoming, Ill., May 13, 1904; s. Edward Kellogg and Ella Jane (Austin) W.; B.S., U. Ill, 1926; m. Virginia Elizabeth Burroughs, Mar. 14, 1931 (dec.); children—Lawrence Burroughs (dec.), Guy James. Appraiser farm loan div. John Hancock Mut. Life Ins. Co., Chgo., 1926-31; appraiser, agrl. cons. Central Trust Co., Topeka, 1931-35; farm mgr., loan correspondent, Met. Life Ins. Co., Oklahoma City, 1935-45; dist. mgr. farm ranch loan dept. Mutual of N.Y., Oklahoma City, 1945-69; pvt. practice agrl. consulting, Oklahoma City, 1969—; agrl. cons. and advisor Farmer & Stockmen's Bank, Clayton, N.Mex., 1969-74. Mem. Oklahoma City C. of C. (chmn. livestock com. 1945-47), Oklahoma City Farm Club (pres. 1955-57), Okla. Partners of the Americas (pres. 1960-62). Republican. Episcopalian. Clubs: Oklahoma City Petroleum, Chinese-Am. Author: The Answers, 1972; contbr. articles in field to profl. jours. Home: 1726 Coventry Ln Nichols Hills OK 73120 Office: 1500 City Nat Bank Tower Oklahoma City OK 73102

WILLES, RALPH ALVIN, civil engr.; b. Salt Lake City, Sept. 16, 1919; s. Hyde Alvin and Sadie (Thornton) W.; student Utah State Coll., 1937-39; B.S. in Civil Engring., U. Utah, 1943; m. Reva Stocking, Jan. 16, 1942; children—Brian Ralph, Arlene Willes Butterworth. Jr. engr. Curtiss-Wright Corp., Columbus, Ohio, 1943-45; house designer Fuller Houses, Wichita, Kans., 1946; structural test engr. Beech Aircraft Corp., Wichita, 1946-47; constrn. engr. Utah Constrn. Co., Salt Lake City, 1947-55; facilities engr. Gen. Electric Co., Evendale, Ohio, 1955-57; missile facilities engr. Martin Marietta Corp., Denver, 1957-68; designer supersonic airplane Boeing Co., Seattle, 1968-71; city engr. City of Prineville, Oreg., 1971-74; sr. asso. Planning Research Corp., Huntsville, Ala., 1974-76; chief engr. Spaceair Aluminum Industries, Huntsville, 1976-78; cons. engr., Houston, 1979—. Sec., Prineville Planning Commn., 1971-74. Recipient Aluminum Extrusion Design Merit award, 1977; registered profl. engr., Ohio, Utah, Colo., Oreg., Ala., Tex.; registered land surveyor, Oreg. Mem. Nat. Soc. Profl. Engrs. (v.p. Oreg. 1974), Am. Inst. Aeros. and Astronautics, Tau Beta Pi. Mem. Ch. of Jesus Christ of Latter-Day Saints. Club: Kiwanis (award 1973). Author: Conventional and Circular House Designs, 1946, 50; Nuclear Power Plant Design, 1957. Home: 1351 M'ardi Ln Houston TX 77055 Office: 2525 N Loop W Suite 122 Houston TX 77056

WILLETT, HELEN ECKMAN, govt. ofcl.; b. Uniontown, Ky., Mar. 12, 1929; d. Andrew M. and Ruby P. (VanSickle) Eckman; student Lockyear's Bus. Coll., Evansville, Ind., 1947, Henderson (Ky.) Community Coll.; m. Maurice C. Willett, Nov. 28, 1953; children—Kerry Michael, Gregory Scott, Sara Kaye. Sec., Lensing Bros. Wholesale, Evansville, 1947; sec. Union County Farm Bur., Morganfield (Ky.) Agrl. Extension Service, 1948; county exec. dir. U.S. Dept. Agr., Union County Agrl. Stablzn. and Conservation Service, Morganfield, 1949—. Mem. Nat. Assn. County Office Employees, Ky. Assn. County Office Employees (dir., Profl. Improvement award 1975), Morganfield Bus. and Profl. Women (v.p.). Roman Catholic. Home: Route 2 Box 96 Morganfield KY 42437 Office: 217 N Court St Morganfield KY 42437

WILLIAMS, ADA ANGELYNE, social worker; b. Mobile County, Ala., July 30, 1952 d. Benjamin Franklin and Ada Angelyne (Everett) W.; B. Social Welfare, U. Ala., 1973, postgrad., 1975-76, M.S.W., 1979. Counselor, Gateway Children's Home, Birmingham, 1973; compensation analyst The Rust Engring. Co., Birmingham, 1974-76; dir. social services East End Meml. Hosp., Birmingham, 1976—; mem. adv. bd. Home Health Care of N. Ala. Center for Study of Aging U. Ala. grantee, 1979. Mem. Am. Soc. Hosp. Social Work Dirs., Nat. Assn. Social Workers, Ala. Soc. Hosp. Social Workers (treas. 1978-79), Jefferson County Med. Social Service Orgn. Democrat. Baptist. Home: 3812 S 5th Ave Apt 206 Birmingham AL 35222 Office: 7916 2d Ave S Birmingham AL 35206

WILLIAMS, ALLAN THOMAS, county ofcl.; b. LaGrange, Ga., Sept. 28, 1947; s. Thomas Earle and Melba Jane (Mitcham) W.; student Reinhardt Coll., 1965-66; Oxford Coll., 1966-67; B.A. with high honors (Woodrow Wilson fellow, Earhardt fellow), Emory U., 1969; M.A. in Public Adminstrn., U. Va., 1976; cert. in mgmt. devel., U. Richmond, 1974; m. Virginia Gee Tuthill, Aug. 24, 1968; children—Allan Augustus Tuthill, Mary Wilson Mitcham. Dir. social services, Madison County, Va., 1970-74; county adminstr. Buckingham County, Va., 1974-76, Montgomery County, Va., 1976—; adj. prof. county mgmt. Va. Poly. Inst. and State U., 1978—. Mem. Buckingham County Bicentennial Com., 1974-76; founder, vice chmn. Madison County Bicentennial Com., 1972-74. Mem. Am. Soc. Public Adminstrn., Internat. City Mgmt. Assn., Va. Assn. County Adminstrs. (v.p. 1979-80), Va. League Social Services Dirs. (dir.). Methodist. Clubs: Brightwood Ruritan (v.p. 1973), Buckingham Ruritan (sec. 1976), Christiansburg Lions. Home: 140 Baldwin Ln Christiansburg VA 24073 Office: Court House Christiansburg VA 24073

WILLIAMS, ANN ELISE YOCHEM, chemist, lab. mgr.; b. Key West, Fla., Sept. 16, 1952; d. August S. and Evelyn June (Seely) Yochem; B.S. in Biology, Queens Coll., 1974; m. Carter Layne, Jan. 27, 1977. Analytical chemist water pollution lab. Mecklenburg County (N.C.) Environ. Health Dept., Charlotte, 1974-76; analytical lab. mgr., head chemist Charles T. Main Inc., Charlotte, 1976—, designer water labs., instr. waste treatment operators and technicians. Office: Charles T Main Inc 5950 Fairview Rd Charlotte NC 28210

WILLIAMS, AUDREY ARTHUR, JR., architect; b. Dallas, Mar. 25, 1925; s. Audrey Arthur and Helen Myrtle (Stark) W.; B.S. in Archtl. Constrn., Tex. Agrl. and Mech. U., 1951; m. Martha Louise Thomas, July 2, 1943; 1 dau., Sally Ann (Mrs. James Richard Hewell, Jr.). Architect, Art Williams Jr. & Assos., Architects, Dallas, 1954—. Owner, Art Williams Jr. Interiors; owner Motor Hotel Consultants; pres., dir. Standard Constrn. Co. Waco (Tex.), Am. Motor Inns, Inc., Americana Mortgage & Leasing Corp.; designer numerous bldgs. including motor hotels, restaurants. Served with USAF, 1942-45; ETO. Mem. Nat., Am. insts. architects, Constrn. Specification Inst., Tex. Soc. Architects. Republican. Home: 14140 Rawhide Pkwy Dallas TX 75234 Office: 2880 LBJ Freeway Dallas TX 75234

WILLIAMS, AVON NYANZA, JR., lawyer, state senator; b. Knoxville, Tenn., Dec. 22, 1921; s. Avon Nyanza and Carrie Belle Williams; A.B., Johnson C. Smith U., Charlotte, N.C., 1940; LL.B., Boston U., 1947, LL.M., 1948; m. Joan Marie Bontemps, 1956; children—Avon Nyanza, Wendy Janette. Admitted to Mass. bar, 1948, Tenn. bar, 1949, U.S. Supreme Ct. bar, 1963; practice law, Knoxville, 1949-53; partner firm, Nashville, 1953-69; individual practice law, Nashville, 1969—; mem. Tenn. State Senate, 1968—; prof. dental jurisprudence Meharry Med. Coll., 1970—. Founding mem. Tenn. Voters Council, 1966—, chmn., 1966—; founding mem. Davidson County Ind. Polit. Council, 1962—, pres., 1962-66; mem. State Dem. Steering Com., 1964; del. Nat. Dem. Conv., 1972; mem. exec. com. Nashville br. NAACP, 1953—; trustee St. Andrews Presbyn. Ch., Nashville, 1966—; mem. appeals and rev. com. Meharry Med. Coll., 1970—; bd. dirs. So. Regional Council, 1968—, Family and Children's Service, 1956-60. Served to lt. col., JAGC, U.S. Army Res. Recipient certs. of achievement for civil rights legal work. Mem. Am. Bar Assn., Am. Judicature Soc., Omega Psi Phi, Sigma Pi Phi. Home: 1414 Parkway Towers Nashville TN 37219

WILLIAMS, BETTYE JEAN, educator; b. Pine Bluff, Ark., July 2, 1946; d. Eunice Williams and Dorothy M. (Willingham) W.; B.A., U. Ark., 1968; M.A., Kans. State Coll., 1969; postgrad. Old Dominion U., 1972, Central State U., 1974, 78. Instr. dept. English, U. Ark., Pine Bluff, 1969—. Vol. for entertaining children living with foster parents, 1977—. Mem. Ark. Tchrs. English, Nat. Council Tchrs. English, Ark. Philol. Assn., Sigma Tau Delta. Baptist. Club: Order Eastern Star. Home: 1203 Brentwood Dr Pine Bluff AR 71601 Office: English Dept U Ark Pine Bluff AR 71601

WILLIAMS, CALVIT HERNDON, JR., chemist; b. Houston, Dec. 28, 1936; s. Calvit Herndon and Julia Eloise (Tybor) W.; B.A., U. St. Thomas, 1958; Ph.D., Brown U., 1964; m. Margaret Florence Jeter, Dec. 27, 1959; children—Sabina Anne, Terence Jeter, Russel Herndon, Damon Andrew. AEC postdoctoral fellow Rice U., Houston, 1964-66; research asso. Sandia Labs., Albuquerque, 1966-70; tchr. St. Pius High Sch., Albuquerque, 1970-71; prof. chemistry U. Campinas, Sao Paulo, Brazil, 1971-76; lab. dir., cons. Aer-Aqua Labs., Inc., Houston, 1976-77; sr. scientist Radian Corp., Austin, Tex., 1977—. Cert. in indsl. hygiene Am. Bd. Indsl. Hygiene. Fellow Am. Inst. Chemistry; mem. Am. Chem. Soc., Am. Soc. Mass Spectrometry, Am. Indsl. Hygiene Assn., Sigma Xi, Delta Epsilon Sigma. Contbr. articles to profl. jours. Home: 1800 Cresthaven Dr Austin TX 78704 Office: 8500 Shoal Creek Rd Austin TX 78766

WILLIAMS, CARL SMITH, elec. engr.; b. San Augustine, Tex., Mar. 12, 1920; s. William Matthew and Maude Ethel (Knight) W.; B.S. in Elec. Engring., Tex. A. and M. U., 1953; m. Wanda Jean Cole, Dec. 24, 1945; children—David K., Wendy F. Williams Love, Leola A. Williams Krueger. Chief engr., gen. mgr. Hensarling Electric Co., Bryan, Tex., 1958-68; system elec. engr. Tex. A. and M. U. System, College Station, 1968—; cons. archtl. cos. Mem. elec. bd. City of College Station. Served with Signal Corps, U.S. Army, 1940-45; ETO. Decorated Fourragere (Belgium); Bronze Star. Registered profl. engr., Tex. Mem. Nat., Tex. socs. profl. engrs., IEEE, Am. Soc. Heating, Refrigeration and Air Conditioning Engrs. Methodist. Clubs: Tex. A. and M. Univ. Century, Elks. Home: 2414 Morris Ln Bryan TX 77801 Office: PO Box 219 College Station TX 77846

WILLIAMS, CHARLES HANSEL, accountant; b. Tifton, Ga., Sept. 2, 1938; s. Amos McKendall and Hattie Idella (Allen) W.; student Ga. Inst. Tech., 1956, Ga. State Coll., 1965, B.B.A., 1965; M.Profl. Accountancy, Ga. State U., 1970; m. Celia Carolyn Trammell, June 27, 1970; 1 son, Trammell Allen. With So. Bell Tel. and Tel. Co., Atlanta, 1957-60; staff accountant William A. Freeman, C.P.A., Atlanta, 1960-63; cons. Chuck Shields Advt. Agy., Atlanta, 1963, U.S. Plastics Co., Inc., Atlanta, 1963; student summer missionary So. Bapt. Home Mission Bd., Ill., 1963, Ariz., 1964; student staffer Glorieta (N.Mex.) Bapt. Assembly, 1964; state auditor State of Ga., Dept. of Audits, Atlanta, 1965-69; sr. staff accountant Touche, Ross, Bailey & Smart, Atlanta, 1970; pvt. practice pub. accounting, Atlanta, 1970; accounting instr. Abraham Baldwin Agrl. Coll., Tifton, Ga., 1970-71; mng. partner Allen & Williams, C.P.A.'s, Tifton, 1971-78; pvt. practice public acctg., Newnan, 1978—. Pres., Ga. State Coll. Bapt. Student Union, 1962-64; enlistment chmn. Ga. Bapt. Student Union, 1963-64; bd. dirs. Hansel & Gretel Nursery Sch., Inc., Atlanta, 1963—, Abraham Baldwin Agrl. Coll. Found., 1972-78, Flint River council Girl Scouts U.S.A., 1973-76, Tifton Concert Assn., 1974-78, United Givers Fund, 1975—; chmn. Wiregrass Arts and Crafts Show, Tifton, 1976; councilman Ga. State U. Student Govt. Council, 1964-65. Served with U.S. Army, 1956-57. C.P.A., Ga., 1969. Mem. Am. Inst. C.P.A.'s, Ga. Soc. C.P.A.'s, Tiftarea Ducks Unltd. Baptist. Clubs: Exchange (bd. dirs. 1974-76), Tifton; Newnan Kiwanis; Springhill Country. Home: 13 Hawthorn Dr Newnan GA 30263 Office: 44 Jefferson St PO Box 2323 Newnan GA 30264

WILLIAMS, CHARLES IVAN, dentist; b. Dallas, Dec. 29, 1943; s. John Groce and Emma Virginia (Fox) W.; student So. Meth. U., 1961-63, Arlington State Coll., summers 1961-63, Dental Sch. U. Tex., 1963-65; D.D.S., Baylor U., 1967; m. Mary Catherine Hollingsworth, Nov. 25, 1965; children—Charles Ivan II, Rachel Dawn, Virginia Eileen. Gen. practice dentistry, Mexia, Tex., 1967-77, Dallas, 1974-78, Ferris, Tex., 1978—; mem. dental staff Meth. Hosp., Dallas, Meth. Charlton Hosp., Dallas; former mem. staff Gen. Mexia Hosp., sec. staff, 1969-77; former cons. dentist Mexia State Sch. for Mentally Retarded, Wortham Hosp.; real estate broker. Recipient Clinic award Dallas Mid-Winter Dental Clinic, 1967. Mem. Am., Tex. dental assns., Am. Orthodontic Soc., Acad. Gen. Dentistry, Tex. Assn. Realtors. Mem. Ch. of Nazarene. Home: 1126 Angela Cedar Hill TX 75104 Office: 213 W 6th St Ferris TX 75125

WILLIAMS, CHARLES SAMUEL, electric safety equipment co. exec.; b. Phoenix, Jan. 3, 1932; s. Charley and Delitha May (Bezonia) W.; B.S., Ariz. State U., 1955; m. Carolyn Nelson, Aug. 28, 1952; children—Stacee Lee, Cynthia Lyn, Sheryl Ann. Mgr. Ramada Inns, Phoenix, 1961-65; properties dir. T.I.M.E.-DC, Inc., Lubbock, Tex., 1965-71; pres. Kineticon Corp., Lubbock, 1971—, also dir. Served in USAF, 1955-60. Mem. AMORC, Order of Essenes. Patentee. Home: 4013 49th St Lubbock TX 79413 Office: PO Box 16466 Lubbock TX 79490

WILLIAMS, CHARLES WESLEY, copy machines sales co. exec.; b. Timmonsville, S.C., July 13, 1941; s. J.B. and Hattie Landis (Martin) W.; A.A. in Bus., Wingate (N.C.) Jr. Coll., 1961; m. Judy Kaye Ramage, Aug. 7, 1966; children—Angela Darlene, Charles Wesley, Judy Ashley. Collection coordinator Ford Motor Credit Corp., 1962-65; major account rep. Xerox Corp., 1965-74; pres. Copy Systems, Inc., Savannah, Ga., 1974—. Active local Little League Baseball. Mem. Nat. Office Machines Dealer Assn., Nat. Skeet Shooters Assn. Methodist. Clubs: German Country, Kiwanis, Shriners (chmn. fund raising for crippled children), Forest City Gun. Home: 136 Cardinal St Savannah GA 31406 Office: 227 W Victory Dr Savannah GA 31403

WILLIAMS, DARRELL WAYNE, petroleum engr., oil co. exec.; b. West Union, W.Va., Nov. 20, 1942; s. I. Wayne and Irene Davis W.; B.S., W.Va. U., 1964; postgrad. George Washington U., Hampton, Va., 1971-72; m. Diana Moore, Nov. 30, 1963; children—Amy, Matthew. Petroleum engr. Exxon Corp., 1963-66; drilling engr. Tenneco Oil Co., Lafayette, La., 1966-68; sr. design engr. Deep Sea Ventures, Gloucester Point, Va., 1968-71; v.p. ops. Sedco Inc., Dallas, 1971-78; pres. Baker Well Services, Inc., Dallas, 1978—; lectr. in field. Active Young Republicans. Registered profl. engr., Tex., W.Va. Mem. Sigma Gamma Epsilon, Pi Epsilon Tau. Contbr. articles to profl. publs. Patentee in field. Office: Baker Well Services Inc 2974 LBJ Freeway Suite 300 Dallas TX 75234

WILLIAMS, DAVID BRUCE, state ofcl.; b. Louisville, Jan. 30, 1948; s. Richard Forrest and Ester Mildred (Sparkman) W.; B.A. cum laude in Psychology (Ind. U. Found. scholar, NSF grantee), Ind. U., 1970; M.P.A., Ky. State U., 1974. Asst. dir. planning Ky. Dept. Corrections, Frankfort, 1971-73: policy and fin. analyst Ky. Dept. Human Resources, Frankfort, 1973-74; legis. budget analyst Ky. Legis. Research Commn., Frankfort, 1974-76; dep. dir. Office Adminstrn., Ky. Dept. Energy, Lexington, 1976—. Active YMCA, Big Bros. Lexington. Mem. Am. Mgmt. Assn. Office: PO Box 11888 Lexington KY 40578

WILLIAMS, DAVID GENE, mfg. co. exec.; b. Galveston, Tex., Dec. 9, 1938; s. Cecil Donald and Gladys Margaruite (Kinser) W.; student Alvin Jr. Coll., 1956-60; A.A.S., Coll. of Mainland, 1975; m. Maria Irma Garcia, Dec. 20, 1975; children—Tammy Joe, Ronald Denton. Sr. offset operator Monsanto Co., Texas City, Tex., 1959-63, asst. supr. office services, 1964-76, field safety insp., 1976-77, safety insp., 1977-78, safety supr., 1979—; faculty Coll. of Mainland, 1975-78. Scoutmaster, Boy Scouts Am., 1959-67; Sunday sch. tchr. Baptist Ch., Algoa, 1960-70; mem. tax equalization bd. Santa Fe Sch. Dist., 1962; sec. Santa Fe PTA, 1964; mem. Algoa Vol. Fire Dept., 1963-74, asst. fire chief, 1967. Eagle Scout with bronze palm; mem. Order of Arrow. Mem. Nat. Safety Mgmt. Soc., Tex. Safety Assn., Nat. Safety Council, Am. Soc. Safety Engrs. Democrat. Home: 1403 Melody Dr LaMarque TX 77568 Office: 1300 Post Oak Tower 5051 Westheimer St Houston TX 77056

WILLIAMS, DAVID MUNROE, computer services co. exec.; b. Chgo., Mar. 13, 1921; s. Ralph and Cora Amaline (Schroff) W.; student Aero. U., 1940, Fla. So. U., 1950, U. Omaha, 1957; B.S., U. Md., 1963; m. Virginia A. Simpson, Jan. 15, 1943; children—Barbara Jean, Cynthia Renee, Wende Dianne. Commd. 2d lt. USAAC, 1942, advanced through grades to col., 1957; ret., 1967; U.S. Def. and Air attache, Bonn, W. Ger., 1963-66, market research mgr. Aerospace Group, The Boeing Co., Seattle, 1967-71; v.p. Nat. Data Corp., 1971-74, group v.p., 1974—, gen. mgr., exec. v.p. Nat. Billing Systems, Inc., subs., 1972-75, pres. subs., 1975—. Mem. Atlanta Postal Adv. Council, 1974—. Decorated Order Patriotic Warfare (Russia), Grosse Verdienstkreuz (Germany); Legion of Merit with oak leaf cluster, D.F.C., Air medal with 3 oak leaf clusters, Air Force Commendation medal. Mem. Electronics Industries Assn., Air Force Assn., Optical Character Reading Assn., Ret. Officers Assn., Air Force Hist. Assn., Second Schweinfurt Meml. Assn., 91st BQ Meml. Assn. Methodist. Club: Atlanta Navy Flying (pres.).

WILLIAMS, DAVID WILLARD, educator; b. Venedocia, O., Aug. 20; s. David W. and Elizabeth J. (Morgan) W.; B.S.A., Ohio State U., 1915; M.Sc., U. Ill., 1916; postgrad. A. and M. Coll. Tex., 1923, postgrad. U. Chgo., summers, 1927-28; Ingeniero Agronomo, U. Coahuila, Mexico, 1957; LL.D., Austin Coll., 1957; m. Magdalene Rees, Aug. 18, 1921; children—Margaret Ann Cardwell, Ruth Elizabeth (Mrs. Bruce B. Lawrence), David Willard. Extension animal husbandman U.S. Dept. Agr., Clemson Agrl. Coll., 1917-19; asso. prof. Tex. A. and M. U., 1919-20, prof., 1920-22, head dept. animal sci., 1922-46, v.p. for agr., 1946-48, vice chancellor for agr., 1948-58, acting pres., 1956-57, vice chancellor emeritus, 1962—. Cattle rancher, 1932-79; cons. U. Ceylon, 1958-62; dir. Bryan Bldg. & Loan. Dept. supt. Southwestern Expn. and Fat Stock Show, 1920-43, chmn. adv. com., 1946-58; pres. Am. Soc. Animal Sci. rep. Internat. Livestock Breeding Congress, Zurich, Switzerland, 1939; agrl. cons. ECA, Germany, 1949; personnel cons. Fgn. Agr. Service, 1949-58; instnl. rep. Ark., White, Red River Interagy. Com., 1951-58; mem. U.S.-Mexico Joint Tech. Agr. Exchange Com., 1951; cons. to Morocco for AID, 1962; councilor Tex. A. and M. Research Found.; cons. Rockfeller Found., Colombia, 1951; cons. ICA, East Pakistan Agr. and Edn.; cons. agr. Escuela Superior De Agricultura, Mexico, 1954. Hon. v.p. State Fair Tex. Served with CWS, 1918, lt. col. U.S. 1943, 46. Fellow AAAS, Tex. Acad. Sci., Am. Soc. Animal Sci. (past pres.); mem. Tex. Southwestern Cattle Raisers Assn., Tex. Agrl. Workers Assn., Am. Quarter Horse Breeders Assn. (past adv. com.), Bryan C. of C. (past pres.), Ceylon Assn. Advancement Sci. (pres. agr. sect. 1958-59), Nat. Collegiate Athletic Assn. (past v.p. councilman at large), Southwest Athletic Conf. (past pres.), Am. Legion, Sigma Delta Chi, Alpha Gamma Rho (past pres. Ohio), Lambda Gamma Delta, Alpha Zeta. Presbyterian (elder). Clubs: Nat. Block and Bridle, Saddle and Sirloin (past pres. Ohio), Masons, Rotary. Author: Beef Cattle in the South, 1941; co-author: Livestock and Poultry, 1925; Agriculture in the Southwest, 1940. Home: 500 Fairview St College Station TX 77840

WILLIAMS, DOLORES L., banker; b. Valley City, N.D., June 7, 1932; d. Edgar S. and Evelyn B. (Taylor) Freborg; grad. sch. Bank Adminstrn., U. Wis., 1978; m. Billy Joe Williams, Jan. 15, 1977; children—Stephen, Cheryl, Daniel, Shawn. With First Nat. Bank, Portland, Oreg., 1950-55, First Nat. Bank, Denver, 1955-61, Central Bank, Denver, 1961-68, Jefferson Bank & Trust Co., Lakewood, Colo., 1971-72; with S. Denver Nat. Bank, 1972-74, asst. v.p., personnel adminstr., asst. to pres., 1972-74; v.p., cashier Comml. Nat. Bank, Longview, Tex., 1974—; lectr. in field. Active fund raising local YMCA. Recipient award Denver Jr. Achievement, 1965. Mem. Am. Inst. Banking (dir., instr.), Nat. Assn. Bank Women, Am. Mgmt. Assn., Democrat. Mem. Christian Ch. (Disciples of Christ). Home: 1205 Columbia Dr Longview TX 75601 Office: PO Box 8349 Longview TX 75602

WILLIAMS, DONNA KAYE, rehab. counselor; b. Fort Worth, May 11, 1949; d. James Henry and Dorothy Frances (Toombs) Williams; student Tex. Women's U., 1968, Mary Hardin-Baylor Coll., 1969-70; B.S., Hardin-Simmons U., 1974; M.A. in Guidance and Counseling, So. Meth. U., 1976. Counselor, mem. pub. relations staff Dallas Soc. for Crippled Children, 1974-76; owner, operator Handicapped Assistance by D. Williams, Dallas, 1979—; cons., 1977—; cons. counseling of handicapped, Dallas, 1976—, Tex. A. and M. U., 1978—; lectr. in field. Project dir. life enrichment program United Cerebral Palsy of Tex. Gulf Coast, 1978-79. Named Tex. Easter Seal Child, 1952. Mem. Am. Personnel and Guidance Assn., Am. Rehab. Counseling Assn., 500 Inc. of Dallas, Innovators. Baptist. Home: 11307 Chicot St Dallas TX 75230 Office: 6200 N Central Expressway Suite 306 Dallas TX 75206

WILLIAMS, DORIS MOSS, educator; b. Washington, July 13, 1931; d. William Alfred and Lila Lee (Elliott) Moss; R.N., Howard U., 1953; B.A., Am. U., Washington, 1960; M.A., U. Chgo., 1962; Ph.D., U. Ala., 1977; m. Lionel Therron Williams, Aug. 10, 1963; children—Lionel Therron, Leah Telesyandra. Program dir. Chgo. Youth Centers, 1963-65; family counselor Family Counseling Assn., Birmingham, Ala., 1965-68; dir. student tng. U. Ala. Med. Sch., Birmingham, 1968-74; asso. dean, dir. M.S.W. degree program U. Ala., University, 1975—, cons. Mgmt. Tng. Inst., 1974—; cons. group counseling VA, 1975—. Mem. women's com. Birmingham Symphony Assn., 1977—. Named Woman of Distinction, Iota Phi Lambda, 1977; U. Chgo. fellow, 1960-62. Mem. Nat. Assn. Social Workers (exec. bd.), Council Social Work Edn. (del.), Women's Polit. Caucus, Phi Delta Kappa, Kappa Delta Pi. Democrat. Baptist. Clubs. Imperial, Federated. Home: 3817 Jefferson Ave SW Birmingham AL 35221 Office: PO Box 1935 University AL 35486

WILLIAMS, DURWARD RAY, land surveyor; b. Winters, Tex., Feb. 2, 1928; s. Andrew Lee and Sarah Ola (Puckett) W.; student Tex. Tech. U., 1944-46, Colo. Sch. Mines, 1969; m. Patricia Dwayne Hallford, Mar. 1, 1952; children—Macqueline Kay, Janice Raye. Clk. Colo. Interstate Gas Co., Masterson, Tex., 1953-55, instrument man, Amarillo, Tex., 1955-68, party chief, Colorado Springs, Colo., 1968-71, Amarillo, 1971—. Farmer, rancher, Canyon, Tex., 1964—. Served with USAF, 1950-53. Democrat. Baptist. Home: Route 1 Box 130 Canyon TX 79015 Office: 3505 Olsen Blvd Amarillo TX 79109

WILLIAMS, EARL CRANSTON, JR., state ofcl., engr.; b. Corbett, Md., Dec. 26, 1920; s. Earl Cranston and Mildred Cedelia (Nimmo) W.; B.C.E., U. Md., 1950; postgrad. Northwestern U., 1952-54, Yale U., 1954-55; m. Billie Leona Harris, Mar. 11, 1945; children—Andrea Williams Perkerson, Linda Williams Putney, Janet Williams Bauer, Earl Cranston. With Wichita Falls (Tex.) Pub. Works Dept., 1950-59, city traffic engr., 1952-59; chief traffic engring. div. Montgomery County, Md., 1959-62; state traffic engr. Tenn. Dept. Transp., Nashville, 1962-77, research engr., 1977—. Served with USAAF, World War II. Recipient Vol. award 1979. Registered profl. engr., Tenn., Tex. Fellow ASCE, Inst. Transp. Engrs. (pres. So. sect. 1969-70 sec. rep. to dist. 5 bd. 1973, dir. dist. 5, 1979—); mem. Transp. Research Bd., Am. Assn. State Hwy. Ofcls., Nat. Advisory Com. Uniform Traffic Control Devices, Nat. Soc. Profl. Engrs. (pres. North Central Tex. chpt.). Democrat. Unitarian. Home: 3629 Central Ave Nashville TN 37205 Office: 550 Doctors Bldg 702 Church St Nashville TN 37203

WILLIAMS, EDWARD HANFORD, cardiovascular surgeon; b. N.Y.C., Feb. 5, 1942; s. Edward Hanford and Mary Elizabeth (Vodopivce) W.; B.A., Lehigh U., 1964; M.D., U. Pa., 1969; m. Dorothy Judith Baker, June 7, 1969; children—Susan Lynn, Edward Hanford. Intern, Hosp. U. Pa., 1969-70, resident, 1970-71, Milton S. Hershey Med. Center, Pa. State U., 1971-75, research asso., 1975-76, asst. prof. surgery, 1976-77; asst. prof. surgery U. Tex., Galveston, 1977-79, asso. prof., 1979—, dir. cardiovascular research, 1977—, chief div. cardiovascular and thoracic surgery, 1980—; cons. USPHS. NIH grantee, 1979—; recipient Nat. Research Service award, 1976. Fellow A.C.S., Am. Coll. Cardiology, Am. Coll. Angiology; mem. Assn. Academic Surgery, Agnew Surg. Soc., Singleton Surg. Soc. Republican. Roman Catholic. Home: 29 Lakeview Dr Galveston TX 77551 Office: Div Cardiovascular and Thoracic Surgery U Tex Med Br Galveston TX 77550

WILLIAMS, EDWARD LIKANDER, research and tng. orgn. exec.; b. Quincy, Mass., Aug. 30, 1931; s. Edward Likander and Agnes Elizabeth (Fuge) W.; A.B., Duke U., 1953; M.B.A., Northwestern U., 1959; m. Mollie Nelson, June 27, 1959; children—Gretchen Kristi, Bridget Alyson, Rebecca Elizabeth. With Pacific Lumber Co., San Francisco and Chgo., 1956-66; v.p. Kendall Coll., Evanston, Ill., 1966-69; dir. spl. and deferred gifts Northwestern U., Evanston, 1969-71; dir. resources Nat. 4-H Found., Chevy Chase, Md., 1971-75; asso. dir. Rural Advancement Fund, Washington, 1975-76; program officer Winrock Internat., Morrilton, Ark., 1976—. Served with U.S. Army, 1953-56. Mem. Am. Mgmt. Assn., Nat. Intercollegiate Soccer Ofcls. Assn., Nat. Council Univ. Research Adminstrs. Congregationalist. Club: Univ. (N.Y.C.). Home: 1414 E View St Morrilton AR 72110 Office: Winrock Internat Petit Jean Mountain Morrilton AR 72110

WILLIAMS, ELLIS, law enforcement officer; b. Raymond, Miss., Oct. 27, 1931; s. Currie and Elise (Morrison) W.; B.A. in Criminology, Loyola U. South, New Orleans, 1972, M.Ed., 1974; m. Priscilla Norman, Jan. 9, 1954; children—Debra, Rita, Claude, Lathan, Glenn, Zelia. Patrolman, dept. police City of New Orleans, 1964-77, police sergeant, asst. platoon comdr., 1977-79, police lt., platoon comdr., 1979—; asso. minister Historic 2d Baptist Ch., New Orleans. Cert. fingerprint identification technician; cert. polygraphist Am. Polygraph Assn. Mem. Fraternal Order Police, Am. Law Enforcement Officers Assn., Police Mut. Benevolent Assn., Internat. Assn. Identifications, La. Assn. Identification, Am. Polygraph Assn., La. Polygraph Assn., Kappa Delta Pi. Democrat. Club: Mason. Home: 3108 Metropolitan St New Orleans LA 70126 Office: 715 S Broad St New Orleans LA 70119

WILLIAMS, ELYNOR ALBERTA, public relations specialist; b. Baton Rouge, La., Oct. 27, 1946; d. Albert Berry and Naomi Theresa (Douglas) W.; B.S., Spelman Coll., 1966; M.S., Cornell U., 1973. Home econs. tchr. Eugene Butler Jr.-Sr. High Sch., Jacksonville, Fla., 1966-68; publicist, pkg. editor, copy editor Gen. Foods Corp., White Plains, N.Y., 1968-71; writer, researcher Expanded Nutrition Edn. program Cornell U., summer 1972, tutor, com. on spl. edn. projects, 1972-73; communication specialist N.C. Agrl. Ext. Service, N.C. A & T State U., Greensboro and N.C. State U., Raleigh, 1973-77; public relations specialist Western Electric, Greensboro, 1977—. Vice-chmn. adv. com. dept. communication arts Cornell U., 1978-79. Bd. dirs. Greensboro Drug Action Council, 1977—; mem. Carolina Theatre Commn., 1977—; mem. steering com. Guilford County Women's Coalition, 1978; agy. bd. mem. solicitor United Way Campaign, 1977—; issues chmn. Triad council Girls Scouts Am., 1979; mem. Mayor's Energy Conservation Commn., 1977-78. Recipient Cornell U. Grad. Sch. fellowship, 1972-73, United Negro Coll. Fund scholarship, 1962-66. Mem. Internat. Assn. Bus. Communicators, Am. Women in Radio and TV. Democrat. Methodist. Home: 1115-B W Bessemer Ave Greensboro NC 27408 Office: Western Electric PO Box 25000 Greensboro NC 27420

WILLIAMS, ETHEL PATTERSON, guidance counselor; b. Lillington, N.C., May 10, 1918; d. Junious Merrimon and Mattie Mae (Shaw) Patterson; B.S., Shaw U., Raleigh, N.C., 1939; M.S., N.C. A&T State U., 1955, M.S. in Guidance, 1975; postgrad. Case Inst. Tech., 1960, N.C. State U., 1965-70; m. Booker T. Williams, Oct. 11, 1945; children—Booker Talieferro, Reynauld Merrimon. Tchr. math. high schs. in N.C., 1939-65; guidance counselor high schs. in N.C., 1965—; guidance counselor Harnett Central High Sch., Angier, N.C., 1977—. Sec. Shawtown Community Recreation Program, Lillington, 1965-70; pres. Women's Progressive Club, Lillington, 1960-68. Named Tchr. of Yr. in Harnett County, 1974. Mem. Am. Personnel and Guidance Assn., NEA, Am. Assn. Coll. Women, Non-White Personnel and Guidance Assn., N.C. Edn. Assn., Zeta Phi Beta. Democrat. Mem. A.M.E. Zion Ch. Home: Route 1 Box 515 Lillington NC 27546

WILLIAMS, FRANK MATHEWS, ophthalmologist; b. Bartow, Fla., Jan. 14, 1938; s. Earnest R. and Ruby (Mathews) W.: B.S. summa cum laude, Yale U., 1960; M.D. cum laude, Harvard U., 1964; m. Jacqueline Mary Rixon, Sept. 13, 1963; children—Christopher Lee, Andrew R. Intern, Harvard Med. Service-Boston City Hosp., 1964-65; resident in ophthalmology Wilmer Ophthalmol. Inst., Johns Hopkins Hosp., Balt., 1965-68; chief ophthalmol. services USPHS Hosps., Detroit, 1968-70; mem. staff Bascom Palmer Eye Inst., Miami, Fla., 1970; practice medicine specializing in ophthalmology, Clearwater, Fla., 1971—; chief ophthalmology dept. Morton F. Plant Hosp., Clearwater. Mem. sch. health adv. council Pinellas County (Fla.). Diplomate Am. Bd. Ophthalmology. Fellow A.C.S., Am. Acad. Ophthalmology; mem. Am. Intraocular Implant Soc., Fla. Ophthal.

Soc., Fla., Pineallas County med. socs. Home: 210 Harbor View Ln Largo FL 33540 Office: Suite 5 430 Pinellas St Clearwater FL 33516

WILLIAMS, FRANKLIN SPRINGER, mgmt. scientist, educator; b. Cin., Feb. 17, 1912; s. John F. and Everella (Springer) W.; B.S., Kent State U., 1933; M.B.A., U. Chgo., 1944; Ph.D., U. Ark., 1957; m. Elizabeth Bassett, Aug. 28, 1945; children—Jeffrey S., Christopher B., Philip F. Tchr. public schs., Conneaut, Youngstown and Akron, Ohio, 1935-43; mktg. researcher, market analyst Chgo. Assn. Commerce, 1944-45, Link-Belt Co., Chgo., 1945-46; asst. prof. mgmt. U. Ark., Fayetteville, 1946-48, now prof. mktg. and mgmt.; dir. mag. research Antioch Rev., also asst. prof. bus. adminstrn. Antioch Coll., Yellow Springs, Ohio, 1948-49; asst. prof. mktg. U. Okla., Norman, 1949-53; asst. prof. mgmt. U. Ark., Little Rock, 1953-58, asso. prof., 1958-59; pub. Red Lion Books of Fayetteville, 1979—; cons. mktg., mgmt., 1946—. Named outstanding tchr. U. Ark., 1946, 76, 77. Mem. Am. Acad. Mgmt., Ozark Econ. Assn., Am. Mktg. Assn., Blue Key, Alpha Delta Sigma, Alpha Kappa Psi, Beta Gamma Sigma, Sigma Iota Epsilon. Author: Survivors, Heroes, 1979. Researcher psychol. survivor tng. Home: Knerr Rd PO Box 25 Fayetteville AR 72701

WILLIAMS, FRED ALTON (AL), JR., coll. adminstr.; b. Paris, Tex., June 13, 1923; s. Fred Alton and Mary Catherine (Gilliland) W.; B.B.A., U. Tex., Austin, 1950; m. Patsy Ruth Williams, Dec. 17, 1954; children—Marilyn, Carol. Partner, Williams Air Activities, Civilian Flight Sch., Sales & Service Tyler, Tex., 1946-52; partner, v.p. Williams Marine Co., Tyler, Holiday Marina-Resort, Inc., Lake Tawakoni, Tex., 1952-65; recruiter Tyler Comml. Coll., 1965-70, exec. dir., 1970-76; dir. fin. aid and secretarial studies Northwood Inst. Tex., Cedar Hill, 1976-79, dir. ops., 1979—; cons. in field; coordinator workshops in field. Served with USAF, capt. Res. ret. Mem. Nat., Tex., Southwestern assns. student fin. aid adminstrs., Southwestern Pvt. Comml. Sch. Assn. (past dir.), Kappa Sigma. Baptist. Club: Lions. Home: 127 Rowland Pl Tyler TX 75701 Office: PO Box 58 Cedar Hill TX 75104

WILLIAMS, FRED DONALD, univ. adminstr.; b. Glasgow, Ky., July 1, 1944; s. Cander and Jessie Vera (Lawson) W.; B.A., Ky. State U., 1969; M.A., Eastern Ky. U., 1975; m. America Ann Pace, Apr. 4, 1969; 1 dau., Tonya Annette. Social worker Bur. Public Assistance, Burkesville, Ky., 1969-71; unit housing dir. Ky. State U., Frankfort, 1977, dir. student recruitment, 1977-78, asst. dir. admissions, 1978—. Pres., Bridgeport Elem. PTO, 1978-79. Recipient Outstanding Young Man of Am. award Nat. Jaycees, 1979. Mem. Am. Personnel and Guidance Assn., Am. Assn. Coll. Registrars and Admissions Officers, Assn. Non-White Concerns in Personnel and Guidance (pres. Ky. chpt. 1978—). Home: 102 Redwood Dr Frankfort KY 40601 Office: Ky State U Frankfort KY 40601

WILLIAMS, GEORGE, educator; b. Cardwell, Mo., Sept. 6, 1919; s. Ira D. and Myrtle Mae (Howe) W.; B.S., Ark. State U., 1949; M.Ed., U. Miss., 1952; m. Fay Kelley, Nov. 23, 1944; 1 son, George D. Tchr. high sch., Steele, Mo., 1949-53; prin. secondary schs., Braggadocio, Mo., 1953-59; tchr. bus. Fort Myers (Fla.) High Sch., 1968—, chmn. dept., 1969—. Chmn. econ. devel. com., Fort Myers; chmn. Democratic Exec. Com., Lee County, Fla., 1974—; exec. officer Manpower Council Fort Myers. Mem. Am. Fedn. Tchrs. (Fla. state treas. 1969-74, exec. dir. Local 1983, pres. Central Labor Council), NEA (tchrs. advisory com.), Phi Delta Kappa (pres. 1972-73). Democrat. Methodist. Clubs: Masons, Shriners. Editor The Reporter, 1969-76, Fla. Federationist, 1969-74. Home: 4355 Cypress Ln Fort Myers FL 33905

WILLIAMS, GEORGE AUBREY, physician, educator; b. Furman, Ala., July 14, 1901; s. Simeon W. and Mattie Mae (Bender) W.; B.S., Emory U., 1922, M.D., 1924; m. Virginia Stone Williams, June 4, 1927; children—George A., Jonathan Stone. Intern, Grady Meml. Hosp., Atlanta, 1924-25, resident in gen. surgery and urology, 1925-26; clin. prof. gynecology and obstetrics Emory U.; mem. staff Grady Meml., Northside, Doctors Meml., Crawford W. Long Meml. hosps., St. Joseph's Infirmary. Recipient Outstanding Clin. Prof. award, 1966. Mem. Med. Assn. Atlanta, Med. Assn. Ga., AMA, Atlanta, S. Atlantic, Ga. obstet. and gynecol. socs., ACS, Am. Coll. Obstetricians and Gynecologists, Internat. Soc. for Study of Vulrar Disease. Methodist. Club: Ansley Golf. Contbr. articles in field to profl. jours. Home: 135 Montgomery Ferry Dr NE Atlanta GA 30309 Office: 401 W Peachtree St NE Atlanta GA 30308

WILLIAMS, GEORGE GARDNER, JR., educator; b. Dallas, Aug. 1, 1921; s. George Gardner and Teresa (Kestner) W.; B.A., B.B.A., So. Meth. U., 1948; M.B.A., U. Tex., 1949; M.A., So. Meth. U., 1968; m. Betty Sue Thornton, June 3, 1967; children—Teresa Susan, Simon Phillip, Deborah Lynn, Lisa Ann. Civilian instr. Air Force, Harlingen, Tex., 1950-53; acct. Amoco Chems. Corp., Stanolind Oil Co., Standard Oil of Ind., Brownsville, Tex., Fort Worth, 1953-59; asso. prof. dept. econs. Tex. Wesleyan Coll., Fort Worth, 1959—. Served with U.S. Army, 1942-45. Decorated Purple Heart. Mem. AAUP, Am. Econ. Assn., Nat. Assn. Bus. Economists, Mem. Ch. of Christ, Science. Soc. Preservation and Encouragement Barbershop Quartet Singing in Am. Home: 1200 Ravenwood Dr Arlington TX 76013 Office: Tex Wesleyan Coll Fort Worth TX 76105

WILLIAMS, HARRY JOHN, accountant; b. West Frankfort, Ill., June 21, 1900; s. George Harry and Lydia (Morgan) W.; student U. Ill., 1920-22; ; m. Helita Eubanks Durham, Oct. 24, 1922; children—Harry John, Patricia (Mrs. Reynold H. Richaud). With Peat, Marwick, Mitchell & Co., C.P.A.'S, 1922-63, partner, 1943-63; accounting adviser Internat. Finance Corp., 1963-67, accounting cons., 1967—. Instr. City Coll. Law and Finance, St. Louis, 1927, Loyola U. of South, New Orleans, 1935. Chmn., Sea Transp. Industry Com., 1952-63; mem. Petroleum Industry Com., 1948-63, chmn. subcom. accounting procedures, 1955-63; mem. Internat. Com. Accounting Cooperation, 1966-72, treas., 1966-67; mem. accountants div. Nat. Fund for Med. Edn., 1955-64; mem. Trade Mission to Orient, 1961. Bd. dirs. Internat. House, New Orleans, 1958-63. C.P.A., Mo., La. Mem. Am. Inst. C.P.A.'s, La. Soc. C.P.A.'s (pres. 1941-42), Nat. Assn. Accountants (pres. New Orleans 1942-43), New Orleans Power Squadron, Grand Isle Tarpon Rodeo (chmn. boat com. 1958-63), Sigma Lambda Epsilon (hon.). Republican. Presbyn. Mason (K.T.). Clubs: Big Ten Universities (pres. 1938), Pickwick, Southern Yacht, Country (New Orleans). Author pamphlets in field.

WILLIAMS, HARRY JOHN, JR., accountant; b. Marion, Ill., Mar. 10, 1924; s. Harry John and Helita (Durham) W.; B.B.A., Tulane U., 1948; m. Joanne Elizabeth Schwartz, Nov. 1, 1947; children—Kathleen Anne Trenchard, Marianne Elizabeth (Mrs. Eugene A. Antoine, Jr.), Barbara Helen (Mrs. Richard L. Moose), Harry John III. With Peat, Marwick, Mitchell & Co., St. Louis, 1948-53; pvt. practice accounting, New Orleans, 1953-76; mng. partner Harry Williams & Co., 1976—; lectr. Tulane U., 1953-56; co-founder Asso. Regional Accounting Firms, chmn., 1969-71. Served with USNR, 1943-46. Mem. Am. Inst. C.P.A.'s, Soc. La. C.P.A.'s (pres. New Orleans chpt. 1964-65, parliamentarian 1971-72, dir. 1964-65, 71-72, mem. trial bd., 1972-75, chmn. 1972-73, chmn. numerous coms.), Accounting Research Assn., New Orleans Estate Planning Council (treas. 1970-71), New Orleans Bd. Trade, Greater New Orleans C. of C., Econ. Devel. Council, Com. of 50, Pi Kappa Alpha. Clubs: Pickwick, Southern Yacht, Internat. House (dir. 1975—, v.p. 1980—) (New Orleans). Methodist. Democrat. Editor: La. C.P.A., 1961-62. Contbr. articles to profl. jours. Home: 6824 Vicksburg St New Orleans LA 70124 Office: 5110 One Shell Sq New Orleans LA 70139

WILLIAMS, HERMAN EDISON, instl. exec.; b. Baker, Fla., Oct. 29, 1931; s. Jesse Diamond and Evie Lue (Smith) W.; student Chipola Jr. Coll., 1963, Pensacola Jr. Coll., 1955-57; B.S., Fla. State U., 1959; m. Margaret M. Talton, June 12, 1955; children—Sue Rene, Diane Katherine. Chief accountant Sunland Tng. Center, Marianna, Fla., 1962-65, bus. mgr. I, Miami, Fla., 1965-68, adminstrv. services dir. I, Fort Myers, Fla., 1968-69; bus. mgr. II, Fla. Sch. for Boys, Okeechobee, 1969—. Served with USN, 1952-54. Methodist. Clubs: Elks, Toastmasters. Address: Florida School for Boys Route 2 Box 250 Okeechobee FL 33472

WILLIAMS, HOSEA LORENZA, state legislator, clergyman, civil rights activist; b. Attapulhus, Ga., Jan. 5, 1926; B.A. in Chemistry, Morris Brown Coll., Atlanta, 1950; postgrad. Atlanta U., 1952; m. Juanita Terry Williams; children—Barbara Jean, Elizabeth LaCedia, Hosea Lorenza, Andre Jerome, Yolanda Felicia. High sch. tchr., 1951-52; research chemist U.S. Dept. Agr., 1952-63; pub. Chatham County Crusader, 1961-63; pres. Kingwell Chem. Corp., Atlanta, 1974; ordained to ministry Baptist Ch., 1971; pastor People's Ch. of Love, Atlanta, 1972—; mem. Ga. Ho. of Reps. from 54th Dist., 1974—; owner Southeastern Chem. Mfg. & Distbg. Co. Spl. projects dir. SCLC, 1970, regional v.p., 1970, nat. program dir., 1971, organizer Met. Atlanta chpt., 1971, nat. bd. dirs., 1972—; mem. Black Promoters Survival Council; organizer Poor People's Union Am., 1973. Recipient service and leadership awards, also certificates appreciation. Served with AUS, 1964-66. Mem. Nat. Black Coalition. Minority Mfrs. Assn., Nat. Com. Black Churchmen, DAV, VFW, Am. Legion, NAACP, Met. Summit, Ga. voters leagues, Phi Beta Sigma. Democrat. Club: Masons. Home: 8 E Lake Dr NE Atlanta GA 30317 Office: 1959 Boulevard Dr SE Atlanta GA 30317

WILLIAMS, J. FRED, ednl. adminstr.; b. Jacksonville, Ala., Dec. 11, 1936; s. Frederick Alfonzo and Dora Belle (Johnston) W.; B.S., Ohio State U., 1964; M.A., Ball State U., 1971; m. Doris Elaine Vermeulen, Dec. 2, 1958; children—Mark, Christopher, Gregory. Commd. 2d lt. U.S. Air Force, 1964, advanced through grades to maj., 1974; fighter/bomber aircraft project mgr. Hdqrs. Europe, 1968-72; asst. prof. aerospace studies U. Louisville, 1972-75; insp., cons. Insp. Gen., Maxwell AFB, Ala., 1975-76; dir. logistics Hdqrs. Air U., Maxwell AFB, 1976-78; ret., 1978; headmaster River Falls Christian Acad., Jeffersonville, Ind., 1978—. Mem., AAUP, Air Force Assn. Republican. Club: Toastmasters. Home: 1256 Eastern Pkwy Louisville KY 40204 Office: PO Box 786 Jeffersonville IN 47130

WILLIAMS, JACK DARYL, data processing exec.; b. Brenham, Tex., Jan. 15, 1948; s. Roudolph Aurel and Alida Minna-Martha (Cordes) W.; B.S. in Bus., U. Houston, 1975; m. Jane Ellen Williams, Mar. 11, 1967; children—John Kevin, Mark Edward. Computer operator Houston Light & Power, 1970-72; programmer, 1972-74; programmer/analyst Milchem, Houston, 1974-75; analyst, programmer Nat. Steel, Houston, 1975-76; data processing mgr. Gen. Homes, Houston, 1976—. Served with USAF, 1966-70. Mem. Data Processing Mgmt. Assn., Am. Mgmt. Assn. Roman Catholic. Home: 156 Dogwood St Sugarland TX 77478 Office: 4434 Bluebonnet St Stafford TX 77477

WILLIAMS, JAMES ALLISON, educator; b. Bailey, N.C., Sept. 20, 1929; s. Marshall and Pattie Pearl W.; B.S. in Spanish and English, East Carolina U., 1953, M.A. in Edn., 1958, M.A. in English, 1967; m. Juanita Loftin Stokes, Aug. 10, 1955; children—James David, Paul Loftin. Tchr. Spanish and English, Lyons (Ga.) High, 1953-54, Ellerbe (N.C.) High, 1954-57; tchr. English and dramatics Hope Mills (N.C.) High, 1958-59; tchr. English and Spanish Williams High, Burlington, N.C., 1959-62; prof. English Louisburg (N.C.) Coll., 1962—. Active Boy Scouts Am.; pres. Franklin County Council Arts, Inc., 1979-80. Democrat. Methodist. Club: Lions (pres. 1975-76). Home and Office: Box 935 Louisburg NC 27549

WILLIAMS, JAMES ARTHUR, musician; b. Columbia, S.C., May 9, 1939; s. George H., Sr., and Ophelia (Taylor) W.; A.B., Allen U., 1960; M.S., U. Ill., 1964; postgrad. Columbia U., 1978; m. Dorothy L. Bostic, June 9, 1961; children—Angela, Melody, James Arthur. Choral dir. C.A. Johnson High Sch., Columbia, 1960-69; minister of music Sidney Park Christian M.E. Ch., Columbia, 1960-69; dept. head, choral dir. Stillman Coll., Tuscaloosa, Ala., 1969—; vis. prof. Morris Coll., Sumter, S.C., 1965-68; cons. black choral music; choral and vocal adjudicator. Recipient Disting. Service award, West Lawn Jr. High Sch., 1979, Dixon Mills (Ala.) Public Schs., 1978. Mem. Am. Choral Dirs. Assn., Am. Guild Organists, Nat. Assn. Negro Musicians, Ala. Coll. Music Adminstrs., Alpha Phi Alpha (Disting. Service award), Omega Psi (Disting. Service award). Home: 1 Geneva Dr Tuscaloosa AL 35403 Office: PO Box 4891 Stillman College Tuscaloosa AL 35403

WILLIAMS, JAMES CHRISTIAN, foundry ofcl.; b. Appomattox County, Va., May 31, 1938; s. Rankin and Madeline Sally (Snell) W.; electronics technician cert. E.C. Glass Vocat. Sch., 1965; B.S. in Social Sci., Va. Sem. and Coll., 1972; m. Edna K. Banks, Sept. 18, 1979. With Lynchburg Foundry Co. div. Mead Corp. (Va.), 1959—, process controlman, 1963-72, foundry leadman, 1972-74, maintenance repair and operating supplies buyer purchasing dept., 1974—. Solicitor, United Way of Central Va.; treas., deacon, mem. pulpit com., trustee Chestnut Grove Bapt. Ch., Lynchburg. Served with U.S. Army, 1956-58. Recipient citation for community services United Way Central Va., 1976, 79. Mem. Purchasing Mgmt. Assn., VFW, Phi Beta Sigma. Home: 1045 Timberlake Dr Lynchburg VA 24502 Office: 620 Court St Lynchburg VA 24505

WILLIAMS, JAMES ELMER, JR., physician; b. Benton, La., Nov. 16, 1923; s. James Elmer and Vera Ethel (Garrett) W.; B.S., La. State U., 1947, M.S., 1948, M.D., 1952; m. Kaye Wilson, Aug. 17, 1974; children—James Elmer, Gregory Mark, David Brian. Intern, N. La. Sanitarium, 1952-53; gen. practice medicine, Timpson, Tex., 1953-55, Baton Rouge, 1955-72; resident in phys. medicine and rehab. Baylor Med. Center, 1972-74; practice medicine specializing in phys. medicine and rehab., Ft. Worth, 1976—; med. dir. dept. phys. medicine and rehab. St. Joseph's Hosp. Bd. dirs. Ft. Worth Easter Seals. Served with USNR, 1943-46. Diplomate Am. Bd. Phys. Medicine and Rehab. Mem. AMA, Tex. Med. Assn., Tarrant County Med. Soc., Am. Acad. Phys. Medicine and Rehab., Tex. Soc. Phys. Medicine and Rehab. (sec.), Alpha Omega Alpha, Omicron Delta Kappa. Episcopalian. Club: Masons. Home: 1002 Whispering Oak Ct Arlington TX 78012 Office: 1400 S Main St Suite 202 Fort Worth TX 76104

WILLIAMS, JAMES H., II, govt. ofcl.; b. Ocala, Fla., June 17, 1926; B.A., U. Fla., 1966; m. Louise Oxner, 3 children. Citrus grower, cattle rancher; mem. Fla. Senate, 1968-74; lt. gov. State of Fla., 1975-79; dep. sec. agr., Washington, 1979—. Served with USAAF, World War II. Recipient Allen Morris award, 1973. Mem. Marion County (Fla.), Marion County Jr. Chambers Commerce, Marion County Cattlemen's Assn. Democrat. Methodist. Office: Office of Sec US Dept Agr Washington DC 20250

WILLIAMS, JAMES HOWARD, research exec.; b. Wheat, Tenn., Dec. 19, 1920; s. William Wess and Sallie (Shelton) W.; A.B., Carson-Newman Coll., 1942; M.A., George Peabody Coll., 1947; Ph.D., Vanderbilt U., 1956; m. Mary Helen Mewshaw, Aug. 31, 1946; children—James Howard, Edward Robert, Nancy Jean. Instr. dept. sociology U. S.C., 1950-55; asst. dir. Nat. Inst. Mental Health Project, Vanderbilt U. 1956-58; asst. prof. social welfare and sociology Fla. State U., 1958-61; research dir. Fla. Bur. Alcoholic Rehab., Avon Park, 1961-75; research asso. Fla. Aging and Adult Services, 1975-76; planner, evaluator Fla. Alcoholic Rehab. Program, Tallahassee, 1976—. Social sci. cons. City of Columbia (S.C.) Planning Comm., 1950-55. Served to lt. USNR, 1942-46. Mem. N.Am. Assn. Alcohol Programs, So. Sociol. Soc., Soc. Study Social Problems, Am. Sociol. Assn., Nat. Rehab. Assn., Population Assn. Am., Fla. Acad. Sci. Kiwanian (pres. Avon Park club 1970-71, 74-75). Contbr. articles to profl. jours. Home: 1537 Woodgate Way Tallahassee FL 32312 Office: 1323 Winewood Blvd Tallahassee FL 32301

WILLIAMS, JAMES NEWTON, psychiatrist; b. Richmond, Va., Aug. 29, 1904; s. Samuel Newton and Frances (Kolbe) W.; A.B., Washington and Lee U., 1926; M.D., Med. Coll. Va., 1930; m. Dorothy Henrietta Behle, Aug. 29, 1933; children—James Newton, Dorothy M. Resident psychiatry Med. Coll. Va., Richmond, 1932-35; pvt. practice psychiatry, 1936—; dir. Va. Bd. Mental Hygiene, Richmond, 1935-41; chief neuropsychiat. service U.S. Naval Hosp., Portsmouth, Va. and Newport, R.I., 1950—; dir. Portsmouth Area Counseling and Guidance Clinic, 1950-54, Atlantic Mental Hygiene Center, Virginia Beach, Va., 1960; mem. adv. bd. Atlantic Mental Health Center, Virginia Beach, 1960—, dir.-psychiatrist, 1962-73. Mem. adv. bd. Child and Family Service and Travelers Aid, Portsmouth, 1961—, Portsmouth Mental Hygiene Assn., 1960—. Served from lt. to capt., M.C., USNR, 1941-62. Fellow A.C.P., Am. Psychiat. Assn.; mem. AMA, Royal Coll. Psychiatrists (London, Eng.), Med. Soc. Va., C. of C. (exec. bd.). Rotarian (past pres). Contbr. numerous articles to profl. jours. Home: 717 Cardinal Rd Virginia Beach VA 23451

WILLIAMS, JEAN TAYLOR, artist; b. Town Creek, Ala., Mar. 27, 1912; d. Woodie Richard and Ella Ross (Harrison) Taylor; B.S., U. Montevallo, 1933; student Chgo. Art Inst., 1936; student of Robert Brackman, Noank, Conn., 1958-60; m. James Hayes Williams, June 18, 1935; children—James Richard, Hayes Taylor, Jean Williams Johnson. Art tchr. high sch., Ala., 1933-35; tchr. pvt. classes own studio, Birmingham, Ala., 1976—; art chmn. Mountain Brook Jr. High Sch., Birmingham, 1965; one-woman shows: Samford U., Nat. Soc. Arts and Letters; exhibited work in Jerome Hines Exhbn., 1977; represented in numerous pvt. collections. Recipient Grand award in Oil Painting, State of Ala., 1961. Mem. Am. Artists Profl. League, Nat. League Am. Pen Women, Nat. Soc. Arts and Letters, Ala. Art League, Birmingham Art Assn. Presbyterian. Clubs: Vestavia Country, Turtle Point Yacht and Country, The Club. Address: 2801 Mountain Brook Pkwy Birmingham AL 35223

WILLIAMS, JEFFREY HOWARD, air force officer; b. Washington, Aug. 31, 1954; s. John H. and Thelma (McGuffin) W.; B.S.B.A., Drake U., 1976, M.B.A., 1977. Commd. 2d lt. USAF, 1976, advanced through grades to 1st lt., 1979; missile combat crew comdr. Titan Missiles, Little Rock AFB, Ark., 1979—; pres. Diamondback Cons., Inc., Des Moines, 1977—; sales asso. Century 21, North Little Rock, 1979—; tutor U. Ark., Little Rock, 1977-79. Mem. Assn. M.B.A. Execs., Nat. Realtors Assn., Kappa Alpha Psi. Home: 172 Randall Dr Jacksonville AR 72076

WILLIAMS, JOANNE VANN, accountant; b. Sampson County, N.C., Nov. 8, 1933; s. Hugh Swinton and Pauline Lee (Baggett) V.; diploma U. N.C., Greensboro, 1952; m. Joseph Henry Williams, June 14, 1952; children—Mary Jo, Steven Paul. Bookkeeper, Sampson County Schs., Clinton, N.C., 1962-65; controller Sampson Tech. Inst., Clinton, 1965—. Mem. N.C. Assn. Ednl. Office Personnel (sec. 1969-70, v.p. 1971-72, pres. 1972-74, chmn. profl. standards com., dist. pres. 1968-69), N.C. Employees Assn., Assn. Community Coll. Bus. Ofcls., Nat. Assn. Ednl. Office Personnel, N.C. Assn. Sch. Adminstrs., Nat. Soc Magna Charta Dames, Plantagenet Soc., DAR. Democrat. Methodist. Home: Rt 1 Clinton NC 28238 Office: PO Drawer 318 Clinton NC 28238

WILLIAMS, JOHN BRAXTON, JR., real estate devel. exec.; b. Indpls., Aug. 10, 1933; s. John Braxton and Jeanette Jane (Webb) W.; B.S. in Civil Engring., So. Meth. U., 1957; 1 son, John Kevin. Pres., co-owner Isles Constrn. Co., Dallas, 1955-58; chief civil engr. Wyatt C. Hedrick Architect/Engr., Dallas, 1958-60; asso., Don Fleming & Assos. Architects/Engrs., Dallas, 1961-62; constrn. engr., overseas projects, M.W. Kellogg Co., N.Y.C., 1963-65; constrn. mgr. J.C. Penney Co., Atlanta, 1966-79; chmn. bd. Arco Properties Inc., Atlanta, 1971—; dir. Trader Investment Co., Dallas, Creative Properties, Atlanta/Dallas Trans-Atlanta Properties, Atlanta. Republican. Unitarian. Contbr. articles to engring. jours. Home: 926 G Waverly Way NE Inman Park Atlanta GA 30307 Office: Box 54032 Atlanta GA 30308

WILLIAMS, JOHN MICHAEL, computer co. exec.; b. Los Angeles, Aug. 17, 1938; s. Earl Bryan and Genevieve (Donovan) W.; student U. Hawaii, 1957-59, U. Calif., Los Angeles, 1959-60; m. Roxanne Rosse O'Leary, May 24, 1969; children by previous marriage—Brian, Genevieve, Paul, John. Mgr. UNIVAC systems programming product devel. UNIVAC div. Sperry UNIVAC Co., Los Angeles, 1956-62, Honolulu, 1957-60, Washington, 1962-65, nat. account rep., Washington, 1965-67; sr. computer scientist Computer Scis. Corp., Falls Church, Va., 1967-77; mgr. computer security research and devel. System Devel. Corp., McLean, Va., 1977—, now dir. info. security tech. programs. Cert. in data processing, cert. in computer programming Inst. for Cert. of Computer Profls. Mem. Assn. Computing Machinery, IEEE (sr. mem., tech. com. chmn. 1979), Armed Forces Communications Electronics Assn., AAAS. Home: 6210 Leeke Forest Ct Bethesda MD 20034 Office: 7929 Westpark Dr McLean VA 22102

WILLIAMS, JOHN RYON RODNEY, polit. scientist, educator; b. Detroit, Nov. 21, 1919; s. Ralph Hill and Myrtle Anna (Ryon) W.; A.B. summa cum laude, Lawrence Coll., 1944; M.A. (Johnston fellow), Johns Hopkins, 1947; Ph.D. (Univ. fellow), Duke, 1951; John Randolph Haynes and Dora Haynes Found. fellow, London Sch. Econs. and Polit. Sci., 1951-52; m. Madeleine Louise Josephine Cremilliac, Aug. 28, 1952; children—Jacques Ralph Andre, Mark Thinh Tien. Instr. polit. sci. Wellesley (Mass.) Coll., 1947-49; asst. prof. polit. sci. W.Va. U., Morgantown, 1949-56, asso. prof., 1956-61, prof., 1961—, chmn. dept. polit. sci., 1961-72, coordinator Univ. Honors Program, 1972—; vis. prof. polit. sci. Waynesburg Coll., 1963-64, Fayette campus Pa. State U., summer 1966, 67-68; acad. visitor London Sch. Econs. and Polit. Sci., 1972. Named Outstanding Prof., W.Va U., 1967. Fellow, Duke U. Commonwealth Studies Center, 1956, Australian Nat. U., Canberra, 1958-60; Fulbright research grantee 1958-60. Mem. Am., Australasian, Canadian, W.Va. (pres. 1968-69) polit. sci. assns., Am. Acad. Polit. and Social Sci., Am.

Friends of London Sch. Econs., A.A.U.P., Assn. for Canadian Studies in U.S., Australian Inst. Polit. Sci., Internat. Platform Assn., London Sch. Econs. Soc., Univ. Profs. for Acad. Order, Phi Beta Kappa, Delta Tau Delta, Pi Sigma Alpha. Conservative. Anglican. Clubs: Monarchist League; Conservative and Unionist Assn. Author: The Conservative Party of Canada, 1956; John Latham and the Conservative Recovery from Defeat, 1969. Columnist, Dominion Post. Contbr. articles to profl. jours. Home: 1498 Eastern Av Morgantown WV 26505 also 165 Marine Ct St Leonards on Sea Sussex TN 38 ODZ England Office: Polit Sci Dept W Va U Morgantown WV 26506

WILLIAMS, JOHN WILLIAM, bookstore exec.; b. Red Hill, Va., Nov. 24, 1918; s. John William and Louise Gray (Anderson) W.; grad. Tarleton Bus. Coll., 1936; student U. Va., 2 yrs.; grad. LaSalle U., 1947; m. Laura Elizabeth Kegley, Nov. 6, 1937; children—Elizabeth Byrd (Mrs. Charles Cortez Abbott), Martha Hayes (Mrs. Ward W. Anderson). Asst. gen. mgr. Anderson Bros. Bookstores, Inc., Charlottesville, Va., 1940-41, v.p., 1941-62, pres., treas., gen. mgr., 1962—; sec.-treas. Anderson Realty Corp., 1969—, also dir.; dir. Va. Nat. Bank. Asst. varsity, head freshman boxing coach U. Va., 1941-43, head boxing coach, 1953—. Mem. Va. Hosp. Bd., 1963—, vice chmn., 1969-71; mem. Albemarle County Bd. Pub. Welfare, 1949-61; chmn. Va. Bd. Welfare, 1974—; treas. bd. trustees U. Va. Med. Alumni Assn., 1978—; bd. dirs. U. Va. Med. Center Found., 1979—. Mem. Albemarle County Sch. Bd., 1946-49; mem. Albemarle County Bd. Suprs., 1949-64, chmn., 1957-64; a.d.c. to gov. of Va., 1959—; chmn. SSS, Charlotteville, 1970—. Pres. Young Democratic Clubs Va., 1953-55; sec. 8th Congl. Dist. Dem. Com., 1956-66; mem. Va. Dem. Central Com., 1956—, mem. steering com., 1969—; chmn. 7th Congl. Dist. Dem. Com., 1969. Gen. vice chmn. devel. com. U. Va. Grad. Sch. Bus. Served to 1st lt. AUS, 1943-46, col. Va. State Guard. Mem. Va. Coll. Stores Assn. (pres. 1971-72), Nat. Intercollegiate Boxing Coaches Assn. (pres. 1957), Assn. Va. Counties (pres. 1960), U. Va. Alumni Assn., Albemarle Hist. Soc. (pres. 1969), Am. Legion. Rotarian. Clubs: Monticello Guard, Farmington Country. Home: Meadowbrook Heights Charlottesville VA 22901 Office: 1541 W Main St Charlottesville VA 22901

WILLIAMS, JOHNNIE BEATRICE, educator; b. Homer, La., Feb. 15, 1943; d. John Benjamin and Maggie Mae (Flucas) Bursey; B.S. in Bus. Edn., Grambling State U., 1964; M.S. in Bus. Edn., Ind. U., 1969; postgrad. La. Tech. U., 1974, U. Santa Clara, 1974, So. U., Baton Rouge, La., 1974; m. Edward L. Williams, Aug. 28, 1971. Chmn. bus. dept. Mansfield (La) DeSoto High Sch., 1964-69; asst. prof. bus., dept. office adminstrn. So. U., Shreveport-Bossier campus, 1969—, dir. coop. edn., 1976-80. Sec., David Raines Community Council, David Raines Community Center, 1972-73, receptionist, 1971-72; campaign asst. Representative Alphonse Jackson, 1974-75; vol. asst. satellite program-drug abuse Shire House, 1973-74; relief office asst. La. Bank & Trust Co., 1978, Beaird-Poulan div. Emerson Electric Co., 1978; vol. campaign asst. Buddy Roemer, 1978, June Phillips, 1979; mem. community adv. com. Gen. Motors, 1978-79; sec. Queensborough in Action, 1980. Mem. Am. Fedn. Tchrs., La. Fedn. Tchrs., Ind. Alumni Assn., Grambling Alumni Assn., Delta Sigma Theta. Democrat. Baptist. Home: 3441 Sunset Dr Shreveport LA 71109 Office: 3050 Cooper Rd Shreveport LA 71107

WILLIAMS, JOSEPH HILL, diversified industry exec.; b. Tulsa, June 2, 1933; s. David Rogerson and Martha Reynolds (Hill) W.; B.A., Yale U., 1956, M.A. (hon.), 1977; postgrad. Sch. Pipeline Tech. U. Tex., 1960; m. Terese T. Ross, May 7, 1977; stepchildren—Margot Ross, Jennifer Ross; children—Joseph Hill Jr., Peter B., James C. Field employee domestic constrn. div. Williams Cos., Tulsa, 1958-60, project coordinator engring. div., 1960-61, project supt., Iran, 1961-62, asst. resident mgr., Iran, 1962-64, project mgr., 1964-65, resident mgr., 1965-67, exec. v.p., 1968-71, pres., chief operating officer, 1971-78, chmn., chief exec. officer, 1978—, also dir.; chmn. Fed. Res. Bank of Kansas City, dir. Parker Drilling Co. Bd. dirs. Industries for Tulsa, Tulsa Area United Way, Okla. C. of C.; mem. adv. com. Jr. Achievement; trustee and fellow Yale Corp. Served with AUS, 1956-58. Mem. Am. Petroleum Inst. (dir.), Young Pres.'s Orgn., Nat. Petroleum Council, Conf. Bd., Assn. Oil Pipe Lines, Pipe Line Contractors Assn., Nat. Petroleum Refiners Assn., Council on Fgn. Relations, Met. Tulsa C. of C. (dir.). Episcopalian. Clubs: St. Anthony (N.Y.C.); Southern Hills Country (bd. govs.), Summit, Tulsa, Yale (sec.), Tulsa Polo and Hunt (Tulsa); Springdale Hall (Camden, S.C.); Augusta (Ga.) Nat. Golf; Grandfather Golf and Country (Linville, S.C.). Office: One Williams Center Tulsa OK 74103

WILLIAMS, JOSEPH NEVILLE, ins. co. exec.; b. Albuquerque, May 16, 1932; s. Joseph Neville and Bertha W.; student Amarillo Jr. Coll., 1955-57, W. Tex. State U., 1957-58; m. LaRue Faye McAmis, Mar. 28, 1959; children—Connie, Terri, Ami, Staci. Agt., South Coast Life, 1960-63, supt. agys., 1963-69; agy. dir. Petroleum State Ins. Co., Beaumont, Tex., 1969-70; with Great Nat. Life, Dallas, 1970—, v.p. adminstrn., 1973-77, sr. v.p. adminstrn., 1977—. Served with USAF, 1951-55. Mem. Tex. Life Ins. Assn., Am. Coll. C.L.U.'s, Nat., Tex. assns. life underwriters. Home: 2905 Teakwood Circle Plano TX 75075 Office: 6500 Harry Hines Blvd Dallas TX 75235

WILLIAMS, KENNETH HAROLD, ins. co. exec.; b. E. Bernstadt, Ky., Apr. 16, 1944; s. Bobby Harold and Cleo (Gabbard) W.; student Lee Coll., 1964-65; m. Shirley M. Davis, May 18, 1972; children—Michelle Lorie, Kimberly Dawn. Agt., Liberty Nat., Cleveland, Tenn., 1967-72, sales mgr., 1972-75; with Am. Gen. Ins. Co., Cleveland, Tenn., 1975-77; owner Williams Ins. Agy., Cleveland, Tenn., 1977—; chmn. for organizing Life Underwriters Training Council, Cleveland area, 1974. Mem. Bradley County Ambulance Bd., 1976—, chmn. budget and fin. com., 1977—. Recipient Liberty Nat. Dist. Leader award, 1971, 73; Am. Gen. Legion of Am. Gen's award, 1976; Am. Gen. Pres.'s award, 1976, Am. Gen. Century Club award, 1977; Nat. Quality Award, Nat. Assn. Life Underwriters, 1973, 74, 75, 76, Nat. Sales Achievement award, 1972, 74, 75, 76, 77; Sertoma Club Gem award, 1974, Centurian Award, 1977, Order of Pres.'s award, 1976. Mem. Nat. Assn. Life Underwriters, Tenn. Assn. Life Underwriters, Cleveland Assn. Life Underwriters (pres. 1977-78), Lee Coll. Alumni Assn. Republican. Ch. of God. Clubs: Lee Coll. Century, Ocoee Sertoma (pres. 1976-77). Composer: A Man Like Him, 1969. Office: PO Box 1354 Cleveland TN 37311

WILLIAMS, KENNETH TIMOTHY, ins. co. exec.; b. East Liverpool, Ohio, Apr. 7, 1949; s. Harold Kenneth and Ruth Ann (Parker) W.; student U. Tenn. at Knoxville, 1967-69; B.S., U. Tenn. at Chattanooga, 1973; student Am. Coll., 1976—; m. Jeri Rebecca Arledge, June 6, 1970. Group contract underwriter Provident Life & Accident Ins. Co., Chattanooga, 1969-73, group service rep., Savannah, Ga., 1973-75; asst. to field v.p. John Hancock Mut. Life Ins. Co., Atlanta, 1975-76, home office rep., 1976—; fin. planning cons., Ga., N.C., S.C. Served with Tenn. Army N.G., 1970-73, Ga. Air N.G., 1973-77. Mem. Atlanta Assn. of Group Ins. Reps., Atlanta Assn. Life Underwriters (J.H. prodn. leader 1978), Delta Tau Delta. Republican. Episcopalian. Home: 4332 Executive Dr Stone Mountain GA 30083 Office: 5775 Peachtree-Dunwoody Rd Suite 210-A Atlanta GA 30342

WILLIAMS, LAVERNE AUGUST, architect; b. Sidney, Nebr., Feb. 28, 1943; s. Carl D. and Leota (Knackstedt) W.; student McPherson Coll., 1961-63; B.Arch., U. Houston, 1971; m. Linda Beth McCoy, Feb. 22, 1963; 1 dau., Dana Elizabeth. Archtl. coordinator Denny & Ray AIA, Houston, 1967-71, Broadnax & Phenix AIA, 1971-72, Ressler & Applebaum AIA, 1972-73; project architect Lawrence Bernstein Assos., AIA, Houston, 1973-74; propr. LaVerne A. Williams, Architect/Energy Conservation Cons., Houston, 1975—; chmn. bd., sec. treas. Environment Assos. Houston, 1978—. Bd. dirs. Post Oak Family YMCA, 1975-78; mem. adv. com. Gov.'s Energy Adv. Council, 1976-77, Tex. Energy Adv. Council, 1977—. Mem. Houston Solar Energy Soc. (founder, dir. 1976—), Constrn. Industry Council (solar energy com.), AIA (chmn. energy com. Houston), Tex. Soc. Architects, Tex. Solar Energy Soc. (founding mem.). Club: Houston Met. Racquet. Office: 2777 Allen Pkwy Suite 207 Houston TX 77019

WILLIAMS, LEAH ANN, biologist; b. Clarksburg, W.Va., July 20, 1932; d. George Woodbridge and Marguerite (Shanabarger) W.; A.B., W.Va. U., 1954, M.S., 1958, Ph.D., 1970. Instr. zoology Pa. State U., 1958-59; instr. biology W.Va. U., Morgantown, 1959-68, asst. prof., 1968-74, asso. prof., 1974—, asso. chmn. dept. biology, 1975-77. USPHS predoctoral fellow, 1967-68; NSF sci. faculty profl. devel. grantee, 1977-78. Mem. Soc. Developmental Biology, Am. Soc. Zoologists, AAAS, Internat. Soc. Cell Differentiation, P.E.O., Order Eastern Star, Sigma Xi, Kappa Delta. Presbyterian. Office: Biology Dept West Virginia U Morgantown WV 26506

WILLIAMS, LEAH MILDRED, physician; b. Union, W.Va., Apr. 8, 1917; d. Raymond and Golda (Carlisle) W.; B.S., Marshall Coll., 1943; M.D., Med. Coll. Va., 1947. Intern, Med. Coll. Va. Hosp., Richmond, 1947-48; health service tchr. U. Ill., Champaign, 1948-49; gen. practice medicine, Charlestown, W.Va., 1949—; mem. staff Charlestown Gen. Hosp., Ransom, W.Va., chief of staff, 1963-64; coroner Jefferson County (W.Va.), 1954—; chmn. Bd. Health Jefferson County, 1957—; mem. Health Adv. Bd. Jefferson County, 1956--. Mem. Eastern Panhandle Med. Soc. Address: 115 W Congress St Charlestown WV 25414

WILLIAMS, LEAH ROSE, social worker; b. Wilmington, N.C., Feb. 15, 1942; d. Duvall McClellan and Maria Ernestina (Benavides) W.; A.B., Meredith Coll., 1963; M.S.W., Tulane U., 1965. Instr. child psychiatry Duke U. Med. Sch., 1967-68; tng. supr. masters program La. State U., 1972-78, Tulane U., 1972-78; pvt. practice psychiat. social work, New Orleans, 1972—; clin. asst. prof. dept. psychiatry La. State U., 1969-78; cons. River Oaks Hosp., 1975-77, Brentwood Sch., 1974—, Children's Hosp., 1976—. Bd. dirs. tutorial program Christ Ch., New Orleans. Certified social worker, La. Mem. Nat. Assn. Social Workers, Acad. Certified Social Workers. Republican. Home: 318 Henry Clay St New Orleans LA 70118 Office: 1419 Amelia St New Orleans LA 70115

WILLIAMS, LOUIS BOOTH, coll. pres.; b. Paris, Tex., Oct. 15, 1916; s. William Louis and Maggie Jo (Booth) W.; A.A., Paris (Tex.) Jr. Coll., 1935; B.B.A., U. Tex., 1937; M.B.A., E. Tex. State U., 1961; LL.D. (hon.), Tex. Wesleyan U., 1976; m. Mary Lou Newman, Oct. 13, 1939; children—Joanne Williams Click, Louis Booth. Profl. local C. of C. exec., Austin, Navasota and Parts, Tex., 1938-44; mgr. Bireley's Beverages, Denison, Tex., 1946-49; asst. to pres. Paris Jr. Coll., 1949-52, pres., 1967—; personnel mgr. Paris Works, Babcock & Wilcox Co., 1952-67; dir. Liberty Nat. Bank, Paris, 1980. Recipient Silver Beaver award Boy Scouts Am., 1957; Paul Harris fellow Rotary Internat., 1974. Mem. Am. Assn. Community Jr. Colls., Assn. Tex. Jr. Colls. Democrat. Methodist. Club: Rotary. Author: The Organization, Functions, and Administration of a Local Chamber of Commerce, 1937. Home: 3170 Louvel Ln Paris TX 75460 Office: Paris Jr Coll Clarksville St Paris TX 75460

WILLIAMS, LUTHER FRANCIS, educator, minister; b. Etowah, Tenn., May 14, 1932; s. Frelon Charles and Mattie Lee (Gentry) W.; Asso. Sci., Freed Hardeman Coll., 1957; B.S., Tenn. Wesleyan Coll., 1964; M.M. Math., U. S.C., 1967; Ed.D., U. Tenn., 1977; m. Barbara Ann Gibson, July 20, 1950; children—Carol Ann, Patricia Lynn, Barbara Kay. Ordained to ministry Church of Christ, 1951; minister Dublin (Ga.) Ch. of Christ, 1957-61; tchr. math. Meigs High Sch., Decatur, Tenn., 1961-66; instr. math. Cleveland (Tenn.) State Community Coll., 1968-74, 75-77, dir. instl. research, 1977—; minister Central Ch. of Christ, Athens, Tenn., 1969-72, Calhoun, Tenn., 1973-75, Etowah, Tenn., 1976—. Chmn. bd. dirs. Cleveland State Christian Student Center, 1978—; bd. dirs. Richmond-Tatum Christian Sch., 1979. Mem. NEA, Nat. Council for Research and Planning, E. Tenn. Edn. Assn., Cleveland State Community Coll. Edn. Assn., Southeastern Assn. Coll. Researchers, Phi Delta Kappa. Republican. Home: Box 41 Route 5 Athens TN 37303 Office: PO Box 1205 Cleveland TN 37311

WILLIAMS, MARIA EMMA, nursing adminstr.; b. San Benito, Tex., Nov. 17, 1934; d. Federico and Rosa (Rodriquez) W.; grad. St. Mary's Sch. Nursing, 1957; m. John Edwin Williams, June 16, 1957; children—John Edwin III, Sandra Maria, Debra Jean, Frederick Samuel, Kathleen Marie. Staff nurse St. Mary's Hosp., Galveston, Tex., 1957-59, 61-62, head nurse, 1962-69, asst. adminstr. nursing, 1969—; staff nurse Coatesville (Pa.) Hosp., 1959-60. Mem. Am. Nurses Assn., Tex. Nurses Assn., Tex. Soc. Nursing Service Adminstrs. Club: Noon Opti-Mrs (Galveston, Tex.). Home: 17 South Shore Dr Galveston TX 77550 Office: 404 8th St Galveston TX 77550

WILLIAMS, MARK LANE, nuclear engr.; b. Monroe, La., Jan. 3, 1951; s. Marshall M. and Polly Marie (Roan) W.; B.S., La. State U., 1973; M.S., Ga. Inst. Tech., 1974; Ph.D., U. Tenn., 1979; m. Gayle Elizabeth Pardue, Oct. 2, 1976. Research asst. Ga. Inst. Tech., Atlanta, 1973-74; nuclear engr. Oak Ridge (Tenn.) Nat. Labs., 1974—. NE La. U. Found. scholar, 1969-70; La. State U. scholar, 1970-73; AEC fellow, 1974. Mem. Am. Nuclear Soc., Phi Kappa Phi, Tau Beta Pi, Pi Mu Epsilon, Lambda Chi Alpha. Democrat. Baptist. Contbr. articles to tech. jours. Home: 10826 Dundee Rd Knoxville TN 37922

WILLIAMS, MARK THOMAS, landscape contractor; b. Houston, Sept. 13, 1951; s. Raymond Thomas and Delores Marion (Thorson) W.; student Austin Coll., 1970-71, Tex. A&M U., 1971-74; m. Deborah Anne Veale, May 31, 1975. Mem. sales staff Van Waters & Rogers, Dallas, 1974-75; retail mgr. Fairview Nursery, McKinney, Tex., 1975-76; pres. Pecan Bend Landscape Co., Garland, Tex., 1976—; pres. Pecan Bend Nursery, Inc.; dir. Mt. Wheeler Devel. Corp. Cert. nurseryman, Tex. Mem. Assn. Am. Nurserymen, Am. Landscape Contractors Assn., Tex. Assn. Nurserymen. Home: 2104 Fairfax Circle Richardson TX 75081 Office: 2013 Holford Rd Garland TX 75081

WILLIAMS, MARSHA RHEA, computer systems engr.; b. Memphis, Aug. 4, 1948; d. James Edward and Velma Lee (Jenkins) W.; B.S., Beloit Coll., 1969; M.S. in Physics, U. Mich., 1971; M.S. in Computer Sci., Vanderbilt U., 1976, postgrad., 1976-78. Asst. transmission engr. Ind. Bell Telephone Co., Indpls., 1971-72; systems analyst, instr. physics Memphis State U., 1972-74; mem. tech. staff Hughes Research Labs., Malibu, Calif., 1976-78; asso. systems engr. IBM Corp., Nashville, 1978—. Editor in chief newspaper Pilgrim Emanuel Bapt. Ch., 1975-76, adv. Chi Rho Youth Fellowship, Temple Bapt. Ch., 1975—. Mem. Data Processing Mgmt. Assn., Assn. Computing Machinery, NAACP.

WILLIAMS, NANCY HEAD, food service dir.; b. Springfield, Tenn., Dec. 7, 1924; d. James Herbert and Edna (Lawrence) Head; B.S., Tenn. Tech. U., 1945; M.A., Peabody Coll., 1950; postgrad. Austin Peay U., U. Tenn., Peabody Coll.; m. W. Royce Williams, Oct. 20, 1946; children—Nancy Melinda, W. Royce. Tchr. home econs. Bell High Sch., Adams, Tenn., 1945-46, Coopertown (Tenn.) High Sch., 1946-64, Springfield (Tenn.) High Sch., 1964-76; dir. food service Robertson County Schs., Springfield, 1976—; adv. FHA, 1945-64. Bd. dirs. Robertson County Fair. Mem. NEA, Tenn. Ednl. Assn., Middle Tenn. Edn. Assn., Am. Sch. Food Service Assn., Robertson County Edn. Assn., Tenn. Sch. Food Service Assn. (treas.). Baptist. Home: 134 N Sequoia Dr Springfield TN 37172 Office: Robertson County Schs Springfield TN 37172

WILLIAMS, NELSON LEE, communications co. exec.; b. Tampa, Fla., June 18, 1926; s. George Winchell and Anne Olive (Nelson) W.; B.S. in Civil Engring., N.C. State U., 1950; grad. USAF Air Command and Staff Sch., 1951; postgrad. U. of N.C., 1974-75; m. Gretchen Van Loon, July 25, 1953 (div.); children—David Nelson, Peter Stroud. Enlisted aviation ordnance USN, 1944-46; commd. 2d lt. USAF, 1950, advanced through grades to capt., 1959; geodetic control officer, research and development officer, USAF, P.R. and Alaska, 1950-52; outside plant engr. Southern Bell Telephone & Telegraph Co., N.C., 1952-56; distributor Executone-Triad, Inc., Greensboro, N.C., 1956-79; invited lectr. on communications to N.C. colleges, 1958-77. Sgt.-at-arms, Crescent Rotary Club, Greensboro, 1975-79, v.p., pres. elect 1979-80). Served res. duty with USN, 1944-46, USAF, 1950-59. Mem. Carolina Interconnect Telephone Asso. (sec. 1975-79). Democrat. Christian Scientist (1st reader, pres., chmn. bd.). Clubs: Greensboro City, Sportime Racquet, Mason (32 deg.). Home: 1014 Guilford Ave Greensboro NC 27401 Office: 1308 E Wendover Ave Greensboro NC 27405

WILLIAMS, OLIN FRANKLIN, educator; b. Georgetown County, S.C., June 8, 1935; s. Jacob Westley and Lula Mae (Baxley) W.; A.A., North Greenville Coll., 1953-55; student Coker Coll., 1956; B.S., Pfeiffer Coll., 1957; M.A.T., The Citadel, 1972, Ed.S., 1980. Tchr. Clarkton (N.C.) High Sch., 1957-58, Massey Hill High Sch., Fayetteville, N.C., 1958-62, Wicomico Sr. High Sch., Salisbury, Md., 1962-63; instr. Palmer Coll., Charleston, S.C., 1963-73, Trident Tech. Coll., Charleston, 1973-76, instructional coordinator secretarial sci., dept. head, Palmer Campus, 1976—. Asst. Appalachian State U., summer 1957. Mem. AAUP, Nat. Bus. Edn. Assn., Internat. Soc. Bus. Educators, So. Bus. Edn. Assn., Am. Vocat. Assn., S.C. Vocat. Assn., S.C. Bus. and Office Edn. Assn., S.C. Tech. Edn. Assn., Nat. Trust for Hist. Preservation, S.C. Hist. Soc., Preservation Soc. Charleston, Am. Heritage Soc. Republican. Baptist. Home: 70 Bull St Charleston SC 29401 Office: 125 Bull St Charleston SC 29401

WILLIAMS, OLIVER CORRY, postal exec.; b. Rockwall, Tex., Feb. 16, 1925; s. Tim Oliver and Grace Inez (Bufkin) W.; grad. pub. schs.; m. Catherine Beard, Apr. 17, 1943; children—Ronald, Judy, Cathy; m. 2d, Janice Williams, Mar. 7, 1963; children—Rebecca, Ronell. With U.S. Post Office Dept., Mesquite, Tex., 1948—, asst. sectional center mgr., 1965-72, asst. postmaster, 1972-75, mgr. customer services, 1975—. Mem. Mesquite (Tex.) City Charter Commn., 1953. Served with USMCR, 1943-46. Mem. Nat. Assn. Postal Suprs. Republican. So. Baptist. Home: 213 Caraway Dr Mesquite TX 75149 Office: 120 E Grubb Dr Mesquite TX 75149

WILLIAMS, PAUL X., fed. judge; b. Booneville, Ark., Feb. 19, 1908; s. Charles X. and Sally Ethel (Cruce) W.; B.A., U. Ark., 1928, J.D., 1930; m. Elizabeth Hays, May 16, 1935; children—Paul X., Charles David, Elizabeth Williams Danielson, Sarah Virginia, John Roger. Admitted to Ark. bar, 1931, practiced in Ark.; chancery judge of Ark., 1948-67; judge U.S. Dist. Ct., Western Dist. of Ark., Ft. Smith, 1967—, now chief judge. Served with USNR, 1942-45. Rotarian. Home: 815 Kennedy St Booneville AR 72927 Office: US Courthouse PO Box 1623 Fort Smith AR 72901

WILLIAMS, RANDALL ALAN, orthopaedic surgeon; b. Chattanooga, Apr. 7, 1936; s. Fred Madison and Ethelyn (Smtih) W.; student U. Chattanooga, 1954-56; M.D., Tulane U., 1960; m. Adelle Crowell, Dec. 28, 1957; children—Laura W. Bergeron, E. Kelley. Intern, Charity Hosp., New Orleans, 1960-61, resident in orthopedic surgery, 1961, 63-67; instr. orthopaedic surgery Tulane U. Sch. Medicine, New Orleans, 1967-69, clin. asst. prof. orthopaedic surgery, 1978—; emergency med. advisor Jefferson Parish Sheriff's Office, 1974—, Jefferson Levee Dist. Police, 1976—; bd. dirs. Emergency Med. Services of S.E. La., 1978—; active staff E. Jefferson Gen. Hosp., Metairie, So. Bapt. Hosp., New Orleans, Lakeside Hosp., Metairie; examiner Am. Bd. Cert. in Orthotics and Prosthetics, 1967, 68, 69; NIH co-clinic chief Juvenile Amputee Clinic for U.S. and Can., New Orleans, 1967-73; chief scoliosis clinic Crippled Children's Program, State of La., New Orleans, 1967-73; cons. orthopaedic surgery VA Hosp., Pineville, La., 1967-70, Huey P. Long Charity Hosp., Pineville, 1967-70, Lallie Kemp Charity Hosp., Independence, La., 1967-69; emergency med. advisor Kenner (La.) Police Dept., 1974—, Jefferson Levee Dist. Police, 1974—; instr. cardiopulmonary resuscitation Am. Heart Assn. of La., 1977—. Served with USAF, 1961-63. Diplomate Am. Bd. Orthopaedic Surgery. Fellow A.C.S., Am. Acad. Orthopaedic Surgeons; mem. La. Med. Soc., So. Med. Assn., La. Orthopaedic Assn., Jefferson Parish Med. Soc. La., Greater New Orleans Orthopaedic Soc., New Orleans Grad. Med. Assembly. Episcopalian. Contbr. articles to profl. jours. Address: 3939 Houma Blvd Suite 16 Metairie LA 70002

WILLIAMS, RICHARD BRUCE, endocrinologist; b. Melbourne, Australia, July 3, 1947; came to U.S., 1978; s. Benjamin Arnold and Norma Merle W.; B.Sc., U. Melbourne, 1968, M.B.B.S., 1973; m. Krystyna Alimurka, Feb. 14, 1975. Intern, Toronto Western Hosp., 1973-74; resident U. Toronto, 1973-78; practice medicine specializing in endocrinology, Chattanooga, 1978—. Fellow Royal Coll. Physicians Can.; mem. A.C.P., AMA, Tenn. Med. Assn., Chattanooga and Hamilton County Med. Assn. Office: 628 Morrison Springs Rd Red Bank TN 37413

WILLIAMS, RICHARD LINWOOD, civil engr.; b. Norfolk, Va., Feb. 7, 1933; s. Hersey Linwood and Helen Susan W.; B.S., Va. Poly. Inst., 1959; m. Martha Lawson Buchanan, Jan. 21, 1961; 1 son, Robert Linwood. Partner, Shumate, Williams, Norfleet & Eddy, Cons. Engrs., Roanoke, Va., 1965-71, Smithey & Boynton, Architects and Engrs., Roanoke, 1971-72; owner, pres., operator Richard L. Williams, Cons. Engr., Inc., Roanoke, 1973—; lectr. in field. Engr. rep. Roanoke County Elec. Bd., 1976—. Served with U.S. Army, 1953-55. Mem. Am. Cons. Engrs. Council, Va. Cons. Engrs. Council (pres. 1979-80), Va. Water Pollution Control Assn. Methodist. Home: 5350 Roselawn Rd Roanoke VA 24018 Office: 4919 Colonial Ave Roanoke VA 24018

WILLIAMS, RICHARD WAYNE, telephone co. exec.; b. Los Angeles, Aug. 21, 1945; s. Orville and Mary Augusta (Ellinghouse) W.; A.A., Phoenix Coll., 1965; B.A., Ariz. State U., 1968, postgrad.,

1968-69; postgrad. Northeastern Okla. State U., 1972; m. Kathleen Louise Jones, Mar. 21, 1970; children—Ryan August, Rachael Kathleen. Tchr. English, Phoenix Union High Sch. Dist., 1968-69; coll. mktg. rep., field editor Holt, Rinehart & Winston, Tulsa, 1969-70; with Southwestern Bell Telephone Co., Tulsa, 1970—, account exec., 1978—. Precinct chmn. Republican party, 1979—. Mem. Am. Soc. for Tng. and Devel., Data Processing Mgrs. Assn., Am. Mgmt. Assn., Tulsa Econs. Club, World Future Soc. Presbyterian. Clubs: Masons, Kiwanis. Home: 339 N Fir St Jenks OK 74037 Office: Southwestern Bell Telephone Co 9810 E 42d St Suite 200 Tulsa OK 74145

WILLIAMS, ROBERT, musician; b. Clarcona, Fla., Aug. 13, 1941; s. Alonzo and Carrie Bell (Coley) W.; B.A., Bethune Cookman Coll., 1963; Mus.M., U.S. Fla., 1968; Ph.D., Fla. State U., 1973; m. Betty Jean Smith, June 23, 1973; 1 dau., Amber Tariell. Dir. choir Carver Jr. High Sch., Orlando, Fla., 1963-67, Central Jr. High Sch., West Palm Beach, Fla., 1968-71; mem. faculty Bethune Cookman Coll., Daytona Beach, Fla., 1973—, prof. music; owner, mgr. Williams Sch. Music; minister music Mt. Carmel Bapt. Ch. Recipient Alumni award, Outstanding Faculty award Bethune Cookman Coll. Mem. Music Educators Nat. Conf., Fla. Music Educators Assn., NAACP. Democrat. Club: Masons. Home: 332 Ellsworth St Daytona Beach FL 32014 Office: Bethune Cookman Coll Daytona Beach FL 32015

WILLIAMS, ROBERT EUGENE, restaurant exec.; b. Biloxi, Miss., July 9, 1945; s. Robert Wilder and Jean Leanore (Egle) W.; student San Antonio Coll., 1965-67, 70-72, S.W. Tex. State U., 1972-73; m. Dorothy Jean Brock, Dec. 27, 1969; 1 son, Matthew Allan. Office mgr. acctg. dept. Frontier Enterprises, San Antonio, 1974—; sec.-treas. HMC Corp. Served with USAF, 1966-70. Mem. Nat. Restaurant Assn. Republican. Baptist. Home: 4735 Guadalajara San Antonio TX 78233 Office: 8520 Crownhill Blvd San Antonio TX 78209

WILLIAMS, ROBERT HILLIS, tool and die co. exec.; b. Wytheville, Va., Jan. 26, 1929; s. Sherman Harkrader and Annie Laurie (Martin) W.; student Wytheville public schs.; m. Ann Elizabeth Cox, Jan. 15, 1956; children—Bobbiann, Robert Hillis, Dixie Susan. Welder, Wythe County Motors, 1943-45, Empire Motor Co., Wytheville, 1946-48; part owner Duck Williams & Son, Wytheville, 1948-61; fire controller U.S. Forest Service, 1950-57; owner sawmill, Wytheville, 1956-58; plant supt. Wytheville Block Co., 1961-63; pres. Williams Mfg. Corp., Wytheville, 1963—. Republican. Presbyterian. Home: 855 N 16th St Wytheville VA 24382 Office: 215 E Marshall St Wytheville VA 24382

WILLIAMS, ROBERT MICHAEL, auditor; b. Balt., Mar. 1, 1949; s. Robert E. and Miriam W.; B.B.A., N. Tex. State U., 1971; m. Dianne Starr, Apr. 14, 1973. Constrn. accountant Redman Devel. Co., Dallas, 1971-72; auditor J.C. Penney Co., Dallas, 1972-74, 76-77, sr. auditor, 1977, field audit coordinator, 1977-78, area audit mgr. adminstrn. and tng., 1978—; systems and fin. auditor Sanger Harris-Federated Dept. Stores, Dallas, 1974-76. Mem. Inst. Internal Auditors. Office: J C Penney Co PO Box 2405 Dallas TX 75221

WILLIAMS, RODNEY PHILLIP, psychiat. social worker; b. Garden City, Kans., Feb. 17, 1948; s. Lewis Edgar and Elizabeth Mary (Hurst) W.; A.S., Garden City Community Jr. Coll., 1968; B.S. in Edn., Kans. State U., Pittsburg, 1970; M.S.W., U. Tenn., Nashville, 1974; m. Janey Sue Pritchett, Oct. 27, 1974; 1 son, Gabrian Troy. Welfare worker Coffey County Welfare Dept., Burlington, Kans., 1970-72; field placement caseworker Cath. Social Services, Nashville, 1972-73, Family and Children's Services, Nashville, 1973-74, social worker, 1974-76; dir., social worker Lexington-Henderson County Counseling Center, Lexington, Tenn., 1976-78; dir. group care Monroe Harding Children's Home, Nashville, 1978-79; psychiat. social worker Lexington-Henderson County Counseling Center, 1979—, dir., 1980—. Active Webloes, Boy Scouts Am. Cert. Acad. Cert. Social Workers. Mem. Nat. Assn. Social Workers. Home: Route 4 Box 39V Lexington TN 38351 Office: 107 E Church St Lexington TN 38351

WILLIAMS, ROGER COURTLAND, lawyer, arbitrator; b. Atlanta, June 11, 1944; s. Ralph Roger and Newell Beatrice (Hill) W.; student Tulane U., 1962-63; B.S., U. Ala., 1966, J.D., 1969; m. Jo Ann Davenport, June 9, 1968; children—Melissa Michelle, Kimberly Ann, Roger Courtland. Admitted to Ala. bar, 1969; partner firm Williams & Williams, P.C., Tuscaloosa, Ala., 1969-73, v.p., 1973—; panel arbitrator Am. Arbitration Assn., 1970—, Fed. Mediation and Conciliation Service, 1972—; v.p., dir. Ala. Law Book Co., Inc., 1971—. Bd. govs. Nat. Labor-Mgmt. Found.; bd. dirs. Tuscaloosa County Assn. for Mental Health, 1975—, Tuscaloosans for Internat. Understanding, 1976—, Boy's Club, Tuscaloosa, 1975—. Served with U.S. Army, 1969-71. Mem. Am., Tuscaloosa County bar assns., Ala. State Bar (exec. council young lawyer's sect 1976-77), Assn. Trial Lawyers Am., Ala., Tuscaloosa trial lawyers assns., Am. Judicature Soc., Am. Arbitration Assn., Nat. Acad. Arbitrators, Farrah Law Soc., Tuscaloosa C. of C. (dir. 1975-76), SAR (pres. Robertson chpt. 1976—), Ala. Jaycees (pres. 1978-79, internal v.p. 1977-78, Outstanding Spoke award 1973), Tuscaloosa Jaycees (pres. 1975-76, chmn. bd. 1976-77, Jaycee of Yr. award 1976), U.S. Jaycees (asso. legal counsel 1979-80), Phi Alpha Delta, Sigma Chi (charter pres. Tuscaloosa alumni chpt. 1976—). Methodist. Clubs: Tuscaloosa Kiwanis (dir. 1973-75), Tuscaloosa Toastmasters (pres. 1972-73, Best Toastmaster award 1972, 73). Home: 124 Covey Chase Tuscaloosa AL 35404 Office: PO Box 2690 2628 8th St Tuscaloosa AL 35403

WILLIAMS, ROGER DAVIS, surgeon; b. Charlotte, N.C., May 26, 1924; s. Edward E. and Lucy Caroline (Davis) W.; B.S.M., Duke U., 1944, M.D., 1947; M.M.Sc., Ohio State U., 1951; m. Martha Jeane Wiedeman, Sept. 7, 1957; children—Diana Lynn, Roger Davis, George Monroe. Intern, Duke Hosp., Durham, N.C., 1947-48; resident Ohio State U. Hosps., Columbus, 1949-54; asst. prof. surgery Ohio State U., Columbus, 1954-59, asso. prof., 1959-62, prof. surgery, 1962-65; prof., chmn. dept. surgery U. Tex. Med. Br., Galveston, 1965-67; clin. prof. surgery U. Miami (Fla.), 1968—; practice medicine, specializing in surgery, Ft. Lauderdale, 1968—; mem. staff Broward Gen. Hosp., Imperial Point Hosp.; pres. Fisher-Williams Surg. Assn., Ft. Lauderdale, 1974—, All-World Auto Parts, Inc., Ft. Lauderdale, 1975—. Mem. Com. of 100, Broward County, Fla., 1976—. Served with USNR, 1949-53. Decorated Bronze Star medal. Mem. Am. Surg. Assn., Am. Gastroenterol. Assn., Soc. Surgery Alimentary Tract, Soc. Univ. Surgeons, Western Surg. Soc., Central Surg. Soc., Internat. Surg. Soc. Republican. Presbyterian. Contbr. articles to med. jours. Home: 2211 SE 20th St Fort Lauderdale FL 33316 Office: 500 SE 17th St Fort Lauderdale FL 33316

WILLIAMS, RONALD JOHN, elec. engr., educator; b. Blue Ash, Ohio, Dec. 14, 1927; s. John Wolfe and Ethel Virginia (Scheve) Williams; B.S., Okla. A. and M. Coll., 1949; M.S., Okla. State U., 1963; Ph.D., Tex. A. and M. U., 1969; m. Patricia Whelan, Aug. 10, 1946; children—Carolyn Virginia (Mrs. Dan Roy Byrne), Eamonn Timothy. Asst. dean applied scis. Del Mar Coll., Corpus Christi, Tex., 1969-71, chmn. engring. tech., 1967-70, prof. engring. tech., 1968—; vis. prof. engring. tech. Tex. A. and M. U., 1971-72; cons. in field. NSF-Sci. Faculty fellow, 1964-65; named tchr. of year Tex. Jr. Coll., 1969; AEC trainee, 1965. Mem. IEEE, Nat., Tex. socs. profl. engrs., Am. Nuclear Soc., ASME, Soc. Mfg. Engrs., Sigma Xi, Eta Kappa Nu, Tau Beta Pi. Democrat. Roman Catholic. Home: PO Box 6027 Corpus Christi TX 78411

WILLIAMS, RUBY MARION, guidance counselor; b. Coldsprings, Tex., Sept. 13, 1938; d. Albert and Iona (Hines) Elmore; B.S. in Elementary Edn., Prairie View (Tex.) A. and M. U., 1958, M.Ed. in Guidance, 1971; m. Artice J. Williams, Mar. 16, 1969; 1 dau., Mario L. Darden. Elementary sch. tchr. Lincoln High Sch. Coldsprings, 1958-66; elementary sch. tchr., then middle sch. tchr. math. and sci. N. Forest Ind. Sch. Dist., Houston, 1966-76, acad. counselor Northwood Middle Sch., 1976—. Del., Tex. Democratic Conv., 1974, sec. 6th senatorial dist.; chmn. econs. resource planning com. N.E. Community Project Funds, Houston, 1974; bd. dirs., 1975—. Grantee U.S. Office Edn., 1971-72, NSF, 1972-73. Mem. Tex., N. Forest (pres. 1966-77; Outstanding Community Service award 1976) classroom tchrs. assns., NEA, Tex., N. Forest tchrs. assns., Am., Houston personnel and guidance assns., Prarie View A and M. U. Alumni Assn. Baptist. Home: 6203 Antha St Houston TX 77016 Office: 10750 Homestead Rd Houston TX 77016

WILLIAMS, STANLEY DALE, electronics co. exec.; b. Woodson County, Kans., Aug. 15, 1936; s. Jack and Thurnelda (Wise) W.; student Kans. State Tchrs. Coll., 1954-56; A.B., U. Kans., 1961; M.A., U. Mo., 1963; postgrad. U. Houston, 1967-68; m. Roberta Ann Wethington, July 22, 1958; children—Celeste Lynn, Stanley Dale, Heather Simone. Engr., Midland Mfg. Co., Kansas City, Kans., 1958-61; computer programmer Bendix Corp., Kansas City, Mo., 1961-64; research engr. Lockheed Missiles & Space Co., Huntsville, Ala., 1964-66, Lockheed Electronics Co., Houston, Tex., 1966—. Mem. Assn. Computing Machinery. Contbr. articles on optimization and thermodynamics to profl. jours. Home: 18415 Point Lookout Dr Houston TX 77058 Office: Lockheed Electronics Co Mail Code B14 1830 NASA Rd 1 Houston TX 77058

WILLIAMS, THEODORE HARVEY, hosp. adminstr., air force officer; b. York, Pa., Jan. 26, 1944; s. Rodger and Kathryn Mae (Landis) W.; B.S., U. Nebr., 1970; M.Sc., Troy State U., 1976; M.Th., Marantha Bible Sem., 1976; Psy.D., Neotarian Coll. Philosophy, 1976, D.D., 1975; m. Ruth Faye Renzell, Jan. 22, 1977. Ordained to ministry Ministry of Christ Ch., 1975; commd. 2d lt., U.S. Air Force, 1961, advanced through grades to capt., 1973; commdr. 3796 Student Squadron, USAF Sch. Health Care Scis., 1971-73; comdr. Med. Squadron sect. Griffiss AFB, N.Y., 1973-74; hosp. adminstr. U.S. Forces Europe, Incirlik, Turkey, 1974-76; team chief health professions recruiting, Balt., 1976-78; chief health professions recruiting Robins AFB, Ga., 1978—; med. adminstrv. cons. Decorated Meritorious Service medal, AF Commendation medal, Armed Forces Expeditionary medal, Nat. Def. Service medal; named Spokane Armed Forces Man of Year, 1964, USAF Top Med. Recruiter, 1978; cert. and lic. clin. psychotherapist. Fellow Am. Acad. Med. Adminstrs.; mem. Am. Coll. Hosp. Adminstrs. (nominee), Assn. Mil. Surgeons U.S., Am. Public Health Assn., Am. Hosp. Assn., Nat. Psychiat. Assn., VFW. Democrat. Club: Pen and Sword. Home: 575A Pine St Robins AFB GA 31098 Office: 3503 USAF Recruiting Group RSH Robins AFB GA 31098

WILLIAMS, THOMAS EUGENE, pediatric hematologist-oncologist; b. Texarkana, Ark., May 13, 1936; s. Thomas Earle and Franki Jo (Garner) W.; B.A., Yale, 1958; M.D., U. Tex. Southwestern Med. Sch., 1962; m. Peggy Jane O'Neill, May 31, 1958; children—Thomas Eugene, Elizabeth Anne, James David. Rotating intern Hermann Hosp., Houston, 1962-63; pediatric resident Children's Med. Center, Dallas, 1963-65; fellow pediatric hematology U. Va. Sch. Medicine, Charlottesville, 1967-68; research asso. Cancer Research Lab., U. Va., Charlottesville, 1968-69; asst. prof. pediatrics and pathology U. Tex. Health Sci. Center at San Antonio, 1969-72, asso. prof. pediatrics and asst. prof. pathology, 1972-73, asso. prof. pediatrics and asso. prof. pathology, 1973-79; med. dir. Santa Rosa Children's Hosp. Cancer Research and Treatment Center, 1974-79; med. dir. S. Tex. Comprehensive Hemophilia Center, 1977-79; sr. clin. research scientist Burroughs Wellcome Co., 1979—; clin. asso. prof. pediatrics U. N.C. Sch. Medicine, 1979—, Duke U. Sch. Medicine, 1980—. Served to lt. comdr. USN, 1965-67. Named Intern of the Year, Hermann Hosp., 1962-63; Am. Cancer Soc. Advanced Clin. fellow, 1968-69, 70-72; Am. Soc. Pharmacology and Exptl. Therapeutics travel awardee, 1968; diplomate Am. Bd. Pediatrics. Mem. World Fedn. Hemophilia, Am. Soc. Clin. Oncology, Am. Soc. Hematology, Am. Assn. for Cancer Edn., Am. Fedn. Clin. Research, Am. Acad. Pediatrics. Episcopalian. Contbr. articles to med. jours. Office: 3030 Cornwallis Rd Research Triangle Park NC 27709

WILLIAMS, THOMAS HARRIS, JR., physician; b. Wetumpka, Ala., Nov. 12, 1919; s. Thomas Harris and Jessie (Moody) W.; A.B., U. Ala., 1941; M.D., Vanderbilt U., 1943; m. Julie Ann Paul, Aug. 26, 1949; children—Amy, Thomas III, Julie, Ray, Barbara. Intern, U. Chgo., Clinics, 1944; resident in surgery U. Iowa Hosps., Iowa City, 1944-45, resident in urology, 1947-49; practice medicine specializing in urology, Montgomery, Ala., 1949—; sr. partner Williams & Reed, P.A., Montgomery, 1970—; chief staff Jackson Hosp. & Clinic, Montgomery, 1958-59; pres. staff Montgomery Baptist Med. Center, 1969-70; pres. bd. dirs. Tyson Manor, Inc., Montgomery, 1962—; chmn. Montgomery County Bd. of Health, 1965-66. Pres. Salvation Army Adv. Bd., 1963. Served to capt. M.C., AUS, 1945-47; to col. USAR, 1947-63. Recipient Durrance award Phi Gama Delta, 1967; diplomate Am. Bd. Urology. Fellow ACS, Soc. Pediatric Urology, Am. Fertility Soc.; mem. Am. Urol. Assn., So. Med. Assn., Pan Pacific Surg. Assn., Ala. Urol. Soc. (pres. elect 1977-78), Am. Soc. Clin. Urologists, Internat. Phi Gamma Delta (Archon pres. 1974-76), Phi Beta Kappa, Alpha Epsilon Delta. Methodist. Clubs: Montgomery Country, Capitol City, Willow Point Country, Montgomery Rotary, (pres. 1963), Vanderbilt Club (pres. 1959-60). Home: 2912 Jamestown Dr Montgomery AL 36111 Office: 1111 E South Blvd Montgomery AL 36116

WILLIAMS, THOMAS THACKERY, educator; b. N.C., Mar. 13, 1925; s. George and Eliza Williams; B.S., Agrl. & Tech. U. N.C., 1948; M.S., U. Ill., 1949; Ph.D. (sr. research asst. 1952-54), Ohio State U., 1955; postgrad. Case Inst. Tech., 1957; 2 children. Instr. agrl. econs. Tuskegee (Ala.) Inst., 1949-50, asst. to dean agr., 1950-52; asst. prof., chmn. agrl. econs. So. U., Baton Rouge, 1955-66, prof., chmn. agrl. econs. and dir. research and devel., 1959-66, adminstrv. asst. and prof. agrl. econs., 1969—, dir. Inst. for Internat. Econ. Devel., 1972—, prof. and adminstrv. asst. for fed. programs, 1972—; OEO Title III program coordinator, 1969-76; cons. in field. Vice pres. Baton Rouge Sister City Internat., 1978, chmn., 1977; mem. Baton Rouge Bd. Christian Giving to Disadvantaged Children, 1976; mem. Scotlandville Devel. Adv. Council, 1976; pres. So. Heights Property Owners Assn., 1970, Baton Rouge Human Relations Com., 1970; mem. Fulbright Selection Com. for Manpower, 1966; La. Manpower Adv. Com., 1969; nat. Fulbright adv. bd. Inst. Internat. Edn., 1970, others. Farm Found. grantee, Russia, 1970, Brazil, 1973; Fulbright Travel grantee, 1967; Ford Found. grantee, 1967-68; AID grantee, 1968; CIES Fulbright Lecture grantee, Tel Aviv, 1967; USOE Fulbright Teaching grantee, Serdang, Malaysia, 1966-67; Fulbright Travel grantee, 1966; Equitable Life Assurance Soc. grantee, 1961; others. Mem. Am. Assn. Agrl. Econs., Nat. Council Social Studies, Acad. Polit. Sci., So. Assn. Profl. Workers, Southwestern Social Sci. Assn., Internat. Devel. Assn. Institutors, Nat. Assn. Land Grant Colls. and State Univs., Assn. Black Economists, Assn. U.S. Univ. Dirs. of Internat. Agrl. Programs, Am. Agrl. Econs. Assn., Western Econs. Assn., Am. Assn. Univ. Adminstrs., SE Consortium for Internat. Devel., Omega Psi Phi named Man of Yr., Omega Psi Phi, 1964, Regional Man of Yr., 1969; Sigma Pi Phi. Club: Kiwanis. Contbr. articles to profl. jours. Address: 2857 77th Ave Baton Rouge LA 70807

WILLIAMS, W. R., acctg. firm exec.; b. Lena Station, La., Mar. 15, 1930; s. Eddie S. and Edna (Rashall) W.; B.S., U. Ark., 1956; m. Lovene Arlene Parker, June 30, 1956; children—Julie Marie, Janet Lynn. Mng. partner Peat, Marwick, Mitchell & Co., Tulsa, 1959-74, sr. partner, Frankfurt, Germany, 1974-78, vice chmn.-S.W., Houston, 1978—; gen. chmn. Tulsa U. Acctg. Conf., 1972-73. Charter mem. Okla. State U. Devel. Council of Tulsa County, 1973-74; mem. governing bd. Houston Grand Opera Assn., 1979—. Served with USAF, 1948-52. Mem. Am. Inst. C.P.A.'s, Okla. Soc. C.P.A.'s (pres. Tulsa chpt. 1969-70) Nat. Assn. Accountants, Am. Acctg. Assn., U. Ark. Alumni Assn., (life). Beta Gamma Sigma, Beta Alpha Psi, Alpha Kappa Psi. Clubs: Houston, Houston Athletic, Houston Racquet, Brae-burn, Houstonian, Toastmasters. Office: 4300 One Shell Plaza Houston TX 77002

WILLIAMS, WILLIAM DUANE, mktg. exec.; b. Long Beach, Calif., Feb. 7, 1944; s. William Leroy and Marjory (Brooks) W.; A.A., Coll. of Orlando, 1969; B.S. in Bus. Adminstrn., U. Central Fla., 1972; m. Jacqualin E. Carver, Nov. 24, 1971; children—John Paul, David Michael, Michael Anthony. Cons., Met. Life Ins. Co., 1971-72; nat. rep. Windsor Publs., 1972-74; account exec. Sun World Broadcasters, 1974; dir. advt. and mktg. Fla. Engring. Soc., Orlando, 1974-78; pres. I.M. Mktg. Group, Inc., Orlando, 1978—; partner Indsl. Mktg. Group, Orlando, 1978—; dir. Williams Diversified. Bd. dirs. Orange County Republican Exec. Com., 1971-72. Served with USAF, 1964-68; Vietnam. Recipient Pres.'s M.D.R.T., 1973; Salesman of Year award Sun World Broadcasters, 1974; Outstanding Achievement award Windsor Publs., Internat., 1973. Mem. Am. Advt. Fedn. Lutheran. Club: Toastmasters. Home: 8605 Caracas Ave Orlando FL 32807 Office: I M Mktg Group Inc 2317 E South St Orlando FL 32803

WILLIAMS, WILLIAM WALTER, JR., banker; b. Savannah, Ga., Jan. 28, 1927; s. William Walter and Anna Laura (Rackley) W.; B.S., Ga. Tchrs. Coll., 1949; M.A., Ga. Peabody Coll., 1953; m. Barbara Hester Burdette, July 17, 1954; children—Walter, Ann, Jane. Various positions to v.p. Citizens and So. Newnan Bank (Ga.), 1954-66, pres., 1967, also dir.; v.p. Citizens and So. Nat. Bank, Atlanta, 1966-67. Pres., Newnan-Coweta Community Chest and Council, 1964. Served with U.S. Army, 1945-46; PTO. Named Young Man of Year for Newnan and Coweta County Jr. C. of C., 1962. Mem. Newnan-Coweta C. of C. (pres. 1965), Am., Ga. (exec. council 1973-74) bankers assns. Democrat. Baptist. Clubs: Newnan Country, Newnan Rotary (pres. 1976-77). Home: 131 Woodbine Circle Newnan GA 30263 Office: 17 Greenville St Newnan GA 30263

WILLIAMS, WILLIE LETHAIT, ednl. adminstr.; b. Perry, Ga., Mar. 26, 1946; s. Willie and Ethel Mae (Bynum) W.; M.S., Fort Valley State Coll., 1974; m. Mary Jean Moore, Feb. 21, 1969; children—Keary Deron, Latonya Meandrea. Tester, Ednl. Testing Service, Atlanta; counselor, asst. dir. fin. aid Fort Valley State Coll., Fort Valley, Ga., 1978—. Served with U.S. Army, 1969-73. Decorated Air Medal. Mem. Am. Personnel and Guidance Assn., Am. Sch. Counselors Assn., Nat. Assn. Student Fin. Aid Adminstrs., So. Assn. Student Fin. Aid Adminstrs., Am. Taekwondo Assn., Kappa Alpha Psi, Alpha Sigma Mu. Clubs: Mason. Home: 101 Monteigo Ct Centerville GA 31028 Office: Box 1125 Fort Valley State Coll Fort Valley GA 31030

WILLIAMS, WINTON HUGH, civil engr.; b. Tampa, Fla., Feb. 14, 1920; s. Herbert DeMain and Alice (Grant) W.; student U. Tampa, 1948; B.C.E., U. Fla., 1959; grad. U.S. Army Res. Asso. Command and Gen. Staff Coll., Ft. Leavenworth, U.S. Army Logistics Mgmt. Center; m. Elizabeth Walser Seelye, Dec. 18, 1949; children—Jan, Dick, Bill, Ann. Constrn. engr. air fields C.E., U.S. Army, McCoy AFB, Fla., 1959-61, Homestead AFB, Miami, Fla., 1961-62; civil engr. C.E., Jacksonville (Fla.) Dist. Office, 1962-65, chief master planning and layout sect., 1965-70; chief master planning and real estate div. Office of Engr. Hdqrs. USARSO, Ft. Clayton, C.Z., 1970-75; spl. asst. for master planning and mil. constrn. programming air bases eastern area Marine Corps Air Sta., Cherry Point, N.C., 1975—. Troop com. chmn. Boy Scouts Am., Explorer Scouts, Curundu, C.Z. Served with U.S. Army, World War II, Korean War; ETO, Africa, PTO, Korea; col. Res. Decorated Breast Order of Yun Hi (Republic China); presdl. citation (Republic Korea). Registered profl. engr., N.C., Fla., Panama, C.Z., Republic Panamá. Mem. Nat. Soc. Profl. Engrs., ASCE, Prestressed Concrete Inst., Res. Officers Assn. (v.p. chpt. 1972-73, v.p. Central and S. Am. 1975-77, dept. pres. 1974-75), Soc. Am. Mil. Engrs., Am. Legion, U. Tampa Alumni Assn. (nat. council), Theta Chi. Presbyn. (bd. ushers). Lion (dir., scouting instl. rep., v.p. 1975-76), Elk. Clubs: Fort Clayton Riding (pres. 1973-74), Balboa Gun, Gamboa Golf and Country. Home: 4408 Coral Point Dr Morehead City NC 28557 Office: Office of Dir Installations and Logistics Marine Corps Air Sta Cherry Point NC 28533

WILLIAMSON, ALBERT NICHOLSON, JR., physicist; b. Greenwood, Miss., Dec. 25, 1934; s. Albert Nicholson and Edith Marion (Henderson) W.; B.S., Millsaps Coll., Jackson, Miss., 1956; m. Charlotte Ann Becker, Oct. 4, 1958; children—Jeffrey Allen, Thomas Albert, Michael Bert. Sr. field engr. Hughes Aircraft Co., Culver City, Calif., 1956-61; mgr. electronic dept. Sch. Pictures Inc., Jackson, 1961-63; research physicist Waterways Experiment Sta., C.E., U.S. Army, Vicksburg, Miss., 1963—. Mem. Interagency Com. Landsat Ground Systems, 1976—; chmn. com. Boy Scouts Am.; chmn. adminstrv. bd. Christ United Meth. Ch., Jackson, Miss., also chmn. staff-parish relations com.; chmn. tech. session 5th Ann. W.F. Pecora Meml. Symposium, Sioux Falls, S.D., 1979. Mem. Am. Soc. Photogrammetry, SAR. Methodist. Contbr. articles to profl. publs. Home: 1825 Hillview Dr Jackson MS 39211 Office: PO Box 631 Vicksburg MS 39180

WILLIAMSON, ANORA, hosp. adminstr.; b. Mullins, S.C., June 5, 1953; d. Ralph and Azile Clemmons W.; B.S., Campbell Coll., 1975. Tchr. elem. lang. arts Harkers Island (N.C.) Elem. Sch., 1975-76; in-service edn. dir. personnel Maria Parham Hosp., Henderson, N.C., 1976—. Asst. Cadette leader Pines council Girl Scouts Am., 1978-79; pres. membership com. N.C. Symphony, 1978—. Mem. Carolinas Soc. Health Edn. and Trainers (indsl. relations com.). Republican. Episcopalian (women's aux., hosp. guild). Club: Henderson Jr. Woman's (arts dept. chmn. 1978, pres. 1979). Home: 518 Waddill St Henderson NC 27536 Office: PO Drawer 59 Henderson NC 27536

WILLIAMSON, DARLENE SWANSON, speech pathologist; b. Lockport, N.Y., June 15, 1948; d. Francis Leonard and Norma May (Murphy) Swanson; student Ohio U., 1966-67; B.S., Purdue U., 1970; M.A., U. Ill., 1973; m. James Paul Williamson, June 27, 1970; children—Jeffrey Mark. Speech pathologist Paxton (Ill.) Community Unit Sch., 1970-73, Montgomery County (Md.) Public Schs.,

1973-74, Fairfax County (Va.) Public Schs., 1974-75; chief speech pathology Washington Hosp. Center, 1975-76; speech pathologist D.C. Cancer Soc., Washington, 1973-79; pvt. practice speech pathology, Houston, 1979—; lectr. in field. Mem. Am. Speech and Hearing Assn. (cert. clin. competency), Internat. Assn. Laryngectomies. Home: 2618 Teague St Houston TX 77080

WILLIAMSON, FLETCHER PHILLIPS, real estate broker; b. Cambridge, Md., Dec. 16, 1923; s. William Fletcher and Florence M. (Phillips) W.; student U. Md., 1941, 42; m. Betty June Stoker, Apr. 1943; 1 son, Jeffrey Phillips; m. 2d, Helen B. Morris, Aug. 28, 1972. Test engr. Engring. Lab. Glen Martin Co., 1942-43; with Corkran Ice Cream Co., Cambridge, 1946-50; real estate broker, 1950—; pres. Williamson Real Estate, Dorchester Corp.; dir., v.p. Cargo Handlers, Inc., Colonial Consultants Ltd., WCEM, Inc.; dir. Cam-Storage, Inc.; dir., chmn. bd. Nat. Bank Cambridge; co-receiver White & Nelson, Inc. Pres., Cambridge Hosp., United Fund Dorchester County. Served with Ordnance Tech. Intelligence, AUS, 1943-46; U.S., ETO. Mem. Md. Assn. Realtors (gov. 1956-60), Outdoor Writers Assn., Nat. Rifle Assn., Am. Ordnance Assn., Cambridge Dorchester C. of C. (dir. 1955—), Power Squadron (comdr. 1954-56). Methodist. Mason (Shriner). Clubs: Explorers, Shikar Safari, Camp Fire, Soc. of the South Pole, Chesapeake Bay Yacht, Md., Tred Avon Yacht. Home: 310 Wildwood Dr E San Antonio TX 78212 Office: The Point US 50 PO Box 715 Cambridge MD 21613

WILLIAMSON, HORACE HAMPTON, architect; b. Butts County, Ga., May 4, 1924; s. Hampton Daughtry and Pearl (Griffin) W.; B.S., Ga. Inst. Tech., 1951, B.Arch., 1952; M.S., M.Arch., Rensselaer Poly. Inst., 1969; Ph.D. in Psychology, U. Utah, 1975; m. Doris Stewart, Nov. 27, 1947; children—Tom S., Larry M., J. Douglas. Draftsman, Aeck Assos., Atlanta, 1948-49; chief designer Woodward and Robert, Spartanburg, S.C., 1952-58; pvt. archtl. practice, Highlands, N.C., 1958-71; from instr. to asso. prof. Clemson (S.C.) U., part-time 1959-71; asso. prof. architecture Tex. Tech. U., Lubbock, 1973—; pvt. archtl. practice, Lubbock, 1978—; campus planning officer Clemson U., 1960-71; design and planning cons. TVA, 1963-65; design cons. psychology dept. Fisk U., Nashville, 1974—; prin. works include Spartanburg Sr. High Sch., Catholic Mission Chapel competition, Park Hills Elem. Sch., Spartanburg. Served with USMC, 1943-46. Recipient 1st prize Louisville Home Show nat. residence competition, 1960, citation Nat. High Sch. design competition, 1958, elem. sch. design competition, 1953; NIMH fellow, 1971-73. Mem. AIA, Am. Psychol. Assn., Southwestern Psychol. Assn., Tex. Psychol. Assn., Tex. Soc. Architects, Nat. Assn. Realtors, Lubbock Bd. Realtors. Methodist. Club: Lake Ridge Country (Lubbock). Co-author: Creativity in the Home, 1973; contbr. articles to profl. publs. Home: 2122 53d St Lubbock TX 79412 Office: 3403 73d St Lubbock TX 79423

WILLIAMSON, JAMES FENELON, physician; b. Inez, Ky., Nov. 15, 1933; s. Russell and Nolda (Cassady) W.; B.S., Georgetown Coll., 1953; M.D., U. Louisville, 1957; m. Lavonne Heath, Aug. 21, 1955; children—Nanci Lynn, Karen Jo, Susan Beth. Intern, St. Elizabeth Hosp., Covington, Ky., 1957-58; resident in obstetrics and gynecology U. Louisville Hosps., 1958-62; practice medicine specializing in obstetrics and gynecology, Ashland, Ky., 1962—; asst. clin. prof. U. Louisville, 1973—; chief of staff Kings Dau. Hosp., 1975; pres. Ashland Med. Arts Inc., 1975; dir. Inez Deposit Bank, Bellefonte Land Co. Bd. dirs. Cerebral Palsy Assn. Eastern Ky. Served with U.S. Army, 1966-68. Diplomate Am. Bd. Obstetrics and Gynecology. Mem. Am. Coll. Obstetricians and Gynecologists, A.C.S., AMA, Ky. State, Boyd County med. socs. Republican. Baptist. Club: Rotary. Home: 2725 Auburn Ave Ashland KY 41101 Office: 2301 Lexington Ave Ashland KY 41101

WILLIAMSON, JOHN ROBERT, lawyer; b. Tuscaloosa, Ala., Oct. 7, 1947; s. Robert Lander and Annie Lou (Howell) W.; A.B., Birmingham-So. Coll., 1969; J.D., U. Ala., 1972; m. Marilyn Florence King, Aug. 23, 1970; children—Joan King, Rachel King. Admitted to Ala. bar, 1972; v.p., gen. counsel Williamson Oil Co., Inc., 1972—. Bd. dirs. Ala. ACLU, 1971-72. Served to capt. U.S. Army Res. Mem. Am., Ala. bar assns., Nat. Oil Jobbers Council. Democrat. Home: PO Box 502 Fort Payne AL 35967 Office: PO Box 575 Fort Payne AL 35967

WILLIAMSON, JOHNNY MACK, ins. co. exec.; b. Middlesboro, Ky., Apr. 15, 1932; s. Henry D. and Retta E. (Ausmus) W.; B.B.A., Lincoln Meml. U., 1957; m. Myrta Charlotte Lindmark, Sept. 1, 1956; children—Debra Lynne, Shawn Mack. Foreman, Middlesboro Tanning Co., 1959-60; mgr. Cumberland Bowling Lanes, Middlesboro, 1960; partner and gen. mgr. Big Sandy Lanes, Paintsville, Ky., 1960-63, Pimingo Lanes, Williamson, W.Va., 1963-65; gen. mgr. Can Run Lanes, Louisville, 1965-69; ins. agt. Caroom & Black Benefits (formerly Blair, Follin, Allen & Walker, Inc.), Louisville, 1969—, account mgr. 1977—; account mgr. Caroom & Black, Louisville, 1977—; dir. Ky. Bowling Inc., 1963-65. Mem. high sch. football team, 1944-49; mem. Louisville Jefferson County Youth Commn., 1966-68; Republican precinct capt., Louisville, 1974-77. Served with USMC, 1951-54; Korea. Mem. Nat., Ky., Louisville assns. life underwriters, Nat. Rifle Assn., Nat. Security Council. Republican. Baptist. Home: Mt Olivet Rd Route 3 LaGrange KY 40031 Office: 1939 Goldsmith Ln Louisville KY 40218

WILLIAMSON, NEIL SEYMOUR, III, army officer; b. Dumont, N.J., Jan. 5, 1935; s. Neil Seymour and Mary Louise (Bittenbender) W.; B.S., U.S. Military Acad., 1958; M.S., U. Mich., 1963; m. Janice Porter Tukey, Aug. 3, 1978; children—Deborah D., Lisa L., Neil S., Dirk A., Wendy L. Commd. lt., U.S. Army, 1958, advanced through grades to col., 1976; asso. prof. dept. earth space and graphic sci. U.S. Mil. Acad., 1965-68; comdr. 27th maintenance battalion, Vietnam, 1969-70; chief edn. sect. ordnance br., Washington, 1971-72; mem. staff Office of Asst. Sec. of Def., 1974-75; chief advanced systems concept office, Ala., 1976-77; comdr., dir. Small Caliber Weapon Systems Lab., Dover, N.J., 1977-78; project mgr. TOW, Dragon, Ala., 1978—. Decorated Legion of Merit, Bronze Star, Purple Heart, and others. Mem. Soc. Automotive Engrs., Assn. Grads. of U.S. Mil. Acad., Army Aviation Assn., Am. Def. Preparedness Assn., Assn. Indsl. Coll. Armed Forces, U. Mich. Alumni Assn. Roman Catholic. Home: 4 Wadsworth Dr Redstone Arsenal AL 35808

WILLIAMSON, PAMELA DANIEL, nurse, educator; b. Waynesville, N.C., Mar. 29, 1949; d. Hugh Sidney and Ruby (Donald) Daniel; B.S. in Nursing, East Carolina U., 1972; m. Donald Kent Williamson, Apr. 1, 1972; children—Ramie, Donald Kent II. Staff nurse New Hanover Meml. Hosp., Wilmington, N.C., 1972-73; instr. nursing Sampson Tech. Inst., Clinton, N.C., 1973-75, James Sprunt Inst., Kenansville, N.C., 1975—. Registered nurse, N.C. Mem. N.C. Council Asso. Degree Nursing Programs, Nurses Assn. of Am. Coll. Obstetricians and Gynecologists, Faculty Assn. N.C. Community Coll. System. Republican. Presbyterian. Home: Route 1 Box 243-A Rocky Point NC 28457 Office: James Sprunt Inst PO Box 398 Kenansville NC 28349

WILLIAMSON, ROYCE BRUCE, state legislator; b. Winston County, Miss., Oct. 22, 1944; s. A.B. and Vera (Reed) W.; B.S., Miss. State U., 1967; m. Julia Coalson, May 29, 1965; children—Tammy, Pamela, Elizabeth. Dairyman, farmer, farm cons., Louisville, Miss., 1965—; mem. Miss. Ho. of Reps. from 20th Dist., 1972—. Named Outstanding Young Farmer, Louisville Jaycees, 1972, 73, Winston County Farm Bur., 1974. Mem. Farm Bur., Miss. Cattlemen's Assn., Winston County Ednl. Found., Winston County Soil Conservation Council. Democrat. Baptist. Clubs: Shriners, Nanih Waiya Hunting, Nanih Waiya Booster. Address: Box 310 Route 3 Louisville MS 39339

WILLIAMSON, VIRGINIA KATHERINE TOPPINS, educator; b. San Antonio, Aug. 14, 1928; d. John Monroe and Emily Fasche (Evans) Toppins; B.S., Trinity U., San Antonio, 1952, M.Ed., 1955; m. David Crowell Williamson, Nov. 28, 1957; children—Michael, Carolyn, Thomas. Asst. personnel dir. Sears, Roebuck & Co., San Antonio, 1947-55; tchr. social studies Page Jr. High Sch., San Antonio, 1955-58; tchr. English, Am. Sch. in Japan, Tokyo, 1964-66; counselor cons. San Antonio Ind. Sch. Dist., San Antonio, 1975—. Mem. Am., Tex. personnel and guidance assns., Internat. Transactional Analysis Assn. Republican. Presbyterian. Home: 5515 Wales St San Antonio TX 78223 Office: 141 Lavaca St San Antonio TX 78223

WILLIAMSON, WALTER ERNEST, JR., physician, surgeon; b. St. Louis, Aug. 16, 1930; s. Walter Ernest and Lucile Burgette (Miller) W.; B.A., Baylor U., 1951, M.D., 1956; postgrad. U. Okla., 1951-52; m. Maxine Elaine Dunn, June 27, 1953; children—Mark Weldon, Leslie Elaine, Jon Walter. Intern USPHS Hosp., New Orleans, 1956-57, gen. surgery resident, 1958-60, 61-62; mem. surg. staff USPHS Hosp., Detroit, 1957-58, chief surgery, 1967-68; research fellow cardiovascular surgery Tulane Med. Sch., 1960-61; asst. chief surgery USPHS Hosp., San Francisco, 1962-64, dep. chief surgery, 1964-67; practice medicine specializing in thoracic, vascular and gen. surgery, Clarskburg, W.Va., 1968—, Bridgeport, W.Va., 1976—; med. dir. Consol. Gas Supply Corp., Clarksburg; instr. Tulane Med. Sch., 1960-61. Pres. Harrison County Heart Assn., 1975-77; pres. Harrison County Cancer Assn., 1973; trustee Alderson-Broaddus Coll., Philippi, W.Va., 1972-75. Diplomate Am. Bd. Surgery. Fellow A.C.S.; mem. Assn. Mil. Surgeons U.S., AMA, Am. Occupational Med. Assn., Harrison County Med. Soc. (pres. 1977-78). Home: 514 Hillcrest Circle Bridgeport WV 26330 Office: 901 W Main St Bridgeport WV 26330

WILLIFORD, WILLIAM BAILEY, publishing co. exec.; b. Sanford, Fla., July 12, 1921; s. William Francis and Frances Elizabeth (Williford) Bailey; student U. Florence (Italy), 1945, U. Tenn., 1946, 46-47, U. Ga., 1947-48, U. Wis., 1960; m. Julia (Benton) Swann Miller, June 23, 1969; 1 son by previous marriage—Lawrence Brumby Williford. Pub. relations exec. with various corps. and govt. agys., 1949-68; pres. Cherokee Pub. Co., Atlanta and Covington, Ga., 1968—. Lectr. creative writing Emory U., Atlanta, 1964. Mem. bd. counselors Oxford Coll., 1972-78. Served with USAAF, 1942-46, USAF, 1950-52; maj. USAF Res. ret. Recipient spl. award Dixie Council Authors and Journalists, 1976. Named Ky. Col., 1968. Mem. Ga., Atlanta (trustee 1960-66), Newton County (trustee 1971-75, chmn. bd. 1971-73) hist. socs., SAR, Ga. Trust for Historic Preservation, Sumter Historic Preservation Soc., Phi Delta Theta. Episcopalian (lay reader 1954-62, vestryman 1972-75). Clubs: Commerce, Capital City (Atlanta); Highlands (N.C.) Country. Author: Americus Through the Years, 1960, rev. edit. 1975; Williford and Allied Families, 1961; Peachtree Street, Atlanta, 1962; The Glory of Covington, 1973. Home: 1164 Floyd St Covington GA 30209 Office: 1151 Monticello St Covington GA 30209

WILLIG, BILLY WINSTON, machine shop, foundry exec.; b. Temple, Tex., Mar. 11, 1929; s. Bruno William and Mary (Barth) W.; student San Angelo Jr. Coll., 1946-47; B.S. in Mech. Engring., U. Tex., 1951; m. Lanelle Brooks, Sept. 11, 1951; children—Bruce Wayne, Jana Lynn. With Western Iron Works, Inc., San Angelo, Tex., 1951—, gen. mgr., pres., chmn. bd., 1971—. Skipper, Sea Scout Ship 22, Boy Scouts Am., 1965—; chmn. Lake Nasworthy Adv. Bd., 1968-70, Area Environ. Council, 1973-74. Trustee, San Angelo Ind. Sch. Dist., 1966—, v.p., 1969, 72, sec., treas., 1968, 71, 73, pres., 1975, 76. Bd. dirs. San Angelo Govtl. Computer Center; bd. dirs. YMCA San Angelo, 1977, v.p., 1979, pres., 1980, chmn. bldg. com., 1979; v.p. San Angelo Industries, 1975-76, pres., 1976-79, dir., 1970—; pres. W. Tex. Indsl. Devel. Corp., 1980—; mem. bd., exec. com. bd. Concho Valley council Boy Scouts Am., v.p. exploring, 1974-78, council commr., 1978-80, recipient Silver Beaver award, 1975. Served with C.E., AUS, 1952-54. Mem. Tex. Mfrs. Assn., Tex. Assn. Bus., Tex. Assn. Sch. Bds. (exec. com. 1975-80), Nat. Rifle Assn., C. of C. (dir. 1976-77, chmn. mfrs. com. 1976—, exec. bd. 1976—, pres. 1978; Citizen of Year 1979), Am. Foundry Soc., Tex. PTA (hon. life). Presbyn. (deacon, elder, clk. session 1968-71, 76-77, 79-80). Mason (Shriner), Rotarian (sec. San Angelo 1973-74, v.p. 1978, pres. 1979-80). Club: Concho Yacht (past commodore San Angelo). Home: 1618 Shafter St San Angelo TX 76901 Office: 21 E 6th St San Angelo TX 76901

WILLIMON, EDWARD LLOYD, architect, educator; b. Florence, S.C., June 8, 1919; s. Walter Eugene and Lee Oliver (Gregg) W.; B.S., Clemson U., 1942; M.S., Columbia, 1947; M.S., So. Meth. U., 1970; m. Janette Sims, June 20, 1943; children—Laura, Vicki, Mary, Jenny. Archtl. draftsman George Christensen, Architect, 1948-50; self-employed as architect, Dallas, 1950—; asst. prof. geology Bishop Coll., Dallas, 1961—, U. Tex. at Arlington, 1979-80. Bd. dirs. Greater Dallas Housing Opportunity Center. Served with AUS, 1942-46. Fellow Tex. Acad. Sci.; mem. AAUP, Paleontol. Soc., Nat. Assn. Geology Tchrs., AIA, AAAS, Am. Legion (comdr. 1949-51), Oak Cliff Gem and Mineral Soc. Prin. archtl. works include Brass Craft Western, Lancaster, Tex., Tex. Color Printers, Dallas, Nat. Chemsearch Corp., Irving, Tex. Home: 111 Royal Oak Dr Duncanville TX 75116 Office: 2450 N Beckley Lancaster TX 75146

WILLIS, CHARLES HENRY, JR., elec. mfg. co. exec.; b. Linden, N.C., Nov. 22, 1943; s. Charles Henry and Lucy (Williams) W.; B.S. in Social Studies, Fayetteville (N.C.) State U., 1966; m. Emma McEachern, Aug. 7, 1966. Tchr., Cumberland County (N.C.) schs., 1966-71; adminstrv. asst. Cumberland County Community Action, 1971-73; personnel asst. Rohm and Haas N.C., Inc., 1973-76; asst. personnel mgr. Burlington Industries Inc., Raeford, N.C., 1976-79; personnel relations supr. control center div. Westinghouse Electric Corp., Fayetteville, 1979—. Bd. dirs. Occupational Industrialization Center, Fayetteville; trustee, pres. jr. usher bd. St. Luke Pentecostal Holiness Ch., Fayetteville. Mem. Southeastern Personnel Assn., Christian Businessmen's League, NAACP. Home: 6951 Ramsey St Fayetteville NC 28301 Office: 2900 Doc Bennett Rd PO Box 64909 Fayetteville NC 28301

WILLIS, DANIEL WILLARD, ins. agt.; b. Spartanburg, S.C., July 16, 1911; s. Milton Lee and Martha Ann (Wilburn) W.; A.B., Wofford Coll., 1932; postgrad. Bus. Adminstrn., Harvard, 1932-33; m. Harriet Bliss Talbot, Feb. 19, 1938; 1 dau., Ann Talbot. With products control Pacific Mills, S.C., 1933; trainee in cost control U.S. Soil Conservation Service, Spartanburg, 1933; with claims dept. sch. Liberty Mutual Ins. Co., Boston, 1934, claims adjuster, N.Y.C., 1935, field claims adjuster, Ky., 1936; dist. mgr. State Farm Ins. Co., Greenville and Spartanburg, 1939-49; owner, operator Willis Ins. Agency, Spartanburg, 1949-61, name changed to Correll-Willis Agency, 1961-70, name changed to Correll Willis-Smith & Assos., Inc., 1970—. Pres. Spartanburg chpt. United Cerebral Palsy, 1957, Sch. for Exceptional Children; bd. dirs. Civitan Community Rehab. Facility, 1968—; mem. United Fund Dr. Allocations Com., 1977—. Served to maj., U.S. Army, 1941-46, 1951-52. Mem. Spartanburg Assn. Fire and Casualty Agts. (pres. 1968), S.C., Nat. Big "I" agts., Carolina Assn. Mutual Ins. Agts. (treas., exec. bd. 1972—, dir. 1966-69, nat. dir., 1969-72;) Nat. Assn. Profl. Ins. Agts., Am. Mgmt. Assn., VFW, Delta Sigma Phi. Republican. Baptist. Clubs: Spartanburg Country, Inter-Club Srs. Golf Assn., K.P., Elks. Contbr. articles to profl. jours. Home: 1235 Partridge Rd Spartanburg SC 29302 Office: 440 E Kennedy St Spartanburg SC 29304

WILLIS, DELMAR ALEXANDER, advt. agy. exec.; b. Bridgeport, Ohio, Mar. 7, 1909; s. James Arthur and Jessie Mae (Payne) W.; A.B., Atlanta U., 1931; postgrad. Atlanta U., 1944-48; m. Margaret Elizabeth Johnson, Dec. 26, 1936; children—Norma J., Elizabeth O. Tchr., Pendleton County schs., Franklin, W.Va., 1931-42; with prodn. control dept. Blaw-Knox Steel Co., Martins Ferry, Ohio, 1942-45; co-owner Angier Ave. Cleaners, Atlanta, 1945-47; mktg. rep. Carling Brewing Co., Cleve., 1948-73, mgr. spl. markets, 1962-73; owner Dawn Advt., Birmingham, Ala., 1976—. Bd. dirs. Cedar Branch YMCA, Cleve., 1966-69, 4th Ave Branch YMCA, 1975—. Recipient certificate Am. Mgmt. Assn., 1969. Mem. Birmingham Press Club. Mem. United Church of Christ. Home: 836 Jasper Rd Birmingham AL 35204 Office: PO Box 35111 Birmingham AL 35211

WILLIS, DENNIS DARYL, cons. mining engr.; b. Norton, Va., Apr. 29, 1948; s. Virgil Hyman and Reva May (Hubbard) W.; B.S. in Civil Engring., Va. Poly. Inst. and State U., 1970; m. Elizabeth J. Short, July 15, 1967; children—Kristi René, Kimberly Denise. Project engr. Island Creek Coal Co., Keen Mountain, Va., 1970-73; design engr. Wiley & Wilson, Inc., consultants, Lynchburg, Va., 1973-74; v.p., dir., head mining div. Thompson & Litton, Inc., consultants, Wise, Va., 1974—; pres. Highland Land & Mineral Co., Inc. Recipient Cons. Engrs. Council/Va. engring. design excellence award for Sediment Structure, 1979. Registered profl. engr., Va., Ky., Tenn., W.Va. Mem. ASCE, Cons. Engrs. Council, Soc. Mining Engrs., Profl. Engrs. in Pvt. Practice, Nat. Soc. Profl. Engrs., Va. Surface Mine and Reclamation Assn. (dir.), Wise Jaycees (sec. 1974-75), Va. Soc. Profl. Engrs. Presbyn. (Sunday sch. tchr. 1974—, elder). Club: Lions. Contbr. articles to profl. publs. Home: 513 Chestnut St Norton VA 24273 Office: PO Box 1307 Wise VA 24293

WILLIS, DOYLE, state legislator Tex.; b. Kaufman, Tex., Aug. 18, 1908; s. Alvin and Eliza (Phillips) W.; B.A., B.S., U. Tex., 1934; LL.B., Georgetown U., 1938; m. Evelyn McDavid, Feb. 25, 1942; children—Doyle, Dan, Dina, Dale. Admitted to D.C. bar, 1937, Tex. bar, 1938; practice in Ft. Worth, 1938—; mem. Tex. Ho. of Reps. from Tarrant County, 1947-52, 69, 72—, Tex. Senate from 10th Dist., 1952-62, pres. Tex. Senate, 1961; mem. Ft. Worth City Council, 1963-64; chmn. W. Tex. Legis. Del., 1977-79 Served to maj. USAAF, World War II. Decorated Bronze Star. Mem. Tex., Tarrant County bar assns., VFW (past comdr. Tex.), Res. Officers Assn. (past pres.), Am. Legion (past post comdr.), G.I. Forum, Sons of Republic of Tex., Sons of Confederate Vets. Democrat. Methodist. Clubs: Lions, Masons, Shriners, K.P., Odd Fellows. Home: 3316 Browning Ct Fort Worth TX 76111 Office: Sinclair Bldg Fort Worth TX 76102

WILLIS, GLENN HARRY, oil co. exec.; b. Magnolia, Ark., Apr. 18, 1922; s. Bernard B. and Irene (Thornton) W.; B.S. in Petroleum Engring., U. Okla., 1950; m. Louise McKinney, May 11, 1948; children—Stephen, Susan, Mary Lynn, Glenda. Oil buyer Standard Oil of Ind., New Orleans, 1950-55; oil buyer Clark Oil & Refining Corp., Dallas, 1955-66; v.p. crude oil supply and transp. dept., 1966-76; chmn. bd., pres. Dorchester Petroleum Co., 1977—; exec. v.p. Clark Maritime Inc.; dir. Southcap Pipe Line Co., Chgo. Pipeline Co., Clark Pipeline Co., Gravcap, Inc. Active precinct worker Democratic party 1959—. Served with AUS, 1940-45. Decorated Combat Infantryman's badge. Mem. Am. Inst. Mining Engrs. Clubs: Petroleum of Dallas, Dallas Athletic; Austin (Tex.). Home: 11084 Erhard Dr Dallas TX 75228 Office: 1906 Southland Center Dallas TX 75201

WILLIS, HAROLD W., ednl. adminstr.; b. Kountze, Tex., Mar. 18, 1918; s. O.E. and Georgia (Wooley) W.; B.B.A. in Accounting, Lamar U., Beaumont, Tex., 1955; M.Ed. in Ednl. Adminstrn., Stephen F. Austin U., Nacogdoches, Tex., 1965; married; children—Wayne, Dale, Kenneth. Tchr., Kountze (Tex.) Ind. Sch. Dist., 1957-65, jr. high sch. prin., 1965-67, bus. mgr., 1967—. Mem. Tex. Edn. Assn., Tex. State Tchrs. Assn., Tex. State Assn. Adminstrs., Tex. Assn. Sch. Bus. Ofcls. Home: Route 1 Box 297 Kountze TX 77625 Office: PO Box 460 Kountze TX 77625

WILLIS, ISAAC, dermatologist; b. Albany, Ga., July 13, 1940; s. R. L. and Susie (Miller) W.; B.S., Morehouse Coll., 1961; M.D., Howard U., 1965; m. Alliene Horne, June 12, 1965; children—Isaac Willis, Alliric Willis. Intern, Phila. Gen. Hosp., 1965-66; resident in dermatology Howard U., 1966-67, U. Pa., 1967-69; asso. in dermatology U. Pa. Sch. Medicine, 1969-70; asst. attending physician Phila. Gen. Hosp., 1969-70; research asso., clin. instr. U. Calif. Sch. Medicine, San Francisco, 1970-72; asst. prof. dermatolgoy Johns Hopkins U. Sch. Medicine, 1972-73; asst. prof. dermatology Howard U. Coll. Medicine, 1972-75; asst. prof. dermatology Emory U. Sch. Medicine, 1973-75; chief dermatology VA Hosp., Atlanta, 1973—; asso. prof. dermatology Emory U. Sch. Medicine, 1975—. Chmn. bd. med. dirs. Atlanta Lupus Erythematosus Found. Mem. Soc. Investigative Dermatology, Am. Soc. Photobiology, Am. Acad. Dermatology, Nat. Med. Assn., AMA, Am. Fedn. Clin. Research, Internat. Soc. Tropical Dermatology, So. Med. Assn., Atlanta Dermatol. Assn., Am. Dermatol. Assn., Phi Beta Kappa. Contbr. articles to med. jours.; contbr. chpts. to textbooks. Home: 1141 Regency Rd NW Atlanta GA 30327 Office: 3312 Piedmont Rd NE Suite 275 Atlanta GA 30305

WILLIS, JANE MARLOW, newspaper editor; b. Brandenburg, Ky., Mar. 8, 1942; d. James Mercer and Thelma (Marlow) Willis; B.A., So. Meth. U., 1964; postgrad. (Mark Ethridge fellow), U. N.C., 1966; B.S. in Fire Prevention, Eastern Ky. U., 1979. Mem. staff Meade County Messenger, Brandenburg, 1964—, editor, 1966—, now also pub. Former den mother local Cub Scouts; mem. drive com. Patton Museum Fund, 1965; mem. local com. Ky. Bicentennial, 1973; patron Pioneer Playhouse, Danville, Ky., 1972; mem. Brandenburg Vol. Fire Dept., 1975; com. chmn. Brandenburg Unity Festival, 1975-76; patron Actors Theatre Louisville Les Boutiques de Noel, 1976; chmn. Fireman's Ball, 1977. Named Ky. col. Mem. Ky., Western Ky. (pres. 1971) press assns., Nat. Newspaper Assn., Internat. Soc. Fire Service Instrs., Mensa, Women of Moose, Sigma Delta Chi. Democrat. Methodist. Editor: Since April Third, 1974; Happy Holidays Cookbook, 1975; Summertime and the Cookin' is Easy, 1977. Home: 321 Main St Brandenburg KY 40108 Office: Box 612 Brandenburg KY 40108

WILLIS, LYNWOOD GRAYSON, architect; b. Savannah, Ga., Sept. 17, 1931; s. Charles Wesley and Valeria (Grayson) W.; B.S., Ga. Inst. Tech., 1956; B.Arch., 1957; m. Jane Thompson, July 7, 1954; children—Ellen Kathleen, Linda Jane, Julia Ann, Ashley Grayson. Partner, Willis & Veenstra, Atlanta, Washington, and Jacksonville,

Fla., 1960—, Willis & Veenstra Investment Co., Atlanta, Jacksonville, 1968; v.p. Crowder, Hammack, Nicolaides & Willis, Inc., Architects and Engrs., Jacksonville, Atlanta, Tampa and Kaiserslautern, Germany, 1974; owner apt. complexes, Jacksonville, Orlando. Mem. Com. of 100, Jacksonville, 1965-71. Mem. Democratic Club, Washington. Founder, Jacksonville Episcopal High Sch., 1966-67. Served with USAF, 1950-51. Recipient Cleve. Found. Structural Design award, 1957, Distinguished Service award Jacksonville Jr. C. of C., 1966. Mem. AIA (Merit award 1971), Alpha Tau Omega. Democrat. Clubs: University, Deerwood, Ponte Vedre, River (Jacksonville); Chatham (Savannah). Archtl. works include: Fla. Jr. Coll., 1971, U.S. Post Office, 1971, Bapt. Towers, 1971, Jacksonville Gen. Hosp., 1971, Pablo Towers, 1972, 1st Bapt. Ch., 1973 (honor award for design 1976), Trinity Bapt. Elementary and High sch., 1972, Intermedic Gen. Hosp., 1973, Piney Island Devel., 1973, Vocat. Tech. Sch., 1975 (all Jacksonville); U.S. Post Office and Fed. Office Bldg., Waycross, Ga., 1971; Caritas Apts., 1975, Stevens Creek Town Houses, 1975 (both Augusta); Camp Riley for handicapped children, Indpls., 1975; Heidelberg (W.Ger.) Dental Clinic, 1976; Bunnell (Fla.) Hosp., 1977; Child Care Centers, Pirmasens and Mannheim (W. Ger.), 1979, N. Am. Shrine Hdqrs. Bldg., Tampa, 1979. Home: 10411 Deerwood Club Rd Jacksonville FL 32216 Office: 415 E Monroe St Jacksonville FL 32202 also 81 Poplar St Atlanta GA 30303 also 1111 C St SE Washington DC 20003

WILLIS, MARTHA ROGERS, psychologist; b. Startex, S.C., Mar. 7, 1946; d. Rodeheaver Homer and Pauline (Cook) Rogers; B.S. (Univ. scholar), Furman U., 1968, M.A., 1969; Ph.D., U. S.C., 1976; m. William David Willis, Jr., Nov. 24, 1967. Tchr. public schs. in S.C. and Va., 1967-73; teaching asst. U. S.C., 1973-75; asso. dir. social services Warren Meml. Hosp., Front Royal, Va., 1975-78; adj. asso. prof. psychology Lord Fairfax Community Coll., Middletown, Va., 1976-79; asst. prof. psychology, dir. secondary edn. Shenandoah Coll. and Conservatory Music, Winchester, Va., 1976—; leader workshops, cons. in field. Mem. Soc. Hosp. Social Work Dirs., Va. Social Sci. Assn., Delta Kappa Gamma. Home: 728 Woodland Ave Winchester VA 22601 Office: Shenandoah Coll and Conservatory Music Winchester VA 22601

WILLIS, ROBERT BERRY, research co. adminstr.; b. Montgomery, Ala., July 11, 1931; s. Berry and Marie Willis; B.S. in Math., Fla. State U., 1953; M.S. in Systems Mgmt., Fla. Inst. Tech., 1970; m. Idella M. Parker, Aug. 29, 1953; 1 dau., Dianne Marie Willis Caylor. Flight test engr. Convair Ft. Worth, 1956-58, Lockheed Aircraft, Marietta, Ga., 1959-61; test engr. Pratt & Whittney Aircraft, West Palm Beach, Fla., 1961; mgr. electronic data reduction RCA, Patrick AFB, Fla., 1961-70; criminal justice coordinator Brevard County (Fla.), 1970-76; ct. planner Jud. Council, Atlanta, 1976-77; adminstr. Dawson Research Corp., Orlando, Fla., 1978-80, v.p., 1980—. Sec., Brevard County (Fla.) Criminal Justice Coordinating Com., 1972-76. Served with USAF, 1953-56. Republican. Baptist. Office: PO Box 8272 Orlando FL 32856

WILLIS, ROBERT ERWIN, financial exec.; b. Atlanta, Jan. 2, 1942; s. William Leslie and Margaret Louise (Nail) W.; B.S., So. Ill. U., Edwardsville, 1968; m. Sherrin Newsome, Oct. 26, 1973; children—Robert Erwin II, William Eugene, Valerie Lorene. Supr. mail service So. Ill. U., 1962-66; accountant Prince Gardner Co., St. Louis, 1966-68; controller Northwestern Constrn. Co., Chamblee, Ga., 1968-69; sr. accountant Touche Ross & Co., Charlotte, N.C., 1969-72; controller Savannah Foods & Industries (Ga.), 1972-78; corporate group controller Rollins, Inc., Atlanta, 1978—. C.P.A., Ga., N.C. Mem. Nat. Assn. Accountants (pres. chpt. 1975—), Am. Inst. C.P.A.'s, Am. Accounting Assn. Home: 2761 Breckenridge Ct Atlanta GA 30345 Office: 2170 Piedmont Rd Atlanta GA 30324

WILLIS, WARREN WAITE, clergyman, camp dir.; b. Milw., Nov. 22, 1911; s. Philip Bliss and Ethel Blanche (Waite) W.; B.A., Fla. So. Coll., 1938, D.D., 1980; B.D., Emory U., 1943, M.Div., 1970; m. Georgie Evelyn Loudy, May 29, 1940; children—Frances Jane (Mrs. Denny Ragsdale), Grace Eileen (Mrs. Richard Wills), Warren Waite, Jr., Mary Diane, Walter Towner (dec.). Ordained to ministry Methodist Ch., 1943; pastor Dunedin (Fla.) Methodist Ch., 1943-45; dir. Fla. Conf. Youth and Camp, United Methodist Ch., Lakeland, Fla., 1945-67, dir. Fla. Conf. Camps, 1968—. Bd. dirs. Lakeland YMCA, 1975—. Bd. trustees Fla. So. Coll., 1961-70. Mem. Am. Camping Assn. (pres. Fla. sect. 1951, 65). Mason, Rotarian. Home: 515 E Beacon Rd Lakeland FL 33803 Office: 1140 E McDonald St Box 3767 Lakeland FL 33801

WILLIS, WILLIAM EARL, hosp. adminstr.; b. Chase City, Va.; B.S., Va. Commonwealth U., 1951; postgrad. U. Richmond, 1953-54, Sch. Hosp. Adminstrn., Med. Coll. Va., 1955-56; m. Mary Jane Bowers, Mar. 1959; children—Elizabeth Ann, Ros Richardson. With bur. hosps. and nursing homes Va. Health Dept., 1954-55; asst. adminstr. Roanoke Meml. Hosp., 1957-60; adminstr. Southside Community Hosp., Farmville, Va., 1960-63; adminstr. Gen. Hosp. Virginia Beach (Va.), 1963—, v.p., 1969—, dir., 1974—. Mem. Mayor's Com. Jobs for Vets. Task Force; bd. dirs. Virginia Beach Beautification Com.; past chmn. bd. deacons, elder First Presbyterian Ch., Virginia Beach; v.p. Central YMCA, 1978; bd. dirs. Neptune Festival, pres., 1975. Fellow Am. Coll. Hosp. Adminstrs.; mem. Va. Hosp. Assn. (dir. 1973-79, past pres.), Tidewater Hosp. Council (past pres.), Md.-Va.-D.C. Hosp. Assn. (dir., pres.-elect), Med. Coll. Va. Alumni Assn. (pres. Tidewater chpt. 1977), Am. Public Health Assn., Va. Public Health Assn., Royal Soc. Promotion Health, Am. Mgmt. Assn., Am. Acad. Health Adminstrs., Virginia Beach C. of C. (dir., mem. exec. com., past pres.). Club: Princess Anne Country. Office: Gen Hosp of Virginia Beach 1060 First Colonial Rd Virginia Beach VA 23454

WILLIS, WILLIAM PASCAL, state ofcl.; b. Anadarko, Okla., Oct. 17, 1910; s. Robert Garnet and Lulu (Wyatt) W.; B.A., E. Central State Coll., Ada, Okla., 1935; M.A., Tulsa U., 1948; m. Zelma M. Bynum, Sept. 19, 1935; children—Diane, Joyce (Mrs. Gerlad Browder), Billie Jean (Mrs. Alvon Crosslin), Zelma (Mrs. David Bailey), Herbert, William Pascal, Doak. Prin. Spaulding (Okla.) High Sch., 1935-36, Mill Creek High Sch., 1936-37; mayor Locust Grove, 1937-44; mem. Okla. Ho. of Reps., 1958—, speaker, 1973-74, 75—. Owner, operator Willis Merc., Tahlequah, 1937-56. Served with AUS, 1944. Recipient Tahlequah Outstanding Citizen award Tahlequah Star Citizen, 1965. Mem. Cherokee Hist. Soc. (Bd. dirs.), C. of C. Mason (Shriner), Kiwanian. Address: 1 Valley St Tahlequah OK 74464

WILLIS, WILLIE JAMES, counselor; b. Birmingham, Ala.; s. Oliver and Annie Bell (Amerson) W.; A.B., Rust Coll., Miss., 1965; M.S., Kans. State Tchrs. Coll., 1970; m. Rose Mae Purdy, July 22, 1965; children—Willie James, Timothy Wayne, Gregory Antonio, Sherita Devonne, Frederick. Tchr., Rosenwald High Sch., Osceola, Ark., 1965-69; instr. Rust Coll., 1970-73; counselor Blytheville AFB, Ark., 1973-76, 78—, RAF Mildenhall AFB, Eng., 1976-78; mem. part-time faculty U. Nebr. Omaha Overseas Program, Eng., 1977-78. Served with USAF, 1961-62. Mem. Am. Personnel and Guidance Assn., Rust Coll. Alumni Assn. (regional v.p. 1979), Phi Beta Sigma. Address: 511 E Calhoun St Luxora AR 72358

WILLISTON, CHRISTOPHER LINCOLN, IV, assn. exec.; b. St. Louis, Jan. 12, 1921; s. Christopher Lincoln, III, and Berenice Marie (Wirfs) W.; B.S., U. Ill., 1942; m. Jane Ann Leucht, July 5, 1947; children—Christine Williston Rhodes, Jayne Ann Williston Miller, Christopher Lincoln, V. Sports writer Evening Courier, Champaign and Urbana, Ill., 1942; staff writer News-Gazette, Champaign/Urbana, 1946-47; mgr. office public info. U. Ill., Chgo. Profl. Colls., 1947-54; exec. dir. Tex. Med. Assn., Austin, 1954—; mem. Seton Med. Center, 1956, chmn. bd. advs., 1966-68. Served with USAAF, 1942-46. Named Boss of Yr., Tower Lights chpt. Am. Bus. Women's Assn., 1975; recipient Sigma Delta Chi award, 1942. Mem. Tex. Soc. Assn. Execs. (pres. 1976-77), Am. Soc. Assn. Execs. (dir. 1977—), Am. Assn. Med. Soc. Execs. (pres. 1963-64), AMA, Public Relations Soc. Am. (pres. Central Tex. chpt. 1958), Tex. Technol. U. Dads Assn. (pres. 1970-71). Roman Catholic. Club: Rotary (chpt. pres. 1960-61) (Austin). Contbr. articles on public relations and assn. mgmt. to profl. jours. Office: 1801 N Lamar Blvd Austin TX 78701

WILLISTON, FREDERICK FRANCIS, mfg. co. exec.; b. Kingwood, W.Va., Apr. 24, 1945; s. John Dee and Evelyn Elizabeth (Borgman) W.; B.S., W.Va. U., 1968; postgrad. Websters Coll., 1979—; m. Carol Ann Greaser, Aug. 31, 1968; children—Matthew, Samuel; 1 adopted dau., Theresa. Salesman, Mut. of Omaha, Kingwood, 1973-74; sales mgr. Ocean One Sales Inc., Myrtle Beach, S.C., 1976-77; salesman Fry-Garris & Assos., real estate, Myrtle Beach, 1978-79; sr. account mgr. AVX Ceramics, Myrtle Beach, 1978—. Served with USAF, 1968-73. Decorated D.F.C. with 2 oak leaf clusters, Air medal (26), others. Served to maj. USAFR, 1973—. Mem. Mensa, Air Force Assn., Res. Officers Assn., VFW, Grand Strand Amateur Radio Club. Republican. Roman Catholic. Home: 5047 Watergate Dr Myrtle Beach SC 29577 Office: PO Box 867 Myrtle Beach SC 29577

WILLNER, EUGENE BURTON, liquors exec.; b. Chgo., July 27, 1934; s. Fred and Mae (Goodhartz) W.; B.A., Northwestern U., 1956; m. Karen Nell Kaye, Feb. 22, 1962; children—Tracy Fran, Kelly Kaye. Pres., World Wide Fisheries Inc., Chgo., 1956-60; merchandiser Edison Bros. Stores Inc., St. Louis, 1960-66; v.p. Mo. Supreme Life Ins. Co., St. Louis, 1966-67; exec. v.p. Exec. Agys., Inc., St. Louis, 1966-67; pres. Bluff Creek Industries, Inc., Ocean Springs, Miss., 1967-69, Purse String Stores, Inc., Miami, Fla., 1968-69, World Wide Fisheries, Inc., Miami, Fla., 1969-73, Universal Fisheries, Inc., Miami, 1974-76, Ronwill Seafoods, Inc., 1979—; chmn. bd. Astral Liquors, Inc., Foxy Laidy Lounges, Prime Universal Seafood Corp., Miami, also Key West, Fla., Caracas, Venezuela, San Juan del Sur, Nicaragua, Quito, Ecuador. dir. Mo. Supreme Life Ins. Co., Lite Am. Corp. Clubs: Kingsbay Country, Jockey, Crickett. Home: 8400 SW 146th St Miami FL 33158 Office: 6507 SW 40th St Miami FL 33155 also PO Box 570326 Miami FL 33157

WILSON, ABNER WORLEY, oil field equipment co. exec.; b. Madisonville, Tex., Dec. 5, 1932; s. Lee Roy and Cecil (Forehand) W.; B.S., U. Tex., 1956; m. Joy Frances Bendily, Aug. 24, 1963; children—Derek Roy, Cynthia Ann. Sales rep. Swaco, New Orleans and Lafayette, La., 1959-62, div. sales mgr., 1962-67; div. mgr. Lower Coast Corp., Harvey, La., 1967-69; pres. Parker Internat. Corp., Harvey, 1969—, also dir. Served with U.S. Army, 1956-58. Mem. AIME. Democrat. Methodist. Clubs: Timberlane Country, Petroleum (New Orleans). Home: 417 Fairfield Ave Gretna LA 70053 Office: Parker Internat Corp 2612 4th St Harvey LA 70058

WILSON, ADRIENNE DENISE, auditor; b. Houston, Aug. 5, 1952; d. London and Jewell (Thigpen) W.; B.A. in Bus. Adminstrn., Fisk U., 1974; postgrad. Tex. So. U., 1974—. Auditor I, audit div. Tex. Dept. Human Resources, Houston, 1975-77, auditor II, 1977-79, auditor III, 1979—. Mem. Nat. Assn. Black Accts. Democrat. Methodist. Office: Audit Div Tex Dept Human Resources 2472 Bolsover Room 460 Houston TX 77005

WILSON, ARTHUR L., minister; b. Elmore County, Ala., Aug. 28, 1928; s. John Wesley and Fannie Mae (Miles) W.; student Ala. State U., 1973; D.D., Free Pentecostal Sch. Religion, 1973, Tuskegee Inst.; m. Nancy Mae Brown, Aug. 8, 1948; children—Vandy, Linda Diane, Carolyn Ann (Mrs. Donald J. Williams Sr.), Barbara Nell (Mrs. James Robert Frazier Jr.), Arthurine, Michael Larvell. Ordained to ministry African Methodist Episcopal Zion Ch., 1954; pastor Harris chapel African Meth. Episcopal Zion Ch., Elmore, Ala., Soloman chapel, Tuskegee, Ala., 1954, Oak Street Ch., Montgomery, Ala., 1957, Thompson chapel, Opelika, Ala., 1964, Shiloh Ch., Opelika, Ala., 1964—. Mem. Montgomery (Ala.) Improvement Assn., 1964—. Pres. Lee County chpt. Ala. Dem. Conf., 1971—, Lee County Voter's League, 1964—. Mem. Opelika (Ala.) City Adv. Bd. Edn., 1972—. Served with USNR, 1944. Trustee Clinton Coll., 1972—. Mem. NAACP, Lee County Ministers Alliance (treas. 1974—). Home and office: 605 Torbert Blvd Opelika AL 36801

WILSON, BILLY JOE, accountant; b. Cleveland, Tenn., Nov. 25, 1933; s. William L. and Nell D. (Davis) W.; A.A. in Bus., Tenn. Wesleyan Coll., 1954; B.B.A. in Accounting, Ga. State U., 1968; LL.B., John Marshall U., 1972. With tax dept. Touche, Ross, Bailey & Smart, C.P.A.'s, Atlanta, 1967-68; accounting supr. Lockheed-Ga. Co., Marietta, 1968-80; pvt. practice accounting, Tucker, Ga., 1972—. Treas., pres. Laurel Ridge PTA. Served in USMCR, 1955-58. Mem. Nat. Assn. Enrolled Agts. (nat. pres. 1977, 78, dir.), Nat. Soc. Pub. Accountants, Ga. Assn. Pub. Accountants, Sigma Delta Kappa (life), Sigma Phi Epsilon (life), Sigma Delta (pres.). Clubs: Masons, Lions (fin. sec.). Home: PO Box 33458 Decatur GA 30033 Office: 4387 Hwy 78 Loganville GA 30249

WILSON, CAROLYN BOWLING, pharmacist; b. Rockwood, Tenn., May 30, 1943; d. William Albert and Helen Elizabeth (Dossett) Bowling; B.S. in Pharmacy, U. Tenn., Memphis, 1966; m. Douglas Edward Wilson, July 3, 1965; children—Susan, Charles Edward. Owner, operator Wilson Drug Co., Rockwood, 1967—; chief pharmacist Chamberlain Meml. Hosp., Rockwood, 1968—; mem. Tenn. State Bd. Pharmacy, 1978—. Mem. Tenn. Soc. Hosp. Pharmacists, Tenn. Pharm. Assn., Nat. Assn. Retail Druggists, Bus. and Profl. Women's Club. Democrat. Baptist. Home: 219 W Rockwood St Rockwood TN 37854 Office: 241 S Chamberlain Ave Rockwood TN 37854

WILSON, CHARLES, congressman; b. Trinity, Tex., June 1, 1933; student Sam Houston State U., Huntsville, Tex., 1951-52; B.S., U.S. Naval Acad., 1956; m. Jerry Carter, 1963. Commd. ensign U.S. Navy, 1956, advanced through grades to lt.; ret., 1960; mem. Tex. Ho. of Reps., 1960-66; mem. Tex. Senate, 1966-72; mem. 93d-96th congresses from 2d Dist. Tex. Mgr. lumber yard. Democrat. Office: 1214 Longworth House Office Bldg Washington DC 20515

WILSON, CHARLES HOWE, surgeon; b. Amarillo, Tex., Jan. 31, 1919; s. George Keene and Lucile (Howe) W.; student U. Tex., 1937-40; M.D., U. Tex. Med. Sch., Galveston, 1942; m. Rosagne Walker, Jan. 1, 1943; children—Mary Evelyn (Mrs. John Cockrell), Charles Robbins. Intern, U.S. Naval Hosp., San Diego, 1943; resident surgery Wichita Falls (Tex.) Clinic, 1947-49, preceptor, 1949, 51; practice medicine specializing in surgery, Wichita Falls, 1952—; instr. anatomy U. Tex. Med. Sch., Galveston, 1949. Mem. exec. bd. Am. Cancer Soc.; bd. dirs. North Tex. Regional Planning Commn.; mem. founding bd. Tri-Region Health Systems Agy., 1976-77; chmn. TEXPAC, 1978. Diplomate Am. Bd. Surgery. Fellow A.C.S., Tex. Surg. Soc.; mem. Wichita Falls Bd. Commerce and Industry, Tex. Med. Assn. (pres. dist. 1968, bd. counselors 1972-76, v.p. 1978-79), Wichita County Med. Soc. (pres. 1975). Methodist (past chmn. bd. dirs.). Club: Kiwanis (pres. 1965). Home: 2602 Bretton Rd Wichita Falls TX 76308 Office: 1635 10th St Wichita Falls TX 76301

WILSON, CLAUDE RAYMOND, JR., lawyer; b. Dallas, Feb. 22, 1933; s. Claude Raymond and Lottie (Watts) W.; B.B.A., So. Methodist U., 1954, LL.B., 1956, LL.M., 1958; m. Barbara Jean Cowherd, Apr. 30, 1960; 1 dau., Deidra Nicole. Admitted to Tex. bar, 1956, practiced in Dallas, 1956-60, 65—; lawyer Tex. & Pacific R.R. Co., Dallas, 1958-60; sr. trial atty., chief counsel IRS, Washington, 1960-65; mem. firm Golden, Potts, Boeckman & Wilson, Dallas, 1965—. Mem. State Bar Tex., Am., Dallas (chmn. sect. taxation 1971-72, chmn. com. unauthorized practice law 1975-76) bar assns., Tex. Soc. C.P.A.'s (dir. 1973—, sec. 1978-79, exec. com. 1980—, dir. Dallas chpt. 1971-72) Delta Sigma Phi, Delta Theta Phi. Republican. Episcopalian. Mason (K.T., 32 deg., Shriner, Jester). Clubs: Chaparral, Dallas Gun, Willow Bend Hunt and Polo. Home: 4069 Hanover Dallas TX 75225 Office: 2300 Republic Bank Tower Dallas TX 75201

WILSON, DANNY RAY, broadcasting exec.; b. Brady, Tex., Apr. 1, 1943; s. Chester Ray and Aurilla Belle (Copeland) W.; B.A. in Math., Angelo State U., 1973; m. Nettie Ann Carr, July 31, 1964 (div.); 1 dau., Catherine Ann. Staff announcer KNEL Radio, Brady, 1963-64; chief engr. Sta. KTEO, San Angelo, Tex., 1964-65; chief engr. KIXY-AM-FM, San Angelo, 1965—, ops. mgr., 1967, news dir., asst. gen. mgr., 1978—; gen. mgr. stas. KIXY and KQSA, 1980—; v.p. news and engring. Solar Broadcasting Co., Inc., San Angelo, to 1978. Recipient Best Documentary award AP, 1978; Best Newscast award Tex. AP Broadcasters, 1979. Mem. San Angelo Press Club. Methodist. Office: KIXY-AM-FM 115 W 1st St City Hall Plaza San Angelo TX 76903

WILSON, DAVID ALLEN, elec. engr.; b. Pitts., July 8, 1942; s. Willard N. and Betty V. (Burns) W.; A.A.S., DeVry Tech. Inst., 1962; B.S. in Elec. Engring., SUNY, Buffalo, 1971; m. Gail K. Smith, June 25, 1968; children—Gordon Daniel, Patrick Wayne. Electro-mechanic The Boeing Co., Seattle, Great Falls, Minot, N.D., 1962-64; engring. aide Westinghouse Electric Co., Buffalo, 1966-67; self-employed as elec. engr./contractor, Bristol, Va., 1971-72; supr. Westinghouse Electric Co., Abingdon, Va., 1972; engr., tech. services engr. Westinghouse Electric Co., Abingdon, 1972—. Served with U.S. Army, 1964-66. Mem. IEEE. Republican. Methodist. Clubs: Amateur Radio, Square Dancing. Office: PO Box 869 Abingdon VA 24210

WILSON, DON ALLEN, radiologist; b. Blackwell, Okla., Dec. 22, 1942; s. Lloyd George and Frances Marie (Bradley) W.; student Ariz. State U., 1960-63; M.D., U. Okla., 1967; m. Julie Stephens, Sept. 5, 1975; children—Cinthia, Kristen, David. Intern, Portsmouth (Va.) Naval Hosp., 1967-68; resident in radiology Okla. U. Health Scis. Center, Oklahoma City, 1971-74, acad. radiologist, 1974—, asso. prof. radiology, 1979—, chief sect. diagnostic ultrasound, physician in charge computerized tomograph, body scanning Okla. Children's Meml. Hosp., 1978—. Served to lt. comdr., M.C., USN, 1967-71. Diplomate Am. Bd. Radiology. Mem. Am. Coll. Radiology, Radiol. Soc. N. Am., Am. Inst. Ultrasound in Medicine, AMA, Soc. Pediatric Radiology, Computerized Tomography Soc., Am. Soc. Echocardiography. Republican. Author monograph: Ultrasound - Applications in the Pediatric Heart and Abdomen, 1978; contbg. editor The New Physician, 1975—. Home: Route 6 Box 635 Edmond OK 73034 Office: Ultrasound Sect Okla Children's Meml Hosp PO Box 26307 Oklahoma City OK 73126

WILSON, DONLY JOYCE, educator; b. Jefferson City, Mo., Aug. 26, 1939; d. Donald Raymond and Agnes Lorene (Hager) W.; B.S.E., Ark. State U., 1961, M.S., 1969. Tchr. bus. edn. Weiner (Ark.) Sch. Dist., 1961-71; instr. Central Coll., Texarkana, Tex., 1971-72; jr. acct. Eslinger Firm, Texarkana, 1972; asst. prof. bus. Texarkana Community Coll. 1973—; co-owner Clothes Shack, Inc., Texarkana, Clothes Shack of Conway, Inc. (Ark.). Baptist. Home: Rt 4 Box 305 D 8 Texarkana AR 75502 Office: 2500 N Robinson Rd Texarkana AR 75501

WILSON, DULCIE KEEPERS, artist; b. Wetmore, Kans., Oct. 2, 1902; d. Stephen Ellsworth and Laura Belle (Randall) Keepers; student Denver U., Farsons Sch. Art; m. Harry Cotter, 1924; 1 son, Bill; m. 2d, James Virgel Wilson, Mar. 6, 1957; stepchildren—Jim, Noel, Linda, Thomas, Wilma. Tchr. pub. schs., Colo., 1921-24; milliner A.T. Lewis, Denver, 1924; designer Dulcie Shop, Denver, 1932; instr. pvt. art classes, Denver; with Remington Arms, Denver; instr. Shelton Coll., Cape May, N.J., 1963-65; co-founder Clearwater (Fla.) Christian Coll., 1965-71; painter stillife, portraits, landscapes, Ripley, Okla., 1971—; exhibited with Am. Painters in Paris, 1976. Mem. Ripley C. of C., Denver Art Club (charter mem.; pres. 1948-50), Stillwater Art Guild, Internat. Soc. Artists. Author booklet: Art in the Home, 1972; prepared Christian program shows throughout U.S., 1964. Home and office: Route 1 Ripley OK 74062

WILSON, DURWARD EARL, steel co. exec.; b. Macon, Ga., Sept. 23, 1925; s. Sam and Eunice (Scoggins) W., B.S. in Indsl. Engring., Ga. Inst. Tech., 1950; m. Sara Ann Saunders, Dec. 20, 1946; children—Beth, Jan, Mark, John. Indsl. engr. E.I. duPont Co., Chattanooga, 1950-54, div. prodn. asst., Wilmington, Del., 1954-56; sr. mgmt. cons. John M. Avent & Assn., Atlanta, 1956-58; planning mgr. Tex. Steel Co., Ft. Worth, 1958-59, asst. v.p., 1959-66, v.p., 1966-72, exec. v.p., 1972-75, pres., 1975—; pres., chmn. bd. Tex. Steel Co. Can., Ltd., St. Stephen, N.B.; pres., dir. L & M Mfg. Co., Steel Casting Machine Co., S.W. Steel Casting Co., Bus. Communications, Inc.; dir. Liberty Mfg. Co. Tex., Armstrong Oil & Land Co. Served with USAAF, 1943-46. Mem. Steel Founders' Soc. Am. (pres., dir.), Cast Metals Fedn. (bd. dirs., chmn. environ. com., Tex. chmn. governmental affairs), Nat. Foundry Assn. (dir.), Am. Foundrymen's Soc., Concrete Reinforcing Steel Inst., Steel Bar Mill Assn., Am. Iron and Steel Engrs. Republican. Episcopalian. Clubs: Shady Oaks Country, Ridglea Country, Century II, Fort Worth. Home: 1 Bounty Rd W Fort Worth TX 76132 Office: 3901 Hemphill St Fort Worth TX 76110

WILSON, E. C., JR., machinery co. exec.; b. Richlands, Va., Feb. 6, 1940; s. E. C. and Buelah M. (Newberry) W.; Asso. Nat. Bus. Coll., Roanoke, Va., 1964; m. Hazel Loretta Billings, May 5, 1962; children—Michael Anthony, Matthew Scott. Owner, E.C. Wilson & Co., C.P.A.'s, Richland, 1971-73; treas. Pyott-Boone, Inc., Tazewell, Va., 1973-74; exec. v.p. Pyott-Boone Machinery Corp., Saltville, Va., 1974-75; pres. Wil-Jon Machinery Corp., Saltville, 1975—; chmn. bd. Miners & Mfrs. Ins. Co.; dir. Denson Corp. Mem. Sequoyah council Boy Scouts Am., 1976; treas. Tazewell County Republican Party, 1972; mem. town council, Cedar Bluff, Va., 1970; bd. visitors Emory (Va.) and Henry Coll., 1977; mem. Smyth County Planning Commn., 1976. Served with AUS, 1957-60. C.P.A., Va. Mem. Am. Inst. C.P.A.'s, Va. Soc. C.P.A.'s. Presbyterian. Clubs: Rotary, Shriners. Address: Box 1321 Richlands VA 24641

WILSON, EDWIN JACKSON (BUD), lawyer; b. Birmingham, Ala., June 28, 1947; s. Edwin Jackson and Catherine (Samuel) W.; student Kennesaw Coll., 1970-72; A.B.J. cum laude, U. Ga., 1974, J.D., 1977. Law intern Presdl. Clemency Bd., The White House, Washington, summer 1975; admitted to Ga. bar, 1977; individual practice law, Marietta, Ga., 1977-79; asst. dist. atty. Augusta Jud. Circuit Dist. Atty.'s Office, Augusta, Ga., 1979—; bd. dirs., counsel Apt. Renters Assn., Inc. County coordinator Smith Foster Congl. campaign, 1978; leader Explorer Scouts. Served to capt. inf. U.S. Army, 1966-70. Decorated Bronze Star. Mem. Am. Bar Assn., Nat. Dist. Attys. Assn., State Bar Ga., Central Savannah River Area Law Enforcement Assn., Phi Alpha Delta, Digamma Kappa. Democrat. Methodist. Club: Lions. Home: 3515 Edgeworth Dr Hephzibah GA 30815 Office: Suite 500 The 500 Bldg Augusta GA 30902

WILSON, FRANK C., mgmt. cons.; b. Hogansville, Ga., June 8, 1928; s. Homer B. and Louise V. Wilson; B.S., Auburn U., 1949; M.S. in Indsl. Engring., Ga. Inst. Tech., 1961; postgrad. N.Y. U.; m. Anne Richardson Jones, June 29, 1951; children—Lynn G., Frank C. In various bus. mgmt. positions in industry; pres. Internat. Mgmt., Gainesville, Ga., 1963—; mem. faculty Piedmont Coll., Ga. Inst. Tech. Republican candidate for chmn. Hall County (Ga.) Commn., 1968. Served to 1st lt. C.E., U.S. Army, 1945-46, 51-53. Registered profl. engr.; registered land surveyor. Mem. Nat. Assn. Profl. Engrs., Am. Inst. Indsl. Engrs., Am. Assn. Cost Engrs., Am. Prodn. and Inventory Control Soc., Assn. Mgmt. Consultants. Presbyterian. Author: Industrial Cost Controls; Short-Term Financial Management, 1975; Production Planning and Inventory Control Handbook, 1980; contbr. articles to profl. publs. Office: 711 Green St # 120 So Bell Bldg Gainesville GA 30501

WILSON, FRANK LYNDALL, surgeon; b. Atlanta, Oct. 29, 1926; s. Frank L. and Elizabeth Smith (Peeples) W.; student U. N.C., 1945-46; B.S., Emory U., 1948, M.D., 1952; m. Eva Jeanette Johnson, Dec. 19, 1951; children—Frank Lyndall III, Patricia Lee. Intern in surgery Western Res. Hosp., Cleve., 1952-53; asst. resident, resident Grady Meml. Hosp., Atlanta, 1955-59; practice medicine specializing in surgery, Atlanta, 1959—; mem. staff Piedmont Hosp., Atlanta, chief outpatient surgery, 1974—; mem. staff Crawford W. Long Hosp., Atlanta; asso. in surgery Emory U., Atlanta, 1959—. Trustee Lovett Sch., Atlanta, 1971—. Served with USNR, 1944-46, as lt. M.C. 1953-55. Diplomate Am. Bd. Surgery Fellow A.C.S. (pres. Ga. chpt. 1976—); mem. AMA, Med. Assn. Atlanta (trustee chmn. bd., pres. elect 1979), Med. Assn. Ga. (del.), A.C.S. (pres. 1976-78), Ga. Surg. Soc. Presbyterian. Club: Piedmont Driving. Home: 3300 Rockingham Dr NW Atlanta GA 30327 Office: 35 Collier Rd NW Atlanta GA 30309

WILSON, FRANK WILEY, judge; b. Knoxville, Tenn., June 21, 1917; s. Frank Caldwell and Mary E. (Wiley) W.; A.B., U. Tenn., 1939, LL.B., 1941; m. Helen E. Warwick, Apr. 6, 1942; children—Frank Carl, William Randall. Admitted to Tenn. bar, 1941, since practiced in Oak Ridge; county atty., Anderson County, Tenn., 1948-50; city atty., Norris, Tenn., 1950-61, U.S. dist. judge Eastern dist. Tenn. So. Div., Chattanooga, 1961—, chief judge, 1970—. Vice pres., dir. Bank of Oak Ridge, 1952-63. Pres. Community Chest; mem. Oak Ridge Bd. Edn. Trustee Siskin Meml. Found. Served with USAAF, 1941-46; MTO. Mem. C. of C. (pres.), Am. Legion (condr.), Order of Coif, Phi Delta Phi, Phi Kappa Phi. Rotarian (past pres.). Home: Stratford Ln Burnham Woods Signal Mountain TN 37377 Office: US Dist Court Chattanooga TN 37402

WILSON, GEORGE RAYMOND, JR., educator; b. Shawnee, Okla., Oct. 22, 1927; s. George Raymond and Blodwen Paulus (Jones) W.; B.M.E., Okla. Bapt. U., 1952; M.R.E., Southwestern Bapt. Theol. Sem., 1954, D.R.E. with honors, 1957; m. Elizabeth Dell Schreiber, June 5, 1948; children—Sarah Elizabeth, Pamela Denise, George Raymond, James Dale. Prof. religious edn. Hong Kong Bapt. Theol. Sem., 1958-72, acting pres., 1965-66, dean of studies, pres., 1979—; acting v.p., dean studies Hong Kong Bapt. Coll., 1958-59, 63-64, dean academic affairs, 1971-72; vis. prof. Midwestern Bapt. Theol. Sem., 1967-68; prof. religious edn. Okla. Bapt. U., 1968-69; vis. prof. Southeastern Theol. Sem., 1972-73; prof. religious edn. Southwestern Bapt. Theol. Sem., Ft. Worth, 1973—. Served with USAF, 1946-47. Named an Outstanding Educator Am., 1975. Mem. Assn. Profs. and Researchers in Religious Edn., So., Southwestern Bapt. religious edn. assns. Democrat. Baptist. Author: Teaching Guide: The Purpose and Plan of Baptist Brotherhood, 1979; contbr. How to Improve Bible Teaching and Learning in Sunday School, 1977.

WILSON, GINNY CHARLOTTE, educator; b. Luverne, Ala., Jan. 26, 1951; d. Charlie and Florelle (Buck) W.; B.S., Troy (Ala.) State U., 1972; M.Ed., Auburn U., Montgomery, Ala., 1976. Elem. sch. tchr. Crenshaw County (Ala.) Bd. Edn., 1972-79; student counselor Highland Home (Ala.) Sch., 1976—, neuropsychiat. unit Farview Med. Center, Montgomery, 1978—; vol. counselor Cadet Center, Montgomery, 1979; elementary sch. tchr. Highland Home Sch., also student counselor div. continuing edn. Auburn U., Montgomery, 1979--. Lic. psychometrist, tchr., Ala. Mem. NEA, Am. Personnel and Guidance Assn., Coll. Student Personnel Assn., Ala. Edn. Assn., Ala. Personnel and Guidance Assn., Crenshaw County Edn. Assn. Democrat. Mem. Ch. of Christ. Home: Route 1 Highland Home AL 36041 Office: Highland Home Sch Highland Home AL 36041

WILSON, GREGORY BRUCE, educator; b. Columbus, Ohio, Oct. 15, 1948; s. Bruce Norman and Miriam Joyce (Allen) W.; B.A. in zoology, UCLA, 1971, Ph.D. in Biology, 1974. Research asst. dept. biology UCLA, 1972, 73-74, Nat. Cystic Fibrosis Research Found. research fellow, postdoctoral scholar, 1974, research asst. dept. microbiology and immunology, sch. medicine, 1972-73; Nat. Cystic Fibrosis Research Found. research fellow, postdoctoral scholar sect. immunology, dept. medicine U. Calif., San Francisco, 1974-75; asso. dept. basic and clin. immunology and microbiology, colls. medicine and dental medicine Med. U. S.C., Charleston, 1975-76, asst. prof., 1976-79, asso. prof., 1979—, mem. univ. coms.; med. adv. bd. Nat. Found. March of Dimes; chmn. med. adv. bd., bd. dirs. Cystic Fibrosis Found.; exec. bd. S.C. Council Ind. Health Orgns.; invited speaker, lectr., vis. scientist, panel participant and chmn. profl. confs., seminars, univs., lay orgns. U.S., Can., No. Ireland, Eng., 1978-79. Basil O'Connor grant awardee, Nat. Found. March of Dimes, 1976-79. Mem. AAAS, Soc. Exptl. Biology and Medicine, Am. Fedn. Clin. Research, Reticuloendothelial Soc., N.Y. Acad. Scis., Sigma Xi. Contbr. articles to profl. publs. Home: 2706 Cameron Blvd Isle of Palms SC 29451 Office: 171 Ashley Ave Charleston SC 29403

WILSON, HAROLD SANFORD, ins. brokerage co. exec.; b. Calhoun Falls, S.C., Mar. 1, 1920; s. Benjamin Clyde and Lila Irene (Bell) W.; B.Elec. Engring., Clemson A. and M. Coll., 1941; postgrad. Ga. Inst. Tech., 1947-48; m. Edith Vane Lloyd, Oct. 28, 1950; children—Frances Caroline, Sanford Lloyd. Safety engr. Liberty Mut. Ins. Co., 1946-58, bus. salesman, 1958-64; adminstrv. sales mgr. Hardwick Stove Co., Cleveland, Tenn., 1964-67; regional loss control mgr. Alexander & Alexander, Inc., Chattanooga, 1967-68, mng. v.p., 1979—; v.p. Ins. Buyer's Counsel, Inc., Atlanta, 1968-72; sr. v.p. R. B. Jones Ins., Chattanooga, 1972-79. Served with U.S. Army, 1941-46. Decorated Bronze Star. Mem. Ret. Officers Assn. (sec. Chattanooga chpt.), Assn. Ind. Ins. Agts., Profl. Ins. Agts. Tenn. Republican. Episcopalian. Club: Walden (Chattanooga). Home: 4711 Robinwood Dr Chattanooga TN 37416 Office: 6100 Bldg Eastgate Center Chattanooga TN 37411

WILSON, HENRY ALLEN, mathematician, guidance counselor; b. Ruston, La., Aug. 18, 1923; s. Allen and Blanche Jessina (Washington) W.; B.S., Grambling Coll. of La., 1959; M.Ed., N.E. La. U., Monroe, 1974, Ed.S., 1978; m. Daisy Mae Stewart, Apr. 13, 1974. Supr., U.S. Naval Depot, Oakland, Calif., 1950-55; tchr. math. New Orleans Public Sch. System, 1959-70; dir. Transylvania Math. Labs. (La.), 1970—; community counselor, Lake Providence, La.; owner, operator Wilson Ins. Agy.; mem. com. for upgrading math. curriculum La. Bd. Edn.; guidance counselor N.E. La. Student Assistance Counselor. Past mem. Career Edn. Council of La.; sec. Voters Amalgamation, Tallulah, La., 1970-71. Served with AUS, 1943-46. Decorated Bronze Star; Math. Research grantee N.E. La. U., 1970. Mem. NEA, La. Assn. Educators, East Carroll Assn. Educators, Nat. Council Tchrs. Math., Am. Personnel and Guidance Assn., La. Guidance Assn., J.K. Haynes Legal Found., Inc., N. La. Health Services Assn. Democrat. Baptist. Clubs: Masons; K.T.; Grambling State U. Alumni; N.E. La. U. Alumni; Grambling Scholarship Boosters; Esquire of La. Home: 706 First St Lake Providence LA 71254 Office: 505 W Green St Tallulah LA 71282

WILSON, JAMES JOHN, constrn. and real estate exec.; b. N.Y.C., Apr. 18, 1933; s. Daniel J. and Mary (O'Donnell) W.; B.C.E., Manhattan Coll., 1955; m. Barbara A. Wilson, July 27, 1957; children—Kevin John, Elizabeth Ann, Thomas Brian, Mary Patricia, James Michael, Brian Joseph. Pres., chmn. Interstate Gen. Corp., Hato Rey, P.R., 1965—; pres., chmn. Wilson Securities Corp.; chmn. Interstate Land Devel. Co., Inc.; dir. Va. Stallion Sta. Inc.; dir. Va. Stallion Sta. Inc. Mem. New Communities Council, Urban Land Inst., Young Pres. Orgn., Manhattan Coll. Alumni Assn. Clubs: Caparra Country; N.Y. Athletic (N.Y.C.); University (Washington). Middleburg (Va.) Tennis; Banker's. Home: Dresden Farm Box 392 Middleburg VA 22117 also Buck Hill Falls PA Office: 336 Post Office Rd St Charles MD 20601 also Box 3908 San Juan PR

WILSON, JERRE WAYNE, civil engr.; b. Moulton, Ala., Oct. 26, 1940; s. George Woodrow and Kathleen (McMillan) W.; student Florence (Ala.) State Coll., 1958-59, Tex. Christian U., 1959; B.S. in Civil Engring., U. Tenn., 1963; m. Nina Jean Phillips, Aug. 29, 1964; children—Jay Weston, Holly Lynette. With TVA, Knoxville and Chattanooga, 1964—, dep. mgr. power office, Chattanooga, 1975—. TVA mgmt. co-chmn. Combined Fed. Campaign; gen. chmn. WATTEC Nat. Energy Conf., 1979; chmn. bd. dirs. TVA Employee Credit Union; elder Westminister Presbyterian Ch., Knoxville. Registered profl. engr., Tenn. Mem. ASCE (named outstanding young engr. Tenn. Valley sect. 1973), Nat. Mgmt. Assn. (profl. devel. award 1976), Knoxville Tech. Soc., U.S. Com. Large Dams, Sigma Phi Epsilon, Chi Epsilon, Tau Beta Pi. Club: Masons. Home: 5320 Inlet View Hixson TN 37343 Office: 500A Chestnut St Tower II Chattanooga TN 37301

WILSON, JOHN ROSS, lawyer; b. Memphis, Aug. 8, 1920; s. Charles Monroe and Lida Scott (Christenberry) W.; student Tex. U., Austin, 1939-41; B.B.A., So. Meth. U., 1943, LL.B., 1948; m. Anne Woodruff Talley, Feb. 7, 1944; children—Margaret Anne, Andrew Ross. Admitted to Tex. bar, 1948, Waco-McLennan County bar, 1948, Am. bar, 1958; asst. prof. Baylor U., 1948-51, asso. prof., 1951-55, prof., 1955—. Served to lt. USNR, 1943-46. Mem. Assn. Trial Attys., Am. Judicature Soc., Tex, Am. bar assns., Delta Theta Phi. Methodist. Author: Cases on Judicial Remedies, 1966; contbr. articles to law revs. Home: 9022 Oriole St Waco TX 76710 Office: Morrison Constn Hall Baylor U Waco TX 76703

WILSON, JOHN TRUESDELL, banker; b. Faubush, Ky., July 23, 1898; s. William Floyd and Doretta (Combest) W.; student Jefferson Sch. Law, 1929-31, Stonier Grad. Sch. Banking, Rutgers U., 1956-68; m. Evangeline Cooper, Apr. 28, 1917; children—John Dave (dec.), James Truesdell, Eva Elizabeth (Mrs. Ollie Caplin, Jr.). Partner Truesdell Wilson Sales & Service, Somerset, Ky., 1945-52; farmer, Ky., 1921-49; salesman Swift & Co., Somerset, 1923-24; plant mgr., engr. Wood-Mosiac Co., Monticello, Ky. and Louisville, 1931-35; with First Farmers Nat. Bank, Somerset, 1933—, pres., 1961-73, chmn., 1973—, also dir.; dealer Chevrolet Co., Somerset, 1937-39, Chrysler Co., Somerset, 1945-52; owner, pres., operator Ky. Oil Co., Somerset, 1935-52. Dir., pres. Farmers Tobacco Warehousing Corp., 1948—, Peoples State Bank, Monticello, Ky., 1934-35. Mgr. various Democratic campaigns, 1935-58. Bd. dirs. Somerset-Pulaski County Airport, 1948—, chmn., 1952—. Mem. Am., Ky. bankers assns., Ky. (dir. 1950-69), Somerset-Pulaski County (pres. 1957) chambers of commerce. Clubs: Masons, Kiwanis (pres. 1955, lt. gov. 1958). Author: History of Banking in Pulaski County, 1970. Home: Dutton Hill Somerset KY 42501 Office: One Fountain Sq Somerset KY 42501

WILSON, LLOYD LEE, housing co. exec.; b. Elkton, Md., Sept. 14, 1947; s. Clifton Laws and Betty Raye (Bare) W.; B.S., M.I.T., 1969, M.S., 1977. Bus. mgr. med. clinics Mass. Gen. Hosp., Boston, 1970-73; partner Willow Co., mgmt. cons.'s, Cambridge, Mass., 1974-77; dir. community relations Wilson Neuropsychiat. Hosp., Charlottesville, Va., 1977-78; exec. dir. Jefferson Area United Transp. Inc., Charlottesville, 1978-80, Va. Mountain Housing Inc., Blacksburg, 1980—. Bd. dirs. Interfaith Housing Corp., 1975-77, treas., 1976-77; mem. corp. Cambridge Friends Sch., 1970-77; mem. permanent bd. New Eng. Yearly Meeting of Friends, 1975-77, human resources assembly, 1978—; regional exec. com. Am. Friends Service Com., 1975-77; ednl. council MIT, 1978—. Mem. Human Resources Assn. Charlottesville. Home: Box 94 Newport VA 24128 Office: Va Mountain Housing Inc 209 N Main St Blacksburg VA 24060

WILSON, LOGAN, assn. exec.; b. Huntsville, Tex., Mar. 6, 1907; s. Samuel Calhoun and Sammie (Logan) W.; student Sam Houston Coll., 1923-26; A.M., U. Tex., 1927; postgrad. So. Meth. U., 1933-34; A.M., Harvard U., 1938, Ph.D., 1939, LL.D. (hon.), 1963; LL.D. (hon.), Tulane U., 1953, Tex. Christian U., 1955, U. R.I., 1961, Washington U., St. Louis, 1962, Oakland U., Mercer U., Del. State Coll., Franklin and Marshall Coll., 1964, U. Del., 1966, Mich. State U., Loyola U., Chgo., U. Colo., 1968, U. Md., 1970, U. Ky., 1971; Litt.D. (hon.), Northeastern U., 1963; D.H.L. (hon.), U. Pitts., 1970; L.H.D. (hon.), U. Ark., 1970; m. Myra Marshall, Dec. 27, 1932; children—Marshall, Reed Calhoun, Asst. prof. English, East Tex. State Tchrs. Coll., 1928-30, 32-36; research asso. Mass. Community Project, 1936-37; tutor in sociology Harvard U., 1937-39; asso. prof. sociology U. Md., 1939-41; prof., head dept. sociology Tulane U., 1941-43; prof., head dept. sociology U. Ky., 1943-44; dean Newcomb Coll., Tulane U., 1944-51; v.p., provost Consol. U. N.C., 1951-53; pres. U. Tex., 1953-60, chancellor, 1960-61; pres. Am. Council Edn., 1961-71, pres. emeritus, 1972—; chmn. Am. Conf. Acad. Deans, 1950-51; mem. Nat. Commn. Accrediting, 1954-55, Coll. Grants Adv. Com., 1955-56, com. Utilization Coll. Teaching Resources, Fund for Advancement Edn., 1955-56; trustee Center Advanced Study in Behavioral Scis., 1956-75, Carnegie Found. Advancement Teaching, 1958-61; adv. com. social scis. NSF, 1959-62; adv. com. study govt. and higher edn. Carnegie Found., 1960-62; mem. nat. rev. bd. East-West Center, 1964-68; mem. adv. council Marshall Scholarship Scheme, 1967-72; mem. Ednl. Testing Service, 1961-71. Recipient Disting. Service medallion Assn. Tex. Colls. and Univs., 1966; hon. citation Am. Alumni council, 1968; Centennial award U. Akron, 1970; named Disting. Alumnus, U. Tex., 1954, Sam Houston State U., 1974. Fellow AAAS; mem. So. Univ. Conf., Assn. Am. Colls. (commn. liberal edn.), State Univs. Assn. (exec. com.), Nat. Assn. State Univs., Am. Council Edn. (chmn. com. problems and policies 1960-61), Am. Sociol. Soc., Com. Econ. Devel., Philos. Soc. Tex. (hon. trustee), Inst. Internat. Edn., Council So. Univs. (pres. 1953-54), So. Assn. Colls. (commn. higher ins.), Phi Beta Kappa (senator at large 1964-72), Alpha Kappa Delta, Sigma Tau Delta, Alpha Tau Omega. Clubs: Cosmos, Univ. (Washington); Town and Gown. Author: The Academic Man, 1942; Twentieth Century Sociology (contbr. to symposium), 1945; (with W.L. Kolb) Sociological Analysis, 1949; Shaping American Higher Edn., 1972; American Academics: Then and Now, 1979; editor The State University: Emerging Patterns in American Higher Edn.; editor, contbr.: The College and the Student; contbr. numerous articles to profl. publs.

WILSON, LOWELL HENRY, real estate broker; b. Grundy County, Mo., May 24, 1932; s. Harry Wayne and Henrietta Alice (Hladky) W.; student Drake U., 1951-52; m. Joan Ann, July 27, 1959; children—Joel Lee, Jeff Allen. With Builder's Supply Co., Des Moines, 1953-56; founder, owner La Pizza Casa, Des Moines, 1957-59; founder Leisure Land Devel., Inc., Trenton, Mo., 1959—; pres., chmn. bd. Cabin Point, Inc., Mt. Holly, Va., 1975—; Fla. state mgr. Continental Western Life Ins., Des Moines, 1973—; pres. Ken Logan Buick Inc., Des Moines, 1973—; real estate broker, Mo., 1962. Mem. Jupiter-Tequesta Athletic Assn. (pres. 1976-77). Club: Masons (32 deg.), Shriners (past potentate). Home: 217 Fairway St W Tequesta FL 33458 Office: PO Box 16 Mount Holly VA 22524

WILSON, MARTHA DAWSON, energy systems cons.; b. Houston, Apr. 24, 1931; d. Terris Neal and Clara (Nixon) Dawson; B.A., So. Meth. U., 1953; tchr.'s cert. S.W. Tex. State U., 1977; 1 son, John Daniel. Statis. sec. Exxon Corp. (formerly Humble Oil & Refining Co.), Houston, 1953-62; corp. sec. Gruy Fed., Inc., Houston, 1977—. Mem. Delta Gamma. Presbyterian. Home: 10388 Hammerly Houston TX 77043 Office: 2900 Tanglewilde Suite 150 Houston TX 77063

WILSON, MARTHA ELIZABETH, counselor; b. Mweka, Zaire, May 7, 1952; d. Robert Henry and Bessie (Hancock) W.; B.A., Taylor U., 1974; M.Ed., Ga. State U., 1977, Ed.S., 1978. Intern, Metro Atlanta Youth for Christ, 1974-75, mem. staff Campus Life, 1975-76, dir. counseling ser., 1978—. Mem. Christian Assn. Psychol. Studies, Am. Personnel and Guidance Assn. Presbyterian. Home: 1135 Woodland Ave #T-2 Atlanta GA 30324 Office: 215 Church St Suite 203 Decatur GA 30030

WILSON, MARY ROSS, nurse, hosp. ofcl.; b. Burlington, N.C., Feb. 18, 1932; d. Ottis Holt and Litsey Tryphenia (Isley) Ross; grad. Macon (Ga.) Hosp. Sch. Nursing, 1953; m. Carl T. Wilson, June 17, 1951; children—Stephen Ross, David Carl. Staff nurse operating room Macon Hosp., 1953-56, head nurse operating room, 1956-70, supr., 1970; surgery dept. supr. Coliseum Park Hosp., Macon, 1970-79, dir. surgery dept., 1979—. lectr., adviser in field; adj. instr. nursing edn. Ga. Coll., 1975-76; mem. panels Operating Room Research Inst. Named employee of yr. Coliseum Park Hosp., 1972. Mem. Assn. Operating Room Nurses (profl. adviser chpt. 1973-79, pres. Middle Ga. chpt. 1978), Operating Room Buying Service, Macon Hosp. Alumnae Assn. (pres. 1967-71), Southeastern Surg. Nurse Assn., Republican. Methodist. Clubs: Riverside Golf and Country, DAR. Home: 2339 Kensington Rd Macon GA 31211 Office: Coliseum Park Hosp 350 Hospital Dr Macon GA 31201

WILSON, MICHAEL WORTH, banker; b. Charlotte, N.C., Apr. 27, 1949; s. Floyd Worth and Hilda W.; m. Elizabeth Anne Stuckey, Sept. 23, 1973; 1 son, Michael Brett. Mgmt. trainee 1st Nat. Bank of S.C., 1974-75, asst. cashier, 1976-78, asst. v.p. charge corp. support services dept., 1978—. Area commr. Boy Scouts Am. Served to 1st lt. AUS, 1972-74. Decorated Army Commendation medal. Mem. Cash Mgmt. Assn. S.C. Methodist. Club: Dutch Fork Civitan (pres.). Home: 1634 Fairhaven Dr Columbia SC 29210

WILSON, MILLARD FILLMORE, educator; b. Sanderson, Fla., Oct. 16, 1911; s. George Washington and Martha Christopher (Houston) W.; B.E., U. Fla., 1939, M.Ed., 1940; postgrad. Duke, 1941; m. Helen P. Brown, Sept. 20. Instr. Andrew Jackson Sch., Jacksonville, Fla., 1940-44, dean of men, 1944-48; asso. prof. commerce Catawba Coll., Salisbury, N.C., 1948-79, prof. emeritus, 1979—, dir. placement office, 1948-78, chmn. dept. commerce, 1950-79. Pres. Rowan County Inter-Civic Council; active Rowan County Friends of Library; mem. nat. speakers bur. Boy Scouts Am., vice chmn. Rowan County council. Named Rowan County Man of Year, 1967. Mem. Am. Acad. Polit. and Social Sci., So. Econ. Assn., Adminstrv. Mgmt. Soc. (pres.), Sales-Mktg. Execs. Club (exec. Salisbury), Am. Accounting Assn., Soc. Advt. Mgmt., Acad. Mgmt., Am. Mktg. Assn., N.C. Bus. Edn. Council, Internat. Platform Assn., Acad. Certified Adminstrv. Mgrs., Kappa Delta Pi. Mason (K.T., Shriner), Lion (pres. Salisbury, zone chmn., dist. gov., internat. counselor). Club: Salisbury Country (dir.). Address: Catawba Coll Salisbury NC 28144

WILSON, NANCY CAROL, educator; b. Brighton, Tenn., July 11, 1940; d. John Calvin and Lillie Mai (Coates) W.; B.B.A., Memphis State U., 1963, M.Ed., 1968; student Lambuth Coll., 1958-59. Tchr. bus. Grand Junction (Tenn.) High Sch., 1963-64; tchr. Munford (Tenn.) Elem. Sch., 1964-66; tchr. bus., head bus. dept. Munford High Sch., 1966-71; asso. prof. secretarial adminstrn. U. Ky./Hopkinsville Community Coll., 1971—. Recipient Great Tchr. award U. Ky./Hopkinsville Community Coll.. 1977. Mem. Nat. Bus. Edn. Assn. (Ky. membership dir. 1974-76), Internat. Soc. Bus. Edn., So. Bus. Edn. Assn. (Ky. rep. 1974-76, chmn. basic bus. div. 1974, chmn. secretarial div. 1975, chmn. community and jr. coll. div. 1977, sec. exec. bd. 1979), Ky. Bus. Edn. Assn. (exec. bd. 1973-76, pres. 1974-75), Nat. Collegiate Assn. Secs. (nat. publicity dir. 1976-78, nat. 1st v.p. 1978-80), Nat. Secs. Assn., Delta Pi Epsilon. Presbyterian. Home: University Heights Apts #8 Talbert Dr Hopkinsville KY 42240 Office: Dept Secretarial Adminstrn U Ky/Hopkinsville Community Coll Hopkinsville KY 42240

WILSON, NELSON EDWARD, mfg. co. ofcl.; b. Groesbeck, Tex., Jan. 31, 1918; s. John Abe and Iler Inez (Ridge) W.; student SW Tex. State Tchrs. Coll., 1938; m. Margie Ruth Franklin, Aug. 27, 1938; children—Carlton Edward, Anita Gail. With Central Producers Oil Co., Freer, Tex., 1940-44; staff Lane Wells Co., 1944-48, sta. mgr., McAllen, Tex., 1948-52, area supt., Alice, Tex., 1952-54, mgr., 1954-58; mgr. Dresser Industries, McAllen, 1958-60, sta. mgr. Atlas div., Luling, Tex., 1960-66, sr. mech. technician, Houston, 1966-76, prodn. supt., mech. assembly, 1976—. Home: 2814 Westerland Houston TX 77063 Office: Dresser Atlas Div Dresser Industries PO Box 6504 Houston TX 77005

WILSON, PAT LEIGHTON, title co. exec.; b. Falfurias, Tex., May 21, 1939; s. Buel Woodrow and Joyce Etoy (Moore) W.; student Baylor U., 1957-58; A.A., San Antonio Coll., 1964; B.B.A., St. Mary's U., 1966; m. Esther Epstein, Oct. 11, 1958; children—Angela, Mark, Lisa. Staff acct. Lewis & Montag, C.P.A.'s, San Antonio, 1966-70; tax specialist Haskins & Sells, C.P.A.'s, San Antonio, 1970-73; chief fin. officer Alamo Title Co., San Antonio, 1973—, sec.-treas., 1974—; dir. Quality Title Co. Served with USNR, 1958-63. C.P.A., Tex. Mem. Am. Inst. C.P.A.'s, Tex. Soc. C.P.A.'s, San Antonio C.P.A.'s, Fin. Execs. Inst., Tex. Land Title Assn., San Antonio Estate Planners Council, Profit Sharing Council. Home: 7538 Blue Mist Mountain San Antonio TX 78255 Office: Alamo Title Co 107 E Travis St San Antonio TX 78205

WILSON, PAULA ANN, speech/lang. pathologist; b. Alexander City, Ala., Oct. 12, 1954; d. William Paul and Sara Ann (Causey) W.; B.A. with honor, Auburn U., 1976, M. Speech Communication, 1978. Post-master's intern speech pathology Center for Developmental and Learning Disorders, U. Ala., Birmingham, 1978-79; clin. pathologist speech/lang. Pappas and Baldwin, M.D., P.A., Birmingham, 1979—. Cert. clin. competence speech pathology. Mem. Am. Speech and Hearing Assn., Speech and Hearing Assn. Ala., Phi Kappa Phi. Baptist. Home: 512 Golden Crest Circle Birmingham AL 35209 Office: Pappas and Baldwin PA 3608 Clairmont Ave Birmingham AL 35222

WILSON, PETER HAMILTON, indsl. hygienist; b. New London, Conn., Aug. 20, 1947; s. Walter Kenneth and Mary Louise (Taliaferro) W.; B.S. in Chemistry, James Madison U., 1969; M.S. in Environ. Health Sci., Temple U., 1973; m. Vicki Marie Brandt, June 10, 1970. Tchr. chemistry Norfolk (Va.) Cath. High Sch., 1969-71; air pollution chemist Va. Air Pollution Control Bd., Richmond, 1972-76; mgr. occupational health and safety A.H. Robins Co., Richmond, 1976—; cons. Va. Environ. Endowment. Cert. indsl. hygienist Am. Bd. Indsl. Hygiene. Mem. Am. Indsl. Hygiene Assn., Am. Acad. Indsl. Hygiene, Am. Chem. Soc. Roman Catholic. Home: 4222 Seminary Ave Richmond VA 23227 Office: A H Robins Co 1407 Cummings Dr Richmond VA 23220

WILSON, RALPH SLOAN, retinal surgeon; b. El Dorado, Ark., Nov. 12, 1937; s. George Evander and Lauree Eta (Doss) W.; A.B., Davidson Coll., 1959; B.S., U. Ark., 1963, M.D. (Research fellow), 1963; m. Sarah Mignon Ross, Dec. 27, 1958; children—Ralph Sloan, William Gregory, Steven Robert. Intern, U. Ark. Hosps., Little Rock, 1963-64; postgrad. opthalmology Harvard Med. Sch., Boston, 1964-65; resident ophthalmology U. Ark. Hosps., 1965, U. Tex. Med. Br., Galveston, 1965-67; Heed fellow of retinal pathology and surgery Mass. Eye and Ear Infirmary, Harvard Med. Sch., Boston, 1969: asst. prof. and dir. retina services dept. ophthalmology U. Ark. Med. Center, Little Rock, 1970-75, asso. prof., 1975-77, acting chmn. ophthalmology dept., 1974-75; practice medicine specializing in retinal surgery Retinal Group, LTD., Little Rock, 1975-77; dir. Retina Service, U.S. VA Hosp., Little Rock; vice chmn. surg. staff, chmn. surg. controls com., exec. com. Drs. Hosp.; dir. Ritchie Grocer Co., S.W. Trading Corp. Bd. dirs. Ark. Eye & Kidney Bank, Ark. Soc. for Prevention of Blindness. Served to lt. comdr. USNR, 1967-69. Diplomate Am. Bd. of Ophthalmology; Hoffmann La Roche grantee, 1966-67; recipient AMA Physicians Recognition awards, 1969, 75. Mem. . Acad. of Ophthalmology and Otolaryngology, Assn. for Research and Vision in Ophthalmology, AMA, Ark., Pulaski County med. socs., Am., Ark. assns. of ophthalmology, AAUP, Research to Prevent Blindness, Ark. Soc. for the Prevention of Blindness (bd. dirs.), So. Med. Assn., Pan Am. Soc. of Ophthalmology, Sociedad Boliviana de Oftalmologia, New Orleans Acad. of Ophthalmology, U. Tex. Med. Br. Ophthalmology Alumni Assn. (pres. 1970-72), Univ. Med. Group, Soc. of Heed Fellows, Little Rock Acad. of Surgery, Retina Soc., Ark. Acad. of Ophthalmology (pres. 1975-76), Ark. Found. for Med. Care, Assn. of VA Ophthalmologists, Ark. Ophthalmology sect. of Ark. Med. Soc. (pres. 1977-78), Assn. Mil. Surgeons, Alpha Omega Alpha, Sigma Xi. Contbr. articles in field to profl. jours., holder patents in field. Home: 120 N Woodrow St Little Rock AR 72205 Office: Doctors Bldg Suite 519 500 S University St Little Rock AR 72205

WILSON, RAYMOND CLARK, health care exec.; b. Birmingham, Ala., July 8, 1915; s. Raymond Clyde and Lida Pearl (Gay) W.; student Oglethorpe U., 1933-34, U. Ga., 1934-37, Tulane U., 1947-48; D.B.A. (hon.), William Carey Coll., 1976; m. Sara Elizabeth Paris, Feb. 17, 1940; children—Margery Jo, Richard Clark, Sara Elizabeth, Raymond Paul. Office mgr. C. R. Justi, Gen. Contractor, Atlanta, 1934-41; paymaster J. A. Jones Constrn. Co., Brunswick, Ga., 1942-45; asst. supt. So. Bapt. Hosp., New Orleans, 1946-53, adminstr., 1953-68, exec. dir., 1968-77; exec. dir. Bapt. Meml. Hosp., Jacksonville, Fla., 1974-77; pres. Affiliated Bapt. Hosps., New Orleans, 1977-80; pres. Health Care Cons. and Mgmt. Services, Inc., New Orleans, 1977—; mem. bd. dirs, exec. com. La. Health & Indemnity Co., 1976—. Served in USAAF, 1945-46. Fellow Am. Coll. Hosp. Adminstrs. (bd. regents 1972-75); mem. Am. Hosp. Assn. (del. 1972-75), New Orleans Hosp. Council (pres. 1954-55), La. Hosp. Assn. (pres. 1956), Bapt. Hosp. Assn. (pres. 1964-65), Southeastern Hosp. Conf. (pres. 1963). Baptist. (deacon, trustee). Club: New Orleans Rotary. Home: Box 1456 HW W Sunnybrook Rd Carriere MS 39426 Office: Suite 402 135 Saint Charles Ave New Orleans LA 70130

WILSON, ROBERT GODFREY, radiologist; b. Montgomery, Ala., Mar. 18, 1937; s. Robert Woodridge and Lucille (Godfrey) W.; B.A., Huntingdon Coll., 1957; M.D., Med. Coll. Ala., 1961; m. Dorothy June Waters, Aug. 31, 1957; children—Amy Lucille, Robert Darwin, Robert Woodridge II, Lucy Elizabeth. Intern, Letterman Gen. Hosp., San Francisco, 1961-62; resident in radiology U. Okla. Med. Center, Oklahoma City, 1965-68, clin. instr. in radiology, 1968—; practice medicine specializing in diagnostic and therapeutic radiology, nuclear medicine, Shawnee, Okla., 1968—; mem. med. staff Shawnee Med. Center, Mission Hill Meml. Hosp., Shawnee, 1968—. Served to capt. M.C., USAF, 1960-65. Diplomate Nat. Bd. Med. Examiners, Am. Bd. Radiology, Am. Bd. Nuclear Medicine. Mem. AMA, Okla., Pottawatomie County med. socs., Okla., Greater Oklahoma City radiol. socs., Am. Coll. Radiology, Soc. Nuclear Medicine, Radiol. Soc. N.Am. Methodist. Home: 26 Sequoyah St Shawnee OK 74801 Office: 605 Fed Nat Bldg Shawnee OK 74801

WILSON, ROBERT LEE, JR., mathematician, educator; b. Auburn, Ala., Jan. 3, 1942; s. Robert Lee and Anna Katherine (Fulton) W.; B.A., Ohio Wesleyan U., 1962; M.A., U. Wis., 1963; Ph.D., 1969; m. Elsie May Hickey, June 4, 1962; children—Anna Katherine, Julia Maria. Asst. prof. math. U. Wis., Madison, 1969-75; asso. prof. math. Washington and Lee U., Lexington, Va., 1975—. Bd. dirs. Rockbridge Presbyn. Children's Home, 1977—. NSF grantee, 1965-77. Mem. Am. Math. Soc., Math. Assn. Am., AAAS, AAUP, Sigma Xi, Phi Beta Kappa, Pi Mu Epsilon. Presbyterian. Contbr. articles to math. jours. Home: Route 5 Box 346 Lexington VA 24450 Office: Washington and Lee U Lexington VA 24450

WILSON, RODNEY FREEMAN, engr.; b. Anadarko, Okla., Dec. 16, 1950; s. Woodrow Wilmon and Lillian Marie (Goombi) W.; B.S. in Chem. Engring., Okla. State U., 1973. With Warren Petroleum Co., 1974—, plant engr. Maysville, Okla., 1975-77, Waddell plant, Crane, Tex., 1977-79, Azalea plant, Midland, Tex., 1979-80, plant supr. Shackleford plant, Albany, Tex., 1980—. Mem. Am. Inst. Chem. Engrs. Democrat. Baptist. Club: Kiowa Gourd Clan. Home: Gen Delivery Albany TX 76430 Office: Box 991 Breckenridge TX 76024

WILSON, ROSE WILLOVENE CONFER, counselor, resource specialist; b. Brackenridge, Pa., June 14, 1924; d. Irven J. and Marguerite Rose (Kelley) Confer; B.A., McNeese State U., 1963, M.Ed., 1971, Edn. Specialist, 1974, Ed.D., 1979; m. Clarence Wilson Jr., Feb. 27, 1945 (dec. Feb. 1955); children—Michael Carson Thomas, Clarence Patrick, James Robert, Marguerite Rose, Stephen Timothy. Tchr., LaGrange Middle Sch., Lake Charles, La., 1963-73, career edn. counselor, 1973-75; grad. asst., instr. counseling McNeese State U., Lake Charles, 1975-76, vis. lectr., 1977-78; guidance counselor Alfred M. Barbe High Sch., Lake Charles, 1976-77; guidance counselor Calcasieu Parish Schs., Lake Charles, 1963—, coordinator occupational readings, 1978-79, resource specialist, 1979—. Pres. SW La. Health Counseling Services, 1971-74, bd. dirs., 1974-79; mem. profl. adv. bd. La. Epilepsy Assn., 1979—; chmn. Mayors Com. Employment of Handicapped, Southwest La., 1979-80; lay minister of Eucharist St. Margaret Roman Catholic Ch., Lake Charles, 1977—, mem. parish council, 1976-80, sec., 1978-80. Recipient Freedoms Found.'s Valley Forge Tchrs. Medal, 1970, keys to City of Lake Charles from Mayor James Sudduth, 1973, woman of yr. award Quota Club Lake Charles, 1975, outstanding Public Servant award Calcasieu Council 1207, 1978. Mem. La. Edn. Research Assn., Am., La. personnel and guidance assns., Am., La. sch. counselors assn., Am. Rehab. Counseling Assn., Assn. Counselor Edn. and Supervision, Nat. Vocat. Guidance Assn., Calcasieu Counselors Assn., La., Calcasieu tchrs. assns. La., Calcasieu assns. classroom tchrs., Cath. Daus. Am. (vice-regent 1972-73), Alpha Delta Kappa, Phi Delta Kappa. Researcher career edn., in-service tng. for counselors. Home: 1529 Tennessee St Lake Charles LA 70605 Office: 1120 W 18th St Lake Charles LA 70601

WILSON, ROWAN SCOTT, mfg. co. exec.; b. Flushing, N.Y., Mar. 31, 1940; s. Walter Pyle and Francis (Kurz) W.; B.A., Taylor U., 1961; children—Wendy Meredith, Marshall Scott. Field rep., sales tng. instr., real estate rep. Mobil Oil Corp., N.Y.C., 1961-66; mgr. prodn. Avon Products Co., Rye, N.Y., 1966-68; with Gilbarco, Inc., Greensboro, N.C., 1968-73, dist. sales mgr., 1968-72, mgr. mktg. adminstrn., 1973; with Dresser Industries, Inc., Atlanta, 1974—, sales mgr. S.E. region, 1978—. Bd. dirs. Therapy, Inc., Gainesville, Fla.; regional dir. United Fund, 1968; area dir. Heart Fund, 1970; dir. Republican Club, West Chester County, N.Y., 1968. Served with USAR, 1962-67. Mem. Ga. Oilmens Assn., N.C. Oil Jobbers Assn., Tenn. Oil Marketers Assn., Fla. Petroleum Marketers Assn., Nat. Fire Protection Assn., Sales Mktg. Execs. Inc. Atlanta, Ala. Petroleum Marketers Assn. Club: Elks. Home: 8601 Roberts Dr Atlanta GA 30338 Office: Suite 380 244 Perimeter Centre Pky Atlanta GA 30346

WILSON, RUPERT DWIGHT, III, florist; b. Gadsden, Ala., July 5, 1943; s. Rupert Dwight and Elsie Carol (Plank) W.; B.S. in Bus. Adminstrn., Auburn U., 1966; m. Joyce Law, Apr. 26, 1969; 1 dau., Margaret Anne. Salesman Rosemont Gardens Wholesale Florist Inc., Montgomery, Ala., 1966-72; credit mgr. Patersons Rosemont Gardens Inc., Montgomery, 1972—, partner, 1978—. Served with USAF, 1966-67. Mem. Ala. Assn. Credit Execs., Montgomery Credit Mgrs. Assn. (pres. 1974-75, chmn. bd. 1976), Montgomery Jaycees (dir. 1967-70, Spoke of Year 1967). Presbyterian. Club: Kiwanis (dir. 1978-80) (Montgomery). Home: 3113 Fitzgerald Rd Montgomery AL 36106 Office: 2210 Rosemont Pl Montgomery AL 36106

WILSON, SHIRLEY BURGESS, ednl. adminstr.; b. South Norfolk, Va., July 3, 1925; d. Richard Leonard and Sarah Ednad (Harvey) Burgess; B.S. in Secondary Edn., Old Dominion U., Norfolk, 1963; M.S. in Bus. Edn., Va. Poly. Inst. and State U., 1967, Ed.D. in Vocat. Edn., 1976; m. George W. Wilson, Jr.; children—Pamela Wilson Zanaveld O'Brien, Lynne Delle Wilson Rosso, George W. Clk., Naval Supply Center, Norfolk, 1950-55; tchr., coordinator, Pub. Schs., Chesapeake, Va., 1963-66; supr. bus. edn. Pub. Schs. Norfolk, 1966-74, acting dir. vocat. edn., 1974-75, supr. bus. edn., 1976-77, prin. Norfolk Tech. Vocat. Center, 1977-78, asst. supt. Region I, 1978—. Chmn. Va. Adv. Council for Vocat. Edn., 1972-74. Recipient Community Service award Internat. Assn. Public Employment Services, 1979. Mem. Va. Vocat. Assn. (pres. 1972-74, Outstanding Service award 1975), Va. Bus. Edn. Assn. (sec. 1965-66, pres. 1967-68, Spl. Recognition award 1968), Am. Assn. Sch. Adminstrs., Va. Assn. Sch. Adminstrs., Assn. Supervision and Curriculum Devel., Norfolk C. of C., Pilot Club of Norfolk, Va. Fedn. Women's Clubs (treas. Tidewater Dist.), Phi Delta Kappa, Delta Pi Epsilon Clubs: Indian Rive Home Demonstration (pres.), Norfolk County Home Demonstration (pres.), Mary Calcott Women's (pres.). Home: 4211 Goldcrest Dr Chesapeake VA 23325 Office: 800 E City Hall Ave Norfolk VA 23510

WILSON, STEPHEN K., hosp. adminstr.; b. Atlanta, Aug. 3, 1931; s. Henry Louie and Alma (Lewis) W.; student U. Fla., 1948-50, 55-57; B.S., Fla. State U., 1959; M.H.A., Washington U., 1961; m. Patricia Ann Copeland, Aug. 17, 1957; children—Tania Elaine, Stephanie Diane, Krista Ann, Stephen Patrick. Asst. adminstr. Gadsden County Hosp., Quincy, Fla., 1958-59; adminstr. Cape Canaveral Hosp., Cocoa Beach, Fla., 1961-73; adminstr. Ormond Beach (Fla.) Hosp., 1974-78; asst. exec. dir. St. Luke's Hosp., Jacksonville, Fla., 1978—. Mem. exec. com. East Central Fla. Hosp. Council, 1969—, pres., 1973. Vice pres., bd. dirs. Volusia County Emergency Med. Services, 1974-78; pres., bd. dirs. Volusia-Flagler Heart Assn., 1975-76; pres. Canaveral div. Am. Heart Assn., bd. dirs. Fla. affiliate, 1976-79; bd. dirs. Workmen's Compensation Hosp. Trust; adv. com. Bethune-Cookman Coll. Nursing Sch., Daytona Beach Community Coll. Nursing Sch., 1977—. Served with USN, 1951-55. Mem. Fla., Am. hosp. assns., Am. Coll. Hosp. Adminstrs., Daytona Beach (com. of 100), Ormond Beach chambers commerce. Rotarian (treas. 1965-66, v.p. 1966-67, pres. 1967-68, dir. 1968-69, bull. editor 1969-70, 75-76, sec. 1975-79, Paul Harris fellow 1979). Home: 6241 Riviera Manor Dr Jacksonville FL 32216 Office: St Luke's Hosp 1900 Blvd Jacksonville FL 32206

WILSON, SUSAN LYNN, mktg. exec.; b. Pensacola, Fla., Dec. 31, 1952; d. Colonel Howard Elmore and Alyce Velma (White) Wilson; B.F.A., So. Meth. U., 1974. Info. specialist Am. Heart Assn., Dallas, 1975-76; mgr. pub. relations Tex. Instruments Credit Union, Dallas, 1976-77; mktg. services coordinator Henry C. Beck Co., and editor Beck Bull., Dallas, 1977—. Adv. bd. Children's Arts and Ideas, Dallas, 1980—; vol. Dallas Ind. Sch. Dist., 1978-80; mem. The 500 Inc. Dallas, 1979-80. Recipient Vol. Service award Dallas Ind. Sch. Dist., 1977-80. Mem. Internat. Assn. Bus. Communicators, Kappa Delta. Home: 5717 Del Roy Dr Dallas TX 75230 Office: 4600 First Nat Bank Bldg Dallas TX 75202

WILSON, THOMAS PRESSLEY, paving co. exec.; b. Oxford, N.C., Feb. 22, 1922; s. John Shelton and Rose Ellen (Blair) W.; student U. Florence (Italy), 1945; m. Jacqueline Bowles, Apr. 17, 1951; children—Carmen Tomasina, Jacqueline Terasa, Thomas P., Angela Karen, Jeanne Ellen. Served with U.S. Army, 1940-57; ret., 1957; supt. in charge asphalt Ames & Webb Inc., Norfolk, Va., 1957-72; pres. Asphalt Paving Co. Inc., Chesapeake, Va., 1972—. Pres. Snug Harbor Property Assn., 1976—. Decorated Purple Heart, Bronze Star. Mem. Am. Legion, VFW. Democrat. Roman Catholic. Club: K.C. Home: 1428 Gust Ln Chesapeake VA 23323 Office: Asphalt Paving Co Inc 1435 Gust Ln Chesapeake VA 23323

WILSON, TIMOTHY MICHAEL, physicist, educator; b. Columbus, Ohio, Aug. 3, 1938; s. Eugene H. and Loretta G. (Dumas) W.; A.A., St. Petersburg Jr. Coll., 1958; B.S. in Chemistry, U. Fla., 1961, Ph.D., 1966; m. Elaine Marie McCoy, Apr. 5, 1974; 1 son, Michael Joseph. Mem. research staff solid state div. Oak Ridge Nat. Lab., summers 1971-76; asst. prof. physics and chemistry U. Fla., Gainesville, 1968-69; asst. prof. physics Okla. State U., Stillwater, 1969-72, asso. prof. physics, 1972-78, asst. dir. Coll. Arts and Scis. Extension, 1977—, prof. physics, 1978—; cons. Pratt & Whitney Research Labs., Middletown, Conn., 1969-70, Mitre Corp., McLean, Va., 1977-78, Oak Ridge Nat. Lab., 1971—. DuPont Teaching fellow, 1965-66, NSF fellow, 1966-68; NSF Travel grantee, 1976. Mem. Am. Phys. Soc., Am. Assn. Physics Tchrs., Okla. Community Edn. Assn., Okla. Adult and Continuing Edn. Assn., Nat. U. Extension Assn., Sigma Xi, Sigma Pi Sigma. Democrat. Contbr. articles on quantum mechanics to sci. jours. Office: Arts and Sciences Extension Okla State Univ Stillwater OK 74074

WILSON, VERNON EARL, univ. adminstr.; b. Kingsley, Iowa, Feb. 16, 1915; s. Willie Earl and Elizabeth Pearl (Kinney) W.; B.S., U. Ill., 1950, M.S., 1952, M.D., 1952; m. Ula R. Rhone, July 1, 1947; children-William Earl, Carla Jean. Asst. dean U. Kans., Lawrence, 1957-59, asso. dean, asst. prof., 1957-59, acting dean, acting dir. med. center, 1959; dean, dir. med. center U. Mo., Columbia, 1959-74, prof. pharmacology, 1966-68, coordinator Mo. regional med. program, 1966-68, exec. dir. for health affairs, 1967-68, v.p. for acad. affairs, 1968-70; adminstr. health services and mental health adminstrn. HEW, 1970-72; prof. community and med. practice U. Mo., Columbia, 1973-74; v.p. med. affairs, prof. med. adminstrn. and preventive medicine Vanderbilt U., Nashville, 1974—; cons. Appalachian regional hosps. to Appalachian Regional Commn., 1975; cons. Nat. Bur. Standards, 1974-76. Served with USN, 1942-46. Named Physician of Year, Mo. Acad. Family Physicians, 1965; Golden Apple, Am. Med. Student Assn., 1967; diplomate Am. Bd. Family Practice, mem., 1962-74. Fellow Am. Acad. Family Physicians; mem. AMA (council on med. edn. 1967-75), Am. Assn. History and Medicine. Am. Assn. Med. Colls. (exec. council 1961-67), Nashville Acad. Medicine, Am. Acad. Family Physicians, Soc. for Health and Human Values, Sigma Xi, Alpha Kappa Kappa, Alpha Omega Alpha, Pi Kappa Epsilon. Presbyterian. Home: 1912 Cromwell Dr Nashville TN 37215 Office: D3300 Med Center Vanderbilt U Nashville TN 37232

WILSON, WESLEY CAMPBELL, coll. adminstr., former army officer; b. Phila., Nov. 29, 1931; s. Wesley and Emily Edith (Campbell) W.; B.S. in Edn., Morgan State U., 1954; Ed.M., Coll. William and Mary, 1974, cert., 1978; m. Elaine Epps, Dec. 26, 1954; children—Carl B., Wayne K., Michael K., Eric W. Commd. 2nd lt. U.S. Army, 1954, advanced through grades to lt. col., 1967; parachutist 82d Airborne Div., Ft. Bragg, N.C., 1955; fixed wing aviator 9th Inf. Div., Ft. Carson, Colo., 1956, rotary wing aviator, 1957; combat pilot 1st Cavalry Div., Korea, 1958-59; aviator HHC/AVNBN, Ft. Richardson, Alaska, 1961-63; company comdr. A/501st Aviation Bn., Vietnam, 1964-65; bn. exec. officer Armed Helicopter Units, Vietnam, 1967-68; dep. group comdr. 325th Aviation Bn., Vietnam, 1972-73; bn. comdr. 38th Transp. Bn., Ft. Eustis, Va., 1973-74; chief research and devel. Logistics Systems and Readiness Agy., Newcumberland, Pa., 1968-70, ret., 1974; asst. to pres. Coll. William and Mary, Williamsburg, Va., 1974—; cons. in staff devel. various sch. systems, 1974—; partner, v.p. C&W Associates, Newport News, Va., 1976—; workshop designer to various ednl. instns. and civic orgns., 1975—. Chmn. Gov.'s Com. on Equal Employment Opportunity, Va., 1976-78; chmn. Newport News Sch. Bd., 1977—; mem. Va. Democratic Com., Newport News, 1974—, Newport News Polit. Action Com., 1974—; mem. exec. bd. 1st Dist. Black Caucus, 1975—; bd. dirs. Peninsula Vocat.-Tech. Edn. Center, 1975-77. Decorated Legion of Merit, Air Medal, D.F.C., Air Medal with twenty one oak leaf clusters, Bronze Star; Cross of Gallantry (Vietnam); named Citizen of Yr., Newport News, 1977. Mem. Am. Personnel and Guidance Assn., Va. Personnel and Guidance Assn., Peninsula Personnel and Guidance Assn., Am. Soc. for Testing and Devel., Va. Assn. for Specialists in Group Work, Va. Coll. Placement Assn., Am. Assn. for Affirmative Action, Va. Assn. for Non-White Concerns, Ret. Officers Assn., NAACP, Omega Psi Phi (pres. Newport News chpt. 1974-76). Democrat. Presbyterian. Contbr. articles on ednl. adminstrn. to profl. publs. Home: 51 Rexford Dr Newport News VA 23602 Office: College of William and Mary Williamsburg VA 23185

WILSON, WILBURN MARTIN, radio exec.; b. Cerulean, Ky., Mar. 13, 1930; s. Robert Estill and Verdya Marie (Shanks) W.; grad. high sch.; m. JoAnn Campbell, May 23, 1954; children—Donna Jo and Deborah Gay (twins). With Princeton Broadcasting Co., Princeton, Ky., 1951-66, news and sports dir., 1955-65; founder WKDZ Am, Cadiz, Ky., 1966, WKDZ FM, 1972, gen. mgr., 1966—. Served with USN, 1951-55. Recipient Communications award Ky. State Farm Bur., 1975. Mem. Cadiz Trigg County C. of C. (past dir.), Ky. AP Broadcasters (past pres.). Baptist (deacon, Sunday Sch. tchr.). Club: Civitan (past pres.). Home: Route 6 Sunset Circle Cadiz KY 42211 Office: Will Jackson Rd Cadiz KY 42211

WILSON, WILLIAM, assn. exec.; b. Hayworth, Okla., Dec. 19, 1929; s. Jubel H. and Anna (Metoxen) W.; B.B.A., Central State U., Edmond, Okla., 1972; m. Joan Crawford; children—Ricky, JoAnna Renee, Tammy Lynn. Regional mgr. Olivetti Underwood Corp., Midland, Tex., 1959-70; tribal econ. devel. specialist Okla. Indian Affairs Commn., 1970-73; exec. dir. Assn. Am. Indian Physicians, Oklahoma City, 1974—; cons. Indian Health Service; bd. dirs. Oklahoma City Urban Indian Health Clinic; vice chmn. Indian Self-Determination Council, 1975; chmn. Am. Indian Health Manpower Devel. Consortium; mem. nat. health ins. council Nat. Indian Health Bd.; rep. on Indian health care improvement act Nat. Congress Am. Indians. Served with USMCR, 1951-53. Mem. Pi Kappa Alpha. Democrat. Baptist. Club: Masons. Author, editor in field. Office: 6801 S Western St Suite 206 Oklahoma City OK 73139

WILSON, WILLIAM ARNEE, JR., ednl. adminstr.; b. Washington, July 14, 1937; s. William Arnee and Lois Rebecca (Freeman) W.; B.A., City Coll. U. City N.Y., 1969; M.A., Tchrs. Coll. Columbia U., 1970, Ed.D. (Coll. fellow), 1974; m. Doris Phillips-Siegh, Feb. 25, 1966; children—Craig-William, Christopher-William, Chandler Phillips. Musician, U.S. and abroad, 1961-71; counselor U. City N.Y., 1969-70; asst. dir. career planning and placement Chgo. State U., 1970-72; lectr. Hostos Community Coll., 1973-74; asso. dean students Bloomfield Coll., 1974-75, dean students, 1975-77; dir. project now Trenton State Coll., 1977-78; dir. counseling, student devel. Mountainview Coll., Dallas, 1978—. ednl. cons. Bergen County (N.J.) Urban League Served with USAF, 1955-56. Recipient Achievement award Mountain View Coll., 1979. Mem. Am. Personnel and Guidance Assn., Am. Coll. Personnel Assn., Nat. Assn. Student Personnel Adminstrs. Methodist. Composer: Now and Forever, Fish and Chips; contbr. articles to profl. jours. Office: 4849 W Illinois Ave Dallas TX 75211

WILSON, WILLIAM FEATHERGAIL, petroleum co. exec.; b. San Antonio, Dec. 25, 1934; s. Glenn Caldwell and Marion (Hord) W.; B.A., U. Tex. Austin, 1957, B.S. with honors, 1960, M.A., 1962; m.

Elizabeth Gail Harmison, Mar. 17, 1979; children—Douglas Hord, Clayton Hill, Wendy Elanore. With dept. geology U. Tex., 1958-61, Texaco, Inc., 1961-65, El Paso Natural Gas Co., 1965-66; ind. petroleum geologist, rancher, real estate exec., 1966-70; environ. geologist Alamo Area Council Govts., 1970; account exec. Merrill Lynch Fenner & Smith, 1970-74; sr. exploration geologist Tesoro Petroleum Corp., San Antonio, 1974, exploration mgr. Tex. dist., 1974-76, Eastern hemisphere, 1976-78; exploration mgr. Placid Oil Co., San Antonio, 1978—; adj. instr. geology U. Tex., San Antonio, 1976—. Mem. Am. Assn. Petroleum Geologists (cert.), Geol. Soc. Am., Assn. Profl. Geol. Scientists (cert.), S. Tex. Geol. Soc. (pres., editor bull. 1976—), AAAS, Sigma Gamma Epsilon. Contbr. stories to San Antonio mag., articles to profl. jours. Home: 422 Fantasia San Antonio TX 78216 Office: 1635 NE Loop 410 Suite 803 San Antonio TX 78209

WILSON, WILLIAM HARRY, employment co. exec.; b. Buffalo, July 14, 1923; s. William H. and Laura W.; B.A., Williams Coll., 1947; m. Karin B. Gerke, Dec. 28, 1968; children—Christopher, Tanya; children from previous marriage—William H., Jeffrey T. Buyer dept. store, Buffalo, 1947-60; stockbroker Walston & Co., Houston, 1961-65; div. mgr. Manpower Inc., Buffalo, 1965-68, br. mgr., Erie, Pa., 1968-69, br. mgr., Dallas, 1969-78, area mgr., 1978—. Served with AUS, 1943-45. Mem. Soc. Advancement Mgmt. (regional v.p., pres.), Adminstrv. Mgmt. Soc. (dir.), Dallas Personnel Assn., Sales and Mktg. Execs. Republican. Club: Kiwanis. Home: 15711 Overmead Circle Dallas TX 75248 Office: 411 N Akard St Dallas TX 75201

WILT, TOBY STACK, investment co. exec.; b. Chgo., Nov. 29, 1944; s. Ted and Ruth (Nettlehorst) W.; B.Engring., Vanderbilt U., 1967; m. Joanne Cliffe Fleming, Sept. 2, 1967; children—Sam Fleming, Joanne Cliffe, Toby Stack. Engr., Steel Service Co., Nashville, 1967-68; auditor Ernst & Ernst, Nashville, 1969-72; analyst, research and corp. fin. depts. J. C. Bradford & Co., Nashville, 1972-73; pres. Hillsboro Enterprises, Inc., Nashville, 1973—; chmn. bd. Breeko Industries, Inc., Nashville, 1973. Mem. fin. com. Gov. Alexander's gubernatorial election, 1974, Congressman Boner, 1978; bd. dirs. Leadership Nashville, 1977-78; treas. Mayor's reelection com., Nashville, 1979. Served with USAF, 1968-69. C.P.A., Tenn. Mem. Am. Inst. C.P.A.'s, Young Presidents Orgn. (dir. 1980), Nashville C. of C. (bd. dirs.). Presbyterian. Clubs: Belle Meade Country, Cumberland, Rotary. Office: 1300 3d Nat Bank Bldg Nashville TN 37219

WILTON, CAROL ANN BALLENGEE, hosp. ofcl.; b. Charleston, W.Va., Apr. 2, 1944; d. George Halley and Daisy Fern (Aliff) Ballengee; grad. Stout Sch. of Music, 1962, Charleston Meml. Hosp. Sch. for Operating Room Technicians, 1966; m. William James Wilton, Jr., Nov. 22, 1962; children—William Randolph, James Russell. Surgery operating room technician Livingston Meml. Hosp., Columbus, Ohio, 1966, Charleston Meml. Hosp., Glenview Hosp., Ft. Worth, 1968; emergency room supr. Lancaster-Pittard Profl. Assn., Grapevine, Tex., 1968-72; surgery operating room technician Grapevine Meml. Hosp., 1972-79, supr. central supply, 1976-79, inservice coordinator, 1976—, dir. materiel mgmt., 1978—. Hosp. campaign mgr. United Way, 1978; loaned exec. United Way of Tarrant County, 1979; bd. dirs. Am. Heart Assn. Certified surg. technologist Nat. Assn. Surg. Technologists. Mem. Nat. Assn. Surg. Technologists, Assn. Surg. Technologists Ft. Worth, Am. Mgmt. Assn., Internat. Material Mgmt. Soc., Tex. Hosp. Assn. Office: Grapevine Meml Hosp 1600 W College St Grapevine TX 76051

WILTSHIRE, CORA BROWN, home bldg. co. exec.; b. Houston, July 18, 1948; d. James A. and Burnett (Grant) Brown; B.B.A., N. Tex. State U., 1970; m. Raymond S. Wiltshire, Jr., June 23, 1973; children—Sean Avery, Marc Sinclair. Sec., Mobil Oil Corp., Dallas, 1970-72; sr. compensation analyst Aetna Ins. Co., Hartford, Conn., 1972-76; personnel dir. U. S. Home Corp., Houston, 1976-78, v.p. sales, 1978—; participant recruiting seminar Fla. A&M U. Recipient 1st place sales award U.S. Home Corp., 1978, 79. Office: US Home Corp 8415 Hearth Dr Houston TX 77054

WIMBERLY, CLARENCE WILLIAM, JR., physician; b. Summerville, S.C., Oct. 12, 1943; s. Clarence William and Alma F. (Infinger) W.; B.S., Wofford Coll., 1965; M.D., Med. U. S.C., 1969; m. Patricia Gayle Huber, Feb. 27, 1971; children—Christopher William, Jason Andrew, Mark Patrick. Intern, Med. U.S.C., Charleston, 1970, resident in family practice, 1970-72; practice medicine specializing in family practice, Summerville, S.C., 1974—; mem. staff North Trident Regional Hosp.; cons. Civic Cancer Soc. Bd. dirs. S.C. Profl. Standards Rev. Orgn.; mem. adminstrv. bd. Summerville Meth. Ch., Dorchester County Mental Retardation Bd. Served with M.C., USAF, 1972-74. Diplomate Am. Bd. Family Practice. Mem. AMA, S.C. Med. Assn., Am. Assn. Family Physicians, S.C. Acad. Family Physicians (com. mem.), Summerville C. of C. (dir.). Republican. Methodist. Clubs: Masons, Sertoma. Contbr. articles to Jour. Family Practice; med. articles to Summerville Jour. Home: 119 President Circle Summerville SC 29483 Office: 435 N Cedar St Summerville SC 29483

WIMBISH, GARY HAROLD, toxicologist; b. Waxahachie, Tex., Jan. 23, 1943; s. Talbert Oglesby and Dorothy Elouiese (Pinkston) W.; B.S., Tex. A&M U., 1966; Ph.D. (fellow), Ind. U., 1973; m. Arveal Jean Ecker, Nov. 28, 1968; children—Gregory Paul, John Harold, Wendy Orlene. Pesticide residue chemist Tex. A&M U., College Station, 1965-66; cons. RSR Corp., Dallas, 1968-69; forensic and analytical chemist Terrell's Lab., Ft. Worth, 1966-69; dir. dept. toxicology Pathology Asso. of Tex., Ft. Worth, 1973-75; cons. S.W. Med. Lab., Dallas, 1975—; asso. prof. Inst. Forensic Medicine, Tex. Coll. Osteo. Medicine, Ft. Worth, 1975—; toxicology cons. Damon Med. Labs., 1975—; toxicologist Poison Control Center, Cook Children's Hosp., 1975—. Advisor, Tarrant Council on Alcoholism and Drug Abuse, 1976—; chmn. Substance Abuse Com. Tarrant County, 1976—. Named Citizen of Year, Ft. Worth, Internat. Assn. Fire Fighters, 1979; diplomate Am. Bd. Forensic Toxicology. Fellow Am. Acad. Forensic Sci.; mem. Internat. Assn. Forensic Toxicologists, Am. Chem. Soc., Southwestern Assn. Toxicologists, Sigma Xi. Contbr. articles to profl. jours. Home: 7429 Meadowbrook Dr Fort Worth TX 76112 Office: Tex Coll Osteo Medicine Camp Bowie at Montgomery Fort Worth TX 76107

WIMMER, ROBERT ALLEN, acct.; b. Narrows, Va., Apr. 13, 1945; s. Allen Berkley and Mary Ellen W.; B.S., Va. Poly. Inst. and State U., 1973; m. Carol Joan Conner, July 3, 1965; children—Allen, Paula. Sr. auditor Ernst & Ernst, 1973-75; supr. gen. acctg. Sealand Services, Inc., subs. RJR Industries, Inc., Winston-Salem, N.C., 1975-76, mgr. gen. acctg., 1976-77, mgr. cost acctg., 1977—. Served with USNR, 1965-69. Mem. Am. Inst. C.P.A.'s, N.C. Soc. C.P.A.'s. Baptist. Club: Masons. Home: 1400 Woodford Rd Clemmons NC 27012 Office: RJ Reynolds Industries Main St Winston Salem NC 27102

WIMPRESS, GORDON DUNCAN, JR., educator, found. exec.; b. Riverside, Cal., Apr. 10, 1922; s. Gordon Duncan and Maude A. (Waldo) W.; B.A., U. Ore., 1946, M.A., 1951; Ph.D., U. Denver, 1958; LL.D., Monmouth Coll., 1970; L.H.D., Tusculum Coll., 1971; m. Jean Margaret Skerry, Nov. 30, 1946; children—Wendy Jo, Victoria Jean, Gordon Duncan III. Dir. pub. relations, instr. journalism Whittier (Cal.) Coll., 1946-51; asst. to pres. Colo. Sch. Mines, Golden, 1951-59; pres. Monticello Coll., Alton, Ill., 1959-64, Monmouth (Ill.) Coll., 1964-70, Trinity U., San Antonio, 1970-77; vice chmn. bd. govs. S.W. Found. Research and Edn., San Antonio, 1977—. Bd. dirs. Am. Inst. Character Edn.; mem. Burlington No. Scholarship Selection com. Trustee Mind Sci. Found., San Antonio Med. Found.; bd. dirs. Southwest Research Inst.; trustee Sigma Phi Epsilon Found., World Bus. Council; bd. govs. Southwest Found. for Research and Edn.; vice chmn. Bd. Fgn. Scholarships. Served to 1st lt. AUS, 1942-45. Decorated Bronze Star. Mem. Am. Acad. Polit. and Social Sci., Am. Assn. Higher Edn., Am. Inst. for Character Edn., Aircraft Owners and Pilots Assn., Council Advancement and Support Edn., Greater San Antonio C. of C., Pilots Internat. Assn., San Antonio Pilots Assn., Assn. Am. Colls., Am. Council on Edn., Mensa, Sigma Delta Chi, Sigma Delta Pi, Sigma Upsilon, Pi Gamma Mu, Sigma Phi Epsilon. Presbyn. Clubs: Rotary (gov.'s rep.), Argyle, Newcomen, St. Anthony, San Antonio Country. Author: American Journalism Comes of Age, 1950. Office: PO Box 28147 San Antonio TX 78284

WINCHESTER, RICHARD LEE, JR., lawyer; b. Memphis, May 21, 1924; s. Cassius Lee and Harriet Haywood (Bond) W.; LL.B., U. Tenn., 1949, J.D., 1965; m. Bette Anne Thompson, July 15, 1944; children—Robin Ann, Richard Lee Jr., John Thompson. Admitted to Tenn. bar, 1949; partner firm Winchester, Marshall, Huggins, Charlton, Leake & Brown, Memphis, 1972—; Shelby County atty., 1961-64; city atty., Germantown and Arlington, Tenn., 1966—. Gen. counsel, dir. Quality Concrete Products Co., Ind.; owner Holiday Inn frachise, El Dorado, Ark.; sec. Beachfront Condos, Inc., N.Fla.; chmn. bd. Bank of Germantown. Chmn., Germantown Planning Commn., 1958-61; mem. Gov.'s Commn. on Human Relations, 1962-68. Vice chmn., treas. Memphis and Shelby County Democratic Exec. Com., 1958-72; state exec. com., pres. Tenn. Young Democrats, 1960-61; del. state and nat. Dem. Convs., 1964-68; nat. elector from Tenn., 1960-72. Pres., bd. dirs. Mid-South Fair Assn.; bd. dirs. Sheltered Occupational Shop, A.R.C.; trustee Episcopal Girls Home, U. Tenn., 1976; trustee U. Tenn.; pres. Episcopal Planning Commn. Served to capt. inf. AUS, 1942-46; PTO. Mem. Am. (past del.), Tenn. (past pres. jr. sect.), Memphis and Shelby County (past pres. jr. sect.) bar assns., Am. Judicature Soc., Nat. Assn. Legal Aid and Pub. Defenders, Am. Legion (past post comdr., past state vice comdr.), 40 and 8, V.F.W. (past post vice comdr.) U. Tenn. Alumni Assn. (past bd. govs., 9th Dist. rep.), Sigma Alpha Epsilon, Phi Eta Sigma, Phi Kappa Phi, Omicron Delta Kappa. Episcopalian. Mason (32 degree, Shriner, Jester), Kiwanian. Club: Tennessee. Bd. editors Tenn. Law Rev., 1948-49. Home: 2121 Pete Mitchell Rd Germantown TN 38138 Office: 1st Tenn Bank Bldg Memphis TN 38103

WINDEGGER, FRANK ROBERT, athletic dir.; b. St. Louis, Jan. 12, 1934; s. Frank Anthony and Ruth Elizabeth Windegger; B.S., Tex. Christian U., 1957; m. Barbara Ann Leatherman, Apr. 10, 1958; children—Sherry, Dana. Mem. athletic staff Tex. Christian U., 1959—, head baseball coach, 1962-75, athletic dir., 1975—. Served with AUS, 1957-59. Decorated Commendation medal. Mem. Nat. Assn. Collegiate Dirs. Assn. Mem. Christian Ch. (Disciples of Christ). Clubs: Colonial Country, Ridglea Country. Office: Athletic Dept Tex Christian Univ Box 400A Fort Worth TX 76129

WINDELL, GEORGE GORDON, educator; b. Seattle, Feb. 24, 1920; s. George Allen and Grace Estelle W.; A.B., U. Tulsa, 1940; M.A., U. Mo., 1941; Ph.D., U. Minn., 1953; m. Marie Elizabeth George, June 14, 1942. Instr., asst. prof., asso. prof. history U. Del., Newark, 1948-69; prof. history U. New Orleans, 1970—; producer, host Opera Hall, Sta. WWNO, New Orleans, 1972—. Served with U.S. Army, 1942-45. Sr. Fulbright fellow, Germany, 1954-55; Am. Philos. Soc. grantee, 1961. Mem. Am. Hist. Assn., So. Hist. Assn., Conf. Group for Central European History. Author: The Catholics and German Unity, 1866-1871, 1954; contbr. sects. to books, anthology. Office: Dept History U New Orleans New Orleans LA 70122

WINDHAM, BERNARD MOORE, JR., state ofcl.; b. Carthage, Miss., May 11, 1942; s. Bernard Moore and Mildred (Henry) W.; B.A. in Math., Miss. State U., Starkville, 1964; M.S. in Math., La. State U., Baton Rouge, 1967; M.S. in Statistics, Fla. State U., Tallahassee, 1971, postgrad., 1971-74; m. Patricia Ann Wood, Dec. 28, 1974. Reliability engr. Autonetics div. N.Am. Aviation Co., Anaheim, Calif., 1964-65; instr. math. Randolph Macon Coll., Ashland, Va., 1967-69; data analyst Fla. Bd. Regents, Tallahassee, 1974; planning, research specialist Fla. Dept. Community Affairs, Tallahassee, 1974-79, legis. analyst, 1979—. Pres., mgr. Apalachee Recycle Center, Tallahassee, 1973—; pres. Fla. Appropriate Tech., Inc.; adv. com. Leon County (Fla.) Resource Recovery, 1977—; active Common Cause. Mem. Population Assn. Am., Am. Statis. Assn., Big Bend Sierra Club (chairperson urban affairs 1977—), Audubon Soc., Environ. Def. Fund. Fellow Am. Mus. Natural History, Fla. Conservation Fund, Zero Population Growth. Methodist. Home: Route 2 Box 385A Tallahassee FL 32301 Office: 2571 Exec Center Circle E Tallahassee FL 32301

WINDHAM, EULA HEARD, librarian; b. Tifton, Ga.; d. William Guy and Eula Beall (Wilson) Windham; A.B., Ga. State Coll. for Women, 1940; postgrad. So. Baptist Theol. Sem., 1945-47; M.R.E., 1950; M.L.S., Emory U., 1956. Tchr. pub. schs. Tifton, 1940-44; bookkeeper State Nat. Bank, Sheffield, Ala., 1944; caseworker Ga. Dept. Pub. Welfare, Tifton, 1945; state jr. leader Ga. Baptist Sunday Sch. Dept., Atlanta, 1947-55; circulation and reference librarian Hardin-Simmons U., Abilene, 1957-60. asst. librarian, 1960-61; librarian Middle Ga. Coll., Cochran, 1961—. Mem. ALA, Tex., Southwestern, Abilene, Ga. (exec. bd. 1963-65, chmn. resources and tech. services div. 1964-65), Southeastern library assns., Ga. Assn. Jr. Colls. (chmn. library div. 1963, 69), Ga. Assn. Educators (local chmn. 1967), Pilot Internat. Clubs: XXI (sec. 1960-61), Cochran Women's (chmn. bicentennial com.), Cochran Pilot (dir. 1977). Compiler: Library Handbook, 1962, rev., 1973. Contbr. articles to profl. jours. Office: Middle Ga Coll Cochran GA 31014

WINDHAM, JAMES MULDROW, lawyer; b. Manning, S.C., July 28, 1909; s. James Manly and Louise Muldrow (Richbourg) W.; B.S., U. S.C., 1932, LL.B., 1934; m. Sarah Louise Askins, June 8, 1935; 1 dau., Carol Ann (Mrs. David Tomlinson). Admitted to S.C. bar, 1934, Supreme Ct. S.C., 1934, U.S. Supreme Ct., 1959, U.S. Tax Ct., 1970; title atty. U.S. Dept. Agr., Charleston, 1934-36; trial atty. S.C. Pub. Service Authority, Charleston, 1940-42; dist. div. atty. Office of Rent Stblzn., Charleston, 1942-52; gen. counsel S.C. Tax Commn., Columbia, 1952-66, also asst. atty. gen. State of S.C., 1952-66; mem. firm Herbert, Dial & Windham, Columbia, 1966-76; partner firm Dial, Jennings, Windham, Thomas & Roberts, Columbia, 1976—. Mem. Am., S.C., Richland County bar assns., Nat. Tax Assn. (dir. 1965-68), Nat. Assn. Tax Adminstrs. (chmn. legal sect. 1964-65), Am. Judicature Soc., Blue Key, Phi Delta Phi. Baptist. Mason, Rotarian. Clubs: Forest Lake; Summit. Contbr. articles to profl. jours. Home: 926 Arbutus Dr Columbia SC 29205 Office: Barringer Bldg Suite 707 Box 1792 Columbia SC 29211

WINDLE, JANE WELCH, hosp. nursing adminstr.; b. Columbus, Miss., Oct. 15, 1950; d. Willie Ervin and Mary Verla (Studdard) Welch; R.N. diploma Druid City Hosp. Sch. Nursing, Tuscaloosa, Ala., 1973; m. Albert Earl Windle, Nov. 17, 1971; children—Jason Earl, Brian Wesley. With Columbus (Miss.) Hosp., 1969-68, 70—, inservice dir., 1974-75, dir. nursing service, 1976—. Named Outstanding Nurse of Year, VFW, 1979. Mem. Miss. Nurses Assn. (dir.), Am. Nurses Assn. (dir.), ARC, Am. Heart Assn. Mem. Churches of Christ. Club: Soroptimists. Office: 1[illegible]01 Main St Columbua MS 39701

WINEBRENNER, MILTON R., valve mfg. co. exec.; b. New Gulf, Tex., Aug. 27, 1936; s. Nelson Milton and Essie Lorene (Von Cannon) W.; B.A., U. Houston, 1973; m. Irene Valigur, Dec. 28, 1956. Supr. inquiry analysis and quotations W-K-M Valve div., ACF Industries, Inc., Houston, 1970-74, mgr. indsl. sales adminstrn., 1974-77, mgr. mktg. adminstrn., 1977-79, dir. mgr. sales adminstrn., 1979—. Served with U.S. Army, 1959-61. Mem. Nat. Mgmt. Assn. (pres. Tex. Gulf Coast Council 1977—, pres. W-K-M div. chpt. 1980, outstanding service award 1976, 77), Democrat. Club: Toastmasters. Home: 8839 Stroud Dr Houston TX 77036 Office: W-K-M div ACF Industries Inc PO Box 2117 Houston TX 77001

WINEGARDNER, ROY EUGENE, plumbing contractor; b. Springfield, Mo., Nov. 15, 1920; s. Sam J. and Frona (Day) W.; student public schs.; m. Alicia Pardo, Dec. 19, 1974; children—Jane Kay, Jill, Nicky, Diego. Self-employed plumbing and heating contractor; dir. First Tenn. Banking Corp., Memphis; contractor and developer Holiday Inn franchise, 1959—; chmn. bd., chief exec. officer Holiday Inns, Inc., 1979—. Bd. dirs. Nat. Jr. Achievement. Served with U.S. Mcht. Marines, 1943-45. Address: Holiday Inns Inc 3742 Lamar Ave Memphis TN 38195

WINFIELD, JOHN BUCKNER, physician; b. Kentfield, Calif., Mar. 19, 1942; s. Richard Buckner and Margaret Genevive (Katterfield) W.; B.A., Williams Coll., 1964; M.D., Cornell U., 1968; m. Teresa Lee McGrath, Mar. 21, 1969; children—Ann Gibson, John Buckner, Virginia Lee. Intern N.Y. Hosp., 1968-69; staff asso. NIH, Bethesda, Md., 1969-71; resident in medicine U. Va. Sch. Medicine, Charlottesville, 1971-73; postdoctoral fellow Rockefeller U., N.Y.C., 1973-75; asst. prof. medicine U. Va. Sch. Medicine, 1975-76, asso. prof. medicine, 1976-78; asso. prof. medicine, chief div. immunology and rheumatology U. N.C. Sch. Medicine, Chapel Hill, 1978—. Active state and nat. arthritis programs. Served with USPHS, 1969-71. Diplomate Am. Bd. Internal Medicine. Fellow ACP; mem. Am. Fedn. Clin. Research, Soc. Soc. Clin. Investigation, Am. Assn. Immunologists, Am. Rheumatism Assn. Republican. Episcopalian. Contbr. articles in field to med. and sci. jours. Home: 801 King's Mill Rd Chapel Hill NC 27514 Office: U NC Sch Medicine Chapel Hill NC 27514

WINFREE, JEANETTE, phys. therapist; b. Orange, Tex., Dec. 13, 1937; d. Jesse Laurence and Gladys Inez (McDonald) W.; B.S., Sam Houston State Tchrs. Coll., 1960; B.S., U. Tex., 1961; M.Ed., Stephen F. Austin State U., 1971. Staff phys. therapist - lab. instr. and research asst. U. Tex. Med. Br., Galveston, 1962-64; cons. Clinic of Internal Medicine, 1966; cons. City of Galveston Medicare program, 1966-71, Moody House Retirement Community, 1965—, Home Health-Home Care, 1974—, Orthopedic Clinic of Galveston, 1966—; adj. instr. U. Tex. Med. Br. Sch. Allied Health Scis., 1974—; clin. edn. supr. Emory U., Atlanta, 1977—; owner, dir. Phys. Therapy Services, Galveston, 1964—; lectr. in field. Fin. chmn. Denman (Tex.) Sch. Bd., 1973; sec. Galveston County Com. on Aging, 1965-68; survey team Galveston Hist. Found., 1973; profl. adv. council Home Health-Home Care, Inc., 1974—; fund worker Am. Heart Assn., 1971; membership capt. Civic Music Assn., 1967-70; mem. Galveston County Cultural Arts Council. Recipient Annual Service award, Am. Phys. Therapy Assn., 1974, 78. Mem. Am. Phys. Therapy Assn. (pres. 1974-78, dir. 1978-81), Nat. Rehab. Assn., Am. Personnel and Guidance Assn., Am. Rehab. Counseling Assn., U. Tex. Phys. Therapy Alumni Assn., I.S. Racquetball Assn., Nat. Women's Polit. Caucus, Tex. Hist. Soc., Orange Keys, Alpha Chi, Kappa Delta Pi. Democrat. Baptist. Author: Oh, My Aching Back, 1973; A Home Program for the Shoulder, 1973 (slide-tape presentations). Home: 1619 Bayou Shore Dr Galveston TX 77550 Office: 422 9 St Galveston TX 77550

WINFREY, DORMAN HAYWARD, state librarian; b. Henderson, Tex., Sept. 4, 1924; s. Luke Abel and Linnie (Fears) W.; B.A., U. Tex., 1950, M.A., 1951, Ph.D., 1962; m. Ruth Carolyn Byrd, June 12, 1954; children—Laura, Jennifer. Social sci. research asso. Research in Tex. History, Tex. Hist. Assn. at U. Tex., 1946-58; state archivist, 1958-60; archivist U. Tex., 1960-61; dir., librarian Tex. State Library, 1962—. Chmn. State Bd. Library Examiners, 1962—; chmn. State Records Preservation Adv. Com., 1965—; mem. Tex. 1986 Sesquicentennial Commn.; bd. dirs. Internat. Festival Inst. at Round Top; adv. bd. Tex. Hist. Records. Served with AUS, 1943-46, ETO. Clara Driscoll scholar for research in Tex. history, 1952-54. Fellow Tex. Hist. Assn. (exec. council, pres. 1971-72), Soc. Am. Archivists (council), Am. Assn. for State and Local History (council), mem. Tex. Inst. Letters, Philos. Soc. Tex. (sec., editor procs. 1976—), Am. Assn. State Libraries (planning com.), ALA, Tex. Library Assn., Am., Tex., So. hist. assns., Tex. Travel Trails Com., Bicentennial Assn. Tex., Phi Alpha Theta, Pi Sigma Alpha. Mem. Disciples of Christ Ch. Author, editor: Texas Indian Papers, 1825-1843, 1959; Texas Indian Papers, 1844-1845, 1960; Texas Indian Papers, 1846-1859, 1961; A History of Rusk County, Texas, 1961; Julien Sidney Devereux and His Monte Verdi Plantation, 1964; Indian Papers of Texas and the Southwest, 1825-1916 (5 vols.), 1966; Arturo Toscanini in Texas; The 1950 NBC Symphony Orchestra Tour, 1967; spl. editor Tex. Ency. for Young People, 1964; asso. editor Jr. Historian mag., 1951-58; Seventy-Five Years of Texas History: The Texas State Historical Association, 1897-1972, 1975. Home: 6503 Willamette Dr Austin TX 78723 Office: Tex State Library Box 12927 Capitol Sta Austin TX 78711

WINFREY, ELISHA WILLIAM, III, physician; b. Richmond, Va., June 10, 1932; s. Elisha William and Lee (Jones) W.; student Washington and Lee U., 1948-50; A.B., U. Va., 1952, M.D., 1956; m. Sylvia Wallace, Sept. 15, 1973; children—Catherine Layne, Rebecca Lee. Intern, U. Va. Hosp., Charlottesville, 1956-57; resident Vanderbilt U. Hosp., Nashville, 1959-63; resident George Washington U. Hosp., Washington, 1963-65, instr. surgery, 1963-65; practice medicine specializing in thoracic and cardiovascular surgery, Newport News, Va., 1965—; mem. staff Hampton Va. VA Hosp., 1965—. Mem. adv. council U. Va., 1966—. Served with USN, 1956-59. Diplomate Am. Bd. Surgery, Am. Bd. Thoracic and Cardiovascular Surgery. Fellow A.C.S.; mem. So. Thoracic Surgery Assn., Flying Physicians Assn., Aircraft Owners and Pilots Assn., S.E. Va. Radio Control Group, Am. Radio Relay League. Contbr. articles to profl. jours. Home: 25 Douglas Dr Newport News VA 23601 Office: 719 J Clyde Morris Blvd Newport News VA 23601

WINGFIELD, MERVYN WALLER, accountant, educator; b. Alleghany County, Va., Aug. 19, 1926; s. James Edlow and Christine Dole (Higgins) W.; A.B., Coll. William and Mary, 1949; M.S., U. Richmond, 1957; Ph.D., U. Ill., 1963. Staff accountant J.A. Daniels, Newport News, Va., 1952-55; instr. accounting U. Ill., Urbana, 1957-60; acting chmn. dept. accounting U. Richmond (Va.), 1960-62; prof. U. S.C., Columbia, 1962-70; chmn. dept. accounting Va. Commonwealth U., Richmond, 1970—. Served with USAAF, 1945. C.P.A., Va., S.C. Mem. Am. Acctg. Assn. (S.E. regional v.p. 1974-75),

Am. Inst. C.P.A.'s, Va. Soc. C.P.A.'s, Inst. Internal Auditors, Nat. Assn. Accountants, Planning Execs. Inst., Assn. Govt. Accts., Mcpl. Fin. Officers Assn., Beta Gamma Sigma, Beta Alpha Psi, Omicron Delta Epsilon. Presbyterian. Club: Farmington Country. Editor: (with Edward N. Coffman) Collected Papers 1975 Annual Meeting Southeast Regional Group American Accounting Assn., 1975. Contbr. articles to profl. jours. Home: 1407 Confederate Ave Richmond VA 23227 Office: Dept Accounting Virginia Commonwealth U Richmond VA 23284

WINGO, JUDITH LYNETTE, counselor; b. Houston, Dec. 11, 1946; d. Mack and N. Vivian (Tomlinson) Akey; B.A. with honors in Spanish, U. Tex., Arlington, 1968; M.Ed., N. Tex. State U., 1974; m. Dennis A. Wingo, Feb. 14, 1969; children—Melissa Shay, Keith Alan. Tchr. Spanish and Tex. history Central Jr. High Sch., Euless, Tex., 1968-69; teaching asst. Spanish, N. Tex. State U., Denton, 1972-73; counselor Tex. Christian U., Ft. Worth, 1974-77; instnl. counselor VA Guidance Center, Tex. Christian U., 1977—; cons. career counseling, job hunting skills, resume writing, standardized testing. Club leader Camp Fire Girls. Provisionally cert. secondary tchr. Mem. Am. Personnel and Guidance Assn., North Central Tex. Personnel and Guidance Assn., Sigma Delta Pi. Mem. Ch. of Christ. Club: N.E. Bus. and Profl. Woman's of Ft. Worth (2d v.p. 1978-79). Home: 1029 Inwood Dr Hurst TX 76053 Office: PO Box 29730A Texas Christian University Fort Worth TX 76129

WINKEL, ERWIN CHARLES, urologist; b. Houston, July 7, 1934; s. Erwin Charles and Annie (Walther) W.; B.A., Baylor U., 1956, M.D., 1959; m. Jacquelyn Yvonne Watson, Sept. 3, 1960; children—Erwin Charles III, Carolyn, Todd. Intern, Hermann Hosp., Houston, 1959-60, resident in urology, 1960-62, 64-66; practice medicine specializing in urology, Houston, 1966—; a founder N. Central Gen. Hosp., Houston, 1974, chief of staff, 1974-75; a founder Houston N.W. Med. Center Hosp., 1973, chief of staff, 1977-78; mem. staffs Meml. Hosp. System, Hermann, Sam Houston, Parkway, Citizens Gen., Spring Branch Meml., Rosewood hosps. clin. asso. in urology U. Tex. Med. Sch., Houston, 1967—. Committeeman Troop 9, Boy Scouts Am., 1952—, instl. rep., 1960-66, merit badge counsellor, 1967-71; mem. adv. bd. Volunteers of Am., 1968-76. Served with U.S. Army, 1962-64. Diplomate Am. Bd. Urology. Fellow Internat. Coll. Surgeons, ACS; mem. AMA (Physicians Recognition award 1969, 72, 75, 77), Am. Urol. Assn., Am. Assn. Clin. Urologists, Tex. Med. Assn., Am. Fertility Soc., Am. Geriatrics Soc., Am. Assn. Physicians and Surgeons, World, So. med. assns., Nat. Kidney Found., Harris County Med. Soc., Houston Urol. Socs., Houston Acad. Medicine. Republican. Methodist. Home: 5523 Foresthaven St Houston TX 77066 Office: 710 FM 1960 West Suite D Houston TX 77090

WINKELMAN, BETTY JANE, nurse, med. adminstr.; b. Albert Lea, Minn., Jan. 20, 1931; d. Milton Charles and Lillian M. (Ausenhus) W.; R.N., Iowa Luth. Hosp. Sch. Nursing, 1953; student Palomar Coll., San Marcos, Calif., 1956-57, U. Wis., Madison, summer 1962. Nurse operating room Iowa Luth. Hosp., Des Moines, 1953-54; staff nurse Madison (Wis.) Gen. Hosp., 1957-58, head nurse central supply, 1958-60, supr. emergency room, student health employee health service and central supply, 1960-63, supr. phys. medicine-rehab. unit, 1963; supr. inhalation therapy dept., 1964-69, supr. operating room and central supply, 1969-72; staff nurse emergency room Baptist Med. Center, Jacksonville, Fla., 1973, asst. dir. materials mgmt., 1973-74, dir. materials mgmt., 1974—, acting dir. operating room, 1979—; cons. in field. Served to lt., Nurse Corps, USNR, 1955-57. Mem. Am. Soc. Hosp. Central Services of Am. Hosp. Assn., Internat. Materials Mgmt. Soc. Episcopalian. Club: Altrusa (pres. Jacksonville 1978-80). Home: 8223 Altama Rd Jacksonville FL 32216 Office: Baptist Med Center 800 Prudential Dr Jacksonville FL 32207

WINKLER, JOHN BENNETT, foundry exec.; b. Harriman, Tenn., May 16, 1949; s. Paul Frank and Estelle (Pye) W.; B.S., U. Tenn., Chattanooga, 1971. Buyer-expediter, corporate engring. dept. Mead Corp., Dayton, Ohio, 1974-76, field cost controller Lynchburg Foundry div., Lynchburg, Va., 1976-77, capital equipment buyer Lynchburg Foundry div., 1977—. Served with Mil. Police Corps, U.S. Army, 1972-74. Presbyterian. Clubs: Central Va. Ski, Oakwood Country. Home: 333 Sumpter St Lynchburg VA 24503 Office: PO Drawer 411 620 Court St Lynchburg VA 24505

WINKLER, JONNY KENT, juvenile probation officer; b. Charleston, W.Va., Jan. 17, 1949; s. William Edward and Vera Ray (Justice) W.; student W.Va. U., 1966-69; B.A. in English, Marshall U., 1971, M.A. in Counseling and Rehab., 1975. With div. traffic engring. W.Va. Dept. Hwys., Charleston, 1972-73; social service worker foster care unit W.Va. Dept. Welfare, Huntington, 1975-78; juvenile probation officer W.Va. State Supreme Ct., 1978—. Mem. Am. Personnel and Guidance Assn., Pub. Offender Counselor Assn., W.Va. Assn. Probation Officers, Phi Delta Kappa. Republican. Baptist. Home: 926 Eutaw Pl Huntington WV 25701 Office: Cabell County Courthouse Huntington WV 25701

WINKLER, JOSEPH AUGUSTINE, III, marketing exec.; b. West Monroe, La., July 19, 1942; s. Joseph A. and Margaret L. (Grace) W.; B.S. in Biochemistry, La. State U., 1965, M.S., 1966; postgrad. Fla. State U., 1966-67, Loyola U., 1967-70, U. Southwestern La., 1970—. Asst. dir. NSF Secondary Sci. Tng. Program, summers 1966, 67-71; v.p. mktg. Phoenix Computer Systems, Inc., 1976—; instr. computer sci. U. Southwestern La., 1978-79. Mem. Assn. Computing Machinery, Aircraft Owners and Pilots Assn., Exptl. Aircraft Assn., Sigma Xi, Alpha Chi Sigma, Tau Kappa Epsilon. Democrat. Roman Catholic. Home: 201 S Locksley Dr Lafayette LA 70508 Office: 3305 W Pinhook Rd Lafayette LA 70508

WINN, LANELLE MILDRED, home-sch. coordinator; b. Amarillo, Tex., Aug. 13, 1929; d. Henry Alton and Mildred Phyllis (Schoening) Bassett; B.A., W.Tex. State U., 1951, M.Ed., 1968; student Our Lady of the Lake U., 1975; m. Cecil Munger Winn, Mar. 13, 1953; children—Gregory Wayne, Cecelia Jean, Sharon Gail. Teacher, Lazbuddy (Tex.) Pub. Schs., 1949-50, Carlsbad (N.M.) Pub. Schs., 1951, Amarillo (Tex.) Pub. Schs., 1952-53; research asst. W.Tex. State U., 1965-67, field rep. Talent Search, 1968; instr. Amarillo Coll., 1969; vocat. counselor Bay City (Tex.) Ind. Sch. Dist., 1970-73; family counselor; cons. sch. personnel, San Antonio, Tex., 1973—. Mem. Am., Tex., S.Tex. personnel and guidance assns., Vis. Teacher Assn. Tex., Alamo Area Vis. Teacher Assn., Nat. Edn. Assn., Tex. State Teacher Assn., Harlandale Tchrs. and Supportive Services Assn. So. Baptist. Home: 159 De Chantle St San Antonio TX 78201 Office: 102 Genevieve St San Antonio TX 78214

WINN, ROGER EUGENE, hosp. adminstr.; b. Wichita, Kans., Apr. 6, 1940; s. Bill Ross and Anne Elizabeth (Madden) W.; B.A., Wichita State U., 1965; postgrad. U. Nebr., 1974-78, M.A., 1978; m. Sandra Mae Arp, Oct. 10, 1962; children—Ross Edward, Scott Hayward, Amy Kathleen. Profl. recruiter Cessna Aircraft, Wichita, 1965-69; wage and salary adminstr. Research Hosp. and Med. Center, Kansas City, Mo., 1969-70, dir. personnel, 1970-72; dir. personnel Lincoln Gen. Hosp., Lincoln, Nebr., 1972-77, adminstrv. dir. personnel, tng., risk mgmt. and mgmt. engring., 1977-79; dir. human resources, personnel and tng. Morton F. Plant Hosp., Clearwater, Fla., 1979—. Mem. Greater Kansas City Area Personnel Dirs. Assn. (pres. 1970-71), Am. Hosp. Assn., Soc. Hosp. Personnel Adminstrn., Hosp. Personnel Assn. Midlands. Republican. Episcopalian. Club: Masons. Home: 10820 Hammock Dr Largo FL 33540 Office: 323 Jeffords St Clearwater FL 33517

WINNINGHAM, ANNIE RUTH, educator; b. E. Tallassee, Ala., July 10, 1926; d. Richard Hubbard and Vera Donie (Oliver) W.; B.S., Auburn U., 1948; M.S., Med. Coll. Ga., 1968. Staff technologist/chief technologist Med. Center, Columbus, Ga., 1949-54; chief technologist Cobb Meml. Hosp., Phenix City, Ala., 1954-57; research technologist U. Miami (Fla.) Sch. Medicine, 1957-65; grad. fellow/instr. Med. Coll. Ga., Augusta, 1965-75, asso. prof., Sch. Allied Health Scis., Sch. Grad. Studies, Dept. Med. Tech., 1975—. Named Med. Technologist of the Year, Ga. Soc. Med. Tech., 1977. Mem. Ga. Soc. Med. Tech. (pres. 1972-74, sec. 1969-71), Am. Soc. Med. Tech., Ga. Soc. Allied Health Professions, Central Savannah River Area Soc. for Med. Lab. Personnel, Alpha Eta, Omicron Sigma. Democrat. Methodist. Hematology book reviewer, Am. Jour. Med. Tech., 1974—; author: Hematology Manual for Med. Tech. Students, vols. I and II, 1975, 79—. Home: Route 2 Box 259G Thomson GA 30824 Office: Dept Med Tech Med Coll Ga Augusta GA 30912

WINSLOW, PHILLIP HUDSON, urologist; b. Norman, Okla., Feb. 25, 1940; s. David Clinton and Mary Josephine W.; B.S., Okla. State U., 1961; M.D., Jefferson Med. Coll., 1965; m. Susan Anne Wasson, June 13, 1965; children—Matthew, Paul. Intern, Cooper Hosp., Camden, N.J., 1965-66; resident in urology U. Mo., 1969-73; practice medicine specializing in urology, Ponca City, Okla., 1973—; mem. staffs St. Joseph's Hosp., Ponca City; bd. dirs. Kidney Found. Okla. Served with USN, 1966-69. Diplomate Am. Bd. Urology. Fellow A.C.S.; mem. AMA, Am. Urol. Assn. Okla. State Med. Assn. Club: Lions. Office: 304 Fairview Ave Ponca City OK 74601

WINSTEAD, GEORGE ALVIS, librarian; b. Owensboro, Ky., Jan. 14, 1916; s. Robert Lee and Mary Oma W.; B.S., Western Ky. U., 1938; M.A., George Peabody Coll., 1940, M.A. in L.S., 1957, M.Ed., 1958; postgrad. in law Vanderbilt U.; m. Elisabeth Weaver, July 8, 1943. Prof. chemistry Vanderbilt U., Nashville, asso. law librarian, 1958-76; librarian Tenn. State Law Library, Nashville, 1976—; dir. Tenn. State Law Libraries, 1975—. Fellow Am. Inst. Chemists. Served with USAF, 1943-46. Home: 3819 Gallatin Rd Nashville TN 37216 Office: Tenn State Law Library Supreme Ct Bldg 104 7th Ave Nashville TN 37219

WINSTEAD, HELEN CAPPS, counseling adminstr.; b. Benson, N.C., Sept. 14, 1936; d. John David and Tobitha Florence (Creech) Capps; B.S., Pembroke State U., 1964; M.Ed., N.C. State U., 1968; Ed.D., Nova U., 1979; div.; children—Ronald J., Stephen D., Richard C., Gregory M. Teacher, Cumberland County Schs., Fay, N.C., 1964-68; dir. guidance services Pine Forest Sr. High Sch., Fayetteville, N.C., 1968-70; counselor Fayetteville Tech. Inst., 1970-75, dir. counseling services, 1975—. Mem. Am., N.C. personnel and guidance assns., Am., N.C. coll. personnel assns., Nat. Assn. Women Deans, Adminstrs., Counselors, Am. Assn. Specialists in Group Work, N.C. Community Coll. Student Personnel Services Assn., Phi Delta Kappa. Democrat. Presbyn. Home: 608 Pilot Ave Fayetteville NC 28303 Office: Fayetteville Tech Inst PO Box 35236 Fayetteville NC 28303

WINSTON, HUBERT MELVIN, chem. engr.; b. Washington, May 29, 1948; s. Hubert and Helen Elaine (Simmons) W.; B.S., N.C. State U., 1970, M.S., 1973, Ph.D., 1975. Asst. prof. chem. engring. N.C. State U., Raleigh, 1975-77; research engr. Exxon Prodn. Research Co., Houston, 1977—. Staff worker, gubernatorial campaign H. Lee, 1976. Served with AUS, 1974. Mem. Am. Inst. Chem. Engrs., Smithsonian Assos., Nat. Orgn. Advancement Black Chemists and Chem. Engrs. Contbr. articles to profl. jours. Home: PO Box 22612 Houston TX 77027 Office: Exxon Prodn Research Co Box 2189 Houston TX 77001

WINSTON, IVAN HARRY, JR., bus. services co. exec.; b. Roanoke, Va., Nov. 14, 1946; s. Ivan Harry and Dollie (Gallagher) W.; B.S., Appalachian State U., 1968; postgrad. U. Va., 1969-70; m. Gerry Dickson, Nov. 1, 1968; children—Hollie Marie, Gregory Porter. Tchr., Roanoke County (Va.) Pub. Schs., 1968-70, Lynchburg (Va.) Pub. Schs., 1970-72; v.p., exec. property mgr. Fralin & Waldron, Inc., Roanoke, 1972—. Mem. Nat. Assn. Home Builders (registered apt. mgr.), Inst. Real Estate Mgmt. (certified property mgr.), Am. Mgmt. Assn. Home: 3022 Merino Dr Roanoke VA 24018 Office: PO Box 4652 Roanoke VA 24015

WINSTON, JOHN HENRY, surgeon; b. Montgomery, Ala., Aug. 7, 1928; s. John H. and Frankie Lee (Madison) W.; B.S., Ala. State U., 1949; M.A., Columbia, 1951; M.D., Meharry Med. Coll., 1956; m. Betha Moore, Mar. 30, 1956; children—Gwyneth, Joni, Dina, Terri, John Henry, III. Intern, St. Margaret's Hosp., Hammond, Ind., 1957-58; resident surgery VA Hosp., Tuskegee, Ala., 1957-61; practice medicine, specializing in surgery, Tuskegee, 1961-63, Montgomery, 1963—; mem. staffs St. Margaret's Hosp., Fairview Med. Center. Mem. Montgomery County Bd. Edn., 1964-66. Bd. dirs. Home Health Services, 1964-66, YMCA, 1962-79, Boy Scouts Am., 1965-79, Community Action of Montgomery County, 1960-64; mem. adv. bd. Ala. State U., 1962-66; trustee Lomax Hannon Coll., 1960-66. Served with USAF, 1951-52. Fellow ACS; mem. AMA, Nat. Med. Assn., Am. Coll. Abdominal Surgeons, Ala. Med. Soc. (pres. 1960-64), Capital City Med. Soc., Alpha Phi Alpha. Home: 1521 Robert Hatch Dr Montgomery AL 36106 Office: 1156 Oak St Montgomery AL 36108

WINTER, LEONARD MARCUS, educator; b. Chgo., Sept. 30, 1920; s. Joseph and Eleanor (Grossman) W.; B.S. in Mil. Sci., U. Md., 1955; M.B.A., Babson Coll., 1960; D.P.A., Nova U., 1978; m. Shirley Glaser Winter, July 5, 1946; children—Becky Gail, Stephen Michael, Elizabeth Ann. Enlisted U.S. Army, 1940; advanced through grades to col., 1970; asst. dir. proc. and prod. USA Weapons Command, Rock Island, Ill., 1961-64; sr. adviser, Viet Nam, 1971-72; asst. dep. chief. of staff 7th Army and comdr. 66 Maint. Bn., Germany, 1964-68; dir. proc. and prod. USA Safeguard Systems Command and USA Missile Command, Redstone Arsenal, Ala., 1972-75; ret., 1975; resident dir. Fla. Inst. Tech., Redstone Arsenal Ala. Grad. Center, 1976—; pres. Winter and Assos., Huntsville, Ala., 1975—; sec., dir. Gulf Airpark Estates, Inc. Decorated Legion of Merit, Bronze Star, D.S.M., Named Outstanding indsl. engr., Am. Soc. Profl. Engrs., 1976. Mem. Am. Inst. Indsl. Engrs. (past pres.), Nat. Contract Mgmt. Assn., Soc. Logistics Engrs., Assn. U.S. Army, Am. Soc. Pub. Adminstrn., Am. Def. Preparedness Assn. Jewish. Clubs: Masons, Shriners. Home: 4005 Piedmont Dr SE Huntsville AL 35802 Office: Bldg 7446 Redstone Arsenal AL 35809

WINTER, WILLIAM FORREST, gov. of Miss., lawyer; b. Grenada, Miss., Feb. 21, 1923; s. William Aylmer and Inez (Parker) W.; B.A., U. Miss., 1943, LL.B., 1949; m. Elise Varner, Oct. 10, 1950; children—Anne, Elise, Eleanor. Admitted to Miss. bar, 1949; practice in Grenada, 1949-58, Jackson, Miss., from 1968; partner Watkins, Pyle, Ludlam, Winter and Stennis, 1968-80; mem. Miss. Ho. of Reps., 1948-56; state tax collector, 1956-64; state treas., 1964-68; lt. gov. Miss., 1972-76; gov. State of Miss., 1980—. Pres. bd. trustees Miss. Dept. Archives and History; trustee Belhaven Coll., Columbia Sem.; bd. dirs. Lamar Soc., Miss. Found. Ind. Colls. Served with AUS, 1943-46, 51. Recipient Margaret Dixon Freedom of Info. award AP, 1972. Mem. Am., Miss., Hinds County bar assns., Phi Delta Phi, Omicron Delta Kappa (Outstanding Alumnus U. Miss. 1975). Phi Delta Theta. Democrat. Presbyterian. Club: Univ. (Jackson). Editor-in-chief U. Miss. Law Jour., 1948-49. Office: Office of Gov New State Capitol 400 High St Jackson MS 39202

WINTER, WILLIAM RAYMOND, ret. elec. engr.; b. Worthington, Ohio, Dec. 5, 1913; s. Thomas Raymond and Ada Eltra (Snell) W.; Chem. Engr., Rensselaer Poly. Inst., 1936; postgrad. Columbia, 1937, 40, 46, U. Va., 1955; m. Kathryn Virginia Morgan Winter, Dec. 14, 1940 (dec. June 1978); children—John Staats, Jean Carolyn (Mrs. Gerald K. Bliss). Sales engr. Bklyn. Union Gas Co., 1936-42, dept. head coke oven and light oil plant, 1946-47; sr. engr. research and devel. Cabot Carbon Co., Pampa, Tex., 1947-49; design engr. heating equipment Silent Automatic div. Timken Corp., Jackson, Mich., 1950-55; with Westinghouse Electric Corp., Staunton, Va., 1955-74, mgr. engring. sect. air conditioning equipment, 1957-74. Served to lt. USNR, 1942-45. Mem. Air-Conditioning and Refrigeration Inst. (mem. gen. standards com. 1973-74), Am. Soc. Heating, Refrigeration and Air Conditioning Engrs. (mem. various tech. coms.), IEEE (mem. tech. com. electric space heating and air conditioning 1968-70), Nat. Elec. Mfrs. Assn. (mem. tech. com. electric comfort heating equipment sect. 1961-66). Lion. Club: Stauton Country (pres. 1969-70). Patentee in field. Address: 2806 Raintree Dr New Port Richey FL 33552

WINTON, EDWARD, broadcasting co. exec.; b. N.Y.C., May 30, 1931; s. Edward and Violet W.; student CCNY, 1950-52; m. Linda Diets, Jan. 7, 1967; children—Rhonda, Lance. Program and sta. mgr. Sta. KELP, El Paso, Tex., 1955-57, Sta. KLIF, Dallas, 1954-55; pres. Connie B. Gay Broadcasting Co., Washington, 1960-66; pres. Sta. WGAY AM/FM, Washington, 1960-66; pres. WOCN, Miami, 1966-76; pres. Sta. WWBA AM/FM, St. Petersburg, Fla., 1968—. Served with U.S. Army, 1951-53. Mem. Tampa Bay Broadcasters Assn. (v.p. 1978-79), Museum of Broadcasting, Miami Radio Broadcasters Assn. (past pres.). Office: Suite 200 Koger Executive Center Saint Petersburg FL 33742

WINTON, GEORGE PETERSON, JR., historian, ret. army officer; b. Knoxville, Tenn., June 17, 1918; s. George Peterson and Dorothy (Calhoun) W.; B.S., U.S. Mil. Acad., 1939; M.A., George Washington U., 1962; Ph.D., U. S.C., 1972; m. Lucille Cutchin, Dec. 13, 1941; children—Margaret Cutchin Winton Engvall, George Beverly. Commd. 2d. lt. U.S. Army, 1939, advanced through grades to col., 1957, served field artillery, ret., 1969; asst. dean Coll. Humanities and Social Scis., instr. in history U. S.C., Columbia, 1973-78, lectr. in history, 1978—. Decorated Legion of Merit, Cross of War Merit (Italy). Mem. Assn. Grads. U.S. Mil. Acad., Am. Mil. Inst., Am. Hist. Assn., So. Hist. Assn., Orgn. Am. Historians, 88th Inf. Div. Assn. Episcopalian. Asst. editor, prin. author: A Short Military History of World War I with Atlas, 1950. Home: 4841 Oakhill Rd Columbia SC 29206 Office: History Dept University of South Carolina Columbia SC 29208

WINTON, HOWARD PHILLIP, optometrist; b. Springfield, Mo., June 23, 1925; s. George Lecoumpt and Emma Pearl (Schoonover) W.; D.Optometry, No. Ill. Coll. Optometry, 1949; postgrad. Mid West Sch. Optics, 1949-50; L.H.D., Ill. Coll. Optometry, 1965; m. Frances Jeanne Zellweger, June 29, 1946; children—Susan (Mrs. C. A. Rossetter, Jr.), James, Stephen, Gary, Carolyn. Pvt. practice optometry, Jacksonville, Fla., 1950-51, Melbourne, Fla., 1951—; nat. cons. to surgeon gen. U.S. Air Force, 1979. Chmn. Brevard Econ. Devel. Council. Trustee So. Coll. Optometry, 1966-67; bd. dirs. Minit Saver, Inc., Better Vision Inst. Served with USNR, 1943-46. Fellow Royal Soc. Health, Am. Acad. Optometry, Am. Optometric Assn. (pres. 1975-76, distinguished mem.); mem. Am. Optometric Student Assn. (hon. life), Fla. (Fla. Optometrist of Year 1970, pres. 1965-66), Indian River (pres. 1953, 79-80) optometric assns., So. Council Optometrists (pres. 1970-71), Melbourne C. of C. (pres. 1963-64); hon. mem. Internat. Orthokeratology sect. Nat. Eye Research Found. Democrat. Methodist (mem. adminstrv. bd. 1967-72). Rotarian (Outstanding Rotarian 1961-62). Club: Eau Gallie Yacht (Melbourne). Home: 30 E Melbourne St Melbourne FL 32901 Office: PO Box 278 Melbourne FL 32901

WINTTER, ARCHIE HERMAN, mech. engr.; b. Hueytown, Ala., June 25, 1920; s. John Arnold and Ruth (Kinnett) W.; student Birmingham So. Coll., 1946-47; B.S. in Mech. Engring., Auburn U., 1949; m. Helen Eloise West, Aug. 12, 1950; children—Archie Kent, Helen Sue. With Woodward Iron Co. (Ala.), 1949-53, draftsman, 1950-53; with Fairfield (Ala.) works U.S. Steel Corp., 1953-70, head design draftsman, 1963-70; engr. Woodward Co. div. Mead Corp., 1970-71, chief draftsman, 1971-74; plant engr. Koppers Co., Inc., 1974-76; pres. XW Engring. Co., Inc., 1974-76; project engr. Ala. By-Products Corp., 1976-77; mech. designer Joy Mfg. Corp., 1977—; sr. designer Goslin div. Envirotech, 1978; mech. engr. Connors Steel, 1979. Served with USAAF, 1941-45. Decorated Air medal. Registered profl. engr., Ala., Tenn. Mem. Pi Tau Sigma. Home: 507 Charleston Dr Bessemer AL 35020 Office: Connor's Steel Co 101 50th St S Birmingham AL 35212

WIORKOWSKI, GABRIELLE KAY, data processing cons.; b. Tulsa, Nov. 10, 1943; d. Marshall Frank and Iva Ann (Johnson) Patterson; B.A. summa cum laude, St. Mary's U., 1971; M.S., U. Tex., Dallas, 1979; m. John J. Wiorkowski, June 4, 1966; 1 dau., Fleur. Adminstrv. asst. Stritch Sch. Medicine, Loyola U., Chgo., 1963-67; sr. programmer Corn Products Co., Chgo., 1967-68; mgr. data communications Jewel Co., Chgo., 1971-74; ind. data processing cons., Dallas, 1975—; lectr. U. Tex., Dallas, 1980—. Mem. Richardson Assn. Gifted and Talented (treas. 1979-80), Assn. Computing Machinery, Nat. Computer Conf. (publs. chmn., steering com. 1977), Delta Epsilon Sigma, Pi Gamma Mu. Republican. Presbyterian. Author chpt. in book; also articles. Home and office: 428 Bedford Dr Richardson TX 75080

WIORKOWSKI, JOHN JAMES, educator; b. Chgo., Sept. 30, 1943; s. John Stanley and Harriet Elizabeth (Bedra) W.; B.S., U. Chgo., 1965, M.S., 1966, Ph.D., 1972; m. Gabrielle K. Hollis, June 4, 1966; children—Fleurette Anne. Research asso. U. Chgo., 1972; asst. prof. Pa. State U., University Park, 1973-74; asso. prof. U. Tex. at Dallas, Richardson, 1975, asso. prof. and program head Math Scis. Program, 1979—; cons. to Fed. Energy Adminstrn., 1975, Tex. Instruments, 1977, Frito-Lay Inc., 1977-78, Republic Nat. Bank, 1979. Served to capt. U.S. Army, 1968-71. Decorated Army Commendation medal. NSF grantee, 1975—. Mem. Am. Statis. Assn. (chpt. pres. 1974, v.p. 1977, chpt. pres. 1978), AAAS, Inst. Math. Stats., Biometric Soc., Sigma Xi. Presbyterian. Contbr. articles to profl. jours. Home: 428 Bedford St Richardson TX 75080 Office: U Tex at Dallas Box 688 Richardson TX 75080

WIPF, AMOS SAMUEL, educator; b. Onida, S.D., Mar. 7, 1924; s. Sam S. and Justina (Pollman) W.; B.A., Huron Coll., 1950; student U. Nebr., summer 1949; postgrad. U. S.D., 1950-51; M.A., Bob Jones U.,

1956; M.Ed., Clemson U., 1962; postgrad. Mont. State U., summer 1963; M.B.S., U. Colo., 1964; D.Arts, U. No. Colo., 1970; m. Joyce Ivaleen Walter, June 29, 1951; children—Anita Joy, Amy Janine, Alice Janelle. Tchr., Claremont (S.D.) Public Schs., 1952-53; faculty Bob Jones U., Greenville, S.C., 1956-63; tchr., chmn. sci. dept. Tehachapi (Calif.) Unified Sch., 1966-72; prof., chmn. div. natural sci. and math. Liberty Baptist Coll., Lynchburg, Va., 1972—, council acad. affairs, 1972—, sec. council, 1978-79, chmn. profl. growth and faculty welfare, 1973-80, sponsor sci. club, 1973-79. Video operator Old Time Gospel Hour TV program, Lynchburg, Va., 1973—; sponsor youth dept. First Baptist Ch., Tehachapi, 1970-72, choir dir. and song leader, 1971-72; Sunday sch. tchr., Boulder, Colo., 1963-64, Greeley, Colo., 1964-67; 4-H Club leader, Onida, S.D., 1942-43; pres. Huron Coll. YMCA, 1947-58; prs., v.p., co-founder World Missionary Aviation Found., Lynchburg. Served in M.C., U.S. Army, 1945-46. NSF fellow, summer 1963, 1963-64. Mem. Am. Chem. Soc., World Future Soc., World Missionary Aviation Found., Am. Legion, Phi Delta Kappa, Pi Kappa Delta, Lambda Sigma Tau. Home: 126 Kirkley Pl Forest VA 24551 Office: Liberty Baptist College Lynchburg VA 24506

WIRGES, MANFORD FRANK, energy resource co. exec.; b. Beatrice, Nebr., Jan. 18, 1925; s. Frank Jessie and Leta Irene (Coon) W.; B.S. in Chem. Engring., U. Okla., 1943, M.S., 1945; m. Joan Audrey Kelly, Sept. 3, 1949; 1 dau., Kelly Marie. Research chem. engr. Cities Service, Bartlesville, Okla., 1946-49, process engr. Ark. Fuel Corp., 1949-52, chief process engr., 1952-54, asst. to mgr., 1954-56; mgr. nat. gas div. Ark. Fuel Corp., 1957-60, chief engr., Tulsa, 1960-61; mgr. chem. devel. sect. Cities Service, N.Y. 1961-62, asst. gen. mgr. Lake Charles Refining Div., 1962-65, mgr. corporate planning, Tulsa, 1965-68, v.p. research and corporate planning, N.Y., 1968-72, v.p. research and tech. div., 1972-78, v.p. tech., Tulsa, 1978—; pres. Cities Service Research and Devel. Co., Tulsa, 1978—. Adv. bd., Coll. Engring., U. Tulsa, 1976—, St. John Med. Center, Tulsa, 1975—; mem. Found. for Excellence Bd., Sch. of Chem. Engring., U. Okla., 1979—. Standard Oil Devel. Co., fellow, 1944-45. Mem. Am. Inst. Chem. Engrs., Am. Petroleum Inst., Inst. Mgmt. Scis., Frontiers of Sci. Found.-Okla.'s Future, Inc. Club: Twenty-Five Yr. of Petroleum Industry, Summit (Tulsa). Home: 3208 E 69 St Tulsa OK 74136 Office: PO Box 300 Tulsa OK 74102

WIRTZ, NORMAN RICHARD, bottling co. exec.; b. Phila., May 23, 1944; s. Joseph and Laura Marie (Runner) W.; B.S. in Commerce and Engring. Scis., Drexel U., 1966; M.B.A., Lehigh U., 1970; m. Mary Jane Knoll, Oct. 18, 1969; children—Susan Michelle, Jeffrey Andrew. Project cost analyst Air Products & Chems. Inc., Allentown, Pa., 1966-69, supr. project cost control, 1969-70, mgr. welding products acctg., 1970-72, mgr. project acctg., 1972-76, mgr. fin. planning, 1976-77; dir. planning analysis, beverage div. Gen. Cinema Co., Miami, Fla., 1977—. Mem. Planning Execs. Inst. (sec. Allentown chpt. 1977, v.p. South Fla. chpt. 1979). Home: 5530 SW 109th Ave Fort Lauderdale FL 33328 Office: Gen Cinema Co PO Box 593577AMF 7777 NW 41st St Miami FL 33328

WISDOM, HAROLD WALTER, forest economist; b. Clarkston, Wash., Oct. 18, 1933; s. Roy D. and Meta T. Wisdom; B.S., U. Idaho, 1960; M.S., Syracuse U., 1964, Ph.D., 1967; m. Carmen J. Del Coro, Aug. 17, 1963; 1 son, John R. Research economist N.E. Forest Expt. Sta., Dept. Agr., Princeton, W.Va., 1965-67; sr. economist Clapp & Mayne, Inc., San Juan, P.R., 1967-69; econ. and planning advisor Govt. of Panama, 1969-71; v.p. Clapp & Mayne, Inc., San Juan, 1971-76; asso. prof. forest econs. Va. Poly. Inst. and State U., Blacksburg, 1976—. Served with USAF, 1953-57. Mem. Soc. Am. Foresters, Xi Sigma Pi. Research on internat. trade in forest products, forestry econs., internat. devel. Office: Dept of Forestry Virginia Polytechnic Institute and State University Blacksburg VA 24061

WISE, BELINDA JO, engring. corp. exec.; b. Kermit, Tex., Jan. 30, 1948; d. William Orvin and Joanne (Barnett) Pigman; student public schs., Tex.; m. Charles Cleveland Wise, Apr. 12, 1978; children by previous marriage—Brandin Rex Presley, Shea Delaina Presley. With Otis Engring. Corp., Dallas, 1968—, supr. engring. records, 1976-77, coordinator engring. info. and systems coordinator, 1977—. Mem. Nat. Micrographic Assn., Assn. Records Mgrs. and Adminstrs. (past sec., dir. Dallas 1975-78), Otis Skeet and Trap League (sec. 1976, 80). Home: 2038 Eagles Nest Pass Lewisville TX 75067 Office: 1001 Crosby Rd Carrollton TX 75006

WISE, GEORGE EWING, JR., state govt. exec.; b. Hinton, W.Va., June 16, 1926; s. George Ewing and Anna May (Mollish) W.; A.S., Beckley Coll., 1950; children—Paula Sue Kester, Georgianna Lynn, Joni Bett. Conservation officer Summers County, W.Va. Dept. Natural Resources, 1950-52, wildlife mgr. Bluestone Pub. Hunting and Fishing Area, 1952-67, land agt. planning and devel. div., Charleston, 1967-75, chief planning and devel. div., Charleston, 1975-77; chief pub. assistance Gov's. Disaster Recovery Office, Charleston, 1977-79; adminstr. abandoned mine reclamation W.Va. Dept. Natural Resources, 1979—. Leader 4-H Club, 1957-61; life rank Appalachian council Boy Scouts Am., 1938-44; bd. dirs. W.Va. Water Festival, Inc., 1966-77; co-chmn. nat. Stock outboard races Am. Power Boat Assn., 1969, 70, 76, 77. Served with USN, 1944-46, with Air N.G., 1955—. Recipient certificate of appreciation for patriotic civilian service C.E., 1977, service certificate Dept. Natural Resources, 1977, certificate of appreciation for flood recovery assistance, 1978. Mem. Am. Right of Way Assn., Soil Conservation Service Soc., W.Va. Planners Assn., Air Force Sgts. Assn. Democrat. Baptist. Clubs: Hinton Lions (pres. 1962-63), Hinton Elks, Hinton Moose. Home: 1604 C Smith Rd Charleston WV 25314 Office: 2002 Quarrier St Charleston WV 25305

WISE, LINDA FLORENCE, counselor, lawyer; b. Waco, Tex., Mar. 13, 1947; d. Herbert Earl and Velma Mlae (Rodman) W.; B.A., Baylor U., 1969; M.Ed., Trinity U., San Antonio, 1973; J.D., S. Tex. Coll. Law, 1978. Tchr., Alamo Heights High Sch., San Antonio, 1969-73; counselor Clear Creek High Sch., League City, Tex., 1973—; admitted to Tex. bar, 1978; individual practice law, Houston, 1978—. Del., Tex. Gov.'s Conf. on Youth and Children, 1970; sr. counselor Tex. Girls State, 1974; coordinator Clear Creek's activities in Houston Bi-Centennial Youth Fair, 1976; 3d. v.p. NASA Area Democrats, 1979; steering com. Greater Houston Area Closeup. Mem. Am. Bar Assn., Tex. Bar Assn., Bay Area Bar Assn., Women in Law, Am. Personnel and Guidance Assn., Women in Communications, NEA, Tex. Tchrs. Assn., Clear Creek Educators Assn., Phi Alpha Delta. Mem. Ch. of Christ. Home: 2002 San Sebastian Ct A-322 Nassau Bay TX 77058

WISE, PATRICIA DIANE TAYLOR, speech pathologist; b. Memphis, Aug. 3, 1951; d. Tommie and Collie Jane Taylor; B.A. in Edn., U. Miss., 1973, M. Communicative Disorders, 1976; m. Mark Wise, June 5, 1971; children—Crystal Diane, April Renee. Speech pathologist Jackson (Miss.) Public Schs., 1974-78, New World Consultant Firm, Jackson, 1978-79; speech pathologist, cons. Community Devel. Enterprises, Jackson, 1979—, dir., pres. New Dimensions in Learning, Inc., Jackson, 1979—. Bd. dirs. Valley N. YMCA, 1978—; active Women for Progress, 1978—, Faith Center; pres. PTA. Named speech pathologist of year, Jackson Public Schs., 1978. Mem. Am. Fedn. Teachers, Am. Speech and Hearing Assn., Central Miss. Speech and Hearing Assn., Nat. Black Assn. Speech and Lang. Pathologist, Zeta Phi Beta (Zeta of year award 1979), Alpha Delta Zeta. Baptist. Address: 5940 Huntview Dr Jackson MS 39206

WISEMAN, BERNARD, artist, author; b. Bklyn., Aug. 26, 1922; s. Abraham Zalman and Yetta Leah (Goldstein) W.; student Art Students League, 1946; m. Susan Levin Cranis; 1 stepson, Peter Franklin Cranis; 1 son, Michael Avram. Cartoonist, New Yorker mag., 1948-57; now artist, illustrator, author. Served with USCG, 1941-46. Author: Boatniks, 1962; Irwin the Intern, 1963; (juveniles) Morris Goes to School, 1970, Morris and Boris, 1974; Iglook's Seal, 1977; Billy Learns Karate, 1977; Morris Has a Cold, 1978; Bobby and Boo, 1978; many others. Illustrator own books, also James Michener's The Boy Who Found Christmas, 1966. Contbr. Sir Nervous Norman stories to Boys' Life mag., 1968—; also contbr. numerous cartoons to maj. mags. in U.S., to Punch mag., Eng. Address: 2640 Lake Hill Rd West Eau Gallie Melbourne FL 32935

WISEMAN, CHARLES LOUIS, physician, educator; b. Los Angeles, Feb. 8, 1944; B.S. (Regents scholar), UCLA, 1965, M.D. (Regents scholar), 1969; m. Barbara Hanauer; children—Joshua Brian, Ari Joel. Intern, U. Utah Hosps., 1969-70; resident in internal medicine Washington U. Hosp., St. Louis, 1970-72; fellow oncology dept. developmental therapeutics M.D. Anderson Hosp. and Tumor Inst., Houston, 1972-73, sr. fellow U. Tex. System Cancer Center, 1975-76, asst. prof. dept. medicine and asst. internist, also chief med. breast div. basic research program, 1976—, asst. prof. dept. molecular carcinogenesis and virology, 1979—. Am. Cancer Soc. fellow, 1972-73. Diplomate Am. Bd. Internal Medicine. Mem. A.C.P., Am. Soc. Clin. Oncology, Am. Assn. Cancer Research, AMA, Tex. Med. Assn., Harris County Med. Soc., Sigma Xi, Phi Beta Kappa, Phi Lambda Upsilon. Contbr. articles to profl. jours. Office: Univ Texas System Cancer Center MD Anderson Hospital and Tumor Inst Texas Med Center 6723 Bertner St Houston TX 77030

WISEMAN, THOMAS ANDERTON, JR., judge; b. Tullahoma, Tenn., Nov. 3, 1930; s. Thomas Anderton and Vera Seleta (Poe) W.; B.A., Vanderbilt U., 1952, LL.B., 1954; m. Emily Barbara Matlack, Mar. 30, 1957; children—Thomas Anderton, Mary Alice, Sarah Emily. Admitted to Tenn. bar; practice law, Tullahoma, 1956-63; partner firm Haynes, Wiseman & Hull, 1963-71; state treas., State of Tenn., 1971-74; partner firm Chambers & Wiseman, 1974-78; U.S. Dist. judge, Middle Dist. of Tenn., Nashville, 1978—; mem. Tenn. Ho. of Reps., 1964-68; Democratic candidate for gov., Tenn., 1974. Chmn. Tenn. Heart Fund, 1973; chmn. Middle Tenn. Heart Fund, 1972. Served with U.S. Army, 1954-56. Mem. Am. Bar Assn., Tenn. Bar Assn. Presbyterian. Clubs: Amateur Chefs of Am., Masons, Shriners. Asso. editor Vanderbilt Law Rev., 1953-54. Office: 824 US Courthouse Nashville TN 37203

WISHARD, BETTY JANE, bank exec.; b. Detroit, Oct. 12, 1948; d. George Leo and Helen Pijut; B.S., Mich. State U., 1971. Asst. buyer accessories Charles A. Stevens, Chgo., 1971-72, corp. dir. tng. and devel., 1972-75; mgr. sales, human relations tng. No. Trust Co., Chgo., 1975-78; asst. v.p., corp. dir. tng. and devel. Hibernia Nat. Bank, New Orleans, 1978—; cons. St. Louis Hotel, St. Ann Hotel, Orleans Transp., New Orleans, 1979; mgmt. devel.-adv. bd. Bus. and Civic Leaders, New Orleans, 1979. Election judge Republican party, Cook County, Chgo., 1972; account exec. United Fund, 1979; bd. dirs. Martha Washington Home for Dependent Crippled Children. Mem. Am. Soc. Tng. and Devel. (dir. La. chpt. 1978—), Nat. Assn. Bank Women, Am. Inst. Banking, Nat. Assn. Female Execs., Am. Soc. Profl. and Exec. Women. Roman Catholic. Home: 3025 Prytania St New Orleans LA 70115 Office: 313 Carondelet St New Orleans LA 70130

WISHNIE, THEODORE BERNARD, restaurant chain exec.; b. N.Y.C., Apr. 4, 1935; s. Joseph and Nettie (Becker) W.; B.S. in Mgmt., N.Y. U., 1957; m. Ethna M.; 2 children. Personnel dir. Jordan Marsh Co., North Miami Beach, Fla., 1971-72; dir. ops. Lillie Rubin Inc., Miami Beach, Fla., 1972-73; v.p. Kapok Tree Inns Corp., Clearwater, Fla., 1973-76, pres., 1977—, also dir. Mem. Nat. Restaurant Assn. Office: 923 S R 593 Clearwater FL 33519

WIST, ABUND OTTOKAR, computer scientist; b. Vienna, Austria, May 23, 1926; s. Engelbert Johannes and Augusta Barbara (Ungewitter) W.; B.S., Tech U. Graz, 1947; M.Ed., U. Vienna, 1950, Ph.D., 1951; m. Suzanne Gregson Smiley, Nov. 30, 1963; children—John Joseph, Abund Charles. Research and devel. engr. Hornyphon AG, Vienna, 1952-54, Siemens & Halske AG, Munich, Germany, 1954-58; dir. research and devel. Brinkman Instruments Co., Westbury, N.Y., 1958-64; sr. scientist Fisher Sci. Inc., Pitts., 1964-69; mem. faculty U. Pitts., 1970-73; asst. prof. computer sci. Va. Commonwealth U., Richmond, 1973—, adj. prof. chemistry, 1977—; gen. chmn. Symposium Computer Applications in Med. Care, Washington, 1977, 78, 79. NASA/Am. Soc. Engring. Edn. faculty fellow, summer 1975. Mem. IEEE (sr.), ASTM, Am. Chem. Soc., N.Y. Acad. Scis., AAAS, Richmond Computer Club (pres. 1977, 78, 79). Roman Catholic. Patentee in electronic and lab. instrumentation. Contbr. articles to profl. jours. Home: 9304 Farmington Dr Richmond VA 23229 Office: 1101 Marshal St N Richmond VA 23298

WITENGIER, MARY JOAN, educator; b. Worchester, Mass., Mar. 26, 1915; d. George H. and Joanna V. (Crowley) MacGilvray; B.S. In Phys. Edn., Boston U., 1938; M.Ed. in Edn. Exceptional Student, U. Fla., 1966; m. Andrew Witengier; children—Mariann, George A., Jan Stephen, Vicent Henry. Chief therapist, Harry Anna Home, Umatilla, Fla., 1940-43, 44-46; coordinator therapy Forrest Park Sch., Orlando, 1950-68; tchr. exceptional student edn. Seminole County Schs., Sanford, Fla., 1968—. Mem. Council Adminstrs. Spl. Edn., Fla. Adminstrn. and Suprs. Assn. (council adminstrs. of spl. edn.), Assn. Childhood Learning Disabilities, Council Exceptional Children. Cert. in phys. edn., phys. therapy, spl. edn., adminstrn. and supervision. Home: 3513 Mayflower Ln Apopka FL 32703 Office: 1211 Mellonville Ave Sanford FL 32771

WITHROW, JON RICHARD, geologist; b. Seminole, Okla., Jan. 8, 1933; s. Richard Dean and LoLeta (Carroll) W.; student Seminole Jr. Coll., 1950-51; B.S. in Petroleum Engring., U. Okla., 1954, M.Geol. Engring., 1963; postgrad. U. Tex., 1958; m. Carol Ann Ferguson, Nov. 21, 1960 (div. Nov. 1968); 1 stepdau., Ann Todd. Mem. engr. tng. program Humble Oil & Refining Co., Odessa, Tex., 1954, petroleum engr., asst. to dist. engr., Andrews, Tex., 1954-55, Wink, Tex., 1955-56, petroleum engr., Midland, Tex., 1956-57, Houston, 1957, Midland, 1957-58; petroleum engr., geologist Montgomery Oil Co., El Dorado, Ark., 1959-60; self-employed petroleum engr., geologist, Oklahoma City, 1960-62; mgr. geol. and engring. dept. Sarkeys Enterprises, Oklahoma City, 1962-65; mgr. geol. and engring. dept. Sarkeys, Inc., Oklahoma City, 1965-72, v.p., 1966-72; ind. petroleum geol. engr., 1972—; pres. Sundance Oil Co., Oklahoma City, 1977—. Registered profl. engr., Okla. Mem. Am. Inst. Mining, Metall, and Petroleum Engrs., Am. Assn. Petroleum Geologists, Nat., Okla. socs. profl. engrs., Oklahoma City Geol. Soc., Oklahoma City Assn. Petroleum Landmen, Oklahoma City Tennis Assn., SAR, Oklahoma City C. of C., Sigma Nu, Tau Beta Pi, Pi Epsilon Tau. Republican. Methodist. Clubs: Oklahoma City Ski, Woodlake Racquet. Home: 6412 Galaxie Terr Oklahoma City OK 73132

WITKIN, JEFFREY KRAEMER, mgmt. cons.; b. Chgo., Jan. 7, 1946; s. Arthur Jerome and Gertrude (Kraemer) W.; B.S., Babson Coll., 1967; M.B.A., U. Chgo., 1973. Mem. adminstrv. service staff Arthur Anderson & Co., Chgo., 1973-75; audit mgr. R.R. Donnelley, Chgo., 1975-78; mgr. mgmt. adv. services dept. Eskew & Gresham, Louisville, 1978; pres. EDP Auditors Assos., Louisville, 1978-79; mgmt. cons., 1980—. Served with U.S. Army, 1969-71. Mem. EDP Auditors Assn., Am. Econ. Assn., Ky. C.P.A.'s, Am. Inst. C.P.A.'s. Home: 2319 Tavener Dr Louisville KY 40222

WITT, CHARLES TILLMAN, JR., mfg. co. exec.; b. Grandfield, Okla., Jan. 10, 1934; s. Charles Tillman and Rachael LaVerne (Kinzer) W.; student Okla. U., 1952, Midwestern U., 1953, Cameron U., 1975, 76; m. Margaret Fay Montgomery, May 15, 1955; children—Rory Dion, Charles Mark, Cindy Joy, Leslie Denise. Engr., LTV, Inc. Continental Electronics div., 1962-67; program adminstr. contracts F&M Systems Co., Dallas, 1967-69; pres. SPS, Inc., Greenville, Tex., 1969-71; owner Witt Service Co., Grandfield, Okla., 1972-75; v.p. Brantly Mfg. Co., Frederick, Okla., 1975—; dir. SPS, Inc. Disaster chmn. ARC; adv. Jr. Achievement; coach Little League; mgr. polit. campaigns, local, state, nat. Served with AUS, 1953-56. Mem. Farm Equipment Mgrs. Assn. Democrat. Lutheran. Author: Garden of the Mind, 1974; contbr. articles to profl. jours. Home: 615 W 2d St Grandfield OK 73546 Office: 516 W Grand St Frederick OK 73542

WITT, ROBERT EDWARD, oil co. exec.; b. El Dorado, Ark., June 28, 1909; s. Edward Nathan and Lula Rebecca (Rankin) W.; student Davidson Coll., 1926-27, 29-30, Washington U., 1927-28; A.B., U. Ark., 1934; M.A., 1934; m. Zoe Elizabeth O'Ferrall, Feb. 22, 1938; 1 dau., Zoe Ann. Chemist, Lion Oil Co., El Dorado, 1934-36, with asphalt sales dept., 1936-56, mgr. asphalt sales dept., 1956-58; pres. Witt Oil Prodn. Co., Shreveport, La., also El Dorado, 1957—. Pres., El Dorado Community Chest Bd., 1955; chmn. Community Chest Campaign, 1953; pres. Sr. Teen Age Club Bd., 1956, El Dorado Community Concert Assn., 1956, El Dorado Library Bd., 1946-76. Trustee Sem. of Southwest, 1965—, mem. exec. com., 1965-69; mem. corp. Warner Brown Hosp.; trustee U. South, 1952-55; vice chmn. Sewanee All Saint Campaign, 1952-54; chmn. dept. finance Exec. Council Diocese Ark., 1953-54, mem. steering com., 1958—; dep. gen. conv. Episcopal Ch., 1953, 56; bd. dirs., exec. v.p. Shreveport Symphony Soc. Mem. Am. Petroleum Inst., Ind. Petroleum Assn. Am. (Ark. v.p. 1960-63, exec. com., 1963-67, dir. 1967-69), Asphalt Inst. (mem. mgmt. com. Div. III 1950-58), Petroleum Adminstrn. War (mem. asphalt sub-com. 1942-44), Shreveport C. of C., Assn. Asphalt Paving Technologists, Sigma Chi, Sigma Upsilon. Democrat. Episcopalian. Clubs: Shreveport, Shreveport Petroleum. Author: Another Autumn and Other Poems, 1977. Home: 710 N Madison Ave El Dorado AR 71730 Office: Commercial Nat Bank Bldg Shreveport LA 71101

WITT, SANDRA, nurse; b. Wingate, Tex., May 5, 1941; d. Edward Stroud and Mary Ezelle (Hurley) W.; B.S.N., U. Tenn., 1973; M.S.N., U. Calif., San Francisco, 1975; postgrad. nursing U. Ala., Birmingham, 1978—; Pediatric head nurse Baptist Hosp., Memphis, 1962-68; dir. nursing service Arlington (Tenn.) Developmental Center, 1969-72; nurse practitioner LeBonheur Children's Hosp., Memphis, 1973-74; instr. nursing Meth. Sch. Nursing, 1975-78; regional genetics nurse Lab. of Med. Genetics, U. Ala., Birmingham, 1979—; cons. in field. Mem. nurse recruitment com. Memphis chpt. ARC, 1975-78. Mem. Am. Nurses Assn., Tenn. Nurses Assn., Council Pediatric Nurse Practitioners, Am. Assn. Mental Deficiency, Sigma Theta Tau. Baptist. Home: 2313 Locke Ln Birmingham AL 35226 Office: Lab of Med Genetics U Ala 1720 7th Ave S Birmingham AL 35294

WITTEN, BARBARA JOYCE, rehab. psychologist; b. Boston, Dec. 28, 1945; d. Joseph and Eleanor (Reithman) W.; A.B., Brown U., 1967; M.Ed., Pa. State U., 1972; Ph.D., Syracuse U., 1980. Research asst. Ednl. Testing Service, Princeton, N.J., 1967-71; asst. regional dir. Community Services, Pa. Bur. Correction, Harrisburg, 1972-74; dir. research and evaluation Pa. Bur. Correction, Camp Hill, 1974-75; asst. dir. grad. programrehab. counseling U. Ky., Lexington, 1979—. HEW Rehab. Services Adminstrn. fellow, 1978-79. Mem. Am. Personnel and Guidance Assn., Am. Rehab. Counselor Assn., Public Offender Counselor Assn. (exec. bd. 1974-77), Nat. Rehab. Assn., Nat. Rehab. Counselors Assn., Nat. Rehab. Adminstrn. Assn., AAUW. Jewish. Contbr. articles to profl. jours. Home: 2900 Yellowstone Pky Lexington KY 40502 Office: Taylor Bldg U Ky Lexington KY 40506

WITTEN, THOMAS DAVID, food service co. exec.; b. Washington, Dec. 6, 1943; s. Schurl George and Ruth Rollins W.; m. Brenda Jane Pope, Feb. 4, 1967. Salesman, J.M. Mathis Co., Durham, N.C., 1966-67; asst. mgr. Marriott Corp., Washington, 1967-68, food service dir., Easton, Md., 1968-75, food service dir., Kingsport, Tenn., 1975-76, dist. mgr. health care, southeast region, Atlanta, 1976—. Talbot County chmn. Nat. Cancer Com., 1974; coach, exec. com., pres. Talbot Little League Football, 1971-75; bd. dirs. Chesapeake Rehab. Center; bd. advisers Chowan Jr. Coll. Served with N.C. NG, 1965-71. Mem. Am. Hosp. Assn. of Hosp. Food Service Dirs., Exec. Chef Soc., Nat. Pilot Assn. Democrat. Roman Catholic. Clubs: Elks, Kiwanis (pres. Easton, lt. gov.-elect dist. 15, 1975). Home: 1910 Ardsley Dr Marietta GA 30062 Office: Marriott Corp 2814 New Spring Rd Suite 208 Atlanta GA 30339

WITTENBERG, PHILIP, lawyer; b. Cleve., Feb. 4, 1928; s. Samuel Monroe and Rhea (Shapiro) W.; A.B., U. Mich., 1948, J.D., 1950; m. Mary Berry Rion, Apr. 16, 1963; stepchildren—Madelyn B. Butts, James Rion Bourgeois, John E. Bourgeois; 1 dau., Mindy Rochelle Wittenberg Lawandales. Admitted to S.C. bar, 1950; individual practice law, Columbia, S.C., 1953-62; partner Levi & Wittenberg, Sumter, S.C., 1962-78, pres., 1978—. Served to 1st lt. U.S. Army, 1951-53. Mem. Am. Bar Assn., S.C. Bar Assn., Sumter County Bar Assn., Richland County Bar Assn., Am. Judicature Soc., S.C. Trial Attys. Assn., S.C. Def. Bar, Comml. Law League Am., Sumter C. of C. Democrat. Jewish. Club: Kiwanis. Home: 7 Paisley Park Sumter SC 29150 Office: Levi & Wittenberg PA PO Drawer 730 Sumter SC 29150

WITTNER, TED PHILIP, ins. exec.; b. Tampa, Sept. 17, 1928; s. Jacob and Helen (Goldman) W.; B.S. in Bus. Adminstrn., U. Fla., 1950; m. Sylvia Heller, Apr. 3, 1954 (dec. May 1975); children—Sharyn (Mrs. Richard Jacobson), Pamela Anne; m. 2d, Jean Giles, Mar. 5, 1979. Mgr., Bell Luggage Co., 1953-54; pvt. life ins. agt., 1955-56; gen. agt. Crown Life Ins. Co., St. Petersburg, Fla., 1956-64; pres. Ted P. Wittner & Assos., 1964-67; chmn. Wittner & Co., 1968— (both St. Petersburg.); pres. Crown Life Brokerage Gen. Agts. Assn., 1968-70; chmn. bd. Profit Programs Co., St. Petersburg, Nat. Bank St. Petersburg, Pinellas State Bank; profl. office developer, 1969—. Bd. dirs. Com. of 100 Pinellas County; mem. St. Petersburg Civic Adv. Com.; bd. dirs. Pinellas Assn. Retarded Children; bd. dirs., sec.-treas. Menorah Center. Served to 2d lt. USAF, 1950-53. Life and qualifying mem. Million Dollar Round Table. Mem. Gen. Agts. and Mgrs. Conf. (pres. St. Petersburg chpt. 1957), Nat. Assn. Life Underwriters, St. Petersburg Area C. of C. (v.p. 1969-72), Fla. Blue Key. Jewish. (pres. congregation 1966-68, chmn. bd. 1964-66). Club: Commerce (pres. 1973-75), St. Petersburg. Home: 1220 Park St N St Petersburg FL 33710 Office: 5999 Central Ave St Petersburg FL 33710

WOELFEL, GEORGE ERNEST, SR., power transmission equipment and goods distbn. co. exec.; b. San Antonio, Nov. 4, 1913; s. John and Martha Emma (Mueller) W.; m. Norma Marie Balzen, June 18, 1939; children—Margaret Evelyn, George E., Martha Jane. Supt. ops. Union Feed Co., San Antonio, 1933-48; owner, mgr. Griesenbeck Belts & Pattern Works, San Antonio, 1948-52; owner San Antonio Belting & Pulley Co., 1952-74, pres., 1974—. Mem. San Antonio C. of C. Lutheran. Club: Hermann Sons of Tex. Home: 430 Alexander Hamilton Dr San Antonio TX 78224 Office: 211 W Cevallos St San Antonio TX 78204

WOFFORD, BENJAMIN HARLAND, JR., plastic surgeon; b. Athens, Ga., Sept. 24, 1937; s. Benjamin Harland and Annie (Puckett) W.; B.S. in Chemistry, U. Ga., 1959; M.D., Med. Coll. Ga., 1962; m. Sandra Odom, July 22, 1966; children—Wendy Elizabeth, Alison Anne, Laura Lea. Intern, USPHS, Balt., 1962-63; resident in gen. surgery Med. Coll. Ga., 1963-67; resident in plastic surgery U. Tex. Med. Br., 1967-70; practice medicine, specializing in plastic surgery, Marietta, Ga., 1970—; staff, Kennestone Hosp., Windy Hill Rd. Hosp. (both Marietta), Cobb Gen. Hosp., Smyrna, Ga. Fellow ACS; mem. Am. Soc. Plastic and Reconstructive Surgeons, Southeastern Soc. Plastic and Reconstructive Surgeons, Ga. Soc. Plastic Surgeons, Cobb County Med. Soc. Methodist. Office: 684 Cherokee St Marietta GA 30060

WOFFORD, GRACE KIRK, journalist; b. Grenada, Miss., Dec. 9, 1914; d. William Hester and Ella Inez (Jones) Kirk; student Grenada Jr. Coll., 1932; B.A., Blue Mountain Coll., 1934; postgrad. U. Chgo., 1936-37, U. Miss., 1937; m. George Conger Wofford, Aug. 6, 1939; children—Martha Kirk (Mrs. John R. Pleasant, Jr.), Susan Elizabeth (Mrs. Riley H. Lunn), Alice Louise (Mrs. Charles R. Hallford), Sarah Margaret (Mrs. James R. Love). High sch. tchr., Ripley, Miss., 1934-36, Louisville, Miss., 1937-39, Cleveland, Miss., 1965-66; mgr. central warehouse Miss. Dept. Pub. Welfare, U.S. Dept. Agr., Drew, 1966-74; journalist Sunflower County News, Drew, 1966; columnist Drew Leader and Ruleville Record, 1968-70; freelance feature writer, photographer; feature writer Grenada County Weekly, 1974—. Leader, Girl Scouts U.S.A., Drew, 1951-72, neighborhood chmn. 1951-79, recipient thanks badge N.W. Miss. council, 1974. Recipient Woman of Achievement award Bus. and Profl. Woman's Club, 1969. Mem. Nat. League Am. Pen Women (pres. Delta br. 1956-58, 78-80, state pres. 1958-60, 70-72, mem. nat. letters bd. 1973-74, nat. corr. sec. 1974-76, nat. rec. sec. 1976-78, nat. chaplain), Woman's Soc. Christian Service (life, pres. 1951-52, sub. dist. pres. 1952-54, dist. rec. sec. 1954-58), Miss. Poetry Soc., Blue Mountain Coll. Alumni Assn. (nat. alumni bd. 1960-64, v.p. 1972-74). Methodist (mem. adminstrv. bd. 1956—). Author: Lyric Poems, 1964. Editor anthology Young Delta, 1972. Contbr. poetry and feature articles under names Eva Gray and Evelyn Hope to numerous anthologies, mags. including Miss. Poetry Jour., Pen Woman. Home: 123 N 3d St Drew MS 38737 Office: Box 188 Drew MS 38737

WOJTALIK, THOMAS ANTHONY, environ. scientist/environ. engr.; b. Akron, Mich., Nov. 1, 1940; s. Anthony and Stella W.; B.S. (Mich. Dept. Conservation fellow, 1961-62), Mich. State U., 1962, M.S., 1963; postgrad. U. Minn., 1963-68; m. Mary Jack Bramblett, Oct. 2, 1970; 1 dau., Amanda Paige; step-children—Morgan, Shari. Limnologist, TVA, Chattanooga, 1968-69, supr. aquatic biology, Muscle Shoals, 1969-71, br. ecologist, 1971-72, staff biologist, Chattanooga, 1972-78, environ. scientist, 1978-80, environ. engr., 1980—; cons. U. North Ala., 1970-72, U.S. Pesticides Working Group, 1970-73, Atomic Indsl. Forum Environ. Coms. NSF research fellow, 1963-66. Mem. Am. Fisheries Soc., Brit. Ecol. Soc., Nat. Mgmt. Assn., Am. Nuclear Soc., Phi Kappa Phi. Office: 323 Chattanooga Bank Bldg Chattanooga TN 37401

WOLF, CLARENCE, JR., stockbroker; b. Phila., May 11, 1908; s. Clarence and Nan (Hogan) W.; student Pa. Mil. Prep. Sch., 1921; grad. Swarthmore (Pa.) Prep. Sch., 1923; m. Alma C. Backhus, Sept. 11, 1942. Founder French-Wolf Paint Products Corp., Phila., 1926, pres. until 1943; admitted to Phila.-Balt. Stock Exchange, 1937; asso. Reynolds Securities Inc. (name now Dean Witter Reynolds Inc.), 1944—, rep., Miami Beach, Fla., 1946-63, spl. rep., 1963-77, v.p. sales, 1977, v.p. investments, 1977—; dir., vice chmn. bd., mem. exec. com. Amcord, Inc.; dir. George S. MacManus Co., Rand Broadcasting Co., owners radio and TV stas., also hotels, 1946-68. Pres. Normandy Isles Improvement Assn., Miami Beach, 1952-53; mem. Presidents Council Miami Beach, 1952—. Mem. Alumnus Assn. Pa. Mil. Coll. (Fla. dir. 1961—). Clubs: Clermont (London, Eng.), Variety, Standard (Miami, Fla.). Home: Jockey Club Apt 901-2 Biscaya Point 11111 Biscayne Blvd Miami FL 33161 Office: care Dean Witter Reynolds Inc 700 Brickell Ave 6th Floor Miami FL 33131

WOLF, JOHN CHARLES, psychologist; b. St. Louis, Sept. 29, 1943; s. Howard August and Wilda Lucille (French) W.; B.S., Stephen F. Austin State U., 1964, M.A., 1967, M.Ed., 1969; Ph.D. (NDEA fellow), N. Tex. State U., 1976; m. Carole Sue Bruce, Oct. 21, 1967; children—Allan Bruce, Anne Elizabeth. Staff psychologist Lufkin (Tex.) State Sch. for Mentally Retarded, 1966-67; instr. psychology Stephen F. Austin State U., 1967-68; dir. rehab. services Goodwill Industries, Ft. Worth, 1969-70; counselor VA Guidance Center, Tex. Christian U., Ft. Worth, 1970-73; officer in charge, counseling psychologist U.S. VA, Lubbock, Tex., 1973—; adj. instr. psychology and human services South Plains Coll., Lubbock, 1973—. Mem. Lubbock County Com. on Employment of Handicapped. Certified and lic. psychologist, Tex. Mem. Am., Southwestern psychol. assns., Am. Personnel and Guidance Assn., Am. Rehab. Counseling Assn., NW Tex. VA Psychol. Assn. (pres. 1979-80), Tex. Personnel and Guidance Assn., Assn. Measurement and Evaluation in Guidance, Tex. Assn. Measurement and Evaluation in Guidance (sec. 1979-80), Psi Chi, Kappa Delta Pi. Contbr. to publs. in field. Home: 3312 40th St Lubbock TX 79413 Office: Federal Bldg Room 122 Lubbock TX 79401

WOLF, MARTA SUSAN, librarian; b. Newark, Mar. 25, 1946; d. John Andrew and Gertrude Agnes (Kane) Turk; B.S., Bowling Green U., 1968; M.L.S., U. Tex., 1977; Library asst. serials dept. Bowling Green (Ohio) U. Library, 1968; sch. librarian Brooks Jr. Secondary Sch., Powell River, B.C., Can., 1968; asst. librarian U. Mich. Libraries, Ann Arbor, 1970-72; br. librarian Social Work Library, Gen. Libraries, U. Tex., Austin, 1972-73, cons. Center Social Work Research, Sch. Social Work, 1974-75, dir. info. services, 1975-79; research librarian Library Devel. Div., Tex. State Library, Austin, 1980—; mem. Nat. Accreditation Com. for Info. and Referral Agys., 1977—; mem. Statewide Devel. Bd. for Establishment Tex. Info. and Referral Orgn., 1976. Mem. Spl. Libraries Assn., Am. Soc. Info. Sci., Alliance Info. and Referral Systems (mem. exec. com. Tex., mem. nat. standards com.), ALA, Tex. Library Assn., Austin On-Line Users Group. Mem. editorial bd. Info. and Referral, Jour. Alliance Info. and Referral Systems, 1978—; editor Library Devels., jour. Tex. State Library, 1980—. Home: 7600 Wood Hollow #218 Austin TX 78731 Office: Library Devel Div Tex State Library PO Box 12927 Austin TX 78711

WOLF, ROLAND ORVILLE, plastic surgeon; b. Ft. Dodge, Iowa, Oct. 5, 1938; s. Gottlieb Frederick and Ida Louella (Gold) W.; B.S., Tex. Luth. Coll., 1962; M.A., U. Tex., 1963, M.D., 1964; m. Jan Pittman Haley, June 19, 1964; children—Jonathan Andrew, Mary Ann, Roland Orville. Intern, St. Joseph's Hosp., Ft. Worth, 1964-65; resident in gen. surgery La. State U., New Orleans, 1967-71; resident in plastic surgery U. Tex. Med. Br., Galveston, 1971-74; practice medicine, specializing in plastic surgery, Abilene, Tex., 1974—; asst. prof. plastic surgery Tex. Tech., Lubbock, 1974-78. Pres., Taylor PTA, 1976-77, Eastern Little League, 1977-78; v.p. Boy Scouts Am., Abilene, 1976-77. NIH grantee, 1960; Am. Cancer Soc. fellow, 1972. Diplomate Am. Bd. Surgery, Am. Bd. Plastic Surgery. Mem. Taylor Jones County Med. Soc., Tex. Surg. Soc., A.C.S., Am. Med. Assn., Tex. Med. Assn., Am. Soc. Plastic and Reconstructive Surgeons. Republican. Lutheran. Club: Abilene Country. Contbr. articles in field to profl. jours. Home: 1501 Hillview St Abilene TX 79601 Office: 1100 N 19th Suite 4-A Abilene TX 79601

WOLFE, ALLEN EUGENE, state ofcl.; b. Marion, Va., Apr. 9, 1930; s. John Tyler and Aubrey Louise (Richardson) W.; A.A., Marion Coll., 1951; B.Sc., Va. Poly. Inst. and State U., 1957; m. Julia Ann Otis, Aug. 16, 1958; children—Louise Ann, John Allen, Michael Ernest, James Thomas. Acct., Southwestern State Hosp., Marion, Va., 1957-59; dir. adminstrv. services Petersburg Tng. Sch. and Hosp. (Va.), 1959-61; asst. supt. Va. Treatment Center for Children, Richmond, 1961-66; asst. supt. No. Va. Mental Health Inst., Falls Church, 1966-71; dir. adminstrv. services central office Va. Dept Mental Health and Mental Retardation, Richmond, 1971, asst. commr. adminstrn., 1971—. Served with U.S. Army, 1951-54. Mem. Am. Acad. Med. Adminstrs., Nat. Assn. Mental Health, Assn. Retarded Citizens. Clubs: Masons, K.T., Shriners, Nat. Sojourners, Heroes of 76, Elks. Address: Va Dept Mental Health and Mental Retardation 109 Governor Box 1797 Richmond VA 23214

WOLFE, ANN MARGARET, real estate broker; b. Quincy, Mass., Feb. 25, 1926; d. Ernest James and Marie Antoinette (Pineau) Murphy; grad. pub. schs.; children—Dorothy Ann, Nancy Marie. Shelter salesman Gen. Devel. Corp., Port Charlotte, Fla., 1970-74, suburban shelter sales mgr., 1974, broker mgr., asst. v.p. Fla. Home Finders Inc. subsidiary, 1974—. Mem. Charlotte County C. of C., Multiple Listing Service, Punta Gorda-Port Charlotte Bd. Realtors, Fla. Assn. Realtors, Nat. Inst. Real Estate Brokers, Nat. Assn. Realtors. Democrat. Presbyn. Mem. Order Eastern Star. Home: 1279 Fletcher St Port Charlotte FL 33952 Office: 205 Tamiami Dr NW Port Charlotte FL 33952

WOLFE, ERNEST CELVESTER, III, mgmt. cons.; b. Houston, Oct. 28, 1947; s. Ernest Celvester and Betty Jo (Tisinger) W.; B.B.A., U. Houston, 1972; M.B.A., Stephen F. Austin State U., 1979; m. Carolyn Rebecca Dorman, Jan. 21, 1973; children—David Allen, Daniel Douglas. Gen. mgr. J.D. Dorman Restaurants, Palestine, Tex., 1972-74, partner, 1976-77; sr. investigator Mo. Pacific R.R., Palestine, 1974-76; sec.-treas., dir. Down Mexico Way, Inc., Athens, Tex., 1977-78; mgmt. cons., Palestine. Mem. troop planning com. Boy Scouts Am., 1968; alternate del. Tex. Democratic Conv., 1972; 1st reader First Ch. of Christ, Scientist, Palestine, 1975-79, bd. dirs., 1976, chmn. ch. fin. audit com., 1979. Served with inf. U.S. Army, 1969-71; Vietnam. Decorated Bronze Star. Mem. Am. Mgmt. Assn., Assn. M.B.A. Execs., M.B.A. Assn., Omicron Delta Epsilon. Republican. Office: 307 5th St Palestine TX 75801

WOLFE, JOHN ALLEN, mining firm exec.; b. Riverton, Ia., June 3, 1920; s. Asa Allen and Alice (Thomas) W.; Geol. Engr., Colo. Sch. Mines, 1947, M.S., 1954; children—James Perry, Cynthia Wolfe Burke; m. 2d, Lenora Irvin, 1969. Dir. exploration Ideal Cement Co., Denver, 1948-65; geol cons., P.I., Latin Am., 1965-68; pres. Mineral Resources Cons., Houston, 1968-75; partner Schoenike, Wolfe & Assos., Houston, 1970-75; v.p., gen. mgr. Lobo Mines, Inc., Manila, Philippines, 1970-75; pres. Taysan Copper, Inc., Manila, 1973—. Lectr., cons. in field; mem. Colo. Mining Industry Devel. Bd., 1963-65. Fellow Geol. Soc. Am.; mem. Am. Mining Congress (gov. 1963-65), Colo. Mining Assn. (pres. 1963), Am. Inst. Mining Engrs., Soc. Econ. Geologists, Am. Inst. Profl. Geologists, Am. Geophys. Union, Assn. Geologists for Internat. Devel., Geol. Soc. Philippines. Republican. Contbr. articles to profl. jours. Home: care Taysan Copper Inc CCPO Box 1868 Makati Metro Manila Philippines Office: 5133 Richmond Ave Suite 1 Houston TX 77027

WOLFE, LARRY DUANE, metallurgist; b. Pampa, Tex., Feb. 26, 1944; s. Joseph George and Wilsie Ruth (Anderson) W.; A.A., Frank Phillips Jr. Coll., 1964; B.S., U. Houston, 1973; m. Shirley Joyce Daugherty, Jan. 15, 1965; children—Ingrid Kristine, Maegan Rhea. Chemist, Cameron Iron Works, Houston, 1967-73; chief chemist Gulf Chem. & Metall. Co., Texas City, Tex., 1973-75; primary metallurgist Georgetown Tex. Steel Corp., Beaumont, 1975—; instr. Coll. of Mainland, 1975. Del. Tex. Democratic Conv., 1972. Mem. AIME, Am. Inst. Chemists, Am. Chem. Soc., Am. Soc. Metals, Soc. Applied Spectroscopy, Smithsonian Assos., Am. Mus. Natural History (asso.), Houston Astron. Soc. Mem. Ch. of Christ. Home: 3111 Oak Ave Groves TX 77619 Office: 435 Bowie St Beaumont TX 77704

WOLFE, NELSON LEE, research chemist; b. Des Moines, July 10, 1938; s. Leo Nelson and Ruth Adelle (Brown) W.; B.S., Luther Coll., 1962; M.S., N.Mex. Highlands U., 1966; Ph.D., Kans. State U., 1971; m. Janet Kay Heckner, June 4, 1961; children—Kent Lee, Kurt Lee. Teaching asst. N.Mex. Highlands U., 1964-66, Kans. State U., 1966-71; research chemist environ. processes br. EPA, Athens, Ga., 1971—. Served with U.S. Army, 1962-64. Mem. Am. Chem. Soc., Sigma Xi. Methodist. Contbr. articles to profl. jours. Home: 105 Richard Way Athens GA 30601 Office: College Station Rd Athens GA 30605

WOLFE, TOWNSEND DURANT, III, arts center exec.; b. Hartsville, S.C., Aug. 15, 1935; s. Christian Townsend and Elizabeth Seignious (Bryant) W.; B.F.A., Atlanta Art Inst., 1958; M.F.A., Cranbrook Acad. Art, Bloomfield Hills, Mich., 1959; cert. art adminstrn., Harvard U., 1970; m. Jane Rightor Lee, Aug. 28, 1968; children—Julliette Fielding, Mary Bryan, Townsend Durant, Zibilla Lee. Instr., Memphis Acad. Art, 1959-64, Scarsdale (N.Y.) Studio Workshop, 1964-65; dir. Wooster Community Art Center, Danbury, Conn., 1965-68; art dir. Upward Bound Project, Danbury, summers 1966-68; exec. dir. Ark. Arts Center, Little Rock, 1968—; adv. council Contemporary Art/Southeast, 1976-80; sec. Ark. Arts Center Found., 1973—; lectr. art U. Ark., Little Rock, 1969-79; bd. dirs. Arts in Edn., 1975-80; cons. in field, 1969—; work reps. pvt. and public collections. Recipient Purchase prize Okla. Printmakers Soc., 1961, M.J. Kaplan prize Nat. Soc. Painters in Casein, 1965, Silvermine Guild award painting, 1967, 1st Winthrop Rockefeller Meml. award, 1973. Mem. Am. Assn. Museums (council 1978-80), Southeastern Museums Conf. (pres. 1978-80), Asso. Council Arts. Episcopalian. Home: 2102 S Louisiana St Little Rock AR 72206 Office: Ark Arts Center PO Box 2137 Little Rock AR 72203

WOLFF, THOMAS WILLIAM, hand surgeon; b. Plymouth, Ind., Feb. 5, 1943; s. Eric Walter and Ruth Lucille (Poore) W.; B.S., Purdue U., 1965; M.D., Ind. U., 1969; m. Geraldine W. Wilson, Nov. 8, 1975; children—Jason T., Erica A., Leon D. Intern, South Bend (Ind.) Meml. Hosp., 1969-70; resident in orthopedic surgery Charlotte, N.C., 1972-76; Christine Kleinert fellow in hand surgery Hand Surgery Assos., Louisville, 1976-77; practice medicine specializing in hand surgery, Louisville, 1976—; partner Hand Surgery Assos., Louisville, 1977—; clin. instr. surgery U. Louisville, 1978—. Served with Spl. Forces, U.S. Army, 1970-72. Diplomate Am. Bd. Orthopedic Surgery. Mem. Am. Acad. Orthopedic Surgeons, Am. Soc. Surgery of the Hand. Contbr. articles to med. jours. Home: 2007 High Canyon Rd Louisville KY 40207 Office: Suite 1001 250 E Liberty St Louisville KY 40202

WOLFSON, MITCHELL, corp. exec.; b. Key West, Fla., Sept. 13, 1900; s. Louis and Rose (Gruner) W.; student Columbia U., 1918; LL.D., U. Miami, 1955; m. Frances Louise Cohen, Jan. 27, 1926; children—Louis (dec.), Frances Wolfson Cary, Mitchell. Founder, pres., chmn. Wometco Enterprises, Inc., Miami, Fla., 1925—; chmn. Fin. Fed. Savs. and Loan Assn., Miami Beach, 1958—. Trustee, Miami-Dade Community Coll., 1957—, chmn., 1968-78; chmn. City of Miami Off-Street Parking Authority, 1961—; trustee Mt. Sinai Med. Center, Miami Beach; adv. trustee Fla. House, Washington; mem. Miami Beach City Council, 1939-43, mayor Miami Beach, 1943. Served to lt. col. AUS, World War II. Decorated Bronze Star, Croix de Guerre; recipient Walt Disney Humanitarian award Nat. Assn. Theatre Owners, 1972; Alfred I. DuPont award for broadcasting journalism Columbia U., 1972; Leonard L. Abess human relations award Anti-Defamation League B'nai B'rith, 1975; Humanitarian award Miami Heart Inst., 1976; Gov.'s award Miami chpt. Nat. Acad. TV Arts and Scis., 1978; Mitchell Wolfson Pier Park dedicated by City of Miami Beach, 1977. Mem. Nat. Assn. Theatre Owners (exec. bd.). Clubs: Masons, Rotary, Elks, Shriners. Office: 306 N Miami Ave Miami FL 33128

WOLFSON, MORTON, educator; b. N.Y.C., May 30, 1922; s. Louis and Marie Jeanette (Wilson) W.; B.A., U. Fla., 1964, M.A., 1967; grad. Brit. Staff Coll., Camberly, Eng., 1955; m. Helen Rose Svacak, Nov. 6, 1947; children—Linda V., Morton L., Robert S. Enlisted man U.S. Army, 1940-42; commd. 2d lt., inf., 1942, advanced through grades to lt. col., 1959; ret., 1961; asst. prof. comprehensive logic U. Fla., Gainesville, 1965-74, asst. prof. behavioral studies, 1974-80; advisor U. Fla. Mortar Bd. Decorated Bronze Star with 2 oak leaf clusters, Army Commendation Medal with 2 oak leaf clusters; named Tchr. of Year, Univ. Coll., U. Fla., 1975-76, Coll. Liberal Arts and Scis., 1978-79; Thomas Jefferson fellow, 1976. Mem. Fla. Blue Key, Omicron Delta Kappa, Phi Kappa Phi, Alpha Kappa Delta, Phi Alpha Theta, Phi Delta Kappa, Kappa Delta Pi, Order of Omega. Clubs: Masons, Kiwanis. Contbg. author to Creative and Critical Thinking (W. Edgar Moore), 1967. Office: 429 Winston W Little Hall Gainesville FL 32611

WOLLANGK, SANDRA JEANNE, speech pathologist; b. Valprisо, Fla., July 5, 1949; d. Arden and Janet (Smith) W.; B.A., U. S. Ala., 1971; M.A., U. Houston, 1972; postgrad. U. Houston, Clear Lake, 1977, S. Tex. Coll. of Law, 1978—. Dir. speech pathology St. Anthony Center, Houston, 1972—, St. Joseph Hosp., Houston, 1977—; med. risk mgr./safety officer St. Anthony Center, Houston, 1979—; clin. supr. U. Houston Grad. Studies at St. Anthony Center, 1972—. Co-chmn. Nursing Task Force on Stroke, Am. Heart Assn., 1975-76; sec. Houston Area Assn. Communication Disurpers, 1975-76; mem. health services task force Houston-Galveston area Council, 1976. U. Houston grad. fellow, 1971-72. Mem. Am. Speech and Hearing Assn., Am. Bar Assn. (student mem.), Am. Coll. Hosp. Adminstrs. Assn. (student mem.). Lutheran. Home: 1809 Stoney Brook St #201 Houston TX 77063 Office: 6301 Almeda St Houston TX 77021

WOLSFELT, GERALD ROBERT, ind. ins. agt.; b. Aurora, Ill., Aug. 7, 1942; s. Gerald and Marie Jeanette (Sigler) W.; A.A., Daytona Beach Jr. Coll., 1964; student Aurora Coll., 1964; student U. Fla., 1964-65; B.A., Fla. Atlantic U., 1966, M.Ed., 1967; postgrad. Ins. Inst., U. Ga., 1976; m. Mary Alice Victoria Chubb, Apr. 24, 1966; children—Victoria Edith, Martha Katherine, Gerald Russell, Peter Van Fleet. Substitute tchr. public schs., Boca Raton, Fla., 1966-67; tchr. history, guidance counselor Douglass High Sch., Thomasville, Ga., 1967-68; agt. Met. Life Ins. Co., Thomasville, 1968-70; ind. ins. agt. Caldwell & Langford Ins. Agy., Thomasville, 1970—. Pres., ARC, Thomasville, 1974-76. disaster chmn., 1975—; div. chmn. United Way, Thomasville, 1977-79; deacon 1st Presbyn. Ch., 1979-80; active Cancer Crusade, 1975, 76, 77; soccer coach YMCA, Thomasville; referee Little League Football, YMCA, jr. high sch., Thomasville. Recipient award United Way, 1976. Mem. Ind. Ins. Agts. Assn. Clubs: Beachton Yacht, Glen Arven Country, Kiwanis, Exchange, Gator of S.W. Ga. (pres.). Office: 320 N Broad St Thomasville GA 31792

WOMACK, BENJAMIN HUNTER, banker; b. Nashville, Jan. 29, 1951; s. Benjamin Franklin and Eloise (Hunter) W.; B.S., Middle Tenn. State U., 1973; grad. Tenn. Young Bankers Sch., 1979; m. Melanie Page Watts, May 20, 1978. Mgmt. trainee Murfreesboro Bank & Trust Co. (Tenn.), 1973-75, asst. cashier, 1975-76, opns. officer, 1976-78, br. mgr., 1978—. Fund raiser Boy Scouts Am.; notary public Rutherford County, Tenn. Mem. Tenn. Young Bankers Assn., Middle Tenn. State U. Alumni Assn., Fraternal Order Police (asso.), Sigma Chi. Democrat. Methodist. Home: 909B Maple Dr Smyrna TN 37167 Office: Box 100 Murfreesboro TN 37130

WOMACK, DAVID L., stock broker; b. Sonora, Tex., Aug. 11, 1952; s. Douglas R. and Betty L. (Cole) W.; B.S., Trinity U., 1974. Engr., Kelly AFB, San Antonio, 1974-78; account exec. Merrill Lynch, San Antonio, 1978—. Br mgr. Combined Fed. Campaign, 1977; mem. 60th Anniversary Planning Com., Kelly AFB, 1977, Armed Forces Week Planning Com., 1977; vice chmn. precinct Republican party, 1968-74, mem. 200 com., 1977—; mem. Blue Ribbon com. Bexar County Hosp.; chmn. grants com. San Antonio Little Theatre. Mem. Tex. Soc. Engrs (asso.), Am. Chem. Soc., Air Force Assn., Am. Mgmt. Assn., Greater San Antonio C. of C., Mil. Affairs Council, Mensa, Concerned Conservatives Group, 1st Wednesday Group. Club: Plaza. Home: 411 Beverly St San Antonio TX 78228 Office: 319 N Saint Mary St San Antonio TX 78205

WOMACK, MORRIS FARRELL, mech. seal mfg. co. exec.; b. Houston, Sept. 8, 1937; s. John Harvey and Georgia Katherine (Richardson) W.; student U. Tex., 1956-61; m. Bettie Jean Martin, Aug. 20, 1958; children—Debbie, Morris M., Laurie, Kathie. Field agt., staff mgr. Nat. Life & Accident Ins. Co., Austin, Houston, 1961-66; agy. supr. Gen. Am. Life Ins. Co., Houston, 1966-67; regional mgr. Pilot Life Ins. Co., Houston, 1967-68; field sales engr. Argo Internat. Corp., Houston, 1968-69; staff sales engr. World Industries, Houston, 1969-71; owner, pres. All Seals Tex., Inc., Houston, 1971—. Vice pres. White Oak Bend Utility Dist., 1978—; del. S.W. area White House Conf. on Small Bus., 1980. Mem. Nat. Am. Small Bus., C. of C. of U.S. Republican. Home: 2206 Airline Dr Friendswood TX 77546 Office: 17400 El Camino St Houston TX 77058

WOMACK, PATRICIA, speech pathologist; b. Florence, S.C., Sept. 24, 1949; d. Charles Hollis and Winifred Elder (Fisher) W.; A.B., Converse Coll., 1971; M.Ed., U.S.C., 1972. Coordinator speech therapy services Beaufort County Dept. Edn., Beaufort, S.C., 1972-79; speech pathologist Richmond County Bd. Edn., Augusta, Ga., 1979—; cons. Low Country Dist. Health Dept., 1975-79, Headstart Child Devel. Program, Ridgeland, S.C., 1978-79. Mem. Am. Speech and Hearing Assn., S.C. Speech and Hearing Assn.

Home: 3188 Skinner Mill Rd 11-A Augusta GA 30909 Office: 3146 Lake Forest Dr Bldg 316 Augusta GA 30909

WONG, BETTY JEAN, ednl. adminstr.; b. Leland, Miss., Mar. 15, 1949; d. Suey Henry and Pon Chu (Lam) Wong; B.S., Miss. State U., 1971; M.Ed., Delta State U., 1973. Asst. gen. mgr. Sta. WJPR, Greenville, Miss., 1973-74; career devel. specialist Greenville Municipal Sch. Dist., 1974-76; career edn. curriculum specialist Miss. State U., Jackson, 1976—, research/curriculum specialist, 1976—; coordinator vocat. research, curriculum and tchr. edn., Miss. State Dept. Edn., 1979—; cons. field career edn. Mem. Am., Miss. (exec. bd., chmn. profl. devel. task force, chmn. conv. 1980) personnel and guidance assns., Am., Miss. vocat. assns., AAUW (handbook chairperson 1975-77). Baptist. Contbr. articles to profl. publs.; also handbook. Home: 1137 Woodfield Dr Jackson MS 39211 Office: PO Box 771 Vocat Div Jackson MS 39205

WONG, JULIUS PAN, mech. engr., educator; b. Shanghai, China, May 8, 1937; s. Kai Shu and Po Ling (Hsu) W.; came to U.S., 1960, naturalized, 1973; B.S., Hong Kong Baptist Coll., 1960; M.S., La. Tech. U., 1962; Ph.D., Okla. State U., 1966. Analytical specialist Energy Controls div. Bendix Corp., South Bend, Ind., 1966-69; asso. prof. mech. engring. Speed Sci. Sch., U. Louisville, 1970—. Recipient Outstanding Faculty award Tau Beta Pi. Registered profl. engr., Ky. Mem. Am. Soc. Mech. Engrs., Am. Acad. Mechanics, Soc. Engring. Sci., Am. Soc. Engring. Edn., AAUP, Soc. Indsl. and Applied Maths. Contbr. articles to profl. pubis., papers profl. orgns. Home: 7104 Bearcreek Dr Louisville KY 40207 Office: Speed Sci Sch U Louisville Louisville KY 40208

WONG, VIVIAN ANNIE, restaurant exec.; b. Hong Kong, Oct. 21, 1940; came to U.S., 1965, naturalized, 1972; d. Kenny Lai-Hang and Suk-Yin (Sin) Kwan; diploma Eton Bus. Coll., 1961; diploma London C. of C.; student Furman U., 1972-74; m. Thomas K. F. Wong, Oct. 29, 1961; children—Madeline, Madina, Michele, Anita. Founder, owner Dragon Den Restaurant chain, Greenville, S.C., 1969—; founder, owner Wong Enterprises, Inc., Greenville, exec. v.p., 1969—. Mem. Internat. Food Services, Nat. Restaurant Assn. Episcopalian. Home: Route 2 Roper Mountain Rd Greenville SC 29607 Office: Wong Enterprises Inc 420 N Pleasantburg Dr Greenville SC 29607

WONNACOTT, JAMES BRIAN, physician; b. Charlottetown, P.E.I., Can., Feb. 24, 1945; came to U.S., 1978; s. Earl Lepage and Eunice Deborah (Eaton) W.; honors diploma, Prince of Wales Coll., 1964; B.Sc. with honors in Biology, Dalhousie U., 1966, M.D., 1972. Intern, Victoria Gen. Hosp., Halifax, N.S., Can., 1971-72; gen. practice medicine, Summerside, P.E.I., 1975-78; practice medicine specializing in family practice, Floydada, Tex., 1978-80, San Antonio, 1980—; civil aviation med. examiner; mem. staff Meth. Hosp. Served with RCAF, 1967-75. Diplomate Coll. Family Physicians of Can. Mem. Tex. Med. Assn., AMA, Am. Acad. Family Physicians, Aerospace Med. Assn., Civil Aviation Med. Assn., Am. Geriatrics Soc. Methodist. Clubs: San Antonio Rotary, Univ. Lodge of Halifax. Office: SW Med Group PA 4499 Medical Dr Suite 260 San Antonio TX 78229

WOO, JOHN C. H., cons. transportation, profl. engr.; b. Kaesung, Korea, June 23, 1930; s. Sang Joon and Chong (Mo) W.; M.S. in Transp., Purdue U., 1968; M.S. in Operation Research, Poly. Inst. Bklyn., 1972; m. Cecilia Y.W. Woo, Apr. 4, 1961; children—Joseph, Violet, Lillian. Pres., Trans-Systems Corp., Vienna, Va., 1976—; sr. transp. cons., engr. DeLeuw, Cather & Co., Washington, 1974-76, Northrop Airport Devel. Corp., Vienna, 1972-74, Gen. Applied Sci. Labs., Westbury, N.Y., 1967-70, Airborne Instrument Lab, Farmingdale, N.Y., 1967-70. Recipient internat. scholdrship Ohio State U., 1953-54, Purdue U., 1955-56; registered profl. engr., Va. Sr. mem. Am. Inst. Indsl. Engrs.; asso. mem. Inst. Transp. Engrs., Ops. Research Soc. Am.; mem. Transp. Research Bd. Methodist. Contbr. articles in field. Home: 1905 Contralto Ct Vienna VA 22180

WOOD, ALFRED MCCREARY, ret. sales exec.; b. Wildie, Ky., Nov. 1, 1896; s. Henry Hugh and Eliza (Stewart) W.; student U. Ky., 1916-17; B.A., Harvard U., 1921; m. Mary Swain, Mar. 11, 1958. With Procter & Gamble Co., 1921-61, salesman, gen. salesman, Kansas City, asst. to gen. sales mgr., Cin., sales supr., Phila., gen. sales supr., N.Y. dist. mgr., Boston, spl. assignment, Dallas, 1921-48, div. mgr., Cin., 1949-61. Served to ensign USN, 1918-19; from maj. to lt. col., USAAF, 1942-45. Decorated Bronze Star, Croix de Guerre with palm. Mem. Am. Acad. Polit. and Social Sci., Newcomen Soc. N.Am., Dallas Council World Affairs (dir.), Sigma Alpha Epsilon. Republican. Presbyterian. Harvard (Dallas), Dallas Country, Dallas. Home: 3525 Turtle Creek Blvd Apt 12E Dallas TX 75219

WOOD, BETTE JEAN, coll. dean; b. Ullin, Ill., Oct. 15, 1933; d. James Arthur and Josie Thomas (Holman) Hiatt; student Mt. Vernon Community Coll., 1968-70; B.S., Eastern Ill. U., 1970, M.S., 1975; m. Don Allen Wood, Dec. 20, 1955; children—Jeffrey Allen, Julie Ann. Tchr. art Unity High Sch., Tolono, Ill., 1970-75; sec. to pres. 1st Nat. Bank, Arcola, Ill., 1976-77; dean women Liberty Bapt. Coll., Lynchburg, Va., 1977—. Mem. Am. Personnel and Guidance Assn., Nat. Assn. Women Deans, Adminstrs. and Counselors, Va. Nat. Identification Program for Advancement of Women in Higher Edn. Adminstrn., Am. Legion. Republican. Mem. Ch. Nazarene. Home: 15 Edgeway Dr Lynchburg VA 24502 Office: Box 1111 Lynchburg VA 24502

WOOD, CURTIS RICHARD, physicist; b. Atlanta, May 8, 1943; s. Curtis Melvin and Annie Elizabeth (Kimbell) W.; B.S., Ga. State U., 1971; M.S., Ga. Inst. Tech., 1972, M.S. in Elec. Engring., 1980; m. Teresa Lynn Joiner, Dec. 2, 1966; children—Brian Scott, Tasca Shalon. Physicist guns and rocket br. Armament Devel. Test Center, Eglin AFB, Fla., 1972-73, project scientist electro-optically guided missiles 1973-76, program mgr. modeling and analysis of electro-optics system, 1976—. Active Stage Crafters, community theater. Served with U.S. Army, 1967-68. Mem. IEEE, Am. Def. Preparedness Assn., Am. Phys. Soc., Sigma Pi Sigma. Republican. Home: 112 Pinewood Terr Fort Walton Beach FL 32548 Office: Armament Devel Test Center/DLMT Eglin AFB FL 32542

WOOD, DAVID DEWAYNE, auditor; b. Franklin, Pa., Feb. 13, 1947; s. Charles DeWayne and Theresa Blanche W.; A.A., Palm Beach (Fla.) Jr. Coll., 1971; B.B.A. in Acctg., Fla. Atlantic U., 1973; m. Kathleen Bell, Oct. 14, 1978. Staff acct. Coopers & Lybrand, West Palm Beach, Fla., 1973-75; internal auditor City of West Palm Beach, 1975-76, Boca Raton (Fla.) Community Hosp., 1976—. Served to 1st lt., AUS, 1966-69. Decorated Bronze Star, Air medal. C.P.A., Fla. Mem. Hosp. Fin. Mgmt. Assn., Am. Inst. C.P.A.'s, Fla. Inst. C.P.A.'s, Inst. Internal Auditors, EDP Auditors Assn. Home: 2536 Griffin Sq West Palm Beach FL 33406 Office: 800 Meadows Rd Boca Raton FL 33432

WOOD, FRANK OSBORNE, trade assn. exec.; b. Utica, N.Y., Dec. 9, 1921; s. Frank Wilson and Frances Lucretia (Osborne) W.; B.S. in Chemistry, Rutgers U., 1950, M.S. in Chemistry, 1956; m. Dorothy Elizabeth Angelstein, Sept. 29, 1951; children—Frank O., Carol E. With Hercules Powder Co., Kenvil, N.J., 1950-53, Wilmington, Del., 1953-55; devel. and research chemist, tech. service Diamond Alkali Co., Painesville, Ohio, 1955-60; tech. service engr. Allied Chem. Co., Syracuse, N.Y., 1960-66; tech. dir. Salt Inst., Alexandria, Va., 1966—. Pres. North Syracuse Little League, 1964-66; mem. exec. com. Nat. Safety Council. Served with USAAF, 1942. Mem. Am. Chem. Soc., ASTM, Nat. Assn. Corrosion Engrs. Republican. Clubs: Masons (Shriner), Toastmasters. Contbr. article on salt and salt production to Ency. Brit. Home: 8509 Cyrus Pl Alexandria VA 22308 Office: Salt Inst 206 N Washington St Alexandria VA 22314

WOOD, JAMES HORACE, acct.; b. Greene County, Tenn., Sept. 9, 1947; s. Jay Enoch and Betty Jean W.; cert. bookkeeping State Area Vocat. Tech. Sch., Crossville, Tenn., 1974; Asso. Sci., Vol. State Community Coll., 1979; m. Thelma Louise Howell, Jan. 25, 1972; children—Villa, Olivia, Jennifer. Sink mfg. Dayton Products Co. (Tenn.), 1974-75; mail clk. Watts Bar Nuclear Plant TVA, Spring City, Tenn., 1975-76, supr. mail and reprodn. service Hartsville (Tenn.) Nuclear Plant, 1976-79, acctg. officer trainee cost office, 1979—. Served with USNR, 1966-70. Decorated medal of Honor. Mem. DAV, PTA. Republican. Baptist. Home: PO Box 46 Castalian Springs TN 37031

WOOD, JAMES JOSEPH, aircraft service and fuel co. exec.; b. Springfield, Ohio, Sept. 27, 1909; s. Frank Edward and Mary Annette (Cavanaugh) W.; student Notre Dame U., 1926-30; m. Dorothy Mae Rainalter, Aug. 16, 1957. Gen. agt., Cleve., Columbus, Cin. Motor Freight Lines, Columbus, Ohio, 1931-36; sr. corr. Home Owners Loan Corp., Columbus, Ohio, 1936-38; credit mgr. Ohio Finance Co., Columbus, 1938-43; comml. agt. Keeshin Motor Express, Columbus, Ohio, 1943-44; civilian head Transp. br. U.S. Navy, Washington, 1946-54; founder Internat. Fueling Co., Inc., also IFC Aviation Co., Alexandria, Va., 1954, pres., 1954—, dir., 1954—; dir. Nat. Service Corp., Alexandria, Va., 1970—. Served with USN, 1944-46. Elected to Aviation Hall of Fame. Republican. Roman Catholic. Club: Westwood Country. Instituted and initiated current land transp. system for U.S. Navy. Home: 7004 Duncraig Court McLean VA 22101 Office: 612 N Washington St Alexandria VA 22314

WOOD, JAMES POWERS, physician; b. Clinton, Miss., Dec. 29, 1920; s. Arthur Eugene and Anne (Powers) W.; B.A. with distinction, Miss. Coll., 1941; M.D., Tulane U., 1950; m. Carroll Bullock, June 14, 1943; children—James Powers, Anne Carroll, Louise Dampeer, Marshall Bullock. Intern Charity Hosp., New Orleans; gen. practice medicine, Waynesboro, Miss., 1951-53, State Line, Miss., 1953-66, Waynesboro, Miss., 1966—; mem. staffs Wayne Gen. Hosp., Waynesboro, Miss., 1951—, Washington County Hosp., Chatom, Ala., 1953—; trustee Greene County Hosp., Leakesville, Miss., 1958-60. Dir., Consumers Wirebound Box Co., Waynesboro, 1957-58; chmn. bd. AGM Drug Co. Miss., Jackson, Miss.; organizer, chmn. bd. 1st Nat. Bank Way, 1966-68. Chmn. bd. trustees State Line High Sch., 1957-59; mem. Greene County Bd. Edn., 1963-66, Miss. Hosp. Commn., 1964-72, Miss. Oil and Gas Bd., 1970-77. Served with USAAF, 1943-46. Decorated Air medal with oak leaf cluster. Hon. col. Miss. Gov.'s staff, 1960-72. Fellow Am. Acad. Family Physicians; mem. Am., Miss. med. assns., So. Miss. Med. Soc., Miss. Acad. Gen. Practice, Alpha Kappa Kappa. Baptist. Home: McIlwain Dr Waynesboro MS 39367 Office: 709 Chickasawhay St Waynesboro MS 39367

WOOD, JANET BOWYER, nurse; b. Bedford, Va., Dec. 10, 1943; d. Charles Roy and Thelma Payne B.; diploma Va. Bapt. Hosp., Lynchburg, 1965; B.S., Lynchburg Coll., 1978, M.A. in Adminstrn., 1981; m. Cecil Glenn Wood, Oct. 16, 1965; children—Michael Glenn, Angela Leigh. Nurse, Bedford County Meml. Hosp., 1965—, operating room supr., 1974—. Pianist, Longwood Ave. Bapt. Ch., 1965-77. Mem. Assn. Operating Rm. Nurses (dir., pres.-elect, chpt. del. 1972, 80), Bedford Bus. and Profl. Woman's. Club: Little Town Players. Contbg. editor Point of View, 1974-79, Today's O.R. Nurse, 1979. Home: Rt 2 Box 94 Bedford VA 24523 Office: Box 688 Bedford VA 24523

WOOD, JOEL EVERETT, county ofcl.; b. York, S.C., Sept. 12, 1945; s. Meek Everett W.; A.S. in Civil Engring., Gaston Coll., 1965; B.A. in Econs., Winthrop Coll., 1975; m. Anne Baker, Aug. 19, 1967; children—Christopher Everett, Andrew Baker. With Davis and Floyd Engrs. Inc., Greenwood, S.C., 1965-66, Williams Engring. Inc., Rock Hill, S.C., 1966-77; dir. public works, county engr. York County, York, 1977—. Registered profl. engr., S.C., N.C. Mem. Am. Public Works Assn., Nat. Soc. Profl. Engrs., S.C. Soc. Profl. Engrs. (pres. Catawba chpt., state dir.). Presbyterian. Home: 9 Brookwood St York SC 29745 Office: PO Box 66 York SC 29745

WOOD, JOHN (LEWIN), mech. engr.; b. Valdivia, Chile, Sept. 20, 1943 (Brit. citizen); came to U.S., 1971; s. George F. and Kathleen J. W.; B.S.M.E., Catholic U., Valparaiso, Chile, 1968; M.S.M.E., Ga. Inst. Tech., 1974; m. Patricia Rochefort, June 19, 1971; children—John R., Alexander R., Christopher R. Plant engr. Crysler Internat. subs. Nun y German, Santiago, Chile, 1969-71; engring. cons. Coca-Cola Export, Atlanta, 1974-75; mgr., plant engr. Sci. Atlanta, 1975—. Chmn. work setting com. Dekalb Health Dept., Atlanta. Mem. ASME. Roman Catholic. Home: 792 Windy Dr Stone Mountain GA 30087 Office: 3845 Pleasantdale Rd Atlanta GA 30340

WOOD, JOHN MICHAEL, underwater contracting co. exec.; b. Mpls., Dec. 15, 1946; s. Donald and Lucille (Jones) W.; student public schs., Council Bluffs, Iowa; m. Ellen Sue Grienke, Jan. 5, 1970; children—Stacia Lucille, John Michael and Michelle Jean (twins). With Union Pacific R.R., Council Bluffs, 1968; with James Dean Divers, Morgan City, La., 1969; diver Fluor Ocean Services, Morgan City, 1972-75; supr. Santa Fe Divers, Houma, La., 1975, Oceaneering Internat., Morgan City, 1976, estimator, asst. operations mgr., 1977, div. ops. mgr., 1978; area mgr. Sub Sea Internat., Morgan City, 1979—; cons. in field. Served with USN, 1965-68. Recipient UNICEF Appreciation award, 1960. Mem. Under Seas Med. Soc., Am. Petroleum Inst., Nat. Assn. Underwater Instrs., VFW, Bass Angler Sportsman Soc. Republican. Club: Morgan City Bassmasters. Contbr. articles to profl. jours. Home: 211 Hebert St Berwick LA 70342 Office: Box 61780 1600 Canal St New Orleans LA 70161

WOOD, LOREN EDWIN, aerospace exec.; b. Taunton, Mass., Dec. 25, 1927; s. Elmer Roe and Alice Eleanor (Philbrick) W.; A.B. magna cum laude, Brown U., 1949; A.M., Cornell U., 1950; m. Ann Hamilton, Aug. 6, 1952; children—Joan, Alice, Scott, Carol. Analytical engr., statistician U.S. Army Ordnance Corps, Aberdeen Proving Ground, Md., 1950-54; project analyst group leader U.S. Air Force, 1954-56; sect. head test planning and evaluation TRW Systems, Redondo Beach, Calif. and Seattle, 1956-61; dept. mgr., Gemin system testing Aerospace Corp., El Segundo, Calif., 1961-66; mgr. tech. planning TRW space program support to NASA, Houston, 1966—. Mayor pro-tem, City of Friendswood, Tex., 1977—; mem. City Charter Commn., Friendswood, 1971. Served with USAF, 1954-56. Asso. fellow AIAA (nat. award chmn. outstanding AIAA sect. Houston 1975-76); mem. Am. Mgmt. Assn., Phi Beta Kappa, Sigma Xi. Home: 905 Coward's Creek Dr Friendswood TX 77546 Office: TRW 1110 NASA Rd 1 Houston TX 77058

WOOD, LUCILLE, educator; b. Louisville, Miss., Jan. 9, 1931; d. George S. and Collie Edna (Myres) W.; A.A., East Central Jr. Coll., 1951; B.S., U. So. Miss., 1953, M.A., 1955. Instr. phys. edn., basketball, tennis coach Copiah-Lincoln Jr. Coll., Wesson, Miss., 1953-56; mem. phys. edn. dept. East Central Jr. Coll., Decatur, Miss., 1956—, chmn. dept., 1961-78, coach women's basketball, tennis, 1968—. Named E. Central Jr. Coll. Alumnus of Year, 1964, Miss. Jr. Coll. Women's Basketball All-Star Coach, 1978, Miss. Assn. Coaches Coach of Year, 1979. Mem. Jr. Coll. Miss. Women's Basketball Coaches (pres.), NEA, Miss. Assn. Educators, Miss. Jr. Coll. Faculty Assn., Miss. Folklore Soc., Nat. Jr. Coll. Coaches Assn., Delta Kappa Gamma. Coach champion teams, 1968, 70, 73, 76, 79. Home: Rt 2 Box 303 Louisville MS 39339 Office: East Central Jr Coll Decatur MS 39327

WOOD, MARY LOVEY, speech pathologist; b. McAllen, Tex., Oct. 9, 1942; d. David Gregg and Florella (Salter) Wood; B.A. in Speech, U. Tex., 1964, M.A. in Communication Disorders (Vocat. Rehab. Adminstrn. grantee), 1966, Ph.D., 1976. Chief dept. speech pathology Cerebral Palsy Center, Austin, Tex., 1965-67; supr. U. Tex. Speech and Hearing Clinic, Austin, 1967-71; co-dir., owner, speech pathologist Austin Speech, Lang., and Hearing Center, 1971—; cons. in field; mem. adv. com. Child and Family Service; mem. task force on autism interagy. div. Tex. Gov's. Adv. Com. on Developmental Disabilities; pres. Tex. Com. Orgns. for Handicapped; mem. Tex. delegation White House Conf. for Handicapped. Fellow Am. Speech and Hearing Assn. (certified in clin. competence, legis. council); mem. Tex. Speech and Hearing Assn. (exec. council, pres.), Tex. Com. of Orgns. for Handicapped, Phi Kappa Phi, Alpha Delta Pi. Methodist. Contbr. articles to profl. pubs. Office: 1209 W 34th St Austin TX 78705

WOOD, R. VICTOR H., JR., restaurant franchise co. exec.; b. Bryn Mawr, Pa., Aug. 12, 1933; s. Ralph V.H. and Edith T. (Thomas) W.; B.A. in Econs., Washington and Jefferson Coll., 1955; postgrad. in bus. adminstrn. Duquesne U., 1963. Sales rep., real estate rep., real estate office mgr. Mobile Oil Corp., 1959-67; real estate negotiator Marriott Corp., 1967-69; with McDonald's Corp., 1969-77, nat. dir. real estate, internat. dir. real estate, to 1977; sr. v.p. devel., in charge of real estate, real estate legal, franchising, constrn. and architecture, Burger King Corp., Miami, Fla., 1977—. Served to comdr. USNR. Mem. Nat. Assn. Corp. Real Estate Execs. (group pres. restaurant group), Res. Officer Assn., Naval Res. Assn. Club: Union League (Phila.). Office: 9200 S Dadeland Blvd Miami FL 33156

WOOD, ROBERT WILLIAM, JR., plastic surgeon; b. Virden, Ill., Jan. 10, 1931; s. Robert W. and Mary J. (Peters) W.; M.D., U. Ill., 1955; m. Sarah Norman, Oct. 12, 1957; children—Robert William III, James Norman, John Willard Guy. Intern Baylor U. Hosp., Dallas, 1955-56; resident Christ Hosp., Cin., 1963-65; practice medicine specializing in aesthetic and plastic surgery; mem. active staff Meth. Hosp., Herman Hosp., Park Plaza Hosp., Diagnostic Hosp., St. Luke's Texas Childrens Hosp.; clin. asst. prof. Baylor U. Med. Sch., Houston, clin. asso. U. Tex. Med. Sch., Houston. Basso Profendo in Dallas Civic Opera Co., 1960-63, Houston Grand Opera Co., 1966-71. Served to capt., M.C., USAF, 1956-58. Diplomate Am. Bd. of Plastic Surgery. Mem. Internat. Soc. of Aesthetic Plastic Surgery, Internat. Soc. of Clin. Plastic Surgery pres. 1977—), Am. Cleft Palate Assn., Am. Burn Assn., Am. Assn. Cosmetic Surgeons (pres. 1979), Houston Soc. of Plastic Surgeons (v.p. 1977—), Tex. Med. Assn., Harris County Med. Soc., Houston Surg. Soc., Am. Soc. of Plastic and Reconstructive Surgeons, Tex. Soc. of Plastic Surgery (v.p. 1977-78, pres. 1978—). Methodist. Clubs: University, Briar (Houston); Tarry House (Austin). Contbr. numerous articles on plastic and reconstructive surgery to profl. jours.; producer (films) on plastic surgery. Home: 15 Pinehill Houston TX 77019 Office: 1213 Hermann Dr Suite 885 Houston TX 77004

WOOD, ROSS JOSEPH, math. statistician; b. Jackson, Mich., July 15, 1926; s. Ross Joseph and Iva Nichols (Dodge) W.; B.A., U. Mich., 1954, M.B.A., 1955; M.A., U. Minn., 1962, Ph.D., 1965; m. Gloria Elaine Pritchard, May 31, 1945; children—Kimberly, Kristopher, Lauren, Anthony. Statistician, Sperry Rand Univac, St. Paul, 1955-63; mgr. statistics Battelle Meml. Inst., Richland, Wash., 1963-67; sr. statistician Dikewood Corp., Albuquerque, 1967-71; chief cons. statistician Center for Disease Control, Atlanta, 1971—; cons. FDA. Served with USNR, 1944-46, 50-51. Mem. Am. Statis. Assn., AAAS, Biometric Soc., IEEE. Contbr. articles to profl. jours. Home: 4865 Longchamps Dr NE Atlanta GA 30319 Office: 1600 Clifton Rd NE Atlanta GA 30333

WOOD, SHELTON EUGENE, army officer; b. Douglas, Ga., May 20, 1938; s. Shelton and Mae Lillie (Pheil) W.; A.A., St. Johns U., 1958; B.A., U. Nebr., 1969; M.Ed., Coll. William and Mary, 1971; Ph.D., Nova U., 1975; M.A., Central Mich. U., 1977; m. Edna Louise Tanner, Aug. 25, 1958; children—Shelton John, Deirdre Louise. Area mgr. Marshall Fields Corp., Fla., 1957-58; transp. supr. Greyhound Corp., Jacksonville, Fla., 1959-62; commd. lt. U.S. Army, 1962, advanced through grades to lt. col., 1977; with Redstone Readiness Group, 1977—; now chief Tng. Mgmt. and Devel. Office. Active Boy Scouts Am., 1977—; lay leader United Meth. Ch., Falls Church, Va., 1977-79. Decorated Bronze Star with 2 oak leaf clusters, Air Medal with 3 oak leaf clusters, Purple Heart. Fellow Sussex Coll., 1969-70. Mem. Am. Soc. Trainers and Developers (pres. S.E. chpt. 1974-75), Am. Def. Preparedness Assn., NEA, Phi Kappa Delta, Phi Delta Kappa. Clubs: Masons, Shriners. Author: An Analysis of Incoming Freshmen at NSC, 1975; Choice of College Factors, 1976; numerous articles and handbooks in field of mil. tng. and mgmt. Address: US Army Redstone Readiness Group PO Box 1500-A Huntsville AL 35807

WOOD, STANLEY DAVID, project engr.; b. Davidson, Sask., Canada, Apr. 24, 1928; s. Stanley Nixon and Elizabeth Marigold (Musselman) W.; came to U.S., 1967; B.Sc., U. B.C., 1952; M.E., Va. Poly. Inst. and State U., 1976; m. Beverly Grace Bryson, Sept. 8, 1951; children—Grace Elizabeth, Colleen Beverly, Cynthia Anne, Allison Ruth. Tech. asst. Canadian Industries Ltd., Kingston, Ont., 1952-54; devel. engr. DuPont of Can., Kingston, 1954-59, devel. supr., 1959-67; process engr. Allied Chem. Corp., Hopewell, Va., 1967-73, sr. project engr., 1973—. Mem. Kingston Twp. Sch. Bd., 1964-67. Mem. Assn. Profl. Engrs. Ont., Soc. Plastics Engrs. Mem. United Ch. of Canada. Club: John Rolfe Players Club Inc. (past pres.). Patentee in field. Home: 12617 Petersburg St Chester VA 23831 Office: Allied Chemical Corp PO Box 831 Hopewell VA 23860

WOOD, STEPHEN WRAY, clergyman, educator, author, musician; b. Winston-Salem, N.C., Oct. 6, 1948; s. Dock Wesley and Annie Lee (Harris) W.; B.A., Asbury Coll., 1973; Th.B., John Wesley Coll., 1970; Th.D., Clarksville Sch. Theology, 1977; M.A., U. N.C. Greensboro, 1980; D.Min., Luther Rice Sem. Internat., 1979; m. Rebecca Starr Smith, June 18, 1978. Edn. aide R.J. Reynolds High Sch., Winston-Salem, 1970; admissions counselor John Wesley Coll., High Point, N.C., 1975-76, asso. dir. admissions, 1976-77, dir. admissions and financial aid, 1977—, instr. history and edn., 1975—; ordained to ministry Religious Soc. Friends; minister music Poplar Ridge Friends Meeting, High Point, 1978-79; asso. pastor Glenwood Friends Meeting, Greensboro, N.C., 1979—; dir. admissions and fin. aid, asst.

acad. dean John Wesley Coll., 1979—; pres. Triad Christian Counseling, Inc., Greensboro, 1978—; pres. Remnant Assos., 1977—; ednl. and mus. cons. Served with U.S. Army, 1970-71. Freedom Found. scholar, 1977. Mem. Am. Hist. Assn., Orgn. Am. Historians, Am. Soc. Ch. History, Wesleyan Theol. Soc., Evang. Theol. Soc., Conf. on Faith and History, N.C. Adult Edn. Assn., Broadcast Music, Inc. (writer affiliate), Phi Alpha Theta. Republican. Author: Grace and Race, 1979; Billy Sunday and John Wesley: A Study in Comparative Evangelism, 1979; History of John Wesley College, 1980; rec. artist Travelin Troubador, 1977, Titusoverture, 1979. Home: 812 Circle Dr High Point NC 27260 Office: John Wesley Coll 924 Eastchester Dr High Point NC 27260

WOOD, SUSAN DARST, fin. corp. exec.; b. Sandwich, Ill., June 21, 1953; d. Dwain E. and Wilma J. (Darst) W.; B.B.A. magna cum laude, Memphis State U., 1975. Staff auditor Ernst & Ernst, Memphis, 1975-76; fin. asso. Sun Co., Inc., Dallas, 1977-78, staff internal auditor, 1978—. Chmn. blood drive Am. Cancer Soc., 1979—; supporter Protect Baby Sales, 1978—. C.P.A., Tex. Mem. Am. Inst. C.P.A.'s, Tex. Soc. C.P.A.'s, Nat. Assn. Accts., Sun Tennis Assn., Beta Alpha Psi, Beta Gamma, Alpha Lambda Delta, Phi Kappa Phi. Club: Mountain People Ski. Home: 2131 Trellis St Richardson TX 75081 Office: Sun Co Inc PO Box 2880 Dallas TX 75231

WOOD, THOMAS WESLEY, JR., editor, reporter, educator; b. Hugo, Okla., Mar. 16, 1920; s. Thomas Wesley Wood and Alma Elora (Rogers) Daniel; B.A., U. Tulsa, 1951, M.A., 1953; M.S., Northwestern U., 1953; Ph.D., U. Okla., 1966; m. L. Deloris Gray, May 31, 1968; children—John, Thomas. Reporter, City News Bur. Chgo., 1952-54; mem. faculty U. Tulsa, 1954-73, So. Ill. U., Carbondale, 1973-76, Am. U., Cairo, Egypt, 1976-78; vis. prof. U. Ark., Little Rock, 1978—; reporter Tulsa World, 1954—, Phila. Inquirer, summer 1956, Chgo. Sun-Times, summer 1960, Oil & Gas Jour., 1976-78, Egyptian Gazette, 1977-78; founder, pub., pres. Lost Generation Jour. Inc., Lit. Enterprises Inc.; free lance editor, reporter, photographer. Served with USAF, 1942-46. Recipient two teaching certificates of merit Am. U., Cairo. Mem. Assn. for Educators in Journalism, N.Y. Overseas Press Club, Tulsa Press Club, Am. Hist. Soc., Egyptian Press Assn., Ark. Press Women, Sigma Delta Chi, Pi Alpha Mu, Phi Alpha Theta, Kappa Tau Alpha. Democrat. Author: An Outline History of American Journalism, 1961; Basic Production Equipment and Processes for Letter Press, 1960; Tulsa University Editing Handbook, 1955; Tulsa University Reporting Handbook, 1955; contbr. biographies of journalists and writers to Ency. World Biography, 1973, Lost Generation Jour. Home: 5805 Butler Rd Little Rock AR 72209 also Route 5 Box 134 Salem MO 65560 Office: University of Arkansas at Little Rock Journalism Dept 33rd and University Little Rock AR 72204

WOOD, VIVIAN POATES, mezzo-soprano, coll. dean, educator; b. Washington, Aug. 19, 1928; d. Harold P. and Mildred G. (Patterson) Wood; student Antioch Coll., 1953-55; student of Denise Restout, Saint-Leu-La-Fôret, France and Lakeville, Conn., 1960-62, 64-70, Paul Ulanowsky, N.Y.C., 1958-68, Elemer Nagy, 1965-68, Vyautas Marijosius, Hartford, Conn., 1967-68, Paul A. Pisk, 1968-71; Mus.B., Hartt Coll. of Music, 1968; postgrad. (fellow), Yale, 1968; Mus.M. (fellow), Washington U., St. Louis, 1971, Ph.D. (fellow), 1973. Debut in recital series Ohio-Jeunesse Musicals Arts Festival, Yellow Springs, 1953; mezzo-soprano soloist with numerous orchestras including: solo fellowship Boston Symphony Orch., Berkshire Music Center, Tanglewood, 1964, St. Louis Symphony Orch., 1969, Washington Orch., 1959, Bach Cantata Series Berkshire Chamber Orch., 1964, Yale Symphony Orch., 1968; appearances in numerous operas, radio and TV programs, 1953-68; appeared as soloist in Internat. Harpsichord Festival, Westminister Choir Coll., Princeton, N.J., 1973; appeared as soloist in meml. concert, Landowska Center, Lakeville, 1969; prof. voice U. So. Miss., Hattiesburg, 1971—, asst. dean Coll. of Fine Arts, 1974-76, acting dean, 1976-77; gastprofessor in Hochschule für Musik, München, Ger., 1978-79; Miss. coordinator Alliance for Arts Edn., Kennedy Center Performing Arts, 1974-76. Mem. Gov.'s Adv. Panel for Gifted and Talented Children, State of Miss., 1974—; mem. 1st Gov.'s Conf. on the Arts, State of Miss., 1974—; bd. dirs. Miss. Opera, 1974—. Recipient Young Am. Artists Concert award N.Y.C., 1955; Wanda Landowska fellow, 1968-72. Mem. Nat. Assn. Tchrs. of Singing, Am. Musicological Soc., Mu Phi Epsilon, Delta Kappa Gamma, Tau Beta Kappa (hon.), Pi Kappa Lambda. Democrat. Episcopalian. Author: Poulenc's Songs: An Analysis of Style, 1979. Home: 212 N 25th Ave Hattiesburg MS 39401 Office: South Station Box 8264 Coll Fine Arts U So Miss Hattiesburg MS 39401

WOOD, WALTER WYVILL, mech. engr.; b. Louisville, Feb. 5, 1928; s. George Twyman and Louise Fairfax (Robertson) W.; B.M.E., U. Louisville, 1954, M.Engring., 1972; m. Caroline Shelburne Crone, Dec. 29, 1956; children—Victoria Armistead, Walter Wyville. Product devel. engr. Gamble Bros. Inc., Louisville, 1954-56; sales engr. Air Reduction Sales Co., Louisville, 1956-61; with Naval Ordnance Sta., Louisville, 1962—, dir. engring. dept., 1973-74, dir. gun systems engring. center, 1974-78, dir. gun systems engring. dept., 1978—. Served with AUS, 1950-52; lt. col. Res. Decorated Meritorious Service medal; recipient Outstanding Citizens award City of Louisville, 1977; named Ky. col., 1969; registered profl. engr., Ky. Mem. Am. Welding Soc. (past chmn. Louisville sect.), Am. Soc. Naval Engrs., Louisville Engr. and Sci. Councils Soc., Louisville Habor Assn. (pres. 1979-80), Theta Tau. Democrat. Episcopalian. Club: River Rd. Country (Louisville). Home: 209 Kennedy Ct Louisville KY 40206 Office: Naval Ordnance Station Southside Dr Louisville KY 40214

WOOD, WILLIAM JARMER, ophthalmologist; b. Lexington, Ky., May 14, 1943; s. William Clark Hewitt and Ruth Anthony (Jarmer) W.; A.B., U. Ky., 1966, M.D., 1970; m. Ruth Hunt Peck, Oct. 6, 1978; 1 dau., Lucy Gay. Intern, U. Ky. Med. Center, Lexington, 1966-70, clin. instr., 1975-78, asso. clin. prof., 1978—; resident in ophthalmology Wilmer Inst., Johns Hopkins U. Hosp., Balt., 1971-74; retinal fellow Harvard U., Mass. Eye & Ear Infirmary, Cambridge, 1974-75; practice medicine specializing in ophthalmology, Lexington, Ky. Bd. dirs. Lexington Diabetes Assn. Served to capt. U.S. Army, 1970-76. Diplomate Nat. Bd. Med. Examiners, Am. Bd. Ophthalmology. Mem. Am. Assn. Ophthalmology, AMA, Ky. Med. Assn., Fayette County Med. Soc., Lexington Acad. Eye Physicians and Surgeons (pres. 1980, 81), Ky. Acad. Eye Surgeons and Physicians. Episcopalian. Club: Idle Hour Country. Contbr. articles in field to profl. jours. Office: 135 E Maxwell St Lexington KY 40508

WOOD, WILLIAM MCBRAYER, lawyer; b. Greenville, S.C., Jan. 27, 1942; s. Oliver Gillan and Grace (McBrayer) W.; B.S. in Accounting, U. S.C., 1964, J.D. cum laude, 1972; LL.M. in Estate Planning (scholar), U. Miami, 1980; m. Nancy Cooper, Feb. 17, 1973; children—Margaret, Walter, Lewis. Admitted to S.C. bar, 1972, D.C. bar, 1973, U.S. Tax Ct. bar, 1972, U.S. Ct. Claims bar, 1972, U.S. Supreme Ct. bar, 1977, Fla. bar, 1979; intern Ct. of Claims sect., Tax Div., U.S. Dept. Justice, 1971; law clk. to chief judge U.S. Ct. Claims, Washington, 1972-74; partner firm Edwards Wood, Duggan & Reese, Greer and Greenville, 1974-78, asst. prof. law Cumberland Sch., Samford U., Birmingham, Ala., 1978-79; faculty Nat. Inst. Trial Advocacy, N.E. Regional Inst., Hofstra U., 1979; asso. firm Shutts & Bowen, Miami, Fla., 1980—. Pres. Piedmont Heritage Fund, Inc., 1975—. Served in USAF, 1965-69; Vietnam. Decorated Air Force Commendation medal; recipient Am. Jurisprudence award in real property and tax I, 1971; winner Grand prize So. Living Mag. travel photo contest, 1969. Mem. Am., S.C., Fla. bar assns., Greer (pres. 1977, Outstanding Leadership award 1976), Greater Greenville (dir. 1977) chambers commerce, Order Wig and Robe, Omicron Delta Kappa. Episcopalian. Clubs: Lions, Masons. Office: Shutts & Bowen Attys 10th Floor SE 1st Nat Bank Bldg Miami FL 33131

WOODALL, CHARLES DANIEL, elec. engr.; b. Jersey City, Dec. 9, 1940; s. Charles William and Mary Ellen (Laverty) W.; Asso. Sci., Newark Coll. Engring., 1961. Engring. asso. Western Electric Co., Newark, 1961-66, Columbus, Ohio, 1966, Newark, 1966-72; staff asst. New Eng. Telephone Co., Boston, 1972-74; engr. So. Bell Telephone Co., Ft. Lauderdale, Fla., 1974—. Democrat. Roman Catholic. Clubs: PPC Users (Santa Ana, Calif.); Whale and Porpoise (Ft. Lauderdale). Home: 777 S Federal Hwy Pompano Beach FL 33062 Office: 6451 N Federal Hwy Ft Lauderdale FL 33308

WOODALL, RONALD STEVEN, retail food co. exec.; b. Gadsden, Ala., Sept. 19, 1953; s. Ronald Grady and Mary Ellen (Hartzog) W.; B.A. in Bus. Mgmt. and History, Houston Baptist U., 1975; m. Rebecca Kay Waldrep, Nov. 18, 1972; children—Jennifer Noel, Ronald Steven, Amy Michelle, Robert Brandon. Sales clk. Foley's Dept. Store, Houston, 1970-72; with Ron's Krispy Fried Chicken, Houston, 1972—, exec. v.p., 1977—, also dir. Pres. Thunderbird West Homeowners Assn., 1978; mem. mktg. and distbrv. edn. adv. bd. Houston Ind. Sch. Dist.; mem. adv. com. PACE, Missouri City, Tex. Mem. Am. Mgmt. Assn., Nat. Restaurant Assn., Tex. Restaurant Assn., Greater Houston Conv. Council, Internat. Franchise Assn. Baptist. Clubs: Chancellors Racket, Quail Valley Country. Home: 3303 Rolling Green Ln Missouri City TX 77459 Office: 10101 Fondree Rd Suite 300 Houston TX 77096

WOODARD, BARBARA CHARLENE CHESNEY, nurse; b. Rocky, Okla., Feb. 8, 1930; d. Charles and Edna Holman (Sanders) Chesney; B.S. in Nursing, Tex. Women's U., 1960, M.A. in Counseling, 1962; Ed.D. in Counseling and Personnel Adminstrn., N. Tex. U., 1971. Dir. nursing services Wichita Gen. Hosp., Wichita Falls, Tex., 1962-63; nurse adminstr. Flow Meml. Hosp., Denton, Tex., 1963-65; dir. nursing services Presbyterian Med. Center, Dallas, 1965—; mem. State of Tex. Bd. Nurse Examiners. Mem. Tex. Hosp. Assn., Dallas C. of C., Tex. Soc. Hosp. Nursing Service Adminstrn., Am. Heart Assn. (dir. 1971-78, chairwoman profl. ednl. com. 1971-72). Presbyterian. Editor: Newsletter Tex. Soc. Hosp. Nursing Service Adminstrn., 1972-73; Cardiac Output for Nurses, Am. Heart Assn. Tex. Affiliate, Inc., 1975-76. Office: 8200 Walnut Hill Ln Dallas TX 75231

WOODARD, BLONDENA SABRINA, acct.; b. Wilson, N.C., Apr. 23, 1940; d. Jesse B. and Pauline H. (Hardy) W.; B.S., Va. State U., 1976; M.A., So. Conn. U., 1977; M.A. in Econs., Va. State U., 1979. Acct., Value Engring. Co., Alexandria, Va., 1972-73; bus. services officer United Community Efforts, Los Angeles, 1967-71; sr. acct. United Community Progress, Inc., New Haven, 1964-65; acct. United Planning Orgn., Washington, 1965-67; owner Tico Tax and Bus. Mgmt. Service, Richmond, Va., 1974—; fin. coordinator, cons. Trust Inc., Richmond, 1971-73. Active, Jackson Ward Civic Assn., 1975-77, Westover S. Civic Assn., 1976-79, Chesterfield County YWCA, 1974-79. Mem. Va. Assn. Realtors, Young Profls., Va. Black Caucus, NAACP, Nat. Assn. Realtors, Am. Bus. Woman's Assn., Alpha Kappa Alpha. Democrat. Baptist. Home: 418 Erich Rd Richmond VA 23225 Office: 1202 Oak St Richmond VA 23222

WOODEN, CHARLES MICHAEL, health care exec.; b. Madison, Tenn., Apr. 25, 1951; s. Charles Talmadge and Louise (Holliman) W.; B.S. in Bus. Mgmt., Carson-Newman Coll., Jefferson City, Tenn., 1973; M.B.A., U. Tenn., 1977; m. Judy Gail Meeks, Nov. 23, 1974. Bus. analyst State of Tenn., 1973-77; dir. profl. relations Hosp. Corp. Am., Nashville, 1977—. Named Outstanding Young Man of Yr., City of Lakewood (Tenn.), 1976. Mem. Am. Mgmt. Assn., Am. Soc. Personnel Adminstrn., Med. Group Mgmt. Assn., Am. Soc. Public Adminstrn., Am. Acad. Public and Social Sci., Am. Hosp. Assn. (personnel sect.), Nashville Area Bd. Realtors. Baptist. Home: 385 Willow Bough Ln Old Hickory TN 37138 Office: Hosp Corp Am 1 Park Plaza Nashville TN 37203

WOODIN, MARTIN DWIGHT, univ. pres.; b. Sicily Island, La., July 7, 1915; s. Dwight E. and Gladys Ann (Martin) W.; B.S., La. State U., 1936; M.S., Cornell U., 1939, Ph.D., 1941; m. Virginia Johnson, Sept. 7, 1939 (dec.); children—Rebecca Woodin Johnson, Pamela Woodin Nelson, Linda Woodin Middleton; m. 2d, Elisabeth Wachalik, Oct. 8, 1968. Mem. faculty La. State U., 1941—, prof. agrl. econs., head dept., 1956-59, dir. resident instruction Coll. Agr., 1959-60, dean at Alexandria, La., 1960-62, exec. v.p. at Baton Rouge, 1962-72, pres. univ. system, 1972—; mem. pres.'s council Am. Assn. State Univs., 1972—; pres. Council So. Univs., 1975-76. Dep. dir. La. CD Agy., 1961-72; v.p., exec. com. United Givers Baton Rouge, 1962-63; mem. Arts and Humanities Council Greater Baton Rouge, 1974—; mem. La. Constn. Rev. Commn.; sec. La. State U. Found., 1962-72; mem. council trustees Gulf South Research Inst., 1972—. Served with USNR, 1942-46; PTO. Mem. Am. Agr. Econ. Assn., So. Assn. Land Grant Colls. and State Univs. (pres. 1977—), Am. Mktg. Assn., Am. Legion (post comdr.), Internat. House New Orleans, Sigma Xi, Omicron Delta Kappa, Phi Kappa Phi, Beta Gamma Sigma, Phi Eta Sigma, Gamma Sigma Delta, Alpha Zeta, Pi Gamma Mu. Presbyterian. Clubs: Elks, Rotary. Author articles in field. Home: 2959 E Lakeshore Dr Baton Rouge LA 70810

WOODMAN, BRUCE WAYNE, fgn. missions exec.; b. Joliet, Ill., June 8, 1931; s. George William and Evelyn H. (Harder) W.; student Bethel Coll., 1949-52, Nyack Missionary Tng. Inst., 1953-54; B.Music, Manhattan Sch. Music, 1956; M.A., Columbia U., 1957; m. Margaret J. Adare, Jan. 17, 1936; children—Bruce, Jeffrey, Christine, Sherrie. Ordained to ministry Evang. interdenominational ch., 1956; founder, exec. dir. S. Am. Crusades Inc., Boca Raton, Fla., 1959—; dir. Evangelism Outreach and Music, radio and TV sta. HCJB, Quito, Ecuador, 1962-67; creator radio program Cruzada, 1964—; creator, dir. daily program Impacto!, 1974—; Spanish music editor Zondervan Corp. Pubs., Grand Rapids, Mich., 1979—. Mem. Interdenominational Fgn. Missions Assn. Republican. Composer 70 musical works, 2 hymnals in Spanish; author 2 records in English, 4 records in Spanish. Home: 1910 Coral Shores Dr Fort Lauderdale FL 33306 Office: Box 2530 Boca Raton FL 33433

WOODMAN, ROBERT EDWIN, radio sta. exec.; b. Ruston, La., May 27, 1940; s. Longino Alphonse and Farris Jean (Armstrong) W.; B.A., U. Tex., Austin, 1963. News dir. KNOW-AM, Austin, 1967-78, advt. sales exec., 1968-70, advt. sales mgr., 1970-71; v.p., gen. mgr. KVIC-AM, KCWM-FM, Victoria, Tex., 1971—. Chmn., Victoria Conv. and Visitors Bur. Commn., 1977—; pres. Victoria Symphony Soc., 1976-77; bd. dirs. S. Tex. Zool. Soc., 1972-79. Served with USN, 1963-69. Mem. Tex. Assn. Broadcasters (past dir.), Victoria C. of C. (dir. 1973-75), Nat. Assn. Broadcasters. Roman Catholic. Club: Rotary. Home: 1806 E Lawndale St Victoria TX 77901 Office: Box 3487 Victoria TX 77901

WOODRUFF, EDWIN CUSHING, geophysicist; b. N.Y.C., July 22, 1926; s. George Percy and Margaret (Neville) W.; student Princeton U., 1947-50; B.S. in Geology, Marietta Coll., 1953; A.M., U. Mo., 1954; 1 dau., Anne Elizabeth. With Geophys. Service, Inc., Merced, Calif., 1953 grad. asst. U. Mo., Columbia, 1953-54; seismologist Shell Oil Co., Hobbs, N.Mex. and Midland, Tex., 1954-59, geophysicist, party chief, 1959-65, sr. geophysicist, Midland, 1969-71; sr. geophysicist Basin Geophys. Inc., Midland, 1971-73; chief geophysicist Am. Quasar Petroleum Co., Midland, 1973—; instr. Permian Basin Grad. Center, Midland, 1972-77; pres. Lee chpt. Am. Field Service, Midland, 1966-68, liaison v.p., 1969-70. Served with USN, 1944-46. Mem. Am. Assn. Petroleum Geologists, West Tex. Geol. Soc. (chmn. geothermal survey 1969-72), Soc. Exploration Geologists, Houston, Denver, Southeastern, Permian Basin (membership chmn. 1968-70) geophys. socs., Gamma Alpha, Delta Upsilon. Unitarian. Club: Kiwanis. Home: 2900 W Illinois St Midland TX 79701 Office: 1000 Mid National Bank Twr Midland TX 79701

WOODRUFF, JEAN LEIGH, educator; b. Smithfield, N.C., Sept. 19, 1950; d. Alton Lee and Jean Eloise (Woody) W.; B.A. in History, U. N.C., Greensboro, 1972; M.B.A., Emory U., 1974; postgrad. U. Ga., 1977—. Instr. mktg. Clemson U., 1974—, chairwoman in mgmt. Office Profl. Devel. Adv., Jr. Troop Old 96 council Girl Scouts U.S.A. Named Young Careerist of Yr., Anderson Bus. and Profl. Women's Club, 1978; an Outstanding Young Woman Am., 1978; Clemson U. grantee, 1977. Mem. Am. Mktg. Assn., So. Mktg. Assn., Inst. Mgmt. Sci., AAUW, Phi Gamma Nu. Democrat. Baptist. Clubs: Civitan, Univ. Women's (Clemson). Contbr. articles to profl. jours.; asst. editor Textile Mktg. Letter, 1975—; research in textile mktg., catalog buyers. Home: PO Box 561 Clemson SC 29631 Office: 420 Sirrine Clemson U Clemson SC 29631

WOODRUFF, MARGUERITE, educator; b. Weston, Ga., July 11, 1919; d. Charles Ezekiel and Rossie U. (Stephens) W.; A.B., Tift Coll., 1940; Th.M., Southwestern Bapt. Theol. Sem., 1947, Th.D., 1949. Faculty Mary Hardin-Baylor Coll., Belton, Tex., 1949-52; faculty Mercer U., Macon, Ga., 1952—, prof. sociology, 1968—. Pres. Mental Health Assn. Central Ga., 1963-65, treas., 1967-77, state bd. dirs., 1972-78; active LWV. NSF grantee in anthropology, 1963; Title IVA teaching grantee, 1978-79. Mem. So. Sociol. Soc., Ga. Sociol. Assn. (pres., 1976), Beta Sigma Phi (hon.). Democrat. Baptist. Contbr. chpt. to book. Home: 1347 Adams St Macon GA 31201 Office: Box 57 Mercer University Macon GA 31207

WOODRUM, ARTHUR, physicist, educator; b. Statesboro, Ga., Mar. 20, 1942; s. Walter Grover and Elise (Nessmith) W.; B.S., Ga. Inst. Tech., 1964, M.S., 1966, Ph.D. in Physics, 1968; m. Mary Alice Blackwell, May 1, 1964; children—David Arthur, Alan Thomas. Instr. (research) Sch. Aerospace Engring., Ga. Inst. Tech., Atlanta, 1966-68; research physicist U.S. Navy Mine Def. Lab., Panama City, Fla., 1968-69; asst. prof physics Ga. So. Coll., Statesboro, 1969-72, asso. prof., 1972—, head dept., 1975—, mem. arts and scis. adv. com. to dean, 1975—, chmn. curriculum subcom., 1978—; mem. physics acad. adv. com. Bd Regents State of Ga., 1975—, chmn. subcom., 1977-78. Chmn., Canoochee Dist. Explorers, Boy Scouts Am., 1972-74; judge various sci. fairs; sec.-treas. Statesboro Primitive Baptist Ch. Brotherhood, 1974-76; mem. Statesboro Home Builders Assn., 1977—, bd. dirs., 1977—, 2d v.p., 1979-80; mem. com. to develop subdiv. regulations for Bulloch County, 1979. NASA grantee. Mem. Ga. Acad. Sci. (sec. physics, math. and engring. sect. 197778, chmn. sect. 1978-79, state councilor sect. 1979—), Soc. Physics Students (chpt. faculty adv. 1974-76), Am. Assn. Physics Tchrs., Am. Geophys. Union, Sigma Xi, Sigma Pi Sigma, Phi Kappa Phi, Phi Eta Sigma, Tau Beta Pi. Democrat. Contbr. articles to sci. jours. Home: Route 3 Statesboro GA 30458 Office: Ga So Coll Statesboro GA 30458

WOODS, ANDRE VINCENT, state ofcl.; b. Charleston, S.C., Feb. 21, 1947; s. Delbert Leon and Thelma Ruth (Hamilton) W.; B.A. in History and Govt., St. Augustine's Coll., 1975; cert. S.C. Trident Tech. Coll., 1977; m. Angela Evangeline Edwards, June 22, 1975; 1 dau., Charity Laverne. Program coordinator migrant camps S.C. Farm Commn., summer 1973; adminstrv. analyst S.C. State Ports Authority, Charleston, 1977-79, accounts analyst, 1979—. Mem. transp. adv. com. S.C. Trident Tech. Coll.; bd. dirs. Neighborhood Legal Services Corp., 1977—, Commn. Redevel. and Preservation, 1977—; mem. budget allocation bd. Trident United Way, Inc., 1979-81; mem. citizens adv. com. Charleston Area Transp. Study; exec. bd., chmn. press and publicity NAACP, Freedom Fighter award, 1973. Recipient cert. achievement in leadership devel. Trident C. of C., 1976. Episcopalian. Periodic columnist Charleston Evening Post newspaper. Home: 236 Ashley Ave Charleston SC 29403 Office: PO Box 817 Concord St Charleston SC 29403

WOODS, BARRY ALAN, lawyer; b. N.Y.C., Nov. 21, 1942; s. Harry E. and Lillian (Breath) W.; B.S., N.Y. U., 1965, LL.M. in Taxation, 1969; J.D., Bklyn. Law Sch., 1968; m. Elizabeth Geller, Sept. 8, 1968; children—Meredith Rose, Pamela Brett. Admitted to N.Y. State bar, 1968, P.R. bar, 1970, U.S. Tax Ct., 1969, U.S. Dist. Ct. P.R., 1971; partner firm Baker & Woods, Santurce, P.R., 1970-76; mng. partner Woods & Woods, Hato Rey, P.R., 1976—. Spl. cons. Tax Mgmt., Inc.; mem. Bur. Nat. Affairs, Adv. Bd. Internat. Taxation. Mem. Am. Soc. Internat. Law, Am. Bar Assn., Colegio de Abogados de P.R. Clubs: Caribe Hilton Swimming and Tennis, Pan Am. Gun, Bankers of P.R., N.Y. U. Author: United States Business Operations in Puerto Rico; Repatriation of Puerto Rico Source Earnings-Implication of Proposed Section 936; other publs. in field. Home: Coral Beach Condominium Isla Verde PR 00911 Office: PO Box 10165 Santurce PR 00908

WOODS, BRIAN ANTHONY, engring. constrn. co. exec.; b. New Orleans, June 20, 1946; s. Louis Raymond and Wylene Leontine (Darengsbourg) W.; B.A., So. U., 1973; postgrad. bus. adminstrn. Loyola U., 1977-78; m. Diana Burrell, Aug. 17, 1974; children—Brian Anthony, Devin. Psychiat. counselor dePaul Mental Hosp., New Orleans, 1971-74; employee relations analyst Shell Oil Co., Norco, La., 1974-78; corp. personnel rep. J. Ray McDermott & Co., New Orleans, 1978-79, corp. salary adminstr., 1979—. Served as sgt. USMC, 1964-68; Vietnam. Decorated Combat Air medal with 2 stars; cert. compensation profl. Mem. Am. Mgmt. Assn., Am. Compensation Assn., Am. Soc. Personnel Adminstrn., Personnel Mgmt. Assn., So. Coll. Placement Assn., Alpha Phi Omega. Democrat. Roman Catholic. Home: 3267 Cheateau Blvd Kenner LA 70062 Office: PO Box 60035 New Orleans LA 70160

WOODS, DONALD ROY, chemist; b. Huntington, W.Va., Dec. 22, 1932; s. Roy Celo and Florence (Maxwell) W.; B.S., Marshall U., 1955; m. Aug. 3, 1953; children—Beverly Gail, Karen Sue. Analyst, Nitrogen Div., Allied Chem. & Dye Co., South Point, Ohio, 1954; with Ashland Petroleum Co. div. Ashland Oil, Inc., (Ky.), 1955—, research chemist, 1971, sr. research chemist, 1978—. Data processing coordinator, telephone worker Contact of Huntington (W.Va.), 1975—; deacon First Presbyn. Ch., Huntington, 1969-73, ruling elder, 1975-79. Mem. ASTM. Republican. Home: 1903 12 Ave Huntington WV 25701 Office: PO Box 391 Ashland KY 41101

WOODS, GERALD WAYNE, lawyer; b. Durham, N.C., Sept. 15, 1946; s. Paul Virgil and Trannie (Ellis) W.; B.S., U. N.C., 1968; J.D., Emory U., 1973. Retail mgmt. Sears, Roebuck & Co., Atlanta, 1968-70; summer intern Ga. Dept. Revenue, Atlanta, 1972-73; asst. to exec. sec. Bd. Regents Univ. System Ga., Atlanta, 1973-76, asst. exec. sec., 1976-78; admitted to Ga. bar, 1973; asst. to pres. Med. Coll. Ga., Augusta, 1978—. Mem. Nat. Assn. Coll. and Univ. Attys. (co-chmn. sect. on health scis. 1979—), Ga. State Bar, Augusta Bar Assn., Am. Bar Assn., Ga. Soc. Hosp. Attys., Am. Soc. Hosp. Attys., Nat. Health Lawyers Assn. Clubs: Augusta Young Lawyers, Kiwanis. Editorial adv. bd. Jour. Coll. and Univ. Law. Home: 3007 Cardinal Dr Augusta GA 30909

WOODS, HERBERT PIERSON, naval officer, naval architect, engring. cons.; b. Montainair, N.M., Jan. 29, 1932; s. William Henry and Wanda Marie (Lyman) W.; B.S., U.S. Naval Acad., 1956; M.S., Webb Inst. Naval Architecture, 1966, U. So. Calif., 1977; m. Marsha Scariano, June 1, 1956; children—Deborah Marie, Charles Garland. Enlisted USN, 1950, commd. ensign, 1956, advanced through grades to comdr., 1969, destroyer duty USS Halsey Powell, submarine duty USS Trumpetfish and USS Raton, engring. duty Mare Island, Da Nang, Vietnam, project mgr. USN Deep Submergence Submarine Rescue Program, 1974-76, dep. dir. dept. systems mgmt., faculty mem. Def. Systems Mgmt. Coll., Ft. Belvoir, Va., 1976-77; head marine dept. Gilbert Assos., Inc., Architects and Engrs., 1977-78; dir. So. ops. Gilbert/Commonwealth, 1978; engring., mgmt. cons. Dept. Def., other govt. agys., fgn. countries, 1970—. Supt., Mare Island Ch. Sch., 1969; chmn. Philippine/Am. Fiesta, 1973; pres. Subic PTA, 1972. Decorated Legion of Merit; registered profl. engr. Mem. Soc. Naval Architects and Marine Engrs., Am. Soc. Naval Engrs., Am. Def. Preparedness Assn., Sigma Xi. Democrat. Clubs: Masons, Shriners. Home: 5024 Cockney Ct Annandale VA 22003 Office: Gilbert Assos Inc 102 Fairbanks Rd Oak Ridge TN 37830

WOODS, LARRY DAVID, lawyer, educator; b. Martinsburg, W.Va., Sept. 10, 1944; s. Allen Noel and Loyce LaVerne (Dillingham) W.; B.A., Emory U., 1966; J.D., Northwestern U., 1969; children—Rachel Bishop, Allen Noel II, Sarah Katherine. Pres., Debate Research Assos., pubs., Chgo., 1966-69; admitted to Tenn. bar, 1969, Ga. bar, 1970; staff atty. Atlanta Legal Aid Soc., Inc., 1969, dir. litigation, 1970-71; asso. dir. Mcpl. Ct. Legal Defender Project, Atlanta, 1970; mem. firm Woods, Bryan & Thomas, Nashville, 1971—; asso. prof. criminal justice dept. Tenn. State U., Nashville, 1972—; lectr. Taft Inst., U. Tenn., 1972—; asst. dir. forensics Emory U., Atlanta, 1969-71. State youth dir. Hooker for Gov., 1966; campaign mgr. Allen for Mayor, 1971, Clement for Pub. Service Commn., 1972; mem. coordinating com. Tenn. Young Democrats, 1971; dir. Tenn. Democratic Telethon, 1972. Chmn., Berkley Forum Found., 1972-74; bd. dirs. Tenn. Civil Liberties Union, Nashville Panel Am. Women. Finalist, Nat. Debate Tournament, 1964-66; nat. pres. DSR-TKA, 1965-66. Ford Found. fellow for legal research, 1968. Mem. Tenn. (ho. dels.), Ga. bar assns., Nat. Assn. Criminal Def. Lawyers, Nat. Legal Aid Defender Assn., Tenn. Consumer Alliance, AAUP. Methodist. Author: (with Fowler) Crime and Investigation, 1967, Compulsory Service and the Alternatives, 1968; The Strategy of Intervention, 1969; Pollution: Problems and Proposals, 1970. Office: 121 17th Av S Nashville TN 37203

WOODS, MARTHA HITCHCOCK, assn. exec.; b. Olean, N.Y., Aug. 26, 1939; d. Leo E. and Erma L. (Butler) Hitchcock; student U. Rochester (N.Y.), 1961; B.S., Barry Coll., Miami, Fla., 1980; m. David L. Woods, Oct. 23, 1971; children—Kevin, Dennis, Cynthia. Adminstrv. asst. Secrytime Corp., Rochester, N.Y., 1968-70; legal asst. Miller & Miller, Miami, 1970-75; service coordinator North Miami Found. for Sr. Citizens Services, North Miami, Fla., 1975-77, exec. dir., 1977—. Active PTA, 1970-78; phone supr. telethon, Muscular Dystrophy, Miami, 1972-76; active Boy Scouts Am., 1973-74. Congregationalist. Home: 520 NW 144th St Miami FL 33168 Office: North Miami Found for Sr Citizens Services 860 NE 126th St North Miami FL 33161

WOODS, MAURICE G(LENN), resource recovery co. exec.; b. Oklahoma City, Oct. 31, 1926; s. Roy G. and Esther C. (Marrs) W.; B.S., Okla. U., 1950; m. Teresa Jean Wright, Feb. 20, 1968; children—Pamela, Virginia, Robert, Brooke, Maurice G., Tyler. Pres., Wedgewood Amusement Park, Oklahoma City, 1954-69, Clean Air Ator Corp., Oklahoma City, 1969-74, Waste Systems, Inc., Oklahoma City, 1975—. Deacon, elder First Christian Ch., Oklahoma City; pres. Greater Oklahoma City United Cerebral Palsy; bd. dirs. Oklahoma City Open Golf Tournament. Served with U.S. Army, 1945-47, USAF, 1950-51. Mem. Sigma Chi (life). Republican. Clubs: Rotary (dir.) (Oklahoma City); Oak Tree Golf. Patentee incinerator with afterburner, solid waste disposal energy recovery system. Home: 6420 N Hillcrest Oklahoma City OK 73116 Office: 2601 NW Expressway Oklahoma City OK 73112

WOODS, PAUL JOSEPH, historian, educator; b. Champaign, Ill., Nov. 11, 1916; s. William Francis and Mary Margaret (Casserly) W.; B.A., U. Ill., 1938, M.A., 1940, Ph.D., 1941; m. Ruth Ellen Hackleman, July 25, 1942; children—Lorrie, Mike. Mem. faculty Tex. A&M U., College Station, 1946-50, 52-60; prof. history Tex. Tech U., Lubbock, 1960—. Served to maj. U.S. Army, 1942-46, 50-52. Decorated Croix de Guerre (France); Forragere (Belgium). Mem. Am. Hist. Assn., Third Armored Div. Assn., Phi Kappa Phi. Democrat. Roman Catholic. Home: 2521 61st St Lubbock TX 79413 Office: Dept History Tex Tech U Lubbock TX 79409

WOODS, PENDLETON, ednl. adminstr., author; b. Ft. Smith, Ark., Dec. 18, 1923; s. John Powell and Mabel (Hon) W.; B.A. in Journalism, U. Ark., 1948; m. Lois Robin Freeman, Apr. 3, 1948; children—Margaret, Paul Pendleton, Nancy. Editor, asst. pub. mgr. Okla. Gas & Electric Co., Oklahoma City, 1948-69; dir. Living Legends of Okla., Okla. Christian Coll., Oklahoma City, 1969—. Bd. dirs. Campfire Girls Council, Okla. Jr. Symphony (past pres.), Boy Scout Council, Okla. Found. Epilepsy, Central Park Neighborhood Assn., Zoo Amphitheater of Oklahoma City, Keep Okla. Beautiful, Will Rogers Centennial Commn.; past pres. Oklahoma City Mental Health Clin.; pub. relations chmn. Oklahoma County chpt. A.R.C.; past chmn. Western Heritage award Nat. Cowboy Hall of Fame; past pres. Variety Health Center; dir. Am. Freedom Council; exec. dir. Oklahoma City Bicentennial Commn. Served with AUS, World War II and Korean; col., state historian Okla. N.G. Named Outstanding Young Man of Year, Oklahoma City Jr. C. of C., 1953; Silver Beaver award Boy Scouts Am., 1963; also 3 honor medals Freedoms Found. Mem. Soc. Asso. Indsl. Editors (past v.p.), Advt. Fedn. Am. (past dist. dir.), Central Okla. Indsl. Communicators (past pres., hon. life mem.), Okla. Jr. C. of C. (hon. life; past internat. dir.), Okla. Distributive Edn. Clubs (hon. life), Oklahoma City Advt. Club (past pres.), Okla. Zool. Soc., Okla. Geneal. Soc. (past pres.), Okla. Hist. Soc. (publ. editor), Okla. Heritage Assn. (publ. editor), Oklahoma City Beautiful (publ. editor), Oklahoma County Hist. Soc. (dir.), 45th Inf. Div. Assn. (dir.), Okla. City Hist. Preservation Commn., Sigma Delta Chi, Kappa Sigma (nat. commr. publs.). Author: You and Your Company Magazine, 1950; Church of Tomorrow, 1964; Myriad of Sports, 1971; This Was Oklahoma, 1979. Recorded Sounds of Scouting, 1969; Born Grown, 1974 (Western Heritage award Nat. Cowboy Hall Fame). Home: 541 NW 31st St Oklahoma City OK 73118

WOODS, POWELL, lawyer; b. Ft. Smith, Ark., Jan. 19, 1922; s. John Powell and Mabel Fairfax (Hon) W.; B.A., U. Ark., 1948; LL.B., U. Ark. at Little Rock, 1950; m. Lola Lavoy Keener, June 18, 1954; children—Lola Lavoy, John Powell. Admitted to Ark. bar, 1950; practiced in Ft. Smith, 1950-58; individual practice law, Siloam Springs, 1958—. City atty., Siloam Springs, 1960-62; municipal judge, Siloam Springs, 1963-64. Sec.-treas. Siloam Springs Salvation Army, 1962—. Served with AUS, 1943-45. Mem. Am., Ark., Benton County bar assns., Comml. Law League, Nat. Rifle Assn., C. of C., N.W. Ark. Geol. Soc., Isaac Walton League. Rotarian. Home: 411 S Britt St Siloam Springs AR 72761 Office: 207 S Broadway Siloam Springs AR 72761

WOODSIDE, MARTHA ANN DURBIN, state ofcl.; b. Shelbyville, Tenn., Dec. 30, 1936; d. Carl and Alene Victoria (Henslee) Durbin; student Ky. State U., 1971-72; m. William David Woodside, Sept. 11, 1954; children—William David, Richard, Leslee Dawn, Victoria Dale. Jr. acctg. clk. Dept. Personnel, Commonwealth Ky., Frankfort, 1957-66, acct. Dept. Ins., 1966-71, sr. acct. Dept. Human Resources, 1971-75, adminstrv. supr. Ky. Dept. Energy, 1975—. Mem. Women's Internat. Bowling Congress, Nat. Assn. Ins. Women, Frankfort Assn. Ins. Women (pres. 1971-72, 79-80), Internat. Personnel Mgmt. Assn. Democrat. Baptist. Office: Ky Dept Energy Capital Plaza Frankfort KY 40601

WOODSON, MELBA LUCILLE GRIMES, sch. counselor; b. Texarkana, Tex., Feb. 11, 1921; d. William Wallace and Harriet McMaster (Henry) Grimes; B.S., N. Tex. State Tchrs. Coll., 1941; M.Ed., N. Tex. State U., 1966; m. Marion (Chink) Woodson, Mar. 14, 1942; children—Nona Ruth, Wallace Marion. Sec., U.S. Army, Ft. Sam Houston, Tex., 1941-42, U.S. Navy, Corpus Christi, Tex., 1942-44; soc. editor Grand Prairie Daily News, 1946-47; sec. Lone Star Boat Co., 1947-49; tchr. first grade Miss Waggoner's Pvt. Sch., Grand Prairie, Tex., 1959-60; math. tchr. Irving (Tex.) Ind. Sch. Dist., 1960-67, high sch. counselor, 1967—. Certified elementary tchr., high sch. tchr., counselor. Mem. Am., N. Tex., Tex. State personnel and guidance assns., Nimitz High Sch., Tex., Nat. PTA's, Tex. State Tchrs. Assn., Assn. Tex. Educators, Nat. Vocat. Guidance Assn., Am. Sch. Counselors Assn., N. Tex. State U. Alumni Assn., Assn. Humanistic Edn. and Devel. Democrat. Baptist. Contbr. articles on genealogy to profl. jour. Home: 1801 Glen Valley St Irving TX 75061 Office: Nimitz High School 100 Oakdale St Irving TX 75060

WOODWARD, HENRY ERNEST, cons. engr.; b. Atlanta, June 27, 1926; s. Henry Thomas and Icie (Green) W.; B.C.E., Ga. Inst. Tech., 1949; student U. Va., 1944; m. Frances Evelyn Puckett, June 13, 1949; children—Scott, Jane, Katherine. Dist. mgr. Worthington Corp., Cin., 1948-56; engring. liaison Trane Co., N.Y.C., 1956-59; mech. contractor Kerby Saunders, Inc. and Alvord & Swift, N.Y.C., 1959-64; prin., chief mech. engr. Tampa Bay Engring., St. Petersburg, Fla., 1964-68; pres. Woodward Air Balance, St. Petersburg, 1968—. Mem. St. Petersburg Planning and Zoning Commn., 1973-75. Named Engr. of Yr., Fla. Engring. Soc., 1972-73, Disting. Service award, 1975. Fellow Fla. Engring. Soc. (pres. elect. 1979); mem. Asso. Air Balance Council, Fla. Inst. Cons. Engrs., ASHRAE, Am. Cons. Engrs. Council, Nat. Soc. Profl. Engrs. Democrat. Mem. United Ch. of Christ. Home: 5165 Dover St NE Saint Petersburg FL 33703 Office: 6536 Lincoln Way N Saint Petersburg FL 33702

WOODWORTH, HAROLD CYRIL, health officer; b. Wells, Minn., Sept. 23, 1920; s. Harry Clark and Martha Meta (Weicking) W.; A.B., Dartmouth Coll., 1942; M.D., Harvard U., 1944; Ph.D., Yale U., 1958; m. Evelyn Eileen Mahon, Aug. 17, 1944; children—Richard, Carl. Intern, Mary Hitchcock Hosp., Hanover, N.H., 1944-45; resident internal medicine, White River Junction, Vt., 1947-48; practice family medicine, Bristol, Vt., 1948-52; chief Microbiology Lab., Center Disease Control, USPHS, Atlanta, 1958-68; county health officer Colbert and Lauderdale Counties, Ala., 1968-75; regional health officer N.W. Ala. Regional Health Dept., Tuscumbia, 1975—. Served with USN, 1945-46, 52-54. Recipient Physician's Recognition award AMA, 1979-82; USPHS postdoctoral fellow, 1955-57, Howard Hughes Med. Inst. fellow, 1957-58. Mem. Med. Assn. Ala., Colbert County Med. Soc. Episcopalian. Club: Civitan (Florence, Ala.). Home: 3808 Chisholm Rd Florence AL 35630 Office: PO Box 30 108 N Water St Tuscumbia AL 35674

WOODWORTH, NORMAN EUGENE, assn. exec.; b. Veedersburg, Ind., Mar. 6, 1933; s. James Dyer and Rosa Mildred (Ferguson) W.; ed. high sch.; m. Judith Aline Fair, Jan. 12, 1952; children—Michael Dwyer, Mark Lee, Gregory F. Staff, United Farm Bur. Ins. Co., Indpls., 1951-66; dist. sales mgr. Ind. Ins. Co., Indpls., 1966-69; v.p. underwriting Fla. Farm Bur. Ins. Co., Gainesville, 1969-74; staff So. Farm Bur. Ins. Co., Jackson, Miss., 1974-77; v.p. systems and adminstrn. Nat. Assn. Ins. Mgrs., Jacksonville, Fla., 1978—. Lic. surplus lines, fire and casualty, life ins. numerous states. Democrat. Methodist. Clubs: Masons, Shriners. Home: 10126 Oakisle Rd W Jacksonville FL 32217 Office: Nat Assn Ins Mgrs 427 Gulf Life Tower Jacksonville FL 32207

WOOFTER, ANDREW CURRENCE, physician; b. Weston, W.Va., Oct. 15, 1907; s. Jesse Aldred and Anna W.; B.S., W.Va. Wesleyan U., 1929; M.D., U. Mich., 1933; m. Martha Woofter, June 12, 1935 (dec.); children—Andrew Currence, Joseph C. Intern, Mercy Hosp., Toledo, 1933-34; practice medicine specializing in cardiology, Parkersburg, W.Va., 1935—; mem. staff Camden Clark Meml., St. Joseph hosps. Served with USPHS, 1942-46. Diplomate Am. Bd. Internal Medicine. Fellow A.C.P., Am. Coll. Cardiology., Parkersburg Acad. Medicine (past pres.), W.Va. Med. Assn., W.Va. Heart Assn. (past pres., hon. dir.), Wood County Heart Assn. (past pres., hon. dir.). Club: Rotary. Home: 1810 Washington Ave Parkersburg WV 26101 Office: 219 10th St Parkersburg WV 26101

WOOLARD, GILBERT GARLAND, educator; b. Greenville, N.C., Sept. 23, 1929; married, 3 children. B.S. in Sci., E. Carolina U., 1951, M.A. in Sch. Adminstrn., 1951; Ed.D. in Community Coll. Adminstrn., N.C. State U., 1973. Founding dir. Kershaw County Vocat. Center, Vocat. Adult Edn., Sch. Dist. of Kershaw County 28, Camden, S.C., 1968—; adj. prof vocat. and adult edn. U. S.C. and Clemson U.; ednl. cons. U.S. Office of Edn. Mem. S.C. Assn. Vocat. Dirs. (past pres.), Am. Assn. School Adm., Am. Vocat. Assn., S.C. Vocat. Assn. (named Adult Educator of Yr. 1976, Vocat. Educator of Yr. 1979, pres. 1979). Cert. supt., prin., tchr. distributive edn., flight instr. Recipient Distinguished Service awards, C. of C., Vocat. Dirs. Assn. Directed numerous projects in field. Author: Master Craftsman-Master Teacher, 1979; author, editor publs. on vocat., adult, career edn. adminstrn. Home: 108 Valley Ct Camden SC 29020 Office: Route 4KCVC Hwy 1 N Camden SC 29020

WOOLARD, GILBERT GARLAND, JR., educator; b. Greenville, N.C., Sept. 23, 1929; s. Gilbert Garland and Inez (Van Dyke) W.; B.S., East Carolina U. 1951, M.A. 1951; Ed.D. (EPDA fellow), N.C. State U. 1973; m. Betty Ethel Heath, Dec. 19, 1950; children—Gilbert Garland III, Becky Marie, David Lee. Prin., Bushy Fork Sch., Roxboro, N.C., 1951; mgr. retail store Woolard Furniture, Williamston, N.C., 1956-63, Kimbrell Furniture Co., Camden, S.C., 1964-68; dir. Kershaw County Vocat. Center, Camden, 1968—; ednl. cons. to schs., industry, govt. agys., fgn. countries; adj. prof. adult and indsl. edn. U. S.C. and Clemson U., 1973—. Scoutmaster Boy Scouts of Am., Williamston, 1956-63; pres. Mchts. Council, Camden 1966-67; pres. United Fund of Williamston, 1960, Williamston C. of C. 1960-61; dep. for cadets CAP, 1968-72. Served as pilot USAF, 1951-56; Korea. Named Young Man of Yr., Williamston Jaycees, 1960; recipient Silver Beaver award Boy Scouts Am., numerous distinguished service awards civic orgns.; S.C. Legislature Commendation, 1976; Am. Aviation award, 1978; named Adult Edn. Dir. of Yr., S.C. Office Adult Edn., 1976, Vocat. Educator of Yr., 1978; designated pilot examiner FAA 1968-72, safety counselor, 1974—; comml. pilot, flight instr. Mem. Am., S.C. (pres. 1973-74) vocat. dirs. assns., S.C. Manpower Council, S.C. Adv. Council on Career Edn., Am., S.C. (pres. 1978) vocat. assns., Am. Aerospace Edn. Council, Am. Acad. Polit. and Social Sci., Am. Assn. Sch. Adminstrs., Adult Edn. Assn. U.S., Nat. Assn. Pub., Continuing and Adult Edn., Assn. Community Edn., S.C. Adult Edn. Assn., S.C. Assn. Adult Edn. Dirs., Phi Delta Kappa. Democrat. Methodist. Clubs: Kiwanis, Masons. Author: Some Got to Try—Some Got to Fly, 1980; Master Craftsman-Master Teacher, 1979; author career edn. monograph 1973; author 4 S.C. state guides on vocat-adult edn. 1972-73, mag. articles, research in field. Home: 108 Valley Ct Camden SC 29020 Office: Kershaw County Vocat Center Hwy 1-N Route 4 Camden SC 29020

WOOLARD, WILLIAM LEON, lawyer; b. Bath, N.C., Aug. 26, 1931; s. Archie Leon and Pearl Irene (Boyd) W.; A.B., Duke U., 1953, LL.B., 1955, J.D., 1955; m. Virginia Harris Stratton, June 17, 1961; children—William Leon, Margaret Anne. Admitted to N.C. bar, 1955; dist. mgr. Chrysler Corp., Charlotte (N.C.) region, 1956-60; partner Jones, Hewson & Woolard, Charlotte, 1960—; pres., dir. Armature Winding Co., Inc.; v.p., dir. Power Products Mfg. Co.; dir. Lawyers Title Co. Trustee, Lawyers Ednl. Found., Inc.; pres. bd. dirs. Lions Ednl. Found., Inc. Angier B. Duke scholar, 1949-53, Carnegie Endowment fellow Duke U., 1951-52. Mem. Am., N.C. bar assns., Am. Judicature Soc., Phi Kappa Sigma, Delta Theta Phi. Democrat. Methodist. Clubs: Masons, Shriners, Lions (dist. gov. 1978-79), Charlotte Athletic. Home: 638 Hempstead Pl Charlotte NC 28207 Office: 1000 Law Bldg Charlotte NC 28202

WOOLF, KENNETH HOWARD, architect; b. N.Y.C., Aug. 19, 1938; s. Howard Walter and Elizabeth Ann (Levy) W.; B.Arch., Cornell U., 1961; m. Elizabeth Adair Rainwater, July 3, 1965; children—Robert Gregg, Susan Adair, Jennifer Adair. Staff architect Look & Morrison, Architects, Pensacola, Fla., 1965-72; pvt. practice architecture, Pensacola, 1972—; instr. architecture Pensacola Jr. Coll., part-time 1967—. Chmn., Pensacola Archtl. Rev. Bd., 1970—; mem. Gulf Breeze Planning Bd., 1976—. Served with USN, 1961-65. Named Jaycee of Year, 1970. Mem. AIA (sec. N.W. Fla. chpt. 1976-77, 1977-78 Comml. Design Honor award 1975). Unitarian. Club: Rotary. Prin. works include: Coca-Cola Bottling Co. Plant, Pensacola, 1974, Twin Towers Profl. Office Bldg., Pensacola, 1976, addition Baptist Hosp., 1977, facilities Rehab. Inst., 1977; The Village, Housing for Elderly, 1978, Sylvan Lake Retirement Community Complex, 1979. Home: 15 N Sunset Blvd Gulf Breeze FL 32561 Office: 100 W Gadsden St Pensacola FL 32501

WOOLF, PHILIP LUTHER, educator; b. Elmira, N.Y., Dec. 2, 1946; s. Luther Ernest and Leona F. (Bellis) W.; B.S., Cornell U., 1969; M.S. in Edn., Elmira Coll., 1971; postgrad. Va. Poly. Inst. and State U., 1973-78, Nova U., 1979—; m. Peggy Gene Jarvis, Mar. 12, 1977. Instr. biology Corning (N.Y.) Community Coll., 1969-72; dir. human kidney procurement Med. Coll. Va., Richmond, 1972-73; asst. prof. anatomy and physiology John Tyler Community Coll., Chester, Va., 1973—; cons. McManis Assos., ednl. cons.'s; ednl. cons. for nursing and related health career programs. Recipient Community Service award Allied Chem. Corp., 1978; cert. CPR instr. Am. Heart Assn. Mem. Nat. Sci. Tchrs. Assn., Am. Heart Assn. Republican. Methodist. Club: Masons. Home: 3140 Klondike Rd Richmond VA 23235 Office: Route 301 Chester VA 23831

WOOLFENDEN, RAYMOND WILSON (COUSIN RAY), broadcasting exec.; b. Kopp, Va., Sept. 15, 1916; s. Raymond Mardsen and Hattie Mae (Abel) W.; student public schs.; m. Doris Mae Lynch, Feb. 15, 1953; children—Mabel Irene, Raymond Wilson, Reginald Dale, Raynee Casmo, Casmere Sharlene, Ranier Dorine. Band musician on radio in Va., Ohio, N.C. and Miss., 1925—; route supr. for bakeries and dairies, 1933-40; owner grocery store, restaurant and service station, Groveton, Va., 1940-46; pres., owner sta. WPWC, Dumfries, Va., 1974—. Served with AUS, 1945-46. Recipient various service awards, including Citizens award Cumberland County, N.C. and Yalobusha County, Miss. Mem. Assn. Country Entertainers, Nat. Assn. Broadcasters, Va. Broadcasters Assn., Mt. Vernon Lee C. of C., Prince William County C. of C., Greater Manassas C. of C., Country Music Entertainers and Musicians Benevolent Assn., VFW, Am. Legion, Assn. U.S. Army. Clubs: Moose, Odd Fellows. Office: 214 S Main St PO Box 189 Dumfries VA 22026

WOOLFLEY, FRANCIS AUGUSTUS, army officer; b. New Orleans, Apr. 30, 1893; s. Franklin Flanders and Mary Florence (Kessler) W.; grad. Inf. Sch., Ft. Benning, Ga., 1926. Command and Gen. Staff Coll., Ft. Leavenworth, Kan., 1935, Army War Coll., Washington, 1938, Chem. Warfare Sch., Edgewood Arsenal, Md., 1938; m. Rosalie Elizabeth Dufour, June 16, 1920; children—Francis Augustus, Rosalie Elizabeth (Mrs. Allen Henry Johness), Horace Louis Dufour. Commd. 2d lt. U.S. Army, 1917, advanced through grades to brig. gen., 1943, inf. advisor to Turkish Army and chief of staff U.S. Army Group, Joint Am. Mil. Mission for Aid to Turkey, Ankara, 1949-52, ret., 1953; dir. La. Civil Def. Agy., 1953-56; asst. adj. gen., dir. La. Civil Def. and dir. Office Emergency Planning for La., 1960-64. Decorated Silver Star with oak leaf cluster, Bronze Star with oak leaf cluster, Legion of Merit, Air medal; Croix de Guerre with palm, chevalier Legion of Honor (France); Croix de Guerre with palm (Belgium); Croix de Guerre (Luxemburg). Mem. SAR (past pres. La. Soc.), Soc. Colonial Wars, Soc. War 1812, Mil. Order World Wars (past comdr.), Am. Legion, Civil War Round Table New Orleans (past pres.), Thackery Soc., Mil. Order Fgn. Wars, Royal Soc. St. George.

Club: Pendennis (New Orleans). Home: 932 Solomon Pl New Orleans LA 70119

WOOLLEY, CLIFTON WARD, pediatrician; b. Tuscaloosa, Ala., Jan. 15, 1910; s. David Zacchaeus and Mary Benthall (Davis) W.; student Memphis State U., 1930-33; B.S., Union U., 1935; M.D., U. Tenn., 1939; m. Mary Selden Prescott, Sept. 5, 1940; children—Elizabeth Woolley Bennett, Martha, John, James. Intern, John Gaston Hosp., Memphis, 1939-40, resident, 1941-42, chief resident, 1946; resident Children's Meml. Hosp., Chgo., 1941-42; pub. health officer Maringo County (Ala.), Linden, 1940-41; practice medicine specializing in pediatrics, Memphis, 1947—; mem. staffs Baptist Meml., Meth., St. Joseph, John Gaston, LeBonheur hosps. (all Memphis); instr. U. Tenn. Coll. Medicine, 1951—; v.p., dir. Die Supplies, Inc., 1963—; physician athletic dept. Memphis State U., 1954—; bd. dirs. Greater Memphis State, Inc., 1970-76; physician athletic dept. Shelby State Community Coll., 1972—. Bd. advisers Hannibal-LaGrange Coll., 1973—, World Evangelism Found., Dallas, 1970—; mem. fgn. mission bd. So. Bapt. Conv., 1966-72; trustee Woolley Ednl. Found., Tenn. Bapt. Children Homes, Luther Rice Sem., Jacksonville, Fla. Served to maj. AUS, 1942-45. Decorated Silver Star (Luzon); named to Memphis State U. Football Hall of Fame, 1978; recipient Golden Tiger award, 1978. Diplomate Am. Bd. Pediatrics. Fellow Am. Acad. Pediatrics; mem. Am., Tenn., Memphis and Shelby County med. socs., Memphis Pediatrics Soc. (pres. 1952), Shelby Bapt. Assn. (missions com. 1966-70, fin. com. 1970-72), Gideons Internat. Contbr. articles to profl. publs. Home: 3604 Midland Ave Memphis TN 38111 Office: 3181 Poplar Ave Memphis TN 38111

WOOLLY, JAMES MAX, supt. schs.; b. Quitman, Ark., Jan. 5, 1914; s. James Otis and Mildred (Ward) W.; B.A., Hendrix Coll., Conway, Ark., 1936, LL.D. (hon.), 1970; M.S., U. Ark., 1941; m. Kathlyn White, Dec. 23, 1937; children—James Max, William Robert, David Allen. Tchr. schs. in Charleston and Warren, Ark., 1936-39; prin. Ark. Sch. Blind, Little Rock, 1939-47, supt., 1947—; v.p. bd. trustees Am. Found. Blind. Recipient Anne Sullivan Centennial award, 1966, Migel medal, 1978. Mem. Assn. Edn. Visually Handicapped (past pres.), Am. Assn. Workers Blind, Ark. Assn. Ednl. Adminstrs., Council Exceptional Children, Phi Delta Kappa. Methodist. Clubs: Pulaski Heights Lions (past pres.), Masons. Home: 2600 W Markham St Little Rock AR 72203 Office: PO Box 668 Little Rock AR 72203

WOOLRICH, SARAH WEAVER, ednl. adminstr.; b. Donna, Tex., June 6, 1919; d. Walter Gerald and Sarah (Sanborne) W.; B.A. in History and Govt., U. Tex., Austin, 1939; postgrad, elementary edn. m. Willis Raymond Woolrich, Jr.; children—Willis Raymond, Sarah Catherine Woolrich Dikeman. Tchr., Pub. Schs., Austin, Tex., Spring Branch Pub. Schs., Houston, 1954-58; headmistress St. Francis Episcopal Day Sch., Houston, 1959—. Mem. Tchr. Center Adv. Bd., Mem. Tex. Assn. Episcopal Schs. (pres. bd., 1968-71), Southwestern (pres., 1968-71), Nat. (bd. govs.), Assn. Episcopal Schs. American Association of University Women, Houston Bapt. U.; community service worker Internat. Inst. Edn. Orton Soc. Houston (dir.), DAR, Eta Chi (pres.), Delta Kappa Gamma. Home: 12826 Tosca St Houston TX 77024 Office: 345 Piney Point Houston TX 77024

WOOLRIDGE, JAMES LOUIS, educator, co. exec.; b. Covington, Ky., June 23, 1947; s. Carl Lewis and Helen (Connley) W.; B.A., U. Ky., 1970; m. Deborah Ann Kleier, Aug. 22, 1970. Asst. mgr. Greater Lexington (Ky.) Aquatic Club, 1967-71, exec. dir., 1972-76; tchr. Covington Ind. Sch. System, 1977—; pres., chief exec. officer Alistair Corp., 1977—; store owner Baskin Robbins; lectr. in field. Mem. Swim Facility Operators Assn. Am. (dir. 1975-76), AAU (1st v.p. 1976), Am. Cichlid Assn. (trustee 1976-77, conv. chmn. 1976), Central Ky. Aquarium Soc. (pres. 1975-76), Greater Cin. Cichlid Assn., Lambda Chi Alpha. Republican. Episcopalian. Contbr. articles to profl. jours. Home: 1002 Parkvale Ct Park Hills KY 41011

WOOLUMS, LYNN ALAN, advt. exec.; b. St. Petersburg, Fla., Apr. 13, 1948; s. Norman Carlisle and Marjorie Dorothy (Mumford) W.; A.A., St. Petersburg Jr. Coll., 1972; B.A., U. South Fla., 1974; m. India Louise Williams, Feb. 24, 1974; 1 dau., Erin Elizabeth. Retail mgr., asst. buyer Mr. Man, Inc., Tampa, 1970-74; advt. dir., 1974-75; account exec. E.J. Hughes Co., St. Petersburg, 1975-76, David Togie Advt., Tampa, 1976, Brown, Dowling & Kitten, Inc., St. Petersburg, 1976-78; pres. Woolums & Assos., Inc., St. Petersburg, 1978—. Mem. Suncoast Better Bus. Council (chmn., dir. public relations 1978—), St. Petersburg Sales and Mktg. Execs., St. Petersburg Advt. Fedn. Office: 337 22d Ave N Suite 114 Saint Petersburg FL 33704

WOOSLEY, ELIZABETH JARRELL MOORE, hist. preservationist; b. Shelbyville, Tenn., Oct. 2, 1930; d. Donald Wells and Elizabeth (Jarrell) Moore; student Va. Intermont Coll., Bristol, 1948-50; B.A., George Peabody Coll., Nashville, 1952; M.S., Vanderbilt U., Nashville, 1953; children—William Bryant III, Edward Jarrell. Audiologist, Augusta (Ga.) Jr. League Sch., 1954-55; originator speech and hearing program Shelbyville City Schs., 1956; coordinator Nashville Bicentennial, for Metro Hist. Commn. of Nashville, 1977—; dir. Jenkins Lutheran Chapel Hist. Site; mem. Tenn. Hist. Commn.; chmn. Shelbyville Beautification Commn., 1971-73, Shelbyville Landmarks, Inc., 1975-78; bd. dirs. Assn. Preservation Tenn. Antiquities; chmn. PTA Horse Show; vice chmn. Shelbyville Library Bd. Mem. Nat. Trust for Hist. Preservation, Ladies Hermitage Assn. (life), Peabody Aid (life), Hist. Belmont Assn., DAR, Alpha Psi Omega, Phi Theta Kappa. Baptist. Clubs: Chgo. Great Books, Town and Country Garden. Painter. Address: 4400 Belmont Park Terrace Nashville TN 37215

WOOTEN, JAMES BYRON, retail exec.; b. Oxford, Miss., July 25, 1938; s. G.B. and Emma Mirl (Green) W.; B.S., Memphis State U., 1961, M.B.A., 1970; m. Mary Ann Johnson, Dec. 23, 1971; 1 dau., Elizabeth Ann. Controller, Redman Industries, Dallas, 1970-72; tax mgr. Opticks, Inc., Dallas, 1972-73; controller, chem. div. Southland Corp., Dallas, 1973-74, sr. fin. analyst, 1974—. C.P.A., Tenn., Tex. Mem. Am. Inst. C.P.A.'s. Democrat. Episcopalian. Home: 2013 Rock Creek Grand Prairie TX 75050 Office: Southland Corp 2828 N Haskel St Dallas TX 75204

WOOTEN, JOHN DAVID, JR., finance exec.; b. Columbia, S.C., Oct. 2, 1930; s. John David and Martha Ann (Mikell) W.; A.A., City Coll. of San Francisco, 1951; B.B.A., Golden Gate Coll., 1955; m. Shirley Ann Gilbert, Dec. 22, 1951; children—David Mikell, Stephen George, Daniel Myer, Timothy Lee, Philip Edward. Jr. accountant C.E. Elbertson & Co., Winston-Salem, N.C., 1956; sr. accountant Wilson-Hosick & Co., Winston-Salem, 1956-58; audit supr. Ernst & Ernst, Winston-Salem, 1958-72; controller Carolina Mirror Corp., North Wilkesboro, N.C., 1973-75; v.p. fin. and adminstrn. Pilot Freight Carriers, Inc., Winston-Salem, 1975—; pres., dir. Transport Clearings East, Charlotte, N.C.; tchr. Wilkes Community Coll., Wilkesboro, N.C. Second v.p. Wilkes County United Way, 1974. Served with U.S. Army, 1951-53. Decorated Bronze Star; C.P.A., N.C. Mem. Nat. Accounting and Finance Council, Am. Inst. C.P.A.'s, N.C. Assn. C.P.A.'s, Nat. Accounting Assn. Democrat. Baptist. Club: Lions. Home: 2315 Palo Verde Dr Winston Salem NC 27106 Office: PO Box 615 Winston Salem NC 27102

WOOTTEN, JOHN ROBERT, investor; b. Chickasha, Okla., Feb. 5, 1929; s. Henry Hughes and Ella Gayle (Ditzler) W.; B.S., Colo. A. and M. U., 1953; m. Mary Lou Schmausser, Mar. 15, 1952 (div.); children—Pamela Jean, Robert Hughes. Sec., S.W. Radio and Equipment Co., Oklahoma City, 1953-55; pres. Belcaro Homes, Inc., 1955-60; pres. Bob Wootten Ford, Yukon, Okla., 1960-68; pres. Bus. Data Systems, 1968-72; chmn., chief exec. officer 1st Nat. Bank, Moore, Okla., 1970-72; pres. Communications Enterprises, Inc., Liberal, Kans., 1967—; pres. Trebor Leasing Co., 1965—; pres. Okla. Sch. Book Depository, Inc., Oklahoma City, 1976—; pres. S.W. Sch. Book Depository Inc., Dallas, 1976—; chmn., chief exec. officer Exchange Nat. Bank Del City (Okla.), 1976-78. Pres. Okla. chpt. Am. Cancer Soc., 1966-67; pres. Okla. chpt. Arthritis Found., 1973-76; pres. Lyric Theater Okla., 1976-77; chmn. bd. trustees Bone and Joint Hosp., 1976—; bd. dirs. Okla. Theater Center, Dallas Theater Center; trustee Oklahoma City U.; pres. Last Frontier council Boy Scouts Am., 1968-70. Recipient Silver Beaver award Boy Scouts Am., 1971. Mem. Ind. Bankers Assn., Am. Bankers Assn., Tex. Bookmans Assn., Navy League. Republican. Episcopalian. Clubs: Econ. of Okla., Masons, NW Oklahoma City Rotary (pres. 1963-64). Home: 6784 E Northwest Hwy Dallas TX 75231 Office: 130 NE 38th St Oklahoma City OK 73105 also 9259 King Arthur Dr Dallas TX 75247

WORCESTER, CURTIS WAYNE, real estate investor; b. Boston, July 20, 1940; s. Lawrence P. and Willa Mae (Curtis) W.; grad. Dean Jr. Coll., Franklin, Mass., 1961; B.S., Emerson Coll., Boston, 1963; m. Joyce Offerd, Dec. 16, 1977; 1 son by previous marriage, Eric. With Crawford and Co. Ins. Adjusters, Atlanta, 1966-76, supr., Los Angeles, 1972-76, supr., Chgo., 1967-72; adjuster, Boston, 1966-67; self-employed as real estate investor, Boca Raton, Fla., 1976—. Republican. Clubs: Boca Raton Hotel, Bankers (Boca Raton, Fla.). Home: 2000 N Ocean Blvd Apt 606 Boca Raton FL 33432

WORDEN, ALLEN JAMES, coll. dean; b. West Allis, Wis., July 19, 1934; s. Foss R. and Mildred (Oehmcke) W.; student Fresno State Coll., 1965-67; B.S., U. Wis., La Crosse, 1959; M.S., U. Wis., Milw., 1965; Ph.D., U. No. Colo., 1972; m. Norma Voss, Apr. 16, 1960; children—Michael, Timothy. Tchr. pub. schs., West Allis, 1959-61, counselor, 1961-62; adminstrv. asst. pub. schs., Hanford, Calif., 1965-68; dir. registration U. Wis., Oshkosh, 1968-70; asst. dean students U. No. Colo., Greeley, 1970-72; dean student devel. Tarrant County Jr. Coll., Fort Worth, 1972-78, dean instrn., 1978—; adj. asst. prof. edn. Tex. Christian U., Fort Worth. Bd. dirs. Fort Worth Sch. for Mental Retardation, 1977—, Career Devel. Center, Arlington, Tex., 1975—, Nat. Paraplegia Found., 1979—. Served with AUS, 1954-56. U. No. Colo. fellow, 1971; Calif. PTA scholar, 1966; recipient Outstanding Young Educator award U. Chgo., 1965. Mem. Jr. Coll. Student Personnel Assn., Tex. (dir. 1976—), S.W., Nat. assns. student personnel adminstrs., Nat. Soc. Study Edn., Tex., Am. personnel and guidance assns., Am. Coll. Personnel Assn., Nat. Council Student Devel., Phi Delta Kappa. Home: 6009 Wormar Fort Worth TX 76133 Office: 5301 Campus Dr Fort Worth TX 76119

WORDEN, EDSON ALLEN, elec. and mech. engr.; b. N.Y.C., July 21, 1935; s. Edson Giffen and Madelene (Belcher) W.; B.M.E. (Parshelsky grantee 1957-60), Union U., Schenectady, 1957; postgrad. CCNY, 1960-63; m. Florence Adelaide Warren, Jan. 28, 1961; children—Faith Adelaide, Edson Warren. Staff engr. Kollsman Instrument Co., Elmhurst, N.Y., 1960-63; sr. engr. Brown Engring. Co., Huntsville, Ala., 1963-65; research engr. Boeing Co., 1965-74; engr. Ala. Power Co., Birmingham, 1974—; dir. Ala. Rail Supply Co. Bd. dirs. ednl. div. Ala. Symphony Orch. Served to capt. USAF, 1957-59. Recipient Eagle Scout and Silver award Boy Scouts Am., 1953. Registered profl. engr., Ala.; cert. welding insp., Am. Welding Soc. Mem. Nat. Watch and Clock Collectors Assn., Am. Orchid Soc., Nat. Model R.R. Assn., Phi Sigma Kappa. Episcopalian. Club: Elks. Author, patentee in field. Home: 601 Eastwood Pl Vestavia Hills AL 35216 Office: 600 N 18th St Birmingham AL 35291

WORDEN, LUCILLE WALL, educator; b. Snyder, Tex., July 4, 1920; d. Grover James and Hattie Elizabeth (Ball) Wall; B.S. in Home Econs., Harding Coll., 1947; B.A. in Elem. Edn., U. Fla., 1970; m. Thomas Ray Sparkman, Mar. 18, 1947 (dec. 1965); children—Elizabeth Rae Sparkman Leavell, Thomas Ray; m. 2d, Amos Worden, Apr. 5, 1976. Tchr. vocat. home econs., 1949-61; basketball coach, 1949-53; co-owner, mgr. Lucille's Food Mart (later IGA Foodliner), 1958-65; elem. tchr., 1965-78; tchr. Crystal River (Fla.) Middle Sch., 1979—; tchr. adult vocat. clothing constrn., 1972-73; mem. Com. on State Math.-Lang. Arts Student Assessment Standards. Tchr. Sunday sch. Ch. of Christ; co-organizer Teentown, 1948; chmn. youth center; Westside cancer chmn., 1952; county adv. Girl Scouts U.S.A., 1958; den mother Cub Scouts, 1970. Named Tchr. of Yr., Citrus County Sch. Bd., 1972, 78. Mem. Citrus County Edn. Assn., Am. Craft Club, Crystal River Garden Club (charter, past sec., pres.). Democrat. Club: Jr. Woman's (charter). Home: Route 2 Box 636 Crystal River FL 32629 Office: Crystal River Middle Sch 705 NE 3d Ave Crystal River FL 32629

WORKMAN, NOEL PHILLIP, advt. co. exec.; b. Watseka, Ill., Jan. 17, 1940; s. Noel Estes and Ruth (Ehard) W.; B.S., U. Ill., 1962; m. Elizabeth Ann Frank, Dec. 30, 1961; children—Ann Elizabeth, Noel Phillip. Editor, Delta Rev. Mag., Memphis, 1965-67; mgr. public relations Graflex div. Singer Co., Greenville, Miss., 1967-69; v.p. Delta Design Group, Greenville, 1969-76, pres., 1976—; pres. Delta Typesetting Service, Greenville, 1974—; dir. Big River Broadcasting, Travel Unlimited. Mem. exec. com. Washington County (Miss.) Democratic 1975—; v.p. Greenville Symphony, 1979—, pres. elect, 1980; bd. dirs. Delta Children's Mus., 1978—. Served to 1st lt. USAF, 1962-65. Mem. Miss. Assn. Advt. Agencies, Greenville C. of C., Alpha Delta Sigma, Sigma Nu. Democrat. Episcopalian. Clubs: No Name Dinner, Cypress Hills Tennis. Contbg. editor Miss. Architect Mag., 1970—, Jour. Miss. Dental Assn., 1975—, Delta Scene Mag., 1975—, Miss. Mag., 1978—. Home: 421 S Washington Ave Greenville MS 38701 Office: 518 Central Ave Greenville MS 38701

WORKMAN, WILLIAM DOUGLAS, III, indsl. relations exec.; b. Charleston S.C., July 3, 1940; s. William Douglas, Jr., and Rhea (Thomas) W.; B.A., The Citadel, 1961; postgrad. U. S.C., 1962; m. Marcia Mae Moorhead, Apr. 23, 1966; children—William Douglas IV, Frank Moorhead. Reporter, Charleston News & Courier, 1964-66, Greenville (S.C.) News, 1966-68; tchr., adminstr., dean allied health scis. Greenville Tech. Coll., 1968-75; exec. asst. to Govt. of S.C., Columbia, 1975-78; dir. area labor market analysis Daniel Internat. Corp., Greenville, 1978—. Adminstrv. bd. Methodist Ch.; bd. trustees Sch. Dist. Greenville County, 1969-75, also vice chmn.; chmn. mgmt. bd. YMCA Camp Greenville, 1973—; chmn. S.C. Health Coordinating Council, 1976-78; founder S.C. Literacy Assn., 1969-73; pack master Cub Scouts, 1978—. Served with AUS, 1962-64; lt. col. Res. Decorated Army Commendation medal with oak leaf cluster; named Outstanding State Chmn., S.C. Jaycees, 1969. Mem. Res. Officers Assn., Assn. U.S. Army. Republican. Clubs: Greenville Country, Beaux Arts of Greenville (past pres.), Greenville-Piedmont Citadel (past pres.). Home: 30 Craigwood Rd Greenville SC 29607 Office: Daniel Bldg Greenville SC 29607

WORLEY, JOHN ALLEN, physician; b. Fort Worth, July 8, 1920; s. Cleon M. and Mildred S. W.; B.S., La. State U., 1941, M.D., 1944; m. Barbara West, Jan. 31, 1940; children—Susan Christine, John Allen. Intern, Charity Hosp., New Orleans, 1944-45, resident, 1945-46; practice medicine specializing in internal medicine, 1944—; mem. staff St. Frances Cabrini Hosp., Marksville Gen. Hosp., Dr.'s Hosp. of Tioga, Rapides Gen. Hosp., Winnfield Gen. Hosp.; cons. England AFB, Alexandria, La., 1976—; asso. dept. medicine Tulane U. Sch. Medicine, 1978-79. Chmn. Civil Service Commn. for the Firemen and Policemen for the City of Alexandria, 1975-79. Served to capt. MC U.S. Army, 1946-48. Diplomate Am. Bd. Internal Medicine. Fellow A.C.P., Am. Coll. Chest Physicians; mem. Royal Soc. Medicine. Democrat. Episcopalian. Home: 601 City Park Blvd Alexandria LA 71301 Office: 2219 Worley Dr Alexandria LA 71301

WORRELL, DENNIS LEE, publisher; b. Indpls., Nov. 22, 1938; s. Herman A. and Vivian A. (Anderson) W.; B.A., Columbia U., 1960, postgrad. in Bus., 1960-62 m. Marie Haspel, June 5, 1958; 1 son, Scott Harrison. Various exec. positions R.H. Macy & Co. Inc., N.Y.C., 1961-67; sr. v.p. Neiman Marcus Co., Dallas, 1967-73, Carter Hawley Hale Stores Inc., Los Angeles, 1973-77; exec. v.p. Haydn Cutler Co., Ft. Worth, 1977-79; owner Eagle Point Press, Inc., Ft. Worth, 1979—; editor Key Mag., Ft. Worth Ad Club News. Active Dallas Grand Opera Assn.: bd. dirs. Dallas Symphony Orch. Guild. Mem. Nat. Retail Mchts. Assn. (dir. 1971-76). Club: Pips Internat. (Los Angeles). Home: Route 9 Box 242 Fort Worth TX 76179 Office: PO Box 1636 Fort Worth TX 76101

WORTH, SIMMONS HOLLADAY, musician; b. Raleigh, N.C., May 17, 1950; d. Hal Venable and Mary Simmons (Andrews) Worth; A.B., U. N.C., 1972; Mus.M., East Carolina U., 1975; m. Glenn Wessell Potter, Apr. 15, 1978 (div.). Tchr. strings, New Hanover County Schs., Wilmington, N.C., 1972-74; tchr. Greenville City Schs., part time 1974-75; tchr. strings New Hanover County, 1975-76, tchr. strings, orch., music theory, 1976-79, Fairfax County (Va.) Schs., Alexandria, 1979—. Music coordinator Thalian Assn., 1976-77; mem. Fairfax Symphony Orch., 1978-79. Mem. Music Educators Nat. Conf. (pres. dist. 1975-77), Va. Music Educators Assn., Nat. Sch. Orch. Assn., Am. String Tchrs. Assn. Democrat. Episcopalian. Club: Jr. League.

WORTHINGTON, ELLIOTT ROBERT, psychologist, army officer; b. New Milford, Conn., May 5, 1937; s. Elmer Harry and Mildred Knight W.; B.A., Dartmouth Coll., 1961; M.A., No. Ariz. U., 1970; Ph.D., U. Utah, 1973; M.A. in Bus. Adminstrn., Webster Coll., 1978; m. Anita Elliott, Sept. 3, 1959; children—Susan Lee, Julie Ann, Karen Lisa. Served as enlisted man U.S. Marine Corps, 1957-59; police officer, Hanover, N.H., 1960-61; commd. 2d lt. inf., U.S. Army, 1961, advanced through grades to maj., 1968, discharged, 1969; counseling psychologist No. Ariz. U., 1970-71; postdoctoral psychology fellow Beaumont Army Med. Center, El Paso, Tex., 1973-74; commd. maj. Med. Service Corps U.S. Army, 1973, advanced through grades to lt. col., 1977; chief consultation service, Ft. Polk, La., 1974-75; psychology cons. U.S. Army Health Service Command, 1975—; chief psychology service Brooke Army Med. Center, Ft. Sam Houston, Tex., 1976-78, dir. community mental health service, 1978—; partner Worthington & Worthings Mgmt. Cons., San Antonio; adj.prof. Trinity U., St. Mary's U. Mem. adv. com. substance abuse council St. Mary's U., 1976—, mem. adv. com. Family Life Center, 1976—. Decorated Bronze Star with oak leaf cluster, Army Commendation medal with 2 oak leaf clusters, Purple Heart; recipient Pres.'s award St. Mary's U., 1979. Mem. Am. Psychol. Assn., Am. Mgmt. Assn., Am. Soc. Personnel Adminstrn., Aircraft Owners and Pilots Assn., Phi Kappa Psi, Phi Kappa Phi. Home: 904 Canterbury Hill San Antonio TX 78209 Office: Community Mental Health Service Brooke Army Med Center San Antonio TX 78234

WORTMAN, FRED AUSTON, JR., accountant; b. Dyersburg, Tenn., Feb. 23, 1947; s. Fred Auston and Carolyn (Reaves) W.; B.S., U. Tenn., 1976; m. Marilyn Ann Cox, June 9, 1973; children—Fred Auston, Lara Kelley. Staff accountant Cheeseman Thompson & Co., Union City, Tenn., 1975-76; owner Fred A. Wortman, Jr., C.P.A., Ridgely, Tenn., 1977—; instr. Dyersburg State Community Coll., 1977-78. Treas. First United Meth. Ch., Ridgely, 1978-79. Served to 1st. lt. U.S. Army, 1967-69. Mem. Am. Inst. C.P.A.'s, Tenn. Soc. C.P.A.'s, U. Tenn. Alumni Assn. (v.p. Ridgely). Democrat. Clubs: Rotary (pres.), Moose, Masons. Home: 403 S Main St Ridgely TN 38080 Office: 108 S Main St Ridgely TN 38080

WRAY, THOMAS ERWIN, naval officer; b. Roanoke, Va., Sept. 12, 1948; s. Charles Irvin and Ruby Jewel (Kinsey) W.; B.A. in History, Lynchburg Coll., 1970; m. Margaret Augusta Hess, June 19, 1971; 1 dau., Daphne Morgan. Enlisted U.S. Navy, 1972, commd. ensign Supply Corps, 1976, advanced through grades to lt., 1980; auditor Naval Audit Service, Norfolk, Va., 1979—. Mem. Am. Hist. Assn., Blue Key. Lutheran. Home: 5219 Powhatan Ave Norfolk VA 23508 Office: Naval Audit Service Naval Air Station Norfolk VA 23501

WREN, RUTH MARIE, govt. ofcl.; b. Graham, Tex., July 17, 1930; d. Marshall Edward and Flora Lee (Lindley) Brown; student public schs., Tex.; m. Bobby Joe Wren, July 31, 1948; children—Robert, Russell, Lee Roy, Marilyn. Operator, Southwestern Bell Tel. Co., 1948; asst. dietitian Southwestern Gen. Hosp., El Paso, Tex., 1967-71; asst. kitchen mgr. Providence Hosp., El Paso, 1963-64; consumer health insp. El Paso City-County Health Unit, 1971-78, edn. supr., 1978—; mem. adv. council bd. Tech. Vocat. Edn. Tex., 1978—. Mem. Infectious Disease Control Practitioners Council, Trans Pecos Health Career Conf. (exec. com.), Am. Mgmt. Assn., Tex. Public Health Assn. Democrat. Methodist. Home: 5809 Tautoga St El Paso TX 79924 Office: 222 S Campbell St El Paso TX 79901

WRENN, ETTA FLORENCE, guidance counselor; b. Chatham County, N.C., Sept. 15, 1942; d. Henry Delbert and Lucy Birteene (Foust) Wrenn; B.S., Guilford Coll., 1964; M.Edn., U. N.C., 1972. Tchr. math. W. Montgomery High Sch., Mt. Gilead, N.C., 1964-68, guidance counselor and head Guidance Dept., 1968—. Recording clk. Friends United Meeting, 1978—, asst. recording clk., 1975-78; presiding clk. Western Quarterly Meeting on Ministry and Counsel, 1976—; recording clk. N.C. Yearly Meeting on Ministry and Counsel, 1976-77. Gen. Electric Guidance fellow, U. S.C., 1970; recipient cert. of Appreciation U.S. Army, 1978. Mem. N.C. Personnel and Guidance Assn. (chpt. sec.-treas. 1978-79), N.C. Assn. Educators, NEA, Am. Personnel and Guidance Assn., N.C. Sch. Counselor Assn., Am. Sch. Counselor Assn., Montgomery Choral Soc. Republican. Home: Route 4 Siler City NC 27344 Office: Route 3 PO Box 228 Mount Gilead NC 27306

WRIGHT, ALFRED SNEED, med. adminstr.; b. Kansas City, Mo., Apr. 3, 1925; s. Sneed and Dollie Osborne (Warford) W.; student U.S. Armed Forces Inst., 1946-59; m. Virginia Mae Sisco, July 15, 1950; children—Joyce Ann, Scott Allen. Served with U.S. Army, 1946-67; personnel dir. Sparks Regional Med. Center, Ft. Smith, Ark., 1968-69; adminstrv. asst. for personnel, St. Joseph's Mercy Med. Center, Hot Springs Nat. Park, Ark., 1969—; cons. in field. Bd. dirs. United Way of Garland County, Ark., 1970-76; mem. Hot Springs/Garland County Ambulance Service Commn., 1980—; mem. sheriff's res. Garland County, 1976-78. Decorated Dept. of Army Commendation with 2 oak leaf clusters, Combat Infantryman's Badge. Mem. Am. Soc. Hosp. Personnel Adminstrs., Ark. Assn. Hosp. Personnel Dirs. (pres. 1970-71). Home: 833 Bellaire Dr Hot Springs Nat Park AR 71901 Office: St Joseph's Mercy Med Center 100 Whittington Ave Hot Springs Nat Park AR 71901

WRIGHT, ALMA MCINTYRE, publishing co. exec.; b. Knoxville, Tenn., July 31, 1909; d. William Mobry and Theresa (Biagiotti) McIntyre; B.S. in Edn., U. Tenn., 1932; m. Robert Oliver Wright, Feb. 17, 1931; 1 son, Robert Oliver. Writer stories, articles on African violets, house plants, 1947—; editor African Violet mag., 1947-63; exec. dir. African Violet Soc. Am., Inc., 1960-63; pres. Indoor Gardener Pub. Co., Inc., Knoxville, 1963—; editor Gesneriad-Saintpaulia News, 1963—. Mem. Am. Hort. Soc. (hon. v.p. 1954), African Violet Soc. Am. (hon. life, rec. sec. 1946-48, nat. pres. 1948-49, membership sec. 1953-63), Saintpaulia Internat. (editor publs., rec. sec. 1963—). Editor: Master List of African Violets, 1962; editor for Am., Gesneria Soc. Home: 7914 Gleason Rd Apt 1075 Knoxville TN 37919 Office: 1800 Grand Ave Knoxville TN 37901

WRIGHT, BENJAMIN WARD, JR., historian; b. Richmond, Va., Aug. 17, 1935; s. Benjamin Ward and Ellen Douglas (Moody) W.; B.A., Randolph-Macon Coll., 1957; M.A., U. Va., 1962. Instr. history Randolph-Macon Coll., 1959-60; instr. Randolph-Macon Woman's Coll., part time, 1966-67; asst. prof. U. Va., Lynchburg, 1962-67; asso. prof. history Central Va. Community Coll., Lynchburg, 1967—; vis. asso. prof. World Campus Afloat, 1969-70; cons. Nat. Endowment of Humanities. Pres., Lynchburg Hist. Found., 1973-75; mem. open space and recreation com. Central Va. Planning Commn., 1974-76; bd. dirs. Lynchburg Community Concerts, 1975—, Lynchburg City Museum System, 1976-78, Dance div. Lynchburg Fine Arts Center, 1978—. Recipient Merit cert. Lynchburg Vol. Bur., 1976-77, Community Service certificate City of Lynchburg, 1978, 15 Year Service award Commonwealth of Va., 1977. Mem. AAUP, Va. Soc. History Tchrs., So. Hist. Assn., Am. Hist. Assn., Orgn. Am. Historians, Va. Social Sci. Assn., Lynchburg Civil War Round Table (pres. 1979—), Lynchburg Fine Arts Center, Va. Mus. Contbr. articles, revs. to hist. jours. Home: 3837 Peakland Pl #7 Lynchburg VA 24503 Office: History Dept Central Va Community Coll PO Box 4098 Lynchburg VA 24502

WRIGHT, BILLIE ELLIS, oil field equipment sales co. exec.; b. Olney, Tex., Oct. 21, 1927; s. Ed and Lena Belle (Ellis) W.; B.S. magna cum laude, Abilene Christian Coll., 1951; M.B.A., U. Tex. of Permian Basin, 1977; m. Mary Jo Green, Aug. 16, 1953; 1 dau., Gay Lyn. With Continental-Emsco Co. subs. LTV Co., 1951—, br. mgr., Abilene, Tex., 1954, St. Louis, 1970-72, sales rep., Midland, Tex., 1972-79, mgr. sales office, sr. sales rep., 1979—. Bd. dirs. West Central Tex. Waterflood Assn., Abilene, Tex., 1967. Served with U.S. Army, 1946-47; Japan. Mem. Am. Petroleum Inst. Democrat. Mem. Churches of Christ. Club: Petroleum of Midland. Home: 4651 Oakwood Odessa TX 79761 Office: 500 Wall Tower W Midland TX 79702

WRIGHT, BURTON, sociologist; b. Detroit, Jan. 31, 1917; s. Burton and Hazel Marie (Thomas) W.; A.A., Canal Zone Coll., 1944; B.A., U. Wash., Seattle, 1947, M.A., 1949; Ph.D., Fla. State U., 1972; m. Marie Fidelis Gallivan, Jan. 22, 1942; children—Burton III, Catherine Margaret (dec.). Enlisted U.S. Navy, 1937, commd. and advanced through grades to comdr., 1957; dir. Naval Res. Recruiting, 1960-64, ret., 1964; mem. faculty U. Wash., 1947-49, Northwestern U., summers 1956-59, George Washington U., Washington, 1954-60, Rollins Coll., Winter Park, Fla., 1966-69; cons. Ford Found., 1951, Dept. Air Force, 1955, U.S. Army Chem. Corps, 1956; prof. dept. sociology U. Central Fla., Orlando, 1972—. Decorated Navy Commendation medal. Fellow Am. Anthropol. Assn.; mem. Am. Sociol. Assn., Soc. Psychol. Study Social Problems, AAUP, Am. Acad. Arts and Scis., Soc. Study Social Problems, So. Sociol. Soc., North Central Sociol. Soc. Roman Catholic. Club: Univ. (Winter Park, Fla.). Author: (with John P. Weiss and Charles M. Unkovic) Perspective: An Introduction to Sociology, 1975; (with Vernon Fox) Criminal Justice and the Social Sciences, 1978; (with John P. Weiss) Social Problems, 1980. Home: 640 London Rd Winter Park FL 32792 Office: Dept Sociology U Central Fla Box 25000 Orlando FL 32816

WRIGHT, CHARLES WESLEY, educator; b. Ft. Worth, Sept. 26, 1937; s. Lewis Weldon and Mattie Ola (Dixon) W.; B.B.A., Tex. So. U., 1966, M.B.A., 1971; m. Sandra Louise Polk, Dec. 15, 1968; children—Raquel Elizabeth, Charles Wesley. Compliance officer U.S. Dept. Labor, Houston, 1966-70; counselor/cons. Small Bus. Devel. Center, Houston, 1970-72; dir. Urban Bus. Devel. Orgn., Houston, 1972-73; head dept. acctg. Prairie View (Tex.) A. and M. U., 1976-77; instr. acctg. Houston Community Coll., 1977—. Served with USAF, 1957-61. Home: 5339 Fairgreen Ln Houston TX 77048

WRIGHT, CLINTON FOSTER, veterinarian; b. Trenton, N.J., Mar. 20, 1931; s. Clinton Hamilton and Mary (Wainwright) W.; B.S.A., U. Fla., 1953; D.V.M., Auburn U., 1970; m. Barbara Ann Thomas, Oct. 26, 1963; 1 son, Thomas Foster. Salesman, Acme Insecticides, Atlanta, 1955-58, Sun Oil Co., Jacksonville, Fla., 1962-63; veterinarian Univ. Blvd. Animal Hosp., Jacksonville, Fla., 1970-72, Ft. Caroline Animal Clinic, Jacksonville, 1972—; chmn. bd. Jacksonville Vet. Emergency Clinic. Trustee N. Fla. Leukemia Soc., 1973—, pres., 1976-77. Served to 1st lt. AUS, 1953-55. Mem. Am., Fla., Jacksonville (pres. 1975) vet. med. assns. Mason (32 deg., Shriner). Club: University. Home: 5226 Atlantic Blvd Jacksonville FL 32207 Office: 5844 Ft Caroline Rd Jacksonville FL 32211

WRIGHT, DAVID BLAINE, chem. engr.; b. Kingsport, Tenn., Feb. 12, 1952; s. Blaine Mac and Nadine Campbell (Gillenwater) W.; B.A. in Chemistry, King Coll., 1974; B.S., U. Tenn., 1975, M.S., 1977; m. Cornelia Lucille Haislip, June 21, 1975; 1 son, Daine Michael. Grad. teaching asst. U. Tenn., Knoxville, 1975-77; devel. engr. Olin Chems. Group Process Technology Charleston, Tenn., 1977—. Mem. Am. Inst. Chem. Engrs., Sigma Xi. Home: 413 Seminole Dr NW Cleveland TN 37311 Office: Olin Chems Box 248 Charleston TN 37310

WRIGHT, DIANNE HAMBY, librarian; b. Lowndes County, Ga., May 4, 1941; d. Alvin D. and Kathryn Elizabeth (Morris) Hamby; B.S., Valdosta State Coll., 1966; M.S., Fla. State U., 1970; m. Nov. 24, 1963. Catalog reviser Ariz. State U., Tempe, 1967; tchr. Valdosta (Ga.) Jr. High Sch., 1968-69; reference librarian Valdosta State Coll., 1970-72, asst. prof., serials librarian, 1972—. Mem. ALA, Southeastern Library Assn., Ga. Library Assn., Beta Phi Mu. Office: Library Valdosta State Coll Valdosta GA 31601

WRIGHT, EDWIN QUISENBERRY, JR., mfg. co. exec.; b. Balt., Apr. 3, 1937; s. Edwin Quisenberry and Anne (Ritchie) W.; B.A., W.Va. U., 1959; M.B.A., James Madison U., 1979; m. Delores Emmagene Mayle, Aug. 28, 1965; children—Elizabeth Lee. Data center mgr. Gen. Dynamics/Electric Boat, Groton, Conn., 1963-68; mgr. systems and procedures Fiber Industries, Inc., Salisbury, N.C., 1968-73; project mgr. Celanese Corp., Charlotte, N.C., 1973-75; dir. mgmt. info. systems ITT-CBC Morton Frozen Foods, Charlottesville, Va., 1975—. Served with U.S. Army, 1960-62. Mem. Inst. Mgmt. Acctg. Republican. Presbyterian. Club: Farmington Country (Charlottesville). Home: 1825 Yorktown Dr Charlottesville VA 22901 Office: 1 Morton Dr Charlottesville VA 22906

WRIGHT, GABRIELA FESSENDEN, mental health counselor; b. Hanau, West Germany, Oct. 28, 1952; d. Gisela Hens; came to U.S., 1955, naturalized, 1970; student U. South Fla., 1971-73; B.S. in Broadcasting, U. Fla., 1975, M.S. and Ed.S., 1979; m. Paul Glen Wright, June 10, 1978. Student asst. U. Fla., Gainesville, 1973-75, sec. III, 1975-76, student asst. IFAS Dist. Agts. Office, 1976-77, grad. asst. Office Student Services, 1977-78; mental health counselor children's program Community Counseling Center of Levy, Gilchrist and Dixie Counties (Fla.), 1979—. Bd. dirs. Univ. United Methodist Ch., 1977—, sr. high Sunday sch. tchr., 1977-78, asst. dir. Youth Fellowship, 1977-78; leader Brownie troop Girl Scouts U.S.A., 1975-76; vol. counselor Corner Drug Store, Gainesville, 1976-78; active U. Fla. Fine Arts Com., 1976-77. Mem. Am. Personnel and Guidance Assn., Alachua County Mental Health Assn. Democrat. Club: Bus. and Profl. Women. Home: 5417 SW 78 Terr Gainesville FL 32601

WRIGHT, GEORGE BYRON, educator; b. Hartford, Conn., Nov. 21, 1943; s. Milton Carlisle and Erna (Mueller) W.; B.S., U. Houston, 1971, M.Ed., 1975; m. Susan Emery Williams, Mar. 5, 1966; children—Laurel Emery, Ian Elizabeth. Nuclear reactor operator U.S. Navy, 1963-69; instr. dept. electronic tech. Alvin (Tex.) Community Coll., 1971-76, dir. computer and info. systems, 1976—; adj. prof. computer sci. U. Houston, Clear Lake City, 1979; dir., sec. GROW Interests, Inc., Friendswood, Tex., 1974. Served with USNR, 1970. Mem. IEEE, IEEE Computer Soc., Assn. Computing Machinery, Tex. Jr. Coll. Tchrs. Assn., Phi Kappa Phi, Tau Alpha Phi. Club: Lions. Address: 3110 Mustang Rd Alvin TX 77511

WRIGHT, GLEN LAVERE, chem. mfg. co. exec.; b. Walton, W.Va., May 28, 1933; s. Opie Presley and Oleta Mesa (Cottrell) W.; B.S., Morris Harvey Coll., 1963; m. Lois Jean Fisher, June 23, 1956; 1 son, Stephen Lee. Lab. technician Union Carbide Corp., S. Charleston, W.Va., 1955-58, sr. lab. technician, 1959-62, research chemist, 1963-66, tech. rep., Charlotte, N.C., 1967-69, area rep., 1970-72, account rep., 1973-74, regional mgr., Tarrytown, N.Y., 1974-77, mgr. contract formulations, Jacksonville, Fla., 1977—. Served in U.S. Army, 1952-55. Mem. Assn. Textile Colorists and Chemists (sr.), Am. Chem. Soc. (sr.), Alpha Chi Sigma. Republican. Baptist. Clubs: Optimists, Lions, Masons, Shriners. Home: 4440 Charter Point Blvd Jacksonville FL 32211 Office: 7825 Baymeadows Way Jacksonville FL 32216

WRIGHT, HARRY HERCULES, physician; b. Charleston, S.C., Jan. 4, 1948; s. Harry Vernon and Agnes Lucile (Simmons) W.; B.S., U. S.C., 1970; M.D., U. Pa., 1976, M.B.A., 1976. Resident in psychiatry Wm. S. Hall Psychiat. Inst., Columbia, S.C., 1977-79; adminstrv. fellow in psychiatry NIMH, Rockville, Md., 1979; fellow in child psychiatry William S. Hall Psychiat. Inst., 1979—. Treas., Kitani Found., 1977-78; bd. dirs. Columbia Area Sickle Cell Anemia Found., 1977. Falk fellow, 1977-79; laughlin fellow, 1979; recipient Freed award Hall Psychiat. Inst., 1978. Mem. AAAS, Am. Public Health Assn., Am. Hosp. Assn., Am. Chem. Soc., Am. Psychiat. Assn., So. Med. Assn., Com. to Combat Huntington's Disease, Riverbank Zool. Soc., Sigma Xi. Methodist. Contbr. articles to profl. jours. Home: PO Box 12474 Columbia SC 29211 Office: PO Box 119 Columbia SC 29202

WRIGHT, JAMES C., JR., congressman; b. Ft. Worth, Dec. 22, 1922; s. James C. and Marie (Lyster) W.; student Weatherford Coll., U. Tex.; m. Betty Hay, Nov. 12, 1972; children by previous marriage—Jimmy, Virginia Sue, Patricia Kay, Alicia Marie. Mem. Tex. Ho. of Reps., 1947-49; mayor City of Weatherford (Tex.), 1950-54; mem. 84th-96th congresses from 12th Tex. Dist., majority leader, 1976—, mem. pub. works and transp. com., 1955-76, mem. budget com. Chmn., Commn. on Hwy. Beautification; mem. Nat. Commn. Water Quality; mem. Ho. of Reps. del. to U.S.-Mex. Interparliamentary Conf., 1963-79. Served with USAAF, World War II. Decorated D.F.C., Legion of Merit; named outstanding young man Tex. Jr. C. of C., 1953; named Most Respected Mem. of Ho. of Reps. in survey taken by U.S. News & World Report, 1980. Mem. League Tex. Municipalities (pres. 1953). Presbyterian. Author: You and Your Congressman, 1965; The Coming Water Famine, 1966; Of Swords and Plowshares, 1968; co-author Congress and Conscience, 1970. Address: 2459 House Office Bldg Washington DC 20515

WRIGHT, JERRY PEYTON, ins. and investment co. exec.; b. Houston, Tex., Dec. 19, 1939; s. George Peyton and Ruby Lee (Nolen) W.; B.B.A., U. Houston, 1967; postgrad. Perkins Sch. Theology So. Meth. U., 1968-69; m. Peggy Thomas, June 21, 1963; children—Jennifer, Joan, Jami. Real estate salesman, Tex., 1960-69; partner Robert Bye & Assos., Houston, 1969-74; owner, pvt. practice ins. and investments co., Houston, 1974—; appeared videotape training films for life ins. sales. Named Rookie of the Yr., New England Life, 1968; recipient various ins. sales awards. Mem. Nat. Assn. of Chartered Life Underwriters, Million Dollar Round Table, Nat. Assn. of Security Dealers, Tex. Assn. of Real Estate Brokers, Houston Fin. and Estate Forum, Leaders Assn. New Eng. Life. Contbr. articles on life inst. to trade publs. Office: PO Box 10193 Houston TX 77206

WRIGHT, JERRY SMITH, lawyer; b. Houston, Oct. 18, 1942; s. Ethridge R. and Betsy (Smith) W.; B.B.A., Lamar U., 1965; J.D., U. Tex., 1969; m. Elizabeth Louise Tolliver, Nov. 23, 1974; 1 dau., Shannon Leigh. Admitted to Tex. bar, 1968; mem. tax staff Alexander Grant & Co., C.P.A.'s, 1969; v.p., trust officer trust div. Houston Nat. Bank, 1969-78; v.p., trust officer 1st Security Bank of Beaumont (Tex.), 1978—. Mem. Beaumont Estate Planning Council (v.p.), Houston Estate and Fin. Forum, Am. Bar Assn., Houston Bar Assn., Jefferson County Bar Assn. Baptist. Clubs: Lions, Beaumont Knife and Fork (pres.). Office: PO Box 3391 Beaumont TX 77704

WRIGHT, JOHN EVANS, clergyman, county ofcl.; b. Falling Waters, W.Va., Dec. 24, 1932; s. William Eugene and Rosemary Boarman W.; A.B., Shepherd Coll., 1956; M.Div., Wesley Theol. Sem., 1959; m. Fay Deeds, June 21, 1959; children—Paul Warner, Jon Brantly. Ordained to ministry, United Methodist Ch., 1959; pastor Camp Hill United Meth. Ch., Harpers Ferry, W.Va., 1959-63; Bedington United Meth. Ch., Martinsburg, W.Va., 1963-73; Inwood (W.Va.) United Meth. Ch., 1973—; chaplain W.Va. Air N.G. Mem. Berkeley County (W.Va.) Commn., 1968—, pres., 1972, 73, 76-79. Served to lt. col. W.Va. Air N.G., 1953-79. Mem. Nat. Guard Assn. U.S., Nat. Guard Assn. W.Va., Mil. Chaplains Assn., Nat. Assn. Counties, Farm Bur. Republican. Home: PO Box 139 Inwood WV 25428 Office: Berkeley County Community Court House Martinsburg WV 25401

WRIGHT, JOHN ROBERT, health physicist; b. Heber Springs, Ark., Apr. 14, 1931; s. Henry Harrison and Nola (Rhode) W.; student Hanford Sch. Nuclear Engring., Richland, Wash., 1953-57; m. Patricia Ann Vanderburg, June 12, 1954; children—John Daniel, Deborah Ann, Vivian Sue, Tracy Lynn. Health physics technician Hanford Atomic Ops. Co., Richland, 1953-57, Lockheed Aircraft Corp., Dawsonville, Ga., 1958-60; health physicist Todd Shipyard's Corp., Galveston, Tex., 1960-63; health physicist in nuclear research Ga. Inst. Tech., 1963-73; chemistry and radiation protection engr. Fla. Power Corp., Crystal River, 1973—; adviser Sch. Radiol. Health Ocala Jr. Coll.; cons. Dynatomics Co.; corp. radiation protection mgr. Fla. Power Corp.; mem. health physics task force Edison Electric Inst. Served with USAF, 1950-53. Mem. Health Physics Soc. (chmn. com. pub. relations Fla. chpt.), Internat. Radiation Protection Agy. Democrat. Baptist. Clubs: Lions, Masons. Contbr. articles on radiol. health to profl. jours.; patentee tritium control device for neutron generator. Home: PO Box 1303 Crystal River FL 32629 Office: PO Box 1228 Crystal River FL 32629

WRIGHT, LINDA HAMLETT, foundry ofcl.; b. Charlotte County, Va., May 15, 1942; d. Emmett Linwood and Beulah (Nash) Hamlett; student Central Va. Community Coll., 1970—; m. James Edward Wright, Nov. 4, 1961; 1 son, Gregory E. Sec., Burlington Industries, Inc., Drakes Branch, Va., 1960-64, Lynchburg (Va.) Tng. Sch. and Hosp., 1964-73, Central Va. Community Coll., Lynchburg, 1973-74; adminstrv. asst. Lynchburg Foundry Co., 1975-78, human resources asso., 1978-80, employee services mgr., 1980—; guest lectr. local colls. and other industries, 1973—. Active various coms. United Way, Lynchburg, 1976-79; adv. Jr. Achievement, Lynchburg, 1978. Mem. Personnel Assn. Central Va. (sec.). Home: 42 Mistletoe Dr Forest VA 24551 Office: Lynchburg Foundry Co Box 411 Lynchburg VA 24505

WRIGHT, MARGARET ADA BENNETT, bus. exec.; b. Camden, N.J., Dec. 20, 1918; d. John Henry and Margaret Catherine (Bloxsom) Bennett; B.S., Glassboro State Coll., 1940; M.A., St. Mary's U. 1970; Ph.D., U., Tex., 1976. Tchr. elementary and secondary schs., N.J., 1940-42, 46-48, Tex., 1966-70; adminstr. student aid library and counseling center Minnie Stevens Piper Found., San Antonio, Tex., 1970-73; counselor Incarnate Word Coll., San Antonio, 1974-75; exec. dir. Tex. Personnel and Guidance Assn., Austin, 1976-79; pres. New Outlook Inc., 1979—; editor, managing editor for counselors' newsletters and profl. jours. Active grad. com. for the instl. self-study St. Mary's U., 1970-72; coll. key person St. Francis Episcopal Ch., 1974-75; bd. dirs. St. Mary's U. Alumni Assn., 1974-77. Served with USNR (WAVES), 1942-46. Certified tchr., N.J., Tex.; profl. life counselor certificate, Tex. Mem. Am. Personnel and Guidance Assn., Nat. Vocat. Guidance Assn., Adult Edn. Assn. of USA. Republican. Contbr. articles in field to profl. jours. Home: PO Box 29221 San Antonio TX 78229

WRIGHT, MARY RUTH, psychologist; b. St. Louis, Apr. 2, 1922; d. Leon Carl and Gwendolyn (Travis) Brown; R.N., Washington U., St. Louis, 1944; B.S., U. Houston, 1966, M.A., 1967; Ph.D., Union Grad Sch., 1978; m. William Kemp Wright, Feb. 10, 1945; children—Gwendolyn, Veronica, Victoria, Jennifer. Instr., U.S. Cadet Nurse Corps, USPHS, 1944; instr. surgery Washington U. Sch. Nursing, 1944-45; instr. pediatrics Children's Meml. Hosp., Chgo., 1945-46; instr. S. Tex. Jr. Coll., Houston, 1967-70; mental health cons. St. Joseph Mental Hosp., Houston, 1966-67; staff psychol. services Almeda Clinic, Houston, 1966-70; pvt. practice marriage and family counseling, Houston, 1970—; med.-psychol. researcher and writer, 1970—; psychologist Houston Health Dept., 1971—; clin. asst. prof. psychology dept. otorhinolaryngology and communicative scis. Baylor Coll. Medicine. Recipient Spl. award Security Agy. Mem. Am. Psychol. Assn., Am. Assn. Marriage and Family Counselors, Am. Assn. Sex Educators and Counselors, Internat. Council Psychologists, Nat. Council Family Relations, Nat. Assn. Social Workers, Mental Health Assn. Houston and Harris County (dir.). Contbr. articles to profl. jours.; speaker U.S. and abroad on psychol. implications of cosmetic surgery. Home: 3671 Del Monte St Houston TX 77019 Office: 633 Hermann Profl Bldg Houston TX 77030

WRIGHT, MYRON A., corp. exec.; b. Blair, Okla., 1911; ed. Okla. State U.; married. With Exxon Co. U.S.A., 1933-76, chmn., chief exec. officer, 1966-76, exec. v.p., dir. Exxon Corp. until 1976; chmn. bd., pres. Cameron Iron Works, Inc., Houston, 1977—, also dir.; mem. exec. com., dir. Am. Gen. Ins. Co., 1st City Bancorp. Tex., Inc. Office: Cameron Iron Works Inc 13013 Northwest Freeway Box 1212 Houston TX 77001

WRIGHT, PARKE, diversified industry exec.; b. Buffalo, 1921; student U. Buffalo; m. Almeria Lykes Holmes, 1944; 1 son, Parke, IV. With Nat. Airlines, 1945-52, regional mgr. Northeastern U.S., until 1952; with Lykes Bros. Inc., 1952—, sr. v.p., 1965—; chmn. exec. com. Freedom Fed. Savs. & Loan Assn., Tampa, Fla.; chmn. bd. Second Nat. Bank, Tampa; dir., mem. exec. com. Gen. Telephone Co. Fla. Past chmn. Fla. State Fair Authority; pres. Fla. State Fair Assn.; chmn. trustees St. Joseph's Hosp., Tampa exec. com. Tampa Com. 100; co-chmn. I-75 Now Task Force; exec. bd. Gulf Ridge council Boy Scouts Am.; chmn. Gov. Fla. Adv. Council Econ. Devel. Named Tampa's Outstanding Citizen, Tampa Civitan Club, 1972; recipient Top Mgmt. award Sales and Mktg. Execs. Assn., 1972. Mem. Fla. C. of C. (pres. 1976-77). Address: 5105 Longfellow Ave Tampa FL 33609

WRIGHT, PHILLIP EUGENE, II, orthopedic hand surgeon; b. Loris, S.C., Oct. 16, 1940; s. Eugene Phillip and Dorothy (Boyd) W.; B.S., Fla. So. Coll., 1963; M.D., U. Miami, 1967; m. Linda Leigh Wright, June 25, 1965; children—Laura, Brian, David. Intern, Jackson Meml. Hosp., Miami, Fla., 1967-68; resident in orthopedic surgery Campbell Found., U. Tenn., 1972-75, fellow in hand surgery, 1975, asst. prof. dept. orthopedic surgery Coll. Medicine, 1978—; fellow in microsurgery Franklin Hosp., San Francisco, 1975. Served with M.C., USN, 1969-72. Mem. Memphis Orthopedic Soc., Memphis and Shelby County Med. Soc., Tenn. Med. Assn., AMA, So. Med. Assn., Mid-South Jour. Club., Tenn. Orthopedic Soc., Am. Acad. Orthopedic Surgeons, Am. Soc. for Surgery of Hand, A.C.S. Office: 869 Madison Memphis TN 38104

WRIGHT, R(ALEIGH) LEWIS, neurosurgeon; b. Roanoke, Va., Apr. 16, 1931; s. Raleigh Lewis and Mary Lillian (Major) W.; B.A., U. Richmond, 1951; M.D., Med. Coll. Va., 1955; m. Sarah Bird Grant, Sept. 7, 1963; 1 son, Alexander Grant. Intern, Duke U. Hosp., 1955-56, surg. resident, 1956-57; neurosurg. resident Mass. Gen. Hosp., Boston, 1959-63; practice medicine specializing in neurosurgery, Boston, 1964-70, Richmond, Va., 1970—; mem. staff St. Mary's, Retreat, Richmond Met., Stuart Circle hosps., Med. Coll. Va.; faculty Harvard Med. Sch., Boston, 1962-70; asst. clin. prof. neurosurgery Med. Coll. Va., 1970—. Trustee Episcopal Book Store, Richmond, 1974—. Served with M.C., USNR, 1957-59. King Trust Fund fellow, 1963-64. Diplomate Am. Bd. Neurol. Surgery, Nat. Bd. Med. Examiners. Fellow A.C.S.; mem. Am. Assn. Neurol. Surgeons, Congress Neurol. Surgeons, Southern Neurosurg. Soc., English-Speaking Union, Am. Acad. Neurology, Med. Soc. Va., Assn. for Research in Nervous and Mental Diseases, Richmond Acad. Medicine. Episcopalian. Club: Commonwealth. Author: Postoperative Craniotomy Infections, 1966; Septic Complications of Neurosurgical Spinal Procedures, 1970. Contbr. articles to profl. jours. Home: 3505 Old Gun Rd Midlothian VA 23113 Office: 4908 Monument Ave Richmond VA 23230

WRIGHT, RICHARD, state legislator, lawyer, farmer; b. Loris, S.C., Oct. 8, 1944; s. Ottis Richard and Olive (Battle) W.; A.B., U. N.C., 1967, J.D., 1971; m. Jeannette McKinnon, Sept. 24, 1977; 1 dau., Elizabeth Armstrong. Admitted to N.C. bar, 1971; partner firm McGougan & Wright, Tabor City, 1971—; owner Flat Bay Farm, Tabor City, 1973; mem. N.C. Ho. of Reps. from 19th Dist., 1975—; mem. N.C. State Democratic Exec. Commn. Bd. dirs. Columbus County Arts Council; chmn. for Columbus County, John Motley Morehead Found.; bd. dirs. Columbus Cotillion, Strike at the Wind; presdl. elector, 1976. Recipient Founders award Heart Fund, State of N.C. Mem. N.C., 13th Jud. (dir.) bar assns., N.C. Tobacco Producers Assn. (dir.), S.C. Geneal. Soc., Phi Beta Kappa. Methodist. Clubs: Civitan (pres. Tabor City 1974), Flat Bay Racquet. Home: 6 Orange St Tabor City NC 28463 Office: 202 Lewis St Tabor City NC 28463

WRIGHT, ROBERT OLIVER, publishing co. exec.; b. Natick, Mass., Apr. 2, 1903; s. Albert John and Rose (Oliver) W.; M.E., Worcester Poly. Inst., 1926; m. Alma McIntyre, Feb. 19, 1931; 1 son, Robert Oliver. Engring. salesman Sullivan Machinery Co., Claremont, N.H., 1926-46; dir., partner Power Equipment Co., Knoxville, 1946-59; v.p., treas. Indoor Gardener Pub. Co., Knoxville, 1964—, also dir. Recipient Service and Performance award Saintpaulia Internat. and Am. Gesneriad Soc., 1976. Clubs: Knoxville Men's Garden, Cherokee Country. Art dir., illustrator, writer Gesneriad Saintpaulia News, 1964-78. Home: 7914 Gleason Rd The Meadows Apt 1075 Knoxville TN 37919 Office: 1800-1802 Grand Ave Knoxville TN 37901

WRIGHT, SHIRLEY ANN BAIN, ins. co. exec.; b. Luling, Tex., Aug. 11, 1935; d. Eldridge and Bessie Delesdinear (Neill) Bain; student pub. schs., Luling. m. George Bonham Wright, Feb. 6, 1954; children—Julia Elizabeth, Kathryn Sue, Martin Eldridge. Cashier, credit clk. Gen. Motors Acceptance Corp., Austin, Tex., 1960-62; ch. sec. Ballaire Bapt. Ch., San Antonio, 1966-71; bookkeeper Harlandale State Bank, San Antonio, 1972-73; acctg. supt. U.S. Fidelity & Guaranty Co., San Antonio, 1973—. Democrat. Baptist. Home: 946 E Petaluma St San Antonio TX 78221 Office: 300 Tower Life Bldg San Antonio TX 78205

WRIGHT, THELMER EUGENE, mfg. co. exec.; b. Oklahoma City, Mar. 30, 1930; s. Thelmer W. and Mary Inza (Ogle) W.; student Okla. U., 1971, S.W. Oklahoma City Jr. Coll., 1973; m. Katherine Julia West, May 9, 1948; children—Terril Eugene, Cheri Lyn. Photocopy operator Midwest Photo Copy Co., Oklahoma City, 1946-51; foreman Riley Reprodns. Co., Midland, Tex., 1951-58; forman Archer Photo Copy Co., Oklahoma City, 1958-61; mgr. office services Kerr McGee Corp., Oklahoma City, 1961—. Scoutmaster Frontier council Boy Scouts Am., 1959-64; mem. players and mgrs. council Amateur Softball Assn. of Am., 1975-79. Recipient Improved Service award U.S. Post Office, 1973; cert. graphic communication mgr. Mem. In Plant Printing Mgmt. Assn. (internat. v.p. 1976-77). Mem. Disciples of Christ Ch. Home: 2023 Minne Ln Oklahoma City OK 73127 Office: 123 Robert S Kerr Ave Oklahoma City OK

WRIGHT, THOMAS H(ENRY), JR., chem. mfg. exec.; b. Wilmington, N.C., Dec. 19, 1918; s. Thomas Henry and Eleanor (Gilchrist) W.; grad. Woodberry Forest Sch., 1937; A.B. in Chemistry, U. N.C., 1941; m. Margaret Guest Taylor, Aug. 10, 1946 (dec. 1956); children—Margaret T., Thomas H. III; m. 2d, Elizabeth Devereux Labouisse, Oct. 9, 1959; children—Elizabeth, Eleanor G. Chmn. bd. Wright Chem. Corp., Acme Station, Riegelwood, N.C., 1959—; pres. Wright Realty Co., 1952—; pres., dir. Shell Island Corp.; pres. Chandler's Wharf, Wilmington; dir. Wachovia Bank and Trust Co., Wachovia Corp. Pres., St. John's Art Gallery, 1963-66; trustee U. N.C., Wilmington; bd. dirs. Wilmington Parking Commn.; pres., bd. dirs. Hist. Wilmington Found., Inc., 1966—; U.S.S. N.C. Battleship Commn.; pres. Thalian Hall Commn.; trustee Woodberry Forest Sch., 1965-71, Cape Fear Acad., 1968-75, Lenoir Rhyne Coll., 1967-71; pres. Babies Hosp., 1957-66; pres., trustee Wrightsville Marine Research Found., 1962—; bd. dirs. Historic Wilmington Tours, 1976—. Served to lt. comdr. USNR, 1941-45. Recipient DAR medal of honor, 1977, Ruth Coltrane Cannon award, 1978. Episcopalian (sr. warden). Home: 2232 Acacia Dr Wilmington NC 28401 Office: Acme Sta Riegelwood NC 28456

WRIGHT, WALTER THOMAS, JR., hosp. ofcl.; b. Augusta, Ga., July 22, 1947; s. Walter Thomas and Thomasena (Walker) W.; student S.C. State Coll., 1965-67; B.A., Ga. State U., 1975; m. Andrea Jackson, Sept. 3, 1967; children—Walter Travis, Wandrea Tenice. Unit mgr. Med. Coll. Ga., Augusta, 1970-73, Wesley Homes, Inc., Atlanta, 1973-74; dir. materials mgmt. Southwest Community Hosp., Atlanta, 1974-77, dir. central services, 1977—. Bd. dirs. Entertainment Atlanta for All Seasons, 1978-79; cubmaster Cub Scout Pack 331, Boy Scouts Am., 1977—. Served with U.S. Army, 1969-70. Mem. Am. Soc. Purchasing Agts., Met. Atlanta Soc. Purchasing Agts., Southeastern Soc. Purchasing Agts., Met. Atlanta Soc. Central Service Personnel (pres. 1976-78), Am. Soc. Central Service Personnel. Office: Southwest Community Hospital 501 Fairburn Rd SW Atlanta GA 30331

WRIGHT, WILSON WALKER, lawyer, state ofcl.; b. Washington, Jan. 26, 1930; s. Chester Maynard and June (Walker) W.; student U. Fla., 1948-52; LL.B., U. Miami, 1954; certificate Fla. State U., 1960; m. Patricia Anne Davis, May 14, 1955; children—Randahl June, Lee Anne. Admitted to Fla. bar, 1954; asst. state's atty. gen. State of Fla., Tallahassee, 1957—. Past pres. Leon County Cancer Soc. pres. Leon High Sch. PTA, 1973. Past pres. Young Democrats Leon County; state pres. Young Dem. Clubs Fla., 1961-62. Served from 2d lt. to capt., USAF, 1954-57. Named One of Fla.'s 5 Outstanding Young Men, 1961; recipient Good Govt. award Talahassee Jr. C. of C., 1967. Mem. Am., Fla. Govt. bar assns., Fla. Bar, U.S. (past dir.), Fla. (past sec., past editor news), Tallahassee (past pres.) jr. chambers commerce, Fla. Blue Key, Sigma Alpha Epsilon, Phi Alpha Delta, Alpha Kappa Psi. Democrat. Kiwanian (past pres. Tallahassee, lt. gov. Fla.). Elk. Contbr. articles to profl. jours. Home: 2628 Lucerne Dr Tallahassee FL 32303 Office: 217 S Adams St Tallahassee FL 32304

WRIGHTMAN, CAROLINE MCGHEE, nurse, mental health counselor; b. Portland, Oreg., Mar. 14, 1942; d. William Hanen and Lola Jeanette (Oberg) McGhee; B.S. in Nursing, Loma Linda U., 1965; M.Nursing in psychiat. nursing, UCLA, 1975; m. Larry Keith Wrightman, Mar. 24, 1974. Head nurse mental health unit Glendale (Calif.) Adventist Med. Center, 1966-68, Loma Linda (Calif.) U. Med. Center, 1968-69; asst. supr. Glendale Adventist Med. Center, 1969-70; instr. nursing Pacific Union Coll., Glendale, 1970-72, Los Angeles County Hosp. Sch. Nursing, 1972-74; mental health counselor Los Angeles County-San Gabriel Valley Mental Health Center, 1976-80; dir. psychiatry Fla. Hosp., Orlando, 1980—. Mem. Loma Linda U. Sch. Nursing Alumni Assn., UCLA Sch. Nursing Alumni Assn. Mem. Ch. of Adventist Fellowship. Home: 4295 N Goldenrod Rd Orlando FL 32807 Office: 601 E Rollins St Orlando FL 32803

WRIGLEY, JOHN EVELETH, historian; b. Phila., Sept. 7, 1919; s. Edmund John and Mary Elizabeth (Suder) W.; B.A., St. Charles Sem., 1942, M.A., 1952; Ph.D., U. Pa., 1965; m. Ruth Leymeister Ditchey, June 12, 1970. Lectr., Villanova U., 1952-54; lectr. LaSalle Coll., Phila., 1954-65, asst. prof., 1965-70; asso. prof. grad. div. St. Charles Sem., Phila., 1967-68; mem. faculty U. N.C., Charlotte, 1970—, prof. history, 1974—, chmn. dept. history, 1975—. Fulbright fellow, 1967; Am. Philos. Soc. grantee, 1966, 75. Mem. Am. Hist. Assn., Am. Cath. Hist. Assn., Phi Alpha Theta. Roman Catholic. Contbr. articles in field to profl. jours. Home: 3732 Pomfret Ln Charlotte NC 28211 Office: Dept History U NC Charlotte NC 28223

WROTEN, PEGGY ANN, educator; b. Corinth, Miss., May 23, 1945; d. Charles Harmon and Minnie V. Rainey; B.S., Blue Mountain Coll., 1967; M.Ed., Miss. State U., 1971; postgrad. U. Miss., 1972-79; m. John Richard Wroten, Dec. 20, 1975; 1 dau., Elizabeth Rainey. Tchr., Head Start, Corinth, 1967, elem. tchr., 1967-73; sixth grade tchr. Elliston Acad., Memphis, 1973-74; prof. psychology N.E. Miss. Jr. Coll., Booneville, 1974—. Active Alcorn County March of Dimes Mothers March, Prentess County Community Fund, Prentiss County Heart Fund. Named one of four top tchrs. Alcorn Tchrs. Assn., 1968-69. Mem. Miss. Educators Assn., Nat. Reading Tchrs., Miss. Reading Tchrs., Miss. Jr. Coll. Reading Tchrs. (treas.), Kappa Kappa Iota (v.p.). Mem. Church of Christ. Club: Booneville Bus. and Profl. Home: 103 Comer St Booneville MS 38829 Office: NE Miss Jr College Booneville MS 38829

WROTENBERY, CARL R., librarian; b. Mt. Pleasant, Tex., Dec. 14, 1929; s. Preston H. and Gertrude (Cates) W.; B.A., Baylor U., 1951; M.Div., Southwestern Baptist Theol. Sem., 1954, Th.D., 1964; M.L.S., U. Tex., Austin, 1969; m. Julia Winn, July 27, 1952; children—Alan, Martha. Ordained to ministry So. Bapt. Conv., 1954; minister chs., Tex., Kans., 1954-61; prof. religion U. Corpus Christi, 1962-68, dir. library, 1962-68, acad. dean, 1969-73, univ. librarian, 1972-80; dir. libraries Houston Bapt. U., 1980—; cons. in field. Mem. Tex. Library Assn., Coastal Bend Library Assn. (chmn.), Home: 12226 Creekhurst Houston TX 77099 Office: 7502 Fondren Rd Houston TX 77074

WU, JOSEPH TAU CHANG, structural engr.; b. Tainan, Taiwan, June 8, 1938; s. Joseph N.H. and Margaret S.S. (Chen) W.; came to U.S., 1964, naturalized, 1970; B.S. in Civil Engring., Chung Yuan Christian Coll. Sci. and Engring., 1962: M.S. in Civil Engring., Va. Poly. Inst. and State U., 1966; m. Cecilia Lee, Sept. 10, 1964; children—David, Daniel, Karen Ann. Constrn. engr., airport constrn., 1962-64; bridge design engr. B., Va. Dept. Hwys., 1965-69; project engr. Rummel Klepper & Kahl, cons. engrs., Mechanicsburg, Pa., 1969-73; head structural dept. Blauvelt Engring. Co., Richmond, Va., 1973-75; sr. structural engr. St. Clair, Callawaye & Frye, engrs., Richmond, 1975-77; structural engr., bridge div., region 15 Fed. Hwy. Adminstrn., Arlington, Va., 1977—. Elder, Christ Presbyterian Ch., Camp Hill, Pa., 1972-73, Three Chopt Presbyn. Ch., Richmond, Va., 1975-77, Kirkwood Presbyn. Ch., Springfield, Va., 1980—. Registered profl. engr., Va., Pa. Fellow ASCE; mem. Nat., Va. socs. profl. engrs. Club: Hunter Valley Community. Home: 7126 Galgate Dr Springfield VA 22152 Office: 1000 N Glebe Rd Arlington VA 22201

WU, KATHLEEN GIBBS JOHNSON, philosopher, educator; b. Jacksonville, Fla., June 17, 1940; d. Norman Dudley and Kathleen Maria (Gibbs) Johnson; A.B. with honors in Philosophy, Bryn Mawr Coll., 1963; M.A., Yale, 1967, Ph.D., 1970; m. Hsiu Kwang Wu, Aug. 17, 1968. Teaching fellow Yale, 1967-68; mem. faculty U. Ala., 1972—, asso. prof. philosophy, 1975—. Woodrow Wilson fellow, 1963-64. Mem. Am. Philos. Assn., Assn. Symbolic Logic. Author articles, chpt. in book. Home: 27 Arcadia Dr Tuscaloosa AL 35404 Office: Dept Philosophy PO Box 6289 Univ Ala University AL 35486

WU, YEEN-KUEN, educator; b. Peking, China, Feb. 19, 1933; came to U.S., 1957, naturalized, 1971; s. Tun-li and Shu-yung (Yang) W.; B.A., Nat. Taiwan U., 1955; M.A., Atlanta U., 1964; m. Teh-Fanh Chen, Sept. 1, 1967; children—George Chi-tai, Michael Chi-kong. Fin. officer Chu-Nan Oil Co., Taiwan, 1956-57; mem. faculty U. Ark., Pine Bluff, 1964—, asso. prof. acctg., bus., econs. and stats., 1968—, acting chmn. dept. bus. and econs., 1965-68; cons. to industry. Fellow NSF, 1975, So. Found., 1967-68, Gen. Electric Co., 1976; named Most Dedicated Prof. in acctg. U. Ark., Pine Bluff, 1973; grantee NSF, 1977. Mem. Am. Econ. Assn., Am. Acctg. Assn., Am. Advanced Mgmt. Soc., Ark. Coll. Tchrs. Econ. and Bus. Assn., Mo. Valley Econ. Assn., So. Econ. Assn., Chinese Assn. Ark. (adv.), Chinese Assn. Central Ark. (v.p. 1977-78), Internat. Club-UAPB (treas. 1976—). Author papers, reports in field. Home: 2 Cromwell Cove Pine Bluff AR 71603 Office: Dept Bus and Econs Univ Ark Pine Bluff AR 71601

WUESTE, MATTHEW EDWARD, govt. ofcl.; b. San Antonio, Sept. 23, 1937; s. Gus Daniel and Ann Marie (Fox) W.; B.S. in Indsl. Engring., St. Mary's U., 1961; m. Marcella Frances Wick, Oct. 28, 1961; children—Matthew, Kathleen, John, Thomas. Indsl. engr. Ed Friedrich Refrigeration, San Antonio, 1962-64; indsl. engr. San Antonio Air Logistic Center, Kelly AFB, Tex., 1964-71, systems specialist, 1971-77, job enrichment specialist, 1977—. Mem. Soc. Mfg. Engrs. (v.p. 1962-70), Air Force Assn. Roman Catholic. Clubs: K.C. (Grand Knight 1961), Alhambra. Home: 10811 Cedar Elm San Antonio TX 78230

WUKASCH, DORIS LUCILLE STORK, educator, counselor; b. Somerville, Tex., Dec. 30, 1924; d. Edwin William and Clara Rofine (Fuchs) Stork; B.A. with high honors, U. Tex., 1944, M.Ed., 1969; m. Joe Eugene Wukasch, July 7, 1945 (div. 1971); children—Linda, Susan, Jean (Mrs. Richard P. Mihalik), Jonathan. Chemist Tex. Dept. Health, Austin, 1944-45; microbiologist Terrell Labs., Ft. Worth, 1946-47; exec. sec. Wukasch Architects and Engrs., Austin, 1954-66; editorial asst. Steck-Vaughn Pubs., Austin, 1966; rehab. caseworker, job counselor Mary Lee Sch., Austin, 1969-70; spl. tchr. career edn. Austin Ind. Sch. Dist., 1970—. Instr. A.R.C., 1972—; vol. tchr. Austin State Sch., 1958-68. Area chmn. Am. Cancer Soc., 1970; mem. Women's Archtl. Guild, 1954-71, pres., 1964; mem. Tex. Fine Arts Assn., 1960—, Smithsonian Assos., 1972—, Wycliffe Assos., 1973—. HEW grantee, 1968-69. Certified rehab. counselor. Mem. Austin Mental Health Assn., Nat. Rehab. Counselors Assn., Nat., Tex. State tchrs. assn., Am. Judicature Soc., Nat. Trust Historic Preservation, Christian Bus. and Profl. Women's Council, Nat. Orgn. Women, Assn. Supervision and Curriculum Devel., Phi Beta Kappa. Lutheran. Contbr. poems and articles to mags. and newspapers. Home: 2500 Inwood Place Austin TX 78703 Office: 6100 Guadalupe Austin TX 78752

WURSTER, MARGUERITE RAY SMITH, ret. librarian; b. Ocala, Fla., Sept. 7, 1916; d. William Edward and Inez (Ray) Smith; B.A., U. Fla. 1963; M.A., U. South Fla., 1972; m. Hal Crockett Batey, Jr., Feb. 20, 1933 (div. June 1948); children—Hal Smith, Marilyn (Mrs. James Lynn Holeman), Diana Ed (Mrs. David Miller Pettengill); m. 2d, Robert Frederick Wurster, June 6, 1965. Library asst., library U. Fla., 1952-58; librarian, div. plant industry Fla. Dept. Agr., Gainesville. 1958-63; asst. to dir. library Fla. Inst. for Continuing U. Studies, Gainesville, 1963-65; asst. dir. Extension Library, U. South Fla., Bay Campus, St. Petersburg, 1965-71; asst. dir. State Univ. System of Fla., Extension Library, 1971-79. Mem. Spl. Librarian Assn. (pres. Fla. chpt. 1970-71), Fla. Southeastern library assns., D.A.R., Y.W.C.A., Kappa Delta Pi, Delta Kappa Gamma (legis. coordinator). Methodist. Club: University South Florida Women's. Home: 6514 27th Ave N St Petersburg FL 33710

WURZ, JOHN ARNOLD, architect; b. Clarksdale, Miss., Feb. 11, 1936; s. Arnold George and Mildred (Whittle) W.; B.S., Ga. Inst. Tech., 1958, B.Arch., 1959; m. Sally Cooper Fortson, Mar. 20, 1958 (div. July 14, 1973); children—Valli Elizabeth, Susan Priscilla, John Arnold; m. 2d, Janice Beauchamp, Dec. 22, 1973. Project mgr. Rich's, Inc., Atlanta, 1962-65; project mgr. Heery & Heery Architects & Engrs., Atlanta, 1963-65, asso. architect, 1965-67, partner, 1967-77; v.p. Cadre Corp., 1977—. Served to capt. USAF, 1959-62, Res., 1962-72. Registered architect, 20 states. Mem. Atlanta Art Assn. (bd. dirs.), Bldg. Research Adv. Bd., Nat. Acad. Sci., Ga. Indsl. Devel. Assn., Ga. Tech. Alumni Assn., AIA, Sigma Nu Alumni Assn. Club: Cherokee Town and Country. Home: 401 Arbor Trail Marietta GA 30067 Office: PO Box 47837 Atlanta GA 30362

WYANT, WILLIAM DEXTER, educator; b. Weston, W.Va., Sept. 1, 1936; s. John Frederick and Evelyn Isabelle (Mount) W.; B.S., Morris Harvey Coll., 1966, postgrad., 1966-67; M.S.E. (NASA fellow), W.Va. U., 1969, M.P.A. (NASA fellow), 1972; m. Norma Ruth Arnold, Feb. 4, 1961; children—Sara Lynn, William Christopher. Engring. technician W.Va. Dept. Hwys., Weston and Charleston, 1954-67; research engr., instr. dept. civil engring. W.Va. U., 1970-72, engring. scientist dept. indsl. engring., 1975-76, research asso. regional med. program, 1972-75, research asso., asst. prof. community medicine, 1976—; cons. in grant and public adminstrn., planning and evaluation to govtl. and pvt. non-profit health orgns. Served with U.S. Army, 1959-61. Mem. Am. Soc. Public Adminstrn. (pres. W.Va. chpt. 1979), Res. Officers Assn. U.S. (life), Sigma Xi, Chi Epsilon, Pi Sigma Alpha. Author research reports on emergency med. services, hosp. and long-term care systems characteristics and use. Home: 505 Overhill St Morgantown WV 26505 Office: 258 Stewart St Morgantown WV 26505

WYATT, JOSEPH P., JR., congressman; b. Victoria, Tex., Oct. 12, 1941; ed. Victoria Coll.; B.A., U. Tex., 1968; postgrad. U. Houston Law Sch. Former mem. staff Tex. Senator William N. Patman, U.S. Rep. Clark W. Thompson, Vice Pres. Lyndon B. Johnson; former auditor Tex. Alcoholic Beverage Commn., Austin; former dir. community affairs Safety Steel, Inc., Voctoria, Tex.; mem. Tex. Ho. of Reps., 1971-79; mem. 96th Congress from 14th Congressional Dist. Tex.; former mem. So. Legis. Conf., Nat. Conf. State Legislatures. Served with USMCR, 1966-70. Named Outstanding Young Man of Yr., Victoria Jaycees, 1976. Mem. Victoria C. of C., Port Lavaca C. of C., Tex. Farm Bur., McNamara-O'Conner Hist. and Fine Arts Mus., Ducks Unltd., Pi Kappa Alpha. Democrat. Roman Catholic. Club: Mid-Coastal Sportsmen's. Office: Room 1730 Longworth House Office Bldg Washington DC 20515*

WYATT, WILSON WATKINS, JR., tobacco co. ofcl.; b. Louisville, Dec. 3, 1943; s. Wilson Watkins and Anne Kinnaird (Duncan) W.; student U. of South, 1965; m. Jane Clay, Aug. 25, 1964 (dec.); children—Carol Alexander, Wilson Watkins III, Sarah Duncan. Reporter, Louisville Courier-Jour., 1964-66; pub. relations account exec. Doe-Anderson Advt., Louisville, 1966-68; account exec. Zimmer-McClaskey-Lewis Advt., Louisville, 1968-70; partner Bennett & Wyatt Pub. Relations, Louisville, 1970-71; rep., vice chmn. appropriations and revenue com. Ky. Legislature, 1970-72; exec. dir. Louisville Central Area, Inc., 1971-77; asst. for corporate affairs Brown & Williamson Tobacco Corp., Louisville, 1977—; urban devel. cons., 1972-77. Mem. Atlantic Inst. Young Leaders' Conf., 1967-68; del. N. Atlantic Treaty Assn., 1967; chmn. Leadership Effort for All Democrats, Louisville, 1967-68; Economic Devel. Commn. Jefferson County (Ky.), 1976—; vice chmn. Louisville Meml. Commn., 1976—; exec. com. Louisville Central Area, Inc., 1977—; mem. So. Growth Policies Bd. of Regional Programs Council, 1977—. Named Louisville outstanding young man of year, 1972, marketing man of year, 1973; Ky. Outstanding Young Man of Yr., 1973. Mem. Pub. Relations Soc. Am. Presbyterian. Clubs: Louisville Country, Pendennis, Jefferson. Home: 2425 Cherokee Pkwy Louisville KY 40206 Office: 1600 W Hill St Louisville KY 40232

WYATT, WILSON WATKINS, SR., lawyer; b. Louisville, Nov. 21, 1905; s. Richard H. and Mary (Watkins) W.; J.D., U. Louisville, 1927, LL.D. (hon.), 1948; LL.D. (hon.), Knox Coll., 1945, Centre Coll. of Ky., 1979; m. Anne Kinnaird Duncan, June 14, 1930; children—Mary Anne, Nancy Kinnaird, Wilson Watkins. Admitted to Ky. bar, 1927; trial atty. City of Louisville, 1934; partner law firm Peter, Heyburn, Marshall & Wyatt, 1935-41; mayor Louisville, 1941-45; housing expediter, adminstr. Nat. Housing Agy., 1946; sr. partner law firm Wyatt, Grafton & Sloss, 1947—; lt. gov. Ky., 1959-63; presdl. emissary from Pres. U.S. to Pres. Indonesia for oil negotiations, Tokyo, 1963; mem. law faculty Jefferson Sch. Law, 1929-35; dir. Courier Jour. and Louisville Times Co., WHAS, Inc., Standard Gravure Co., Forest Farmers Assn. Spl. rep. Bd. Econ. Warfare, N. Africa, 1943; chmn. Louisville Met. Area Def. Council (twice awarded Citation of Merit), 1942-45; pres. Am. Soc. Planning Ofcls., 1943-44, Ky. Municipal League, 1944, Am. Municipal Assn., 1945, Louisville Area Devel. Assn., 1944-45; adv. bd. U.S. Conf. Mayors, 1942-45; v.p. Nat. Municipal League, 1945-72, pres., 1973-75, chmn. nat. conf. on govt., 1975-80, chmn. council, 1978—; chmn. Ky. Econ. Devel. Commn., 1960-63, mem. exec. com., 1975; mem. Commn. on Future of South, 1974. Commn. on Operation of U.S. Senate, 1975-76; chmn. U.S. Circuit Judge Nominating Com., 6th Circuit Panel, 1977—. Trustee U. Louisville, 1950-58, chmn. 1951-55; chmn. bd. Regional Cancer Center Corp., 1977—; chmn. Leadership Louisville Found., 1978—; Ky. chmn. Treasury adv. com. U.S. Savs. Bonds Program, 1948-55; trustee Bellarmine Coll., 1974—, vice chmn., 1977-79, chmn., 1979—; bd. dirs. Ky. Center for Arts Endowment Fund, 1980; 1st pres. Young Democrats Club, Louisville-Jefferson County; nat. chmn. Jefferson-Jackson Day Dinners, 1948, 49; del.-at-large nat. convs., 1944-68; personal campaign mgr. for Adlai E. Stevenson, 1952, 56; mem. Dem. Nat. Com. Ky., 1960-64. Recipient Kentuckian of Year award WHAS, 1952; Distinguished Service award U.S. Treasury, 1955; Citizen of Year award Louisville Jaycees, 1972; Man of Year award Louisville Advt. Club, 1974; Brotherhood award NCCJ, 1974; Gold Cup for community service Louisville Area C. of C., 1975; Gov.'s Disting. Service medallion Commonwealth of Ky., 1980. Mem. English Speaking Union U.S. (nat. dir.), Ky. (dir. 1974—), Louisville Area (pres. 1972) chambers commerce, World, Am., Fed. Communications, Ky. (sec. 1930-34, commr. 1958), Louisville bar assns., Am. Law Inst. (life). Democrat. Presbyterian. Clubs: Rotary; Pendennis, Wynn-Stay, Louisville Country, Jefferson; Century (N.Y.C.). Home: 1001 Alta Vista Rd Louisville KY 40205 Office: 28th Floor Citizens Plaza Louisville KY 40202

WYCKOFF, JAMES CLARENCE, JR., adminstr./planner; b. Washington, Aug. 14, 1938; s. James Clarence and Lena Lake (Steffey) W.; B.A., E. Tenn. State U., 1961; postgrad. Harvard Grad. Sch. Design, 1977; children—Whitney Von Lake, Courtney Dayna. Exec. dir. Fairfax County (Va.) Planning Commn., 1971—. Chmn. City of Fairfax Bd. Archtl. Review, 1970—; past vice chmn. Fairfax County Redevel. and Housing Authority. Recipient numerous civic and profl. awards. Mem. Va. Citizens Planning Assn. (dir.), Am. Inst. Planners, Internat. City Mgmt. Assn., Methodist. Clubs: Jaycees (past pres. Fairfax, ambassador), Elks. Home: PO Box 1 Fairfax Station VA 22039 Office: Massey Bldg 10th Fl 4100 Chainbridge Rd Fairfax VA 22030

WYERS, GEORGE DANIEL, wholesale distbn. co. ofcl.; b. Mountain Top, Ark., Aug. 29, 1932; s. Theodore Rosevelt and Otha Emaline (Pipkins) W.; B.S. in Physics and Math. with honors, Coll. of Ozarks, 1957; m. Anna Belle Baskin, Sept. 5, 1953; children—Daniel, Diane, Pamela, Mark, Lisa. Tech. staff spl. aerospace projects Hughes Aircraft, Culver City, Calif., 1957-62; engring. specialist Avionics LTV Aerospace Corp., Dallas, 1962-68; contractor, cons., Ft. Smith, Ark., 1968-72; gen./sales mgr. Westernaire Inc., Dallas, 1972—. Original charter commn. Bedford, 1965; chmn. Bedford City Planning and Zoning Commn. Served with USAF, 1950-54. Recipient profl. recognition for service to U.S. Dept. Def., 1959. Designer for environ. control; contbr. exptl. research paper to profl. jour. Home: 124 Stonegate Ct Bedford TX 76021 Office: 3137 Halifax St Dallas TX 75247

WYLAND, BEN F., clergyman; b. Harlan, Iowa, Mar. 16, 1882; s. Frank and Mary (Griffith) W.; Ph.B., U. Iowa, 1905; B.D., Yale, 1908, M.Div., 1971; Litt.D., Edward Waters Coll., 1954; m. Ada D. Beach, Jan. 14, 1909; children—Gordon B., Hugh C., Robert B., Molly G.; m. 2d, Mildred E. Oeschger, May 5, 1955. Ordained to ministry Congl. Ch., 1908; pastor, Worcester, Mass., 1918-26, Lincoln, Neb., 1926-36, Bklyn., 1936-39; radio pastor Sta. KFAB, 1926-36; exchange pastor to Eng., 1933; in charge ch. relations for Herbert Hoover's Campaign, Food for Small Democracies, 1940-41; exec. sec. United Chs. Greater St. Petersburg (Fla.), 1948-56, Fla. Council Racial Cooperation, St. Petersburg, 1956—. Chmn. Com. To Preserve Negro Rights; founder Negro Girls Welfare Home, St. Petersburg, St. Petersburg Helping Hand for Sr. Citizens; chmn. United Negro Coll. Fund. Recipient citation from Maj. Gen. Philip Hayes, 3d Service Command; B'nai B'rith Brotherhood award, St. Petersburg, 1954; recipient Oscar, Community Chest dr., 1955; citation Met. Council, Inc., 1958; Bethune Cookman Coll., Edward Waters Coll. Mem. Am. Relief Assn. (dir.), Am. Com. Christian Refugees in Bklyn. (exec. sec.), Bklyn. Fedn. Chs., (dir.), Crime Prevention Soc. (dir.), N.Y.C. Assn. Chs. (pres. bd. dirs.), Congl. Ministers (pres.), Americanization Com. (chmn.), Food Commn. (chmn.), Delta Sigma Phi, Alpha Chi Rho. Mason (32 deg., K.T.), Kiwanian. Home: Apt 107 1898 Shore Dr S St Petersburg FL 33707

WYLES, HENRY EDMUND, JR., electro-acoustic engr.; b. Newark, Nov. 3, 1948; s. Henry Edmund and Ruth Edna (Baudendistel) W.; B.S.E.E., 1968, M.S. in Physics, 1970, Sc.D. in Physics, 1977. Retail div. mgr. Lafayette Radio Electronics, Syosset, N.Y., 1969-70; asst. mdse. mgr. Campbell Music Co., Washington, 1970-71; exec. v.p. Shrader Sound, Inc., Washington, 1971-72; chmn. bd. 410 Systems, Inc., Washington, 1972—, Hawke Rec. Co., Boston, 1970—; pres., chmn. bd. DHD Engring. Corp., Harrison, N.J., 1968—; audio-visual cons. U.S. Army Audio-Visual Agy., Washington, 1974—; spl. cons. to bd. dirs. Blue Ridge Alliance of Performing Arts, 1976-77, dir., 1978—, adminstrv. v.p., 1978—. Recipient commendations Dept. Army, 1975, U.S. Armed Forces Bicentennial Band, 1975. Mem. Audio Engring. Soc., Soc. Motion Picture and TV Engrs., Soc. Audio Cons.'s, Acoustical Soc. Am., Soc. Photog. Counselors, Am. Theater Assn., Army Theater Arts Assn., IEEE, U.S. Inst. Theater Tech., Soc. Broadcast Engrs., Mensa. Club: N. Jersey Radio League (founder, pres., 1965-69). Author: Theater Sound Design, 1974; Basics of Sound Reinforcement for Theater, 1975; contbr. spl. report to FTC, 1970. Home: 3906 Estel Rd Fairfax VA 22031 Office: PO Box 6033 Arlington VA 22206

WYLIE, WILLIAM TERRANCE, retail exec.; b. Providence, Jan. 20, 1940; s. Ernest A. and Helen M. (Geagan) W.; grad. Pinkerton Acad., 1963; m. Jane L. Allen, Apr. 25, 1959; children—Kevin D., Keith D., Kelley D. Store mgr. McCrory-McLellan Stores, New Eng., 1957-61, W.T. Grant Co., New Eng., 1961-75; dist. mgr., regional mdsc. mgr. Stone Mfg. Co., Greenville, S.C., 1975-78, v.p., gen. mgr. retail div., 1978—. Mem. Nat. Retail Mchts. Assn. Roman Catholic. Office: Stone Mfg Co 1500 Poinsett Highway Greenville SC 29608

WYLLIE, JAMES JOSEPH, JR., lawyer, educator; b. Orange, Tex., Nov. 26, 1948; s. James Joseph and Edna Mae (Allen) W.; B.S., Loyola U., 1971, J.D., 1974; M.P.H., Tulane U., 1976. Admitted to La., Ark. bars; individual practice law, New Orleans, 1975—; asst. prof. grad. program in health systems adminstrn. Tulane U., New Orleans, 1977—. Katz scholar; La. Heart Assn. research grantee. Mem. Am. Bar Assn. and Forum on Health Law, Ark. Bar, La. Bar, Nat. Health Lawyers Assn., Am. Soc. Law and Medicine, Am. Soc. Hosp. Attys., St. Thomas More Law Soc., Blue Key. Contbr. articles to profl. publs. Office: 1430 Tulane Ave New Orleans LA 70112

WYLLIE, SAMUEL DUFFIN, mfg. co. exec.; b. Phila., Sept. 23, 1930; s. James and Margaret (Duffin) W.; B.S., Pa. State U., 1956; postgrad. U. Richmond, 1973, Harvard U., 1977; m. Larita Ann King, Sept. 11, 1954; children—Donna Lynn Wyllie Bailey, Kevin Main, Dennis Ray, Virginia Ann. With Scott Paper Co., Columbus, Ohio, 1956-58; with Reynolds Metals Co., 1958—, v.p., gen. mgr. consumer div., Richmond, Va., 1978—. Served with U.S. Army, 1948-52. Mem. Nat. Assn. Convenience Stores, Grocery Mfrs. Am., Gen. Mdse. Distbrs. Council. Club: Masons. Home: 200 El Dorado Dr Richmond VA 23229 Office: Reynolds Metals Co Consumer Div 6603 W Broad St Richmond VA 23261

WYRICK, ROBERT KECK, social worker; b. Sharps Chapel, Tenn., Aug. 17, 1936; s. William Latham and Lori Esther (Keck) W.; B.S., Lincoln Meml. U., 1960; M.S. in Social Work, U. Tenn., Knoxville, 1964; m. Sally Ann Pope, Dec. 31, 1961; children—Robert Jeffrey, Thomas Aaron. Child welfare worker Dept. Human Services of Tenn., 1978; dir. community services Regional Mental Health Center, Oak Ridge, 1978—; mem. faculty U. Tenn.; cons. Brushy Mountain Prison. Bd. dirs. Community Services for Exceptional Citizens, Oak Ridge, Morgan County Med. Center, Wartburg, Tenn. Mem. Nat. Assn. Social Workers. Democrat. Baptist. Club: Masons. Home: Route 3 Box 66 Clinton TN 37716 Office: 240 W Tyrone Rd Oak Ridge TN 38230

YABLONSKY, ALAN DONALD, cons. co. exec.; b. Providence, Apr. 22, 1938; s. Louis Harry and Lillian Ruth (Kotlen) Y.; B.A., U. Fla., 1960; M.B.A., Fla. Atlantic U., 1973; m. Robin Aleen Dubbin, June 5, 1966; children—Marla Rose, Michael Jacob. Personnel supr. Boeing Co., Cocoa Beach, Fla., 1966-68; personnel supr. Systems Engring. Labs., Ft. Lauderdale, Fla., 1968-69; personnel mgr. Airpax Electronics, Ft. Lauderdale, 1969-71; personnel and tng. mgr. Atlantic Fed. Savs. & Loan, Ft. Lauderdale, 1972-74; v.p. personnel Hollywood Fed. Savs. & Loan Assn. (Fla.), 1974-79; pres. Shea/Yablonsky Assos., Inc., Ft. Lauderdale, 1979—; instr. principles of mgmt. Broward Community Coll., Nova U.; instr. principles of supervision and human behavior Inst. of Financial Edn. Mem. advisory com. for savs. and loan Broward Community Coll., 1975-77; mem. personnel advisory com. City of Plantation (Fla.), 1977-79. Served in USNR, 1962-65. Mem. Am. Soc. for Personnel Adminstrn. (accredited exec. in personnel), Inst. of Financial Edn. (past dir. Suncoast chpt.), Fla. Savs. and Loan League, (chmn. personnel com. 1978), S. Fla. Savs. and Loan Personnel Assn. (charter mem., past pres.), U.S. League of Savs. Assns., Personnel Assn. Broward County (pres. 1979). Home: 7500 SW 15th St Plantation FL 33317 Office: 3045 N Federal Hwy Fort Lauderdale FL 33306

YADAO, ALEX PERALTA, physician and surgeon; b. Naguilian, La Union, Philippines, Jan. 20, 1938; s. Leo Santos and Felisa Boquirin (Peralta) Y.; came to U.S., 1964, naturalized, 1975; M.D., U. Santo Tomas, Manila, 1963; m. Nilda Zorrilla Alcasabas, Oct. 21, 1967; children—Albert, Glynn, Melissa, Cherie. Rotating intern Vet.'s Meml. Hosp., Philippines, 1962-63; surg. intern Sinai Hosp., Balt., 1964, resident, 1965; surg. resident Washington Hosp. Center, 1965-68, chief resident, 1968-69; surg. house officer Fairfax (Va.) Hosp., 1969-73; pvt. practice gen. and vascular surgery, pres., dir. Potomac-Triangle Med. Assos., Ltd., Triangle, Va., 1973—; mem. staff Potomac, Commonwealth Doctors', Jefferson, Prince William County, Alexandria hosps.; corp. mem. Potomac Hosp. and Alexandria Hosp. Corp. Mem. Nat. Capitol Area council Boy Scouts Am., also dist. advancement chmn. Served with Philippine Army, 1959-60. Recipient Physician Recognition award AMA, 1969, 72, 75. Fellow Internat. Coll. Surgeons, Am. Coll. Internat. Surgeons, Am. Soc. Abdominal Surgeons (life); mem. Am. Trauma Soc. (founding), Assn. Philippine Practicing Physicians in Am. (life), Philippine Heritage Fedn. (pres. 1980—), Am. Soc. Bariatric Physicians, Fairfax, Prince William County, Alexandria med. socs., Va. Assn. Philippine Physicians (pres. 1977-79), Soc. Philippine Surgeons in Am. (life), Va. State Med. Arbitration Bd. (panel mem.), Congress Filipino-Am. Citizens (state dir.), No. Va. Found. Med. Care, Am. Coll. Internat. Physicians. Roman Catholic. Clubs: K.C., Optimist (dir.). Home: 9323 Old Mt Vernon Rd Alexandria VA 22308 Office: 18700 Old Triangle Rd Triangle VA 22172 also 6345 S Kings Hwy Alexandria VA 22306

YAGER, KENNETH JAMES, TV sta. exec.; b. Detroit, May 12, 1935; s. Kenneth Richard and Clarissa Evangeline (Poppen) Y.; grad. Colgate U., 1957; postgrad. Wayne State U., 1957-58; m. Patricia Talbert, Dec. 29, 1961; children—Kenneth R., Hilary Power. Sales promotion and mdse. mgr. Sta WIS-TV, Columbia, S.C., 1960-61, gen. mgr., 1968; mem. spl. group Broadcasting Co. of the South, 1961-62; dir. planning and devel. Cosmos Broadcasting Co., Columbia, 1962-65, v.p., 1965-70, sr. v.p., from 1970; gen. mgr. Cosmos Cablevision Corp., Columbia; sr. v.p., gen. mgr. Sta. WDSU-TV, New Orleans, 1974—; guest prof. U. S.C., 1972-74. Promotion chmn. United Way, 1977; bd. dirs. Urban League, New Orleans, 1975—, Better Bus. Bur., New Orleans. Served with U.S. Army, 1958-60. Mem. New Orleans C. of C., La. Assn. Broadcasters (dir. 1977), Sigma Chi. Episcopalian. Clubs: Internat. House, New Orleans Country, Plimsoll. Office: 520 Royal St New Orleans LA 70130

YANCEY, BRUCE JON, draftsman; b. Paterson, N.J., Apr. 28, 1949; s. Jon Keith and Juliette Matillda (Dhondt) Y.; B.S. in Trade and Indsl. Edn., Okla. State U., 1972; m. Marsha Elaine Copley, Dec. 28, 1975. Mech. design draftsman Howard Samis Porch, Oklahoma City, 1972-75; drafting and design instr. O.T. Autry Area Vocat. Tech. Center, Enid, Okla., 1975—; tchr. solar energy courses Okla. State U., summer 1977; designer custom houses; owner Achievement Dynamics Co., motivational and self-improvement tng., human resource devel. Mem. NEA, Okla. Edn. Assn., Am. Soc. Heating, Refrigerating and Air-Conditioning Engrs., U.S. Jaycees, Am. Vocat. Assn., Red Red Rose, Iota Lambda Sigma, Phi Kappa Theta. Roman Catholic. Club: K.C. Home: PO Box 132 Hunter OK 74640 Office: 1201 W Willow St Enid OK 73701

YANCEY, ROBERT EARL, oil refinery exec.; b. Cleve., July 15, 1921; s. George Washington II and Mary (Gutzwiller) Y.; B.E., Marshall U., 1943; m. Mary Estelline Tackett, July 25, 1941; children—Robert Earl, Susan Carol. With Ashland Oil, Inc. (Ky.), 1943—, successively process engr., project engr., operating supt., coordinator sales and refining, gen. supt. refineries, 1943-56, v.p. in charge mfg., 1956-59, adminstrv. v.p., 1959-65, sr. v.p., 1965-72, pres., 1972—, chief operating officer, 1969—; pres. Ashland Chem. Co., 1967-69, Ashland Petroleum Co., 1969—. Mem. Nat. Petroleum Refiners Assn. (pres. 1969-70), Nat. Petroleum Assn. (mfg. com.), Am. Petroleum Inst., Ky. Soc. Profl. Engr. Protestant. Home: 102 Lycan Dr Bellefonte Ashland KY 41101 Office: Box 391 Ashland KY 41101

YANCEY, WILLIAM EUGENE, family physician; b. Springfield, Ky., June 19, 1927; s. William Sale and Martha Frances (Moore) Y.; B.S., U. Louisville, 1949, M.D., 1952; m. Justine Marie Stinner, July 12, 1951 (div. 1978); children—Patrice, Katherine, Martha, Bill, Jon. Intern, St. Joseph Infirmary, Louisville, 1952-53; group practice medicine specializing in family medicine, William E. Yancey Louisville, 1953—, sr. asso.; asst. clin. prof. dept. family practice U. Ky. Sch. Medicine. Dir. Jefferson Fed. Savs. and Loan Assn., Louisville. Trustee Union Coll., Barbourville, Ky.; adv. bd. Jeffersontown Vocat. Sch., Ky.; adminstrv. bd. St. Paul's Methodist Ch., Louisville. Served with C.E., U.S. Army, 1945-47. Diplomate Am. Bd. Family Practice. Mem. AMA, Am. Acad. Family Physicians, Ky., Jefferson County med. socs. Democrat. Methodist. Office: 4825 S 3d St Louisville KY 40214

YANCY, WILLIAM SAMUEL, pediatrician; b. Pittsboro, Miss., Aug. 17, 1939; s. Lester Truman and Maxyne (Lindsey) Y.; B.A., Duke U., 1961, M.D., 1965; m. Susan Elizabeth Guest, June 19, 1965; children—Amy Lynn, William Samuel, James Michael. Pediatric intern Duke U. Med. Center, Durham, 1965-66, pediatric resident, 1967-68; pediatric resident and fellow in adolescent medicine and behavioral pediatrics U. Rochester (N.Y.) Med. Center, 1966-67, 70-71; practice medicine specializing in pediatrics Durham (N.C.) Child Care Center, 1971—; pediatric staff Watts Hosp., Durham, 1971-75, Duke U. Med. Center, 1971—; pediatric staff Durham County Gen. Hosp., 1975—, asst. chmn. dept. pediatrics, 1977—; asst. clin. prof. depts. pediatrics Duke Med. Center, 1971—, asst. clin. prof. dept. psychiatry, 1977—, dir. youth clinic, 1971—, dir. W.T. Grant Tng. Program in Behavioral Pediatrics, 1978—. Bd. dirs. Child Advocacy Commn. of Durham, 1973-76, 79—, pres. 1973; bd. dirs. Durham Community Guidance Clinic, 1974-76, v.p., 1976; bd. dirs. Family Counseling Service of Durham, 1976-77, Durham Health Care, 1976—. Served to lt. comdr. M.C., USNR, 1968-70. Diplomate Nat. Bd. Med. Examiners, Am. Bd. Pediatrics. Fellow Am. Acad. Pediatrics; me. Soc. for Adolescent Medicine (exec. sec. 1978—), N.C. Pediatric Soc., Am. Med. Assn., N.C. Med. Soc., Durham-Orange County Med. Soc. Contbr. articles in field to profl. jours. Home: 59 Kimberly Dr Durham NC 27707 Office: 306 S Gregson St Durham NC 27701

YANKO, JOHN BERNARD, actuary; b. Aurora, Ill., Jan. 1, 1935; s. John Joseph and Sophie Delores (Kroptovich) Y.; B.A., Wabash Coll., 1957; M.S., Northeastern U., 1964; M.B.A., So. Meth. U., 1979; m. Jeananne Yanko, Aug. 26, 1956; children—Alan, Karen. Group actuary Am. United Life, Indpls., 1962-71; v.p., actuary Nat. Investors Life, Little Rock, 1971-75; sr. v.p., chief actuary Fidelity Union Life Ins. Co., Dallas, 1975—. Fellow Soc. Actuaries; mem. Internat. Actuarial Assn., Am. Acad. Actuaries, Actuaries Club of the SW (enrolled actuary), Actuaries Club of the SE. Home: 5826 St Marks Circle Dallas TX 75230 Office: PO Box 500 Dallas TX 75221

YARBOROUGH, GORDON WILSON, mfg. co. exec.; b. Lexington, N.C., Dec. 27, 1940; s. Walter G. and Hattie (Latista) Y.; A.A., Wingate Coll., 1962; B.S. in Psychology and Phys. Edn., High Point Coll., 1974; m. Martha Huggin, July 1, 1967; children—Preston, Scott. Salesman, Ragan Hardware Co., High Point, N.C., 1964-66; founder Yarborough & Co., High Point, N.C., 1968, pres., 1968—. Bd. dirs. Central YMCA, 1973—, chmn. youth com., 1974-75; bd. dirs. ARC, 1975—; bd. dirs. Am. Cancer Soc., 1975—, pres., 1978-79; bd. dirs. N.C. Cancer Bd.; mem. adv. bd. Salvation Army, 1979. Named Alumnus of the Year, High Point Coll., 1979. Mem. High Point C. of C., Am. Bus. Club (dir. 1973, chmn. 1973). Democrat. Methodist. Home: 1717 W Lexington Ave High Point NC 27260 Office: 1111 Redding Dr High Point NC 27261

YARBROUGH, CHARLES ROBERT, automobile dealership exec.; b. Shreveport, La., Sept. 14, 1940; s. Robert Franklin and Charlene Y.; B.S. in Bus., Centenary Coll., Shreveport, 1962; m. Pamela Dell, June 22, 1963; children—Charles Robert, Bradford Odell. Salesman, Prescott Motor Co., Prescott, Ark., 1967-69, parts mgr., 1969-70, sales mgr., 1970-73, gen. mgr., 1973—, v.p., 1970—. Served with USAF, 1962-67. Mem. Nevada County State Parks Assn. (pres.). Methodist. Clubs: Prescott Kiwanis (pres. 1975-76, dir. 1970-73), Shreveport Country. Office: PO Box 639 Prescott AR 71857

YARBROUGH, SELENE MESSICK, nurse; b. Coffee County, Tenn., Aug. 27, 1941; d. Horace Newton and Annie Jane (Bush) Messick; diploma St. Thomas Hosp. Sch. Nursing, 1962; B.S.N., U. Tenn., 1966; M.N. (Fed. Nurse trainee), Emory U., 1967; m. James M. Yarbrough, Oct. 17, 1970; 1 dau., Hallie Andrea. Staff nurse St. Thomas Hosp., Nashville, 1962-64, Hotel Dieu Hosp., New Orleans, 1964, Henrietta Egleston Hosp., Atlanta, 1967-68, Ga. Mental Health Inst., Atlanta, 1968; clin. nurse specialist Ga. Dept. Public Health, Atlanta, 1969; asst. dir. nursing Ga. Retardation Center, Atlanta, 1969-75, coordinator nursing services, 1975—. Project dir. Spalding Neighbors Garden Club; bd. dirs Occupational Edn. Center, Dekalb County, Ga. Mem. Am. Nurses Assn., Nat. League for Nursing, Ga. League for Nursing (sec.), Am. Assn. Mental Deficiency. Home: 355 Spalding Lake Ct Atlanta GA 30340 Office: Ga Retardation Center 4770 N Peachtree Rd Atlanta GA 30338

YARBROUGH, TERRY LEROY, data processing exec.; b. Meridian, Miss., Jan. 18, 1947; s. Leroy and Willie Ruth (Moore) Y.; postgrad. Meridian Jr. Coll., 1976; m. Winifred Frances Long, Dec. 21, 1966; children—William, Lamar, Michael Kevin. Stock clk. Pepsi Cola Co., 1965, route salesman, 1965-66; computer operator So. Pipe & Supply Co., Meridian, 1969-71, sr. operator, 1971-74, sr. operator-programmer, 1974-75; mgr. Rush Found. Hosp./Rush Med. Group, Meridian, 1975-76, dir. data processing, 1976—. Served with U.S. Army, 1966-69. Mem. Data Processing Mgmt. Assn., Meridian Jaycees. Baptist. Clubs: Miss. Bowhunters Assn., Miss. Wildlife Assn., Queen City Bowhunters Assn. Home: 6304 Oakland Park St Meridian MS 39301 Office: 1314 19th Ave Meridian MS 39301

YASSINI-FARD, HOSSEIN, physician; b. Teheran, Iran, Apr. 4, 1935; came to U.S., 1967, naturalized, 1972; s. Mahmood and Soghra (Lajevardi) Yassini-F.; M.D., Med. Sch., U. Teheran (Iran), 1961; m. Matar Parviz, Mar. 15, 1963; children—Patrick, Roya. Intern, St. Paul Hosp., Saskatoon, Sask., Can., 1964; resident, Ottawa (Ont., Can.) Civic Hosp., 1965; practice medicine, specializing in family practice, Wheeling, W.Va., 1977—; staff Ohio Valley Gen. Hosp., Wheeling, 1977—; preceptor in teaching family practice residents Wheeling Hosp.; coll. physician West Liberty (W.Va.) State Coll., 1969—. Recipient Physician Recognition award AMA, 1969, 72, 75, 78. Mem. AMA, Am. Acad. Family Practice, W.Va. Med. Assn., So. Med. Assn., Ohio County Med. Soc., Islamic Med. Assn., W.Va. Acad. Family Practice. Democrat. Moslem. Club: Masons (32 deg.). Author: Urogenital Hygiene, 1961. Home: 1130 National Rd Wheeling WV 26003 Office: 1132 National Rd Wheeling WV 26003

YATES, ERNEST JONAH, lawyer; b. Tallahassee, Apr. 27, 1945; s. Ernest Norton and Itara (McAllister) Y.; A.B., Valdosta (Ga.) State Coll., 1967, J.D., U. Ga., 1970; m. Marsha Spurlock; children—Jessica Lynn, Marnie McAllister. Admitted to Ga. bar, 1970; asso. firm Reinhardt, Whitley & Sims, prof. corp., Tifton, Ga., 1970-76; individual practice, 1976—. Pres. Len Lastinger PTA, Tifton, 1974; bd. dirs. Tift County chpt. Am. Cancer Soc.; bd. dirs. Tift Area YMCA, 1974—, incorporator, 1974. Recipient Am. Jurisprudence Scholastic award Lawyer's Coop. Pub. Co., 1968. Mem. Tifton (pres. 1974), Am. bar assns., State Bar Ga., Am. Judicature Soc., Comml. Law League, Conf. Personal Fin. Law, Tift County C. of C., Tifton Sertoma Club, Tifton Jaycees (spoke award 1972, spark plug award 1973, sec. 1972-73, dir.), Valdosta State Coll. Alumni Soc. (dir. 1974—), Sigma Phi Epsilon, Phi Alpha Delta. Baptist. Clubs: Elks, Kiwanis (pres. Tifton 1973-74, v.p. 1978-79). Home: 125 Lewis St Tifton GA 31794 Office: 408 Tift N Ave Tifton GA 31794

YATES, PAUL LEE, ins. agt.; b. Dallas, July 12, 1945; s. Harold Crawford and Eleanor Catherine (Jackson) Y.; B.B.A., U. Tex., Austin, 1967; postgrad. Baylor U. Sch. Law, 1976-77; m. Connie Gayle Crow, Feb. 16, 1976. Mgr., Harold C. Yates Agy., Waco, Tex., 1971-76; owner, operator Southwestern Ins. Assos., Waco, 1974-78; regional mgr. Ins. Adminstrv. Services, Inc., Houston, 1978-79; spl. agt. Transamerica Ins. Group, Waco, 1979—. Past pres. exec. com., legis. chmn. Muscular Dystrophy Assn.; mem. adv. bd. restored houses Historic Waco Found. Mem. Nat. Assn. Life Underwriters, Tex. Assn. Life Underwriters, Waco Assn. Life Underwriters, Am. Mgmt. Assn., Hedonia. Conservative Republican. Episcopalian. Home: 4408 Westchester St Waco TX 76710 Office: Transamerica Ins Group 813 Lake Air St Waco TX 76710

YAWN, DAVID HOUSTON, physician; b. Angleton, Tex., Feb. 12, 1943; s. Quincy T. and Grace (Graham) Y.; B.A. in Biology and German summa cum laude, Rice U., 1965; M.D., Baylor U., 1969. Intern in pathology Johns Hopkins Hosp., Balt., 1969-70, resident and fellow in pathology, 1970-71; rotating intern in medicine and surgery Baylor Affiliated Hosps., Houston, 1971-72; resident in pathology U.S.S. Hope, Brazil, summer, 1973, Baylor Affiliated Hosps., Houston, 1972-74; practice medicine specializing in pathology; chief hematopathology sect. Lab. Harris County Hosp. Dist., Houston, 1976—; asst. attending staff Methodist Hosp. Houston, 1976—; asso. pathologist Tex. Children's Hosp., Houston, 1979—; asst. prof. pathology Baylor Coll. Medicine, Houston, 1976—; civilian expert, clin. lab. Johnson Space Center, NASA, Houston, 1978—. Served to lt. comdr. M.C., USN, 1974-76. Diplomate Am. Bd. Pathology. Fellow Am. Soc. Clin. Pathologists; mem. Houston Soc. Clin. Pathologists, Tex. Soc. Pathologists, Tex. Med. Assn., Tex. Soc. Pathologists, AMA, Harris County Med. Soc. Contbr. articles on pathology to profl. jours. Home: 5451 Whispering Creek Houston TX 77017 Office: Dept of Pathology Baylor College of Medicine 1200 Moursund Houston TX 77030

YEAMAN, JAMES OSCAR, trade assn. exec.; b. Dothan, Ala., Feb. 21, 1942; s. James Edward and Mildred (Reeves) Y.; B.A., Auburn U., 1966; m. Carole Conniff, Aug. 27, 1966 (div.); children—Jamie Elisabeth, Ashley Michele. Producer, dir. Ala. ETV Network, 1965; dir. radio and television service dept. univ. relations Auburn U., 1966-67; dir. conv. and visitor promotion div. Montgomery Area C. of C., 1967-69; pub. relations dir. Ala. Edn. Assn., 1969-73; exec. v.p. Automotive Wholesalers Assn. of Ala., Montgomery, 1973—. Bd. dirs. Salvation Army. Served with Ala. N.G., 1959-65. Cert. assn. exec. Mem. Pub. Relations Council Ala. (named Practitioner of Yr. 1980), Automotive Wholesalers' Assn. Execs. (v.p.), Automotive Service Industry Assn. (tng. and edn. com.), Montgomery Area C. of

C. (chmn. conv. and visitor promotion council), Ala. Council Assn. Execs. (past pres.), Am. Soc. Assn. Execs. (membership com.), Phi Eta Sigma, Omicron Delta Kappa, Phi Gamma Delta. Episcopalian. Club: Montgomery Capital Rotary (pres.). Home: 3423 Malabar Rd Montgomery AL 36101 Office: 958 S Perry St Montgomery AL 36104

YEARGIN, ROBERT ARNOLD, acct., fin. cons.; b. Nashville, June 27, 1944; s. Arnold E. and Margaret (Dobbs) Y.; B.S., Middle Tenn. State U., 1966; M.B.A., U. Tenn., 1977; m. Mary C. Eskew, July 1, 1978; children—Robert Arnold, Kimberly J. Controller, Anchor Wire Corp., Goodlettsville, Tenn., 1970-73; asst. dir. fiscal services State of Tenn., Nashville, 1973-76; dir. spl. projects-fin. mgmt. Vanderbilt U. Med. Center, Nashville, 1976-77; owner Yeargin & Asso., Nashville, 1977—; dir. Nat. Bldg. Corp., Nashville, 1977-78; lectr. in field. Pres., M.B.A. Student Body, U. Tenn., Nashville, 1976-77; chmn. bd. Nat. Hemophilia Found., 1977. Named Jaycee of the Year, 1974-75; numerous other state, regional, nat. awards. Mem. Franklin Rd. Jaycees (v.p. 1975-76), Middle Tenn. State U. Acctg. Soc., Alpha Kappa Psi. Home: 4626 Shy's Hill Rd Nashville TN 37215 Office: 814 19th Ave S Nashville TN 37203

YEARY, DANIEL JOHN, clergyman; b. Miami, Okla., Dec. 28, 1938; s. John Wesley and Eileen M. (Briggs) Y.; B.A., Hardin-Simmons U., 1961; M.R.E., Southwestern Bapt. Theol. Sem, 1965; m. Melinda Mae Millican, Mar. 31, 1961; children—John Weston, Melissa Kaye, Doak Daniel. Ordained to ministry Baptist Ch., 1963; with Ky. Bapt. Conv., 1965-67; coll. minister First Bapt. Ch., Lubbock, Tex., 1967-72; asso. pastor S. Main Bapt. Ch., Houston, 1972-75; pastor Univ. Bapt. Ch., Coral Gables, Fla., 1975—. Mem. bd. of young assos. Hardin-Simmons U.; mem. Youth Adv. Bd. City of Coral Gables; bd. dirs. Youth Center; youth football coach and baseball Pop Warner. Contbg. author: The Church's Mission to the Campus, 1969. Office: Univ Bapt Ch 624 Anastasia Ave Coral Gables FL 33134

YEATTS, COLEMAN BENNETT, JR., lawyer; b. Danville, Va., Dec. 28, 1942; s. Coleman B. and Grace Ruth (Cook) Y.; B.A., Richmond Coll., 1965; M.A., T.C. Williams Sch. Law, 1969; m. Caryl Elizabeth Hogg, July 6, 1968. Instr. in govt. Hargrave Mil. Acad., Chatham, Va., 1967; law clk. Coleman B. Yeatts, Sr., Chatham, 1969-72; instr. govt. Danville (Va.) Community Coll., 1971; admitted to Va. bar, 1973; asso. firm Coleman B. Yeatts, Sr., Chatham, 1973-74; partner firm Yeatts, Overbey & Yeatts, Chatham, 1974—; town atty. Town of Gretna (Va.), 1975—; JAG officer U.S. Army Res., Martinsville, Va., 1975—. Bd. deacons Chatham Baptist Ch., 1975—; chmn. Chatham Area Heart Fund Dr., 1978; mem. Danville-Pittsylvania Mental Health and Mental Retardation Services Bd., 1978—, Danville-Pittsylvania Heart Unit, 1978—. Served with U.S. Army, 1967-68, to capt. USAR, 1967—. Decorated USAR achievement medal, Armed Forces Res. campaign and service medals. Mem. Am., Va., Pittsylvania County bar assns., Va. Trial Lawyers Assn., Res. Officers U.S., Res. Officers Assn., Hargrave Mil. Acad. Alumni Assn. (pres. 1975-77), Chatham C. of C. (pres. 1977—, dir. 1975-77). Democrat. Baptist. Clubs: Chatham Rotary (v.p. 1977-78, pres. 1978, dir. 1975-80), Cedars Country (dir. 1974-76) Westwood Racquet, Stratford Tennis (dir. 1977-79), Danville Execs. Home: PO Box 364 Chatham VA 24531 Office: PO Drawer 459 Yeatts Overby & Yeatts Chatham VA 24531

YEH, PU-SEN, engr., educator; b. Taiwan, China, July 7, 1935; s. Fua-Eang and Chin-Mei L.; M.S., U. Ill., 1962; Ph.D. in Mech. Engring., Rutgers U., 1967; m. Grace Yeh, June 6, 1964; children—Flora, Felice, Gilbert. Research, teaching asst. U. Ill., 1961-64; research asst. Rutgers U., 1964-67; asso. prof., head computer sci. and engring. Jacksonville (Ala.) State U., 1978—. Mem. Am. Soc. Engring. Edn., ASME. Presbyterian. Office: Dept Computer Sci and Engring Jacksonville State Univ Jacksonville AL 36265

YEH, RAYMOND WEI-HWA, architect, educator; b. Shanghai, China, Feb. 25, 1942; s. Herbert Hwan-Ching and Joyce Bo-Ding (Kwan) Y.; came to U.S., 1958, naturalized, 1976; student Whitman Coll., 1961-63; B.A., U. Ore., 1965, B.Arch., 1967; M.Arch., U. Minn., 1969; m. Hsiao-Yen Chen, Sept. 16, 1967; children—Bryant Po-Yung, Clement Chung-Yung, Emily Su-Yung. Designer, draftsman Naramore-Bain-Brady-Johanson, Seattle, 1967, Cerny Asso., Mpls., 1967-68; asst. architect Winston Close, FAIA, U. Minn., Mpls., 1968; design architect Ellerbe Architects, Mpls., 1968-70; asst. prof., then asso. prof. architecture U. Okla., Norman, 1970-78, prof., 1978—; v.p., dir. design Sorey-Hill-Binnicker, Oklahoma City, 1973-74; prin. architect Raymond W. H. Yeh and Asso., Norman, 1975—; lectr. in field. Profl. advisor Neighborhood Conservation and Devel. Center, Oklahoma City, 1977—. Nat. Endowment for Arts fellow, 1978-79; recipient Nat. Design award, Guild of Religious Arch., 1978. Cert. Nat. Council of Archtl. Registration Bd., 1972; lic. architect, Calif., Tex., Okla. Mem. AAUP, AIA, Internat. Alumni Assn. (dir. 1978—), Alumni Assn. U. Minn., Alumni Assn. U. Oreg. Christian Ch. Contbr. articles in field to profl. jours. Home: 501 Trenton Rd Norman OK 73069 Office: 180 W Brooks St Norman OK 73069

YEH, WALTER HUAI-TEH, educator, composer; b. Shanghai, China, Jan. 7, 1911; s. Ziang Tsung and Pei-Yu (Huang) Y.; came to U.S., 1944, naturalized, 1955; A.B., St. John's U. (China), 1933; grad. summa cum laude Nat. Conservatory of Music (China), 1935; M.A. and Mus. M., Eastman Sch. Music, U. Rochester, 1945; A.M., Harvard, 1948, researcher, 1951-54; Ph.D., U. Rochester, 1949; m. Moong Yue, Aug. 8, 1942; children—Peter Wen-chun, Arthur Cho-chun. Prof. flute Nat. Conservatory of Music, China, 1940-44; prof. music, chmn. joint music dept. Allen U and Benedict Coll., Columbia, S.C., 1954—, chmn. humanities div. Allen U., 1957-60, 63-79, chmn. div. fine arts and drama Benedict Coll., 1968-71, 72-74, interim pres. Allen U., 1973. Bd. dirs. Columbia Lyric Theatre, 1972-75. Fellow Internat. Inst. Arts and Letters. Rotarian. Composer: Concerto Grosso in F for Oboe, String Quartet and Harp with String Orchestra, 1944; Symphony in D, 1944; Chinese Suite, 1945; Chinese Symphony, 1948; (madrigal) Come Away, Come Away, Death!, 1957; The Cuckoo Chorus, 1958; Hymn for Peace, 1960; And Ruth Said: Intreat Me Not to Leave Thee, 1962; The Solitary Reaper, 1964; She Never Told Her Love, 1965; This Glorious Christmas Night, 1967; Gloria Patri and Kyrie, 1968; The Pattering Rain, 1968; The Lord's Prayer, 1969; We Shall Overcome, 1970; A Tombstone Epitaph, 1971; Alleuia, May Peace Be on Earth, 1972; Farewell for Ever!, 1972; All Glory, Praise and Honor, 1973; Echoes from on the Great Wall, 1974; He Who Loves God Loves All People, 1975; Last Night, 1975; Oh Slide and Stamp!, 1976; For Dust Thou Art, and Unto Dust Shalt Thou Return, 1977; Think! Think! Think!, 1977; Long, Long Ago, 1977; Farewell Alma Mater Dear! God Be With You Till We Meet Again, 1977; Concerto Ecclesiastico, 1979; Orientalia string quartet, 1980; composer orchestral and choral works, other compositions. Home: 710 Heidt St Columbia SC 29205

YEH, YUN-CHI, biochemist; b. Hwalien, China, Oct. 16, 1930; s. Pu-Lun and Sei-Mei Y.; B.S., Nat. Taiwan U., 1954; Ph.D., U. Calif. at San Francisco, 1964: m. Hsing-Wu Cheng Yeh, Oct. 10, 1930; children—John, I-Tien, Davida, Ann. Research asso. Med. Sch., U. Mich., Ann Arbor, 1964-67; asst. prof. Med. Sch. U. Ark., Little Rock, 1967-72, asso. prof. biochemistry, 1972-79, prof., 1979—; vis. asso. prof. molecular biology Salk Inst., LaJolla, Calif., 1975-76. Recipient grants NIH, Am. Cancer Soc. Mem. Am. Soc. Biol. Chemists, Am. Soc. Microbiology, Am. Chem. Soc., Internat. Platform Assn., Sigma Xi. Club: Lions. Home: 11120 Shenandoah Valley Dr Little Rock AR 72212 Office: 4301 W Markham St Little Rock AR 72201

YEILDING, KENNETH DUANE, educator; b. Gatesville, Tex., Mar. 30, 1936; s. Hollis Clinton and Margaret Evelyn (Boyd) Y.; B.S. magna cum laude, Hardin-Simmons U., 1957; M.A., U. Tex., El Paso, 1962; Ph.D., Tex. Tech. U., 1973; m. Patsy Ann Hicks, June 22, 1957; children—Lisa Lynn, Suzanne Renee, Bethalyn Carol. Tchr., Lincoln Jr. High Sch., Abilene, Tex., 1957-58, Boynton Jr. High Sch., Ithaca, N.Y., 1960-62, Ysleta Jr. High Sch., El Paso, Tex., 1962-64, Abilene High Sch., 1964-66; instr. Odessa (Tex.) Coll., 1966-68, prof. history and govt., 1970—, pres. acad. senate, 1979-80; part-time instr. Tex. Tech. U., Lubbock, 1968-70; spl. asst. to city mgr., Odessa, 1974; spl. researcher census and stats. subcom. Post Office and Civil Service Com., U.S. Ho. of Reps., Washington, 1974; spl. research asst. Hon. Dan B. Hemphill, Mayor, City of Odessa, 1975-78; cons. corp. history project El Paso Products Co., Odessa, 1976—; Mem. Friends Ector County Library, 1970—, 2d. v.p., 1974-75; bd. dirs. Odessa Shakespeare Globe of Great Southwest, 1976-77, Odessa Arts and Humanities Commn., 1975-77; vice chmn., mem. exec. com. Heritage Odessa Bicentennial Commn., 1973-77; dir. Presdl. Mus., 1967—, mem. exec. bd., 1967-78; mem. exec. com. Democratic Party Ector County, 1970—, vice chmn., 1979-80; del. State Dem. Party Convs., 1968, 70, 72, 74, 76, 78. Served with U.S. Army, 1958-60. Mem. Am. Hist. Assn., Am. Polit. Sci. Assn., Orgn. Am. Historians, Tex. State Hist. Assn., Tex. Jr. Coll. Tchrs. Assn., Tex. Mus. Assn., Tex. Tech. U. Alumni Assn., U. Tex. El Paso Alumni Assn., West Tex. Hist. Assn., Western History Assn., Ft. Stockton Hist. Soc., El Paso Hist. Soc., Southwest Polit. Sci. Assn., Llano Estacado Heritage (dir. 1976—), C. of C., Hardin-Simmons U. Alumni and Ex-Student Assn. (chpt. pres. 1973—), Phi Kappa Phi, Pi Gamma Mu, Phi Alpha Theta, Pi Kappa Delta, Phi Delta Kappa. Baptist. Clubs: Masons (Shriner) (treas. 1979-80), Rotary. Contbr. numerous articles to various publs. Home: 2904 Nabors Ln Odessa TX 79762 Office: Odessa Coll 214 W University Odessa TX 79760

YEITER, ROBERT MARION, newspaper exec.; b. Lafayette, Ind., Apr. 28, 1922; s. Claude Robert and Della Lucille (Rutherford) Y.; grad. high sch.; m. Ruby Inez Robinett, Apr. 1, 1944; children—George Marion, Jerry Elmo. With newspapers in Columbus, Ga., 1946-55, Oklahoma City, 1955-57, Savannah, Ga., 1957-60, Portland, Oreg., 1960-62, Pasco, Wash., 1962-69; prodn. mgr. Biloxi-Gulfport (Miss.) newspapers, 1969—. Served with U.S. Army, 1942-46, 52. Mem. Am. Legion, DAV. Republican. Mormon. Home: 2319 Middlecoff Dr Gulfport MS 39501 Office: PO Box 4567 Biloxi MS 39531

YENAWINE, DAVID LEROY, engr.; b. El Campo, Tex., July 10, 1934; s. George Leroy and Beatrice Maude (Hicks) Y.; B.S. in Ceramic Engring., U. Tex., 1960, Ph.D. in M.E., 1970; M.S. in Metall. Engring., Rensselaer Poly. Inst., 1963; m. Mae Beth Knapp, June 22, 1958; children—Dallas Lee, King Allan, Dean Alden. Sr. metallurgist Pratt & Whitney Aircraft, Middletown, Conn., 1960-64; materials and process engr. Douglas Aircraft Co., Charlotte, N.C., 1964-65; sect. mgr. materials devel. group Tracor, Austin, Tex., 1967-71; tech. dir. failure analysis and materials engring. Tex. Instruments, Dallas, 1971—. Served with U.S. Army, 1954-56. Registered profl. engr., Tex. Mem. Am. Soc. Metals, Am. Ceramic Soc., Nat. Inst. Ceramic Engrs., Am. Electroplating Soc., Am. Inst. Mining, Metall. and Petroleum Mech. Engrs., Phi Theta Kappa, Pi Tau Sigma. Patentee in field. Home: 1234 Briarcove Dr Richardson TX 75081 Office: PO Box 6015 Dallas TX 75222

YERGER, JOHN HENRY, cons.; b. Reading, Pa., Jan. 4, 1914; s. John Henry and Anna (Long) Y.; A.B., Muhlenberg Coll., 1935; M.S. in Social Service, Boston U., 1942; cert. advanced mgmt. U. Chgo., 1972; m. Christine Helen Fegley, June 12, 1937; 1 dau., Pamela Louise Zarab. Supr., Pa. Dept. Pub. Assistance, Reading, 1935-40; exec. ARC, Boston, Cape Cod, Worcester, Mass., Hudson County, N.J., 1942-50, Niagara Falls (N.Y.) Community Chest, 1950-51; exec. dir. Ottawa (Ont., Can.) Community Chest, 1951-55, United Appeal Met. Toronto (Ont.), 1955-72; v.p. United Way of Am., Alexandria, Va., 1972-77; cons., 1977—; lectr. Harvard U., 1941-42, Clark U., 1946-47, Cornell U., 1950-51, Boston U., 1942, U. Toronto, 1962-72; cons. community orgn. to nat. orgns. and U.S. and Canadian cities, 1945—; chmn. nat. com. bus. leaders Canadian Community Funds, 1964-70, chmn. nat. com. to improve pub. relations, 1964; chmn. Internat. Conf. Community Funds and Councils, Los Angeles, 1972. Mem. Mayor's Civic Com., Toronto, 1958-70; founder Cape Cod Council, 1943; bd. dirs. Canadian Welfare Council, 1955-72, Met. Toronto Social Planning Council, 1955-72, Boca Atlantic Homeowners Assn., 1977—; chmn. bd. elders St. Paul Lutheran Ch., Boca Raton, 1977-79. Served with USCGR, 1943-45. Decorated Most Venerable Order of Hosp. of St. John of Jerusalem in Brit. Realm; Letters of The Kings At Arms, City of Ottawa; recipient citation ARC, 1946, Distinguished Service award United Community Fund, 1959, Canadian Red Cross, 1971, Boy Scouts Can., 1971, City of Toronto, 1971. Fellow Royal Soc. Health; mem. Acad. Certified Social Workers, Nat. Assn. Social Workers (chmn. Worcester chpt. 1944-45), Nat. Assn. Fund Raisers, Phi Kappa Tau, Tau Kappa Alpha. Clubs: Nat., Canadian (Toronto); Kiwanis of Boca Raton (v.p.). Author: CPM for United Ways, 1977. Contbr. articles to tech. mags. Home: Apt 2105 Chalfonte North 500 S Ocean Blvd Boca Raton FL 33432 Office: 801 N Fairfax St Alexandria VA 22314

YESNER, BERNARD, family physician; b. N.Y.C., Nov. 10, 1915; s. Jacob and Anna (Schweiger) Y.; B.S., U. Ark., 1936, M.D., 1940; m. Annette Sara Lasky, Feb. 15, 1950; children—Leslie Joyce, Alan Jay, Judi Marcia. Intern, Mary Immaculate Hosp., Jamaica, N.Y., 1940-41; practice family medicine, Jamaica, 1943-49, Miami, Fla., 1949—; mem. faculty Sch. Medicine, U. Miami, 1956—, clin. asso. prof. dept. family medicine, 1974—; pres. med. staff South Miami Hosp., 1975. Served as capt. M.C., AUS, 1941-43. Recipient Pfizer award U.S. CD Council, 1967; Shalom award State of Israel, 1971; diplomate Am. Bd. Family Practice. Fellow Am. Acad. Family Physicians; mem. Am. Physicians Fellowship of Israel Med. Assn., Fla., Dade County med. assns., Am., Am.-Israel numis. assns., Israel Numis. Soc. Greater Miami, Am. Philatelic Soc., Jewish War Vets, Tau Epsilon Phi. Jewish. Clubs: Masons, Shriners. Home: 422 Luenga Coral Gables FL 33146 Office: 7540 S W 61st Ave South Miami FL 33143

YETT, FOWLER REDFORD, educator; b. Johnson City, Tex., Oct. 18, 1919; s. James William, Sr. and Rebecca Jane (Stribling) Y.; B.S. in Chem. Engring. (Univ. scholar), U. Tex. at Austin, 1943, M.A. in Math., 1952; Ph.D., Iowa State U., 1955; m. Mary Sue Lytle, June 17, 1945; children—Jane Marie, Rebecca (Mrs. Thomas Moore Root), Mary Wester. Research chemist, research chem. engr. Manhattan Project, U. Chgo., 1943-44, Richland, Wash., 1944-45; owner, mgr. Camera Supplies of Houston, 1946-49; teaching fellow math. U. Tex. at Austin, 1949-52, asst. prof., 1956-65; instr. math. Iowa State U., Ames, 1952-55; asst. prof. math. Long Beach (Calif.) State Coll., 1955-56; prof. math. U. So. Ala. at Mobile, 1965—, chmn. dept., 1965-68; sr. research engr. N.Am. Aviation, Inc., Downey, Calif., summers 1956-57, 59; faculty research asso. Boeing Co., Seattle, summer 1958; chmn. bd. Home Security Systems, Inc.; pres. Dr. Fowler Redford Yett & Daus., Inc. Active all Lyndon Baines Johnson election campaigns, 1937-68. Recipient Excellence in Teaching awards U. Tex. at Austin, 1958, U. So. Ala. at Mobile, 1975. Mem. Am. Math. Soc. Methodist (tchr. Sunday sch. 1970-71). Office: Math Dept U So Ala Mobile AL 36688

YETTER, CHAUNCEY RUSSELL, steel corp. exec.; b. Tulsa, Aug. 9, 1924; s. George Daniel and Jessie Evelyn Yetter; B.S. in Bus. Adminstrn., Tulsa U., 1951; system certificate Brandon Sch., 1961; 1 dau., Cathy Sue Yetter Gilbert. Operator, Pub. Service Co. of Okla., 1947-50; asst. data mgr. Brit.-Am. Oil Co., 1951; asst. data mgr., analyst Jones & Laughlin Steel Corp., Houston, 1951—. Served with C.E., AUS, 1943-46. Mem. Data Processing Mgmt. Assn. Democrat. Methodist. Home: 3113 Esquire Ln Garland TX 75042 Office: 1810 Commerce St Dallas TX 75032

YIANNOPOULOS, ATHANASSIOS NICHOLAS, lawyer, educator; b. Thessaloniki, Greece, Mar. 13, 1928; s. Nicholas A. and Areti T. (Alvanos) Y.; came to U.S., 1953, naturalized, 1963; LL.B., U. Thessaloniki, 1950, M.C.L., U. Chgo., 1954; LL.M. (Walter Perry Johnson fellow in law 1954-56), U. Cal. at Berkeley, 1955, J.S.D., 1956; J.D., U. Cologne (Germany), 1961; m. Carolyn Crawford, Nov. 17, 1967; children—Maria, Nicholas. Admitted to Greek bar, 1958; prof. law La. State U, Baton Rouge, 1958-79, W.R. Irby prof. law, 1979—, charge revision of La. Civil Code at La. State U. Law Inst., 1962—. Pres. Baton Rouge Symphony Assn., 1972-83; mem. bd. Chamber Music Soc., 1961—. Served to 2d lt., inf. Greek Army, 1950-53. Mem. Phi Alpha Delta. Greek Orthodox. Club: Baton Rouge City, Author: Civil Law Property, 1966, 2d edit., 1980; Personal Servitudes, 1968, 2d edit., 1978. Home: 662 Sunset Blvd Baton Rouge LA 70808 Office: Tulane U Sch Law New Orleans LA 70118

YIANTSOU, CHRIS GUS, physician; b. Imroz Island, Turkey, Oct. 23, 1947; came to U.S., 1967, naturalized, 1978; s. Athanasios Moutzakas and Pinelopi Trigoni; A.A., Frank Phillips Jr. Coll., 1969; B.S. cum laude in Pharmacy, U. Houston, 1972; M.D., Tex. Technol. U., 1975; m. Barbara Tibbets, Dec. 28, 1974. Intern, St. Paul Hosp., Dallas, 1975-76, resident in medicine, 1976-78, resident in gastroenterology, 1978-79; resident in gastroenterology VA Hosp., Dallas, 1979; practice medicine specializing in gastroenterology, Bedford, Tex., 1979—. Mem. AMA, A.C.P., Rho Chi, Phi Kappa Phi, Phi Theta Kappa. Greek Orthodox. Club: Soto Grande Tennis Center. Home: 2525 Lakeview Dr Bedford TX 76021 Office: 2600 Tibbets Dr Bedford TX 76021

YING, SHUH-JING, mech. engr., educator; b. Shaohing, China, July 5, 1930; came to U.S., 1958, naturalized, 1972; s. Kao-Sun and Yeen-Yuen (Fann) Y.; B.S., Cheng-Kung U., 1958; M.S., Brown U., 1961; Ph.D., Harvard U., 1965; m. Shun-si Shiu, Nov. 10, 1962; children—Sue, Lily, Jean, June, Howard. Asst. prof. Cath. U. Am., Washington, 1965-63; asso. prof. Wayne State U., Detroit, 1968-71; prof. Detroit Inst. Tech., 1971-78; asso. prof. mech. engring. U. South Fla., Tampa, 1978—, acting chmn. dept. mech. engring., 1977-78. Served with Chinese Air Force, 1954-58. Recipient Outstanding Faculty award Engring Coll., Detroit Inst. Tech., 1976; registered profl. engr., Fla. Mem. ASME, Soc. Automotive Engrs., Combustion Inst., Am. Geophys. Union, Orgn. Chinese Ams. (dir. 1977-79, chmn. cultural and ednl. com. 1976-79), Sigma Xi. Christian. Contbr. articles to profl. jours. Home: 5008 The Riviera Tampa FL 33609 Office: Energy Conversion Mech Design U South Fla Tampa FL 33620

YOAKUM, ANNA MARGARET, chemist; b. Loudon, Tenn., Jan. 13, 1933; d. Hugh L. and Emily (Watkins) Yoakum; A.B., Maryville Coll., 1954; M.S., U Fla., 1956, Ph.D., 1960. Chief chemist, lab. supr. Greenback Industries, Inc., 1956-59; research chemist Chemstrand Research Center, Inc., 1960-64; research staff Oak Ridge Nat. Lab., 1964-69, exec. v.p., lab dir. Stewart Labs., Inc., Knoxville, 1969—, also dir.; sec.-treas., dir. Royal Powdered Metals, 1978—. Recipient Alumni citation Maryville Coll., 1979. Fellow Am. Inst. Chemists; mem. ASTM, Am. Chem. Soc., Soc. Applied Spectroscopy (sect. sec., treas. 1965-68), N.Y. Acad. Scis., Phi Beta Kappa, Sigma Xi, Phi Kappa Phi, Gamma Sigma Epsilon. Methodist. Club: Knoxville Executives. Home: Route 4 Box 324 Twin Coves Lenoir City TN 37771 Office: 5815 Middlebrook Pike Knoxville TN 37921

YODER, DAVID, real estate devel. co. exec.; b. Meyersdale, Pa., Oct. 10, 1931; s. Ernest and Lena (Bender) Y.; B.A., Goshen (Ind.) Coll., 1957; postgrad. W.Va. U., 1957-65, U. Vienna, 1962, U. Graz (Austria), 1965; m. Ruby Jeanell Shenk, Sept. 6, 1964; children—Jon, Robert. Exec. v.p. Allegheny Devel. Corp. Inc., Morgantown, W.Va., 1966—; pres. Pineview Realty, Inc., Morgantown, 1970—; sec., treas. Allegheny Realestate Sales, Morgantown, 1975—; dir. Allegheny Devel. Corp., Inc., Pineview Realty, Inc., Allegheny Realestate Sales. Mem. Morgantown Area C. of C., N. Central W.Va. Home Builders Assn. (v.p. 1976, pres. 1977-80), Home Builders Assn. of W.Va. (v.p. 1980). Home: Winona Ct Morgantown WV 26505 Office: 1225 Pineview Dr Morgantown WV 26505

YODER, HILDA (MRS. ALBERT FRANCIS GARROU), ednl. adminstr.; b. Hickory, N.C., Jan. 1, 1903; d. Ellis Hampton and Elizabeth (Frye) Whitener; B.S., Lenoir Rhyne Coll., 1924, L.H.D., 1955; M.A., Tchrs. Coll., Columbia U., 1945; m. Luther Glenn Yoder, July 7, 1928 (dec. Oct. 1940); m. 2d, Albert Francis Garrou, Nov. 3, 1956 (dec. Nov. 1978). Tchr., supr. high sch., N.C., N.J., 1926-45; research anti-convulsive clinic psychiat, and neurol. dept. U. Va. Hosp., 1945-47; founder, dir. Yoder Sch., N.Y.C., 1949—; lectr. postgrad. Sch. Ophthalmology, N.Y. U., Bellevue Med. Center, 1950-53. Dir. Reading Clinic Inst. Ophthalmology, Columbia-Presbyn. Med. Center, 1950-56; bd. dirs. So. Appalachian Highlands Conservancy; bd. devel. Lenoir Rhyne Coll. Mem. Daus. Am. Colonists, D.A.R. Presbyterian. Author: Help a Child To Be a Better Reader, 1977. Home: Valdese NC 28690

YOIST, MICHAEL WAYNE, mental health adminstr.; b. Alexandria, La., Mar. 2, 1946; s. Francis Moore, Jr., and Mary (LeDoux) Y.; student La. State U., Alexandria, 1964-66; B.A., La. Coll., Pineville, 1969; M.S.W., U. Ark., 1975; m. Michelene Alletag, Aug. 27, 1967; children—Michael Wayne, Kimberly Michelle. Clin. social worker Alexandria Mental Health Center, 1975-78, adminstr. adult services, 1979—; acting adminstr. Leesville (La.) Mental Health Clinic, 1978-79; social services cons. Bio-Med. Assn., Naomi Heights Nursing Home, Rehab. Center Rapides Parish; adj. asst. prof. Northwestern State U.; adj. instr. La. State U. Sunday Sch. tchr. 1st Baptist Ch., 1977—; mem. People for People, 1976—, Mental Health Assn. La., 1977—, Human Resources Council Vernon Parish, 1978-79. Served with USAF, 1970-74. Decorated Am. Spirit Honor Medal; named Weather Observer of Yr., USAF 5th Weather Wing, 1971; recipient stipend NIMH, 1974; cert. social worker, La. Mem. Nat. Assn. Social Workers, Acad. Cert. Social Workers, La. Assn. Mental Health and Substance Abuse Adminstrs. Baptist. Research on premature unilateral client termination at Elizabeth Mitchell Children's Center. Home: 3229 Cloverland Dr Pineville LA 71360 Office: PO Box 7473 Alexandria LA 71306

YOKELY, RONALD EUGENE, research co. exec.; b. High Point, N.C., Feb. 7, 1942; s. Clarence Eugene and Grayce (Waddy) Y.; B.S. in Mech. Engring., N.C. State U., Raleigh, 1963; m. E. Joanne Williams, July 6, 1963; children—Rhonda Lynette, Rene Michelle. Test engr. McDonnell Douglas Corp., St. Louis, 1963-67; task leader Simulation Products div. Singer Co., Houston, 1967-68, engring. group supr., 1968-71, engring. sr. supr., sect. mgr. for Skylab.-Command Module simulator, 1971-73; engring. mgr. Philco-Ford Corp., Houston, 1973-75, mgr. earth resources tech. applications studies Aeroneutronic Ford Corp. (formerly Philco-Ford Corp.), Houston, 1975-76; ind. cons. in mgmt. and systems engring., Houston, 1975-76; sr. v.p., dir. mktg. Onyx Corp., Atlanta, 1976-78; pres. Acumenics Research & Tech., Inc., Bethesda, Md., 1978—. Registered profl. engr., Tex. Mem. Am. Inst. Aeros. and Astronautics, Nat. Soc. Profl. Engrs., IEEE, Omega Psi Phi. Episcopalian. Author: A Proposed Aviation Energy Conservation Program for the National Aviation System, 4 vols., 1977; The Impact of Microcomputers on Aviation, 2 vols., 1977; Microcomputers to the Year 2000 A.D., 1978; Microcomputers: A Technology Forecast and Assessment to the Year 2000, 1980. Home: 11453 Purple Beech Dr Reston VA 22091 Office: 4340 East-West Hwy Bethesda MD 20014

YONGE, JOHN JOSEPH, chem. co. exec.; b. Savannah, Ga., Feb. 5, 1948; s. Arthur Dunham and Mac Agnes (Armstrong) Y.; student U. Tex., Austin, 1970. Teaching asst. U. Tex., 1966-70; lab. supr. Forrest and Cotton, Austin, 1968-70; shift supr. Dow Tex. div., Freeport, 1973-74; lab. supr. Shintech Inc., Freeport, 1974-78, environ. control supr., 1978—. Advisor Jr. Achievement, Lake Jackson, Tex., 1973—; high adventure post advisor Bay Area Council Boy Scouts Am., Lake Jackson. Mem. ASTM, Vinyl Chloride Safety Assn., Brazosport Mcpl. Fire Instrs. Assn., Tex. Chem. Council. Roman Catholic. Office: 5618 E Hwy 332 Freeport TX 77541

YONKER, THOMAS FREDERICK, JR., gas co. exec.; b. Ranger, Tex., Aug. 20, 1930; s. Thomas Frederick and Edith M. (Thompson) Y.; student Tex. Coll. of Arts and Industries, 1947-49; m. Frana Lajean Barrett, Nov. 1, 1969; children—Thomas Frederick III, Timothy H., Patricia S., Steven R. Fogle (stepson). Sr. dispatcher Transcontinental Gas Pipeline, Houston, Tex., 1950-62; mgr. Alamo Gas Supply Co., San Antonio, Tex., 1962-63; mgr. Coastal States Gas Corp., Corpus Christi, Tex., 1963-74; v.p. of ops. La. Intrastate Gas Corp., Alexandria, 1974—; lectr. Tex. A. and I. U., 1971; cons. in natural gas measurement, 1971—. Mem. Alexandria C. of C., ASME, Petroleum Industry Elec. Assn., Mid-State Radio Control Soc. Republican. Roman Catholic. Author: Gas Control Manual, 1967. Contbr. short stories to various mags. Home: 123 Choctaw Dr Pineville LA 71360 Office: PO Box 1352 Alexandria LA 71301

YORK, ELIZA RUTH, counselor; b. Brazoria, Tex., July 5, 1936; d. Anderson and Blanche (Lee) Goode; B.S., Tex. So. U., 1961, M.A., 1970, cert. in supt. adminstrn., 1979; Marshall Henry York, June 22, 1957; children—Gwendolyn Marie, Stephanie Cezanna, Marshall. Tchr., N. Forest Sch. Dist., Houston, 1964-66; tchr. Houston Ind. Sch. Dist., 1966-77; counselor, Bellaire, Tex., 1977—. Mem. NEA, Am. Personnel and Guidance Assn., Houston Tchrs. Assn. Baptist. Home: 12514 Sorsby St Houston TX 77047 Office: 5100 Maple St Bellaire TX 77401

YORK, J. STEVEN, psychologist; b. Murfreesboro, Tenn., June 7, 1947; s. Ether Norman and Nora (Moore) Y.; B.S., Middle Tenn. State U., 1969; M.A., Ohio State U., 1972, Ph.D., 1975; m. Glenda June Sharp, Dec. 27, 1968; 1 son, Brett Steven. Psychology trainee Nisonger Center, Ohio State U., Columbus, 1973-74; instr. Columbus Tech. Inst., 1974; tchr. spl. edn. Columbus pub. schs., 1969-73; coordinator psychol. services, Devel. Disability Center for Children, La. State U. Med. Center, New Orleans, 1974-78, also asst. prof., chmn. interdisciplinary work group, 1979—; individual practice child clin. psychology, 1975—; mem. NOARC Human Rights Advisory Bd.; cons. in field. Grantee Developmental Disability Council La., 1977. Mem. Am. Psychol. Assn., Am. Assn. Mental Deficiency, Am. Assn. Psychiat. Services Children, Soc. Research in Child Devel., Am. Orthopsychiat. Assn., Council Exceptional Children, Nat. Soc. Autistic Citizens, Nat. Assn. Retarded Citizens. Contbr. author: Play Therapy with Developmentally Disabled Children, 1980; also articles. Editorial bd. Jour. Child Clin. Psychology. Home: 1815 Audubon St New Orleans LA 70118 Office: 1100 Florida Ave Bldg 138 New Orleans LA 70119

YORRA, DAVID IAN, constrn. and devel. co. exec.; b. Boston, Mar. 30, 1923; s. Joseph and Mary (Becker) Y.; B.S., Mass. Coll. Optometry, 1946, O.D., 1947; m. Lila Joyce Sable, Dec. 20, 1954; children—Lesley, Bruce, Allison. Gen. practice optometry, Clinton, N.C., 1947-53; pres. Cresthaven Enterprises, Inc., Pompano Beach, Fla., 1953—; dir. S.E. Bank of Broward (Fla.), 1959—. Served with USAAF, 1942-46. Named Palm Beach County (Fla.) Developer of Year Condominium News, 1975; licensed optometrist, N.C., Ky., Mass. Mem. Nat. Assn. Home Builders, Home Builders Assn. South Fla. Jewish religion. Home: 610 Cypress Blvd Pompano Beach FL 33060 Office: 1620 NE 36th St Pompano Beach FL 33064

YORSTON, LUCILLE ELIZABETH NOYES, program analyst; b. Campbellton, Tex., June 6, 1928; d. Tom Harvey and Ollie Elizabeth (Stockhorst) Roane; student S.W. Tex. State U., 1945-47; B.A. in Economics, Trinity U., San Antonio, 1975; m. Dale L. Noyes, Mar. 28, 1958 (dec.); 1 son, Craig Lowell; m. 2d, Alfred Yorston, Jr., May 12, 1979. Clk., Dept. of Army, San Antonio, 1944-45; sec., bookkeeper W.R. Quin Oil Co., San Antonio, 1947-49; clerk-typist Dept. Air Force, Kelly AFB, Tex., 1950-53; clerk-steno Humble Oil and Refining Co., Houston, 1953; clerk-typist, statis. clerk Dept. of Army, Ft. Sam Houston, Tex., 1953-63, budget analyst, 1963-67, program analyst, 1967-73, program analysis officer, 1973—. Active Boy Scouts Am., Tex. Folklife Festival. Recipient various Dept. Army achievement certificates and performance awards. Mem. Assn. Govt. Accountants (pres. San Antonio chpt.), Am. Soc. Mil. Comptrollers, Nat. Assn. Parliamentarians, Internat. Platform Assn., Toastmistress Club, Zonta Internat., Fed. Woman's Program. Methodist. Clubs: Order Eastern Star, Daughters of Nile. Home: 5842 Winding Ridge San Antonio TX 78239 Office: Directorate of Plans Training and Security Headquarters Fort Sam Houston TX 78234

YOST, CHARLES ANTHONY, engring. exec.; b. Boston, July 10, 1933; s. Charles William and Winnie (Tuminski) Y.; B.S. in Aero. Engring., Northrop U., 1962; m. Sandra G. Thacker, Apr. 15, 1978; children—Robin William, Julie Ann, Susan Leigh. Research engr. Convair div. Gen. Dynamics, San Diego, Calif., 1951-53; systems dynamics engr. Apollo, N. Am. Rockwell, Downey, Calif., 1962-67; dynamics engr. Stencel Aero Engring. Corp., Asheville, N.C., 1968-73; pres. Dynamics Systems, Inc., Leicester, N.C., 1974—; aerospace cons. Served with AUS, 1953-55. Recipient award for tech. devels. NASA, 1975. High energy elec. research. Home and Office: Route 2 Box 182B Leicester NC 28748

YOST, WILLIAM EDWARD, JR., electronics engr.; b. Washington, Mar. 7, 1920; s. William Edward and Hortense Jeanette (Zeh) Y.; student Rensselaer Poly. Inst., 1937-39; certificate radio engring., U. Md., 1941; m. Evelyn Wyatt Pritchett, May 20, 1975; children—Lynn, Camilla, David, Brenda; stepchildren—William, Gloria, Barry, Cindy. Engaged in family retail appliance bus., 1945-51; With Engring. & Research Corp., Riverdale, Md., 1951-53; sr. engr. Page Communications Engrs. Inc., Washington, 1953-55; v.p. engring. Datronics Engrs. Inc., Bethesda, Md., 1959-61, Scateer Communications Inc., Bethesda, 1957-59; gen. mgr. Bethesda div. Radio Engring. Labs., div. Dynamics Corp. Am., 1961-65; cons., 1965-70; chief radar br., electronic systems div. U.S. Army Fgn. Sci. and Tech. Center, Charloeesville, Va., 1970—; cons. in field. Pres. Montgomery County (Md.) Council Better Edn., 1958-61. Served with U.S. Army, 1941-45. Registered profl. engr., Md. Sr. mem. IEEE; mem. AAAS. Club: Kiwanis. Address: 105 King George Circle Charlottesville VA 22901

YOUMAN, ALFRED ELIOT, educator; b. Miami, Fla., Mar. 3, 1933; s. Alfred Gillespie and Elizabeth (Risinger) Y.; B.A., Yale U., 1955, Ph.D., 1959; m. Katherine May Small, June 12, 1956; children—Basil Eliot, Farley Hayes. Tchr., Hopkins Grammar Sch., New Haven, 1959-60; asst. prof. Union Coll., Schenectady, 1961-64; with Mercer Coll., Macon, Ga., 1964—, prof. dept. class. langs., 1980—. Tchr. Sunday sch. Cherakee Methodist Ch., Macon. Mem. Classical Assn. Midwest and So. States. Club: Macon Tennis. Contbr. articles to profl. jours. Home: 1789 Adams St Macon GA 31206 Office: Mercer U Coleman Ave Macon GA 31207

YOUMANS, E. GRANT, sociologist; b. Elling, N.D., Oct. 2, 1907; s. George and Jennie (Perchie) Y.; A.B., U. Chgo., 1937, A.M., 1938; Ph.D., Mich. State U., 1953; m. Elsie Markesi, Aug. 2, 1945; children—Douglas, Beverly. Instr. social sci. Mich. State U., East Lansing, 1946-51; mgmt. analyst Fed. Govt., Washington, 1951-53; research sociologist NIMH, Bethesda, Md., 1953-57; sociologist, prof. U. Ky., Lexington, 1957-68, emeritus prof., 1977—; cons. various colls. and hosps. Recipient Certificate of Merit, U.S. Dept. Agr., 1969; NIMH grantee, 1969, U.S. Dept. Agr. grantee, 1961-75. Mem. Am. Sociol. Assn., Gerontol. Soc., Am. Assn. Ret. Persons, Nat. Assn. Ret. Fed. Employees. Club: U. Ky. Editor: Older Rural Americans, 1967; contbr. articles on social aspects of aging to profl. jours. Home: 1226 Scoville Rd Lexington KY 40502 Office: Dept Sociology U Ky Lexington KY 40506

YOUMANS, JOSEPH LEE, power co. exec.; b. New Orleans, May 11, 1922; s. Ferris Ferman and Bertha Almyra (Urquhart) Y.; B.E.E., U. Fla., 1949; m. Barbara Marie Stewart, May 4, 1946; 1 dau., Marta Marie. Jr. elec. engr. Gulf Power Co., Pensacola, Fla., 1949-51, office engr., 1951-53, dist. engr., 1953-55, dist. supt. ops., 1955-61, mgr. transmission distbn., 1961-63, mgr. distbn. ops., 1963-65, mgr. co. relations, 1965-67, mgr. Western div., 1967-71, mgr. purchasing, stores, 1971-78, dir. purchasing and gen. services, 1978—. Served with U.S. Army, 1940-45; ETO. Certified mgr. Inst. Certified Profl. Mgrs. Mem. Pensacola C. of C. Roman Catholic. Clubs: Gulf Power Co. Mgmt., Lions (1st v.p. Pensacola 1975). Home: 824 Ash Dr Pensacola FL 32503 Office: PO Box 1151 Pensacola FL 32520

YOUNG, BEVERLY SUE, psychologist, educator; b. Oskaloosa, Iowa, Sept. 11, 1925; d. George Floyd and Alta Bernice (Stephen) Garner; B.A., William Penn Coll., 1961; M.A. U. No. Iowa, 1964; Ph.D. (Univ. fellow), State U. Iowa, 1968; m. William Thomas Young, Feb. 12, 1960; children—Rebecca, Rolfe, Thomas, David, Jennifer. Tchr. elem. public schs., New Sharon, Iowa, 1945-60, reading supr., 1964-65; sch. psychologist public schs., Poweshiels County, Iowa, 1965-66; prof. elem. edn. Stephen F. Austin State U., 1968—, dir. Learning Center, 1970—; cons., adv. on reading programs to public schs., Tex.; psychol. cons. Community Action Program, Nacagdoches, Tex., 1972-75; participant in orgn. and devel. numerous reading clinics in public schs. Eastern Tex., 1970-77. Chmn. commn. on edn. United Methodist Ch., Nacogdoches, 1976-78. Cert. elem. and spl. edn. adminstr., tchr., Iowa, Tex. Mem. Am. Psychol. Assn., Tex. Assn. Profs. Reading, Tex. Assn. Coll. Tchrs., Tex. Assn. Improvement Reading (exec. council 1975-79), Stone Ft. Reading Council, Am. Ednl. Research Assn., Internat. Reading Assn. (chmn. reading clinic panel Tex. council 1977-78), Delta Kappa Gamma. Author: Bibliography of High Interest, Low Vocabulary Books, 1968; Reading Handbook, 1972; Reading—How and Why, 1976.

YOUNG, BILLY WARREN, coal co. exec.; b. Trafford, Ala., May 13, 1927; s. Willie E. and Mulree V. (Padgett) Y.; student pub. schs., Ala.; m. Linda L. Slatton, Jan. 12, 1951; children—Rhonda Young Bibb, Kathy Sharon, Billy Warren Jr. With Ala. By-Products Corp., 1948-51, U.S. Steel Corp., 1951-58; self-employed in mining, 1958-75; pres. Baty Coal Co., Inc., Trafford, 1975—; v.p. Trafford Indsl. Devel. Bd., 1970—. Mem. City Council, 1968-72. Served with AUS, 1946-47. Clubs: Civitan (sec. 1971—), Civic (pres 1976) (Trafford). Address: Box 127 Trafford AL 35172

YOUNG, BOB F., oil co. exec.; b. Muldoon, Tex., Oct. 10, 1931; s. Ancil Edward and na Katherine (Kelley) Y.; B.B.A., U. Ga., 1958; LL.B., U. Tex., 1961; m. Faye Estelle Harris, Mar. 3, 1956; children—Robert Ancil, Joseph Kelley, Barry Allan, Alicia Carol. Served with U.S. Air Force, 1949-59, capt. USAR, 1961-71, ret., 1971; admitted to Tex. bar, 1961; atty. Sinclair Oil & Gas Co., Midland, Tex., 1962-66; chief counsel, sec., Tex. Oil & Gas Corp., Dallas, 1967-72, gen. counsel, sec., 1972-76, v.p., gen. counsel, sec., 1976—. Active youth programs, Dallas, 1966-72. Mem. State Bar of Tex., Am. Soc. Corp. Secs. Contbr. article to legal jour. Home: Route 4 Box 570 Rockwall TX 75087 Office: 3100 Fidelity Union Tower Dallas TX 75201

YOUNG, C. B. FEHRLER, oil refinery exec.; b. Birmingham, Ala., May 13, 1908; s. Francis B. Fehrler and Lena Edna Young; B.S. in Chemistry, Howard Coll., 1930, M.S. in Chem. Engring., 1932; Ph.D. in Electrometallurgy, Columbia U., 1934; m. Lois Frances Ellis, Dec. 31, 1934; children—Charles Ellis, Frank Bernard, James T. Cons. to various cos. in N.E., 1932-44; exec. v.p. Nat. So. Products Corp., 1942-52; pres. Warrior Asphalt Corp., 1949-54, Cytho Corp., 1949—, Ala. So. Warehouse Corp., 1949—, Metals Recycling Corp., 1974—; chmn. bd. King Hardware Co., 1974—, Energy Explorations, Inc., 1976—; chmn. bd., So. Fed. Savs. & Loan. Mem. Douglas County (Ga.) Planning Bd., 1958-59; bd. dirs. Greater United Fund, Atlanta, 1975-77; hon. bd. dirs. Ga. Engring. Found., 1975—. Mem. Am. Inst. Chem. Engrs., AAAS, Chemists Club. Mem. Ch. of Christ. Author: Surface Acting Agents, 1945; Chemistry for Electroplating, 1947; contbr. articles to profl. jours. Patentee in field. Home: 1688 Caron Ln Douglasville GA 30134 Office: PO Box 796 Douglasville GA 30133

YOUNG, C. W. BILL, congressman; b. Harmarville, Pa., Dec. 16, 1930; m. Marian Ford; children—Pamela Kay, Terry Lee, Kimber. Mem. Fla. Senate, 1960-70; mem. 92d-96th Congresses from 6th Dist. Fla. Mem. Fla. Constn. Revision Commn., 1965-67; chmn. So. Hwy. Policy Com., 1966-68; del. Rep. Nat. Conv., 1968; mem. Electoral Coll., 1968. Served to sgt. Fla. N.G., 1948-57. Named One of Outstanding Young Men Am., U.S. Jr. C. of C., 1965, Most Valuable Senator, Capitol Press Corps, 1969. Methodist. Office: 2453 Rayburn House Office Bldg Washington DC 20515

YOUNG, CHARLES EDWARD, ednl. adminstr.; b. New Orleans, Dec. 25, 1942; s. Edward Jacob and Rita Honora (Gross) Y.; B.S., Loyola, New Orleans, 1964; m. Sandra Mary Krebs, Aug. 6, 1966; children—Melissa, Amy, Pamela. Sportswriter New Orleans States Item, 1964-67; asst. dir. devel. Loyola U., New Orleans, 1967-68; mem. community relations dept. New Orleans Pub. Service Inc., 1968-70; dir. pub. relations and devel. Mercy Hosp. New Orleans, 1970-74; v.p. mktg. and opns. New Orleans Fed. Savs. & Loan Assn., 1974-78; v.p. instl. advancement Loyola U., New Orleans, 1978—; mem. faculty Loyola U., 1970-72, Our Lady Holy Cross Coll., 1974-78; mem. pres. council Loyola U., 1975-78. Pres., Lakeview Civic Improvement Assn., 1976-77; founding bd. dirs. La. Right to Life, 1970-72. Mem. Jesuit Advancement Adminstrn., Bus. Boosters New Orleans (past pres.), Internat. Assn. Bus. Communicators, New Orleans League Savs. and Loans (exec. com. 1977), Loyola Alumni Assn. (pres. 1975-76), Upsilon Beta Lambda. Democrat. Roman Catholic. Club: K.C., Krewe of Alhambra. Home: 6101 Louisville St New Orleans LA 70124 Office: PO Box 139 6363 St Charles Ave New Orleans LA 70118

YOUNG, CHESTER RAYMOND, historian; b. Garlin, Ky., July 2, 1920; s. Joseph Alexander and Girtie May (Cole) Y.; A.B., Berea Coll., 1943; M.Div., So. Bapt. Theol. Sem., 1949, Th.M., 1959; M.A., U. Hawaii, 1964; Ph.D., Vanderbilt U., 1969; m. Florence Alice Baird, Aug. 7, 1947; children—Charlotte May, Chester Raymond, Virginia Ruth. Ordained to ministry Bapt. Ch., 1947; mission pastor Columbia (Ky.) Bapt. Ch., 1947-49; missionary So. Bapt. Fgn. Mission Bd., Honolulu, 1949-64; asso. prof. history Cumberland Coll., Williamsburg, Ky., 1967-69, prof. history, 1969—, head dept. history and polit. sci., 1970—. Scoutmaster, Boy Scouts Am., Honolulu, 1945-46, 50-54; asst. to Protestant chaplain Oahu Prison, Honolulu, 1959-64; exec. com. Kalihi-Palama Community Council, Honolulu, 1959-64, 2nd v.p. 1963-64. Served with U.S. Army, 1943-45. Mem. Soc. Am. Archivists, Orgn. Am. Historians, Am. Hist. Assn., Va. Hist. Soc., Ky. Hist. Soc., So. Bapt. Hist. Soc., Ky. Council Archives, Ky. Assn. Tchrs. History. Republican. Contbr. articles in field to profl. jours. Home: 658 College Station Williamsburg KY 40769 Office: 658 College Sta Williamsburg KY 40769

YOUNG, DAVID NELSON, journalist, filmmaker, photographer; b. Baton Rouge, Nov. 12, 1953; s. Nelson Joseph and Agnes Eugenie (LeBlanc) Y.; student La. State U., 1971-73, U. Southwestern La., 1974-76, Nikon Sch. Photography, Baton Rouge, 1976; m. Michele Jeanine Bedel, May 7, 1977; 1 son, Jason Nicholas. Gen. assignment reporter Gonzales (La.) Weekly, 1971-73, news and photog. editor, 1977—; producer, dir. Sta. WBJ-TV U. Southwestern La., Lafayette, 1975-76; news dir. Sta. KRVS, Lafayette, 1975-76; chief news film photographer Sta. KATC-TV, Lafayette, 1976-77; founder, pres. Media-Magic Communications Group, Inc., Gonzales, 1979—; contbg. editor KSMI-FM, Donaldsonville, La.; talk show host WSLG-AM, Gonzales; freelance journalist and photographer. Dir. public relations and photography Council for Devel. of French in La.; apptd. Goodwill Ambassador to France, City of Gonzales, 1978. Recipient Cystic Fibrosis Vol. award, 1977, 78; Ofcl. Commendation for outstanding reporting of local issues Gonzales Mayor and Council, 1979. Mem. La. Press Assn., Nat. Geog. Soc., Internat. Platform Assn., Profl. Photographers Assn., Nat. Hist. Soc., Nat. Writers Club, Gonzales C. of C. Democrat. Roman Catholic. Club: Art and Photography Guild Gonzales. Founder Sportsman, a community outdoor publ., 1971. Home: 514 N Marchand Ave Gonzales LA 70737

YOUNG, DENNIS ALLEN, mortgage co. exec.; b. Marion, Ohio, Nov. 11, 1946; s. Waller Raymond and Louise (Tibbles) Y.; B.S. in Bus. Adminstrn., East Carolina U., 1969; m. Ellen Linda Gowens, July 14, 1968; children—Mari Allison, Dennis Allen. Sr. acct. A.M. Pullen & Co., Winston Salem, N.C., 1969-72; exec. vp., treas. Atlantic Mortgage & Investment Co., Winston Salem, 1972—; pres. Atlantic Comml. Sales, Inc. Served with USAR, 1969-70. C.P.A., N.C.; lic. real estate broker, N.C., S.C. Mem. N.C. Assn. C.P.A.'s, Am. Inst. C.P.A.'s, Republican. Baptist. Home: Route 3 Advance NC 27006 Office: 2000 W 1st St Winston Salem NC 27104

YOUNG, FLOY WOODUL, educator; b. Hope, Ark.; d. John Henry and Lou (Wylie) Woodul; student with Silvio Scionti, Chgo. Musical Coll., 1935, 36, 37, North Tex. Tchrs. Coll., Denton, 1942-49; m. Benjamin Richard Young, Sept. 13, 1924 (dec.); 1 son, John Richard. Field rep., guest tchr. in progressive series of piano Art Pub. Soc., St. Louis, 1926-28; pvt. tchr. piano, Shreveport, La., 1929—; organist Broadmoor Baptist Ch., Shreveport, 1938-78. Certified piano tchr., Music Tchrs. Nat. Assn. Mem. Am. Coll. Musicians, Nat., La. State, Greater Shreveport music tchrs. assns. Democrat. Address: 902 Anniston St Shreveport LA 71105

YOUNG, FRANK PAUL, research adminstr.; b. Cleve., Aug. 17, 1950; s. Frank Paul and Letha Lena (Mackey) Pulaski; B.S., Ga. State U., 1972, M.A., 1974. Research planner Dept. Community and Human Devel., Atlanta, 1971-72; research asso., mgmt. dept. Ga. State U., 1972-73, research asso. Sch. Urban Life, 1973-74; research cons. James Wright & Assos., 1974; research dir. Dept. Parks, Libraries, Cultural and Internat. Affairs, 1974-76; social scientist Inst. Urban Research and Service, Atlanta, 1976-77. Named One of Five Outstanding Young Men, Atlanta Jaycees, 1978. Mem. Lambda Iota Tau, Phi Alpha Theta. Roman Catholic. Author: (with William Nash) Church-Community Relations in Transition Neighborhoods, 1974; The Import of the Political System in Regard to Legislative Innovation in the American States, 1974; (with Carlton Rochell) Atlanta's Neighborhoods, 2 vols., 1975; Community Participation Information Systems, 1975; contbr. articles to profl. jours. Home: 2021 Briarcliff Rd Atlanta GA 30329 Office: 1540 Stewart Ave Atlanta GA 30310

YOUNG, FREDERICK LE, JR., architect, engr., missionary; b. Dallas, Dec. 30, 1925; s. Frederick L. and Lillie P. Y.; B.S., U. Tex., 1953, M.S., 1960; m. M. Sue Box, Nov. 28, 1953; children—Martha Sue, Kathryn Ann. Engr., Shell Oil Co., Corpus Christi, Tex., 1952-58; chief architect, engr. Meth. Bd. Missions, Lahore, Pakistan, 1959-66; environ. engr. Forrest and Cotton, Inc., Dallas, 1966-69; v.p. Snell Environ. Group, Lansing, Mich., 1969-72; water and waste water coordinator for constrn. mgmt. City of Austin (Tex.), 1972-75; pres. Constrn. Arts Assn., 1975—; v.p. Snell Engring.; spl. studies EPA. Bd. dirs. Operation Bootstrap. Served with USN, 1945-46. Recipient commendation for United Christian Hosp. design and constrn. from Pakistan, 1965. Mem. ASCE, Nat. Soc. Profl. Engrs., Water Pollution Control Fedn., AIA, Earth Awareness Found. Club (pres.). Democrat. Water, wastewater treatment inventions; contbr. articles in field to Civil Engring. Home: PO Box 19471 Dallas TX 75219 Office: EPA Region 6 Dallas TX 75270

YOUNG, GEORGE CRESSLER, chief judge; b. Cin., Aug. 4, 1916; s. George Phillip and Gladys (Crassler) Y.; student Rollins Coll., 1934; A.B., U. Fla., 1938, LL.B., 1940; postgrad. Harvard Coll. Law, 1947; m. Iris June Hart, Oct. 6, 1951; children—George Cressler, Barbara Ann. Admitted to Fla. bar, 1940; asst. city attt., Winter Haven, Fla., 1941-42; asso. in law firm Smathers, Thompson, Maxwell & Dyer, Miami, Fla., 1947; adminstr., also legislative asst. to Senator George Smathers, Fla., 1948-52; asst. U.S. atty., 1952; partner law firm Knight, Kincaid, Young & Harris, 1953-61; U.S. dist. judge Fla., 1961—, now chief judge. Mem. com. adminstrn. Fed. Magistrates System. Bd. dirs. United Cerebral Palsy Jacksonville, 1953-60. Served from ensign to lt. USNR, 1942-46, ETO, PTO. Mem. Am. (mem. spl.

com. adminstrn. criminal justice 1975-76), Jacksonville (past pres.) bar assns., Fla. Bar (bd. govs. 1961), Am. Law Inst., C. of C. (chmn. nat. affairs com. 1956-57), Order of Coif, Phi Beta Kappa, Phi Kappa Phi, Phi Delta Phi, Fla. Blue Key, Sigma Alpha Epsilon. Home: 2424 Shrewsbury Rd Orlando FL 32803 Office: US Ct House Orlando FL 32801

YOUNG, HENRY ARCHIE, educator; b. West Monroe, La.; s. Eddie and Arniece Marguerite (Gordon) Y.; B.A., So. U., 1955; M.A., La. State U., 1963; Ph.D., Kans. State U., 1973; m. Evelyn M. Stamper, Dec. 24, 1957; children—Ronald Paul, Darryl Wayne, Ericka Arniece. Speech correctionist Iberville Parish (La.) Sch. Bd., 1957-61; supervising tchr. speech and theatre So. U., Baton Rouge, 1961-70, asso. prof., 1973-77, prof., dir. communication skills center, 1977—; teaching asst. Kans. State U., Manhattan, 1971-73. Served with U.S. Army, 1955-57. Mem. Speech Communication Assn., Assn. Supervision and Curriculum Devel., Phi Delta Kappa, Kappa Phi Kappa, Alpha Psi Omega, Alpha Phi Alpha. Democrat. Baptist. Club: Conquistodors Social and Civic. Home: 1187 Bayberry Ave Baton Rouge LA 70807 Office: So U PO Box 11406 Baton Rouge LA 70813

YOUNG, JAMES CHARLES, engring. co. exec.; b. Shawnee, Okla., Nov. 25, 1931; s. James Carl and Evelyn Lucille (McEwen) Y.; student Oklahoma City U., 1949-50; B.B.A., Ga. State U., 1963; m. Carol Ann Gesford, Feb. 22, 1958; children—James Charles, Jennifer Lynn. Asst. exec. dir. Kappa Alpha Order, Atlanta, 1956-63; dir. info. and edn. Okla. Restaurant Assn., Oklahoma City, 1963-64; mgr. communications Oklahoma City aero comdr. div. North Am. Rockwell Co., 1964-68; dir. pub. relations Star Mfg. Co., Oklahoma City, 1968-72; dir. mktg. communications C-E Natco, Combustion Engring., Inc., Tulsa, 1972—. Div. chmn. Oklahoma City United Appeal, 1969-71; mem. fund raising com. Oklahoma City Jr. Achievement, 1970; mem. budget com. Tulsa United Way, 1977. Served with inf. U.S. Army, 1950-52; Japan, Korea. Recipient B. L. Semptner Meml. award Oklahoma City United Appeal, 1969, 70; Named Editor of Yr., Oklahoma City chpt. Indsl. Editors, 1967; recipient 1st Pl. Advt. awards Oklahoma City and Tulsa Advt. Clubs, 1969, 72, 73, 75-77, 79, award of Excellence, Dist. V Internat. Council Indsl. Editors, 1968. Mem. Pub. Relations Soc. Am. (accredited), Bus./Profl. Advertisers Assn. (cert. bus. communicator), Internat. Bus. Communicators (pres. Oklahoma City chpt.). Republican. Presbyterian. Clubs: Lakeview Country (Oklahoma City); The Summit, Tulsa Press (Tulsa); Admiral's, Masons, Kappa Alpha Order (Ct. of Honor 1959, exec. council 1974-77). Editor Kappa Alpha Jour., 1959-71, Midsouthwest Foodservice Mag., 1963-64. Home: 7423 E 70th St S Tulsa OK 74133 Office: PO Box 1710 Tulsa OK 74101

YOUNG, JAMES GIVENS, food processing exec.; b. Florence, S.C., Aug. 6, 1921; s. Thomas Benton and Mary Evelyn (Brown) Y.; B.S., Clemson U., 1942; m. Florence Hunter, Nov. 21, 1942; children—Marian Young Howard, Elizabeth Young Gilbert, Mary Miles Young Swink. Pres. Young Pecan Shelling Co., Inc., Florence, 1945—, Young Pecan Sales Corp., Florence, 1963—, Calhoun Pecan Co., Inc., Florence, 1968—; dir. Florence Peoples' Fed. Savs. & Loan Assn.; mem. adv. bd. S.C. Nat. Bank, Florence, 1956—. Trustee McLeod Meml. Hosp., Florence, 1959-79, chmn. bd., 1975-79; trustee James F. Byrnes Acad., Florence, 1965-79, Coker Coll., Hartsville, S.C., 1977—; trustee New McLeod Regional Med. Center, Florence, 1975—, chmn. bd., 1975—. Served to capt. AUS, 1942-45. Decorated Silver Star, Bronze Star, Purple Heart with oak leaf cluster; recipient Distinguished Alumni award Clemson U., 1975; Greater Florence C. of C. award, 1975; Service to Mankind award Sertoma Clubs Florence, 1976. Mem. Nat. Pecan Shellers Processors Assn. (pres. 1959-61, dir. 1950—), Food Industry Assn. S.C. (pres. 1972-74, dir. 1974-75). Presbyterian (deacon). Club: Rotary. Home: 1704 Highland Ave Florence SC 29501 Office: PO Drawer 5779 Young Pecan Shelling Co 1200 Pecan St Florence SC 29501

YOUNG, JAMES HARVEY, pharmacist, air force officer; b. Homerville, Ga., July 27, 1948; s. James Leon and Alice Jean (Corbitt) Y.; A.S., S. Ga. Coll., 1968; B.S. in Pharmacy, Mercer U., 1971; m. Nancy Lindsey Grant, July 14, 1968; 1 dau., Dawn Renee. Pharmacist, Eckerd Drugs, Valdosta, Ga., 1972-74; owner, operator Economy Drugs, Valdosta, 1974-78; commd. 1st lt. USAF, 1978, advanced to capt., 1978; chief of outpatient pharmacy USAF Regional Hospital, Maxwell AFB, Ala., 1978—. Bd. dirs. Lowndes chpt. Kidney Found. of Ga., 1977; chmn, steering com., pres., chmn. bd. Lowndes Diabetes Assn., 1976-77, bd. dirs. Ga. chpt., 1977-78. Mem. Tri-County Pharm. Assn. (pres.), Ga. Pharm. Assn. (v.p. 8th Dist.). Baptist. Clubs: Shriners, Masons. Home: 607A 7th St Maxwell Air Force Base AL 36113 Office: USAF Regional Hospital SGHP Maxwell Air Force Base AL 36112

YOUNG, JAMES HILLIARD, coll. adminstr.; b. Rocky Mount, N.C., Jan. 29, 1946; s. John Wesley and Lois Sessoms Y.; B.S. in English, East Carolina U., 1968, M.A. in Guidance and Counseling, 1974; Ed.D. in Adult and Community Coll. Edn., N.C. State U., 1977; m. Rebecca Barrow, June 1, 1968; children—Laura, Lisa. Acting asst. dean men East Carolina U., Greenville, N.C., 1968, dir. sports info., 1971-72; dir. Farmville br. Pitt Tech. Inst., Greenville, 1969-71, asst. to pres., 1972-75; dir. instnl. devel. Pitt Community Coll., Greenville, 1977—; doctoral intern N.C. Bd. Edn., 1975-77; adj. grad. prof. higher and adult edn. George Washington U.; adj. grad. prof. adult and community coll. edn. N.C. State U.; v.p. Edu-Tec, Inc., alt. energy co.; cons. grants, resource devel., mgmt. and evaluation to various jr. and community colls.; mem. Nat. Council for Resource Devel. of Am. Assn. Community and Jr. Coll., 1973—, bd. dirs., 1977—. Mem. N.C. Community Coll. Adult Edn. Assn., N.C. Assn. for Research in Edn. Democrat. Presbyterian. Editorial asst. Community Coll. Rev., 1975-77. Home: 1900 E 6th St Greenville NC 27834 Office: Pitt Community Coll PO Drawer 7007 Greenville NC 27834

YOUNG, JAMES ROBERT, city ofcl.; b. Lubbock, Tex., Jan. 15, 1947; s. Henry Ephraham and Ella Faye (Hickman) Y.; student San Jacinto Coll., 1976-78; m. Linda Marie Tate, July 24, 1976; 1 dau., Angela Dee. Reporter, KWFR AM-FM, San Angelo, Tex., 1971; news dir. KORA AM-FM, Bryan, Tex., 1972; news anchorman KULF AM-FM, Houston, 1973-77; regional mgr. public info. Tex. Office Traffic Safety, Houston, 1978; asst. dir. communications Office of Mayor, Houston, 1979—. Served with USN, 1966-70. Mem. Tex. Public Relations Assn., Public Relations Found. Tex. (charter life), Phi Theta Kappa. Office: 900 Bagby St Houston TX 77001

YOUNG, JANICE GAIL ROBERTS, interior designer; b. Monroe, Ga., July 18, 1947; s. John Lee and Melba Louise (Richardson) Roberts; B. Interior Design, Auburn U., 1969. Designer, adminstrv. asst. So. Wholesale Furniture/Denrell Contract, Inc., Jacksonville, Fla., 1971-74; dir. interior design, asst. v.p. Kemp, Bunch & Jackson Architects, Inc., Jacksonville, 1974—; exhibit designer Arts Festival '78, Jacksonville Art Mus., Friends of Mus., Jacksonville Children's Hosp., Antiques Show. Mem. Am. Soc. Interior Designers (Area III sec. 1976-77, Fla. North sec., dir. 1978, service award 1978). Democrat. Episcopalian. Home: 1624 River Rd Jacksonville FL 32207 Office: 1320 Seaboard Coastline Bldg Jacksonville FL 32202

YOUNG, JERRY LYNN, educator; b. Crystal Springs, Miss., May 11, 1942; s. Bervy Arthur and Edna Earl (Crawford) Y.; B.S., U. So. Miss., 1964; M.A. (NDEA fellow), U. South Ala., 1971; Ed.D. (NDEA fellow), U. Ala., 1973; m. Lynn Dudley Carter, Nov. 26, 1965; 1 dau., Lynnell. Tchr. math. St. Tammany Parish (La.) Sch. Bd., 1964-66, Baldwin County (Ala.) Sch. Bd., 1966-71; dir. project Learning Activity Package, Title III-NDEA. Demopolis (Ala.) City Schs., 1973-74; curriculum specialist Ala. Boys Indsl. Sch., Birmingham, 1974-75; asso. prof. curriculum and instrn. U. So. Miss., Hattiesburg, 1975—; cons. in field. Sunday Sch. tchr. So. Baptist Ch., Robertsdale, Ala., 1966-71, deacon, 1969-71; lay leader, tchr. United Meth. Ch., Hattiesburg, 1977-78; bd. dirs. Hattiesburg Travelers Aid Soc. Mem. Assn. for Supervision and Curriculum Devel., Miss. Assn. for Supervision and Curriculum Devel., Assn. Miss. Tchr. Educators, Phi Delta Kappa. Home: 106 Mary Circle Hattiesburg MS 39401 Office: Dept Curriculum and Instruction U So Miss So Sta Box 9293 Hattiesburg MS 39401

YOUNG, JESS WOLLETT, lawyer; b. San Antonio, Sept. 16, 1926; s. James and Zetta (Alonso) Y.; student Southwestern U., 1944, U. Tex., 1946-49; B.A., Trinity U., 1956; LL.B., St. Mary's Sch. Law, 1958; m. Mary Alma Keeter, Apr. 17, 1954; children—Zetta, Imogen. Admitted to Tex. bar, 1957; practiced in San Antonio, 1957—; mem. firm, pres., dir. Young & Richards, Inc., 1978—; dir. Dean L. Leeper Co., Dallas; county judge Bexar County (Tex.), 1964; city atty. Olmos Park (Tex.), 1965-70, Poteet (Tex.), 1975—. Precinct committeeman, San Antonio, 1964-76; state Democratic committeeman, 1970-72. Served with USNR, 1944-46. Mem. Am., San Antonio bar assns., State Bar Tex., Delta Theta Phi. Club: San Antonio Gun (dir. 1958-63). Republican. Home: 321 Thelma Dr San Antonio TX 78212 Office: 107 W Mistletoe Ave San Antonio TX 78212

YOUNG, JOE ASBURY, retailer, real estate broker; b. Easley, S.C., July 15, 1936; s. Gartrell Asbury and Irene Elaine (Boggs) Y.; student Am. U., 1969-70, U. Notre Dame, 1971; m. Brenda Jean Walker, May 10, 1972; 1 dau., Esther Arlene. Owner, mgr., drive-in restaurant, Easley, S.C., 1956-59; salesman, Jamison Furniture Co., Easley, 1959-62; store mgr., Bridges Furniture Co., Greenville, S.C., 1962-68; mgr. Magnavox store, Greenville, 1968-69; owner, operator, Young's Inc., and real estate broker, Easley, 1969—. Pres. Easley Church Softball Leagues, 1960-64; pres. Easley C. of C., 1971-72; pres. Easley Ch. of God Young People's Assn., 1959-64. Recipient service award, Easley C. of C., 1971, spl. newspaper advt. awards, 1971, 72; named Gibson appliance retailer of year in S.C., 1970, 71. Mem. Town and Country Plaza Merchants Assn. (pres.), Easley C. of C. (pres. 1979-80). Clubs: Lions (pres. Easley fellowship, 1963-64); Easley Rotary. Inventor spl. bookkeeping system for major appliance retail stores. Home: Route 1 Liberty SC 29657 Office: Town and Country Plaza Easley SC 29640

YOUNG, JOHN, former congressman; b. Corpus Christi, Tex., Nov. 10, 1916; B.A., St. Edward's U., 1937, LL.D., 1961; student law, U. Tex., 1940; m. Jane F. Gallier, Jan. 21, 1950 (dec.); children—Catherine Gaffney, Nancy Rae, John Andrew, Robert Harold, Mary Patricia. Admitted to Tex. bar, 1940, U.S. Supreme Ct. bar; asst. county atty. Nueces County (Tex.), 1946; asst. dist. atty. Nueces County, 1947-50, county atty., 1951-52, county judge, 1953-56; mem. 85th-95th Congresses from 14th Tex. Dist. Served in USNR, 1941-45. Decorated Presdl. Unit Citation. Mem. Tex., Nueces County bar assns., VFW, Am. Legion, DAV. Clubs: K.C., Elks, Moose. Home: 941 Delaine St Corpus Christi TX 78411

YOUNG, JOHN HARLEY, electronics engr.; b. Springfield, Mo., May 10, 1944; s. Louis L. and Clarinda Elizabeth (Kelly) Y.; A.B., Drury Coll., 1966; M.S., Purdue U., 1975; m. Pamela Sue Larkin, Aug. 10, 1965; 1 son, John Edward. Broadcast engr. Ind. Broadcasters, Inc., Springfield, 1964-67; engr. Magnavox Gov. & Indsl. Electronics Co., Ft. Wayne, Ind., 1967-74, sr. engr., 1974-77; sr. engr. LaBarge Electronics, Tulsa, 1977-78; engr. Century Geophys. Corp., Tulsa, 1978—. Music dir. Calvary Ind. Baptist Ch., Ft. Wayne, 1974-76. Mem. IEEE, Internat. Soc. Hybrid Microelectronics, Automatic Test Equipment Assn., Creation Research Soc., Phi Alpha Beta, Phi Eta Sigma. Editor Okla. Trumpet, 1979—; patentee in field. Office: 6650 E Apache Tulsa OK 74115

YOUNG, JOHN RANDOLPH, JR., physician; b. Greenwood, Miss., Aug. 30, 1936; s. John Randolph and Nancy Hathorn (Statham) Y.; B.S., Tulane U., 1958, M.D., 1961; m. Eleanor Minor Eustis, Oct. 18, 1963. Intern, Charity Hosp. La., New Orleans, 1961-62; resident otolaryngology New Orleans Eye, Ear, Nose and Throat Hosp., 1962-65; fellow gen. surgery Oshsner Found. Hosp., New Orleans, 1965-66; chief otolaryngology USAF Hosp., Dyess AFB, Tex., 1966-68; pvt. practice ltd. to otolaryngology, Natchez, Miss., 1968—; mem. staff Natchez Community, Jefferson Davis Meml., Natchez Charity hosps.; clin. instr. U. Miss. Sch. Medicine, Tulane Sch. Medicine; dir. 1st Natchez Bank; mem. Miss. Comprehensive Health Planning Council, 1972-75. Trustee Miss. Eleemosynary Instns., 1972—, chmn., 1976—. Served to capt. USAF, 1966-68. Diplomate Am. Bd. Otolaryngology. Fellow A.C.S.; mem. AMA, Am. Acad. Ophthalmology and Otolaryngology, Miss. Med. Assn., La.-Miss. Ophthalmol. and Otolaryngol. Soc., Am. Acad. Facial Plastic and Reconstructive Surgery, Soc. War of 1812, Phi Delta Theta. Episcopalian. Clubs: Rotary, Pickwick, Pendennis (New Orleans). Contbr. articles to profl. jours. Home: The Hedges Route 3 Natchez MS 39120 Office: 55 Sergeant Prentiss Dr Natchez MS 39120

YOUNG, LARRY TRUMAN, retail mcht.; b. Abilene, Tex., June 24, 1943; s. Zearl Truman and Dolly Dimple Y.; student N.Mex. Mil. Inst., 1958-62, U. Minn., 1962-63; m. Patricia Sue Baker, Jan. 30, 1962; children—Serena M., Sabra M., Stacy M. Vice pres., sales mgr. Zearl T. Young, Inc., Hobbs, N.Mex., 1963-74; pres. Furniture Land, Inc., Hobbs, 1965—, also owner, operator Levelland True Value Hardware (Tex.), 1975—. Dir. Hobbs Miss N.Mex. Pageant, 1964-66; pres. Levelland United Fund, 1976-78. Mem. Levelland C. of C. (dir. 1976-78), Nat. Fedn. Ind. Bus., S.W. Hardware Assn., Am. Bus. Club (pres. Hobbs 1969). Republican. Club: Masons. Home: 2033 Longhorn St Levelland TX 79336 Office: 1709 Ave H Levelland TX 79336

YOUNG, LAWRENCE EUGENE, physician; b. Waterville, Ohio, Mar. 18, 1913; s. William Edward and Ruth Elizabeth (Farnsworth) Y.; B.A., Ohio Wesleyan U., 1935, D.Sc. (hon.), 1967; M.D., U. Rochester, 1939; D.Sc. (hon.), Med. Coll. Ohio, Toledo, 1977; m. Annette Briggs, May 25, 1940; children—Carolyn Ann, Beverly Jane, Marjorie Briggs, Anderson Briggs. Intern, Strong Meml. Hosp., Rochester, N.Y., 1939-40, asst. resident, 1940-41, chief resident in medicine, 1942-43, physician-in-chief, 1957-74; asst. in bacteriology Johns Hopkins U., asst. in medicine Johns Hopkins Hosp., Balt., 1941-42; instr. U. Rochester, 1943-44, fellow, 1946-47, asst. prof., 1948-50, asso. prof., 1950-57, Dewey prof., chmn. dept., 1957-74, Alumni Disting. Service prof., 1974-78, emeritus, 1978—; disting. vis. prof. medicine U. South Fla., Tampa, 1978—; dir. U. Rochester Asso. Hosps. Program in Internal Medicine, 1974-78; bd. dirs. Genesee Valley Med. Care, 1956-59, Genesee Valley Group Health Assn., Rochester, 1977-78; chmn. planning com. Rochester Regional Med. Program, 1965-70; bd. dirs. clin. scholars program Robert Wood Johnson Found., 1978—. Served to lt. M.C., USNR, 1944-46. Recipient Gold medal U. Rochester Med. Alumni Assn., 1973, citation to faculty, 1978, Albert D. Kaiser award Rochester Acad. Medicine, 1978; diplomate Am. Bd. Internal Medicine. Master A.C.P. (bd. govs. Upstate N.Y. 1959-61, regent 1972-78, v.p. 1976-77); mem. Am. Soc. Hematology, Internat. Soc. Hematology, Am. Soc. Clin. Investigation, Assn. Am. Physicians (pres. 1973-74), Assn. Profs. of Medicine (pres. 1966-67, Robert H. Williams Disting. Chmn. Medicine award 1976). Mem. editorial bd. Jour. Clin. Investigation, 1954-58, Am. Jour. Medicine, 1961-74; contbr. articles to med. jours., chpts. in books. Home: 5216 El Toro Ct Apt 124 Tampa FL 33603 Office: 12901 N 30th St Tampa FL 33612

YOUNG, MARGARET ALETHA MCMULLEN (MRS. HERBERT WILSON YOUNG), social worker; b. Vossburg, Miss., June 13, 1916; d. Grady Garland and Virgie Aletha (Moore) McMullen; B.A. cum laude, Columbia Bible Coll., 1949; grad. Massey Bus. Coll., 1958; M.S.W., Fla. State U., 1965; postgrad. Jacksonville U., 1961-62, Tulane U., 1967, Miss. U. for Women, 1976; m. Herbert Wilson Young, Aug. 19, 1959. Dir. Christian edn. Eau Claire Presbyn. Ch., Columbia, S.C., 1946-51; tchr. Massey Bus. Coll., Jacksonville, Fla., 1954-57, office mgr., 1957-59; social worker, unit supr. Fla. div. Family Services, St. Petersburg, 1960-66, dist. casework supr., 1966-71; social worker, 1971-77; project supr. Project Playpen, Inc., 1977—. Mem. Acad. Certified Social Workers, Nat. Assn. Social Workers (pres. Tampa Bay chpt. 1973-74, chmn. state nominating com. 1974-76, registered clin. social worker), Fla. Assn. on Children Under Six. Democrat. Presbyn. Rotary Ann (pres. 1970-71). Home: 330 Roebling Rd N Belleair Clearwater FL 33516 Office: 4140 49th St N Saint Petersburg FL 33709

YOUNG, MARJORIE WILLIS, writer, journalist, lectr.; b. Mansfield, Ohio; d. John Edgar and Mary Adelle (Reiter) Willis; student agr. Cornell U., 1924; student Art Students League, 1925-27, Cooper Union, 1925-27, Columbia U., 1927, 43, Sorbonne, U. Paris, 1928-30, Japanese Lang. Sch., Tokyo, 1934-35, N.Y. U., 1944; m. James Russell Young, Oct. 2, 1934; 1 son, Willis Patterson. Columnist in Far East, Internat. News Service, 1938-41; feature writer King Features Syndicate, 1939, Saturday Pictorial Rev., 1941-45; asst. tech. dir. motion picture Behind the Rising Sun, 1943; research dept. Believe It or Not, 1946-43; feature editor and columnist The Sunday Star, Wilmington, Del., 1946-48; promotion dir. David McKay Pub. Co., 1945-48; lectr. Nat. Concert and Artists Corp., 1942-43; feature writer Anderson (S.C.) Independent, 1949-73; feature writer Anderson Daily Mail, 1949-73, asso. editor The New South, ann. spl. edit. of Daily Mail, 1966-73; editor The Safety Jour., Anderson, 1953—; program moderator Decorating for a Holiday, Sta. WAIM-TV, 1953-54, safety program moderator WAIM-TV, 1953—, program moderator How to Cut and Sew, 1954-55, travel feature program WAIM-WCAC-FM, 1973—; travel editor Quote mag., 1977—; editor Vets. of Safety news page, What's What monthly; dir. Capitol City Communications, Inc. Spl. scroll dir. Chinese War Orphans Relief, 1941-45; publicity dir. Crusade for Children, State of Del., 1948; publicity chmn. S.C. Indsl. Nurses Assn., 1953; dir. S.C. 4-H Club TV Safety Program, 1953; coordinator Ann. S.C. State Landmark Conf., 1979. Bd. dirs. Anderson Heritage, Inc. Recipient various awards for safety activities including Distinguished Service award S.C. Occupational Safety Council, 1973. Mem. U. S.C. Caroliniana Soc., Writers Assn. Am., Am. Women in Radio and TV, Nat. Recreation Assn., S.C. Recreation Soc. (v.p. and program dir. 1954-56), Anderson County Hist. Soc. (pres. 1978-80), Am. Soc. Safety Engrs., Vets. Safety Internat., (pres. 1979), DAR. Episcopalian. Clubs: Am. Newspaper Women's, Washington Press (Washington); Overseas Press of Am.; Cornell Women's (N.Y.C.). Author: Decorating for Joyful Occasions, 1952; It's Time for Christmas Decorations, 1957; Fodor's Tour Guide of South Carolina, 1966-68, Tour Guide of Georgia, 1966-67; Japanese American Cook Book, 1972; The Cateechee Trail, 1975; South Carolina's Women Patriots of the American Revolution, 1975. Editor: Textile Leaders, 1963. Home: 2003 Laurel Dr Anderson SC 29621 Office: Safety Jour PO Box 4189 Anderson SC 29622

YOUNG, PATRICK JEN HWA, architect; b. Shanghai, China, Mar. 17, 1930; s. Andrew A.J. and Helen (Loh) Y.; came to U.S., 1967, naturalized, 1972; Diplom Ingenieur, Architekt, Technische Hochschule, Darmstadt, Ger., 1962; m. Hildegard Luise Vassmer, Sept. 6, 1958. Architect, 1967—. Mem. AIA, Am. Inst. Physics, Acoustical Soc. Am. Address: PO Box 2396 Jackson MS 39205

YOUNG, RAYMOND VICTOR, chem. engr.; b. Johnson City, Tenn., Feb. 1, 1940; s. Raymond and Doris Marie (Range) Y.; B.S. in Chem. Engring., U. Tenn., 1963. Process design engr. Sinclair Research, Inc., Harvey, Ill., 1963-66; process engr. Sinclair-Koppers Co., Port Arthur, Tex., 1966-70, sr. process engr., 1970-75; chief environ. engr. Arco Polymers, Inc., Port Arthur, 1975—. Mem. City of Port Arthur Clean Air Com., 1978—, air quality adv. com. SE Tex. Regional Planning Commn., 1978. Recipient Distinguished Indsl. Achievement award Lamar U., 1975. Mem. Am. Inst. Chem. Engrs., Water Pollution Control Fedn., Tex. Water Pollution Control Assn., Port Arthur C. of C. (environ. com. 1974-76, air quality task force 1978—), Air Pollution Control Assn., Port Arthur Little Theatre, Tau Beta Pi. Home: 4117 Gulfway Port Arthur TX 77640 Office: PO Box 848 Port Arthur TX 77640

YOUNG, RICHARD ALAN, athletic dir.; b. Columbus, Ohio, Jan. 3, 1932; s. Harry H. and Christine A. (Wickline) Y.; B.S. (Big Ten scholar athlete 1954 All-Am. Scholarship Team 1954), Ohio State U., Columbus, 1955, M.A., 1959; Ph.D. (Outstanding Achievement award), Bowling Green (Ohio) State U., 1975; m. Alexandra Waddell, Mar. 22, 1954; children—Timothy, Pamela, Alyson. Prof. health and phys. edn., head baseball coach Bowling Green State U., 1959-71, athletic dir., 1971-78; athletic dir. Okla. State U., Stillwater, 1978—; bd. visitors U.S. Sports Acad. Served as aviator USN, 1955-58. Mem. Nat. Collegiate Athletic Assn., Nat. Assn. Collegiate Dirs. Athletics. Office: Athletic Dept Okla State Univ Stillwater OK 74074

YOUNG, ROBERT ALEXANDER, marine geologist; b. Boston, Jan. 8, 1942; s. Frank A. and Joyce E. Y.; B.S., Bklyn. Coll., 1969; M.S., M.I.T., 1972, Ph.D., 1975; m. Rosemary Masure, June 26, 1966; children—Susanna, Nicole. Research asst. Woods Hole Oceanographic Inst., 1972-75; research oceanographer Atlantic Oceanographic and Meteorol. Labs., NOAA, Miami, Fla., 1975—; adj. prof. marine geology U. Miami. Served with U.S. Army, 1959-63. Mem. Am. Geophys. Union, Geol. Soc. Am. Office: Atlantic Oceanographic and Meteorol Labs NOAA 15 Rickenbacker Causeway Miami FL 33149

YOUNG, ROBERT ELI, social worker, educator; b. Phila., Apr. 18, 1931; s. Nathan C. and Clara K. (Silverman) Y.; B.A., Pa. State U., 1953; M. Social Service, Bryn Mawr Coll., 1957; D.S.W., U. Pa., 1971; m. Emily Kimball, Apr. 6, 1958; children—Joshua, Kim, Susan; m. 2d, Marguerite Ulrich, Sept. 12, 1975. Lectr., Sch. Social Work, U. Pa., 1966-70; asst. prof. Sch. Social Work, Va. Commonwealth U., Richmond, 1970-73; dir. consultation and edn. Community Mental Health Center, Norfolk, Va., 1973—; asso. prof. dept. psychiatry and behavioral sci. Eastern Va. Med. Sch., Norfolk, 1973—; clinician Community Mental Health Center, Norfolk, 1973—. Served with U.S. Army, 1955-57. Lic. clin. social worker, Va. Mem. Nat. Assn.

Social Workers, Acad. Cert. Social Workers, AAUP, Council Social Work Edn., Va. Council Social Welfare. Home: 3426 Dandelion Crescent Virginia Beach VA 23456 Office: 721 Fairfax Ave Norfolk VA 23510

YOUNG, ROGER STACY, horticulturist; b. Ft. Wayne, Ind., Sept. 27, 1920; s. Roy and Jessie (Barr) Y.; B.S., Purdue U., 1942; M.S., Mich. State U., 1949, Ph.D., 1951; m. Margaret Ann Leutzinger, July 18, 1948; children—Susan M., SethT., LeRoy W., Anne L. Horticulturist, U. Ark., Fayettville, 1949-51; farm mgr. V-M Corp., Benton Harbor, Mich., 1951-63; agrl. scientist-horticulture Univ. Exptl. Farm, W.Va. U., Kearneysville, 1963—. Vice pres. program Berkeley County Youth Fair, 1970-79; camping and activities chmn. Shenandoah Area council Potomac dist. Boy Scouts Am., 1965—. Served with U.S. Army, 1942-45. Recipient Silver Beaver award Boy Scouts Am., 1979. Mem. Am. Soc. Horticulture Sci., Weed Sci. Soc. Am., Internat. Dwarf Fruit Tree Assn., Plant Growth Regulator Working Group. Presbyterian. Home: 503 Edgemont Terr Martinsburg WV 25401 Office: Experiment Farm WVa U Kearneysville WV 25430

YOUNG, SIDNEY BEAUFORD, educator; b. Tildon, Ala., July 18, 1921; s. Samuel Ulysses and Ervia Bulah (Marsh) Y.; B.S., Hampton Inst., 1950, M.A., 1963; postgrad. U. Minn., Mpls., Am. U., Washington; m. Fredricka Robinson, Apr. 12, 1952; children—Lyndon Anthony, Deborah Denise. Tchr. math., instrumental music, dir. band Wilson High Sch., Florence, S.C., 1950-60; coll. instr. instrumental music, orchestration, dir. marching and concert bands Claflin Coll., Orangeburg, S.C., 1960—; guest conductor Santee (S.C.) Conf. Band; adjudicator band festivals S.C. Cub scoutmaster Central S.C. Council. Served with USN, 1942-45. Recipient Silver Beaver award Boy Scouts Am., 1978. Mem. Danforth Found., Phi Delta Kappa. Democrat. Methodist. Home: 2025 Myers Rd SE Orangeburg SC 29115 Office: Claflin Coll Orangeburg SC 29115

YOUNG, WALTER CROSTON, state legislator; b. Rochester, N.Y., Mar. 2, 1922; s. James and Mary Y.; B.S., Niagara U., 1949; M.S., Barry Coll., 1957; Ed.D., U. Miami, 1965; m. Dorothy Foresberg, Sept. 11, 1953; children—Nancy (Mrs. Robert Dasho), Jane, Dorothy. Faculty, grad. continuing edn. Fla. Atlantic U., Barry Coll., Fla. Mem. Pres.'s Com. Hiring of Handicapped. Bd. govs. YMCA; active Boy Scouts Am. Served with USAF; PTO. Trustee Broward Community Coll. Mem. Pembroke Pines (Fla.) City Council, 1962—, pres., 1963; mem. Pembroke Pines Zoning Bd., Pembroke Pines Bd. Adjustment; mem. Fla. Ho. of Reps. from Broward-Dade County, 1972—, mem. edn. com., bus. regulation com., environmental protection com., mem. joint conf. com. on edn., 1973, chmn. edn. com., 1980—, chmn. primary edn. council; mem. Fla. Energy Com., 1973—. Mem. Dade County Classroom Tchrs. Assn. (Sch. Bell award 1973). Lutheran (sec. bd., chmn. edn. bd., tchr. Sunday sch.). Lion (dir. Fla. eye bank). Home: 1311 SW 68 Bldg Pembroke Pines FL 33023 Office: PO Box 4647 Hollywood FL 33023

YOUNG, WALTER LEWIS, JR., bank holding co. exec.; b. Roanoke, Va., Oct. 23, 1934; s. Walter and Virginia Agnes (Wiltsee) Y.; B.S. in Physics, Coll. William and Mary, 1956; postgrad. Johns Hopkins U., 1956-59; M.B.A., Va. Poly. Inst. and State U., 1978, postgrad., 1979—; m. Doris Marie Stultz, Aug. 26, 1961. Analyst Appalachian Power Co., Roanoke, 1959-65; systems analyst 1st Nat. Exchange Bank Va., Roanoke, 1965-66, dir. data processing services, 1966-70, v.p., 1970-73; v.p., mgr. data processing Dominion Bankshares Corp., Roanoke, 1973, v.p., dir. research, 1973—, on leave, 1976—; lectr. computer sci. Roanoke Coll., Salem, Va., 1968-69. Mem. energy conservation com. Roanoke Valley C. of C., 1975. Cert. Data Processing Inst. Certification of Computer Profls. Mem. Data Processing Mgmt. Assn. (cert. in data processing), Am. Inst. Physics, Am. Phys. Soc., Am. Inst. Banking. Club: Jefferson. Home: 5009 Youngwood Dr NW Roanoke VA 24017 Office: PO Box 13327 Roanoke VA 24040

YOUNG, WALTER RICHARD, accountant; b. Danville, Ky., Aug. 7, 1947; s. Harold Basil and Dorothy (Devine) Y.; B.S. in Acctg., Western Ky. U., 1969; M.S. (Haggin fellow), U. Ky., 1972; m. Lisette Rowley, June 19, 1971; children—Walter Richard, Ralph Martin. With Price Waterhouse & Co., 1972—, audit mgr., Little Rock, 1977—. Treas. Friends Ark. Ednl. TV, 1978—, chmn. acctg. div. for festival, 1978, 79, 80. Served with USAR, 1969-71. Decorated Army Commendation medal; C.P.A., Ark., Tenn. Mem. Am. Inst. C.P.A.'s, Ark. Soc. C.P.A.'s, Tenn. Soc. C.P.A.'s, Inst. Internal Auditors, Hosp. Fin. Mgrs. Assn., Western Ky. U. Alumni Assn., U. Ky. Alumni Assn. Democrat. Baptist. Club: Western Ky. U. Ark. (pres. 1978—). Home: 1014 Chepstow Ln Sherwood AR 72116 Office: 650 Tower Bldg Little Rock AR 72201

YOUNG, WILLIAM JOHN, elec. mfg. co. exec.; b. New Castle, Pa., Jan. 18, 1920; s. Joseph A. and Mary J. (Kearns) Y.; student St. Fidelis U., 1939-41; B.S. in Psychology, Duquesne U., 1949; M.S. in Indsl. Psychology, Western Res. U., 1951; m. Bettye Jean Day, May 24, 1952; children—Joseph, William, Christopher, Mary Beth, Michael, Margaret. Chief vocat. counselor, John Carroll U., Cleve., 1950-51; with Westinghouse Electric Corp., 1951—, mgr. profl. devel., Lima, Ohio, 1951-68, personnel relations mgr., Pitts., 1968-70, Orlando, Fla., 1970—; guest lectr. Air Force U., 1960-68. Bd. dirs. Ohio State U., Lima; sponsor Orlando Jr. Achievement. Served with U.S. Army, 1941-45. Mem. Orlando Area C. of C., Am. Personnel and Guidance Assn., Am. Psychol. Assn., Nat. Vocat. Guidance Assn. Republican. Roman Catholic. Clubs: Elks, KOFC. Contbr. article to mag. Home: 204 Ranger Blvd Winter Park FL 32792 Office: 1200 W Colonial Dr Orlando FL 32804

YOUNG, WILLIAM LEE, III, physician; b. Danville, Va., June 20, 1947; s. William Lee and Dorothy Adkins Y.; B.A., U. Va., 1969, M.D., 1974; m. Patricia Flint, May 3, 1975; children—Scott, Day, Will. Resident in family practice U. Va., Charlottesville, 1974-77, chief resident, 1976-77; practice family medicine Family Practice Assos., Hickory, N.C., 1977—; mem. staff Glen R. Frye Meml. Hosp., sec. staff, 1980. Bd. dirs. N.C. Cancer Soc., 1979, Catawba Cancer Soc., 1978—; commr. Public Housing Authority, Hickory, 1978-79; adminstrv. bd. St. Lukes Meth. Ch., 1980—; bd. dirs. Catawba Valley Hospice, 1979—. Named Boss of Yr., Am. Assn. Med. Assts., 1979. Fellow Am. Acad. Family Practice; mem. Med. Soc. Va., N.C. Med. Soc., Catawba County Med. Soc., Phi Kappa Psi. Club: Rotary (dir. 1979—, v.p. 1980-81). Home: 367 6th St NW Hickory NC 28601 Office: 210 13th Ave Pl NW Hickory NC 28601

YOUNGER, HAROLD BURRNELL, dentist; b. Morgan, Tex., Sept. 20, 1906; s. Williamson Henry and Stella (McKisick) Y.; D.D.S., Baylor U., 1927; postgrad. So. Methodist U., 1943-44; m. Lois Hortense King, Feb. 21, 1935 (dec. Feb. 1975); 1 dau., Suzanne (Mrs. Aubrey Benjamen/Pinnell, Jr.); m. 2d, Rubye Frances Jameson, June 16, 1979. Practice dentistry, Dallas, 1927—. Mem. staff Children's Med. Center, Dallas, 1928—, chief dental service, 1935-67, chief emeritus, 1967—; asso. dental research Baylor U., Dallas, 1941-50, lectr., 1957-62, asso. prof., 1962-63, clin. prof., 1963-69; columnist Your Teeth and You, Dallas Morning News, 1960—; mem. Dallas Pub. Health Bd., 1962; chmn. Dallas Health Council, 1956-58; dir. Freeman Meml. Clinic, Dallas, 1953—. Mem. City-County Civil Def. Commn; chief Dallas County (Tex.) Sheriff's Res., 1950-70. Bd. dirs. Dallas Council Social Agys., 1956-60, Dallas Community Chest, 1959-60. maj. gen. Tex. State Guard ret. Fellow Am. Coll. Dentists (pres. Tex. sect. 1957-58); mem. Am. (clinician), Tex., Nebr. (hon., clinician), Colo. (clinician), N.Mex. (clinician) dental assns., Dallas County Dental Soc. (pres. 1959-60), Tex. Acad. Dental Practice Adminstrn.; Southwestern Soc. Oral Medicine (pres. 1953-54), Am. Acad. Dental Practice Adminstrn., Omicron Kappa Upsilon, Delta Sigma Delta. Methodist. Kiwanian (distinguished service award Dallas 1953, pres. Dallas 1969). Contbr. articles and chpts. to profl. publs. Home: 3615 Fairmount St Dallas TX 75219

YOUNGREN, HARRISON, educator; b. Altona, Ill., Nov. 27; s. David N. and Esther F. (Quick) Y.; A.B., Knox Coll., 1936; M.A., So. Ill. U., 1967, Ph.D., 1975; m. Margaret Rue Stansfield, June 24, 1972. Sales and market researcher Wander Co., 1936-41; commd. 1st lt. U.S. Army, 1941, advanced through grades to lt. col.; ret., 1962; editor Mt. Carmel (Ill.) Daily Republican Register, 1962-64; mem. faculty dept. journalism U. Wis.-Oshkosh, 1969-73; prof. journalism Angelo State U., San Angelo, Tex., 1973—, head dept., 1973-74, 78-79; adviser in mass communications Republic of Korea, 1956-57, Laos, 1958-61; cons. in field. SerMem. Knox Coll. Alumni Adv. Com., 1962—. Mem. Assn. Edn. in Journalism, Tex. Journalism Edn. Council (treas.), San Angelo Press Club (dir.), Kappa Tau Alpha. Democrat. Lutheran. Home: 2425 Lindenwood Ct San Angelo TX 76901 Office: Dept Journalism Angelo State Univ San Angelo TX 76909

YOUNKIN, C. GEORGE, archivist; b. Great Bend, Kan., Oct. 13, 1910; s. Charles Franklin and Nannie Sylvia (Wilson) Y.; student Washburn U., 1932-35, Southeastern U., Washington, 1936-37; m. Ruth Ward, Dec. 27, 1939; children—Karen (Mrs. John R. Postma), Eleta (Mrs. Stephen B. McElroy), Cheryl (Mrs. Thomas R. Gamble), Chip G. With U.S. Dept. Agr., Washington, 1935-51; with Nat. Archives, Ft. Worth, 1951-75, regional archivist for Ark., La., N.Mex., Okla. and Tex., 1968-75; ret., 1975; pres. S.W. Archives Cons., 1975—; archive cons. Kiowa Hist. and Research Assn., Carnegie, Okla. Mem. council exec. com. Boy Scouts Am., Ft. Worth, 1975—; mem. Gov.'s Adv. Com. on Aged for Tarrant County, 1976-80. Served with AUS, 1943-45. Recipient Silver Beaver award Boy Scouts Am., 1966, Order of Arrow, Boy Scouts Am., 1966; pub. service award GSA, 1967, spl. service award Fed. Bus. Assn., 1967. Fellow Tex. State Geneal. Soc.; mem. Soc. S.W. Archivists (sec.-treas.), Internat. Council Archives, Am. Indian Hist. Soc., Soc. Am. Archivists (regional activities com.), Nat. Trust Historic Preservation, Kiowa Tia-Piah Soc. Carnegie (Okla.), Westerners Internat., Western History Assn., Tex. Hist. Assn. Dir., Llano Estacado Heritage Quar., 1974—. Home and Office: 3501 Quail Ln Arlington TX 76016

YOUNKINS, DANIEL, II, mfg. co. exec.; b. Connellsville, Pa., Oct. 21, 1934; s. Victor Daniel and Florence (Woodmansee) Y.; B.B.A., Emory U., 1956; postgrad. Fla. State U., 1968-69; m. Beverly Hayes, Nov. 23, 1974; children—Victor, Scott, Leslie. Br. mgr. IBM, 1961-70, Computer Scis. Corp., 1970-72; dist. mgr. Martin Marietta Co., 1972-73, Boeing Computer Services, 1973-74; v.p. Wheelabrator Cleanfuel Corp. subs. Wheelabrator-Frye, Inc., Washington, 1974-78; pres. Am. Fine Wire Corp., Selma, Ala., 1978--; pres., dir. Phoenix Service Industries, Inc. Vice pres. Sales and Mktg. Execs. Internat., 1970-72; pres. Am. Businessmen's Assn., 1971-72. Served to lt. USNR, 1957-60. Episcopalian. Clubs: The Club, Inverness Country (Birmingham, Ala.). Contbr. articles on energy, coal and hospitality industry to profl. jours. Home: 9225 Huntcliff Trace Atlanta GA 30338 Office: 907 Ravenwood Dr Box 966 Selma AL 36701

YOUNT, GORDON ADOLPHUS, educator; b. Tarboro, N.C., Nov. 25, 1926; s. Gordon A. and Annie E. (Whichard) Y.; B.S., Lenoir Rhyne Coll., 1947; M.A. (NSF fellow), U. N.C., 1964; m. Martha V. Cline, July 14, 1957; children by previous marriage—James F., William B. Tchr., West Nottingham Acad., 1947; analyst nylon div. E. I. duPont Co., 1948; grad. asst. U. S.C., 1949; metall. insp. Buick div. Gen. Motors Co., 1955; indsl. engr. distbn. transformer div. Gen. Electric Co., 1956-60; engr. Superior Cable Corp., 1961; tchr. sci. Newton-Conover High Sch., Newton, N.C., 1961-63; prof. physics and math. Catawba Valley Tech. Inst., 1964—; cons. physics manuscripts several pub. cos.; mem. Unifour Pollution Control Adv. Council; tech. cons. to area law enforcement units, mfrs. non-ferrous wire. Served with USNR, 1943-44, U.S. Army, 1949-54; ETO. Mem. N.C. Assn. Educators, N.C. Vocat. Assn., NEA, Am. Vocat. Assn., N.C. Edn. Assn., N.C. Vocat. Assn., Soc. 40 and 8, Non-Ferrous Wire Engrs. Assn., Carolina Geol. Soc., Catawba Fair Assn. (dir. and v.p. emeritus), Am. Legion (comdr. post 1963—), Phi Delta Kappa. Democrat. Methodist. Club: Gideons. Author: Elementary Wave Physics, 1967; A Guide to Self-Instruction in Applied Mechanics, 1970. Home: 42 30th Ave NW Hickory NC 28601 Office: Hwy 64-70 SE Hickory NC 28601

YOUNTS, CHARLES ROLPHI, ret. petroleum exec.; b. Pineville, N.C., July 7, 1895; s. William E. and Eunice (Bell) Y.; grad. Bairds U., 1912; L.H.D., Erskine Coll., 1962; m. Willie Antoinette Camp, Mar. 12, 1930. With Standard Oil Co. of N.J. and affiliates, 1912-60; pres. Plantation Pipe Line Co., 1941-59, chmn. bd., 1960. Past moderator Gen. Synod Asso. Ref. Presbyn. Ch., also trustee, mem. session, Doraville, Ga., treas. retirement plan; bd. dirs. Blue Ridge Assembly, Inc.; past pres. Churches Homes for Bus. Girls, Inc., Atlanta; bd. dirs., past chmn. Atlanta chpt. ARC; dir. So. Indsl. Relations Conf.; past trustee Erskine Coll., Due West, S.C., Met. Atlanta YMCA. Served from pvt. to 1st sgt. U.S. Army, 1917-19. Mem. Newcomen Soc., SAR. Clubs: Masons, Rotary (Atlanta Armin Maier award for 1949-50), Piedmont Driving, Capital City (Atlanta). Home: 3018 Habersham Rd NW Atlanta GA 30305 Office: 913 Healey Bldg 57 Forsyth St NW Atlanta GA 30303

YOUNTS, MILLARD STEPHEN (MITT), radio broadcasting exec.; b. Pinehurst, N.C., May 9, 1950; s. Jack Spurgeon and Elizabeth (Mendenhall) Y.; B.A. in Journalism, Washington and Lee U., 1972; M.A. in Communications, U. N.C., Chapel Hill, 1978. With Sta. WEEB, Southern Pines, N.C., 1973—, sta. mgr., 1974-79; v.p. Sandhill Community Broadcasters, Inc., Southern Pines, 1974-79, pres., gen. mgr., 1979—. Mem. Nat. Assn. Broadcasters, Daytime Broadcasters Assn. (v.p., dir.), Sigma Delta Chi, Sigma Nu, C. of C., Ducks Unlimited. Presbyterian. Clubs: Overseas Press (N.Y.C.); Country of N.C., Elks, Kiwanis. Home: Box 265 Southern Pines NC 28387 Office: Box 570 Midland Rd Southern Pines NC 28387

YOURITZIN, GLENDA GREEN, artist; b. Weatherford, Tex., Feb. 4, 1945; d. Allen and Alma Green; B.F.A. magna cum laude with honors in Painting, Tex. Christian U., 1967; M.A. in Art History (Kress fellow 1967-70), Tulane U., 1970; m. Victor Koshkin Youritzin, Aug. 20, 1970. Research asst. to dir. Kimbell Art Mus., Ft. Worth, 1968-69; curator collections Newcomb Art Sch., Tulane U., 1968-72, instr. art history, 1969-72; guest artist U. Okla., 1972-75, vis. instr. art history, 1973-76; artist-in-residence Okla. Arts and Humanities Council, 1977-78; mem. acquisition and edn. coms. Okla. Mus. Art, Oklahoma City, 1978—; one-woman exhbns.: Okla. Art Center, 1978, Philbrook Art Center, Tulsa, 1978, Central State U., Edmond, Okla., 1973, N.Tex. State U., Denton, 1974, U. Okla. Mus. Art, 1975, Mus. Southwest, Midland, Tex., 1975, Okla. Mus. Art, 1976, U. Okla., 1977; participant regional and nat. exhbns., 1967—; represented in permanent collections Nat. Mus. History and Tech., Mus. City N.Y., Williams Coll. Mus. Art, State Okla. Art Collection, U. Okla., Tex. Christian U., also pvt. collections. Adv. trustee George Lynn Cross Acad., Norman, Okla., 1978—. Mem. Coll. Art Assn. Am. Home: 1721 Oakwood Dr Norman OK 73069

YOURITZIN, VICTOR KOSHKIN, educator; b. N.Y.C., Dec. 20, 1942; s. Basil and Tatiana (Koshkin) Y.; B.A. cum laude, Williams Coll., 1964; postgrad. Columbia U., 1964-65; M.A. in Art History, Inst. Fine Arts, N.Y. U., 1967; cert. in mus. tng. N.Y. U. and Met. Mus. Art, 1969; m. Glenda Allen Green, Aug. 29, 1970. Ford Found. fellow, Met. Mus. Art, N.Y.C., 1967-68; instr. art history Vanderbilt U., Nashville, 1968-69, Newcomb Coll., Tulane U., New Orleans, 1969-72; asst. prof. history of art, U. Okla., Norman, 1972-80, asso. prof., 1980—, contbg. editor/regional corr. Art Voices/South, 1978—; cons. advanced placement exam. in art history Ednl. Testing Service, Princeton, N.J., 1974; lectr. in field; judge art exhbns.; asst. coordinator art exhibits USIA, Vanderbilt U. Tulane U., 1969-72, others. Trustee, Okla. Mus. Art, Oklahoma City, 1978—; mem. steering and planning com. arts and humanities enrichment program Norman Public Schs., 1977-79; adv. trustee George Lynn Cross Acad., Norman, 1978—. Noble fellow, 1964-65; IBM fellow, 1965; U. Okla. faculty research travel grantee, 1978, 79. Mem. Coll. Art Assn. Am., Am. Assn. Museums, Okla. Mus. Assn., Midwest Art History Soc. Contbr. articles in field to profl. jours.; editor, designer: The Poetry of the Body: Paintings by Paul Peck, 1970. Home: 1721 Oakwood Dr Norman OK 73069 Office: Sch of Art U Okla 520 Parrington Oval Norman OK 73019

YU, PETER SHU-KUEN, thoracic surgeon; b. Canton, China, Oct. 23, 1934; s. Yat-Sum and Lai-Ching (Wong) Y.; B.A., Westminster Coll., 1959; M.D., St. Louis U., 1963; m. Susan Carolyn Benedict, Oct. 15, 1966; children—Nancy Lynn, David Michael. Intern, Charity Hosp., New Orleans, 1963-64; resident in gen. surgery La. State U. Med. Center and Charity Hosp., 1964-68; resident in cardiovascular and thoracic surgery Charlotte (N.C.) Meml. Hosp., 1968-70; cardiovascular and thoracic surgeon Hamoet Hosp., Erie, Pa., 1970-73; practice medicine specializing in cardiovascular and thoracic surgery, Huntsville, Ala., 1973—; mem. staff Huntsville Hosp., Med. Center Hosp., Crestwood Hosp.; cons. Redstone Arsenal Hosp., 1974—; clin. asst. prof. surgery U. Ala. at Huntsville Sch. Primary Medicine, 1974—. Bd. dirs. Am. Heart Assn., N. Pa., 1971-73, Madison County chpt. Ala. Heart Assn., 1975-76. Diplomate Am. Bd. Surgery, Am. Bd. Thoracic Surgery. Fellow ACS, Am. Coll. Cardiology, Am. Coll. Angiology, Soc. Thoracic Surgery, So. Thoracic Soc.; mem. AMA, Ala., Madison County med. socs., James Rives Surg. Soc. Presbyterian. Home: 1006 Appalachee Dr Huntsville AL 35801 Office: 2102 Franklin St Huntsville AL 35801

YUDIN, LEE WILLIAM, social services adminstr.; b. Bklyn., Jan. 26, 1937; s. Irving and Dorothy Yudin; B.B.A., CCNY, then M.S. in Clin. Psychology; Ph.D., U. Mass., 1964; m. Jeanne Carter, Apr. 26, 1975; children—Daniel Arthur, Rachel Miriam, John Richard. Clin. intern Inst. of Living, Hartford, Conn., 1963-64; sr. staff psychologist Irving Schwartz Inst. for Children and Youth, Phila. Psychiat. Center, 1964-67; asst. dir. research and evaluation West Philadelphia Community Mental Health Consortium, 1967-69, dir., 1969-76; dir. research and evaluation Northside Community Mental Health Center, Tampa, Fla.. 1976-77, asso. dir. community and center services. 1977-78; cons. Mvers Consulting, 1978. Fla. Mental Health Inst.. 1978; exec. dir. El Paso (Tex.) Center for Mental Health and Mental Retardation Services 1978—. USPHS fellow. 1961-63. Mem. El Paso Psvchol. Assn.. Am. Psvchol. Assn.. Fla. Psychol. Assn., Assn. of Mental Health Adminstrs., Human Services Center of Phila. Soc. Clin. Psychologists (sec. bd. dirs. 1975-76), Sigma Xi, Psi Chi. Contbr. numerous articles on mental health to profl. jours. Home: 621 Lakeway Dr El Paso TX 79932 Office: 1801 Wyoming Ave El Paso TX 79902

YUEN, LAWRENCE KOON YEE KAIKALA, govt. ofcl.; b. Honolulu, Nov. 24, 1932; s. Frank K. and Alice Y.A. (Au) Y.; B.A., U. Hawaii, 1955; postgrad. U. San Fernando, 1971-73; m. Gloria Jean Diaz, June 19, 1965; children—Catherine M.N., Elizabeth M.Y., Lawrence S.L. Research chemist Am. Latex Products Corp., El Segundo, Calif., 1960-62; research chemist VA Med. Center, Sepulveda, Calif., 1962-66, research chemist is psychopharmacology research, 1966-75, adminstrv. officer, research and devel., Birmingham, Ala., 1975—. Served with USN, 1955-59. Mem. Am. Chem. Soc., Soc. Research Adminstrs. Democrat. Roman Catholic. Contbr. articles to profl. jours. Home: 453 Westchester Dr Birmingham AL 35215 Office: VA Medical Center 700 S 19th St Birmingham AL 35233

YUHASZ, GEORGE WILLIAM, govt. ofcl.; b. Meadville, Pa., Oct. 8, 1946; s. George Andrew and Gladys Lorraine (Hornstein) Y.; B.A., Am. U., 1968; M.S., U. No. Colo., 1979; m. Anne L. Coll-Pardo, Oct. 23, 1971; 1 son, George William. Urban community developer U.S. Dept. State, Dominican Republican, 1968-69; police officer Washington Met. Police Dept., 1969-70; spl. agt. U.S. Bur. Narcotics and Dangerous Drugs, Balt., Miami and Caribbean Islands, Latin Am., 1970-73; consumer protection specialist FTC, Washington, 1973-75; investigator in charge Consumer Product Safety Commn. U.S., Miami, 1975-77; spl. agt. U.S. Dept. Def., Miami, 1977—. Vol. counselor Dade County (Fla.) Public Schs. Recipient Outstanding Performance award Consumer Product Safety Commn., 1976. Mem. Am. Personnel and Guidance Assn., Fed. Criminal Investigators Assn., Dade County Mental Health Assn., Phi Sigma Kappa. Republican. Roman Catholic. Office: 6595 NW 36th St Miami FL 33166

YUNICE, ANIECE ANDY, biochemist, educator; b. Rahbeh-Akkar, Lebanon, Jan. 2, 1925; s. Asad Makkoul and Mona Nickola (Khouri) Y.; came to U.S., 1954; naturalized, 1962; B.A., Am. U., Beirut, Lebanon, 1949; M.S., Wayne State U., 1958; Ph.D., Okla. U., 1970; m. Lillian M. Saleeby, Aug. 5, 1959; children—Carla, Paula, Laurie. Tchr., Am. High Sch., Tripoli, Lebanon, 1949-53; research asst. in medicine, Wash. U., St. Louis, 1958-69, VA Hosp., St. Louis, 1958-69; asst. prof. research medicine Okla. U., Oklahoma City, 1970—, asso. prof. physiology and biophysics, 1979—. Dir. trace metals research labs. VA Hosp., Oklahoma City, 1970—; prin. high sch., Bishmizine, Lebanon, 1953-54. NIH Research grantee, 1971, VA Research Support grantee, 1973. Mem. Am. Soc. Exptl. Biology and Medicine, Internat., Am. socs. nephrology, Gerontol. Soc., AAAS, Am. Chem. Soc., Am. Fedn. Clin. Research, Sigma Xi. Contbr. articles on biochem. role of trace metals in chronic diseases to profl. jours. Home: 2325 Morgan Dr Norman OK 73069 Office: 921 NE 13th St Oklahoma City OK 73104

YURMAN, HERMAN WALTER, fin. planner; b. Bklyn., Feb. 4, 1920; s. Samuel and Fannie (Margolis) Y.; grad. James Madison High Sch., Bklyn., 1938; B.S. in Bus. Adminstrn., M.S. in Fin. Planning, Calif. Nat. Open U., 1977; hon. doctorate in fin. adminstrn. U. Sarasota, 1978; m. Phyllis Loretta Corino, June 9, 1945; children—Lynda Yurman Pite, Bruce D. Registered rep., prin. Raymond James, St. Petersburg, Fla., 1966-70; v.p. Planning Corp.

Am., St. Petersburg, 1968-70; pres. Delta Planning Corp., St. Petersburg, 1970-71; v.p. Petro-Lewis Securities Corp., Denver, 1970-73; pres. Alpha/Omega Planning Corp., St. Petersburg, 1973—; sr. fellow, bd. dirs. Am. Inst. Fin. and Mgmt. Vice chmn. academics Coll. for Fin. Planning, also bd. regents; chmn. bd. Coll. Fin. Planning Found. Served with U.S. Army, 1941-45. Decorated Bronze Star. Mem. Internat. Assn. Fin. Planners (chmn., dir.), Inst. Certified Fin. Planners. Republican. Jewish. Author: A Financial Planner's Guide, 1972; The Basics of Financial Planning, 1976; The Basics of Conceptual Financial Planning, 1978. Home: 4008 Overlook Dr NE St Petersburg FL 33703 Office: 9450 Koger Blvd Suite 127 St Petersburg FL 33702

ZACHARIAS, DONALD WAYNE, univ. pres.; b. Salem, Ind., Sept. 28, 1935; s. William Otto and Estelle Mae (Newlon) Z.; B.A., Georgetown (Ky.) Coll., 1957; M.A., Ind. U., 1959, Ph.D., 1963; m. Tommie Kline Dekle, Aug. 16, 1959; children—Alan, Eric, Leslie. Asst. prof. communication and theatre Ind. U., 1963-69; asso. prof. communication U. Tex., Austin, 1969-72, prof., 1972-79, asst. to pres., 1974-77; exec. asst. to chancellor U. Tex. System, 1978-79; pres. Western Ky. U., 1979—; cons. savs. and loan leagues. Bd. dirs. Little League, Austin, 1977-78. Served with U.S. Army, 1959-60. Recipient Teaching award Ind. U. Found., 1963, Cactus Teaching award U. Tex., 1971. Mem. Speech Communication Assn., Internat. Communication Assn., Am. Assn. Higher Edn., Phi Kappa Phi (pres. 1978). Democrat. Episcopalian. Author: In Pursuit of Peace: Speeches of the Sixties, 1970. Office: Office of Pres Western Ky U Bowling Green KY 42101

ZACHARIAS, WILLIAM PAUL, mgmt. cons.; b. Tucson, Ariz., Nov. 25, 1930; s. William Paul and Mary Lou (Boyd) Z.; student So. Ill. U., 1948-50; B.A., U. Denver, 1957; m. Beverly Smith, June 5, 1971; children by previous marriage—William D. Zacharias, Janet L. Zacharias, James M., Beverly Dianne, Charles E. Calhoun. Tchr., Denver pub. schs., 1957-59; dir., therapist Easter Seal Rehab. Center, Albany, Ga., 1959-64; exec. sec. S.W. Ga. Soc. for Crippled Children and Adults, Inc., Albany, 1960-64; personnel adminstr. Lilliston Corp., Albany, 1964-71; corporate dir. employee relations Builders Homes, Inc. div. Am. Standard, Inc., Dothan, Ala., 1971-72, W.C. Bradley Co., Columbus, Ga., 1972-76; pres. Zacharias & Assos., Inc., mgmt. cons., Columbus, 1976—; pres. Preferred Placements, Inc., Columbus, Employee Relations Concepts, 1978—; also lectr. Chmn. advisory com. for vocational-tech. edn. Musoogee County Sch. System; past pres., chmn. bd. Jr. Achievement of Columbus (Ga.), Jr. Achievement of Phenix City (Ala.); mem. personnel rev. bd. Consol. Govt. of Columbus; mem. Commn. on Status of Women, Commn. on Employment of Handicapped, Ga. Employer-Employee Relations Council. Served in USAF, 1950-54. Recipient Leadership award Jr. Achievement of Am., 1976, 77; numerous awards from various charitable and health orgns. Mem. Am. Soc. for Personnel Adminstrn. (accredited personnel diplomate), Am. Mgmt. Assn., Am. Arbitration Assn., Am. Soc. for Tng. and Devel., C. of C. U.S., Ga., Columbus, Cordele, LaGrange chambers commerce, Columbus Personnel Assn. Methodist. Clubs: Sertoma (Columbus); One Hundred. Contbr. articles to profl. periodicals. Home: 1853 F Dyke Rd Marietta GA 30067 Office: PO Drawer 4408 Columbus GA 31904 also 1 Piedmont Center Suite 400 3565 Piedmont Rd NE Atlanta GA 30305

ZACHERT, VIRGINIA, psychologist, educator; b. Jacksonville, Ala., Mar. 1, 1920; d. Rev. R. E. and Cora H. (Massee) Z.; student Norman Jr. Coll., 1937; A.B., Ga. State Woman's Coll. (now Valdosta State Coll.), 1940; M.A., Emory U., 1947; Ph.D., Purdue U., 1949. Statistician, Davison-Paxon Co., Atlanta, 1941-44; research psychologist Mil. Contracts, Auburn Research Found., Ala. Poly. Inst.; indsl. and research psychologist Sturm & O'Brien, cons. engrs., 1958-59; research project dir. Western Design, Biloxi, Miss., 1960-61; self-employed cons. psychologist, Norman Park, Ga., 1961-71, Good Hope, Ga., 1971—; research asso. med. edn. Med. Coll. Ga. Augusta, 1963-65, asso. prof., 1965-70, prof., 1970—, chief learning materials div., 1973—; mem. Ga. Bd. Examiners of Psychologists, 1974-79, v.p., 1977, pres., 1978. Mem. adv. bd. Comdr. Gen. ATC, USAF, 1967-70; bd. dirs., sec. Health Center Credit Union, 1980—. Served as aerologist USN, 1944-46, aviation psychologist USAF, 1949-54. Named Alumna of Yr., Valdosta State Coll., 1980; diplomate Am. Bd. Profl. Psychologists. Fellow Am. Psychol. Assn.; mem. Am. Statis. Assn., AAUP (chpt. pres. 1978-80), Sigma Xi. Baptist. Author: (with P. L. Wilds) Essentials of Gynecology-Oncology, 1967, Applications of Gynecology-Oncology, 1967. Home: 1126 Highland Ave Augusta GA 30904 Office: Dept Obstetrics and Gynecology Med Coll Ga Augusta GA 30912

ZACHRY, CHARLES CANDLER, JR., ins. co. exec.; b. Nashville, Apr. 28, 1942; s. Charles Candler and Harriet Louise (Campbell) Z.; B.S.E.E., Tenn. Tech. U., 1964; M.B.A., U. Ala., Birmingham, 1976; m. Sherry Marie Wilding, Jan. 13, 1968; children—Elizabeth Marie, Cara Louise. Student supr. South Central Bell Telephone Co., Nashville, 1964-65, facilities supr., 1967-69, asso. facilities adminstr., 1970-71, traffic mgr., Humboldt, Tenn., 1969-71, traffic staff supr., Nashville, 1971-72, staff specialist, Birmingham, Ala., 1972-78; dir. network engring. Ins. Systems Am., Atlanta, 1978—. Served with Signal Corps, U.S. Army, 1965-67. Registered profl. engr., Ala. Mem. Mil. Affiliate Radio Systems, V F W, Res. Officers Assn., Tau Beta Pi, Omicron Delta Epsilon. Home: 6805 Hunters Trace Circle Atlanta GA 30328 Office: 6855 Jimmy Carter Blvd PO Box 47975 Atlanta GA 30362

ZACK, GEORGE, orch. condr. and music dir.; b. Pine Bluff, Ark., July 8, 1936; s. George Peter and Eugenia (Trianddfilou) Z.; Mus.B. cum laude, Wichita State U., 1958; Mus.M., U. Mich., 1960; Ph.D., Fla. State U., 1960; viola student Robert Courte; postgrd. Yale U., 1970-71; m. Kerry Sheehan, Oct. 4, 1970; children—Katherine Eugenia, Melissa Sheehan. Instr. in music theory U. Mich., 1962-64; asso. prof. music Hiram Coll., 1964-72; condr., music dir. Wooster (Ohio) Symphony, 1965-67, Warren (Ohio) Chamber Orch., 1968—, Lexington (Ky.) Philharmonic Orch., 1972—; vis. artist-in-residence Eastern Ky. U., 1976; artist-in-residence James Madison U., 1978; bd. dirs. Central Ky. Youth Music Soc., 1974—, also acting music dir., condr. symphony orch.; mem. Arts Council, 1972—; conducting student Am. Symphony Orch. League Conducting Inst., summers. grad. asst. Fla. State U., 1960-62; community adv. bd. WEKU-FM, 1979—. Recipient Orpheus award Phi Mu Alpha Sinfonia, 1975. Mem. Am. Fedn. Musicians, Am. Symphony Orch. League, Nat. Assn. Arts, Letters (chmn. membership Ky. chpt.). Greek Orthodox. Author: The Music Dramas of Manolis Kalomiris, 1972. Home: 237 Woodspoint Rd Lexington KY 40502 Office: PO Box 838 Lexington KY 40587

ZACK, SAM GENE, newspaper pub.; b. Haines City, Fla., Dec. 17, 1929; s. P.J. and Dorothy Fern (Lancaster) Z.; A.A., Massey Bus. Coll., 1950; student Nat. Acad. Broadcast, 1952; m. Constance Horne, Nov. 5, 1954; children—Julie E., Angela D. Pitcher profl. baseball, 1950-51; radio announcer, ops. mgr., mgr. radio stas., Jacksonville, Fla., New Orleans, Los Angeles, 1955-68; newspaper account exec. Fla. Pub. Co., Jacksonville, 1969-70; pub. Jacksonville Herald, 1973—. Served with USAF, 1947-50; Alaska. Mem. Bradford County C. of C. (v.p. 1957-59). Democrat. Clubs: Am. Legion, Elks. Home: 3208 Fruitwood Ln Jacksonville FL 32211 Office: 1332 University Blvd N Jacksonville FL 32211

ZAGURSKY, GEORGE PALMER, nuclear engr.; b. N.Y.C., Dec. 14, 1943; s. George and Kathryn (Hreneczko) Z.; B.S. in Nuclear Engring. (NSF scholar), Miss. State U., 1968; M.B.A., U. Miami, 1975; postgrad. Nova U., 1977—; m. Jacquelyn Susan Hayden, Aug. 29, 1969; 1 son, Adam Hayden. Test engr. Turkey Point nuclear plant Fla. Power & Light Co., 1968-71, mech. start-up engr., hot functional coordinator Turkey Point nuclear plant, 1971-73, plant supr. integrated leak rate coordinator Turkey Point nuclear plant, 1973-75, sr. engr., power plant engring. dept., gen. office, Miami, 1975-76, supervising engr. mech. and nuclear specialists, gen. office, 1976—. Mem. Am. Nuclear Soc., ASME, Good Govt. Mgmt. Assn., U. Miami Alumni Assn. Republican. Lutheran. Club: Masons. Home: 9041 SW 140th St Miami FL 33176 Office: Fla Power & Light Co PO Box 529100 Miami FL 33152

ZAINO, RUSSELL BRUCE, banker; b. Louisville, July 10, 1948; s. Louis Frederick and Mabel Christine (Hickey) Z.; B.S.C., U. Louisville, 1974, M.B.A., 1976, postgrad. 1980—; m. Sherrie Arla Warren, Dec. 31, 1975. Supr., Manpower Inc., Louisville, 1972-74; asst. cashier Liberty Nat. Bank, Louisville, 1974-76, asst. v.p. mktg. 1977-78, v.p. mktg., 1978—; cons., lectr. in field. Active Third Century, (revitalization of inner city), Louisville, 1977—. Served with U.S. Army, 1967-71. Decorated Army Commendation medal, Purple Heart, Bronze Star medal. Mem. Bank Mktg. Assn., Sigma Delta Kappa. Home: 1740 Harvard Dr Louisville KY 40205 Office: 416 W Jefferson St Louisville KY 40202

ZAISER, KENT AMES, lawyer; b. St. Petersburg, Fla., June 10, 1945; s. Robert Alan and Marion Llewellyn (Brown) Z.; A.B., Duke U., 1967; J.D., U. Fla., 1972; student U. Calif., Berkeley, 1971. Admitted to Fla. bar, 1973; asst. to pres. Sea Pines Co., Hilton Head Island, S.C., 1968-70; law clk., bus. mgr. law firm Michael L. Bryant & James O. Birr, Gainesville, Fla., 1972-73; research aide Fla. Supreme Ct., 1973-75, adminstrv. asst., 1975-76; asst. dept. atty. Fla. Dept. Natural Resources, 1976-80; asst. atty. gen. Fla. Dept. Legal Affairs, 1980—; pres. Equity Holdings, Inc., St. Petersburg, 1975-78. Campaign mgr. Vince Fechtel for Fla. State Rep., 1972. Served with USNR, 1963-66, USAR, 1969-75. NROTC scholar, 1963. Mem. Fla. Bar Assn., Am. Bar Assn., Tallahassee Bar Assn., Fla. Govt. Employees Bar Assn., U. Fla. Alumni Assn. Democrat. Episcopalian. Home: 3278 Longleaf Rd Tallahassee FL 32304 Office: Capitol Bldg Tallahassee FL 32301

ZAKAIB, PAUL, JR., lawyer, former state legislator; b. Los Angeles, Oct. 20, 1932; s. Paul and Hazel (Rahal) Z.; B.A., Morris Harvey Coll., Charleston, W.Va., 1955; LL.B., W.Va. U., 1958; m. Maria Lucia DeRito, Mar. 12, 1967; children—Paul III, Stefan Andrew. Admitted to W.Va. bar, 1959; non legal clk., adminstrv. div. Dept. Justice, Washington, 1958; atty. W.Va. Tax Commn., 1958-59, W.Va. Dept. Employment Security, 1959-60, W.Va. Econ. Devel. Agy., 1960; atty. exec. asst. W.Va. Dept. Commerce, 1960-62; individual practice law; mem. W.Va. Ho. of Reps., 1967-75; minority counsel W.Va. Senate, 1979, 80. Del. Republican Nat. Conv., 1976. Served with AUS, 1952-54; Korea. Mem. Am. Bar Assn. (state rep. local govt. law sect.), Am., W.Va. assns. trial lawyers, Phi Delta Phi. Mem. Greek Orthodox Ch. (trustee). Home: 4102 Virginia Ave SE Charleston WV 25304 Office: 209 Blvd Tower Charleston WV

ZAKI, OMAR SHAHID, physician; b. Lahore, Pakistan, Apr. 15, 1945; came to U.S., 1967; s. Mohammad and Bashir-Un-Nisa Z.; M.D., King Edward Med. Sch. (Pakistan), 1967; m. Anne Louise Ross, July 23, 1977. Intern, Beth Israel Med. Center, N.Y.C., 1967-68; resident, Lenox Hill Hosp., N.Y.C., 1968-69; practice medicine, specializing in internal medicine, Falls Church, Va., 1976—; staff, Arlington (Va.) Hosp., Peter Bent Brigham Hosp. Boston fellow, 1973. Mem. Fairfax County Med. Soc. Home: 8615 Georgetown Pike McLean VA 22102 Office: 7700 Leesburg Pike Suite 417 Falls Church VA 22043

ZALE, DONALD, retail exec.; b. 1933; student Tex. A. and M. Coll.; B.B.A., So. Meth. U., 1953. With Zale Corp., Dallas, 1954—, asst. treas., 1961-63, treas., 1963-64, exec. v.p., 1964-71, formerly pres., now vice chmn. and chief exec. officer. Office: Zale Corp 3000 Diamond Park Dr Dallas TX 75247

ZANVILLE, ROSE LYN, advt. co. exec.; b. Cleve., May 5, 1944; d. Robert N. and Edith S. (Urman) Zanville; B.A. in English, Lindenwood Coll. for Women, 1966; M.F.A. in Broadcast-Film Art, So. Meth. U., 1972. Writer, Glenn Advt. Agy., Dallas, Tex., 1969-71, Tracy-Locke, Inc., Dallas, 1971-73; sr. writer Bloom Agy., Dallas, 1973-74; sr. writer/producer Glenn, Bozell & Jacobs, Inc., Dallas, 1974-75; writing supr. nat. advt. campaign Am. Heart Assn., Dallas, 1975-76; creative dir. Lacy, Skloss & Pleuckhahn, Inc., Austin, Tex., 1976-77; pres. Warren-Lawrence Advt. Inc., Austin, 1977, Lyn Zanville, Inc., Dallas, 1977—; instr. Acad. of Visual Communications, So. Meth. U., 1974-76; exhibited advt. art N.Y. Art Dirs. Club, 1974, 58th Exhbn., 1979, 59th Exhbn., 1980, Dallas-Ft. Worth Soc. of Visual Communications, 1972, 74, CA-79 Communication Arts mag., 1979. Vol., Parkland Hosp. and Children's Med. Center, 1969-70. Recipient Bronze award, Ft. Worth Soc. of Visual Communications, 1972, Gold medal, 1974; Cert. of Excellence, Art Dirs. Club of Houston, 1979. Mem. Dallas C. of C., Dallas Advt. League (1st pl. 1967). Office: PO Box 25443 Dallas TX 75225

ZAPOLEON, MARGUERITE WYKOFF, cons., lectr., author; b. Cin., Aug. 18, 1907; d. Fred Clark and Elizabeth (Voth) Wykoff; B.A., engring. degree, U. Cin., 1928; postgrad. Geneva Sch. Internat. Studies, 1927, N.Y. Sch. Social Work, 1928-29, London Sch. Econs. and Polit. Sci., 1932; M.A., Am. U., 1938; m. Louis B. Zapoleon, Oct. 2, 1937 (dec. Dec. 1969). Began career as vocation counselor Cin. Pub. Schs., 1929-35; chief of counseling div. D.C. Employment Center, 1935-39; specialist occupational info. and guidance service U.S. Office Edn., 1939-43; tng. specialist Hdqrs. ASF, 1943-44; chief employment opportunities br. Women's Bur., Dept. Labor, 1944-51, spl. asst. occupational outlook service Bur. Labor Statistics, 1951-55, spl. asst. to dir. Women's Bur., 1955-60; cons. on labor econs. and vocat. guidance, 1960—; lectr., workshop leader, instr. vocat. guidance and occupational research colls., univs., AAUW adult counseling project, 1965; adv. com., panel asso. Assn. Appraisers Earning Capacity, 1964-70; mem. tech. coms., recorder employment sect. White House Conf. on Aging, 1971. Bd. dirs. Am. Soc. Econometric Appraisers, 1967-70; bd. dirs. Friends of Everglades, Broward County, chmn. 1972—, Environ. Council of Broward County, 1979—; trustee Fla. Council Aging, 1973-75. Mem. Nat. Vocat. Guidance Assn. (trustee 1945-51), Council Guidance and Personnel Assn. (v.p. 1947-48), Alliance for Guidance Rural Youth (2d v.p. 1952-60), Am. Personnel and Guidance Assn. (del. Assembly 1951-60), Am. Econ. Assn., Indsl. Relations Research Assn., AAUW, Nat. League Am. Pen Women, AAAS, Am. Statis. Assn., Internat. Platform Assn., Nature Conservancy (rec. sec. Fla. chpt. 1972-78), Fla. Wildlife Fedn., Fairchild Gardens, Cousteau Soc., Am. Forestry Assn., Gerontol. Soc., Kappa Kappa Gamma (alumni achievement award 1968). Presbyterian. Author: (with Louise Moore) Reference and Related Information: Vocational Guidance for Girls and Women, 1941; Community Occupational Surveys, 1942; The College Girl Looks Ahead to Her Career Opportunities, 1956; Occupational Planning for Women, 1961; Girls and Their Futures, 1963, rev. edit., 1978; Wrongful Death of Housewife and Mother, 1965; Economic Aspects of Counseling Adult Women, 1966; also author of numerous govermental pamphlets on occupations and vocational guidance edn. and tng.; contbr. articles to profl. jours.; editor Vocat. Guidance Quar., 1953-54. Home: 816 SE Riviera Isle Fort Lauderdale FL 33301

ZARIN, JERALD LAWRENCE, pediatrician; b. N.Y.C., Feb. 21, 1942; s. Emanuel Bernard and Esther (Feldman) Z.; B.S., Rensselaer Poly. Inst., 1962; M.D., Albert Einstein Coll. Medicine, 1966; m. Aileen Carole Singer, May 24, 1970; children—Jason Scott, Randall Jeffrey, Marni Dee. Intern in pediatrics Univ. Hosps. of Cleve., 1966-67, resident, 1967-69; practice medicine specializing in pediatrics, Houston, 1971—; asst. clin. prof. pediatrics Baylor Coll. Medicine, Houston, 1976—; chief pediatrics Meml. Hosp. Houston, 1979-80; mem. staff Tex. Children's Hosp., Spring Br. Meml. Hosp., Parkway Hosp., Hermann Hosp., St. Luke's Hosp., Meth. Hosp., Tex. Women's Hosp. (all Houston). Mem. Meml. area com. Jewish Community Center, Houston, 1976-78; trustee Congregation Beth Am, Houston, 1976-78; v.p. Frostwood Sch. PTA, Houston, 1980—. Served with USAF, 1969-71. Diplomate Am. Bd. Pediatrics, Nat. Bd. Med. Examiners. Fellow Am. Acad. Pediatrics; mem. Tex. Med. Assn., Houston Pediatric Soc., Harris County Med. Soc. Home: 12330 Boheme Dr Houston TX 77024 Office: 8230 Antoine Dr Suite A-4 Houston TX 77088

ZARO, LYNN KERBY, ednl. cons.; b. Atlanta, Dec. 10, 1949; d. Wilford Dixon and Martha Dunn Kerby; B.A., Furman U., 1971; m. Guillermo Eduardo Zaro, Sept. 6, 1977. Spl. edn. tchr. Baker's Chapel Elementary Sch., Greenville, S.C., 1971-72; teller, personnel asst., mgr. tng. and devel First Fed. Broward, Fort Lauderdale, Fla., 1972-79; performance cons. Results Unlimited, Fort Lauderdale, 1979; cons. Broward County Sch. System, 1978; mem. adv. bd. Youth Bus. Devel. Project, 1978-79; instr. Inst. Fin. Edn., 1976-80. Mem. Am. Soc. Tng. and Devel., Fla. Com. on Tng. and Devel. Club: Toastmaster's. Home: 3730 NW 39th St Lauderdale Lakes FL 33309 Office: 263 Harbor Dr Lauderdale-by-the-Sea FL 33308

ZASTOUPIL, MARK ALAN, indsl. engr.; b. Madison, Wis., Aug. 29, 1951; s. Arthur John and Ruth June (Grimm) Z.; B.S., U. Wis., 1973; diploma in bus. mgmt. LaSalle Ext. U., 1976; m. Margaret Jean Holtz, May 26, 1973; 1 dau., Jeanna Kay. Jr. indsl. engr. Green Giant Co., Lafayette, Ind., 1973-74, indsl. engring. rep., Belvidere, Ill., 1974-75, corp. indsl. engr., LeSueur, Minn., 1975-78; corp. indsl. engr. Doric Foods Corp., Mt. Dora, Fla., 1978—. Mem. Am. Inst. Indsl. Engrs., Am. Assn. Cost Engrs. Republican. Methodist. Club: Rotary. Home: 1424 E 5th Ave Mount Dora FL 32757 Office: PO Box 986 Mount Dora FL 32757

ZAUBER, RAYMOND G., editor; b. Jellico, Tenn., June 25, 1918; s. Milton H. and Mollie Rose (Garber) Z.; student Guilford Coll., 1940-41, U. N.C. at Chapel Hill, 1934-36; m. Eloise Ruth Horstmann, Sept. 30, 1944 (div. Mar. 1968); children—Glenn, Kim, Vonn; m. 2d, Mary Huggins Stout, Jan. 19, 1975; stepchildren—Michael, Mary Elizabeth. With Dallas Times Herald, 1945-46, WBAP News, 1946, Dallas News, 1946-47; pub. Oak Cliff Tribune and subsidiaries, Dallas, 1947—; editor, pub. Grand Prairie Banner, 1948-51, Irving Herald Index, 1948-51; chmn. bd. Newspaper Enterprises, Inc., Dallas and Oklahoma City, 1958-65; pub. County Courier, 1974—, Lancaster Leader, 1977—, Oak Cliff Advertiser; ltd. partner Cable Log, Storer Cable TV. Founder, commr.'s adv. bd. Dallas Bapt. Coll., 1966-70. Mem. Airport Bd., 1945-74; mem. Interregional Hwy. Council, 1971—, Central Hwy. Com., 1970—. Bd. dirs. Circle council Boy Scouts Am., 1948-50, Oak Cliff YMCA, 1959-62. Served to lt. inf. AUS, World War II; PTO. Recipient cited by Altrusa, Jr. C. of C., and others. Mem. Am. Legion (vice comdr. 1946—), C. of C. (chmn. hwy. com. 1971—), Cedar Crest Golf Assn. (past pres.), Sigma Delta Chi. Kiwanian (Spl. Man of Yr. award). Clubs: Press, Oak Cliff Country, Top o' the Cliff, Exec. 100 (dir.), Cosmopolitan, Singing Hills Country (dir.). Home: 5760 Talbot Dallas TX 75232 Office: 4575 S Westmoreland Dallas TX 75224

ZEARS, RUSSELL WINFRED, computer field engr.; b. Gainesville, Ga., Dec. 13, 1951; s. Russell Winfred, Jr., and Hilda (Clark) Z.; B.S. in Elec. Engring. and Computer Sci. (Ill. State scholar), U. Ill., 1973; M.S. in Computer Sci. and E.E., U. Calif., Berkeley, 1975. Mem. tech. staff Bell Telephone Labs., Naperville, Ill., 1973; systems analyst U. Tex. Med. Br., Galveston, 1975-78; computer field engr. Hewlett-Packard, Houston, 1978—; cons., tchr. Pres. Homeowners Assn., 1978. Mem. Assn. Computing Machinery. Mem. Ch. of Religious Science. Author: (with others) Computers in Nutrition, 1979; contbr. articles to periodicals, chpt. in book. Office: 10535 Harwin Dr Houston TX 77036

ZEBROWSKI, JOHN HOST, educator; b. Wyandotte, Mich., Nov. 3, 1914; s. Jozef Host and Wladyslawa (Napierkowska) Z.; B.A., U. Mich., 1936, M.A. (Univ. scholar), 1938; postgrad. law U. Detroit, 1940, cinema U. So. Calif., 1960; m. Louise Myers, 1962. Ednl. dir. Fisher Body div. Gen. Motors Corp., 1940-42; account exec. Visual Tng. Corp, 1943-44; co-organizer, dir., sales and advt. mgr. Regal Mfg. Corp., 1944-47; owner, mgr. advt. agy., Calif., 1948-61; lectr. U. Tampa, 1962-65; asso. prof. English, Inter Am. U. P.R., Hato Rey, 1965—, founder, dir. Inter Am. U. Press, 1970—; founder, editor Revista/Rev. Inter Americana, 1971—. Mem. Caribbean Studies Assn. (gov. council 1977-80, sec.-treas. 1980—), Coll. English Assn. (founder chpt.). Internat. Assn. Scholarly Pubs., Soc. Scholarly Pubs. Author: Uncle Bruno (short stories), 1972; contbr. articles to profl. jours. Office: GPO Box 3255 San Juan PR 00936

ZEFF, STEPHEN ADDAM, educator; b. Chgo., July 26, 1933; s. Roy David and Hazel (Sex) Z.; B.S., U. Colo., 1955, M.S., 1957; M.B.A., U. Mich., 1960, Ph.D., 1962. Instr. U. Colo., 1955-57; teaching fellow instr. U. Mich., 1958-61; asst. prof. acctg. Tulane U., New Orleans, 1961-63, asso. prof., 1963-67, prof., 1967-78; prof. acctg. Rice U., Houston, 1978—; vis. asso. prof. U. Cal., Berkeley, 1964-65, U. Chgo., 1966; vis. prof. Instituto Tecnológico y de Estudios Superiores de Monterrey (Mexico), 1969, Victoria U., Wellington, N.Z., 1976; spl. lectr., also hon. sr. Fulbright scholar Monash U., Australia, 1972. Mem. Am. Accounting Assn., (dir. edn. 1969-71), Am. Econ. Assn., Nat. Assn. Accountants, Fin. Execs. Inst., AAUP. Author: Uses of Accounting for Small Business, 1962, American Accounting Assn. Its First 50 Years, 1966; Forging Accounting Principles in Five Countries: A History and an Analysis of Trends, 1972; Forging Accounting Principles in Australia, 1973. Editor: Business Schools and the Challenge of International Business, 1968; Asset Appreciation, Business Income and Price-Level Accounting: 1918-1935, 1976. Co-editor: Financial Accounting Theory, Vol. I, 1964, rev., 1973, Vol. II, 1969. Book rev. editor Accounting Rev., 1962-66. Founder, editor Boletin Interamericano de Contabilidad, 1968-71. Contbr. articles to profl. jours. Home: 4545 Acacia Bellaire TX 77401

ZEGAN, PETER JAMES, airline exec.; b. Perth Amboy, N.J., Sept. 4, 1938; s. Peter Joseph and Helen (Rusin) Z.; B.S. in Physics, Ind. Inst. Tech., 1952; M.S., U. Fla., 1970; m. Gari Louise Dunne, Jan. 17,

1962; children—Shannon, Sara, Jill, Lauren. Instr., Physics Lab., Ind. Inst. Tech., Ft. Wayne, 1959-62; engr. Philco Corp., Phila., 1962; research engr. N. Am. Rockwell Corp., Downey, Calif., 1962-65, mem. tech. staff III, Cocoa Beach, Fla., 1965-68; sr. tech. specialist Eastern Air Lines, Inc., Miami, Fla., 1968-69, mgr. schedule performance and analysis, 1969-72, dir. ops. group systems/schedule performance, 1972-77, dir. systems design and analysis, 1977—; adj. prof. Fla. Internat. U., Miami, 1972—, N.Y. Inst. Tech., Eastern Air Lines Degree program, Miami, 1976-78, Nova U., Ft. Lauderdale, Fla., 1977; instr. indsl. engring. U. Miami, Coral Gables, 1968-74; instr. computer sci. Fla. Inst. Tech., Melbourne, 1967-68; instr. math. West Coast U., Orange, Calif., 1963-65; cons. ADI Transp. Systems, Woodbury, N.Y., 1979—; cons. Transp. Data Systems, Brookline, Mass., 1977—; cons. FAA, Washington, 1976—. Served with USAF, 1955-59. Mem. Nat. Mgmt. Assn., Eastern Airlines Mgmt. Council, Assn. for Systems Mgmt., Nat. Acad. Sci. Transp. Research Bd. Republican. Christian Ch. Contbr. articles to profl. jours. Home: 9650 Red Rd Miami FL 33156 Office: Eastern Air Lines Miami Internat Airport Miami FL 33148

ZEIGLER, GORDON EDWARD, photographic equipment retail store exec.; b. Plainview, Tex., Mar. 2, 1949; s. Roland Scaife and Frances Sophronia (Crowther) Z.; B.A., Tex. Tech. U., 1971, postgrad. 1975-76. Chief photographer, gen. reporter Plainview (Tex.) Daily Herald, 1971-73; regional editor Lubbock Avalanche Jour., 1973-76; v.p. Zeiglers' Camera Shop, Plainview, 1976—; instr. photography S. Plains Coll. Recipient Young Taxan of Month award Optimists, 1966. Mem. S. Plains Profl. Photographers Assn., Sigma Delta Chi, Alpha Phi Omega. Democrat. Presbyterian. Clubs: Optimist, Plainview Camera, W.Tex. Amateur Athletic Union. Office: 1713 W 7th St Plainview TX 79072

ZEIGLER, JEANINE BAHRAM PATTON, guidance counselor; b. Chgo., Nov. 9, 1928; d. Lester H. and Florence (Toney) Bahram; B.A., Mich. State U., 1965, M.A., 1969; m. Daniel J. Patton, Jr. (dec.); children—Daniel J., Deborah J., Denise J.; m. 2d, Lamar Henry Zeigler, June 19, 1971. Successively elementary tchr., sch. social worker, elementary sch. prin. Battle Creek (Mich.) public schs., 1965-77; guidance counselor So. U., New Orleans, 1977—. Chmn. bd. dirs. Bethany Day Care Center, New Orleans, 1978—; hon. chmn. Battle Creek Cancer Crusade, 1976; bd. dirs. Y Center, Battle Creek, 1974-77. Recipient various service awards. Mem. Assn. Supervision and Curriculum Devel., Am. Personnel and Guidance Assn., Am. Coll. Personnel Assn., Am. Assn. Non-White Concerns, AAUW (pres. Battle Creek chpt. 1974-76), La. Assn. Coll. and Univ. Student Personnel Adminstrs., Urban League, Delta Sigma Theta. Methodist. Clubs: Nat. Smart Set, Internat. Y's Men (New Orleans). Office: 6400 Press St New Orleans LA 70126

ZEIGLER, (DENNIS) STEVEN, environ. scientist; b. Galesburg, Ill., June 19, 1942; s. Tillman W. and Else Minnie Z.; B.S. in Chemistry, Central State U., 1971. Pollution control specialist Okla. Water Resources Bd., Oklahoma City, 1971-74; chemist Weyerhaeuser Co., Valliant, Okla., 1974-75, environ. chemist, 1975-76, regional environ. scientist, Hot Springs, Ark., 1976—. Mem. Source Evaluation Soc., Am. Chem. Soc. Republican. Baptist. Contbr. article to profl. publ. Office: PO Box 1060 Hot Springs AR 71901

ZEILINGER, RICHARD, social worker; b. Vienna, Austria, Jan. 8, 1925; came to U.S., 1967, naturalized, 1979; s. Gustav and Hermine (Laufer) Z.; student London Sch. Econ. and Polit. Sci., 1951-53; B.A., U. Western Ont. (Can.), 1962; M.S.W., McGill U. (Can.), 1967; m. Agatha Trigilio, Dec. 24, 1949; 1 son, Lawrence David. Counselling coordinator UNNRA-IRO, Italy, 1947-51; supr. Children's Aid Soc., London, Ont., Can., 1953-63; asst. exec. dir. Baron de Hirsch Inst., Montreal, Que., Can., 1963-67; exec. dir. Children's Bur. of New Orleans, 1967—; field work instr. Tulane U., New Orleans, 1968-75, La. State U., New Orleans, 1969-78. Vice pres. New Orleans Area Health Agy., 1971-74. Served with Brit. Army, 1944-47. Mem. Nat. Assn. Social Workers (Social Worker of Yr. 1977). Club: Canadian (New Orleans). Home: 5853 Oxford Pl New Orleans LA 70114 Office: 226 Carondelet St New Orleans LA 70130

ZELENY, MARJORIE PFEIFFER (MRS. CHARLES ELLINGSON ZELENY), psychologist; b. Balt., Mar. 31, 1924; d. Lloyd Armitage and Mable (Willian) Pfeiffer; B.A., U. Md., 1947; M.S., U. Ill., 1949, postgrad., 1951-54; m. Charles Ellingson Zeleny, Dec. 11, 1950; children—Ann Douglas, Charles Timberlake. Vocational counseling psychologist VA, Balt., 1947-48; asst. U. Ill., Urbana, 1948-50, research asso. Bur. Research, 1952-53; chief psychologist dept. neurology and psychiatry Ohio State U. Coll. Medicine, Columbus, 1950-51; research psychologist, cons., Tucson, Washington, 1954—. Mem. Am., D.C. psychol. assns., AAAS, Soc. for Psychol. Study Social Issues, D.A.R., Mortar Bd., Delta Delta Delta, Sigma Delta Epsilon, Psi Chi, Sigma Tau Epsilon. Roman Catholic. Home: 6825 Wemberly Way McLean VA 22101

ZEMP, JOHN WORKMAN, coll. dean, biochemist; b. Camden, S.C., Sept. 28, 1931; B.S., Coll. Charleston, 1953; M.S., Med. U. S.C., 1954; postgrad. Stanford U., 1954-56, Harvard U., 1960-63; Ph.D. (NSF fellow), U. N.C., 1966; m. Lois Dewitt, Dec. 20, 1958; children—John, Virginia, Blake, DeWitt. Asst. prof. dept. biochemistry U. N.C., Chapel Hill, 1967-68; asst. prof. biochemistry and psychiatry Med. U. S.C., Charleston, 1969-70, asso. prof., 1970-74, prof. biochemistry and psychiatry, 1974—, asso. dean acad. affairs Coll. Medicine, 1973-76, acting v.p. acad. affairs, 1974-75, dean Coll. Grad. Studies, 1977—, asst. to pres. for interinstitutional devel., 1976-77. Chmn. Task Force on Orgn. of Higher Edn. for S.C. State Reorganization Com., 1977; mem. Diocesan Council, Episcopal Diocese of S.C., 1978—; bd. dirs. Trident 2000, 1978, chmn., 1978—; bd. dirs. Coll. Preparatory Sch., Charleston, 1977—, chmn., 1977—; trustee Health Scis. Found., 1977—; bd. dirs. St. John's Episcopal Mission Center, 1970—, chmn., 1972-75. Served with USN, 1956-63. NSF fellow, 1966-67. Mem. Am. Chem. Soc., S.C. Acad. Sci., Soc. for Exptl. Biology and Medicine, Internat. Soc. Neurochemistry, Am. Soc. Neurochemistry, AAAS, S.C. Hist. Soc., S.C. Art Assn., Navy League, Coll. Charleston Alumni Assn. (pres. 1978—), Trident C. of C. (mem. human resources com. 1978—), Omicron Delta Kappa. Contbr. numerous articles on neurochemistry to sci. jours. Home: 95 Lenwood Blvd Charleston SC 29401 Office: Medical Univ of South Carolina 171 Ashley Ave Charleston SC 29403

ZEPP, RICHARD GARDNER, research photochemist; b. Bklyn., Nov. 20, 1941; s. Harry M. and Jessie (Gardner) Z.; B.S., Furman U., 1963; Ph.D., Fla. State U., 1968; m. Mary Ann Loeb, Aug. 2, 1968; 1 dau., Joanne. Research asso. dept. chemistry Mich. State U., 1969-70; research photochemist Athens (Ga.) Environ. Research Lab., EPA, 1971—. Woodrow Wilson fellow, 1963-64. Mem. Am. Chem. Soc. (sec. N.E. Ga. sect.), Am. Soc. Limnology and Oceanography, Chem. Soc. Royal Inst. Chemistry. Democrat. Methodist. Contbr. articles to profl. jours. Home: 465 Crestwood Dr Athens GA 30605 Office: EPA College Station Rd Athens GA 30605

ZERFOSS, LESTER FRANK, mgmt. cons., educator; b. Mountaintop, Pa., Nov. 2, 1903; s. Clinton and Mabel (Wilcox) Z.; B.A. cum laude, Pa. State U., 1926, M.Ed., 1934, D.Ed., 1958; m. Harriet Mildred Cary, Dec. 21, 1928; children—Patricia Anne (Mrs. Thomas Sitben), Clinton Cary, Robert Williamson. Coll. tchr., pub. sch. adminstr., Pa., 1928-41; supr. design, devel. Gen. Motors Inst., 1942-46; head supervisory devel. Detroit Edison Co., 1946-52; corporate tng. dir. Am. Enka Corp. (N.C.), 1952-59, dir. indsl. relations, mgmt. services, 1952-66, mgmt. cons. for managerial and tech. devel., 1966-68; asso. prof. psychology Asheville-Biltmore Coll., 1966-68; research prof. developmental psychology, dir. mgmt. devel. programs U. N.C. at Asheville, 1968-74, prof. mgmt. and psychology, chmn. dept. mgmt., 1974-76, prof. emeritus, 1976—; pres. L.F. Zerfoss Assos., Inc., 1977—. Mem. bd., head mgmt. devel. com. N.C. Personnel Bd., 1966-70; cons. to gov. for mgmt. devel., 1970-73; mem. Southeastern Regional Manpower Adv. Com., 1966-70, N.C. Adv. Com. for Community Colls. Trustee Brevard Coll., Asheville-Buncombe Tech. Inst. Recipient Distinguished Service award U. N.C., 1976. Mem. Am. Mgmt. Assn. (lectr. mgmt. for seminars), Nat. Soc. Advancement Mgmt. (profl. mgr. citation 1962), Am. Soc. Tng. and Devel., Phi Delta Kappa, Kappa Phi Kappa, Kappa Delta Pi, Delta Sigma Phi. Rotarian. Author: Developing Professional Personnel in Business, Industry and Government, 1977. Contbg. author: Training and Development Handbook, 1968; Management Handbook for Plant Engineers, 1978; Psychology in Action, 1978. Contbr. articles to profl. jours. Home: 3911 Lovett Circle Charlotte NC 28210 Office: Box 386 Liberty SC 29657

ZETER, NORMAN CARL, utility co. exec.; b. Lincoln, Ill., Feb. 21, 1934; s. Carl Alvin and Helen (Hoelscher); student U. Ill., 1952-55; B.S. in Engring., Bradley U., 1969; postgrad. Va. Commonwealth U., 1977-78; m. Sandra Lee Ball, July 5, 1959; children—Gregory Todd, Jeffrey Scott. Design draftsman then research design engr., Caterpillar Tractor Co., Peoria, Ill., 1955-62; with constrn. equipment div. Wabco, Peoria, 1962-72, mgr. parts sales and mktg., 1967-72; prin., exec. v.p. James River Equipment Co., Richmond, Va., 1972-77; dir. mktg. and bus. devel. Bremner, Youngblood and King, Inc., cons. engrs., Mechanicsville, Va., 1977-78; dir. transp. Va. Electric & Power Co., 1979—. Bd. dirs. Burkewood Recreation Assn., 1973-80; pres. Peoria Area Council Chs., 1968-72; elder Fairmount Christian Ch., Richmond, 1973—, chmn. ch. bd., 1979-80; v.p. Golden Age Christian Homes, Inc., 1975—; mem. Hanover County (Va.) Sch. Bd., 1975-79, vice chmn., 1978-79. Served with U.S. Army, 1957. Mem. U. Ill. Alumni Assn. (life), Phi Kappa Sigma. Home: 2 Pebblebrook Dr Mechanicsville VA 23111

ZETLIN, THALIA, internat. trade/distbn. exec.; b. Ithaca, N.Y., Mar. 18, 1952; d. Lev and Eve (Shmueli) Z.; B.A., N.Y. U., 1974; P.A.S., U. Miami Sch. Bus., 1975; M.B.A., Fla. Atlantic U., 1980; m. Mitchell J. Beer, May 21, 1972. Computer programmer Lev Zetlin Assos., Inc., N.Y.C., 1972-73, mktg. coordinator, 1973-75; account exec. Whittelsey Woods, Miami, Fla., 1975-76; pres. Zetlin-Beer-Liu, Inc., Ft. Lauderdale, Fla., 1977—; v.p., dir. Zetlin-Argo Liaison & Guidance Corp., N.Y.C., 1978—; dir. Thalia B. Linen Boutique, Hallandale, Fla.; export cons. Polar Chips Internat. Mem. Fla. team Internat. Challenge Cup, 1978—. Mem. Mensa, Intertel, Phi Kappa Phi, Internat. Backgammon Assn. Home: 6615 Racquet Club Dr Lauderhill FL 33319 Office: 5901 SW 43 St Davie FL 33314

ZICHI, JOSEPH DAMIAN, social worker; b. Bklyn., Jan. 14, 1948; s. Joseph and Frances (Asaro) Z.; B.A., U. Mich., 1969; M.S.W., Waterloo Luth. U., 1973; m. Gretchen Gray, Apr. 29, 1978; 1 dau., Jennifer Lee. Psychiat. social worker Cath. Children's Aid Soc., Toronto, Can., 1969-71, 73-74, Family and Children's Services, Kalamazoo, 1974-75; boys' cottage dir. Daniel Meml., Inc., Jacksonville, Fla., 1975-79; dir. Meth. Family Services, Jacksonville, 1979—; adj. prof. U. North Fla., 1979; mem. planning com. Comprehensive Emergency Services for Children, 1976-78. Cert. Acad. Cert. Social Workers. Mem. Nat. Assn. Social Workers (treas. N.E. Fla. unit 1977-78). Home: 2929 Searchwood Dr Jacksonville FL 32211 Office: Methodist Family Services 1640 Jefferson St Jacksonville FL 32209

ZIDEK, BERNICE LOUISE (MRS. STEPHEN P. ZIDEK), wire mfg. exec.; b. Chgo., Oct. 10, 1906; d. Albert and Bessie (Kaberna) Vonder; diploma Englewood (Ill.) Secretarial Coll., 1923; m. Stephen Paul Zidek, July 22, 1925; children—Louise Ann Zidek Pavlin, Charles Edward. Asst. to asst. mgr. Emerson Drug Co., Chgo., 1923-24; office mgr. Van Dyke Industries, Chgo., 1936-38; partner Midland Metal Products Co., Chgo., 1941—. Troop leader to leader trainer Lone Tree Area council Girl Scouts U.S.A., 1938-68. Recipient Thank You award Girl Scouts U.S.A., 1957. Mem. Nat., Fla. State assns. parliamentarians, Am. Guild Flower Arrangers, Floralia, Nat. Council State Garden Clubs (life), Fla. Fedn. Garden Clubs (life), Nat. Council Flower Show Judges (certified judge), Parliamentary Law Unit Pompano Beach (pres. 1979—), Coral Springs Cultural Soc., Freedoms Found. at Valley Forge. Republican. Roman Catholic. Clubs: Bauhinia Garden Circle (pres. 1965-67), Federated Garden Circles of Ft. Lauderdale (pres. 1974-75), Coral Springs Garden, Midwest, Lighthouse Bonsai, Amateur Fencers, Ikebana Internat. (chpt. pres. 1978-80), Moraine Valley (Ill.) Parliamentary Unit, Women's Civic Coral Ridge Yacht (Ft. Lauderdale); Coral Springs Golf and Tennis; Riverside (Ill.) Golf. Home: 2791 NW 112th Ave Coral Springs FL 33065 also 250 N Delaplaine Rd Riverside IL 60546

ZIEGLER, FREDERICK GENE, cons. engr.; b. Camden, N.J., Nov. 21, 1942; s. Frederick Otto and Irene M. (Bard) Z.; B.E., Vanderbilt U., 1965, M.S., 1966, Ph.D., 1969; m. Victoria B. Ganser, June 4, 1966; children—Laura Lee, Carol Cathleen. Cons. engr. Asso. Water and Air Resources Engrs., Inc., Nashville, 1971, dir. air pollution studies, project engr., 1971, cons. engr., asso. and dir. of air and water resource engring., project mgr., 1972—; guest lectr. Vanderbilt U., Dept. Environ. and Water Resources Engr., Nashville, 1972—, adj. asst. prof., 1974-75; cons. in field. Bd. dirs. Nashville Tech. Inst. of Chem. Engring. Dept., 1974—; mem. Stewardship com. Our Savior Luth. Ch., 1974-75. Served to lt. comdr., USNR, 1969-71. Registered profl. engr., Pa., N.J., Fla., N.C., Tenn. Mem. Ala. Water and Pollution Control Assn., Air Pollution Control Assn., Ky.-Tenn. Water Pollution Control Assn., Water Pollution Control Fedn., Internat. Assn. on Water Pollution Research, Soc. Profl. Engrs., Air Pollution Control Assn., Sigma Nu., Chi Epsilon, Tau Beta Pi. Lutheran. Club: Md. Farms Racket. Home: 2004 Stonehurst Dr Nashville TN 37215 Office: PO Box 40284 Nashville TN 37204

ZIEGLER, JOHN ALAN, polit. scientist; b. Belleville, Ill., Jan. 28, 1933; s. John Wendell and Georgia Elizabeth (Reppel) Z.; B.S., So. Ill. U., Carbondale, 1955, M.S., 1956; Rotary Found. fellow, St. Andrews (Scotland) U., 1956-57; Ph.D., Syracuse (N.Y.) U., 1970; m. Carol Ruth Alcorn, June 15, 1963; children—Mimi, Robin. Asst. prof. polit. sci. and social sci. Calif. State U., Hayward, 1966-72; lectr. Am. civilization Calif. State Poly. U., Pomona, 1972-74; asso. prof., head social sci. area, chmn. dept. polit. sci. and history Hendrix Coll., Conway, Ark., 1974—. Served with AUS, 1957-60. Mem. Am. Polit. Sci. Assn., AAUP, Friends London Sch. Econs., Friends Churchill Meml., Am. Friends Wilton Park. Mem. United Ch. Christ. Home: 14 Oakdale Dr Conway AR 72032 Office: Hendrix Coll Conway AR 72032

ZIEHE, CARL ALBERT, mfg. co. exec.; b. Fort Worth, July 29, 1925; s. Paul Frederick and Helen Marie (Hoffman) Z.; student N. Tex. Agrl. Coll., 1946-47; Tex. Christian U., 1943, 54-55, George Washington U., 1947; m. Mabel Luella Wilke, Aug. 18, 1948; children—David Carl, Susan Marie, Frederick William. Jr. engr., prodn. foreman Nat. Electronics Lab., Alexandria, Va., 1948-49, electronic equipment engr., 1949-50, employment interviewer, 1950-51; wage and salary analyst Gen. Dynamics Corp., Fort Worth, 1951-53, labor relations rep., 1953-55, wage and salary rep., 1955-61, wage and salary adminstr., 1961-68, mgr. mgmt. compensation and devel., 1968-71, corp. mgr. salary compensation, 1971-73, mgr. mgmt. relations and ednl. programs, 1973—; guest speaker in field. Served with USAF, 1943-46; CBI. Mem. Am. Compensation Assn., Gen. Dynamics Mgmt. Assn., Nat. Mgmt. Assn. Lutheran. Home: 4524 Quail Hollow Ct Fort Worth TX 76133 Office: PO Box 748 Fort Worth TX 76101

ZIEMANN, ROBERT LEWIS, accountant; b. Southwick, Idaho, Jan. 23, 1927; s. Gus H. and Wilda (Keeney) Z.; student Oreg. State Coll., 1945-46, U. Idaho, 1948-49; B.B.A., U. Houston, 1952. Accountant, Briscoe, House & Stovall, C.P.A.'s, Houston, 1954, Mattison & Riquelmy, C.P.A.'s, Houston, 1954-61, Harris, Kerr, Forster & Co., C.P.A.'s, Houston, 1961-65; self-employed as C.P.A., Houston, 1965—. Served with USAAF, 1946-47. Elk. Home: 14803 Cypress Meadow Cypress TX also PO Box 66681 Houston TX 77006 Office: 8705 Katy Freeway Houston TX 77024

ZIERER, THOMAS KATONA, oil co. exec.; b. Hungary, Oct. 23, 1943; s. Andre R. and Agotha Katona; came to U.S., 1962, naturalized, 1970; Bacca Laureate, U. Chile, 1962; B.S. and M.S. Indsl. Engring., U. Calif., Berkeley, 1968; m. Kenna Ruth Howell, Nov. 15, 1975. Bus. mgr. The Daily Californian, 1963-67; with Shell Oil Co., Houston, 1968—, sr. transp. specialist, 1972-77, sr. supplies specialist, 1977—; instr. Houston Community Coll., 1975-77. Class of 1902 scholar, 1964—. Mem. Inst. Internat. Edn., Houston Jaycees, L'Alliance Francaise, Ops. Research Soc. Am., Internat. Assn. Energy Economists. Club: Toastmasters. Home: 6224 Willers Way Houston TX 77057 Office: One Shell Plaza Rm 2620 Houston TX 77002

ZIESCHE, SHIRLEY STEEB, ednl. adminstr.; b. Pitts., June 27, 1923; married. B.A. in Sociology, U. Pitts., 1944, M.Ed. in Elem. Edn., 1965. Tchr. presch., 1952-62; tchr., Shady Side Acad., Pitts., 1962-68; tchr. Bd. Public Instrn., Sarasota County, Sarasota, Fla., 1968-71, elem. math. specialist, 1971-74, supr. math. K-12, 1974—. Judge, clk. Local Election Bd., 1952-53. Cert. in sch. supervision. Mem. Sarasota Council Tchrs. Math. (v.p. 1972-74), Nat., Fla. councils tchrs. math., Assn. Supervision and Curriculum Devel., Fla. Assn. Supervision and Curriculum Devel., Fla. Assn. Sch. Adminstrs., Childhood Edn. Internat. Sarasota (v.p.), Fla. Assn. Math. Suprs. (sec.-treas. 1976-78, pres.-elect 1979-80), Internat. Council Edn. of Tchrs., Assn. Supervision and Curriculum Devel., Delta Kappa Gamma. Author: Birds: Activity Books I and II; Understanding Place Value, A.T., 1970. Home: 5529 Cape Leyte Dr Sarasota FL 33581 Office: 2418 Hatton St Sarasota FL 33577

ZIGLAR, NADINE HAYS, charitable orgn. exec.; b. Butler, Pa., Feb. 9, 1952; d. Robert Vernon and Marian (Logan) Hays; B.A. in Religion and Philosophy, Maryville (Tenn.) Coll., 1974; div. With Walton Manor Furniture Industries, Maryville, 1975; exec. dir. United Cerebral Palsy of Central Fla., Inc., Orlando, 1975—. Bd. dirs., sec. T.H.E. Wayfarer, Inc., Orlando, 1978—; vice chmn. Coalition for Citizens with Disabilities, Orlando, 1978—. Mem. Orange County Vol. Health Assn., Brevard County Vol. Health Assn., Am. Bus. Woman's Assn. (named Boss of Yr., City Beautiful chpt. 1978). Democrat. Presbyterian. Office: 506 E Colonial Dr Orlando FL 32803

ZIGMONT, LAWRENCE JOSEPH, data processing auditor; b. Chgo., Apr. 24, 1943; s. William Joseph and Frances Ann (Pocius) Z.; student St. Edward's U., Austin, Tex., 1961-65, U. Wis.-Madison, 1973-75; grad. Sch. Bank Adminstrn. Grad. Program, U. Wis., 1976; m. Celine Mary Barrett, Mar. 20, 1967; 1 dau., Jennifer Marie. Staff auditor S.E. Banking Corp., Miami, Fla., 1966-68, sr. staff auditor, 1968-69, adminstrv. audit asst., 1969-71, auditing officer, 1971-72, asst. auditor, 1972-73, 74-78, asst. to gen. auditor, 1978—; cashier S.E. Bank of Dadeland, Miami, 1973-74. Instr. Office of Comptroller of Currency, Washington, 1975-76, Am. Inst. Banking, 1974—; chmn. Burroughs Bank EDP Auditors Group, 1972-73. Served with USAF, 1965-71. Certified internal auditor, data processing auditor. Mem. Eastern States Assn. Bank Data Processing Auditors (dir.), Am. Inst. Banking, Inst. Internal Auditors (pres. 1976-77, internat. research com. 1977—), EDP Auditors Assn., Data Processing Mgmt. Assn., Bank Adminstrn. Inst. Roman Catholic. Club: K.C. Home: 1315 NE 136 St North Miami FL 33161 Office: 100 S Biscayne Blvd Miami FL 33131

ZIMMER, PAUL THOMAS, electronics co. exec.; b. Monroe, La., Aug. 31, 1934; s. Charles F. and Anna Marie (Sitton) Z.; B.S.E.E., U. Southwestern La., 1962; m. Connie Avant Prevost, Nov. 24, 1962; children—Maria, Rebecca, Patrice, Felicia. Chief engr. Genisco Tech. Corp., Compton, Calif., 1967-71; dir. engring. and reliability The Potter Co., Inglewood, Calif., 1971-73; engring. supr. AVX, San Diego, 1973-76; pres., dir. Tex. Spectrum Electronics, Inc., Dallas, 1976—. Served in USMC, 1955-59. Mem. U.S. C. of C., Nat. Fedn. Ind. Businessmen. Republican. Club: St. Francis Assisi Cath. Ch. Home: 904 Peach Ln De Soto TX 75115 Office: 619 Mercury Ave Duncanville TX 75137

ZIMMERLY, ARTHUR WEAVER, hosp. engr.; b. Hope, Ark., June 6, 1918; s. Charles P. and Louisa Freida (Steinknog) Z.; student Coll. of Mines, El Paso, Tex., 1948-49, Internat. Corr. Schs., 1964-66, Tex. A&M U., 1966-69, U. Tex., 1970-71; m. Cleo Katherine Johnson, Mar. 14, 1940; children—Mary Gail Zimmerly May, Delbert Ray. Elec. apprentice, 1933-37; plumbing apprentice, 1937-41; supt. hosp. constrn. A. W. Johnson Co., Texarkana, Ark., and Benco, Inc., Texarkana, 1941-58; dir. engring. and security Wadley Hosp., Texarkana, Tex., 1958-80; cons. hosp. engring., Texarkana, Ark., 1980—; chmn. adv. com. for engring. Tri-States Shared Services; mem. adv. bd. Tex. State Tech. Inst., Waco, 1975—. Life mem. bd. dirs., past pres. Texarkana Boys' Club; bd. dirs. Tri-States chpt. ARC, 1970—; mem. bldg. com. Texarkana Hist. Soc. and Mus., 1971—; bd. dirs. United Way; deacon Community Baptist Ch. Fellow Ark. Assn. Hosp. Engrs. (pres. 1966-67); mem. Am. Soc. for Hosp. Engrs. (charter, dir. 1969-72), Tex. Assn. Hosp. Engrs. (pres. 1966-67), Ark. Hosp. Assn. (life). Club: Optimist (past dir.). Home: 1903 Senator St Texarkana AR 75502 Office: 2212 Florida St Texarkana AR 75502

ZIMMERMAN, EUGENE WALTER, developer, investor, owner motor hotels; b. nr. Jenner Twp., Pa., Mar. 23, 1909; s. Robert and Amanda A. (Walter) Z.; student pub. schs.; m. Eleanor Witt, Apr. 8, 1930 (div. Oct. 1965); children—Doris Joan Zimmerman Mapes, Ronald E., Rosalie Eleanor Zimmerman Johnson; m. 2d, Irene Fabian, May 23, 1966. Developer, owner Zimmerman Motor Co., Somerset, Pa., 1938-45, Roof Garden Motor Hotel, 1941-52, Ella-Gene Apts., Ft. Lauderdale, Fla., 1946-49, Motel Harrisburg, Pa., 1950-57 (now known as Holiday Motor Hotel-East), 1957—; developer, owner Holiday Motor Hotel, West, Harrisburg, Pa., 1952—, Holiday Inn Town, 1962—; owner Gene Zimmerman's Automobilorama and

Mus., Holiday West, 1965—; ofcl. staff editor Clissold Pub. Co., Chgo. Cons. to motor hotel industry. Recipient Hall of Fame award Am. Motel Mag., Chgo., 1961, Merit Resolution, Pa. Ho. of Reps., 1968. Mem. Am. Hotel Assn., Pa. Motel Assn. (pres. 1953-54, dir. master hosts 1955—, ambassador master hosts 1961, 62), Am. Motor Hotel Assn., (v.p., dir. 1956), Pa., Central Pa. restaurant assns., Nat. Assn. Travel Orgn., Hotel Sales Mgrs. Assn., Hotel Greeters Am., Inter-Am., Internat. hotel assns., Hammond Organ Soc., Tall Cedars Leganon, Harrisburg C. of C., Am. Airlines (Admiral), Acacia, Antique Automobile Club Am. (sr. judge), Classic Car Club Am., Horseless Carriage Club, Vets. Motor Car Club, Auburn-Cord-Duesenberg Club, Pierce-Arrow Soc., Rolls Royce Owners Club, S.A.R., Am. Soc. Travel Agts., Pa. Soc. Republican. Lutheran. Mason (K.T., Shriner), Rotarian. Clubs: TWA Ambassador (life), American Airlines Admiral (life) (N.Y.C.); Matson Mariners' (hon. navigator) (San Francisco) Curved Dash Owners (New Hope, Pa.); Executives, Zembo Luncheon (Harrisburg); Le Club International (Fort Lauderdale); Red Carpet of United Airlines; Chub Cay (The Bahamas). Internat. editor: Am. Motel mag., 1962—. Home: 2567 Mercedes Dr Fort Lauderdale FL 33316 Office: Automobilorama Inc 1500 SE 17th St Fort Lauderdale FL 33316

ZIMMERMAN, KENT WILLIAM, fin. analyst; b. Tampa, Fla., Jan. 26, 1948; s. G. Floyd and Dorthy (Johns) Z.; B.S. in B.A., Fla. Tech. U., 1978; m. Candace Cheryl Pinder, Jan. 4, 1969; children—Kent William, Michelle Renea. Program adminstr., Harris Corp., Palm Bay, Fla., 1968-72, dept. adminstr. 1972-78, fin. analyst, 1978—. Served with USAR/USCGR, 1969—. Mem. Am. Mgmt. Assn., Spacecoast Swim Assn. (treas. 1979—). Methodist. Home: 220 W Fee Ave Melbourne FL 32901 Office: PO Box 37 Melbourne FL 32901

ZIMMERMAN, RAYMOND ERNEST, cons. energy engr.; b. Pitts., Oct. 10, 1903; s. Corwin Ernest and Katherine Louise (Moran) Z.; B.C.S., Pa. State U., 1926, M.S., 1928, E.M., 1930; m. Loretta Frances Markle, Sept. 29, 1945; children—Robert, Patricia, David, Barbara, Gail. Dir. research Pitts. Coal Carbonization Co., 1930-40; prof., head dept. mineral engring. Pa. State U., 1946-50; dir. coal preparation U.S. Steel, 1951-54; v.p., cons. engr. Paul Weir Co., Chgo., 1954—. Served to lt. col. AUS, 1940-46; ETO, CBI. Decorated Legion of Merit; registered profl. engr., Can. Fellow Inst. Mining and Metallurgy (U.K.), Mineral Preparation Soc. (U.K.); mem. Am., Can. insts. mining engrs., AAAS, Sigma Xi, Phi Lambda Upsilon, Sigma Gamma Epsilon, Pi Kappa Phi. Republican. Clubs: Tower (Chgo.); Masons (32 deg.). Author: (with others) Coal Preparation, 1977; asso. editor World Coal, 1975—; contbr. articles to profl. jours. Home: 4803 Sunset Cts Cape Coral FL 33904

ZIMMERMAN, RAYMOND JOHN, biologist, educator; b. Millville, N.J., Sept. 9, 1946; s. Raymond John and Doris Ruth Z.; B.A., Pfeiffer Coll., 1968; M.S., N.C. State U., 1974, Ph.D., 1976; m. Lawanna Carr, Apr. 8, 1978; children—Nancy Beth, Laurie Jean (by previous marriage). Tchr. biology and chemistry, varsity coach Millville (N.J.) Sr. High Sch., 1968-72; asst. prof. biology U. S.C., Aiken, 1976—. NIH trainee in genetics, 1972-76; NSF grantee, 1978. Mem. AAAS, Am. Soc. Microbiology, Sigma Xi. Methodist. Home: 3320 Forest Dr Aiken SC 29801 Office: Biology Dept U SC 201 N 171 University Pkwy Aiken SC 29801

ZIMMERMAN, ROBERT EUGENE, mfg. co. exec.; b. Jay County, Ind., Jan. 1, 1923; s. Forrest John and Mildred Ruth (Life) Z.; cert. Ball State U.; m. Mary Elizabeth Jackson, May 5, 1943; 1 dau. Suzanne K. With Warner Machine Products, Inc., Muncie, Ind., 1941-71, treas., officer mgr., 1965-71, also dir.; sales coordinator Muncie Parts Mfg. Co., Inc., 1971-76, mgr., Atlanta, 1976—. Bd. dirs., treas. Vis. Nurses' Assn., 1963-68, pres., 1968; bd. dirs. sec. Muncie Boys Club, 1964-76; treas. Delaware County (Ind.) Cancer Soc., 1964-70; trustee Earlham Coll., Richmond, Ind., 1968-76. Served with USNR, 1943-46. Republican. Quaker. Club: Optimist (pres. 1958-59). Home: 3406 Mill Stream Ln Marietta GA 30060 Office: 1100 La Grange Blvd SW Atlanta GA 30336

ZIMMERMAN, ROBERT LOUIS, physicist; b. Yonkers, N.Y., June 17, 1929; s. Percy W. and Patti Z.; B.S., Rensselaer Poly. Inst., 1951; M.S., Ga. Inst. Tech., 1969; m. Doris Viola Toy, Sept. 23, 1961; 1 dau., Melissa Caroline. Physics trainee duPont, Oak Ridge, 1951-52, health physics supr., Savannah River, 1952-59; mgr. health physics Republic Aviation Corp., 1959-61; radiological safety officer Ga. Inst. Tech., Atlanta, 1961-73, also asso. chief nuclear and biol. scis. div.; pres. Phoenix Technology Corp. cons. med. and indsl. users radiation, Decatur, Ga., 1973—. Certified in health physics Am. Bd. Health Physics. Mem. Health Physics Soc., Am. Nuclear Soc., Soc. Nuclear Medicine, Am. Indsl. Assn. Home: 1863 Bedfordshire Ct Decatur GA 30033 Office: 2256 Northlake Pky Suite 305 Tucker GA 30084

ZIMMERMAN, SAMUEL LEE, SR., ednl. adminstr.; b. Anderson, S.C., Apr. 28, 1923; s. W. L. Zimmerman; B.A. in Elementary Edn., Benedict Coll., 1960; postgrad. Furman U., 1965-67; m. Blanche Carol; 1 son, Samuel Lee. Tchr. reading, elementary sch. Greenville (S.C.) Sch. Dist., 1960-70, adminstrv. asst. for sch. community relations, 1960-70, dir. sch.-community relations, 1973—; editorial writer, Black affairs reporter The Greenville Piedmont, 1970-73. Bd. dirs. Greenville Urban League, 1970-76, United Way, 1975-77; chmn. drive Multiple Schlerosis, 1976; bd. dirs. Family Counseling Services, 1974-77, Easter Seal Soc. Crippled Children and Adults, 1974-77; mem. S.C. Commn. for Blind, 1974—, v.p.-at-large, 1979—. Mem. Greenville County Edn. Assn., S.C. Edn. Assn., NEA, Nat. Sch. Public Relations Assn. Home: 6 Allendale Ln Greenville SC 19607 Office: Box 2848 Greenville SC 29602

ZIMNY, MARILYN LUCILE, anatomist; b. Chgo., Dec. 12, 1927; d. John and Lucile (Andryske) Zimny; A.B., U. Ill., 1948; M.S., Loyola U., Chgo., 1951, Ph.D., 1954. Asst. prof., Med. Center, La. State U., New Orleans, 1954-59, asso. prof., 1959-64, prof., 1964-75, prof. and acting dept. head, 1975-76, prof. and dept. head, 1976—. Grantee NIH, 1958-72, La. Chpt. Arthritis Found., 1969-72, Schlieder Ednl. Found., 1972-75, Frost Found., 1975—. Mem. Am. Assn. Anatomists, Am. Physiol. Soc., Orthopedic Research Soc., Electron Microscopic Soc. Am., La. Soc. Electron Microscopy (pres. 1975), Omicron Kappa Upsilon. Roman Catholic. Home: 1106 Burgundy St New Orleans LA 70116 Office: 1542 Tulane Ave New Orleans LA 70112

ZINK, EVELYN JEANNETTE, govt. ofcl.; b. Duncan, Okla., Dec. 16, 1948; d. Leroy and Betty Jo (Williams) Z.; B.A., U. Okla., 1971, M.Ed., 1975. Asst. to fin. aid dir. Office of Student Fin. Aid. Okla. U., Norman, 1972, fin. aid counselor, 1972-75; fin. aid adv. Office of Student Fin. Aid, N.Mex. State U., Las Cruces, 1975-79, asst. dir., 1978-79, asso. dir., 1979; edn. program specialist Office Edn., HEW, Dallas, 1979—. Mem. Am. Coll. Personnel Assn. (state rep. to women's task force 1976—), Am. Personnel and Guidance Assn., Nat., SW, N.Mex. (treas. 1978-79) assns. student fin. aid adminstrs., Assn. U. Okla. Profl. Employees, Omicron Nu. Office: Box 1200 Main Tower Bldg Dallas TX

ZINN, ELIAS PAUL, retail audio exec.; b. Houston, Nov. 7, 1954; s. Julius and Harriett (Dubinski) Z.; student U. Tex., 1972-74; m. Janis Ann Turboff, Aug. 7, 1977. Salesman, Custom Hi Fi Discount Center, Houston, 1971-72, mgr., 1972-73, v.p. sales, 1974—, v.p. sales and operation, 1974-75, pres., 1975-76, pres., chief exec. officer, chief operating officer, 1976—. Advisor, Better Bus. Bur., Houston, 1976-79. Mem. C. of C. Democrat. Jewish. Club: Emanuel Brotherhood. Home: 10630 Sandpiper St Houston TX 77096 Office: 11231 Southwest Freeway Houston TX 77096

ZINSMASTER, ROBERT FREDERICK, utilities ofcl.; b. Pitts., Aug. 16, 1939; s. Robert Charles and Estella Clara (Koehler) Z.; student Valencia Community Coll., 1977-79, Mid-Fla. Tech. Inst., 1975; m. Helen Heide, Dec. 21, 1962; children—Robert David, Kelly Ann. With Howard Johnson's, Pitts., 1961-62, Holiday Inns Am., Pitts and Tyler, Tex., 1963-64; heavy equipment operator Shaler Twp., Pitts., 1964-68; with Walt Disney World, Orlando, Fla., 1970-72; chief draftsman Orlando Utilities Commn., 1972—; serviceman Automatic Controls, Pitts. Sec., St. Charles Sch. Bd., Orlando, 1977-78; co. rep. United Fund, 1977-78. Served with USN, 1957-60. Recipient Cert. of Achievement, Engring. Reprographics Soc., 1978. Mem. Engring. Reprographics Soc., Am. Mgmt. Assn. Republican. Roman Catholic. Club: Bass Masters. Home: 1016 N Palm Ave Orlando FL 32804 Office: PO Box 3193 Orlando FL 32802

ZINTGRAFF, EDWARD FORREST, hosp. adminstr.; b. Ft. Lauderdale, Fla., Dec. 21, 1950; s. Paul Edward and June Rose (Zent) Z.; B.A. in Econs. and Govt., U. Redlands, 1973; M.Ed. in Adminstrn. (Tex. Assn. Sch. Bus. Ofcls. scholar 1976), Tex. Tech. U., 1976; m. Pamela Diann Dean. Asst. bus. mgr. Central Plains Regional Hosp., Plainview, Tex., 1977-78; adminstr. Garza Meml. Hosp., Post, Tex., 1977-79, City-County Ambulance Ser., Post, 1978-79, Yoakum County Hosp., Denver City, Tex., 1979—; emergency med. technician, instr. Mem. Tex. Hosp. Assn., N.W. Tex. Hosp. Assn., Garza County Emergency Med. Ser. Assn., Am. Cancer Soc., A.R.C., Post C. of C. Presbyterian. Club: Post Rotary. Home: 506 W Elm St Denver City TX 79323 Office: 612 W 4th St Denver City TX 79323

ZION, CAROL LEE, coll. adminstr.; b. N.Y.C., Aug. 1 1932; d. Benjamin and Ruth (Shotlender) Leventhal; B.A., U. Miami, 1952, M.S., 1953; Ph.D., Fla. State U., 1965. Instr. philosophy Miami-Dade Community Coll., 1960-61, head philosophy dept., 1961-63, dir. humanities, 1965; dean instrn. El Centro Coll., 1966-67; specialist in ednl. planning Dallas County Community Coll. Dist., 1967-68; dir. staff and orgn. devel. Miami-Dade Community Coll., 1968—; pvt. cons. agys., univs. Recipient Dallas Time-Herald Woman of Year award, 1968. Mem. Am. Assn. Higher Edn., Am. Mgmt. Assn., Am. Soc. Tng. and Devel., Profl. Orgn. Devel. Network (core com. 1979—), Psi Chi, Alpha Lambda Delta, Phi Kappa Phi, Mortar Board. Co-author and editor: Miami-Dade Community Coll. Staff Devel. Handbooks, Vol. I-V, 1973; contbr. articles to profl. jours., chpts. to books. Home: 6565 SW 93d Ave Miami FL 33173 Office: Miami-Dade Community Coll 11380 NW 27th Ave Miami FL 33167

ZIRKO, LOUIS JOHN, roofing mfg. co. exec.; b. Elgin, Ill., Dec. 10, 1953; s. Louis John and Mary Elizabeth (Krewson) Z.; student U. Ky., Wake Forest U., 1971, Murray State U., 1972; A.A.S. in Mgmt. Tech., Madisonville Community Coll., 1975. Mem. rates and tariffs staff Ligon Specialized Haulers, Madisonville, Ky., 1972-75; mem. personnel staff Goodyear Tire & Rubber Co., Madisonville, 1975-79, editor Wingfoot Clan, 1975-79; mgr. personnel and safety Elk Corp. Ala., Tuscaloosa, 1979—. Commr., Hopkins County (Ky.) Indsl. Basketball League, 1976-79; bd. dirs. Hopkins County chpt. ARC, 1977-79; fin. chmn. Hopkins County Young Republicans, 1979. Mem. Internat. Assn. Bus. Communicators, Tuscaloosa Mgmt. Assn., Tuscaloosa Personnel Assn., Am. Soc. Personnel Adminstrs., Bass Anglers Sportsman's Soc., Evansville Aquarium Soc. Roman Catholic. Clubs: Goodyear Bass, Sons Am. Legion; Rotary (Tuscaloosa). Office: PO Box 2450 Old Sanders Ferry Rd Tuscaloosa AL 35403

ZODHIATES, SPIROS GEORGE, assn. exec.; b. Cyprus, Mar. 13, 1922; s. George and Mary (Toumazou) Z.; student Am. U. Cairo, 1941-45; B.Th., Shelton Coll., 1947; M.A., N.Y. U., 1951; Th.D., Luther Rice Sem., 1978; m. Joan Carol Wassel, Jan. 10, 1948; children—Priscilla, Lois Ann, Philip, Mary. Came to U.S., 1946, naturalized, 1949. Gen. sec. Am. Mission to Greeks, Inc., Ridgefield, N.J., 1946-65, pres., 1965—. Served with Brit. Army, 1943-45. Recipient Gold medal Greek Red Cross, 1957. Baptist. Author: Behavior of Belief, 1959; Was Christ God?, 1966; The Pursuit of Happiness, 1966; A Christian View of War and Peace, 1966; To Love Is to Live, 1967; Conquering the Fear of Death, 1970; The Song of the Virgin, 1973; Tongues!?, 1974; The Perfect Gift, 1974; A Revolutionary Mystery, 1974, others; editor-in-chief: Pulpit Helps; (in Greek) Voice of the Gospel. Daily radio broadcaster. Home: 8927 Villa Rica Circle Chattanooga TN 37421

ZOHDI, MAGD ELDIN, educator; b. Cairo, Apr. 18, 1933; came to U.S., 1964, naturalized, 1971; s. Ismail Abdella and Nemat (Rizk) Z.; diploma Cairo U., 1954, B.S., 1962; M.S., U. Kan., 1965; Ph.D., Okla. State U., 1969; m. Omnia Elmenshawy, Sept. 17, 1964; children—Tarek, Mona. With Maintenance Machinery, Cairo, 1954-60; instr. Cairo U., 1962-64; grad. teaching asst. Okla. State U., Stillwater, 1966-69; asso. prof. La. State U., Baton Rouge, 1969-75, prof., 1975—, coordinator engring. mgmt. program, 1976—; pres. Am. Contracting and Trading Corp., Baton Rouge, 1978. Fulbright scholar, 1964; recipient Excellence in Undergrad. Teaching award Standard Oil Found., 1971; Presdl. Honor award Okla. State U., 1968. Mem. Soc. Mfg. Engrs., Am. Inst. Indsl. Engrs., Sigma Xi, Tau Beta Pi. Contbr. articles to profl. jours. Home: 5050 S Chalet Ct Baton Rouge LA 70808 Office: 3132 Ceba Bldg La State Univ Baton Rouge LA 70803

ZOLTEWICZ, JOHN ANDREW, chemist; b. Nanticoke, Pa., Dec. 5, 1935; s. John Francis and Anne M. (Turchin) Z.; A.B., Princeton U., 1957, Ph.D., 1960; m. Susan Wier, Aug. 17, 1965; children—Jennifer Ann, Joanna Sue, John Andrew. NATO postdoctoral fellow U. Munich (Ger.), 1960-61; NIH and Shell Fund postdoctoral fellow Brown U., 1961-63; prof. Organic Chemistry U. Fla., 1963—; Fulbright Sr. scholar, Australia, 1976. Recipient Research award Sigma Xi, 1973. Mem. Am. Chem. Soc. Research, numerous publs. in chemistry. Home: 2609 SW 9th Dr Gainesville FL 32601 Office: Dept Chemistry U Fla Gainesville FL 32611

ZONGOR, ENDRE B., mfg. co. exec.; b. Budapest, Hungary, Sept. 23, 1943; came to U.S., 1951, naturalized, 1956; s. Endre Tibor and Eniko (Telkes) Z.; B.S., U. Ill., 1965; m. Irene R. Tykvart, June 24, 1967; children—Michael, Steven, Kenneth. Research asst. dept. pathology Michael Reese Hosp., Chgo., 1965-67; formulator Sherwin Williams, Chgo., 1967; corrosion engr. Union Tank Car, East Chicago, Ind., 1967-70; sales rep. Amoco Chems. Corp., Chgo., 1970-73; v.p. mktg. Nat. Polymer Co., Memphis, 1973-75; v.p. Prime Colorants, Franklin, Tenn., 1975—. Mem. Nat. Assn. Corrosion Engrs., Protective Coatings Com., Soc. Plastics Engrs. (dir.), Tennessee Valley Soc. Plastics Engrs. (pres. 1975, 78). Home: 1112 Dickinson Ln Franklin TN 37064 Office: PO Box 427 Alpha Dr Franklin TN 37064

ZONTINE, DAVID HERBERT, neurologist; b. Pitts., Nov. 6, 1938; s. Clarence William and Eleanor Mary (Foley) Z.; B.A., St. Vincent Coll., 1960; M.D., U Pitts., 1964; m. Patricia Ann Lynch, Aug. 27, 1964; children—Carrie Beth, Matthew David. Intern, Mercy Hosp., Pitts., 1964-65; resident U. Va., Charlottesville, 1968-71, chief resident, 1971; instr. neurology U. Mich. Med. Center, Ann Arbor, 1971-74; asst. chief neurology VA Hosp., Ann Arbor, 1971-74; clin. asst. prof. neurology U. Va. Med. Sch., 1974—; practice medicine specializing in neurology, Winchester, Va., 1974—; mem. staffs Winchester Meml. Hosp., Loudoun Meml. Hosp., King's Daus. Hosp., City Hosp., Martinsburg, W.Va., Warren Meml. Hosp., Front Royal, Va. Served with USNR 1966-68. Jesse Clark fellow, U. Pitts., 1960-61; diplomate Am. Bd. Psychiatry and Neurology (examiner 1975-77). Mem. Am. Acad. Neurology, Va. Neurol. Assn., No. Va. Med. Soc., Soc. Clin. Neurologists, Winchester-Frederick County Hist. Soc., Preservation of Historic Winchester. Republican. Roman Catholic. Home: 614 Tennyson Ave Winchester VA 22601 Office: 125 Medical Circle Winchester VA 22601

ZOPF, EVELYN LANOEL MONTGOMERY, guidance counselor; b. Laurel, Miss., July 10, 1932; d. Arthur LaNoel and Ruby Lee (Lewis) Montgomery; Mus.B. in Edn., U. So. Miss., 1953, M.A., 1954; m. Paul Edward Zopf, Jr., Aug. 5, 1956; 1 son, Eric Paul. Guidance counselor U. So. Miss., 1953-54, U. Fla., 1954-56; tchr. New Orleans City Schs., 1956-57; pub. sch. music tchr., band dir., choral dir. Putnam County Schs., Fla., 1957-59; pvt. music tchr. voice, pino, clarinet and trumpet, 1953-61; substitute tchr. Guilford County Schs., 1959—; mem. arts series com. Guilford Coll., 1973-77; interim choir dir. New Garden Friends Meeting, 1961, chmn. music com., 1974-76. Vol., ARC, Boy Scouts Am.; adviser to fgn. students, 1954-56, 59-62; precinct del. County Democratic Conv., 1977, 79, precinct worker, 1980, campaign worker, 1980; bd. dirs. Greensboro Friends of Music, 1970-71. Recipient Best Citizen award Miss. So. Coll., 1953. Mem. United Soc. of Friends Women (pres. 1979-81), Guilford Coll. Community Chorus, Phi Mu. Clubs: Women's Soc. (dir. 1978—), Guilford Coll. Women (past pres.), Guilford Coll. Arts Appreciation (v.p. 1980—), Guilford Gourmet. Home: 815 George White Rd Greensboro NC 27410

ZORN, EUGENE CHRISTIAN, JR., bank economist; b. N.Y.C., Jan. 17, 1916; s. Eugene Christian and Charlotte (Bode) Z.; B.B.A., CCNY, 1937; M.S., Columbia U., 1942; m. Elizabeth Orban, Aug. 11, 1956; children—Barbara Jean, Robert Eugene. Dep. mgr., dir. research Am. Bankers Assn., N.Y.C., 1952-60; v.p., economist Republic Nat. Bank, Dallas 1960-66, sr. v.p., economist, 1966—, also mem. exec., trust, trust investment and fund mgmt. coms.; mem. faculty Southwestern Grad. Sch. Banking, Stonier Grad. Sch. Banking; mem. cons. com. bank economists U.S. Comptroller of Currency, 1964-77, chmn., 1973-77. Bd. dirs. Tex. Research League, 1965-74, Tex. Council Econ. Edn., 1968-72; mem. adv. com. and tech. subcom. Tex. Energy Adv. Council, 1977—; mem. fin. adv. council Tex. Tech. U., 1979—; conferee and essayist Goals for Dallas, 1966, mem. econ. potentials com., 1967-71, chmn. tech. adv. group of economists, 1967-71, mem. task force on economy of Dallas, 1976-78, mem. economy goals achievement com., 1978—; mem. econ. research com. Greater Dallas Planning Council, 1970, mem. environ. and urban design com., 1979—; mem. family and children's panel Community Council Greater Dallas, 1966-68; chmn. Spl. Dallas Citizens Council Study Com. on Philanthropy, 1963-65. Served to capt. USAAF, 1943-46. Recipient Alumni Achievement award CCNY, 1968. Mem. Am. Bankers Assn. (econ. adv. com. 1970-74; urban devel. com. 1974-77, chmn. 1976-77; governing council 1976-77), Nat. Planning Assn. (bus. com. on nat. policy 1972—), Am. Econ. Assn., Am. Mgmt. Assn., Am. Statis. Assn., Am. Fin. Assn., Nat. Assn. Bus. Economists, Nat. Economists Club, Southwestern Social Sci. Assn., So. Fin. Assn., Fin. Mgmt. Assn., Dallas Council World Affairs, Dallas Press Club, Dallas Art Assn., Alliance Française, Newcomen Soc., U.S. C. of C. (banking, monetary and fiscal affairs com. 1967-76), Dallas C. of C. (bus. and econ. research com. 1963-69, chmn. 1968, 69; subcom. gen. aviation 1968-69), Beta Gamma Sigma. Club: Northwood (Dallas). Home: 4647 Hallmark Dr Dallas TX 75229 Office Republic Nat Bank PO Box 225961 Dallas TX 75265

ZSCHAU, JULIUS JAMES, lawyer; b. Peoria, Ill., Apr. 1, 1940; s. Raymond Ernst and Rosamond Lillian (Malicoat) Z.; B.S. in Commerce, U. Ill., 1962, J.D., 1966; LL.M., John Marshall Law Sch., 1978; m. Leila Joan Krueger, Aug. 7, 1971; children—Kristen Elisabeth, Kimberly Erna, Kira Jamie. Admitted to Ill. bar, 1966, U.S. Supreme Ct. bar, 1973, Fla. bar, 1975; atty. Ill. Central R.R. Co., Chgo., 1966-68; asso. firm Coin & Sheerin, Chgo., 1968-70, Snyder, Clarke, Dalziel, Holmquist & Johnson, Waukegan, Ill., 1970-72; counsel Ill. Center Corp. Chgo., 1972-74; v.p., gen. counsel, sec. Am. Agronomics Corp., Tampa, Fla., 1974-75; pres. firm Sorota & Zschau, P.A., Clearwater, Fla., 1975—; dir. Holopeter & Post Inc., 1974-76, SE States Mortgage Ic., 1975-77; v.p., gen. counsel, sec. Am. Internat. Land Corp., 1974-75. Candidate Ill. Constl. Conv., 1969. Served to comdr. USNR, 1962-64. Mem. S.A.R., Am., Ill., Chgo., Fla., Clearwater bar assns. Republican. Mem. United Ch. Christ. Clubs: Countryside Country, Masons, Shriners. Home: 1910 Saddlehill Rd N Dunedin FL 33528 Office: 2515 Countryside Blvd Suite A Clearwater FL 33515

ZSOHAR, JULIUS, artist, educator; b. Kisrakos, Hungary, Apr. 23, 1912; came to U.S., 1950, naturalized, 1956; s. Michael and Ethel (Batha) Z.; Cert. in Teaching, State Tchrs. Coll. (Budapest), 1932; Ph.D., U. Budapest, 1941; m. Elizabeth Padanyi, July 22, 1940; children—Elizabeth, Julius, Helen, Zoltan, Julia, Isabel, Leslie. Tchr. public schs., Budapest, 1933-44; asst. to prof. U. Budapest, 1941-44; advt. artist Flexsteel Furniture Co., Waxahachie, Tex., 1959-60; designing artist Superior Decals Co., Dallas, 1960-63; part-time faculty art Hill Jr. Coll., Hillsboro, Tex., 1964—, instr., 1973—, Cleburne Extension, 1970—; lectr. art appreciation, water color, oil painting; owner Dr. Zsohar's Sch. Art and Gallery, Dallas, 1960—; group shows: Dallas Artists and Craftsmen Associated, 1963, 64, 65, 66, 67, 68, 69, 78, 79, Coppini Acad. Fine Arts, San Antonio, 1978-79, Southwestern Watercolor Soc., Dallas, 1979; represented in permanent collections: Hill Jr. Coll., Tex. Dept. Parks and Wildlife, also pvt. collections. Mem. Artists and Craftsmen Associated Dallas (pres. 1970), Southwestern Watercolor Soc., Coppini Acad. Fine Arts. Presbyterian. Contbr. articles to profl. jours.; author: Teacher's Guide Book Teaching Nature Science, 1944. Home: 1400 E Marvin Ave Waxahachie TX 75165 Office: 8420 Ames St Dallas TX 75225

ZUCKER, LEON WILLIAM, financial exec.; b. N.Y.C., May 7, 1921; s. Benjamin and Helen (Schellerman) Z.; B.B.A., Coll. City, N.Y., 1940; postgrad. Stanford, 1943-44; m. Arline Davidson, June 17, 1947; children—Harold G., Ricki S. Treas., Sealand Dock and Terminal Corp., Fed. Stevedoring Co., Inc., Bklyn., 1947-59, treas., dir. Containerships, Inc., N.Y.C., 1959-61; treas. Erie & St. Lawrence Corp., 1959-61; asst. treas. Meml. Sloan-Kettering Cancer Center, Sloan-Kettering Inst. for Cancer Research, Meml. Hosp. for Cancer and Allied Diseases, 1961-66, v.p. fin., 1966-76; v.p. fin. Pub. Health Trust of Dade County (Fla.), 1976—; pvt. practice C.P.A., 1940-42, 45-47; adj. prof. U. Miami, 1978—. Cons. U.S. Dept. Health, Edn. and Welfare, 1969—. Bd. dirs. Nassau Center for Emotionally Disturbed Children, 1965-70, treas., 1966-69, pres., 1969-70; bd. dirs. Pride of

Judea Treatment Center, 1974-76; mem. U.S. Com. for Israel Environment; trustee Arnold and Marie Schwartz Coll. Pharmacy and Health Scis., L.I. U., 1976-77; vice chmn. State of Fla. Medicaid Adv. Council; mem. United Way of Dade County, 1978. Mem. Am. Inst. C.P.A.'s, Financial Execs. Inst. (dir.), N.Y. State Soc. C.P.A.'s, Hosp. Financial Mgmt. Assn., Fla. Inst. C.P.A.'s. Home: 3650 N 36th Ave Hollywood FL 33021 Office: 1611 NW 12th Ave Miami FL 33136

ZUCKERMAN, JOHN VITTO, educator, mgmt. cons.; b. Chgo., Sept. 15, 1918; s. Nathan and Tillie (Vitto) Z.; student U. Chgo., 1939, 42; M.A., Stanford U., 1948, Ph.D., 1951; postgrad. Bates Coll. Law, U. Houston, 1976-80; 1 son from previous marriage, John Bruce. Research scientist Air Force and U.S. Army, Washington, 1950-55; dir. personnel and indsl. relations Ampex Corp., Redwood City, Calif., 1955-60; mgr. mktg. Ampex Corp., Washington, 1960-61; dep. and acting dir. Bur. Internat. Bus. Ops., Dept. Commerce, 1961-63; asso. prof. mgmt., dir. research and devel. mgmt. program U. So. Calif., 1963-69; prof. mgmt. U. Houston, 1969—, dep. dir. Energy Inst., 1973-75; mgmt. cons., 1951—. Vice pres., then pres. Peninsula Symphony Assn., 1956-60; v.p. Brentwood Symphony Assn., 1964-69; mem. Houston Center for Humanities, 1979—. Served with AUS, 1943-46. Lic. psychologist, Tex. Fellow Am. Psychol. Assn.; mem. Acad. Mgmt., Acad. Applied Sci., Indsl. Relations Research Assn., Houston C. of C., Sigma Xi, Beta Gamma Sigma. Contbr. articles to profl. jours. Office: Dept Mgmt Univ Houston Houston TX 77004

ZUHDI, MOHAMED NAZIH, physician; b. Beirut, Lebanon, May 19, 1925; s. Omar and Lutfiye (Atef) Z.; came to U.S., 1950; B.A., Am. U., Beirut, Lebanon, 1946, M.D., 1950; children by previous marriage—Omar, Nabil; m. 2d, Annette McMichael; children—Adam, Leyla, Zachariah. Intern St. Vincent's Hosp., N.Y.C., 1950-51, Presbyn.-Columbia Med. Center. N.Y.C., 1951-52; resident Kings County State U. N.Y. Med. Center, N.Y.C., 1952-56, fellow, 1952-53; resident U. Hosp., Mpls., 1956, Oklahoma City, 1957-58; practice medicine specializing in cardivocascular and thoracic surgery, Oklahoma City, 1958—; active thoracic Bapt., Mercy, St. Anthony hosps.; asst. instr. surgery State U. N.Y., 1955-56. Named Hon. Citizen Brazil. Diplomate Am. Bd. Surgery, Am. Bd. Thoracic Surgery. Fellow A.C.S.; mem. Am., Okla. thoracic socs., Am., So., Okla. med. assns., Internat., Am. colls. angiology, Am. Coll. Chest Physicians, Oklahoma City C. of C., Oklahoma County Med. Soc., Oklahoma City Clin. Soc., Okla. Surg. Assn., Southwestern Sug. Congress, Am. Coll. Cardiology, Am. Soc. Artificial Internal Organs, Soc. Thoracic Surgeons (founder mem.), Am. Assn. for Thoracic Surgery, Internat. Cardiovascular Soc., Okla. Heart Assn., Osler Soc., Am. Assn. Thoracic Surgery, La Sociedad Colombia de Cardiologia (hon.). Contbg. author Cardiac Surgery. Contbr. numerous articles to profl. jours.; developer numerous med. devices and techniques. Home: 7528 NW 150 Route 2 Edmond OK 73034 Office: 3400 NW Expressway Oklahoma City OK 73112

ZUKER, RAYMOND FREDERICK, univ. adminstr.; b. Dothan, Ala., Dec. 30, 1945; s. Raymond Francis and Naomi Amanda (Clark) Z.; B.A., Duke U., 1967, M.Ed., 1975, postgrad., 1975—; m. Su Young Lee, May 15, 1971; children—Sonya Lee, Julianna Marie. Asst. dir. admissions undergraduate, Duke U., Durham, N.C., 1971-77; instr. health and phys. edn., 1973-77; asso. dir. admissions Tulane U., New Orleans, 1977-79, dir. admissions, 1979—; coordinator community edn. Durham County Schs., 1975-76. Bd. dirs. Carrington Community Edn. Center, Inc., 1976-77; county chmn. Howard Lee for Lt. Gov., 1976. Served with U.S. Army, 1968-71. N.C. Inst. Politics fellow, 1974. Mem. Am., N.C. psychol. assns., Am., N.C. personnel and guidance assns., Nat. Assn. Coll. Admissions Counselors, Am. Assn. Collegiate Registrars and Admissions Officers, Nat. Assn. Fgn. Student Affairs. Author: (with Karen C. Hegener) Peterson's Guide to College Admissions—How to Put the Odds on Your Side, 1976. Home: 9239 4th St River Ridge LA 70123 Office: Office Admissions Tulane Univ New Orleans LA 70118

ZUMBERGE, JAMES H., univ. pres.; Ph.D., U. Minn.; LL.D., Grand Valley State Coll., Allendale, Mich.; L.H.D., Nebr. Wesleyan U.; m. Marilyn Edwards, 1947; children—John, JoEllen, James, Mark. Instr. Duke, 1946-47, U. Minn., 1947-50; mem. faculty U. Mich., 1950-62; pres. Grand Valley State Coll., Allendale, Mich., 1963-68; dean U. Ariz., 1968-72; chancellor U. Nebr., Lincoln, 1972-75; pres. So. Meth. U., Dallas, 1975—; dir. Gardner-Denver Corp., Dallas Power and Light Co., Bankers Life Nebr. Chmn. com. polar research Nat. Acad. Scis., 1972—. Recipient Antarctic Service medal, 1966; U. Minn. Outstanding Alumni Service award, 1972. Mem. Geol. Soc. Am., Am. Geophys. Union, Soc. Econ. Geologists, Glaciol. Soc., AAAS, Sigma Xi. Clubs: Cosmos (Washington). Author: Lakes of Minnesota, 1952; Elements of Geology, 1957, 63, 72; Laboratory Manual for Physical Geology, 1951, 57, 67, 73. Home: 3721 Potomac St Dallas TX 75205 Office: So Meth U Dallas TX 75275

ZURICH, RICHARD PETER, marine retail exec.; b. Freeport, N.Y., Oct. 11, 1947; s. John Peter and Pearl Marie (Bode) Z.; B.S. in Math., SUNY, 1969; M.B.A. with high honors, Fla. Inst. Tech., 1976; m. Elizabeth Ann Stein, Feb. 14, 1970; children—Jennifer Leigh, Brett Frederick. Service rep. Fla. Power & Light Co., Stuart and Ft. Pierce, 1972-77; pres. Casa Rio Boat & Motor Sales, Inc., Jensen Beach, Fla., 1977—; adj. instr. mgmt. Fla. Inst. Tech., also mem. curriculum devel. com. for marine devel. Mem. Vestry St. Mary's Ch., Stuart. Served with USN, 1969-70. Mem. Marine Industries Assn. (past treas.), Stuart C. of C., Jensen Beach C. of C. (dir.), Episcopalian. Clubs: Stuart Rotary (past dir., community service award, 1976), Stuart Sailfish. Home: 1112 NE St Lucie Terrace Jensen Beach FL 33457 Office: 1050 NE Dixie Highway Jensen Beach FL 33457

ZUSSMAN, BERNARD MAURICE, physician; b. N.Y.C., Apr. 26, 1906; s. Julius and Ida (Finkelstein) Z.; B.S., City U. N.Y., 1925; M.A., Columbia U., 1926; M.D., N.Y. U., 1930; m. Jane Erdman, Feb. 10, 1945. Intern, St. Mark's Hosp., N.Y.C., 1930-31, Coney Island Hosp., Bklyn., 1931-32; resident Montefiore Hosp. & Research Center, Bronx, and Mt. Sinai Hosp., N.Y.C., 1932; sr. clin. asst. medicine Beth Israel Hosp. & Research Center, 1932-41, adj. in medicine, 1933-41; practice internal medicine, N.Y.C., 1932-41; practice internal medicine specializing in allergy, Memphis, 1944—; sr. clin. prof. Dept. Medicine, U. Tenn. Center for Health Scis., Memphis; cons. Bapt. Meml. Hosp., USPHS Hosp., LeBonheur Children's Hosp., Meth. Hosp. Bd. dirs. Memphis Arts Council; trustee, regional co-chmn. Nat. Jewish Hosp./Nat. Asthma Center, Denver. Served to 1st lt. M.C., U.S. Army and Med. Reserve Corps, 1939-41, 41-44. Recipient Merit award Am. Coll. Allergists, 1977; Philanthropic Service award Nat. Jewish Hosp. & Research Center/Nat. Asthma Center, 1979. Fellow Am. Acad. Allergists, Am. Coll. Allergists, Am. Geriatrics Assn.; mem. Am. Bd. Internal Medicine (diplomate), Am. Bd. Allergy and Immunology (diplomate), Royal Soc. Health, Internat. Assn. Allergology, N.Y. Acad. Sci., AAAS, Cert. Allergists Assn., N.Y. U. Alumni Assn. (pres. Memphis chpt.). Clubs: Petroleum, Ridgeway Country, Sertoma (dir.). Contbr. articles to profl. jours. Home: 321 Greenway Rd Memphis TN 38107 Office: 40 N Pauline St Memphis TN 38105

ZWEIACKER, PAUL LEON, elec. equipment corp. exec.; b. Walters, Okla., Oct. 18, 1941; s. Leo and Anna Marie Z.; B.S., Okla. State U., 1963, Ph.D., 1971; M.S., U. S.D., 1967; m. JoAnn Robinson, Aug. 17, 1963; 1 son, Gregory Paul. Head biology dept. Putman City Public Schs., 1964-66, Consol. Edison Co., N.Y.C., 1970-72; program mgr. Tex. Instruments Inc., Dallas, 1974-77, dir. tech. staff ecol. services, 1977-78, br. mgr., 1978—; environ. cons., 1969—. Sustaining mem. Republican Nat. Com., 1977—. Mem. Am. Fisheries Soc., Hudson River Environ. Soc., Okla. Scenic Rivers Assn., Am. Inst. Fishery Biologists, Okla. Acad. Sci. Lutheran. Contbr. articles to profl. lit. Home: 929 Blue Lake Circle Richardson TX 75080 Office: Tex Instruments Ecol Services PO Box 225621 MS 3949 Dallas TX 75265

ZWEIBAN, SOFIA TOPPER, speech and lang. pathologist; b. Stockholm, Sweden, Dec. 27, 1947; d. Judah and Ethel (Kalb) Topper; came to U.S., 1951, naturalized, 1959; B.A., City Coll., City U. N.Y., 1968, M.A., 1969; m. Glenn Alan Zweiban, June 13, 1976; children—Shannon Lee, Lauren Nicole. Speech-lang. pathologist St. Charles Hosp., Port Jefferson, N.Y., 1969-70, Wassaic (N.Y.) State Sch., 1970-71; pvt. practice speech and lang. pathology, Rome, N.Y., 1971-73; speech-lang. pathologist Denton (Tex.) State Sch., 1973-76, United Cerebral Palsy Assn., Dallas, 1976-77; part-time pvt. practice speech and lang. pathology, Dallas, 1977—; cons. speech and lang. pathology. Mem. Am. Speech and Hearing Assn., Am. Assn. Mental Deficiency. Contbr. articles to profl. jours. Address: 12202 Wightman Pl Dallas TX 75243

ZWEIG, PETER JAY, architect, educator; b. N.Y.C., July 26, 1948; s. Sol M. and Harriet S. (Salpeter) Z.; B.A., Syracuse U., 1971, B.Arch., 1971, M.Arch., 1972; m. Linda Warren, May 28, 1977. With Paolo Soleri, Architect, Scottsdale, Ariz., 1970-71; co-dir. Site Inc., N.Y.C., 1972; with Matthew Lambert, Architect and Engr., Jericho, L.I., 1972-73, Carl Puchall, Architect, N.Y.C., 1973-74, Claude Samton, Architect, N.Y.C., 1974; asst. prof. Tex. A. and M. U., College Station, 1974-78, asso. prof. architecture, 1978—; architect, College Station, 1974—; lectr. in field. Tex. A. and M. U. grantee, 1977, 74; Tex. Archtl. Found. grantee, 1976; Spl. Merit award Am. Plywood Assn., Progressive Architecture, Better Homes and Gardens, 1979; registered architect, N.Mex., Tex. Mem. Nat. Council Archtl. Registration Bds., Internat. Solar Energy Soc. (Australia), Tex. Solar Energy Soc., World Future Soc., AIA, Tex. Soc. Architects. Contbr. articles to profl. jours.; archtl. works include: Walden House, Ga., 1976, Zweig Residence, College Station, Tex., 1977, Pahlavi Nat. Library, Iran, 1978, Siegal House, N.Y., 1975, Brazos Valley Art Center, Bryan, Tex., 1975, Rough Rock Demonstation Sch., Chinle, Ariz., 1973, Shinkenchiku Residence, Japan, 1979, Les Halles Neighborhood proposal, Paris, 1979. Home: 2509 Fitzgerald St College Station TX 77840 Office: Tex A and M Univ Dept Arch College Station TX 77843

ZWICK, CHARLES JOHN, banker; b. Plantsville, Conn., July 17, 1926; s. Louis Christian and Mabel (Rich) Z.; B.S. in Agrl. Econs., U. Conn., 1950, M.S., 1951; Ph.D. in Econs., Harvard U., 1954; m. Joan Wallace Cameron, June 21, 1952; children—Robert Louis, Janet Ellen. Instr., U. Conn., 1951, Harvard U., 1954-56; head logistics dept. RAND Corp., 1956-63, mem. research council, 1963-65; asst. dir. U.S. Bur. Budget, 1965-68, dir., 1968-69; pres., SE Banking Corp., Miami, 1969—; dir. SE 1st Nat. Bank Miami, SE Mortgage Co., So. Bell Tel. & Tel. Co., Johns-Manville Corp. Chmn., Pres.'s Commn. Mil. Compensation, 1977-78; mem. Controller Gen.'s Cons. Panel; mem. panel econ. advisors U.S. Congress Congressional Budget Office; mem. council Internat. Exec. Service Corps; bd. dirs. Fla. Council 100; trustee Carnegie Endowment Internat. Peace. Served with U.S. Army, 1946-47. Mem. Econ. Soc. So. Fla. (dir.), Assn. Res. City Bankers, Conf. Bd., Greater Miami C. of C., Am. Hist. and Cultural Soc. (dir.). Home: 4210 Santa Maria St Coral Gables FL 33146 Office: Southeast Banking Corp 100 S Biscayne Blvd Miami FL 33131

Who's Who in America

Biographees of the South and Southwest

The following biographees of the South and Southwestern regions have sketches appearing in the 41st edition of *Who's Who in America.*

Aaron, Chloe Wellingham
Aaron, Danny Doyle
Aaron, Harold Robert
Aaron, Henry
Aaron, Henry
Aaron, Ira Edward
Aaronson, Robert Jay
Abbey, Richard Sargent
Abbot, William Wright
Abbott, Edward Leroy
Abbott, Lynn DeForrest, Jr.
Abbott, Preston Sargent
Abbott, Robert Tucker
Abbott, William Harvey
Abdnor, James
Abell, Murray Richardson
Abell, Thomas Henry
Abelson, Philip Hauge
Abely, Joseph Francis, Jr.
Abernathy, Jack Harvey
Abernathy, Mabra Glenn
Abernathy, Maurine Howard
Abernathy, Ralph David
Abernathy, Robert Shields
Abernethy, George Lawrence
Abernethy, Robert Gordon
Abersfeller, Heinz Andrew
Abess, Leonard Leroy
Abhau, William Conrad
Abney, Frederick Sherwood
Abourezk, James G.
Abraham, Henry Julian
Abrams, Bernard William
Abrams, Earl Bernard
Abrams, Edward Marvin
Abramson, Hyman Norman
Abramson, Morrie Kaplan
Abshire, David Manker
Absolon, Karel B.
Acheson, David Campion
Achhammer, Bernard George
Achilles, Theodore Carter
Achinstein, Asher
Achinstein, Peter Jacob
Acito, Daniel Joseph
Ackell, Edmund Ferris
Acker, Joseph Edington, Jr.
Acker, Nathaniel Hull
Acker, Robert Flint
Ackerman, Lennis Campbell
Ackerman, Raymond Basil
Ackerman, Richard Henry
Ackman, Fredric C.
Acuff, Roy Claxton
Adair, Charles Robert, Jr.
Adair, James Edward
Adams, Alexander Pratt, Jr.
Adams, Alfred Hugh
Adams, Andrew Joseph
Adams, Andrew Stanford
Adams, Andrew Wilson
Adams, Anne Hutchinson
Adams, Apollonia Fischer Olson (Mrs. Edward Everett Adams)
Adams, Arthur Harvey
Adams, Donald Croxton
Adams, Edward Beverle
Adams, Edward James
Adams, Edwin Melville
Adams, Elie Maynard
Adams, Elijah
Adams, Francis L(ee)
Adams, James Blackburn
Adams, James Norman
Adams, John Allan Stewart
Adams, John Berry
Adams, John Evi
Adams, John Franklin
Adams, John Gibbons
Adams, John Hanly
Adams, John Wesley, Jr.
Adams, Joseph Peter
Adams, Kenneth Stanley, Jr.
Adams, Laurence Joseph
Adams, Leonard C.
Adams, Leslie Bunn, Jr.
Adams, Non Quincy
Adams, Norman Ilsley, Jr.
Adams, Paul DeWitt
Adams, Ralph Edwin
Adams, Ralph Wyatt, Sr.
Adams, Ranald Trevor, Jr.
Adams, Richard Leon
Adams, Richard Newbold
Adams, Richey Darell
Adams, Rob L.
Adams, Rob Lee
Adams, Robert Franklin
Adams, Robert Waugh, Jr.
Adams, Russell B(aird)
Adams, Samuel Clifford, Jr.
Adams, Scott
Adams, Theodore Floyd
Adams, Walter Harris
Adams, Ware
Adams, Warren Sanford, 2d
Adams, William Hensley
Adams, William Hester, III
Adams, William Jackson, Jr.
Adams, Wright Rowe
Adamson, Terrence Burdett
Adcock, Willis Alfred
Addison, Francis Girault, III
Addison, Walter John
Addlestone, Nathan Sidney
Adduci, Vincent James
Ade, Erwin Jerome
Ades, Robert O.
Adkerson, J(oseph) Carson
Adkins, Cecil Dale
Adkins, Elijah Dale, Jr.
Adkins, James Calhoun
Adkins, John Nathaniel
Adkins, Paul Charles
Adkinson, Burton Wilbur
Adkisson, Perry Lee
Adkisson, Richard Blanks
Adler, Charles
Adler, Gary
Adler, Howard, Jr.
Adler, James Barron
Adler, John Hans
Adler, Larry
Adler, Lawrence
Adler, Louis Kootz
Adler, Michael H.B.
Adomian, George
Adreon, Harry Barnes
Adriani, John
Aeck, Richard Leon
Affronti, Lewis Francis
Agan, Arthur Columbus, Jr.
Agan, Sam Wilkerson
Agee, Warren Kendall
Agee, William Cameron
Agger, Donald George
Agnew, Allen Francis
Agnew, Bruce Andras
Agnew, Donald Charles
Agnew, Spiro Theodore
Agnew, Theodore Lee, Jr.
Agosin, Moises Kankolsky
Agus, Jacob Bernard
Ahearne, John Francis
Ahern, Timothy Ignatius
Ahlberg, Thorsten Jacob
Ahlgren, Frank Richard
Ahlquist, Raymond Perry
Ahmad, Sharon Erdkamp
Ahmann, James Henry
Ahmann, Mathew Hall
Ahrens, Maurice Russell
Aiken, Thomas Worthen
Aikens, Joan Deacon
Ailes, Stephen
Ainbinder, Seymour
Ainsworth, Mary Dinsmore Salter
Ainsworth, Oscar Richard
Ainsworth, Robert Andrew, Jr.
Ainsworth, Stanley Humphreys
Airis, Thomas Fergrieve
Aitken, Alexander Philip
Ajemian, Robert Myron
Akaka, Daniel Kahikina
Akens, David Strode
Akers, Albert Bayliss
Akers, Fred Sanford
Akers, John McCorkle
Akers, William Walter
Akin, Henry David
Alaimo, Anthony A.
Alatis, James Efstathios
Albaugh, Kenneth Clocker, Jr.
Alberger, William Relph
Albert, Alfred Gerhardt
Albert, Carl
Albert, John
Albertson, Fred W(oodward)
Albosta, Donald Joseph
Albrecht, Harold L.
Albrecht, Milton C.
Albright, Arnold DeWald
Albright, George Franklin
Albright, Joseph Medill Patterson
Albright, Penrose Lucas
Albright, Raymond Jacob
Albritton, Claude Carroll, Jr.
Albritton, Robert Bynum
Albritton, William Harold, III
Albus, James Sacra
Alden, Douglas William
Alden, John Richard
Alderman, James E(lliott)
Alderman, Louis Cleveland, Jr.
Aldrich, Clarence Knight
Aldridge, Mary Hennen Dellinger
Alexander, Andrew Lamar, Jr.
Alexander, Cecil Abraham
Alexander, Chalmers Whitfield
Alexander, Charles Haynes
Alexander, Charles Thomas
Alexander, Chauncey A.
Alexander, Clifford L., Jr.
Alexander, Donald Crichton
Alexander, Eben, Jr.
Alexander, Frederick Americo
Alexander, George Moyer
Alexander, Holmes
Alexander, Irving Emanuel
Alexander, James Henry
Alexander, Jimmy Euel
Alexander, John Davis
Alexander, Joseph Kunkle, Jr.
Alexander, Judith Ann
Alexander, Melton Lee
Alexander, Myrl Early
Alexander, Robert Baldwin
Alexander, Sydenham Benoni
Alexander, Theodore Martin
Alexander, Welborn Excell, Jr.
Alexander, William Brooks
Alexander, William Henry
Alexander, William Marvin
Alexander, William Olin
Alexander, William Owen
Alexander, William Vollie, Jr.
Alexander, Willis Walter
Alexeff, Igor
Alexich, Milton Pivar
Alexopoulos, Constantine John
Alford, Bobby Ray
Alford, Charles Aaron, Jr.
Alford, Frederick Fergus, Jr.
Alford, John Morris
Alford, John Warner, Jr.
Alford, Neill Herbert, Jr.
Alfultis, Richard Joseph
Alimanestianu, Calin
Allain, William A.
Allaire, Edwin Bonar, Jr.
Allan, Barry David
Allan, Virginia Rachel
Allard, David Henry
Allard, William Albert
Allbeck, Willard Dow
Allbritton, Joe Lewis
Allen, Alfred Keys
Allen, Anita Ford
Allen, Arthur Beverly
Allen, Arthur Wright, Jr.
Allen, Charles Livingstone
Allen, Charles Mengel
Allen, Charles Robert
Allen, Clarence Milton
Allen, Clifton Judson
Allen, Don Lee
Allen, Donald Clinton
Allen, Duane David
Allen, Dwight William
Allen, Edward Lawrence
Allen, Elbert Enrico
Allen, Ernest Mason
Allen, Francis Pitcher
Allen, Frank Carroll
Allen, Fred Cary
Allen, Harry
Allen, Herbert
Allen, Ivan, Jr.
Allen, Jack
Allen, James Albert
Allen, James Caldwell
Allen, James Harrill
Allen, John Eldridge
Allen, John Stuart
Allen, Joseph Percival
Allen, Kenneth Dale
Allen, L. Calhoun, Jr.
Allen, L. Scott
Allen, Lawrence A.
Allen, Lee Norcross
Allen, Lew, Jr.
Allen, Maryon Pittman
Allen, Newton Perkins
Allen, Nicholas Eugene
Allen, Robert Scott
Allen, Robert Sharon
Allen, Rumley Worden, Jr.
Allen, Thomas Oscar
Allen, Turner Wharton
Allen, Willard Myron
Allen, William Hayes
Allen, William Payne
Alley, James William
Allgood, Clarence William
Allinger, Norman Louis
Allison, Fred, Jr.
Allison, Hansell Jack
Allison, Henry Barden, II
Allison, Irl
Allison, Junius Landrum
Allison, Robert Arthur
Allison, Robert James, Jr.
Allison, Stanley Frederick
Allman, Conrad Scott
Allman, Gregory LeNoir
Allyn, Arthur Cecil
Alm, Alvin L.
Almand, Bond
Almon, Clopper
Almon, Reneau Pearson
Almond, Carl Harman
Almond, James Lindsay, Jr.
Alper, Jerome Milton
Alper, Melvin Gustavus
Alpiner, Jerome Gerald
Alsop, Joseph Wright
Alston, Annie May
Alston, Philip Henry, Jr.
Altazan, John Edward
Alter, David Emmet, Jr.
Altman, Marvin Harold
Altmann, Andrew Taylor
Alto, Vincent Richard
Altschul, Aaron Mayer
Altshuler, Kenneth Z.
Altshuler, Nathan
Alvarado-Torres, Thilda Iris
Alvary, Lorenzo
Alvey, Edward, Jr.
Alvis, John Hubbard
Alyea, Edwin Pascal
Amadeo, Jose H.
Amaral, Jesus Eduardo
Amateis, Edmond Romulus
Ambler, Ernest
Ambro, Jerome A.
Ambrose, Myles Joseph
Ames, Fisher
Ames, Frank Anthony
Ames, Joseph Lynn
Ames, Milton Benjamin, Jr.
Ames, William Francis
Amirikian, Arsham
Amis, Edward Stephen
Amling, Frederick
Ammarell, John Samuel, Jr.
Ammon, James E.
Amory, Robert, Jr.
Amos, Dennis Bernard
Amos, James Lysle
Amos, John Beverly
Amos, John Ellis
Amos, Larry Charles
Amos, Marvin Cyril
Amram, Philip Werner
Amspoker, James Mack
Amundson, Neal Russell
Amussen, Theodore Smith
Anastos, George
Ances, I. G(eorge)
Andelson, Robert Vernon
Anderson, Andrew Broadus, Jr.
Anderson, Arnold Herbert
Anderson, Bette B.
Anderson, Bill
Anderson, Bruce Murray
Anderson, Carl Wilson
Anderson, Carolyn Jennings
Anderson, Charles Burroughs
Anderson, Clifton A.
Anderson, Cortland Edwin, Jr.
Anderson, David Prewitt
Anderson, Donald Benton
Anderson, E. Karl
Anderson, Edward Clifford
Anderson, Elmer Ebert
Anderson, Floyd Edward
Anderson, Frank Abel
Anderson, George Frederick
Anderson, George Harding
Anderson, George McClintock
Anderson, George W., Jr.
Anderson, Glenn Elwood
Anderson, Glenn Malcolm
Anderson, Harry Robert
Anderson, Howard Clevenger
Anderson, Howard Stone
Anderson, Hugh Hansen
Anderson, Hurst Robins
Anderson, Ira Dennis
Anderson, Irving Charles
Anderson, Jack Northman
Anderson, Jack Roy
Anderson, James Byrd, Jr.
Anderson, James Richard
Anderson, James William, III
Anderson, John Bayard
Anderson, John David, Jr.
Anderson, John Weir
Anderson, Lee Stratton
Anderson, Leonard Gustave
Anderson, Marion Cornelius
Anderson, Neil Martin
Anderson, Peyton Tooke, Jr.
Anderson, Philip Sidney
Anderson, Ralph Alexander, Jr.
Anderson, Richard Davis
Anderson, Richard Edmund
Anderson, Richard L(oree)
Anderson, Robbin Colyer
Anderson, Robert
Anderson, Robert Cletus
Anderson, Robert Henry
Anderson, Robert Jewell
Anderson, Robert John
Anderson, Robert Theodore
Anderson, Stanley James
Anderson, Stanley Joseph
Anderson, Stanley Robert
Anderson, Thomas Dunaway
Anderson, Thomas Jefferson
Anderson, Wallace Ervin
Anderson, Walter
Anderson, William (Albion), Jr.
Anderson, William Arnold Douglas
Anderson, William Evan
Anderson, William Len
Anderson, William Page
Anderson, William Pinckney, III
Anderson, William Robert
Anderson, Wilton Thomas
Anderson, Winston Faine
Andersson, Theodore
Anderton, Farris Norman
Andolsek, Ludwig John
André, Oscar Jules
Andreoli, Kathleen Gainor
Andres, Reubin
Andrew, Charles Curtis
Andrews, Archie Moulton
Andrews, Burton Howell
Andrews, Charles Edward
Andrews, Emmet Charles
Andrews, Glenn
Andrews, Ike Franklin
Andrews, James Edgar
Andrews, Jay D.
Andrews, John Charles
Andrews, John Frank
Andrews, John Robert
Andrews, John Stewart
Andrews, Lavone D.
Andrews, Mark
Andrews, Mark Edwin
Andrews, Robert Vincent
Andrews, T. Coleman
Andrews, Thelma
Andrews, Theodore Henderson
Andrews, William Cooke
Andrews, William Francis
Andrews, William Henry, Jr.
Andringa, Calvin Bruce
Andriole, Stephen John
Andriot, John Leo
Andrus, Cecil D.
Andrus, Gerald Louis
Andujar, John J.
Andy, Orlando Joseph
Anfinsen, Christian Boehmer
Angel, Grover LaMarr
Angel, John Lawrence
Angulo, Albert William
Anlyan, William George
Annis, Edward Roland
Annunzio, Frank
Ansel, Howard Carl
Ansley, Bradford Dunham, Jr.
Anson, Abraham
Anson, Charles Phillips
Anthony, Beryl F., Jr.
Anthony, Guy Mauldin
Anthony, Ray Taylor
Antman, Stuart Sheldon
Anton, David Michael
Anton, John Peter
Anton, Nicholas Guy
Apel, Harold William
Aponte, Juan Bautista
Aponte Martinez, Luis
Appelbaum, Joseph
Apple, Jay Lawrence
Apple, William Shoulden
Applebaum, Edmond Lewis
Applebee, Frank Woodbury
Applegate, Harry Alvin
Applegate, Oral Lester
Appleton, Arthur Ivar
Appleton, Francis Henry, III
Appleton, Joseph Hayne
Appleton, Julius Henry
Appley, Lawrence A.
Appling, Hugh Guernsey
Apstein, Maurice
Aragon, Joseph William
Aramony, William
Arango, Jorge Sanin
Aranson, Mike Elliott
Arant, William Douglas
Arbour, Harold Cyril
Arceneaux, Thomas Joseph
Arceneaux, William
Archambault, George Francis
Archer, Bill
Archer, David R.
Archer, Edmund Minor
Archer, Glenn LeRoy
Archer, James Elson
Archey, William Thomas
Archibald, A. Edward
Ard, Harold Jacob
Ardery, Philip Pendleton
Ardis, Mark Burkett
Ardoin, John Louis
Ardoyno (Dorr), Dolores
Arduser, Raymond A.
Areen, Judith Carol
Arena, Jay M.
Arendall, Charles Baker, Jr.
Arensmeyer, Robert Mark
Arent, Albert Ezra
Arents, Chester Abbo
Argue, John Clifford
Armacost, Michael Hayden
Armaly, Mansour F(arid)
Armbrecht, Frank Maurice
Armbrecht, William H.
Armbrecht, William Henry, III
Armel, Thomas Nathaniel
Armistead, Moss William, III
Armistead, Theus Nicholson
Armistead, Willis William
Armour, Lloyd Rowland
Armstrong, Alfred Ringgold
Armstrong, Anne Legendre (Mrs. Tobin Armstrong)
Armstrong, Garner Ted
Armstrong, George Robert
Armstrong, George Thomson
Armstrong, James Elwood, III
Armstrong, Jane Botsford
Armstrong, John Dale
Armstrong, Lloyd, Jr.
Armstrong, Oliver Wendell
Armstrong, Richard Burke
Armstrong, Robert Baker
Armstrong, Robert Markle
Armstrong, Robert Plant
Armstrong, Victor Adelbert
Armstrong, Walter Preston, Jr.
Armstrong, William L.
Armstrong, Willis Coburn
Arnall, Ellis Gibbs
Arnett, Ross Harold, Jr.
Arnett, Warren Grant
Arnim, Sumter Smith
Arnold, Elting
Arnold, Frank Delwin
Arnold, Frederic Eberhard, Jr.
Arnold, G. Dewey, Jr.
Arnold, Gary Howard
Arnold, Margaret Long (Mrs. Dexter Otis Arnold)
Arnold, Philip Mills
Arnold, Richard Keith
Arnold, Richard Sheppard
Arnold, Robert Oliver
Arnold, Terrell E. S.
Arnold, Tom
Arnold, Walter Martin
Arnold, William Strang
Arnott, Howard Joseph

REGIONAL LISTING—SOUTH-SOUTHWEST 838

Arnow, Winston Eugene
Arnwine, Don Lee
Aron, William
Aronoff, Billie Louis
Aronovitz, Sidney Myer
Aronson, Bernard William
Arrington, Richard
Arrol, John
Arrowsmith, William Ayres
Arthur, Thomas Donnelly
Artinian, Artine
Arvey, Martin Dale
Asbill, Mac
Asbill, Mac, Jr.
Aschaffenburg, E. Lysle
Aschheim, Joseph
Ash, Fred Calbert
Ash, Mary Kay Wagner
Ash, Robert
Ashbrook, John Milan
Ashby, Eugene Christopher
Ashcroft, Herbert
Asheim, Lester Eugene
Asher, Lila Oliver
Asher, Robert Eller
Ashler, Philip Frederic
Ashley, Thomas William Ludlow
Ashmore, Henry Ludlow
Ashmore, Robert Thomas
Ashwell, George Gilbert
Ashworth, Kenneth Hayden
Ashworth, Maynard Richard
Askew, Reubin O'Donovan
Aspin, Les
Assousa, George Elias
Astin, Allen Varley
Aston, James William
Atcheson, James Edward
Atchison, William Franklin, computer scientist, educator; b. Smithfield, Ky., Apr. 7
Atchley, Bill Lee
Atherton, Charles Henry
Atherton, James Kenneth Ward
Atkeson, Timothy Breed
Atkins, C(arl) Clyde
Atkins, Chester B.
Atkins, James Frederick
Atkins, Orin Ellsworth
Atkinson, Carroll Holloway
Atkinson, Eugene Vincent
Atkinson, Frederick Griswold
Atkinson, Gordon
Atkinson, Henry Troy, Jr.
Atkinson, Richard Chatham
Atlas, David
Atterholt, Frank Marion
Attinello, John Salvatore
Attinger, Ernst Otto
Attwell, Kirby
Atwater, Franklin Simpson
Atwater, John Spencer
Atwell, Anthony
Atwell, Robert Herron
Atwood, Edward Charles, Jr.
Atwood, John Brian
Atwood, Paul Williams
Atwood, Rollin Salisbury
Atwood, Sanford Soverhill
Auberger, Kenneth James
Aubry, Eugene Edwards
Auchincloss, Samuel Sloan
AuCoin, Les
Auer, Bernhard Machold
Auerbach, Mark
Auerbach, Seymour
Auerbach, Stanley Irving
Auerbach, Stuart Charles
Augsburger, Aaron Donald
Augustine, Norman Ralph
Auld, David Vinson
Aust, Joe Bradley
Austell, Edward Callaway
Austern, Herman Thomas
Austin, Charles John
Austin, Frederick Pasqua, Jr.
Austin, Harry Guiden
Austin, James William
Austin, John Paul
Austin, Patricia
Austin, Robert Carter
Austin, Robert Eugene, Jr.
Austin, T. Louis, Jr.
Austin, Tom Noell
Austin, Walter James
Auten, John Harold
Authement, Ray
Autian, John
Avalle-Arce, Juan Bautista
Averch, Harvey Allan
Averitt, Jack Nelson
Avery, Benjamin Franklin
Avery, Frederick Fifield
Avery, William Henry
Avery, William Hinckley
Avery, William Turner
Avirett, John Williams, 2d
Avram, Henriette Davidson
Axelrod, Julius
Axene, Dean Lane
Axton, William Fitch
Ayars, Albert Lee
Ayars, Albert Lee
Aycock, Ezra Kenneth
Aycock, William Brantley
Ayers, Archie Raymond
Ayers, Richard Winston
Ayers, Thomas Dudley
Aylward, Thomas James, Jr.
Ayres, Robert Moss, Jr.
Ayres, William Hanes
Azar, Henry Amin
Babb, Thomas Adams
Babcock, Hope Madeline
Babcock, Richard Joseph
Babin, Claude Hunter
Baccus, Ira Bishop
Baccus, Robert Lee
Bachman, Kenneth Leroy
Bachman, Leonard
Bachmeyer, Robert Wesley
Bachus, Walter Otis
Back, Kurt Wolfgang
Backas, James Jacob
Backlund, Ralph Theodore
Backus, Milo Morlan
Bacon, Donald Walter
Bacon, Louis Albert
Bacon, Phillip
Bacon, Richard Franklin
Bader, Henri
Bader, Michael Haley
Badham, Robert E.
Badley, Ronnie Dale
Badura-Skoda, Paul
Baeder, Donald Lee
Baer, David Clyde
Baer, Henry
Baer, Robert Jacob
Baetjer, Anna Medora
Bafalis, Louis Arthur
Bageant, Kenneth Edmond
Bagge, Carl Elmer
Baggett, Agnes
Baggott, James Lee
Bagley, William Thompson
Bagwell, Ross Kennedy
Bahakel, Cy N.
Bahr, Gunter F.
Bailar, John Christian, III
Bailey, Amos Purnell
Bailey, Byron James
Bailey, Cecil Cabaniss
Bailey, Elizabeth Ellery
Bailey, George Gilbert
Bailey, Glenn Waldemar
Bailey, Hugh Coleman
Bailey, Jack Blendon
Bailey, Joel Furness
Bailey, John Martin
Bailey, John Milton
Bailey, Kenneth Kyle
Bailey, (John) Larrie
Bailey, Oscar Wilson
Bailey, Paul Clinton
Bailey, Philip Sigmon
Bailey, Ruth Domincovich (Mrs. John A. Bailey)
Bailey, Ryburn Hancock
Bailey, Scott Field
Bailey, Stuart L.
Bailey, Wilford Sherrill
Bailey, William John
Bailey, William Stuart
Baily, Nathan Ariel
Bain, Chester Ward
Bain, Helen Pate
Bain, James Arthur
Bainbridge, Frederick Freeman, III
Bains, Lee Edmundson
Bainum, Peter Montgomery
Bair, Scott Slaybaugh
Baird, James Catchings, Jr.
Baird, William David
Baisler, Perry E.
Baker, Alton Wesley
Baker, Arthur Alan
Baker, Benjamin May
Baker, Broughton Leonard
Baker, Burke, Jr.
Baker, Edwin Clarence
Baker, Ernest Beasley, Jr.
Baker, Frank Hamon
Baker, George Ivan
Baker, George Walter
Baker, Halmer Loren
Baker, Henry S., Jr.
Baker, Hollis MacClure
Baker, Howard Henry, Jr.
Baker, James Edward
Baker, James Kendrick
Baker, James Wimberly
Baker, John Alexander, Jr.
Baker, John Austin
Baker, Lenox Dial
Baker, Leonard Stanley
Baker, Lisle, Jr.
Baker, Melvin C.
Baker, Merl
Baker, Paul
Baker, Paul, Jr.
Baker, R. Robinson
Baker, Raymond Charles
Baker, Rex Gavin, Jr.
Baker, Robert Allen, Jr.
Baker, Robert Ernest, Jr.
Baker, Robert Henry
Baker, Robert Leon
Baker, Roger Denio
Baker, Russell Tremaine, Jr.
Baker, Sarah Marinda
Baker, William Roy, Jr.
Baker, Willie Arthur, Jr.
Bakes, Philip John, Jr.
Baklanoff, Eric Nicolas
Balassa, Bela
Balch, Clyde Wilkinson
Balch, Samuel Eason
Baldinger, Milton Irving
Baldus, Alvin James
Baldwin, Bernard Coleman, Jr.
Baldwin, Charles Franklin
Baldwin, David Merrill
Baldwin, Garza, Jr.
Baldwin, Henry Furlong
Baldwin, Horace Strow
Baldwin, Jack Norman
Baldwin, John Wesley
Baldwin, Phillip Benjamin
Baldwin, Robert Wilton
Baldwin, William Russell
Balen, Samuel Thomas
Bales, Richard Henry Horner
Balin, Howard
Ball, Billy Joe
Ball, Frank Jervey
Ball, Lewis Edwin, II
Ball, Mary Margaret
Ball, Rex Martin
Ball, Robert M.
Ball, Vaughn Charles
Ball, William Kenneth
Ballance, Paul Salen
Ballantine, Thomas Austin, Jr.
Ballantyne, Robert Jadwin
Ballard, Edward Brooks
Ballard, Edward Goodwin
Ballard, Frederick Armstrong
Ballard, Stanley Sumner
Ballard, Wiley Perry
Ballinger, Robert Irving, Jr.
Ballman, Frederick Carl
Balows, Albert
Balsley, Howard Lloyd
Balsley, Philip Elwood
Balter, Robert Brandon
Bambas, Karl John
Bandeen, William Reid
Bandy, Moe
Bandy, William Thomas, Jr.
Bane, David Morgan
Bane, Frank
Banes, Daniel
Bang, Frederik Barry
Bangdiwala, Ishver Surchand
Bangs, John R.
Banister, John Robert
Bank, Merrill Lee
Banker, Paul Albert
Bankhead, Walter Will
Banks, John Houston
Banks, Richard Austin
Banks, Robert Louis
Banner, Donald Witte
Banner, William Augustus
Bannerot, Frederick George, Jr.
Banning, Margaret Culkin
Bannister, Dan Wesley
Banta, James Elmer
Banzhaf, John F., III
Bar-Adon, Aaron
Barall, Milton
Baranowski, Frank Paul
Baratz, Morton Sachs
Barber, Arthur Whiting
Barber, James David
Barber, John Merrell
Barber, Perry Oscar, Jr.
Barber, Raymond H.
Barber, Richard Leslie
Barchet, Stephen
Barclay, Harriet George
Barclay, James Ralph
Bard, Allen Joseph
Bardolph, Richard
Bardon, Jack Irving
Bardon, Marcel
Barelare, Bruno
Bares, Rudolph, Jr.
Barfield, Rufus Lenro
Barfield, Thomas Harwell
Barge, Daniel Bythewood, Jr.
Barger, Benjamin
Barger, Herman H.
Barham, Mack Elwin
Barham, Richard Wendell
Barhyte, Donald James
Baringer, Richard E.
Barkalow, Frederick Schenck, Jr.
Barker, Hal Burnett
Barker, John Grove
Barker, Robert Whitney
Barker, Samuel Booth
Barker, Stephen Francis
Barker, Stonie, Jr.
Barker, Walter William
Barksdale, Hiram Collier
Barksdale, Richard Dillon
Barlass, Jack S.
Barley, Frank Jay
Barley, Robert Arthur
Barlow, Joel
Barnard, Druie Douglas, Jr.
Barnard, Robert C.
Barnebey, Kenneth Alan
Barnebey, Malcolm Richard
Barnes, Allan Campbell
Barnes, B. Don
Barnes, Benjamin Shields, Jr.
Barnes, Carl Belton
Barnes, Jay William, Jr.
Barnes, Michael Darr
Barnes, Thomas Joseph
Barnes, William Anderson (Andy)
Barnes, William P.
Barnes, Wilson King
Barness, Lewis Abraham
Barnet, Ann Birnbaum
Barnett, Arthur Doak
Barnett, Benjamin Lewis, Jr.
Barnett, Burleigh Francis
Barnett, David Leon
Barnett, Herman L.
Barnett, M. Robert
Barnett, Robert James
Barnett, Robert Warren
Barnett, Walter Michael
Barnette, Newton Hall
Barney, Charles Lester
Barnhardt, William Horace
Barnhardt, Zeb Elonzo, Jr.
Barnhart, Charles Elmer
Barnhart, William Rupp
Barno, Peter Sanden
Barnstone, Howard
Barnum, John Wallace
Baroff, George Stanley
Baron, Frederick David
Baron, Martin Raymond
Baron, Samuel
Baron, Samuel Haskell
Baroni, Geno C.
Baroody, William Joseph
Baroody, William Joseph, Jr.
Barr, Alfred Lowell
Barr, Harry George
Barr, Howard Raymond
Barr, Irwin Robert
Barr, John Watson, III
Barr, Joseph Walker
Barredo, Maniya
Barrett, Clifton Waller
Barrett, James Emmett
Barrett, Joe Clifford
Barrett, Richard David
Barrett, William Riker
Barrick, Nolan Ellmore
Barrineau, Edwin
Barringer, Paul Brandon, II
Barringer, Philip E.
Barron, Bryton
Barron, Dean James
Barron, Dempsey J.
Barron, Donald H.
Barron, Norman Macdonald
Barron, Roger L.
Barrow, Allen Edward
Barrow, Charles Wallace
Barrow, Frank Pearson, Jr.
Barrow, George Terrell
Barrow, John Curtis
Barrow, Robert George
Barrow, Robert Hilliard
Barry, Marion Shepilov, Jr.
Barry, Richard Francis, III
Barry, Richard Francis, III
Barry, Robert Louis
Barshop, Samuel Edwin
Barstis, Leonard
Barta, Frank Rudolph, Sr.
Bartch, Carl Edward
Bartel, Herbert Herman, Jr.
Barter, Robert Henry
Barth, John Simmons
Barth, Max
Barth, Michael Carl
Barth, Pius Joseph
Barthelme, Donald
Bartimo, Vincent J(oseph)
Bartlett, Charles Leffingwell
Bartlett, Claude Jackson
Bartlett, James Vincent
Bartlett, Paul Doughty
Bartlett, Thomas Alva
Bartling, Theodore Charles
Bartnoff, Judith
Bartnoff, Judith
Bartocha, Bodo
Barton, Alan Raymond
Barton, Jackson Mounce
Barton, Nelda Ann (Mrs. Harold Bryan Barton)
Barton, Paul Booth, Jr.
Barton, Richard Fleming
Barton, Robert Thomas, Jr.
Barton, William Blackburn
Bartscht, Heri Bert
Bartter, Frederic Crosby
Baruch, Jordan Jay
Baruch, Morton Arnold
Barwick, Eugene Thomas
Bascom, Perry Bagnall
Bashful, Emmett Wilfort
Baskerville, Charles Alexander
Baskette, Floyd Kenneth, Jr.
Baskin, Robert Edward
Baskir, Lawrence M.
Basler, Roy Prentice
Bass, Allan Delmage
Bass, James Orin
Bass, John Fred
Bass, Joseph Alonzo
Bass, Perry Richardson
Bass, Roy Byrn
Bass, Shailer Linwood
Bass, William Marvin, III
Bassett, Harry Hood
Bassett, John Edwin
Bassett, Woodson William, Jr.
Bassin, Jules
Bassin, Robert Harris
Bastian, James Harold
Bateman, Durward Franklin
Bateman, Fred Willom
Bates, Carl ElKanah
Bates, Cornelius John Lighthall, Jr.
Bates, John Wesley
Batson, Blair Everett
Batson, Charles Alvin
Batson, Randolph
Batson, Richard Neal
Battaglia, Anthony Sylvester
Batte, George Albert, Jr.
Batten, Frank
Batten, James Knox
Battestin, Martin Carey
Battey, Bryan M.
Battista, Orlando Aloysius
Battle, Allen Overton, Jr.
Battle, Jean Allen
Battle, Lucius Durham
Battle, Mark Garvey
Battle, William Rainey
Battle, William Robert
Baucus, Max S.
Baudhuin, Ralph Julian
Bauer, Charles Kurt
Bauer, Charles Theodore
Bauer, Frederick Christian
Bauer, Henry Hermann
Bauer, Richard H.
Bauer, Siegfried Josef
Bauersfeld, Carl F.
Baughman, Ernest Theodore
Baughman, George Fechtig
Baughman, George W.
Baukhages, Frederick Edwin
Bauknight, Clarence Brock
Bauknight, William Cooper
Baum, Siegmund Jacob
Baum, Warren C.
Baum, Werner A.
Baum, Cardinal William
Bauman, Jerome Alan
Bauman, Robert Edmund
Bauman, Robert Poe
Baumeister, Theodore
Baumgartner, Robert Murdock
Bawden, James Wyatt
Baxter, Batsell Barrett
Baxter, L.C.
Baxter, M. Richard
Baxter, Michael John
Baxter, Raymond Carlos
Baxter, Robert Hampton, III
Baxter, Samuel Newman, Jr.
Baxter, Stephen Bartow
Baxter, William MacNeil
Bayh, Birch Evans, Jr.
Baylen, Joseph Oscar
Bayless, James Leavell
Baylin, George Jay
Baynes, Harold Losey
Baynes, Thomas Edward, Jr.
Bayse, David Duke
Baze, Roy Allen
Bazelon, David Lionel
Beach, Cecil Prentice
Beach, Leonard Brothwell
Beach, William Waldo
Beacham, Woodard Davis
Beachley, Michael Charles
Beaird, Charles T.
Beale, Betty (Mrs. George K. Graeber)
Beall, Arthur Charles, Jr.
Beall, George
Beall, Paul Rensselaer
Beals, Loren Alan
Beam, Charles Grier
Beam, Walter Raleigh
Beaman, Chester Earl
Beaman, Marvin Lee, Jr.
Beame, Abraham David
Beamesderfer, John William
Beamguard, Elizabeth Parks
Bean, Alan L.
Bean, Robert Beveridge
Bean, William Bennett
Beane, Alpheus C.
Beanstock, Sam
Bear, Richard Scott
Beard, Charles Ronald
Beard, Daniel Perry
Beard, Edward Peter
Beard, Elizabeth Letitia
Beard, Leo Roy
Beard, Richard Leonard
Beard, Robin
Beard, Thomas Rex
Beard, Winston Clingan
Bearden, James Hudson
Bearden, Joyce Alvin
Beardslee, William Armitage
Beasley, B. Rex
Beasley, Cecil Ackmond, Jr.
Beasley, George Garland
Beasley, John Michael
Beasley, John Snodgrass, II
Beasley, Kenneth Ephraim
Beasley, Rex
Beasley, Theodore Prentis
Beatley, Charles Earle, Jr.
Beattie, Donald Sherman
Beattie, Richard Irwin, Jr.
Beatty, Kenneth Orion, Jr.
Beatty, Richard Scrivener
Beatty, Samuel Alston
Beaty, Orren, Jr.
Beauchamp, Richard Agustas
Beauchamp, William Ellsworth
Beaver, Lucile Elizabeth
Beaver, Paul Chester
Bechill, William Daniel
Bechtel, William Russell
Beck, Abe Jack
Beck, Clifford Keith
Beck, Earl Ray
Beck, Guenter Joseph
Beck, Stanley Clifton
Beckelhymer, Paul Hunter
Beckenstein, Myron
Becker, Charles Steve
Becker, George J., Jr.
Becker, Ralph Elihu
Becker, William Watters
Beckett, William Wade
Beckham, William, Jr.
Beckjord, Philip Rains
Beckman, Aldo Bruce
Beckman, Norman
Beckmann, Robert Bader
Beckstead, Dan John
Beckwith, William Hunter
Beddall, Thomas Henry
Beddow, Thomas John
Bedell, Berkley Warren
Bedell, George Chester
Bedini, Silvio A.
Bednarek, Alexander Robert
Bedwell, Theodore Cleveland, Jr.
Beebe, Hamilton Keller
Beebe, William Bovell
Beebe, William Thomas
Beecherl, Louis Arthur, Jr.
Beeman, Alice Lee
Beer, Michael
Beery, Bruce Arnold
Beery, John Replogle
Begg, John Murray
Beggs, Thomas Montague
Begley, Michael J.
Begtzos, John, Jr.
Behnke, Roy Herbert
Behr, Lyell Christian
Behr, Robert McLean
Behrens, William Wohlsen, Jr.
Behringer, Marjorie Perrin
Behrman, Jack Newton
Beidler, Lloyd Mumbauer
Beightler, Charles Sprague
Beilenson, Anthony Charles
Beisel, William Robert
Belanger, William Joseph
Belcher, John Cheslow
Belden, Clark
Belen, Frederick Christopher
Belew, John Seymour
BeLieu, Kenneth Eugene
Belk, Irwin
Belk, John Montgomery
Bell, Bernard R.
Bell, C(lyde) Ritchie
Bell, Clyde Roberts
Bell, Eugene Gibbs
Bell, Griffin B.
Bell, Henry Herbert
Bell, Henry Marsh, Jr.
Bell, Howard Holman
Bell, Howard Hughes
Bell, James Finley
Bell, James Frederick
Bell, James Frederick
Bell, John Oscar
Bell, Kenneth John
Bell, Robert Eugene
Bell, Stephen Scott (Steve)
Bell, Thomas Alvin
Bell, Victor Altmark, Jr.
Bell, William Jack
Bellamy, William Butler
Bellard, Emory Dilworth
Bellino, Carmine Salvatore
Bellmon, Henry
Bellows, Everett Hollis
Bellows, Thomas John
Belmont, August
Belton, William
Beman, Deane Randolph
Bement, Arden Lee, Jr.
Benade, Leo Edward
Benario, Herbert William
Benatar, Leo
Benbow, Charles Clarence
Benbow, Charles Frank
Benbrook, Paul
Bender, Morton Alvin
Bender, William Ernest
Bendetsen, Karl Robin
Benedek, Martin Henry
Benedetto, Francis Aristide
Benedick, Richard Elliot
Benedict, Andrew Bell, Jr.
Benedict, Robert Clyde
Benerito, Ruth Rogan (Mrs. Frank H. Benerito)
Benfey, Otto Theodor
Benfield, William Avery, Jr.
Benham, David Blair
Benitez, Mario Antonio
Benjamin, Adam, Jr.
Benjamin, Albert, III
Benjamin, Edward Bernard, Jr.
Benn, Nathan Herman
Bennet, Douglas Joseph, Jr.
Bennett, Charles Edward
Bennett, Conner Leeman
Bennett, Dale Gordon
Bennett, Edward Owen
Bennett, (Silas) Fleming
Bennett, Harry
Bennett, Harry Jackson
Bennett, Henry Stanley
Bennett, Howard Clifton
Bennett, James Jefferson
Bennett, Joe Claude
Bennett, John Fisher
Bennett, Josiah Whitney
Bennett, Louis Lowell
Bennett, Marion Tinsley
Bennett, Robert Leo, Jr.
Bennett, Ronald Thomas
Bennett, Walter Hartwell
Bennett, Willard Harrison
Bennett, William Ralbert
Bennett, William Tapley, Jr.
Bennison, Bertrand Earl
Bennsky, George Michael
Bensinger, Peter Benjamin
Benson, Elizabeth Polk
Benson, George Stuart
Benson, Lawrence Kern
Benson, Nettie Lee
Benson, Oliver Earl
Benson, Robert Dale
Benson, Roy Stanley
Benson, William Edward Barnes
Benstock, Gerald Martin
Bent, Donn Newberry
Bent, Willard Osborn
Bentley, Helen Delich (Mrs. William Roy Bentley)
Bentley, Hershel Paul, Jr.
Bentley, James Luther
Bentley, Kenton Earl
Benton, George Stock
Benton, Hugh Arthur

839 REGIONAL LISTING—SOUTH-SOUTHWEST

Benton, Joseph Nelson, Jr.
Benton, Morris Carey, Jr.
Benton, Raymond Stetson
Bentsen, Kenneth Edward
Bentsen, Lloyd
Ben-Veniste, Richard
Benz, John Stephen
Berenda, Carlton Warren
Berendzen, Richard Earl
Berenson, Gerald Sanders
Beresford, Spencer Moxon
Bereston, Eugene Sydney
Bereuter, Douglas Kent
Berfield, Morton Lang
Berg, Ericson
Berg, Irwin August
Berg, Joseph Wilbur, Jr.
Berg, Norman Alf
Berg, Robert Raymond
Berg, Rodney Kenneth
Berg, Thomas
Berger, Harold
Berger, Louis
Berger, Patricia Wilson
Bergeron, Wilbur Lee
Bergman, Harry
Bergmann, Fred Heinz
Bergmann, Otto
Bergold, Harry Earl, Jr.
Bergquist, Gregory David
Bergquist, Robert Louis
Bergsma, Stuart
Bergsten, C. Fred
Beringer, William Ernst
Berkey, Barry Robert
Berkman, William Roger
Berkowitz, Leon
Berkowitz, Marshall
Berl, Walter George
Berlin, Ira
Berlin, Kenneth Darrell
Berlin, Seymour Sanford
Berman, Alan
Berman, Edgar Frank
Berman, Harry Louis
Berman, Louise Marguerite
Berman, Milton Schooler
Bernard, Hugh Yancey, Jr.
Bernard, Lola Diane
Bernard, Spencer Thomas
Bernard, William G.
Bernardo, Charles Michael
Bernay, Betti
Bernd, Joseph Laurence
Bernd-Cohen, Max
Berne, Robert Matthew
Berner, Lewis
Bernhard, Berl
Bernhardt, John Bowman
Bernheim, Frederick
Bernier, Joseph Leroy
Bernstein, Carl
Bernstein, George Kaskel
Bernstein, Joel
Bernstein, Karl Joseph
Bernstein, Robert
Berrier, James Joseph
Berrigan, Philip Francis
Berry, Charles Oscar
Berry, Chuck (Charles Edward Anderson Berry)
Berry, Harold A.
Berry, James D.
Berry, Keehn W.
Berry, Levette Joe
Berry, Mary Frances
Berry, Max Nathan
Berry, Nancy Michaels
Berry, Robert Lee
Berry, Sidney Bryan
Berry, Thornton Granville, Jr.
Berry, Wendell
Berry, William Wells
Berryhill, Henry Lee, Jr.
Berryman, Macon Moore
Berson, Robert Chambliss
Bert, Charles Wesley
Bertalan, Frank Joseph
Berte, Neal Richard
Berthel, John Hallock
Bertrand, Alvin Lee
Bertrand, Anson Rabb
Bertrand, John Raney
Bertrand, Joseph Aaron
Besbekos, George Angelo
Besch, Everett Dickman
Beshany, Philip Arthur
Beshear, Steven L.
Besing, Ray Gilbert
Besley, Lowell
Bessette, Joseph Thomas
Bessman, Maurice Jules
Bessom, Malcolm Eugene
Best, Eugene Crawford, Jr.
Best, Hugo Monroe
Betchkal, James Joseph
Bethune, Edwin R., Jr.
Bethune, Thomas Reese, Jr.
Beto, George John
Bettersworth, John Knox
Bettmann, Otto Ludwig
Betts, Austin Wortham
Betts, Doris June Waugh
Betts, Emmett Albert
Betts, Ernest Claire, Jr.
Betts, James Franklin
Betzig, Edward
Bevan, John Morgan
Bevan, Wendell Lowell, Jr.
Bevan, William
Beveridge, George David, Jr.
Bevill, Tom
Bevington, E(dmund) Milton
Bevis, Joseph C.
Bewkes, Eugene Garrett
Beyer, Robert Carlyle
Bezou, Henry Charles
Bhaskar, Surindar Nath
Biaggi, Mario
Bibb, Peyton Dandridge
Bibby, Douglas Earl
Bible, Frances Lillian
Bickel, Clarence Alois
Bickel, Herbert Jacob, Jr.
Bickel, John Henry, III
Bickham, Thomas Marion, Jr.
Bickley, William Elbert
Biddington, William Robert
Biddle, Eric Harbeson
Biddle, James
Biddle, Livingston Ludlow, Jr.
Biden, Joseph Robinette, Jr.
Biedenharn, Lawrence Christian, Jr.
Biederman, Kenneth Robert
Biegel, Herman Charles
Bieging, David Arthur
Biemiller, Andrew John
Bienvenu, Bernard Jefferson
Bienvenu, Rene Joseph
Bieri, John Genther
Bierley, John Charles
Bierstedt, Robert
Biery, John Carlton
Biesele, John Julius
Bigelow, Donald Nevius
Biggers, William Joseph
Biggs, Thomas Jones
Biggs, Wellington Allen
Bighinatti, Enso Victor
Bildersee, Barnett
Billingham, John Eugene
Billingham, Rupert Everett
Billings, Dorothy Baker
Billings, Frederic Tremaine, Jr.
Billings, Harold Wayne
Billings, William Dwight
Bills, Robert Edgar
Billups, Rufus Lee
Bilpuch, Edward George
Binda, H. Jeffrey
Binder, Leonard James
Binford, Chapman Hunter
Bing, R.H.
Bingaman, David Paul
Bingham, Barry
Bingham, Charles Tiffany, Jr.
Bingham, Eula
Bingham, George Barry, Jr.
Bingham, George Barry, Jr.
Bingham, Mary Caperton (Mrs. Barry Bingham)
Bingham, Rebecca Josephine Taylor (Mrs. Walter D. Bingham)
Bingham, Walter D.
Bininger, Clem Edward
Binion, Willie Clayte, Jr.
Binkert, Alvin John
Binkley, James Samuel
Binkley, Olin Trivette
Binswanger, Milton S., Jr.
Bird, Agnes Thornton
Bird, Francis Marion
Bird, John Adams
Bird, Robert James
Birdsong, William Herbert, Jr.
Birely, William Cramer
Birkenstock, James Warren
Birkhoff, Robert D.
Birney, Robert Charles
Bisbee, Royal Daniel, Jr.
Bischoff, Charles Michael
Bischoff, Robert Michael
Bisher, James Furman
Bishop, Calvin Thomas
Bishop, Charles Edwin
Bishop, Gene Herbert
Bishop, Jim
Bishop, Luther Doyle
Bishop, Samuel Worth
Bishop, Wayne Staton
Bishopric, Karl
Bishton, Robert Arthur
Bissell, Charles Overman
Bissell, Jean Galloway
Bisset, John Thomas
Bissett, James Robert
Bistline, James Adams
Bitter, John
Bittinger, Donald S.
Bittles, William John, Jr.
Bittman, William Omar
Bixler, Ray Herbert
Black, Brady Forrest
Black, Charles Alvin
Black, Creed Carter
Black, Darrell Lacy
Black, Emilie Annabelle
Black, Fischer Sheffey
Black, Hugo Lafayette, Jr.
Black, James Hay
Black, Kenneth, Jr.
Black, Martin Lee, Jr.
Black, Peter
Black, Ralph
Black, Robert Bruce
Black, Robert Coleman
Black, Robert Duncan
Black, Robert Perry
Black, Thomas Bentley
Black, Walter Evan, Jr.
Blackard, Embree Hoss
Blackburn, Charles Lee
Blackburn, Francis Marion
Blackburn, John Oliver
Blackburn, Robert McGrady
Blackburn, William Martin
Blackerby, Philip Earle
Blackford, Benjamin
Blackledge, William Wesley
Blackman, Charles Franklin
Blackmun, Harry Andrew
Blackstock, LeRoy
Blackstock, Robert William
Blackwell, Cecil
Blackwell, Gordon Williams
Blackwell, John Davenport
Blackwell, Lloyd Phalti
Blackwell, Randolph Talmadge
Blackwell, William Allen
Blackwood, Walser Arthur
Blades, William Hamlet
Blair, Calvin Patton
Blair, Charles Stanley
Blair, Forbes Wesley
Blair, Fred Edward
Blair, Glenn Myers
Blair, James Pease
Blair, Leon Borden
Blair, Samuel Rufus
Blair, Warren Emerson
Blair, William Draper, Jr.
Blair, William Franklin
Blair, William McCormick, Jr.
Blair, William Mellville
Blake, Frederick Julius
Blake, Gerald Rutherford
Blake, James J.
Blake, John Ballard
Blake, Peter Jost
Blake, Richard Wilson
Blake, Robert Rogers
Blakeburn, Roy Ellsworth
Blakely, Florence Ella
Blakley, George Robert, Jr.
Blalock, Joseph Rogers
Blanchard, George Samuel
Blanchard, James J.
Blanchard, Lawrence Eley, Jr.
Blanchard, Robert Treat
Blanche, Fred A., Jr.
Blanchette, James Grady, Jr.
Bland, Chester
Blandford, John Russell
Blandford, Sister Margaret Vincent
Blankenheimer, Bernard
Blanshard, Paul
Blanton, Edward Lee, Jr.
Blanton, Jack Sawtelle
Blass, Noland, Jr.
Blau, Theodore Hertzl
Blayney, Keith Dale
Blecher, Melvin
Blechman, Barry M.
Bleckwell, Edgar Hale
Bledsoe, Lafayette Felix
Blee, Myron Roy
Blessey, Walter Emanuel
Blevins, Robert Winston
Bleymaier, Joseph Sylvester
Blinick, George
Blinken, Maurice Henry
Blinn, Keith Wayne
Blinn, Robert D.
Bliss, Daniel
Bliss, Robert Harms
Blitch, James Buchanan
Blitzer, Charles
Bliznakov, Milka Tcherneva
Blizzard, Robert M.
Bloch, Ingram
Bloch, Milton Joseph
Bloch, Richard Isaac
Bloch, Thomas Moffat
Block, Herbert Lawrence (Herblock)
Block, Seymour Stanton
Block, Stanley Byron
Blocker, Truman Graves, Jr.
Blodgett, John Quigg
Blodgett, Ralph Hamilton
Blomquist, Harry Laurentz, Jr.
Blomquist, Richard Frederick
Blomster, Ralph Norman
Bloodworth, James Nelson
Bloom, Joseph Duitch
Bloom, Walter Lyon
Bloomer, John Wellman
Blossman, Alfred Rhody, Jr.
Blough, Carman George
Blough, Glenn Orlando
Blough, Roy
Blouke, Pierre
Blount, Clarence William
Blount, John Bruce
Blount, Robert Haddock
Blount, Winton Malcolm
Blow, George
Blue, George R.
Blue, William L(acy)
Blum, Barbara Davis
Blum, Jacob Joseph
Blum, John Curtis
Blumberg, Joe Morris
Blumberg, Richard Winston
Blume, Jack Paul
Blumenfeld, Michael
Blumenthal, Robert Louis
Blunck, Herbert Christopher
Blunt, William Williams, Jr.
Blyholder, George Donald
Blythe, David Knox
Blythe, Robert Douglass
Blythe, William Brevard
Blythe, William LeGette
Boak, Ruth Alice
Boardman, Richard Stanton
Boatner, James Gowen
Bobbitt, Oliver Beirne, Jr.
Bobbitt, William Haywood
Bobo, Donald Arthur
Bobo, James Robert
Bobrow, Davis Bernard
Bochner, Salomon
Boddiger, George Cyrus
Bode, Albert William
Bode, Carl
Bodenstein, Dietrich H. F. A.
Bodensteiner, Wayne Dean
Bodey, Gerald Paul
Bodian, David
Bodie, Belin Voorhees
Bodman, Richard Stockwell
Boeker, Paul Harold
Boerrigter, Glenn Charles
Boes, Warren Norman
Bogardus, Carl Robert, Jr.
Bogardus, John Robert
Bogart, Frank Arthur
Bogdan, Victor Michael
Boger, Lawrence Leroy
Boggess, Mildred Morford Andrews
Boggs, Corinne C. (Lindy)
Boggs, Jack Aaron
Boggs, James Ernest
Boggs, Thomas Hale, Jr.
Bogle, Hugh Andrew
Bogley, Samuel Walter, III
Bogusch, Edwin Robert
Bohannon, Richard Leland
Bohanon, Luther L.
Boisfontaine, Curtis Rich
Boke, Norman Hill
Boland, Christopher Thomas, II
Boland, Edward P.
Bolduc, Lucien Eugene, Jr.
Bolen, Amos Alonzo
Bolen, David B.
Bolender, Carroll Herdus
Boles, C. E.
Bolger, William Frederick
Boling, Edward Joseph
Bolinger, John C., Jr.
Bolles, Edmund Blair
Bolling, Alexander Russell, Jr.
Bolling, Landrum Rymer
Bollum, Frederick James
Bolster, Archie Milburn
Bolsterli, Margaret Jones
Bolté, Brown
Bolton, Arthur K.
Bolton, Preston Morgan
Bolton, Robert Harvey
Boman, John Harris, Jr.
Bomar, William Purinton
Bonansea, Bernardino Maria
Bonbright, James Cummings
Bond, Calhoun
Bond, Cornelius Combs, Jr.
Bond, Joseph Francis
Bond, Julian
Bond, Langhorne McCook
Bond, Lewis Honyman
Bond, Niles Woodbridge
Bond, Robert McGehee
Bond, Thomas Jackson
Bond, William Robert
Bonds, B. Hancel
Bonds, William Kenneth
Bondurant, Emmet Jopling, II
Bonelli, Anthony Eugene
Boner, Marian Oldfather
Bonet, Frank Joseph
Boney, Leslie Norwood, Jr.
Bonior, David Edward
Bonjean, Charles Michael
Bonker, Don L.
Bonner, Francis Wesley
Bonner, Oscar Davis
Bonner, Walter Joseph
Bonner, William Neely, Jr.
Bonner, Zora David
Bonney, Hal James, Jr.
Bonney, Herbert Staats, Jr.
Bonney, Samuel Robert
Bonnyman, George Gordon
Bonosaro, Carol Alessandra
Bonsack, Samuel Elliott, III
Bonsal, Philip Wilson
Bonsall, Joseph Sloan, Jr.
Bonsignore, Joseph John
Bonte, Frederick James
Bontoyan, Warren Roberts
Bookalam, Alex Charles
Booker, Lewis Thomas
Bookholt, William John
Bookout, John Frank, Jr.
Bookstaver, Alexander
Boomershine, Donald Eugene
Boone, Charles Chaffin
Boone, Edgar John
Boone, George Clark, Jr.
Boone, Gray Davis
Boone, James Buford, Sr.
Boone, Jerry Neal
Boone, Michael Mauldin
Boone, Oliver Kiel
Boone, Walter Fredrick
Boonstra, Clarence A.
Boorstin, Daniel J.
Boose, Arthur John
Boote, Howard Sherry, Jr.
Booth, Charles Loomis
Booth, Irvin Stanley
Booth, Windsor Peyton
Boothe, Armistead Lloyd
Boothe, Leon Estel
Boothman, Claud Otho
Bootle, William Augustus
Booton, John Roller
Boozer, Howard Rai
Boozer, Robert Charles
Borden, Craig Warren
Borders, William D.
Boreman, Herbert Stephenson
Boren, Benjamin N.
Boren, David Lyle
Boren, Hollis Grady
Boren, William Meredith
Borg, Alfred Francis
Borg, Charles Arthur
Borget, Lloyd George
Borglum, James Lincoln de la Mothe
Borgmeyer, Sister Bernard Marie
Boring, John Wayne
Borklund, Carl Wilbur
Borkowski, Francis Thomas
Borman, Frank
Bornstein, Sam
Boroughs, Lewis Edward
Borsari, George Robert, Jr.
Borsody, Benjamin Frank
Bosch, Gulnar Khairallah
Bosch, Jorge Jose
Boschung, Herbert Theodore, Jr.
Boschwitz, Rudy
Boshell, Buris Raye
Boskey, Bennett
Boslow, Harold Meyer
Bosomworth, Peter Palliser
Bosserman, Joseph Norwood
Bossier, Albert Louis, Jr.
Bostian, Carey Hoyt
Boswell, Victor Rickman
Bosworth, Robinson, Jr.
Bothe, Elsbeth
Bottorff, Dennis C.
Botts, Guy Warren
Botts, Truman Arthur
Boucher, William, III
Boudreaux, Warren Louis
Bougas, Stanley John
Boult, Reber Fielding
Boulware, Lemuel Ricketts
Bouquard, Marilyn Lloyd
Bourgeois, Andre Marie Georges
Bourne, Geoffrey Howard
Bourne, Henry Clark, Jr.
Bourne, Peter Geoffry
Bousquet, Thomas Gourrier
Bouvier, John Andre, Jr.
Bovay, Harry Elmo, Jr.
Bovet, Claude J.
Bowden, Edwin Turner
Bowden, Henry Lumpkin
Bowden, Jesse Earle
Bowdler, William G.
Bowdoin, Wilmoth Bowen
Bowen, David Reece
Bowen, Harold Gardner, Jr.
Bowen, James Milton
Bowen, Ted
Bowen, W.J.
Bowers, Elliott Toulmin
Bowers, Fredson Thayer
Bowers, Karl S.
Bowers, Wayne Alexander
Bowersock, Justin Dewitt, III
Bowery, Thomas Glenn
Bowles, Aubrey Russell, Jr.
Bowles, Aubrey Russell, III
Bowles, Grover Cleveland, Jr.
Bowles, Jesse Groover
Bowles, Walter Donald
Bowley, Albert John
Bowling, John William
Bowman, A. Smith
Bowman, Albert Hall
Bowman, Barbara Hyde
Bowman, Ben Cook
Bowman, George Shepard, Jr.
Bowman, Philip Irvin
Bowman, Richard Carl
Bowmer, Jim Dewitt
Bown, Oliver Hutchins
Bowron, Richard Anderson
Bows, Albert Julius, Jr.
Bowsher, Charles Arthur
Box, Dwain D.
Box, John Harold
Boy, John Buckner
Boyce, Benjamin
Boyce, Carroll Wilson
Boyce, Donald Nelson
Boyce, Edward Wayne, Jr.
Boyce, Ernest F.
Boyce, Joseph Canon
Boyce, Joseph Nelson
Boyd, Alan Stephenson
Boyd, Clarence Elmo
Boyd, Earl Neal
Boyd, Edward Lee
Boyd, Elizabeth Margaret
Boyd, George Edward
Boyd, Harper White, Jr.
Boyd, Howard Taney
Boyd, J(esse) Cookman, Jr.
Boyd, Joseph Arthur, Jr.
Boyd, Joseph Aubrey
Boyd, Louis Jefferson
Boyd, Robert
Boyd, Robert Osborn
Boyd, Thomas Munford
Boyer, Ernest LeRoy
Boyer, Robert Ernst
Boyes, Jon L.
Boyette, Joseph Greene
Boykin, Lykes M.
Boykin, Robert Heath
Boykins, Ernest A., Jr.
Boyle, John Joseph
Boyle, Robert Patrick
Boynton, Willard Harold
Boyson, William Albert
Brace, John Wells
Brachman, Malcolm K.
Brachman, Philip Sigmund
Brack, Reginald Kufeld, Sr.
Brack, William Dennis
Bracken, Clyde Earl, Jr.
Brackley, William Lowell
Bracy, Terrence Lester
Braddy, Haldeen
Braddy, Minton Venner
Brademas, John
Braden, Charles Hosea
Braden, David Rice
Braden, Emmett Wade
Braden, Thomas Wardell
Braden, Waldo W.
Brader, Walter Howe, Jr.
Braderman, Eugene Maur
Bradford, A. Lee
Bradford, Addison Morton, Jr.
Bradford, Harold Keith
Bradford, James Cowdon
Bradford, Leland Powers
Bradford, Peter Amory
Bradford, Reagan Howard
Bradham, Gilbert Bowman
Bradlee, Benjamin Crowninshield
Bradley, Bill
Bradley, Francis Xavier
Bradley, Francis Xavier
Bradley, Gene Elliott
Bradley, Harold Whitman
Bradley, Holbrook
Bradley, Hugh Wilson
Bradley, John Andrew
Bradley, John Paul
Bradley, Lee Carrington, Jr.
Bradley, Omar Nelson
Bradley, Ralph Allan
Bradley, Ronald Calvin
Bradley, Sterling Gaylen
Bradshaw, Barbara Robinson
Bradshaw, Charles Marvin
Bradshaw, Lillian Moore
Bradsher, Charles Kilgo
Bradsher, Henry St. Amant
Brady, Joseph Vincent
Brady, Morris Joseph
Brady, Roscoe O.
Brady, Rupert Joseph
Bragdon, Clifford Richardson
Bragg, John Mackie
Brahms, Thomas Walter
Brailsford, James Moncrief
Brainard, Harry Gray
Bramlett, Edwin Chandler, Jr.
Brammer, Kurt William
Branch, Harllee, Jr.
Branch, James Elliott
Branch, Joseph
Brand, Donald Dilworth
Brand, Edward Cabell
Brand, Joseph Lyon
Brand, Paul Wilson
Brand, Vance Devoe
Brandborg, Stewart Monroe
Brandell, Roy A.
Brandenburg, David John
Brandenburg, John Nelson
Brandis, Henry Parker, Jr.
Brandon, Alfred Northrup
Brandon, Arthur Leon
Brandon, David Calvin
Brandon, (Oscar) Henry
Brandon, Inman
Brands, Allen Jean
Brandstatter, Arthur Frank
Brandt, Edward Newman, Jr.
Brandt, Richard Martin
Brandt, Warren William
Branham, Henry Craig
Brann, William Paul
Brannan, Eulie Ross
Brannan, Robert Russel
Brannon, Clifton Woodrow
Brannon, Russell Herbert
Branscomb, Ben Vaughan
Branscomb, Bennett Harvie
Branscomb, Harvie
Branson, Branley Allan
Brantley, Oliver Wiley
Branton, Wiley Austin
Brasfield, Evans Booker
Brashares, William Charles
Braswell, A. Glenn
Braswell, Arnold Webb
Braswell, Louis Erskine
Braswell, Robert Neil
Bratton, James Henry, Jr.
Bratton, Joseph Key
Braudy, Leo Beal
Brauer, Alfred T(heodor)
Brauer, Ralph Werner
Braun, Edward Joseph
Braun, Kurt
Braun, Matitiahu
Braunstein, Jules
Braver, Rita Lynn
Braverman, Nathan Norman
Brawner, Lee Basil
Bray, Charles William, III
Bray, Leslie William, Jr.
Brazeal, Brailsford Reese
Brazell, Carl Crane, Jr.
Brazier, Don Roland
Breathitt, Edward Thompson
Breaux, John B.
Breazeale, Mack Alfred
Breazile, James Edward
Brebbia, John Henry
Brecher, Gerhard Adolf
Breck, Howard Rolland
Breck, Louis William
Breck, Luther Adams
Breckinridge, Charles Edward, Jr.
Bredenberg, Paul Arnold
Breder, Charles Marcus, Jr.
Bree, Germaine
Breed, Allen Forbes
Breeden, Edward Lebbaeus, Jr.
Breedlove, William Davis
Breen, John Edward

REGIONAL LISTING—SOUTH-SOUTHWEST 840

Breen, John Francis
Breen, John William
Breese, George Richard
Breeskin, Adelyn Dohme
Breeskin, Barnett
Breffeilh, Louis Andrew
Breggin, Peter Roger
Bregman, Jacob Israel
Brehm, William Keith
Breitbach, Harry Franklin
Breitenfeld, Frederick, Jr.
Brement, Marshall
Bremermann, Herbert John, Jr.
Brenkert, Karl, Jr.
Brennan, Charles Michael
Brennan, Edward Thomas
Brennan, James G.
Brennan, Joseph Benjamin
Brennan, William Joseph, Jr.
Brenner, Edward John
Brenner, William Edward
Brent, Andrew Jackson
Brent, William Cary, Jr.
Brentlinger, William Brock
Bresee, James Collins
Bresler, Emanuel Harold
Bresnahan, William Alman
Brewer, Albert Preston
Brewer, Benjamin Eddins, Jr.
Brewer, George Madison
Brewer, Marion Carey
Brewer, Norman (Craig), Jr.
Brewer, Thomas Bowman
Brewster, Carroll Worcester
Brewster, Robert Charles
Brewster, Robert Gene
Brian, Alexis Morgan, Jr.
Brian, Harry Findley
Brice, Ashbel Green
Brice, Bill Eugene
Brickel, James Russell
Brickell, Edward Ernest, Jr.
Bricker, Donald Lee
Brickfield, Cyril Francis
Bridgers, John Dixon
Bridgewater, Herbert Jeremiah, Jr.
Bridwell, Bob S.
Briggs, F. Norman
Briggs, Garrett
Briggs, Harold Melvin
Briggs, Lloyd Arnold
Briggs, Robert LeRoy
Briggs, Shirley Ann
Briggs, Wallace Neal
Bright, Harold Frederick
Bright, Harvey R.
Bright, John
Bright, Margaret
Bright, Simeon Miller
Brightmire, Paul William
Bril, Jacques L.
Briley, Clifton Beverly
Brill, Daniel Herbert
Brimmer, Andrew Felton
Brinberg, Herbert Raphael
Bringhurst, John Henry, Jr.
Brinker, John Henry, Jr.
Brinker, Norman Eugene
Brinkerhoff, Philip Richard
Brinkhous, Kenneth Merle
Brinkley, David
Brinkley, Homer Lee
Brinkley, Jack Thomas
Brinkley, William Clark
Brinton, Edgar Harry
Briscoe, John Hanson
Bristow, Robert O'Neil
Britt, David M.
Britt, Henry Middleton
Britt, Rolland W.
Britten, Gerald Hallbeck
Brittin, Norman Aylsworth
Britton, Willard P.
Brixey, John Clark
Broach, Wilson James
Broadbent, Smith Dudley, Jr.
Broadwater, Robert James
Broce, Thomas Edward
Broches, Aron
Brock, Harry B., Jr.
Brock, Horace Rhea
Brock, James Daniel
Brock, Paul Warrington
Brock, Pope Furman
Brock, Ray Leonard, Jr.
Brock, Ventress Nolan
Brock, Walter Edgar
Brock, William E.
Brockenbrough, Henry Watkins
Brockett, Oscar Gross
Brockway, William Robert
Brockwell, Charles Wilbur, Jr.
Brode, Marvin Jay
Broder, David Salzer
Brodhead, William McNulty
Brodie, Bernard Beryl
Brodine, Charles Edward
Brody, Eugene Bloor
Broersma, Sybrand
Brogan, John Andrew, III
Brogdon, Byron Gilliam
Brokaw, Charles Hugh
Bromage, Philip Raikes
Bromberg, Alan Robert
Bromberg, Henri Louie, Jr.
Bromberg, John Edward
Bronars, Edward Joseph
Bronfenbrenner, Martin
Bronson, Oswald Perry
Brooke, Edward William
Brooke, Francis John, 3d
Brooker, Marvin Adel
Brookhouse, Christopher
Brooks, David William
Brooks, Elbert Daniel
Brooks, Eugene Howard
Brooks, Frank Carothers
Brooks, Frederick Phillips, Jr.
Brooks, George Daniel
Brooks, George Henry
Brooks, George William
Brooks, Herman Edgar
Brooks, Jack Bascom
Brooks, James Elwood
Brooks, Lyman Beecher
Brooks, Richard Boynton
Brooks, Roger Leon
Brooks, Seth Rogers
Brooks, Thomas Joseph, Jr.
Broom, Vernon Herrin
Brooman, John Cresswell
Broome, George Calvin, III
Broquist, Harry Pearson
Brosman, Catharine Hill Savage
Bross, John Adams
Brotzman, Donald Glenn
Broughton, Thomas Robert Shannon
Broussard, Joseph Otto, III
Broussard, Joseph Otto, III
Browdy, Alvin
Brower, Charles Nelson
Brown, Albert Linwood
Brown, Alexander Joseph, Jr.
Brown, Arthur
Brown, Arthur Morton
Brown, Arthur Wayne
Brown, Aubrey Neblett, Jr.
Brown, Bailey
Brown, Bart A., Jr.
Brown, Ben Hill, Jr.
Brown, Benjamin A.
Brown, Bernard Loam, Jr.
Brown, Bertram S.
Brown, Bob Burton
Brown, Bob Marion
Brown, Bruce K.
Brown, Butler Malloy
Brown, Calvin Smith
Brown, Charles Arthur
Brown, Charles Carter
Brown, Charles Freeman
Brown, Charles Henry
Brown, David Springer
Brown, Dee Alexander
Brown, Dennison Robert
Brown, Donald Arthur
Brown, Donald David
Brown, Dorothy Lavinia
Brown, Earl Appleton, Jr.
Brown, Earl Ivan, II
Brown, Edward McLain, Jr.
Brown, Elizabeth Ann
Brown, Ellsworth Howard
Brown, Elvin J.
Brown, Ephraim Taylor, Jr.
Brown, Ernest Joseph
Brown, Eugene Hill
Brown, Firman Hewitt, Jr.
Brown, Francis Taylor
Brown, George Bosworth
Brown, George Rufus
Brown, George Wayne
Brown, Harlan Craig
Brown, Harold
Brown, Harry Matthew
Brown, Horace Brightberry, Jr.
Brown, Hubert Jude
Brown, Ivan Willard, Jr.
Brown, J(oseph) Gordon
Brown, J(ames) Hyatt
Brown, Jack Harold Upton
Brown, James Andrew
Brown, James Barrow
Brown, James Edward (Jim Ed)
Brown, James Grady
Brown, James H., Jr.
Brown, James Harvey
Brown, James Leon
Brown, James Monroe, III
Brown, James Raphael, Jr.
Brown, James Seay
Brown, James Wilson
Brown, Jean William
Brown, John Carter
Brown, John Elward, Jr.
Brown, John Lackey
Brown, John Robert
Brown, John Y.
Brown, Jon Thomas
Brown, Kenneth James
Brown, Lee Patrick
Brown, Leon
Brown, Leonard Franklin, Jr.
Brown, LeRoy
Brown, Leslie Eugene
Brown, Lester Russell
Brown, Lewis Arnold
Brown, Lewis Dean
Brown, Madison Baldwin
Brown, Mark
Brown, Michael Arthur
Brown, Myrtle Irene
Brown, Paul Marvin, Jr.
Brown, Peter Gilbert
Brown, Philip Bransfield
Brown, Richard Fargo
Brown, Richard Lee
Brown, Richard Rolland
Brown, Robert Joseph
Brown, Robert Lee
Brown, Robert Lyle
Brown, Rodgers N.
Brown, Ronald
Brown, Russell Wilfrid
Brown, Samuel W., Jr.
Brown, Sarah Cole
Brown, Sterling Wade
Brown, Thomas Andrew
Brown, Thomas Carl
Brown, Thomas McPherson
Brown, Thomas Philip, III
Brown, Virginia Mae
Brown, Weir Messick
Brown, William Albert
Brown, William Ernest
Brown, William Holmes
Brown, William Lee Lyons, Jr.
Brown, William Randall
Brown, William Russell
Brown, Wilson Gordon
Brown, Winthrop Gilman
Brown, Wood
Browne, Francis Cedric
Browne, John Robinson
Brownell, Philip Curtis
Browning, Cecil Oba
Browning, Chauncey Hoyt, Jr.
Browning, Grayson Douglas
Browning, Henry Prentice
Brownlee, Jerry L.
Brownlee, Robert Calvin
Brownlee, Thomas Marshall
Brownley, Floyd Irving, Jr.
Brownson, Charles Bruce
Brownson, Robert Henry
Brownstein, Philip Nathan
Broyhill, James Thomas
Broyles, James Edward
Broyles, John Franklin
Broyles, William Dodson, Jr.
Brubaker, Lauren Edgar
Bruccoli, Matthew Joseph
Bruce, E(stel) Edward
Bruce, Elmer Ivan
Bruce, Imon Elba
Bruce, Robert Rockwell
Bruce, Thomas Allen
Bruce, William Rankin
Bruch, Hilde
Bruck, Stephen Desiderius
Brueck, Robert Paul
Brueckheimer, William Rogers
Bruesch, Simon Rulin
Bruhn, John Glyndon
Brumback, Charles Tiedtke
Brumbaugh, John Maynard
Brumley, Robert Julian
Brummet, Richard Lee
Brummett, Marvin Kight
Brundett, George Lee, Jr.
Bruner, William Wallace
Brunhild, Gordon
Brunini, Joseph Bernard
Brunner, Richard Francis
Bruno, Harold Robinson, Jr.
Bruno, Harold Robinson, Jr.
Bruno, Vincent John
Bruns, Franklin Richard, Jr.
Brunson, Joel Garrett
Brush, Lucien Munson, Jr.
Brusilow, Anshel
Bruton, James DeWitt, Jr.
Bryan, Albert V(ickers)
Bryan, Clarence Russell
Bryan, Colgan Hobson
Bryan, David Tennant
Bryan, George T.
Bryan, J(oseph), III
Bryan, Jacob Franklin, III
Bryan, James Edward
Bryan, John Alexander
Bryan, John Leland
Bryan, Joseph McKinley
Bryan, Paul Robey, Jr.
Bryan, Robert Armistead
Bryan, Robert Fessler
Bryan, Wright
Bryant, Anita Jane (Mrs. Robert Einar Green)
Bryant, Arthur Herbert, II
Bryant, Billy Finney
Bryant, Boudleaux
Bryant, Britain Hamilton
Bryant, Cecil Farris
Bryant, Celia Mae Small
Bryant, Donald Loudon
Bryant, Edward Kendall
Bryant, Felice
Bryant, Hubert Hale
Bryant, James William
Bryant, John Harland
Bryant, Oscar Sims, Jr.
Bryant, Robert Parker
Bryant, Thomas Edward
Bryant, William B.
Bryson, Brady Oliver
Brzezinski, John Charles
Brzezinski, Zbigniew
Buchanan, Donald Duane
Buchanan, James McGill, Jr.
Buchanan, John Donald
Buchanan, John Donald, Jr.
Buchanan, John Hall, Jr.
Buchanan, Patrick Joseph
Buchanan, Wallace Davis
Buchanan, Wesley Evans
Buchanan, Wiley Thomas, Jr.
Buchanan, William
Buchanan, William Walter
Buchel, August Reynolds
Buchen, Philip William
Bucher, Robert Monroe
Buchholz, Donald Alden
Buchwald, Art
Buchwald, Jules
Buck, Alfred Andreas
Buck, Ervin Oscar
Buck, John Bonner
Buck, Morison
Buck, Thomas Randolph
Buckingham, Charles Edward
Buckingham, Clay Thompson
Buckley, Emerson
Buckley, Frank Wilson
Buckley, Helen Ann
Buckley, John Lee, Jr.
Buckley, Joseph
Buckley, Joseph Paul
Buckley, William Elmhirst
Buckman, Robert Erwin
Buckner, George Walker, Jr.
Buckner, John Hugh
Bucy, Paul C.
Budalur, Thyagarajan Subbanarayan
Budd, Louis John
Budd, Philip Joseph
Buddendorf, Bobby Eugene
Budig, Gene Arthur
Bue, Carl Olaf, Jr.
Bueding, Ernest
Buergenthal, Thomas
Buescher, Edward Louis
Buesseler, John Aure
Bueter, Arnold Gerhard
Buffington, Ralph Meldrim
Buffkins, Archie Lee
Buford, Edwin Rucker
Bugg, James Luckin, Jr.
Buhler, Jean Emil
Bukantz, Samuel Charles
Bulger, Roger James
Bulkeley, John Duncan
Bull, William Earnest
Bullard, Edgar John, III
Bullard, K(ennedy) C(ornelius)
Bullerjahn, Eduard Henri
Bullock, Henry Morton
Bullock, Maurice Randolph
Bullock, Orin Miles, Jr.
Bumgarner, John Carson, Sr.
Bumpers, Dale Leon
Bunch, Franklin Swope
Bundy, Charles Alan
Bunker, Edmund Cason
Bunker, Ellsworth
Bunnelle, Robert Ellsworth
Bunten, John Richard
Buntin, Thomas Eugene, Jr.
Bunting, Cyrenus Garritt
Bunting, James Whitney
Bunting, Josiah
Bunzl, Rudolph Hans
Burch, Dean
Burch, Francis Boucher
Burch, George E.
Burch, Lucius Edward, Jr.
Burch, Robert Ray
Burchard, Charles
Burchell, Herbert Joseph
Burchfield, Harry Phineas, Jr.
Burck, Arthur Albert
Burdett, Allen Mitchell, Jr.
Burdette, Walter James
Burdick, Harold Eugene
Burdick, Quentin Northrop
Burge, William Lee
Burgener, Clair W.
Burger, Warren Earl
Burgess, Alfred Franklin
Burgess, Charles Harry
Burgess, Isabel Andrews
Burgess, Kenneth Alexander
Burgess, Roger
Burgoon, Norman Aaron, Jr.
Burgos-Calderon, Rafael
Burguieres, Philip Joseph
Burguieres, Philip Joseph
Burk, Alfred E.
Burk, Creighton A.
Burk, Dean
Burk, Marguerite Catherine
Burke, Frederick A.
Burke, J. Herbert
Burke, Kelly Howard
Burke, Thomas Edward
Burke, William Temple, Jr.
Burkett, Lowell Abner
Burkhalter, David A.
Burkhardt, Francis Xavier
Burkhart, Lynne C.
Burky, Howard Fred
Burleson, Elizabeth (Mrs. Gamewell David Burleson)
Burleson, Ira Lee
Burleson, Omar
Burlison, Bill D.
Burmaster, David Elton
Burmeister, Clifton Alvin
Burnam, Paul Wayne
Burnett, Arthur Louis
Burnett, Carey Corley
Burnett, George Wesley
Burnett, Henry
Burnett, William Clyde, Jr.
Burney, Cecil Edward
Burnham, David Bright
Burns, Arthur Edward
Burns, Arthur Frank
Burns, Carroll Dean
Burns, David Mitchell
Burns, Gerald Phillip
Burns, John Howard
Burns, Kathleen Marie
Burns, Mary Ann Theresa
Burns, Mitchel Anthony
Burns, Norman
Burns, Robert Whitehall
Burns, William A.
Burns, William S.
Burnside, Maurice Gwinn
Burnside, Waldo Howard
Burr, Donald Calvin
Burr, Helen Gunderson (Mrs. Horace Burr)
Burr, Helen Gunderson (Mrs. Horace Burr)
Burr, John Green
Burrell, Donald Samuel
Burrill, Meredith Frederic
Burroughs, John Andrew, Jr.
Burroughs, Raymon
Burrow, Harold
Burrow, William Fite, Sr.
Burrows, Charles Robert
Burrus, John N(ewell)
Burson, George Allen, Jr.
Burson, Phyllis S.
Burson, Sherman LeRoy, Jr.
Burt, Alvin Victor, Jr.
Burtner, Edwin Russell
Burton, Charles Henning
Burton, Dwight Lowell
Burton, Glenn Willard
Burton, John Flack
Burton, John Lowell
Burton, Phillip
Burton, Ralph Joseph
Burwell, Clayton L.
Burwell, James Robert
Burwell, Lewis Carter, Jr.
Burzlaff, Donald Frederick
Burzynski, Norman Stephen
Busbee, George Dekle
Busby, David
Busch, Arthur Winston
Busch, Harris
Busey, James Buchanan, IV
Bush, Dorothy Vredenburgh
Bush, George Herbert Walker
Bush, Herman Spencer
Bush, Jean Evans
Bush, John William
Bush, Robert Cecil
Bushel, Arthur
Bushnell, John Alden
Bussard, Clarence Lease
Busse, Ewald William
Bussmann, Charles Haines
Bustamante, Rodrigo Antonio
Busteed, Robert Charles
Butcher, (Charles) Philip
Butcher, Reginald William
Butchman, Alan Archer
Butenhoff, Robert Lowell
Butkus, Dick
Butler, Bernard Yvo
Butler, Broadus Nathaniel
Butler, Charles Randolph
Butler, Edward Scannell
Butler, Eugene
Butler, Frederick George
Butler, George Harrison
Butler, Jack Lawrence
Butler, James Frederick
Butler, Lee David
Butler, Manley Caldwell
Butler, Philip Alan
Butler, Richard Colburn
Butler, Robert Neil
Butler, Roy Francis
Butler, Sydney Johnston
Butler, Wendell Pace
Butler, William Robert
Butler, William Thomas
Butner, Fred Washington, Jr.
Butson, Alton Thomas
Butt, Charles C.
Butt, Howard Edward
Butt, Howard Edward, Jr.
Butterfield, Samuel Hale
Butters, Thomas Arden
Butterworth, Charles Edwin, Jr.
Butterworth, James Donald
Buttle, Edgar Allyn
Button, Jack Blair
Buttrill, Sidney Eugene
Butts, David Phillip
Butts, Herbert Clell
Butts, William A.
Butz, Karl Theodore
Butzner, John Decker, Jr.
Buxeda, Roberto
Byars, Edward Ford
Byars, Walter Ryland, Jr.
Byerly, Theodore Carroll
Byers, Buckley Morris
Bynum, Arlen Dean
Byrd, Benjamin Franklin, Jr.
Byrd, Charles Lee
Byrd, Conley F.
Byrd, David Lamar
Byrd, Donald Arthur
Byrd, Harry Flood, Jr.
Byrd, Isaac Burlin
Byrd, James Adon
Byrd, Jerome W.
Byrd, John Baxter
Byrd, Robert Carlyle
Byrd, Robert Gray
Byrne, John Carr Clarke
Byrne, John Joseph, Jr.
Byrnes, Arthur F.
Byrnes, John W.
Byrnside, Oscar Jehu, Jr.
Byron, Beverly Butcher
Bywaters, Jerry
Cacheris, Plato
Caddell, John A.
Caddell, John Allen
Cade, James Robert
Cade, Lawrence
Cadenhead, Alfred Paul
Cady, Edwin Harrison
Caffey, Guy Hamilton, Jr.
Cahill, Charles Leslie
Cahill, Fred Virgil
Cahn, Charles, II
Cahn, Jean Camper
Cahn, John Werner
Cahn, Julius Norman
Cahn, Robert
Cahoon, Stuart Newton
Cain, Byron Wilson
Cain, Donald Ezell
Cain, E. Lee
Cain, Harry Pulliam, II
Cain, J. Frederick
Cain, Joseph Alexander
Caine, Walter Eugene
Cairnes, Joseph Francis
Cairns, Huntington
Calamaro, Raymond Stuart
Calame, Gerald Paul
Calder, Iain Wilson
Calderhead, William Dickson
Caldwell, Charles Gambill
Caldwell, Frank Hill
Caldwell, Garnett Ernest
Caldwell, Harold Dwane
Caldwell, Hugh Harris, Jr.
Caldwell, John Tyler
Caldwell, Joseph Morton
Caldwell, Lafayette Hardwick, Jr.
Caldwell, Thomas Allison, Jr.
Caldwell, Thomas Jones, Jr.
Caldwell, Wayne Eugene
Caldwell, William Burns, III
Cale, Edgar Barclay
Calfee, William Howard
Calhoon, Richard Percival
Calhoon, Thomas Bruce
Calhoun, Calfrey C.
Calhoun, Frank Wayne
Calhoun, Harold
Calhoun, John C., Jr.
Calhoun, Sister Mary Dorothy
Calhoun, Milburn Eugene
Calhoun, Walter Bowman
Califano, Joseph Anthony, Jr.
Calingaert, Michael
Calio, Anthony John
Calkins, Charles Richard
Calkins, Earl C., Sr.
Calkins, Francis Joseph
Calkins, Gary Nathan
Calkins, Kingsley Mark
Calkins, Robert De Blois
Callaham, Thomas Hunter
Callaham, Thomas Hunter
Callahan, Daniel Joseph, III
Callahan, North
Callander, Bruce Douglas
Callaway, Fuller Earle, Jr.
Callaway, Jasper Lamar
Callaway, Paul Smith
Callaway, William Howard
Callen, Earl Robert
Callen, Irwin R.
Callihan, E. L.
Callison, George Preston
Callmer, James Peter
Calloway, David Wayne
Calogero, Pascal Frank
Calver, James Lewis
Calverley, John Robert
Calvert, Delbert William
Calvert, Gordon Lee
Camacho, Alvro Manuel
Cambel, Ali B.
Cameron, Benjamin Franklin, Jr.
Cameron, Charles Clifford
Cameron, Charles Franklin
Cameron, Charles Metz, Jr.
Cameron, Duncan Hume
Cameron, John Lansing
Cameron, Richard Ray
Cameron, Rondo
Camm, Frank Ambler
Camp, David Bennett
Camp, James Leonidas, Jr.
Camp, Joseph Shelton, Jr.
Camp, Lawrence Hicks
Campaneris, Dagoberto Blanco
Campbell, Alan Keith
Campbell, Archie James
Campbell, Bruce Emerson, Jr.
Campbell, Carroll Ashmore, Jr.
Campbell, Colin
Campbell, Donald Alfred
Campbell, Edmund Douglas
Campbell, George Emerson
Campbell, George Wilbur
Campbell, Herbert Peterkin
Campbell, James Fromhart
Campbell, James Philander, Jr.
Campbell, James Wayne
Campbell, John Lloyd
Campbell, John Morgan
Campbell, John Tucker
Campbell, Laurence Randolph
Campbell, Leonard Gene
Campbell, Maria Bouchelle
Campbell, McCoy Clempson, III
Campbell, Norman William
Campbell, Robert Neal
Campbell, Rolla Dacres
Campbell, Stuart Bland, Jr.
Campbell, Thomas Corwith, Jr.
Campbell, Thomas Nolan
Campbell, Wallace Justin
Campbell, Wilburn Camrock
Campbell, William J.
Campbell, William J.
Campion, Donald Richard
Campobasso, Thomas Anthony
Canales, Jose Antonio
Candler, John Slaughter, II
Canfield, Edward Francis
Canfield, Frederick Weber
Cangelosi, Vincent Emanuel
Canham, Robert Allen
Cannon, Edmund Rasha
Cannon, Henry Cecil, Jr.
Cannon, Howard Walter
Cannon, Isabella Walton
Cannon, Joseph Harris

841 REGIONAL LISTING—SOUTH-SOUTHWEST

Cannon, Kenneth Dean
Cannon, Mark Wilcox
Cannon, William John
Cannon, William Ragsdale
Cantarino, Vicente
Canter, Milton Ernest
Cantey, James Willis
Cantrell, Clyde Hull
Cantrell, Robert Wendell
Cantrell, William Allen
Canup, William Caleb
Capen, Charles Herbert
Capers, Charlotte
Capers, Gerald Mortimer, Jr.
Caperton, Charles Lee
Caplan, Fred Harry
Caplin, Mortimer Maxwell
Caplow, Theodore
Capone, Lucien, Jr.
Capp, Glenn Richard
Cappiello, Frank Anthony, Jr.
Capps, Benjamin Franklin
Capps, Ethan LeRoy
Capwell, Richard Leonard
Carameros, George Demitrius, Jr.
Carbone, Robert Frank
Carden, Arnold Eugene
Cardenas, Blandina
Cardin, Benjamin Louis
Cardozo, Manoel
Cardozo, Michael Hart
Cardus, David
Cardwell, Alvin Boyd
Cardwell, Horace Milton
Carey, Charles Jeremiah
Carey, Francis E.
Carey, Gerald John, Jr.
Carey, Harvey Locke
Carey, Richard Edward
Carey, Thomas Devore
Carey, William Daniel
Carey, William Nelson, Jr.
Cargill, Ian Peter M.
Cargo, William Ira
Carithers, Hugh Alfred
Carius, Robert Wilhelm
Carle, Leland Lester
Carle, Wilfred Fred
Carleton, Willard Tracy
Carley, Charles Team, Jr.
Carliner, David
Carlisle, William Aiken
Carlitz, Leonard
Carlos, James Paul
Carlson, Albin Edmund
Carlson, James Gordon
Carlson, John Swink
Carlson, Natalie Savage
Carlson, Norman A.
Carlson, Robert Lee
Carlson, Robert Scott
Carlson, William Samuel
Carlsson, Percy Allan
Carlton, Dean
Carlton, Donald Morrill
Carlucci, Frank Charles, III
Carmack, George
Carman, George Henry
Carmel, Alan Stuart
Carmichael, Emmett Bryan
Carmichael, Mary Mulloy
Carmichael, William Jerome
Carmody, Martin Doan
Carnahan, Ralph Herbert
Carnell, Paul Herbert
Carnes, James Robert
Carnes, Wilson Woodrow
Carney, Chesney M.
Carney, Price Felts
Carney, Robert Forrest
Carney, Robert Joseph
Carnicero, Jorge
Carpenter, Charles Congden
Carpenter, Clifford Earl
Carpenter, Delma Rae, Jr.
Carpenter, Elizabeth Sutherland
Carpenter, John Wilson, III
Carpenter, Malcolm Breckenridge
Carpenter, Robert Eddy
Carpenter, Stanley Sherman
Carpenter, Thomas Earl
Carpenter, William Levy
Carr, Archie F.
Carr, Chalmers Rankin
Carr, Charles Jelleff
Carr, David Turner
Carr, Frederick Louis
Carr, George C.
Carr, Gerald Paul
Carr, Howard Earl
Carr, Jerome Harris
Carr, Joe Cordell
Carr, Kenneth Monroe
Carr, Lawrence Edward, Jr.
Carr, M. Robert
Carr, Milton L.
Carr, Richard
Carr, Waggoner
Carr, William George
Carretta, Albert Aloysius
Carrico, Harry Lee
Carrier, Glass Bowling, Jr.
Carrier, Ronald Edwin
Carriere, Charles Montbrun
Carriger, John Shields
Carrington, Paul
Carrington, Paul DeWitt
Carrion, Jose Luis
Carrion, Rafael, Jr.
Carroll, Billy Price
Carroll, Chester Coen
Carroll, David Shields
Carroll, Dewey Eugene
Carroll, Edwin Winford
Carroll, Frances Laverne
Carroll, George Joseph
Carroll, James Conrad
Carroll, John Bissell
Carroll, Julian Morton
Carroll, Lewis Andrew
Carroll, Mark Sullivan
Carroll, Marshall Elliott
Carroll, Matthew Eugene
Carroll, Richard Scott
Carroll, Thomas Charles
Carroll, (John) Wallace
Carrow, Milton Michael
Carruth, Charles Weldon
Carruthers, Paul Matthew
Carson, Dale George
Carson, Robert Gordon, Jr.
Carswell, Robert
Cartagena, Rafael
Carter, Alan
Carter, Barry Edward
Carter, Boyd George
Carter, Curtis Harold
Carter, Dan T.
Carter, Don Earl
Carter, Donald Clayton
Carter, Dotian
Carter, Everett Charlie
Carter, George Francis
Carter, Gwendolen Margaret
Carter, Harlon Bronson
Carter, Harry Tyson
Carter, (William) Hodding, III
Carter, Hugh Alton, Jr.
Carter, Jaine Marie
Carter, James Clarence
Carter, James Johnston
Carter, Jay Boyd
Carter, Jimmy (James Earl, Jr.)
Carter, John Boyd, Jr.
Carter, John Coles
Carter, Joseph Carlyle, Jr.
Carter, Lamore Joseph
Carter, Lester Clyde
Carter, Lisle Carleton, Jr.
Carter, Rex Lyle
Carter, Rosalynn Smith
Carter, Tim Lee
Carter, Walter Colquitt
Carter, Wilbur Lee, Jr.
Carter, William Beverly, Jr.
Carter, William Gilbert
Carter, William Hodding, III
Carter, William Minor
Carter, William Thomas, III
Carter, William Walton
Carter, Willis Merle
Cartlidge, Alva Ray
Cartwright, Jan Eric
Cartwright, Walter Joseph
Cartwright, William Holman
Carusi, Eugene Cassin
Caruthers, Robert Mack
Carver, Dale Ringwalt
Carver, George Allen
Cary, Freeman Hamilton
Cary, James Donald
Cary, John Hale
Case, Charles Carroll
Case, Clifford Philip
Case, Richard Werber
Casey, Albert Vincent
Casey, Edward Dennis
Casey, Ethel Laughlin
Casey, Eugene Bernard
Casey, Joe Dixon
Casey, John Joseph
Casey, Maurice Francis
Casey, Ralph Edward
Cash, Claybourne Allison
Cash, James Barrett, Jr.
Cash, June Carter
Cash, Polk Wright
Cash, William Bradbury
Cashen, Henry Christopher, II
Cashin, James A.
Cason, Charles Monroe
Cason, Robert Benjamin
Casper, Willie Ragan
Cass, A. Carl
Cass, Millard
Cassata, John T.
Cassedy, Marshall Royal
Cassel, Fred Carl, Jr.
Cassell, George Louis
Casselli, Henry Calvin, Jr.
Casselman, William E., II
Cassibry, Fred James
Cassidy, James Joseph
Cassidy, Richard Thomas
Cassin, William Bourke
Castellan, Gilbert William
Castelli, Alexander Gerard
Castillo, Leonel Jabier
Castle, Emery Neal
Castle, John Raymond, Jr.
Castleberry, Vivian Lou Anderson (Mrs. Curtis Wales Castleberry)
Catania, Anthony Charles
Cate, Wirt Armistead
Cater, Douglass
Cater, John Thomas
Cates, Don Tate
Cates, MacFarlane Lafferty, Jr.
Cather, Donald Warren
Cathey, Cornelius Oliver
Cathey, Oliver Edward
Catledge, Richard Carroll
Catlett, Leon Bidez
Catola, Stanley Guy
Catravas, George Nicholas
Catto, Henry Edward, Jr.
Cattoi, Robert Louis
Caudill, Harry Monroe
Caudill, Robert Paul
Caudle, Jones Richard, Jr.
Causey, Norman Michael
Cauthen, Baker James
Cauthen, Irby Bruce, Jr.
Cavanagh, Denis
Cavanaugh, Gordon
Cavanaugh, John Joseph
Caveny, Elmer Leonard
Cavin, F. G.
Cavin, Wade Leonard
Cavin, William Pinckney
Cawley, Edward Philip
Cawley, Francis Riggs
Cawthon, William Connell
Cazort, Ralph Jerry
Cecil, Ode Vaughan
Cederberg, Elford Albin
Cedrone, Louis Robert, Jr.
Celeste, Richard F.
Cella, Francis Raymond
Celli, Vittorio
Cerf, Vinton Gray
Cerf, Vinton Gray
Cernan, Eugene A.
Cerveny, Frank Stanley
Chabon, Steve
Chacko, George Kuttickal
Chaddock, Jack Bartley
Chadenet, Bernard
Chadick, T. C.
Chadwick, Donald Roger
Chadwick, George Albert, Jr.
Chafee, John Hubbard
Chafetz, Morris Edward
Chaffin, Verner Franklin
Chait, William
Challinor, David
Chamberlain, Charles Ernest
Chamberlain, Donald Frank
Chamberlain, Joseph Wyan
Chamberlin, Ward Bryan, Jr.
Chambers, David Smith
Chambers, Fred
Chambers, James Floyd, Jr.
Chambers, Justice Marion
Chambers, S. James
Chambliss, John Randolph
Champion, John E.
Champlin, Richard H.
Chandler, Albert Benjamin
Chandler, Daniel Brooks
Chandler, Daniel Brooks
Chandler, James Elkins
Chandler, James Williams
Chandler, (Robert) Lewis
Chandler, Reuben Carl
Chandler, Stephen S.
Chandler, Wallace Lee
Chandler, Wyeth
Chane, George Warren
Chaney, David Webb
Chaney, Vincent Verlando
Chang, Chung Mou (Morris)
Chang, Henry Chung-Lien
Chang, Jeffrey Peh-I
Channell, Donald Everett
Channer, Earle Adare
Chantilis, Peter Samuel
Chapanis, Alphonse
Chapel, Dewey Elbert
Chapin, William Sellew
Chapman, Alan Jesse
Chapman, Alvah Herman, Jr.
Chapman, Christian Addison
Chapman, Donald D.
Chapman, Grosvenor
Chapman, Harry Moulton
Chapman, Hugh McMaster
Chapman, James Alfred, Jr.
Chapman, James Lee
Chapman, John Edmon
Chapman, John Stewart
Chapman, Joseph Edgar, Jr.
Chapman, Leonard Fielding, Jr.
Chapman, Robert B., III
Chapman, Robert DeWitt
Chapman, Robert Foster
Chapman, Samuel Greeley
Chapman, Thomas William
Chapoton, John Edgar
Chappell, Clovis Gillham, Jr.
Chappell, James Wilbert
Chappell, Robert Harvey, Jr.
Chappell, Warren
Chappell, William Venroe, Jr.
Chardon, Carlos Eugenio
Charles, Jack
Charles, Philipp Lambert
Charry, Michael
Chartouni, Adib Elias
Chartrand, Robert Lee
Charyk, Joseph Vincent
Chase, Anthony Goodwin
Chase, Charles Henry
Chase, Gilbert
Chase, Goodwin
Chase, Harold William
Chase, John Saunders
Chase, Nicholas Joseph
Chase, Richard
Chase, Robert Willard
Chase, Thomas George
Chase, Thomas Newell
Chase, William Thomas, III
Chaseman, Joel
Chasen, Robert E.
Chastain, Elijah Denton, Jr.
Chattin, Chester Coles
Chayes, Abram
Chayes, Antonia Handler
Chayes, Felix
Cheaney, Philip Norbourne
Cheatham, John Bane, Jr.
Cheatham, John McGee
Checchi, Alfred Attilio
Checchi, Vincent
Cheek, Charles Wall
Cheek, James Edward
Cheek, James Howe, III
Cheek, King Virgil, Jr.
Chen, Wayne H.
Chenery, Hollis Burnley
Cheney, Elliott Ward
Cheney, Frances Neel
Cheng, Tsung O.
Chennault, Anna Chan (Mrs. Claire Lee Chennault)
Chenoweth, Alice Drew
Cheraskin, Emanuel
Cherner, Marvin
Chernoff, Amoz Immanuel
Cherry, Gwendolyn Sawyer
Cherry, Wendell
Cherry, William Ashley
Cheshire, Richard Duncan
Chesley, Harry Woolford, Jr.
Cheslock, Louis
Chesney, John Raymond
Chesnut, Donald Blair
Chesnut, Franklin Gilmore
Chess, Sammie, Jr.
Chesteen, John Saffell
Cheston, Charles Edward
Chewning, Lewis Garland
Cheyney, William James
Chezem, Curtis Gordon
Chiarello, Donald Frederick
Chieri, Pericle Adriano C.
Chilcote, Lugean Lester
Chilcote, Samuel Day, Jr.
Chilcote, Thomas Franklin
Childers, Robert Lee
Childs, Barton
Childs, David Magie
Childs, James Rives
Childs, Marquis William
Childs, Selma Bart
Chiles, Lawton Mainor
Chilton, Horace Thomas
Chilton, Robert Carter
Chilton, Samuel Blackwell
Chilton, St. John Poindexter
Chilton, William Edwin, III
Chinn, Herman Isaac
Chisholm, Leslie Lee
Chisholm, Tommy
Chitty, Arthur Benjamin, Jr.
Chitwood, Robert Hodson
Choate, Robert Burnett
Choppin, Gregory Robert
Chopra, Kuldrip Prakash
Chow, Rita Kathleen
Chrencik, Frank
Christ, Carl Finley
Christen, Arnold Buhl
Christenberry, George Andrew
Christensen, Ernest Edward
Christensen, James Philip
Christensen, Kenneth Serenus
Christensen, William Harold
Christian, Almeric Leander
Christian, Betty Jo
Christian, Charles Clifford
Christian, Ernest Silsbee, Jr.
Christian, George Eastland
Christian, John Catlett, Jr.
Christian, John Kenton
Christian, Robert Henry
Christian, Sherril Duane
Christiansen, Ted Leo
Christianson, Alden Henig
Christie, Alden Bradford
Christie, George Custis
Christie, John Milton
Christie, Marion Francis
Christie, Thomas Philip
Christman, John Francis
Christoph, Karl John, Jr.
Christopher, Thomas Weldon
Christopher, Warren Minor
Christopher, Wilford Scott
Christopherson, William Martin
Christy, James Walter
Chrysler, Walter P., Jr.
Chubb, John Everson
Chubb, Talbot Albert
Church, Dale Walker
Church, Frank
Church, John Trammell
Church, Martha Eleanor
Churchill, Irving Lester
Churchill, James A(llen)
Chytil, Frank
Ciereszko, Leon Stanley
Civileti, Benjamin R.
Cizauskas, Albert Charles
Cizek, Eugene Darwin
Cizik, Robert
Clabaugh, Stephen Edmund
Clack, Charles Gilbert
Cladouhos, Harry William
Clague, Ewan
Claiborne, Jerry David
Claiborne, John Wellons
Clancy, Joseph Patrick
Clapp, Roger Alvin
Clapp, Roger Howland
Clapp, William Jacob
Clapsaddle, Gerald Leon
Clark, Alfred
Clark, Arthur Watts
Clark, Blake
Clark, C. Kenneth
Clark, Champ
Clark, Charles
Clark, Chester William
Clark, Clifton Bob
Clark, David Barrett
Clark, Dick Clarence
Clark, Donald Otis
Clark, Earl Wesley
Clark, Edward
Clark, Eliot Candee
Clark, Eloise Elizabeth
Clark, Eugenie
Clark, Frank Rinker, Jr.
Clark, George McMurry
Clark, Gilbert Edward
Clark, Gordon Haddon
Clark, H. Sol
Clark, Harold Florian
Clark, Howard Longstreth
Clark, James Benton
Clark, James Mott
Clark, John Conrad
Clark, John Hallett, III
Clark, John Richard
Clark, John Russell
Clark, John Steven
Clark, John Walter, Jr.
Clark, Leigh Mallet
Clark, Leonard Vernon
Clark, Lynwood Edgerton
Clark, Melvin Eugene
Clark, Meredith Kaye Plier (Mrs. Philip C. Clark)
Clark, Ralph Leigh
Clark, Randolph Lee
Clark, Raymond Skinner
Clark, Robert Edward
Clark, Robert Lloyd, Jr.
Clark, Robert Phillips
Clark, Roy
Clark, Sherman Rockwell
Clark, Teunison Cary, Jr.
Clark, Thomas Barron
Clark, Thomas Dionysius
Clark, Ward Christopher
Clark, William Henry, III
Clark, William Kemp
Clarke, Bowman Lafayette
Clarke, Clifford Montreville
Clarke, Erwin Bennet
Clarke, Frank Eldridge
Clarke, Frederic B., III
Clarke, Frederick James
Clarke, J. Calvitt, Jr.
Clarke, Jack Wells
Clarke, John Frederick Gates
Clarke, Mary Elizabeth
Clarke, Thomas Hal
Clarke, Walter Sheldon
Clarke, William Henry
Clarkson, John Donald
Clarkson, Julian Derieux
Clarkson, Mark H.
Clarkson, Thomas B.
Clarson, John Julius
Clary, Howard Leonard
Classen, John Newell
Claud, Joseph Gillette
Claude, Inis Lothair, Jr.
Clausen, Don Holst
Clausen, Hugh Joseph
Clauss, Carin Ann
Clawson, David Kay
Clawson, Marion
Claxton, Philander Priestley, Jr.
Clay, Albert Greene
Clay, Diskin
Clay, John William
Clay, Lyell Bufington
Clay, Orson C.
Clay, William Dane
Clay, William Lacy
Claybrook, Joan B.
Claydon, Sister Margaret
Clayton, Billy Wayne
Clayton, Carl Cleveland, Jr.
Clayton, Donald Delbert
Clayton, Frances Elizabeth
Clayton, James Edwin
Clayton, John B., III
Clayton, Preston Copeland
Clayton, William Howard
Claytor, Robert Buckner
Claytor, William Graham, Jr.
Cleary, James Roy
Cleary, Robert Edward
Cleary, Timothy Finbar
Cleaveland, Frederic Neill
Cleaver, Vera Allen
Cleaver, William Joseph
Cleino, Edward Henry
Cleland, John Robin Davis
Cleland, Joseph Maxwell
Clement, Alvis Macon
Clement, Joseph Dale
Clement, Robert William
Clement, William Alexander
Clements, Charles L.
Clements, Charles Lane, Jr.
Clements, James David
Clements, Vassar Carlton
Clements, William Perry, Jr.
Clements, Woodrow Wilson
Clendinen, James Augustus
Clepper, Henry Edward
Cleveland, Ambrose Gamble, Jr.
Cleveland, Forrest Fenton
Cleveland, James Colgate
Cleveland, Robert Gran
Cleverdon, Ernest Grove
Clewlow, Carl William
Cliburn, Van (Harvey Lavan, Jr.)
Cliett, Charles Buren
Clifford, Alan Frank
Clifford, Alfred Hoblitzelle
Clifford, Clark McAdams
Clifford, Earle Winchester, Jr.
Clifford, Edward
Clifford, Frederick Burr
Clifford, John Fenn
Clifford, Paul Arthur
Clifford, Thomas Edward
Clifton, Chester Victor, Jr.
Clifton, Lucille Thelma
Clignet, Remi P(ierre)
Clinch, John Houstoun McIntosh
Cline, Clarence Lee
Cline, Marjorie Ann
Cline, Paul Charles
Cline, Ray Steiner
Clinger, William Floyd, Jr.
Clinton, William J.
Cloar, Carroll
Clodius, Robert LeRoy
Cloney, James Maurice
Close, David Palmer
Close, Hugh William
Clotworthy, John Harris
Cloud, Bruce Benjamin
Cloud, Stanley Wills
Clough, Ralph Nelson
Clough, Susan Sebesta
Clower, Jerry
Clowes, Royston Courtney
Clubb, Bruce Edwin
Clusen, Ruth Chickering
Clute, Robert Eugene
Cluverius, Wat Tyler, IV
Clymer, Ludwick M.
Coady, Arthur Bernard
Coates, Jesse
Coates, Joseph Francis
Coats, David Samuel
Cobb, Alton Bernard
Cobb, G. Elliott, Jr.
Cobb, Gary Donald
Cobb, George Hamilton
Cobb, Henry Van Zandt
Cobb, James Outterson
Cobb, Stanwood
Cobb, William Lyman
Cobb, William Montague
Cobb, William Warren
Coble, Ted Columbus
Cochran, Alexander Smith
Cochran, Douglas Eugene
Cochran, Garland Perry
Cochran, George Moffett
Cochran, James Francis, III
Cochran, Kendall Pinney
Cochran, Les
Cochran, Lewis W.
Cochran, Robert Glenn
Cochran, Thad
Cochran, Wendell
Cochrane, William Henry
Cocke, Erle, Jr.
Cockerham, Columbus Clark
Cockrel, Clement Lee
Cockrell, Lila May
Cockrill, John Long
Cody, Morrill
Cody, Thomas Gerald
Cody, Walter James Michael
Cody, Wilmer St. Clair
Coe, Paul Francis
Coe, Robert Vernon
Coe, Vincent
Coe, Ward Baldwin, Jr.
Coelho, Tony
Coerper, Milo George
Coey, John Smiley
Cofer, Charles Norval
Coffee, Linda Nellene
Coffee, Roy Clarence, Jr.
Coffey, Donald Straley
Coffey, Rufus
Coffey, Thomas Francis, Jr.
Coffield, William Howard
Coffin, Tristram
Coffman, Amos James
Coffman, Charles DeWitt
Cogan, David Glendenning
Cogburn, Edmund Lewis
Coggeshall, Peter Collin
Coggin, Walter Arthur
Coggins, Homer Dale
Cogswell, Dorothy McIntosh
Cohee, James Joseph
Cohen, Benjamin Victor
Cohen, David
Cohen, Edwin Samuel
Cohen, Eugene Erwin
Cohen, George Leon
Cohen, Herman
Cohen, Herman Jay
Cohen, Isadore T.
Cohen, Jules Simon
Cohen, Kalman Joseph
Cohen, Lester
Cohen, Lewis Isaac
Cohen, Lois Ruth Kushner
Cohen, Louis David
Cohen, Nehemiah Myer
Cohen, Philip
Cohen, Robert Abraham
Cohen, Sheldon Stanley
Cohen, Stanley
Cohen, Wallace M.
Cohen, William Sebastian
Cohn, David Herc
Cohn, Herbert B.
Cohn, Isidore, Jr.
Cohn, Jess Victor
Cohn, Marcus
Cohn, Norman Stanley
Cohn, Samuel Maurice
Cohn, Sherman Louis
Cohn, Victor Edward
Coiner, Richard Tide, Jr.
Coke, Henry Cornick, Jr.
Coker, Elizabeth Boatwright (Mrs. James Lide Coker)
Colaianni, Joseph Vincent

REGIONAL LISTING—SOUTH-SOUTHWEST 842

Colberg, Marshall Rudolph
Colbert, Charles Ralph
Colbert, Lester Lum
Colbert, Robert B., Jr.
Colbourn, Trevor
Colburn, Charles Buford
Colburn, John H.
Colby, Ethel
Colby, William Egan
Coldwell, Philip Edward
Cole, Alan Y.
Cole, Benjamin Richason
Cole, Benjamin Theodore
Cole, Clyde Curtis, Jr.
Cole, Donald Charles
Cole, Fred Carrington
Cole, George David
Cole, Gordon Henry
Cole, Harry A.
Cole, Houston
Cole, John Owen
Cole, John Pope, Jr.
Cole, Ray Martin
Cole, Robert Bates
Cole, Robert Taylor
Cole, Sterling
Colean, Miles Lanier
Coleman, Almand Rouse
Coleman, Amoss Lee
Coleman, Edmund Benedict
Coleman, Francis Carter
Coleman, George Melchiades
Coleman, Henry Crim
Coleman, Howard S.
Coleman, James Edwin, Jr.
Coleman, James Julian
Coleman, James Plemon
Coleman, James Samuel, Jr.
Coleman, John Marshall
Coleman, John Sherrard
Coleman, John Winston, Jr.
Coleman, Lynn R.
Coleman, William Thaddeus, Jr.
Coles, John William
Coli, Guido John, Jr.
Coliton, William Peter
Colker, Marvin Leonard
Coll, Helen F.
Colledge, Charles Hopson
Collens, John Wharton, III
Collet, Marjen Henry (Bud)
Collette, John Edwin
Colley, John Leonard, Jr.
Collie, Marvin Key
Collier, Everett Dolton
Collier, Felton Moreland
Collier, Hampden Fischer
Collier, Robert Arthur
Collinge, Robert Joy
Collings, John Kempthorne, Jr.
Collins, Arthur Sylvester, Jr.
Collins, Beulah Stowe
Collins, Cardiss Robertson
Collins, Clair Joseph
Collins, Forres McGraw
Collins, Frank Charles, Jr.
Collins, Frederic William
Collins, George Bryan
Collins, Harker
Collins, Harold Ray
Collins, Henry Bascom
Collins, Henry James, III
Collins, James Foster
Collins, James Lawton, Jr.
Collins, James Mitchell
Collins, LeRoy
Collins, LeRoy, Jr.
Collins, Lester Albertson
Collins, Martha Layne
Collins, Michael
Collins, Michael James
Collins, Norman James
Collins, Philip Reilly
Collins, Robert Frederick
Collins, Royal Eugene
Collins, Samuel Cornette
Collins, Theodore Clyde, Jr.
Collins, Thomas Asa
Collins, Truman Edward
Collins, Vincent Patrick
Collins, W(illiam) Leighton
Collins, (George) Willard
Collins, William Edgar
Collins, William Edward
Collis, Charles
Colman, William Gerald
Colodny, Edwin Irving
Coloney, Wayne Herndon
Colowick, Sidney Paul
Colquitt, Landon Augustus
Colsky, Jacob
Colson, Charles Wendell
Colson, Earl M.
Colston, James Allen
Colter, Jessi (Jennings, Mirriam Joan Johnson)
Colton, Sterling Don
Colvard, Dean Wallace
Colvert, Clyde Cornellus
Colvin, Burton Houston
Colvin, (Otis) Herbert, Jr.
Colvin, Milton
Colwell, Rita Rossi
Colwin, Arthur Lentz
Combes, Frank Charles
Combs, Bert Thomas
Comer, Donald, Jr.
Comer, Donald, III
Comfort, John
Comini, Alessandra
Comiskey, James August
Comissiona, Sergiu
Compton, Ann Woodruff
Compton, Asbury Christian
Compton, Bryan Whitfield, Jr.
Compton, John Joseph
Comstock, George Wills
Conant, Allah B., Jr.
Conaway, Orrin Bryte
Concordia, Charles
Conder, Maxine
Condit, Gex Pullen, Jr.
Condit, Ross Rowland, Jr.
Condom, Jaime Ernesto
Condon, Lester Patrick
Cone, Carl Bruce
Cone, Clarence Newton
Confrey, Eugene A.
Conger, Clement Ellis
Conklin, Clarence Robert
Conklin, Hugh Randolph
Conklin, Kenneth Edward
Conley, Carroll Lockard
Conley, Eugene
Conley, Paul Agnew
Conn, Frederick James, Jr.
Conn, Jack Trammell
Conn, Jerome W.
Conn, Rex Boland, Jr.
Connally, John Bowden
Connell, John Gibbs, Jr.
Connell, Lawrence
Connelly, Charles Edward
Conner, John Davis
Conner, Pierre Euclide, Jr.
Conner, Troy Blaine, Jr.
Connolly, Arthur Guild
Connolly, Charles Huntley
Connor, James Thomas
Connor, Seymour Vaughan
Connor, Thomas Byrne
Connors, Robert Michael
Conole, Clement Vincent
Conover, Harry
Conrad, Hans
Conrad, Harold Everett
Conrad, Paul Ernest
Conrad, Walter Allan Grenville
Conroy, David James
Conroy, Sarah Booth
Conselman, Frank Buckley
Constable, Stuart
Constantin, James Alford
Conta, Lewis Dalcin
Conte, Silvio O.
Contney, John J.
Conway, Dwight Colbur
Conway, Hobart McKinley, Jr.
Conway, James Valentine Patrick
Conway, John Harold, Jr.
Conway, Martha Bell
Conyers, John, Jr.
Cook, A. Samuel
Cook, Ann Jennalie
Cook, Benjamin Hopson
Cook, C. Richard
Cook, Camille Wright
Cook, Cecil Newton
Cook, Charles Wilkerson, Jr.
Cook, Charles William
Cook, Chauncey William Wallace
Cook, Clarence Sharp
Cook, Earl Ferguson
Cook, Edward Willingham
Cook, George Thomas
Cook, Harold Dale
Cook, Harry Clayton, Jr.
Cook, James Fielder
Cook, James Joseph
Cook, John Logan, Jr.
Cook, M. L.
Cook, Michael Coleman
Cook, Milton Olin
Cook, Richard Wallace
Cook, Samuel DuBois
Cook, Walter McQueen
Cook, Wayne Michael
Cook, William Holmes
Cooke, David Ohlmer
Cooke, Dennis Hargrove
Cooke, Edward William
Cooke, Eileen Delores
Cooke, Jack Kent
Cooke, Richard Dickson, Jr.
Cooke, William Latimer
Cooley, David William
Cooley, Denton
Cooley, Robert Nelson
Coolidge, Edwin Channing
Coon, Carleton Stevens, Jr.
Coon, Robert William
Cooney, David Martin
Cooney, James Patrick
Cooney, Ray Howard
Cooper, Arthur Darrah
Cooper, Benjamin F.
Cooper, Bernard Richard
Cooper, Charles Howard
Cooper, Donald Lee
Cooper, Frederick Eansor
Cooper, Grace Rogers
Cooper, Gustav Arthur
Cooper, Irving S.
Cooper, Jerome A.
Cooper, Jerome Maurice
Cooper, John Alfred, Jr.
Cooper, John Allen Dicks
Cooper, John Crossan, Jr.
Cooper, John Sherman
Cooper, Kenneth Ezelle
Cooper, Leroy Gordon, Jr.
Cooper, Paul
Cooper, Richard Melvyn
Cooper, Richard Newell
Cooper, Robert Elbert
Cooper, Robert Shanklin
Cooper, Thomas Luther
Cooper, Walter Elmore
Cooper, Weldon
Cope, William Henry
Copeland, Hunter Armstrong
Copeland, James Isaac
Copeland, James William
Copeland, Joseph J.
Copeland, Morris Albert
Copeland, Murray M.
Copeland, Norman Arland
Copenhaver, John Thomas, Jr.
Copenhaver, Wilfred Monroe
Copenhaver, William Pierce
Copp, James Harris
Copping, Allen Anthony
Corber, Robert Jack
Corbett, Bradford Gary
Corbett, Bradford Gary
Corbett, Leo Joseph
Corbin, Arnold
Corbin, Claire (Mrs. Arnold Corbin)
Corbin, Kendall Brooks
Corcoran, Howard Francis
Corcoran, John Joseph
Corcoran, Thomas Gardiner
Cordell, Howard William
Cordell, Joe B.
Corder, Jim W.
Corea, Luis Felipe
Corfman, Philip Albert
Coriden, Guy Edward
Corley, Donald Earl
Corliss, John Ozro
Corman, James Charles
Cormier, Milton Joseph
Corn, Ira George, Jr.
Cornblath, Marvin
Cornelius, Charles Edward
Cornelius, Helen Lorene
Cornell, John Bilheimer
Cornell, Samuel Douglas
Cornely, Paul Bertau
Cornett, Richard Orin
Cornette, James P.
Cornish, Edward Seymour
Cornwall, John Michael
Cornwell, Eugene Howe, Jr.
Corpe, Raymond Francis
Corr, James Vanis
Corrada, Baltasar
Corradi, Peter
Corrick, Ann Marjorie
Corrigan, James Henry, Jr.
Corrigan, Paul James, Jr.
Corrigan, Robert Foster
Corrin, Brownlee Sands
Corrsin, Stanley
Corse, John Doggett
Corson, John Jay
Cortada, James N.
Cosenza, Arthur George
Cosgrove, John Edward
Cosgrove, John Patrick
Costa, Jasper Silva
Costa, Victor Charles
Costanzo, Henry John
Costello, John (Jack) Francis, Jr.
Costello, Joseph Mark, III
Costes, Nicholas Constantine
Costle, Douglas M.
Costrell, Louis
Cothen, Grady Coulter
Cotlow, Lewis Nathaniel
Cottam, Howard Rex
Cotten, Marion deVeaux
Cotter, Francis Patrick
Cotter, William Joseph
Cottingham, Harold Fred
Cotton, Frank Albert
Cotton, John Pierce
Cotton, Maurice Edward
Cotton, Richard
Cotton, William Davis
Cottone, Benedict Peter
Cottrell, Leonard S., Jr.
Cottrell, Rufus Hester, Jr.
Couch, Alan Jay
Couch, J.O. Terrell
Couch, Jesse Wadsworth
Couch, John Nathaniel
Couch, Robert Barnard
Couch, Virgil Lee
Coughlin, John Thomas
Coughlin, Leo Daniel, Jr.
Coughlin, Richard James
Coughlin, Robert Lawrence, Jr.
Coughran, Tom Bristol
Coulling, Sidney Baxter
Coulter, Ellis Merton
Coulter, James Bennett
Coulter, Kirkley Schley
Coulter, Norman Arthur, Jr.
Counts, James Curtis
Coupal, Joseph Richard, Jr.
Couper, Louise Pettigrew
Courshon, Arthur Howard
Courshon, Jack Robert
Courtenay, Joseph Kenneth
Courts, Richard Winn
Cousins, Margaret
Cousins, Thomas Grady
Covey, Charles William
Covey, Cyclone
Covey, Milton H.
Covi, Dario Alessandro
Coville, Cabot
Covington, Harold Douglas
Covington, Hubert Wilson
Cowan, Dwaine Oliver
Cowan, Edward
Cowan, Finis Ewing
Cowan, Irving
Cowan, Richard Sumner
Cowan, Walter Greaves
Cowart, Elgin Courtland, Jr.
Cowden, Dudley Johnstone
Cowden, Thomas Kyle
Cowell, Charles Herbert
Cowell, Fred J.
Cowen, Donna Ruth
Cowen, Eugene Sherman
Cowen, Robert Henry
Cowen, Wilson
Cowen, Wilson Walker
Cowhill, William Joseph
Cowles, Milly
Cowley, Alan Herbert
Cowley, Luis M.
Cowling, Ellis Brevier
Cox, Calvin Kennedy
Cox, Charles Clemmons
Cox, Clair Edward, II
Cox, Headley Morris, Jr.
Cox, Herman Grahme, Jr.
Cox, James Talley
Cox, Julius Grady
Cox, Kenneth Allen
Cox, Owen DeVol
Cox, Warren Jacob
Cox, Wilbert Louis
Cox, William Harold
Cox, William Plummer
Coyle, William
Cozan, Lee
Crabtree, Beverly June
Crabtree, John Henry, Jr.
Craddock, Billy Wayne (Crash Craddock)
Craf, John Riley
Craft, Harold Dumont, Jr.
Craft, Harvey Milton
Craft, John Richard
Crager, Jay Cecil, Jr.
Cragwall, Joseph Samuel, Jr.
Craig, Cornelius Abernathy, II
Craig, James Barkley
Craig, Mack Wayne
Craig, Paul Max, Jr.
Craig, William Garrott
Craighead, Claude C.
Craighill, Francis Hopkinson, III
Craighill, George Bowdoin, Jr.
Craigie, Walter Williams, Sr.
Crain, Bluford Walter, Jr.
Crain, J. Wendell
Cram, Ira Higgins
Cramer, Dale Lewis
Cramer, John Scott
Cramer, Maurice Browning
Cramer, Robert Eli
Cramer, William Cato
Cramer, William Smith
Crampton, Bruce Sidney
Crampton, Scott Paul
Crane, Andrew Jones
Crane, Daniel B.
Crane, John Bever
Crane, Leo Stanley
Crane, Neal Dahlberg
Crane, Philip Miller
Crane, Radford Raymond
Crank, James Eldon
Cranston, Alan
Crary, Albert Paddock
Crass, Maurice Frederick, Jr.
Crater, Robert Winfield
Craven, James Braxton, III
Cravens, Kathryn
Cravens, Raymond Lewis
Crawford, David Coleman
Crawford, Earl Boyd
Crawford, H(azle) R(eid)
Crawford, John Calvin, Jr.
Crawford, Joseph Paul, Jr.
Crawford, Kenneth Charles
Crawford, Kenneth Gale
Crawford, Lester Mills, Jr.
Crawford, Meredith Pullen
Crawford, Norman Crane, Jr.
Crawford, Stanley Everett
Crawford, Thomas Hilliard, Jr.
Crawford, Vernon D'Orsay
Crawford, Walter Hamilton
Crawford, William Avery
Crawford, William Donham
Crawford, William Rex, Jr.
Crawford-Mason, Clare Wootten
Crawley, Thomas Edward
Creech, Danten Dayle
Creech, Fulton Hunter
Creech, Glenwood Lewis
Creech, Wilbur Lyman
Creekmore, Marion Virgil, Jr.
Creel, Joe
Creel, Luther Edward, III
Creer, Philip Douglas
Creiger, Edward
Creighton, William Forman
Crenshaw, Ben
Crenshaw, Craig Moffett
Crenshaw, Francis Nelson
Crenshaw, Gordon Lee
Crenshaw, Jack
Crenshaw, Marion Carlyle, Jr.
Cress, George Ayers
Cress, Paul Williams
Cressman, George Parmley
Creviston, Robert Helms
Crew, John L.
Crews, Harry Eugene
Crihfield, Brevard Ewing
Crikelair, George Francis
Crim, Alonzo A.
Criser, Marshall
Crisman, Thomas Lynn
Crisp, Porter Lee
Crispell, Kenneth Raymond
Crispin, Andre Arthur
Crist, Frederic Eugene
Criswell, W.A.
Critchfield, Jack B.
Crittenberger, Willis Dale, Jr.
Crittenden, William
Critz, Harry Herndon
Crocker, Diane W.
Crockett, Gibson M.
Crockett, Jerry Bruce
Croft, Harry Allen
Crohn, Max Henry, Jr.
Cromiller, Harold Lee
Cromley, Allan Wray
Cromley, Raymond Avolon
Cromwell, Edwin Boykin
Cromwell, William Kennedy, III
Cronin, Thomas Dillon
Cronvich, James Anthony
Crook, Dorothy
Crook, William Grant
Crooker, John H., Jr.
Crosby, John Campbell
Crosby, Kenneth McCorkle
Crosby, Oliver Sexmith
Crosby, Philip Bayard
Crosland, Edward Burton
Cross, Charles Tenney
Cross, Eason, Jr.
Cross, George Lynn
Cross, Gordon Bismarck
Cross, Lenora Routon
Cross, Richard
Cross, Robert Brandt
Cross, Robert Dougherty
Cross, Sam Young, Jr.
Crossette, George
Crossfield, Albert Scott
Crouch, Thomas Gene
Crout, J(ohn) Richard
Crow, Duward Lowery
Crow, James Sylvester
Crow, Jane Hanes
Crow, Lester Donald
Crow, William Langstaff
Crowder, Walter Frederick
Crowe, Eugene Bertrand
Crowe, Guthrie Ferguson
Crowell, Gentry
Crowell, Thomas Irving
Crowley, James Worthington
Crown, David Allan
Crowther, James Earl
Croxton, Fred(erick) E(mory), (Jr.)
Crudup, Josiah
Cruikshank, Nelson Hale
Cruikshank, Thomas Henry
Crum, James Merrill
Crum, John Kistler
Crumbo, Woodrow Wilson
Crump, Harold Craft
Cruse, Julius Major, Jr.
Crutcher, James Carroll
Crutchfield, Charles Harvey
Crutchfield, Finis Alonzo, Jr.
Cruz-Aponte, Ramon Aristides
Crysler, Frederick Safford
Csonka, Larry Richard
Cua, Antonio S.
Cuatrecasas, Pedro Martin
Culbertson, Horace Coe
Culbertson, Katheryn Campbell
Culbertson, Robert Elmore
Culbertson, Walter LeRoy
Culbreath, Hugh Lee, Jr.
Cullen, Abbey Boyd, Jr.
Cullen, George
Culley, Perry Hager
Cullins, Peter Kendall
Cullom, William Otis
Culp, Ralph Borden
Culpepper, Fred Carroll, Jr.
Culver, Barbara Green
Culver, John C.
Culverhouse, Hugh Franklin
Cumerford, William Richard
Cuming, George Scott
Cumming, Hugh Smith, Jr.
Cumming, Joseph Bryan
Cumming, William Patterson
Cummings, Frank C.
Cummings, Martin Marc
Cummings, Milton Curtis, Jr.
Cummings, William Bruce
Cummins, Bobby Dean
Cummiskey, Charles Joseph
Cundiff, Edward William
Cundiff, Paul Arthur
Cuneo, Ernest L.
Cuninggim, (Augustus) Merrimon
Cunniff, Patrick Francis
Cunningham, Bruce Thomas
Cunningham, Carl Robert
Cunningham, Emory O.
Cunningham, George Woody
Cunningham, Jacques
Cunningham, James Everett
Cunningham, John Edward
Cunningham, Keith Allen
Cunningham, Leon William
Cunningham, Morris
Cunningham, R. Walter
Cunningham, William Alexander, III
Cunningham, William Palmer
Cureton, Edward Eugene
Curl, Robert Floyd, Jr.
Curl, Samuel Everett
Curley, John Joseph, Jr.
Curran, Edward Matthew
Current, Richard Nelson
Current-Garcia, Eugene
Currie, Charles Leonard
Currie, Clifford William Herbert
Currie, James Bradford
Currie, James Sloan
Currie, Overton Anderson
Currier, Albert Eldred
Currier, Robert David
Curris, Constantine William
Curry, Bill
Curry, Stowers Leigh, Jr.
Curry, Thomas Harvey
Curtin, Philip De Armond
Curtin, Sharon Rose
Curtin, Terrence Michael
Curtin, William Joseph
Curtis, Carl Thomas
Curtis, Doris S. Malkin
Curtis, James Michael
Curtis, Joseph
Curtis, Josiah Montgomery
Curtis, Marcia
Curtis, Morton Landers
Curtis, Robert McNown
Curtiss, Roy, III
Cushman, Martelle Loreen
Cushman, Robert Earl
Cusimano, Charles Vincent
Custis, Donald L.
Cutchins, Clifford Armstrong, III
Cuthrell, Carl Edward
Cutler, Bernard Joseph
Cutler, Edward I.
Cutler, Lloyd Norton
Cutler, M. Rupert
Cutler, Robert H.
Cutler, Robert Ward
Cutler, Walter Leon
Cutlip, Scott Munson
Cutright, Duane Edwin
Cutright, Phillips
Cutter, Charles Richard, III
Cuttino, John Tindal
Cuykendall, Trevor Rhys
Cypert, Jimmie Dean
Daane, James Dewey
Dabbs, Jack Autrey
Dabney, Hovey Slayton
Dabney, Virginius
Dabney, Watson Barr
Dadisman, Joseph Carrol
Daeschner, Charles William, Jr.
Daeuble, Louis
Dahlgren, John Onsgard
Dahlstrom, William Grant
Daigle, O'Neil James, Jr.
Dail, Joseph Garner, Jr.
Daisley, William Prescott
Dakan, Norman Eugene
Dake, Marcia Allene
Dale, Al
Dalehite, Thomas Hiram
Daley, John Edward
Daley, John (Bud) Joseph, Jr.
Dallas, Sherman Forbes
Dalley, George Albert
Dallman, Paul Jerald
Dalrymple, Gordon Bennett
Dalrymple, Guy Harold
Dalton, Albert Joseph
Dalton, Donald H.
Dalton, George Ronald
Dalton, Harry Jirou, Jr.
Dalton, Harry Lee
Dalton, James Edward
Dalton, John Howard
Dalton, John Nichols
Dalton, Ted
Dalvit, Lewis David, Jr.
Daly, James Joseph
Daly, Owen, II
D'Amours, Norman Edward
Dampier, Joseph Henry
Damtoft, Walter Atkinson
Dancy, John Albert
Danforth, Louis Fremont
Daniel, Charles Dwelle, Jr.
Daniel, Dan
Daniel, Harben Winfield
Daniel, Hawthorne
Daniel, James Wilson
Daniel, Jaquelin James
Daniel, Joseph Carl, Jr.
Daniel, Kenneth Rule
Daniel, Robert Hugh
Daniel, Robert Williams, Jr.
Daniel, Victor James, Jr.
Danieley, James Earl
Daniels, Charlie
Daniels, Charlie
Daniels, Draper
Daniels, Elmer Harland
Daniels, Frank Arthur
Daniels, Frank Arthur, Jr.
Daniels, George Goetz
Daniels, Jonathan Worth
Daniels, Myra Janco (Mrs. Draper Daniels)
Daniels, Ralph
Daniels, Stanley Lee
Daniels, Stanley Lee
Daniels, William Ward
Danielson, George Elmore
Danielson, Wayne Allen
Danneman, Fred Charles
Dannemeyer, William Edwin
Dannenberg, Martin Ernest
Danton, Raymond
D'Antonio, Nicholas
Danzig, Richard Jeffrey
Da Parma, Edward Ulysses
D'Arezzo, Joseph Paul
D'Arista, Robert Augustus
Darling, Robert Edward
Darrah, Louis James, Jr.
Darrow, Robert Arthur
Dart, Charles Edward

843 REGIONAL LISTING—SOUTH-SOUTHWEST

Darwent, Basil de Baskerville
Dascal, Charles
Daschbach, Richard Joseph
Daschle, Thomas Andrew
Dash, Leon DeCosta, Jr.
Dash, Samuel
Dauer, Manning Juilan, Jr.
Daughdrill, James Harold, Jr.
Daugherty, Alfred Clark
Daugherty, Franklin W.
Daugherty, Frederick Alvin
Daugherty, Fredrica
Daugherty, Robert Allen
Daugherty, Samuel Edwin
Daughtry, DeWitt Cornell
Daughtry, John Cary
Davenport, Chester
Davenport, Dona Lee
Davenport, Gwen (Mrs. John Davenport)
Davenport, Joan Mariarenee
Davenport, John Sidney, III
Davenport, Manuel Manson
Davenport, Milton Monroe
Davey, Charles Bingham
Davey, Winthrop Newbury
David, Henry
David, Paul Theodore
Davidson, Bruce Merrill
Davidson, Chalmers Gaston
Davidson, Charles Edward
Davidson, Gordon Byron
Davidson, Hugh Maccullough
Davidson, Jack Leroy
Davidson, James Frederic
Davidson, James Joseph, Jr.
Davidson, Lorimer Arthur
Davidson, Philip Grant, Jr.
Davidson, Rita Charmatz
Davidson, Robert Franklin
Davidson, Thomas Maxwell
Davidson, Vanda Arthur, Jr.
Davidson, Waid J., Jr.
Davie, Donald Alfred
Davies, Archibald Donald
Davies, David George
Davies, David R.
Davies, Gordon Kenneth
Davies, Marion Elizabeth
Davies, Richard Townsend
Davies, Thomas Daniel
Davies, William David
Davis, Archibald Hilliard
Davis, Archibald Kimbrough
Davis, Artemus Darius
Davis, Arthur Quentin
Davis, Benjamin Oliver, Jr.
Davis, Bennie Luke
Davis, Bertram Hylton
Davis, Burke
Davis, Cabell Seal, Jr.
Davis, Charles Francis, Jr.
Davis, Courtland Harwell, Jr.
Davis, Daniel Walter
Davis, Danny (George Joseph Nowlan)
Davis, Darrey Adkins
Davis, David Oliver
Davis, Dorland Jones
Davis, Drexel Reed
Davis, Edwin Adams
Davis, Ernest B.
Davis, Evelyn Y.
Davis, Finis E.
Davis, Frank Bell
Davis, Frank Elwood
Davis, Frank Faville
Davis, Gene Bernard
Davis, George Kelso
Davis, Gertrude Elizabeth Coddington (Mrs. William L. Davis)
Davis, Gifford
Davis, Glenn Robert
Davis, Harold Eugene
Davis, Harold Fenimore
Davis, Harry
Davis, Harry Willard
Davis, Hartwell
Davis, Hartwell
Davis, Henry Jefferson, Jr.
Davis, Herbert Lowell
Davis, Horance Gibbs, Jr.
Davis, Howard
Davis, Howard Eckert
Davis, Jacqueline Marie Vincent (Mrs. Louis Reid Davis)
Davis, James Burnam
Davis, James Elsworth
Davis, James H. (Jimmie)
Davis, James Hornor, III
Davis, James Paxton
Davis, Jefferson
Davis, Jefferson Clark, Jr.
Davis, Joe William
Davis, John
Davis, John Anderson
Davis, John Cordon
Davis, John Henry
Davis, John Michael
Davis, John Park
Davis, Karen Padgett
Davis, Lambert
Davis, Leonard McCutchan
Davis, Lewis Berkley
Davis, Louis Freeman
Davis, Lynn Etheridge
Davis, Mack Parker
Davis, Marian Belle
Davis, Mattie Belle Edwards
Davis, Mendel Jackson
Davis, Mendell McLillian
Davis, Milton Wickers, Jr.
Davis, Morgan Jones
Davis, N(oah) Knowles
Davis, Norris Garland
Davis, Oscar Hirsh
Davis, Paul Ford
Davis, Raymond Edward
Davis, Rex Lloyd
Davis, Richard Beale
Davis, Richard Francis
Davis, Richard Joel
Davis, Robert Aldine
Davis, Robert Houser
Davis, Robert Leach
Davis, Robert Thomas, Jr.
Davis, Ronello Melzar
Davis, Ross Dane
Davis, Roy Wright
Davis, Ruth Margaret (Mrs. Benjamin Franklin Lohr)
Davis, Samuel Beverly, III
Davis, Sid
Davis, Thomas Henry
Davis, Tine Wayne
Davis, True
Davis, Vincent
Davis, William Columbus
Davis, William Duncan, Jr.
Davis, William Evans
Davis, William Prather
Davis, William Robert
Davis, William Virginius
Davis, Wylie Herman
Davison, Charles Marshall, Jr.
Davison, Denver N.
Davison, Frederick Corbet
Davison, Joseph Wade
Davison, Roderic Hollett
Davison, Vernon Gill
Dawalt, Kenneth Francis
Dawes, Richard Irving
Dawkins, Ben C., Jr.
Dawley, Melvin Emerson
Dawson, Giles Edwin
Dawson, Howard Athalone, Jr.
Dawson, Ray Fields
Dawson, Raymond Howard
Dawson, Robert Oscar
Dawson, Samuel Cooper, Jr.
Dawson, Wallace Douglas, Jr.
Dawson, William Levi
Day, Daniel Edgar
Day, J(ames) Edward
Day, James Vincent
Day, James Warren
Day, John Franklin
Day, LeRoy Edward
Day, Maurice Jerome
Day, Melvin Sherman
Day, Richard Earl
Day, Robert James
Day, William Edwin
Dayhoff, Margaret Oakley
Days, Drew Saunders, III
Dazey, William Boyd
Deacon, John Campbell
Deaderick, Lucile
Deakin, James
Deal, David Vernon
Deal, Ernest Linwood, Jr.
Deal, George Edgar
Deal, James Dennison
Deal, William Brown
Dealey, Joseph MacDonald
Dean, Alan Loren
Dean, Beale
Dean, David
Dean, Dewey Hobson, Jr.
Dean, Frances Childers
Dean, Jack Pearce
Dean, John Gunther
Dean, Lydia Margaret Carter (Mrs. Halsey Albert Dean)
Dean, Paul Regis
Dean, Stanley Rochelle
Dean, Walter Raleigh, Jr.
Deane, Frederick, Jr.
Dearhart, Earl Louis
Deasy, William Edward
De Bakey, Lois
De Bakey, Michael Ellis
De Bardeleben, Bailey Thomas
de Blij, Harm Jan
De Bremaecker, Jean-Claude
de Brier, Donald Paul
DeBusk, Edith M.
DeBusk, Manuel Conrad
de Butts, John Dulany
Decher, Rudolf
Deckard, H. Joel
Deckelbaum, Nelson
Decker, Alonzo Galloway, Jr.
Decker, John Laws
Deckert, Gordon Harmon
DeClaris, Nicholas
DeConcini, Dennis
DeConcini, John Cyrus
DeCosta, Laler Cook
De Curtis, David Samuel
Dederich, Susan Russell
Dedmon, Donald Newton
Deering, Ferdie Jackson
Dees, Morris Seligman, Jr.
Deese, James Earle
Deevey, Edward Smith, Jr.
Deffer, Philip Augustus
deFord, Sara Whitcraft
De Frank, Vincent
DeGrandi, Joseph A.
DeHaven, Oren Edwin
DeHay, John Carlisle, Jr.
Dehoney, William Wayne
Deiss, William Paul, Jr.
Dekle, Clayton Barnett
De Lacey, J. Gibson
de la Colina, Rafael
de la Garza, E(kika)
Delaney, Edward Norman
Delaney, Patrick James
Delaney, Steve
Delano, Victor
Delany, Kevin F.X.
de la Parte, Louis Anthony, Jr.
Delaplaine, Edward Schley
Delappe, Irving Pierce
de la Sierra, Angello
Delaune, Elton Joseph, Jr.
Delchamps, O.H., Jr.
Delcher, Edwin G.
De Leeuw, Samuel Leonard
De Leon, Antonio Carmelo, Jr.
Delevoryas, Theodore
Delgado, Jaime Nabor
Dell, Donald Lundy
Dellenback, John Richard
Dellinger, Walter Estes, III
Delliquadri, Pardo Frederick
Dellums, Ronald Vernie
Delmar, Eugene Anthony
del Mar, Roland Haddaway
Delmore, John Robert
de Loach, Anthony Cortelyou
del Regato, Juan Angel
DeLuca, Patrick Phillip
Delzell, Charles Floyd
Demartini, Robert John
Dembling, Paul Gerald
De Mello, Walmor Carlos
Demos, John Theodore
Dempsey, Bruce Harvey
Dempsey, Charles Lade
Dempsey, James Raymon
Dempsey, William Henry
Dempsey, William James
Demuth, Richard Holzman
Denegre, George
Denemark, George William
Denison, Edward Fulton
Denius, Franklin Wofford
Denius, Homer Rainey
Denker, Arnold
Denman, Ben Pittman
Denman, Charles Frank
Denman, Eugene Dale
Denman, Joe Carter, Jr.
Dennard, Cleveland Leon
Dennen, William Henry
Dennery, Moise Waldhorn
Denney, George Covert, Jr.
Dennis, Donald Daly
Dennis, Henry Arnold
Dennis, James Leon
Dennis, James Loudon
Dennis, Joe
Dennis, John Murray
Dennison, Alfred Dudley
Dennison, Charles Stuart
Dennison, John Manley
Dennison, Robert Lee
Dennstedt, Frederick DeVere
Denny, Floyd Wolfe, Jr.
Denny, J(ames) William
Denny, Robert Stanley
DeNoyer, John Milford
Dent, Albert Walter
Dent, Frederick Baily
Dent, James Norman
Dent, Vincent Val Jean
Denton, Chauncey Lovelace, Jr.
Denton, Herbert Howard, Jr.
Denton, James G.
Denton, Jeremiah Andrew, Jr.
DePaulo, J. Raymond
Deprit, Andre Albert
DePuy, William Eugene
Derian, Patricia Murphy
Dermer, Otis Clifford
DeRosier, Arthur Henry, Jr.
Derrick, Butler Carson, Jr.
Derrick, William Sheldon
Derryberry, William Everett
Derthick, Lawrence Gridley, Sr.
Derzon, Robert Alan
de Saint Phalle, Thibaut
Desan, Wilfrid
Desautels, Claude John
De Selm, Henry Rawie
de Serres, Frederick Joseph
Desiderio, Dominic Morse, Jr.
De Simone, Daniel V.
Desloge, Edward Augustine
Desmond, John Jacob
Despalj, Pavle
Dessart, Donald Joseph
Dessauer, Herbert Clay
Dessler, Alexander Jack
de Stwolinski, Gail Rounce Boyd
de Tonnancour, Paul Roger Godefroy
Dettbarn, Wolf-Dietrich
Dettinger, Garth Bryant
Detwiler, William Clifford
Deusing, Murl
Deutch, John Mark
Deutsch, Robert William
Deutsch, Stanley
Devan, Christopher Bartram
De Vault, Virgil Thomas
Devening, Robert Randolph
Devin, William Augustus, Jr.
Devine, James Brendan
Devine, Samuel Leeper
DeVito, Mathias Joseph
Devlin, Michael Coles
De Vore, George Warren
de Vyver, Frank Traver
Dewar, Michael James Steuart
Dewberry, Lawrence Glenn, Jr.
de Weldon, Felix Weihs
deWette, Frederik Willem
De Witt, Lew Calvin
De Witt-Morette, Cécile
DeWolf, L. Harold
Dewsbury, Donald Allen
Dexter, John Bondy
DeYoung, Russell
Diaforli, LaRue C.
Dial, William Henry
Diamond, Leo Aaron
Diamond, Murray Allen
Diamond, William
Diaz, Horacio
Diaz, John Francis
Dibbs, Edward George (Eddie)
Dibner, David Robert
Di Bona, Charles Joseph
Dickens, Milton
Dickerson, Billy Ray
Dickerson, Elbert Lee
Dickerson, George William
Dickerson, Nancy Hanschman
Dickerson, Norvin Kennedy
Dickerson, Thomas Milton
Dickey, Francis George
Dickey, Frank Graves
Dickey, Imogene Bentley
Dickey, James
Dickey, Parke Atherton
Dickey, Raymond Roosevelt
Dickinson, Alfred James
Dickinson, Charles Bruce
Dickinson, Frank Herman
Dickinson, Joshua Clifton, Jr.
Dickinson, Roger Allyn
Dickinson, William Boyd, Jr.
Dickinson, William Louis
Dickison, Walter Lee
Dicks, John Barber
Dicks, Norman De Valois
Dickson, Herbert Jackson
Dickson, Paul
Dickson, William Petty, Jr.
Dickstein, Sidney
Diddle, Albert Washington
Diener, Theodor Otto
Diercks, Chester William, Jr.
Diercks, Frederick Otto
Diers, Hank
Dies, Douglas Hilton
Diesel, John Phillip
Dieter, George E., Jr.
Dietrich, John Erb
Dietsch, Robert William
Diettrich, Sigismond de Ruedesheim
Dietz, Cecil Eugene
Dietz, Hanns-Bertold
Dietz, James Reginald
Dietze, Gottfried
Diggs, Charles C., Jr.
Diggs, Lemuel Whitley
Diggs, Walter Whitley
Dilday, William Horace, Jr.
Dillahunty, Wilbur Harris
Dillard, Dudley
Dillard, Hardy Cross
Dillard, Joey Lee
Dillard, Katherine Shannon Rawlings (Mrs. Tom Clinton Dillard)
Dillard, Robert Lionel, Jr.
Dillman, Grant
Dillon, Conley Hall
Dillon, James Lee
Dillon, John Andrew, Jr.
Dillon, Oscar Wendell, Jr.
Dillon, Robert Morton
Dillon, Thomas Andrew
DiLuzio, Nicholas Robert
Dilworth, Edwin Earle
Dilworth, Richard Hanson
Dince, Robert Reuben
Dingell, John David, Jr.
Dingledy, Paul George
Dingman, Milford Howard, Jr.
Dinklage, Ralph Dietrich
Dinneen, Gerald Paul
Dircks, William Joseph
Dirks, Kenneth Ray
Di Sabato, Louis Roman
DiSalle, Michael Vincent
Discher, Sister Martha
Disharoon, Leslie Benjamin
Disher, John Howard
Dittert, J. Lee, Jr.
Dittman, Duane Arthur
Ditzen, Lowell Russell
Ditzler, John William
Divers, William Keeveny
Divine, Robert Alexander
Diwoky, Roy John
Dix, Fred Andrew, Jr.
Dixon, James Payson, Jr.
Dixon, James William, Jr.
Dixon, Jeane L.
Dixon, John Allen, Jr.
Dixon, John Wainwright
Dixon, Julian Carey
Dixon, Paul Rand
Dixon, Roger Coit
Dizard, Wilson Paul, Jr.
diZerega, Thomas William
Djerejian, Edward Peter
Dlesk, George
Dobbins, Charles Gordon
Dobbs, Henri Talmage, Jr.
Dobbs, Hubert Lee
Dobbs, Theodore Burrell
Dobelle, Evan Samuel
Dobriansky, Lev Eugene
Doby, John Thomas
Dockeray, James Carlton
Dockray, George Henry
Docter, Charles Alfred
Dodd, Christopher J.
Dodd, Ed(ward Benton)
Dodd, Lamar
Dodd, William Joseph
Doder, Dusko
Dodge, Charles Granville
Dodge, Guy Howard
Dodson, Edward Griffith, Jr.
Doenges, Byron Frederick
Doenges, William Conrad
Doerr, Arthur Harry
Doerr, John Spurr
Doerre, Karl Harold
Doetsch, Raymond Nicholas
Doggett, Aubrey Clayton, Jr.
Doheny, David Armour
Doherty, Edward Denvir, II
Doherty, Herbert Joseph, Jr.
Doherty, James Edward, III
Doherty, Josephine Kristan
Doherty, William Thomas, Jr.
Doke, Marshall J., Jr.
Dolan, Edward William
Dolan, William David, Jr.
Dolansky, E.F.
Dolar, Raymond Edward
Dole, Elizabeth Hanford
Dole, Hollis Mathews
Dole, Malcolm
Dole, Richard Fairfax, Jr.
Dole, Robert J.
Dollmeyer, Walker George
Dolmetsch, Carl Richard, Jr.
Dolson, Charles Herbert
Doluisio, James Thomas
Domenici, Pete V(ichi)
Dominik, Jack Edward
Domit, Moussa Majed
Domokos, Gabor
Donachie, Robert James
Donahue, Hayden Hackney
Donahue, Thomas Reilly
Donaldson, Jeff Richardson
Donaldson, Robert Ward
Donaldson, Samuel Andrew
Donato, Anthony
Donavan, George Edgar
Donchian, Richard Davoud
Donelan, Joseph Francis, Jr.
Donlan, Charles Joseph
Donnahoe, Alan Stanley
Donnellan, Thomas A.
Donnelley, Dixon
Donnelly, Brian J.
Donnelly, Joseph Lennon
Donnelly, Marjorie Morrison (Mrs. James Ford Donnelly, Jr.)
Donner, Martin Walter
Donovan, Charles Joseph
Donovan, David Gerard
Donovan, James Albort, Jr.
Donovan, Jerome Francis
Donovan, Paul F.
Donovan, Paul Thomas
Donovan, Robert John
Doole, George Arntzen
Dooley, Edwin Benedict
Doolin, John B
Doolittle, Jesse William, Jr.
Doran, Adron
Dorcy, William Leo
Doremus, Ogden
Doris Ann (Doris Ann Scharfenberg)
Dorman, Gladys M.
Dorn, William Jennings Bryan
Dornan, Robert Kenneth
Dorough, Charles Dwight
Dorsett, Tony Drew
Dorsey, Bob Rawls
Dorsey, Earl A.
Dorsey, John Russell
Dorsey, John Wesley, Jr.
Dorsey, Rhoda Mary
Dorst, John Phillips
Doskocil, Karl Vaclav
Dotson, Robert Charles
Doty, Arthur Murphy
Doty, Donald D.
Doty, James Edward
Doub, William Offutt
Doubleday, Van Courtlandt
Douce, William Clark
Dougal, Arwin Adelbert
Dougherty, Charles F.
Dougherty, John Chrysostom
Dougherty, Joseph Calton, Jr.
Dougherty, Jude Patrick
Dougherty, Russell Elliott
Dougherty, William H.
Douglas, Cathleen Curran Heffernan (Mrs. William O. Douglas)
Douglas, Charles Francis
Douglas, Clarence James, Jr.
Douglas, G. Bruce
Douglas, James Nathaniel
Douglas, John Harold
Douglas, Leslie
Douglas, Mervyn Lee
Douglas, Robert Alden
Douglass, Carl Dean
Douglass, John William
Dovat, Ernest Charles
Dove, George Naff
Dover, James Burrell
Dow, Louis Arnold
Dow, Robert Nesbitt, Jr.
Dowben, Robert Morris
Dowd, Thomas Nathan
Dowdey, Clifford Shirley, Jr.
Dowdle, Walter Reid
Dowdy, George Winston
Dowdy, John Wesley
Dowdy, Lewis Carnegie
Dowell, Dudley
Dowell, John Carson
Dowgray, John Gray Laird, Jr.
Dowling, Harry Filmore
Dowling, Roderick Anthony
Downey, Mortimer Leo, III
Downing, Thomas Nelms
Downs, Anthony
Downs, Harry
Doyle, David Kyte
Doyle, Edward Allen
Doyle, Frederick Joseph
Doyle, Katherine Lee Lee
Doyle, Marion Wade (Mrs. Henry Grattan Doyle)
Doyle, Michael
Doyle, Roger Hart
Dozier, Carroll Thomas
Dozier, Craig Lanier
Dozier, Ollin Kemp
Drachman, Daniel Bruce
Dragoo, Donald Wayne
Dragt, Alexander James
Drain, Lee
Drake, Clifford Barnes
Drake, George Lenton, Jr.
Drake, John Walter
Drake, Raleigh Moseley
Drake, Richard Bryant
Drake, Robert Mortimer, Jr.
Drake, William Earle
Draper, Daniel David, Jr.
Draper, Earle Sumner
Drayton, William
Drazek, Stanley Joseph
Dreger, Ralph Mason
Drennan, Merrill William
Drennen, William Miller
Drescher, John Mummau
Dresser, Donald Markham
Dresser, Laurence L.
Dressler, Robert Eugene
Drew, Katherine Fischer
Drew, Russell Cooper
Drewes, Werner
Drewry, Guy Carleton
Drewry, John Eldridge
Driehuys, Leonardus Bastiaan
Driesell, Charles Grice
Driessnack, Hans Helmuth
Drinkard, Donald
Driscoll, Clement Joseph
Driver, Lottie Elizabeth
Driver, William Joseph
Droessler, Earl George
Drosdoff, Daniel Aaron
Drossos, Angelo John
Drucker, Bertram Morris
Drucker, Darrell Irving, Jr.
Drucker, Miriam Koontz
Drumm, Streuby Lloyd
Drummond, Roscoe
Drummond, William Joe
Drummond, Winslow
Drury, Thomas Joseph
Dryburgh, Bruce Sinclair
Dryden, Franklin Bridges
Drysdale, Douglas D.
Duba, John Gorman
Du Bar, Jules Ramon
Dublin, Thomas David
Du Bois, Jack Edwin
DuBois, Robert Lee
Ducrest, Willis Francis
Dudek, Richard Albert
Dudgeon, Farnham Francis
Dudley, Eastham Waller
Dudley, Elford Samuel
Dudley, Guilford, Jr.
Dudley, James Hudson
Dudley, Tilford E.
Dudman, Richard Beebe
Dudrick, Stanley John
Dudrow, Louis Albert
Duemer, Walter Corliss
Duff, Fratis Lee
Duffey, Frank Marion
Duffey, Joseph Daniel
Duffy, Francis Daniel
Du Flon, Henry A.
Dugan, Donovan Paul
Dugan, Robert Perry, Jr.
Dugas, Louis, Jr.
Duggan, Ben O., Jr.
Duggan, Herbert Garrison
Dugger, Gordon Leslie
Dugger, Ronnie E.
Dukas, Peter
Duke, Douglas
Duke, James Alan
Duke, Paul Robert
Dukes, David Virgil
Dukler, Abraham Emanuel
Dulan, Harold Andrew
Dulaney, Woodford Hector
Dull, Carl Arey, Jr.
Dulles, Avery
Dulles, Eleanor Lansing
Duma, Richard Joseph
Dumas, Lawrence
Dunaway, Charles (Chuck) Ray
Dunbar, Charles Edward, III
Dunbar, John Burton
Dunbar, Lemuel Cotton
Dunbar, Robert Standish, Jr.
Dunbar, Wallace Huntington
Duncan, A. Baker
Duncan, Buell Gard, Jr.
Duncan, Charles Tignor
Duncan, Charles William, Jr.
Duncan, David Beattie
Duncan, Donald
Duncan, Francis
Duncan, Irma Wagner
Duncan, James Loughlin
Duncan, James Russell
Duncan, John Bonner
Duncan, John James

Duncan, John Lapsley
Duncan, Joseph Wayman
Duncan, Pope Alexander
Duncan, Robert Blackford
Duncan, William Adolphus, Jr.
Duncan-Peters, Stephen James
Duncombe, Raynor Lockwood
Dunham, Roy Henry
Dunham, William Barrett
Dunhill, Robert
Dunkle, William Frederick, Jr.
Dunlap, Charles Edward
Dunlap, E. T.
Dunlap, James Anderson
Dunlap, Richard Freeman
Dunn, Clark Allan
Dunn, Edgar Hart, Jr.
Dunn, Edward Clare
Dunn, Ellen Catherine
Dunn, H. Stewart, Jr.
Dunn, John Michael
Dunn, Parker Southerland
Dunn, R. Walter
Dunn, Robert Francis
Dunning, James Henry Fitzgerald
Dunphy, Donal
Dunton, Edward Albert
Dunwody, William Elliott, Jr.
Dunworth, John
Duplantier, Adrian Guy
DuPont, Robert L., Jr.
DuPree, Billy Joe
Dupree, Franklin Taylor, Jr.
DuPuis, Robert Newell
Dupuy, Trevor Nevitt
Duquemin, Gordon James
Dur, Philip Francis
Durand, John Donald
Durant, Frederick Clark, III
Durant, John
Durbin, James E.
Durbin, Richard Louis
Durden, Robert Franklin
Duren, William Larkin, Jr.
Durenberger, David Ferdinand
Durfee, Harold Allen
Durfey, Robert Walker
Durham, Clarence Ray
Durham, Norman Nevill
Durham, Ronald Oatis
Durieux, Caroline Wogan
Durig, James Robert
Durkee, Arthur Bowman
Durkee, William Carl
Durkee, William Porter
Durkin, John A.
Durland, Jack Raymond
Durrett, James Frazer, Jr.
Duscha, Julius Carl
Dussich, John Peter Joseph
Dustan, Harriet Pearson
Dutcher, Clinton Harvey
Dutro, John Thomas, Jr.
Dutta, Sisir Kamal
Dutton, Donnell Wayne
Dutton, Frederick Gary
Dutton, Wilmer Coffman, Jr.
DuVal, Miles P., Jr.
Dwight, James Scutt, Jr.
Dwyer, Jean Agnes Ferguson
Dwyer, John Bartholomew
Dyal, William M., Jr.
Dybczak, Zbigniew Wladyslaw
Dyck, Walter Peter
Dye, Bradford Johnson, Jr.
Dye, Thomas Roy
Dyer, David William
Dyer, Everett Dixon
Dyer, Herbert Lincoln
Dyer, Irby Lloyd
Dyer, John Martin
Dyer, Newman Houghton
Dyer, Wayne Walter
Dyess, Bobby Dale
Dyess, William Jennings
Dyke, Delbert Ammon
Dykes, Charles Edwin
Dykes, Jefferson Chenowth
Dykstra, Francis Earl
Dykstra, Vergil Homer
Dymond, Lewis Wandell
Dynes, Russell Rowe
Eades, James Beverly, Jr.
Eads, Ora Wilbert
Eager, John Howard, III
Eagleburger, Lawrence Sidney
Eagles, Eldon Lewis
Eagles, Sidney Smith, Jr.
Eagleson, Halson Vashon
Eakin, Charles Edward
Eakin, Robert Edward
Earl, Lewis Harold
Earle, Kenneth Martin
Earll, Jerry Miller
Early, Jack Jones
Early, James
Earnest, Jack Edward
Earnshaw, Virginia Watson
Earthman, William Fletcher
Eason, Robert Gaston
East, Charles E.
East, Richard Clayton
Easterling, Crawford Alan, Jr.
Easterling, William Ewart, Jr.
Easterly, Harry Watkey, Jr.
Easterwood, Henry Lewis
Eastham, Jerome Fields
Eastham, Thomas
Eastin, Keith E.
Eastland, James O.
Eastwood, Richard Truman
Eaton, Conrad Paul
Eaton, Gordon Pryor
Eaton, Joe O.
Eaton, Leonard James, Jr.
Eaton, Samuel Dickinson
Eaton, William James
Eaves, James Clifton
Eberhard, John Paul
Eberly, John Wilgus
Ebert, James David
Ebert, Richard Vincent
Eblen, Amos Hall
Eby, Helen Marie
Eckel, Paul Edward
Eckelmann, Frank Donald
Ecker, Harry Allen
Eckerman, Jerome
Eckert, Robert Ray
Eckhardt, Robert Christian
Eckley, Frederick Ralph, Jr.
Eckman, David Walter
Economos, George Themistocles
Eddleman, Elvia Etheridge, Jr.
Eddleman, William Glenn
Eddleman, William Roseman
Eddy, Charles P(hillips)
Eddy, George Amos
Eddy, John Paul
Edelcup, Norman Scott
Edelman, Marian Wright (Mrs. Peter B. Edelman)
Edelman, Peter Benjamin
Eden, Murray
Eden, William Gibbs
Edenfield, Berry Avant
Edens, Donald Keith
Edens, Henry Harman
Edens, James Drake, Jr.
Edes, Nik Bruce
Edgar, Robert William
Edge, Findley Bartow
Edge, Robert Laneer
Edgerton, Milton Thomas, Jr.
Edgerton, Norman Edward
Edgett, William Maloy
Edidin, Michael Aaron
Edinger, Lois Virginia
Edington, Robert Sherard
Edisen, Clayton Bryon
Edison, Robert Donald
Edlund, Milton Carl
Edminster, Talcott W.
Edmison, Marvin Tipton
Edmisten, Rufus Ligh
Edmonds, Frank Norman, Jr.
Edmondson, Jeannette B.
Edmondson, William Brockway
Edmonson, Dan Hutcheson
Edmonson, Munro Sterling
Edmunds, Frances Ravenel
Edmunds, John Ollie
Edmunds, Robert Larry
Edozien, Joseph Chike
Edris, Paul Milburn
Edwards, A. Wilson
Edwards, B.C.
Edwards, Billy Matt
Edwards, Charles Hayden
Edwards, Don
Edwards, Edgar Owen
Edwards, Edmund Barber
Edwards, Edwin Washington
Edwards, Ernest Preston
Edwards, George Alva
Edwards, Gilbert Franklin
Edwards, Hardy Malcolm, Jr.
Edwards, Harold Mills
Edwards, Howard Dawson
Edwards, Hugh Stephenson
Edwards, Jack
Edwards, Jack Donald
Edwards, James Burrows
Edwards, James D.
Edwards, James Donald
Edwards, Jarlath O'Neill (J.O.)
Edwards, Joseph Daniel, Jr.
Edwards, Julia Spalding
Edwards, Lillian Brown
Edwards, Louis Ward, Jr.
Edwards, Marshall Henry
Edwards, Marvin H. Mickey
Edwards, Max Nixon
Edwards, Presley William
Edwards, Robert Cook
Edwards, Roy Vernell
Edwards, Steve
Edwards, Willard
Edwards, William F.
Eek, Nathaniel Sisson
Eells, John Shepard, Jr.
Efferson, John Norman
Efron, Samuel
Egan, Michael Joseph
Egan, Robert Lee
Egeberg, Roger Olaf
Egerton, John Walden
Egeth, Howard Elliott
Egger, George Edward
Eggert, Lowell Franklin
Eglevsky, Marina
Egozi, David
Ehle, John Marsden, Jr.
Ehlers, Joseph Henry
Ehmann, William Donald
Ehre, Edward
Ehrenhaft, Peter David
Ehrenpreis, Irvin
Ehrensberger, Ray
Ehrlich, Gertrude
Ehrlich, Morton
Ehrlich, S(aul) Paul, Jr.
Ehrlich, Thomas
Eichelberger, Robert John
Eichhorn, George Carl
Eichhorn, Gunther Louis
Eichhorn, Roger
Eidman, Kraft Warner
Eidson, John Olin
Eikleberry, Robert Woodrow
Einkauf, Oscar Ernest, Jr.
Einspruch, Norman Gerald
Eisel, Leo Martin
Eisele, Albert Alois
Eisele, Donn Fulton
Eisele, Garnett Thomas
Eisenberg, Kenneth Sawyer
Eisenberg, Meyer
Eisenberg, Phillip
Eisenbies, Ray Fred
Eisenbraun, Edmund Julius Johannes
Eisenhower, Milton Stover
Eisenstein, Julian Calvert
Eitel, Hubert Messinger
Eizenstat, Stuart E.
Ekman, Anders Lundin
Ekstrom, William Ferdinand
Elam, Harper Johnston, III
Elam, Lloyd Charles
Elam, Theodore Marinus
El-Baz, Farouk
Elberson, Robert Evans
Elbin, Paul Nowell
Elconin, Victor A.
Elder, John Howard, Jr.
Elder, Robert Lee
Elder, Samuel Adams
Elder, Stewart Taylor
Eldredge, William Augustus, Jr.
Eldridge, David Carlton
Eldridge, John Cole
Eldridge, Josiah Baker
Eldridge, Marie Delaney
Elebash, Hunley Agee
Elfin, Mel
Elgin, Edwin Stevens
Eliason, Norman Ellsworth
Eliel, Ernest Ludwig
Elion, Gertrude Belle
Elisburg, Donald Earl
Eliscu, Frank
Elkins, Francis Clark
Elkins, James Anderson, Jr.
Elkins, Lloyd Edwin
Elkouri, Frank
Ellin, Marvin
Ellington, Charles Ronald
Elliot, Robert Sherrard, Jr.
Elliott, Benjamin Paul
Elliott, Edward
Elliott, Frank Wallace
Elliott, Grover Sager
Elliott, Harold Edward
Elliott, Howard Clyde, Jr.
Elliott, James Robert
Elliott, Lloyd Hartman
Elliott, Martin Anderson
Elliott, Warren G.
Ellis, Aileen Virginia
Ellis, Anthony Thornton
Ellis, Billy Joe
Ellis, Clarke Norton
Ellis, Don Edwin
Ellis, Edward Evan
Ellis, Edward Evan
Ellis, Elmo Israel
Ellis, Fred Wilson
Ellis, Harry Bearse
Ellis, James Edward
Ellis, James Watson
Ellis, John
Ellis, John Tracy
Ellis, Leslie Lee, Jr.
Ellis, Michael
Ellis, Richard Archie
Ellis, Robert Arthur
Ellis, Robert Ford, Jr.
Ellis, Spencer Percy
Ellis, Sydney
Ellis, Van Calvin
Ellis, William Harold
Ellis, William Leigh
Ellison, Fred Pittman
Ellison, Samuel Porter, Jr.
Ellsberg, Edward
Ellsworth, Robert Fred
Elman, Philip
Elmer, William Morris
Elmore, Stancliff Churchill
Elrod, Ben Moody
Elsasser, Robert William
Elsasser, Walter Maurice
Elsberg, Milton Leonard
Elsberg, Stuart Michael
Elsey, George McKee
Elson, Edward Elliott
Elwell, Harry Howard, Jr.
Elwood, Hugh McJunkin
Ely, Northcutt
Embry, Robert Campbell, Jr.
Embry, Thomas Eric
Emerich, Donald Warren
Emerson, David Frederick
Emerson, Horace Mann, III
Emerson, Robert Kennerly
Emerson, William Allen
Emery, David Farnham
Emiliani, Cesare
Emken, Robert Allan
Emmanuel, Constantinos Basil
Emmanuel, Michel George
Emme, Eugene Morlock
Emmer, John Wiltz
Enders, Richard Warren
Enfield, Clifton Willis
Engel, Melvin M.
Engel, Paul Bernard
Engel, Paul Huber
Engel, Ralph
Engel, William King
Engelder, Theodore Carl
Engelhardt, Hugo Tristram, Jr.
Engen, Donald Davenport
Enger, Walter Melvin
Engert, Cornelius Van H.
England, Anthony W.
England, Arthur Jay, Jr.
Englander, Harold Robert
Englert, Roy Theodore
Englesmith, Tejas
English, Glenn
English, Paul Ward
English, Spofford Grady
Englund, Ralph Caldwell
Engman, Lewis August
Engstrom, Alfred Garvin
Enix, Agnes Lucille
Enloe, Robert Ted, III
Ennis, Billy Mack
Ennis, Thomas Elmer, Jr.
Eno, Charles Franklin
Enoch, Jay Martin
Ensign, William Lloyd
Ensley, Grover William
Ensminger, Luther Glenn
Entorf, Richard Carl
Entwisle, George
Ephraim, Charles
Ephron, Nora
Epley, Lewis Everett, Jr.
Epley, Marion Jay, Jr.
Eppler, William Burgess
Epps, Anna Cherrie
Epps, Augustus Charles
Epps, Ernest Allen, Jr.
Epps, William Monroe
Epstein, Arthur William
Epstein, Barry R.
Epstein, David Gustav
Epstein, Edward S.
Epstein, Eleni Sakes (Mrs. Sidney Epstein)
Epstein, Lionel Charles
Epstein, Robert Marvin
Epstein, Sidney
Erdos, Ervin George
Erekson, Paul Webb
Erfft, Kenneth Reynders
Ericksen, Ephraim Gordon
Ericksen, Jerald Laverne
Erickson, Ernst Walfred
Erickson, James Huston
Erickson, LeRoy Alexander
Erickson, William Clarence
Ericson, Richard Ferdinand
Erlandson, Ray Sanford
Erlenborn, John Neal
Ernst, Richard James
Ernst, Robert Craig
Ersek, Robert Allen
Ertel, Allen Edward
Ervin, Robert Marvin
Ervin, Samuel James, Jr.
Erwin, Frank William
Esch, Marvin L.
Escobar, Rodolfo Rene
Eskenazi, Jacob Victor
Eskew, Rhea Taliaferro
Eskridge, John Ira
Esposito, Albert Charles
Esposito, Alfred Lewis
Espy, Charles Clifford
Estabrook, Ronald Winfield
Estes, Carl L., II
Estes, Edward Harvey, Jr.
Estes, Gerald Walter
Estes, Howard Mitchell, Jr.
Estes, Howell Marion, Jr.
Estes, Joe Ewing
Esteves, Vernon Rafael
Estrada, Rodney Joseph
Etheredge, Robert Foster
Etheridge, Jack Paul
Etherington, Edwin Deacon
Ethridge, Samuel Broughton
Ethridge, Thomas Ramage
Etter, Betty
Eubank, Alvah Hovey, Jr.
Eubanks, Luther Boyd
Eugere, Edward Joseph
Eure, Spurgeon Bryant
Eure, Thad
Eustace, Robert Joseph
Evans, Billy Lee
Evans, Carleton Cannon
Evans, Clifford
Evans, Clifford Jesse
Evans, David Walter
Evans, Edward Parker
Evans, Edward Steptoe, Jr.
Evans, Edwin Curtis
Evans, Emory Gibbons
Evans, Frank Edward
Evans, Frank Owen
Evans, George Heberton, Jr.
Evans, Grose
Evans, Harry Lee
Evans, Hawthorne Clough, Jr.
Evans, James Clarence
Evans, Joseph Patrick
Evans, Mark Lewis
Evans, Medford Stanton
Evans, Ormond Keister, Jr.
Evans, Paul Lewis
Evans, Philip Morgan
Evans, Ray Marshall
Evans, Rowland, Jr.
Evans, Walter Fontaine
Evans, William Buell
Evarts, Edward Vaughan
Eveland, Harmon Edwin
Evelyn, Douglas Everett
Evenden, Frederick George
Everett, Boyd Nixon
Everett, Donald Edward
Everett, Durward R., Jr.
Everett, Houston Spencer, Jr.
Everett, Roberts
Everingham, Roger J(ames)
Evers, James Charles
Evert, Christine Marie (Chris)
Evinrude, Ralph
Ewalt, Jack Richard
Ewell, Vincent Fletcher, Jr.
Ewen, David
Ewers, John Canfield
Ewing, Frank Marion
Ewing, George H.
Ewing, George McNaught
Ewing, John Alexander
Ewing, John Arthur
Ewing, Ky Pepper, Jr.
Ewing, Oscar Ross
Ewing, Richard Tucker
Ewing, Samuel Daniel, Jr.
Ewing, Samuel Evans
Ewing, Sidney Alton
Exum, James Gooden, Jr.
Eyre, John Douglas
Eyster, William Bibb
Ezekiel, Walter Naphtali
Ezell, John Samuel
Ezell, Kerry Moore
Fable, Robert Cooper, Jr.
Fackler, Benjamine Lloyd
Fadner, Frank Leslie
Fadum, Ralph Eigil
Fagg, John Edwin
Fahringer, Catherine Hewson
Fain, Jim
Fair, James Rutherford, Jr.
Fairbank, Henry Alan
Fairbanks, Charles Herron
Fairbanks, Douglas Elton, Jr.
Fairbanks, Harold Vincent
Fairchild, James Delano
Fairgrieve, William Robertson
Fairley, Albert Langley, Jr.
Fairley, Francis Hilliard
Falck, Edward
Falco, Mathea
Falk, Bernard Henry
Falk, Eugene Hannes
Falk, Harold Frank
Falk, James H.
Faller, Theodore Sylvester
Fallows, James Mackenzie
Fancher, George Homer
Fang, Bertrand Tien-Chueh
Fang, Joong
Fanning, Barry Hedges
Fanning, John Harold
Fanning, Robert Allen
Fanseen, James Foster
Fantle, Sheldon William
Fanucci, Jerome Benedict
Farabow, Ford Franklin, Jr.
Farbach, Carl Frederick
Farber, James Polk
Fargo, Donna
Faricy, William Thomas
Faries, Belmont
Farinholt, Larkin Hundley
Faris, Esron McGruder
Faris, Jesse Edwin, Jr.
Farley, Joseph McConnell
Farley, Richard Alan
Farlow, J. Binford
Farmakides, John Basil
Farmer, Donald Edwin
Farmer, Frances
Farmer, Guy
Farmer, James
Farmer, Joe Sam
Farmer, Thomas Albert, Jr.
Farmer, Thomas Laurence
Farmer, Thomas Wohlsen
Farmer, Welford Stuart
Farnham, Emily
Farnsley, Charles Rowland Peaslee
Farnsworth, Alan Coyle
Farnsworth, Jerry
Farquhar, Norman
Farr, Walter Greene, Jr.
Farrell, John Joseph
Farrell, Paul Edward
Farrell, Robert Emmet
Farris, Jefferson Davis
Farris, Milton Glenn
Farthing, Barton Roby
Farver, Alvin D.
Farwell, Albert Edmond
Farwell, F. Evans
Fary, John G.
Fascell, Dante B.
Fashena, Gladys Jeanette
Fasser, Paul James, Jr.
Fauber, Joseph Everette, Jr.
Faubus, Orval Eugene
Faulconer, Robert Jamieson
Faulders, Cyril Thomas, Jr.
Faulk, Lloyd Buford
Faulk, Odie B.
Faulkner, Avery Coonley
Faulkner, Claude Winston
Faulkner, Elizabeth Coonley
Faulkner, James Hardin
Faulstich, Albert Joseph
Fauntroy, Walter E.
Faust, John William, Jr.
Faver, Dudley Ervin
Faw, Charles Dennis
Fay, Albert Bel
Fay, Frederic Albert
Fay, Peter Thorp
Fay, William Michael
Fazio, Vic
Fearey, Robert Appleton
Feaster, George Erwin
Featherston, C. Moxley
Feaver, John Clayton
Fedder, Joel David
Federa, Henry Appleton
Feehan, Thomas Joseph
Feffer, James Joseph
Fehr, Carl August
Feibleman, James Kern
Fein, John Morton
Feinbloom, Abraham
Feingold, S. Norman
Feland, John J.
Felber, Everett Henry Fred
Feld, Alan David
Feld, Irvin
Feld, Werner Joachim
Feldbaum, Carl B.
Feldman, Clarice Rochelle
Feldman, Edmund Burke
Feldman, Martin L. C.
Feldman, Melvin J.
Feldman, Myer
Feldman, Roger B.
Feldmann, Edward George
Felker, Richard Reeves
Fellendorf, George William
Fellers, James Davison
Fellner, William John
Fellowes, Frederick Gale, Jr.
Fellows, Russell Coleman
Fels, Rendigs
Felsenfeld, Gary
Feltner, Richard Lee
Felton, Gordon H.
Felton, Lurton Eugene
Felts, William Robert, Jr.
Fender, Freddy (Baldemar Huerta)
Fendler, Oscar
Feninger, Claude
Fenn, Charles Van Orden
Fenner, Mildred Sandison (Mrs. Ernest G. Reid)
Fenter, Felix West
Fenton, Edward A.
Fenwick, Millicent Hammond
Fenyvesi, Charles
Feragen, Robert White
Ferebee, Stephen Scott, Jr.
Ference, Michael, Jr.
Ferguson, Allen Richmond
Ferguson, Arthur Bowles
Ferguson, Charles Ray
Ferguson, Chester Howell
Ferguson, Frederick Palmer
Ferguson, James
Ferguson, James A.
Ferguson, James Sharbrough
Ferguson, Jo McCown
Ferguson, Joseph Gantt
Ferguson, Milton Carr, Jr.
Ferguson, Oliver Watkins
Ferguson, Phil Moss
Ferguson, Robert Louis
Ferguson, Robert Willi
Ferguson, Thomas William, Jr.
Ferkiss, Victor Christopher
Ferman, Irving
Fern, Alan Maxwell
Fernandez, Eustasio, Jr.
Fernandez, Manuel J.
Fernandez, Mariano Hugo
Ferrand, Jean Claude
Ferrara, Ralph Carmine
Ferrari, Alfred J.
Ferrari, Herbert Alfred
Ferraro, Geraldine Anne
Ferre, Antonio Luis
Ferre, Gustave Adolf
Ferre, Jose Antonio
Ferre, Maurice Antonio
Ferrell, James K.
Ferrell, William Wilson
Ferren, John Maxwell
Ferris, Charles Daniel
Ferris, George Mallette
Ferris, George Mallette, Jr.
Ferris, Robert Edmund
Ferry, Andrew Peter
Ferry, Robert Dean
Fetter, Bernard Frank
Fetter, William Hutchinson
Fettig, Lester Alan
Feuer, Lewis S.
Feuer, Samuel Gustave
Feuerlein, Willy John Arthur
Feuerzeig, Henry Louis
Feuille, Richard Harlan
Fichenberg, Robert Gordon
Fichter, Joseph H.
Ficklen, Jack Howells
Fickling, William Arthur, Jr.
Fiddler, Thomas Robert
Fidler, William Perry
Field, Elois Rachel
Field, Henry
Field, James Bernard
Field, John A., Jr.
Field, Lamar
Field, Thomas Parry
Fielden, Clarence Franklin, Jr.
Fielder, John Thomas
Fielder, Parker Clinton
Fielding, Elizabeth M(ay)
Fields, Emmett B.
Fields, Ralph Raymond
Fields, William Henry
Fields, William Straus
Fields, Wilmer Clemont
Fifield, Gary Morton
Fifield, Willard Merwin
Figg, Robert McCormick, Jr.
Fike, Claude Edwin
Filby, Percy William
Filiatrault, Alfred Charles, Jr.
Finberg, Donald Richard
Finch, James Harrison
Finch, Raymond Lawrence
Finch, Ronald M., Jr.
Finch, Thomas Austin, Jr.
Finch, Walter G.

845 REGIONAL LISTING—SOUTH-SOUTHWEST

Finch, William George Harold
Fincher, Cameron Lane
Fincher, John Albert
Fincher, Julian Hayes
Fine, Morton Samuel
Fine, Stanley Sidney
Fineg, Jerry
Finegan, Thomas Aldrich
Finerty, John Charles
Finger, Harold B.
Finger, Homer Ellis, Jr.
Finger, Kenneth Franklin
Finger, Leonard Zindler
Fini, Frank Caesar
Fink, Arthur Emil
Fink, Diane Joanne
Fink, Lyman Roger
Fink, Richard Walter
Finkel, E. Jay
Finkelstein, David
Finklea, John Furman
Finley, James Edward
Finley, Sara Crews
Finley, Wayne House
Finn, Gene Leroy
Finn, William Goebel
Finnegan, Marcus Bartlett
Finneran, John Glennon
Finnerty, Frank Ambrose
Finney, Joseph Claude Jeans
Finney, Redmond Conyngham Stewart
Finney, Ruth (Mrs. Robert Sharon Allen)
Fintel, Norman Dale
Fiore, Louis Robert
Fiorenza, Joseph Francis
Firestone, George
Firm, Ruth M.
Fischbach, Henry
Fischel, David
Fischer, Carl Castle
Fischer, George Herman, III
Fischer, James Lee
Fischer, LeRoy Henry
Fish, Hamilton, Jr.
Fish, Howard Math
Fish, Stanley Eugene
Fish, Stewart Allison
Fishburn, Howard DeWitt
Fishel, Peter Livingston
Fisher, Alfred Foster
Fisher, Allan Carroll, Jr.
Fisher, Allan Herbert, Jr.
Fisher, Benjamin Chatburn
Fisher, Benjamin Coleman
Fisher, Carl Frederick
Fisher, Charles Frederick
Fisher, Charles Harold
Fisher, Dale John
Fisher, Donald Dale
Fisher, Edward
Fisher, Frederick Ellis
Fisher, George Wescott
Fisher, Granville Chapman
Fisher, Jack Carrington
Fisher, James Lee
Fisher, James William
Fisher, Joel Hilton
Fisher, John Hurt
Fisher, John Morris
Fisher, John Richard
Fisher, Joseph Jefferson
Fisher, Joseph Lyman
Fisher, Leslie Robert
Fisher, Louis Joseph
Fisher, Miles Mark, IV
Fisher, Rayburn Jerome
Fisher, Robert Henry
Fisher, Russell Sylvester
Fisher, Seymour
Fisher, Thomas Francis, Jr.
Fisher, William Earl
Fisher, William Lawrence
Fisher, Yule
Fishko, Sol
Fishwick, John Palmer
Fiske, Richard Sewell
Fitch, Alva Revista
Fitch, David Robnett
Fite, Daniel Harley
Fite, Elwin
Fite, George Liddle
Fite, Gilbert Courtland
Fite, Julian Kroh
Fithian, Floyd
Fitt, Alfred Bradley
Fitts, James Walter
Fitzgeorge, Harold James
Fitzgerald, Edwin Roger
Fitzgerald, Eugene Francis
Fitzgerald, Raphael Vincent
Fitz Gerald, William Henry Gerald
Fitzgibbons, David John
Fitz-Hugh, Glassell Slaughter
Fitzmorris, James Edward, Jr.
Fitzpatrick, John J.
Fitzsimmons, Frank E.
Flack, James Monroe
Flack, Joe Fenley
Flack, Roberta
Flanagan, Edward Michael, Jr.
Flanagan, Michael Kendall
Flanagan, William Robert
Flannagan, William Hamilton
Flannery, Thomas
Flannery, Thomas Aquinas
Flannery, William Louis
Flathman, Richard Earl
Flatt, William Perry
Flawn, Peter Tyrrell
Flax, Alexander Henry
Fleischer, Michael
Fleishman, Joel Lawrence
Fleming, Denna Frank
Fleming, Edward Stitt
Fleming, Foy Burwell
Fleming, George McMillan
Fleming, John West
Fleming, Lawrence Durwood
Fleming, Mack Gerald
Fleming, Rex James
Fleming, Richard Carl Dunne
Fleming, Robben Wright
Fleming, Robben Wright
Fleming, Robert Henry
Fleming, Robert Wright
Fleming, Samuel M.
Fleming, William Adam
Fleming, William Cary
Fleming, William Herbert
Fleming, William Wright, Jr.
Flemming, Arthur Sherwood
Flemming, Harry S.
Fletcher, Charles William
Fletcher, Cliff
Fletcher, Cyril Scott
Fletcher, Frank Utley
Fletcher, Gilbert Hungerford
Fletcher, Hugh, Jr.
Fletcher, James Chipman
Fletcher, Jesse Conrad
Fletcher, John Caldwell
Fletcher, Lloyd
Fletcher, Robert Irving
Fletcher, Stewart Gailey
Fletcher, William Henry
Flett-Francis, William Justus
Flewellen, William Crawford, Jr.
Flickinger, Charles John
Flieger, Howard Wentworth
Flinn, Edward Ambrose, III
Flinn, Thomas Hance
Flinner, Charles Frederick
Flippo, Ronnie Gene
Flittie, William Jorgen
Flom, Edward Leonard
Flom, Samuel Louis
Florio, James J.
Flory, Daisy Parker
Flory, Walter S., Jr.
Flory, William Evans Sherlock
Flowers, Charles Ely, Jr.
Flowers, Langdon Strong
Flowers, Walter
Flowers, William Howard, Jr.
Floyd, Carlisle
Floyd, Edwin Earl
Floyd, Hugh Jackson
Floyd, Jack William
Floyd, Raymond
Floyd, Robert Lester
Fluke, Donald John
Flynn, Paul Bartholomew
Flynn, Thomas Francis
Flynn, William H.
Flynt, John James, Jr.
Foa, Joseph Victor
Foard, Susan Lee
Fobes, John Edwin
Focht, John Arnold, Jr.
Focke, Arthur Bernard
Foege, William Herbert
Foelber, Charles Hepburn
Foft, John William
Fogarty, William Thomas
Fogelman, Morris Joseph
Fogelson, David
Fogle, Richard Harter
Fogleman, John Albert
Fogleman, Julian Barton
Foil, Robert Rodney
Foisie, Philip Manning
Foland, Howard Lane
Foley, Henry Arthur
Foley, Patrick Martin
Foley, Thomas Stephen
Foley, William Edward
Folger, John Clifford
Folger, Lee Merritt
Folk, Robert Louis
Folkers, Karl August
Folley, A.J.
Folmar, Laurie Worth
Folsom, John Roy
Folsom, Robert S.
Folwell, William Hopkins
Fonda, Avery Hunt
Fones, William Hardin Davis
Fong, Peter
Fonken, Gerhard Joseph
Fontaine, Richard Kern
Fontenot, Elvina Sebastien
Foote, George Wilson, Jr.
Foote, Guy Myrph
Foote, Marcelle K.
Foote, Shelby
Forbes, John Douglas
Forbes, John Ripley
Forbes, Theodore McCoy, Jr.
Ford, Archie W.
Ford, Frederick Wayne
Ford, Gordon Buell, Jr.
Ford, Harold Eugene
Ford, Jesse Hill
Ford, Joe Thomas
Ford, John Gilmore
Ford, John Joseph
Ford, John William
Ford, Johnny Lawrence
Ford, Joseph
Ford, Lyman Sedgwick
Ford, Richard Donald
Ford, Richard Edmond
Ford, Thomas Robert
Ford, Wendell Hampton
Ford, William David
Fordham, Christopher Columbus, III
Fordyce, Phillip Randall
Foreman, Carol Lee Tucker
Foreman, Spencer
Foresman, Bob
Forest, Herbert Leon
Forester, John Gordon, Jr.
Forkner, Claude Ellis
Forman, H(enry) Chandlee
Forman, L. Ronald
Forrest, Herbert Emerson
Forrest, Hugh Sommerville
Forrest, John Franklin
Forrester, Bruce Millar
Forsberg, Edward Carl Albin
Forsee, Joe Brown
Forster, Robert
Forstman, Henry Jackson
Forsythe, Earl Andrew
Forsythe, Edwin B.
Fortas, Abe
Fortenbach, Ray Thomas
Fortenberry, Charles Nolan
Fortin, Luis Horacio
Fortune, Porter Lee, Jr.
Foscue, Henry Armfield
Foshee, John G.
Fossum, Kyle Kingman
Fossum, Robert Ross
Foster, Charles Howell
Foster, Elizabeth Connell
Foster, Eugene Lewis
Foster, Gerald Len
Foster, Gordon William
Foster, Joe Bill
Foster, John Strickland
Foster, Lawrence
Foster, Luther Hilton
Foster, Mark Gardner
Foster, Norman Ross
Foster, Paul David, Jr.
Foster, Paul Marvel
Foster, Robert Francis
Foster, Robert Lawson
Foster, Robert Watson
Foster, Ruel Elton
Foster, Susan Elizabeth
Foster, William Chapman
Foster, William Edwin (Bill)
Foulis, Ronald Jamieson
Foulkes, William Wilkinson, Jr.
Fountain, L.H.
Fountain, Peter Dewey, Jr.
Fouty, William Joseph
Fowinkle, Eugene W.
Fowler, Ben B.
Fowler, Conrad Murphree
Fowler, Daniel Eison
Fowler, David Wayne
Fowler, Henry Hamill
Fowler, Joseph William
Fowler, Raymond Dalton, Jr.
Fowler, Richard Edmond Lee
Fowler, Richard Gildart
Fowler, Samuel Benjamin
Fowler, William Wyche, Jr.
Fowlie, Wallace
Fox, Carroll Lawson
Fox, Cecil Edward
Fox, Edward Jackson
Fox, Frank
Fox, Henry Jackson
Fox, Jean Ann
Fox, John David
Fox, John George
Fox, John Michael
Fox, Lawrence Aaron
Fox, Matthew Ignatius
Fox, Michael Wilson
Fox, Paul Harris
Fox, Randall Louis
Fox, Robert Hamlon
Fox, Samuel Mickle, III
Fox, Sidney Walter
Fox, Vernon Brittain
Fox, William Robert
Foy, Joe Hardeman
Foy, Joseph Gerard
Foyt, A(nthony) J(oseph), (Jr.)
Frackelton, William Hamilton
Fragomen, Austin Thomas
Fraker, Elmer L.
France, Newell Edwin
Francis, Bill Dean
Francis, Darryl Robert
Francis, David Livingston
Francis, John Darrell
Francisco, Clyde Taylor
Francisco, George Joseph
Franck, Lawrence Joseph
Franck, William Francis
Franco, Johan (Henri Gustave)
Frank, Curtiss E.
Frank, Eli, Jr.
Frank, Elke
Frank, Isaiah
Frank, Jerome David
Frank, Michael M.
Frank, Richard Asher
Frank, Richard Horton, Jr.
Franklin, Alan Douglas
Franklin, Hardy R.
Franklin, Jon Daniel
Franklin, Omer W., Jr.
Franklin, Richard Ewell
Franklin, Robert Dumont
Franklin, Thomas Chester
Franks, Charles Leslie
Frantz, Ray William, Jr.
Fraser, Charles Elbert
Fraser, George Broadrup
Fraser, Kenneth William, Jr.
Fraser, Powell Alexander
Fraser, Thomas Augustus, Jr.
Frasure, Carl Maynard
Frates, William Snow
Frazer, Arthur Watson
Frazer, James Nisbet
Frazier, Dallas June
Frazier, Owsley Brown
Fread, Danny Lee
Freas, Frank Kelly
Frederick, Anthony Peter
Frederick, Joseph Francis, Jr.
Frederickson, Arman Frederick
Frederickson, Evan Lloyd
Fredine, Clarence Gordon
Fredland, John Roger
Fredrick, Laurence William
Fredrickson, Donald Sharp
Fredrickson, Jay Warren
Freed, David Clark
Freedberg, Irwin Mark
Freedman, Solomon
Freedman, Stanley Marvin
Freedman, Walter
Freehling, William Wilhartz
Freeland, T. Paul
Freeman, Corinne
Freeman, David Lynn
Freeman, Elsa S.
Freeman, George Clemon, Jr.
Freeman, George Lester
Freeman, Harry Lynwood
Freeman, Howard Lee, Jr.
Freeman, Joe Bailey, Jr.
Freeman, Kester St. Clair, Jr.
Freeman, (George) Lester
Freeman, Meredith Norwin
Freeman, Milton Victor
Freeman, Montine McDaniel
Freeman, Neal Blackwell
Freeman, Raymond Lee
Freeman, Richard C.
Freeman, Richard Merrell
Freeman, Richard West
Freeman, Robert L.
Freeman, Robert Turner, Jr.
Freeman, Rowland Godfrey, III
Freeman, Ruth Benson
Freeman, Simon David
Freeman, William Ernest, Jr.
Freemyer, Howard Ross
Freeze, James Donald
Freidberg, Sidney
Freireich, Emil J
Freis, Edward David
Freitag, Robert Frederick
Freling, Richard Alan
French, Bevan Meredith
French, Charles Ezra
French, Judson Cull
French, Robert Warren
French, William Daniel
Frenkil, Victor
Frenzel, Bill
Freret, Julian Payne
Freshley, Dwight Lowell
Fretwell, Elbert Kirtley, Jr.
Freudenberg, Boris
Freudenheim, Tom Lippmann
Freudenthal, Steven Franklin
Frey, Gerard Louis
Frey, James McKnight
Frey, Robert Ketterman
Freyberg, Richard Harold
Freyhan, Fritz Adolf
Fri, Robert Wheeler
Fricke, Howard Rudolph
Friday, Herschel Hugar
Friday, William Clyde
Fridlund, H(ilmer) Maurice
Fridovich, Irwin
Fried, Edward R.
Fried, Herbert Daniel
Fried, Melvin
Friedberg, Wallace
Friederich, Werner Paul
Friedewald, William Frank
Friedheim, Jerry Warden
Friedl, Ernestine (Mrs. Harry L. Levy)
Friedman, Alan Warren
Friedman, Alvin
Friedman, Ben Ignatius
Friedman, Edward David
Friedman, Herbert
Friedman, Joseph Bivens
Friedman, Louis Frank
Friedman, Malcolm
Friedman, Mark Willard
Friedman, Martin Jay
Friedman, Marvin Pushin
Friedman, Milton Arthur
Friedman, Myles Ivan
Friedrich, Lawrence William
Friedrichs, George Shelby
Friend, Edward Malcolm, Jr.
Frierson, John Burton, Jr.
Fries, Vollmer Walter
Frisbee, John Lee
Frischknecht, Lee Conrad
Frist, Thomas Fearn
Fritchey, Clayton
Frith, James Robert
Fritschler, A(llen) Lee
Frizzell, Kent
Froehlich, S. Charles
Froehlke, Robert Frederick
Frommhold, Lothar Werner
Fronterhouse, Gerald Wayne
Frosch, Robert Alan
Frost, Ellen Louise
Frost, Jonas Martin
Frost, Morris McCampbell
Frost, Norman Cooper
Frost, Shirley David (Dave)
Frost, Thomas Clayborne, Jr.
Frucci, Richard Lawrence
Fruit, Melvyn Herschel
Fruit, Melvyn Herschel
Fry, Arthur James
Fry, Edward Irad
Fry, Louis Edwin, Sr.
Fry, Malcolm Craig
Fry, Thomas Albert, Jr
Fry, William James
Fryar, Russell McKenzie
Frye, John H., Jr.
Frye, John William, III
Frye, Keith Nale
Frymire, Richard Lamar, Jr.
Fubini, Eugene Ghiron
Fudenberg, H. Hugh
Fuentealba, Victor William
Fuermann, George Melvin
Fugate, Douglas Brown
Fuhrman, Ralph Edward
Fulbright, James William
Fulcher, Martin Clay
Fulgham, John Rawles, Jr.
Fullenweider, Donn Charles
Fuller, Hoyt William
Fuller, Lawrence Joseph
Fuller, Marvin Don
Fuller, Melvin Stuart
Fuller, Morris Greenleaf
Fuller, Parrish
Fuller, Reginald Horace
Fuller, Robert Byron
Fuller, Robert Garfield
Fuller, William Sidney
Fullerton, Charles Gordon
Fullmer, Harold Milton
Fulmer, Robert M.
Fulton, Charles B.
Fulton, Conrad Hobart
Fulton, George Pearman, Jr.
Fulton, James Street
Fulton, Richard Alsina
Fulton, Richard Harmon
Fulton, Robert Burwell
Fulton, Thomas
Fulwiler, Robert Neal
Fumich, George M.
Funk, James (Ellis)
Funk, Paul Eugene
Funkhouser, A. Paul
Funkhouser, Richard Nelson
Fuqua, Don
Fuqua, John Brooks
Furbacher, Stephen A.
Furchtgott, Ernest
Furcolow, Michael Leo
Furey, Francis James
Furgurson, Ernest Baker, Jr.
Furino, Antonio
Furlong, Edward Colson, Jr.
Furlong, Raymond Bernard
Furman, Martin William
Furniss, Warren Todd
Furst, Lilian Renee
Furth, Hans Gerhard
Fuselier, Louis Alfred
Fuster, Jaime Benito
Gabhart, Herbert Conway
Gabianelli, Vincent James
Gable, G. Ellis
Gabriel, Charles Alvin
Gaddis, Paul Otto
Gade, Marvin Francis
Gadsden, Elmer Lewis, Jr.
Gadsden, Richard Hamilton
Gaebelein, Frank Ely
Gaffney, Thomas Edward
Gafford, Frank Hall
Gagliano, Frank Joseph
Gaglio, Sam Peter
Gagne, Robert Mills
Gaguine, Benito
Gailey, Franklin Bryan
Gailey, James Reed
Gaillard, John Palmer, Jr.
Gainer, Ronald Lee
Gaines, Alan McCulloch
Gaines, Alexander Pendleton
Gaither, Robert Barker
Gajdusek, Daniel Carleton
Galbraith, Francis Joseph
Galbraith, James Garber
Galbreath, Richmond Brierre
Gale, Robert L(ee)
Galinsky, Gotthard Karl
Galkin, Elliott Washington
Gall, Lawrence Howard
Gallagher, Hubert R.
Gallagher, James John
Gallagher, Michael Timothy
Gallagher, Walter Edward
Gallaher, Art, Jr.
Galland, Diana Baker
Gallander, Cathleen Sparks
Galler, Sidney Roland
Galliano, Vernon Frederick
Gallie, Thomas Muir, Jr.
Galligan, Clarence Joseph
Gallo, Robert Charles
Gallopo, Charles Peter
Galloway, Marion Barritt
Galloway, Mitchell Olin
Galloway, William Jefferson
Galphin, Bruce Maxwell
Galt, Barry J.
Galvin, Charles O'Neill
Galvin, Hoyt Rees
Gamble, Joseph Graham, Jr.
Gamble, Robert Dale
Gambrell, Barmore Pepper
Gambrell, David Henry
Gambrell, Enoch Smythe
Gamer, Saul Richard
Gammage, Robert Alton
Gammon, William Hugh
Gamser, Howard G.
Gandal, Alvin Harry
Gandy, Edythe Evelyn
Gangel, Kenneth Otto
Gannon, John Deane
Gano, John
Gant, James Lamar
Gant, Norman Ferrell, Jr.
Ganter, Bernard J.
Ganus, Clifton Loyd, Jr.
Garber, Paul Edward
Garbis, Marvin Joseph
Garcia, James David
Garcia, Julio Hernan
Garcia, Robert
Garcia-Palmieri, Mario Ruben
Gard, Robert Gibbins, Jr.
Gardiner, Donald Andrew
Gardiner, William Cecil, Jr.
Gardner, Alvin Frederick
Gardner, Clifford Speer
Gardner, Gene Pritchard
Gardner, Hilary Cherry
Gardner, Hoyt Devane
Gardner, Hy
Gardner, James Barrington
Gardner, John William
Gardner, Lucien Dunbibbin, Jr.
Gardner, Marshall C.
Gardner, R. H. (Rufus Hallette III)
Gardner, Robin Pierce
Gardner, Warner Winslow
Garelick, Martin
Garets, Wallace Earl
Garfinkel, Herbert
Garg, Devendra Prakash
Garibaldi, James Joseph
Garland, Robert DeWitt, Jr.
Garman, Willard Hershel
Garn, Edwin Jacob
Garner, Alto Luther
Garner, Henry Thomas
Garner, John Michael
Garner, Mildred Maxine
Garner, Samuel Paul
Garner, Stanton Berry
Garner, William Simpson
Garonzik, Jarrell
Garretson, Henry David
Garrett, Arthur Sellers
Garrett, Bernard Robert
Garrett, David Clyde, Jr.
Garrett, Edward Robert
Garrett, Ethel Shields
Garrett, Wilbur Eugene
Garrett, William Ray
Garrigus, Wesley Patterson
Garriott, Owen K.
Garrison, Lemuel Alonzo
Garrison, Marion Ames
Garrison, Mark Joseph
Garrison, Truitt B.
Garrison, William Carl
Garrity, James Franklin
Garrou, Louis William
Garsaud, Marcel, Jr.
Gart, Murray Joseph
Garthoff, Raymond Leonard
Gartland, William Joseph, Jr.
Garvey, Edward Robert
Garvey, John Leo
Garvey, Robert Robey, Jr.
Garwood, William Lockhart
Garwood, Wilmer St. John
Gary, Charles Lester
Gary, Theodore Sauvinet
Garza, Reynaldo G.
Gasch, Oliver
Gaskell, James Shields, Jr.
Gaskill, Richard Tillman
Gastler, Harold Lee
Gaston, David Aiken
Gaston, Gerald Nicholas
Gastwirth, Joseph Lewis
Gates, Charles Bernard, Jr.
Gates, Dillard Herbert
Gates, Howard Perry, Jr.
Gates, James David
Gates, Leslie Clifford
Gates, Theodore Ross
Gates, William Fred, Jr.
Gates, William Lewis
Gatewood, Willard Badgett, Jr.
Gathright, Joseph Radford
Gatlin, Larry Wayne
Gauch, Eugene William, Jr.
Gauer, Charlotte Edwina
Gault, Thomas Gower
Gault, Willis Manning
Gauthier, Victor Arthur, Jr.
Gautreaux, Marcelian Francis, Jr.
Gavazzi, Aladino A.
Gavenda, J(ohn) David
Gaver, Mary Virginia
Gay, J. Edwin
Gay, William Ingalls
Gayle, Gibson, Jr.
Gayles, Joseph Nathan Webster, Jr.
Gaylord, Charles Nelson
Gaylord, Edward Lewis
Gaynor, Florence Small
Gazin, Charles Lewis
Gazzolo, Dorothy Haven
Geber, Anthony
Gee, Lynn LaMar
Gee, Thomas Gibbs
Geeker, Nicholas Peter
Geer, Ronald Lamar
Geer, William Dudley
Geerdes, James (Divine)
Gehrig, Leo Joseph
Gehring, Mary Louise
Gehron, William Jules
Geib, Philip Oldham
Geiberger, Allen L.
Geiger, Robert Keith
Geis, Duane Virgil
Geisert, Gene A.
Geisert, Wayne Frederick

REGIONAL LISTING—SOUTH-SOUTHWEST 846

Gelb, Leslie Howard
Gelband, Stephen Laurence
Gelboin, Harry Victor
Gelfand, Meyer
Gelfand, Meyer
Geller, Henry
Gellhorn, Ernest Albert Eugene
Gelsey, Stephen Ian
Geltz, Charles Gottlieb
Gemmill, Henry
Gennetti, William Thomas
Gentile, Arthur Christopher
Gentry, Bern Leon
Gentry, Dwight Lonnie
Gentry, John N.
Gentry, Robert Vance
George, Austin Herbert
George, Beauford James, Jr.
George, Claude Swanson, Jr.
George, Marcus Benjamin
George, Ronald Baylis
George, Scott
George, Walter Eugene, Jr.
Georgiade, Nicholas George
Georgiades, William Den Hartog
Geraghty, John James
Gerald, Barry Elmo
Gerard, Forrest J.
Gerber, Joseph Newton
Gerber, William
Gerbermann, Hugo Mark
Gerbino, John
Gerhardt, Harrison Alan
Gericke, Paul William
Germany, Thomas Gordy
Gerschefski, Edwin
Gershon, Elliot Sheldon
Gerstel, Dan Ulrich
Gert, Gerard Martin
Gervasi, Frank
Gesell, Gerhard Alden
Geshwiler, Joseph Elton
Gessow, Alfred
Getman, Frank Newton
Gettemy, James Noah
Getting, Vlado Andrew
Gettys, Thomas Smithwick
Gevantman, Lewis Herman
Gewin, Walter Pettus
Geyer, Alan
Geyer, Charles Edgar
Geyer, Georgie Anne
Geyer, John Charles
Geyer, Richard Adam
Ghiardi, John Felix Linus
Gholson, Cecil Jack
Ghormley, Ralph McDougall
Ghormley, William Kerr
Giaimo, Robert Nicholas
Giannini, Valerio Louis
Gianturco, Delio E.
Gibbard, Harold Allan
Gibbens, James Cottingham
Gibbons, John Howard
Gibbons, Joseph John
Gibbons, Paul Coy, Jr.
Gibbons, Sam Melville
Gibbs, Alan John
Gibbs, Charles Haskell
Gibbs, Delbridge Lindley
Gibbs, Hubert Smith
Gibbs, Raymond Douglas
Gibian, Thomas George
Giblin, Patrick David
Gibson, Arrell Morgan
Gibson, Charles Merritt, Jr.
Gibson, Dale Lynn
Gibson, David Argyle
Gibson, Everett Kay, Jr.
Gibson, Foye Goodner
Gibson, George Dandridge
Gibson, Glenn Venning
Gibson, Harold Burton, Jr.
Gibson, Jerry Leigh
Gibson, Ralph Edward
Gibson, Sam Thompson
Gifford, Porter William
Gifford, William Leo
Gil, Federico Guillermo
Gilbart, Arthur William
Gilbert, Allan H.
Gilbert, Anne Wieland
Gilbert, Ben William
Gilbert, Charles Richard Alsop
Gilbert, Harold Stanley
Gilbert, Leonard Harold
Gilbert, Perry Webster
Gilbert, Robert Randle, III
Gilbreth, Frank Bunker, Jr.
Gildenhorn, Joseph Bernard
Giles, Alexander Wetheral, Jr.
Giles, Norman Henry
Giles, Thomas D.
Gilinsky, Victor
Gilkerson, Yancey Sherard
Gill, Atticus James
Gill, George Norman
Gill, Samuel Lafayette, Jr.
Gill, William Albert, Jr.
Gillen, William Albert
Gillenwater, James E.
Gillenwater, Jay Young
Giller, Edward Bonfoy
Giller, Norman Myer
Gillespie, Edward Malcolm
Gillespie, Robert Gill
Gillette, Hyde
Gilley, James Ray
Gilley, Mickey Leroy
Gillham, Nicholas Wright
Gilliam, Carroll Lewis
Gilliam, John Charles
Gilliam, John Rally
Gilliland, Charles Herbert, Sr.
Gilliland, William Elton
Gillilland, Whitney
Gillingham, William James
Gilliom, Judith Carr
Gillis, Everett Alden
Gillman, Leonard
Gillon, John William
Gilman, Donald Lawrence
Gilman, Lauren Cundiff
Gilmer, B. von Haller
Gilmer, Robert William, Jr.
Gilmore, Gordon Leonard
Gilmore, Harry Bassett, Jr.
Gilmore, Jerry Carl
Gilmore, Voit
Gilreath, Esmarch Senn
Gilruth, Robert Rowe
Gimenez-Munoz, Miguel Angel
Gingrich, Newton Leroy
Ginn, Olin Winton
Ginn, Ronald (Bo)
Ginn, Ronn
Ginsberg, Leon Herman
Ginsberg, Milton
Ginsberg, Reuben M.
Ginsberg, Stewart Theodore
Ginsburg, Charles David
Ginsburg, Marcus
Ginsburg, Robert Nathan
Ginsburgh, Robert Neville
Ginzburg, Yankel Jacob
Giordano, Andrew Anthony
Giordano, John Read
Girand, Charles Andrew
Girard, Louis Joseph
Girard, René Noel
Giroir, Charles Joseph, Jr.
Girone, Vito Anthony
Girvin, Eb Carl
Giss, Vernon Jacob
Gist, Howard Battle, Jr.
Githens, Sherwood, Jr.
Givens, Johnnie Esther
Givens, Joseph Edwin
Givens, Paul Ronald
Glade, William Patton, Jr.
Gladieux, Bernard Louis
Glancy, Walter John
Glaser, Michael Lance
Glaser, Vera Romans
Glasgow, Jesse Edward
Glasier, Charles Henry
Glass, Bryan Pettigrew
Glass, Carson McElyea
Glass, Henry Edward
Glass, Thomas Franklin, Jr.
Glassell, Alfred Curry, Jr.
Glasser, Otto John
Glasser, Paul Harold
Glasser, Robert Gene
Glassie, Henry Haywood
Glassman, Armand Barry
Glassman, Edward
Glazer, Esther
Glazer, Frederic Jay
Glazer, Larry Sylvester
Gleason, Jackie
Gleason, Ralph Newton
Gleazer, Edmund John, Jr.
Gleckner, Robert Francis
Glenn, Charles Melancthon, Jr.
Glenn, James Francis
Glenn, Michael Douglas
Glenn, Norval Dwight
Glenn, Terrell Lyles
Glennan, Thomas Keith
Glick, Jacob Ezra
Glick, Paul Charles
Glick, Philip Milton
Glick, Richard Edwin
Glick, Warren W.
Glickman, Daniel Robert
Glidden, Robert Burr
Glindeman, Henry Peter, Jr.
Glines, Carroll Vane, Jr.
Glocker, Theodore Wesley, Jr.
Gloster, Hugh Morris
Glover, Charles Carroll, III
Glover, Clifford Clarke
Gloyna, Earnest Frederick
Gluckstern, Robert Leonard
Goade, William Richard
Goald, Harold Jerome
Godard, James McFate
Godbold, Jake Maurice
Godbold, John Cooper
Godchaux, Frank Area, III
Goddard, Joseph Paul
Godding, George Arthur
Godenne, Ghislaine Dudley
Godfrey, Garland Alonzo
Godfrey, James Logan
Godley, Gene Edwin
Godshall, Henry Stites
Godwin, Charles William
Godwin, Mills Edwin, Jr.
Goeden, James Peter
Goedicke, Hans
Goeglein, Richard John
Goekjian, Samuel Vahram
Goellner, Jack Gordon
Goelz, Paul Cornelius
Goers, Melvin Armand
Goethert, Bernhard Hermann
Goff, Regina Mary
Goff, Robert Burnside
Goforth, Foy Nelson
Goglia, Gennaro Louis
Goglia, Mario Joseph
Goin, Lauren Jackson
Going, Allen Johnston
Goizueta, Roberto Crispulo
Goland, Martin
Gold, Bill (William Emil)
Goldberg, Arthur Joseph
Goldberg, Arthur Samuel
Goldberg, Chaim
Goldberg, Harold
Goldberg, Herman Raphael
Goldberg, Irving Loeb
Goldberg, Joel
Goldberg, Seymour
Goldburg, Norman Michael
Golden, Harry
Golden, Hawkins
Golden, Leon
Golden, Max
Golden, William Lee
Goldfarb, Ronald Lawrence
Goldfield, Edwin David
Goldhaber, Jacob Kopel
Goldhurst, William
Golding, Martin Philip
Golding, Stuart Samuel
Goldman, Aaron
Goldman, Joseph Bernard
Goldman, Joseph Elias
Goldman, Ralph
Goldman, Richard Franko
Goldner, Herman Wilson
Goldner, Joseph Leonard
Goldschmidt, Neil Edward
Goldsmith, Jack Landman
Goldsmith, John Alan
Goldsmith, Robert Hillis
Goldsmith, Samuel Lunt, Jr.
Goldstein, Allan Leonard
Goldstein, Burton Jack
Goldstein, Carl Liptner
Goldstein, Elliott
Goldstein, Harold
Goldstein, Lewis Charles
Goldstein, Louis Lazarus
Goldstein, Murray
Goldstein, Robert Arnold
Goldthwait, Richard Parker
Goldwater, Barry Morris, Jr.
Goldwater, Leonard John
Golembiewski, Robert Thomas
Golemon, Albert Sidney
Gollattscheck, James Franklin
Gollmar, Richard Jacob
Golodner, Jack
Gomez, Rudolph
Gomezplata, Albert
Gompf, Arthur Milton
Gong, Edmond Joseph
Gonzales, Brother Alexis (Joseph M. Gonzales)
Gonzales, John Edmond
González, Abelardo
Gonzalez, Henry B.
Gonzalez, Jose Alejandro, Jr.
Gonzalez, Nancie Loudon
Gonzalez, Richard Joseph
Gonzalez-Oliver, Wallace
Gooch, James Thomas
Good, Dale Edward
Good, Laurance Frederic
Good, Leonard Phelps
Good, Mary Lowe (Mrs. Billy Jewel Good)
Goodale, Fairfield
Goodall, Leon Steele
Goodby, James Eugene
Goodchild, Chauncey George
Goode, Lewis Bouldin, Jr.
Goode, Mackarness Hutchins
Goode, Marian Elizabeth
Goode, Richard Benjamin
Goodell, Charles Ellsworth
Goodell, Sol
Gooden, Reginald Heber
Goodling, William F.
Goodman, Benjamin
Goodner, Dwight Benjamin
Goodner, James Ernest
Goodrich, George Herbert
Goodrich, Nathaniel Herman
Goodrich, Richard Lane
Goodridge, Marjorie A. Stewart (Mrs. George Goodridge)
Goodson, Carl Edward
Goodson, James Butler
Goodson, Louie Aubrey, Jr.
Goodson, Walter Kenneth
Goodstein, Barnett Maurice
Goodwin, Andrew Jackson
Goodwin, Claude Elbert
Goodwin, Craufurd David
Goodwin, Frederick King
Goodwin, George Evans
Goodwin, Merrill Harry
Goodwyn, Ulysses Vincent
Goodykoontz, Charles Alfred
Goodykoontz, Harry Gordon
Goolsbee, Charles Thomas
Goott, Daniel
Goralski, Robert
Gordh, George Rudolph
Gordon, Charles
Gordon, Eugene Andrew
Gordon, H. Stephan
Gordon, Harold
Gordon, Harry Bernard
Gordon, Jack David
Gordon, Jack Murphy
Gordon, James Braund
Gordon, James Fleming
Gordon, Joseph Elwell
Gordon, Lincoln
Gordon, Richard Edwards
Gordon, Robert Charles Frost
Gordon, Robert Sirkosky, Jr.
Gordon, Samuel Cantey, Jr.
Gordon, Thomas Christian, Jr.
Gordon, William Edwin
Gordon, William Talbott
Gordy, Walter
Gore, Albert, Jr.
Gore, Albert Arnold
Gore, George William, Jr.
Gore, Jack Worter
Gore, Willis Carroll
Goren, Charles Henry
Gorham, William
Gorin, George
Gorman, Burton William
Gorman, Cornelius Eugene
Gormley, William Clarke
Gorodetzky, Charles William
Gorovitz, Samuel
Gorrell, Frank Cheatham
Gorsline, George William
Gorsuch, George Edward
Gorwitz, Bertram Kall
Gose, Wulf Achim
Gosling, John Alfred
Gosnell, Harold Cornelius
Goss, James Walter
Gossett, Ed
Gossick, Lee Van
Gossman, Francis Joseph
Gott, Vincent Lynn
Gottfried, Brian Edward
Gottlieb, A(braham) Arthur
Gottlieb, Bertram
Gottschalk, Carl William
Gottschalk, Charles Max
Gottschalk, John Simison
Gottschalk, Mary Therese
Gottwald, Bruce Cobb
Gottwald, Floyd Dewey, Jr.
Gotwals, Charles Place, Jr.
Gould, Bernard Albert
Gould, Gordon
Gould, Kenneth Lawrence
Gould, Samuel Brookner
Goulden, Charles Evans
Goulden, Joseph Chesley
Goulding, Phil G.
Gouraud, Jackson S.
Gourley, Desmond Robert Hugh
Gourley, James Edwin
Gouse, S. William, Jr.
Govan, James Fauntleroy
Govan, Mary Christine Noble
Grace, William Porter
Gracida, Rene Henry
Graddick, Charles Allen
Grady, Thomas J.
Graebner, Norman Arthur
Graf, LeRoy Philip
Graff, William
Graffis, Herb
Grafton, Martha Stackhouse (Mrs. Thomas H. Grafton)
Grafton, Thurman Stanford
Gragg, Williford
Graham, Cameron Russell
Graham, Charles Passmore
Graham, Clarence R.
Graham, D. Robert (Bob)
Graham, Daniel Arthur
Graham, David Anthony
Graham, Donald Edward
Graham, Ford Mulford
Graham, Fred Patterson
Graham, George Adams
Graham, George Gordon
Graham, Gordon Marion
Graham, Hugh Davis
Graham, James Bernard
Graham, James Herbert
Graham, John Borden
Graham, Katharine
Graham, William Edgar, Jr.
Graham, William Franklin
Gram, Harvey B., Jr.
Grambs, Jean Dresden
Gramley, Dale Hartzler
Gramley, Lyle Elden
Gramm, William Philip
Grand, John Louis Rochon
Grandfield, Gerald Boyd
Grandy, Cyrus Wiley
Grange, David Ellsworth, Jr.
Graning, Harald Martin
Grant, Byron Eldredge
Grant, Daniel Ross
Grant, Edward Donald
Grant, James Pineo
Grant, Joseph Moorman
Grant, Lindsey
Grant, Murray
Grant, Verne Edwin
Grantham, Dewey Wesley
Grantham, George Leighton
Grantham, Roy Emery
Graser, Clarence Francis
Grassie, Joseph Roberts
Grassley, Charles E.
Grattan, Clinton Hartley
Gratz, Pauline
Graue, Fremont David
Gravel, Camille Francis, Jr.
Gravel, Mike
Gravenstein, Joachim Stefan
Graves, Allen Willis
Graves, Austin Taylor
Graves, Benjamin Barnes
Graves, Edward S.
Graves, Ernest, Jr.
Graves, Harold Nathan, Jr.
Graves, Lawrence Lester
Graves, Lawrence P.
Graves, Thomas Ashley, Jr.
Graves, Walter Albert
Gray, C. Vernon
Gray, David Lawrence
Gray, Duncan Montgomery, Jr.
Gray, Edward Zigmund
Gray, Elizabeth Stuart
Gray, Frank Truan
Gray, Fred David
Gray, Frederick Thomas, Jr.
Gray, Gordon
Gray, James Alexander
Gray, John Edmund
Gray, Myles McClure
Gray, Oscar Shalom
Gray, Robert Keith
Gray, Robert Steele
Gray, Robin Bryant
Gray, Warren Philips
Gray, William H., III
Graybeal, Sidney Norman
Graybiel, Ashton
Graydon, Augustus Tompkins
Grays, Mattelia Bennett
Grayson, Cary Travers, Jr.
Grayson, Charles Jackson, Jr.
Grayson, James McDonald
Grayson, Walton, III
Grayson, Walton George, III
Greacen, Thomas Edmund, II
Greaves, Thomas Guy, Jr.
Grecco, William Louis
Greeley, Arthur White
Greeley, John Bernard, III
Green, Al
Green, Alice
Green, Asa Norman
Green, Bert Franklin, Jr.
Green, Cecil Howard
Green, Ernest Gideon
Green, Fitzhugh
Green, Frances Marian
Green, Gareth Montraville
Green, James Collins
Green, James Wyche
Green, Jerome George
Green, Joe Morris, Jr.
Green, John Cawley
Green, Joyce Hens
Green, June Lazenby
Green, Laurence Burton
Green, Leon, Jr.
Green, Lucien Astor
Green, Margaret
Green, Mark Joseph
Green, Marshall
Green, Norman Kenneth
Green, Paul Eliot
Green, Richard Alan
Green, Richard James
Green, Robert Edward, Jr.
Green, S. William
Green, Thomas Fitzgerald
Green, Wallace Orpheus
Green, William Paul
Greenaway, Donald
Greenbacker, John Everett
Greenbaum, Lowell Marvin
Greenberg, Bernard George
Greenberg, Frank S.
Greenberg, Howard
Greenberg, Isidore M.
Greenberg, Melvin Nathaniel
Greenberg, Michael John
Greenberg, Oscar Wallace
Greenberg, Paul
Greenberg, Sanford David
Greenberger, Martin
Greenblatt, Robert Benjamin
Greene, A(lvin) C(arl)
Greene, Charles Herbert
Greene, Charles Jerome
Greene, Francis Thornton
Greene, George Benjamin, Jr.
Greene, Harold H.
Greene, Harris
Greene, Jack Phillip
Greene, John William, Jr.
Greene, Joseph Arthur, Jr.
Greene, Jule Blounte
Greene, Lamont Robert
Greene, Lee Seifert
Greene, Mark Richard
Greene, Michael Joseph Lenihan
Greene, Raleigh Williams, Jr.
Greene, Robert Zemon
Greenfield, Alfred M.
Greenfield, Joseph Cholmondeley, Jr.
Greenfield, Lazar John
Greenfield, Meg
Greenfield, Taylor Hatton
Greenfield, Wilbert
Greenhill, Eleanor Simmons
Greenhill, Joe R.
Greenhut, Melvin Leonard
Greenlaw, Ralph Weller
Greenspan, Donald
Greenspan, Martin
Greenwalt, Lynn Adams
Greenwood, James, Jr.
Greenwood, Pat Minter
Greenwood, Robert Ewing
Greenwood, William Frank
Greenwood, William Thomas
Greer, Edward
Greer, Germaine
Greer, Joseph Moss
Greer, Melvin
Greer, Thomas Upton
Greer, Thomas Vernon
Gregg, Arthur James
Gregg, James Calvin
Gregg, Walter Emmor
Gregory, Bettina Louise
Gregory, Edward Wadsworth, Jr.
Gregory, George Tillman, Jr.
Gregory, John Mason Moody, Jr.
Gregory, Robert Earle, Jr.
Gregory, Robert Todd
Gregory, Thorne
Gregory, Walton Carlyle
Gregory, William Hamilton
Greiner, Morris Esty, Jr.
Gremillion, Curtis Lionel, Jr.
Grenga, Helen Eva
Grenier, Arthur Sylvester, Jr.
Gresham, Newton
Gresham, Perry Epler
Gresham, Robert Coleman
Gressette, Lawrence Marion
Gressman, Eugene
Greulich, Richard Curtice
Greve, Donald Joe
Grevelle, James Vernon
Grey, James David
Gribble, Lloyd Raymond
Gribbon, Daniel McNamara
Grider, George William
Grier, Joseph Williamson, Jr.
Grier, Paul Livingston
Gries, George Alexander
Griese, Robert Allen
Griessman, Benjamin Eugene
Grieves, Robert Belanger
Griffen, Ward Orin, Jr.
Griffenhagen, George Bernard
Griffies, Hiram Farrell
Griffin, Benjamin Ernest
Griffin, Gerald Duane
Griffin, Henry Ludwig
Griffin, John Howard
Griffin, John Toole
Griffin, Marvin Anthony
Griffin, Oscar O'Neal, Jr.
Griffin, Ralph Harrell
Griffin, Robert Thomas
Griffin, Tom
Griffin, William Hancock
Griffing, Clayton Allen
Griffith, Edwin Claybrook
Griffith, Ernest Stacey
Griffith, James William
Griffith, Oran Heaton
Griffith, Wayland Coleman
Griffiths, Charles Henry
Griffiths, Victor Segismundo
Griffy, Thomas Alan
Grigg, Milton LaTour
Grigg, William Humphrey
Griggy, Kenneth Joseph
Grigorieff, Wladimir W.
Grigsby, Margaret Elizabeth
Grim, Jerry
Grim, Samuel Oram
Grimball, William Heyward
Grimditch, William Henry, Jr.
Grimes, Stephen Henry
Grimsley, James Alexander, Jr.
Grimson, Keith Sanford
Grisham, Frank Phillips
Grisham, Joe Wheeler
Grisham, Wayne R.
Grissom, J. David
Griswold, Benjamin Howell, III
Griswold, Erwin Nathaniel
Grobel, Olaf
Groebli, Werner Fritz (Mr. Frick)
Grollman, Arthur
Groner, Frank Shelby
Groner, Pat Neff
Gronouski, John Austin
Groom, Dale
Grooms, Harlan Hobart
Gropp, Armin Henry
Grose, Robert Warfield
Groseclose, Elgin
Gross, Bernard Joseph
Gross, Charles Wayne
Gross, Dean Cochran
Gross, George Myron
Gross, John Birney
Gross, Patrick Walter
Gross, Paul
Gross, Samson Richard
Grosslight, Joseph Henry
Grossman, Lawrence
Grossman, Lawrence Kugelmass
Grossman, Robert George
Grosvenor, Gilbert Melville
Grosvenor, John Homer, Jr.
Grosvenor, Melville Bell
Grothmann, Carl Ellis
Grotz, William Arthur
Grove, Brandon Hambright, Jr.
Grove, Edward Ryneal
Grovenstein, Erling, Jr.
Grover, Eve Ruth
Grover, Norman LaMotte
Grover, Robert Lawrence
Groves, George L., Jr.
Groves, Harry Edward
Grub, Phillip Donald
Grubb, Donald Hartman
Grubb, H. Dale
Grubb, Wilson Lyon
Grubbs, William Eugene, Jr.
Gruber, Fredric Francis
Gruber, William Edward
Gruenberg, Ernest Matsner
Gruenberg, Robert
Gruenberg, Robert Pershing
Gruene, Hans Friedrich
Grumbach, Doris
Grunwald, Joseph
Grzybowski, Kazimierz
Guandolo, John
Guard, Ray Wesley
Guarino, Armand John
Gubelmann, Walter Stanley
Gude, Gilbert
Gudger, Lamar
Guenther, Jack Egon
Guerin, Dean Patrick

Guerin, John William
Guernsey, James Meredith
Guernsey, Joseph Shedd
Guerrero, E.T.
Guess, Wallace Louis
Guest, Maurice Mason
Guffin, Gilbert L.
Gugelot, Piet Cornelis
Guice, John Thompson
Guidry, George Joseph, Jr.
Guidry, Marion Antoine
Guidry, Ronald Ames
Guild, Nelson Prescott
Guild, Walter Rufus
Guilds, John Caldwell, Jr.
Guillot, Robert Miller
Guin, Junius Foy, Jr.
Guinn, Dick Henry
Guinn, George Earl
Guittar, Lee John
Gulick, Clarence Swift
Gulick, John
Gull, Cloyd Dake
Gullander, Werner Paul
Gulley, Warren L.
Gulley, Wilbur Paul, Jr.
Gulliver, Harold Strong
Gully, Arnold Jarvis
Gummere, Walter Cooper
Gumpert, Gunther
Gunn, Hartford Nelson, Jr.
Gunning, John Thaddeus
Gunter, Annie Laurie
Gunter, Gordon
Gunter, William Dawson, Jr.
Gupta, Om Prakash
Gurin, Samuel
Gurney, Edward John
Gurney, James Thomas
Gurtner, Wendell Jones
Gushman, John Louis
Gussman, Herbert
Gustafson, Dwight Leonard
Guste, William Joseph, Jr.
Gutermuth, Clinton Raymond
Guth, Donald John
Guth, Paul Spencer
Guthe, Alfred Kidder
Gutheim, Frederick
Gutheim, Robert Julius
Guthrie, Eugene Harding
Guthrie, Frank Edwin
Guthrie, John Conaughty
Guthrie, John Reiley
Guthrie, Randolph Hobson
Guthrie, Robert Lee
Guttman, Helene Nathan
Guy, Charles Walker
Guyer, Tennyson
Guyton, Arthur Clifton
Guyton, Jack Smallwood
Guyton, Robert Pool
Guzman, Ralph
Gwaltney, Jack Merrit, Jr.
Gwathmey, Owen
Haag, William George
Haar, James (Edward)
Haas, Frederick Peter
Haas, George Aaron
Haas, Josef
Haas, Joseph F.
Haas, Joseph Marshall
Haas, Lester Carl
Haas, Paul Raymond
Haas, Warren James
Haber, Francis Colin
Habermann, Helen Margaret
Hack, John Tilton
Hack, Marvin H.
Hackel, Donald Benjamin
Hackel, Stella Bloomberg
Hackerman, Norman
Hackethorn, Harry Bert
Hackl, Alphons J.
Haddad, Eugene
Haddon, William, Jr.
Haddy, Francis John
Haden, Charles H., II
Hadlow, Earl Bryce
Hadsel, Fred Latimer
Haeckel, Gerald Burseth
Haeffner, Fred Albert
Haehnel, William Otto, Jr.
Haffer, Louis Paul
Hafstad, Lawrence Randolph
Hagadorn, Irvine Rey
Hagan, Clifford Oldham
Hagan, John Aubrey
Hagan, Robert Leslie
Hagan, Wallace Woodrow
Hagedorn, Judy Wright
Hagedorn, Thomas Michael
Hagemeyer, Hugh John
Hagemeyer, Richard Herman
Hager, George Philip
Hager, Lawrence White, Sr.
Haggerty, Patrick Eugene
Hagman, Robert Thomas
Hagood, Annabel Dunham
Hagood, Charles Lyman
Hahn, Gilbert, Jr.
Hahn, James Maglorie
Haile, James Francis
Haiman, Robert James
Hain, Bruce Valentine
Haines, Lewis Francis
Hairston, Guy Edward, Jr.
Hairston, John Thomas, Jr.
Hairston, Nelson George
Hairston, William Russell, Jr.
Haizlip, Henry Hardin, Jr.
Halbach, Joseph James
Halberstam, Michael Joseph
Halbouty, Michel Thomas
Haldeman, Joe William
Hale, Joseph Rice
Hale, Laurence Swart
Hale, Lucius Melvin
Hale, Mason Ellsworth, Jr.
Hale, Nancy
Hale, Oron James
Hales, David Foster
Haley, James Andrew
Haley, Roger Kendall
Halford, Robert Lavelle
Hall, A. James
Hall, Albert Carruthers
Hall, Arthur Raymond, Jr.
Hall, Charles Washington
Hall, Charles William
Hall, Donald Perry
Hall, E. Eugene
Hall, Edward Byron
Hall, Elisha Anderson, Jr.
Hall, Ernest E.
Hall, Esther Jane Wood
Hall, Frank Dawson
Hall, Hal Ogden
Hall, Harold Emile
Hall, Hugh David
Hall, James Curtis
Hall, Joe Beasman
Hall, John Lewis
Hall, John Richard
Hall, Joseph Edgar
Hall, Kenneth Keller
Hall, Miles Lewis, Jr.
Hall, O. Glen
Hall, Ogden Henderson
Hall, R(oyal) Glenn
Hall, Robert Bruce
Hall, Robert Howell
Hall, Robert Thallon
Hall, Rufus George
Hall, Sam Blakeley, Jr.
Hall, Thomas Oscar, Jr.
Hall, Thor
Hall, Tom T.
Hall, Tony P.
Hall, Warren Esterly, Jr.
Hall, William Charles
Hall, William Darlington
Hall, William Stone
Halladay, Daniel Whitney
Halle, Katherine Murphy
Halleck, Charles White
Haller, Ellis Metcalf
Halley, James Harvey
Hallgren, Richard Edwin
Halliburton, Gus Gordon
Hallman, Grady Lamar, Jr.
Halloran, Bernard Thorpe
Halloran, Richard Colby
Hallowell, John Hamilton
Hallstein, D. Wayne
Halperin, Samuel
Halperin, Victor
Halpern, James Bladen
Halpine, Stuart Francis
Halsema, James J(ulius)
Halsey, Ashley
Halsey, James A.
Halsey, James Herron, Jr.
Halsted, John Mac Harg
Haltom, Elbert Bertram, Jr.
Ham, Joe Strother, Jr.
Hamall, Thomas Kenny
Hamarneh, Sami Khalaf
Hamblet, Newman
Hamburg, Carl Heinz
Hamburg, David A.
Hamburg, Joseph
Hamel, Dana Bertrand
Hames, Clifford Moffett
Hamff, Leonard Harvey
Hamilton, Charles Henry
Hamilton, Earle Grady, Jr.
Hamilton, George E., Jr.
Hamilton, George Hege, IV
Hamilton, George Henry, Jr.
Hamilton, Grace Towns
Hamilton, Harold Philip
Hamilton, Herman Lynn, Jr.
Hamilton, Howard Laverne
Hamilton, James Buford
Hamilton, Joseph Hants, Jr.
Hamilton, Joseph Heberling
Hamilton, Lee Herbert
Hamilton, Peter Bannerman
Hamilton, Robert Morrison
Hamilton, Robert Woodruff
Hamilton, Thomas Earle
Hamilton, William Berry, Jr.
Hamilton, William Cowles
Hamit, Harold Francis
Hamlet, James Frank
Hamlet, Kenneth Bruce
Hamlett, Samuel Barksdale
Hamlin, James Turner, III
Hamlin, Robert Henry
Hamm, Charles John
Hamm, Edward Frederick, Jr.
Hammaker, Paul M.
Hamme, Donald George
Hammer, Carl
Hammer, Philip Gibbon
Hammerschmidt, John Paul
Hammerschmidt, William Warner
Hammett, John William, Jr.
Hammock, Joseph Culver
Hammock, Leon Russell
Hammond, Edwin Hughes
Hammond, Guyton Bowers
Hammond, Harold Francis
Hammond, John Payne
Hammond, Lawrence Austin
Hammond, William Rogers
Hammonds, George Hamilton
Hampton, Ambrose Gonzales
Hampton, Mark Garrison
Hampton, Robert Norris
Hamrick, Claude Meredith
Hamrick, John Asa
Hamrick, John Asa
Hanahan, Donald James
Hanau, Richard
Hanbury, George Lafayette, II
Hance, Kent R.
Hanchey, Richard Howard
Hancock, Ian Francis
Hancock, M(arion) Donald
Hand, Charles Connor
Hand, W.G.
Hand, William Brevard
Handin, John Walter
Handler, Philip
Handley, Leon Hunter
Handyside, Holsey Gates
Haneman, Vincent Siering, Jr.
Hanes, David Gordon
Hanes, Frank Borden
Hanes, Fred William
Hanes, Gordon
Hanes, John Wesley, Jr.
Hanfling, Robert Irwin
Hanford, William Edward
Hanft, Ruth S. Samuels (Mrs. Herbert Hanft)
Hanigan, John Leonard
Hanke, Byron Reidt
Hanke, Steven Harold
Hankenson, E. Craig, Jr.
Hankins, Jack Franklin
Hankins, James Edwin (Mike)
Hankins, Richard Poole
Hanks, Nancy
Hanks, Robert Jack
Hanle, Paul Arthur
Hann, J. David
Hann, Roy William, Jr.
Hannah, John Henry, Jr.
Hannah, Norman Britton
Hannan, Philip Matthew
Hannaway, Owen
Hannay, Allen Burroughs
Hanneman, Richard Harvey
Hannum, Erwin Charles
Hanrahan, Edward Stephenson
Hanrahan, Robert Joseph
Hanscom, Daniel Herbert
Hansen, George Vernon
Hansen, Herbert Edwin
Hansen, Hobart Garfield
Hansen, John Paul
Hansen, Morris Howard
Hansen, Niles Maurice
Hansen, Orval
Hansen, Peter Sijer
Hansen, Richard Alan
Hansen, Zenon Clayton Raymond
Hanson, Angus Alexander
Hanson, Carl Thor
Hanson, Clarence Bloodworth, Jr.
Hanson, Duane Elwood
Hanson, Durwin Melford
Hanson, Roger Wayne
Hanson, Victor Henry, II
Hapala, Milan Ernest
Harbaugh, Jane Worth
Harbaugh, William Henry
Harbert, John Murdoch
Harbin, John Pickens
Harbin, Wayne DeWitt
Harbison, William James
Hardaway, Robert Morris, III
Hardberger, Phillip Duane
Hardeen, Theodore, Jr.
Harden, John William
Harden, Richard Martin
Harder, Frederick Eugene John
Harder, Hudson Orlan
Hardesty, Boyd Archer
Hardesty, Charles Howard, Jr.
Hardie, Robert Howle
Hardiman, Joseph Raymond
Hardin, Dale Wayne
Hardin, Eugene Brooks, Jr.
Hardin, George Cecil, Jr.
Hardin, Hal D.
Hardin, Harold Frank, Jr.
Hardin, Joseph Walker
Harding, Fann
Harding, Harold Friend
Harding, Hurshel Rudolph
Harding, Warren Gamaliel
Hardison, Osborne Bennett, Jr.
Hardman, William Edward
Hardre, Jacques
Hardway, Wendell Gary
Hardwick, John Harold
Hardy, George
Hardy, James Daniel
Hardy, Paul Jude
Hardy, Thomas Cresson
Hare, Francis Hutcheson
Hare, Raymond Arthur
Hare, Woodrow Wilson
Harford, Carol Vivian
Harger, Robert Owens
Hargrave, Rudolph
Hargraves, J. Archie
Hargrove, James Ward
Hargrove, Linda
Haring, Ellen Stone (Mrs. E.S. Haring)
Harkaway, William Irving
Harkey, Ira Brown, Jr.
Harkey, John Norman
Harkin, Thomas R.
Harkins, James Archibald
Harkness, Mary Lou
Harkrader, Carleton Allen
Harkrader, Charles Johnston, Jr.
Harlan, James Clarke
Harlan, John Frederick, Jr.
Harlan, Roma Christine
Harlan, Ross Edgar
Harlan, W. Glen
Harley, William Gardner
Harllee, John
Harlow, Harold Eugene
Harlow, James Gindling, Jr.
Harman, Alexander M(arrs)
Harman, Charles Morgan
Harman, Walter James
Harman, William Boys, Jr.
Harmel, Merel Hilber
Harmon, Gary Lee
Harmon, Lindsey Richard
Harmon, Reginald Carl
Harms, Robert Thomas
Harned, David Baily
Haro, Michael Samuel
Harper, Cordie Lee
Harper, Edward J.
Harper, George Mills
Harper, Harlan, Jr.
Harper, Howard Vincent
Harper, Laura Jane
Harper, Lawrence
Harper, Robert Alexander
Harper, Robert Allan
Harper, Terrell Ray
Harper, Thomas
Harper, Thomas Gerald
Harper, William Lloyd
Harpham, Virginia Ruth
Harr, Karl Gottlieb, Jr.
Harr, Luther Armstrong
Harrar, Helen Joanne
Harrawood, Paul
Harrell, Billy Earl
Harrell, David Edwin, Jr.
Harrelson, Walter Joseph
Harrer, Gustave Adolphus
Harrigan, Anthony Hart
Harriman, Edward Eugene
Harriman, William Averell
Harrington, John Vincent
Harrington, Marion Ray
Harrington, Walter Joel
Harrington, William Fields
Harris, Albert Claude
Harris, Bill J.
Harris, Byron P.
Harris, Carl Vernon
Harris, Carleton
Harris, Carmon Coleman
Harris, Charles David
Harris, Charles Frederick
Harris, Charles Upchurch
Harris, Clifford Allen
Harris, Don Victor, Jr.
Harris, Fred Earl
Harris, Harwell Hamilton
Harris, Henry Hiter, Jr.
Harris, Henry Wood
Harris, Herbert E., III
Harris, Hugh Pate
Harris, Jean Louise
Harris, Jerome Sylvan
Harris, Jesse Graham, Jr.
Harris, John David, Jr.
Harris, Julian Hoke
Harris, Martin Harvey
Harris, Milton
Harris, Nell
Harris, Oren
Harris, Patricia Roberts
Harris, Rae Lawrence, Jr.
Harris, Reed
Harris, Robert Harry
Harris, Robert Jennings
Harris, Robert Louis
Harris, Ronald David
Harris, Rufus Carrollton
Harris, Ruth Bates
Harris, Sanford Arnold
Harris, Shearon
Harris, Thomas Cunningham
Harris, Thomas Everett
Harris, Vincent Madeley
Harris, William Gibson
Harris, William James, Jr.
Harrisberger, Edgar Lee
Harrison, Albertis Sydney, Jr.
Harrison, Benjamin Leslie
Harrison, Clifford Joy, Jr.
Harrison, Frank
Harrison, Frank Russell, III
Harrison, Horace Hawes
Harrison, John Armstrong
Harrison, John Francis
Harrison, John Raymond
Harrison, Marion Edwyn
Harrison, Milton M.
Harrison, Richard Donald
Harrison, T. Felton
Harrison, W. Earl
Harrison, William Allen
Harrison, William Neal
Harrison, William Wright
Harriss, Julius Welch
Harrold, David Ernest
Harrold, Orville Goodwin, Jr.
Harron, Brian Gregory
Harrop, William Caldwell
Harry, Thomas
Harsanyi, Janice
Harshbarger, Boyd
Harshbarger, Sam Ross
Hart, Donald John
Hart, Frederick Donald
Hart, Gary
Hart, George Luzerne, Jr.
Hart, Patrick Joseph
Hart, Richard Banner
Hart, Robert Gordon
Hart, William Milton
Hart, William Sebastian
Harte, Edward Holmead
Harte, Houston Harriman
Hartford, Ellis Ford
Hartigan, Grace
Hartin, John Sykes
Hartlage, Lawrence Clifton
Hartle, Richard Eastham
Hartman, George Eitel
Hartman, Howard Carl
Hartman, Howard Levi
Hartman, James Theodore
Hartman, Philip
Hartman, Ralph Maxwell
Hartman, Richard Leon
Hartmann, Gregory Kemenyi
Hartmann, Robert Carl
Hartmann, Robert Trowbridge
Hartmann, William Herman
Hartranft, Joseph Beckwith, Jr.
Hartshorne, Charles
Hartt, Frederick
Hartt, Julian Norris
Hartwell, Stephen
Hartzman, Carl Edwin
Harvey, Abner McGehee
Harvey, Alexander, II
Harvey, Curran Whitthorne, Jr.
Harvey, Donald Phillips
Harvey, Edwin Malcolm
Harvey, F. Barton Jr.
Harvey, Frank W.
Harvey, James Douglas
Harvey, James Lawrence
Harvey, Jasper Elliott
Harvey, John Collins
Harvey, Paul Henry
Harvey, Robert Dixon Hopkins
Harvey, Robert Otto
Harvey, Watkins Proctor
Harvey, William Brantley, Jr.
Harvin, Lucius Herman, Jr.
Harvin, William Charles
Harwell, Edwin Whitley
Harwell, Kenneth Edwin
Harwell, Richard Barksdale
Harwood, Douglas Amend
Harwood, Richard Lee
Harwood, Richard Roberts, Jr.
Haserick, John Roger
Haskew, Laurence DeFee
Haskins, Caryl Parker
Haskins, Jack Burton
Haslam, Charles Linn
Hassler, Francis Jefferson
Hastie, Reid William
Hastings, David Canfield
Hastings, Lawrence Vaeth
Hatch, David Lincoln
Hatch, Harold Arthur
Hatch, Mary Gies
Hatch, Orrin Grant
Hatch, Robert Norris
Hatcher, Charles Ross, Jr.
Hatcher, William Hamilton
Hatcher, William Julian, Jr.
Hatchett, Joseph Woodrow
Hatfield, Mark
Hatfield, W.C.
Hatfield, William Emerson
Hathaway, Dale Ernest
Hathaway, Walter Murphy
Hauberg, Robert Engelbrecht
Hauck, John Joseph
Hauck, William Francis
Haugerud, Howard Edward
Haught, James Albert, Jr.
Haughton, Kenneth Elwood
Haughton, Ronald Waring
Hauser, Michael George
Haverty, John Rhodes
Haverty, Rawson
Haviland, Fred Russ, Jr.
Haviland, John Kenneth
Haviland, Virginia
Hawkins, Augustus Freeman
Hawkins, Francis Glenn
Hawkins, Merrill Morris
Hawkins, Osie Penman, Jr.
Hawkins, Rebecca Bowles
Hawley, Wheeler
Haworth, Michael Elliott, Jr.
Hawthorne, Frank Howard
Hawver, Carl Fullerton
Hay, Jess Thomas
Hay, Raymond A.
Hay, William Winn
Hayakawa, Samuel Ichiye
Hayden, Carlos Keith
Hayden, Donald Eugene
Hayes, Charles Leonard
Hayes, Elvin
Hayes, James Joseph
Hayes, John Briggs
Hayes, John Patrick
Hayes, John S.
Hayes, Joseph
Hayes, Joseph Claude
Hayes, Mark Stephen
Hayes, Nathaniel Perkinson
Hayes, Ray Hogan
Hayes, Richard Lloyd
Hayes, Robert Bruce
Hayes, Robert Samuel
Hayes, Robert Wesley
Hayes, Samuel Perkins
Hayes, Sarah Hall
Hayes, Wayland Jackson, Jr.
Hayman, Harry
Haymes, Harmon Hayden
Haymes, Robert C.
Haynes, Boyd Withers, Jr.
Haynes, Donald
Haynes, Douglas Martin
Haynes, John Jackson
Haynes, Kenneth George
Haynes, Robert Vaughn
Haynie, Hugh
Haynie, Roscoe George
Haynsworth, Clement Furman, Jr.
Haynsworth, Harry J., IV
Hays, Brooks
Hays, Donald Osborne
Hays, Marguerite Thompson
Hays, Ronald Jackson
Hays, Steele
Hays, Virgil Wilford
Hays, William Lee
Hayward, Thomas Bibb
Haywood, Charles Foster
Haywood, Egbert Lynch
Haywood, H(erbert) Carl(ton)
Haywood, Oliver Garfield
Haywood, Theodore Joseph
Hayworth, Don
Hazard, John Beach
Hazard, John Wharton
Hazelrigg, Charles Tabb
Hazen, Sally Sue
Hazlehurst, Franklin Hamilton
Hazlett, James Stephen
Hazlett, Robert Cummins
Head, Holman
Head, Mary Johnston
Heady, James Kenneth
Heald, Don Elliot
Heald, Milton Tidd
Healey, James Francis
Healey, James Stewart
Healy, George Robert
Healy, George William, Jr.
Healy, Patrick, III
Healy, Paul Francis
Healy, Robert Edward
Healy, Robert William
Healy, Timothy Stafford
Heard, (George) Alexander
Heard, Jerry Michael
Heard, Wilbur Wright
Hearin, Robert Matlock
Hearing, Vincent Joseph
Hearn, Edell Midgett
Hearn, Thomas K., Jr.
Hearth, Donald Payne
Heath, Alfred Oswald
Heath, Jesse Boyd, Jr.
Heath, Peter Lauchlan
Heath, Robert Galbraith
Heatherington, J. Scott
Hebb, Malcolm Hayden
Hecht, Alan Dannenberg
Hecht, Robert Earl, Sr.
Hechtman, Robert Aaron
Heck, James Baker
Heck, L. Douglas
Heckelmann, Charles Newman (pen name Charles Lawton)
Heckerling, Philip Ephraim
Heckler, Margaret Mary
Heckman, James William, Jr.
Hector, Louis Julius
Hederman, Thomas Martin, Jr.
Hedge, George Albert
Hedges, Ralph Richard
Hedges, William Leonard
Hedlund, Floyd Frederick
Hedmeg, Andrew
Hedrick, David Warrington
Hedrick, Floyd Dudley
Hedrick, Frederic Cleveland, Jr.
Heebe, Frederick Jacob Regan
Heedy, Henry Glen, Jr.
Heelan, Bernard Francis
Heer, John Edward, Jr.
Heeschen, David Sutphin
Heffelfinger, Thomas Browning
Heffelfinger, William Stewart
Heffernan, John William
Heffernan, Paul Malcolm
Heffernan, Wilbert Joseph
Heffron, Howard (Alvin)
Hefler, Richard James
Heflin, Howell Thomas
Hefner, Thomas Reeder
Hefner, W. G. (Bill)
Heft, Arnold Abraham
Heftel, Cecil
Heginbotham, Erland Howard
Hegsted, David Mark
Heid, Charles Christian, Jr.
Heiligbrodt, Ludolph William
Heilman, Earl Bruce
Heilmeier, George Harry
Heilpern, George Seymour
Heilprin, Laurence Bedford
Heine, Walter Norman
Heineman, Benjamin Walter, Jr.
Heinen, Erwin
Heinfelden, Curt H.G.
Heinl, Robert Debs, Jr.
Heinly, David Reed
Heins, Maurice Haskell
Heiple, Loren Ray
Heise, Herman Albrecht
Heiser, Arnold Melvin
Heiser, Joseph Miller, Jr.
Heisler, Kenneth Glenn
Heisler, Philip Samuel
Hejtmancik, Milton Rudolph
Held, Joe Roger
Held, Philip
Heldenfels, Frederick William, Jr.
Heldman, Alan Wohl
Helland, George Archibald, Jr.
Hellegers, Andre E.
Heller, Harold William
Heller, Jack Isaac
Heller, William Mohn

Hellman, Louis M.
Hellmuth, William Frederick, Jr.
Hellwig, Langley Roberts
Helm, Lewis Marshall
Helm, Robert Meredith
Helman, Gerald Bernard
Helmbold, F. Wilbur
Helmerich, Walter Hugo, III
Helms, Fred Bryan
Helms, Jesse
Helrich, Martin
Helwig, Elson Bowman
Hemba, Alton W(oodley)
Hembree, Hugh Lawson, III
Hemphill, Robert Witherspoon
Hemphill, William Edwin
Hempstone, Smith, Jr.
Hemry, Jerome Eldon
Hemry, Leslie Plumb
Henderson, Albert John
Henderson, Donald Ainslie
Henderson, Douglas Boyd
Henderson, Edwin Harold
Henderson, Freddye Scarborough
Henderson, Henry Lorenzo
Henderson, Horace Edward
Henderson, Howard DeWeese
Henderson, Hubert Platt
Henderson, James Henry Meriwether
Henderson, James Marvin
Henderson, John Batty
Henderson, John Brown
Henderson, John Burns, Jr.
Henderson, Lenneal Joseph, Jr.
Henderson, Loy Wesley
Henderson, Madeline Mary Berry
Henderson, Merlin Theodore
Henderson, Milton Arnold
Henderson, Robert Dean
Henderson, Robert Waugh
Henderson, Stanley Dale
Henderson, Warren Stanley Patrick
Henderson, William E.
Hendley, Dan Lunsford
Hendon, Robert Caraway
Hendon, Robert Randall
Hendrick, James Pomeroy
Hendricks, Charles Henning
Hendricks, Donald Duane
Hendricks, Ernest L.
Hendricks, Sterling B.
Hendrickson, Warren Edwin
Hendrie, Joseph Mallam
Hendrix, Dennis Ralph
Hendrix, James Harvey, Jr.
Hendrix, Thomas Russell
Heneman, Harlow James
Henican, Caswell Ells
Henington, David Mead
Henize, Karl Gordon
Henke, Emerson Overbeck
Henkel, Lee Hampton, Jr.
Henkin, Daniel Zwie
Henle, Peter
Henley, Ernest Justus
Henley, Vernard William
Henley, William Branch, Jr.
Henn, Richard Leonard, Jr.
Henneke, Ben Graf
Henneman, Dorothy Hughes
Hennessy, Daniel Kraft
Hennings, Josephine Silva (Halpin)
Henry, David Howe, II
Henry, Donald Lee
Henry, E. L.
Henry, Herman Luther, Jr.
Henry, John Bernard
Henry, John Case
Henry, John Frederick
Henry, Joseph Ward
Henry, Marion Lucas
Henry, Waights Gibbs, Jr.
Henry, Walter Lester, Jr.
Henry, William Oscar Eugene
Hensel, H. Struve
Henshaw, Edmund Lee, Jr.
Henshaw, Francis Harold
Hensley, Marble John
Henson, Walter DeRossette
Henton, Willis Ryan
Henze, Calvin Rudolph
Henze, Paul Bernard
Heppner, James Paul
Hepting, George Henry
Herberg, John Clifford
Herbers, Tod Arthur
Herbert, Edward
Herbert, George Richard
Herbert, Ira C.
Herbert, James Arthur
Herbich, John Bronislaw
Herbig, Gunther
Herbst, Robert LeRoy
Herd, Charles Felix
Herd, Ruby Helm
Hereford, Frank Loucks, Jr.
Herge, Henry Curtis, Sr.
Herge, J. Curtis
Hering, Anthony Joseph, Jr.
Herling, John
Hermach, Francis Lewis
Herman, Abe Mitchell
Herman, Alexis M.
Herman, Charles Robert
Herman, Daniel Harold
Herman, George Edward
Herman, Kenneth Neil
Herman, Robert
Hermann, Robert Jay
Hermanowski, Charles C.
Hermanson, Gordon Elmer
Hernandez, Frank P.
Herndon, Claude Nash
Herndon, James Francis
Herndon, (Claude) Nash, III
Herndon, Terry Eugene
Herndon, William Cecil
Herold, Donald George
Heroman, John Basil, Jr.
Heron, Duncan
Herrick, Allyn Marsh
Herrick, H.T.
Herrick, Kenneth Whitman
Herring, Charles Ferguson
Herring, Jack William
Herring, Leonard Gray
Herring, Robert Ray
Herrmann, Donald Joseph
Herron, Robert Ernest
Hersey, David Floyd
Hersh, Seymour M.
Hershman, Jacob Earl
Hersman, Marion Frank
Herstand, Theodore
Hertz, Kenneth Theodore
Hertz, Roy
Hervey, Frederick Taylor
Herz, Martin Florian
Herz, Werner
Herzberg, Donald Gabriel
Herzog, Robert
Hess, Eugene Lyle
Hess, George Kellogg, Jr.
Hess, Seymour Lester
Hess, Stephen
Hesse, William R.
Hesseltine, Henry Close
Hesser, Leon Francis
Hessler, Curtis Alan
Hessman, James David
Hester, James Lynn
Hester, Robert William
Heuberger, Oscar
Heuer, Robert Maynard, II
Heuer, Scott, Jr.
Heumann, Karl Fredrich
Heuson, William Georges
Hewes, Laurence Ilsley, Jr.
Hewes, Laurence Ilsley, III
Hewett, Arthur Edward
Hewins, Kenneth F.
Hewitt, John Arnot, Jr.
Hewitt, Robert Lee
Hewlett, C(ecil) James
Hewlett, Frank West
Hewlett, Richard Greening
Heymann, Philip B.
Heyssel, Robert Morris
Hiaasen, Carl Andreas
Hibbard, Edwin Davis
Hibbard, Walter Rollo, Jr.
Hibbs, Leon
Hibbs, Richard Guythal
Hibel, Edna (Mrs. Theodore Plotkin)
Hickey, Robert Cornelius
Hicklin, Robert McLean
Hickman, Cleveland Pendleton, Jr.
Hickman, Darrell David
Hickman, James Blake
Hicks, Byron Adna
Hicks, Clifford Byron
Hicks, James Robert, Jr.
Hicks, Kenneth William
Hicks, Leslie Hubert
Hicks, Marshall Monroe
Hicks, Virginia Sybil Drake
Hidalgo, Edward
Hiebert, Ray Eldon
Hieronymus, Clara Booth Wiggins
Hierth, Harrison Ewing
Higbee, Dallas Clay
Higginbotham, Fred Caswell, Jr.
Higginbotham, Patrick Errol
Higginbotham, Sanford Wilson
Higgins, Howard
Higgins, John Thomas
Higgins, Lois Lundell
Higgins, Robert Louis
Higginson, R. Keith
High, George Borman
Higham, John
Highland, Cecil Blaine, Jr.
Highsaw, James Leonard, Jr.
Highsaw, Robert Baker
Highsmith, Shelby
Highsmith, William Edward
Hightower, Jack English
Hightower, William Harrison, Jr.
Higley, Bruce Wadsworth
Higley, Robert Joseph
Hilborne, Tom George
Hild, Walther Johannes
Hileman, Donald Goodman
Hill, Albert Gordon
Hill, Allen Edward
Hill, Benjamin Harvey, Jr.
Hill, Benjamin Harvey, Jr.
Hill, Bobby Lee
Hill, Carl McClellan
Hill, Charles Strunk
Hill, Clyde Cecil, Jr.
Hill, Donald Walter
Hill, Dumond Peck
Hill, Edwin Hollis, Jr.
Hill, George Watts
Hill, Harold Nelson, Jr.
Hill, Isaac William
Hill, James A.
Hill, James Clinkscales
Hill, James Daniel
Hill, James L.
Hill, Jerry Gifford
Hill, Jimmie Dale
Hill, John Alexander
Hill, John Gillespie, Jr.
Hill, John Hub
Hill, John Luke
Hill, John Rutledge, Jr.
Hill, John William
Hill, Joseph MacGlashan
Hill, Kenneth Martin
Hill, Lucius Gordon, Jr.
Hill, Melvin James
Hill, Richard Keith
Hill, Robert Lee
Hill, Robert Leland
Hill, Samuel Richardson, Jr.
Hill, Terrell Leslie
Hill, Thomas Bowen, Jr.
Hill, Thomas Bowen, III
Hill, Wendell Talbot, Jr.
Hill, William Calvin
Hill, William Leon
Hill, Wilmer Bailey
Hillard, James Milton
Hillerich, John Andrew, III
Hilliard, James Henning
Hilliard, Pauline
Hilliard, Robert Glenn
Hilliard, Sam Bowers
Hillis, Elwood Haynes
Hills, Carla Anderson
Hills, Lee
Hills, Roderick M.
Hilsman, William Joseph
Hilton, Howard Judd
Hilton, Mary Nelson
Hilton, Ordway
Himel, Chester Mora
Himelstein, Philip Nathan
Himmelblau, David Mautner
Hinckley, Elmer Dumond
Hinden, Stanley Jay
Hindle, Brooke
Hinds, Charles Franklin
Hinds, Jackson Ceivers
Hine, Gilbert Clarendon
Hiner, Louis Chase
Hines, Andrew Hampton, Jr.
Hines, Howard Harry
Hines, James Herman
Hines, Merrill Odom
Hines, Ralph Howard
Hines, William Meredith, Jr.
Hinich, Melvin Jay
Hinkle, Walter C., Jr.
Hinnant, A(ugustus) Ray(mond)
Hinshaw, Carroll Elton
Hinshaw, Lerner Brady
Hinshaw, William Russell
Hinson, Howard Houston
Hinson, Jon Clifton
Hintikka, Kaarlo Jaakko
Hipp, Francis Moffett
Hipp, Herman Neel
Hipp, William Hayne
Hipple, James Blackman
Hirsch, Charles Bronislaw
Hirsch, Eric Donald, Jr.
Hirsch, Maurice
Hirsch, Reginald Alfred
Hirschberg, Joseph Gustav
Hirschfield, Howard J.
Hirschowitz, Basil Isaac
Hirsh, Allan Thurman, Jr.
Hirst, Julian Fravel
Hirt, Al
Hitchcock, Billy
Hitchcock, Henry Perry
Hitching, Harry James
Hitchings, George Herbert
Hite, James Tillman, III
Hitt, David H.
Hitt, Harold Hamilton
Hitt, Homer Lee
Hittle, James D.
Hixon, Robert Charles
Hjort, Howard Warren
Hlass, I. Jerry
Hoadley, Irene Braden (Mrs. Edward Hoadley)
Hoag, Arthur Howard, Jr.
Hoagland, Jimmie Lee
Hobbs, Edward Henry
Hobbs, Estel Milton
Hobbs, Grimsley Taylor
Hobbs, Herman Hedberg
Hobbs, Horton Holcombe, Jr.
Hobbs, Marcus Edwin
Hobbs, Michael Edwin
Hobbs, Nicholas
Hobbs, Robert Wesley
Hobbs, William Calvin
Hobbs, William David
Hobby, Oveta Culp (Mrs. William P. Hobby)
Hobby, William Pettus
Hoberecht, Earnest
Hobgood, William P.
Hoblitzell, Alan Penniman, Jr.
Hochbaum, Godfrey Martin
Hochberg, Bayard Zabdial
Hochberger, Simon
Hoche, Philip Anthony
Hocker, Jon Christopher
Hocott, Claude Richard
Hoctor, Thomas Francis
Hocutt, Max Oliver
Hodes, Philip Jacob
Hodge, Jerry H.
Hodge, Raymond Joseph
Hodge, Verne Antonio
Hodgell, Murlin Ray
Hodges, Donald Clark
Hodges, Henry Raiford, Jr.
Hodges, John Raymond
Hodges, Joseph Howard
Hodges, Luther Hartwell, Jr.
Hodges, Ralph B.
Hodges, Ralph Dore, Jr.
Hodges, Thompson Gene
Hodges, William Terrell
Hodgson, Daniel Blake
Hodgson, Matthew Marshall Neil
Hodnett, Edward
Hodnette, Robert Edward, Jr.
Hodous, Robert Power
Hodson, Kenneth Joe
Hoeffding, Wassily
Hoehler, Fred Kenneth, Jr.
Hoehn, Elmer L.
Hoekenga, Earl Nelson
Hoel, Lester A.
Hoelscher, John Henry
Hoenack, August Frederick
Hoeveler, William M.
Hoff, Ebbe Curtis
Hoff, Gerhardt Michael
Hoffacker, Lewis
Hoffberger, Jerold Charles
Hoffberger, LeRoy Edward
Hoffberger, Stanley Alan
Hoffman, Calvin
Hoffman, Edwin Karl
Hoffman, George W(alter)
Hoffman, Harold Wayne
Hoffman, Irwin
Hoffman, Philip Guthrie
Hoffman, Thomas Henry
Hoffman, Walter Edward
Hoffmann, Ludwig Carl
Hoffmeyer, Dan
Hoffstrom, Piercy J. (P. J. Hoff)
Hofheinz, James Fred
Hogan, Bartholomew William
Hogan, Ernest Lynn, Jr.
Hogan, Henry Leon, III
Hogarth, Charles Pinckney
Hogg, William Richey
Hoggard, Lara Guldmar
Hoglund, Forrest Eugene
Hoglund, Richard Frank
Hogness, John Rusten
Hogue, Alexandre
Hohenberg, John
Hohstadt, Thomas Dowd
Holberg, Ralph Gans, Jr.
Holbrook, Hollis Howard
Holbrooke, Richard Charles Albert
Holcomb, George Ruhle
Holcomb, M. Staser
Holcomb, William A.
Holcombe, James Vance
Holden, John Bernard
Holden, Raymond Thomas
Holden, Reuben Andrus
Holder, Harold Douglas
Holder, Lee
Holderman, James Bowker
Holdridge, Barbara
Holgate, Jeanne
Holguin, Alfonso Hudson
Holik, William Veazey, Jr.
Holladay, Charles Edwin
Holladay, Wendell Gene
Hollaender, Alexander
Holland, Charles Donald
Holland, Clarence Adrian
Holland, Daniel E.
Holland, David Scott
Holland, Kenn
Holland, Laurence Bedwell
Holland, Lyman Faith, Jr.
Holland, Park, Jr.
Holland, Robert Carl
Holland, Robert Debnam
Holland, Robert Lee
Hollander, Edwin Paul
Hollander, Morton Joseph
Hollander, Richard Allen
Hollander, Richard Isaac
Holle, Henry August
Hollen, Donald Edward
Hollenbeck, Harold Capistran
Hollender, Marc Hale
Hollenshead, Clyde Willys
Holley, Edward Gailon
Holley, Howard Lamar
Holliday, Raymond Middleton
Holliman, Joe Milton
Hollings, Ernest Frederick
Hollingsworth, Borden Benton, Jr.
Hollingsworth, Max Harold
Hollingsworth, Robert Edmund
Hollinshead, Ariel Cahill
Hollis, Charles Carroll
Hollis, Harris Whitton
Hollis, Howell
Hollis, Mark D.
Hollister, William Gray
Holloway, Albert Weston
Holloway, Bruce Keener
Holloway, Clarke Lee
Holloway, Frederic Ancrum Lord
Holloway, John Thomas
Holloway, Leonard Leveine
Holloway, William, Jr.
Holm, Jeanne Marjorie
Holman, Benjamin F.
Holman, Clarence Hugh
Holman, Gerald Hall
Holman, Jack Philip
Holman, M. Carl
Holman, William Roger
Holmberg, Albert William, Jr.
Holmberg, Ruth Sulzberger
Holmes, Ann Hitchcock
Holmes, Bert Otis E., Jr.
Holmes, Broox Garrett
Holmes, Edward Warren
Holmes, George Washington, III
Holmes, Henry Allen
Holmes, Major Joe
Holmes, Marjorie Rose
Holmes, Nicholas Hanson, Jr.
Holmes, Oliver Wendell
Holmes, Preston Turner
Holmes, Thomas Vinton, Jr.
Holmes, Urban Tigner, III
Holmgren, Harry D.
Holmquest, Donald Lee
Holscher, Franz Foster
Holsti, Ole Rudolf
Holt, Charles Carter
Holt, David Earl
Holt, Don S.
Holt, Everett William
Holt, John B.
Holt, Joseph Frank
Holt, Marjorie Sewell
Holt, Ralph Manning, Jr.
Holt, Robert LeRoi
Holt, William E.
Holth, Henry
Holtman, Darlington Frank
Holton, A. Linwood, Jr.
Holton, James Leo
Holton, Raymond William
Holtzclaw, Benjamin Clark
Holtzman, Elizabeth
Holtzman, Wayne Harold
Holub, Fred Paul
Holway, William Rea
Honemann, Daniel Henry
Honey, Richard David
Honeycutt, Earl Moore
Honeycutt, Thomas Edison
Honig, Orie Charles
Honkala, Fred Saul
Hood, Dorothy
Hood, Robin Lee
Hook, Edward Watson, Jr.
Hook, Harold Swanson
Hooker, Charles Wright
Hooker, Dan
Hooker, John Jay, Jr.
Hooks, William Gary
Hoole, William Stanley
Hooper, Edith Ferry
Hooper, Frank Arthur
Hooper, Gilman Stanley
Hooper, Samuel Edward
Hoopes, John Eugene
Hoopes, Townsend Walter
Hoopes, Townsend Walter
Hoover, Charles William
Hoover, Francis Louis
Hoover, Herbert William, Jr.
Hoover, John Elwood
Hoover, Joseph Samuel
Hoover, Linn
Hoover, Roland Armitage
Hope, Clarence Caldwell, Jr.
Hope, Garland Howard
Hope, Henry Radford
Hope, Samuel Howard
Hopkins, Dan Walton
Hopkins, Ernest Loyd
Hopkins, Everett Harold
Hopkins, Frank Snowden
Hopkins, George Mathews Marks
Hopkins, John Isaac
Hopkins, Larry J.
Hopkins, Milo Brancroft
Hopkins, Samuel
Hopkins, Thomas Matthews
Hoppenstein, Joel Manuel
Hopper, Grace Brewster Murray
Hopper, William David
Hoppess, Karl Coulter
Hopps, Hope Elizabeth Byrne
Horadam, Weyman Wilson
Horan, Hume Alexander
Horan, Leo Gallaspy
Horger, Edgar Olin, III
Horkey, William Richard
Hormats, Robert David
Horn, Carl, Jr.
Horn, Myron Kay
Horn, Roger Alan
Hornaday, Harold Preston
Hornback, Joseph Hope
Hornbeak, Mack Haynes
Hornbeck, David Wallace
Hornbostel, Peter Anthony
Hornbostel, Victor Otto
Horne, Homa Judson
Horne, James Grady
Horne, John E.
Horne, Walter Batcheller
Horner, Charles Thompson, Jr.
Horner, Garnett Denton
Horner, Lorenzo David, III
Horner, William Harry
Horner, William Ludwig
Hornung, Lenora Virginia
Horovitz, Samuel Bertram
Horowitz, Daniel L.
Horowitz, Harold
Horrigan, Alfred Frederic
Horrigan, Edward A., Jr.
Horsky, Charles Antone
Horstmyer, Kenneth Leroy
Horten, Carl Frank
Horton, Claude Wendell
Horton, Frank
Horton, George Roswell
Horton, James Wright
Horton, Paul Bradfield
Horton, Thomas Edward, Jr.
Horvat, John James
Horvath, Ronald Joseph
Horvitz, Wayne Louis
Hosea, Addison
Hosea, Rufus Haywood
Hosenball, S. Neil
Hosmer, Craig
Hosner, John Frank
Hotz, Robert Bergmann
Houbolt, John Cornelius
Houbrick, Richard Stephen
Hougen, Joel Oliver
Hough, Eldred Wilson
Hough, George Anthony, III
Houghton, Arthur Amory, Jr.
Houghton, Woodson Plyer
Houk, Allen Ramsey
Hounshell, Charles David
House, Robert William
Houser, William Douglas
Housewright, Riley Dee
Housewright, Wiley Lee
Houska, Charles Robert
Housman, Arthur Lloyd
Houston, Benjamin Franklin
Houston, Howard Edwin
Houston, John Coates, Jr.
Houston, Kenneth Ray (Ken)
Houston, Ralph Hubert
Houstoun, Lawrence Orson, Jr.
Houtmann, Jacques
Houtz, Duane Talbott
Houze, Robert Alvin
Hover, William A.
Hovey, Justus Allan, Jr.
Hovey, Richard Bennett
Hovey, Rolf Eggerichs
Howard, Alan M.
Howard, Arthur Ellsworth Dick
Howard, Daggett Horton
Howard, Dana Douglas
Howard, Gene Claude
Howard, George Salladé
Howard, Harry Nicholas
Howard, J. Woodford, Jr.
Howard, Jack
Howard, James J.
Howard, Joseph Harvey
Howard, Lee Milton
Howard, Milo Barrett, Jr.
Howard, Paul Noble, Jr.
Howard, Rhea
Howard, Thomas Bailey, Jr.
Howard, William Allen
Howard, William Sugg
Howard, Willie Thomas, Jr.
Howarth, Thomas
Howe, Calderon
Howe, Fisher
Howell, Almonte Charles, Jr.
Howell, Arthur
Howell, Everette Irl
Howell, Hilton Hatchett
Howell, James Theodore
Howell, John McDade
Howell, Ralph Rodney
Hower, Frank Beard, Jr.
Howison, John McCoul
Howland, Richard Hubbard
Howland, Wilfred Glenroy
Howorth, Lucy Somerville
Howrey, Edward F.
Howsam, Robert Basil
Howse, Harold Darrow
Howze, Harry Clayton
Howze, Joseph Lawson Edward
Hoy, Harry Eugene
Hoy, William Ivan
Hoyme, Chad Earl
Hoyt, George Washington
Hoyt, Homer
Hoyt, Kenneth Boyd
Hoyt, Mary Finch
Hrones, John Anthony
Hsie, Abraham Wuhsiung
Hsu, Tao-Chiuh
Hsueh, Chun-tu
Huang, Chen-Jung
Hubbard, Carroll, Jr.
Hubbard, Frank Muldrow
Hubbard, John Barry
Hubbard, Paul Stancyl, Jr.
Hubbard, Perry
Hubbard, Rudolph Trezvant
Hubbard, Samuel Walton, Jr.
Hubbell, Lester Earle
Hubbert, Marion King
Huber, Leonard Eldon
Hubert, Frank William Rene
Hubley, George Wilbur, Jr.
Hubschman, Henry A.
Huck, William Frederick
Huckaby, Thomas Jerald
Huddleston, Walter Darlington
Hudiburg, John Justus, Jr.
Hudnall, Jarrett, Jr.
Hudson, Anthony Webster
Hudson, George Elbert
Hudson, Herbert Edson, Jr.
Hudson, Hinton Gardner
Hudson, Jack William, Jr.
Hudson, James Jackson
Hudson, Jesse Tucker, Jr.
Hudson, John Allen
Hudson, John Lester
Hudson, John Stephen
Hudson, Ralph Percy
Hudson, Robert Douglas
Hudson, William Thomas
Hudson, Winthrop Still
Hudspeth, Chalmers Mac
Hudspeth, Emmett LeRoy
Huebner, John Stephen
Huebner, Robert Joseph

849 REGIONAL LISTING—SOUTH-SOUTHWEST

Huebner, Thomas Edgar
Huerta, John Edmund
Huestis, Charles Benjamin
Huey, Stanton Ennes
Hufbauer, Gary Clyde
Huff, William Nathan
Huffman, Delton Cleon, Jr.
Huffman, George Garrett
Huffman, Jack Daphen
Huffman, William Charles
Huffstetler, Palmer Eugene
Huggins, Sara Espe
Huggins, William Herbert
Hughes, Carl Wilson
Hughes, Edwin R(oss)
Hughes, H(arry) Herbert
Hughes, Harry Clarence
Hughes, Harry Roe
Hughes, Joseph Kenneth
Hughes, Leo
Hughes, Lynn Nettleton
Hughes, Marija Matich
Hughes, Phillip Samuel
Hughes, Ray Harrison
Hughes, Sarah Tilghman
Hughes, Thomas Joseph
Hughes, Thomas Lowe
Hughes, Thomas Raymond
Hughes, Vester Thomas, Jr.
Hughes, William Anthony
Hughes, William Lewis
Hughlett, Robert Brooks
Hughs, Robert Nathaniel
Hughston, Harold Vaughan
Hugus, Z Zimmerman, Jr.
Huheey, F. Thomas
Huie, William Bradford
Huie, William Orr
Huie, William Stell
Hull, Norman James, Jr.
Hulse, Frank Wilson
Hulse, Stewart Harding, Jr.
Hultgren, Warren Curtis
Hultman, Charles William
Humann, Walter Johann
Hume, Alexander Britton
Hume, David
Hume, David Lang
Hume, John Chandler
Hume, Patrick Henry
Hume, Paul Chandler
Humelsine, Carlisle Hubbard
Humes, Bernard James
Humphrey, Gordon John
Humphrey, Hubert Ben, Jr.
Humphrey, William Grey
Humphreys, Mabel Gweneth
Humphreys, Robert Russell
Humphries, Jack Wood
Humphries, John O'Neal
Hund, James Madden
Hundley, Frank Temple
Huneke, Harold Vernon
Hungate, Joseph Irvin, Jr.
Hunt, David Ford
Hunt, Donald R.
Hunt, Douglass
Hunt, E(verette) Howard, Jr.
Hunt, Earl Gladstone, Jr.
Hunt, George Pinney
Hunt, Jacob Tate
Hunt, James Baxter, Jr.
Hunt, James Calvin
Hunt, Leamon Ray
Hunt, Ray
Hunt, William Dudley, Jr.
Hunter, Bynum Merritt
Hunter, Dean Dwight, Jr.
Hunter, Edgar Hayes
Hunter, Edwin Ford, Jr.
Hunter, Grover Cleveland, Jr.
Hunter, J(ohn) Robert
Hunter, John Anderson
Hunter, John Terrence
Hunter, Kermit Houston
Hunter, Leland Clair, Jr.
Hunter, Margaret King
Hunter, Morgan
Hunter, Robert Frank
Hunter, Robert Grams
Hunter, Thomas Harrison
Huntley, Robert Edward Royall
Huntley, Robert Ross
Huntsman, Stanley Houser
Hunziker, Don Allen
Hurd, John Gavin
Hurlbutt, John Alba
Hurley, Ruby
Hurley, Willard Lee
Hurson, Daniel L.
Hurst, John Emory, Jr.
Hurst, John Willis
Hurst, Robert Winn
Hurst, Vernon James
Hurst, Victor
Hurwitz, Lawrence Neal
Husby, Donald Evans
Huseman, Richard C.
Huskins, J. Frank
Husky, Ferlin
Hussey, Hugh Hudson
Hussey, Ward MacLean
Hussin, Vincent Gerard
Husted, John Edwin
Huston, Edwin Allen
Huston, Harris Hyde
Huston, James Alvin
Huston, John Wilson
Hutchens, George Burt
Hutchens, Raymond Paul
Hutcheson, James Byron
Hutcheson, Joseph Chappell, III
Hutcheson, Richard Gordon, III
Hutcheson, Thaddeus Thomson, Jr.
Hutcheson, Thomas Barksdale, Jr.
Hutchins, Ross Elliott
Hutchinson, Everett
Hutchinson, J. Edward
Hutchinson, James Gordon
Hutchison, David William
Hutchison, Joseph Carson
Hutchison, Victor Hobbs
Hutchison, William Leete
Hutt, Peter Barton
Hutto, Earl
Hutto, James Calhoun
Hutto, James Cecil
Hutton, Robert Franklin
Hutts, Joseph Clair, Jr.
Hutzler, Albert David, Jr.
Hyde, Edwin
Hyde, Henry van Zile
Hyde, Isabel Emily
Hyde, Laurance Mastick, Jr.
Hyer, Frank Perry
Hyman, Albert Lewis
Hymoff, Edward
Hynning, Clifford J(ames)
Hyson, Charles David
I'Anson, Lawrence Warren
Idema, James Mead
Iglehart, Louis Tillman
Ignatius, Paul Robert
Igusa, Jun-Ichi
Ikard, Frank Neville
Ikenberry, Henry Cephas, Jr.
Ikle, Fred Charles
Ilchman, Alice Stone
Ilchman, Warren Frederick
Illig, Carl
Illig, James Michael
Imhoff, John Leonard
Ince, Eugene St. Clair, Jr.
Ingalls, Daniel Henry Holmes
Ingerson, Fred Earl
Ingols, Robert Smalley
Ingraham, Edward Clarke, Jr.
Ingraham, Joe McDonald
Ingram, Alvin John
Ingram, Charles Clark, Jr.
Ingram, Conley
Ingram, Denny Ouzts, Jr.
Ingram, Edith Jacqueline
Ingram, Frederic Bigelow
Ingram, James Carlton
Ingram, Roy Lee
Ingram, Sam Harris
Ingram, William Emmett
Ingram, William Thomas, Jr.
Inman, Bobby Ray
Inman, Harry Ansel, II
Inouye, Daniel Ken
Irby, Richard Logan
Ireland, Andy
Ireland, Charles W(illiam)
Ireland, Harry Bert, Jr.
Irigaray, Pedro Jose
Irion, Mortimer Raguet
Irish, Leon Eugene
Irish, Marian Doris
Irizarry-Yunque, Carlos Juan
Irons, Evelyn Christine
Irons, George Vernon
Irvin, Joseph Logan
Irvin, Tinsley Hoyt
Irvine, Francis Sprague
Irving, James Bruce
Irving, John Stiles, Jr.
Irving, Thomas Herbert
Irwin, George Rankin
Irwin, James Wesley
Irwin, John Valeur
Irwin, Leo Howard
Irwin, Pat
Irzyk, Albin Felix
Isaac, William H.
Isaacs, Edgar E.
Isaacs, Rufus Philip
Isaacs, Russell Lowell
Isbell, Horace Smith
Isbell, Robert
Isbister, James David
Iselin, Donald Grote
Isenberg, Abraham Charles
Isenbergh, Max
Isenhour, Thomas Lee
Isham, Sheila Eaton
Israel, George Matthew, III
Israel, Sam, Jr.
Israelson, Max Roth
Ivash, Eugene Vasily
Iverson, Francis Kenneth
Ives, George Skinner
Ives, Stephen Bradshaw, Jr.
Ivey, James Burnett
Ivins, James Elbert
Ivory, Peter B.C.B.
Izlar, William Henry, Jr.
Jachimczyk, Joseph Alexander
Jack, William Harry
Jackson, Allen Keith
Jackson, Bettina Adeline Bush (Mrs. Daniel F. Jackson)
Jackson, Blyden
Jackson, Carmault Benjamin, Jr.
Jackson, Clayton LeRoy
Jackson, D. Brooks
Jackson, Daniel Francis
Jackson, David Munro
Jackson, Dempster McKee
Jackson, Donald William
Jackson, Dudley Pennington
Jackson, Elmer Martin, Jr.
Jackson, Eugene Bernard
Jackson, Francis Charles
Jackson, Francis Xavier
Jackson, George Woodrow
Jackson, Gerald Audron
Jackson, Harry Cook
Jackson, Hezekiah
Jackson, J. Harry
Jackson, Jacquelyne Johnson
Jackson, James Wyly, Jr.
Jackson, Jay Marion
Jackson, John Burton
Jackson, John Ellett
Jackson, John Nelson
Jackson, Julian Ellis
Jackson, Kern Chandler
Jackson, Larry Artope
Jackson, Laura (Riding)
Jackson, Maynard Holbrook
Jackson, Nyle M.
Jackson, Philip Chappell, Jr.
Jackson, R(oy) Graham
Jackson, Robert Cecil
Jackson, Robert William
Jackson, Roy
Jackson, Samuel Charles
Jackson, Thomas Searing
Jackson, William Calhoun (Decker), Jr.
Jackson, William David
Jacobi, Eileen M.
Jacobs, Andrew, Jr.
Jacobs, Barbara Beaman
Jacobs, Bradford McElderry
Jacobs, James Albert
Jacobs, John Clayton
Jacobs, Melvin
Jacobs, Norman Ernest
Jacobs, Roger Francis
Jacobs, Sydney
Jacobs, Walter William
Jacobs, Woodrow Cooper
Jacobsen, John Charles
Jacobsmeyer, John Henry, Jr.
Jacobson, Antone Gardner
Jacobson, David
Jacoby, Robert Bird
Jacoby, William Jerome, Jr.
Jadot, Jean Lambert Octave
Jaeger, Leonard Henry
Jaeke, Harold Theodore
Jaffe, Harold
Jaffe, Leonard Sigmund
Jagoda, Barry Lionel
Jahn, Laurence Roy
Jain, Sagar Chand
Jalonick, George Washington, III
Jamail, Joseph Dahr, Jr.
James, Allix Bledsoe
James, Charles A.
James, Clifford Cyril
James, D(orris) Clayton
James, Daniel J.
James, Floyd Benjamine
James, Forrest Hood, Jr. (Fob)
James, Franklin Ward
James, Fred Calhoun
James, Jack Milton
James, John V.
James, Joseph B.
James, Mark (Francis Rodney Zambon)
James, Robert Milton
James, Thomas Naum
Jamieson, Graham A.
Jamieson, John Kenneth
Jamieson, John Kenneth
Jamieson, Robert John
Jamison, John Ambler
Jamison, Richard Melvin
Jandl, Henry Anthony
Jandt, Elizabeth Carrie
Janeway, Ray Curtis
Janeway, Richard
Janis, Jay
Janney, Stuart Symington, Jr.
Janning, Mary Bernadette
Jantzen, Alice Catherine
January, Don
Jaques, Thomas Francis
Jaques, William Everett
Jaquith, Richard Herbert
Jaramillo, Mari-Luci
Jarman, Walton Maxey
Jarmolow, Kenneth
Jarnagin, Richard Calvin
Jaroszewicz, Mark T.
Jarrard, Jerald Osborne
Jarrard, Leonard Everett
Jasinowski, Jerry Joseph
Jaskot, John Joseph
Jasper, David Westwater
Jasper, Martin Theophilus
Jaspersen, J. William
Jaszi, George
Jatras, Stephen James
Jauchem, Clarence Ralph
Jaworski, Leon
Jayne, Benjamin Anderson
Jayson, Lester Samuel
Jeffers, John Leroy
Jeffers, William Armand
Jeffery, Geoffrey Marron
Jeffett, Frank Asbury
Jeffries, James E.
Jeffries, McChesney Hill
Jeffries, William Worthington
Jeffris, Ronald Duane
Jehlik, Paul Joseph
Jelks, Joseph William, Jr.
Jencks, Francis Haynes
Jenerick, Howard Peter
Jenkins, Alfred le Sesne
Jenkins, Daniel Edwards, Jr.
Jenkins, Edgar Lanier
Jenkins, Ferguson Arthur
Jenkins, Harry Earle
Jenkins, Iredell
Jenkins, John Smith
Jenkins, Kempton Boyce
Jenkins, Leo Warren
Jenkins, Robert Ellsworth, Jr.
Jenkins, Ruben Lee
Jenkins, William Robert
Jenks, Thomas Elijah
Jenks, William Alexander
Jennings, Albert Ray
Jennings, Alston
Jennings, James Monroe, II
Jennings, John Melville
Jennings, Joseph Ashby
Jennings, Lewellyn A.
Jennings, Richard Louis
Jennings, Robert Burgess
Jennings, W. Croft
Jennings, Waylon
Jenrette, John Wilson, Jr.
Jensen, Howard Francis
Jensen, Marvin Eli
Jensen, Paul Harold
Jenson, Sherman Milton
Jentz, Gaylord Adair
Jenzano, Anthony Francis
Jepsen, Roger William
Jernigan, James Coffey
Jernigan, Kenneth
Jerome, William Travers III
Jerrard, Jerry
Jerrick, Stephen Joseph
Jeschke, Channing Renwick
Jeskey, Harold Alfred
Jesse, Mary Jane
Jessen, George Eli
Jessup, Joe Lee
Jesurún, Harold Méndez
Jetton, Clyde Thomas
Jewell, Malcolm Edwin
Jewell, Robert Burnett
Jimenez, Jorge Jaime
Jobe, Larry Alton
Jobe, Sharon Cannon
Jöbsis, Frans Frederik
Johansen, Eivind Herbert
Johanson, Stanley Morris
John, Peter William Meredith
John, Ralph Candler
Johns, John Edwin
Johns, Richard James
Johnsen, Russell Harold
Johnson, Alan Arthur
Johnson, Alvin Carl
Johnson, Belton Kleberg
Johnson, Benjamin Franklin, Jr.
Johnson, Berkeley Daniels
Johnson, Bert Willard
Johnson, Bruce Connor
Johnson, Cecil C.
Johnson, Cecil Earl
Johnson, Charles Christopher, Jr.
Johnson, Charles Sidney, Jr.
Johnson, Clark Everette, Jr.
Johnson, Corwin Waggoner
Johnson, David Livingstone
Johnson, David Simonds
Johnson, Davis Gilman
Johnson, Douglas Elliott
Johnson, Elliott Amos
Johnson, Elmer Douglas
Johnson, Elvis Eugene
Johnson, Ernest Wiley
Johnson, Eugene Ingwall
Johnson, Everett Ramon
Johnson, Francis Severin
Johnson, Frank Minis, Jr.
Johnson, Frederick Charles
Johnson, George, Jr.
Johnson, George William
Johnson, George William
Johnson, Gerald White
Johnson, Gifford K.
Johnson, Glendon E.
Johnson, Gove Griffith, Jr.
Johnson, Graham Madden
Johnson, Harold T.
Johnson, Haynes Bonner
Johnson, Herbert Alan
Johnson, Herbert Frederick
Johnson, Homer Fields
Johnson, Hugh Bailey
Johnson, Hunter
Johnson, Ivan Earl
Johnson, J. Donald, Jr.
Johnson, James
Johnson, James Arthur
Johnson, James Douglas (Jim)
Johnson, James Gibb
Johnson, James Glover
Johnson, James P.
Johnson, James Terence
Johnson, John A.
Johnson, John Harold
Johnson, John William, Jr.
Johnson, Johnny Ray
Johnson, Joseph Benjamin
Johnson, Joseph Eggleston, III
Johnson, Joseph Yandell
Johnson, Karl McKibben
Johnson, Kenneth Oscar
Johnson, Kenneth Owen
Johnson, Kermit Douglas
Johnson, Lady Bird (Claudia Alta Taylor) (Mrs. Lyndon Baines Johnson)
Johnson, Lee Harnie
Johnson, Lincoln F., Jr.
Johnson, Lloyd Kenneth
Johnson, Lynwood Albert
Johnson, Marvin Richard Alois
Johnson, Maurice DeVere Sanford
Johnson, Nicholas
Johnson, Norman
Johnson, Philip Carl
Johnson, Phillip Eugene
Johnson, Rafer Lewis
Johnson, Raymond Edward
Johnson, Rex D.
Johnson, Richard Abraham
Johnson, Richard Clayton
Johnson, Richard James Vaughn
Johnson, Richard Tenney
Johnson, Richard Tidball
Johnson, Robert Calvin, Jr.
Johnson, Robert Gerald
Johnson, Robert Hugh
Johnson, Robert Merrill
Johnson, Ronald Carl
Johnson, Russell Simms
Johnson, Ruth Carter
Johnson, Sam
Johnson, Searcy Lee
Johnson, Stanley Herbert, Jr.
Johnson, Terry Walter, Jr.
Johnson, Vernon Arthur
Johnson, Victor Samuel, Jr.
Johnson, Vinton Charles
Johnson, Warren Richard
Johnson, Wayne D.
Johnson, Wendell Eugene
Johnson, William Alexander
Johnson, William McKinley, Jr.
Johnson, William Rudolph
Johnston, Edward Allan
Johnston, Ernest B., Jr.
Johnston, Everett Dale
Johnston, Frank Randolph
Johnston, George Washington
Johnston, J. Bennett, Jr.
Johnston, James Jordon
Johnston, Joseph Forney
Johnston, Joseph Forney, Jr.
Johnston, Paul
Johnston, Richard Smith
Johnston, Robert Atkinson
Johnston, Thomas Alexander, III
Johnston, William Noel
Johnstone, Edmund Frank
Johnstone, Edward Huggins
Johnstone, Harry Inge
Johnstone, Leo Haskell, Jr.
Johnstone, Paul Meredith
Johnstone, Robert Lawrence
Joklik, Wolfgang Karl
Jolley, Homer Richard
Jolson, Marvin Arnold
Jonassen, Hans Boegh
Jones, Albert
Jones, Alfred William
Jones, Alma West
Jones, Bertram Hays
Jones, Billy Mac
Jones, Bob, Jr.
Jones, Catesby Brooke
Jones, Charles Franklin
Jones, Claiborne Stribling
Jones, D. Paul, Jr.
Jones, David Allen
Jones, David Charles
Jones, Douglas Epps
Jones, Ed
Jones, Edith Augusta
Jones, Edward Faucett
Jones, Edward Marshall
Jones, Edwin Lee, Jr.
Jones, Eric Wynn
Jones, Ernest Carl
Jones, Euine Fay
Jones, Frank Cater
Jones, Franklin Ross
Jones, Gordon
Jones, Gorman Robinson, Jr.
Jones, Halbert McNair
Jones, Harry Lee, II
Jones, Harry LeRoy
Jones, Henry Earl
Jones, Horace Charles
Jones, Howard Leon
Jones, Howard St. Claire, Jr.
Jones, Howard Wilbur, Jr.
Jones, J. Benton, Jr.
Jones, J. Kenley
Jones, J. Knox, Jr.
Jones, James Arthur
Jones, James Beverly
Jones, James R.
Jones, James Rees
Jones, Jameson Miller
Jones, Jenkin Lloyd
Jones, John Barclay, Jr.
Jones, John Evan
Jones, John Harris
Jones, John Martin, Jr.
Jones, John Paul
Jones, John Tilford, Jr.
Jones, Joseph West
Jones, Lawrence McCeney, Jr.
Jones, Lawrence Neale
Jones, Leo Bond
Jones, Lois Mailou (Mrs. V. Pierre-Noel)
Jones, Lyle Vincent
Jones, Madison Percy, Jr.
Jones, Malcolm Gwynne
Jones, Marshall (Louis) (Grandpa Jones)
Jones, Marshall Robertson
Jones, Milton Samuel
Jones, Otis Hunter
Jones, Philip Howard
Jones, Ralph Wood
Jones, Ray Lockwood
Jones, Rayford Scott
Jones, Raymond Allen, Jr.
Jones, Richard L.
Jones, Robert Edwards
Jones, Robert Gean
Jones, Robert Lawton
Jones, Robert Lee
Jones, Robert Marion
Jones, Roderic Miller
Jones, Roy Winfield
Jones, Samuel
Jones, Sarah Dowlin
Jones, Sidney Lewis
Jones, Stanley Llewelyn
Jones, Theodore Lawrence
Jones, Thomas L.
Jones, Virginia Lacy (Mrs. E.A. Jones)
Jones, Walter Beaman
Jones, Warren LeRoy
Jones, Wayne Van Leer
Jones, William Benjamin, Jr.
Jones, William Bowdoin
Jones, William Cecil
Jones, William Kenefick
Jones, William Maurice
Jones, Woodrow Wilson
Jones. Anne Patricia
Jonsson, Bjarni
Joost, Nicholas Teynac
Jordan, Barbara C.
Jordan, Bryce
Jordan, Carl Frederick
Jordan, Castle William
Jordan, Charles Lemuel
Jordan, Edward Daniel
Jordan, George Lyman, Jr.
Jordan, George Royal, Jr.
Jordan, Hamilton (William Hamilton McWhorter Jordan)
Jordan, Howard, Jr.
Jordan, James Dempsey
Jordan, James Phillip
Jordan, Jerry Niles
Jordan, John Richard, Jr.
Jordan, Joye Esch
Jordan, Kenneth Louis, Jr.
Jordan, Robert Elijah, III
Jordan, Robert Henry
Jordan, Robert Smith
Jordan, William Bryan, Jr.
Jordan, William Ditmer
Jordan, William Stone, Jr.
Jordan, Willis Pope, Jr.
Jorden, William John
Jordin, Marcus Wayne
Jorgensen, Matt Lawrence
Jorgenson, Wallace James
Jortberg, Robert Francis
Jory, Stephen Godfrey
Joseph, James Alfred
Joseph, Samuel Israel
Joslin, G. Stanley
Jova, Henri Vatable
Jova, Joseph John
Joyce, Harry Alexis Jones
Joyce, James Daniel
Joyner, Leon Felix
Joyner, Roy Elton
Joyner, Upshur Tucker
Joyner, Weyland Thomas
Judd, Brian Raymond
Jude, James Roderick
Judson, Jay Richard
Judy, Hubert Stonewall
Juhasz, Stephen
Juliana, James Nicholas
Julin, Joseph Richard
Jung, Rodney C.
Jurgensen, Christian Adolph, III
Jurgensen, Warren Peter
Jurkiewicz, Maurice John
Just, Carolyn Royall
Justice, (David) Blair
Justice, William Wayne
Kaelin, Eugene Francis
Kafka, Alexandre
Kafoed, E. J.
Kahan, Barry Donald
Kahler, Elizabeth Sartor
Kahler, Woodland
Kahn, Edwin Leonard
Kahn, Edwin Leonard
Kahn, Gordon Barry
Kahn, Herman Bernard
Kahn, Herman Heywood
Kahn, Tom
Kain, Ronald Stuart
Kainen, Jacob
Kaiser, Fred
Kaiser, Herbert
Kaiser, Philip M.
Kaiser, Robert Greeley
Kalergis, James George
Kalkus, Stanley
Kallsen, Theodore John
Kalman, Rudolf Emil
Kalmus, Henry Paul
Kalter, Seymour Sanford
Kaludis, George
Kamats, George Michael
Kamenetz, Herman Leo
Kamenske, Bernard Harold
Kamerow, Martin Laurence
Kamin, Henry
Kaminer, Hampton Glenn
Kamm, Linda Heller
Kamm, Robert B.
Kamm, Robert William
Kamm, Thomas Allen
Kampelman, Max M.
Kamphoefner, Henry Leveke
Kampmeier, Rudolph Herman
Kamrath, Karl
Kane, Charles Joseph
Kane, James Stewart
Kane, John Dandridge Henley, Jr.

REGIONAL LISTING—SOUTH-SOUTHWEST 850

Kanes, William Henry
Kanter, Joseph Hyman
Kantner, Arthur Henry
Kantner, John F.
Kantor, Harry Simkha
Kantor, Seth
Kaplan, Arthur Mark
Kaplan, Lewis David
Kaplan, Marshall L.
Kaplan, Sheldon Z.
Kaplow, Herbert Elias
Kappe, Stanley Edward
Kappel, Frederick Russell
Kapuscinski, Lucian
Karayanis, Plato
Karger, Delmar William
Kargon, Robert Hugh
Karl, Frederick Brennan
Karle, Isabella Lugoski
Karle, Jerome
Karlen, Delmar
Karlik, John R.
Karmel, Roberta S.
Karmin, Monroe William
Karner, Herbert Rudolf
Karnow, Stanley
Karson, Samuel
Karzon, David Theodore
Kash, Don Eldon
Kashiwa, Shiro
Kasriel, Robert Herman
Kass, Benny Lee
Kass, Julius
Kasserman, Kreel Wayne
Kasten, Paul Rudolph
Kasten, Robert W., Jr.
Katahn, Martin
Katell, Sidney
Katims, Milton
Katlic, John Edward
Kattawar, George Williford
Katz, Abraham
Katz, Herbert Marvin
Katz, Julius Louis
Katz, Samuel Lawrence
Katzen, Jay Kenneth
Katzman, Daniel
Kauderer, Bernard Marvin
Kauffman, David Lin
Kauffman, Kenneth Mark
Kaufman, Frank Albert
Kaufman, Herbert
Kaufman, Herbert Edward
Kaufman, Joseph W.
Kaufman, Nathan
Kaufman, Paul
Kaufman, Raymond Henry
Kaufman, Ronald Paul
Kaufmann, Ralph James
Kaulback, Frank Sanford, Jr.
Kautz, Lynford English
Kautz, Norman John
Kavalek, Lubomir
Kay, Albert
Kay, Joel Phillip
Kay, Saul
Kayser, Elmer Louis
Kazen, Abraham, Jr.
Keady, William Colbert
Keane, Mark Edward
Kearl, Wayne
Kearney, Lester T., Jr.
Kearney, Richard David
Keat, James Sussman
Keating, Louis Clark
Keats, Harold Alan
Keats, Theodore Eliot
Keay, James William
Kee, Walter Andrew
Keeble, Sydney Frazer, Jr.
Keech, Richmond B.
Keefe, William Carroll
Keegan, George Joseph, Jr.
Keeley, Robert Vossler
Keeling, Thomas Callender, Jr.
Keener, Bruce, III
Keener, Irby Arthur, Jr.
Keeney, Arthur Hail
Keeney, John C.
Keeny, Spurgeon Milton, Jr.
Keeton, Morris Teuton
Kehlbeck, Joseph Henry
Keiper, Bernard Stephen
Keiser, Harry Robert
Keith, Donald Raymond
Keith, Julian Faison
Keith, Robert Drake
Keith, Warren Gray
Keith-Lucas, Alan
Kelch, David Erdman
Kellam, Richard B.
Kelleher, Harry Bartlett
Kelleher, Herbert David
Keller, Charles, Jr.
Keller, Christoph, Jr.
Keller, Clarence Christian
Keller, Edward Clarence, Jr.
Keller, Robert Alexander, III
Keller, Robert Franklin
Keller, Stanley Ellis
Keller, Thomas Franklin
Kellerman, Karl Frederic
Kelley, Albert Benjamin
Kelley, Daniel Francis, Jr.
Kelley, Daniel Francis, Jr.
Kelley, Estel Wood
Kelley, Everette Eugene
Kelley, Helen
Kelley, Kitty
Kelley, Noble Henry
Kelley, Timothy Edward
Kelley, Vernon Edward
Kellison, James Bruce
Kelln, Albert Lee
Kellogg, Charles Edwin
Kellogg, Marion Knight

Kelly, Douglas, Jr.
Kelly, James Francis
Kelly, James Joseph
Kelly, Luther Wrentmore, Jr.
Kelly, Michael John
Kelly, Milton
Kelly, Orris Eugene
Kelly, Paul L.
Kelly, Richard
Kelly, Robert Emmett
Kelly, Robert Gorrell
Kelly, Samuel Edgar, Jr.
Kelly, Thomas C.
Kelly, Thomas Paine, Jr.
Kelly, Timothy Michael
Kelly, William Clark
Kelly, William Watkins
Kelsey, Frances Oldham, (Mrs. Fremont Ellis Kelsey)
Kelso, John Hodgson
Kemble, Charles Robert
Kemp, Emory Leland
Kemp, Francis Bolling, III
Kemp, Harris Atteridge
Kemp, Jack F.
Kemp, Lebbeus Courtright, Jr.
Kempf, Cecil Joseph
Kempner, Isaac Herbert, III
Kempner, Walter
Kempster, Norman Roy
Kendall, William Hersey
Kenderdine, John Marshall
Kendig, Edwin Lawrence, Jr.
Kendig, Perry Fridy
Kendrick, Caldwell Chappelear
Kendrick, Herbert Spencer, Jr.
Kendrick, John Jesse, Jr.
Kenelly, John Willis, Jr.
Kenley, James Bunting
Kennamer, Lorrin Garfield, Jr.
Kennan, Kent Wheeler
Kennedy, Cornelius Bryant
Kennedy, Davis Lee
Kennedy, Donald Sipe
Kennedy, Edward Moore
Kennedy, Ethel Skaker
Kennedy, Eugene Richard
Kennedy, Frances
Kennedy, George Alexander
Kennedy, John Wesley
Kennedy, Matthew Washington
Kennedy, Richard Thomas
Kennedy, Robert Edgar
Kennedy, Robert Emmet
Kennedy, Roger George
Kennedy, Thomas James, Jr.
Kennedy, William Jesse, III
Kenner, William Hugh
Kennerly, David Hume
Kenney, Howard Washington
Kenney, John Andrew, Jr.
Kenney, Richard Alec
Kenney, W. John
Kenney, William Richardson
Kenshalo, Daniel Ralph
Kent, Calvin Albert
Kent, Frederick Heber
Kent, George Cantine, Jr.
Kent, Robert Hutton
Kentera, George Richard
Kenyon, Carleton Weller
Kenyon, Hewitt
Keough, Donald Raymond
Kepley, James Spencer
Kepner, Woody
Kern, Bernard Donald
Kerney, James, Jr.
Kernodle, Rigdon Wayne
Kerr, Baine Perkins
Kerr, Dorothy Marie Burmeister
Kerr, Frank John
Kerr, Hawley Coe
Kerr, Robert S.
Kersh, Kenneth George
Kershaw, Joseph
Kershner, Howard Eldred
Kerwin, Joseph Peter
Kerxton, Alan Smith
Kessler, Edwin
Kessler, George William
Kessler, Karl Gunther
Kessler, Richard Callie
Kessler, Ronald Borek
Kester, John Gordon
Kester, Stewart Randolph
Kesting, Theodore
Kestner, Neil Richard
Ketcham, Alfred Schutt
Ketcham, Bruce Valenline
Ketcham, Howard
Ketcham, Orman weston
Ketchum, Harry Wilbur
Ketelsen, James Lee
Ketner, Ralph Wright
Keulegan, Garbis Hovannes
Keuper, Jerome Penn
Key, David McKendree
Key, Joe Lynn
Key, Marcus M(alvin)
Key, Milton Eugene
Key, Robert Edward Lee
Keyes, William C.
Kezios, Stothe Peter
Khadduri, Majid
Kharasch, Robert Nelson
Kibbe, Milton Homer
Kibler, David Burke, III
Kice, John Lord
Kidd, Charles Vincent
Kidd, Gene
Kidd, Roy Walter
Kidde, John Frederick
Kidder, James Hugh
Kieffer, Jarold Alan

Kiepper, Alan Frederick
Kier, Porter Martin
Kierce, James Brunson, Jr.
Kiernan, Owen Burns
Kiesling, Ernst Willie
Kiger, Joseph Charles
Kiker, Billy Frazier
Kiker, Ralph Douglas, Jr.
Kiker, Ralph Douglas, Jr.
Kilberg, Barbara (Bobbie) Greene
Kilberg, William Jeffrey
Kilborne, Robert Stewart
Kilby, Jack St. Clair
Kilcline, Thomas John
Kilgore, Ann Hitch
Kilgore, James Alford
Kilgore, Joe Madison
Kilgore, John Edward, Jr.
Kilgore, William Jackson
Kilian, Michael D.
Killebrew, James Robert
Killin, Charles Clark
Killinger, George Glenn
Killorin, Edward Wylly
Killpack, Larry Movell
Kilpatrick, Charles Otis
Kilpatrick, George H.
Kilpatrick, James Jackson, Jr.
Kilpatrick, James Lowe
Kilpatrick, S. James, Jr.
Kilroy, James Francis
Kim, Thomas Kunhyuk
Kimatian, Stephen H.
Kimball, Allyn Winthrop
Kimball, Arthur Alden
Kimball, Aubrey Pierce
Kimball, Solon Toothaker
Kimball, Thomas Lloyd
Kimball, Vera F.
Kimberly, John Robbins
Kimble, Gregory Adams
Kimbrel, Monroe
Kimbrough, Emory Calloway Landon, Jr.
Kimbrough, Ralph Bradley
Kimbrough, William Adams, Jr.
Kimche, Leila Iris
Kimelman, Henry L.
Kimerer, Neil Banard, Sr.
Kimmons, George Harvey
Kinard, Hargett Yingling
Kincaid, Hugh Reid
Kincaid, John Franklin
Kincheloe, James Benjamin
Kinder, Harold M.
Kindsvater, Carl Edward
King, Algin Braddy
King, Arnold Kimsey
King, August Allen
King, Benjamin Chamberlin
King, Benjamin Franklin, III
King, Billy Lee
King, Charles Erwin
King, Clyde Richard
King, Colbert Isaiah
King, Coretta Scott (Mrs. Martin Luther King, Jr.)
King, Elmer Richard
King, Francis Michael
King, Frederick Alexander
King, George Harold
King, George Harold, Jr.
King, Glen Doyle
King, Huger Sinkler
King, James F.
King, James Lawrence
King, John Francis
King, John Harry, Jr.
King, John Quill Taylor
King, Joseph Bertram
King, Joseph H.
King, Marian
King, Peter
King, Peter Cotterill
King, Preston Cloud, Jr.
King, Richard Adams
King, Robert Augustin
King, Robert Bruce
King, Robert Bruce
King, Robert Desmond
King, Robert Leroy
King, Robert Thomas
King, Rufus
King, Sol
King, Susan Bennett
King, Theodore Matthew
King, Thomas Joseph
King, Thomas Slater
Kingdon, Henry Shannon
Kingsbury-Smith, Joseph
Kingsley, Daniel Thain
Kingsley, Thomas Drowne
Kinlaw, Dennis Franklin
Kinnard, William James, Jr.
Kinne, Frances Bartlett
Kinnear, George Espy Ridgeway, II
Kinnebrew, Thomas Richard
Kinney, Douglas Merrill
Kinney, Sterling Edward
Kinoshita, Jin Harold
Kinsolving, Charles Lester
Kintner, Earl Wilson
Kintner, Edwin Earl
Kiplinger, Austin Huntington
Kipp, Dean Carl
Kirbo, Charles Hughes
Kirby, George Francis
Kirby, James Cordell, Jr.
Kirchheimer, Waldemar Franz
Kirchman, Robert Lester
Kirk, Alan Goodrich, II
Kirk, James Curtis
Kirk, James Lawrence, II

Kirk, Robert L.
Kirk, Roger Mann
Kirkbride, Chalmer Gatlin
Kirkendall, Ernest Oliver
Kirkendall, Walter Murray
Kirkland, John David
Kirkland, Joseph Lane
Kirklin, John Webster
Kirkpatrick, Evron Maurice
Kirkpatrick, Forrest Hunter
Kirkpatrick, Jeane Duane Jordan
Kirkpatrick, John Elson
Kirkpatrick, Milo Orton
Kirkpatrick, Richard Bogue
Kirksey, Charley Darwin
Kirmss, Frank, Jr.
Kirsch, Edward
Kirschstein, Ruth Lillian
Kirsner, Robert
Kirwan, William English, II
Kiser, Clyde Vernon
Kiser, James Webb
Kiser, Robert Wayne
Kissinger, Henry Alfred
Kit, Saul
Kitchen, Delmas Kendall
Kitchens, Alton Walter
Kitchin, Alvin Paul
Kitt, Loren Wayne
Kittleson, Henry Marshall
Kittrell, Flemmie Pansy
Kittrie, Nicholas N(orbert Nehemiah)
Kitzman, John Anthony
Kizer, Bernice Lichty
Kizer, John Oscar
Kizziar, Janet Wright
Kjellstrom, John Alfred
Klaerner, Curtis Maurice
Klagsbrunn, Hans Alexander
Klamon, Lawrence Paine
Klappert, Peter
Klaus, Kenneth Blanchard
Klein, Bernard
Klein, Elias
Klein, Melvyn Norman
Klein, Milton Martin
Klein, Raymond Walter
Kleinberg, Howard J.
Kleine, Herman
Kleinert, Harold Earl
Klement, Jerome Joseph
Klemt, Calvin Carl
Kleppe, Thomas S.
Klerman, Gerald Lawrence
Kletter, Edward
Kley, John Arthur
Kliewer, Edward Albert, Jr.
Kline, Billy Dan
Kline, Claire Benton, Jr.
Kline, David Gellinger
Kline, Gordon Mabey
Kline, Jacob
Kline, John William
Kline, Raymond Adam
Kline, Robert Reeves
Klinefelter, James Louis
Kling, William
Klingberg, Frank Wysor
Klintworth, Gordon Kenneth
Klip, Willem
Klippstatter, Kurt L.
Klitzke, Theodore Elmer
Klocko, Richard Phillip
Klopman, William Allen
Klostermeyer, Howard Randolph
Klotter, John Charles
Klotz, Bill W.
Klotz, Herbert Werner
Klotz, John Wesley
Kluge, Ralph Wendel
Klutznick, Philip M.
Knapp, Charles B.
Knapp, Daniel C.
Knapp, David Hebard
Knapp, Dennis Raymond
Knapp, George Lawrence, Jr.
Knapp, Joseph Grant
Knapp, Richard Bruce
Knauer, Virginia Harrington Wright (Mrs. Wilhelm F. Knauer)
Knebel, John Albert
Knecht, Charles Daniel
Knecht, Louis Bernard
Knickerbocker, Kenneth Leslie
Knight, Alfred Bishop
Knight, Franklin Willis
Knight, H. Stuart
Knight, Herbert Borwell
Knight, James Allen
Knight, James L.
Knight, John Allan
Knight, John Francis
Knight, John Lowden
Knight, John W.
Knight, Samuel Bradley
Knight, Vernon
Knight, Walker Leigh
Knight, William Edwards
Knipp, Helmut
Knisely, William Hagerman
Kniskern, Maynard
Knoblauch, Harold Carl
Knobloch, Carl William, Jr.
Knoedler, Elmer L.
Knoizen, Arthur Kenneth
Knoll, Jerry
Knoop, Werner Caldwell
Knopf, Irwin Jay
Knorr, Klaus Eugene
Knorr, Norman John
Knott, Francis Xavier
Knott, Henry Joseph

Knott, James Robert
Knowles, Jack Oliver
Knowles, Malcolm Shepherd
Knowles, Pete
Knowles, William Leroy
Knowlton, Charles Wilson
Knox, Bernard MacGregor Walker
Knox, C. Neal
Knox, Carl Warner
Knox, Ernest Rudder
Knox, John Marshall
Knutson, Ronald Dale
Kobayashi, Riki
Koch, Adolph Meyer
Koch, George William
Koch, Peter
Kochakian, Charles Daniel
Kochendorfer, Fred Daniel
Kochman, Andrew John
Kocurek, Louis Joe
Koehler, John Theodore
Koehler, Robert Earl
Koehler, Robert Earl
Koenig, Charles Louis
Koenig, Paul Edward
Koenig, Virgil
Koeppe, Roger Erdman
Koetter, Gunter William
Kogstad, Arthur Woodrow
Kohler, Charlotte
Kohler, Foy
Kohler, Peter Ogden
Kohlmeier, Louis Martin, Jr.
Kohn, John Peter, Jr.
Kohno, Toshiko
Koile, Earl
Koisch, Francis Paul
Kojian, Miran Haig
Kolb, Nathaniel Key, Jr.
Kole, John William
Kolenda, Konstantin
Koller, Herbert Richard
Kollmorgen, Leland Stanford
Kolodey, Fred James
Koltnow, Peter Gregory
Komer, Robert William
Komodore, Bill G.
Kondonassis, Alexander John
Konopnicki, Emil Leon
Kontos, Constantine William
Koomen, Jacob, Jr.
Koonts, Jones Calvin
Koop, Theodore Frederick
Koppel, Ted
Koppelman, Ray
Koren, Henry Joseph
Korn, David
Korn, Gerald Edward
Kornberg, Warren Stanley
Kornegay, Horace Robinson
Kornfeld, Julian Potash
Kornfeld, Lewis F., Jr.
Korologos, Tom Chris
Korth, Fred
Kory, Ross Conklin
Kosanke, William Henry
Kosberg, J. Livingston
Koski, Walter S.
Kossack, Carl Frederick
Kossiakoff, Alexander
Kostuik, Stephen Paul
Kotas, Robert Vincent
Kotcher, Emil
Kothe, Charles Aloysius
Kothe, Charles Aloysius
Kotschnig, Walter Maria
Kotz, Nathan Kallison (Nick)
Kotz, Samuel
Kouchoukos, Nicholas Thomas
Kouri, Donald Jack
Kousoulas, Dimitrios George
Kovach, Eugene George
Kovach, Francis Joseph
Kovasznay, Leslie Stephen George
Kowarski, Chana Rose (Mrs. Avinoam Kowarski)
Kozlowski, Ronald Stephan
Kozmetsky, George
Kraehe, Enno Edward
Kraemer, Charles Edgar Stanberry
Kraemer, William S.
Kraft, Christopher Columbus, Jr.
Kraft, Erwin Otto
Kraft, Joseph
Kraft, Tim
Krahl, Nat Wetzel
Krakower, Bernard Marvin
Kramer, Alex
Kramer, Amihud
Kramer, James Joseph
Kramer, Kenneth Bentley
Kramer, Morton
Kramer, Paul Jackson
Kramer, Reuben Robert
Kramer, Robert
Kramer, Robert Ivan
Kramish, Arnold
Krantz, Palmer Eric, III
Krantz, Sanford Burton
Kranzberg, Melvin
Kraslow, David
Krastin, Karl
Kratochvil, L(ouis) Glen
Kraus, Alfred Paul
Kraus, Gerard
Kraus, Sister Irene
Krause, Harry Norman
Krause, Manfred Otto
Krause, Richard Arthur
Krause, Richard Michael
Krause, William Austin
Krausse, Daniel Marston

Kravitch, Phyllis A.
Kravitz, Lawrence Charles
Krebs, Max Vance
Krebs, Rockne
Kreeger, David Lloyd
Kreider, Thomas McRoberts
Krementz, Edward Thomas
Krentzman, Ben
Kreps, Juanita Morris (Mrs. Clifton H. Kreps, Jr.)
Kress, Paul Frederick
Kress, Roy Alfred
Kretchmer, Norman
Kreyling, Edward George, Jr.
Krieger, Robert Lyman
Krigbaum, William Richard
Krisch, Adolph Oscar
Krisch, Joel
Krislov, Samuel
Krispyn, Egbert
Kristiansen, Magne
Krogdahl, Wasley Swen
Kroll, Milton Paul
Krombein, Karl vonVorse
Kromhout, Robert Andrew
Kronstadt, Arnold Mayo
Kruger, Gustav Otto, Jr.
Kruger, Jerome
Kruger, Rudolf
Krulitz, Leo Morrion
Krumholz, Louis Augustus
Kruse, Cornelius Wolfram
Kruse, Heeren Samuel Eilts
Kruse, Paul Robert
Krusen, Edward Montgomery
Krusen, Henry Stanley
Krutchkoff, Richard Gerald
Kucera, Anthony Lee
Kuechenberg, Robert John
Kuehn, Ronald L(awrence), Jr.
Kuenzler, Edward Julian
Kugel, Robert Benjamin
Kuhlthau, Alden Robert
Kuhn, Albin Owings
Kuhn, Charles E.
Kuhn, Gus David, Jr.
Kuhn, Jack Weil
Kulczycki, Lucas L.
Kullback, Solomon
Kulski, Julian Eugeniusz
Kulski, Wladyslaw Wszebor
Kulynych, Petro
Kumpe, Roy Franklin
Kunstadter, Ralph Hess
Kuntz, Eugene Oscar
Kuntz, Marion Lucile Leathers
Kuntz, Paul Grimley
Kunz, George James
Kunze, George William
Kunzig, Robert Lowe
Ku Pei-Moo
Kupfer, Carl
Kupperian, James Edward, Jr.
Kupperman, Robert Harris
Kurk, George John
Kursunoglu, Behram
Kurth, Walter Richard
Kurtz, Jerome
Kurtz, Samuel Mordecai
Kurtzke, John Francis
Kurzhals, Peter Ralph
Kurzman, Stephen
Kusch, Polykarp
Kushner, David Zakeri
Kushner, Lawrence Maurice
Kuss, Henry John, Jr.
Kuttas, George
Kutz, Joseph Edward
Kuykendall, Jerome Kenneth
Kwiatkowski, Gordon Jerome
Kyl, John Henry
Kyle, John Hamilton
Kyle, William J., Jr.
LaBarge, Mary Jane
LaBarre, Carl Anthony
La Berge, Walter Barber
Laborde, Alden James
Lacey, Howard Elton
Lachs, John
Lack, Fredell
Lack, Leon
Lackey, Robert (Shields)
Lacovara, Philip Allen
Lacy, Alexander Shelton
Ladd, David Lowell
Ladd, Ernest Fleetwood, Jr.
Ladin, Eugene
Ladner, Heber A.
La Falce, John Joseph
Lagather, Robert B.
Lagomarsino, Robert John
Lagowski, J(oseph) J(ohn)
LaGrone, Alfred Hall
LaGrone, Cyrus Wilson, Jr.
LaHood, Charles George, Jr.
Laingen, Lowell Bruce
Laird, E. Ruth
Laird, Melvin R.
Laise, Frederic Stevens
Laitin, Joseph
Laitinen, Herbert August
Lake, I. Beverly
Lake, John Byron
Lake, Richard Harrington
Lake, W(illiam) Anthony Kirsopp
Lalley, John Spalding
Lallinger, E. Michael
Lally, Francis Joseph
Lally, Richard Francis
Lamas, Jose Ramon
Lamb, George Thomas
Lamb, Jamie Parker, Jr.
Lamb, Lawrence Edward
Lambert, Jeremiah Daniel
Lambert, Olaf Cecil

851 REGIONAL LISTING—SOUTH-SOUTHWEST

Lambert, Robert Gilbert
Lambert, Robert Stansbury
Lambooy, John Peter
Lamborn, Robert Louis
Lamkin, William Pierce
Lamm, Lester Paul
Lammons, Aubrey Owen
Lamon, Harry Vincent, Jr.
Lamone, Rudolph Philip
Lamont, Elizabeth Carrington Brown
La Motte, Clyde Wilson
Lampl, Peggy Ann
Lampton, Robert Benjamin
Lamy, Peter Paul
Lanahan, John Stevenson
Lancaster, Billy Jack
Lancaster, Bruce Morgan
Lancaster, Joseph Lawrence, Jr.
Lancaster, Robert Samuel
Lance, Thomas Bertram
Land, Aubrey Christian
Land, Francis LaVerne
Land, Malcolm Louis
Landa, Alfonso
Landa, William Robert
Landau, Brooksley Elizabeth
Landauer, Jerry Gerd
Landen, Robert Geran
Landis, Lewis Rex
Landmann, Wendell August
Landolt, Arlo Udell
Landon, Robert Kirkwood
Landrieu, Moon
Landrith, Harold Fochone
Landry, Tom (Thomas Wade)
Landstrom, Karl Sigurd
Lane, Alvin Huey, Jr.
Lane, Bernard Bell
Lane, Charles William, III
Lane, Edward Eliot
Lane, Edward Wood, Jr.
Lane, James Franklin
Lane, James Garland, Jr.
Lane, John Dennis
Lane, John Michael
Lane, Louis
Lane, Lyle Franklin
Lane, Mark
Lane, Montague
Lane, Richard N.
Lane, William Guerrant
Lane, William H.
Laney, James Joseph
Laney, James Thomas
Lang, Arthur Wilson, Jr.
Lang, Cecil Yelverton
Lang, Erich Karl
Lang, John Sanford
Langbaum, Robert Woodrow
Langbein, Walter B.
Langdale, Noah Noel, Jr.
Langdell, Robert Dana
Langdon, James Lloyd
Lange, Frederick Matthew
Lange, James Braxton
Lange, Phil C.
Langenberg, Frederick Charles
Langenderfer, Harold Quentin
Langenkamp, R. Dobie
Langer, James John
Langford, Ernest
Langford, Irvin James
Langford, Kenneth Royston
Langford, Thomas Anderson
Langhetee, Edmond Joseph, Jr.
Langhoff, Severin Peter, Jr.
Langholz, Robert Wayne
Langlinais, Joseph Willis
Langman, Jan
Langstaff, George Quigley, Jr.
Langston, James Horace
Langston, Paul T.
Langston, Roy A.
Langston, Russell Lee
Lanham, Benjamin Tillman, Jr.
Lanham, Elizabeth
Lanier, John Hicks
Lanier, Joseph Lamar, Jr.
Lanier, Sartain
Laning, Robert Comegys
Lank, Robert Byron
Lankford, Francis Greenfield, Jr.
Lannan, J. Patrick
Lanouette, William John
Lansdale, Robert Tucker
Lansden, Merle
Lanzillotti, Robert Franklin
Lapidus, Morris
Lapsley, William Winston
Laqueur, Walter
Laramore, Don Nelson
Large, John Willard
Larkin, Brian James
Larkin, Richard Xavier
Larkins, John Davis, Jr.
Larner, Joseph
Laro, Arthur Emmett
LaRocca, Joseph Paul
La Rocque, Gene Robert
Larrabee, Carroll Burton
Larrabee, Donald Richard
Larrabee, Martin Glover
Larry, R. Heath
Larsh, Howard William
Larsh, John Edgar, Jr.
Larson, Clarence Edward
Larson, Godfrey Edward
Larson, Harold Vernon
Larson, Jess
Larson, Kermit Dean
Larson, Paul Frank
Larson, Thomas Bryan
Lasater, Hubert L.
Lascara, Vincent Alfred
Lashinsky, Herbert
Lashof, Joyce R. Cohen
Lasky, Victor
Lasley, James Bernard
Lassiter, Charles Albert
Lassiter, Ronald Corbett
Lasslo, Andrew
Laswell, Troy James
Latane, James Wilson
Latham, Gary Vincent
Latham, Jean Lee
Latham, William Peters
Latimer, Allie B.
Latimer, John Francis
Latimer, Murray Webb
Latimer, Paul Henry
Latta, Delbert L.
Latta, Gordon Eric
Lattin, Clark Parker, Jr.
Latting, Patience Sewell (Mrs. Trimble B. Latting)
Latto, Lawrence Jay
Lauderdale, Frank, Jr.
Laufe, Leonard Edward
Laufman, Sidney
Laughery, Jack Arnold
Laughlin, Charles Vaill
Lauinger, Philip Charles
Launius, Melvin Ray
Laupus, William Edward
Laurence, Dan H.
Laurent, Don
Laurent, Lawrence Bell
Laurent, Ronald P.
Lavender, Robert Eugene
Laverge, Jan
Lavery, William Edward
Lavis, Rick Comstock
Law, Lloyd William
Lawhon, John E., III
Lawler, Beverley Rhea
Lawler, Bruce Gibbs
Lawler, Charles Alton
Lawrence, Charles Barnes, Jr.
Lawrence, Charles Edmund
Lawrence, George H.
Lawrence, Harding Luther
Lawrence, James Harold, Jr.
Lawrence, John Miller
Lawrence, Kenneth Morrison
Lawrence, Philip Signor
Lawrence, Richard Day
Lawrence, Walter, Jr.
Lawrence, Walter David
Lawrence, William Porter
Laws, Robert Julian
Lawson, Juan Otto
Lawson, Richard Henry
Lawson, Richard Laverne
Lawson, Robert Barrett
Lawson, Robert William, Jr.
Lawson, Thomas Sawyer
Lawson, William David, III
Lawton, Alfred Henry
Lawton, George Albert
Lawton, Robert Oswald
Lawwill, Theodore
Laxalt, Paul
Lay, Herman Warden
Lay, Kenneth Lee
Lay, Norvie Lee
Layden, Andrew James
Laymon, Charles Martin
Layne, James Nathaniel
Layton, Emmet John
Lazarus, Kenneth Anthony
Lazenby, Fred Wiehl
Lea, Scott Carter
Lea, Tom
Leach, Daniel Edward
Leach, Edward Curtis
Leach, Joseph Lee
Leach, Maurice Derby, Jr.
Leachman, Robert Briggs
League, Archie William
Leahy, Patrick Joseph
Leak, Robert E.
Leake, George Junius
Lear, William Edward
Leard, John Earnshaw
Learey, Fred Don
Leary, James Francis
Leary, John Charles
Leary, Lewis
Leary, Thomas Samuel
Leath, James Marvin
Leavell, Byrd Stuart
Leavell, Jerome Fontaine
Leavengood, Victor Price
Leaverton, Paul Emmett, Jr.
Leavitt, Joan Kazanjian
Leavitt, Joseph
Leavitt, Milo David, Jr.
Leban, Michael Eugene
LeBaron, Edward Wayne, Jr.
Lebensohn, Zigmond Meyer
Leber, Walter Philip
Lebow, Irwin Leon
Lechowich, Richard Victor
Leclerc, Ivor
Ledbetter, Calvin (Cal) Reville, Jr.
Lederer, Raymond Francis
Lederman, Leonard Lawrence
Ledford, Hubert Francis
Ledogar, Raymond Anthony
LeDoux, Harold Anthony
Ledyard, Robins Heard
Lee, Addison Earl
Lee, Allan Wren
Lee, Armistead Mason
Lee, Blair, III
Lee, Brenda
Lee, Charles Robert
Lee, Chester Maurice
Lee Ching Wen
Lee, Frederick Billings
Lee, Frederick Yuk Leong
Lee, Gary A.
Lee, Gary Edwin
Lee, Gus Charles
Lee, James Gillis
Lee, James Michael
Lee, Joe R.
Lee, Norman Ray
Lee, R(aymond) William, Jr.
Lee, Robert E.
Lee, Ronald Barry
Lee, Sidney Phillip
Lee, Sul Hi
Lee, Thomas Edison
Lee, William Franklin, III
Lee, William James
Lee, William John
Lee, William States
Lee, Yung-Keun
Leech, Robert Milton
Leech, William McMillan, Jr.
Leeds, William Latham
Leedy, Daniel Loney
Leek, Sybil
Leer, John W.
Leestma, Robert
Lefevre, Elbert Walter, Jr.
Leff, Arthur
Leff, Carl
Leff, Julius Jack
Leffall, LaSalle Doheny, Jr.
Leflar, Robert Allen
LeFlore, Byron Louis
Leftwich, Richard Henry
Legerton, Clarence William, Jr.
Legg, William Jefferson
Leggett, Robert Louis
Lehman, Arnold Lester
Lehman, Harvey Eugene
Lehman, William
Lehmann, Winfred Philipp
Lehne, Henry
Lehninger, Albert Lester
Lehrer, James Charles
Lehrer, Robert Nathaniel
Lehrman, Irving
Leibold, Arthur William, Jr.
Leidesdorf, Arthur David
Leidinger, William John
Leiferman, Irwin Hamilton
Leiferman, Silvia Weiner (Mrs. Irwin H. Leiferman)
Leigh, Donald Charles
Leigh, Monroe
Leigh, Thomas Watkins
Leigh, Walter Henry
Leighton, David Keller, Sr.
Leigon, Ralph Arthur
Leiper, Harper
Leiss, James Elroy
Leith, Carlton James
Leith, John Haddon
Leitzell, Terry Lee
Le Jeune, Francis Ernest, Jr.
Lejeune, Michael Leonard
Lejins, Peter Pierre
Leland, George Thomas (Mickey)
Lemaistre, Charles Aubrey
Lemann, Thomas Berthelot
LeMieux, Henry Fisher
Lemlich, Robert
Lemon, Frank Raymond
Lemos, Ramon Marcelino
Lenaburg, Alvin Edward
Lenchuk, Paul, Jr.
Lenfant, Claude Jean-Marie
Leng, Shao Chuan
Lenihan, Joseph Leo
Lennarz, William Joseph
Lensen, George Alexander
Lenski, Gerhard Emmanuel
Lent, George Eidt
Lentz, Harold Herbert
Lentz, Leslie Lawrence
Leon, Leonard
Leonard, Hugh Randolph
Leonard, James Fulton
Leonard, James Joseph
Leonard, Jerris
Leonard, Rodney Edwin
Leonard, Walter Jewell
Leonard, Walter Raymond
Leonard, Will Ernest, Jr.
Leonard, William Augustus, II
Leonard, William Norris
Leone, Charles Abner
Leone, Fred Charles
Leonhardt, William Stroup
Lerch, Richard Heaphy
Lerner, Abba Ptachya
Lerner, Abram
Lerner, Louis Abraham
Lerner, Louis C.
Lerner, Warren
LeRoy, L. David
Lesch, George Henry
Lesch, James Richard
Lesesne, Joab Mauldin, Jr.
Lesh, Janet Rountree
Lesher, Richard Lee
Leshner, Zane
Lesikar, Raymond Vincent
Leslie, Gerald Ronnell
Leslie, Henry Arthur
Leslie, John Walter
Leslie, John William
Lesnik, Max
Lessard, Raymond W.
Lessenberry, D. D.
Lester, Antalo David
Lester, Barnett Benjamin
Lester, Charles Turner
Lester, Edward
Lester, Garner McConnico
Lester, Malcolm
Lester, Richard Garrison
Lester, Robert Leonard
Lester, Virginia Laudano
Lester, William Dale
Lethbridge, Francis Donald
LeTourneau, Richard Howard
Letson, John Walter
Letton, Alva Hamblin
Leva, Marx
Le Van, C. J.
Levatino, Anthony Samuel
Levenson, Jacob Clavner
Levenson, Seymour
Leventhal, Carl M.
Leverenz, Oscar Taylor
Levey, Gerrit
Levi, Robert Henry
Levin, Carl
Levin, Carl
Levin, David
Levin, Gilbert Victor
Levin, Harold Arthur
Levin, Ruben
Levin, William Cohn
Levine, David Lawrence
Levine, Irving Raskin
Levine, Jerome
Levine, Robert Sidney
Levine, Samuel Gale
Levine, Saul
Levison, Robert Henry
Levit, George E.
Levitan, Sar A.
Levitas, Elliott H.
Levitine, George
Levitz, Ralph
Levy, Benjamin Hirsch
Levy, David
Levy, David Alfred
Levy, Harold Rochelle
Levy, Michael Richard
Levy, Robert Isaac
Lewenthal, Reeves, Sr.
Lewicki, Ann Maria
Lewin, George Forest
Lewinsohn, Joann
Lewis, Arthur Dee
Lewis, Boyd De Wolf
Lewis, Ceylon Smith, Jr.
Lewis, Charles William, Jr.
Lewis, Daniel Curtis, Jr.
Lewis, Edward Grey
Lewis, Edward Sheldon
Lewis, Emanuel Raymond
Lewis, Floyd Wallace
Lewis, Frank Russell
Lewis, George Russel
Lewis, Hal Graham
Lewis, Harold Gregg
Lewis, Harold Walter
Lewis, Harvey Shelton
Lewis, Henry Wilkins
Lewis, Herman Willian
Lewis, James Eldon
Lewis, James Pitcher
Lewis, James Woodrow
Lewis, Jerry
Lewis, John Gideon, Jr.
Lewis, Jordan David
Lewis, Matthew, Jr.
Lewis, Morris, Jr.
Lewis, Oren Ritter
Lewis, Richard Stanley
Lewis, Robert George
Lewis, Sydney
Lewis, Walter David
Lewis, William Walker
Ley, Herbert Leonard, Jr.
Lhotka, John Francis
Liberto, Joseph Salvatore
Licht, Sidney
Lichtenstein, Lawrence Mark
Lichtwardt, Richard Donald
Liddle, Grant Winder
Lide, Theodore Ellis, Jr.
Lidtke, Vernon LeRoy
Lieb, Irwin Chester
Liebenow, Robert C.
Liebenow, Robert C.
Liebert, John Granville
Liebmann, George William
Liebowitz, Harold
Liedtke, John Hugh
Liedtke, John Hugh
Lierman, James Darwin
Lietzke, Milton Henry
Light, Arthur Heath
Lightner, Jerry Preston
Lijinsky, William
Lilienfeld, Abraham Morris
Lilienfield, Lawrence Spencer
Lill, Gordon Grigsby
Lilley, Tom
Lilly, Hugh Tucker
Lilly, James Epling
Lilly, Thomas Gerald
Lilly, William Eldridge
Lincoln, C(harles) Eric
Lindemann, Oscar Curtis
Linder, Allen James
Linder, Bruno
Linder, Forrest Edward
Linder, Isham Wiseman
Linder, James Benjamin
Lindholm, William Lawrence
Lindley, Denton Ray
Lindley, James Gunn
Lindquist, Clarence Bernhart
Lindquist, Richard Frederick
Lindquist, Robert Stewart
Lindsay, Bryan Eugene
Lindsay, David Breed, Jr.
Lindsey, Henry Carlton
Lindsey, James Russell
Lindsey, John Horace
Lindsey, John Morton
Lindsey, Robert Sears
Linduska, Joseph Paul
Linehan, John Andrew
Linehan, Kathleen Mary
Ling, James J.
Link, David Merrill
Link, Edwin Albert
Link, Mae Mills (Mrs. S. Gordden Link)
Link, Marilyn Calmes
Link, S. Gordden
Linowitz, Sol Myron
Linton, Calvin Darlington
Lion, Donor
Lion, Paul Michel, III
Lipman, Ira Ackerman
Lipnick, Elton Starley
Lippincott, Joseph Wharton, Jr.
Lippitt, Gordon Leslie
Lipscomb, Edward Lowndes
Lipsett, Mortimer Broadwin
Lipshie, Joseph
Lipshutz, Robert Jerome
Lipshy, Ben Allen
Lipson, Harry Aaron, Jr.
Lipton, Morris Abraham
Liquori, Martin William, Jr.
Lisanby, James Walker
Liska, George
Lissim, Simon
Lister, Thomas Mosie
Litchfield, John Thomas, Jr.
Litke, Arthur Ludwig
Litschgi, Albert Byrne
Litt, Nahum
Littell, Gale Patterson
Littell, Norman Mather
Littell, Wallace William
Littig, Lawrence William
Little, C(harles) Edward, Sr.
Little, Edward Southard
Little, Elbert Luther, Jr.
Little, Jack Denver
Little, James Maxwell
Little, Joseph Alexander
Little, Larry Chatmon
Little, Loyd Harry, Jr.
Little, Robert Colby
Little, Robert Narvaez, Jr.
Little, Walter Francis, Jr.
Little, William Frederick
Littlefield, John Walley
Littlejohn, Cameron Bruce
Littlejohn, Oliver Marsilius
Littleton, Harvey Kline
Littleton, Isaac Thomas, III
Littman, Earl
Lively, Edwin Lowe
Lively, Pierce
Livezey, William Edmund
Livick, Malcolm Harris
Livingston, Boynton Parker
Livingston, J. Sterling
Livingston, James Archibald, Jr.
Livingston, James Craig
Livingston, Robert Edward
Livingston, Robert Linlithgow, Jr.
Livingston, William Samuel
Livingstone, Ray(mond) S.
Ljungdahl, Lars Gerhard
Llewellyn, James Bruce
Llewellyn, John Anthony
Lloyd, Arthur Young
Lloyd, Hermon
Lloyd, Hugh Adams
Lloyd, Jim
Lloyd, Ralph Waldo
Lloyd-Jones, Donald J.
Loader, Jay Gordon
Loar, Peggy Ann Wahl
Lobanov-Rostovsky, Oleg
Locke, Edwin Allen, III
Locke, John Robinson
Locke, Louis Glenn
Locke, Walter Michael
Locke, Wendell Vernon
Lockett, Aubrey Lee
Lockhart, Vance Elvis
Lockhead, Gregory Roger
Lockwood, Lee
Lockwood, Richard Allen
Loeffler, Thomas G.
Loehlin, John Clinton
Loerke, William Carl
Loesch, Harrison
Loeser, Norma Maine
Loevinger, Lee
Loewenstein, Werner Randolph
Loftin, Marion Theo
Loftis, John Landrum, Jr.
Logan, John A.
Logan, Lowell Alvin
Logan, Mathew Kuykendall
Logan, Rayford W.
Logan, William Boyd
Lokey, Hamilton
London, George
Londrey, James Leslie
Long, Bob G.
Long, Charles Houston
Long, Clarence Dickinson, Jr.
Long, Donlin Martin
Long, Eugene Hudson
Long, Gillis William
Long, Herbert Elwood
Long, Homer Samuel, Jr.
Long, Maurice Wayne
Long, Meredith J.
Long, Robert Clark
Long, Robert Radcliffe
Long, Russell Billiu
Longaker, Richard Pancoast
Longcrier, Henry Leslie, Jr.
Longenecker, Herbert Eugene
Longfellow, M. Tom
Longley, James Baird
Longworth, Alice Lee Roosevelt
Loomis, Henry
Loomis, John Edward
Loomis, Philip Albert, Jr.
Looney, William Boyd
Looper, Charles Eugene
Loos, John Louis
Loosbrock, John Francis
Lopez de Victoria, Juan de Dios
Lopez-Morillas, Juan
Lord, Anthony
Lord, Charles Edwin
Lord, Douglas Robert
Lord, Glenn Richard
Lord, Henry Robbins
Lord, William Jackson, Jr.
Lorensen, Willard Dean
Lorentz, George G.
Lorenz, John George
Lorenz, John Robbins
Lorenzo, Francisco A.
Lorinczi, George Gabriel
Lorsung, Thomas Nicholas
Loser, Joseph Carlton
Lotito, Ernest Arthur
Lott, Kench Lee, Jr.
Lott, Kench Lee, Jr.
Lott, Trent
Lott, William Cato
Lotz, Walter Edward, Jr.
Loucks, Charles Ernest
Loudermilk, John D.
Loughery, Richard Miller
Louis, Paul Adolph
Louis, William Roger
Lourie, Reginald Spencer
Louttit, Richard Talcott
Love, Benton F.
Love, Charles Marion, Jr.
Love, Franklin Sadler
Love, James Franklin, Jr.
Love, James Lowrey
Love, Richard Harvey
Love, Robert William, Jr.
Love, Tom Jay, Jr.
Love, Warner Edwards
Lovelace, Alan Mathieson
Loveland, Edward Henry
Loveland, Eugene Franklin
Loveless, Herschel Cellel
Lovell, James A., Jr.
Lovell, James Frederick
Lovell, Malcolm Read, Jr.
Lovern, James Chessel
Lovett, H(enry) Malcolm
Loving, George Gilmer, Jr.
Lovvorn, Roy Lee
Lovvorn, Wilmer Lamar
Low, Edmon
Low, Emmet Francis, Jr.
Low, John Thomas Cuyama
Low, Joseph
Low, Peter Weeks
Low, Stephen
Lowance, Carter O.
Lowd, Judson Dean
Lowe, Betty Ann
Lowe, Dewey Kwoc Kung
Lowe, Harry
Lowe, Harry J.
Lowe, M. David
Lowe, Sam Franklin, Jr.
Lowe, Thomas Parker
Lowe, William Alexander
Lowens, Irving
Lowenstein, Irwin Lang
Lowenstein, James Gordon
Lowenstein, Ralph Lynn
Lowery, Joseph E.
Lowrey, Ernest James
Lowry, Charles Wesley
Lowry, Mike
Lowry, Ralph Addison
Loy, Frank Ernest
Loyd, Harold Lynn
Lozzio, Bismarck Berto
Lubar, Jeffrey Stuart
Lubell, Harold
Lubick, Donald Cyril
Lucas, Aubrey Keith
Lucas, Edwin Fleming, Jr.
Lucas, J. Richard
Lucas, William Blair
Lucas, William Devaughn
Lucas, William Ray
Lucey, Charles Emmet
Lucey, Charles Timothy
Luchsinger, Vincent Peter, Jr.
Lucier, Francis Paul
Luck, Georg Hans Bhawani
Luckhart, Elton Wagner
Luckie, Robert Ervin, Jr.
Lucy, William
Ludeke, Carl Arthur
Ludeman, Douglas Henry
Ludlum, John Charles
Ludlum, Robert Phillips
Ludwick, William R.
Ludwig, George Harry
Ludwig, John McKay
Ludwig, Louis
Ludwigson, John Ormont
Lueck, James Ferguson, Jr.
Luecke, Sister Janemarie
Luetkemeyer, John Alexander
Lugar, Richard Green
Luhrs, Albert Weigand
Luibel, George Joseph

REGIONAL LISTING—SOUTH-SOUTHWEST 852

Luigs, Charles Russell
Luikart, Fordyce Whitney
Lujan, Manuel, Jr.
Lukash, William Matthew
Luke, Norman John
Luke, Robert Alfred
Luken, Thomas A.
Lukens, Alan Wood
Lukin, Philip
Lukowsky, Robert Owen
Lumpkin, Alva Moore
Lumpkin, John Henderson
Lumpkin, Thomas Dunlap
Lund, Wendell Luther
Lundeberg, Philip Karl
Lundelius, Ernest Luther, Jr.
Lundell, Cyrus Longworth
Lundine, Stanley Nelson
Lundquist, Charles Arthur
Lundquist, Clarence Theodore
Lunger, Irvin Eugene
Lunin, Martin
Lunn, Robert Joseph
Lunney, Glynn Stephen
Lunnon, Betty Sheehan
Luper, Harold Lee
Luper, Oral Leon
Lupton, Charles Hamilton, Jr.
Lush, Gerson Harrison
Luss, Dan
Lutey, John Kent
Luther, Herbert Adesla
Lutken, Donald C.
Luton, Johnston Edward
Lutz, Hartwell Borden
Lutz, Raymond Price
Luvisi, Lee
Luxenberg, Malcolm Neuwahl
Lyall, Katharine C(ulbert)
Lydman, Jack Wilson
Lyght, Charles Everard
Lykes, Joseph T., Jr.
Lyle, James Albert
Lyle, Robert Edward, Jr.
Lyle, Robert Simpson
Lyles, William Gordon
Lynch, Corwin James, Jr.
Lynch, Creighton Brooks
Lynch, Edward Michael
Lynch, John Brown
Lynch, John Ellsworth
Lynch, John F.
Lynch, Thomas Patrick
Lynch, William Walker
Lyng, Richard Edmund
Lynn, Henry Sharpe
Lynn, James Thomas
Lynn, Kenneth Schuyler
Lynn, Loretta Webb (Mrs. Oliver Lynn, Jr.)
Lynn, Thomas Neil, Jr.
Lynn, William Sanford, Jr.
Lynn, Yen-Mow
Lynne, Seybourn Harris
Lyon, Eugene Davisson
Lyon, George Marshall
Lyon, Scott Calvin
Lyons, Champ, Jr.
Lyons, Charles A., Jr.
Lyons, Clifford Pierson
Lyons, Dennis Gerald
Lyons, Ellis
Lyons, Francis Joseph
Lyons, George Sage
Lyons, James Aloysius, Jr.
Lyons, John H.
Lyons, John W(inship)
Lyons, Thomas William
Lysinger, Rex Jackson
Lystad, Mary Hanemann (Mrs. Robert Lystad)
Lystad, Robert Arthur
Lythcott, George Ignatius
Lytle, Andrew Nelson
Ma, Michael
MacArthur, Donald Malcolm
MacArthur, Gloria
Macaulay, Hugh Holleman, Jr.
MacCallan, W(illiam) David
Mac Corkle, Stuart Alexander
Macdaniel, Gibbs, Jr.
Macdonald, Cynthia Lee
Mac Donald, Gordon James Fraser
Macdonald, H. Malcolm
Macdonald, James Ross
MacDonald, John Dann
MacDonald, Kevin John
Mac Donald, Malcolm Murdoch
Macdonald, Ray Woodward
Macdonald, Robert Rigg, Jr.
MacDonald, Thomas Cook, Jr.
MacDonnell, Robert George
Mace, David Robert
Macer, Dan Johnstone
Macesich, George
Macey, Morris William
Macfarlan, Duncan
MacFarland, Lonsdale Porter, Jr.
MacGowan, Charles Frederic
MacGregor, Clark
Machemer, Robert
Macht, Robert
MacIntyre, A(lfonso) Everette
Mack, Edward John
Mack, Julia Cooper
Mack, Raymond Francis
Mack, William Paden
Mackall, Laidler Bowie
Mac Kaye, William Ross
Mackenzie, John
MacKenzie, Richard Stanley
Mackey, Howard Hamilton, Sr.
Mackey, Louis Henry
Mackey, William Sturges, Jr.
Mackin, Bernard John
Mackin, Catherine
Mackin, Cooper Richerson
MacKinnon, Cyrus Leland
MacKinnon, George E.
Mackle, Francis Elliott, Jr.
Macklin, Gordon Stanley
Mackmull, Jack Vincent
Macksey, Richard Alan
MacLamroc, James Gwaltney Westwarren
Mac Laury, Bruce King
MacLean, Hector
MacLean, John Ronald
Maclean, Malcolm Roderick
MacLean, Paul Donald
MacLean, William
Macleay, Donald
MacMahon, Charles Hutchins, Jr.
MacMillan, James Murdock
Macmillan, William Hooper
Macnamara, Thomas Edward
MacNaughton, Donald Sinclair
MacNaughton, James Robert
MacNeil, Grace M. S. McKittrick (Mrs. Douglas H. MacNeil)
MacNelly, Jeffrey Kenneth
Macon, Joseph Allston
Macon, Seth Craven
MacPherson, Herbert Grenfell
MacRae, Duncan, Jr.
MacRae, Edith Krugelis (Mrs. Duncan MacRae, Jr.)
Macrae, John, Jr.
Macy, John Williams, Jr.
Madden, David
Madden, Murdaugh Stuart
Madden, Wales Hendrix, Jr.
Maddox, Alva Hugh
Maddox, Jesse Cordell
Maddox, Lester Garfield
Maddox, Robert Nott
Maddux, James Frederick
Madigan, Edward R.
Madigan, Richard Allen
Maechling, Charles, Jr.
Maehl, William Henry, Jr.
Maffin, Robert William
Maffitt, Theodore Stuart, Jr.
Magee, Warren Egbert
Mager, Gerald
Magill, Bradford Steele
Maglione, Ralph John, Jr.
Magner, George William
Magnuson, Warren Grant
Maguire, Andrew
Mahaffey, John
Mahan, Archie Irvin
Maher, John Richard
Maher, Patrick Joseph
Mahesh, Virendra Bushan
Mahey, John Andrew
Mahlmann, John James
Mahon, Eldon Brooks
Mahon, James Samuel
Mahon, John Keith
Mahoney, William Grattan
Mahood, Stephen Carroll
Mai, Klaus Ludwig
Mai, Ludwig Hubert
Maiden, Conde George
Mains, Gilbert Joseph
Mainwaring, Thomas Lloyd
Maisch, Louis William
Major, James Russell
Major, Winfield Watson
Mak, Dayton Seymour
Malarkey, Martin Francis, Jr.
Male, Roy Raymond
Malec, William Frank
Malek, Frederic Vincent
Maley, Donald
Malhotra, Jagadish Chandra
Malina, Joseph Francis, Jr.
Malkin, Myron Samuel
Mallette, Malcolm Francis
Malley, John Wallace
Malley, Robert Joseph
Mallick, Earl William
Malloy, John Cyril
Malone, Dumas
Malone, Edwin Scott, III
Malone, James (Richard)
Malone, Lee Harrison Brown
Malone, Moses
Malone, Richard Henry
Malone, Wex Smathers
Maloney, Charles Garrett
Maloney, Frank Edward
Maloney, John Alexander
Maloney, Joseph Patrick
Maloy, Richard Joseph
Maloy, Robert Michael
Malzahn, Ray Andrew
Mamatey, Victor Samuel
Man, Eugene Herbert
Manasco, Carter
Manatos, Andrew Emanuel
Manatos, Mike
Manchin, A. James
Mandel, H(arold) George
Mandelkern, Leo
Mandell, Leon
Mandelstam, Robert Stanley
Mandil, I. Harry
Mandrell, Barbara Ann
Manell, Abram E.
Manes, Nella Cellini
Maney, Michael Mason
Manful, Melvin Lawrence
Mangan, Robert Martin
Manganaro, Francis Ferdinand
Mangaroo, Jewellean Smith (Mrs. Arthur S. Mangaroo)
Manhard, Philip Wallace
Manier, Miller
Manigault, Peter
Manire, George Philip
Manire, James McDonnell
Mankiewicz, Frank Fabian
Mankin, Charles John
Mankoff, Ronald Morton
Manley, Albert Edward
Manley, Frank
Manley, Harold Wheatley
Manley, William Tanner
Mann, Charles August
Mann, Charles Kenneth
Mann, David Emerson
Mann, Edward Beverly
Mann, Fletcher Cullen
Mann, Forbes
Mann, Frank Eugene
Mann, Gerald C.
Mann, James Harold
Mann, James Robert
Mann, Jewell Russell (Mrs. John Henry Clay Mann)
Mann, Lowell Kimsey
Mann, Lyle Eugene
Mann, Marion
Mann, Robert Trask
Mann, Stanley Jay
Mann, Thurston Jefferson
Mann, Walter
Manne, Henry Girard
Manners, George Emanuel
Manning, Alfred Paul
Manning, Arthur Brewster
Manning, Francis Scott
Manning, John Thomas
Manning, Noel Thomas (Tommy)
Manning, William Raymond
Manning, William Sinkler
Mannoni, Raymond
Manring, Edward Raymond
Manship, Charles Phelps, Jr.
Manship, Douglas
Manson-Hing, Lincoln Roy
Mantell, Murray Irwin
Mantle, Mickey Charles
Mapp, Alf Johnson, Jr.
Maran, Stephen Paul
Maravich, Pete
Marbury, William Luke
Marbut, Robert Gordon
March, Frederic Clifton
Marchand, Leslie Alexis
Marco, Guy Anthony
Marcotte, Robert Seraphin
Marcuccio, Phyllis Rose
Marcus, Richard Cantrell
Marcus, Stanley
Marcus, Walter F., Jr.
Marcuss, Stanley Joseph
Marcy, Carl Milton
Maren, Thomas Hartley
Margach, Clarence Stuart
Margain, Hugo B.
Margileth, Andrew Menges
Margolin, Edward
Margrave, John Lee
Margulies, Harold
Mariella, Raymond P.
Marienthal, George
Maril, Herman
Marinaccio, Anthony
Marino, Amerigo Angelo
Marino, Eugene Antonio
Marino, Samuel Joseph
Marinos, Peter Nick
Marion, Andrew Burnet
Marion, Cecil Price, Jr.
Marion, William Francis
Mark, David Everett
Mark, Hans Michael
Mark, Peter Alan
Mark, Stewart Winston
Markey, Edward John
Markey, Gene
Markey, Howard Thomas
Markey, Lucille Parker
Markley, Rodney Weir
Markman, Sidney David
Marks, Charles
Marks, Charles Caldwell
Marks, Dorothy Louise Ames (Mrs. Leonard H. Marks)
Marks, Leonard Harold
Marks, Marc Lincoln
Marks, Meyer Benjamin
Markun, Patricia Maloney (Mrs. David Joseph Markun)
Marlatt, Abby Lindsey
Marlenee, Ronald Charles
Marlowe, Donald E.
Marmion, William Henry
Maroney, Daniel Vincent, Jr.
Marquis, Robert Henry
Marr, David Francis
Marra, Edward Francis
Marriott, Alice Sheets (Mrs. John Willard Marriott)
Marriott, John Willard
Marriott, John Willard, Jr.
Marriott, Richard Edwin
Marsh, Burton Wallace
Marsh, Quinton Neely
Marsh, Thad Norton
Marshak, Robert Eugene
Marshall, Charles Burton
Marshall, Charles Louis
Marshall, J. Howard, II
Marshall, John Richard
Marshall, John Sedberry
Marshall, Keith Cooper
Marshall, Kneale Thomas
Marshall, Lane Lee
Marshall, Ray
Marshall, Robert Creel
Marshall, Robert Gerald
Marshall, Robert Herman
Marshall, Sarah Catherine Wood (pen name Catherine Marshall)
Marshall, Stanley
Marshall, Sylvan Mitchell
Marshall, Terrell
Marshall, Thomas Oliver, Jr.
Marshall, Thurgood
Marshall, Victor Fray
Marshall, William, Jr.
Marshall, William Jefferson
Marston, Robert Quarles
Martell, Arthur Earl
Martens, Robert John
Martin, Abner Broadwater
Martin, Alfred
Martin, Charles Wallace
Martin, Clarence Eugene, Jr.
Martin, David Nathan
Martin, Dean Frederick
Martin, Donald Ray
Martin, Edward Dana
Martin, Edwin Wilson, Jr.
Martin, Fowler Ward
Martin, George Clarke
Martin, George Wilbur
Martin, Guy
Martin, Guy Richard
Martin, Harold Harber
Martin, Hunter Lenon, Jr.
Martin, James Blakely
Martin, James Grubbs
Martin, James Mordecai
Martin, James Robert, Jr.
Martin, John Andrew
Martin, John Butlin
Martin, John Gilbert
Martin, John Joseph
Martin, Kenneth Douglas
Martin, Lockett Brooks
Martin, Louis Emanuel
Martin, Mark
Martin, Monroe Harnish
Martin, Norman Marshall
Martin, Otis Orval
Martin, Paul Edward
Martin, Robert Bruce
Martin, Robert Finlay, Jr.
Martin, Robert Richard
Martin, Theodore Krinn
Martin, Thomas Stephen
Martin, Wilbur Forrest
Martin, William Frederick
Martin, William Henry, III
Martin, William McChesney, Jr.
Martin, William Robert
Martin, William Royall, Jr.
Martinez, Arabella
Martinez, Luis Aponte
Martinez-Lopez, Jorge Ignacio
Martz, Walter Atlee
Maruyama, Yosh
Marvin, Murray Joseph
Marvin, Oscar McDowell
Marx, George L.
Masey, Jack
Masiko, Peter, Jr.
Mason, Aaron S.
Mason, Barry Jean
Mason, Brian Harold
Mason, David Dickenson
Mason, David Ernest
Mason, Franklin Rogers
Mason, George Robert
Mason, Henry Lloyd
Mason, Jimilu
Mason, John Clarke
Mason, John Russell
Mason, Joseph Barry
Mason, Lowell Blake
Mason, Paul Joseph
Mason, Paul Warren
Mason, Raymond Adams
Mason, Ronald Lawrence
Mason, Thomas Boyd
Masoro, Edward Joseph, Jr.
Masquelette, Philip Abbott
Massel, Mark S.
Massell, Sam
Massey, Charles Knox, Jr.
Massey, Harold Wallace
Massey, Peyton Howard, Jr.
Massey, Richard Walter
Mast, James William
Masten, John Talbot
Masters, Charles Day
Masterson, Harris
Masterson, Kleber Sandlin
Masterson, Thomas Robert
Mata, Eduardo
Mate, Hubert Emery
Mather, Bryant
Mather, Katharine
Mather, William Green, Jr.
Mathes, Rachel Clarke
Mathews, Arthur Francis
Mathews, Charles Drayton
Mathews, Ferrin Young
Mathews, George Donald
Mathews, Harlan
Mathews, James Kenneth
Mathias, Charles McCurdy, Jr.
Mathis, Luster Doyle
Mathis, M. Dawson
Mathis, Robert Couth
Mathis, William Lowrey
Matkin, George Garrett
Matlock, Clifford Charles
Matlock, Jack Foust, Jr.
Matlock, Kenneth Jerome
Matloff, Maurice
Matricciani, Joseph Stephen
Matsen, Frederick Albert
Matson, Greta
Matson, Sigfred Christian
Matsunaga, Spark Masayuki
Mattern, Donald Heckman
Matthews, A(lan) Bruce
Matthews, Alfred St. John, Jr.
Matthews, Burnita Shelton
Matthews, Charles Arnold
Matthews, Clark J(io), II
Matthews, David
Matthews, Donald Ray Billy
Matthews, Gary Nathaniel
Matthews, Mary Jean O'Leary
Matthews, Robert Emil
Matthews, Wilbur Lee
Matthews, William Lewis, Jr.
Matthias, Willard C.
Mattil, Edward La Marr
Mattingly, Thomas K.
Mattison, George Augustus, Jr.
Mattox, James Albon
Mattox, Richard Benjamin
Mattson, Joe Oliver Philip
Matula, Richard Allen
Matzke, Frank J.
Mauck, Elwyn Arthur
Mauck, Henry Page, Jr.
Mauer, Alvin Marx
Mauldin, Robert Ray
Maumenee, Alfred Edward
Maupin, Armistead Jones
Maurer, Fred Dry
Maurer, Harold Maurice
Maurer, Richard Scott
Mautz, Robert Barbeau
Mauzy, Oscar Holcombe
Mavroules, Nicholas
Maxa, Rudolph Joseph, Jr.
Maxfield, James Robert, Jr.
Maxfield, John Frank
Maxheim, John Howard
Maxson, A. L.
Maxson, William Leslie, Jr.
Maxwell, Chester Arthur
Maxwell, David F.
Maxwell, Fowden Gene
Maxwell, James Livingston
Maxwell, John Crawford
Maxwell, Otis Allen
Maxwell, Robert Earl
Maxwell, William David
May, Daniel
May, Francis Barns
May, John Lawrence
May, Orville Edward
May, Ronald Alan
May, Timothy James
Mayda, Jaro
Mayer, Fred Christian
Mayer, Frederick Miller
Mayer, Jack Farley
Mayer, Manfred Martin
Mayer, Morris Lehman
Mayer, Paul Gustav Wilhelm
Mayer, William Dixon
Mayes, Wendell Wise, Jr.
Mayfield, Charles Herbert
Mayfield, Richard Heverin
Mayfield, Thomas Brient, III
Mayhew, Kenneth Edwin, Jr.
Maynard, Don Rogers
Maynard, Donald Nelson
Maynes, Charles William
Maynor, Hal Wharton, Jr.
Mayo, James Wellington
Mayo, Louis Harkey
Mayo, Selz Cabot
Mayo, Thomas Tabb, IV
Mayor, John Roberts
Mayor, Richard Blair
Mays, Benjamin Elijah
Mays, Gerald Avery (Jerry)
Mays, L. Lowry
Mays, Marshall Trammell
Mays, Roy Mark
Mayson, Joseph Douglas
Maytag, Lewis B.
Mazan, Walter Lawrence
Maze, Clarence, Jr.
Mazo, Earl
Mazzoli, Romano L.
McAdam, Charles Vincent
Mc Adams, Herbert Hall
Mc Adoo, Donald Eldridge
McAfee, Kenneth Emberry
McAfee, William
Mc Alester, Arcie Lee, Jr.
Mc Alister, Ernest Elmo, Jr.
Mc Alister, Luther Durwood
Mc Alister, Robert Carter
Mc Allister, Gerald Nicholas
Mc Allister, Kenneth
Mc Allister, Walter Williams
McAllister, Walter Williams, Jr.
Mc Allister, Walter Williams, III
Mc Alpin, Kirk Martin
McAnulty, William Noel
McArdle, Paul Francis
Mc Ardle, Richard Edwin
McArthur, George
Mc Auliffe, Dennis Philip
Mc Bay, Henry Cecil
McBean, Alexander Marshall
Mc Bee, James Leonard, Jr.
McBride, Earle Francis
Mc Bride, John Alexander
Mc Bride, Raymond Andrew
Mc Bride, Thomas Frederick
Mc Cabe, Cynthia Jaffee
Mc Cabe, Edward Aeneas
Mc Cabe, Gerard Benedict
McCabe, William Gordon, Jr.
McCaffrey, Joseph Francis
McCain, William David
Mc Cain, William David, Jr.
Mc Call, Abner Vernon
Mc Call, Daniel Thompson, Jr.
Mc Call, Hobby Halbert
Mc Call, Jerry Chalmers
McCalla, Gary Edward
McCallick, Hugh Ernest
Mc Callum, Charles Alexander
Mc Callum, Robert D.
McCally, Charles Thomas
McCamant, William Cyrus
McCameron, Fritz Allen
McCammon, Curtis Paul
Mc Candless, Bruce, II
Mc Candless, Robert Cecil
McCandlish, Fairfax Sheild
Mc Candlish, Robert John, Jr.
Mc Cann, Samuel McDonald
Mc Cardell, Adrian LeRoy, Jr.
Mc Carn, Grace Hayden
McCarter, Charles Vernon
Mc Carthy, Alfred Lee
McCarthy, Charles Joseph
McCarthy, David Jerome, Jr.
McCarthy, Edward Anthony
Mc Carthy, Edward D.
Mc Carthy, Eugene Joseph
McCarthy, John Edward
McCarthy, Joseph Walton
Mc Carthy, Stephen Anthony
Mc Cartin, Thomas Ronald
McCarty, Bruce
McCarty, Kenneth Scott
McCarty, Robert Lee
Mc Caskey, Ambrose Everett, Jr.
McCauley, Alfred Robert
McCauley, John Corran, Jr.
McCauley, R. Paul
McCausland, Thomas Gerome
McCay, Myron Stanley
McCay, Percy Luzenberg
McClain, William Asbury
McClain, William Harold
McClatchey, Devereaux Fore
Mc Clellan, Albert Alfred
McClellan, Carole Keeton
McClellan, Thomas Marcus, Jr.
McClelland, Walter Moore
McClendon, Charles Youmans
Mc Clendon, Sarah Newcomb
Mc Clendon, William Hutchinson, III
McClennan, William Howard
McClennan, William Howard, Jr.
McClenney, Byron Nelson
McCleskey, James Milton, Jr.
McClintock, David William
Mc Clinton, Donald G.
Mc Clinton, Robert Brock
McCloskey, Paul N., Jr.
Mc Closkey, Peter Francis
Mc Clung, Jim Hill
Mc Clung, Norvel Malcolm
McClung, Roy Cornelius
McClure, Brooks
Mc Clure, Harlan Ewart
McClure, James A.
McClure, William Pendleton
McColl, Hugh Leon, Jr.
Mc Collister, John Charles
McCollom, Kenneth Allen
Mc Collough, Newton Clark, III
McCollum, John Isaac, Jr.
McComas, James Douglas
McCombs, G. B.
McConagha, Alan
McConn, James Joseph
McConnell, David Moffatt
Mc Connell, Edward Bosworth
Mc Connell, Freeman Erton
McConnell, John William, Jr.
Mc Connell, Robert Chalmers
McCord, Kenneth Armstrong
McCord, Larry Reed
McCord, Marshal
McCord, William Charles
Mc Cord, William Mellen
McCormack, Larry Warren
McCormack, Mike
McCormick, Donald Bruce
Mc Cormick, William Frederick
McCormick, William Morgan
McCorquodale, Joseph Charles, Jr.
McCorquodale, Joseph Charles, Jr.
McCowan, Robert Taylor
McCown, Hal Dale
Mc Coy, Charles Wallace
McCoy, Charlie
McCoy, Jerome Dean
McCoy, John Milton, II
McCoy, Wesley Lawrence
McCracken, George Herbert
McCracken, Jarrell Franklin
Mc Cracken, Ralph Joseph
McCrady, James David
McCree, Wade Hampton, Jr.
McCrimmon, James McNab
Mc Crory, Thomas Milton
Mc Crossan, John Anthony
McCubbin, Melvin A.
McCue, Carolyn Moore
McCulloch, Frank W.
McCullough, Gerald W.
Mc Cullough, Ralph Clayton, II
McCullough, Ray Daniel, Jr.
McCullough, Robert Dale
McCullough, Roland Alexander

853 REGIONAL LISTING—SOUTH-SOUTHWEST

Mc Cune, Shannon
McCurdy, Harold Grier
Mc Curley, Robert Lee, Jr.
Mc Cuskey, George
Mc Dade, Joseph Edward
Mc Dade, Joseph Michael
Mc Daniel, Charles Pope
McDaniel, Earl Wadsworth
Mc Daniel, Jesse Wood, Jr.
McDaniel, Raymond Lamar
McDavid, Joel Duncan
McDermott, Albert Leo
Mc Dermott, Edward Aloysious
McDermott, John Joseph
McDevitt, Joseph Bryan
Mc Dill, Edward Lamar
Mc Donald, Andrew J.
McDonald, Atwood
McDonald, Donald Fiedler
Mc Donald, Frank Bethune
McDonald, James Benjamin
McDonald, John Clifton
McDonald, John Warlick, Jr.
Mc Donald, Lawrence P.
McDonald, Leslie Ernest
McDonald, Marshall
McDonald, O. V.
McDonald, Patrick Hill, Jr.
Mc Donald, Roy
Mc Donald, Stephen Lee
McDonald, Walter J.
Mc Donald, Walter Joseph
McDonald, Walter Scott
McDonald, Wesley Lee
McDonald, William G(erald)
Mc Donnell, John Thomas
McDonough, George Francis, Jr.
McDonough, Robert Paul
McDonough, Thomas Joseph
McDougal, Milford Merlyn
McDow, John Jett
McDowell, Charles Eager
McDowell, Elmer Hugh
McDowell, William Ralston
McDuff, Odis Pelham
McEachern, Edward Merritt, Jr.
McEachern, Wilbur Washington
McElhaney, James Harry
McElheny, John Daniel
McEllistrem, Marcus Thomas, Jr.
McElroy, James Russell
McElwain, William E.
McElwaine, Robert Marshall
Mc Elwee, William Henry
McEnany, Michael Vincent
Mc Enery, John Winn
McEwan, Oswald Beverly
McEwen, Robert Cameron
McFadden, Frank Hampton
McFadden, G. Bruce
McFadden, Thomas Bernard
Mc Farland, Frank Eugene
McFarland, Marvin Wilks
Mc Fee, Arthur Storer
Mc Fee, Thomas Stuart
McGanity, William James
Mc Gannon, Donald Edward, Jr.
Mc Garity, Edmund Cody, Jr.
Mc Garr, Paul Rowland
Mc Garrah, William Erwin, Jr.
Mc Gaughan, Alexander Stanley
Mc Gaughy, John Bell
Mc Gavock, William Gillespie
McGeachy, John Alexander, Jr.
Mc Gee, Dean Anderson
McGee, Gale
Mc Gee, John Frampton
McGee, William Sears
McGehee, Benjamin Harris
McGehee, Carden Coleman
McGehee, Larry Thomas
McGhee, George Crews
McGhee, Nancy Bullock (Mrs. Samuel C. McGhee)
McGhee, Robert Barclay
McGiffert, David Eliot
Mc Giffert, John Rutherford
McGimsey, Charles Robert, III
McGinnis, Charles Irving
Mc Ginnis, James Michael
McGinnis, Robert Campbell
McGinty, James Shiver
Mc Ginty, John Milton
Mc Glothlin, James Harrison
McGlynn, Sean Patrick
McGough, Bobby Cornelius
McGovern, George Stanley
McGovern, John Phillip
McGovern, Joseph James
McGowan, Carl
McGowin, Nicholas Stallworth
McGrath, William Loughney
Mc Graw, Darrell Vivian, Jr.
Mc Graw, Walter John
Mc Gregor, Donald Thornton
McGrory, Mary
McGuigan, Frank Joseph
Mc Guigan, Frank Joseph
McGuigan, James Edward
McGuire, Edward Perkins
McGuire, Francis Thomas
Mc Guire, Marie C.
Mc Guirk, William Edward, Jr.
Mc Gurn, Barrett
McGurn, John Martin
Mc Hale, Inez Pecore
Mc Hugh, Paul (Rodney)
Mc Hugh, Robert Paul
McHugh, Simon Francis, Jr.
McIlvaine, Robinson
Mc Ilwain, William Franklin
McIlwaine, Ellen
Mc Ilwaine, William Andrew
McIndoe, Darrell Winfred
McInerney, James Eugene, Jr.
McInnes, William Charles
McIntosh, James Eugene, Jr.
McIntyre, James Talmadge, Jr.
Mc Intyre, Jane O'Neill Mahady
McIntyre, John Armin
McIntyre, John Edward
McIntyre, Lamar Calvert
McIsaac, George Scott
McKaig, Dianne L.
McKay, Arthur Raymond
McKay, Douglas, Jr.
Mc Kay, Douglas William
McKay, John G., Jr.
McKay, John Harvey
McKay, Vernon
McKean, Hugh Ferguson
McKean, Roland Neely
McKee, Arthur, Jr.
McKee, Calvin Charles
McKee, Fran
Mc Kee, Jewel Chester, Jr.
Mc Kee, Kinnaird Rowe
Mc Kee, Patrick Allen
McKee, Robert Smith
McKee, William F.
Mc Keen, Chester M., Jr.
Mc Kelvey, Vincent Ellis
Mc Kenna, Gerald Clair
McKenna, Hugh Franklin
McKenna, James Aloysius, Jr.
McKenna, James Edward
Mc Kenney, Walter Gibbs, Jr.
McKenny, Jere Wesley
Mc Kenzie, Harold Cantrell, Jr.
Mc Kenzie, Harold Jackson
Mc Kenzie, William H.
Mc Ketta, John J., Jr.
McKhann, Guy Mead
McKibbin, John Mead
Mc Kie, James Warren
McKillop, David Holmes
McKim, Paul Arthur
Mc Kinley, Gordon Wells
Mc Kinney, James Carroll
Mc Kinney, James William
McKinney, Joseph F.
McKinney, Robert Moody
McKinney, Stewart B.
McKinnon, Michael D.
McKnew, Thomas Willson
McKnight, Colbert Augustus
Mc Knight, John Lacy
Mc Kusick, Victor Almon
Mc Lain, Joseph Howard
McLain, Maurice Clayton
Mc Larnan, Charles Walter
McLaughlin, Francis
McLaughlin, John D.
McLaughlin, Marvin Louis
McLaurin, James W.
Mc Lean, George Francis
Mc Lean, John William
Mc Lean, Robert Thomas
Mc Lean, Thomas Edwin
McLean, Thomas Neil
Mc Lean, William Hugh
Mc Lemore, Robert Henry
McLendon, Charles A.
McLendon, Ruth Ann
McLeod, Daniel Rogers
McLeod, John Wishart
McLeod, Walton James, Jr.
Mc Leod, William Eugene
McLindon, Gerald Joseph
Mc Loughlin, Ellen Veronica
Mc Lucas, John Luther
Mc Mahan, Robert Chandler
McMahen, Charles Edwin
Mc Mahon, Donald Aylward
McMahon, F. Gilbert
Mc Manaway, Herman Blair
Mc Manus, Charles Anthony, Jr.
McManus, Harold Lynn
McManus, Joseph Forde Anthony
Mc Manus, Philip Daniel
Mc Manus, Samuel Plyler
McManus, Walter Leonard
Mc Math, Sidney Sanders
Mc Michael, Jane Pierson
McMillan, Charles William
McMillan, Donald Edgar
Mc Millan, George Duncan Hastie, Jr.
McMillan, James Bryan
Mc Millen, Wheeler
McMullen, Charles Haynes
McMullen, James Ernest, Jr.
Mc Mullen, Thomas Henry
McMullian, Amos Ryals
McMullin, Carleton Eugene
Mc Murry, Idanelle Sam
Mc Nab, Maxwell Douglas
McNair, Champney Adams
Mc Nair, Robert Evander
McNally, Frank J.
Mc Namara, Francis Terry
McNamara, Rieman, Jr.
Mc Namara, Robert Strange
Mc Naughton, William Hugh
Mc Neal, Archie Liddell
Mc Neeley, Harry Drake
McNees, James Lafayette, Jr.
Mc Neese, Aylmer Green, Jr.
Mc Neil, Gomer Thomas
Mc Neil, Neil Venable
McNeill, Ishmael Eugene
Mc Neill, Robert Eugene
McNeill, Robert L.
Mc New, Bennie Banks
McNish, Charles Otis
McNulty, Chester Howard
Mc Nutt, Dolly Hite
McPhail, Andrew Tennent
Mc Phee, Henry Roemer
McPheeters, Edwin Keith
Mc Pherson, Alice Ruth
Mc Pherson, Frank Alfred
Mc Pherson, Harry Cummings, Jr.
Mc Pherson, James Alan
Mc Pherson, John Barkley
Mc Pherson, Robert Donald
McPherson, Robert Grier
McPherson, William Alexander
Mc Quade, Henry Ford
McQueen, Marvin Duncan
Mc Quillan, Joseph Michael
Mc Quown, O. Ruth
Mc Rae, Hamilton Eugene, Jr.
Mc Rae, Robert Malcolm, Jr.
Mc Rae, Thomas Kenneth
Mc Rorie, Robert Anderson, Jr.
Mc Spadden, George Elbert
Mc Swain, Angus Stewart, Jr.
McVerry, Thomas Leo
Mc Vicker, Jesse Jay
Mc Voy, James David
Mc Wherter, Ned R.
Mc Whorter, Hezzie Boyd
Mc Williams, John Michael
Mc Williams, Ralph David
McWilliams, William Jameson
Meacham, Standish, Jr.
Meacham, William Feland
Mead, Gilbert D(unbar)
Mead, Gordon V.
Meade, Edwin Baylies
Meade, Richard Andrew
Meade, Roy Hampton
Meader, Jonathan Grant
Meador, Clifton Kirkpatrick
Meador, Daniel John
Meadows, Daniel Thomas
Meadows, Robert Merle
Meads, Manson
Meads, Walter Frederick
Meagher, Mark Joseph
Meaney, Donald Vincent
Means, Marianne Hansen
Mears, Walter Robert
Meason, George Hollingsworth
Mebane, John Harrison
Mecimore, Charles Douglas
Mecom, John W., Jr.
Medalie, Richard James
Medaris, John Bruce
Medina, Jose Enrique
Medina, William A.
Medlin, John Grimes, Jr.
Medvecky, Robert Stephen
Meek, Paul Derald
Meek, Phillip Joseph
Meeker, David Olan, Jr.
Meeker, James Julian
Meeker, Leonard Carpenter
Meeks, Curtis Leo
Meem, James Lawrence, Jr.
Meffen, James Douglas
Megahan, John Bruce
Megan, Thomas Ignatius
Megarr, Edward John
Megaw, Robert Neill Ellison
Meggers, Betty J(ane)
Mehren, George Louis
Mehrtens, William Osborne
Meier, David Edward
Meierotto, Larry Edward
Meijer, Paul Herman Ernst
Meima, Ralph Chester, Jr.
Meininger, Leigh Richard
Meirose, Leo Harry
Meirovitch, Leonard
Meisch, Adrien Ferdinand Joseph
Meiselman, David Israel
Meiser, Robert Newman
Meiser, Robert Newman
Meissner, Charles F.
Meissner, Doris Marie
Meitzen, Manfred Otto
Meixner, John
Melcher, John
Melchert, James Frederick
Mellen, William Robert
Mellon, Paul
Mellor, John Edward
Melnick, Joseph L.
Meloy, Guy Stanley, III
Melson, William Henry, Jr.
Melton, Buckner Franklin
Melton, Charles Estel
Melton, Howell Webster
Melton, John Derrel
Melville, Robert Seaman
Melvin, Norman Cecil
Menard, Henry William, Jr.
Mencher, Bruce Stephan
Mendell, M(ordecai) Lester
Mendeloff, Albert Irwin
Mendeloff, Henry
Mendelson, Wallace
Mendenhall, Edward Emerson, Jr.
Mendonsa, Arthur Adonel
Meneely, George Rodney
Menius, Arthur Clayton, Jr.
Menkes, Joshua
Menter, Sanford
Mentschikoff, Soia
Mercure, Alex P.
Meredith, Charles Eymard
Meredith, Henry McGaughy
Meredith, Howard Voas
Meredith, Hugh Stockdell
Meredith, James Howard
Merhige, Robert Reynold, Jr.
Meriwether, Charles Minor
Meriwether, James Babcock
Meriwether, W. Delano
Merker, Frank Ferdinand
Mermel, Thaddeus Walter
Merriam, William Rush
Merrick, Robert Graff
Merrill, Arthur Jesse
Merrill, Edward Clifton, Jr.
Merrill, Hugh Davis
Merrill, James Allen
Merrill, John Calhoun
Merrill, Joseph Melton
Merrill, Maurice Hitchcock
Merrill, Philip
Merrill, Richard Austin
Merrill, Richard Glen
Merrill, Walter James
Merritt, Arthur Donald
Merritt, Doris Honig
Merritt, Gilbert Stroud
Merritt, Jack Neil
Merritt, James Harmer
Merriwether, Duncan
Merryman, James Harold
Mersereau, Hiram Stipe
Merwin, Charles Lewis
Merwin, John David
Merzbacher, Eugen
Meschan, Isadore
Messing, Frederick Andrew, Jr.
Mester, Jorge
Meszar, Frank
Metcalf, Joseph, III
Metcalf, William Henry, Jr.
Metcalfe, Tom Brooks
Metrakos, Robert Arthur
Metz, Charles Baker
Metz, Mary Clare
Metzenbaum, Howard Morton
Metzger, Sidney
Mew, Thomas (Tommy) Joseph, III
Mewborn, Ancel Clyde
Mewborne, William Burke, Jr.
Meyer, Armin Henry
Meyer, Arthur B.
Meyer, Ben Franklin
Meyer, Edward C.
Meyer, Frederick Ray
Meyer, George Gotthold
Meyer, Harry M., Jr.
Meyer, Howard Raymond
Meyer, Johannes Horst
Meyer, John Edward
Meyer, Max Bernhardt
Meyer, Randall
Meyer, Sylvan Hugh
Meyer, Walter Leslie
Meyer, Wayne Eugene
Meyerhoff, Joseph
Meyers, Ishmael Alexander
Meyers, John Francis
Meyers, Michael (Ozzie)
Meyers, Sheldon
Mica, Daniel A.
Michael, Ludwig Alexander
Michael, Max, Jr.
Michael, Sherwood Albert
Michael, William Herbert, Jr.
Michaelis, Frederick Hayes
Michaelis, John Hersey
Michaelis, Michael
Michaels, Willard A.
Michaelson, Julius
Michaux, Henry McKinley, Jr.
Michel, F. Curtis
Michel, Harding Boehme Owre (Mrs. John F. Michel)
Michel, Paul Redmond
Michels, Agnes Kirsopp Lake (Mrs. Walter C. Michels)
Michels, Eugene
Michelson, Edward J.
Mickel, Ernest Preston
Mickey, Paul Fogle
Mickle, Jack Pearson
Micks, Don Wilfred
Middendorf, William Henry
Middleton, Christopher
Middleton, Edwin Gheens
Middleton, Frank Walters, Jr.
Middleton, Harry Joseph
Miele, Angelo
Miele, Anthony William
Mielke, Donald Craig
Migeon, Claude Jean
Mighell, Kenneth John
Mikita, Joseph Karl
Miklos, Jack C.
Miklozek, Frank Louis
Mikulak, Daniel, Jr.
Mikulski, Barbara Ann
Mikva, Abner Joseph
Miles, A. Stevens
Miles, Ernest Percy, Jr.
Milhorat, Thomas Herrick
Milhouse, Paul William
Milk, Benjamin Lechtman
Millar, Jeffery Lynn
Millar, John Donald
Millard, Charles Warren, III
Millard, David Ralph, Jr.
Miller, Andrew Pickens
Miller, Arnold Ray
Miller, Ben Neely
Miller, Ben Robertson
Miller, Bennett
Miller, C. Arden
Miller, Carroll Lee Liverpool
Miller, Charles Edmond
Miller, Charles O.
Miller, Clarence E.
Miller, Claude Rue
Miller, David Philip
Miller, Dean Harold
Miller, Delmas Ferguson
Miller, Edward Kirkbride
Miller, Edwin Frederick
Miller, Elfer Buel
Miller, Eugene Leslie
Miller, Fred Hunter
Miller, G(eorge) William
Miller, Gene Edward
Miller, George David
Miller, Harriet Evelyn
Miller, Harry Charles, Jr.
Miller, Henry Louis
Miller, Herbert Elmer
Miller, Herbert John, Jr.
Miller, Hope Ridings
Miller, Jack Richard
Miller, Jack Wayne
Miller, James Grier
Miller, James Halyburton
Miller, James Hugh, Jr.
Miller, James Rogers, Jr.
Miller, James Roland
Miller, Jarrell Etson
Miller, Jarvis Ernest
Miller, Jesse Edward
Miller, Jody
Miller, Joe Leon
Miller, John Albert
Miller, John Eldon
Miller, John Elvis
Miller, John Francis
Miller, John Richard
Miller, John Ulman
Miller, Kenneth Roy
Miller, Lambert H
Miller, Leonard
Miller, Loye Wheat
Miller, Loye Wheat, Jr.
Miller, Lynn Harvey
Miller, Mahlon Albert
Miller, Michael Shaffer
Miller, Nathan
Miller, Newton Edd, Jr.
Miller, Norman Charles, Jr.
Miller, Norman Clark
Miller, Oscar Lee, Jr.
Miller, Paul A.
Miller, Paul George
Miller, Philip R.
Miller, Reuben George
Miller, Robert James
Miller, Robert L.
Miller, Robert Lee
Miller, Sanford Arthur
Miller, Saul
Miller, Thomas Burk
Miller, Thomas Hulbert, Jr.
Miller, Thomas Marshall
Miller, Wallace, Jr.
Miller, William Franklin
Miller, William Jack
Miller, William Owen
Miller, William Scott, Jr.
Miller, Zell Bryan
Millett, John David
Millett, Ralph Linwood, Jr.
Millican, Charles Norman
Milligan, Glenn Ellis
Milligan, Mancil Wood
Milligan, Michael Roy
Milligan, W(infred) O(liver)
Milliken, Callie Faye
Milliken, Roger
Millin, Henry Allan
Million, Elmer Mayse
Millis, James H.
Mills, David Harlow
Mills, Earl B.
Mills, George Alexander
Mills, Jesse Cobb
Mills, Lev Timothy
Mills, Ray Jackson
Mills, Robert Lee
Mills, William Andrew
Mills, William Hayes
Millsaps, Fred Ray
Millsaps, Knox
Millson, Warner Lee
Milner, Philip H.
Milnes, Roger Farnam
Milnor, William Robert
Milsap, Ronnie
Milsten, David Randolph
Milsten, Robert B.
Mims, Lambert Carter
Mims, Thomas Jerome
Miner, Walter Francis
Mineta, Norman Y.
Mingay, John Inman
Minikes, Stephen Michael
Minish, Joseph George
Mink, John Robert
Minker, Jack
Minor, Charles Venable
Minor, George Gilmer, Jr.
Minor, Hugh Calvin
Minor, James Beryll
Minor, Wilson Floyd (Bill)
Mintener, James Bradshaw
Minter, Charles Floyd
Minter, James Gideon, Jr.
Minton, Jerry Davis
Minton, John Dean
Minton, Paul Dixon
Mintz, Albert
Mintz, Morton Abner
Mintz, Saul Aaron
Mintz, Seymour Stanley
Mintz, Sidney Wilfred
Mintzes, Joseph
Mirkin, Abraham Jonathan
Mirkin, Melvin J.
Mirman, Irving R.
Mirse, Ralph Thomas
Mischo, Othmer Joseph
Mish, Charles Carroll
Mishtowt, George Illarion
Miskovsky, George
Mitchell, Clarence M., Jr.
Mitchell, Donald J.
Mitchell, Edward Lee
Mitchell, Herbert Hall
Mitchell, James Lowry, II
Mitchell, John Edward
Mitchell, John Murray, Jr.
Mitchell, Joseph A.
Mitchell, Julia L.
Mitchell, Lansing Leroy
Mitchell, Nicholas Pendleton
Mitchell, Parren James
Mitchell, Richard Frank
Mitchell, Richard Scott
Mitchell, Robert Edward
Mitchell, Wylie Whitfield
Mitchell-Bateman, Mildred
Mithoefer, John Caldwell
Mittenthal, Freeman Lee
Mixson, John Wayne
Miya, Tom Saburo
Mize, Joe Henry
Mizell, Merle
Mizell, Walter Sherman
Mizwa, Tad (Thaddeus) S(tephen)
Moakley, John Joseph
Mobberley, David George
Moberly, Robert Blakely
Mochrie, Richard Douglas
Mock, Lawrence Edward
Modell, Jerome Herbert
Moder, Joseph John
Modlin, George Matthews
Modlin, Philip Hodgin
Moe, Richard
Moffat, Jay P.
Moffatt, Katherine Louella
Moffett, Anthony Toby
Moffett, Harry Lee
Moffett, James Davis
Mogabgab, William Joseph
Mohammed, M. Hamdi Abdelhakim
Mohan, Robert Paul
Mohler, Daniel Nathan
Mohney, Ralph Wilson
Mohrhardt, Foster Edward
Mokrasch, Lewis Carl
Moler, Edward Harold
Moll, William Gene
Mollenhoff, Clark Raymond
Molleur, Richard Raymond
Mollohan, Robert Homer
Molloy, Patrick Haggin
Molloy, Robert Thomas
Molony, Michael Janssens, Jr.
Moment, Gairdner B(ostwick)
Monaghan, Bernard Andrew
Monaghan, Hugh Joseph, II
Monahan, William Gregory
Monas, Sidney
Moncure, James Ashby
Moncure, John Lewis
Mondale, Joan Adams
Mondale, Walter Frederick
Mondello, Anthony Louis
Money, John William
Mongan, James John
Monger, Albert Jackson
Monlux, Andrew W.
Monnett, Victor Brown
Monroe, Archie Lee
Monroe, Edwin Wall
Monroe, Gerald Morgan
Monroe, Herman Eugene
Monroe, James Harrison
Monroe, Malcolm Logan
Monroe, Robert Rawson
Monroe, William Blanc, Jr.
Monroe, William Smith
Monroney, Michael
Monsky, John Bertrand
Montalbano, William Daniel
Montalvo, Mario J.
Montes, Leopoldo Feliciano
Montesi, John W.
Montgomery, Billy Glen
Montgomery, David Campbell
Montgomery, Edward Benjamin
Montgomery, Gillespie V.
Montgomery, Jeff
Montgomery, Jim
Montgomery, Joseph Webster, Jr.
Montgomery, Robert Morel, Jr.
Montgomery, Ruth Shick
Montgomery, Theron Earle, Jr.
Monty, Kenneth James
Moody, Raymond Avery, Jr.
Moody, Tom Rush, Jr.
Moody, Whitson Jarvis
Moody, Willis Elvis, Jr.
Moon, James E.
Moon, James Lindsay
Mooney, John Bradford, Jr.
Mooney, Richard J.
Moor, Manly Eugene, Jr.
Moore, Arthur Cotton
Moore, Beverly Cooper
Moore, Bob Stahly
Moore, Bruce
Moore, Carl Henry
Moore, Charles Arthur

REGIONAL LISTING—SOUTH-SOUTHWEST 854

Moore, Charles Ellet, Jr.
Moore, Dan Killian
Moore, Daniel Algernon
Moore, David Channing
Moore, David Graham
Moore, Dorothy Marie
Moore, Eugene Bedford, Jr.
Moore, Fletcher Brooks
Moore, Frank
Moore, Frank Stanley
Moore, Fred Holmsley
Moore, Gene Carroll
Moore, George Mansfield
Moore, Harvin Cooper
Moore, James Alfred
Moore, James Mendon
Moore, James Norman
Moore, James Robert
Moore, James Wallace
Moore, Joe Farnham
Moore, John Lovell, Jr.
Moore, John Norton
Moore, John Robert
Moore, John Travers
Moore, John Wilson
Moore, Joseph Curtis
Moore, Marc Anthony
Moore, Sister Marie
Moore, Maurice Edwin
Moore, Merrill Dennis, Sr.
Moore, Rayburn Sabatzky
Moore, Raymond Thomas
Moore, Richmond, Jr.
Moore, Robert Arle
Moore, Robert Edward
Moore, Robert Leslie
Moore, Robert Luston
Moore, Robert Stuart
Moore, Roy Dean
Moore, Thomas Justin, Jr.
Moore, Walter Leon
Moore, Walter Loton
Moore, Whayne Ray
Moore, William Grover, Jr.
Moore, William Henson
Moore, William Henson, III
Moore, William J.
Moore, William Moultrie, Jr.
Moore, William Theodore, Jr.
Moore, William Whitney, Jr.
Moore, Withers McAlister
Moores, Richard Arnold
Moores, Russell Ray
Moorhead, Carlos J.
Moorhead, Ernest John
Moorhead, Sylvester Andrew
Moorhead, William Singer
Moorman, Charles Wickliffe
Moorman, James W.
Moorman, Kay
Moos, Malcolm Charles
Moose, Richard M.
Mooz, Ralph Peter
Morabito, Rocco
Morales-Sanchez, Julio
Moran, Garland Ernest, Jr.
Moran, Neil Clymer
Moran, Robert Daniel
Moran, W(illiam) Dean
Moran, William Edward
Morch, Ernst Trier
More, Philip Jerome
Moreau, Arthur Stanley, Jr.
Morehead, James Caddall, Jr.
Moreland, Allen Barwick
Moreton, Robert Dulaney
Moretz, William Henry
Morey, George Ellers, Jr.
Morgan, Andrew Wesley
Morgan, Bruce Ray
Morgan, Charles, Jr.
Morgan, Edward P.
Morgan, Edward Pierpont
Morgan, George Allen
Morgan, Henry Joshua
Morgan, Herbert Roy
Morgan, James Lauder
Morgan, John Davis, Jr.
Morgan, Joy Elmer
Morgan, Karl Ziegler
Morgan, Lewis Render
Morgan, Lucy Shields
Morgan, Marabel
Morgan, Patrick Monroe
Morgan, Perry Eugene
Morgan, Robert Burren
Morgan, Robert Marion
Morgan, Roy Leonard
Morgan, Wesley K.
Morgan, William Donald
Morgan, William Newton
Morgan, Winfield Scott, III
Morgenroth, William Mason
Morial, Ernest Nathan
Morin, Alexander Joseph
Morin, James Brendon
Morkovsky, John Louis
Morley, Felix Muskett
Morley, Nicholas H.
Moroney, John Rodgers
Moroney, Robert Emmet
Morphos, Panos Paul
Morrill, William Kelso, Jr.
Morring, Carl Augustus, Jr.
Morris, Andrew Jackson
Morris, Barton Wistar, Jr.
Morris, Ben Rankin
Morris, Buckner Stuart
Morris, Carloss
Morris, Charles Robert
Morris, Earle Elias, Jr.
Morris, Edward Karrick
Morris, Edward Stanton
Morris, Edwin Alexander
Morris, Edwin Thaddeus
Morris, Glenn Berns
Morris, Harry A.
Morris, Jack Austin, Jr.
Morris, Jack Pershing
Morris, Jack Rector
Morris, James Aloysius
Morris, John (Jack) Holmes, III
Morris, John Woodland
Morris, Joseph Wilson
Morris, Kelso Bronson
Morris, Louis Harold
Morris, Max King
Morris, Michael Boris
Morris, Owen Glenn
Morris, Patrick Francis
Morris, Samuel Solomon, Jr.
Morris, Seth Irwin
Morris, Thomas Dallam
Morris, Walter Scott
Morris, William Shivers, III
Morrison, Bayard Hunter, III
Morrison, Francis Secrest
Morrison, Jack Sherman
Morrison, James Carleton
Morrison, Kenneth Douglas
Morrison, Morris Robert
Morrison, William Fowler, Jr.
Morrissette, Maurice
Morrow, Andrew Glenn
Morrow, Giles
Morrow, John Charles, III
Morse, Joshua Marion
Morse, Stanley Bear
Morton, Azie Taylor
Morton, Ben L.
Morton, Herbert Charles
Morton, John Wayland
Morton, Leland Clure
Morton, Thruston Ballard
Morton, Tommie Winston
Mosbacher, Robert Adam
Mosby, Henry Sackett
Moseley, Vince
Moser, Donald Bruce
Moser, Hugo Wolfgang
Moses, Robert Keen, Sr.
Moses, Warren Gustave
Mosher, Charles Adams
Mosher, Frederick Camp
Mosher, Sol
Moskowitz, Jay
Moskowitz, Samuel Zouri
Mosley, Donald Crumpton
Mosley, Zack Terrell
Mosmiller, Joseph William
Moss, Charles Malcolm
Moss, Clement Murphy, Jr.
Moss, James Mercer
Moss, James Paisley
Moss, Joe Albaugh
Moss, Lawrence Kenneth
Mossner, Ernest Campbell
Most, Woodrow Lloyd
Mostoff, Allan (Samuel)
Mott, Ralph Oliver
Mott, William Chamberlain
Motta, John Richard
Motter, David Calvin
Mottl, Ronald Milton
Motto, Anna Lydia (Mrs. John R. Clark)
Moudy, James Mattox
Moulder, Peter Vincent, Jr.
Moulthrop, Edward Allen
Moultrie, Fred
Moultrie, H. Carl
Mouly, George Joseph
Mountain, Clifton Fletcher
Mountcastle, Paul
Mountcastle, Vernon Benjamin, Jr.
Mountz, Wade
Mourelatos, Alexander Phoebus Dionysiou
Moursund, M. Waddell
Mouse, Stanley Garrison
Mouser, Paul Watson
Mow, Douglas Farris
Mowry, George Edwin
Mowry, Robert Wilbur
Moxley, John Howard, III
Moye, Charles Allen, Jr.
Moyles, William Philip
Moynahan, Bernard Thomas, Jr.
Moynihan, Daniel Patrick
Moyse, Hermann, Jr.
Mrozowski, Stanislaw
Muchmore, Harold Gordon
Mudd, John Philip
Mudd, Roger Harrison
Muehlberger, William Rudolf
Mueller, Arno William, Jr.
Mueller, Edward Albert
Mueller, Helmut Charles
Mueller, Robert
Mueller, William Randolph
Mugnolo, Anthony F.
Muir, J. Dapray
Muir, Warren R.
Muirhead, Peter Parker
Mulcahy, Edward William
Muldowney, Joseph John
Mulhern, Francis James
Mulkey, Jack Clarendon
Mullaney, Sister Michael Leo
Mullen, Robert Rodolf
Mullen, William Thomas
Mullens, William Reese
Muller, Henry John
Müller, Ronald Ernst
Muller, Steven
Muller, William Henry, Jr.
Mulligan, James Kenneth
Mulligan, Joseph Francis
Mullinax, Otto B.
Mullins, Jonas Fred
Mullins, Lorin John
Multhauf, Robert Phillip
Mumaw, John Rudy
Mumford, John Becker
Mumford, L. Quincy
Mumma, Michael Jon
Mund, Vernon Arthur
Mundie, William Lade
Munford, Dillard
Munger, Frank James
Munisteri, Joseph George
Munitz, Barry Allen
Munn, Cecil Edwin
Munn, Robert Ferguson
Munroe, Pat
Munsell, Albert Lowell
Munsey, Virdell Everard, Jr.
Munson, Paul Lewis
Munves, William
Murad, John Louis
Murayama, Makio
Murcer, Bobby Ray
Murchison, Charles Holton
Murchison, David Claudius
Murchison, Spencer Mayo
Murdoch, Bernard Constantine
Murfee, Latimer
Murfin, Mark
Muro, James Joseph
Muroff, Lawrence Ross
Murphey, William Mills
Murphy, Austin John
Murphy, Betty Jane Southard (Mrs. Cornelius F. Murphy)
Murphy, Calvin
Murphy, Charles Haywood
Murphy, Charles S.
Murphy, Daniel Joseph
Murphy, Eugene William
Murphy, Harold Loyd
Murphy, Hugh Cornelius
Murphy, James Bryson, Jr.
Murphy, James Daniel
Murphy, James Gary
Murphy, James Russell
Murphy, James Sherman
Murphy, John Carter
Murphy, John Damian
Murphy, John Francis
Murphy, John Henry, III
Murphy, John Joseph
Murphy, John Michael
Murphy, Joseph Stephen
Murphy, Michael Emmett
Murphy, Morgan Francis
Murphy, Patrick Vincent
Murphy, Ralph Frederick, Jr.
Murphy, Robert C(harles)
Murphy, Robert Drown
Murphy, Robert Joseph, Jr.
Murphy, Thomas Austin
Murphy, Thomas Bailey
Murr, Brown Lewis, Jr.
Murray, David George
Murray, George Mosley
Murray, Grover Elmer
Murray, Herbert Frazier
Murray, J. Ralph
Murray, James Daniel
Murray, John Einar
Murray, Joseph Edward, Jr.
Murray, Raymond LeRoy
Murray, Robert Fulton, Jr.
Murray, Royce Wilton
Murray, Russell, II
Murray, Vanderhosrt Bonneau, Jr.
Murray, William David
Murrill, Paul Whitfield
Murtagh, John Anthony, Jr.
Murtha, John Patrick
Muse, McGillivray
Muse, William Van
Musgrave, F. Story
Musgrave, Thea
Mushkin, Selma Jay
Muskat, Irving Elkin
Muskie, Edmund Sixtus
Muslow, Ike
Muss, Joshua Alan
Musselman, Vernon Armor
Musser, A. Wendell
Musser, William Wesley, Jr.
Musslewhite, David Carroll
Muster, Douglas Frederick
Mustian, Middleton Truett
Mut, Stuart Creighton
Mutch, Thomas Andrew
Muth, George Edward
Muuss, Rolf Eduard
Myers, Albert G., Jr.
Myers, Albert Ray
Myers, Alice Christine
Myers, Clark Everett
Myers, Eugene Ekander
Myers, Fred Arthur
Myers, Gail Eldridge
Myers, Ira Lee
Myers, Israel
Myers, Jack Edgar
Myers, James Lawrence
Myers, Jonathan Phillip
Myers, Michael (Ozzie)
Myers, Norman Allan
Myers, Orie Eugene, Jr.
Myers, Paul Walter
Myers, Richard Thomas
Myers, Robert Durant
Myers, Robert John
Myers, Robert Julius
Myers, Robert Manson
Myers, Ronald Elwood
Myers, Samuel Lloyd
Myers, William Sims, Jr.
Myers, Wyckoff
Myrbeck, Sven Gunnar
Myrberg, Arthur August, Jr.
Myren, Richard Albert
Myrvik, Quentin Newell
Myshak, Richard John
Myskowski, Walter Joseph
Nabors, James Douglas
Nabrit, Samuel Milton
Nace, Barry John
Nachman, Merton Roland, Jr.
Nachmanoff, Arnold
Nader, Ralph
Naess, Michael Ragnar
Naftalin, Micah Harry
Nagel, Paul Chester
Nagel, Robert Hamilton
Nagler, Benedict
Naka, Fumio Robert
Nakarai, Toyozo Wada
Nalen, Craig Anthony
Nall, Torney Otto, Jr.
Nam, Charles Benjamin
Namboodiri, Narayanan Krishnan
Namorato, Cono Rocco
Nance, Cecil Boone, Jr.
Nance, H. Hart
Nance, James Wilson
Nance, Joseph Milton
Nance, Milligan Maceo, Jr.
Nance, Walter Elmore
Nanz, Robert Hamilton
Napier, James Voss
Narwold, Lewis Lammers
Nash, Bernard Elbert
Nash, Bradley DeLamater
Nash, Henry Warren
Nash, Michaux, Jr.
Nash, Michaux, Jr.
Nash, Peter Gillette
Nash, Robert Johnson
Nash, Thomas Gibson, Jr.
Nashman, Alvin E.
Nassikas, John Nicholas
Natcher, William Huston
Nathan, Robert Roy
Nathans, Daniel
Nation, Warren Busby
Nau, Carl August
Naugle, John Earl
Naugle, Thomas Earl
Nauheim, Ferdinand Alan
Naumann, Oscar Edward
Naumoff, Philip
Nave, Henry John
Navratilova, Martina
Naylor, Aubrey Willard
Naylor, John Thomas
Naylor, Lewis Cecil
Naylor, Thomas Herbert
Nazareth, Vasco Philip
Neal, Frances Potter
Neal, Harry Edward
Neal, Julian Spencer
Neal, Marcus Pinson, Jr.
Neal, Phil Hudson, Jr.
Neal, Roger Lee
Neal, Stephen Lybrook
Neale, William F.
Neary, William Leonard
Nebeker, Frank Quill
Nechay, Bohdan Roman
Nedderman, Wendell Herman
Nedzi, Lucien Norbert
Neel, James Merrill
Neel, Richard Eugene
Neel, Samuel Ellison
Neel, Spurgeon Hart, Jr.
Neel, William Charles
Neely, Charles Lea, Jr.
Neely, Edgar Adams, Jr.
Neely, Richard
Nees, Bernard Joseph
Neese, C.G.
Nef, Evelyn Stefansson
Nef, John Ulric
Neff, Donald Lloyd
Negron-Garcia, Antonio S.
Negroponte, John Dimitri
Nehmer, Stanley
Neibel, John Brewster
Neikirk, Joseph Randolph
Neikirk, William Robert
Neilan, Edwin Peter
Neill, John Edmonds
Neill, Rolfe
Neiman, Fraser
Neimark, Sheridan
Neimeyer, Richard Dawe
Nejelski, Paul Arthur
Neldner, Curtis Edward
Nell, O. Leslie
Nelligan, William David
Nelson, Bill
Nelson, Bruce Warren
Nelson, Carl Roger
Nelson, Charles J.
Nelson, Curtis Andrew
Nelson, David
Nelson, Dotson McGinnis, Jr.
Nelson, Edward Gage
Nelson, Edward Sheffield
Nelson, Erland Randall
Nelson, Gaylord Anton
Nelson, Ivan
Nelson, John Howard
Nelson, John Marbury, III
Nelson, Kottom Ray
Nelson, Leonard C.
Nelson, Lewis Bailey
Nelson, Milton Eugene
Nelson, Norman Crooks
Nelson, Richard Copeland
Nelson, Robert Louis
Nelson, Roland Hill, Jr.
Nelson, Russell Andrew
Nelson, Thomas Joseph
Nelson, Thomas William
Nelson, Waldemar Stanley
Nelson, Wallace Boyd
Nelson, William Clark
Nelson, William Richard
Nemecek, Albert Duncan, Jr.
Nemetz, Anthony Albert
Nemirow, Samuel Benjamin
Nenno, Robert Peter
Neptune, Robert Herndon
Neptune, William Everett
Nesbitt, Charles Rudolph
Nesbitt, Tom Edward
Ness, Evaline (Mrs. Arnold A. Bayard)
Ness, Frederic William
Ness, Julius B.
Ness, Norman Frederick
Neter, John
Nethercut, Philip Edwin
Nethercut, William Robert
Netterville, John Thomas
Nettles, Bert Sheffield
Nettles, John Barnwell
Neuhaus, Julius Victor, III
Neuhaus, Philip Ross
Neuhaus, William Oscar
Neuhoff, Roger Alan
Neumann, Alfred Robert
Neumann, Henry Matthew
Neumann, Robert Gerhard
Neustadt, David Harold
Neva, Franklin Allen
Neviaser, Robert Jon
Neville, James Francis
New, John Calhoun
New, Noah Carroll
New, William Neil
Newberry, William Marcus
Newcomb, Paul Kerry
Newcomb, Robinson
Newcomb, Thomas Finley
Newcomb, William Wilmon, Jr.
Newell, Guy Rene
Newell, Oswald, Jr.
Newell, Paul Haynes, Jr.
Newfield, Mayer Ullman
Newhall, David Sowle
Newland, Chester Albert
Newland, Thomas Wills
Newman, Charles
Newman, Guy Douglas
Newman, Herbert Ellis
Newman, James Blakey
Newman, James Heflin
Newman, Marcel K.
Newman, Peter Kenneth
Newman, Richard Oakley
Newman, Robert Jacob
Newman, Samuel Raphael
Newman, Theodore R., Jr.
Newman, William
Newman, William Louis
Newman, William Stein
Newport, John Paul
Newport, Marvin Gene
Newsom, David Dunlop
Newsome, George Lane, Jr.
Newsome, Paul Albert
Newton, Alexander Worthy
Newton, Blake Tyler, Jr.
Newton, Carl Davidson
Newton, Charles Martin
Newton, Derek Arnold
Newton, Frank Richards, Jr.
Newton, Robert Park, Jr.
Nexsen, Julian Jacobs
Ney, Jerome M.
Ney, Robert Leo
Niblock, Walter Raymond
Nicandros, Constantine Stavros
Nice, Charles Monroe, Jr.
Nichol, Henry Ferris
Nicholas, Louis Thurston
Nicholls, Robert Perry
Nichols, Edwin James
Nichols, Eugene Douglas
Nichols, Franklin Allen
Nichols, Frederick Doveton
Nichols, Henry Louis
Nichols, Horace Elmo
Nichols, James Richard
Nichols, Kenneth David
Nichols, Philip, Jr.
Nichols, Robert Leighton
Nichols, Shuford Reinhardt
Nichols, Thomas S.
Nichols, William
Nicholson, John Burton, Jr.
Nicholson, Patrick James
Nicholson, Roy S.
Nicholson, William Lloyd, III
Nickerson, Dorothy
Nickerson, James Findley
Nicklas, Robert Bruce
Nicklaus, Jack William
Nickon, Alex
Nicks, Oran Wesley
Nickson, James Joseph
Nicol, Joseph Arthur Colin
Nicol, William Kennedy
Nida, Jane Bolster (Mrs. Dow Hughes Nida)
Nidecker, John E.
Niebell, Paul Milton, Sr.
Niedergeses, James D.
Niederlehner, Leonard
Nielsen, Aldon Dale
Nielsen, Alvin Herborg
Nielsen, Einer
Nielsen, Niels Christian, Jr.
Nielsen, Otto R.
Nielson, James Melvin
Niemann, Kurt Max Walter
Niess, Robert Judson
Nigh, George
Nightingale, Earl Clifford
Nigro, Felix Anthony
Niles, Henry Edward
Niles, John Jacob
Nimetz, Matthew
Nirenberg, Marshall Warren
Nisbet, Robert A.
Nitze, Paul Henry
Nix, James Kelly
Nixon, Frank Leslie
Nixon, Jack Lowell
Nixon, Walter Louis, Jr.
Noakes, Edward Henry
Noble, Ernest Pascal
Nobles, Edward Burgess
Nobles, Lewis
Nobles, William Lewis
Noce, Robert Henry
Nodine, William Edward
Noel, James Latane, Jr.
Noel, Philip Jordan, Jr.
Noël Hume, Ivor
Noer, Rudolf J.
Noetzel, Grover Archibald Joseph
Nolan, James Parker
Nolan, John Edward, Jr.
Nolan, John Lester
Nolan, John Stephan
Nolan, Patrick Joseph
Nolan, Paul Thomas
Nolan, Richard
Nolan, Richard Charles
Nolan, Thomas Brennan
Noland, James Terry
Noland, Lloyd U., Jr.
Noland, Royce Paul
Nolen, Calvin Cleave
Nolte, James Adam
Nolte, Roger Emerson
Noojin, Ray O.
Noonan, Patrick Francis
Noonan, William James
Noonkester, James Ralph
Nooter, Robert Harry
Norbeck, Edward
Norberg, Charles Robert
Nord, Alan Andrew
Nordby, Gene Milo
Norfleet, Morris Lee
Norman, Albert George, Jr.
Norman, George Emerson, Jr.
Norman, LaLander Stadig
Norman, Lewis Sheppard, Jr.
Norman, Philip Sidney
Norman, Ralph Louis
Norman, Ralph Vernon, Jr.
Norris, Arthur Hughes
Norris, John Windsor, Jr.
Norris, William Elmore, Jr.
North, Cecil Jackson
North, Harper Qua
North, John Ringling
North, Phil Record
North, Robert Hugh
North, Warren James
North, William Haven
Northcutt, Clarence Dewey
Northcutt, Jesse James
Northcutt, Travis J., Jr.
Northrop, Edward Skottowe
Northrop, Monroe
Northup, Robert Edgar
Norton, Andre Alice
Norton, Clarence Clifford
Norton, Eleanor Holmes
Norton, Howard Melvin
Norton, Hugh Stanton
Norton, Joseph Randolph
Norwood, Bernard
Norwood, George McIntosh, Jr.
Norwood, Janet Lippe
Nosenzo, Louis Vincent
Notman, Donald Douglas
Novak, Anthony
Novak, Arthur Francis
Novak, Michael (John), (Jr.)
Novak, Robert David Sanders
Nover, Naomi (Goll)
Novik, Ylda Farkas (Mrs. David Novik)
Novosal, Paul Peter
Nowak, Henry James
Nowlan, Hiram Merrill, Jr.
Noyes, Guy Emerson
Noyes, Ward David
Noyes, William Albert, Jr.
Nuckolls, Robert Theodore
Nuesse, Celestine Joseph
Nugent, Bill Allen
Nugent, Brother Gregory
Nugent, Richard Joseph, Jr.
Nuland, James Greenbury
Nunn, Grady Harrison
Nunn, Louie B.
Nunn, Sam
Nunneley, Emory Trufant
Nuss, Eldon Paul
Nutting, Charles Bernard
Nyirjesy, Istvan
Nystrom, Harold Charles
Nystrom, John Warren
Oakar, Mary Rose
Oakes, Herbert Lee
Oakes, John Cogswell
Oakley, Owen Horace
Oakley, Robert Bigger
Oates, John Alexander, III
Oates, John Francis
Obel, Arne
Ober, Frank Benedict
Oberbeck, Arthur William
Oberdorfer, Louis F.

Oberhelman, Harley Dean
Oberlin, David Wright
Oberst, Paul
Obey, David Ross
O'Boyle, Patrick Aloysius
O'Brien, Darcy
O'Brien, Edward William
O'Brien, James Joseph
O'Brien, Michael
O'Brien, Thomas Stanley, III
O'Brien, Tim Andrew
O'Brien, William Howard
O'Bryan, Samuel Oliver, Jr.
O'Bryan, William Monteith
O'Byrne, John Coates
O'Callaghan, Jerry Alexander
Ochs, Elmer Raymond
Ochs, Robert David
Ochsner, Alton
O'Connell, Brian
O'Connell, Daniel Kevin
O'Connell, Donald William
O'Connell, Jeffrey
O'Connell, Joseph James, Jr.
O'Connell, Quinn
O'Connor, Harry Thomas
O'Connor, James Patrick
O'Connor, John Albert, Jr.
O'Connor, John Joseph, Jr.
O'Connor, John Martin
O'Connor, Karl William
O'Connor, Lawrence Joseph, Jr.
O'Connor, Ralph Sturges
O'Connor, Rod
O'Connor, William Charles
O'Daniel, Finis Arch
Oddis, Joseph Anthony
O'Dea, Thomas Emmett
Odell, Arthur Gould, Jr.
O'Dell, Charles Robert
Odell, Patrick Lowry
O'Dell, William Francis
Odenheimer, Kurt John Sigmund
O'Doherty, Desmond Sylvester
Odom, Alfred Dargan, Jr.
Odom, John Pershing
O'Donnell, Alice Louise
O'Donnell, Bernard Joseph
O'Donnell, James Francis
O'Donnell, John Daniel
Oechsli, Leonard Paul
Oehlert, Benjamin Hilborn, Jr.
Oehser, Paul Henry
Oestreich, Charles Henry
Oettinger, Katherine Brownell
Offutt, George Quentin
Ogan, Russell Griffith
Ogburn, Charlton
Ogden, Frederic Dorrance
Ogden, Schubert Miles
Ogden, Squire Redmon
Ogilvy, Stewart Marks
Oglesby, Daniel Kirkland, Jr.
Ognibene, Andre J(ohn)
O'Hair, Madalyn Mays (Mrs. Richard Franklin O'Hair)
Ohanian, Mihran Jacob (Jack)
O'Hara, James Grant
O'Hara, Mary
O'Hare, James Raymond
O'Haren, James Francis
Ohlke, Clarence Carl
O'Kane, Robert Maxwell
O'Keefe, Michael Hanley
O'Keefe, Michael Thomas
O'Keefe, Robert James
O'Keeffe, Charles B(enjamin), Jr.
O'Kelley, Grover Davis
O'Kelley, Joseph Charles
O'Kelley, William Clark
O'Konski, A.E.
Oksenberg, Michel Charles
Okun, Arthur M.
Okun, Daniel Alexander
Olan, Levi Arthur
Old, Jonathan Whitehead, Jr.
Olds, Elizabeth
Oleck, Howard L.
Oleksiw, Daniel Philip
Oler, Wesley Marion, III
Oliphant, Patrick
Olivarez, Graciela
Olive, Lindsay Shepherd
Oliver, Allen Laws, Jr.
Oliver, Alvin E.
Oliver, James Henry
Oliver, James Willard
Oliver, Mary Wilhelmina
Oliver, William Albert, Jr.
Olkowska, Krystyna Maria Nardelli
Oller, William Maxwell
Olling, Edward Henry
Olmstead, Ralph W.
Olmsted, George Hamden
Olsen, Merrill Elvin
Olson, Harvey S.
Olson, John Victor
Olson, Loren Keith
Olson, Merlin Iver
Olson, Roy Edwin
Olson, Sylvester Irwin
Olson, William Clinton
Olsson, Nils William
Olsson, Sture Gordon
O'Mahoney, Robert M.
O'Malley, Bert William
O'Malley, Jerome Francis
Omang, Joanne Brenda
Omata, Robert Rokuro
Omberg, Arthur Chalmers
Omenn, Gilbert Stanley
Omer, Daniel Oliver
Omer, Guy Clifton, Jr.
Omran, Abdel Rahim
O'Neal, Arthur Daniel, Jr.
O'Neal, John Milton, Jr.
O'Neal, Michael Leonard
O'Neal, Robert Munger
O'Neal, William Bainter
O'Neil, John
O'Neill, Albert Clarence, Jr.
O'Neill, Brian Edward
O'Neill, James Edward
O'Neill, John Joseph, Jr.
O'Neill, Thomas P.
O'Neill, William T.
Ooms, Van Doorn
Opala, Marian P(eter)
Oppenheim, Saul Chesterfield
Oppenheimer, Carl Henry
Oppenheimer, Franz Martin
Oppenheimer, Reuben
Oppenlander, Robert
Opper, Franz Frederick
O'Quinn, Silas Edgar
Ordile, Joseph Robert
Ordway, Frederick Ira, III
O'Reilly, Phillip Andrew
Oren, John Birdsell
Orfila, Alejandro
Orgain, Benjamin Darby
Orgel, Stephen Kitay
Orloff, Jack
Orman, Leonard Arnold
Orme, Keith Martell
Ormes, Robert Verner
Ormsby, Robert Benzein, Jr.
Orn, Clayton Lincoln
Oro, Juan
O'Rourke, Lawrence Michael
Orovitz, Max
Orr, Clyde, Jr.
Orr, Clyde, Jr.
Orr, Clyde Lynn
Orr, Daniel
Orr, Kenneth Dew
Orr, Paul Glenn
Orrick, Norwood Bentley
Orsy, Ladislas
Ortega, James McDonough
Ortique, Revius Oliver, Jr.
Ortiz, Francis Vincent, Jr.
Ortiz Mena, Antonio
Orton, Stewart
Orton, William Rolen, Jr.
Ortwein, Mathias Joseph
Osberg, James William
Osborn, Donald Keith
Osborn, Marvin Griffing, Jr.
Osborn, Prime Francis, III
Osborn, Retus Woodruff, III
Osborn, Stellanova (born Stella Brunt)
Osborne, Dee S.
Osborne, John
Osborne, Sonny
O'Shea, Horace William, Jr.
O'Shields, Richard Lee
Osius, Larry Clark
Osmalov, Robert
Osmer, Margaret
Osnos, Peter Lionel Winston
Ostar, Allan William
Oster, Patrick Ralph
Osterhout, Suydam
Ostlund, H. Gote
Ostwalt, Jay Harold
O'Sullivan, James Lawton
Oswald, Rudolph A.
Otero, Manuel Jesus
Othersen, Henry Biemann, Jr.
Otis, Arthur Brooks
Otis, Jack
O'Toole, Allan Thomas
Ott, David Ewing
Ott, Stanley Joseph
Ott, William Vits
Ottaway, David Blackburne
Ottenheimer, Edwin
Ottenheimer, Gus
Otth, Edward John, Jr.
Otto, Kenneth Lee
Oulahan, George McCall Courts
Ould, Edward Hatcher, Jr.
Oulliber, John Andrew
Outler, Albert Cook
Overall, John E.
Overbeck, Gene Edward
Overbeck, Henry West
Overby, George Robert
Overcash, Reece A., Jr.
Overstreet, Bonaro Wilkinson
Overton, Ben Fredrick
Overton, Edward Franklin
Overton, Joseph Allen, Jr.
Overton, Stanley D.
Overton, William Ward, Jr.
Owen, David Rogers
Owen, George E.
Owen, George Earle
Owen, Henry
Owen, Howard Malcolm
Owen, John Atkinson, Jr.
Owen, John Pipkin
Owen, Ralph
Owen, Robert Hubert
Owen, Thomas Barron
Owen, Thomas John
Owens, Bob R.
Owens, Hugh Franklin
Owens, Robert Hunter
Owens, Wilbur Dawson, Jr.
Owens, William Abbott, Jr.
Oxford, Charles William
Oxley, John Thurman
Ozmon, Howard
Pabst, William Richard, Jr.
Pace, Stephen Shell
Pace, Warren M.
Pack, David Massey
Packard, George Randolph
Packard, Robert Gay
Packer, Arnold Herman
Packer, Leo S.
Packwood, Bob
Paddock, Austin Joseph
Padgett, Inman
Padilla-Escabí, Salvador M.
Pafford, Ward
Page, Addison Franklin
Page, Charles Greenleaf
Page, George Keith
Page, George Matthews
Page, Harry Robert
Page, Richard S.
Page, Robert Henry
Page, Robert Wesley
Page, Thornton Leigh
Page, William Marion
Page, Willis
Paige, Hilliard Wegner
Paik, Kwanik Kenneth
Pain, Charles Leslie
Paine, Louis Burr, Jr.
Painter, Mary Ella
Painton, Ira Wayne
Palastra, Joseph Thomas, Jr.
Palermo, Joseph
Paletti, Arthur Valentine
Pallot, E. Albert
Palmer, Archie M(acInnes)
Palmer, Edward Jackson
Palmer, Forrest Charles
Palmer, Frederick Fraser
Palmer, Harold Bruce
Palmer, James Alvin
Palmer, Jeffress Gary
Palmer, Milton Meade
Palmer, Philip Isham, Jr.
Palmer, Richard Emery
Palmer, Sandra Jean
Palmer, Stephen Eugene, Jr.
Palmore, John Stanley, Jr.
Palms, John Michael
Palter, Robert Monroe
Palumbo, Frank A.
Pan, Elizabeth Lim
Panichas, George Andrew
Pankey, George Atkinson
Panoff, Robert
Papa, Anthony Emil
Papper, Emanuel Martin
Papper, Solomon
Paradiso, Louis John
Paramore, Edwin Lee
Parcher, James Vernon
Pardee, Arthur E., Jr.
Pardee, John (Jack) Perry
Pardes, Herbert
Parelman, Samuel Theodore
Parham, Paul Morris
Paris, Demetrius Theodore
Paris, Leonard Alton
Parish, Archie Gale
Parish, Robert Underwood
Parisi, William Edward
Parker, Alfred Browning
Parker, Austin Smith
Parker, B. B.
Parker, Bobby Eugene, Sr.
Parker, Brant Julian
Parker, Bruce Covell
Parker, Clea Edward
Parker, Daniel
Parker, Franklin
Parker, George Conrad
Parker, George Frederick
Parker, Harold Talbot
Parker, Harry S., III
Parker, Israel Frank
Parker, John Crump
Parker, Joseph B., Jr.
Parker, Joseph Orville
Parker, Kenneth Whitten
Parker, Robert Allan Ridley
Parker, Robert Hutson
Parker, Rodger Duane
Parker, Roy Turnage
Parker, Walter Burr
Parkes, Ed
Parkhurst, Charles
Parkins, Frederick Milton
Parkinson, Thomas Carter
Parkman, Paul Douglas
Parks, Albert (Fielding)
Parks, Harold Francis
Parks, Henry Emslie
Parks, Madelyn N.
Parks, Paul Franklin
Parks, Seigle Wilson
Parmer, Jess Norman
Parnell, James Quincy, Jr.
Parnell, Thomas Alfred
Paro, Tom Edward
Parr, Robert Ghormley
Parr, Royse Milton
Parra, Francisco José
Parris, James Leonard
Parris, Robert
Parrish, Alvin Edward
Parrish, Charles Milton, III
Parrish, Chester Warner
Parrish, Eugene Milton
Parrish, Frank Jennings
Parrish, Herbert Charles
Parrish, James Milton
Parrish, Lemar
Parrott, Raymond Cleo
Parrott, Thomas Curtis
Parry, Albert
Parry, Ernest Bruce
Parry, Hugh Jones (James Cross)
Parsons, Albert L.
Parsons, Ervin Ivy, Jr.
Parsons, Henry McIlvaine
Parsons, Irene
Parsons, James Wilson, Jr.
Parsons, Malcolm Barningham
Parsons, Vinson Adair
Parsons, William Simeon
Partain, Edward Allen
Partee, John Charles
Parten, Jubal R.
Parthemos, George Steven
Parthemos, James
Partridge, Lloyd Donald
Parzen, Emanuel
Pasch, Alan
Paschal, Joel Francis
Paschall, James Ernest
Pasewark, William Robert
Pashayan, Charles, Jr.
Paskusz, Gerhard Frederick
Paslay, Le Roy Clay
Paslay, Paul Robert
Pasmanick, Kenneth
Pasqua, Pietro F.
Passano, Edward Magruder
Passano, William Moore
Passey, George Edward
Past, Raymond Edgar
Pasta, John Robert
Pastore, Peter Nicholas
Pate, Jerome Kendrick
Pate, John Ralston
Paterson, Katherine Womeldorf
Paterson, Robert Andrew
Pati, Jogesh Chandra
Paton, David
Paton, William Dunning
Patrick, Carl Lloyd
Patrick, John
Patrick, John Vernon, Jr.
Patten, Edward James
Patten, Gerland Paul
Patterson, Carrick Heiskell
Patterson, Donald Hamilton
Patterson, Donald Hamilton
Patterson, Eugene Corbett
Patterson, Hugh Baskin, Jr.
Patterson, James Nelson
Patterson, Jerry Mumford
Patterson, John Malcolm
Patterson, John McCready
Patterson, John Miles
Patterson, Joseph Redwine
Patterson, Lyman Ray
Patterson, Marcel
Patterson, Mary Marvin Breckinridge (Mrs. Jefferson Patterson)
Patterson, Neville
Patterson, Ray Albert
Patterson, Robert Youngman, Jr.
Patterson, Ronald Glen
Patterson, William Robert
Patteson, Roy Kinneer, Jr.
Pattillo, Charles Curtis
Pattillo, Cuthbert Augustus
Pattillo, Manning Mason, Jr.
Patton, David U.
Patton, George Smith
Patton, James Godfrey
Patton, James Richard, Jr.
Patton, James William, Jr.
Patton, Larry Dixon
Patton, Macon Glasgow
Patton, Mitchell
Patton, Selma Hicks (Mrs. Curry Patton)
Patton, Wendell Melton, Jr.
Patty, Claibourne Watkins, Jr.
Patty, Clarence Wayne
Patz, Arnall
Patz, Edward Frank
Paul, Donald Ross
Paul, Gabriel (Gabe)
Paul, James Robert
Paul, Robert Henry, Jr.
Paul, Ron
Paul, William Dewitt, Jr.
Paul, William George
Pauley, Stanley Frank
Paulson, Donald Lowell
Paulson, Moses
Pauly, John Edward
Pavlik, William Bruce
Paycheck, Johnny (Don Lytle)
Payne, M. Lee
Payne, Melvin Monroe
Payne, Tyson Elliott, Jr.
Payne, William Jackson
Payne, William Walker
Paynter, Harry Alvin
Payton, Carolyn Robertson
Peabody, Robert Lee
Peach, William Bernard
Peach, William Nelson
Peacock, Erle Ewart
Peacock, Franklin Kellogg
Peacock, James Lowe
Peacock, Lamar Batts
Peacock, Lelon James
Peacock, Leslie Clark
Peacock, Markham Lovick, Jr.
Peacock, Peter Bligh
Peacock, William Eldred
Peal, William Hugh
Peapples, George Alan
Pearce, Edwin McKigney, Jr.
Pearce, William Martin
Pearl, Martin Herbert
Pearl, Minnie (Sarah Ophelia Colley Cannon)
Pearman, Jean Richardson
Pearne, John Frederick
Pearsall, George Wilbur
Pearsall, Marion
Pearson, Charles Thomas, Jr.
Pearson, Daniel S.
Pearson, David Gene
Pearson, Donald Emanual
Pearson, Drew
Pearson, Henry Charles
Pearson, James Blackwood
Pearson, Jerre Leonadis
Pearson, Jim Berry
Pearson, John Earle
Pearson, Roger
Pease, James Norman, Jr.
Peaslee, Margaret Mae Hermanek
Pechman, Joseph Aaron
Peck, Dallas Lynn
Peck, James Stevenson
Peck, Richard Hyde
Peckham, Howard Henry
Pedelahore, Joseph Earl
Peden, Katherine Graham
Pedersen, Thomas August
Pedersen, Wesley Niels
Peebles, Dick
Peebles, Fred Neal
Peele, Roger
Peele, Talmage Lee
Peeples, William Dewey, Jr.
Peery, Allison Boyd
Peery, Thomas Martin
Peet, Richard Clayton
Peirce, Brooke
Peirce, Neal R.
Pejovic, Ilija
Pelczar, Michael Joseph, Jr.
Pell, Claiborne
Pell, Walden, II
Pell, William Hicks
Pellegrino, Edmund Daniel
Pellerzi, Leo Maurice
Pelletier, S. William
Peltason, Jack Walter
Pemberton, Harrison Joseph, Jr.
Pena, William Merriweather
Pendell, Elmer
Pender, Pollard Eugene
Pendergrass, Webster
Pendleton, Eugene Barbour, Jr.
Pendleton, Sumner Alden
Penegar, Kenneth Lawing
Penland, John Thomas
Penn, John Garrett
Penna, Richard Paul
Penniall, Ralph
Penniman, Abbott Lawrence, Jr.
Penniman, Howard Rae
Pennington, James Cloy
Pennington, Paul Jordan
Pennington, William Herbert
Penny, Charles Richard
Pennybacker, Albert Mitchell, Jr.
Penrod, Kenneth Earl
Penry, James Kiffin
Penz, Anton Jacob
Penzer, Mark
Peoples, John Arthur, Jr.
Peoples, Thomas Edward
Pepitone, Byron Vincent
Pepper, Claude Denson
Pepperdene, Margaret Williams
Peppler, Albert Patterson
Pequegnat, Willis Eugene
Percival, Walter Clement
Percy, Charles Harting
Percy, Walker
Peretz, Martin
Perez, Gines
Perini, Vincent Walker
Perkins, Bob(by) F(rank)
Perkins, Carl D.
Perkins, Carl L.
Perkins, Courtland Davis
Perkins, Cyrus Lee
Perkins, Raymond Lamont
Perkins, Richard Sturgis
Perlik, Charles Andrew, Jr.
Perlin, Seymour
Perlis, Leo
Perlman, Harvey Stuart
Perlmutter, Jack
Perlmutter, Jerome Herbert
Perlyn, Donald Laurence
Permutt, Solbert
Perot, H. Ross
Perrin, Fred Smith
Perrin, James
Perrine, Laurence
Perros, Theodore Peter
Perrot, Paul Norman
Perry, Benjamin Luther, Jr.
Perry, Charles E
Perry, Gaylord Jackson
Perry, John Holliday, Jr.
Perry, Margaret Nutt
Perry, Marvin Banks, Jr.
Perry, Murvin Henry
Perry, Percival
Perry, Robert William
Perry, Rufus Patterson
Perry, Russell H
Perry, Seymour Monroe
Perry, William James
Perry, Yvonne Scruggs
Pershing, Francis Warren
Persons, Clayton Henry
Pertschuk, Michael
Perusse, Roland Irving
Pervin, William Joseph
Pesquera, Hernan G.
Pestana, Carlos
Peter, Edward Compston, II
Peter, Phillips Smith
Peterkin, George Alexander, Jr.
Peters, Bruce Harry
Peters, C. Wilbur
Peters, Emil Edward
Peters, Henry Buckland
Peters, Henry John
Peters, James Alexander
Peters, John Donald
Peters, Ralph Martin
Peters, Robert Lee
Peters, Robert Revedd
Peters, William Henry
Petersdorf, Robert James
Petersen, Forrest Silas
Petersen, Frank Emmanuel, Jr.
Peterson, Carl Rudolf
Peterson, Dean Freeman, Jr.
Peterson, Edward Adrian
Peterson, Esther
Peterson, Floyd Delner
Peterson, Frank Dewey
Peterson, Fred McCrae
Peterson, James Byron
Peterson, James Robert
Peterson, Lysle Henry
Peterson, Mendel Lazear
Peterson, Merrill Daniel
Peterson, Oscar James, III
Peterson, Roger Ernest
Peterson, Victor Herbert
Peterson, William Herbert
Petranek, Stephen Lynn
Petrazio, Edward Glenn
Petree, William Horton
Petri, Thomas E(vert)
Petrik, Eugene Vincent
Petrone, Rocco A.
Petry, Herbert Charles, Jr.
Petteway, Samuel Bruce
Pettigrew, Richard Allen
Pettijohn, Francis John
Pettit, Arch Paull
Pettit, Joseph Mayo
Pettit, Manson Bowers
Pettit, Rowland
Pettit, William Schuyler
Pettit, William Thomas
Pettus, Erle, Jr.
Pettway, George Holmes
Petty, Charles Sutherland
Petty, Dan Sherman
Petty, Richard
Petty, Travis Hubert
Petty, Wilbert Cornelius
Pfaff, William Wallace
Pfeffer, Richard Lawrence
Pfeifer, Susan Elizabeth (Mrs. Anastasios C. Soutzos)
Pfeiffer, Eric Armin
Pfister, Edward Joseph
Pfouts, Ralph William
Phair, George
Phaup, Bernard Hugo
Pheiffer, Chester Harry
Phelan, Harold Leon
Phelps, Ashton
Phelps, James Carl
Phelps, Joseph Barnwell
Phelps, Joseph William
Phelps, Malcom Elza
Phelps, Thomas William
Phifer, Kenneth Galloway
Philbin, John Arthur
Philipp, Alicia Anne
Philipp, Howard John
Philips, Abram Lewis, Jr.
Philips, John Nash
Philipson, Herman Louis, Jr.
Phillabaum, Leslie Ervin
Phillips, A(ndrew) Craig
Phillips, Channing Emery
Phillips, Charles Emory
Phillips, Charles Franklin, Jr.
Phillips, Christopher Hallowell
Phillips, Claude Frank
Phillips, David Shelby
Phillips, Dean
Phillips, Frances Marie
Phillips, Guy Berryman, Jr.
Phillips, Harry
Phillips, Ivan Edward
Phillips, James Dickson, Jr.
Phillips, James Paul, II
Phillips, Jerry Juan
Phillips, John Davisson
Phillips, John Gurley
Phillips, Kevin Price
Phillips, Laughlin
Phillips, Louie Martin
Phillips, Loyal
Phillips, Oail Andres (Bum)
Phillips, Owen Martin
Phillips, Pressly Craig
Phillips, Richard Idler
Phillips, Richard Myron
Phillips, Rufus Colfax, III
Phillips, Ruth H.
Phillips, Silas Bent, Jr.
Phillips, Walter Ray
Phillipy, Lester Newton
Philos, Conrad Donald
Philpott, Harry Melvin
Phinney, William Charles
Phipps, John H. (Ben)
Pianka, Eric Rodger
Piatt, William McKinney, III
Piazza, Marguerite
Picirilli, Robert Eugene
Pickard, John Benedict
Pickard, Lowery Blaine
Pickels, Donald George
Pickens, Marshall Ivey
Pickens, Thomas Boone, Jr.
Pickerell, James Howard

REGIONAL LISTING—SOUTH-SOUTHWEST 856

Pickering, John Harold
Pickering, Thomas Reeve
Pickett, Betty Horenstein
Pickett, George Eastman
Pickett, George Edward
Pickle, J.J.
Pickral, George Monroe
Pickrell, Kenneth LeRoy
Pico, Rafael
Picon, Leon
Picott, John Rupert
Pieper, Samuel John Louis, Jr.
Pierce, Alan Kraft
Pierce, Charles Curry
Pierce, Claude Connor, Jr.
Pierce, George Foster, Jr.
Pierce, Harvey Fenn
Pierce, Kenneth Ray
Pierce, Lovick
Pierce, Margaret Hunter
Pierce, Robert Nash
Pierotti, Robert Amedeo
Pierpoint, Robert Charles
Pierre, Percy Anthony
Pierson, Earl Wendell
Pierson, Gordon Keith
Pierson, Leon H.A.
Pierson, Robert James, Jr.
Pierson, William Michel
Pike, Kenneth Lee
Pilkey, Orrin H.
Pilkinton, James Harvey
Pillard, Charles Harry
Pimentel, George Claude
Pincock, Carolyn Snyder
Pincoffs, Edmund Lloyd
Pincus, George
Pincus, Joseph
Pincus, Walter Haskell
Pinion, Dwight James
Pinkham, Frederick Oliver
Pinkney, James Faulkner
Pinkston, John William, Jr.
Pinney, Edward Lee
Pinnix, Robert Henry
Pinsky, Lawrence Steven
Piper, Don Courtney
Pipes, Samuel Wesley, III
Piquet, Howard S.
Pirie, Robert Burns, Jr.
Pirkle, Earl Charnell
Pirone, Thomas Pascal
Pirrung, Gilbert Robinson
Pisacano, Nicholas Joseph
Pisani, Joseph Michael
Pishkin, Vladimir
Pistor, Charles Herman, Jr.
Pitchell, Robert J.
Pitkin, Robert Bolter
Pitman, Benjamin Franklin, Jr.
Pitt, Harvey Lloyd
Pitt, Robert Healy, II
Pittinger, Charles Bernard
Pittle, R. David
Pittman, James Allen, Jr.
Pittman, Richard Frank, Jr.
Pittman, Steuart Lansing
Pittman, Virgil
Pitts, Curtis Hardaman
Pitts, Lloyd Frank
Pitts, Nathan Alvin
Pitts, William Reid
Pitzner, A. Frederick
Pixley, Charles Calvin
Pizer, Donald
Plasberg, Coen Christian
Plaskett, Thomas George
Plass, Gilbert Norman
Plaxico, James Samuel
Pledger, Thomas
Pletcher, Eldon
Plotkin, Harry Morris
Plotkin, Manuel D.
Plum, Charles Walden
Plumb, John Jay
Plummer, Frank Arthur
Plummer, Risque Wilson
Plunk, James Harold
Plym, Lawrence John
Poage, William Robert
Poats, Rutherford Mell
Pocock, John Greville Agard
Podshadley, Arlon George
Poe, Luke Harvey, Jr.
Poe, William Frederick
Poff, Richard Harding
Poffenberger, Paul Routzahn
Poggemeyer, Herman, Jr.
Poggio, Gian Franco
Pogue, Forrest Carlisle
Pogue, Lloyd Welch
Pogue, William Reid
Pohl, Herbert Ackland
Poillon, Arthur Jacques
Poindexter, Charles Weber
Poindexter, Hildrus Augustus
Poindexter, Robert Downs
Pointer, Sam Clyde, Jr.
Poirier, Jacques Charles
Poister, Arthur (William)
Pojeta, John, Jr.
Pokempner, Joseph Kres
Polack, Joseph Albert
Politz, Alfred
Polk, Charles Henry
Polk, Hiram Carey, Jr.
Polk, James Hilliard
Polk, James Ray
Pollack, Herman
Pollack, Joseph
Pollack, Reginald Murray
Pollak, Harry Hamilton
Pollak, Stephen John
Pollard, David Edward
Pollard, George Marvin
Pollard, James Joseph
Pollard, Thomas Dean
Pollard, William Sherman, Jr.
Pollin, Abe
Pollin, William
Polomé, Edgar Charles
Pomeroy, Edward Coffin
Pond, Robert Barrett, Sr.
Ponder, Thomas C.
Poole, Daniel Arnold
Poole, Frazer Glendon
Poole, James Edwin
Poole, John Jordan
Poole, Richard William
Poovey, William Arthur
Pope, Andrew Jackson (Jack), Jr.
Pope, Generoso Paul, Jr.
Pope, John Alexander
Pope, John Edwin, III
Pope, Thomas Harrington
Pope, William Kenneth
Popper, David
Popper, David Henry
Porch, Ralph Douglas, Jr.
Porretto, John Paul
Porter, Clyde Henry
Porter, Dudley, Jr.
Porter, Dwight Johnson
Porter, Elsa Allgood
Porter, Felix Nathaniel
Porter, Gene Huntley
Porter, Henry Homes, Jr.
Porter, John Edward
Porter, John Finley, Jr.
Porter, John Wesley, Jr.
Porter, Katherine Anne
Porter, Robert George
Porter, Robert William
Porterfield, James H.
Porterfield, William Wendell
Portes, Alejandro
Portman, John Calvin, Jr.
Portnoy, William Manos
Portugal, Decoroso M.
Posey, Eldon Eugene
Posey, Rollin Bennett
Posner, Michael Louis
Posner, Victor
Post, Allen
Post, Gerald Joseph
Post, Jackie Edith
Post, Richard Saint Francis
Postma, Herman
Poston, Ersa Hines
Poston, Gretchen
Poston, Met Ray
Poteat, William Hardman
Poteete, Robert Arthur
Poth, Edgar Jacob
Potter, Bradley Orville
Potter, William Bartlett
Pottinger, John Stanley
Potts, Albert Mintz
Potts, Ramsay Douglas
Potvin, Raymond Herve
Pou, Emily Hotchkiss Quinn
Poulos, Michael James
Pourciau, Lester John, Jr.
Povich, Shirley Lewis
Powell, Alan
Powell, Allen Larue
Powell, Benjamin Edward
Powell, Benjamin Harrison, IV
Powell, Bolling Raines
Powell, Boone
Powell, Charles Gregory, Jr.
Powell, Drexel Dwane, Jr.
Powell, Edward Angus
Powell, Edwin Lloyd, Jr.
Powell, Evan Arnold
Powell, Hampton Oliver
Powell, Harvard Wendell
Powell, James Frederick
Powell, James Milton
Powell, Joseph Lester, Jr. (Jody)
Powell, Julius Cherry
Powell, Leslie Charles, Jr.
Powell, Lewis Franklin, Jr.
Powell, Norborne Berkeley
Powell, Richard Pitts
Powell, Robert Morgan
Powell, Sumner Chilton
Powell, William Arnold, Jr.
Powell, William Rossell, Jr.
Power, John Francis
Power, Joseph Thomas
Powers, Darden
Powers, Edward Latell
Powers, Edward Lawrence
Powers, Gene Roy
Powers, Georgia Montgomery Davis
Powers, Hugh William
Powers, James Bascom
Powers, James Joseph Aloysius
Powers, Samuel Joseph, Jr.
Powley, George Reinhold
Poyner, James Marion
Pozen, Walter
Prasil, Antone George
Prather, Elbert Charlton
Pratt, Arnold W.
Pratt, James Reece
Pratt, John Helm
Pratt, Norman Twombly, Jr.
Pratt, Philip Chase
Predmore, Richard Lionel
Prengle, Herman William, Jr.
Prentice, Norman Macdonald
Prescott, John Mack
Prescott, Kenneth Wade
Present, Richard David
Present, Robert Tucker
Presley, Bobby Wayne
Press, Frank
Pressler, Herman Paul
Pressler, Larry
Prestage, Jewel Limar
Preston, Conrad Smith
Preston, Edward Francis
Preston, Frances W.
Preston, Hubert Max
Preston, Philip Cottle
Preston, Wilbur Day, Jr.
Preston, Will Manier
Prestwood, Alvin Tennyson
Prettyman, Elijah Barrett, Jr.
Preyer, L. Richardson
Price, Alvin Audis
Price, Bruce Hays
Price, C. Jack
Price, David Deakins
Price, David Edgar
Price, Edgar Hilleary, Jr.
Price, Edward Warren
Price, Frank James
Price, Harold Lafler
Price, Harry Borum, Jr.
Price, Harvey Earl
Price, J(ohn) William
Price, Jackson Ernest
Price, James Hardy, Jr.
Price, James Ligon, Jr.
Price, Karl Rhorer
Price, Marion Woodrow
Price, Melvin
Price, (Noble) Ray
Price, Raymond Kissam, Jr.
Price, Reynolds
Price, Richard
Price, Robert Dale
Price, Robert Eben
Price, William James
Price, William James, IV
Prichard, Edgar Allen
Pride, Charley
Priest, Melville Stanton
Priestman, Brian
Prigmore, Charles Samuel
Prina, L(ouis) Edgar
Prince, David Chandler
Prince, Gregory Smith
Prince, Julius Samuel
Prince, Philip Hunter
Pritchard, Joel M.
Probert, Walter
Procter, John Ernest
Procter, Russell
Proctor, Donald Frederick
Proctor, Jesse Harris, Jr.
Proctor, John Franklin
Proctor, Richard Culpepper
Proctor, Samuel
Proffitt, William Lloyd
Prokop, Ruth Timberlake
Promisel, Nathan E.
Prophet, William Forbes
Prothro, James Warren
Proxmire, William
Pruett, James Daniel
Pruett, James Worrell
Prugh, Jeffery Douglas
Pruitt, Basil Arthur
Pruitt, Dean Garner
Prunty, Merle Charles
Prussing, Ellis Moulton
Pryor, David Hampton
Pryor, Harold S.
Pryor, John Paul
Pryor, Joseph Ehrman
Pryor, William Austin
Puckette, Stephen Elliott
Pugh, George Willard
Pugh, Herbert Lamont
Pugh, Olin Sharpe
Pullen, Thomas Granville, Jr.
Pulley, Charles Henson
Puls, Fritz L.
Purcell, Arthur Henry
Purcell, Dale
Purcell, Francis Eugene
Purcell, Joe Edward
Purcell, William Paul
Purdom, Thomas James
Purdy, Laurence Henry
Purdy, Rob Roy
Purnell, Maurice Eugene, Jr.
Pursell, Carl Duane
Purvis, George Frank, Jr.
Purvis, Hugh Frank
Pusey, William Webb, III
Pustay, John Stephen
Putnam, Carleton
Putnam, George W., Jr.
Putnam, Howard Dean
Putnam, Richard Johnson, Sr.
Putzel, Constance Kellner
Putzel, William L.
Putzell, Edwin Joseph, Jr.
Pyatt, Everett Arno
Pye, August Kenneth
Pyles, Thomas
Quagliano, James Vincent
Quainton, Anthony Cecil Eden
Qualls, Robert L.
Qualls, Youra Thelma
Quarles, Carroll Adair, Jr.
Quarles, James Cliv
Quarles, Joseph Very, III
Quay, Herbert Callister
Quealy, William Harrison
Queenan, John Thomas
Quehl, Gary Howard
Quest, Charles Francis
Quillen, James Henry
Quillian, William Fletcher, Jr.
Quinn, Charles Nicholas
Quinn, Jarus William
Quinn, John Fenton
Quinn, Robert William
Quinn, Sally
Quinn, William Wilson
Quintana, Ronald Preston
Quirarte, Jacinto
Quittmeyer, Charles Loreaux
Raach, Frederick Raymond
Raad, Virginia
Raaen, John Carpenter, Jr.
Raba, Ernest Aloysius
Rabb, Ellis
Rabin, Edward William, Jr.
Rabin, Herbert
Rabinovitsj, Max
Rabinow, Jacob
Rabinowitch, Victor
Rabinowitz, Stanley Samuel
Raborn, William Francis, Jr.
Rabson, Alan Saul
Race, George Justice
Rachmeler, Louis
Rackley, Audie Neal
Rackley, Clifford Walker
Rackow, Leon Lionel
Radcliffe, George Grove
Radcliffe, Redonia Wheeler
Radcliffe, S. Victor
Rader, Lloyd Edwin
Rader, Louis T.
Radewagen, Fred
Radomski, Jack London
Radomsky, William
Radow, Ray Saul
Rady, Joseph James
Rafferty, Max
Raffety, Thomas Alva, Jr.
Rafshoon, Gerald Monroe
Raftery, Sylvester Frank
Ragan, Samuel Talmadge
Ragano, Frank Paul
Raggio, Louise Ballerstedt (Mrs. Grier H. Raggio)
Raggio, Thomas Louis
Ragone, Stanley
Ragsdale, Carl Vandyke
Rahall, Nick, II
Rahn, Richard William
Railton, William Scott
Rain, Robert Eley, Jr.
Rainer, Rex Kelly
Rainey, Edward Carr
Rainwater, Crawford Veazey
Rall, David Platt
Rall, Joseph Edward
Ralls, Katherine
Ramazani, Rouhollah Karegar
Ramberg, Walter Dodd
Ramey, Cecil Edward, Jr.
Ramey, Estelle R.
Ramirez, Mario Efrain
Ramm, Hans Henry
Rampey, Denver Lee, Jr.
Ramsay, John Erwin
Ramsay, Rex Carlyle, Jr.
Ramseur, Fred H., Jr.
Ramsey, Charles Eugene
Ramsey, Claude Swanson, Jr.
Ramsey, Ira Clayton
Ramsey, Joseph Robert
Ramsey, Lloyd Brinkley
Ramsey, Marjorie Elizabeth
Ramsey, Norman Park
Ramsey, William Ray
Ramwell, Peter William
Randall, William Madison
Randle, Marvin Herbert
Randolph, Arthur Raymond, Jr.
Randolph, Jennings
Randolph, John Hager, Jr.
Randolph, Kenneth Vincent
Rangel, Charles Bernard
Rankin, George Carlson
Rankin, James
Rankin, James A.
Rankin, Judith Torluemke
Rankin, Karl Lott
Ransom, Harry Howe
Ranson, Guy Harvey
Ransone, Coleman Bernard, Jr.
Ranta, Hugo Armas
Ranta, Hugo Armas
Raper, William Burkette
Raphel, Arnold Lewis
Rapmund, Garrison
Rapoport, Daniel
Rapp, Dennis Arthur
Rapuano, Albert John
Rarick, Joseph Francis, Sr.
Raridon, Richard Jay
Rash, Bryson Brennan
Rasmussen, L.V.
Raspberry, William James
Rassman, Emil Charles
Rast, Loy Edmund
Rather, Henry Lee
Ratliff, Charles Edward, Jr.
Ratliff, William Durrah, Jr.
Ratner, Milton Dunne
Rauh, Carl Stephen
Rauh, Joseph L., Jr.
Raullerson, Calvin Henry
Raum, Arnold
Raunborg, John Dee
Rauscher, John Howard, Jr.
Rauth, J. Donald
Ravasz, Laszlo Antal
Ravel, Joanne Macow
Ravenholt, Reimert Thorolf
Ravich, Abraham
Raviolo, Victor Gino
Rawalt, Marguerite
Rawitscher, Jack Joseph
Rawlings, Paul C.
Rawls, John Samuel
Rawls, Joseph Leonard, Jr.
Rawls, Wendell Lee, Jr.
Rawson, Ralph William
Ray, C(larence) Thorpe
Ray, Dennis Fred
Ray, Donald P.
Ray, Edgar Wayne
Ray, Edgar Wayne, Jr.
Ray, George Einar
Ray, H. M.
Ray, James Davis, Jr.
Ray, Jeter Seehorn
Ray, Richard Archibald
Ray, Royal Henderson
Raymer, Steven Laurence
Raymond, Harvey Francis
Rayson, Edwin Hope
Raywid, Alan
Rea, Bryce, Jr.
Read, Alexander Louis
Read, Benjamin Huger
Read, William Lawrence
Reade, Richard Sill
Reagan, Billy Reece
Reagan, Sydney Chandler
Reap, Elizabeth
Reardon, Timothy James, Jr.
Reasoner, Harry Max
Reaves, Charles Durham
Reaves, Kelsie Loomis
Reavley, Thomas Morrow
Rebozo, Charles Gregory
Recer, Paul Herbert
Rechcigl, Miloslav, Jr.
Reck, Andrew Joseph
Reckard, Edgar Carpenter, Jr.
Rector, John Michael
Redd, George Nathaniel
Reddell, William Jennings
Redden, Kenneth Robert
Redden, Lawrence Drew
Reddick, DeWitt Carter
Reddoch, James Wilson
Reddy, William John
Redetzki, Helmut Max
Redfern, John Joseph, Jr.
Redford, Emmette Shelburn
Redman, John C.
Reece, Joe Wilson
Reed, Adrian Faragher
Reed, Alfred
Reed, Charles Foster
Reed, Charles Hancock
Reed, David Benson
Reed, Fredric Wilson
Reed, George Francis
Reed, George Franklin
Reed, George Joseph
Reed, Hugh, Jr.
Reed, Jerry
Reed, John Alton
Reed, John Franklin
Reed, John Hathaway
Reed, Lester James
Reed, Paul Allen
Reed, Scott
Reed, Sidney George, Jr.
Reed, Stanley Forman
Reed, Stanley Foster
Reed, Theodore Harold
Reed, Travis Dean
Reed, Vincent Emory
Reed, Walter Dudley
Reed, William Edward
Reed, William LaForest
Reed, William Vernon
Reed, Willis
Reeder, James Pryor
Reeder, Oliver Howard
Reeder, William Glase
Reep, Edward Arnold
Rees, Frank William, Jr.
Rees, Paul Stromberg
Rees, Sherrel Jerry Evans
Rees, Thomas Mankell
Reese, Jack Edward
Reese, Jay Rodney
Reese, Kenneth Wendell
Reese, Lymon Clifton
Reesing, John Palmer, Jr.
Reeve, Edward Wilkins
Reeves, Frank Blair
Reeves, Franklin Delano (Dell)
Reeves, George Paul
Reeves, Robert Grier LeFevre
Reeves, William Boyd
Regeimbal, Neil Robert, Sr.
Regenstein, Louis
Regula, Ralph Straus
Rehm, John Bartram
Rehm, Warren Stacey, Jr.
Rehnquist, William Hubbs
Reich, Alan Anderson
Reich, Robert Sigmund
Reichardt, Paul Edward
Reid, Donald Sidney
Reid, George Willard
Reid, Harold Wilson
Reid, Jackson Brock
Reid, Joseph Edmondson
Reid, Robert Newton
Reid, Toy Franklin
Reid, Willard Malcolm
Reifsnyder, Charles Frank
Reighard, Homer Leroy
Reilly, David Henry
Reilly, Gerard Denis
Reimer, Melvin Adolph
Reindollar, Robert Mason, Jr.
Reinhard, Erwin Arthur
Reinhardt, John Edward
Reinhart, Bruce Lloyd
Reinheimer, Robert, Jr.
Reinsch, Emerson Gerald
Reinsch, James Leonard
Reiss, Eric
Reistle, Carl Ernest, Jr.
Reistrup, Jeanne Moss
Reistrup, Paul Hansen
Reith, Carl Joseph
Reitz, J(ulius) Wayne
Relic, Peter Donald
Rembert, William Adair, Jr.
Remke, Robert Lang
Rendtorff, Robert Carlisle
Renick, Ralph Apperson
Renner, John Wilson
Rentenbach, Thomas Joseph
Rephan, Jack
Replogle, Thomas Harvey
Resler, Rexford Adrian
Resnik, Harvey Lewis Paul
Resnik, Michael David
Reston, James Barrett
Reston, Thomas Busey
Rettgers, Forrest I.
Reuschlein, Harold Gill
Reuter, Frank Theodore
Revercomb, Everett Eugene
Reville, Charles Oliver, Jr.
Rew, Thomas Frederick
Rey, William Kenneth
Reyburn, Harold Orbra
Reyer, Randall William
Reyner, Anthony Stephen
Reynolds, Andrew Jackson
Reynolds, Charles McKinley, Jr.
Reynolds, Dana Drummond
Reynolds, David Parham
Reynolds, Edward Storrs
Reynolds, Edwin Louis
Reynolds, Emmett Robinson
Reynolds, Frank Miller
Reynolds, Herbert Hal
Reynolds, Joseph Allen, Jr.
Reynolds, Joshua Paul
Reynolds, Julian Louis
Reynolds, Norman Eben
Reynolds, Orr Esrey
Reynolds, Richard S., Jr.
Reynolds, Robert Lester
Reynolds, Thomas Lee
Reynolds, Virgil Lloyd
Reynolds, Wiley Richard
Reynolds, Wiley Richard
Reynolds, William Walter
Rhame, William Thomas
Rhinehardt, Fred Hinton
Rhinelander, Frederic William Templeton
Rhoads, James Berton
Rhodes, Allen Franklin
Rhodes, Donald Henry
Rhodes, Donald Robert
Rhodes, John Jacob
Rhodes, William Luther, Jr.
Rhyne, Charles Sylvanus
Ribeiro, Lenor de Sa
Ribicoff, Abraham A.
Rice, Dorothy Pechman (Mrs. John Donald)
Rice, Elroy Leon
Rice, Frederick Anders Hudson
Rice, George Washington
Rice, Michael Stephen
Rice, Richard Lee
Rich, Arthur Lowndes
Rich, Charles Allan
Rich, Giles Sutherland
Rich, John Henderson
Rich, Linvil Gene
Rich, Paul Ian
Richard, John Benard
Richard, Ralph Stephenson
Richards, Darrie Hewitt
Richards, Jeanne Herron
Richards, John Raymond
Richards, Ralph Julian, Jr.
Richards, Richard Davison
Richards, Robert Wadsworth
Richardson, Brittain David
Richardson, Elliot Lee
Richardson, James Abner, III
Richardson, James Milton
Richardson, Jean
Richardson, John, Jr.
Richardson, John Marshall
Richardson, John William, Jr.
Richardson, Lloyd Merritt
Richardson, Mark Edwin, II
Richardson, Richard Judson
Richardson, Robert Charlwood, III
Richardson, Rupert Norval
Richardson, Sylvia Onesti
Richardson, William Alan
Richardson, William Rowland
Richert, Earl Harvey
Richey, Charles R.
Richey, Charles Robert
Richman, Robert Maxwell
Richmond, David Walker
Richmond, James Ellis
Richmond, Samuel Bernard
Richter, George Holmes
Rickey, Gerard Brandon
Rickover, Hyman George
Riddell, Joseph Murray, Jr.
Ridder, Walter Thompson
Riddle, Hugh, Jr.
Riddleberger, Hugh Compton
Ridenhour, Joseph Conrad
Rider, Rowland Vance
Ridgely, Joseph Vincent
Ridgeway, James Fowler
Riedel, Alan Ellis
Riegel, Kurt Wetherhold
Riely, John William
Rifenburgh, Richard Philip
Rigau, Marco Antonio
Riggs, Arthur Jordy
Riggs, Robert Owen
Rigler, Patricia Hanges

Riley, Daniel Edward
Riley, James Edwin
Riley, Janet Mary
Riley, Jeannie C. Stephenson (Mrs. Mitchell E. Riley)
Riley, Joseph Harry
Riley, Paul Harbert
Riley, Paul Hunter
Riley, Ray Allen
Riley, Richard Wilson
Rill, James Franklin
Rinaldo, Matthew J.
Ringer, Jules Jacob
Ringham, Rodger Falk
Ringler, Robert Lloyd
Rink, Wesley Winfred
Rinker, Marshall Edison
Rinta, Eugene Fridolph
Rioch, David McKenzie
Riopelle, Arthur Jean
Riordan, Dale Patrick
Ripley, Sidney Dillon, 2d
Ripley, Thomas Huntington
Ripperger, Eugene Arman
Ripstein, Charles Benjamin
Risi, Louis J., Jr.
Risser, James Vaulx, Jr.
Risser, Paul Gillan
Ritchie, John
Ritchie, Reeves Estes
Ritter, Alfred Francis, Jr.
Ritterman, Stuart I.
Rivera-Dueno, Jaime
Rivers, Eurith Dickinson, Jr.
Rivers, Marie Bie
Rives, Albert Gordon
Rives, Richard Taylor
Rivet, Charles Landry
Riviere, Paul Franklin
Rivinus, Edward Florens
Rivlin, Alice Mitchell
Rixey, Charles Woodford
Rizzoli, Hugo V(ictor)
Roach, James Robert
Roach, Wesley Linville
Roache, Milton Oris, Jr.
Roaden, Arliss Lloyd
Roark, Elijah Buck, Jr.
Rob, Charles Granville
Robb, Charles Spittal
Robb, Felix Compton
Robb, Lynda Johnson
Robb, Roger
Robbie, Joseph
Robbins, Anthony
Robbins, Jerry Hal
Robbins, Marty (Martin David Robinson)
Robbins, Paul Hebert
Robbins, Ray Charles
Robbins, Warren Murray
Roberson, Nathan Russell
Roberts, Bonny K.
Roberts, Chalmers McGeagh
Roberts, Charles Riles
Roberts, Doris Emma
Roberts, Elliott Clifton
Roberts, Elmer A.
Roberts, Frances Cabaniss
Roberts, Francis Warren
Roberts, Irving
Roberts, Jack
Roberts, James Milnor, Jr.
Roberts, Jeanne Addison
Roberts, Kenneth Lewis
Roberts, Marguerite
Roberts, Merrill Joseph
Roberts, (Granville) Oral
Roberts, Ray
Roberts, Ray Crouse, Jr.
Roberts, Robert, Jr.
Roberts, Royston Murphy
Roberts, Steven Victor
Roberts, Warren Austin
Roberts, William C.
Robertson, David Wyatt
Robertson, Frank Lewis
Robertson, George Leven
Robertson, Gerald Leslie
Robertson, Horace Bascomb, Jr.
Robertson, James David
Robertson, James Irvin, Jr.
Robertson, John Marshall, Jr.
Robertson, Joseph Moorman
Robertson, Lawrence Vernon, Jr.
Robertson, Marion Gordon
Robertson, Richard Bentley
Robertson, Robert Roy, Jr.
Robertson, Stokes Vernon
Robertson, Sydenham Brooks
Robertson, William Dixon, Jr.
Robertson, William Franklin
Robins, E. Claiborne
Robins, Gerald Burns
Robinson, Alice Gram
Robinson, Allyn Preston, Jr.
Robinson, Aubrey Eugene, Jr.
Robinson, Bob Leo
Robinson, Brooks Calbert, Jr.
Robinson, David Adair
Robinson, Dean Wentworth
Robinson, Donald Walter
Robinson, Florence Claire Crim
Robinson, Frank
Robinson, Gon Zala
Robinson, H. Elmo
Robinson, Hampton Carroll, Jr.
Robinson, Harold Frank
Robinson, Harold Nyle
Robinson, Harry Maximilian, Jr.
Robinson, Howard Olis
Robinson, Hugh Granville
Robinson, Ira Charles
Robinson, James Anthony
Robinson, James Arthur
Robinson, James Kenneth
Robinson, James William
Robinson, John Beckwith
Robinson, Len (Truck)
Robinson, Mary Frances McFeeters
Robinson, Milton Bernidine
Robinson, Paul Irwin
Robinson, Peter Clark
Robinson, Prezell Russell
Robinson, Robert Alexander
Robinson, Roscoe Ross
Robinson, Ruth Olevia
Robinson, Spottswood William, III
Robinson, Walter McLaren, Jr.
Robinson, William Edward, Jr.
Robinson, William Peters
Robison, Andrew Cliffe, Jr.
Robison, G(eorge) Alan
Robitscher, Jonas
Robsion, John Marshall, Jr.
Roch, Robert Hoover
Rochberg, Samuel
Rochester, Dudley Fortescue
Rochlin, Paul R.
Rockefeller, Edwin Shaffer
Rockefeller, John Davison, IV
Rockler, Walter James
Rockwell, Theodore, III
Rockwood, Ruth H.
Roddis, Louis Harry, Jr.
Rodemacher, W.D.
Roderick, Dorrance Douglas
Rodes, Elmer Owen, Jr.
Rodgers, Frank
Rodgers, Joann Ellison
Rodgers, William Woodson
Rodino, Peter Wallace, Jr.
Rodman, Nathaniel Fulford, Jr.
Rodnick, David
Rodriguez, John Raul Davis
Rodriguez, Juan Guadalupe
Rodriguez, Mario Edgardo
Rodriguez-Bou, Ismael
Roe, Ina Lea
Roe, Thomas Anderson
Roe, Thomas Coombe
Roedel, Philip Morgan
Roehm, MacDonell, Jr.
Roehr, Juergen Hermann
Roels, Oswald Albert
Roesler, Robert Harry
Roesner, Larry August
Roessler, Robert Louis
Roessler, Ronald James
Roessner, Roland Gommel
Roethel, David Albert Hill
Roettger, Norman Charles, Jr.
Rogat, Morris Edward
Rogers, Adrian P(ierce)
Rogers, Archibald Coleman
Rogers, C. B.
Rogers, Charles McPherson Aduston, III
Rogers, Donald Lee
Rogers, Ernest Paul
Rogers, Frank Waters
Rogers, Franklyn Christopher
Rogers, Gaines Madison
Rogers, Hamilton
Rogers, James Frederick
Rogers, John James William
Rogers, Jon Guy
Rogers, Jon Guy
Rogers, Lewis Henry
Rogers, Lockhart Burgess
Rogers, Lorene Lane (Mrs. Burl Gordon Rogers)
Rogers, M(aynard) L(ivingston), Jr. (Tex)
Rogers, Mac Edwin
Rogers, Nathaniel Sims
Rogers, Paul Grant
Rogers, Ralph B.
Rogers, Richard Raymond
Rogers, Robert Francis
Rogers, Scott A(rthur), Jr.
Rogers, Stephen Douglas
Rogers, Theodore Courtney
Rogers, Warren Joseph, Jr.
Rogers, William Pierce
Roget, Einar Leonard
Rogg, Nathaniel H.
Rogovin, Mitchell
Roher, William Carl
Rohlich, Gerard Addison
Rohner, Ralph John
Rohrbaugh, Albert Howard
Rojas, Richard Raimond
Roland, Charles Pierce
Rolf, Howard Leroy
Roller, Duane Henry DuBose
Rolleston, William Francis
Rollins, Alfred Brooks, Jr.
Roman, Nancy Grace
Romanell, Patrick
Romanowitz, Byron Foster
Romansky, Monroe James
Romero-Barceló, Carlos Antonio
Romine, Thomas Beeson, Jr.
Rommel, Wilfred H.
Romney, Carl F.
Ronald, Peter
Rone, William Eugene, Jr.
Roney, Jay Louis
Roney, Paul H.
Rooney, Fred B.
Rooney, Kevin Davitt
Rooney, William Richard
Roorda, John Francis, Jr.
Roos, Philip
Roosa, Stuart
Roosevelt, Archibald Bulloch, Jr.
Root, William Alden
Roper, Clyde Forrest Eugene
Roper, John Lonsdale, II
Roper, John Lonsdale, III
Roper, Paul Holmes
Ropp, Theodore
Rorie, Conrad Jonathan
Rorschach, Harold Emil, Jr.
Rorschach, Richard Gordon
Rosan, Richard Adams
Rosberg, David William
Roscopf, Charles Buford
Rose, Beatrice Schroeder (Mrs. William H. Rose)
Rose, Charles Grandison, III
Rose, Christopher Walcott
Rose, David Shepherd
Rose, Frank Anthony
Rose, James McKinley, Jr.
Rose, John Charles
Rose, Mary Carman (Mrs. Alexander Grant Rose)
Rose, Michael David
Rose, Nicholas John
Rose, Robert Marc
Rose, William Alfred
Roseberg, Carl Andersson
Roseman, Saul
Rosen, Bernard
Rosen, Martin M.
Rosen, Milton William
Rosenbaum, Harold Dennis
Rosenberg, David Howard
Rosenberg, Dennis Melville Leo
Rosenberg, Henry A., Jr.
Rosenberg, Jay Frank
Rosenberg, Leonard B.
Rosenberg, Maurice
Rosenberg, Steven Aaron
Rosenberger, Homer Tope
Rosenblatt, Peter Ronald
Rosenblatt, Roger
Rosenbloom, Arlan Lee
Rosenbloom, Morris Victor
Rosenblum, Donald Edward
Rosenblum, Marvin
Rosengarten, Theodore Harvey
Rosenkranz, Stanley William
Rosenquist, James Albert
Rosenson, Leonard Henry
Rosenstein, Claude Houston
Rosenstein, Samuel Murray
Rosensweig, Stanley Harold
Rosenthal, Aaron
Rosenthal, Douglas Eurico
Rosenthal, Gerald David
Rosenthal, Stanley Lawrence
Rosenthal, William J.
Rosky, Theodore Samuel
Rosomoff, Hubert Lawrence
Ross, Alan
Ross, Allan Anderson
Ross, Billy Irvan
Ross, Bradford
Ross, Clarence Hopkins
Ross, David, III
Ross, Glenn Robert
Ross, Griff Terry
Ross, John Stoner
Ross, Joseph Comer
Ross, Marion Collier
Ross, Richard Starr
Ross, Sherman
Ross, Stanford G.
Ross, Stanley Robert
Ross, Thomas Bernard
Ross, William Dee, Jr.
Ross, William Jarboe
Rosse, Wendell Franklyn
Rosser, Charles D.
Rossini, Frederick Dominic
Rossiter, Frank Raymond
Rossmiller, George Eddie
Rosson, Glenn Richard
Rost, Duane Delbert
Rostker, Bernard Daniel
Rostow, Elspeth Davies
Rostow, Walt Whitman
Rostropovich, Mstislav
Roth, George Leith, Jr.
Roth, Jesse
Roth, L(inwood) Evans
Roth, Myron Alfred
Roth, Raymond Edward
Roth, Robert
Roth, Robert Earl
Roth, Sanford Irwin
Roth, William V., Jr.
Rothenberg, Allen W.
Rothman, Donald Nahum
Rotholz, Max B.
Rothschild, Alan Friend
Rothschild, Amalie Rosenfeld
Rothschild, Louis Samuel
Rottman, Ellis
Rouland, Jay Thomas
Rourke, Francis Edward
Rous, Stephen Norman
Rousakis, John Paul
Rouse, Roscoe, Jr.
Rouse, Roy Dennis
Rouse, Stanley Harry
Rousselot, John Harbin
Routh, Porter Wroe
Rowan, Carl Thomas
Rowan, John Robert
Rowden, Marcus Aubrey
Rowe, Charles Spurgeon
Rowe, Herbert Joseph
Rowe, James Henry, Jr.
Rowe, James W.
Rowe, Joseph Everett
Rowe, Wallace Prescott
Rowen, Hobart
Rowland, Arthur Ray
Rowland, Richard Creswell
Rowley, James Walton
Rowley, Worth
Rowntree, Gradie Raymond
Rowny, Edward Leon
Roy, Elsijane Trimble
Roy, Robert Hall
Royal, Darrell K.
Royall, Robert Venning, Jr.
Roybal, Edward R.
Royer, John Everett
Royer, Robert Lewis
Roylance, D.C.
Royster, Vermont (Connecticut)
Royster, Wimberly Calvin
Rubenstein, Martin
Rubenstein, Richard Lowell
Rubin, Alvin Benjamin
Rubin, Louis Decimus, Jr.
Rubin, Seymour Jeffrey
Rubinstein, Hyman Solomon
Rubottom, Roy Richard, Jr.
Ruby, Russell (Glenn)
Rucci, Eustine Paul
Rucker, Tinsley White, III
Rucks, Joseph Gibson
Rudd, Eldon
Rudd, Robert William
Rudner, William Barnett
Rudolph, Robert Edmund
Rudow, David Barry
Ruefli, Timothy Walter
Ruenheck, Jerome B.
Rufa, Robert Henry
Ruff, Charles F. C.
Ruffin, Albert Leslie, Jr.
Ruge, Daniel August
Ruggiero, John Salvator
Ruhl, Robert Henry
Ruiz, Aldelmo
Rumaggi, Louis Jacob
Rumble, Richard Edwards
Rumbough, Stanley Maddox, Jr.
Rumford, Beatrix Tyson
Rundles, Ralph Wayne
Runkle, Lowe Winfield
Runnels, Harold Lowell
Runyan, John William, Jr.
Ruppe, Philip E.
Ruscio, Domenic Richard
Rush, Fletcher Gray, Jr.
Rush, James Avery, Jr.
Rush, Kenneth
Rushing, Jane Gilmore
Rushing, Joe Bob
Rushton, William James
Rushton, William James, III
Rusk, Dean
Russell, Albert Richard
Russell, Dan M., Jr.
Russell, Donald Glenn
Russell, Donald Stuart
Russell, Edgar Poe, Jr.
Russell, Fred McFerrin
Russell, George
Russell, Harold Louis
Russell, James Alvin, Jr.
Russell, James Webster, Jr.
Russell, John Clifford
Russell, Josiah Cox
Russell, Lao (Mrs. Walter Russell)
Russell, Mark
Russell, Paul Farr
Russell, R. Robert
Russell, Richard Olney, Jr.
Russell, Thomas Dameron
Russell, Thomas Triplett
Russell, William Joseph
Russo, Alexander Peter
Russo, Martin A.
Rust, William Fitzhugh, Jr.
Rutenberg, Charles
Rutherford, F(loyd) James
Rutherford, James J.
Rutherford, John Sherman, III (Johnny)
Rutland, Robert Allen
Rutstein, David W.
Ruttenberg, Stanley Harvey
Ruud, Millard Harrington
Ryals, Clyde de Loache
Ryan, Allan A.
Ryan, Cornelius O'Brien
Ryan, John William
Ryan, Louis Farthing
Ryan, Malcolm Edward, Jr.
Ryan, Nolan
Ryan, Thomas Joseph
Ryder, Frank Glessner
Ryder, John Douglas
Rye, Joe Terry
Rylance, George Austin
Rymer, S. Bradford, Jr.
Ryor, John
Ryschkewitsch, George Eugene
Sabatella, Joseph John
Sabel, John Burke
Sabin, Albert Bruce
Sabine, Gordon Arthur
Sabiston, David Coston, Jr.
Sabrosky, Curtis Williams
Sachar, Howard Morley
Sachs, Alan Richard
Sachs, Raymond Joseph, Jr.
Sachs, Sidney Stanley
Sachs, Stephen Howard
Sachse, Harry Rubenstein
Sachse, Victor A., Jr.
Sack, Sylvan Hanan
Sackett, Albert Monroe
Sackett, Leland Russell, Jr.
Sackett, Ross DeForest
Sackett, Walter Wallace, Jr.
Sadik, Marvin Sherwood
Safer, John
Saff, Edward Barry
Saffiotti, Umberto
Saffir, Herbert Seymour
Safire, William
Sagalkin, Sanford
Sagar, William Clayton
Sage, Andrew Patrick, Jr.
Sager, Merel Seaman
Sagerholm, James Alvin
Sagle, Robert Franklin
St. Clair, Nelson Lewis, Jr.
St. Clair, Rita Erika
St. Jean, Joseph, Jr.
St John, Adrian, II
St. John, John
Salant, Walter S.
Salatka, Charles Alexander
Salik, Julian Oswald
Salis, Andrew Edmond
Salley, John Jones
Salmon, Joseph Thaddeus
Salmon, Louis
Salmon, Paul Blair
Saltarelli, Gerald C.
Salvaggio, John Edmond
Salvaggio, Tony Joe
Sam, Joseph
Samford, Frank Park, Jr.
Samford, Thomas Drake, III
Samford, Yetta Glenn, Jr.
Sammet, George, Jr.
Sammet, Jean E.
Sampson, A(rthur) Clarence
Sampson, Arthur Francis
Sams, Herbert William
Sams, W(iley) Mitchell, Jr.
Samson, Charles Harold, Jr.
Samuchin, Michael George
Samuel, Howard David
Samuels, Sheldon Wilfred
Sanchez, Adel
Sanchez, Rafael Camilo
Sandefur, Joseph Thomas
Sanderlin, John Boswell
Sanders, Aaron Perry
Sanders, Carl Julian
Sanders, Charles Lionel
Sanders, Harland
Sanders, Harold Barefoot, Jr.
Sanders, Howard
Sanders, Joe William
Sanders, John Lassiter
Sanders, Leonard Marion, Jr.
Sanders, Murray Jonathan
Sanders, Oliver Paul
Sanders, Paul Hampton
Sanders, Thomas Alfred, Jr.
Sanders, William Evan
Sanderson, Fred Hugo
Sanderson, Walton White
Sandground, Mark B.
Sanditen, Edgar Richard
Sandlin, Joseph Ernest
Sandmeyer, Robert Lee
Sandoloski, Sandy Moise
Sandor, George Nason
Sandridge, Sidney Edwin
Sands, Robert Kenneth
Sands, Thomas John
Sanfelici, Arthur Hugo
Sanford, John Berkshire, Jr.
Sanford, Terry
Sanford, Valerius
Sanger, Herbert Shelton, Jr.
Sangster, William McCoy
Sanroma, Jesus Maria
Sansom, Richard E.
Santarelli, Donald Eugene
Santelmann, Paul William
Santini, James David
Santos, George Wesley
Sapienza, John Thomas
Sapir, Philip
Sapp, Walter William
Sappington, Thomas Asbury
Sarasin, Ronald A.
Saraw, Arnold F.
Sarbacher, Robert Irving
Sarbanes, Paul Spyros
Sarber, Raymond William
Sargent, Frederick, II
Sarnoff, Stanley Jay
Sarosdy, Louis Robert
Sarpy, Leon
Sarro, Ronald Armand
Sasser, James Ralph
Satchler, George Raymond
Sato, Frank Saburo
Sattee, Andrew L.
Satterfield, David Edward, III
Satterfield, Grey Wilson, Jr.
Satterfield, John Creighton
Satterthwaite, Cameron B.
Satterwhite, William Thomas
Saucier, Walter Joseph
Sauers, Clayton Henry
Saul, B. Francis II
Saunders, Charles Baskerville, Jr.
Saunders, Harold Henry
Saunders, Harris, Jr.
Saunders, Jack Palmer
Saunders, James Henry
Saunders, Joseph Benjamin, Jr.
Saunders, Joseph Francis
Saunders, Ralph Scott
Savage, Charles Francis
Savage, Henry, Jr.
Savage, James Francis
Savage, Robert Stanley
Savage, Wallace Hamilton
Savage, William Woodrow
Savell, Edward Lupo
Saville, Lloyd (Blackstone)
Saville, Thorndike, Jr.
Savit, Carl Hertz
Savitz, Gerald Samuel
Sawhill, Isabel Van Devanter
Sawhill, John Crittenden
Sawyer, Granville Monroe
Sawyer, Harold S.
Sawyer, Helen Alton
Sawyers, John Lazelle
Saxe, Harry Charles
Saye, Albert Berry
Sayre, Robert Marion
Sayre, Thomas Henry
Scaggs, Howard Irwin
Scaglione, Aldo Domenico
Scaglione, Frank
Scales, James Ralph
Scali, John Alfred
Scammon, Richard Montgomery
Scandalios, John George
Scarborough, Robert Bowman
Scarborough, Robert Henry, Jr.
Scarbrough, Cleve Knox, Jr.
Scarlett, John Donald
Scarton, Bennie, Jr.
Schaaf, C(arl) Hart
Schachtel, Hyman Judah
Schad, Theodore George, Jr.
Schaefer, Henry Frederick, III
Schaefer, Robert Ellsworth
Schaefer, Robert Wayne
Schaefer, William Donald
Schaefer, William Goerman, Jr.
Schaeffer, Leonard David
Schaeffer, Wendell Gordon
Schafer, John Henry
Schafer, Lothar
Schaffer, William Gray
Schaffner, Robert Michael
Schally, Andrew Victor
Schank, Stanley Cox
Schapery, Richard Allan
Schaub, James Hamilton
Schechter, Edmund
Schechter, Robert Samuel
Scheel, Paul Joseph
Scheeler, Charles
Scheeler, James Arthur
Scheer, Julian Weisel
Scheer, Milton David
Scheer, Stuart Charles
Scheffer, Walter Francis
Scheibe, Fred Karl
Scheibel, Kenneth Maynard
Scheibner, Edwin Joseph
Schein, Philip Samuel
Scheinberg, Peritz
Scheiner, Samuel
Schell, Braxton
Schelling, John Paul
Schenkel, James Milton
Schenkkan, Robert Frederic
Scheps, Clarence
Scherer, Lee Richard, Jr.
Scherer, Raymond Lewis
Scherer, Robert W.
Scherich, Edward Baptiste
Schersten, H. Donald
Schetz, Joseph Alfred
Scheuer, James Haas
Scheving, Lawrence Einar
Schiebler, Gerold Ludwig
Schiering, Harry Calvin
Schiller, Everett Lyle
Schiller, Milton S.
Schilling, Ralph Franklin
Schindler, Albert Isadore
Schindler, Clayton Moss
Schkade, Lawrence Louis
Schlagel, Richard Harold
Schlaretzki, Walter Ernest
Schlenger, Jacques Thompson
Schlesinger, James Rodney
Schlesinger, Theodore
Schlezinger, Julius
Schloegel, George Anthony
Schlom, Jeffrey Bert
Schluter, Fredric Edward
Schmeling, Gareth
Schmeltzer, Edward
Schmick, William Frederick, Jr.
Schmid, Bernard Francis
Schmid, John Samuel
Schmidt, Carl Frederic
Schmidt, Harold Eugene
Schmidt, Joseph William, Jr.
Schmidt, Ralph Leopold William
Schmidt, Richard Marten, Jr.
Schmidt, Robert Louis
Schmidt, Terry Lane
Schmidt, Wilson Emerson
Schmidt-Nielsen, Knut
Schmieder, Frank Joseph
Schmitt, Harrison Hagan
Schmitt, Karl Michael
Schnader, Donald Dixon
Schnaitman, William Kenneth
Schneider, John Hoke
Schneider, Kenneth Albert
Schneider, Louis
Schneider, Mark Lewis
Schneider, Roy Lester
Schneider, Vernon Earl
Schneider, William Charles
Schneiders, Gregory Stephen
Schnering, Philip Blessed
Schnittker, John Alvin
Schnitzer, Martin Colby
Schoelkopf, Dean Harold
Schoenbaum, Alex

Schoenbaum, Samuel
Schoeneman, Richard Howard
Schoenleb, Edwin Christian
Schoep, Arthur Paul
Scholtes, Robert Martin
Schonk, Robert Martin
Schoolar, Joseph Clayton
Schooley, Allen Heaten
Schopler, Eric
Schorr, Daniel Louis
Schorr, Lisbeth Bamberger
Schorre, Louis Charles, Jr.
Schotland, Roy Arnold
Schottstaedt, William Walter
Schrader, Bernard William
Schrader, George Robert
Schrader, Harry Christian, Jr.
Schram, Martin Jay
Schramm, Texas E.
Schrank, Auline Raymond
Schreiber, Fred James, Jr.
Schreiber, Melvyn Hirsh
Schriever, Bernard Adolph
Schroeder, Leon William
Schroeder, Sister M. Rita (Viola)
Schroeder, Patricia Scott (Mrs. James White Schroeder)
Schruben, John Henry
Schuck, Victoria
Schuette, Oswald Francis
Schull, William Jackson
Schuller, Gordon Joseph
Schulman, Ivan Albert
Schulman, Joseph Daniel
Schulman, Robert Arnold
Schulte, Rainer
Schultz, Franklin M.
Schultz, Frederick Henry
Schultz, James Clement
Schultz, Leslie P.
Schultz, Milton John, Jr.
Schultz, Stanley George
Schultze, Charles Louis
Schulz, Robert L(udwig)
Schulze, Richard Carl
Schulze, Richard Taylor
Schumacher, Carl J., Jr.
Schurman, Joseph Rathborne
Schussheim, Morton Joel
Schust, Ralph Henry
Schuster, Gary Francis
Schuster, Herman Frederick
Schuster, Joseph Lawrence
Schwab, John Joseph
Schwait, Allen Louis
Schwartz, Abba Philip
Schwartz, Charles, Jr.
Schwartz, Charles Frederick
Schwartz, David
Schwartz, Donald Edward
Schwartz, Harry Kane
Schwartz, Kessel
Schwartz, Lloyd Marvin
Schwartz, Michael Averill
Schwartz, Victor Elliot
Schwarz, Joseph Edmund
Schwarz, Michael Jay
Schwarzschild, William Harry, Jr.
Schwarzwalder, John Carl
Schwebel, Stephen Myron
Schweiker, Richard Schultz
Schweitz, Robert Edwin
Schweitzer, George Keene
Schweitzer, H. George
Schwend, Fred Seaton
Schwendeman, J(oseph) R(aymond)
Schwert, George William
Schwetman, Herbert Dewitt
Schwiebert, Leslie Nordean
Schwing, Charles Edward
Schwinghamer, Robert John
Scifres, Robert E.
Scisson, Sidney E.
Scofield, Henry Harland
Scotese, Peter G.
Scott, Alastair Ian
Scott, Charles Ray
Scott, Charles Waldo
Scott, Charley
Scott, David Bytovetzski
Scott, Edward William, Jr.
Scott, Frederick Isadore, Jr.
Scott, Henry L.
Scott, Henry William, Jr.
Scott, Hugh
Scott, Irene Feagin
Scott, Jessie M.
Scott, Joan Wallach
Scott, John Alden
Scott, John Dilworth
Scott, John Edward
Scott, John Irving Elias
Scott, John Winfield, Jr.
Scott, Lewis Pennington, III
Scott, Nathan Alexander, Jr.
Scott, Nauman S.
Scott, Ralph Mason
Scott, Robert Cooper
Scott, Robert Vernon
Scott, Roland Boyd
Scott, Tasso Harold
Scott, Tom Burkett, Jr.
Scott, Tom Keck
Scott, Walter Coke
Scott, Willard Philip
Scott, William Lloyd
Scott, Wilton Elege
Scoville, Herbert, Jr.
Scowcroft, Brent
Scribner, Louie Lorraine
Scriggins, Larry Palmer
Scripps, Edward Wyllis
Scriven, L. Edward
Scruggs, Earl Eugene
Scruggs, John Dudley
Scurlock, Arch Chilton
Scurlock, Eddy Clark
Seager, Robert, II
Seagondollar, Lewis Worth
Seal, John Ridley
Seals, Woodrow
Sealy, Tom
Sealy, Will Camp
Seamans, James McGeery
Sear, Morey Leonard
Searcy, Albert Wynne
Searle, Philip Ford
Searles, Dewitt Richard
Searls, Frederick Taylor
Sears, Earl Wayne
Sears, John Patrick
Sears, John Raymond, Jr.
Sears, Leslie Ray, Jr.
Sears, William Gray (Will)
Seaton, William Russell
Seatz, Lloyd Frank
Seay, Edward Ward
Seay, William H.
Sebastian, Rex Arden
Sebes, Joseph Schobert
Sebesta, Charles Joseph, Jr.
Sebrell, William Henry, Jr.
Sederbaum, William
Sedwick, (Benjamin) Frank
Seeburg, Noel Marshall, Jr.
Seeger, Michael
Seegmiller, Ray Reuben
Seelye, Talcott Williams
Seemann, Ernest Albright
Seib, Charles Bach
Seiberlich, Carl Joseph
Seiberling, John F.
Seibert, Russell Jacob
Seibold, Martin
Seidler, I. Marshall
Seidman, Bert
Seifert, Lee Roe
Seiferth, Solis
Seigel, Stuart Evan
Seigenthaler, John Lawrence
Seigle, John William
Seignious, George Marion, II
Seiler, Lewis P.
Seiler, Robert Edward
Seinsheimer, Joseph Fellman, Jr.
Selby, Henry Anderson
Selby, John Edward
Selby, Richard Roy
Selden, Joseph Wixson
Selden, Richard Thomas
Selecman, Charles Edward
Self, David Wilson
Self, James Cuthbert
Self, Raymond Weaver
Selig, John Samuel
Seliger, Howard H.
Selin, Ivan
Selkirk, James Kirkwood
Sell, Edward Scott, Jr.
Sell, Kenneth Walter
Sellers, James Earl
Sellers, Richard Morgan
Sellers, Robert Vernon
Sellinger, Joseph Anthony
Sells, Saul B.
Sellstrom, Albert Donald
Semans, Truman Thomas
Semrod, T. Joseph
Sener, Joseph Ward
Sener, Joseph Ward, Jr.
Senkus, Murray
Senseman, Ronald Sylvester
Sentell, James Oscar
Senter, L. T.
Senter, William Oscar
Serber, Robert
Serfass, Earl James
Serralles, Felix J.
Serris, Nicholas Harry
Service, James Edward
Servies, James Albert
Sessions, Cicero Columbus
Sessions, Cliff
Sessoms, Stuart McGuire
Seto, Yeb Jo
Settle, Mary Lee
Settlemyer, Claude Harold
Sevareid, Arnold Eric
Sevel, Bernard Jerome
Severino, Alexandrino Eusebio
Sevik, Maurice
Seward, Ralph Theodore
Seward, Richard Bevin
Seward, William Ward, Jr.
Sewell, Ben Gardner
Sewell, Duane Campbell
Sewell, James Leslie
Sewell, Winifred
Sexton, Irwin
Seydell, Mildred
Seymour, Ernest Richard
Seymour, Thaddeus
Shaara, Michael Joseph, Jr.
Shaefer, Richard Francis
Shaeffer, Charles Wayne
Shafer, W. O.
Shaffer, Charles Norman
Shaffer, Guy Henry Baskerville
Shaffer, James Travis
Shaffer, John Hixon
Shaffer, Mary L.
Shahan, Ewing Pope
Shaheen, Michael Edmund, Jr.
Shaklee, William Eugene
Shalala, Donna Edna
Shalowitz, Erwin Emmanuel
Shamburek, Roland Howard
Shanahan, Edward P.
Shanahan, Eileen
Shands, William Ridley, Jr.
Shane, Bob
Shank, Clare Brown Williams
Shanker, Albert
Shanklin, J. Gordon
Shanks, Eugene Baylis
Shanks, Hershel
Shannon, David Allen
Shannon, Donald Hawkins
Shannon, Edgar Finley, Jr.
Shannon, Gail
Shannon, Margaret Rutledge
Shannon, Thomas Alfred
Shannon, Thomas Francis
Shanor, Leland
Shapere, Dudley
Shapiro, Albert
Shapiro, David Israel
Shapiro, Maurice Mandel
Shapiro, Myron Frederick (Mike)
Shapiro, Ronald Maurice
Shapiro, Sam
Shapiro, Samuel Bernard
Shapiro, Sumner
Sharp, Aaron John
Sharp, Bert Lavon
Sharp, Charles Frederick
Sharp, David Earl
Sharp, Jere Worth
Sharp, Paul Frederick
Sharp, Philip R.
Sharp, Susie Marshall
Sharp, William
Sharp, William Harry
Sharpe, Keith Yount
Sharpe, Robert Francis
Sharpe, Ruel Yount
Sharpe, William Norman, Jr.
Sharples, Wynne
Sharpley, John Miles
Sharry, John Joseph
Shatto, Gloria McDermith
Shattuck, Roger Whitney
Shaver, Jesse Milton
Shaw, Arnold Franklin
Shaw, Bernard
Shaw, E. Clay, Jr.
Shaw, Edward Andrew
Shaw, Henry King
Shaw, Henry Overstreet
Shaw, John Sherman, Jr.
Shaw, Margery Wayne Schlamp
Shaw, Robert
Shaw, Rodrick Lucian
Shaw, Russell Burnham
Shaw, Steven John
Shaw, Thelma Skaggs
Shaw, William Frederick
Shaw, William Henry
Shaw, William Whitfield
Shea, Francis Michael
Shea, John Joseph
Sheard, William James
Shearer, John Clyde
Shearer, Otis Claude, III
Shearer, Richard Eugene
Shearin, Jess Stewart, Jr.
Sheehan, Edward James
Sheehan, Helen Lee
Sheehan, John Eugene
Sheehan, John Wight
Sheehan, Neil
Sheen, Robert Tilton
Sheets, Donald Guy
Sheetz, Richard LaTrelle
Sheffey, Fred Clifton, Jr.
Sheffield, Roy Dexter
Sheffield, William Johnson
Shefler, Stephen Alan
Shehan, Lawrence Joseph
Sheinberg, Israel
Sheinfeld, Myron
Shelby, Richard Craig
Sheldon, Georgiana Hortense
Shelesnyak, Moses Chaim
Sheline, Raymond K.
Shell, Owen G.
Shellhase, Leslie John
Shelokov, Alexis
Shelton, David Howard
Shelton, George Calvin
Shelton, Karl Mason
Shelton, Larry Brandon
Shelton, Lewis Samuel
Shelton, Raymond Orris
Shelton, Travis Duane
Shenaut, John Frederick
Shenefield, John Hale
Shenkir, William Gary
Shepard, Adrian Bruce
Shepard, Alan Bartlett, Jr.
Shepard, Charles Carter
Shepard, Jean
Shepard, Robert Earl
Shepard, Tazewell Taylor
Shepherd, Cybill
Shepherd, Mark, Jr.
Shepherd, Robert Ashland
Shepley, James Robinson
Sheppard, Albert Parker, Jr.
Sheppard, Charles Stewart
Shepperd, John Ben
Sheps, Cecil George
Sher, Stanley Owen
Sherard, John Holmes, IV
Sherburne, Donald Wynne
Sherer, Lewis Michael, Jr.
Sheridan, Patrick Michael
Sheridan, Stan Roger
Sheriff, Hilla
Sheriff, Seymour
Sherman, Alice E.
Sherman, Jerome Kalman
Sherman, John Foord
Sherman, Merritt
Sherman, Richard Freeman
Sherman, Stuart Holmes, Jr.
Sherman, William Courtney
Sherrer, James Wylie, Sr.
Sherrer, Wayman Gray
Sherrill, William W.
Sherrod, Robert Lee
Sherry, William James
Sherwood, Aaron Wiley
Sherwood, Bette Wilson
Sherwood, Sidney
Shevin, Robert Lewis
Shewmake, Charles Burrel
Shewmaker, Russell Newton
Shick, George Barton, Jr.
Shields, John Harold
Shiels, Eugene F.
Shiffman, Bernard
Shifley, Ralph Louis
Shih, Chia Shun
Shih, J. Chung-wen
Shilling, Kenneth
Shilling, Roy Bryant, Jr.
Shillito, Barry J.
Shine, Henry Joseph
Shinn, Allen Mayhew
Shipley, Vergil Alan
Shipman, Furney George
Shippen, Zoe
Shirley, David Allen
Shive, William
Shively, John Adrian
Shivers, Allan
Shivler, James Fletcher, Jr.
Shneiderov, Anatol James
Shock, Nathan Wetherill
Shockley, Thomas Dewey
Shoemake, Shockley Taliaferro
Shoemaker, Don(ald Cleavenger)
Shoemaker, Gradus Lawrence
Shoemaker, Robert Morin
Shon, Frederick John
Shores, Janie Ledlow
Shores, Louis
Short, Byron Elliott
Short, David Gaines
Short, Walter Joseph
Shory, Naseeb Lein
Shosid, Joseph Lewis
Shotts, Bryan Meeks
Shotzberger, Martin Luther
Showalter, English
Shower, Robert Wesley
Showers, Donald McCollister
Shreeve, Charles Alfred, Jr.
Shriver, Eunice Mary Kennedy (Mrs. Robert Sargent Shriver, Jr.)
Shriver, Garner Edward
Shriver, Harry Clair
Shriver, Robert Sargent, Jr.
Shropshire, Walter, Jr.
Shuford, Harry Alexander
Shula, Don Francis
Shull, Fremont Adam, Jr.
Shull, Leon
Shulman, Arnold
Shulman, Marshall Darrow
Shulman, Stephen Neal
Shults, Robert Luther, Jr.
Shumaker, Thomas Paine
Shuman, Frederick Gale
Shuman, Samuel Irving
Shumate, Joseph Davenport
Shumate, Stuart
Shupert, George Thomas
Shurick, Edward Palmes
Shurrager, Phil Sheridan
Shuster, Bud
Shuval, Andrew Jackson
Shytle, John David
Sibal, Abner Woodruff
Sibley, Harper, Jr.
Sibley, James Malcolm
Sibley, John Adams
Sibley, John Meares, Jr.
Sibley, William Arthur
Sidbury, James Buren
Sidebottom, John Herbert
Sidell, William
Sidey, Hugh Swanson
Sidimus, Joysanne
Sidransky, Herschel
Sieber, Harry Charles
Siegel, Arthur
Siegel, Laurence
Siegel, Max
Siegel, Milton P.
Siegel, Peter Vincent
Siegel, Robert Ted
Siegel, Samuel
Siegel, Samuel
Siegel, Thomas Louis
Siegelman, Don Eugene
Siegler, Howard Matthew
Siemer, Deanne C.
Siena, James Vincent
Siepi, Cesare
Sierakowski, Robert Leon
Siess, Charles Preston, Jr.
Sievering, Nelson Frederick, Jr.
Sievers, Robert H.
Sieverts, Frank Arne
Sigel, M(ola) Michael
Sigel, Stanley Jordan
Sigerson, David Kinley
Sihler, William Wooding
Sikes, Charles Renford
Sikes, G. Griffin
Sikes, Robert L.F.
Silas, Cecil Jesse
Silberman, Lou Hackett
Silberman, Peter Henry
Silbert, Earl J.
Siler, Eugene Edward, Jr.
Silver, Charles Hal
Silver, James Wesley
Silver, Samuel Manuel
Silverlight, Irwin Joseph
Silverman, Alvin Michaels
Silverman, Joseph
Silvers, Earl Reed, Jr.
Silverstein, Leonard Lewis
Silverstone, Harris Julian
Simecheck, Don Mac
Simes, Dimitri Konstantin
Simes, Frank James
Simkins, Leon Jack
Simmonds, James Henry
Simmons, Charles Ferdinand
Simmons, Darrell Aubrey
Simmons, David Arthur
Simmons, Edwin Howard
Simmons, Grant G., Jr.
Simmons, John Kaul
Simmons, Mabel Clarke
Simmons, Richard Morgan, Jr.
Simmons, Sherwin Palmer
Simmons, Thomas Jefferson
Simmons, William Pinckney
Simms, Arthur Benjamin
Simms, Leroy Alanson
Simms, Richard Lee, Jr.
Simms, Robert D.
Simokaitis, Frank Joseph
Simon, Alex Joseph
Simon, Dolph B(ertram) H(irst)
Simon, Ernest Robert
Simon, Joel Norman
Simon, Paul
Simon, Stanley Cornelius
Simone, Joseph Vincent
Simonpietri, Andre C.
Simons, Albert, Jr.
Simons, Charles Earl, Jr.
Simons, Charles J.
Simons, Elwyn LaVerne
Simons, Gordon Donald, Jr.
Simons, Howard
Simons, Lawrence B.
Simons, Lewis Martin
Simons, Thomas Cunningham
Simonson, Roy Walter
Simpson, Alan Kooi
Simpson, Charles Reagan
Simpson, Fred Bryan
Simpson, Gordon
Simpson, Harrell Abner
Simpson, James Shores
Simpson, Joanne Malkus
Simpson, John Arol
Simpson, John Wistar
Simpson, Lewis Pearson
Simpson, Robert Edward
Simpson, Zelma Alene
Simrall, Harry Charles Fleming
Sims, Bennett Jones
Sims, Edward Howell
Sims, James Redding
Sims, Joe
Sims, John Rogers, Jr.
Sims, John William
Sims, Joseph Sherrer
Sims, Wilson
Sinai, Arthur
Sinclair, Alford Charles
Sinclair, John Taylor, Jr.
Sinclair, Rolf Malcolm
Sineath, Timothy Wayne
Sinel, Norman Mark
Singer, Armand Edwards
Singer, Maxine Frank
Singer, Robert Norman
Singer, S(iegfried) Fred
Singer, Sanford R.
Singletary, Clarence Edward
Singletary, Otis Arnold, Jr.
Singleton, Charles Southward
Singleton, Edward Marion
Singleton, John Paul
Singleton, John Virgil, Jr.
Sinkford, Jeanne Craig
Sinks, Lucius Frederick
Sintz, Edward Francis
Sippel, John Parker
Sirica, John J.
Sis, Raymond Francis
Sisco, Joseph John
Sisk, John Kelly
Sisler, Harry Hall
Sisson, Joseph Andrew
Sistrunk, James Dudley
Sitton, Claude Fox
Sizer, Phillip Spelman
Sjoberg, Sigurd Arnold
Skallerup, Walter Thorwald, Jr.
Skehan, Patrick William
Skelton, Alan Gordon
Skelton, Byron George
Skelton, John Frederick, Jr.
Skelton, Robert Beattie
Skibell, Carl Albert
Skibine, George Boris
Skibine, Marjorie Louise Tallchief
Skiff, Robert Woltz
Skiles, Elwin Lloyd
Skinner, Dorothy M.
Skinner, Truman Arnold
Skirving, John Lionel
Sklenar, Herbert Anthony
Skolnik, Barnet David
Skornia, Harry Jay
Skorski, Roman
Skubitz, Joseph
Slaatte, Howard Alexander
Slack, Derald Allen
Slack, John M., Jr.
Sladen, William Joseph Lambart
Slamecka, Vladimir
Slappey, Sterling Greene
Slate, Joe Hutson
Slater, Courtenay Murphy
Slater, Ellis Dwinnell
Slater, Oliver Eugene
Slattery, Sister Margaret Patrice
Slaughter, Adolph James
Slaughter, Edward Ratliff, Jr.
Slaughter, Frank G.
Slaughter, Harrison T.
Slavin, Arthur Joseph
Slawsky, Zaka Israel
Slay, Alton Davis
Slayton, Donald Kent
Slayton, William Larew
Sledd, Herbert Davis
Sledd, James Hinton
Sledd, Marvin Banks
Sledge, Clarence Linden
Sleeper, Sherwin James
Slepian, Paul
Slick, William Thomas, Jr.
Sliepcevich, Cedomir M.
Slifer, Luther Walter, Jr.
Sliger, Bernard Francis
Slingluff, Thomas Rowland, Jr.
Slitor, Richard Eaton
Slivinsky, Cornell J.
Sloan, Frank Keenan
Sloan, LeRoy (Mike) Hendrick
Sloan, Maceo Archibald
Sloan, Robert Dye
Sloan, Stephen Charles
Sloane, George Harvey Ingalls
Slocombe, Walter Becker
Sloman, Marvin Sherk
Sloss, Robert Lee
Slover, George, Jr.
Slowinski, Walter Aloysius
Small, George Milton
Small, Parker Adams, Jr.
Small, Ray
Small, Robert Scott
Small, William Edwin, Jr.
Smalley, Harold Eugene, Sr.
Smart, Clifton Murray, Jr.
Smart, Jacob Edward
Smart, John Kenneth
Smartt, Charles Hinkley
Smathers, Bruce Armistead
Smathers, George A.
Smathers, James Burton
Smeda, Ralph
Smedberg, William Renwick, IV
Smiddy, Joseph Charles
Smiley, Joseph Royall
Smith, A. Robert
Smith, Agnes (Mrs. Richard Bruce Parrish)
Smith, Albin William
Smith, Alexander Goudy
Smith, Alexander Wyly, Jr.
Smith, Alfred Glaze, Jr.
Smith, Alfred Goud
Smith, Andrew Cannon
Smith, Angie Frank, Jr.
Smith, Anthony Wayne
Smith, Arthur
Smith, Arthur Alvin
Smith, Betty Faye
Smith, Bettye Jane
Smith, Bryan Francis
Smith, Bunnie Othanel
Smith, Burton Joseph (B. J.)
Smith, Byron Charles
Smith, C(harles) Carney
Smith, Carol Castlemen, Jr.
Smith, Cece
Smith, Charles Alphonso
Smith, Charles Anderson
Smith, Charles Edward
Smith, Charles Isaac
Smith, Charles Sydney, Jr.
Smith, Charles Thomas
Smith, Clyde Fuhriman
Smith, Cullen
Smith, Cyril James
Smith, Cyrus Rowlett
Smith, DaCosta, Jr.
Smith, David Coles
Smith, David Edmund
Smith, David Lee
Smith, David Shiverick
Smith, David Thornton
Smith, Dean Edwards
Smith, Donald Houston
Smith, Donald Kaye
Smith, Donald Nickerson
Smith, Donn L.
Smith, Douglas
Smith, Douglas Rathbone
Smith, Earl E.T.
Smith, Edward Byron
Smith, Edward Samuel
Smith, Elwyn Allen
Smith, Estus
Smith, Ewell Lee, Jr.
Smith, Floyd Rodenback
Smith, Foster Lee
Smith, Frank Edward
Smith, Frederick George Walton
Smith, Gardner Watkins
Smith, George Dee
Smith, George Edwin
Smith, George Emmett
Smith, George Franklin, Jr.
Smith, George Maynard
Smith, George Patrick, II
Smith, George Rose

Smith, George Van Riper
Smith, Gordon Hunt
Smith, Gordon Laidlaw, Jr.
Smith, Grover Cleveland
Smith, H. Everett
Smith, Hamilton Othanel
Smith, Harlan James
Smith, Harmon Lee, Jr.
Smith, Harold Colby
Smith, Harry Alcide
Smith, Harvey Liss
Smith, Hedrick Laurence
Smith, Herbert Livingston, III
Smith, Horace Lilburn, Jr.
Smith, Howard Kingsbury
Smith, Howard McQueen
Smith, Hugh Montgomery
Smith, Ivan Huron
Smith, James Albert
Smith, James C.
Smith, James Kirby
Smith, James Raymond
Smith, James Roswell
Smith, Jean Chandler
Smith, Jeffrey Bordeaux
Smith, Jeffrey Greenwood
Smith, Jesse Graham, Jr.
Smith, Jessie Carney
Smith, Jim Allison
Smith, Joe Dorsey, Jr.
Smith, John Bertie
Smith, John Joseph
Smith, John Lee, Jr.
Smith, John Lewis, Jr.
Smith, John Lucian, Jr.
Smith, John Sylvester
Smith, John Wayne
Smith, Joseph James
Smith, Joseph Newton Smith, III
Smith, Joseph Wilson
Smith, K(ermit) Wayne
Smith, Kenneth Myers
Smith, Kenneth Wright
Smith, Lanty L(loyd)
Smith, Lee Herman
Smith, Lee Keith, Jr.
Smith, Lemuel Augustus, Jr.
Smith, Leo Clifford
Smith, Leslie Raymond
Smith, Lloyd Hilton
Smith, Marion Pafford
Smith, Marvin Hugh
Smith, McNeill
Smith, Michael Brackett
Smith, Myron George
Smith, Myron John, Jr.
Smith, Neal Edward
Smith, Norman Cutler
Smith, Numa Lamar, Jr.
Smith, Orma Rinehart
Smith, Paul Traylor
Smith, Peter Garthwaite
Smith, Phillip Nolan, Jr.
Smith, Pomeroy
Smith, Quentin Miller, Jr.
Smith, R. G.
Smith, Ralph Lee
Smith, Rankin McEachern
Smith, Rankin McEachern, Jr.
Smith, Ray Winfield
Smith, Raymond D(aniel)
Smith, Richard Thomas
Smith, Richard Thomas
Smith, Robert Earl
Smith, Robert Leo
Smith, Robert Sellers
Smith, Robert Steen
Smith, Ronald Bromley
Smith, Ronald Lee
Smith, Ronald Lynn
Smith, Russell B.
Smith, Russell Hunt
Smith, Russell Jack
Smith, Ruth Dabney Camp
Smith, Ruth Lillian Schluchter
Smith, Samuel Boyd
Smith, Sherwood Draughon
Smith, Sherwood Hubbard, Jr.
Smith, Sidney Oslin, Jr.
Smith, Stanley Roger
Smith, Stuart Seaborne
Smith, Talbot Merton
Smith, Terence Fitzgerald
Smith, Thomas Crampton, Jr.
Smith, Timothy Lawrence
Smith, Tom Eugene
Smith, Walker William
Smith, Walstein Bennett, Jr.
Smith, Walter Douglas
Smith, Walter Joseph, Jr.
Smith, Walter Lee
Smith, Walter Rhea
Smith, Walter Tilford
Smith, Warner Taliaferro
Smith, Wendell Ross
Smith, Wilbur Stevenson
Smith, Wilburn Jackson, Jr.
Smith, William Burton
Smith, William Clifford
Smith, William Harold
Smith, William Joseph
Smith, William Lewis
Smith, William Reece, Jr.
Smith, William Stanford
Smith, William Vick
Smith, Zachary Taylor, II
Smithdeal, William Fralin
Smitherman, Gustavus Scott
Smithson, John Royston
Smoluchowski, Roman
Smutz, Morton
Smylie, John Edwin
Smythe, Cheves McCord
Smythe, Mabel Murphy
Smythies, John Raymond

Snakard, Robert F.
Snapp, Roy Baker
Snavely, Brant Rittenhouse
Snavely, Tipton Ray
Snavely, William Pennington
Snavely-Dixon, Mary Margaret
Snead, George Murrell, Jr.
Snead, Jesse Carlyle
Sneed, Earl
Snell, Absalom West
Snell, Esmond Emerson
Snell, Ralph Ronald
Snellgrove, Harold Sinclair
Snelling, George Arthur
Snider, Edwin Wallace
Snider, John Joseph
Snider, Robert Larry
Snider, William Davis
Snively, Harvey Bowden, Jr.
Snodgrass, Alan Carl
Snook, John Lloyd
Snow, George Abraham
Snow, Hank (Clarence Eugene Snow)
Snow, William Hayden
Snowden, Frank Martin, Jr.
Snowe, Olympia J.
Snyder, Edwin Knowlson
Snyder, Harry Martin
Snyder, John Joseph
Snyder, John Wesley
Snyder, Marlon Gene
Snyder, Robert Martin
Snyder, Roy Dietrich, Jr.
Snyder, Solomon Halbert
Snyder, Wahl John
Snyder, William Russell
Sober, Sidney
Soderbergh, Peter Andrew
Soenneker, Henry Joseph
Soffen, Gerald Alan
Sohn, Michael N(orman)
Sokal, Joseph Emanuel
Sokatch, John Robert
Sokel, Walter Herbert
Sokmensuer, Adil
Solarz, Stephen Joshua
Solem, Delmar E.
Solender, Robert Lawrence
Soles, William Roger
Sollenberger, Howard Edwin
Solomon, Allan Bernard
Solomon, Harold Charles
Solomon, Henry
Solomon, Neil
Solomon, Richard Allan
Solomon, Robert
Solomon, Syd
Solomon, William Tarver
Solomonson, Charles D.
Solzbacher, William Aloysius
Somerville, Ormond
Somerville, William B.
Somjen, George Gustav
Sommer, Alphonse Adam, Jr.
Sommer, John Robert
Sommerfeld, Raynard Matthias
Sommers, James Bainbridge
Sones, Charles Gaylon
Sonfield, Robert Leon, Jr.
Song, Pill-Soon
Sonne, Clarence Melvin, Jr.
Sonnemann, Harry
Sonnenfeldt, Helmut
Sonnenreich, Michael Roy
Sontag, James Mitchell
Sorensen, Allan Chresten
Sorkin, Gerald B.
Sortor, Harold Edward
Sostrin, Morey
Sottile, James
Sottile, James, III
Soule, George
Soupart, Pierre
South, Charles Sumner
Southard, Frank Allan, Jr.
Southard, Rupert Barron, Jr.
Southard, Shelby Edward
Souther, Roy Hobart
Southerland, Louis Feno, Jr.
Southwick, Paul
Southwood, John Eugene
Sovey, Louis Terrell
Sowers, George Frederick
Sowers, William Armand
Spach, Jule Christian
Spach, Madison Stockton
Spain, Frank Edward
Spain, James Donald
Spain, James William
Spalding, Jack Johnson
Spalding, John Robert, Jr.
Spang, Ralph McCurdy
Spaniol, Joseph Frederick, Jr.
Spanjer, Ralph Howard
Spann, William Bowman, Jr.
Sparber, Byron Lee
Sparkman, Brandon Buster
Sparkman, Robert Satterfield
Sparks, Claud Glenn
Sparks, David Stanley
Sparks, Henry Alvy
Sparks, Thomas Everett
Spaulding, Asa Timothy
Spaulding, Charles Clinton, Jr.
Spaw, Louis David, Jr.
Speake, Margaret
Speakes, Larry Melvin
Speakman, Edwin Aaron
Spear, William Wilson
Spears, Adrian Anthony
Spears, Alexander White, III
Spears, Franklin Scott
Spears, Monroe Kirk
Spears, Robert Wright
Specht, Charles Alfred

Speck, John King
Speck, Marvin Luther
Spector, Louis
Spector, Melbourne Louis
Speece, Herbert Elvin
Speed, Billie Cheney (Mrs. Thomas S. Speed)
Speed, Edwin Maurice
Speer, David Gordon
Speer, Eugene Eaven, Jr.
Speer, Talbot Taylor
Speidel, John Joseph
Speizman, Morris
Spellings, James McIntosh
Spellman, Eugene Paul
Spellman, Gladys Noon
Spence, Clyde Wadsworth, Jr.
Spence, Floyd Davidson
Spence, Harry Metcalfe
Spence, Janet Taylor
Spence, Richard Dee
Spencer, Daniel Lloyd
Spencer, Edgar Winston
Spencer, Harold Garth
Spencer, Harry Chadwick
Spencer, James Jacob
Spencer, Melvin Joe
Spencer, Samuel
Spencer, Samuel Reid, Jr.
Spencer, Thomas Morris
Spencer, Warren Frank
Spencer, William Albert
Spencer, William Micajah, III
Spengler, Joseph John
Sperling, Godfrey, Jr.
Spezzano, Vincent Edward
Spicer, Robert Thurston
Spiers, Ronald Ian
Spilhaus, Athelstan
Spilman, Robert Henkel
Spindel, William
Spingarn, Jerome H.
Spingarn, Stephen J.
Spinks, Leon
Spiro, Herbert John
Spiro, Robert Harry, Jr.
Spitzer, John J.
Spivak, Alvin A.
Spivak, Lawrence Edmund
Spivey, Herman Everett
Spivey, Robert Atwood
Spock, Benjamin McLane
Spofford, William Benjamin, Jr.
Spohr, Clifford Ernest
Spong, William Belser, Jr.
Sponsler, George Curtis, III
Sporn, Michael Benjamin
Spragens, Thomas Arthur
Spragens, William Henry, Jr.
Sprague, Charles Cameron
Sprague, Irvine Henry
Sprague, L(loyd) Dean
Sprague, William Wallace, Jr.
Spreiregen, Paul David
Spring, David
Springer, Jack G.
Springer, Stanley G.
Springfield, James Francis
Springsteen, George Stoney, Jr.
Sproull, James Edward
Spruce, Everett Franklin
Spurlock, Jeanne
Spurr, Stephen Hopkins
Squires, Arthur Morton
Squires, William Randolph, Jr.
Srere, Paul Arnold
Staats, Elmer Boyd
Staats, William Ferdinand
Stabile, Benedict Louis
Stabler, Lewis Vastine, Jr.
Stacey, Weston Monroe, Jr.
Stack, Edward J.
Stadtler, John Walmsley
Stadtman, Earl Reece
Stafford, Donald Gene
Stafford, Edward Stephen
Stafford, Elvin Andrew
Stafford, George Millard
Stafford, J. Francis
Stafford, Martin Douglas
Stafford, Robert Theodore
Stafford, Thomas Patten
Stafford, William Henry, Jr.
Stage, Thomas Benton
Stagg, Tom
Staggers, Harley Orrin
Stahl, David Edward
Stahl, Lesley R.
Stahl, Sidney
Stahmer, Harold Martin, Jr.
Stair, Frederick Rogers
Stair, Lois Harkrider
Stakem, Thomas Edward, Jr.
Stalcup, Joe Alan
Staley, Thomas Fabian
Stall, James Lamar
Stallings, (Charles) Norman
Stallones, Reuel Arthur
Stalnaker, John Marshall
Stamper, Joe Allen
Stancil, James Whitehurst
Stanford, Dennis Joe
Stanford, Henry King
Stanger, Frank Bateman
Stanger, Russell
Stanley, Julian Cecil, Jr.
Stanley, Steven Mitchell
Stanley, Thomas Bahnson, Jr.
Stanley, Timothy Wadsworth
Stanley, William Hubert
Stanley, William Oliver, Jr.
Stannett, Vivian Thomas
Stansberry, James Wesley
Stanton, Curtis Henderson
Stanwick, Tad
Stapel, Paul Frederick

Staples, Albert Franklin
Staples, Eugene Leo
Stapp, Dan Ernest
Starfield, Barbara Helen
Stark, Fortney Hillman, Jr.
Starke, Walter Marcellus
Starling, James Holt
Starnes, Earl Maxwell
Starnes, Richard
Starnes, Stancil Rose
Starnes, William Love
Starr, Benjamin Fred, Jr.
Starr, Henry Frank, Jr.
Starr, Jason Leonard
Starr, Luther Wade
Starr, Richard Cawthon
Starr, Steven Dawson
Starr, Wilmarth Holt
Starry, Donn Albert
Statland, Edward Morris
Staub, August William
Staubach, Roger Thomas
Stead, Eugene Anson, Jr.
Stead, William White
Steadman, Charles Walters
Steadman, John Montague
Steakley, Zollie Coffer, Jr.
Stearns, David W.
Stearns, Richard Gordon
Steber, Alan Barnes
Steed, Tom
Steel, William Carlton
Steele, Allen Mulherrin
Steele, Earl Larsen
Steele, Ernest Clyde
Steele, Jack
Steele, James Harlan
Steele, James Patrick, Jr.
Steele, John Lawrence
Steele, Joseph Lee
Steele, Lendell Eugene
Steele, Margaret Therese
Steele, Richard Harold
Steele, William Taylor, Jr.
Steelman, Alan Watson
Steely, Will Frank
Steen, Hugh Fleming
Steer, Alfred Gilbert, Jr.
Steere, David D.
Steers, Newton Ivan, Jr.
Stefan, Joseph
Stefany, John Edgar
Steffy, David Louis
Steg, J(ames) L(ouis)
Steger, Byron Ludwig
Steger, Meritt Homer
Steger, William Merritt
Steglich, Winfred George
Steiger, William A.
Steimel, Edward Joseph
Steimle, Edmund Augustus
Stein, Herbert
Steinbach, Frank Ward
Steinberg, Lawrence Edward
Steincrohn, Peter Joseph
Steiner, Gilbert Yale
Steiner, Richard Lewis
Steiner, Robert Frank
Steinfeld, Jesse Leonard
Steinfink, Hugo
Steinhardt, Ralph Gustav, Jr.
Steinhaus, John Edward
Steinhoff, Dan
Stellings, Ernest George
Stelson, Paul Hugh
Steltenpohl, Joseph Aloysius
Stembler, John Hardwick
Stembridge, Vernie A(lbert)
Stempler, Jack Leon
Stenholm, Charles W.
Stennis, John Cornelius
Stephansky, Ben Solomon
Stephens, Arial Avant
Stephens, Denny
Stephens, George Gayle
Stephens, Jack Thomas, Jr.
Stephens, Jackson Thomas
Stephens, Jackson Thomas
Stephens, John Calhoun, Jr.
Stephens, John Fred
Stephens, Louis Cornelius, Jr.
Stephens, Ralph Haygood
Stephens, Robert F.
Stephens, Robert Grier, Jr.
Stephens, Rothwell Clifford
Stephens, Roy Malcolm
Stephens, William Theodore
Stephens, William Thomas
Stephenson, Harold F.
Stephenson, James Bennett
Stephenson, Samuel Edward, Jr.
Sterban, Richard Anthony
Sterenbuch, Martin
Sterling, Robert R.
Stern, Aaron
Stern, Alfred
Stern, Arthur Cecil
Stern, Carl Leonard
Stern, Philip Van Doren
Stern, Samuel Alan
Stern, William Louis
Sternberg, Daniel Arle
Sternberg, Marvin John
Sterne, Augustus Herrington
Sterne, Joseph Robert Livingston
Sterner, Michael Edmund
Sternfeld, Reuben
Sterns, Sydney S.
Sterrett, Samuel Black
Stetler, C. Joseph
Stetler, Russell Dearnley, Jr.
Stetson, John
Stetson, John Charles
Stetson, Nathaniel

Stetten, DeWitt, Jr.
Stevens, Boswell
Stevens, George, Jr.
Stevens, John Paul
Stevens, Milton Lewis, Jr.
Stevens, Phineas
Stevens, Preston Standish
Stevens, Ray (Harold Ray Ragsdale)
Stevens, Robert David
Stevens, Roger L.
Stevens, Russell Bradford
Stevens, Theodore Fulton
Stevens, William Tristram
Stevens, William Wilson
Stevenson, A. Brockie
Stevenson, Adlai Ewing, III
Stevenson, Ben
Stevenson, Eric Van Cortlandt
Stevenson, James Rufus
Stevenson, Joseph Donald
Stevenson, Lloyd Grenfell
Stevenson, William Edwards
Stever, Horton Guyford
Stewart, Anne English
Stewart, Carl Jerome, Jr
Stewart, Carleton M.
Stewart, Charles David
Stewart, Chester Larry
Stewart, Cornelius James, II
Stewart, David Hugh
Stewart, David Marshall
Stewart, Donald Wilbur
Stewart, Easton
Stewart, Edgar Allen
Stewart, Eugene Lawrence
Stewart, George Ray
Stewart, Harold Leroy
Stewart, Harris Bates, Jr.
Stewart, Irvin
Stewart, John Daugherty
Stewart, Larry S.
Stewart, Meryle Richard
Stewart, Potter
Stewart, Robert, Jr.
Stewart, Robert Edwin
Stewart, Robert Gordon
Stewart, Robert H., III
Stewart, Robert Ivey
Stewart, Roma J.
Stewart, Thomas James, Jr.
Stewart, Ward
Stewart, William Donald
Stewart, William Franklin
Stice, James Edward
Sticht, J. Paul
Stickley, John Leon
Stidham, Wofford H.
Stief, Louis John
Stiff, John Sterling
Stiff, Robert Martin
Still, Clyfford
Still, Richard Ralph
Stilo, Anthony Joseph
Stilwell, Richard Dale
Stingel, Donald Eugene
Stinnette, Charles Roy, Jr.
Stinson, Louis, Jr.
Stitt, Edward Sonny
Stjernholm, Rune Leonard
Stockard, James Alfred
Stockdale, James Bond
Stocker, Arthur Frederick
Stocking, Hobart Ebey
Stockman, David Allen
Stockton, Ernest Looney
Stockton, Ralph Madison, Jr.
Stockwell, Benjamin Eugene
Stockwell, George Lewis
Stockwell, Oliver Perkins
Stoddard, Burdett Clark
Stoecker, Karl A.
Stokely, Murray Marvin
Stokes, Arnold Paul
Stokes, B. R.
Stokes, Colin
Stokes, George Alwin
Stokes, John Lemacks, II
Stokes, Louis
Stokes, Mack (Marion) Boyd
Stokley, Robert Willson
Stokoe, William Clarence
Stollerman, Gene Howard
Stone, Albert Lynn
Stone, Charles Rivers
Stone, Charles Turner
Stone, Edward Durell, Jr.
Stone, Edward Harris, II
Stone, Elizabeth Wenger
Stone, Eugene E., III
Stone, Ferdinand Fairfax
Stone, Franklin Martin
Stone, H. Lowell
Stone, I. F. (Isidor Feinstein)
Stone, James M.
Stone, Jeremy Judah
Stone, Kenneth Eugene, Jr.
Stone, Kirk Haskin
Stone, Leon
Stone, Marvin Jules
Stone, Marvin Lawrence
Stone, Patsy Ruth Schnibben
Stone, Richard Bernard
Stone, Robert Samuel
Stone, Williard Everard
Stoneburner, Roger Whitney
Stonecipher, David Allen
Stoner, James Lloyd
Stophlet, Donald Victor
Storer, Morris Brewster
Storey, Charles Porter
Storey, Frederick George
Storey, Robert Gerald
Storey, Woodrow Wilson
Storin, Edward Michael
Stormont, Richard Mansfield

Storrs, Eleanor Emerett
Storrs, Thomas Irwin
Stotler, Roger Grant
Stottlemyer, David Lee
Stoup, Curry Wardell
Stovall, S. J.
Stovall, Thelma L.
Stover, Carl Frederick
Stover, James Howard
Stover, Phil Sheridan, Jr.
Stowe, David Henry
Stowe, Harold Crosby
Stowe, Robert Lee, Jr.
Stowe, William McFerrin
Stradley, Fred Sill
Straiton, Archie Waugh
Strake, George W., Jr.
Straley, H. W., III
Strand, Kaj Aage Gunnar
Strange, Jack Roy
Strasser, Gabor
Strasser, William Carl, Jr.
Stratton, Harold Duane
Stratton, James David
Straub, Peter Thornton
Straubel, James Henderson
Straus, Ellen Sulzberger
Straus, R. Peter
Straus, Robert
Strauss, Elliott Bowman
Strauss, Robert Schwarz
Straw, H. Thompson
Strawser, Neil Edward
Strean, Bernard M.
Street, Clarence Parke
Street, Edward Robert
Street, Frank Tandy, Jr.
Street, William Ezra
Streeter, Donald Vinton
Streett, Alexander Graham
Streibich, Harold Cecil
Streit, Clarence Kirshman
Streng, William Paul
Strickert, Roland Rudolf
Strickland, James Tyler
Strickland, Maurice Alexander
Strickland, Nellie B.
Strickland, Robert
Strickland, Robert Louis
Strickland, Thomas Joseph
Strickler, Thomas David
Striner, Herbert Edward
Stringfield, Hezz, Jr.
Stringham, Luther Winters
Strittmatter, Cornelius Frederick, IV
Strobel, Fredric Andrew
Strobel, Howard Austin
Strobel, James Walter
Strode, William Hall, III
Strong, Henry
Strong, Jack Perry
Strongin, Theodore
Strothman, Dale Roy
Stroud, John Fred, Jr.
Stroud, Robert Malone, Sr.
Stroupe, Henry Smith
Strout, Richard Lee
Struby, Chester Albert, Jr.
Struckhoff, Eugene C(harles)
Struckle, Joe J.
Strudler, Robert Jacob
Struelens, Michel Maurice Joseph Georges
Strupp, Hans Hermann
Struyk, Raymond Jay
Stuart, George Rogers Clark
Stuart, Harold Cutliff
Stuart, James Alexander
Stuart, Jesse Hilton
Stuart, Johannes
Stuart, John Thomas, III
Stuart, Walter Bynum, III
Stubblefield, Page Kindred
Stubbs, James Carlton
Stuckey, Walter Jackson, Jr.
Stuhlinger, Ernst
Stump, Bob
Stump, Forest J.
Stump, John Sutton
Stumpf, Samuel Enoch
Stupar, Branko
Sturc, Ernest
Sturgeon, Charles Edwin
Sturm, Albert Lee
Sturtevant, Brereton
Sturtevant, William Curtis
Stutzman, Vernon Charles
Suarez, Raleigh Anthony, Jr.
Suarez, Roberto J.
Suarez-Murias, Marguerite C.
Sublett, Henry Lee, Jr.
Sudarshan, Ennackal Chandy George
Suderburg, Robert Charles
Sugarman, Jule M.
Sugarman, Norman Alfred
Sugg, Robert Perkins
Suggs, John Thomas
Sugihara, Thomas Tamotsu
Sugioka, Kenneth
Suitor, Jesse Hale
Suki, Wadi Nagib
Sulkin, Sidney
Sullivan, Carl Rollynn, Jr.
Sullivan, Charles Andrew
Sullivan, Edward Cuyler
Sullivan, Francis Charles
Sullivan, George William, Jr.
Sullivan, Glenn Ray
Sullivan, Harold Joseph
Sullivan, James Lenox
Sullivan, John Daniel
Sullivan, John McGrath
Sullivan, Joseph V.
Sullivan, Leonard, Jr.

REGIONAL LISTING—SOUTH-SOUTHWEST 860

Sullivan, Margaret Patricia
Sullivan, Sister Marie Celeste
Sullivan, Mark, Jr.
Sullivan, Max William
Sullivan, Philip Burt
Sullivan, Roger Winthrop
Sullivan, Thomas James
Sullivan, Thomas Michael
Sullivan, Walter Francis
Sulser, Jack Arnold
Sulzby, James Frederick, Jr.
Summer, Albioun F.
Summer, Virgil Clifton, Jr.
Summerford, Ben Long
Summers, Earl Taliaferro
Summers, Edward Lee
Summers, Frank William
Summers, Frank Wynerth
Summers, James Warfield
Summers, John Benjamin
Summers, Ray
Summersell, Charles Grayson
Sumner, Billy Taylor
Sumner, Theodore Bynum, Jr.
Sumser, Raymond Joseph
Sundberg, Alan Carl
Sundberg, Carl Oscar
Sunderlin, Charles Eugene
Sundquist, James Lloyd
Sunley, Emil McKee
Sunshine, Donald Raymond
Suojanen, Waino W.
Surawicz, Borys
Surface, James Richard
Surface, Thomas James
Surrency, Erwin Campbell
Surrey, Walter Sterling
Susman, Stephen Daily
Sussex, James Neil
Sussman, Barry
Sussman, Bernard Jules
Sussman, Jerry
Suter, Cary Grayson
Suter, Emanuel
Sutherland, William Anderson
Sutherlund, David Arvid
Suttle, Dorwin Wallace
Suttle, William Wayne
Suttles, William Maurrelle
Sutton, Barrett Boulware
Sutton, Berrien Daniel
Sutton, George Miksch
Sutton, Harry Eldon
Sutton, John Floyd, Jr.
Sutton, Joseph Thomas
Sutton, Ottis Alton
Svendsen, LeRoy William, Jr.
Swain, James Obed
Swalin, Benjamin Franklin
Swall, Ross Forrest
Swaney, Hugh Frantz
Swanke, Albert Homer
Swankin, David Arnold
Swanson, August George
Swanson, Bert Elmer
Swanson, Daniel Cramer
Swanson, Joel Oliver
Swanson, Lawrence Wilbur
Swanson, Rune E.
Swanson, Wallace Martin
Swantz, Alexander
Swearingen, Eugene Laurel
Sweeney, Arthur Hamilton, Jr.
Sweeney, James Daniel
Sweeney, Joseph Modeste
Sweeney, Robert Joseph
Sweet, John Howard
Sweet, Norman Leland
Sweigart, John Winfield, Jr.
Swesnik, Robert Malcolm
Swetnam, Monte Newton
Swett, Albert Hersey
Swezey, Robert Dwight
Swidler, Joseph Charles
Swift, Al
Swift, Clifford J., Jr.
Swift, Frank Meador
Swigart, Theodore Earl
Swindler, William Finley
Swinford, John Walker
Swintosky, Joseph Vincent
Switzer, Barry
Sykes, Conwell Shoup
Sykes, Gresham M'Cready
Sykes, Melvin Julius
Sykes, William Maltby
Sylvester, George Howard
Symes, George James
Symington, James Wadsworth
Symington, Lloyd
Symmes, Harrison Matthews
Symms, Steven Douglas
Symons, James Martin
Synan, Joseph Alexander, Sr.
Synar, Mike Lynn
Szabo, Daniel
Szabo, Stephen Lee
Szebehely, Victor G.
Szmant, Alina Margarita
Szulc, Tad
Szymanski, Richard Frank
Tabatznik, Bernard
Taber, Robert Clinton
Tabor, Herbert
Tabor, John Kaye
Tabor, Neil
Tackaberry, Thomas Howard
Tacker, Edgar Carroll
Tade, George Thomas
Taeni, John Ignatius
Taeni, Madeleine Renata Weigner (Mrs. John Taeni)
Taeuber, Conrad
Taff, Charles A.
Taft, Paul E.
Taft, Richard George
Taggart, Glen Laird
Taishoff, Lawrence Bruce
Taishoff, Sol Joseph
Tait, Edward Thomas
Talalay, Paul
Talbert, Preston Tidball
Talbot, John Mayo
Talbot, Richard Burritt
Talbott, Frank, III
Talbott, John Harold
Talbott, Orwin Clark
Talbott, Strobe
Taliaferro, Francis Tournier
Talkington, Perry Clement
Talley, Charles Richmond
Talley-Morris, Neva Bennett
Tally, John Benton
Talmadge, Herman Eugene
Tamm, Edward Allen
Tanenbaum, Bernard Jerome, Jr.
Tanford, Charles
Tang, Anthony Matthew
Tanguy, Charles Reed
Taniguchi, Alan Yamato
Tank, Martin Marcus
Tankersley, James Odell
Tannenwald, Theodore, Jr.
Tanner, E(leanor) J(ane)
Tanner, Leonard Roscoe, III
Tanner, Raymond Lewis
Tansill, Frederick Riker
Tanzer, Lester
Tape, Gerald Frederick
Tapley, Byron Dean
Tapley, James Leroy
Taquey, Charles Henri
Taranik, James Vladimir
Tarbell, Dean Stanley
Tarbutton, Lloyd Tilghman
Tarleau, Thomas Nicholas
Tarrant, John Edward
Tarrants, William Eugene
Tarver, Jackson Williams
Tate, Albert, Jr.
Tate, Grayson D., Jr.
Tate, Harold Simmons, Jr.
Tate, Joe Tom
Tate, Ralph Bryant
Tate, S. Shepherd
Tate, Willis McDonald
Tatel, David Stephen
Tatum, Donald Edwards
Tatum, Samuel Cameron
Taulbee, John Earl
Taylor, Arthur Canning, Jr.
Taylor, Benjamin Franklin
Taylor, Carl Ernest
Taylor, Charles
Taylor, Charles Forbes
Taylor, Charles Perry
Taylor, David Wyatt Aiken
Taylor, Eldon Donivan
Taylor, Estelle Wormley
Taylor, Eugene Charles
Taylor, Foster Jay
Taylor, Gene
Taylor, George Vanderbeck
Taylor, George Winston, Jr.
Taylor, Harold Ralph
Taylor, Harold Wayne
Taylor, Henry Hamilton, Jr.
Taylor, Herman, Jr.
Taylor, Hobart, Jr.
Taylor, Howard M., Jr.
Taylor, J(ames) Herbert
Taylor, Joe Clinton
Taylor, Joseph Henry
Taylor, Lauriston Sale
Taylor, Lynnette Dobbins
Taylor, Marshall Bennett
Taylor, Maxwell Davenport
Taylor, Nelson Ferebee
Taylor, Nettie Barcroft
Taylor, Paul Peak
Taylor, Peter Hillsman
Taylor, Prentiss Hottel
Taylor, Raymond Mason
Taylor, Richard William
Taylor, Robert Clark
Taylor, Robert Cleveland
Taylor, Robert Edward
Taylor, Robert L.
Taylor, Robert Lee
Taylor, Theodore Brewster
Teaff, Grant Garland
Teague, Barry Elvin
Teague, Robert Sterling
Teague, Wayne
Teal, Gordon Kidd
Tease, James Edward
Teed, John Edson
Teele, Arthur Earle
Teer, Nello Leguy, Jr.
Teeters, Nancy Hays
Teicher, Morton Irving
Telesca, Francis Eugene
Telford, Ira Rockwood
Telkes, Maria
Tell, William Kirn, Jr.
Tellepsen, Howard Tellef
Temerlin, Liener
Temko, Stanley Leonard
Temple, Gray
Temple, Jerome Balaam Pound, Jr.
Temple, Joseph George, Jr.
Templeton, Arleigh Brantley
Templeton, Robert Earl
Tennenbaum, Robert
Tennent, Charles Gaillard
Tenny, Francis Briggs
Tenzel, Richard Ruvin
ter Horst, Jerald Franklin
Terrel, Charles Lynn
Terrell, Arthur P.
Terrell, Charles William
Terrell, Norman Edwards
Terrell, Tol
Terrill, Clair Elman
Terry, James Anderson
Terry, Ronald Anderson
Terzick, Peter Edward
Tesseneer, Ralph Athen, Jr.
Teverbaugh, Harold Garland
Tewell, Joseph Robert, Jr.
Texter, E(lmer) Clinton, Jr.
Thacher, Henry Clarke, Jr.
Thagard, Warren Thomas, III
Thaler, William John
Thalhimer, William B., Jr.
Tharpe, Frazier Eugene
Thatcher, Charles Manson
Thatcher, Richard Cassin, Jr.
Thaxton, Carlton James
Thaxton, Marvin Dell
Thayer, Edwin Cabot
Thayer, Paul
Thayer, Robert Helyer
Theberge, James Daniel
Theis, John William
Theismann, Joseph Robert
Theon, John Speridon
Thibault, Conrad
Thibaut, Charest deLauzon, Jr.
Thie, William Archibald
Thieblot, Robert Jean
Thies, Austin Cole
Thiessen, Delbert Duane
Thigpen, Alton Hill
Thigpen, Joseph Jackson
Thigpen, Richard Elton
Thimmesch, Nicholas Palen
Thomas, Adeeb Elias
Thomas, Andrew Johnston
Thomas, Ann Van Wynen
Thomas, Arthur Lawrence
Thomas, B(illy) J(oe)
Thomas, Bert Lester
Thomas, Carl Henry
Thomas, Colin Gordon, Jr.
Thomas, Dan Anderson
Thomas, Daniel Holcombe
Thomas, Gary Lynn
Thomas, George Edward
Thomas, Helen A. (Mrs. Douglas B. Cornell)
Thomas, Herbert Leon, Jr.
Thomas, Joab Langston
Thomas, John Edwin
Thomas, John Eugene
Thomas, John Kellinger
Thomas, Joyce Kilmer
Thomas, Larry Lee
Thomas, Lee Baldwin
Thomas, Nathaniel Charles
Thomas, Payne Edward Lloyd
Thomas, Ralph Stephens
Thomas, Robert
Thomas, Robert Eggleston
Thomas, Robert Wilburn
Thomas, Thomas A.
Thomas, Walter Ivan
Thomason, James R.
Thompson, Allison Garnett
Thompson, Beverley Venable, Jr.
Thompson, Clark Wallace
Thompson, Cyrus Welter
Thompson, Drury Blair
Thompson, Fred Priestly, Jr.
Thompson, George Louis
Thompson, George Wesley
Thompson, Harvey Wesley
Thompson, James C.
Thompson, James Charles
Thompson, James Chilton
Thompson, James Elliott
Thompson, James Harry
Thompson, James Howard
Thompson, James Mason
Thompson, John Burton
Thompson, John Daniel
Thompson, John Murray
Thompson, John P.
Thompson, Kenneth W(infred)
Thompson, Lawrence Sidney
Thompson, Lee Bennett
Thompson, Milton Douhan
Thompson, Philip Anthony
Thompson, Ralph Gordon
Thompson, Robert Charles
Thompson, Thomas Edward
Thompson, Thomas Franklin, Jr.
Thompson, Victor Alexander
Thompson, W. Blake
Thompson, William Donald
Thompson, William Reid
Thompson, William Taliaferro, Jr.
Thompson, William Young
Thompson, Willis Herbert, Jr.
Thompson, Yewell Reynolds
Thomsen, Charles Burton
Thomsen, Roszel C.
Thomson, James Robert, Jr.
Thomson, Paul Rice, Jr.
Thomson, Vernon Wallace
Thon, Robert William, Jr.
Thor, Daniel Einar
Thorington, Robert Dinning
Thorn, Frank Josef
Thornberry, William Homer
Thorndike, Charles Jesse (Chuck)
Thorndike, Richard King
Thornell, Jack Randolph
Thornton, Charles Victor
Thornton, J. Edward
Thornton, O. Frank
Thornton, Ray Hudson
Thornton, Raymond Hoyt, Jr.
Thornton, Robert Ambrose
Thornton, Spencer P.
Thornton, Sue Bonner
Thornton, William E.
Thornton, William James, Jr.
Thornton, William Norman, Jr.
Thorpe, Merle, Jr.
Thorson, Oswald Hagen
Thorson, Phillip Thorwald
Thorup, Oscar Andreas
Thrall, Robert McDowell
Thrash, Edsel E.
Threefoot, Sam Abraham
Threlkeld, William Berry
Thrift, Charles Tinsley, Jr.
Throop, Allen Eaton
Thrower, Randolph William
Thuesen, Gerald Jorgen
Thumann, Albert
Thurber, James Perry, Jr.
Thurman, Henry Louis, Jr.
Thurman, John Royster, III
Thurmond, Strom
Thurston, Carl Givens
Thurston, George Butte
Thurston, James Norton
Thurston, Raymond LeRoy
Thurstone, Fredrick Louis
Thursz, Daniel
Tice, Raphael Dean
Tichenor, Donald Keith
Tidball, M(ary) Elizabeth Peters (Mrs. Charles S. Tidball)
Tiede, Tom Robert
Tiemann, Norbert Theodore
Tiemeyer, Christian
Tietjens, Norman Orwig
Tighe, Mary Ann Scarangello (Mary Ann Hidalgo)
Tihany, Leslie Charles
Tillack, Thomas Warner
Tiller, Frank Monteray
Tillis, Mel(vin)
Tillman, Rodney
Tilman, Robert Oliver
Tilson, Hugh Hanna
Timberg, Sigmund
Time, Fred
Timko, Stephen
Timm, Everett Leroy
Timmerberg, Paul Miller
Timmerman, George Bell, Jr.
Timmerman, Robert McFee
Timmerman, Robert Phinizy
Timmons, Bascom N.
Timmons, Edwin O'Neal
Timmons, William Evan
Tims, Eugene Francis
Tindall, Charles William, Jr.
Tindall, George Brown
Tinlin, Ronald Glenn
Tinsley, Thomas A.
Tinstman, Robert Mechling
Tipler, Frank Jennings
Tippit, Clifford Carlisle
Tipton, Isabel Hanson
Tipton, John Howard, Jr.
Tipton, Samuel Ridley
Tirana, Bardyl Rifat
Tiryakian, Edward Ashod
Titkemeyer, Charles William
Tjoflat, Gerald Bard
Tobin, Robert Lynn Batts
Toburen, Lawrence Richter
Tocker, Phillip
Todaro, George Joseph
Todd, Alexander Calhoun, Jr.
Todd, Anderson
Todd, John Dickerson, Jr.
Todd, William Burton
Todd, William Kenneth
Todd, William Russell
Toland, William Gipsy
Tolbert, Charles Madden
Tolbert, James R., III
Toledano, Ralph de
Toledo, Jose Victor
Toler, James Larkin
Toler, Loomis Harvey
Tolk, Roy
Toll, John Sampson
Tolles, Walter Edwin
Tolleson, John Carter
Tolley, Aubrey Granville
Tolson, Hillory Alfred
Tolson, John Jarvis, III
Tomaselli, Julius Louis
Tomjanovich, Rudy
Tomlin, Daniel Otis
Tomlinson, Gus
Tomlinson, John Doren
Tomlinson, Milton Ambrose
Tomlinson, William D. (Frank)
Tompkins, James McLane
Tompkins, Robert George
Tompsett, Ralph
Tompson, Carroll Gray
Tomskey, Gilbert Charles
Tonkin, Leo Sampson
Tonsmeire, Arthur C., Jr.
Tontz, Robert L.
Toole, Albert Julius, III
Toole, James Francis
Toombs, Kenneth Eldridge
Toomey, Robert E.
Toomey, Thomas Murray
Toon, Malcolm
Toone, Elam Cooksey, Jr.
Topazio, Virgil William
Topol, Sidney
Topping, Peter (William)
Torbert, Clement Clay, Jr.
Torgersen, Paul Ernest
Torgerson, Fernando Gordon
Torrance, Ellis Paul
Torrence, Andrew Pumphrey
Torres, Esteban Edward
Torres-Rigual, Hiram
Toth, Robert Charles
Totter, John Randolph
Toulmin, Priestley, III
Toulouse, Robert Bartell
Toups, John Melburn
Tousey, Richard
Toussaint, Allen Richard
Touster, Oscar
Towe, Peter M.
Towell, William Earnest
Tower, Donald Bayley
Tower, John Goodwin
Towers, Charles Daughtry, Jr.
Towill, John Bell
Townsend, Frank Marion
Townsend, John William, Jr.
Townsend, Lee Hill
Townsend, Maurice Karlen
Townsend, Richard Marvin
Trachtman, Paul
Tracy, Warren Francis
Train, Harry Depue, II
Trainor, Bernard Edmund
Trantham, William Eugene
Trask, David Frederic
Trask, Frederick Kingsbury, Jr.
Trautmann, Robert Dale
Traviesas, Herminio
Travis, Leola Elizabeth Madison
Travis, Merle Robert
Travis, Stephen Michael
Traxler, Bob
Traylor, Orba Forest
Traynor, Harry Sheehy
Treadwell, Mary
Trecker, Harleigh Bradley
Tredinnick, George Donald
Treen, David Conner
Trefonas, Louis Marco
Trefry, Richard Greenleaf
Trelease, Allen William
Trelogan, Harry Chester
Treml, Vladimir Guy
Trent, Buck
Trentin, John Joseph
Tressler, Josef Snyder
Tretick, Stanley
Trevas, Simon Harrison
Trevillian, Wallace Dabney
Trevino, Lee Buck
Trezise, Philip Harold
Trezza, Alphonse Fiore
Trias-Monge, Jose
Trias-Monge, Jose
Trible, Paul Seward, Jr.
Trible, William MacLohon
Trier, William Cronin
Triggiani, Leonard Vincent
Trimble, Preston Albert
Trimble, Vance Henry
Trimble, William Cattell, Jr.
Trimmer, Harold Sharp, Jr.
Trocin, Robert Edward
Troester, Carl Augustus, Jr.
Trogdon, Dewey Leonard, Jr.
Trogdon, William Oren
Trohan, Walter
Trombino, Roger A.
Trombley, Kenneth Edward
Trooboff, Peter Dennis
Trotter, Frederick Thomas
Trotter, Samuel Eugene
Trotter, Thomas Fallon
Trotter, Virginia Yapp
Trotti, John Boone
Troup, Thomas James
Trout, Maurice Elmore
Troutman, Holmes Russell
True, Roy Joe
Trueschler, Bernard Charles
Truesdell, Clifford Ambrose, III
Truett, Bob
Truex, Dorothy Adine
Truitt, Anne Dean
Trumbull, Richard
Trump, Benjamin Franlin
Trump, Guy Winston
Trussel, Jacque
Trussell, Charles Tait
Trustman, Benjamin Arthur
Tryon, Lawrence Edwin
Trythall, Harry Gilbert
Tsantes, John Frank
Tschantz, Bruce Allen
Tschoepe, Thomas
Tsiapera, Maria
Tso, Tien Chioh
Tsongas, Paul Efthemios
Tsutsui, Minoru
Tubb, Ernest Dale
Tubb, James Clarence
Tuch, Hans Nathan
Tuck, Grayson Edwin
Tuck, William Munford
Tucker, Allan
Tucker, Frank Mayer, Jr.
Tucker, John Andrew, III
Tucker, John Hellums, Jr.
Tucker, Laurey Dan
Tucker, Lem (Lemuel)
Tucker, Morrison Graham
Tucker, Robert Warren
Tucker, Stefan Franklin
Tucker, Sterling
Tucker, William Earle
Tucker, William Edward
Tucker, William Thomas
Tucker, Willis Carleton
Tucker, Woodie
Tuckson, Coleman Reed
Tufts, Eleanor May
Tull, David Adolphus
Tullis, Edward Lewis
Tullis, Richard Barclay
Tullock, Gordon
Tullos, John Baxter
Tully, Albert Julian
Tully, Andrew Frederick, Jr.
Tumin, David Ullman
Tumulty, Philip Anthony
Tungate, Mace, Jr.
Tunick, Stanley Bloch
Tunstall, Edmund Joseph
Tuohy, John Joseph
Turano, Emanuel Nicolas
Turbeville, William Jackson, Jr.
Turbyfill, John Ray
Turk, James Clinton
Turley, Stewart
Turley, (Ronald) Windle
Turlington, Edgar Lawrence, Jr.
Turnage, William Albert
Turnbull, Benjamin Walton
Turner, (Henry) Arlin
Turner, Billie Lee
Turner, Donald Frank
Turner, Edward Mason
Turner, Evan Hopkins
Turner, Halcott Mebane
Turner, Herbert David
Turner, James Castle
Turner, James Philip
Turner, James Steven
Turner, John Brister
Turner, John Sidney, Jr.
Turner, John Walter
Turner, Malcolm Elijah, Jr.
Turner, Robert Edward, III (Ted)
Turner, Stansfield
Turner, Vernon Magruder
Turner, Victor Witter
Turner, William Wilson
Turner, Willie
Turney, Charles
Turnmeyer, George Earl
Turrentine, Robert Cleveland
Turvey, Charles Robert
Tuthill, John Beakes
Tuttle, Elbert Parr
Tuttle, Harris Benjamin, Sr.
Tuve, Merle Antony
Twaddell, William Hartshorne
Twigg, Bernard Alvin
Twinam, Joseph Wright
Twisdale, Harold Winfred
Twiss, John Russell, Jr.
Twitty, Conway
Twitty, James Watson
Twomey, David Malone
Twyman, Joseph Paschal
Tydings, Joseph Davies
Tygrett, Howard Volney, Jr.
Tyl, Noel Jan
Tyler, Anne (Mrs. Taghi M. Modarressi)
Tyler, David Earl
Tyler, Max Ezra
Tyler, Morgan Seymour, Jr.
Tyler, Ottis Jan
Tyler, Ronnie Curtis
Tyner, George S.
Tyner, Mack, Jr.
Tyree, David Merrill
Tyree, Sheppard Young, Jr.
Tyrer, John Lloyd
Tyson, Kenneth Robert Thomas
Uberall, Herbert Michael Stefan
Udall, Morris King
Udall, Stewart Lee
Uelsmann, Jerry Norman
Uhde, George Irvin
Uhl, Edward George
Uhrig, Robert Eugene
Ulich, Willie Lee
Ulinski, John Anthony, Jr.
Ullman, Albert Conrad
Ulmer, Melville Jack
Ulry, Orval Lee
Umlauf, Charles Julius
Undercofler, Hiram K.
Underhill, Francis Trelease, Jr.
Underwood, Cecil H.
Underwood, Milton R.
Unger, David Grant
Unger, Ferdinand Thomas
Ungerman, Irvine E.
Ungerman, Maynard Ivan
Unitas, John Constantine
Unklesbay, Athel Glyde
Unna, Warren W.
Unruh, Henry Cornelius
Unsell, Lloyd Neal
Unterkoefler, Ernest
Upchurch, Theron Acriel
Upston, John Edwin
Upthegrove, William Reid
Upton, Arthur Canfield
Upton, Arvin Edward
Upton, Eldon Claggett, Jr.
Urban, Carlyle Woodrow
Urban, Eugene Willard
Urban, Gilbert William
Urban, James Arthur
Urbanski, James Francis
Urbina, Ricardo Manuel
Urofsky, Melvin Irving
Ursano, James Joseph
Usdane, William Miller
Usdin, Gene Leonard
Utermohle, Charles Edward, Jr.
Utiger, Robert David

Utnik, William Joseph
Utterback, Priscilla Wooten
Utting, Mary Emogene
Utz, John Philip
Vacca, John Joseph
Vaccara, Beatrice Newman
Vadakin, James Charles
Vaeth, Joseph Gordon
Vahan, Richard
Vail, Charles Brooks
Vail, Charles Rowe
Vail, Peter Robbins
Vaill, Peter Brown
Vaky, Viron Peter
Valdes-Dapena, Marie Agnes
Valenti, Jack Joseph
Valentine, Dorris Lynn
Valentine, Foy Dan
Valentine, Herman Edward
Valeriani, Richard Gerard
Valk, Henry Snowden
Vallbona, Carlos
Vallotton, William Wise
Valtin, Rolf
Van, George Paul
Van Allen, William Kent
van Aller, Robert Thomas
Van Arsdall, Clyde James, Jr.
Van Arsdall, Robert Armes
Van Artsdalen, Ervin Robert
Vanatta, John Crothers, III
Van Baalen, Chase
Van Buren, Martin Leroy
Van Buskirk, Alden Lothrop
Van Caspel, Venita Walker (Mrs. Jacob T. Van Caspel)
Vance, Cyrus Roberts
Vance, James Earbee
Vance, Robert Smith
Vance, Sheldon Baird
Vance, Stanley Charles
Vance, William Silas
Van Cleve, Ruth Gill
Van Deerlin, Lionel
Vande Hey, James Michael
Vande Linde, Vernon David
Vandell, Robert Frank
Van Dellen, Theodore Robert
Vandemark, Robert Goodyear
Van der Heuvel, Gerry Burch
Vander Jagt, Guy
Vanderpool, Robert Lee, Jr.
Vanderryn, Jack
Vandersall, John Henry
Vanderslice, Joseph Thomas
Vanderveld, John, Jr.
Vandervoort, Benjamin Hays
Vanderwerf, Calvin Anthony
Vandeventer, Braden
Vandiver, Frank Everson
Vandiviere, H(orace) Mac
Van Dore, Wade (Kivel)
Van Dusen, Bruce Buick
Van Eseltine, William Parker
Van Fleet, James Alward
Van Gelderen, Barbara
vanHaeften, Carl Frederick
Van Heuvelen, Willis H.
Van Hoek, Robert
Van Horn, Verne Hile, III
Van Horne, Ralph Richard
Van Houweling, Cornelius Donald
VanLandingham, William J.
Van Lopik, Jack Richard
Vann, David Johnson
Vannoy, Walter Monroe, Jr.
Van Pelt, John Robert, Jr.
VanPoole, Thomas Bennett, Jr.
van Rensburg, Willem Cornelius Janse
Van Riper, Paul Pritchard
VanSant, Nicholas
Van Seters, John
Van Siclen, DeWitt Clinton
Van Slyke, Helen
Van Smith, Howard
Vanstrum, Paul Ross
Van Wazer, John Robert
Van Wickler, John Henry
Van Woerkom, Dorothy O'Brien
Van Wyk, Judson John
Van-Zant, Ronald Wayne (Ronnie)
Varnadore, Donald Gene
Varner, Robert Edward
Varnum, Laurent Kimball
Varrone, Angelo Robert
Vasek, Richard Jim
Vaslef, Irene
Vasta, Bruno Morreale
Vath, Joseph G.
Vaughan, Eugene H., Jr.
Vaughan, John Thomas
Vaughan, Joseph Lee
Vaughan, Odie Frank, Jr.
Vaughey, William Meagher
Vaughn, Jack Joseph
Vaughn, Rufus Mahlon
Vaught, Jack Thomas
Vaught, James Benjamin
Vazquez, Alberto M.
Vazsonyi, Andrew
Veach, Henry Harrell
Veeder, William John
Velder, Eli
Veletsos, Anestis Stavrou
Veltri, Robert William
Vento, Bruce Frank
Ventulett, Thomas Walker, III
Verheyen, Egon
Verity, George Luther
Verlander, William Ashley
Vernberg, Frank John
Verner, Hugh David
Verner, James Melton
Vernon, Weston (Wes), III
Veron, Earl Ernest
Verplanck, William Samuel
Verrill, Charles Owen, Jr.
Verrill, F. Glenn
Verwoerdt, Adriaan
Vescolani, Fred Julius
Vesic, Aleksandar Sedmak
Vest, George Southall
Vestal, Lucian LaRoe
Vette, James Ira
Vetter, Betty McGee
Vetter, James George, Jr.
Vickery, Edward Downtain
Vickrey, James Frank, Jr.
Vicroy, Frank Marion
Victor, Mary O'Neill
Vierbuchen, Richard Carl
Vierling, Bernard Julius
Vigness, David Martell
Vigtel, Gudmund
Viguerie, Richard Art
Villarreal, Carlos Castaneda
Vincent, Hal Wellman
Vincent, Harry Fleming
Vincent, Joseph Scott
Vincent, Lloyd Drexell
Vine, Richard David
Vines, Dwight Delbert
Vinson, Bailie Walsh
Vinson, Fred Moore, Jr.
Viola, Herman Joseph
Viorst, Milton
Vitale, Alfred William
Vivian, Cordy Tindell
Vliet, Rollin Dale
Voegeli, Victor Jacque
Vogeli, Henry Elliott
Vogel, Herbert Davis
Vogel, Howard H., Jr.
Vogtle, Alvin Ward, Jr.
Voisinet, James Raymond
Voland, Kenneth Lee
Volker, Joseph Francis
Volkmer, Harold L.
Volner, Jill Wine
Volny, James George
Volpe, Erminio Peter
Volz, Charles Harvie, Jr.
Volz, Marlin Milton
vom Baur, Francis Trowbridge
von Bomhard, Moritz
Vonderhaar, William Purcell
von der Mehden, Fred R.
Von Eckardt, Wolf
von Euler, Leo Hans
vonGrossmann, Frederic Richard (Fritz)
von Hoffman, Nicholas
Von Kann, Clifton Ferdinand
von Mering, Otto Oswald
Vontress, Clemmont Eyvind
Voorde, Frances
Vorderburg, Marvin Franklin
Vorsanger, Fred S.
Vosbeck, Robert Randall
Vosbeck, William Frederick, Jr.
Vosburgh, Frederick George
Voss, Carl Hermann
Voss, William Charles
Voth, Ben
Vredenburgh, John Culloden
Vrenios, Anastasios
Vykukal, Eugene Lawrence
Waalkes, T. Phillip
Wachtman, John Bryan, Jr.
Wackenhut, George Russell
Wackenhut, Ruth J. (Mrs. George R. Wackenhut)
Wacker, Fred P.
Wacker, John August
Wactor, James Wesley
Waddell, William Joseph
Wade, Adelbert Elton
Wade, Charles Byrd, Jr.
Wade, John Webster
Wade, John William
Wade, Robert Hirsch Beard
Wade, Robert Paul
Wade, William Hampton
Wadkins, Charles LeRoy
Wadley, Ellen Pearl
Wadlington, Walter James
Wadsworth, Joseph Allison Cannon
Wadsworth, Philip Adrian
Waechter, Arthur Joseph, Jr.
Wagener, James Wilbur
Wager, Willis Joseph
Waggener, Robert Glenn
Wagman, Robert John
Wagner, Charles W.
Wagner, Clarence J.
Wagner, Edward Frederick
Wagner, Frederick Earl
Wagner, Frederick William (Bill)
Wagner, Harvey Maurice
Wagner, Henry Nicholas, Jr.
Wagner, James Dennis
Wagner, Louis Carson, Jr.
Wagner, Peter Ewing
Wagner, Philip Marshall
Wagner, Robert Earl
Wagner, Robert Roderick
Wagner, Stanley Paul
Wagner, William Frederick
Wagoner, Porter
Wagoner, William Hampton
Waid, James Bynum
Waidelich, Charles J.
Wainerdi, Richard Elliott
Wainwright, Bill C.
Waite, Mary George Jordan
Waite, Norman
Wakefield, Benton McMillin, Jr.
Wakefield, Stephen Alan
Wakeham, Helmut Richard Rae
Wakeland, Henry H.
Wakelin, James Henry, Jr.
Wakley, James Turner
Walbert, David Eugene
Walbesser, Henry Herman, Jr.
Walborsky, Harry M.
Walbridge, Smith Starr
Walbridge, Willard Eugene
Walburn, Roswell Lee
Wald, Haskell Philip
Wald, Patricia McGowan
Wald, Robert Lewis
Walden, Omi Gail
Walden, Philip Michael
Waldo, Albert Leon
Waldo, (Clifford) Dwight
Waldo, Tommy Ruth Blackmon (Mrs. Selden Fennell Waldo)
Waldrop, Francis Neil
Walgren, Doug
Walk, Frank Humphrey
Walker, Agesilaus Wilson, Jr.
Walker, Aubrey Max
Walker, Barth Powell
Walker, Charls Edward
Walker, David Tutherly
Walker, Edward Bullock, III
Walker, Ernest Winfield
Walker, Estellene Paxton
Walker, Everitt Donald
Walker, Floyd Lee
Walker, Fred Collins
Walker, George Thomas
Walker, Glenn David
Walker, H(erbert) Leslie, Jr.
Walker, Harry Grey
Walker, Henry Gary
Walker, James Benjamin
Walker, James Calvin
Walker, James Kenneth
Walker, Jerald Carter
Walker, John Alexander
Walker, John Byrnes
Walker, John Luther
Walker, John Moore
Walker, John Mort, Jr.
Walker, John Rex
Walker, John T.
Walker, Josephine Denning
Walker, Lannon
Walker, LeRoy Tashreau
Walker, Luther Loneith
Walker, M. Lucius, Jr.
Walker, Oliver Mallory
Walker, Richard David
Walker, Richard Louis
Walker, Robert Harris
Walker, Robert Kirk
Walker, Robert Smith
Walker, Ronald H.
Walker, Vincent Henry
Walker, Wade Hampton
Walker, Warren Stanley
Walker, Wesley M.
Walker, Wilbur Gordon
Walker, William
Walker, William Bond
Walker, William Delany
Walker, William Laurens
Walkup, John Harper
Wall, Bennett Harrison
Wall, Matthew Joseph
Wall, Maurice Stanley
Wall, Nathan Sanders
Wallace, Andrew Grover
Wallace, Carl S.
Wallace, George Corley
Wallace, George Magoun, II
Wallace, George Roberts
Wallace, Harold Lew
Wallace, Joan Edaire Scott
Wallace, John Howard
Wallace, John R.
Wallace, Robert Glenn
Wallace, Thomas P.
Wallace, Wesley Herndon
Wallace, William Ray
Walleigh, Robert Shuler
Waller, John Henry
Waller, Michael Reginald
Waller, Richard Conrad
Waller, William
Waller, William Weaver
Wallich, Henry Christopher
Walling, Robert Harold
Wallis, Carlton Lamar
Wallop, Malcolm
Walls, Carmage
Walls, Dwayne Estes
Walls, Martha Ann Williams (Mrs. B. Carmage Walls)
Walser, Mackenzie
Walsh, Bryan O.
Walsh, Cornelius Stephen
Walsh, Ethel Bent
Walsh, Grace Jayne Kelleher (Mrs. John Edward Walsh)
Walsh, James Louis
Walsh, James Paul
Walsh, John Joseph
Walsh, John Walter
Walsh, Julia Margaret Curry (Mrs. Thomas M. Walsh)
Walsh, Maurice David, Jr.
Walsh, Patrick Craig
Walsh, Ulysses (Jim)
Walsh, William Bertalan
Walske, M(ax) Carl, Jr.
Waltemeyer, Robert Victor
Walter, James W.
Walter, Richard Lawrence
Walters, David McLean
Walters, Frederick J(ames)
Walters, Geoffrey King
Walters, George Merle
Walters, John Sherwood
Walters, Johnnie McKeiver
Walters, Morgan Leigh
Walters, Robert Levi
Walton, Charles Milton
Walton, Francis Ray
Walton, John
Walton, Miller
Walton, William Bowen
Waltrip, Darrell Lee
Walts, Robert Warren
Walvoord, John Flipse
Wampler, Charles Edwin
Wampler, G. V.
Wampler, William Creed
Wampold, Charles Henry, Jr.
Wanders, Hans Walter
Wang, Paul Pao-Shih
Wang, Shih Yi
Wannamaker, William Whetstone, Jr.
Wanty, Vernon
Ward, Bernard James
Ward, Douglas Alan
Ward, George Thorpe
Ward, Harry Pfeffer
Ward, Hiram Hamilton
Ward, James Muncie
Ward, James Myron
Ward, Jasper Dudley, III
Ward, John Wesley
Ward, Judson Clements, Jr.
Ward, Lee
Ward, Robert
Ward, Thomas Greydon
Ward, Virgil Scott
Ward, Walter Leroy, Jr.
Warden, Richard Dana
Wardlaw, Frank Harper, Jr.
Wardropper, Bruce Wear
Ward-Smith, Kenneth
Ware, Henry Hall, Jr.
Ware, Thaddeus Van
Warfield, Charles Horace
Warfield, Edwin
Warner, Arthur E.
Warner, Harry Hathaway
Warner, John Andrew
Warner, John William
Warner, John William
Warner, Seth L.
Warner, Volney F.
Warner, William Whitesides
Warnke, Paul Culliton
Warren, Albert
Warren, Earl Francis
Warren, Ferdinand E.
Warren, Frederick Hayes
Warren, Frederick Marshall
Warren, John Rush
Warren, Lucian Crissey
Warren, Matthew
Warren, Richard Moore
Warren, Thomas Wayne
Warren, Willis Burney
Warriner, David Dortch
Warshaw, Stanley Irving
Warth, Robert Douglas
Warthen, Harry Justice, Jr.
Warwick, William Bertram
Washburn, Abbott McConnell
Washburn, Wilcomb Edward
Washington, Bennetta Bullock
Washington, Walter
Washington, Walter E.
Waskow, Arthur Irwin
Wasserman, Paul
Waters, David Rogers
Watkin, Virginia Guild
Watkins, Carlton Gunter
Watkins, Ellis Herrin
Watkins, Jerry West
Watkins, Ralph James
Watkins, Robert Dorsey
Watkins, Wesley Wade
Watlington, John Francis, Jr.
Watson, Arthel Lane (Doc)
Watson, Arthur Richard
Watson, Barbara M.
Watson, Clarence Joseph
Watson, George Henry
Watson, Jack H., Jr.
Watson, James Edgar
Watson, John R.
Watson, K. Bert
Watson, Max Powell
Watson, Robert Fletcher
Watson, Robert Tanner
Watson, Robert Winthrop
Watson, Sterl Arthur, Jr.
Watson, William
Watt, George Willard
Watt, Graham Wend
Watt, William Joseph
Wattenberg, Ben J.
Watters, Frank Carleton
Watts, Charles DeWitt
Watts, Charles Henry, II
Watts, Daniel Thomas
Watts, Glenn Ellis
Watts, Olin Ethredge
Waugh, Butler Huggins
Waugh, William Howard
Waxman, Henry Arnold
Wayland, Russell Gibson, Jr.
Wearn, Wilson Cannon
Weatherbee, Donald Emery
Weatherford, Willis Duke, Jr.
Weatherly, Robert Stone, Jr.
Weaver, A. Vernon
Weaver, Adele Tombrink (Mrs. James Baird Weaver)
Weaver, Carlton Davis
Weaver, Charles Edward
Weaver, Charles Hadley
Weaver, Charles Steele
Weaver, Douglas Williams
Weaver, Earl Sidney
Weaver, Galbraith McFadden
Weaver, Jim
Weaver, John Boyd
Weaver, Kenneth Newcomer
Weaver, Narvin Blake
Weaver, Warren, Jr.
Weaver, Warren Eldred
Weaver, Winston Odell
Webb, Charles Albert
Webb, Donald Arthur
Webb, Harry Charles
Webb, Jack M.
Webb, James Edwin
Webb, James Lewis Adrian
Webb, Julian
Webb, Omri Kenneth, Jr.
Webb, Robert Kiefer
Webb, Ross Allan
Webb, William Loyd, Jr
Webb, William Robert, III
Webb, Wilse Bernard
Weber, Eugene William
Weber, LaVern E.
Webster, George Drury
Webster, Henry deForest
Webster, James C.
Webster, Lee Davis
Webster, Luther Denver, Jr.
Webster, Marion Elizabeth
Webster, Ronald Lee
Webster, William Hedgcock
Weddig, Lee J(ohn)
Weddington, Sarah Ragle
Wedel, Cynthia Clark
Wedemeyer, Albert Coady
Weed, Maurice James
Weedon, William Stone
Weeks, David Lee
Weeks, Roland, Jr.
Weens, Heinz Stephen
Weersing, Marc Calvin
Wegner, Helmuth Adalbert
Wehner, William E.
Wehrle, Russell Schilling
Weichsel, Hans Milton, Jr.
Weicker, Lowell Palmer, Jr.
Weidenfeld, Edward Lee
Weidman, Hazel Hitson
Weidman, Jerome
Weiger, Robert William
Weigle, Richard Daniel
Weil, Frank A.
Weil, Stephen Edward
Weilenmann, Richard Armin
Weimer, Richard George
Weinberg, Alvin Martin
Weinberg, Edward
Weinberg, Gerhard Ludwig
Weinberg, Harry Bernard
Weinberg, Robert Leonard
Weiner, Arnold Murray
Weiner, Morton David
Weinert, Donald G(regory)
Weingarten, Bernard Louis
Weingarten, Murray
Weingartner, H(ars) Martin
Weinhardt, Carl J., Jr.
Weinhauer, William Gillette
Weinlein, Anthony Gerard
Weinmann, John Giffen
Weinstein, Myron I.
Weintraub, Joseph
Weintraub, Russell Jay
Weir, Donald William
Weise, Frank Earl, Jr.
Weisert, John Jacob
Weisiger, Felix Mann
Weiskittel, Ralph Joseph
Weismiller, Edward Ronald
Weisner, Maurice Franklin
Weiss, Leonard
Weiss, Leonard
Weiss, Milton
Weiss, Paul
Weiss, Peter Josef
Weiss, Seymour
Weiss, Shirley F.
Weiss, Stanley I.
Weiss, Stephen Joel
Weisskopf, Bernard
Weitzel, Edwin Anthony
Welch, Arnold D(eMerritt)
Welch, Bernie Burnette
Welch, Byron Eugene
Welch, Donald Wilton
Welch, Harry Scoville
Welch, John David
Welch, Louie
Weldon, Norman Ross
Wellendorf, Theodore Eugene
Weller, Robert Norman
Wellford, Harry Walker
Wellman, Arthur Ogden
Wellman, Richard Vance
Wells, Harry Kennady
Wells, James Howard
Wells, Joel Reaves, Jr.
Wells, Kenneth Dale
Wells, Kitty (Muriel Deason Wright)
Wells, Leonard Nathaniel David, Jr.
Wells, Maxwell Warnock
Wells, William Calvin
Welsch, Glenn Albert
Welsh, Robert Edward
Welsh, Ronald Arthur
Welsh, Thomas Hammond, Jr.
Welsh, Thomas J.
Welsh, William Brownlee
Welsh, William Joseph
Welting, Ruth Lynn
Weltner, William, Jr.
Welton, Arthur Dorman
Welton, James Richard
Welty, Eudora
Wen, Chin Yung
Wendelstedt, Harry Hunter, Jr.
Wender, Simon Harold
Wendlandt, Wesley William
Wendling, Donald Brand
Wendorf, Denver Fred, Jr.
Wendt, Lloyd
Wenkert, Ernest
Wenner, William Watkins
Wentsch, George Maurice
Werbow, Stanley Newman
Werle, Ira Charles
Werner, John Bailey
Wert, James Junior
Wertheim, Mitzi Mallina
Wertz, David Frederick
Wesberry, James Pickett
Wesler, Oscar
Wessel, Carl John
Wessel, Herbert William, Jr.
Wessell, Nils Yngve
Wesson, Robert Laughlin
West, Bobby Bowlus
West, Edwin Nelson
West, Elmer Gordon
West, Felton
West, Gail Berry
West, James LeRoy
West, John Carl
West, John Oliver
West, Lee Roy
West, Lewis Harmon
West, Millard Farrar, Jr.
West, Philip William
West, Quentin Mecham
West, Richard Luther
West, Robert Cooper
West, Robert Van Osdell, Jr.
West, Stanley LeRoy
West, Togo Dennis, Jr.
West, Warren Reed
West, William Beverley, III
West, William Lionel
Westbrook, James Edwin
Westbrook, Joel Whitsitt, III
Westby, Gerald Holinbeck
Wester, E. Truman
Wester, William Daniel
Westerhout, Gart
Westfall, Thomas Dale
Westphal, Ulrich Friedrich
Westrom, Frederick Nicholas
Westwood, Albert Ronald Clifton
Wetherby, Lawrence Winchester
Wethington, John Abner, Jr.
Wetmore, Thomas Trask, III
Wetter, Edward
Wetzel, Frank Harry
Wetzel, William Joseph
Wexler, Anne
Wey, Herbert Walter
Weybrew, Joseph Arthur
Weyrauch, Walter Otto
Whalen, Charles William, Jr.
Whalen, Richard James
Whalen, William Jerome
Whaley, Storm Hammond
Whaley, Thomas Gaines
Whaley, W(illiam) Gordon
Whaling, Anne
Whang, Yun Chow
Wharton, Elizabeth Austin
Wharton, James Henry
Whatley, Brown Lee
Whatley, Thomas Jewel
Whatmore, Marvin Clement
Whayne, Tom French
Whedon, George Donald
Whedon, Margaret Brunssen
Wheelen, Thomas Leo
Wheeler, Charles Vawter
Wheeler, Clayton Eugene, Jr.
Wheeler, Edward Kendall
Wheeler, John Archibald
Wheeler, John Perry, Jr.
Wheeler, Marshall Ralph
Wheeler, Otis Bullard
Wheeler, Raymond Milner
Wheeler, Roger Milton
Wheeler, Ruric E.
Wheeler, Towson Ames
Wheelock, Arthur Kingsland, Jr.
Whelan, William Joseph
Whiddon, Frederick Palmer
Whillock, Carl Simpson
Whipple, Royson Newton
Whisenton, Andre Carl
Whitaker, Bruce Ezell
Whitaker, Joseph McSwain
Whitbread, Thomas Bacon
White, Alan George Castle
White, B. Frank
White, Bob Jon
White, Byron R.
White, Charles Safford
White, Christian Sherwood
White, David Manning
White, David Meade, Jr.
White, Frederic Randolph
White, George Malcolm
White, Gordon Eliot
White, Jack Edward
White, James H.
White, James Robert
White, Jean Marie

REGIONAL LISTING—SOUTH-SOUTHWEST 862

White, Jerry Max
White, John Arnold
White, John C.
White, John Jamieson, Jr.
White, John Patrick
White, John Vernon, Jr.
White, John William
White, Jon Burran
White, Joseph Addison, Jr.
White, Julius
White, Lee C.
White, Lowell E., Jr.
White, Margita Eklund
White, Mark Wells, Jr.
White, Mastin Gentry
White, Paul Ellis
White, Perry Merrill, Jr.
White, Ray Edward, Jr.
White, Raymond Petrie, Jr.
White, Reginald Pace
White, Richard Crawford
White, Robert Arthur
White, Robert Lee
White, Robert Mayer
White, Samuel Walter, Jr.
White, Steven Angelo
White, Thomas Justin, Jr.
White, Thurman James
White, Warren Keith
White, Warren Travis
White, William D.
White, Zebulon Waters
Whiteford, William Hamilton
Whitehead, Charles Oliver
Whitehead, Don
Whitehead, Ennis Clement, Jr.
Whitehead, Thomas Hillyer
Whitehead, Walter Dexter, Jr.
Whitehorn, William Victor
Whitehurst, George William
Whitehurst, Robert Neal
Whiteley, Johnnie B.
Whitelock, Alfred Theodore
Whiteman, Harold Bartlett, Jr.
Whitenack, Carolyn Irene
Whitener, Basil Lee
Whiteside, Daniel Fowler
Whiteside, Stansell Eugene
Whitham, (George) Warren, Jr.
Whiting, Albert Nathaniel
Whiting, Basil John, Jr.
Whitley, Charles Orville
Whitley, Joseph Efird
Whitley, Wyatt Carr
Whitlock, Baird Woodruff
Whitlock, Bennett Clarke, Jr.
Whitlock, Foster Brand
Whitman, Reginald Norman
Whitman, William Tate
Whitmore, John Edwin
Whitner, George Crabtree
Whitney, A(delbert) Grant
Whitney, John Edward
Whitsett, Wesley Gavin
Whitson, James Norfleet, Jr.
Whitt, David Virgel
Whitt, Richard Ernest
Whittaker, Philip Newbold
Whittemore, Robert Clifton
Whitten, Dolphus, Jr.
Whitten, Jamie Lloyd
Whitten, Leslie Hunter, Jr.
Whittenburg, Samuel Benjamin
Whittier, Charles Taylor
Whittinghill, George David
Whittington, Verle Glenn
Whittle, Alfred James, Jr.
Whittum, Charles H., Jr.
Whitworth, Kathrynne Ann
Whorton, Judson Seaborn
Whyte, James Primrose, Jr.
Whyte, William George
Wick, Robert Senters
Wickens, Aryness Joy
Wicker, John Jordan, Jr.
Wickham, John Adams, Jr.
Wickstrom, Jack Kenneth
Wickstrom, Karl Youngert
Widener, Hiram Emory, Jr.
Widman, Richard Gustave
Widner, Ralph Randolph
Wiebush, Joseph Roy
Wieczynski, Frank Robert
Wiedeman, Geoffrey Paul
Wiegering, William Hice
Wiegert, Henry Thomas
Wieghart, James Gerard
Wielage, Robert Cecil
Wienandt, Elwyn Arthur
Wiener, Louise Weingarten
Wiernik, Peter Harris
Wiggers, Harold Carl
Wiggins, Norman Adrian
Wigginton, Madison Smartt
Wigley, Willard Robert
Wilbourn, High Randolph, Jr.
Wilbur, Cornelia Burwell
Wilbur, William Hale
Wilcox, Arthur Manigault
Wilcox, Francis Orlando
Wilcox, Harry Hammond
Wilcox, Harvey John
Wilcox, James Henry
Wilcox, Marion Walter
Wilcox, William Harry
Wilder, John Shelton
Wilder, Pelham, Jr.
Wildhack, William August
Wilen, Stanley Herbert
Wiles, Charles Preston
Wiley, Bell Irvin
Wiley, John Preston, Jr.
Wiley, Richard Emerson
Wilhelmi, Alfred Ellis
Wilhite, Jim
Wilhoit, James Cammack, Jr.
Wilkens, Harold Louis
Wilkerson, Leo Carl
Wilkey, Malcolm Richard
Wilkie, Valleau, Jr.
Wilkins, (George) Barratt
Wilkins, Robert C.
Wilkinson, Albert Mims, Jr.
Wilkinson, Donald Ellsworth
Wilkinson, Glen Anderson
Wilkinson, Harry Edward, Jr.
Wilkinson, Howard Preston
Wilkinson, James Harvie, III
Wilkinson, James Richard
Wilkinson, John Burke
Wilkinson, John Paul, Jr.
Wilkinson, Vernon Lee
Wilkinson, William Durfee
Wilkowski, Jean Mary
Will, George F.
Willard, Ralph Lawrence
Willauer, Whiting Russell
Wille, Frank
Willenbrock, Frederick Karl
Willi, George
Williams, Arthur
Williams, Arthur Middleton, Jr.
Williams, Arvin Samuel
Williams, Barbara Jean May
Williams, Ben T.
Williams, Beverly Chan
Williams, Bryan
Williams, Charles David
Williams, Charles Laval, Jr.
Williams, Charles Stanley, Jr.
Williams, Charles Wiley
Williams, Clifford David
Williams, Clyde Michael, Jr.
Williams, Cratis Dearl
Williams, Dan C.
Williams, David Alan
Williams, Don R.
Williams, Eddie Nathan
Williams, Edward Bennett
Williams, Edwin Gantt
Williams, Ernest Going
Williams, Fielding Lewis
Williams, George Middleton
Williams, George Rainey
Williams, Glen Morgan
Williams, Godwin, Jr.
Williams, Harold Ellis
Williams, Harrison Arlington, Jr.
Williams, Harry John
Williams, Harvey Ladew
Williams, Hiram Draper
Williams, Hulen Brown
Williams, Jack Kenny
Williams, James Alexander
Williams, James Earl
Williams, James Edward, Jr.
Williams, James H., II
Williams, James Kelley
Williams, Jerre Stockton
Williams, John Clifton
Williams, John Cornelius
Williams, John Grouille, Jr.
Williams, John Horter
Williams, John Rodney
Williams, Joseph Hill
Williams, Judson Finlon
Williams, Kenneth Raynor
Williams, Langbourne Meade
Williams, Lawrence Harvey
Williams, Linwood Roger
Williams, Lloyd Pyron
Williams, Louis Gressett
Williams, Marjorie J. (Mrs. Bill H. Williams)
Williams, Martin
Williams, Mary Pearl
Williams, Melvin John
Williams, Miller
Williams, Murat Willis
Williams, Owen Wingate
Williams, Parham Henry, Jr.
Williams, Pat
Williams, Paul Whitcomb
Williams, Paul X.
Williams, Percy Don
Williams, Preston Clark, Jr.
Williams, Ralph Watson, Jr.
Williams, Randall Lee
Williams, Ray W.
Williams, Reginald Lamar
Williams, Richard Blondell
Williams, Robert Gainsford Wynne, Jr.
Williams, Robert Hope, Jr.
Williams, Robert Leon
Williams, Robert Ray
Williams, Robert Townsend
Williams, Roger John
Williams, Ronald Lorainne
Williams, Ross Norman
Williams, Shirley
Williams, Susan J.
Williams, Ted (Theodore Samuel)
Williams, Thomas Ffrancon
Williams, Thomas Rhys
Williams, Thomas Rice
Williams, Timothy Glyne
Williams, Troy Davis
Williams, Walker Alonzo
Williams, Walter Charles, Jr.
Williams, Walter Waylon
Williams, William Lane
Williams, William Lawrence
Williams, William Ralston
Williams, William Reginald
Williams, William Thomas, Jr.
Williamson, Burke
Williamson, Ernest Lavone
Williamson, Merritt Alvin
Williamson, Peter David
Williamson, Rene de Visme
Williamson, Sam
Williamson, Samuel Ruthven, Jr.
Williford, Donald Bratton
Willig, Winston Armin
Willingham, Clark Suttles
Willis, Clayton
Willis, Glen O.
Willis, Henry Stuart Kendall
Willis, Paul Allen
Willis, William Darrell, Jr.
Willis, William Hillman
Willis, William Scott
Willmott, Peter S.
Willocks, Robert Max
Willoughby, William Francis
Wills, Garry
Wills, Riley James
Wills, Sidney Hayward
Willson, James Hardin
Wilmerding, John
Wilmot, William Vernon, Jr.
Wilner, Morton Harrison
Wilson, Alexander Erwin, Jr.
Wilson, Allen Barnum
Wilson, Alma Dorothy Bell (Mrs. William A. Wilson)
Wilson, Almon Chapman
Wilson, Bernard Edgar
Wilson, Bruce Page
Wilson, Charles
Wilson, Charles Banks
Wilson, Charles Glen
Wilson, Charles H.
Wilson, Charles William
Wilson, Claude Raymond, Jr.
Wilson, Colon Hayes
Wilson, Coyt Taylor
Wilson, David James
Wilson, Donald Hurst, Jr.
Wilson, Earl Stevenson, Sr.
Wilson, Edgar Hunter
Wilson, Edward Converse, Jr.
Wilson, Elmer Dee
Wilson, Ernest Raymond
Wilson, Everett Dale
Wilson, Frank Wiley
Wilson, Fred Talbott
Wilson, Gary Lee
Wilson, George Angus
Wilson, George Howard
Wilson, Hillsman Vaughan
Wilson, Howard Bagby, Jr.
Wilson, Ian Robert
Wilson, J. Tylee
Wilson, James Hargrove, Jr.
Wilson, James William
Wilson, Jean Donald
Wilson, John Cowles
Wilson, John D.
Wilson, John Eric
Wilson, John Johnston
Wilson, Kemmons
Wilson, Leland Leslie
Wilson, Louis Hugh
Wilson, Luther
Wilson, M(athew) Kent
Wilson, Marjorie Price
Wilson, Maurice Julius
Wilson, Milner Bradley, III
Wilson, Milton
Wilson, Orme, Jr.
Wilson, Ralph Edwin
Wilson, Ralph Erdman, Jr.
Wilson, Raymond Clark
Wilson, Richard Harold
Wilson, Robert Alexander
Wilson, Robert Andrew
Wilson, Robert Henry
Wilson, Robert James
Wilson, Robert Lee
Wilson, Roy Kenneth
Wilson, Ruby Lelia
Wilson, Rufus Harold
Wilson, Russell Howard
Wilson, Samuel, Jr.
Wilson, Vernon Earl
Wilson, William Preston
Wiltshire, Raymond Stanley
Wiltshire, Richard Watkins
Wiman, David Wayne
Wimberly, John Harry
Winckler, Charles Edwin
Windal, Floyd Wesley
Windham, Charles Wyatt
Wine, James Wilmer
Winegardner, Roy Eugene
Wineland, Fred L.
Winer, Harold
Winer, Ward Otis
Winesanker, Michael Max
Winfrey, Dorman Hayward
Winger, Maurice H., Jr.
Wingfield, Clyde Joye
Winikates, Charles John
Winn, Albert Curry
Winn, Edward Burton
Winn, Edward Lawrence, Jr. (Larry)
Winn, Ellene
Winnefeld, James Alexander
Winpisinger, William P.
Winship, Charles Thiot
Winstead, Nash Nicks
Winstead, Raymond Landon
Winston, Carey
Winter, Arch Reese
Winter, David Leon
Winter, Harrison L.
Winter, Harvey John
Winter, Rolf Gerhard
Winter, William Forrest
Winters, J. Otis
Winters, J(ohn) Sam
Winters, John Wesley
Winters, Leo
Winwar, Frances (Francesca Vinciguerra)
Winzenried, Jesse David
Wire, William Shidaker, II
Wirges, Manford Frank
Wirth, Timothy Endicott
Wirth, William Collins
Wirths, Theodore William
Wirtz, William Willard
Wisdom, John Minor
Wise, Bill McFarland
Wise, Charles Conrad, Jr.
Wise, Edmund N.
Wise, Erbon Wilbur
Wise, Gene
Wise, George Schneiweis
Wise, Henry Erle
Wise, John Hice
Wise, Louis Neal
Wise, Marvin Jay
Wise, Milton B.
Wise, Sherwood Willing
Wise, Watson William
Wiseman, Thomas Anderton, Jr.
Wissler, John George
Witek, James Eugene
Witherspoon, Gibson Boudinot
Withrow, Frank Burdon, Jr.
Witkop, Bernhard
Witmer, John Albert
Witmer, William Kern
Witt, Norbert Albert
Witt, Raymond Buckner, Jr.
Witten, David Melvin
Wodlinger, Mark L.
Woehle, Fritz
Woerthwein, Arthur Theodore
Wohlschlag, Donald Eugene
Wolbrecht, Walter Frederick
Wolbrink, James Francis
Wolf, Clarence, Jr.
Wolf, Dallas Richard
Wolf, George Van Velsor
Wolf, Gordon Joseph
Wolf, Harold Arthur
Wolf, Harry Charles, III
Wolf, John Baptiste
Wolf, Larry M.
Wolf, Richard Charles
Wolfe, Alexander McWhorter, Jr.
Wolfe, Charles Jordan
Wolfe, Gregory Baker
Wolfe, Townsend Durant, III
Wolfe, William Gerald
Wolfe, William Roy, Jr.
Wolff, Lester Lionel
Wolffer, William Aubrey
Wolfowitz, Jacob
Wolfowitz, Paul Dundes
Wolfson, Mitchell
Wolfson, Richard Frederick
Wolking, Joseph Anthony
Wolkomir, Nathan Tully
Woll, Joseph Albert
Wolle, William Down
Wollenberg, J. Roger
Wolma, Fred John, Jr.
Wolman, Abel
Wolman, M. Gordon
Wolpe, Howard Eliot
Wolper, Marshall
Wolter, Allan Bernard
Woltz, Charles Killian
Wolverton, Robert Earl
Womach, Emily Hitch
Womble, George Morgan
Womble, William Fletcher
Wood, Benjamin Olando, Jr.
Wood, Cliff Calvin
Wood, Don James
Wood, Donald Euriah
Wood, Edmund Reynolds
Wood, Frank Bradshaw
Wood, Frank Preuit
Wood, George F.
Wood, Harry Eugene
Wood, Howard Graham
Wood, Jack Calvin
Wood, James Allen
Wood, James Ralph, Jr.
Wood, Jeanne Clarke
Wood, John Edward, III
Wood, John Lewis
Wood, John Wayne Headlee
Wood, Philip W.
Wood, Raymond Harland
Wood, Reuben Esselstyn
Wood, Robert Hart
Wood, Thomas Hermon
Woodall, Norman Eugene
Woodall, William Clements, Jr.
Woodbury, Max Atkin
Woodbury, Wendell Wilfred
Woodfin, Gene Mack
Woodhouse, John Frederick
Woodin, Martin Dwight
Woodland, Don L.
Woodliff, George Franklin
Woodroe, William May
Woodrow, Robert Henry, Jr.
Woodruff, Frank George
Woodruff, George Robert
Woodruff, James Arthur
Woodruff, James Donald
Woodruff, Judson Sage
Woodruff, Judy Carline
Woodruff, Robert Paul
Woodrum, Patricia Ann
Woods, Charles Ellerbe
Woods, Henry
Woods, John William
Woods, John Witherspoon
Woods, Rose Mary
Woods, Samuel Hubert, Jr.
Woods, William Sledge
Woodside, Gilbert Llewellyn
Woodson, Herbert Horace
Woodson, Warren Brooks
Woodward, Albert Young
Woodward, Cleveland Landon
Woodward, Edward Roy
Woodward, Halbert Owen
Woodward, Harman
Woodward, Lewis Klair, Jr.
Woodward, Madison Truman, Jr.
Woodward, Ralph Lee, Jr.
Woodward, Robert Forbes
Woodward, Robert Upshur
Woodward, Theodore Englar
Woolam, Gerald Lynn
Wooldridge, Charles William
Woollen, Charles Russell
Woolley, George Walter
Woolman, Myron
Woolsey, Frederick William
Woolsey, Robert James, Jr.
Woolsey, Samuel Mitchell
Wooten, Louis Ernest
Wooten, Oscar Smith
Woozley, Anthony Douglas
Worcester, Donald Emmet
Worden, Alfred Merrill
Worden, Penn William, Jr.
Work, Henry Harcus
Work, William
Workman, William Douglas, Jr.
Workman, William Gatewood
Worley, Bland Wallace
Worley, Evelyn L.
Worley, James Samuel
Worth, Gary James
Wortham, John Lilburn
Worthy, K(enneth) Martin
Worthy, Patricia Morris
Worzel, John Lamar
Wouk, Herman
Wozencraft, Frank McReynolds
Wragg, Joanna DiCarlo (Mrs. Otis Oliver Wragg III)
Wrapp, Henry Edward
Wray, Charles Williamson, Jr.
Wray, Frank Junior
Wray, William Robert
Wright, Carroll
Wright, Charles Alan
Wright, Cheryl Frances
Wright, Christopher
Wright, Floyd Vernon
Wright, Frank Cookman, Jr.
Wright, Harry Forrest, Jr.
Wright, Helen Patton
Wright, Howard Emory
Wright, James C., Jr.
Wright, James Edward
Wright, James Lee
Wright, James Roscoe
Wright, James Skelly
Wright, John Charles Young
Wright, John Collins
Wright, John Dean, Jr.
Wright, John Emerson
Wright, John MacNair, Jr.
Wright, John Peale
Wright, Leslie Stephen
Wright, Louis Booker
Wright, Marcellus Eugene, Jr.
Wright, Marvin Eugene, Jr.
Wright, Myron Arnold
Wright, Nathalia
Wright, Paul, Jr.
Wright, Paul McCoy
Wright, Randolph Earle
Wright, Richard Earl, III
Wright, Richard Newport, III
Wright, Richard Warren
Wright, Robert Dean
Wright, Robert Lee
Wright, Robert Ross, III
Wright, Samuel Lee
Wright, Stanley Robert
Wright, Stephen Junius
Wright, Thomas Henry
Wright, Thomas William Dunstan
Wright, Tom Z.
Wrightsman, Charles Bierer
Wroth, James Melvin
Wu, Hsiu Kwang
Wu, James Chen-Yuan
Wu, Jin
Wurf, Jerry
Wurtzel, Alan Leon
Wyant, Dominique Homan
Wyatt, Edward Avery, IV
Wyatt, Forest Kent
Wyatt, Forest Kent
Wyatt, Jack Miller
Wyatt, Joseph Peyton, Jr.
Wyatt, Oscar S., Jr.
Wyatt, Robert Eugene
Wyatt, Wilson Watkins
Wyckoff, Peter Hines
Wygal, Benjamin Raymond
Wyland, Robert Brooks
Wylie, Albert Sidney
Wylie, Chalmers Pangburn
Wylie, Clarence Raymond, Jr.
Wylie, William Earl
Wyly, Charles Joseph
Wyly, Lemuel David
Wyman, Marvin Eugene
Wyndham, Herbert Bernard, Jr.
Wynette, Tammy
Wyngaarden, James Barnes
Wynn, Sproesser
Wynn, William Harrison
Wynne, Brian James
Wynne, Richard Blitch
Wynne, William Joseph
Wyss, Orville
Yablonski, Joseph Andrew
Yager, Joseph Arthur, Jr.
Yaghjian, Edmund
Yanagisawa, Samuel Tsuguo
Yancey, Asa Greenwood
Yancey, Benjamin Walmsley
Yancey, Clarence Langston
Yancey, Robert Earl
Yancey, William Burbridge, Jr.
Yang, Joseph Houng-Yu
Yankovich, James Michael
Yannello, Judith Ann
Yannuzzi, William A(nthony)
Yantis, John Marshall
Yarborough, Ralph Webster
Yarborough, Richard Warren
Yarborough, William Caleb
Yarborough, William Pelham
Yarbrough, James Richard
Yard, Rix Nelson
Yardley, John Finley
Yardley, John Howard
Yardley, Jonathan
Yarmolinsky, Adam
Yarnell, Richard Asa
Yarnell, Sam Igou
Yasinski, Philip H.
Yates, Charles Richardson
Yates, Ella (Mae) Gaines
Yates, Sidney Richard
Yatron, Gus
Yeager, C. Robert
Yeager, Joseph Henry
Yeagley, J. Walter
Yeargan, Percy Baxter
Yeargin, Robert Harper
Yeates, Zeno Lanier
Yeh, Raymond Tzuu-Yau
Yeilding, Frank Brooks, Jr.
Yeldell, Joseph Philip
Yelton, Chestley Lee
Yeoman, Wayne Allen
Yepremian, Garo Sarkis
Yerger, Ralph William
Yerkes, David Norton
Yerks, Robert George
Yestadt, James Francis
Yielding, K. Lemone
Yingling, Gary Lee
Yochelson, Ellis L(eon)
Yochelson, Leon
Yochum, Philip Theodore
Yock, Robert John
Yoder, Edwin Milton
Yoder, Hatten Schuyler, Jr.
Yoe, Harry Warner
Yon, Joseph L.
Yordan, Carlos Manuel
York, Colon Wesley
York, E. Travis, Jr.
York, Frank Snyder, Jr.
Yost, Charles Woodruff
Yost, George
Yost, L. Morgan
Yost, Paul Alexander, Jr.
Youel, Kenneth
Young, Ardell Moody
Young, Arthur Chiles
Young, Barney Thornton
Young, Bryant Llewellyn
Young, Burton
Young, C. W. Bill
Young, Dean Wayne
Young, Donald Alan
Young, Donald E.
Young, Franklin Woodrow
Young, George Cressler
Young, Glen Murphy
Young, Henry Ben
Young, James Fred
Young, James Harvey
Young, John Donald
Young, John Paul
Young, John Watts
Young, Kenneth
Young, Kenneth Evans
Young, Lawrence Eugene
Young, Louise Merwin (Mrs. Ralph A. Young)
Young, Martin D.
Young, Milton Earl
Young, Oran Reed
Young, Ralph Aubrey
Young, Raymond Alfred, III
Young, Richard Donald
Young, Richard Mortimer
Young, Robert Alan
Young, Robert Anton
Young, Robert Bunnell
Young, Robert Lyle
Young, Samuel Doak
Young, Stephen M.
Young, Thomas Daniel
Young, Warren Howard
Young, William Glenn, Jr.
Young, William Tandy, Jr.
Young, William Thompson
Youngblade, Charles John
Youngdahl, James Edward
Youngdahl, Paul David
Yount, Ernest Harshaw, Jr.
Yount, Florence Jane
Yowell, Grover McClelland, Jr.
Yuan Shao Wen
Yunis, Adel Assad
Yust, Harold Robert
Yzaguirre, Raul Humberto
Zaban, Erwin
Zacharias, Donald Wayne

Zachert, Martha Jane
Zachert, Virginia
Zachry, Henry Bartell
Zack, Albert Joseph
Zacks, Shelemyahu
Zagoria, Sam
Zahl, Paul Arthur
Zahrn, Fred J.
Zakhartchenko, Constantine Leo
Zallen, Harold
Zamora, Mario Dimarucut
Zane, Edward Raymond
Zassenhaus, Hiltgunt Margret
Zausner, L. Andrew
Zavist, Algerd Frank

Zdanis, Richard Albert
Zech, Robert Francis
Zechman, Fred William, Jr.
Zedek, Mishael
Zeferetti, Leo C.
Zeiberg, Seymour Lawrence
Zeidman, Philip Fisher
Zeigler, Rowland Franklin
Zeiller, Warren
Zelby, Leon Wolf
Zeldin, Mary-Barbara
Zelikoff, Murray
Zeller, Earnest Jerome
Zelnick, Carl Robert
Zelnik, Melvin
Zemp, John Workman

Zen, E-an
Zenke, Larry Lynn
Zeppa, Robert
Zerman, William Sheridan
Zeugner, Orland Kump
Ziebarth, Karl Rex
Ziegler, Daniel Martin
Ziegler, Ronald Louis
Zierler, Kenneth
Ziff, Robert Paul
Zim, Herbert Spencer
Zimmer, Donald William
Zimmer, Paul Howard
Zimmer, William Louis, III
Zimmerer, Ann(a) Morgan
Zimmerman, Edward K.

Zimmerman, Edwin Morton
Zimmerman, Hyman Joseph
Zimmerman, John Richman
Zimmerman, Joseph Dale
Zimmerman, M. Paul
Zimmerman, Richard Gayford
Zimmerman, Warren Eugene
Zimmerman, William Dudley
Zimmermann, Bernard
Zimmermann, Robert Walter
Zimny, Marylin Lucile
Zinner, Paul
Ziperman, H. Haskell
Zirkind, Ralph
Zischke, Douglas Arthur
Zisfein, Melvin Bernard

Zisk, Richard Walter
Zlatkis, Albert
Zodhiates, Spiros George
Zoghby, Linda Victoria
Zook, Donovan Quay
Zorinsky, Edward
Zorn, Eugene Christian, Jr.
Zorthian, Barry
Zubrod, Charles Gordon
Zuck, Alfred Miller
Zucker, Alexander
Zuckman, Harvey Lyle
Zuelzer, W. W.
Zuidema, George Dale
Zuk, William
Zukel, William John

Zumas, Nicholas Harry
Zumberge, James Herbert
Zumwalt, Richard Dowling
Zumwinkle, Robert Gordon
Zurcher, Louis Anthony, Jr.
Zurkowski, Paul George
Zwanzig, Robert Walter
Zwemer, Raymund Lull
Zwick, Charles John
Zwolinski, Bruno John
Zylstra, Roger Edward